A CHRONOLOGY OF AMERICAN MUSICAL THEATER

A CHRONOLOGY OF AMERICAN MUSICAL THEATER

Richard C. Norton

VOLUME I

OXFORD
UNIVERSITY PRESS
2002

OXFORD
UNIVERSITY PRESS

Oxford New York
Auckland Bangkok Buenos Aires Cape Town Chennai
Dar es Salaam Delhi Hong Kong Istanbul Karachi Kolkata
Kuala Lumpur Madrid Melbourne Mexico City Mumbai Nairobi
São Paulo Shanghai Singapore Taipei Tokyo Toronto
and an associated company in Berlin

Published by Oxford University Press, Inc.
198 Madison Avenue, New York, New York 10016
www.oup.com

Library of Congress Cataloging-in-Publication Data
Norton, Richard C., 1953-
A chronology of American musical theater / Richard C. Norton
Includes indexes
ISBN 0-19-508888-3 (set: cloth : alk. paper) – ISBN 0-19-515565-3 (v. 1: cloth : alk. Paper)
1. Musical theater—New York (State)—New York—Chronology. I. Title.
ML 1711.8.N3 N67 2002
782.1'4'097471—dc21 2001055710

EDITORIAL AND PRODUCTION STAFF
Project Editor: Mark Mones
Production Director: John Sollami
Indexes: Prepared by Magic Fingers
Book Designer: Joan Greenfield
Composition: General Meador, Inc.
Publisher: Karen Day

1 3 5 7 9 8 6 4 2

Printed in the United States of America
on acid-free paper

CONTENTS

PREFACE

The purpose of these volumes is to assemble a comprehensive picture of the popular American Musical Theatre as presented on first-class stages in New York City, from 1850 to the present, seen through the details of its theatre programs. Selected productions from 1750–1850 are also included because of their importance to future theatre, and as informed by Gerald Bordman's *American Musical Theatre: A Chronicle,* published by Oxford University Press in 2001 and years prior, to which these volumes are meant as a companion. While Mr. Bordman and I have made every effort to reconcile and correlate the information presented, I have included a number of insignificant revivals, return engagements, early farces, burlesques, and plays with musical content which he may have chosen to omit or else preferred to include as plays in his volumes on *American Theatre: A Chronicle of Comedy & Drama, 1869–1969,* also published by Oxford University Press, Inc. He has also elected to include early musical productions produced outside New York which are not to be found in my volumes.

HOW TO USE THIS BOOK

All productions appear in chronological order by season (1 June–31 May). If you do not know when a show opened, refer to the Alphabetical Title Index in Volume 3 for the production's opening date and index number. Each production is assigned an index number within the calendar year in which it opened. Thus A ROUND OF PLEASURE (1897.25) is the 25th production in this book to open in the calendar year of 1897. Every effort has been made to reproduce the principal credits for every production as they appear in the programs. Volume 3 also contains a Chronological Title Index, an Index of Songs, and an Index of Persons.

If an extant New York opening night or opening week program is unavailable, I have reconstituted as much detail as possible using alternative sources such as *Variety,* the *Dramatic Mirror, New York Clipper, Billboard,* the *New York Times,* the *New York Herald,* the *New York Tribune,* and Odell's *History of the New York Theatre* (1750–1894). Full cast lists including chorus and dance ensemble (when known) are given, followed by details of acts and scenes, and a comprehensive list of songs, sketches, dances, specialties, etc. In the opening paragraph of production credits, I have also added pertinent information which does not appear in programs, including the opening and closing dates, change of venue, return engagements and number of performances.

SHOW TITLE

Variant show titles have been included for ease of use, so that both PO-CA-HON-TAS and POCAHONTAS, FOLLIES OF 1907 and ZIEGFELD FOLLIES OF 1907, BEAUTY AND THE BEAST and DISNEY'S BEAUTY AND THE BEAST will be found. If a show's title changed during the course of its run, that will be both footnoted and cross-indexed (THE MYSTERY OF EDWIN DROOD, 1985, became DROOD!; PIGGY, 1927, became I TOLD YOU SO).

If a production was substantially revised, reconstructed, or presented in a second edition during its *continuous* run, the detail will appear at the end of the show's first entry. For example, HUMPTY DUMPTY (10 March 1868, Olympic Theatre) proved so successful that its reconstructed version was introduced 15 June 1868, whose details warrant only a footnote. HUMPTY DUMPTY: Second Edition, Bound to Please, was introduced as part of the production's continuous run on 25 January 1869, the program details of which immediately follow the entry for the first edition. As a further example, BALIEFF'S CHAUVE-SOURIS (4 February1922, 49th St) was presented in four consecutive editions during a continuous run in two theatres, program details of which immediately follow the first edition. CRAZY WITH THE HEAT proved such a failure in its 14 January 1941 opening that it was withdrawn after one week, and revised, and re-opened at the same theatre under different auspices 30 January 1941; complete program details for both versions appear consecutively in Volume 2. Conversely, if a show closed and later reopened in a revised version or under a different title (SWEET AND LOW, 17 November 1930, 46th Street, later became BILLY ROSE'S CRAZY QUILT, 19 May 1931, 44th Street), the production credits will appear separately according to opening date, rather than consecutively; the correlation between the two productions will be footnoted.

Principal credits which do **not** appear in the program, but which in my opinion are essential to a full understanding of a show's origins and presentation, have been added in parentheses. For example, the program credits for POOR JONATHAN (14 October 1890, Casino Theatre) read "Adapted from the original German by Hugo Wittmann and Julius Bauer." For further clarification I have added both the title of the original German work and that of its French source, which information appears in parentheses: Adapted from the original German (operette 'Der arme Jonathan,' libretto) by Hugo Wittmann and Julius Bauer (based on the French comedy 'Les Deux Anglais' by P-F Merville).

A production is typically described in its program as a musical comedy, operetta, revue, burlesque, etc.; variant descriptions will appear afterwards in parentheses. In some instances a program identifies a production only by its title and not by type. In such cases I have identified it in the way it was advertised and/or reviewed. In many instances, a work first produced and published in France as an opéra-comique may have been advertised in New York as a comic opera or musical farce. This change in nomenclature had less to do with the nature of the work than it did with marketing a production to the New York public. Once the term "comic opera" was deemed old-fashioned or prejudicial in the 1890s, terms such as music drama or musical comedy or romantic drama were freely used in programs and advertisements. Rodgers and Hammerstein popularized the term "musical play" in the 1940s in order to suggest a work less frivolous than musical comedy. Since 1970, the term "musical comedy" is less frequently used than the simpler term "a new musical." Such terms and definitions are no longer as strictly observed as they once were.

If a work is presented in one, two, three, or more acts, and however many scenes, whether or not so billed on the title page, I have identified it as such in the opening credits. Many programs neglect to list individual scenes, which should not be interpreted to mean that a show was presented with only one set. Performance numbers have been calculated and checked against a production's advertised performance schedule. Other sources may vary substantially from the numbers presented here. Some productions in the 1850–1870 era were presented in repertory, and it is not possible to verify the exact number of performances, given nightly variations. For example, last-minute changes to the announced production schedule typically led to the substitution of one work for another in Maurice Grau's opéra comique company. Initially Wallack's company performed six nights a week, while matinees were used to introduce new works. Niblo's Garden typically added Saturday matinees to attract women and children. Harrigan and Hart's company for a time offered Tuesday and Friday matinees for an 8-performance week. In the nineteenth century I have chosen to exclude benefit performances, which typically included excerpts from many different plays and musicals. Even though I verified performance schedules for Kelly & Leon's and Koster & Bial's, among other venues, parenthesized (50) performance numbers indicate that they are a best estimate. Nineteenth-century theatrical producers often advertised special souvenirs to commemorate the 50th or 100th performance of a production; for example, in the instance of the original production of THE PIRATES OF PENZANCE I discovered such claims included a company's cumulative performances in Brooklyn and outside Manhattan.

PERFORMERS AND OTHER CREATIVE PERSONNEL

Principal cast members have been capitalized to distinguish them from featured performers. All **principal** performers listed in a program's cast list have been indexed in Volume 3. Where first names were omitted, as was common practice in the nineteenth century, full names or initials have been added in the body of the text where authoritatively known. In order to contain the size of the index, **ensemble** or **chorus** persons have **not** been indexed, except where they also appear with a given character name, or else if their subsequent fame warrants inclusion in the index. I have capitalized the names of the principal players in an effort to identify principal roles (not necessarily stars) in a production's cast list, even if all performers were granted the same billing in the program. **Cast changes are not included in this book**, with a few notable exceptions: (1) if dual performers alternated in a role, the principal actor or the first actor reviewed in the role appears first, (2) if a production plays a return engagement, a change in principal actors is usually noted by separate cast list, or else footnote, and (3) when new songs or specialties are introduced into a production by a new actor/actress not in the original company, his or her full name will appear opposite the song he or she introduced.

In the nineteenth century, cast lists generally listed men and women actors separately, men first, without regard for the gender of the role played, in descending order of stardom or stature. Mid–nineteenth-century programs often described the characters in elaborate detail with puns and wordplay. For example, the cast list for FORTUNIO AND HIS GIFTED SERVANTS (3 June 1872) reads:

CAST: *Hon. Miss Myrtina*, youngest daughter of the Baron Dunover, afterwards called Fortunio, by Royal Fairy license: Mrs. JAMES A. OATES. *Miss Pertina, Miss Flirtina*, her elder sisters: Nellie Allen, Miss Thorpe. *Baron Dunover*, a distressed Knight, who having invested his bottom dollar at 162 1/2 on "Black Friday," finds himself without means to procure a substitute for the Army, but is relieved from his dilemma by the exercise of "Women's Rights": H. E. ANDREW. *King Alforite*, the reigning sovereign of any place, best suited to the imagination of the audience, having had a little unpleasantness with his neighbor and came out second best, is just now in great distress for want of men and money to carry on the war: WILLIAM H. CRANE.

In this book, the character names appear in program order, are *in italics*, and followed by whatever descriptive detail appeared; then the actor/actress's name appears after a colon. Late in the nineteenth century, some programs freely mixed men and women in the cast list, often in order of appearance. Only in the instance of some musical revues lacking character names following World War I does a proper cast list not appear in programs; in such instances I have had to assemble the cast list from the title and content pages. Members of the chorus are inconsistently identified according to the whim of the producer, sometimes only by full name, last name, or mere number, or the early term "numerous auxiliaries." In the nineteenth century program credits may also include the machinist, properties (man), costume designer, scene painters, gas or calcium lights (man), etc., in addition to playwright, composer, director, choreographer, musical director or conductor, and producer. Conversely the playwright, producer and director are often not identified! A director may often be the playwright uncredited, the stage manager as billed, or in the case of actor-managers like George Fox, the star himself. In many instances there are no program credits for scenery or costumes, in which case these may have been rented, or re-used from earlier productions. The musical director or conductor named will be that person who conducted the show on an on-going basis, although it was not unusual for the composer to conduct a show's opening night. Up until World War I, many major theatres, whether housing a drama, comedy, or musical, maintained a separate house orchestra and house conductor apart from the orchestra and conductor for a musical show. This house orchestra would present light classical music before and after the performance and during intermission, and their repertoire was sometimes listed in the program, and should not be confused with that of the theatrical entertainment itself.

A stage name when known may be followed by an individual's other name, maiden name, etc. for purposes of clarification, in brackets [ ]. Often a performer would change his or her name over the course of a career, as Fannie Brice became Fanny Brice; they might add Jr. or Sr. to their stage name, or else a middle initial, or often the letter "e." Archie Leach becomes Cary Grant, Virginia Earl becomes Virginia Earle, Grace Van Studdiford becomes Grace Studdiford, etc. Maiden names are often succeeded by married names. I make no claim for being able to catch all of these variations, but have in good faith attempted to cite as many as possible.

Beginning in the 1960s and 1970s, the title pages of programs have for contractual reasons also included many more production credits, which previously appeared in fine print at the back of the program. For example, I have chosen to omit credits for general manager, press representative, hair stylist, marketing consultant, and music contractor. While I intend no lack of professional respect for these individuals' generous, necessary, and creative contributions, this inflation of production credits obscures the principal creative credits which, for comparative reasons, I wish to emphasize: book, music, lyrics, direction, choreography, costumes, scenery, lighting, orchestration, conductor, sound, music and/or dance arrangements, producers, associate producers.

SONGS

All songs that appear in quotation marks in the text have been indexed (for example, "Erbie Fitch's Twitch" or "Which Switch Is the Switch, Miss, for Ipswich?"), including variant titles, which appear in parentheses alongside the original title. Thus the song "Merely Marvelous" as it appears in the program for REDHEAD will also appear in the index as "I Feel Merely Marvelous," since its sheet music was published under that title; in the body of the book, it will also appear as "(I Feel) Merely Marvelous." The original SHOW BOAT program contains both "Ol' Man River" and "Old Man River." Generic entries such as Song, Specialty, Finale, Dance, and Trio are not indexed. Overtures and Entr'actes are not listed in the book, whether or not listed in the program, as they were as often performed as not.

To distinguish songs from sketches in revues, sketches appear without quotation marks. In THE GIRLS AGAINST THE BOYS (1959), scenes 3 and 5 are sketches, scene 4 is a song:

Scene 3
Can We Save Our Marriage?
Counselor: D. Van Dyke. *Stella*: J. L. Walker. *Harry*: B. Lahr.
Scene 4
"I Gotta Have You"
I. DeMartin, R. France, C. Abney, S. Devlin, R. Pointer, N. Schwartz
Scene 5
Home Late (based on an idea by Robert Mott)
Husband: D. Van Dyke. *Wife*: B. Halliday.

Sketch titles are not indexed. Only dance numbers with specific titles (Slaughter on Tenth Avenue, from ON YOUR TOES, 1936) are indexed.

Until 1920 it was common practice for some musical entertainments, particularly comic operas, not to include song lists in programs. Nonetheless, known song titles appear in published libretti, piano vocal scores, vocal selections, individually published song sheets, biographies, production manuscripts, prompt books, newspaper reviews, etc. I have footnoted these alternate sources. I ask the reader to accept the limitations of such an assumption, insofar as the musical work actually performed may have varied from the published version, in terms of revisions, interpolations, excisions, or vocal attributions, the details of which are now lost. For example, consider a British comic opera or French opéra-comique presented in New York; we may only know the song list from the published British or French piano vocal score, where no American edition or manuscript has been published or found. Such scores or libretti were published in many editions and revised by many hands over a musical's popular life. Whereas there may be many extant English translations, for example, of von Suppé's BOCCACCIO, I have not listed musical numbers unless I can be certain that the published translation was indeed the one performed. With a nod to the conventions of grand opera, musical numbers from early romantic and comic operas were often identified simply as Aria, Duet, Couplet, etc., with the opening lyric parenthesized. These have **not** been indexed, unless they are widely recognized song titles. While I have made every attempt to uncover and disclose known variations and interpolations, the reader must accept the limitations of extant source materials. All songs are listed **in performance order** except where noted; however, producers, authors and performers often freely cut songs, interpolated new songs or revised the running order, which I have noted in the text, where known.

In those musical productions, particularly revues, where individual songs are written by many hands, every effort has been made to identify the correct writers. Likewise the authors, and composers, where known, of additional songs, interpolated into book musicals have been included, whether or not such detail appears in the program. This information can be found in published song sheets, piano vocal scores, copyright files, and even occasionally on recordings.

With regard to musical numbers in early burlesques, new lyrics were often fitted to existing popular songs. For example, consider MUCH ADO ABOUT A MERCHANT OF VENICE (1858):

Aria, 'L'Elisir d'Amore' (I am starving! I am starving!)
Miss E. Allen
Trio (Better service can we offer)
Misses E. Allen, E. Germon, E. Newton
Duet, 'Nora Creina' (We shall have a Jew de spree)
Miss E. Newton, J. Brougham
Song (If you ever should deceive me)
J. Brougham
Song, 'The Sea' (The key! The key!)
Mrs. L. Eckhardt

The first entry is an aria, set to the known melody 'L'Elisir d'Amore,' but fitted with new lyrics whose opening lines in the libretto are 'I am starving! I am starving!' The next entry is a Trio, with the opening lyric 'Better service we can offer,' set either to original or uncredited music. Often such opening lyrics are the only means of identifying the song performed.

Most of the songs in these volumes have been written explicitly for a stage production. However, many popular songs not intended for the theatre have been interpolated by performers, producers, or writers into theatrical productions, and I have made no attempt to distinguish them as such. Consider, for example, the jazz or blues classics "Take the 'A' Train" or "St. Louis Blues," or "New York, New York" from the film of the same name. If an interpolated musical number has been introduced previously in another musical production or film, I have parenthesized such source information for the convenience of the reader. Consider for example the musical numbers interpolated into Act 1 of the revue MUSIC! MUSIC! (1974):

Scene 1
"Basin Street Blues"
(*Music and Lyrics by* Spencer Williams.)
"When the Saints Go Marching In" (traditional)
Scene 2
"The Merry Widow Waltz" (from THE MERRY WIDOW)
(*Music by* Franz Lehár.)
"Yankee Doodle Dandy" (from LITTLE JOHNNY JONES)
(*Music and Lyrics by* George M. Cohan.)

I make no claim for catching all such interpolations, but it is safe to say that the theatre has introduced as many or more songs into popular culture as it has borrowed for theatrical interpolation.

If you are searching the song index for "Wouldn't It be Loverly?" from MY FAIR LADY, for example, it will be indexed only at 1956.01, and not under its 1964, 1968, 1976, 1981 or 1993 revivals. "Hello, Young Lovers" is not only indexed under its 1951 premiere in THE KING AND I (1951.12), but also under 1973.19, when it was interpolated into AN EVENING WITH JOSEPHINE BAKER.

REVIVALS

Revivals were seldom billed as such in programs. Consequently, I have indicated when a production is a revival in the opening paragraph of credits. In the nineteenth century many comic operas were presented first in their original French or German, then later in one or more English adaptations, often uncredited; some were advertised by their original language title (DIE FLEDERMAUS), but performed in English. To facilitate ease of comparison, the opening date, theatre, and number of performances for the original production will be footnoted. Where the scene list and/or song lists are substantively the same as the original production, I prefer to spare the reader the redundancy of repeated information, and any change in the list of scenes or songs has been footnoted. When a production is substantively different from the original production, I will include the completely revised scene and/or song list.

CRITERIA

My criteria for inclusion in these volumes have been as broad as possible, namely every musical, musical play, musical comedy, operetta, opérette, opéra comique, opéra bouffe, comic opera, burlesque, musical revue, comedy revue, dance drama, pantomime, farce comedy, extravaganza, rock opera, etc., whether performed in English or a foreign language, in a major New York City venue, beginning 1 January 1850. Prior to 1850, there was an abundance of comic operas, burlesques, burlettas, spectacles, etc. presented in New York City, not included in this book. Despite many scholarly advocates I do not believe that the modern musical theatre may be said to have begun simply with either THE BEGGAR'S OPERA, THE ARCHERS, THE BLACK CROOK, H.M.S. PINAFORE, ADONIS, SHOW BOAT, or OKLAHOMA!, despite each historic work's indisputable creative impact. The collaborative evolution of musical theatre has been complex, revolutionary, conservative, reckless, fickle, depressed, mercenary, and creative, in terms that defy simple categorization. For every rule, assumption, or generalization, there will be an exception.

Prior to 1865, most New York theatres changed their bills nightly; a typical evening's entertainment might include a short fore-piece, the evening's main entertainment, and an after-piece, occasionally interspersed with music or comic specialties. Indeed in the eighteenth and nineteenth centuries live music was an integral part of all theatrical entertainments, and efforts to force any non-musical or musical categorization upon these works would be misleading. In consultation with Mr. Bordman, I have included an introductory chapter of several, but by no means all, significant pre-1850 works, which, because of their authors, performers, or subsequent revival post-1850, warranted inclusion. For readers and researchers eager to know more about this period, there are William Dunlap's "History of the American Theatre" (J. & J. Harper, New York, 1832; republished by Burt Franklin, New York, 1963); George C. D. Odell's *Annals of the New York Stage* in fifteen volumes to 1894 (Columbia University Press, New York, 1927–49); Joseph N. Ireland's *Records of the New York Stage 1750–1860* in two volumes (originally 1866–7; republished by Burt Franklin, New York, 1968); and Julian Mates' *The American Musical Stage before 1800* (Rutgers University Press, New Brunswick, New Jersey, 1962).

The decision to include or exclude some pre-1900 borderline entries has been at my discretion, and no doubt many unintended omissions will emerge. For the twentieth century, inclusion in or exclusion from this volume bears no relation to the entries in the Best Plays series or Theatre World annuals, Tony Award eligibility, NY Drama Critics Circle Award eligibility, Actors Equity/American Guild of Variety Artists membership; all of these criteria and sources have been weighed and considered independently. I have excluded most plays with fewer than three or four incidental musical numbers. Inclusion in this volume is not intended to confer or deny a work's legitimacy as musical theatre.

Shakespearean plays, such as A Midsummer Night's Dream, which commonly feature incidental songs, have been excluded except when fully adapted into new musical form or a musical burlesque. Grand opera, however significant its impact on the popular musical theatre, has likewise been excluded because by definition it lies outside the popular theatrical forms defined above. Despite occasional overlap, the history, repertoire, and artistic personnel of grand opera encompass a different universe from popular musical theatre and is better documented elsewhere. Therefore no entries appear for the Metropolitan Opera productions of DIE FLEDERMAUS, GIUDITTA, THE MERRY WIDOW, or PORGY AND BESS, even though these works would be included had they been presented in another venue. In a few instances, the Metropolitan Opera House has been used for outside commercial bookings of musical entertainments which are therefore included (THE LADIES PARADISE, MASS, EVERY GOOD BOY DESERVES FAVOR). Minstrel shows, another popular musical theatrical form of the nineteenth century, have for the most part been excluded from this volume, insofar as their content changed daily or weekly. However, several early minstrel companies (Kelly & Leon, San Francisco Minstrels, etc.) began presenting elaborate musical burlesques or farces as theatrical after-pieces, preceded by the traditional minstrel olio or variety program. I have selectively included them as significant transitional pieces in the evolution of musical theatre. Similarly, Harrigan & Hart and Weber & Fields began their legendary careers in vaudeville and variety with one-act comic sketches. As these evolved into ever more elaborate farces with larger casts, the variety or olio portion of the evening's entertainment gradually shrank in importance.

VENUE

With regard to venue, I have included only popular musical entertainments presented in Manhattan. This is not intended to diminish the exceptional contributions from our contemporary regional theatres, be they Boston, Philadelphia, or Chicago, or many other American cities or towns which have had their own indigenous, vibrant, creative contribution to musical theatre over the 150 years of this book. Such works and the necessary information about them are so widely dispersed that their inclusion falls beyond the reasonable scope of this book. I have also not included Off-Broadway, Brooklyn, Harlem, tryouts, shows that closed in preview, workshop or showcase productions, benefits, or staged readings. Consequently THE FANTASTICKS (1960), the longest running musical in American history from Off-Broadway, perversely does not appear in this book. Nor are the recent revivals of Broadway musicals presented by the popular Encores Series at New York City Center included; this series began originally as staged readings with full orchestra, and has gradually evolved into ever more elaborate stagings. Were I to include Encores, then I would have to include all other concert stagings of musicals. Next edition, perhaps.

The geographic center of the commercial theatre has migrated slowly northward along the axis of Broadway during the 150 years examined here. Early venues (1850–1870) such as the Olympic (622 Broadway), Wallack's, the Standard, the Bowery, and Niblo's Garden were concentrated below 14th Street. A few, such as Pike's Opera House, later known as the Grand Opera House, lay as far north as Eighth Avenue at 23rd Street. By the 1890s the theatrical community was centered along Broadway between Union Square (14th Street) and Herald Square (34th Street). Theatres such as the Casino (39th Street and Broadway) marked the northernmost location. Former first class venues such as the Bowery, Grand Opera House, Olympic, 14th Street, Niblo's Garden, which began as principal venues, fall to second-class status, become combination houses, and finally become variety venues or film houses. Beginning 1900–1920 the city's traditional theatrical center relocated to the former Longacre Square, now Times Square, along Broadway from 40th to 59th Street, with the building of theatres along 42nd Street (New Amsterdam, Harris, Selwyn, Times Square, Liberty, Apollo, etc.) and beyond. During the depression of the 1930s, when talkies overtook the 42nd Street houses, the locus shifted slightly north and became concentrated from 44th to 53rd Streets. This book includes all such venues and occasional upstarts. Hammerstein's Theatre Republic on West 42nd Street opposite the New Amsterdam, was once a first class Broadway venue, but now operates as the new Victory Theatre presenting visiting non-for-profit companies under a distinctly non-Broadway contract. As an Off-Off-Broadway venue it launched IT AIN'T NOTHIN' BUT THE BLUES (1999) which managed a subsequent Broadway transfer. Some venues appear only once, as the Bamboo Isle did in 1922 at the corner of 57th Street and 8th Avenue, for OH JOY! Combination houses from 1890–1910 (American, Murray Hill, Third Avenue, Harlem Opera House, Columbus, Metropolis, etc.) briefly developed as second-tier venues which played primarily touring plays and musicals for one week engagements.

Beginning with the New York City Center (at 55th St) in 1944 and then the New York City Opera, not-for-profit productions emerge in prolific number, adding to the artistic and commercial mix of musical entertainments. Now Lincoln Center Theatre Company and the Roundabout Theatre Company may be joined by such traditional Off-Broadway producers as the Public Theatre and Manhattan Theatre Club in presenting revivals and new work on Broadway.

For our own times, I have omitted preview dates and performances; some shows may have given as many as 50 previews before their press opening, and some shows, such as SARAVA (1979), never designated a press opening at all. Venues such as Radio City Music Hall, the Beacon Theatre, or Madison Square Garden, previously regarded as non-Broadway venues, have in recent years presented Broadway-style entertainment, such as THE WIZ, A CHRISTMAS CAROL, AND PORGY AND BESS, and I have therefore included them. Shows with irregular performance schedules such as A CHRISTMAS CAROL, with 12 performances weekly, are duly noted; otherwise most contemporary Broadway shows under Equity contract give 8 performances a week. When a Broadway production was previously presented Off-Broadway, in a showcase or nightclub, I have footnoted variant dates, cast, and performance details.

Many productions, whether commercial or non-profit, may be announced for limited runs of several nights, one or several weeks. Length of run is, however, a crude and inexact measure of a play's success. I offer no comment as to a producer's intent, limited or open run strategy, nor any estimate of its artistic or commercial success. Many touring productions have enjoyed enormous success outside of New York, playing as little as one week's engagement of 8 performances in New York. Yet PICKWICK and OLIVER!, regarded by most observers as a failure and a hit, respectively, famously recouped their capital before reaching New York. Whereas a 100–performance New York run was considered successful at the beginning of the twentieth century, the 657 performance run of A TRIP TO CHINATOWN was regarded as a phenomenon in 1891. Nowadays some productions fail to recoup their capital after nearly 1,000 New York performances (RAGTIME, SUNSET BOULEVARD, WOMAN OF THE YEAR, KISS OF THE SPIDER WOMAN, for example). Subsidiary revenues from later productions or tours may yet render these productions profitable in accounting terms.

GENRE

What emerges over time and gradual study of the musical entertainments contained in this volume is their mutual interdependence in form, reference, and evolution. The rise and fall of burlesque, extravaganza, opéra comique, operetta, ragtime and jazz, revue as spectacle, the musical play, intimate revue, rock opera, etc. may be traced through these pages. What constituted musical entertainment in the nineteenth century was far less formalized than it is today. Grand opera and classical drama formed the basis for many of the burlesques and comic sketches in the nineteenth century; contemporary audiences recognized and celebrated their favorite operas, dramas, and performers burlesqued in ways that would be incomprehensible to today's audiences. Such topical burlesque references or idioms dominated THE BLACK CROOK (1866), Kelly & Leon's THE GRAND DUTCH S (1868), ADONIS (1884), and Weber & Fields' FIDDLE-DEE-DEE (1900). Today grand opera is both celebrated and ridiculed in PHANTOM OF THE OPERA (1988).

BURLESQUE AND REVUE

The long-standing theatrical tradition of gender reversal, be it a lady in a trouser role or a man as female impersonator, was as common to Tony Hart in THE MULLIGAN GUARDS' SURPRISE (1880), Lillian Russell in THE LITTLE DUKE (1895), and Julian Eltinge in THE LAUGHING HUSBAND (1914) as in this era's LA CAGE AUX FOLLES (1983), THE MYSTERY OF EDWIN DROOD (1985), or DAME EDNA: THE ROYAL TOUR (1999). Throughout the book I use the term "burlesque" in its original form, to denote contemporary parody, and not as it evolved into its mid–twentieth-century usage for strip shows. Early forms of minstrel olio and variety are the logical progenitor of the musical revue, be it Laura Keene's VARIETY, or the Picture Gallery (1857), EYES AND EARS IN LONDON (1880), the first PASSING SHOW (1894) leading to all of the ZIEGFELD FOLLIES (1907–1957) or SUGAR BABIES (1979). Note that early musical revues, like book musicals, often attempted to sustain an incoherent plot with its central characters traveling through a loosely connected series of adventures, for example THE PASSING SHOW (1894), but also THE PLEASURE SEEKERS (1913) or THE DANCING GIRL (1923). Later revues have eschewed plot altogether and have instead become retrospectives of a songwriter, as in AIN'T MISBEHAVIN'

(1978), a director-choreographer JEROME ROBBINS' BROADWAY (1989), or music genre IT AIN'T NOTHIN' BUT THE BLUES (1999). Off-Broadway's FORBIDDEN BROADWAY (1982–present) perpetuates the long-standing burlesque tradition of both celebrating and skewering current musical shows.

OPERETTA AND MUSICAL COMEDY

America's musical theatre often created or followed popular crazes beginning with a fascination for all things European. A simple program credit in the nineteenth century, "Costumes from Paris" or "Entire production as presented at the Theatre Royal, Drury Lane," were seen as legitimizing credentials to a sophisticated public which presumed a European cultural superiority over all things American. **Offenbach**'s oeuvre, for example, achieved worldwide success, whether presented in New York in its original French, as LA GRANDE DUCHESSE DE GÉROLSTEIN (1867) or in English (Lydia Thompson's LA PRINCESSE DE TRÉBIZONDE in 1871) or American adaptations (YE LEGEND OF YE GRAND QUEEN BESS! in 1867), or in burlesque form, Kelly & Leon's LA BELLE L.N. (1868). Offenbach's contemporary appeal today is less potent, despite the New York City Opera's revivals in English of ORPHEUS IN THE UNDERWORLD (1956) and THE GRAND DUCHESS OF GÉROLSTEIN (1982). **W. S. Gilbert and Arthur Sullivan**'s impact can be seen by the proliferation of competing, and many unauthorized, productions of H.M.S. PINAFORE (1879), not only in English, but also with juvenile casts, a Philadelphia Church choir, or an all-black or German-speaking company! Beginning in 1879 Gilbert and Sullivan set the standard for comic opera until the advent of the new century and the emergence of American talents. The unprecedented success of THE MIKADO (1885) spawned many imitations with exotic Far Eastern plots and settings, among the most successful being the London-originated FLORODORA (1900), or the American originals THE WIZARD OF THE NILE by Victor Herbert (1895) and the Messrs. Shubert's FANTANA (1905).

America developed its own **indigenous musical theatre talents** with the early local farces of Edward Harrigan and Tony Hart (music by David Braham) from 1876–1890. The nineteenth century genre of farce comedy, loosely built around the talents of a star (May Irwin, James T. Powers, Nat Goodwin) or writer (Charles H. Hoyt, with his A TRIP TO CHINATOWN in 1891), with incidental song interpolations, predates the form and structure of American musical comedies like HELLO, DOLLY! (1964). Joseph Weber and Lew Fields further expanded the musical farce with a highly trained ensemble of stars in their musical farce extravaganzas, HURLY BURLY (1898), WHIRL-I-GIG (1899), FIDDLE-DEE-DEE (1900), HOITY TOITY (1901), etc. The emergence of indigenous American song writers at the turn of the century, to match and then usurp the dominance of the Europeans, started with Victor Herbert, Jerome Kern, and Irving Berlin, followed by the great heyday of musical theatre writers, with Richard Rodgers & Lorenz Hart, Cole Porter, George and Ira Gershwin, Oscar Hammerstein II, Alan Jay Lerner and Frederick Loewe, and Stephen Sondheim among many others, all of whom have been given biographical treatment in substantial detail elsewhere.

Historical and economic trends have likewise had a precipitous impact upon New York theatrical productions. The outbreak of World War I in 1914 effectively banished all Viennese and German operettas from popular favor; the Messrs. Shubert resorted to extraordinary means to conceal the Viennese or German origins of such works as: THE BLUE PARADISE (1915), HER SOLDIER BOY (1916), THE RIVIERA GIRL (1917), MAYTIME (1917), BLOSSOM TIME (1921). The introduction of recorded sound, in particular cylinders and then 78rpm discs, was at first regarded warily as unwelcome competition for the theatre-going audience. Jerome Kern insisted that his musical score for SITTING PRETTY (1924) be heard live, and thus its music went unrecorded at the time. The emergence first of radio and then motion pictures with sound (1929) was initially feared to be a great threat to live musical theatre; wisdom in hindsight has demonstrated that sound recordings, radio, film and television could be used to promote, exploit and expand the audience for live musical theatre entertainment. Apart from brief cyclical blips in theatrical production (the Iroquois Theatre fire in Chicago 30 December 1903, influenza epidemic in 1918, economic recessions in 1873, 1893, 1903, 1911), the great depression of the 1930s had the most severe creative and statistical impact in the absolute decline of musical theatre productions.

Dramatic **motion pictures** were often adapted into musical theatre form, beginning with THE LITTLE WHOPPER (1919). Gabriel Pascal's film of *Pygmalion* more than Shaw's own play, formed the inspiration for MY FAIR LADY (1956), and the film of *Anna and the King of Siam* was equally instrumental in inspiring Rodgers and Hammerstein to create THE KING AND I from Margaret Landon's historical novel. Consequently film becomes source material for Broadway musical theatre as well an ancillary life for musical theatre after its stage production. The films of THE GAY DIVORCE, OKLAHOMA, WEST SIDE STORY, THE SOUND OF MUSIC and THE ROCKY HORROR SHOW, among many others, have all contributed generously to the perpetuation of musical theatre as a genre. Until the appearance and later dominance of rock and roll music in the late 1950s, much of the best in American Popular Music came from its theatrical composers. Despite many great artistic, commercial and long-running successes since then, musical theatre has ceased to dominate popular music in the way that OKLAHOMA! (1943), MY FAIR LADY (1956) and HELLO, DOLLY! (1964) once did. Despite the welcome arrival of pop song writers like Elton John, Pete Townshend and The Who, Paul Simon and Andrew Lloyd Webber in the musical theatre, it is increasingly true that what works best on the musical theatre stage is no longer necessarily what the public listens to on the radio or in the home.

These challenges to the contrary, the musical theatre continues to re-invent and redefine itself in ways unimaginable to earlier generations. While much of that experimentation now occurs beyond the traditional confines of Broadway, the last decade has witnessed renewed efforts to re-marry popular music to the theatre and to woo a younger audience, whether in adapting film musicals to the stage, with the mixed results of TOMMY (1995), FOOTLOOSE (1998), and SATURDAY NIGHT FEVER (1999); assembling pop music revues like SMOKY JOE'S CAFÉ (1994) and LEADER OF THE PACK (1985); or inviting new work written for the theatre, such as RENT (1996), and THE CAPEMAN (1998). Risk-averse producers have increasingly turned to revivals of proven musical theatre classics, or else stage adaptations of film musicals, including GIGI (1973), 42ND STREET (1980 and 2001), SEVEN BRIDES FOR SEVEN BROTHERS (1982), SINGIN' IN THE

RAIN (1985), STATE FAIR (1995), and THE LION KING (1997). The latest trend has been to reproduce the literal film experience live onstage.

HISTORY OF PROGRAMS

Not only have the forms of musical theatre evolved over the 150 years I examined, but also the chosen format, language and nomenclature of musical theatre **programs** have changed according to popular taste and expectations. Early theatre programs (approximately 1850–1890) were printed on newsprint quality paper, measured roughly 10 × 14, and included theatrical and non-theatrical copy and advertising. They were usually 4 pages, roughly the size of our contemporary tabloid newspaper, folded in half. Concurrently, many programs were also printed without advertising or news, on one-sided gallery sheets roughly 6 × 14, and there were many, many variations from these typical formats. Some of the production credits I examined were in fact broadsheets or posters. A new musical production might be billed thus (1855):

PO-CA-HON-TAS,
or, The Gentle Savage

An Original, Aboriginal, Erratic, Operatic, Semi-Civilized and Demi-Savage Extravaganza in Two Acts, being a perversion of ye trew and wonderfulle Hystorie of ye Renounede Pryncesse.

Rather than identifying this production as a burlesque as contemporary critics and advertising did, the program often included such humorous, fanciful and witty descriptive copy. Many productions up until the 1890s were subtitled, with the main title in bold face print, and the subtitle in smaller print below.

Frequently the playwright and/or composer were not identified, for a variety of reasons, inconceivable as that may be to our own generation of theatregoers! Among the many reasons: (1) English and European works could be freely produced, adapted, or revised because copyright control was lax, (2) Theatre owners and managers could commission work for hire without credit, (3) An actor-manager may have conceived a play or role for himself/herself and thus wish to conceal the vanity origins of the work presented, (4) The music may often be borrowed, revised, arranged or adapted from popular songs of the day, often without credit. In many instances the theatre owner was the producer of the play, which information may not be readily apparent from the playbill, or else the actor-manager star of the production may function as his own producer, with a business manager as agent. Usually the librettist is presumed to be the work's lyricist as well as book-writer, unless otherwise stated.

In the nineteenth century, comic operas, extravaganzas and spectacles often listed a synopsis of scenes replete with plot cues, specialties and spectacular tableaux. Consider the revival of Balfe's THE ENCHANTRESS (1854) for example:

Act 1, Scene 1: The Hermitage of "Our Lady of the Wood." Mountains in the distance. Descent amidst the rocks. *Scene 2:* The Pirates' Cave. Entrance of the Enchantress. *Scene 3:* Rocky Pass and Gorge. *Scene 4:* Abode of the Enchantress; State-room of the Pirate Queen; Sylvio's Dream; Greek Slaves Tableau.

Act 2, Scene 1: Sylvio's richly draperied tent; disaffection of the Soldiery, and timely arrival of an unknown friend; Destruction of the Regent's Fleet. *Scene 2:* Rich Apartment in the Palace; Vestibule of the grand hall of Audience. *Scene 3:* Sumptuous Palace Scene. The scene is thrown back, forming an immense amphitheatre for a Grand Bal Masque. *Scene 4:* The Pavilion of Myrtles.

Act 3, Scene 1: Exterior of a Sicilienne Inn. Vineyard adjacent; Arched Interior; Visit of the Senators to Don Silvio; the Enchantress still maintains the Ascendancy, and Don Sylvio is proclaimed King. *Scene 2:* Shore of Palermo, by Moonlight; Church of St. Marie Majeure; the Nuptials of the Enchantress, and the Fulfillment of the Vow. Magnanimity of Ramir, the Pirate Chief; his pardon; Sylvio and Stella, King and Queen of Sicily. Chorus and Tableau.

I have included this same information where I think it may be insightful and instructive. Often the musical numbers were not identified, except as Song, Chorus or Specialty. Ballets and Grand Transformation Scenes were, however, often described in elaborate detail.

Beginning about the 1890s, theatre programs began to assume a booklet form of up to a dozen or more pages, measuring at first 8 × 10, then narrowing somewhat to 6 × 9 at the turn of the century. With the advent of the New York Theatre Program Corporation and its successor, Playbill, which has dominated the theatre program market since the 1910s, the contents and configuration of theatre programs have remained remarkably constant. In the 1910–1930 era, programs were generally 5 × 7.5, expanding with the depression to 7 × 9.5, then shrinking gradually after World War II to the present size of 5.25 × 8.5. The proliferation of advertising and added copy has increased the number of pages from 10–20 in the 1940s to as many as 100 during the present winter holidays.

It is my hope that these volumes will prove indispensable, and that they will answer your questions and provoke the need for further research and reflection. Although the information contained herein is as thorough and complete as I have been able to find it, no doubt you and I will find errors and omissions! Musical theatre is a varied and constantly changing field both in contemporary creative terms and in historically documented terms. Long may it prosper and flourish.

ACKNOWLEDGMENTS

I would have been unable to attempt to document this vast musical theatre history without the help of many scholars, colleagues, and friends. This project was originally conceived by Gerald Bordman and Sheldon Meyer some ten years ago, and their persistence and vision of what these volumes ought to contain were an inspiration to me at all times. Contractually we first anticipated three years' work; given the elusive dispersal of pre-World War I programs and other primary sources, what I imagined as a five-year project soon expanded to seven-year labor of love. Little did we know that the final text would contain over a million proper names, with approximately 100,000 persons and almost 50,000 songs indexed.

I'd like to thank the Research Divisions of the New York City Public Library at Lincoln Center—in particular, Theatre, Music, Dance and Recorded Sound—for their efforts on my behalf, as well as curators Ric Wilson (present) and Jeanne Newlin (past) and Annette Fern of the Theatre Collection at Harvard's Houghton Library, who helped me in a thousand ways. I'm grateful to my personal friends—Dan Langan, Kurt Gänzl, and Gerald Bordman—for their critical perusal of parts of the manuscript and their resourceful suggestions and corrections. Thanks to Gary Schocker for his unquestioned support and tolerance of the disarray of paper and research materials that have overwhelmed two households. I also offer my love and thanks to my parents, Alexandra and Dick Norton, who have always supported me in pursuit of my ambitions and dreams.

Special thanks to my picture researcher Frank Vlastnik, who selected the illustrations for these volumes, chosen with a particular eye for the unfamiliar image. My editors at Oxford University Press through these years—Sheldon Meyer, Cathy Gouldner, Claude Conyers, Jeffrey Edelstein, Matt Giarratano, and finally, Mark Mones—deserve particular thanks for seeing this project through to its fruition. Many individuals also helped me with advice from their private collections—in particular Rex Bunnett, Bradley Bennett, Ken Bloom, Jack Raymond, Ron Spivak, Richard Traubner, Christophe Mirambeau, Paul Newman, and Jeffrey Dunn, among many. To Susan Leelike, whose Magic Fingers prepared the endless index so integral to this project, I offer my warmest appreciation. I'd also like to thank Michael Frazier, Joan Cullman, and Lori Schmidt, whose production office I share and whose support I have appreciated. Among those predecessors who've documented the musical theatre so thoroughly, I pay particular tribute to George C. Odell, Gerald Bordman, Kurt Gänzl, Stanley Green, Robert Kimball, Jack Raymond, Dave Hummel, Ken Bloom, Robert Kimball, and Don Stubblebine. All of the New York City daily and weekly general interest newspapers, as well as *Variety*, *Dramatic Mirror*, *Clipper*, and *Billboard*, proved of inestimable value in determining dates and confirming production credits. To the Library of Congress, Boston Public Library, and the many other useful collections and databases accessed via the Internet, I am immensely grateful. I'm certainly the first to recognize the limitations, errors, and omissions in this project, and I welcome substantive comments and corrections from my peers.

Richard C. Norton
New York City
January 2002

A CHRONOLOGY OF AMERICAN MUSICAL THEATER

1750–1850 SEASONS

John Brougham
Billy Rose Theatre Collection, New York Public Library for the Performing Arts

1750–1850 SEASONS

1750.01 THE BEGGAR'S OPERA

A Ballad Opera in Three Acts. Libretto by John Gay. Overture composed and tunes arranged and harmonized by Dr. John Christopher Pepusch. Managers, Messrs. Walter Murray and Thomas Kean. Opened 3 December 1750 at the Theatre in Nassau Street; repeated 10 December 1750, 15 January 1751, 21 January 1751, 18 February 1751, closing 13 May 1751 after 5 performances; season ended 8 July 1851.

CAST: *Peachum, Lockit, Macheath, Filch. Macheath's Gang (8): Jemmy Twitcher, Crook-finger'd Jack, Wat Dreary, Robin of Bagshot, Nimming Ned, Harry Padington, Mat 'o the Mint, Ben Budge: Beggar, Player. Constables, Drawer, Turnkey, &c.* Messrs. WALTER MURRAY, THOMAS KEAN, JOHN TREMAIN, Charles Somerset Woodham, Jago, Scott, Leigh, Smith, Moore, Marks, Master Dickie Murray.

Mrs. Peachum, Polly Peachum, Lucy Lockit, Diana Trapes. Women of the Town (8): Mrs. Coaxer, Dolly Trull, Mrs. Vixen, Betty Doxy, Jenny Diver, Mrs. Slammekin, Suky Tawdry, Molly Brazen. Misses Osborn, Nancy George; Mrs. Taylor, Leigh, Davis.

Act 1: Peachum's House. (London, 1728.)

Act 2: A Tavern near Newgate.

Act 3: Newgate.

ACT 1[1]

"Through all the Employments of Life" (Air 1)
[Peachum]
"'Tis Woman that seduces all Mankind" (Air 2)
[Filch]
"If any Wench Venus's Girdle wear" (Air 3)
[Mrs. Peachum]
"If Love the Virgin's Heart invade" (Air 4)
[Mrs. Peachum]
"A Maid is like the golden Oar" (Air 5)
[Mrs. Peachum]
"Virgins are like the fair Flower in its Lustre" (Air 6)
[Polly]
"Our Polly is a sad Slut! nor heeds what we have taught her" (Air 7)
[Mrs. Peachum]
"Can Love be controul'd by Advice?" (Air 8)
[Polly]
"O Polly, you might have toy'd and kist" (Air 9)
[Mrs. Peachum, Polly]
"I, like a Ship in Storms, was tost" (Air 10)
[Polly]
"A Fox may steal your Hens, Sir" (Air 11)
[Peachum]
"Oh, ponder well! Be not severe" (Air 12)
[Polly]
"The Turtle thus with plaintive crying" (Air 13)
[Polly]
"Pretty Polly, say" (Air 14)
[Macheath, Polly]
"My Heart was so free" (Air 15)
[Macheath]
"Were I laid on Greenland's Coast" (Air 16)
[Macheath, Polly]
"O what Pain it is to part!" (Air 17)
[Polly, Macheath]
"The Miser thus a Shilling sees" (Air 18)
[Macheath, Polly]

ACT 2

"Fill ev'ry Glass, for Wine inspires us" (Air 19)
[Matt o' the Mint, Chorus]
"Let us take the Road" (Air 20)
[Matt o' the Mint, Chorus]
"If the Heart of a Man is deprest with Cares" (Air 21)
[Macheath]
"Youth's the Season made for Joys" (Air 22)
[Macheath, Ladies' Chorus]
"Before the Barn-door crowing" (Air 23)
[Jenny Diver]
"The Gamesters and Lawyers are Jugglers alike" (Air 24)
[Jenny Diver]
"At the Tree I shall suffer with pleasure" (Air 25)
[Macheath]
"Man may escape from Rope and Gun" (Air 26)
[Macheath]
"Thus when a good Huswife sees a Rat" (Air 27)
[Lucy]
"How cruel are the Traytors" (Air 28)
[Lucy]
"The first time at the Looking-glass" (Air 29)
[Macheath]
"When you censure the Age" (Air 30)
[Lockit, Peachum]
"Is then his Fate decreed, Sir?" (Air 31)
[Lucy]
"You'll think e'er many days ensue" (Air 32)
[Lockit]
"If you at an Office solicit your Due" (Air 33)
[Macheath]
"Thus when the Swallow, seeking Prey" (Air 34)
[Polly]
"How happy could I be with either" (Air 35)
[Macheath]
"I'm bubbled" (Air 36)
[Polly, Lucy]
"Cease your Funning" (Air 37)
[Polly]
"Why how now, Madam Flirt?" (Air 38)
[Lucy, Polly]
"No Power on Earth can e'er divide" (Air 39)
[Polly]
"I like the Fox shall grieve" (Air 40)
[Lucy]

ACT 3

"When Young at the Bar you first taught me to score" (Air 41)
Lucy]
"My Love is all Madness and Folly" (Air 42)
[Lucy]
"Thus Gamesters United in Friendship are found" (Air 43)
[Lockit]
"The Modes of the Court so common are grown"[2] (Air 44)
[Macheath]
"What Gudgeons are we Men!" (Air 45)
[Lockit]
"In the Days of my Youth I could bill like a Dove, fa, la, la, &c." (Air 46)
[Mrs. Trapes]
"I'm like Skiff on the Ocean tost" (Air 47)
[Lucy]
"When a Wife's in her Pout" (Air 48)
[Lucy]
"A Curse attends that Woman's Love" (Air 49)
[Polly, Lucy]
"Among the Men, Coquets we find" (Air 50)
[Polly]
"Come, sweet Lass" (Air 51)
[Lucy]
"Hither, dear Husband, turn your Eyes" (Air 52)
[Polly, Lucy]
"Which way shall I turn me?—How can I decide?" (Air 53)
[Macheath]
"When my Hero in Court appears" (Air 54)
[Polly]
"When he holds up his Hand arraign'd for his Life" (Air 55)
[Lucy]

[1]No New York program found. Scene and songs list prepared from a reproduction of the Second Edition, published 1728 in London, England, "printed for John Watts, at the Printing Office in Wild-Court, near Lincoln's-Inn-Fields, as reproduced in THE BEGGAR'S OPERA by John Gay, Edited by Peter Lewis (Barnes & Noble, New York, 1973).

[2]Later productions and recordings have sometimes placed this song as No. 20 following the opening of Act 2.

"Our selves, like the Great, to secure a Retreat" (Air 56)
[Lockit]
"The Charge is prepar'd; The Lawyers are met" (Air 57)
[Macheath]
"O cruel, cruel, cruel Case" (Air 58)
[Macheath]
"Of all the Friends in time of Grief" (Air 59)
[Macheath]
"Since I must Swing,—I scorn, I scorn to wince or whine" (Air 60)
"But now again my Spirits sink" (Air 61)
"But Valour the stronger grows" (Air 62)
"If thus—A Man can die" (Air 63)
"So I drink off this Bumper.—And now I can stand the Test" (Air 64)
"But can I leave my pretty Hussies" (Air 65)
"Their Eyes, their Lips, their Busses" (Air 66)
"Since Laws were made for ev'ry degree" (Air 67)
"Would I might be hang'd!" (Air 68)
[Lucy, Polly, Macheath, Chorus]
"Thus I stand like the Turk, with his Doxies around" (Air 69)
[Macheath, Chorus]

MAY DAY IN TOWN, or, New York in an Uproar

1787.01

An Opera Trifle (Play and lyrics) by Royall Tyler. Music compiled from the most eminent masters, with an Overture and Accompaniments. Prologue (spoken) by Mrs. Morris. Produced by Thomas Wignell. Opened and closed 19 May 1787 at the John Street Theatre after 1 performance.

MUSICAL NUMBERS[3]

"May Day in Town"
"Be Deaf to her Tongue"
"Pompey's Complaint"
"Ye Strains of Soft Murmurs"
"Fly to His Arms"
"Love, Mighty Love"
"May Morning in Town"
"I Thank Her for Her Care"
"A Tender Feeling Heart"
"Never More Removing" (Finale)

NEEDS MUST, or, The Ballad Singers

1793.01

A Musical Trifle by Mrs. Pownall and Mrs. (Anne Julia) Hatton[4]. Produced by the Old American Company (John Henry, Lewis Hallam). Opened 26 December 1793 at the John Street Theatre in repertory.

CAST: *Hoardwell*: Mr. W. H. PRIGMORE. *Anthony*: Mr. Martin. *Rushbrook*: Mr. Bergman. *Delia*: Mrs. (Lewis) Hallam. *Marian*: Mrs. POWNALL.

TAMMANY, or, The Indian Chief/ The Agreeable Surprise

1794.01

A Double Bill of Operas. Produced by the Old American Company (John Henry, Lewis Hallam). Opened 3 March 1794 at the John Street Theatre closed 11 April 1794 after 4 performances in repertory; season ended 28 June 1794.

PART 1

TAMMANY, or, The Indian Chief. An Operatic Spectacle in Three Acts, a Prologue and an Epilogue. Libretto by Mrs. (Anne Julia) Hatton. Overture and Accompaniments composed by James Hewitt. Prologue by Richard B. Davis. New scenery, dresses and decorations. Scenery by Messrs. (Charles) Ciceri and Robins.

CAST: *Tammany*: Mr. (JOHN) HODGKINSON. *Perez*: Mr. King. *Ferdinand*: Mr. (JOHN) MARTIN. *Wegaw*: Mr. (W. H.) PRIGMORE. *Columbus*: Mr. (LEWIS) HALLAM. *Indian Dancers*: Messrs. Durang, Miller. *Indians*: Messrs. Richards, Robbins, West, Bisset. *Spaniards*: Messrs. Hammond, O'Reilly, Kenna, etc. *Rhema*: Mrs. (Lewis) Hallam. *Zulla*: Mrs. Hamilton. *Manana*: Mrs. (JOHN) HODGKINSON. *Indian Women*: Mrs. Lang, Mrs. Kenna, Mrs. Miller, Mrs. King, etc.

ACT 1[5]

Prologue (Whence glows in each Columbian breast that flame)
Mr. J. Hodgkinson
Air (Refulgent pow'r! whose gladsome ray)
Mrs. J. Hodgkinson
Air (Dear woods! beneath whose spreading bows)
Mrs. J. Hodgkinson
Air (At early dawn to rouse the chase)
Mrs. J. Hodgkinson
Air (When dark and cheerless is the sky)
Mrs. J. Hodgkinson
Chorus of Indians (Neer Or'noco's limpid stream)
Men, Mrs. Hamilton, Mrs. J. Hodgkinson

ACT 2

Air (For the deep sups of this liquor I swear)
Mr. W. H. Prigmore
Song (Sweet simple maid dispel each fear)
Mr. J. Martin
Air (See! the orb of night appears)
Mrs. J. Hodgkinson
Air (Pale chilly fear my heart assails)
Mrs. J. Hodgkinson
Chorus (Joy and mirth dispel, the pensive tears of grief)
Chorus

ACT 3

Air (Fury swells my aching soul)
Mr. J. Hodgkinson
Air (From they dear brow that frown remove)
Mrs. J. Hodgkinson
Air (Soft peace, alas! from us is flown)
Mrs. J. Hodgkinson
Duet, altered from the old Indian song (The sun sets in night and the stars shun the day)
Mr. and Mrs. J. Hodgkinson
Air (Now let's forget each woe that's past)
Mr. and Mrs. J. Hodgkinson, Chorus
Duet (Yes, he deserv'd our warmest praise)
Mr. and Mrs. J. Hodgkinson
Chorus (Oh Hero! sunk alas thy might)
Indian Priests
Chorus (You whose souls with virtue burn)
Indians, Spaniards
Chorus (Indian maids your voices raise)
Chorus of Women
Chorus (While we rear the standard high)
Chorus
Epilogue (The Drama over—'t has been long the vogue)
Mr. Martin

PART 2

THE AGREEABLE SURPRISE. A Revival of the Comic Opera in Two Acts[6]. Libretto by John O'Keeffe. Music by Samuel Arnold.

CAST: *Lingo*: Mr. (JOHN) HODGKINSON. *Eugene*: Mr. Martin. *Sir Felix Friendly*: Mr. King. *Chicane*: Mr. Ashton. *Mr. Cudden*: Mr. Ryan. *John*: Mr. O'Reily. *Thomas*: Mr. Durang. *Compton*: Mr. Woolls. *Laura*: Mrs. King. *The Widow Cheshire*: Mrs. Miller. *Fringe*: Mrs. Hamilton. *Cowslip*: Mrs. (JOHN) HODGKINSON.

[3]No program found. The original script and score have been lost; only Tyler's lyrics are extant. List prepared from a bicentennial 1987 production at the Royall Tyler Theatre, Vermont, wherein Tyler's lyrics were retained, not necessarily in 1787 performance order.

[4]Preceded by a fore-piece SUCH THINGS ARE, featuring Mr. Hodgkinson and Mrs. Melmoth.

[5]Cast detail from Yankee Doodle-Doo: A Collection of Songs of the Early American Stage, compiled with an introduction and notes by Grenville Vernon. (Payson & Clarke, New York City, 1927). Vernon adds that an Indian Dance was performed by Messrs. Durang and Miller, a Procession was performed by the Company. List of musical numbers prepared from typescript on deposit at New York City Public Library, Performing Arts, Music Division.

[6]Previously presented 29 November 1793 at the John Street Theatre as an after-piece to the comedy, NOTORIETY.

THE ARCHERS, or, The Mountaineers of Switzerland

1796.01

A Dramatic Piece in Three Acts, interspersed with songs, choruses, &c., 13 Scenes[7]. Libretto by William Dunlap, founded on the story of William Tell[8]. Music by Benjamin Carr. Scenery by (Charles) Ciceri. Leader of the orchestra, James Hewitt. Produced by the Old American Company (Lewis Hallam, John Hodgkinson). Opened 18 April 1796 at the John Street Theatre, repeated again 22 April 1796 and closed after 3 performances in repertory.

CAST: *William Tell*, Burgher of Altdorf, Canton of Uri: Mr. (JOHN) HODGKINSON. *Walter Furst* of Uri: Mr. (JOHN) JOHNSON. *Werner Staffach*, of Schweitz: Mr. Lewis Hallam, Jr. *Arnold Melcthal*, (Chief) of Underwalden: Mr. (JOSEPH) TYLER. *Gesler*, Austrian Governor of Uri: Mr. Cleveland. *Lieutenant* to Gesler: Mr. (JOSEPH) JEFFERSON. *Burgomaster of Altdorf*: Mr. (W. H.) Prigmore. *Conrad*, a seller of wooden ware, in Altdorf: Mr. (LEWIS) HALLAM. *Leopold*, Duke of Austria: Mr. King. *Bowmen* (of Uri): Messrs. Lee, Durang, &c. *Pikemen* (of Schweitz): Messrs. Munto, Tomkins, &c. *Burghers*: Messrs. Des Moulins, Woolls, &c. *Austrian Soldiers*: Messrs. Leonard, McKnight, &c.

Portia, Tell's wife: Mrs. MELMOTH. *Rodolpha*, Walter Furst's daughter: Miss BROADHURST. *Cecily*, a basket-woman: Mrs. (JOHN) HODGKINSON. *Female Archers*: Miss Brett, Mrs. Tompkins, Mde. Val, Mrs. Durang, Made. Gardie, &c. (*Boy*, Tell's Son: Miss Harding. *Maidens of Uri*: Madame Gardie, Madame Val, Miss Brett &c.)

Act 1, Scene 1: A street in Altdorf, Switzerland. *Scene 2*: (Entrance of William Tell.) *Scene 3*: By the side of a Piece of Water, on the other side the sublime Hills, hanging Rocks, and various appropriate Beauties of the Lake of Uri.

Act 2, Scene 1: In front of the Castle of Altdorf. *Scene 2*: The Town Hall of Altdorf. — Burghers meeting. *Scene 3*: The Castle of Altdorf. *Scene 4*: Inside the Governor's Palace. *Scene 5*: The Mountains, a Water-Fall, and a distant View of a part of the Lake.

Act 3, Scene 1: (In front of the) Castle of Altdorf. *Scene 2*: The Mountains—Violent Storm, Wind, Rain and Thunder. *Scene 3*: The Castle of Altdorf. *Scene 4*: The Field of Battle, surrounded by Mountains. *Scene 5*: Another Part of the Field.

ACT 1[9]

Prologue (We tell a tale of Liberty to-night)

Scene 1

Duet (Come who'll buy my baskets?)
Mrs. J. Hodgkinson

Song (Here are bowls by the dozen, and spoons by the gross)
L. Hallam

Duet (If a man would a faithful follower have) Mrs. J. Hodgkinson, L. Hallam

Trio (The soldiers are devilish kind)
J. Jefferson, L. Hallam, Mrs. J. Hodgkinson

Scene 2

Song (Forever lives the patriot's fame)
J. Hodgkinson

Scene 3

Chorus of Bowmen of Uri (Genius of our pine-clad hills)
Mr. Lee, Chorus

Song (Uri's sons, with open arms)
Bowmen

Song (To the war-horn's loud and solemn blast)
Pikemen

March (March our bold yeomen dauntless to the field)
Mr. Johnson

Song, "Why, Huntress, Why, (wilt thou thy life expose)?"
J. Tyler

Song (At trumpet's clang, or the war-horn's sound)
Miss Broadhurst

Chorus (Let every act, let every thought)
Chorus of the Whole

ACT 2

Scene 1

Duet (How happy is a soldier's life)
J. Jefferson, L. Hallam

Song (While thus with mind infirm and limbs unnerved)
Miss Broadhurst

Scene 3

Song (Come, Conrad, awake from your trance!)
Mrs. J. Hodgkinson

Song (Come all ye pretty maidens)
Mrs. J. Hodgkinson

Ballad (There lived in Altdorf city fair)
Mrs. J. Hodgkinson

Scene 5

Song (While man, with high-wrought impious pride)
J. Tyler

Trio and Chorus (Dear is the homely cot, and dear the shed)
Miss Broadhurst, Messrs. J. Tyler, Lee, Chorus of the Whole

ACT 3

Scene 2

Song (Hark! from the mountain's awful head)
J. Tyler

Song (Haste, my Maidens, haste with me!)
Miss Broadhurst

Song (He comes! he comes! the victor comes)
Miss Broadhurst, Mr. J. Tyler, Chorus

Duet (In storied page where shall we find)
Miss Broadhurst, J. Tyler

Scene 3

Song (Good mistress, kind lady, my thanks receive)
Mrs. J. Hodgkinson

Glee and Dance (Come, my maidens, haste away!)
Miss Broadhurst, Mr. J. Tyler, Mrs. J. Hodgkinson

Scene 5

Song (When heaven pours blessings all around)
J. Hodgkinson, J. Tyler, Miss Broadhurst, Mrs. J. Hodgkinson, Chorus of the Whole

THE SICILIAN ROMANCE, or, The Spectre of the Cliffs

1796.02

A Comic Opera in Two Acts, 13 Scenes[10]. Libretto by Henry Siddons, based on a novel by Ann Ward Radcliffe. Music by William Reeve. Produced by the Old American Company (Lewis Hallam, John Hodgkinson). Opened 27 April 1796 at the John Street Theatre.

CAST: *Ferrand*, Marquis of Otranto: Mr. CLEVELAND. *Don Lope de Viega*, his Uncle: Mr. (John) Johnson. *Lindor*: Mr. (Joseph) Tyler. *Martin*, his Servant: Mr. (Joseph) Jefferson. *Prior* of the Convent: Mr. (Stephen) Woolls. *Vincent*: Mr. Munto. *Jaques, Sancho*, Servants: Messrs. Durang, M'Kenzie. *Gerbin*, the Porter: Mr. (JOHN) HODGKINSON. *Banditti*: Messrs. Lee, Leonard, McKnight, etc. *Alinda*: Miss BROADHURST. *Clara*, her Maid: Miss Brett. *Julia*, Ferrand's child: Master Stockwell. *Adelaide*, Lady of Otranto: Mrs. CLEVELAND. *Guards, Friars, Soldiers and Messengers.*

Act 1, Scene 1: A Wood, and a Tower of the Castle, with the Door. The Lights down, and the Moon shining. *Scene 2*: A Servant's Hall. *Scene 3*: A Chamber. *Scene 4*: Pieces of Rock, with a Tower, and a Blue Light burning in the Window.

Act 2, Scene 1: An Iron Door, fastened with a Chain. *Scene 2*: A Grove. A Monastery in View. *Scene 3*: The Inside of a Convent. *Scene 4*: A Small parapet before the Convent. *Scene 5*: An Aisle of the Convent.

Act 3, Scene 1: A Gothic Hall in the Castle. *Scene 2*: The Interior Part of the Convent. A Tomb-stone, or Altar in the Middle. *Scene 3*: A Wood. *Scene 4*: The Infernal Rock.

ACT 1[11]

Scene 1

Air (Borne on hope's deluding gale)
Mr. J. Tyler

---

[7]Followed by a dramatic tale, EDGAR AND EMMELINE, as an after-piece.

[8]In Mates' "The American Musical Stage Before 1800," music critic John Tasker Howard remarks that the libretto is an adaptation of Schiller's "Wilhelm Tell."

[9]Details of scenes and musical numbers prepared from published libretto, printed by T. J. Swords, New York, 1797, and Julian Mates' volume, "The American Musical Stage Before 1800" (Rutgers University Press, New Brunswick, New Jersey, 1962).

[10]Preceded by a tragedy, ROMAN FATHER, or, The Deliverer of His Country, and a comic dance, Devil Upon Two Sticks, by Mr. Francisquy. Later performances were given under the title The CASTLE OF OTRANTO, as per Pelissier's Columbian Melodies (A-R Editions, Inc., Madison, Wisconsin, 1984.)

[11]Musical numbers not listed in programs. List prepared from published English libretto, as THE SICILIAN ROMANCE; or, The Apparition of the Cliffs (printed for J. Barker, Dramatic Repository, London, 1794).

Scene 3
Air (Kind zephyr waft my passing sighs)
Miss Broadhurst
(*Music by* Victor Pelissier.)
Song (Nature, provident in all)
Miss Brett
Scene 4
[Incantation] Spirit of this dread abyss
Mr. J. Hodgkinson
ACT 2
Scene 5
Song (Were I as free as once I was)
Mr. J. Jefferson
ACT 3
Scene 3
Song (Thus, when stormy skies are over)
Miss Broadhurst
Scene 4
Finale (Now ev'ry fear and danger past)
Mr. J. Tyler, Misses Broadhurst, J. Jefferson, Chorus

EDWIN AND ANGELINA, or, The Banditti

1796.03

An Opera (Musical Drama) in Three Acts, based on Oliver Goldsmith's ballad "The Hermit" (found in "The Vicar of Wakefield"). Libretto by Elihu Hubbard Smith. Songs partly from Goldsmith, and partly original. Music by Victor Pelissier. Scenery by (Charles) Ciceri. William Dunlap, Manager. Opened and closed 19 December 1796 at the John Street Theatre after 1 performance.

CAST: *Sifrid*: Mr. (JOHN) HODGKINSON. *Edwin*: Mr. (JOSEPH) TYLER. *(Earl) Ethelbert*: Mr. (JOHN E.) MARTIN. *Walter*: Mr. Crosby. *Edred*: Mr. Munto. *Hugo*: Mr. Miller. *Banditti*: —. *Angelina*: Mrs. (JOHN) HODGKINSON.

Time: That of the Representation.

Act 1: A Forest, on the northern extremity of England.

Act 2: Another part of the Forest.

Act 3: The Entrance of a Hermitage in the Forest. The Inside of the Cavern. The Hermitage.

ACT 1[12]
When wars surround, and dangers rife
Mr. Munto, Banditti
The generous heart, distressed with shame
Mr. J. Hodgkinson
When'er Oppression dares to urge
Mr. J. Hodgkinson
ACT 2
The lover, journeying to his fair
Mr. J. E. Martin
The bird, when summer charms no more
Mrs. J. Hodgkinson
The mother, anxious for her child
Mr. J. Hodgkinson
Sweet are the fleet and flying hours (Duet)
Messrs. J. Hodgkinson, J. E. Martin
ACT 3
O Memory! Thou fond deceiver
Mr. J. Tyler
Turn gentle hermit of the dale
Mrs. J. Hodgkinson
Then turn, my son, and freely share
Mr. J. Tyler
When, in our youth, a friend we find
Mr. J. Hodgkinson
But mine the sorrow, mine the fault
Mrs. J. Hodgkinson
Turn, Angelina, ever dear
Mr. J. Tyler
Now burst the shout of joy around
Chorus, (All)

[12]Detail of scenes and musical numbers prepared from published libretto, printed by T. & J. Swords, New York, 1797.

TOM & JERRY, or, Life in London

1823.01

An Extravaganza Burletta of Fun, Frolic, Fashion and Flash, in Three Acts, 21 Scenes[13]. Play by W. T. Moncrieff, adapted from Pierce Egan's work of the same name. Scenery, dresses by Messrs. Evers and Robins. Produced by Edmund Simpson and Joseph Cowell. Opened 3 March 1823 in repertory at the Park Theatre and closed 4 July 1823[14].

CAST: *Corinthian Tom*: Mr. EDMUND SIMPSON. *Jerry Hawthorn*: JOSEPH COWELL. *Squire Hawthorn*: Mr. Nexsen. *Bob Logic*: Mr. WATKINSON. *Hon. Dick Trifle*: Mr. Richings. *Jemmy Green*: Mr. Bancker. *O'Boozle*: Mr. Anderson. *Tattersall*: Mr. Woodhull. *Tartar*: Mr. Phillips. *Tom Crib*: Mr. Foot. *Mac*: Mr. Kent. *Regular*: Mr. Wheatley. *Mr. Lightfoot*: Mr. Tatin. *O'Boozle*: Mr. Anderson. *Sir Harry Blood*: Mr. Lamb. *Dusty Bob*: Mr. Broad. *Little Jemmy*: Mr. Olliff. *Ragged Jack*: Mr. Stuart. *Seedy*: Mr. Durie. *Marker*: Mr. Went. *African Sal*: Mr. Thompson. *Sportsmen, Jockeys, Noblemen, Fancy lads, Watchmen, Beggars, Debtors, Masqueraders*: Rest of the Company, aided by auxiliaries.

Kate, otherwise the *Hon. Miss Trifle*, otherwise Sir *Jeremy Brag*, otherwise *Nan*, the Match Girl: Mrs. BANCKER. *Sue*, otherwise the *Hon. Miss Trifle*, otherwise *Captain Swaggery*, otherwise *Poll*, the Ballad Singer: Miss JOHNSON. *Jane*, otherwise the *Hon. Miss Trifle*, otherwise *Mrs. Mummery*, the Fortune Teller, otherwise *Sal*, the Pretty Singer: Mrs. (Harriet) HOLMAN. *Mrs. Tartar*: Mrs. Wheatley. *Mrs. Devis*: Miss Chamberlain. *Miss Lightfoot*: Miss I. Durang. *Pirouette*: Miss C. Durang. *Miss Waltzini*: Miss Brundage. *Dancers, Ladies, Beggars*: Rest of the Company.

Act 1, Scene 1: Life in the Country. Sportsman's Cabinet. *Scene 2*: Life in Love. *Scene 3*: Life in Training. Chaffing Crib in Corinthian House. *Scene 4*: Life on Foot. (Evers.) *Scene 5*: Life on Horseback. Interior of Tattersals. (Robins.) How to sell a Horse. *Scene 6*: Life in preparation. *Scene 7*: Life in the West. Almack's Rooms, brilliantly illuminated. (Evers.)

Act 2, Scene 1: Life in Fancy. Cribb's Parlour. (Evers.) *Scene 2*: Life in the Dark. Boxing a Charley. *Scene 3*: Life in the Street. Logic Floor'd—Grand Row. *Scene 4*: Life in St. Dustan's. Interior of Watchhouse. (Evers.) *Scene 5*: Life in a Modern Hell. Gaming House in St. James'. *Scene 6*: Life in Rags. Beggar's Hall in St. Giles'. (Evers.) *Scene 7*: Life in Limbo.

Act 3, Scene 1: Life in Bond Street. Jackson's Rooms. *Scene 2*: Life in the Stars. Interior of Fortune Teller's Garret. *Scene 3*: Life in the East. (Evers.) *Scene 4*: Life in a Nonplus. Logic's Chambers in the Albany. *Scene 5*: Life in a Lark. Masqueraders passing to the Carnival. *Scene 6*: Life in a Mask. *Scene 7*: Grand Carnival. Stage illuminated; and a Beautiful transparency of the Corinthian Column. (Robins and Evers.)

ACT 1
Scene 7
A Minuet and Waltz
Mr. Tatin, Miss C. Durang
A Quadrille and Waltz
Members of the Company
ACT 3
Scene 1
A Scientific Set-to
Mr. Fuller, an amateur
Scene 3
A Pas de Deux
Messrs. Thompson, Broad
Scene 4
A Waltz
Mr. Tatin, Miss I. Durang
Scene 7
Masquerade and Dance
The Characters

MATHEWS AT HOME!/ THE COMIC ANNUAL

1834.01

A Lecture on Men, Manners and Peculiarities, and his last new entertainment, the Comic Annual for 1833, embellished with humorous cuts, eccentric portraits and numerous head and tale pieces. Produced by Stephen Price and Edmund Simpson. Opened 13 October 1834 at the Park Theatre in repertory and closed 31 October 1834.

[13]Accompanied by a varying program of fore-pieces, usually a ballet, and concluding with an after-piece, usually a drama.
[14]Revived 2 October 1823 at the Park Theatre, 9 October 1824 at Chatham Garden Theatre, 16 September 1825 at Chatham Garden Theatre, etc.

CAST: CHARLES MATHEWS

ACT 1[15]

Title Page
Address to the House
Contrasted Characters
Messrs. Verjuice and Honey
The Sun in London
Song—"Humors of a Country Fair"
Embellishment
Josephus Jollyfat, a Gastronomer Astronomer
Lecture on the Solar System to his nephew, and directions for dinner to his cook
Embellishment
The Old Scotch Lady's Leetle Anecdote
A Kirk Story
Sandy Anderson
Cheapside in an uproar
"A Police Report," abridged and described in Song
Mansion House
Embellishment
Double Bedded Room
Living Night Mare
Pie Crust
'What can possibly keep me awake?'
This impression—in sheets

ACT 2

Embellishment
Half Length of a Lady, Mrs. Digby Jones
Conversazione—
Malaprop-riation of Scientific words; new writs
Visits to the Hustings
Song—"General Election"
Shopboard disquisition
Scotch and Irish Opinions upon poetry and poets, Burns, Byron, Scott, Shakespeare
Song—Street Melodists, (a medley) including Welsh, French, Scottish, Irish, Indian, Swiss and English Airs, with Embellishments
Monsieur Tonson

THE DEEP, DEEP SEA,
or, The Sea Serpent!

1834.02

An Original, Mythological, Aquatic, Equestrian Burletta in One Act, 4 Scenes.[16] Play by Charles Dance and James Robinson Planché. Musical yarns strung together and dedicated nauti-cally disposed and Amphitrite in particular, (some of them being handed Over-to-her), by way of Overture, by Mr. William Penson. New scenery by Mr. Evers. Opened 15 November 1834 at the Park Theatre in repertory and closed 4 July 1835 after (18+) performances in repertory. Revived 19 August 1835, 15 December 1835 at the Park Theatre, 23 September 1837 at the Olympic Theatre, 29 July 1839 at the Park Theatre.

CAST[17]: Immortals: *Neptune*, Captain of the Ocean: Mr. (W. H.) LATHAM. *Triton*, his first Lieutenant: Mr. (THOMAS) PLACIDE. *Ditto of the Minnows*, or Middies: Master Kneass. *Amphitrite*, the Captain's Lady: Mrs. Vernon. *Minerva*: Mrs. Durie. *Nereides*, a fair sample of the Sisterhood so-called, ladies who, mirabile dictu!, candidly owned to being fifty: Mesdames Archer, Turnbull, J. Turnbull, E. Turnbull, Simms, Conway, etc. *"Ut sent divorum, Mars, Bacchus, Apollo," etc.*: Messrs. King, Johnson, Harvey, Lackaday, Simms, Case, etc.

Mortals: *Cepheus*, King of Ethiopia, a very fair Monarch considering: Mr. (John) FISHER. *Phineas*, his brother, in love with Andromeda: Mr. T. H. BLAKELEY. *Perseus*, Son of Jupiter and Danae—Ditto with Ditto: Mrs. S. CHAPMAN. *Attendant*: Mr. Johnson. *Cassiope*, the fair Queen of Ethiopia: Mrs. Archer. *Andromeda*, Daughter of Cepheus and Cassiope, bound to her uncle and chained to a rock, but attached to Perseus: Mrs. GURNER. *Black Cook of "The Ocean"*, a white-livered runagate: Mr. Russell. *Great American Sea Serpent*, a Yankee-Doodle come to town—'half man,' with an azure mane, and 'half-alligator,' with an endless tale: Mr. (HENRY) PLACIDE. *Pegasus*: A Real Poney. *Priests of Jupiter, Soldiers, etc.*

Scene 1: The Sub Marine Villa of Neptune. *Scene 2*: Hall in the Palace of King Cepheus. *Scene 3*: Fig Tree Court, Temple of Jupiter Ammon. *Scene 4*: Coast of Ethiopia.

THE SAW MILL,
or, A Yankee Trick

1834.03

A Comic Opera in Two Acts, 13 Scenes. (Libretto) Written and (Music) composed by Micah Hawkins. Orchestra accompaniments by James Hewitt. Scenery and Machinery designed by Mr. H. Reinagle. Dresses characteristic of the country. Produced by H. B. Barrière. Opened 29 November 1834 at the Chatham Garden Theatre and closed 5 February 1835 after (5) performances in repertory.

CAST: *Baron Scharfdenduyvel*[18]: Mr. Morrison. *Count Phlegm*: Mr. Spiller. *Bloom*: Mr. Blake. *Herman*: Mr. Petrie. *(Uncle) Stodoff*: Mr. A. Simpson. *Jacob (Kinner)*: Mr. ROBERTS. *Elna*: Mrs. Allen. *Louisa*: Mrs. Waring. *Norchee*: Mrs. Walstein. *Servants, Canal Lockmen, Workmen on the Saw-Mill, Ladies and Gentlemen, Rustics, &c. Corps de Ballet.*

The action is set first at Rome, afterward at Oneida Creek. State of New York.

Act 1, Scene 1: A library in Bloom's house. *Scene 2*: A Rural Spot. *Scene 3*: Bloom's House and Gardens. In the distance, a pleasant view of Country, &c. *Scene 4*: A mountainous country, through which runs the Grand Canal having a lock in view. *Scene 5*: A room in Baron Scharfdenduyvel's house. *Scene 6*: Same as Scene 3, excepting it is now night, and Bloom's house is brilliantly illuminated.

Act 2, Scene 1: A room in Bloom's house. *Scene 2*: An end and side view of Baron Scharfdenduyvel's house, which is of Holland architecture, and very magnificent. On the left, a large barn, with a number of out-buildings of various sizes and shapes. *Scene 3*: A kind of covert situation, —a copse through which runs a lively stream of water. The place is strewed about with pieces of timber, slabs, shingles, chips, &c. indicative of a spot where a building is being put up. In the foreground a high stump, on which lays a writing book, open. *Scene 4*: A pathway through a forest. *Scene 5*: A room in the Baron's house. *Scene 6*: A sort of blind footpath through a woody retreat, the prominent feature of which is a kind of hovel, composed of decaying logs carelessly thrown together. *Scene 7*: Night. A mountainous and extremely romantic situation. On the right a mill-dam, over part of which the water from the mill-pond tumbles in great luxury. The part of the dam farthest from the audience has attached to it a Saw-Mill, with every necessary appurtenance, tail-race, &c. A Bridge crossing both the tail-race and the sheet of water which rolls over the dam, connects the back with the fore-ground. On the left, through the trees, appear many buildings &c. seemingly of a direct relation with the improvements immediately in view. The extreme distance is bounded by a section of the Grand Canal with a Lock, &c. The fore-ground represents a kind of rude alcove, brilliantly lit up—having tables sumptuously stored with a profusion of every thing. Seats arranged alongside of them, on which is discovered many well-dressed persons of both sexes.

ACT 1[19]

Scene 1
"Richard Bloom, Esq." (Air)
Mr. Roberts
"What joy breaks forth" (Rondo)
Mr. Roberts

Scene 2
"The world forbids it" (Song)
Mrs. Allen

Scene 3
"We will be merry" (Glee)
Messrs. Roberts, Blake, Petrie

Scene 4
Grand Canal Chance Medley
Messrs. Keene, Spiller, Petrie, Roberts, Blake, Collins, Simpson, Wray, etc.
"Cease my heart" (Rondo)
Mrs. Waring

Scene 5
"Rum-Nose Ben" (Duet)
Messrs. Blake, Petrie

[15]First produced in London as THE DEEP, DEEP SEA, or: Perseus and Andromeda.

[16]Mathews further revised the bill on 15 and 20 October 1834 with short farces and sketches.

[17]No program found for beginning of the run. Cast principals from Odell, supporting cast and ensemble from program dated 10 February 1835.

[18]In the published libretto, the character is named Baron Schaffderduval.

[19]Scenes and additional detail of Musical Numbers listed in published libretto (J. & J. Harper, New York, 1824).

Scene 6
"Oh! Yes by Day" (Song)
*Mr. Roberts
"Peace unto this dwelling" (Duet and Trio)
Mrs. Waring, Mrs. Walstein, Mr. Roberts

ACT 2[20]

Scene 1
"Historians and Poets" (Song)(Scotch Air)
Mr. Blake

Scene 2
"Whilst roughest Mountain Tops" (Song)
Mrs. Allen

Scene 3
"Oh! Love sends its Vot'ries on wild expeditions" (Song)
Mrs. Waring

Scene 4
"Thus love doth bind us firm together" (Quartette)
Mrs. Waring, Mrs. Walstein, Messrs. Roberts, Petrie

Scene 7
Waltz
Messrs. Simpson, Saunders
"We read that at the hallowed time" (Song)
Mr. Roberts
Dance (Tune, Possum Up a Gum Tree)
Corps de Ballet
Finale Solo (And long may this saw-mill saw)
Mr. Roberts
[Chorus Characters]

1836.01

NORMAN LESLIE

A Play in Four Acts, 16 Scenes. Adapted by Louisa H. Medina, formed on facts that occurred in this city many years back, on which the novel of the same name by Theodore S. Fay is founded. Scenery by Mr. F. Grain. Dresses by Mr. Lewis. Music by St. Luke. Dances by Mr. Parker. Produced by T. S. Hamblin. Opened 11 January 1836 at the Bowery Theatre in repertory, closing 30 August 1836 after (26+) performances. Revived 17 April 1836 at the Bowery Theatre, 30 July 1838 at the Franklin Theatre, (13) November 1839 at the Bowery Theatre, 4 May 1840 at the Bowery Theatre, 23 January 1842 at the Bowery Theatre, 5 December 1842 at the Chatham Theatre, 11 March 1843 at the Bowery Theatre.

CAST: *Norman Leslie*: Mr. T. S. HAMBLIN. *Mr. Frederick Morton*: Mr. Flynn. *Count Clairmont*: Mr. PICKERING. *Mr. Moreland*: Mr. Woodhull. *Mr. Howard*: Mr. Lewis. *Mr. Romaine*: Mr. Addis. *Mr. Germaine*: Mr. Jackson. *Marquis de Medici*: Mr. Jones. *Conte Bondelmonte*: Mr. Hinckings. *Marquis Torrini*: Mr. Ames. *Raffaelo*: Mr. Baldock. *Footman*: Mr. Beckwell. *Mr. Smith*: Mr. Flint. *Officer of Police*: Mr. Ross. *Crime*: Mr. Bruns. *First Assassin*: Mr. Hayden. *Second Assassin*: Mr. Smith. *Mountebank*: Mr. Strickland. *First Gentleman*: Mr. Hepburne. *Second Gentleman*: Mr. Brough. *Third Gentleman*: Mr. Hill. *Fourth Gentleman*: Mr. Woodley.
Madame Louise: Mrs. Flynn. *Rosalie Romaine*: Mrs. HERRING. *Flora Temple*: Miss Woodhull. *Miss Howard*: Miss BELL. *Fanny Strickland*: Mrs. Farren. *Page*: Miss Turner. *First Lady*: Mrs. Moore. *Second Lady*: Miss Moore.

Act 1, Scene 1: Broadway by the American Hotel. Several calls on Count Clairmont. Leslie introduced by Miss Howard—inspection of diamonds—ring missed—sleighing—Louise, fair Italian, and child, rescued by Norman Leslie. *Scene 2*: A magnificent Ball Room—Quadrille party, which will consist of the most fashionable and popular dances, as now danced in private circles, such as Quadrilles, Waltzes and Gallopades—Morton making love to Flora Temple—quarrels with Count Clairmont and retires. *Scene 3*: Room in City Hotel—Morton sends for Norman Leslie and informs him he will challenge the Count—Leslie gives good reasons for his not doing so—Count enters—dispute between him and Leslie. *Scene 4*: Chamber in Mrs. Temple's—Gentlemen discovered after dinner—quarrel with Leslie and Clairmont.

Act 2, Scene 1: The house of Mrs. Romaine at Bloomingdale—a chamber in which Rosalie is seen reclining on a sofa—she remains full dressed, as if just returned from the Ball. *Scene 2*: A dark wood on the North River—Mr. Romaine's house in the distance (Grain.)—interview with her and Clairmont—Rosalie meets Leslie. *Scene 3*: A room—Norman Leslie arrested for the murder of Rosalie Romaine. *Scene 4*: Lock-up room in Bridewell—Leslie confined—affecting interview between him and Moreland. *Scene 5*: Interior of the City Hall—Trial by jury—Norman Leslie pleads his own cause.

Act 3: Norman Leslie wanders despised and shunned by all—Fall of the thunderbolt—Mr. Temple's house on fire—Flora Temple in imminent peril—Leslie rescues her. [Six years are supposed to elapse between the third and fourth acts.]

Act 4, Scene 1: Italian Palazzo, and Gardens by Sunset—Grain.)—Stage gaily adorned with rural garlands—Peasants Dancing and Singing—Louise descends splendidly attired—she walks up—Peasants arrange in line and sing as Norman enters, "To the land where amorous Petrarch sighed." *Scene 2*: A room with sliding door concealed in panel—(Grain). *Scene 3*: Church of St. Peters. Grand Square and Statue of St. Leo—(Grain.) Procession of White Novices—Hymn. "Ave Maria! Virgo blest."—Procession of Monks. *Scene 4*: A Street—(Grain.). *Scene 5*: Carnival Masquerade. In order to give full space for the spectacle, the Mazeppa scaffolding is pulled down, and every inch of this immense space thrown open for the following groups of characters: Alexander and Queens—Shylock—Richard III—Hamlet-—Falconbridge—Falstaff—Two Dromios—Othello—Virginius—Julius Caesar —Cardinal Woolsey—Timon of Athens—Orestes—Achilles—Pylades—Macbeth—Macduff—Tippoo Saib—Ali Pacha—Mahomet—Soothsayers—Knight Templars— Richard Coeur de Lion—Archduke of Austria—Nicholas of Russia—Polish officers—Virgins of the Sun—Arab Rovers—Conrad the Corsair—Indian Chiefs, Black Hawk and Red Jacket—Minstrels—Jews—Banditti—Alessandro Massaroni —Brigands—Gondoliers, Celebrated Russian Dance, entitled the "Mazourka," which will be performed by 16 Ladies and Gentlemen in full costume. Spanish Dance with Castanets by Madame Trust. Arrival of a Company of Morice Dancers, who will go through an entire new Comic, Laughable Extravaganza, arranged expressly for this occasion by Mr. Parker, entitled The Humors of a Country Wake, with a style of dresses never seen before in this country. *Scene 6*: Coliseum in Ruins—Marble Arches—Broken Colonades through which Moonlight shines. Grand Denouement! Fearful mystery explained.

1838.01

AMILIE, or, The Love Test

An Opera in Three Acts, 4 Scenes. Libretto by J. T. Haines. Music by William Michael Rooke. Scenery by Mr. Bengough. Chorus and orchestra under the direction of Penson. Produced by J. W. Wallack. Opened 15 October 1838 at the National Theatre in repertory, season closing 28 June 1839. Revived 14 October 1839 at the National Theatre, Broadway, adjoining Niblo's Garden, 12 October 1842 at the Olympic Theatre.

CAST: *Count von der Teimer*: Mr. (EDWARD) SEGUIN. *Jose Spechbacker*: Mr. (JOHN) WILSON. *Brenner*: Mr. Horncastle. *Gervaise Grenadot*: Mr. W. H. Williams. *Paul Pesta*: Mr. A. Andrews. *Jean Piednoir*: Mr. Blakeley. *Hans Meyer*: Mr. Duggan. *Babet*: Mrs. Cantor. *Amilie*: Miss (JANE) SHIRREFF. *Lelia*: Mrs. W. Penson. *Chorus*: Misses Mary Taylor, Singleton, etc.

Act 1: The Village of Winklern. Exterior of the Church.

Act 2: A vaulted cavern, supposed to be on the side of the great Glochner. The Valley of Eysach far below.

Act 3, Scene 1: Gardens of the Château de Rosen, and part of the castle with steps. *Scene 2*: Another part of the garden.

ACT 1[21]

Introduction
Recitative and Air, "'Tis now the hour 'ere darkness flies"
"Come, gather, brave hunters"
A. Andrews, J. Wilson
Recitative and air, "The ice-clad alp"
"Who has not mark'd"
J. Wilson
Hymn to the Dead: "Rest. Spirit. Rest"
J. Shirreff, Chorus
Recitative, Air and Polonaise: "Oh, Love art thou true"
"Thou Art Gone"
"O, love, thou'rt near me"
J. Shirreff

[20]Contrary to the program, the published libretto contains the following at the opening scene to Act 2:
I won't,—I will, I will but say
Mr. Roberts
"Historians, poets, painters all" appears in the middle of Act 2, Scene 3. Appearing in the published libretto in Act 2, Scene 3, is the following dialect song:
Yenkeetutels come to town
A. Simpson

[21]Musical numbers not listed in programs. List of Scenes and Musical Numbers prepared from published libretto (Abbott & Co., Melbourne, Australia, 1864).

Song, "To the Vine-feast"
Mrs. W. Penson
Recitative and solo "My Boyhood's home"
E. Seguin
Finale to Act 1: Recitative and air: "O fatal; chance"
J. Shirreff, J. Wilson
Quintette "Should I reveal"
J. Shirreff, J. Wilson, E. Seguin, Mrs. W. Penson, Mr. Duggan
Solo, "Beware, that hour"
E. Seguin

ACT 2
Grand scena, "By passion toss'd"
"Time, time thou cheat of human bliss"
Recitative, "Thou shrouded fiend"
Air, "Yes, methinks I see her smiling"
J. Wilson
Duet
J. Wilson, [Pierre]
Recitative, "What juggling fiend bows to thy power?"
Air, "When the red star hath risen o'er the lake and o'er the lea"
Chorus of Hunters, "To the mountain (away)"
Solo, "What is the spell which in manhood's dawn"
E. Seguin
Recitative and solo, "Though, sun thou fliest"
J. Shirreff
"When the morning first dawns"
Finale, "It looks the picture of good nature"

ACT 3
Scene 1
Recitative, "Still as death"
[Pierre, Wilhelm]
Chorus of Gipsies, "Tarry not, brother"
Solo, "Under the tree, 'neath the merry green tree"
[Pierre]
Solo, "Oh! I remember"
J. Shirreff
Trio, "We swear - thus joined - we swear"
E. Seguin, J. Wilson, A. Andrews

Scene 2
Finale "Farewell, O thou world"
Quartette "To this heart where love ne'er dieth"
J. Shirreff, E. Seguin, Mrs. W. Penson, [Anderl]

1839.01 THE STRANGE GENTLEMAN/ THE ROOF SCRAMBLER

A Multiple Bill of a Comic Burletta and a Burlesque Ballet Opera[22]. Produced by William Mitchell. Opened 16 December 1839 at the Olympic Theatre in repertory; season closed 30 May 1839.

THE STRANGE GENTLEMAN!, a comic burletta by Boz [Charles Dickens]. Returned 21 September 1840 to the Olympic Theatre in repertory.

CAST: *The Strange Gentleman*: Mr. (J. S.) BROWNE. *Tom Sparks*: Mr. (WILLIAM) MITCHELL. *John Johnson*: Mr. (HENRY) HORNCASTLE. *Owen Overton*: Mr. ANDERSON. *Charles Tomkins*: Mr. RUSSELL. *Mary Wilson*: Mrs. Plumer. *Julia*: Miss Randolph. *Fanny Wilson*: Miss Fitzgerald. *Mrs. Noakes*: Mrs. Jones.

THE ROOF SCRAMBLER, a grand burlesque ballet opera on "La Sonnambula"[23]. Musical director, George Loder. Presented in repertory for 34 performances during the season. Returned 1 October 1840 to the Olympic Theatre in repertory.

CAST[24]: *Swelvino*, a Sexton: Mr. (HENRY) HARDCASTLE. *Rodolpho*, Inspector of Police: Mr. RUSSELL. *Notary*: Mr. Everard. *Bobbo*, a Fool: Mr. Johnson. *Molly Brown*, a greasy roamer over the tops of houses as originally performed by him in London: Mr. (WILLIAM) MITCHELL. *Lizzy*: Miss Randolph. *Therese*: Mrs. Jones.

1840.01 LA MUSQUITOE

A Comic Burlesque Ballet in Two Scenes[25]. Music has been begged, borrowed and stolen from all sorts of Operas and Ballets, in the most impudent and free and easy style—by the music director George Loder. Produced by William Mitchell. Opened 21 May 1840 at the Olympic Theatre in repertory; season closed 30 May 1840, resumed 10 June-1 July 1840.

CAST: *Low-Dickey*: Mr. RUSSELL. *Doctor Low-Belia*: Mr. Johnson. *Low-Retta*: Mr. (WILLIAM) MITCHELL. *Low-thea*, Mother of Low-Retta: Mrs. Penson. *Signora Low-Rinde*: Mrs. JONES.

This Ballet is founded upon the well-known properties of the Musquitoe, whose bite renders the patient exceedingly impatient, and throws him into a fit of scratching, slapping and swearing delirium, technically termed the "Cacoethes Scratchedni," causing the unfortunate sufferer to cut capers enough for several legs of mutton.

The scene now lies in Hoboken.

Low-Dickey loves Low-Retta.

(Scene 1) An awful accident happens—Abduction of La Signora Low-Rinde by Shad-Fishers. Low-Dicky assembles his friends. Invocation to cowhides—they rush to her rescue-Success of their virtuous and valorous efforts—Gratitude of Low-Rinde—She retires to take a Nap.

A Traveler who has come all the way from the other side of the North River now appears—the bombastic and wealthy Doctor Low-Belia, whose wife fell overboard on the passage. He professes ardent affection for Low-Retta—She considers him an old fool and retires, declaring her love for Low-Dicky.

An unexpected occurrence unexpectedly occurs—Low-Rettta rushes on frightened and shaking like several Skaters—Low-Dicky has been bitten by a Musquitoe—and she describes his delirium—his slapping, scratching and panting agony. The old Doctor refuses to cure Low-Dicky unless Low-Retta will consent to marry him—Low-Retta to save Low-Dicky consents, and is led away in an awful stew.

Scene 2. The plot thickens into the consistence of a London Fog—Low-Retta does all sorts of things—so-do-all the other people—until at last a circumstance occurs which settles the Doctor's love-making—and Low-Retta is united to her beloved Low-Dicky, and the piece ends with a Saltatorial Exhibition of extraordinary and overwhelming beauty. The view of Hoboken is from an original sketch taken on the spot.

1840.02 1940!, or, Crummles in Search of Novelty

A Local Extravaganza in One Act, 3 Scenes[26]. (Play by A. Allan.) Scenery by Mr. Bengough. Produced by William Mitchell. Opened 15 October 1840 at the Olympic Theatre in repertory, closing 24 November 1840 after 35 consecutive performances; resumed 30 November 1840 in repertory, with season ending 5 June 1841.

CAST: *Crummles*, formerly manager of the Portsmouth Theatre, now of the Olympic: Mr. (WILLIAM) MITCHELL. *Mr. Alleyn*, a scribe: Mr. RUSSELL. *Miss Thomasina Bell*, a female auctioneer: Mr. (GEORGE) GRAHAM. *Wriggle*, an un-natural philosopher: Mr. (WILLIAM) EDWIN. *Isaac Walton*, an angler: Mr. ROBERTS. *Schneiderkin*, a Tailor: Mr. Barnett. *Grub Up*, an antique Antiquary: Mr. CUNNINGHAM. *Anna Maria Josephine Kicksey*, a female Groom: Miss FLYNN. *Fancy*, a flight-y lady: Mrs. Timm. *Time* 'thou cheat of human bliss': Mrs. Strebor. *Melpomene*, the Tragic muse: Mrs. Watts. *Thalia*, the Comic muse: Miss Turnbull. *Clotho, Lachaesis, Atropos*, the Fates (3): Misses Randall, Singleton, Mrs. Baldock. *Miss Alexina Black*, Clerk at Tatter's-sale Room: Mrs. MONTGOMERY. *Mermaids*: Mere Maids, Matrons & Other Queer Fish.

Scene 1: (1840) Crummles puzzled. Novelty announced but not come-at-ible. Invocation to, & sudden appearance of fancy. Crummles starts on a voyage of discovery.

Scene 2: 1940! Tatter's-sale Room, a Mart for the sale of Men Martryrs. Ladies in the Ascendant—"Going! Going!! Gone!!!" Niblo's a Hundred years hence. "Can such

---

[22]The order of the program on Opening night was: THE STRANGE GENTLEMAN, the petite opera MATRIMONY, THE ROOF SCRAMBLER, and a drama 347 BROADWAY.

[23]Suggested by the famous opera by Vincenzo Bellini.

[24]The roles of Lizzy and Therese did not appear in the program until the second performance.

[25]Inspired by the highly publicized appearance of ballet artiste Fanny Ellsler 14 May 1840 at the Park Theatre. LA MUSQUITOE was accompanied on opening by The Waterman, La Crack-a-Vein! (a burlesque Ellsler's ballet 'La Cracovienne'), and The Tiger at Large; or, The Cad of the "Buss." Following LA MUSQUITOE was an after-piece, UNFORTUNATE MISS BAILEY.

[26]Presented as one of a program of three or four pieces, usually farces or burlettas. Beginning 1 January 1841 the production was retitled, 1941! Or. .Crummles in Search of Novelty.

things be?" The March of Miracles. Improvements in Railroads and Balloons—Tall Travelling! The Mermaids' Cave. "Where the rocks of Coral grow." *Scene* 3: Return to the present Time! 1840! A Well Known Fashionable Resort! Crummles between Tragedy and Comedy! Behold and make your choice! Grand Tableau Vivant. The Trial of Queen Catherine. Comic Tableau. Thalia must reign! Finale!

1840.03 BUY-IT-DEAR, 'TIS MADE OF CASHMERE

A Burlesque Operatic Ballet in One Act (inspired by the popular ballet "La Bayadère, or The Maid of Cashmere"). (Burlesque by James Henry Horncastle.) Produced by William Mitchell. Opened 2 November 1840 at the Olympic Theatre, closing 5 December 1840 after 30 consecutive performances; resumed in repertory during the season which closed 5 June 1841.

CAST: *The Unknown*, afterwards discovered to be the celebrated ———: Mr. (WILLIAM) EDWIN. *Brutus Bumble*, an amatory old overseer: Mr. (GEORGE) GRAHAM. *Chopitda*, a Soup-erior officer: Mr. CUNNINGHAM. *Snivellum*, a ringing, singing, jingling, tingling noisy old bellman: Mr. ROBERTS. *Guards, Slaves, Porters and Officers.*

Mad'lle. Tinker, the head of the Buy-a-Brooms, telling Chloe's *tale* in a song; Mrs. TIMM. *La Belle Fatty-ma*, an oleaginous beauty: Mr. RUSSELL. *Chloe*, the Terpsichorean Saltatorial leader of the dancing Buy-a-Brooms: Miss TURNBULL. *Antique Anna*, an elderly lady: Mrs. Watts. *The Buy-a-Brooms (6)*: *Plumpa*: Mrs. Baldock. *Pootypet*: Miss Singleton. *Longy*: Miss Randall. *Dumpy*: Miss Flynn. *Fatiste*: Mrs. Barnett. *Peeky*: Mrs. Montgomery.

MUSICAL NUMBERS

"Here on the Stoop" (Opening Chorus)
"Active am I" (Recitative and Aria)
"Broom Buy a Broom" (Chorus)
"Vait Sare and hear von little story" (Song from LE POSTILLON)
"Charming little Broom Girl" (Song)
"This Thimble take" (Song)
"My heart is torn asunder" (Solo and Grand Chorus)
"Life, long life" (Chorus)
"Beats there a heart?" (Song)
"When Chloe awakens" (Song)
"I love her, I love her" (Song)
"I beg your pardon" (Trio)
"Oh! Happy Cat and Bagpipes" (Duet)
"Kind wishes waft over you" (Grand Finale)

DANCES

Entrée of the Buy-a-Brooms
Grand Broom Dance
Procession of the Palanquin
Grand Trial Dance

1840.04 THE CAT'S IN THE LARDER, or, The Maid with a Parasol

A Burlesque, Operatic Burletta on "La Gazza Ladra, or The Maid of Palaiseau," in One Act, 5 Scenes. Play by James Henry Horncastle after the opera by Gioacchino Rossini). Music arranged by George Loder. Scenery by Mr. Bengough. Stage arrangements by Mr. (William) Mitchell. Opened 23 December 1840 in repertory at the Olympic Theatre, closing 24 January 1841 after 27 consecutive performances; resumed in repertory throughout season ending 5 June 1841.

CAST: *Fernando Villyebilly*, an old soldier of the U.S. Army—with his old martial cloak around him: Mr. (WILLIAM) MITCHELL. *Fitzfritto Velscore*, Master of the "Friends Retreat," a hotel formerly upon the Harlem Road: Mr. CUNNINGHAM. *William Velscore*, his son vacated for the vacation and the main instrument in bringing on the 'cat-as-trophe' of the piece: Mr. RUSSELL. *Ikey Ikey*, a clock-maker, a very distant relation to Stan Slick: Mr. (GEORGE) GRAHAM. *Blazes*, a gentleman of color, and a waiter at the "Friends Retreat;" Mr. Roberts. *Mr. Leary Roche*, a Justice of the Peace—punishing the passion of other people, but able to control his own: Mr. (WILLIAM) EDWIN. *Anthony*, his clerk embodying the old adage: Mr. Clarke. *The Tom Cat*: Le Petit Inconnu. *Guests, Constables, etc.*

Mrs. Fitzfritto Velscore, a shrewd woman, but a bitter shrew: Mrs. WATTS. *Janetta*, a bar-maid, daughter of Villyebilly—virtuous, and persecuted orthodoxically: Mrs. TIMM. *Miss Kookensnivey*, a young lady wot dances: Miss TURNBULL. *Ladies, Guests, etc.*

Scene: New York and its environs.

MUSICAL NUMBERS[27]

Scene 1

Opening Chorus (Air of 'Let's haste to the wedding')(Let us haste to the wedding)
Chorus
Recitative (Air of 'Di pacer mi balza il cor')(Deep in the chair)
Mrs. Timm
Aria (Air of 'Oh, you will come today')
Mrs. Timm
Song (Air of "Clar de Kitchen')(Clocks, clocks, clocks, who'll buy my clocks?)
Mr. Graham
Song (Air from 'PAUL AND VIRGINIA')(What sound strikes my ear?)
Mrs. Timm
Dance (The Xaleo de Xeres)
Miss Turnbull
Grand Scena (Air of 'Bow, wow, wow!')(Last night, just as the sun, behind)
Mr. Mitchell
Ballad (Air of 'My Pretty Jane')(My pretty Jane, my bar-maid Jane)
Mr. Edwin
Song (Air of 'She wore a wreath of roses')(He wore upon his person)
Mrs. Timm
Trio (Air of "Oh nume benefico')(Thank fate; I am hither sent)
(Air changes to 'Mrs. Sneak and I')
Messrs. Mitchell, Edwin, Mrs. Timm

Scene 2

Sestette and Grand Chorus (Airs from LA GAZZA LADRA)
(Oh hear a red-rosed feather)
Messrs. Mitchell, Edwin, Graham, Mrs. Timm, [Mrs. Ikey], Chorus

Scene 3

Ballad (Air of 'The Bridal Ring')(I dreamed, last night of my early days)
Mr. Edwin
Trio (Air of 'Hark! Tis the Indian Drum')(Yes like the Indian drum)
Mrs. Timm, Messrs. Edwin, Russell

Scene 4

Song (Air of 'Kelvin Grove')(Yes, I'll haste to Centre Street)
Mr. Mitchell

Scene 5

Finale, Solos and Chorus (Airs of LA GAZZA LADRA)
(Farewell, Janetta's sorrow)
All

1841.01 THE NAIAD QUEEN, or, The Mysteries of the Lurlie Berg!

A Mythological and Romantic Drama (Legendary Ballet Spectacle) in Four Acts[28]. Play by W. E. Burton. Original music by Mr. Woolf. Produced under the direction of Joseph Foster. Armor, dresses, banners, trophies and appointments by Mr. Foster. Scenery by Messrs. J. R. Smith, Hiester. Musical director, Mr. Duggan. Dances designed by Madame Petit and Mr. D. Oakey. Produced by W. E. Burton. Opened 21 April 1841 at the National Theatre and closed 22 May 1841 after 24 performances in repertory.

CAST: *Sir Rupert*, the Fearnought, a Knight of Fortune: Mr. SHAW. *Companions-in-arms of Sir Rupert, the Fearnought (6)*: *Winkleman*: Mr. Byrne. *Almagro*: Mr. Stanley. *Roland*: Mr. Sherman. *Manfrid*: Mr. Philips. *Calmar*: Mr. Boulard. *Siegefried*: Mr. Ford. *The Baron of Lorchhausen*: Mr. H. LEWIS. *Greinwald, Rodolph*, his Castellians: Messrs. Green, Newton. *Schnapps*, Sir Rupert's Squire: Mr. W. E. BURTON. *Amphibeo*, the Demon Sprite of the Rhine: Mr. D. OAKEY. *Rithen, Rual*, Dwarf Demons of the Lurlie Berg: Masters Reed, Foster. *Demons of the Dark Submarine Cavern of Lurlie*: Messrs. Nelson, B. Williams, C. Williams, Reed, Gleson, Keyser, Paullin, Lewis, King, Romaine, Wilson, Shepherd.

[27]Cast list and list of musical numbers prepared from published libretto (William Applegate, New York, 1840).

[28]Beginning 28 April 1841, THE NAIAD QUEEN was accompanied by a short farce, either as fore-piece or after-piece.

English Companions of Sir Rupert: *Sir Albert de Tracy*: Mr. Cowley. *Sir Reginald Volt*: Mr. Jones. *Sir Egbert Harold*: Mr. Wiley. *Sir Alfred de Bracey*: Mr. Smith. *Sir Thomas de Clifford*: Mr. Anderson. *Sir Hugh de Montfort*: Mr. Bracy.

French Knights, Companions of the Fearnought: *Sir Jean de Moreau*: Mr. Sweeney. *Alvitz*, the Knight of Bouleau: Mr. Green. *Sir Reine de Calvez*: Mr. Prosser. *Sir Attamount of Orgaleau*: Mr. Harbright. *Marquis de Villecour*: Mr. Hanker. *Richemont*, a Knight of Chalons: Mr. King.

German Knight Companions of Sir Rupert: *Sir Albert Roustan*: Mr. Gray. *Sir Roderick Revault*: Mr. Miller. *Sir Trewalt de Ritzberg*: Mr. Caleraft. *The Landgrave of Inspruck*: Mr. Nathewson. *Sir Guy the Bold*, Count of Malvert: Mr. Haines. *The Margrave of Anspack*, surnamedthe Black Knight of the Rock: Mr. Hagert.

Soldiers, Attendants of the Fearnought, and the Baron of Lorchhausen, Warders of the Castle, Banner Bearers, Pages, etc.: Numerous train of Auxiliaries.

The Naiad Queen: Miss (CHARLOTTE) CUSHMAN. *Coraline*, her Favorite Naiad: Miss Randolph. *Fluvine*: Miss Josephine Shaw. *Idex*, a Dancing Naiad: Miss CELESTE WILLIAMS. *Jona*, companion to Idex: Miss Jones. *The Lady Una of Lorchhausen*: Mrs. H. ISHERWOOD. *Bridget*, the Housekeeper of Lorchhausen Castle: Mrs. Rivers. *Naiads, Water Nymphs, and submarine spirits*, subservient to the power of The Naiad Queen: Mesdames Ferrers, A'Becket, Foster, Brooks, Ribas, Higgs, Knight, Johnson, Stubbs, Murray, Hilson, Andrews, Jones, Misses Jones, Collingborne, Blunt, Ince, Warner, Carpenter, King, Norman, Pitt, Weston, Bryan, Cooke, Honor, Haggerty, Holloway, Aaron, Sherwood, Mann, Hill, Peters, Smith, Simpson, Thompson, Hargreeve, Johnson, Andrews, Fisher, Joy, Cooper, Whitney, Wilson, Stuart, Power, Andrews, Stohwasser, Patterson.

Act 1: Hall in the Castle of St. Goar; the Mysteries of Lurlie Berg; The Bath of Beauty!. (Heister.)

Act 2: The Adamantine Chamber; Grand Stalactistic Hall. (Heister.)

Act 3: Sumptuous Banquet in the Castle of Lorchhausen (Smith); Gothic Hall with Painted Windows (Smith); Crystal Palace of the Naiad Queen (Heister); Chamber in Lorchhausen Castle (Heister); Submarine Hall; Gothic Hall (Smith); The Palace of Terraces (Smith).

ACT 1

"One Cheer More Will Add to the Score" (Glee and Chorus)
Mr. Shaw, Chorus

ACT 2

The Demons' Dance
Messrs. Oakey, Foster, Reed

Ballet

Beautiful Scarf Movement
Nymphs

Pas Seul

Pas de Naiade

Classic Tableau—Lighted by Colored Fire

ACT 3

Song
Miss Randolph

Song
Mr. Burton

Military Evolutions
50 Female Warriors

Double Procession of the Sons of the Earth and the Daughters of the Deep

1844.01 THE BOHEMIAN GIRL

A Grand Opera in Three Acts, 5 Scenes[29]. (Libretto by Alfred Bunn, after Jules-Henri Vernoy de Saint-Georges' and Mazilier's ballet-pantomime "La Gypsy," adapted from the story "La Gitanella" by Cervantes). Music by Michael William Balfe. Scenery by Mr. Hillyard. Costumes and decorations by Mr. Dejonge. Machinery by Mr. Speyers. Maître de Ballet, Monsieur Martin. Musical director and conductor, Mr. Chubb. Opened 25 November 1844 at the Park Theatre and closed 14 December 1844 after 17 performances in repertory.

CAST: *Thaddeus*, a proscribed Pole: Mr. FRAZER. *Devilshoof*, Chief of the Gipsey Tribe: EDWARD SEGUIN. *Count Arnheim*, Governor of Presburg: A. Andrews. *Florestein* his nephew: S. Pearson. *Captain of the Guard*: Mr. Kneass. *Officer*: Mr. Freeland. *Gipsey*: Mr. Anderson.

Arline, the Count's Daughter, in Acts 2, 3: Mrs. ANNE SEGUIN. *Arline*, Act 1: Miss Dyott. *Buda*, her attendant: Mrs. John Dyott. *Queen of the Gipsies*: Mrs. KNIGHT.

Chorus (of Nobles, Huntsmen, Gipsies, etc.): Messrs. Pearson, Pearson, Jr., Holman, Van Pragg, Selle, Colman, Sardoff, Litch, Gallot, Kneass, Schneph, Kavanagh, Leach, Harris, Povey, Gourlay, etc. Mesdames Boulard, Barton, Hiffart, Wiesa, Burrows, Griffith, Jacobson, Willis, etc. .

Principal Dancers: Misses JULIA TURNBULL, Mons. MARTIN, assisted by Misses St. CLAIR, COHEN and a Corps de Ballet. Messrs. King, Charles, Wilson, Henrique, Whalan, Joseph, Hoffman, Emilius. Misses Jacobs, Yates, (Mrs.) Gallot, Rosa, Delia, Augusta, Clara, Ritter.

Act 1: The Castle and Grounds of Count Arnheim on the Danube near Presburg.

Act 2, Scene 1: A Street in Presburg, by moonlight. The tent of the Queen of the Gipsies. Twelve years later. *Scene 2*: Another street in Presburg, daylight. *Scene 3*: A Grand Fair in the Public Square of Presburg.

Act 3: A splendid salon in the Castle of Count Arnheim.

ACT 1[30]

"Up with the banner" (Opening Chorus)
Chorus

"A soldier's life" (Solo)
A. Andrews

"Without friends" (Recitative)
Mr. Frazer

"'Tis sad to leave our fatherland" (Cavatina)
Mr. Frazer

"In the gipsy's life you read" (Chorus)
Gipsies

"Comrade, your hands" (Duet)
Mr. Frazer, E. Seguin

"Is no succour near at hand?" (Solo)
S. Pearson

"What means this alarm?"
Mr. Frazer

"Down with the daring slave" (Concerted Piece)
Mr. Frazer, E. Seguin, A. Andrews, S. Pearson, Chorus

"What sounds break on the ear?" (Ensemble)
Chorus

"Thou in might supreme" (Prayer)

"Follow, follow" (Finale)

ACT 2

"Silence, silence! The lady moon" (Solo and Chorus)
Mrs. Knight, S. Pearson, E. Seguin, Gipsies

"I dreamt I dwelt in marble halls" (Ballad)
A. Seguin

"The wound upon thine arm" (Duet)
A. Seguin, Mr. Frazer

"What is the spell hath yet effaced" (Recitative)
A. Seguin

"Listen, while I relate the hope of a gipsy's fate" (Concerted Piece)
A. Seguin, Mrs. Knight, E. Seguin, Mr. Frazer, etc.

"In the gipsy's life you read" (reprise)
Gipsies

"'Tis gone—the past was all a dream"
Mrs. Knight

"This is thy deed" (Duet)
Mrs. Knight, Mr. Frazer

"In the gipsies' life. ."/"Come with the gipsy bride" (Tambourine Song)
Chorus, A. Seguin

"Life itself is at the best" (Chorus)
Chorus

"From the Valleys and Hills" (Quartette)
A. Seguin, Mrs. Knight, etc.

"Sir Knight and Lady, Listen" (Solo)
A. Seguin

"Shame! Shame!" (Concerted Piece)
Principals, Chorus

[29]Followed by a farce, GONE TO TEXAS; the after-piece was changed repeatedly during the run.

[30]Musical numbers not listed in programs. List prepared from published piano vocal score (Boosey & Hawkes, London, 1843), recordings.

"The heart bow'd down" (Song)
A. Andrews
"Hold! hold!"
A. Seguin, A. Andrews, S. Pearson, A. Andrews, etc.

ACT 3
Introduction/"The past appears to me but a dream"
A. Seguin
"Then you'll remember me" (Ballad)
Mr. Frazer
"Through the world thou wilt fly, love" (Trio)
A. Seguin, Mr. Frazer, E. Seguin
"Welcome the present" (Concerted Piece)
A. Seguin, Mrs. Knight, S. Pearson, A. Andrews
"Though every hope be fled" (Quartette)
A. Seguin, Mrs. Knight, Mr. Frazer, S. Pearson, A. Andrews
"See at your feet a suppliant one" (Solo)
A. Seguin
"When the fair land of Poland" (Song)
Mr. Frazer
"Pity for one in childhood torn" (Solo)
Mr. Frazer
"The feuds of a nation's strife" (Solo)
A. Andrews
"Let not the soul for sorrows grieve" (Trio)
A. Seguin, Mr. Frazer, A. Andrews
"Oh, what full delight" (Finale)
A. Seguin, Chorus

1845.01 THE BOHEA-MAN'S GIRL

A Local Burlesque (of Balfe's "The Bohemian Girl") in One Act, 2 Scenes. Written by B. A. Baker. Music arranged by George Loder. Scenery by Mr. Bengough. Stage arrangements by Mr. (William) Mitchell. Properties by Mr. Roberts. Machinery by Mr. Burns. Produced by William Mitchell. Opened 11 March 1845 at the Olympic Theatre in repertory, closing 25 April 1845 after (20) performances; returned 10 November 1845 to the Olympic Theatre in repertory; revived 29 November 1849 at the Olympic Theatre in repertory.

CAST: *Mr. Harniem*, a retired tea merchant: Mr. (BENEDICT) DeBAR. *Floorstain*, his hopeful nephew: Mr. (CHARLES M.) WALCOT. *Thady*, an exiled tea merchant from the Bowery: Mr. DENNISON. *M.P.*, of the New Police: Mr. Levere. *Hoopincough*, a Ragpicker Chieftain: Mr. EVERARD. *Jake Jenkins*, Mr. Rea. *Mr. Oldschool*, a liberal minded man: Mr. Bleeker. *Arline*, a fine specimen of young Harlem: Miss EMMA TAYLOR. *Arline*, twelve years older and supposed to be the same individual: Miss MARY TAYLOR. *Mrs. Quin*, Landlady of the "Hotel de Ragpickers": Mr. (JOHN) NICKINSON. *Buder*, a very Careless Nurse: Miss ROBERTS.

Ragpickers, Visitors, Roulette Man, Thimble Rig, &c.: Messrs. Rosenthal, Lee, Clark, Roberts, Smith. Mesdames Everard, Isherwood, Dunn, Webb, Pray, Selwyn, Phillips, &c.

Scenes: 12 years is supposed to have elapsed between the first and second scenes.

MUSICAL NUMBERS
"Hurrah for Bowery Tea" (Opening Chorus)
Neighbors
"Through all my life" (Song)
Mr. DeBar
"Bless the Bohea-Man's Name" (Chorus)
Neighbors
"'Tis Sad to Leave a Business Grand" (Song)
Mr. Dennison
"Thus we pick up in the Street" (Chorus)
Ragpickers
"Good gracious! Is any one Near" (Song)
Mr. Walcot
"I Dreamt I had Money to Buy a Shawl" (Song)
Miss Taylor
"That scratch upon thy Nose" (Duet)
Mr. Dennison, Miss Taylor
Ragpickers Attend (Concerted Piece)
Miss Taylor, Messrs. Nickinson, Everard, Chorus
"Now I'm Dear Thady's Bride" (Song and Chorus)
Miss Taylor, Ragpickers
"Bad luck, I've lost my Thad" (Song)
Mr. Nickinson
"This is the Place for Fun" (Chorus)
Citizens
Song
Miss Taylor
"When e'er I on the Canvas look" (Song)
Mr. DeBar
"Once I knew a Pretty Girl" (Song)
Mr. Everard
"When other Gents" (Song)
Mr. Dennison
"Fly thro' the Window with me" (Trio)
Mr. Dennison, Miss Taylor, Mr. Everard
"A Store in the Bowery" (Song)
Mr. Dennison
Finale
All the Characters

1846.01 THE ENCHANTRESS

A Grand Operatic Drama (Light Opera) in Three Acts and a Prologue. Libretto by Alfred Bunn, adapted from a text by J. H. Vernoy de Saint-Georges. Music by Michael William Balfe and Mr. Cunnington. Scenery by Mr. Wiser. Produced under the direction of J. Foster. Opened 25 May 1846 at the Chatham Theatre and closed 6 June 1846 after ?12 performances.

CAST: *Ramir*: Mr. DeBAR. *Don Sylvio*: Mr. J. BOOTH, JR. *Doctor Mathanasius*: Mr. BELLAMY. *Forte Bracchio*: Mr. REA. *Nuegez*: Mr. Dennison. *Pietro*: Mr. Van Stavoren. *Duc d'Acquila*: Mr. Jackson. *Galca*, minister: Mr. Van Stavoren. *Mumbo Jumba*: Mr. Resor. *Pamba Puncho*: Mr. Greene. *Zenofoco Puncho*: Mr. Winans. *Goliah Puncho*: Mr. Foster. *Slendor Puncho*: Susan Dennin. *Mushroom*, Cook to the Palace: Mr. Crouta. *First Greek*: Mr. Bradshaw. *Second Greek*: Mr. Foster. *Alexis*: Mr. Stafford. *Fisrt Officer*: Mr. Matthews. *Second Officer*: Mr. Barnett. *First Senator*: Mr. Matthews. *Second Senator*: Mr. Van Stavoren. *Third Senator*: Mr. Williams. *Foruth Senator*: Mr. Jones. *Assasin*: Mr. Bradshaw. *Dancing Demons*: Messrs. Resor, Bradshaw, Barnett, Jones, Hart, Williams. *Greek Peasants*: Messrs. Matthews, Williams, Barnett. *First Citizen*: Mr. Barnett. *Second Citizen*: Mr. Williams. *Neva*, Stella's companion: Mrs. (Harriet) Phillips. *Inissala*: Mrs. LaForest. *Child in Prologue*: Miss Dennin.

Stella, the Enchantress: Mrs. FLYNN. *Spirit of Evil*: Mr. C. FOSTER. *Spirit of Good*: Miss COHEN. *Senators, Magistrates, Heralds, Pursuivants, Esquires, Royal Guards, Priests, Citizens, Dominoes, Maskers, Minstrels, Popualce, Servants, Bridesmaids, Attendants, Pages, Greek Slaves, Assassins*. Equestrian Cavalcade by 12 Horses.

Prologue: On board the Pirates' Ship at Anchor. Fifteen years before Act 1.

Act 1, Scene 1: The hermitage of "Our Lady of the Woods." *Scene 2*: The Pirates' Cave. *Scene 3*: Rocky Pass and Gorge. *Scene 4*: Abode of the Enchantress.

Act 2, Scene 1: Colonnade in the Duke's Palace. *Scene 2*: Sylvio's Richly Draperied Tent. *Scene 3*: A Rich Apartment in the Palace. Vestibule of the Grand Hall of Audience. Sumptuous Palace Scene or Saloon, in which is given the Grand Ducal Fete. *Scene 5*: Picturesque Garden by Moonlight. *Scene 6*: The Pavilion of Myrtles.

Act 3, Scene 1: Exterior of an Sicilian Inn. *Scene 2*: Arched Interior, Stained Glass Doors of Great Magnitude. *Scene 3*: Kitchen of the Palace. *Scene 4*: Shore of Palermo by Moonlight. *Scene 5*: Church of St. Marie Majeure. *Scene 6*: A Full-sized vessel under sail nears the shore, the Decks and Masts crowded with Pirates.

PROLOGUE
"By the Gleaming Stars" (Chorus of Pirates)
(*Music by* Mr. Cunnington.)
"However Bright" (Song)
Mr. Dennison
"Pirates' Prayer"
(*Music by* Mr. Cunnington.)
"See where the Golden Sun" (Solo)
Mr. DeBar
(*Music by* Mr. Cunnington.)
"Comrades be Silent" (Chorus)
(*Music by* Mr. Cunnington.)
"Oh! Rage, Oh! Wild Despair" (Chorus)
(*Music by* Mr. Cunnington.)

"To Pillage and to death" (Song)
Mr. Dennison
(*Music by* Mr. Cunnington.)
"Comrades this pledge behold" (Song and Chorus)
Mr. Dennison
(*Music by* Mr. Cunnington.)

ACT 1

"Behold before high heaven" (Invocation)
(*Music by* Mr. Cunnington.)
"See where the Vapors of morn arise" (Song)
Mr. DeBar
"Where earth is troubled" (Chorus)
Ballet d'Ensemble with Flute Solo
Miss Cohen (Specialty), Ballet
"On her fiend accounts" (Chorus)
(*Music by* Mr. Cunnington.)
"Comrades and Friends" (Chorus)
(*Music by* Mr. Cunnington.)
"At early dawn" (Solo)
Mr. Dennison
(*Music by* Mr. Cunnington.)
"We've sworn to defend her" (Chorus)
(*Music by* Mr. Cunnington.)
"Ever be happy" (Pirates' Chorus)
"Our Presence Still" (Chorus and Solo)(Finale)
Mrs. Phillips
(*Music by* Mr. Cunnington.)

ACT 2

"Down in Sparkling Glass" (Four Voices)
(*Music by* Mr. Cunnington.)
"Woman's Heart" (Song)
Mrs. Phillips
"Give us bread" (Chorus)
(*Music by* Mr. Cunnington.)
"The Young Nadir" (Song)
Mrs. Phillips
"Honor's Homage" (Finale)
(*Music by* Mr. Cunnington.)

ACT 3

"Happy Days of Life" (Song)
Mr. DeBar
"Hither we come" (Chorus)
(*Music by* Mr. Cunnington.)
"Ever be happy" (Pirates' Chorus)
"Who has not heard" (Cavatina)
Mr. Phillips
(*Music by* Mr. Cunnington.)
"Our Presence Still" (Finale)
All the characters
(*Music by* Mr. Cunnington.)

A GLANCE AT NEW YORK IN 1848

1848.01

A Local Sketch in Two Acts, 12 Scenes. Play by Benjamin A. Baker. Music arranged by Mr. E. Woolf. Scenery by Mr. Bengough. Machinery by Mr. Burns. Dresses by Mr. Roberts. Produced under the direction of Mr. (William) Mitchell. Produced by William Mitchell. Opened 15 February 1848 at the Olympic Theatre (24 performances) in repertory; revised version with additional characters opened 15 March 1848, closing 23 May 1848 after an additional 26 performances in repertory. Total: 50 performances.

CAST: *Mose*, a true specimen of one of the B'hoys (a New York Fire Boy): Mr. F. S. CHANFRAU. *Harry Gordon*, a Gothamite: Mr. G. J. ARNOLD. *George Parsells*, a Green-horn: Mr. G. CLARK. *Jake*, a Sharper, and Proprietor of Loafer's Paradise: Mr. W. CONOVER. *Mike*, a Sharper: Mr. Bleecker. *Major Gates*, a Literary Loafer: Mr. Levere. *Mrs. Morton*, President of the "Ladies Bowling Saloon": Mrs. HENRY. *Mary*, her daughter: Miss Phillips. *Jane*, a young girl from the country: Miss C. Roberts. *Members of the 'Ladies Bowling Saloon'*: Misses Mealing, Garvey, E. Barber, M. Barber, Elton, Maberly, Mrs. LeBrun. *Cabmen, Applewomen, Loafers, Newsboys*: Members of the Company.

New Characters: *Sykesee*: Mr. J. Seymour. *Mr. Morton*: Mr. Henry. *Ben*, peripatetic vender of News: Mr. Seymour. *Sam* a young Thief: Master Drew. *Eliza Stebbins* (Lizey), one of the Gals: Miss MARY TAYLOR. *Jenny Bogert*, her friend: Miss M. Barber.

Act 1, Scene 1: View of Steamboat Pier, foot of Barclay Street. (New York City.) *Scene 2*: Front Street, Broadway. *Scene 3*: Ladies' Bowling Saloon. Bar at back. *Scene 4*: Front Street. *Scene 5*: Loafer's Paradise. A dirty bar-room. Large stove in the center, with Pipe off wing. *Scene 6*: Front Street. Music hurry. Dark Stage.

Act 2, Scene 1: [Same as at close of Act 1]. *Scene 2*: New Street. Lights up house. *Scene 3*: Front Street. St. Paul's Church. *Scene 4*: A Mock Auction Store. Counter and Rostrum. Placards about Store. *Scene 5*: Front Street. *Scene 6*: Vauxhall Garden. Arches of Variegated Lamps. Refreshment Tables.

ACT 1[31]

Scene 1

Air 'Jolly Young Waterman' (The folks are all wanting to see the fast steamer)
Opening Chorus

Scene 3

Chorus from FRA DIAVOLO, Act 2 (For pleasure there's no denying)
Chorus

Scene 4

Song 'Bow-wow-wow' (I'm sure the world can't blame a man)
W. Conover

Scene 5

Irish Air (Here we are, a precious crew, that's always on hand)
Chorus

ACT 2

Scene 1

Trio 'Canadian Boat Song' (Go, Major, go, for half the night's past)
Messrs. Bleecker, Levere, [Joe]

Scene 2

Song "Lovely Mae"
M. Taylor

Scene 5

Duet 'Oh, Lud, Galls' (Here we are, as you diskivir)
M. Taylor, M. Barber

MET-A-MORA, or, the Last of the Pollywogs

1848.02

A Grand Tragical Comical Burlesque (of John A. Stone's tragedy, Metamora, or the Last of the Wampanoags) in Two Acts, 6 Scenes. Play by John Brougham. Produced by Edmund Simpson. Opened 6 March 1848 at the Park Theatre in repertory; returned 22, 29 April 1848 at the Broadway Theatre for 2 additional performances.

CAST: *Anglo-Saxons*: *Pappy Vaughan*, an influential early settler, early settled: Mr. Bridges. *Lord Fitzfaddle*, a highly-to-be-envied individual, who has the honor to die by Metamora's knife: Mr. A. ANDREWS. *Master Walter*, not the hunchback, but over head and ears in love: Mr. McDouall. *Bad-Enough*, a most unpleasant individual: Mr. Bernard. *Worser*, much the same, only more so: Mr. Heath. *Oceana*, old Vaughan's daughter, a chip off the old block: Mrs. FRARY.

Pollywogs: *Metamora*, the ultimate Pollywog, an aboriginal hero, and a favorite child of the FORREST: Mr. JOHN BROUGHAM. *Kantshine*, a friend, who gives excellent advice, and is treated as are all who do it: Mr. Povey. *Old Tar*, Indian interpreter, from the Junk, half savage, half sailor: Mr. S. Pearson. *Whiskee Toddi*, skilled in talk, so we are informed: Mr. King. *Anaconda*, a recreant red man, rather serpentine: Mr. Barton. *Tapiokee*, La Belle Sauvage, the squalling Squaw of Metamora, killed with kindness: Mrs. JOHN BROUGHAM. *Pappoose*, being the last of the Last of the Pollywogs: Miss —.

Act 1, Scene 1: A Wood. *Scene 2*: Kitchen. *Scene 3*: Chamber. Center doors, fourth grooves. Table with books, paper, pen and ink.

Act 2, Scene 1: Wood in third grooves. *Scene 2*: Front wood. *Scene 3*: Landscape, fifth groove. Bridge across stage with return piece.

ACT 1[32]

Scene 2

Air, 'O slumber, my darling' (O, slumber, my pappoose!)
Mrs. J. Brougham

---

[31]Musical numbers and scenes not listed in programs List prepared from published prompt book (Samuel French, New York, (1858?).

[32]Scenes and Musical Numbers not listed in programs. List prepared from published promptbook (Samuel French, New York, (1858).

Scene 3
Chorus, 'Dan Tucker' (We can hardly suppress our laughter)
Chorus
Tableau, Metamora seizes Vaughan

ACT 2
Scene 3
Song (Hush-a-by, baby, on the tree top)
Mrs. J. Brougham
Burlesque Combat
Chorus, 'We're all nodding' (We're all dying, die, dying)
Chorus
Solo (You're all lying, lie, lie, lying)
Mr. J. Brougham
Finale (If you would look out for pleasure)
Mr. J. Brougham
Chorus (Pollywog, Polly, Polly, Pollywog)
Chorus
Comic Dance and Tableau

1848.03

NEW YORK AS IT IS

A Local Extravaganza in One Act[33]. Play by Benjamin A. Baker. Produced by F. S. Chanfrau. The whole produced under the supervision of Stage manager, R. J. Jones. Scenery by Mr. Cuthbert. Machinery by Mr. Briggs. Properties by Mr. Sherman. Dresses by Mme. DeGrouche. Opened 17 April 1848 at the Chatham Theatre and closed 25 July 1848 after 47 performances in repertory.

CAST: *Mose*, one of the B'hoys, the great original: Mr. (F. S.) CHANFRAU. *Joe*, a Catharine Market Loafer: Mr. (JOHN) WINANS. *Charles Meadows*, a New Yorker: Mr. Stafford. *William Twill*, his cousin from the country: Mr. (John) Herbert. *Charley Bates*, a person who lives by duping innocent countrymen: Mr. Rea. *Sam Sharp*, his partner: Mr. W. Hield, Jr. *Mr. Meadows*, a citizen: Mr. (H.O.) PARDEY. *Hugh*, a candidate for Sing Sing: Mr. Salisbury. *Tom Small*, proprietor of the Soup House: Mr. Varrey. *Old Man*: Mr. W. Taylor. *Andrew*, vulgarly called "Andy," an old gentleman of color, who throws the dices in a style peculiarly his own: Mr. Barnett. *Jack*, a negro, and dancer for eels: Mr. Johnson. *Katy*, a lady's maid, betrothed to Mose: Mrs. J. B. BOOTH, JR. *Kitty*, a cook: Miss Julia Miles. *Emily Meadows*: Miss E. Hildreth. *Susan Meadows*: Mrs. W. (Fanny) Isherwood. *Ruth*, an orphan, Hugh's niece, forced by him to beg in the streets: SUSAN DENIN. *Citizens, Male and Female, Loafers, Fishermen, Market Women*: Members of the Company.

Scene 1: Views of Chatham Square and Chatham Theatre. *Scene 2*: View of the Old Dutch Church. *Scene 3*: Interior of the Soup House. *Scene 4*: City Hall; A Chamber in the house of Meadows. *Scene 5*: Chamber in the House of Mr. Meadows. *Scene 6*: Catharine Fish Market. *Scene 7*: A Street in New York. *Scene 8*: A Ladies' Gynmasium. *Scene 9*: The Old Bowery in flames, with Mose and the Fire Company in operation. Grand Tableau.

MUSICAL NUMBERS
Scene 1
"What delight to roam this great city" (Chorus of Citizens)
Scene 3
"We have a good party here to-night" (Chorus of Paupers)
Scene 4
General Fight
Scene 5
"Come Miss, Stir Your Stumps" (Duet)
"Ah, Mosey I am yours for life"
Mrs. Booth
Scene 6
Race between the Steamers Oregon & Vanderbilt
"To the Market" (Chorus)
Nigger Dance for eels
Scene 7
"Oh here I am chuck full of woe" (Song)
Mr. Winans
Scene 8
"Rise old Napper" (Chorus)

[33]A sequel to A GLANCE AT NEW YORK IN 1848 which opened 15 February 1848 and A NEW GLANCE AT NEW YORK which succeeded it 15 March 1848, both at the Olympic Theatre.

Scene 9
Arrival of Mose and his Fire Company. Mose dashes into the burning building, appears at the window with the child in his arms. She is saved. Grand tableau.

1848.04

MARITANA

A Light Opera in Three Acts, 4 Scenes[34]. Libretto by Edward Fitzball. Based on the play "Don César de Bazan" by Adolphe d'Ennery and Philippe Dumanoir. Music by William Vincent Wallace. Produced by T. S. Hamblin. Opened 4 May 1848 at the Bowery Theatre and closed 6 May 1848 after 3 performances.

CAST: *Don Caesar de Bazan*: Mr. GARDNER. *Don José de Santarem*: EDWARD SEGUIN. *Charles II*: Mr. SAURE. *The Marquis di Montefiore*: Mr. Warden. *The Alcalde*: Mr. Schneff. *Captain of the Guard*: ?. *The King*: ?. *Lazarillo*: Miss LICHTENSTEIN. *Maritana, Gitana*: Mrs. ANNE SEGUIN. *The Marchioness di Montefiore*: Mrs. J. Stickney. *Chorus of Soldiers, Gipsies, and Populace*.

Act 1: A Square in Madrid.

Act 2, Scene 1: Interior of a Fortress. *Scene 2*: A Saloon in the Palace of the Marquis di Montefiore.

Act 3: A magnificent apartment.

ACT 1[35]
"Sing, pretty maiden, sing" (Opening Chorus)
Chorus
"It was a Knight of princely mien" (Romance)
A. Seguin, Chorus
"'Tis the harp in the air" (Romance)
A. Seguin
"Angels that around us hover" (Angelus)
Chorus
"Of fairy wand had I the power" (Duet)
A. Seguin, E. Seguin
"All the world over" (Song)
Mr. Gardner
"See the culprit" (Quartett and Chorus)
Miss Lichtenstein, Messrs. Gardner, [Captain], E. Seguin
"Pretty Gitana" (Chorus)
Chorus
"Farewell, my gallant Captain" (Finale)
A. Seguin, Miss Lichtenstein, Messrs. Gardner, E. Seguin, Chorus

ACT 2
Scene 1
"Alas! Those chimes so sweetly stealing" (Romance)
Miss Lichtenstein
"Hither as I came" (Duet)
Mr. Gardner, Miss Lichtenstein
"Turn on, old Time" (Trio)
Mr. Gardner, Miss Lichtenstein, E. Seguin
"Yes! let me like a Soldier fall" (Song)
Mr. Gardner
"In happy moments day by day" (Ballad)
E. Seguin
(*Lyrics by* Alfred Bunn.)
"Health to the Lady" (Quartett and Chorus)
A. Seguin, Miss Lichtenstein, Messrs. Gardner, E. Seguin
Scene 2
"Oh! what pleasure" (Chorus)
Waltz
"The Mariner in his barque" (Song)
[King]
"There is a flower that bloometh" (Song)
Mr. Gardner

[34]Accompanied on its first night by an after-piece, LA CHISELLE, a burlesque extravaganza, in which the following appeared: *Chiselle*: Mr. BURKE. *Mr. Albert Duck*: Mr. Warden. *Mrs. Albert Duck*: Mrs. Hart.
[35]Musical numbers not listed in programs. List prepared from published English piano vocal score (W. Johnson, London, 1845).

"Ah! confusion!" (Quartett)
Mrs. J. Stickney, Messrs. Gardner, E. Seguin, Warden
"That voice! That voice!" (Finale)
A. Seguin, Messrs. Gardner, E. Seguin, Chorus

ACT 3
"How dreary to my heart" (Recitative)
A. Seguin
"Scenes that are the brightest" (Ballad)
A. Seguin
(*Lyrics by* Alfred Bunn.)
"This heart by woe o'ertaken" (Song)
E. Seguin
"I am the King of Spain" (Duet)
Mr. Gardner, [King]
"Oh, Maritana!" (Duet)
A. Seguin, Mr. Gardner
"Sainted Mother" (Prayer)
A. Seguin, Miss Lichtenstein
"Remorse and dishonor" (trio)
A. Seguin, Mr. Gardner, [King]
"With rapture glowing" (Finale)
A. Seguin, Chorus

1850–1860 SEASONS

"The Laura Keene Schottisch" (Autographed Sheet Music, 1856)
Museum of the City of New York, Gift of Harry Shaw Newman, 40.160.1064

1850–1860 SEASONS

1850.01 SHE'S COME! JENNY'S COME!

An Extravaganza in One Act, with several startling situations, grand processions, romantic songs and other curiosities[1]. Produced by William Burton. Opened 2 September 1850 at Burton's Theatre in repertory.

CAST: *Mr. Blarneyem*, Jenny Lind's Manager and Proprietor of a Museum: Mr. WILLIAM BURTON. *The Mayor of the City*: Mr. Bland. *A couple of Aldermen*: Messrs. Henry, Keyser. *Ichabod Longface*, opposed to theatrical amusements: Mr. Skerrett. *Mr. von Humbug*, Blarneyem's assistant: Mr. HOLMAN. *The Drunkard*: Mr. Barton. *The Anaconda*: Mr. Levere. *The Spotted Nigger*: Mr. Wise. *Tom Thumb*: Master Henry. *The Two Fat Boys*: Messrs. Wilson, Jeffries. *Music Director*, neat as imported: Mr. Frédéric. *Newsboy*: Master Raphael. *Waiter*: Mr. Parsloe. *The Nightingale*: Herr von JANSEN.

1851.01 FAUSTUS, or, The Demon of the Drachenfels

A Revival of the Grand Romantic Spectacle in Three Acts, 14 Scenes[2]. (Play by George Soane.) Songs, duets and concerted music by Sir Henry Bishop. Melo-dramatic music composed, selected and arranged by Mons. Perot. Scenery designed by George Heister. Carnival and ballet dances produced under the direction of Mons. Schmdt. Machinery and mechanical changes by E. Speyre. Costumes, decorations, properties and appointments by S. Wallis. Produced by E. A. Marshall. Opened 13 January 1851 at the Broadway Theatre and closed 22 February 1851 after 36 performances; reopened 16 May 1851 at the Broadway Theatre and closed 21 May 1851 after 5 additional performances. Total: 41 performances.

CAST: *Faustus*, the German Doctor: Mr. DYOTT. *Mephistopheles*, the ________: Mr. CONWAY. *Count de Casanova*, Father of Rosolia: Mr. WHITING. *Count Orsini*, a young Venetian, in love with Adine: Mr. HILL. *Montolio*, *Antonio*, Venetians and friends of Enrico: Messrs. Shaw, Reynolds. *Wagner*, a young German student: Mr. W. DAVIDGE. *Enrico*, a gallant Soldier, and brother of Adine: Mr. HARRIS. *Marco*, a Venetian officer: Mr. Hind. *Grognoso*, Innkeeper and Father to Lucetta: Mr. Mathews. *Brevillo*, a Servant of the Inn, and in love with Lucetta: Mr. Scharf. *Officers*: Messrs. Wright, Wise, Cleverly, Williams. *Paolo*: Mr. Parry. *Luco*: Mr. Wharton. *Officers of the Inquisition*: Messrs. Keimes, Marhler, Herman, Hart.

Adine, Sister to Enrico: Mme. [Elizabeth] PONISI. *Rosolia*, Daughter of the Count de Casanova, and betrothed to Montolio: Mrs. ABBOTT. *Lucetta*, Grognoso's Daughter, and in love with Wagner: Miss CAPEL. *Lords and Ladies, Attendants, Officers, Chamberlains, Guards, Banner Bearers, Male and Female Peasants.*

Janet: Miss Olivia. *Lisette*: Miss Josephine Gougenheim. *Liza*: Miss Adelaide Gougenheim. *Manette*: La Petite Carman. *Principal Danseuse*: Miss Adeline. *Principal Grotesque Dancer*: Mr. Checkeni. *Choristers, Dancers, Masqueraders, Comic Pantomime Performers, Grotesque Figures*: Ladies and Gentlemen of the Company. Chorus and Supernumerary Force of 150.

Act 1, Scene 1: On the Drachenfels. *Scene 2*: Carnival in Venice. *Scene 3*: A Churchyard by moonlight. *Scene 4*: Exterior of an Inn. *Scene 5*: A room in the Inn. *Scene 6*: A Moonlight Garden and the Mansion of the Count de Casanova.

Act 2, Scene 1: A Splendid Apartment. *Scene 2*: Rosalia's Apartment in the Count de Casanova's Palace.

Act 3, Scene 1: Gorgeous Room in Faustus' Palace. *Scene 2*: Before the Inn, as in Act 1. *Scene 3*: Interior of a Prison. *Scene 4*: Ante-room of a Royal Chamber. *Scene 5*: A Street in Naples. *Scene 6*: Illuminated Banquet Hall in the Palace.

ACT 1
Scene 1
Chorus of Fishermen (Home! There's a storm in the whistling blast)
Chorus of Hunters (The wild bird is rocking in his nest)
Chorus of Peasants (Now for the fireside's cheerful blaze)
The Secret Charm (I've the charm, which. .)
The Invocation (Spirits of darkness, I invoke thee)
Invisible Chorus of Demons, and Sudden Appearance of ________!!!
Incantation (Pass earth, pass sky)
Scene 2
Grand Ballet (Carnival in Venice)
Principal Brigand: Mlle. Adeline.
La Mère Gigonde
a most prolific character
Character Dance
La Petite Carman
Grand Pas
Mons. Chickeni
Grand Galop
All the characters
Scene 4
Song (I'm a young German scholar)
Mr. Davidge
Scene 5
Trio (Now prithee your laughing give over)
Mr. Whiting, Miss Capel, Mr. Davidge
Song (Lucy, Lucy, dear Lucy! wake to the spring)
Miss Capel

ACT 2
Scene 1
Song (Oh, sweetly the noon day's ending)
Mme. Ponisi
Scene 2
Finale and Chorus (Magic wild, and dire delusion)
Messrs. Whiting, Davidge, Dyott, Servants, Officers of Inquisition, Demons, etc.

ACT 3
Scene 1
First Vision (A Cemetery); Second Vision (Interior of a Church); Third Vision (The Bay of Naples)
Scene 4
Invisible Chorus of Demons (Rejoice, rejoice)
Grand Procession and Chorus (The morn is up)
Lords, Ladies, Guards, etc.
Scene 5
Duet
Mr. Davidge, Miss Capel
Scene 6
The Fete
Chorus from LEONORA (Fill up, fill up, the vine-wreathed cup)
(*Music by* Mr. Fry.)
Grand Greek Divertissement
Recitative and Air (Oh Saul, oh King)
Terrific denouement!

1851.02 THE ANDALUSIAN, or, The Young Guard

A Petite Opera in One Act[3]. Libretto by George Loder. Music by Edward Loder. Arranged for this establishment by George Loder. Stage manager, Harry Lynne. (Scene painters, Charles Thorne and Mr. Roberts. Costumes, G. Taylor.) Musical director, George Loder. Produced by John Brougham. Opened 15 January 1851 at Brougham's Lyceum Theatre and closed January 1851 in repertory.

CAST: *Don Guzman*, a General Officer in the service of Queen Christina: Mr. LYSTER. *Don Alvarez*, a Carlist: Mr. Dunn. *Captain Miguel*: M. (Stephen) Leach. *Pedro*, a Sergeant: Mr. Thompson. *Mendez*, a Corporal: Mr. Saurin (Lyster). *Estella*, disguised as a wandering Minstrel Boy: Miss (JULIA) GOULD. *Donna Olympia*, sister to Don Alverez, disguised as a Female Minstrel: Mrs. GEORGE LODER. *Soldiers, Soldiers' Wives, Sutlers, etc.* (*Dance Specialty*: Mlle. DUCY-BARRE, Messrs. G. W. Smith, Fletcher, Miss Tayleure.)

---

[1]Inspired by P. T. Barnum's extravagant promotion of Jenny Lind, the Swedish Nightingale, in her New York debut in September 1850. Presented as an after-piece to Boucicault's comedy, London Assurance, and other plays.

[2]First produced 11 October 1827 at the Park Theatre. This revival was preceded by the popular farce, My Young Wife and Old Umbrella; replaced 20 January by a new comedy, The Husband of My Heart; replaced 27 January by a new comedy, My Heart's Idol; replaced 31 January by the petite comedy Faint Heart Never Won Fair Lady, etc. For the return engagement, the fore-piece was The Fair One with the Golden Locks. On successive nights The Rough Diamond was presented, or Who Speaks First.

[3]Preceded by a stage adaptation of Charles Dickens' David Copperfield.

MUSICAL NUMBERS

Tarantella (Scene 1)

Mlle. Ducy-Barre, Messrs. G. W. Smith, Fletcher, Miss Tayleure

THE WORLD'S FAIR, or, Columbia in the Clouds

1851.03

An original, aboriginal, logical and mythological, opposite and apporistic anonymosity in One Act[4]. Stage manager, Henry Lynne. Musical director, George Loder. Produced by John Brougham. Opened 10 February 1851 at Brougham's Lyceum and closed 6 March 1851 after 20 performances in repertory; returned in a new edition 20 March 1851.

CAST: *Jove*, the original Don Joveanni, an uncontroverted Pagan of very doubtful repute, famous for his attachment to the fair of all nations: Mr. (JOHN) BROUGHAM. *Apollo*, God of Music and Phisic, Inventor of Derogatory Type, and regular publisher of "the Sun" daily: Mr. DUNN. *Mercury*, the winged footman of Olympus, Star of Wall street, and patron of pickpockets—in a respectable phase: Miss JULIA GOULD. *Bacchus Lyceus*, conductor and professor of Geology—a loose character, and consequently "tight": Mr. Leach. *Mars*, a professed pugilist and great expounder of the "Hyer" law: Mr. Lyster. *Neptune*, a "Fishmonger," Ruler of the Ocean, and a "heavy swell" occasionally: Mr. Saurien. *Ganymede*, Jove's cupbearer, "a heavenly body," although not in the Solar System: Miss E. Taylor. *Vulcan*, Founder of the "Smith" family, and originator of "Old Sledge," a great forger: Mr. Gaylor. *Herr Hercules*, the King of Clubs, a Deuce of a Fellow, and a very strong trump: Mr. Hunt. *Cupid*, a Knave of Hearts, a Court Card: Mr. Thompson. *Esculapius*, a Son of Apollo, the first Regular Practitioner Licensed to Kill—secundem artem: Mr. Bristoll. *Nox*, a dark Knight: Mr. Baker. *Columbia*, a democratic and access-ible genius, liable to be "hailed" by everybody, making a flying visit to the clouds, "just for a flyer," with a few notes of introduction from the gentle Jenny, and a parody upon Pardi: Miss MARY TAYLOR. *Juno Februalia*, the Oxeyed spouse of Jove, a bit of a bully: Mrs. W. R. BLAKE. *Other Gods, Goddesses, Semi-semi-deities, attendants, etc. and characters in the tableaux*: Rest of the Company, Corps de Ballet.

MUSICAL NUMBERS, SPECIALTIES[5]

In the Clouds. Jove not at all social.

Opening Chorus, a rather miserable glee ("Oh this dolce far niente")

Familiar conversation touching sublunary affairs. Apollo defines his position and sings

"I Love To See a Red, Red Nose"

Mr. Dunn

Mars waxes egotistical, hints at Mexico, and on the strength of his warlike deeds, speculates on the presidency. Arrival of the Extra SUN. Great news from Earth. The Deities indulge in a few satirical remarks, not over complimentary to human kind. Another arrival. The sky open. The first Balloon of the Season. Scarcity of Lightning satisfactorily accounted for. Extraordinary intrusion of COLUMBIA to the consternation of the Celestials. She introduces herself, and a Medley:

"I'm Columbia, understand"

M. Taylor

In which she sings a brief autobiography, ending with a grand Anglo-Saxon-Italiano Scena Furioso:

"When I first saw Parodi"

M. Taylor

to the astonishment of the Orchestra, and the satisfaction of all parties. Jove presents her to the Crowd. Brandy smash suggested, but "No Mint." Columbia brags on City Ordinances. Mysterious disappearance of the SIGNS OF THE TIMES, an Essay on new Brooms, Clean Streets, and of course, "The Sweep Song." Cupid and Columbia have a chat. The former tells a few secrets not far from the truth, and the latter informs the assembled Celestials of the approaching WORLD'S FAIR. Jove determines not to be outdone, and resolves that he must have one also. Malapropos Entrance of Juno, who naturally and jealously confounds the FAIR of all Nations, having had sufficient cause heretofore, Confusion, misconception, general anger, and a terrific sound, (musical). By way of variety they sing a "Polka." The action walks to the ELYSIAN FIELDS, a little ABOVE Hoboken. Mercury enters, and as he is in a hurry, stops and sings. Bacchus takes the liberty of sending a mysterious message to Liberty-Street, N. Y., in return for which he sings:

"A Horn, a Horn"

Mr. Leach

Juno, unquiet, pumps Mercury, who prevaricates. The two fixed stars are ultimately in a fix, from which they extricate themselves effectually. Jove grumbles with Columbia, who gives him "the Mitten." Sudden return of Mercury with THE WORLD'S FAIR, leading to scene last, Frame work of Celestial Society. Jove sold. Exhibition of the Fair (sex) from THE FOUR QUARTERS OF THE GLOBE in a series of brilliant tableaux, ending with Grand Allegorical Scene, Homage to Columbia. Three quarters of the Globe. Ending with a regular (Sky) Lark.

[4]Preceded by a farce, Betsey Baker.

[5]In the third week of the run, a new scene was added, Columbia's tribute to the great Washington.

THE WORLD'S FAIR, or, London in 1851

1851.04

A Cosmopolite Pre-maturity (the Favorite Burletta) in One Act[6]. (Scenic artist, Mr. George Heilge. Costumes, Mr. Keyser.) Produced by William E. Burton. Opened 15 February 1851 at Burton's Theatre and closed March 1851 in repertory.[7]

CAST: *William Waggles*, principal managing director of the great Fair of all nations: WILLIAM E. BURTON. *Count Kanouski*, from the Russian Empire: Mr. JORDAN. *Mynheer Swyzeldam*, from Rotterdam: Mr. (T. B.) Johnston. *The Original John Smith*: Mr. (George) Holman. *Ching Loo*, a mild Mandarin, from the Celestial Empire: Mr. Howard. *The Bosjeman*, from the Cape Country: Mr. Bland. *Bill Wilkes*, errand boy at a lodging house: Mr. (George) SKERRETT. *Colonel Laforet*, a French Republican: Mons. Frederic. *Amin Bey*, from Constantinople: Mr. Henry. *We-Peek, Lo-Po-Te-Kuk*, Cherokee Chiefs: Messrs. Charles T. Parsloe, Jr., Levere. *Sambo*, a negro: Mr. Gourlay. *Don Pedro*, a Spaniard: Mr. Moore. *Pete Gotobed, Esq.*, from Vermont, Barnum's agent: Mr. Johnston. *A Pair of Esquimaux Indians*: Mr. M. Keyser, Miss Wilson. *Pelgrino*, an Italian: Mr. G. Barton. *Father Time*, his first appearance on the boards of a Theatre: Mr. Howard. *Mrs. Smudge*, keeper of a London Lodging house: Mrs. (Esther) HUGHES. *Miss Smudge*, her daughter, beloved by John Smith: Mrs. (George) SKERRETT. *Madame Cherinski*: Miss (Annie) Walters. *Fatima*, escaped from a Harem: Mrs. (George) Holman. *The Greek Slave*: Miss Jane Hill [Mrs. Burton]. *Signorina Francesca*: Miss Weston. *The Light of the Morning*: Miss Day. *Mrs. Jones*: Mrs. Henry. *Fair Star*, a Squaw: Miss Cooke. *Arabian Girl*: Mrs. Bell.

THE SPIRIT OF THE AIR, or, The Enchanted Star

1851.05

An Operatic Romance in Two Acts, 8 Scenes. Adapted from the French by John Brougham. New and original music composed and directed by George Loder. Stage manager, Harry Lynne. Scene painter, Charles Thorne. Costumes, G. Taylor. Mechanical effects, Mr. DeMilt. Produced by John Brougham. Opened 7 April 1851 at Brougham's Lyceum and closed 24 April 1851 after 13 performances in repertory.

CAST: *Aerials*: *Asteria*, the Child of the Air: Miss MARY TAYLOR. *Uranice* (Urania), the Planet Queen: Miss JULIA GOULD. *Iris*, the Spirit of the Rainbow: Miss E. Taylor. *Oriana*: Miss Marie Tayleure.

Attendant Stars: *Aeria*: Miss Lyster. *Cerulia*: Miss Bishop. *Pleida*: Miss Marlan. *Stella*: Miss Ostrander. *Zephyra*: Miss Osborne. *Psyche*: Miss Hart. *Millia*: Miss Bell. *Euphia*: Miss Reives.*Cynthia*: Miss Huntley. *Boreas*, the North wind: Mr. LEACH. *Flutter*, a Southern breeze: Mr. DUNN.

Demons: *Astaroth*: FRED LYSTER. *Attendant Demons*: Messrs. Thonton, Hopes, Hunt, Sourien, Fletcher, Bristol, Baker, Scherpff, Gimber, etc.

Mortals: *Roland*, a young Wood-cutter, in love with Asteria: Mr. Palmer. *Weizler*, in love with Lisette: Mr. RAYMOND. *Dame Marguerite*: Mrs. Dunn. *Lisette*: Mrs. GEORGE LODER.

Act 1, Scene 1: Home of the Stars. *Scene 2*: The young wood-cutter (Roland) and his intended bride. *Scene 3*: Interior of Roland's Cottage. *Scene 4*: The Magic Oak. *Scene 5*: The Wizard's Grove.

Act 2, Scene 1: Fairy Grotto. *Scene 2*: Woody landscape. *Scene 3*: Cottage of Roland, a storm at hand.

ACT 1

Scene 1

Chorus and Cavatina (Ever merrily glancing)

M. Tayleure

Cavatina (To quit the skies)

M. Taylor

Quartette and Chorus (Fly, sister, fly)

J. Gould, M. Taylor, Messrs. Dunn, Leach

[6]Preceded by the comedy The Hypocrite; followed by an after-piece, Sent to the Tower.

[7]No musical numbers or specialties listed in programs. A rival production, THE WORLD'S FAIR, or, Columbia in the Clouds, was also presented 10 February 1851 at Brougham's Lyceum.

Scene 2
Entrance of Weizler (Make us thoughtful)
Mr. Raymond, Palmer, M, Taylor
Descriptive Scena (I am the mighty God of wind)
Mr. Leach
Scene 4
Cabaletta (Seek me, seek me, where I glide)
M. Taylor
Scene 5
Phantom Chorus and Dance of Demons
Solo (Help, help, my senses fail)
M. Taylor
Ensemble (The Star is lost)
M. Taylor, Messrs. Dunn, Leach, Chorus
Chorus (The Star alone we duty owe)

ACT 2
Scene 1
Aria Scene (What new sensations fill my breast)
M. Taylor
Scene 2
Ballad (When woman led by fashion)
Mrs. G. Loder
Scene 3
Chorus of Friends (Rejoice, rejoice)
Rondeau Finale (Your cheering smiles)
M. Taylor, Quartette, Chorus

1851.06 THE VISION OF THE SUN

A Revival of the Romantic, Fairy Operatic Spectacle in Three Acts, 16 Scenes[8]. Scenery by George Heister. Machinery by Mr. Speyers. Costumes and decorations by S. Wallis. Dances arranged by Mons. Schmidt. Produced by E. A. Marshall. Opened 7 April 1851 at the Broadway Theatre and closed 15 May 1851 after 30 performances.

CAST: *Koran*, a supposed peasant: Miss ANDERTON. *Tacmar*, his supposed father: Mr. WHITING. *Oultanpac*: Mr. Harris. *Oratzuma*: Mr. Hill. *Huainatapac*, King of Cusco: Mr. Fredericks. *Tycobroc*, a dumb slave: Signor Carlo. *Genii of the Harp*: Miss OLIVIA. *Genii of the Ebon Wand*: Mr. Reynolds. *King of Silence*: Mr. Matthews. *Guard*: Mr. Davis. *Soldier*: Mr. Byrne. *Knights, Imps, Citizens of Peru, Peruvian Youths, Virgins, Priests, etc.*

Runac, Princess of Cusco: ADELAIDE GOUGENHEIM. *Ocella*, her friend: JOSEPHINE GOUGENHEIM. *Cassana*: Mrs. Isherwood. *Nymphs, Attendants*: Corps de Ballet. (*Premiere Danseuse*: Mlle. Therese.)

Act 1, Scene 1: Distant Hills and Mountains in Peru. *Scene 2*: The Magician's Abode on the isle of Uxi. *Scene 3*: The City of Cusco and the Royal Palace. *Scene 4*: The Golden Lake and Golbac's Castle.

Act 2, Scene 1: A Splendid Pavilion. *Scene 2*: The Grand Square of Cusco. *Scene 3*: The Exterior of a Peruvian House. *Scene 4*: The Palace of Nuptials.

Act 3, Scene 1: Lake, with distant city of Cusco. Most brilliant palace rises out of the water. A gorgeous grotto. *Scene 2*: The Palace of Cusco. *Scene 3*: Chamber of Enlightenment. *Scene 4*: Dazzling Colonnade. Rock of Porphery. *Scene 5*: Entrance to the Hall of the Enchanter. *Scene 6*: The Prison Chamber. *Scene 7*: The Blighted Grove. *Scene 8*: Temple of the Lions, and the Pedestal with the Talismanic Lance. The Vision of the Sun.

ACT 1
Scene 1
Genii's Task (Koran, though obscure and lowly bred)
Miss Olivia
Scene 2
Chorus (Spirits of great Oultanpac)
Imps, etc.
Scene 4
Song of the Genii of the Harp (Agents of my power attend)
Miss Olivia
Invisible Chorus (Thy potent voice we hear)
Pas Seul and Corps de Ballet des Fées

ACT 2
Scene 1
Song (Say what is more dear to the breast of the brave)
A. Gougenheim
Scene 2
Grand Triumphal Procession
Peruvian Soldiers, Nobles, Officers, Slaves, Youths, etc.
Chorus (Rend the air, sons of Peru)
Chorus (Joy, joy, happy glorious day)
Marche Chivalesque and Pas de Deux
Mlle. Therese, M. Schmidt, Corps de Ballet
Scene 4
Bridal Procession (Mighty Capac, hear our prayer)
Priests, Virgins, Youths

ACT 3
Scene 1
Procession of Nymphs and Sea Deities
Scene 3
Pas de Offrandes
Mlle. Therese, 24 Odalesques
Scene 7
Ariel Voices (Koran, Koran, one trial more)

1851.07 AZAEL, THE PRODIGAL

A Romantic and Operatic Spectacle in Three Acts, 5 Scenes[9]. Translated from the French ('L'Enfant Prodigue' of Eugène Scribe) by an American dramatist[10]. Music by Daniel Auber. Scenery by George Heister. Machinery by Speyer. Dresses from the original drawings, received from Paris, expressly for this theatre by S. Wallis. (Dance) Divertissements by Mons. Schmidt. Produced by E. A. Marshall. Opened 2 June 1851 at the Broadway Theatre and closed 24 June 1851 after 19 performances.

CAST: *Azael*, the prodigal: Mr. F. CONWAY. *Reuben*, his father (Chief of a Tribe of Israelites): Mr. N. B. CLARKE. *Amenophis*, a traveller: Mr. Shaw. *Bocharis*, a High Priest of Isis: Mr. WHITING. *Nimrod* (Nemroud), a camel-driver: Mr. MATTHEWS. *Canopi, Manethon*, Priests of Isis: Messrs. Hind, Byrne. *Egyptians*: Messrs. Parry, Roberts. *Jephtele*, niece to Reuben, and betrothed to Azael: Miss ANDERTON. *Nefti*, companion of Amenophis: Mrs. Abbott. *Lia*, principal dancer of the tribe of Almees: Mlle. THÉRÈSE.

Jews: Messrs. Byrne, Roberts, Hart, Herman, Keenan, Wharton, Franks, Williams, Robertson, I. Stone, Wright, J., Bradley, C. Matthews, Marhler, R. Hamilton, Thomas Richardson, R. Thomas, J. Charles, W. Norton, etc. *Jewesses*: Mesdames Conways, Adelaide Goughenheim, Josephine Gougenheim, Olivia Carman, Brock, Wilson, Lefore, Kelly, Johnson, Anderson, Simms, J. Hill, M. Richardson, A. Wallis, M. Norton, E. Norton, Fell, Hamilton, Miles, Smilee, Mitchell, Huntley, Hallas, Rice, Norval, Macbeth, Thompson, Wench, Wharton, Lewis, Gallot, Bishop, Walby, Darcy, Sherwood, Deane, etc. *Egyptians, Guards, Ethiops, Egyptian Danseuses, Priests, Priestesses, Harlots of the King, Slaves, Pages, Military Chiefs*: Augmented Auxiliary Force.

Act 1, Scene 1: Interior of the Tent of Reuben the Patriarch, through which is discovered a Sunset View of the Rich Valley of Gessen. *Scene 2*: Grand Square in the mighty city. A Festal Day at Memphis.

Act 2: Stupendous Interior of the Temple of Isis.

Act 3, Scene 1: The Desert home of the Camel-Drivers. *Scene 2*: The Luxurious valley of Gessen.

ACT 1
Scene 2
Sacred Procession of the Ox Apis
Pas de Fascination
Mlle. Thérèse, Full Corps de Ballet

ACT 2
Grand Drinking Chorus of Revellers, and Goblet Dance

[8]First produced in New York as THE VISION OF THE SUN, or, The Orphan of Peru, 3 October 1825 at the Park Theatre. Authorship in 1825 and 1851 uncredited.

[9]Preceded each evening by 'a favorite farce:' for example, The Rough Diamond; Betsey Baker; Shocking Events; Thumping Legacy.

[10]A previous English translation by Edward Fitzball no doubt figured largely in the American adaptation.

Pas de Poignards
Mlle. Thérèse, Full Corps de Ballet

ACT 3
Scene 1
Chorus (Harks their clear Bells ring)
Chorus (Yea, in Araby a merry life we lead)
Scene 2
Grand Chorus of Prayers and Imposing Denouement

1851.08
AZAEL, THE PRODIGAL

A Revival of the Romantic Spectacle in Three Acts, 9 Scenes[11]. Adapted from the French original ('L'Enfant Prodigue' of Eugène Scribe) by Mrs. A. Carman. Music by Daniel Auber. Stage arrangements by Mr. Stevens, Stage Manager. Music under the supervision of W. T. Peterschen. Ballet department under the supervision of Mons. Schmidt. Scenery by Mr. Lamb. Machinery by Mr. Lamb. Dresses by Mr. Matthews. Properties by Mr. Milons. Decorative painting by Messrs. Richardson, Thompson. Gas fixtures by Thomas W. Newton. Produced by Thomas S. Hamblin. Opened 21 July 1851 at the Bowery Theatre and closed 2 August 1851 after 12 performances.

CAST: *Azael*, the Prodigal: Mr. E. EDDY. *Reuben*, Azael's father: Mr. JOHN GILBERT. *Amenophis*, a merchant: Mr. Tilton. *Nemroud*, a desert dweller: Mr. M. W. LEFFINGWELL. *Citizens and Gamblers of Memphis (4)*: *Pylates*: Mr. Bowes. *Dato*: Mr. Wharton. *Emor*: Mr. Fracks. *Rudac*: Mr. Geary. *Sethos*, novice of the Temple: Mr. Moore. *Bucharis*, high priest of Isis: Mr. C. L. STONE. *Jeroam*: Mr. H. C. Jordan. *Ishmael*: Mr. Gouldson. *Jephtele*, the affianced of Azael, and Reuben's niece: Miss ANDERTON. *Nefte*, sister to Amenophis: Mrs. C. L. Stone. *Lia*, the enchanted Almee: Annie Walters. *Ceanea*, her companion: Mrs. Leffingwell. *Spirit of the Desert*: Miss Herring. *Zenita*: Miss Hiffert.

Priests, Dignitaries of the Temple: Messrs. Matterson, LeClerq, Smithers, Marks, Waters, G. Wharton, Senoir, James Williams, Denaud, Bosden, Barlowe, Deniclar, Showdowne, W. Smith, Wilkinson, LeMare, Swartz, Dunkarder, Reynolds, C. Senoir. *Jewesses*: Mesdames Barnard, Fielding, Barnes, Bishop, LeFowle, Kelley, M. Hall, Waltby, S. Hill, Hamilton, Fell, Sherwood, Dering, J. King, Fisk, Wilson, Myers, Anderson, Broadley, Hart, Needham, Williams, I. Williams, O'Connor, Josephine. *Guards, Numidian Slaves, Citizens, etc.*

Act 1: Abode of Reuben.

Act 2, Scene 1: The Golden City. *Scene 2*: The Vicinity of Memphis. *Scene 3*: Exterior of a Temple. *Scene 4*: Temple of Isis.

Act 3, Scene 1: The Burning Desert. *Scene 2*: The Tent of Nemroud. *Scene 3*: The Valley. *Scene 4*: The Wanderer's Home.

ACT 1
Opening Chorus (Fly the Distaff)
Camel Driver's Chorus
Azael's Farewell
Chorus (Now we merrily haste away)

ACT 2
Scene 1
Festival Chorus (Shout, boys, shout)
Triumphal Entry of Azael and Amenophis in their Glittering Car
Grand Procession of Sacrifice
A brilliant Pas de Fascination
A. Walters, Corps de Ballet
Scene 3
The Funeral Train
Chant (Pray for the stranger)
Scene 4
The Poignard Dance
A. Walters
The Oath of Vengeance (We swear)
Chorus

ACT 3
Scene 2
Vision of the Prodigal
Invisible Chorus (Holy spirit hear our prayer)
Scene 3
Chorus of Welcome (Hail, travellers, hail)
Scene 4
The Prodigal Azael!
Grand Finale

1852.01
PAUL CLIFFORD

A Grand Operatic and Dramatic Spectacle in Three Acts, 13 Scenes[12]. Play by Edward Fitzball (adapted from Edward Bulwer Lytton's novel). Scenery by George Heister. Costumes by Mrs. S. Wallis. Machinery by Mr. Speyers. Decorations by Mr. Wallis. Chorus master, Mr. Lyster. Musical director, Mr. Roberts. Ballet department under the direction of Signor Neri. Produced by E. A. Marshall. Opened 19 January 1852 at the Broadway Theatre and closed 7 February 1852 after 18 performances.

CAST: *Paul Clifford*: Mr. (JOHN) COLLINS. *Lord Manleverer*: Mr. REYNOLDS. *Sir William Brandon*: Mr. Barry. *Long Ned*: Mr. A. W. Fenno. *Augustus Tomlinson*: Mr. Pope. *Scarlet Jack*: Mr. Brunton. *Dummie Dunnicker*: Mr. W. Davidge. *Dennis O'Hooney*: Mr. Hind. *Gentleman George*: Mr. Barrett. *Valentine*, Valet to Lord Manleverer: Mr. Gourlay. *Police Officer*: Mr. Wright. *Doctor Slopperton*: Mr. WHITING. *Chorus*: Messrs. Keimes, Wharton, Lyster, Bride, Geary, Liverati, Grosse, Moult, Thimes, Kiepelback, Baker, Mueller, Farrar, Schneff, Willis, George. Mesdames Carman, Liverati, Gubeli, Mowe, Brook, Wilson, Norton, Smith, Jackson, etc. *Ballet*: Misses Price, Josephine, Lafoie, Fell, Wrench, Lewis, West, Celeste, Miles, McCormick, Johnson, Carter, Walter, Willis, Foster, etc.

Lucy Brandon: Miss JULIA GOULD. *Miss Terpsichore Slopperton*: Mme. PONISI. *Mrs. Slopperton*: Mrs. Vernon. *Mrs. Margery Lobkins*: Mrs. John Sefton. *Sally Rosemary*: Miss Kate Horn. *Principal Dancers*: Signor Neri, Mlle. Adeline. *Guests, Hiughwaymen, Soldiers, Sailors, Watchmen, Lasses, etc.*

Act 1, Scene 1: Interior of the Mug. *Scene 2*: London Bridge, at Night. *Scene 3*: Outside of Covent Garden Theatre, at night. *Scene 4*: Doctor Slopperton's Lodgings. *Scene 5*: Bridewell Yard and Garden with Environs (double scene).

Act 2, Scene 1: The Jolly Angler. *Scene 2*: Doctor Slopperton's Parlor. *Scene 3*: Landscape by Moonlight. *Scene 4*: The Tunnel in the Hollow Way.

Act 3, Scene 1: A Magnificent Hall. *Scene 2*: Chamber at Lord Manleverer's. *Scene 3*: The Home of Misery. *Scene 4*: View near the Tower of London, with the River Thames and Shipping, in the background.

ACT 1[13]
Scene 1
"Pass the Parting Goblet Round"
Full Chorus
"Mother Give your boy a Buss" (Song)
Mr. J. Collins
Scene 2
"Oh, for a cot by a Silvery lake" (Song)
Mr. Brunton
Scene 3
"Light, light, your honor" (Chorus)
Chorus
"What a Lovely Creature" (Solo)
Mr. J. Collins
"Still my heart is beating" (Solo)
Miss J. Gould
"This degradation" (Concerted Piece)
Mr. J. Collins, Miss J. Gould, Chorus
Scene 4
"These men are all deceivers" (Song)
Miss J. Gould

[11]A rival production and different translation was produced under different management 2 June 1851 at the Broadway Theatre for 18 performances. This production was preceded by a comedy, Husband's Secret (24 July 1851), etc.

[12]Preceded by a short comedy: Mr. and Mrs. Lillywhite; The Dumb Bell, etc.

[13]Interpolated during the run, as per programs:
Overture to DUC d'OLONNE by Auber
Ingomar Polka, introducing the air sung in that play by Mme. Ponisi
New Quadrilles "Paul Clifford"

Scene 5
"All is ready" (Concerted Piece)
Principals, Chorus

ACT 2
Scene 1
"Laughing at Sorrow" (Air and Chorus)
"The Stirrup Cup" (Song and Chorus)
Mr. J. Collins, Chorus
Scene 2
"Phillis have you seen my love" (Air)
Mme. Ponisi
"I saw him but once" (Song)
Miss J. Gould
Scene 3
"Hurra for the road" (Song)
Mr. J. Collins
Scene 4
"Good night, my Lord" (Chorus)

ACT 3
Scene 1
Grand Fancy Dress Ball
"Weave the Fairy Round" (Chorus)
Grand Pas de Deux (in French costume)
Signor Neri, Mlle. Adeline
Grand Cotillion and Polka
32 Characters
"By the Light" (Rondo)
Miss J. Gould
Scene 2
"Maiden, I'll ne'er deceive thee" (Song)
Mr. J. Collins
Scene 4
"Hurra for the Bowl" (Chorus of Sailors)
"Heaven Shield the Soldier" (Finale)

1852.02 THE MAGIC DEER, or Princess Sweetlips

A Serio-Comico-Tragico-Operatical-Heroical-Extravaganzical-Burletical Tale of Enchantment, in Two Acts[14]. (Libretto by Alfred Bunn.[15]) Produced by A. H. Purdy. Opened 8 March 1852 at the National Theatre and closed 12 March 1852 after 5 performances.

CAST: *Ding Dong Bell*, King of the Island of Jewels: Mr. C. W. TAYLOR. *Count Tinculum*, Lord High Chamberlain: Mr. HERBERT. *Prince Saffronhill*, heir to the crown of the Saffron Island: Mr. BRADSHAW. *Tristam*, his valet, and confidential ambassador to the Island of Jewels: Mr. L. Fox. *Rich-in-craft*, a mischievous Spirit: Harry Seymour. *Carl*, a peasant: Mr. Toulmin. *Little Red Courier*, of fairy creation: Master Murray. *The Fairies' Gardener*: Mr. Mack. *Officer of the Red Guard*: Mr. Barnett. *Page to Queen Jonquilla*: Miss Barry. *Black Carriers*: Messrs. Barry, Morrison, Mitchell, Blunt. *Blood O'Nouns*, a large Frog: Mr. Marsh. *Officer*: Mr. Cline. *Soldiers, Citizens, Courtiers, heralds, Banner Bearers, etc.*

Princess Sweetlips, Daughter of King Ding Dong Bell: Mrs. H. F. NICHOLS. *Carabossa*, Spirit of the Fountain: Mrs. W. G. JONES. *Fairy of the Lake*: Miss M. CHARLES. *Fairy of the Moonbeam*: Miss Williams. *Pixeapple*, Fairy of the Grove: Miss LUDLAM. *Finetta*: Miss MARTINE. *Queen Jonquilla*, of the Saffron Island: Mrs. HAUTONVILLE. *Rougetta*, Queen of the Red Island, in love with Prince Saffronhill: Miss COLBURN. *Nurses to the Infant Sweetlips*: Mrs. Barnett, Miss Miller. *Dancing Girls, Peasants, etc.*: Ladies of the Ballet.

ACT 1: A Beautiful Lake and Exterior of the Palace of King Ding Dong Bell, on the Island of Jewels. Chorus, "Come Bustle Lads, about." The Fairy of the Lake arrives in a Car of Shells; the Fairy of the Groves appears in her Foliage Bower; the Fairy of the Moonbeam descends in a Brilliant Star; unexpected arrival of an uninvited guest; Mysterious Warning; sudden appearance of the fairy of the Fountain; condemnation of the Princess to remain One and Twenty years without seeing the light of day.

Twenty years have now elapsed. Haunted Ruin on the borders of a forest. The Fairy Well; a Rough and Tumble between the Frog and Imp. Interior of the Magic Tower, in which the Princess Sweetlips has been confined for Twenty Years, though the malice of the Fairy of The Well. The Spirit of Evil is victorious—Tableau.

ACT 2: A Tranquil Lake and Woodman's Lodge; the Prince pulls the fatal trigger, the poor animal falls wounded. Sudden Transformation of the whole Scene to a Splendid Palace. Exterior of Dungeons in the Palace of Queen Rougetta. Palace of the Red Queen. The marriage procession approaches. The Palace Bell tolls the hour; the Sun has set; the White Deer is lost to the sight, and the Princess Sweetlips stands foreward in her own proper person; she sets all her enemies at defiance and trusts to Die Game; a happy termination. Tableau and Finale.

1852.03 THE ENCHANTRESS

A Revival of the Light Opera in Three Acts[16]. (Libretto by Alfred Bunn, adapted from a text by J. H. Vernoy de Saint-Georges.) Music by Michael William Balfe. Scenery by Henry Isherwood. Musical director, Signor LaManna. Manager, John Sefton. Opened 31 May 1852 at Niblo's Garden and closed 4 June 1852 after 3 performances in repertory.

CAST: *Stella*, the Enchantress: Mme. ANNA THILLON. *(Don) Sylvio*: Mr. HUDSON. *Ramir*, a Pirate, disguised as a Hermit: Mr. LEACH. *Mathanasius*: A. Andrews. *Chief of the Senate*: Mr. Martin. *Duke D'Aguila*, Regent of Sicily: Mr. Howard. *Nuguz*: Mr. Lyster. *Forte Brochio*, a Pirate: Mr. Rea. *Don Pedro*: Mr. Trevor. *Don Hervero*: Mr. Wilson. *Torrero*: Mr. French. *Don Miguel*: Mr. Wharton. *Gurno*: Mr. Gonzalez. *Theobaldo*: L. Vincent. *Sacripanto*: A. Vincent. *Pacheco*: Mr. Conyers.

1852.04 THE ENCHANTRESS

A Return Engagement of the Grand Romantic Opera (Light Opera) in Three Acts[17]. Libretto by Alfred Bunn, adapted from a text by J. H. Vernoy de Saint-Georges. Music by Michael William Balfe. Stage manager, J. P. Cartlitch. Scenery by Minard Lewis. Costumes by G. Taylor. Machinery by Mr. Tunison. Properties and appointments by Mr. Cabin. Ballet arranged by Mr. Evain. Orchestra under the direction of Mr. Wyatt. Produced by Charles R. Thorne. Opened 30 August 1852 at the New York Theatre, Astor Place[18], for 1 performance.

CAST: *Stella*, the Enchantress: Mlle. ANNA THILLON. *Don Sylvio*: Mr. HUDSON. *Ramir*, a Pirate disguised as the Hermit Fra Antonio: Mr. MEYER. *Duke de Aquila*, Regent of Sicily: Mr. Henderson. *Doctor Mathanasius*: E. B. Williams. *Nuguez*: Mr. Terry. *Forte Brachio*: Mr. Lewis. *Chief of the Senate*: Mr. Bensall. *Galeas*: Mr. Brand. *Torrero*: Mr. Weymss. *Don Miguel*: Mr. Davis. *Pacheco*: Mr. Howarde. *Gurno*: Mr. Love. *Theobaldo*: Mr. Evain. *Don Pedro*: Mr. Thompson. *Don Horvero*: Mr. Brown. *Sacripanto*: Mr. Williams. *Chief of Assassins*: Mr. Whitman. *Senators, Officers, Soldiers, Pirates, Peasants, Assassins, Pages, Attendants, Female Peasants, Dancers, Bridesmaids, etc.*

1852.05 THE PERI, or, The Enchanted Fountain

A Grand Romantic Opera in Three Acts, 9 Scenes[19]. (Libretto by S. J. Burr.) Taken from a story in Washington Irving's 'History of Columbus.' Music by James Gaspard Maeder. Scenery by George Heister. Costumes by Mrs. Wallis. Decorations by Mr. Wallis. Machinery by Mr. Speyers. Musical conductor, James G. Maeder. Leader of orchestra and Chorus master, Mr. Roberts. Stage management, Mr. Barry. Produced by E. A. Marshall. Opened 13 December 1852 at the Broadway Theatre and closed 25 December 1852 after 12 performances.

---

[14]THE WHITE DEER was proceded by a drama, The Female Highwayman, and followed by a farce, The Bonnycastles.

[15]When produced in London as 'The Princess who was changed to a deer,' the musical score was credited to R. Hughes, and in its previous Paris production to M. Pilati.

[16]Previously produced in New York 25 May 1846 at the Chatham Theatre for 12 performances. For Musical Numbers, see original 1846 production.

[17]Previously produced in New York 25 May 1846 at the Chatham Theatre for 12 performances. For Synopsis of Scenes and Musical Numbers, see original 1846 production. THE ENCHANTRESS was followed by the petite comedy, Faint Heart Never Won Fair Lady, with the Misses Raymond, Herring, Mrs. Penson, and Messrs. Marchant and Bellamy.

[18]Commonly known as the Astor Place Opera House.

[19]Preceded by a farce, Married & Settled; 2 Bonnycastles; Petticoat Government; Ladies Beware, etc.

CAST: *Fluvia*, the Peri, Queen of the Fairies: Miss CAROLINE RICHINGS. *Aquilla*, an Indian Girl in love with Miguel: Miss EMELINE REED. *Nanorkee*, an Indian witch: Miss PONISI. *Principal Dancing Fairies*: Misses Price, Josephine. *Ponce de Leon*, formerly Governor of Porto Rico: Mr. T. BISHOP. *Miguel*, his Lieutenant: Mr. PETER RICHINGS. *Pantro*, his Servant: Mr. W. DAVIDGE. *Alonzo, Pedro*, Soldiers: Messrs. Wright, Vincent. *Velasquez, Gomez*, Sailors: Messrs. Lyster, Keimes. *Razylcraft*, a Wizard: Mr. ROEHR. *First Witch*: Mr. Matthews. *Chorus of Soldiers, Sailors and Witches*: Messrs. Reinard, Miller, Meyers, Geery, Snefft, Kuselbach, Bonsiguis, Berenger, Albertazzi, Ximenes, Krensi, Vaux, Clevely, Foster, Michael, etc. Mesdames Gould, Weiderhold, J. Weiderhold, Berans, Albertazzi, Gerald, Meyer, Duchworth, Fell, Lewis, Brock, Carman.

Act 1, Scene 1: View of Castle and Harbor of Porto Rico. *Scene 2*: View of the Town of Porto Rico. *Scene 3*: Interior of Chapel.

Act 2, Scene 1: Panoramic view of the passage of the Fairy Bark to the Island of Bimini. The Wizard's Lair in the Enchanted Island. *Scene 2*: Landscape on the Enchanted Island. The Magic Chamber. View in the Island. *Scene 3*: The Enchanted Fountain and Fairy Land.

Act 3, Scene 1: Haunt of the Fairies. A Wood. *Scene 2*: Magic Hall and Visions. *Scene 3*: The Coral Bower. Scene of Enchantment.

ACT 1
Scene 1
Chorus (The foe is fled)
Song (Thoughts that have for years been sleeping)
T. Bishop
Cavatina (A Queen am I)
C. Richings
Concerted Piece (Do you believe)
Song (Why should anguish)
T. Bishop
Trio (Why despair)
Invisible Chorus of Fairies (Come to the Fountain Brink)
Quartette (Come and stay awhile)
Scene 2
Sailors' Chorus (Yoho! Yoho!)
Scene 3
Concerted Piece (Holy, Holy)
Chorus (See, see the Spell)
Finale (See, see, the Bark Invites)

ACT 2
Scene 1
Chorus of Witches (Ours is the storm)
Recitative (I'd have a storm)
Mr. Rohr
Grand Scena and Recitative (What care I?)
Mr. Rohr
Scene 2
Recitative and Air (My Beautiful)
T. Bishop
Cavatina (Mine it is at Midnight)
C. Richings
Song (Come back to the Forest)
E. Reed
Scene 3
"An Old Man is a Youth Again" (Home of my youth)
[T. Bishop]
Finale (What change, what bliss)

ACT 3
Scene 1
Chorus (Lightly let each Merry Note)
Solo (There are Sports in the Air)
C. Richings
Chorus (Love is the case)
Duet (Once more shall I behold her)
C. Richings, T. Bishop
Ballad (Gayer the Scene)
E. Reed
Song (Name not the wretch)
P. Richings
Scene 2
Descriptive Ballad (A maiden Sleeps)
C. Richings
Song (Dark Eyes)
Mr. Rohr
Trio (Who art thou)
Scene 3
Grand Finale (Joy, joy, let earth and main)

1852.06 THE BASKET MAKER'S WIFE

A Comic Opera in Two Acts[20]. (Libretto by Alfred Bunn, adapted from the ballad opera "The Devil to Pay" by Charles Coffey.) Music by Michael William Balfe. New dresses and transformations. Produced by William Niblo. Opened 17 December 1852 at Niblo's Garden and closed 23 December 1852 after 3 performances in repertory.

CAST: *Count Wallenberg*: Mr. ALLEYNE. *Albert*: Mr. J. B. Bentley. *Herman*: JAMES HUDSON. *Lunastro*: FRED LYSTER. *Maestro Hans*: Mr. Müller. *Carlo*: Mr. Rea. *Guthman*: Mr. G. Howard. *Vincent*: Mr. Convers. *Letty*: Mme. ANNA THILLON. *The Countess of Wallenberg*: Mrs. [Clara Fisher] MAEDER. *Bridget*: Mrs. Conover. *Stammitz*: Mr. McNesbit. *Stralheim*: Mr. Bracciani. *Vol Venz*: Mr. Wilson. *Ludwig*: Mr. Hoffman. *Fiendz*: Mr. Schlein.

1852.07 THE BOHEMIAN GIRL

A Revival of the Light Opera in Three Acts[21]. Libretto by Alfred Bunn, after Jules-Henri Vernoy de Saint-Georges' ballet-pantomime "The Gypsy." Music by Michael William Balfe. Produced by Thomas S. Hamblin. Opened 22 December 1852 at the Bowery Theatre and closed 31 December 1852 after 9 performances.

CAST: *Arline*: ADA PLUNKETT. *Thaddeus*: Mr. JAMES DUNN. *Count Arnheim*: Mr. HAMILTON. *Buda*: Mrs. YEAMANS. *Austrian Dance*: Miss G. Dawes, Mr. Fletcher. Also Drum Polka.

1853.01 THE REVIEW, or, The Wags of Windsor

The Revived Musical Farce in One Act[22]. Produced by James W. Wallack. Opened 1 February 1853 at Wallack's Theatre and closed 13 May 1853 in repertory.

CAST: *Caleb Quotem*: Mr. CHARLES WALCOT. *John Lump*: Mr. Hale. *Looney Mac Twoulter*: Mr. JOHN BROUGHAM. *Deputy Bull*: Mr. Chippendale. *Captain Brangard*: Mr. Reynolds. *Dubbs*: Mr. Durant. *Grace Gaylove*: Mrs. Hale. *Lucy*: Mrs. STEPHENS. *Martha*: Miss Tayleure. Also Messrs. Rea, Lyster, Trevor, Oliver, Brown.

MUSICAL NUMBERS
"A poor little Gipsey" (Song)
Mrs. Stephens
"Life's a Bumper" (Glee)
Messrs. Walcot, Rea, Lyster, Trevor, Oliver, Brown
"Oh, Whack!" (Song)
Mr. J. Brougham
"I'm Parish Clerk"
Mr. Walcot
Briskly beat the Hollow Drum" (Finale)
All the characters

---

[20]Previously produced in England as THE DEVIL'S IN IT.
[21]First produced in New York 25 November 1844 for 17 performances in repertory at the Park Theatre. For Synopsis of Scenes and Musical Numbers, see original 1844 production. Followed by The Irish Lion, with Mr. Eddy as Tim Moore, Mrs. Grattan as Mrs. Fitzgig, with singing and dancing. Also The Smuggler of the Mill, with Messrs. Hamilton, Bowes, Miss Heron, Mrs. Grattan.
[22]Performed as an after=piece to E. B. Lytton's drama, The Lady of Lyons.

1853.02 FIRST COME—FIRST SERVED

An Operetta in Two Acts[23]. Music by Adrien Boïeldieu. New scenery and costumes. Produced by James W. Wallack. Opened 21 February 1853 at Wallack's Theatre and closed 2 March 1853 after 6 performances in repertory.

CAST: *Marquis de Valmont*: Mr. FRED LYSTER. *Frontin*, his valet, assuming his name: CHARLES M. WALCOT. *Bailie*: Mr. Rea. *François*: Mr. Trevor. *Blaize*: Mr. Alleyne. *Villagers, Servants, etc. Nanette*: Miss JULIA GOULD.

ACT 1

Introduction
Messrs. Rea, Trevor, Alleyne, Miss J. Gould
"This wine you say" (Duet)
Messrs. Walcot, Alleyne
"For one day I'm master" (Song)
C. Walcot
"Oh you've rights" (Duet)
Miss J. Gould, C. Walcot
"Now with shouts of joy" (Finale)
All the characters

ACT 2

"Just like Julius Caesar" (Duet)
Messrs. Rea, Lyster
Song and Chorus
Miss J. Gould, Characters
Finale
All the characters

1853.03 THE PET OF THE PETTICOATS!

A Revival of the Comic Operetta in Three Acts[24]. Play by John Baldwin Buckstone (adapted from the French vaudeville Vert-Vert by de Leuven and Desforges.) Produced by James W. Wallack. Opened 25 March 1853 at Wallack's Theatre and closed (25 April 1853) in repertory.

CAST: *Paul*, nicknamed 'Poll the Pet': Miss LAURA KEENE. *Mons. Zephyr*, Dancing Master to the Convent: Mr. CHARLES WALCOT. *Job*, the Convent Gardener: H. B. Phillips. *Officers of Dragoons (8): Chevalier St. Pierre*: Mr. REYNOLDS. *Colonel Belair*: Mr. FRED LYSTER. *Captain Cannonade*: Mr. REA. *Ensign Bannier*: Mr. Alleyne. *Captain Achille*: Mr. Trevor. *Lieutenant Victor, Captain Fuzee Ensign Cadet, Lieutenant Cisar*: Gentlemen of the Chorus. *Tobie*, Landlord of the Golden Lion: Mr. Durant.

Lady Superior of the Convent: Mrs. Rea. *Sister Vinaigre* Mrs. Cramer. *Mimi*, a Boarder: Mrs. Stephens. *Julia, Emma*, Boarders at the Convent and married to St. Pierre and Belair: Mrs. Hale, Miss Tayleure. *Madame Bravura*, an opera singer: Miss JULIA GOULD. *Babet*, Chambermaid at the Golden Lion: Miss Osborne. *Zoe, Lison, Dorothée*, Boarders: Ladies of the Chorus. *Travelers, Waiters, Officers of Dragoons, etc.*

Act 1: A Convent Garden.

Act 2: The Interior of the Golden Lion at Nevers.

Act 3: The Convent Garden, same as Act 1.

ACT 1[25]

Concerted Piece (Come hither, come,—come hither, come)
Mrs. Stephens, Mrs. Hale, Miss Tayleure, Boarders
Concerted Piece (Why do you fly from us, pretty Poll?)
All the Girls, L. Keene, Mrs. Stephens, Zoe
Finale and Crying Chorus (Goodbye, sisters, dry your tears)
L. Keene, Mrs. Stephens, All the Girls

ACT 2

Opening Chorus (Women, gaming, drinking)
Mr. Rea, F. Lyster, Chorus
Song (In the gay French guards a solider, I)
Mr. Reynolds
Song (Away with all water wherever I come)
Mr. Rea
(Lyrics from Leigh Hunt's translation of Redi's poem of 'Bacchus in Tuscany.')
Song (The pious child who loves to walk)
L. Keene
Song (Sweet eyes, how beautiful you are!)
L. Keene
Song (Let the butterfly be constant to the blossom of the bell)
F. Lyster
(*Lyrics by* S. M. Dowling.)
Song (A health to thee, my sweetest)
L. Keene
Finale (Sweetest lady, now adieu)
L. Keene, J. Gould, All

ACT 3

Song (Love's a little pet, wild and overwhelming)
Mrs. Stephens
Concerted Piece (You naughty, wicked, dreadful, horrid, cruel, little man)
Mrs. Stephens, All
Finale (The conqueror love smiles on us now)
Mr. Reynolds, Mrs. Stephens, L. Keene, Chorus, All

1853.04 THE BOHEMIAN GIRL

Mme. Anna Thillon's English Opera Company in a Revival of the Light Opera in Three Acts[26]. Libretto by Alfred Bunn, after Jules-Henri Vernoy de Saint-Georges' ballet-pantomime "The Gypsy." Music by Michael William Balfe. Scenery by Mr. Henry Isherwood. Orchestra under the direction of Signor LaManna. Produced by William Niblo. Opened 20 July 1853 at Niblo's Garden in repertory; season closed 16 August 1853.

CAST: *Thaddeus*: Mr. J. J. FRAZER. *Devilshoof*: Mr. JAMES HUDSON. *Count Arnheim*: Mr. STEPHEN LEACH. *Arline*: Mme. ANNA THILLON. *The Gipsy Queen*: Mrs. [Clara Fisher] MAEDER. Full Chorus and Corps de Ballet.

1853.05 SHYLOCK: A Jerusalem Hearty Joke

An entirely new reading of Shakespeare, from an edition hitherto undiscovered by modern authorities, and which it is hoped may be received as the stray leaves of a Jerusalem Hearty-Joke (A Musical Burlesque in One Act)[27]. Play by Francis Talfourd, founded on William Shakespeare's "The Merchant of Venice." Scenery, Mr. George Heilge. Musical director, J. Cooke. Stage manager, John Moore. Produced by William E. Burton. Opened 29 October 1853 at Burton's Theatre in repertory and closed 9 November 1853 after 4 performances.

CAST: *Judge Deukeroennis*: Mr. Moore. *Mr. Prince of Morocco*, black as the soot which he prefers to Portia, who prefers Bassanio's suit to his: Mr. LAWSON. *Shylock*, a Jew, who does not on this occasion conduct himself as a Gentile-man: Mr. T. B. JOHNSTON. *Portia*, a rich Heiress—a Lady called to the Bar for a Maiden Assize: Miss (Emeline) RAYMOND. *Jessica*, Shylock's "One fair Daughter, and—something more: Mrs. BURTON.

---

[23]Preceded by a comedy by Poole, Twould Puzzle a Conjuror; in later performances The Lady of Lyons, Road to Ruin or The Rivals were the fore-pieces.

[24]First produced in New York 21 May 1835 at the Park Theatre.

[25]Musical numbers prepared from published prompt book (Samuel French, New York, [1853]). Additional interpolations listed in program: "The Pious Child" (Song) performed by Laura Keene, and a song performed by Miss J. Gould.

[26]First produced in New York 25 November 1844 for 17 performances in repertory at the Park Theatre. For Synopsis of Scenes and Musical Numbers, see original 1844 production.

[27]No program found for this production. For Synopsis of Scenes and Musical Numbers, see the later revival of 27 July 1857 at Wallack's Theatre from which prompt book a list was prepared. SHYLOCK was accompanied by a varying program of after-pieces, The Young Actress, and The Serious Family, on the opening performance; Parents and Guardians, and My Uncle's Card, at a later performance.

FAUSTUS,

1854.01 or, the Demon of the Drachenfels

A Revival of the Grand Romantic Spectacle in Three Acts, 14 Scenes[28]. (Play by George Soane. Songs, duets and concerted music by Sir Henry Bishop. Melo-dramatic music composed, selected and arranged by Mons. Perot.) Stage manager, John B. Wright. Scenery designed by George Heister. Carnival and ballet dances produced under the direction of Prof. B. Yates. Machinery by John Furze. Decorations by S. Wallis. Dresses by Mrs. Wallis. Music under the immediate direction of Mr. Roberts. Produced by E. A. Marshall. Opened 29 May 1854 at the Broadway Theatre and closed 17 June 1854 after 18 performances.

CAST: *Faustus*, the German Doctor: Mr. C. POPE. *Mephistopheles*, the ________: Mr. CONWAY. *Count de Casanova*, Father of Rosolia: Mr. WHITING. *Count Orsini*, a young Venetian, in love with Adine: Mr. SANDFORD. *Montolio, Antonio*, Venetians and friends of Enrico: Messrs. Lanergan, McDouall. *Wagner*, a young German student: Mr. W. DAVIDGE. *Enrico*, a gallant Soldier, and brother of Adine: Mr. GROSVENOR. *Marco*, a Venetian officer: Mr. Walters. *Grognoso*, Innkeeper and Father to Lucetta: Mr. Matthews. *Brevillo*, a Servant of the Inn, and in love with Lucetta: Mr. Fisk. *Officers*: Messrs. Wright, Goldston, Cleverly, Williams. *Paolo*: Mr. Vincent. *Luco*: Mr. Cutter. *Officers of the Inquisition*: Messrs. Keimes, Marhler, Herman, Hart.

Adine, Sister to Enrico: Mme. PONISI. *Rosolia*, Daughter of the Count de Casanova, and betrothed to Montolio: ADELAIDE GOUGENHEIM. *Lucetta*, Grognoso's Daughter, and in love with Wagner: JOSEPHINE GOUGENHEIM. *Lords and Ladies, Attendants, Officers, Chamberlains, Guards, Banner Bearers, Male and Female Peasants.*

Janet: Miss Barnet. *Liza*: Miss Williams. *Manette*: Miss Richardson. (*Principal Dansers*: Misses Adelaide Price, Leeder, Signor Doubledenee.) *Choristers, Dancers, Masqueraders, Grotesque Figures*: Ladies and Gentlemen of the Company. Chorus and Supernumerary Force of 150.

Carnival Scene, Comic Specialties: *Little Old Man*: Master Wallis. *Little Old Woman*: Miss Wallis. *Giantess*: Mrs. Cutter. *Punchinello*: Prof. B. Yates. *Dwarf Dance*: Original One. *Harlequin*: Mr. J. Bath. *Clown*: Mr. C. Bacon. *Pantaloon*: Mr. T. Coleman. *Fishwoman*: Imoggins. *Columbine*: Miss Adelaide Price.

1854.02 THE ENCHANTRESS

A Revival of the Light Opera in Three Acts[29]. Libretto by Alfred Bunn, adapted from a text by J. H. Vernoy de Saint-Georges. Music by Michael William Balfe. Musical director, Signor LaManna. Produced by Charles R. Thorne. Opened 4 July 1854 at Niblo's Garden in repertory; season closed 5 August 1854.

CAST: *Stella*, the Enchantress: Mme. ANNA THILLON. *Don Sylvio*: Mr. J. J. FRAZER. *Ramir*: Mr. Meyer. Company also included Mr. FRED LYSTER, Mr. Reynolds, A. Andrews, and Mrs. [Clara Fisher] MAEDER, CONOVER.

1854.03 THE BOHEMIAN GIRL

A Revival of the Light Opera in Three Acts[30]. (Libretto by Alfred Bunn, after Jules-Henri Vernoy de Saint-Georges' ballet-pantomime "The Gypsy.") Music by Michael William Balfe. Stage manager, G. H. Barrett. Musical director and conductor, Signor LaManna. Produced by E. A. Marshall. Opened 12 October 1854 at the Broadway Theatre in repertory; season closed 17 February 1854.

CAST: *Thaddeus*, a proscribed Pole: Mr. WILLIAM HARRISON. *Devilshoof*, Chief of the Gipsy Tribe: Mr. CAMOENS. *Count Arnheim*, Governor of Presburg: Mr. BORRANI. *Count Florestein*, his nephew: Mr. W. Reeves. *Captain of the Guard*: Mr. Vincent. *First Gipsy*: Mr. Bernard. *Second Gipsy*: Mr. Wright. *Officer*: Mr. Allen. *Arline*, the Bohemian Girl: Miss LOUISA PYNE. *Queen of the Gipsies*: Miss (SUSAN) PYNE.

1854.04 APOLLO IN NEW YORK

A Local Piece of Satire in One Act, 4 Scenes.[31] Play by Dion Boucicault. Stage manager, John Moore. Music arranged by J. Cooke. Scenic artist, Mr. Heigle. Produced by William E. Burton. Opened 11 December 1854 at Burton's Theatre and closed 6 January 1855 after 18 performances in repertory.

CAST: *Jupiter*, God of Thunder, disguised as Sandy Hook, a pilot: Mr. (WILLIAM E.) BURTON. *Apollo*, or Apollonini, a grand Italian tenor: Miss (MARIAN) MACARTHY. *Mars*, as a Bowery fireman: Mr. A. ANDREWS. *Mercury*, as a Penny-a-Liner: Mr. HOLMAN. *Cupid*, as a News Boy: Miss KATE SAXON. *New York*, one side as Fifth Avenue, one side as Bowery, and one side as—something else: Mr. T. JOHNSTON. *Reporters*: Messrs. Russell, Gardener, etc. *Newsboys*: Mr. C. Parsloe, etc. *Butcher*: Mr. Gourlay. *Policemen*: Messrs. Lawson, Paul. *Cabman*: Mr. Macarthy. (*Chatham Street Auctioneer*: Mr. WILLIAM E. BURTON.) *Vistors*: Messrs. Wenslee, Hempstead, etc.

Juno, alias Hell Gate: Mrs. HOLMAN. *Venus*, a French modiste: Mrs. HOUGH. *The Mysterious Mrs. Coutts*: Mr. Frederic. *Mrs. Partington*: Sandy Hook [Mr. WILLIAM E. BURTON.]

Members of the Woman's Rights Convention: *The Reverend Antoinette Blue*: Miss Florence. *Mrs. Screecher Crowe*, with a protegee: Mrs. COOKE. *Abby Fulsome*: Miss WALTERS. *Rs. Hook Smith*: Miss M. Cooke. *Mrs. Bloomer*: Miss Terry. *Lucretia Pott*: Miss Farren. *Lucy Rock*: Miss Connor. *Anne Royal*: Mrs. Bell.

Scene 1: Sandy Hook, with the Lighthouses. *Scene 2*: Staten Island Ferry. *Scene 3*: A Tavern and Mock Auction in Chatham Street. *Scene 4*: Woman's Rights Convention.

MUSICAL NUMBERS

Scene 1
- Landing of Venus and Apollo
- "Wait for the Wagon" (Song)

Scene 2
- Public Reception of the Great Tenor
- "How do you like the country"
- The White lady and the Singer
- "I own I am seducing" (Air)
- "The Four Leaved Shamrock" (Air)

Scene 3
- Apollo proposed as Mayor of New York
- "You'll remember me" (Air)
- Present State of New York, with its Incumbrances
- Wonderful Effects produced by a Know Nothing Hat
- Sale of Unredeemed Pledges
- Sandy Hook rather shaky on the Liquor Question
- "The Know Nothing" (Song)

Scene 4
- Mrs. Partington in the Chair
- The Passwords and Signs of the Secret Order
- Beautiful American Tableau
- Yankee Doodle Finale

1854.05 MONSIEUR JACQUES

A Musical Drama in One Act.[32] Play by Morris Barnett. Music composed by John Barnett. Produced by William E. Burton. Opened 18 December 1854 at Burton's Theatre and closed 21 December 1854 after 2 performances in

---

[28]First produced 11 October 1827 at the Park Theatre; revived 13 January 1851 at the Broadway Theatre for 36 performances. For Synopsis of Scenes and Musical Numbers, see 1851 production. This revival was preceded by a farce: Antony and Cleopatra; Faint Heart Never Won Fair Lady, etc. Specialties added for the Carnival Scene in this revival:

Spanish Dance, El Jaleo de Xeres
Mlle. Leeder

La Jota Arragonese
B. Yates, Vincent, Misses Price, Josephine, E. Wallis, Osborne, Richardson, Pentland

Three Legged Polka
Signor Doubledenee

La Neapolitain
Prof. B. Yates, Miss Adelaide Price

Grand Gallop
Pantomime Characters

[29]Previously produced in New York 25 May 1846 at the Chatham Theatre for 12 performances. For Synopsis of Scenes and Musical Numbers, see original 1846 production.

[30]First produced in New York 25 November 1844 at the Park Theatre for 17 performances in repertory. For Synopsis of Scenes and Musical Numbers, see original 1844 production. Followed by a farce: To Oblige Benson, etc.

[31]APOLLO IN NEW YORK was preceded by a comedy, Loving Too Fast, or a Twelvemonth's Honeymoon, and followed by a farce, A Blighted Being; these were replaced by a play, The Upper Ten and the Lower Twenty. In the thrid wek of the run, a new character was added for Mr. Burton by the name of Bonhomme.

[32]MONSIEUR JACQUES was preceded by Mr. Barnett's comedy, The Serious Family, and followed by the farce, A Blighted Being.

repertory; returned 2 March 1855 to the Broadway Theatre for 1 performance in repertory; returned 15 May 1855 to the Metropolitan Theatre in repertory.

CAST: *Monsieur Jacques* (his original character): Mr. MORRIS BARNETT. (Mr.) *Sequence*: Mr. Andrews. *Vivid*: Mr. Marchant. *Anthony (Antonio)*:— —-. *Nina*: Miss E. RAYMOND.

Scene: An attic. Dover, England.

MUSICAL NUMBERS[33]

Air "To-morrow, To-morrow"
M. Barnett

Song "Palermo's Bell"
Miss E. Raymond

Romance "A noble's daughter loved to madness"
Miss E. Raymond

Still cheer thee youth
Miss E. Raymond

1854.06 THE BEGGAR'S OPERA

A Revival of the Comic Opera (Ballad Opera)[34]. Libretto by John Gay. Adapted to the modern stage by William Harrison. Musical conductor, Signor LaManna. Produced by the (Louisa) Pyne-(William) Harrison Troupe. Presented by E. A. Marshall. Opened 20 December 1854 at the Broadway Theatre in repertory; season closed 17 February 1855.

CAST: *Captain Macheath*: Mr. WILLIAM HARRISON. *Peachum*: Mr. D. WHITING. *Lockit*: Mr. France. *Mat o' the Mint*: Mr. (Joseph) Grosvenor. *Filch*: Mr. W. P. DAVIDGE. *Ben-Budge*: Mr. Scheff. *Crook-fingered Jack*: Mr. Wood. *Jemmy Twitcher*: Mr. Rea. *Wat Dreary*: Mr. Horton. *Nimming Ned*: Mr. Allen. *Harry Paddington*: Mr. Hayes. *Robin of Bagshot*: Mr. Vincent. *Drawer*: Mr. Barnet.

Polly: LOUISA PYNE. *Lucy*: Miss JOSEPHINE GOUGENHEIM. *Mrs. Coaxer*: Mrs. Henry. *Jenny*: Mrs. James Seymour. *Mrs. Peachum*: Mrs. France.

Prologue and Epilogue: *The Player*: Mr. McDouall. *The Beggar*: Mr. M. W. Leffingwell.

MUSICAL NUMBERS

"Through all the employments of life" (Song)
Mr. Whiting

"'Tis woman that seduces all mankind" (Song)
Mr. W. Davidge

"Like the fair flower in its lustre" (Song)
L. Pyne

"Can love be controlled by advice" (Song)
L. Pyne

"Oh! Polly" (Duet)
Mr. Whiting, L. Pyne

"Like a ship in storms" (Song)
L. Pyne

"Oh! ponder well" (Song)
L. Pyne

"Pretty Polly, say" (Song)
W. Harrison

"My heart was so free" (Song)
W. Harrison

"Were I laid" (Duet)
W. Harrison, L. Pyne

"The miser still a shilling sees" (Duet)
W. Harrison, L. Pyne

"Fill every glass" (Solo and Chorus)

"Let us take the road" (Air and Chorus)

"If the heart of a man" (Song)
W. Harrison

"At the tree I shall suffer with pleasure" (Song)
W. Harrison

"How happy could I be with either?" (Song)
W. Harrison

"I'm bubbled" (Duet)
L. Pyne, J. Gougenheim

"Cease your funning" (Air with celebrated Variations)
L. Pyne

"Madame Flirt" (Duet)
L. Pyne, J. Gougenheim

"I'm like a skiff" (Song)
J. Gougenheim

"Come sweet lass" (Song)
J. Gougenheim

"The Charge is prepared" (Song)
W. Harrison

"Oh! cruel, cruel case" (Medley)
W. Harrison

"Would I might be hanged" (Trio)
L. Pyne, J. Gougenheim, W. Harrison

Finale—A General Dance, arranged expressly for the characters

1854.07 THE ENCHANTRESS

A Revival of the Grand Opera and Spectacle (Light Opera) in Three Acts, 10 Scenes[35]. (Libretto by Alfred Bunn, adapted from a text by J. H. Vernoy de Saint-Georges.) Music by Michael William Balfe. Scenery by George Heister. Properties, Appointments, Banners by S. Wallis. Machinery by John Furze. Ballet under the direction of Mr. Wiethoff. Musical conductor, Signor LaManna. Produced by the (Louisa) Pyne-(William) Harrison Troupe. Presented by E. A. Marshall. Opened 25 December 1854 at the Broadway Theatre in repertory closing 17 February 1855.

CAST: *Don Sylvio*: Mr. WILLIAM HARRISON. *Duke D'Aquila*, Regent of Sicily: Mr. MEYER. *Doctor Mathanasius*, Tutor of Don Sylvio: D. WHITING. *Galeas*, Prime Minister: Mr. Sanford. *Ramir*, Chief of the Pirates: Mr. BORRANI. *Chief of the Senate*: Mr. Walters. *Nuguez*, Ramir's Lieutenant: Mr. McDouall. *Forte Brachio*, a Pirate: Mr. Horton. *Chief of the Assassins*: Mr. Barnard. *Jose*: Mr. Vincent. *Don Henrique*, an Officer: Mr. Cutter. *Seneschal*: Mr. Smith. *Don Mathias*: Mr. G. Rae. *Pacheo*: Mr. Wright. *Sancho*: Mr. Allen. *Pages*: Master Wright, Miss Furze. *Nobles, Cardinals, Lords, Ladies, Soldiers, Pirates, Greek Slaves, etc.*

Stella (the Enchantress): LOUISA PYNE. *Black Domino*: Miss Portland. *Blue Domino*: Mrs. Barnard. (*Ballet*: Mlle. ZOE, Misses Henry, Price; Messrs. B. Yates, Wiethoff. Corps de Ballet.)

Act 1, Scene 1: The Hermitage of "Our Lady of the Wood." Mountains in the distance. Descent amidst the rocks. *Scene 2*: The Pirates' Cave. Entrance of the Enchantress. *Scene 3*: Rocky Pass and Gorge. *Scene 4*: Abode of the Enchantress; State-room of the Pirate Queen; Sylvio's Dream; Greek Slaves Tableau.

Act 2, Scene 1: Sylvio's richly draperied tent; disaffection of the Soldiery, and timely arrival of an unknown friend; Destruction of the Regent's Fleet. *Scene 2*: Rich Apartment in the Palace; Vestibule of the grand hall of Audience. *Scene 3*: Sumptuous Palace Scene. The scene is thrown back, forming an immense amphitheatre for a Grand Bal Masque. *Scene 4*: The Pavilion of Myrtles.

Act 3, Scene 1: Exterior of a Sicilienne Inn. Vineyard adjacent; Arched Interior; Visit of the Senators to Don Silvio; the Enchantress still maintains the Ascendancy, and Don Sylvio is proclaimed King. *Scene 2*: Shore of Palermo, by Moonlight; Church of St. Marie Majeure; the Nuptials of the Enchantress, and the Fulfillment of the Vow. Magnanimity of Ramir, the Pirate Chief; his pardon; Sylvio and Stella, King and Queen of Sicily. Chorus and Tableau.

MUSICAL NUMBERS, SPECIALTIES[36]

Grand Bal Masque (from the opera GUSTAVUS)

Grand March
Characters

Punchinello
B. Yates

Pas des Follies
Misses Henry, Price, Corps de Ballet

Grand Pas de Intrigue
Mlle. Zoe, Mons. Wiethoff

[33]Musical numbers and Scenes not listed in programs. List prepared from published libretto (J. Duncombe & Co., London, (1836)].

[34]First produced in New York 3 December 1750 at the Theatre in Nassau Street for 5 performances in repertory. This revival was preceded by a comedy, A Lady & Gentleman.

[35]Previously produced in New York 25 May 1846 at the Chatham Theatre for 12 performances. For Synopsis of Scenes and Musical Numbers, see original 1846 production. Preceded by the farce, To Oblige Benson.

[36]Musical numbers not listed in programs. Only this new ballet specialty was detailed.

Greek Polka
Misses Price, Henry, Mr. B. Yates
La Sicilienne
Mlle. Zoe, Mons. Wiethoff
Grande Gallope
All the Characters

GUY MANNERING, or, the Gipsy's Prophecy

1855.01

A Revival of the Romantic Musical Drama in Three Acts, 10 Scenes[37]. Play by Daniel Terry, adapted from Sir Walter Scott's novel of the same name. (Music by Sir Henry R. Bishop, John Davy, Messrs. Thomas Attwood and Whittaker.) Stage manager, G. H. Barrett. Scenery by George Heister. Properties by S. Wallis. Machinery by John Furze. Musical conductor, Signor LaManna. Produced by the (William) Harrison-(Louisa) Pyne Troupe. Presented by E. A. Marshall. Opened 1 January 1855 at the Broadway Theatre in repertory; season closed 17 February 1855.

CAST: *Colonel Mannering*: Mr. Graee. *Henry Bertram*: WILLIAM HARRISON. *Dominie Sampson*: Mr. W. DAVIDGE. *Dandie Dinmont*: Mr. Whiting. *Dirk Hatteraick*: Mr. Hanchett. *Gilbert Glossin*: Mr. M. W. LEFFINGWELL. *Bailie Mucklethrift*: Mr. France. *Gipsies (3)*: *Sebastian*: Mr. Rae. *Gabriel*: Mr. Borrani. *Franco*, a boy: Miss Wallis. *Jack Jabos*, Ostler to Mrs. M'Candlish: Mr. Cutter. *Sergeant M'Crae*: Mr. Allen. *Farmers*: Messrs. Rae, Lyster, Keimes, Franks, etc. *Villagers, Gipsies, Soldiers, Chorusters, etc.*

Julia Mannering: LOUISA PYNE. *Lucy Bertram*: Miss ADELAIDE GOUGENHEIM. *Meg Merrilies*: Mme. PONISI. *Mrs. M'Candish*: Mrs. France. *Flora*: Miss Joey [Josephine] Gougenheim.

Act 1, Scene 1: M'Candlish's Inn. Scotland. *Scene 2*: Another room in the Inn.

Act 2, Scene 1: Miss Mannering's Boudoir in the House at Woodburne. *Scene 2*: A desolate Heath between Woodburne and Kippletringan. *Scene 3*: A wilder and more romantic part of the chase, or forest. A sort of scattered copse wood, with branches of one or two decayed oaks. A cliff or two rising behind them. Hills in the distance. *Scene 4*: A wild landscape. *Scene 5*: A sort of Dell or Passe, with cliffs rugged or broken; shaggy underwood growing on each side.

Act 3, Scene 1: Ellangowan. The Seashore, with the Castle on the rocks. *Scene 2*: A apartment in Woodburne House. *Scene 3*: The cavern near the Tower of Dorncleugh.

ACT 1[38]
Scene 1
Glee (The winds whistle cold)
Mr. and Mrs. France, Farmers
Scene 2
Air (Ye dear paternal scenes, farewell!)
Miss A. Gougenheim
Finale (The fox jumpt over the parson's gate)
Mr. W. Davidge
Trio (Away with old Care)
Misses L. Pyne, A. Gougenheim, Mr. W. Davidge, Chorus
ACT 2
Scene 1
Air (Oh! slumber, my darling)
Miss A. Gougenheim
Air (Oh, tell me, love, the dearest hour)
Miss. A. Gougenheim, Mr. W. Harrison
Song (Be mine, dear maid!)
Mr. W. Harrison
Air (In ancient times, in Britain's isle)
Miss L. Pyne
Scene 2
Duet (Without a companion, what's life but a heath)
Messrs. Whiting, W. Harrison
Scene 3
Gipsey Glee and Chorus (The chough and crow to roost are gone)
Miss Wallis, Gipsey Woman, Mr. Borrani
Air (Oh! hark thee, young Henry)
Mme. Ponisi
Spoken (Listen, youth, to words of power)
Mme. Ponisi
Scene 4
Song (Follow him, nor fearful deem)
Mr. Borrani
Scene 5
Song and Chorus (Now fill the glass, and let it pass)
Messrs. Whiting, Allen, Chorus
ACT 3
Scene 1
Air (Oh! blame me not, that such high worth)
Miss. A. Gougenheim
Scene 3
Finale and Chorus (Oh! let your hands assure the youth)
Misses A. Gougenheim, L. Pyne, Mr. W. Harrison, Chorus
MUSICAL NUMBERS[39]
"Bonnie Prince Charlie"
L. Pyne
"Home Sweet Home"
L. Pyne
"Now hope, now fear" (The celebrated Echo Duet)
L. Pyne, W. Harrison
"The Thorn"
W. Harrison
"Without a Companion"
W. Harrison, Mr. Whiting

CINDERELLA, or, The Little Glass Slipper

1855.02

A Grand Opera and Fairy Spectacle in Three Acts, 13 Scenes[40], (from the fairy tale by Charles Perrault). Stage manager, G. H. Barrett. Scenery by George Heister. Appointments, tricks and decorations by S. Wallis. Machinery by John Furze. Costumes by Mrs. Wallis. Dances arranged by Mr. B. Yates. Musical conductor, Signor LaManna. Produced by the (Louisa) Pyne-(William) Harrison Troupe. Presented by E. A. Marshall. Opened 15 January 1855 at the Broadway Theatre in repertory closing 17 February 1855.

CAST: *Prince Felix*: WILLIAM HARRISON. *Alidoro*, his Tutor: Mr. (HENRY) HORNCASTLE. *Dandini*, the Prince valet: Mr. BORRANI. *Baron Pompolino*: Mr. WHITING. *Pedro*, the Baron's servant: Mr. W. DAVIDGE. *Clorinda*: Miss (SUSAN) PYNE. *Thisbe*: CARLOTTA POZZONI. *Fairy Queen*: Mrs. REEVES. *Fairies, Sylphs, Cupids, Lords, Ladies, etc.*: Numerous Auxiliaries. *Cinderella*: Miss LOUISA PYNE.

Act 1, Scene 1: The Fairy Haunt. Enchanted Fountain. *Scene 2*: Vision. Magical appearance of Cinderella. *Scene 3*: Prince overcome sinks on a bank of flowers, and the clouds pass and repass; the scene changes to a beautiful landscape. *Scene 4*: A Gothic Apartment in the Baron's Castle.

Act 2, Scene 1: An Ante-chamber in the Palace. *Scene 2*: The Kitchen of the Baron. *Scene 3*: Magical change to a Moonlight View of the Prince's Castle in the distance. *Scene 4*: The Coach and Four makes the Circuit of the Stage.

Act 3, Scene 1: A Grand Corinthian Palace; the Prince's Ball. *Scene 2*: Pedro and the Mysterious Pumpkin. *Scene 3*: The Kitchen; Return of Cinderella and Pedro. *Scene 4*: The Baron's Apartment; the Proclamation of the Prince. *Scene 5*: Audience Chamber of the Prince. Magical change of scene, discovering the Fairies' abode with the Temple of Love, surrounded by revolving Suns.

[37]Previously produced in New York 18 September 1816 at the Park Theatre. This production of GUY MANNERING was accompanied by Francis Talfourd's burlesque Ganem, or The Slave of Love, in which Mr. Davidge sang "Will they remember me," and Misses Henry and Price performed the Trial Dance from La Bayadere. After GUY MANNERING, Mr. Yates also performed his Comic Pas Seul (The Solider and the Sailor), and Mr. Seymour sang a Comic Song.

[38]Musical numbers not listed in programs, apart from interpolations below. List prepared from published prompt book (William Taylor & Co., New York, [1849]).

[39]Interpolations listed in program, not in performance order.

[40]No authors credited. Concluding with a farce, The Irish Tutor; Bona Fide Travelers, etc.

ACT 1
Scene 1
Chorus and Dance of Fairies and Sylphs (While the sunbeams are glancing)
Song (Morning its sweets are flinging)
Concerted Piece (Music floats the air)
W. Harrison, Chorus
Scene 3
Chorus (What wild sounds)
Solo (Soft, behold!)
Mr. Borrani
Chorus (Our noble Prince is found)
Scene 4
Trio (With steps so light)
L. Pyne, C. Pozzoni, Mrs. Reeves
Chorus and Quartette (Back from his morning chase)
Song (Ye tormentors)
Mr. Whiting
Recitative and Duet
W. Harrison, L. Pyne
Finale, Act 1
L. Pyne, W. Harrison, Messrs. Borrani, Horncastle, Chorus
ACT 2
Scene 1
Duet (Softly, Softly)
W. Harrison, Mr. Borrani
Duet (Sir, a secret most important)
Messrs. Whiting, Borrani
Scene 2
Invisible Chorus; Sudden appearance of the Fairy Queen through the Chimney; The Wonderful Pumpkin; The Mouse Trap; The Rat Trap.
Scene 3
The Fireplace becomes a Fountain; the Pumpkin, a Beautiful Real Miniature Coach; the Mice into Real Ponies, and the Rat a Coachman; and the Lizzards, Footmen.
Miniature Coach with Four Shetland Ponies.
Scene 4
Finale, Act 2 (Delightful hours of rapture)
ACT 3[41]
Scene 1
Opening Chorus and Gallop (In Light Tripping Measure)
The Prince's Ball:
Neapolitan
Misses Price, Henry, Mr. Yates
Polka Quadrille and Waltz
Corps de Ballet
Transformation of Cinderella and Pedro
The Little Glass Slipper
Air and Chorus (What Demon's Opposing Malice)
Scene 5
The Trial of the Slipper
Finale (Now with Grief no Longer Bending)

1855.03 THE MARRIAGE OF GEORGETTE

An Operetta in One Act. (Original French libretto to "Les Noces de Jeannette" by Michel Carré and Jules Barbier.) English libretto by William Harrison. Music by Victor Massé. Conductor, George F. Bristow. Produced by the (Louisa) Pyne-(William) Harrison Company. Opened 9 April 1855 at Niblo's Garden for 1 performance; returned 8 October 1855 to Niblo's Garden in repertory.

CAST: *Georgette*: Miss LOUISA PYNE. *Jacques*: Mr. WILLIAM HARRISON.

MUSICAL NUMBERS
"At length I am alone, and here I am at home" (Recitative and Air)
W. Harrison
"Amongst the Village Swains" (Air)
Miss L. Pyne
"Stay there if you please" (Duet)
Miss L. Pyne, Mr. W. Harrison
"Ah! you can better know, my dear" (Song)
W. Harrison
"Tell him thus the love lingers in the heart" (Ballad)
Miss L. Pyne
"The Nightingale" (Air and Variations, with Flute Obligato)
Miss. L. Pyne
"Sit down, 'tis my wish" (Duet)
Miss L. Pyne, W. Harrison
"There is no human joy" (Finale)
Miss L. Pyne

1855.04 MARITANA

A Revival of the Light Opera in Three Acts[42]. (Libretto by Edward Fitzball. Based on the play "Don César de Bazan" by Adolphe d'Ennery and Philippe Dumanoir.) Music by Vincent Wallace. Scenery by Mr. H. Hillyard. Musical director, George F. Bristow. Produced by the (Louisa) Pyne-(William) Harrison Company. Opened 25 May 1855 at Niblo's Garden in repertory; season closed 3 November 1855.

CAST: *Charles II*, King of Spain: Mr. HORNCASTLE. *Don Caesar de Bazan*: Mr. WILLIAM HARRISON. *Don José de Santarem*: Mr. BORRANI. *Marquis de Montefiore*: Mr. RUSSELL. *Alcalde*: Mr. Paul. *Captain of Guard*: Mr. Swan. *Old Man*: Mr. Jones. *Boatman*: Mr. Lawson. *Lazarillo*: Miss (Susan) Pyne. *Maritana*: Miss LOUISA PYNE. *Marchioness de Montefiore*: Miss Florence. Full Chorus.

1855.05 THE BOHEMIAN GIRL

A Revival of the Light Opera in Three Acts[43]. (Libretto by Alfred Bunn, after Jules-Henri Vernoy de Saint-Georges' ballet-pantomime "The Gypsy.") Music by Michael William Balfe. Scenery, Act 2, by Mr. H. Hillyard. Musical director, George F. Bristow. Produced by the (Louisa) Pyne-(William) Harrison Company. Opened 2 June 1855 at Niblo's Garden in repertory; season closed 3 November 1855.

CAST: *Thaddeus*: Mr. WILLIAM HARRISON. *Count Arnheim*: Mr. BORRANI. *Florestein*: Mr. HOLMAN. *Devilshoof*: Mr. HORNCASTLE. *Captain of the Guard*: Mr. Jones. *Officer*: Mr. G. Lawson. *Gipsy*: Mr. Swan. *Servant*: Mr. Paul. *Arline*: Miss LOUISA PYNE. *Gypsy Queen*: Miss (Susan) PYNE. *Buda*: Miss France. *Child*: Miss Henry. Full Chorus.

1855.06 THE DAUGHTER OF ST. MARK

An Operetta Novelty (Grand Opera) in Three Acts, 7 Scenes. Libretto by Alfred Bunn (after St. Georges)[44]. Music by Michael William Balfe. Scenery by Messrs. H. Hillyard, George Heilge. Machinery by Messrs. Phalan, Runyan. Costumes and Armours by Mr. G. Taylor. Accessories by Mr. C. Sylvestre. Dances by Mr. Fredericks. Musical director, George F. Bristow. Produced by the (Louisa) Pyne-(William) Harrison Company. Opened 18 June 1855 at Niblo's Garden and closed 28 June 1855 after 10 performances.

[41]In Act 3, Miss L. Pyne will introduce a new aria composed by Julius Benedict:
"The Skylark"
L. Pyne

[42]First produced in New York 4 May 1848 at the Bowery Theatre for 3 performances. For Synopsis of Scenes and Musical Numbers, see original 1848 production.

[43] First produced in New York 25 November 1844 for 17 performances in repertory at the Park Theatre. For Synopsis of Scenes and Musical Numbers, see original 1844 production.

[44]Program note: The following extract taken from the sketches of Venetian history, vol. 2 page 124, furnished a warrant for the title of this opera, in order to satisfy the rigid law which forbade the marriage of any Venetian of noble birth, with a foreigner, the destined bride was solemnly "Adopted by the State" and declared a "Daughter of St. Mark."

CAST: *Lusignano*, King of Cyprus: Mr. GEORGE HOLMAN. *Andrea Connaro*, a Patrician of Venice: Mr. BORRANI. *Moncenigo*, one of the Council of Ten: Mr. HORNCASTLE. *Adolphe de Courcy*, a French Knight: Mr. WILLIAM HARRISON. *Strozzi*: Mr. Chambers. *Catarina Cornaro*: Miss LOUISA PYNE. *Marian*, Page to the King: Miss Calla. *Principal Herald*: Mr. G. Rea. *Assassins*: Messrs. Lawson, Paul, France. *Archbishop, Bishops, Priests, Penitents, Officers, Guards, Standard Bearers, Knights, Esquires, Gentry, Estradists, Municipal Body, etc. Nobility, Maids of Honor, Bridesmaids, Venetian Suite, Flower Girls, etc.*

Act 1: Hall in the Villa Andrea. Venice, 1469.

Act 2, Scene 1: The Oratory of Catarina. *Scene 2*: Apartments in the Moncenigo Palace. *Scene 3*: The Battlements of the Palace of Famagosta in Cyprus, with a view of the port seen under them, taken from an original sketch.

Act 3, Scene 1: The Gardens of a Casino at Nicosia in Cyprus. *Scene 2*: Ante-room in the Palace. *Scene 3*: Public place in Nicosia.

ACT 1[45]

"There's sunlight in Heaven"
[Sereande], W. Harrison
"Be this mont the brightest" (Duet)
L. Pyne, W. Harrison
"The home I loved so, leaving" (Duet)
L. Pyne, W. Harrison
"To thee whose wisdom is the guiding star" (Trio)
L. Pyne, Messrs. W. Harrison, Borrani
"One of the Council placed within my halls" (Recitative)
Messrs. Borrani, Horncastle
"As pure in ray as early day" (Bridal Chorus)
First Air de Ballet
"The altar is prepared" (Finale)
Chorus
"What means these words?"
Chorus

ACT 2

"There's not a sound however light"
Gondoliers' Chorus
"The Gondolier" (Song)
L. Pyne
"Oh! when thus they've bereft me" (Scena and Prayer)
L. Pyne
"The sorrow heaped on thee" (Recitative)
Mr. Borrani
"When all around our path is dreary" (Ballad)
Mr. Borrani
"Enchantress of my life" (Duet)
L. Pyne, W. Harrison
"My bark which o'er the tide" (Barcarole)
W. Harrison
"My dream is realized" (Recitative)
Mr. Horncastle
"O, what hopes at their height" (Song)
Mr. Horncastle
"Hail to this joyous day" (Chorus)
Chorus
Second Air de Ballet
"People of Cyprus" (Proclamation and Chorus)
Grand March and Finale

ACT 3

"The world is only after all" (Opening Chorus)
"Sad exile on the stranger's shore" (Duet)
Messrs. W. Harrison, G. Holman
"The cannon rebounding" (Duet)
Messrs. W. Harrison, G. Holman
"Oh, smile as thou wert wont to smile" or "We may be happy yet" (Ballad)
W. Harrison
"Before these bursting eyes" (Duet)
Messrs. Borrani, G. Holman
"Pray for the soul's repose" (Chorus)
Chorus
"If true his tale" (Canon)
Messrs. Borrani, G. Holman, Horncastle
"There is no human joy" (Rondo Finale)
L. Pyne, Chorus

[45]Musical numbers not listed in programs. List prepared from published English piano vocal score (Chappell, London, 1844).

1855.07 A QUEEN OF A DAY

A Comic Opera in Two Acts. Libretto by J. B. Buckstone. Music by Edward Fitzwilliam. Scenery by H. Hillyard. Musical director, George F. Bristow. Dances arranged by Mr. Fredericks. Produced by the (Louisa) Pyne–(William) Harrison Company. Opened 2 July 1855 at Niblo's Garden in repertory; season closed 3 November 1855.

CAST: *Sir Henry Vere*, a royalist: Mr. (GEORGE) HOLMAN. *Timothy Turnwell*: Mr. BORRANI. *Walter*, a young sailor in the coasting trade: Mr. WILLIAM HARRISON. *The Sheriff*: Mr. Chambers. *First Sailor*: Mr. G. Rea. *Second Sailor*: Mr. Hayes. *Abel (Strongitharm), Gideon*: Puritan Troopers: Messrs. Paul, Lawson. *Lords, Soldiers, Sailors, etc.)*

Lady Oldcourt: Mrs. HOLMAN. *Cicily*: Miss (SUSAN) PYNE. *Janet*: Miss France. *Lucy Lovelace*, a milliner: Miss LOUISA PYNE. *Ladies, Lasses, etc.*

Act 1: Market Place, Dover. (England) 1660.

Act 2: Turnwell's Inn, Rochester.

ACT 1[46]

Glee (Just landed from the raging main)
Sailors' Chorus
Song (Farewell, I cannot think of thee)
W. Harrison
Song (Amid the songsters of the grove)
S. Pyne
Cavatina (Returning from a foreign shore)
L. Pyne
Duet (An April day, a storm at sea)
S. Pyne, L. Pyne
Duet (Follow your fancy dream no more)
W. Harrison, L. Pyne
Song (Tra la la, my heart's gaily beating)
L. Pyne
Finale (Joy, joy, joy!)
Chorus

ACT 2

Song (When cavaliers shall bear the sway)
Mr. Borrani
Scena Recitative (A Queen at length behold me)
L. Pyne
Aria (Soon this golden vision over)
L. Pyne
Chorus (Hail to our Queen)
Chorus
Ballad (O ask me not to tell the charms that won my roving heart)
W. Harrison
Scene (Guard well the door)
Messrs. Chambers, Borrani, L. Pyne, Chorus
Song and Chorus (The valiant trooper, free from care)
Mr. Borrani, Chorus
Grand Finale
L. Pyne, Company

[46]Musical numbers not listed in programs. List prepared from published libretto (J. H. Eastburne's Press, Boston, 1855). Interpolated as per program:
Morris Dance (Act 1)
Interpolated as per reviews:
"The Skylark"
L. Pyne

1855.08

THE BEGGAR'S OPERA

A Revival of the Comic Opera (Ballad Opera) in Three Acts[47]. Libretto by John Gay. Adapted to the modern stage by William Harrison. Musical director, George F. Bristow. Produced by the (Louisa) Pyne-(William) Harrison Company. Opened 14 September 1855 at Niblo's Garden in repertory; season closed 3 November 1855.

CAST: *Captain Macheath*: Mr. WILLIAM HARRISON. *Peachum*: Mr. HORNCASTLE. *Lockit*: Mr. France. *Mat o' the Mint*: Mr. Hayes. *Filch*: Mr. Miller. *Ben Budget*: Mr. Ghor. *Crook-fingered Jack*: Mr. Warre. *Jemmy Twitcher*: Mr. Edwards. *Wat Drury*: Mr. Atkins. *Nimming Ned*: Mr. Graff. *Harry Paddington*: Mr. Chambers. *Robin of Bagshot*: Mr. Klebs. *Drawer*: Mr. Dailey.

Polly: Miss LOUISA PYNE. *Lucy*: Mrs. HALE. *Mrs. Coaxer*: Miss Calla. *Jenny Driver*: Miss France. *Mrs. Peachum*: Mrs. H. P. Grattan.

Prologue and Epilogue: *The Player*: Mr. Swan. *The Beggar*: Mr. Setche.

1855.09

RIP VAN WINKLE

A Comic Opera in Three Acts, 12 Scenes. Libretto by J. Howard Wainwright. Music by George F. Bristow. Scenery by H. Hillyard and Charles Thorne. Costumes by Mr. Taylor. Propreties by Mr. Silvester. Musical director, George F. Bristow. Produced by the (Louisa) Pyne-(William) Harrison Company. Opened 27 September 1855 at Niblo's Garden and closed 23 October 1855 after 17 performances in repertory.[48]

CAST: *Rip Van Winkle*, a farmer resident among the Kaatskill Mountains: Mr. STRETTON. *Nicholas Vedder*, Landlord of the Inn: Mr. Hayes. *Derrick Van Brummel*, Schoolmaster: Mr. Setchell. *Spirit of (Hendrik) Hudson*: Mr. Atkins. *A Spirit*, one of Hendrik Hudson's crew: Mr. Bee. *Edward Gardenier*, a Captain in the Continental Army, betrothed to Alice: Mr. WILLIAM HARRISON. *Frederick Vilcoeur*, enamoured of Alice: Mr. Horncastle. *Young Rip Van Winkle* (Act 1): Master France. *Alice Van Winkle* (Act 1): Miss Gourlay. *Young Rip* (Acts 2 and 3): Mr. Miller. *Sergeant* of the Continental Army: Mr. Chambers. *Sheriff*: Mr. Swan. *Dame Van Winkle*, Rip's wife: Miss SUSAN PYNE. *Anna*, a Village Maiden: Mrs. Hood. *Alice Van Winkle*, now grown up (Act 2): Miss LOUISA PYNE. *Dame Van Duzer*, an old woman: Mrs. HOOD. *Male and Female Villagers, Spirits, Soldiers, etc.*

The action is set in the northern part of the State of New York, partly among the Kaatskill Mountains and partly on the Saratoga Plains.

Act 1, Scene 1: The Village of Kaatskill, with the Village Inn sign of 'George III.' Autumn of 1763. Mid-day. (Thorne.) *Scene 2*: The Village of Kaatskill from the mountains. (Hillyard.) *Scene 3*: Interior of Rip's house. (Thorne.) *Scene 4*: View on the peaks of the Kaatskill mountain. (Hillyard.) *Scene 5*: Falls of Kaatskill. (Hillyard.)

Act 2, Scene 1: The Village of Kaatskill with the Village Inn sign of 'George Washington.' Autumn of 1777. (Thorne.) *Scene 2*: Interior of Rip's house. *Scene 3*: Jessup's Landing and the Bivouac of the Continental Army. The Old Pine Tree and the Rattlesnake Flag.

Act 3, Scene 1: The Peaks of Kaatskill with distant view of the Village of Kaatskill and the River Hudson. Autumn of 1783. (Hillyard.) *Scene 2*: A Street in the Village of Kaatskill. (Thorne.) *Scene 3*: The Village on the Mountain with the sign of the New Inn, 'George Washington." The Liberty Pole, from which floats the banner bearing Thirteen Stars and Stripes, emblematic of the Original Confederacy of Independent States.

ACT 1[49]
Scene 1
Chorus (The summer has faded fast away)
Chorus
Solo (Then gather round the village green)
Mrs. Hood, Chorus
Song (The gentry may talk of their excellent wine)
Mr. Stretton
Concerted Piece (What, sir! are you here again?)
Miss. S. Pyne, Mr. Stretton, Chorus
Ensemble (Oh! dear! my greatest plague in life)
Mr. Stretton, Miss S. Pyne, Chorus
Ensemble (A bachelor would had I tarried)
Mr. Stretton, Miss. S. Pyne, Chorus
Scene 3
Duet and Ensemble (Whither art thou going)
Mr. Stretton, Miss S. Pyne
Scene 4
Recitative (What sound is that?)
Mr. Stretton
Scene 5
Chorus of Spirits (Evening is falling o'er meadow and lea)
Mr. Atkins, Chorus of Spirits
Recitative (What would'st thou here)
Messrs. Atkins, Stretton
Chorus (Quick on its course, like the warrior horse)
Chorus of Spirits
Song (The day is done, the setting sun)
Mr. Stretton
Incantation (Chant we now in mystic numbers)
Chorus of Spirits

ACT 2
Scene 1
Opening Chorus (The time has come when tyrant's power)
Chorus
Recitative and Aria (I cannot wait his coming in the house)
Miss S. Pyne
Recitative (I hear a step)
Miss. S. Pyne, Mr. Horncastle, W. Harrison
Solo and Ensemble (Though I've wandered in many a place, love)
W. Harrison, Miss S. Pyne, Mr. Horncastle, Chorus
Song (Nay, do not weep my Alice, dear)
W. Harrison
Scena, Recitative and Prayer (He's gone, and now the wild wood rose)
Miss. S. Pyne
Solo and Chorus (Come, my brave comrades)
W. Harrison, Chorus
Scene 2
Ballad (When circled round in youth's glad spring)
Miss. S. Pyne
Scene 3
Camp Song (Hurra for the life the soldier leads)
Soldiers (Chorus)
Solo (We station the watch, lest the foe should come)
W. Harrison
Song (Gladly I accept the place)
Miss S. Pyne
Recitative (He is here to share your defeat!)
Mr. Horncastle, W. Harrison, Miss S. Pyne
Concerted Piece (At last, proud girl, I have thee in my power)
Mr. Horncastle, W. Harrison, Miss S. Pyne
Chorus and Curse (The foe has retreated, the warfare is done)
Miss S. Pyne, Chorus

ACT 3
Scene 1
Chorus of the Daughters of the Morning (Wake, sleeper, wake)
Chorus
Scene 2
Recitative (Who speaks? Who calls? Where am I? Speak once more!)
Mr. Stretton
Song (The dew of night I am afraid)
Mr. Stretton
Scene 3
Chorus (Spread our banners to the wind)
Chorus
Recitative (Well met, dear friends, I greet you once again)
W. Harrison, Miss S. Pyne

[47]First produced in New York 3 December 1750 at the Theatre in Nassau Street for 5 performances in repertory. For Synopsis of Scenes and Musical Numbers, see original 1750 production. This adaptation previously presented in New York 20 December 1854 at the Broadway Theatre in repertory. For Synopsis of Musical numbers, see 1854 production.

[48]The tableaux in Act 1 are after the celebrated etchings of Rip Van Winkle by F. O. C. Darley.

[49]Musical numbers not listed in programs List prepared from published libretto (Wardle Corbyn, New York, 1855).

Solo (When, dearest, far from thee away)
W. Harrison
Recitative (Oh what a joyous day is this to me)
Miss S. Pyne, Mr. Stretton, Chorus
Ballad (Alone, all alone, in this wide world of sorrow)
Mr. Stretton
Recitative (Come, tell us who thou art?)
Messrs. Swan, Stretton, All
Finale: Solo (List! the merry bells are ringing)
Miss S. Pyne

KING CHARMING, or, The Blue Bird of Paradise

1855.10

A Grand Comic Fairy Extravaganza in Two Acts, 9 Scenes[50]. Play by James Robinson Planché. Founded on the popular story "L'Oiseau Bleu" by Countess D'Aulnoy. Stage manager, W. B. Blake. Musical director and composer, J. Cooke. Scenery by George Heister. Dresses by Mrs. Wallis. Properties, Tricks, Banners and Unique Appointments by Mr. S. Wallis. Machinery by Messrs. Squires, Gurnsey, Bogert. Tableaus and evolutions by Mons. Monplaisir. Produced by E. A. Marshall. Opened 24 December 1855 at the Broadway Theatre, closing 12 January 1856 after 18 performances; returned in alternating repertory 21 January 1856 with 'The Sea of Ice" for (12) additional performances, closing 16 February 1856.

CAST: *Charming the First*, King of the Fan-Sea Isles, an immortal personage: Mrs. H. C. WATSON. *Henpeckt the Hundredth*, King of Cockayne: Mr. D. WHITING. *Tyrana*, his Queen and second wife: Mme. ELIZABETH PONISI. *Princess Florina*, Daughter of King Henpeckt, by his first wife: Miss JOS. MANNERS. *Princess Troutina*, Daughter of Queen Tyrana, by her first husband: Mrs. Littell. *Tinsel*, Ambassador from King Charming: Mr. B. T. Ringgold. *Pretty*, King Charming's Page: Miss E. Wallis. *Natty*, his Valet: Mr. Seymour. *Knobby*, his Porter: Mr. Walters. *Chamberlain to King Henpeckt*: Mr. Harcourt. *Usher*: Mr. Allen. *Hocus Pocus*, a Magician, Friend and Physician Extraordinary to King Charming: Mr. CARROLL. *Sal-Volatile, Spirit of Nitre, Spirit of Hartshorn, Sprit of Ether, etc., his assistant Bottle-Imps*: Messrs. VINCENT, Wright, Cutter, etc. *Azurine*, (Fairy) Godmother to Charming: EMMA HARDINGE. *Soussio*, (Fairy) Godmother to Troutina: Miss DUCKWORTH. *Blue-Bell*, Azurine's attendant: Miss A. Price. *Nobles, Ladies of the Court, Guards, Servants, etc.*: Over 100 Auxiliaries.

Act 1, Scene 1: Hall of Audience in the Castle of King Henpeckt. *Scene 2*: Garden of the Castle. *Scene 3*: Abode of the Fairy Soussio. Florina's Chamber. *Scene 4*: The Cypress Grove, with a Nec-romantic and Panoramic Excursion to the Fan-Sea Islands.

Act 2, Scene 1: Haunt of the Fairies. Fairy Legion summoned by their Chief; Warlike Spirit of the Feminines; Tableaus, Marches and Evolutions by Forty Ladies. *Scene 2*: Gates of King Charming's Palace. *Scene 3*: Whispering Gallery and Hall of Echoes in the Palace. *Scene 4*: King Charming's Cabinet. *Scene 5*: [The Whispering Gallery-dark] A Scene of Destruction, succeeded by the glorious restoration of King Charming to the throne of Fan-Sea. Denouement of Dazzling Grandeur!

ACT 1[51]
Scene 1
Air, 'With a betwiching mean, ah.' by Rossini (What a bewitching queen, ah!)
D. Whiting
Morceau d'Ensemble, Air-'St. Petersburg Polka' (We by our counsel must be guided)
H. C. Watson, D. Whiting, E. Ponisi, J. Manners, Mrs. Littell
Air, 'Vaga Luna, or Katy Darling' (O Florina, my dear, my duck, my darling!)
H. C. Watson
Scene 2
Air, 'When the heart of a man' (For the heart of the man, A fig I don't care)
E. Ponisi
Scene 3
Trio, Air from NORMA (O fie for shame, you naughty man!)
Miss Duckworth, Mrs. Littell, H. C. Watson
Scene 4
Air, 'The Cavalier' (What a pitiful plight!)
Miss J. Manners
Duet, 'Over the hills and far away' (Were I perch'd on Greenland's coast)
Miss J. Manners, H. C. Watson
Air, 'Lady Bird, Lady Bird, fly away home'
(Pretty bird, pretty bird, blue as the sky)
H. C. Watson, Miss J. Manners
Air, 'My own Blue Bell' (My own blue bird, my pretty blue bird)
Miss J. Manners
Scene 5
Song, 'The King of Cannibal Islands' (Hocus Pocus is his name)
Mr. Vincent, Chorus of Spirits

ACT 2
Scene 1
Address A-La-Rolla
E. Hardinge
Fairy Amazonian March
Air, 'Lady Bird, Lady Bird, fly away home' (Pretty bird, pretty bird, blue as the sky)[reprise]
Miss J. Manners
Air, Over the water and over the sea
Miss J. Manners
Scene 2
Sing a Song of Sixpence (Nursery Rhyme)
24 Blackbirds
Scene 3
Air, 'Pretty Mocking Bird' (Friendly echo—By your leave)
Miss. J. Manners
Scene 4
Air, 'Go Away black man' (As I stole out one very dark night)
H. C. Watson
Air, 'Come down the back stairs'[same]
Mr. Seymour
Scene 5
Duet, 'Suono il trombe intrepida' (So now we'll trump intrepidly)
H. C. Watson, Miss J. Manners
Finale, 'Morris Dance' (Our trials o'er, but one fear more)
H. C. Watson, Miss J. Manners

PO-CA-HON-TAS, or, The Gentle Savage

1855.11

An Original, Aboriginal, Erratic, Operatic, Semi-Civilized and Demi-Savage Extravaganza (Burlesque) in Two Acts, 3 Scenes[52], being a perversion of ye trew and wonderfulle Hystorie of ye Renounede Pryncesse. Burlesque by John Brougham. Music entirely dislocated and re-set [composed and arranged] by James G. Maeder. Orchestra leader, Signor La Manna. Scenery by Henry Isherwood, Mr. Wallace. Costumes by T. Flanry. Machinery by Mr. Demilt. Properties by Mr. Timmany. Indian Dances, Marches choreographed by Professor B. Yates. Stage manager, Mr. Lester. Produced by James W. Wallack. Opened 24 December 1855 at Wallack's Lyceum Theatre and closed 25 February 1856 in repertory; re-opened 28 May 1856 at Wallack's Lyceum Theatre and closed 11 June 1856; re-opened 28 July 1856 at the Bowery Theatre (paired with "The Pirates of the Mississippi") and closed 16 August 1856.

CAST: *Of Ye English*: *Captain John Smith*, the undoubted Original, vocal and instrumental, in the settlement of Virginia, in love with Pocahontas, according to this story, though somewhat at variance with his story: Mr. CHARLES M. WALCOT. *Lieutenant Thomas Brown*, Second in Command, a hitherto neglected Genius, whose claims on

[50]Preceded by a varying program of burlettas or farces: To Paris And Back For £5 (24 December 1855); My Neighbor's Wife (27 December 1855); Don't Judge By Appearances (1 January 1856), and Catching A Mermaid (7 January 1856), etc.
[51]Musical numbers not listed in programs. List of Scenes and Musical numbers prepared from published prompt book (Samuel French, New York, 1856).

[52]The other short bills joining PO-CA-HON-TAS included X. Y. Z. (forepiece), and the farce, The Secret, or a Hole in the Wall (after-piece). Later bills included The Little Treasure; Pauline; Bachelor of Arts; A Gentleman from Ireland; Out for a Holiday The Bold Dragoons.

posterity are now for the first time acknowledged, as is but right: Mr. Phillips. *William Jones*, sometimes called Bill, another of the same sort left: Mr. Simpson. *Mynheer Rolff*, the real Husband of Pocahontas, but dramatically divorced contrary to all law and fact: Mr. PETERS.

Splicers of main-braces, shiverers of timbers, anathematizers of eyes and limbs, promiscuously general dealers in single combats and double hornpipes, and altogether, amazingly nautical people: *Benjamin Brace*: Mr. Hare. *John Junk*: Mr. Thompson. *Henry Halyard*: Mr. Johns. *William Buntline*: Mr. Reddy. *Barnabas Binancle*: Mr. James.

Of Ye Savages: *His Imperial Majesty, Pow-Ha-Tan I*, King of the Tuscaroras—a crotchety Monarch, in fact, a Semi-Brave: Mr. JOHN BROUGHAM. *The Right Hon. Quash-al-Jaw*, Speaker of the Savage House of Lords—straightener of unpleasant kinks, and oiler of troubled waters, unraveller of knotty points, adjuster of pugnacious difficulties, and Grand Eye Parliamentary Factotum and Fugleman: Mr. Burke. *O-po-dil-doc*, One of the Aboriginal F. F. V's[53], an indignant dignitary: Mr. Levere. *Col-o-gog*, another warm-hearted and headed Son of Old Virginia: Mr. Stoddart. *Jin-go*, Sergeant-at-Arms, a friend to swear by: Mr. Jeffries. *Kreen-Fay-Sloon*, Bearer of Dispatches, and news-carrier in ordinary: Mr. Harrison.

Medicine Men, of the Saultz and Sennaca Tribe: *Ip-pah-kak*: Mr. Oliver. *Sas-sy-pril*: Mr. Samuels. *Kod-liv-Royl*: Mr. Reynolds. *Kal-o-mel*: Mr. Carver.

H. R. H. Princess Po-Ka-Hon-Tas, the Beautiful, and very properly undutiful, daughter of King Pow-Ha-Tan, married, according to the ridiculous dictum of actual circumstances, to Master Rolff, but the author flatters himself much more advantageously disposed of in the Acting edition: Miss GEORGINA HODSON. *Poo-tee-pet, Di-mun-di*, Interesting offshoots from aristocratic stock, anterior to the first Families of Virginia: Mrs. STEPHENS, Mrs. H. B. PHILLIPS. *Wee-cha-ven-da, Kros-as-kan-bee*, Embodying the rigid principles of the Tuscarora Fashionable Finishing School: Mrs. Sylvester, Mrs. Thompson.

Their "dear charges," for whom they don't forget to charge dear enough for in the Quarterly Bills: *Dah-Lin-Duck*: Miss Melville. *O-you-Jewel*: Mrs. Thompson. *Lov-lie-kreete*: Miss Pine. *Oso-char-ming*: Miss Carman. *Lum-Pa-Shuga*: Mrs. Stewart.

Dro-may-jah, a high official: Mrs. Norton. *Soldiers, Sailors, Indians, Members of the Tuscarora Light Guard, etc.*

Act 1, Scene 1: King Pow-Ha-Tan's Summer Palace[54]. *Scene 2*: A Playground in a Tuscarora Ladies' School, with a bird's-eye view of one of the principal streets, public buildings, etc.

Act 2, Scene 1: Interior of a Wigwam. (Isherwood.) *Scene 2*: School grounds as before. *Scene 3*:

ACT 1[55]

Scene 1

Opening Chorus: Air-'King of the Cannibal Islands' (Oh how absurd of people to prate)
J. Brougham, Chorus

Song: Air-'Widow Machree' (Oh, wid a dhudieen I can blow away care)
J. Brougham

Song and Chorus: Air-'Rosin the bow' (Come forward here every rapscallion)
J. Brougham, Chorus

Grand Scena Complicato in the Anglo-Italiano Style (As you are o)
C. M. Walcot, Chorus

Concerted Piece: (Grab away While you may)
All

Song (It is of a French actress I am going to tell)
C. M. Walcot, Chorus

Scene 2

Chorus of Emancipated Maidens (Sing-sing away!)
Chorus

Song (I wish my Pa would send for me! Oh dear!)
Mrs. Stephens, Mrs. H. B. Phillips

International Scena: Recitavo—Italiani doloroso (Sport am I of fortune); Inter-Aria Nigroquæ (Where the idlers now are shopping); Cantata Varioso (Scenes that are the brightest)
Miss G. Hodson

Intrusive Chorus (Oh! what a beau)
Chorus

Duet (My love is like a raging hot volcano)
C. M. Walcot, G. Hodson

Grand Finale—Affettuoso—Furioso—E. Conglomeroso (Come let us now like watch-dogs bark)
C. M. Walcot, G. Hodson, J. Brougham, Chorus

ACT 2

Scene 1

Duetto Impetuoso (Now Ma'am I have a notion)
J. Brougham, G. Hodson

Grand Scena Perturbato:

Aria 'Hibernoso affettuosamente'
G. Hodson

Cantata 'Giojoso et amoroso'
Mr. Peters

Song 'Doloroso et petulento'
J. Brougham, G. Hodson, Mr. Peters

Song: "With Tyrolean Fixins" (Like the Tyrolese singers)
Mr. Peters

Quartette (Fill now a flowing glass)
J. Brougham, C. M. Walcot, Mr. Peters, G. Hodson

Scene 2

Air-'Pop Goes the Weazel' (As we're going on a train)
Chorus

Scene 3

Air-'Hark 'tis the Indian drum' (Hark 'tis the ingine bell)
Chorus

Air—Nocturne, Grazioso vel Filosofoso (Oh, some are right)
G. Hodson

Duet "Prima Donna Waltz" (Although a bird am I)
C. M. Walcot, G. Hodson

Recitative (Not I, such an alliance would be a lie)
J. Brougham, Mrs. Stephens

Characteristic Concerted Piece (Now for a jolly encounter at High, Low, Jack and the Game)
J. Brougham, C. M. Walcot, G. Hodson, Chorus

Grand Finale—A la Grec (And now we've done our duty here)
J. Brougham, C. M. Walcot, Chorus

1856.01

NOVELTY

A Novel Rhythmical, Musical, Political, Scenic, Dramatic, Artistic, Serio-comico, Rational and National Extravaganza, founded upon facts and systemized and developed by the combined talent of the various persons comprising the Company of the Varieties, in One Act, 10 Scenes[56]. Stage manager, Mr. H. Hall. Musical director and composer, Mr. Thomas Baker. Scenery, very old and incorrect. Machinery, warranted to work slowly. Dresses, out of all character. Music, borrowed from street organs. Properties, beyond description. (Maitre de Ballet, Mons. Monplaisir. Scenery by J. R. Smith. Machinery by John Furze. Costumes by R. Williams.) Produced by Laura Keene. Opened 22 February 1856 at Laura Keene's Varieties and closed 3 May 1856 in repertory.

CAST: *The Directress*: LAURA KEENE. *Fashion*: Mrs. LESDERNIER. *Novelty*, with songs: ROSALIE DURAND. *Fortune*: KATE REIGNOLDS.

Messrs. T. B. Johnston, Mr. Chandler, F. Rea, Carpenter, Tree, Watson, F. Trevor, Tillman, Master Kelly. Misses Annie Walters, Annie Lee, Clara Jonson, F. Kelly, Wilson, M. Wells, James, Tree, Eames, Castles, McDonogh, V. Franck, N. Tillman, Mrs. (Lotty) Hough, Mrs. Carpenter.

SCENES and MUSICAL NUMBERS

Scene 1

Toodles (by a gentleman who once "twinned" with the great original)
Mr. Hall

Scene 2

Rachel in 'Phedre'
A. Walters

Scene 3

Mr. Barney Williams: T. B. Johnston. *Mrs. Barney Williams*: Lotty Hough.
"Bobbing Around"/"Whiskey in the Jug"

Scene 4

Undine
Mlle. V. Franck, Mlle. N. Tillman, Mons. Tillman.

---

[53]First Family of Virginia.

[54]The prompt book lists this scene as Palace of Weramocomoco.

[55]Musical numbers not listed in programs. List prepared from published prompt book (Samuel French, New York, n.d.).

[56]Sharing the bill as a fore-piece was a comedietta, The Balance of Comfort; and as an after-piece the farce, The Lottery Ticket.

Scene 5

Pauline

Mr. Lester: Mr. Chandler. *Stewart*: F. Rea. *Mr. Lyster*: Mr. Carpenter. *Mr. Bernard*: Mr. Tree. *Mr. Trevor*: Mr. F. Trevor.

"With much Care and Thought" (Song)

R. Durand

Scene 6

A Midsummer Night's Dream

Titania: Miss A. Lee. *Oberon*: Miss C. Jonson. *Puck*: Miss F. Kelly. *Indian Boy*: Master Kelly.

"I show a Bank" (Song)

L. Keene, R. Durand

Scene 7

Shakespeare: Mr. F. Rea

"Thou art gone from my gaze" (Song)

R. Durand

Scene 8

Uncle Tom

Topsey: Mrs. Carpenter. *Eva*: Miss Wilson. *Uncle Tom*: Mr. Watson.

Scene 9

Herne, the Hunter

Mister Herne, with a daring act of Horsemanship and Terrific Leap: T. B. Johnston.

The Tragic Music

Lady Macbeth, 200 years since: Miss M. Wells.

Scene 10

The Apotheosis of Washington

Columbia: Miss Jonson. *Fame*: Miss James. *Liberty*: Miss Tree. *Peace*: Miss Eames. *Justice*: Miss Castles. *Hope*: Mrs. Hough. *Plenty*: Miss McDonogh.

Shade of Washington

LIFE IN NEW YORK,
1856.02 or, Tom and Jerry on a Visit

A Local Operatic Pantomimic Drama illustrative of the present time (Adapted from W. T. Moncrieff's play "Tom and Jerry, or Life in London") in Two Acts, 7 Scenes[57]. Dances and stage business by B. Yates. Scenery by H. Hillyard and Gaspard Maeder. Machinery by W. Demilt. Properties by Mr. Campbell. (Produced by John Brougham.) Opened 18 August 1856 at the Bowery Theatre and closed 30 August 1856 after 12 performances; re-opened 15 September 1856 at the Bowery Theatre (on a bill with MET-A-MORA) and closed 20 September 1856 after an additional 6 performances.

CAST: *Corinthian Tom*: Mr. FISHER. *Jerry Hawthorn*: Mr. JAMES C. DUNN. *Bob Logic*: Mr. CANOLL. *Tom Smith*: Mr. JOHN BROUGHAM. *Captain the Hon. Fitzgammon Bowlingreen*: Mr. JOHN BROUGHAM. *Laporte*: Mr. Whiting. *Count Marie Sulpice Sebastian Nybobbe*: Mr. Whiting. *James Trollop Fidler Dickens Greene*: Mr. James Seymour. *Skinneflynte Codfishe, Esq.*: Mr. Bellamy. *Harry Manly*: Mr. Grosvenor. *Cubbe Codfishe*: Mr. Haviland. *Jollie Brycke*: Mr. T. Hodges. *Slimm Shanghai*: Mr. Baker. *Lejeune Rooster*: Mr. Randall. *Thinshanke*: Mr. Denham. *Lieutenant Simpson*: Mr. Carpenter. *Four Cent Man*: Mr. Lingard. *Cuffee*: Mr. Bogart. *Apple Woman*: Mr. Post. *Newsboys*: J. Moore, W. Bogart. *Hackmen, Street Celebrities, etc.*: Messrs. Bunbee, Oliver, Smith, Jones, etc.

Corinthian Kate: Mme. (ELIZABETH) PONISI. *Sue Hawthorn*: Miss KATE REIGNOLDS. *Clementina Victorina Codfishe*: Miss EMMA TAYLOR. *Celestina Eugenia Codfishe*: Miss McDonough. *Fanny*: Miss F. Denham. *Mrs. Codfishe*: Mrs. Dunn. *Visitors, Dancers*: Corps de Ballet.

Act 1: Life at the Landing. *Scene 1*: Collins Wharf; Canal Street. *Scene 2*: A Room at the Astor. *Scene 3*: Magnificent ball-room at Mrs. Codfishe's Mansion.

Act 2: Life among the Humble. *Scene 1*: Codfishe's Place of Business. *Scene 2*: Life among the Breakers. *Scene 3*: A view of Tryon Row and part of Centre Street. *Scene 4*: View of City Hall, on 4 July.

ACT 1

Scene 1

Opening Chorus (Cheer boys, cheer, and raise the jolly chorus)

Life in New York begins (Come away-come away)

Scene 3

New Danse de Société, introducing the Polka, Varsovienne, Schottische, Mazourka, Redowa

ACT 2

Scene 3

Saturday Night Carnival:

Brilliant Display of Fireworks

MET-A-MO-RA,
1856.03 or, the Last of the Pollywogs

A Revival of the Amusical, Musical, Mimical Pantomimical, Historical Reminiscence (a Burlesque of John A. Stone's tragedy, Metamora, or the Last of the Wampanoags) in One Act[58]. Play by John Brougham. Music under the direction of C. Dodworth. Produced by John Brougham. Opened 15 September 1856 at the Bowery Theatre and closed 20 September 1856 after 6 performances.

CAST: Anglo Saxons: *Pappy Jenks*, an influential early settler, early settled: Mr. Whiting. *Lord Fitzfaddle*, a highly to be envied individual, who has the honor to die by Met-a-mo-ra's knife: Mr. Barry. *Master Walter*, not the hunchback, but over head and ears in love: Mr. JAMES DUNN. *Badenough*, a most unpleasant individual: Mr. Randall. *Worser*, much the same, only more so: Mr. Post. *Oceana*, old Jenks' daughter, and chip of the old block: Miss F. DENHAM.

Pollywogs: *Met-a-mo-ra*, the ultimate Pollywog, an Aboriginal Hero, and favorite (child) of the Forrest: Mr. JOHN BROUGHAM. *Kantshine*, a friend who gives excellent advice, and is treated as all are who do: Mr. Smith. *Old Tar*, an Indian interpreter, from the Junk, half savage—half sailor: Mr. Denham. *Whiskee Todde*, skilled in talk, so we are informed: Mr. Bilby. *Anaconda*, a recreant red man, rather serpentine: Mr. Baker. *Tapiokee*, La Belle Sauvage, the squalling squaw of Met-a-mo-ra, killed with kindness: Miss KATE REIGNOLDS. *Papoose*, being the last of the Pollywogs: Miss Lizzie Wallis.

HIAWATHA,
1856.04 or, Ardent Spirits and Laughing Water

An Atrocious Outrage (a Burlesque) in Two Acts, 6 Scenes[59]. Play by Charles Melton Walcot. Stage manager, Mr. Lester. Scenic artist, Henry Isherwood. Music arranged by Signor LaManna. Costumes by Mr. Flannery. Machinist, Mr. Landers. Produced by James W. Wallack. Opened 25 December 1856 at Wallack's Lyceum Theatre and closed 21 January 1857 after 24 performances; re-opened 13 July 1857 at Wallack's Theatre and closed 18 July 1857 after an additional 6 performances.

CAST: *Hiawatha*, a character strikingly more in the style of a School-boy than of a Long-fellow: Mr. CHARLES MELTON WALCOT. *Nukkleundah*, a creation, à la Frankenstein: Mr. W. H. REYNOLDS. *Gitchi-Manito*, viewed as a spirit, but as a part, a "Small Potato": Mr. LEVERE. *Wabun*, a down-East Indian: Mr. H. B. Phillips. *Kabikonokka*, of the North: Mr. G. S. Lee. *Shawondasee*, of the South: Mr. Harrison. *Yenadizzi*, the original "Young New York": Mr. C. Stuart. *Dammidortur*, a-n-arrow-minded person, father of Minnehaha: Mr. Owen. *Minnehaha*, surnamed "Laughing Water", and eminently calculated (when she has a good chance) to infect her audience to the immediate danger of sundry bands and strings: Mrs. JOHN WOOD. *Poohpoohmammi*, an indescribable self-willed young lady, in fact, a sort of "Gennesee Squaw": Miss MARY GANNON. *No-go-miss*, Hiawatha's grandmamma: Mr. G. Holland. *Hianakite*, Poohpoohmammi's mother: Mr. Peters. *Indians*: Messrs. Harrison, Rea, Bee, Oliver, Cotton, DeSilveria, Hill, James, Mason, etc. *Squaws*: Mesdames Carman, Thompson, Hall, Pyne, Peters, Bishop, DeVoe, Browne, Carter, etc.

---

[57]LIFE IN NEW YORK was followed by a program by the French dancers:

"I Know a Bank" (Duet)

Emma and Georgina Reignolds

Grand Pas de Bouquet

B. Yates, Ernestine Henrarde

Pas Seul

Miss M. Partington

La Truandise

Ernestine and Annie Henrarde

And an after-piece, PO-CA-HON-TAS, an original, aboriginal, erratic, operatic, semi-civilized and demi-savage extravaganza. In the second week, PO-CA-HON-TAS was played first.

[58]First produced in New York 6 March 1848 at the Park Theatre in repertory. For synopsis of Scenes and Musical Numbers, see original 1848 production.

[59]HIAWATHA was preceded by a comedietta by Morton, Rights and Wrongs of Woman, and followed by a capital holiday piece, Out for a Holiday.

Act 1, Scene 1: The Great Red Pipe Stone Quarry on the Mountains of the Prairie. *Scene 2*: Interior of Dammidortur's Wigwam or Lodge. *Scene 3*: Romantic landscape.

Act 2, Scene 1: A Wood. *Scene 2*: An Indian Village. *Scene 3*: Landscape.

ACT 1[60]

Scene 1

Solo and Chorus (The Fox and Crow for moose are gone)
Mr. Levere, Chorus

Song (I popped my head out of the door)
C. M. Walcot

Song (Air-'Root, Hog, or Die') (Now boys from the South)
C. M. Walcot, Chorus

Scene 2

Symphony of Cuckoo Song

Song (It can't be denied, because 'tis true)
Mrs. J. Wood

Scene 3

Song (Now, my lads, since we're bent on a bender)
W. H. Reynolds

Chorus (Hip! hip! hip! Hurrah! hurrah! hurrah!)

Duet (Oh, here's a go! this fellow broke my heart)
[Sturgeon], C. M. Walcot

Aria (Air, 'Tu Vedrai') (Do but try and venture arter)
C. M. Walcot

Trio ('Tis a very funny thing here to wait and sing)
C. M. Walcot, Mrs. J. Wood, M. Gannon

Finale (from LA GAZZA LADRA) and Laughing Trio
(Air 'Vadasi via de Qua')

(See what dreadful small potato)
Mrs. J. Wood, M. Gannon, C. M. Walcot, Omnes

ACT 2

Scene 2

Chorus (Air-AMILIE) (Hiawatha! Hiawatha! and Minnehaha)

Two Part Song (in imitation of London beggar Singers)

(Oh, my love he is a saileur)
Mrs. J. Wood, C. M. Walcot

Scene 3

Recitative and Air (All is lost now)
C. M. Walcot

Duet (Air-'Suoni la tromba') from I PURITANI (If you're the trump I think you are)
W. H. Reynolds, C. M. Walcott

Song (from "The Maniac")(I see him leap the garden wall)
Mrs. J. Wood

Fragment from LUCIA, Mad Scene
Mrs. J. Wood

Symphony of Finale
Mrs. J. Wood (spoken)

Finale (Air-L'ELISIR D'AMORE)
Mrs. J. Wood

Moral
C. M. Walcot

YOUNG BACCHUS, or, Spirits and Water

1857.01

A Burlesque Extravaganza[61] in One Act, 5 Scenes. Music composed, adapted and arranged by Thomas Baker. The piece under the immediate personal supervision of Laura Keene. Scenery by Charles J. Hawthorne and Oscar F. Almy. Dresses by Mrs. Stafford. Properties and decorations by Mr. W. Deverna. Produced by Laura Keene. Opened 5 January 1857 at Laura Keene's Theatre and closed 28 January 1857 in repertory.

CAST: *Gods, Goddesses and Common People: Bacchus*, a smart boy, at the age of sixteen, on the best of *understanding* himself and everybody else, Except Juno, who, to corner him, tried to pass a *Lick-er* law by *Maine* force. Having been nearly burnt to death before he was born, he is continually surrounded by *flames* afterwards. He sailed with the Nymphs of *Nysa*, because he knew no nicer Nymphs. The true *Republican* ticket for the next Presidential campaign: Miss LAURA KEENE. *Jupiter*, the Napoleon of the sky—no relation to the present Emperor of France, though equally given to strong measures: Mr. J. G. BURNETT. *Momus*, God of Mirth, Father of Fun, and the Joe Miller of Olympus—son of Nox from whom he received many in his youth. A Satirist and Buffoon, attached to Bacchus, eaps and *belles*. A *rum* fellow, with a fine flow of *spirits*: Mr. C. WHEATLEIGH. *Hymen*, God of marriage—the original Blacksmith of the Olympian Gretna Green: Miss Cornelia Jefferson. *Mars*, God of War— the General Scot-*free* of heathen mythology. Head of fillibusters: Mr. Hayes. *Silenus*, son of pan, foster-father and boon companion of Bacchus. Inventor of the *Cellar*-ius waltz: Mr. H. McDougall. *Pan*, the original Mr. Pipes, and inventor of Puffs, always blowing himself up, and endeavoring to give himself new *h-airs*. Formerly attached to every great gun, but not known to any revolver: Mr. B. Yates. *Mercury*, the Olympian postman, and "Express Messenger." God of Orators, merchants, and thieves. A taking character, unacquainted with the laws of *meum* and *tuum*, but quite familiar with those of *melt-em* and *do-em*: Miss Josephine Manners. *Apollo*, God of Music, with a *lyre* in his hand and another by his side, as much disposed to "gammon" as the "*gamut*": Miss Stella. *Cadmus*, Prince of Phoenicia, grand-dad of Bacchus. Inventor of the first sixteen letters of the alphabet, who never could come to his *p's* and *q's*. The original sower of Dragon's Teeth in the Crimea: Mr. J. H. Stoddart. *Ampuleus*, a hunter of the *dears* and deer, with an *i-dea* or two of his own: Mr. Alleyne. *Vulcan*, a striking character, *an-vil*-lainous: Mr. Donelson. *Cupid*, a mischievous young gentleman, known to everybody: Miss Clara Taylor.

Phoenicians, Satyrs, Fauns, etc.: *Juno*, wife of Jupiter, the original celestial "Mrs. Candle," a strong-minded woman, given to *strong* waters and *strong* measures, with a *penchant* for combing Jupiter's ambrosial locks: Mrs. W. H. SMITH. *Ariadne*, widow of Theseus, who helped her first husband out of the Cretan labyrinth with a string, to enter that of Love with her second. Being the daughter of *Minos*, she thought to marry a proper *minor*, so took young Bacchus, who for short calls her "Ariad," and when particularly jolly abbreviates it to Polly: Miss JULIA GOULD. *Venus*, Goddess of Love and Beauty. Vulcan's wife, and wooed by many; renowned for her *faux pas*, and attached to her "Mars": Miss Alleyne. *Dirce*, a lady of an uncertain age, in love with all who have the manly form divine; always in tears, and though a *wet* subject, dry nurse to Bacchus: Mr. T. B. JOHNSTON. *Flora*, Goddess of Flowers, and celestial bouquet maker: Mrs. T. B. JOHNSTON. *Hebe*, Goddess of Youth, Jove's daughter and cup hearer; a general dispenser of "smiles and smashes," "jokes and juleps," "curtseys and cobblers": Miss Howell. *Calliope*, Goddess of heroic poetry: Miss Winnie. *Diana*, Goddess of the cashe, who being much run-after, is of course chaste: Miss Gray. *Iola*, whom Momus having loved long, called Io, for shortness: Mrs. J. H. Stoddart. *Ceres*, Goddess of agriculture, who "Owns up the corn,"—the very "Mapes" of Olympus in usefulness, by practically farming and lecturing—originator of the "Model Farm": Miss Mairs. *Olio*, one of the muses in this museum: Mrs. Harry Wall. *Other Nymphs of Nysa*: Several ladies of the company, than whom, none can be nicer.

Scene 1: Cloudy Realms of Olympus. *Scene 2*: Bower of Bacchus; Shores of the isle of Naxos—Sunrise. (Hawthorne.) *Scene 3*: Moonlight. (Almy.) *Scene 4*: Diana's Hunting Grounds. *Scene 5*: Realms of Juno; Triumphal Car of Bacchus, realizing the celebrated picture of the Triumph of Bacchus.

THE ELVES, or, The Statue Bride

1857.02

An Operatic, Romantic Semi-Burlesque Burletta in Two Acts, 8 Scenes[62]. Play by Charles Selby, founded on "Les Elfes" (a ballet-fantasie in Three Acts by J. H. Vernoy de St. Georges and N. Mazilliev. Music by the Count N. Gabrielli.) Music composed and arranged by Thomas Baker. Scenery by Oscar F. Almy. Costumes by Mr. Bulloch, Mrs. Bevis, Mrs. Hawthorne. Dances selected and arranged by Mr. B. Yates. Mechanical effects by Mr. Smart. Properties by W. Deverna. Play arranged and produced under the immediate supervision of Laura Keene. Opened 16 March 1857 at Laura Keene's Theatre and closed 6 May 1857 after 50 performances.

CAST: *Prince Pomp*, a Grand Palatine: Mr. Stoddart. *Prince Lubin Jocky Club*, a beau jeune homme: Miss KATE REIGNOLDS. *Count Coldstreamer*, an old beau: Mr. C. WHEATLEIGH. *Toadylor, Soft Sowder, Chringis*, Courtiers: Messrs. J. A. Smith, Alleyne, Hayes. *Hyacinthe*: Mr. McDouall. *Colin*, a romantic tailor: Mr. T. B. JOHNSTON. *Corin*: Mr. Jackson. *Arcader*: Mr. B. Yates. *Colantha*: Mr. Harcourt. *Eglantor*: Mr. Benson. *Argentor*: Mr. Reeve. *Sylva*, the Statue Bride: LAURA KEENE. *Princess Jonquil*: Miss MANNERS. *Phillis*, a Miller's Daughter: Miss Jefferson. *Eoline*, Queen of Elves: Mrs. T. B. Johnston. *Madame Chloe*, Mother of Colin: Mrs. H. P. GRATTAN. *Daphne, Phoebe, Iphis, Grundyne*, Ladies of the Court: Misses Stoddart, Alleyne, Julia Gould, Atwood. *Zephyr*: Miss Stella. *Florinis*: Miss Berkowitz. *Blondin*: Miss West. *Myrtilis*: Miss Alice. *Melantha*: Miss Alford. *Grimalkin*, Colin's cat: Master Thomas.

---

[60]List of Scenes and Musical Numbers prepared from published prompt book (Samuel French, New York, 1856).

[61]Also billed as "an entirely new, decidedly original, and particularly plotless Mythological, Local, Political, Tragical, Social, Comical, Satirical, Farcical, Paradoxical, Musical and—the Directress thinks—Capital Burlesque Extravaganza." Accompanied by a short drama 'Second Love'.

[62]THE ELVES preceded by a short drama, The Black Book.

Act 1, Scene 1: Interior of Colin's Cottage. *Scene 2*: Bosky Glade in a Forest. *Scene 3*: Hawthorn Dell in another part of the forest.

Act 2, Scene 1: Grand Saloon and Boudoir (in the Princess' Palace.) *Scene 2*: The Miller's Wine Cellar. *Scene 3*: Gardens and Exterior of the Prince's Palace. *Scene 4*: A Prison. *Scene 5*: A Hall of Statues; The Elfin Change; Magic Star and Fairy Bower.

ACT 1

Scene 1

The influence of Spirits on a romantic imagination. Awful scene of clock rapping. and cat-erwauling.

Scene 2

Rendezvous de la chasse

The Huntsmen's Chorus, a long way after Der Freischutz.

The old and young sportsmen. The aspect of the world at twenty and at forty. Lamentable case of premature "used up."

Scene 3

Song (If a Fairy Elf you'd see)
(Chorus)

The course of curiosity, like that of true love, never running smooth. The determination of the romantic Tailor to avail himself of the above, bewildering invitation—is interrupted by an unexpected incident. The Hunters who have searched in van for a Stag, discover a statue of a Wood Nymph. The Linden Tree, and the Wishing Well. Appearance of the Queen of the Elves in a Crystal Fountain and Animation of the Statue! The folly of buying a "pig in a poke," and the advantage of possessing beauty without mind. The Butterfly! The Dove! The Hare! The Four Magic Roses. The proverb of "Old Fools" verified—Love rules alike the Palace and the Cottage. Determination of the Prince appropriate to the statue. Reappearance of the Elves.

ACT 2

Scene 1

Introduction of a "Beautiful Young Princess" to the "Marble Halls" of the Ancestors of her Betrothed. The Toilet of Beauty. Though Shakespeare has recorded that it is fruitless "to paint the lily, and add a perfume to the violet," it is not to be supposed that pretty faces and forms are not to be improved by the labors of a Parisian Modute. The Statue is again endowed with life. The force of example: The Fan! The Train! The Feathers! The great Relation and the cold Colation.

Scene 2

Love's Stratagem. The Demon Daughter. Cupid in tatters, the Victim of Fatal Curiosity. Women's fascination and Man's infatuation. Who can resist the artillery of beauty! The Romantic Tailor succumbs to the Demon Daughter; but he finds, when too late, that flirting with Demon Daughters is like playing with fire; he is invited to sign the usual bond, and take a dose of Patent Go-to-Sleep-Nine, which he in horror refuses, and after a scene of fearful mental torture, effects a miraculous escape.

Scene 3

"Fie ladies, don't be fond of scandal."

Grand Fête du Champêtre in honor of the Princess Catamaranski; the Lords and Ladies of the Court, as is usual on such occasions, express their joy in a

Danse à la Cour

Pas de Deux, à la Lanliers

The shades of night appear. The Statue having life but during the day, returns to its Marble Shroud.

Scene 4

The Romantic Tailor, who is in chains and misery, is visited by the Demon Daughter who relates the history of her love, and makes him her prisoner of love forever.

Scene 5

The return of Day restores the Statue to life; the Prince claims her for his bride, but is opposed by the Court, who asserts a prior right. Fatal Encounter and Mortal Death of Sylva, who again becomes marble; the Elfin Queen appears. Elfin Change and Fairy Bower.

1857.03 VARIETY, or, The Picture Gallery

An Extravaganza in One Act, 12 Scenes[63]. (Scenery by Charles J. Hawthorne, O. F. Almy. Ballet master, Mons. Montplaisir.) Music arranged by Thomas Baker. Scenery by Mr. Charles Hawthorne, Oscar F. Almy. The whole produced under the personal supervision of Laura Keene. Opened 11 May 1857 at Laura Keene's Theatre in repertory and closed 27 June 1857 after 48 performances.

CAST: Messrs. Ringgold, Harcourt, Reeve, Benson, Leslie, Alleyne, Hayes, Yates, Brown, S. Brown, T. B. Johnston, F. M. Kent; Misses KATE REIGNOLDS, JOSEPHINE MANNERS, JULIA GOULD, Stella Mairs, Clifton, Mrs. Stoddart.

Scene: The Temple of the Modern Standard Drama in a Woeful Plight.

PROGRAM

Scene 1

Ruin Temple of the Drama, with Melpomne and Crato
Spirit of Drama: K. Reignolds. *Romeo*: Mr. Ringgold. *Juliet*: Miss S. Mairs. *Hamlet*: Mr. Harcourt. *Ophelia*: Miss S. Mairs. *Othello*: Mr. Reeve. *Iago*: Mr. Benson. *Apothecary*: Mr. Leslie. (*Scenery by* Hawthorne.)

Scene 2

Sagas-cious appearance of Puff, the Hope of the Living Drama

Puff, a fashionating portion of the Theatrical World: J. Manners.

Scene 3

Fancy, Backed up by Apollo
Fancy, she's all my fancy painted her: J. Gould. (*Scenery* by Almy.)

"We Met by Chance" (Ballad)
J. Gould

Scene 4

The Three Witches and Three Macbeths
Scene: The Blasted Heath. (*Scenery by* Hawthorne.)
Kean: Mr. Leslie. *Garrick*: Mr. Ringgold. *Forrest*: Mr. Hayes. *First Witch*: Mr. Brown. *Second Witch*: Mr. Alleyne. *Third Witch*: Mrs. Brown.

Solo and Glee from Locke's celebrated music of MACBETH
Messrs. Brown, Hayes, Alleyne, Miss Gould, Mrs. Brown

Scene 5

Rivals of the Legitimate (Modern Stars)
Comedy: Miss Clifton. *Spectacle*: Mrs. Stoddart. *Burlesque*: Mr. T. B. Johnson. *Punch*: Mr. Yates.

"O Happy Pair, or the load stars"
(*Music* by Shields.)Mrs. Stoddart

Punchinello Dance
Mr. Yates

Scene 6

Daughters of the Stars
Miss Stella, all the Ladies of the Ballet

"Elphin Home" (Duet)
Miss J. Gould, Mrs. Stoddart
Scene: Moonlight Haunt. (*Scenery by* Hawthorne.)

Scene 7

The Phantom, or the Modern Sheridan
The Phantom: Mr. Alleyne.

"Sally in Our Alley" (Song)
Mr. Alleyne

Scene 8

Melo Drama: Grand Appalling Combat
Melo Drama, No. 1: Mr. T. B. Johnston. *Melo Drama, No. 2*: Mr. F. M. Kent.

---

[63]Also billed as "a highly original, miscellaneous, ancient, modern, high-storical, upperatical, musical semi-burlesque, and wholly scenic extravagant extravaganza (the most villainous perpetrated this season) having been translated from the English, stolen from the German, borrowed from the French, begged from Planché and Co., imported from California and Australia, written, compiled and rendered indigenous to the locality of New York, with the aid of a pastepot and a pair of scissors, by that highly talented and universally quiguitous individual, a Gentleman of New Jersey, who has taken refuge in that benighted land, for the purpose of escaping from that most horrible catastrophe, the destruction of the United States by the Comet." VARIETY was preceded by a short comedy by H. J. Conway, Nature and Art; this was succeeded on 25 May by A Bird in the Hand Is Worth Two in the Bush; 8 June, Life's Troubled Tides; 17 June, Plot and Passion.

Scene 9
Young America
Yankee Girl: Miss S. Mairs.
"Independence Day" (Song)
S. Mairs
Scene 10
The Queen of the Roses
Queen: Miss Stella. And all the Ladies of the Ballet.
"London Apprentice"
Mrs. Alleyne
"Sally in our alley"
Mrs. Alleyne
Scene 11
Hippodrome[64] (Hippodrama)
Mme. Floirneau, with the grand double act of Horsemanship on a single horse: Mlle. T. B. Johnston. (*Scenery by* Hawthorne.)
"Should auld acquaintance be forgot" (Glee)
Scene 12
The Sunlit Grove of palms
The Floral Bouquet—Three Graces—The Magic Scarfs
Scene: The Shower of Gold. (*Scenery by* Hawthorne.)

OLYMPIANA,
1857.04 or, A Night with Mitchell

A musical, whimsical, spiritual, farcical burlesque burletta (Local Burlesque) in One Act, 8 Scenes[65]. Play by Charles Gayler. Music composed and arranged by Anthony Reiff. Costumes by Mons. deGrouche. Properties by Mr. Leach. Scenery by Mr. Wallack. Machinery by Mr. Drew. Produced by T. W. Meighan. Opened 13 July 1857 at the Olympic Theatre and 5 August 1857 after 21 performances in repertory.

CAST: T. B. JOHNSTON, CHARLES HOWARD, F. S. CHANFRAU, W. TRYON, T. W. MEIGHAN, Messrs. ALFORD, FRANCE, NICHOLS, Harry Hall, Master Bogart, James Seymour, Messrs. Baker, Levick, Tate, F. Hodges, Edeson; Mrs. France, Seymour, Mrs. Charles Howard, Kate Pennoyer, Sarah Howell, Miss F. France.

PROGRAM OF SCENES
Scene 1
Introduction
Stage Manager: H. Hall. *Prompter*: Prompter. *Shade of Mitchell*: J. Seymour. *Call Boy*: Master Bogart. *Mrs. Charles Howard*, with a song: Mrs. C. Howard. *Sarah Howell*: S. Howell.
Song
Mrs. C. Howard
Scene 2
'Buy-It-Dear'
Master of the Workhouse: Mr. Alford. *Mr. Bumble*: Mr. France. *The Unknown*: Mrs. C. Howard. *Miss Tinker*: Miss Howell. *Principal Broom Girl*: K. Pennoyer. *Chorus of Paupers, Broom Girls, etc.*: Choristers (a long way from the Italian opera).
Scene 3
'Amilie'
Wilson: F. S. Chanfrau. *Seguin*: Mr. Nichols. *Miss Shireff*: Mrs. C. Howard.
"To the Mountain"
Chorus of Chamois Hunters
"As I vos a Valliking" (Song)
J. Seymour

Scene 4
The Hunchback
Master Walter, Editor of the "_____": T. B. Johnston. *Julia*, a lone and unprotected girl: Mrs. C. Howard.
Scene 5
'Camille'
Camille, with a song and a cough: Mrs. C. Howard. *The Retired Physician*, 'whose sands of life have nearly run out' by a: Veteran Philanthropist. *The Rest of the Characters*: Competent Individuals.
Song
Mrs. C. Howard
Scene 6
Man-Fred[66]
Man-Fred: T. B. Johnston. *Spirit of Alderman*: Mr. France.
In this scene will be introduced a striking novelty—a pile of mud—and terrific denouement.
Scene 7
'Where's the Police?'
First Policeman: Mr. Baker. *Second Policeman*: Mr. Levick. *Third Policeman*: Mr. Tate. *Fourth Policeman*: F. Hodges. *Fifth Policeman*: Mr. Edeson. *Stephen H. Branch*, with a biography: T. B. Johnson.
Scene 8
'The Future'[67]
Mr. Meighan, the wealthy proprietor: T. W. Meighan. *Mr. Chanfrau*, the millionaire: F. S. Chanfrau. *Mr. W. Tryon*, the independent treasurer: W. Tryon. *Thalia*, Mrs. C. Howard. *Terpsichore*: K. Pennoyer. *Fame*: F. France. *Gods, Goddesses, Knights, Lords, Ladies and Gentlemen (of the ballet)*: Auxiliaries.
Shower of Gold with Grand Terpsichorean display
Whole Company
Overflowing Finale, to say nothing of a Grand Display of Fireworks!

SHYLOCK,
1857.05 or, The Merchant of Venice Preserved

(A Revival of) An entirely new reading of Shakespeare, from an edition hitherto undiscovered by modern authorities, and which it is hoped may be received as the stray leaves of a Jerusalem Hearty-Joke (A Musical Burlesque in One Act, 5 Scenes)[68]. Play by Francis Talfourd, founded on William Shakespeare's "The Merchant of Venice." Scenery by Henry Isherwood. Dresses by Mr. Flannery. Mechanical effects by Mr. Landers. Appointments by Mr. Timmony. Musical director, J. Cooke. Stage manager, H. B. Phillips. Produced by Mr. William Stuart. Opened 27 July 1857 in repertory at Wallack's Theatre and closed 17 August 1857 after 14 performances in repertory.

CAST: *Shylock*, a Jew, who does not on this occasion conduct himself as a Gentleman: Mr. JOHN WOOD. *Tubal*, his convenient "Friend in the City": Mr. Holmes. *Duke of Venice*, and Lord Chief Baron of the Judge and Jury Society, Venice: Mr. Oliver. *The Prince of Morocco*, black as the soot which he prefers to Portia, who prefers Bassanio's suit to his: Mr. DeSilveria. *Ditto of Aragon*, author of his own Rejected Addresses: Mr. Laporte. *Antonio*, would-be importer of the merchandize, for the loss of which the Merchant dies; whose solid flesh is to melt, thaw, and resolve itself into a Jew: Mr. Peters. *Bassanio*, his Friend and Pitcher into the misfortune above alluded to: Mr. Levere. *Gratiano*, a Footman, very much out of place: Mr. A. H. DAVENPORT. *Lorenzo*, the small trump who follows suit to Jessica's heart: Mr. G. Rea. *Launcelot*, a Page, who tears himself out of Jessica's good books: Mr. H. B. Phillips. *Portia*, a rich Heiress—a Lady called to the Bar for a Maiden Assize: Mrs. JOHN WOOD. *Nerissa*, Handmaid to a Belle, with herself a had made to a ring: Miss JOSEPHINE MANNERS. *Jessica*, Shylock's "One fair Daughter, and—something more: Miss EMILY MILTON. *Other people of both sexes*: The company and numerous supernumeraries of Superlative and Supernatural abilities.

Act 1, Scene 1: Interior of a Pawnbroker's Shop (Shylock's place of business). *Scene 2*: Drawing-room in the house of Portia. *Scene 3*: Exterior of Shylock's house and shop. *Scene 4*: A street in Venice. *Scene 5*: The Judge and Jury Society, Venice.

ACT 1[69]
Scene 2
Medley: Air, 'Nelly Bligh' (Vainly I cast my eye everywhere to see)/

[64]Added to this scene during the run:
Signor Nixenini: B. Ringgold. *Signor Ricco*: B. Yates.
"Oh happy fair" (Solo and Quartette)
J. Gould, others

[65] A program note adds that it is founded upon events of recent and long past occurence. It is not adapted from the French, translated from the Kamschatkian, stolen from the German, or altered from the Russian. It is purely original. OLYMPIANA was preceded by the musical farce, THE LOAN OF A LOVER, with Mrs. C. Howard, T. B. Johnson, Messrs. Levick, Baker, France, and Mrs. Seymour; this fore-piece was changed to a farce early in the run.

[66]This scene was dropped in the second week of the run.

[67]This scene was dropped in the second week of the run.

[68]Previously produced in New York 29 October 1853 at Burton's Theatre for 4 performances in repertory.

[69]Musical numbers not listed in programs. List prepared from published prompt book (Samuel French, New York, n.d.)

Air—'O Santa Melodia' (If I could only see-e her)/
Air—'Low Back'd Car' (When I first saw Nerissa)
Mr. Davenport
Duet, Air—'To the West, to the West' (You had best, you had best, while you can, get off free)
Miss J. Manners, Mr. Davenport
Trio, 'The One Horse Shay' (Since wedding life you want)
Mrs. J. Wood, J. Manners, Mr. Davenport
Duet, Air—'Brindisi' from LUCRETIA BORGIA (There's a chance tho' to make you feel easy)
Miss J. Manners, Mrs. J. Wood
Air, 'Lord Lovel' (Lord love you, I'll bring to the garden gate)
Mr. Davenport
Air, 'A Master I Have' (A mistress I have and I am her maid)
Miss J. Manners

Scene 3
Air, 'The Ghost Melody' from CORSICAN BROTHERS (Though alive oh!—still I strive to)
Mr. Phillips
Song, 'Life of a Valet'. Air, 'Think of Your Head in the Morning' (I was once a buttons, but now have grown up)
Mr. Davenport
Song, Air—'Young Lord Lochinvar' ('Neath lock, bolt, and bar you'll be safe in your nest)
J. Wood
Song, Air—'On Yonder Rock Reclining' from FRA DIAVOLO (In yonder house is dining)
Mr. G. Rea, Miss E. Milton
Duet and Dance, Air—"Pop goes the weazel' (Long I've loved you, dearest maid)
Mr. G. Rea, Miss E. Milton

Scene 4
Song, Air—'The Maniac' by H. Russell (There's some one comes this way)
J. Wood
Song, Air—'Tippety Witchet' (from my first floor window handy)
J. Wood

Scene 5
Chorus, Air—'The Roast Beef of Old England' (When the new law procedure reformers can boast)
Judge and Jury Society of Venice, the Senate (Chorus)
Finale, Air—'Non Più Mesta' (Some few misters can't abide to laugh)
Miss J. Manners, Chorus

1857.06 THE KING OF CONEY ISLAND

A Disconnected Piece of Absurdity (Burlesque) in One Act, 5 Scenes.[70] Music arranged by Anthony Reiff. Costumes by Mons. deGrouche. Properties by Mr. Leach. Scenery (selected from the best in the house) by Herr Von Whitewashbrush. Machinery by Mons. Uptosnuff. Produced by T. W. Meighan. Opened 30 July 1857 at the Olympic Theatre and closed 31 July 1857 after 2 performances in repertory.

CAST: *New Yorkers*: *Frank Fudge*, an author, in failing circumstances: Mr. RINGOLD. *Corney O'Callaghan*, a ditto, and more so still: JAMES SEYMOUR.

Nondescripts: *Djim-Kro-Ryce*, a Demon from the Wheelabout: T. B. JOHNSTON. *Sea-Serpent*, from Cape Cod, and other oriental parts: Mr. Baker.

Coney Islanders: *Muffin CXVII*, King of Coney Island, a wide-awake, but much tormented monarch: HARRY HALL. *Lord Yawn*, first stick in waiting: Mr. France. *Duke of Nod*, a silent prime minister: Mr. Neville. *Baron Grab*, Lord High Constable of the realm: Mr. Edeson. *Hon. Mr. Grip*, High Sheriff of the County: Mr. Tate. *Coney Islander*, an alarmed native: Mr. Edwards. *Boy*, from the nearest Lager Beer Saloon: Master Bogart. *Princess Darling*, a young lady wanting a young lord, with airs, graces and a mad scene: Mrs. CHARLES HOWARD. *Countess Tootsey*, first lady in waiting: Miss SALLIE PARTINGTON.

Scene 1: An author's chamber, scantily furnished. *Scene 2*: Immense Forest in Coney Island. *Scene 3*: Audience Chamber of King Muffin. *Scene 4*: Street in the capital of Coney Island. *Scene 5*: Apartments (one of them) of the Princess.

MUSICAL NUMBERS, INCIDENTS

Scene 1
Incantation and mysterious appearance of the dark Demon of the Wheelabout.
The Magic Boot and the Unhallowed Brush!
"Jim Crow"
Orchestra

Scene 2
Entrance of a great Ocean Monster. The Sea-Serpent is subdued.
"We Heroes Bold" (Solo)
J. Seymour
"Triumph" (Chorus)
Islanders

Scene 3
"If you think that a King" (Solo)
H. Hall
A King with three troubles; a Princess with one. Stately procession of the nation's defenders, to the inspiring strains of martial music.
March of the 6th Regiment, N.Y.S.M.
Orchestra
Royal munificence. Introduction of three mugs of Real lager!!! The Princess in love. The Princess denied. The Princess goeth mad.
"General Jackson had a Snuff-box" (Solo)
Mrs. C. Howard
The King is put to sleep.

Scene 4
"Oh, Paddy Mahon" (Song)
J. Seymour
The voyagers rescued by means of the Magic Boot, from the Official Philistines.

Scene 5
"With troubled filled and sorrow laden" (Song and Duet)
Mrs. C. Howard, S. Partington
Elopement prevented by the timely appearance of an enraged father. Effects of the Demon's power. The hot Muffin cools. The whole terminating by a great stampede, with postures to match, having no connection with the piece, but meant as a wind-up and break-down.
"Keep one thumb and a finger" (Chorus)
Everybody
Grand Finale de Uproar!

1857.07 THE CORSAIR/ THE LOAN OF A LOVER

A New Nautical, Poetical and Melo-Dramatical Burlesque Extravaganza, preceded by a revival of the Musical Farce, A Loan of a Lover. Scenery by Henry Isherwood. Dresses by Mr. Flannery. Mechanical effects by Mr. Landers. Appointments by Mr. Timmony. Musical director, J. Cooke. Stage manager, H. B. Phillips. Produced by Mr. William Stuart. Opened 10 August 1857 at Wallack's Theatre and closed 14 August 1857 after 4 performances in repertory.

THE LOAN OF A LOVER A Revival of Musical Farce in One Act by James Robinson Planché[71].

CAST: *Peter Spyk*: Mr. JOHN WOOD. *Swyzel*: H. B. Phillips. *Captain Amersfort*: Mr. Levere. *Delve*: Mr. Holmes. *Gertrude*, with songs: Mrs. JOHN WOOD. *Ernestine Rosendaal*: Mrs. H. B. Phillips.

THE CORSAIR A Nautical, Poetical and Melodramatic Burlesque in One Act by William Brough.[72]

CAST: *Conrad*, the Corsair, Notable Pirate, and Salt Water Thief, gloomy, Misanthropical, Ironical and Byronical: Mrs. JOHN WOOD. *Birbanto*, his lieutenant, an Officer, but not a Gentleman: Mr. JOHN WOOD. *Seyd*, or Seedy Pasha, a terrible

[70]Preceded by the laughable burletta, The Rough Diamond, and followed by a screaming farce, The Limerick Boy. For the second performance, THE KING OF CONEY ISLAND was presented as a fore-piece to Olympiana.

[71]First produced in New York 7 April 1835 at the Park Theatre.

[72]Previously produced in London as CONRAD AND MEDORA.

Turk: H. B. Phillips. *Syng Smani*, a General Officer—Major Domo, Pead Cock and Bottle Washer to the Pasha: Mr. Holmes. *Yussuf*, in his own country Joseph, or familiarly, Old Joe, a renegade slave merchant: Mr. PETERS. *Hassan*, a Boatswain: Miss Holmes. *Medora*, a Grecian maiden, Niece and Ward to Yussuf, a scared pledge intrusted to her uncle: Miss JOSEPHINE MANNERS. *Gulnare*, the reigning Beauty of the Pasha's Harem, his favorite, and most other people's, it is hoped, including the audience: Mrs. Vernon. *Zuleima*, a light of other days, a little faded: Mrs. Cook. *Submarina*, the Fairy Guardian of the Deep, Deep Sea. Chief Inspector of the Ocean Police, and Deputy Ruler of the Waves: Mrs. H. B. PHILLIPS. *Serena*, the Fairy of the bottom of the sea: Miss EMILY MILTON. *Corsairs, Slaves, Odalisques, Almas, Water Nymphs, Fairies, Guards, Attendants, etc.*

Scene 1: Naiad's Coralline Temple. *Scene 2*: Corsair's on Shore. *Scene 3*: Terrific Storm at Sea. *Scene 4*: The Pirate's Cave. *Scene 5*: The Harem and Gardens of the Pasha. *Scene 6*: The Corsair's Cell. *Scene 7*: Home of the Naiads.

SPECIALTIES, MUSICAL NUMBERS

Comic Song by a Melodramatic Ruffian (Scene 2)

Terrific Combat à la Coney and Blanchard (Scene 4)
Mr. & Mrs. John Wood

"Bobbin' Around" (Finale)(Scene 7)
All the characters

1857.08 COLUMBUS EL FILIBUSTERO!!

A New and Audaciously Historico-Plagiaristic, Ante-National, Pre-Patriotic, and Omni-Local Confusion of Circumstances, running through Two Acts and Four Centuries (a Burlesque in Two Acts, 4 Scenes). Play by John Brougham. Produced by John Brougham and William E. Burton. Opened 30 December 1857 at Burton's Theatre in repertory and closed February 1858; played a return engagement[73] 13 July 1858 at Niblo's Garden in repertory; returned 9 July 1860 at Niblo's Garden for one week's additional performances.

CAST: *Ferdinand*, King of Aragon—an aggressive and progressive monarch, of rather a speculative turn, with a good many irons on the fire, besides an eye on Castile: MARK SMITH. *Juan Rodérigues de Fonseca*, Archdeacon of Seville, keeper of the King's conscience, (a handsome sinecure,) and court spiritual adviser generally, therefore, naturally opposed to Columbus and the spread of knowledge: Mr. HOLMAN. *Fernando de Talavera*, an old picture, very much improved by time: Mr. Barrett. *Luis de St. Angel*, a contented office-holder, pursuing the even tenor of his way: Mr. Alleyne. *Alonzo de Quintanella*, a courtier of much lower note: Mr. Gledhill. *Don Christoval Colon*, alias *Columbus*, a clairvoyant voyager, whose filibustering expedition gave rise at the time to a world of speculation: JOHN BROUGHAM. *Diego*, a semicolon among the King's pages: Miss JOSEPHINE ORTON.

Distinguished Members of the Historical Society, now meeting together for the first time (4): *Vasco Nunez*: Mr. Hurley. *Hernando Cortez*: Mr. Atkins. *Amerigo Vespucci*: Mr. Paul. *Ponce de Leon*: Mr. Lawson.

A noisy crew of mutinous Seapoys (4): *Sancho Ruis*: Mr. McRae. *Pedro Nino*: Mr. Bishop. *Bartolomeo*: Mr. Hayes. *Juan Perez*: Mr. Bruce. &c., &c.

Isabella, wife of Ferdinand, possessor of half-a-crown by marriage rite, and a whole one by right of having to carry its weight on her own shoulders: Mrs. HOLMAN. *Columbia*, a national debutante, her first appearance on any stage: Mrs. L. W. DAVENPORT. *Little Miss Kansas*, a discordant element: Miss Taylor. *Members of Reception Committee, Aldermen, Discontented Politicians, Independent Voters, and other natural curiosities*: Competent Representatives. *Full-grown States, Juvenile Territories, etc.*: Energetic Host of Auxiliaries.

Act 1, Scene 1: King Ferdinand's Royal Reception Room. *Scene 2*: A modest and retiring apartment in the Palace. *Scene 3*: A Highly Concentrated View of the Atlantic from the deck of the *Santa Maria*.

Act 2: Same palace at Seville, but in an empty state.

ACT 1[74]

Scene 1

Complimentary Chorus, 'GUSTAVUS' (Hail! oh, King of Aragon!)

Laughing Chorus, 'DER FREISCHUTZ' (Such madman's words, how shall we style 'em?)

Ecco Italiani, 'TROVATORE' (Scizzerrere!)
Mr. Holman, Chorus

Biographic Cantata:

Introductory Recitative (Mio simplissima storio dost thou requesto)

Aria Familiaria (My name it is Columbus, I was born in Genoa)

Sleepy Chorus, Fonseca (We are so nappy that to bed we must start)

Duetto Cordiali: Sonny, all right, good night
Messs. M. Smith, J. Brougham

Scene 2

Song, 'Star-Spangled Banner' (Oh, say, shall I see, ere my soul takes its flight)
J. Brougham

Scene 3

Striking Chorus of Mutinous Mariners, taken from miscellaneous sources (Our captain swears he'll have his fling)
Chorus, J. Brougham

Finale—Dis-concerted piece, by the antagonistic politicians:

Chorus, 'GUSTAVUS,' Vive le Roi (Swearing death to all who cave)

ACT 2

Singular vocal melange, 'ROBERT LE DIABLE' (Gold, gold, gold, is no chimera)
M. Smith

Choral interruption, 'RIGOLETTO' (Hard times, bard times, we've suffered)
Chorus

Selfish and unprincipled solo, 'Poor Soldier' (Now the money panic)
Mr. Holman

Solo, 'THE QUAKER'S WIFE" (Father and I are both in town)
Miss J. Orton

Her Majesty signifies her intentions, 'JEANNETTE AND JEANNOT" (Oh! I'll have such brilliant parties now as never yet were seen)
Mrs. Holman

Song, 'LUCY NEAL' (And all you will see kneel)
Mrs. Holman

Trans-Atlantic Procession flies in

Finale, 'Hail Columbia' (Hail Columbia's honored band)

1858.01 DALILAH

The French Theatre in a Drama with Songs in Five Acts, in French. Play by Octave Feuillet. Stage manager, C. Sage. Producer, Frederick Widdows. Opened and closed 22 June 1858 at the Wallack's Theatre after 1 performance in repertory.

CAST: *La Princesse*: Mlle. ELISA PITRON. *Roswein*: M. Tallot. *Carmoli*: Mons. THIÉRY. *Marthe*: Mlle. Juliette. *La Comtesse*: Mlle. Tallot. *Calish*: Mons. EDGARD.

1858.02 LES DEUX AVEUGLES

A Bouffonnerie Musicale in One Act, in French[75]. Libretto by Jules Moinaux. Music by Jacques Offenbach. Stage manager, C. Sage. Producer, Frederick Widdows. Opened 26 August 1858 at the Metropolitan Music Hall [French Theatre] in repertory.

CAST: *Giraffier*: Mons. EDGARD. *Patachon*: Mons. THIÉRY.

Scene: Un pont . . . Paris au fond.

MUSICAL NUMBERS[76]

Scene (Dans sa pauvre vi' malheureuse)
Mons. Thiéry

Duo (Justinien, ce monstre odieux)
Messrs. Edgard, Thiéry

Boléro (La lune brille, Le Ciel scintilla)
Messrs. Edgard, Thiéry

Duo (Ah! fort. . . . Viens je . . .)
Messrs. Thiéry, Edgard

---

[73]For the return engagement, principal cast members were: *Ferdinand*: Mr. WHEATLEIGH. *Juan Rodérigues de Fonseca*: A. H. DAVENPORT. *Columbia*: ADA CLIFTON. *Isabella*: IDA VERNON. *Columbus*: JOHN BROUGHAM.

[74]No program found. List of musical numbers prepared from published prompt-book (Samuel French, New York, n.d. [1858].

[75]In the program examined (3 September 1858), LES DEUX AVEUGLES was preceded by a comédie vaudeville in 2 Acts, Le Gamin de Paris.

[76]Musical numbers not listed in programs. List prepared from published French piano vocal score and libretto (G. Brandus et S. Dufour, Paris, 1855).

1858.03

THE BOHEMIAN GIRL

A Revival of the Light Opera in Three Acts[77]. (Libretto by Alfred Bunn, after Jules-Henri Vernoy de Saint-Georges' ballet-pantomime "The Gypsy.") Music by Michael William Balfe. Musical director, Edmund Reyloff. Produced by the Lucy Escott Opera Troupe. Opened 6 October 1858 at Burton's Theatre and closed 9 October 1858 after 4 performances in repertory.

CAST: *Count Arnheim*, Governor of Presburg: CHARLES DURAND. *Thaddeus*, a proscribed Pole: HENRY SQUIRES. *Florestein*, nephew to the Count: BROOKHOUSE BOWLER. *Devilshoof*, chief of the Gipsy tribe: (Thomas) AYNSLEY COOK. *Captain of the Guard*: Mr. Gonzales. *Officer*: J. Hurley. *First Gipsy*: Mr. Hayes. *Second Gipsy*: Mr. Gledhill. *Arline*: LUCY ESCOTT. *Buda*, her attendant: Harriet Payne. *Queen of the Gipsies*: Emma Heywood. *Nobles, Soldiers, Gipsies, Retainers, Peasants, etc.*

At the closing performance, an afterpiece, THE WATERMAN, or The First of August, a Musical Farce was also presented 9 October 1858.

CAST: *Tom Tug*: BROOKHOUSE BOWLER. *Bundle*: Mr. MOORE. *Robin*: (Thomas) AYNSLEY COOK. *Mrs. Bundle*: Mrs. Dunn. *Miss Wilhelmina*: Miss HEYWOOD.

MUSICAL NUMBERS

"Did you ever hear tell of a Jolly Young Waterman"
B. Bowler

"Then farewell my trimbuilt Wherry"
B. Bowler

"The Bay of Biscay"
B. Bowler

"Cherries and Plums" (Mock Bravura)
A. Cook

"I canna like ye, gentle sir" (Scotch Ballad)
Miss Heywood

"Terence's Farewell to Kathleen" (Irish ballad by Lady Dufferin)
Miss Heywood

1858.04

MEDEA

A Classical Burlesque in One Act[78]. Stage manager, George L. Fox. Acting manager, J. W. Lingard. Leader of orchestra, H. Beissenherz. Produced by George L. Fox and J. W. Lingard. Opened and closed 4 December 1858 at the Bowery Theatre in repertory.

CAST: *Jason*: Miss A. HATHAWAY. *Orpheus*: Miss FANNY HERRING. *Creon*: Mr. Oakley. *Lycaou*: Miss Gourlay. *Melanthe*: Miss Thomas. *Medea*, the only successful rival of Miss Matilda Heron: Mr. GEORGE L. FOX. *Creusa*: Miss Keough. *Sairee*: Mrs. Henry. *First Citizen*: Mr. Stanton. *Second Citizen*: Mr. Bradshaw. *Third Citizen*: Mr. Mitchell. *Fourth Citizen*: Mr. Holland.

MUSICAL NUMBERS

"Old Girl I left behind me" (Song)
A. Hathaway

"Decamp I will to Glory" (Duet)
F. Herring, A. Hathaway

Medley Quartette
G. L. Fox, F. Herring, Miss Keough, [Nurse]

"Polly, won't you try me now" (Duet)
F. Herring, Miss Keough

"City Grenadiers" (Song)
A. Hathaway

"Robinson Crusoe" (Duet)
G. L. Fox, A. Hathaway

"Young May Morn" (Solo and Chorus)
F. Herring, Characters

"West Country air" (Solo)
G. L. Fox

"One Horse Shay" (Finale)
G. F. Fox, Characters

---

[77]First produced in New York 25 November 1844 for 17 performances in repertory at the Park Theatre. For Synopsis of Scenes and Musical Numbers, see original 1844 production.

[78]Presented as an after-piece to a drama, Ida May, or the Kidnapped Child, followed by the farce The Four Mowbrays. MEDEA was followed by a comic pantomime, The Magic Trumpet.

1859.01

ROB ROY

An Operatic Drama (Grand Spectacular Romance with songs and dances) in Four Acts, 12 Scenes. Founded on Sir Walter Scott's novel. (Adaptation by Isaac Pocock. Music composed and arranged by Henry Bishop.) New costumes scenery, properties. Produced by E. Eddy. Opened 9 May 1859 at Niblo's Garden and closed 21 May 1859 after 14 performances; returned 3 June 1859 to Niblo's Garden for 1 additional performance.

CAST: *Diana Vernon*: LUCY ESCOTT. *Rob Roy Macgregor*: Mr. E. EDDY. *Francis Osbaldistone*: Mr. DAVID MIRANDA. *Rashleigh Osbaldistone*: N. B. Clarke. *Sir Frederick Vernon*: Mr. Moore. *Mr. Owen*: Mr. McCloskey. *Bailie Nicol Jarvie*: Mr. HARRY PEARSON. *Captain Thornton*: Mr. Grosvenor. *Major Galbraith*: Mr. DAVIDGE. *Dougal*: H. Bland. *Mr. Stuart*: Mr. Barrett. *Saunders Wylie*: Mr. Wright. *Jobson*: Mr. Stuart. *Mr. Vittie*: Mr. Fielding. *Andrew Fairservice*: Mr. Pike. *Sergeant of the Guard*: Mr. Willis. *Lancie*: Mr. Peterson. *Willit*: Mr. Tammia. *Robert, Hamish*, Rob Roy's sons: Masters J. Blake, T. Blake. *Helen Macgregor*: Mme. PONISI. *Mattie*: Miss Keough. *Martha*: Miss Osborne. *Jean McAlpine*: Mrs. Germon. *Hostess*: Mrs. Wilson. *Soldiers, Villagers, Highlanders*: Numerous Auxiliaries, Chorus expressly engaged for this occasion. (*Scotch Ballet Specialty*: Mlle. DUCY BARRE.

Act 1, Scene 1: Osbaldistone Hall and exterior of Roadside Inn. *Scene 2*: Chamber in the House of Sir Frederick Vernon. *Scene 3*: Room in Bailie Nicol Jarvie's House, Glasgow. *Scene 4*: Glasgow—Moonlight. *Scene 5*: Hall in the Tolbooth. *Scene 6*: Cell in the Tolbooth.

Act 2, Scene 1: College Gardens, Glasgow. *Scene 2*: Room in Osbaldistone Hall. *Scene 3*: Interior of Jean M'Alpine Change House, in the Clachan to Aberfoyle. *Scene 4*: The Clachan of Aberfoyle.

Act 3: Pass of Lochard.

Act 4, Scene 1: Interior of Inn. *Scene 2*: Scene in the Neighborhood of Aberfoyle. *Scene 3*: Rob Roy's Cave, Moonlight.

ACT 1

Scene 1

"Soon the Sun will gae to rest"
Chorus

"My love is like the red, red rose" (Song)
D. Miranda

Scene 2

"Tho' you leave me now in sorrow" (Duet)
L. Escott, D. Miranda

"Auld Robin Grey" (Song)
L. Escott

Scene 6

"Hark! from St. Mungo's Tower" (Finale)

ACT 2

Scene 2

"A highland lad, my love was born" (Song)
L. Escott

Scene 3

"A famous man was Robin Hood" (Song and Chorus)
Mr. Davidge

"Auld lang Syne" (Song and Chorus)
D. Miranda

Scene 4

March and Tramp Chorus
Entire Company

ACT 3

Grand Battle Tableau between English Soldiers and Highlanders

"O! hone a me" (The Lament)

"Roy's Wife of Aldivalloch" (Chorus and Dance)

Grand Scotch Ballet
Mlle. D. Barre and characters

ACT 4

Scene 2

Song
L. Escott

"Forlorn and broken hearted" (Song)
D. Miranda, L. Escott

Scene 3

"Pardon now the bold Outlaw" (Finale)
All the characters

1859.02

THE WATERMAN

A Revival of the Operetta (Musical Farce) in One Act[79]. Produced by Mr. E. Eddy. Opened 1 June 1859 at Niblo's Garden and closed 2 June 1859 after 2 performances.

CAST: *Miss Wilhelmina*: Miss LUCY ESCOTT. *Tom Tug*: Mr. D. MIRANDA. *Mr. Bundle*: Mr. BLAND. *Mrs. Bundle*: Mrs. Germon. *Robin*: Mr. DAVIDGE.

1859.03

THE BOHEMIAN GIRL

A Revival of the Light Opera in Three Acts, 5 Scenes[80]. (Libretto by Alfred Bunn, after Jules-Henri Vernoy de Saint-Georges' ballet-pantomime "The Gypsy.") Music by Michael William Balfe. Conductor, St. Luke. Leader of orchestra, Julian Wyeth. Produced by Mr. E. Eddy. Opened 6 June 1859 at Niblo's Garden and closed 11 (matinee) June 1859 after 5 performances in repertory.

CAST: *Thaddeus*, a proscribed Pole: Mr. DAVID MIRANDA. *Devilshoof*, Chief of the Gipsy Tribe: Mr. HARRY PEARSON. *Count Arnheim*, Governor of Presburg: Mr. FRANK REA. *Florestein*, his nephew: Mr. McCLOSKEY. *Overhoof*: Mr. HUTCHINS. *Burian*: Mr. Sapho. *Captain of the Guard*: Mr. Converse. *First Officer*: Mr. Schlim. *Second Officer*: Mr. Benscoten. *First Peasant*: Mr. Jones. *First Gipsy*: Mr. —. *Arline*, the Bohemian Girl: Miss LUCY ESCOTT. *Gipsey Queen*: Miss (EMMA) HEYWOOD. *Buda*: Miss Keough. *Retainers, Gipsies, Nobles, Soldiers, Peasants, etc.*

1859.04

THE BEGGAR'S OPERA

A Revival of the Comic Opera (Ballad Opera)[81]. (Libretto by John Gay.) Compressed and adapted for the occasion. Produced by Mr. E. Eddy. Opened 9 June 1859 at Niblo's Garden as an afterpiece in repertory; closed 10 June 1859 after 2 performances.

CAST: *Polly Peachum*: Miss HEYWOOD. *Captain Macheath*: Mr. DAVID MIRANDA. *Mr. Peachum*: Mr. W. DAVIDGE. *Mat o' the Mint*: Mr. HARRY PEARSON. *Filch*: Mr. McCloskey. *Ben-Budge*: Mr. Pike. *Lockit*: Mr. Bland. *Crook-fingered Jack*: Mr. Higgins. *Lucy*: Miss KEOUGH. *Mrs. Peachum*: Mrs. Germon.

1859.05

CINDERELLA

A Burlesque Extravganza in One Act, 9 Scenes.[82] Play by William and Robert Brough (from the fairy tale by Charles Perrault). (Scenery, Minard Lewis. Ballet master, Mons. Montplaisir.) Music arranged by Thomas Baker. Produced by Laura Keene. Opened 15 June 1859 at Laura Keene's Theatre and closed 4 July (matinee) 1859 after 11 performances in repertory.

CAST: *Cinderella*: ADELAIDE GOUGENHEIM. *Prince Rodolph*: JOSEPHINE [Joey] GOUGENHEIM. *Baron Soldoff*: Mr. Burnett. *Capillaire*: Mr. C. Peters. *Seneschal*: Mr. B. Brown. *Rumpelstiltskin, the Red Man of Agar*: Mr. Zavistowski. *Baroness Soldoff*: Mrs. Booth, Jr. (C. DeBar). *Rondoletia*: Ida Vernon. *Patchoulia*: Miss C. Howard. *Queen of the Fairies*: Miss White. *Attendants, Guests, Fairies, etc.* (*Specialties*: ZAVISTOWSKI'S JUVENILE BALLET TROUPE, including Alice, Christine, Petite Emeline, Petit Henry.)

Scene 1: View of an Old Town. *Scene 2*: Hall in the Baron's Mansion. *Scene 3*: A Terrace and View of the Baron's House. *Scene 4*: A Kitchen in the Baron's Mansion. *Scene 5*: Inner Court of the Baron's Mansion. *Scene 6*: Entrance Hall to the Palace. *Scene 7*: Grand Hall in the Palace. *Scene 8*: A Room in the Palace. *Scene 9*: The Silver Halls of Dazzling Light. Grand change to The Fairy Home, revealing the Golden Corridors of the Aerial Amphitheatre.

BALLETS, SPECIALTIES

"Fill, my jolly Boys"[83] (Duet)(Scene 1)
Messrs. Burnett, C. Peters
Serenade, à la Don Pasquale (Scene 1)
Mr. Burnett
Grand Scena, Fra Pocca (Scene 2)
A. Gougenheim
Grand Pas d'Ensemble (Scene 2)
Juvenile Troupe, led by A. Zavistowski
Poor Dog Tray (Scene 2), discussed by
A. Gougenheim, Mr. Burnett
"Come the Dinner's Waiting" (Quintette and Chorus)(Scene 2)
"Oh! Pa, do let us go" (Musical entreaty)(Scene 5)
Misses I. Vernon, C. Howard
"Home, sweet home" (Scene 5)
A. Gougenheim
Red Man of Agar (Specialty)(Scene 5)
Mons. Zavsitowski
Pas des Arab (Scene 5)
Eugenia, Clara, Emeline, Fanny
Pas de Deux, Comic (Scene 5)
Clara, Henry
La Madrilène (Scene 5)
A. Zavsitowski
Pas Seul (Scene 5)
Petite Emeline
Chorus—Finale (Scene 9)
All the Characters

1859.06

MASSANIELLO,
Hero and Martyr of Italian Liberty

A Burlesque in One Act, 6 Scenes[84]. Play by William and Robert Brough. Inspired by the opera Masaniello by Daniel Auber. Music arranged and conducted by Thomas Baker. Scenery painted by Oscar F. Almy. Pyrotechnics by Messrs. J. G. & J. Edge. Produced by Laura Keene. Opened 27 June 1859 at Laura Keene's Theatre and closed 9 July 1859 after 12 performances.

CAST: *Massaniello*, fishmonger and general dealer. Country orders attended to on the shortest notice, &c. (vide card.) The greatest plebian of the common lot: JOSEPHINE ["Joey"] GOUGENHEIM *Susanna*, a waiting maid—waiting to be asked in marriage: ADELAIDE GOUGENHEIM. *Alphonso*, Prince of somewhere else, attached to the Spanish Embassy at the Court of Naples, also to Elvira: Mr. C. Stuart. *Elvira*, Princess of somewhere else, the locality being uncertain, attached to the attaché above alluded to: Ida Vernon. *Lorenzo*, friend to Alphonso: Mr. C. Peters. *Rowers in the same boat with Massaniello (3)*: *Pietro*: Mr. Burnett. *Borella*: Mr. Brown. *Coreno*: Mr. Evans. *Selva*, otherwise 7, of the B division, the myridon of a despotic government: Mr. DAVIDGE. *Doggia, Billibarlo*, Gamens of Naples: Messrs. Thompson, Williams. *First Policeman*: Mr. Muneret. *Fenella*, the Fisho'man of Naples, a young lady suffering from a severe attack of blighted affections, but who never told her love because she couldn't—played, on this occasion as on all others, by a Dummy: Mlle. CHRISTINE. *Ladies of the Halle (3)*: *Tolla Contadini*: Mrs. C. DeBar. *Guidi Galigani*: Miss White. *Betta Martini*: Miss Everett. (*Ballet Specialty*: Mons. ZAVISTOWSKI.)

Scene 1: The Union of a Pair of Flats. *Scene 2*: The Bay of Naples. *Scene 3*: A Room in the Viceroy's Palace. *Scene 4*: A Violent Outbreak. *Scene 5*: Interior of Massaniello's Cabin. *Scene 6*: Banqueting Hall in the Palace, with Mount Vesuvius in the Distance.

SPECIALTIES[85]

Pas L'Espagnol (Scene 1)
Mlle. Christine
Grand Pas de Fascination (Scene 2)
Mlle. Christine
Grand Pas de Deux, La Sicilienne (Scene 4)
Mlle. Christine, Mons. Zavistowski
Equestrian Act (Scene 5)
J. Gougenheim
Grand Eruption of Mount Vesuvius (Scene 6)

---

79 Previously presented in New York 9 October 1858; for Musical Numbers, see previous production. Presented on a triple bill with Ingomar, the Barbarian, a play in five acts; following THE WATERMAN, a ballet in 2 tableaux, La Vedova Scattro was presented.

80 First produced in New York 25 November 1844 for 17 performances in repertory at the Park Theatre. For Synopsis of Scenes and Musical Numbers, see original 1844 production.

81 First produced in New York 3 December 1750 at the Theatre in Nassau Street for 5 performances in repertory. This revival was preceeded by a comedy, A Lady & Gentleman.

82 Preceded by a farce, A Model of a Wife, then later in the run, Ladies Beware.

83 Dropped during the run.

84 Preceded by Buckstone's farce, Shocking Events.

85 Announced on 4 July was a new song "The Song of the Union" performed by the sisters Gougenheim.

1859.07

THE INVISIBLE PRINCE

A Revival of the Exquisite Extravaganza in One Act[86]. Play by James Robinson Planché. Music arranged and conducted by Thomas Baker. Scenery painted by Oscar F. Almy. Produced by Laura Keene. Opened 11 July 1859 at Laura Keene's Theatre and closed 13 July 1859 after 3 performances.

CAST: *Prince Leander*, lineally descended from the Native Kings of Allaquiz: Miss JOEY GOUGENHEIM. *Apricotina*, own maid to the Princess of the Island of Tranquil Delights: Miss ADELAIDE GOUGENHEIM. *Prince Furibond, only son of Blouzabella and extra-ORDINARY Prince*: Mr. DAVIDGE. *Marquis Anysidos*, Major Domo: Mr. BURNETT. *Don Moustachez de Haro y Barbios*, Captain of the Guard: Mr. C. Stuart. *Count Palava Torquemova*, introducer of Ambassadors: Mr. B. Brown. *Sambo*: Mr. Evans. *Princess Xquisitelittlepet*: Miss LAURA HONEY. *Queen (Blouzabella)* of Allaquiz, a city somewhere on the Spanish main: Mrs. C. DeBAR. *Fairy Gentilla*: Miss Morton. Chorus of Auxiliaries.

Scene 1: Gallery in the royal castle of Allaquiz, a château en Espagne nouvelle. *Scene 2*: Garden of an old Hunting Lodge, Leander's family seat. *Scene 3*: A Forest. *Scene 4*: Sea shore and distant view of the Palace of Pleasure on the Island of Tranquil Delights somewhere in the Pacific Ocean. *Scene 5*: Throne room in the Palace of Pleasure. *Scene 6*: Grotto in the Palace Gardens, with pose plastique of Apollo. *Scene 7*: Camp of Furibond. *Scene 8*: Palace of Pleasure.

MUSICAL NUMBERS

Scene 1
- Air, 'I'd rather have a guinea than a one pound note' (Tis a shame I declare)
  Chorus
- Song, 'Bonny laddie' (Bow ye venal servile train)
  Mr. Davidge
- Round (The Indian Drum)
- Catch, 'Twas you that kissed the pretty girl' (How now, sir)
  B. Brown, Mr. Davidge, J. Gougenheim, Mr. Evans
- Trio, 'Poor soldier' (Out of my sight)
  Mrs. C. Debar, Mr. Davidge, J. Gougenheim
- Air, from LA SONNAMBULA (When I played those tricks so charming)
  J. Gougenheim

Scene 3
- Duet, 'Over the mountain' (The sweetest youth I e'er did see)
  Misses Gougenheim

Scene 4
- Song, 'The Bold Dragoon' (There was a fairy queen)
  A. Goughenheim

Scene 5
- Duet, 'Oh come to me when daylight sets' (I must be gone e're daylight sets)
  Misses Gougenheim
- Chorus, 'Cellarius'
- Duet from THE BEGGAR'S OPERA (Pretty Polly say)
  J. Gougenheim, L. Honey
- Song, 'Old Dan Tucker' (In my blue cat I take a pride)
  L. Honey, Chorus
- Air and Chorus, 'Buffalo Gals' (As I was flying down the street)
  Misses Gougenheim, L. Honey, Chorus

Scene 6
- Grand medley scena:
- Recitative (A child no more)
  L. Honey
- Air, 'The power of love' from SATANELLA (Love has power)
  L. Honey, J. Gougenheim
- Song, 'Wait for the wagon'
- Air, 'The Standard Bearer' (A flag of truce)
  J. Gougenheim
- Duet, 'Charming Judy Callaghan' (Ye terrible sisters three)
  A. Gougenheim, L. Honey

Scene 7
- Song, 'The Dashing White Sergeant' (He's a donkey I know)
  Mr. Davidge
- Air, 'Sally come up' (He's let the daylight through me clear)
  Mr. Davidge
- Finale (In my cap kindly place a new feather)
  Misses Gougenheim, L. Honey, Mr. Davidge, Chorus

[86]THE INVISIBLE PRINCE was performed as an after-piece to a three-act drama, Giralda, or Which is My Husband. THE INVISIBLE PRINCE, or, The Island of Tranquil Delights was first performed in New York 26 April 1847 at the Park Theatre. No program found for this revival; detail of Scenes and Musical Numbers prepared from prompt book, as revised for this 1859 revival.

1859.08

LALLA ROOKH, or, The Fire Worshippers

A New and Entertaining pièce de circonstance (a Burlesque) in One Act, an Introduction and 7 Scenes[87] Entire production under the direction of Mr. W. J. Florence. Music, new and selected by John Cooke. Scenery by Messrs. Culbert, Oscar F. Almy, Wallace, Jeffries. Dresses by Miss Georgianna Flannery. Machinery by Mr. Bishop, Mr. J. Johnson. Properties by James T. Timmony. Produced by Mr. & Mrs. W. J. Florence. Opened 18 July 1859 at Wallack's Theatre and closed 20 August 1859 after 30 performances.

CAST: Introduction: *Baulky Colt, Railer, Drysticks, Grumbling Authors*: Messrs. Jeffries, Langdon, Ralyea. *Columbia*, the Gem of the Ocean: Mrs. W. J. FLORENCE. *Manager*, in distress of course: Mr. Floyd. *The Shade of Shakespeare*: Mr. Grosvenor. *The Shade of Byron*: Mr. Flourants. *The Shade of Milton*: Mr. Stoddart. *The Temple of Liberty*: Mr. Jeffries.

Khorsanbad, Chief of the Gheber's Fire Department: Mr. W. J. FLORENCE. *Skihroket*: Mr. Ralyea. *Ghebers and Fire Worshippers at large (4)*: *Torpedo*: Mr. Tree. *Dublehedher*: Mr. Oliver. *Pihnweels*: Mr. Coburn. *Hafed*: Mr. Grosvenor.

Hamoune, the banished Peri: Miss Kate Edwards. *Laloute*, first Peri to the Court: Miss J. Gourlay. *Peris (4)*: *Nice Lyti-sing*: Miss M. Evercott. *Taffi-Kandigh*: Miss G. Monk. *Sitrate-Magneeshuh*: Miss S. Perring. *Tootai-Poop-psi*: Miss Masse.

Lalla Rookh, a spoiled child: Mrs. W. J. FLORENCE. *Fadladeen*, the Grand Vizier: Mr. STODDART. *Ferramorz*: Mrs. STODDART.

Arongzebe, King of Kantellyu: Mr. Sidney Smith. *Sum-thing*, the Chinese Ambassador: Mr. Floyd. *Jon Bawliver*, the Ambassador of Cashmere: Mr. Parsloe. *Hinda*, maid in waiting to Lalla: Mrs. Floyd. *Bayaderes, Chinese Bell Hangers, Treasure Bearers, etc.*

Colonel Lalla Rookh: Mrs. W. J. FLORENCE. *Lieutenant Colonel Hinda*: Mrs. Floyd.

Introduction: The Cavern of Despair. (Jeffries.) *Act 1, Scene 1*: The Astor House and Park. (Almy.) *Scene 2*: The Banished Peri. *Scene 3*: Lalla in Her Tent. The Veiled Prophet of Khorasson. *Scene 4*: The Hall of Reception. *Scene 5*: Street in New York. *Scene 6*: Niagra Falls. *Scene 7*: Camp of the Amazons on Staten Island. Grand change to the Fairy Aquarium.

MUSICAL NUMBERS

Introduction
- "When managers are fighting" (Solo and Chorus)
- "I've Wandered over many lands" (Song)
  Mrs. W. J. Florence
- "He's no money, so you see" (Song)
  Mrs. W. J. Florence

Scene 1
- "Now, now, now" (Song and Chorus)
- "Joy, Ghebers, joy" (Song and Chorus)
  Mr. Grosvenor, Ghebers

Scene 2
- "Out, Miss" (Song and Chorus)
  Miss J. Gourlay, Chorus

Scene 3
- "Polly, will you try me" (Duet)/
- "Rose tree in full bearing" (Duet)
  Mrs. W. J. Florence, Mrs. Stoddart

Scene 4
- "Pray, Daddy, please to moderate" (Song)
  Mrs. W. J. Florence
- "Old Dorg Tray" (Song and Chorus)
  Mrs. W. J. Florence, Ladies

Scene 7
- March of the Seventy-First Regiment of the Amazonian Guard
- Grand Fete; La Bayadère; Lalla Rookh

[87]Preceded by a fore-piece, The Irish Lion, which was later replaced by Temptattion, or, The Irish Emigrant, which was replaced by Mr. Florence's comic farce, The Yankee Housekeeper, which was later replaced by The Irish Mormon, or, Brian O'Lynn.

"Gaily, the minstrel boy" (Song)
Mrs. Stoddart
"Robinson Crusoe" (Song)
Mrs. W. J. Florence
Grand Finale
All the characters

1859.09 NEVER JUDGE BY APPEARANCES/ DIAMOND CUT DIAMOND

A Double Bill of English Parlor Operas in One Act. Orchestra under the direction of M. Vaillant. (Produced under the supervision of Henri Drayton.) Produced by George A. Wells. Opened 12 October 1859 at the French Theatre in repertory[88]; NEVER JUDGE BY APPEARANCES returned 8 November 1859 to the New Opera House in repertory on a double bill with LOVE'S LABOR LOST; DIAMOND CUT DIAMOND returned 2 December 1859 to the New Opera House on a double bill with NOTHING VENTURE NOTHING HAVE.

CAST: Mr. HENRI DRAYTON; Mrs. HENRI DRAYTON [Susanna Lowe].

ACT 1

NEVER JUDGE BY APPEARANCES. An English Parlor Opera (Operetta) in One Act. Written by Henri Drayton. Music by E. J. Loder.

CAST: *Louise*, Countess de Belleville: Mrs. HENRI DRAYTON. *Oscar*, Count de Belleville: Mr. HENRI DRAYTON.

MUSICAL NUMBERS

"I've loved thee long, Louise" (Song)
Mrs. H. Drayton
"Good husband" (Duet)
Mr. and Mrs. H. Drayton
"He's gone; once more I am alone" (Recitative)/
"If I but dared to tell how much I loved" (Ballad)
Mrs. H. Drayton
"I've said it, sir, and law my will must be" (Duettino)
Mr. and Mrs. H. Drayton
"Ah! yes, as in the play" (Recitative)/
"Happiness, joy divine" (Grand Air)/
"How oft in fancy have I heard" (Melody)
Mr. H. Drayton
"Good night" (Duet)
Mr. and Mrs. H. Drayton
"Dear Oscar, I am thine alone" (Recitative)/
"When in solitude, I ponder" (Cantabile)/
"Hope now brightly beaming" (Cabaletta)
Mr. and Mrs. H. Drayton
"Leave me, I pray" (Duet)/
"Madame, I know all" (Duet)/
"What vengeance, what fury, within thee doth burn" (Finale)
Mr. and Mrs. H. Drayton

ACT 2

DIAMOND CUT DIAMOND. An Operatic Proverb Bouffe (Operetta) in One Act. Written by Henri Drayton. Music by Grisar.

CAST: *Josephine*, a waiting woman: Mrs. HENRI DRAYTON. *Countess de Valdenne*: Mrs. HENRI DRAYTON. *Victor*, a valet: Mr. HENRI DRAYTON. *Captain Sanspeur*: Mr. HENRI DRAYTON. *Simon Sabot*: Mr. HENRI DRAYTON.

MUSICAL NUMBERS

"Behold Victor" (Air)
Mr. H. Drayton
"Behold this, Victor" (Recitative)/
"Good Sir" (Duo)/
"Yes I see clearly now" (Stretta)
Mr. and Mrs. H. Drayton
"Soon all must obey" (Song)
Mrs. H. Drayton
"Who dares brave me" (Grand Duo)/
"Ah, no man I'll fear" (Ensemble)
Mr. and Mrs. H. Drayton
"Yes, we must part" (Ballad)
Mrs. H. Drayton
"Ah, from this hour" (Ensemble)/
"This, Victor, I've been told" (Duo)
Mr. and Mrs. H. Drayton
"With her I will ever" (Ensemble)/
"With me you will ever" (Ensemble)
Mr. and Mrs. H. Drayton
"Too Late" (Song)
Mrs. Drayton
(*Music by* John R. S. Pratten.)
They will also introduce:
"Simon the Cellarer"
Mr. H. Drayton
(*Music by* John Hatton.)
"When a Little Farm We Keep"
Mr. and Mrs. H. Drayton

1859.10 TOINETTE ET SON CARABINIER

An Operette (Opéra-Bouffe) in One Act, in French[89]. Libretto by Michel Delaporte. Music by Hervé. Opened 13 October 1859 at the Théâtre Français and closed 15 October 1859 after 2 performances in repertory.

CAST: *Toinette*, Cuisinière: Mlle. DARCY. *Pandore*, Carabinier: Mons. JUIGNET. *Biscotin*, Ecrivain public: Mons. EUGÈNE LOIRET.

MUSICAL NUMBERS[90]

Chanson (Carabinier rempli de zèle)
Mons. Juignet
Couplets (Le diable qui s'en empara)
Mons. Juignet
Air (Ecrivain, rédacteur c'est ma plume féconde)
Mons. Loiret
Romance (Quand j'obtenais une sortie)
Mlle. Darcy
Duetto (Carabinier, que tu m'affliges)
Mlle. Darcy, Mons. Juignet
Trio (Oui tirons vengeance de la manignance)
Tous
Canon Final (Croyez-moi, monsieur Biscotin)
Tous

1859.11 CHAMOONI III

A Musical, Fantastic, Historical Piece of Extravaganze (a Burlesque) in One Act, representing the adventures of three unfortunate Americans, cast away upon an unknown shore. (Play by Dion Boucicault[91].) Scenery by Mr. W. Hayes. Produced by William Stuart and Dion Boucicault. Opened 19 October 1859 at the Winter Garden in repertory.

CAST: *Chamooni III*, Autocrat of all the Mozambiques: Mr. HARRY PEARSON. *Harico*, his Mandarin: Mr. GEORGE HOLLAND. *Jamaica Gravesend*, from New York, an operator on the sewing machine, a young person of great enterprises: Miss AGNES ROBERTSON. *Yonkers*, a kerbstone operator, late of William Street, N. Y., but now on a speculative trip to Shanghai: Mr. JOSEPH JEFFERSON. *Cattaraugus*

[88]The Double Bills of English Parlor Operas were presented on Monday, Wednesday and Friday evenings, alternating with a program of French plays.

[89]TOINETTE ET SON CARABINIER was preceded by a varying program of fore-pieces, Tambour Battant; Levreux Braconnier; Brutus Lache Caesar; Un Caprice; Qui Se Ressemble Se Gene. The premiere announced for 11 October appears to have been cancelled.

[90]No program found for this production. List of musical numbers prepared from published French piano vocal score, (Théâtre des Folies Nouvelles, Heu, Editeur, Paris, 1856).

[91]Author uncredited in programs; Odell identifies Boucicault as the author.

Gravesend, his late partner, an ardent, but weak admirer of Mr. Yonkers' abilities: Mr. T. B. JOHNSTON. (*Dance Specialty*: Mme. DEULIN.)

Wives of Chamooni: *Zemzem*: Miss Clinton. *Lulu*: Miss Fielding. *Mishmish*: Miss Burke. *Koo-koo*: Miss Secor. *Kooz-Kooz*: Miss Denham. *Weeneel*: Miss Gimber. *Kisskiss*: Miss Morton. *Oma-e-toot*: Miss Tuomy. *Toot-o-mac*: Miss Walters.

Time and Place: This evening, on the stage.

Scene: The Celestial Gardens (from a sketch on the spot).

MUSICAL NUMBERS

"Yonder in extremis lying"
Chorus
Jamaica accepts with philosophy her bloomers and cap, but objects to lose her head—The Death of the Premier of Mozambiques—Terror of the Minister, Harico—Who shall inform the Shah—The opinion of the Ladies of Mozambique upon the Geographical Position of America—They settle the Question—The procession of the Corpus.

"Recollections of Gotham" (Song)
A. Robertson
The Arrival of the American Embassy in the Celestial Gardens—Utter Ignorance of the People of All Diplomatic Etiquette—The Envoys learn the Only Conditions on which they may be admitted to Trade—Acceptance of the Terms—Terrible Condition of the Travelers—They prepare to die like True Americans—They postpone the Inconvenience—Yonkers resolves to Meet and Defeat the College of Mandarins.

Medley (Song)
J. Jefferson
Entrance of the Shah—His Reception of the Mission—The Arkansas Traveler—A "Bar"—The Magnificent Performance of Cattaraugus—His first appearance in the part, but not his first in the character—Triumph of the Strangers

"Jordan" (Solo on the Accordion)

Polka Rowdyova
A. Robertson, T. B. Johnston
Mashallah! The Shah has an idea, in which Cattaraugus does not coincide—Vamos—The Fête.

"I'm Monarch Here" (Song)
H. Pearson
The Incarnation of Cattaraugus—Duet between two cages:

"Oh, don't despair" (from DON PASQUALE)
The Terrible Appearance of the Rival Minister—Two heads better than one—The conspiracy to take the Shah's head—Arrival of his truculency—Fearful condition of the ministry—Yonkers is put to it—He accounts philosophically for the condition of his party—It won't do—Despair of Jamaica—The heads of the offenders are laid at the Shah's feet—Superb conclusion.

The Fête in the Celestial Gardens

The Nautch Dance; The Almee
Mme. Deulin

The Arkansas Beraika-Douna
A. Robertson, J. Jefferson, T. B. Johnson
Triumph of American Terpshickory and General Illumination

Immense Enthusiasm of Spectators

1859.12 NEVER DESPAIR

An English Parlor Opera in One Act. Written by Henri Drayton. Founded upon the well-known story of 'Pauvre Jacques.' Music by J. F. Duggan. Orchestra under the direction of M. Vaillant. (Produced under the supervision of Henri Drayton.) Produced by George A. Wells. Opened 19 October 1859 at the French Theatre in repertory[92]; returned 11 November 1859 to the New Opera House (Hope Chapel) in repertory[93]; season closed 31 December 1859.

CAST: *Jacques*, an old Musician: Mr. HENRI DRAYTON. *Marie*: Mrs. HENRI DRAYTON [Susanna Lowe]. *Fraulein Von Baeirn*: Mrs. HENRI DRAYTON. *Leonie*: Mrs. HENRI DRAYTON.

MUSICAL NUMBERS[94]

"At night upon the moonlit tide" (Serenade)
"The musical authority" (Air bouffe)
"Now, Marie, I prithee hear me" (Duet)
"Sweet Sleep, in visions thou dost bring" (Grand Air)
"Haste, love, to me" (Cabaletta)
The Story
"Oh! kaufen sic ein besen" (German Song)
"Love laughs at locksmiths" (Song)
"My old spinette" (Song)
"But here! no! yes!" (Recitative)
"At Venice, when the moon shone bright" (Romance)
"Heaven o'er doth shield us with its care, and seems to say—Never Despair!" (Finale)

1859.13 BETTER LATE THAN NEVER!

An English Parlor Opera in One Act. Written by Henri Drayton. Music by W. G. F. Beale. Orchestra under the direction of M. Vaillant. (Produced under the supervision of Henri Drayton.) Produced by George A. Wells. Opened 26 October 1859 at the French Theatre in repertory[95]; returned 14 November 1859 to the New Opera House (Hope Chapel) in repertory with NEVER DESPAIR; season closed 31 December 1859.

CAST: *Jeannot*: Mr. HENRI DRAYTON. *Jeannette*: Mrs. HENRI DRAYTON [Susanna Lowe].

MUSICAL NUMBERS[96]

"As all alone, now every day"
Mrs. H. Drayton
"Hola! hola! house here"
Mr. H. Drayton
"Come here, Mam'selle"
Mr. and Mrs. H. Drayton
"A good old man indeed was he" (Melody)
Mrs. H. Drayton
"No! no! though for a moment" (Duet)
Mr. and Mrs. H. Drayton
"Then I am rich" (Arietta)
Mr. H. Drayton
"Oh! tis charming" (Finale)
Mrs. Drayton will also introduce the celebrated and favorite song "Home, Sweet Home."

1859.14 GOING IT BLIND

A Comic Music Duality in One Act.[97] Original French libretto to the bouffonerie musicale "Les Deux Aveugles" by Jules Moinaux. English adaptation by Maria Grace Walcot. Music by Jacques Offenbach. Music arranged by Robert Stoepel. Scenery by Mr. Henry Isherwood. Stage manager, Lester Wallack. Produced by Mr. James W. Wallack. Opened 31 October 1859 at Wallack's Lyceum Theatre and closed 9 November 1859 after 9 performances.

---

[92]The Double Bills of English Parlor Operas were presented on Monday, Wednesday and Friday evenings, alternating with a program of French plays; NEVER DESPAIR replaced NEVER JUDGE BY APPEARANCES.

[93]Presented as a fore-piece to a musical adaptation of LOVE LABOR LOST; see entry below at that date.

[94]Added to the production 22 December 1859:
"The Drayton Polka Song"
Mrs. H. Drayton
(*Music and Lyrics by* Francis H. Brown.)

[95]The Double Bills of English Parlor Operas were presented on Monday, Wednesday and Friday evenings, alternating with a program of French plays; all the Parlor Operas alternated with one another in repertory.

[96]Added during the run:
"Simon the Cellarer" (Song)
Mr. H. Drayton

[97]GOING IT BLIND followed a drama in Three Acts, Fast Men of the Olden Time.

CAST: *Bogus*, a blind magician: Mr. CHARLES M. WALCOT. *Buncomb*, ditto, a little more ditto: Mr. JOHN BROUGHAM.

Scene: Central Park, from the entrance at 79th Street.

MUSICAL NUMBERS

"Both Blind and poor dears" (Aria, accompanying himself on trombone)
J. Brougham

"A drop for me" (Lament)
Trombone

"He prevents me, 'po my soul" (Aria)
C. M. Walcot
(Accompanying himself on violincello, with Mr. Brougham on trombone)

Due Concertante, Trombone and Violincello
Messrs. Brougham, Walcott

"How many beans make five"?" (Duo di Voce, Instrumental)
Messrs. Brougham, Walcott, Trombone, Violincello

Grand Finale
All the characters, accompanied by the Central Park Orchestra

1859.15 LOVE'S LABOR LOST

A New Version of Shakespeare's "Love's Labour Lost" in One Act. Written by Henri Drayton. Music selected from Balfe, Dibdin, Lee, Hatton, Lover, Donizetti, Verdi, etc. (Produced under the supervision of Henri Drayton.) Musical director, Henri Drayton. Produced by George A. Wells. Opened 8 November 1859 at the New Opera House (Hope Chapel) in repertory; season closed 31 December 1859.

CAST: *Pat Donalan*: HENRI DRAYTON. *General Firelock*: HENRI DRAYTON. *Sir Charles Ramrod*: HENRI DRAYTON. *Zadekiah Heat*, a Yankee dentist: HENRI DRAYTON. *Old Anthony Grumble*: HENRI DRAYTON. *Fanny Sparkle*: Mrs. HENRI DRAYTON [Susanna Lowe]. *Meggy O'Callagan*: Mrs. HENRI DRAYTON. *Grace Smoothtongue*: Mrs. HENRI DRAYTON. *Sairey Gamp*: Mrs. HENRI DRAYTON.

MUSICAL NUMBERS

"I'll be no submissive wife" (Song)
Mrs. Drayton

"When all the world's asleep" (Serenade, from the celebrated 'Misere' in IL TROVATORE)
Mr. and Mrs. Drayton

"Father Malloy" (Song)
Mr. Drayton

"When gentlemen a-courting go" (Song)
Mrs. Drayton

"Old age and gout" (Air)
Mrs. Drayton

"Without more ado" (Duet)(Senza tanti complementi)
Mr. and Mrs. Drayton

"If ever I should have a wife" (Song)(Yankee Doodle)
Mr. Drayton

"I am not she" (Duet)(from THE ROSE OF CASTILE)
Mr. and Mrs. Drayton
(*Music by* Michael William Balfe.)

"When the lads of the village" (Song)
Mr. Drayton

1859.16 LOVE IS BLIND/ NE'ER TOO LATE TO MEND

An Operetta in Two Acts written and composed by Val Morris. (Produced under the supervision of Henri Drayton.) Musical director, Henri Drayton. Produced by George A. Wells. Opened 17 November 1859 at the New Opera House (Hope Chapel) in repertory; season closed 31 December 1859.

CAST: *Captain Ravensworth*: Mr. HENRI DRAYTON. *Julia Beauchamp*: Mrs. HENRI DRAYTON [Susan Lowe]. *Julia Middleton*: Mrs. HENRI DRAYTON.

ACT 1: LOVE IS BLIND

"I've seen the battle field" (Scena)
Mr. Drayton

"Fond memory oft" (Ballad)
Mrs. Drayton

"He's positively crazed" (Ensmble)
Mr. and Mrs. Drayton

"What strange emotion" (Recitative)
Mr. Drayton

"When first eighteen" (Aria)
Mr. Drayton

"Women of all ranks and station" (Cabaletta)
Mr. Drayton

"Your frankness no one can deny" (Recitative)
Mrs. Drayton

"Since first we parted" (Andante)
Mrs. Drayton

"The harp and the piano, etc." (Recitative, à la John Parry)
Mrs. Drayton

"On horseback, I've no fear" (Galop)
Mrs. Drayton

"I'm not ugly, I'm not old" (Waltz)
Mrs. Drayton

"Thus the gauntlet down I throw" (Ensemble)
Mr. and Mrs. Drayton

"Oh! fond moment of delight" (Ensemble)
Mr. and Mrs. Drayton

"Will you so obliging be" (Finale)
Mr. and Mrs. Drayton

"For journies when preparing" (Stretta)
Mr. and Mrs. Drayton

"My parcels gently bearing" (Ensemble)
Mr. and Mrs. Drayton
In this operetta, Mrs. Drayton will introduce the celebrated "Cavatina" from Balfe's new opera, THE ROSE OF CASTILE.

ACT 2: NE'ER TOO LATE TO MEND

"Woman's smile" (Romance)
Mr. Drayton

"The fay of the forest" (Cavatina)
Mrs. Drayton

"The singing lesson" (Buffo Duet)
Mr. and Mrs. Drayton

"You love, at least, andc." (Grand Duo)
Mr. and Mrs. Drayton

"Forgive me, Julia" (Melody)
Mr. Drayton

"He's caught at last" (Ensemble)
Mr. and Mrs. Drayton

"No more can love" (Andante)
Mrs. Drayton

"Oh happy moment" (Finale)
Mr. and Mrs. Drayton
In this operetta, Mr. Drayton will introduce the Patriotic National Song "The Star Spangled Banner."

1859.17 NOTHING VENTURE NOTHING HAVE, or, A Courtship in 1640

An Operatic Proverb in One Act written and composed by Henri Drayton. Music by Gaetano Donizetti. (Produced under the supervision of Henri Drayton.) Musical director, Henri Drayton. Produced by George A. Wells. Opened 2 December 1859 at the New Opera House (Hope Chapel) in repertory; season closed 31 December 1859.

CAST: *Gustave*, Marquis de Belisle: Mr. HENRI DRAYTON. *Clarisse De Lindor*: Mrs. HENRI DRAYTON [Susan Lowe].

MUSICAL NUMBERS

"Here in silence" (Recitative)
Mr. and Mrs. Drayton

"I have gone too far, I Fear" (Ensemble)
Mr. and Mrs. Drayton
"Adieu Marquis" (Recitative)
Mr. and Mrs. Drayton
"A maiden e'er loves to torment" (Allegro)
Mr. and Mrs. Drayton
"Whene'er a Lover only sighs" (Romance)
Mrs. Drayton
"How I have lov'd thee" (Recitative)
Mr. Drayton
"On days gone by we poonder" (Ballad)
Mr. Drayton
"Not gone yet, I perceive" (Recitative)
Mr. and Mrs. Drayton
"Is he honest" (Andante)
Mr. and Mrs. Drayton
"Trasting now to my own invention" (Allegro)
Mr. and Mrs. Drayton
"Ah how often have I, sighing" (Grand Air)
Mrs. Drayton
"This once my plan succeeding" (Recitative)
Mrs. Drayton
"For me what joy, what happiness" (Allegro)
Mrs. Drayton
"We no more will disagree" (Duo Finale)
Mr. and Mrs. Drayton

THERE'S A SILVER LINING TO EVERY CLOUD, or, The Sonnambulist

1859.18

An Operatic Proverb (Parlor Opera) of Bellini's 'La Sonnabula" in One Act. Written by Henri Drayton. (Produced under the supervision of Henri Drayton.) Music by Vincenzo Bellini[98]. Musical director, Henri Drayton. Conductor, Herr L. Engelke. Produced by George A. Wells. Opened 5 December 1859 at the New Opera House (Hope Chapel) in repertory, with BETTER LATE THAN NEVER presented as an after-piece; season closed 31 December 1859.

CAST: *Amina*: Mrs. HENRI DRAYTON [Susanna Lowe]. *Corporal Ransfeldt*, alias Count Rodolpho: HENRI DRAYTON.

MUSICAL NUMBERS

Overture
Mrs. Drayton
"When daylight's going" (Descriptive Romance)
Mrs. Drayton
"Dearest companions" (Recitation)
Mrs. Drayton
"Oh! love for me" (Air)
Mrs. Drayton
"While this heart" (Cabaletta)
Mrs. Drayton
"Good night" (Duettino)
Mr. and Mrs. Drayton
"The mill there" (Recitative)
Mr. Drayton
"As I view now" (Andante)
Mr. Drayton
"Yes! that form" (Recitative)
Mr. Drayton
"Maid, those bright eyes" (Air)
Mr. Drayton
"Whats ee I?" (Recitative)
Mr. and Mrs. Drayton
"Oh! Heaven aid me now" (Duo)
Mr. and Mrs. Drayton
"Hear me swear now" (Grand Duo)
Mr. and Mrs. Drayton
"The ring he gave me" (Recitative)
Mr. and Mrs. Drayton
"Such return" (Stretta)
Mr. Drayton

THE STORY
"Do not mingle" (Finale)
Mrs. Drayton

BLUE BEARD, or, The Punishment of Curiosity

1860.01

Nixon's Equestrian Troupe in a Revival of the Romantic Equestrian Spectacle in One Act, 10 Scenes, followed by Equestrian Scenes of Horsemanship. Magnificent Processions of Horse and Foot, original Music, Songs, Duets, Choruses, Corps de Ballet, new costumes, banners and appointments. Music arranged under the direction of the leader, John Cooke. Produced by J. M. Nixon. Opened 7 May 1860 at Niblo's Garden and closed 19 May 1860 after 16 performances.

CAST: *Abomelique, Blue Beard*: JAMES CARROLL. *Shacabac*, his slave: CHARLES HALE. *Ibrahim*, Major Domo to the Bashaw, with three tails: JOSEPH O. SEFTON. *Selim*, Chief of Spahis: L. H. EVERETT. *Hassan*: Mr. Ellington. *Hafed*: Mr. Parton. *Hali*: Mr. Ruggles. *Haroun*: Mr. Pastor. *Nazrad*: Mr. Jones. *Talathan*: Mr. Rogers. *Hassarac*: Mr. Kincade. *Hamet*: Mr. Davenport. *Moloch*: Mr. Thomson. *Kapan*: Steele. *Ali*: Mr. Craft. *Monctar*: Mr. Grant. *Fatima*: MARIAN MACARTHY. *Irene*: Mrs. Eliza Place. *Beda*: Georgina Reignolds. And the Hanlons, Zoyara, Robinson. Linda Windel. (*Court Jester*: J. Pentland.)

Scene 1: A Romantic Mountainous Country. Ibrahim's home in the valley—sunrise. *Scene 2*: Gallery in the Seraglio. *Scene 3*: The Gardens of the Seraglio. *Scene 4*: Interior of the Seraglio. *Scene 5*: The Terrible Blue Chamber. (Maeder.) *Scene 6*: The Seraglio. *Scene 7*: A Turret of the Castle of Blue Beard. *Scene 8*: The Spahis. Attack on the Castle. *Scene 9*: Interior of the Sepulchre. *Scene 10*: Ruins of Blue Beard's Castle in flames.

MUSICAL NUMBERS, SPECIALTIES

Scene 1
"Twilight Glimmers" (Opening Duet)
M. Macarthy, L. H. Everett
Grand March of Horse and Foot
Arrival of Blue Beard mounted on an elephant
"Mark his approach with thunder" (Grand Chorus)

Scene 2
"Yes, Beda, this Beda" (Duet)
C. Hale, G. Reignolds
"Abomelique's Wives"
C. Hale
"While pensive I thought of my love"
M. Macarthy

Scene 3
A brilliant fête; Opening tableau
"Lowly we bend in duty" (Chorus)
Grand Pas de Scarf
L. Windel, Ladies of the Ballet Corps

Scene 4
"Captive Greek Girl" (Song)
M. Macarthy

Scene 5
"All is hushed" (Duet)
M. Macarthy, E. Place

Scene 7
"Look from the turret, sister dear" (Concerted Piece)
M. Macarthy, E. Place, C. Hale

Scene 10
Thrilling Tableau; Union of Fatima and Selim

[98]The original and beautiful Airs, Melodies, Duets, etc. of the celebrated opera have been retained.

1860.02

THE BRONZE DONKEY

An Entirely New and Original Operatic, Dramatic, Spasmodic Burlesque with songs, duets and choruses, in One Act[99]. Play by C. W. Taylor (inspired by the opera Le Cheval de Bronze by Daniel Auber). Stage manager, George L. Fox. Produced by George L. Fox and James W. Lingard. Opened 7 May 1860 at the New Bowery Theatre and closed 19 May 1860 after 12 performances.

CAST: *Zamma*, Prince of China: Miss FANNY HERRING. *Ping Sing*, a Mandarin: GEORGE L. FOX. *Katyong*, the Bronze champion: CHARLES K. FOX. *Yang Ko*, Chamberlain of household: Mr. M. Pike. *Tchin Wang*, a China farmer: Mr. D. Oakley. *Kayan Tea Chan*, lover of Pecki: Mr. S. Bradshaw. *The Cloud King*: Mr. J. McCloskey. *Peco Nor, Ski Ki, Bootcher*, attendants on the Prince: Messrs. S. Wright, W. Mitchell, J. Lewis. *Villagers, Guards, Mandarins, Officers, etc.*

Margelia, Princess of Pow Wow, under the influence of the Cloud King: Miss FISHER. *Peeki Weeki*, betrothed to Ping Sing: Miss F. FRANCE. *Kar Yan*, Foruth wife to Ping Sing: Mrs. France. *Lo Marghi*: ——.

In the course of the piece, numerous startling and absorbing incidents and effects, etc. too numerous for description, amongst which are a Grand Eastern Encampment (by Starlight), Japanese Embassy—arrival of the Prince (not of Wales, but) of Vicklafoggle, amidst a copious shower of Vocal Notes, and a side illustration of the "Ratcatcher's Daughter." Eclipse of a Planet and its interesting contents. Sympathies of love (at a distance). A Mandarin's quintette in matrimony. Terrific flight of live donkey into the realm of cloud-dom, laden with royal freight and wafted up by a succession of agreeable airs. International Fight for the Championship and Belt [Burlesque of the Heenan and Sayers fight, *Heenan*: GEORGE L. FOX. *Sayers*: CHARLES K. FOX.] exhibiting a wondrous display of Sinew, Pluck, Muscle, Game, Plugging, Mugging and going to grass generally. "The Boy" proclaimed and acknowledged to be Champion of the World! Rejoicings and congratulations. A stewed Mandarin. "Extras" and "Expresses" forwarded per Aerial Flight of the Live Donkey to the azure Firmament, announcing the result, wafted upwards by the sledge hammer harmonies of the Trovotorean Anvil Chorus, mingled with chromatic shouts, Forte Flourishes, Red Lights, Picturesque Tableaux, and other sundries used on such occasions.

1860.03

THE INVISIBLE PRINCE, or, The Island of Tranquil Delights

A Revival of the Burlesque in One Act, 9 Scenes[100]. Burlesque by James Robinson Planché. Music arranged by Thomas Baker. Stage manager, James Simmonds. Scenic artist, W. Hayes. Produced by Joseph Jefferson. Opened 16 May 1860 at Laura Keene's Theatre and closed 2 June 1860 after 18 performances in repertory.

CAST: *Furibond*: JOSEPH JEFFERSON. *Count Palava*: Mr. THORNE. *Marquis Amysidos*: Mr. Stoddart. *Don Moustachez*: Mr. Wall. *First Lord*: Mr. Collins. *Second Lord*: Mr. Thorne. *Sambo*: Mr. C. Goodrich. *Mr. Stilletto*: Mr. Brown. *Desperado*: Mr. Cline. *Mr. Ruffino*: Mr. Hurley. *Sanquino*: Mr. Jones. *Diego*: Mr. Albert.

Leander: Mrs. JOHN WOOD. *Abricotina*: Miss (Cornelia) JEFFERSON. *Princess*: Mrs. (F. S.) CHANFRAU. *Queen*: Miss WALKER. *Fairy Gentilla*: Miss Burke. *Tax a Tittle Tattle*: Miss Gimber. *First Lady*: Miss Clinton. *Second Lady*: Miss Howe.

Scene 1: Interior of Royal Castle of Allaquiz. *Scene 2*: Garden of an Old Hunting Lodge and Bower. *Scene 3*: Forest, five miles from Hicks Hall. *Scene 4*: View of the Palace of Pleasure, on the Island of Tranquil Delights. (Hayes.) *Scene 5*: Interior of the Palace of Pleasure. *Scene 6*: Moonlight Grotto and Magic Shell. (Hayes.) *Scene 7*: Landscape. *Scene 8*: Encampment of Furibond's Host and Tents of the "Shower of Gold." (Hayes.) *Scene 9*: Magic Transformation to Island of Tranquil Delight and the Fairy Realm. (Hayes.)

MUSICAL NUMBERS

"'Tis a Shame I Declare" (Opening Chorus)

"Bow ye Venal Servile Train"
J. Jefferson

"The Indian Drum" (Round)

"'Twas You That Kissed the Pretty Girl"
Mr. Thorne, J. Jefferson, Mrs. J. Wood, Mr. Goodrich, Chorus

"The Poor Soldier" (Trio)
Miss Walker, Mrs. J. Wood, J. Jefferson

"When I Played those Tricks so Charming" (Air)
Mrs. J. Wood

"Over the Mountain" (Duet)
Miss Jefferson, Mrs. J. Wood

"The Bold Dragoon" (Song)
Miss Jefferson

"O Come to Me When Daylight Sets" (Duet)
Mrs. J. Wood, Miss Jefferson

"Celarius"—"Of all the pleasures here so various" (Chorus)

"Celarius" (Air)
Mrs. Chanfrau

"Beggar's Opera" (Duet)
Mrs. Chanfrau, Mrs. J. Wood

Solo and Chorus
Mrs. Chanfrau, Ladies

"Buffalo Girls" (Air and Chorus)
Mrs. J. Wood, Mrs. Chanfrau, Miss Jefferson, Ladies

Grand Medley Scena
Mrs. Chanfrau

"Oh fairest maid beneath the Sun" (Air)
Mrs. J. Wood

"The Standard Watcher" (Air)
Mrs. J. Wood

"Charming Judy Callaghan" (Duo)
Mrs. Chanfrau, Miss Jefferson

"If I Had a Beau" (Air)
J. Jefferson

"One Bumper at Parting" (Finale)
Mrs. J. Wood, Mrs. Chanfrau, Miss Jefferson, J. Jefferson, Chorus

[99]Presented with a fore-piece, the drama in Three Acts by G. L. Aiken, titled Harry Blake, the Man that travels on his Muscle. The evening concluded with the roaring comic farce, How's Your Uncle?. The fore-piece and after-piece changed repeatedly during the run.

[100]First produced in New York 26 April 1847 at the Park Theatre. This revival was preceded by the fore-pieces, An Affair of Honor, and A Duel in Drugs; later after-pieces were The Benicia Boy, and the farce Lend Me Five Shillings.

1860–1865 SEASONS

Sallie Holman (Holman Troupe) (Photo: Trask)
Billy Rose Theatre Collection, New York Public Library for the Performing Arts

1860–1865 SEASONS

1860.04 JENNY LIND/ OUR JAPANESE EMBASSY

A Double Bill of a Musical Farce and an Extravaganza[1]. Stage manager, James Simmonds. Scenic artist, Mr. W. Hayes. Musical director, Thomas Baker. Produced by Joseph Jefferson. Opened 4 June 1860 at Laura Keene's Theatre and closed 30 June 1860 after 24 performances.[2]

JENNY LIND. A Musical Farce in One Act.

CAST: *Jenny Leatherlungs*: Mrs. JOHN WOOD. *Granby Gag*: JOSEPH JEFFERSON. *Baron*: J. G. Burnett. *Spitoon*: Mr. Collins. *Meerchaum*: Mr. Wall. *Canaster*: Mr. Thorne. *Leatherlungs*: Mr. Stoddart. *Sour Krout*: Mr. C. Goodrich. *Spek*: Mr. Gledhill. *Snuph*: Mr. Hurly.

OUR JAPANESE EMBASSY. Extravaganza by H. Plunkett.

CAST: *Letty Laurel*, a pleasant graft from the undying wreath of fame, singing her native wooden notes wild, and indulging in a dance: Mrs. JOHN WOOD. *C. T. Item*, a paragraphist, poetiser, projector and penny-a-liner: JOSEPH JEFFERSON. *Mr. Conservative Codfish*, a Wall Street brick, (we beg his pardon—broker) with the metamorphosian power of becoming a "bull" or a "bear" as may suit his convenience: J. H. STODDART. *Mr. Veracius White*, a Goshen Geraud, not a Numedian, but a New York lion catcher: J. G. BURNETT. *Mister Mawley, hevery hinch a Henglishman, you know, but hentirely hunprejudiced, you know*: James Simmons. *Swag*, a man of few words: Mr. Goodrich. *St. Julian*, a French valet: Mr. Brown. *Mr. Byron Thackery Moore Green*, a splendid illustration of his name: Mr. Wall. *Mr. Napoleon Bonaparte Wellington Smith*, a gentleman who having fulfilled his mission of coloring his meerchaum in despair turns his attention to Minerva and matrimony: C. R. THORNE, JR. *Mrs. Conservative Codfish*, one of the upper-ten, with a peculiar penchant for illustrious Exiles and exclusive Exotics: Mrs. H. VINING. *Miss Penelope Codfish*, a devotee to burnt cork melody: IONE BURKE. *Miss Minerva Codfish*, considerably higher in the scale of song, full of Auber and the Opera: HETTY WARREN. *Ladies and Gentlemen.*

1860.05 THE TYCOON, or, Young American in Japan

A Burlesque in One Act, 7 Scenes[3]. Play by O'Brien and Rosenberg, founded on the Arabian Nights story of Camaralzeman and Badura. Music composed and arranged by Thomas Baker. Scenic artist, W. Hayes. Produced by Joseph Jefferson. Opened 2 July 1860 at Laura Keene's Theatre and closed 21 July 1860 after 18 performances.

CAST: *Persimmons*, a fast youth of modern times, kept fast locked by his father, which has a tendency to make him faster, addicted to Japan ware: Mrs. JOHN WOOD. *The Tycoon*, addicted to having his own way, putting his subjects out of the way, and bringing up a wayward daughter: JOSEPH JEFFERSON. *Young Coon*, a distant relative of Old Zip Coon, and Nephew of Tycoon: JAMES SIMMONDS. *Koniac*, a third class spirit, i. e. a dojinn, a sort of bottle Imp, much addicted to poker, a connoisseur in the fine arts, in short a regular Japanese Bohemian: J. G. BURNETT. *Floxi*, keeper of the half-way house in the clouds, consequently only a half-way spirit: Mr. Hurley. *Chamberlain*, keeper of the rod, one of which is always in pickle for himself: C. Goodrich.

Allura, a young lady, who resists all attempts to allure her (to rallura): Miss CORNELIA JEFFERSON. *Begonia*, a first class spirit, addicted to falling in love with mere mortals and meeting a mortal repulse: Mrs. F. S. CHANFRAU. *Myrtilla*, a pure spirit: Miss HETTY WARREN. *Faddle*, a young lady retained for the express purpose of administering a pill: Ione Burke. *Guards, Officers, Lantern Bearers, Amazons and Female Attendants.*

Scene 1: A Highway and Temple in the Clouds. *Scene 2*: Magic change to Persimmons Mansions. Murray Hill, New York. *Scene 3*: Trip to Japanese Dominions. The Imperial Gates. Interior of the Imperial Palace. *Scene 4*: Street and Court in Japan, Jeddo City. *Scene 5*: Grand Archway and Gates to the Palace. *Scene 6*: The Coral Grotto, Home of Begonia. *Scene 7*: The Walls of the City.

MUSICAL NUMBERS

"Carnival de Venice" (Chorus)
Ladies

"Jenny Jones" (Song)
Mrs. F. S. Chanfrau

"Some Leave to Roam" (Song)
J. G. Burnett

"In Jeddo's City" (Duet)
Mrs. F. S. Chanfrau, J. G. Burnett

"Fly not yet" (Duet)
Mrs. F. S. Chanfrau, J. G. Burnett

"I'm a Regular New York Stunner" (Song)
Mrs. J. Wood

"Swiss Boy" (Song)
J. G. Burnett

"Young Agnes" (Song) (from FRA DIAVOLO)
Mrs. J. Wood
(*Music by* Daniel Auber.)

"The Sea"/"Brindisi" (Medley from LA TRAVIATA)(College Hornpipe and Dance)
Mrs. J. Wood
(*Music by* Giuseppe Verdi.)

Recitation and Aria from LA BAYADERE
J. Jefferson
(*Music by* Daniel Auber.)

"Gay Cavalier" (Song)
Mr. Simmonds

Recitative and Duet from LUCIA DI LAMMERMOOR
J. Jefferson, C. Jefferson
(*Music by* Gaetano Donizetti.)

"Cruiskeen Lawn" (Song and Chorus)
J. Jefferson

"Spirto Gentil"/"Little More Cider"/"SOMNAMBULA" (Medley)
Mr. Simmonds, J. Jefferson

"Sprig of Shillelah" (Song)
Mrs. J. Wood

"Pretty Girl Milking Her Cow" (Song)
Mrs. J. Wood

Chorus from MACBETH
Company
(*Music by* Giuseppe Verdi.)

Duet and Chorus from CINDERELLA
Mrs. J. Wood, J. Jefferson, Company

"Buy a Broom"/"Copenhagen"/"Never Talk to Me of Waltzing"/

German Waltz (Quartette)

Chinese Dance
All the Characters

March of the Lanterns

Finale, THE BRONZE HORSE

1860.06 THE SEVEN SISTERS!

An Operatic, Spectacular, Diabolical, Musical, Terpsichorean Farcical Burletta (Romantic Burlesque) in Three Acts, 13 Scenes[4]. Play by Robert Jones, founded on the old German play "The Seven Daughters of Satan." New music by Thomas Baker. Produced under the immediate personal supervision of Laura Keene. Scenery by James M. Roberts. New costumes, new properties, etc. Zouave marches and drills arranged by Frederick Cook, of the 71st Regiment. Produced by Laura Keene. Opened 26 November 1860 at Laura Keene's Theatre, revised 1 January 1861, 11 February 1861 and closed 10 August 1861 after 253 performances.

CAST: Mortals: *Arthur Stunner*, a dramatist and artist in crayon H. F. DALY. *Snail*, his friend: Mr. BARTON. *Catchem*, a Phenomenal Policeman, always in the way when wanted, with aids: Mr. Wren. *Mary Springleaf*: Mrs. J. H. ALLEN.

---

[1]JENNY LIND was succeeded by the farce The Governor's Wife for the week beginning 18 June 1860, and by the comedietta The Quack Doctor for the week beginning 25 June 1860.

[2]Musical numbers not identified in programs, apart from an "original Japanese melody by a native discomposer, pronounced "Th-eak-ura-te, St-ilto-n."

[3]Preceded by Slasher and Crasher, then the farce My Young Wife and My Old Umbrella, and then later in the run Poole's comedy, Paul Pry.

[4]For its subsequent tour, the play acquired a subtitle, The Birth of the Butterfly in the Bower of Ferns. Musical numbers not listed in programs, apart from the Zouaves' Song and Grand Zouave March and Drill at the opening of Act 2.

Immortals: *Pluto*, King of Hades, the Elysian Fields and all low countries generally, a monarch by no means so black as he is painted, though probably not nearly so good as he will appear by the representation of: DAN LEESON. *Astaroth*, an old friend with a new face, once a great favorite with an indulgent public, whose reappearance, it is hoped, will fully sustain his past reputation: T. B. Johnson. *Demonos*, another old friend with a new face, and a striking likeness, also hoping to impress the public favorably: Milnes Levick. *Cuffee*, one of the original sable brothers, an unmitigated nuisance, in everybody's way, and never accomplishing anything good—in fact, so very bad that his black father, Pluto, won't have him in Hades at any price: J. G. Burnett. *Cornerlot, Red Eye*, not bad spirits by any means, but who, while on earth, managed effectually to misrepresent their constituents in the corporation councils: Messrs. Wall, Goodrich.

The Seven Sisters, Daughters of Satan: *Diavoline*, first of the Seven Sisters, raising a revolt in Hades and a breeze on Earth, afterwards the Angel —, afterwards Tom Highboy, afterwards the Murderous Mother, afterwards Flora, Goddess of Flowers, afterwards Captain Highboy, of the Feminine Zouaves, afterwards Flora, his sister, which disguises she assumes in the vain endeavor to mislead Arthur: LAURA KEENE. *Plutella*, the second sister, a chip of the old block, out for a holiday, afterwards the Angel —, afterwards Bob Highboy, afterwards Psyche, afterwards Lieutenant Highboy, of the feminine Zouaves, afterwards Miss Angeline Highboy, a fashionable belle, afterwards a bootblack, always assisting her sister, and occasionally speculating a little on her own account: POLLY MARSHALL. *Tartarine*, the third sister, another lignum vitae chip, also out for a holiday, afterwards the Angel —, afterwards Jerusha Highboy, afterwards Lieutenant Highboy, of the feminine Zouaves, afterwards Mehitable Highboy, a fashionable belle, afterwards a hot corn girl, following in the footsteps of her illustrious predecessors in all particulars: LOTTY HOUGH. *The remaining four of the Seven Sisters who, in the most able manner, assist the diableries of their sisters, assuming a variety of characters for that purpose*: *Sulphurine*: Mrs. H. Vining. *Farcinella*: Miss Couldock. *Satanella*: Miss Melvyn. *Cantabile*: Miss Willoughby.

Mrs. Pluto, formerly called Proserpine, the one fair daughter of Ceres, originally borne to her by Jupiter, and subsequently borne from her by Pluto, which fact sufficiently accounts for her appearing in this connection: CHARLES PETERS. *Ceres*, an estimable lady, considerably younger than her daughter above alluded to, and introduced solely for the purpose of introducing the last scene: Miss Everett. *Spirit of Arthur's Sister*: Miss Frances.

During the piece will be represented A Very Serious Tragedy in One Act, and a series of tableaux, called the "Murderous Mother, or the Devoted Daughter." *The Remorseless Tyrant*: G. F. Browne. The remaining characters will be sustained by the various persons connected with the play.

Act 1, Scene 1: A Breakfast Room in Hades. *Scene 2*: The Poor Author's Home. *Scene 3*: A Street in New York. *Scene 4*: Behind the Scenes at Laura Keene's.

Act 2, Scene 1: The Zouave Armory. *Scene 2*: Our old friend again; he hears from Sam. *Scene 3*: The Poor Author's Home again. *Scene 4*: A Street in New York. *Scene 5*: The American Cremorne.

Act 3, Scene 1: Canal Street. *Scene 2*: The Poor Author's Home. *Scene 3*: A Council Chamber in Hades. *Scene 4*: Grand Transformation Scene of the Birth of the Butterfly in the Bower of Ferns.

1861.01 HARLEQUIN JACK, THE GIANT KILLER

A Grand Comic Pantomime in One Act, 16 Scenes.[5] Written and composed by George L. Fox. Stage manager, George L. Fox. Scenery painted by R. S. Smith, H. Hilliard. Leader of orchestra, H. Beissenherz. Produced by George L. Fox and J. W. Lingard. Opened 4 February 1861 in repertory at the New Bowery Theatre, suspended 12 February 1861, resumed 18 February 1861 and closed 16 March 1861 (matinee) after (26) performances.

CAST: *Ralpho*, a blacksmith apprentice: GEORGE L. FOX. *Jack*, the Giant Killer: W. STANTON. *Hudibras*, a blacksmith: CHARLES K. FOX. *Gorgibuster*, a Giant: Mr. BRADSHAW. *Gem*, of the Lower Region: Mr. Pike. *Sybil*: Miss A. PRICE. *Queen Bee*: Mrs. Marden. *Truth*: Miss Archer. *Innocence*: Miss Adair. *Jack's Mother*: Mrs. Beane.

Transformation: *Clown*: GEORGE L. FOX. *Pantaloon*: CHARLES K. FOX. *Harlequin*: W. STANTON. *Columbine*: Miss A. PRICE. *Barber*: Mr. Shavequick. *Peasants*: Messrs. Clod, Spade. *Waiter*: Mr. Standstill. *Passenger*: Mr. Goquick. *Policemen*: Messrs. Grabem, Catchem. *Porter*: Mr. Stout. *Fairies, Attendants*: Numerous Train of Auxiliaries.

Scene 1: Fairy Abode of Queen Bee and Magical Change to the Village of Normandy. (Smith.) *Scene 2*: The Village of Normandy. *Scene 3*: The Giant Gorgibuster's Castle. (Smith.) *Scene 4*: Interior of the Giant's Castle. (Smith.) *Scene 5*: Queen Bee's Palace of Pleasure. (Hilliard.) *Scene 6*: Panoramic View of New York Harbor. (Smith.) *Scene 7*: Interior of Hotel, no where's in particular. *Scene 8*: Rail Road Depot, Bergen. (Smith.) *Scene 9*: Rustic View. *Scene 10*: Cigar Store in Chatham Street. (Smith.) *Scene 11*: Clute's Hat Store and Zacharie's Perfume Store in the Bowery. (Smith.) *Scene 12*: Interior of Varick's Hair Dressing Saloon, New Bowery Theatre. (Smith.) *Scene 13*: Baldwin's Clothing Store, Bowery. (Smith.) *Scene 14*: The Garden of Poses. (Smith.) *Scene 15*: Moonlight View. *Scene 16*: The Bower of Queen Bee and the Abode of the Fairies. (Hilliard.)

BALLETS, SPECIALTIES

"Queen of the Magical Islands" (Grand Ballet and Chorus)(Scene 1)
"Dixie's Land"[6] (Scene 3)
Chorus
Grand Transformation (Scene 5)
Mazurka (Scene 7)
W. Stanton, A. Price
Grand Fairy Tableau (Scene 16)

1861.02 ORPHEUS IN DER UNTERWELT

A Burleske Oper in Two Acts, 4 Scenes, in German. Original French libretto by Hector Crémieux. German adaptation by Johann Nestroy. Music by Jacques Offenbach. Leader of orchestra, Fr. Herwig. Opened 6 March 1861 at the New Yorker Stadt-Theatre for (9+) performances in repertory.

CAST: Company included MEAUBERTS, KRILLING, KLEIN, and Fräulein Scheller.

1861.03 CINDERELLA

A Musical Extravaganza in One Act, 7 Scenes[7]. Play by Charles Dawson Shanley (from the fairy tale by Charles Perrault). New music composed and arranged by Charles Koppitz. Scenery by C. S. Getz. Machinery by Wilson. Costumes by Mrs. Bokannon. Properties and accessories by Zeites. Lights by Messrs. Clark, Ellis. Produced by A. W. Jackson. Opened 9 September 1861 at the Winter Garden and closed 5 October 1861 after 24 performances.

CAST: *Cinderella*, a Young lady who soon leaves the ashes for the great: Mrs. JOHN WOOD. *Miss Patchoulia*, one of the Cantankerous Sisters—more given to idle ways than good books: ADA CLIFTON, *Miss Rondelitia*, the other Cantankerous Sister: Mrs. GEORGE SKERRETT. *The Baroness Soldoff*, made after the pattern of Mrs. Caudle—a copy from Punch: Mrs. W. R. BLAKE. *Fairy Queen*: Miss Lothian. *Fancy*, in tears: Miss Bennet. *The Prince Rodolph*, a reformed young man, as regards latch keys and cocktails. No relation to Prince Napoleon: A. H. DAVENPORT. *The Baron Soldoff*, very nearly sold himself: LEWIS BAKER. *Capillaire*, a corpulent young gentleman, recently returned from a country retreat: HARRY PEARSON. *Rumplestiltskin*, the great German Gnome and Prestidigitatem: Mons. Szollosy. *The Seneschal*: Mr. Clark. *The Flunkeys*: Messrs. Galloway, Thompson, Clower, Skidder. *The Baron's Band*: Messrs. Fendel, Lester. *Choristers*: Messrs. Rae, Melville, etc. *Fairies, Hunters, Sprites, Amazons, Lackeys, etc.*

Scene 1: Ruins of the Chateau of the Countess D'Anois. *Scene 2*: Exterior of the house of Baron Soldoff—with a view of old street and popular saloon. *Scene 3*: Hall of the old mansion, from "Nash's Views." *Scene 4*: Courtyard of the Baron's House. *Scene 5*: Garden of the Baron's House. Mysterious Transformation. *Scene 6*: Corridor of the Palace. *Scene 7*: Grand Ballroom in the Palace, opening upon the gardens and grounds.

MUSICAL NUMBERS

Scene 1
"Come Bustle, Little Elves" (Song, Burlesque)
Scene 2
"We won't go home till morning" (Duet)
L. Baker, H. Pearson
"O for Contracts in I'll go" (Song)
L. Baker
Scene 3
"Once a King" (Song)
Mrs. J. Wood
"Faint and Wearily" (Duet)
L. Baker, Mrs. J. Wood

[5]Preceded by the farce Cool as a Cucumber; later fore-pieces included the petite drama The Cross of Gold; the after-piece at the opening was a melodrama Therese, the Orphan of Geneva; later after-pieces included the domestic drama, Woman's Love.

[6]Billed as an old tune to a new song.

[7]Preceded by a comedietta, Cool as a Cucumber, with Lewis Baker, J. H. Stoddart, Mr. Cline, Misses Bennet, Lothian.

"All around is silent" (Recitative)
A. H. Davenport
"Put on this cap" (Duet)
A. H. Davenport, H. Pearson
"The Prince is a Coming" (Quartette)
"Come, the Dinner's Waiting" (Concerted Polka)
All the characters
Scene 4
"Thou chid by the" (alias La ci darem)(Duet)
A. H. Davenport, Mrs. J. Wood
"This heart no more is mine" (Duet)
A. H. Davenport, Mrs. J. Wood
"Oh! Pa, let us go" (Duet)
A. Clifton, Mrs. G. Skerrett
Scene 5
"Home, Sweet Home" (Song with flute accompaniment)
Mrs. J. Wood
Scene 6
"Bacon and Greens and a Drop of Good Beer" (Medley)
H. Pearson
"Libertad" (Duet)
L. Baker, H. Pearson
Scene 7
Un Ballo in Maschera, as it ought to have been!
Triple Polka
A. H. Davenport, A. Clifton, G. Skerrett
Grand Pas d'Extase
Mrs. J. Wood, Mons. Szollosy
"Oh Joy Unbounded" (from DINORAH)(Finale)
Mrs. J. Wood

1861.04 THE SEVEN SONS!

A New and Indescribable Curiosity of Literature, comprising comedy, farce, burlesque, spectacle, melodrama, opera, ballet, etc. in Three Acts, 10 Scenes. Music composed and arranged by Thomas Baker. Scenery by James M. Roberts, Minard Lewis. Machinery by John M. Smart. Properties and appointments by Mr. Henry. Produced by Laura Keene. Opened 23 September 1861 at Laura Keene's Theatre, reconstructed 3 December 1861 and closed 21 December 1861 after 96 performances.

CAST: *Diavoline*, an old favorite, one of the Seven Sisters: LAURA KEENE. *Columbia*: Mrs. J. H. ALLEN. *Satanella*, another of the Seven Sisters: SARA STEVENS. *Tartarus*, afterwards Ike, a Yankee boy, and Hezekiah Peabody, a Yankee pedlar: LOTTY HOUGH. *Asmodeus*, afterwards Hank, a fast boy, afterwards Mlle. Marie, a French lady: Mrs. F. S. CHANFRAU. *Diavolus*, afterwards Tim Toggles, an imported tiger, afterwards Dr. Dashaway, an equestrienne: IONE BURKE. *Molasses*, afterwards Jack, a sailor: Miss Frances. *Rhadamanthus*, afterwards Harry, a news boy: Mrs. Dillon. *Sulphurus*, afterwards Hans, a Dutch boy, afterwards the Fraulein pumper neckel: Mrs. Owen Marlowe. *Mephistopheles*, afterwards a young man about town: Miss Robertson. *Pluto*, King of Hades, afterwards Cuffee, irrepressible as ever, in everybody's way, continually breaking out in a new place, with a new Union song: J. G. Burnett. *Caesar*, afterwards Dr. Fussall, special war correspondent of the Thunderer, fully impregnated with the belief that he who don't fight but runs away will certainly have the best chance to fight: Milnes Levick. *Jake Butt*, a New York boy, other than which no description is necessary: H. F. Daly. *Fred Flutter*, an English fop, formerly an officer in the Crimea: Owen Marlowe. *Mickey McGinniss*, one of the great unwashed, a Sixth Ward Politician: Mr. Dillon. *Machiavelli*, afterwards Sleekwit, an unmitigated abolitionist: J. H. Stoddart. *Alexander*, afterwards Von Slyck, a gentleman of Teutonic original, who has been spoiled by his appetite: Mr. C. Burnett. *Imp*: J. D. Bilby. *Mrs. Pluto*, mother of the Seven Sons, as well as the maternal parent of the Seven Sisters: CHARLES PETERS.

Pollywogs: Misses Everett, Harris, Valentine, Burt, Erving, Clifford, Scott, Dix, Brown, Smith, Welsh, Jones, Galway, Pitt, Webb, Pratt, Wells, Smart, Young, Black, Baker, Blake, Wood, Orton, King, Price, Marks, Horton, Arthur, Clarke, Mackey, Burke, Pond, Parks, Lewis, Leigh, Newton, Matthews, Markham, Lillie, Jackson, Hall, Hills, Derby, Franks, Lake, Ladd, Barilly, Ludlow, Clay.

Act 1, Scene 1: A Dell in the Catskills. (Roberts.) *Scene 2*: The Gates of Hades. (Roberts.) *Scene 3*: Columbia's Home. A House of Mourning. A Picture of Anarchy. The Spirit of '76. The Battle of Bunker Hill. (Lewis.) *Scene 4*: A New York Hotel. *Scene 5*: Coral Cave. (Roberts.)

Act 2, Scene 1: A Skating Pond. (Roberts.) *Scene 2*: A Street in New York. *Scene 3*: Columbia's Retreat. A Sequestered Nook in the Depths of the Forest. The Peerless Pool of Water Lilies. Ascent of the Spirits of the Lake. (Lewis.)

Act 3, Scene 1: . A Federal Picket Camp on the South Bank of the Potomac. (Lewis.) *Scene 2*: The Hall of Justice in the Elysian Fields. (Lewis.) The Great Watteau Scene of Arcadian Nymphs amongst their flocks, by the Mountain Torrent of real water. (Roberts.)

ACT 1[8]
Dance of the Follies (Scene 1)
The Fairy Pollywogs (Scene 5)
Pas de Deux of the Coral Nymphs (Scene 5)
Mlles. Augusta, Marie
Drill of the Pollywogs (Scene 5)

ACT 2
"Hi, Hi, Hi!" (Song and Dance)(Scene 1)
Bully Boys of New York
A Yankee Song (Scene 2)

ACT 3
Drill of the Emerald Greens (Scene 1)

1861.05 LES NOCES DE JEANNETTE

An Opéra-comique in One Act, 14 Scenes, in French.[9] Libretto by Michel Carré and Jules Barbier. Music by Victor Massé. Musical director and conductor, Signor Muzio. Opened 28 October 1861 at the Academy of Music for 1 performance.

CAST: *Jean*, the Bridegroom: Signor DUBREUIL. *Jeannette*, the Bride: CLARA LOUISE KELLOGG. Other roles by Mlle. Elena and Signor Mazzini.

Scene: Un Village.

MUSICAL NUMBERS[10]
Air (Ouf! Je l'échappe belle)
Signor Dubreuil
Romance, Chanson, Allegro
(Parmi tant d'amoureux empressés à me plaire)
C. L. Kellogg, Signor Dubreuil, Chorus
Duo (Halte là s'il vous plaît)
C. L. Kellogg, Signor Dubreuil
Couplets (Ah! vous ne savez pas, ma chère)
C. L. Kellogg, Signor Dubreuil
Romance de l'Aiguille, et Air des Meubles
(Cours, mon aiguille dans la laine)
C. L. Kellogg
Air du Rossignol (Au bord du chemin)
C. L. Kellogg
Duo (Allons! je veux qu'on s'assoie)
Signor Dubreuil, C. L. Kellogg
Final (Eh dites donc là-bas, ne vous déranger pas!)
All

1861.06 ONDINA!, or, The Spirit of the Waters

A Fairy Spectacular Drama in Four Acts, Numerous Tableaux[11]. Play by a popular author. Drama entirely produced by E. F. Taylor. Music, choruses

[8]Program also announced a Fairy Minuet, a new Medley Quadrille on popular melodies of the day, with solos for all the principal instruments, a new Military Galop, "Napoleon," with solo for bells. During the run were added "Tunes for the Million," "Belle Brandon" (for solo cornet), "Hazel Dell" (for 2 violins), "Widow Machree" (for solo flute), the Sailor Boy with imitation of Jem Bags' famous clarinet solo; Gig, played on the wood and straw instruments, Bells, Bagpipes, and the new and popular "Laura Keene Waltz," and El Zapada de Callaga (Spanish Dance).

[9]Paired with Donizetti's opera, Betly. No program available; detail prepared from cast announcement in program from preceding week.

[10]Musical numbers not listed in programs. List prepared from the published Academy of Music French-English libretto (Palmer & Co., New York, 1861)

[11]A revised version of the popular spectacle THE NAIAD QUEEN. Beginning 27 January 1862 the production was billed as ONDINA, or, The Naiad Queen. Numerous specialties were interpolated between Acts 3 and 4.

and marches composed and arranged by W. T. Peterschen. Scenery by George Heilge. Armours and wardrobe by R. and T. Walker. Machinery by Charles Burns. Dances by Mlle. Deulin; marches by F. N. Cook, 71st Regiment. Augmented orchestra led by W. T. Peterschen. (Produced by Phineas T. Barnum.) Opened 23 December 1861 at Barnum's Museum and closed 1 March 1862 after (114) performances[12].

CAST: *Mortals*: *C. Huldbrand*, of the Cross: J. E. NAGLE. *Rinaldo*: J. H. CLARKE. *Rudolph*, a fisherman: Mr. BRIDGMAN. *Carl*, Esquire to Sir Huldebrand: Mr. HADAWAY. *Hans Speyenhausen*: Mr. Haviland. *Bartle Olfinger*, a Peasant: G. Brooks. *Lady Una*: Miss Douglas. *Dame Marguerite*: Mrs. France. *Olinda*, Waiting Maid at the Castle: Miss C. Allford. *Retainers, Soldiers, Guests.*

Immortals: *Khulebhorn*, the Forest Demon: W. L. JAMIESON. *Abeo, Zoro, Fareo, Doro*, his attendants: Messrs. Cunningham, Hughes, Anderson, Brogan. *Ampieno*, a deformed dwarf, afterwards Sprite of the Forest: Mr. CHAPMAN.

Naiad Court: *Ondina*, Queen of the Waters, endowed with Mortal Spirit: Mrs. J. J. PRIOR. *Coralia*: Miss JENNIE WALTERS. *Nouralia*: Mrs. ROSA FRANCE. *Soto*: Miss Pearson. *Chrystalline*: Miss H. WALBY. *Sylphia*: Miss Chapman. *Pearlina*: Miss Drew. *Coral Leaf*: Addie LeBrun. *Dew Drop*: Emma LeBrun. *Aloyd*, a Dancing Naiad of the Deep: Mlle. DEULIN. *Naiads, Water Nymphs, etc*: Numerous Auxiliaries.

Act 1: Leafy Dell and Enchanted Lake. Dark and Gloomy Wood. Vestibule of the Castle. Interior of Rudolph Cottage. Glade in the Enchanted Forest. Rock of the Lurleiberg by Moonlight.

Act 2: Landscape. Water Cavern beneath the Rhine. Coral Cavern of Ondina. Abode of the Naiads.

Act 3: Hall in Huldbrand's Castle. Naiads' Cavern. Dark Chamber. Slatadite Cave and River View.

Act 4: Spacious Apartment and Hall of the Audience. Bower of Beauty in the Enchanted Forest. (Mechanical scene by Randall.) Abode of the Fairies.

ACT 1

- Chorus of Naiads
- Dance
  - H. Walby
- Recitative (I'm coming to you laden with treasures of pearly dew)
  - Mrs. J. J. Prior
- Invisible Chorus of Naiads

ACT 2

- Duet (Let's stray through the weedy groves)
  - Mr. Hadawy, Miss J. Walters
- Chorus (Hail to our Queen, her request we attend)
- Grand Ballet by Nymphs of the Rhine
- Pas seul "La Sylphide"
  - Mlle. Deulin
- Pas Ondine
  - A. LeBrun
- Chorus (Oh! 'tis sweet in a Fairy boat, over the silvery stream to float)

ACT 3

- Song
  - Mr. Hadaway
- Chorus (Unto the fight with hearts of flame)
- Grand March and Evolutions
  - Fairy Body Guard of Ondina

ACT 4

- Departure of the Queen for the Bower of Beauty in the Enchanted Forest

SADAK AND KALASRADE!, or, The Waters of Oblivion

1862.01

An Oriental Fairy Spectacle in Four Acts, based on an Eastern Tale. Music composed and arranged by W. T. Peterschen. Scenery by George Heilge. Machinery by Charles Burns. Costumes by R & T. Walker. Stage appointments by C. Deice. Dances by Mlle. Deulin. Produced under the direction of E. F. Taylor. Produced by Phineas T. Barnum. Opened 3 March 1862 at Barnum's Museum and closed 5 April 1862 after 60 performances[13].

CAST: *Amurath*, Sultan of Persia: J. E. NAGLE. *Sadak*, Leader of the Forces: Mrs. J. J. PRIOR. *Misnar*, Grand Vizier: Mr. HAVILAND. *Semack*, a Ghebar Chieftain: W. L. JAMIESON. *Dum Dum*, Sadak's Arab Slave: E. F. TAYLOR. *Mustapha*, a Cadi: Mr. BRIDGMAN. *Rainbow Broadcloth*, as Tailor: Mr. HADAWAY. *Mahoud*: J. H. CLARKE. *Smutta*, a Black Slave: G. BROOKES. *Cordan*, son of Sadak: Addie LeBrun. *Guards, Banner Bearers, Citziens, etc. Kalasrade*, Wife of Sadak: Miss C. ALFORD. *Sultana Hemjuna*: Miss Jennie Walters. *Adehe*: Miss R. France. *Hobaddan*: Miss (Emma) LeBrun. *Odez*: Miss Walby. *Nowrenhi*: Miss Jones. *Fairy Gentilla*, Guardian of the waters of Oblivion: Miss Douglas. *Dancing Girls, Ladies of the Court, etc. Specialties*: Commodore (Rodnia) NUTT[14].

Act 1: Kiosk and Garden of Sadak. Grand Divan or Hall of Audience. Exterior of Tailor's Shop. Sadak's Dwelling.

Act 2: Apartment in the Harem. Forest of Palms. Battlefield and Triumph of the Persians. The Defeat and Field of Battle by Moonlight. Rainbow's Cottage. Grand Street of the City.

Act 3: Hall of the Audience. Street. Dungeon. Vestibule of the Palace. Valley of the Waters of Oblivion.

Act 4: Anti-Chamber of the Palace. Bower of Beauty in the Enchanted Forest, and Abode of the Fairies.

ACT 1

- Eastern Dance
  - Corps de Ballet
- Chorus (Weave the gay garland sing the lay, 'Tis our master's natal day)

ACT 2

- Fairy Invisible Chorus (Joy! Joy! Joy! Our fairy Queen is free!)
- Fairy Chorus (Thro' the sparkling milky way, where the elves and fairies play)
- Chorus of Warriors (Might Sadak comes, Persia's conquering son)
- Procession of Citizens and Soldiery
- Grand March and Drill of Sadak's Body Guard

ACT 3

- Javelin Dance
  - Mlle. Deulin

ACT 4

- Brilliant Finale

HOP O' MY THUMB, or, The Ogre and the Dwarf!

1862.02

A New Play (with Songs) in Five Acts, 11 Scenes. (Play by Albert Smith, with alterations and additions to suit the times[15].) Original music by W. T. Peterschen. Produced under the entire superintendence of E. F. Taylor. Produced by Phineas T. Barnum. Opened 7 April 1862 at Barnum's American Museum and closed 2 May 1862 after 46 performances.[16]

CAST: *King Cole*, a powerful Monarch, more inclined to social harmony than warfare, with songs: Mr. BRIDGMAN. *Lord Thomas Noddy*, his Secretary, always writing what the King does wrong: Mr. HAVILAND. *Robin*, a woodcutter, who would cut more if he could, with songs: J. H. CLARKE. *Solomon*, one of the agricultural classes, wishing to enter into a union with Margery, with a Duet: Mr. G. BROOKS. *Figaro*: Addie LeBrun. *Arty, Marmy, Franky, Jemmy, Tommy, Harry*, the woodcutter's 6 sons, with little bodies but enormous stomachs: Misses (Emma) LeBrun, James, Smith, McCormick, E. McCormick, etc. *Hop 'o My Thumb*, a tarnation cute little brick, first rate to go ahead, and no mistake, with songs, dances and drum solo: Commodore

---

[12]Performed twice daily.

[13]Performed twice daily; specialties were changed frequently.

[14]In Act 1 Commodore Nutt will appear in the Grecian Statues, Hercules struggling with the Nemean Lion; Romulus; Remus; Ajax defying lightning; Achilles; The Slave Emoleur; The Child's Prayer. Between Acts 3 and 4, Commodore Nutt will sing a patriotic song, dance the Schottische with Addie LeBrun, sing "Billy Barlow," the orchestra will play the Commodore Nutt Schottische, and he will dance the Sailor's Hornpipe.

[15]The published prompt book (Wynkoop, Hallenbeck & Thomas, Steam Printers, New York, 1862) credits the late playwright Albert Smith, whose earlier English version was produced and published in London in 1846 as HOP-O'-MY-THUMB; or, The Seven League Boots, a romance of nursery history. Song list and additional scene detail prepared from published prompt book.

[16]Performed twice daily. During the run short comediettas were added to close the program.

(Rodnia) NUTT. *Grimgriffinhoff*, a mighty Ogre, a descendant of the King of the Cannibal Islands: Monsieur BIHIN (the great French giant). *Herald*: Mr. Cunningham. *King Cole's Three Fiddlers*: Messrs. Minim, Critchet, Quaver. *Drummer*: Mr. Poundwell. *Soldiers, Courtiers, Peasants*: Legion of Supernumerary Artists. *King Cole's Steed*: a well made Jerusalem Pony.

Fairy Court: *Oberon*, the Fairy King, and not a bad looking one either: Miss DOUGLAS. *Friar Rush*, a mischievous sprite: Miss ROSA FRANCE. *Moth*, the Queen's Remembrancer: Miss H. Walby. *Fairies*: Misses Chapman, Morton, Franklin, Atkins, C. Howard, etc. *Grabolotta*, the Ogre's wife, with all the pride of being wife to such a great man: Mrs. France. *Bridget*, Robin's partner, a rural Mrs. Candle: Miss LeBrun. *Margery*, about to marry, and quite ready, with a Duet: Miss JENNIE WALTERS. *Emmy, Flossy, Bessy, Polly, Rosey, Annie*, the Ogre's daughters: Misses Brown, Lopez, Dallry, Antell, Shearsly, Thomas. *Peasant Girls, etc.*

Act 1, Scene 1: Sylvan Glade and Fairy Abode of Oberon by Moonlight. *Scene 2*: Robin's Cottage. *Scene 3*: Gloomy Wood and Mammoth Tree.

Act 2, Scene 1: Ogre's Castle. *Scene 2*: A Country Landscape. *Scene 3*: Wood. *Scene 4*: Ante-chamber in the Palace.

Act 3: Fairy Garden of Oberon, Flowers, Fountains, Spring. Interior of Hop o' My Thumb's Drawing Room.

Act 4: Gardens of Happy Land and Oberon's Bower.

Act 5, Scene 1: Grand Hall of Audience in the Palace of King Cole. *Scene 2*: Tapestried Chamber. Bower of Beauty in the Enchanted Forest, and Abode of the Fairies.

ACT 1

Scene 1

Opening Chorus (Air-'Follow the Drum')
Chorus

Scene 2

"Ri tooral, looral" (Robin's Song)
J. H. Clarke

"Lucy Long" (Song)
Commodore Nutt

Sailor's Hornpipe, à la E L. Davenport
Commodore Nutt

Drum Solo; March
Commodore Nutt

Scene 3

Post Horn Galloppe à l'umbrella
G. Brooks, J. Walters

Grand Procession
Commodore Nutt, Fairies

ACT 2

Scene 1

"Boys and girls come out to play" (Nursery Air)
Chorus

"Oh, slumber my darling" (Air)
Mrs. France

"The Roast Beef of Old England" (Music)

"Down amongst the Dead Men" (Music)

Scene 3

"Bye baby bunting" (Music)

ACT 3

"Where the Bee lurks" (Air)

"If you're waking call me early" (Music)

"Lass of Richmond Hill" (Air)

"I love her, how I love her" (Air)

"Largo al factotum" (Air)

ACT4

Martial Chorus (Let him be ever happy and gay)(Air, Pirates' Chorus, from THE ENCHANTRESS)
Fairies
(*Music by* Michael William Balfe.)

March and Drill of Fairy Warriors
Hop 'o My Thumb's Amazonian Infantry

ACT 5

Grand Triumphal March

Chorus from NORMA (Now let the brazen trumpets clang)
(*Music by* Vincenzo Bellini.)

1862.03 THE ENCHANTRESS!

A Revival of the Grand Operatic Spectacle in a Prologue and Three Acts, 16 Scenes[17]. (Libretto by Alfred Bunn, adapted from a text by J. H. Vernoy de Saint-Georges.) Music by Michael William Balfe and Dr. Cunnington[18]. Produced under the stage direction of Peter Richings. Stage director, Leon J. Vincent. Scenery by J. H. Selwyn. Machinery by Runyon, Demilt. Costumes by Mons. Phillipe (New York), Watson (Philadelphia), Joyce (Boston). Ballet under the direction of Mons. Tophoff. Decorations and banners by George Letzinger. Orchestra under the direction of John Cooke. Produced by E. L. Davenport, Henry C. Jarrett and William Wheatley. Opened 14 April 1862 at Niblo's Garden and closed 7 June 1862 after 48 performances.

CAST: Prologue, Pirates: *Ramir*: E. L. DAVENPORT. *Forte Braccio*: Mr. BOUDINOT. *Nuguez*: JAMES DUNN. *Julio*: GEORGE REA. *Pietro*: Mr. VAN DERREN. *Sacripante*: Mr. Daly.

Act 1: *Ramir*, disguised as the Hermit, Friar Antonio: E. L. DAVENPORT. *Don Sylvio*: WILLIAM WHEATLEY. *Dr. Mathanasius*: PETER RICHINGS. *Duke d'Aquila*, a Regent: J. W. Collier. *Galeas*: Mr. Blaisdell. *Busiris*: Mr. Williams. *Mushroom*: Harry Pearson. *Pambo Poncho*, Regent's servant: Mr. Scallan. *Mumbo Jumbo*: W. S. LENNOX. *Alexis*: Mr. J. Maeder. *Page*: Miss Denham. *First Citizen*: Mr. Gledhill. *Captain of the Guard*: Mr. Daly. *First Officer*: Mr. Germon. *Spirit of Evil*: Mr. Tophoff. *Stella*, the Enchantress: CAROLINE RICHINGS. *Spirit of Good*: ANNETTA GALLETTI. *Vision*: Mlle. Helene. *Dream*: Mlle. Katrine. *Slumber*: Josephine Henry. *Nobles, Ladies, Peasants, Pirates, Senators, Royal Guards, Heralds, Soldiers, Slaves, Pursuivants, Bridesmaids, Dancers, Demons, Pages, Masqueraders, etc.* (*Ballet*: Mons. Tophoff.)

Prologue: Deck of the Pirate Ship.

Act 1, Scene 1: Fifteen years later. Mt. Helicon and Hermitage of Our Lady in the Woods. *Scene 2*: The Pirates' Cavern. *Scene 3*: Mountain Pass. *Scene 4*: Abode of the Enchantress!

Act 2, Scene 1: Vestibule at the Regent's Palace. *Scene 2*: The Tent of Silvio. *Scene 3*: Vestibule of the Palace. *Scene 4*: Grand Hall of Honor in the Regent's Palace. *Scene 5*: Hall of Myrtles. *Scene 6*: Gardens of the Palace. *Scene 7*: The Palace on Fire!

Act 3, Scene 1: A Lonely Sicilian Inn. *Scene 2*: The King's Cabinet. *Scene 3*: Rocky Pass near the Shore. *Scene 4*: Sea Side and Church of St. Marie Majure. The Pirate Ship under full sail!

PROLOGUE

"By the Gleaming Stars" (Chorus and Solo)
J. Dunn, Pirates
(*Music by* Dr. Cunnington.)

"Thou who when Winds" (Prayer and Finale)
(*Music by* Dr. Cunnington.)

ACT 1

"Bend before High Heaven" (Invocation)
(*Music by* Dr. Cunnington.)

"She is seen" (Song and Chorus)
E. L. Davenport
(*Music by* Michael William Balfe.)

"Hark to that Omen" (Chorus)
(*Music by* Dr. Cunnington.)

"Ever be Happy" (Celebrated Pirates' Chorus)
(*Music by* Michael William Balfe.)

Celebrated Variations[19]
C. Richings
(*Music by* Michael William Balfe.)

Grand Ballet (Strife between spirits of good and evil)
Mlles. A. Galletti, Helene, Katrine, Mr. Tophoff, Corps de Ballet

Finale
C. Richings, Chorus
(*Music by* Dr. Cunnington.)

ACT 2

"La Sicilienne" (Grand Air from LES VÊPRES SICILIENNES)
C. Richings
(*Music by* Giuseppe Verdi.)

---

[17]Previously produced in New York 25 May 1846 at the Chatham Theatre for 12 performances.
[18]Cunnington's interpolations were for this American revival.
[19]Dropped for subsequent tour.

"Drown in the Mantling Glass"[20] (Glee)
(*Music by* Dr. Cunnington.)
"Woman's Heart" (Song)
C. Richings
(*Music by* Michael William Balfe.)
"The Young Nadir" (Legend)
C. Richings
(*Music by* Michael William Balfe.)
Grand Masquerade
J. W. Collier, Courtiers
Procession
Grand Pas Seul "Favorita"
Chinese Dance
Cymbal DanceCorps de Ballet
Grand Equestrian Scene
"Honor and Homage" (Finale)
C. Richings, Chorus
(*Music by* Dr. Cunnington.)

ACT 3[21]
"Hither we Come" (Introductory Chorus)
(*Music by* Dr. Cunnington.)
"Who has not heard" (Cavatina)
C. Richings
(*Music by* Dr. Cunnington.)
Finale (Chorus)
C. Richings, E. L. Davenport
(*Music by* Michael William Balfe.)

1862.04 THE SYREN

An Operatic Romance in Three Acts, 4 Scenes. Expressly adapted for Miss Richings from the French comic opera 'La Sirene' with libretto by Eugene Scribe[22]. Music by Daniel Auber. (Produced under the stage direction of Peter Richings.) Scenery by J. H. Selwyn. Decorations by George Letzinger. Machinery by Runyon and Demilt. Costumes by Mons. Phillippe. Produced by E. L. Davenport, Henry C. Jarrett and William Wheatley. Opened 9 June 1862 at Niblo's Garden and closed 21 June 1862 after 12 performances.

CAST: *Scopetto*, Chief of the Smugglers: E. L. DAVENPORT. *Duke di Popoli*, Governor of the Abruzzi: JOHN GILBERT. *Bolbaya*, the Neapolitan Manager: PETER RICHINGS. *Scipio*, a young Sailor: L. R. Shewell. *Pecchione*, Scopetto's sub-lieutenant: Mr. Boudinot. *Pietro*, Scopetto's sub-lieutenant: James Dunn. *Captain of Chausseurs*: Mr. Maeder. *Officer*: Mr. Germon. *Mathea*, a Servant: Mrs. J. MAEDER (Clara Fisher). *Zerlina*, Scopetto's Sister, the Syren: CAROLINE RICHINGS. *Chasseurs, Smugglers, Marines, Servants.*

Act 1: Interior of a Priest's dwelling house in the village of Cartel di Sangro in the Abruzzi mountains. 1790.

Act 2: A wild and picturesque view—high and mountainous. The Interior of a lonely Inn, under the mountain, with the forest and rugged foot-path over the rocks, leading to the Smuggler's Retreat.

Act 3, Scene 1: A rich saloon in the Palace of the Duke of Popoli. *Scene 2*: The open sea, with the Tower and balcony of the Castle. The barque *Etna* appears in the offing in full sail, bearing Scopetto in triumph, amidst the exultation of his crew.

ACT 1
"When in silence the day is dying" (Song and Refrain)
Mrs. J. Maeder, C. Richings
"Thou, who canst all depict" (Refrain)
C. Richings
Barcarole
J. Dunn, Mr. Boudinot, Chorus

ACT 2
"If your Life's Moments" (Entr'acte and Chorus)
"The Mountain maid who Wooeth" (Song)
C. Richings
"With the High Dreams of Childhood" (Romance)
C. Richings
"No, I dare not sing" (Cavatina)
C. Richings
Finale (Fortune now sustains us)
C. Richings, J. Dunn, Mr. Boudinot, P. Richings, Chorus

ACT 3
"Throw aside all sorrow" (Entr'acte and Chorus)
"When the sun in full splendor" (Acte and Chorus)
C. Richings
"The Ray of Hope" (Cavatina)
C. Richings
Finale (Oh, yonder descry)
Characters, Chorus
"Thou, who canst all depict" (Barcarole)(reprise)

1862.05 THE WIZARD'S TEMPEST, or, The King of the Magical Island

A Spectacular, Magical Burlesque (of William Shakespeare's 'The Tempest' and 'A Midsummer Night's Dream') in a Prologue, Two Acts, 7 Scenes, with magnificent scenery, gorgeous costumes, songs, choruses and dances, grand processions and enchanting tableaux. Play by Charles Gayler. Stage manager, James G. Burnett. Scenery by Mr. Hayes. Produced by Professor J. H. Anderson. Opened 9 June 1862 at the Winter Garden and closed 30 June 1862 after 21 performances[23].

CAST (Prologue): *Children of Shakespeare's Brain, and the offspring of his fancy, with a deep sympathy for their suffering Pa (6)*: *Oberon*: Miss Hackett. *Puck*: Little Mary Bullock. *Ariel*: IONE BURKE. *Mustardseed*: Mlle. Virginie. *Peas-blossom*: Mlle. Melanie. *Titania*: Mrs. Mark Smith. *Hecate*, a blustering beldame, with a grand incantation: CHARLES HALE. *Shade of Shakespeare*, who having something on his mind, revisits the "glimpses of the moon in his habit as he lived," for the purpose of having his say, and suggesting the burlesque: A. D. BRADLEY. *The Wizard of the North*: Professor J. H. ANDERSON.

CAST (Burlesque): *Neapolitans, Usurpers, Secessionists, Filibusters, and discontented Papers generally*: *Alonzo*, one of the crowned heads of Europe, a snivelling tyrant, and the head of his house, in search of its heir: John Nickinson. *Antonio*, a bogus Duke, and president of the C.S.I.—the prototype of the bogus president of the C.S.A.: George Chaplin. *Ferdinand*, the Prince of Italian W(h)ales, in his own estimation, but in reality a sardine: Louisa Anderson. *Sebastian*, who takes to the sea, to make the seizure of his crown sure: Henry Russell. *Gonzalo*, a member of Antonio's cabinet (not illusion's) with a lingering longing for "the old flag": Mr. Evans. *Stephano*, an ancient butler, purveyor of the royal grog, and concoctor of the Prince's cocktails: CHARLES HALE. *Trinculo*, the great Neapolitan clown, with the usual number of "Here we are's!" and "Old Jo's": Mr. Jeffries. *Captain Cuttle*, a gay mariner, and commander of the galley *"The Skimmer of the Seas"*: T. E. Morris. *Jack Bunsby*, his boatswain , and a man "as can give an opinion": C. Burnett.

Inhabitants of the Uninhabited Island: *Prospero*, a wizard who rules the waves by the wave of his wand, who though a constitutional sovereign, waves no constitutional right, and who, driven from his throne, wanders with his wand, performing wanders: J. H. ANDERSON, J. G. BURNETT (Which is which? "You pays your money and you takes your choice."). *Ariel*, the Wizard's confederate, a tricksy spirit, fly to all sorts of tricks and up to all sorts of traps: IONE BURKE. *Miranda*, the Wizard's little treasure, whom he loves passing well, with a weakness for Ferdinand and the latest fashions; also a heroine of the first water: EMILY THORNE. *Caliban*, a monster, neither fish, flesh nor fowl; a thoroughly irrepressible contraband, and a secessionist of the blackest dye, continually howling for freedom, and a proof that "where there is a great cry there is (a) little wool: S. HEMPLE. *Fairies, Spiritual Vivandières, Amazons, Demons, and various Magical Spirits of assorted colors. Lords and other "bloated aristocrats."*

Prologue: Inside the cave of Eolus. The Churchyard of Stratford-upon-Avon, with view of Stratford Church.

Act 1, Scene 1: Bay of Naples. Deck of Galley. Gorgeous panorama of the Mediterranean, from Naples to Gibraltar, painted by Mr. Hayes on 30,000 square feet of canvas, displaying Vesuvius in a state of eruption, and all the places of enduring interest on the far famed and classic shores of the Sea of Italy. The Open Sea, with pass-

[20]Dropped for subsequent tour.
[21]Restored for subsequent tour to Act 3, after "Who has not heard" (Cavatina):
"Ever be happy" (Pirates' Chorus)
(*Music by* Michael William Balfe.)
[22]English adaptation uncredited.

[23]No songs listed in programs (apart from incantations and fairy choruses), nor credits for music.

ing vessels. There's a Tempest Brewing! The Tempest brewed. The Ship sinks (in this scene the whole back of the stage disappears.) *Scene* 2: Landscape on Prospero's Magical Island. *Scene* 3: Prospero's Cave with a view of the sea. Floral Psychomanteum of Professor Anderson. The Grand Magic Seance by Professor Anderson with the magic, Psychical Second Sight, illustrated by Miss E. M. Anderson.

Act 2, *Scene* 1: Rocky Pass on the Magical Island. *Scene* 2: Magnificent Landscape. *Scene* 3: Coral Cave by the Sea Shore. *Scene* 4: Miraculous Metamorphosis. Prospero's Return and the Flight of Ariel.

1862.06

MRS. PARTINGTON,
or, Home for the Holidays

The Holman National Opera Troupe in a Comic Operetta in One Act[24], accompanied by a laughable vaudeville and an opening program of operatic ballads and songs. Music original and selected. Presented by Phineas T. Barnum. Opened 14 July 1862 at Barnum's Museum and closed 26 July 1862 after 24 performances.[25]

CAST: Holman National Opera Troupe: (Miss) Sallie Holman, (Infant) Julia Holman, Master Alfred Holman, Master Benjamin Holman.

Opening Program

"Gentle Jenny Gray" (Solo and Chorus)
S. Holman, Troupe

"Annie o' the banks O'Dee' (Scotch ballad)
John Holman

"Ridin' in a Railroad Kerr" (Comic Song)
Infant Julia Holman

"Lawks John you flatter" (Comic Rustic Duett en costume)
S. Holman, A. Holman

La Zingarella (Dance)
Infant Julia Holman

Wondrous Drum Performance, giving correct imitations of the March to Battlefield, The Battle, the Explosion of a Shell, The Booming of Artillery, the Rattle of Musktery. Also his famous Railroad trip, Getting under way, Sixty Miles an hour, and arrival at the terminus, on which occasion he will wear his Prize Silver Drum Sticks, presented by the 71st Regiment, N.Y. S. M.

"The Bird of Beauty" (Aria) (Contralto and Soprano)
S. Holman

Pas de Deux
Litlle Julia Holman, S. Holman

"Ever of Thee" (Duett)
B. Holman, A. Holman

Patriotic Medley
S. Holman

"Johnny came courting me" (Eccentric Song)
J. Holman

"Plantation" (Solo and Chorus)
A. Holman, Troupe

MRS. PARTINGTON

CAST: *Mrs. Partington*, the great original, in all her pristine purity and unsophisticated simplicity: Miss SALLIE (HOLMAN). *Ike*, her Grandson, a precocious youth, full of fun, and who declared, in a vocal way that he "Loves a bit of mischief ever dearly O!": Little JULIA (HOLMAN). *Roger*, an old bachelor, who "was in love once," but who came to an exemplary conclusion to let the women alone: Master ALFRED (HOLMAN). *Rattle*, Grandson No. 2, "Home for the Holidays" and "In for a Spree": Master ALFRED (HOLMAN). *Monsieur Lignumvitae*, a distinguished member of "zee-tee-a-tree" and a celebrated horn player "in a horn": Master ALFRED (HOLMAN). *Farmer Fallowfield*, a bluff sort of bumpkin with a bad memory: Master ALFRED (HOLMAN). *Ebeneezer Snow*, a crusty old cove and a complainant of Ike: Master BENJAMIN (HOLMAN). *Molly Malone*, a sprig of the Emerald Isle, and the fond "parient" of a "bieutiful boys that's the every image of his mother": Master BENJAMIN (HOLMAN). *Coddington*, Grandson No. 3 to Mrs. P., —also "Home for the Holidays" and "In for a Spree": Master BENJAMIN (HOLMAN).

[24]Authorship uncredited, though "written expressly for the Holman Troupe."
[25]Performed twice daily. Also performed, as per broadsheets:

Commodore Nutt in his various performances (after Opening Program)

Swiss Warbler in imitations of various birds, animals, etc.

"Dost Thou Love Me" (Duet)(after MRS. PARTINGTON)
J. Holman, Commodore Nutt

1862.06

THE SCHOOLMASTER ABROAD,
or, The Frolics of Fitzfoolzleums.
A Vaudeville.

CAST: *Mr. Micky Magra*, professor of things but master of none in particular, with the song "The Fine Ould Irish Gentlemean": Master ALFRED (HOLMAN). *Master Phineas Phipps Fitzfoolzleum*, a bright sprig of humanity: Master BENJAMIN (HOLMAN). *Miss Fanny Fitzfoolzleum*, fond of a little bit of fun, under the rose, in which she will dance the Donnybrook Jig with Master Alfred: Miss SALLIE (HOLMAN). *Miss Titania Phips Fitzfoolzleum*, who sees more than some folks like: Little JULIA (HOLMAN). During the piece, a Double Dance by Little Julia and Miss Sallie.

For the second week 21-26, July 1862, Edwin Kelly, tenor and light comedian, and Master (Francis) Leon, The Ethiopian Cubas, joined the production. The opening program above, was dispensed with; following MRS. PARTINGTON, the program continued as follows:

1862.06

LA VIVANDIÈRE,
A Comic Operetta

(by Edwin Kelly and Francis Leon).

CAST: *Frank*, a Zouave: EDWIN KELLY. *Jenny*, afterwards the Vivandière: Master (FRANCIS) LEON.

MUSICAL NUMBERS

"The Dream of Love"

"Kiss Me Good Night, Mother"

"Captain with His Whiskers"

Duet from the opera "I MASNADIERI"
(*Music by* Giuseppe Verdi)

Dance, Grand Melange, by the Ethiopian Cubas
Master (Francis) Leon

1862.06

WANTED, A FAMILY,
or, Three Too Many

A laughable operetta written expressly for the Holman Troupe.

CAST: *Mr. Morton*, a retired old bachelor, tired of his single blessedness, and determined to adopt a family of small children: Master ALFRED (HOLMAN). *Washington Napoleon Scott Morton*, a dashing young American Zouave: Miss SALLIE (HOLMAN). *Gourmand Morton*, a small boy with a large appetite: Miss SALLIE (HOLMAN). *Decatur Morton*, a genuine Yankee Tar, who discourses on his tarry "toplights": Miss SALLIE (HOLMAN). *Alice*, only daughter of Mr. Frank Morton, a discarded niece of old Morton, a trump card, and in the end more than a match for the four, old Morton has set his heart upon: Miss SALLIE (HOLMAN). *Jerusha*, a cute Yankee to help old Morton: Miss JULIA (HOLMAN). *Pat*, Irish Help to old Morton, a bright particular specimen of the Emerald Isle: Master BENJAMIN (HOLMAN).

1862.06

THE PRIMA DONNA FROM THE COUNTRY,
An Ethiopian Burlesque

Illustrating the airs of Prima Donnas in general, and none in particular.

CAST: *Mademoiselle Patti de fois gras*, a would-be prima donna: Master (FRANCIS) LEON. *Signor Marrowfat Barrell Ullman*, an anxious manager: EDWIN KELLY.

1862.07

THE PET OF THE PETTICOATS!

A Revival of the Comic Operetta in Three Acts[26]. Play by John Baldwin Buckstone (adapted from the French vaudeville Vert-Vert by de Leuven and Desforges). Produced by Maggie Mitchell. Opened 14 July 1862 at Laura Keene's Theatre and closed 15 August 1862 after 2 performances in repertory.

CAST: *Paul*, nicknamed 'Poll the Pet': MAGGIE MITCHELL. *Mons. Zephyr*, Dancing Master to the Convent: A. H. DAVENPORT. *Job*, the Convent Gardener: J. H. STODDART. *Officers of Dragoons (8)*: *Chevalier St. Pierre*: J. W. Collier. *Colonel Belair*: —. *Captain Cannonade*: Charles T. Parlsoe, Jr. *Ensign Bannier*: Mr. Brown. *Captain Achille*: Mr. Bilby. *Lieutenant Victor*: Mr. King. *Ensign Cadet*: Mr. Williams. *Lieutenant Fusée*: Mr. Thomas. *Tobie*, Landlord of the Golden Lion: Mr. D. C. Little.

[26]First produced in New York 21 May 1835 at the Park Theatre; for Synopsis of Scenes and Musical Numbers, see 25 March 1853 revival at Wallach's Theatre.

Julia, Emma, Boarders at the Convent and married to St. Pierre and Belair: Misses Nelson, Mitchell. *Sister Vinaigre* Mrs. A. Hind. *Lady Superior*: Miss Monell. *Mimi*: Mrs. J. H. STODDART. *Zoe*: Miss F. Monell. *Dorothy*: Miss Julia Monell. *Liza*: Miss Walker. *Lady Boarders at the Convent, Officers, etc.*

KING COTTON, or, The Exiled Prince

1862.08

A New, National, Quizzical, Local, Farcical, Musical, Dramatical Burlesque Extravaganza in One Act, 9 Scenes, suitable to the times, slightly altered from something else in plot, and outrageously original in material[27]. Play by Charles Chamberlain, Jr. Music director, Mr. E. Mollenhauer. Produced by W. M. Fleming. Opened 21 July 1862 at the Winter Garden and closed 26 July 1862 after 5 performances in repertory.

CAST: *Don Pluribustah*, an exiled Federal Prince, on a visit to Secessia: Miss FANNIE BROWN. *Jeff Davis the First*, King of Cotton, and Monarch of an indefinite and portable Kingdom: J. M. WARD. *Don Wigfall*, Captain of the King's body guard, and Chief Controller of Contrabands: GEORGE D. CHAPLIN. *Don Thompson, Don Cobb*, well-known ministers of King Cotton's Court, who need no introduction: Messrs. G. L. AIKEN, D. Myron. *Ponce de Leon*, the Prince of Florida: L. F. RAND. *Dig Deep*, King Cotton's Gardener, and Patentee of the last ditch: E. EBERLE. *Don Floyd*, too well known to everybody: J. H. Evans. *Columbia*, the fascinating Princess of the Federal Isles: (ISABELLA) FREEMAN. *The Fairy Goodwill*, an accomodating Spirit, with a large stock in trade: Miss Emma Morton. *Toosweettolookat, Nearlysweetenoughtokiss*, Ladies in Waiting on the Princess: Misses Alice Douglas, L. Wood. *Members of the Court, Ladies in Waiting, Amazons, Body Guards, Black Guards, etc.*

Scene 1: Court of Jeff Davis, the Cotton King. *Scene 2*: The Garden of King Cotton's Palace. *Scene 3*: Which is the way to the Capitol? *Scene 4*: A Sylvan Retreat. *Scene 5*: Hall in the Fairy Palace. *Scene 6*: Garden of the Palace. *Scene 7*: King Cotton's Pavilion. *Scene 8*: Court Yard of the Fairy Palace. *Scene 9*: Lawn in front of Palace.

MUSICAL NUMBERS

Opening Chorus (He's the Cotton King we know)(Scene 1)
Grand Entry of King Cotton (Scene 1)
"A Prince here you see" (Song)(Scene 2)
Grand Chorus and Dance of the Fairies (Scene 5)
Entrance of the Confederate Guard (Scene 5)
"Since I've been in the Army" (Song)(Scene 6)
Grand Entry of the Secession Army (Scene 9)
Chorus of Federals (Oh, Jeff Davis, have we caught you!)(Scene 9)
Grand Apotheosis; Grand Chorale Finale (Scene 9)

BLONDETTE, or, The Naughty Prince and Pretty Peasant

1862.09

An Original Fairy Spectacle (Extravaganza, scenical, comical and whimsical) in Three Acts, 12 Scenes (adapted from the French féerie Rothomago). Music composed and arranged from the works of Myerbeer, Weber, Mendelssohn, Rossini, Verdi, Auber, etc. by Thomas Baker. Scenery by Minard Lewis, aided by Howard Rogers. Machinery and novel mechanical tricks by W. Sanders. Dresses by Mons. and Mme. Tilson. Stage appointments by J. H. Bilby. The whole produced under the immediate direction of Laura Keene. Musical director, Thomas Baker. Produced by Laura Keene. Opened 25 November 1862 at Laura Keene's Theatre and closed 3 January 1863 after 42 performances.

CAST: *King Merlin*, the senior partner of the house of Merlin and Son, the celebrated dealers in necromancy: Mr. J. H. STODDART. *Prince Merlin*, his son, very naughty, very pretty, and owner of the Magic Watch: Miss EMMA TAYLOR. *Lubin*, a peasant, a fortunate one, the finder of the Magic Watch: Mr. J. T. RAYMOND. *Gambille*, nephew to the great Rampage and friend of Lubin's, who shares his good and evil fortune: Mr. WALTER LENNOX. *Trufio*, a deaf old Shepherd, a little tainted with Romance: Mr. Stuart Robson. *Picklewitz*, a Page: Miss Thompson. *Fe-fi-fo-fum*, a great Irish Ogre, the old-fashioned terror of naughty Boys and Girls, and half cousin to Blondette: Mr. Xtensive. *Count Shilabala*: Mr. Morgan. *Lord Hocuspocus*: Mr. Florence. *Lady Hocuspocus*: Mrs. Fielding. *Mr. and Mrs. Bogle*: Mr. and Mrs. Bugbear. *The Princess Blondette*, a wayward child because she always had her own way and always her own way of having it: Mrs. SEDLEY BROWN. *Urla, Ina*, her Maids of Honor: Misses Isabella Nickinson, Clara Leigh. *The Fairy Rampage*, a terrible person, especially when on the rampage: Mrs. ROBERTSON. *Mignonette*, the meek and beautiful, rescued by Prince Merlin from the horrid Pirates, 290 maybe: Miss IONE BURKE. *Rosette, Jolliette*, Village maidens and Bridesmaids to Mignonette: Mrs. J. H. Stodddart, Miss Everett.

The Twelve Hours: *Hour of Love*: Miss Isabelle Nickinson. *Hour of Ball*: Miss Tirrel. *Hour of Prayer*: Miss Thompson. *Hour of Dinner*: Miss Clara Leigh. *Hour of Sleep*: Miss E. Thomson. *Hour of Midnight*: Miss A. Merry. *Hour of Work*: Miss H. Mosely. *Hour of Mirth*: Miss Hosmer. *Hour of Indolence*: Miss Troy. *Hour of Supper*: Miss Irving. *Hour of Pain*: Miss Blake. *Hour of Misery*: Miss Wheeler. *Pages, Lady Attendants on the Palace of Lace, Visitors to Palace of Diamonds*: Numerous Corps de Ballet.

Act 1, Scene 1: The Bride's Boudoir. *Scene 2*: The Terrace and Gardens of the Palace of King Merlin. *Scene 3*: Cottage of Mignonette. The Kingdom of the Hours. *Scene 4*: Grotto of Love.

Act 2, Scene 1: A Corn Field. *Scene 2*: Cottage of Mignonette. *Scene 3*: Gardens of the Palace. *Scene 4*: The Palace of Lace. The Palace of Diamonds.

Act 3, Scene 1: Chamber of an Inn. *Scene 2*: The Devil's Crossing and Fairy Grove. *Scene 3*: Yard of a Sheep Fold. *Scene 4*: Mignonette's Cottage. The Crystal Kingdom of the Magic Watch.

ACT 1
Scene 1
Chorus of Bridesmaids
"All of a sudden her Godmama" (Song)
Entrance of the Fairy Rampage
Scene 2
King Merlin's History (Recitation)
"Cruel fate why thus pursuing" (Solo and Chorus)
Scene 3
The Kingdom of the Hours
"Power of Love" (Song)

ACT 2
Scene 1
"The Father of Little Ninette" (Song)
W. Lennox
The Rival Prestidigitators
Scene 2
"Long live Prince Lubin" (Song)
Mrs. S. Brown
Scene 4
Blondette Polka
Corps de Ballet of Laces
"The Perfect Cure"
All the characters

ACT 3
Scene 2
Ballet of Beauty
Scene 4
Crystal Kingdom of the Magic Watch (Finale)

JENNY LIND/ THE INVINCIBLES!

1863.01

A Double Bill of Comedy and Song. Stage director, Ben A. Baker. Musical director, Thomas Baker. Produced by Mrs. John Wood. Opened 5 January 1863 at Laura Keene's Theatre and closed 10 January 1863 after 6 performances; THE INVINCIBLES! returned on a bill with THE LOAN OF A LOVER 2 February 1863.

ACT 1

JENNY LIND, a Revival of the Operatic Bagatellry in One Act.

CAST: *Jenny Leatherlungs*, in which character she will give her celebrated imitations of Brignoli, Amodio, Grisi and Patti: Mrs. JOHN WOOD. *Mr. Granby Gag*, a London manager in search of a star: Mr. WALTER LENNOX. *Baron Swigitoff Beery*, a Student, surnamed the "Cock of the College:" Mr. STUART ROBSON. *Mr. Lawrence Leatherlungs*, a Tanner, on a tour: Mr. J. H. STODDART.

German students: *Herr Kanaster*: Mr. J. H. Bilby. *Herr Cheroot*: Mr. Duel. *Herr Spittoon*: Mr. Mosgun. *Herr Koff*: Mr. Andrews. *Herr Sneeze*: Mr. Wilson. *Herr Splutter*: Mr. Martin. *Herr Stammer*: Mr. Breen. *Herr Meerschaum*: Mr. Palmer. *Landlord*: Mr. Florence.

ACT 2

THE INVINCIBLES!, a Comic Musical Burletta in One Act.

[27]Preceded by the fourth act, or celebrated trial scene, of Shakespeare's The Merchant of Venice. KING COTTON was followed by an after-piece, the farce, Paddy Miles' Boy.

CAST: *Victoire*, Sergeant of the Invincibles: Mrs. JOHN WOOD. *Captain Florville*: Mr. H. F. DALY. *General Verdun*: Mr. J. H. STODDART. *Invalids commanding Fort Rivage (3)*: *Sergeant Brusque*: Mr. STUART ROBSON. *Corporal O'Flash*: Mr. J. T. RAYMOND. *Private Tactique*: Mr. WALTER LENNOX. *Frivolle*, a valet: Mr. J. H. Bilby. *Porter*: Mr. Florence.

The Invincibles: *Juliette*: Miss IONE BURKE. *Sophie*: Miss Thompson. *Emilie*: Miss Gilmar. *Therese*: Miss Rossit. *Elise*: Miss Kaster. *Marie*: Miss Robinson. *Eugenia*: Miss Pillow. *Augusta*: Miss Mosely. *Nannette*: Miss Irving. *Jacquette*: Miss Duel. *Louise*: Miss Hoffman. *Officers, Maskers, Servants, etc.*

MUSICAL NUMBERS

"Let's all speak our minds" (Song)
Mrs. J. Wood

"Fall not in love" (Song)
Mrs. J. Wood

"When first I heard" (Song and Chorus)
Mrs. J. Wood, Invincibles

"Sweet Spirit, hear my Prayer" (Aria)
Miss I. Burke

"When Bullets we trade in" (Finale)
All the characters

1863.02 THE PET OF THE PETTICOATS!

A Revival of the Comic Operetta in Three Acts[28]. (Play by John Baldwin Buckstone [adapted from the French vauldeville Vert-Vert by de Leuven and Desforges].) Stage director, Ben A. Baker. Musical director, Thomas Baker. Produced by Mrs. John Wood. Opened 26 January 1863 at Laura Keene's Theatre and closed 7 February 1863 after 6 performances in repertory.

CAST: *Paul*, the Pet: Mrs. JOHN WOOD. *Mons. Zephyr*, Dancing Master to the Convent: Mr. STUART ROBSON. *Job*, the Convent Gardener: Mr. J. H. STODDART. *Officers in the French Army (8)*: *Chevalier St. Pierre*: Mr. H. F. Daly. *Colonel Belair*: Mr. Marlowe. *Captain Cannonade*: Mr. Williams. *Ensign Bannier*: Mr. Florence. *Captain Achille*: Mr. Arthur. *Lieutenant Victor*: Mr. Maxwell. *Ensign Cadet*: Mr. Duel. *Lieutenant Fuzee*: Mr. Morgan. *Tobie*, Landlord of the Golden Lion: Mr. J. H. Bilby.

Minnie: Mrs. SEDLEY BROWN. *Julia, Emma*, Boarders at the Convent and married to St. Pierre and Belair: Misses Emma Taylor, Isabella Nickinson. *Madame Bravusa*, an Opera Singer: Mrs. J. H. STODDART. *Sister Vinagre* Mrs. A. Hind. *Lady Superior*: Mrs. Tyrrell. *Zoe*: Miss M. Thompson. *Emily*: Miss Gilmer. *Dorothea*: Miss Costar. *Liza*: Miss Mosely. *Therese*: Miss C. Thompson. *Louise*: Miss Hoffman. *Babet*, bar maid at the Inn: Miss Alice Merry. *Lady Boarders at the Convent, Officers, etc.*: Numerous Corps de Ballet.

MUSICAL NUMBERS[29]

"The Pious Child"
Mrs. J. Wood

"Sweet Eyes"
Mrs. J. Wood

"Farewell Sisters" (Sestette)
Mrs. J. Wood

"Dear friends around me smiling"
Mrs. J. Wood

"Vive la Companie" (Finale)
Mrs. J. Wood

"Home Sweet Home"
Mrs. S. Brown

1863.03 THE LOAN OF A LOVER

A Revival of the Musical Comedietta in One Act[30]. (Play by James Robinson Planché.) Stage director, Ben A. Baker. Musical director, Thomas Baker. Produced by Mrs. John Wood. Opened 30 January 1863 at Laura Keene's Theatre in repertory.

CAST: *Gertrude*: Mrs. JOHN WOOD. *Peter Spyk*, a Farmer: Mr J. T. RAYMOND. *Captain Amersfort*: Mr. H. F. DALY. *Swyzle*, Steward at the Castle: Mr. STUART ROBSON. *Delve*, a Gardener: Mr. J. H. Bilby. *Ernestine Rosendaal*: Miss Emma Taylor.

MUSICAL NUMBERS

"I don't think I'm ugly" (Song)
Mrs. J. Wood

"I've no money" (Song)
Mrs. J. Wood

"To-morrow will be Market Day" (Duet)
Mrs. J. Wood, Mr. J. T. Raymond

"My years with sweet contentment bless" (Duet)
Mrs. J. Wood, Mr. S. Robson

1863.04 THE FAIR ONE WITH THE GOLDEN LOCKS

A New Version of James Robinson Planché's celebrated Fairy Extravaganza in One Act, 4 Scenes[31]. Compiled and revised by Charles M. Walcot. New music compiled and arranged by J. G. Maeder and Thomas Baker. Stage director, Ben A. Baker. Scenery by Minard Lewis. Machinery by W. Sanders. Costumes by Mons. and Mme. Tillson. Properties by J. H. Bilby. Musical director, Thomas Baker. Produced by Mrs. John Wood. Opened 9 February 1863 at Laura Keene's Theatre and closed 14 March 1863 after 30 performances.

CAST: *Queen Lucidora*, surnamed the "Fair one with the Golden Locks," and really a very Fair Queen, considering how she could "go it" if she were just to wear a wig, and sell her hair at 160: Mrs. JOHN WOOD. *Pitchin*, commonly called Plucky Pitchin, Page of Prince Naryred; on the staff of General D. Light and proved capable of controlling hundreds of thousands through never failing campaigns: Mrs. JOHN WOOD. *Original Jacobs*, a travelling merchant, a connection of Moses in the School for Scandal, introduced expressly to prove Mrs. Wood's devotion to the legitimate drama: Mrs. JOHN WOOD. *King Lachrymoso*, author of "rejected addresses" to the Fair one with the Golden Locks: Mr. CHARLES M. WALCOT, Sr. *Prince Naryred*, Heir to the Realms of Notacop, in love with Queen Lucidora; taken in by Count Pleniposo, and done for by the Queen: Mrs. SEDLEY BROWN. *Count Pleniposo*, Master of State and Ambassador, very extraordinary to the fair one with the Golden Locks: Mr. J. T. RAYMOND. *Viscount Verysoso*, Grand Chamberlain to the King: Mr. Marlowe. *Marquis Fiddlefaddle*, Grand Chamberlain to Queen Lucidora: Mr. J. H. STODDART. *Lord Cut*, a creature of Count Pleniposo, but anything but a comfort to Prince Naryred: Mr. WALTER LENNOX. *Lord Thrust*, a ditto, ditto, to match: Mr. STUART ROBSON. *Captain of the King's Guard*: Mr. J. H. Bilby. *Mollymopsa*, Housemaid of Honor to the Queen: Miss IONE BURKE. *Pappilotina*, first lady's maid in Waiting: Miss Isabella Nickinson. *Mantillina*, Mistress of the Robes: Miss Alice Merry. *Gallifron*, a gigantic Giant, standing nearly twelve feet, besides the two in his shoes: THE ARAB GIANT. *A Carp*, an odd fish completely out of water: Mr. Scaly. *A Crow*, an old acquaintance: Mr. Williams. *An Owl*, an illustrious foreigner: Mr. Hooter. *Fairy Windup*: Miss M. Thompson. *Second and Third Fairies*: Misses Koster, Hoffman. *Maids of Honor, Courtiers, Guards*: Powerful Chorus and Corps de Ballet.

Scene 1: Laracenic Hall from the Palace of the Alhambras. *Scene 2*: Fairy Lake and Landscape. *Scene 3*: Palace of King Lachrymoso. *Scene 4*: Abode of the Guardian Sprites.

MUSICAL NUMBERS[32]

"Lucidora, surnamed the Fair one" (Opening Chorus)
Courtiers, Ladies, etc.

"There are ladies who dwell" (Medley)
Mrs. J. Wood

"Comb it genteely" (Aria and Chorus)
Mrs. J. Wood, J. T. Raymond, Mrs. S. Brown, Courtiers

"Fair Queen, I beg my suit you'll grant" (Three Part Song)
Mrs. S. Brown, J. T. Raymond, Mrs. J. Wood

"Madam, with all humility" (Duet)
Mrs. S. Brown, Mrs. J. Wood

"Lucidora, the pride of this heart" (Song)
Mrs. S. Brown

"Ills so great, oh!" (Brindisi)
Mrs. J. Wood

"See, here comes the King" (Chorus)
Courtiers, Guards, etc.

"Simple as A.B.C." (Trio)
Mrs. J. Wood, C. M. Walcot, J. T. Raymond

"Begone, Sir" (Duet and Chorus)
C. M. Walcot, Mrs. J. Wood, Chorus

---

[29]Preceded by a comedy, Mr. & Mrs. White. First produced in New York 21 May 1835 at the Park Theatre.
[30]Not in performance order.
[31]First produced in New York 7 April 1835 at the Park Theatre in repertory.

[31]Preceded by a comedietta, Regular Fix, with much the same cast excepting Mrs. Wood.
[32]Song added during the run: "How Are You Greenbacks?"

"Sir, a secret" (Duet)
Mrs. J. Wood, C. M. Walcot
"Here's a go!" (Concerted Piece)
C. M. Walcot, Mrs. J. Wood, J. T. Raymond, Mrs. S. Brown, Courtiers
Note: This piece is a novelty never before attempted. The characters sing a celebrated Overture.
"From these Coves could I fly, love" (Trio)
Mrs. S. Brown, Mrs. J. Wood, C. M. Walcot
"Now our rivalry is o'er" (Finale)
Mrs. J. Wood, Chorus

1863.05 LA ROSE DE SAINT-FLOUR

An Opera Bouffe (Operette) in One Act, in French[33]. Libretto by Michel Carré. Music by Jacques Offenbach. Manager, Mr. Juignet. Produced by the Théâtre Français. Opened 14 February 1863 at Niblo's Saloon in repertory.

CAST: *Marcachu*: Mons. ?. *Chapaillou*: Mons. ?. *Pierrette*: Mlle. ANNA HAMBURG. Company included Messrs. JUIGNET, EDGARD.

Scene: Auvergne.

MUSICAL NUMBERS[34]

Couplets (Entre les deux mon coeur balanche)
A. Hamburg
Air (Chette marmite neuve)
[Marcachu]
Récit (Ah! que cette maison est triste)
[Chapaillou]
Couplets (Pour les petits pieds)
[Chapaillou]
Grand Duo (Eh! farceur)
A. Hamburg, [Marcachu]
Duetto (Monsieur de Marcachu)
[Chapaillou, Marcachu]
Trio (Ah! comm' nous nous amujames)
A. Hamburg, [Chapaillou, Marcachu]
Couplets (C'était la noch' de Thomas)
A. Hamburg, [Chapaillou, Marcachu]
Trio (Je vous épouse)
A. Hamburg, [Chapaillou, Marcachu]
Final (Ah! comm' nous nous amujames)(reprise)
A. Hamburg, [Chapaillou, Marcachu]

1863.06 SATANELLA, or, the Power of Love

A Comic Opera in Four Acts. (Libretto by Edmund Falconer and Augustus Harris, revised.) Music by Michael William Balfe. Scenery by James E. Hayes and J. H. Selwyn. Dresses by Mons. Phillipe. Appointments by S. Wallis. Mechanical effects by Runyon and Demilt. Ballet under the direction of Signor Ronzani. Augmented orchestra under the direction of Harvey B. Dodworth. Produced by the Richings Opera Company. Presented by William Wheatley. Opened 23 February 1863 at Niblo's Garden and closed 14 March 1863 after 18 performances.

CAST: *Satanella*, the Spirit of Beauty: CAROLINE RICHINGS. *Julian*, the Demon Page: CAROLINE RICHINGS. *Arimane*, the Master Fiend: PETER RICHINGS. *Hernando*, Fabio's Tutor: PETER RICHINGS. *Malius*, the Imp of Mischief, afterwards "Flick": Mons. MARZETTI. *Fabio*: L. R. SHEWELL. *Marquis Leoni*: Mr. Buck. *Count Cassabella*: J. W. Blaisdell. *Vincentio Rozzoli*: Mr. DeForrest. *Juan Rovero*: Mr. Rendle. *Giacomo*: Edward Lamb. *The Cadi*: George Andrews. *Mooly Hassam*: C. H. Wilson. *Seyed Hassam*: Mr. Owens. *Nobles, Guards, Guests, etc.*

Countess Florabella: Mrs. Skerrett. *Jeannet*: Mrs. L. R. Shewell. *Lelia*, a Peasant: Mrs. F. S. CHANFRAU. *Beatrice*, an old Housekeeper: Mrs. H. P. Grattan. *Fairy Queen*: Miss C. Reed. *Nymphaleo*: Miss LeBrun. *Fairies, Flower Girls, etc.*

Ballet: Mlles. ANNETTA GALLETTI, KATRINE, MARZETTI, Mons. MARZETTI. Corps de Ballet.

Act 1: Pleasure Ground of the Countess Floribella.

Act 2: Dilapidated Apartment in Fabio's Chateau.

Act 3: The Slave Market, Tunis.

Act 4: Apartment in Fabio's Chateau.

ACT 1

Introduction and Opening Chorus
Grand Ballet:
Introduction
Corps de Ballet
Pas de Trois
Mlle. Galletti, Marzetti, Katrine, Corps de Ballet
Gambling Song
Mr. Buck, Chorus
Fairy Incantation
Orchestra

ACT 2

Aerial Chorus
Chorus
"The Power of Love" (Song)
C. Richings
"The Vintage of Champagne" (Drinking Song)
C. Richings

ACT 3

"Let Not the World" (Ballad)
C. Richings
"Merry Tunis" (Slave Market Chorus)
Chorus
Grand Ballet
Introduction
Corps de Ballet
Spanish Dance
Corps de Ballet
Romanica
Mlles. Marzetti, Katrine
Pas de l'Escharpe
Mlle. Galletti, Corps de Ballet
Grand Finale
"Anelta Sultana Zuleima"
C. Richings, Chorus
Grand Air and Cabuletta
C. Richings, Chorus

ACT 4

"Oh Could I But His Heart Enslave" (Cavatina)
C. Richings
"I am here, behold!" (Incantation)
C. Richings
"Vengeance, Vengeance" (Demon Chorus)
"The Power of Love" (Finale)
C. Richings, Chorus

1863.07 THE ENCHANTRESS!

A Revival of the Grand Operatic Spectacle in a Prologue and Three Acts, 15 Scenes[35]. (Libretto by Alfred Bunn, adapted from a text by J. H. Vernoy de Saint-Georges.) Music by Michael William Balfe and Dr. Cunnington[36]. Produced under the stage direction of Peter Richings. Stage director, Leon J. Vincent. Scenery by J. H. Selwyn. Machinery by Runyon, Demilt. Costumes by Mons. Phillipe (New York), Watson (Philadelphia), Joyce (Boston). Ballet under the direction of Signor Ronzani. Decorations and banners by George Letzinger. Orchestra under the direction of Harvey B. Dodworth. Produced by the Caroline Richings Opera Company. Presented by William Wheatley. Opened 16 March 1863 at Niblo's Garden and closed 28 March 1863 after 11 performances.

CAST: Prologue, Pirates: *Ramir*: PETER RICHINGS. *Nugues*: Mr. Birch. *Forte Braccio*: GEORGE REA. *Julio*: Mr. Rendle. *Pietro*: Mr. G. Clarke. *Sacripante*: Mr. Hurley. *Stella*, 3 years old: Miss LeBrun.

Act 1: *Ramir*, the Pirate Chief disguised as the Hermit, Friar Antonio: PETER RICHINGS. *Don Sylvio*: L. R. SHEWELL. *Dr. Mathanasius*: Mr. E. LAMB. *Forte*

[33]Followed by Un Caprice, Margot ou Les Benefaits de l'Education.
[34]No New York program found. Musical numbers not listed in programs. List prepared from published French piano vocal score (Ph. Maquet, Ancien Maison Brandus, Paris, n.d.).

[35]Previously produced in New York 25 May 1846 at the Chatham Theatre for 12 performances.
[36]Cunnington's interpolations were for this American revival.

Braccio: GEORGE REA. *Galeas*: Mr. J. Blaisdell. *Brisiris, Alexis*, Greeks: Messrs. Thompson, Flood. *Mushroom*: Harry Pearson. *Pambo Poncho*, Regent's servant: Mr. George Andrews. *Numba Jumba*, a Negro: C. W. Wilson. *Captain of the Guard*: Mr. Post. *First Officer*: Mr. Lloyd. *First Citizen*: Mr. Leman. *Pages*: Master and Miss Herne. *Spirit of Good*: ANNETTA GALLETTI. *Spirit of Evil*: Signor Ronzani. *Stella*, the Enchantress, assuming the characters of the Fairy Queen, the Greek Page and the Sultana: CAROLINE RICHINGS. *Vision*: Mlle. MARZETTI. *Dream*: Mlle. KATRINE. (*Nobles, Ladies, Peasants, Pirates, Senators, Royal Guards, Heralds, Soldiers, Slaves, Pursuivants, Bridesmaids, Dancers, Demons, Pages, Masqueraders, etc.*)

1863.08

TIB, or, The Cat in Crinoline

A Spectacular Burlesque in Three Acts[37]. Music by Thomas Baker. Scenery by Minard Lewis. Costumes by Mme. Tillson. Properties by W. H. Bilby. The whole produced under the personal supervision of Laura Keene and Milnes Levick. Musical director, Thomas Baker. Produced by Laura Keene. Opened 4 May 1863 at Laura Keene's Theatre and closed 5 May 1863 after 2 performances.

CAST: *Tib*, originally Fargeau's mouser, transformed by Titania, the Fairy Queen, into a rather pretty woman, who, though entirely too long a cat to be quite at home in crinoline, still manages to purr-severe in her part: Miss LAURA KEENE. *Frederick*, foster son of Fargeau, the miller, rightfully heir of Rudolph, nephew to the Duke, as is shown in the cat-astrophe—a very nice young man, master of Tib and Lover of Alice: Mr. H. F. DALY. *Christian*, the second son of the defunct Fargeau, a practical mortal and a man of entirely too much common sense to make much of a figure: Mr. STUART ROBSON. *Hans*, a disciple of Pythagoras, third and youngest son of the aforesaid Fargeau, inherits his father's donkey and purr-sists in running against feline and any other claws: Mr. CHARLES PETERS. *Duke*, a miserly usur-purr, equally addicted to gold and gastronomy, who, after managing to circumvent others for a long while, is finally circumvented himself, and cat-ches it ultimately with a vengeance: Mr. CHARLES WALCOT. *Fritz*, Cat-er cousin and confidante, sadly in want of a cat, a pleasure for a mind diseased, addicted to lapping on the sly: Mr. J. H. STODDART. *Molkers*, the Court Cat-e-chiser: Mr. Rouse. *Alice*, stepdaughter of the Duke, and like all stepdaughters, very much unlike her dad. She is romantic enough to prefer love to lucre, but sensible enough not to object to the union of both. In fact she is a young lady of very strong and decided union proclivities: Miss LAURA LEIGH. *The Donkey*, afterwards Jenny or Jennette (a young lady with a mews-i-cal hee-haw): Miss IONE BURKE.

Immortals: *Titania*, see Shakespeare. Not quite what she was in better days and something the worse for wear, but still able to wield her wand to some purpose: Miss Isabella Nickinson. *Oberon*, see Shakespeare. A respectable gentleman, very much hen-pecked, and not much in a game of chess, but who manages to come out strong in the last heat: Mrs. Tyrrell. *Fairies, Cats, Mice, Rabbits and other Nondescripts.*

1863.09

BROTHER AND SISTER

A Revival of the Musical Burletta in Two Acts, 7 Scenes.[38] Libretto by William Dimond. Music by Sir Henry Bishop. Scenery by James E. Hayes. Costums by Cornelia Flannery. Director, Charles M. Walcot. Musical director, Thomas Baker. Produced by Mrs. John Wood. Opened 8 October 1863 at the Olympic Theatre and closed 17 October 1863 after 9 performances.

CAST: *Don Christoval de Tormes*: J. H. STODDART. *Don Sylvio*: GEORGE BECKS. *Pacheco*: W. DAVIDGE. *Bartolo*: FRANK REA. *Isidora*: Mrs. MARY SEDLEY BROWN. *Camilla*: ELSIE FOLSOM. *Rosanthe*: Mrs. JOHN WOOD.

Vestals Misses Norton, Elmore, Gilmer, Evans, Lloyd, A. Henrie, E. Henrie, Prestige, Jackson.

Act 1, Scene 1: Hall in Isidora's Castle. *Scene 2*: Garden of the Castle. *Scene 3*: Room at Donna Camilla's. *Scene 4*: The Castle Hall.

Act 2, Scene 1: Gallery in the Castle. *Scene 2*: Shrubbery in the Castle Grounds. *Scene 3*: Saloon in the Castle.

MUSICAL NUMBERS

"A Band of True Virgins" (Opening Chorus)(Act 1, Scene 1)

"Taste, oh, taste this spicy wine" (Song)(Act 1, Scene 1)
Mrs. J. Wood

"What airy Sounds" (Song)(Act 1, Scene 2)
Mrs. M. S. Brown

"Welcome, welcome cavaliers" (Chorus)(Act 1, Scene 4)

"One Vow I've taken" (Finale)(Act 2, Scene 3)

1863.10

PO-CA-HON-TAS, or, Ye Gentle Savage

A Revival of the Extravaganza (Burlesque) in Two Acts[39]. by John Brougham. Orchestra leader, Signor La Manna. Scenery by James E. Hayes. Costumes by Cornelia Flannery. Properties by William Henry. Director, Charles M. Walcot. Musical director, Thomas Baker[40]. Produced by Mrs. John Wood. Opened 19 October 1863 at the Olympic Theatre and closed 31 October 1863 after 12 performances.

CAST: *Of Ye Englishe*: *Captain John Smith*, the undoubted Original, vocal and instrumental, in the settlement of Virginia, in love with Pocahontas, according to this story, though somewhat at variance with his story: Mr. GEORGE BECKS. *Lieutenant Thomas Brown*, Second in Command, a hitherto neglected Genius, whose claims on posterity are now for the first time acknowledged, as is but right: Mr. Wyndham. *William Jones*, sometimes called Bill, another of the same sort left: Mr. Evans. *Mynheer Rolff*, the real Husband of Pocahontas, but dramatically divorced contrary to all law and fact: Mr. THOMAS EVANS.

Splicers of main-braces, shiverers of timbers, anathematizers of eyes and limbs, promiscuously general dealers in single combats and double hornpipes, and altogether, amazingly nautical people: *Benjamin Brace*: Mr. Jonas. *John Junk*: Mr. Williams. *Henry Halyard*: Mr. Shields. *William Buntline*: Mr. Dale.

Of Ye Savages: *His Imperial Majesty, Pow-Ha-Tan I*, King of the Tuscaroras—a crotchety Monarch, in fact, a Semi-Brave: Mr. W. DAVIDGE. *The Right Hon. Quash-al-Jaw*, Speaker of the Savage House of Lords—straightener of unpleasant kinks, and oiler of troubled waters, unraveller of knotty points, adjuster of pugnacious difficulties, and Grand Eye Parliamentary Factotum and Fugleman: Mr. Frank Rea. *O-po-dil-doc*, One of the Aboriginal F. F. V's[41], an indignant dignitary: Mr. G. H. Clarke. *Col-o-gog*, another warm-hearted and headed Son of Old Virginia: Mr. N. Forrester. *Jin-go*, Sergeant-at-Arms, a friend to swear by: Mr. Charles T. Parsloe, Jr. *Kreem-Fay-Sloon*, Bearer of Dispatches, and news-carrier in ordinary: Mr. Bruciani.

Medicine Men, of the Saultz and Sennaca Tribe: *Ip-pah-kak*: Mr. Gledhill. *Sas-sy-pril*: Mr. Brogan. *Kod-liv-Royl*: Mr. Taylor. *Kal-o-mel*: Mr. Boyd.

H. R. H. Princess Po-Ca-Hon-Tas, the Beautiful, and very properly undutiful, daughter of King Pow-Ha-Tan, married, according to the ridiculous dictum of actual circumstances, to Master Rolff, but the author flatters himself much more advantageously disposed of in the Acting edition: Mrs. JOHN WOOD. *Poo-tee-pet, Di-mun-di*, Interesting offshoots from aristocratic stock, anterior to the first Families of Virginia: Mrs. SEDLEY BROWN, V. GRATTAN. *Wee-cha-ven-da, Kros-as-kan-bee*, Embodying the rigid principles of the Tuscarora Fashionable Finishing School: Mrs. Walcot, Mrs. Wilkinson.

---

[37]Program note: Compiled from the German of the illustrious Ludwig Tieck's "Der Gestiefelte Kater," with an introduction from an unpublished and unacted tragedy by the great French dramatist, Johannes Crosseau entitled "Minette;" and also Auber's opera of "La Chatte Sage," Mozart's alteration of the same, and Dion Boucicault's amalgamation of the whole of the above, and also expanded from that primitive and delightful cosmopolitan fairy tale known as "Puss in Boots," and also enriched with occasional selections from the "Sokeontala" of the Sanscrit dramatist, and also containing fragments of the lost "Pompholugopehlasmata" of Aristophanes, and a small amount of original matter being the joint productions of those mammoth brains that conceived those classical dramas, "The Seven Sisters" and "Uncle Sam's Magic Lantern." The above gifted authors distinctly wish it to be understood they have pur-pussly avoided seeking any assistance from those mediocre compilers whose milk and water effusions culminated in "The Seven Sons." Some loud caterwalling and tender mews-ic will be given by our own Thomas Baker. Scenery has been catered for from numerous and midnight observations on the tiles by Minard Lewis. Madame Tiles-on has caught a severe cat-arrh in the cat-acombs, in her desire to furnish the sleekest coats and continuations, according to defunct authorities. Mr. Bilby will furnish twelve live cat-aphracts, and twelve fiery, untamed chargers, from the mews of Wilson, Crosby St.

[38]First produced in New York 5 January 1816 at the Park Theatre in repertory. This revival was presented as an after-piece to the comedietta in two acts, Married Daughters.

[39]First produced in New York 24 December 1855 at Wallack's Lyceum Theatre in repertory; re-opened 28 May 1856 at Wallack's Lyceum Theatre; re-opened 28 July 1856 at the Bowery Theatre. For Synopsis of Scenes and Musical Numbers, see original 1855 production. This revival was preceded by a comedietta, My Preserver.

[40]The original 1855 production credit for music read "Music entirely dislocated and re-set by James G. Maeder." Precisely how much music was retained or substituted by Thomas Baker for this revival is not known.

[41]First Family of Virginia.

Their "dear charges," for whom they don't forget to charge dear enough for in the Quarterly Bills: *Dah-Lin-Duck*: Miss Jennie Walters. *O-you-Jewel*: Mrs. Adele Grattan. *Luv-lie-kreeta*: Miss Morton. *Oso-char-ming*: Miss Louisa Carman. *Lum-Pa-Shuga*: Mrs. F. Rea.

Dontiwishit: Miss Augustine. *Woodificud*: Miss Prestige. *Hafaspooti*: Miss Elmore. *Dro-may-jah*, a high official: Miss Harris. *Target Bearer*: Master Doublequick. *Soldiers, Sailors, Indians, Members of the Tuscarora Light Guard, etc.*

1864.01 LES DEUX AVEUGLES

A Revival of the Bouffonnerie Musicale in One Act[42], in French. Libretto by Jules Moinaux. Music by Jacques Offenbach. Produced by the Théâtre Français. Opened 9 January 1864 at Niblo's Saloon in repertory; season closed 30 April 1864.

CAST: *Giraffier*: *Patachon*: Company included Messrs. ERNEST GRAVIER, EDGARD, CHOL, ROCHE, DONATIEN, FAYE; Mmes. LEVASSEUR, ANNA HAMBURG, MAILLET, DONATIEN.

1864.02 THE HOUSE THAT JACK BUILT, or, Harlequin and the Fairy Generous

A Comic, Fairy and Trick Pantomime in One Act, by James S. Maffit, preceded by an Olio. The piece abounding in Funny Tricks, Mechanical Changes, Startling Transformations, Tableaux, Choruses, &c. Stage manager, Mons. LaThorne. Ballet under the direction of Mons. Paul Brillant. Musical director, Ferd. Von Olker. Scenic artist, J. H. Wallack. Costumer, Mons. Toled. Manager, R. W. Butler. Opened 11 January 1864 at the American Theatre (444 Broadway) and closed 30 January 1864 after 21 performances.

Olio: Fancy Pas Seul by Miss Mary Blake. Song and Dance by Master Tommy. La Cellarius, by Miss Frank Nixon. Countryman's Visit: *Ike Stevenson*: Bob Hart. *James*: J. Wambold. *Little Gus*: Master Tommy. La Manola, Miss Viro Farrand. The Happy Old Man, by Charles E. Collins. Double pas Styrienne, Misses Annetta and Lottie LaPoint. The Veteran's Return, with Add Weaver and Bob hart. Crytsal Caverns; or, The Daughters of the Danube, the beautiful Oriental Spectacular Divertissement composed by Mons. Paul Brillant, with Misses Lizzie Schultze, Millie Flora, Annetta and Lottie LaPoint, Frank Nixon, Mary Blake, Viro Farrand, Florence Wells, Julia Melville, Clara Bogart and Jennie Lorraine. Song, Miss Adelaide Nixon. Malicious Trespass, with Charley White, Bob Hart, J. Wambold. The Cure, an original eccentric and amusign scene, with Mr. Charles E. Collins. Pas La Ariel, Miss Millie Flora. Banjo Solo and Song, James F. Wambold. Cracovienne, Miss Frank Nixon. Bumpology Explained: *Professor Fowler*: Bob Hart. *Ditimus Grubbs*: Add Weaver. *Jasper*: Charley White. Tarantella, Miss Lottie LaPoint. Song and Dance, Nigger Brigade, Add Weaver. English Jig, Miss Florence Wells. Song, Miss Adelaide Nixon. Cremorne Polka, with Misses Lizzie Schultze, Millie Flora, Annetta and Lottie LaPoint, Frank Nixon, Mary Blake, Viro Farrand, Florence Wells, Julia Melville, Clara Bogart and Jennie Lorraine. The Dumb Savoyard of Gin-oa, with Charley White and James Wambold. The Active Boy, an original Medley Song and Dance, Mr. Charles E. Collins. Fancy Dance, Miss Millie Flora.

Pantomime CAST: *Farmer Jack*, afterward Clown: JAMES S. MAFFIT. *Roger*, afterwards Pantaloon: BOB [Robert] HART. *The Man all tattered and torn*, afterwards Harlequin: Miss ANNETTA LaPOINT. *The Maiden all forlorn*, afterwards Columbine: Miss LIZZIE SCHULTZE. *The Fairy Generous*: Miss JULIA MELVILLE. *The Fairest all shaven and shorn*: Add Weaver. *Rat that ate the Malt*: A 4-legged animal. *Dog that worried the Cat*: Mr. Bark. *Cow with the Crumpled Horn*: Miss Cream. *Cat that killed the Rat*: Miss Scratch. *Cock that crowed in the Morn*: A Live Rooster. *John*: Mr. James Wambold. *Thomas*: Mr. Morris. *Car Driver*: Mr. J. Myers. *Bed Carrier*: Mr. Smith. *Beer Woman*: Miss Bogart. *Dick*: Mr. Williams. *Harry*: Master Tommy. *Negro*: Mr. Sullivan. *Tinker*: Mr. Lewis. *Waiting Maid*: Miss Millie Flora. *Demons, Peasants, Villagers*: The Company. *Brillant's Great Ballet Troupe*.

[42]On a triple bill, preceded by Les Pièges Dorés" by de Beauplan and "L'Histoire d'un Sou" by Clairville. LES DEUX AVEUGLES was first produced in New York 26 August 1857 at the Metropolitan Hall in repertory. For Synopsis of Scenes and Musical Numbers, see original 1857 production.

1864.03 TROMB-AL-CA-ZAR, ou, Les Criminels dramatiques

A Bouffonnerie musicale in One Act, in French[43]. (Libretto by Charles Dupeuty and Ernest Bourget.) Music by Jacques Offenbach. Directeurs. Produced by the Théâtre Français. Opened 12 January 1864 at Niblo's Saloon in repertory; season ended 30 April 1864.

CAST: *Beaujolais*: Mons. ?. *Vert-Panné*: Mons. ?. *Gigolette/Simplette*: Mlle. ?. *Ignace*: Mons. ?. Company included Messrs. ERNEST GRAVIER, EDGARD, CHOL, ROCHE, DONATIEN, FAYE; Mmes. LEVASSEUR, ANNA HAMBURG, MAILLET, DONATIEN.

Scene: Une auberge des Basses-Pyrénées.

MUSICAL NUMBERS[44]

- Recitative et Air (Ô rage, ô desespoir!) [Beaujolais]
- Trio (Le crocodile en partant pour la guerre) [Gigolette, Beaujolais, Vert-Panné]
- Trio (Détaillons) [Gigolette, Beaujolais, Vert-Panné]
- Couplets (La gitana, ah! croyez bien) [Gigolette]
- Trio (Un jambon de Bayonne) [Gigolette, Beaujolais, Vert-Panné]
- Quattuor (Un beau jour) [Gigolette, Beaujolais, Ignace, Vert-Panné]
- Introduction, valse
- Reprise du Trio du jambon [Gigolette, Beaujolais, Vert-Panné]

1864.04 THE BOHEMIAN GIRL

A Revival of the Light Opera in Three Acts[45]. (Libretto by Alfred Bunn, after Jules-Henri Vernoy de Saint-Georges' ballet-pantomime "The Gypsy.") Music by Michael William Balfe. Director of cast, chorus and orchestra, Theodore Thomas. Produced by Harrison's English Opera Troupe (Gabriel Harrison, Manager). Opened 13 January 1864 at Niblo's Saloon in repertory[46]; season closed February 1864.

CAST: *Arline*: Mme. COMTE BORCHARD. *Gypsey Queen*: Miss REYNOLDS. *Thaddeus*: Mr. WILLIAM CASTLE. *Count Arnheim*: Mr. S. C. CAMPBELL. *Devilshoof*: Mr. GEORGE REA. *Florestein*, his nephew: Mr. M. B. PIKE. *Captain of the Guard*: Mr. Florence. *Tambourine Dance*, Act 1: Miss Jennie Gourlay. *Gipsies, Peasants, Retainers, etc.*: Ladies and Gentlemen of the Chorus and Corps de Ballet.

1864.05 MAZEPPA, or, the Untamed Rocking Horse

A Revival of the Burlesque in One Act, 5 Scenes[47], founded (a very little) on a rather celebrated poem (by George Noel Gordon, Lord Byron), and a great deal on a noted Equestrian Drama[48]. Burlesque by H. J. Byron. Scenery by James E. Hayes. Director, Charles M. Walcot. Musical director, Thomas Baker. Produced by Mrs. John Wood. Opened 18 January 1864 at the Olympic Theatre and closed 6 February 1864 after 18 performances.

CAST: *Mazeppa*, alias Cassimir, a Child of Mystery: FRANK DREW. *Olinska*, the Pearl of Poland: Mrs. JOHN WOOD. *The Castellan of Laurinski*, a stern parient, and

[43]Accompanied by a dance by Pauline Grossi, La Fascination, boufonnerie choreographique by Messrs. Edgard and Chol, and "La Joie Fait Peur," comédie by Mme. Elide Girardin.

[44]Musical numbers not listed in programs. List prepared from published French piano vocal score (G. Brandus, Dufour et Cie., Paris, [1856]).

[45]First produced in New York 25 November 1844 for 17 performances in repertory at the Park Theatre. For Synopsis of Scenes and Musical Numbers, see original 1844 production.

[46]English opera was presented twice weekly, Wednesday and Friday, or else Tuesday and Thursday. On alternate nights, a season of light opera was presented at the Park Theatre, Brooklyn.

[47]Preceded by the comedy by Charles Mathews, A Bull in a China Shop. MAZEPPA, or The Fiery, Untamed Rocking Horse was first produced in New York 14 January 1861 at the Winter Garden.

[48]Mazeppa, or the Wild Horse of Tartary, various adaptations by Andrew Ducrow or H. M. Milner.

an upright Pole: ?. *Arder Khan*, King of Tartary, a khan in very low water indeed: *Count Premislas*, Last of his race, and sole prop of an ancient line: *Drolinski*: *Rudzoloff*: *Thamar*, a rebellious chieftain: *Koscar, Kadac, Zemba*, regular Tartars: *Zemilla*, Olinska's tiring, not to say fatiguing, maid: . *Oneiza*, the maid with the milking pail: ?.

Scene 1: Courtyard of Laurinski Castle. *Scene 2*: The Saloon in the Laurinski Castle. *Scene 3*: The Wilds of Tartary. *Scene 4*: A Very Pretty Pass. *Scene 5*: Downfall of Evil and the final curtain.

1864.06 THE HOUSE THAT JACK BUILT

A Pantomime in ? Acts[49]. Play written and directed by George L. Fox. Music arranged and composed by A. Tyte. Scenery by J. R. Smith, R. S. Smith, R. L. Weed. Machinery by William Crane. Costumes by C. and A. Phillips. Properties by Nelse Waldron. Produced George L. Fox. Opened 25 January 1864 at Fox's Old Bowery Theatre and closed 5 March 1864 after 36 performances; returned 9 May 1864 to Fox's Old Bowery Theatre and closed 21 May 1864 after an additional 12 performances.

CAST: *Simon Slendershanks*, afterwards Clown: GEORGE L. FOX. *Boss Trowel*, afterwards Pantaloon: CHARLES K. FOX. *Jack Stout*, afterwards Harlequin: TONY DENIER. *Angelina*, afterwards Columbine: LOUISA BROWNE. *Other characters*: G. L. Fox's troupe of pantomimists. *Gnomes, Fairies, etc.*: Lilliputian Family.

1864.07 MARITANA

A Revival of the Light Opera in Three Acts[50]. (Libretto by Edward Fitzball. Based on the play "Don César de Bazan" by Adolphe d'Ennery and Philippe Dumanoir.) Music by Vincent Wallace. Director of cast, chorus and orchestra, Theodore Thomas. Produced by Harrison's English Opera Troupe (Gabriel Harrison, Manager). Opened 5 February 1864 at Niblo's Saloon in repertory[51]; season closed February 1864.

CAST: *Maritana*: Mme. COMTE BORCHARD. *Don Caesar de Bazan*: WILLIAM CASTLE. *Don José de Santarem*: Mr. S. C. CAMPBELL. *Charles II*, King of Spain: Mr. GEORGE REA. *Marquis de Montefiore*: R. G. FRANCE. *Lazarillo*: Miss Myers. *Captain of Guard*: Mr. Somers. *Lopez*: Mr. Florence. *Alcalde*: Mr. Post. *Marchioness de Montefiore*: Mrs. Burroughs. *Citizens, Gipsies, Lords and Ladies, Soldiers*: Full Chorus and Corps de Ballet.

1864.08 LE MARIAGE AUX LANTERNES

An Opérette in One Act, in French[52]. Libretto by Michel Carré and Léon Battu. Music by Jacques Offenbach. Produced by the Théâtre Français. Opened 6 February 1864 at Niblo's Saloon in repertory; season closed 30 April 1864.

CAST: *Guillot*: *Denise*: *Catherine*: *Fanchette*:
Company included Messrs. ERNEST GRAVIER, EDGARD, CHOL, ROCHE, DONATIEN, FAYE; Mmes. LEVASSEUR, ANNA HAMBURG, MAILLET, DONATIEN.

MUSICAL NUMBERS[53]

Couplets (Que dirait l'oncle Mathurin)
[Guillot]

Couplets (Mon cher mari)
[Catherine, Fanchette]

Trio (Eh bien, Guillot, quoi vous ne lisez pas!)
[Fanchette, Catherine, Guillot]

Chanson à boire (Quand les moutons sont dans la plaine)
[Guillot]

Duet (Ah! la fine, fine mouche)
[Fanchette, Catherine]

Quatuor de l'angélus (Voici l'angélus qui sonne)
[Denise, Guillot, Fanchette, Catherine]

Finale (Messieurs, la pièce est terminée)
Tous

1864.09 ILL TREATED IL TROVATORE!, or, The Mother, The Maiden and The Musicianer

An Original Burlesque, Extravagant Extravaganza founded on the famous but confusing opera of that name, in Two Acts[54]. Play by H. J. Byron. New music, including all the principal Gems from the Real Opera, arranged by Thomas Baker. Stage manager, J. H. Selwyn. Costumes by Cornelia Flannery. Musical director, Thomas Baker. Produced by Mrs. John Wood. Opened 8 February 1864 at the Olympic Theatre and closed 13 February 1864 after 6 performances.

CAST: *Manrico*, the original wandering minstrel, a real good fellow, though a true-bad-doer: Mrs. JOHN WOOD. *Count di Luna*, Count di Magistrate: Mr. W. DAVIDGE. *Fernando*, his creature: Mr. N. C. LAPAUGH. *Guard*: Mr. Peck. *The Kinchen*, a Gypsy thief, a Ticket of Leave: Mr. CHARLES T. PARSLOE, Jr. *Ruiz*: Mr. Walton. *Gipsy*: Mr. Bruccaini. *Azucena*, an elderly Gypsy party, with a great deal on her mind: Mr. FRANK DREW. *Leonora*, a ward of DiLuna's, eventually awarded to Manrico: Mrs. SEDLEY BROWN. *Inez*, Leonora's confidential Tire Woman: Miss Harris. *Gypsies, Guards and Attendants*.

Act 1: Exterior of the Count's Palace. By the Bay of Biscay.

Act 2: A Wood near a Finishing Academy. The Prison.

SPECIALTIES

Grand Terpsichorean Melange of Vengeance and Castanets (Act 1)

Grand Tarantella (Act 1)
Mrs. J. Wood, Mr. F. Drew

1864.10 LE VIOLONEUX

Légende bretonne (Opérette) in One Act[55], in French. (Libretto by Eugène Mestépès and Émile Chevalet.) Music by Jacques Offenbach. Produced by the Théâtre Français. Opened 11 February 1864 at Niblo's Saloon in repertory; season closed 30 April 1864.

CAST: *Le Père Mathieu*, violoneux: Mons. DONATIEN. *Pierre*, sabotier: Mons. EDGARD. *Reinette*, filleule du père Mathieu: Mlle. MAILLET.

MUSICAL NUMBERS[56]

Couplets (Je suis conscrit, conscrit)
Mons. Edgard

Mélodrame (La la la la)
Mons. Edgard

Couplets et Duo (J'sais bien que c'n'est pas l'usage)
Mlle. Maillet, Mons. Edgard

Ronde (Le violoneux du village)
Mons. Donatien

Duo (Le clarion sonne à la parade)
Mlle. Maillet, Mons. Donatien

Duo (Que vois-je ici que vois-je ici)
Mlle. Maillet, Mons. Edgard

Couplets (Je t'apporte la délivrance)
Mons. Donatien

Mélodrame et Final (Tout petit dans le village)
Tous

---

[49]A rival and altogether different production from that of the same name playing the American Theatre. Preceded by a drama, and followed by a farce.

[50]First produced in New York 4 May 1848 at the Bowery Theatre for 3 performances. For Synopsis of Scenes and Musical Numbers, see original 1848 production.

[51]English opera was presented twice weekly, Wednesday and Friday, or else Tuesday and Thursday. On alternate nights, a season of light opera was presented at the Park Theatre, Brooklyn.

[52]Followed by two after-pieces, Le Pour et Le Contre, a proverbe in one act by Octave Feuillet, and Le Caporal et La Payse, folie vaudeville in one act by Paul de Keck and Varin.

[53]Musical numbers not listed in program. List prepared from published French piano vocal score (Heugel, Paris, 1857).

[54]Suggested by the opera Il Trovatore, Music by Giuseppe Verdi. Preceded by a fore-piece, the petite comedy, Follies of a Night, with many of the same cast.

[55]On a triple bill, followed by La Ferme de Primrose, a comédie-vaudeville in one act by Cormon, and La Femme qui se Jette par la Fenêtre, a comédie-vaudeville in one act by Eugène Scribe.

[56]Musical numbers not listed in programs. List prepared from published French piano vocal score (Brandus et Cie., Paris, 1855).

1864.11

BA-TA-CLAN

Chinoiserie Musicale in One Act, in French[57]. Libretto by Ludovic Halévy. Music by Jacques Offenbach. Produced by the Théâtre Français. Opened 25 February 1864 at Niblo's Saloon in repertory; season closed 30 April 1864.

CAST: *Fé-ni-han*, Souverain de Ché-i-no-or: ?. *Ko-ko-ri-ko*, Capitaine des gardes de Fé-ni-han and Chef de la Conspiration: ?. *Ké-ki-ka-ko* de la suite de Fé-ni-han: ?. *Fé-an-nich-ton* de la suite de Fé-ni-han: ?. *Choeur des Conjurés*.

Virginie: *Alfred*: Company included Messrs. ERNEST GRAVIER, EDGARD, CHOL, ROCHE, DONATIEN, FAYE; Mmes. LEVASSEUR, ANNA HAMBURG, MAILLET, DONATIEN.

MUSICAL NUMBERS[58]

Choeur et Quatuor Chinois (Cloc Clock, moc mock, cloc clock)
Toutes les principals, Les Choeurs

Romance (J'étais aimable, élégante)
[Fé-an-nich-ton]

Duo (Te souviens-tu de la maison dorée)
[Fé-an-nich-ton, Ké-ki-ka-ko]

Couplets de Florette (Etes vous pauvre et plein d'ardeur)
[Fé-an-nich-ton]

Duo Italien (Morto morto infamio infamio morto)
[Fé-ni-han, Ké-ki-ka-ko]

Trio Bouffe (Je suis français)
[Fé-an-nich-ton, Fé-ni-han, Ké-ki-ka-ko]

Le Ba-ta-clan (Marseillaise chinoise)(Le chapeau chinois)
Tous, Les Chœurs

1864.12

LOYALINA,
or, Brigadier-General Fortunio, and His Seven Gifted Aides-de-Camp

An Extravaganza in Two Acts, 8 Scenes, adapted, adopted and conformed to Olympic wants, without leave or license from James Robinson Planché[59]. Music, selected and original, composed and arranged by Thomas Baker. Stage manager, J. H. Selwyn. Scenery by James E. Hayes. Costumes by Miss Cornelia Flannery. Properties by W. Henry. Machinery by C. Long. Produced by Mrs. John Wood. Opened 11 April 1864 at the Olympic Theatre and closed 30 April 1864 after 18 performances.

CAST: *Loyalina*, Daughter of Ex-Alderman Gotham, and afterwards Brigadier General Fortunio: MRS. JOHN WOOD. *Ex-Alderman Gotham*, too old to fight and much too poor to pay: Mr. T. OWENS. *Flirtina, Pertina*, two more of his amiable and fashionable daughters: Miss J. Walters, Mrs. Grener. *Fairy Policeman*, a Guardian of the Piece: Mrs. SEDLEY BROWN. *King Alwaysrite*, a King, not bad look-King: Mr. FRANK DREW. *Princess Vindietta*, sister to her brother the King: Miss A. Harris. *Prime Minister*: Mr. Berry. *Lord in Waiting*: Mr. Peck. *Florida*, own maid to the Princess: Mrs. Young. *Emperor Shoddy*, mixed up with contracts (rebel brother of King Alwaysrite): Mr. W. DAVIDGE. *Lord Chamberlain*: Mr. France. *Princess Volante*, with dance: Mrs. G. Browne.

The Seven Gifted Aides: *Lightfoot*: Mr. Charles T. Parsloe, Jr. *Strongback*: Mr. Neel. *Bositerer*: Mr. Vosburgh. *Sharpshooter*: Mr. Edwards. *Tippler*: Mr. Brucianni. *Fine Ear*: Mr. Hill. *Gormand*: Mr. Boys.

Act 1, Scene 1: Provost Marshal's Headquarters. *Scene 2*: Corridor in the Castle of King Alwaysrite. *Scene 3*: Roadway through Central Park. *Scene 4*: Castle of King Alwaysrite. *Scene 5*: Exterior of Castle and Fountain.

Act 2, Scene 1: Hall of the Emperor Shoddy. *Scene 2*: The Race Course. *Scene 3*: Reconciliation and Denouement.

ACT 1

"Brave Volunteers you must enroll" (Chorus)
Citizens

"When this cruel war is over" (Song)
Mrs. J. Wood

"Central Parkish Lawn" (Song)
Mrs. S. Brown

"Northern Refrain" (Song)
Mrs. J. Wood

"To the King's Court" (Chorus)
Mrs. J. Wood, Mrs. S. Brown, Aides

Medley Song
F. Drew

"The days when we went Typsying in" (Song)
F. Drew

"Sir, you can't refuse me" (Duet)
Mrs. J. Wood, Miss A. Harris

"The Dragon is coming" (Chorus)
Citizens

"Go where glory waits thee" (Concerted piece)
Mrs. J. Wood, F. Drew, Chorus

"Come fill every flagon" (Chorus)
Citizens

"She will of me a martyr make" (Finale)
Mrs. J. Wood, F. Drew, Citizens

ACT 2

Dance of the Princess Volante
Mrs. G. Browne

"I'm King of the Shoddy Contractors" (Song)
W. Davidge

"Brave Blue Coats" (Song)
Mrs. J. Wood

"The Bread Brigade" (Concerted)

"Come again tomorrow night" (Finale)

1864.13

FRA DIAVOLO,
or, The Beauty and the Brigands/ Thrice Married

A Laughable Burlesque Burletta in One Act, preceded by a comedietta. Burlesque by H. J. Byron. Music, mostly original, by John T. Cooke. Scenery by Mr. Bartholomew. Costumes by Mr. Bohannon. Properties by Mr. Sylvester. Machinery by Mr. Morgan. Produced by Mr. and Mrs. W. J. Florence. Opened 23 May 1864 at the Winter Garden and closed 18 June 1864 after 24 performances.

THRICE MARRIED, a protean comedietta written by Mrs. W. J. Florence.

CAST: *Vivian Ripple*, a painter: W. J. FLORENCE. *Horace Waddles*, a retired Ballet Master: Mr. Morris. *Jack Quaverly*, an Old Music Teacher: Mr. Hind. *Carlotta*, a Bal Masque Costumer, with the songs "Captain with his Whiskers," and "The Young Recruit": Mrs. W. J. FLORENCE. *Victorine Le Page*, An Opera Singer, with French song, "Les Yeux," and German song, "Dre Federn": Mrs. W. J. FLORENCE. *Senora Perea Nena*,a Spanish Dancer, with Grand Spanish Dance, La Sequadilla: Mrs. W. J. FLORENCE. *Gustavus Vasa*, a Cadet of the Zouave school: Mrs. W. J. FLORENCE. *Vivian's friends (8)*: Messrs. Howard, Jennings, Wilmot, Lecroix, Riley, Walsh, Dennison, Daly.

FRA DIAVOLO CAST: *Fra Diavolo*, alias the Marquis di Centre Market, an amiable and captivating Brigand, such as are seen nowhere save on the stage: Mrs. W. J. FLORENCE. *Beppo*, a particularly heavy ruffian, not troubled with the faintest outline of a conscience, or indeed anything but the hoarseness peculiar to melo-Dramatic Brigands: Mr. W. J. FLORENCE. *Lorenzo*, an officer of the Police, in fact an inn spectre, as he haunts the Inn collecting his sweetheart: VINING BOWERS. *Matteo*, landlord of the "Jolly Brigand:" E A. EBERLE. *Lord Allcash*, an English nobleman, making a tour of pleasure, and himself as agreeable as possible—the invariable custom of travelling Britons—the amiable darlings: T. E. Morris. *Giacomo*, a promising young Bandit: A. H. DAVENPORT. *Francesca*, an extensive young Farmer: Mr. Dennison. *Antonio*, a discontented paper: Mr. Riley. *Redwhiska*, another: Mr. Riley. *Zerlina* the Village Beauty, and Barkeeper at the "Jolly Brigand:" Mrs. F. CHANFRAU. *Lady Allcash*, a lady making her first tour, and though F—a D—o's, wiles her first trip: Mrs. Floyd. A *full corps de ballet* led by Miss Pulman.

MUSICAL NUMBERS

Opening Chorus, from FAUST
V. Bowers, E. A. Eberle, Carbineers

"There's a Monster who lives" (Descriptive Song and Chorus)
V. Bowers, Chorus

"Don't annoy me, oh!" (Duet)
T. E. Morris, Mrs. Floyd

---

[57]Followed by On Demande un Gouverneur, a comédie vaudeville in two acts by Decourcelle.

[58]Musical numbers not listed in programs. List prepared from published French piano vocal score (Léon Escudier, Paris, 1855).

[59]Preceded by a comic drama, Our Wife, or The Rose of Amiens, by J. M. Morton, Esq. In Two Acts.

"I'm in a dreadful state of mind" (Aria)
Mrs. Chanfrau
"Daylight Love" (Romanza)
Mrs. W. J. Florence
Drinking Song, from the opera THE PURITAN'S DAUGHTER
Mrs. W. J. Florence
(*Music by* Michael William Balfe.)
"On yonder rock reclining" (Duet)
Mrs. W. J. Florence, Mrs. Chanfrau
"'Tis hard to put the hand" (Duet)
Mr. W. J. Florence, A. H. Davenport
"Do not Jingle" (Concerted Piece)
All Hands
"Ah Key Lay" (Song)
A. H. Davenport
"Pop goes his Weasel" (Song)
Mr. W. J. Florence
"Gentle Zerlina" (Song)
Mrs. Chanfrau
"Hoopen de dooden do" (Concerted Piece)
Mrs. Chanfrau, Mr and Mrs. W. J. Florence
"Nelly Bly" (Concerted Piece)
Mrs. Chanfrau, T. E. Morris, Mrs. Floyd
"Let us leave Italy" (Duet)
T. E. Morris, Mrs. Floyd
Grand Chorus, "La Kermesse" from FAUST
(*Music by* Charles Gounod.)
Clothers' Chorus
Mr. W. J. Florence, A, H. Davenport, [Hurliani, Iberli]
"Dark girl dressed in blue" (Song)
Mrs. W. J. Florence
"Let me kiss him Yankee Doodle" (Song)
V. Bowers
Finale—U. S. G.
Everybody

1864.14

MISS LOTTA

Miss Lotta (Crabtree) the California Sensation (in a varying program of One-Act musical plays). Produced by Lotta (Crabtree). Acting manager, Harry Jordan. Opened 1 June 1864 at Niblo's Saloon and closed 4 June 1864 after 4 performances.

CAST: *Jenny Lind*, with songs, dances, etc.: Miss LOTTA (CRABTREE). *Granby Gag*: HARRY JORDAN. *Baron Swigitoff Beery*: A. W. Fenno. *Leatherlungs*: F. Rea. *Herr Scheroot*: J. E. Irving. *Herr Kanaster*: S. Johnston. *Students, etc.*

On 1 June 1864, Miss Lotta appeared in THE MYSTERIOUS CHAMBER, with songs and dances, and a Revival of the Operatic Burletta JENNY LIND[60]. Prior to JENNY LIND, Miss Lotta will perform a new local song and an Irish jig.

On 2 June 1864 Miss Lotta appeared in A DAY AFTER MARRIAGE, with banjo solos, and songs, followed by JENNY LIND.

On 3 June 1864 Miss Lotta appeared in A WIFE'S LESSON, with comic song, and Chinese Song, followed by OUR JEMIMY, with songs.

One 4 June 1864 Miss Lotta appeared in OUR JEMIMY, with Miss Lotta as Miss Topsey, in song and dance, followed by THE MAID OF MUNSTER.

1864.15

ALADDIN, or, The Wonderful Lamp

A Revival of the Grand, Romantic, Spectacular, Musical, Mechanical and Pantomimical Drama in Three Acts, 8 Scenes. Based on that ancient history of the Arabians, "The Thousand and One Nights." Music, Real, Descriptive and Pantomimical, composed and arranged on sound principles, expressly for the piece, by Thomas Baker. Scenery by James E. Hayes. Machinery by Charles Long. Costumes by Miss C. Flannery. Properties and Appointments by William Henry. Gas work by Martin O'Brien. Produced by Mrs. John Wood. Opened 2 June 1864 at the Olympic Theatre and closed 2 July 1864 after 27 performances.

CAST: *Aladdin*, his mother's pet, and an Anomaly, for though a "lively youth," he is a sad boy: Mrs. JOHN WOOD. *Abenazer*, a Magician in search of the Lamp: W. DAVIDGE. *The Grand Cham*, mighty Emperor of all Chinas: T. OWENS. *Azack*, the Vizier's son, enamoured of the Princess: GEORGE H. CLARKE. *The Vizier*: Mr. Boyd. *Kasrac*, the Dumb Slave: CHARLES T. PARSLOE, JR. *Orlock*: Mr. Berry. *Slave of the Lamp*: Mr. Fosburgh. *Slave of the Ring*: Miss C. Young. *Princess Badroulbadour*, this Princess was, in fact, a most beautiful brunette, &c., &c. vide "Arabian Nights": Miss J. WALTERS. *Zobyad*, her attendant, "her eyes were large, well-placed and full of fire," &c., &c.: Mrs. SEDLEY BROWN. *Amron*: Miss Mabel Giffort. *Widow Jing Jolly Gong*, Aladdin's mother, who, to quote the "Arabian Nights," was rather old, and who even in her youth had not possessed much beauty: J. H. STODDART.

Act 1, Scene 1: Cave of the Magician, Abenazer. *Scene 2*: Street in Pekin. *Scene 3*: Apartment of the Princess Badroulbadour. *Scene 4*: The Blasted Cedar and Mountains of the Moon. *Scene 5*: The Jewelled Cavern.

Act 2, Scene 1: Cottage of the Widow Jing Jolly Gong. *Scene 2*: The Royal Baths; the Bridges of the Grand Cham.

Act 3: Exterior of Aladdin's Palace. Egypt, and interior of Aladdin's palace. Return of the Palace to China.

SPECIALTIES, MUSICAL NUMBERS
Grand Procession of Aladdin and his Suite (Act 2, Scene 2)

1864.16

MARITANA

A Revival of the Light Opera in Three Acts[61]. (Libretto by Edward Fitzball. Based on the play "Don César de Bazan" by Adolphe d'Ennery and Philippe Dumanoir.) Music by Vincent Wallace. Manager, Ben A. Baker. Musical director, Anthony Rieff. Produced by Mrs. John Wood. Opened 4 July 1864 at the Olympic Theatre in repertory; closed 9 July 1864 after 6 performances.

CAST: *Maritana*: Mme. COMTE BORCHARD. *Don Caesar de Bazan*: WILLIAM CASTLE. *Don José de Santarem*: S. C. CAMPBELL. *Charles II*, King of Spain: Mr. J. CLARK. *Marquis de Montefiore*: WARREN WHITE. *Lazarillo*: Miss LOUISA MYERS. *Marchioness de Montefiore*: Mrs. M. E. BURROUGHS. Full Chorus.

1864.17

MAZULM, or, The Night Owl

A Revival of the Ballet Pantomime in One Act. Ballet master, M. A. Grossi. Scenery by George Heilge. Properties by Robert Cutler. Machinery by Charles Burns. Wardrobe by Robert Walker. Gas effects by William Wilson. Produced by Phineas T. Barnum. Opened 11 July 1864 at Barnum's Museum and closed 6 August 1864 after 48 performances.[62]

Previous to the pantomime, J. H. Clifford, Negro Melodist, will appear in new song and dance.

CAST: *Barriano*: CHARLES K. FOX. *Emile*: GEORGE DAVENPORT. *Maclou*: TONY DENIER. *Doctor Dunderberg*: M. A. GROSSI. *Cavoussa*: J. Lewis. *Mazulm*, the Night Owl: J. M. HUGHES. *Pasto*: Mr. Anderson. *Pedro*: Mr. Castello. *Gasco*: Mr. Davis. *Lopez*: Mr. Leman. *Jean*: Mr. Wilcox. *François*: Mr. Hunter. *Antoine*: Mr. Stevens. *Mariana*: Miss Dulany. *Julie*: Mlle. ERNESTINE. *Janet*: Miss Law. *Ladies, Nuns, Market Women*: Numerous Corps de Ballet.

Clown: TONY DENIER. *Pantaloon*: C. K. FOX. *Harlequin*: GEORGE DAVENPORT. *Columbine*: Mlle. ERNESTINE.

Scenes: Cemetery of a Cathedral changing to a Grand Palace of Pillars. Road near Cadiz. Neapolitan Market Scene. Restaurant and Picture Gallery. Abode of Mazulm, the Night Owl. Resplendent Halls of Light and Abode of Happiness. Gorgeous Pantomimic Tableau.

---

[60]Preceded by the petite comedy, The Mysterious Chamber, with A. W. Fenno, G. Metkiff, Harry Jordan, J. E. Irving, Mrs. H. Jordan, and Mrs. Mark Smith.

[61]First produced in New York 4 May 1848 at the Bowery Theatre for 3 performances. For Synopsis of Scenes and Musical Numbers, see original 1848 production.

[62]Performed twice daily; no credits for music, etc.

FRA DIAVOLO, or, The Inn of Terracina

1864.18

A Revival of the Romantic Opera in Three Acts[63]. Original French libretto (to the Opéra-comique 'Fra Diavolo, or L'Hotellerie de Terracina') by Eugène Scribe. English adaptation by Rophino Lacy. Music by Daniel Auber. Manager, Ben A. Baker Musical director, Anthony Rieff. Produced by Mrs. John Wood. Opened 11 July 1864 at the Olympic Theatre in repertory; closed 16 July 1864 after 6 performances.

CAST: *Zerlina*: Mme. COMTE BORCHARD. *Lady Allcash*: Miss LOUISA MYERS. *Fra Diavolo*, disguised as the Marquis San Carlo: WILLIAM CASTLE. *Lorenzo*: WALTER BIRCH. *Lord Allcash*: Mr. J. W. NEEL. *Beppo, Giacomo*, Two Italian bandits: Messrs. S. C. Campbell, Warren White. *Matteo*, Zerlina's father: J. Clarke. *First Carbineer*: Mr. W. Skaats. *Francisco*: Mr. Peck. *Carbineers, Villagers, Male and Female*: Ladies and Gentlemen of the Chorus and Corps de Ballet.

THE BOHEMIAN GIRL

1864.19

A Revival of the Light Opera in Three Acts[64]. (Libretto by Alfred Bunn, after Jules-Henri Vernoy de Saint-Georges' ballet-pantomime "The Gypsy.") Music by Michael William Balfe. Manager, Ben A. Baker. Musical director, Anthony Rieff. Produced by Mrs. John Wood. Opened 18 July 1864 at the Olympic Theatre in repertory; closed 26 July 1864 after 8 performances.

CAST: *Arline*: Mme. COMTE BORCHARD. *Thaddeus*: Mr. WILLIAM CASTLE. *Count Arnheim*: Mr. S. C. CAMPBELL. *Florestein*, his nephew: Mr. WALTER BIRCH. *Devilshoof*: Mr. WARREN WHITE. *Captain of the Guard*: Mr. Peck. *Gypsey Queen*: Miss LOUISA MYERS. *Buda*: Mrs. M. E. Burroughs. (*Dance Specialty*, Pas Seul: Miss Anna Kreuger.) *Gipsies, Peasants, Retainers, etc.*: Ladies and Gentlemen of the Chorus and Corps de Ballet.

THE ROSE OF CASTILE

1864.20

A Romantic Opera in Three Acts. Libretto by Augustus Harris and Edmund Falconer. Music by Michael William Balfe. Manager, Ben A. Baker. Musical director, Anthony Rieff. Produced by Mrs. John Wood. Opened 27 July 1864 at the Olympic Theatre in repertory; season closed 30 July 1864 after 4 performances.

CAST: *Elvira*, the Rose of Castile: Mme. COMTE BORCHARD. *Donna Carmen*: Miss LOUISA MYERS. *Beatrice*, Duchess of Calatrava: Mrs. M. E. Burroughs. *Manuel*, a Muleteer: WILLIAM CASTLE. *Don Pedro*: S. C. CAMPBELL. *Don Florio de Santa Cruz*: W. H. LEAK. *Don Sallust*: WALTER BIRCH. *Pablo*: Mr. J. Clark. *Dance Specialty*: Miss ANNA KRUGER. *Ladies of Honor, Nobles, Conspirators, Guards, Peasants, etc.*

Act 1: The Court Yard of a Spanish Posada.

Act 2: Throne Room of the Palace of Valladolid.

Act 3: The Queen's Oratory in the Palace.

ACT 1[65]

Solo and Chorus (List to the gay castanet)
J. Clark, Chorus

Duettino (Your pardon, Señors)
C. Borchard, L. Myers

Scherzo (Yes, I'll obey)
C. Borchard, Chorus

Song (I am a simple muleteer)
W. Castle

Song (Keep thy heart for me)
W. Castle

Duet (Dost thou fear me?)
C. Borchard, W. Castle

Bacchanalian Trio (For wine's sake)
W. Birch, W. H. Leak, S. C. Campbell

Quartet (In every feature like the Queen)
C. Borchard, W. Birch, W. H. Leak, S. C. Campbell

Rondo Mauresque (Oh, were I the Queen of Spain)
C. Borchard, W. Birch, Don W. H. Leak, Don S. C. Campbell

Finale (Decide! Decide!)
Principals, Chorus

ACT 2

Chorus and Solo (The Queen's in the Palace)

Ballad (Though fortune o'er me darkly frowns)
S. C. Campbell

Chorus and Solo (Hail! All honor to our Queen)
C. Borchard, W. Birch, W. H. Leak, S. C. Campbell, Chorus

Ballad (The Convent Cell)(Of girlhood's happy days I dream)
C. Borchard

Concerted Piece (We are alone)
C. Borchard, W. Castle, L. Myers, Mrs. M. E. Burroughs, Chorus

Buffo Duet (Go quickly, bring the maid)
W. H. Leak, S. C. Campbell

Aria di Bravura (I'm but a simple peasant maid)
C. Borchard

Finale (Fear not, tho' danger threaten you)
Principals, Chorus

ACT 3

Ballad (Though love's the greatest plague in life)
L. Myers

Duet (The Queen my presence doth require)
L. Myers, W. H. Leak

Recitative and Aria (At last I'm Sov'reign here)
C. Borchard

Ballad ('Twas rank and fame that tempted thee)
W. Castle

Recitative and Aria (Hark! the clarion sounding)
S. C. Campbell

Finale (Assembling all, assembling all)
Principals, Chorus

THE ROSE OF CASTILE

1864.21

A Revival of the Comic Musical Drama (Romantic Opera) in Two Acts[66]. Libretto by Augustus Harris and Edmund Falconer. Music by Michael William Balfe. Stage manager, J. H. Selwyn. Scenery by James E. Hayes. Costumes by W. Bullock. Properties by W. Henry. Mechanical department by W. Sanders. Orchestra under the direction of Thomas Baker. Produced by Mrs. John Wood. Opened 2 November 1864 at the Olympic Theatre in repertory.

CAST: *Don Pedro*: T. B. BERRY. *Don Scipio*: T. J. HIND. *Count Torribio de Pompolo*: WILLIAM HOLSTON. *Manuel*, a Muleteer: B. T. RINGGOLD. *Pablo*, Keeper of a Posado: Mr. Williams. *Jose*: Mr. Rockwell. *Elvira*, Queen of Murcia (the Rose of Castile): Mrs. JOHN WOOD. *Donna Carmen*, her confidante: Miss LOUISA MYERS. *Countess de Pompolo*, Principal Lady of the Bedchamber: Mrs. G. H. GILBERT. *Dance Specialty*, Act 2: Miss ANNA KRUGER. *Courtiers, Ladies, Officers, Peasantry, etc.*

THE RING OF FATE, or, Fire, Air, Earth and Water

1864.22

A Musical Fairy Romance in Three Acts, interspersed with Diablerie, Enchantment, Dances, Music and Startling Effects, preceded by a variety program. New and original music composed by F. W. Peterschen. Scenery by George Heilge. Properties by Robert Cutler. Mechanism by Charles Burns. Wardrobe by Robert S. Walker. Calcium and gas effects by J. Wilson.

[63]First produced in New York in English as The Devil's Brother 20 June 1833 at the Park Theatre.

[64]First produced in New York 25 November 1844 for 17 performances in repertory at the Park Theatre. For Synopsis of Scenes and Musical Numbers, see original 1844 production.

[65]Musical numbers not listed in programs. List prepared from published English piano vocal score (Cramer & Co., London, 1858).

[66]First produced in New York 27 July 1864 at the Olympic Theatre in repertory; for Synopsis of Scenes and Musical Numbers, see entry at that date. Preceded by a farce in two acts, Bull in a China Shop.

Produced under the entire direction of E. F. Taylor. Produced by Phineas T. Barnum. Opened 26 December 1864 at Barnum's Museum, closing 14 January 1865; resumed 6 February 1865 and closed 11 February 1865 after (40) performances in repertory[67].

Opening variety: Miss Jennie Stone, the Scottish Queen, aged 18, 24 inches high. The Indians in their War Dances and Songs. W. B. Harrison, the celebrated comic and extemporaneous figure, in hist at the times and people. Sawnee, the Musical Contraband will appear in his imitation of an organ, hurdy gurdy, thrashing machines, etc.

CAST: *Mortals: Arnulph*, Knight of Bohemia: W. L. JAMIESON. *Rodolph*, Knight of Nassau: B. C. PORTER. *Rupert*, Knight of Britain: J. BRIDGEMAN. *Otto*, Knight of Saxony: E. HAVILAND. *Adolph, Conrade, Edric and Louis*, their Esquires: Messrs. Anderson, Keppel, Stevens, Richmond. *Herbert*, a Page as the Minstrel of Cassel: Mrs. J. J. Prior. *Franco*, his Brother, a Charcoal Burner: L. J. Mestayer. *Jonas Barefoot*, a Yankee: R. France. *Bibo*, a host: Mr. Brown. *Peasants, Yankees, Indians, Quakers, Firemen*: Numerous Auxiliaries. *Princess Eveline*, under the spells of Godah: Jennie Cleaver. *Lecia*, her attendant, an Enchantress Enchanted: Mrs. W. L. Jamieson. *Indian Squaws*: Misses Law, Thompson. *Sicilian Peasants, American Ladies*: Corps de Ballet.

Spirits of the Coral Cave: Coralie, the Naiad: Harriet Walby. *Attendant Maids*: Misses C. Monell, Addie LeBrun, Fenton, Germaine, Anson, Law, Evers, Burts, etc. *Fairy Haida*, Spirit of the Ring of Fate: LAURA GRAHAM. *Whirlibug*, Spirits of the Ring: TONY DENIER.

Immortals: Godah, Wizard of the Four Elements: MILNES LEVICK. *Oscaloosa*, an Indian Chief: MILNES LEVICK. *Isaac of Brescia*, a Pedlar: MILNES LEVICK. *Storm Spirit of Niagara*: Nannie Kook. *Friends of Elna, Gnomes of the Diamond Cavern, Water Monsters*: Messrs. Hunter, Stevens, Keppel, Anderson, Chatterson, Richmond, James, Beebe, etc. *Black Knight*, a Magician: [MILNES LEVICK].

Scenes: Sicilian Landscape, Elna in the distance. Caverns of the Brazen Hand, Illuminated Temple of the Ring of Fate. Charcoal Burners' Hut. Realms of Godah, the Fire King. Lava Hills of Etna and Burning Mountain. Falls of Niagara and Abode of the Mist Spirit which changes by a mechanical illusion to the Grotto Palace of the Naiads and Lake of Translucent Light. Cave of Gems in the Valley of Diamonds. Fairy Staircase and Elfin Gallery. Italian Vineyard—Forest of the Rider Cloud Palace of the Fairy World abode of the elements and Temple of Revolving Lights. Fire! Air!! Earth!!! and Water!!!!

ACT 1

"Tho' we are worsted" (Solo)
W. L. Jamieson
"The Stirrup Cup" (Chorus)
"Minstrel of Cassel" (Song)
Mrs. J. J. Prior
"It is! It is! That child of Song" (Chorus)
"Master! Master! We are ready" (Demonical Chorus)
"What fury rends his heart" (Quartette and Chorus)
"Despair! Despair!" (Grand Chorus)

ACT 2

"Floating o'er yon silvery tide" (Quartette of Fairy Chorus)

ACT 3

"Laugh, Brothers, Laugh" (Chorus of Gnomes)
"Gianetta" (Song)
Mrs. W. L. Jamieson
"Up with the Sun" (Solo)
Mr. Bridgman
"Deeds of Death" (Chorus)
"Hail to the Beauteous and the Bold" (Grand Finale)

1864.23 HARLEQUIN BLUEBEARD, or, The Good Fairy Preciosa and the Bad Demon Rustifusti

An Original, Comical, Oratorical, Quizzical, Farcical, Diabolical, Allegorical Christmas Pantomime in Two Acts, 7 Scenes, preceded by an Equestrian and Gymnastic program. Musical conductor, Mr. H. Wayrauch. Director of Amusements, James M. Nixon. Opened 26 December 1864 at the Hippotheatron and closed 11 February 1865 after 56 performances.

ACT 1: Equestrian and Gymnastic Divertissement

Grand Equestrian Entrée, 'Knights and Ladies of Palestine'
Ten Star Riders
Gymnastic, 'Grand Drawing Room Act'
Le Petit Giorga and François Siegrist
Juggling on Horseback
Mr. N. Austin
Acrobatic, 'Ground and Lofty Tumbling Act'
Company
Equestrian, 'Graceful and Classical Act on a Bare-backed Steed'Mme. Louise Tournaire
Equine Intelligence and Education, exemplified by the highly trained horse, General Scott
Calisthenic, 'La Tranca Espagnol'
Mr. James Cooke
Equestrian, 'Grand Somersault Act'
Mr. R. Stickney
Grand Equestrian Act, 'La Haute École de la Manège'
Mme. Louise Tournaire.

ACT 2

HARLEQUIN BLUEBEARD CAST: *Abomelique, The Abominable*, commonly called Blue Beard, for the cogent reason that his beard was blue; the great original lady-killer, in esse and posse, alternately uxorious and furious; the inventor of Polygamy and Mormonism, who having arrived at the Matrimonial years of discretion, and dispatched twenty-one wives, takes unto himself Mrs. B. No. 22, and finds her too many for him (afterwards Clown): Mr. N. AUSTIN. *Rustifusti, the Wicked Wizard*, Blue Beard's Backer, the indispendable Evil One of all pantomimes, the terror of all good wives and marriageable maidens, and the consequent friend of flinty-hearted husbands, who put Abomelique up to snuff and then deserts him at a pinch: Mr. R. ELLINGHAM. *Electra*, his head Devil, with a phosphoric tail, the original man with a black bag: Mr. J. HANKINS. *Secon Devil*, in the kitchen cabinet: Mr. C. Devere. *Ibrahim*, the jolly old Turkish gardener, father of Fatima, the sair and fat, who has one eye on Blue Beard as a son-in-law, and the other on carrots, without any fear of B.B. severing his daughter's caroti-id artery: Mr. JOHN FOSTER. Afterwards, *Pantaloon*: Mr. FRANÇOIS SIEGRIST. *Selim*, Miss Fatima's young man, who is remarkably sweet upon her, and is naturally disgusted with the idea of her becoming Mrs. B No. 22, is therefore bent on cooking Abomelique's goose in the most approved fashion: Mr. J. COOK. Afterwards, *Harlequin*: M. CARRON. *Preciosa*, the good Fairy, very precious indeed to all young lovers, the paternal protectress of injured innocence, and though a good fairy Blue Beard's evil genius: Miss JULIA. *Fatima*, Ibrahim's "one of two fair daughters," violently attached to young Selim, but detached from him by her father's mandate, who has sold her to Blue Beard, which she regards as a very cruel sell indeed; the beau-ideal of her sex, curiosity included—a young lady much given to stopping out o'nights (in the paternal balcony,) hooking it there whilst her dad is smoking his hookah and taking his hot tod; a model miss, who loves both well and wisely, and is never better pleased than when her lover sings "Fat-am-I, Fat-am-I, See-limbs here, dost thou not hear love's call?": Mrs. SOYER. Afterwards *Columbine*: MARIETTA ZANFRETTA. *Mrs. Bluebeard No. 1*, a model spiritual wife, minus her head, which she carries in her market basket: Miss LYONS. *Blue Beard's other twenty defunct wives by as many eligible young ladies. Blue Beard's twenty-one children, various sized PLEDGES of affection left in pawn by his defunct wives to be redeemed by Mrs. Blue Beard No. 22, each of them the very image of his cruel father. Fairies, Imps of darkness, with heller-itish ways, Guards, Slaves, Ambassadors, Palanquin Bearers, Men-at-Arms with good legs, banner Bearers, etc.*: Corps de Ballet of Fifty Ladies and Gentlemen.

Characters in the Comic Scenes: Harlequin: M. CARRON. *Columbine*: MARIETTA ZANFRETTA. *Pantaloon*: FRANÇOIS SIEGRIST. *Clown*: N. AUSTIN. *Sprite*: Master R. STICKNEY. *Santa Claus*: Herr Knickerbocker. *Fishermen, Bakers, Piemen, Dandies, Hodmen, Soldiers, Vegetable Merchants, Young Ladies, Servant Girls, New York Mounted Policemen, Tar Men, Butchers, Sedan Chairmen, Crying Babies, etc.*: Company and Auxiliaries. *The Mad Bull*, in a furious rage: Sig. Taurus.

Act 1, Scene 1: The Winter Quarters of Rustifusti. *Scene 2*: Exterior of Blue Beard's Castle, and outside view of the Blue Chamber.

Act 2, Scene 1: Grand Magical Transformation. *Scene 2*: A Hotel, good accomodation for man and beast. *Scene 3*: A well known street. *Scene 4*: A comfortable kitchen. *Scene 5*: Barber's Shop.

1865.01 OLD DAME TROT AND HER COMICAL CAT

A Comic Pantomime in One Act, 12 Scenes.[68] Pantomime by George L. Fox. New scenery and costumes. The whole produced under the supervision

[67]Performed twice daily in its initial engagement, evenings only on its return engagement

[68]Accompanied by a drama, Michael Erle.

and direction of the author, George L. Fox. Produced by George L. Fox. Opened 30 January 1865 at Fox's Bowery Theatre and closed 25 March 1865 after 56 performances.

OLD DAME TROT CAST: *Sappy Saponaceous*, alias "John, the Piper's Son, who stole a Pig and away he run"—afterwards Clown: GEORGE L. FOX. *Antiquated Solderwell*, alias "Jack Sprat, who could eat no fat"—afterwards Pantaloon: CHARLES K. FOX. *John Stout*, alias "The Little Boy Blue, come blow your horn"—afterwards Harlequin: Mons. BAPTISTINE. *Little Bo-Peep*, "Who lost her sheep, and don't know where to find them"—afterwards Columbine: Mlle. MARTINETTI. *Old Dame Trot*: J. McCLOSKEY. *Flibberty Gibbet*, her Comical Cat, and a capital Mouser: Master TIMOTHY. *Mother Hubbard*: Miss Ward. *Mother Goose*: Miss Law. *Robin, the Bobbin*, "The big-bellied Ben, who ate more meat than four-score men": J. Coburn. *Pat O'Brien*, an Irishman: S. Bradshaw. *Lunch*, a Landlord: J. Bilchler. *Ben Cat-Head*, a Blockade Runner: H. Johnstone. *Jack Bobstay, Harry Bluff, Bill Adams*, Sailors of the Union: Messrs. Hammond, Sanford, F. Hofele. *Wheatley*, a dusty Miller, native of Flour-sack-ony: Mr. May. *Laidupinport*, host of the Sailor's Home: Mr. Waxemall. *Grass*, the Straw man: Mr. Bailey. *Nigger Joe*, the Soup man: J. Lewis. *Holdfast*, a Policeman: Mr. Whitmore. *V. Cutlet*, a dealer in Meat: Mr. Suit. *Greens*, a dealer in Vegetables: Mr. Weed. *Look-alive, Tusty, Toby of Ale, 'Alf and 'Alf*, waiters: —. *Peasants, Witches, Passengers, etc.*

Columbia, the Gem of the Ocean: Miss S. WILLIAMS. *Love*: Miss Wall. *Joy*: Miss Fenton. *Mirth*: Miss Finton. *Happiness*: Miss Allyne. *Hope*: Miss Josephs. *Dame Fridgetswither*: Miss Jaw. *Helen Urether Snowdrop*: Miss Fair. *Janet*: Miss Martin.

Scene 1: The Caverns of Gloom, near the Slough of Despond, in the Regions of Despair. *Scene 2*: Harvest Home, Katonah, the residence of the Faithful Lovers. Grand Transformation. *Scene 3*: Street. *Scene 4*: Interior of Hotel. *Scene 5*: Gold-Beaters' Street. *Scene 6*: Bull' Head. *Scene 7*: Rustic Street. *Scene 8*: Hotel. *Scene 9*: Village Landscape. *Scene 10*: Market. *Scene 11*: Blue Cave. *Scene 12*: Enchanted Temple in the Realms of Fairyland; Concentrations of Flying Corrusctions, surrounded with Rays of Prismatic Light; The Crystal Globe; Home of the Flying Mercury.

BALLETS, SPECIALTIES

Dance Characteristic (Scene 1)

Pas de Deux (Scene 2)
Mlle. Martinetti, Mons. Baptistine

Village Hornpipe (Scene 2)
Mlle. Martinetti

Transformation and Grand Tableau (Scene 12)

MOTHER GOOSE! and the Fairy Legend of the Golden Egg

1865.02

A Comical, Oratorical, Quizzical, Farcical, Diabolical, Allegorical Pantomime in One Act, 9 Scenes[69]. Conductor, H. Wayrauch. Produced by James M. Nixon. Opened 13 February 1865 at the Hippotheatron and closed 27 March 1865 after 49 performances.

CAST (in the Opening): *Papillon*, the Fairy Queen: Miss JULIA, afterwards changed to *Mother Goose*: Mr. ELLINGHAM. *Rosebud*, Captain of the fairy Light Guard: Miss Soyer. *Colinette*, the maid of many Lovers, afterwards Columbine: MARIETTA ZANFRETTA. *Squire Avaro*, an Avaricious Old Hunks, in love with Colinette, a leading gold speculator, more "Bear than Bull:" Mr. FOSTER. *Colin*, a nice young Man, Colinette's own true Loveyer," afterwards Harlequin: Mr. ODELL. *Pedro*, another "Loveyer" of Colinette, afterwards Pero: M. CARRON. *Father Miller*, Colinette's Guardian, who buys a Goose and Gets sold himself: FRANÇOIS SIEGRIST. *Bumble*, the Beadle: Mr. C. Devere. *The Wonderful Goose*, all Fuss and Feathers, ever laying the Golden Egg, a high priced article in the Poultry Line: Mons. BAPTISTE. *The Fairy Light Guard*, who support Arms, and are great on their legs, never refusing to Toe the mark, by a Full Corps de Ballet of Lightning Eyed Young Ladies.

CAST (in the Comic Scenes): *Clown*: M. CARRON. *Harlequin*: Mr. ODELL. *Senor Pontoloon*; FRANÇOIS SIEGRIST. *Columbine*: MARIETTA ZANFRETTA. *The Great Rush-in-Giant*: Scount Scarem-off. *Milly*, "The Maid with the Milking Pail:" Mlle. ANGELIQUE. *The Great Bear, Ursus Major*: Master Burt. *The Mob*: The Guard Mob-ile.

Scene 1: The Home of the Fairies in the Asteroid Hemisphere of the Milkey Whey. *Scene 2*: The Mill and the Millers. *Scene 3*: A Farm Yard and a Valuable Haystack. *Scene 4*: The Private Library of a Bibliotheque. *Scene 5*: A Public Market. *Scene 6*: A Cosey Kitchen. *Scene 7*: The Paternal Home of "My Uncle." *Scene 8*: A Well-Known Street. *Scene 9*: The Realms of Light. The Magic Railroad. Effulgent Temple of the Fairy Queen and her Radiant Court. Grand Allegorical Tableau. The Bower of Beauty and the Home of Love.

[69]Preceded by a variety program of equestrian acts.

BALLETS, SPECIALTIES

Grand Fairy Ballet (Scene 1)
Fairy Light Guard, led by Mlle. Angelique

The Magical Transformation (Scene 1)

Fairy Chorus of Invisible Singers (Scene 2)

Magic Transformation of the Haystack to Fairy Bower of Roses (Scene 3)

The Harlequinade Transformation (Scene 3)

Grand Allegorical Tableau (Scene 9)

PETROLIAMANIA, or, Oil on the Brain

1865.03

A Local Burlesque in One Act, 4 Scenes, preceded by an Olio. Play by Charles Gayler. Stage manager, Cool White. Conductor, F. R. Mollenhauer. Scenery by Gaspard Maeder. Produced by Henry Wood. Opened 6 March 1865 at Wood's Minstrel Hall and closed 13 May 1865 after 51 performances[70].

Olio: Opening Chorus, Semiramide, Wood's Minstrels. Rock Me to Sleep, Mother, W. D. Corrister. Drafted into the Army, J. W. Glenn. The Song of Enoch Arden, C. G. Lockwood. The Peace Commissioners, S. S. Purdy. The Prisoner's Hope, C. Henry. Guard Finale, Wood's Minstrels.

Varieties: Happy Uncle Tom!, Frank Bower, accompanied on the banjo by Frank Converse. Grand Pas Seul, "La Bayadère," M. Lewis. Looney Napoleon, S. S. Purdy. Come Where My Love Lies Dreaming, C. Henry, C. G. Lockwood, J. W. Glenn, H. Schwicardi. Banjo Obligato, with imitations of the chimes of the Trinity Church Bells, Frank Converse. Mississippi, Fling, S. S. Purdy. Favorite Dance, M. Lewis.

CAST: *Pete Trollem*, the Demon King of the Oil Regions: FRANK BROWER. *Oleagenons Trap*, a Darkey that's struck Ile, a Millionaire, formerly a Boot Black: COOL WHITE. *Chic N. West*, a heavy dealer in stocks: S. S. PURDY. *Job S. Turkey*, an unfortunate speculator, "bought over his margin": J. W. GLENN. *Michigan Central, Cumberland Coal, Mariposa*, Oil speculators: Messrs. C. Henry, F. Converse. H. Schwicardi. *Johannes Jerome*, Pete's favorite Imp, and Superintendant of the Oil Works in the Lower Regions: C. G. Lockwood. *The Red Spirit*, Petroleum Imp, with Demon Dance: M. Lewis. *The Green Monster*: W. D. Corrister. *Specialty*: Sheridan and Mack.

Scene 1: William Street. Merchants' Exchange. *Scene 2*: A Cave. Pete's Ante-chamber. *Scene 3*: Swamp Angel Crevice. *Scene 4*: Petrolia.

MUSICAL NUMBERS, SPECIALTIES

Scene 1
"Bulls and Bears come get along" (Song)
"I've struck Ile" (Song)
"I'm Hunkey Dorey" (Song and Chorus)
"I know, I spose, whar de Oil Well flows" (Duet)
"Johnny, how do you flow?" (Chorus)

Scene 2
"How are you, Old Petroleum?" (Chorus)

Scene 3
"I'se Johannes Jerome, oh! oh!" (Song and Dance)

Scene 4
"Grease 'em, squeeze 'em" (Chorus)
"We're pumping up de Ile" (Chorus)
Grand Tableau

THE FAIRY PRINCE O'DONOUGHUE, or, the White Horse of Killarney

1865.04

An Entirely New, Grand Spectacular and Comic Pantomime in One Act, 9 Scenes, preceded by an Equestrian and Gymnastic Divertissement. Music composed and arranged by H. Wayrauch. Processions, Dances and Marches by Signor Ronzani. Scenery by Mr. Bruce. Costumes by Mrs. Lehman. Properties and appointments by Mr. Wallace, Mr. Hodo. Machinery by Mr. Demilt. Magical Tricks and Transformations by M. Lehman. Produced (and

[70]All New York Theatres closed following the assassination of President Lincoln on 14 April 1865; performances resumed 26 April 1865.

conceived) under the stage direction of M. Lehman. Conductor, H. Wayrauch. Director of Amusements, James M. Nixon. Opened 3 April 1865 at the Hippotheatron and closed 13 May 1865 after 36 performances[71].

ACT 1: Equestrian and Gymnastic Divertissement

Equestrian, 'Grand Oriental Entre'
Company

Gymnastic, 'The Athlete and his Pupil'
François Siegrist, La Petite Giorga

The Olympians
George Batchelor, Mr. Hankins

Equilibria, 'The Corde Tendue'
Marietta Zanfretta

Equestrian, 'Great Hurdle Act'
Young Carpenter

Gymnastic, 'The Mid-Air Trapeze'
The Delavanti Brothers

Equestrian, 'Great Barebacked Act'
Eaton Stone

ACT 2

THE FAIRY PRINCE O'DONOUGHUE CAST: *O'Donoughue*, the Fairy Prince: Mlle. ROSA CERITO. *Coralina*, the Fairy Equery of the Coral Stables: Miss JULIA. *Potheen*, the Evil Spirit: Mr. J. RIVERS. *The Hag of Mischief*: Mr. J. FOSTER. *Dermot Asthore*, afterwards Harlequin: M. CARRON. *Lord Bullfrog*, afterwards Clown: Mr. N. AUSTIN. *Blousabella Brisket*, afterwards Pantaloon: Mr. HARTLAND. *Kathleen Mavourneen*, afterwards Columbine: MARIETTA ZANFRETTA.

The Demon Toads, Staff Officers of the Hag of Mischief: Masters Henry, Charles, James, William, Edward and Thomas. *Fiends*: Messrs. Webbe, Carpenter, Smith, Messenger, Bachelor, Ashton. *Huntsmen*: Messrs. Oliver, Huntley, August and Barton. *The Amazonian Guard*: Grand Corps de Ballet of 24 Ladies.

Scene 1: The Glen of Mischief. *Scene 2*: The Coral Home of O'Donoughue. *Scene 3*: Lodge of Lord Bullfrog's House. *Scene 4*: May Day in the Hills of Killarney. *Scene 5*: The Encampment of the Fairy Light Guard. Comic Pantomimic Transformation. Comic Scenes: *Scene 6*: Lord Bullfrog's Mansion; a new suitor for Kathleen's hand; a bold warrior; a great Don: Gyges explained. *Scene 7*: Grand Masquerade and Carnival; Harlequin and Columbine in Masque; Columbine turns up Giantess; Rescue by the Don; Harlequin changes to Dwarf; comic Manquet; Harlequin condemned to be shot; How to escape the draft; the fiends leap with Columbine; Clown turns Pugilist; gets one "on the Smeller," à la Heenan. *Scene 8*: A Restaurant; Dinner for two; portrait gets hungry; first of May; moveable furniture; patent press and its effects; a prize Doctor; no cure, no pay; New Way to Pay Old Debts; the Doctor's Ghost. *Scene 9*: Uncle Moses' Institution; Clown on guard; Food for an Italian; caught by a red back; wanted a loan; "Oh! my prophetic soul, my Uncle;" bad digestion; Uncle Sam's Protectors; Harlequin in a tight space; Powder Telegraph; effects of sticking plaster; The Lovers caught; Bad Spirit on Hand; appearance of O'Donoghue. Grand Finale. O'Donoghue's Body Guard; Grand Fairy Ballet.

[71]All New York Theatres closed following the assassination of President Lincoln on 14 April 1865; performances resumed 26 April 1865.

1865–1866 SEASON

BARNUM'S MUSEUM.

Engagement of the Great American Artist

MR. G. L. FOX,

WHO WILL APPEAR IN HIS

Comic Pantomime

OF

JACK & GILL,

Produced on a scale of

MAGNIFICENT SPLENDOR.

The Introductory and Explanatory Dialogue by G. C. HOWARD.

Entered according to Act of Congress, in the year 1866, by G. C. HOWARD, in the Clerk's Office of the District Court of the United States, for the Southern District of New York.

Barnum's Museum, JACK AND GILL, with Mr. G. L. Fox, Comic Pantomime (1866)
Museum of the City of New York

1865–1866 SEASON

THE GREEN MONSTER,

1865.05 or, The White Knight and the Giant Warrior

Barnum's Combination Pantomime Company in a Spectacular Fairy and Comic Pantomime in One Act, 12 Scenes, full of magical tricks, marvellous tranformations and comic incidents. Orchestra under the direction of F. W. Peterschen. Produced under the direction of Mons. A. Grossi. Produced by Phineas T. Barnum. Opened 10 July 1865 at Barnum's Museum, closing 12 July 1865[1]; re-opened 22 July 1865 at Barnum's Museum at the Winter Garden, and closed 29 July 1865 after (20) performances.

CAST: *The White Knight*, surnamed the Terrible: TONY DENIER. *Chevalier LeGrand*, the Giant Warrior: CHARLES K. FOX. *Chevalier Marco*: Mons. BAPTISTINE. *The Green Monster*: Master TIMOTHY. *Chief of the Sorcerers*: M. ANTONIO. *Carbone*: Jean Lewis. *Herald of the Giant Warrior*: Mr. Stevens. *Herald of the Chevalier Marco*: Mr. Scott. *Harlequin*: Leon Chenat. *Baron Miroque*: Mr. ANDERSON. *The White Genii*: T. F. Edwards. *Herald of the White Knight*: Mr. Hunter. *Landlord*: Mr. Howell. *Waiter*: Mr. Martin. *Rosalie*, Daughter of the Baron Miroque: Mlle. AURIOL (Mrs. Tony Denier). *Gertrude*, her Governess: Miss C. Monell. *Landlady*: Miss A. Anson. *Countess Ulla*: Miss J. Fenton. *Countess Des Milles Fleures*: Miss M. Henry. *Countess Azella*: Miss Davenport. *Countess Aurora*: Miss Georgianna. *Countess Batilda*: Miss Walker. *Countess Eugenia*: Miss Fenton. *Countess Elgitha*: Miss Thompson. *Countess Norissa*: Miss J. Monell. (*Ballet*: Mlle. Auriol, Emma Schell, Mons. Baptistine, Corps de Ballet.)

Grossi, the Ballet Master: *Clown*: TONY DENIER. *Pantaloon*: CHARLES K. FOX. *Harlequin*: LEON CHENAT. *Columbine*: Mlle. Auriol. *Specialties*, before the Pantomime: Rosina Richardson (fat woman), Anna Swan (Nova Scotia giantess), the Circassian Family (Zuruby Hannum, Zuluma Agra, Azela Pacha), and W. B. Harrison (comic and extemporaneous songs).

Scene 1: The Sorcerer's Cave. *Scene 2*: A Garden. *Scene 3*: The Palace of Miroque. *Scene 4*: The Arena. *Scene 5*: Picturesque landscape. *Scene 6*: Saloon in a Hotel. *Scene 7*: Street. *Scene 8*: Chateau and Tower of the White Knight. *Scene 9*: Rue de Diable. *Scene 10*: Ancient Ruins by Moonlight. *Scene 11*: Grand Transformation. *Scene 12*: The Unfathomable Caves of Ocean.

BALLETS, SPECIALTIES

Pas Seul (Scene 4)
E. Schell

Pas de Deux (Scene 4)
Mlle. Auriol, Mons. Baptistine

Grand Club Combat (Scene 4)
T. Denier, C. K. Fox

Concert à la Julien (Scene 8)

Grand Tableau Aquatique (Scene 12)

ARRAH-NA-POGUE,

1865.06 or, The Wicklow Wedding

A Grand Spectacular (Irish) Drama in Three Acts. Play by Dion Boucicault and E. H. House. Stage manager, L. J. Vincent. Musical director, Harvey B. Dodworth. Scenic artists, H. Hilliard; Charles Thorne, Charles Witham. Produced by William Wheatley. Opened 12 July 1865 at Niblo's Garden and closed 16 September 1865 after 66 performances; returned 15 November 1865[2] to Niblo's Garden in repertory, closing 23 December 1865 after an additional 24 performances. Returned 25 December 1865[3] to the New Bowery Theatre and closed 6 January 1866 after an additional 12 performances. Produced under the direction of Mr. B. Deane. Original music by C. Levy. Total: 102 performances.

CAST: *Shaun the Post*, a Wicklow Carman: T. H. GLENNEY. *Colonel Bagenal O'Grady*, the O'Grady: J. G. BURNETT. *Beamish McCoul*, the McCoul: W. E. SHERIDAN. *Major Coffin*, an English officer: J. W. Blaisdell. *The Secretary*: W. H. Norton. *The Sergeant*: E. B. Holmes. *Michael Feeny*: W. SCALLAN. *Winterbottom*, the Valet: CHARLES PETERS. *Oiny Farrell*: W. L. Jamieson. *Andy Regan*: Mr. Murphy. *Lanagan*: W. H. Danvers. *Patsy*: Mr. H. A. Rendle. *Tim Cogan*: CHARLES T. PARSLOE, JR.

Arrah Meelish, nicknamed by the peasantry 'Arrah Na Pogue," or Arrah of the Kiss: JOSEPHINE ORTON. *Fanny Power*, of Cabinteely: MARIA MAEDER. *Katty*: Mary Wells. *Peasants, Peasant Girls, Soldiers, Beggars, etc.*

Act 1: Glendalough by Moonlight. 1798. Arrah's Cabin. The Armory. (Hilliard.) The Barn. (Thorne, Witham.)

Act 2: The Devils's Glen. A Room in Ballybetagh. (Hilliard) The Prison. (Thorne.) Ballybetagh Castle. The Justice Hall. (Hilliard.)

Act 3: The Secretary's Room. Ballybetagh Castle. Night. The Prison. The Keep. The Ivywall. (Hilliard) The Watch Tower. (Thorne, Witham.) The Summit. (Hilliard).

ACT 1[4]

"Cushla Agus Machree"
J. Orton
(*Music by* Benjamin E. Woolf.)

"The Barn Door Jig"
C. T. Parsloe, Jr.

"The Wearing of the Green"
T. H. Glenney
(*Lyrics by* Dion Boucicault and E. H. House.)

ACT 3

"From My Love Parted"
J. Orton
(*Music by* Benjamin E. Woolf.)

THE BEAUTY OF SEVILLE/ ROBERT AND BERTRAND

1865.07

Barnum's Combination Pantomime Company in a Double Bill of a Ballet and a Comic Pantomime, accompanied by a variety program. Arranged by Mons. A. Grossi. Orchestra under the direction of F. W. Peterschen. Produced by Phineas T. Barnum. Opened 31 July 1865 at Barnum's Museum at the Winter Garden and closed 5 August 1865 after 12 performances.

THE BEAUTY OF SEVILLE, a Beautiful and Characteristic Ballet in One Act.

CAST: *Don Basilio*: TONY DENIER. *DON JUAN*: Mons. BAPTISTINE. *Don Pedro*: LEON CHENAT. *Don Inacio*: Jean Lewis. *Don Octavio*: M. Vigotty. *Don Pacchio*, father of Rosita: Mr. Anderson. *Don Pirez*: Mr. Scott. *Don Miguel*: Mr. Stevens. *Lords, Citizens, Guards, etc.*

Rosita, the Beauty of Seville: Mlle. AURIOL. *Pepita*, the Coquette: EMMA SCHELL. *Juanita*: Miss C. Monell. *Theresina*: Miss Davenport. *Isabella*: Mlle. Georgianna. *Conchita*: Miss J. Fenton. *Mariquetta*: Miss M. Henry. *Pequita*: Miss Thompson. *Govita*: Miss S. Fenton. (*Corps de Ballet*: Mlle. AURIOL, EMMA SCHELL, Mons. BAPISTINE, Master Timothy, Corps de Ballet. *Specialty*: Nicolo Brothers.)

BALLETS, SPECIALTIES

Introduction
Corps de Ballet

Rosita Waltz
E. Schell, L. Chenat

Spanish Dance
Corps de Ballet

Pas de Step
Mons. Baptistine

Punch in Good Humor, Dance and Drunken Scene on Stilts
Master Timothy

The Fighting Gladiators
Nicolo Brothers

La Sevillena
Mlle. Auriol, Mons. Baptistine

[1]Fire destroyed the building on 13 July 1865.

[2]For return engagement, new and original music was credited to C. Levy. The following cast changes were made: *Arrah Meelish*: AGNES PERRY. *Beamish McCoul*: D. E. Ralton. *Secretary*: J. Nunan. *Sergeant*: B. B. Holmes. *Winterbottom*: George Becks. *Oiny Farrell*: W. H. Danvers. *Andy Regan*: Mr. Alfred. *Lanagan*: Mr. Neel. *Tim Cogan*: Mr. Nolan. *Corporal*: Mr. Welsh.

[3]Returned 25 December 1865 to the New Bowery for an additional 2 weeks. Cast: *Shaun*: T. H. GLENNEY. *Arrah Meelish*: Mrs. Jones. *The O'Grady*: G. W. THOMPSON. *Beamish McCoul*: GEORGE LINGARD. *Michael Feeny*: J. Winter. *Fanny Power*: Miss Simmons. For the last 2 performances, only Act 1 was presented, preceded by a full-length presentation of Boucicault's drama The Colleen Bawn.

[4]Also performed, as per published sheet music:
"Pat Malloy"
(*Music arranged by* John P. Crook. *Lyrics by* Dion Boucicault.)

Pas d'Ensemble
T. Denier, L. Chenat, J. Lewis, Mlle. Auriol
Comic and Characteriustic Solo
T. Denier
Cachucha and Zapateo
Mlle Auriol
Finale
Characters, Corps de Ballet

ROBERT AND BERTRAND, or, The Two Fugitives, a Comic Pantomime in One Act.

CAST: *Jacques Strop*: TONY DENIER. *Robert Macaire*: CHARLES K. FOX. *Beaufort*: LEON CHENAT. *Mons. LaRoche*: Mr. Stevens. *Dumont*: Mr. Anderson. *Pierre*: Jean Lewis. *Sergeant Loupy*: Mons. Vigotty. *Baton*: Mr. Scott. *Flonflon*: Mr. Whitmore. *Bagnette*: Mr. Bailey. *Fusee*: Mr. Jerrold. *Adelaide*: Miss J. Monell. *Crignette*: Miss C. Monell. *Peasants, etc.*

BALLETS, SPECIALTIES
French Quadrille
All the characters

THE MIDNIGHT ASSAULT,
or, The Italian Brigands/ Love Amongst the Bonnets!

1865.08

Barnum's Combination Pantomime Company in a Double Bill of a Sensational Pantomime Ballet and a Laughable Ballet Pantomime accompanied by a variety program. Arranged by Mons. A. Grossi. Orchestra under the direction of F. W. Peterschen. Produced by Phineas T. Barnum. Opened 7 August 1865 at Barnum's Museum at the Winter Garden and closed 12 August 1865 after 12 performances.

THE MIDNIGHT ASSAULT, or The Italian Brigands, a Sensational Pantomime Ballet in One Act, 6 Scenes. Founded upon circumstances which actually occurred in France in 1804, the original pictures of which cost the Government 28,000 francs.

CAST: *Coc*, a Simple Lad of all work: TONY DENIER. *Mazzuolo*, the Brigand Chief: CHARLES K. FOX. *Gaston*, the Intendant: LEON CHENAT. *Followers of Mazzuolo (5)*: *Gonsalvo*: Jean Lewis. *Phillario*: Mr. Anderson. *Francisco*: Mons. Vigotty. *Antonio*: Mr. Scott. *Pietro*: Mr. Bailey. *Captain of the Commandant*: Mr. Stevens. *Musket*, the Sentry: Mr. Campbell. *Soldiers, Brigands, Peasants, etc.*
Mme. Bedouin: Miss C. Monell. *Franc*, her son: Master Kellino.

Scene 1: The Brigands' Success. *Scene 2*: The Forced Entrance. *Scene 3*: The Burglary and Attempt at Murder. *Scene 4*: The Surprise by the Soldiers. *Scene 5*: The Assault. *Scene 6*: The Defeat of the Brigands by the Soldiers, and the Triumph of Coco, who saves the life of his Master's Son. Death of the Brigand Chief.

BALLETS, SPECIALTIES
Grand Divertissement—Magic Ladders
Nicolo Brothers
Greek Hornpipe
E. Schell
La Polonaise
Chenat
Pas de Deux
Mlle. Auriol, Mons. Baptistine
Pas de Chinois
Master Timothy

LOVE AMONG THE BONNETS!, a Laughable Ballet Pantomime in One Act.

CAST: *Simon*, the Footman: TONY DENIER. *Longitude*, an Ardent Student: CHARLES K. FOX. *Hungarians (3)*: *Ernest*: Mons. BAPTISTINE. *Alfred*: LEON CHENAT. *Hector*: Mons. Vigotty. *Varnish*, a Painter: Jean Lewis. *Julia Varnish*: Miss C. Monell. *Mary*: Miss F. Monell. *Jenny*: EMMA SCHELL. *Louisa*: Mlle Georgianna. *Susan*: Miss Anson.

BALLETS, SPECIALTIES
Quadrille
Mons. Baptistine, L. Chenat, E. Schell, F. Monell
Mirror Dance
Mons. Baptistine
Comic Pas de Trois
C. K. Fox, E. Schell, F. Monell

THE WITCH OF THE BLACK CAVERN,
or, The Golden Pills of Magic

1865.09

Barnum's Combination Pantomime Company in a Grand Fairy and Comic Pantomime (accompanied by a variety program). Produced with new scenery, costumes, appointments and magical transformations under the entire direction of Mons. A. Grossi. Produced by Phineas T. Barnum. Opened 14 August 1865 at Barnum's Museum at the Winter Garden and closed 19 August 1865 after 12 performances.

Variety program: A Grand Divertissement: Character Dance, Emma Schell. Comic Dance on Stilts, Master Timothy. The celebrated comic and extemporaneous singer, W. B. Harrison, in comic and impromptu songs; Hits at the Times and Peoples. The Lion-Hearted Talleen Brothers of the Nicolo Troupe, together with Young Nicolo, the Child Wonder, will appear on aerial bars.

CAST: *Dandy Grinaldo*, a Pink of perfection: TONY DENIER. *Poltroon*, his Valet: CHARLES K. FOX. *Vangirard*, a Rival to Grinaldo: Mons. BAPTISTINE. *Don Pancho*, a rich apothecary: Mr. Stevens. *Red Spirtit*: T. L. Edwards. *Garonbio*: Mr. Scott. *Mariano, Zoaken*, Gamblers: Messrs. Vigotty, Anderson. *First Gnome*: Master Small. *Second Gnome*: Master Hughes. *Notary*: Mr. Campbell. *Landlord*: Mr. Bailey. *Frog*: Master Timothy. *Waiter*: Mr. Jerrold. *Citizens, Lords, Demons, etc.*
Elvina: Mlle. AURIOL. *Ortensia*, Hostess of the Inn: Miss Walker. *Myrrah*, Witch of the Black Cavern: Miss C. MONELL. (*Specialty in Character*: Miss ANNA SWAN, the Nova Scotia Giantess.)

BALLETS, SPECIALTIES
Pas de Deux
Mlle. Auriol, Mons. Baptistine

JOCKO,
or, The Brazilian Ape

1865.10

Barnum's Combination Pantomime Company in a Laughable Pantomime in One Act preceded by a variety program. Scenery by George Heilge. Produced by Phineas T. Barnum. Opened 28 August 1865 at Barnum's Museum at the Winter Garden and closed 2 September 1865 after 12 performances.

Variety program: Grand Divertissement: Magic Ladders, Nicolo Troupe; Sailor's Hornpipe, Miss Davenport; La Zingaro, Emma Schell; Revolving Globes, The Active Talleens. The celebrated comic and extemporaneous singer, W. B. Harrison, in comic and impromptu songs; Hits at the Times and Peoples. The fearless youth, Young Nicolo, the Wonder of the World, on the perilous flying trapeze.

CAST: *Pipo*, Servant to Lorenzo: TONY DENIER. *Lorenzo*, on a Travelling Tour: CHARLES K. FOX. *Jocko*, the Ape: Master TIMOTHY. *Fernandez*: Mons. Vigotty. *Pedro*, an Overseer: Mr. Stevens. *Sancho*: Mr. Anderson. *First Planter*: Mr. Scott. *Cora*: Mlle. Auriol. *Inez*, Fernandez' wife: Miss C. Monell. *Child*: Master Kellino.

Scenes: View of a Plantation on the Sea Coast of Brazil. Thunderbolt strikes the Vessel. Jocko's Cave.

BALLETS, SPECIALTIES
Galop
Corps de Ballet
Character Dance
E. Schell

SINBAD THE SAILOR,
or, The Valley of Diamonds

1865.11

A Pantomimic Spectacular Drama in Three Acts, 10 Scenes[5]. Produced under the able direction of George L. Fox. Music, new and selected, by Alexander Tyte. Scenery by J. Johnson, Jr. Machinery by William Crane. Properties by Nelse Waldron. Dresses by Keyser. Produced by George L. Fox. Opened 27 November 1865 at Fox's Old Bowery Theatre and closed 16 December 1865 after 18 performances.

CAST: Mortals: *Sinbad the Sailor*, with songs: FANNY HERRING. *Kabob*, the Ship's Steward: GEORGE L. FOX. *Koniah*, Captain of the Vessel, and Merchant trading with the Dwarfs at Salabat: J. McCLOSKEY. *Hamet*, a decayed merchant: C. FOSTER. *Zaco Knocknoe*, the Auctioneer: J. Coburn. *Guffarat, Gasna*, Diamond Merchants: Messrs. T. Cherry, Sanford. *Ali*, Mate of the "*Matchless Pearl*": W.

[5]Preceded by a favorite drama.

Mitchell. *Wabelo*, a Slave: F. Hofele. *First Merchant*: Mr. Whitmore. *Merchants, Sailors, etc. Leila*, daughter of Hamet, beloved by Sinbad: Miss S. WILLIAMS.

Cannibals: *Almorac*, Giant King of Salabat: Mr. Francis. *Casgar*, Chief of the Dwarfs: J. Lewis. *Hobnob, Gimessack*, Attendant Dwarfs: Messrs. Bailey, Gay. *The Old Man of the Sea*: S. BRADSHAW. *Dwarfs, etc.*

Genii: *Yelcobrac*, Slave of the Star, and Guardian Sprite of Sinbad: Master TIMOTHY. *Kalmoran*, the Genii: F. Ashbury.

Act 1, Scene 1: An Eastern Port. *Scene 2*: A Rocky Shore. *Scene 3*: Sea Covers the Stage.

Act 2, Scene 1: The Gate of King Salabat's Palace. *Scene 2*: A Grand Hall and Kitchen of the Giant King. *Scene 3*: The Shore of the Island of Salabat.

Act 3, Scene 1: The Valley of the Diamonds. *Scene 2*: Another Part of the Island. *Scene 3*: A Port. *Scene 4*: Deck of Koniah's Vessel. Appearance of Sinbad's Ship. A battle ensues.

SPECIALTIES, BALLETS

Solo and Chorus
All the characters

"Thou Art the Star"
F. Herring

"Her Bright Smile Haunts Me Still"
F. Herring

Grand Tableau and Triumphant Termination

1866.01 THE BLACK DOMINO/ BETWEEN YOU AND ME AND THE POST

A Double Bill of a Musical Comedy, followed by a Musical Burlesque. Acting manager, H. H. Davis. Stage manager, James Schonberg. Orchestra under the leadership of Henry Tissington. Produced by Lucy Rushton. Opened 29 January 1866 at Lucy Rushton's New York Theatre; BETWEEN YOU AND ME AND THE POST closed 24 February 1866 after 24 performances; THE BLACK DOMINO closed 3 March 1866 after 30 performances.

ACT 1

THE BLACK DOMINO A Musical Comedy in One Act. New scenery and appointments.

CAST: *Horace de Massarena*: J. K. Mortimer. *Count Julian*: C. W. Clarke. *Lord Elfort*: W. S. Higgins. *Gil Perez*: Mr. Gourlay. *The Black Domino*, with songs: LUCY RUSHTON. *Jacintha*: Mrs Maeder. *Bridget*: Mrs. Mark Smith. *Sister Ursuler*: Lucia Dean. *Sister Gertrude*: Miss K. Dudley. *Guests, Masqueraders, Nuns, etc.*

MUSICAL NUMBERS

"The Spirit of the Good"
L. Rushton

"Guard My Steps"
L. Rushton

"The Black Domino Polka"

ACT 2

BETWEEN YOU AND ME AND THE POST, a Musical Burlesque in One Act founded upon the drama Arrah na Pogue (by Dion Bouciault and E. H. House). Play by James Schonberg. Music arranged and composed by Jonathan P. Cooke. Scenery by George Evans. Appointments, mechanical effects by T. Morgan.

CAST: *Arrah Meelish*, of the Kiss, with songs: ROSA COOKE. *Fanny Power*, of the Affections: MARK SMITH. *Shaun*, of the Post, with songs: H. PEARSON. *Feeny*, of the Law: W. S. Higgins. *McCoul*, of the Rebels: W. A. Mestayer. *Colonel O'Grady, Sergeant, Officers, Soldiers, etc.*, of the Military: Messrs. Russell, Gourlay, Folwell, others. *Reagan and Peasants*, of the Emerald Isle: Mr. Thompson, others.

Scene 1: Glendalough, Ireland. *Scene 2*: Arrah's Cabin. *Scene 3*: The Barn. *Scene 4*: One seen before. *Scene 5*: The Court Room. *Scene 6*: Ballybetagh Castle. *Scene 7*: The Prison.

1866.02 JACK AND GILL WENT UP THE HILL

A Comic Pantomime in 11 Scenes and Illuminated Tableaux.[6] Spectacle written and invented by George L. Fox. Stage direction by George L. Fox. New music, original and selected, by Alexander Tyte. Scenery by J. Johnson. Costumes by Keyser. Elaborate transformations and machinery by William Crane. Properties, appointments and decorations by N. Waldron. Ballet arranged by Mons. Grossi. Calcium lights and illuminations by Thomas Newton. Produced by George L. Fox. Opened 19 February 1866 at Fox's Bowery Theatre and closed 28 April 1866 after 70 performances; re-opened 9 July 1866 at Barnum's Museum and closed 11 August 1866 after 35 additional performances. Total: 105 performances.

CAST: *Jackdaw Jaculation*, known throughout the country as Troublesome Jack, afterwards Clown: GEORGE L. FOX. *Mistress Jurisprudence Gill*, afterwards Pantaloon: CHARLES K. FOX. *Little Jack Horner*, the good boy of the village, afterwards Harlequin: Master TIMOTHY. *Little Mary Marigold*, afterwards Columbine: Mlle. MARTINETTI[7]. *Fleece*, Mary's favorite lamb: A Real One. *Luminous*, the Sun Spirit, protector of Little Jack Horner and Mary: C. Foster. *Smaller Luminaries*, but closely connected with the Sun Spirit (4): *Sun Beam*: Miss Law. *Sun Rise*: Miss Fenton. *Sun Set*: Miss S. Follwell. *Sun Shine*: Miss J. Follwell. *King Icicle Icy*, Grand Ruler of the Frozen Waters: F. Ashbury. *His Satellites and Guardian Sprites of the Magic Icebergs (4)*: *Frostiano*: T. Cherry. *Wintry Winds*: Mr. Sanford. *Frozen rain*: F. Hofele. *Sleetyhailall*: W. Mitchell. *Squire Arrogant*, a rich but haughty person: J. Coburn. *Oppressor Arrogant*, his son, "a chip off the old block": Mr. Gay. *Farmers who take after the old song (5)*: *Rogueingrain*: Mr. Baily. *Wheaten*: Mr. Whitman. *Barleycorn*: Mr. Jerrold. *Oatcake*: Mr. Goodwin. *Grist*: Mr. Truman. *P. T. Poor*: Mr. Thomas. *H.T. Blind*: Mr. Banks. *P.O. Bummer*, a beggar: Mr. Stout. *Short Cake*, a baker: Mr. Yest. *Freedman Bureau Bill*, a black boy: Master William.[8] *Tag, Rag and Bobtail*: By any amount of Ragged Urchins. *Levy Stickemall*, a merchant offering "Two segars for five cents": Mr. Simons. *One-for-pork Two-for-mutton*, a pieman: Mr. Murray. *Mike O'Rafferty*, a Yankee peddler: S. Bradshaw. *Grabem, Catchem*, policemen: Messrs. Murray, S. Bradhsaw. *Yourordersir*, a waiter: Mr. Burden. *Dontknowhisname*, an organ grinder: Mr. Birchler. *Bagetelle*, a monkey: A Real One. *Howmanyyards*, a dry goods clerk: Mr. Davis. *Cheap John*, of the Yankee Notions: Mr. Davis. *Farmers, Policemen, Shopsellers, etc. Old Mother Widdle Waddle*: Mr. J. Lewis. *Susan Waitonthedoor*, a maid: Miss Cranfield. *Madame Anybody*, a shoplifter: Miss Follett.

Scene 1: The Frozen Regions (near the North Pole). Grand Transformation. *Scene 2*: Foxborough, near Valentine Plantation. *Scene 3*: Village Green. *Scene 4*: Tobacco and Wine Store. *Scene 5*: Room in a Hotel. *Scene 6*: Music Store. *Scene 7*: Dry Goods and Variety Store. *Scene 8*: The Grant Oak. *Scene 9*: The Double Bedded Room. *Scene 10*: Tennyson's Tower. *Scene 11*: Grotto of the Dancing Waters and the Shower of Gold.

SPECIALTIES, BALLETS

Grand Tableau and Illuminated Pictures (Scene 1):
Sir John Franklin and Doctor Kane, the Great Explorers; Washington Crossing the Delaware; Our Country's Glory, General Grant.

Character Dance; Grand Transformation (Scene 2)

The Wearing of the Green; Poor John Bull (Scene 6)

Retreat of the Sun Spirit (Scene 11)

1866.03 CINDERELLA E LA COMARE, or, The Lover, The Lackey, and the Little Glass Slipper

A Fairy Burlesque Extravaganza in One Act[9] (adapted by H. J. Byron from the fairy tale by Charles Perrault). Music, new and selected, by Thomas Baker. Scenery by Joseph Hayes. Machinery by W. Sanders. Properties by W. Henry. Costumes by J. Bullock. Gas by M. O'Brien. Produced by Mrs. John Wood. Opened 26 February 1866 at the Olympic Theatre and closed 31 March 1866 after 30 performances.

CAST: *Prince Poppetti*, Prince of Salerno, and of pretty Fellows: Miss ELIZA NEWTON. *Dandini*, his Valet, and a very deep one: C. H. MORTON. *Alidoro*, his Tutor: T. J. HIND. *The Baron Balderdash*, a slightly damaged edition of the "Last of the Barons," bound in calf, three vols. In one, by no means lettered, and very generally cut: J. H. STODDART. *Buttoni*, a Page of the "Last of the Barons:" James Lewis. *Clorinda*, the Baron's eldest Daughter, an oldish young person of the gushing order, very hard upon Thisbe, but soft on the Prince: GEORGE FAWCETT ROWE. *Thisbe*, the Baron's second Daughter: Miss AMILIE HARRIS. *Cinderella*, the Baron's youngest Daughter:

[6] Accompanied by a farce, Marriage at Any Price.

[7] For return engagement at Barnum's Museum, this role was assumed by KATE PENNOYER.

[8] For return engagement at Barnum's Museum, this role was assumed by Master George Topack.

[9] Preceded by the play Used Up, which was succeeded by Doing for the Best, and later Robert Macaire, or, The Roadside Inn.

Mrs. JOHN WOOD. *The Fairy Queen*, Cinderella's Godmother: LOUISA MYERS. *Honeydew*, a Fay: Miss Caroline Lee. *Harebell*: Miss Nellie Fox. *Lords, Ladies, Lackeys, Fairies, etc.*

1866.04

THE LOAN OF A LOVER

A Revival of the Musical Comedietta in One Act.[10] (Play by James Robinson Planché.) Acting manager, H. H. Davis. Stage manager, James Schonberg. Orchestra under the direction of Henry Tissington. Produced by Lucy Rushton. Opened 1 March 1866 at Lucy Rushton's Theatre and closed 10 March 1866 after 9 performances.

THE LOAN OF A LOVER CAST: *Captain Amersfort*: W. A. MESTAYER. *Peter Spyk*, with Song: H. PEARSON. *Swyzzle*: W. S. Higgins. *Delve*: Mr. Gourlay. *Ernestine*, with Song: LUCIA DEANE. *Gertrude*, with Songs: ROSA COOKE.

1866.05

VALIANT VALENTINE

A Spectacular Burlesque in One Act.[11] Play by James Schonberg. Music by Henry Tissington. Scenery by George Evans. Machinery by Matt Morgan. Appointments by J. Lundy. Costumes by H. Seymour. Dances arranged by M. Grossi. Grand Transformation scene invented and arranged by Lucy Rushton and H. H. Davis. Orchestra under the direction of Henry Tissington. Produced by Lucy Rushton[12]. Opened 27 March 1866 at Lucy Rushton's Theatre and closed 8 April 1866 after 12 performances.

CAST: *Mortals*: *Valiant Valentine*, a Knight of the Day, sans peur et sans reproche, a study from the life, and a most loquacious likeness, with Songs, Dances and Delight: LUCY RUSHTON. *King Pippin*, a monarch of all he surveys, when it is his, and although a King, a subject subjected to all the necessities of the Drama: C. W. CLARKE. *Henry*, a cozening cousin of Valentine's: G. L. PARKES. *Hautrey*, a ditto ditto of ditto's: Mr. Russell. *Hugo*, an unlettered quarto page of Valentine's: W. S. Higgins. *Agramont*, an Erring Knight of Green, a Sorcerer who feels sore-sir!: H. Seymour. *Blandiman*, a Writing Master, who plumes himself upon his style: Mr. Gourlay. *Orson*, The Beast of Orelans, a wood-cut picture of the saying 'De Gustibus non est disputandem': H. Pearson. *The Bear*, a Star of the Ursu Major order, after much consideration: The Most Discontented Man of the Company. *The Policeman*, by the kind permission of Secretary Stanton: ——. *The Herald*, a popular Reporter of Current Items, and one of the famed trumps of Fame: Mr. Burke. *Eglantine*, a young Pippin, daughter of a King, and aching to find a sweetheart, when she happily receives a Valentine: LUCIA DEANE. *Florimonda*, another King's daughter, in the clutches of Agramont, whom she aggravates: Miss Henry. *Belisanta*, the original School marm, and although not apparent, the parent of a Hero, who—but to say who would only—and therefore—we need say no more: Mrs. MAEDER. *Agatha*, a waiting maid, or a maid awaiting Eglantine's orders: Miss Mosston. *The Valentine Brigade*: Ladies of the Ballet. *Knights, Courtiers, Citizens, Peasants, Men-at-Arms, Monks, Pages, Nuns, Standard-Bearers, Trumpeters, Heralds, Others*: Auxiliaries, Super-Superior Supers.

Immortals: *The Fairy Queen*, a matter of Moonshine, a cobweb of the brain, immaterailly considered; yet not materially rendered by: Miss MOWBRAY. *Puck*, a well-known creation; in this instance as Minister to Orleans, a ministering Angel to Valentine: Mrs. MARK SMITH. *Gossamer, Cobweb, Mushroom, Fern-Seed, Moss, Lichen, Anemone, Gauze-wing, Verbena, Chrysalina, Convoyulus, Daisy and Others, being attendant Fairies*: Ladies of the Ballet.

Scenes: Moonlight Glade near a Silver Lake. Public Square in the City of Orleans. Vestibule in Pippin's Palace. The Forest of Orleans. Orleans Grand Trunk Junction. King Pippin's Palace. The Camp of Agramont. The Sphynx! Grand Transformation to the Prismatic Home of Queen Crystal.

BALLETS, SPECIALTIES

Grand Procession (Valentine's Entry)

Duett
L. Rushton, H. Pearson

Grand Ballet
Mlle. Windell, Corps de Ballet

Song
L. Rushton

Triumphant Reception of Valiant Valentine

1866.06

THE ELVES, or, The Statue Bride

A Revival of the Serio-Comic Spectacular Extravaganza in Two Acts, 10 Scenes[13]. Play by Charles Selby, founded on the French grand ballet spectacle "Les Elfes."[13] Stage manager, Ben A. Baker. Acting manager, Samuel Colville. Leader of orchestra, H. Beisenhertz. Scenic artist, Robert Grain. Produced by George Wood. Opened 30 April 1866 at Wood's Theatre and closed 2 June 1866 after 35 performances; returned 16 July 1866 to Wood's Theatre in repertory.

CAST: *Sylvia*, the Statue Bride: SOPHIE WORRELL. *Prince Lubin*, "Jockey Club," a beau jeune homme: IRENE WORRELL. *Phillis*, a Miller's Daughter: JENNIE WORRELL. *Count Coldstream*: MYRON W. LEFFINGWELL. *Colin*, a Romantic Tailor: G. C. DAVENPORT. *Prince Pompolino*: WELSH EDWARDS. *Princess Jonquil*: Miss LUCIA DEANE. *Toadylor*, a Courtier: Miss Alice Seidler. *Grimdyne*, a demon: Mr. James. *Madame Chloe*: Mrs. E. Wright. *Madam Chloe*: Mrs. E. Wright. *Eoline*, Queen of the Elves: Miss Annie Merry. *Daphne*, maid in waiting: Miss Jenny Gilmer. *Elves, Lords, Ladies of the Court*: Ladies and Gentlemen. (*Ballet*: Mlle. STREBINGER, Corps de Ballet.)

Act 1, Scene 1: Madame Chloe's Dwelling. *Scene 2*: The Entrance of the Count and Huntsmen. *Scene 3*: The Hawthorn Dell.

Act 2, Scene 1: Saloon and Boudoir of the Princess. *Scene 2*: The Miller's Daughter. *Scene 3*: The Gardens of the Palace. *Scene 4*: The Count again. *Scene 5*: Colin in chains. *Scene 6*: The Hall of Statues. *Scene 7*: The Elfin Grotto.

ACT 1
Scene 1
"Bobbing Around" (Song)
G. C. Davenport
Scene 2
"Thou art the Star" (Song)
I. Worrell
Scene 3
Grand Pas des Elves
Mme. Strebinger, Corps de Ballet
"Sing, Birdie, Sing" (Song)
S. Worrell
"Ever be Happy" (Tableau and Chorus)
All the characters

ACT 2
Scene 1
"Guillerette" (Aria)
L. Deane
Scene 2
"Mother has Gone Away" (Song)
J. Worrell
Clog Dance
J. Worrell
Scene 3
The Fête
"Come away, Elves" (Duet)
I. Worrell, S. Worrell
Pas de Deux
I. Worrell, S. Worrell
"Charlie is my Darling" (Song)
L. Deane
Scene 4
"Out of my sight" (Duet)
G. C. Davenport, L. Deane
Scene 5
Double Hornpipe
G. C. Davenport, J. Worrell

[10]THE LOAN OF A LOVER was first produced in New York 7 April 1835 in repertory. This revival was preceded by a comedy, Giralda! with Mrs Maeder, Lucy Rushton, Messrs. W. A. Mestayer, Pearson, Higgins and Clarke.

[11]Preceded by a comedietta, The Guardian Angel.

[12]In order to increase the attractiveness of the mis-en scène, Miss Rushton has secured the services of Mlle. Lina Windell, celebrated danseuse.

[13]First produced in New York 16 March 1857 at Laura Keene's Theatre for 50 performances in repertory. Preceded by the comedietta, Nan, The Good for Nothing, featuring Jennie Worrell. In the second week, this was succeeded by Crossing the Line, featuring Irene and Jennie Worrell. Later fore-pieces included The Fool of the Family.

[14]Les Elfes, a ballet-fantasie in Three Acts, by J. H. Vernoy de St.-Georges an N. Mazillier. Music by the Count N. Gabrielli.

Scene 6
"Shubert's Serenade" (Song)
S. Worrell
Scene 7
Happy Denouement

1866.07 THE DOCTOR OF ALCANTARA

A Comic Opera (Opéra-bouffe) in Two Acts. Libretto by Benjamin E. Woolf. Music by Julius Eichberg. Stage manager, George F. Ketchum. Conductor, Julius Eichberg. Produced by the English Comic Opera Company. Opened 28 May 1866 at the Théâtre Français (New French Theatre) in repertory; season closed 3 July 1866.

CAST: *Doctor Paracelsus*: EDWARD SEGUIN. *Señor Balthazar*: GEORGE F. KETCHUM. *Carlos*, his son: WILLIAM CASTLE. *Don Pomposo*, alguazil: HENRY C. PEAKES. *Perez, Sancho*, porters: James Peakes, Mr. Danks. *Inez*: CAROLINE RICHINGS. *Donna Lucrezia*, Wife to Doctor Paracelsus: SOPHIE MOZART. *Isabella*, her daughter: ZELDA HARRISON. *Serenaders, Citizens, etc*,

Scene: Alcantara, in the house of Doctor Paracelsus.

ACT 1[15]
"Wake, Lady, Wake" (Serenade)
W. Castle, Chorus
"You Saucy Jade" (Quarrel Trio)
S. Mozart, C. Richings, Z. Harrison
"He Still Was There" (Romanza)
Z. Harrison
"When a Lover Is Poor" (Arietta)
C. Richings
"Away Despair" (Duettino)
Z. Harrison, C. Richings
"Buenos Noches"
J. Peakes, Mr. Danks
"Love's Cruel Dart" (Cavatina)
W. Castle
"The Knight of Alcantara" (Ballad)
S. Mozart
"I Love, I Love" (Duetto)
W. Castle, S. Mozart
"I'm Don Hypolito Lopez Pomposo" (Bass Song)
H. C. Peakes
Finale
E. Seguin, C. Richings, S. Mozart, Z. Harrison, H. C. Peakes, Chorus

ACT 2
Scena and Bolero[16]
Z. Harrison
"Senor, Senor" (Trio)
W. Castle, E. Seguin, C. Richings
"Here You Must Repose" (Cabaletta)
W. Castle, E. Seguin, C. Richings
"So Strange a House"[17] (Stretta)
W. Castle, E. Seguin, C. Richings
"Good Night Senor Balthazar" (Quartette)
E. Seguin, C. Richings, S. Mozart, Z. Harrison
Finale:
"I Tremble o'er with Fear" (Finale-Duo)
E. Seguin, C. Richings
"Oh! Where am I?" (Trio)
W. Castle, E. Seguin, C. Richings
"Is He Your Son?" (Quintette)
Z. Harrison, W. Castle, E. Seguin, C. Richings, S. Mozart
"Hope Ever Smiling" (Quintette)
Ensemble

[15]Musical numbers not listed in New York programs. List prepared from published piano vocal score (Oliver Ditson & Co., Boston, 1862), revised according to a Boston program dated 1 April 1865. The appendix in the published libretto included the following additional songs:
"Doctor's Song" (Good people all, behold in me)[Doctor]
"Day Dreams of Love"
Scena and Bolero—Recitivo (Ah, woe is me!) (see Act 2 above)

[16]Appears in Boston program but not in vocal score.
[17]Appears in Boston program but not in vocal score.

1866–1867 SEASON

Maria Bonfanti in THE BLACK CROOK
Museum of the City of New York, The S. P. Sherwood Collection, 36.440.1477

1866–1867 SEASON

1866.08
THE INVISIBLE PRINCE, or, The Island of Tranquil Delights

A Revival of the Burlesque in One Act, 9 Scenes[1]. Burlesque by James Robinson Planché. Stage manager, Ben. A. Baker. Acting manager, Samuel Colville. Leader of orchestra, H. Beisenhertz. Scenic artist, Robert Grain. Produced by George Wood. Opened 4 June 1866 at Wood's Theatre, closing 16 June 1866 after 14 performances; returned 25 June 1866 to Wood's Theatre and closed 30 June 1866 after an additional 7 performances.

Acrobatic Program: Perilous Ladder Feats, by the Nicolo Troupe. Terpsichorean Flights, by Mlle. DeWilborn. Sports of Atlas, Brothers Tallace. The Flying Trapeze, by Young Nicolo, Boy Wonder.

THE INVISIBLE PRINCE CAST: *Prince Leander*, the rightful King of Allaquiz: SOPHIE WORRELL. *Princess Pretty Pet*, of the Island of Tranquil Delights: IRENE WORRELL. *Abricotina*, maid in waiting on the Princess: JENNIE WORRELL. *Furibond el Filisbustero*, usurping the Crown of Allaquiz: Mr. M. W. LEFFINGWELL. *Don Mustachios*, his Prime Minister: W. James. *Marquis of Anysidos*: J. C. Walsh. *Lord Squeezwicks*: Mr. Newton. *Count Veryoso*: J. S. Goodman. *Gardener*: Mr. Fielding. *Sambo*, Ambassador from the Catspaw Indians: Mr. Peck. *Ruffino, Desperado, Sanguino, Stilletto*, Banditti of the Old School: Messrs. Wilson, Luke, Sartrin, Riley. *Queen Dolalolla*: Miss Mary Everett. *Fairy Queen*: Miss Alice Seidler. *Huntsmen, Courtiers, Ladies of the Court, etc.*

1866.09
LE VIOLONEUX

A Revival of the Legende Bretonne (Opérette) in One Act[2], in French. Libretto by E. Mestépès and E. Chevalet. Music by Jacques Offenbach. Conductor, Auguste Predigam. P. Juignet, C. Drivet, Directeurs. Opened 12 June 1866 at the Théâtre Français in repertory.

CAST: *Le Père Mathieu*, violoneux: Mons. FLEURY. *Pierre*, sabotier: Mons. HARNDOFF. *Reinette*, filleule du père Mathieu: Mme. FLEURY.

1866.10
THE ROSE OF CASTILE

A Revival of the Romantic Opera in Three Acts[3]. Libretto by Augustus Harris and Edmund Falconer. Music by Michael William Balfe. Produced by Caroline Richings English Comic Opera Company. Opened 13 June 1866 at the Théâtre Français for 1 performance in repertory; season closed 30 June 1866; returned 28 January 1867 to the Olympic Theatre and closed 31 January 1867 after 2 additional performances in repertory.

CAST: *Manuel*, a Muleteer, disguised King of Castile: Mr. WILLIAM CASTLE. *Conspirators* (3): *Don Pedro*: Mr. S. C. CAMPBELL. *Don Florio de Santa Cruz*: Mr. EDWARD SEGUIN. *Don Sallaste*: D. B. WYLIE. *Pablo*: Mr. JAMES G. PEAKES. *Elvira*, the Rose of Castile, Queen of Spain: CAROLINE RICHINGS. *Donna Carmen*: Miss ZELDA HARRISON (Seguin). *Beatrice*, Duchess of Calatrava: Mrs. Boudinot. *Ladies of Honor, Nobles, Conspirators, Guards, Peasants, etc.*

1866.11
THE 3 SISTERS!

A New and Original Mythological, Allegorical, Local and Musical Extravaganza in One Act, 10 Scenes, written expressly for the Worrell Sisters[4]. Produced under the stage direction of Stage manager, Ben. A. Baker. Acting manager, Samuel Colville. Leader of orchestra, H. Beisenhertz. Scenic artist, Robert Grain. Machinery by Levi Guernsey. Appointments, Mr. Peterson. Produced by George Wood. Opened 18 June 1866 at Wood's Theatre and closed 23 June 1866 after 8 performances.

CAST: Immortals: *Hygeia*, the Goddess of Health, assuming the characters of Harry Thorne, a young man about town; Senorita La Scala, a Spanish Danseuse; Jem Stokes, member of a Base Ball Club; Frau Vanderheysen, a Dutch Woman: Miss SOPHIE WORRELL. *Callirhoe*, Goddess of Wealth, assuming the characters of Joe Havens, a fast young man; Senorita Pepita, from the Teatro La Scala, Milan; Billy Peters, one of the Base Ball Nine; Frauleen Chummy, from Lion Park: Miss IRENE WORRELL. *Mnemosyne*, Goddess of Mirth, assuming the characters of Tom Quirk, Jr., one of the young sports; Senorita Isabella, from sunny Spain; Dick Catcher, the pet of the Atlantics; Susette Switzercase, from Faderland: Miss JENNIE WORRELL. *Jove* (him of the Thunderbolt): J. B. CURRAN. *Juno*, his better half: Mrs. E. Wright. *Gods, Goddesses, etc.*

Mortals: *Jabez Strong*, a Philanthropist: M. W. LEFFINGWELL. *Phelim O'Pake*, from Gowanus: T. L. DONNELLY. *Augustus*: Mr. W. James. *Lollypop*: Mr. Reed. *Maleflirt*: Mr. Newton. *Karl*, keeper of a Lager Beer Saloon: J. S. Goodman. *Mary Melville*, an Orphan: Miss ALICE SEIDLER. *Ladies and Gentlemen, Base Ball Players, Visitors*: Members of the Company and Corps de Ballet.

Scene 1: Olympus. *Scene 2*: Harlem Railroad Depot, 27th Street and Fourth Avenue. *Scene 3*: Lager Beer Saloon. *Scene 4*: City Hall. *Scene 5*: Mall in Central Park. *Scene 6*: Union Square. *Scene 7*: Base Ball Ground, Brooklyn. *Scene 8*: Room in Mary's House. *Scene 9*: Room in the Hotel. *Scene 10*: The Feast of Flowers. Tableau: Shower of Gold!

SPECIALTIES, MUSICAL NUMBERS

Scene 1
- "Jove he has gone" (Chorus of Gods and Goddesses)
- The Three Sisters, Health, Wealth and Mirth (Grand Tableau)
- "Come away!" (Chorus)
- "Over the clouds and far away!" (Trio)
  Worrell Sisters

Scene 2
- "Old Ireland, you're my darling" (Song)
  M. W. Leffingwell

Scene 3
- "Brindisi" (Drinking Song)
  I. Worrell
- Banjo Solo
  J. Worrell
- Irish Jig
  T. L. Donnelly

Scene 5
- "Guard March" (Music)
- "Jota de los Toreros" (Duet)
  S. Worrell, I. Worrell
- El Jota Aragonaise
  Worrell Sisters

Scene 6
- Song
  T. L. Donnelly

Scene 7
- The Favorites of the Field (Baseball specialty)
- Double Clog Dance
  J. Worrell, I. Worrell

Scene 9
- "Turn on, Old Time!" (Trio)
  Worrell Sisters

Scene 10
- "Chink of Gold" (Song)
- "Hail to Jove, our King" (Finale)
  All the characters

1866.12
THE SHEEP'S FOOT!

The Buislay Family in a Laughable Extravaganza (Burlesque Drama) in Three Acts[5]. (Adapted from the French "Le Pied du Mouton" by Frères

[1]First produced in New York 26 April 1847 at the Park Theatre. Musical numbers and scenes not listed in programs. THE INVISIBLE PRINCE was preceded by a play, Crossing The Line, in which Misses Irene and Jennie Worrell introduce their Double Clog Dance; later in the run, this was replaced by the comedietta Mr. and Mrs. Peter White, in which Jennie Worrell and Mr. Leffingwell sing a duet, and dance the Mock Minuet de la Cour. Also an acrobatic program, detail above.

[2]On a bill with La Veuve aux Camélia, and Les Femmes qui Pleurent. LE VIOLONEUX was first produced in New York 11 February 1864 at the Théâtre Français in repertory. For Synopsis of Scenes and Musical Numbers, see original 1864 production.

[3]First produced in New York 27 July 1864 at the Olympic Theatre in repertory. For Synopsis of Scenes and Musical Numbers, see original 1864 production.

[4]Preceded by the comedietta Too Much for Good Nature, in which M. W. Leffingwell plays Mr. Romeo Taffler Jenkins, with supporting cast.

[5]Although advertised as LE PIED DU MOUTON, or, The Sheep's Foot, the actual program offers the title in English only.

Cogniard, Henri Cremieux and M. Delaporte.) New music by Prof. Charles Schultz. Scenery by Mr. H. Hilliard. Mechanical effects by T. Morgan. Conductor, Charles Schultz. Ballets under the direction of Mons. Grossi. Stage manager, J. Schonberg. Produced by J. Schonberg and C. H. Platt. Opened 18 June 1866 at the New Bowery Theatre and closed 30 June 1866 after 16 performances.

CAST[6]: *Don Guzman*, a Favored Lover: Miss SALLIE HINCKLEY. *Don Syllione*, a Persecuted Suitor: Mr. FREDERICK WOODHULL. *Don Lopez*, Leonora's Guardian: Mr. GEORGE BECKS. *Don Gonzalez*, Guzman's friend: Mr. GEORGE ROUNDY. *Lazarillo*, Syllione's servant: Mr. ALFRED BECKS. *Donna Leonora*, betrothed to Guzman, with songs: Miss ALICIA THORNE. *Antidota*, a Good Fairy, with songs: Miss BLANCHE CHAPMAN. *Cupid*, the God of Love: JOAQUIN BUISLAY. *Vulcan*, the God of Fire: Mr. Wright. *Duennas, Musicians, Fairies, Demons, Sprits, Gnomes, Valets, Guestrs, and Soldiers.*

Specialties: THE BUISLAY FAMILY (Etienne, Adolphe, Auguste, Julio, Grenet, Justin, Master Joaquin, Mlle. Luisa. Miss CARRIE A. MOORE (The Ice Queen). Mme. STREBINGER (Premiere danseuse). Complete Corps de Ballet, Skating Troupe.

SPECIALTIES, BALLETS, MUSICAL NUMBERS

The Buislay Family will introduce their Wonderful Niagara Leap, their graceful and daring act, The Persian Throne. They will be assisted by Miss Carrie A. Moore, The Ice Queen. Mme. Strebinger, Première danseuse, Full Dramatic Company, Complete Corps de Ballet, and a Skating Troupe.

1866.13 PO-CA-HON-TAS, or, The Gentle Savage

A Revival of the Extravaganza (Burlesque) in Two Acts, 3 Scenes[7], being a perversion of ye trew and wonderfulle Hystorie of ye Renounede Pryncesse. Play by John Brougham. Music entirely dislocated and re-set [composed and arranged] by James G. Maeder. Orchestra leader, Robert Stoepel. New scenery, costumes and appointments. Produced by John Brougham. Opened 18 June 1866 at the Winter Garden and closed 7 July 1866 after 18 performances; returned 6 August 1866 to the Winter Garden on a bill with JENNY LIND and closed 11 August 1866 after an additional 6 perfomances.

CAST: *Of Ye English*: *Captain John Smith*, the undoubted Original, vocal and instrumental, in the settlement of Virginia, in love with Pocahontas, according to this story, though somewhat at variance with his story: Mr. J. C. DUNN. *Lieutenant Thomas Brown*, Second in Command, a hitherto neglected Genius, whose claims on posterity are now for the first time acknowledged, as is but right: Mr. J. MILOT. *William Brown*, sometimes called Bill, another of the same sort left: Mr. DUN BROWN. *Mynheer Rolff*, the real Husband of Pocahontas, but dramatically divorced contrary to all law and fact: Mr. C. M. WALCOT, JR.

Splicers of main-bracers, shiverers of timbers, anathematizers of eyes and limbs, promiscuously general dealers in single combats and double hornpipes, and altogether, amazingly nautical people: *Benjamin Brace*: Mr. Go-Ahead. *John Junk*: Mr. Come-Up. *Henry Halyard*: Mr. Sparr. *William Buntline*: Mr. Mast Head.

Of Ye Savages: *His Imperial Majesty, Pow-Ha-Tan I*, King of the Tuscaroras—a crotchety Monarch, in fact, a Semi-Brave: Mr. JOHN BROUGHAM. *The Right Hon. Quash-al-Jaw*, Speaker of the Savage House of Lords—straightener of unpleasant kinks, and oiler of troubled waters, unraveller of knotty points, adjuster of pugnacious difficulties, and Grand Eye Parliamentary Factotum and Fugleman: Mr. T. J. Leigh. *O-po-dil-doc*, One of the Aboriginal F. F. V's[8], an indignant dignitary: Mr. H. Fawcett. *Col-o-gog*, another warm-hearted and headed Son of Old Virginia: Mr. W. S. Andrews. *Bi-Jin-go*, Sergeant-at-Arms, a friend to swear by: Mr. Waddleton.

Medicine Men, of the Saultz and Sennaca Tribe: *Ip-pah-kak*: Mr. L. Carland. *Sas-sy-pril*: Mr. J. Bull. *Kod-liv-Royl*: Mr. A. Fish. *Kal-o-mel*: Mr. A. Gew.

H. R. H. Princess Po-Ka-Hon-Tas, the Beautiful, and very properly undutiful, daughter of King Pow-Ha-Tan, married, according to the ridiculous dictum of actual circumstances, to Master Rolff, but the author flatters himself much more advantageously disposed of in the Acting edition: Miss EMILIE MELVILLE. *Poo-tee-pet, Di-mun-di*, Interesting offshoots from aristocratic stock, anterior to the first Families of Virginia: Miss FANNY STOCQUELER, Miss Dunn. *Wee-cha-ven-da, Kros-as-kan-bee*, Embodying the rigid principles of the Tuscarora Fashionable Finishing School: Misses Mary Carr, Moore.

Their "dear charges," for whom they don't forget to charge dear enough for in the Quarterly Bills: *Dah-Lin-Duck*: Miss Jennie Morton. *O-you-Jewel*: Miss E. Howard. *Lov-lie-kreete*: Miss A. Ryan. *Oso-char-ming*: Miss S. Williams.

1866.14 A NIGHT IN ROME

An Operetta (Opéra-bouffe) in Two Acts. Libretto and music by Julius Eichberg. Stage manager, George F. Ketchum. Conductor, Julius Eichberg. Produced by the English Comic Opera Company. Opened 25 June 1866 at the New French Theatre (Théâtre Français) in repertory; season closed 30 June 1866.

CAST: *Pietro*, a gondolier: S. C. CAMPBELL. *Moccoloni*, a Village Barber: D. B. WYLIE. *Beppo*: JAMES PEAKES. *Grand Judge*: GEORGE K. KETCHUM. *Coro*: (Henry C.) PEAKES. *Giuglio*: GEORGE F. KETCHUM. *Ninetta*, an Orphan: CAROLINE RICHINGS. *Masqueraders, Policemen, Citizens, Gondoliers*: Chorus.

Scene: Street in Rome, with a view of the river Tiber and St. Peter's in the distance.

MUSICAL NUMBERS[9]

"Come fill the Bowl with Sparkling Wine"
Chorus

"Dearest Friends, my Ardent Love"
S. C. Campbell

"Rely on Our Assistance"
Chorus

Serenade
D. B. Wylie, Chorus

Proclamation
S. C. Campbell

"Forehead low, but full of cunning" (Ensemble)
S. C. Campbell, D. B. Wylie, J. Peakes, Chorus

"When still the Night, when o'er the Waves" (Ballad)
C. Richings

"O Moment of Bliss" (Comic Duo)
C. Richings, S. C. Campbell

"H'm, H'm, H'm" (Duettino Bouffe and Pantomime)
Coco, G. F. Ketchum

"Strapanzoni il Banditto" (Grand chorus and Ensemble)
C. Richings, S. C. Campbell, G. F. Ketchum, D. B. Wylie, J. Peakes, Chorus

"Lisette's a Fresh and Charming Maid" (Couplets)
C. Richings

"How do ye do, Signor Moccoloni? How do you do, Senor Moccolo?"
Chorus

Finale
All the characters, Chorus

1866.15 FRA DIAVOLO

A Burlesque Burletta (suggested by the opera by Daniel Auber) in One Act, 5 Scenes[10]. Stage manager, Ben. A. Baker. Acting manager, Samuel Colville. Leader of orchestra, H. Beisenhertz. Scenic artist, Robert Grain. Produced by George Wood. Opened 2 July 1866 at Wood's Theatre and closed 14 July 1866 after 16 performances.

CAST: *Fra Diavolo*, alias the Marquis di Cranbourne Alli, an amiable and captivating creature, with a weakness for jewelry and flirtation—although a large price set upon him, decidedly not to be sold: SOPHIE WORRELL. *Zerlina*, the Beauty of the Village, and Barmaid of the "Jolly Brigands:" IRENE WORRELL. *Lady Allcash*, a Lady making her first tour, and through F-A-D-O's wiles, very nearly her first trip: JENNIE WORRELL. *Beppo*, a particularly heavy Ruffian, not troubled with the faintest outline of a consicience, or indeed with anything but the conventional hoarseness peculiar to melodramatic Brigands: M. W. LEFFINGWELL. *Lord Allcash*, An English nobleman, making the grand tour and himself as agreeable as possible—the invariable custom of travelling Britons: J. B. CURRAN. *Matteo*, Landlord of the "Jolly Brigands," who refuses to allow his child to marry a man of no means—the monster!: J. S. GOODMAN. *Lorenzo*, an Offcier of Police, who haunts the Tavern, containing his sweetheart—in fact, an inn-spectre—a youth whose figure will prevent his attaining any height in his profession: T. L. DONNELLY. *Giacomo*, a promising young bandit: Mr. Beekman. Francesco, an extensive young farmer: Mr. Reed. *Antonio*, 1858, Z: Mr. James. *Peasants, Peelers, Pretty Girls, Prigs and Populace.*

Scene 1: Exterior of "The Jolly Brigands"—The stern parient—A Carbinier's Carol—Fashionable arrivals—Nerves and their consequences—"3,000 Francs for the capture of Fra Diavolo!"—A ray of hope on the lonely peeler's path—Arrival of Heavy Swell of the period—Matteo has a Full House, but plenty of Orders—Sudden appearance of unprepossessing strangers—Extraordinary instance of Brute Taming by Fra Diavolo, not Mr.

---

[6]Also billed in advertisements, but not billed in program, Messrs. L. R. Benneux, J. R. Pemberton.

[7]First produced in New York 24 December 1855 at Wallack's Lyceum Theatre in repertory. For Synopsis of Scenes and Musical Numbers, see original 1855 production.

[8]First Families of Virginia.

[9]Musical numbers not listed in programs; no published score found. List prepared from Boston program dated 1 April 1865.

[10]Performed with a fore-piece, a two-act comedy entitled Brother Sam, starring Barton Hill.

Rarey's plan—Jealousy, Jewelry and Joy—Restitution, Revenge and Rage. *Scene 2*: Another. Evil consequences of a strike—Beppo possessed of an iron will, and Giacomo proves the legacy—Operatic Selections. *Scene 3*: Zerlina's chamber. An expensive Bust and a Shilling fair—Case of cupboard admiration—Zerlina indulges in a Soliloquy, a Song and a Pas Seul—The Sword which hangs above her prevented from failing by a single Air—Disgraceful appearance of the bridegroom—Sudden vision of a nobleman in trepidation and a Nightcap. *Scene 4*: Another part of the premises. This scene is introduced entirely for the domestic felicity of Lord and Lady Allcash, who become reconciled to their own, and (it is hoped) to the public, satisfaction. *Scene 5*: Gardens at "The Jolly Brigands." Chorus of Brigands, who certainly have no right to be there, but being a very pretty troupe, and having exceedingly nice dresses, must appear at some time—Diavolo himself again—Rejected addresses—Beppo recognizes an old acquaintance—Uncomfortable position of the Brigands—The Ballet turns out a no—Diavolo's descent upon the tin foiled—Lorenzo throws himself on Diavolo, who throws himself on the tender mercies of an enlightened American public. Unalloyed happiness of everybody.

SPECIALTIES, MUSICAL NUMBERS

A Carbinier's Carol (Scene 1)

Operatic Selections (Scene 2)

Soliloquy, Song, Pas Seul (Scene 3)
I. Worrell

Chorus of Brigands (Scene 5)

Grand Pas de Recollection (Scene 5)
M. W. Leffingwell, Mr. Beekman

Ballet (Scene 5)

1866.16 COLUMBUS RECONSTRUCTED

A Revised Version of the Burlesque (Columbus El Filibustero!!) in Two Acts, 7 Scenes[11]. Play by John Brougham. Music by Robert Stoepel. Scenery by Messrs. Charles W. Witham and H. Hillyard. Dresses by Mrs. Bohannon. Machinery by A. Wright. Appointments by H. Duell and Mr. Murray. Produced by John Brougham. Opened 9 July 1866 at the Winter Garden and closed 4 August 1866 after 24 performances.

CAST: *Ferdinand* King of Arragon, an arrogant, aggressive and progressive monarch, of rather a speculative turn: J. C. DUNN. *Cardinal de Fonseca*, keeper of the King's consience, and court spiritual advisor generally, therefore naturally opposed to Columbus and the spread of knowledge: J. G. BURNETT. *Fernando de Talavera*, an old picture very much improved by time: W. S. ANDREWS. *Luis de St. Angel*, a contented office-holder, pursuing the even tenor of his way: J. Hurley. *Alonzo de Quintanella*, a courtier of much lower note: Mr. Gledhill. *Don Christoval Colon, alias Columbus*, a clairvoyant voyager, whose filibustering expedition gave rise to a world of speculation: JOHN BROUGHAM. *Diego*, a semi-colon among the Queen's pages: Miss E. JOHNSON. *Distinguished Members of the Historical Society*, now meeting again for the first time (4): *Vasco Nunez*: J. Oliver. *Hernandez Cortez*: Mr. Hill. *Amerigo Vespucci*: R. Sutton. *Ponce de Leon*: Mr. Hogan. *A noisy crew of Mutineers (4)*: *Sancho Ruis*: Mr. Duell. *Pedro Nino*: Mr. Waddleton. *Bartolomeo*: Mr. Leighs. *Juan Perez*: Mr. Davis. *Isabella*, wife of Ferdinand, possessor of half-a-crown by marriage rite, and a whole one by right of raving to carry its weight on her own shoulders: Miss E. Andrews. *Columbia*, a national debutante, her first appearance on any stage: Miss EMILIE MELVILLE. *Little Miss Colorado*, rather precocious: Miss Carline. *Manhatta*: Miss J. Morton. *Demon of Discord*, a Secessionalist: Mr. N. Decker. *Members of Reception Committee, Aldermen, Discontented Politicians, Independent Voters, and other natural curiosities*: Competent representatives. *Full grown States, Juvenile Territories, etc.*: Energetic Host of Auxiliaries.

Act 1: Speculation. *Scene 1*: A Royal Chateau en Espagne. *Scene 2*: A Part of another apartment in the Palace. *Scene 3*: Deck of the *Santa Maria*. *Scene 4*: Coney Island.

Act 2: Realization. *Scene 1*: The Same Palace in an Empty State. *Scene 2*: Anywhere—the same being a topographical necessity. *Scene 3*: Pyramidic tableau of American Worthies.

ACT 1

Scene 1

"Hail! Oh King of Aragon" (Grand Complimentary Chorus of Courtiers)

"Bound to be a Sailor Boy" (Biographic cantata of Columbus)

"We are so happy" (Chorus of Sharehodlers, narcotic)

Scene 2

"Star Spangled Banner" (Verse)

Scene 3

"Fling him in the briny" (Chorus of deaf mutineers)

"Columbia"

Scene 4

"Swearing death to all who cave" (Grand Demonstrative Finale)

ACT 2

Scene 1

"Gold, gold, is no chimera" (Vocal melange by the whole court)

Medley of Harmonious Airs

Genial March

Scene 3

Pyramidic Tableau of American Worthies; Martial Epochs 1775 and 1865. Brilliant Pyrotechnic Apotheosis.

1866.17 JENNY LIND

A Revival of the Musical Farce in One Act[12]. Produced by John Brougham. Opened 30 July 1866 at the Winter Garden and closed 11 August 1866 after 12 performances.

CAST: *Jenny Leatherlungs*: Miss EMILIE MELVILLE. *Baron Swigitoff Beery*, with a song: J. C. Dunn. *Granby Gagg*: W. S. Andrews. *Lawrence Leatherlungs*: Mr. Adams. *Herr Kanaster*: Mr. N. Decker. *Herr Sheroot*: Mr. Hurley. *Herr Spittoon*: Mr. Waddleton. *Herr Koff*: Mr. Gledhill. *Herr Sneeze*: Mr. Oliver. *Herr Splutter*: Mr. Hill. *Herr Stammer*: Mr. Hogan. *Herr Meerschaum*: Mr. Sutton. *Landlord*: Mr. Duell.

MUSICAL NUMBERS

"I'll Be No Submissive Wife"
E. Melville

Il Bacio—The Kiss
E. Melville

"The Ratcatcher's Daughter"
E. Melville

A Famous Jig (dance)
E. Melville

Song
J. C. Dunn

1866.18 THE BLACK CROOK

An Original, Grand, Romantic Magical and Spectacular Drama in Four Acts, 17 Scenes. Play by Charles M. Barras. Music by Thomas E. Baker. Produced under the immediate direction of William Wheatley. Ballets directed by Davide Costa. Scenery by Richard Marston, J. E. Hayes, R. S. Smith, D. A. Strong, F. W. Seaver, W. Wallack, Brothers Drew. Costumes by M. Phillipe and Madame Costa. Properties and appointments by S. Wallis. Gas contrivances by Charles Murray. Calcium lights by Charles Seward. Conductor, Harvey B. Dodworth. Produced by Henry Jarrett and Harry Palmer, by arrangement with William Wheatley. Opened 12 September 1866 at Niblo's Garden, reconstructed 27 May 1867[13], 30 September 1867 and closed 4 January 1868 after 475 performances.

---

[11]First produced in New York in an earlier version as COLUMBUS EL FILIBUSTERO!! 30 December 1857 at Burton's Theatre in repertory. As an after–piece, A Pretty Piece of Business was presented for the first two weeks of the run; in the third week, Time Tries All, a play by J. Courtney, took its place; for the final week Miss Emelie Melville assumed the title role in the operetta JENNY LIND.

[12]Performed as a fore-piece to COLUMBUS (Reconstructed) for the first week, and to PO-CA-HON-TAS! for the second week.

[13]Introduced in January 1867:

"Fairyland's Daughters" (Aria)(Act 2)
A. K. Bowler
(*Music by* Harvey B. Dodworth.)

"Now let the glorious Sun of Joy" (Cavatina)(Act 2)
A. K. Bowler
(*Music by* Harvey B. Dodworth.)

Dance de Tartufo (Act 3)
Mlles. Sangalli, Mazzeri (2), Zuardi, Zuccoli
For the May 1867 revision, Jarret & Palmer offered new scenery by Richard Marston of a magnificent ball-room scene (Act 4), and new ballets, "The Bouquet" (Act 1), "The Water Lily" and "Pas de Demon" (both Act 2). The Grand Carnival in the Ballroom (Act 4) featured new ballets: Galop, La Postillon, Deborah; Punchinello, La Tarantella, La Folie and Pas Chinois.

Added in late July 1867, replacing her 2 other songs:

"Some Fairy Hand" (Cavatina)
A. K. Bowler

The September revision featured:

"Tapping at the Window" (Song)
Lizzie Willmore [Carline]

CAST: *Count Wolfenstein*: J. W. BLAISDELL. *Rodolphe*, a poor artist: GEORGE C. BONIFACE. *Von Puffengruntz*, the Count's steward: J. G. BURNETT. *Hertzog*, the Black Crook, an alchymist and sorcerer: C. H. MORTON. *Greppo*, his drudge, with duet and dance: GEORGE ATKINS. *Zamiel*, the arch-fiend: E. B. HOLMES. *Wolfgar*, a gypsy ruffian: E. Barry. *Bruno*, his companion: F. Ellis. *Casper*, a peasant: H. Weaver. *Red Glare*, the Recording Demon: F. Clark. *Skuldawelp*, familiar to Hertzog: Mr. Rendle. *Jan*: Frank Little.

Amphibea (8): *Dragonfin*: Hernandez Foster. *Hackletooth*: Mr. Weaver. *Sharkskin*: Mr. Ellis. *Splayfoot*: Mr. Miles. *Stickleback*: Mr. Pray. *Mulletmug*: Mr. Evans. *Eeleye*: Mr. Willis. *Cuttlekonk*: Mr. Snowden.

Gnomes (6): *Golddust*: Mr. Webb. *Nuggetnose*: Mr. Tuttle. *Yellowscale*: Mr. Gage. *Spangleneck*: Mr. West. *Smelterface*: Mr. Wells. *Pinchback*: Mr. Law. *Villagers, Peasants, Guards, Attendants, Demons, Monsters, Apparitions, Skeltons, Gnomes, etc.*

Stalacta, Queen of the Golden Realm, Prima Donna Contralta, with songs: ANNIE KEMP (BOWLER). *Her Attendants* (8): *Crystaline*: Miss Richardson. *Rubyblossom*: Miss Moseley. *Sapphire*: Miss Atkins. *Emeraldine*: Miss Consoll. *Scintilla*: Miss Josephine. *Amythysta*: : Miss McLean. *Coralbud*: Miss Brown. *Garnet*: Miss Hodges. *Amina*, betrothed to Rodolphe: ROSE MORTON. *Dame Barbara*, her foster mother: Mary Wells. *Carline*, with songs and dance: MILLY CAVENDISH. *Rosetta*, a peasant: Miss C. Whitlock. *Fairies, Sprites, Naiads, Submarine Monsters, etc.*

Parisienne Ballet Troupe: Mlles. MARIE BONFANTI, RITA SANGALLI (Première Danseuses Assoluta), BETTY RIGL, Louisa and Giovana Mazzeri, Amelie and Eugenia Zuccoli, Guiseppe, Luisidi, Marie Duclos, Paulina, Zuardi. Signor DAVIDE COSTA. *Coryphées*: Mlles. Rose Delval, Elise, Helene Delval, Emilie Rigl, Armande, Nathile, Urban, Marie Doche, Lacroix, Fleur Jollie, Portois, Leoni Portois, St. Bertrand, Artois, Marie, Rose Cheri, Helene, etc.

The action takes place in and around the Hartz Mountains, about 1600.

Act 1, Scene 1: A Valley at the foot of the Hartz Mountains. (Hayes.) *Scene 2*: A Woody Pass. (Seaver.) *Scene 3*: Laboratory of the Black Crook. (Smith.) *Scene 4*: An Apartment in the Castle of Wolfenstein. (Carline.) *Scene 5*: A Wild Glen in the heart of the Brocken. (Smith.) Cataract of Real Water and River of Blood. (Marston.)

Act 2, Scene 1: Subterranean Vault in the Castle of Wolfenstein. (Smith.) *Scene 2*: Lobby in the Castle of Wolfenstein. (Smith.) *Scene 3*: A Wild Pass in the Hartz Mountains. (Strong.) *Scene 4*: The Grotto of Stalacta. (Marston.)

Act 3: Illuminated Garden of Wolfenstein by Moonlight. (Smith.)

Act 4, Scene 1: An Apartment in the Castle of Wolfenstein. *Scene 2*: The Retreat of Rudolphe in the Forest. (Wallack.) *Scene 3*: A Forest. *Scene 4*: A Burning Forest. (Marston.) *Scene 5*: Another part of the Forest. *Scene 6*: Pandemonium. (Seaver.) *Scene 7*: The Palace of Dew Drops. (Drew.)

ACT 1[14]
Scene 1
"Early in the Morning" (Song)
M. Cavendish
Grand Ballet: Pas de Sabot
Mlles. Delval, Paulina, Elise, Helene, Marie, Rose, Cheri, Helene, Duclos
Pas de Fleurs
Mlles. Bonfanti, Sangalli, Rigl,
Mazzeri (2), Zuccoli (2), Guiseppe, Luisidi, M. Duclos, Paulina, Full Corps
Scene 4
"Naughty, Naughty Man" (You Naughty, Naughty Men)(Song)
M. Cavendish
(*Music by* G. Bicknell. *Lyrics by* T. Kennick.)
Scene 5
Grand Incantation! Introducing many Weird and Startling Effects

ACT 2
Scene 4
Splendid Pas de Naide
Mlle. Sangalli, Full Ballet
"Flow On, Silver Stream" (Song)
A. K. Bowler
"(The) Power of Love" (Song)
A. K. Bowler
March of Fishes and Dance of Mermaids
Corps de Ballet
Pas de Demons
Mlles. Bonfanti, Rigl, Zuccoli, Zuardi, Mazzeri; Signor D. Costa

ACT 3
The Bal Masque:
Pas Espagnole
Mlle. Sangali, Eight Second Premiers
Pas de Hongroise
Mlles. Mazzeri (2), Zucoli, Zuardi
An Original and Grand Dance de Amazons
Mlle. Bonfanti, Full Corps

ACT 4
Scene 2
Triple Sword Combat
Scene 5
Duet and Dance
M. Cavendish, G. Atkins
Scene 7
Dazzling Transformation Scene, revealing the Nymphs of the Golden Realm, terminating with Stalacta's Happiness and Joy.

1866.19 THE DOCTOR OF ALCANTARA

A Revival of the Comic Operetta (Opéra-bouffe) in Two Acts[15]. Libretto by Benjamin E. Woolf. Music by Julius Eichberg. (Directed by Jules Eichberg. Musical director, Julius Eichberg. Produced by the English Comic Opera Company.) Opened 13 September 1866 at the Théâtre Français and closed 25 September 1866 in repertory.

CAST: *Isabella*: MINA GEARY. *Lucrezia*: LIZZIE ALLEN. *Inez*: FANNIE STOCKTON. *Carlos*: W. F. HILL. *Doctor (Paracelsus)*: E. DUCHESNE. *Pomposo*: M. Montrose. *(Señor) Balthazar*: E. Warden. *Chorus*.

1866.20 THE TWO DOVES/HIPPODROME!

Kelly & Leon's Minstrels in a Minstrel Program in Two Acts. Stage director, Edwin Kelly. Scenic artist, Ludovico Malmsha. Leader of orchestra, T. McNally. Produced by (Edwin) Kelly and (Francis) Leon's Great Western Minstrels. Opened 1 October 1866 at Kelly & Leon's Minstrel Hall and closed 6 October 1866 after 6 performances.

CAST: EDWIN KELLY, FRANCIS LEON, FRANK MORAN, JOHN ALLEN, JOHN F. OBERIST, T. McNALLY, Messrs. Jackson, J. F. Dunnie, Shattuck, E. B. Fairbanks, Solomons, Devereux, H. Mudge, Sterling, J. Rainforth, Thompson, A. S. Parks, Sam Price, C. Williams, J. Grant.

ACT 1
Opening Operatic Chorus (Selection from Sicilian Vespers)
Minstrels
"When the Moon with Glory Brightens"
Mr. Jackson
"S.T. 1860"
J. Allen
"Marion Lee"
E. Kelly
"Finnegan's Wake"
F. Moran
"Mountain Song'
J. F. Oberist
"When I Courted Miss Kidd"
E. Kelly, J. Allen, F. Moran, Company
(*Music and Lyrics by* Francis Leon.)

Footnote 13 (continued)

New Dances (Act 3); La Guarde Imperiale (with 150 children); La Petite Ravel; Belle Vivandiere, Hungarian Pas Nationale; Carnival de Venice; Harlequinade; Grand Amazonian March.

Mechanical Donkey (Act 4)

[14]Much music was published from various editions of THE BLACK CROOK. "The Black Crook Galop" and "Transformation Polka" were both credited to Thomas Baker. Baker's own piano selection included the titles Bonfanti, Sangalli, Betty Regal [Rigl], evidently excerpted ballet specialty music. Piano arrangements of the "March of the Amazons," "Black Crook Waltes," "Mazzari Mazurka," "Costa Polka" and "Water Nymphs Galop" were also published by permission of Signor Davide Costa.

[15]Accompanied by a farce, Wanted, 1,000 Milliners. THE DOCTOR OF ALCANTARA was first produced in New York 28 May 1866 at the Théâtre Français in repertory. For Synopsis of Scenes and Musical Numbers, see original 1866 production.

ACT 2

L'Ariel

F. Leon

Quartette

Messrs. Jackson, Oberist, Dunnie, Fairbanks

The Active Boy

J. Allen

Solo, Clarionet

Mr. Solomons

THE TWO DOVES, an operetta by Francis Leon.

Mr. Peregrine Dove: E. Kelly. *Mrs. Peregrine Dove*: F. Leon.

Solo, Clog

H. Mudge

Oxygenated Air!

Demonstrator of the same: F. Moran. *Victims to Prejudice*: J. Allen, J. F. Oberist, Dunnie, Jackson.

The Cow-bell-o-gians, from their native mountains

HIPPODROME!, Kelly & Leon's great burlesque, introducing eight highly trained and magnificent Arabians, the Busy Family, Hand-a-lones, and other celebrities.

1866.21 THE DOCTOR OF ALCANTARA

A Revival of the Opéra-bouffe in Two Acts[16]. Libretto by Benjamin E. Woolf. Music by Julius Eichberg. Assistant stage manager, E. F. Taylor. Scenery by Richard Farren. Musical director, Julius Eichberg. Managers, Lewis Baker and Mark Smith. Opened 3 October 1866 at the New York Theatre and closed 20 October 1866 after 16 performances in repertory.

CAST: *Doctor Paracelsus*: MARK SMITH. *Señor Balthazar*: WILLIAM GOMERSAL. *Carlos*, his son: JOHN FARLEY. *Don Pomposo*: Joseph Weinlich. *Perez*: Mr. Caldwell. *Sancho*: Mr. Chapman. *Inez*: Mrs. WILLIAM GOMERSAL. *Donna Lucrezia*, Wife of Doctor Paracelsus: Mrs. SOPHIE MOZART. *Isabella*, her daughter: MARIA NORTON. *Serenaders, Citizens, etc.*: Full and Efficient Chorus.

ACT 1

"Wake, Lady, Wake" (Serenade)

J. Farley, Chorus

"You Saucy Jade" (Quarrel Trio)

Mrs. W. Gomersal, M. Norton, S. Mozart

"He Still Was There" (Romanza)

Miss M. Norton

"If a Lover Is Poor" (Arietta)

Mrs. W. Gomersal

"Away Despair" (Duettino)

M. Norton, Mrs. W. Gomersal

"Buenos Noches" (Porter's Song)

Messrs. Caldwell, Chapman

"Day Dreams of Love" (Ballad)

J. Farley

"The Knight of Alcantara" (Romanza)

S. Mozart

"I Love, I Love" (Duo)

S. Mozart, J. Farley

Scena and Bolero

J. Weinlich, M. Smith, M. Norton

Finale

S. Mozart, M. Norton, Chorus

ACT 2

"Senor, Senor" (Trio)

J. Farley, M. Smith, Mrs. W. Gomersal

"Here You Must Repose" (Cabaletta)

J. Farley, M. Smith, Mrs. W. Gomersal

"So Odd a House" (Stretta)

J. Farley, M. Smith, Mrs. W. Gomersal

"Good Night" (Quartette)

W. Gomersal, Mrs. W. Gomersal, M. Smith, S. Mozart, M. Norton

Finale:

"I Tremble o'er with Fear" (Duo)

M. Smith, Mrs. W. Gomersal

"Oh! Where am I?" (Trio)

J. Farley, M. Smith, Mrs. W. Gomersal

"Is He Your Son?" (Quintette)

M. Norton, J. Farley, M. Smith, Mrs. W. Gomersal, S. Mozart

"Hope Ever Smiling" (Concerted)

Ensemble

1866.22 THE DOCTOR OF ALL-CAN-TEAR-HER!

Kelly & Leon's Minstrels in a Burlesque (of Eichburg's The Doctor of Alcantara) in One Scene, preceded by an Olio. (Written by Edwin Kelly and Francis Leon.) Stage director, Edwin Kelly. Scenic artist, Ludovico Malmsha. Leader of orchestra, T. McNally. Produced by (Edwin) Kelly and (Francis) Leon's Minstrels. Opened 8 October 1866 at Kelly & Leon's Opera House in featured repertory.

CAST: EDWIN KELLY, FRANCIS LEON, GEORGE CHRISTY, DICK SANDS, G. W. JACKSON, John Allen, John F. Oberist, George Guy, Willie Guy, E. B. Fairbanks, L. H. West.

ACT 1

Opening Operatic Chorus

Minstrels

"Annie O' the Banks O' Dee"

G. W. Jackson

"Why Don't They Do So Now"

G. Christy

"Maid of Beauty, Fond and True"

E. Kelly

"The Feller That Looks Like Me"

J. Allen

"Mountain Song"

J. F. Oberist

The Darkey at the Play

E. Kelly, G. Christy, J. Allen

ACT 2

Pas des Anglais

The Wonderful (Francis) Leon

Ballad

G. W. Jackosn

Double Song and Dance

G. Guy, W. Guy

MATRIMONY, an Operetta by Edwin Kelly

Mr. Goodheart: E. B. Fairbanks. *Frank Duval*: E. Kelly. *Clara Duval*: F. Leon.

Champion Clog Dance

D. Sands

Fifth Avenue Help

G. Christy, J. Allen, J. F. Oberist

Solo, Flageolet

L. H. West

My-De-Ar Res-Tore-Her (Leon in his Great Living Photograph)

Nicodemus Johnson (Specialty)

J. Allen

THE DOCTOR OF ALL-CAN-TEAR-HER! (a Burlesque of the Comic Opera by Julius Eichberg and Benjamin E. Woolf).

CAST: *Grand-ma All-can-tear-her*: GEORGE CHRISTY. *Grand-pa All-can-tear-her*: JOHN F. OBERIST. *Car Lost*: EDWIN KELLY. *Hearherbeller*: FRANCIS LEON. *Serenaders, Citizens, etc.*

1866.23 LE MAÎTRE DE CHAPELLE

An Opéra-Comique in One Act[17], in French. (Comédie by Alexandre Duval. Paroles by Mme. Sophie Gay.) Music by Ferdinando Paër. Costumes

[16]First produced in New York 28 May 1866 at the Théâtre Français in repertory. For Synopsis of Scenes and Musical Numbers, see original 1866 production. Advertisements claim that the composer had added a Tenor Romanza and Duo for Soprano and Tenor, expressly for this revival production.

[17]On a bill with Le Mari de la Veuve and La Consigne est de Ronfler.

by Mons. H. Deligne. Conductor, Auguste Predigam. P. Juignet, C. Drivet, Directeurs. Opened 11 October 1866 at the Théâtre Français in repertory.

CAST: *Barnabé*, Maître de Chapelle: Mons. WILHELM. *Benetto*, son neveu: Mons. EDGARD. *Gertrude*, servante de Barnabé: Mlle. LAURENTIS.

Scene: The home of Mons. Barnabé, in a village near Milan.

MUSICAL NUMBERS[18]

Trio (Paix! Chut!)
Mlle. Laurentis, Messrs. Wilhelm, Edgard

Scene (Ah! quel plaisir de presenttir sa gloire!)
Mons. Wilhelm

Duo (Comment comment comment voulez-vous que je chante)
Mlle. Laurentis, Mons. Wilhelm

1866.24

A NIGHT IN ROME

A Revival of the Operetta Bouffe in One Act[19] Libretto and music by Julius Eichberg. Scenery by Richard Farren. Costumes by R. Williams. Machinery and properties by Denham and Lundy. Musical director, Julius Eichberg. Managers, Lewis Baker and Mark Smith. Opened 17 October 1866 at the New York Theatre and closed 18 October 1866 after 2 performances.

CAST: *Pietro*, a gondolier: C. F. Shattuck. *Moccoloni*, a Village Barber: Mr. JOHN FARLEY. *Beppo*: ?. *Grand Judge*: ?. *Coro*: ?. *Giuglio*: ?. *Ninetta*, an Orphan: Mrs. WILLIAM GOMERSAL. *Masqueraders, Policemen, Citizens, Gondoliers*: Chorus.

Company included Mr. CALDWELL, Mr. CHAPMAN, Mr. PERCY and a strengthened chorus. During the opera, a ballet and a new feature, the Dance of the Jumping Jacks, The Knaves of Diamonds, Hearts, Spades and Clubs, will be introduced.

1866.25

LE TORÉADOR

An Opéra-Bouffon in Two Acts in French (on a bill with LE MAÎTRE DE CHAPELLE). Libretto by Mons. T. Sauvage. Music by Adolphe Adam. Costumes by Mons. H. Deligne. Conductor, Auguste Predigam. P. Juignet, C. Drivet, Directeurs. Opened 18 October 1866 at the Théâtre Français in repertory.

CAST: *Don Belfor*, Toréador en retraite: Mons. VERT. *Coraline*, sa femme: Mlle. NADDIE. *Tracolin*: Mons. ANTHELME.

Scene: Barcelona, Spain.

ACT 1[20]

Scène (Tandis que tout sommeille)
Mlle. Naddie

Couplets (Je tremble et doute)
Mlle. Naddie

Trio (La voila là la voila)
Mlle. Naddie, Messrs. Vert, Anthelme

Air (Oui la vie oui la vie)
Mons. Vert

Couplets (Vous connaissez)
Mons. Anthelme

Trio (Ah! vous dirais–je maman)
Mlle. Naddie, Messrs. Vert, Anthelme

Duo (Qu'est cela)
Mlle. Naddie, Mons. Vert

ACT 2

Air (Avec son petit air)
Mlle. Naddie

Air (Dans vos regards)
Mons. Anthelme

Trio Final (Oh! tremblez)
Mlle. Naddie, Messrs. Vert, Anthelme

1866.26

DOMESTIC BLISS!/ DODGING FOR A WIFE

Kelly & Leon's Minstrels in an Operetta and Farce each in One Scene, accompanied by an Olio. (Written by Edwin Kelly and Francis Leon.) Stage director, Edwin Kelly. Scenic artist, Ludovico Malmsha. Leader of orchestra, T. McNally. Produced by (Edwin) Kelly and (Francis) Leon's Minstrels. Opened 22 October 1866 at Kelly & Leon's Minstrels in featured repertory.

CAST: EDWIN KELLY, FRANCIS LEON, G. W. Jackson, John Allen, Frank Moran, John Oberist, Dick Sands, George and Willie Guy, E. B. Fairbanks, Mr. Dunnie.

ACT 1

"Lucretia" (Grand Opening Chorus)
Minstrels

"Annie O' the Banks O' Dee"
G. W. Jackson

"The Fenian ball"
J. Allen

"Little Barefoot"
E. Kelly

"Gal with the Hood On"
F. Moran

"Swiss Mountain Song"
J. Oberist

Queer, Querious and Inquisitive Questions (written by Francis Leon)
E. Kelly, F. Moran, J. Allen

ACT 2

Pas des Anglais
The Wonderful (Francis) Leon

The Two Gaylies!
G. Christy, E. Kelly, F. Moran, J. F. Oberist

Broadway News Boy, with Imitations
J. Allen

DOMESTIC BLISS!, an Operetta by Francis Leon.

CAST: *Mr. Bliss*: E. Kelly. *Mrs. Bliss*: F. Leon.

Champion Clog Dance
D. Sands

Laughing Gas!
Demonstrator of the same: F. Moran. *Victims to prejudice*: J. Allen, J. Oberist, Messrs. Dunnie and Jackson.

Double Song and Dance
G. Guy, W. Guy

DODGING FOR A WIFE, a Farce by Francis Leon.

CAST: *Mr. Schnapps*: J. F. Oberist. *Slimkia Sason*: E. Kelly. *Lollypop*: G. Christy. *Policeman*: E. B. Fairbanks. *Sally Schnapps*: (F.) Leon. &c., &c., &c.

1866.27

LE CHÂLET/ LES NOCES DE JEANNETTE

A Double Bill of Opéra-comique, in French. Costumes by Mons. H. Deligne. Conductor, Auguste Predigam. P. Juignet, C. Drivet, Directeurs. Opened 23 October 1866 at the Théâtre Français in repertory.

LE CHÂLET. An Opéra-comique in One Act, in French. Libretto by Eugène Scribe and A. H. J. Mélesville. Music by Adolphe Adam.

CAST: *Daniel*, jeune fermier: Mons. de SURMONT. *Max*, soldat Suisse: Mons. VERT. *Bettly*, soeur de Max: Mlle. LAURENTIS. *Choeurs de soldats, paysans, paysannes*.

Scene: Switzerland, in the canton of Appenzel.

[18]Musical numbers not listed in programs. Published in France as LE MAÎTRE DE CHAPELLE, ou Le Souper Imprévu. List prepared from published French piano vocal score (Emile Gallet, Paris, 1824). A later two-act version introduced the characters Firmin, Sans Quartier and Coelénie.

[19]First produced in New York 25 June 1866 at the Théâtre Français in a two act version. Followed by an after-piece, a Comedietta , Wanted a Thousands Milliners, with Mark Smith and dramatic company.

[20]Musical numbers not listed in programs. List prepared from published French piano vocal score (Brandus et Cie., Paris, 1849).

MUSICAL NUMBERS[21]

Introduction (Déjà dans la plaine)
Choeur
Air (Elle est à moi c'est ma compagne)
Couplets (Dans ce modeste et simple asile)
Air (Arrêtons-nous ici)
Mons. Vert
Ensemble (Par cet étroit sentier)
Mons. Vert, Mlle. Laurentis, Choeur
Couplets (Dans le service de l'Autriche)
Mons. Vert, Mlle. Laurentis
Duo (Prêt à quitter ceux que l'on aime)
Mlle. Laurentis, Mons. de Surmont
Duo (Il faut me céder ta maitresse)
Messrs. de Surmont, Vert
Romance (Adieu vous que j'ai tant chérie)
Mons. De Surmont, Mlle. Laurentis
Trio (Soutiens mon bras Dieu que j'implore)
Messrs. Vert, de Surmont, Mlle. Laurentis

LES NOCES DE JEANNETTE. A Revival of the Opéra-comique in One Act[22], in French. (Libretto by Michel Carré and Jules Barbier.) Music by Victor Massé.

CAST: *Jean*: Mons. WILHELM. *Jeannette*: Mlle. NADDIE. *Le Petit-Pierre*: Mlle. ALPHONSINE. *Paysans*.

1866.28

JACK AND GILL WENT UP THE HILL

A Revival of the Comic Pantomime in 11 Scenes[23]. Spectacle written and invented by George L. Fox. Opening and Explanatory dialogue by G. C. Howard. Stage direction by George L. Fox. New music, original and selected, by Alexander Tyte. Scenery by J. Johnson. Costumes by Keyser. Elaborate transformations and machinery by William Crane. Properties, appointments and decorations by Nelse Waldron. Ballet arranged by Mons. Grossi. Calcium lights and illuminations by Thomas Newton. Produced by George L. Fox. Opened 12 November 1866 at Fox's Bowery Theatre and closed 1 December 1866 after 22 performances.

CAST: *Jackdaw Jaculation*, known throughout the country as Troublesome Jack, afterwards Clown: GEORGE L. FOX. *Mistress Jurisprudence Gill*, afterwards Pantaloon: CHARLES K. FOX. *Little Jack Horner*, the good boy of the village, afterwards Harlequin: Master TIMOTHY. *Little Mary Marigold*, afterwards Columbine: Mlle. MARTINETTI[24]. *Fleece*, Mary's favorite lamb: A Real One. *Luminous*, the Sun Spirit, protector of Little Jack Horner and Mary: C. Foster. *Smaller Luminaries*, but closely connected with the Sun Spirit (4): *Sun Beam*: Miss Dulany. *Sun Rise*: Miss Douglas. *Sun Set*: Miss Forrest. *Sun Shine*: Miss Shelden. *King Icicle Icy*, Grand Ruler of the Frozen Waters: G. Malmberg. *His Satellites and Guardian Sprites of the Magic Icebergs* (4): *Frostiano*: Mr. Thomas. *Wintry Winds*: Mr. Sanford. *Frozen rain*: F. Hofele. *Sleetyhailall*: W. Mitchell. *Squire Arrogant*, a rich but haughty person: J. B. Howland. *Oppressor Arrogant*, his son, "a chip off the old block": J. Baker. *Farmers* who take after the old song (5): *Rogueingrain*: Mr. Baily. *Wheaten*: Mr. Whitman. *Barleycorn*: Mr. Jerrold. *Oatcake*: Mr. Goodwin. *Grist*: Mr. Truman. *P. T. Poor*: Mr. Thomas. *H.T. Blind*: Mr. Banks. *P.O. Bummer*, a beggar: Mr. Stout. *Short Cake*, a baker: Mr. Yeast. *Freedman Bureau Bill*, a black boy: Master William.[25] *Tag, Rag and Bobtail*: By any amount of Ragged Urchins. *Levy Stickemall*, a Merchant offering "Two segars for five cents": Mr. Simons. *One-for-pork Two-for-mutton*, a pieman: Mr. Murray. *Mike O'Rafferty*, a Yankee Peddler: Mr. Jones. *Grabem, Catchem*, Policemen: Messrs. Myers, Odwell. *Yourordersir*, a waiter: Mr. Burden. *Dontknowhisname*, an organ-grinder: Mr. Birchler. *Bagetelle*, his monkey, an inmate of the college: A Real One. *Howmanyyards*, a dry goods clerk: Mr. Davis. *Cheap John*, of the Yankee Notions: Mr. Davis. *Farmers, Policemen, Shopsellers, etc. Old Mother Widdle Waddle*: Mr. J. Lewis. *Susan Waitonthedoor*, a maid: Miss Crand. *Madame Anybody*, a shoplifter: Miss Canby.

[21]Musical numbers not listed in programs. List prepared from published French piano vocal score (Schonenberger, Paris, 1834).
[22]First produced in New York in French 28 October 1861 at the Academy of Music in repertory. For Synopsis of Scenes and Musical Numbers, see original 1861 production.
[23]First produced in New York 19 February 1866 at Fox's Bowery Theatre for 70 performances; re-opened 9 July 1866 at Barnum's Museum for 35 additional performances. This revival was accompanied by a Farce or Drama.
[24]For return engagement at Barnum's Museum, this role was assumed by KATE PENNOYER.
[25]For return engagement at Barnum's Museum, this role was assumed by Master George Topack.

1866.29

L'AMOUR QUE QU'C'EST QU'ÇA?/ LES DEUX AVEUGLES

A Double Bill of Opéra-comique[26], in French. Costumes by Mons. H. Deligne. Conductor, Auguste Predigam. P. Juignet, C. Drivet, Directeurs. Opened 24 November 1866 at the Theatre Français in repertory.

LES DEUX AVEUGLES. A Revival of the Bouffonnerie Musicale in One Act, in French[27]. (Libretto by Jules Moineaux.) Music by Jacques Offenbach.

CAST: *Patachou*: Mons. EDGARD. *Girafier*: Mons. FRANCIS.

L'AMOUR QUE QU'C'EST QU'ÇA?. A Vaudeville-Opérette in One Act, in French.[28] Libretto by Clairville. Music by Julien Nargéot.

CAST: *Blezinet*, Meunier: Mlle. ROSA SAUNIER. *Pitou*, Garçon de Moulin: Mons. FRANCIS. *Le père Toby*, vieux Berger: Mons. DELIGNE. *François*, Garçon de Moulin: Mons. LUCIEN. *Suzanne*: Mlle. Caruel. *Zerline*: Mlle. Dambrun. *Jacqueline*: Mlle. Solange. *Garçons, Meuniers et Filles de Moulin*.

1866.30

TROMB-AL-CA-ZAR

A Revival of the Bouffonnerie Musicale in One Act, in French[29]. (Libretto by Charles Dupeuty and Ernest Bourget.) Music by Jacques Offenbach. Costumes by Mons. H. Deligne. Conductor, Auguste Predigam. P. Juignet, C. Drivet, Directeurs. Opened 3 December 1866 at the Théâtre Français in repertory.

CAST: *Gigolette*: Mlle. LAURENTIS. *Beaujolais*: Mons. EDGARD. *Vert-Panné*: Mons. Chol. *Simplette*: Mlle. LAURENTIS. *Ignace*: Mons. Francis. *Comédiens et Comédiennes*.

1866.31

TOM-TOM, THE PIPER'S SON
Stole a Pig and Away he Run

A Comic Pantomime in One Act, 8 Scenes.[30] Music composed and arranged by B. Deane. Scenery by William Wallack. Machinery by J. Connaughty. Tricks and appointments by Nelse Waldron. Dances and ballet by W. Stanton. Proprietor, J. W. Lingard. Opened 3 December 1866 at the New Bowery Theatre and closed 14 December 1866 after 11 performances.

CAST: Opening: *Tom, Tom, the Piper's Son*: W. STANTON. *Old Towzer*: Mr. (Andrew) GLASSFORD. *Grim Griffling*: Mr. PEARSON. *John Oblong*: LITTLE MAC. *Margery Daw*: KATE GLASSFORD.

Immortals: *Fairy Goodwill* Sallie Steele. *Amethyst*: Miss Fowell. *Diamond*: Miss Fenton. *Ruby*: Miss Barnes. *Emerald*: Nellie Davenport. *Coral*: Frank Davenport. *Garnet*: Sayers. *Amber*: Syirice. *Agate*: Eliza Glassford.

Transformation: *Harlequin*: W. STANTON. *Clown*: LITTLE MAC. *Pantaloon*: (Andrew) GLASSFORD. *Columbine*: KATE GLASSFORD.

Scene 1: Abode of the Fairies. *Scene 2*: A Street. *Scene 3*: The Blasted Heath. *Scene 4*: Quiet Street. *Scene 5*: Interior of Hotel. *Scene 6*: A Grove. *Scene 7*: Dark Regions. *Scene 8*: Magic Change to Revolving Temple, and the Abode of the Fairies.

[26]With the comedy 500 Francs de recompense! performed after LES DEUX AVEUGLES.
[27]First produced in New York in French 31 August 1857 at the Metropolitan Music Hall.
[28]Musical numbers not listed in programs; no published piano vocal score found.
[29]Accompanied by Rosier's Croque-Poule and Scribe's Les Premiers Amours, then later Massé's opera Galathée, and Ambrose Thomas' opera buffa The Caïd. TROMB-AL-CA-ZAR was first produced in New York 12 January 1864 at Théâtre Français (Niblo's Saloon).
[30]Author not credited. Preceded by a nautical drama My Poll and My Partner Joe, and followed by a drama The Vagrant, his Wife and Family. In the second week of the run, an Irish drama Invasion of Ireland opened the performance; the pantomime was followed by a comedy, Mrs. Green's Grocery Store, or, The Amorous Policeman.

BALLETS, SPECIALTIES
"Listen, Fairies" (Scene 1)
Chorus
"Tom, Tom, The Piper's Son" (Scene 1)
Chorus
"See Saw" (Scene 1)
Chorus
Grand Transformation Scene (Scene 3)
Dance (Scene 4)
W. Stanton, K. Glassford
Zingarilla (Scene 5)
W. Stanton, K. Glassford
Shadow Pantomime (Scene 5)
Dance (Scene 6)
W. Stanton, K. Glassford
"Stout Boy Wanted" (Scene 7)

1866.32 MATRIMONY/ THE BLACK STATUE

An Operetta in One Scene, and a Burlesque in One Scene, accompanied by an Olio. (Written by Edwin Kelly and Francis Leon.) Stage director, Edwin Kelly. Scenic artist, Ludovico Malmsha. Leader of orchestra, T. McNally. Produced by (Edwin) Kelly and (Francis) Leon's Minstrels. Opened 3 December 1866 at Kelly & Leon's Minstrels in featured repertory.

MATRIMONY, an Operetta in One Scene, by Edwin Kelly.

CAST: *Mr. Goodheart*: W. Butler. *Frank Duval*: EDWIN KELLY. *Clara Duval*: FRANCIS LEON. Introducing the Trio from ATTILA, "Tu sol quest' anima." (*Music by* Giuseppe Verdi.)

THE BLACK STATUE, a Burlesque in One Scene.

CAST: *Jake*: GEORGE CHRISTY. *Pete*: EDWIN KELLY. *Dr. Pilgarlic*: William H. Brockway. *Old Squintum*: John F. Oberist. *Mrs. Squintum*: Sam Price. *Rose*, her daughter: [FRANCIS] LEON.

1866.33 ORPHEUS IN DER UNTERWELT

A Revival of the Burleske Oper in Two Acts, 4 Scenes[31], in German. Original French libretto by Hector Crémieux. German adaptation by Johann Nestroy. Music by Jacques Offenbach. Opened 12 December 1866 at the Stadt-Theater in repertory, closing 1 January 1867.

CAST: *Diana*: JEANETTE REIFFARTH. *Orpheus*: Herr KLEIN. *Die öffentliche Meinung* (Public Opinion): Frau HOYM. *Eurydice*: Frau STEGLICH-FUCHS. *Aristæus*: Herr Brügmann. *Pluto*: *Jupiter*: Herr Knorr. *Apollo*: Herr Lennert. *Mars*: Herr Stemmler. *Cupido*: Fraulein Ebert. *Minerva*: Fraulein Irschick. *Venus*: Frau Becker-Grahn. *Juno*: Frau Hübner. *Neptun*: Herr Piperti. *Merkur* (Mercury): Herr Fortner. *Hebe*: Frau Unger. *Styx*: Herr Reiffarth.

1866.34 CENDRILLON

The Parisian Fairy Spectacle in Five Acts, 16 Scenes. Translated from the French by L. E. Beneux (from the fairy tale by Charles Perrault). New and appropriate music composed and arranged by Henry Tissington. Scenery and wardrobe under the supervision of Sallie A. Hinckley. Production under the direction of Sallie A. Hinckley. Ballet under the direction of Signor Grossi. Scenery by Griffith Morgan, George Heilge, Minard Lewis. Managers, Lewis Baker and Mark Smith. Produced by Sallie A. Hinckley. Opened 13 December 1866 at the New York Theatre and closed 28 January 1867 after (36) performances.

CAST: *Prince Charming*: ELIZA NEWTON. *Cendrillon*: Mrs. WILLIAM GOMERSAL. *Urania de la Houspignolle*: Mrs. MARIE WILKINS. *Javotte*: SAIDEE COLE. *Madelon*: ALICIA MANDEVILLE. *Luciola*, Fairy of the Glow-worms: SALLIE A. HINCKLEY. *Oculi*: ANNIE YEAMANS. *President of Cupid's Court*: Mrs. H. Bland. *Aurora*: Rosa St. Clair. *Queen of the Sun*: Ada Devere. *Queen of the Night*: Annie Kreuger. *King Hurly Burly XIX*: MARK SMITH. *Mons. De la Pinchonnière*: LEWIS BAKER. *Jolicoco*, Prime Minister: WILLIAM GOMERSAL. *Riquiqui*: F. Percy. *Farhulaz*: H. Bland. *Maclou*: F. Chapman. *Usher*: C. Newton. *Marteau*: F. Williams.

[31]Previously produced in German March 1861 at the Stadttheater in repertory.

The Five Senses: *Princesses of the Isle of Flowers*: *Princesses of the Butterflies*: *Princesses of the Crystal Grottoes*: *Princesses of the Volcanic Isles*: *Officers of the Court, Hussars, Amazons, Diamondtines, Lords, Ladies, Peasants, Fire Demons, Glow-worms, the Court of Cupid, etc.*: Corps de Ballet of 50 Ladies and a Host of Auxiliaries.

Act 1, Scene 1: De la Pinchonnière's Manor. (Morgan.) *Scene 2*: The Gardens of Cupid's Court. (Morgan.) *Scene 3*: Corridor in the Manor House. *Scene 4*: The Kitchen. (Heilge.) *Scene 5*: Riquiqui becomes a courtier. *Scene 6*: The Obscure Grotto. (Morgan.) *Scene 7*: The Grotto of Glow-worms. (Lewis.)

Act 2, Scene 1: The Conservatory of the Royal Palace. (Morgan.) *Scene 2*: Saloon in the Palace. (Morgan.) *Scene 3*: The Gardens of the Palace. (Morgan and Heilge.)

Act 3, Scene 1: The Royal Park. (Morgan.) *Scene 2*: The Platform of the Mountain. Grand Transformation. The Flaming Craters of the Fire Mountain. (Morgan.)

Act 4, Scene 1: The Return to the Manor House. *Scene 2*: State Chamber in the Palace. (Morgan.)

Act 5, Scene 1: Cendrillon lost in the woods. *Scene 2*: The Fairy Kingdom. (Morgan.)

ACT 1
Scene 1
The Wedding Party
"The reverenced name of Mother" (Solo)
Mrs. Gomersal
"Oh, Scandal, Infamy" (Concerted Piece)
Mrs. Gomersal, Mrs. M. Wilkins,
L. Baker, S. Cole, A. Mandeville, W. Gomersal
Scene 2
Grand March of Cupid's Guards
"Search and you may find me" (Recitative)
Mrs. Gomersal
Scene 3
"Once a King there chanced to be" (Solo)
Mrs. Gomersal
Scene 4
"Oh, daughters high and fair" (Solo)
W. Gomersal
Scene 5
"The Running Footman" (Solo)
F. Percy
Scene 7
Apotheosis

ACT 2
Scene 1
The Ball at the Royal Palace
"Sneezing Song" (Solo)
M. Smith
The Musical Handkerchief
Scene 2
"A sweet, a nameless charm" (Duet)
E. Newton, Mrs. Gomersal
"Celestial Emanations" (Solo)
Mrs. M. Wilkins
"Dansez Princesses" (Solo)
Mrs. Gomersal
"Once More to Find Her" (Solo)
E. Newton
Scene 3
The Lantern Galop
Apotheosis

ACT 3
Scene 1
Quartette
L. Baker, Mrs. M. Wilkins, S. Cole, A. Mandeville
Scene 2
Grand Transformation

ACT 4
Scene 2
"The Magic Slipper" (Solo)
E. Newton
Grand Procession of the Aspiring Princesses
Military Evolutions of the Diamondtines
Grand Ballet Tableau

ACT 5
Scene 1
Duet
Mrs. Gomersal, E. Newton
Scene 2
Solo
Mrs. Gomersal
Grand Apotheosis

1866.35 CHIP OF THE OLD BLOCK!

A Burlesque in One Scene, accompanied by an Olio and Comic Sketches. (Written by Edwin Kelly and Francis Leon.) Stage director, Edwin Kelly. Scenic artist, Ludovico Malmsha. Leader of orchestra, T. McNally. Produced by (Edwin) Kelly and (Francis) Leon's Minstrels. Opened 24 December 1866 at Kelly & Leon's Minstrels and closed 29 December 1866 after 6 performances.

CAST: The Only (FRANCIS) LEON, EDWIN KELLY, JOHN ALLEN, G. W. Jackson, Nelse Seymour, John F. Oberist, William H. Brockway, George and Willie Guy, Sam Price, Little Mac.

ACT 1
"Morning Is Breaking" (Opening Chorus)
"Jennie Who Lives in the Dell" (Ballad)
G. W. Jackson
Baby Show
N. Seymour
"Happy Thoughts" (Ballad)
E. Kelly
Dutch Barber
J. Allen
The Styrian Herdsman
J. F. Oberist
The City Cars (Written by Francis Leon)
N. Seymour, J. Allen, W. H. Brockway, J. F. Oberist, Company
ACT 2
Schmitt mit a Y
F. Leon
Bachelor's Troubles
J. Allen, S. Price, J. F. Oberist
Essence of Ole Virginny
Little Mac!
A CHIP OF THE OLD BLOCK!, a Burlesque (Domestic Operetta) written by Francis Leon.

CAST: *Mr. Cady Stanton*: EDWIN KELLY. *Mrs. Cady Stanton*: FRANCIS LEON. *Old Mrs. Fred Doug*: W. F. Brockway. *Old Mr. Fred Doug*: J. F. Oberist.
Parepa Waltz, "L'Estasi" (The Ecstasy)
F. Leon
Johnny's Gone Away
J. Allen
Ici L'on Parle Français
Madame D. B.: W. H. Brockway. *Mons. Garlic*: Nelse Seymour. *Jocko*, Mischievous Monkey: LITTLE MAC.

Anthony Snow, written by (and with the kind persion of) Charley White.

Anthony Snow: Sam Price. *Colonel Flutter*: EDWIN KELLY. *Frippon*: John F. Oberist. *Larry O'Brien*: N. Seymour. *Mrs. Morton*, a Widow: William H. Brockway. *Fanny*, her maid: [FRANCIS] LEON.

1867.01 $7,000

A Burlesque in One Act[32], accompanied by an Olio. Produced by Edwin Kelly and Francis Leon. Stage director, Edwin Kelly. Scenic artist, Ludovico Malmsha. Leader of orchestra, T. McNally. Produced by (Edwin) Kelly and (Francis) Leon's Minstrels. Opened 7 January 1867 at Kelly & Leon's Opera House and closed 12 January 1867 after 6 performances.

Olio: The Musical Twins. Soirée Ethiope. Schmit Mitt a Y. The City Cars. Mr. Jack Cade. Grand Trio (from LUCRETIA BORGIA).

[32]No program found.

CAST: EDWIN KELLY. FRANCIS LEON. With Messrs. H. Kelly, John Allen, Nelse Seymour, Sam Price, Butler.

1867.02 CINDER-LE-ON!

The Excruciating Fairy Spectacle (a Burlesque of L. E. Beneux's Cendrillon) in One Act, accompanied by an Olio. (Written by Edwin Kelly and Francis Leon.) Stage director, Edwin Kelly. Scenic artist, Ludovico Malmsha. Costumes by Smyth. Leader of orchestra, T. McNally. Produced by (Edwin) Kelly and (Francis) Leon's Minstrels. Opened 14 January 1867 at Kelly & Leon's Opera House and closed 19 January 1867 after 6 performances.

CAST: *Cinder-le-on*, not from Théâtre Châtelet, Paris, or Astley's, London, in appropriate primitive costume: FRANCIS LEON. *Kellifanti*: EDWIN KELLY. *Seymourgalli*: Mr. Nelse Seymour. *Allenalli*: Mr. John Allen. *Pricini*: Mr. Sam Price. And the celebrated Madagascar Ballet Troupe.

1867.03 MARITANA

A Revival of the Light Opera in Three Acts[33]. (Libretto by Edward Fitzball. Based on the play "Don César de Bazan" by Adolphe d'Ennery and Philippe Dumanoir.) Music by Vincent Wallace. Manager, Mr. Leonard Grover. Musical director, W. H. Dietrich. Produced by the Caroline Richings English Opera Company. Opened 15 January 1867 at the Olympic Theatre and closed 30 January 1867 after 2 performances in repertory.

CAST: *Charles II*, King of Spain: HENRY C. PEAKES. *Don Caesar de Bazan*: WILLIAM CASTLE. *Don José de Santarem*: S. C. CAMPBELL. *Marquis de Lazarillo*: Mrs. ZELDA HARRISON (Seguin). *Maritana*: Miss CAROLINE RICHINGS. Full Chorus. Company also included EDWARD SEGUIN, D. B. WYLIE, ARNOLD HARRISON.

1867.04 FRA DIAVOLO, or, The Inn of Terracina

A Revival of the Romantic Opera in Three Acts[34]. Original French libretto (to the Opéra-comique 'Fra Diavolo, or L'Hotellerie de Terracina') by Eugène Scribe. English adaptation by Rophino Lacy. Music by Daniel Auber. Manager, Mr. Leonard Grover. Musical director, W. H. Dietrich. Produced by the Caroline Richings English Opera Company. Opened 16 January 1867 at the Olympic Theatre and closed 25 January 1867 after 3 performances in repertory.

CAST: *Zerlina*: CAROLINE RICHINGS. *Fra Diavolo*, disguised as the Marquis San Carlo: WILLIAM CASTLE. *Lorenzo*: EDWARD SEGUIN. *Lord Allcash*: ARNOLD HARRISON. *Lady Allcash*: Mrs. ZELDA HARRISON (Seguin). *Beppo*, *Giacomo*, Two Italian bandits: S. C. CAMPBELL, HENRY C. PEAKES. *Matteo*: ?. *Soldiers, Peasants, Bandits, etc.*

Act 1: The entrance porch of an Italian Inn.

Act 2: A sleeping chamber in the Inn.

Act 3: An extensive and romantic landscape, (including) an outward door to the Inn, a leafy arbor, a patch of arbute trees. Towards the horizon, a large mountain on whose summit rises a small hermitage-chapel with a belfry.

ACT 1[35]
Introductory Chorus (Drink! For, joy bestowing)
E. Seguin, Carbineers
Song (Vainly, alas! Thoud'st soothe the pang I feel)
E. Seguin
Concerted Piece (Give us help!—they're at hand)
A. Harrison, Z. Harrison, E. Seguin, C. Richings, [Matteo], Carbineers
Duet (I don't object, I don't object)
A. Harrison, Z. Harrison
Quintet (Oh, rapture unbounded!)
W. Castle, A. Harrison, Z. Harrison, C. Richings, [Matteo]

[33]First produced in New York 4 May 1848 at the Bowery Theatre for 3 performances. For Synopsis of Scenes and Musical Numbers, see original 1848 production.
[34]First produced in New York in English as The Devil's Brother 20 June 1833 at the Park Theatre.
[35]Musical numbers not listed in programs. List prepared from published libretto "as presented by the Caroline Richings Opera Company," (Philadelphia Ledger Job Printing Office, 1867).

Song (On yonder rock reclining)
C. Richings, W. Castle
The Barcarole (The gondolier, fond passion's slave)
W. Castle
Trio (By music I'm ever delighted)
A. Harrison, Z. Harrison, W. Castle
Finale (Hark! Those sounds!)
Principals, Chorus

ACT 2
Song (Oh, hour of joy! From restraint I am now free!)
C. Richings
Trio (Let us, I pray, good wife, to rest!)
A. Harrison, Z. Harrison, C. Richings
Serenade (Young Agnes, beauteous flower)
W. Castle
Cavatina and Concerted Piece ('Tis to-morrow—yes, to-morrow)
C. Richings, W. Castle, S. C. Campbell, H. C. Peakes
Finale (Would it not be as well, Sir Brigadier)
Principals, Chorus

ACT 3
Recitative (My companions are warn'd and our plans fitly laid)
W. Castle
Martial Air (Proudly and wide my standard flies)
W. Castle
Cavatina (We never aught demand from the fair—)
W. Castle
Rondeau (Then since life glides so fast away)
W. Castle
Chorus and Concerted Piece (Hail! Blessed morning)
Villagers, Peasants
General Chorus (Oh, Holy Virgin! Bright and fair)
[Matteo], Chorus of Youths and Maidens
Song (I'm thine! I'm thine! She oft would say)
E. Seguin
Concerted Finale (Come Captain, let's no longer stay)
Principals, Chorus
Quintet (With gratitude now blended)
C. Richings, E. Seguin, A. Harrison, Z. Harrison, [Matteo]

1867.05 ORPHÉE AUX ENFERS

An Opéra-bouffon in Two Acts, 4 Scenes[36], in French. Libretto by Hector Crémieux. Music by Jacques Offenbach. Opened 17 January 1867 at the Théâtre Français in repertory; season closed 14 February 1867.

CAST: *Orpheus* (Orphée): Mons. ARMAND. *Eurydice*: Mlle. LAURENTIS, *Aristaeus* (Aristée): ?. *Pluto* (Pluton): Mons. de SURMONT, *Public Opinion* (L'Opinion Publique): ?. *Jupiter*: Mons. KERPEL. *Diana* (Diane): Mlle. NADDI. *John Styx*: Mons. VERT. *Mercury* (Mercure): ?. *Bacchus*: ?. *Venus*: ?. *Cupid* (Cupidon): ?. *Juno* (Junon): ?. *Minerva* (Minerve): ?. Company included Mlles. Bonconsiglio, Dembrun, Maria, Wilhelm, Messr. Lucien.

Act 1, Scene 1: The Peaceful Abode of Orphée. *Scene 2*: The Olymp.

Act 2. Scene 1: Pluton's Boudoir. *Scene 2*: L'Enfers.

ACT 1[37]
Scene 1
Mélodrame et Couplets d'Eurydice (La femme dont le coeur rêve)
[Eurydice]
Duo (avec Solo de Violon)(Ah! c'est ainsi!)
[Eurydice, Orpheus]
Chanson Pastorale (Moi, je suis Aristée)
[Aristaeus]
Couplets (Le Mort d"Eurydice)(La mort m'apparaît souriante)
[Eurydice]
Mélodrame et Duettino (Viens, viens, viens)
[Public Opinion, Orpheus]
Scene 2
Choeur de Sommeil (Dormons, dormons)
Choeur
Couplets de Diane (Ah! rien n'également tourment)
[Diane]
Choeur de la Révolte (Aux armes! Dieux et demi-dieux)
[Diane, Venus, Cupidon], Choeur
Rondeau/Couplets (Pour séduire Alcmène la fière)
[Diane, Venus, Cupidon, Minerve, Pluton]
Final (Il approche! Il s'avance!)
[Diane, Cupidon, Venus, Junon, Orpheus, Pluton, Jupiter, Morphée, Mercure, Public Opinion], Choeur

ACT 2
Scene 1
Couplets du Roi de Béotie (Quand j'étais roi de Béotie)
[John Styx]
Duo de la Mouche (Il me semble sur mon épaule)
[Eurydice, Jupiter]
Scène Finale (Bel insecte à l'aile doré)
[Eurydice, John Styx, Pluton]
Scene 2
Choeur Infernale (Vive le vin, vive Pluton)
[Eurydice, Diane, Junon,Minerve, Cupidon, Pluton, Mercure, John Styx, Jupiter], Choeur
Hymne à Bacchus (J'ai vu le Dieu Bacchus)
[Eurydice, Diane, Cupidon], Choeur
Menuet (Maintenant je veux)
[Jupiter, Diane, Minerve, Junon, Mercure, Morphée, Mars]], Choeur
Galop Infernale (Ce bal est original)
Tous a l'unison
Final (Ne regarde pas en arrière)
[Public Opinion, Diane, Cupidon, Venus, Junon, Minerva, Jupiter], Chœur

1867.06 THE DOCTOR OF ALCANTARA

A Revival of the Comic Opera (Opéra-bouffe) in Two Acts[38]. Libretto by Benjamin E. Woolf. Music by Julius Eichberg. Manager, Mr. Leonard Grover. Musical director, W. H. Dietrich. Produced by the Caroline Richings English Opera Company. Opened 19 January 1867 at the Olympic Theatre and closed 2 February 1867 after 2 performances in repertory.

CAST: *Doctor Paracelsus*: EDWARD SEGUIN. *Señor Balthazar*: WILLIAM CASTLE. *Carlos*, his son: D. B. WYLIE. *Don Pomposo*, alguazil: HENRY C. PEAKES[39]. *Perez, Sancho*, porters: S. C. CAMPBELL, ARNOLD HARRISON. *Inez*: CAROLINE RICHINGS. *Donna Lucrezia*, Wife to Doctor Paracelsus: ?. *Isabella*, her daughter: ZELDA HARRISON (Seguin). *Serenaders, Citizens, etc.*

1867.07 THE BOHEMIAN GIRL

A Revival of the Light Opera in Three Acts[40]. (Libretto by Alfred Bunn, after Jules-Henri Vernoy de Saint-Georges' ballet-pantomime "The Gypsy.") Music by Michael William Balfe. Manager, Mr. Leonard Grover. Musical director, W. G. Dietrich. Produced by the Caroline Richings English Opera Company (Caroline Richings, Directress). Opened 21 January 1867 at the Olympic Theatre and closed 2 February 1867 after 4 performances in repertory.

CAST: *Count Arnheim*: Mr. S. C. CAMPBELL. *Thaddeus*: Mr. WILLIAM CASTLE. *Devilshoof*, Chief of the Tribe: Mr. EDWARD SEGUIN. *Florestine*, Nephew to the Count: Mr. D. B. WYLIE. *Captain of the Guard*: Mr. J. Gordon. *Officer*: Mr. Hill. *First Gipsey*: Mr. Neal. *Second Gipsey*: Mr. Oliver. *Arline*: Miss CAROLINE RICHINGS. *Buda*: Miss Burnett. *Queenof the Gipsies*: Miss Arnold. *Nobles, Soldiers, Retainers*: Full Chorus.

[36]French language premiere in New York; previously produced in German as ORPHEUS IN DER UNTERWELT March 1861 at the Stadttheater in repertory. No program found for this engagement.
[37]Musical numbers not listed in programs. List prepared frm published French piano vocal score, Edition Bouffes Parisiens (Heugel et Cie., Paris 1858).

[38]First produced in New York 28 May 1866 at the Théâtre Français in repertory. For Synopsis of Scenes and Musical Numbers, see original 1866 production. No program found for this engagement.
[39]Henry C. Peakes was announced to appear, but his younger brother James was reviewed in the role.
[40]First produced in New York 25 November 1844 at the Park Theatre for 17 performances in repertory. For Synopsis of Scenes and Musical Numbers, see original 1844 production.

1867.08 A BIRD OF PARADISE

A Romantic and Spectacular Drama in Four Acts, 7 Scenes. Adapted from the French by Alfred Thompson. New and appropriate music composed and arranged by Henry Tissington. Scenery by Griffith Morgan. Wardrobe by R. Williams. Corps de ballet under the direction of Signor A. Grossi. Produced under the stage direction of Sallie A. Hinckley. Managers, Lewis Baker and Mark Smith. Opened 29 January 1867 at the New York Theatre and closed 9 February 1867 after 15 performances.

CAST: *Djina*: Mlle. (IDA) DeVERE. *Stella*: Mlle. (IDA) DeVERE. *Clotilde de Villerville*: Mlle. (IDA) DeVERE. *Phenicia*: Mlle. (IDA) DeVERE. *Mousseline*: Mrs. (WILLIAM) GOMERSAL. *Paquita*: Annie Yeamans. *Baroness de Trouville*: Mrs. Bland. *Nikobar*: MARK SMITH. *Short Boots*: LEWIS BAKER. *Karaboul*: WILLIAM GOMERSAL. *Don Fernand*: SALLIE A. HINCKLEY. *Zelmis*: Miss Saidie Cole. *Alienor*: F. Chapman. *Marquis d'Aguilar*: Harry Wall. *Lord Sylvain*: C. Newton. *Sackemor*: H. Bland. *Panca-Plata-Flores*: F. Chapman. *Brahmin Chief*: E. Jones. *Harpagus*: F. Williams. *Don Felix*: William Massey.

Act 1, Scene 1: The Magician's Cave. (Farren.) *Scene 2*: The Gardens of the Pagoda.

Act 2: The Black Forest of Germany.

Act 3, Scene 1: An Antechamber in the Chateau de Sceaux, France. *Scene 2*: The Palace of Dreams.

Act 4, Scene 1: A Street in Grenada. *Scene 2*: The Return to India. Grand Apotheosis; Dreamland.

BALLETS, SPECIALTIES

Grand Ballet of Fauns (Act 1, Scene 2)
Flight of the Bird of Paradise (Act 1, Scene 2)
Grand Ballet: The Bohemian Wedding (Act 2, Scene 1)
Grand Ballet of Action (Act 3, Scene 2)
Grand Ballet (Festival) (Act 4, Scene 1)
Death of the Bird of Paradise (Act 4, Scene 2)

1867.09 THE BLIND MAN'S DAUGHTER

A Beautiful Musical Drama in One Act[41]. Libretto by T. Haynes Bayley. Manager, Mr. Leonard Grover. Musical director, W. H. Dietrich. Produced by the Caroline Richings English Opera Company. Opened 1 February 1867 at the Olympic Theatre for 1 performance in repertory.

CAST: *Major Wilson*: PETER RICHINGS. *Lady Somerville*, with song "Mother, Dear Mother": CAROLINE RICHINGS.

1867.10 KENILWORTH, or, Ye Queene, Ye Earle and Ye Maydenne

A Historical Burlesque (Comic Operatic Extravaganza) in One Act[42]. Burlesque by Andrew Halliday and Frederic Lawrence, founded on Walter Scott's novel of the same name. New and magnificent scenery, gorgeous dresses and effects. Managers, Lewis Baker and Mark Smith. Opened 18 February 1867 at the New York Theatre and closed 2 March 1867 after 12 performances.

CAST: *Queen Elizabeth*, a Virgin Queen, verging on fifty, the original strong-minded woman, quite a rough character at any rate, a character in ruff, with a great deal of hoop, and a little doo-den-doo: Mr. MARK SMITH. *Earl of Leicester*, a premier of the period, by no means Leicester Square in his policy, who, studying to please his mistress, sold his stud, and in consequence wears a ruffled front: LADY DON. *Amy Robsart*, an unprotected female, very much in distress, who, while making herself agreeable to others, will make herself very disagreeable to her husband: Mrs. WILLIAM GOMERSAL. *Sir Walter Raleigh*, a gent, but a youth of great cape-ability, who, having taken a Bird's eye view of the world, discovers tobacco, and returns to England: SAIDEE COLE. *Tressalian*, a blighted being, who, having missed his Aim-y, wishes to take a random shot at himself—the whole of his property having gone to the dogs, he is not even an Kennel-worth: J. Dunn. *Duke of Sussex*, a leader of the opposition, a wag-in-waiting, to be sent for with a party eager to take a ride on the seats of office: Mrs. ANNIE YEAMANS. *Janet*, a waiting maid, waiting for a husband, in the blues in consequence of the heartless conduct of her particular baker, who has joined the line: Mrs. Bland. *Varney*, Leicester's Master of the Horse, quite a sinecure under the circumstances, a villain with one eye to business, and another I to rhyme with Tressilian: Mr. WILLIAM GOMERSAL. *Wayland Smith*, Bank Director, Doctor, Horse-Tamer, Poor Stroller, Rogue and Vagabond—but why repeat synonymous terms?—everything by turns and nothing long: Mr. LEWIS BAKER. *Michael Lambourne*, a swash-buckler—whatever that may be—from the Spanish main, main fond of a drop of summat, and consequently not bound to the Maine liquor law: Mr. Williams. *Tony Forster*, alias Fire-the-Fagot, a turncoat in religion, a turnkey in business, a party who has no compassion for a female in distress, and consequently unworthy of the name of, etc: Mr. Chapman. *Giles Gosling*, a landlord, so hard at work in bringing beer to his customers, that he almost brings himself to his bier: Mr. Newton. *Beef Eater*: Messrs. Risk, Burns. *Two Small Beef Eaters*: Messrs. Gresham, Baird. *Banner Bearers*: Messrs. Fenwick, Smith. *Maids of Honor*: Misses Jones, Sentanler. *Two Heralds*: Messrs. Chapman, Glen. *Courtiers, Poets with nothing to Chaw-Sir, Private Soldiers so excited that the officers can't keep a private still, Beef Eaters, in name only, and others too numerous to mention in detail, but who will be found in de-tale itself.*

The Burlesque will terminate with a Grand Allegorical Tableau representing Britannia and Columbia joined by the Atlantic Cable! Neptune and his Tritons, with the Genius of Peace, which ends the piece.

MUSICAL NUMBERS, SPECIALTIES

"Good Bye, Sweetheart, Good Bye"
Lady Don
Famous "Garter Song"
Lady Don

SCENES AND MUSICAL NUMBERS[43]

Scene 1: A Handsome Chamber of the Elizabethan period at Cunmer Place—richly furnished. *Scene 2*: Road to London. *Scene 3*: Greenwich. View of the Palace, the river, the Great Harry, Courtyard of the Queen's Palace. *Scene 4*: Road to Kenilworth. View of the Village of Kenilworth in the distance. An Inn, sign projecting, bearing the picture of two arms, inscribed "Leicester's Arms," finger post, with road to Kenilworth. *Scene 5*: Kenilworth Gardens at Sunset. *Scene 6*: Dark Corridor in the Castle. *Scene 7*: Kenilworth Gardens by Moonlight.

Scene 1

Duet, Air 'My Pretty Page' (My pretty maid look out afar)
[Amy, Janet]
Duet, Air 'When the heart of a man' (When the heart of a woman's on fire)
[Amy, Janet]
Song, Air 'Why did my master sell me' (Why did my Amy leave me?)
[Tressilian]
Duet, 'Pen and ink polka' (Go away, ugly man, don't you come a-nigh me)
[Amy, Varney]
Duet, 'M'apparì tout amour' (from MARTHA) (*Music by* Friedrich von Flotow) (A lady at a fair, in the guise of servant lass)
[Leicester, Amy]
Song, Air 'The Ratcatcher's Daughter' (Long, long ago in Westminster)
[Leicester]

Scene 2

Song, Air 'Uncle Ned' (I was once much bigger, but now I'm growing thin')
[Tres]
Song, Air 'Friar of Orders Grey' (from MERRY SHERWOOD) (*Music by* William Reeve) (I am a fellow that's always fly)
[Wayland, Tressilian]
Duet, Air 'Little Dorrit Polka' (Come, strike hands)
[Wayland, Tressilian]
Song, 'The Bob o' Dumblane'
[Varney]

Scene 3

Ballet of Sailors, 'Red, white and blue'
Duet, Air 'Dudah' (Pray don't pull a face so long)
[Raleigh, Tressilian]

---

[41]Accompanied by a scene from the opera Norma, and Act 2 of the opera Martha.

[42]Preceded by Selby's comic drama, Peggy Greene, with Lewis Baker, William Gomersal, Mr. Hind, Lady Don, Mrs. Wilkins, Yeamans, Cave, S Cole., etc. For the second week of the run, Peggy Greene was replaced for the second week by The Pretty Horse Breaker with songs "I Love the Merry Sunshine" and "The Hour of Chase."

[43]Scene List and extended List of Musical Numbers prepared from the published acting edition from original *London* production dated 27 December 1858 (Thomas Hailes Lacy, London, n.d.). Whereas the cast list and its companion descriptions match the American production, the musical numbers and specialties were undoubtedly adjusted to the talents of the American company. The following list should therefore be regarded as representative of what was actually performed. "Good Bye, Sweetheart, Good Bye" and the famous "Garter Song" were no doubt American interpolations to suit the talents of the visiting English star, Lady Don.

Comic Dance, 'Black Sal and Dusty Bob'

Trio, Air 'I am not the Queen' (from THE ROSE OF CASTILE) (*Music by* Michael William Balfe.) (Mind I'm the Queen—Ha, ha!)

[Queen, Leicester, Sussex]

Quintette, Air 'Hoop de dooden doo' (And now, my liege, my story's done)

[Varney, Tressilian, Sussex, Queen]

Concerted Piece, Air 'Suoni la Tromba' (from I PURITANI) (*Music by* Vincenzo Bellini.) (Mind that you do not deceive me)

[Queen, Sussex, All]

Scene 4

Chinese music, Willow Pattern Plate

Music, 'Down among the dead men,' 'Ivy Green'

Duet and Dance, Air 'Billy Taylor' (A noble lord, the Earl of Leicester)

[Amy, Wayland]

Scene 5

Chorus, March (from WILLIAM TELL) (*Music by* Gioachino Rossini.) (Fill, fill, fill, fill, fill, until the cup runs o'er)

[Chorus]

Music from THE BRONZE HORSE

Song, Air 'How happy I could be with either' from THE BEGGAR'S OPERA (How happy I could be with—neither)

[Queen]

Tambourine Dance, 'Golden Stream Varsoviana'

[Amy]

Scene 6

Fight (One, two, buckle my shoe)

Scene 7

Grand Transformation Scene

Finale, First Chorus (from LUCREZIA BORGIA) (*Music by* Gaetano Donizetti.) (And now ends our little play)

1867.11 NORMA ON THE HALF SHELL

A Burlesque Operetta (of Bellini's opera "Norma") in Two Scenes, accompanied by an Olio[44]. (Written by Edwin Kelly and Francis Leon.) Stage director, Edwin Kelly. Scenic artist, Ludovico Malmsha. Leader of orchestra, T. McNally. Produced by (Edwin) Kelly and (Francis) Leon's Minstrels and Burlesque Opera Troupe. Opened 25 March 1867 at Kelly & Leon's Minstrels and closed 6 April 1867 after 12 performances.

Olio: Travellers Trials. Cinder-leon. Burlesque of The Black Crook. Screaming Legacy. The Druids.

CAST: *Norma à La Titiens*: FRANCIS LEON. *Pole-io*: EDWIN KELLY. *Flavio*: ?. *Orovoso*: ?. *Druids, Signors, etc.*

1867.12 LITTLE BOY BLUE, or, Hush-A-Bye Baby and Patty and Her Pitcher

A Comic Pantomime in One Act, 15 Scenes[45]. Play by George L. Fox. New overture and appropriate music composed, arranged and selected by Alexander Tyte. Scenery by J. Johnson, Jr. and R. L. Weed. Machinery, practical tricks and traps by William Crane. Appointments, properties, masks, devices by John G. Williams. Costumes by Keyser. Ballet arranged by Mons. A. Grossi. Calcium lights and illuminations by Thomas Newton. Produced by George L. Fox. Opened 1 April 1867 at the Bowery Theatre and closed 11 May 1867 after 36 performances; returned 29 July 1867[46] to the Barnum and Van Amburgh Museum and Menagerie and closed 17 August 1867 after 36 additional performances. Total: 72 performances.

CAST: *Disturbance Discomfiture*, alias Hush-a-Bye, a rising young gardener, who would like to attend to his business, but being of a musical turn of mind, finds more comfort in disturbing his neighbors, afterwards Clown: GEORGE L. FOX. *Ungrateful Ingratitude*, supposed to be a farmer, but hard to tell; like all stern patients, will not let children have their own way, afterwards Pantaloon: CHARLES K. FOX. *Little Boy Blue*, a romantic young shepherd, afterwards Harlequin: Master T. CALLIGNE. *Pretty Patty*, a pattern for all good Girls, Sanita's especial favorite, afterwards Columbine: Mlle. MARTINETTI. *Sanita*, the Genius of General Harmony, whose compass it is hoped will reach the high C's—as far as the eyes see and further: Miss G. REIGNOLDS. *Mephistopheles*, the Demon of Evil: H. CUNNINGHAM. *Spiderion*, author of Cobwebs to Catch Horse Flies: G. Malmberg. *Reptile*: J. B. Howland. *The Tarantula*, Destroyer General of the peace of families—an individual especially obnoxious to the Sweeping Act: Master Legg. *Nature's Noblemen that earn their bread by the seat of their brows (5)*: *Yokel*: B. Bailey. *Pumpkin*: J. Gay. *Whackstraw*: S. Whitmore. *Chawbacon*: D. Jerrold. *Hedge*: T. Goodwin. *Village Orchestra, belonging to an independent association (3)*: *Rosin Catgut*: F. Hofele. *H. Blower*: N. Banks. *P. Flute*: J. Stout. *Sergeant Ramrod*, a Recruiting Officer: J. L. Lewis. *Unrelenting Birch*, the Schoolmaster: J. Coburn. *Lardandpaste*, a waffleman: W. Mitchell. *Tobias Mainspring*, a watchmaker: L. Benedict. *Prideall Lookatme*, a N. Y. Gent of '67: J. Birchler. *Tom Tyremall*, Host of "The 3 Sisters": A. Clapp. *Daub Smearwell*, an artist: T. Daisy. *Check*, a waiter: S. Burden. *Felt*, a hatter: L. Ernest. *Molherrio*, an artist's assistant: J. Crow. *Carrot*, dealer in vegetables: M. Murray. *Buckram*, a Tailor: G. Broadcloth. *Moweatwithme*, a Landlord: T. Laury. *Flutemygilder, Cadwallerder*, Policemen, "Clubs are trumps": Messrs. Roberts, Myers. *Shells*, a Chestnut Vender: J. Thomas.

Members of the Great American Base Ball Club, by the celebrated Muffin Players: *Sure*, the Pitcher. *Fly*, the Catcher. *Lengthy*, 1st base. *Shorty*, 2nd base. *Active*, 3rd base. *Meadows*, R. Field. *Creek*, L. Field. *Old Rocks*, C. Field. *Spring*, Short Stop.

Masterdon Behemoth, fond of the game of B.B.: S. Healthy. *Schoolboys (5)*: *Master Lanky*: Master Carson. *Master Pranky*: Master James. *Master Dodgy*: Master Reuben. *Master Thinny*: Master George. *Master Teaser*: Master Topack. *Villagers, Soldiers, Policemen, Sprites, Reptiles, Nondescripts, Vipers*: Numerous Auxiliaries.

Dame Dowager: Miss Dulany. *Blanche*: Miss Maywood.

Scene 1: Realms of Reptiles. *Scene 2*: Storm of Clouds. *Scene 3*: Mountainous Landscape. *Scene 4*: Franklin Academy and National Yacht Club House. *Scene 5*: Exterior of a Jeweler's and Library. *Scene 6*: Interior of a Picture Gallery. *Scene 7*: High Road to Truly Rural. *Scene 8*: Library. *Scene 9*: Landscape. *Scene 10*: Base Ball Ground. *Scene 11*: Up and Down Street. *Scene 12*: The Magic Bed Chamber. *Scene 13*: Storm Clouds. *Scene 14*: The Ruined Temple by Moonlight. *Scene 15*: The Prismatic Bower of Astral Glory in the Glittering Retreat of the Genius of Purity.

SPECIALTIES, BALLETS

Grand Transformation (Scene 2)

[G. L. Fox, C. K. Fox, Master Calligne, Mlle. Martinetti]

Grand Transformation (Scene 14)

1867.13 ALADDIN, or, The Wonderful Scamp/ Cinderella

A Double Bill Revival of the Burlesques, each in One Act by Henry J. Byron. Stage director, Ben A. Baker. Scenic artist, Joseph S. Schell. Musical director, Herr Eckhardt. Produced by the Worrell Sisters (Jennie, Sophie, Irene). Opened 6 May 1867 at the Worrell Sisters' New York Theatre; ALADDIN closed 8 June 1867 after (15) performances in repertory; CINDERELLA closed 8 June 1867 after (31) performances in repertory.

ALADDIN CAST: *Aladdin*, an Anomaly, for although he is considered by every one to be a "Lively Youth," he is universally looked upon as a "Sad Boy": JENNIE WORRELL. *Pekoe*, The Vizier's hope and his own pride: SOPHIE WORRELL. *Princess Badroulboudour*: IRENE WORRELL. *The Sultan*: T. L. DONNELLY. *The Vizier*: WELSH EDWARDS. *Abanazar*: J. C. Dunn. *Te-To-Tum*: W. Sullivan. *The Slave of the Lamp*: Miss Gay. *The Genius of the Ring*: J. O'Neal. *The Widow Twankey*: Mrs. E. Wright. *Ballet*: Mlle. MARTINETTI, Corps de Ballet.

MUSICAL NUMBERS

Duets and Operatic Gems

S. Worrell, I. Worrell

Clog Dances

J. Worrell

Grand Cure Dance

J. Worrell, Company

Pas de Chinois

Mlle. Martinetti, Corps de Ballet

CINDERELLA CAST: *Prince Poppetti*: SOPHIE WORRELL. *Dandini*: JENNIE WORRELL. *Cinderella*: IRENE WORRELL. *Clorinda*: T. L. Donnelly. *Thisbe*: Mrs.

[44]No program found for this engagement.

[45]Preceded by a short comedy or drama: Perfection! (5 April 1867); Favorite Pieces! (8 April 1867); Betsey Baker (12 April 1867, with The Purse, preceding); The Seaman's Legacy (26 April 1867, with Bamboozling!, preceding).

[46]Performed twice daily.

T. W. Davey. *Alidora*: T. E. Owens. *Fairy Queen*: Miss Gay. *Dew Drop*: Miss Cave. *Harebell*: Miss Dunn. *Baron balderdash*: WELSH EDWARDS. *Butroni*: J. C. Dunn

In the course of the piece, songs, duets, quartettes, jigs, reels, break downs, clog dances, etc.

Clog Dance
J. Worrell
Double Irish Jig
J. Worrell, T. L. Donnelly

1867.14 THE ELVES, or, The Statue Bride

A Revival of the Burlesque in One Act[47], (followed by the burlesque CINDERELLA). Play by Charles Selby, founded on "Les Elfes" (a French ballet-fantasie in Three Acts by J. H. Vernoy de St. Georges and N. Mazillier. Music by the Count N. Gabrielli.) Stage director, Ben A. Baker. Scenic artist, Joseph S. Schell. Musical director, Herr Eckhardt. Produced by the Worrell Sisters (Jennie, Sophie, Irene). Opened 13 May 1867 at the Worrell Sisters' New York Theatre, closing 18 May 1867; returned 3 June 1867 on a double bill with ALADDIN and closed 5 June 1867 after (9) performances in repertory.

CAST: *Prince Lubin*, "Jockey Club," a beau jeune homme: IRENE WORRELL. *Sylvia*, the Statue Bride: SOPHIE WORRELL. *Phillis*, a Miller's Daughter: JENNIE WORRELL. *Colin*, a Romantic Young Tailor: T. L. DONNELLY. *Count Coldstream*, la home blaze: J. C. Dunn. *Prince Pomp*: WELSH EDWARDS. *Toadylor*, a Courtier: Mr. O'Neal. *Grimdyne*, a demon: Mr. Williams. *Princess Jonquil*: Mrs. E. Wright. *Madame Chloe*: Mrs. Davey. *Eoline*, Queen of the Elves: Miss Gay. *Huntsmen, Lords, Ladies, Fairies*: Ladies and Genlemen. (*Ballet*: Mlle. MARTINETTI, Corps de Ballet.)

MUSICAL NUMBERS
Pas des Elves
Mlle. Martinetti
Duets and a pas de Deux
S. Worrell, I. Worrell

1867.15 THE INVISIBLE PRINCE, or, The Island of Tranquil Delights

A Revival of the Musical Extravaganza in One Act[48], (followed by the burlesque CINDERELLA). Extravaganza by James Robinson Planché. Stage director, Ben A. Baker. Scenic artist, Joseph S. Schell. Musical director, Herr Eckhardt. Produced by the Worrell Sisters (Jennie, Sophie, Irene). Opened 27 May 1867 at the Worrell Sisters' New York Theatre and closed 1 June 1867 after (7) performances in repertory.

CAST: *Don Leander*, lineally descended from the Kings of Allaquiz: SOPHIE WORRELL. *Xquisitelittlepet*, Princess of the Island of Tranquil Delights: IRENE WORRELL. *Abricotina*, her Maid in Waiting: JENNIE WORRELL. *Furibond*, el Filibustero: T. L. DONNELLY. *Count Palaoa Torquemova*: Mr. Corrister. *Marquis of Anysidos*: Mr. Hurley. *Don Mustachios*: Mr. Williams. *First Lord*: Mr. Sullivan. *Second Lord*: Mr. Knowles. *Sambo*: Mr. O'Neal. *Fairy Gentilla*: Miss Gay. *Queenblousabella*: Miss Cary. *Ruffians of the first class order (4)*: *Ruffino*: Mr. Fierce. *Desperetta*: Mr. Strong. *Sanguino*: Mr. Bold. *Stilletto*: Mr. Dauntless. *Lord, Ladies, Fairies, Attendants*: Company. (*Ballet*: Mlle. MARTINETTI, Corps de Ballet.)

MUSICAL NUMBERS
Double Clog Dance
I. Worrell, J. Worrell
Grand Pas Seul
Mlle. Martinetti
Waltz
Corps de Ballet

[47] First produced in New York in a two-act version 16 March 1857 at Laura Keene's Theatre for 50 performances. For Synopsis of Scenes and Musical Numbers, see original 1857 production.

[48] First produced in New York 26 April 1847 at the Park Theatre.

1867–1868 SEASON

Lotta Crabtree in LITTLE NELL AND THE MARCHIONESS, Carte de Viste (March 4, 1877)
Museum of the City of New York, Gift of Richard B. Kent, 43.426.16

1867–1868 SEASON

FAUST, or, The Demon, the Doctor and the Devil's Draught

1867.16

A Local Burlesque in One Act, 7 Scenes, written expressly for the Worrell Sisters.[1] Stage director, Ben A. Baker. Scenic artist, Joseph S. Schell. Musical director, Henry Tissington. Produced by the Worrell Sisters (Jennie, Sophie, Irene). Opened 10 June 1867 at the Worrell Sisters' New York Theatre and closed 29 June 1867 after (21) performances in repertory.

CAST: *Faust*, an elderly Astrologer, Inventor of Printing, hence Father of the Sun, and other diurnal journals, who literally "raises the Devil," and by striking a bargain, becomes striking-ly young and handsome—The fact of his being a printer is a proof that he will make a good impression: SOPHIE WORRELL. *Mephistopheles*, the original colored gentleman, with a good address and a bad residence, who, though making a monster demon-stration, will be found quite "a charming little devil": JENNIE WORRELL. *Rosenheim*, a dashing young "beau, who for a soldier would go," but who, "the cruel war" being over, returns from hard tack and hard attacks to peace and pea-soup: IRENE WORRELL. *Wagner*, a boild solider Boy, so successful in the war-cry that he finally gets engaged as town-crier: J. C. Dunn. *Brattner*, a Veteran from Schleswig Holstein, who, failing to fill a bier in battle, returns to get his fill o' bier at home: WELSH EDWARDS. *Kreutzer*, a Speculator of the period: Mr. O'Neill. *Fritz*, a Politician of the ditto: Mr. Sullivan. *Karl*, a Sporting Man of the likewise: Mr. Corrister. *Albert*, a Mechanic of the same: Mr. Williams. *Werner*, a Broker of the aforesaid: Mr. Hurley. *Marguerite*, a young and interesting female, with a penchant for Faust, the Ballet, Rosenheim and dollar Jewelry, a nice Belle to ring: Mr. T. L. DONNELLY. *Martha*, her nurse, a careful Dame, with a character to sustain, which she does very well, as also the character she sustains in the piece: Mrs. E. WRIGHT. *Fairy Queen*, the usually intensely uninteresting, but handsomely-dressed young lady, who always appears at the right moment: JENNY GILMER. *Rose*: Miss Cave. *Lisette*: Miss Dunn. *Emma*: Miss King. *Soldiers, Peasants, Citizens, Scandal-hunters, etc.* (*Ballet*: Mlle. MARTINETTI, Corps de Ballet.)

Scene 1: Laboratory of Faust. *Scene 2*: Exterior of the Theatre of the Period. *Scene 3*: Market Place and Armory of the Seventh Regiment. *Scene 4*: Marguerite's Boudoir. *Scene 5*: Illuminated Gardens. *Scene 6*: Street. City Residence of Marguerite. *Scene 7*: The very pleasant aerial retreat of the Fairies.

MUSICAL NUMBERS

The Midnight Chorus (Scene 1)
Chorus to a popular air (Scene 3)
Rosenheim takes a long farewell of his lady love in the usual operatic manner (Scene 3)
I. Worrell
Jig (Scene 3)
J. Worrell
Air (Scene 4)
T. L. Donnelly
Song and Dance, à la Mins. Trel de Corque (Scene 4)
The Liederkranz Ball (Scene 5)
Galop du Diable (Scene 5)
Mlle. Martinetti

BETWEEN YOU AND ME AND THE POST

1867.17

A Revival of the Musical Burlesque in One Act[2], founded upon the drama 'Arrah-na-Pogue' (by Dion Boucicault and E. H. House). Play by James Schonberg. Music arranged and composed by Jonathan P. Cooke. Scenery by Joseph S. Schell. New Appointments. Mechanical effects by J. Denham. Orchestra under the direction of Henry Tissington. Produced by the Worrell Sisters. Opened 1 July 1867 at the Worrell Sisters' New York Theatre and closed 6 July 1867 after (5) performances in repertory.

CAST: *Beemish McCoul*, of the Rebels: SOPHIE WORRELL. *Arrah Meelish*, of the Kiss, with songs: IRENE WORRELL. *Shaun*, of the Post, with songs: JENNIE WORRELL. *Fanny Power*, of the Affections: Miss Lizzie Davey. *Michael Feeney*, of the Law: T. L. DONNELLY. *Colonel O'Grady*: WELSH EDWARDS. *Captain Bullet*: J. C. Dunn. *Regan*: W. Sullivan. *Officer*: W. Corrister. *Officers of the Military*: Messrs. McLean, Barnum, Scott, Atwell, others. *Peasants of the Emerald Isle*: Mr. O'Neal, others.

1867.18 COLUMBUS RECONSTRUCTED

A Revival of the Revised Version of the Historical Extravaganza (the Burlesque Columbus El Filibustero!!) in Two Acts, 4 Scenes[3]. Play by John Brougham. Stage manager, Thomas E. Morris. Produced by John Brougham. Opened 22 July 1867 at the Olympic Theatre and closed 3 August 1867 after 12 performances.

CAST: *Ferdinand* King of Arragon, an arrogant, aggressive and progressive monarch, of rather a speculative turn: H. S. MURDOCK. *Cardinal de Fonseca*, keeper of the King's consience, and court spiritual advisor generally, therefore naturally opposed to Columbus and the spread of knowledge: Mr. T. Hampton. *Fernando de Talavera*, an old picture very much improved by time: Mr. Foster. *Luis de St. Angel*, a contented office-holder, pursuing the even tenor of his way: Mr. Hill. *Alonza de Quintanela*, a courtier of much lower note: Mr. Gonzales. *Don Critoval Colon, alias Columbus*, a clairvoyant voyager, whose filibustering expedition gave rise to a world of speculation: JOHN BROUGHAM. *Diego*, a semi-colon among the Queen's pages: Miss ALICE BARRISON. *Distinguished Members of the Historical Society*, now meeting again for the first time (4): *Vasco Nunez*: F. Stall. *Hernandez Cortez*: E. Wilks. *Amerigo Vespucci*: J. Henderson. *Ponce de Leon*: N. Smith. *A noisy crew of Mutineers (4)*: *Sancho Ruis*: Mr. Oliver. *Pedro Nino*: Mr. Waddleton. *Bartolomeo*: Mr. Burke. *Juan Perez*: Mr. E. T. Sinclair. *Isabella*, wife of Ferdinand, possessor of half-a-crown by marriage rite, and a whole one by right of raving to carry its weight on her own shoulders: Mrs. ELDRIDGE. *Columbia*, a national debutante, her first appearance on any stage, with song, "Shout for one glorious Star Spangled Banner" written expressly for her by Charles Gaylor: Miss EMILY THORNE. *Little Miss Colorado*, rather precocious: Bella Green. *Manhatta*: Miss Flora Lee. *Demon of Discord*, a Sece-sionalist: Mr. Decker. *Members of Reception Committee, Aldermen, Discontented Politicians, Independent Voters, and other naturtal curiosities*: Comptenent representatives. *Full grown States, Juvenile Territories, etc.*: Energetic Host of Auxiliaries.

Act 1: Speculation. *Scene 1*: A Roytal "Chateau en Espagne." *Scene 2*: A part of another apartment in the Palace. *Scene 3*: Deck of the *Santa Maria*.

Act 2: Realization. *Scene 1*: The same palace in an empty state. *Scene 2*: Anywhere—the same being a topical necessity. *Scene 3*: Pyramidic Tableau of American Worthies. Gorgeous culmination of Causes and Effects, terminating in a brilliant pyrotechnic apotheosis.

ACT 1
Scene 1
"Hail! Oh, King of Aragon" (Grand Complimentary Chorus of Courtiers)
"Bound to be a Sailor Boy" (Biographic Cantata)
J. Brougham
"We are so happy" (Chorus of Shareholders, narcotic)
Scene 2
"The Star Spangled Banner" (Admonitory words)E. Thorne
Scene 3
"Fling him in the briny" (Striking chorus of deaf mutineers)
"Columbia" (Song)
"Swearing death to all who cave" (Grand Demonstrative Finale)

ACT 2
Scene 1
"Gold, gold is no chimera" (Vocal Melange)
The whole court
Medley of harmonious Airs from all points of the compass
"Children in arms not admitted" (Genial March)

[1]Preceded by a comedietta The Last Legs. During the run, The Last Legs was replaced for the second week by A Kiss in the Dark, which was replaced mid-week by Naval Engagements! which remained the after-piece for the balance of the run.

[2]First produced in New York 29 January 1866 at Lucy Rushton's New York Theatre for 24 performances. For Synopsis of Scenes, see original 1866 production. Preceded by the comedietta, The Irish Lion.

[3]First produced in New York in an earlier version as COLUMBUS EL FILIBUSTERO!! 30 December 1857 at Burton's Theatre in repertory. This adaptation previously presented in New York 9 July 1866 at the Winter Garden for 24 performances. A fore-piece was presented, The Fast Man, by W. Leman Rede; for the second week of the run, a comedy in 2 acts by Fitzjames O'Brien, Gentleman from Ireland.

Scene 3
The Showman speaks; Brilliant pyrotechnic apotheosis

1867.19 THE PET OF THE PETTICOATS!/ FAMILY JARS

A Double Bill of a Revivals: THE PET OF THE PETTICOATS, the Operatic Comedy in Three Acts by John Baldwin Buckstone[4], followed by FAMILY JARS, the Musical Farce. Produced by Clifton Tayleure. Opened 29 July 1867 at Wallack's Theatre and closed 13 August 1867 after 14 performances; returned 17 February 1868 to Barney Williams' Broadway Theatre and closed 22 February 1868 after an additional 6 performances. Total: 20 performances.

PET OF THE PETTICOATS CAST: *Paul*, nicknamed Poll: LOTTA (CRABTREE). *Job*, Porter of the Convent: George Holland. *Mons. Zephyr*, Dancing Master to the Convent: J. C. WILLIAMSON. *Officers of the Royal Guard (9): Chevalier St. Pierre*: B. T. Ringgold. *Colonel Belair*: J. W. Leonard. *Captain Carmonade*: E., Milton. *Captain Achille*: Mr. Graham. *Captain Fusée*: Mr. Kenway. *Lieutenant Victor*: Mr. Ward. *Lieutenant Cisar*: Mr. Minton. *Ensign Bauier*: Mr. Peilford. *Ensign Cadet*: Mr. Morrison. *Landlord*: Mr. Cashin.

The Superior of the Convent: Miss Carman. *Sister Vinaigre* E. Andrews. *Convent Boarders (8)*: *Mimi*: Annie Ward. *Julie*: W. Winter. *Emma*: Miss Scott. *Zoe*: Miss Day. *Lison*: Miss Clarke. *Dorothee*: Miss Williams. *Jacquelaine*: C. Timony. *Lucie*: Miss Thomas. *Mad. Bravura*, an Opera Singer: Miss L. Carman. *Babet*: Miss Timony.

During the comedy, Miss Lotta will sing "Cupid, the Little Archer."

FAMILY JARS CAST: *Liddy Laregan*: LOTTA (CRABTREE). *Emily*: Mrs. W. Winter. *Delph*: George Holland. *Diggory Delph*: J. C. WILLIAMSON. *Porcelain*: J. W. Leonard. *Benedick*: E. Milton. *Joe*: Mr. Cashin.

During the farce, Lotta will sing "Mickey is Gone Away," dance "Mrs. McGowan's Reel," and play a banjo solo.

1867.20 LITTLE NELL AND THE MARCHIONESS

A Drama in Four Acts, 14 Scenes. Suggested by an episode in "The Old Curiosity Shop" by Charles Dickens, adapted by John Brougham. Produced by Clifton Tayleure. Opened 14 August 1867 at Wallack's Theatre and closed 12 September 1867 after 26 performances.[5]

CAST: *Little Nell*: LOTTA (CRABTREE). *The Marchioness*: LOTTA (CRABTREE). *Old Grandfather Trent*: T. HIND. *Dick Swiveller*: J. C. WILLIAMSON. *Daniel Quilp*: E. COLEMAN. *Sampson Brass*: J. W. LEONARD. *Ned Trent*: E. Milton. *Mr. Slum*: T. Graham. *Corkey Jack*: G. F. Browne. *Reuben Kadger*: G. F. Kenway. *Foxy Joe*: T. Ward. *Higgins*: C. Wilson. *Burton*: H. Powell. *Showman*: W. H. Pope. *Abdallah*: E. Cashin.

Mrs. Quilp: Mrs. W. Winter. *Mrs. Jarley*: Miss Annie Ward. *Mrs. Jenevir*: Miss L. Carman. *Sally Brass*: Miss E. Andrews. *Mrs. George*: Miss Clarke. *Mrs. Simmons*: Miss Carman. *Villagers, Morris Dancers, Guests, Showmen, etc.*

Act 1, Scene 1: Quilp's House. *Scene 2*: Dick Swiveller and His Friends (Street in London). *Scene 3*: Brass' House.

Act 2, Scene 1: The Old Curiosity Shop. *Scene 2*: The Marchioness and her spelling book. (Room in Brass' House). *Scene 3*: The Old Curiosity Shop.

Act 3, Scene 1: Street (in London). *Scene 2*: Dick Swiveller's Apartment. *Scene 3*: A landscape (The Road to Highgate). *Scene 4*: The Fair at Highgate.

Act 4, Scene 1: The Kitchen of the Ale House, and Little Nell's Bedroom. *Scene 2*: Brass' House. *Scene 3*: Quilp in his glory. *Scene 4*: Swiveller's Wedding Party. (*Apotheosis*: The Grave of Little Nell, and the Apotheosis of Innocence.)

SPECIALTIES

Song and Banjo Solo (Act 1, Scene 3)
Lotta, J. C. Williamson

Song; Unrivalled Clog Dance (Act 3, Scene 4)

Morris Dance (Act 4, Scene 2)

Duet and Dance (Act 4, Scene 2)
Lotta, J. C. Williamson

Wedding Party and Apotheosis (Act 4, Scene 4)

[4]First produced in New York 21 May 1835 at the Park Theatre.
[5]Lotta and Company departed New York for 13-14 September performances at the Brooklyn Academy of Music.

1867.21 KILL TROVATORE!

A Burlesque in Three Acts, preceded by an Olio. (Suggested by Verdi's opera 'Il Trovatore'.) Written by Edwin Kelly and Francis Leon. Scenic effects by Ludovico Malmsha. Orchestra under the direction of Fred Hoffman. Produced by Kelly & Leon's Minstrels. Opened 26 August 1867 at Kelly & Leon's Minstrels and closed 28 September 1867 after 30 performances.

CAST: *The Dutch-Cheese Leon-Hurra*, well known in New York at the present day from her peculiar excellence in the arts, Vocal, Dramatic, Terpsichorean and Tragic, in love with a Knight of the green cloth, by whom she is induced to take *Pies on*, and *pastes* her fate to his, before she is *brushed* off in the finale: [FRANCIS] LEON. *Ma-han-her-echo*, a gentle Fenian Knight, a gay and festive youth, who is frequently victor in his *gambols* on the *green*, and successfully resists all calls from the *Tombs*, until he comes in contact with an M.P. club, when it is necessary for the *peace* to drop the curtain on his career: EDWIN KELLY. *Looney*, who *counts* in the Opera, among the most ancient of the *Luna-tick* family, is smitten at Central Park with a desire to become famous, and volunters at once to become a member of the Broadway toothpick brigade, doing guard duty at all the principal Hotel entrances, and falls at last nobly beneath a swarm of *locusts*: WILLIAM H. BUTLER. *As You've Seen Her*, a very prominent feature in this burlesque, a fearful desecrator of brick piles and fences, a regular visitor to Ann Street, with the proper spoils of her nightly raids. The last scene of her exploits is a (sell) which the audience will find: GEORGE GUY. *Fair-Hand-Oh!*, who deals largely in the service of the Looney Family, and is on the threshold of a successful career, which is suddenly closed by a *colt* at a festival given by the Knight of the green: WILLIAM H. BROCKWAY. *I-Nose*, an agent of the congressional smelling committee, who is in New York to *con over* the affairs of the Dutch Cheese Leon Hurra, and thinks its *right* to *let-her* alone, and she has a Pard-in Ma-han-her-echo, wo would rather see the *ash-ly* on her, than see her betrayed, concludes her *washing-done* and returns to Washington: W. Guy. *Camp followers, Monks, Musicians, Blacksmiths, Gypsies, Nuns, etc.*

Act 1: The Scene is laid in with a white ground, and is full of life.

Act 2: This scene is a great secret, but everybody will come to see it.

Act 3: Being the great Monk Scene. The audience are politely requested to keep as quiet possible, so as to enjoy the grand musical effects of the affecting Finale.

1867.22 CINDERELLA, or, The Lover, the Lackey, and the Little Glass Slipper

A Musical Burlesque Extravaganza in One Act[6]. Play by Henry J. Byron (from the fairy tale by Charles Perrault). Musical director, Napoleon Gilles. Produced by Garland's Burlesque and Comedy Company (Manager, C. H. Garland). Opened 2 September 1867 at the Fifth Avenue Theatre and closed 7 September 1867 after 7 performances; returned 21-26 October 1867 to the Fifth Avenue Theatre on a double-bill with FRA DIAVOLO for an additional 7 performances; returned 28 October-13 November 1867 to the Fifth Avenue Theatre on a double-bill with SHYLOCK.[7]

CAST: *Clorinda*: M. W. LEFFINGWELL. *Cinderella*: Mrs. SEDLEY BROWN. *Dandini*: MILLIE SACKETT. *Thisbe*: Miss MARY MADDERN. *Theadora*: LINA EDWIN. *Aldioro*: SOL SMITH, JR. *The Prince*: Mrs. LEFFINGWELL. *Fairy Queen*: Alice Vane. *Baron*: E. A. EBERLE. *Buttoni*: Maurice B. Pike.

1867.23 FRA DIAVOLO!, or, The Beauty and the Brigands

A Burlesque Extravaganza of Auber's opera 'Fra Diavolo' in One Act[8] Burlesque by Henry J. Byron. Musical director, Napoleon Gilles. Produced by Garland's Burlesque and Comedy Company (Manager, C. H. Garland). Opened 9 September 1867 at the Fifth Avenue Theatre and closed 5 October 1867 after 28 performances; returned 21-26 October 1867 to the Fifth Avenue Theatre in a double bill with CINDERELLA for an additional 7 performances.[9]

[6]Followed by an after-piece, Too Much for Good Nature.
[7]Original programs contain no list of scenes or musical numbers, apart from the note "interspersed with songs, duets, etc."
[8]Followed by an after-piece Too Much for Good Nature. Other programs not from this engagement identify five scenes: Exterior of the "Jolly Brigands"; Garden of the Inn; Corridor; Front Chamber; Tea Gardens at the "Jolly Brigands."
[9]Scenes and songs not identified in programs.

FRA DIAVOLO CAST: *Beppo*, a particularly heavy ruffian, not troubled with the faintest outline of conscience, or indeed, with anything but the conventional hoarseness peculiar to melodramatic brigands: MYRON W. LEFFINGWELL. *Fra Diavolo*, alias the Marquis di Cuanbournealli, an amiable and captivating creature, with a weakness for Jewellery and Flirtation—although a large price set upon him, decidedly unlikely to be sold: Mrs. SEDLEY BROWN. *Matteo*, Landlord of the Jolly Brigands, who refuses to allow his child to marry a man of no small means—the monster: J. B. McCLOSKEY. *Lorenzo*, an Officer of Police, who haunts the Tavern containing his sweetheart—in fact an Inn-Spectre—a youth whose figure will prevent his attaining any height in his profession: SOL SMITH, JR. *Lord Allcash*, an English nobleman, making the Grand Tour and himself as agreeable as possible—the invariable custom of traveling Britons: E. A. EBERLE. *Giacomo*, a promising young bandit: Maurice B. Pike. *Francesco*, an extensive young Farmer: Miss LINA EDWIN. *Antonio*, 1860z: Mr. Brown. *Zerlina*, the Beauty of the Village, and Barmaid of the Jolly Brigade: MILLIE SACKETT. *Lady Allcash*, a Lady making her first tour, and through Fra Diavolo's wiles, very nearly her first trip: Mrs. M. W. LEFFINGWELL. *(Brigands, Carabiniers, Villagers, etc.)*

TOO MUCH FOR GOOD NATURE!, a Laughable Extravaganza by E. Falconer.

CAST: *Romeo Jaffier Jenkins*, a romantic youth: MYRON W. LEFFINGWELL. *Matilda J. Chummy*, the beloved of Jenkins: Mrs. SEDLEY BROWN. *Mrs. (Louisa) Adolphus*: Mrs. M. W. Leffingwell. *Mrs. Chummy*, an irascible old lady: Miss MARY MADDERN. *Miss Precise*, her aunt: Miss Lina Edwin. *Mrs. Spalding*, a lady quite independent of "Female Protectionary Laws": J. B. McCloskey. *Betty*, chambermaid of no little consequence: Miss M. Sackett. *Mrs. Jones*, a stupid woman, averse to science: Alice Vane. *Miss Jones*: Miss Whisper. *Mr. Spalding*, not the Glue Man, but a Mesmeric Experimentalist: E. A. Eberle. *Mr. Adolphus*, a very good-natured Gentleman: SOL SMITH, JR.

1867.24 LA GRANDE-DUCHESSE DE GÉROLSTEIN

An Opèra-bouffe in Three Acts, 4 Scenes, in French. Libretto by Henri Meilhac and Ludovic Halévy. Music by Jacques Offenbach. Conductor, Mons. Lefevre. Scenery by George Evans. Produced by H. L. Bateman's Opéra Bouffe Company. Opened 24 September 1867 at the Théâtre Français and closed 25 March 1868 after 156 performances in repertory.

CAST: *La Grande-Duchesse de Gérolstein*: LUCILLE TOSTÉE. *Fritz*, soldat: Mons. GUFFROY. *Prince Paul of Steis-Stein-Steis-Laper-Bottmoll-Schorstenburg*: Mons. LEDUC. *Baron Puck*, précepteur de la Grande-Duchesse: Mons. LAGRIFFOUL. *Général Boum*: Mons. DUCHESNE. *Baron Grog*, diplomate: Mons. Valter. *Nepomuc*, aide de camp: Mons. Monier. *Officer*: Mons. Chopin. *Wanda*, fiancée de Fritz: Mlle. de FELCOURT. *Les demoiselles d'honneur (4)*: *Iza*: Mlle. Borgars. *Amélie*: Mlle. Monier. *Olga*: Mlle. Mathilde. *Charlotte*: Mlle. Suzanne. *Ladies in Waiting*: Mlles. Duchesne, Bertha, Faustine, Boudinot. *Lords, Ladies, Soldiers, Peasants, etc.*

Act 1: A Military Encampment. (Campement de Soldats.)

Act 2: Saloon in the Ducal Palace. (Une Salle dans le Palais.)

Act 3, Scene 1: Old Gothic Apartment. (Le Chambre Rouge-Vielle Salle Gothique.) *Scene 2*: A Military Encampment. (Campement de Soldats.)

ACT 1[10]

Choeur de soldats (En attendant que l'heure sonne)

Chanson de Fritz (Allez, jeunes filles, dansez et tournez!)
Mons. Guffroy

Piff Paff Pouff (À cheval sur la discipline)
Messrs. Guffroy, Duchesne, Choeur

Choeur de sortie (Et Piff, paff, pouff, et Tara papa poum)
Messrs. Guffroy, Duchesne, Choeur

Duo de Fritz et Wanda (Me voici, me voici)
Mons. Guffroy, Mlle. de Felcourt

Choeur (Portez armes!)
Messrs. Guffroy, Lagriffoul, Duchesne

Rondo de la Grande-Duchesse (Ah! que j'aime les militaires)

Chanson de régiment (Ah! C'est un fameux régiment)
Mme. L. Tostée, Mons. Guffroy, Mlle. de Felcourt, 4 Ladies in Waiting, Messrs. Lagriffoul, Monier, Choeur

Choeur de sortie (Sonnez donc la trompette)
Choeur

Chronicle de la *Gazette de Hollande* (Pour épouser une princesse)
Mme. L. Tostée, Mons. Leduc

Choeur de soldats (Ils vont tous partir)

Couplets de sabre (Voici le sabre de mon père)
Mme. L. Tostée, Messrs. Guffroy, Lagriffoul, Monier, Duchesne

Départ de l'armée (Vous pouvez sans terreur)

ACT 2

Choeur de demoiselles d'honneur (Enfin, la guerre est terminée)
Mlles. Borgars, Monier, Mathilde, Suzanne

Couplets des lettres (Je t'ai sur mon coeur)
Mlles. Borgars, Monier, Mathilde, Suzanne, Choeur

Sortie des demoiselles d'honneur (Ah! lettre adorée)

Retour de la guerre (Après la victoire)
Mons. Guffroy, Mme. L. Tostée, Choeur

Rondo de Fritz (En très bon ordre, nous partîmes)
Mons. Guffroy

Choeur de sortie (La, la, la, la, la)
Choeur

Duetto et déclaration (Oui, général/Dites-lui qu'on l'a remarqué)
Mme. L. Tostée, Mons. Guffroy

Mélodrame

Trio bouffe et Ballade (Ne devinez-vous pas?/Max était soldat de fortune)
Messrs. Lagriffoul, Leduc, Duchesne

Mélodrame et finale

ACT 3
Scene 1

Duetto (O grandes leçons du passé!)
Mme. L. Tostée, Mons. Duchesne

Conjuration (Sortez, sortez de ce couloir)
Messrs. Lagriffoul, Leduc, Monier, Duchesne

Chant des rémouleurs (Tournez, tournez, manivelles)
Messrs. Duchesne, Lagriffoul, Leduc, Monier

Mélodrame

Chant nuptial (Nous amenons la jeune épouse)
Choeur

Nocturne (Bonne nuit, monsieur!)
Mlle. de Felcourt, Messrs. Guffroy, Lagriffoul, Leduc, Monier, Duchesne, Valter, Choeur

Couplets des mariés (Faut-il, mon Dieu, que je sois bête!)
Mlle. de Felcourt, Mons. Guffroy

Sérénade (Musique militaire dans la coulisse)
Mons. Guffroy, Mlle. de Felcourt, Messrs. Guffroy, Lagriffoul, Leduc

A cheval! (A cheval! vite, monsieur le général!)
Messrs. Lagriffoul, Leduc, Duchesne, Choeur

Scene 2

Choeur de noce (Au repas comme à la bataille)
Messrs. Lagriffoul, Leduc, Monier, Duchesne, Valter, Choeur

Légende du Verre (Il était un de mes aïeux)
Mme. L. Tostée, Messrs. Leduc, Monier, Duchesne, Valter, Choeur

Retour et complainte de Fritz (Voici revenir mon pauvre homme/ Eh bien, Altesse, me voilà!)
Mme. L. Tostée, Messrs. Monier, Duchesne, Valter, Choeur

Finale (Enfin, j'ai repris la panache)

1867.25 THE DEVIL'S AUCTION, or, The Golden Branch

A Grand Spectacular Féerie in Three Acts. Play by Arthur Cuyas Arnengol. New music by Auguste Predigam. Mis en scène by John DePol. Properties and costumes from Paris. Mechanical effects by Messrs. Hood & Wilson. Ballets under the direction of Mons. Ronzani. Stage manager, Henry DePol. Scenery by Hannibal Calyo & Sons. Produced by John DePol. Opened 3 October 1867 at Banvard's Opera House, moved 3 December 1867 to the Academy of Music in repertory with a program of grand opera and closed 14 December 1867 after 73 performances.[11]

[10]Musical numbers not listed in programs. List prepared from published French piano vocal score (M. Lévy, frères, Paris, 1867), and American French-English libretto (John A. Gray & Green, New York, 1868).

[11]Original programs contain no list of scenes or musical numbers. Subsequent touring productions include different characters, specialties and ballets too numerous to list. Academy of Music repertory schedule of 4 performances weekly included Tuesday, Thursday and Saturday evenings, Wednesday matinees, for the first week, 6 performances for the second week.

CAST: *Jack*, a Donkey, afterwards transformed to a man—with song: ROBERT McWADE. *Count of Dyspring*: H. B. PHILLIPPS. *Uncle Boniface*: M. C. DALY. *Arnold*, a poor shepherd: G. F. METKIFF. *Mr. Ransack*, a Notary: D. W. Miller. *Mr. Knockemdown*, an Auctioneer: S. B. DUFFIELD. *Peter*: Mr. Harris. *Robert*, a Villager: J. THOMPSON. *Rosemary*, in love with Jack, with song, and in five different characters: FANNY STOCQUELER. *Constance*, beloved by Arnold: FANNY REEVES. *Lily*, the Good Fairy: EMMA SOMERS. *Villagers, Servants, Nymphs, Syrens, Indian Guards, Warriors, Amazons, Inhabitants of El Dorada, Pages, Bacchantes, Fairies, Angels, etc.*

Ballet: Mlles. GIUSEPPINA MORLACCHI, ELISA BLASINA, AUGUSTA SOHLKE, ERMESILDA DIANI, EUGENIA LUPO, AURELIA RICCI, CARLOTTA LAPOINTE; Mons. GIOVANNI LUPO, Corps de Ballet.

Act 1: El Dorado.

Act 2: The Marine Grotto.

Act 3: Realms of Bacchus.

ACT 1

Danse Champêtre
Corps de Ballet

Syren Dance
Mlles. E. Blasina, E. Lupo, C. Lapointe, Ladies of the Company

Grand Introduction, Pas Seul
Mlle. G. Morlacchi

Valse Brilliant
Corps de Ballet

Pas à Deux
Mlle. G. Morlacchi, Mons. G. Lupo

ACT 2

Grand March
Indian Guards, Amazons and Warriors,
preceding the Queen of El Dorado, her Ministers and Court

Grand Pas Imperial à Trois
Mlle. E. Blasina, A. Sohlke, Mons. G. Lupo

Grand Evolution Guerrière
Corps de Ballet

ACT 3

Danse de Bacchantes
Principals, Coryphées

Song
(*Music by* Signor Tamaro.)
F. Stocqueler

Visit of Terpsichore and her Pupil to Bacchus

Invitation to the Dance

Pas à Deux
Terpsichore: E. Diani. *Her Pupil*: A. Sohlke.

Inebriation Dance
Mlle. L. Baretta, 16 Young Ladies
Bacchus: L. Baretta.

Pas Seul, the celebrated and renowned Bee Dance
Mlle. G. Morlacchi

Hungarian Polka
Mlle. A. Sohlke

Inebriation Scene
Principals, Coryphées

Galop Finale

Transformation

The Cascade of Wine

1867.26 ALADDIN, THE WONDERFUL SCAMP!

A Laughable and Excitable Burlesque Extravaganza[12]. Play by Henry J. Byron. Musical director, Napoleon Gilles. Produced by Garland's Burlesque and Comedy Company (Manager, C. H. Garland). Opened 7 October 1867 at the Fifth Avenue Theatre and closed 19 October 1867 after 14 performances; returned 14-30 November 1867 to the Fifth Avenue Theatre on a varying double bill.

CAST: *Widow Twankey*: MYRON W. LEFFINGWELL. *Aladdin*, the Scamp: Mrs. SEDLEY BROWN. *Pekoe*: MILLIE SACKETT. *Princess Badroulbadour*: Mrs. LEFFINGWELL. *Emperor*: SOL SMITH, JR. *Vizier*: E. A. EBERLE. *Abanazer*: MAURICE B. PIKE. *Genii of the Ring*: J. B. McCloskey. *Slave of the Lamp*: LINA EDWIN. *Teetotum*: Jennie Wallace.

[12]Followed by an after-piece, Too Much for Good Nature by E. Falconer.

1867.27 SHYLOCK, or, The Merchant of Venice Preserved

An Improvement of Shakespeare's story (a Burlesque of Shakespeare's "The Merchant of Venice") followed by the extravaganza CINDERELLA.[13] Burlesque by Francis Talfourd. Incidental and descriptive music arranged by Charles Koppitz. Musical director, Napoleon Gilles. Produced by Garland's Burlesque and Comedy Company (Manager, C. H. Garland). Opened 28 October 1867 at the Fifth Avenue Theatre and closed 13 November 1867 after 18 performances; returned 4-9 December 1867 to the Fifth Avenue Theatre for an additional 7 performances[14].

CAST: *Duke of Venice*, Lord Chief Baron of the Judge and Jury Society of Venice: Mr. Smith. *The Prince of Morocco*, black as soot which he prefers to Portia, who prefers Bassanio's suit to his: JENNY WALLACE. *Ditto of Aragon*, author of his own rejected addresses: JENNIE GILMER. *Antonio*, would-be importer of the merchandise, for the loss of which the merchant dies; whose solid flesh is to melt, thaw, and resolve itself into a Jew: E. A. EBERLE. *Bassanio*, his friend and pitcher into the misfortune above alluded to: Miss MARY MADDERN. *Gratiano*, a Footman very much out of place: Mrs. SEDLEY BROWN. *Shylock*, a Jew, who does not on this occasion conduct himself as a Gentile-man: MYRON W. LEFFINGWELL. *Tubal*, his convenient "Fiend in the City": J. B. McCloskey. *Lorenzo*, the small trump who follows suit to Jessica's heart: Maurice B. Pike. *Launcelot*, a page, who tears himself out of Jessica's good books: SOL SMITH, JR. *Portia*, a rich heiress—a lady called to the bar for a maiden assize: MILLIE SACKETT. *Nerissa*, handmaid to a belle, with herself a hand made to a ring: Mrs. M. W. Leffingwell. *Jessica*, Shyock's "one fair daughter" and—something more: LINA EDWIN. *Other people of both sexes, by the company, and numerous supernumeraries of superlative and supernatural ablities, who will be seen when required, and who must be seen to be appreciated.*

1867.28 FAUST

A Burlesque in One Act, preceded by an Olio. (Suggested by Charles Gounod's opera and the play by Goethe.) Written by Edwin Kelly and Francis Leon. Produced by Kelly & Leon's Minstrels. Opened 4 November 1867 at Kelly & Leon's Opera House and closed 30 November 1867 after 24 performances.

CAST: *Marguerite*, with golden locks: FRANCIS LEON. *Mephisto*, with the golden calf: EDWIN KELLY. [Brass Band orchestra, supporting company]

MUSICAL NUMBERS, SPECIALTIES[15]

Jewel Song
F. Leon

Flower Song
F. Leon

Gold Song
E. Kelly

Kermesse

Italian Opera Chorus

Grand Fanfare Militaire

Transformation Abode of the Fairy Elves of Tritonia

Submarine Finale

1867.29 MEDEA!, or, The Best of Mothers with a Brute of a Husband

A Musical Burlesque Extravaganza of Euripides' tragedy in One Act, 3 Scenes.[16] Play by Robert B. Brough. New music arranged by Napoleon Gilles. Musical director, Napoleon Gilles. Produced by Garland's Burlesque and Comedy Company (Manager, C. H. Garland). Opened 18 November 1867 at the Fifth Avenue Theatre and closed 30 November 1867 after 14 performances.

[13]See production and cast detail above at 2 September 1867.

[14]Followed by a musical farce, Jenny Lind.

[15]No program found for this engagement. List prepared from newspaper advertisements in the New York Herald; not in performance order.

[16]Followed by a comedy, Fit to be a Duchess.

CAST: *Medea*, a conjugal lesson, surpassing in intensity anything of a similar descip-tion attempted even at this Establishment, an awful warning to every single individual: Mr. M. W. LEFFINGWELL. *Creusa*, a more agreeable prospect from the same point of view: MILLIE SACKETT. *Jason*, a hero of antiquity, of fabulous courage, about to marry the second time without the slightest hesitation: Mrs. CHARLES HOWARD WATKINS. *Orpheus*, his intolerably good-natured friend, first fiddle at the ancient concerts, Corinth: Mrs. M. W. LEFFINGWELL. *Creon*, King of Corinth, a tyrant of the old school, a genuine Greek, but nevertheless a terrible Turk: SOL SMITH, JR. *A Corinthian* of excitable temperament: Jennie Gilmer. *Lycaon, Melanthe*, two miniature souvenirs of Jason, left for Medea to keep: Misses Kate Nagle, Fortesque. *Sairee*, Creusa's nurse, combining the antique virtues of the good old body and the jolly old soul: Miss MARY MADDERN.

Allegorical Group representing the Gems of the American Stage, executed by Griffin Morgan: Miss Charlotte Cushman as Meg Merriles; Mr. Edwin Forrest as Spartacus; Mr. Edwin Booth as Hamlet; Miss Maggie Mitchell as Fanchon; Miss Lotta as The Widow McGowan's Reel; Mr. John Owens as Solon Shingle; Mr. Joe Jefferson as Rip Van Winkle. Ferocious Transformation of the Statue of Saturn to a well-known character.

Scene 1: A Palace near Corinth. *Scene 2*: Classic Interior. *Scene 3*: Banqueting hall in the Palace of Creon.

1867.30 LA ROSE DE SAINT FLOUR

A Revival of the Opérette in One Act, in French.[17] (Libretto by Michel Carré.) Music by Jacques Offenbach. Acting manager, Adolphe Birgfeld. Conductor, Mons. Lefevre. Produced by H. L. Bateman's Opera Bouffe Company. Opened 23 November 1867 at the Théâtre Français in repertory.

CAST: *Marcachou*: Mons. LAGRIFFOUL. *Chapailloux*: Mons. LEDUC. *Pierrette*: Mlle. ISABELLA ARMAND.

1867.31 YE LEGEND OF YE GRAND QUEEN BESS!

A Burlesque in Two Acts[18], inspired by "La Grande-Duchesse de Gérolstein." Libretto by Edward Falconer. Offenbach's music arranged by Professor Eckhardt. Musical director, Napoleon Gilles. Produced by Garland's Burlesque and Comedy Company (Manager, C. H. Garland). Opened 9 December 1867 at the Fifth Avenue Theatre and closed 1 January 1868 after 25 performances.

CAST: *Ye Grand Queen Bess*, who whether historically or ristorically rendered, has no will but her own—a Virgin Queen, verging upon the other thing: Mr. MYRON W. LEFFINGWELL. *Lady Sariah Howard*, a model wife, who prefers her first love—whom she didn't marry—to her second—whom she did—and blessed in the usual way: Mrs. M. W. LEFFINGWELL. *Ladies of Honor*, by the greatest courtesy of the author of the bill—a bill which it is hoped the audience will not dishonor: Lina Edwin, Jenny Wallace, Katy Nagle. *Ye Earl of Essex*, as famous for his marches as for its marshes—O, such a nice young man—the first love of Lady Sariah and the ninety-ninth of the Virgin Queen, and rather in a fix how to fix the two: Mrs. CHARLES HOWARD WATKINS. *Ye Earl of Burleigh*, the traditional wearer of a wig, in which there was a large quantity of powder and very little brains—Ye Prime Minister of Queen Bess, and, of course, most liberal in tendering advice which she never takes: E. A. EBERLE. *Ye Sir Francis Bacon*, Ye Philosopher, not more nice than wise, and by some wiseacres imagined to be the surreptitious author of Shakespeare: MILLIE SACKETT. *One Davison*, Ye Secretary, a first rate penman, but slightly shakey in his orthography: M. B. Pike. *James the First of England and Sixth of Scotland*—the Latter must have been partial to rulers of that type, seeing that the former wouldn't endure a second edition or even a reprint—a hungry Highlander, partial to English cattle: J. B. McCloskey. *Don Diego de Mendoza*—Ye Spanish Ambassador and ye great original performer of Guy Faux, a most mendacious Mendoza: Sol Smith, Jr. *A Beef Eater*—A mythical personage with a very complimentary title, as he was originally an Irish super—a Murphy, and of course, never ate anything but potatoes: Jenny Gilmer. *Ye Lord Howard of Effingham*—Ye Lord High Admiral on the Seas, although very low down in the cast—so great a man that, being in pawn to his honor, he is obliged to be represented by a duplicate: M. B. Pike. *Ye Regiment of Ye Great Queen Bess*—a very noted Regiment for running away at the sight of the enemy.

[17]Accompanied by Le Supplice d'une Femme by E. Girardin, and La Pluie et le Beau Temps by Leon Gozlan; later accompanied by Le Bourreau des Crânes, comédie-vaudeville by Messrs. Lafarge and Siraudin, and a vaudeville Edgard et sa bonne by Labiche and Marc-Michel.

[18]Billed as a new and original burlesque, of the composite order, inasmuch as it is built of Italian Marble and Plaster of Paris, while the Embellishments are of Irish, English and American growth. "More true to history than that dear ristori. A little Tostéeficated, which means, of course, a little elevated."

1867.32 LITTLE DEW DROP, or, The Fairies' Home in the Palace of Neptune

A Grand Fairy Spectacular Pantomime in One Act, 11 Scenes[19]. Written and arranged by Harry Gilbert. New and original music by Prof. Krakaner. Entirely new and splendid scenery by George Heilge. New and costly dresses by Mr. R. Walker. Magnificent properties by Robert Cutler. Startling mechanical effects by D. Pratt. Gas and calcium effects by J. Wilson. The whole under the immediate supervision of Harry Gilbert and Milnes Levick. Produced by P. T. Barnum. Opened 23 December 1867 at The Barnum & van Amburgh Museum and Menagerie and closed 11 January 1868 after 36 performances.

CAST: *Simple Johnny*, the pest of the Village—afterwards Clown: HARRY GILBERT. *Honest Harry*, according to his name he should be honest—therefore interesting—afterwards Harlequin: WINTHER RAVEL. *Daddy Hines*, the Miller, a cruel Parient—afterwards Pantaloon: T. E. JACKSON. *Tim Forge*, the Blacksmith, father of Johnny—afterwards Sprite: W. HENDERSON. *Hary Hines*, the Miller's Daughter—afterwards Columbine: FLORENCE WELLS. *Little Dew Drop*, God-mother to Mary, one of those convenient persons that Dew-drop-in just at the proper time: LITTLE CARRIE. *Zircon*, the Fairy King: IRENE GAY. *Young Neptune*, a See King wot never was: General Grant, Jr. *Mr. Dough*, a Baker: Mr. Knead. *Mr. Shears*, a Tailor: Mr. Clip. *Mr. Apron*, a Waiter: Mr. What-l-you-have. *Mr. Barrel*, a Cooper: Mr. Whoop. *Mr. Soldier*, a Tinker: Mr. Tin-ware-to-mend. *Mr. Smoke*, a Cigar Keeper. Mr. Puff. *Mr. Fielder*, a Base-ball maker: Mr. Pitcher. *Miss Tend Baby*, a Nurse: Miss Attention. *Miss Malone*, a Cook: Miss Understand.

Base-ball Players: Messrs. Shortstop, Pitcher, Catcher, First Base, Second Base, Umpire, Third Base, Centre Field, Right Field, Left Field. *Villagers, Citizens, Irrepressibles, etc.*

Scene 1: The Village—Early morning. *Scene 2*: A Street. *Scene 3*: Base Ball Emporium. *Scene 4*: Interior of a Tailor Shop. *Scene 5*: Wood. *Scene 6*: Magnificent Palace, Home of Terpsichore. *Scene 7*: Street. *Scene 8*: Bakery. *Scene 9*: Leow Bridge Street. *Scene 10*: Moonlight Abbey. *Scene 11*: Fairies' Home in the Palace of Neptune.

SPECIALTIES, MUSICAL NUMBERS

Village Festival Dance (Scene 1)

Tarantella
F. Wells

Pas de Matelot
W. Ravel

Transformation "Here we are" (Scene 2)

Novel Bear Dance on 5 Legs (Scene 6)

"Oh! don't yer wish yer was me" (Song and Dance)(Scene 6)
H. Robinson

La Gazelle (Scene 6)
F. Wells, W. Ravel

Grand Transformation (Scene 11)

1868.01 THE LILY OF KILLARNEY, or, The Colleen Bawn

A Romantic Opera in Three Acts, 8 Scenes. Libretto by John Oxenford and Dion Boucicault. Based on the play "The Colleen Bawn" by Dion Boucicault, adapted from the novel "The Collegians" by Gerald Griffin. Music by Julius Benedict. Stage director, J. G. Peakes. Costumes by Mrs. M. Thornton and sister. Musical director, W. C. Dietrich. Produced by Richings' English Opera Company (Caroline Richings, Directress). Opened 1 January 1868 at the Academy of Music and closed 2 January 1868 after 2 performances in repertory; season closed 18 January 1868; returned 22 May 1868 to the Théâtre Français for 1 additional performance in repertory.

CAST: *Eily O'Connor*, the Colleen Bawn: Miss CAROLINE RICHINGS. *Anne Chute*, the Heiress: Mrs. EDWIN SEGUIN. *Sheelah Mann*: Mrs. M. Smith. *Mrs. Cregan*, Hardress' Mother: Mrs. J. A. Arnold. *Hardress Cregan*: WILLIAM CASTLE. *Danny Mann*: S. C. CAMPBELL. *Myles Na Coppaleen*: PIERRE BERNARD. *Father Tom*: H. C. Peakes. *O'Moore*, a Magistrate: D. B. Wylie. *Mr. Corrigan*: J. A. Arnold. *Bridesmaids, Boatmen.*

Act 1, Scene 1: Banqueting Hall at Tore Cregan. *Scene 2*: Pass in the Gap of Dunloe. *Scene 3*: Interior of the Colleen Bawn's Cottage.

[19]Preceded by a pleasing comedietta: A Day after the Wedding, with Messrs. Levick, G. Mitchell, J. J. Prior, G. W. Malburg, T. Atkins, Mrs. Massen.

Act 2, Scene 1: Exterior of Tore Cregan. *Scene 2*: Exterior of Eily's Cottage. *Scene 3*: The Water Cave.

Act 3, Scene 1: Exterior of Myles-na-Coppaleen's Cottage. *Scene 2*: Ball-room in Castle Chute.

ACT 1[20]

Introduction ("Another cheer")
D. B. Wylie, W. Castle, Chorus

Duet (I come, I come)("The moon has raised his lamp above")
W. Castle, S. C. Campbell

Quartet ("Ah, never was seen")
Mrs. J. A. Arnold, W. Castle, J. A. Arnold, S. C. Campbell

Recitative ("From Inchigela")
P. Bernard

Air ("It is a charming girl")
P. Bernard

Recitative ("Far o'er the lake")
C. Richings

Romance ("In my wild mountain valley")
C. Richings

Quartet ("Let the farmer praise his grounds")
C. Richings, Mrs. M. Smith, P. Bernard, H. C. Peakes

Finale ("With this treasure I must part")
C. Richings, W. Castle, P. Bernard, H. C. Peakes

ACT 2

Hunting Chorus ("Tally-ho!")
Chorus

Solo ("No, no, this morning Hardress leaves")
Mrs. E. Seguin

Air ("The eye of love is keen")
Mrs. E. Seguin

Duet ("Ah, never may that faithful heart")
Mrs. E. Seguin, W. Castle

Trio ("Villain, you dare!)
Mrs. J. A. Arnold, W. Castle, J. A. Arnold

Duet ("Trust me")
Mrs. J. A. Arnold, S. C. Campbell

Scene ("A lowly peasant girl")
S. C. Campbell

Air ("The Colleen Bawn")
S. C. Campbell

Air ("I'm alone")
C. Richings

Melodrame

Duet ("I give the best advice")
C. Richings, P. Bernard

Finale ("Across the broad waters")
Chorus of Boatmen

ACT 3

Air ("Your slumbers")
P. Bernard

Trio ("Blessings on that reverend land")
C. Richings, P. Bernard, H. C. Peakes

Chorus with Solos ("The wedding day has come at last")
Mrs. E. Seguin, Mrs. J. A. Arnold, H. C. Peakes

Chorus of Bridesmaids ("Let the mystic Orange flowers")
Bridesmaids

Ballad ("Eily, mavourneen")
W. Castle

Concerted Piece ("Mother, what means those looks so wild?")
Mrs. E. Seguin, Mrs. J. A. Arnold, W. Castle, D. B. Wylie, J. A. Arnold

Finale ("Stop, to put an end to everything")
P. Bernard, W. Castle, D. B. Wylie, H. C. Peakes, Mrs. E. Seguin, Chorus

Rondo Finale ("By sorrow tried severely")
C. Richings, Chorus

[20]Musical numbers not listed in programs. List prepared from published English piano vocal score (Boosey & Co., London and New York, 187?, as produced in 1862).

1868.02

THE DESERT FLOWER

A Romantic Opera in Three Acts. Libretto by A. Harris and T. J. Williams. Music by William Vincent Wallace. Stage director, J. G. Peakes. Costumes by Mrs. M. Thornton and sister. Musical director, W. C. Dietrich. Produced by Richings' English Opera Company (Caroline Richings, Directress). Opened 13 January 1868 at the Academy of Music and closed 15 January 1868 after 2 performances in repertory; season closed 18 January 1868.

CAST: *Captain Maurice*, an officer in the Dutch service: WILLIAM CASTLE. *Major (Hector) von Pumpernickel* of the Dutch service: EDWARD SEGUIN. *Sergeant Peterman*: J. A. Arnold. *Casgan*, an Indian chief disguised as a trapper: S. G. CAMPBELL. *Juanita* (Oanita), Queen of the Indian tribe Anakowtas: Miss CAROLINE RICHINGS. *Eva*, owner of a plantation: Mrs. J. A. ARNOLD.

Act 1: The scene is set in Surinam, Dutch Guiana.

Act 2: A luxuriant forest with a rocky pass.

Act 3: A tropical rainforest.

ACT 1[21]

Introduction (Hark! the loud voic'd cannon's roar)
Mrs. J. Arnold, Peters, E. Seguin, Chorus

"Through the Pathless Forest Drear" (Song)
W. Castle

"'Tis Oanita" (Ensemble)
Mrs. J. Arnold, S. G. Campbell, W. Castle, E. Seguin, C. Richings, Chorus

"Swift as Dart" (Air)

"See! yonder stands our Beauteous Foe" (Trio)
W. Castle, C. Richings, E. Seguin

"The Wood-Bird's Song"C. Richings

Finale (Ne'er will we brook the stranger's sway)
Principals, Chorus

ACT 2

Introduction (The golden sun sinks fast to rest)
S. G. Campbell, Chorus

"The Pangs of Unrequited Love" (Romance)
S. G. Campbell

"Why did I leave my Country Dear" (Song)
E. Seguin

"Away, Away!" (Trio and Chorus)
Peters, W. Castle, E. Seguin, Chorus

"Though Born in Woods" (Ballad)
W. Castle

March

"The Eagle of Battle" (War Song)
W. Castle, C. Richings, Indian Maidens

Indian Chorus and Ballet

March

"Why Throbs this Heart with rapture New" (Ballad)
C. Richings

Finale (Our place of meeting hard by)
Principals, Chorus

"Ah! Happy Hour" (Duettino)
W. Castle, C. Richings

ACT 3

"Warrior Prepare" (Grand Scena)
S. G. Campbell

Indian March and Chorus (Our sacred idol comes this way)

"I make thee King" (Solo and Chorus)
C. Richings, Chorus

"No mortal power can now avail" (Trio and Chorus)
S. G. Campbell, W. Castle, C. Richings

"My Loved Home I shall ne'er see more" (Romance)
W. Castle

"What is it I Hear" (Duet)
S. G. Campbell, C. Richings

Finale ('Mid vengeful flames soon shall expire the impious wretch)
Principals, Chorus

Rondo (No joy can e'er Bliss exceed)
C. Richings

[21]Musical numbers not listed in program. List prepared from published piano vocal score (Hall, New York, 1869).

1868.03

THE WHITE FAWN

A Fairy Burlesque Spectacular Extravaganza in a Prologue and Four Acts. Play by James Mortimer (from the fairy tale "La Biche au Bois" by Countess d'Aulnoy[22]). Music by Howard Glover. Stage manager, L. J. Vincent. Ballets by Signor (Davide) Costa. Scenery by Richard Marston, D. Strong, Sachetti of Paris. Costumes by S. W. Laureys and Madame Costa. Mechanical effects, John Froude, J. Leo. Gas and calcium lights by Charles Murray. Musical director, E. Mollenhauer[23]. Produced by Henry Jarrett and Harry Palmer. Opened 17 January 1868 at Niblo's Garden, reconstructed 13 April 1868 and closed 11 July 1868 after 176 performances.

CAST: *King Dingdong*, the Magnificent Monarch of Belle Isle, with songs: MARK SMITH. *Count Tinculum*, Lord High Chamberlain: E. B. HOLMES. *Prince Leander*, Heir Apparent of the Yellow Kingdom: LUCY EGERTON. *Lord Twaddledum*, his Esquire: VINING BOWERS. *Abdalla*, the Enchanter: Hernandez Foster. *King Salmon*, Sovereign of the Fishes: Mr. Martin. *Queen Safronilla*, Sovereign of the Yellow Kingdom: MARY WELLS. *Princess Graceful*, Heiress of King Dingdong: Jennie DeLacey. *Finetta*, her Waiting-woman: LIZZIE WILMORE. *Princess Aika*, Queen of the Ebony Islands: Lena Montague. *Aquilina*, Fairy of the Lake: FANNY STOCKTON. *Fairies (3): Ruby*: Kate Palmer. *Turquoise*: Miss Colson. *Emerald*: Miss LeClaire. *Courtiers, Chamberlains, Pages, Amazons, Soldiers, Bayaderes, Ladies, etc.*

Parisienne Ballet Troupe: Mlles. MARIE BONFANTI, AUGUSTA SOHLKE, LOUISE BILLON, Pagani, Setti, Fontana, M. Van Hamme, Jarrett & Palmer's Parisian Ballet Troupe, etc.

Prologue: The Bell Kingdom outside the Palace of King Dingdong. (Sachetti.)

Act 1: Sixteen years later. A Hall in the Palace of Safronilla. (Marston.) Interior of the Dark Tower. (Strong.) An Enchanted Lake in the Forest of Sycamores. (Sachetti.)

Act 2: The Bowels of the Earth (Strong.) The Yellow Drawing-Room. (Marston.) The Kingdom of Fishes.

Act 3: The Royal Kitchen in the Palace of Aika. The Dungeon. The Palace of Aika.

Act 4: The Bright Realms of the Dragon-Fly. (Marston.)

BALLETS, SONGS AND SPECIALTIES[24]

Grand Ballet: Pas de Sonnett (Prologue)
Mlles. Billion, Fontani, Sohlke;
Mons. Van Hamme, Principals, Full Corps

Grand Ballet of Fire-Flies (Act 1)
Mlle. Bonfanti, Principals, Full Corps

Grand Procession (Act 1)
J. Delacy, the White Fawn

Grand Procession of the Finny Tribe: (Act 2)

Danse de Poissons
Mlles. Bonfanti, Mons. Costa, Principals, Full Corps

Nettle-Fish Dance (Arr. by Van Hamme)
Mlles. Sohlke, Billion; Mons. Van Hamme, Principals

Imposing Procession: (Act 3)

Grand Ballet: (arr. Costa)

Dance d'Alemées and Bayadères
Principals, Full Corps

Egyptian Dance
Corpyphées

Pas de Cinq, "La Perle"
Mlles. Bonfanti, Billion, Sohlke, Fontani, Mons. Van Hamme

Grand March: Ballet d'Aika
Principals, Full Corps

"I'm King Ding Dong"[25] (Song)
M. Smith

"King Supreme"[26] (Song)
M. Smith

"Prince Leander Is My Name" (Song)
L. Egerton

"Waking Early at Dawn"[27] (Song)
L. Egerton

"I'll Never Ride Again" (Song)
V. Bowers

Trio
M. Smith, L. Wilmore, V. Bowers

"When You Win a Maiden's Heart"[28] (Song)
L. Wilmore
(*Music by* Holder.)

Duet
L. Wilmore, M. Smith

"I Love the Military" (from THE GRAND DUCHESS OF GÉROLSTEIN)
L. Wilmore
(*Music by* Jacques Offenbach.)

Song
F. Stockton

Mazurka[29]
F. Stockton

[22]Presumably adapted without credit from the French "La Biche au bois" by Frères Cogniaud, and the English "The White Fawn" by F. C. Burnand.

[21]Succeeded after the opening by Howard Glover, who interpolated songs of his own authorship and selections from TAM O'SHANTER.

[22]Not in performance order. Added during the run:

The Loves of Martha and Lionel (Comic Ballet) (Act 2)

"Now Our Little Game Is Ended" (Polka—Quarette and Chorus)(Act 3)
Company
(*Music by* Howard Glover.)

Songs added for subsequent tour:

"Willow Glen" (Song)
Rachel Noah (Finetta)
(*Music by* Napier Lothian.)

1868.04

LITTLE NELL AND THE MARCHIONESS

A Return Engagement of the Melodrama in Four Acts, 14 Scenes[30]. Suggested by an episode in the novel "The Old Curiosity Shop" by Charles Dickens, adapted by John Brougham. Scenery by George Dayton. Costumes by Williams. Accessories by Charles DeForrest. Machinery by Levi Guernsey. Opened 27 January 1868 at Barney Williams' Broadway Theatre and closed 15 February 1868 after 18 performances.

CAST: *Little Nell*: LOTTA (CRABTREE). *The Marchioness*: LOTTA (CRABTREE). *Old Grandfather Trent*: J. H. JACK. *Dick Swiveller*: GEORGE STODDARD. *Daniel Quilp*: C. HALE. *Sampson Brass*: J. MOORE. *Ned Trent*: Mr. Stuart. *Mr. Slum*: F. Evans. *Corkey Jack*: Mr. Wilson. *Reuben Kadger*: Mr. Peck. *Fogy Joe*: Mr. Goodman. *Higgins*: Mr. Beekman. *Burton*: Mr. Jordan. *Showman*: Mr. James. *Abdallah*: Mr. Lancer. *Mrs. Quilp*: Isabel Freeman. *Mrs. Jarley*: Mrs. H. Chapman. *Mrs. Jeniwin*: Mrs. W. H. Reeves. *Sally Brass*: Mrs. G. H. GILBERT. *Mrs. George*: Miss Smith. *Mrs. Simmons*: Miss Blaisdell. *Villagers, Morris Dancers, Guests, Showmen, Minstrels, etc*: Numerous Auxiliaries., including a Troupe of Acrobats and Minstrels.

SPECIALTIES

Song and Banjo Solo (Act 1, Scene 3)
G. Stoddard, L. Crabtree

Morris Dance (Act 3, Scene 4)

Song; Unrivalled Clog Dance (Act 3, Scene 4)
L. Crabtree

Duet and Dance (Act 4, Scene 2)
G. Stoddard, L. Crabtree

Wedding Party and Apotheosis (Act 4, Scene 4)

[25]Replaced after opening by:
"Who's King Dingdong" (Song)
M. Smith
(*Music by* Howard Glover.)

[26]Replaced after opening by:
"Piff, Paff, Pouff" (from LA GRAND DUCHESS OF GÉROLSTEIN)
M. Smith

[27]Dropped during the run.

[28]Replaced during the run by:
"What a Thing Is Love" (Song)
L. Willmore
(*Music by* Howard Glover.)

[29]Replaced during the run by:
"Bridal Morn" (Song)
F. Stockton
(*Music by* Howard Glover.)

[30]First produced in New York 14 August 1867 at Wallack's Theatre for 26 performances. For Synopsis of Scenes, see original 1867 production.

1868.05 (Leon's Own) GRAND DUTCH "S"

An Operatic Burlesque of Offenbach's "La Grande Duchesse de Gérolstein" in One Act, 5 Scenes, preceded by an Olio. Music by Jacques Offenbach. Libretto by Edwin Kelly. Scenery by Simonds. Machinery and props by Fred Bowen. Costumes by Mme. LaFontaine. Leader of orchestra, Prof. Fred W. Zaulig. Produced by Kelly and Leon's Minstrels. Opened 3 February 1868 at (Edwin) Kelly and (Francis) Leon's Minstrels and closed 6 June 1868 after (162) performances; returned 19 October 1868 to Kelly & Leon's Minstrels and closed 31 October 1868 after an additional 12 performances.

CAST: *The Grand Dutch (S)*, a fascinating young Lady, of Warlike Proclivities, much attached to her army, believes in rapid promotion, does everything à la Militaire—by her Papa's (not Bateman's)—Sword in a very musical manner, in French, (in which language it will be found less offensive to ears polite), in which after careful rehearsals, she is effectively aided by her Courtiers and Army: FRANCIS LEON. *Fritz*, a full private, afterwards Baron Von Saurschweitzerlimburgerkasekraut, in love with Miss Wanda—no wonder that he makes no miss of her—but Mrs. her in the third scene, as will be seen by their entering the United States where they join a merry can-can dance to amuse the audience: WILLIAM H. BROCKWAY. *Papa's Sword*, a necessity of the opera, without which there would be no point to the plot, no fame to the Artists, no receipts for Bateman, nor revenue for Uncle Sam: An original Damascus blade made in Chicopee. *Prince Paul and Virginia*, a Graduate of the Yellow-Covered Literature College—and as some Men-ken say, addicted to Dumas—waiting his own Ma's consent to an Orthodox attachment, with a view of Ma-rriage, his age approaching do-tage: NELSE SEYMOUR. *General Boum*, supposed to be the originator of the Dutch Gap Canal and other highly successful specimens of military strategy, pacificator of the Indian village of Mine-hate-on during elections, desirous of being Grand Political and High Military Cock-o-lorum of his country, thrives on Spoon diet and successful in defeating women and children: G. W. H. GRIFFIN. *Baron Puck*, a special ambassador von Deutschland, our Vaderland, in hard luck, a Statesman, anxious for the hand of his Mistress and the Tammany Nomination, but not being a Bismarck does not make his mark: S. S. Purdy. *Bear-on Grog*, keeps a Matrimonial Alliance Agency, has the Dutch (S) on his books, but not being on her books, is, of course, book'd by everybody a failure, and is last seen in a-last-car, traveling toward the pole-ar regions of Jersey: John Hogan. *Nip and Tuck*, very much flurried and in great haste, City Messenger in the Grand Army, recently saved from death by the Cars Under the Gaslights, being excited the audience are asked to excuse his usual hurried manner: Richard Hughes. *Wanda*, a Bashful Young Milliner, introduced by the author for the purpose of Frenchifying the plot and to save Fritz from being left out in the cold: SAM PRICE. *Statesmen, Counsellors, Officers (MPs), Newsboys, Pugilistic Emigrants and Crossing Sweepers, etc.*

Scene 1: Encampment of Soldiers. Quarantine Grounds. *Scene 2*: Boudoir of the Grand Dutch (S). *Scene 3*: Gorgeous Red Chamber. *Scene 4*: Another Encampment on Staten Island. *Scene 5*: Hudson River by Night. The Night Express. Terrific explosion of two boats!

MUSICAL NUMBERS[31]

"Voici le Cheese-Knife"

1868.06 HUMPTY DUMPTY

A Spectacular Ballet Pantomime in One Act[32], 16 Scenes. Play by George L. Fox[33]. Music composed, arranged and directed by A. Reiff, Jr. Produced under the immediate supervison of George L. Fox. Maitre de Ballet, M. Jambone. Scenery by Minard Lewis, J. A. Johnson. Caricatures by Thomas Nast. Costumes by R. Hamilton. Machinery by W. Sanders. Tricks by William Crane. Properties by W. Henry. Gas and calcium lights, O'Brien, Caffrey and Wilson. Produced by George L. Fox. Opened 10 March 1868 at the Olympic Theatre; re-constructed 15 June 1868[34], 25 January 1869 (as The Second Volume, Bound to Please; detail below) and closed 15 May 1869 after 483 performances.

CAST: *Humpty Dumpty*, or Pestiferous Perturbation, a destructive lad, brought up by nobody, taken care of by somebody, always unlucky (you must bear in mind that this pestilential youth is the one mentioned in ye ancient nursery legend); afterwards *Clown*: GEORGE L. FOX. *Avaricious Fearfulness*, called Ole One, Tow, Buckle my shoe, an obstinate father (very luxurious, but at times excessively furious, and then highly injurious); afterwards *Pantaloon*: CHARLES K. FOX. *Tommy Tucker* (everybody knows and adores; to be loving and brave at the same time, makes up a fine character) afterwards *Harlequin*: Mr. E. LACY. *Little Goody Two Shoes* (a bright divinty, with a kind and loving heart, but in this instance the victim of an attachment to a handsome youth); afterwards *Columbine*: Mlle. EMILIE RIGL. *King Lavender*, otherwise Burlesque. "Slap! also "Bang!" and likewise "Here again." I always use slang phrases of the day, Familiar, I admit, but that's my way: ALICE HARRISON. *Romance*—"Truly, Romance is sad in her cell; Once delighted, she recited What in the way of travelers fell, in woods who got benighted." This person is out of date at the present day: Mrs. C. EDMONDS.

Romance's Attendants in Exile (7): *Holmes "Guardian Angel"*: Mr. Whitmore. *Cooper's "Red Rover"*: T. Sanford. *"Lucille" of Bulwer*: G. Bailey. *"Leaves of Grass" Walt Whitman*: C. Gay. *Dickens' "Little Nell"*: Mr. Williams. *Sylvanus Cobb's "Pirate Chief"*: T. Hyde. *"Gnawwood," (Beecher's)*: Master Grey.

Ill News and Good News: Mr. McClough West Foote. *Burlesque's Supporters (4)*: *Lightfoot*: Miss Julia Fenton. *Breakdown*: Miss Sarah Fenton. *Quickstep*: Miss E. Germain. *Fandango*: Miss A. Herne. *Dr. Nitrous Oxide Gas Cureall*, a Quack Physician on a perigrination through the country: Mr. E. TARR. *Blowquick*, his Valet: Mr. Gannzman. *Hon. Grandeur Dignify*, fond of a sporting life, but still fonder of little Goody Two Shoes: J. B. HOWLAND. *Sickle, Rake, Ploughshare, Yokle, Evergreen*, attached to the Farm of Plenty: Messrs. Laidlaw, Nott, Selby, Fletcher, Hulson. *Napkin*, a waiter: Mr. Roberts. *Upton Tactic*, a Sergeant—a Great Disciplinarian: Mr. M. Quinlan. *Penny Gaff*, a Proprietor of a Peep Show: T. Ross. *Peeler Copp*, a Policeman: Mr. Wilson. *Gutter Snipe*, a Ragpicker: Mr. Moorhouse. *Rounds*, a Lamplighter: Mr. Burt. *Second Edition*, a Newsboy: W. Sanders. *Frosty Rink*, of the Grand Skating Pond: Mr. Silver. *Gnome Cobbler*: Master George Topack. *Living Gorilla*, the only one in captivity, escaped from Barnum's Museum for this occasion: Mr. T. Calligne. *Burden*, a Porter: Mr. Banks. *Beverage*, a fancier of dogs, from a small Black and tan to a large Siberian Bloodhound: Mr. Toby. *Paste Bucket*, a Bill Poster: Mr. Stick. *Roomstolet*, a Landlord: Mr. Tusky. *Guyon, McDefeat*, Champion Billiard Players: Messrs. Chalk, Cue. *All Right, Japanese Tommy*, Ambassadors from Japan: Masters John, George. *Hosschesnutz*, a Prosperous Lager Bier Saloon: J. F. Lewis. *Peasants, Soldiers, Policemen, Foot Passengers, Venders, Schoolboys, Firemen, Gnomes, etc.*

Miss Elegance Custom, a fashionable young lady: Miss Gay. *Liza Laffenhausen*, a Dutch Girl: Miss Naylor. *Bridget O'Donoghue*, an Apple Woman: Miss Jarrard. *Cora Shade*, (colored) Hot Corn Woman: Miss Thomas. *Nymphalia*, Queen of the Nixes, or River Fairies: Miss Laura. *Pipalu*, her Elfin Chief: Miss P. Germain. *Nixes*—"Know you the Nixes gay and fair, With their beaming eyes and their golden hair?:" Corps de Ballet. *Europe, Asia, Africa, America*, the Four Quarters of the World: Misses Jones, G. Germain, Mr. E. Gillet, Miss Flora Lee. *New Jersey*, somewhere about the 4 quarters: Mr. E. T. Sinclair.

Ballet: Mlles. RITA SANGALLI, BETTY RIGL; Mons. BAPTISTAN; Mlles. Laurent, Schell, Blake, Lillie Whiting, Corps de Ballet. *Specialties*: Miss CARRIE A. MOORE, JOHN ENGLER, JR., C. E. LOVETT (skaters).

Scene 1: Retreat of Romance by Moonlight. Transformation of Characters. (Lewis.) *Scene 2*: The Farm of Plenty. In the Valley of Fertility. (Lewis.) *Scene 3*: Subterranean Grotto (of the Nixes). (Lewis.) *Scene 4*: Roadside Inn. (Johnson.) *Scene 5*: Exterior of Broadway Dining Room. (Johnson.) *Scene 6*: Enchanted Garden. (Lewis.) *Scene 7*: The Olympic Theatre by Night. (Johnson.) *Scene 8*: German Billiard Saloon. (Johnson.) *Scene 9*: A Broadway Candy Store. (Johnson.) *Scene 10*: Skating Pond by Moonlight. (Lewis.) *Scene 11*: City Hall Park. (Johnson.) *Scene 12*: A Street by Moonlight. (Johnson.) *Scene 13*: The New Court House. (Johnson.) *Scene 14*: Room in a Hotel. (Johnson.) *Scene 15*: The Dell of Ferns. (Lewis.) *Scene 16*: Retreat of the Silver Sprites. Grand Transformation Scene. (Lewis.)

BALLETS AND SPECIALTIES

Character Dance
F. Lacy, E. Rigl

Transformation of Characters (Scene 2)

Contra Dance (Scene 2)
Characters

Grand Ballet—The Grotto Dance (Scene 3)
Mlles. Sangalli, Mlles. Schell, Laurent, Blake, L. Whiting, Mons. Cellini, Full Corps of Coryphées

Grand Ballet—Garden Dance (Scene 6)

The Coquette
Mlles. B. Rigl, Laurent, Schell, Blake, L. Whiting, Mons. Baptistan

Pas Seul
Mlle. Laurent

Grand Pas de Deux (La Tarantella)
Mlle. Sangalli, Mons. Baptistan

Polish National Dance (Scene 10)
Mlle. R Sangalli, Mons. Baptistan, Mlles. Laurent, Schell, Blake, L. Whiting

Grand Carnival on Skates (Scene 10)
C. A. Moore, J. Engler, Jr., C. E. Lovett

Grand Transformation Scene; Epilogue (Scene 16)

HUMPTY DUMPTY(reconstructed 15 June 1868):

CAST: *Humpty Dumpty*, or Pestiferous Perturbation, a destructive lad, brought up by nobody, taken care of by somebody, always unlucky (you must bear in mind that this

[31]Musical numbers not listed in programs; single title quoted in reviews.
[32]Ten days after opening, the production was divided into Two Acts with an Interval following Scene 6.
[33]Laurence Senelick in his biography "The Art and Stage of George L. Fox" identifies Clifton Tayleure as the play's true author.
[34]For the first reconstruction, new tricks, new scenery, new music, new costumes, a new skating scene, new dances and a new drop curtain by Minard Lewis were advertised. The program also includes two new characters in the burlesque opening scene: *Burlesque*, with Medley Song: ALICE HARRISON. *Romance*: Mrs. C. EDMONDS.

pestilential youth is the one mentioned in ye ancient nursery legend), afterwards Clown: GEORGE L. FOX. *Avaricious Fearfulness*, called Old One, Two, Buckle My Shoe, an obstinate father (very luxurious, but at times excessively furious, and then highly injurious); afterwards Pantaloon: CHARLES K. FOX. *Tommy Tucker*, everyone knows and adores; to be loving and brave at the same time, makes up a fine character) afterwards Harlequin: F. LACY. *Little Goody Two Shoes*, a bright divinity, with a kind and loving heart, but in this instance the victim of an attachment to a handsome youth, afterwards Columbine: EMILIE RIGL. *Kig Lavender*, other wise Burlesque, "Slap!" also "Bang!" and likewise "Here again." I always use slang pharses of the day, Familiar I admit, but that's my way: ALICE HARRISON. *Romance*, "Truly, Romance is sad in her cell; once delighted, she recited What in the way of travelers fell, In woods who got benighted." This person is out of date at the present day: Mrs. C. Edmonds.

Romance's Attendants in Exile (7): *Holmes' Guardian Angel*: Mr. Whitmore. *Cooper's Red Rover*: T. Sanford. *Lucille, of Bulwer*: G. Bailey. *Leaves of Grass, Walt Whitman*: C. Gay. *Dickens' Little Nell*: Mr.Williams. *Sylvanus Cobb's Pirate Chief*: T. Hyde. *Gnawwood (Beechers)*: Master Grey. *Ill News and Good News*: Mr. McClough West Foote. *Burlesque's Supporters (4)*: *Lightfoot*: Julia Fenton. *Breakdown*: Sarah Fenton. *Quickstep*: E. Germain. *Fandango*: A. Herne. *Dr. Nitrous Oxide Gas Cureall*, a Quack Physician on a perigrination through the country: E. TARR. *Blowquick*, his Valet: Mr. Gannzman. *Hon. Grandeur Dignify*, fond of a sporting life, but still fonder of his Little Goody Two Shoes: J. B. HOWLAND. *Attached to the Farm of Plenty (5)*: *Sickle*: Mr. Laidlaw. *Rake*: Mr. Nott. *Ploughshare*: Mr. Selby. *Yokle*: Mr. Fletcher. *Evergreen*: Mr. Hulson. *Napkin*, a waiter: Mr. Roberts. *Upton Tactic*, a sergeant—a great disciplinarian: Mr. M. Quinlan. *Penny Gaff*, a Proprietor of a Peep Show: T. Ross. *Peeler Copp*, a Policeman: Mr. Wilson. *Gutter Snipe*, a Ragpicker: Mr. Moorhouse. *Rounds*, a Lamplighter: Mr. Burt. *Second Edition*, a Newsboy: W. Sanders. *Frosty Rink*, of the Grand Skating Pond: Mr. Silver. *Gnome Cobbler*: Master George Topack. *Living Gorilla*, the only one in captivity, escaped from Barnum's Museum for this occasion: Mr. T. Calligne. *Burden*, a Porter: Mr. Banks. *Beverage*, a fancier of dogs, from a small Black and Tan to a large Siberian Bloohound: Mr. Toby. *Paste Bucket*, a Bill Poster: Mr. Stick. *Roomstolet*, a Landlord: Mr. Tusky. *Guyon, McDefeat*, Champion Billiard Players: Mr. Chalk, Mr. Cue. *All Right, Japanese Tommy*, Ambassadors from Japan: Masters John, George. *Hosschesnutz*, a Prosperous Lager Bier Saloon: J. F. LEWIS. *Peasants, Soldiers, Policemen, Foot Passengers, Venders, Schoolboys, Firemen, Gnomes, etc. Miss Elegance Custom*, a fashionable young lady: Miss Gay. *Liza Laffenhausen*, a Dutch girl: Miss Naylor. *Bridget O'Donoghue*, an Apple Woman: Miss Jarrad. *Cora Shade*, (colored) Hot Corn Woman: Miss Thomas. *Nymphalia*, Queen of the Nixes, or River Fairies: Miss Laura. *Pipalu*, her Elfin Chief: Miss P. Germain. *Nixes*, "know you the Nixes gay and fair, with their beaming eyes and golden hair?:" Corps de Ballet. *The Four Quarters of the World*: *Europe*: Miss Jones. *Asia*: Miss G. Germain. *Africa*: Mr. E. Gillet. *America*: Miss Flora Lee. *New Jersey*, somewhere about the 4 Quarters: E. T. SINCLAIR (Champion Skater of All America). *Ballet*: Mlles. RITA SANGALLI, BETTY RIGL; Messrs. BAPTISTAN, J. Zucchi; Mlles A. Laurent, M. Blake, E. Schell.

Act 1, Scene 1: Retreat of Romance by Moonlight. Transformation of Characters. (Lewis.) *Scene 2*: The Farm of Plenty, in the Valley of Fertility. (Lewis.) *Scene 3*: Subterranean Grotto (of the Nixes). (Lewis.) *Scene 4*: Roadside Inn. (Johnson.) *Scene 5*: Exterior of Broadway Dining Room. (Johnson.) *Scene 6*: Enchanted Garden. (Lewis.)

Act 2, Scene 1[35]: The Olympic Theatre by Night. (Johnson.) *Scene 2*: German Billiard Saloon. (Johnson.) *Scene 3*: Wild's Candy and Walstein's Optician Stores, Broadway. (Johnson.) *Scene 4*: Skating Pond by Moonlight. (Lewis.) *Scene 5*: View of City Hall Park. (Johnson.) *Scene 6*: A Street by Moonlight. (Johnson.) *Scene 7*: The New Court House. (Johnson.) *Scene 8*: Room in a Hotel. (Johnson.) *Scene 9*: The Dell of Ferns. (Lewis.) *Scene 10*: Retreat of the Silver Sprites. Grand Transformation Scene. (Lewis.)

BALLETS AND SPECIALTIES[36]

Contra Dance (Act 1, Scene 2)
Characters

Transformation of Characters (Act 1, Scene 2)

Grand Ballet—The Grotto Dance (Act 1, Scene 3)
Mlles. Sangalli, Mlles. Schell, E. Rigl, Blake, L. Whiting, Mons. Baptistan, Full Corps of Coryphees

Ballet Divertissement[37] (Act 1, Scene 6)
Mlle. B. Rigl, Mons. Baptistan; Mlles. Laurent, Blake, Schell, L. Whiting

[35]Running order of Scenes in Act 2 revised during the run.
[36]During the run the following were added:
Character Dance (Act 1, Scene 2)
F. Lacy, E. Rigl
Burlesque Can Can (Act 1, Scene 1)(added October 1868)
Chorus and Dance (Act 1, Scene 2)(added October 1868)
The Dancing Lesson (New Italian Can-Can)(Act 1, Scene 4)
Mlle. Sangalli; G. L. Fox, Messr. Baptistan, Coryphées
Zuave Drill, "La Tarantella"
Carrie and Charles Austin, Full Corps de Ballet
Trick Scenes: Act 1, Scenes 4, 5; Act 2, Scenes 1, 2, 3, 5, 6, 7.
[37]Replaced during the first run by"La Tarantella" (Grand Pas de Deux)
Mlle. Sangalli, Messr. Baptistan

Polish National Dance (Act 2, Scene 4)
Mlle. R Sangalli, Mons. Baptistan, Mlles. Laurent, Schell, L. Whiting

HUMPTY DUMPTY

The Comic and Spectacular Pantomime in Two Acts, 19 Scenes. Second Volume Bound to Please, Arranged and Compiled from Traditional Facts, Dilapidated Scraps, Memory and Imagaination by George L. Fox. Music composed and conducted by A. Reiff, Jr. Scenery by J. A. Johnson. Machinery by William Saunders. Tricks by Robert Cutler. Ballets and classical groupings by Signor Davide Costa. Costumes by Mme. Costa. Caricatures by Thomas Nast. Stage director, E. F. Taylor. (Produced by George L. Fox. James E. Hayes, Lessee and Manager) Reconstruction opened 25 January 1869.[38]

CAST: *Humpty Dumpty*, revised and corrected (despite his incorrigibility), later Clown: GEORGE L. FOX. *The Venerable One Two Buckle My Shoe*, rather too late to mend, later Pantaloon: CHARLES K. FOX. *Tommy Tucker*, a Nursery Acquaintance, later Harlequin: FRANK LACY. *Little Goody Two Shoes* of time-honored origin, later Columbine: Mlle. A. LAURENT. *The Genii of Enterprise*: MILLY SACKETT. *The Genii of Fortune*: Mrs. C. Edmunds. *Brother Jonathan*, with an eye to both geniies: E. T. SINCLAIR. *Vulcan*, the original Smith, and the only honest Forger of that name: J. B. HOWLAND. *Deputy Vulcan*, a forger of less acoount than the one above him: Mr. M. Quinlan.

Act 1, Scene 1: Vulcan's Court of Quarter Sessions. *Scene 2*: Farm of Plenty. *Scene 3*: Arcadian Haunt of Fancy. *Scene 4*: The Labyrinth of Love in the Bower of Beauty. *Scene 5*: A Glade in Fairyland. *Scene 6*: Country Inn and Blacksmith's Shop. *Scene 7*: Tobacco and Dry Goods Emporium. *Scene 8*: The Lawn. *Scene 9*: Harlequin's Residence. *Scene 10*: Railway Tunnel.

Act 2, Scene 1: Transmogrification of Eatables. *Scene 2*: Mossy Glen. *Scene 3*: Boot and Shoe Store, and Young Ladies' Seminary. *Scene 4*: Interior of an Artist's Home. *Scene 5*: Pastoral Landscape. *Scene 6*: An Elegant Boudoir. *Scene 7*: Liquor Store and Private House. *Scene 8*: A Surprisingly Frightful Pass. *Scene 9*: Entirely New and Original Transformation Scene.

BALLETS AND SPECIALTIES

Arcadian Haunt of Fancy (Act 1, Scene 3)

La Sylphide (Grand Ballet)(Act 1, Scene 4)
Mlle. R. Sangalli, Mons. Costa, Full Corps de Ballet

Transformation of Characters to Harlequinade (Act 1, Scene 5)

Scandinavian Polka (Act 1, Scene 8)
Mlle. R. Sangalli, George L. Fox, Ladies of the Ballet

Signor Costa's Fancy Dress Ball of Deportment (Act 1, Scene 9)
Mlle. R. Sangalli, Full Corps de Ballet

Transformation Scene/Georgeous Fairy Scene (Act 2, Scene 9)

1868.07 LA BELLE HÉLÈNE

An Opéra-bouffe in Three Acts, in French. Libretto by Henri Meilhac and Ludovic Halévy. Music by Jacques Offenbach. Stage manager, Mons. V. Guffroy. Conductor, Mons. Lefevre. Scenery by Minard Lewis. Costumes by Nonon (Paris) and Toledo (New York). Appointments by John D. Lundy. Stage machinery by Henry Drew. Produced by Harold L. Bateman's Parisian Opera Company. Opened 26 March 1868 at the Théâtre Français and closed 2 May 1868 (matinee) after 37 performances.

CAST: *Hélène*, Queen of Sparta: Mlle. LUCILLE TOSTÉE. *Paris*, Son of King Priam: Mons. V. GUFFROY. *Ménélas*, King of Sparta: Mons. LEDUC. *Agamemnon*, King of Kings: Mons. DUCHESNE. *Calchas*, Grand Augur of Jupiter: Mons. LAGRIFFOUL. *Achilles*, King of Phthiotis: Mons. Valter. *Ajax I*, King of Salamis: Mons. Benedick. *Ajax II*, King of the Locrians: Mons. Monier. *Orestes*, Son of Agamemnon: Mlle. deFelcourt. *Bacchis*, Attendant of Hélène: Mlle. Juliani. *Parthoenis*: Mlle. Marguerite. *Loena*: Mlle. Mathilde. *Philocomes*, servant of Calchas: Mons. Hamilton/Brabant. *Euthycles*, a Blacksmith: Mons. Fleury. *A Slave*: Mons. Perrigueur. *Princess and Princesses, Courtiers, Mourners of Adonis, Helen's Attendants, Guards, People, Slaves, etc.*

Act 1: Exterior of the Temple of Jupiter, at Sparta.

Act 2: Hall in the Palace.—The Game of Goose.

Act 3: Sea Shore at Nauplia.—The Newport of Ancient Greece. The Galley of Venus.

ACT 1[39]

Choeur (Vers tes autels, Jupin)
Choeur

[38]Scenery uncredited.
[39]Musical Numbers not listed in programs. List prepared from published libretto (J. A. Gray & Green, New York, 1868) "as presented by H. L. Bateman at the French Theatre in March 1868."

Choeur des jeunes filles (C'est le devoir des jeunes filles)
Mlle. L. Tostée, Choeur de Femmes
Air d'Hélène (Amours divins)
Mlle. L. Tostée
Ronde d'Orphée (Ce cygne traqué par un aigle)
Mons. Lagriffoul
Couplets (Au cabaret du Labyrinthe)
Mlle. DeFelcourt, Mons. Lagriffoul, Choeur
Fabliau: Le Jugement de Paris (Au mont Ida trois déesses)
Mon. V. Guffroy
Marche et Choeur (Voici les rois de la Grèce!)
Messrs. Benedick, Monier, Choeur
Couplets des Rois (Ces Rois remplis de vaillance)
Messrs. Benedic, Monier
Entrée d'Achille (Je suis le bouillant Achille)
Mons. Valter, Choeur
Entrée de Ménélas (Je suis mari de la reine, Le Roi Ménélas)
Mons. Leduc, Choeur
Entrée d'Agamemnon (Le roi barbu qui s'avance)
Mons. Duchesne, Choeur
Final (Gloire! Gloire! au berger victorieux!)
Tous

ACT 2
Choeur (O reine, en ce jour il faut faire)
Choeur
Invocation à Venus (Nous naissons toutes soucieuses)
Mlle. L. Tostée
Marche de L'Oie (Le voici, le roi des rois)
Choeur
Morceau d'Ensemble/Scène du jeu (Craignez Calchas!)
Messrs. Lagriffoul, Duchesne, Leduc, Benedic, Monier, Mlles. deFelcourt, Tostée
Couplets (En couronnes tressons roses)
Mlle. deFelcourt, Choeur
Duo du rève (C'est le ciel qui m'envoie)
Mlle. Tostée, Mons. V. Guffroy
Finale (A moi! Rois de la Grèce, à moi!)
Tous
Couplets (Un mari sage)
Mlle. L. Tostée

ACT 3
Choeur (Dansons! aimons! buvons! chantons!)
Choeur
Rondo (Venus au fond de nos âmes)
Mlle. DeFelcourt
Couplets (Là! Vrai, je ne suis pas coupable)
Mlle. L. Tostée
Trio Patriotique (Lorsque la Grèce est un champ de carnage)
Messrs. Duchesne, Lagriffoul, Leduc
Choeur Général (La galère de Cythère)
Choeur
Prière (La Grèce entière suppliante)
Choeur
Air Tyrolienne (Et tout d'abord)
Mon. V. Guffroy, Mlle. deFelcourt, Choeur
Finale/Choeur Générale (Elle vient! C'est elle!)
Tous

PARIS AND HELEN, or, The Grecian Elopement

1868.08

An Original Adaptation of the Opéra-bouffe[40]. English adaptation by Molyneux St. John. Based on the opéra-bouffe "La Belle Hélène," (French libretto by Henri Meilhac and Ludovic Halévy). Music by Jacques Offenbach. Acting manager, M. L. Finch. Stage manager, Ben A. Baker. Scenic artist, Joseph S. Schell. Leader of orchestra, Henry Tissington. Opened 13 April 1868 at the New York Theatre and closed 16 June 1868 after 65 performances.

CAST: *Helen*, the fairest of the fair—in most things but not towards Menelaus. Mistress of Sparta and Society but not of herself. Though a Queen in Greece, she flies to Paris, embarks on a Gal(l)ey and goes off as gaily as possible, though she knows that in the loss of his Helen, Menelaus must find the (k)nell of his happiness: SOPHIE WORRELL. *Paris*, the pride of La Belle Helene (not La Belle France), a Prince, a Poet, and although a Shepherd, by no means a Cowherd (coward). Like the Sunday Mercury he is a good judge of beauty. Being asked by Menelaus to take something, he does so, and takes his Host's Wife, and behaves very shabbily, but is altogether a very fashionable and fascinating fellow: IRENE WORRELL. *Orestes*, a sweet youth in the estimation of his mother, and indeed, of young ladies in the neighborhood. Though green in costume, he is by no means so in nature, and is said to have made his enemies look remarkable blue on more than one occasion: JENNIE WORRELL. *Menelaus*, King of Sparta and husband to Helen, a Monarch who, though bought off by Venus, is given to jealousy, and eventually sold by his wife: J. C. DUNN. *Agamemnon*, King of Myconœ, a gentleman who betrayed his sympathy with the exiled Royal Family of France by his partiality for a Bourbon whenever he saw one: GEORGE LINGARD. *Calchas*, High Priest of Jupiter, a regular Down East Greek, who would have sold wooden nutmegs if his congregation had possessed any money to pay for them. As it is he takes what he can and growls at not getting more. Proprietor of the Bogus Thunder and Lightning: WELSH EDWARDS. *Achilles*, King of Thessaly, a Grecian Commander, who, dipped in the Styx by his mother, was made invulnerable except in his heel, the part by which she held him. In this spot he was wounded, and as his heel could not be healed, he died and his mother was sol(e)d: S. B. Villa. *Ajax I*, King of Salamis, another Grecian commander, who though living in Greece, failed to strike "Ile": J. Hurley. *Ajax II*, King of Locris, one more Grecian commander, and partner of Ajax I. He resided in ancient Jersey, and was a teetotaller. Hence his story of defying the lightning: W. Corrister. *Philocomes*, Property man to Calchas. A good performer on the Sheet Iron Thunder Machine: J. O'Neal. *Glauce*, a lady-in-waiting—for a husband, as well as for the Queen's left-off robes. She has ot much to say, but what she has is well said by: Lizzie Davey. *Lœna*, a young girl, whose part is rather lœner, than that of Glauce. She cherishes hope of lœna-ing on Orestes for life. If we know Orestes rightly, she will be mistaken: Agnes Wallace. *Parthœnis*, one of those nice little girls, who speak only when they are spoken to: J. Wakeman. *Chorus, Worshippers, Guards, etc, all as Large as Life and Infinitely more Natural.*

MUSICAL NUMBERS
"I'm on a Spree, Sir" (Solo)
J. Worrell
"Sing la La"
Chorus
"Oh! Love Divine!" (Solo)
S. Worrell
"Judgement of Paris" (Solo)
I. Worrell
"Fair Helen of Sparta" (Solo)
S. Worrell
"For Jollity, now let's away" (Solo)
J. Worrell
"Yes, 'Tis a Dream" (Duet)
S. Worrell, I. Worrell
"When Husbands go to Crete, you know" (Solo)
"Venus Commands, we will Obey" (solo)
J. Worrell
"I've Nothing to Confess" (Solo)
S. Worrell
"Tyroliene" (Solo with Chorus)
I. Worrell, Chorus

MARITANA

1868.09

A Revival of the Light Opera in Three Acts[41]. (Libretto by Edward Fitzball. Based on the play "Don César de Bazan" by Adolphe d'Ennery and Philippe Dumanoir.) Music by William Vincent Wallace. Musical director, W. G. Deitrich. Produced by the Caroline Richings English Opera Company (Caroline Richings, Directress; A. S. Pennoyer, Business Manager). Opened 12 May 1868 at the Théâtre Français for 1 performance in repertory; season closed 23 May 1868.

[40]After two weeks, an after-piece comedietta, Too Much for Good Nature was addded to the bill.

[41]First produced in New York 4 May 1848 at the Bowery Theatre for 3 performances. For Synopsis of Scenes and Musical Numbers, see original 1848 production.

CAST: *Charles II*, King of Spain: HENRY C. PEAKES. *Don Caesar de Bazan*: WILLIAM CASTLE. *Don José de Santarem*: S. C. CAMPBELL. *Marquis de Montefiore*: EDWARD SEGUIN. *Lazarillo*: Mrs. EDWARD SEGUIN (Zelda Harrison). *Maritana*: Miss CAROLINE RICHINGS. *Marchioness de Montefiore*: Mrs. J. A. Arnold. Full Chorus.

1868.10 FRA DIAVOLO, or, The Inn of Terracina

A Revival of the Romantic Opera in Three Acts[42]. Original French libretto (to the Opéra-comique 'Fra Diavolo, or L'Hotellerie de Terracina') by Eugène Scribe. English adaptation by Rophino Lacy. Music by Daniel Auber. Musical director, W. G. Deitrich. Produced by the Caroline Richings Opera Company (Caroline Richings, Directress; A. S. Pennoyer, Business Manager). Opened 16 May 1868 (matinee) for 1 performance in repertory at the Théâtre Français; season closed 23 May 1868.

CAST: *Fra Diavolo*, disguised as the Marquis San Carlo: WILLIAM CASTLE. *Lorenzo*: ARNOLD HARRISON. *Lord Allcash*: EDWARD SEGUIN. *Beppo, Giacomo*, Two Italian bandits: S. C. CAMPBELL, HENRY C. PEAKES. *Matteo*, Zerlina's father: ?. *Zerlina*: CAROLINE RICHINGS. *Lady Allcash*: Mrs. EDWARD SEGUIN (Zelda Harrison). *Soldiers, Peasants, Bandits, etc.*

1868.11 THE DOCTOR OF ALCANTARA

A Revival of the Comic Opera (Opéra-bouffe) in Two Acts[43]. Libretto by Benjamin E. Woolf. Music by Julius Eichberg. Musical director, W. G. Deitrich. Produced by the Caroline Richings English Opera Company (Caroline Richings, Directress; A. S. Pennoyer, Business Manager). Opened 16 May 1868 at the Théâtre Français and closed 23 May 1868 after 2 performances in repertory.

CAST: *Doctor Paracelsus*: EDWARD SEGUIN. *Señor Balthazar*: ?. *Carlos*, his son: WILLIAM CASTLE. *Don Pomposo*, alguazie: HENRY C. PEAKES. *Perez, Sancho*, porters: ??, ??. *Inez*: CAROLINE RICHINGS. *Donna Lucrezia*, Wife to Doctor Paracelsus: ?. *Isabella*, her daughter: ZELDA HARRISON (Mrs. E. Seguin). *Serenaders, Citizens, etc.* Company included S. C. CAMPBELL. D. B. WYLIE. ARNOLD HARRISON. Pierre Bernard. J. A. Arnold. J. Murphy. Mrs. J. A. Arnold. Mrs. Dallimeur.

1868.12 THE BOHEMIAN GIRL

A Revival of the Light Opera in Three Acts[44]. (Libretto by Alfred Bunn, after Jules-Henri Vernoy de Saint-Georges' ballet-pantomime "The Gypsy.") Music by Michael William Balfe. Musical director, W. G. Deitrich. Produced by the Caroline Richings English Opera Company (Caroline Richings, Directress; A. S. Pennoyer, Business Manager). Opened 20 May 1868 at the Théâtre Français and closed 23 May 1868 after 2 performances in repertory.

CAST: *Thaddeus*: WILLIAM CASTLE. *Count Arnheim*: S. C. CAMPBELL. *Florestein, nephew to the Count*: D. B. WYLIE. *Devilshoof*, chief of the tribe: EDWARD SEGUIN. *Captain of the Guard*: Arnold Harrison. *Officer*: Pierre Bernard. *Gipsies*: J. A. Arnold, J. Murphy. *Arline*: CAROLINE RICHINGS. *Gypsy Queen*: Mrs. J. A. Arnold. *Buda*: Mrs. Dallimeur. Full Chorus.

[42]First produced in New York in English as THE DEVIL'S BROTHER 20 June 1833 at the Park Theatre.

[43]First produced in New York 28 May 1866 at the Théâtre Français in repertory. For Synopsis of Scenes and Musical Numbers, see original 1866 production. No program found for this production.

[44]First produced in New York 25 November 1844 at the Park Theatre for 17 performances in repertory. For Synopsis of Scenes and Musical Numbers, see original 1844 production.

1868–1869 SEASON

Lydia Thompson in FORTY THIEVES
Billy Rose Theatre Collection, New York Public Library for the Performing Arts

1868–1869 SEASON

1868.13 ORPHÉE AUX ENFERS

A Revival of the Opéra-bouffon in Four Acts[1], in French. Libretto by Hector Crémieux. Music by Jacques Offenbach. Scenery by Messrs. Hannibal Calyo, Smith and Hill. Musical director, Mons. Ysaye. Produced by Messrs. Alhaiza and Calabresi (Directors of the New Orleans Opera House). Opened 4 June 1868 at the Théâtre Français and closed 13 (matinee) June 1868 after 8 performances in repertory.

CAST: *Eurydice*: Mlle. ALINE LAMBÈLE. *Orphée*: Mons. DECRE. *Public Opinion*: Mons. THOLER. *Aristée*: Mons. GOUGEON [Goujon]. *Pluto*: Mons. GOUGEON. *Jupiter*: Mons. EDGARD [Edyard]. *John Styx*: Mons. Gilbert. *Mercury*: Mons. Aurenson. *Mars*: Mons. Mederick. *Time*: Mons. Charlotte. *Bacchus*: Mons. Serlet. *Diana*: Mlle. THOLER. *Junon*: Mlle. Decre. *Venus*: Mlle. CADIC. *Cupidon*: Mlle. ESAI [Isai]. *Minerva*: Mlle. Duhamel.

1868.14 LEON'S LA! BELL-L.N.

A Burlesque of Offenbach's "La Belle Hélène" in One Act, 6 Scenes, preceded by an Olio. Libretto by Francis Leon. Music by Jacques Offenbach, adapted and arranged by Prof. Fred W. Zaulig. Produced under the supervision of Francis Leon. Scenery and machinery by Edward Simmons. Stage alterations and properties by Charles Brown. Produced by Edwin Kelly and Francis Leon. Opened 6 June 1868 at Kelly & Leon's Minstrels and closed 24 June 1868 after 21 performances.[2]

CAST: *Helen*, fond of Paris, which is not strange, seeing that L.N. is Supreme Ruler of that moral European city. According to mythological tradition—Helen was the daughter of Tyndarus and Leda—but not as tender as the Music of the Leader, or she would not have left her husband money-less and gone on her Paris-ian excursion to Troy: FRANCIS LEON. *Paris*, a Son of old Prima, not morally prime, but mentally, vocally and physically very prime, originator of boat travel to Troy and author of the Trojan row, yet not a rowdy: EDWIN KELLY. *Cal-Chase*, High Priest of the Temple of Jupiter and Soothsayer to the Temple of Impeachment, considered very game—at cards: ADD RYMAN. *All-Gamon*, King of Kings, Generalissimo at Troy of the Armies of Greece during the Southern rebellion, where he opened a recruiting office and dedicated a Temple to King Pharo: G. W. G. GRIFFIN. *Money-Less*, a King of Sparta, husband of Helen, a regular tartar, the first in those days to furnish plots for odern plays: W. H. BROCKWAY. *A-Killer*, a King of Greece, who, in his infancy, was washed in the Hudson River and was thereby rendered forever invulnerable to cleanliness. After serving as a volunteer in the Trojan row, he was killed by an ar-row from Paris' bow: John F. Oberist. *A-Jacks No. 1*, Son of Tel-a-mon, a distinguished Prince of Grease judging from his avordupois—he killed himself because he could be a killer, in which he made a vile hit, and for which he was changed to a violet: Charles Stuart. *A-Jacks No. 2*, Greasier than No. 1—couldn't kill himself, 'twould take too long: Alex. Stuart. *Arrest-Us*, Son of All-Gammon and Clytemnestra, whose desire to be an orphan was so great that when old Gammon died, he killed his mamma and then peddled statues of Diana to the benighted denizens of Fulton Market: S. S. Purdy. *Filopena*, daughter of a King of Athens, a very voluble young lady, who, after being deprived of her tongue, was compelled to sing te Nightingale Waltzes. The audience need not be alarmed, she will not sing now: C. Heywood. *Looney*, a Priestess of Bacchus, always ready to back-us with her voice or Boots: Foley McKeiver. *To-Bac-chus*, a Son of Jupiter and Semele—or Smile eh?—a favorite expression at Delmonico's, the Palace of this famous God. His appearnce in the Burlesque is to remind his disciples that the bar is closed at 12: W. Guy. *Herald*, not New York—very useful in furnishing Greeks with intelligence: George Guy. *Men at arms, Grecians, Trojans, Ladies of the Court*: Large Corps of Auxiliaries.

Scene 1: Temple of Venus—Front Door. *Scene 2*: Mulberry Street, Sparta. *Scene 3*: Helen's Boudoir in Palace. *Scene 4*: Greek Street with Nicholson Pavement. *Scene 5*: Garden of the Hellespont, 69th Street. *Scene 6*: Galley of Venus, Pier 41.

[1]Previously produced in French in New York 17 January 1867 at the Théâtre Français. For Synopsis of Scenes and Musical Numbers, see original 1867 production.

[2]Musical numbers not listed in programs. Returned 2 May 1870 to Kelly & Leon's for 1 week, and 11 July 1870 to Kelly & Leon's for an additional week.

1868.15 LA GRANDE-DUCHESSE DE GÉROLSTEIN

A Revival of the Opèra-bouffe in Three Acts[3], in French. Libretto by Henri Meilhac and Ludovic Halévy. Music by Jacques Offenbach. Scenery by Messrs. Hannibal Calyo, Smith and Hill. Musical director, Mons. Ysaye. Produced by Messrs. Alhaiza and Calabresi (Directors of the New Orleans Opera House). Opened and closed 13 June 1868 at the Théâtre Français after 1 performance.

CAST: *La Grande-Duchesse de Gérolstein*: Mlle. ALINE LAMBÈLE. *Fritz*: Mons. DECRE. *General Boum*: Mons. EDGARD. *Baron Puck*: Mons. ROSAMBEAU. *Prince Paul*: Mons. GOUJON. *Nepomuc*: Mons. GILBERT. *Baron Grog*: Mons. AURENSON. *Wanda*: Mlle. THOLER. *Isa*: Mlle. Isaye. *Amelia*: Mlle. Duhamel. *Olga*: Mlle. Cadic. *Charlotte*: Mlle. Isaye.

1868.16 THE GRAND DUCHESS OF GÉROLSTEIN

A Revival of the Opèra-bouffe in Three Acts[4]. Original French libretto to "La Grande Duchesse de Gérolstein" by Henri Meilhac and Ludovic Halévy. Adaptation from the French expressly for the Worrell Sisters by Ben A. Baker. Music by Jacques Offenbach. Acting manager, M. L. Finch. Stage manager, Ben A. Baker. Scenic artist, J. S. Schell. Leader of orchestra, Henry Tissington. Produced by the Worrell Sisters. Opened 17 June 1868 at the New York Theatre and closed 18 July 1868 after 33 performances.

CAST: *La Grande-Duchesse de Gérolstein*: SOPHIE WORRELL. *Wanda*, betrothed to Fritz: IRENE WORRELL. *Prince Paul* , a suitor for the hand of the Duchess: JENNIE WORRELL. *Fritz*, a private soldier in the army of the Grand Duchess: JAMES C. DUNN. *General Boum*, Commander-in-Chief of the army of the Grand Duchess: WELSH EDWARDS. *Baron Puck*, Prime Minister and Tutor to the Grand Duchess: George Lingard. *Nepomuc*, Aide-de-Camp to the Grand Duchess: S. B. Villa. *Baron Grog*, Special Envoy to the Court of the Grand Duchess: F. B. Chapman. *Snider, Switzer, Sloppen*, Soldiers in the army of the Grand Duchess: Messrs. Hurley, Corrister, Neil. *Maids of Honor attending the Grand Duchess (4)*: *Irza*: Agnes Wallace. *Amelia*: J. Wakeman. *Olga*: Mary Everett. *Charlotte*: Kate Dunn. *Soldiers, Officers, Peasants, Ladies of Honor.*

1868.17 LISCHEN ET FRITZCHEN

A Saynète (Conversation Alsacienne) in One Act, in French. Libretto by Paul Boisselot. Music by Jacques Offenbach. Produced by Harold L. Bateman. Opened and closed 25 June 1868 at the Academy of Music after 1 performance[5]; returned 30 November 1868 to Pike's Opera House (on a bill with BARBE BLEU) and closed 5 December 1868 after 7 additional performances.

CAST: *Lischen*, Alsacienne, Mde. de balais: Mlle. LUCILLE TOSTÉE. *Fritzchen*, Alsacien, domestique: Mons. V. GUFFROY[6].

MUSICAL NUMBERS[7]

Couplets (Me chasser, me forcer)
V. Guffroy

Chanson (P'tits balais, p'tits balais)
L. Tostée

Duo (Je suis alsacienne)
L. Tostée, V. Guffroy

[3]Previously produced in French in New York 24 September 1867 at the Théâtre Français for 156 performances. For Synopsis of Scenes and Musical Numbers, see original 1867 production. No program found for this engagement

[4]English language premiere in New York. Previously produced in French in New York 24 September 1867 at the Théâtre Français for 156 performances.

[5]American premiere. Act 1 of La Grande Duchesse de Gérolstein preceded Lischen et Fritzchen in the benefit program; Act 2 of La Belle Hélène followed.

[6]Succeeded by Mons. DARDIGNAC for the Pike's Opera House engagement.

[7]Musical numbers not listed in programs. List prepared from published French piano vocal score (G. Brandus et S. Dufour, Paris, 1864).

Fable (Un jour un rat de ville)
L. Tostée
Final et Duo (Quoi! Fritzchen)
L. Tostée, V. Guffroy

1868.18 BARBE-BLEUE

An Opèra-bouffe (Bluebeard) in Four Acts, in French. Libretto by Henri Meilhac and Ludovic Halévy. Music by Jacques Offenbach. Director, Harold L. Bateman. Ballets by Davide Costa. Scenery by Minard Lewis and G. Strong. Costumes by Mons. Marage (Paris). Conductor, H. Dennery. Produced by Harold L. Bateman's Opéra Bouffe Company. Opened 13 July 1868 at Niblo's Garden and closed 8 October 1868 after 81 performances; returned 16 November 1868 to Pike's Opera House and closed 5 December 1868 after an additional 21 performances[8]; returned 7 April 1869 to the Fifth Avenue Theatre under the auspices of James Fisk, Jr. and closed 11 June 1869 after 17 additional performances in repertory. Total: 119 performances.

CAST: *Boulotte*: Mlle. IRMA. *Princess Hermia*: Mlle. LAMBÈLE. *Queen Clementine*: Mlle. JEANNE DUCLOS. *Heloise*: Mlle. Rose. *Rosalinde*: Mlle. Mathilde. *Isaure*: Mlle. Cadix. *Blanche*: Mlle. Desenfants. *Eleonore*: Mlle. Lemoine. *Barbe-Bleu*: Mons. AUJAC. *Prince Saphir*: Mons. DARDIGNAC. *Count Oscar*: Mons. LAGRIFFOUL. *King Bobeche*: Mons. FRANCIS. *Popolani*: Mons. DUCHESNE. *Alvarez*: Mons. EDGARD. *Sheriff*: Mons. Hamilton. *A Page*: Mlle. Louise. *A Peasant-woman*: Mme. Hamilton. *A Boy*: Master George. *Jarrett and Palmer's Parisian Ballet Troupe*: Mlle. DeROSA, Signor DAVIDE COSTA; Mlles. Giovani, Mazzeri, Pagani, Invernezzi, Francisco, Elena Francisco, Setti, Sisters Negri, Cataneo. *Peasants, Guards, Nobles, Pages, Mexicans, Bohemians, etc.*

Act 1: A Village in Brittany, during the Crusades. Bluebeard's Castle in the distance.

Act 2: Palace of King Bobeche.

Act 3: The Alchemist's Cave.

Act 4: The Royal Wedding.

ACT 1[9]

Recit et Duo (Dans la nature tout se réveille)
Mons. Dardignac, [Fleurette]
Couplets (Y'a p't-êtr' des bergers dans le village)
Mlle. Irma
Choeur (Sur la place il faut nous rendre)
Choeur
Proclamation (J'apporte les volontés)
Mons. Duchesne, Choeur
Choeur de la loterie (Ah! prends mon nom)
Choeur des femmes
Couplets de la rosière (V'la z'encor de drol's)
Mlle. Irma
Choeur (Boulotte! saperlotte!)
Mons. Duchesne
Choeur du palanquin (Montez sur ce palanquin)
Choeur
Légende de Barbe-Bleu (Ma première femme)
Mons. Aujac, Choeur
Final (Honneur! Honneur à Monseigneur)
Messrs. Aujac, Duchesne, Mlle. Irma, Choeur

ACT 2

Introduction, Choeur et Couplets (C'est un métier difficile)
Mons. Laggrifoul, Choeur
Choeur de sortie (Qu'un bon courtisan s'incline)
Rondo (On prend une ange d'innocence)
Mlle. J. Duclos
Quatuor (C'est mon berger!)
Mlles. Lambèle, Choeur
Ran, plan, plan
Messrs. Francis, Dardignac, Mlles. J. Duclos, Lambelé
Final (Voici cet heureux couple!)
Choeur
Couplets (J'ai, la dernière semaine)
Mons. Aujac, Mlle. Irma, Choeur
Ensemble General (Partez, partez!)
Tous

ACT 3

Cantabile (Le voilà donc, le tombeau)
Mons. Aujac
Duo (Vous avez vu ce monument)
Mons. Aujac, Mlle. Irma
Les aveux (Pierre, un beau jour, parvint)
Mons. Aujac, Mlle. Irma
Trio (Hola! Hola! Ça me prend là!)
Messrs. Aujac, Duchesne, Mlle. Irma
Final (Salut à toi)
Mlles. Irma, Rose, Mons. Duchesne, Les Cinq Femmes
Couplets (Mortes, sortez de vos tombeaux)
Mlle. Irma

ACT 4

Choeur nuptial (Hymenée! Hymenée!)
Choeur
Lamento (Madame, Ah! Madame)
Mons. Aujac, Choeur
Duel
Choeur nuptial (reprise)
Choeur des Bohémiens (Nous arrivons à l'instant même)
Choeur
Ballade de la Bohémienne (Nous possédons)
Mlle. Irma
Final (Idée heureuse, ingénieuse)
Messrs. Aujac, Duchesne, Lagriffoul, Mlles. Irma, Lambèle, Chœur

[8]In the final week of the Pike's Opera House engagement, LISCHEN AND FRITZCHEN was added to the program.

[9]Musical numbers not listed in programs. List prepared from published English-French libretto, as performed by Bateman's Parisian Opera Company (John A. Gray & Green, New York, 1868). Libretto credits Adolf Birgfeld as conductor. According to program, the following specialty not listed in libretto was performed in Act 4:
Grand Mexican Ballet Divertissement
Full Ballet

1868.19 FIRE FLY, or, The Friend of the Flag

A Military Drama in Five Acts, 17 Scenes. Play by Edmund Falconer (adapted from Ouida's novel "Under Two Flags"). Original music by Mr. Thomas Baker. Stage director, J. G. Hanley. Scenery by Messrs. H. Isherwood, Evans. Costumes by Mr. Benschoten. Machinery by Mr. H. Butler. Appointments by Mr. James Timmony. Music conductor, Thomas Baker. Produced by Lotta Crabtree. Opened 10 August 1868 at Wallack's Theatre and closed 5 September 1868 after 24 performances.

CAST: *Fire Fly*, the Friend of the Flag: LOTTA (CRABTREE). *Harold Cecil*, passing as Louis Victor: CHARLES FISHER. *Duke of Lyonnaise*, Friend to Harold: B. T. RINGOLD. *Berkley Cecil*, Brother to Harold: C. H. ROCKWELL. *Ben Arslan*, a Zouave: George Holland. *Rake*, Harold's own man: E. Lamb. *Colonel Chateauroy*: Theodore Hamilton. *Marshall McDonald*: T. J. Hind. *Shadrick Levi*: R. McWade. *Claude Chaurillon*: T. Milton. *Alcide*: J. Hogan. *Beauchamp*: W. J. Leonard. *Millbank*: W. H. Pope. *Barbe Grise*: H. George. *Arab Sheik*: L. J. Williams. *First Arab*: P. H. Wilson. *Officer*: H. Jacobs. *Orderly*: J. McGee. *Aid-de-Camp*: J. Quigley. *Tata Leroux*: J. T. Ward. *Venetia*, Princess of Corona: Miss LeClaire Phillips. *Marquise de Renardière*: Miss Mary Barrett. *French Soldiers, Passengers, Servants, Arabs, News Venders, etc.*

Act 1, Scene 1: The Quay or Landing Place on the Mole at Algiers. *Scene 2*: A Street in Algiers. *Scene 3*: The Café of the Chasseurs.

Act 2, Scene 1: The Chambree or Barrack Room. Two years later. *Scene 2*: A Street in Algiers. *Scene 3*: The Ruins (of a Mosque) in the Desert. *Scene 4*: The Salle de Danse in the Café of the Chasseurs.

Act 3, Scene 1: The Tent of the Princess in the Camp on the Desert. *Scene 2*: On the outskirts of the Camp. *Scene 3*: The Outpost. (The Bivouac. The Battle.)

Act 4, Scene 1: The Parade Ground. (A Plain in front of the camp.) *Scene 2*: Outskirts of the Camp. *Scene 3*: The Tent of the Princess.

Act 5, Scene 1: A Street in Algiers. *Scene 2*: The Head-Quarters of the Marshall. *Scene 3*: The Desert. *Scene 4*: The Parade Ground. Military Execution. Unexpected and Impressive Denouement.

SPECIALTIES, MUSICAL NUMBERS

Song ("Bright Champagne") and Mad Dance (Act 2, Scene 4)
Lotta

Celebrated Song and Solo on the Snare Drum (Act 4, Scene 1)
Lotta

1868.20 MARRIAGE BY LANTERNS/66

A Double Bill of One Act Comic Operas[10]. Stage manager, J. B. Curran. Scenic artists, Robert Grain, Joseph B. Ayers. Musical director, Henry Hahn. George Wood, Proprietor. Opened 31 August 1868 at Wood's Museum and Metropolitan Theatre and closed 26 September 1868 after 20 matinee performances[11].

ACT 1

MARRIAGE BY LANTERNS. (Original French libretto to "Le Mariage aux Lanternes" by Michael Carré and Léon Battu, adapted from "Le Tresor à Mathurin" by Léon Battu.) Music by Jacques Offenbach.

CAST: *Fanchette*, with introduced song: SUSAN GALTON. *Guillot*, a young Farmer: THOMAS WHIFFEN. *Denise*, his Cousin: BLANCHE GALTON. *Catherine*, a Widow: Mrs. SUSAN PYNE GALTON.

ACT 2

66. (Original French libretto to "Le 66" by Pittaud de Forges and M. Laurencin [P. A. Chapelle].) Music by Jacques Offenbach.

CAST: *Grittley*, a Wandering Minstrel: SUSAN GALTON. *Frantz*: THOMAS WHIFFEN. *Berthold*, a Pedlar: CONWAY COX.

1868.21 BAR-BER BLU

A Burlesque of Offenbach's "Barbe-Bleu" in One Act, 5 Scenes, preceded by an Olio. (Burlesque by Edwin Kelly and Francis Leon.) Music by Jacques Offenbach. Musical director, Professor Fred W. Zaulig. Produced by Kelly & Leon's Minstrels (Edwin Kelly, Manager). Opened 31 August 1868 at Kelly & Leon's Minstrels and closed 17 October 1868 after 42 performances.

CAST: *Bullyette*, a lovely creature, à la Fanchon, simple in manner, dress and appearance, until she draws a prize in the Lottery of Life, that affects her with the blues, but produces the opposite effect on the audience, who appreciate the fact that she will not "git" as her predecessors Heloise, Blanche, Isaura and others have done before her: FRANCIS LEON. *Barber Blu*, a namesake of the burlesque, full of fun and matrimony, an original Mormon Chief, who adds Bullyette to the number of the faithful, very gallant, but finally yields his hand, heart and Beer-d—Blues and all, to the little arch Gipsy, Bullyette: EDWIN KELLY. *Princess Her-me-ah*, a prepossessing and stylish young lady, just out: Leon Mayer. *Queen Clem*, a matronly lady of despotic tendencies: J. C. Campbell. *Prince Say Fire*, a nice young man whose numerous disguises and invariably seen through: William H. Brockway. *Count O'Scar*, a scion of the ancient Celtic noblesse: George Guy. *Pop O'Linn*, an ancient combination of Cagliostro and the Wizard of the Sun: G. W. H. Griffin. *B. O'Beech*, a fossil of Royalty, who experiences little clemency from his Queen Clem: W. White. *Lords Ladies, Pages, Peasants, Halberdiers, Men-at-arms, Heralds, Tinkers, Soldiers, Sailors, Scrubs, Gipsies and Camp Followers*: A large corps of Enthusiastic Vocalists and Auxiliaries.

Scene 1: Inaccessible Mountains, with Barber-Blu's house in the distance. *Scene 2*: A Grand Palace. *Scene 3*: A Cavern. *Scene 4*: A Gorgeous Chamber in Bar-Ber Blu's residence. *Scene 5*: The Home of the Modern Bar-Ber Blu on the Pacific Slope. The City of the Saints in the Desert, with a new and novel outburst and Amazonian March of the Wives! Introducing an Original and Exciting Finale.

1868.22 LITTLE NELL AND THE MARCHIONESS

A Return Engagement of the Melodrama in Four Acts, 14 Scenes[12]. Suggested by an episode in the novel "The Old Curiosity Shop" by Charles Dickens, adapted by John Brougham. Produced by Lotta Crabtree. Opened 7 September 1868 at Wallack's Theatre and closed 12 September 1868 after 7 performances.

CAST: *Little Nell*: LOTTA (CRABTREE). *The Marchioness*: LOTTA (CRABTREE). *Old Grandfather Trent*: T. Hind. *Dick Swiveller*: C. FISHER. *Daniel Quilp*: H. COLEMAN. *Sampson Brass*: J. W. LEONARD. *Ned Trent*: E. Milton. *Mr. Slum*: C. Rockwell. *Corkey Jack*: H. Meredith. *Reuben Kadger*: J. McGee. *Fogy Joe*: T. Ward. *Higgins*: J. Quigley. *Burton*: H. Powell. *Showman*: W. H. Pope. *Abdallah*: E. Cashin. *Mrs. Quilp*: Mrs. W. Winter. *Mrs. Jarley*: Miss LeClaire Phillips. *Mrs. Jeniwin*: Miss L. Carman. *Sally Brass*: Miss C. Carman. *Mrs. George*: Miss Clarke. *Mrs. Simmons*: Miss J. Day. *Villagers, Morris Daners, Guests, Showmen, Minstrels, etc*: Numerous Auxiliaries, including a Troupe of Acrobats and Minstrels.

1868.23 IXION!, or, the Man at the Wheel

A Burlesque Extravaganza in One Act, 6 Scenes. Play localized and adapted by F. C. Burnand. New music arranged and composed by Michael Connolly. Scenery designed by Robert Grain. Machinery by Levi Gurnsey. Properties by Charles DeForrest. Dresses by Mrs. Huther (Liverpool) and Mr. Williams (New York). Musical director, Michael Connolly. Produced by George Wood. Opened 28 September 1868 at Wood's Museum and Metropolitan Theatreand closed 26 December 1868 after 104 performances; returned in a shortened form with ERNANI, or, the Horn of a Dilemma 18 January 1869 to Wood's Museum and Metropolitan Theatre and closed 30 January 1869 after 16 additional performances.

CAST: Prologue, Mortals: *King Ixion*, ex-King of Thessaly, but though a King with the prefix of an "X", it does not alphabetically follow that he has a wise head on his shoulders: LYDIA THOMPSON. *Tondapameibomenos, Prosephe, Podasokus*, three Thessalians who would be these aliens if they weren't these natives; calumious conspirators, dreadful democrats, members of several secret societies who demand the right of free speaking in a state of free-dumb: Messrs. Deboney, Cook and Marsden. *A young Grecian*, first class from the Sixth Ward: H. Stewart. *Queen Dia*, Ixion's disloyal wife, who leads the Revolutionists, and proposes to be a tanner of her husband as well as a Dyer, and tramples on her regal diadem in order to become a regal Democrat: Mr. BARNES. *Crowd of Red Republicans, Un-Read Republicans, Avengers, Scavengers, Greeeks, Sneaks, and Female Furies, appropriately crowned with mob caps*, by Messrs. Torch, Firebrand, Flame, Riot, Ruin, Famine, Disorder, etc.

Immortals: *Jupiter*, King of the Gods, and the most finished Gentleman in Olympus: ADA HARLAND. *Mercury*, the celestial telegraph boy: LISA WEBER. *Ixion*, who being bankrupt and sadly in want of change, is, in spite of his bad character in his former situation, "taken" up by Jupiter and patronized by the "upper ten": LYDIA THOMPSON. *Juno*, Queen of the Gods and Jove's spouse, described by Poets as the Ox-eyed Lady, and consequently of a mettlesome temperament; fond of peacocks that sing Pea-hens of joy while drawing her car: ALICE LOGAN. *Venus*, the Goddess of Beauty; still a spinster, although it has been said by a great authority that "Venus orta Mari," which being translated in "Venus ought to marry": PAULINE MARKHAM. *Cupid*, the son of Venus, who will at once be recognized as Love at First Sight: GRACE LOGAN. *Minerva*, Goddess of Wisdom, a remarkably strong-minded lady, the defender of her own rights and woman's wrongs: HARRY BECKETT. *Apollo*, secretary to the Imperial Sun Fire Insurance Company (Ltd.): AGGIE WOOD. *Bacchus*, promoter and chief director of the Celestial Whiskey Ring Association: Mr. Mestayer. *Mars*, Commander-in-Chief, as Ma's generally are: C. Daley. *Ganymede*, Jupiter's beautiful "Buttons," a nice active lad, the original Fat Boy who may be described as Ganny-mede and Ganny-purse un too: Sol Smith, (Jr.).

The Three Graces, duchess in their own right: —. *The Nine Muses*: *Calliope*: Miss Herring. *Melpomene*: Miss Jackson. *Polly Hymnia*: Miss Boneau. *Clio*: Miss Smith. *Erato*: Miss West. *Urania*: Miss Lyon. *Euterpe*: Miss Brown. *Terpsichore*: Miss Kellogg. *Thalia*: Miss Burk.

Scene 1: Ruins of a Doric Temple. *Scene 2*: The Royal Distillery in the Sky. *Scene 3*: Juno's Reception Hall. *Scene 4*: Apollo's Sun Light, Fire and Insurance Office. *Scene 5*: Cupid's Castle in the Air. *Scene 6*: The Milky Way.

MUSICAL NUMBERS

Revolutionary Chorus (Scene 1)

Grand Demonstration in Honor of Ixion's Visit (Scene 3)

Chorus and Break Down (Scene 3)

Topical Song (Scene 4)
L. Thompson

Allegorical Tableau (Scene 6)

Grand Selections from IL TROVATORE by the orchestra (Scene 6)
(*Music by* Giuseppe Verdi.)

Burlesque on the nursery rhyme "Taffy the Welshman"[13]
A. Harland, P. Markham, L. Weber, H. Beckett, S. Smith, Jr.

---

[10]English language premiere in New York. Previously produced in New York in German 18 March 1860 at the Stadttheater; in French 6 February 1864 at Theatre Français/Niblo's Saloon.

[11]Performed at weekday matinees only, not including Saturdays; the play LORLE, adapted from the German by J. H. Rosewald, played the regular schedule.

[12]First produced in New York 14 August 1867 at Wallack's Theatre for 26 performances. For Synopsis of Scenes and Musical Numbers, see original 1867 production.

[13]Not listed in programs or on posters, but discussed at length in the Times 1 October 1868.

LA GRANDE-DUCHESSE DE GÉROLSTEIN

1868.24

A Revival of the Opéra-bouffe in Three Acts, in French[14]. Libretto by Henri Meilhac and Ludovic Halévy. Music by Jacques Offenbach. Scenic artist, Hannibal Calyo. Regisseur, Paul Juignet. Musical director and conductor, Robert Stoepel. Produced by Jacob Grau. Opened 5 October 1868 at the Théâtre Français and closed 17 October 1868 after 12 performances.

CAST: *La Grande-Duchesse de Gérolstein*: ROSE BELL. *Fritz*: Mons. CARRIER. *General Boum*: Mons. BECKERS. *Prince Paul*: Mons. GOBY. *Baron Puck*: Mons. GENOT. *Baron Grog*: Mons. BOURGOIN. *Nepomuc*: Mons. Mussay. *Wanda*: Mlle. FONTANEL. *Iza*: Mlle. Rosa. *Amelie*: Mlle. Villiers. *Olga*: Mlle. Clementine. *Charlotte*: Mlle. Mariebriot. *Officer*: Mons. Chopin. *Lords and Ladies, Soldiers, Peasants, etc.*

LA GRANDE-DUCHESSE DE GÉROLSTEIN

1868.25

A Revival of the Opéra-bouffe in Three Acts, in French[15]. Libretto by Henri Meilhac and Ludovic Halévy. Music by Jacques Offenbach. Musical director, A. Birgfeld. Conductors, Édouard Colonne, H. Dennery. Scenery by William Voegtlin and Ludovico Malmsha. Machinist, Bensen Sherwood. Properties by John Lundy. Costumes by Mr. Toledo. Produced by Harold L. Bateman's Opera Bouffe Company. Opened 14 October 1868 at Pike's Opera House and closed 31 October 1868 after 18 performances; returned under the auspices of James Fisk to the Fifth Avenue Theatre 6 April 1869 for 1 additional performance.[16]

CAST: *La Grande-Duchesse de Gérolstein*: Mlle. LUCILLE TOSTÉE. *Fritz*: Mons. AUJAC. *General Boum*: Mons. DUCHESNE. *Baron Puck*: Mons. LAGRIFFOUL. *Prince Paul*: Mons. LEDUC. *Baron Grog*: Mons. DARON. *Nepomuc*: Mons. Guidon. *Wanda*: Mlle. LAMBÈLE. *Iza*: Mlle. Rose. *Olga*: Mlle. Mathilde. *Amelia*: Mlle. Laruelle. *Charlotte*: Mlle. Arsène. *Ladies in Waiting*: Mlles. Bertha, Boudinot. *Officers, Vivandiers, Lords, Ladies, Soldiers, Peasants.*

GENEVIÈVE DE BRABANT

1868.26

An Opéra-bouffe in Three Acts, 9 Scenes, in French. Libretto by Hector Crémieux and Étienne Tréfeu. Music by Jacques Offenbach. Regisseur, Paul Juignet. Scenic artist, Hannibal Calyo, Mons. Cambon (Paris), Mons. Fromant (Paris). Costumes by Mlle. Blanche Armand (New York), Mme. Gervais (Paris). Musical director, Robert Stoepel. Produced by Jacob Grau. Opened 22 October 1868 at the Théâtre Français in repertory; season closed 16 February 1869.

CAST: *Sifroy*, Duke of Curaçao: Mons. CARRIER. *Golo*, his favorite courtier: Mons. Goby. *Vanderprout*, Borgomaster of the City: Mons. GENOT. *Charles Martel*: Mons. BECKERS. *Grabuge*, Sergeant-at-Arms: Mons. BOURGOIN. *Pitou*, common soldier: Mons. GABEL. *Narcisse*, Poet to Sifroy: Mons. Petit. *Péterpip*, First Alderman: Mons. Mussay. *Saladin*: Mons. Rousseau. *Don Quixote*: Mons. Lefevre. *Renaud de Montauban*: Mons. Charrière. *The Hermit of the Ravine*: Mons. Mussay.

La Folie Aspieres: Mlle. Briot. *La Folie Bougival*: Mlle. Musier. *First Sapper*: Mlle. Rosa. *Dulcinea*: Mlle. Breton. *Drogan*, Page to Geneviève: Mlle. ROSE-BELL. *Geneviève de Brabant*, Wife of Sifroy: Mlle. MARIE DESCLAUZAS. *Brigitte*, her confidante: Mlle. GUERETTI. *Isolina*, Wife of Golo: Mlle. CLEMENTINE. *Christine*: Mlle. Maurice. *Gudule*: Mlle. Rosa. *Faroline*: Mlle. Rachel. *Houblonne*: Mlle. Breton. *Dorothea*: Mlle. Emelie. *Gretchen*: Mlle. Briot. *Yolande*: Mlle. Solanges. *Griselis*: Mlle. Desenfants. *Rosemonde*: Mlle. Briot. *Armide*: Mlle. Rachel. *Bradamante*: Mlle. Villiers. *The Four sons Aymon, lords, chevaliers, aldermen, citizens, pages, pastry cooks, drummers, musicians, chantes, sappers, boatmen, populace, etc.*

Act 1, Scene 1: The City of Curaçao in Brabant. (Cambon.) *Scene 2*: Geneviève's Boudoir. (Fromant.) *Scene 3*: Sifroy's Sleeping Apartment. (Calyo.) *Scene 4*: Northern Railway Station. (Fromant.)

Act 2, Scene 1: The Ravine. (Calyo.) *Scene 2*: The Apparition. (Calyo.) *Scene 3*: (A Banquet in the grand gallery of the clock-tower in) The Chateau of Aspières. (Fromant.)

Act 3, Scene 1: The Forest. (Cambon.) *Scene 2*: The Grand Hall of the Palace. (Cambon.)

ACT 1[17]

Scene 1

Choeur (Flammands de tous les pays)

Couplet (Vos échevins, vos édiles)
Mons. Genot

Entrance of Drogan and Rondeau (Salut, salut, noble assemblée)
Mlle. Rose-Bell, Tous

Serenade du Page (En passant sous la fenêtre)
Mlles. Rose-Bell, M. Desclauzas

Choeur (Curaçoïens, que la victoire couronne)

Air (Il m'a mis sur le front sa toque de satin)
Messrs. Goby, Petit

Couplets de la Poule
Messrs. Carrier, Goby, Tous

Scene 2

Scene (Travaillons commes des fées)
Mlles. Maurice, Rosa, Emelie, Briot, Breton, Faroline, Choeur

Ronde (Cet habit-là ne lui va point)
Mlle. Gueretti, Rose-Bell, Tous

Trio (Ah! Madame, Vous qui brillez sur le trône)
Mlles. Rose-Bell, M. Desclauzas, Gueretti

Couplets du Pate (Ah! de mon coeur un trouble s'empare)
Mons. Carrier, Mlle. M. Desclauzas

Scene 3

Couplet (Je ne connais rien au monde)
Mons. Carrier

Couplet (J'arrive armé de pied en cap!)
Mons. Beckers

Scene (Ciel! qu'ai-je appris, que vient-on de me dire?)
Mlle. M. Desclauzas, Messrs. Carrier, Goby, Tous

Scene 4

Final (Le clairon qui sonne)
Mons. Beckers, Tous

ACT 2

Scene 1

Scene (Fuyons, fuyons, l'orage gronde)
Mlles. Rose-Bell, M. Desclauzas, Gueretti

Couplets (Protéger le repos des villes)
Messrs. Bourgoin, Gabel

Scene 2

Trio (Allons, madame, il faut mourir)
Mlle. M. Desclauzas, Messrs. Bourgoin, Gabel

Scene 3

Choeur (Chantez, chantez Cocodettes. .)
Mlles. Briot, Rachel, Villiers, Choeur

La Ronde des infidèles (Pour combattre le Sarrasin)
Mons. Beckers, Carrier, Mlle. Clementine, Choeur

Chanteurs tyroliens (L'aube naît, on y voit)
Mmes. Gueretti, Bageard, Mons. Chopin; Mons. Carrier, Chopin, Raphael

Farandole (Place pour la farandole)
Choeur général

Les Folies (Ohé, de canot!)
Mlles. Briot, Musier, Villiers, Les Tyroliens

Danse Generale

Couplets de la Mèche (Geneviève était blonde)
Mlle. Rose-Bell

---

[14]Previously produced in New York in French 24 September 1867 at the Theatre Français for 156 performances; in English 17 June 1868 at the New York Theatre. For Synopsis of Scenes and Musical Numbers, see September 1867 production.

[15]Previously produced in New York in French 24 September 1867 at the Theatre Français for 156 performances; in English 17 June 1868 at the New York Theatre. For Synopsis of Scenes and Musical Numbers, see September 1867 production.

[16]Stage director uncredited.

[17]Musical numbers not listed in programs. List prepared from published English/French libretto (Metropolitan Printing and Engraving, New York, 1868).

ACT 3
Scene 1
Couplets (Quand on possède une bîche)
Mlle. Gueretti
Quatuor de Gardes-chasse (Allons, en chasse!)
Mlles. Rose-Bell, Messrs. Goby, Genot, Mussay
Scene (Je viens de la Turquie)
Messrs. Carrier, Beckers
Scene 2
Choeur (Curaçoïens! que la victoire)
Complainte (Golo, monstre plein de crimes!)
Mlle. Rose-Bell, Tous
Choeur Final (Chantons, chantons pour Geneviève)

1868.27 LA BELLE HÉLÈNE

A Revival of the Opèra-bouffe in Three Acts, in French[18]. Libretto by Henri Meilhac and Ludovic Halévy. Music by Jacques Offenbach. Musical director, A. Birgfeld. Conductors, E. Colonne, H. Dennery. Scenery by William Voegtlin and Ludovico Malmsha. Machinist, S. Wallis. Properties, John Lundy. Costumes by Mr. Toledo. Produced by Harold L. Bateman's Opéra Bouffe Company. Opened 2 November 1868 at Pike's Opera House and closed 14 November 1868 after 14 performances; returned 10 April 1869 to the Fifth Avenue Theatre under the auspices of James Fisk, Jr. and closed 30 April 1869 after 4 additional performances in repertory.

CAST: *La Belle Hélène*: Mlle. LUCILLE TOSTÉE. *Orestes*: Mlle. de Felcourt. *Paris*: Mons. DECRÉ. *Agamemnon*: Mons. DUCHESNE. *Calchas*: Mons. LAGRIFFOUL. *Ménélaus*: Mons. LEDUC. *Ajax I*: Mons. Houdin. *Ajax II*: Mons. Guidon. *Achilles*: Mons. Daron. *Bacchis*: Mlle. Arsene. *Parthoenis*: Mlle. H. Rose. *Loena*: Mlle. Marguerite. *Philocomes*: Mons. Aurere. *Euthycles*: Mons. Plainville. *Slave*: Mons. Piperno.

1868.28 ORPHÉE AUX ENFERS

A Local Sensation (Operatic) Burlesque in One Act[19], introducing the entire music of Jacques Offenbach, and all the peculiarities, oddities, whims and idiosyncracies of the times, by (Francis) Leon. With new and gorgeous costumes, magnificent scenery, marvelous transformations and novel effects. Manager, Edwin Kelly. Opened 2 November 1868 at Kelly & Leon's Minstrels and closed 26 (matinee) November 1868 after 25 performances.

Olio: The Only Leon's "Bend." R. M. Carroll. Leslie and Traynor, the California Comedians.

CAST: *Eurydice*: FRANCIS LEON. *Orpheus*: EDWIN KELLY.

1868.29 TAME CATS

A Piquant Musical and Pantomimic (Burlesque) Extravaganza in One Act[20], by Francis Leon. The music in the "scena dansante" selected from "Le Juif Erant" (The Wandering Jew), the local music from popular operas. During the progress of the piece African scenery of great beauty will be introduced. The burlesque costumes will be of the oddest character, and great attention has been given to the properties and pantomimic effects. Opened 30 November 1868 at Kelly & Leon's Opera House and closed 26 December 1868 after 25 performances.

CAST: EDWIN KELLY. FRANCIS LEON. And Company.

1868.30 LES BAVARDS

An Opéra-Bouffe in Two Acts, in French. Libretto by Charles Nuitter, based on the intermezzo "Los Habladores" by Cervantes. Music by Jacques Offenbach. Musical director, Adolph Birgfeld. Conductors, H. Dennery, Edouard Colonne. Produced by Harold L. Bateman. Opened 9 December 1868 at Pike's Opera House and closed 2 January 1869 after 26 performances; returned 9 April 1869 to the Fifth Avenue Theatre under the auspices of James Fisk, Jr. on a bill with LA CHANSON DE FORTUNIO and closed 23 April 1869 after 3 additional performances in repertory.

CAST: *Roland*, a Young Nobleman: Mlle. IRMA. *Sarmiento*, Uncle of Inès: Mons. DUCHESNE. *Cristobal*, Alcalde: Mons. LAGRIFFOUL. *Torribio*, Sheriff: Mons. LEDUC. *Pedro*, Servant: Mons. Brunet. *Inès*: Mlle. LAMBÈLE. *Béatrix*, Aunt of Inès: Mlle. DUCLOS. *(Creditors, etc.)*

Scene: Spain.

ACT 1[21]
Introduction, Choeur (Cherchons, cherchons bien)
Choeur
Scène (Vit on jamais par tous les diables)
Mlle. Irma
Romance (Sans aimer, ah! peut on vivre)
Mlle. Irma
Couplets (Ce sont d'étranges personnages)
Mlle. Lambèle
Duetto (Et maintenant il faut que je vous quitte)
Mlles. Lambèle, Irma
Air (C'est bien reconnu)
Mlle. Duclos
Chanson (Partout on chercherait en vain)
Messrs. Lagriffoul, Leduc
Duo Bouffe (Quel bavard insupportable)
Mlle. Irma, Mons. Duchesne
Choeur (Seigneur alcade)
Choeur
Scène (La paix, la paix)
Messrs. Lagriffoul, Leduc, Choeur
Couplets (C'est moi qui le rase)
Choeur
Ensemble (Vous nous avez bien entendus)
Messrs. Lagriffoul, Leduc, Choeur
Choeur (Mes amis, faisons diligence)
Choeur
ACT 2
Couplets (Ouf! Quel métier)
Mlle. Duclos
Quatuor (À table, à table)
Mlles. Duclos, Lambèle, Irma, Mons. Duchesne
Chanson (C'est l'Espagne qui nous donne)
Mlle. Irma
Causerie (Ah! quel repassans égal)
Mlle. Irma
Ensemble (J'étouffe de colère)
Mlles. Duclos, Lambèle, Irma, Mons. Duchesne
Trio (Taisons nous, pas un mot)
Mlles. Lambèle, Duclos, Irma
Ensemble (Vos factures, cher seigneur)
Mlle. Irma, Mons. Lagriffoul, Choeur
Final (Il est un bruit plus doux encore)
Mlle. Irma, Tutti

[18]First produced in New York 26 March 1868 at the Theatre Français for 37 performances. For Synopsis of Scenes and Musical Numbers, see original 1868 production.
[19]No program found.
[20]No program found. From an advertisement in the New York Herald: "The pantomime was played two years in London, Vauxhall Gardens, in a pantomime entitled "Harlequin Aurora," and later "A Midsummer Night's Dream;" will also introduce DuChaillou's Scenes in Africa. The whole to conclude with a burlesque transformation, including 100 new artists, Five with Golden Hair all their own." Beginning 14 December, TAME CATS was joined by BARBER BLU, a burlesque of Offenbach's "Barbe Bleue" in which Edwin Kelly appeared as Barber Blu; Blue Edwin appeared as Barber Kelly; Barber Kelly appeared as Edwin Blu. Messrs. Leveridge and Meyer, of London, also appeared in BARBER BLU. Francis Leon also appeared as Bullyet in a burlesque sketch of 'Boulotte.' During the remaining two weeks of the run, TAME CATS shrunk in billing, and BARBER BLU became the principal draw.
[21]Musical numbers not listed in programs. List prepared from published French piano vocal score (G. Brandus & S. Dufour, Paris, [1863]).

1868.31 LA CHANSON DE FORTUNIO

An Opéra Comique in One Act, in French.[22] Libretto by Hector Crémieux and Ludovic Halévy. Music by Jacques Offenbach. Musical director, Adolph Birgfeld. Conductors, H. Dennery, Edouard Colonne. Produced by Harold L. Bateman. Opened 21 December 1868 at Pike's Opera House and closed 2 January 1869 after 14 performances; returned 9 April 1869 to the Fifth Avenue Theatre on a double bill with LES BAVARDS under the auspices of James Fisk, Jr. and closed 23 April 1869 after an additional 3 performances in repertory.[23] Total: 17 performances.

CAST: *Valentin*: Mlle. IRMA. *Laurette*, Fortunio's wife: Mlle. ALINE LAMBÈLE. *Maitre Fortunio*: Mons. FRANCIS. *Friquet*: Mons. LEDUC. *Babet*: Mlle. Mathilde. *Guillaume*: Mlle. Rose. *Landry*: Mlle. Marie. *Saturnin*: Mlle. Arsène. *Sylvain*: Mlle. Anna.

Scene: A Garden in France at the time of Louis XV.

MUSICAL NUMBERS[24]

Couplets de Laurette (Prenez garde à vous)
Mlle. A. Lambèle

Ensemble (Du pain et des pommes)/

Chanson à boire (La belle eau claire)
Mlles. Irma, Rose, Marie, Arsène, Anna

Couplets du petit Friquet (C'est moi qui suis le petit clerc)
Mons. Leduc

Ronde des Clercs (Autrefois, aujourdhui)
Mlles. Rosa, Marie, Arsène, Anna

Couplets de Valentin (Je t'aime)
Mlle. Irma

Duo, Ensemble et Couplets (Par devant maître)
Mlle. Irma, Mons. Leduc

Valse des clercs (Toutes les femmes sont à nous)
Mlle. Irma, Mons. Leduc

Duo et Chanson de Fortunio (Allons, allons, venez là, pres de moi!)
Mlles. Irma, A. Lambèle

Scène Finale (Si vous croyez que je vais dire)
Tutti

1868.32 ERNANI, or, The Horn of a Dilemma

An Original Burlesque Extravaganza in One Act[25]. Play by William Brough. New music arranged and composed by Michael Connolly. Scenery designed by Robert Grain. Machinery by Levi Gurnsey. Properties by Charles DeForrest. Dresses by Mrs. Huther (Liverpool) and Mr. Williams (New York). Musical director, Michael Connolly. Produced by George Wood. Opened 28 December 1868 at Wood's Museum and Metropolitan Theatre and closed 30 January 1869 after 40 performances.

CAST: *Ernani*, alias Don John of Arragon—an outlaw, whose wrongs the author finds impossible to write: Miss LYDIA THOMPSON. *Don Carlos*, Charles the First of Spain—and Fifth of the German Empire—a "Merry Monarch, though a "Sad Fellow," sowing his wild oats in a sow-sow course of life: Miss LISA WEBER. *Followers of Ernani (3): Scampa*: W. J. Hill. *Roguey*: M. C. Daly. *Vagabondi*, a Vagabond: J. Barnes. *Don Ruy Gomez de Silva*, an old Castilian Noble, Guardian of the wealthy heiress Elvira, induced by principle to stick to his word, and by interest to stick to his ward: Mr. LOUIS MESTAYER. *Jago*, his Squire—who, though a man at arms, generally prefers trusting to his legs as being better in the long run: HARRY BECKETT. *Ricardo*, First Lord in Waiting, Commander-in-Chief, Head Cook and Bottle Washer, or something or other to the King: Kate Mortimer. *Donna Elvira*, DeSilva's ward—a high-born maiden, who in spite of her haughty culture, despises her Guard(i)an—Ernani having planted a tender passion flower in her heart: Miss ADA HARLAND. *Jacinta*, a Duenna, appointed to take care of Elvira, but by no means disinclined to take care of herself: Mary Wells. *Juana*, Elvira's waiting maid and confidante: Kate Logan. *Brigands, Rebels, Outlaws, Conspirators, and other highly objectionable characters, Nobles, Guards, Retainers, Peasants and other highly respectable personages*: Talented Corps of Auxiliaries. *Ladies of the Ballet.*

1868.33 GIN-NEVIEVE de GRAW

An Operatic Burlesque of 'Geneviève de Brabant' in One Act, by Francis Leon. All the original music by Jacques Offenbach. New scenery and properties. Manager, Edwin Kelly. Opened 28 December 1868 at Kelly & Leon's Minstrels and closed 9 January 1869 after 13 performances.[26]

Olio: Saucy Sal, by Francis Leon. St. Anthony's Dance; Twice Married. Loveliest on Earth. All by the Company. The Tyrolean Hamburgers.

CAST: *Drogan*, in imitation of Rosa Bell: FRANCIS LEON. *Gin-Nevieve de Graw*: EDWIN KELLY. With Gendarmes, and Messrs. J. H. Surridge and William H. Brockway.

1869.01 LA PÉRICHOLE

An Opèra-bouffe in Three Acts, in French. Libretto by Ludovic Halévy and Henri Meilhac. Based on "Le Carosse du Saint-Sacrament" by Prosper Mérimée. Music by Jacques Offenbach. Manager of the opera, Adolph Birgfeld. Conductors, Messrs. A. Birgfeld, Edouard Colonne, H. Dennery. Produced by Harold L Bateman[27]. Opened 4 January 1869 at Pike's Opera House and closed 6 February 1869 after 35 performances; returned 5 April 1869 to the Fifth Avenue Theatre and closed 19 June 1969 after an additional 19 performances in repertory. Total: 44 performances.

CAST: *La Périchole*, a Street Singer: Mlle. IRMA. *Piquillo*, a Street Singer: Mons. AUJAC. *Don Andrès de Ribeira*, Viceroy of Peru: Mons. LEDUC. *The Count (Miguel) of Panatellas*, First Gentleman of the Bed Chamber: Mons. LAGRIFFOUL. *Don Pedro de Hinoyosa*, Governor of the City of Lima: Mons. EDGARD. *The Marquis of Tarapote*: Mons. Francis. *First Notary*: Mons. Hamilton. *Second Notary*: Mons. Guidon. *First Drinker*: Mons. Brabant. *Second Drinker*: Mons. Brunet. *The Three Cousins: Guadalena*: Mlle. Rose. *Berginella*: Mlle. Tholer. *Mastrilla*: Mlle. Cadic. *The Maids of Honor to the Viceroy: Frasquinella*: Mlle. Arsene. *Brambilla*: Mlle. Mathilde. *Ninetta*: Mlle. Anna. *Manuelita*: Mlle. Carmen. *Lords and Ladies of the Court, Peruvians, Indians, Pages, Ushers, Soldiers of the Viceroy's Body Guard, Jugglers, Clerks, etc.*

Act 1: Public Square in Lima. (Lima, sur la place publique, devant le cabaret des Trois Couisnes.)

Act 2: The Palace. (Le palais du Vice-Roi.)

Act 3: The Dinner. (Le palais du Vice-Roi.)

ACT 1[28]

Choeur (Du vice-roi, c'est aujourd'hui la fête)
Mlles. Rose, Tholer, Cadic, Choeur

Chanson des Trois Cousines (Promptes à servir la pratique)
Mlles. Rose, Tholer, Cadic

Reprise du choeur (Ah! qu'on y fait gaiement glou glou)
Mlles. Rose, Tholer, Cadic, Mons. Edgard, Choeur

Choeur (C'est lui, c'est notre vice-roi)
Choeur

Couplets de l'Incognito (Sans en rien souffler à personne)
Mons. Leduc

Marche indienne et Entrée des chanteurs
Mlle. Irma, Mons. Aujac

Complainte: L'Espagnol et la jeune Indienne (Le conquérant dit à la jeune Indienne)
Mlle. Irma, Mons. Aujac

Séguidille: Le muletier et la jeune personne (Vous a-t-on dit souvent)
Mlle. Irma, Mons. Aujac

Choeur des saltimbanques (Levez-vous et prenez vos rangs)
Choeur

---

[22] Followed by LES BAVARDS.

[23] No credits in programs for the new costumes, scenery or stage direction. Between the operas, Mlles. DeRosa, R. Francisco, M. Francisco and Mons. Cellini performed a Pas de Quatre. For the return engagement, Mlle. Tostée assumed the role of Valentin.

[24] Musical numbers not listed in programs. List prepared from published French piano vocal score (Heugel et Cie., Paris, 1861).

[25] Preceded by a comedy, The Quiet Family; beginning 18 January 1869, The Quiet Family was dropped, and ERNANI shared the bill with a shortened version of IXION.

[26] No program found.

[27] James Fisk, Jr. acquired H. L. Bateman's Opera Bouffe Company on 9 January 1869, per Odell. The theatre was then renamed The Grand Opera House.

[28] Musical numbers not listed in programs. List prepared from published French piano vocal score (C. Joubert, Paris, 1868).

La Lettre de la Périchole (O mon cher amant, je te jure)
Mlle. Irma
Mélodrame
Choeur et duetto des notaires (Holà! hé! holà! de là-bas)
Mlles. Rose, Tholer, Cadic, Choeur
Griserie-Ariette (Ah! quel dîner je viens de faire)
Mlle. Irma, Choeur
Duetto de Mariage (Je dois vous prévenir, Madame)
Mlles. Irma, Rose, Tholer, Cadic, Messrs. Aujac, Lagriffoul, Leduc, Edgard, Choeur
Final et marche des palanquins (Qu'on se hâte et qu'on les marie)
Mlles. Rose, Tholer, Cadic, Messrs. Lagriffoul, Leduc, Edgard, Hamilton, Guidon, Choeur

ACT 2
Chanson des dames de la cour (Cher seigneur, revenez à vous)
Mlles. Carmen, Arsene, Mathilde, Anna, Dames de la Cour
Cancans-Couplets (On vante partout son sourire)
Mlles. Carmen, Arsene, Mathilde, Anna, Dames de la Cour
Choeur des seigneurs (Quel marché de bassesse)
Tenors, basses
Couplets: Les Femmes il n'y a qu'ça (Et là, maintenant que nous sommes seuls)
Messrs. Aujac, Lagriffoul, Edgard
Choeur de la présentation (Nous allons donc voir un mari)
Mlle. Irma, Messrs. Aujac, Lagriffoul, Leduc, Edgard, Francis, Choeur
Couplets: Ah! que les hommes sont bêtes (Que veulent dire ces colères?)
Mlle. Irma
Rondo de bravoure (Écoute, ô Roi, je te présente)
Mons. Aujac
Galop d l'Arrestation (Sautez dessus! sautez dessus!)
Mons. Leduc, Choeur
Ronde des Maris (Conduisez-le, bons courtisans)
Mons. Leduc, Choeur, Tous

ACT 3
Couplets de l'Aveu (Tu n'es pas beau, tu n'es pas riche)
Mlle. Irma
Couplet (Aie donc confiance)
Mlle. Irma, Mons. Aujac
Le couvert du roi (Son Altesse, à l'heure ordinaire)
Choeur
Entrée des chanteurs
Séguidille (Un roi se promenant)
Mlle. Irma, Mons. Aujac
Finale (Tous deux, au temps de peine et de misère)
Mlle. Irma, Mons. Aujac, Choeur

THE PAGE'S REVEL, or, the Summer Night's Bivouac/ Nicodemus

1869.02

A Corygraphic Extravaganza (Burlesque), accompanied by a ballet, variety and comic pantomime. Play by Henry B. Farnie. Incidental music by Signor Giuseppi Operti. Scenery and mechanical effects by Messrs. (William) Voegtlin, (Felix) Slowman. Costumes by Mr. S. W. Laureys. Ballet Divertissement by Mons. Carlo Carle. Produced by the Tammany Amusement Company (Messrs. Henry Jarrett and Harry Palmer, proprietors; Leonard Grover, managing director). Opened 4 January 1869 at the Tammany, Grand Theatre and closed 16 January 1869 after 14 performances.

ACT 1
"Wreath of Roses" (Ballad)
R. Green
LES FOLIES, a Grand Ballet d'Action, arranged by Monsieur Carle.
(*Music by* Provine.)
Incidental Grand Solo
Mlle. Marie Bonfanti
Incidental Grand Pas de Trois
Mlles. Bonfanti, Carle, Mons. C. Carle
Madrigal Chorus—Men of Harlich
(*Music by* Bishop.)Quartette, Chorus of Youths
Comic Topsy Toy Song
Mr. Ernee Clarke
Character Songs—The Merry Lass
Miss Lizzie Dashwood
Wooden Shoe Dance
J. Maffit, W. A. Bartholomew

ACT 2
THE PAGE'S REVEL; or, the Summer Night's Bivouac, written for the Tammany by Henry B. Farnie.

CAST: *Ernest St. Pol*, Captain of the Pages: Miss ALICE HARRISON. *Victor*: Miss LIZZIE KELSEY. *Tristan*: Miss SALLIE MADDOX. *Marechal de Longueville*: Mr. Robert Green. *Captain Coquelonchon*, Aid: Mr. Barry. *Pierre St. Paul*, Maitre d'Armes: J. Hatter. *Toulerou, Miller and Mayor*: Ben Maginley. *Mère Gobo*, Duenna: F. Kent. *Valentina*, the Marechal's daughter: BESSIE SUDLOW. *Babette*, Sister of Toulerou: Lillie Whiting. *A Hussar*: Mr. Bernard. (*Ballet*: Mesdames MARIE BONFANTI, EMMA CARLE, Corps de Ballet.) *Pages, Grenadiers, Millers, Peasants, etc.*

Scene: A French Hamlet in the olden times. Sunset.

SYNOPSIS OF ACTION, SPECIALTIES
The return from the vineyards. The Angleus rings. Toulerou and his millers descend from the windmill. The gallantry of the Mayor and what happened with Mère Gobo. Valentina and Babette exchange confidences. Hark! a bugle.
Procession and Chorus of the Pages
Ernest finds that the course of true love is as rough as usual, and Toulerou reads an address. What happened thereat, and how Babette makes up for lost time. The carousal.
"The glorious vintage of Champagne"
The village en fête. Lucette's wedding. The bridal procession; the peasants and soldiers fraternize.
Sabot Dance and Grand Military Ballet
Mlles. Bonfanti, Carle, Corps de Ballet
Pas de Deux des Sabots
J. Maffit, W. A. Bartholomew
The alarm! Cannon shots! Coquelonchon and St. Pol to support the outposts. How the Maire armed himself to die for his country, and finally concluded that he wouldn't. The assignation with Valentina at the balcony. Babette in hot water.
Pitching the Tents
The moonlight serenade. How to get down from a balcony. Toulerou at cross-purposes with the Marechal.
"I am the Maire, I do declare"
The Marechal falls on a new detective system. Ernest discovered. A counter strategem. Daybreak. The pages in disgrace. The confession of Ernest and the return of Coquelonchon's party. Grand denouement and happy termination of the loves of Ernest and Valentina. Toulerou is also mated. The word of command 'Fall in,' and the Farewell to "The Hamlet smiling in the vale."

ACT 3[29]
Madrigal Chorus

[29]After the opening, the Madrigal Chorus, "Mother Land," and the Pas de Deux were replaced by:
Morceaux Descriptifs—Gladiateur (by Signor Giuseppi Operti)
The Derby Day. A troupe of Negro delineators at Lord Dundreary's carriage. Meeting of a loving couple. Call for saddling. Placing of the horses. Clear the course. They're off!! Flirtations between Ladies and Swells of the first-water. Betting at the Grand Stand. The field against Gladiateur. Anxiety of individuals who have large bets and no money. Distant view of the horses—last struggle, and immense speed of Gladiateur. Voices—"Here they come!" Gladiateur carrying the victory. Hurrah! Hurrah!
Grotesque Stilt Dance
C. Parker
Pas de Shamrock
L. Kelsey, S. Maddox

"Mother Land" (by Farnie)
Quartette, Chorus of Youths
Pas de Deux
Misses L. Kelsey, S. Maddox
Comic Duet-The Broadway Swell and the Brooklyn Belle
Messrs. Sheridan and Mack
AFTER THE DUSK, a parody on Dion Boucicault's 'After Dark,' a Protean burlesque by Mr. and Mrs. Valentine Love:
Dicey Coleman Morris, of Chatham Street, and Niblo's Garden: V. Love. *Old Tom Bang*, dirty but virtuous: V. Love. *George Meadows*, a Cab-man and barrownite: Mrs. V. Love. *Fitzgerald Bellingham, Esq.*, a wicked stock broker, though not holding much *ear-ie*: Mrs. V. Love. *Eliza Louisa Moore*, who leaves the Boxes in Tiers: Mrs. V. Love.
Grand Transept Flight
Mons. and Mlle. Senyah

ACT 4
NICODEMUS, a comic pantomime by James Maffit.
CAST: *Nicodemus*, a clown: JAMES MAFFIT. *M. Garrotte*, a gardener: WILLIAM A. BARTHOLOMEW. *Old Crusty*, a baker: C. Parker. *François*, a young lover: Mr. HENRY RAVEL. *Villagers (3)*: *Jean Victor*: Mr. Charles. *Pierre Alphonse*: Mr. Adams. *Emile Pietro*: Mr. Mack. *Dame Garrotte*: M. Kent. *Annette*, her daughter: Mlle. Armande. *Peasants, Villagers, etc.*

SPECIALTIES
Incidental Ballet
Auxiliary Corps
Character Pas de Deux
Lascelle Sisters (Fannie, Rose)
Grand Triple Trapeze
Brothers Victorelli (William, Matthew, Antoine)
Getz's Grand Allegorical Scene—Birth of New Year
(by Charles S. Getz, assisted by Sommer Getz and John W. Sommer)
The veil of the Allegory discloses Christmas followed by the birth of the New Year, who summons the Seasons, Spring, Summer, Autumn and Winter. Pomona and Flora precede Aurora with attendant sprites.
Star Spangled Banner
Brass and Reed Bands

1869.03

L'OEIL CREVÉ

An Opéra Bouffe (Folie Musicale) in Three Acts, in French. Libretto and music by Hervé. Regisseur, Paul Juignet. Scenery by Hannibal Calyo. Costumes by Blanche Armand (New York), Mons. Phillipe. Musical director, Robert Stoepel. Produced by Joseph Grau. Opened 11 January 1869 at the Théâtre Français and closed 30 January 1869 after 21 performances.

CAST: *Dindonnette*, the belle of the village, in love with Alexandrivore: Mme. ROSE-BELL. *Fleur-de-Noblesse*, daughter of the Marquis, in love with Ernest: Mlle. MARIE DESCLAUZAS. *Marchioness*: Mlle. Clementine. *Alexandrivore*, the best marksman in the village, Dendonette's lover: Mons. CARRIER. *Le Marquis d'en Face*, father of Fleur-de-Noblesse: Mons. BECKERS. *Géromé*, a gendarme: Mons. GABEL. *Bailiff*: Mons. GÉNOT. *Ernest*, a young mechanic in love with Fleur-de-Noblesse: Mons. E. Petit. *Duc d'en Face*, the Duke from over the way: Mons. MUSSAY. *Archers (4)*: *Chavassus*: Mons. Charrière. *Copeau*: Mons. Brag. *Boussin*: Mons. Lefevre. *Dufour*: Mons. Emile. *Sentinel*: Mons. Chopin. *Clerk*: Mons. Caralp. *Eclosine*, innkeeper: Mlle. Villiers. *Mariette, Françoise*, waitresses: Mlles. Briot, Rosa. *Crossbowmen, Peasants, Peasant Girls, Nobles, Servants of the Marquis.*

Act 1: Courtyard of the Inn. (The Belle Eclosine, Wineshop.)

Act 2: Gardens of the Chateau and Target Ground.

Act 3: Platform of the Castle; The Tower and Prisoner's Cell.

ACT 1[30]
Ronde (Qu'ils sont gentils, qu'ils sont coquets)
Mlle. Briot, Rosa, Villiers, Ensemble
Romance (Ma pauvre Dindonette)
Mme. Rose-Bell, Mlle. Villiers
Choeur (Allons, gai chasseur)
Mons. Charriere, Choeur
Duo (Déjà tout mon sang bouillonne)
Mons. Carrier, Mme. Rose-Bell
Couplets (Sur les rives d l'Adour)
Mons. Beckers, Mme. Rose-Bell
Choeur Final (If faut partir)
Mons. Carrier, Mme. Rose-Bell, Mlles. Villiers, Briot, Rosa, Les Chasseurs

ACT 2
Rondeau (Menuiserie, charpenterie, font de ma vie)
Mlle. Desclauzas
Trio (Quoique je paraisse joyeux)
Mons. E. Petit, Mlle. Desclauzas, Mons. Génot
Chanson de Géromé (Pour les braves militaires)
Mons. Gabel, Mons. Génot
Choeur (Fête nouvelle en ce lieu nous appelle)
Choeur
Septuor (Quel est donc le chasseur?)
Mons. Carrier, Mlle. Briot, Mons. Génot, Mlle. Desclauzas, Choeur
Chanson/La Polonaise et l'Hirondelle
(Un jour, passant par Meudon)
Mons. Carrier, Mlle. Desclauzas
Choeur (Ah! quel accident!)
Choeur
Choeur Final (En prison! A la tour du Donjon!)
Choeur

ACT 3
Air (Tristes amours! folles chimères!/Mille canons)
Mons. Gabel
Romance (A mes regards voilés)
Mons. Carrier
Duetto (Te voilà, mon bibi!)
Mons. Carrier, Mme. Rose-Bell
Choeur de docteurs (Nous voici tous, savants docteurs)
Choeur
Romance (Une femme est à plaindre)
Mlle. Desclauzas, Choeur
Couplets (Croyez-en mon expérience)
Mme. Rose-Bell
Duo Final (Public charmant, Excuse un peu notre bizarrerie)
Mlle. Desclauzas, Mme. Rose-Bell, Chœur

1869.04

THE DRAMATIC REVIEW FOR 1868

The First Edition of a Series of somewhat personal, but the compiler hopes, not unpardonable reflections upon the ablities and notabilities of the past season, containing amongst other injunctionable mattter, sundry audacious and unjustifiable infringements upon existing patent rights. (A Review in a Prologue and Eight Illustrations, by John Brougham[31]. Production staged by John Brougham.) Scenery by C. J. Hawthorne, Richard Marston, Louis Duflocq, A. Wheatley. Wardrobe, Miss Flannery. Machinery, W. W. Demilt. Properties, J. Williams. Leader of orchestra, H. Eckhardt. Produced by John Brougham. Opened 25 January 1869 at Brougham's Theatre and closed 20 February 1869 after 24 performances.

CAST: *Manhatta*, the favorite daughter of Columbia, by her union with a highly respectable Dutch settler named Niew Amsterdam, progenitor of all the subsequent dams, except McComb's, whose patronymic sufficiently indicates its oriental origin: ANNIE FIRMIN. *Brooklyna*, the eldest of her numerous family, a remarkably forward young lady, proud, pious and independent, holding but ferry little intercourse with her Ma, and that she means to abridge: Miss LYLE. *Newjersia*, another of Manhatta's offspring, but having been unfortunately born, out of the Union, not in complete communion with her sisters: Miss Lizzie Mahon. *North Rivero*, a fluent individual, whose certificate of character consists of his running from Albany: Mr. HURLEY. *East Rivero*, the Janitor of Hell Gate, rather shallow in spots, but sound in the main: Mr. C.

[30]Musical numbers not listed in programs. List prepared from published French/English libretto (John A. Gray & Green, New York, 1869) "as performed for the first time in New York under the direction of J. Grau."

[31]Preceded by a comedy "Better Late Than Never" by John Brougham, which was replaced for the last two weeks by "An Irish Stew, or the Mysterious Widow of Long Branch."

HILLYARD. *Mademoiselle Fashion*, from Paris, Manhatta's dearest friend; general dealer in darling Dry Goods, ducks of diamonds, and other indispensable necessities to the disconsolate people who have "nothing to wear": EFFIE GERMON. *Public Opinion*, the great "Sir Oracle" of social life, whose judgement wise men reverence, fools fear, and knaves deride: ELIZA NEWTON. *Melpomene*, an old and much neglected melancholy Muse, who has seen better days, and brags about them, which she has every right to do, poor soul: Mrs. Prior. *Captain Jinks*, of the naval Equestrian service: EFFIE GERMON.

(*Additional principals in the Illustrations*: Messrs. C. Edmonds, Corrie Crosbie, Arthur Matthison, Grossi, Alexander, Charles Hale, E. Lamb, H. Peck, Gray; Misses Thomas, Hearn, Amy Ames, Clara Fisher, Belle Fisher; Mrs. Lizzy Eckhardt.)

Plate First: Allegorical Group, New York. (Duflocq.)

TABLE OF CONTENTS[32]

Illustration 1

Subject, The Emerald Ring

Dedlight, the Vyllan: C. Edmonds. *Mike*, the Avenger: C. Crosbie. *Geraldine*, the Persecuted: Miss Thomas. *Maggie*, the Resolute: Miss Hearn.

Illustration 2

Subject, Barbe Bleue, After Dark

Barbe Bleue: A. Matthison. *Boulotte*: Miss E. Ames. *The "One More Unfortunate"*: —. *Homeless Wanderers, Appalled Spectators and Blackfriars Archers generally.*

Illustration 3

Subject, The Fox's Nest (Humptumtyidiotics)

Humpty Dumpty, The Illimittable: C. Crosby. *Pantaloon*, an excellent pair to wear: M. Grossi. *Harlequin*, the Velocipdeal: Mr. Alexander.

Illustration 4

Subject, A Plate of Bouffe, à la Mode

Queen Elizabeth Ristori: Mrs. J. J. Prior. *Pitou*, the Lachrymoe: C. Hale. *Gabauche*, the Inflexible: E. Lamb. *Drogan*, the Invisible: Mrs. L. Eckhardt. *Tyrolean*: A. Matthison. *Tyroleanesses*: Mrs. L. Eckhardt, Miss C. Fisher.

Illustration 5

Subject, The Lancashire Lasses

A Party by the Name of Johnson: C. Edmonds. *Dick*, the Slippery: H. Peck.

Illustration 6

Subject, The Men at the Wheel

Ixion, the Inimitable: Miss C. Fisher. *Venus*, the Irresistible: Miss B. Fisher. *Mercury*, the Irrepressible: Miss E. Ames. *Minerva*, the Impregnable: Mr. Hurley.

Illustration 7

Subject, Pike's Grand Palace

Grande Duchesse No. 1: E. Germon. *Grande Duchesse No. 2*: Mrs. L. Eckhardt. *Fritz*, the Embarassed: A. Matthison.

Illustration 8

Subject, The Deep Sea Depot. (*Transformation Scene by* Marston.)

Neptune, Conductor of the Ocean Telegraph: Mr. Gray. *Surrounded by Submarine Operators*: All Diving Belles.

1869.05 FLEUR DE THÉ

An Opéra-bouffe in Three Acts, in French. Libretto by Alfred Duru and Henri Chivot. Music by Charles Lecocq. Regisseur, Paul Juignet. Ballets arranged by Mons. Baptistan. Scenic artists, Hannibal W. Calyo; Mons. Fromont (Paris). Machinist, H. J. Drew. Costumes designed by Mons. Stop, Drauer and Berthat (Paris). Properties, appointments and illuminations designed by Mons. Saqui (Paris). Musical director, Robert Stoepel. Chorus director, Mons. Gambogi. Produced by Jacob Grau. Opened 1 February 1869 at the Théâtre Français and closed 3 March 1869 (matinee) after (18) performances in repertory.

CAST: *Césarine*, a French Vivandière, wife of Pinsonnet: Mlle. DESCLAUZAS. *Fleur de Thé*, a Chinese Belle, daughter of Tien-Tien: Mlle. RIZARELLI. *Eustache Pinsonnet*: Mons. CARRIER. *Tien-Tien*, Mandarin with the Zinc Bells; Chief of Police at Pekin: Mons. BECKERS. *Kaolin*, Captain of the Tigres: Mons. PETIT. *Corbillon*, Boatswain of *La Pintade*: Mons. Carriere. *Ha-Va-Le-Tou Kru*, Officer of the Fire-Eaters: Mons. Lefevre. *Midshipmen (5)*: *Grain-de-Sel*: Mlle. Villiers. *Garroche*: Mlle. Rosa. *Touche-a-Tout*: Mlle. Briot. *Vive-la-Joie*: Mlle. Rachel. *Va-la-Bon-Coeur*: Mlle. Breton. *French Soldiers and Sailors, Midshipmen, Vivandières, Mandarins, Chinese Populace, Slaves, Fire-Eaters, etc.*

Ballet: Mlles. HEDWIG SCHLAEGER, MARIE ADRIEN, Pauline Martinetti, Emma Schell, Lillie Whiting, Lizzie Whelpley; Mons. BAPTISTAN. Corps de Ballet.

Act 1: The French in Pekin. Franco-Chinese canteen in Pekin, with a view of the bay and French man-of-war at anchor. (Calyo.)

Act 2: Marriage Fête in China. Grand illuminated Chinese interior. (Calyo.)

Act 3: The Law of Tsing. A Grandee's palace and pleasure garden in the celestial empire. Richly decorated pavilion, terraces, exotica, Chinese pagoda, etc. (Fromont.)

BALLETS, SPECIALITIES

The French in Pekin (Act 1)

Sailors, Vivandières, Midshipmen, Chinese

Pas de Matelot (Act 1)

Mlles. Schlaeger, Adrien, Martinetti, Schell, Whiting, Whelpley

Marriage Fête in China: Grand Illuminations, Processions, Cortege, Grand Divertissement Oriental (Act 2)

Introduction Ensemble

Mlles. Martinetti, Schell, Whiting, Whelpley

Variations

Mlle. Schlaeger, Mons. Baptistan

Solo

Mlle. Adrien

Grand Variation

Mons. Baptistan, Coryphées

Tableau Finale

Principals, Coryphées

The Law of Tsing (Act 3)

French and Chinese (Act 3)

Vive la France (Act 3)

Kan Kan Franco-Chinese (Act 3)

Grand Rondo Finale (Act 3)

Cliquot Champagne (Act 3)

ACT 1[33]

Scène (À boire, à boire, à boire)

Mons. Carriere, Marins, Soldats, Mlle. Desclauzas

Couplets (J'ai couru grossir la foule)

Mons. Carrier

Duo (A l'éviter j'ai réussi)

Mlle. Rizarelli, Mons. Carrier

Ensemble (O ciel! qu'elle est jolie)

Mons. Carrier, Mlle. Rizarelli

Couplets (Depuis longtemps avant l'envie)

Mlle. Rizarelli, Mons. Carrier

Ensemble (O pauvre Fleur-de-Thé)

Mlle. Rizarelli, Mons. Carrier

Choeur de Chinois (Vive le grand Tien-tien)

Messrs. Beckers, Petit, Carrier; Chinois, Chinoises, Marins Français

Couplets (Je suis clairvoyant comme un sphinx!)

Messrs. Beckers, Petit

Quarette (Ah! Quelle affreuse aventure!)

Messrs. Beckers, Petit; Mlles. Rizarelli, Desclauzas

Final (Avançons avec prudence)

Les Six Esclaves, Messrs. Beckers, Petit, Carrier

---

[32]The running order was revised after the opening. The Barbe-Bleue and After Dark 'Illustrations" were divided, and Barbe-Bleue appeared as Illustration 1, followed by The Emerald Ring, The Fox's Nest, then After Dark. Late in the run Barbe Bleue was replaced by:

Subject, Madmadrigals, à la "What Oh!"—"Here in the Cool Grot"

Colin: A. Matthison. *Phillis*: Mrs. H. Eckhardt. *Corydon*: Mr. F. Gough. *Chloe*: Miss Eloise Allen.

The Lancashire Lasses and The Men at the Wheel were dropped; a New Illustration #7 was added:

Subject, The Cancanibalistics

La Petite Morlacchi, Le Petite Runnels

[33]Ballet, specialties listed in programs; musical numbers not listed. List prepared from published English-French libretto (John A. Gray & Green, New York, 1869) "as presented at Théâtre Français by J. Grau in February 1869."

ACT 2

Trio (La loi du Tssing est fort claire)
Messrs. Becker, Carrier, Petit

Couplets (Je suis né dans le Japon)
Mons. Petit

Scène (Au son du gong de la cythere)
Choeur, Messrs. Petit, Carrier, Mlle. Rizarelli

Couplets (En tous pays l'home est un être)
Mlle. Desclauzas

Final (L'astre aux rayons d'opale)
Les jeune filles, Messrs. Petit, Beckers, Carrier; Mlles. Desclauzas, Rizarelli

ACT 3

Couplets (Césarine, à mes voeux docile)
Mons. Carrier

Duo (Rappelle-toi, ma chère ami)
Mons. Carrier, Mlle. Desclauzas

Choeur (Place au gardien de nos familles)
Choeur

Couplets (Ce n'est pas un vin de carême)
Mlle. Desclauzas, Tous, Messrs. Carrier, Petit, Beckers

Final (Oui, buvons, buvons!)
Tous

1869.06 THE FORTY THIEVES, or, Striking Oil in Family Jars!

Lydia Thompson Burlesque Troupe in a Gorgeous, Oriental, Fairy, Spectacular Burlesque Extravaganza in Two Acts, 10 Scenes. Play by Henry B. Farnie. Music selected and arranged by Michael Connelly. Produced under the direction of L. J. Vincent. Scenery by Minard Lewis. Machinery and mechanical effects by Benson Sherwood. Costumes by S. W. Laureys and Miss Lewis. Properties, appointments and masks by Benedict. Incidental divertissements by Mons. Carle. Produced by Henry Jarrett and Harry Palmer. Opened 1 February 1869 at Niblo's Garden; reconstructed 5 April 1869, and closed 28 May 1869 after 136 performances.

CAST: Infernal: *Orchobrand*, the enchanting enchanter of the Silver Forest, groundlandlord of the 40 Thieves: EMMA GRATTAN. Supernal: *The Fairy Queen*, Supernatual, and we don't wonder at it: BELLE LAND. *Exiles from their native land; but how people could have the heart to—well! No matter! (4)*: *American Fay*: Annie Byron. *German Fay*: Fraulein Schroetter. *English Fay*: Miss Forrest. *French Fay*: Mlle. Carre Geddes. Mortal: *Ali Baba*, a first chop-dealer in Cordwood, who finds out the occasional advantage of caving in: W. J. HILL. *Ganem*, his son—or rather not to mix metaphors, a chip off the old block. A favorable specimen of young Bagdad—sweet on Amber though Morgy tries hard to gain 'em: LYDIA THOMPSON. *Cassim*, Ali's well-to-do brother, wh deals in measures, not men, and finds his account therein: GEORGE F. KETCHUM. *Cogia*, Ali's rib, whom he well could spare; but you will judge for yourself: J. W. BRUTONE. *Amber*, daughter of Cassim—with such and such, but we anticipate: LIZZIE KELSEY. *Morgiana*, a blonde beauty of the basement; help to Cogia and hindrance to Ganem. Despite unrequited love for that young man, she strikes 40 others all in a heap: LISA WEBER. *Abdallah*, Captain of the 40, swell to Hassarac's shady cove—an Arabian Knight—not a thousand and one, but one in a thousand: PAULINE MARKHAM. *Hassarac*, a regular Eastern terror; not like your Sultan Az-iz, but your bandit as was, in the palmy days of the drama—Lieutenant of the 40, and a regular rough'un: HARRY BECKETT. *The Cadi*, an Eastern Judge. Thanks goodness! they don't exist in the glorious West: Mr. Bruton. *The Forty Thieves*: By Ladies; not only light-fingered, but light-footed; and let us hope that they will steal nothing more than a march. *The Bagdad Police*: By members of the Police Force. Active, intelligent, etc. etc. 'Twasn't their fault if etc, etc. No blame is to be attached to etc. Expected to make a big strike. *The Donkey*, from Fifth Avenue, expressly engaged for the piece. He can a tail unfold. *Little Nigs and Big Nigs in confusion, by no means niggardly. Billiardists, Barkeepers, Cooks, Barbers and other young Shavers.*

Act 1, Scene 1: A Ravine in the Forest of Bagdad. *Scene 2*: The Silver Forest at Dawn. *Scene 3*: A Glade in the Wood. *Scene 4*: House of Ali Baba.

Act 2, Scene 1: The Cave of the Forty Thieves. *Scene 2*: Exterior of Ali's House. *Scene 3*: The Court of Ali's House by moonlight. *Scene 4*: A Street in Bagdad. *Scene 5*: The Cadi's Court. *Scene 6*: Change to Paris!

BALLETS, SPECIALTIES[34]

"I'd Like to Be a Swell!"
L. Thompson

"Swinging Round the Circle"
L. Weber

"The Bashful Girl"
P. Markham

"Nonsense Rhymes" (Quartet)
L. Thompson, P. Markham, H. Beckett, J. W. Hill

Quadrille, Waltz, Galop

Grand Finale (Act 1, Scene 3)

Grand Finale (Act 2, Scene 3)

Can Can (Act 2, Scene 6)

[34]Not in performance order. Musical numbers not listed in programs. Titles taken from published sheet music notice in programs.

1869.07 PLUTO

A Burlesque in One Act, preceded by a drama[35]. Play by Henry B. Farnie, adapted from H. J. Byron's 'Orpheus and Eurydice.' Music by David Braham. Costumes by Samuel May, of London. Scenery by Richard Marston. Properties and appointments by Nelse Waldron and Mr. Donnelly. Stage manager, George C. Boniface. Musical director, David Braham. Produced by William Horace Lingard. Opened 1 February 1869 at the Theatre Comique; reconstructed by William Horace Lingard 26 April 1869, and closed 5 June 1869 after 128 performances.

CAST: *Orpheus*: ALICE DUNNING. *Aristaeus*: ETHEL NORMAN. *Apollo*: Miss DICKIE LINGARD. *Eurydice*: LINA EDWIN. *Proserpine*: Miss Lillie Hall. *Pluto*: WILLIAM HORACE LINGARD[36]. *Clotilda*: George Atkins.

Reconstructed: *W. H. Seward*: Owen Fawcett. *Columbia*: Maggie Boniface. *John Bull*: Conway Cox. *Charon*: Conway Cox. *Cerberus*: Master Fred Strepo. *The Three Fates*: Misses Earle, Green, and Aggie Wood. *The Three Furies*: Messrs. Sinclair, Tyson, Brooks. *Rhadamanthus*: Messrs. Newton and Claire. *Imps, Gods, Goddesses, Demons, and other auxiliaries too numerous to mention.*

MUSICAL NUMBERS reconstructed, all new

"The Sunny Side"
A. Dunning

"Riding on a Velocipede"
A. Dunning, D. Lingard

"Good-bye, Dear Orpheus"
L. Edwin

"I'm a Nobby Little Swell"
E. Norman

"Baby, you're a Nasty Little Elf"
G. Atkins

"Farewell forever, Deceitful Old Wretch"
L. Hall, L. Edwin, C. Cox

"Now One and All"
A. Dunning

"I'm a Jolly Old tar'
C. Cox

"Tell Me where My Wife has gone"
A. Dunning, E. Norman

"Come and be Jolly in a moderate way"
A. Dunning, D. Lingard

"How to Hades, I'm off Slick"
A. Dunning, E. Norman, C. Cox, G. Atkins

"Pretty Tillie, if you Love me"
D. Lingard, E. Norman, G. Atkins

"The Old Woman and her Pig"
A. Dunning, E. Norman, G. Atkins, C. Cox

[35]William Lingard appeared in his celebrated Comic Sketches and Living Statues, followed by: The Married Rake. Beginning 8 February, Two Can Play at That Game; beginning 8 March, Don Caesar de Bazan; beginning 29 March 1869, Time Tries All!; beginning 3 May 1869, A Silent Protector, beginning 31 May 1869, The Jacobite.

[36]Succeeded by J. C. Williamson for the reconstructed version.

1869.08 THE FIELD OF THE CLOTH OF GOLD

A Burlesque in One Act, 5 Scenes. Play by William Brough, re-constructed (for America) by W. J. Florence. Music composed, selected and arranged by Howard Glover. Scenery by Robert Grain, L. W. Seavey. Machinery by Levi Guernsey. Properties and appointments by Charles LaForrest. Costumes by R. W. Williams. Orchestra under the direction of Henry Hahn. Produced by George Wood. Opened 1 February 1869 at Wood's Museum and closed 27 February 1869 after 28 performances[37].

ACT 1

THE FIELD OF THE CLOTH OF GOLD CAST: *Francis I*, of France, a monarch who though in reality a French Franc thinks himself quite equal to the English Sovereign alluded to below: Mr. W. J. FLORENCE. *Lady Constance de Grey*, an English heiress, and a Ward in Chancery—a living ward in a dead-lock, making a bolt of it: Mrs. W. J. FLORENCE. *Earl Darnley*, a Banished English Peer, his character shamefully misrepresented at first, but having justice done him at last by the misrepresentation of: ROSE MASSEY. *Henry VIII*, of England, surnamed the "Bluff King Hal," on a visit to France, English Sovereigns being always acceptable on the Continent: LOUIS MESTAYER. *Sir Guy*, the Cripple, a Hunchback, denounced by Constance as crookeder in the mind than body and denounced by Darnley as a traitor: SOL SMITH, JR. *The Duke of Suffolk*, master of Ceremonies in the English Court; "a heavy swell," such as is often met crossing the Channel: Miss ROSE COOK. *La Sieur de Boissy*, Master of the Ceremonies to the French Court; like the last character, a swell as well: Miss LILLIE ELDRIDGE. *Tete Veau*, High Constable of Calais, with a Staff of Specials improvised by himself, the materials for his constable's staff being produced out of his own head: Fred G. Maeder. *Members of a German Band*, and therefore of necessity, producers of all sorts of discords Block (3): *Von Schlascher*: J. Deboney. *Von Kroscher*: H. Stuart. *Von Smascher*: J. Barnes. *A Citizen of Credit and renown*: George Mitchell. *Queen Katharine*, one of King Henry's many "better halves"—who, when aggrieved, thinks it were better to "ha(l)ve out:" Mr. M. C. Daley. *Anne Boylan*, chief Maid of Honor—destined to succeed Queen Katharine and it is hoped no less as: Alice Logan. *Rose de Lafox*: Kate Logan. *Herald of the English Court*: Annie Mortimer. *Herlad of the French Court*: Aggie Wood. *English Pages*: Misses Grey, Garber, Lewis, Page. *French Pages*: Miss Robertson, Smith, Robertson, Brown. *Special Constables, Lords and Ladies in Waiting, Gold, Silver and other Sticks, Guards, Rogues, Vagabonds, etc.* (*Ballet Specialty*: Mlle. GIUSEPPINA MORLACCHI, Corps de Ballet.)

(The action takes place in England and France during the reign of King Henry VIII, 1519-1520.)

Scene 1: The Quay at Calais. *Scene 2*: The Woods and Forests! *Scene 3*: The Field of the Cloth of Gold. *Scene 4*: Ante-Chamber in King Henry's Pavilion. *Scene 5*: The Tournament.

SPECIALITIES, MUSICAL NUMBERS

- Song (Scene 1)
- Mull-a-dramatic Situation (Scene 2)
- Great Demonstration in honor of the Anglo-French Alliance (Scene 3)
- Hair-Dressing by Machinery (Scene 4)
- The Roped Arena: the French Chicken vs. the British Infant (Scene 5)
- La Diadem (Grand Sensational Ballet)(Scen 5)
  - Mlle. G. Morlacchi, Corps de Ballet
- "A Good and Lasting Piece" (Scene 5, Finale)

ACT 2

L'ALMÉE, an Asiatic Ballet Divertissement arranged by Signor Constantine.

CAST: *L'Almée*, the favorite: Mlle. GIUSEPPINA MORLACCHI. *Zuliska*: Mlle. G. Mazzeri. *Verdiana*: Mlle. Beretta. *Linda*: Mlle. L. Mazzeri. *Medora*: Mlle. M. Albertin. *Hermasita*: Mlle. Panzere. *Nahdir*, a Young Sultan: Signor Constantine. *El Hebur, Grand Vizier, Attendants, Khedives, Slaves, etc.*: Corps de Ballet.

BALLETS

- Pas des Odalisques
  - Principals, Corps de Ballet
- Entrée Dansante
  - Mlle. G. Morlacchi
- Grand Adagio
  - Mlle. G. Morlacchi
- Variations
  - Mlles. G. Morlacchi, L. Mazzeri, Albertin, Panzere, Signor Constantine, Corps de Ballet
- Pas de Almée
  - Mlle. G. Morlacchi
- Grand Finale
  - Mlle. G. Morlacchi, Principals, Corps de Ballet

[37]Presented with a fore-piece LITTLE TOODLEKINS by Charles Mathews, and an afterpiece ballet divertissement, L'ALMÉE. Beginning 15 February 1869 the burlesque of FRA DIAVOLO replaced LITTLE TOODLEKINS as the fore-piece, and Mlle. Morlacchi in her ballet L'ALMÉE, was dropped.

1869.09 LES DEUX AVEUGLES

A Revival of the Bouffonnerie Musicale in One Act[38], in French (as a curtain-raiser before LA PÉRICHOLE). Libretto by Jules Moinaux. Music by Jacques Offenbach. Manager, Adolph Birgfeld. Conductor, H. Dennery. Produced by James Fisk, Jr. Opened 3 February 1869 at the Grand Opera House and closed 6 February 1869 after 6 performances.

CAST: *Giraffier*: Mons. LEDUC. *Patachon*: Mons. LAGRIFFOUL.

1869.10 ORPHÉE AUX ENFERS

A Revival of the Opéra Bouffon in Four Acts, in French[39]. Libretto by Hector Crémieux. Music by Jacques Offenbach. Manager, Adolph Birgfeld. Conductor, H. Dennery, Edouard Colonne. Produced by James Fisk, Jr. Opened 8 February 1869 at the Grand Opera House and closed 20 February 1869 (matinee) after 13 peformances; returned 8, 15 April 1869 to the Fifth Avenue Theatre for 2 additional performances in repertory.

CAST: *Eurydice*: Mlle. LUCILLE TOSTÉE. *Orphée*: Mons. DECRÉ. *Aristée*: Mons. LEDUC. *Pluton*: Mons. LEDUC. *Jupiter*: Mons. DUCHESNE. *John Styx*: Mons. GUIDON. *Merucry*: Mons. LAGRIFFOUL. *Diane*: Mlle. DUCLOS. *Junon*: Mlle. Mathilde. *Minerve*: Mlle. Delphine. *Venus*: Mlle. Cadix. *Cupidon*: Mlle. Rose. *L'Opinion Public*: Mlle. Arsene. *Gods, Goddesses, Followers of Diane and Minerve, Peasants, Guards of the Olympe, Demons.*

1869.11 LUCRETIA BORGIA, M.D., La Grande Doctresse

The Elise Holt Burlesque Troupe in an Operatic Burlesque in One Act, 5 Scenes[40]. Play by Henry J. Byron. (Inspired by the grand opera 'Lucrezia Borgia" by Gaetano Donizetti.) Music arranged and adapted by Napier Lothian. Production directed by Harry Wall. Scenery by J. S. Schell. Orchestra under the direction of Fred W. Zaulig. Produced by G. T. Reeder. Opened 17 February 1869 at the Waverley Theatre and closed 30 March 1869 after 42 performances; returned 19 April 1869 to the Waverley Theatre and closed 24 April 1869 after an additional 7 performances. Total: 49 performances.

CAST: *Gennaro*, a student of medicine, on a reading tour with his fellow pupils—one who is very nearly dying early in the piece, but who eventually turns out to be one of those pupils who die-late: ELISE HOLT. *Orsini*, his friend and philosopher: EMILY PITT. *Young medical puppies who will someday be dog-tors* (3): *Lireotto*: Fanny Prestige. *Petrucca*: Minnie Jackson. *Vitelli*: Mary Pitt. *The Dook*, a poor creature, but not to be confounded with the "Ducal Creaure" in Rob Roy, inasmuch as he is of Italian parent-

[38]First produced in New York 26 August 1857 at Metropolitan Hall in repertory.

[39]First produced in New York in French 17 January 1867 at the Theatre Français for 14 performances. For Synopsis of Scenes and Musical Numbers, see original 1867 production.

[40]Preceded by a comedietta, A Pretty Piece of Business, which was later replaced by Who's to Win Him? Musical numbers not listed in programs, except:

- The New Can-Can
  - E. Holt, B. Rigl, E. Rigl, Entire Company
- Burlesques of Offenbach and Lancashire Lass (Scene 4)

age: HARRY WALL. *Lucretia Borgia*, Duchess of Ferrara—a lady who has "gone in" for medicine, and "come out" with honors, who always dosing the ministry may be considered a "piller" of the state, a Fer-"rara avis in terris," mistress of her art but not her heart, which is not the Dook's but somebody else's: JAMES LEWIS. *Rustighello*, always to be found when wanted (?): Charles T. Parsloe, Jr. *Jubetta*, Lucretia's psychic boy, who has so eager a taste for Medical Literature that he is always taking in his mistress' Compositions: Belvil Ryan. *First Page*: Carrie Williams. *Second Page*: Annie Campion. *Third Page*: Emma Bell. *Guests, Serenaders and Attendants, the Noblest Ladies and Gents in New York.* (*Specialty*: BETTY RIGL, EMILY RIGL.)

Scene 1: At Venice. *Scene 2*: Apartment at the Ducal Palace. *Scene 3*: Lucretia's Surgery. *Scene 4*: Ante-chamber in the Ducal Palace. *Scene 5*: Ducal Palace.

MUSICAL NUMBERS

"Up in a Balloon" (Scene 5)
E. Holt

1869.12 MONSIEUR CHOUFLEURY

An Operette (Monsieur Choufleuri Restera chez lui le (24 Janvier 1833)) in One Act, in French. (Libretto by le Duc de Morny, et al). Music by Jacques Offenbach. Manager, Adolph Birgfeld. Conductor, H. Dennery. Produced by James Fisk, Jr. Opened and closed 20 February 1869 at the Grand Opera House after 1 performance (preceded by Act 2 of LA BELLE HÉLÈNE); returned 6-8 May 1869 on a double bill with "Le Mariage aux Lanternes" at the Fifth Avenue Theatre for 3 performances in repertory; returned 15, 29 May 1869 on a double bill with MONSIEUR LANDRY to the Fifth Avenue Theatre for 2 additional performances in repertory.

CAST: *Ernestine, fille de Choufleury*: Mlle. LUCILLE TOSTÉE. *Chrysodule Babylas*, jeune compositeur: Mons. LEDUC. *Monsieur Choufleury*: Mons. DUCHESNE. *Peterman*, domestique de Choufleury: Mons. DECRÉ. *Mme. Balandard*, une invitée: Mons Guidon. *Mons. Balandard*, un invité: Mons. Lagriffoul. *Guests (Les invités), etc,*

Scene: À Paris, au Marais, en 1833.

MUSICAL NUMBERS[41]

Couplet (J'étais vraiment très ignorante)
Mlle. L. Tostée

Bolero (En naissant, chacque créature)
Mlle. L. Tostée. Mons. Leduc

Trio (Babylas! Babylas! Babylas!)
Mlle. L. Tostée, Messrs. Leduc, Duchesne

Ensemble (Le plaisir miniscule)
Messrs. Lagriffoul, Guidon, Decré, Choeur

Trio (Italia la bella! Mia bella patria!)
Mlle. L. Tostée, Messrs. Leduc, Duchesne

Final (Vraiment, votre petite fille)
Mlle. L. Tostée, Messrs. Leduc, Duchesne, Guidon, Lagriffoul, Choeur

1869.13 PO-CA-HON-TAS, or, The Gentle Savage

A Revised Edition of the Original, Aboriginal, Erratic, Operatic, Semi-Civilized and Demi-Savage Extravaganza (A Burlesque) in Two Acts[42]. Libretto by John Brougham. Scenery by C. J. Hawthorne, Richard Marston, Louis Duflocq, A. Wheatley. Wardrobe, Miss Flannery. Machinery, W. W. Demilt. Properties, J. Williams. Leader of orchestra, H. Eckhardt. Produced by John Brougham. Opened 22 February 1869 at Brougham's Theatre and closed 6 March 1869 after 12 performances.

CAST: Of Ye Englishe: *Captain John Smith*, the undoubted Original, vocal and instrumental, in the settlement of Virginia, in love with Pocahontas according to this story, though somewhat at variance with his story: Miss ELIZA NEWTON. *Lieutenant Thomas Brown*, second in command, a hitherto neglected genius, whose claims on posterity are now for the first time acknowledged, as is but right: Mr. Florence. *William Jones*, sometimes called Bill, another of the same sort left: Mr. J. Peck. *Mynheer Rolf*, the real husband of Pocahontas, but dramatically divorced contrary to all law and fact: Mr. C. Hale. *Splicers of main braces, shiverers of timbers, anathematizers of eyes and limbs, promiscuously general dealers in single Combats and double Hornpipes, and altogether amazingly nautical people (5)*: *Benjamin Brace*: Mr. Cough. *John Junk*: Mr. Johnson. *Henry Halyard*: Mr. Gray. *Wiliam Buntline*: Mr. Newan. *Barnabas Binnacle*: Mr. Hall.

Of Ye Salvages: *H. J. Pow-Ha-Tan I*, King of the Tuscaroras, a crotchety Monarch, in fact a semi-Brave: JOHN BROUGHAM. *The Right Hon. Quash-al-Jaw*, Speaker of the savage House of Lords, straightener of unpleasant kinks and oiler of troubled waters, unraveller of knotty points, adjuster of pugnacious difficulties, and Grand Eye Parliamentary Factotum and Fagleman: Mr. J. HURLEY. *O-po-dil-doc*, One of the Aboriginal F. F. V.'s, an indignant dignitary: Mr. C. Hilyard. *Col-o-gog*, another warm-hearted and headed Son of Old Virginia, the untiring: Mr. C. Edmunds. *Jin-go*, Sergeant-at-Arms, a friend to swear by: C. Crosbie. *Kreem-fay-sloon*, Bearer of Despatches and News Carrier in ordinary: —. *Medicine Men, of the Saultz and Senna-ca Tribe (4)*: *Ip-pah-kak, Sassy-Pril, Kod-liv-royl, Kal-o-mel*: Efficient Chorus. *H. R. H. Princess Po-Ca-Hon-Tas*, the Beautiful and very properly undutiful Daughter of King Pow-ha-tan, married, according to the ridculous dictum of actual circumstane, to Master Rolff, but the author flatters himself, much more advantageously disposed of in the acting edition: Miss EFFIE GERMON. *Interesting offshoots from aristocratic stock, anterior to the First Families of Virginia, embodying the rigid principles of the Tuscarora Fashionable Finishing School (3)*: *Poo-tee-pet*: Miss Annie Firmin. *Di-mun-di*: Miss Lizzie Mahon. *Wee-Cha-Ven-Da*: Miss E. Andrews. *Their "dear charges" for whom they don't forget to charge dear enough for in the Quarterly Bills (5)*: *Dah-lin-duk*: Miss Eloise Allen. *O-you-jewel*: Miss Belle Fisher. *Luv-lie-kreeta*: Miss Clara Fisher. *Oso-char-ming*: Miss E. Ames. *Lum-pa-shuga*: Miss E. Lyle. *Soldiers, Sailors, Indians, Members of the Tuscarora Light Guard, etc.*

1869.14 THE HORSE MARINES/ NICODEMUS

A Spectacular Burlesqular, Extravaganzacular Odd-ditty (Burlesque)[43] in One Act, 5 Scenes, accompanied by a ballet, variety and comic pantomime. Stage mamaner, Ben A. Baker. Musical director, Signor Giuseppe Operti. Produced by the Tammany Amusement Company (Messrs. Henry Jarrett and Harry Palmer, proprietors; Leonard Grover, managing director). Opened 1 March 1869 at the Tammany, Grand Theatre and closed 24 April 1869 after 56 performances.

ACT 1

"The White Squall" (Song)(by Barker)
Mr. Robert Green
The Carlo Brothers (George, Fred) in their great Gymnastic Act, introducing Muscular and Antipodean Performances

"The Syren and Friar" (Duet)
Miss Bessie Sudlow, Mr. R. Green

Duet
The Dashwood Sisters

Character Song
Harry Raynor

ACT 2

THE HORSE MARINES. A simple domestic story of some people who, having to sing, are naturally hoarse, and being Hoarse Mare'en, the simple music which comes so Oftenback that everybody is familiar with it. In accordance with the custom of the day, stolen from various sources, and not particularly well-stolen. Music arranged by Signor (Giuseppe) Operti.

CAST: *George Jinks*, Captain of the Horse Marines, victim of circumstances: Miss ALICE HARRISON. *Madame Jinks*, his Mama, proprietress of a young ladies' school: Mr. BEN MAGINLEY. *Ruth*, the Lancashire Lass, pupil of Madame Jinks and of course in love with George: Miss HENRIETTA TEMPLE. *Peggy*, young lady of the period: Miss LILLIE WHITING. *Susie*, delicate creature of Upper Tendom: SALLIE MADDOX. *Old Tom*, the sensation Drama

[41]Musical numbers not listed in programs. List prepared from published French piano vocal score (Paris: E. Gérard et Cie., 1861).

[42]First produced in New York 24 December 1855 at Wallack's Theatre; rturned 28 May 1856 to Wallack's Theatre; returned 28 July 1856 to the Bowery Theatre. PO-CA-HON-TAS was accompanied by a comedy "A Gentleman from Ireland" by Fitzjames O'Brien For the second week of the run, "A Gentleman from Ireland" was replaced by Angus Reach's vaudeville of Jenny Lind!, which was later combined with a shortened form of "An Irish Stew."

[43]Also billed as "a simple domestic story of some people who, having to sing, are naturally hoarse, and being Hoarse Mare'en, the music which comes so Oftenback that every body is familiar with it."

Man, Plotter, Counter Plotter, and General Fire Eater, with a disposition to get Tom full o'rye, naturally commits a little tomfollery: Mr. W. DONALDSON. *Joseph Baxter*, Not for Joe—but why not?: Mr. A. Bascom. *Champagne Charley*, doing penance: Mr. C. Fisher. *Enfant perdu*, lost in livery: Mr. ROBERT GREEN. *Policeman of the Period*: Mr. Freeman. *Waiter at the Bellevue*: Mr. J. W. Wesley. *Hermit*: Mr. J. F. SHERIDAN.

Scene 1: Madame Jinks' School. Teaching young ladies how to dance. *Scene 2*: Street in Marinedom. Conspiracy to kick Jinks out of the Army. *Scene 3*: Bellevue Garden. Shoving the queer. *Scene 4*: Prison. Reminiscience of Genevieve to save a wait. *Scene 5*: Realm of the Marines. Review of the Horse Marines.

SPECIALTY

Pas de Fleur—Divertissement Brilliante des Bataillons (Scene 3)
Mlle. E. Carle, Mons. Carle
With Misses Whiting, Maddox, Strondell, Therese, Gabrielle, Caroline, Colson, Hopgood, Delaflamina, etc.

ACT 3

"Palm Leaf" (Waltz)
P. Stanhager
The Carlo Brothers (George, Fred), Musical Clowns introducing curious and wonderful antics while playing on two violins.

"Di Provenza" (Song)
Mr. Robert Green

"The Love of a Prince" (Protean Burlesque)
Dashwood Sisters

La Dame aux Camélias (Grand Ballet d'Action)(Music arranged by Sig. Operti.)

Adagio and Solo-La Dame aux Camélias
Mlle. Emma Carle

Divertissement
Mons. Charles Carle

Allegretto

Corps de Ballet

Galop Finale
Mlle. E. Carle, Corps de Ballet

The Japanese Fiddle, on one string
Harry Raynor

Comic Metamorphosis: "My Old Wife and I," "Pat McCann," and "The Nerves"
Johnny Sheridan, James Mack

ACT 4

NICODEMUS, a comic pantomime by James Maffit.[44]

CAST: *Nicodemus*, a clown: JAMES MAFFIT. *M. Garrotte*, a gardener: WILLIAM A. BARTHOLOMEW. *Old Crusty*, a baker: J. W. Wesley. *François*, a young lover: Mons. Carlo Carle. *Villagers (3)*: *Jean Victor*: Mr. Charles. *Pierre Alphonse*: Mr. Adams. *Emile Pietro*: Mr. (James) Mack. *Annette*, her daughter: Mlle. (Emma) Carle. *Peasants, Villagers, etc.*

1869.15 MUCH ADO ABOUT A MERCHANT OF VENICE

(A Burlesque on Shakespeare's "Merchant of Venice" in Three Acts, 4 Scenes)[45] From the Original Text—a Long Way. Play by John Brougham. Music by the most celebrated composers, unblushingly appropriated, disconnected and placed in unaccustomed positions. Scenery from sketches taken on the spot. Costumes copied from Fashion Plates of the Period. Tableaux and Incidental Choreographics. Produced by John Brougham. Opened 8 March 1869 at Brougham's Theatre and closed 3 April 1869 after 24 performances.

CAST: *Shylock*, a shamefully ill-used and persecuted old Hebrew gentleman, in fact, an Israelite of other days, whose character was darkened by Christian contemporaries simply to conceal their own nefarious transactions, victimized, as he was, by sundry unjustifiable confidence operations: Mr. JOHN BROUGHAM. *Lorenzo*, a fast young Venetian swell, who swindles Shylock out of his duck of a daughter, and his ducats as well, and by so doing ultimately catches Jesse: Miss EFFIE GERMON. *Bassanio*, another interesting youth without an atom of principle, but being anatomically attractive, secures a wealthy heiress in a tricky kind of way: Miss ELIZA NEWTON. *Antonio*, the gay and sportive Merchant of Venice, who narrowly escapes venisection at the hands of Shylock, who has a lien upon his chest: Mr. ARTHUR MATTHISON. *Tubal*, a Christianized Hebrew Serf, in fact, a converted bondman: Mr. Charles Hale. *Gratiano*, a remarkably stylish serving gentleman, out of livery, attached provisionally to Bassanio, being on board wages: Miss Annie Firman. *Launcelot*, Shylock's man of all work, and only domestic; a hungry hack discontented with his fare: Miss E. ALLEN. *Chief Justice* of the high old Court of Venice, with a heavy charge, which he discharges at the Jury: Mr. GEORGE W. STODDART. *Asscoiated Judges* of mixed nationality: Messrs. Gossi, Crosby. *Page to Portia*, a patient annunciator: Miss CLARA FISHER. *The Prince of Aragon*, an arrogant individual, and a suitor to Portia, who does not suit her: Mr. E. Edmunds. *King Theodore of Abyssiania*, the adorer of Portia, also, who is likewise referred to the door: Mr. F. Gough. *Crier of the Court*, an important, imported functionary: Mr. W. J. Hurley. *Policeman of the period*: Mr. Jones. *Portia*, a well-proportioned heiress, with a tendency towards the tender passion and practical conundrums: Mrs. J. J. Prior. *Jessica*, the Jew's undutiful daughter, who makes a jubilee of her sire's sorrows, and gives further proof that love laughs at shy-locksmiths: Mrs. LIZZIE ECKHARDT. *Nerissa*, Portia's Irish hand-maid, distressingly in love; evidently a Bridget of Sighs: Miss Amy Ames. *Ladies, Gentlemen, Masqueraders, Men-at-Arms and other Medieval Personnages.*

Act 1: Street in Venice.

Act 2: Portia's Drawing Room.

Act 3, Scene 1: Front Chamber. *Scene 2*: The High Old Court of Venice.

ACT 1[46]

Opening Chorus (Merry maskers, merry maskers)
Chorus

"Milkman's Song" (Original)
Miss E. Germon

"Pitiful Plaint" (Recititavo)
Miss E. Allen

Aria, 'L'ELISIR D'AMORE' (I am starving! I am starving!)
Miss E. Allen
(*Music by* Gaetano Donizetti)

Trio (Better service can we offer)
Misses E. Allen, E. Germon, E. Newton

"I Know a Bank" (Double Duet)
Mr. A. Matthison, Misses E. Germon, E. Allen, Mrs. L. Eckhardt

Duet, 'Nora Creina' (We shall have a Jew de spree)
Miss E. Newton, J. Brougham

Song (If you ever should deceive me)
J. Brougham

Song, 'The Sea' (The key! The key!)
Mrs. L. Eckhardt

Lamentation, from "JEANNETTE AND JEANNOT" (She has vamoosed far away)
J. Brougham

ACT 2

Cantata Disconsolata, 'Wearing of the Green' (Oh! Tubal, did you not hear)
J. Brougham

Concerted Piece of Antagonistic Harmonies (Now let us have a jolly spree)
Chorus, Mr. A. Matthison, Miss E. Newton, E. Germon, Mrs. L. Eckhardt

Finale (There's my man, arrest him, take him hence!)
J. Brougham

ACT 3

Scene 2

Finale
J. Brougham, All

[44]Previously presented at Tammany 4 January 1869, accompanying THE PAGE'S REVEL.

[45]Preceded by a comedietta, Perfection, which was replaced during the second and third weeks of the run by A Gentleman from Ireland; in the fourth and last week of the run, the fore-piece was His Last Legs.

[46]Musical numbers not listed in programs. List prepared from published prompt book (Samuel French, New York, n.d.)

1869.16

LA VIE PARISIENNE

An Opéra-bouffe in Four Acts, 5 Scenes, in French. Libretto by Henri Meilhac and Ludovic Halévy. Music by Jacques Offenbach. Regisseur, Paul Juignet. Scenery by Hannibal Calyo. Machinist, Mr. Drew. Costumes by Mme. Armand and Mons. Philippe. Conductor, Robert Stoepel. Chorus director, Mons. Gambogi. Produced by Jacob Grau. Opened 29 March 1869 at the Théâtre Français and closed 13 April 1869 after 11 performances in repertory.

CAST: *Un Brésilien*: Mons. CARRIER. *Frick*: Mons. CARRIER. *Prosper*: Mons. CARRIER. *Le Baron de Gondremarck*: Mons. BECKERS. *Bobinet*: Mons. MUSSAY. *L'Amiral Suisse*: Mons. Mussay. *Raoul de Gardefeu*: Mons. DELIGNE. *Urbain*: Mons. GENOT. *Le General de Porto Ricco*: Mons. Genot. *Joseph*: Mons. Bourgoin. *Alphonse*: Mons. Rivenez. *Gontran*: Mons. Paul Juignet. *Railway Employe*: Mons. Brag. *Gabrielle*: Mlle. ROSE BELL. *Métella*: Mlle. MARIE DESCLAUZAS. *La Baronne de Gondremarck*: Mlle. GUERETTI. *Pauline*: Mlle. RIZARELLI. *Madame de Folleverdue*: Mlle. Bageard. *Leonie*: Mlle. Victoria Maurice. *Clara*: Mlle. Briot. *Justine*: Mlle. Estephe. *Louise*: Mlle. Villiers. *Adele*: Mlle. Rosa. *Julie*: Mlle. Rachel. *Railway Employees, Travelers, Guests, Servants—male and female, Masks, Waiters, etc.*

Act 1: La gare Saint-Lazare.

Act 2: A Little Hotel in the Grand Hotel.

Act 3: Une Soirée dans le quart de monde.

Act 4, Scene 1: A Parisian Restaurant. *Scene 2*: Le Jardin Mabille with the Pavillon de Danse. Grand Fête.

ACT 1[47]

Introduction (Nous sommes employés)

Choeur (Le ciel est noir il va pleuvoir)

Couplets de la Parisienne (Elles sont tristes les marquises)
Mlle. R. Bell

Triolets (Ce que c'est pourtant que la vie)
Mons. Deligne

Final (A Paris nous arrivons en masse)

Rondeau (Je suis Brésilien, j'ai de l'or)
Mons. Carrier

ACT 2

Duo (Entrez, entrez jeune fille à l'oeil bleu)
Mons. Carrier, Mlle. R. Bell

Couplets (Dans cette ville toute pleine)
Mons. Beckers

Rondeau de la lettre (Vous souvient-il, ma belle)
M. Desclauzas

Couplets du Major (Pour découper adroitment)
Mons. Carrier

Final (Nous entrons dans cette meure)
Choeur

Couplets (Je suis veuve d'un colonel)
Mlle. R. Bell

Air Tyrolien (Auf der Berliner)
Mlle. R. Bell, Tous

ACT 3

Introduction (Il faut nous dépècher ville)
Choeur

Septuor (Donc je puis me fier à vous)
Messrs. Mussay, Genot, Mlle Rizarelli, Les Serviteurs

Duo (L'amour c'est une échelle immense)
Mlle. Rizarelli, Mons. Beckers

Couplets (On va courir on va sortir)
Mlle. R. Bell

Ensemble (Votre habit a craqué dans le dos!)
Mlle. Rizarelli, Messrs. Beckers, Mussay, Carrier

Final (Soupons, soupons, c'est le moment)

Chanson à boire (En endossant mon uniforme)
Messrs. Mussay, Carrier, Genot, Mlle. R. Bell, Tous

ACT 4

Scene 1

Rondeau (Je suis encore toute éblouie)
Mlle. Gueretti

Couplets (Quoi ces messieurs pourraient, ma chère)

Reprise de l'ensemble (Vengeons nous, il faut nous venger)

Final (Tout tourne, tourne, tourne)

Scene 2

Choeur (Bien bichonnés et bien rasés)

Couplets (Avant toute chouse il faut être mystérieux)

Rondeau (C'est ici l'endroit redouté)
Mlle. M. Desclauzas

Mélodrame

Couplets et ensemble (Je te connais! Tu me connais!)
Mons. Beckers, Mlle. Gueretti, Bageard

Choeur (En avant les jeunes femmes)

Duo de la gantière et du Brésilien (Hier à midi la gantière)
Mlle. R. Bell, Mons. Carrier

Mélodrame (sortie des invités)

Final (Par nos chants et par nos cris)
Mlle. R. Bell, Gueretti, M. Desclauzas, Mons. Carrier, Tous

Couplets (En cherchant dans la ville)

1869.17

IVANHOE

Elise Holt's Burlesque Troupe in a Powerful Burlesque in One Act, 6 Scenes.[48] Play by Henry J. Byron. Production directed by Harry Wall and Asa Cushman. Scenery by J. S. Schell. Dresses by Minnie Moore. Properties by Mr. Brockway. Orchestra under the direction of Howard Glover. Produced by G. T. Reeder. Opened 31 March 1869 at the Waverley Theatre and closed 17 April 1869 after 19 performances.

CAST: *Wamba*, "a fool by right of descent, the son of Witless, who was the son of Weatherbrain, who was the son of an Alderman," Clown to the Circle of Cedric's acquaintance: MAGGIE DESMOND[49]. *The Palmer*, otherwise Sir Wilfred, of Ivanhoe, the only son of Cedric, banished from his father's house in consequence of Miss Rowena and misconduct: MINNIE JACKSON. *The Lady Rowena*, "her complexion was exquisitely fair; her profuse hair, of a color betwixt brown and golden, was arranged in a fanciful and graceful manner in numerous ringlets, to a form which Art had probably misled "Nature," a distant relative of Cedric's and the betrothed of the absent Ivanhoe: EMILY PITT. *Prince John*, a bad relation who seizes the Crown and Sceptre in England, while his eldest brother Richard, Coeur de Lion, is attacking the Sarecen's head in Palestine: MARY PITT. *Rebecca*, "the figure of Rebecca might indeed have compared with the proudest beauties of England": JAMES LEWIS. *Isaac of York*, "a tall, thin, old man, who, howver, had lost, by the habit of stooping, much of his actual height." Outfitter, Army Clothier and General Dealer. The best prices given for ladies' and gentlemen's cast off garments: E. Coleman. *Sir Brian de Bois Gilbert*, a Knight Templar. "His expression was calculated to impress a degree of awe, if not of fear, upon stranger": GEORGE BECKETT. *Cedric the Saxon*: "It often appeared, however, from the countenance of this proprietor, that he was of a hasty and choleric temper—Master of Botherwood but not of himself": Belvil Ryan. *The Black Knight*, a dark Knight, finishing with a prolonged reign; a mysterious volume in black letter, illustrated on steel; and most successful with the public, in consequence of a good education: CHARLES T. PARSLOE, Jr. *DeBracy*, Toady in ordinary to Prince John: Fanny Prestiiage. *Oswald*, Cedric's Major Domo: Annie Campion. *Ladies, Knights, Peasants, Courtiers, and Attendants.* (*Specialty*: BETTY RIGL, EMILY RIGL.)

Scene 1: Banqueting Hall in Botherwood. *Scene 2*: Road to Ashby-de-La-Zouche. *Scene 3*: The Lists of Ashby. *Scene 4*: Sherwood Forest, Sunset. *Scene 5*: Apartment at Isaac's. *Scene 6*: Turret Chamber at Torquilstone.

[47]Musical numbers not listed in programs. List prepared from published French piano vocal score (E. Heu, Paris, 1866) and English-French libretto published to accompany Jacob Grau's New York premiere.

[48]Preceded by a farce, Quiet Family.

[49]Following an illness, Elise Holt assumed her starring role as Wamba on 12 April 1869.

SPECIALTIES

Pas de Deux[50] (Scene 3)
Rigl Sisters

Unalloyed Happiness of Everybody, and a little of Orpheus to wind up (Scene 6)

1869.18 LA GRANDE-DUCHESSE DE GÉROLSTEIN

A Revival of the Opèra-bouffe in Four Acts, in French[51]. Libretto by Henri Meilhac and Ludovic Halévy. Music by Jacques Offenbach. Proprietor, James Fisk, Jr. Stage manager, L. Benedick. Conductor, Edouard Colonne. Opened 6 April 1869 at the Fifth Avenue Theatre and closed 4 May 1869 after 5 performances in repertory.

CAST: *The Grand Duchesse*: Mlle. LUCILLE TOSTÉE. *Fritz*: Mons. AUJAC. *Prince Paul*: Mons. LEDUC. *Baron Puck*: Mons. LAGRIFFOUL. *Général Boum*: Mons. DUCHESNE. *Baron Groge*: Mons. Hamilton. *Nepomuc*: Mons. Guidon. *Wanda*: Mlle. DUCLOS. (*Les demoiselles d'honneur (4)*:) *Iza*: Mlle. Tholer. *Amélie*: Mlle. Rose. *Olga*: Mlle. Mathilde. *Charlotte*: Mlle. Arsene. *Ladies in Waiting*: Mlles. Bertha, Boudinot. *Officers, Vivandiers, Lords, Ladies, Soldiers, Peasants, etc.*

1869.19 MONSIEUR LANDRY/ LE MAÎTRE DE CHAPELLE

A Double Bill of One Act Opéras, in French. Manager, Adolph Birgfeld. Stage manager, L. Benedick. Conductor, Edouard Colonne. Produced by James Fisk, Jr. Opened 24 April 1869 at the Fifth Avenue Theatre and closed 29 April 1869 after 2 performances in repertory; MONSIEUR LANDRY returned 29 May 1869 for 1 performance on a bill with Monsieur Choulfleuri.

ACT 1

MONSIEUR LANDRY. An Opérette Bouffe (M'sieu Landry) in One Act, in French. Music by Jules Duprato. Libretto by Camille du Locle.

CAST: *Madame Parfait*, Javotte: Mlle. TOSTÉE. *Monsieur Landry*: Mons. DARDIGNAC. *Monsieur Parfait*: Mons. DUCHESNE. *Suzanne*: Mlle. Rose.

MUSICAL NUMBERS[52]

Duo (Après six mois de mariage)
Mons. Duchesne, Mlle. Tostée

Couplets (M'sieu Landry su l'dos d'son grison)
Mlle. Rose

Rondo (A la foire de Bayeux)
Mons. Dardignac

Duo (Comme l'éclair ouvrant au ciel de flamme)
Mons. Dardiganc, Mlle. Tostée

Couplets (De ton mari pauvre Javotte) Mons. Duchesne

Finale
Tous

ACT 2

LE MAÎTRE DE CHAPELLE. A Revival of the Opéra Comique in One Act[53], in French. Libretto by Mme. Sophie Gay. Music by Ferdinando Paër.

CAST: *Barnabé*, Maître de Chapelle: Mons. THOLER. *Benetto*, son neveu: Mons. DECRE. *Gertrude*, servante de Barnabé: Mlle. DUCLOS.

[50]Replaced during the run by a Tarantella.

[51]First produced in New York 24 September 1867 at the Théâtre Français for 156 performances in repertory. For Synopsis of Scenes and Musical Numbers, see original 1867 production.

[52]Musical numbers not listed in programs. List prepared from published French piano vocal score (E. Heu, Paris, 1857).

[53]First produced in New York in French 11 October 1866 at the Théâtre Français in repertory. For Synopsis of Scenes and Musical Numbers, see original 1866 production.

1869.20 ROBINSON CRUSOE AND HIS MAN FRIDAY!

A Grand Pantomime Burlesque in Two Acts, 7 Scenes, accompanied by a ballet, variety and pantomime. Stage manager, B. A. Baker. Musical director, Signor Giuseppi Operti. Scenery by Ludovico Malmsha, William Voegtlin; Charles Thorne. Mechanical effects by J. Denham. Produced by the Tammany Amusement Company (Henry Jarrett and Harry Palmer, proprietors; Leonard Grover, managing director). Opened 26 April 1869 at the Tammany, Grand Theatre and closed 22 May 1869 after 28 performances.

ACT 1

"Annie Dear, Good bye" (Song by Wallace)
Robert Green

L'École Gymnase
The Carons

"Lovely Nancy Brown" (Song and Dance)
Messrs. McDermott, O'Dowd

Musical Parterre
Messrs. Zanfretta, Caron

Classic Trapeze
Mlle. Zuleila, Mons. Ventini

ACT 2 and 3

ROBINSON CRUSOE AND HIS MAN FRIDAY!

CAST: *Robinson Crusoe*: WILLIAM H. BARTHOLOMEW. *Captain Will Atkins*: LOUIS MESTAYER. *Daddy Pigtail*: Mr. Barry. *Cutpurse*: Mr. Fielding. *Gouge Eye*: J. W. Wesley. *Bunting*: R. Talbot. *Bowline*: H. Richards. *Friday*: JAMES S. MAFFIT. *King of the Cannibal Islands*: T. E. Jackson. *Hokee Pokee*: C. Vincent. *Wanky Fum*: J. Freeman. *Jenny Pigtail*: ALICE HARRISON. *The Elf Prince*: BESSIE SUDLOW. *Fairy Queen*: Lillie Whiting. *Farfalletto*: Sally Maddox. *Picalli*: JOSE ZANFRETTA. *The Monkey*: Alex. Zanfretta. *The Cat*: Master W. Caron. *Sprite*: Mr. Caron. *Landlord, Waiters, Sailors, Indians, Sisters of the Sorosis of Elf Land, Fairies, etc.*
(*Ballet*: Mlles. AUGUSTA BARETTA, ANGELIQUE, EMMA CARLE; Mons. CHARLES CARLE. Misses Lascelles, Strudel, Gabrielle, Therese, Caroline, Delatimania, Hopgood, West, etc. *Specialty*: Rizarelli Brothers.)

Act 2, Scene 1: The Island of Sorosis. (Malmsha.) *Scene 2*: Rocky Shore of the Island. (Malmsha.) *Scene 3*: London in the Olden Times. (Malmsha.)

Act 3, Scene 1: Forest Dell. (Malmsha.) *Scene 2*: The Island Home of Robinson Crusoe. (Voegtlin.) *Scene 3*: Further into the Untrodden Forest. (Voegtlin.) *Scene 4*: The Shore of the Island. (Malmsha.)

DANCES, SPECIALTIES

Grand Ballet (Pipe the Main Brace and Fore and Aft)(Act 2, Scene 3)

Pas de Deux
Mlles. Baretta, Angelique

Grand Caribbean Ballet (Act 3, Scene 4)
Corps de Ballet

Caprice Indienne
Mlles. Baretta, Angelique,
with Misses Lascelles, Strudel, Gabrielle, Therese, Caroline, Delatimania, Hopgood, West, etc.

ACT 4

Pantomime and Harlequinade in 9 Scenes.
Scene 1: Scene on the Island. *Scene 2*: A Woody Wood. (Malmsha.) *Scene 3*: Post Office and Isaac Abrams. (Thorne.) *Scene 4*: Seamen's Home. (Malmsha.) *Scene 5*: The Arena. *Scene 6*: A Shady Grove. *Scene 7*: The Model Farm Yard. Transformation to the Model Kitchen. (Thorne.) *Scene 8*: Pyrotechnical Laboratory and Pawn Shop. *Scene 9*: Cavern of Gloom in the Regions of Dark Despair. Change to the Golden Realm!

SPECIALTIES

Transformation of the Characters (Scene 1)
Clown: J. S. Maffit. *Pantaloon*: W. H. Bartholomew. *Harlequin*: Mons. Carlo Carle. *Columbia*: Mlle. Emma Carle.

Polka Mazurka
Mons. C. Carle, Mlle. E. Carle

Hornpipe (Scene 4)
Mons. C. Carle, Mlle. E. Carle

Amazonian March (Scene 5)

Terrific Comat
J. S. Maffit, W. H. Bartholomew

Variations
Mlle. Augusta Baretta

Octangularum, the Great Trapeze Act
Rizarelli Brothers

Dance Polka (Scene 6)
Mons. C. Carle, Mlle. E. Carle

Trip (Scene 8)
Mons. C. Carle, Mlle. E. Carle

1869.21 PARIS, or, The Judgement

The Elise Holt Burlesque Company in a Burlesque in One Act, 5 Scenes. Adapted from F. C. Burnand's burlesque of the same name, by C. R. Rattray. New music selected by Elise Holt, arranged and instrumentalized by Howard Glover. Stage manager, Asa Cushman. Scenery by J. S. Schell. Produced by G. T. Reeder. Opened 28 April 1869 at the Waverley Theatre and closed 8 May 1869 after (12) performances; returned 17-19 June 1869 to the Waverley Theatre for 4 additional performances.[54]

CAST: *Paris*: ELSIE HOLT. *Oenone*: JAMES LEWIS. *Venus*: VIOLA CROCKER. *Orion*: HARRY WALL. *Mercury*: EMILY PITT. *Juno*: MARY PITT. *Minerva*: Fanny Prestige. *Jupiter*: Minnie Jackson. *Cupid*: Belvil Ryan. *Castor*: Charley Parsloe. *Pollux*: T. Waddleton. *Psyche*: Kate Dunn. *Ganymede*: Emilie Bell.

Scene 1: Cupid's Tea Rose Gardens. *Scene 2*: Interior of Oenone's Cottage. *Scene 3*: On Mount Ida. The Gods at a Picnic. *Scene 4*: Mercury's General Post and Telegraph Office. *Scene 5*: Grounds of the Palace of Venus in Cythera during a Fête Champêtre.

1869.22 LE MARIAGE AUX LANTERNES

A Revival of the Operette in One Act[55], in French (presented on a double bill with "Monsieur Choufleury.") Libretto by Michael Carré and Léon Battu (adapted from "Le Tresor à Mathurin" by Léon Battu). Music by Jacques Offenbach. Stage manager, L. Benedick. Scenery by R. Smith. Costumes by Mons. Marat (Paris). Musical director, Edouard Colonne. Produced by James Fisk, Jr. Opened 6 May 1869 at the Fifth Avenue Theatre and closed 8 May 1869 after 3 performances in repertory.

CAST: *Fanchette*: *Guillot*: *Denise*: *Catherine*:
Cast included Mlle. IRMA, Mlle. LUCILLE TOSTÉE.

1869.23 ROBINSON CRUSOE

A Burlesque Pantomime in One Act, 9 Scenes, adapted from Daniel Defoe's celebrated romance[56]. Music composed, selected and arranged by Fred W. Humphrey. The whole under the personal supervision of Mercer H. Simpson. Stage manager, Joseph Irving. Scenery by James Roberts. Appointments, masks and properties by Mr. Brunton, of Covent Garden. Costumes from London and Paris. Machinery by R. Smith. Leader of the orchestra, H. W. Humphreys. Produced by George Wood, by arrangement with M. H. Simpson. Opened 8 May 1869 at Wood's Museum and closed 12 June 1869 after 81 performances[57].

CAST [in order of appearance]: *An Elf*, an adventurous spirit, smart enough to take care of his-elf: MARION TAYLOR. *Submarina*, the sedate Fairy of the Enchanted Island: BELLA PATEMAN. *Robinson Crusoe*, a nautical youth whose wreckular habits secure for him a fling afloat and a cast ashore: MARIE LONGMORE. *Will Atkins*, who is a Wilun, and downright wrong doer. A mute-in-here! But a noizy fellow else-where: JOSEPH IRVING. *Polly Mainbrace*, the Lass who loves a Sailor. A Mainbrace that any fellow would like to splice: Mrs. J. Irving. *The Parish Beadle*, a pillar of the Constitution: Mr. Bloated Boy. *Friday*, Crusoe's servant of all work, and no pay. A "Nigger Heir" of captive'ating manners: ROBERT PATEMAN. *Kickeraboo-The First*, a black king without polish, who tries his hand at a rub with Crusoe, and puts his foot in!: Mr. J. J. WALLACE. *Little Snowball*, the King's favorite Squaw: Miss Chapman. (*Ballet Specialty*: Mlle. JULIE FEDER, Corps de Ballet.)

Scene 1: The Enchanted Island. *Scene 2*: Town of Hull, in the year 1659. *Scene 3*: The Island of Juan Fernandez. The Wreck. The Raft. The Arrival. *Scene 4*: Another part of the Island. *Scene 5*: Interior of Crusoe's Hut. The Dog. The Cat. The Goat. The Parrot. *Scene 6*: A Tangled Brake. Grand Transformation. *Scene 7*: A Nice Country Villa. *Scene 8*: Doctors' and Bakers'. *Scene 9*: Shadow and Sunshine.

MUSICAL NUMBERS, SPECIALTIES

Frolic of the Fairies (Ballet)(Scene 1)
Mlle. J. Feder, Corps de Ballet

Grand Procession of the Tribes (Scene 3)

Entrance of the King and Squaw in their Alligator Chariot, surrounded by their Court, composed of Ostrich Cavalry, Minstrel Troupe, Amazon Warriors, Indian Guards, Negro Guards, Cymbal Dancers, Native Warriors, etc.

"My own, my native Isle" (Soliloquy)(Scene 4)
M. Longmore

Grand Tranformation (Scene 6)
Columbine: Mlle. Julie FEDER. *Harlequina*: Miss CHAPMAN. *Harlequin*: ROBERT PATEMAN. *Pantaloon*: Mr. T. CHAPMAN. *The Bobby*: Mr. Chrisdee. *Clown*: Mr. C. ABBOTT.

Grand Characteristic Polka (Scene 7)
Ladies of the Ballet

Irish Jig (Scene 8)
Mlle. J. Feder, R. Pateman

Song without Words for the Orchestra (Scene 9)

1869.24 LES DRAGONS DE VILLARS, or, The Hermit's Bell

An Opéra-comique in Three Acts[58], in French. Libretto by Lockroy [Joseph Simon] and Eugène Cormon. Music by Aimé Maillart. Stage manager, L. Benedick. Scenery by R. Smith. Costumes by Mons. Marat (Paris). Musical director, Edouard Colonne. Produced by James Fisk, Jr. Opened 10 May 1869 at the Fifth Avenue Theatre and closed 4 June 1869 after 15 performances in repertory.

CAST: *Rose Friquet*, a Peasant Girl: Mlle. IRMA. *Sylvain*, First Farm Hand: Mons. DECRE. *(Sergeant) Belamy*, Officer of Dragoons: Mons. THOLER. *Thibaut*, a Rich Farmer: Mons. LAGRIFFOUL. *Georgette*, his wife: Mlle. DUCLOS. *A Pastor*: Mons. Hamilton. *A Dragoon*: Mons. Rousseau. *A Lieutenant*: Mons. Brunet. *Dragoons, Male and Female Peasants.*

Scene: Un village de la montagne d l'Esterel, vers 1704, à la fin de la guerre des Cévennes.

ACT 1[59]

Introduction

Choeur (Heureux enfants de la Provence)
Mlle. Duclos, Messrs. Lagriffoul, Tholer, 1st & 2nd dessus

Chanson Provençale (Blaise qui partait)
Mlle. Duclos, Choeur

Ariette Militaire (Quand le dragon a bien trotté)
Mons. Tholer

[54]Musical numbers not listed in programs, apart from the notice that Miss Holt's songs were published, and the production features new songs, dances, music, etc.
[55]First produced in New York 6 February 1864 at the Théâtre Français in repertory. For Synopsis of Scenes and Musical Numbers, see original 1864 production.
[56]In its third week, ROBINSON CRUSOE was divided into two acts, with an interval ofter Scene 6, which combined a Tangled Brake with Shadow and Sunshine, including the Song without Words. Act 2 consisted of the Pantomime and remaining scenes, concluding with a new Grand Tableau descriptive of the Ascent of Columbia.
[57]Performed twice daily. Authorship uncredited in programs and posters.

[58]French language premiere in New York. Previously produced in German 22 April 1868 at the Stadttheater.
[59]Musical numbers not listed in programs. List prepared from published French piano vocal score (G. Brandus et S. Dufour, Paris, 1857).

Air (Maître Thibaut vos mules sont charmantes)
Mlle. Irma

Romance (Ne parle pas Rose je t'en supplie)
Mons. Decre

Duo (Allons ma chère)
Mlle. Irma, Mons. Tholer

Couplets de l'ermite (Grace à ce vilain ermite)
Mlle. Duclos

Final (Le bouteselle)
Tous

ACT 2

Scène et Pastorale (Ah! tra la ah! tra la)
Mlle. Irma, Mons. Decre

Duo (Moi, jolie?)
Mlle. Irma, Mons. Decre

Trio (C'est là, c'est là, voilà)
Mlles. Irma, Duclos, Mons. Tholer

Musique Scènique

Prière et Final (Marchons, marchons, sans bruit)
Mlle. Irma, Messrs. Decre, Hamilton, Choeur

ACT 3

Choeur (Vous savez la nouvelle)
Mlle. Duclos, Mons. Lagriffoul

Chanson à boire (Le sage qui s'éveille)
Mons. Tholer

Air (Il m'aime)
Mlle. Irma

Choeur et Ensemble (Allons la belle fiancée)
Mlles. Irma, Duclos, Messrs. Decre, Lagriffoul, Choeur

Musique Scènique

Final (Sonne, sonne toujours)
Tous

PYGMALION,

1869.25 or, The Peerless & Beautiful Statue

A New and Original Burlesque in One Act, 6 Scenes, by William Brough[60]. New music, new dances, new dresses, new scenery, new properties. Scenery by J. S. Schell. Musical director, Howard Glover. Produced by London Burlesque Combination (G. T. Reeder, Proprietor; T. E. Morris, Manager). Opened 15 May 1869 at the Waverley Theatre and closed 25 May 1869 after 10 performances.

CAST: Immortals: *Venus*, the Goddess of Love and Beauty, a character too well-known to require description: Miss EMILY PITT. *Cupid*, her son, another well-known party: Miss LIZZIE WILLMORE. *Psyche*, the same to her and many of them: Miss MARY PITT. *Prettiphare, Verenyce*, Nymphs attendant upon Venus: Misses Emma Bell, Katie Dunn.

Mortals: *King Astyages*, a heavy father with a daughter on his hands, whom he is anxious to "get off"—tryting to light the torch of hymen with the very worst of matches: Mr. CHARLES T. PARLSOE, JR. *Harpagus*, General of the King's Army, an old Soldier, who having seen much service in the wars, now hopes to be of some service in the piece: Mr. JAMES C. DUNN. *Pygmalion*, a renowned sculptor, an artist averse to matrimony—in fact, a confirmed bachelor of Arts—avoiding all women in real life, and even cutting them in marble: Miss MINNIE JACKSON. *Cambyses*, his apprentice, an aspiring youth, who commencing with dreams beyond his station, ultimately attains a station beyond his dreams: Mr. FELIX ROGERS. *Phlunkeyon, Menialides*, Pygmalion's servants, of whom (both being wretched parts) the less the author says the better: Messrs. T. Waddleton, J. Collins. *The Princess Mandane*, an old maid whose pater is anxious to mate her: Mr. BELVIL RYAN. *Mopsa*, a Maid of all work and no play—till now—the present play being the first she has appeared in: Miss ANNIE CAMPION. *(Ballet Specialty*, the Pas de Scarf: Miss BETTY and EMILY RIGL, Corps de Ballet.) *Guards, Lords, Attendants, Shepherds, Pesants, Shepherdesses, etc.*

Semi-Mortal: *The Statue*, Pygmalion's most successful work, an unmistakable "hit" which afterwards becomes an equally unmistakable "miss" made for sale by the Sculptor, but really soul'd by Psyche: Miss JENNY WILLMORE.

Scene 1: The home of Venus on the island of Cyrus. Dance of the Nymphs, their harmony interrupted by a rapid movement in be sharp to escape a discord—the Goddess of love and her ngligent naughty boy—Cupid promises to be, for the future, a good son, and a good darter. *Scene 2*: The Sculptor's Studio. The Artist's Soul—its longings—its shortcomings—in fact, the long and short of it. Royal Visit to the Gallery of Statues. King Astyages is anxious his daughter should not marry too well, although he wants her to get married very badly. A rising lad takes a step up the rising ladder—Pygmalion scorning to Love, Cupid's arrow makes a very pointed attack on him, and brings him to the scratch. Pygmalion and the Statue Fair. *Scene 3*: The Festival of Venus. Merry-making of the peasantry—The Artist's Soul aspires more than ever—approaching marriage in high life. The Goddess of Love and her revenge—Pygmalion's prayer. The Living Statue. *Scene 4*: A Landscape Somewhere Thereabouts. Cupid and Psyche—Their love-making interrupted by the boy's mamma. The departure of the ma celebrated by the execution of a pas—Pygmalion, finding his loved statue without a mind, nearly goes out of his own—The beggar woman! The Soulless Statue! The Kiss and its Consequences! *Scene 5*: Throne Room in the Palace. The wedding breakfast—Singular interruption, followed by very plural interruptions of the marriage festivities—The jilted one—The deserted one—The saved one—The rejected one—The accepted one—General reconciliation, and universal pairing off, by the drawing of several prizes in the Heart Union. *Scene 6*: Up in the clouds. Venus enraged—Cupid however, proving himself a little love, and Psyche a good soul, she concludes, it is hoped a lasting piece, in a Grand Allegorical Tableau "Love's Triumph!" Apotheosis of Pygmalion and the Statue.

HICCORY DICCORY DOCK,

1869.26 or, Harlequin Jack of the Beanstalk!

A Grand Magical, Comical, Pastoral and Peculiarly Pantomimical Pantomime, founded on "Ye Ancient Nursery Rhymes" in Two Acts, 19 Scenes. Play by George L. Fox. Music selected, arranged and conducted by Mons. F. Strebinger. The whole produced under the immediate supervision of George L. Fox. Ballets by Signor Davide Costa, Kiralfy Troupe. Scenery by James E. Hayes, J. A. Johnson. Machinery, tricks, transformations and properties by Robert Cutler. Costumes by Mme. Costa. James E. Hayes, Manager. Opened 18 May 1869 at the Olympic Theatre and closed 4 September 1869 after 110 performances.

CAST: *Hiccory Diccory Dock*, the individual who was called for, when the mouse ran up the clock: GEORGE L. FOX. *Mistress Ancientry Spratt*, the consort of Jack Spratt, who could eat no fat: CHARLES K. FOX. *Jack of the Beanstalk*: FRANK LACY. *Little Red Riding Hood*: Mlle. A. LAURENT. *The Giant Gorgibustor Swallowallup*, a heavy-weight on a large scale: E. T. SINCLAIR. *Trilateraltriptote*, the Three-legged Ogre: Bipeds. *Squire Zenodorus Zoophyte*, of the Manor Born: J. L. LEWIS. *Zenodorus*, the Infant: Miss Raggs. *Fairy Queen of the Beanstalk*: Miss S. SACKETT. *The Lady Zoophyte*, the Squire's better half: Miss Dubious. *Jack's Mother*, who is describedin this somewhat disrespectful manner, from th fact of no chronicler having given Jack's surname: FLORA LEE. *Attenderina*, the Giant's wife: Miss Jackson. *Fullweight*,a Grocer: L. Birchler. *Parlsey*, a Farmer: Mr. Jones. *O. Country*, an Ice Cream Dealer: S. Wright. *Spirit of Mountain Dew*, "in a Scotch Mist": Mr. Connerly. *Spigott*, mine host of Ye "Excise." This individual plays the part of Barrel Organ: M. Quinlan. *Substance Shaver*, a Barber: Mr. Louis. *Slaughter*, a Butcher: J. B. Howland. *Allwaysup*, a Landlord: X. Zeitner. *Judge Correct*, of his own District: E. S. TARR. *Burnemail*,a Lawyer: Mr. Brown. *Yeast*, a Baker: Mr. Thompson. *Steerage*, a Ferryman: Mr. Smith. *Limpy*, a Beggar: Mr. Barney. *Gnawebone, Seizem*, Policemen: Messrs. Peeler, Burns. *Bruin, by the Celebrated Performing Bear, Nondescript*: Master George Topack. *Farmers, Villagers, Townsmen, Police, Soldiers, etc. (Specialty*: Mr. W. C. Ravel.)

Ballet: Mlle. SANGALLI, Signor DAVIDE COSTA; The KIRALFY TROUPE (Imre, Bolossy, Mlle. Haniola Kiralfy; Mlles. Ida, Edelka, Jonka, Susy, Amalli, Katiska, Roska, Nemea); Corps de Ballet.

Act 1, Scene 1: Exterior of Mistress Spratt's Cottage, with Rural Landscape in the Distance. *Scene 2*: The Brazen Castle. *Scene 3*: Interior of the Giant's Castle. *Scene 4*: Turrets and Terrace of the Giant's Castle. *Scene 5*: The Farm Yard. *Scene 6*: Ice Cream Saloon and Grocery Store. *Scene 7*: The Haunt of Fancy. *Scene 8*: Public House and Gold Beater's Establishment. *Scene 9*: The Court Room. *Scene 10*: In the Street. *Scene 11*: "On the Beach."

Act 2, Scene 1: Ruins of an Ancient Abbey. Magic change from Grave to Gay! *Scene 2*: Palace of Dazzling Light. *Scene 3*: In the Hotel. *Scene 4*: The Moonlit Lake. *Scene 5*: Outside the Barber's Shop. *Scene 6*: A Parlor. *Scene 7*: Drawing Room. *Scene 8*: The Streets by Night. Sudden Transformation to the Happy Home of the Fairy of the Beanstalk. Hiccory Diccory's Aerial Voyage by the First "Flying Velocipede" ever known, and his remarkable experiments in airy station, carrying him far beyond the bounds of probability.

[60]Preceded by a fore-piece, the farce, Ici on parle Français, with Miss Jennie Willmore as Anna Maria, and Mr. Felix Rogers as Mr. Spriggins, and supporting cast.

SPECIALTIES, BALLETS[61]

Grand Magical Metamorphosis: (Act 1, Scene 5)

Clown: GEORGE L. FOX. *Pantaloon*: CHARLES K. FOX. *Harlequin*: FRANK LACY. *Columbine*: Mlle. A. LAURENT. *Sprite*: Mr. W. C. RAVEL.

Grand Ballet (Act 1, Scene 7)

The Coral Nymphs

Entire Corps de Ballet

Original and Classical Dance "The Lily"

Mlle. Sangalli

La Tartuffo (Dance)(Act 2, Scene 2)

Mlle. Sangalli

Grand Fancy Dress Ballet (Act 2, Scene 2)

Corps de Ballet

"Our Nations" (Patriotic Song) (Act 2, Scene 2)

W. Neville, Chorus

(*Music and Lyrics by* G. C. Howard.)

Grand Transformation and Hiccory Diccory's Aerial Voyage by the First Flying Velocipede (Act 2, Scene 8)

CLORINDA!
The Girl of the Period/
PETER GRAY,
or, Ding Dong Din

1869.27

A Burlesque in Two Acts, 6 Scenes, followed by an after-piece. Play by Henry J. Byron (from the fairy tale by Charles Perrault). Stage manager, S. H. Verney. Musical director, Signor Giuseppi Operti. Scenery by Ludovico Malmsha. Costumes by S. W. Laureys. Mechanical effects by Denham. Produced by the Tammany Amusement Company (Henry Jarrett and Harry Palmer, proprietors; Leonard Grover, managing director). Opened 24 May 1869 at the Tammany, Grand Theatre and closed 11 June 1869 after 20 performances.

ACT 1

CLORINDA CAST: *Clorinda*, the Baron's eldest daughter, an oldish young person, of the gushing order, very hard upon Thisbe, but remarkably soft upon the Prince: Mr. M. W. LEFFINGWELL. *Prince Poppetti*, Prince of Salerno and of pretty fellows: ALICE HARRISON. *Dandino*, his valet, and a very deep one: EMMA GRATTAN. *Cinderella*, the Baron's youngest daughter—now the story is out: LEONA CAVENDER. *The Baron Balderdash*, a slightly damaged edition of "Last of the Barons": LOUIS MESTAYER. *Buttoni*, a page of the "Last of the Barons": J. J. Wallace. *Alidoro*, the tutor to the Prince: F. Barry. *Thisbe*, the Baron's second daughter: Mrs. W. ANDREWS. *The Fairy Queen*, godmother to all good little girls: Miss Blanche Bradshaw. *Harebell*, a Fay: Miss Laura West. *Honeydew*, one more left of the same sort: Miss Rose Hopgood. *Lords, Ladies, Hunters, Lackeys, Reatiners, Fairies, Mice, Rats, Pumpkins, But why particularize? Ballet*: Mlle. BARETTA. Corps de Ballet.

Act 1, Scene 1: A Forest Dell. *Scene 2*: Apartment at the Baron's.

Act 2, Scene 1: Another Apartment at the Baron's. *Scene 2*: The Baron's Kitchen. *Scene 3*: Corridor in the Prince's Palace. *Scene 4*: Grand Ballroom at the Palace.

ACT 2

Zanfretta's Comic Pantomime[62], PETER GRAY, or, Ding Dong Din, a combination of old Story and Mother Goose, Blow you in the morning, Blow, ye winds, high ho, Blow, blow, blow. Pussy's in the well; who put her in? Many people will be stupid enough to say that this is the Old Ravel Pantomime of Vol au Vent, but they say the same of everything else.

PETER GRAY CAST: *Peter Gray*, creature of mischief: Mr. ALEXANDER ZANFRETTA. *Simple Simon*: Mr. JOSEPH CARON. *Johnny Green*, the one who put her in: Mlle. J. ZANFRETTA. *Annetta*, a sly puss, who would not be put in the well: Mlle. VIOLETTA ZANFRETTA. *John*, son of the Piper: Mr. John W. Wesley. *Peter Piper*, not even permitted to pick his company: Mr. J. Freeman. *Boy Blue*, "If you was I, and I was you," this was that other one: Beppo Zanfretta. First time of Mlle. ZULALIA's Challenge Transept Flight.

IXION!,
or, the Man at the Wheel

1869.28

A Revival of the Burlesque Extravaganza in One Act, 6 Scenes[63]. Play localized and adapted by F. C. Burnand. Scenery by J. S. Schell. Machinery and mechancial effects by Robert Brown. Properties and decorations by Mr. Brockway. New dresses by Mrs. Minnie Moore. Musical director, Harry Widmer. Produced by the London Burlesque Combination (G. T. Reeder, Proprietor; T. E. Morris, Manager). Opened 26 May 1869 at the Waverley Theatre and closed 12 June 1869 after 19 performances.

CAST: Prologue, Mortals: *King Ixion*, ex-King of Thessaly, but though a King with the prefix of an "X", it does not alphabetically follow that he has a wise head on his shoulders: JENNIE WILLMORE. *Tondapameibomenos, Prosephe, Podasokus*, three Thessalians who would be these aliens if they weren't these natives; calumious conspirators, dreadful democrats, members of several secret societies who demand the right of free speaking in a state of free-dumb: Messrs. T. Waddleton, Jones, Collins. *A young Grecian*, first class from the Sixth Ward: H. Stewart. *Queen Dia*, Ixion's disloyal wife, who leads the Revolutionists, and proposes to be a tanner of her husband as well as a Dyer, and tramples on her regal diadem in order to become a regal Democrat: Miss BELL.

Immortals: *Jupiter*, King of the Gods, and the most finished Gentleman in Olympus: Mrs. SEDLEY BROWN. *Mercury*, the celestial telegraph boy: MINNIE JACKSON. *Ixion*, who being bankrupt and sadly in want of change, is, in spite of his bad character in his former situation, "taken" up by Jupiter and patronized by the "upper ten": JENNIE WILLMORE. *Juno*, Queen of the Gods and Jove's spouse, described by Poets as the Ox-eyed Lady, and consequently of a mettlesome temperament; fond of peacocks that sing Pea-hens of joy while drawing her car: LIZZIE WILLMORE. *Venus*, the Goddess of Beauty; still a spinster, although it has been said by a great authority that "Venus orta Mari," which being translated in "Venus ought to marry": ANNIE CAMPION. *Cupid*, the son of Venus, who will at once be recognized as Love at First Sight: MARY PITT. *Minerva*, Goddess of Wisdom, a remarkably strong-minded lady, the defender of her own rights and woman's wrongs: FELIX ROGERS. *Apollo*, secretary to the Imperial Sun Fire Insurance Company (Ltd.): Miss EMILY PITT. *Bacchus*, promoter and chief director of the Celestial Whiskey Ring Association: BELVIL RYAN. *Mars*, Commander-in-Chief, as Ma's generally are: CHARLES T. PARSLOE, JR. *Ganymede*, Jupiter's beautiful "Buttons," a nice active lad, the original Fat Boy who may be described as Ganny-mede and Ganny-purse un too: JAMES C. DUNN. *Diana*: Miss Dunn. *Vista*: Miss Sheldon. *Ceres*: Miss Tayleure. *Clerk of the Weather*: Mr. Perry. *Citizen*: Mr. Smith. *Apollo's Tiger*: Master Johnny Denham. *Dance Specialty*: Misses BETTY and EMILY RIGL.

SINDBAD THE SAILOR,
or, The Ungenial Geni and the Little Cabin Boy!!

1869.29

The Lydia Thompson Troupe in a Gorgeous Arabian Night-mare-ish Burlesque Extravaganza in Two Acts, 13 Scenes. Play by Henry B. Farnie. Music selected and arranged by Michael Connelly. Produced under the direction of L. J. Vincent. Scenery by William Voegtlin. Machinery and mechanical effects by Benson Sherwood. Costumes by S. W. Laureys, Miss Lewis. Properties and appointments by Benedict. Produced by Henry Jarrett and Harry Palmer. Opened 29 May 1869 at Niblo's Garden and closed 31 July 1869 after 64 performances.

CAST[64] (in order of appearance): *The Messenger Gnome*: Mr. DeSolla. *Dress, Pleasure,Wine, Cards, Turf*, Spirits: Misses Strickland, Whitlock, Dutton, Crossen, Lyndwood. *The Fairy, Hope*: Clara Thompson. *The Ungenial Geni*: HARRY BECKETT. *Sindbad*: LYDIA THOMPSON. *El Capitano Judh-kintz*: ***. *The Chief Cook*

---

[61]Added after opening (June 1869):

Magyar Csardás (Grand Sensational Hungarian Divertissement)(Act 1)

Kiralfy Troupe

"Sailors Ashore" Dance

Kiralfy Troupe

[62]PETER GRAY was replaced shortly by M W. Leffingwell as Romeo Jaffier Jenkins, in a nonsense specialty, Too Much for Good Nature, with Messrs. J. J. Wallace, J. Freeman, Louis Mestayer, Misses Emma Grattan, Leona Cavender, Blanche Bradshaw, E. Andrews, A. Robertson, Rose Hopgood, Willis.

[63]First produced in New York 28 September 1868 at Wood's Museum and Metropolitan Theatre for 2 engagements totalling 120 performances. For Synopsis of Scenes and Musical Numbers, see original 1868 production.

[64]The asterisks in the program below are as they appear in the original programs.

and Bottle-Washer: Mr. Burke. *The Sheriff of Bagdad*: George F. Ketchum. *Hafiz, Selim*, Swells of the Period: Bessie Harding, Maggie Desmond. *Ali Ben Drygoods*: Mr. Cahill. *Koh-i-noor*, his daughter: PAULINE MARKHAM. *The Hadji Blimber*, a College Don: W. J. HILL. *Stevedores*, loading the steamer: Messrs. Gripit, Rollit, Hoistit, Loreit, Bangit, Haulit, Shuntit, etc. *General Baboobangabout: A Native with a Toothache: Full Privates*: Gobble, Hobble, Nobble, Bobble, Black, Dirty, Grim, Shady, Umbrageous and other cannibals in the service of Queen Sootyphiz. *Queen Sootyphiz*, an amiable Cannibal: ***. *The Old Man of the Sea*: ***. *His Pirate Band*: Messrs. Prowl, Skulk, Shirk, Stab, etc. *The Pigmy Champion*: ***. *7000 Pigmy Soldiers*: Whose names we refrain from giving in detail. *The Sultan*: Mr. DeSolla. *A Turkish Matrimonial Agent*: ***. *Bul-Bul*, the Imperial favorite: ***. *The Chief of the Eunuchs*: ***. *Subsidiary Eunuchs*: ***. *The Grand Viziere*: ***. *The Auctioneers's Clerk*: ***. *A fat believer*: Mr. Chapman. *1st—Circassian*: ***. *2nd—Circassian*: ***. *3rd—Houri*: ***. *4th—Opportunity*: ***. *5th—Catch*: ***. *Demons, Imps, Gnomes, Negro Pages, Paseengers, for Parts Unknown, Ladies of the Seraglio, Attendants, Musselmans, Palaanquin-Bearers, Troops, Slaves, etc.*

THE CLODOCHE TROUPE, Specialty from Paris: Messrs. Clodoche, Flageolet, Normande, La Comete.

Act 1, Scene 1: The Demons' Rendezvous, near the Bassorah Shore. *Scene 2*: The Port of Bassorah. *Scene 3*: The Main-Deck of the Ocean Steamer. *Scene 4*: Shore of the Savage Island. Distant view of the Wreck. *Scene 5*: The Bamboo Palace of Queen Sootyphiz. *Scene 6*: The Diamond Valley of Alaska.

Act 2, Scene 1: The Pirates' Lair on the Coast of Pigmy Island. *Scene 2*: The Pigmy Capital. *Scene 3*: The Hollow Vine Wood in the Pigmy Island. *Scene 4*: A Corridor in the Imperial Harem, Constantinople. *Scene 5*: The Matrimonial Market of the Period. *Scene 6*: The Gardens of the Seraglio, by moonlight! *Scene 7*: Interior of the Harem!! Moonlit Groves of the Palace of Sweet Waters!

BALLETS, SPECIALTIES[65]

"Go A-head!"
H. Beckett

"The Great Velocipede Song"
L. Thompson

Song (Act 1, Scene 1)
C. Thompson, H. Beckett

Grand Hornpipe (Act 1, Scene 3)
L. Thompson

Soliloquy (Act 1, Scene 4)
L. Thompson

The Clodoche Troupe (Act 2, Scene 7)

[65]Songs not listed in programs. Not in performance order. List prepared from published sheet music, etc.

1869–1870 SEASON

Jennie Worrell
Billy Rose Theatre Collection, New York Public Library for the Performing Arts

1869–1870 SEASON

1869.30 CHILPÉRIC

An Opéra-bouffe in Three Acts, 4 Scenes, in French. Libretto, music and lyrics by Hervé. Régisseur, Paul Juignet. Scenery by Hannibal Calyo. Costumes by Mme. Armand and Mons. Philippe. Conductor, Robert Stoepel. Chorus director, Mons. Gambogi. Produced by Jacob Grau. Opened 1 June 1869 at the Théâtre Français and closed 7 June 1869 after 6 performances in repertory.

CAST: *Chilpéric*, King of France: Mons. CARRIER. *Ricin*, Royal Physician: Mons. BECKERS. *Sigebert*, Chilpéric's brother: Mons. GINOT. *Le Grand Légendaire* (Great Historian), Chilpéric's factotum: Mons. BOURGOIN. *Don Nervoso*: Mons. Francis. *Leucaste*: Mons. Deligne. *Major Domo*: Mons. Brag. *Diviaticus*, Chief of the Druids: Mons. CHOPIN. *Frédégonde*: Mlle. ROSE-BELL. *Galsuinthe*, betrothed to Chilpéric: Mlle. DESCLAUZAS. *Brunehaut*, Sigebert's wife: Mlle. GUERETTI. *Landry*, peasant: Mlle. Rizarelli. *Fana*, priestess: Mlle. Gueretti. *Alfred*, first page: Mlle. V. Maurice. *Mad. Chapuis*: Mlle. Mussay. *Pages (7)*: *Gustave*: Mlle. Villiers. *Charles*: Mlle. Rosa. *Ernest*: Mlle. Rachel. *Emile*: Mlle. Victorine. *Hector*: Mlle. Vandamme. *Edouard*: Mlle. Faustine.

Act 1: Lethéâtre represente un forêt.

Act 2: Une grande salle du Palais à Soissons.

Act 3, Scene 1: La Chambre Nuptiale de Galsuinthe. *Scene 2*: Camp de Chilpéric.

ACT 1[1]
- Solo (Prêtres d'Ésus)
  - Mons. Chopin
- Druids' Chorus (Coupe le gui selon nos usage)
  - Chorus
- Grand Ensemble (Prêtres d'Esus)
  - Mons. Chopin, Chorus
- Légende du Chilpéric (Voyze cette figure)
  - Mlle. Rose-Bell
- Choeur des Chasseurs (Que nos voix dans les bois)
  - Chorus of Hunters
- Chanson du Jambon (Un jour le grand Pharamond)
  - Mons. Carrier, Chorus
- Quatuor (Divine Frédégonde)
  - Messrs. Carrier, Ginot, Mlles. Gueretti, Rose-Bell
- Final (A ton désir nous nous rendons)
  - Messrs. Chopin, Carrier, Druids, Druidesses

ACT 2
- Couplets (Je suis nerveuse)
  - Mlle. Mussay
- Choeur de Pages (Il est dix heures, c'est l'instant)
  - Mlle. V. Maurice
- Romance (Dans la grandeur)
  - Mlle. Rizarelli
- Chanson du Petit Papillon Bleu (Petit papillon bleu volage)
  - Mons. Carrier
- Air (En tout affaire)
  - Mons. Beckers
- Chant du Pastour (Sur les côteaux, pauvre pastour)
  - Mlles. Rizarelli, Gueretti
- Scene (O ciel! que vient-on de m'apprendre?)
  - Mlle. Rose-Bell, Mons. Carrier
- Scene (Je viens vous annonçer le Grand Légendaire)
  - Mons. Carrier, Chorus
- Boléro (À la sierra Morena)
  - Mlle. Desclauzas, Chorus
- Lamentations de Frédégonde (Loin de ces lieux)
  - Mlle. Rose-Bell
- Chorus (Ah! que c'est donc amusant)
  - Chorus

ACT 3

Scene 1
- Rondo (Chantons, buvons! Vidon les flacons)
  - Pages
- Couplets (Passerez-vous la nuit tranquille?)
  - Mlle. V. Maurice
- Trio (De Singapour au Kamtschatka)
  - Messrs. Beckers, Bourgoin, Mlle. V. Maurice
- Air (Nuit fortunée)
  - Mlle. Rose-Bell, Chorus
- Duetto (Loin des armes, du bruit)
  - Mlle. Desclauzas, Mons. Carrier
- Fandango (De pampelune à Saragosse)
  - Mlle. Desclauzas
- Choeur des Pages (O! surprise! O! crainte!)
  - Pages

Scene 2
- Marche de l'Armée Gauloise (L'ennemi fuit éperdu)
  - Chorus
- Chant Gauloise (Cors et cymbles)
  - Mons. Carrier, Chorus
- Final Général (Cors et cymbales)
  - Mons. Carrier, All

1869.31 IXION!, or, the Man at the Wheel

A Revival of the Humorous Mythological Burlesque in One Act, 5 Scenes[2]. Scenery designed by William Scheaffer, Mr. Weed. Machinery by William Crane. Appointments and mountings by Frank Farrel. Costumes by Mr. Keyser. Illuminated effects by Thomas W. Newton. Musical director, B. Deane. Produced by W. B. Frelich. Opened 7 June 1869 at the Bowery Theatre and closed 18 June 1869 after 9 performances in repertory.

Ixion: FANNY HERRING. *Minerva*: Mr. GEORGE BROOKES. *Mercury*: Miss JENNY CLIFFORD. *Jupiter*: Miss CASSIE TROY. *Venus*: MAGGY PARKER. *Cupid*, the Boy with the Dart: Miss ANNIE NEWMAN. *Juno*: Miss KATE COLLINS. *Apollo*: Miss Fenton. *Queen Dia*, a Queen as is a Queen: Mr. WALSH. *Ganymede*, on a Strike: Mr. J. McCLOSKY. *Bacchus*: Mr. J. H. BOWERS. *Mars*: Mr. Seabert. *Tondapameibomenos*: Mr. SEABERT. *Podasokeesdoeay*: Mr. Murray. *Prosphe*: Mr. Kirk. *Diana*: Mr. Frank Davenport. *Clerk of the Weather*: Mr. Mason. *Vesta*: Miss Crompton. *Apollo's Tiger*: Mr. Taylor. *Ceres*: Nelly Davenport.

Scene 1: Ruins of a Temple of Jupiter in Thessaly. *Scene 2*: The Vault of the Sky. *Scene 3*: Juno's Drawing Room. *Scene 4*: Apollo's Private Room in the Olympian Government's Sun Light Fire and Insurance Office. *Scene 5*: Cupid's Chateau d'Espagne.

1869.32 BEPPO

A Rollicking Burlesque of (Daniel Auber's) 'Fra Diavolo' in One Act[3], 5 Scenes, by Henry J. Byron. New scenery, new dresses, new songs, new dances. Stage manager, S. H. Verney. Musical director, Signor Giuseppe Operti. Produced by the Tammany Amsuement Company (Messrs. Henry Jarrett and Harry Palmer, proprietors; Leonard Grover, managing director). Opened 12 June 1869 at the Tammany, Grand Theatre and closed 19 June 1869 after 8 performances.

CAST: *Beppo*, a particularly heavy Ruffian, not troubled with the faintest outline of a conscience, or indeed, with anything but the conventional hoarseness peculiar to melodramatic Brigands (in a sanguinary and ferocious caricature of Edwin Forrest, Esq.): M. W. LEFFINGWELL. *Fra Diavolo*, an amiable and captivating creature with a weakness for Jewelry and Flirtation, although a large price is set upon him, decidedly unlikely to be sold: Miss EMMA GRATTAN. *Lorenzo*, an Officer of Police who haunts

[1]List of musical numbers, scenes and additional cast detail prepared from published French-English librettto for Jacob Grau's production at the Théâtre Français (New York, 1869).

[2]First produced in New York in different version by F. C. Burnand 28 September 1868 at Wood's Museum for 120 performances in 2 engagements.

[3]First produced in London in 1858 as FRA DIAVOLO, or The Beauty and the Brigands. Followed by Leffingwell's great comic specialty, Romeo Jaffier Jenkins, in the comedy, Too Much for Good Nature, with supporting cast. After which, Classic Trapeze with Mons. Ventini and Mlle. Zuleila, and the Challenge Transept Flight of 120 Feet, by Mlle. Zuleila.

theTavern containing his sweetheart. In fact, an Inn-Spectre—a youth whose figure will prevent his attaining any height in his profession: Mr. LOUIS MESTAYER. *Lord Allcash*, an English Nobleman, making the Grand Tour and himself as agreeable as possible—the invariable custom of travelling Britons: Mr. J. J. Wallace. *Francesco*, an extensive young Farmer: Miss A. Robertson. *Matteo*, Landlord of the Jolly Brigands, who refuses to allow his child to marry a man of no small means—the monster: Mr. F. Barry. *Giacomo*, a promising young Bandit: Mr. J. Westley. *Antonio*: Mr. J. Freeman. *Zerlina*, the Beauty of the Village, and Barmaid of the Jolly Brigands: Miss LEONA CAVENDER. *Lady Allcash*, a lady making her first Tour: Miss BLANCHE BRADSHAW. *Caribineers, Male and Female Peasants.*

Scene 1: Exterior of the 'Jolly Brigands.' *Scene 2*: Another. *Scene 3*: Zerlina's Chamber. *Scene 4*: Another part of the premises. *Scene 5*: At the 'Jolly Brigands.'

SPECIALTIES, MUSICAL NUMBERS

Operatic Selections (Scene 2)

A Soliloquy, a Song and a Pas Seul (Scene 3)
Miss Cavender

Grand Pas de Recollection (Scene 5)
M. W. Leffingwell, Mr. Westley

ARRAH-NA-POGUE,
1869.33 or, The Wicklow Wedding

A Revival of the Grand Spectacular (Irish) Drama in Three Acts[4]. Play by Dion Boucicault and E. H. House. Stage manager, L. J. Vincent. Musical director, Signor Giuseppe Operti. Scenic artist, William F. Voegtlin. Mechanical effects, Benson Sherwood, J. Leo. Costumes by S. W. Laureys. Appointments by Benedict. Produced by Henry Jarrett and Harry Palmer. Opened 2 August 1869 at Niblo's Garden and closed 4 September 1869 after 30 performances.

CAST: *Shaun the Post*, a Wicklow Carman: DAN BRYANT. *Colonel Bagenal O'Grady*, the O'Grady: ALEX. FITZGERALD. *Beamish McCoul*, the McCoul: JAMES CARDEN. *Major Coffin*, an English officer: C. H. Rockwell. *The Secretary*: J. R. Healy. *The Sergeant*: G. F. Ketchum. *Michael Feeny*: DOMINICK MURRAY. *Winterbottom*, the Valet: J. W. BRUTONE. *Oiny Farrell*: G. C. Charles. *Andy Regan*: N. McIntyre. *Lanagan*: W. Daly. *Patsy*: G. Chapman. *Tim Cogan*: J. LYNCH.

Arrah Meelish, nicknamed by the peasantry 'Arrah na Pogue," or Arrah of the Kiss: ROSE EYTINGE. *Fanny Power*, of Cabinteely: JOSEPHINE FIDDES. *Katty*: J. Burke. *Peasants, Peasant Girls, Soldiers, Beggars, etc.*

ACT 1

"The Barn Door Jig"
J. Lynch, J. Burke, D. Bryant

"The Wearing of the Green"
D. Bryant
(*Lyrics by* Dion Boucicault and E. H. House.)

LALLA ROOKH,
1869.34 or, The Prophet Unveiled

The Great London Burlesque in Two Acts by Ben A. Baker. Stage manager, Ben A. Baker. Scenery by Joseph B. Ayers. Properties by George Denham. Leader of orchestra, Fred W. Zaulig. Produced by George Wood. Opened 2 August 1869 at Wood's Museum and closed 21 August 1869 after 18 performances.

CAST: *Lalla Rookh*, the Beautiful: JENNIE WORRELL. *Feramorz*, a Troubadour: SOPHIE WORRELL. *Khossenbad*: Edward Coleman. *Aurungzebe*: Charles H. Morton. *Fadladeen*: George Lingard. *Nogo*: J. P. Johnson. *Trybac*: Mr. Hurley. *Hafed*: Miss Kate O'Neil. *Hinda*: Miss Hattie O'Neil. *Namonne*: Carmelyte Aiken. *Laloute*: Miss Page. *Ret-chid*: Mr. Johnson. *No-grayt-shakes*: Mr. Hagan. *Lazie Bones*: Mr. Haley. (*Ballet Specialty*: Mlle. EUGENIE OBERTI, Mons. BAPTISTIN.) *Ghebers, Fire Worshippers, Ambassadors, Soldiers, Fairies*: Corps of Auxiliaries.

BALLETS, SPECIALTIES

Pas Comique (Act 1)
Mlle. E. Oberti

Grand Pas de Deux (Act 2)
Mlle. E. Oberti, Mons. Baptistin

THE QUEEN OF HEARTS,
or, Harlequin, the Knave of Hearts,
who stole the Tarts, and
1869.35 the Old Woman that Lived in a Shoe

A Spectacular Fairy Extravaganza and Pantomime in Three Acts, 14 Scenes. Scenery by L. Malmsha, William F. Voegtlin, and Hannibal Calyo. Costumes by S. W. Laureys. Properties by Talfourd and Lane. Ballets arranged by John Lauri. Water calciums and gas under the direction of John Silvester. Machinist, J. C. Denham. Stage management and direction, S. H. Verney. Orchestra under the direction of Richard Arnold. Produced by the Tammany Amusement Company (Messrs. Henry Jarrett and Harry Palmer, proprietors). Opened 16 August 1869 at the Tammany, Grand Theatre and closed 2 October 1869 after 48 performances.

CAST: *King of Hearts*, a Potentate and great card: J. B. CURRAN. *Queen of Hearts*, Wife of his buzzum: LOUIS MESTAYER. *Prince Euchre*, who goes it alone: ALICE HARRISON. *Right Bower, Left Bower*, Her Pages: Misses Annie Cornforth, May Robinson. *Knight of the Ugly Mug*, the very bad one: A. H. Sheldon. *Florizel*, the rightful heir: PAULINE MARKHAM. *Sairah*, for whom the bells go ringing: Maggie Desmond. *Water Lily*, a Good Fairy: Ida Geddes. *Knave of Hearts*, who stole the Tarts: CHARLES LAURI. *The Old Woman*, who lived in a shoe: HENRY LAURI. *Mother Redcap, Mother Bunch*, full-blown Witches: Messrs. Hatfield, Harry St. Clair. *Chamberlain*, Supreme Lunkhead: Mr. Snodgrass. *Generalissimo*: Mr. Vining. *King-at-arms, Herald, Ring Master, and Rag, Tag, Bobtail, the (3) Progeny of the Old Woman, etc.*: Mr. Freeman's students. (*Ballet*: John, Charles and Harry Lauri, Mme. Lauri, Corps de Ballet.)

Act 1, Scene 1: Broomstick Glen by Moonlight. *Scene 2*: Home of the Water Lily. (Voegtlin.) *Scene 3*: A Lone Glade in the Haunted Wood. (Malmsha.) *Scene 4*: Boudoir of the Princess Euchre. (Malmsha.) *Scene 5*: Card Castle. (Malmsha.)

Act 2, Scene 1: A Lonely Forest Path. *Scene 2*: The Brown Leather High Stoop Shoe. (Malmsha and Denham.) *Scene 3*: Village Street. *Scene 4*: On the Beach at Long Branch. (From a sketch by Calyo.)

Act 3, Scene 1: Ramparts of the Ugly Mug Castle. (Malmsha.) *Scene 2*: The Lists (Malmsha.) *Scene 3*: Harlequin Villa and Pantaloon Home. *Scene 4*: A Séance with the Spirits. *Scene 5*: Home of the Fairy Water Lily.

ACT 1

Scene 1

"Hark! Hark! The dogs do bark. The Witches are coming to town"
Chorus

Scene 2

Shells of the Ocean (Grand Ballet)

"I Gathered shells from day to day"
J. Lauri, Mme. Lauri, Grand Corps de Ballet

Scene 5

Game at Cards (Grand Ballet)

Pas de Quatre Comique
Four Knaves (4 Lauris), Corps de Ballet

ACT 2

Scene 2

The Old Woman Who Lived in a Shoe
The Old Woman That Lived in a Shoe: H. Lauri. *Bobby*: Charles Lauri. *Tommy*: E. Lauri. *Rest of the Troublesome Children.*

Scene 4

Grand Croquet Ballet
Girls of the Period

ACT 3

Scene 2

Double Skating Act (The beginners)
Moe and Goodrich

"The Rosebud" (Song and Dance)
Grand Corps of Comic Dancers, arranged by Robert Newcomb

Fricassee Dance
Corps de Ballet

Agonizing Melee/Transformation
Harlequin: John Lauri. *Columbine*: Madame Lauri. *Clown*: Charles Lauri. *Paantaloon*: Henry Lauri. *Policeman*: Edward Lauri. *Swell*: H. St. Clair.

[4]First produced in New York 12 July 1865 at Niblo's Garden for 66 performances; returned 15 November 1865 to Niblo's Garden for an additional 24 performances; returning 25 December 1866 to the New Bowery Theatre for an additional 12 performances. Total: 102 performances. For Synopsis of Scenes, see original 1865 production.

Scene 3
Trombone Solo by Lauri
Scene 4
A Séance with the Spirits
E. Lauri

1869.36 MASANIELLO

A Local and Musical Burlesque in One Act, preceded by a burletta. Burlesque by the Zavistowski Sisters. Scenery by Joseph B. Ayers. Properties by Charles LaForrest. Produced under the direction of C. W. Barry. Orchestra by Professor Yonkers. Produced by George Wood. Opened 13 September 1869 at Wood's Museum and closed 18 September 1869 after 6 matinee performances; returned in shortened form 11-16 October 1869 on a bill with WIP WAN WINKLE for an additional 6 performances.

KOLIN, a Laughable Burletta.

CAST: *Kolin*: EMMELINE ZAVISTOWSKI. *Father Philip*: Mr. Rooeny. *Rinaldo*: Mr. barnes. *Eliza*: ALICE ZAVISTOWKSI. *Governess*: Miss Jackson. Incidental to the farce, a duet by Emmeline and Alice Zavistowski.

MASANIELLO CAST: *Aristocrats*: *Alphanso*, Prince of Somewhere—Attached to the Spanish Embassy at the Court of Naples, also to Elvira: Miss ALICE ZAVISTOWSKI. *Lorenze*, his friend: Miss Lisette Bernard. *Elvira*, Princess of Somewhere Else (the locality being uncertain)—Attached to the Attaché above alluded to: Mr. Morton.

Plebians: *Masaniello*, Fishmonger and General Dealer. "Whitebait dinner provided. Country orders attended to on the shortest notice." (Vide Card.) The Greatest Plebian of the Common Lot: Miss EMMELINE ZAVISTOWKSI. *Fenella*, the Fisho'man of Naples—a Young lady suffering from a severe attack of blighted affections, but who never told her love, because she couldn't—Played on this occasion, as on all previous ones, by a dummy: Miss CHRISTINE ZAVISTOWSKI. *Pietro, Borella, Coreno*, Rowers in the same boat: Messrs. Marsden, DeBoney, Collins. *Selva*, otherwise 7 of the B Division—the myrmidon of a Despotic Government: G. C. Charles. *Billibario, Doggia*, Gamins of Naples: Misses Thompson, Jackson. *Suzanna* a waiting Maid, Waiting to be asked in marriage: Miss A. Logan. *Tolla Contadini, Guida Galigani, Betta Martini*, Ladies of the Halle: Misses Teresa Wood, DeWitt, Brown.

1869.37 WIP WAN WINKLE

A new and by no means somnolent Cats-kill-ian Burlesque in Three Acts, with new and startling effects, brilliant dialogue, sparkling songs, fantastic dances, original tableaux and thrilling incidents. Play by James Barnes (suggested by Joseph Jefferson's drama 'Rip Van Winkle.') Scenery by Joseph B. Ayers. Properties by Charles LaForrest. Produced under the direction of C. W. Barry. Orchestra by Professor Yonkers. Produced by George Wood. Opened 20 September 1869 at Wood's Museum and closed 16 October 1869 after 18 performances[5].

CAST: *Wip-Wan-Winkle*, the Original Loafer, a young Rip, who comes to grief by sleeping from home, and who, as a sleeper, justly claims the Champion Belt: Miss EMMELINE ZAVISTOWSKI. *Willie-Von-Swillen*, a young Dutch gallant, considered by the ladies a festive cuss, and in his own estimation the prince of lady killer: Miss ALICE ZAVISTOWSKI. *Erieifiskiana*, the Demon of the Kaatskill, the name being "Irish," will be new of course to people of our day, but children of 80 summers will remember having to read of his awful doings in the year 1, in Bergh's Book on 'Crulety to Animals': GEORGE C. CHARLES. *Dann-der-Hedder*, a block head of a Landlord, who glories in having evaded the Excise Law: James Collins. *King Arthur*, the unfortunate victim of the Round Table, a mythical cuss: George A. Archer. *Q-Rius-Duphar*, avery inquisitive cove, in pursuit of knowledge: JAMES BARNES. *Gripsack Von Smith, Sweitzer Case, Von Bluffenberg*, (3) Big Headed Dutchmen: Messrs. A. J. DeBoney, Broderip, McGregor. *Zephyr*, the Fairy Queen, *a very airy creature, and champion masher of Fairy Land*: Miss CHRISTINE ZAVISTOWSKI. *Katarina Von Sassell*, Rip's early love, and cause of all his troubles: Miss T. WOOD. *Bertha*, Willie's Darling, a being to be loved and cherished: LISETTE BERNARD. *Gretchen*, Willie's worser half, a decidedly Dutch importation, as observed "Walking Down Broadway:" Mr. John Morton. *Lillybell*, a Fairy Sprite: Miss C. Thompson. *Fairies, Peasants, Demons, etc.*

Between Acts 1 and 2, 20,000 years are supposed to elapse. Between Acts 2 and 3, another long relapse. During the piece, A. J. DeBoney's Great Franco-German-American Clod-Hoche Troupe from Penn-Yan, will appear. These unrivalled Artistes receive such immense salaries and wear such gorgeous apparel, that they must be seen to be appreciated. The piece will terminate with the great novel American Can-Can, by Misses Emmeline, Alice and Christine Zavistowski.

[5]In its final week 11-16 October 1869, WIP WAN WINKLE and MASANIELLO shared the evening bill in shortened form.

1869.38 FLICK FLOCK

A new delightful and highly Sensational Pantomime Burlesque Fairy Extravaganza in Three Acts, adapted expressly for the American stage by Mlle. Rita Sangalli. Music arranged by Signor J. Aberle. Whole production under the direction of Mlle. Rita Sangalli, and Mr. C. W. Barry. Stage Manager. Scenery by Joseph B. Ayers and Robert Grain. Preperties by Charles LaForrest. Costumes by M. Lafont and Williams. Illusions and effects by Signor Sangalli. Produced by George Wood. Opened 18 October 1869 at Wood's Museum and closed 6 November 1869 after 18 performances.

CAST: *Djini*: Mlle. RITA SANGALLI. *Stella*: Mlle. RITA SANGALLI. *Clotilde de Villarville*: Mlle. RITA SANGALLI. *Queen of Dreams*: Mlle. RITA SANGALLI. *Phenicia*, Première Danseuse: Mlle. RITA SANGALLI. *Sangalli Troupe*: Mlles. Rachel De Francesco, Marie De Francesco, Josephine Strodel, Bertha Rupert, Josephine Micheline, Rosa Albertini.

Don Fernand, a young Naval Lieutenant: T. W. KEENE. *Nikobar*, a Brahmin Alchemist: FRANK EVANS. *Flick*, taking the disguises of Alcindor, Vivargenti, Cibouk: Mr. J. M. WARD. *Flock*: JAMES BARNES. *Marquis d'Arguilar*: George A. Archer. *Sakemor*, Chief of the Gipsies: W. J. Fleming. *Mahut Ali Pacha*, Oriental Major: George Charles. *Chief Brahmin*: J. S. Rooney. *A French Lord*: Mr. J. Collins. *Fly's Wing*: J. DeBoney. *Raouki*, a Young Gipsy: H. D. Lisle. *Mousseline*, a Young Indian Maiden, in the service of Nikobar: Olivia Rand. *The Baroness*: Miss Noble. *Jedda*, Oriental Hostess: Comte Thompson. *Forresters, Wood Cutters, Soldiers, Brahmins, Mutes, Slaves, Lords, Students, Gipsies*, Numerous Corps of Auxiliaries.

SPECIALTIES

"La Sangalli" (Singing a new set of Waltzes composed expressly for Mlle. Sangalli by Signor Paolo Giorza)

1869.39 ALADDIN, or, The WonderfuL Scamp

A Screaming Burlesque in One Act[6]. Produced by George Wood. Opened 15 November 1869 at Wood's Museum and closed 27 November 1869 after 11 performances.

CAST: *Aladdin*: CLELIA HOWSON. *Sultan*: J. M. Ward. *Vizier*: John Morton. *Pekoe*: Therese Wood. *Abanazar*: James Barnes. *Teto Tum*: Mr. J. Collins. *Slave of the Lamp*: Mr. J. deBoney. *Genius of the Ring*: Miss C. Thompson. *Widow Twankay*: Mr. JOHN J. HOWSON. *Princess Badroulboudour*: ALICE LOGAN. *Maidens, Mandarins and Mob.*

1869.40 FIRE-FLY!

A Revival of the Military Drama in Five Acts, 17 Scenes[7]. Play by Edmund Falconer (adapted from Ouida's novel "Under Two Flags"). Stage manager, L. J. Vincent. Scenery by William Voegtlin. Costumes, effects and appointments by Laureys, Benson Sherwood and H. Benedict. Musical conductor and composer, Signor Giuseppe Operti. Produced by Henry Jarrett and Harry Palmer. Opened 22 November 1869 at Niblo's Garden and closed 4 December 1869 after 14 performances.

CAST: *Fire-Fly*, the Friend of the Flag: LOTTA (CRABTREE). *Harold Cecil*, passing as Louis Victor: J. H. TAYLOR. *Duke of Lyonnaise*, friend to Louis: GEORGE AIKEN. *Berkley Cecil*: FRED MAEDER. *Ben Arslan*, a Zouave: H. A. Rendle. *Rake*, Harold's own man: Felix A. Vincent. *Colonel Chateauroy*: George Metkiff. *Marshall McDonald*: A. D. BRADLEY. *Shadrick Levi*: Edward Coleman. *Claude Churillon*: A. S. Vaughan. *Alcide*: E. Collier. *Beauchamp*: E. Kidder. *Milbanks*: A. S. Carpenter. *Barbe Grise*: W. Daly. *Arab Sheik*: J. T. Ward. *First Arab*: J. Williams. *Orderly*: G. Green. *Tata Leroux*: J. W. Brutone. *Venetia*, Princess of Corona: KATE NEWTON. *Marquise de Renardier*: Miss Edwards. *Attendant*: Miss Strickland. *French Soldiers, Passengers, Servants, Arabs, News Venders, etc.*

In the course of the piece, Lotta will sing two new songs, composed expressly for her by Signor (Giuseppe) Operti, Musical Conductor, entitled "Up to G" and "Fire-Fly." The Band will perform a new Military Overture by the same composer.

[6]Presented in the evenings only the first week, and weekday matinees the second week. Followed by an after-piece, Pretty Horsebreaker, with Clelia and John Howson and Company. No additional detail in programs.
[7]First produced in New York as FIREFLY, or, The Friend of the Flag, 10 August 1868 at Wallack's Theatre for 24 performances. For Synopsis of Scenes and Musical Numbers, see original 1868 production. Some programs appear as FIRE-FLY!, others merely as FIRE FLY.

1869.41 THE BOHEMIAN GIRL

A Revival of the Light Opera in Three Acts[8]. Libretto by Alfred Bunn (after Jules-Henri Vernoy de Saint-Georges' ballet-pantomime "The Gypsy"). Music by Michael William Balfe. Stage director, James G. Peakes. Conductor, S. Behrens. Costumer, Martha Thornton. Produced by Caroline Richings Bernard English Opera Company (A. S. Pennoyer, Business Manager). Opened 22 November 1869 at the Grand Opera House in repertory; season closed 11 December 1869.

CAST: *Count Arnheim*: HENRY DRAYTON. *Thaddeus*: HENRY HAIGH. *Devilshoof*: HENRY C. PEAKES. *Florestine*: Walter Birch. *Captain of the Guard*: J. Murphy. *Arline*: CAROLINE RICHINGS BERNARD; Mrs. HENRY DRAYTON; EMMA HOWSON. *Queen of the Gipsies*: Anna Mischka. *Buda*: Miss Massen. *Nobles, Soldiers, Retainers, Chorus, etc. Ballet*: RITA SANGALI BALLET TROUPE, assisted by Mons. E. Van Hamme, Six Premières.

KENILWORTH,
1869.42 or, Ye Queene, Ye Earle and Ye Maydenne

A Revival of the Historical Burlesque in One Act, 7 Scenes[9]. (Burlesque by Andrew Halliday and Frederic Lawrence, founded on Walter Scott's novel of the same name.) Music arranged by Mr. Yonkers. Produced under the direction of C. W. Barry, Stage Manager. Produced by George Wood. Opened 29 November 1869 at Wood's Museum and Menagerie and closed 1 January 1870 after 39 performances[10].

CAST: *Queen Elizabeth*, a Virgin Queen, verging on fifty, the original strong-minded woman, quite a rough character at any rate, a character in ruff, with a great deal of hoop, and a little doo-den-doo: Mr. JOHN MORTON. *Earl of Leicester*, a premier of the period, periodically in trouble, constantly studying to please a mistress of the period, hunts shoo flies of the period which causes a sale of his stud, and induces him to wear a ruffled front: Miss OLIVIA RAND. *Amy Robsart*, an unprotected female, very much in distress, who, while making herself agreeable to others, will make herself very disagreeable to her husband, but very pleasing to the audience: Miss ROSA RAND. *Sir Walter Raleigh*, a gent, but a youth of great cape-ability, who, having taken a Bird's eye view of the world, discovers tobacco, and returns to England: Miss THERESA WOOD. *Tressalian*, a blighted being, who, having missed his Aim-y, wishes to take a random shot at himself—the whole of his property having gone to the dogs, he is not even an Kennel-worth: Miss Lizette Bernard. *Duke of Sussex*, a leader of the opposition, a wag-in-waiting, to be sent for with a party eager to take a ride on the seats of office: Miss CONNIE THOMPSON. *Janet*, a waiting maid, waiting for a husband, in the blues in consequence of the heartless conduct of her particular baker, who has joined the line: Miss Agnes Robertson. *Varney*, Leicester's Master of the Horse, quite a sinecure under the circumstances, a villain with one eye to business, and another I to rhyme with Tressilian: Mr. G. C. CHARLES. *Wayland Smith*, Bank Director, Doctor, Horse-Tamer, Poor Stroller, Rogue and Vagabond—but why repeat synonymous terms?—everything by turns and nothing long: Mr. J. M. WARD. *Michael Lambourne*, a swash-buckler—whatever that may be—from the Spanish main, main fond of a drop of summat, and consequently not bound to the Maine liquor law: Mr. JAMES BARNES. *Tony Foster*, alias Fire-the-Fagot, a turncoat in religion, a turnkey in business, a party who has no compassion for a female in distress, and consequently unworthy of the name of, etc: Mr. J. DeBoney. *Giles Gosling*, a landlord, so hard at work in bringing beer to his customers, that he almost brings himself to his bier: Mr. J. Collins. *Large Beef Eaters, Two Small Beef Eaters, Banner Bearers on Broadway, Maids of Honor, Two Heralds*, latest edition. *Courtiers, Poets with nothing to Chaw-Sir, Private Soldiers so excited that the officers can't keep a private still, Beef Eaters, in name only, and others too numerous to mention in detail, but who will be found in de-tale itself. (Specialty*, Champion Artistic and Brilliant Execution of the "Manual of Arms," embracing Upton's Manual and the Lightning Zouave Drill, using the genuine Springfield Musket: Sergeant BURK. *Combat Specialty*: Mr. Varney, Wayland Smith.)

The Burlesque will terminate with a Grand Demonstration on the recent influx of Shoo Flies.

MUSICAL NUMBERS

Scene 1
- "My Pretty Page" (Duet)
  R. Rand, Miss Jackson
- "The Merriest Girl That's Out" (Song)
  R. Rand
- Comic Medley
  O. Rand
- "Garter Song"
  O. Rand
- "The Sunset"
  Misses R. Rand, O. Rand
  (*Written especially for the Rand Sisters by* Stephen H. Massett.)(Jeemes Pipes)

Scene 2
- "Irishman's Rambles" (Song)
  J. M. Ward
- "Hardware Line" (Duet)
  J. M. Ward, L. Bernard
- "Have You Seen Her Lately" (Song)
  G. C. Charles

Scene 3
- "Why do I Dream" (Song)
  L. Bernard
- "Dudah" (Duet)
  T. Wood, L. Bernard
- "I'm the Queen of England" (Song and Chorus)
  J. Morton
- "Bat-a-clan" (Concerted Piece)
  Misses Rand, Wood, Bernard, J. Morton, etc.

Scene 4
- "Crossing on the Ferry" (Song)
  T. Wood
- "Sally Comes Home" (Song)
  J. Collins
- "Air, Billy Taylor" (Duet)
  R. Rand, J. M. Ward

Scene 5
- The Lightning Drill (Specialty)
  Sergeant Burk
- Grand Equestrian Act
  G.C. Charles and his Celebrated Charger
- "Pat McCann," Walk 'round and Break Down (Concerted Piece)
  The Characters

Scene 6
- Terrific Combat
  Messrs. Varney, Wayland Smith

Scene 7
- "The Velocipede"
  O. Rand
- "Shoo Fly," Grand Finale
  All the characters

1869.43 BAD DICKEY

A Burlesque in Two Acts, a Prologue and 8 Scenes[11]. Founded on F. C. Burnand (burlesque of) "Richard the Third." Music by Richard Arnold. Scenery by D. A. Strong. Costumes by S. W. Laureys. Machinist, Mr. Denham. Properties by Mr. Delavan. Orchestra under the direction of Richard Arnold. Produced by the Tammany Amusement Company (Henry Jarrett and Harry Palmer, proprietors). Opened 6 December 1869 at the Tammany, Grand Theatre and closed 29 January 1870 after 56 performances.

CAST(Prologue): *Genius of Despair*: Alfred Stewart. *Genius of Novelty*: Lillie Whiting. *The Watcher*: Miss Wells. *The Gamester*: Mr. Henry. *Desperate Manager*: Mr. S. H. Verney. *Call Boy*: Master Mortimer. *Stage Manager*: Mr. Bidwell. *Carpenter*: Mr. Perkins. *Artist*: Mr. Wilkins. *Choristers, Imps, etc.*

CAST (Burlesque): *Duke of Gloster—Bad Dickey* (Richard III): M. W. FISKE. *Henri, Earl of Richmond*: Miss Fanny Herring. *Lord Stanley*: S. H. Verney. *Duke of Buckingham*: Miss Lizzie Kelsey. *Sir John Catesby*: Miss BESSIE SUDLOW. *Tyrrel*: Mr. A. H. Sheldon. *Lord Mayor of London*: Mr. Alfred Stewart. *The Recorder*: Miss Lillie Whiting. *The Mace*: Miss May Robinson. *Pages of History*: Misses Howard, Brooks, Haines, Graham, Elise, Wesner, Sully, Caroline. *Princess Elizabeth*: Miss ALICE HARRISON. *Lady Anne*: Miss MAGGIE DESMOND. *Duchess of York*: LOUIS MESTAYER. *Knights, Courtiers, Armies of York and Lancaster.*

---

[8]First produced in New York 25 November 1844 at the Park Theatre for 17 performances in repertory. For Synopsis of Scenes and Musical Numbers, see original 1844 production.

[9]Previously produced in New York 18 February 1867 at the New York Theatre for (23) performances in repertory.

[10]Performed twice daily for the first two weeks of the run, then matinees Monday to Friday thereafter.

[11]Preceded by a comedietta, The Eton Boy, with Rose Massey, Louis Mestayer, A. H. Sheldon, Alfred Stewart, Maggie Desmond.

Act 1, Scene 1: Cave of Despair. *Scene 2*: The Manager's Office. *Scene 3*: The Gardens of the Duke of Gloster. *Scene 4*: Gothic Apartments at Lord Stanley's.

Act 2, Scene 1: Ancient Palace on the Banks of the Thames, or anywhere else. *Scene 2*: Landscape on the way. *Scene 3*: Tent of Bad Dickey. *Scene 4*: The Original Field of Bosworth.

ACT 1
Scene 1
"Let all come who feel despair"
Chorus
The Tableaux
Miss Wells, Mr. Henry, S. H. Verney
Scene 3
"Twinkling stars are laughing Love"
B. Sudlow, L. Kelsey
"She's a gal of mine"
B. Sudlow
"How do you do"
M. Desmond, M. W. Fiske, L. Kelsey, B. Sudlow, Chorus
"Humpty Dumpty Man"
M. W. Fiske, L. Kelsey, B. Sudlow, M. Desmond, Chorus
Scene 4
"An Angel of Innocence"
A. Harrison
"Medley"
F. Herring
"Pretty Betty, if you love me"
A. Harrison, M. W. Fiske, F. Herring, L. Mestayer
"The Rhapsody"
M. W. Fiske, L. Mestayer, A. Harrison, B. Sudlow, Chorus
"Shoo Fly, don't bodder me" (Grand Finale, Act 1)

ACT 2
Scene 1
"Tyrolienne"
M. W. Fiske, A. Harrison, L. Mestayer, B. Sudlow
"Here take the sword, King Richard"
A. Harrison, M. W. Fiske, L. Mestayer, B. Sudlow
Scene 2
"An Irish Refrain"
M. W. Fiske
"Three Bad Boys"
All and Every One
Scene 3
"Blow, blow the trump, &c."
A. Harrison, M. W. Fiske, B. Sudlow, Chorus
Scene 4
Grand Finale

1869.44 THE LITTLE DETECTIVE/ AN OBJECT OF INTEREST

A Double Bill of a Drama in Three Acts, 8 Scenes, arranged especially for Lotta, sustaining six different characters, with songs, dances, etc., and a Farce after-piece. Stage manager, L. J. Vincent. Conductor, Signor Giuseppe Operti. Produced by Lotta Crabtree. Presented by Henry Jarrett and Harry Palmer. Opened 6 December 1869 at Niblo's Garden and closed 18 December 1869 after 14 performances.

THE LITTLE DETECTIVE CAST: *Florence Langton*: LOTTA (CRABTREE). *Grizzle Gutteridge*, a country girl, with song: LOTTA (CRABTREE). *Mrs. Gammage*, an old woman: LOTTA (CRABTREE). *Pat (McCann)*, an Irish boy, with Irish Medley and Shillelah Jig: LOTTA (CRABTREE). *Jack Rackett*, a fast young man: LOTTA (CRABTREE). *Gaunse-a-Shaney-Josephen-a-ch-te-Lager-Lodovic-a*, a Dutch Girl, with Tyrolean song: LOTTA (CRABTREE).

Sir Gervaise Langton, father to Florence: J. W. BRUTONE. *Barry Mallison*, alias Percy Allen, an adventurer seeking Una Langton in marriage: J. H. TAYLOR. *Ludovic Stuyvesant*, a German sharper and swindler: FELIX A. VINCENT. *Phoebus Rockaway*, his associate—light-hearted and light-fingered: FRED MAEDER. *Mr. Roderick Tracy*, a Bow Street runner in disguise: A. D. BRADLEY. *Stephen Hardcliffe*, a foremer accomplice of Barry Mallinson: George Metkiff. *Dozey*, a London watchman: T. Edwards. *Nap & Snooze*, his companions in vigilance: Messrs. Ellis, Thomas. *Captain Gustave Koenig*, of the Baden-Baden City Guard: C. Green. *Madame Ritzdorf*, a wealthy merchant's widow: Mrs. Bradshaw. *Stella*, her daughter, travelling with her mother for the benefit of her health: KATE NEWTON. *Una Langton*, sister to Florence, betrothed to Barry Mallison: LIZZIE EDWARDS.

Act 1: Evening at Baden-Baden.

Act 2, Scene 1: Garden at Baden-Baden. *Scene 2*: Lane near the Mansion. *Scene 3*: Boat-house on the Lake.

Act 3, Scene 1: Street in London. *Scene 2*: Thieves' Den in London. *Scene 3*: Street in London. (Same as Scene 1) *Scene 4*: Ruined Castle.

MUSICAL NUMBERS
"You Needn't Tell Your Mother" (Song)(Act 1)
L. Crabtree (as Grizzle Gutteridge)
Irish Medley and Shillelagh Jig (Act 2)
L. Crabtree (as Pat McAnn)
Tyrolean Song (Act 3)
L. Crabtree (as Dutch Girl)

AN OBJECT OF INTEREST, a Roaring Farce in One Act.

CAST: *Fanny Gribbles*, with Banjo Solos: LOTTA (CRABTREE). *Barney O'Dwyer*: FELIX A. VINCENT. *Mr. Sydenham Simmerton*: Fred Maeder. *Major Hildebrand Culverin*: J. W. Brutone. *Mrs. Marmaduke Primrose*: A. D. Bradley. *Mrs. Trevor Newton*: KATE NEWTON. *Mrs. Major Culverin*: Mrs. Bradshaw.

1869.45 DORA BELLA, the Minstrel, the Mission, the Miss, the Mill and the Misery, or, The Dyed Hair and the Turned Head!

A Comical, Tragical, Pastoral, Scenical, Musical, Mimical, Topical, Pantomimical, Burlesque Extravaganza in One Act, 5 Episodes[12]. (Adapted from "The Fair One with the Golden Locks.") Produced by George Wood. Opened 13 December 1869 at Wood's Museum and Menagerie and closed 1 January 1870 after 21 performances.

CAST: *Court of King Blubberoso*: *Blubberoso*, surnamed the Ugly, King of the Lachrymoso Islands: Mr. J. M. WARD. *Count Pleniposo*, surnamed the Haughty, first walking stick in waiting: Miss THERESA WOOD. *Captain Killingoso*, surnamed the Slashing: Miss LILLIE HALL. *Niceyoso*, surnamed the Brave, King Blubberoso's Minstrel and prime favorite: Miss LISA WEBER. *Spiceyoso*, surnamed the Saucy, Blubberoso's Jester: Miss ADA HARLAND. *Dashingoso Guards, Courtiers, Pages, etc.*

Court of Queen Dora Bella: *Dora Bella*, surnamed Golden Hair, Queen of the Flirtilla Islands: Mr. EDWARD RIGHTON. *Papillotina*, surnamed the Butterfly, Dora Bella's Maid of Honor: Miss LIZZIE WILLMORE. *Hookandeyeina*, Dora Bella's Hand Maid: Mr. Marsden. *Mantlewrapina*, Dora Bella's Foot Maid: Mr. J. Deboney. *Hairpinfixina*, Dora Bella's Head Maid: Mr. Florence. *Staylacepalina*, Dora Bella's Cloak Maid: Mr. Cook. *Pages, Amazons, etc.*

Immortals: *Queen Carp*, Queen of all the Salmon Tribe: Miss Alice Logan. *An Owl*, a distinguished foreigner, an ould acquaintance: Mr. J. Collins. *A Crow*, ancestor of the Immortal Jim: Mr. James Barnes. *A Monster*, the sight of whom makes the brave mon stir: Mr. G. A. Archer.

Episode 1: The Minstrel. *Episode 2*: The Mission. *Episode 3*: The Miss. *Episode 4*: The Mill. *Episode 5*: The Misery.

1869.46 PLUTO, or, The Magic Lyre

A Revival of the Burlesque in One Act[13], preceded by a drama[14] and program of sketches. Play by Henry B. Farnie, adapted from H. J. Byron's 'Orpheus and Eurydice.' Costumes by Samuel May, of London. Musical director, Henry Tissington. Produced by William Horace Lingard. Opened 13 December 1869 at the Grand Opera House in repertory and closed 15 January 1870 after 21 performances.

[12]Followed by an after-piece, Mr. & Mrs. Peter White.

[13]First produced in New York 1 February 1869 at the Theatre Comique; reconstructed 26 April 1869, closing after 128 performances. For Synopsis fo Scenes and Msuical Numbers, see original 1869 production.

[14]The fore-piece was a drama in two acts, All That Glitters Is Not Gold, by Thomas and J. Maddison Morton. Midway through the week, this replaced by the comedy, A Day After the Wedding, or, A Wife's First Lesson.

Original Sketches written and performed by William Horace Lingard: Fifth Avenue; A Young Widow; Dutch Onion Vendor; Romping Nellie; Par Excellence; Walking Down Broadway; Charles Dickens; Mayor Hall; President Grant; Robert Lee; B. F. Butler; Horace Greeley. (Added during the run: Mr. Muddlebrian, with after-dinner speech. Jay Gould, Esq. James Fisk, Jr.)

CAST: *Pluto*, King of a region which is unmentionable to ears polite, the deepest monarch of his day: WILLIAM HORACE LINGARD. *Orpheus*, a very poor young author, with scarcely any symptom of a beard, so that he is hard up before he is soft down: ALICE DUNNING. *Aristaeus*, a sporting party, fast and loose, in fact a regular swell: Miss DICKIE LINGARD. *Eurydice*, Orpheus' pretty wife, a reformed flirt, who was once flighty abroad, but who now's stayed at home: LINA EDWIN. *Apollo*, a very fascinating celestial, very fond of dancing: Miss AGGIE WOOD. *Proserpine*, Queen of the same place as Pluto's, every inch an in(ch)ured queen: Miss Amilie Harris. *Clotilda*, called Tilly, Eurydice's nurse, cook, housemaid and drudge, one who dies very often: Mr. W. M. Paul. *Charon*, ferryman of the Styx, a regular old tar: Mr. A. D. Billings. *Rhadamanthus*: Mr. H. Sinclair. *The Three Fates*: Misses Nettie Hicks, Nannie Egbert, Flora Robinson. *First Fury*: Mrs. J. M. Henry.

1869.47 THE MAID AND THE MAGPIE

A New and Original Burlesque Burletta in One Act, preceded a comedy[15], a selection of songs, impersonations, and sketches. Burlesque by Henry J. Byron. Produced by William Horace Lingard. Opened 20 December 1869 at the Grand Opera House and closed 25 December 1869 after 7 performances in repertory.

Mr. and Mrs. HOWARD PAUL in a Selection of Songs and Impersonations from their celebrated entertainment:

Mrs. Howard Paul will sing the "Drinking Song" from THE GRAND DUCHESS, introducing her funny little "ping", and also the Famous French "Sneezing Song"

Mr. Howard Paul as a "Carpet Warrior of the period" with song to the immortal melody of "Jinks," entitled "Captain Vane of the Life Guards Pink."

Mrs. Howard Paul will sing Henry Russell's great Scena, "The Dream of the Reveller."

Mr. Howard Paul as an old man of four score, with song, by (Jacques) Offenbach "When George the Third Was King."

Mrs. Howard Paul as Miss Anna Maria Grym, will deliver a Red Hot Lecture on "Woman's Rights" and sing a song called "Brother the Men."

Mr. Howard Paul will give a fantastic portrait (from a sketch by Gustave Doré) of the "Coming Swell," and sing "What New York Swells are coming to!"

Original Sketches written and performed by William Horace Lingard: Fifth Avenue; A Young Widow; Dutch Onion Vendor; Mr. Muddlebrian, with after-dinner speech; Par Excellence; Walking Down Broadway; Mayor Hall; President Grant; Robert Lee; B. F. Butler; Horace Greeley; Jay Gould, Esq.; James Fisk, Jr.

Mrs. Howard Paul in her extraordinary imitation of Mr. Sims Reeves, the celebrated English tenor, in his famous ballad, "Come into the Garden, Maud."

THE MAID AND THE MAGPIE CAST: *Ninetta*: WILLIAM HORACE LINGARD. *Pippo*: Miss ALICE DUNNING. *Giannetto*: Miss DICKIE LINGARD. *Lucia*: Miss AGGIE WOOD. *Elvira*: Miss Nettie Hicks. *Louisa*: Miss Nannie Egbert. *Fernando*: Mr. E. Coleman. *Magistrate*: Mr. A. D. Billings. *Isaac*: Mr. W. M. Paul. *Fabrizio*: Mr. C. J. Edmonds.

1870.01 WITHOUT A NAME

A New Traditional, Sensational, Operatical, Allegorical, Historical and somewhat love-sick-i-cal Spectacular Extravaganza in One Act. Scenery by Joseph B. Ayers. Wardrobe imported expressly from Paris. Properties and effects by Charles LaForrest. Produced under the stage direction of C. W. Barry, Stage Manager. Proprietor, George Wood. Opened 3 January 1870 at Wood's Museum and Menagerie and closed 22 January 1870 after 15 performances[16].

[15]The comedy fore-piece was A Day After the Wedding; or, a Wife's First Lesson, with Alice Dunning and supporting cast.

[16]WITHOUT A NAME was performed for weekday matinees in repertory with IXION which was performed in the evenings.

CAST: *King of Grenada*, a Moorish Monarch, who has consulted an astrologer and is sorry for it: G. CHARLES. *Prince Ahmed*, his Son, a sick lov-yer, a Pil-grim, not addicted to sports or pastimes, like Vanderbilt and Stewart, dis-card-ed by Cupid, with a scarred heart, although in stage parlance, a flowery card for writing on in burlesque: OLIVIA RAND. *Ebben Bonabeen*, his Tutor, described in the Legend as one of the wisest and driest of Arabian Sages: J. M. WARD. *The Parrot*, formerly in the law, but at present the victim of circumstancs: JAMES COLLINS. *Evil Genius*, exceedingly evil: J. DEBONEY. *Good Fairy*, with equal power: THERESA WOOD. *Sir John Smith*, an English Lord: LIZETTE BERNARD. *Twig*, his faithful valet: JAMES BARNES. *Suitors for the hand of Princess Aldegonda (4)*: *Mons. de Phalon*: T. Florence. *Count de Hubert Ainsley*: T. Manley. *Baron Grog*: G. A. Archer. *Menelaus*: Fred Marsden. *King of Toledo*, an exceedingly fond (not to say foolish) father, who can forgive anything but having his wishes crossed in the slightest degree: JOHN MORTON. *The Herald*, eventually a Mourning Herald and by no means Weakly, as he can stand a very powerful blow: CONNIE THOMPSON. *An Allopathic Doctor, a Homeopathic Doctor*, Physicians in Ordinary, very ordinary to the Court: Messrs. H. Broderick, J. P. Cooke. *Princess Aldegonda*, a youthful Princess in the bloom and sweetness of her years: ROSA RAND. *Jacinta*, her attendant: ALICE LOGAN. *Moors, Mutes, Merry-Makers, Men-at-arms, and Mob in General.*

MUSICAL NUMBERS

Duet from LA BELLE HÉLÈNE (*Music by* Jacques Offenbach)
O. Rand, J. Deboney

"Immensikoff" (Trio)
O. Rand, J. Collins, T. Wood

"How's That for I" (Song and Dance)
Miss Bernard

"The Lady Killer" (Duet)
Mr. Barnes, Miss Bernard

"Pretty Jemima" (Quartette)
Miss Bernard, Mr. Collins, Mr. Barnes, O. Rand

"Bow Wow" (Song)
R. Rand

Comic Medley
O. Rand

Soirée à la Negro (Grand Opening Chorus)

"Dearest May" (Song)
Mr. Collins

"Banjo Solo
J. Debonay

"Linger not, Darling" (Song)
R. Rand

"Railroad Smash up" (Grand Finale)
Company

"Music in the Air"
L. Myers

Trio from GENEVIEVE DE BRABANT (*Music by* Jacques Offenbach)
O. Rand, R. Rand, Mr. Collins

"Di Quella Pira" (Song from IL TROVATORE)
R. Rand
(*Music by* Giuseppe Verdi.)

"We're All Dodging" (Song)
J. M. Ward

"Kayser do you want to buy a Dog" (Song)
O. Rand

Medley Duet
O. Rand, J. M. Ward

Squeak Family of Bell Ringers (Specialty)

Incidental to the Tournament, Terrific Combat of Six:

Chorus and Walk Around
All the Characters

"Par Excellence" (Song)
J. Collins

Pas de Caprice (Dance)
T. Wood

The Celebrated "Sneezing Song" (from GENEVIEVE DE BRABANT)
O. Rand

Finale from LA BELLE HÉLÈNE (*Music by* Jacques Offenbach)
All the Characters

1870.02

IXION!, or, the Man at the Wheel

A Revival of the Burlesque in One Act, a Prologue and 6 Scenes[17]. Play by F. C. Burnand. Musical director, Michael Connolly. Produced by George Wood. Opened 10 January 1870 at Wood's Museum and Menagerie and closed 5 February 1870 after 24 performances.

CAST: Prologue, Mortals: *King Ixion*, ex-King of Thessaly, but though a King with the prefix of an "X", it does not alphabetically follow that he has a wise head on his shoulders: BELLE HOWITT. *Tondapameibomenos, Prosephe, Podasokus*, three Thessalians who would be these aliens if they weren't these natives; calumious conspirators, dreadful democrats, members of several secret societies who demand the right of free speaking in a state of free-dumb: Messrs. Deboney, Cook and Marsden. *A young Grecian*, first class from the Sixth Ward: Mr. Collins. *Queen Dia*, Ixion's disloyal wife, who leads the Revolutionists, and proposes to be a tanner of her husband as well as a Dyer, and tramples on her regal diadem in order to become a regal Democrat: Mr. BARNES. *Crowd of Red Republicans, Un-Read Republicans, Avengers, Scavengers, Greeks, Sneaks, and Female Furies, appropriately crowned with mob caps*, by Messrs. Torch, Firebrand, Flame, Riot, Ruin, Famine, Disorder, etc.

Immortals: *Jupiter*, King of the Gods, and the most finished Gentleman in Olympus: ADA HARLAND. *Mercury*, the celestial telegraph boy: LISA WEBER. *Ixion*, who being bankrupt and sadly in want of change, is, in spite of his bad character in his former situation, "taken" up by Jupiter and patronized by the "upper ten": BELLE HOWITT. *Juno*, Queen of the Gods and Jove's spouse, described by Poets as the Ox-eyed Lady, and consequently of a mettlesome temperament; fond of peacocks that sing Pea-hens of joy while drawing her car: LIZZIE WILLMORE. *Venus*, the Goddess of Beauty; still a spinster, although it has been said by a great authority that "Venus orta Mari," which being translated in "Venus ought to marry": EMILY PITT. *Cupid*, the son of Venus, who will at once be recognized as Love at First Sight: CLARA FISHER. *Minerva*, Goddess of Wisdom, a remarkably strong-minded lady, the defender of her own rights and woman's wrongs: EDWARD RIGHTON. *Apollo*, secretary to the Imperial Sun Fire Insurance Company (Ltd.): LILLIE HALL. *Bacchus*, promoter and chief director of the Celestial Whiskey Ring Association: Mr. Charles. *Mars*, Commander-in-Chief, as Ma's generally are: Mr. Morton. *Ganymede*, Jupiter's beautiful "Buttons," a nice active lad, the original Fat Boy who may be described as Ganny-mede and Ganny-purse un too: Mr. J. Ward.

The Three Graces, duchess in their own right: Messrs. Earle, Mason,—. *The Nine Muses*: *Calliope*: Miss Herring. *Melpomene*: Miss Jackson. *Polly Hymnia*: Miss Bonneau. *Clio*: Miss Smith. *Erato*: Miss West. *Urania*: Miss Lyon. *Euterpe*: Miss Brown. *Terpsichore*: Miss Kellogg. *Thalia*: Miss Burk.

1870.03

LA GRANDE-DUCHESSE DE GÉROLSTEIN

A Revival of the Opéra-bouffe in Three Acts, in French[18]. Libretto by Henri Meilhac and Ludovic Halévy. Music by Jacques Offenbach. Stage manager, Mons. Duchesne. Scenery by Hannibal Calyo. Costumes by Wirz and Jacoby. Chef d'orchestra, Robert Stoepel. Produced by C. A. Byrne and Starr. Opened 24 January 1870 at the Théâtre Français and closed 5 February 1870 (matinee) after 13 performances.

CAST: *La Grande-Duchesse de Gérolstein*: Mrs. HOWARD PAUL. *Fritz*: Mons. GEREBEUCK. *General Boum*: Mons. DUCHESNE. *Prince Paul*: Mons. FRANCIS. *Baron Puck*: Mons. GENOT. *Baron Grog*: Mons. EDGARD. *Nepomuc*: Mons. ROUSSEAU. *Wanda*: Mme. GUILLEMOT. *Iza*: Mme. Victoria. *Amelia*: Mme. Briot. *Charlotte*: Mme. Charles. *Olga*: Mme. Arsene. *First Officer*: Mlle. Fanny Kellogg. *Second Officer*: Mlle. Louise Kellogg. *Ladies, Pages, Soldiers, Peasants, etc.*

1870.04

THE GLORIOUS 7

An Original Extravaganza in Three Acts, 15 Scenes. Play by John F. Poole. Music by Richard Arnold. Scenery by David Strong, Smith. Costumes by S. W. Laureys. Machinery and mechanical effects, J. C. Denham. Properties by Delevan. Gas and fixtures by W. O'Neill. Incidental dances arranged by Signor Costa. Stage manager, S. H. Verney. Orchestra under the direction of Richard Arnold. Produced by the Tammany Amusement Company (Henry Jarrett and Harry Palmer, proprietors). Opened 31 January 1870 at the Tammany, Grand Theatre and closed 19 February 1870 after 21 performances.

CAST (Immortals): *Proteana*: ETHEL NORMAN. *Fairy Leda*: ETHEL NORMAN. *Adolphus Dawdle*: ETHEL NORMAN. *Olive*: ETHEL NORMAN. *Tom Tittle*: ETHEL NORMAN. *Fruitina*, Berry Girl: ETHEL NORMAN. *Stalacta*: ALICE HARRISON. *Jerusha Jane Flapjack*: ALICE HARRISON. *Fraulein Pretzel*: ALICE HARRISON. *Captain Dashaway*: ALICE HARRISON. *Katie*, Hot Corn: ALICE HARRISON. *Luxurine*: LIZZIE KELSEY. *Fairy Caleyo*: LIZZIE KELSEY. *Solomon Slashaway*: LIZZIE KELSEY. *Aspasia*: LIZZIE KELSEY. *Rob Racket*: LIZZIE KELSEY. *Lieutenant Cringle*: LIZZIE KELSEY. *The Mint Girl*: LIZZIE KELSEY. *Imperia*: BELLE LAND. *Fairy Zycleta*: BELLE LAND. *Apollo Fitzdaddle*: BELLE LAND. *Coraline*: BELLE LAND. *Bill Tompkins*: BELLE LAND. *Seregant Smithers*: BELLE LAND. *The Bouquet Girl*: BELLE LAND. *Asmodine*: MAGGIE DESMOND. *Fairy Valiote*: MAGGIE DESMOND. *Pat Maguire*: MAGGIE DESMOND. *Sergeant Fite*: MAGGIE DESMOND. *Bob*, Last Edition: MAGGIE DESMOND. *Fadladina*: Anna Stanton. *Fairy Peyea*: Anna Stanton. *Agatha*: Anna Stanton. *Bob Simpkins*: Anna Stanton. *Corproral Jones*: Anna Stanton. *Shine 'em*: Anna Stanton. *Malevola*: May Robinson. *Fairy Manta*: May Robinson. *Cecelia*: May Robinson. *Harry Lyons*: May Robinson. *Corporal Nip*: May Robinson. *Dick*, Five o'clock: May Robinson. *Liberty*: Lillie Whiting. *Edith*, a Spirit: Annie Cornforth. *Tyranny*: Harry Thomas. *Mrs. Mephisto*: M. W. FISKE. *Moll Maguire*: M. W. FISKE. *Mlle. Zulelia*, a Coryphée: M. W. FISKE. *Clorinda*, Girl of Period: M. W. FISKE. *Mr. Mephisto*: J. J. WALLACE. *Bullanbear*: ALFRED STEWART. *Brownstone*: Mr. Danielson.

CAST (Mortals): *Frederick Flash*: ROSE MASSEY. *Sylvester Slipper*: LOUIS MESTAYER. *Augustus Arlington Makeweight*: S. H. VERNEY. *Ginger*: A. H. SHELDON. *Alice Hawthorne*: EDITH CHALLIS. And Forty graceful beauties.

Act 1: The place where the bad niggers go. Likewise the place where they come from. *Scene 1*: Apartment in Hades. *Scene 2*: Corner (of) Chamber and Chatham (Streets). *Scene 3*: Author's Home. *Scene 4*: Tammany Theatre, Fourteenth Street. *Scene 5*: Masquerade.

Act 2: Combat for a Soul .*Scene 1*: The author at work. *Scene 2*: Trials of Life. *Scene 3*: The Match. *Scene 4*: On the Watch. *Scene 5*: The Counterplot. *Scene 6*: Rocky Glen.

Act 3: Defeat of Inferno. *Scene 1*: Street Arabs. *Scene 2*: To the rescue. *Scene 3*: Resolution made to be kept. *Scene 4*: Return to Hades.

ACT 1

Scene 1

Revels of the inhabitants—Breakfast for one—Return of the Master—Stalacta, the Fortune Teller—Husband and wife on matters in general—The Vision as shown—Sorrows of Youth—In Heaven her spirit rests—Desire to visit Earth—Danger—The Book of Fate—The Candidates—The Resolve—Preparation for the Visit—Chorus

Scene 2

The pursuit—Used up—The Author—The Creditor—5 Cents is all.

Scene 3

The D—l takes a cigar—Author despondent—The Friend—Companions—The Invisible—Vision of the 7—Angel of my dream—The Yankee Girl—Song—Broadway Swell—The Sister's Spirit protects the Poor Author

Scene 4

Africa and Ireland—Song—Only 10 cents

Scene 5

The Temptress—Protesting Spirit—The colored Attendant—Ireland and America—The Irish Tilt, Stalacta and Asmodine—Cupid à la Bayadère—Consternation—Tableau

ACT 2

Scene 1

The visit—No comfort—A woman's hand—The Caller—The Spirit comes to comfort

Scene 2

Stalacta as a Deitcher Vrow—Song—Base Ball Challenge—Invitation

Scene 3

Out on a Fly—Down at first base—Tableau

Scene 4

Pa around—Determination—Summons from Home—The vision of the Victim

Scene 5

Ma as the Girl of the Period

[17]First produced in New York 28 September 1868 at Wood's Museum and Metropolitan Theatre for 2 engagements totalling 120 performances. For Synopsis of Scenes and Musical Numbers, see original 1868 production.

[18]Previously produced in New York in French 24 September 1867 at the Theatre Français for 156 performances; in English 17 June 1868 at the New York Theatre. For Synopsis of Scenes and Musical Numbers, see June 1868 production.

Scene 6
The hour of vengeance—Reconoitering—The Rescue—Thrilling Tableau

ACT 3
Master Mark Sniffen in his specialties

Scene 1
Darkey as a gentleman, new role—Discovery—The father, versus mother and daughters—The threat—The temptress once more—Skirmish, tableau

Scene 2
Police victory

Scene 3
The forger—Office of Check—The temptress foiled—The Guardian Angel—The doom of death thwarted by Spirit—Happiness—The friend?—Conundrum

Scene 4
Ma elevated—Sudden appearance of Pa—The accusation—The seven nephews—Several marriages intended but don't come off—Ma's veto—The Fifteenth Amendment—Who struck Billy Patterson—The charge—Liberty appears

Moral of the Extravaganza. Allegorical Tableau.

Combat of the Fiends for Freedom. Temple of Liberty shattered. Peace and Good Will.

Restoration of the Free.

1870.05 THE TWELVE TEMPTATIONS!

A Spectacular and Legendary Romance in Four Acts, 21 Scenes. Play by Joseph C. Foster and John E. McDonough, founded on the popular German legend "Walpurgis Eve." Ballets by Davide Costa. Music arranged by Henry Tissington. Scenery by George W. Dayton, Louis Duflocq, Richard Marston, Cardoni, W. E. Deverna. Costumes by Miss Knapp. Produced by James Fisk, Jr. Opened 7 February 1870 at the Grand Opera House and closed 9 July 1870 after 154 performances.

CAST: *Ulric*, the Lost Soul: GEORGE C. BONIFACE. *Rudolph*, the Tempter: E. L. TILTON. *Eric*, Ulric's Foster Brother: G. Maxwell. *Petreuse*, surnamed the Timid: Lewis Baker. *Kalig*, the spirit of Evil assuming many forms: W. Davidge, Jr. *Eblis*, the King of Fire: J. V. DALY. *Gnomelob*, his Prime Minister: T. WARD. *Gnomelob, Scourgeall*, of legendary fame: G. T. Wilson, L. Sanders. *Prince Bauodin*, surnamed the Just: J. R. HEALY. *Michael Braun*, Minister of Justice: G. W. Marcellus. *Pietro*, Captain of the Guard: A. Enos. *Sir Anthony of Italy*: G. Laforest. *Sir James of Spain*: F. Levasseur. *Emperor of Germany*: T. Pendleton. *Beaufour*, a Herald: G. B. Douglas. *Bishop of Flanders*: F. Gordon. *Executioner of the Ape*: T. Williamson. *Executioner of Fire*: J. W. Benton. *Orchus*, an Egyptian Warrior: M. B. Pike. *Busirus*, the Ruthless: J. Taylor. *Metcalf*, Keeper of the Royal Beetles: M. C. Daly. *Twelve Knights of the Round Table, Courtiers, Demons, Mummies, Priests of Ibis, Egyptians, etc. Two Hundred Auxiliaries*: Assisted by a Powerful Chorus.

Janette, Mother of Ulric: Mme. PONISI. *Niocelle*, in love with Eric: Mrs. GEORGE C. BONIFACE. *Margaretta*, with song "The Vesper Hymn": NULLY PIERIS. *Princess O'Dwyle*: F. CLARABEL. *Justice*: Fanny Lovelace. *Faith*: Nannie Egbert. *Hope*: Flora Leland. *Charity*: Nellie Jarman. *Purity*: Marion Herbert. *The Graces*: Misses Fortescue, Jordan, Sylvester. *The Muses*: Misses Clairville, Benton, Morehouse. *The Senses*: Misses Chlemsford, Jeffreys and Evans. *Ladies of the Court, Peasants*: Corps of Female Choristers. *Dancing, Almes, Pages, Amazons, etc.*

Ballet: Mlles. ROZE, BRUNETTI (Premier Danseuses Assoluto); Mons. AJAX (the famous Grotesque); Mlles. Rachel Francesca, Marie Francesca, Josephine Strudel, Antonina Corsi, Coryphées, Corps de Ballet.

Act 1, Scene 1: Ruins of an Ancient Convent. (Dayton.) *Scene 2*: Mill of St. Donatius. (Dayton.) *Scene 3*: Studio of Eblis, in the Kingdom of Despair. (Duflocq.)

Act 2, Scene 1: The Grove of Illusion by Sunrise. (Duflocq.) *Scene 2*: The Demons' Hunting Ground, and Cateract of Terror by Sunset. (Marston.) *Scene 3*: Interior of Arundel's Tent. (Dayton.) *Scene 4*: The Port of Flanders. (Dayton.) *Scene 5*: The Lists of Flanders, and Festival of Reason. (Duflocq.)

Act 3, Scene 1: Saloon in the Palace of Bauodin. (Dayton.) *Scene 2*: Ulric's Sleeping Chamber. (Dayton.) *Scene 3*: Road to Flanders. (Dayton.) *Scene 4*: Triumphant Arch and Cathedral. (Dayton, Duflocq, Cardoni, etc.)

Act 4, Scene 1: Dungeons of Inquisition. (Dayton.) *Scene 2*: View near Flanders. (Dayton.) *Scene 3*: Interior of Temple of Ibis. (Dayton.) *Scene 4*: Egyptian Ruins. (Dayton.) *Scene 5*: View of the Pyramids and the Colossal Sphinxes. (Dayton.) *Scene 6*: Illuminated Egyptian Gardens. (Martson.) *Scene 7*: The Desert and Distant View of the City in Flames. (Dayton.) *Scene 8*: Dissolving and Clouds gradually ascend. *Scene 9*: Transformation Scene: Three Senses, Five Graces, Temple of the Muses, in the Golden Palace of Contentment, the Home of Virtue, Purity, Love, Joy Peace. (Deverna.)

ACT 1
Scene 2
"The Vesper Hymn" (Chant)
N. Pieris
The Twelve Temptations
Scene 3
Grand Tableau[19]

ACT 2
Scene 1
The First Temptation
Scene 2
The Second Temptation
The Third Temptation
Scene 4
"I'll Never be a Soldier" (Song)
L. Baker
Scene 5
Grand Tournament: Grand Ballet
Introduction and Variations
Mlle. Brunetti
Pas de Folie
Mlle. Roze, Mons. Ajax
Finale
Premières, Secondes, Coryphées, Corps de Ballet
Tableau of Delight and Wonder

ACT 3
Scene 1
The Fourth Temptation
Scene 2
The Fifth Temptation[20]
Scene 4
Tableau of Mercy[21]

ACT 4
Scene 1
The Sixth and Seventh Temptations
Scene 3
The Eighth and Ninth Temptations[22]
Scene 6
The Tenth and Eleventh Temptations
Grand Egyptian Ballet:
Grand Mummy Dance
Mons. Ajax
Characteristic Dances
Mlle. Roze, Brunetti, Francesca, Strudel, Corsi, Coryphées, Full Corps de Ballet
Scene 7
The Twelfth Temptation
Scene 9
Transformation Scene

---

[19]Replaced during the run by:
Demon Can Can
Mlles. Roze, Brunetti, Adriana, Oberti, Rachel and Marie Francesca, Strudelli, Coris, Coryphées and Corps de Ballet

[20]Added during the run:
"Sweet Spirit, Hear my prayer" (Chant, from LURLINE)
N. Pieris
(*Music by* Vincent Wallace.)

[21]Replaced during the run by:
Grand Triumphant March of the Clergy, Knights, Banner Bearers, Soldiers of all Nations.
"Hail to the Beauteous of Flanders" (Chorus of Rejoicing)
J. R. Healy, G. C. Boniface, N. Hicks, Chorus

[22]Added to this scene during the run: Tableau of Victory.

1870.06 FAUST, or, The Vicissitudes of a "Girl of the Period"

A Burlesque Extravaganza in One Act, 6 Scenes[23] Play by F. C. Burnand. New scenery, costumes, etc. Produced by George Wood. Opened 7 February 1870 at Wood's Museum and Menagerie and closed 26 February 1870 after 21 performances.

CAST: *Dr. Faust*, an old Chemist and Druggist, afterwards a very fa(u)st young man: Miss LIZZIE WILLMORE. *Wagner*, his assistant in the Chemical and Drug Department: Miss EMILY PITT. *Valentine*, Marguerite's brother, a soldier bound for the wars, worse luck: Miss LILLIE HALL. *Alonzo*, a chaaracter borrowed from a popular song and introduced here for the purpose of presenting: Miss ADA HARLAND. *Brandt*, his friend, the conventional singing, walking gentleman of the Drama: Miss CLARA FISHER. *Siebel*, a fat page with a good deal of margin, ancestor of the immortal fat boy: J. M. WARD. *Cobbler*: Mr. J. Deboney. *Schwiger*: —. *Schlarger*, Landlord of the Hartz and the Gnomes: —. *Zopritz*, a visible "policeman:" Mr. JAMES BARNES. *Mephistopheles*, a merry devil, who in the language of the promoters of the pneumatic bore might be termed an underground authority: Miss LISA WEBER. *Dame Martha*, who marks out Mephistopheles for her husband, but fails in making a good shot, being a bad dame: John Morton. *Marguerite*, a servant girl of the period, Alonzo is her first love, whom she thinks nothing of ousting for the sake of Faust: Mr. EDWARD RIGHTON. *A German band of comrades, pretty housemaids, soldiers, masqueraders, and all sorts of people.*

Scene 1: Druggist's Store and Library of useless knowledge. *Scene 2*: The Market Place (mark it, please). *Scene 3*: The Garden Wall. *Scene 4*: A kitchen with an airy prospect. *Scene 5*: The old spot. *Scene 6*: Omitted at the Opera and for the first time in America introduced here. The Walpurgis night, or Midsummer night mare.

1870.07 HAMLET

A Burlesque of Shakespeare's play by Thomas Cooper DeLeon, in Two Acts, 6 Scenes. Produced under the supervision of George L. Fox. Stage director, Asa Cushman. Scenery by James E. Hayes, T. Johnson. Costumes by Mme. Trimble. Properties by William Henry. Machinery by James Tate. Director of orchestra, F. Danze. Produced by James E. Hayes. Opened 14 February 1870 at the Olympic Theatre and closed 16 April 1870 after 72 performances.[24]

CAST: *Claudius*, King of Denmark: BEN MAGINLEY. *Hamlet* (H.D.), son of the former and nephew of the present King: GEORGE L. FOX. *Polonius*, Lord Chamberlain: LESTER CAVENDISH. *Horatio*, Friend to Hamlet: Mrs. BLANCHE BRADSHAW. *Laertes*, Son of Polonius: Mrs. MARIE LONGMORE. *Rozencrantz, Guildenstern*, Courtiers: J. M. Charles, George F. Ketchum. *Osric*, a Courtier: Fanny Queen. *Priest*: Mr. Connolly. *Marcellus*, an Officer: G. A. Bean. *Bernardo*, an Officer: Laura Queen. *Ghost of Hamlet's Father*: Mrs. Edward Wright. *First Actor*: H. C. Cunningham. *Second Actor*: S. Wright. *Actress*: Asa Cushman. *Gravedigger*: Julia Queen. *Gertrude*, Queen of Denmark and the mother of Hamlet: Mrs. BRADSHAW. *Ophelia*, Daughter of Polonius: BELLE HOWITT.

SPECIALTIES[25]

Music from FRA DIAVOLO (Scene 1)
(*Music by* Daniel Auber.)

"You'll Remember Me" (by Thomas Moore)(Scene 2)
M. Longmore, B. Howitt

"Look Out for Number One" (Scene 2)
L. Cavendish

"The Girl with the Golden Switch" (Scene 2)
B. Howitt

"Beautiful Night" (Scene 3)
G. A. Bean. L. Queen

"Johnny Fill Up the Bowl" (Scene 3)
Chorus

"I am a Native Here" (Scene 3)
G. L. Fox

"Shoo-Fly" (Finale)

"The Heart Bowed Down" (Act 2, Scene 1)

"Can-Can" (Scene 2)
G. L. Fox, Mrs. Bradshaw, Mrs. E. Wright

Pas de Deux (Scene 2)
M. Longmore, B. Maginley

"Five O'Clock in the Morning" (Scene 3)
J. Queen

"Why Do I Weep for Thee?" (Scene 3)
J. Queen

"Shoo Fly" (Finale) (Scene 3)

1870.08 LE PETIT FAUST

A Burlesque (of Hervé's opéra-bouffe) in One Act, 4 Scenes, preceded by an Olio[26]. Produced by Edwin Kelly and Francis Leon. Opened 14 February 1870 at Kelly & Leon's Minstrels and closed 26 March 1870 after 36 performances; returned 29 August 1870 to Kelly & Leon's Minstrels and closed 10 September 1870 after an additional 12 performances. Total: 48 performances.

CAST: *Doctor Faust*, an old bachelor and venerable gentleman, but discontented with his situation, having an eye for the sweet and fair of this "fleeting show," and like the age somewhat hypocritical: EDWIN KELLY. *Mephisto*: W. H. BROCKWAY. *Valentine*: S. S. PURDY. *Desire*: Cool Burgess. *Siebel*: J. H. Surridge. *Altmeyer*: J. B. Carter. *Monitor*: James Clarke. *Marguerite*: FRANCIS LEON. *Agnes*: Mr. C. R. Clinton. *Lizette*: Mr. Sam Price. *Specialty*: THE CLODHOPPER TROUPE[27]. *Girls, Boys, Soldiers, Policemen, Countrymen, Brothers.*

Scene 1: Dr. Faust's Academy. *Scene 2*: Le Jardin, Mobile. *Scene 3*: Everything works well. *Scene 4*: Mephisto at home.

MUSICAL NUMBERS[28]

"Flower of Purity"
F. Leon

"Vaterland, Oh, Vaterland"
F. Leon

"Cancan Song"
F. Leon

"The Dance of Fate"
F. Leon

"Youth Will Pass Too Soon"
E. Kelly

"Love Has O'ercome Me"
E. Kelly

"Put Your Head In, Valiant Soldier"
Chorus

French Clodhopper Troupe
Chorus

1870.09 WILLIAM TELL

A Musical Burlesque in One Act, 5 Scenes[29]. Produced under the direction of C. W. Barry. Produced by George Wood. Opened 14 March 1870 at Wood's Museum and Menagerie and closed 25 March 1870 after 10 performances (matinees only).

CAST: *William Tell*, a young Patriot, an excellent Marksman who has made his Mark in history by the aid of a bow and arrow, Married to an elderly party with a slight incumbrance: Miss OLIVIA RAND. *Albert*, called Alberto Mia, the slight (but agreeable) incumbrance: Miss ROSA RAND. *Gesler*, the tyrannical governor of Altorf, who exercises his rule in the city, but misses his sway in the Mountains: MOSES W. FISKE. *Sarnem*, a bilious Jailer, with a secret: Mr. J. S. Rooney. *Emma*, the elderly lady, with a slight incumbrance: LOUIS MESTAYER. *Erni*, a Patriot, who, though scarcely ready to die for his country, objects to Erni's living: Miss THERESA WOOD. *Furst, Melchthal, Verner*, Patriots pure and more than usually simple: Misses Jackson, Thompson, Stevens. *Catch'em, Eat'em*, two healthy subjects, up to snuff, in fact a good

[23]Previouslly produced in London in 1864 as FAUST AND MARGUERITE. The burlesque was preceded by a screaming farce, The Maid and the Milking Pail, with Messrs. Rooney, Morton, Barnes, and Miss Rand.
[24]No music credits in program despite the following program notes: "It abounds in capital music, which is exquisitely rendered by several very pretty ladies; it is garnished with an abundance of excellent singing; it furnishes a good share of dancing."
[25]List of specialties and musical numbers prepared from Laurence Senelick's biography "The Age and Stage of George L. Fox."

[26]Added to the Olio during the run, Offenbach's LISCHEN AND FRITZCHEN. See entry below.
[27]A Burlesque on the Clodoche Dancers.
[28]Not in performance order.
[29]Preceded by a comedy, Born To Good Luck!, with the same cast.

pair of snuffers: Messrs. J. Barnes, G. Charles. *Rosetta*, daughter of Sarnem, who thinks a good deal herself, but more of Albert: Miss LIZETTE BERNARD. *Minetta*: Miss C. Moshier. *Finetta*: Miss A. Page. *Baretta*: Miss Westerberg. *Susetta*: Miss Earle. *Peasantry, ready for unpleasantry, Tag, Rag, and Bobtail in reckless profusion.*

Scene 1: Tell's Dwelling, with a View of Switzerland in general. The Proposed Outbreak and Concerted Piece. *Scene 2*: Another part of Switzerland. The Break-Up and the Break-Down. *Scene 3*: Ye Crags and Peaks. A Grand Operatic Scena. *Scene 4*: The Gates of Altorf. Corporal Punishment and General Despair. *Scene 5*: An Open Situation. A final and conclusive HIT!!!

1870.10 LISCHEN ET FRITZCHEN

A Revival of the Saynète in One Act[30], in French. Libretto by Paul Boisselot. Music by Jacques Offenbach. Produced by Edwin Kelly and Francis Leon. Opened 14 March 1870 at Kelly and Leon's Minstrels (on a bill with LE PETIT FAUST) closed 26 March 1870 after 12 performances.

Olio: The Ladder of Fame.

CAST: *Lischen*: FRANCIS LEON. *Fritzchen*: EDWIN KELLY.

1870.11 CHING CHOW HI!, or, a cracked piece of China

A Comic Opera in One Act[31] preceded by an Olio and 'Popsy Wopsy—Leon, the Musical Thief.' Libretto by William Brough and Thomas German Reed. (Adapted from the French Chinoiserie musicale "Ba-ta-clan," libretto by Ludovic Halévy.) Music by Jacques Offenbach. Produced by Edwin Kelly and Francis Leon. Opened 28 March 1870 at Kelly & Leon's Minstrels and closed 16 April 1870 after 18 performances; returned 4-9 July 1870 to Kelly & Leon's Minstrels for an additional 6 performances. Total: 24 performances.

CAST: *Fe-ni-han*, Emperor of China, willing to return to the humble walks of life, yet anxious to crush the rebellion and the new City Charter; having no sympathy with the young Democracy, or any other man: EDWIN KELLY. *Ke-Ki-Ka-Ko*, Chinese Mandarin, a pleasant fellow, fond of pictorial papers—sighing for the odorous dust and whiskey straights of Broadway: S. S. PURDY. *Ko-Ko-Ri-Ko*, Captain of Fe-ni-han's Guards, a Conspirator, an angel of destruction, death on Barber's Poles and Lobby Kings: L. GRAHAM. *Hi-Ki-Ki-Hi*, another of the same sort: J. H. SURRIDGE. *Ko-Fi-Hi-Hi*, a Conspiraor, with a Carpet bag full of useless Police Bills, Charters, etc. always on hand to vote on Rail Road Bills: W. H. BROCKWAY. *Hi-Pe-Kin*, a Conspirator, the man who saw the Angel of Destruction descend on the House in Albany: Sam Price. *Chin-Chin-Chow-der*, a Conspirator, knows all those worth knowing, in fact a knowing fellow: J. B. Carter. *Hi-Fo-Fum-Ki*, a Conspirator, does the outside business, attending to the Grand Sachem Meetings and the German Votes: C. R. Clinton. *Bow-wou-er-y*, a Conspirator, one of the b'hoys, believes in "bracing up" and "getting sick": James Clarke. *Fe-An-ich-ton*, Princess in the suite of Fe-ni-han, a nice young woman, anxious to escape from China and its Rebellions to become a Female Broker, but afraid of a "bad check" being offered to her. Determiendto get away, anyway, and on her arrival in New York, would have no objection to accept an agency for the sale of Cadetships and other fancy stock: FRANCIS LEON. *Guards, Chinese Shop Keepers, Attendants, etc.*: Corps of Supernumeraries.

1870.12 THE WHITE CAT

A Fairy Musical Burlesque Extravaganza in One Act, 9 Scenes. Play adapted from the French by James Barnes. Produced under the direction of Charles W. Barry. Mechanical effects by Joseph B. Ayers. Properties by Charles LaForrest. Produced by George Wood. Opened 28 March 1870 at Wood's Museum and Menagerie and closed 23 April 1870 after 20 performances.[32]

CAST: *King Pippin*, King of Nevermindítsnamia, who though a crab apple at first turns out to be a regular Newtown Pippin: T. W. KEENE. *Count Coincide*, his Prime Minister, and an agreeable one: G. C. CHARLES. *Hikery Pikery*, a Palacial Runner: JAMES BARNES. *Old Mother Hubbard*, an excellent likeness of the old lady, as seen in Nursery Tales: Mr. M. W. FISKE. *Towzer*, the Dame's famous dog: J. L. DEBONEY. *Goat*, a rollicking Ram, another Scion of Dame Hubbard: Master A. Grossi. *Prince Paragon*, a perfect paragon of princes, and the eldest son of King Pippin: OLIVIA RAND. *Prince Precious*, another of the same: LIZETTE BERNARD. *Prince Placid*, another of Pippin's B'hoys: Miss C. THOMPSON. *White Cat*, a lovely princess but now compelled to wear a cat' skin through the malice of Dame Hubbard: ROSA RAND. *Tuberose*, the Fairy Queen, a stunner: Miss E. Moshier. *Jingo*, the Court Fool, but not the fool he appears: THERESA WOOD. *Princess Sugar Candy*, a sweet subject: Miss Westerberg. *Princess Chin Chin*, a Chinese exotic: Miss A. Page. *Tortoise Shell Cat*, a lovely tabby: Miss K. Harrison. *Lively Shrimps, Tom Cats, Black Cats, Mousers, Guards, Courtiers, etc.*

Scene 1: The King's Palace in Well, Neverminditsnamia. *Scene 2*: The Fortune Teller. *Scene 3*: The Enchanted Forest. *Scene 4*: The White Cat's Banquet Hall. *Scene 5*: Old Mother Hubbard's Home. *Scene 6*: The King's Blow Out. *Scene 7*: Garden in the White Cat's Castle. *Scene 8*: The City Gates of Neverminditsnamia. *Scene 9*: The Grand Transformation to a Cat's Paradise, or the Happy land to which all good cats retire after living their nine lives.

MUSICAL NUMBERS

A Wonderful Irish Jig (Scene 2)
T. Wood
Chorus of Invisible Spirits (Scene 3)
Arrival of Mew-sicians; Mew-sic by the Band (Scene 4)
Grand Umbrella March[33] (Scene 4)
Concerted Music and Demon Can Can (Scene 5)
The Walk Around (Scene 6)
Super-Magnificent Procession (Scene 8)
Grand Allegorical Picture and Transformation (Scene 9)

1870.13 PIPPIN, or, The King of the Gold Mines

A Grand Spectacular Burlesque Extravaganza in Two Acts, 9 Scenes. Founded upon one of the celebrated stories of the Brothers Grimm, specially written and adapted to the American stage by Harry Beckett. Music arranged and composed by Michael Connolly. Scenery by William F. Voegtlin. Mechanical effects by Benson Sherwood. Costumes by S. W. Laureys. Properties by Benedict. Musical director, Michael Connolly. Stage manager, L. J. Vincent. Produced by Henry Jarrett and Harry Palmer. Opened 4 April 1870 at Niblo's Garden and closed 30 April 1870 after 28 performances.

CAST: *King Oddsandenz, the 'orrible*, a king of shreds and patches; last of the Tag-Rag-and-Bobtail Dynasty; very hard up: WILLIAM B. CAHILL. *Prince Pippin*, his heir-apparent, who wishes to wed apple-ly. He can't anchor himself to a Princess, and is cant-anker-ous in consequence: LYDIA THOMPSON. *Prince Dollius*, his younger brother. A regular swell, with two splendid eyes in his head, but no double u on his tongue. A second Lord Dundreary, but no Dreary Dun to the Audience: LINA EDWIN. *Baron Nowitz*, Prime Minister, Chancellor of the Exchequer, and in fact, for economy's sake, the entire Ministry: Mr. W. Brutone. *Twiggletto*, Court Detective, a spy who has his finger in everyone's pie: ALICE ATHERTON. ————, alias Thingummy, alias What's-his-name. Known at home by a very few confidential friends as ——. But never mind: HARRY JACKSON. *Flourimugsen*, the dusty miller, a native of Flour-sacks-ony: Mr. T. Chapman. *Dame Flourimugsen*, the miller's better half, or, by comparison, three quarters. Fat and fair to the eye, and very forte to the ear: HARRY BECKETT. *Princess Opalina*, the pride (literally) of a foreign court, on a matter 'o money-al visit to King Oddsandenz: PAULINE MARKHAM. *Lilliken, the Golden Haired*, The Miller's Daughter and a Pretty Spinster. Like many young ladies she can make the money spin, but unlike them, she can make the money by spinning: ELIZA WEATHERSBY. *Grandmother*, a nice old Lady, only 300 years old. Stone deaf, or may we say, Granny-to-deaf: John Dunn. *Baroness Giggle, Countess Sniggle*, Ladies attached to the Princess' train. Sweets to the suite, but not at all superfluous: Misses Robinson, Lippincott. *Hunters*, two little Dears who are game for sport. Being fawned of excitement, they dislike Stag-nation: Misses Hughes, Williams. *Fraulein Smallbrainz, Fraulein Kittenspitz*, Belles of the Village, ready for a ring, who come to the fete without mamma but with their fraud pass: Miss Hamilton, Strickland. *Courtiers, Soldiers, Guards, Policemen, Hunters, Pilgrims, Peasants, Musicians, Millers, Lackeys, Bridesmaids, Pages, Ladies, etc.*

[30]First produced in New York in French 25 June 1868 at the Academy of Music for 1 performance. For List of Musical Numbers, see original 1868 production.

[31]English langauge premiere in New York. First produced in New York in French as BA-TA-CLAN 25 February 1864 at the Theatre Français.

[32]For the first two weeks of the run THE WHITE CAT was presented evenings and Saturday matinees; for the last two weeks of the run as THE WHITE CAT AND KING PIPPIN it was presented for weekday matinees only.

[33]Added during the run.

Act 1, Scene 1: Enchanted Groves in the ——'s Dominions. *Scene 2*: Room in the Palace of King Oddsandenz the 'orrible. *Scene 3*: Exterior of Flourimugsen's Mill. *Scene 4*: On the Road to the Palace. *Scene 5*: Grand Hall of Reception in King Oddsandenz Palace.

Act 2, Scene 1: Ante-chamber in the King's Palace. *Scene 2*: A Street in Germanywhere. *Scene 3*: A Rocky Pass in the ——'s Dominions. *Scene 4*: In the Enchanted Castle.

MUSICAL NUMBERS, SPECIALTIES

"Golden Tresses"
P. Markham
(*Music by* Signor Giuseppe Operti.)

Quartette (Act 1, Scene 4)

Grand Chorus of Umbrellas (Act 2, Scene 2)

Grand Transformation and general jollity of the animated jewels in the house of the King of the Gold Mines (Act 2, Scene 4)

"The Blonde That Never Dyes"
E. Weathersby

1870.14

THE BOHEMIAN GIRL, or, The Merry Zingara

An Operatic "Blonde" Burlesque of the Romantic Opera in One Act, preceded by a farce. (Directed by Felix Rogers.) Produced by George Wood. Opened 11 April 1870 at Wood's Museum and Menagerie and closed 30 April 1870 after 17 performances.[34]

CAST: *Count Arnheim*: LOUIS MESTAYER. *Florestein*, his nephew: LIZETTE BERNARD. *Thaddeus*: ADA HARLAND. *Max*, his valet: Lizzie Wilmore. *Devilshoof*: FELIX ROGERS. *Rudolph*: Miss Neomi. *Arline*, the Count's daughter: JENNY WILLMORE. *Gipsy Queen*: Emily Pitt. *Buda*, Arline's nurse: Aggy Robertson. *Count Steinforth*: Fred Marsden. *Baron Plum-duphe*: G. A. Archer. *Count Tiddlewinki*: J. L. Deboney. *Fritz*, a young detective: James Barnes. *Preitsel, Preissnitz*, assistants on the defective Detective Squad: J. P. Cooke, C. M. Manley.

SPECIALTIES

During the burlesque a Grand Fair Scene will be represented, introducing a number of a Tribe of Genuine Wild Indians, and Living Wild Animals, who will perform extraordinary and thrilling gymnastic feats.

1870.15

MACBETH

A Burlesque of Shakespeare's play in Two Acts, 14 Scenes. Version of George L. Fox. Music by Matthew Locke. Produced by James E. Hayes. Opened 18 April 1870 at the Olympic Theatre and closed 7 May 1870 after 24 perfomances.

CAST: *Duncan*, King of Scotland: J. M. CHARLES. *Malcolm*, his son: JULIA QUEEN. *Generals in the King's Army (3)*: *Macbeth*: GEORGE L. FOX. *Banquo*: H. CUNNINGHAM. *Macduff*: CHARLES K. FOX. *Noblemen of Scotland (3)*: *Rosse*: Fanny Queen. *Monteith*: Miss Newton. *Angus*: Miss Lawson. *Fleance*, Son to Banquo: Master (George) Topack. *Siward*, Earl of Northumberland: W. Eunice. *Seyton*, an Officer attending on Macbeth: Miss Lula Prior. *Physician*: J. L. Lewis. *First Witch*: George Ketchum. *Second Witch*: Mrs. Edward Wright. *Third Witch*: Mr. G. A. Bean. *First Officer*: Mr. Connolly. *Second Officer*: Mr. Knight. *First Murderer*: Mr. Quickly. *Second Murderer*: Ms. Surely. *First Singing Witch*: Laura Queen. *Second Singing Witch*: Mme. Pezzone. *Hecate*: Herr Staudt. *Lady Macbeth*: MARIE LONGMORE. *Gentlewoman*: Sarah Germaine. *Lords Ladies, Officers, Soldiers, Attedants, etc.*: Full and Powerful Chorus.

Act 1, Scene 1: The Heath. *Scene 2*: The Palace at Fores. *Scene 3*: Macbeth's Castle at Inverness. *Scene 4*: The Gates of Inverness Castle. *Scene 5*: The Interior of the Castle. *Scene 6*: The Gallery. *Scene 7*: A Wood on the Skirt of the Heath.

Act 2, Scene 1: The Banqueting Room in the Palace. *Scene 2*: The Open Country. *Scene 3*: The Cave. *Scene 4*: The Country in England. *Scene 5*: Chamber in the Castle at Dunsinane. *Scene 6*: Hall in the Castle. *Scene 7*: The Ramparts.

ACT 1
Scene 7
"Ill Deeds are Seldom Slow"
"When lightning and dread thunder"
"Sometimes like brindled cats"
"Thither the chirping cricket"
"Ah, the Night Raven's Dismal Voice"
"The Echoes"

ACT 2
Scene 2
"Hecate's Call"
"Malkin, my Sweet Spirit"
"We fly by Night"
Scene 3
"Black Spirits and White"
"Around, around, about"

1870.16

FROW-FROW

A Burlesque in Five Acts, suggested by Augustin Daly's society drama 'Frou-Frou;" preceded by an Olio. Burlesque by Tom Donnelly. New and original music by Professor Vogel. Scenery by Simmonds. Produced by Edwin Kelly and Francis Leon. Opened 18 April 1870 at Kelly and Leon's Minstrels and closed 30 April 1870 after 7 performances.[35]

Olio: Francis Leon as 'Fashionable Kate.' Purdy's Balloonist. Hart's African Dwarf Tommy. 'Invaded Studio,' a sketch with Hart , Add Ryman and Sam Price.

CAST: *Henry Sartorys* EDWIN KELLY. *Brigard*: ?. *Comte DeValreas*: W. H. BROCKWAY. *Baron DeCambri*: S. S. PURDY. *Gilberte*: The Only [FRANCIS] LEON. *Louise*, her sister: ?. *Baronne DeCambri*: ?. *Angelique*: ?. *Georgie*: ?.

Act 1: The Home at Les Chamerettes. Love.

Act 2: Paris. Private Theatricals. Marriage.

Act 3: Home in Paris. Separation.

Act 4: Venice. Desertion.

Act 5: Paris

1870.17

LA BELLE L.N.

A Revival of the Burlesque of Offenbach's "La Belle Hélène" in One Act, 6 Scenes, preceded by an Olio[36]. Libretto by Francis Leon. Music by Jacques Offenbach, adapted and arranged by Prof. Vogel. Produced under the supervision of Francis Leon. Scenery and machinery by Edward Simmons. Stage alterations and properties by Charles Brown. Produced by Edwin Kelly and Francis Leon. Opened 2 May 1870 at Kelly & Leon's Minstrels and closed 7 May 1870 after 6 performances; returned 11 July 1870 to Kelly and Leon's Minstrels for an additional 6 performances. Total: 12 performances.

CAST: *Helen*, fond of Paris, which is not strange, seeing that L.N. is Supreme Ruler of that moral European city. According to mythological tradition—Helen was the daughter of Tyndarus and Leda—but not as tender as the Music of the Leader, or she would not have left her husband money-less and gone on her Paris-ian excursion to Troy: FRANCIS LEON. *Paris*, a Son of old Prima, not morally prime, but mentally, vocally and physically very prime, originator of boat travel to Troy and author of the Trojan row, yet not a rowdy: EDWIN KELLY. *Cal-Chase*, High Priest of the Temple of Jupiter and Soothsayer to the Temple of Impeachment, considered very game—at cards: ADD RYMAN. *All-Gamon*, King of Kings, Generalissimo at Troy of the Armies of Greece during the Southern rebellion, where he opened a recruiting office and dedicated a Temple to King Pharo: G. W. G. GRIFFIN. *Money-Less*, a King of Sparta, husband of Helen, a regular tartar, the first in those days to furnish plots for odern plays: W. H. BROCKWAY. *A-Killer*, a King of Greece, who, in his infancy, was washed in the Hudson River and was thereby rendered forever invulnerable to cleanliness. After serving as a volunteer in the Trojan row, he was killed by an ar-row from Paris' bow: John F. Oberist. *A-Jacks No. 1*, Son of Tel-a-mon, a distinguished Prince of Grease judging from his avordupois—he killed himself because he could be a killer, in which he made a vile hit, and for which he was changed to a violet: Charles Stuart. *A-Jacks No. 2*, Greasier than No. 1—couldn't kill himself, 'twould take too long: Alex. Stuart. *Arrest-Us*, Son of All-Gammon and Clytemnestra, whose desire to be an orphan was so great that when old Gammon died, he killed his mamma and then peddled statues of Diana to the benighted denizens of Fulton Market: S. S. PURDY. *Filopena*, daughter of a

[34]For the first two weeks of the run this burlesque was presented evenings and Saturday matinees; for the final week it was a weekday matinee attraction.

[35]No program found.

[36]First produced in New York 6 June 1868 at Kelly and Leon's Minstrels for 21 performances. For Synopsis of Scenes, see original 1868 production.

King of Athens, a very voluble young lady, who, after being deprived of her tongue, was compelled to sing the Nightingale Waltzes. The audience need not be alarmed, she will not sing now: C. Heywood. *Looney*, a Priestess of Bacchus, always ready to back-us with her voice or Boots: Foley McKeiver. *To-Bac-chus*, a Son of Jupiter and Semele—or Smile eh?—a favorite expression at Delmonico's, the Palace of this famous God. His appearnce in the Burlesque is to remind his disciples that the bar is closed at 12: W. Guy. *Herald*, not New York—very useful in furnishing Greeks with intelligence: George Guy. *Men at arms, Grecians, Trojans, Ladies of the Court*: Large Corps of Auxiliaries.

1870.18

FRA DIAVOLO, The Brigand of the Period

A reconstructed and original version of the famous Auberian opera, a very gem of burlesque, with new music, costumes and scenery, in One Act[37]. Produced by George Wood. Opened 2 May 1870 at Wood's Museum and Menagerie and closed 7 May 1870 after 12 performances.

CAST: *Beppo*, a Forrestirn swell: Mr. M. W. LEFFINGWELL. *Fra Diavolo*, alias the Marquis Di Crambournelli, an amiable and captivating creature: Miss OLIVIA RAND. *Zerlina*, the beauty of the village, and barmaid of "The Jolly Brigands:" Miss ROSA RAND. *Lady Allcash*, a lady making her first tour: Miss THERESA WOOD. *Matteo*, Landlord of "The Jolly Brigands:" JAMES BARNES. *Lorenzo*, an officer of Police: LOUIS MESTAYER. *Lord Allcash*, an English nobleman: T. W. KEENE. *Ciocomo*, a promising young bandit: F. Marsden. *Francesco*, an extensive young farmer: Miss C. Thompson. *Antonio*, 1860 Z: G. A. Archer.

1870.19

MOSQUITO/ LA SONNAMBULA

The Lydia Thompson Troupe in a Double Bill of Drama and Burlesque. Stage manager, L. J. Vincent. Produced by Henry Jarrett and Harry Palmer. Opened 2 May 1870 at Niblo's Garden and closed 21 May 1870 after 21 performances.

ACT 1

MOSQUITO, a new and original drama in Three Acts, 10 Scenes, written expressly for Lydia Thompson by Alexandre Dumas, père. Music arranged by Michael Connolly. Scenery by William Voegtlin. Machinery by Benson Sherwood.

CAST: *Olivia*: Miss LYDIA THOMPSON. *Mosquito*, a Creole boy: Miss LYDIA THOMPSON. *Quitan*, otherwise the Marquis Fonseca, a Spanish Émigré and Planter: Mr. M. Lanagan. *Valderrama*, a Spanish painter: Mr. NEIL WARNER. *Pierre LeRouge*, a Buccaneer: Mr. HARRY JACKSON. *Patte de Velours*, a Paris Night-Hawk: Mr. W. B. CAHILL. *M. de Mauleon*, a French nobleman: Mr. Foster. *Matapas*, an old exquisite: Mr. JOHN DUNN. *Partout*, a dramatist: J. W. BRUTONE. *The Regent of New Orleans*: James Marriott. *Leon de Beaulieu*: Mr. McKEE RANKIN. *Bobech, Fil de Fer*, French cuthroats: Messrs. Kidder, T. Chapman. *Tomas, Anton*, Spanish seamen: Messrs. Higgins, Hughes. *Gendarme*: E. Collier. *Diana de Mauleon*: Miss PAULINE MARKHAM. *Madame Dubac*, a parvenu: Mrs. Walcot. *Madame de Lucenay*: Miss LINA EDWIN. *Slaves, Sailors, Colonists, French Peasants, Guests, Masqueraders, Guards du Corps, etc.*

Act 1: A Spanish settlement in South America, 1760. *Scene 1*: The Harbor of Puerta da Santa Maria. *Scene 2*: The Pine Gorge. Sunset. *Scene 3*: The Plantation of Quintana. Moonlight.

Act 2, Scene 1: The Hotel Fonseca at Paris. 1761. *Scene 2*: Corridor in the Hotel. *Scene 3*: The Old Auberge "Le Roi d'Yoetot" at Sunset.

Act 3, Scene 1: Ante-chamber in the Hotel Fonseca. *Scene 2*: The Masque Ball at Versailles. A Royal Fête under Regent of Orleans. *Scene 3*: The wager of battle. *Scene 4*: The Grove of Apollo in the Park of Versailles. Moonlight.

MUSICAL NUMBERS, SPECIALTIES

Nanette's Song (Act 2, Scene 3)

ACT 2

LA SONNAMBULA, a Burlesque of the opera[38] by Henry J. Byron, especially adapted for the Lydia Thompson Troupe.

CAST: *Count Rudolpho*, Misanthropical, Metaphysical, Metaphorical, Dyspeptic, Bilious and Disagreeable: Mr. W. B. CAHILL. *Village Notary*, Marriage Contracts, Paternal Blessings, Title Deeds, Rightful Heirs, and other Stage requirements on the shortest notice: E. Chapman. *Alessio*, the merry Swiss boy, Village-Barber-and-Chatterbox, combining two extreme military ranks, being at once Private Inquirer and General Gossip: Miss ELIZA WEATHERSBY. *Elvino*, the "Nice Young Man" of the village: Miss PAULINE MARKHAM. *A Virtuous Peasant*, by kind permission of the legitimate drama: J. W. Brutone. *Amina*, the Village Beauty: Mr. HARRY BECKETT. *Liza*, Mistress of the Village Inn, buit not of herself, who having been thrown over Elvino, naturally feels considerably upset: Miss LINA EDWIN. *Teresa*, Aunt to Amina. In the opera she is Amina's mother, but in the present drama she arn't: Miss ALICE ATHERTON. *Lisette*: Miss Jennie Hughes. *Peasants and Populace, regardless of Expense.*

1870.20

THE FAIR ONE WITH BLONDE WIG

A Fairy Extravaganza (Burlesque) in Two Acts, 8 Scenes, adapted expressly for the troupe. Selected gems (music) from all the popular operas. Stage manager, JOHN W. Thorpe. Scenery by James E. Hayes. Leader of orchestra, F. Strebinger. Produced by Mrs. James A. Oates Burlesque Company. Presented by James E. Hayes. Opened 16 May 1870 at the Olympic Theatre and closed 11 June 1870 after 32 performances.

CAST: *Graceful*, a Maid of Honor: Mrs. JAMES A. [Alice] OATES. *Princess Ba-be-bi-bo-bu*, the Fair One with the Golden Locks: Mr. H. T. ALLEN. *Leander*, the Rightful Heir: JOHN H. CHATTERSON. *Prince Huckaback*, the Usurper: M. W. FISKE. *Marquis Verysoso*: M. V. Snyder. *Count Prettilittleman*: Jennie Gilmer. *Caliposh*, a Gardiner: J. T. Walters. *Ruffians (4)*: *Drinkhard*: W. R. Hayden. *Eatquick*: H. H. Pratt. *Paynone*: Mr. Bernard. *Graball*: Paul Burges. *The Hon. Sambofromsingsing*: J. H. Jones. *Sugarall*: Ida D'Soyer. *Honeydew*: Miss H. Sloan. *Queen Ti-tum-tilly-silly*: Mrs. E. M. Post. *Fair Lucidora*: Mrs. Pauline Heyden.

Act 1, Scene 1: Grand Hall in the Palace of Allaquiz. *Scene 2*: The Banished Prince. *Scene 3*: Gardens adjoining the Palace. *Scene 4*: A Lonely Roadside. *Scene 5*: Island of Delight in the Distance. *Scene 6*: Interior of the Palace of Tranquil Delights.

Act 2, Scene 1: Grotto in the Garden of Princes. *Scene 2*: Camp of Prince Huckabuck.

ACT 1

Scene 1

"Prince Leander is His Name" (Opening Chorus)

"Quite another story"

"Courtiers are ever bowing"

"Hark, 'Tis the Indian Drum" (Solo and Chorus)

"You rascal, You!"

"How now, Sir"

"Hush! Hush" These Sounds of revelry" (Connected piece)

Scene 2

Ballad (The Banished Prince)
(J. H. Chatterson)

Scene 4

"We Are Villains Double Dyed" (The Conspiracy)
The Klu-Klux

"The Syren and the Friar" (Duet)

"The Time will come"

"Swallows Fly" (Duet)

Scene 5

"There Was a Fairy Queen" (Story)

Scene 6

"They Stole My Child Away" (Solo and Chorus)

"Fetch the Cat" (Duet from NORMA)
(*Music by* Vincenzo Bellini.)

Grand Divertissement:

The Boston Peace Jubilee—Arrival of the Sangerbund

Professor Gilmore
Mr. A. M. Hernandez

Grand Overture

The Tumbleronicon
Prof. M. O'Riordan

The Cowbellogians
Fernandez and Troupe

"Good Night! Shoo Fly, Don't Bodder Me" (Grand Finale)

[37]Performed twice daily; preceded by a laughable farce, Too Much For Good Nature, with the same cast.

[38]Suggested by the opera with music by Vincenzo Bellini, libretto by Felice Romani, after Eugène Scribe's ballet-pantomime 'La Sonnambule.' Byron's burlesque was produced in London under the title, La Sonnambula; or, the Supper, the Sleeper, and the Merry Swiss Boy. No further details in programs.

ACT 2
Scene 1
"She Can Love True"
Trio from ATTILA
(*Music by* Giuseppe Verdi.)
Scene 2
Hernandez Imperials Japs from Hoshkosh
"Here Have I Pitched My Tent"
"When you've won the battle, let me know"
"Larry O'Brien"[39] (Song)
"Hand That Rose Over"
"Seize Her"
"I Think I sees You"
"You've Stuck Me"
"Long Live Leander the True Prince"
Grand Finale

1870.21 THE FORTY THIEVES

Lydia Thompson Burlesque Troupe in a re-constructed version of the Celebrated Burlesque in One Act, 6 Scenes.[40], followed by an after-piece. (Original play by Henry B. Farnie, reconstructed by C. Ware.) New music selected and arranged by Michael Connelly. Stage manager, L. J. Vincent. Produced by Henry Jarrett and Harry Palmer. Opened 23 May 1870 at Niblo's Garden and closed 4 June 1870 after 12 performances.

CAST: *Ganem*, son of Ali, who from his small sighs may scarcely be considered a full groan: LYDIA THOMPSON. *Ali Baba*, an alley who has just gone through the court: WILLIAM B. CAHILL. *Cassim Baba*, a "baa-baa, black sheep": J. W. BRUTONE. *Abdalla*, a polished robber, and leader of the brassiest band imaginable: PAULINE MARKHAM. *Hassarac*, his rebellious lieutenant, and unscrupulous individual, prepared to stick at everything, in general, and nothing in particular—a base performer, whose vice ranges from the faintest pitch and toss to the most prononce manslaughter: HARRY BECKETT. *Mirza*, Penny Plain: Mr. E. Collier. *Hassan*, Twopence Coloured: Mr. E. Chapman. *Orchobrand*, the Enchanter of the Forest: ALICE ATHERTON. *Cogia Baba*, Ali's better half: Jennie Hughes. *Zaide*, Cassim's ditto: Miss James. *Morjiana*, a slave to Cassim and to circumstances: JENNIE WEATHERSBY. *The original Donkey*, forelegs, and hindlegs: Eugene Carpenter, Edmund Glover Rough, Esqs. *Robbers, Thieves, Guests, etc.*

Scene 1: The Forest. *Scene 2*: Interior of Ali Baba's Cottage. *Scene 3*: The Robbers' Cave. *Scene 4*: Street in Bagdad. *Scene 5*: Interior of Ali's House. Verandah. *Scene 6*: Versailles during a fete.

---

[39]Replaced in second week of the run by "Jubilee Jim."

[40]Originally produced in New York in a Two Act, 10 Scene version which opened 1 February 1869 at Niblo's Garden for 136 performances. The after-piece was a farce, To Oblige Benson, with Harry Beckett, Eliza Weathersby, Alice Atherton.

1870–1871 SEASON

George L. Fox as WEE WILLIE WINKIE (Drawn and printed by Charles H. Crosby & Son)
Museum of the City of New York

1870–1871 SEASON

1870.22 HOP O' MY THUMB

An Entirely New and Original Fairy Pantomime in One Act, 12 Scenes. Play by James Schonberg. New scenery, new costumes, new tricks, new transformations. Produced under the direction of the Martinetti Brothers. Produced by George Wood. Opened 6 June 1870 at Wood's Museum and Menagerie and closed 18 June 1870 after 28 performances[1].

CAST: *Father Hardup*, an impecunious individual, who, in wet weather, has seen better days: J. S. ROONEY. *Dame Hardup*, his loving spouse, who espouses her husband's fortunes and approves them: JAMES BARNES. *Hop o' My Thumb*, their last and least child: Master IGNACIO MARTINETTI. *Hop's Eleven Brothers*: *Tofee*, the Gourmand: Master Manley. *Thickhead*, the Dunce: Master Monday. *Tommy*, the Awkward: Master Page. *Grub*, the Hungry: Master Brown. *Prog*, the Voracious: Master Robson. *Swig*, the Thirsty: Master Smithers. *Thinasalath*, the Unsatisfied: Master Shanks. *Suckthumb*, the Luxurious: Master Wilson. *Sugarmouth*, the Epicure: Master Baron. *Stickyfingers*, the Expensive: Master Ryner. *Humguffin*, the Hypocritical: Master Traynor. *The Ogre Smith*, a gentleman of full habit, limited means but expensive and ambitious tastes. One with a relish for cold p(h)easant pie: Mr. T. W. KEENE. *Goldheart*, his favorite Cheyld: Miss Niece. *Goldheart's Eleven Sisters*: *Pugnose*, the Proud: Miss Westerberg. *Iwantit*, the Envious: Miss West. *Don'tbother*, the Grumpy: Miss Stevens. *Sumpumkin*, the Vain: Miss Fradel. *Giveitme*, the Greedy: Miss Travers. *Chatterchatter*, the Loquacious: Miss Barnes. *Suchatemper*, the Vixen: Miss Johnson. *Eversopert*, the Saucy: Miss Parker. *Lunkhead*, the Stupid: Miss Page. *Sotired*, the Lazy: Miss Verner. *Itoldyouso*, the Spiteful: Miss Jackson. *Chamberlain*, and Wooden-Stick-in-Waiting: Mr. G. C. Charles. *Abaddun*, true to his name in every sense of the word: Mr. BLUNT. *Satanella*, for a time his slave, but afterwards translated into *Gentilla*, the Fairy Guardian of Hop's Fortune: Miss THERESE WOOD. *Jasmine, Eglantine, Heartsease, Marigold*, Fairies: Misses Page, Neomi, West, Stevens. *Kerosene, Camphine, Fusiloil, Deltremes*, Demons: Messrs. Morton, Johnson, Orton, Parkhurst. *Fairies, Demons, and other good and bad characters.*

Following characters by THE MARTINETTI TROUPE: *Harlequin*: Mr. Paul. *Clown*: Mr. Julien. *Pantaloon*: Mr. Phillip. *Columbine*: Mlle. Desirée. Other personages by the Martinetti Troupe.

Scene 1: Picturesque prospect of pandemonium. The River Styx in the distance and long may it continue there. *Scene 2*: Hardup's Hut (unfurnished with every convenience). *Scene 3*: The forest and the traditional cut wood. *Scene 4*: Mr. Smith's Brown Stone Ogre's Mansion. *Scene 5*: A Street in a busy neighborhood. *Scene 6*: Another street. *Scene 7*: A modern kitchen. *Scene 8*: The street again. *Scene 9*: A newly furnished bedroom. *Scene 10*: A suburban locality. *Scene 11*: Bay of Naples by moonlight. *Scene 12*: The Volcano in eruption.

SPECIALTIES

- Opening Chorus (Scene 1)
  Abaddun's spirits
- Tableau—The Storm and Shipwreck (Scene 1)
- Danse Infernale (Scene 1)
- Music Tremuloso terrific (Scene 2)
- Grand Magical Transformation (Scene 4)
- Comic, Pantomimic, Acrobatic and Wonderful Feats
  Martinetti Troupe
- Trip "Tarantella" (Scene 5)
- Terrific and brilliant denouement amid Liquid Fire, Molten Lava and Flames (Scene 12)

1870.23 THE DAUGHTER OF THE REGIMENT, or, The 800 Fathers

A Burlesque of the Popular Opera[2], preceded by an Olio. Music selected from popular operas. Stage manager, J. W. Thorpe. Leader of orchestra, F. Strebinger. Produced by Mrs. James A. Oates Burlesque Company. Presented by James E. Hayes. Opened 13 June 1870 at the Olympic Theatre and closed 18 June 1870 after 8 performances.

CAST: *Josephine*, the Adopted Child of the 21st Regiment: Mrs. JAMES A. [Alice] OATES. *Sergeant Scalade*, of the 21st: H. T. ALLEN. *Guillot*, a Tyrolean: J. H. CHATTERTON. *Pumpernickle*, Steward to the Marchioness: M. W. FISKE. *Duke de Grandtete*: H. H. PRATT. *Soldiers (3)*: *Bernard*: W. B. Hayden. *Pierre*: J. H. Jones. *Etienne*: P. Berger. *Stephen*, a Peasant: Miss Germaine. *Valet*: Miss Watson. *The Little Corporal*: Ida DeSoyer. *Marchioness de Berkenfeldt*: Mrs. J. J. PRIOR. *Duchess de Grandtete*: Mrs. W. R. HAYDEN. (*Specialties*: WILLIE EDOUIN, HERNANDEZ' IMPERIAL JAPS, A. M. HERNANDEZ; LEON BROTHERS.)

SPECIALTIES, MUSICAL NUMBERS

- The Dancing Barber! (Farce)
  Narcissus Fitznoodle: W. Edouin.
- Hernandez' Imperial Japs, introducing new tricks
- Guitar Quartette and Triple Perche
  Leon Brothers
- "This is a Famous Regiment"
  (*Music by* Jacques Offenbach.)
- Trio from IL TROVATORE
  (*Music by* Giuseppe Verdi.)
- Trio from ATTILA
  (*Music by* Giuseppe Verdi.)
- "Like a Soldier Fall"
  (*Music by* Vincent Wallace.)
- "Sabre de Mon Pere"
  (*Music by* Jacques Offenbach.)
- "Il Baccio"
  (*Music by* Luigi Arditi.)
- Potpourri from THE GRAND DUCHESS (Concerted Finale)
  (*Music by* Jacques Offenbach.)
- Grand Parisian Ballet:
  Mlle. Marie Bonfanti: W. Edouin. *Signor Novissimo*: H. H. Pratt.
- Hernandez' Grand Orchestra
- The Boston vs. the Beethoven Festival
  Professor Gilmore: A. M. Hernandez.

1870.24 FRITZ, OUR COUSIN GERMAN

A Great Specialty of the German Immigrant (Drama) in Three Acts, 7 Scenes. Play by Charles Gayler. (Produced by Charles Gayler.) Opened 11 July 1870 at Niblo's Garden and closed 10 September 1870 after 63 performances.

CAST: *Fritz Van Vonderblinkinstoffen*: JOSEPH K. EMMET. *Colonel Crafton*, Chief of a Gang of Counterfeiters: CHARLES FISHER. *Bobbit*, Keeper of a Concert Saloon: B. T. RINGGOLD. *Bloker, Smasher*, Emigrant Runners: J. C. Williamson, W. J. Leonard. *Adolphus Jenkins*, a Henglish Hartist you know: E. M. HOLLAND. *Judge Griffin*: C. H. ROCKWELL. *Pat McClure*: J. Peck. *Father Metzler*: Mr. Smythe. *Flint*: J. Quigley. *Little Fritz*: MINNIE MADDERN (Fiske). *Katarina*: GEORGIE LANGLEY. *Moppy*: Miss Chambers. *Paulina*: Miss Abbott. *Angelina*: Miss Fowler. *Julie*: Miss Toyson. *Judy Roche*: Miss Rowe. *Mother Metzler*: EMILY MESTAYER. *La Belle*: Miss Hayden. *Marie*: Miss Blaisdell.

Act 1, Scene 1: A View of the Bay of New York. *Scene 2*: Fritz in search of Katrina. *Scene 3*: The sanctum of Phil Bobbit's nice little establishment.

Act 2, Scene 1: Katrina's place of refuge. *Scene 2*: Justice Griffin's Court Room. *Scene 3*: The Grand International Concert Hall.

Act 3: The Home of Fritz, the Happy Miller.

MUSICAL NUMBERS

- "Valking Dat Broadway Down"[3]
- "Oh, Schneider, How You Vas?"
- "(Emmet's) Lullaby"
  (*Music and lyrics by* Joseph K. Emmet.)

---

[1]Performed twice daily. A fore-piece, the farce THE YOUNG WIDOW, with Messrs. Keene, Mestayer, Monday, Misses A. Logan and T. Wood, was also performed, followed by Mr. Dan Leon (skillful and intrepid gymnast in his successful and astonishing trapeze act) assisted by Paul Martinetti, and then Master Ignacio Martinetti, the infant prodigy in his amusing song and dance, "Love Among the Roses."

[2]LA FILLE DU RÉGIMENT, music by Gaetano Donizetti, libretto by Jules-Henri Vernoy de Saint-Georges and Jean François Alfred Bayard.

[3]Most likely Emmet's own dialect version of the popular song "Walking Down Broadway."

1870.25

EAST LYNNE, or, the Elopement

A New Musical Burlesque founded on the drama (by Mrs. Henry Wood) in ? Act. Burlesque by James Barnes. Produced by George Wood. Opened 25 July 1870 at Wood's Museum and Menagerie and closed 30 July 1870 after 12 performances.

CAST: Misses ROSA RAND, ALICE HARRISON, THERESE WOOD; Messrs. E. LAMB, T. W. KEENE, JAMES BARNES; Mr. Rooney, *Billy*, the fat boy: G. C. CHARLES.

Following the burlesque, the new trick pantomime, THE MAGIC TRUMPET, performed by the Martinetti Troupe.

1870.26

LITTLE FAUST!

An Opera Bouffe in Three Acts. (Original French libretto by Hector Crémieux and Adolphe Jaime.) English adaptation by Henry B. Farnie, arranged by Frank Musgrave. Music by Hervé. Produced under the direction of John E. Macdonough. Scenery by James E. Hayes, J. Johnson. Costumes by Mme. Charlotte. Leader of orchestra, F. Strebinger. Produced by James A. Oates Comic Opera Company. Presented by James E. Hayes. Opened 22 August 1870 at the Olympic Theatre and closed 1 October 1870 after 48 performances.

CAST: *Mephisto*, King of the Netherlands: Mrs. JAMES A. [Alice] OATES. *Martha*, a Spinster who never says die: GEORGE L. FOX. *Marguerite*, a timid young maid: MARION TAYLOR. *Faust*, a young old tenor: H. T. ALLEN. *Valentine*, of the very household troops: WILLIAM CRANE. *Siebel*, Youth of the Period: Charles Drew. *Karl*, alias Herr Hobper, a gentleman of capers: Miss Lula Prior. *Fritz*, a regulation swell: Miss F. Jones. *Buttons*, afterwards Tiger—always spotted: Miss F. Beane. *Arab*[4], alive to coppers, though keeping a broom: Miss Wren. *A Cabman*, Hansom is as hansom does: James W. Thorpe. *The Little Cornet*, a pocket warrior: Miss FLORA LEE.

Lady Gymnasts and Pupils of Martha's Finishing Academy: *Sophonisba*: Miss Flynn. *Mary Jane*: Miss Bauderaux. *Matilda*: Miss Leveni. *Lucy*: Miss Hill. *Jemima Anne*: Miss Topack. *Euphemia*: Miss Melnotte. *Lavinia*: Miss Naylor. *Ross Malagundina*: Miss S. Fenton. *Lischen*: Miss E. Fenton. *Chlorinda*: Miss A. Fenton. *Peasants, Warriors, Ladies of All Nations, etc.*: Numerous Host of Auxiliaries.

Act 1: Grounds of Dame Martha('s Finishing Academy).

Act 2: Illuminated Garden.

Act 3: German Market Place.

MUSICAL NUMBERS, SPECIALTIES[5]

"King of Thule" (Invisible Chorus)(Act 2)
M. Taylor
"Where shall I take my Bride?" (Song)(Act 2)
First appearance of Horse Marines, clad in bristling steel and plenty of boots. (Act 2)
Song and Chorus (Act 2)
Troop
Triple Chorus (Act 3)
Grand Chorus and Magic Transformation to the Home of Mephisto (Act 3)
Finale (Act 3)
"Mephisto Is My Name"
"Song of the Seasons"
"Soldier's Chorus"
"Fatherland"
"Railroad Song"

1870.27

LE PETIT FAUST!

A Revival of the Opéra-bouffe in Three Acts[6]. Libretto by Hector Crémieux and Adolphe Jaime. English adaptation by Kelly and Leon. Music by Hervé. Scenery by R. H. Halley. Produced by Edwin Kelly and Francis Leon. Opened 29 August 1870 at Kelly and Leon's Minstrels and closed 10 September 1870 after 12 performances.

CAST: *Doctor Faust*, an old bachelor and venerable gentleman, but dreadfully discontented with his situation, having an eye for the sweet and fair of this 'fleeting show,' and like the age, somewhat hypocritical: EDWIN KELLY. *Méphisto*, an agent of the dark unknown, like many others, very kind and obliging so long as it suits his purpose, but a devil of a fellow when put out: GEORGE H. COES. *Valentine*, a soldier, brave as a lion, commander of the forces, off to the war, in search of fame, fortune and a good appetite: J. H. SURRIDGE. *Desire*, a mischievous boy, a long time at school, hot tempered but fond of the girls, fond of a fight, and all other luxuries: Luke Schoolcraft. *Sibel*, a bad boy, a wicked boy, a fighting boy, and a general disturber of the peace, but takes care of his clothes, which is a comfort to his parents: E. M. Kayne. *Altmeyer*, another of the same sort, and a tattle-tale, and a cowardly, cowardly custard, eat your father's mustard: Charles Walters. *Monitor*, a muff, down with him: Edwin Lester. *Marguerite*, sister of Valentine, 16 1/2 years, but knows as much as one twice her age, or any other man, a young lady of pugilistic proclivities, an embryo woman's rightist and a veritable "girl of the period": FRANCIS LEON. *Agnes*, a meek and gentle being, pure and lovely as the lily of the valley, with a hankering after boys: J. W. Morton. *Lisette*, an exact counterpart of Agnes, only more so: Wash Norton. *Girls, Boys, Soldiers, Policemen, Countrymen, Brothers.*

MUSICAL NUMBERS

"Put your Head in" (Chorus)
"It is too Bad, your Time to Waste" (Solo, Tenor)
E. Kelly
"Valiant Solders" (Chorus)
"When a good Soldier" (Solo, Tenor)
J. H. Surridge
"Flower of Purity" (Solo, Soprano)
F. Leon
"She is so Good" (Chorus)
"I Am Mephisto" (Solo, Baritone)
G. H. Coes
"Youth and Love" (Chorus)
"Love has O'ercome Me" (Solo)
E. Kelly
"Vaterland, Vaterland" (Solo)
F. Leon
"Liebe, Liebe Freundlin" (Duet)
E. Kelly, F. Leon
"Come Go, Let's Leave" (Chorus)
"The Hours Pass Lightly Away" (Chorus)
"Death by Sister Dear" (Solo)
J. H. Surridge
"Now the Dance of Fate Begins" (Solo)
F. Leon
"Come to the Ball" (Chorus)
"Dance, Dance, Dance" (Chorus, Finale)
E. Kelly, F. Leon, J. H. Surridge, G. H. Coes, Chorus

1870.28

THE GOLDEN BUTTERFLY

A Fairy Musical Extravaganza in One Act, 7 Scenes[7]. Play by James Barnes. Music arranged by William H. Brinkworth. Scenery by Joseph B. Ayers. Costumes by Mr. Toledo. Properties by Charles LaForrest. Produced under the direction of James Barnes, stage director. Musical director, William H. Brinkworth. Produced by George Wood. Opened 5 September 1870 at Wood's Museum and Menagerie and closed 30 September 1870 after 20 weekday matinee performances.

CAST: *King Mulligrub*, a wretched Old Man with an only Son: T. W. KEENE. *Queen Tingertongue*, his worser half but one too many for the King: LOUIS MESTAYER. *Pitty Pat*, their own Darling one of the boys we read of: ALICE HARRISON. *Baron Plumdoph*, the Prime Minister a regular Duffer: J. S. Rooney. *Concertina*, a Rebellious Subject, in fact a *horfull willain*: THERESA WOOD. *Lunkhead*, a simple rustic, with a taste for Hunting Butterflys: J. Barnes. *Scalliwag*, King of the Fire-Flys, a hard hearted Cove, by Jove: G. C. Charles. *Kiskatong*, the Persian Ambassador who gets kicked: H. Stewart. *Lord Knowswho*, the Egyptian Ambassador who likewise is deeply insulted by the King: Miss M. Baratta. *Lord Perriwig*, a sleepy Old Buffer: C. M. Manley. *Lord Nobrains*, another wise Councellor: J. C. Walsh. *Limbo*, a Demon Firefly: T. Barclay.

---

[4]During the run, the role of Arab, a London newsboy, was recast and played by Mrs. James A. Oates in addition to her role as Mephisto.
[5]Not in performance order; last 5 songs contained in program advertisements.
[6]First produced in New York 14 February 1870 at Kelly & Leon's Minstrels.

[7]Preceded by a farce, "Deaf as a Post."

Rosetint, the Golden Butterfly: LIZZIE HALL. *Lillywhite*, the Butterfly Queen: ANNIE FIRMIN. *Gausewing*, an airy subject and as beautiful as a Butterfly: EMMA MOSHIER. *Guards, Courtiers, Bull-frogs, Fire-flies and Croton Water Bugs*: Numerous Ladies and Gents.

Scene 1: The Winning Card. *Scene 2*: The Rebellious Subject. *Scene 3*: The Stern Resolve. *Scene 4*: The King's Vision. *Scene 5*: The Fairy's Revenge. *Scene 6*: The Test of Love. *Scene 7*: The Heart of Gold.

SYNOPSIS OF INCIDENTS, SPECIALTIES

Scene 1

Council Chamber of King Mulligrub. A Sleepy Lot of Wise Men. The King in the Dumps. Oh, by halidame, they swore. Awake, Awake. A Logical Deduction, which is interrupted by "The Queen." "The Queen," a moment of horror. You shall not marry him, Dreadful Noise. The French Wrestlers outdone. My child. My Pitty Pat. Oh Pickles. Delightful Concerted Music and Amazing Dance by the King. Fate shall choose for me. Bring forth the Lucky Bag. Scramble. All black. All Black. No, no all blank. The Butterfly wins, it holds the winning card—an-no—NOT an Ace of Spades. More heavenly music, and Scotch Reel, by all hands.

Scene 2

Revenge! Revenge! The plot at a Song and Dance. The love of a Queen, which finds vent in a comic dance. We Three will do the deed—Stay—the Quartette.

Scene 3

The Valley of Butterflys. The seizure and the consequences. Pitty Pat and the Queen of the Butterflys. Guazewing around. A Stunning Fairy Chorus and Triumphal departure of the Golden Chariot.

Scene 4

A Lunkhead on a Hunting Expedition. A Throne for me! A splendid piece of concerted music and a stunning Dance. The King and the Queen. He sleeps. A horse, a horse! A "walk-around."

Scene 5

The house of the Fire-fly. All's lost. No, no. Pitty Pat on hand. The Duet. The Struggle for Liberty. Terrific Combat of 6-7 and defeat of Scalliwag. Red Fire and Tableau.

Scene 6

Concertino still gloating. A beauteous Lightning Bug. The Green-Eyes Lobster. The King, the King. And Ha, Ha. The Queen and a wonderful melody of "Gibble Gobble."

Scene 7

A Wild Wood Haunt. Sweet Spirit hear my song. My Mother "That Butterfly you'll never see again." Lost, Lost, Seize him! Ha-ha! Gauzewing to the rescue. Everybody saved from despair, and Grand Transformation Scene. The Crystal Bower of Butterflies.

1870.29 THE BABIES OF THE PERIOD

A Comic Opera in One Act, accompanied by an Olio[8]. "First time in America." Produced by Edwin Kelly and Francis Leon. Opened 12 September 1870 at Kelly & Leon's Minstrels and closed 1 October 1870 after 18 performances.

Olio: Leon's new acts: Sweetest of Williams and the Street Singer. The Jealous Husband. The Lost Child. In Central Park, etc.

CAST: *Lucy Smith*: The Only [FRANCIS] LEON. *Henry Clifton Pickles*: EDWIN KELLY. Including the Crying Chorus.

1870.30 LE PETIT FAUST

An Opéra-bouffe in Three Acts, 4 Scenes[9], in French. Libretto by Hector Crémieux and Adolphe Jaime. Music by Hervé. Ballet music composed by Henry Tissington. Stage manager, Mons. Charles Estève. Maitre de ballet, Signor Davide Costa. Scenery by Richard Marston and George Dayton. Costumes imported from Paris by Mrs. A. Knapp, Mons. A. Jacobi. Machinery by G. B. Winnie. Mountings, decorations and general paraphernalia by Samuel Wallis. Calcium effects, illuminations and mediums by J. K. Simpson. Musical director, Carlo Patti. Produced by James Fisk, Jr. Opened 26 September 1870 at the Grand Opera House in repertory; season closed 20 May 1871.

CAST: *Méphisto*: Mlle. LÉA SILLY. *Marguerite*: Mlle. CÉLINE MONTALAND. *(Doctor) Faust*: Mons. CONSTANT GAUSINS. *Valentin*: Mons. PAUL HITTEMANS. *The King, Clothaire VIII*: Mons. Jacques Antony. *A Coachman*: Mons. Alphonse Cayla. *An Usher*: Mons. Adrien Valter. *An Anglo-Saxon*: Mons. Brunet.

Female Pupils (8): *Lisette*: Mlle. Julie Hache. *Aglae*: Mlle. Juliette Jousse. *Clorinde*: Mme. Eloise Lasalle. *Frosch*: Mme. Lagrange. *Charlotte*: Mme. Riotte. *Lischen*: Mme. Elise Darlia. *Dorothée*: Mme. Louise Lesage. *Agnes*: Mme. Emilie Beaumont. *Male Pupils (6)*: *Siebel*: Mlle. Marie Vaudelet. *Frantz*: Mme. Legros. *Fritz*: Mme. Victorine. *Wagner*: Mme. Alda. *Altmayer*: Mme. Pinjean. *Brander*: Mme. Eloise. (*Ballet*: Mlles. Albertina, Lupo, Mazzeri, Rachel and Marie Francesca, Coryphées, Corps de Ballet.) *Soldiers, Students, Old Men and Women, Anglo-Saxons, Russians, Male and Female Demons.*

Act 1: Faust's School Room. (L'École du docteur Faust) (Dayton.)

Act 2: Garden Champêtre. (La closerie des Vergeiss-mein-nicht.) (Marston.)

Act 3, Scene 1: Marguerite's Boudoir. (La chambre virginale.) (Dayton.) *Scene 2*: Palace of Satan. (Le Palais du diable, La nuit de Va-te-Purgis.) (Marston.)

ACT 1[10]

Ensemble (Saute! saute! coup' ta tête)
Mlles. J. Hache, E. Lasalle, Choeur

Scene (Et pour braver quel moment)
C. Gausins

Choeur des Soldats (Vaillants guerriers, sur la terre étrangère)
P. Hittemans, Choeur

Air Tyrolienne (Fleur de candeur, je suis la petite Marguerite)
C. Montaland

Morceau d'Ensemble (Il nous faut un example!)
C. Gausins, C. Montaland, Choeur

Duo (Ah! l'étrange phénomène)
C. Gausins, C. Montaland

Rondeau (Je suis Méphisto, serviteur fidèle)
C. Montaland

Final (Viv' l'amour, la jeunesse)
Mlles. J. Hache, J. Jousse, C. Montaland, C. Gausins, L. Silly, Choeur

ACT 2

Choeur de Cocottes (Cocottes de tous les pays)
Cocottes

Choeur de Vieillards (Nous, nous sommes les vieux noceurs)
Vieillards

Choeur d'Étudiants (Enfants de l'université)
Étudiants

Chanson (Le Satrape et la Puce, ou la Puce elle s'attrape)
L. Silly

Chanson (Oh! je suis un fameux viveur!)
C. Gausins

Scene (Troupe joyeuse et belle)
L. Silly, C. Gausins, les Cocottes

Chanson (Place, place à la voyageuse)
C. Montaland

Chanson (Dans l'ombre d'un rêve)
L. Silly

Duet et Terzetto (Ne permettez-vous pas, charmante mademoiselle)
C. Gausins, C. Montaland

Finale (O ciel! qui donc est tombé là?)
C. Montaland, C. Gausins, P. Hittemans, Choeur

ACT 3

Scene 1

Scene (Séparons-nous, c'est l'heure fortunée)
Choeur

Chanson (Écoutez, gens d'Allemagne)
C. Montaland

Choeur des Jeunes Vierges et Gens (Nous venons, jeunes vestales)
C. Montaland, Choeur

[8]No program found; authorship uncredited in advertisements and reviews.
[9]French language premiere in New York. Previously produced in English 29 August 1870 at Kelly and Leon's.

[10]Musical numbers not listed in programs; list of musical numbers prepared from published French libretti (Ancienne Maison Michel Lévy Frères, Paris, 1881). List of Ballets from programs.

Chanson (Permettez-moi de vous offrir le bouquet d'Adolphe)
L. Silly, Choeur

Scene (Quand un militaire y s' trouv' dans une soupière)
P. Hittemans, C. Montaland, C. Gausins

Trio (Pour les beaux yeux d'un rêveur)
C. Montaland, C. Gausins, P. Hittemans

Scene 2

Finale (Riez, chantez, o cher troupeau maudit)
L. Silly, Choeur

BALLETS

Rondo (Act 1)
Coryphées, Corps de Ballet

Melange: (Act 2)

English
Mlle. Albertina, Coryphées, Corps de Ballet

Italian
Mlle Lupo, Coryphées, Corps de Ballet

French
Mlles. Mazzeri, Rachel and Marie Francesca; Strudelli, Corsi; Coryphées, Corps de Ballet

Javanaise
Mlles. Lupo, Albertina, Coryphées, Corps de Ballet

Finale, Dance Infernale (Act 3, Scene 2)
Mlles. Albertina, Lupo, Mazzeri, Entire Corps de Ballet

HUMPTY DUMPTY JUNIOR, or, The Fairy of the Diamond Mines and the Giant's Festival

1870.31

A Grand Comic Spectacular Trick Pantomime in Two Acts, 12 Scenes.[11] (Entire production conceived and produced by Imre and Bolossy Kiralfy.) Musical director, William H. Brinkworth. Produced by George Wood. Opened 3 October 1870 at Wood's Museum and closed 15 October 1870 after 14 performances.

MAGYAR CSARDAS (Grand Hungarian Sensational Divertissement), by Mlle. Haniola (Kiralfy), and Messrs. Imre and Bolossy Kiralfy, and members of their celebrated troupe.

HUMPTY DUMPTY CAST: *Humpty Dumpty Junior*, afterwards Clown: LITTLE GREAT GRIMALDI KIRALFY. *Hunkidori*, an old farmer, afterwards, pantaloon: LE PETITE CHRISTIE. *Little Red Riding Hood*, afterwrads Columbine: LA PETITE RAVEL. *Toby Toker*, afterwards Harlequin: LE PETITE CAWTHORN. *Nick Nack*, afterwards Sprite: LE PETITE GREEN. *Moonbeam*, Queen of the Fairies, with song: La Petite Belle Green. *Zingarella*, a Gipsey, with song: La Petite Lillie. *Clexus*, a notary: Little Clarence. *Boniface*, the comic footman: Little Frenche. *Bull*, a Butcher: Little Clark. *Baby Policeman*: Master Troupe. Other characters by the Grimaldi Troupe.

Specialties: CHARLES WINTER RAVEL, LA PETITE RAVEL (La Premiere Danseuse). *KIRALFY MONSTER TROUPE*: Company of 60, including Mlle. HANIOLA KIRALFY, Messrs. IMRE and BOLOSSY KIRALFY, Mlles. Olga, Katiska, Paulina, Sophie, Addie, Nemea, Ida, Adelska. *SAXON INFANT BALLET TROUPE*: 40 children, aged 3-7. *Secondas*: Misses Clemence, Henriette, Charlotte, Eleonore, Frenche (Twin Sisters), Cawthorne, Hartman, Kirshbaum, Finn, Greene, Lillie, Minnie, Bella, Gray, Brown, Betz, Hockstader, Clara Hinley, Atkins, Bochell, Black, Lizie, Collins, Strosburg, Arda, Corps de Ballet.

Act 1, Scene 1: Farm at Oxington. *Scene 2*: Segar Store. *Scene 3*: Humpty Dumpty here again. *Scene 4*: Enchanted Garden of the Flowers of the Future.

Act 2, Scene 1: Fishing amusement. *Scene 2*: Music Store. *Scene 3*: The Giants' Festival. *Scene 4*: Grand Fire Scene. *Scene 5*: Bad Baby and Barber's Shop. *Scene 6*: French Boarding and Lodging. *Scene 7*: Humpty Dumpty and Policeman. *Scene 8*: Grand Finale.

ACT 1

Scene 1

Magic Transformation: Clown, Harlequin, Columbine, Pantaloon.

Scene 4

Fleurs et Papillons (Grand Ballet)

Saxon Infant Ballet, La Petite Ravel, Première Danseuse, Secondas

ACT 2

Scene 3

Giants Festival

Comic Dance
C. W. Ravel

Scene 4

Female Fire Brigade
Infant Saxon Troupe

Scene 8

Terrific Battle Tableau
To conclude with, for the first time in the United States, the Grand Characteristic Divertissement, GUERIERES SAUVAGE, with Mlle. Haniola (Kiralfy), Messrs. Imre and Bolossy Kiralfy, Mlles. Paulina, Fannie, Addie, Sophie, Nemea, Ida and Adelka, and Charles Ravel.

RIP VAN WINKLE, or, a 20 Year's Snooze

1870.32

An entirely new somnolent Cats-kill-ian Burlesque in Three Acts[12]. Play by James Barnes (suggested by Joseph Jefferson's drama 'Rip Van Winkle.') Music arranged by William H. Brinkworth. Scenery by Joseph B. Ayers. Costumes by Mr. Toledo. Properties by Charles LaForrest. Stage director, James Barnes. Musical director, William H. Brinkworth. Produced by George Wood. Opened 3 October 1870 at Wood's Museum and closed 14 October 1870 after 10 performances (weekday matinees).

CAST: *Rip-Van-Winkle*, the original Loafer, a young Rip, who comes to grief by sleeping from home, and who as a sleeper, justly claims the Champion Belt: Miss ALICE HARRISON. *Willie-Von-Swillen*, a young Dutch gallant, considered by the ladies a festive cuss, and in his own estimation the prince of lady killers: Miss ANNIE FIRMIN. *Eriefiskiana*, the Demon the Catskill, the name being "Irish," will be new of course to people of our day, but children of 80 summers will remember having to read of his awful doings in the year 1, in Bergh's Book on 'Cruelty to Animals': MOSES W. FISKE. *Dunn-der-Hedder*, a block head of a Landlord, who glories in having evaded the Excise Law: Harry Stewart. *King Arthur*, the unfortunate victim of the Round Table, a mythical cuss: C. M. Manley. *Q-Rius-Duphar*, a very inquisitive cove, in pursuit of knowledge: JAMES BARNES. *Gripsack Von Smith, Sweitzer Case, Von Bluffenberg*, (3) Big Headed Dutchmen: Messrs. J. C. Walsh, T. Barclay, L. Willard. *Zephyr*, the Fairy Queen, a very airy creature, and champion masher of Fairy Land: Miss EMMA MOSHIER. *Katerine Von Sassell*, Rip's early love, and cause of all his troubles: Miss THERESA WOOD. *Bertha*, Willie's Darling, a being to be loved and cherished: Miss LILLIE HALL. *Gretchen*, Willie's worser half, a decidedly Dutch importation, as observed "Walking Down Broadway": Mr. G. C. CHARLES. *Lillybell*, a Fairy Sprite: Miss Marion Westerberg. *Lowena*: Miss Jennie Satterlee. *Seraphina*: Miss Annie Page. *Serena*: Miss E. Palmer. *Angelina*: Miss Lizzie West. *Matilda*: Miss Addie Abbott. *Fairies, Peasants, Demons, etc.*

WEE WILLIE WINKIE

1870.33

A Pantomime in Two Acts, 21 Scenes. Play by George L. Fox. Music composed and arranged by Mon. F. Strebinger. Produced under the direction of George L. Fox. Scenery by James E. Hayes, J. Johnson. Mechanical changes by R. Cutler, Taite. Costumes by Mrs. Trimble and Tilson. Produced by James E. Hayes. Opened 5 October 1870 at the Olympic Theatre and closed 4 February 1871 after 132 performances.

CAST: *Wee Willie Winkie*, man of all work, afterwards Clown: GEORGE L. FOX. *Old Grain*, The Jolly Miller on the River Dee, afterwards Pantaloon: GEORGE BEANE. *Leander*, a youth of Hellespont fame, in love with Blondette, afterwards Harlequin: R. HONEYMOON. *Blondette*, the Miller's pride, flaxen-haired, though not a blonde, yet Leander's affianced, afterwards Columbine: FANNY BEANE. *H.R.H. King De Bobbin*: H. H. PRATT. *Blousabella*, the Queen Consort: Miss E. ROGERS. *Chatterbox*, the Royal Laundry Maid: Miss ANNIE YEAMANS. *Our Fritz*, Captain of

[11]Preceded by a Farce, A SUIT OF TWEEDS, and accompanied by two divertissements.

[12]Previously produced in New York as WIP WAN WINKLE 20 September 1859 at Wood's Museum for 21 performances. Preceded by a farce, A SUIT OF TWEEDS with members of the same cast.

the Royal Guard: J. L. Debonay. *Professor Blotter*, the Royal Cook: T. Atkins. *Florisette*, the Queen of Light and Beauty: LULU PRIOR. *Diamantine*, her Fairy Attendant: FLORA LEE. (*Specialties*: Little JENNIE YEAMANS; PROFESSOR MAXIMILIAN, the Renowned Prestidigitateur.) *Auxiliaries*.

Village Friends of Blondette: *Colin*: Sarah Fenton. *Herman*: Julia Fenton. *Conrad*: Mary Johnston. *Rodolph*: Mary Topack. *Annette*: Katie Melnotte. *Florette*: Maria Hill. *Juliette*: Lizzie Pierce. *Fanette*: Hessie Naylor.

Act 1, Scene 1: Fairy Dell. *Scene 2*: The Village by the Lake. *Scene 3*: King De Bobbins' Castle. *Scene 4*: The Royal Grounds and Castle. *Scene 5*: Arrival of the Fairy Queen. *Scene 6*: Transformation Scene. The Glory of Florisette in the Home of Convolvoli.

Act 2, Scene 1: Snow Scene. *Scene 2*: Dollar Store and Pawnbroker's. *Scene 3*: The Kitchen. *Scene 4*: Straight Street. *Scene 5*: Exterior of Barn. *Scene 6*: Blacksmith Shop. *Scene 7*: Chamber at Hotel, No. 2999 7/8. *Scene 8*: Landscape. *Scene 9*: Cascade by Moonlight. *Scene 10*: View of China. *Scene 11*: Wung Tsi Street, Pekin, China. *Scene 12*: Wine Vaults. *Scene 13*: Dark Scene. *Scene 14*: Regions of Fire. *Scene 15*: Final Transformation. The Realms of Light and Beauty.

MUSICAL NUMBERS, SPECIALTIES

Song (Act 2, Scene 2)
J. Yeamans

Barn Door Jig (Act 2, Scene 5)
A. Yeamans

Policeman's Song (Act 2, Scene 6)
J. Yeamans

Homeward March of the Gallant Ninth (from Longbranch) (Act 2, Scene 8)

Military Tactics, Martial Music, and

"A Drum Major as Is a Drum Major" (Act 2, Scene 8)

Drum Solo and Song (Act 2, Scene 8)
J. Yeamans

Solo Dance (Act 2, Scene 9)
F. Beane [Columbine]

Signor Bosa, the great Fire-Eater, with his interminable ribbons (Act 2, Scene 10)

Ah-Wung, the coming man, with native song and violin accompaniment

(Act 2, Scene 10)
A. Yeamans

1870.34 LITTLE NELL AND THE MARCHIONESS

A Revival of the Melodrama in Four Acts[13]. Suggested by an episode in "The Old Curiosity Shop" by Charles Dickens, adapted by John Brougham. Opened 10 October 1870 at Niblo's Garden and closed 20 October 1870 after 11 performances.

CAST: *Little Nell*: LOTTA (CRABTREE). *The Marchioness*: LOTTA (CRABTREE). *Dick Swiveller*: VINING BOWERS. *Daniel Quilp*: FELIX ROGERS. Cast also included SOL SMITH, A. Fitzgerald, T. H. Morris, John Trainor; Miss Buchanan, Hind, Merrett, LeBrun, J. Brutone. Numerous Auxiliaries, including a Troupe of Acrobats and the Sable Minstrels (Ida Ross in a Highland Fling, The Romelli Family).

1870.35 LURLINE, or, The Knight and the Naiads

A Grand Spectacular Burlesque in Two Acts, a Prologue and 8 Scenes. Play by H. J. Byron. Music composed and arranged by Michael Connolly. Scenery by Joseph B. Ayers. Properties by Charles LaForrest. Costumes by M. Toledo. Mechanical effects by B. Wetmore. Musical director, Michael Connolly. The whole produced under the immediate direction of Lydia Thompson. Produced by the Lydia Thompson Troupe. Opened 17 October 1870 at Wood's Museum and closed 12 November 1870 after 28 performances.

CAST: *Sir Rupert the Reckless*, a very hard up young German, who goes down the Rhine in search of an heiress: LYDIA THOMPSON. *His Seneschal*, still harder up, with very little on his body, but a good deal on his mind: JOHN L. HALL. *Wilfrid, Albert, Rinaldo*, individuals with the strongest objection to manual labor, but who gladly turn their hands to anything not their own: Mr. H. Stewart, ALICE ATHERTON, C. M. Manley. *Baron Witz*, an empty-headed person who is posessed of a fruitful property though barren his tete: W. B. CAHILL. *Count Calimanco*, happy at first, but eventually a good deal cut up: MARIE LONGMORE. *The Family Herald*: ——. *The River Monster*, "neither flesh, fowl nor good red herring": Mr. Morris. *Lurline*, the Naiad Queen—a sweet young syren, and a sad victim of misplaced confidence: PAULINE MARKHAM. *Wavelet*, her Naiad-in-waiting, eventually an Naiad de-camp: WILLIE EDOUIN. *The Lady Una*, Baron Witz's Daughter, a Great Prize in the German Lottery: FANNY PRESTIGE. *Moonbeam, Shadow, Dew Drop*, Fairy Sprites, very pretty and very good: Emma Moshier, Marian Westerberg, Addie Abbott. *Guards, Retainers, Scalawags and Mob in general.*

Ballet: Annie Smiggins, Lizzie West, Marie Holcombe, H. Wilson, L. Johnson, Nellie Stewart, May Stevens, Katie Bell, Addie Blake, E. Coor, E. Simmons, Jackson. . : ELIZA WEATHERSBY.

Prologue: Fairy Grotto and Haunt of the Water Nymphs.

Act 1, Scene 1: Rupert's Dining Hall, with a distant view of the Rhine. *Scene 2*: Strasbourg by moonlight. *Scene 3*: Coral Grotto beneath the Rhine.

Act 2, Scene 1: Hall in the Baron's Castle. *Scene 2*: Crystal Bower of Beauty. *Scene 3*: Lurline's Boudoir. Meeting of the Waters. Rifle Corps. *Scene 4*: Another Apartment in the Castle. The Rows of Cast-Steel! *Scene 5*: Unexpected Interruption. The Set-To. Grand Tableaux. Finale.

BALLETS, SPECIALTIES

Grand Moral Ballet (Act 1, Scene 3)
Harriet Beecher Stowe: A. Smiggins. *Elizabeth Cady Stanton*: L. West. *Anne Dickenson*: M. Stevens. *Mrs. Dr. Walker*: K. Bell. *Jemima*: M. Holcombe. *Jacintha*: H. Wilson. *Ariminta*: A. Blake. *Tabitha Tibbs*: E. Coor. *Mrs. Smith*: L. Johnson. *Mrs. Jones*: N. Stewart. *Mrs. Robinson*: E. Simmons. *Mrs. S. Gamp*: Miss Jackson.

1870.36 LAW! SON-AMBLE-AH!/ CINDERELLA!, or, The Lover, the Lackey and the Little Glass Slipper

A Double Bill of Burlesque. Stage manager, Harry Jackson. Scenic artist, Griffith Morgan. Properties, Mr. Benedict. Machinist, J. H. Butler. Orchestra conducted by Jonathan P. Donniker. Produced by Lina Edwin. Opened 10 October 1870 at Lina Edwin's Theatre and closed 29 October 1870 after 21 performances; CINDERELLA joined the bill 17 October 1870 and closed 22 October 1870 after 7 performances.

ACT 1

LAW! SON-AMBLE-AH!, a Burlesque of the Opera "La Sonnambula" in One Act.[14] (Suggested by the opera with music by Vincenzo Bellini, libretto by Felice Romani, after Eugène Scribe's ballet-pantomime 'La Sonnambule.')

CAST: *Alessio*, the 'Merry Swiss Boy,' Village Barber and Chatterbox, combining two extreme military ranks, being at once private enquirer and general gossip: Miss ELIZA WEATHERSBY. *Aminia*, the Village Beauty, in her own opinion: STUART ROBSON. *Elvino*, the Nice Young Man of the Village: Miss LILLIE ELDRIDGE. *Count Rodolpho*, Misanthropical, Metaphysical, Metaphorical, Dyspeptic, Billious and Disagreeable: Mr. HARRY JACKSON. *Liza*, Mistress of the Village Inn, but not of herself, who having been thrown over by Elvino, naturally feels considerably upset: Mr. HARRY JOSEPHS. *Virtuous Peasant*, by the kind permission of the Legitimate Drama: Miss AGGIE WOOD. *Teresa*, Aunt to Amina, in the opera she is Amina's mother, but in the present drama, she aren't: Miss ADA HERBERT. *Village Notary*, Marriage Contracts, Paternal Blessings, Title Deeds, Rightful Heirs, and other stage requirements, on the shortest notice: Mr. Eugene Eberle. *Ingenious Rustic*: Mr. E. Cauldwell. *A Simple-Minded Villager*: Mr. Klebs. *A Guileless*

[13]First produced in New York 14 September 1867 at Wallack's Theatre for 26 performances. For Synopsis of Scenes, see original 1867 production. Lotta will perform her banjo solos, a new duet, a clog dance, and a Tyrolean Duck Song.

[14]In the second and third weeks of the run, LAW! SON-AMBLE-AH! was retitled simply SONNAMBULA in its theatre programs.

[15]Previously produced in New York 2 September 1867 at the Fifth Avenue Theatre for 14+ performances in repertory.

Clodhopper: Mr. Langenbach. *Elvira, Lisetta*, a pretty pair of Alpine Kids: Misses S. Germaine, A. Germaine. *Ansette*: Miss Katy Doud.

ACT 2

CINDERELLA, or, The Lover, the Lackey and the Little Glass Slipper. A Revival of the Splendid Spectacular Burlesque in One Act, 6 Scenes[15]. (Play by Henry J. Byron, suggested by Charles Perrault's fairy tale.)

CAST: *Clorinda*, the Baron's eldest daughter, an oldish young person of the gushing order, very hard upon Thisbe, but remarkably soft upon the Prince: Mr. STUART ROBSON. *Buttons*, a Page of the "Last of the Barons": Mr. HARRY JOSEPHS. *Alidoro*, Tutor to the Prince: Mr. E. B. Holmes. *Baron Balderdash*, a slightly damaged edition of the "Last of the Barons," bound in calf, three volumes in one, by no means lettered and very generally cut: Mr. EUGENE EBERLE. *Cinderella*, the Baron's youngest daughter: Miss LINA EDWIN. *Prince Popetti*, Prince of Salerno, and of pretty fellows: Miss LILLIE ELDRIDGE. *Dandino*, the prince's valet, and a very deep one: Mrs. LEFFINGWELL. *Thisbe*, the Baron's second daughter: Miss Amelia Harris. *The Fairy Queen*, Cinderella's godmother: Miss AGGIE WOOD. *Honeydew*, a fairy: Miss S. Germaine.

Scene 1: A Forest Dell. *Scene 2*: The Baron's Apartments. *Scene 3*: Great indignation meeting of the Prince with Dandini. *Scene 4*: The Kitchen. *Scene 5*: Corridor in the Palace. *Scene 6*: Grand Ballroom of the Palace.

1870.37 LA GRANDE DUCHESSE!

A Revival of the Opéra Bouffe in Three Acts, in French. Stage manager, Mons. Charles Estève. Musical director, Carlo Patti. Produced by James Fisk, Jr. Opened 19 October 1870 at the Grand Opera House in repertory; season closed 20 May 1871[16].

CAST: *The Grand Duchess*: Mlles. CÉLINE MONTALAND, LÉA SILLY. *Wanda*: Mlle. SUSANNE THAL. *Fritz*: Mons. CONSTANT CAUSINS. *Prince Paul*: Mons. PAUL HITTEMANS. *Baron Puck*: Mons. Adrian Valter. *General Boum*: Mons. Jacques Antony. *Baron Grog*: Mons. Varlet. *Nepomuc*: Mons. Brunot. *Iza*: Mlle. Julie Hache. *Amelia*: Mlle. Juliette Jousse. *Olga*: Mlle. T. Darlia. *Charlotte*: Mlle. L. Darlia. *Lords and Ladies of the Court, Maids of Honour, Pages, Ushers, Soldiers, Vivandières, Peasants*: Auxiliaries.

1870.38 LA ROSE DE SAINT FLOUR

A Comic Opera in One Act[17] preceded by an Olio. Original French libretto to the operette by Michel Carré. Music by Jacques Offenbach. Musical director, Fred W. Zaulig. Produced by Edwin Kelly & Francis Leon. Opened 24 October 1870 at Kelly & Leon's Minstrels and closed 3 December 1870 after 36 performances.

Olio: Kneelson Concert. Fashionable Kate. Tea Party. Kitty from Cork.

CAST: *Lizzette*: FRANCIS LEON. *Brown*: EDWIN KELLY. *Smith*: S. S. PURDY. *Martin*: George Guy. *Peter*: J. H. Surridge. *Alliston*: J. B. Carter. *Andre*: Sam Price. *Reginald*: Daniel Wilson.

MUSICAL NUMBERS

"Between Those Two" (Song)
F. Leon

"Temple of Love" (Recitative)
S. S. Purdy

"For These Little Feet" (Song)
S. S. Purdy

"The New Saucepan" (Song)
E. Kelly

"How you joke" (Grand Duet)
F. Leon, E. Kelly

"Uncle Tom's Wedding" (Trio and Couplet)
E. Kelly, F. Leon, S. S. Purdy

Finale (Chorus)
E. Kelly, S. S. Purdy, F. Leon, Company

"Angelus" (Tableaux)

1870.39 ALADDIN, or, The Wonderful Scamp!/ BLACKEY'D SUSAN/ THE BLIND BEGGARS

A Triple Bill of Burlesque, Comic Opera and Farce Specialty[18]. Orchestra under the direction of William Withers, Jr. Produced by Lina Edwin. Opened 31 October 1870 at Lina Edwin's Theatre and closed 12 November 1870 after 14 performances.

ALADDIN, or, The Wonderful Scamp! A Burlesque in One Act.

CAST: *The Widow Twankey*, Aladdin's mother, who, to quote the Arabian Nights, was rather old, and who, ever in her youth, had not possessed any beauty: HARRY BECKETT. *Aladdin*, an anomaly, for, although he is considered by everyone to be a lively youth, he is universally looked upon as a sad boy: Mrs. LEFFINGWELL. *Princess Badroulboudour*. This princess was in fact the most beautiful brunette that ever was seen; her eyes were large, well-placed and full-of-fire, etc.: KATE O'NEIL. *The Sultan*, a monarch in difficulties, and anything but a rex pecunarium: E. EBERLE. *The Vizier*, who amidst other dirty work is supposed to have cleaned out the exchequer: E. B. HOLMES. *Pekoe*, the Vizier's Hope and his own pride: Miss AGGIE WOOD. *Abanazer*, a magician who has been round the world in search of the lamp, but who finds great difficulty in getting round Aladdin: FRED MARSDEN. *The Slave of the Lamp*: Emma Lewis. *The Genius of the Ring*: Dora Herbert. *Te-to-tum*: Mr. Broughton.

BLACKEY'D SUSAN, or, that 'ere Leetle Bill that was taken Hup. An Amusing Burlesque in One Act.

CAST: *Captain Cariolanus Crosstree*: Mr. STUART ROBSON. *Dog-Grass*: Mr. Eugene Eberle. *Dame Hatley*: Mr. HARRY JOSEPHS. *High Admiral*: Charles T. Parsloe, Jr. *Baker*: Fred Marsden. *Admiral of the Red*: J. H. Broughton. *Admiral of the Blue*: J. Somers. *Admiral of the Black*: T. Everton. *Admiral of the White*: W. King. *Captain of the Fokesell*: Mons. Laugenbach. *Surgeon of the Keel*: Mr. Caldwell. *Head her-to-Winda'ard*: H. Schwickardi. *Bill Mainstay*: T. Krebs. *Susan*, with Song; Miss LINA EDWIN. *William*, with Song: Miss EMMA CLINE. *Hatchet*: Miss AGGIE WOOD. *Dolly Mayflower*: Miss Ellen Lewis. *Gnatbrain*: Miss Dora Herbert. *Sailor of the period*: Miss Kitty Doud.

Bracers of the Cook's Galley, Caewers of Pigtail, several Heavers too, as well as many other fellows who "Shiver their Timbers" "Blast Their Eyes," etc. True-hearted Polls of the Mariners: Misses Susan and Emelie Germaine, Lysle, Caldwell, Lamarchi, and two hundred others. *More Sailors, more Lasses, more Peasants, and a few Horse marines, and any quantity of s(o)upes served out according to the number of their mess.* More names would be placed here but the enumerators (so called) failed to perform their duties.

THE BLIND BEGGARS A Comic Opera in One Act, adapted from Offenbach's "Les Deux Aveugles." (Music by Jacques Offenbach. Original French libretto by Jules Moinaux.)

CAST: *Giraffier*, a Blind Beggar: BLANCHE GALTON. *Patachon*, another B.B., with solos of Trombone and Violin, introducing Lover's celebrated Irish song, "I'm Not Myself at All": THOMAS WHIFFIN.

1870.40 THE GRAND DUCHESS

A Revival of the Opéra Bouffe in Three Acts[19]. (Original French libretto to "La Grande Duchesse de Gérolstein" by Henri Meilhac and Ludovic Halévy.) Music by Jacques Offenbach. Director, Fred Lyster. Musical director, William H. Brinkworth. Produced by George Wood. Opened 14 November 1870 at Wood's Museum and closed 25 November 1870 after 11 performances (weekday matinees).

[16]For the return engagement the following cast changes among the principals: *La Grande Duchesse*: Mlle. MARIE AIMÉE. *Vanda*: Mlle. ROSA TAILLEFEUR. *Fritz*: Messr. GAUSINS. *Prince Paul*: Messr. LEGROS. *Baron Puck*: Messr. Edgard. *General Boum*: Messr. Duchesne. *Iza*: Mlle. Briot. *Olga*: Mlle. Anna. *Charlotte*: Mlle. Vaudelet.

[17]New adaptation in English. First produced in New York in French 14 February 1863 at the Théâtre Français.

[18]The Farce Specialty was ROMEO JAFFER JENKINS. Its cast included Mr. W. Leffingewell, Misses Kate O'Neil, Leffingwell, E. Lewis, A. Wood, S. and E. Germaine, Dora Herbert, Messrs. Broughton, E. Aberle, Henry Josephs.

[19]First produced in New York in English 17 June 1868 at the New York Theatre for 33 performances. English adaptation uncredited for this revival.

CAST: *The Grand Duchess*: EMMA HOWSON. *Wanda*: MINNIE WALTON. *General Boum*: FRED LYSTER. *Fritz*: W. S. BAKER. *Prince Paul*: HARRY STEWART. *Baron Puck*: Mr. Malette. *Baron Grog*: J. P. Cooke. *Nepomuc*: C. M. Manly. *Charlotte*: Emma Moshier. *Amelia*: Miss Westerberg. *Iza*: Mme. Bageard. *Olga*: Miss Andrew. (*Lords and Ladies of the Court, Maids of Honour, Pages, Ushers, Soldiers, Vivandières, Peasants.*)

1870.41 LES BRIGANDS

An Opéra-bouffe in Three Acts, in French. Libretto by Henri Meilhac and Ludovic Halévy. Music by Jacques Offenbach. Stage manager, Mons. Charles Estève. Scenery by Richard Marston, George Dayton. Musical director, Carlo Patti. Produced by James Fisk, Jr. Opened 14 November 1870 at the Grand Opera House in repertory; season closed 20 May 1871.

CAST: *Fiorella*, Falsacappa's daughter: Mlles. LEA SILLY, CÉLINE MONTALAND. *The Princess of Granada*: Mlle. JULIE HACHE. *The Duchess*: Mlle. L. Darlia. *The Marchioness*: Mlle. Legros. *Pipa*, Pipo's wife: Mlle. Lesage. *Pipetta*, Pipo's daughter: Mlle. Watson. *Peasants (4)*: *Zerlina*: Mlle. Victorine. *Fiametta*: Mlle. Vaudelet. *Bianca*: Mlle. Riotte. *Cicinella*: Mlle. Beaumont. *Fragoletto*, a young farmer: Mlle. ELISE PERSINI. *Falsacappa*, the Brigand Chief: Mons. CONSTANT GAUSINS, Mons. Girrebeuk. *Pietro*, his lieutenant: Mons. JACQUES ANTONY. *Duke of Mantua*: Mme. J. DARLIA. *Antonio*, the Duke's treasurer (Le Caissier): Mons. PAUL HITTEMANS. *Baron de Campotasso*, Esquire to the Duke: Mons. Cayla. *Captain of Caribineers*: Mons. Varlet. *Count de Gloria Cassis*, chamberlain to the Princess: Mons. Legros. *Adolph de Valladolid*, page to the Princess: Mme. Jousse. *Tutor* to the Princess: Mons. Oudin. *Pipo*, an innkeeper: Mons. BRUNET. *Brigands (3)*: *Carmagnola*: Mons. Brabant. *Barbavano*: Mons. Valter. *Domino*: Mons. Bastide. *A Courier*: Mons. Victoire. *A Sheriff*: Mons. Beaugard. *Ballet Specialty*, Act 3: Mlles. Lupo, Albertina, Gaugain, Mazzeri. *Brigands, Caribineers, Peasants, Pages, Lords and Ladies of Honor of the Court of Mantua; Pages, Lord and Ladies of the Court of Granada.*

Act 1: The Brigands' Hold.

Act 2: Farmhouse and Wheat Field.

Act 3: Palace and Ball Room.

ACT 1[20]

Introduction:

Choeur des Brigands (Le Cor dans la montagne)
Messrs. Bastide, Valter, Brabant, Choeur des Brigands

Couplets des Jeunes Filles (Déjà depuis une grande heure)
Mlles. Vaudelet, Victorine, Riotte, Beaumont

Couplets de Falsacappa (Quel est celui qui par les plaines)
Messrs. C. Gausins, Brabant, Bastide, Valter,
Mlles. Vaudelet, Victorine, Riotte, Beaumont

Strette
Messrs. Brabant, Valter, C. Gausins, Choeur

Couplets de Fiorella (Au chapeau je porte une aigrette)
Mlle. L. Silly

Morceau d'Ensemble (Nous avons pris ce petit homme)
Mlles. L. Silly, E. Persini,
Messrs. C. Gausins, J. Antony, Brabant, Bastide, Valter, Choeur

Couplets (Quand tu me fis l'insigne honneur)
Mlle. E. Persini

Rondo (Après avoir pris à droite)
Mlles. L. Silly, J. Darlia

Saltarelle (Falsacappa voici ma prise)
Mlle. E. Persini, Messrs. Brabant, J. Antony, Bastide, Valter, Choeur

Final:
Mlles. L. Silly, E. Persini, Les Quatre Jeunes Filles,
Messrs. C. Gausins, Brabant, J. Antony, Bastide, Valter, Varlet, Choeur

Choeur de Réception (Pour cette cérémonie)

Couplets (Vole, vole)

Orgie

Choeur des Carabiniers

Strette

ACT 2

Choeur (Les fourneaux sont allumés)
Mlles. Watson, Lesage, Mons. Brunet, Choeur

Canon (Soyez pitoyables)
Mlles. L. Silly, E. Persini, Messrs. C. Gausins,
J. Antony, Brabant, Bastide, Valter, Les Quatre Jeunes Filles, Choeur

Duetto du Notaire (Hé! la! hé! la!)
Mlles. L. Silly, E. Persini, Les Quatre Jeunes Filles

Choeur de Sortie
Choeur (Tutti)

Trio des Marmitons (Arrête toi donc je t'en prie)
Mlle. E. Persini, Messrs. C. Gausins, J. Antony

Choeur et Mélodrame (A nous holà!)
Mlle. E. Persini, Messrs. C. Gausins, J. Antony, Brabant, Bastide, Choeur

Choeur et Couplets de L'ambassade (Dissimulons)
E. Persini, Vaudelet, Victorine, Mlles. Riotte, Beaumont, Messrs. C. Gausins,
Brabant, J. Antony, Cayla, Bastide, Varlet, Choeur

Choeur

Mélodrame et scène (Entrez là)
Tutti

Couplets des Espagnols (Ja dis vous n'aviez qu'un'patrie)
Mlle. Legros

Couplets (Pourquoi l'on aime)
Mlles. L. Silly, E. Persini, J. Hache, Mme. Jousse

Final
Tutti

ACT 3

Choeur de Fête (L'aurore parait fêtons l'aurore)
Mlles. L. Darlia, Legros, Choeur des femmes

Couplets du Prince (Ja dis régnait un Prince)
Mlle. J. Darlia

Choeur de Sortie

Couplets du Caissier (O mes amours)
Mons. P. Hittemans

Morceau d'ensemble (Voici venir J. Hache)
Mlles. Legros, L. Darlia, Seigneurs et dames de la Cour, Tous les Brigands

Choeur de Sortie

Final
Tutti

1870.42 PARIS, or, The Apple of Discord

A Burlesque in One Act, 5 Scenes[21]. Music selected and arranged by Michael Connolly. Produced under the stage direction of Lydia Thompson. Stage director, James Barnes. Scenery by Joseph B. Ayers. Costumes designed by Lydia Thompson and M. Toledo. Machinery by William B. Carpenter. Appointments and properties by Charles LaForrest. Musical director, Michael Connolly. Produced by Lydia Thompson's Burlesque Troupe. Opened 14 November 1870 at Wood's Museum; reconstructed 19 December 1870 and closed 31 December 1870 after 49 performances.

CAST: Messieurs Celestial: *Jupiter*, King of the Gods, the ever juvenile: MARIE LONGMORE. *Mercury*, the royal tiger: ELIZA WEATHERSBY. *Mars*, General of the Forces: HARRY STEWART. *Apollo*, President of the Royal Academy of Music, fine arts, and post laureate to Olympus: Mary Stevens. *Cupid*, an old love: Jennie Arnott.

Mesdames Celestials: *Juno*, Queen of the Gods and Goddesses: Annie Firmin. *Venus*, the fairest: Minnie Walton. *Minerva*, the Goddess of literary warfare, lady and commander in chief of the blues: Lillie Hall. *Diana*: Lizzie West. *Pomona*: Jennie Satterlee.

Demi-Gods, the solid middle class: *Castor, Pollux*, the gemini sons of Deoda and Jupiter, and half-brothers of the celebrated beautiful Helen Castor, fond of driving; Pollux is a good hand with the gloves: W. B. CAHILL, WILLIE EDOUIN. *Orion*, (Mr. O'Ryan), the only Irish constellation in the skies: ALICE ATHERTON. *Ganymede*, the page of mythology—immortal buttons: Marian Westerberg.

---

[20]Musical numbers not listed in programs. List prepared from published French piano vocal score (Colombier, Paris, 1870).

[21]Especially written and adapted for the Lydia Thompson Troupe, authorship uncredited. Preceded by a farce, My Young Wife and Old Umbrella. As per reviews, included the song:
"Let Me Be"
L. Thompson, H. Becket

Demi-Goddesses: *Psyche*: Emma Moshier. *Hebe*, lady's maid to the goddesses: Marion Holcombe.

An Ordinary Mortal: *Oenone*, a shepherdess, married to Mister Alexander, as mentioned below by us, and by the gods above: HARRY BECKETT.

An Extraordinary Mortal: *Paris*, known among the peasants of Mount Ida, as Alexander the Little, chairman of the Irregular Rips, and G. M. of the Jolly Dogs Club: LYDIA THOMPSON. *First Pleasure*: Annie Page. *Second Pleasure*: Nellie Stewart. *Third Pleasure*: Kate Nelson. *Apollo's Grooms*: Masters Major, Scott. *Appleton's R. R. Guide*: C. Walsh.

Scene 1: Cupid's Tea-Rose Gardens. *Scene 2*: Oenone's Cottage. *Scene 3*: Mount Ida. *Scene 4*: Mercury's Message Office. *Scene 5*: Cythera. Reconciliation of Oenone and Paris. Grand Regatta in celebration of the happy event, inaugurated by Venus rising from the sea.

1870.43 FAUST!/ LOVE AMONG THE ROSES!, or, an Ambassador from Below

A Triple Bill of Musical Extravaganza, Opera Burlesque and Farce Specialty[22]. Orchestra under the direction of William Withers. Produced by Lina Edwin. Opened 21 November 1870 at Lina Edwin's Theatre and closed 26 November 1870 after 8 performances.

LOVE AMONG THE ROSES, or, an Ambassador from Below. A Musical Extravaganza in One Act.[23]

CAST: *Marquis de Brancadour*: THOMAS WHIFFIN. *Fiammetta*, the Gardener's Wife: BLANCHE GALTON. *Mephistopheles*, a young gentleman nearly related to the old one, his first appearance in this world: Miss MARION TAYLOR. *Repite*, the Gardener: Miss MARION TAYLOR. *Honesta*, Marchioness de Brancador: Miss MARION TAYLOR. *Attendants, Servants, etc.*

Scene: The Marquis de Brancadour's Villa near Naples.

FAUST! An entirely original Spectacular Burlesque on the Charming Opera in One Act, 5 Scenes.

CAST: *Faust*: Mrs. JOHN L. HALL. *Mephistopheles*, Père: JOHN L. HALL. *Mephistopheles*, Fils: La Petite ALBERTA. *Dame Martha*: Mr. J. MORRIS. *Sieble*: E. A. EBERLE. *Valemtine*: THOMAS WHIFFIN. *Marguerite*: BLANCHE GALTON. *Annetta*: S. Germaine. *Katrina*: E. Germaine. *Slim Jack*: H. Broughton. *Tonderdasher*: Mr. Somers. *Slick Tom*: Mr. Klebs. *Drammon*: Mr. Caldwell.

Scene 1: Faust's Study. *Scene 2*: Dame Martha's House. *Scene 3*: Exterior of a Garden near the Town Gate. *Scene 4*: Garden attached to Marguerite's dwelling. *Scene 5*: Near Wittemberg. Grand Denouement.

1870.44 THE BLACK CROOK

A Revival of the Original Grand, Romantic, Magical and Spectacular Drama (Musical Extravaganza) in Four Acts, 11 Scenes[24]. Play by Charles M. Barras. Music by Thomas Baker, together with new music arranged and composed by the conductor, Signor Giuseppe Operti. Ballets arranged by Signor Davide Costa. Scenery by William Voegtlin, assisted by Mons. Reitzky. Stage machinery by Bensen Sherwood. Costumes by J. W. Laureys. Properties and appointments by W. Duvernay. Illuminations by C. Murray. Produced by Henry Jarrett and Harry Palmer. Opened 12 December 1870 at Niblo's Garden and closed 8 April 1871 after 122 performances.

CAST: *Count Wolfenstein*: ALEX FITZGERALD. *Rodolphe*, a poor artist: THEODORE HAMILTON. *Von Puffengruntz*, the Count's steward: B. MAGINLEY. *Hertzog*, surnamed the Black Crook, an alchymist: C. H. MORTON. *Greppo*, his Servant: FELIX ROGERS. *Dragonfin*: J. Franklin. *Zamiel*, the arch-fiend: J. Robertson. *Wolfgar*, a gypsy ruffian: E. K. Collier. *Caspar*, a peasant: R. Smith. *Red Glare*, the Recording Demon: F. Clark. *Skudawelp*, familiar to Hertzog: P. Lamb. *Villagers, Peasants, Guards, Attendants, Demons, Monsters, Apparitions, Gnomes, etc.*

Stalacta, Queen of the Golden Realm: PAULINE MARKHAM. *Amina*, betrothed to Rodolphe: Miss RAWLINSON. *Dame Barbara*, her foster mother: Mrs. Edward Wright. *Carline*, Amina's maid: Miss Fanny Prestige. *Rosetta*, a Peasant: Miss Warren. *Fairies, Naiads, etc.*

Ballet: Mlle. MARIETTA BONFANTI (Premiere Danseuse), Signor GIOVANNI NOVISSIMO (Premier Danseur). *Soloists*: Mlles. Cora Adrienne, Rosita Pagani, Rosa Zuardi, Betty Rimmersberg, Marie Rimmersberg, Marie Kurtz, Stritter, Jeannette, Marie, Leotine, Laurent, Guissepina Nini, Louise Langlois. *Coryphées*: Rose, Louise, Vernet, Pauline, Camilla, Clara, Koch, Antonina, Pinzuti, Baretta, Lambert, Stella, Sophie, Arnal, Medina, Brisson, Blanche, Alexandrine, Antoinette, Jenny, Helene, Hortense, Anna, Marie, Cabal, Victoire, Aurelie, Adrienne, Leonie, Jeanne, Eugenie. Corps de Ballet of 100. *Specialties*: The Majiltons (Charles, Henri, Marie; acrobats), Moe and Goodrich (skaters).

Act 1, Scene 1: A Valley at the Foot of the Hartz Mountains. (Reitzky.) *Scene 2*: A Woody Pass. (Voegtlin.) *Scene 3*: Laboratory of the Black Crook. (Voegtlin.) *Scene 4*: An Apartment in the Castle of Wolfenstein. (Reitzky.) *Scene 5*: A Wild Glen in the Heart of the Brocken. (Voegtlin.)

Act 2, Scene 1: Subterranean Vault in the Casle of Wolfenstein. (Voegtlin.) *Scene 2*: Lobby in the Castle of Wolfenstein. (Reitzky.) *Scene 3*: A Wild Pass in the Hartz Mountains. (Voegtlin.) *Scene 4*: The Grocco of Stalacta. Fern Lake of Silver Sheen with the Crystal Cascade. (Voegtlin.)

Act 3: Six months later. Illuminated Golden Terrace of the Castle Wolfenstein. (Voegtlin.)

Act 4: Six months later. Palace of Dew Drops, forming a dazzling transformation scene. A Dazzling Transformation Scene, revealing the Nymphs of the Golden Reams. (Brothers Brew, of London.)

BALLETS, SPECIALTIES, MUSICAL NUMBERS[25]

Pas de Sabot (Wooden Shoe Waltz)(Grand Ballet)(Act 1, Scene 1)
Coryphées
(*Music by* Giuseppe Operti.)

Pas des Fleurs (Flower Dance Mazurka; Act 1, Scene 1)
Mlle. C. Adrienne, Soloists, Full Corps de Ballet
(*Music by* Giuseppe Operti.)

"Naughty, Naughty Man" (He's naughty, but he's nice)(Song)
F. Prestige
(*Music by* Giuseppe Operti.)

"The Mermaid's Song" (from the opera, Oberon) (Act 2, Scene 4)
P. Markham
(*Music by* Karl Maria von Weber. *Lyrics by* James Robinson Planché.)

"The Power of Love" (I Said to My Love)(Ballad) (Act 2, Scene 4)
P. Markham
(*Music by* Giuseppe Operti.)

Grand Ballet Des Ferns (Act 2, Scene 4)
Mlle. M. Bonfanti, Signor Novissimo, Soloists, Coryphées

Grand Candelabra Ballet (Act 3)
Coryphées

Pas de Deux
Mlle. Bonfanti, Signor Novissimo

Nautch Girl's Dance
Mlles. C. Adrienne, R. Pagani

Cantonnière Parisienne
Mlles. R. Zuardi, Rimmersberg, Jeannette

Pas de Follie
Mlles. Stritter, Kurtz, Leontine, Marie, Rimmersberg, Laurent

Les Trois Diables (Act 3)
Wonderful Majiltons

[22]The Farce Specialty was ROMEO JAFFIER JENKINS, the great Leffingwell specialty. CAST: Mr. M. W. Leffingwell, Misses Kate O'Neil, Leffingwell, E. Lewis, A. Wood, S. and E. Germaine, Dora Herbert, Messrs. Broughton, E. A. Eberle, Harry Josephs.

[23]Billed "1st time in this country." Author and composer uncredited; earlier versions of Love Among the Roses, librettist uncredited, have been presented in London since the 1820s, always with different composers.

[24]First produced in New York 12 September 1866 at Niblo's Garden for 475 performances.

[25]Additional musical selections from THE BLACK CROOK composed by Giuseppe Operti and advertised in the theatre program:

"Oh no! not in these boots" (Ballad)
F. Prestige

"Married on Michaelmas' Day" (Bllad)
F. Prestige

"I am waiting for thee" (Ballad)
P. Markham

Lotoz Waltz

Golden Terrace Galop

Messrs. Moe & Goodrich (Act 3)
Comic Song and Duet (Act 3)
F. Prestige, F. Rogers
(*Music by* Giuseppe Operti.)
Grand Amazonian March (Act 3)
(*Music by* Giuseppe Operti.)
Transformation Scene, revealing Nymphs of the Golden Realm (Act 4)

1870.45 BARBE BLEU

A Revival of the Opèra-bouffe in Three Acts[26], 4 Scenes, in French. Libretto by Henri Meilhac and Ludovic Halévy. Music by Jacques Offenbach. Musical director, Carlo Patti. Produced by James Fisk, Jr. Opened 24 December 1870 at the Grand Opera House in repertory; season closed 20 May 1871.

CAST: *Boulotte*: Mlle. MARIE AIMÉE. *Blue Beard*: Mons. CONSTANT GAUSINS. *Count Oscar*: Mons. PAUL HITTEMANS. *Prince Saphir*: Mons. LEGROS. *A Magistrate*: Mons. Brunet. *Popolani*: Mons. Varlet. *King Bobeche*: Mons. DUCHESNE. *Alvarez*: Mons. Valter. *Princess Hermia*: Mlle. JULIE HACHE. *Queen Clementine*: Mlle. SUSANNE THAL. *Heloise*: Mlle. Jousse. *Isaure*: Mlle. L. Darlia. *Blanche*: Mlle. Vandamme. *Peasant Woman*: Mlle. Pingeon. *Eleonore*: Mlle. Lesage. *Rosalinde*: Mlle. Briot. *Dorothée*: Mlle. Alda. *Lords and Ladies, Pages, Guards at the Court of King Bobeche, Men-at-Arms of the Lord Blue Beard, Peasants, etc.*

1871.01 THE 40 THIEVES, or, Striking Oil in Family Jars!

Lydia Thompson Burlesque Troupe in a Revised Version of the Grand Spectacular Burlesque Extravaganza in Two Acts, 7 Scenes[27]. (Original play by Henry B. Farnie. Produced under the direction of Lydia Thompson.) Music selected and arranged by Michael Connolly. Produced by Lydia Thompson. Opened 2 January 1871 at Wood's Museum and closed 7 January 1871 after 7 performances.

CAST: *Ali Baba*, an Alley who has just gone through the Court: WILLIE EDOUIN. *Ganem*, his son, who, from his small sighs, may be scarcely considered a full grown: LYDIA THOMPSON. *Cassim Baba*, 'a baa baa, black sheep': T. W. KEENE. *Abdallah*, a polished robber, and leader of the brassiest band imaginable: ADA HARLAND. *Hassarac*, his rebellious lieutenant, an unscrupulous individual, prepared to stick at everything in general, and nothing in particular—a base performer, whose vice ranges from the faintest pitch and toss to the most pronounced manslaughter: HARRY BECKETT. *The Cadi*: G. C. Charles. *Phizwig*: Harry Stewart. *Sleepy Policeman*: J. C. Walsh. *Mirza*, "Penny Plain": A. Hamilton. *Hassan*, "Twopence Colored": C. M. Manly. *Orchobrand*, the enchanter of the forest: Jennie Arnott. *Cogia Baba*, Ali's better half: ALICE ATHERTON. *Zaide*, Cassim's ditto: Nellie Henderson. *Morgiana*, slave to Cassim, and to circumstances, having no wages she can only save—the entire family: ALICE HARRISON. *Gossimer*, The Fairy Queen: EMMA MOSHIER.

Act 1, Scene 1: A Forest. *Scene 2*: Interior of Ali Baba's Cottage.

Act 2, Scene 1: The Robbers' Cavern. *Scene 2*: Exterior of Ali's House. *Scene 3*: Verandah of Ali's New House. *Scene 4*: The Court. *Scene 5*: Reception room in an Eastern Palace.

1871.02 ST. GEORGE AND THE DRAGON!, or, The 7 Champions of Christendom

A Burlesque Extravaganza in Two Acts, 7 Scenes. Music selected and arranged by Michael Connolly. Scenery by Joseph B. Ayers. Costumes by Lydia Thompson and M. Toledo. Machinery by W. B. Carpenter. Appointments and properties by Charles LaForrest. Produced under the direction of Lydia Thompson. Opened 9 January 1871 at Wood's Museum and closed 21 January 1871 after 14 performances.

CAST: *St. George of England*: LYDIA THOMPSON. *St. Denis of France*: ALICE HARRISON. *St. Patrick of Ireland*: ALICE ATHERTON. *St. Antony of Italy*: EMMA MOSHIER. *St. James of Spain*: Nellie Henderson. *St. Andrews of Scotland*: Annie Firmin. *St. David Of Wales*: Lottie Grant. *Emperor of Morosco*: HARRY BECKETT. *Alektra*, a Sorceress: T. W. KEENE. *Sultan*: WILLIE EDOUIN. *Vizier*: G. C. Charles. *La Sbara, Not de Monpari*: Ada Harland. *Brunette*: Jenny Arnott. *Emilia*: Lizzie West. *Lavinia*: Marion Westerber. *Rosina*: Hattie Lyon. *Julia*: Marion Holcomb. *Angelica*: Jennie Satterlee. *Drum Major*: Harry Stewart. *First Syren*: Hattie Price. *Second Syren*: Kate Devoy. *Pirate Chief*: C. M. Manley. *Dragon*: J. P. Cooke. *Guards, Serpents, Mokes, Syrens, Water Nymphs.*

Act 1, Scene 1: The Island of Alektra. *Scene 2*: Apartment in the Court of the Sultan of Egypt. *Scene 3*: A Harbor in Egypt. *Scene 4*: On board the Emperor's Yacht.

Act 2, Scene 1: Gardens of the Imperial Moorish Seraglio in Spain. Encounter of St. George and the Dragon. *Scene 2*: Before the Gates of Alektra's Castle. *Scene 3*: Infernal Fernery of Alektra's Castle.

1871.03 LA PÉRICHOLE

A Revival of the Opéra-bouffe in Two Acts[28], in French. Libretto by Ludovic Halévy and Henri Meilhac. Based on "Le Carosse du Saint-Sacrament" by Prosper Mérimée. Music by Jacques Offenbach. Musical director, Carlo Patti. Produced by James Fisk, Jr. Opened 18 January 1871 at the Grand Opera House in repertory; season closed 20 May 1871.

CAST: *La Périchole*, a Ballad Singer: Mlle. MARIE AIMÉE. *Piquillo*, a Ballad Singer: Mons. CONSTANT GAUSINS. *Don Andre des Ribeira*, Viceroy of Peru: Mons. DUCHESNE. *Don Pedro de Hinoyosa*, Governor of Lima: Mons. Edgard. *Le Compte de Panatellas*, First Gentleman of the Bedchamber: Mons. Varlet. *Le Marquis de Tarapote*: Mons. Adrian Valter. *The Three Cousins*: *Guadalena*: Mlle. Julie Hache. *Mastrilla*: Mlle. Jousse. *Berginella*: Mlle. J. Darlia. *Ladies of the Court (4)*: *Brambilla*: Mlle. L. Darlia. *Ninetta*: Mlle. Briot. *Manuelita*: Mlle. Legros. *Frasquinella*: Mlle. Taillefer. *Notaries, Soldiers, Courtiers, Indians, Peasants, Guards, Pages, Servants.*

1871.04 RICHELIEU OF THE PERIOD!

A Burlesque in Two Acts of Edward Bulwer Lytton's drama "Richelieu." Play by James Schonberg and T. B. DeWalden. Music composed and arranged by F. Strebinger without respect to the Ancient Masters, but with great regard to the Lays of the Last Minstrel. Scenery by Joseph Hayes and J. Johnson. Costumes by Miss Trimble. Decorative department, R. Cutler. Mechanical effects by James Tate. Lightning conductor, John McComb. Acting manager, John H. Selwyn. Stage manager, E. S. Tarr. Produced by James E. Hayes. Opened 6 February 1871 at the Olympic Theatre and closed 18 March 1871 after 48 performances.

CAST: *George L. Armand Jean Des Etats Unis*, with all the cardinal virtues of the Duc de Richelieu: GEORGE L. FOX. *His Cabinet*: *Secretary of Hymen*: ADA HARLAND. *Secretary of Venus*: LILLIE ELDRIDGE. *François, Secretary of Momus, and Mercury of Richelieu*: Little JENNIE YEAMANS. *Secretary of Olympus*: H. R. TEESDALE. *Secretary of Hades*: ED. COLEMAN.

De Mauprat: ADA HARLAND. *De Baradas*: ED. COLEMAN. *Cardinal G. L. Richelieu*: GEORGE L. FOX. *Joseph*: George Beane. *Huguet*: H. H. Honeywood. *Louis XIII*: H. R. TEESDALE. *Sieur de Berighen*: Lulu Prior. *Gaston*: Fannie Beane. *François*: Little JENNIE YEAMANS. *De Clermont*: Flora Lee. *De Saurdaic*: J. B. Richards. *Longueville*: Samuel Distin. *De Gramont*: E. M. Howard. *Governor of the Bastille*: H. H. Pratt. *Gaoler*: J. L. Debonay. *King's Pages*: Miss Dunham, G. Fenton. *Cardinal's Pages*: Messrs. Pierce, S. O'Neil. *Julie de Mortimar*: LILLIE ELDRIDGE. *Marion De Lorme*: Annie Yeamans. *Courtiers, Musketeers, Arquebussiers, Monks, Cardinals, Guards, King's Guards, Heralds, Pages, Trumpeters, Servants, etc.*

SPECIALTIES, MUSICAL NUMBERS
"Put Me in My Little Bed" (Trio, Act 1, Scene 6)
L. Eldridge, A. Harland, G. L. Fox

[26]First produced in New York in French 13 July 1868 at Niblo's Garden. For Synopsis of Scenes and Musical Numbers, see original 1868 production.
[27]First produced in New York in an earlier, longer version 1 February 1869 at Niblo's Garden; reconstructed 5 April 1869, for 136 performances.

[28]Previously produced in New York in French 4 January 1869 at Pike's Opera House.

1871.05 LUCRETIA BORGIA, or, the Cup of Cold Poison!

A Superb Burlesque Extravaganza in One Act, 5 Scenes[29]. Stage director, James Barnes. Musical director, William H. Brinkworth. Produced by George Wood. Opened 13 February 1871 at Wood's Museum and closed 24 February 1871 after 12 performances; returned 13-17 March 1871 for 5 additional matinees. Total: 17 performances[30].

CAST: *The Dook*: W. B. CAHILL. *Rustighello*: T. W. KEENE. *Gubetta*: GEORGE C. CHARLES. *Jeppo*: HARRY STEWART. *Lucretia Borgia*: LOUIS J. MESTAYER. *Gennaro*: Miss ALICE HARRISON. *Orsini*: Miss THERESA WOOD. *Livretto*: Miss ALICE ATHERTON. *Petrucci*: Miss Emma Moshier. *Vitelli*: Miss Jenny Satterlee. *Guests, Serenaders, Attendants.*

Scene 1: At Venice. A Reading party and Reading Sauce. Arrival of a famous Water Party, and touching interview between Lucretia and Gennaro, resulting in The Mob, The Music and the Malediction. *Scene 2*: Apartment in the Ducal Palace. How the Dook and Rustighello—but no matter. *Scene 3*: Lucretia's Surgery. The Insult. The Poison, and the Antidote. *Scene 4*: Ante Chamber in the Ducal Palace. *Scene 5*: The Ducal Palace. Retribution Justice. The Dook's Punishment. The Climax. Everybody Triumphant.

1871.06 LES GÉORGIENNES

A Grand Military Spectacle and Opéra-bouffe in Three Acts, in French. Libretto by Jules Moinaux. Music by Jacques Offenbach. Scenery by George Dayton. Dresses by Philippi. Appointments, armors by Wallis. Musical director, Carlo Patti. Produced by James Fisk, Jr. Opened 6 March 1871 at the Grand Opera House in repertory; season closed 20 May 1871.

CAST: *Rhodendron*: Mons. CONSTANT GAUSINS. *Jol-Hiddin*: Mons. LEGROS. *Boboli*: Mons. PAUL HITTEMANS. *Poterno*: Mons. Jacques Antony. *Cocobo*: Mons. Varlet. *Férosa*: Mlle. MARIE AIMÉE. *Nani*: Mlle. ELISE PERSINI. *Alita*: Mlle. Juliette Jousse. *Zaida*: Mlle. Julie Hache. *Mileva*: Mlle. Legros. *Nadji*: Mlle. J. Darlia. *Zora*: Mlle. L. Darlia. *Melano*: Mlle. Taillefer. *Mirza*: Mlle. Briot. *Fatime*: Mlle. Lesage. *Nourika*: Mlle. Vaudelet. *Zetuibe*: Mlle. Anna. *First Drummer*: Mlle. Vandam. *Second Drummer*: Mlle. Alda. *First Trumpeter*: Mlle. Riotte. *Second Trumpeter*: Mlle. Gremaud. *Chorus of 100 Young Ladies*. (*Specialty*: The Elephant "Yusuf.")

Act 1: A Vineyard at Djegani in Asiatic Georgia.

Act 2: The General's Tent.

Act 3: Ramparts of Djegani.

ACT 1[31]

Choeur (A pleines corbeilles)
Mlles. E. Persini, J. Hache, Vendageuses

Couplets (Constantinople, ô mon pays)
Mons. P. Hittemans, Choeur

Quintette (Ah! quel malheur, quel sort effroyable!)
Mlles. M. Aimée, E. Persini, J. Hache, J. Jousse, Mons. P. Hittemans, Toutes les femmes

Air (Je suis ce pacha de si grand renom)
Messrs. C. Gausins, P. Hittemans, Varlet

Choeur (Ah! pour nous quel beau jour!)
Messrs. Legros, J. Antony, Quatre Soldats

Couplets (Ah! vraiment C'est charmant)
Mlle. E. Persini

Scene et Choeur (Allons! foulez la grappe)
Mlle. M. Aimée, Choeur

Choeur des Éclopés (Après une guerre funeste)
Messrs. Legros, J. Antony, Les Géorgiennes

Final (Et nous vous accusions)
Messrs. P. Hittemans, Varlet, M. Aimée, Toutes les femmes, Ensemble

ACT 2[32]

Air (Attention, tapins)
Mons. C. Gausins, Tambours, Tous

Couplets (Sous cet uniforme modeste)
Mlle. E. Persini

Duo (Secondez-moi, coquetteries)
Mlle. M. Aimée, Mons. Legros

Chanson (Tin, tin, tin, tin)
Mlle. M. Aimée, Choeur

ACT 3

Choeur des Femmes (Guettez bien tous)

Scene (Empalé, moi, misericorde!)
Messrs. P. Hittemans, C. Gausins

Choeur (Quel bruit, quel escalandre)
Mlles. E. Persini, J. Hache, J. Jousse, Taillefer, Legros, L. Darlia, J. Darlia, Toutes

Air (Allons, femmes, serrons nos rangs)
Mlle. M. Aimée

Ensemble (Nous sommes de pauvres Zingari)
Messrs. C. Gausins, P. Hittemans, Varlet, Legros, J. Antony, Deux Hommes

Reprise du Chant de Guerre (Si vers nous l'ennemi jamais)
Mlle. M. Aimée

[29]Preceded by a charming melodrama, NORAH CREINA, with much the same cast.
[30]In its second week, LUCRETIA BORGIA was performed for 5 weekday matinees.
[31]Musical numbers not listed in programs. List prepared from published French/English libretto prepared for this production (Metropolitan Job Printing and Engraving, New York, 1870).
[32]Triumphal March (*Music by* Carlo Patti.) also performed in Act 2, as per program. Not in published libretto.

1871.07 LA BELLE HÉLÈNE

A Revival of the Opéra-bouffe in Three Acts[33], in French. Libretto by Henri Meilhac and Ludovic Halévy. Music by Jacques Offenbach. Stage manager, Mons. Charles Estève. Musical director, Carlo Patti. Produced by James Fisk, Jr. Opened 13 April 1871 at the Grand Opera House in repertory; season closed 20 May 1871.

CAST: *Hélène*, Queen of Sparta: Mlle. MARIE AIMÉE. *Orestes*, son of Agamemnon: Mlle. ELISE PERSINI. *Bacchis*, attendant on Hélène: Mlle. Julie Hache. *Loena, Parthenis*, Women of Corinth: Mlles. Anna, Briot. *Paris*, son of King Priam: Mons. CONSTANT GAUSINS. *Menelaus*, King of Sparta: Mons. Edgard. *Agamemnon*, King of Greece: Mons. DUCHESNE. *Achilles*, King of Phiotis: Mons. LEGROS. *Ajax I*, King of Salamino: Mons. Brabant. *Ajax II*, King of Locria: Mons. Bastide. *Calchas*, Grand Augur of Jupiter: Mons. Adrien Valter. *Euthecles*, a blacksmith: Mons. Cayla. *Philocomes*, servant to Calchas: Mons. Rafael. *Slave*: Mons. Beauxan. *Guards, Citizens, Slaves*: Male and Female Auxiliaries.

1871.08 THE THREE HUNCHBACKS!

A Grand Spectacular Pantomime in a Prologue, Two Acts, 14 Scenes. Play by J. McClosky, adapted from "The Arabian Nights." Stage manager, A. S. Pennoyer. Musical director, Henry Tissington. Produced by James Fisk, Jr. Opened 22 May 1871 at the Grand Opera House and closed 24 June 1871 after 35 performances.

CAST: *The Three Blue Hunchbacks*: *Cephoni*: J. B. MAGILL. *Ozmoni*: J. R. DAVIS. *Tezmoni*: C. THOMPSON. *Haroun-Al Haschid*, Caliph of Bagdad: J. Webster. *Giaffir*, his Grand Vizier: Harry Saunders. *Giant Ab-ra-ca-dab-ra* of Eagles Nest: A gentleman only 24 feet high. *Molkus, Erebus*, Yellow Sprites, attendants on the Giant: C. Zeltner, J. O. Franklin. *Arab Chieftains, Captives, Black Slaves, Eunuchs, Banner Bearers. Fairy Queen Azureoli*, Guardian of the Blue Dwarfs: ETHEL NORMAN. *Zuelika*, with songs: BELLA HOWITT.

Pantomime: *Clown*: CHARLES ABBOTT. *Harlequin*: J. W. SANFORD. *Pantaloon*: C. CHRISDIE. *Columbine*: Mlle. EMMA. *Specialties*: Mlle. MARIE BONFANTI, Signor NOVISSIMO, Coryphées, Corps de Ballet (ballet); Mr. Levy (Cornet a Piston), Moe and Goodrich (skaters); La Petite Benson.

Prologue: Blue Cavern of the Giant Ab-ra-ca-dab-ra. Living Statues and departure for Zuleika's house at Bagdad. Grand Square of the prophet in Bagdad.

Act 1: Pantomime. *Scene 1*: Old Splorger's Mill. *Scene 2*: Helmbold's New Store. *Scene 3*: Lager Bier Garden.

Act 2, Scene 1: Model Farm Yard. *Scene 2*: A Street. *Scene 3*: Butchers and Bakers. *Scene 4*: A Prison what is a prison. *Scene 5*: Elevated Railroad. *Scene 6*: Grand Skating carnival. *Scene 7*: A street with fun for the million. *Scene 8*: The Magic Chamber.

[33]First produced in New York in French 26 March 1868 at the Théâtre Français. For Synopsis of Scenes and Musical Numbers, see original 1868 production.

Scene 9: Dr. Whackman's House. *Scene 10*: A Cavern. *Scene 11*: Grand Transformation Scene; The Palace of the Azure Fairy and Bower of Bright Delight.

PROLOGUE

Arrival of the Fairy Queen and her attendant train

"It's Naughty but it's Nice" (Song)
B. Howitt

Grand Eastern March

"Pearls of the Orient" (Ballet)
Mlle. M. Bonfanti, Signor Novissimo, Full Corps de Ballet

ACT 1

Scene 1

Grand Transformation of Characters

Scene 3

Buy a Broom Dance
16 Ladies from Deutschland

Double Hornpipe
French Twin Sisters

"Dew d'Andes" (Song)
B. Howitt

Grand Finale

ACT 2

Scene 1

Grand Ladder Dance
C. Abbott

Scene 5

Revels Mexicano (Grand Ballet)
Mlle. M. Bonfanti, Signor Novissimo, Coryphées

Little Song and Little Dance (Specialty)
La Petite Benson

Scene 6

Moe & Goodrich (Skating specialty)

Scene 11

Grand Transformation Scene

1871–1872 SEASON

Marie Aimee in LES BRIGANDS (Photo: Mora)
Billy Rose Theatre Collection, New York Public Library for the Performing Arts

1871–1872 SEASON

THREE BLIND MICE!, or, Harlequin Tell-Tale Tit

1871.09

Fox & Denier Pantomime Troupe in a Pantomime in Two Acts, 12 Scenes. Music composed by A. W. Maflin. Produced by George Wood. Opened 5 June 1871 at Wood's Museum and closed 24 June 1871 after 36 performances[1].

CAST: *Screech Owl*, a knowing and downy old bird, not to be caught with any amount of chaff: TONY DENIER. *Humphrey with his flail*, a dainty sort of chap, who from the moment he stepped on the ground, put his foot in it, afterwards Clown: TONY DENIER. *Ye Terrible Monster*, a cripple, vassal and creature of "nobody": CHARLES K. FOX. *Old Blunderhead*, the Miller, without any son, but with a flourishing daughter: CHARLES K. FOX. *Pantaloon*: CHARLES K. FOX. *Little Boy Blue*, afterwards Harlequin: A. W. MAFLIN. *Little Wee Foot*, afterwards Columbine: Miss LINDA deRHONA. *Fairy Flower*, the Queen: Miss Nellie Sanford. *Miss Sweetapple*: Miss Annie Bond. *Nobody*, an evil genius, who lives no one knows where: B. J. McLAUGHLIN. *Tell Take Tit*, a wicked old witch: B. J. McLAUGHLIN. *Onduty*, a model Policeman: Tom Williams. *Sprightly*, a waiter, always up and doing: Frank Switz. *Old Timbertoe*, a gouty Bachelor: Louis Birchler. *Paddy Carey*, an Irish Emigrant: J. King. *Fearnaught*, the King's Messenger: Jean Louis. *The Soldier with his musket*: R. Durdy. *Pantomime characters by the Entire Company*. (*Specialty*: WOODEN HEADED ACROBATS, Tagge, Wragge and Bobtael, Burlesque Gymnast Artists.)

Act 1, Scene 1: The Haunts of Nobody. *Scene 2*: The home of the Jolly Miller on the river. *Scene 3*: The Fighting Roosters on the road to fun. *Scene 4*: Somebody or other's apartment. *Scene 5*: Cook shop. Nowhere in particular! *Scene 6*: The Abode of the gay and Festive.

Act 2, Scene 1: Interior of International Lodging House. *Scene 2*: Scene in China with the Celestials. *Scene 3*: The Bower of Beauty. *Scene 4*: Hippodrome at Paris. *Scene 5*: Butcher's Bull's Head and Stock Market. *Scene 6*: Wine Vaults.

SPECIALTIES, MUSICAL NUMBERS

Pas de Paysanne (Act 1, Scene 3)
Mlle. Pagani, Corps de Ballet

The Three Blind Mice and Grand Transformation of the Characters (Act 1, Scene 3)

Wonderful Spade Dance (Act 1, Scene 6)
A. W. Maflin

Terpsichorean Aerostations and Homage to Brother Jonathan and his happy family (Act 1, Scene 6)

Three Blind Mice Polka (Act 2)

Juggling Specialty (Act 2, Scene 3)
H. Evans

Juggling a Cannon Ball weighing 20 pounds, a Glass Bottle, and an Egg

Skipping the Rope Redowa (Act 2, Scene 3)
L. deRhona

Wooden Headed Acrobats (Act 2, Scene 4)
T. Denier, Tagge, Wragge, Bobtael

Dancing Ladder (Act 2, Scene 4)
A. W. Maflin

Last scene of all that ends this strange eventful history (Act 2, Scene 6)

PAUL CLIFFORD!

1871.10

A Revival of the Grand, Musical and Spectacular Drama in Three Acts, 13 Scenes. Adapted from Edward G. E. L. Bulwer-Lytton's novel (by B. Webster). Produced under the direction of C. H. Morton. Scenery by William Voegtlin. Mechanical effects by Bensen Sherwood. Properties by A. Benedict. Calcium lights by C. Murray. Costumes by C. Laureys. Orchestra under the direction of Signor Giuseppe Operti. Produced by Henry Jarrett and Harry Palmer. Opened 12 June 1871 at Niblo's Garden and closed 24 June 1871 after 14 performances[2].

CAST: *Paul Clifford* (the Eminent Irish Comedian and Vocalist): JOHN COLLINS. *Long Ned*: GEORGE C. BONIFACE. *Scarlet Jack*: C. A. McMANUS. *Dr. Slopperton*: J. H. JACK. *Dummie Dunaker*: C. H. MORTON. *Sir William Brandon*: J. Foster. *Augustus Tomlinson*: S. B. Duffield. *Lord Manleverer*: T. C. HOWARD. *Dennis O'Holahan*: J. W. Brutone. *Lucy Brandon*: EMMA HOWSON. *Terpsichore Slopperton*: BESSIE SUDLOW. *Mrs. Dr. Slopperton*: Mrs. A. Hind. *Sally Rosemary*: Fannie Burt. *Mrs. Margery Lobkins*: Mrs. J. Brutone. *Highwaymen, Sailors, Watchmen, Ladies and Gentlemen of the Court*: Chorus of 24.

Act 1, Scene 1: Interior of the Pewter Mug Tavern. *Scene 2*: London Bridge by Moonlight. *Scene 3*: Exterior of Covent Garden Theatre. *Scene 4*: Room in Dr. Slopperton's House. *Scene 5*: Interior of Bridewell Prison.

Act 2, Scene 1: The Jolly Angler Tavern. *Scene 2*: Dr. Slopperton's House. *Scene 3*: Hounslow Heath by Moonlight. *Scene 4*: The Tunnel in the holloway of the Bath Road.

Act 3, Scene 1: Illuminated Gardens of Lord Manleverer's Mansion. *Scene 2*: A Chamber in Lord Manleverer's House. *Scene 3*: A Miserable Attic. *Scene 4*: View of the Thames, and Tower of London.

ACT 1

Scene 1

"Cuckoo, cuckoo goes the clock" (Opening Chorus)

"Mother, give your boy a buss" (Song)
J. Collins

Scene 2

"Oh, for a cot by a Silvery Lake" (Song)
C. A. McManus

Scene 3

"Oh what a horrid crowding" (Concerted piece)

"Light, Light, your honor" (Chorus of Linkmen)

"Oh what a Lovely Creature" (Duet)
J. Collins, E. Howson

"This degradation must I endure" (Concerted piece)
J. Collins, E. Howson, Chorus

Scene 4

"These men are all deceivers" (Song)
E. Howson

"Oh promise me by those Bright Eyes" (Duet)
C. A. McManus, B. Sudlow

Scene 5

"All is ready, haste away" (Grand Finale)
J. Collins, G. C. Boniface, C. H. Morton, S. B. Duffield, Chorus

ACT 2

Scene 1

"Laughing at sorrow, Strangers to fear" (Chorus of Highwaymen)

"The Stirrup Cup" (Solo and Chorus)
J. Collins, Highwaymen
(*Music by* Luigi Arditti. *Lyrics by* Henry B. Farnie.)

Scene 2

"Phillis have you seen my love?" (Song)
B. Sudlow

"I saw Him but once" (Song)
E. Howson

Scene 3

"Hurrah for the Road!" (Song)
J. Collins

Scene 4

"Good night, good night, my Lord" (Finale)
J. Collins, Highwaymen

ACT 3

Scene 1

Grand Fete and Fancy Ball

"Weave the Fairy round of Pleasure" (Chorus)

Scene 2

"Maiden, I will ne'er deceive thee" (Ballad)
(J. Collins)

[1]No other credits in programs. Performed twice daily.

[2]Authorship uncredited in programs. Previous adaptations of this novel 19 January 1852 at the Broadway Theatre, and 26 January 1852 at the Bowery Theatre, do not appear to have contained as much music.

Scene 4
"Hurrah for the lads of sea!" (Chorus of Sailors)
"Farewell to old England!" (Grand Finale)
All the characters

HUMPTY DUMPTY, Volume the Third

1871.11

Fox & Denier's Pantomime Troupe in Fox's Great Original Pantomime in Two Acts, 13 Scenes. Everything new. Produced by George Wood. Opened 26 June 1871 at Wood's Museum and closed 1 July 1871 after 12 performances.

CAST: *Humpty Dumpty*, afterwards Clown: TONY DENIER. *Old One Two Buckle My Shoe*, afterwards Pantaloon: CHARLES K. FOX. *Tommy Tucker*, afterwards Harlequin: A. W. MAFLIN. *Goody Two Shoes*, afterwards Columbine: LINDA deRHONA. *Hon, Grandeur Dignity*, fond of a sporting life, but still fonder of Little Goody Two Shoes: F. LOUIS. *Hosschessnutz*, a Dutchman: L. Birchler. *Gnome*, a Cobbler: A. D. Morris. *Sickle, Rake, Ploughshare*, attached to the Farm of Plenty: Messrs. Laidlow, Nott, Selby. *Yokle*, a Country Boy: G. White. *Napkin*, a Waiter: H. Evans. *Upton Tackton*, a Sergeant, a Great Disciplinarian: Mr. Moorhouse. *Burden*, a Porter: Mr. Banks. *Hash*, a Mutton Pie Man: Mr. Catspaw. *Roomstolet*, a Landlord: Mr. Burt. *Rounds*, a Policeman: B. J. McLAUGHLIN. *Peasants, Soldiers, Policemen, Foot Passengers, Venders Firemen, Gnomes, etc.*

Imagination, Queen of the Land of Golden Dreams: Miss NELLIE SANFORD. *Her Retinue (6)*: *Romance*: Miss Mason. *Reverie*: Miss Rose. *Poesy*: Miss Bright. *Fiction*: Miss Brown. *Flight*: Miss Wright. *Fancy*: Miss Davidson. *Miss Elegance Custom*, a fashionable young lady: Miss Gray. *Miss Starch*, Governess at Mrs. Howdydoo's establishment for young ladies: Miss Prideall.

Act 1, Scene 1: Farm of Plenty. *Scene 2*: Inn by the Roadside. *Scene 3*: Young Ladies' Seminary and Dry Goods Store. *Scene 4*: Enchanted Garden. *Scene 5*: Comfortable Apartments. *Scene 6*: The Railroad. The Last Sensation. Midnight Express Locomotive!

Act 2, Scene 1: Interior of Public House. *Scene 2*: Street. *Scene 3*: The Seaside. *Scene 4*: Up and Down Street. *Scene 5*: Street. *Scene 6*: Another Street. *Scene 7*: Happy Home!

SPECIALTIES
Grand Magical Transformation (Act 1, Scene 1)
Clown: T. Denier. *Pantaloon*: C. K. Fox. *Harlequin*: A W. Maflin. *Columbine*: L. deRhona.

THE BELLES OF THE KITCHEN

1871.12

Kelly & Leon's Minstrels in a Musical Burletta in One Scene, preceded by an Olio. (Written by Edwin Kelly and Francis Leon.) Leader of orchestra, G. P. Barnard. Scenic artist, H. W. Wallace. Stage manager, Cool White. Machinist, James Collis. Pianist, Charles E. Pratt. Produced by (Edwin) Kelly and (Francis) Leon's Minstrels. Opened 31 July 1871 at Lina Edwin's Theatre and closed 19 August 1871 after 18 performances.

CAST: EDWIN KELLY, FRANCIS LEON, DON PEDRO DORREGO (guitarist), Billy Rice, Cool White, Dave Wilson, J. K. Campbell, H. T. Mudge, Messrs. Devere and Nelson, H. Nichols, Charles Storme, William D. Corrister, G. P. Barnard (violinist).

Olio: ACT 1
"Don't Be Angry with Me, Darling"
H. Nichols
"Rackety Jack"
D. Wilson
"Yes, I'll Meet Thee, Dearest"
E. Kelly
"The Dry Goods Clerk"
B. Rice
"May Breezes"
C. Storme
"Carry the News to Mary" (Finale)
B. Rice, D. Wilson, C. White, Company

Olio: ACT 2
Grand Carnival of Fun
"Par Excellence" and "Wenn die Shalben"
F. Leon
The Great Musical Wonder (Specialty)
D. P. Dorego
"I Wouldn't Like to Tell" (Song and Dance)
Messrs. Devere & Nelson
The Lawyer's Clerk, a laughable sketch by J. K. Campbell
Tommy Trot, a Lawyer's Clerk: B. Rice. *Mr. Jones*, a Lawyer: J. K. Campbell. *Mr. Flutter*, a Traveler: D. Wilson. *Mr. Loogshanks*, a sensitive young man: J. B. Carter. *Dame trot*, Tommy's mother: W. D. Corrister. *Miss Longshanks*, a lady of fashion: Mr. Nelson.
Medley Clog, Excelsior
H. T. Mudge
THE BELLES OF THE KITCHEN, a Musical Burletta[3] (by Francis Leon).
Criss, the Kitchen Bride: The Only (Francis) Leon. *Peter*, a Footman: E. Kelly. *Dutchers*: D. Wilson. *Doctor*: J. B. Carter. *Mr. Steadfast*, a retired merchant: Mr. Devere. *Susan*, a cook: W. D. Corrister. *Mrs. Steadfast*, the lady of the house: Mr. Nelson.

LITTLE NELL AND THE MARCHIONESS

1871.13

A Revival of the Melodrama in Four Acts[4]. Suggested by an episode in "The Old Curiosity Shop" by Charles Dickens, adapted by John Brougham. Produced by Lotta Crabtree. Opened 14 August 1871 at Booth's Theatre and closed 9 September 1871 after 28 performances.

CAST: *Little Nell*: LOTTA (CRABTREE). *The Marchioness*: LOTTA (CRABTREE). *Old Grandfather Trent*: D. C. ANDERSON. *Dick Swiveller*: JOHN T. RAYMOND. *Daniel Quilp*: ROBERT PATEMAN. *Sampson Brass*: HAROLD FORSBERG. *Ned Trent*: JOHN S. NORTON. *Mr. Slum*: A. W. Fenno. *Reuben Kadger*: N. Decker. *Foxey Joe*: T. F. Brennan. *Higgins*: Marius Turck. *Burton*: F. Monroe. *Corkey Jack*: C. Rosene. *Showman*: G. H. Harris. *Abdallah*: H. Hogan. *Circus Man*: J. Taylor. *Peep Showman*: F. C. Richardson. *Mrs. Quilp*: Miss E. Livingston. *Mrs. Jarley*: Mrs. S. E. McDougall. *Mrs. Jeniwin*: Miss M. Andrews. *Sally Brass*: MARY WELLS. *Mrs. George*: Mary Young. *Mrs. Simmons*: Jennie DeLacy. *Gipsy Girl*: Carrie Whitlock. *Gingerbread Woman*: Jennie Ross. *Dancing Girl*: J. W. Burgess. *Villagers, Morris Dancers, Guests, Showmen, Minstrels, etc.*: Numerous Auxiliaries, including a Troupe of Acrobats and Minstrels.

BLUEBEARD, or, the Mormon, the Maiden and The Little Militaire

1871.14

The celebrated Domestic Tale specially written and adapted for the Lydia Thompson Company (a Burlesque) in One Act, 5 Scenes[5]. Play by Henry B. Farnie. The latest musical novelties from Europe, specially imported, assorted and concerted, by Michael Connolly. Stage manager, Harry Beckett. Scenery by H. Isherwood, G. Evans and J. Hillyard. Costumes designed by Lydia Thompson. Properties by Frank Goodwin. Mechanical effects by H. Butler. Musical director, Michael Connolly. Produced by Lydia Thompson (Management, Alex Henderson). Opened 16 August 1871 at Wallack's Theatre and closing 9 September 1871; returned 18-21 September 1871 to Wallack's Theatre and closed 21 September 1871 after a total of 30 performances.

CAST: *Blue Beard*, the great P'Shaw! A confirmed lady-killer, with cerulean whiskers; but now inclined to Lake—Salt Lake, that is: HARRY BECKETT. *Ibrahim*, the original "Father, come home!": John Bryer. *Fatima*, his daughter; an orient pearl at random strung: CAMILLE DUBOIS. *Sorosister Anne*, an advanced Damsel of the Period,

[3]No doubt inspired by the success of the Vokes Family farce of the same name, previously produced in England and later presented in New York 15 April 1872 at the Union Square Theatre; for detail, see entry below.
[4]First produced in New York 14 August 1867 at Wallack's Theatre for 26 performances. For Synopsis of Scenes and Musical Numbers, see original 1867 production. Incidental to the Fair Scene in Act 3, Acrobatic Feats will be performed by William H. Ashton & Sons, a Scottish Dance by Mrs. J. W. Burgess, and Minstrelsy by Messrs. Robert Smith, James Clark, V. Benjamin and Frank Clark.
[5]Preceded by a farce, Give a Dog a Bad Name!, which was dropped after four nights.

always looking for the "coming man": CARLOTTA ZERBINI. *Selim*, Sous-Lieutenant of Spahis, who, losing his sweetheart, enlists in the "Blues" and eventually turns shepherd, in order to win her by hook or by crook: LYDIA THOMPSON. *Corporal Zoug-Zoug*, of the Turcos, afterwards a heathen Chinee, who talks pigeon English, but declines to be plucked: WILLIE EDOUIN. *Hassan*, the first page—set up in "nonpareil," very "mignon," and doesn't think "small pica" of himself: HETTY TRACY. *The O'Shacabac*, Blue Beard's Buttons, a "Tipperara avis," bedad; pedigree, by Jabers, out of Begorra: H. W. MONTGOMERY. *Fez*, an offier of "Curs," and yet has done good service: Tilly Earle. *Said*, a wild young dog, also in the service—but what's least "Said" is soonest mended: Kate Edgerton. *Beda*. Beda's eye is a "bead as" can sparkle—string for Beda's lead: Nellie Cook.

A set of pages that you won't cut (6): *Zaffo*: Lotta Mira. *Quaffo*: Kate Heathcote. *Chaffo*: Miss Clarke. *Laugho*: Miss Johnson. *Raffo*: Miss McCormack. *Pfaffo*: Miss Roland. *The "Spiritual Wives" of Blue-Beard; the Body Guards (Mamelukes) of the Great P'Shaw; Turkish Girls and Wedding Guests, etc.*

Scene 1: The Village of Bishmillah at Sunset. (Evans.) *Scene 2*: The Zigzag Path to Castle Blue-Beard by moonlight. (Isherwood.) *Scene 3*: Castle Blue-Beard. The Star-spangled Hall of many nuptials. (Hillyard.) *Scene 4*: Portals of the Blue-Room. (Hillyard.) *Scene 5*: The Look-out Towers on the Castle Ramparts. (Isherwood.)

MUSICAL NUMBERS

Grand Finale (Scene 1)

The celebrated Mandolin Song (Scene 2)

Finale (Scene 2)

Unparalleled Finale (Scene 3)

Finale expressive of considerable mental excitement (Scene 4)

Finale (Scene 5)

1871.15 FRITZ, OUR COUSIN GERMAN!

A Revival of the Great Specialty of the German Immigrant (Drama) in Three Acts, 7 Scenes[6]. Play by Charles Gayler. Musical director, Giuseppe Operti. Produced by Henry Jarrett and Harry Palmer. Opened 21 August 1871 at Niblo's Garden and closed 30 September 1871 after 30 performances[7].

CAST: *Fritz Van Vonderblinkinstoffen*, in which character he will introduce his charming characteristic melange, songs, dances and instrumental solos: JOSEPH K. EMMET. *Colonel Crafton*, Chief of a Gang of Counterfeiters: A. H. HASTINGS. *Bobbit*, Keeper of a Concert Saloon: C. H. MORTON. *Bloker, Smasher*, Emigrant Runners: E. K. Collier, P. Stoner. *Adolphus Jenkins*, a Henglish H'artist you know: Mr. HILLIARD. *Judge Griffin*: Mr. Norton. *Lawyer Grim*: J. W. Brutone. *Father Metzler*: Mr. Jarvis. *Julius Snow*: Mr. Havron. *Jacob Callout*: Mr. Morris. *Flint*, a Detective: Mr. Jacobs. *Wintgen*: Mr. Wood. *Mickie Foy*: Mr. Adams. *Little Fritz*: Little MINNIE MADDERN (Fiske). *Katrina*: ROSE EVANS. *Moppy*: ALICE BROOKES. *Paulina*: Kitty Dowd. *Angelina*: Mary Burbank. *Julie*: Miss Richardson. *Judy Roche*: Miss Rowe. *Mother Metzler*: Mrs. (JULIA) BRUTONE. *La Belle*: Mary Benedict. *Marie*: Miss Marquette.

Act 1, Scene 1: A View of the Bay of New York, with the Offices of the Commissioners of Emigration. *Scene 2*: Fritz in search of Katrina. *Scene 3*: The Sanctum of Phil Bobbit's nice Little Establishment.

Act 2, Scene 1: Katrina's place of refuge. *Scene 2*: Justice Griffin's Court Room. *Scene 3*: The Grand Parlor Concert Scene.

Act 3: Seven years later. The Home of Fritz, the Happy Miller.

ACT 2

Scene 3

Charming Character Melange, New Songs and Dances, Solo on the Mouth Harmonicon, with five variations on the popular tune, "Home Sweet Home"
J. K. Emmet

ACT 3

"Oh, Schneider, How You Vas?"
J. K. Emmet

[6]First produced in New York 11 July 1870 at Wallack's Theatre for 63 performances.

[7]For the last week of the run FRITZ, OUR COUSIN GERMAN alternated with CARL, THE FIDDLER in repertory. Scenery, costumes and stage direction uncredited.

1871.16 A TRIP AROUND THE WORLD!

Kelly & Leon's Minstrels in a Grand Panorama with Dioramic Effects in Two Acts. (Conceived and written by Edwin Kelly and Francis Leon.) Stage manager, Cool White. Leader of orchestra, G. P. Barnard. Scenic artist, H. W. Wallace. Produced by Edwin Kelly and Francis Leon. Opened 21 August 1871 at Lina Edwin's Theatre and closed 9 September 1871 after 12 performances.

CAST: EDWIN KELLY, FRANCIS LEON, BILLY RICE, Dave Wilson, Charles Storme, E. M. Kayne, Cool White, J. B. Carter, William D. Corrister, Ben Nevis, Vich Alpine, ROYAL CHRISTY MINSTRELS (Messrs. J. K. Campbell, H. T. Mudge, Master Clarence, Thomas Sully and Henri Stuart).

ACT 1

Preparation for the start. The embarkation on board the good ship *Uncle Sam*. All aboard. The Anchor weighed. Off we go. Departure from Sandy Hook. Return of the pilot boat. The message, 'Love to all at home.' Alone on the ocean.

"A Life on the Ocean Wave" (Song)
E. Kelly

Scenes on the ocean. Vessels passing to and fro. The prostrating effects of seasickness. Bones and Tambo the victims. 'Land ho.' The white cliffs of old Albion. Safe arrival in England. The town and harbor of Woolwich. The debarkation and departure by Railroad in the express train for London. General view of the country. Arrival at London. The Yankees astonished at the sights in London. Hyde Park. Nelson's Monument. The Queen's Guards. National anthem, "God Save the Queen."

Negro Minstrelsy in England
Royal Christy Minstrels

Overture

Opening Chorus "Dinah's Wedding"

"Walk Along John"
J. K. Campbell

Getting thirsty. Give me some lager. No Lager in England. Try "Alf and Alf," or a Pot of Hale.

"The Fine Old English Gentleman" (Song)
E. M. Kayne

Can't stay long in one place. All aboard. Off again for Scotland.

"Annie Laurie" (Song)
E. Kelly

A trip through the highlands. Dinah ye hear the Slogan. The Campbells are coming. View of Loch Lomond. Ben Nevis and Vich Alpine.

A startling proposition. Let us take a trip in a balloon across the Northern Ocean. The proposition agreed to, and venturesome travelers take their flight in the Aerial Ship, passing over Edinburgh, Sir Walter Scott's Monument, etc.

"Coming Through the Rye" (Song)
C. Storme

The Ocean as seen from the Clouds. Coast of France. Cherbourg in the distance. Grand Naval Combat between the *Kearsage* and *Alabama*. Arrival of the Voyagers in Paris.

The Street Singers of Paris
The Only (Francis) Leon, E. Kelly

Hoop La (from LA PÉRICHOLE)

The Cat Duet

The Boulevards. The Palais Royale. The Tuilleries, etc.

"The Marsellaise" (Song)
C. Storme

Off we go again. Arrival in Germany.

"Bingen on the Rhine" German Sports—Lager and Pretzels.

"Cruelty to Johnny" (Duet)
J. K. Campbell, H. T. Mudge

"The Watch on the Rhine" (Song)
C. Storme

Off again and safe arrival in Ireland. Blarney Castle.

St. Patrick's Day
Orchestra

A lively time with the Irish Boys.

Barn Door Jig
J. K. Campbell, H. T. Mudge
Biddy Malloy: J. K. Campbell. *Pat McGlinn*: H. T. Mudge.
"The Irishman's Shanty" (Song)
B. Rice
"The Harp That Once Through Tara's Hall" (Song)
E. Kelly
"There's better days for old Ireland yet"
Departure from the Green Isle and return trip to America.
"Home Again from a Foreign Shore" (Chorus)
Company
Safe arrival in New York City. New York by Gaslight, City Hall, Park, etc.
Grand Finale
"Carry the News to Mary" (The Great Camp Meeting Scene)
B. Rice, D. Wilson, C. White, Company

ACT 2
Grand Carnival of Fun
"Sweetest of Williams" and "The Tipsey Song"
The Only (Francis) Leon
Double Clog Dance
T. Sully, H. Stuart
The Carpet Bagger
Pete Slow: B. Rice. *Jim Fast*: D. Wilson. *Carpet Bagger*: J. K. Campbell. *Mr. Peabody*: C. White. *Mr. Smart*: J. B. Carter.
"They Say I'm So Stylish" (Song and Dance)
T. Sully
A Chip of the Old Block, a Domestic Operetta
Mrs. Cady Stanton: The Only (Francis) Leon. *Mr. Cady Stanton*: E. Kelly. *Old Mr. Fred Doug*: C. White. *Old Mrs. Fred Doug*: W. D. Corrister. *James*: J. B. Carter. *Susy*: E. M. Kayne. Other characters by the company.

1871.17 ON THE TRACK!

A Drama in Three Acts, written for G. Swaine Buckley by a distinguished American author. Music composed and arranged by E. N. Catlin. Orchestra directed by B. J. Deane. Opened 28 August 1871 at the Bowery Theatre and closed 9 September 1871 after 12 performances.

CAST: *Harry Romer*, a young Southern blood: G. SWAINE BUCKLEY. *Biddy Macarthy*, the Irish Woman of the period: G. SWAINE BUCKLEY. *Paul Clifford*, a London swell: G. SWAINE BUCKLEY. *Peleg Slickens*, a Yankee peddler: G. SWAINE BUCKLEY. *Old Rats*: G. SWAINE BUCKLEY. *Mons. Achille Bonbon*, Le Chevalier D'Industrie: G. SWAINE BUCKLEY. *Cuff*, the irrepressible contraband: G. SWAINE BUCKLEY. In which several characters Mr. Buckley will exhibit his excellence upon almost every known musical instrument (10: guitar, piano, English cornet, toy cornet, melophone, violin, banjo, pine sticks, bones, etc.) and give his unequalled Irish humors and witticisms, Yankee stories and yarns, sentimental and comic songs (12), fancy and characteristic dances (6), a Performance unequalled in his specialties.
Sidney Chandos, a Southerner and Adventurer: W. MARDEN. *Philip Romer*, Harry's brother, a young author: E. Barry. *Mr. Merriden*, Clara's father: Charles Foster. *Neros*, a dumb Malay, servant to Chandos: P. Connolly. *Mr. Grabstock*, the Lawyer: C. M. Manley. *Sampson Slink*, ye jack of all trades: L. W. Harris. *Scaley Bob*, a street Arab: Miss Millie Sackett. *The Strange Man*: J. Winter. *Clara Merriden*: Mrs. W. G. Jones. *Amy*: POLLY BOOTH. *Mrs. Sampson Slink*, Mr. S's better (?) half: Mrs. E. B. HOLMES. *Lords and Gentlemen, Bathers, Visitors, Citizens, etc.* (*Specialty*: T. Bolas.)

Act 1: England. Brighton. Railroad Station. On the Lands—Bathing! The storm.

Act 2: America. Photographic Gallery. Agricultural Fair and Cattle Show in Vermont.

Act 3: Down South. The Levee at New Orleans. Cabin of the Creole. On a Plantation.

ACT 1
Song at the Piano
G. S. Buckley [as Harry]
Great Specialty
G. S. Buckley [as Biddy Macarthy]

ACT 2
Fop Song—Cornet Solo
G. S. Buckley [as Paul Clifford]
Agricultural Fair and Cattle Show
Songs, Solos, Speeches, Yankee Stories
G. S. Buckley [as Peleg Slickens]

ACT 3
Melophone Solo and French Songs
G. S. Buckley [as Achille Bonbon]
Comicalities in Black
G. S. Buckley [as Cuff the Darkey]
Plantation Festival
Dutch Songs
T. Bolas

SONGS
"My Soul in One Unbroken Sigh" (love song, accompanying himself)
English Swell Song
"Slickens' Pill" (Yankee Medley)
Song in the French Language
Three Ethiopian Ditties
Six Characteristic Dances

1871.18 HUMPTY DUMPTY

A Revival of the Spectacular Ballet Pantomime in Three Acts, 13 Scenes[8]. Play by George L. Fox. Music composed and selected by F. Strebinger. Stage director, E. S. Tarr. Presented under the personal direction of George L. Fox. Ballets (arranged) by Imre Kiralfy. Musical director, F. Strebinger. Scenery and effects by James E. Hayes, J. A. Johnson. Produced by James E. Hayes. Opened 31 August 1871 at the Olympic Theatre; reconstructed 8 January 1872 and 1 April 1872[9], and closed 11 June 1872 after 333 performances.

CAST: Opening Burlesque: *Tragedy*: Mrs. (ANNIE) YEAMANS. *Burlesque*: LULU PRIOR. *America*: FLORA LEE. *Europe*: Miss K. Melnotte. *Africa*: Mr. Debonnay. *Asia*: Miss H. Naylor. *New Jersey*: GEORGE A. BEANE. *Others*: Messrs. Tyson, Atkins.
Transformation of Characters: *Clown*: GEORGE L. FOX. *Pantaloon*: C. K. FOX. *Harlequins*: IMRE and BOLOSSY KIRALFY. *Columbines*: HANIOLA and EMILIE KIRALFY. *The Sprite*: Herr Willio. *The Beaux and Belles of the Period*: Little JENNIE YEAMANS. *Specialties*: THE MARTENS (Mons. Martens, Mme. Martens, Mlle. Gretchen Martens), THE KIRALFYS (Imre, Bolossy, Haniola, Emilie, Katie), Signor CASSELLI (Invisible Wire Act), Young Adonis and Little Venus (Bicycle Act), "The Zig Zags, or Human Insects" (Mons. Brunaux, Maire, Robert, Rojade; Parisian Grotesques). *Ballet*: Mlles. Adele Paglieri, Marietta Morondo, Clemence Alexandrowa, Derpa, Howe, F. Beane, Richards, Moritz, Mayer, Bohme, Flora Lee, Coryphées and Full Corps de Ballet.

Act 1, Scene 1: The Burlesque. Retreat of Romance. *Scene 2*: Vale of Fertility. *Scene 3*: Subterranean Grotto. *Scene 4*: Roadside Inn. *Scene 5*: Dry Goods Store. *Scene 6*: Market Place.

Act 2: Grand Oriental Palace.

Act 3, Scene 1: Street by Moonlight. *Scene 2*: Establishment for the Sale of Groceries. *Scene 3*: Railroad Crossing and great Moonlight Leap. *Scene 4*: Pastoral Landscape. *Scene 5*: Room in a City Hotel. *Scene 6*: Humpty Dumpty on Police Duty. Grand Final Transformation and Carnival.

BALLETS, SPECIALTIES
Grand Ballet (Act 1, Scene 3)
Full Corps de Ballet
Grand Entrée des Folles (Act 2)
Coryphées, Corps de Ballet
Entrée Des Gnomes (Act 2)
Ladies of the Kiralfy Troupe
Les Eccentricities Tyroliennes (Act 2)
Martens Family
Signor Casselli (Act 2)
The Zig-Zags, or Human Insects ('The Escaped Lunatics')(Act 2)
Young Adonis and Little Venus (Act 2)

[8] First produced in New York 10 March 1868 at the Olympic Theatre for 483 performances.
[9] At the time of the revisions the show was billed as HUMPTY DUMPTY! REMODELLED.

The Cats
Mons. and Mme. Martens
Magyar Csardas[10] (Sensational Hungarian Divertissement)(Act 2)
Kiralfy Family, Troupe

HUMPTY DUMPTY. George L. Fox's new version of his famous pantomime in Three Acts, 9 Scenes, (reconstructed), 8 January 1872:

Sun Spirit: LULU PRIOR. *The Ice King*: GEORGE A. BEANE. *Specialties*: The Carroll Family (R. M. Carroll, and his sons, Dick, Eddie, Bennie in songs, dances, eccentricities), Little JENNIE YEAMANS, THE MARTENS (Mons. Marten, Mme. Marten, Mlle. Gretchen), THE KIRALFYS (Imre, Bolossy, Haniola, Emilie, Katie), Signor CASSELLI (Invisible Wire Act), Mons. Robere and Mlle. Emma; Young Adonis and Little Venus (Bicycle Act), "The Zig Zags, or Human Insects" (Mons. Brunaux, Maire, Robert, Rojade; Parisian Grotesques). *Ballet*: Mlles. Adele Paglieri, Marietta Morondo, Coryphées and Full Corps de Ballet.

Act 1: Fancy's Frolic. *Scene 1*: Moonlit Glen. *Scene 2*: Humpty Dumpty's House. *Scene 3*: Village Post Office. *Scene 4*: In the Streets; Humpty's Shopping Tour. *Scene 5*: View of St. Petersburgh.

Act 2: Palace of the Sun Spirits.

Act 3, Scene 1: Clown and Pantaloon. Humpty's Experiments with Nitro-Glycerine. *Scene 2*: A Question of Digestion. *Scene 3*: Humpty's Boarding House. *Scene 4*: More Trouble for Humpty. Grand Transformation.

BALLETS, SPECIALTIES[11]
The Chrysalis of Pantomime (Act 1, Scene 1)
The Butterfly on Wing (Act 1, Scene 2)
Society Songs and Characterizations (Act 1, Scene 3)
Little J. Yeamans
Twenty Minutes with the Carrolls: Pranks of the Pygmies (Act 1, Scene 4)
King Icicle's Extravaganza (Act 1, Scene 4)
The Zig-Zags, or Human Insects ('The Russian Glide')(Act 1, Scene 5)
J. E. Taylor's Musical and Terpsichorean Skating Act, Character Changes (Act 1, Scene 5)
Russian Songs (Act 1, Scene 5)
Martens Family
Sunbeam Ballet (Act 2)
Mlles. Paglieri, Morando, Coryphées
Les Eccentricities Tyroliennes (Act 2)
Martens Family
The Zig-Zags, or Human Insects ('The Merry Mites')(Act 2)
Antics of the Antipodes, Waltz on the Ceiling (Act 2)
Mons. Robere, Mlle. Emma
The Crystal Maze (Act 2)
Young Adonis and Little Venus (Act 2)
The Cat Duet (Act 2)
Mons. and Mme. Marten
The Legions of the Sun Spirit (Ballet)(Act 2)
Kiralfy Family, Troupe
The Educated Elephant (Act 3)
Grand Transformation (Act 3)

HUMPTY DUMPTY! Remodelled. George L. Fox's new version of his famous pantomime in Three Acts, 14 Scenes, (reconstructed) 1 April 1872:

Humpty Dumpty, the accredited prophet of fun, a famous character: GEORGE L. FOX. *Old One Two*, an arithmetical sum of villainy, and a famed Pantoloonatic: C. K. FOX. *Harlequins*, gandy gentlemen, who are votaries of the saltatorial and sartorial arts—professing sleight of hand, yet practising Sleight of Foot: IMRE KIRALFY, BOLOSSY KIRALFY. *Columbines*, young ladies who do the Fairy business, illustrating the rugged course of true love, and all that sort of thing, you know: Mlles. EMILY KIRALFY, HANIOLA KIRALFY. *Sanita*, the Spirit of Purity and Cleanliness—the representative of wash day, house cleaning and other agreeable domestic sanitary peculiarities—a spirit, whose mission it is to kick up a dust: LULU PRIOR. *Pluto, Jr.*, son of the old boy—junior branch of the well-known house of Pluto and Son, dealers in sulphur, a fashionable fiend of the first society: GEORGE A. BEANE. *Spiderion*, an apprentice of Pluto's, a regular little devil: Master Topack. *The Pitcher*, a Professional among the Juniors, a good player when the Harlequin's at the bat: Master (Thomas) Casselli.

Specialties: Signor Casselli; Kynock & Smith (skaters); Martens Trio (Mons. and Mme. Martens, Mlle. Gretchen); Wilson Brothers.

Act 1, Scene 1: The Burlesque. The Garret of Hades. *Scene 2*: The Heart of Nimbus. *Scene 3*: The Pantomime. Humpty Dumpty's Home. *Scene 4*: The Village Tavern. *Scene 5*: Lunch Room Down Town. *Scene 6*: A Road to Somewhere. *Scene 7*: The Beautiful Snow. *Scene 8*: Another Road to Somewhere Else. *Scene 9*: Fox's Magic Shadows.

Act 2: Humpty's Kaleidoscope.

Act 3, Scene 1: Humpty's Grocery. *Scene 2*: Sailor's Home. *Scene 3*: A Dogmatic View of Things. *Scene 4*: The Genuine Darkness of Erebus. *Scene 5*: The Hall of Statues.

ACT 1
Scene 2
Song
L. Prior
Scene 3
Country Dance
Corps de Ballet
Scene 4
Song
J. Yeamans
Scene 6
Song
T. Casselli
Scene 7
Grand Military Evolutions
Ballet
The Twirls of Mazy; The Giraffe Dance
Kynock & Smith
Scene 8
Duet
Mme. Martens, Gretchen

ACT 2
Grand Ballet
Dreams of Fairyland
The Kiralfy's Great Dance in the Air
The Alphabetical Ballet
Sig. Casselli on the Invisible Wire
The Famed Martens Trio
The Matchless Wilson Brothers (in their pyramid somersaults)
Venus & Adonis on the Velocipede
The Cats
Mons. and Mme. Martens
The Dance of the Sprites and the Famous Shield Tableau!

ACT 3
Scene 1
A Gastronomic Trip
Scene 2
Humpty on Aquatics and Aquatics on Humpty
Scene 5
Humpty's specimens of high art
Living-stone found at last!

---

[10]Replaced during the run by:
Csikos (New Hungarian Divertissement)
Kiralfy Troupe, Ladies, Coryphées, Corps de Ballet

[11]During the run, the specialties in Act 1 Scene 5 were replaced by:
The Dance of the Uhlans
Corps de Ballet
Kynock and Smith (Skating Acts)
Gushes of Melody (Descriptive Duet)
Mme. Marten, Mlle. Gretchen
The Chant of the Celestials
Mrs. A. Yeamans
Triple Tourniquet
Wilson Brothers

Superb marble tableau
"The Rape of the Sabines"
Humpty's Final Splendor

1871.19 THE PRINCESS OF TRÉBIZONDE!

An Opéra-bouffe in Three Acts. Original French libretto ("La Princesse de Trébizonde') by Charles Nuitter and Étienne Tréfeu. Rewritten and adapted into a musical burlesque expressly for Miss Lydia Thompson and her new company by Samuel Harrison. Music by Jacques Offenbach. Stage director, James Schonberg. Scenery by George Evans, H. Isherwood and H. Hillyard. Costumes designed by Lydia Thompson. Musical director, Michael Connelly. Produced by Lydia Thompson. (Management, Alex Henderson.) Opened 11 September 1871 at Wallack's Theatre and closed 16 September 1871 after 7 performances.

CAST: *Regina*: LYDIA THOMPSON. *Cabrioli*: HARRY BECKETT. *Manola*: WILLIE EDOUIN. *Prince Casimir*: HENRY MONTGOMERY. *Dr. Sparadrap*: John Bryer. *The Lottery Keeper*: Mr. Broughton. *Tremolina*: Hetty Tracy. *Zanetta*: Camille Dubois. *Prince Raphael*: Carlotta Zerbini. *Chouffleur*: Millie Cook. *Brocoli*: Lotta Mira. *Flamingo*: Kate Egerton. *Francesco*: Kate Heathcote. *The Public, Peasants, Mountebanks, etc.*

Act 1: A Public Square. (Evans.)

Act 2: The Gardens of a Baronial Hall. (Isherwood.)

Act 3: Apartment in the Chateau. (Hillyard.)

ACT 1
"Now, Gentlemen and Ladies" (Concerted Piece)
H. Tracy, all the characters
"The Broken Nose" (Song)
C. Dubois
"When upon the Tight-Rope Dancing" (Song)
L. Thompson
"The Turtle Doves" (Song)
C. Zerbini
"It was indeed a Splendid Sight" (Concerted Piece)
All the characters
"Farewell, Old Booth" (Quartette and Finale)
H. Beckett, L. Thompson, C. Dubois, H. Tracy, all the characters

ACT 2[12]
"Where is now each merry antic?" (Quintette)
H. Beckett, L. Thompson, H. Tracy, C. Dubois, W. Edouin
"Yonder see, sure 'tis she" (Duo)
C. Dubois, C. Zerbini
"The Lawful Wife of Rustifum" (Finale Rondo)
C. Dubois, all the characters

ACT 3
"Alas, a sad and sorry task" (Chorus)
Pages
"O'er this Youth once so Painted" (Song)
C. Zerbini
"The Toothache" (Song)
L. Thompson
"The Night on Daylights realm encroaches" (Duo)
L. Thompson, H. Tracy
"All in Measure Treading" (Rondo)
Pages
"If the Fair is not Superfine" (Duo)
C. Zerbini, C. Dubois
"When Wed, 'tis good on either side" (Finale)
L. Thompson, all the characters

Incidental to this act will be presented a thrilling drama of the period entitled 'The Rosebud of Stinging Nettle Farm' (by Henry J. Byron) with the following unapproachable cast: Bill Hugly, a convict (Regina), Sir Narcissus Slapdash (Tremolini), Gaffer Turmurfield (Manola), Giles Furrow (Zanetta), Rose Turmurfield (Cabrioli).

[12]The New York Times' critic praises a song in Act 2 entitled "The Turtle Doves."

1871.20 THE PET OF THE PETTICOATS!/ FAMILY JARS

A Double Bill of a (Musical) Comedy, followed by a laughable comedietta. Produced by Lotta Crabtree. Opened 11 September 1871 at Booth's Theatre and closed 16 September 1871 after 7 performances.[13]

THE PET OF THE PETTICOATS. Musical comedy in Three Acts by J. B. Buckstone. CAST: *Paul*, nicknamed Poll the Pet, in which she will sing all the Original Music, and the Beautiful Dream Medley: LOTTA (CRABTREE). *Chevalier St. Pierre*: JOHN S. NORTON. *Job*, the Convent Gardner: JOHN T. RAYMOND. *Mons. Zephyr*, Dancing Master to the Convent: ROBERT PATEMAN. *Col. Belair*: N. Decker. *Captain Cannonade*: Marius Turck. *Tobie*, Landlord of the Golden Lion: Charles Rosene.

FAMILY JARS CAST: *Liddy Larrigan*, with song[14]: LOTTA (CRABTREE). *Porcelain*: A. W. Fenno. *Benedict*, his son: Nelson Decker. *Delph*: JOHN T. RAYMOND. *Diggory*, Delph's son: Charles Rosene. *Emily*, married to Benedict: Miss Theresa Selden.

Lotta's Company this season also included F. Monroe, T. F. Brennan, F. Intropodi, G. N. Harris, Henry Hogan, S. E. Brown, Misses Mary Wells, Teresa Selden, E. Livington, Mary Young, Jennie DeLacy, Jennie Ross, Carrie Whitlock, Charlotte Cove, E. Howard.

1871.21 THE LITTLE DETECTIVE, or, Woman's Curiosity

A Revival of the Melodrama in Three Acts[15]. Produced by Lotta Crabtree. Opened 18 September 1871 at Booth's Theatre and closed 23 September 1871 after 7 performances.

CAST: *Florence Langton*, with song: LOTTA (CRABTREE). *Grizzle Gutteridge*: LOTTA (CRABTREE). *Mrs. Gamage*, an old nurse: LOTTA (CRABTREE). *Harry Rackett*: LOTTA (CRABTREE). *Barney O'Brien*, with new Irish Medley and Shillelagh Jig: LOTTA (CRABTREE). *Gaunse-ash-nee-joseph-e-ne-cli-te-lager-lodovica*, an original Dutch character with a Tyrolean song: LOTTA (CRABTREE).

Roderick Tracy, a Detective: A. W. Fenno. *Barry Mallison*, the Robber: John W. Norton. *Sir Gervaise Langton*, father to Florence: John T. Raymond. *Ludovic Stuvesant*, de honest shentleman Comedian: Robert Pateman. *Phoebus Rockaway*, a gent waiting for something to turn up: Mr. Wilson. *Stephen Hardcliffe*, a Pigeon: N. Decker. *Captain Gustave*, a Policeman: J. Taylor. *Madame Ritzdorf*: Mary Wells. *Stella*: Miss Bella Pateman. *Una*: Teresa Selden.

1871.22 CARL, THE FIDDLER

A Drama in Three Acts. Play and lyrics by Charles Gayler. Original music composed by Giuseppe Operti. Produced under the personal supervision of Charles Gayler. Produced by Henry Jarrett and Harry Palmer. Opened 18 September 1871 at Niblo's Garden and closed 30 September 1871 after 12 performances in repertory.[16]

CAST: *Carl*, a Musician: JOSEPH K. EMMET. *Harper Bates*: A. H. HASTINGS. *Payton Boyd*, his Secretary: Mr. Hilliard. *Dickson Crawl*, a Lawyer: C. H. MORTON. *Hudson Wayne*, his nephew: A. H. DAVENPORT. *Servant*: Mr. Hammond. *Magistrate*: Mr. Bedford. *Officer*: Mr. Moore. *Polly Searles*: IDA VERNON. *Dora Bates*: FRANKIE McCLELLAN. *Mrs. Hasher*: Miss Lizzie Maddern. *Kate Leland*, a Gishing Sappho: Miss Mack. *Hilda*: Little MINNIE MADDERN (Fiske). *Ladies, Gentlemen, etc.*

Act 1: The Lost Darling.

Act 2: The Wanderer.

Act 3: The Lost One Restored.

[13]No program found for this engagement.
[14]Lotta's songs: "Mickey's Gone Away" and "Mrs. Gowan's Reel."
[15]First produced in New York 6 December 1869 at Niblo's Garden for 14 performances. For Musical Numbers, see original 1869 production. No program found for this engagement.
[16]For the two weeks of its run, CARL, THE FIDDLER alternated with FRITZ, OUR COUSIN GERMAN in repertory.

MUSICAL NUMBERS
"Hilda" (Original Song)(Act 1)
J. K. Emmet
"The Wanderer's Serenade" (Act 2)
J. K. Emmet
"The Brother's Lullaby" (Act 2)
J. K. Emmet

1871.23 LA PÉRICHOLE

A Revival of the Opéra-bouffe in Two Acts[17], in French. Libretto by Ludovic Halévy and Henri Meilhac, based on 'Le Carosse du Saint-Sacrement' by Prosper Merimée. Music by Jacques Offenbach. Stage manager, Mons. A. Valter. Costumes by B. Phillips. Leader of orchestra, Mons. Bessières. Opened 9 October 1871 at Lina Edwin's Theatre; season closed 3 February 1872 after (22) performances in repertory.

CAST: *La Périchole*, a Street Singer: MARIE AIMÉE. *Piquillo*: Mons. A. JULIEN. *Don Andrès*, Viceroy of Peru: Mons. DUCHESNE. *Don Pedro*, Governor of Lima: Mons. EDGARD. *Panatellas*, First Gentleman of the Bedchamber: Mons. CAYLA. *Marquis de Tarapote*, Courtier: Mons. Adrien Valter. *Three Cousins*: *Guadalena*: Mlle. Ferd. T. Hache. *Berginella*: Mlle. Dorlia. *Mastrilla*: Mlle. Bessières. *Manuelita*: Mlle. T. Julie Hache. *Ladies of the Court (3)*: *Ninetta*: Mlle. Bessières. *Brambilla*: Mlle. Dorlia. *Frasquinella*: Mlle. Brist. *First Notarie*: Mons. Brag. *Second Notarie*: Mons. Oudin. *Peasants, Guards, Courtiers, Ladies, etc.*

1871.24 FLEUR DE THÉ

A Revival of the Opéra-bouffe in Three Acts[18], in French. Libretto by Alfred Duru and Henri Chivot. Music by Charles Lecocq. Stage manager, A. Valter. Costumes by B. Phillips. Leader of orchestra, Mons. Bessières. Opened 26 October 1871 at Lina Edwin's Theatre; season closed 3 February 1872 after (20) performances in repertory.[19]

CAST: *Césarine*, Pinsonnet's wife: Mlle. MARIE AIMÉE. *Pinsonnet*, Cook on board *La Pintade*: Mons. NOE. *Tien-Tien*, Chief of the Pekin Police: Mons. DUCHESNE. *Ka-o-lin*, Captain of Vigers: Mons. EDGARD. *Fleur-de-Thé*, Tien-Tien's Daughter: Mlle. VANDAMME. *Corbillon*, Boatswain of *La Pintade*: Mlle. Berthon. *French Sailors, Chinese Men and Women, Slaves, etc.*

1871.25 LA GRANDE DUCHESS DE GÉROLSTEIN

A Revival of the Opéra-bouffe in Three Acts[20], in French. Libretto by Henri Meilhac and Ludovic Halévy. Music by Jacques Offenbach. Stage manager, Mons. A. Valter. Scenery by Hannibal W. Calyo. Costumes by B. Phillip and Mme. Colon. Leader of orchestra, Mons. Bessières. Opened 13 November 1871 at Lina Edwin's Theatre; season closed 3 February 1872 after (18) performances in repertory.

CAST: *La Grande-Duchesse de Gérolstein*: Mlle. MARIE AIMÉE. *Fritz*: Mons. F. NOE. *Prince Paul*: Mons. ALBERT JULIEN. *Baron Puck*: Mons. EDGARD. *General Boum*: Mons. DUCHESNE. *Baron Grog*: Mons. Adrien Valter. *Nepomuc*: Mons. Parent. *Wanda*: Mlle. JULIE HACHE. *Dames d'Honneur*: Mlles. Jausse, Bessières, Dorlia, A. Cave. *Guards, Courtiers, Ladies, etc.*

1871.26 LE PONT DES SOUPIRS

An Opéra-bouffe in Four Acts, in French. Libretto by Hector Crémieux and Ludovic Halévy. Music by Jacques Offenbach. Stage manager, A. Valter. Scenery by Hannibal W. Calyo. Costumes by Toledo. Leader of orchestra, Mons. Bessières. Produced by Aimée's French Opera Bouffe Company. Opened 27 November 1871 at Lina Edwin's Theatre; season closed 3 February 1872 after (26) performances in repertory.

CAST: *Catarina Cornarini*, the Wife of the Admiral Doge, a lady of virtuous character, with a tender feeling for her page Amoroso: Mlle. MARIE AIMÉE. *Fabiano Fabiani Malatromba*, Cousin of the Admiral Doge. Expects to succeed him both in state and matrimonial duties: Mons. F. NOE. *Cornarino Cornarini*, Doge of Venice and Great Admiral of the Fleet, the jealous husband of Catarina: Mons. DUCHESNE. *Baptiste*, the devoted Equerry of the Admiral: Mons. EDGARD. *Great Chief of the Council of Ten [Le Conseil des Dix]*, a great philosopher, a great connoisseur of human heart: Mons. ADRIEN VALTER. *Amoroso*, Page of Catarina Cornarini, in love with his mistress: Mlle. DORLIA. *Gascadetto*, Public Crier: Mlle. Vandamme. *Franrusto, Astolfo*, Spies and Shirri of Malatromba: Mlles. Cayla, Julien. *Paillumido*: Mlle. Noriac. *Rigolo*: Mlle. Alberto. *Usher*: Mlle. Guiot. *An Officer*: Mlle. Guerra. *Mesd. Laedice [Laôdice]*, Private Confidante of Catarina Cornarino: Mlle. Briot. *Gondoliers to the Lagune (5)*: *Fiorella*: Mlle. Zousse. *Ninetta*: Mlle. Julie Hache. *Fiammetta*: Mlle. Bessières. *Zerlina*: Mlle. A. Cave. *Marietta*: Mlle. Briot. *Characters of the Carnival (6)*: *Leandre*: Mlle. Jousse. *Columbine*: Mlle. Briot. *Pierrot*: Mlle. Vandamme. *Isabelle*: Mlle. T. Hache. *Harlequin*: Mlle. A. Cave. *Cassandra*: Mlle. Bessières. *Members of the Terrible Council of Ten, Venetian Men and Women, Guards, Bravi, Masks, Gondoliers, etc.*

Act 1: A Piaretta in Venice. 1321.

Act 2: A Hall in Carnarini Palace.

Act 3: The Hall of the Council of Ten.

Act 4: The Lido.

ACT 1[21]
Choeur dans la coulisse (Ah que Venise est belle)
Messrs. Duchesne, Edgard, Choeur
Recit et Barcarolle (Nous voici de retour)
Messrs. Duchesne, Edgard
Sérénade d'Amoroso (Catarina, je chante)
Mlle. Dorlia
Couplets de Catarina
Mlle. M. Aimée
Sérénade de Malatromba
Mons. F. Noe
Ensemble
Mlle. Dorlia, Messrs. F. Noe, Duchesne, Edgard
Complainte de Cornarino (L'amiral Cornarini avec nos vaisseaux)
Mlle. Vandamme, Choeur
Final (L'amiral en vérité)
Choeur

ACT 2
Choeur de femmes (Hélas! noble maîtresse)
Mlle. Briot, Choeur des femmes
La colombe et l'autour (La colombe)
Mons. N. Noe
Quatuor des Poignards (Hélas! mon Dieu! que vont ils faire?)
Messrs. Duchesne, Edgard, Julien, Mlle. Cayla
Terzettino (Ayez pitié! ayez pitié!)
Messrs. F. Noe, Duchesne, Edgard
Le Rêve (Ah! qu'il était doux mon beau rêve)
Mons. F. Noe
Scène de folie (Ah! le Doge!)
Mlle. Aimée, Mons. F. Noe
Bolero (C'est un coin tout petit)
Messrs. F. Noe, Edgard, Duchesne, Mlles. M. Aimée, Julien, Cayla
Scène et choeur des Sires (D'où sortent ces cris)
Messrs. F. Noe, Edgard, Duchesne, Mlles. M. Aimée, Choeur
Final:
Profession de foi (Mes amis, je n'ai d'autre vie)
Messrs. F. Noe, Edgard, Duchesne, Mlles. M. Aimée, Julien, Cayla, Choeur
Marche triomphale (Vive, vive Malatromba)
Mlles. Julien, Cayla, Choeur

[17] First produced in New York in French 4 January 1869 at Pike Opera House. For Synopsis of Scenes and Musical Numbers, see original 1869 production.

[18] First produced in New York in French 1 February 1869 at the Théatre Français. For Synopsis of Scenes and Musical Numbers, see original 1869 production.

[19] No New York program found. Cast list prepared from Boston touring program 14 May 1872.

[20] Previously presented in New York in French 24 September 1867 at the Théatre Français for 156 performances. For Synopsis of Scenes and Musical Numbers, see original 1867 production.

[21] Musical numbers not listed in programs. List prepared from published French piano vocal score, 'nouvelle partition' (Heugel et Cie., Paris, 1868).

ACT 3

Choeur des Gondolières (Vole, vole, vole, ma gondole)
Choeur des gondoliéres

Couplets (Les affairs sont les affairs)
Mons. F. Noe, Choeur

Ensemble (Reconduisez ces demoiselles)
Choeur des gondoliéres

Couplets des Éperons (Ces éperons, ces compagnons de gloire)
Mons. Duchesne

Duettino (Nous sommes deux aventuriers)
Mlles. M. Aimée, Dorlia, Choeur (Conseil des dix)

Marche funèbre

Final (Ah! qu'il est drôle!)
Messrs. F. Noe, A. Valter, Choeur (Conseil des dix)

ACT 4

Le Carnival (En avant pierrots et pierrettes)
Choeur

Couplets des masques (Mon Pierrot)
Mlles. Briot, Vandamme, T. Hache, Choeur

Couplets avec choeur (Le tourbillon)
Mlles. A. Cave, Bessiéres, Briot, Vandamme, T. Hache, Jousse, Choeur

Entrée du Conseil des Dix
Choeur

Le Défi (Cousin traître et parjure)
Messrs. Duchesne, F. Noe, Choeur

Ensemble et Mélodrame (Le sort sera contraire)
Choeur

Boléro final (C'est un coin petit au fin fond des Espagnes)
Mlles. M. Aimée, Dorlia, Messrs. F. Noe, Duchesne, Edgard, Conseils des Dix, Chowur

1871.27 THE BLACK CROOK

A Revival of the Musical Extravaganza in Four Acts, 11 Scenes[22]. Play by Charles M. Barras. Music by Signor Giuseppe Operti. Stage manager, C. H. Morton. Ballet under the supervision of Davide Costa. Scenery by Messrs. Laren, William Voegtlin, Reitzky, George Heister. Prismatic light effects by Professor Smith. Stage architecture and mechanism by Bensen Sherwood. Costumes by Laureys and Auguste & Company. Properties by John Lundy. Musical director, Signor Giuseppe Operti. Produced by Henry Jarrett and Harry Palmer. Opened 18 December 1871 at Niblo's Garden and closed 24 February 1872 after 71 performances.

CAST: *Count Wolfenstein*: E. K. COLLIER. *Rudolphe*, a poor artist: ARTHUR MATTHISON. *Von Puffengruntz*, the Count's Steward: HARRY PEARSON. *Hertzog*, the Count's Steward: C. H. MORTON. *Greppo*, his servant: FELIX ROGERS. *Dragonfin*: Master MARTIN. *Zamiel*, the arch fiend: H. PACKARD. *Wolfgar*, a Gypsy ruffian: F. Beresford. *Caspar*, a Peasant: J. Riley. *Red Glare*, the Recording Demon: A. Fleming. *Skuldawelp*, familiar to Hertzog: W. Hennessy. *Villagers, Peasants, Guards, Attendants, Demons, Monsters, Apparitions, Gnomes, etc.*

Stalacta, Queen of the Golden Realm: KATE SANTLEY. *Amina*, betrothed to Rudolphe: BESSIE SUDLOW. *Dame Barbara*, her foster mother: Mrs. EDWARD WRIGHT. *Carline*, Amina's maid: JENNIE LEE. *Rosetta*, a Peasant: Addie Strickland. *Fairies, Naiads, etc.*

Ballet: Mlles. PIERINA SASSI, CORA ADRIENNE, BEDON FELICITA, BONNI BAMBINA, CLOTILDA MARCHESI, ISRIALDI ANNETTA, Isabella, Leontine, Lehman, Kruger, Josephine, Antoinette, Caroline, Jeanette, Eugenie, Jeanne, Leonie, Adrienne, Aurelle, Victorie, Cabal, Marie, Anna, Hortense, Helene, Jennie, Antoinette, Alexandrine, Blanche, Brisson, Morlet, Medina, Varnal, Sophie, Stella, Lambert, Beretta, Pinzuti, Antonina, Koch, Clara, Camilla, Rose, Pauline, Vernet, Louise, etc. (Ballet of 60) *Specialties*: THE MAJILTONS, Trio of Egyptian Jugglers (Hassan, Anak, Selim); (St. Felix Parisienne) Infant Ballet Troupe; Professor Smith and His Children; Professor Samwell's Troupe of Trained Animals; The Celebrated Clown Dog, Grimaldi.

Act 1, Scene 1: A Valley at the Foot of the Hartz Mountains. (Laren.) *Scene 2*: A Woody Pass. (Voegtlin.) *Scene 3*: Laboratory of the Black Crook. (Voegtlin.) *Scene 4*: An Apartment in the Castle of Wolfenstein. (Reitzky.) *Scene 5*: A Wild Glen in the Heart of the Brocken. (Laren.)

Act 2, Scene 1: Subterranean Vault in the Castle of Wolfenstein. (Voegtlin.) *Scene 2*: Lobby in the Castle of Wolfenstein. (Reitzky.) *Scene 3*: A Wild Pass in the Hartz Mountains. (Voegtlin.) *Scene 4*: The Grotto of Stalacta. (Laren.); The Fountain of Glowing Light. (Smith.)

Act 3: Illuminated Golden Terrace of the Castle of Wolfenstein. (Heister.)

Act 4: The Palace of Dew Drops.

BALLETS AND SPECIALITIES

"I'll Be True to Thee" (Duet)(Act 1, Scene 1)
B. Sudlow, A. Matthison
(*Music and Lyrics by* Stephen Foster.)

Dance de Breton-Sabot Dance (Act 1, Scene 1)
Mlles. Adrienne, Bambina, Felicita,
Clotilda, Marchesi, Isabella, Leontine, Lehman, Kruger, Josephine, Antoinette, etc.

"Fascinating Little Man" (Act 1, Scene 4)
J. Lee

Grand Incantation Scene (Act 1, Scene 5)

"Cupid's Mischief" (Song)(Act 2, Scene 5)
K. Santley
(*Music by* Arthur Sullivan.)

"L'Allegra" (Joy)(Song)(Act 2, Scene 5)
K. Santley
(*Music by* Signor Giuseppe Operti.)

Quartette (Act 2, Scene 5)
K. Santley, J. Lee, A. Matthison, F. Rogers

Polka Diabolique (Act 2, Scene 5)
Infant Ballet Troupe

Ballet, Orgia à Passo Demoni (Act 2, Scene 5)
Mlles. Sassi, Adrienne, Felicita, Bambina,
Marchesi, Isabella, Leontine, Lehman, Kruger, Antoinette, Caroline, Jeanette, Coryphées

The Bath of the Sprites (Act 2, Scene 5)

Bacchanale (Act 3)
Mlle. Sassi, Corps de Ballet

Les Crelots d'Amour
Mlles. Adrienne, Felicita, Bambina, Annetta

Mandolinata
Mlles. Isabella, Lehman, Kruger, Josephine, Antoinette, Caroline, Jeanette
Les Matelots

St. Felix Parisienne Infant Ballet Troupe

La Follia (Passo Fattastique)
Mlle. Sassi, Corps de Ballet

Grand Finale Fatastatique
Entire Corps de Ballet

The Wonderful Majiltons in their peculiar Acte Fantastique (Act 3)

"The Little Pet Jockey" (Song, with Jockey Hornpipe)(Act 3)
J. Lee

Specialties: Prof. Smith and His Children; Prof. Samwell's Troupe of Trained Animals; The Dog, Grimaldi; Egyptian Jugglers (Act 3)

Aria (Act 3)
K. Santley

The March of the Amazons (Act 3)

Dazzling Transformation Scene revealing the Nymphs of the Golden Realm (Act 4)

1871.28 BARBE BLEUE

A Revival of the Opéra-bouffe in Three Acts[23], in French. Libretto by Henri Meilhac and Ludovic Halévy. Music by Jacques Offenbach. Conductor, Professor Fred W. Zaulig. Opened 19 December 1871 at Lina Edwin's Theatre; season closed 3 February 1872 after (12) performances in repertory.

CAST: *Boulotte*: Mlle. MARIE AIMÉE. *Sire de Barbe-bleue*: Mons. COUELITE. *King Bobèche*: Mons. DUCHESNE. *Queen Clémentine*: Mlle. DORLIA. *Count Oscar*: Mons. JULIEN. *Princess Hermia*: Mlle. HACHE. *Prince Saphir*: Mons. Berthon. *Popolani*: Mons. EDGARD. Chorus.

[22]First produced in New York 12 September 1866 at Niblo's Garden for 475 performances.

[23]First produced in New York in French 13 July 1868 at Niblo's Garden. For Synopsis of Scenes and Musical Numbers, see original 1868 production.

1872.01 LES NOCES DE JEANNETTE

A Revival of the Opéra-comique in One Act[24], in French. Libretto by Michel Carré and Jules Barbier. Music by Victor Massé. Conductor, Professor Fred W. Zaulig. Opened 4 January 1872 at Lina Edwin's Theatre; season closed 3 February 1872 after (12) performances in repertory.

CAST: *Jeannette*: Mlle. DUBOIS. *Jean*: ??.

1872.02 LITTLE RED RIDING-HOOD

A Burlesque Extravaganza in One Act[25]. Stage director, James Barnes. Musical director, William H. Brinkworth. Produced by George Wood. Opened 15 January 1872 at Wood's Museum and closed 3 February 1872 after 17 performances.

CAST: *Blondinette*, known as Little Red Riding Hood: Miss BELLE HOWITT. *Colin*, a Model of Constancy: Miss PAULINE MARKHAM. *Baron Reginald DeWolf*, a Heavy Villain: HARRY STEWART. *Diavolo*, his Seneschal: A. H. SHELDON. *Florisette*, a Fairy of the Orthodox Legendary School: Miss Jennie Arnot. *First Peasant*: Miss Nellie Lewis. *Second Peasant*: Miss Jenny Satterlee. *Pertina*, a Fast Little Sprite: Miss ALICE ATHERTON. *Jennie*, a pure-minded puir bodie: Miss THERESA WOOD. *Granny*: R. J. LEWIS. *First Ruffian*: L. R. Willard. *Second Ruffian*: Mr. E. Coyle.

1872.03 LES BRIGANDS

A Revival of the Opéra-bouffe in Three Acts[26], in French. Libretto by Henri Meilhac and Ludovic Halévy. Conductor, Professor Fred W. Zaulig. Music by Jacques Offenbach. Opened 29 January 1872 at Lina Edwin's Theatre; season closed 3 February 1872 after (6) performances in repertory.[27]

CAST: *Fiorella*: Mlle. MARIE AIMÉE. *Fragoletto*, a Young Farmer: Mlle. DUBOIS. *Falsacappa*: Mons. FERNAND NOE. *Pietro*, his Lieutenant: Mons. DUCHESNE. *Count Gloria-Cassis*, Chamberlain to the Princess: Mons. Berthon. *Baron de Campotasso*, Esquire to the Duke: Mons. Julien. *The Captain of the Caribineers*: Mons. EDGARD. *Brigands (3)*: *Carmagnola*: Mons. Salvator. *Barbavano*: Mons. Guiot. *Domino*: Mlle. Parent. *Pipo*, an innkeeper: Mons. Victor. *Le Precepteur*: Mons. Oudin. *Un Courier, Un Huissier*: Mons. Seve. *The Duke of Mantua*: Mons. VANDELET. *Adolphe de Vallodolid*: Mons. Vandamme. *The Princess of Granada*: Mlle. GOMER. *The Duchess*: Mlle. Noemie. *The Marquise*: Mlle. Julien. *The Cashier*: Mlle. Edgard. *Brigands, Caribineers, Peasants, Pages, Lords and Ladies of the Court of Mantua, Pages and Ladies of the Court of Granada.*

1872.04 DICK WHITTINGTON AND HIS CAT

A New Pantomimic Burlesque Extravaganza in One Act, 8 Scenes. Music by William H. Brinkworth. Produced under the supervision of stage director James Barnes. Scenery by John A. Thompson. Machinery by William B. Carpenter. Properties by Charles LaForrest. Costumes by Mons. Toledo. Musical director, William H. Brinkworth. Produced by George Wood. Opened 5 February 1872 at Wood's Museum and closed 16 February 1872 after 10 performances (weekday matinees).

CAST: *Dick Whittington*, The Good Apprentice, who though worried by the Knaves in the pack, at last turns up a trump: Miss BELLE HOWITT. *Alice Fitzwarren*, His Sweetheart, a Rustic Beauty of "Ye Olden Time": Miss PAULINE MARKHAM. *Al-Mi-Hi*, Emperor of the Isle of Wangdoodle, a dark subject with an aversion to Rats: Mr. A. H. SHELDON. *Old Fitzwarren*, Father of Alice, a crusty old parent, with a dislike to Cats: Mr. HARRY STEWART. *Captain Blowhard*, a salt sea rover, with a home on the rolling deep: Mr. R. J. Lewis. *Wideawake*, a sleepy watchman: L. R. Willard. *Rataplan*, King of the Rats: Mr. E. Coyle. *Hokri-Kee*, a sable Ethiopian: Miss Ellen Lewis. *Hokey-Pokey*, another: Miss M. Holcomb. *The Cat*, the feline cause of all Dick's troubles: Miss AGGIE KEENE. *Queen Olivebranch*, a Fairy, light and airy: Miss ALICE ATHERTON. *Cupid* the God of Love: Miss Jennie Arnot. *Princess Up-I-Dee*, a cream-colored Asiatic: Miss THERESA WOOD. *Dame Margery*, Erin go Bragh forever: Miss Jennie Satterlee. *Rats! Cats! Ethiopians! Citizens! Guards and Blackguards!*

Scene 1: Street in old London Citie. *Scene 2*: Milestone on Highgate Hill. *Scene 3*: The Lively Sally. *Scene 4*: An Oriental landscape. *Scene 5*: The Isle of Wangdoodle. *Scene 6*: The Home of Little Alice. *Scene 7*: In the Clouds. *Scene 8*: The Peri's Home in the Palace of Pearls.

SPECIALTIES

"Down in a Coal Mine"; "Eliza Jane"; "Walk Around" (Scene 1)
Terrible Storm and Wreck of the Lively Sally (Scene 3)
Review of the Rat Army (Scene 4)
Arrival of the Royal Cortege (Scene 4)
Pas de Keene (Scene 4)
T. W. Keene
Fierce Combat of the Cat and the Rat (Scene 5)
Laughing Chorus (Scene 6)
Finale (Scene 8)

1872.05 POLL AND PARTNER JOE

A Nautical Burlesque in One Act[28]. Play by F. C. Burnand. Music by William H. Brinkworth. Scenery by John A. Thompson. Produced under the immediate supervision of James Barnes, Stage Director. Machinery by William B. Carpenter. Properties by Charles LaForrest. Costumes by Mons. Toledo. Produced by George Wood. Opened 19 February 1872 (matinee) at Wood's Museum in repertory and closed 2 March 1872 after 10 performances.

CAST: *Mary Maybud* (Poll): Miss PAULINE MARKHAM. *Harry Hallyard*: Miss BELLE HOWITT. *Black Brandon*: Mr. A. H. SHELDON. *Dame Tiller*: ROLLIN HOWARD. *Joe Tiller*: Miss THERESE WOOD. *Snatchem*: Mr. Harry Stewart. *Watchful Waxend*: Mr. A. J. Debonay. *Sam Sculier*: Mr. R. J. Lewis. *Ben Bowse*: Miss Alice Atherton. *Lieut. Manley*: Miss Jennie Arnot. *Abigail*: Miss Nellie Lewis. *First Mate*: Miss Jennie Satterlee. *Landlord*: Mr. L. R. Willard. *Press Gang, Watermen, Sailors.*

1872.06 THE NAIAD QUEEN

A Revival of the Spectacle in Three Acts, 9 Scenes[29]. (Play by W. E. Burton.) Stage manager, C. H. Morton. Scenery by William Voegtlin, Reitzky, George Heister. Produced by Henry Jarrett and Harry Palmer. Opened 26 February 1872 at Niblo's Garden and closed 2 March 1872 after 7 performances.

CAST: Mortals: *Sir Rupert*: ARTHUR MATTHISON. *Schnapps*: WALTER LENNOX. *Rodolpho*: C. M. Lewis. *Rinaldo*: E. L. Parsons. *Manfredi*: William T. Styles. *Albert*: J. S. Norton. *Winkleman*: J. Cole. *Baron of Lochausen*: J. Beresford. *Bridget*: Mrs. Howard. *Lady Una*: Miss Marquette.

Demons: *Amphibeo*: Master Martin. *Carbunelle*: Samuel Barker. *Finback*: James Maxwell. *Sharkeye*: William Barrett. *Phantom Face*: F. Florence. *Scaley Skin*: Mr. Smythe.

Immortals: *The Naiad Queen*: KATE SANTLEY. *Idex*: JENNIE LEE. *Fluvia*: Carrie White. *Sparkle*: Emily King. *Dew-Drop*: Miss Parker. *Iona*: Miss M. F. King. *Limpid*: Miss T. Florence. *Sea Nettle*: Miss P. Connolly. *Polypus*: Miss A. Smith. *Coraline*: Miss Burnett.

Premiere Danseuses: Mlles. JOSEPHINE DEROSA, AMINA VENTUROLI, CORA ADRIENNE, PIERINA SASSI. *Ballet*: Mlles. Bedon Felicita, Bonni Bambina, Clotilda Marchesi; Mlles. Isabella, Leontine, Lehman, Kruger, Josephine, Antoinette, Caroline, Jeannette, Coryphées, Corps de Ballet of 60. *Specialties*: St. Felix Parisienne Infant Ballet Troupe, Professor Samwell's Troupe of Trained Animals, Professor Schmidt and his children, The celebrated Clown Dog, Grimaldi; Alexis, the Great Equestrian Goat; Spanish Minstrels.

Act 1, Scene 1: Interior of Sir Rupert's Castle (Reitzky.) *Scene 2*: Moonlight View of the Rhine. (Heister.) *Scene 3*: Haunt of the Naiads. (Heister.) *Scene 4*: Stalactite Grotto of the Naiad Queen. (Heister.)

---

[24]First produced in New York in English 9 April 1855 at Niblo's Garden as THE MARRIAGE OF GEORGETTE; in French 28 October 1861 at the Academy of Music. For Synopsis of Scenes and Musical Numbers, see original 1861 production. Presented on a double bill with FLEUR DE THÉ.

[25]Followed by the after-piece, TEN NIGHTS IN A BAR-ROOM, with T. W. Keene and Company. For the second and third weeks, LITTLE RED RIDING HOOD became a weekday matinee attraction, paired with a comedy, HIS LAST VICTORY.

[26]First produced in New York in French 14 November 1870 at the Grand Opera House. For Synopsis of Scenes and Musical Numbers, see original 1870 production.

[27]No New York program found; cast list prepared from Boston tour 17 May 1872.

[28]Scenes and Musical Numbers not listed in programs. Presented for daily weekday matinees for the first week of the run. Preceded by the drama WOMAN OF THE WORLD the first week, and OUT AT SEA in the second week.

[29]First produced in New York 21 April 1841 at the National Opera House. For Synopsis of Scenes and Musical Numbers, see original 1841 production.

Act 2: The Grotto.

Act 3, *Scene* 1: Cave of the Nymphs. (Heister.) *Scene* 2: Grand Hall in Rupert's Castle. (Voegtlin.) *Scene* 3: Corridor of the Castle. *Scene* 4: Grand Hall.

ACT 1
Scene 2
"Flow on Silver Rhine" (Aria)
K. Santley
"Had I a Spirit's Wings" (Romance)
K. Santley, A. Matthison
Scene 3
Comic Duet
J. Lee, W. Lennox
Scene 4
Comic Duet, with Chorus
J. Lee, W. Lennox

ACT 2
Aria
K. Santley
Pas de Poissons (Ballet)
Mlles. J. de Rosa, A. Venturoli, C. Adrienne, Ballet, Coryphées
The Cloud-Veil with the Hues of Sunset
Professor Schmidt
The Fountain of Jewels
Professor Schmidt

ACT 3
Scene 1
Song
J. Lee
Scene 3
The Demon Fight
Scene 4
Assault of the Naiads
Mandolinata
Mlles. Isabella, Lehman, Kruger, Josephine, Antoinette, Caroline, Jeannett
Pas de Caledonia
St. Felix Parisienne Infant Ballet Troupe
Hungarian Polka
Mlle. A. Venturoli
Oriental Serpent Dance
Mlle. P. Sassi, and a living anaconda
Grand Finale Fantastique
Entire Corps de Ballet
The Wonderful Majiltons in their Peculiar Acte Fantastique
Spanish Minstrels, from the Royal Alhambra, Madrid
Professor Schmidt's Pupils in their Classical Groupings
The Wonderful Goat, Alexis, in his great Equestrian Act
Professor Samwell's Troupe of Trained Animals. The Dog, Grimaldi.
The March of the Amazons
Aria
K. Santley
Quartette
K. Santley, J. Lee, A. Matthison, W. Lennox
Grand Finale

IXION, or, the Man at the Wheel

1872.07

A Revival of the Burlesque in 6 Scenes, preceded by an Olio[30]. Play by F. C. Burnand. Music by Henry Wannemacher. Scenery by R. L. Weed. Properties and machinery by Nelse Waldron. Orchestra director, Henry Wannemacher. Produced by Josh Hart. Opened 26 February 1872 at the Theatre Comique and closed 16 March 1872 after 24 performances.[31]

CAST: *King Ixion*, an ex-King in distress, invited by Jupiter to visit the skies by Jove, and taken up by Jingo: SOPHIE WORRELL. *Venus*, the Goddess of Beauty, a Lady-like Goddess: IRENE WORRELL. *Mercury*, Jove's Messenger, a Celestial Telegraph Boy, a fast Young Man: JENNIE WORRELL. *Jupiter*, King of Olympus, a Musical Monarch: LILLIE HALL. *Cupid*, Son of Venus, dressed a little more than the cupids we usually see on Valentines: Ada Wray. *Apollo*, Jupiter's private secretary: Jennie Hughes. *Juno*, Queen of the Gods, Jupiter's better half, a perfect Lady in every respect: Kitty Tilstone. *Minerva*, an intensely and immensely strong-minded woman, the impersonified embodiment of Lucy Stone, Susan B. Anthony, Horace Greeley, Harriet Beecher Stowe, Victoria C. Woodhull and other advocates and defenders of woman's rights and woman's wrong: E. D. Gooding. *Mars*, the God of War, the idol of the M. G.: Harry Guion. *Bacchus*, Head Centre of the Celestial Whiskey Ring and opposed to the Excise Law: Larry Tooley. *Ganymede*, the original Active Boy, Special Messenger and Man of All Work: Johnny Wild. *Thrice diabolical conspirators from the Fourteenth Ward (4)*: *Tonomarrowbones*: Charley White. *Paddesoker*: James Bradley. *Prosperus*: G. L. Stoute. *That Young Grecian*: J. Lewis. *Calliope*: Emma Maddux. *Melpomene*: Kitty O'Neil. *Polyhymnia*: Lilly Brice. *Mortals, Immortals, Greeks, Grecians and other Greenhorns*: Much enlightened supernumeraries.

Scene 1: A dark wood near the Kingdom of Ixion. *Scene* 2: The Exterior of Bacchus' saloon in the Sky. *Scene* 3: Juno's Reception Hall in the Kingdom of Jupiter. *Scene* 4: The Head Centre of the Sun. *Scene* 5: Exterior of Juno's Chamber in the Sky. *Scene* 6: The Halls of Jupiter.

LUNA, the Naughty Little Boy who cried for the Moon

1872.08

A Pantomimic Burlesque Extravaganza in One Act, 6 Scenes. Music by William H. Brinkworth. Stage director, James Barnes. Scenery by John A. Thompson. Stage machinery by William B. Carpenter. Properties by Charles LaForrest. Costumes by Mons. Toledo. Musical director, William H. Brinkworth. Produced by George Wood. Opened 4 March 1872 at Wood's Museum and closed 15 March 1872 after 12 performances[32].

CAST: *Endymion*, Prince of the Shepherd Band with matrimonial notions much above his station, the naughty boy who cried for the moon: Miss BELLE HOWITT. *Diana*, Goddess of Hunting, otherwise known as the Moon, in all respects a shining character: Miss PAULINE MARKHAM. *Clymene*, Sister of Endymion, and a more or less assister of the plot: ROLLIN HOWARD. *Putaplasteron*, the Family Doctor, an M. D. by diploma: Mr. A. H. SHELDON. *Aethlius*, Endymion's Father, whose evening of life is contrary to all natural laws, brightened by the glories of his rising Son: Mr. R. J. Lewis. *Actaeon*, Squire Actaeon, who was run by his own hounds, and who trespassing on a celebrated preserve, finds himself in a famous pickle: Mr. HARRY STEWART. *Alphaeus*, a River Deity, a classical type of the "Jolly Young Waterman," a rapid stream in which capacity it is hoped he may long be allowed to run: Miss THERESE WOOD. *Cupid*, God of Love, a mischievous boy, delighting in inspiring a great passion, wherever he finds a little pet: Miss Jennie Arnot. *Pan*, the God of Shepherds and of huntsmen: Mr. J. A. Meade. *Taunion, Phaunion, Harnion*, Satyrs attendant upon Pan: Messrs. A. J. Debonay, Charles Sturges, L. R. Willard. *Stupidon*: Mr. E. Coyle. *Clodoppa*: Mr. S. Fisher. *Arethusa*, Surnamed the Saucy, a favorite nymph: Miss ALICE ATHERTON. *Polydora*: Miss Nellie Lewis. *Nyce*: Miss Jennie Satterlee. *Eudea*: Miss Maron Holcomb. *Coralpso*: Miss Annie Page. *Fairies, Satyrs, Huntsmen, etc.*

Scene 1: Diana's Retreat in the Valley of Gargaphia. *Scene* 2: Borders of the Forest. *Scene* 3: Summit of Mount Latmos. *Scene* 4: The Shepherd's Festival. *Scene* 5: Diana's Bower. *Scene* 6: Endymion's Home. He ascends to the Silver Throne of Luna.

LA BELLE SAUVAGE

1872.09

John Brougham's great burlesque in Two Acts, re-written expressly for this company[33]. (Adapted from his earlier 'Po-ca-hon-tas, or Ye Gentle Savage'[34]) Produced under the immediate supervision of Mrs. John Wood. Presented by Henry Jarrett and Harry Palmer. Opened 4 March 1872 at Niblo's Garden and closed 30 March 1872 after 28 performances.

---

[30]First produced in New York 28 September 1868 at Wood's Museum & Metropolitan Theatre in two engagements for 120 performances.
[31]Program note: Various songs and incidents of the burlesque are too many to enumerate amongst the synopsis.

[32]For the first week, performed evenings and Saturday matinees, with an exhibition of Fijian Cannibals as fore-piece, and the comedy, A Bull in a China Shop as an after-piece. For the balance of the run, LUNA became the weekday matinee entertainment.
[33]Accompanied by a fore-piece, A MODEL OF A WIFE, which was replaced by CHECKMATE
[34]Brougham's burlesque PO-CA-HON-TAS, or, Ye Gentle Savage, was first produced in New York 24 December 1855 at Wallack's Theatre in repertory. For Synopsis of Scenes and Musical Numbers, see original 1855 production. No scenes or musical numbers listed in the Niblo's Garden program.

CAST: *H.R.H. Princess Pocahontas*: Mrs. JOHN WOOD. *Krosascanbe*: Mr. HARRY COX. *Pooteepet*: Miss EMILY WESTON. *Dimundi*: Annie Tyson. *Dahlinduck*: Katie Tyson. *Oujewel*: Miss Florence. *Luvlicreetur*: Miss Richardson. *Osocharmin*: Miss Clarke. *Litelpeste*: Petite Minnie. *H.I.M. King Powhattan*: MARK SMITH. *Count Rolfe*: A. W. YOUNG. *Captain John Smith*: G. W. ANSON. *Lieutenant Thomas Brown*: J. Reilly. *Opodildoc*: JULIAN CROSSE. *Mucmodo*: Mr. Hurley. *Quashaljaw*: Mr. Graham. *Glass O'Grog*: Mr. Johnson. *Jing Go*: Mr. Sandford. *Indians, School Girls, Sailors, etc*: Numerous Auxiliaries.

LALLA ROOKH, or, The Pearl of India!

1872.10

A Grand Spectacular Drama in Four Acts, 18 Scenes. Play by Joseph C. Foster, adapted from the poem by Thomas Moore. Music composed by Henry Tissington. Scenery by Richard Marston, Joseph Schell, George Dayton. Costumes by Anna Foster. Novel accessories and ingenious mechanism by Samuel Wallis. Properties and appointments by Joseph C. Foster. Ballets arranged by Mons. Van Hamme. Orchestra under the direction of Henry Tissington. Produced under the immediate supervision of (directed by) Joseph C. Foster and L. J. Vincent. Produced by John F. Cole. Opened 18 March 1872 at the Grand Opera House and closed 4 May 1872 after 50 performances.

CAST: *Ziraftighan*, Gheber of the Desert: J. B. STUDLEY. *Aliris*, King of Bucharis, disguised as Feramorz, a Minstrel: GEORGE BECKS. *Arunzeba*, Emperor of the Indies: J. R. Healy. *Fadladeen*, a Grand Chamberlain: THOMAS E. MORRIS. *Kali*, Kofo, Tartar Chiefs: C. Nichols, R. Elberts. *Himlah*, Ambassador from Aliris: George Johnson. *Slaves of Fadladeen (4)*: *Pungo*: T. T. Rainey. *Mungo*: L. Burke. *Lumbo*: G. Wells. *Jumbo*: S. Ellis. *Kamboso*, a favorite officer of Arunzeba: S. B. Duffield. *Kalfir*, Captain of the Guard: E. Dennison. *Clip Clap*, Crier of Delhi: M. W. FISKE. Hafed, King of Fire: G. St. George. *Sabithilghan*, Vizier of Bucharia: T. Waddleton. *Theodosius Lional*, a Wild Beast Tamer: MARK BATES. *No-Fum-So*, Ambassador from China: T. Edwards. *Zeorwriff*, Ambassador from Siam: C. West. *Korrassen*, Ambassador from the Burmese Empire: E. Small. *Zeffoadine*, Ambassador from Persia: P. Rose. *Hyder Ali*, Ambassador from Mysore: S. Wells. *Keriru*, a Fire Worshipper: H. DeBarclay. *Rajahs, Sepoys, Tartars, Fire Worshippers, Ghebers, Banner Bearers, Zodiac Bearers, Children, Hindoos, etc.*

Lalla Rookh, the Pearl of India: EDITH CHALLIS. *Pinion*, Lalla Rookh's Favorite Page (with songs and duet with Liskar): SUSAN GALTON. *Liskar*, Clip Clop's Sister (with songs and duet with Pinion): EMMA CLINE. *Indamora*, wife No. 1 to Fadladeen: Miss Everett. *Ladies of the Harem, Bayaderes, Slaves, Arab Dancers, Chinese Dancers, etc.*

Ballet: Mlles. deROSA, ALBERTINA, LOUISE MAZZERI, LUSUARDI, Coryphées, Fifty Dancers. *Coryphées*: Mlles. G. Schrotter, Marie, C. Schrotter, Elise, Strudel, Josephine, Katarina, Waldau.

Act 1, Scene 1: Interior of the Temple of the Sun. (Marston.) *Scene 2*: Distant View of Delhi City. (Dayton.) *Scene 3*: The Palace of the Emperor, Arunzeba. (Dayton.)

Act 2, Scene 1: Corridor in the Palace. (Schell.) *Scene 2*: Clip Clap's House. (Dayton.) *Scene 3*: The Grove of Palms. (Schell.) *Scene 4*: Sand Hills in the Desert. (Schell.) *Scene 5*: The Lake of Pearls. (Marston.)

Act 3, Scene 1: The Jungle. (Schell.) *Scene 2*: The Illuminated Cedar Grove. (Schell.)

Act 4, Scene 1: The Pilgrim's Well. (Dayton.) *Scene 2*: The Royal Tent. (Dayton.) *Scene 3*: The Lake of Terror. (Dayton.) *Scene 4*: The Gates of Bucharia. (Schell.) *Scene 5*: Grand View of the City of Bucharia. (Marston, Dayton.) *Scene 6*: The Palace of Aliris. (Schell.) *Scene 7*: The Panorama, Sinking Boats and City. (Marston.) *Scene 8*: The Fire Gem of Silver Setting! (Marston.)

ACT 1

Scene 1

Chorus of the Fire Worshippers. The Compact.

The Magic Steed.

"From Earth, through Sky, through Air, You fly, you fly, you fly, you fly"

Scene 2

"Ali Pacha" (Song)
S. Galton

Scene 3

Grand Chorus. The Contest for Beauty.

Arab Ballet
Mlles. Albertina, Mazzeri, Lusuardi, Fulls Corps

The Ambassadors of Love

Glittering Procession

"Thine own sweet emblem, Princess fair, a rose without a thorn"

Bucharia's King we do prefer. The Combat. The Horse of Fire. Discomfiture of the Tartar Chief. Tableau.

ACT 2

Scene 1

Wooing Uneasy.

"Love's Greatest Plague in Life" (Song)
E. Cline

Fadladeen and His Mode of Conquest. The Slaves. The Programme. The Journey to Bucharia.

Scene 2

The Youth and Maiden. A Brother in the Way.

"The Lover and the Nightingale" (Song)
S. Galton

The Ancient Briton. The Ladder of Love. A Proclamation.

Song and Chorus
M. W. Fiske, S. Galton, Female Divinity

The Scene ends with some noise and no confusion.

Scene 3

Arrival of the Tartar Chief. The Black Vulture and the Pilgrim's Plan.

Scene 4

How to defend the Passage to the Lake of Pearls. The Emperor prepared to meet the foe.

Scene 5

Grand Cashmere Ballet!
Mlles. DeRosa, Albertina, Mazzeri, Lusuardi, Coryphées, 50 Danseuses

The Poet and his noble mien. The Vulture's fate. Villainy foiled.

The Test and Result! Triumph of Truth!

ACT 3

Scene 1

How the beasts of the forest upset the nerves of Delhi's Crier. The Tower of London's representative. How barbarians are treated by civilians. The three purses of gold have no charm 'gainst the affection of slimy friends.

Scene 2

The Princess and her train. Feramorz and his poetry.

"As by magic at thy sight, To burst in beauteous, radiant light"

The Feast of the Lanterns

Chinese Festival!!! In a brilliant and enchanting fete
Mlles. Albertina, Mazzeri, Lusuardi, Fulls Corps, Celestial Children

The guarded pass and peaceful slumbers of the future Queen.

The maze of Lanterns. The winding Pageant. The sleeping beauty. The mandate we fulfill.

ACT 4

Scene 1

The plotters and their watchers. Poison better than steel. How an eastern Chamberlain takes to his psychic—and humble servitors imitate their betters.

Scene 2

The dawn of Love. The surprise. The Gift and Departure.

Scene 3

How a wild beast tamer takes an observation. Confederates no bar to a trusty friend. Ambition foiled. The Packets. 1, 2, 3, Low Jack and the Game. Mrs. L., the Queen of Trumps.

Scene 4

Pinion and his true love. A ready-made Princess. A black seizure, ending with a duet

"The Perils of Flirting" (Duet)
S. Galton, E. Cline

Scene 5

A father's hope. Grand Procession. Aliris and his Bride. The meeting. The alarm. The enemy at hand. The Despatches. Plunder and Consternation.

Scene 6

"Barcarole Song" (from the opera of LALLA ROOKH[35])

E. Cline

A Royal Pardon to the Crier. The Pacha of many wives—sudden departure of greatness.

Scene 7

Combat of Ghebers and Bucharians. Destruction of Ziraftighan and Triumph of Aliris. Grand Tableau.

Scene 8

The Fire Gem of Silver Setting!

1872.11 POLL AND PARTNER JOE

A Nautical Burlesque in Two Acts[36]. Play by F. C. Burnand. Music selected and arranged by Napier Lothian. Scenery by George Heister. Produced under the immediate supervision of Mrs. John Wood. (Musical director, Napier Lothian.) Presented by Henry Jarrett and Harry Palmer. Opened 1 April 1872 at Niblo's Garden and closed 20 April 1872 after 21 performances.

CAST: *Mary Maybud*: Mrs. JOHN WOOD. *Black Brandon*: Mr. G. W. ANSON. *Harry Hallyard*: Miss JENNIE LEE. *Joe Tiller*: HARRY PEARSON. *Sam Snatchem*: Mr. Charles H. Morton. *Watchful Waxend*: Mr. A. W. Young. *Sam Sculier*: Mr. J. Brutone. *Ben Bowse*: Miss Emily Weston. *Lieut. Manley*: Julian Cross. *Dame Tiller*: Harry Cox. *Bosun*: G. Chorister. *Abigail*: Miss Tyson. *Press Gang, Watermen, Sailors.*

MUSICAL NUMBERS

"His Heart was True to Poll"

Mrs. J. Wood

1872.12 LURLINE, or, The Knight and the Naiads

A Revival of the Grand Spectacular Burlesque Extravaganza in One Act, a Prologue and 8 Scenes[37]. Play by Henry J. Byron. Music by William H. Brinkworth. Scenery by Joseph B. Ayers. Properties by Charles LaForrest. Costumes by M. Toledo. Musical director, William H. Brinkworth. The whole produced under the immediate direction of James Barnes. Produced by George Wood. Opened 1 April 1872 at Wood's Museum and closed 12 April 1872 after 10 (matinee) performances; returned 7, 10 (matinee) 1873 to the Academy of Music for 2 additional performances.

CAST: *Sir Rupert the Reckless*, a very hard up young German, who goes down the Rhine in search of an heiress: Miss BELLE HOWITT. *Lurline*, the Naiad Queen—a sweet young syren, and a sad victim of misplaced confidence: PAULINE MARKHAM. *Wavelet*, a Naiad-in-waiting, eventually an Naid de-camp: Mr. ROLLIN HOWARD. *The Seneschal*, still harder up, with very little on his body, but a good deal on his mind: Mr. A. H. SHELDON. *Baron Witz*, an empty-headed person who is possessed of a fruitful property though barren his tete: Mr. HARRY STEWART. *Captain of the Scalawags*: Mr. R. J. Lewis. *Count Calimanco*, happy at first, but eventually a good deal cut up: Miss THERESE WOOD. *Albert, Wilfrid, Rinaldo*, individuals with the strongest objection to manual labor: Alice Atherton, Charles Sturges, L. R. Willard. *The Lady Una*, Baron Witz's Daughter, a Great Prize in the German Lottery: Miss JENNIE ARNOT. *Moonbeam, Shadow, Dew Drop*, Fairy Sprites, very pretty, very good: Misses Nellie Lewis, Maud Holcomb, Annie Page. *The River Monster*, "neither flesh, fowl nor good red herring": Mr. A. J. Debonay. *The Family Herald*: Miss Alice Atherton. *Ripple*, another Naiad: Miss Jennie Satterlee. *Guards, Retainers, Scalawags and Mob in general.*

1872.13 THE BELLES OF THE KITCHEN

A Laughable Sketch in One Act, preceded by a farce.[38] Play by the Vokes Family. Opened 15 April 1872 at the Union Square Theatre and closed 1 June 1872 after 49 performances in repertory.

CAST: *Lucinda Scrubbs*, a Lady's Maid: JESSIE VOKES. *Mary*, a House Maid: VICTORIA VOKES. *Barbara*, a Kitchen Maid: ROSINA VOKES. *Timotheus Gibbs*, a Doctor's Page: FRED VOKES. *Wiggins*, a Hair Dresser: FAWDON VOKES.

SPECIALTIES

In the course of the piece will be introduced Specimens of High Tragedy!!!, Low Comedy!!!, Opera and Ballet!!

1872.14 IXION, or, the Man at the Wheel

A Revival of the Popular Burlesque Extravaganza in One Act, 6 Scenes[39]. Play by F. C. Burnand. New songs by Rollin Howard. Stage director, James Barnes. Musical director, William H. Brinkworth. Opened 29 April 1872 at Woods' Museum and closed 11 May 1872 after 12 performances[40].

CAST: *Ixion*: Miss BELLE HOWITT. *Tondapameibomenos*: Mr. A. J. Debonay. *Prosephe*: Mr. R. J. Lewis. *Podasokus*: Mr. Charles Sturges. *A Young Grecian*: Mr. L. R. Willard. *Queen Dia*: Mr. HARRY STEWART.

Immortals: *Jupiter*: Miss THERESE WOOD. *Mercury*: Miss ALICE ATHERTON.

Characters in the Drama: *Venus*: Miss PAULINE MARKHAM. *Ixion*: Miss BELLE HOWITT. *Minerva*: Mr. ROLLIN HOWARD. *Mars*: Mr. T W. KEENE. *Ganymede*: A. H. SHELDON. *Bacchus*: Mr. J. J. WALLACE. *Juno*: Miss EMMA MOSHIER. *Jupiter*: Miss THERESE WOOD. *Mercury*: Miss ALICE ATHERTON. *Cupid*: Miss Jennie Arnot. *Apollo*: Miss Jennie Satterlee. *The Three Graces*: Misses Stevens, Harvey and Lavenia.

The Nine Muses: *Calliope*: Miss Annie Page. *Melpomene*: Miss Tillie Lewis. *Pollyhmnia*: Miss Nellie Davenport. *Clio*: Miss Lavenia. *Erato*: Miss Tillie Page. *Urania*: Miss E. Shay. *Euterpe*: Miss Maud Allerton. *Terpsichore*: Miss Fanny Hanwood. *Thalia*: Miss Lottie Kane.

Scene 1: Ruins of a Doric Temple. *Scene 2*: The Royal Distillery in the Sky! *Scene 3*: Juno's Reception Hall. *Scene 4*: Apollo's Sun, Light, Fire and Insurance Office! *Scene 5*: Cupid's Castle in the Air! *Scene 6*: The Milky Way Jove's Awful and Appalling Sentence, Allegorical Tableau, representing FAME, aided by FACT and FICTION.

NEW SONGS

"A Nobby Sport Am I" (New Canzonetta)

B. Howitt

"Dolly Varden" (A New Serio-Comic Song)

R. Howard

1872.15 THE WRONG MAN IN THE RIGHT PLACE

A Comical, Musical and Saltatorial Farce in One Act[41]. Play invented, written, arranged and acted exclusively by the Vokes Family. Opened 27 May 1872 at the Union Square Theatre and closed 30 May 1872 after 6 performances.

CAST: *Emily Merton*, niece to the proprietress of a young ladies' college, near London: JESSIE VOKES. *Clara Staunton*, a romantic young lady, remaining at the college during vacation: VICTORIA VOKES. *Sarah Jane*, a young person desirous of improving her position in life, at present parlor maid to the establishment: ROSINA VOKES. *Benjamin Buttontop*, manager of an unlicensed theatre, at present under a cloud: FRED VOKES. *Sampson Biffles*, footman to the college, formerly a super in a third-class theatre: FAWDON VOKES.

---

[35]Most likely the opéra-comique with music by Félicien César David, lyrics by Michel Carré and Hippolyte Lucas, produced in France in 1862.

[36]A rival production to the earlier New York production which opened 19 February 1872 at Wood's Museum for 11 matinee performances. Scenes and Musical Numbers not listed in programs.

[37]Previously produced in two acts, 17 October 1870 at Wood's Museum for 28 performances. For Synopsis of Scenes, see original 1870 production. Scene 3 featured a Grand Moral ballet, in which Rollin Howard executed a Terrific Snake Dance, à la Sassi. A fore-piece, the comedy, HAPPIEST DAY OF MY LIFE shared the bill.

[38]The farce, My Preserver, with Cast: A. H. Davenport, E. F. Thorne, Harry Hotto, Welsh Edwards, George Atkins, George Coes, Minnie Jackson, Annie Wood, Millie Cook.During the run, the curtain-raiser or fore-piece was frequently changed: My Preserver was succeeded 29 April 1872 by Sketches In India; 13 May 1872 by A Roland For An Oliver; 20 May 1872 by Naval Engagements.

[39]First produced in New York 28 September 1868 at Wood's Museum & Metropolitan Theatre in two engagements for 120 performances.

[40]In the second week of its run, IXION was performed at daily matinees.

[41]Preceded by a farce, 'Phobus Fix.'

SPECIALTIES, MUSICAL NUMBERS[42]

Operatic Duet
V. Vokes, F. Vokes

Leary Dance
R. Vokes

Burlesque Polka
F. Vokes

The Vokes Quadrilles
Vokes Family

[42]Not in performance order.

1872–1873 SEASON

Matilda Vining (Mrs. John) Wood (Photo: Barraud)
Billy Rose Theatre Collection, New York Public Library for the Performing Arts

1872–1873 SEASON

1872.16 FORTUNIO AND HIS GIFTED SERVANTS!

A Comic Operatic Burlesque Extravaganza in Two Acts. Libretto by James Robinson Planché. Music incidental to the piece composed by Frank A. Howson. Scenery and mechanical arrangements by Edward Simmons. Gas and illuminations by William Mackey. Chemical lights by McCaffrey and Wilson. Musical director, Frank A. Howson. Produced by Mrs. James A. Oates Comic Opera and Burlesque Troupe. Opened 3 June 1872 at the Union Square Theatre and closed 20 June 1872 after 18 performances; season closed 2 July 1872.

CAST: *Hon. Miss Myrtina,* youngest daughter of the Baron Dunover, afterwards called Fortunio, by Royal Fairy license: Mrs. JAMES A. OATES. *Miss Pertina, Miss Flirtina,* her elder sisters: Nellie Allen, Miss Thorpe. *Baron Dunover,* a distressed Knight, who having invested his bottom dollar at 162 1/2 on "Black Friday," finds himself without means to procure a substitute for the Army, but is relieved from his dilemma by the exercise of "Women's Rights": H. E. ANDREW. *King Alforite,* the reigning sovereign of any place, best suited to the imagination of the audience, having had a little unpleasantness with his neighbor and came out second best, is just now in great distress for want of men and money to carry on the war: WILLIAM H. CRANE. *Princess Vindicta,* his sister, she with auburn hair, gentle as a dove, frail as the linnet, whose love for Fortunio is only exceeded by her appetite, and immense capacity for vengeance: (Mr.) H. T. ALLEN. *Emperor Fou Fou,* boss of the ring, when first discovered; land owner, contractor, manufacturer of railroad and state bonds, etc., when last scene is, carpet bag in hand, demurely seeking a place of rest; glory and office gone through freedom of the press and losses on the turf: H. H. PRATT. *Prince Elfo,* the fairy and generalissimo of the elfin realms, whose most apparent object is to be on hand when required and explain to the audience what it's all about: CHARLES H. DREW. *Gormand,* with an unhealthy appetite: A. W. Maflin. *Tippler,* the man fish: A. W. Maflin. *Strongback,* the elephant tosser, and splitter of light-wood, noted for beauty of form and feature: A. W. MAFLIN. *Lightfoot,* Goldsmith's maid nowhere: (Mr.) J. H. Jones. *Marksman,* Captain Travis eclipsed: Kate Heathcote. *Fine Ear,* could hear a pin drop in Congress: Kate Heathcote. *Herald,* the first vocalist of the evening, whose introductory lyric effort is invariably followed by vociferous shouts from the bewildered audience of Wachtel! Wachtel!, whose silvery tones are only equalled by the lustre of his golden locks: John Henry. *Princess Ting Sing,* fleetfooted and a natural blonde, easily done, for she has plenty of time for change and not much change—: Miss McClellan. *Karl Form,* Basso Profundo, Prime Minister to the Emperor Fou Fou: E. Horan. *Courtiers, Guards, Citizens, Stock Jobbers, Fugitive Governors, Carpet Baggers, Colored Legislators, etc.*

Act 1: An Ancient Street; The Fairy Dell; Fancy Apartments in the King's Palace; The Royal Gardens.

Act 2: Grand Audience Hall of the Chinese Emperor. The Great Race Scene; Beautiful Moonlight View; Finale—Grand Transformation.

SPECIALTIES[1]

Ladder and Spade Dance
A. W. Maflin

Professor Farber will introduce his Wonderful Talking Machine which speaks in any language, laughs and sings. (Act 2)

1872.17 THE BOHEMIAN GIRL

A Revival of the Light Opera in Three Acts[2]. Libretto by Alfred Bunn, after Jules-Henri Vernoy de Saint-Georges' ballet-pantomime "The Gypsy." Music by Michael William Balfe. Conductor, Anthony Reiff, Jr. Produced by the English Opera Company. Opened 3 June 1872 at Bryant's Opera House and closed 8 June 1872 after 3 performances in repertory; season closed 15 June 1872.

CAST: *Arline*: EMMA HOWSON. *The Gipsey Queen*: Zelda Seguin. *Thaddeus*: BROOKHOUSE BOWLER. *Count Arnheim*: HENRI DRAYTON. *Devilshoof*: EDWARD SEGUIN. *Florestein*: J. H. CHATTERSON. *Buda*: Mrs. Brand. *Captain of the Guard*: Mr. Kinross. *Nobles, Soldiers, Retainers, Chorus, etc.*

1872.18 PRIMA DONNA OF A NIGHT

An Operetta in One Act[3]. Original French libretto to the opérette-bouffe "Monsieur Choufleuri" by Duc de Morny and friends. Music by Jacques Offenbach. Musical director, Frank A. Howson. Produced by Mrs. James A. Oates Comic Opera and Burlesque Troupe. Opened 21 June 1872 at the Union Square Theatre; season closed 2 July 1872 after 7 performances in repertory.

CAST: *Ernestine*: Mrs. JAMES A. OATES. *Monsieur Choufleuri*: H. T. ALLEN. *Chrysodule Babylas*: CHARLES H. DREW. *Peterman*: WILLIAM H. CRANE. *M. Balandard*: J. H. JONES. *M. Busterman*: EDWARD HORAN. *Mme. Balandard*: Mrs. H. T. ALLEN.

1872.19 THE FAIR ONE WITH THE BLONDE WIG

A Revival of the Fairy Extravaganza (Burlesque) in Two Acts, 8 Scenes, adapted expressly for the troupe[4]. Selected gems (music) from all the popular operas. Scenery by James E. Hayes. Musical director, Frank A. Howson. Produced by Mrs. James A. Oates Comic Opera and Burlesque Company. Opened 26 June 1872 at the Union Square Theatre; season closed 2 July 1872 after 5 performances in repertory.

CAST: *Graceful,* a Maid of Honor: Mrs. JAMES A. [Alice] OATES. *Princess Ba-be-bi-bo-bu,* the Fair One with the Golden Locks: Mr. H. T. ALLEN.

Mrs. Oates Company also included A. W. MAFLIN. CHARLES H. DREW, WILLIAM H. CRANE, H. Jones, Edward Horan.

1872.20 THE GRAND DUCHESS

A Revival of the Opéra-bouffe in Four Acts[5]. Original French libretto ("La Grande-Duchesse de Gérolstein") by Henri Meilhac and Ludovic Halévy. Music by Jacques Offenbach. Musical director, Frank A. Howson. Produced by the Howson English Opera Company (T. H. Elliott, Manager). Opened 3 July 1872 at the Union Square Theatre and closed 13 July 1872 after 12 performances.

CAST: *Grand Duchess of Gerolstein*: EMMA HOWSON. *Wanda,* a peasant girl: BLANCHE GALTON. *General Boum*: WILLIAM H. CRANE. *Fritz*: THOMAS WHIFFIN. *Prince Paul*: ALFRED KELLEHER. *Baron Puck,* a Diplomatist: JOHN HOWSON. *Baron Grog*: Warren White. *Nepomuc*: J. H. Jones. *Amelia,* Maid of Honor: Mrs. Boudinot. *Olga,* Maid of Honor: Mrs. Caldwell. *Soldiers, Peasants, Ushers, etc.*

1872.21 ROBIN HOOD, Or, The Maid That Was Arch, and the Youth That Was Archer

A Burlesque in Two Acts, 6 Scenes, specially written and arranged for the Lydia Thompson Troupe. Stage director, James Schonberg. Scenery by George Evans and H. Isherwood. Costumes by Samuel May, of London, and William Wilson. Musical director, Michael Connolly. Produced by Lydia Thompson Troupe Opened 22 July 1872 at Wallack's Theatre and closed 10 August 1872 after 21 performances; returned 8 May 1873 to the Academy of Music for 1 additional performance.

---

[1]Musical numbers not listed in programs; no published score or libretto found for this production.

[2]First produced in New York 25 November 1844 at the Park Theatre for 17 performances in repertory. For Synopsis of Scenes and Musical Numbers, see original 1844 production.

[3]First produced in New York its original French version MONSIEUR CHOUFLEURI 20 February 1869 at the Grand Opera House for 1 performance in repertory. This production marks the work's New York English language premiere; its English adaptation was uncredited. The opera was accompanied by the farce "An Alarming Sacrifice" by John Baldwin Buckstone; for the last two nights of the season this farce was replaced by Morton's "The Two Puddifoots."

[4]First produced in New York 16 May 1870 at the Olympic Theatre for 32 performances. For Synopsis of Scenes and Musical Numbers, see original 1870 production. No program found for this engagement.

[5]English adaptation uncredited. First produced in New York in French 24 September 1867 at the Théâtre Français for 156 performances in repertory. English language premiere (different adaptation) 17 June 1868 at the New York Theatre for 33 performances.

CAST: *Robin Hood*, alias Locksley, the 'Prentice, alias the Earl of Huntingdon, the Merry Outlaw of Sherwood, who first found out that bows were aid of yews—a little party, and fond of A-less: LYDIA THOMPSON. *Maid Marian*, the Guileless Belle of the Village, the cynosure of all eyes, as I know sure: HARRY BECKETT. *Baron Front de Boeuf*, Sheriff of Nottingham, a villain of the deepest dye, though always ready to serve you: WILLIE EDOUIN. *Alice*, daughter of the above, we mean, not the lot, but the Sheriff, and who follows her parent's lead, by "issuing an attachment" on Robin Hood: ELIZA WEATHERBSY. *Coeur-de-Lion*, The Black Knight, who eventually comes to the throne, and makes it all up Dicky with traitors: AMY SHERIDAN. *Blondel*, exactly Blond-elle! which explains itself, always giving himself airs: LOUISE BEVERLEY. *Sir Gilbert Montfalcon*, a pretender to Alice's hand and Robin's title; a Mellow-Dramatic Conspirator, ripe for anything: CAMILLE DUBOIS. *Symmetrical Outlaws and Robin's Lieutenants (3)*: *Little John*: Tilly Earle. *Will Scarlett*: Marie Parselle. *Much*, the Miller's son: Pauline Leslie. *Friar Tuck*, Chaplain to the Forces in the Forest, where also he attends to the Cool-an'-airy Department: JOHN BRIER. *Will o' Wisp*, Usher of the Forest: FANNIE LESLIE. *Citizens, Peasants, Outlaws, Ladies of the Court, etc.*

Act 1, Scene 1: The Market-place of Nottingham in the Olden Time. (Evans.) *Scene 2*: The Deepest Dungeon 'neath the Castle Moat. (Isherwood.) *Scene 3*: Nottingham by night.

Act 2, Scene 1: Sherwood Forest; The Outlaw Camp. (Isherwood.) *Scene 2*: Tapestry Corridor in the Baron's Castle. *Scene 3*: The Archery Gala in the Castle Grounds. (Isherwood.)

BALLETS AND SPECIALTIES

The Village Fair (Act 1, Scene 1)
Finale and Tableau (Act 1, Scene 3)
Tropical Finale (Act 2, Scene 1)
Grand Dolly Varden Skipping-Rope Ballet (Act 2, Scene 3)
Solos (Act 2, Scene 3)
F. Leslie
Grand Finale (Act 2, Scene 3)

1872.22

BLUE BEARD, or, the Mormon, the Maiden and The Little Militaire

A Revival of the Celebrated Domestic Tale (a Burlesque) in Two Acts[6], specially written and arranged for the Lydia Thompson Troupe. (Play by Henry B. Farnie.) Latest musical novelties imported, assorted and concerted by Michael Connolly. Stage director, James Schonberg. Costumes designed by Lydia Thompson. Musical director, Michael Connolly. Produced by Lydia Thompson's Burlesque Company. Opened 12 August 1872 at Wallack's Theatre and closed 31 August 1872 after 21 performances; returned 18 September 1872 to Wallack's Theatre for an additional performance; returned 6-7 December 1872 to the Olympic Theatre for 2 additional performances; returned 5 May 1873 to the Academy of Music for 1 additional performance.

CAST: *Blue Beard*, The great P'Shaw! a confirmed lady-killer, with a cerulean whisker, but now inclined to Lake (Salt Lake, that is): HARRY BECKETT. *Ibrahim*, the original "Father, Come Home": JOHN BRYER. *Fatima*, his daughter; an orient pearl at random strung, and eventually bow-strung: CAMILLE DuBOIS. *Sorosister Anne*, Damsel of the Period, always looking for the "coming man": CARLOTTA ZERBINI. *Selim*, Sous-Lieutenant of Spahis, who, losing his sweetheart, enlists in the "Blues," and eventually turns shepherd, in order to win her by hook or by crook: LYDIA THOMPSON. *Corporal Zoug-Zoug*, of the Turcos, afterwards a Heathen Chinee, who talks "pigeon" English, but declines to be plucked: WILLIE EDOUIN. *Hassan*, the First Page, set up in "nonpareil," very "mignon," doesn't think "small pica" of herself: AMY SHERIDAN[7]. *The O'Shacabac*, Blue Beard's Buttons: ELIZA WEATHERBSY. *Said*, a wild young dog also in the service—but what's leas "Said" is soonest mended: Tilly Earl. *Beda*, Beada's eye is a bead as can sparkle—string for Beada's lead: Miss Halstead[8]. *A set of pages you won't cut (6)*: *Zaffo*: Louise Beverly. *Quaffo*: Miss Imree. *Chaffo*: Miss Blaisdell. *Laugho*: Miss Rowland. *Raffo*: Miss Clark. *Pfaffo*: Miss Clifford. The Spiritual Wives of Blue Beard, the Body Guards (Mamelukes) of the great P'Shaw, Turkish Girls, Wedding Guests, etc.

[6]First produced in New York 16 August 1871 at Wallack's Theatre for 30 performances. For Synopsis of Scenes and Musical Numbers, see original 1871 production. Incidental to Act: "His heart is true to Poll" (Song and Chorus), "If ever I cease to love" (Duet), and the Game of Euchre Scene from Bret Harte's "The Heathen Chinee". Miss Fanny Leslie as 'Strike a Light Dick.'

[7]For return engagement in December, Hassan was played by ALICE ATHERTON.

[8]For return engagement in December, Beda was played by Fanny Leslie.

1872.23

LE ROI CAROTTE

A Grand Spectacular Fairy Opéra-bouffe in Four Acts, 19 Scenes. Original French libretto by Victorien Sardou. Adapted into English expressly for this theatre by Augustin Daly. Music by Jacques Offenbach. (Production staged by Augustin Daly.) Scenery by George Heister, Louis Duflocq, L. W. Seavey, Minard Lewis, George W. Dayton. Costumes imported from Paris. Dances arranged by John Lauri. Machinery by Thomas Kelly and William Smith. Musical director, Robert Stoepel. Produced by Augustin Daly. Opened 26 August 1872 at the Grand Opera House and closed 23 November 1872 after 92 performances.

CAST: *Fridolin XXIV*, the Rightful Prince of Krokodyne; addicted to sport rather than business; although deposed by revolution, believes that "one good term deserves another": ROBERT CRAIG. *King Carrot*, Le Roi Carotte, Monarch of the Vegetable Race, complexion carrotty, yet decidedly raddish, not to be beet at official cabbaging; his motto, "Luttuce have Peas": JOHN BROUGHAM. *Robin Luron*, a good genie, who undertakes to reform the fast Prince; a tough job—but she Wood do it: Mrs. JOHN WOOD. *Coloquinte*, the Wicked Witch, who invented the Carot King and protects him; at the end of the play, finding she don't go down with the people, goes down with the King: ANNIE DELAND. *Rosée du Soir*, the most lovely and interesting Princess seen anywhere out of a Fairy Story, stolen in infancy by the Wicked Witch: ROSE HERSEE. *Princess Cunégonde of Krakhausen*, the sublimated essence of all the fast, fickle and frolicsome Princesses of Operabouffeland: EMMA HOWSON. *Truck the Faithful*, Secretary of magic to Prince Fridolin's Cabinet, sometimes known as "Old Probabilities," Chief of the Signal Service Bureau: Stuart Robson. *Baron Koffre*, another Cabinet Minister, Secretary of the Treasury, and negotiator of Bonds for the Bankrupt Kingdom of Krokodyne: G. F. Ketchum. *Pipertrunk*, another Chief of Police; while the other officials knock down he takes up: J. W. JENNINGS. *Count Schopp*, another Secretary of State, and highest of-fish-al in the Cabinet: Julian Cross. *General Track*, the last of the lot, Secretary of War, a model of his kind: J. G. Peakes. *Wives of the Cabinet and Leaders of Krokodyne Society (4)*: *Mme. Pipertrunk*: Roberta Norwood. *Mme. Schopp*: Ella Dietz. *Mme. Koffre*: Helen Strange. *Mme. Track*: Miss C. Bronte. *Psitt!*, the Chamberlain of the Court of Krokodyne: J. A. Mackay. *Quribibi*, a Magician of more than ordinary experience, 127 years of age, perhaps "the oldest inhabitant" and certainly the greatest necromancer ever seen or heard of: Martin Golden. *The Six Ancestors of Prince Fridolin*, all in complete armor, dead since several centuries but resolved to raise their voices: Messrs. —. *Prebendary at the Inn*: Mr. E. Chapman. *The Landlady*: Mary Stuart. *Lizette*, one of the Students' Mates: Louise Volmer. *Corporal Drum*: Henri Lauri. *Grand Claude*: Clive Hersee. *Mother Wangott*, who went to market and began the Revolt against high prices and King Carrot: Mrs. Yeamans. *Jenny*, the egg seller: Mary Rice. *Captain of Police*: F. Chapman.

Harpax, the Soldier of Jerusalem: James A. Meade. *Corinne*, the Pompeian beauty: Ella Dietz. *Lepida*, the bride: Blanche Hayden. *Gurges*, the Fop: Mr. Clive. *Panza*, the Edile: G. F. Enos. *Medulla*, a Slave: Miss Volmer. *Megadore*, a Poet: Mr. Mackay. *Circulion*, the Bridegroom: Mr. Chapman. *The King of the Monkeys*: Charles Lauri. *The Queen of the Bees*: Miss Predigam. *The Leaders of the Farandole*: Messrs. Lauri.

Specialties: The LAURI Family (John, Charles, Henri, Charles Jr., Fanny pantomimists), The MAJILTONS (3 Acrobats).

Act 1: The Ancestral Armors. *Scene 1*: Outside the City Gates of Krokodyne. (Duflocq.) *Scene 2*: Rosée du Soir. Tower-prison in the ancient palace. (Dayton.) *Scene 3*: The Hall of Armors in the Old Palace of Krokodyne. (Seavey.) *Scene 4*: The Back-door of the Palace. (Dayton.) *Scene 5*: The Kitchen Garden. (Dayton.) *Scene 6*: The Royal Garden and Terrace of the New Palace. (Duflocq.)

Act 2: The Banished Prince. *Scene 1*: The Courtyard of an Inn on the borders of Krokodyne. (Heister.) *Scene 2*: The Roadside. (Dayton.) *Scene 3*: The Laboratory of the Magician Quribibi. (Dayton.) *Scene 4*: The Ruins of Pompeii, A. D. 1872. (Heister.) *Scene 5*: To the city of Pompeii as it existed in the year 76—prior to the eruption which destroyed it. Eruption of Vesuvius. (Heister.)

Act 3: The Iron Ring. *Scene 1*: Royal Apartment of the new incumbent. (Dayton.) *Scene 2*: The darksome Forest. (Lewis.) *Scene 3*: The Island of Monkeys. (Lewis.)

Act 4: The Powder of Discontent. *Scene 1*: The Market Place of Krokodyne. (Seavey.) *Scene 2*: The King's Palace. *Scene 3*: The Haunt of the Insects. (Heister.) *Scene 4*: Apotheosis. (Heister.) *Scene 5*: The New Palace. (Seavey.)

ACT 1

"The Sunset" (Chorus)
Soldiers, Citizens
"Make Way" (Chorus)
Students
"The Student" (Rondo)
Mrs. J. Wood
"I Was But a Little Girl"
E. Howson
"Night Watch" (Scene and Chorus)
R. Craig, Students
"Birds and Flowers" (Romance)
R. Hersee

"The Little Ball of Golden Thread" (Duet)
Mrs. J. Wood, R. Hersee
"The Armors" (Scene and Chorus)
R. Craig, Students
"Happy Day" (Chorus)
Courtiers
"What Noise!" (Chorus)
Courtiers
"I Am King Carrot" (Air)
J. Brougham
Finale
J. Brougham, Mrs. J. Wood, R. Craig, E. Howson, Chorus

ACT 2
"The Gardeners" (Chorus)
Peasants
Faranadole (Dance)
Ballet
"The Ruins of Pompeii" (Quartette)
R. Craig, R. Hersee, Mrs. J. Wood, J. W. Jennings
"Pompeii Restored" (Chorus)
Pompeians
"The Railroad" (Rondo)
Mrs. J. Wood, R. Hersee, R. Craig, J. W. Jennings, S. Robson

ACT 3
"Enter! Enter!" (Chorus)
Chorus
"The Peddlars" (Rondo)
Mrs. J. Wood, R. Hersee, J. W. Jennings
"Love Awakening" (Duet)
R. Craig, E. Howson
"The Five-Leaved Shamrock" (Romance)
R. Hersee

ACT 4
"The Market Place" (Chorus)
Citizens
"The Revolt" (Scene and Chorus)
Citizens, Soldiers
"Down with the Tyrants" (Air)
Mrs. J. Wood
"The Plume"
E. Howson
"The Subterranean Toilers" (March and Chorus)
Insects
"Poor Old King Carrot" (Finale)
Mrs. J. Wood, Chorus

IXION, or, the Man at the Wheel

1872.24

A Revival of the Burlesque Extravaganza in a Prologue and 4 Scenes[9]. Burlesque by F. C. Burnand. Music arranged and composed by Michael Connolly. Scenery by G. Evans. Machinery by Mr. Butler. Properties by Mr. Goodwin. Dresses by Mrs. Wilson, designed by Lydia Thompson. Stage director, James Schonberg. Musical director, Michael Connolly. Produced by Lydia Thompson Troupe Opened 2 September 1872 at Wallack's Theatre and closed 21 September 1872 after 20 performances in repertory.

IXION CAST: Prologue, Mortals: *Ixion*, ex-King of Thessaly, but though a King with the prefix of an "X," it does not alphabetically follow that he had a wise head on his shoulders: LYDIA THOMPSON. *Trondapameibomenos*: Mr. Stowe. *Prosephe*: Mr. Janier. *Podasokus*: Mr. Jones. *A Young Grecian*, first class, from the Bluecoat Boys: Mr. Hunter. *Queen Dia*, Ixion's disloyal wife, who leads the Revolutionists, and proposes to be a tamer of her husband as well as a dyer, and tramples on her regal diadem, in order to become a regal Dia-democrat: Mr. Sparks. Immortals: *Jupiter*, King of the Gods, and the most finished gentleman in Olympus: ROSE COGHLAN. *Mercury*, the celestial telegraph boy—"with wings on his ankles, and wings near his toes, and no time he loses wherever he goes": ELIZA WEATHERBSY. *Ixion*, who being bankrupt and sadly in want of change, is, in spite of his bad character in his former situation, taken up by Jupiter, and patronized by the "upper ten": LYDIA THOMPSON. *Juno*, Queen of the Gods, and Jove's Spouse, described by the Poets as the Ox-eye'd Lady, and consequently of a mettlesome temperament; fond of Pea-cocks that sing Pea-hens of joy while drawing her car: CARLOTTA ZERBINI. *Venus*, the Goddess of Beauty; still a spinster, although it has been said by a great authority, that "Venus orta mari," which being translated, is "Venus ought to marry": AMY SHERIDAN. *Cupid*, the son of Venus, who will be at once recognized as Love at first sight: CAMILLE DUBOIS. *Minerva*, Goddess of Wisdom; a very studious and quiet lady, though generally appearing with an owl; Jupiter's housekeeper and keeper of the royal keys, but not on that account to be confounded with the more modern Mother Bunch: HARRY BECKETT. *Apollo*, Secretary to the Imperial "Sun" Fire Insurance Company (Limited), and, out of his official capacity, author of several scientific works, art critic, adapter of dramas by any foreign hand, and sporting member of the four-in-hand Club: TILLY EARL. *Ganymede*, Jupiter's beautiful "Buttons," a nice, active lad, the original fat Boy, who may be described as a Ganymede and Gany-pursey-un too: WILLIE EDOUIN. *Bacchus*, Promoter and Chief Director of the Celestial Light Wine Association; Patron Deity of Newington Butts; Jove's Butler, who with full power over the Imperial Pints, does not, in consequence of his occupation, lose his tune: JOHN BRYER. *Mars*: Mr. Imrie. *Diana*: Miss Asher. *Vesta*: Miss Hilton. *Clerk of the Weather*: Fannie Leslie. *Winged Genii, Passing Clouds, Shooting Stars, Apollo's Grooms, Jupiter's Satellites, and other heavenly bodies too numerous to mention.*

[9]First produced in New York 28 September 1868 at Wood's Museum & Metropolitan Theatre for 120 performances in two engagements. Preceded by a comedietta, A Happy Pair.

CHOW CHOW, or, A Tale of Pekin

1872.25

A Chinese Burlesque Extravaganza in Two Acts, 6 Scenes. Libretto by James Barnes. Music selected and arranged by W. H. Brinkworth. Scenery by John A. Thompson. Costumes by Mr. Phillippe from Paris. Properties and appointments by Charles LaForrest. Calcium lights by T. Neville. Stage machinery by William B. Carpenter. Production under the supervision of James Barnes. Opened 9 September 1872 at Wood's Museum and closed 5 October 1872 after 24 performances in repertory.

CAST: *Conrad the Corsair*, a notable Pirate Chief: LISA WEBER. *Maimounie*, Queen of the Fairies and mainspring of the plot: PAULINE MARKHAM. *Prince Pretty Pill*, a Young Sport, who cheeks his Pa and Ma, and won't fall in love: BELLE HOWITT. *Medora*, a lovely maiden, entrusted as a pledge to her uncle: EMMA GRATTAN. *Yusetowaz*, King Razman's better half, a regular Nemesis: GEORGE ATKINS. *Razman*, King of—, well no matter where: L. J. Mestayer. *Beebo Bazil*, a discontented and crushed nobleman, reduced to Captain of Marines: A. H. Sheldon. *Mesrour*, Head Cook and Royal Bottle Washer: Harry Stewart. *Chow Chow*, a Chinese pickle: G. C. CHARLES. *Pig-Taili, his shadow*: J. Debonay. *Skidamalink*, a Black and Tan: Charles Sturges. *Bumble Bee*, a Chinese beadle: R. J. Lewis. *Sin Sing*: Frank Langley. *Chebib*: Aggie Wood. *Edid*: Dolly Thonton. *Sari Gampy*, a Chinese nurse: Theresa Wood. *Cupid*, the God of Love: Jennie Arnot. *Glowworm*, Maimounie's Right Bower: ALICE ATHERTON. *Paudeen McCarty*, a Chinese Irishman: Jennie Satterlee. *Soldiers, Fairies, Persians, and Chinese.*

Act 1, Scene 1: King Razman's Palace in Mesoptamia. *Scene 2*: Gardens of the Palace. *Scene 3*: Haunted Well and View of Lake Lovely.

Act 2, Scene 1: The Quay at Pekin. *Scene 2*: Chow Chow's Palace in Pekin. *Scene 3*: Floating in the Air, with a view of the Home of the Peri, and Golden Gates of the Gardens and Perennial Springs.

ACT 1
Scene 1
"Glory to Allah"
"Walk Around"
Scene 2
Terrific Broadsword Combat
'Sixtette' singing Nursery Rhymes
Scene 3
"Listen to the Mocking Bird"
A Trio invites all hands to "Sweet Cider"

ACT 2
Scene 1
Conrad's Counter March
Beebo Bazil and His Army
Maimounie shows Conrad how to "Duet"
P. Markham, L. Weber
Chinese Song and Dance
A. Atherton, T. Wood
Scene 2
Queen Maimounie's Royal Drum Corps

Scene 3
Songs of "Way Down South" C. Sturges

KENILWORTH,
1872.26 or, Ye Queen, Ye Knight and Ye Maiden

A Burlesque of Sir Walter Scott's "Kenilworth" in Two Acts, 9 Scenes. Play by H. S. Murdoch. Music by Michael Connolly. Stage director, James Schonberg. Scenery by John Watson. Elegant appointments by Mr. Goodwin. Costumes designed by Lydia Thompson, prepared by Mrs. Wilson. Mechanism by H. Butler. Musical director, Michael Connolly. Produced by Lydia Thompson's Burlesque Company. Opened 21 September 1872 at Wallack's Theatre and closed 28 September 1872 after 7 performances; reopened 29 November 1872 at the Olympic Theatre and closed 5 December 1872 after 8 performances; returned 6 May 1873 to the Academy of Music for 1 additional performance.

CAST: *Earl of Leicester*: LYDIA THOMPSON. *Queen Elizabeth*, a strong-minded virgin, verging on fifty: HARRY BECKETT. *Amy Robsart*, an agreeable girl, at times disagreeable: ELIZA WEATHERBSY. *Water Raleigh*, a fast boy, who has an eye to his own interest: CAMILLE DuBOIS. *Tressillian*, a blighted being: CARLOTTA ZURBINI. *Duke of Sussex*, a wag in waiting: AMY SHERIDAN[10]. *Janet*, a waiting maid: Miss Johnson. *Varney*, a fit member for Tammany: WILLIE EDOUIN. *Wayland Smith*, rogue, bank director, vagabond, etc.: JOHN BRYER. *Michael Lambourne*, a swashbuckler: TILLY EARL. *Tony Foster*, turncoat, turnkey and traitor generally: Mr. Irwin. *Giles Gosling*, an ambitious politician: FANNY LESLIE. *Courtiers, Beef and Mutton Eaters, Cocktail Drinkers, Private and Public Nuisances, too numerous to detail, but who will be found in de-tale itself.*

ARRAH-NA-POGUE,
1872.27 or, The Wicklow Wedding!

A Revival of the Grand Spectacular (Irish) Drama in Three Acts[11]. Play by Dion Boucicault (and E. H. House). Produced from the original models of the author. Stage direction, D. W. Waller. Musical director, E. Mollenhauer. Scenic artist, Charles W. Witham. Machinery, Jno. W. Dunne. Costumes by Thomas Joyce. Appointments by J. P. Deuel. Produced by Edwin Booth. Opened 23 September 1872 at Booth's Theatre and closed 21 October 1872 after 29 performances; returned 21 April 1873 to Booth's Theatre[12] and closed 8 May 1873 after 14 additional performances. Total: 43 performances.

CAST: *Shaun the Post*, a Wicklow Carman: DION BOUCICAULT. *Michael Feeny*: SHIEL BARRY. *Colonel Bagenal O'Grady*, the O'Grady: JOSEPH WHEELOCK. *Major Coffin*, an English officer: A. W. Fenno. *Beamish McCoul*, the McCoul: C. ALEXANDER. *The Sergeant*: George Becks. *Winterbottom*, the Valet: J. W. BRUTONE. *Oiny Farrell*: G. C. Charles. *Tim Cogan*: J. C. WILLIAMS. *Patsy*: Charles Rosene. *Lanagan*: Sol Smith. *Andy Regan*: M. B. Pike. *Moran*: Nelson Decker. *Lanty*: T. F. Brennan.

Arrah Meelish, nicknamed by the peasantry 'Arrah na Pogue," or Arrah of the Kiss: Mrs. DION BOUCICAULT [Agnes Robertson]. *Fanny Power*, of Cabinteely: MILLIE SACKETT. *Katty*: Mary Wells. *Peasants, Peasant Girls, Soldiers, Beggars, etc.*

Act 1: Glendalough by Moonlight. (1798.) Arrah's Cabin at Laragh. Oak Chamber at Ballybetagh. The Barn.

Act 2: The Prison. Ballybetagh Castle. The Justice Hall.

Act 3: The Deadman's Cell at Ballybetagh. The Watch Tower. The Summit.

MUSICAL NUMBERS, SPECIALTIES

"The Wearing of the Green" (Act 1)
D. Boucicault
(*Lyrics by* Dion Boucicault and E. H. House.)

"Arrah' Song" (Act 3)
Mrs. D. Boucicault

Irish Jig
M. Wells

[10]For return engagement, Duke of Sussex was played by ALICE ATHERTON.
[11]First produced in New York 12 July 1865 at Niblo's Garden for a total of 102 performances. For Synopsis of Scenes, see original 1865 production.
[12]Cast changes: *Arrah Meelish*: BELLA PATEMAN. *Oiny Farrell*: S. W. Glenn. ARRAH-NA-POGUE was followed by Boucicault's 1-Act comedy drama 'Kerry, or Night and Morning.'

1872.28 LA PÉRICHOLE

A Revival of the Opéra-bouffe in Two Acts[13], in Two Acts. Libretto by Ludovic Halévy and Henri Meilhac, based on 'Le Carosse du Saint-Sacrement' by Prosper Merimée. Music by Jacques Offenbach. Musical director, Charles Van Ghele. Produced by Mlle. Marie Aimée and the New Parisian Opera Troupe (C. A. Chizzola & Co., Directors). Opened 14 October 1872 at the Olympic Theatre, closing 4 November 1872 after 6 performances in repertory; returned in repertory the week of 30 December 1872 at the Olympic Theatre and season closed 11 January 1873 after a total of (16) performances in repertory.

CAST: *La Périchole*, a Street Singer: Mlle. MARIE AIMÉE. *Piquillo*: Mons. JUTEAU. *Don Andrès de Ribera*: Mons. DUCHESNE. *Le Comte de Panatellas*: Mons. Julien. *Don Pedro*: Mons. Salvator. *Les Trois Cousines*: *Guadalena*: Mlle. Grenet. *Mastrilla*: Mlle. Juteau. *Berjinella*: Mlle. Vandamme. *Ladies, Pages, Courtiers, etc.*

LA GRANDE-DUCHESSE DE GÉROLSTEIN
1872.29

A Revival of the Opéra-bouffe in Three Acts[14], in French. Libretto by Henri Meilhac and Ludovic Halévy. Music by Jacques Offenbach. Musical director, Charles Van Ghele. Produced by Mlle. Marie Aimée and the New Parisian Opera Troupe (C. A. Chizzola & Co., Directors). Opened 18 October 1872 at the Olympic Theatre and closed 8 November after 7 performances in repertory; returned in repertory the week of 30 December 1872 at the Olympic Theatre and season closed 11 January 1873 after (4) performances in repertory.

CAST: *La Grande-Duchesse de Gérolstein*: Mlle. MARIE AIMÉE. *Baron Puck*: Mons. DUCHESNE. *General Boum*: Mons. LECUYER. *Prince Paul of Steis-Stein-Steis-Laper-Bottmoll-Schorstenburg*: Mons. Marcas. *Fritz*: Mons. JUTEAU. *Wanda*: Mlle. ROLLAND.

1872.30 THE 3 MUS-KE-TEERS

A New Burlesque Extravaganza in Two Acts, 5 Scenes, adapted and arranged by James Barnes, Stage Director. Overture composed and incidental music arranged by William H. Brinkworth. Scenery by John A. Thompson. Costumes by Mons. Phillipe. Properties and appointments by Charles LaForrest. Machinery by William B. Crane. Musical director, William H. Brinkworth. Produced by George Wood. Opened 21 October 1872 at Wood's Museum and closed 1 November 1872 after 12 performances[15].

CAST: *D'Artagnan*, an Adventurer—afterwards Mus-ke-teer—afterwards Hero—afterwards Rebel—but always gay, gallant, debonaire: Miss LIZA WEBER. *Aramis*, an Exquisite of the King's Mus-ke-teers—the crack "Hussars" of that Period, and candidate for huzzahs in this: Miss BELLE HOWITT. *Constance*, Maid-in-Waiting—worth her weight in mating: Miss PAULINE MARKHAM. *Porthos*, Once on a time burly, surly, big, now a girly whirlygig as becomes: Miss EMMA GRATTAN. *Athos*, Another Hussar, not exactly one "cheer" more—though something of a "brayvo"—proud, hasty, discreet, and Count de la Fere, with the sublime family motto, "Little pot soon hot:" Mr. A. H. SHELDON. *Lady de Winter*, Countess de la Fere and Baroness de Sheffield—from the latter title, and her many lovers, supposed to be the original knife with a hundred blades: Mr. GEORGE ATKINS. *Louis XIII*, Father of his "People's love," "father of" his wife affection: LOUIS J. MESTAYER. *Rochefort*, a Spy, seldom heard, although Milady's "creeture:" Miss AGGIE WOOD. *Villiers*, Duke of Buckingham—an English lover at a French court: Miss JENNIE ARNOT. *Pouchet*, in the public line: G. C. Charles. *Peiro, Rocheguyon*, Nobles—crème de la crème: HARRY STEWART, JENNIE SATTERLEE. *Anne of Austria*, in look so meek, in frowns so meagre, in friendship she kissed Villiers: THERESA WOOD. *Coliquet, Molliquet, Jolliquet*, "a bad crowd:" Messrs. Charles Sturges, J. Debonay, A. J. Lewis. *Little Nip*: Miss Aggie Keene. *Peers, Peasants, Merry Manufacturers, Goblet Quaffers, etc.*

[13]First produced in New York in French 4 January 1869 at Pike Opera House. For Synopsis of Scenes and Musical Numbers, see original 1869 production.
[14]Previously presented in New York in French 24 September 1867 at the Théâtre Français for 156 performances; in English 17 June 1868 (in a different version) at the New York Theatre for 33 performances. For Synopsis of Scenes and Musical Numbers, see original 1868 production. No program found for this engagement.
[15]Preceded by a fore-piece, the farce A MAN WITHOUT A HEAD! For the second week of the run, THE 3 MUS-KE-TEERS was performed weekday matinees only.

Act 1, Scene 1: Roadside Auberge in the Bourg of Meung. *Scene 2*: The Picture Gallery. *Scene 3*: Deck of the *Fleur-de-Lys*, off Calais.

Act 2, Scene 1: The Terrace. *Scene 2*: Illuminated Gardens of the Louvre.

1872.31 GENEVIÈVE DE BRABANT

A Revival of the Opéra-bouffe in Three Acts[16], in French. Libretto by Hector Crémieux and Étienne Tréfeu. Music by Jacques Offenbach. Scenery by James E. Hayes. Musical director, Charles Van Ghele. Produced by Mlle. Marie Aimée and the New Parisian Opera Troupe (C. A. Chizzola & Co., Directors). Opened 24 October 1872 at the Olympic Theatre and closed 2 November 1872 after 10 performances in repertory; returned in repertory the week of 30 December 1872 at the Olympic Theatre and season closed 11 January 1873 after (8) performances in repertory.

CAST: *Drogan*, Page to Genevieve: Mlle. MARIE AIMÉE. *Sifroy*, Duke of Curaçao: Mons. JUTEAU. *Geneviève de Brabant*, Wife to Silfroy: Mlle. BONELLI. *Brigitte*, her confidante: Mlle. ROLLAND. *Pitou, Grabuge*, the Gendarmes: Messrs. Gabel, Lecuyer. *Charles Martel*: Mons. DUCHESNE.

1872.32 THE SILVER DEMON!

A New Pantomimic Burlesque Extravaganza in Two Acts, 6 Scenes. Arranged by James Barnes, Stage Director, expressly for this establishment. Produced by George Wood. Opened 4 November 1872 at Wood's Museum, closing 15 November 1872; resuming 18 November 1872 at Wood's Museum and closed 22 November 1872 after 17 performances.

CAST: *The Silver Demon*, appearing on Earth as Prince Tom Tiddlervick—possessed of a secret and wealth which are both alike—untold: Miss LIZA WEBER. *The Princess Beatrix*, Daughter of the Grand Duke, a belle whom the Gnome King seeks to ring: Miss PAULINE MARKHAM. *Count Kubb*, a smart, active lad, willing to make himself useful—if he could: Miss THERESE WOOD. *Hardupp the Hundredth*, Ruler of the Grand Duchy of Tinpotzein: LOUIS J. MESTAYER. *Humguffin*, Lord Chancellor, First Lord of the Treasury: Mr. HARRY STEWART. *Looney Bill*, Clown to the Court: Mr. A. H. SHELDON. *Karl*, an old Miner: G. C. Charles. *Max*, who being under age, has perhaps more right to be called a miner than his father: Miss Emma Grattan. *Gertrude*, Sister to Max: Miss Emma Moshler. *The Lady Greymarenbetterhorssen*, Wife of the Baron Von Heinpectstein: Mr. GEORGE ATKINS. *The Fairy Argentine*: Miss Aggie Wood. *Flipflop*: Miss Jennie Arnot. *Poopoo, Knottagoodun*, Oriental Duffers: Charles Sturges, J. Debonay. *Snarleyou*, a very bad Demon: Mr. R. J. Lewis. *Puffwind*: Miss Jenny Satterlee. *Lords, Soldiers, Little Demons, Miners, etc.*

Act 1, Scene 1: Palace in the Grand Duchy of Tinpotzein. *Scene 2*: Mountainous Landscape and Mouth of the Mine. *Scene 3*: The Silver Mine.

Act 2, Scene 1: Ante-room in the Palace. *Scene 2*: Gardens of the Chateau of Prince Tom Tiddlervich. *Scene 3*: Home of the Dragon Flies and Cascade of Fleeting Shadows.

BALLETS, SPECIALTIES

Destruction of the Silver Demon! and Delectation of Everybody else, leading to the Pantomime (Act 2, Scene 2):
Clown: A. H. Sheldon. *Pantaloon*: R. J. Lewis. *Harlequin*: J. Debonay. *Columbine*: A. Wood.

1872.33 BARBE BLEUE

A Revival of the Opéra-bouffe in Three Acts[17], in French. Libretto by Henri Meilhac and Ludovic Halévy. Music by Jacques Offenbach. Scenery by James E. Hayes. Musical director, Charles Van Ghele. Produced by Mlle. Marie Aimée and the New Parisian Opera Troupe (C. A. Chizzola & Co., Directors). Opened 5 November 1872 at the Olympic Theatre and closed 9 November 1872 after 5 performances in repertory.

CAST: *Boulotte*: Mlle. MARIE AIMÉE. *Princess Hermia*: Mlle. Roland. *Barbe Bleue*: Mons. JUTEAU. *Populuni*: Mons. LECUYER. *Roi Bobèche*: Mons. DUCHESNE. *Count Oscar*: Mons. Marcas. *Prince Saphir*: Mons. Berthon. *Alvarez*: Mons. Salvator. *Le Reine Clémentine*: Mlle. Cantrelle. *Héloise*: Mme. Juteau. *Eleonore*: Mlle. Deschamps. *Isaure*: Mlle. Nardin. *Blanche*: Mlle. Julien. *Rosalinde*: Mlle. Louise.

[16]First produced in New York in French 22 October 1868 at the Théâtre Français 22 October 1868. For Synopsis of Scenes and Musical Numbers, see original 1868 production. No program found for this engagement.
[17]First produced in New York in French 13 July 1868 at Niblo's Garden. For Synopsis of Scenes and Musical Numbers, see original 1868 production.

1872.34 ALADDIN THE SECOND

A Grand Spectacular Burlesque Extravaganza in Two Acts, 8 Scenes[18]. Music composed and arranged by David Braham. Produced under the direction of Harry Beckett. Ballets invented and arranged by John Lauri. Scenery by James E. Hayes, J. A. Johnson. Costumes designed by Lydia Thompson, Mrs. Wilson, Mrs. Tillson. Mechanical effects by James Tate. Properties by D. Ryan. Calcium lights by Caffrey & Wilson. Produced by Lydia Thompson's Burlesque Company. Opened 11 November 1872 at the Olympic Theatre and closed 28 November 1872 after 21 performances; returned 9 May 1873 to the Academy of Music for 1 additional performance.

CAST: *Aladdin the Second*: LYDIA THOMPSON. *The Sultan*: JOHN BRYER. *The Vizier*: CARLOTTA ZURBINI. *Pekoe*: CAMILLE DUBOIS. *Abanazar*: WILLIE EDOUIN. *Te-to-tum*: FANNIE LESLIE. *The Slave of the Lamp*: TILLY EARLE. *The Genius of the Ring*: Jennie Wheatleigh. *The Widow Twankay*: HARRY BECKETT. *Princess Badroulboudour*: ELIZA WEATHERBSY. *Maidens, Mandarins, and Mob. Ballet*: Misses Carrie Haines, Fannie Lucelle, Ida and Carry Ross, Corps de Ballet of 40 Ladies.

Act 1, Scene 1: Hand-Tea Room in the Sultan's Palace. *Scene 2*: A Street in Pekin. *Scene 3*: The Jewelled Cavern. *Scene 4*: Aladdin's Cottage. *Scene 5*: The Sultan's Palace.

Act 2, Scene 1: Exterior of Aladdin's Palace. *Scene 2*: Saloon in the Magic Palace. *Scene 3*: African Palace.

ACT 1
Scene 1
Duet
C. Zurbini, C. Dubois
Ring Chorus and Dance
Scene 2
"Vagabond Boy" (Song)
L. Thompson
Trio Dance
L. Thompson, W. Edouin, H. Beckett
Scene 3
"Walking in the Starlight" (Song and Dance)
L. Thompson
The Grand Procession to the Bath
Scene 4
The Magic Feast
"Local" (The Gendarme's Duet)
L. Thompson, H. Beckett
"My Son" (Song and Chorus)
H. Beckett
Scene 5
Grand Characteristic Ballet Divertissement and Marriage Finale

ACT 2
Scene 1
Characteristic Dance (Solo)
W. Edouin
Flight of the Palace (a Grand Effect)
Scene 2
Quartette and March for Africa
"Cackle Song"
E. Weathersby
Scene 3
Grand Silver and Magic Tree Ballet
Finale

1872.35 ROUND THE CLOCK; or, New York By Dark

A Local Sensational Folly in Four Acts, 13 Scenes. Adapted into English by Augustin Daly (from the original French "La Tour du Cadran" by H. Crémieux and H. Bocage). Scenery by George Dayton, George Heister, L. W. Seavey, Louis Duflocq. Produced by Augustin Daly. Opened 25 November 1872 at the Grand Opera House and closed 18 January 1873 after 57 performances.

[18]Authorship uncredited; totally unrelated to Hervé's burlesque of the same name, Anglicized by Alfred Thompson.

CAST: *Juliana Tartar*, the pretty Baker of Tarts and Pies and ready-maker of tart replies: Mrs. JOHN WOOD. *Roderick Killgobbin*, Esq., a person of many disguises and shrewd surmises; in fact, a man of wax and of whacks—easily kneaded and often needed: JOHN BROUGHAM. *Ernesta Hardacre*, having been "born under a cabbage" is naturally a little green: EMMA HOWSON. *Mr. Abraham Hardacre*, a Wheedler: J. W. HENNINGS. *Lawyer Goddigatt*, a subject for the Bar Association: G. K. KETCHUM. *Joey Lillyburn*, an Innocent from Boston: ELLA DIETZ. *Peter Dodd*, a Dyer—likewise a dire deceiver: James Meade. *Mrs. Peter Dodd*, the Wife of the Dyer, and victim of the deceiver: Annie Deland. *Mr. Mutton*, of Essex Market: Martin Golden. *Alderman Dooley*, a newly-elected gentleman with privileges behind the scenes: E. Pierce.

Borrowed from Niblo's Garden expressly for this play: *The Manager*: J. G. Peakes. *Machinist*: E. Cauldwell. *Property Man*: Mr. Sullivan. *Call Boy*: Master DeVere. *Mme. Sangalli*: Mme. Lauri. *Her Maid*: Cora Cassidy. *Black Crook*: E. Chapman. *Zamiel*: A. G. Enos. *Ladies of the Ballet, Figurantes, Demons, Audience, etc.*

Harry Hill, a popular gentleman: J. A. Meade. *Dooney Harris*, a light-weigh: Dooney Harris. *Johnny Aaron*, a heavy-weight: Johnny Aaron. *Old Bill Tovel*: Himself. *Barkeeper*: C. Hersee. *Black Sal*: John Lauri. *Dusty Bob*: Harry Lauri. *Billy Vatters*: Charles Lauri. *Visitors at Harry Hills, Waiter Girls, etc.*

Roundsman Lafferty: Julian Cross. *Pyrotechnist at Lion Park*: A. G. Enos. *Smack*, a servant: F. Chapman. *Scuttle*, another: Mr. Connolly. *Rascal Sue*, a sketch from nature: Mrs. Yeamans. *Rose*, the tart-seller's clerk: Roberta Norwood. *Relations (3)*: *Mrs. Bowlit*: Miss C. Bronte. *Mrs. Impey*: Miss. Rice. *Kitty Tyrrell*: Louise Volmer. *Queen of Folly*: Helen Strange. *Prince Carnival*: James Peakes. *The Real Majiltons*: The MAJILTONS.

Act 1, Scene 1: The Library in the Residence of the Departed Millionaire. One o'clock. (Dayton.) *Scene 2*: The Grand Union Depot. Three o'clock. (Dayton.) *Scene 3*: Mrs. Tartar's Confectionary and Ice Cream Bazaar in Grand Street. Five o'clock. (Heister.)

Act 2, Scene 1: Moonlight Dance at Lion Park. Eight o'clock. (Seavey.) *Scene 2*: Behind the Scenes at Niblo's Garden. Nine o'clock. (Heister.) *Scene 3*: Back view of "The Black Crook." Half-past nine.

Act 3, Scene 1: At Harry Hill's (Saloon). Ten o'clock. (Dayton.) *Scene 2*: In front of Harry Hill's, with a view of Murderer's Row. *Scene 3*: In front of the Fifth Avenue Hotel. Half-past ten. (Duflocq.) *Scene 4*: Donovan's Alley in the Five Points during a snowstorm. Eleven o'clock. (Duflocq.)

Act 4, Scene 1: The Courtyard of Daddy Hardacres. Twelve o'clock. (Duflocq.) *Scene 2*: Half -past twelve. The Fortune adjudged. *Scene 3*: A glance at the Liederkranz Masquerade at the Academy of Music. One o'clock. (Heister.)

SPECIALTIES

Chorus of Hackmen and Police (Act 1, Scene 2)

Moonlight Dance at Lion Park/Fireworks (Act 2, Scene 1)

The Black Crook Transformation Scene, seen from the rear of the stage (Act 2, Scene 3)

Two Sets of Majiltons (Act 2, Scene 3)

A realistic exhibition of the modus operandi of The Prize Ring (Act 3, Scene 1)

Ernesta's Danger in the Burning Rookery (Act 3, Scene 4)

Retrospective Panorama of the Daughters of Eve as they have dressed for 5,000 years, concluding with a new and original Can-Can, arranged by John Lauri (Act 4, Scene 3)

Lauri Family, the Majiltons, Entire Company

First Era: *Eva*: Cora Cassidy.

Second Era: *The Woman of the Wilderness*: Miss Clifford. *Judith*: Miss Heinds. *Cleopatra*: Miss Costenyra.

Third Era: *Madame Clovis*: Miss Maddox. *Marquinte*, the Provincial: Ada Bell. *The Belle of the Middle Ages*: Miss Adams. *Isabella of Bavaria*: Miss Stewart. *Queen Elizabeth*: Miss Stevens.

Fourth Era: *Madame de Pompadour*: Julia Bell. *Queen Anne*: Kate Cohen. *Hannah Lightfoot*: Miss Mansey. *Charlotte Corday*: Miss Lester. *One of our grandmothers*: Miss Celeste. *A Grecian Bend*: Miss Cohen. *The Girl of the Period*: Miss Hersey.

IXION,

1872.36 or, the Man at the Wheel

A Revival of the Popular Burlesque Extravaganza in One Act, 6 Scenes[19]. Play by F. C. Burnand. Overture composed and incidental music arranged by William H. Brinkworth. Produced under the immediate supervision of stage director, James Barnes. Scenery by John A. Thompson. Costumes by Mons. Phillipe. Properties and appointments by Charles LaForrest. Machinery by William H. Crane. Musical director, William H. Brinkworth. Produced by George Wood. Opened 25 November 1872 at Woods' Museum and closed 29 November 1872 after 5 performances[20].

CAST: *Characters in the Prologue*: *Ixion*: Miss LISA WEBER. *Tondapameibomenos, Prosephe, Podasokus*, Three Thessalians who would these aliens if they weren't these natives: Messrs. A. J. Debonay. R. J. Lewis, Charles Sturges. *A Young Grecian*, first-class, from the 6th Ward: Mr. E. C. Coyle. *Queen Dia*: Jennie Satterlee. *Crowd of Red Republicans, Un-Read Republicans, Avengers, Scavengers, Greeks, Sneaks and Female Furies, appropriately crowned with Mob Caps*: Messrs. Torch, Firebrand, Flame, Riot, Ruin, Famine, and Disorder.

Immortals: *Jupiter*, King of the Gods, and the most finished gentleman in Olympus: Miss THERESE WOOD. *Mercury*, the Celestial Telegraph Boy: Miss EMMA GRATTAN.

Characters in the Drama: *Venus*, the Goddess of Beauty; still a spinster, although it is said by a great authority "Venus orta mari," which, being translated, is "Venus ought to marry": Miss PAULINE MARKHAM. *Ixion*, who being bankrupt and sadly in want of change, is, in spite of his bad character in his former situation, "taken" up by Jupiter, and patronized by the "Upper Ten": Miss LIZA WEBER. *Minerva*, Goddess of Wisdom; a remarkably strong-minded lady, the defender of her own rights and women's wrongs: Mr. GEORGE ATKINS. *Mars*, Commander-in-Chief, as Ma's generally are: Mr. HARRY STEWART. *Ganymede*, Jupiter's beautiful "Buttons," a nice, active lad, who may be described as a Ganny-mede and a Ganny-purse-un too: Mr. HARRY STEWART. *Bacchus*, Promoter and Chief Director of the Celestial Whiskey Association: Mr G. C. CHARLES. *Juno*, Queen of the Gods and Jove's spouse, described by the poets as Ox-ey'd lady, and consequently of a mettle-some temperament; fond of peacocks that sings Pea-hens of joy while drawing her ear: Miss EMMA MOSHIER. *Jupiter*, King of the Gods, and the most finished gentleman in Olympus: Miss THERESE WOOD. *Mercury*, the Celestial Telegraph Boy: Miss EMMA GRATTAN. *Cupid*, the Son of Venus, who will be at once recognized as love at first sight: Miss Jennie Arnot. *Apollo*, Secretary to the Imperial "Sun" Fire Insurance Company, Limited: Miss Aggie Wood. *The Three Graces*: Misses Lavenia, Tillie Lewis, Fanny Mills.

The Nine Muses: *Calliope*: Miss Annie Page. *Melpomene*: Miss Aggie Keene. *Pollyhmnia*: Miss Georgia Leister. *Clio*: Miss Mary Saxe. *Erato*: Miss Tilly Page. *Urania*: Miss Ida Sefton. *Euterpe*: Miss Maud Allerton. *Terpsichore*: Miss Fanny Hanwood. *Thalia*: Miss Lottie Kane.

Characters in the Pantomime: *Clown*: A. H. Sheldon. *Pantaloon*: R. J. Lewis. *Harlequin*: J. Debonay. *Columbine*: Miss A. Wood.

Act 1, Scene 1: Ruins of a Doric Temple. *Scene 2*: The Royal Distillery in the Sky. *Scene 3*: Juno's Reception Hall.

Act 2, Scene 1: Apollo's Sun, Light, Fire and Insurance Office. *Scene 2*: Cupid's Castle in the Air. *Scene 3*: The Milky Way. Allegorical Tableau, representing FAME, aided by FACT and FICTION.

Pantomime Scenes: *Scene 1*: A Street—Clown and Pantaloon in trouble. A Clean Shave. Clown turns Cobbler and sticks to his last. Carrying the Hod under difficulties. A Bad Eye. *Scene 2*: Hotel de Flip May Gilder. A bad night's rest. Lively bedfellows. The tables turned. A safe way to get to Ludlow Street Jail. Clown goes for Diamonds, and Pantaloon gets Raw Carrots. *Scene 3*: Demons' Cave. A Dark Prospect. Sent to Blue Blazes. *Scene 4*: Home of the Dragonflies and Cascade of Fleeting Shadows.

1872.37 LEO AND LOTOS

A Grand Spectacular Dramatic Romance in Four Acts, 13 Scenes[21]. Stage manager, L. J. Vincent. Scenic artist, William Voegtlin. Musical conductor, Michael Connolly. Produced by Henry Jarrett and Harry Palmer. Opened 30 November 1872 at Niblo's Garden, reconstructed 10 March 1873 and closed 29 March 1873 after 120 performances.

CAST: *Prince Leo* of Gaul: Mlle. DIANI. *Kohinoor*, Monarch of the Jewel Kingdom: HENRY COLLARD. *Plutus*, God of Mammon: Mr. Roberts. *Electra*, Spirit of Mischief: Lizzie Kelsey. *Astronomer Royal*: Philip Stoner. *Poet Laureate*: M. W. LEFFINGWELL. *Grand Hereditary Muddle*: B. Maginley. *Emperor Eagle*: Harry Gwinnette. *Fidelio*: Bessie Sudlow. *Gobo*, Groom to Leo: M. W. Fiske. *Princess Lotos Leaf*: Mlle. MARIE ROSETTI. *Babette*: Laura Joyce. *Snowflake*, the Guardian Spirit: OLIVIA RAND. *Satanella*, the Beautiful Fiend: Lulu Prior. *Queen Jewel*, a very large precious-Stun: Mrs. Edward Wright. *Venus*: MILLY COOK. *Ballet*: KATHI LANNIER, Mlle. JEAN PITTERI, Mlle. EUGÉNIA LUPO, Mlle. MARIE ADRIENNE. *Specialty*: E. D. DAVIES (ventriloquist).

Act 1, Scene 1: The Glittering Halls of Mammon. *Scene 2*: The Cool Grotto of the Fairy Snowflake. *Scene 3*: The Cottage of Huberlu in the Woods of Brittany. *Scene 4*: The Palace of the Jewel King.

[19]First produced in New York 28 September 1868 at Wood's Museum & Metropolitan Theatre in two engagements for 120 performances.

[20]In the second week of its run, IXION was performed at daily matinees.

[21]Authorship uncredited in programs and reviews.

Act 2, Scene 1: The Cliffs of the Enchanted Valley. *Scene 2*: The Market Place in the City of Daimios. *Scene 3*: A Suburb of Twitterville! The Wedding of the Canary and the Linnet. *Scene 4*: The Bird Cage Palace.

Act 3, Scene 1: The Boudoir of Venus. *Scene 2*: Paris in Smiles. A Fete Day at St. Cloud. *Scene 3*: A Corridor in the Halls of Venus. *Scene 4*: Paris in Tears!

Act 4: The Nativity of Venus! (Grand Transformation Scene).

BALLETS, SPECIALTIES[22]

Grand Ballet of the Jewels (Act 1, Scene 4)
Mlles. Pitteri, Adrienne, Coryphées, Corps de Ballet

The Triumph of Satanella (Act 1, Scene 4)

The Wedding of the Canary and the Linnet (Act 2, Scene 3)

The Grand Bird Ballet (Act 2, Scene 4)
K. Lannier, Coryphées, Corps de Ballet

The Translation of Lotos (Act 2, Scene 4)

Grand Military Ballet and Divertissement (Act 3, Scene 2)
Mlles. Pitteri, Lupo, Adrienne, Coryphées, Corps de Ballet

Specialties: Child Americus (the coming Mozart); E. D. Davis (ventriloquist); Professor Siegrist and Family in their Classical Parlor Entertainment, after which Professor Siegrist will introduce his celebrated Performing Dogs (Act 3, Scene 2)

Panorama of the city of Paris under the Commune: (Act 3, Scene 4)

Cry Havoc! and let slip the Dogs of War; 'Twixt life and death; the Last Sortie, or, the Forlorn Hope; Destruction of the Column Vendome; Shooting of the Petroleuse; Death, the Real Victor. Ending with the attack on and burning of the Hotel de Ville.

The Victory of Snowflake (Act 3, Scene 4)

The Nativity of Venus! (Grand Transformation Scene)(Act 4)

1872.38 THE GOLDEN BUTTERFLY

A Revival of the Fairy Musical Extravaganza and Pantomime in Two Acts, 11 Scenes[23]. Extravaganza by James Barnes. Music arranged by William H. Brinkworth. Scenery by John A. Thompson. Costumes by Mons. Phillipe. Properties by Charles LaForrest. Produced under the direction of James Barnes, stage director. Musical director, William H. Brinkworth. Produced by George Wood. Opened 2 December 1872 at Wood's Museum and closed 13 December 1872 after 10 (weekday matinee) performances.

CAST: *Rosetint*, the Golden Butterfly: Miss PAULINE MARKHAM. *Pitty Pat*, one of the boys we read of: Miss LIZA WEBER. *Concertina*, a Rebellious Subject, in fact a *horfull willain*: Miss EMMA GRATTAN. *King Mulligrub*, a wretched Old Man with an only Son: LOUIS J. MESTAYER. *Queen Tingertongue*, his worser half but one too many for the King: Mr. GEORGE ATKINS. *Lunkhead*, a simple rustic, with a taste for Hunting Butterflys: A. H. SHELDON. *Scalliwag*, King of the Fire-Flys, a hard hearted Cove, by Jove: Mr. G. C. Charles. *Baron Plumdoph*, the Prime Minister a regular Duffer: H. Stewart. *Lord Perriwig*, a sleepy Old Buffer: Charles Sturges. *Lord Nobrains*, another wise Councellor: John Debonay. *Limbo*, a Demon Firefly: D. Barclay. *Lillywhite*, the Butterfly Queen: Miss THERESA WOOD. *Gausewing*, an airy subject and as beautiful as a Butterfly: Miss EMMA MOSHIER. *Kiskatong*, the Persian Ambassador who gets kicked: Miss Aggie Wood. *Lord Knowswho*, the Egyptian Ambassador who likewise is deeply insulted by the King: Miss Jennie Satterlee. *Guards, Courtiers, Bull-frogs, Fire-flies and Croton Water Bugs*: Numerous Ladies and Gents.

Pantomime: *Clown*: A. H. Sheldon. *Pantaloon*: R. J. Lewis. *Harlequin*: J. Debonay. *Columbine*: Miss A. Wood.

Act 1, Scene 1: The Winning Card. *Scene 2*: The Rebellious Subject. *Scene 3*: The Stern Resolve.

Act 2, Scene 1: The Fairy's Revenge. *Scene 2*: The Test of Love. *Scene 3*: The Heart of Gold.

Pantomime: *Scene 1*: A Street. Gunsmith and Segar Shop. The Pantaloon gets kicked and the Clown shot. Free Lunch. Gone where the Woodbine twineth. Grand Rally. *Scene 2*: The Roadside. Things fearfully mixed. *Scene 3*: Limburger's Hotel. A picture that eats. And several others that cry Ha! Ha! Ha! A Skilligan! A big fat Dutchman. Now we have him. N, we don't. Reading under difficulties. Too much light. *Scene 4*: The Dark Hour. *Scene 5*: Grand Transformation Scene. The Crystal Bower of Butterflies.

[22]Programs note that the producers introduced new songs, music and ballets throughout the run.
[23]Previously produced (without the pantomime) in New York 5 September 1870 at Wood's Museum for 20 matinee performances.

1872.39 LA BELLE HÉLÈNE

A Revival of the Opéra-bouffe in Three Acts[24], in French. Libretto by Henri Meilhac and Ludovic Halévy. Music by Jacques Offenbach. Musical director, Charles Van Ghele. Produced by Mlle. Marie Aimée and the New Parisian Opera Troupe (C A. Chizzola & Co., Directors). Opened 9 December 1872 at the Olympic Theatre and closed 21 December 1872, returned in repertory the week of 30 December 1872 at the Olympic Theatre; season closed 11 January 1873 after (15) performances in repertory.

CAST: *La Belle Hélène*, Queen of Sparta: Mlle. MARIE AIMÉE. *Orestes*: Mlle. ROLLAND. *Paris*, Son of King Priam: Mons. JUTEAU. *Agamemnon*, King of Greece: Mons. DUSCHESNE. *Menelaus*, King of Sparta: Mons. NARDIN. *Calchas*, Grand Augur of Jupiter: Mons. LECUYER. *Achille*, King of Phtiotis: Mons. Julien. *Ajax I*, King of Salamine: Mons. Marcas. *Ajax II*, King of Locria: Mons. Caralp. *Bacchis*: Mlle. Vandame. *Parthenis*, a Woman of Corinth: Mlle. Juteau. *Leona*, a Woman of Corinth: Mmes. Deschamps. (*Guests, Slaves, the Populace, etc.*)

1872.40 THE BABES IN THE WOOD

A Burlesque Extravaganza in Two Acts. Adapted and arranged by James Barnes, Stage Director. Musical director, William H. Brinkworth. Produced by George Wood. Opened 16 December 1872 at Wood's Museum and closed 28 December 1872 after 12 performances[25].

CAST: *Sir Rowland Macassar*, the remorseless "Uncle," in whose care his elder brother has left his pledges: Miss LIZA WEBER. *Maid Marian*, alias Miss Jones, protectoress of the Babes, who using her position as a Cloak to conceal her true feelings, proves herself a regular Ready Made 'Un: Miss PAULINE MARKHAM. *Sir William Macassar*, long lost brother and father of Babes, with nom de plume of Will Scarlet: Miss EMMA GRATTAN. *Robin Hood*, the Bold Outlaw: Miss BELLE HOWITT. *Tommy, Sally*, the two babes referred to, so young, so innocent, yet so ingenious: Messrs. A. H. SHELDON, GEORGE ATKINS. *Smith*, the first Ruffian—a mysterious creature: LOUIS J. MESTAYER. *Brown*, the second Ruffian, a villain of a deeper dye: Mr. HARRY STEWART. *Doctor Pilgarlic*, the Family M.D. from Germany: CHARLES STRURGES. *Slim Slum, Glim Glum*, Gendarmes of the Period, much superior to those in Genevieve: Messrs. R. J. Mills, John Debonay. *Lady Macassar*: G. C. Charles. *Badenough*: R. J. Lewis. *Brilliantina*: Miss Therese Wood. *Little John*: Miss Emma Moshier. *Sir Roderick*: Miss Aggie Wood. *Sir Rupert*: Miss Jennie Satterlee. (*Specialties*: Messrs. DELEHANTY & HENGLER, Song and Dance Artists; Messrs. SHERIDAN and MACK, versatile character change artists; Professor JACOB SHOWLES with his highly educated Trick Mules, Pete and Barney.)

1872.41 LE PETIT FAUST

A Revival of the Opéra-bouffe in Three Acts[26], in French. Libretto by Hector Crémieux and Adolphe Jaime. Music by Hervé. Musical director, Charles Van Ghele. Produced by Mlle. Marie Aimée's New Parisian Opera Troupe (C. A. Chizzola & Co., Directors). Opened 21 December 1872 at the Olympic Theatre in repertory, season closed 11 January 1873 after (4) performances in repertory.

CAST: *Méphisto*: Mlle. MARIE AIMÉE. *Marguerite*: Mlle. BONELLI. *Faust*: Mons. JUTEAU. *Valentine*: Mons. LECUYER. *Un Cocher*: Mons. Marcas. *Un Pion*: Mons. Julien. *Un Anglo Saxon*: Mons. Berthon. Aimée's Company this season also included Mmes. Juteau, Deschamps, Cantrelle, Grenet, Barin, etc.

1872.42 LES CENT VIERGES

An Opéra-bouffe in Three Acts, in French. Libretto by Clairville, Henri Chivot and Alfred Duru. Music by Charles Lecocq. Musical director, Charles Van Ghele. Produced by Mlle. Marie Aimée and the New Parisian Opera Troupe (C A. Chizzola & Co., Directors). Opened 23 December 1872 at the Olympic Theatre; season closed 11 January 1873 after (8) performances in repertory.

[24]First produced in New York 26 March 1868 at the Théâtre Français for 37 performances. For Synopsis of Scenes and Musical Numbers, see original 1868 production.
[25]For its second week, THE BABES IN THE WOOD played weekday matinees.
[26]First produced in New York in English 29 August 1870 at Kelly and Leon's for 12 performances; in French 29 August 1870 at the Grand Opera House. For Synopsis of Scenes and Musical Numbers, see original 1870 production at the Grand Opera House.

CAST: *Gabrielle*, femme du Duc de Quillenbois: Mlle. MARIE AIMÉE. *Eglantine*, femme de Poulardot: Mlle. BONELLI. *Fanny*, niece de Crockley: Mlle. ROLAND. *Dolores*, Espagnole: Mme. Juteau. *Paquebette*, Hollandaise: Mlle. Vandame. *Rettly*, Suissesse: Mlle. Deschamps. *Paoli*, Italienne: Mlle. Marie Nardin. *Lisbeth*, Tyrolienne: Mons. Peraut. *Olga*, Polonaise: Mlle. Cantrelle. *Lysis*, Grecque: Mlle. Julien. *Gilda*, Gitane: Mlle. Barin. *Nadge*, Russe: Mlle. Grenet. *Katerine*, Hongroise: Mlle. Nardin. *Madelon*, Breton: Mlle. Vandelet. *Boscotte*, Picarde: Mlle. Regnault. *Le Duc Anatole de Quillenbois*: Mons. JUTEAU. *Sir Jonathan Pluperson*, Gouverneur de l'Ile Verte: Mons. LECUYER. *Poulardot*, ancien negociant: Mons. DUCHESNE. *Brididick*, Secretaire de Pluperson: Mons. NARDIN. *Crockley*, Tavernier: Mons. Marcas. *Le Capitaine Thompson*: Mons. Julien. *Un Constable*: Mons. Berthon.

Colons Anglaise: *Calsonn*: Mons. Salvator. *Bitter*: Mons. Caralp. *Bristow*: Mons. Davalis. *Jolly*: Mons. Adrocy. *Robinson*: Mons. Guerra. *Duchester*: Mons. Careme. *Monitor*: Mons. Grazzini. *Grospater*: Mons. Victor. *Hosteball*: Mons. Ruffino. *McFarlann*: Mons. Peraut. *Towtenpatt*: Mons. Leclerc. *Grosborn*: Mons. Bragg. *Emigrants, Marines, Soldiers, Colonists, etc.*

Act 1: London.

Act 2: The Green Islands.

Act 3: The Green Islands.

ACT 1[27]

Introduction:

Choeur (Vive le gin, vive le bière)

Mlle. Roland, Mons. Marcas, Cheour

Chanson du Porter (Quel est de toute le terre le plus beau pays)
Mlle. Roland

Choeur de sortie (Qui rend l'existence douce)
Choeur

Ariette (J'ai la tête romanesque)
Mlle. Aimée

Duo (Dans les forêts de l'Amérique)
Mlle. Aimée, Mons. Juteau

Quintette (Un turbot? un turbot?)
Mlles. Aimée, Bonnelli, Messrs. Juteau, Duchesne, Marcas

Morceau d'ensemble et final (Voici le moment de l'enrôlement)
Tous

ACT 2

Couplets (Sans femme l'homme est un corps sans âme)
Messrs. Lecuyer, Nardin, Choeur

Choeur et musique de scène (Sans femme, sans femme, eh bien!)
Choeur

Morceau d'ensemble (Au bonheur, à la joie, aujourd'hui livrez-vous)
Mlles. Aimée, Bonnelli, Messrs. Lecuyer, Nardin, Juteau, Duchesne, Julien

Choeur (Allez, mes tourterelles, allez)
Messrs. Lecuyer, Nardin, Choeur

Quatuor (Silence, silence, si l'on vous entendait)
Mlles. Aimée, Bonnelli, Messrs. Juteau, Duchesne

Grande valse (Je soupire et maudis le destin)
Mlle. Aimée, Choeur

Choeur (Toutes ici, nous nous livrons)
Choeur

Ensemble et Ballade (Deux nouvelles femmes, ici)
Mlle. Aimée, Bonnelli, Messrs. Juteau, Duchesne, Lecuyer, Nardin, Choeur

Final des Mariages (Ah! cette idée est forte jolie)
Tous

ACT 3

Choeur et Ensemble (Pour faire honneur au Gouverneur)
Mlles. Aimée, Bonnelli, Messrs. Juteau, Duchesne, Nardin, Choeur

Quatuor (À table, chassons l'humeur noire)
Messrs. Juteau, Lecuyer, Nardin, Duchesne

Chanson (Un vieux et riche céladon)
Messrs. Juteau, Lecuyer, Nardin, Duchesne

Duetto (Ah! Monsieur le Secrétaire)
Mlles. Aimée, Bonnelli

Déclaration (Je t'aime, je t'aime, mon beau séducteur)
Mlle. Aimée

Final (Vengeance! Vengeance!)
Mlles. Aimée, Bonnelli, Messrs. Juteau, Lecuyer, Nardin, Duchesne, Chœur

[27]Musical numbers not listed in programs. List prepared from published French piano vocal score (C. Joubert, Paris, 1872).

1872.43 JACK; THE GIANT KILLER

A Burlesque Extravaganza in Two Acts, 6 Scenes. Adapted and arranged by James Barnes, Stage Director. Musical director, William H. Brinkworth. Produced by George Wood. Opened 30 December 1872 at Wood's Museum and closed 10 January 1873 after 12 performances[28].

CAST: *The Giant Gorgibuster*, a Giant in intellect if not in size: Miss LIZA WEBER. *Jack*, Queen Bee's especial favorite, and the public's: Miss BELLE HOWITT. *Jack's Mother*, who is described in this somewhat disrespectful manner from the fact of no chronicler having given Jack's surname: Mr. GEORGE ATKINS. *Sybil*, the maid of the Inn. A damsel whose eyes speak volumes, not to say Sybilline books: Miss NELLY LARKELL. *King Arthur*, a character generally conceived on the narrowest historical foundation, but in this instance, on the broadest burlesque basis: Mr. LOUIS J. MESTAYER. *Queen Bee*, a good Fairy, the enemy of all Drones, and the protectoress of those who "improve each shining hour:" Miss EMMA GRATTAN. *Stuffclub*, one of King Arthur's Broadway squad: Mr. A. H. SHELDON. *Sir Single, Sir Gringle, Sir Cringle*, King Arthur's Knight: Misses Emma Moshier, Aggie Wood, Jennie Satterlee. *So-so*, the Giant's cook: Miss THERESE WOOD. *Te-to Tum*: Mr. HARRY STEWART. *Toofat*, an Innkeeper, proprietor of the "Good King Arthur:" Mr. G. C. Charles. *Tremoloso*: Charles Sturges. *Soapfat*, a Rustic Youth: Mr. John Debonay. *Blunderbore*, the Giant's Big Brother: Mr. R. J. Lewis.

Queen Bee's Subjects: *Honeybee*: Miss Tilly Lewis. *Busybee*: Miss Alice Lavenia. *Letmebee*: Miss Fanny Mills. *Bumblebee*: Miss Mary O'Neill. *Jumblebee*: Miss Mertza Parker. *Bullseye*: Miss Ida Sefton. *Queen Bee's Sweets*: *Gingerbread*: Miss Aggie Keene. *Cracker*: Master Joe Hagan. *Bunn*: Miss Mary Saxe. *Peppermint Candy*: Miss Mary Page. *Lollypop*: Miss Georgie Lyster. *Bees, Peasants, Giants, etc.* (*Specialties*: Messrs. DELEHANTY & HENGLER, Song and Dance Artists; Messrs. SHERIDAN and MACK, versatile character change artists; Professor JACOB SHOWLES with his highly educated Trick Mules, Pete and Barney.)

Act 1, Scene 1: Exterior of the "Good King Arthur" Tavern. *Scene 2*: A Street in ancient Rome. *Scene 3*: Jack's 'Umble Roof. *Scene 4*: Hall of Honeycombs, Queen Bee's Hunt, and Home of Perpetual Sweets.

Act 2, Scene 1: The Battlements of the Giant's Castle. *Scene 2*: Gorgibuster's Boudoir.

1873.01 LES BRIGANDS

A Revival of the Opéra-bouffe in Three Acts[29], in French. Libretto by Henri Meilhac and Ludovic Halévy. Music by Jacques Offenbach. Musical director, Charles Van Ghele. Produced by Mlle. Marie Aimée's New Parisian Opera Troupe (C. A. Chizzola & Co., Managers). Opened 6 January 1873 at the Olympic Theatre and closed 11 January 1873 after 6 performances in repertory.

CAST: *Fiorella*: Mlle. MARIE AIMÉE. *Fragoletto*: Mlle. BONELLI. *Duke of Mantua*: Mlle. ROLLAND. *Falsacappa*: Mons. JUTEAU. *Pietro*: Mons. DUCHESNE. *Antonio*: Mons. Marcas. *Chief of Carabineers*: Mons. Lecuyer. *Gloria-Cassis*: Mons. Berthon. *Adolphe de Vallodolid*: Mlle. Deschamps. *Princess of Grenada*: Mlle. Juteau. *The Duchesse*: Mlle. Cantrelle. *The Marchioness*: Mlle. Vendamme. *Carmagnola*: Mons. Salvator. *Pipo*: Mons. Careme. *Barbano*: Mons. Peraut. *Domino*: Mons. Caralp. *The Precepteur*: Mons. Adorci. *Bandits, Courtiers, Cooks, Ladies, Carabineers, etc.*

1873.02 HUMPTY DUMPTY

A Revival of the Spectacular Pantomime in Three Acts, 14 Scenes[30]. Play revised, remodelled and reconstructed by its author George L. Fox. Stage director, E. S. Tarr. Musical director, F. Strebinger. Produced by James E. Hayes. Opened 17 February 1873 at the Olympic Theatre; reconstructed 21 April 1873, and closed 7 June 1873 after 128 performances.

CAST: *Humpty Dumpty*, the Original, the Great Prophet of Fun: GEORGE L. FOX. *Old One Two*, a famed Pantaloonatic: C. K. FOX. *Tommy Tucker*, who everybody knows and adores: C. [Charles] W. RAVEL. *Little Goody-Two Shoes*, a bright divinity: Miss FANNIE BEANE. *King Icicle*, Ruler of the Frozen Regions: G. A. Beane. *Sunbeam*, a Radiant Spirit: Marion Fiske. *Hon. Grandeur Dignity*: S. Roller. *Doctor Cureall*: B. Limer. *Gnome Cobbler*: Master George Topack. *Police Officer*: G. Hildebrande. *Giant Policeman*: A. Copp. Other characters by the great corps of Pantomimists.

[28]For its second week, JACK; THE GIANT KILLER played weekday matinees.

[29]First produced in New York in French 14 November 1870 at the Grand Opera House. For Synopsis of Scenes and Musical Numbers, see original 1870 production.

[30]First produced in New York 10 March 1868 at the Olympic Theatre for 483 performances.

Specialties[31]: Russian Quartette; Alice and Ada Molteno (harp and violin); The Marten Family; the children Venus and Adonis; Senor Casselli (wirewalker), Kynock and Smith (skaters), Bedouin Arabs (10), Professor Nelson & Sons (gymnasts).

Act 1, Scene 1: Fancy's Frolic. Moonlit Glen. *Scene 2*: The place where Humpty Dumpty was born. Transformation of the Characters. *Scene 3*: Post Office; Wayside Inn. *Scene 4*: Dry Goods Emporium and Ladies' Seminary. *Scene 5*: The Auditory. *Scene 6*: Market Place.

Act 2: Humpty's Kaleidoscope.

Act 3, Scene 1: Library. *Scene 2*: Candy Store. *Scene 3*: Street somewhere. *Scene 4*: Street. *Scene 5*: Bed Chamber. *Scene 6*: Another Street. *Scene 7*: Surprise of the Nymphs.

SPECIALTIES

Transformation of Characters (Act 1, Scene 2)
Clown: G. L. Fox. *Pantaloon*: C. K. Fox. *Harlequin*: Winter Ravel. *Columbine*: Miss F. Beane.

"Di Pescatore" (Duet, Harp and Violin) (from LUCREZIA BORGIA)(Act 1, Scene 5)
Misses Molteno
(*Music by* Gaetano Donizetti.)

Dance (Act 1, Scene 6)
C. Ravel, F. Beane

Senor Casselli on the Invisible Wire (Act 2)

Russian Quartette (Musical Specialties) (Act 2)

Professor Nelson & Sons in their classical gymnastic feats (Act 2)

"Tyrolienne" from GENEVIEVE DE BRABANT (Act 2)
Mons. and Mme. Marten, Mlle. Gretchen
(*Music by* Jacques Offenbach.)

Skatorial Evolutions by Messrs. Kynock & Smith (Act 2)

The Infant Venus and Adonis on the Velocipede (Act 2)

Grand Cat Duet (Act 2)
Mons. and Mme. Marten

The Bedouin Arabs (Acrobats) (Act 2)

Surprise of the Nymphs (Act 3, Scene 7)

1873.03

ROUGHING IT!!

A Kaleidoscopic Drama in Four Acts, 11 Scenes and a Transformation. Play by Augustin Daly, adapted from the latest Parisian Spectacular Folly, and embellished with some of the experiences of Mark Twain. Music by Auguste Predigam. Scenery by George Dayton, Joseph De La Harpe, Louis Duflocq, L. W. Seavey, George Heister. Produced by Augustin Daly. Opened 18 February 1873 at the Grand Opera House and closed 15 March 1873 after 27 performances.

CAST: *Mr. Denis Macduffie*, a Gentleman of fortune, with one daughter and no more, living in Arcadia Villa, on the Grand Boulevard, an Elysium of his own creation: JOHN BROUGHAM. *Miss Antonietta Macduffie*, the undescribable and irresistible Sole Hope of the House of Macduffie: MRS. JOHN WOOD. *Jerolomon White, Triptolemus Black*, comprising the eminent firm of White & Black, distinguished detectives doing business at No. 1 City Hall Place J. K. MORTIMER, OWEN FAWCETT. *Mrs. John Wood*, queen of comedy and song. See Small Bills: ANNIE DELAND. *Aubrey von Dollas*, a scion of one of our first families, in love with Antonietta but too poor to face her too Solvent Parents: J. G. PEAKES. *M. Lorreylord von Millens*, a wealthy young stockbroker, who aspires with paternal sanction to the hand of Antonietta: EDMUND PIERCE. *The Amiable Arkansas*: J. W. Jennings. *Slade*, the pale fire eater of Simpson's Bar: J. G. Golden. *Eldorado Johnny*: A. G. Enos. *Mr. Brown*, the Landlord: G. F. Ketchum. *The Chief of the Goshoots*, a lineal descendant of "Lo," and other poor Indians: J. A. Meade. *Tom Barkey*, Macduffie's confidential head Imp: Julian Cross. *Muldoon*: E. Chapman. *"4 11"*, Bellboy at the Metropolitan Hotel: F. Chapman. *The Opium Dreamer*: Mr. Golden. *Florentina*, the romantic Maid of the fair Antonietta: Roberta Norwood. *Mother Terror*, an opium crone: Annie Yeamans. *Arrah na Pogue*, newly arrived at Castle garden: Miss Hyde. *Slipshod*: LOUISE VOLMER. *Italian Street Cleaners, Emigrants of various nationalities, Passengers and Officers at the Grand Union Depot, Roughs at Simpson's Bar, Indians of the Goshoot Tribe, (see Mark Twain) Opium Smokers, United States Cavalry, etc.*: Chorus and Auxiliaries. *The Geunine Mexican Plug* [horse], by the trained steed, Harry Bassett, Jr.

Act 1: A Villa on the Grand Drive or Boulevard, (see Report of the Commissioners of Central Park, Pub. Doc., Vol. 1038, pp. 1000-1.) (Dayton).

Act 2, Scene 1: No. 1, City Hall Place. (De La Harpe.) *Scene 2*: Room No. 499 at the Metropolitan. (De La Harpe.) *Scene 3*: The Comedienne's Parlors at the "Metropolitan." (Duflocq.) *Scene 4*: A glance at Castle Garden. (Dayton.) *Scene 5*: Interior of Grand Union Depot. (Seavey.)

Act 3, Scene 1: The Red Dog Tavern at Simpson's Bar. (De La Harpe.) *Scene 2*: On the borders of civilization. (Dayton.) *Scene 3*: At the foot of the Rocky Mountains. (Duflocq.) An Indian camping ground by starlight.

Act 4, Scene 1: Interior of a Chinese Opium Den. *Scenes 2, 3 , 4 and 5*: An Elaborate Transformation , or Dissolving Vision of the Four Seasons showing an Opium Smoker's Dream. (Heister.)

SPECIALTIES AND MUSICAL NUMBERS

Chorus of happy Big Pipe Men (Act 1)

Arrah na Pogue wants a piano! (Act 2, Scene 4)

Chorus and Dance of Passengers, Conductors, Porters and Breakmen (Act 2, Scene 5)

A Reminiscence of "Alixe" (Act 4, Scene 1)(Burlesque)

1873.04

MASKS AND FACES, or, The Miseries of Midgit!/ LA SOMNAMBULA, The Sleep Walker!

A Double Bill of Burlesque in Two Parts, accompanied by an Olio. New scenery and costumes. Produced by (G. Swaine) Buckley and (Sam) Sharpley's Burlesque Opera Troupe. Opened 3 March 1873 at the St. James' Theatre and closed 15 March 1873 after 12 performances.

ACT 1

MASKS AND FACES, or, The Miseries of Midgit!, a laughable and Original Musical Burlesque in One Act, written expressly for this company. Burlesque by John F. Poole.

CAST: *Old Midgit*, who wants to give a concert: G. B. FROTHINGHAM. *Sam*, his servant, who presumes on his position: SAM SHARPLEY. *Harry*, Midgit's nephew, who wants to occur at the Concert: G. SWAINE BUCKLEY. *Josiah Jonathan Jewhittaker*, a Yankee who occurs: G. SWAINE BUCKLEY. *Mons. Jacques Morbleau*, a Frenchman who dittoes: G. SWAINE BUCKLEY. *Biddy McCarty*, an Irish Apple Vendor, who also dittoes: G. SWAINE BUCKLEY. *Cuffee Crowquill*, who dittoes much: G. SWAINE BUCKLEY.

During the piece, Mr. Buckley will perform upon the following instruments: Guitar, Cornet, Melophone, Violin, Bones, Banjo Zylophone and Chinese Fiddle. Concluding with his Songs and Dances.

After which a delicious bit of Irish comedy, Barney's Courtship! With Fred McEvoy as Mrs. Malone and Barney Dwyer, and Mrs. Fred McEvoy as Molly. Music on the Brain, in which G. Swaine Buckley plays on seven different instruments at one and the same time—original. Banjo-Vial Demonstrations by the original Sam Sharpley, including his latest compositions, Local and Political Hits at Men and Manners, Fashions and Folies of the times.

ACT 2

LA SOMNAMBULA, The Sleep Walker!, A Burlesque Opera[32] in Three Acts (inspired by the opera 'La Sonnambula,' music by Vincenzo Bellini, libretto by Felice Romani, after Eugène Scribe's ballet-pantomime 'La Sonnambule.')

CAST: *Amina* (Dina): Miss EVA BRENT. *Susanna* (Liza): Mrs. Fred McEvoy. *Alezio* (Lazy Joe): SAM SHARPLEY. *Deacon Ducklegs*: Horace Frail. *Elvino* (Jumbo): G. SWAINE BUCKLEY. *Rudolph* (San Tucker): GEORGE B. FROTHINGHAM. *Aunt Sally*: Fred McEvoy. *Cudjo*: T. L. Fitch.

ACT 1

"Viva, Dinah" (Chorus)
Company

"Oh, Susey, let us married be"
S. Sharpley

"While this heart with joy revealing" (Aria)
E. Brent

"Take now this ring" (Duet)
E. Brent, G. S. Buckley

"See, Sir, See" (Chorus)
Company

[31]For the reconstruction: The Wilson Brothers, William and Harry Jee (hat spinners), Americus (violinist), Professor Nelson, Six Russians, etc.

[32]The public is respectfully informed that this production is not like the Burlesques of the present day—but contains all the gems of the original opera, interspersed and enlivened by popular Minstrel Melodies, Laughable Situations and Original Humor.

"As I view now" (Aria)
G. B. Frothingham
"Who is he, say, can you tell?" (Chorus)
Company
"My poor Lucy Neal" (Solo and Chorus)
"Good Night" (Phantom Chorus)
Company

ACT 2
"Such a getting up stairs" (Chorus)
"Oh, look here, oh, look dar" (Chorus)
Company
"We disdain thee" (Chorus)
Company
"Hear me swear" (Quintet)
E. Brent, G. S. Buckley, Chorus
"Such return for love" (Chorus)
"Come day, go day" (Chorus)
Company

ACT 3
"All is lost" (Grand Aria)
"Still so gently"
G. S. Buckley
"Oh, Dinah" (Prayer)
"Sitting on a rail"
E. Brent, Chorus
"Just take a peep" (Chorus)
S. Sharpley, Chorus
"Wake, wake Dinah" (Chorus)
Company
"Do not mingle" (Aria)
E. Brent
Grand Finale

1873.05
LUCREZIA BORGIA

A Burlesque Opera in Three Scenes, followed by an Olio. (Inspired by the opera 'Lucretia Borgia' music by Gaetano Donizetti, with libretto by Felice Romani after Victor Hugo's 'Lucrèce Borgia.') New scenery and costumes. Produced by (G. Swaine) Buckley & (Sam) Sharpley's Excelsior Troupe. Opened 17 March 1873 at the St. James' Theatre and closed 22 March 1873 after 6 performances.

CAST: *Lucrezia Borgia*, the Pizner: Miss EVA BRENT. *Gennaro*, Captain of the Fifty "Black Guards," in love with somebody he don't know, never saw or heard of: G. SWAINE BUCKLEY. *Orsini*, fond of everybody's wine, a spinner of yarns, not confined to truth, a would-be poet, and a fast-friend of Gennaro: SAM SHARPLEY. *Duke Alphonso*, a green-eyed lobster: G. B. FROTHINGHAM. *Gubetta*, a detective spy of Lucrezia, who sees much but says little: HORACE FRAIL. *Polontrova*, a young man fond of seeing the elephant: Monroe Dempster. *Gabbero*, a fast young coon of Venice: William Butler. *Body Guard*, rather slim: Fred McAvoy. *Astolpho Poro Tempo*, consumer of benzine: J. Kane. *Monks, Venetians, Counts (of no account), Gentlemen-at-arms, followers of Gennaro (at dinner time)*: Company.

Olio: "Goodbye to Old Ireland" Fred and Annie McAvoy. Characteristic Song & Dance, G. Swaine Buckley. Comic Banjo Song, Sam Sharpley. "The Sneezing Song", Miss Eva Brent. The Widow Malone, Messrs. Frail and Frothingham. Music on the Brain, G. Swaine Buckley in his original act, playing seven different instruments at one time. The Old Clock (laughable sketch), with Fred McAvoy, Horace Frail, G. B. Frothingham, Mrs. Fred McAvoy.

Scene 1: Venice by Moonlight and Coonlight. *Scene 2*: The Ducal Palace. *Scene 3*: Banquet Chamber.

MUSICAL NUMBERS

Scene 1
"Hail Lovely Venice" (Opening Chorus)
"Music invites us" (Chorus)
"Holy Beauty" (Solo)
E. Brent
"Oh, Heaven" (Duet)
G. S. Buckley, E. Brent
"Deemed of a fisherman's lowly race" (Solo)
G. S. Buckley
"Oh, what fond and fervent love" (Duet)
"What am she, and who's her name?" (Duet)
"'Tis the Borgia" (Tableau)

Scene 2
"Haste then to glut my vengeance" (Solo)
E. Brent
"Aye through the fourth of my husbands" (Duet)
"Guard thee from all emotion" (Trio)
"Hapless Victims" (Duet)
"The Antidote of a doting mother" (Medley)
"Thank heaven, he's saved" (Tableau)

Scene 3
"What's de matter, Susey?" (Opening Chorus)
Exciting Chorus
"It is better to laugh" (Drinking song)
S. Sharpley
Chorus of Monks
"You've all drunk cold pizen"
E. Brent
"Mamma, is this thy welcome" (Duet)
G. S. Buckley, E. Brent
"Todder side of Jordan" (Finale)

1873.06
THE BELLES OF THE KITCHEN

The Vokes Family in a Return Engagement of the Laughable Sketch in One Act[33]. Play by the Vokes Family. Opened 14 April 1873 at Niblo's Garden and closed 19 April 1873 after 8 performances.

CAST: *Lucinda Scrubbs*, a Lady's Maid: JESSIE VOKES. *Mary*, a House Maid: VICTORIA VOKES. *Barbara*, a Kitchen Maid: ROSINA VOKES. *Timotheus Gibbs*, a Doctor's Page: FRED VOKES. *Wiggins*, a Hair Dresser: FAWDON VOKES.

1873.07
THE WRONG MAN IN THE RIGHT PLACE

The Vokes Family in a Return Engagement of the Laughable Sketch in One Act[34]. Play by the Vokes Family. Opened 21 April 1873 at Niblo's Garden and closed 26 April 1873 after 8 performances.

CAST: *Emily Merton*, Niece to the Proprietress of a Young Ladies College near London: JESSIE VOKES. *Clara Staunton*, a Romantic Young Lady, remaining at the college during vacation. Who will sing with Benjamin Buttontop an Operatic Duet: VICTORIA VOKES. *Sarah Jane*, a Young Person desirous of improving her position in life, at present parlor maid to the Establishment, who will introduce her peculiar and original "Leary Dance": ROSINA VOKES. *Benjamin Buttontop*, Manager of an unlicensed Theatre, at present under a cloud. Who will dance his own Burlesque Polka, and sing with Clara Staunton: FRED VOKES. *Sampson Biffles*, footman to the College, formerly a super in a third-class theatre: FAWDON VOKES.

1873.08
AZRAEL; or, The Magic Charm

A Ballet-Spectacle-Pantomime in a Prologue, Three Acts, and 17 Scenes. Music by Michael Connelly. Grand Harlequinade, everything new and original, written and invented by James S. Maffitt. Stage manager, L. J. Vincent. Scenery by William Voegtlin and R. Schell. Mechanism by Benson Sherwood. Costumes, properties and appointments designed and

[33]First produced in New York 15 April 1872 at the Union Square Theatre for 49 performances. For Synopsis of Musical Specialties, see original 1872 production. THE BELLES OF THE KITCHEN was preceded by a comedietta Orange Blossoms, in which the Vokes did not appear.

[34]First produced in New York 27 May 1872 at the Union Square Theatre for 6 performances. For Synopsis of Musical Specialties, see original 1872 production. THE WRONG MAN IN THE RIGHT PLACE was preceded by a drama with George Fawcett Rowe, Micawber, in which the Vokes did not appear.

constructed by William Deverna. Produced by Henry Jarrett and Harry Palmer. Opened 28 April 1873 at Niblo's Garden and closed 7 June 1873 after 47 performances.[35]

CAST: *Gondy*, a Magician: HARRY GWYNETTE. *His Brothers (5)*: *Wilfred*: E. K. Collier. *Bertram*: W. Carpenter. *Carl*: James Freeman. *Ernest*: E. Dennison. *Albert*: C. Bernard. *Waldemar*, with song: Charles Hersee. *Peerschen*: Harry Hotto. *Bertha*: Jennie Arnott. *Dame Lucille*, Bertha's Mother: Mrs. Walcot. *Blanchette*, a Fairy: Millie Cook. *Zelda*, a Witch: Lulu Prior. *Lisette*: Laura Joyce. *Marco*, the Cat: Master Eddie. *Hugo*, a Villager: James Imrie. *Peasants, Demons, Fairies, etc.*

The Harlequinade: The Unequalled Quartette: *Clown*: JAMES S. MAFFITT. *Pantaloon*: W. H. BARTHOLOMEW. *Harlequin*: Mons. E. VELARDE. *Columbine*: Mlle. CLARA LEONTINE. *Ballet*: KATHI LANNER, Mlle. PITTERI. *Specialty*: LULU (the Gymnast).

Prologue, Scene 1: The Alchemist's Laboratory. (Voegtlin.) *Scene 2*: The Village Mill. (Schell.) *Scene 3*: The Forest. *Scene 4*: The Witch's Glen. (Voegtlin.) *Scene 5*: The Road. *Scene 6*: The Mill.

Act 1, Scene 1: Music and Dry Goods Store. *Scene 2*: An Irishman's Shanty. *Scene 3*: New York by Moonlight. (Schell.)

Act 2, Scene 1: Vienna Exposition. *Scene 2*: Post Office and Railway Station. *Scene 3*: Pennsylvania Central Railroad.

Act 3, Scene 1: Pic-nic Garden. (Schell.) *Scene 2*: Masonic Lodge and Stock Brokers. *Scene 3*: Rival Groceries. (Voegtlin.) *Scene 4*: The slough of despond in the regions of despair; Pantomime drawing to a close. *Scene 5*: Grand Transformation Scene. (Voegtlin.) The Grotto of the Coral Queen.

PROLOGUE

Quartette (Scene 2)
J. Arnott, M. Cook, C. Hersee, J. Imrie

The Demon Ballet (Scene 4)
K. Lannier, Coryphées, Corps de Ballet

Song (Scene 5)
L. Joyce

Grand Harlequinade (Scene 6)

ACT 1

Hornpipe (Scene 1)
E. Velarde, C. Leontine

ACT 2

Caledonia Ballet (Scene 1)
Coryphées, Corps de Ballet

Lulu! (Eighth Wonder of the World)

ACT 3

Grand Ballerina (Scene 1)
Mlle. J. Pitteri, Coryphées, Corps de Ballet

Grand Transformation Scene (Scene 5)

[35]No author or director credited in programs.

1873–1874 SEASON

John K. Emmett in FRITZ, OUR GERMAN COUSIN (Photo: Sarony)
Billy Rose Theatre Collection, New York Public Library for the Performing Arts

1873–1874 SEASON

1873.09 FUN IN A FOG

A Musical, Comical, Nautical Extravaganza, invented, written, arranged and acted exclusively by the Vokes Family[1]. Opened 11 August 1873 at the Union Square Theatre and closed 9 September 1873 after 30 performances; returned 26-31 January 1874 to Niblo's Garden for 7 additional performances. Total: 37 performances[2].

CAST: *Percival Postlethwaite*, Captain of the Muddleton Militia, England, on a visit to his cousin in America, in search of adventures: FREDERICK VOKES. *Dan*, his valet, a Cockney, in constant fear of being scalped by the Indians: FAWDON VOKES. *Grace Gaybird*, Percival's American cousin, a young lady with nautical tastes and a mischievous propensity for practical jokes: VICTORIA VOKES. *Ella Hamilton*, her friend and ally, an accomplished interpreter of the Indians' language: JESSIE VOKES. *Janet*, a smart help, ready for fun, and willing to assist in any plot for the discomfiture of Dan: ROSINA VOKES.

1873.10 THE BLACK CROOK!

A Revival of the Musical Extravaganza in Four Acts, 11 Scenes[3]. (Play by Charles M. Barras. Music by Thomas Baker, others.) Stage manager, L. J. Vincent. Ballets invented and arranged by Imre Kiralfy. Scenic artist, William Voegtlin. Properties by William Deverna. Musical director, Michael Connelly. Produced by Henry Jarrett and Harry Palmer. Opened 18 August 1873 at Niblo's Garden and closed 6 December 1873 after 120 performances.

CAST: Mortals: *Count Wolfenstein*: HARRY GWYNNETTE. *Rudolphe*, a poor artist: E. K. COLLIER. *Von Puffengruntz*, the Count's Steward: J. W. BRUTONE. *Hertzog*, surnamed the Black Crook, an alchemist: C. H. MORTON. *Greppo*, his servant: George Atkins. *Dragonfin*: William Martin. *Zamiel*, the Arch-Fiend: H. PACKARD. *Wolfgar*, a Gypsy Ruffian: F. Williams. *Caspar*, a Peasant: J. Riley. *Redglare*, the Recording Demon: W. Carpenter. *Skudawelp*, familiar to Hertzog: Julian Mitchell. *Villagers, Peasants, Guards, Attendants, Demons, Monsters, Apparitions, Gnomes, etc.*

Immortals: *Stalacta*, Queen of the Golden Realm: PAULINE MARKHAM. *Amina*, betrothed to Rudolphe: LIZZIE KELSEY. *Dame Barbara*, her foster-mother: Mrs. Edward Wright. *Carline*, Amina's Maid: BESSIE SUDLOW. *Rosetta*, a Peasant: Addie Pearson. *Fairies, Naiads, etc. Ballet*: Mlles. ADELE BONI, EMILIA GIAVASSI, Mlles. Leontine, Caroline, Marie, Bertha, Gabrielle, Lizette, Dark, Elise, Emily, Jeannette, Strudel, Theresa, Hunt, Joanna, Baretta, Badoni, Bochanna, Premières, Secondas, and Corps de Ballet. Messrs. ARNOLD KIRALFY, IMRE KIRALFY, BOLOSSY KIRALFY; Mlles. HANIOLA KIRALFY, EMILIE KIRALFY, KATI KIRALFY. 120 Auxiliaries.

Specialties: M. Felix Régamey; E. D. Davies; London Madrigal Boys, The Female Swabian Nightingale Quartette; the infant Vaidis (gymnasts in mid-air exploits).

Act 1, Scene 1: A Valley at the foot of the Hartz Mountains. *Scene 2*: A Woody Pass. *Scene 3*: Laboratory of the Black Crook. *Scene 4*: An Apartment in the Castle Wolfenstein. *Scene 5*: A Wild Glen in the heart of the Brocken.

Act 2, Scene 1: Subterranean Vault in the Castle Wolfenstein. Six months later. *Scene 2*: Lobby in the Castle Wolfenstein. *Scene 3*: A Wild Pass in the Hartz Mountains. *Scene 4*: The Grotto of Stalacta.

Act 3: Illuminated Golden Terrace.

Act 4: Grand Allegorical Pictures (Matt Morgan): Wine, Wealth, Women, Power, Fortune in War; Immortality.

ACT 1

"The Political Whip" (Song)(Scene 4)
B. Sudlow

Grand Incantation Scene: (Scene 5)

Martin's Mechanical Head; The Flight of the Imps; The Climbing Skeleton, etc.

ACT 2

"Dare I Tell"[4] (Song)(Scene 4)
P. Markham

"Kissing" (Song)(Scene 4)
P. Markham

Quartette[5] (Scene 4)
P. Markham, B. Sudlow, E. K. Collier, G. Atkins

The Revel of the Sirens!! (Grand Ballet)(Scene 4)
Mlles. A. Boni, E. Giavassi, Corps de Ballet

The Bath of the Sprites—The Fountain of Jewels.

ACT 3

Grand Ballet of All Nations

Dance de Bretagne
Corps de Ballet

Entrée, Persia and Russia
Coryphées

Entrée, Spain
Danseuses Seconda

Magyar Vigado (Hungarian Sensational Pas de Cinq)
Mlles. Haniola, Emilie, Kati Kiralfy; Mons. Imre, Bolossy Kiralfy

La Normandie
Mlle. E. Giavassi

Dance South American
Mons. Martin, A. Kiralfy, Assistants

United States
Mlle. A. Boni

Magyar Solos and Friska
Kiralfy Family and Troupe

Grand Finale, China, Japan, Nations of the World
Premières, Secondas, Coryphées, Corps de Ballet, 120 Auxiliaries

"Spring, Gentle Spring"[6]
London Madrigal Boys
(*Music by* J. Riviere. *Lyrics by* James Robinson Planché.)

The Twin Sisters Verday (Child Gymnasts)

Mons. Felix Régamey (Caricaturist)

E. D. Davies (Ventriloquist, Puppets)

The March of the Amazons—The Combat!

ACT 4

Matt Morgan's Grand Allegorical Pictures

1873.11 LA FILLE DE MADAME ANGOT

An Opéra-comique in Three Acts, in French. Libretto by Clairville, Paul Siraudin and Victor Koning. Music by Charles Lecocq. Stage manager, Mons. C. Lecuyer. Scenery after Parisian models by Joseph De La Harpe. Musical director, Mons. Charles Van Ghele. Aimée French Opera Bouffe Company (C. A. Chizzola, Director) presented by Augustin Daly. Opened 25 August 1873 at Daly's Broadway Theatre and closed 27 September 1873 in repertory; returned 9 March 1874 to the Lyceum Theatre in repertory, closing 4 April 1874.

CAST: *Clairette Angot*: Mlle. MARIE AIMÉE. *Mlle. Lange*: Mlle. ROSINA STANI. *Amaranthe*: Mlle. CANTRELLE. *Javotte*: Mlle. Sophie Gherzi. *Cydalise*: Mlle. JUTEAU. *Mlle. Delaunay*: Mlle. Villiers. *Hersilie*: Mlle. Marie Vandamme. *Babet*: Mlle. Perraut. *Manon*: Mlle. Deschamps. *Thérèse*: Mlle. Nardin. *Herbelin*: Mlle. Marie Nardin. *Ange Pitou*: Mons. JUTEAU. *Larivaudière*: Mons. DUCHESNE. *Trenitz*: Mons. C. LECUYER. *Pomponnet*: Mons. DESCHAMPS. *Louchard*: Mons. DUPLAN. *Cadet*: Mons. Benedick. *Buteux*: Mons. Julien. *Guillaume*: Mons. Nardin. *Un Incroyable*: Mons. Salvator. *Un Officier*: Mons. Davalis. *Un Cabaretier*: Mons. Perraut. *Ports de la Halle, Bourgeois, Grenadiers, Encroyables, Conspirateurs, Hussars, Domestiques, Dames de la Halle, Bougeoises, Merveilleuses*: Choeur (Chorus).

Act 1: Le Marche des Innocents.

Act 2: Salon chez Mlle. Lange.

Act 3: Les Jardins de Calypso.

---

[1]Accompanied by an olio and a curtain-raiser, Old Phil's Birthday, which was replaced 10 September 1873 by Milky Way. For return engagement, the curtain-raiser was Naval Engagements.

[2]No songs listed in programs, nor credits for scenery, costumes, musical direction, etc. Program note: In the course of the piece will be introduced songs, duets, and dances, mystification and merriment.

[3]First produced in New York 12 September 1866 at Niblo's Garden for 475 performances.

[4]Late in the run "Dare I Tell" and "Kissing" replaced by:

Medley, and "Love Behind the Kitchen Door"
B. Sudlow

[5]In later programs identified as "Now I Lay Me Down to Sleep." (*Music by* Arthur D. Walbridge. *Lyrics by* Hattie A. Fox.)

[6]Late in the run replaced by:

"Killarney" and "Scots Wha Ha'e (wi Wallace bled)" (by Robert Burns)
London Madrigal Boys

ACT 1[7]

Introduction—La Noce (Bras dessus, bras dessous)
Choeur
Couplet et Ensemble (Aujourd'hui, prenons bien garde)
Mons. Deschamps, Choeur
Choeur (Beauté, grâce et décence)
Choeur
Romance (Je vous dois tout)
Mlle. M. Aimée, Mons. Deschamps, Choeur
Scène (Un obstacle pour le moment)
Mlle. Cantrelle, Mons. Deschamps, Choeur
Couplets (Marchande de marée)
Mlle. Cantrelle, Choeur
Rondeau (Certainement j'amais Clairette)
Mons. Juteau
Duo (Pour être fort on se rassemble)
Mons. Juteau, Mlle. M. Aimée
Final (Tu l'as promis, tu chanteras)
Choeur
Chanson (Jadis les rois, race proscrit)
Mlle. M. Aimée, Choeur
Choeur Général (Nous ne devons rien entendre)
Messrs. Duplan, Deschamps, Choeur

ACT 2

Choeur des Merveilleuses (Non personne ne voudra croire)
Mlles. Villiers, Juteau, M. Nardin, Choeur
Couplets (Les soldats d'Augereau sont des hommes)
Mlle. R. Stani, Choeur
Couplets (Gloire au pouvoir exécutif!)
Mons. C. Lecuyer
Couplets (Elle est tellement innocente)
Mons. Deschamps
Duo (Jours fortunés de notre enfance)
Mlles. M. Aimée, R. Stani
Duetto (Voyons, monsieur, raisonnons politique)
Mlle. R. Stani, Mons. Juteau
Quintette (Oui je vous le dit, c'est pour elle)
Mlles. R. Stani, M. Aimée, Messrs. Duchesne, Juteau, Duplan
Choeur des Conjurés (Quand on conspire)
Choeur
Scène (Calmez cette frayeur!)
Mlle. R. Stani
Choeur Général (Fatale destinée)
Choeur
Choeur des Soldats (En avant contre la clique)
Choeur
Scène (Tournez, tournez)
Mlle. R. Stani
Final (Du directeur Barras en moi voyez l'amie)
Mlles. R. Stani, M. Aimée, Mons. Juteau, Choeur

ACT 3

Choeur (Place, place! Sur son passage!)
Choeur
Couplets (Vous aviez fait de la dépense)
Mlle. M. Aimée
Duo (Duo des deux forts)
Messrs. Duchesne, Deschamps
Trio, Couplets et Récitatif (Je trouve mon futur charmant)
Mlle. M. Aimée, Messrs. Deschamps, Duchesne
Duo (Cher ennemi que je devrais haïr)
Mlle. R. Stani, Mons. Juteau
Cavatina (Je ne suis rien qu'un rêveur trop sensible)
Mlle. R. Stani
Final (Ah! ah! ah! ah! le beau secret)
Choeur
Quarreling Duet (Ah! c'est donc toi, Madam' Barras)
Mlles. M. Aimée, R. Stani
Dispute Générale (Ah! j'espère/Laissez faire)
Mlles. M. Aimée, R. Stani, Messrs. Deschamps, Duchesne, Juteau, Chœur

[7]Musical numbers not listed in programs. List prepared from published French-English libretto (Metropolitan Printing and Engraving, New York, 1873).

1873.12 MEPHISTO AND THE FOUR SENSATIONS!

A Grand Classical, Mytholical, Mythical, Allegorical, Paradoxical Extravaganza (Burlesque) in Two Acts, 6 Scenes. Libretto by George Fawcett Rowe. Music composed, arranged and selected from the latest Parisian novelties by W. E. Mallandaine. Director, Alex. Henderson. Scenery by J. A. Johnson and J. R. Wilkins. Costumes by Samuel May of London, designed by Lydia Thompson. Mechanical effects by James Tait. Musical director, William Withers, Jr. Produced by Lydia Thompson and Her Burlesque Company (Samuel Colville, Manager). Opened 25 August 1873 at the Olympic Theatre and closed 10 September 1873 after 20 performances in repertory.

CAST: Immortals: *Pluto*, a revered Monarch, the King of — celebrated in all nations under a variety of names, finally turning up as the modern Mephisto, and the elegant d—l of modern society: LYDIA THOMPSON. *Proserpine*, a young goddess of the antique type, drafted on the fashionable fast young Miss of the period: Ada Beaumont. *Æscalpius*, a very important member of the Plutonian troupe, a flying telegram from the infernal regions, a fac-totum in in Tartarus, retaining in his immaterial state all the *material* bad qualities displayed on earth. "look at his *phiz*, you'll recognize the fat boy." Afterwards transformed into the ring-tailed monkey: WILLIE EDOUIN. *Hermes*, the messenger of the Gods, commissioner from the U.S. to the World's Fair at Vienna, concealing his divine origin and his knowledge of the Greek tongue under the Milesian dialect: W. B. Cahill. *The Belle Hélène*, a lady formerly residing in Greece, a troublesome visitor at Troy, enbalmed in Homer: Augusta Stuart. *Camille*, one of the choicest dishes of that famous cook and novelist, Alex Dumas, highly perfumed, delicately tinted, a butterfly in tissue paper, set to exquisite strains by Verdi: Alice Atherton. *Frou-Frou*, a fashionable specimen of the French school of domestic morality: Tilly Earl. *Geneviève de Brabant*, the last, most fascinating and most impudent musical emanation of the fantastic and creative genius of Mons. Offenbach; the latest addition to Pluto's family circle: Alice Mansfield. *Minerva*, the Goddess of Wisdom, who, finding this commodity of little service amongst the heathen, comes to earth, proprietress of a fashionable boarding school for young ladies, Terms:-$5,000 a Quarter, each pupil will bring her own knife and fork, six bottles of The Bloom of Youth, half a dozen towels and a razor: Harry Taylor. *Rhadamanthus*, a Judge upon the earth, and having passed through the Tombs, retains his dignity in Hades: John Bryer. *Minus*, another judge in the inferior Courts: Madeline Santon. *Æachus*, of whom very little is known: James Barrett. *Asbestos*: Dora Temple. *Cerberus*, Pluto's pet poodle: Major Newell.

Mortals: *Robin Adair*, a dweller in the land of fancy, a disingenuous youth, who has never traveled beyond the bounds of propriety, eager to cull the sweets from every flower, to find at last the bitters lie beneath them: ALMA SANTON. *Sacharissa*, an earthly bonbon, a chocolate caramel, compounded of sugar and simplicity, a dweller in the enchanted artless valley, betrothed to Robin Adair: CAMILLE DUBOIS. *Chloe, Melinda, Aspasia, Thyrsis, Sticphon, Colin, Colon, Comma and other Shepherds and Shepherdesses. Quartette*: John Wray, James Barrett, Herbert A. Cripps, Arthur England Miller.

Act 1, Scene 1: Palace of Pluto. *Scene 2*: The Happy Valley. *Scene 3*: The Enchanted Forest.

Act 2, Scene 1: Schoolroom in Minerva's Academy. *Scene 2*: View of the Kitchen Garden and Back Door. *Scene 3*: Elysian Fields (not in New Jersey), concluding with a Glimpse of the Happy Land.

SPECIALTIES

Laughing Song (Act 1, Scene 3)
Major Newell (Song and Dance/Skatorial Phenomenon)(Act 2, Scene 1)

1873.13 THE BELLES OF THE KITCHEN

A Revival of the Celebrated Dramatic, Vocal, Terpsichorean, Farcical Burlesque Entertainment[8], invented, written, arranged and acted exclusively by the Vokes Family. Opened 10 September 1873 at the Union Square and closed 27 September 1873 after 19 performances; returned 5 January 1874 to Niblo's Garden and closed 24 January 1874 after 24 additional performances, returned 14 February 1874 to Niblo's Garden for 1 performance.[9]

[8]Originally produced in New York 15 April 1872 at the Union Square Theatre for 49 performances. For Synopsis of Scenes and Musical Numbers, see original 1872 production. Accompanied by a curtain-raiser, Wilkins Micawber. No credits in programs for costumes, scenery, musical direction, etc.

[9]Program note: In the course of the piece will be introduced original specimens of Tragedy! Comedy! Opera! Farce! Dance and Song!

CAST: *Lucid Scrubb*, a Lady's Maid, who will appear as Juliet and Premiere Danseuse: JESSIE VOKES. *Mary*, a Housemaid, with an eccentric Dance and Song, and the Recitative and Duo from "Il Trovatore": VICTORIA VOKES. *Barbara*, a Kitchenmaid, the Incarnation of Mischief, full of fun and frolic, with a pas seul and sword exercise: ROSINA VOKES. *Timotheus Gibbs*, a Doctor's Assistant, with a Dance Diabolique, a droll duet from Il Trovatore, and Legs ad libitum: FREDERICK VOKES. *Wiggins*, a Barber, with a rapid gig, and some trouble with Barbara: FAWDON VOKES.

1873.14

SINBAD THE SAILOR!

A Revival of the Traveling Edition of the Oriental Burlesque in Two Act, 8 Scenes. Founded very remotely on "The Arabian Nights." Music by Michael Connelly and William Withers, Jr. (Director, Alex. Henderson.) Scenery by J. A. Johnson and J. R. Wilkins. Costumes by Samuel May of London, designed by Lydia Thompson. Mechanical effects by James Tait. Musical director, William Withers, Jr. Produced by Lydia Thompson and Her Burlesque Company (Samuel Colville, Manager). Opened 11 September 1873 at the Olympic Theatre and closed 20 September 1873 after 12 performances in repertory[10].

CAST: *Sinbad*, surnamed the Sailor, but known to his friends as the Canvas-Back Duck: LYDIA THOMPSON. Assuming various disguises, amongst other introducing her new novelty of *The Dancing Quakers*, in conjunction with HENRY TAYLOR. *Ali El Ektro*, Founder of the only original Dollar Store: WILLIE EDOUIN. *Hafiz*, a young man of the period: CAMILLE DUBOIS. *Selim*, another, fast and a little loose: TILLY EARLE. *The Hadji*, their tutor, an Oriental L. L. D., who like the old Scotch Kings, always carries his Harper with him: W. B. CAHILL. *Kohinoor*, afterwards Bulbul, a scrumptious lady, whom all the young gentlemen of the period would get on the brain—if they had any: ADA BEAUMONT. *The Sultan*, a very much married potentate: ALMA SANTON. *The Gory Pirate of the Archipelago*, a bloodthirsty bandit: John Bryer. *A Fat Believer*: Jacob Thorn. *Alaska Fay*: Augusta Stuart. *Tomidod*: Alice Atherton. *Hinda*: Alice Mansfield. *The Sheriff of Bassorah*: John Wray. *Zulienna*: Madeline Santon. *Zobeide*: Dora Temple. *Chief Eunuch*: Mr. Cripps. *Sing Small*: James Barrett. *(Turkish Citizens, Sailors, Pirates, Ladies of the Harem, Guards, Parisians, Masqueraders, etc.)*

Act 1, Scene 1: A Square in Bassora. *Scene 2*: The Quay of Bassora. *Scene 3*: The Deck of the *Lively Polly*.

Act 2, Scene 1: Diamond Valley of Alaska. *Scene 2*: Corridor in the Sultan's Harem. *Scene 3*: The Marriage Market in Constantinople. *Scene 4*: A Street near the Seraglio. *Scene 5*: Interior of the Sultan's Harem.

SPECIALTIES

Nursery Rhymes (Act 2, Scene 3)Quartette

The Dancing Quakers (Act 2, Scene 3)

Skatorial Phenomenon (Act 2, Scene 5)

1873.15

LA GRANDE-DUCHESSE DE GÉROLSTEIN

A Revival of the Opéra-bouffe in Three Acts[11], in French. Libretto by Henri Meilhac and Ludovic Halévy. Music by Jacques Offenbach. Stage manager, Mons. C. Lecuyer. Musical director, Mons. Charles Van Ghele. Aimée French Opera Bouffe Company (C. A. Chizzola, Director) presented by Augustin Daly. Opened 15 September 1873 at Daly's Broadway Theatre and closed 27 September 1873 in repertory; returned under the auspices of C. A. Chizzola 26 March 1874 to the Lyceum Theatre in repertory, closing 4 April 1874.

CAST:: *Fritz*: Mons. JUTEAU. *General Boum*: Mons. DUCHESNE. *Baron Puck*: Mons. LECUYER. *Prince Paul*: Mons. DESCHAMPS. *Baron Grog*: Mons. JULIEN[12]. *Nepomuc*: Mons. Benedick. *La Grande-Duchesse de Gérolstein*: Mlle. MARIE AIMÉE[13]. *Wanda*: Mlle. MARIE ROLAND. *Iza*: Mme. Sophie Gherzi. *Amelie*: Mlle. Villiers. *Olga*: Mlle. Juteau. *Charlotte*: Mlle. Vandamme. *Maids of Honor, Gentlemen, Pages, Ladies of the Court, Officers and Soldiers.*

[10]For the week 22-27 September 1873 Lydia Thompson and Her Burlesque Company performed a combination program consisting of Act 1 of ALADDIN and Act 2 of SINBAD THE SAILOR.

[11]Previously presented in New York in French 24 September 1867 at the Théâtre Français for 156 performances; in English 17 June 1868 at the New York Theatre for 33 performances. For Synopsis of Scenes and Musical Numbers, see original 1867 production.

[12]For return engagement in March, Baron Grog was played by Mons. SALVATOR.

[13]For return engagement in March, the Grand Duchess was played by ROSINA STANI.

1873.16

LA PÉRICHOLE

A Revival of the Opéra-bouffe in Two Acts[14], in French. Libretto by Ludovic Halévy and Henri Meilhac, based on "Le Carosse du Saint-Sacrament" by Prosper Merimée. Music by Jacques Offenbach. General stage manager, Mons. Lecuyer. Stage manager, Mons. Benedick. Musical director, Mons. Charles Van Ghele. Aimée French Opera Bouffe Company (C. A. Chizzola, Director) presented by Augustin Daly. Opened 17 September 1873 at Daly's Broadway Theatre and closed 27 September 1873 in repertory; returned under the auspices of C. A. Chizzola 28 (matinee) March 1874 to the Lyceum Theatre in repertory, closing 4 April 1874.

CAST: *Piquillo*: Mons. JUTEAU. *Don Andrès de Ribeira*: Mons. DUCHESNE. *Comte de Panatellas*: Mons. LECUYER. *Don Hinoyosa*: Mons. Duplan. *Marquis Tarapote*: Mons. Julien. *La Périchole*: Mlle. MARIE AIMÉE. *Three Cousins*: *Guadalena*: Mlle. Juteau. *Mastilla*: Mlle. Marie Vandame. *Berginella*: Mlle. Sophie Gherzi. *Brambilla*: Mlle. Juteau. *Minetta*: Mlle. Sophie Gherzi. *Mannelita*: Mlle. Villiers. *Frasquinella*: Mlle. Mardie Nardin. *Premiere Notaire*: Mons. Brag. *Deuxieme Notaire*: Mons. Perraut. *Ladies of the Court, Gentlemen, Pages, Bohemians, etc.*

1873.17

ALADDIN/ SINBAD THE SAILOR

Lydia Thompson and Her Burlesque Company in Two Burlesques, consisting of Act 1 of ALADDIN and Act 2 of SINBAD THE SAILOR[15]. Musical director, William Withers, Jr. Produced by Lydia Thompson and Her Burlesque Company (Samuel Colville, Manager). Opened 22 September 1873 at the Olympic Theatre and closed 27 September 1873 after 8 performances in repertory.

ACT 1

CAST: *Aladdin*: LYDIA THOMPSON. *The Sultan*: W. B. CAHILL. *The Vizier*: ALMA SANTON. *Pekoe*: CAMILLE DUBOIS. *Abanazar*: WILLIE EDOUIN. *Te-to-tum*: Madeline Santon. *The Slave of the Lamp*: Tilly Earle. *The Genius of the Ring*: Augusta Stewart. *The Widow Twankay*: HARRY TAYLOR. *Princess Badroulbadour*: ADA BEAUMONT. *Maidens, Mandarins and Mob.*

SPECIALTIES

"Gen d'Arms Duet" (localized from GENEVIEVE DE BRABANT)
L. Thompson, H. Taylor

Grotesque Dane and Specialties
W. Edouin

Solo Songs
A. Beaumont, C. Dubois

"Kiss Song" (requested)
L. Thompson

Concerted Music
Company

Nursery Rhymes

The Dancing Quakers

Skatorial Phenomenon (Song and Dance upon Parlor Skates)

1873.18

MME. ANGOT'S CHILD!

An Opéra-comique in Three Acts[16]. Original French libretto, "La Fille de Madame Angot" by Clairville, Paul Siraudin and Victor Koning. English adaptation by Henry J. Byron. Music by Charles Lecocq. Stage director, W. H. Crane. Scenery by J. A. Johnson. Mechanical effects by James Carson. Mechanical effects by James Tait. Musical director, Frank A. Howson. Produced by Mrs. James A. Oates Comic Opera Company (Manager, Tracy W. Titus). Opened 29 September 1873 at the Olympic Theatre and closed 11 October 1873 after 16 performances.

CAST: *Clairette Angot*: Mrs. JAMES [Alice] OATES. *Mlle. Lange*: ANNIE KEMP BOWLER. *Amaranthe*: NELLIE LARKELLE. *Hersilie*: Tracy White. *Ange Pitou*: W.

[14]First produced in New York in French 4 January 1869 at Pike's Opera House. For Synopsis of Scenes and Musical Numbers, see original 1869 production. In Act 2, Mlle. Aimée will sing the "Aimée Waltz" composed by Mons. Charles Van Ghele.

[15] Cast and credits for SINBAD as detailed above. No credits for ALADDIN with regard to authorship, scenery, costumes, music, etc.

[16]This was its New York English language premiere; previously produced in New York in French 25 August 1873 at the Broadway Theatre in repertory.

HAYDON TILLA. *Larivaudière*: W. H. Woodfield. *Trenitz*: J. H. Jones. *Cadet*: J. Haywood. *Captain of the Guard*: William Duane. *Javotte*: Pauline Merritt. *Babet*: Miss T. Vincinia. *Manon*: Miss C. LaGrassa. *Thérèse*: Adele Wood. *Pomponnet*: W. H. CRANE. *Louchard*: Edward Horan. *Guillaume*: J. Williams. *Butueux*: H. Brown. *Incredible*: H. Caldwell. *Mons. Laroux*: M. S. Lane. *Soldiers, Conspirators, Gendarmes, Citizens.*

Act 1: Market Place in Belville.

Act 2: Apartments of Mlle. Lange, the female friend of the Directory.

Act 3: Garden at Belleville.

1873.19 MAX! THE MERRY SWISS BOY

A Musical Romantic Drama in Three Acts, 5 Scenes. Play by Henry J. Byron. Songs composed and selected by Joseph K. Emmet. Stage manager, George F. Devere. Scenery by Joseph De La Harpe. Produced by Joseph K. Emmet. Opened 6 October 1873 at the Broadway Theatre and closed 20 October 1873 after 15 performances.

CAST: *Max*, Mme. Barbette's adopted son: JOSEPH K. EMMET. *Chevalier Rockleigh*, an adventurer: George F. DeVere. *General Graham*, traveling on the continent: G. H. GRIFFITHS. *Bruno*, a ne'r do well: D'Orsay Ogden. *Berthold*, with the story of the Lion of Lucerne: Martin Golden. *Schlopphausen*, an old guide and innkeeper: J. G. Peakes. *Lieutenant Herman*: George Gilbert. *Julius*, General Graham's colored servant: F. Curtis. *Hans*, a servant: G. E. Sands. *Little Yosie*, Max's pet: Carrie Boschell. *Mme. Barbette*, keeper of the Mountain Inn: ANNIE DELAND. *Carline*, her daughter: Minne Walton. *Amy Graham*, the General's niece: Rosa St. Clair. *Minna*: Miss E. Wood. *Fruitsellers, Peasants, Soldiers, Flower Girls, etc.*

Act 1: Alpine Village.

Act 2: Alpine Village, morning, early spring.

Act 3, Scene 1: The Ruined Arches. *Scene 2*: The Road near Schlopphausen's Inn. *Scene 3*: The Eagle's Nest.

ACT 1

"I Come! I Come!"

"I Love the Little Babies"

"Wenk"
(*Music by* Joseph K. Emmet.)

"Wake Out!" (Serenade)
(*Music by* Joseph K. Emmet.)

ACT 2

"Sour Krout" (with banjo)

"Oh, a Jolly Good Time We Have! Oh, Yes, Das So"
(*Music by* Joseph K. Emmet.)

ACT 3

Scene 1

Max's Entertainment
J. K. Emmet

"Come Buy My Flowers"; "Climb Up, Climb Up"; "Who Wants Some Milka"; "Shonnie Vas a Nice Young Man"; "Oh, Joe, Hand Around the Beer."

Scene 3

"That's Where the Laugh Comes In!" (Finale—Song)

1873.20 ARRAH-NA-BROGUE!

A Beautiful Dramatic Burlesque (of the drama Arrah-na-pogue by Dion Boucicault and E. H. House) in One Act, 7 Scenes, preceded by an Olio. Play by John F. Poole. New music by David Braham. Scenery by R. L. Weed. Machinery and effects, Nelse Waldron. Stage manager, G. L. Stout. Orchestra director, David Braham. Produced by Josh Hart. Opened 13 October 1873 at the Theatre Comique and closed 18 October 1878 after 8 performances.

Olio: The Haunted Wig-maker, a laughable sketch with John Wild, James Bardley, J. A. Graver. The Comical Clowns, the Three Jackley Brothers. Serio-Comic Songs, Mrs. John Wild. Beautiful Negro Specialty, After the War!, by (Edward) Harrigan and (Tony) Hart. Beautiful Character Dance, Miss Kitty O'Neill. John Wild's Laughable Interlude, The Trial Dance, with John Wild, J. Bradley, R. Hall. Little Jennie Yeamans, the Child Artiste, in her Character Songs and Changes. Blood Will Tell, a laughable sketch, with Edward Harrigan, Tony Hart, John Wild, James Bradley. The Great Jackley Family in their beautiful act, Elfengeister!, by the Jackley Troupe (11 in number).

ARRAH-NA-BROGUE! CAST: *Shawn* the Wicked Low Postman: FRANK KERNS. *Beamish McCoul*: J. S. CROSSEN. *Mickey Feeney*: Edward Harrigan. *Kernel Mac O'Grady*: D. A. Kelley. *Major Coughing*: G. L. Stout. *Sergeant Slashcutansaberem*: John Wild. *Andy Geoghegan*: G. Lewis. *Danny Grogan*: James Bradley. *Jimmy Garregan*: R. Hall. *Arrah Musha Meelish*: Mrs. John Wild. *Fanny Be the Powers*: Marie Gorenflo. *Mollie Malone*: Kitty O'Neil. *Katy Kilroy*: Tony Hart. *Peasantry, Soldiery and such like.*

Scene 1: A view anywhere in Ireland, with the humble but virtuous cabin of Arrah. *Scene 2*: O'Grady's Front Parlor. *Scene 3*: The Barn Bedad. *Scene 4*: The Prison. *Scene 5*: The Court. *Scene 6*: Cell in the Prison. *Scene 7*: The Ivy Green Tower.

MUSICAL NUMBERS, SPECIALTIES

"All Among the Hay" (Scene 3)

Irish Sports and Pastimes (Scene 3)

Songs, Dances and Diversions (Scene 3)

"The Wearing of the Green" (Scene 3)

Barn Door Reel (Scene 3)
T. Hart, J. Bradley

Grand Procession of Three (Scene 4)

1873.21 THE GRAND DUCHESS

A Revival of the Opéra-bouffe in Three Acts[17]. Original French libretto by Henri Meilhac and Ludovic Halévy. Music by Jacques Offenbach. Stage director, W. H. Crane. Musical director, Frank A. Howson. Produced by Mrs. James A. Oates Comic Opera Company (Manager, Tracy W. Titus). Opened 13 October 1873 at the Olympic Theatre and closed 18 October 1873 after 8 performances in repertory.[18]

CAST: *The Grand Duchess*: Mrs. JAMES [Alice] OATES. *Wanda*: NELLIE LARKELLE. *Fritz*, a Soldier: W. HAYDON TILLA. *General Boum*: W. H. CRANE. *Baron Puck*: J. H. Jones. *Prince Paul*: W. H. Woodfield. *Nepomuc*: H. H. Pratt. *Baron Grog*: Edward Horan. *Olga*: Pauline Merritt. *Iza*: Miss L. Cornell. *Charlotte*: Miss G. Caldwell. *Amelia*: Tracy White. *Soldiers of the Grand Duchess' Army, Vivandières, Ladies of the Courrt, etc.*

1873.22 THE CROOK, or, The Hunchback of Not-er-dam

A New and Original Copyright Burlesque in One Act, 6 Scenes, preceded by an Olio. Play by John F. Poole. New music by David Braham. Scenery by R. L. Weed. Machinery and effects, Nelse Waldron. Stage manager, G. L. Stout. Orchestra director, David Braham. Produced by Josh Hart. Opened 20 October 1873 and closed 25 October 1878 after 8 performances.

Olio: Smoked Out, a laughable sketch by J. C. Stewart, with J. C. Stewart, R. M. Hall, D. A. Kelly, G. L. Stout, J. A. Graver, James Bradley. Serio-Comic songs by baby McDonneld. Ricardo Freary and Nellie Steel in a variety of comic duets and sketches. Beautiful character dance by Miss Kitty O'Neil. Mr. Harry Monroe, the gifted comic vocalist. Eh! What Is It?, a laughable sketch by J. C. Stewart, with J. C. Stewart, John Wild, J. A. Graver, D. A. Kelley, G. L. Stout, James Bradley. Jennie Yeamans in her character songs. (Edward) Harrigan and (Tony) Hart in their very laughable and original sketch, The Mulligan Guards! Mr. James M'Donald, in his entirely new act, Dancing on Skates on a High Pedestal. Miss Grace Harris in her repertoire of serio-comic songs.

THE CROOK CAST: *Quasimodo Hertzog*, the Crook of Not-er-dam: D. A. KELLY. *Zamiel*, a Mephistophelian Character, a Devil of a Fellow, of a Satanical Cast of Character, the sort of fiend we read about but seldom see: J. S. CROSSEN. *Claude Frollo*, Count of Wolfenstein, an Intolerable Bore, represented as bad as he can possibly be: EDWARD HARRIGAN. *Ernest*, now this is a fellow we'd like to say something about, but, it is unnecessary, He speaks for himself: FRANK KERNS. *Wolfgar*, this individual would be a very contemptible creature if it were not for the fact that he is introduced: TONY HART. *Grippo*, the poorly paid servant of Quasimodo Hertzog, who would starve to death were it not for the very liberal salary paid to the author of his being, viz.: JOHN WILD. *Pierre Gringoire*, the Poet, with nothing to say and a very good job too: James Bradley. *Clopin*, another inmate of the Deaf and Dumb Asylum: J. A. Graver. *Dragonfin*, a very respectable local demon: J. Lewis. *Casper*, a Desperate and Determined Free Lunch Fiend: A. Martin. *Rodolfe*, sometimes, but not very often called Captain Phoebus Chateaupiers, but why, no one has the slightest idea,—very handsome, very lively and very musical, very interesting: JOHN WILD. *Esmeralda*, the Dancing Girl, who, by the way, don't dance in the piece, a Mysterious Creature, as she sings "Don't get this confounded with Mysterious Screecher," as it would be doing a great injustice to: Miss JENNIE HUGHES. *Carlina*, Sweet Carlina, an amiable Creature, bodily transported from one Crook to serve in another: JENNIE SATTERLEE. *Stalacta*, a gentle persecuted being, accidentally strayed away from West Flushing and in danger in the city: KITTY O'NEIL.

[17]First produced in New York in French 24 September 1867 at the Théâtre Français; in English 17 June 1868 at the New York Theatre.

[18]No credits in programs for English adaptation, scenery or costumes.

THE NEW CROOK BALLET!: *Premiere Danseuse Assoluta*: Mlle. J. C. Stuartine. [J. C. STEWART]. *Danseuse Première*: Mlle. Frankini Kersini [FRANK KERNS]. *Danseuse Premiere*: Signoriana Johnena Wildano [JOHN WILD]. *Danseuse Premiere*: Senora Eduetta Harrigano [EDWARD HARRIGAN]. *Danseuse Secunda*: Mlle. Toni Hartini [TONY HART]. *Danseuse Secunda*: Mlle. Stevena Rogerini. *Danseuse Secunda*: Fraulein Andea McKeelero. *Premiere Coryphée*: Mlle. Angela Stoutella [G. L. STOUT]. *Premiere Coryphée*: Senoretta Jamaisa Bradleie [JAMES BRADLEY]. *Girls in the Second Row*: Mlles. Maguire, Ryan, Donovan, O'Reilly, Macarthy, Dusenheimer, Schwartzhockler, Maginness.

Scene 1: Wood of Not-er-dam near the Drachenfels, County Cork, Bohemia. *Scene 2*: Rue de Elizabeth. *Scene 3*: Castle of Count Wolfenstein. *Scene 4*: Plaza del Destino-Mullingar. *Scene 5*: View on the Banks of that lone river. *Scene 6*: Grotto of Satalacta.

MUSICAL NUMBERS, SPECIALTIES

Grand Incantation Scene (Scene 1)

The Very-Mad-Regal Boys (Scene 3)

Revel of the Sirens; Wine, Woman, War, Wittles, and such like. (Scene 6)

The Hartini Ballet Troupe (Scene 6)

Fangois, the world-renowned Egyptian juggler, will perform his wonderful feats (Scene 6)

1873.23 MONSIEUR CHOUFLEURI!

A Revival of the Comic Opera (Opérette-bouffe) in One Act[19]. (Original French libretto by Duc de Morny and friends.) Music by Jacques Offenbach. Stage director, W. H. Crane. Musical director, Frank A. Howson. Produced by Mrs. James A. Oates' Comic Opera Company (Manager, Tracy W. Titus). Opened 20 October 1873 at the Olympic Theatre and closed 25 October 1873 after 8 performances.[20]

CAST: *Ernestine*, a School-Girl: MRS. JAMES [Alice] OATES. *Monsieur Choufleuri*: H. T. ALLEN. *Chrysodule Babylas*, in love with Ernestine: W. HAYDON TILLA. *Peterman*, a Dutch servant: W. H. CRANE. *Mons. Balandard*, a wealthy retired banker: J. H. JONES. *Mons. Busterman*: Edward Horan. *Mme. Balandard*: Nellie Allen. *Mme. Busterman*: Adele Wood.

1873.24 FRITZ, OUR COUSIN GERMAN!

A Revival of the Popular Drama in Three Acts, 7 Scenes.[21] Play by Charles Gayler. Stage manager, George F. DeVere. [Produced by J. K. Emmet.] Opened 21 October 1873 at Daly's Broadway Theatre and closed 1 November 1873 after 13 performances.

CAST: *Max*, Our Cousin German: JOSEPH K. EMMET. *Colonel Grafton*, Chief of a Gang of Counterfeiters: GEORGE GRIFFITHS. *Phil Bobbit*, Keeper of a concert saloon: D'ORSAY OGDEN. *Jem Smasher*, *Archie Bloker*, emigrant runners: Frank Curtis, J. Taylor. *Adolphus Jenkins*, a Henglish Hartist, you know: JOHN W. JENNINGS. *Judge Griffin*, a Justice: MARTIN GOLDEN. *Lawyer Grimm*: James G. Peakes. *Jacob Callout*, Clerk of Court: George Gilbert. *Macky Floy*, from the Ould Sod: C. W. Kemble. *Flint*, a Detective: J. W. Gogin. *Katrina*, a young Fraulein: MINNE WALTON. *Moppy*, an object of interest: BELLA GOLDEN. *Devotées of Terpsichore and Apollo in the popular establishment of Bobbit (5)*: *Pauline*: Miss E. Griffiths. *Angelina*: Cora Cassidy. *Marie*: Miss Costignero. *Julie*: Miss Clark. *LaBelle*: Miss Hopgood. *Judy Roche*, an Apple Seller: Miss E. Wood. *Little Fritz*, Son of Fritz and Katrina: Miss Ella Pet. *Emigrants, Runners, Bummers, Citizens.*

Act 1, Scene 1: A View of the Bay of New York. *Scene 2*: Fritz in search of Katrina. *Scene 3*: The sanctum of Phil Bobbit's nice little establishment.

Act 2, Scene 1: Katrina's place of refuge. *Scene 2*: Justice Griffin's Court Room. *Scene 3*: The Grand International Concert Hall.

Act 3: The Home of Fritz, the Happy Miller.

SPECIALTIES

Fritz's Original Character Burlesque, popular songs and dances, solo on the mouth harmonicon (Act 2, Scene 3)
J. K. Emmet

"Oh, Schneider, How You Was!" (Act 3)
J. K. Emmet

1873.25 ROUND THE CLOCK, or, New York by Dark

A Revival of the Popular Spectacular Local Sensational Folly in Three Acts, 11 Scenes[22]. Play by Augustin Daly. (Based on a French farce "La Tour de Cadran" by Hector Crémieux and H. Bocage.) Produced by Augustin Daly. Opened 27 October 1873 at the Grand Opera House and closed 8 November 1873 after 14 performances.

CAST: *Roderick Killgobbin*, Esq., a person of many disguises and shrewd surmises—in fact a man of wax and whacks—easily kneaded and often needed; afterwards assuming the disguise of "A Plug Ugly," "A Bill Sticker," etc.: FRANK HARDENBERG. *Ernesta Hardacre*, having been "born under a cabbage," is naturally green: ADELAIDE LENNOX. *Abraham Hardacre*, a wheedler: CHARLES LECLERQ. *Lawyer Goddigotta* subject for the Bar Association; afterwards assuming the disguise of "A Target" and "Mr. G. L. Fox": G. L. FOX. *Joey Lillyburn*, an innocent from Boston: Mrs. C. M. WALCOT. *Peter Dodd*, a dyer—likewise a dire deceiver; afterwards assuming the disguise of "Harlequin": M. A. Kennedy. *Mrs. Peter Dodd*, the wife of the dyer and victim of the deceiver: Marguerite Chambers. *Mr. Mutton*, of Essex Market: Cyril Searle. *Alderman Dooley*, a newly elected gentleman, with privileges behind the scenes: M. D. Bebus. *Borrowed from the Olympic Theatre, expressly for this play (5)*: *The Manager*: J. H. Howland. *The Machinist*: Tait Herbert. *The Property Man*: Mr. Cutler. *The Call Boy*: Fred. *Mlle. Sangali*: Agnes Lee. *Ladies of the Ballet, Figurantes, Demons, Audiences, etc.*

Harry Hill, a popular gentleman: Mr. Manley. *Jim Kelly*, Champion of Feather Weight, Boston: Himself. *Young Burk*, another: Himself. *Mike Coburn*: Himself. *Ned Mallahan*: Himself. *Visitors at Harry Hill's, Waiter, Girls, etc. Roundsman Laffery*: Mr. Hamilton. *The Pyrotechnist at Lion Park*: Mr. Enos. *Smack*, a servant: Mr. Sullivan. *Rascal Sue*, a sketch from nature: Mary Carr. *Rose*, the tartseller's clerk: Tilly Mitchell. *Mrs. Bowlit*, *Mrs. Impey*, relations: Jennie Clarke, Julia Bell. *Juliana Tartar*, the pretty baker of tarts and pies and ready maker of tart replies; afterwards assuming the disguise of "Columbine" and "Philadelphia Charley": FANNY HEYWOOD.

Act 1: The Reading of the Will. *Scene 1*: The Library in the Residence of the departed Millionaire. One o'clock. *Scene 2*: The Grand Union Depot. Three o'clock. *Scene 3*: Mrs. Tartar's Confectionary and Ice Cream Bazaar in Grand Street.

Act 2: The Revelries of the Night. *Scene 1*: Moonlight Dance at Lion Park. Eight o'clock. *Scene 2*: In front of Harry Hill's. *Scene 3*: At Harry Hill's. Nine o'clock. *Scene 4*: Behind the scenes of the Olympic on a Humpty Dumpty night. Ten o'clock. *Scene 5*: Interior of the Olympic Stage.

Act 3: The Dangers of the Night. *Scene 1*: Donovan's Alley in the Five Points during a snow storm. Eleven o'clock. *Scene 2*: The Courtyard of Daddy Hardacre. Twelve o'clock. *Scene 3*: A glance at The Black Crook and its transformation scene!

1873.26 HUMPTY DUMPTY ABROAD!

A New Grand Trick Pantomime in Three Acts, 13 Scenes. Play by George L. Fox. Music by L. Strebinger. (Staged by Augustin Daly.) Ballet dances by M. E. Kiralfy. Scenery by George Heister, Charles W. Witham, Louis Duflocq, Joseph De La Harpe, L. W. Seavey. Machinery by Thomas J. Kelly. Tricks and properties by Robert J. Cutler. Costumes by Miss M. Finchette. Produced by Augustin Daly. Opened 24 November 1873 at the Grand Opera House and closed 7 February 1874 after 80 performances.

CAST: Opening: *Fairy Badtemper*: Miss ROBERTO NORWOOD. *Spirit of the Pastures*: AGNES LEE. *Oldfyle*, a magician: J. H. HOWLAND. *Docillion*, his son, the owner of the Magic Watch: FANNY HAYWARD. *Humpty Dumpty*, an original: GEORGE L. FOX. *Old One-Two*, "Buckle My Shoe," his great Grand-Uncle: CHARLES K. FOX. *Peter*, a salt-petre of a Sailor: W. H. HAMILTON. *Thomas*, a peasant: Mr. A. G. Enos. *Belline*, the village belle: ADELAIDE LENNOX. *The Princess Admiranda*: IDA TERRANCE.

The Hours (12): *The Hour of Labor*: Marguerite Chambers. *The Hour of Dinner*: Virginia Stewart. *The Hour of Play*: Miss A. Munroe. *The Hour of Rest*: Miss M. Foley. *The Hour of Sleep*: Carrie Hassleberger. *The Hour of Waking*: Tilly Lurch. *The Hour of Dreams*: Miss M. Farrell. *The Hour of the Ball*: Ida Bell. *The Hour of Midnight*: Cora Cassidy. *The Hour of Dawn*: Miss N. Broze. *The Hour of Prayer*: Miss E. Wood. *The Hour of Temptation*: Maggie Brunelle.

Pantomime: *Chwang-Yu-Wang*, Emperor of China: C. MANLY. *Prince Che-Hwang-Te*, his son: J. H. HOWLAND. *How-Chou*, Grand Vizier: R. Sullivan. *Shin Pan-Seen*, Mandarin of the red button: C. Welling. *Yan-Keen*, Mandarin of the yellow button: J. W. Freeth. *Ying-Tsung*, Mandarin of the blue button: A. Welling. *Ching-Te*, Mandarin of the green button: William Welling. *Tei-Tei*, *Kung-Ye*, fan bearers to the Emperor:

[19]First produced in New York in its original French 20 February 1869 at the Grand Opera House for 1 performance in repertory. This English adaptation previously produced in New York 21 June 1872 at the Union Square Theatre by Mrs. Oates for 7 performances as The Prima Donna For A Night. This revival was accompanied by a fore-piece, a farce 'Alarming Sacrifice!.

[20]English adaptation uncredited in programs; no credits for scenery or costumes.

[21]First produced in New York 11 July 1820 at Niblo's garden for 63 performances.

[22]First produced in New York 25 November 1872 at the Grand Opera House for 57 performances. For Synopsis of Scenes and Musical Numbers, see original 1872 production. During the Harry Hill scene, the celebrated California Quartette will appear and sing one of their glees.

Misses Sarah Wallis, Hannah Johnson. *Mung-Teen*, officer of the guard: Mr. H. Thompson. *Tradesmen (3)*: *Ching-Ring*: J. Harris. *Ching-San-Yan*: W. Townsend. *Ching-Wang*: George Topack. *The Widow Sa-Yang-Fu*: Susanna Leigh. *Elves of the burning forest (4)*: *Torchianibus*: J. Brad. *Firebrandibus*: W. Morton. *Steamuppibus*: H. Golden. *Sindereibus*: L. Watson. *Iceberg, Snowstorm*: Natives of the Frigid Zone: Messrs. A. Matthews, Charles Wareham. *Gabriotto*, proprietor of the vineyard: W. H. Mason. *Sergeant Bravelino*, full of bravery and liquor: John Wilson. *Italian Peasants (3)*: *Vincolo*: Harry Knowles. *Gonasaloo*: George Sloan. *Popolino*: S. Hibbard. *Francisca*, daughter of Gabriotto: JENNIE ROGERS. *Wretchedcattiferus*, the Brigand Chief: W. H. HAMILTON. *Brigands with many more (3)*: *Miserablazeo*: K. Kelly. *Coward Hooketo*: S. Shaw. *Whitefeatherino*: T. Weeks. *Sketch*, a poor artiste: C. Coal. *Moneypenny*, a landlord: Mr. Pinch. *Fitzjamesmakeup*, a gent of the Period: J. Howland. *Scrubbing girls (5)*: *Susan*: Miss Kettell. *Polly*: Miss Williams. *Bridget*: Miss Robinson. *Mary Ann*: Miss Wattell. *Jane*: Miss —. *Jack of Clubs*, a policeman always to be found: A. G. Enos. *Smiling Johnny*, of the eating house: P. Balls. *Professor Quills* of the writing academy: Mr. Goldpen. *Gutter*, a street sweeper: Mr. Snipe. *Wicks*, a lamplighter: Mr. Lightning.

Ballets: Misses BETTY AND EMILIE RIGL, Misses Bertha, Lavigne, Verand, Kelsey, Flora Lee Smith, Cook, Hurd, Ross, Bogard Sisters, Esta, White, Hadley, Corps de Ballet. *Specialties*: Martens Family Tyroliennes, the Jackley Troupe, Herr Karl Lind, the California Quarette.

Act 1, Scene 1: Subterraneous Cave of the Fairy Badtemper. (Heister.) *Scene 2*: The Golden Valley. The Cottage of Humpty and Belline. (Duflocq.) *Scene 3*: The Palace of Instruments in the Isle of Harmonie.

Act 2, Scene 1: Celestial Empire. China. (Heister.) *Scene 2*: Outskirts of the City. (Heister.) *Scene 3*: Sunny Italy. Vineyard and View of Naples. (Heister.) Panorama of the Burning Forest—and the North Pole, arriving at the Bay of New York. The Ocean Yacht Race.

Act 3, Scene 1: Painter's Studio, New York. (Seavey.) *Scene 2*: Chamber. (Seavey.) *Scene 3*: Dining Rooms and Writing Academy. (Seavey.) *Scene 4*: Elevated Railroad. (Seavey.) *Scene 5*: Street in Aniplace. (Seavey.) *Scene 6*: Interior of a Boarding House. (Seavey.) *Scene 7*: A Dark and Hideous Glen. (Seavey.) Grand Transformation.

ACT 1

Scene 2

- Duet
  - A. Lennox, F. Heyward
- Wedding Party and Chorus

Scene 3

- Ballet of the Charivari and Instruments
  - (*Designed and arranged by* Mme. Kiralfy)
  - Mlles. B. Rigl, E. Rigl, Misses Bertha, Lavigne, Verand, Kelsey, Flora Lee Smith, Cook, Hurd, Ross, Bogard Sisters, Esta, White, Hadley, Full Corps de Ballet
- The Music Bells
  - 8 Coryphées
- Entree, Pas de Deux
  - Rigl Sisters
- Les Mandolines Animées
  - 8 Coryphées
- Grand Variation
- Grand Finale Charivari
- Herr Karl Lind (Specialty)
- Grand Transformation:
  - *Clown*: G. L. Fox. *Pantaloon*: C. K. Fox. *Harlequin*: K. Lind. *Columbine*: E. Rigl.

ACT 2

Scene 1

- La Fête de Peking (Grand Chinese Divertissement de Danse)
  - (*Designed and arranged by* Mme. Kiralfy)
- Ching Chang
  - Corps de Ballet, Coryphées
- A-O Ping Long
- 8 Native Ladies
- The Pearl of Hong Kong
  - B. Rigl
- Piramide Dances
  - Jackley Troupe, Corps de Ballet
- Grand Brilliant Illuminated Finale/Lantern Festival
  - Entire Ballet Corps

Scene 3

- Italian National Divertissement
  - Coryphées, Corps de Ballet
  - (*Designed and arranged by* Mme. Kiralfy)

ACT 3

Scene 4

- Specialty Acts
- Jackley Family

Scene 7

- Grand Transformation
- The Realm of the Hours
- Martens in their "Cat Duet"
- California Quartette in a program of favorite selections

IXION!

1873.27 or, the Man at the Wheel

A Revival of the Musical Burlesque in One Act, 6 Scenes[23], preceded by an Olio. Play by John F. Poole. New music by David Braham. Scenery designed by R. L. Weed. Properties and Machinery by Nelse Waldron. Musical director, David Braham. Produced by Josh Hart. Opened 1 December 1873 at the Theatre Comique and closed 6 December 1873 after 8 performances in repertory.

Olio: Vinegar Bitters!, a new Ethiopian sketch with J. A. Graver, Charles White, John Wild, J. S. Crossen, G. L. Stout, R. Hall, J. Bradley. Banjo Solo and Song, Little Jennie Yeamans. Beautiful Character Dance, Miss Kitty O'Neil. Irish Hearts, a sketch by Edward Harrigan, with Edward Harrigan, Jennie Hughes. Miss Sophie Elma will sing a collection of new and favorite ballads. The McFadden Family, an Irish sketch, with R. M. Carroll, in new and original songs and dances. Mr. Eph Horn in his original Ethiopian Specialties. Serio-Comic Songs by Miss Jennie Hughes. New and Original Collection of Comic Song by Edward Harrigan. Mr. Tom Harper, the wonderful one-legged dancer, will perform his Essence of Old Virginia.

CAST: *Ixion*, an ex-King in distress, invited by Jupiter to visit the Skies by Jove, and taken up by Jingo: Miss SOPHIE WORRELL. *Venus*, the Goddess of Beauty, a Lady-like Goddess: Miss Jennie Hughes. *Mercury*, Jove's Messenger, a Celestial Telegraph Boy, a Fast Young Man: Miss IRENE WORRELL. *Jupiter*, King of Olympus, a Musical Monarch: Miss JENNIE SATTERLEE. *Cupid*, Son of Venus, dressed a little more than the Cupids we usually see on Valentines: Mrs. JOHN WILD. *Apollo*, Jupiter's private secretary: Miss KITTIE O'NEIL. *Juno*, Queen of the Gods, Jupiter's better half, a perfect lady in every respect: Miss MARIE GORENFLO. *Minerva*, an intensely and immensely strong-minded woman, the impersonified embodiment of Lucy Stone, Susan B. Anthony, Horace Greeley, Harriet Beecher-Stowe, Victoria C. Woodhull, and other advocates and defenders of woman's rights and woman's wrongs: Mr. HARRY PRATT. *Mars*, God of War, the Idol of the M.G.: Mr. J. F. Crosson. *Bacchus*, Head Centre of the Celestial Whiskey Ring and opposed to the Excise Law: Mr. EDWARD HARRIGAN. *Ganymede*, the Original Active Boy, Special Messenger, and Man of All Work: Mr. JOHN WILD.

Thrice Diabolical Conspirators from the Fourteenth Ward (4): *Tonomorrowbones*: Mr. Charley White. *Paddesoker*: James Bradley. *Prosperus*: J. A. Graver. *That Young Grecian*: Mr. R. Hall. *Calliope*: Miss Emma Moore. *Melpomene*: Miss Minnie Lewis. *Polyhymnia*: Lilly Brice. *Mortals, Immortals, Greeks, Grecians, and other Greenhorns*: Much enlightened Supernumeraries.

Scene 1: A Dark Wood near the Kingdom of Ixion. *Scene 2*: The Exterior of Bacchus' Saloon in the Sky. *Scene 3*: Juno's Reception Hall in the Kingdom of Jupiter. *Scene 4*: The Head Centre of the Sun. *Scene 5*: Exterior of Juno's Chamber in the Sky. *Scene 6*: The Halls of Jupiter.

1873.28 THE CHILDREN IN THE WOOD

A Dramatic, Musical, Comical, Fairy Spectacular Extravaganza in a Prologue and Three Acts, 7 Scenes. Play by E. L. Blanchard. Songs composed and arranged by W. C. Levy. Entire spectacle produced under the immediate supervision of Frederick Vokes. Overture and ballet music by Michael Connelly. Scenery by William Voegtlin. Properties, tricks and changes by W. Henry, William Deverna. Costumes by Mr. and Mrs. Vokes. Machinery by John Leo. Illuminations by John Weatherspoon. Ballets and incidental dances arranged by Frederick and Fawdon Vokes. Produced by Henry Jarrett and Harry Palmer. Opened 8 December 1873 at Niblo's Garden and closed 3 January 1874 after 28 performances.

CAST: Prologue: *Columbia*: BESSIE SUDLOW. *Old Father Time*: E. K. COLLIER. *Day*: Annie Wilton. *Week*: Grace Vernon. *Month*: Fannie Lee. *The Twelve Hours*: A dozen Misses of Sweet Sixteen. *Cupid*: Aggie Thorpe. *Invention*: Aggie Thorpe.

---

[23]First produced in New York in another version by F C Burnand, 28 September 1868 at Wood's Museum for 120 performances in 2 engagements.

The Play: *Sir Rowland*, the cruel uncle: FREDERICK VOKES. *Master William*, his nephew: VICTORIA VOKES. *Miss Mary*, his niece: ROSINA VOKES. *Winifred*, the nursery governess: JESSIE VOKES. *Geoffrey*: FAWDON VOKES. *Rufus*, the Ruffian: W. B. CAHILL. *Walter*, the woodman: CHARLES COLLINS. *Gabriel Greybeard*, the Steward: J. W. Brutone. *Queen Mab*: BESSIE SUDLOW. *Cooks, Servants, Retainers, Guards, etc. Ballet*: Mlle. MARIE BONFANTI (Premiere Danseuse Assolute), Coryphées, Corps de Ballet. *Specialties*: The London Madrigal Boys.

Prologue: The Abode of Father Time.

Act 1, Scene 1: Magpie Hall and Grounds by Sunset. *Scene 2*: The Ivory Gate of Dreams leading to the Dominion of Queen Mab.

Act 2, Scene 1: Breakfast Parlor in Magpie Hall. *Scene 2*: Fox-Glove Dell, on Skirts of the Forest. *Scene 3*: The Depths of the Forest.

Act 3: The Bat's Cave. Splendid Transformation Scene to the Home of Queen Mab.

PROLOGUE
"Vicar of Bray" (Song)
E. K. Collier

ACT 1
Scene 1
"Mother Says I Mustn't" (Duet)
V. Vokes, R. Vokes
"Makes Me So Awfully Wild" (Trio)
C. Collins, V. Vokes, R. Vokes
Quartette
F. Vokes, F. Vokes, R. Vokes, V. Vokes
Scene 2
"Harp in the Air" (Song)
B. Sudlow
"Beautiful Dreams" (Song)
V. Vokes
Tableau of Nursery Legends:
Cinderella, Jack the Giant Killer, Blue Beard, Little Red Riding Hood, Aladdin, Puss in Boots, Four and Twenty Black Birds, Old Woman who lived in a shoe.
Scene 3
Gossamer Dreams (Grand Ballet)
Mlle. M. Bonfanti, Coryphées, Corps de Ballet

ACT 2
Scene 1
"Bold Vicious Man" (Duet)
F. Vokes, W. B. Cahill
"I Am So Volatile" (Concerted Song)
V. Vokes, R. Vokes, J. Vokes, F. Vokes, W. B. Cahill
Scene 2
"The Gypsey Tent" (Original Song and Chorus)
London Madrigal Boys
"The Terrible Man" (Song)
W. B. Cahill
"The Pretty Pair" (Song)
C. Collins
Duet
V. Vokes, R. Vokes
Scene 3
The Gathering of the Birds and the Squirrels
The Fall of the Leaf! (Grand Ballet)
Mlle. M. Bonfanti, Coryphées, Corps de Ballet

ACT 3
Transformation Scene

1873.29 GABRIEL GRUB; or, The Story of the Goblins Who Stole the Sexton!

A Fantastical, Farcical, Demoniacal, Comical, Musical, Legendary and Terpsichorean Imagination in a Prologue, Two Acts, 4 Scenes[24]. Adapted to the stage from Charles Dickens' legend of the same name by the Majilton and Raynor families. Dialogue by Fred Lyster. Music by David Braham. Musical conductor, F. Rochow. Produced by George H. Tyler. Opened 22 December 1873 at the Olympic Theatre and closed 17 January 1874 after 34 performances.

CAST:: *The Mysterious Stranger*: EMMA LEWIS. *Polly Dark*, the Sexton's daughter, with two strings to her bow: MARIE MAJILTON. *Polly Grub*, her visionary prototype: MARIE MAJILTON. *Melusine*, Queen of Pandemonium: MARIE MAJILTON. *Thunderbolt*, an Electric Imp: MARIE MAJILTON. *The Saucy Fly*, an Impudent Imp: MARIE MAJILTON. *Nat Dark*, the Village Sexton: HARRY RAYNOR. *Mr. Golightly*, a Monosyllabic Party: HARRY RAYNOR. *Gabriel Grub*, a morose, lonely old man: HARRY RAYNOR. *Marcofax*, King of the Goblins: HARRY RAYNOR. *Luke Twist*, an Eccentric Tobacconist: CHARLES MAJILTON. *Jix*, the Goblin of the Tombstone: CHARLES MAJILTON. *Mistigris*, the Gnome of Earth: CHARLES MAJILTON. *Forcepanto*, a Tarantula: CHARLES MAJILTON. *Anky Slender*, a Poetical tailor, suitor to Polly and rival of Twist: CHARLES RAYNOR. *Xit*, a Goblin: CHARLES RAYNOR. *Antennae*, a Tarantula: CHARLES RAYNOR. *Ghurrh*, Secretary to Marcofax: CHARLES RAYNOR. *Frank Dark*, a sweet youth, brother to Polly: FRANK MAJILTON. *Nip*, a Goblin: FRANK MAJILTON. *Pipifax*, an Imp of Darkness: FRANK MAJILTON. *Mlle. Nadelgewehr*, a French milliner from Berlin: CARRIE MAJILTON. *Goblin Gymnastics*: Professor NELSON & SONS. *Solos, Chorus, etc.*: Russian Quartette. *Christmas Carolers, Guests, Demons, Goblins, Black Spirits and White, Red Spirits and Gray, all the host of—*: Two Hundred Auxiliaries.

Prologue: Christmas Eve at the Old Sexton's.

Act 1, Scene 1: Polly's Dream. The Dark Lane. *Scene 2*: The Old Churchyard. Gabriel's Farm.

Act 2: Pandemonium. And I awoke, and lo! It was a dream.

PROLOGUE
Concertina and Banjo Duet
H. Raynor, C. Raynor
"We Are So Volatile" (Song and Chorus)
H. Raynor, Charles Majilton, C. Raynor, F., Majilton, M. Majilton, Carrie Majilton
Quadrille Domestique
All the Company
Christmas Chimes
H. Raynor, C. Raynor
"A Jolly Christmas Party" (Song)
H. Raynor, Company

ACT 1
"Hark the Vesper Hymn Is Stealing"

ACT 2
Dance Diabolique
M. Majilton
"Our Welcome Guest" (Song)
H. Raynor, Company
"Eccentrique" (Song)
M. Majilton
Japanese Fiddle (Solo, on one string)
H. Raynor
Diabolical Gymnastics
F. Majilton, H. Raynor
Sports Eccentric
Charles Majilton, H. Raynor
Goblin's Revels
Professor Nelson & Sons
"The Spider and the Fly" (Duet Entomologique)
M. Majilton, C. Raynor
Dirge
H. Raynor
And I awoke, and lo! It was a dream!

1874.01 THE GRAND DUCHESS

A Revival of the Opéra-bouffe in Three Acts[25], followed by an Olio. Original French libretto by Henri Meilhac and Ludovic Halévy. English adaptation by George Holman. Music by Jacques Offenbach. Orchestra under the direction of Mrs. Harriet Holman. Produced by Holman's English Opera

[24]Preceded by Charles Selby's comedietta Object of Interest, which was dropped altogether for New Year's week, and replaced after New Year's by a comedy, Family Jars!

[25]Previously presented in New York in French 24 September 1867 at the Théâtre Français for 156 performances; in English 17 June 1868 (in a different version) at the New York Theatre for 33 performances.

Bouffe Troupe. Opened 2 February 1874 at the Olympic Theatre and closed 7 February 1874 for 8 performances in repertory.

CAST: *Grande-Duchesse de Gérolstein*: SALLIE HOLMAN. *Wanda*: JULIA HOLMAN. *Fritz*, in love with Wanda[26]: JOSEPH BRANDISI. *General Boum*: ELLIS RYSE. *Baron Puck*, Prime Minister to the Grand Duchess: A. D. HOLMAN. *Prince Paul*, affianced to the Grand Duchess: GEORGE H. BARTON. *Baron Grog*: Mills Hall. *Nepomuc*: CHARLES J. MIERS. *Rasman*: E. M. Bellen. *Peterman*: G. Bellamy. *Olga*: Emma Phillips. *Amelia*: G. Stradella. *Vivandière*: Ida Carpenter. *Soldiers, Guards*: Numerous Auxiliaries.

1874.02 THE BOHEMIAN GIRL

A Revival of the Romantic Opera in Four Acts[27], followed by an Olio. Libretto by Alfred Bunn. Music by Michael William Balfe. Orchestra under the direction of Mrs. Harriet Holman. Produced by Holman's English Opera Bouffe Troupe. Opened 9 February 1874 at the Olympic Theatre and closed 11 February 1874 after 3 performances in repertory.

CAST: *Arline*: *Thaddeus*: Company included SALLIE HOLMAN. : JULIA HOLMAN. : JOSEPH BRANDISI. : Mrs. HARRIET HOLMAN. ELLIS RYSE. A. D. HOLMAN, GEORGE H. BARTON. Mills Hall. CHARLES J. MIERS. E. M. Bellen. G. Bellamy. Emma Phillips. G. Stradella. Ida Carpenter.

1874.03 HUMPTY DUMPTY AT SCHOOL!

A Revival of the Comic Pantomime in One Act, founded on the celebrated picture of "The School in an Uproar!"[28], preceded by a Fox Specialty and an Olio[29]. Acting manager, George L. Fox. Acting manager, Joseph H. Tooker. Stage manager, J. B. Wright. Produced by Augustin Daly. Opened 9 February 1874 at the Grand Opera House and closed 14 March 1874 after 35 performances.

ACT 1

JACK HARKAWAY AT SEA!, an old and popular George L. Fox Specialty. Incidental to the piece, "Sailor's Song and Chorus" by the California Quartette.

CAST: *Mr. Tobias Shortcut*, a Tobacconist: GEORGE L. FOX. *Captain Harvey Shortcut*: W. H. HAMILTON. *Lieutenant Jack Harkaway*: M. A. KENNEDY. *Bobstay*: J. W. JENNINGS. *Lieut. Grating*: J. H. HOWLAND. *Mr. Foreceps*, Surgeon: A. G. Enos. *Lieut. Wilson*: R. Sullivan. *Marlinspike*: M. D. Bebus. *Sailors*: Messrs. F. Davis, J. Wanham. *Midshipmen*: Misses Cora Cassidy, V. Stewart, E. Byron, C. Martin, C. Hasselberger, Ida Bell. *Mrs. Fidget*: Miss M. Chambers. *Emily*, Jack's affianced: Mrs. C. M. WALCOTT, JR.

ACT 2

Wilson Brothers in their Pyramid Somersaults

Sculptor's Dream!, the famous Taglioni Ballet D'Action in Two Scenes
Betty Rigl, Emily Rigl, Coryphées, Corps de Ballet
(Arranged and produced under the direction of Betty Rigl.)

The Celebrated Martens in Sweet Tyrolean Ballads

J. W. McAndrews, the great Ethiopian Delineator, assisted by Harry Stanwood, in the great act called The Power of Music.

King Sarbro, who will along other perilous feats, walk a rope stretched from the stage to the Family Circle of the Grand Opera House, and descend on one foot while standing erect.

Triple Tourniquet, by the Wilson Brothers

Mr. Harry Stanwood in His Banjo Act

Mr. J. Morris, in his unique, mystical, musical act, entitled The Seven Magical Changes.

The Martens in their famous Cat Duett

ACT 3

HUMPTY DUMPTY AT SCHOOL!, a Comic Pantomime in One Act.

CAST: *Master Bobby Bobbs*, the Big Boy of the School: GEORGE L. FOX. *Doctor Noddy*, the School Master: C. K. FOX. *Monsieur Stepps*, the Dancing Master: CHARLES RAVEL. *Mr. Robert Bobbs, Sr.*: CHARLES MANLEY. *Mr. Easy*, ver complying: W. H. HAMILTON. *Ready for Examination Day (3)*: *Master Easy*: A. G. Enos. *Master Late*: G. Downs. *Master Hookey*: W. Neville. *School Boys, etc.*

Annette, the Maid of all Work: EMILY RIGL. *Madam Stepps*: Agnes Lee. *Mrs. Robert Bobbs*: Ida Bell. *Mrs. Easy*: Cora Cassidy.

1874.04 LES CENT VIERGES

A Revival of the Opérette in Three Acts[30], in French. Libretto by Clairville, Henri Chivot and Alfred Duru. Music by Charles Lecocq. Stage manager, Mons. Benedick. General stage manger, C. Lecuyer. Musical director, Charles Van Ghele. Produced by C. A. Chizzola. Opened 20 March 1874 at the Lyceum Theatre in repertory, season closing 4 April 1874.

CAST: *Gabrielle*, femme du Duc de Quillenbois: Mlle. MARIE AIMÉE. *Eglantine*, femme de Poulardot: Mlle. ROSINA STANI. *Fanny*, niece de Crockley: Mlle. Roland. *Dolores*, Espagnole: Mme. Juteau. *Paquebette*, Hollandaise: Mlle. Vandame. *Retly*, Suissesse: Mlle. Deschamps. *Paoli*, Italienne: Mlle. Marie Nardin. *Lisbeth*, Tyrolienne: Mons. Peraut. *Olga*, Polonaise: Mlle. Cantrelle. *Lysis*, Grecque: Mlle. Louise. *Gilda*, Gitane: Mlle. Barin. *Nadge*, Russe: Mlle. Marais. *Katerine*, Hongroise: Mlle. Nardin. *Madelon*, Breton: Mlle. Augusta. *Boscotte*, Picarde: Mlle. Nardin. *Sir Jonathan Plupersonn*, Gouverneur de l'Ile Verte: Mons. LECUYER. *Le Duc Anatole de Queillenbois*: Mons. JUTEAU. *Poulardot*, ancien négociant: Mons. DUCHESNE. *Brididick*, Secrétaire de Plupersonn: Mons. Nardin. *Crockley*, Tavernier: Mons. Duplan. *Le Capitaine Thompson*: Mons. DAVALIS. *Un Constable*: Mons. Benedick.

Colons Anglais: *Calsonn*: Salvator. *Bitter*: Caralp. *Bristow*: Davalis. *Jolly*: Adrocy. *Robinson*: Guerra. *Duchester*: Careme. *Monitor*: Grazzin. *Grospater*: Victor. *Hosteball*: Ruffino. *McFarlann*: Peraut. *Towtenpatt*: Leclerc. *Grosborn*: Brag. *Emigrants, Marines, Soldiers, Colonists, etc.*

1874.05 LE PETIT FAUST

A Revival of the Opéra-bouffe in Three Acts[31], in French. Libretto by Hector Crémieux and Adolphe Jaime. Music by Hervé. Stage manager, Mons. Benedick. General stage manger, C. Lecuyer. Musical director, Charles Van Ghele. Produced by C. A. Chizzola. Opened 21 March 1874 (matinee) at the Lyceum Theatre in repertory, closing 4 April 1874.

CAST: *Marguerite*: Mlle. MARIE AIMÉE. *Méphisto*: Mlle. ROSINA STANI. *Danseuse*: Mlle. Roland.

Female Pupils (7): *Lisette*: Mlle. Juteau. *Aglae*: Mlle. Briot. *Clorinde*: Mlle. Sophie Gherzi. *Charlotte*: Mlle. Nardin. *Lischen*: Mlle. Peraut. *Dorothée*: Mlle. Bonetti. *Agriel*: Mlle. Cantrelle. *Male Pupils (5)*: *Siebel*: Mlle. Marie Nardin. *Frantz*: Mlle. Marie Vandamme. *Wagner*: Mlle. Marietta. *Altmayer*: Mlle. Deschamps. *Brander*: Mlle. Peraut. *Dr. Faust*: Mons. E. JUTEAU. *Valentin*. Mons. LECUYER. *Le Cocher*: Mons. Duplan. *An Anglo-Saxon*: Mons. Deschamps. *Le Pion*: Mons. Benedick. *Soldiers, Students, Old Men and Women, Anglo-Saxons, Russians, Male and Female Demons.*

1874.06 LA VIE PARISIENNE

A Revival of the Opéra-bouffe in Four Acts[32], in French. Libretto by Henri Meilhac and Ludovic Halévy. Music by Jacques Offenbach. Stage manager, Mons. Benedick. General stage manger, C. Lecuyer. Scenery by Hannibal W. Calyo. Musical director, Charles Van Ghele. Produced by C. A. Chizzola. Opened 23 March 1874 at the Lyceum Theatre in repertory, closing 4 April 1874.

CAST: *Gabrielle*: Mlle. MARIE AIMÉE. *Le Bresilien*: Mons. JUTEAU. *Frick*: Mons. JUTEAU. *Prosper*: Mons. JUTEAU. *Métella*: Mlle. ROSINA STANI. *La Baronne de Gondremarck*: Mlle. Roland. *Mme. de Quimper Karadac*: Mlle. Cantrelle. *Mme. de Folle Verdure*: Mlle. Juteau. *Léonie*: Mlle. Duplan. *Louise*: Mlle. Perraut. *Clara*: Mlle. M. Nardin. *Le Baron de Gondremarck*: Mons. Duplan. *Bobinet*: Mons. LECUYER. *Raoul de Gardefeu*: Mons. Deschamps. *Urbain*: Mons. Benedick. *Joseph*: Mons. Perraut. *Alphonse*: Mons. Salvator. *Gontran*: Mons. Davalis. *Chef de Gare*: Mons. Brag. *Domestiques, Employés, Voyageurs, etc.*

---

[26]In which he will introduce "La Marseillaise."

[27]First produced in New York 25 November 1844 at the Park Theatre for 17 performances in repertory. For Synopsis of Scenes and Musical Numbers, see original 1844 production.

[28]During the run the show was retitled A ROUND OF PLEASURE, which had been the show's previous sub-title.

[29]The Olio and Fox Specialty changed weekly. For the second week, JACK HARKAWAY AT SEA was replaced by another Fox specialty entitled '2450.'

[30]First produced in New York in French 23 December 1872 at the Olympic Theatre for (8) performances in repertory. For Synopsis of Scenes and Musical Numbers, see original 1872 production.

[31]Fist produced in New York in English 29 August 1870 at Kelly and Leon's for (12) performances; in French 29 August 1870 at the Grand Opera House. For Synopsis of Scenes and Musical Numbers, see original 1870 production at the Grand Opera House.

[32]First produced in New York in French 29 March 1869 at the Théâtre Français. For Synopsis of Scenes and Musical Numbers, see original 1869 production.

1874.07

L'ŒIL CREVÉ

A Revival of the Opéra Bouffe (Folie Musicale) in Three Acts[33], in French. Libretto and music by Hervé. Stage manager, Mons. Benedick. General stage manger, C. Lecuyer. Musical director, Charles Van Ghele. Produced by C. A. Chizzola. Opened 27 March 1874 at the Lyceum Theatre in repertory, closing 4 April 1874.

CAST: *Fleur de Noblesse*, demoiselle of the Chateau: Mlle. MARIE AIMÉE. *Dindonette*, a Foundling and local soprano: Mlle. ROSINA STANI. *Géromé*, the Local Posse Comitatus: Mons. LECUYER. *Alexandrivoire*, Champion Crossbowman: Mons. JUTEAU. *Le Marquis*, feudal superior of the village: Mons. Duchesne. *Le Baili*: Mons. Duplan. *Ernest*: Mons. Deschamps. *Le Duc d'Enface*: Mons. Benedick. *La Marquise*, most mystery fraught: Mlle. Cantrelle. *Eclosine*, Hostess of the Bull's Eye Inn: Mme. Juteau. *Mariette*: Mlle. Duplan. *François*: Mlle. Vandamme. *Crossbowmen, Peasants, Physicians and Notables.*

1874.08

MONSIEUR CHOUFLEURI RESTERA CHEZ LUI-LE

A Revival of the Opérette-bouffe in One Act, in French.[34] Libretto by Duc de Morny, etc. Music by Jacques Offenbach. Stage manager, Mons. Benedick. General stage manger, C. Lecuyer. Musical director, Charles Van Ghele. Produced by C. A. Chizzola. Opened 28 March 1874 (evening) at the Lyceum Theatre in repertory, closing 4 April 1874.

CAST: *Ernestine*: Mlle. MARIE AIMÉE. *Monsieur Choufleuri*: Mons. DUCHESNE. *Chrysoldule Babylas*: Mons. JUTEAU. *Petermaine*: Mons. LECUYER. *Balandard*: Mons. DUPLAN. *Monsieur. Balandard*: Mons. Benedick. *Rubensteinoff*: Mons. Deschamps.

1874.09

HUMPTY-DUMPTY AT HOME

A Comic Trick Pantomime in Three Acts, 14 Scenes. Play by George L. Fox. Acting manager, George H. Tyler. Ballets arranged by Mons. A. Grossi. Scenery by J. A. Johnson. Musical director, F. Strebinger. Produced by George L. Fox. Opened 6 April 1874 at Fox's Broadway Theatre and closed 16 May 1874 after 54 performances.

CAST: *Humpty Dumpty*, the Irresistible: GEORGE L. FOX. *Old One-Two*, the inevitable: CHARLES K. FOX. *Tommy Tucker*, the Indispensable: CHARLES WINTER RAVEL. *Little Goody Two Shoes*, the Incontestable: LOUISE BOSHELL. *Aurora*, the dawn, "I always use the phrases of the day": Ida Yerance. *Mannahatta*, of the Empire Isle: Marguerite Chambers. *Hon. Grandeur Dignify*, fond of sport, but still fonder of Goody Two Shoes: CHARLES T. PARSLOE, JR. *Dr. Nitrous Oxide Gas Cureall*, a quack physician: W. H. Hamilton. *Peeler Copp*, a policeman, "when really wanted to be seen": A. G. Enos. *Creamfaceloon*, a milkman: George Topack. *Upton Tactic*, a sergeant, a great disciplinarian: F. Hildebrand. *Attached to the Farm of Plenty (5)*: *Sickle*: Mr. Sage. *Rake*: W. F. Rushmore. *Ploughshare*: M. Glory. *Yokle*: S. Savoury. *Evergreen*: W. Shaff. *Gnome Cobbler*: Master George Downs. *Jimmy* of the Fish Market: Master W. Melville. *Gutter Snipe*, a rag-picker: P. Daniels. *Perch*, landlord of the "Man and Beast": William Henry. *Nimble*, a waiter, always ready: Mr. Stapleton. *Bang Up*, a pieman: M. Coveney. *Mike O'Rafferty*, an Irishman: G. Pritchett. *Horsechestnutz*, a Dutchman: C. Forman. *Freedman Bureau*, a black boy: Master Mustard Seed. *Miss Elegance Custom*, Girl of the Period: Ella Shirley. *Mrs. Sowerby Creamly*, a School-teacher: Sophie Ravel. *Bessy Bluebell*, a country girl: Minnie Parker. *Officer Clubs*, the giant policeman: Robert Cutler. *Peasants, Soldier Boys, Policemen, Venders, Passengers, etc.*

Specialties: Georgie Dean Spaulding, W. P. Spaulding and the Spaulding Bell Ringers; Nellie Daniels; Etta Morgan; Orrin Brothers and Mlle. de Lucia (gymnasts), Prof. J. L. Davis (trained dogs). *Ballet*: Mlles. Augusta LaBella, Enerica Venerin (dancers).

Act 1, Scene 1: The Retreat of Mannahatta by Moonlight. *Scene 2*: The Farm of Plenty. *Scene 3*: Subterranean Grotto. *Scene 4*: Country Inn on the Highway. *Scene 5*: Dry Goods Store and Ladies' Seminary. *Scene 6*: Market-place. Sudden change to Open Sea.

Act 2: Humpty's World of Wonders!

Act 3, Scene 1: Library. *Scene 2*: Exterior of Grocery Store. *Scene 3*: Fireworks Depot and Private House. *Scene 4*: A Rural Home near Pleasantville. *Scene 5*: Model Lodging House (approved by the Board of Health). *Scene 6*: A Dangerous Locality. *Scene 7*: The Enchanted Retreat in the Realms of Fairyland. Happy Denouement.

ACT 1

Scene 3

Roses and Butterflies (Grand Ballet d'Action)
Mlle. Augusta La Bella, Corps de Ballet

Grand Transformation of Characters
Clown: G. L. Fox. *Pantaloon*: C. K. Fox. *Harlequin*: C. W. Ravel. *Columbine*: L. Boshell.

ACT 2

"Home Sweet Home" played upon the Swiss Bells/

Solo for Bass Bells by W. P. Spaulding
Spaulding's Bell Ringers

The Orrin Brothers and Mlle. deLucia in their grand Olympian and Calisthenical Exposition

Harp Solo, Grand Fantasie for Harp—Carnival de Venice, concluding with her celebrated Music Box Imitation
Georgie Dean Spaulding

Wire Volant Equilibriums
Louise Boshell

Musical novelty of the Age
Prof. O'Reardon, famed tumberonicon

"Albanians!" (Grand Grecian Ballet Divertissement)
Mlle. E. Venerina, Corps de Ballet

Quickstep
Ladies Cornet Quartette

Prof. J. L. Davis, his school of educated dogs

ACT 3

Happy Denouement

1874.10

A PARISIAN FOLLY

Schumann's Transatlantic Combination in an Entertainment in Three Acts, involving Pantomime, Ballet and the Latest European Novelties, the whole forming a combination unequalled in America. Opened 6 April 1874 at the Lyceum Theatre, moved 20 April 1874 to Niblo's Garden and closed 2 May 1874 after 28 performances.

ACT 1[35]

A Comic Pantomime in One Act, 3 Scenes, arranged by Thomas Lovell.

CAST: *Jack*, the Doctor's Boy, afterwards Clown: THOMAS LOVELL. *The Policeman*, afterwards Pantaloon: CHARLES ALMONTE. *Quaker Suitor*, afterwards Harlequin: JAMES ALMONTE. *The Brave Grenadier*: Henry Brown. *Old Granny*, whom nobody wants: John Nash. *Susanna*: ADDIE SCARSEY. *Ballet*: Mlle. MARIE BONFANTI.
Scene 1: Susanna's Lovers. *Scene 2*: The Juggler. *Scene 3*: The Shadow Ballet.

ACT 2

The Skatatorial Dancers (Mlle. Fredrika, Mons. Elliott, Mons. Franche, Mlle. Corrie) in their artistically Comical Specialties, as performed at the Grand Opera House, Paris.

Mons. Beckman, the Jongleur, in his famous acts.

J. B. Johnson, the world-famed Champion Swimmer of England, Winner of the Championship Cup of England, in his unrivalled exhibition in a tank of real water.

ACT 3

Herr. A. Schulze, the famous man of masks and faces, in his unrivalled Facial Transformations, including nine peculiar changes of the most surprising character, performed without preparation or deception, and over One Hundred different and distinct Delineations of Face, Character and Person.

The Roussells and Almontes in their peculiar acrobatic specialties.

Don Ferrayra, the man flute, in his unequalled vocalisms.

The Brown Velocipede Combination in a closing scene, The Veil of Laces!, including 8 beautiful female riders, and Professor Henry Brown in feats of daring and surprising balancy on the bicycle, forming a grand Velocipedal Tournament in Unique Groups.

---

[33]First produced in New York in French 11 January 1869 at the Théâtre Français. For Synopsis of Scenes and Musical Numbers, see original 1869 production.

[34]First produced in New York in French 20 February 1869 at the Grand Opera House for 1 performance. This revival was presented as an afterpiece to LA PÉRICHOLE.

[35]Added for the second week of the run:
The Phantoms, a new comic pantomime.
Diana and Her Pet Satyr, a new ballet composed by L. Espinosa, with L. Espinosa and Mlle. Bonfanti.

1874–1875 SEASON

Ione Burke (Photo: Rockwood)
Billy Rose Theatre Collection, New York Public Library for the Performing Arts

1874–1875 SEASON

EVANGELINE, or, The Belle of Acadia

1874.11

An American Extravaganza with original Music in Three Acts, 12 Scenes. Libretto by J. Cheever Goodwin. Suggested by Henry Wadsworth Longfellow's poem "Evangeline." Music by E. Everitt Rice [Edward E. Rice]. Musical director, William Withers, Jr. Produced by Charles R. Thorne, Jr. Opened 27 July 1874 at Niblo's Garden and closed 8 August 1874 after 14 performances.

CAST: *Evangeline*, the heroine (Victim of a misplaced affection, which nearly proves her ruin): IONE BURKE. *Eulalie*, her confidante (Confidently hoping for woman's rights.): MAY ARLINGTON. *Catherine*, Gabriel's mother (Large enough to smother anyone; "fat, fair and two hundred and forty—pounds"): LOUIS MESTAYER. *The Queen*, the king's consort. (Though from the play it would appear that she never cons aught but her fingers.): MAY VERNON. *Gabriel*, Evangeline's worshipper. (A good singer, though you may think that if you wore shipper, he would not be considered good in voice: CARRIE THOMPSON. *LeBlanc*, the Notary. (Although a not-ary coroner, in-quest of some-body, and led to believe there's a good deal in a name: W. H. Crane. *Basil*, the blacksmith. Who believes blacks myths, until convinced to the contrary by Evangeline: JAMES DUNN. *Felician*, Eulalie's adorer (who persists in loving her, though it is sad o'er her wishes thus to ride rough shod): C. A. McIntosh. *Michael*, a violinist. (Supposed to derive inspiration from a vial in his(t) pocket, a victim of fo(u)rtune's, though he knows but one): W. B. Cahill. *The Captain* (A champion of hard tack, which he's always champi(ng) on, and Hardee's tactics): WILLIAM SCALLAN. *King Boorioboola Gha*, a suffering sovereign. The story of whose rule is a story of a reign of peace; sooty, and a kind it is hoped will suit.): E. S. Tarr. *Lo*, the lowest and lonest Indian of them all. Such a dealer in human hair as it is hoped you may ne'er meet on any stage put this): E. K. Collier. *The Reporter*, a genius. Accustomed to report a fire, a robber or men dead. The least said about him because the soonest mended: Florence Lee. *The Policeman*, called by facetious boys "a peeler," possibly because he was never known to heed any appeal a prisoner might make. "Lucus a non," and all that sort of thing: James Martin. *Hans Wagner* (Though corporal, fond of spiritual aid-de-camp; and as de-camp means "leave" the list of characters will be left here): Charles Rosine. *The Lone Fisherman*: J. W. THOMAN.

Act 1: Acadia. *Scene 1*: Exterior view of Basil's house, and a bird's eye view of the sea. *Scene 2*: A Lane. *Scene 3*: Basil's Kitchen.

Act 2: Africa. The Desert of Sahara. *Scene 1*: An inn in the desert. *Scene 2*: The diamond fields. *Scene 3*: The back yard of Boorioboola Gha's Palace. *Scene 4*: The King's Hall of Justice. *Scene 5*: The Prison. *Scene 6*: The Public Square.

Act 3: Arizona. *Scene 1*: The Forest's edge. *Scene 2*: A mountain pass. *Scene 3*: Basil's orchard.

ACT 1

"There's a man" (Opening Chorus)

"Would'st know the way?" (Ballad)
I. Burke

"She's saved! She's saved!" (Choral)

"(Sweet) Evangeline"(Song and Dance)
C. Thompson

"Gorra, the Life Is a Hard One I Lead" (Irish Song)
W. B. Cahill

"A Farmer Lived" (Ditty)
J. Dunn, Chorus

"He Says I Must Go"(Finale)

Evangeline Polka and Last Farewell Waltzes

ACT 2

"Hickory Hacker, Jim Jam" (Chorus of Natives)

"I'm in lofe" (Dutch Song)
W. Scallan

"We Are Off (to Seek for Eva)" (Comic Duet)
L. Mestayer, W. H. Crane

"Where Are Thou (Now), My Beloved?" (Bereft)
I. Burke

"Round about the City's Streets" (Chant of Watchmen)

"Prowling around the Diamond Fields" (Policeman's Narrative)
J. Martin

Evangeline March

"She's Acquitted, (He's Outwitted)" (Finale)

Evangeline Waltzes; Evangeline Polka Mazurka

ACT 3

"Go Not, Happy Day" (Duet)
I. Burke, C. Thompson

"(The) Six Miserable Ruffians" (Sextette)

"Sammy Smug" (Sextette)

"You Wonder Why" (Song and Dance)
I. Burke

"Oh! Ain't this sweet?" (Threble Finale)

LA TIMBALE D'ARGENT

1874.12

An Opéra Comique (Opéra-bouffe) in Three Acts, in French. Libretto by Adolphe Jaime and Jules Noriac. Music by Léon Vasseur. Scenery by Hannibal W. Calyo. Costumes by Mons. Landolff. Properties and appointments by Mr. Williams. Mise en scène by Mons. Valaire. Musical director, Charles Van Ghele. Produced by C. A. Chizzola and Maurice Grau. Opened 24 August 1874 at the Lyceum Theatre and closed 9 September 1874 after 17 performances.

CAST: *Müller*: Mlle. MARIE AIMÉE. *Molda*, niece to Raab: Mlle. LEONTINE MINELLY. *Fichtel*, nephew to Pruth: Mlle. BLANCHE GANDON. *Gaben*: Mme. Dubouchet. *Pola*: Mlle. Briot. *Agathe*: Mlle. Perraut. *Marza*: Mlle. Sivry. *Barnabe*: Mlle. Gherzi. *Anich*: Mlle. Vandelet. *Petit-Pierre*: Mlle. Genot. *Raab*, Judge of the canton Groog-à-l'eau-de-sedlitz: Mons. DUBOUCHET. *Pruth*, Jailkeeper and leader of the singing club: Mons. DEBEER. *Barnabe*: Mons. Guyot. *Wilhelm*: Mons. Perraut. *Valter*: Mons. Salvator. *Gerome*: Mons. Chantal. *Fritz*: Mons. Davalis.

Act 1: Grand concours de la Timbale. Devant la maison du Juge Raab.

Act 2: Les Fiancailles de Muller. Chez Juge Raab.

Act 3: La Tentation. Dans le préau de la prison.

ACT 1[1]

Introduction et Choeur (Chanter et boire)
Mme. Dubouchet, Mons. Perraut, Choeur

Répétition de la Tyrolienne (Sol, la, si, si, re)
Choeur

Couplets de la Timbale (La timbale au somemt)
L. Minelly

Rondo (Voici Molda, qu'elle est jolie)
Mons. Dubouchet, Choeur

Sérénade (Pendant que sur la nappe blanche)
M. Aimée

Trio (Asseyez-vous à cette table!)
M. Aimée, Messrs. Dubouchet, Debeer

Marche et Choeur (Nous arrivons pour le)
M. Aimée, L. Minelly, Mons. Dubouchet, Choeur

Tyrolienne (Quand nous allons dans les)
Mlles. M. Aimée, L. Minelly

Final (Chantons victoire!)
Tutti

ACT 2

Choeur de buveurs (Buvons, buvons à la ronde)
Choeur

Chanson du Postillon (Allons, margot)
L. Minelly

Ronde (Enfants, je m'en vais vous donner)
Mons. Dubouchet, Choeur

Bonne Nuit! (Choeur) (Bonsoir, la demoiselle)
Choeur

Couplets de la porte (Comment, vous me fermez)
M. Aimée

[1]Musical numbers not listed in programs. List prepared from published French piano vocal score (E. Gérard & Cie., Paris, 1872).

Morceau Symphonique

Valse-Sérénade
Choeur

Final (Muller! Muller! affublé de la sorte)
Mlles. M. Aimée, L. Minelly, B. Gandon, Messrs. Dubouchet, Debeer, Perraut, Choeur

ACT 3

Choeur et Scène (Ah! c'est abominable)
Mme. Dubouchet, Mlles. Briot, Perraut, Sivry, Mons. Dubouchet

Choeur de Sortie

Couplets: La Leçon de Coquetterie (Faut lui sourire)
L. Minelly

Duo de la cloche (Grand dieu! qu'avez vous)
Mlles. M. Aimée, Minelly, Mons. Debeer

Final (L'succès est un mât don't l'assaut)
Tutti

THE DELUGE, or Paradise Lost

1874.13

A Grand Parisian Spectacular Drama in Four Acts[2]. (Adapted from the Old Testament.) New and original music by Alex. Artus of Paris, and William Withers, Jr. of Niblo's. Staged by Imre Kiralfy. New and Grand Ballet Marches composed by J. Kiralfy. Scenery by D. B. Hughes & Son. Costumes by Miss Fisher & Prise of London. Armors by Messrs. Srager & Hirsh of Paris. Appointments by Deveny. (Musical director, William Withers, Jr.) Produced by Charles R. Thorne. Opened 7 September 1874 at Niblo's Garden; reconstructed[3] 12 October 1874 and closed 14 November 1874 after 71 performances.

CAST: *Satan*: JULIA SEAMAN. *Eve*: LILLIE MacDONALD. *Noema*: LILLIE MacDONALD. *Abel*: KATTIE NEW. *Mercy*: Kate Fellows. *Adam*: R. P. Steele. *Japhet*: R. P. Steele. *Cain*: George Stretton. *Tubal*, a son of Cain: George Stretton. *Gabriel*: W. A. Davenport. *Satan's Conspirators (7)*: *Molooh*: G. Elliott. *Chamos*: Alfred Court. *Belial*: J. Thurman. *Ormolooh*: Mr. Walters. *Raniel*: Mr. Roony. *Belzebub*: Mr. Johnson. *Simon*: Mr. Leeman. *Old Man*: Mr. Johnson. *Boatman*: Mr. Thurman. *The Mother*: Miss Vernon. *Alexa*: Miss Smith. *Warriors, Demons, Slaves, Good Spirits*.

Dance Specialties: The Kiralfy Sisters, Misses Schrötter, Strudel, Zorner. The Boisset Family. Corps de Ballet of 200. *Specialty*: Le Jeune Bonnay! (xilophone virtuoso).

Act 1: Borders of Bitumin Lake.

Act 2: Garden of Eden.

Act 3: Autumn Glade. Death of Abel.

Act 4: Temple of Enoch.

BALLETS, SPECIALTIES

Great Demon Ballet (Act 1)
Mlles. Shrotter, Strudel, Zorner, Corps de Ballet

Grand Ballet & Bacchanale (Act 4)
Corps de Ballet

"Tubal"[4] (Song)(Act 4)
G. Stretton

Gorgeous Pageant of the People of Enoch and the Sons of Cain (Act 4)

Les Filles d'Eve (Grand Ballet Fantasie)(Act 4)
Kiralfy Sisters, Corps de Ballet, Boisset Family

[2]Author uncredited in programs.
[3]Reconstructed with Betty Remelsberg, Alpine echoists, the Ulm Sisters, the Boisset family and the Kiralfy Sisters.
[4]Dropped after opening.

LA PRINCESSE DE TRÉBIZONDE

1874.14

An Opéra-bouffe in Three Acts[5], in French. Libretto by Charles Nuitter and Étienne Tréfeu. Music by Jacques Offenbach. Scenery by Hannibal W. Calyo. Costumes by Millet of Paris. Mis en scène by Mons. Talaire. Musical director, Charles Van Ghele. Produced by C. A. Chizzola and Maurice Grau. Opened 10 September 1874 at the Lyceum Theatre and closed 3 October 1874 after 25 performances in repertory.

CAST: *Le Prince Raphaël*: *Pages, Chasseurs, Saltimbanques* Mlle. MARIE AIMÉE. *Zanetta*: Mlle. LEONTINE MINELLY. *Régina*: Mlle. BLANCHE GANDON. *Paola*: Mlle. JENNY KID. *Le Prince Casimir*: Mons. DUPLAN. *Cabriolo*: Mons. DUBOUCHET. *Trémolini*: Mons. DEBEER. *Sparadrap*: Mons. GUYOT. *Le Directeur de la Loterie*: Mons. Chantal. *Pages (5)*: *Riccardi*: Mlle. Dubouchet. *Flaminio*: Mlle. Sivry. *Brocoli*: Mlle. Perraut. *Francesco*: Mlle. Vaudelet. *Finochini*: Mlle. Lafontaine. *Paysannes, Paysans, etc.*

Act 1: An open square, on one side the Lottery Office, on the other, the Juggler's Booth.

Act 2: A Terrace in front of a Baronial Castle.

Act 3: Apartment in the Castle.

ACT 1[6]

Introduction (Entrez, messieurs, mesdames)
Les Saltimbanques, Messrs. Dubouchet, Debeer, Chantal, Jeunes Filles

Solo (Messieurs, prêtez-moi vos oreilles)
Mons. Debeer

Couplets (Ah! quel malheur! ô maladresse)
Mlle. L. Minelly

Couplets (Quand je suis sur la corde raide)
Mlle. B. Gandon

Couplets (Une jeune fille passait)
Mlle. M. Aimée

Ensemble Final (Ah! ce spectacle, était charmant!)
Mlles. L. Minelly, B. Gandon, Messrs. Dubouchet, Debeer, Tous

Scène (Voici le moment solonnel)
Mons. Chantal, Tous

Ensemble (Treize cent treize!)
Mons. Dubouchet, Mlles. B. Gandon, L. Minelly, Les Saltimbanques, Le Public

Reprise de l'Ensemble (Tout va changer)
Les Saltimbanques, Le Public

Suite du Final (Adieu, baraque héreditare)
Les Saltimbanques, Tous

ACT 2

Quintette (Où sont nos folles parades)
Messrs. Dubouchet, Debeer, Mlles. L. Minelly, B. Gandon, J. Kid

Choeur de Chasseurs (Au bois on chasse!)
Choeur

Duo (C'est elle! la voilà!)
Mlles. M. Aimée, L. Minelly

Couplets (Me maquillé-je comme on dit!)
Mons. Duplan

Couplets (Elle est admirablement)
Mlle. M. Aimée

Final (Oui, c'est le Prince Casimir!)
Choeur, Mons. Duplan, Dubouchet, Tous

Ronde (Femme du grand Rhotomago, La princesse de Trébizonde)
Mlle. L. Minelly, Tous

[5]French language premiere in the New York. Previously produced in New York in English 11 September 1871 at Wallack's Theatre for 7 performances.
[6]Musical numbers not listed in programs. List prepared from published French-English libretto (Metropolitan Printing Co., New York, 1874).

ACT 3

Choeur des Pages (Ah! quel ennui! quel sot métier!)
Des Pages

Couplets (Cet enfant manquait d'audace)
Mlles. Vaudelet, Perraut

Scène (Fleur qui se fane avant d'éclore)
Mlle. M. Aimée

Choeur (Voici mon seigneur, qu'on se range)
Choeur

Couplets (Je suis satisfait)
Mons. Duplan

Morceau d'Ensemble (D'où vient cette crise soudaine)
Messrs. Duplan, Guyot, Mlles. L. Minelly, M. Aimée

Duo (Moment fatal, hélas! que faire)
Mons. Debeer, Mlle. B. Gandon

Ronde (D'un bout à l'autre du palais)
Des Pages

Scène (Ce sont des amis)
Mlles. M. Aimée, L. Minelly, Messrs. Dubouchet, Debeer

Symphonie Burlesque

Final (Nous allons donc entrer ce soir)
Mlles. L. Minelly, B. Gandon, M. Aimée, Tous

1874.15 LA FILLE DE MADAME ANGOT

A Revival of the Opéra-comique in Three Acts[7], in French. Libretto by Clairville, Paul Siraudin and Victor Koning. Music by Charles Lecocq. Musical director, Charles Van Ghele. Produced by C. A. Chizzola and Maurice Grau. Opened 5 October 1874 at the Lyceum Theatre and closed 17 October 1874 after 10 performances in repertory.

CAST: *Clairette*: Mlle. MARIE AIMÉE. *Mlle. Lange*: Mlle. LEONTINE MINELLY. *Amaranthe*: Mlle. JENNY KID. *Javotte*: Mlle. Gersey. *Cydalise*: Mlle. Dubouchet. *Hersilie*: Mlle. Vandamme. *Mlle. Ducoudray*: Mlle. Duplan. *Babet*: Mlle. Perraut. *Manon*: Mlle. Sivry. *Therese*: Mlle. Briot. *Ange Pitou*: Mons. CHARLES KOLLETZ. *Larivaudière*: Mons. DUBOUCHET. *Pomponnet*: Mons. DEBEER. *Trénitz*: Mons. GENOT. *Louchard*: Mons. DUPLAN. *Gadet*: Mons. GUYOT. *Buteux*: Mons. DAVALIS. *Guillaume*: Mons. Salvator. *Un Incroyable*: Mons. Perraut. *Un Officier*: Mons. Victor. *Un Cabaretier*: Mons. Chantal. *Ports de la Halle, Grenadiers, Incroyables, Conspirateurs, Hussards, Domestiques, Dames de la Halle, Bourgeoisis, Merveilleuses, etc.*

1874.16 LA PÉRICHOLE

A Revival of the Opéra-bouffe in Two Acts, 3 Scenes, in French[8]. Libretto by Ludovic Halévy and Henri Meilhac, based on "Le Carosse du Saint-Sacrament" by Prosper Merimée. Music by Jacques Offenbach. Musical director, Charles Van Ghele. Produced by C. A. Chizzola and Maurice Grau. Opened and closed 16 October 1874 at the Lyceum Theatre after 1 performance; returned 13 May 1875 to the Lyceum Theatre for 1 additional performance.

CAST: *La Périchole*, a Street Singer: Mlle. MARIE AIMÉE. *Piquillo*: Mons. KOLLETZ. Aimée's company this season also included Mlles. LEONTINE MINELLY, BLANCHE GANDON, JENNY, Dubouchet, Sivry, Perraut, Vaudelet, Lafontaine; Messrs. DUPLAN, DUBOUCHET, DEBEER, GUYOT, Chantal.

1874.17 GENEVIÈVE DE BRABANT

A Revival of the Opéra-bouffe in Two Acts, 6 Scenes[9], followed by an olio. (Original French libretto by Hector Crémieux and Étienne Tréfeu.) English adaptation by Henry B. Farnie. Music by Jacques Offenbach. Conductor, Mr. Fred W. Zaulig. Produced by John F. Poole. Opened 19 October 1874 at the Olympic Theatre and closed 31 October 1874 after 16 performances.

CAST: *Socold*, Duke of Curaçao: E. D. Gooding. *Golo*, his Prime Minister: E. W. WARDEN. *Vanderprout*, the Burgomaster: Billy Gray. *Charles Martel*, the Emperor: S. Holdworth. *Graubage, Pitou*, Gens D'Armes: Messrs. A. J. Talbot, James Vincent. *Narcisse*, the Duke's Poet Page: Sarah Montague. *The Hermit*: J. Tracy. *Drogan*, a Pastry Cook: ROSA LEE. *Geneviève de Brabant*, Duchess of Curaçao: ALICE HARRISON. *Brigitte*, her confidante: EMMA HOFFMAN. *Isoline*, Golo's wife: Addie Farwell. *Maids of Honor (6)*: *Christine*: Miss Jackson. *Gudule*: Miss Thornton. *Favoline*: Sadie O'Neil. *Houblonne*: Miss Leon. *Dorothea*: Miss Wilson. *Gretchen*: Miss Martin. *Aldermen, Pages, Peasants, etc.*

Act 1, Scene 1: The Duke's Reception. The Page and His Pie. The Legend of Brabant. The Supper and its Consequences. The Plot of the Jealous Minister. The Crowing Chorus and Court Merriment. *Scene 2*: The Page, the Duke, and the Installation of the new Page. Drogan in love. The Duke in a Dilemma. The arrival of a Crusader. Off to Palestine. *Scene 3*: The departure for Palestine, and farewell of the Duke to battle.

Act 2, Scene 1: The Hermit's Home. The Oracle. The Storm. The Fugitives. The Pursuit of the Gens D'Armes. The Arrest. The Escape of the Burgomaster. The life and death of the two Gens D'Armes. The surprise in the forest, and comic tableau. *Scene 2*: Th Sorrows of the faithful wife. The journey of love. The song of love and Genevieve. The plot in conclusion. The vow of the Conspirators. Keep it dark and we shall triumph. *Scene 3*: The Duke's return. Joy of Brabant. The Troubadour's testimony. The lock of hair. The condemnation of Golo. The Tofty of Genevieve. The verdict of villainy, and love triumphant. Dance of Bells, and tableau of joy and jollification.

Olio: The Marvelous Faust Family; Banjo Eccentricities, with A. J. Leavitt. Intelligence Office!, a sketch with E. D. Gooding, Billy Gray, Master Barney. Excelsior Jig, by Miss Sallie O'Neil. The Living Fountain, or the Bath of the Innocents (Parisian Sensation). GUS WILLIAMS in his Dutch songs and budget of comicalities. Emma Hoffman in her bouquet of melodies. Rickey and Barney's sketch, Casey, the Piper!, with Sam Rickey, Master Barney, E. D. Gooding, Billy Gray, G. W. Reed, E. Miles, A. J. Talbot, Addie Farwell, Misses Thornton and Jackson. Quintessence of Old Virginia, by J. H. O'Neil. The Happy Family!, the laughable sketch, with Gus Williams, G. W. Reed, E. Miles, A. Farwell.

1874.18 GENEVIÉVE DE BRABANT

An Opéra-bouffe in Two Acts, 6 Scenes[10]. (Original French libretto by Hector Crémieux and Étienne Tréfeu.) Rewritten and arranged for the American stage by Emily Soldene. Music by Jacques Offenbach. Stage manager, John Wallace. Acting manager, John Powell. Scenery by Hannibal W. Calyo. Costumes by M. Auguste and Co. (London and Paris). Conductor, George Richardson. Manager of the Soldene Company, Charles Morton. Produced by Maurice Grau and C. A. Chizzola. Opened 2 November 1874 at the Lyceum Theatre and closed 14 November 1874 after 14 performances; repertory season closed 2 January 1875; returned 2 June 1875 for 1 additional performance in repertory at the Lyceum Theatre.

CAST: *Drogan*, Apprentice Pastry Cook: EMILY SOLDENE. *Geneviève de Brabant*, Duchess of Brabant: AGNES LYNDHURST. *Brigitte*, her Confidante: LIZZY ROBSON. *Cocorico*, Duke of Brabant: JOHN WALLACE. *Oswald*, Duke's peculiar page: LAURA CARTHEW. *Golo*, Minister of Police: H. LEWENS. *The Burgomaster of Curaçao*: J. B. RAE. *Charles Martel*, a Saladin: H. LAURENT. *Philibert*, his Esquire: Miss E. St. CLAIR. *Grabuge, Pitou*, the two gendarmes: Edward Marshall, E. D. Beverly. *The Hermit of the Valley*: C. Gibbons. *Pip, Peterkin*, Pages of the Household: Miss Nicholas, Una Brooke.

Maids of Honor: *Christine*: MARIE WILLIAMS. *Gertrude*: JULIA ROBERTS. *Gudule*: RUTH REID. *Houibonne*: Jessie Loftus. *Isoline*: Laura Carthew. *Yolande*: Neillie Reid. *Gretchen*: Helen Travers. *Bradamante*: Clara Gray. *Faroline*: Miss

---

[7]First produced in New York in French 23 August 1873 at the Lyceum Theatre. For Synopsis of Scenes and Musical Numbers, see original 1873 production. At the commencement of Act 3, the highly characteristic national Republican dance "La Fricassee" will be danced by Mlle. Gandon, Mons. Genot, and the whole company

[8]First produced in New York in French 4 January 1869 at Pike Opera House. For Synopsis of Scenes and Musical Numbers, see original 1869 production. No program found for this production. Advertisements noted that Aimée will sing "Pretty as a Picture" in Act 1 and "La Paloma" In Act 3.

[9]English language premiere in New York. First produced in New York in French 22 October 1868 at the Théâtre Français in repertory.

[10]A rival production to the Olympic's English language premiere in New York. First produced in New York in French 22 October 1868 at the Théâtre Français.

Beaumont. *Musketeers of the Guard*: Messrs. Maynard, Cullen, Cooper, Quaine, Hillier, Quinton, Cottrell. *Members of the Council, Apprentice Cooks, Citizens of Curaçao*: Misses Rose Roberts, Kate Chorley, etc.

Act 2, Ladies and Chevaliers of the French Court: *Saint Remy*: Helen Travers. *Sans Terre*: Clara Gray. *De Thionville*: Laura Carthew. *De Nangis*: Miss Williams.

Act 1, Scene 1: The Grand Palace in the City of Curaçao. The Idyll of the Pie. *Scene 2*: Tapestry Chamber in the Palace. The Nocturne interrupted. *Scene 3*: The Departure for Palestine. Eothen.

Act 2, Scene 1: The Hermit's Ravine, near Versailles. Working an Oracle. *Scene 2*: A Bridle Path in the Forest, on the road to the Ball. *Scene 3*: Versailles en fête. The Meeting of the Watteaux! Grand Denouement.

ACT 1[11]

Scene 1

Chorus of Sightseers (We fear that something's going wrong)
Citizens

Song (Good people of Brabant)
L. Robson

The Burgomaster's Song (Thanks to our sage consultation)
J. B. Rae

Song of the Pie (That plàt, O gentlemen and ladies)
E. Soldene, Citizens

Chorus

The Balcony Duet (My devotion she's approiving)
E. Soldene, A. Lyndhurst

Crowing Chorus (Chanticleer upon a wall)
J. Wallace, A. Lyndhurst, E. Soldene, Citizens

Scene 2

Sewing Stanzas (Here are we poor damsels, sewing)
M. Williams, R. Reid, L. Carthew, H. Travers, Maids of Honor

The Toilette Song (This rig, my dears, will never do)
M. Williams, H. Travers, R. Reid, Maids of Honor

"Love in Youth" (Ballad)(Youth has a wisdom of its own)
E. Soldene

Trio of the Purse (A grautity; . . . a grautity!)
E. Soldene, L. Robson, A. Lyndhurst

"The fact is, Duke!" (Trio)(I really don't know what's the matter)
J. Wallace, A. Lyndhurst, E. Soldene

"A cup of tea" (Song and Chorus)
J. Wallace, Pages, Maids of Honor

The Armorer's Ditty (Tap him gently)
H. Laurent, All

Scene 3

Grand Finale (Off the Duke is going!)
All, E. Soldene

ACT 2

Scene 1

Bugle Chorus (The hunt is up!)
Chorus

The Bigotted Crusader (To Saracen land)(Ronde d'escrime)
H. Laurent

Storm Trio (Thunder, wind, rain, all come together!)
E. Soldene, L. Robson, A. Lyndhurst

Sleep Song (Sleep on, sleep on, my Queen!)
E. Soldene

The Gens d'Armes' Duet (We're public guardians, bold, yet wary)
E. Marshall, E. D. Beverly

Trio (A Lady can but die at lost)
E. Marshall, E. D. Beverly, A. Lyndhurst

Quartette (fear not! Mistress mine)
E. Marshall, E. D. Beverly, A. Lyndhurst, L. Robson

Scene 2

Tyrolienne (How bright hath grown the day!)
A. Lyndhurst, E. Soldene, L. Robson

Ballad (Who hath not felt, when sad and lone)
A. Lyndhurst

Scene 3

Farandole and Anacreontic (Dance we now a joyous measure)
Ladies and Chevaliers of the French Court

Romance of the Ringlet ('Tis true her hair was raven black)
E. Soldene

Song of the Witnesses (Fate to shield you now refuses)
E. Soldene, L. Robson, A. Lyndhurst, Chorus

Hope and Love (Finale)(Hope! Unto thee sing we a strain)
E. Soldene, All

[11]Musical numbers not listed in programs. List prepared from published libretto "English version adapted to the American stage as performed by Miss Emily Soldene's English Opera Bouffe Company at the Lyceum Theatre, New York, under the management of Messrs. Maurice Grau and C. A. Chizzola (Metropolitan Printing and Engraving Establishment, New York, 1874).

1874.19 LA FILLE DE MADAME ANGOT

An Opéra-comique in Three Acts[12]. Original French libretto by Clairville, Paul Siraudin and Victor Koning. Music by Charles Lecocq. Stage manager, John Wallace. Acting manager, John Powell. Scenery by Hannibal W. Calyo. Costumes by Samuel May, London. Properties and appointments by Mr. Smith, Covent Garden. Conductor, George Richardson. Manager of the Emily Soldene English Opera Bouffe Company, Charles Morton. Produced by Maurice Grau and C. A. Chizzola. Opened 16 November 1874 at the Lyceum Theatre and closed 28 November 1874 after 15 performances in repertory; season closed 2 January 1875; returned 3 June 1875 for an additional performance in repertory at the Lyceum.

CAST: *Mlle. Lange*: EMILY SOLDENE. *Clairette (Angot)*: LIZZY ROBSON. *Pomponnet*: J. B. RAE. *Ange Pitou*: E. D. BEVERLY. *Larivaudière*: H. LEWENS. *Trénitz*: John Wallace. *Cadet*: J. E. Cullen. (*Buteaux*: Mr. Maynard.) *Louchard*: EDWARD MARSHALL. *Officer*: C. Gibbons. *Amaranthe*: Rose Roberts. *Javotte*: Miss E. St. CLAIR. *Babet*: LAURA CARTHEW. *Hersilie*: Clara Vesey. *Market Men and Women, Conspirators, Hussars, Incredibles, Citizens, etc.*

Act 1: The Market of the Innocents. Paris, 1793. (Market place in Paris under the Directory.)

Act 2: Mlle. Lange at Home. (Drawing room in Mlle. Lange's home.)

Act 3: The Gardens of Calypso, near Paris. (The Calypso Ball at Belleville by night.)

ACT 1[13]

Chorus and Solo (Arm-in-arm, here we come, altogether)
Ensemble

Air (Flow'r so fair, and yet so fleeting)
J. B. Rae

Ensemble (Perfect troth in form and feature)
Ensemble

Romance (I am your child, you've treated me kindly)
L. Robson

Song and Chorus (To sell fish was her calling)("Madame Angot")
E. Soldene

Song (Of course, Clairette I will love ever)
E. D. Beverly

Duet (When seeking out the 'why' and 'whether')
E. D. Beverly, L. Robson

*Duo (So you are Larivaudière?)
E. D. Beverly, H. Lewens

Finale (Come, come, poltroon)
Crowd (Ensemble)

The Sedition Rondo (Time was that monarchy meant plunder)
L. Robson

Tableau of the Arrest (Sir, I swear that you are wrong)
E. D. Beverly, J. B. Rae, Ensemble

ACT 2

Scandal Chorus (Since you say so, we will receive it)
Ineffables (Ensemble)

"The Hussar Song" (Augereau's soldiers are fine fellows!)
E. Soldene

[12]English language premiere in New York, adaptation uncredited. First produced in New York in French 23 August 1873 at the Lyceum Theatre.
[13]Musical numbers not listed in programs. List prepared from published libretto (Metropolitan Printing and Engraving, New York, 1874).

"The Schoolfellows" (Duet)(Dear days of childhood)
E. Soldene, L. Robson
"The Fascination Duet" (How find you politics?)
E. Soldene, E. D. Beverly
Quintette and Ensemble ('Tis the truth I tell!)
E. Soldene, L. Robson, E. D. Beverly, H. Lewens, E. Marshall
Finale (When folk conspire to intrigue and plot)
The Incredibles (Ensemble)
Soldiers' Chant (Down with plots and down with plotters)
Hussars
Valse de Seduction (Whirling whirling)
E. Soldene

ACT 3
Chorus and Song (Spite of bearing, spite of dressing)
Market Folks, J. E. Cullen, R. Roberts
Air (You sent me, at much cost, to school)
L. Robson
"The 'Roughs' Duet" (What do you want? You ass! a cuff?)
J. B. Rae, H. Lewens
Finale (Oh dearest enemy! It is my fate)
E. D. Beverly, E. Soldene
Ensemble (Ah! it is false)
E. Soldene
"The Quarrel Duo" (Ah, now I've trapp'd you, madam, fine)
L. Robson, E. Soldene
Ensemble (Least that's said is soonest mended)
All

1874.20 ROUND THE CLOCK; or, New York By Dark

A Revival of the Local Sensational Folly in Four Acts, 13 Scenes[14]. Adapted into English by Augustin Daly (from the original French "La Tour du Cadran" by Hector Crémieux and H. Bocage). Music by William H. Brinkworth. Machinery by William H. Crane. Properties by J. Timoney. Costumes by Mons. Lewis. Stage director, James Barnes. Musical director, William H. Brinkworth. Produced by Augustin Daly. Opened 23 November 1874 at Wood's Museum and closed 28 November 1874 after 12 performances.

CAST: *Roderick Killgobbin*, Esq., a person of many disguises and shrewd surmises; in fact, a man of wax and of whacks—easily kneaded and often needed, afterwards assuming the disguise of a "A Plug Ugly, a Bill Sticker," etc.: LOUIS ALDRICH. *Juliana Tartar*, the pretty Baker of Tarts and Pies and ready-maker of tart replies: BELLE HOWITT. *Ernesta Hardacre*, having been "born under a cabbage" is naturally a little green: MARION SACKETT. *Mr. Abraham Hardacre*, a Wheedler: M. W. LEFFINGWELL *Lawyer Goddigatt*, a subject for the Bar Association, afterwards assuming the disguise of "A Target": A. H. SHELDON. *Alderman Dooley*, a newly-elected gentleman with privileges behind the scenes: T. L. CONNOR. *Joey Lillyburn*, an Innocent from Boston: THERESA WOOD. *Peter Dodd*, a Dyer—likewise a dire deceiver: Harry Stewart. *Mrs. Peter Dodd*, the Wife of the Dyer, and victim of the deceiver: Florence Stratton. *Mr. Mutton*, of Essex Market: T. J. Martin.

The Manager: W. H. Partello. *Machinist*: W. H. Crane. *Property Man*: J. Timoney. *Call Boy*: D. Sheerin. *Mme. Sangalli*: Kate Harrison. *Borrowed from this theatre expressly for this play: Ladies of the Ballet, Figurantes, Demons, Audience, etc.*

Harry Hill, a popular gentleman: L. R. Birchler. *Visitors at Harry Hills, Waiter Girls, etc. Roundsman Lafferty*: L. R. Willard. *Pyrotechnist at Lion Park*: A. Leonard. *Smack*, a servant: Charles Sturges. *Rascal Sue*, a sketch from nature: Mrs. D. B. Van Deren. *Rose*, the tart-seller's clerk: Nellie Sanford. *Relations (2): Mrs. Bowlit*: Miss McCullough. *Mrs. Impey*: Tillie Page. *Kitty Tyrrell*: Lulu Hillens. *Mrs. Bangs*: Miss E. Shay. *Baskins*: Christie Miller. *Black Crook*: R. J. Lewis. *Impey*: C. Wilson. *Little Boy*: Kate Neville. *Little Girl*: Mary Page.

1874.21 THE BLACK CROOK

A Revival of the Imperial Spectacle (Musical Extravaganza) in Four Acts[15]. (Play by Charles M. Barras. Music by Thomas Baker, others.) Produced and staged by the Kiralfy Brothers (Imre, Bolossy). Opened 25 November 1874 at the Grand Opera House and closed 2 January 1875 after 44 performances.[16]

CAST: Mortals: *Rudolph Werner*, a Young Painter: W. L. STREET. *Count Wolfenstein*: W. A. DAVENPORT. *Hertzog*, The Black Crook": E. K. COLLIER. *Greppo*, his servant: GEORGE ATKINS. *M. Von Puffengruntz*, the Count's Chamberlain: GEORGE E. ELLIOTT. *Wolfgar, Bruno*, Gipsey Ruffians in the pay of Wolfenstein: John Hammond, Pietro Caisi. *Caspar*, a Peasant: Charles Rushton. *Dame Barbara*: Mme. R. Neuville. *Carline*: ANNIE KEMP BOWLER. *Amina*: KATE FELLOWS. *Rosetta*, a Peasant: Sally Pierson. *Peasants, Guards, etc.*

Immortals: *Stalacta*, Queen of the Golden Realm: ELIZA WEATHERSBY. *Dragonfin*, a Sprite: Master Martin. *Zamiel*, the Arch Fiend: R. CHARLES. *Redglare*, Recording Demon: R. Charles. *Skudawelp*: William Crowley.

Ballet: Mlles. MARIE BONFANTI, EUGENIA LUPO, KATHI and EMILY KIRALFY. *Specialties*: THE LENTON FAMILY (acrobats), THE VAIDI'S PERSIAN TWIN SISTERS (trapeze act), Kynock and Smith (skating), The London Madrigal Boys.

Act 1: Hartz Mountains.

Act 2: Grotto of Stalacta.

Act 3: Illuminated Gardens of Wolfenstein.

Act 4: Pandemonium. Zamiel in Council.

BALLETS, SPECIALTIES
Song (Act 1)
A. K. Bowler
Songs (Act 2)
E. Weathersby
"Silver Threads (Among the Gold)" (Act 2)
Quartette
(*Music by* Hart Pease Danks. *Lyrics by* Eben E. Rexford.)
The Demon's Revels (Act 2)
Grand Ballet Infernato (*Composed and arranged by* Imre Kiralfy.)
Mlles. Bonfanti, Lupo, Secondas, Coryphées, Corps de Ballet
Grand Ballet of All Nations (Act 3) (*Composed and arranged by* Imre Kiralfy.)
Grand Entrée, Persia, Russia, Germaina
Coryphées, Corps de Ballet
Fleur d'Espagne
Danseuses Secondaires
Les Sabotiers de Normandy
Ladies of the Ballet
Ensemble and Hongrois
Coryphées
Csardas
Kiralfy Sisters
France
Mlle. Lupo
Friska
Kiralfy Troupe
Grand Finale, Brilliante of China, Japan and All Nations
Premieres, Secondas, Coryphées, Corps de Ballet
Specialties (Act 3)
The London Madrigal Boys
The Vaidi's Persian Twin Sisters in their grand Double Trapeze performance
Messrs. Kynock & Smith in their skating act
The Famous Lenten Family
Grand March of the Diamond Warriors
250 Ladies
Grand Marble Life Tableaux: (Act 4)
Les Fêtes des Gladiateurs (*Arranged by* Imre Kiralfy.)

[14]First produced in New York 25 November 1872 at the Grand Opera House for 57 performances. For Synopsis of Scenes, see original 1872 production.
[15]First produced in New York 12 September 1866 at Niblo's Garden for 475 performances.

[16]No credits for authorship, scenery, costumes or musical director in programs.

1874.22

THE GRAND DUCHESS OF GÉROLSTEIN

A Revival of the Opéra-bouffe in Three Acts[17],. Original French libretto by Henri Meilhac and Ludovic Halévy. Music by Jacques Offenbach. Stage manager, John Wallace. Acting manager, John Powell. Scenery by Hannibal W. Calyo. Conductor, George Richardson. Produced by Maurice Grau and C. A. Chizzola. Manager of the Emily Soldene English Opera Bouffe Company, Charles Morton. Opened 30 November 1874 at the Lyceum Theatre and closed 25 December 1874 after 10 performances in repertory; season closed 2 January 1875.

CAST: *La Grande-Duchesse de Gérolstein*: EMILY SOLDENE. *Fritz*: E. D. BEVERLY. *Prince Paul*: J. B. RAE. *Baron Puck*: EDWARD MARSHALL. *General Boum*: H. LEWENS. *Baron Grog*: HENRI LAURENT. *Nepomuc*, Aid-de-Camp: J. Wallace. *Wanda*, Country Girl: Clara Vesey. *Maids of Honor to the Grand Duchess (4)*: *Iza*: LIZZY ROBSON. *Amelia*: LAURA CARTHEW. *Olga*: MARIE WILLIAMS. *Charlotte*: Miss H. Travers. *Lords and Ladies of the Court, Maids of Honor, Pages, Ushers, Soldiers, Vivandières, Country Girls.*

Period: 1720.

1874.23

CHILPÉRIC

An Opéra-bouffe in Three Acts, 4 Scenes[18]. Original French libretto and music by Hervé. (English adaptation by Richard Mansell, Robert Reece and F. A. Marshall.) Stage manager, John Wallace. Acting manager, John Powell. Scenery by Hannibal W. Calyo. Conductor, George Richardson. Manager of the Emily Soldene English Opera Bouffe Company, Charles Morton. Produced by Maurice Grau and C. A. Chizzola. Opened 9 December 1874 at the Lyceum Theatre and closed 26 December 1874 after 13 performances in repertory; season closed 2 January 1875; returned 31 May 1875 for an additional performance in repertory at the Lyceum Theatre.

CAST: *Chilpéric*, King of the Gauls: EMILY SOLDENE. *Senna*, Court Physician: EDWARD MARSHALL. *Landry*, a Peasant: H. LAURENT. *Fatout*, Grand Chamberlain: J. WALLACE. *Sigebert*, Chilpéric's Brother: H. LEWENS. *Nervoso*, a Spanish Grandee: J. B. RAE. *Divitiaticus*, High Priest of the Druids: T. Quine. *Frédégonde*, a Peasant Girl: AGNES LYNDHURST. *Galsuinda*, a Spanish Princess: LIZZIE ROBSON. *Brunehaut*, Sigebert's Wife: H. Travers. *Alfred*, Chilpéric's Pet Page: Clara Vesey. *Clodomir*, a Noble: Laura Carthew. *Leucaste*, a Noble: Miss E. St. Clair. *Fana*, High Priestess: Miss Carthew.

Pages to Chilpéric (12): *Edward*: Miss R. Roberts. *Hubert*: Miss U. Brooke. *Richard*: Miss Beaumont. *Albert*: Miss N. Reid. *Hector*: Miss R. Reid. *Henry*: Miss Loftus. *Charles*: Miss K. Charley. *William*: Miss Williams. *Ernest*: Miss Grey. *Conrad*: Miss Nichols. *Eustache*: Miss Bell. *Francis*: Miss Carman. *Druids, Druidesses, Huntsmen, Warriors, Lords, Ladies, etc.*

Act 1: A Forest.

Act 2: A magnificent ante-room in the palace of Chilpéric.

Act 3, Scene 1: Chamber in the palace. *Scene 2*: Chilpéric's Camp outside the walls of Soissons.

ACT 1[19]

Opening Chorus (The golden sickle's waiting)
T. Quine, Chorus of Druids

"The Story of Chilpéric" (Mark yon visage appalling)
A. Lyndhurst, Land

Entrance of Chilpéric (Halt, my friends!)
E. Soldene

"The Story of the Ham" (One day the great King Pharamond)
E. Soldene, Chorus

Entrance of Senna (In the hour of need)
E. Marshall

"Queen of My Heart" (None can compare with thee)(Ballad)
E. Soldene

Quartette and Ensemble (Ah! charming Frédégonde)
E. Soldene, H. Lewens, H. Travers, A. Lyndhurst

Entrance of Druids and Druidesses (At your command, behold us here!)
T. Quine, E. Soldene, Chorus

Entrance of Fana (Devilish pretty woman too!)
E. Soldene, Miss Carthew, Chorus

Finale (Come, let us mount and hasten home)
E. Soldene, Miss Carthew, A. Lyndhurst, All

ACT 2

Scene ('Tis ten o'clock, the hour has come)
A. Lyndhurst, H. Laurent, Pages

"Song of the Butterfly" (A Butterfly lived in a garden gay)
E. Soldene, Chorus

Air (As head physician, my high position)
E. Marshall

"The Shepherd's Song" (Ah! Simple youth!)
H. Landry, H. Travers

Couplets (What means this information?)
A. Lyndhurst, E. Soldene

Scene (The Princess is at hand)
J. Wallace, E. Soldene, Chorus

Scene (Welcome from all, with deepest expectation)
E. Soldene, L. Robson

Bolero (In the Sierra Morena)
E. Marshall, L. Robson, Chorus

Finale (My hope is o'er now far away I go)
A. Lyndhurst, Chorus

ACT 3

Scene 1

Opening Chorus (With jest and song the hours we'll prolong)
Pages

Solo (Say will the night pass o'er securely)
A. Lyndhurst

Scene (Ah! night of vengeance hasten on)
A. Lyndhurst, Chorus

Duet (Can you go? leave me so?)
L. Robson, E. Soldene

Fandango! (In Pampelune, near old Toledo)
L. Robson

Chorus (Oh, bother!)
Chorus

Scene 2

Solo (Life is but a brief transition—)
H. Lewens

March of the Gallic Host (Vanquished is the stubborn foe)
Chorus

Finale (Now strife is over)
E. Soldene

1874.24

JACK AND JILL

A Comical, Whimsical, Allegorical, Tragical, Logical (Trick) Pantomime in a Prologue and Three Acts, 18 Scenes. Play written and directed by James S. Maffitt. Mechanical effects, William Deverna. Musical director, William Withers, Jr. Produced by N. D. Roberts. Opened 21 December 1874 at Niblo's Garden and closed 2 January 1875 after 17 performances.[20]

CAST: Prologue: *Science*: KATY FELLOWS. *Art*: Emily Hervert. *Dame Nature*: Imogene Schofield. *Ignorance*: G. F. Williams. *Stupidity*: J. M. Freeman. *Crime*: Harry Hunter. *Prejudice*: Harry Lester. *Conceit*: J. C. Franklin. *Poverty*: William Ennice. *Idleness*: Fred Runnells.

Pantomime: *Jackdaw Jaculation*, known as Troublesome Jack: JAMES S. MAFFITT. *Miss Jemima Dill*, known as Mischievous Jill: HARRY JEE. *Dame Dorothy Dingle*, known as Goody Two-Shoes; CHARLES CHRISTIE. *Old Gridley Grindstone*, the Hard-hearted Miller: GEORGE F. KETCHUM. *Peter Piper*, who picked the Pickled

[17]Previously presented in New York in French 24 September 1867 at the Théâtre Français for 156 performances; in English 17 June 1868 (in a different version) at the New York Theatre for 33 performances. For Synopsis of Scenes and Musical Numbers, see original 1868 production. No credit for English adaptation.

[18]English language premiere in New York. Previously produced in New York in French 1 June 1869 at Théâtre Français for 6 performances.

[19]Musical numbers not listed in programs. List prepared from published libretto (Metropolitan Printing and Engraving Establishment, New York, 1874).

[20]Costumes and scenery uncredited in programs, posters.

Peppers: JAMES W. SANFORD. *Jack Horner*, who once sat in a corner: WASH ANTONIO. *Miss Henrietta Hood*, known as Little Red Riding Hood: Mlle. DEARDON. *Miss Anna Maria Dimple*, known as Dotty Dimple: ADA LAURENT. *Dairy Maids, Villagers, Corps de Ballet, Peasants, Millers, Farm Hands*: Numerous Auxiliaries.

Transformation of Characters: *Clowns*: JAMES S. MAFFITT, HARRY JEE. *Harlequins*: JAMES W. SANFORD, WASH ANTONIO. *Pantaloons*: GEORGE F. KETCHUM, CHARLES CHRISTIE. *Columbines*: ADA LAURENT, Mlle. DEARDON. *Sprites*: William Eunice, Fred Runnells. *Specialties*: GARNELLA BROTHERS (Robert, Little Dick), gymnasts, acrobats; JEE FAMILY (Harry, William, Joseph, and children, Ninnie and Joey); Caron Family; Langlois Brothers (Egyptian Jugglers), Shed LeClair, Kit Carson, John LeClair, Burt Johnson, Frank Barry, John A. Saunders, Davenport Brothers (Edward, Lewis), Ted Almont, Felix Rovetti, Tom Barry, John A. Smyth. *Ballet*: Mlles. MARIE BONFANTI, AMELIA CERUTE; Mons. APPOLON BAPTISTAN. Mlles. Katrina, Emily Crowe, Sophie Ravel, Addie Scarcey, Rose May, Stacy, Lizzie Smith, Evelina, Mars, Frank. Corps de Ballet of 30.

Act 1, Scene 1: Dense Depths of Ignorance. *Scene 2*: The Cave of Dark Despair. *Scene 3*: Dingle Dell Dairy Farm. *Scene 4*: Garnella Brothers. *Scene 5*: Original Dollar Store and Wild Cat Savings Bank. *Scene 6*: Musical Rocks. *Scene 7*: English Farm Yard.

Act 2, Scene 1: Les Nymphs du Lac. *Scene 2*: Bells in the Kitchen. *Scene 3*: Bill Foster's retreat. *Scene 4*: Caron Family. *Scene 5*: Franklin School. *Scene 6*: Langlois Brothers. *Scene 7*: Anywhere Place. *Scene 8*: Squeer's Academy for Ladies. *Scene 9*: Faro Bank. *Scene 10*: Le Grand Trampelin.

Act 3: Transformation Scene.

BALLETS, SPECIALTIES

Transformation of Characters (Act 1, Scene 3)

Garnella Brothers (Act 1, Scene 4)

Jee Brothers (Harry, William)(Act 1, Scene 6)

Les Nymphs Du Lac (Grand Ballet, arranged by Appolon Baptistan)
Mlles. Katrina, E. Crowe, S. Ravel, A. Scarcey, R. May, Stacy, L. Smith, Evelina, Mars, Frank, Corps de Ballet

Jee Brothers (Harry, William)(Act 2, Scene 2)

Caron Family in their pleasing performances (Act 2, Scene 4)

Langlois Brothers (Act 2, Scene 6)

Le Grand Trampolin (Act 2, Scene 10)
S. LeClair, K. Carson, J. LeClair, B. Johnson, F. Barry, W. Jee, J. A. Saunders, W. Eunice, Langlois Brothers, F. Runnells, Davenport Brothers, T. Almont, F. Rovetti, T. Barry, J. A. Smyth

Transformation of Characters (Act 4)

1874.25

FEE-G!

An Original Comical Musical Burlesque in One Act, 5 Scenes, preceded by an Olio. Play by Edward Harrigan. Music by David Braham. Stage manager, G. L. Stout. Scenic artist, D. L. Weed. Orchestra director, David Braham. Costumes, Miss Margaret Devoy. Machinist and Properties, Nelse Waldron. Produced by Josh Hart. Opened 21 December 1874 at the Theatre Comique and closed 26 December 1874 after 9 performances.

Olio: Big Gun and Little Gun, a laughable sketch with Charles White and William Carter. Miss Alice Bennett in her beautiful songs. John Williams in his unequalled Clog Dance. Patrick's Day Parade, an original Irish sketch by Edward Harrigan with music by David Braham, with Edward Harrigan (as Fitzgerald Conroy), Tony Hart (as Johanna McCann), and James Bradley (as Hogarth Higgins). Serio-Comic Songs by Miss Amy Roberts. George H. Adams on the Stilts. Wild and White's very laughable Negro sketch entitled, Going Home Again! John Wild and William Gaylord in their burlesque trapeze. Unparalleled success of Harrigan's laughable musical interlude entitled The Skidmores! performed by Messrs. Harrigan, Hart, Wild, White, Carter, Kelly, Bradley, Gaylord, Williams, Andrews, and Graver. The LeCalvin Brothers with their Crystal Caskets.

CAST: *King Luncher*, who keeps a Map of route: D. H. KELLY. *Prince Dainty*, an eat 'em on the half shell: Miss POLLY BOOTH. *Peter Heathentamer*, a Migrate f rom Brooklyn to the land of the Palm: JOHN WILD. *Mrs. Heathentamer*, his better half, who takes her old tickets for her lecture: Mr. WILLIAM CARTER. *P. T. Barnum*, name is sufficient: J. F. CROSSIN. *Appetizer*, always hungry: J. Bradley. *Watermelon*, always hungry: J. A. Graver. *Vealcutletts*: G. L. Stout. *Policeman*: G. L. Stout. *Ham and Eggs, Corn-Starch*, opposite sex: Mrs. Graver, Miss Kelly Tilstone. *Custardo, Omelet*, opposite sex: Miss Grabs, Miss Lewis. *W. U. T. Co.*: An Emissary. *Bernardo*, a Sligo man, who secures the influences of a King: EDWARD HARRIGAN. *Princess Mutton Chops*, a real Buffalo-William-Indian beauty: Mr. TONY HART.

The action takes place in a restaurant. No checks. Time on slate.

Scene 1: A wet and dark night on the Fee-Gee Group of Islands. *Scene 2*: A Grove similar to Dudley's. *Scene 3*: The Mutual Base-Ball Ground. *Scene 4*: Ward School in the Tropics. *Scene 5*: Ball-Room in King Luncher's Palace.

MUSICAL NUMBERS, SPECIALTIES

Midnight Song and Chorus of Real Vicious Cannibals (Scene 1)

"Muffin Nine" (Duet)(Scene 2)
P. Booth, T. Hart

Grand March of the Dresses (Scene 5)

1874.26

MADAME L'ARCHIDUC

An Opéra-comique in Three Acts. Original French libretto by Albert Millaud. English adaptation by Henry B. Farnie. Music by Jacques Offenbach. Stage manager, John Wallace. Acting manager, John Powell. Scenery by Hannibal W. Calyo. Conductor, George Richardson. Manager of the Emily Soldene English Opera Bouffe Company, Charles Morton. Produced by Maurice Grau and C. A. Chizzola. Opened 29 December 1874 at the Lyceum Theatre and closed 2 January 1875 after 6 performances in repertory; returned 1 and 4 June 1875 for 2 additional performances in repertory at the Lyceum Theatre.

CAST: *Marietta*, Madame L'Archiduc: EMILY SOLDENE. *Fortunato*: LIZZIE ROBSON. *The Countess*: CLARA VESEY. *Giacommetta*: ROSINA ROBERTS. *Archduke Ernest*: EDWARD MARSHALL. *Giletti*: E. D. BEVERLEY. *The Count*: Mr. HILLIERS. *Innkeeper*: F. Charles. *Ricardo*: J. B. RAE. *Beppino*: Mr. Cooper. *Conspirators (4)*: *Scaevola*: HENRI LAURENT. *Cocles*: Mr. Quine. *Themistocles*: Mr. Maynard. *Lycurgus*: Mr. Cullen. *Ministers (4)*: *Piano Dolce*: Mr. Hilliers. *Andantino*: Mr. Quinton. *Tutti Frutti*: Mr. Gibbons. *Chi-lo-sa*: Mr. Cotterill. *Dragoons, Courtiers, Ladies, (Villagers, Retainers, Waiters, Maid-Servants,) etc.*

Act 1: Exterior of a rural Italian Inn.

Act 2: A Hall in the Count's Chateau.

Act 3: Exterior of Chateau at night.

ACT 1[21]

Conspirators' Chorus (S.A.D.E.)
Messrs. H. Laurent, Quine, Maynard, Cullen

Chorus (At last the happy hour is ringing)
Villagers, Waiters, Servant-Maids

Bridal Couplets (To be made man and wife so merry)
E. Soldene, E. D. Beverly, Chorus

The Bridal Tour (I know not where we shall be roving)
E. Soldene

The Waiters' Lament (We have all a family feeling)
Waiters, Maid Servants

Kissing Duet (To think of me ever I'd teach thee—)
Mr. Hilliers, C. Vesey

Song (Your pardon, sir; my lady, pardon!)
E. Soldene

Quartette (She tells the truth)
E. Soldene, C. Vesey, E. D. Beverly, Mr. Hilliers

"The Little Captain" (Who am I? You must come from Siam!)
L. Robson

Nonsense Duet (Pumpernickel ist Deutsches brodt)
Mr. Hilliers, C. Vesey, L. Robson

Dragoons' Chorus (Nous sommes il dragoni del Ernesto Quarto)
L. Robson, E. D. Beverly, C. Vesey, Mr. Hilliers, J. B. Rae, Chorus

Song (A captain, you! and no mustache!)
E. Soldene

Finale (Come on, come on)
Principals, Chorus

ACT 2

Retainers' Chorus (In the halls of their ancestors)
Chorus

Duet (Ah! Ah! 'Tis thou, Marietta!)
E. D. Beverly, E. Soldene

Song (Oh, yes, I can perceive my blunder)
L. Robson

"Alphabet Sextette" (S.A.D.E.)
E. Soldene, E. D. Beverly, Conspirators

---

[21]Musical numbers not listed in programs. List prepared from published libretto (Metropolitan Printing and Engraving Establishment, New York, 1875); Farnie's name does not appear.

Entrance of Duke (Here comes the Duke)
Chorus
Song (Original! Original! I am a true original!)
E. Marshall, Chorus
Chorus (Original! Original! Surely he is original!)
Courtiers, Lords, Ladies, Dragoons, Ministers
Villager's Song ('Tis at night we meet, we're carousing)
E. Soldene, E. Marshall, L. Robson
Chorus (It is the Duke's bell that's ringing)
E. Soldene, E. Marshall, L. Robson, Chorus
Entrance of Conspirators (Here they are—I released them duly)
L. Robson, E. Soldene, E. D. Beverly, E. Marshall, Chorus
Finale (Come, come, it's time to be getting along)
E. D. Beverly, L. Robson, E. Marshall, Chorus

ACT 3
Patrol Chorus (In uniform, we're guardians of the night)
L. Robson, Chorus
Scene (What is that noise, some dread alarm 'tis)
L. Robson, E. Soldene, E. Marshall, Chorus
Duet (Oh! stay a moment more! Ah! stay thee)
L. Robson, E. Soldene
Song (The Duke, with royal kindness)
E. Soldene
Finale (I am no longer Countess)
E. Soldene

1875.01 LE VOYAGE EN CHINE

An Opéra-comique in Three Acts, in French. Libretto by Eugène Labiche and Alfred Delacour. Music by François Bazin. Mis en scène [staged] by M. Valere. Scenery by H. Isherwood, Gaspard Maeder. Chorus and orchestra under the direction of Charles Van Ghele. Produced by William Stuart, in association with C. A. Chizzola and Maurice Grau. Opened 11 January 1875 at the Park Theatre for (11) performances in repertory; season closed 20 March 1875.

CAST: *Henri de Kernoison*: Mons. DeQuercy. *Pompéry*: Mons. DUPLAN. *Alidor de Rosenville*: Mons. DEBEER. *Bonneteau*, Notaire: Mons. Valaire. *Maurice Fréval*: Mons. Chantal. *Martial*: Mons. Victor. *Mme. Marie Pompéry*: Mlle. LEONTINE MINELLY. *Berthe Pompéry*: Mlle. GUERZY. *Caroline*, femme de Pompery: Mlle. ROSE BLONDELET. *Un Domestique*: Mlle. Thulliard. *Un Garçon D'hotel*: Mlle. Davalis. *Baignon, Bagneuses, Matelots.*

Act 1: Salon at Paris, 1874.

Act 2: Salon in Casino, at Cherbourg.

Act 3: Le Voyage en Chine—Deck of the Ship.

ACT 1[22]
Duo (Qu'a-t-elle donc?)
Mlles. Minelly, Guerzy, Blondelet
Chanson Napolitaine (Le ciel bleu se colore)
Mlles. Minelly, Gherzy
Marche at Choeur (C'est jour de fête)
Mlles. Blondelet, Gherzy, Blondelet, Mons. Chantal, [Baptiste], Choeur
Air et Morceau d'Ensemble (Bien tranquille, rênes en mine)
Mons. Duplan, Tous
Morceau d'Ensemble (Je vous présente ici ma femme)
Messrs. Duplan, Debeer, Chantal, Mlles. Gherzy, Blondelet
Boléro (Dans toutes les Espagnes)
Messrs. Debeer, Duplan, Chantal, Mlles. Minelly, Gherzy, Blondelet
Récitatif et Romance (Ah! Je vais donc enfin la revoir)
Mons. DeQuercy
Duo (Ah! quelle amusante folie)
Mlle. Minelly, Mons. DeQuercy
Finale (C'est jour de fête)
Tous

ACT 2
Choeur et Morceau d'Ensemble (Ah! quelle heureuse destinée!)
Messrs. Duplan, Valaire, Mlles. Blondelet, Minelly, Gherzy, Choeur
Ariette (Six cailloux, cinq cailloux)
Messrs. Debeer, Duplan, Valaire, Mlles. Blondelet, Minelly, Gherzy
Choeur et Morceau d'Ensemble (Quel temps effroyable!)
Mlles. Blondelet, Minnely, Gherzy, Messrs. DeQuercy, Duplan, Duplan, Valaire
Duo (Oui, mon coeur est à toi)
Mlle. Minelly, Mons. DeQuercy
Duo (Je suis Breton)
Messrs. DeQuercy, Duplan
Duetto (Oui, dès ce soir, j'en ai l'espoir)
Mlle. Minelly, Mons. DeQuercy
Finale (Grand Dieu! Qu'ai-je entendu?)
Tous

ACT 3
Choeur des Matelots (Voguons, la mer est belle)
Messrs. Victor, Duplan, Valaire, Debeer, Choeur
Choeur du Cidre (Qu'il est bon le cidre de Normandie!)
Mons. Victor, Choeur
Couplets (Quand le soleil sur notre monde)
Mons. Duplan
Récitatif et Air (Il est parti! Rêve d'amour et d'espérance)
Mlle. Minelly
Duo (Cet instant qui me rend mon Henri)
Mlle. Minelly, Mons. DeQuercy
Morceau d'Ensemble (En Chien! en Chine!)
Mlles. Guerzy, Blondelet, Messrs. Debeer, Duplan, Valaire, Victor
Air (La Chine est un pays charmante)
Mons. DeQuercy
Choeur (A bas le capitaine!)
Mons. Victor, Choeur
Couplets (Pour bien fêter notre retour)
Mons. Duplan
Finale (Tin! tin! tin! Qu'ici l'allégresse)
Tous

1875.02 LA FILLE DE MADAME ANGOT!

A Revival of the Opéra-comique in Three Acts, in French[23]. Libretto by Clairville, Paul Siraudin and Victor Koning. Music by Charles Lecocq. Scenery by Messrs. Hannibal Calyo and Weston. Musical director, Mons. Charles Van Ghele. Produced by William Stuart, in association with C. A. Chizzola and Maurice Grau. Opened 22 January 1875 at the Park Theatre for (13) performances in repertory; season closed 20 March 1875.

CAST: *Clairette Angot*: Mlle. BERTHE GIRARDIN. *Mlle. Lange*: Mlle. LEONTINE MINELLY. *Amaranthe*: Mlle. Jenny Kid. *Ange Pitou*: Mons. DeQuercy. *Larivaudière*: Mons. VALAIRE. *Trenitz*: Mons. GENOT. *Pomponnet*: Mons. DAVALIS. *Louchard*: Mons. DUPLAN. *(Ports de la Halle, Bourgeois, Grenadiers, Encroyables, Conspirateurs, Hussards, Domestiques, Dames de la Halle, Bougeoises, Merveilleuses*: Chorus.)

In the Third Act, "La Fricassee," a National Republican Dance of 1797, will be danced by Mlle. Vandame, Mons. Genot and the entire company.

1875.03 TOM AND JERRY, or, Life in London

A Revival of the Burletta Extravaganza in Three Acts, 18 Scenes[24]. Play by W. T. Moncrieff "with new scenery and all the original music." Produced by

[22]Musical numbers not listed in programs. List prepared from published French piano vocal score (Lemoine & fils, Paris, (1865).

[23]First produced in New York in French 25 August 1873 at Daly's Broadway Theatre in repertory; returned 9 March 1874 to the Lyceum Theatre in repertory. For Synopsis of Scenes and Musical Numbers, see original 1873 production.

[24]First produced in New York 3 March 1823 at the Park Theatre. In its last day, the advertised title of the play became CORINTHIAN TOM AND HAWTHORNE JERRY; or, High and Low Life in London. For this revival, the following ballets were performed at the close of Act 1:
Grand Pas de Tros
K. Lanner, Francesco Sisters
Mazourka
K. Lanner, Francesco Sisters
La Galleganda, Pas Espagnole Comique
K. Lanner, G. V. de Francesco

C. R. Thorne. Opened 1 February 1875 at Niblo's Garden and closed 3 February 1875 after 3 performances.

CAST: *Corinthian Tom*: C. L. FARWELL. *Jerry Hawthorn*: LOUIS MESTAYER. *Dr. Logic*, commonly called Bob Logic: Mr. Ketchum. *Squire Hawthorn*: G. Johnson. *Hon. Dick Trifle*: W. H. Hamilton. *Primefit*: W. H. Hamilton. *O'Boozle*: Mr. Waters. *McLush*: J. Reily. *Tartar*, Constable of the Night: G. Johnson. *Jack*, the Gas-Light Man: M. Lewis. *Mace*: Mr. Jones. *Cope*: Mr. Barckley. *Gullum*: Mr. Waters. *Baron Nab 'Em*, alias Mr. Borrowbody: Mr. Fox. *Crib*: Mr. Johnson. *Tattersall*: Mr. Riely. *Regulator*: Mr. Montgomery. *Sir Harry Blood*: Mr. Peters. *Billy Waters*: Mr. Hunsen. *Dusty Bob*: H. Walker. *Little Jerry*: Little Budworth. *Ragged Jack*: Mr. Tilston. *O'Shaughnessy*: Mr. Mathews. *African Sal*: F. Budworth. *Jackson*: Mr. Abrahams. *Shadow*, Confederate: Mr. Paulson. *Kate Corinthian*: Fanny Burt. *Hon. Miss Triffle*: Fanny Burt. *Sir Jeremy Brag*: Fanny Burt. *Match Girl*: Fanny Burt. *Sue*: Kate Quinton. *Hon. Miss Triffle*: Kate Quinton. *Captain Swagger*: Kate Quinton. *Ballad Singer*: Kate Quinton. *Jane*: Elsie Moore. *Hon. Miss Triffle*: Elsie Moore. *Mr. Memerag*, Fortune-Teller: Elsie Moore. *Pretty Beggar*: Elsie Moore. *Mrs. Tartar*: Emily Vernon. *Beggars, Dancers, Ladies of the Ballet. Ballet*: Mlles. KATHI LANNER, RACHEL de FRANCESCO, MARIETTA de FRANCESCO; Signor G. V. de FRANCESCO. *Boxing Specialty*: JAMES KELLY, SEDDONS MOUSE.

1875.04 GIROFLÉ-GIROFLA

An Opéra-bouffe in Three Acts, in French. Libretto by Albert Vanloo and Eugene Leterrier. Music by Charles Lecocq. Scenery by Matt Morgan, Richard Marston, William Voegtlin. Costumes made in Paris by Millet. Mechanical effects by Mons. Burgard, Garbit and Hardy. Chorus and orchestra under the direction of Mons. Charles Van Ghele. Produced by William Stuart, in association with C. A. Chizzola and Maurice Grau. Opened 4 February 1875 at the Park Theatre for (46) performances in repertory; season closed 20 March 1875; re-opened 15 May 1875 at the Lyceum Theatre; season closed 29 May 1875.

CAST: *Giroflé, Girofla*: Mlle. CORALIE GEOFFROY. *Marasquin*: Mlle. LEONTINE MINELLY. *Aurore*: Mlle. Jenny Kid. *Pedro*: Mlle. Esther Dorel. *Paquita*: Mlle. VANDAMME. *Mourzouk*: Mons. DeQuercy. *Don Bolero d'Alcazaros*: Mons. VALAIRE. *Le Chef de Pirates*: Mons. Valter. *Un Danzeur*: Mons. Genot. *Le Parrain*: Mons. Salvator. *Le Notaire*: Mons. Perrault. *Le Precepteur*: Mons. Négre. *L'Oncle*: Mons. Chantal. *Le Garçon d'honneur*: Mons. Duvalis. *La Marraine*: Mlle. Blondelet. *Fernand*: Mlle. Perrault. *Guzman*: Mlle. Julien. *Almazer*: Mlle. Clancey. *Petits cousins, des maries, hommes et dames du palais, demoiselles d'honneur. Pages, Pirates, Moures, de la suit de Mourzouk.*

Act 1: The Jardin and Palais of Bolero. Spain, around 1250. (Morgan.)

Act 2: Grand Salon in the Palais Bolero. (Marston.)

Act 3: Another Salon in the Palais Bolero. (Voegtlin.)

ACT 1[25]

Introduction:
Choeur (Que chacun se compose un visage joyeux)
Ballade (Lorsque la journée est finie)
Mlle. Vandamme
Couplets (Pour un tendre père)
Mons. Valaire
Couplets de Giroflé (Père adoré, c'est Giroflé)
Mlle. C. Geoffroy
Musique de Scène et Couplets de Griroflé
Couplets de Marasquin (Mon père est un très-gros banquier)
Mlle. L. Minelly
Ensemble et Choeur (A la chapelle on vous appelle)
Couplets (O ciel! qu'ai-je ressenti là)
Mlles. L. Minelly, C. Geoffroy
Choeur des Pirates (Parmi les choses délicates)
Duo (C'est fini! le mariage)
Mlles. L. Minelly, C. Geoffroy
Marche Mauresque et Choeur des Maures (Majestueux et deux par deux)
Couplets (Ce matin l'on m'a dit)
Mlle. C. Geoffroy
Finale:
Choeur (Voici l'heure et le moment)
Choeur
Sextuor (Comme elle ressemble à sa soeur)

ACT 2

Choeur des Invités (Nous voici, monsieur le beau-père)
Sortie (À table! à table!)
Duetto (Papa! papa! ça n'peut pas durer comm 'ça)
Mlle. C. Geoffroy, Mons. Valaire
Chanson avec choeur (Nos ancêtres étaient sages)
Mlle. L. Minelly
Galop (Écoutez cette musique)
Quintetto (Matamoros grand capitaine)
Mons. Valaire, Mlles. E. Dorel, J. Kid, C. Geoffroy, Vandamme
Musique de scène
Ensemble (Bon appétit belle cousine)
Brindisi (Le punch scintille)
Mlle. C. Geoffroy
Musique de scène
Finale (Ah! qu'il est bon, qu'il est donc bon)

ACT 3

Aubade (Voici le matin)
Choeur
Duo (En tête-à-tête faire la dinette)
Mlles. C. Geoffroy, L. Minelly
Rondeau (Soyez généreux, soyez magnanime)
Duo (Ma belle Girofla)
Mons. DeQuercy, Mlle. C. Geoffroy
Trio (Il rage, l'animal)
Mons. DeQuercy, Mlles. C. Geoffroy, L. Minelly
Ensemble (Il est temps de se mettre en voyage)
Couplets (Certes, dans toute circonstance)
Mons. DeQuercy
Finale (Matamoros, grand capitaine)
Chœur

1875.05 AROUND THE WORLD IN 80 DAYS

A Spectacular and Realistic Drama in Six Acts, 10 Scenes. Play by Pillet and Connelly. Adapted from the novel by Jules Verne. Music by Benjamin Dean. Scenery by Ferdinand Arrogeni, Samuel Culbert, Richard Farren and John Watson. Mechanical effects by Harry West. Costumes by Louis Carland, Mrs. Pentland. Properties by Ferdinand W. Hofele. Calcium lights by Thomas W. Newton. Production under the immediate supervision of Maurice Pike, Stage Manager. William B. Freligh, Lessee and Manager. Opened 29 March 1875 at the Bowery Theatre and closed 24 April 1875 after 28 performances.[26]

CAST [in order of appearance]: *John Archibald*, an American: EDWIN F. THORNE. *Phileas Fogg*, who makes the bet: W. J. FLEMING. *Jean Passe Partout*, his servant: E. W. MARSTON. *Thomas Bulkley*, a brewer: W. Murray. *Andrew Steward*, an engineer: GEORGE FORRESTER. *Sir Philip Phelps*, a banker: Edwin Barry. *Samuel Fallentin*, a banker: F. J. Post. *Walter Ralph*, director of the Bank of England: W. Lansing. *Servant*, in club house of Eccentrics: S. Halpin. *Nancy*, sweetheart of Jean Passe Partout: MILLIE SACKETT. *John Fix*, a smart detective: Neil Gray. *Mr. Blivens*, English Consular Agent at Suez: John Chamberlain. *Djelnar*, foster-brother to Aouda and Ayeesha: J. B. Brown. *Aouda*, widow of the Rajah, whom they wish to burn: Mrs. W. G. JONES. *Ayeesha*, sister of Aouda: SAIDEE MONTGOMERY. *Priests, Armed Guards, Fakirs, Dervishes, Hindoo Multitude, Amazons. Mr. Obadiah*, a pompous Calcutta magistrate: John Walsh. *Mr. Oysterpuff*, his clerk: F. J. Post. *Secomale, Mabula, Mogula*, Priestesses: Misses Barry, Malvern, Conroy. *Mr. Whitely*, an old '49er: Charles Stokes. *Colonel Law*, another old '49er: W. Murray. *DeLoosely*, an excitable young stock broker: George Beam. *Philip*, the Barkeeper: S. Halpin. *Sammy*, the cool old operator on the little board: F. J. Post. *Second Barkeeper*: Mr. Lansing. *Carver*: Mr. Jones. *Chinamen, Guests and Patrons of Bar and Board. Bill Miles*, keeper of the station in the wilderness: Edwin Fenton. *Tom*, section man on the road: W. A. Murtach. *Conductor*, C.P.R.R.: Mr. Forrester. *Brakeman*: George Beam. *De Je Nonda*, chief of a hostile band of Sioux Indians: J. B. Brown. *Passengers, Indians, First and Second Chiefs. Lieutenant of Dragoons*: Charles Small. *Captain Andrew Speedy*, Master of Steamer Henrietta: John Brooks. *Mate*: W. Murray. *Engineer*: S. Halpin. *Fireman*: Mr. Jones. *Man at Wheel*: W. Lansing. *Sailors, Passengers, etc. Walter Ralph*: W. Lansing. *Telegraph Messenger*: Mr. Lanagan. *Liverpool Policemen*. (*Specialty*: Ouina, the Trained War Elephant.)

[25]Musical numbers not listed in programs. List prepared from the published English/French piano vocal score (Enoch & Sons, London, [1874]).

[26]No musical numbers listed in programs.

Act 1, Scene 1: Grand Saloon in the "Eccentrics" Club-House. (Culbert.) *Scene 2*: Wharf of the Steamship Canal at Suez. (Arrogoni.)

Act 2, Scene 1: An East Indian Bungalow. (Farren.) *Scene 2*: The Pagoda of Pillarye. (Arrogoni.) *Scene 3*: An Oriental Hotel at Calcutta. (Culbert.)

Act 3, Scene 1: The Cave of the Serpents on the Isle of Borneo. (Arrogoni.) *Scene 2*: The Merchants' Exchange, San Francisco, California. (Culbert.)

Act 4, Scene 1: Kearney Station, on the Pacific Railroad. (Farren.) *Scene 2*: The Ginat's Stairway. A Wild, Grand and Picturesque Ravine in the Rocky Mountains. (Farren.)

Act 5, Scene 1: The Cabin of the Steamer "Henrietta." (Watson) *Scene 2*: The Upper-Deck of the Steamer "Henrietta." (Watson.)

Act 6, Scene 1: Room in a Hotel in Liverpool. (Watson.) *Scene 2*: The Club-Room of the Eccentrics.

1875.06 AHMED!

A Great Tale of Enchantment, the Most Spectacular Drama Ever Produced, in Four Acts. Written and invented by Mrs. Julia E. Dunn, taken from a sketch by Washington Irving. Music by William Withers, Jr. Acting manager, Joseph C. Foster. Stage manager, Jerry Taylor. Ballets arranged by Mme. Kathi Lanner. Scenery by Matt Morgan. Music director, William Withers, Jr. Produced by Mrs. Julia E. Dunn. Opened 30 March 1875 at the Grand Opera House and closed 28 April 1875 after 28 performances.

CAST: *Moors: Ahmed*, the Captive Prince: KATIE MAYHEW. *Moulard*, King of Granada: CHARLES WRIGHT. *Eben Bonnaben*, the Prince's Tutor: Mr. Peters. *Himlah*, Captain of the Guard: Mr. W. Major. *Hazab*, a favorite slave: Charles Rosene. *Moorish Guards, Slaves, Nondescripts, etc.*

Birds Of The Air: Philosopher, an aged Owl: WELSH EDWARDS. *Foperina*, a well-bred Parrot: GEORGE ATKINS. *Croker*, a fortune-telling Raven: Mr. Elberts. *Nondescript*, the Raven's Provider: W. R. GREGORY. *Owls, Parrots, Ravens, etc.*: Birds of Good and Evil Omen.

Spaniards: Philip, King of Toledo: JOSEPH WILKS. *Leon, Sylvio*, Heralds of the Court: E. Restof, Frank Crane. *Abenfoulah*, a Magician: George Johnson. *Saledrino*, well versed in Magic: J. C. Archer. *Pedro Manassa, Lopez Sancho*, Physicians to the Court: Messrs. R. Williams, West. *Princess Aldegonda*, Daughter to the King: EDITH OSMOND.

Knights Aspiring To The Hand Of The Princess: Sir Anthony, Knight of Italy: J. C. CHAMBERLAIN. *Knight of the Golden Cross*: Mr. Welling. *Knight of the Conquering Sword*: Mr. Horton. *Knight of Valor and Constancy*: Mr. Fowler. *Knight Devoted to Love and War*: Mr. Decker. *Knight of Courage and Truth*: Mr. Hartwell. *Knight of the Powerful Arm*: Mr. Merrill. *Knight of Tried Fidelity*: Mr. Chapman. *Knight of the Lily of France*: Mr. Palmer. *Knight of the Golden Axe*: Mr. Howard. *Herald, Guards, Banner Bearers, Esquires, Pages, Ladies of the Court, etc.*

Spirits Of Good: Zelva, Spirit of Good, much needed through the world: ANNIE MORTIMER. *Ackbar*, Golden Sprite of the Enchanted Ring, a devoted slave to Zelva: Mr. T. J. Relluf.

Spirits Of Evil: Divetus, a Spirit of Revenge: STEPHEN SAVILLE. *Zamas*, Spirit of Fire: Mr. W. Major. *Furies*: Entire Chorus. *Nymphal Queen of the Enchanted Grotto*: ESTELLE MORTIMER. *Lipeta, Silva, Lorella*, Nymphs devoted to Love: Misses Martin, Emilie, Maria Bogart. *Spirits of Good and Evil, Dancing Girls of Toledo, Moorish Slaves, etc.*: Powerful Corps de Ballet.

Ballet: Mlles. GIUSEPPINA MORLACCHI, ANNETTA GALLETTI, RACHEL de FRANCESCO; Mlles. Karolin Schrotter, Marie Cammara, Johanna, Zoerner, Catrine, Michely, Minnie Holt, Ferrant, Emilie, Hearn, Ester, Julia Fenton, Marie Muller, Marie Schumann, Sophie Hasselberger, Katti Orloff; Secondas, Coryphées, Kathi Lanner's Pupils, Corps de Ballet.

Scene: Luxurious Garden attached to a Moorish Castle in Granada in medieval Spain. The Abode of the captive Prince.

BALLETS AND SPECIALTIES

"Who has not heard the Bird of the Air?" (Song)(Act 1)
K. Mayhew

Grand Divertissement Espagnol (Act 2)
Mlles. Schrotter, Cammara, Johanna, Zoerner, Catrine, Michely, Holt, Ferrant, Emilie, Hearn, Ester, Fenton

Grand Ballet of the Three Graces (Act 3)

Les Trois Graces
Mlles. Morlacchi, Galletti, DeFrancesco

Les Cupido
Kathi Lanner's Pupils

Grand Adagio
Mlles. Morlacchi, Kathi Lanner's Pupils

Valse
Mlles. Shrotter, Cammara, Johanna, Anna, Zoerner, Catrine, Josephine, Michely, Holt, Ferrant

Variation
Mlle. DeFrancesco

Lily Bud Dance
Kathi Lanner's Pupils

Variation
Mlle. Galletti

Variation
Mlle. Morlacchi

Grand Finale
Entire Ballet

Galop, Chorus and Ballet Movement (Act 4)
Coryphées, Corps de Ballet

Pas Espagnol (Act 4)
Kathi Lanner's Pupils

Bolero (Act 4)
Mlles. Schrotter, Cammara, Johanna, Zoerner, Catrine, Michely, Holt, Ferrant, Coryphées

1875.07 LA JOLIE PARFUMEUSE

An Opéra-comique in Three Acts, in French. Libretto by Hector Crémieux and Ernest Blum. Music by Jacques Offenbach. Stage manager, Mons. Schmidt. Scenery by Hannibal W. Calyo. Costumes by Mons. Millet. Musical director, Charles Van Ghele. Produced by C. A. Chizzola and Maurice Grau. Opened 31 March 1875 at the Lyceum Theatre and closed 14 May 1875 after a season in repertory.

CAST: *Rose Michon*: Mlle. MARIE AIMÉE. *Bavolet*: Mlle. NARDYNN. *Clorinde*: Mlle. DUBOUCHET. *Lise*: Mlle. CORAGLIA. *La Julienne*: —. *Mirette*: Mlle. Defrang. *Arthemise*: Mlle. Sivry. *Poirot*: Mons. CHARLES KOLLETZ. *Madelon*: Mlle. Vandelet. *La Cocardière*: Mons. DUBOUCHET. *Justine*: Mlle. Delmas. *Germain*: Mons. Arrigotti. *Waiters, Blind Musicians, Maids of Honor, Chambermaids, etc.*

Act 1: Aux Porcherons. Le jardin-bal.

Act 2: Un salon chez La Cocardière.

Act 3: Le magasin de la jolie parfumeuse.

ACT 1[27]

Choeur (C'est la noce! c'est la noce)

Couplets (Je vous amène aux Porcherons)
Mlle. Dubouchet

Choeur de Noce (Halte! Fixe! Immobiole!)
Messrs. C. Kolletz, Dubouchet, Mlles. Nardynn, [La Julienne], Choeur

Couplets de vertue (Y'a des gens qui s'imagin' bien)
Mlle. M. Aimée

Duetto (Ah! tenez! Monsieur Bavolet!)
Mlles. M. Aimée, Nardynn

Choeur (Du café des Ayeugl' artistes musiciens)

Couplets (Place au grand Verrouillaski)
Mons. C. Kolletz, Choeur

Choeur (Ohé! Marjolaines!)
Mlles. M. Aimée, Nardynn, Choeur

Final (Voici le couvre-feu!)
Tous

ACT 2

Choeur (La bonne aubaine que voilà!)
Mon. Arrigotti, Mlles. Delmas, Coraglia, Choeur

Scène (Salute, madame la mariée!)
Mlle. M. Aimée, Delmas, Coraglia, Choeur

Duo (Puisque plus rien ne t'embarrasse)
Mons. Dubouchet, Mlle. M. Aimée

Couplets de fête (Cher et noble La Cocardière)
Mlle. Dubouchet

Couplets (Mon parrain! ah! mon parrain!)
Mlle. Nardynn, Mons. C. Kolletz

[27]Musical numbers not listed in programs. List prepared from published French/English libretto (Metropolitan Printing and Engraving, New York, 1875).

Ensemble (Allons! le verre en main!)/ Chanson de Bruscambille
Mlles. M. Aimée, Nardynn, Dubouchet, Sivry, Vandelet, Mons. C. Kolletz, Choeur
Duo (Il paraît que dans le grand monde)
Mlles. Nardynn, M. Aimée
Chanson de Bruscambille (À Toulouse en Toulousain)
Mlle. Nardynn, M. Aimée

ACT 3
Choeur (Pan! pan! pan! à la boutique)
Mlles. Nardynn, [La Julienne], Choeur
Rondeau (Soyez donc bon homme)
Choeur
La Lettre (Monsieur, madam' Dorothé Bruscambille)
Mons. C. Kolletz
Duo (À nous deux, ma femme!)
Mlles. Nardynn, M. Aimée
Couplet (Ce qu'il faut me servir)
Mlle. Dubouchet
Final (Où donc as-tu passé la nuit?)
Mlles. Nardynn, M. Aimée, Mons. C. Kolletz, Tous

1875.08 LE PETIT FAUST

A Revival of the Opéra-bouffe in Three Acts[28], in French. Libretto by Hector Crémieux Adolphe Jaime. Music by Hervé. Musical director, Charles Van Ghele. Produced by C. A. Chizzola and Maurice Grau. Opened and closed 11 May 1875 at the Lyceum Theatre for 1 performance in repertory.

CAST: *Marguerite*: Mlle. MARIA AIMÉE. *Méphisto*: Mlle. NARDYNN. *Faust*: CHARLES KOLLETZ. *Valentin*: Mons. DeBEER. *A Coachman*: Mons. Genot. *An Anglo-Saxon*: Mons. Arrigotti.
Female Pupils (4): *Lisette*: Mlle. Cantrelle. *Aglae*: Mlle. Lafontaine. *Clorinde*: Mlle. Delmas. *Frosch*: Mlle. Limat. *Siebel*: Mlle. Vaudelet. *Soldiers, Students, Old Men and Women, Anglo-Saxons, Russians, Male and Female Demons.*

1875.09 LISCHEN ET FRITZCHEN

An Operetta in One Act, in French[29]. Libretto by Paul Boisselot. Music by Jacques Offenbach. Musical director, Charles Van Ghele. Produced by C. A. Chizzola and Maurice Grau. Opened and closed 14 May 1875 at the Lyceum Theatre after 1 performance.

CAST: *Lischen*, Alsacienne, Mde. De Halais: Mlle. MARIE AIMÉE. *Fritzchen*, Alsacien, Domestique: Mons. DeBEER.

MUSICAL NUMBERS[30]
Couplets (Me chasser, me forcer)
Mons. DeBeer
Chanson (P'tits balais, p'tits balais)
Mlle. M. Aimée
Duo (Je suis alsacienne)
Mlle. M. Aimée, Mons. DeBeer
Fable (Un jour un rat de ville)
Mlle. M. Aimée
Final et Duo (Quoi! Fritzchen)
Mlle. M. Aimée, Mons. DeBeer

[28]First produced in New York in French 26 September 1870 at the Grand Opera House for in repertory. For Synopsis of Scenes and Musical Numbers, see original 1870 production.
[29]New York premiere. In its published score, LISCHEN ET FRITZCHEN is billed not as an operetta, but as "conversation alsacienne en un acte." Followed by Act 2 of LA JOLIE PARFUMEUSE and a comedy vaudeville in One Act, La Femme aux Oeufs d'Or, by Dumanoir and Clairvlle, in which Aimée introduced songs in French, Spanish, German and English.
[30]Musical numbers not listed in programs. List prepared from published French piano vocal score (Brandus & Dufour, Paris, 1864).

1875.10 THE TWELVE TEMPTATIONS!

A Revival of the Beautiful Legendary Romance (Extravaganza) in Four Acts, 18 Scenes[31]. Play by Joseph C. Foster. Produced under the direction of Francis R. Foster. Ballets under the direction of Kathi Lanner. Orchestra under the direction of William Withers, Jr. Opened 15 May 1875 at the Grand Opera House and closed 25 May 1875 after 10 performances.

CAST: *Ulric*, the Tempted and Doomed: JOSEPH F. WHEELOCK. *Petreuse*, a Miller, with Songs: CHARLES STANLEY. *Rudolph*, the Tempter and Vampire: CHARLES WAVERLY. *Eblis*, the Spirit of Evil: Edward Dwyer. *Kalig*, the Son of Darkness: Francis Foster. *Eric*, Brother to Ulric: Charles Norris. *Gnomelob*, Prime Minister: George Johnson. *Baudoin*, Prince of Flanders: Charles H. Nichols. *Michael Brenno*, Chief Justice: Walter Glassford. *Captain Pierrepont*, Captain of the Guard: Frank Munro. *Sir Anthony*: R. E. Fulton. *Leon*, Chief Herald: John Reilly. *Archbishop of Flanders*: Francis Rufus. *Metcalf*, Keeper of the Royal Beetles: E. Chapman. *Justin*, the Red Executioner: Mr. Wright. *Paoli*, the Black Executioner: Mr. Jennings. *Egyptian Warriors (4)*: *Orchus*: M. Bellamore. *Busirus*: F. Glanze. *Orestor*: William Fitzallen. *Oleondez*: Henry Sirron. *Knight of Italy*: S. T. Savage. *Knight of France*: John Casey. *Knight of England*: Mr. Monteith. *Knight of Ireland*: Mr. Fitzroy. *Knight of Germany*: William Roberts. *Knight of Flanders*: John Enfield. *Knight of Sicily*: Mr. Dickson.*Warriors of the Cross, Soldiery of Egypt, Servitors of the Empire, Priests of Isis, Banner Bearers, Spirits of Destruction, Witches of the Walpurgis, Pilgrims, Knights, Esquires, Heralds, Pages, Armor Bearers, etc*: 200 Auxiliaries.
Janette, Mother to Ulric: HENRIETTA IRVING. *Niocelle*, her foster child, with songs: LILLIE ANDREWS. *Spirit of Goodness*, with songs: LILLIE ANDREWS. *Princess Odyle*: FLORENCE FOSTER. *Justice*: Alice Boyd. *Faith*: Clara Wilson. *Hope*: Angie Martine. *Charity*: Louise Deverille. *Pages, Tempters, Peasants, Egyptian Maids, etc.*: Extra Ballet of 100. (*Specialties*: Professor NELSON and Sons (Gymnasts), Professor J. L. DAVIS and his dogs. *Ballet*: KATHI LANNER, FAY TEMPLETON.)

Act 1, Scene 1: The Accursed Heath of Desolation surrounding the abode of the Red Fiends. *Scene 2*: Mill of St. Donatus.

Act 2, Scene 1: The Groves of Delusion. *Scene 2*: The Demons' Hunting Ground and Boiling Cataract. *Scene 3*: Pavilion of the Earl of Arundel. *Scene 4*: The Port of Flanders. *Scene 5*: Grand Tournament Scene at the Court of the Prince Baudoin.

Act 3, Scene 1: Salon in the Palace of Baudoin. *Scene 2*: Ulric's Sleeping Chamber on All Soul's Eve. *Scene 3*: A View in Flanders. *Scene 4*: Ancient Street and Alley in Cologne.

Act 4, Scene 1: The Awe-Inspiring Dungeons of the Inquisition. *Scene 2*: Street in the Pays Bas. *Scene 3*: The Temple of Isis. *Scene 4*: View of the Pyramids by Moonlight. *Scene 5*: View of the Nile. *Scene 6*: Gardens of the Egyptian Palace Gorgeously Illuminated. *Scene 7*: The Withered Desert, and distant view of the city of Alexandria in flames. Tableau of Horror and Grandeur. Downfall of Vice and Final Tableau. The Home of the Fairies.

BALLETS, SPECIALTIES
The Demons' Festival (Grand Ballet)(Act 1, Scene 2)
K. Lanner, Corps de Ballet
Danse des Paysannes (Picturesque Ballet)(Act 2, Scene 5)
Fay Templeton, Queen of the Petites ("Sweet Spirit")
Professor J. L. Davis and his dogs
Professor Nelson and Sons (gymnasts) (Act 4, Scene 6)
Grand Ballet Divertissement Egyptian (Act 4, Scene 6)
Corps de Ballet
Final Tableau: Home of the Fairies

1875.11 GIROFLÉ-GIROFLA!

An Opéra Bouffe in Three Acts[32]. Original French libretto by Albert Vanloo and Eugene Leterrier. English adaptation by Campbell Clarke. Music by Charles Lecocq. Scenery by Matt Morgan. Costumes by H. J. Seymour. Musical director, Charles Christrup. Produced by Robinson's English Bouffe Company. Opened 19 May 1875 at Robinson Hall and closed 17 July 1875 after 61 performances.[33]

[31]First produced in New York 7 February 1870 at the Grand Opera House for 154 performances. For Synopsis of Scenes, see original 1870 production.
[32]English language premiere. First produced in New York in French 4 February 1875 at the Park Theatre.
[33]At the start of the fourth week (7 June 1875) the Emily Soldene Troupe of Beautiful Women joined the production, interpolating the famous Parisian Can-Can into the production: Mlles. Nellie Beaumont, Emily St. Clair, Cora Austin, Maude Foster, Helen Travers, Lizzie Wright, Maggie Williams, Kate Hatch.

CAST: *Giroflé, Girofla*, twin daughters of Boléro and Aurora: CLARA FISHER. *Marasquin*, a young banker, and betrothed to Giroflé: LOUISE FRANKLE. *Aurora*, wife of Don Boléro: ANNIE MORTIMER. *Don Boléro d'Alcazaras*, Governor of a Spanish province: GEORGE ATKINS. *Mourzouk*, Chief of the Moors, and betrothed to Girofla: WELSH EDWARDS. *Paquita*, Attendant of Giroflé and Girofla: MARIE HARCOURT. *Pedro*, a Page, in love with Paquita: Edith Osmond. *Cousins of the Family of Boléros (8)*: *Fernando*: Alice M. Kemp. *Alonzo*: Georgiana Davis. *Almanzor*: Julia Wilson. *Juliano*: Sallie Getchell. *Antonio*: Sallie Green. *Alcindor*: Ella Green. *Alvarez*: Clara Campbell. *Henrico*: Annetta Keenan. *Chief of the Pirates*: J. H. Merritt. *Admiral Matamoros*: R. C. Palmer. *Bridesmen, Pirates, Moors, Guests, Pages, etc.*

The action is laid in Spain about 1290.

Act 1: Garden of the Palace of Boléro.

Act 2: Grand Salon in the Palace of Boléro.

Act 3: Another Salon in the Palace of Boléro.

ACT 1[34]

Introduction:
Choeur (Let our voices be glad)
Ballade (The sun has sunk behind the clouds)
M. Harcourt
Couplets (What a happy day for a father kind)
G. Atkins
Couplets de Giroflé (Turn not away, here's Giroflé)
C. Fisher
Musique de Scène et Couplets de Grirоflé
Couplets de Marasquin (My father is a banker old)
L. Frankle
Ensemble et Choeur (The wedding bells begin to play)
Couplets (O dear, my heart goes pit-a-pat)
L. Frankle, C. Fisher
Choeur des Pirates (Of all the charms of our profession)
Duo (All is over, we are married)
L. Frankle, C. Fisher
Marche Mauresque et Choeur des Maures (Make way, ye slaves)
Couplets (Hast forgot how you said)
C. Fisher
Finale:
Choeur (Now's the day and now's the hour)
Chorus
Sextuor (How like she is to Giroflé)
C. Fisher, M. Harcourt, A. Mortimer, L. Frankle, G. Atkins, W. Edwards

ACT 2

Choeur des Invités (Pray accept our congratulations)
Sortie (Away! away!)
Duetto (Papa! papa! I'll not stand this any more)
C. Fisher, G. Atkins
Chanson avec choeur (Fools may jeer)
L. Frankle
Galop (Hark! the bright and festive measure)
Quintetto (The gallant sailor Matamore)
E. Osmond, G. Atkins, A. Mortimer, C. Fisher, M. Harcourt
Musique de scène
Ensemble (Good appetite, good appetite)
Brindisi (See how it sparkles)
C. Fisher
Finale (First rate, first rate, excellent wine)

ACT 3

Aubade (Lo, the dawn is breaking)
Chorus
Duo (Oh, how delightful to breakfast together)
C. Fisher, L. Frankle
Rondeau (Pray have pity now)
Duo (My Girofla, my bride)
W. Edwards, C. Fisher
Trio (My jealous husband here!)
W. Edwards, C. Fisher, L. Frankle
Ensemble (It is time your carpet bag to fasten)
Couplets (The trav'lers lot is always bitter)
W. Edwards
Finale (The gallant sailor Matamore)
Chorus

[34]Musical numbers not listed in programs. List prepared from the published English/French piano vocal score (Enoch & Sons, London, [1874]).

1875.12 LA BELLE GALATEA/ LA MARRIAGE AUX LANTERNS!

A Double Bill of Comic Operas[35]. Manager, Charles S. Gray. Produced by the Park Theatre Opera Company. Opened 25 May 1875 at the Park Theatre and closed 28 May 1875 after (5) performances.

LA BELLE GALATEA. A Comic Opera in Two Acts. (Original German libretto[36] to "Die Schöne Galathée" by 'Poly Henrion.' Music by Franz von Suppé.)

CAST: *Galatea*: LINA WASSMAN. *Pygmalion*, the sculptor: PAUL KIRCHNER. *Ganymede*, a Servant: Amelia Stahl. *Mydas*: Mr. W. Heinrich. *Priests and Priestesses*: Full Chorus.

Acts 1 and 2: Pygmalion's Studio in the Island of Cyprus.

LA MARRIAGE AUX LANTERNS![37] (Marriage by Lanterns). A Revival of the Operetta in One Act. (Original French libretto by Michel Carré and Léon Battu. Music by Jacques Offenbach.)

CAST: *Peter*, a Farmer: PAUL KIRCHNER. *Lisa*, his ward: Miss L. Roettger. *Anna Marie, Katherine*, widows: LINA WASSMAN, AMELIA STAHL. *Beadle*: Julius Engel. *Villagers, Farmer, etc.*

Scene: Peter's Farm in Normandy.

1875.13 BAGATELLE

An Opéra Bouffe (Opéra-comique, opérette) in One Act, in French[38]. Libretto by Hector Crémieux and Ernest Blum. Music by Jacques Offenbach. Musical director, Charles Van Ghele. Produced by C. A. Chizzola and Maurice Grau. Opened and closed 28 May 1875 at the Lyceum Theatre after 1 performance.

CAST: *Bagatelle*: Mlle. CORALIE GEOFFROY. *Georges (de Planteville)*: Mlle. LEONTINE MINELLY. *Finette*: Mlle. Vandamme. *Pistache*: Mons. Valter.

MUSICAL NUMBERS[39]

Couplets de Pistache (Comm'tout être poétique)
Mons. Valter
Rondo de l'amité (L'homme est jeune, la femme est belle)
Mlle. C. Geoffroy
Duo de la Pincette (Ah! ce sang-froid m'irrite)
Mlles. C. Geoffroy, L. Minelly
Rondo (A la campagne avant hier soir)
Mlle. L. Minelly
Nocturne et Trio (Dormons, dormons il faut en finir)
Mlles. C. Geoffroy, L. Minelly, Mons. Valter
Couplets de Javotte (Javotte aimait le gros Mathurin)
Mlle. C. Geoffroy
Scène (Ah! Bagatelle, Bagatelle)
Mlles. C. Geoffroy, L. Minelly
Final (Mon p'tit Mathurin)
Tous

[35]No credits for English language adaptations.
[36]Original Berlin version presented in one act.
[37]As billed; correct French title is LE MARIAGE AUX LANTERNES. Previously produced in New York in French 6 February 1864 at the Théâtre Français in repertory.
[38]New York premiere. Preceded by Act 2 of LA FILLE DE MME. ANGOT and Act 3 of BARBE BLEUE.
[39]Musical numbers not listed in programs. List prepared from published French piano vocal score (Choudens, père et fils, Paris, 1874).

1875.14

THE DONOVANS

A Local Sensational Drama in Four Acts[40], with an Olio as Act Three. (Play by Josh Hart.[41]) Incidental music composed and arranged by Dave Braham. Scenery by Matt Morgan, J. Morris and J. Clare. Fire effects and steam apparatus by Nelse Waldron. Mechanical appliances by H. Butler. Furniture by F. Dorrington. Produced by Lester Wallack. Opened 31 May 1875 at Wallack's Theatre and closed 19 June 1875 after 24 performances.

CAST: *Michael Donovan*, a young Engine Driver seeking his fortune in the New World: EDWARD HARRIGAN. *Norah Donovan*, his wife, aiding in the search: TONY HART. *Reuben Morford*, a Bird of Prey, addicted to piety (on the surface): W. E. SHERIDAN. *Hiram Markot*, of a similar feather, with no pious pretensions: J. W. JENNINGS. *Doctor Chalmers*, of the Old School: WELSH EDWARDS. *Arthur Chalmers*, his Nephew, an Artist of the New School: John W. Norton. *Butt Riley*, a type of a class: E. M. Holland. *James Schlim*, of Diamond's Theatre Variété: G. L. Stout. *A brace of Walling's best (2)*: *Jack Burleigh*: W. J. Leonard. *Tom Boylan*: C. E. Edwin. *Bill Blanneigh, Phil Pitcher*, Members of "Butt" Riley's class: W. Elton, J. Peck. *Members of New York Fire Depatment (5)*: *Rube Meadows*: G. L. Comstock. *Mort Whitney*: T. Morgan. *Walt Tompkins*: H. Ackerman. *"Pud" Granger*: S. Morrison. *Andy Newman*: W. Wilson. *Mr. Frederick Mountjoy*, an English Tourist: C. E. Edwin. *Jacob Brunnen*, a German Tourist: J. Atkins. *Florence Morford*, a Young Widow: Ada Monk. *Mrs. Barton*, with a sad history: Mme. Ponisi. *Kitty Edwards*, addicted to Ledger Literature: Alice Clayton. *Mrs. Gudger*, addicted to Reuben Morford: Mrs. Van Deren. *Lillian Morford*, Florence's child: Little Bessie Vivian. *Firemen, Policemen, Citizens, Hands, Girls, etc.*: Crowds of Auxiliaries.

Olio: Harrigan and Hart in their sketches[42]: St. Patrick's Day Parade (Hibernian sketch), Old Uncle Pete (Plantation Specialty); Peak Family of Bell-ringers; Charles and Carrie Austin (Drill and Bayonet Combat); Miss Nellie St. John (vocalist); Baby Bindley (Child Wonder in songs, dances, character sketches).

Scenes: Villa and Grounds near Fort Washington (Morris); View of Bowling Green and Cunard Block (Clare); The Destruction, by Fire, of a Tenement House; View of the Old Walton Mansion, Pearl Street (Morris): Old Kentucky Home and Plantation (Morgan); Side Cut of New Railroad Wall, Fourth Avenue, with View of Tunnel and Section of Street Bridge (Morris); Railroad Viaduct over Harlem Flats (Clare).

---

[40]During the run, Acts 1 and 2 were combined.

[41]Josh Hart is credited by copyright, but not in programs. Programs say the play was "written expressly for the celebrated specialty artists Harrigan and Hart."

[42]Later in the run the two Harrigan & Hart sketches were "London Comic Singers" and "The Miniature 69th", words by Edward Harrigan, music by Dave Braham

1875–1876 SEASON

Sophie Worrell in NIMBLE NIP
Billy Rose Theatre Collection, New York Public Library for the Performing Arts

1875–1876 SEASON

CHILPÉRIC/ THE ROSE OF AUVERGNE

1875.15

A Double-Bill of an Opéra-bouffe in Two Acts, preceded by an opérette curtain-raiser. New scenery, dresses and appointments. Musical director, Charles Christrup. Produced by Robinson's English Opera Bouffe Company. Opened 19 July 1875 at Robinson Hall; CHILPÉRIC closed 21 August 1875 after 35 performances; THE ROSE OF AUVERGNE closed 14 August 1875 after 28 performances.

ACT 1

THE ROSE OF AUVERGNE, an Opérette in One Act[1]. Music by Jacques Offenbach. (Original French libretto to "La Rose de Saint-Flour" by Michel Carré. English adaptation by Henry B. Farnie.)

CAST: *Fleurette*, Belle of the Village (landlady of a village cabaret): LOUISE HOWARD. *Pierre*, a Blacksmith: Mr. E. O. JEPSON. *Alphonse*, a Shoemaker: HENRI LAURENT.

Scene: The interior of Fleurette's cabaret.

MUSICAL NUMBERS[2]

"Heigh-Ho! Which to Choose" (Song)
L. Howard

"This Stewpan Bright and New" (Song)
E. O. Jepson

"For Her Dear Feet" (Recitative and Romance)
H. Laurent

"Go Along! (Duet)
E. O. Jepson, L. Howard

"You Blacksmith, look you here!" (Duet)
H. Laurent, E. O. Jepson

"The Rustic Wedding" (Trio)
L. Howard, H. Laurent, E. O. Jepson

"My Hand Is Yours!" (Finale)
L. Howard, H. Laurent, E. O. Jepson

On 16 August 1875, THE ROSE OF AUVERGNE was replaced by the operetta LISCHEN AND FRITZCHEN, an Operetta in One Act[3]. Original French libretto by Paul Boisselot. Music by Jacques Offenbach. Closed 21 August 1875 after 7 performances.

CAST: *Lischen*: CLARA FISHER. *Fritzchen*: WALTER H. WOODFIELD.

ACT 2

CHILPÉRIC, a Revival of the Opera-bouffe in Two Acts[4]. Original French libretto and music by Hervé.

CAST: *Chilpéric*, King of the Gauls: HENRI LAURENT. *Frédégonde*, a Peasant Girl: LOUISE HOWARD. *Senna*, Court Physician: GEORGE ATKINS. *Landry*, a Peasant: ELMA MARINI. *Sigebert*, Chilperic's Brother: E. O. JEPSON. *Divitiaticus*, High Priest of the Druids: GEORGE E. MERRILL. *Nervoso*, a Spanish Grandee: GEORGE E. MERRILL. *Fatout*, Grand Chamberlain: FRANK HOWARD. *Brunehaut*, Sigebert's Wife: ANNIE MORTIMER. *Galsuinda*, a Spanish Princess: VENIE G. CLANCY. *Fana*, High Priestess: Sadie Getchell. *Leucaste*, a Noble: Sadie Getchell. *Alfred*, Chilpéric's Pet Page: Emily St. Clair. *Clodomir*, a Noble: Virgie Jackson.

Pages to Chilpéric (12): *Edward*: Miss Alice Kemp. *Hubert*: Miss Minnie Mortimer. *Richard*: Miss Laura Clancy. *Albert*: Miss Amy Julian. *Hector*: Miss M. Delmar. *Henry*: Miss Cora Austin. *Charles*: Miss Cornelia Adams. *William*: Miss Annie Bogart. *Ernest*: Miss Lizzie Wright. *Conrad*: Miss Gussie Turner. *Eustace*: Miss Lillie Townshend. *Francis*: Miss Julia Wilson. *Druids, Druidesses, Huntsmen, Warriors, Lords, Ladies, etc.*

PATCHWORK

1875.16

A Comic Absurdity in One Act[5]. Produced by (Nate) Salsbury's Troubadours. Opened 21 July 1875 at the Union Square Theatre and closed 28 July 1875 after 7 performances.

CAST (Comic Absurdity): *Joseph Jefferson Horn Wallack Spout*, a tearer from the word go, no actor, but an actor of the tonsorial world, a shaver that "cuts" his trade and "beards" you even in the lion's den: NATE SALSBURY. *Peter Tennyson Whittier McClosky Boucicault Short*, "Short" by name, ditto by nature, an author upon the "ragged edge," with a love for free lunch and ambition that soars beyond his abilities: ED MARBLE. *Strathmore Cullinbrain*, an extraordinary gentleman's gentleman, whose brain needs no culling, as he possesses none, being "too sweet to live," and yet is not happy: John Webster. *Hon. Bellhandler*, sparing of words, but makes his appearance in time to bring down the curtain with great eclat: S. R. Reed. *Anastasia Janauschek Grub*, the name settles it!—nothing further need be said: KATIE WILSON. *Betty Spider*, always in the way and no use to anybody, but bound to have her say— —so give the "spider" a chance and the fly will fare well enough in her parlor: NELLIE McHENRY.

Scene: Drawing-room at the mansion of the Hon. Ignatius Bellhandler. Hour, 7:30 in the morning. The family of the arms of Morpheus. Souvenirs of the Masquerade of the previous evening. Servants and their weaknesses. A cloud of mystery—Eureka! The bird that can't sing and will sing, must not be allowed to sing. Appointments as plenty as in Washington. The Stage Manager's duties. A grand dress rehearsal. Servants' squabbles. The performance begins. HOOP-LA DUET, LA PÉRICHOLE'S ANASTASIA AND BETTY. Gayly the Troubadour. A little music from Spout. The crockery suffers by the appearance of a flunkey in its midst. A merited act. The costumes. Servants in a quandary. How shall we get them in? Richard's himself again. A living photograph of Napoleon. GRAND POTPOURRI OF ALL NATIONS by all the characters. Another discovery. The Squeak Family. Recollections from the pasture. Cow-bellogians. Getting into your clothes upside down. That settles it. Gens des Armes Geneviève de Brabant. The bounce. A new way to build a theatre. An appreciative audience. One too many. Recollections of all the great actors. "Ye Centennial Parade." A hundred years ago. The family aroused. Sudden disappearance. The stove hole. The windows—the chimneys of some use. Appearance of the Hon. Bellhandler. Good night!

THE BELLES OF THE KITCHEN/ A BUNCH OF BERRIES/ THE WRONG MAN IN THE RIGHT PLACE

1875.17

The Vokes Family in a revival of their original, musical, saltatorial, operatic, tragical comical extravaganza in One Act[6]. Season opened 2 August 1875 at the Fifth Avenue Theatre and closed 21 August 1875 after 21 performances. Replacing THE BELLES OF THE KITCHEN after 7 performances, A BUNCH OF BERRIES, a farcical extravaganza in One Act by E. L. Blanchard[7], opened 9 August 1875, preceded by His Own Enemy, and closed 19 August 1875 after 11 performances.

---

[1]Previously produced in New York in French 14 February 1863 at the Théâtre Français, and in other English adaptations; this was the New York premiere for this version.

[2]Musical numbers not listed in programs. List prepared from published American piano vocal score (William A. Pond & Co., 1900), THE ROSE OF AUVERGNE; or, Spoiling the Broth, being a reissue of the London edition of 1870, published by Metzler & Co.

[3]English adaptation uncredited.

[4]This revival is a condensed version. CHILPÉRIC was previously produced in New York in English in a Three Act version 9 December 1874 at the Lyceum Theatre for 13 performances in repertory. English adaptation for this revival was uncredited, presumably a reduction of the previous adaptation by Richard Mansell, Robert Reece and F. A. Marshall. Interpolated for this production: The Umbrella Dance (Act 1), and Grand Parisienne Quadrille Grotesque (Act 2), arranged by George Atkins.

[5]Preceded by a comedietta Two Can Play at That Game! CAST: *Lady Arundel*: Rose Massey. *Howard Leslie*: Charles Vandenhoff, Jr. *Charles Arundel*: George D. Chaplin.

[6]Preceded by a comedy, His Own Enemy. This was replaced on 16 August 1875 by a farce, Living Too Fast. Beginning 20 August 1875 THE WRONG MAN IN THE RIGHT PLACE returned to the repertory, with Living Too Fast and Rosina Vokes in NAN, THE GOOD FOR NOTHING.THE BELLES OF THE KITCHEN was first produced in New York 15 April 1872 at the Union Square Theatre for 49 performances. THE WRONG MAN IN THE RIGHT PLACE was first produced in New York 27 May 1872 at the Union Square Theatre for 6 performances. For Synopses of Scenes and Musical Numbers, see original 1872 productions.

[7]Reviewers commented that an opening chorus, a chorus of fairies, a chorus of shepherdesses, a grotesque dance by Fred Vokes, an operatic selection by Fred and Victoria Vokes, and an amateur pantomime of 'Twelfth Night" were prominently featured.

THE BELLES OF THE KITCHEN CAST: *Lucinda Scrubbs*, a lady's maid with "airs and graces:" JESSIE VOKES. *Mary*, a house-maid of "aristocratic inclinations," with Song, Dance and Duet: VICTORIA VOKES. *Barbara*, a kitchen-maid, "the incarnation of fun," full of mirth, merriment and mischief: BESSIE SANSON. *Timethus Gibbs*, a doctor's assistant, and chief bottle-washer, with song, dance and legs ad libitum: FERD VOKES. *Wiggins*, a barber, with Wigs, Jigs, a Waltz and Dance, and trouble with Barbara: FAWDON VOKES.

A BUNCH OF BERRIES CAST: *Sir Gilbert Gooseberry* owner of Hollybush Hall: John Moore. *William Gooseberry*, his son, familiarly called Bill Berry: FAWDON VOKES. *Lord Strawberry*, on a visit: FREDERICK VOKES. *Lady Raspberry*, Sir Gilbert's sister: Miss Sargent. *Sir Gilbert's nieces (3)*: *May Berry*: VICTORIA VOKES. *Rose Berry*: ROSINA VOKES. *Hilda Berry*: JESSIE VOKES. *John Thomas*, servant to Sir Gilbert: I. Daveau. *Harris*, a policeman: E. Chapman.

THE WRONG MAN IN THE RIGHT PLACE CAST: *Emily Merton*, Niece to the Proprietress of a Young Ladies College near London: JESSIE VOKES. *Clara Staunton*, a Romantic Young Lady, remaining at the college during vacation. Who will sing with Benjamin Buttontop an Operatic Duet: VICTORIA VOKES. *Sarah Jane*, a Young Person desirous of improving her position in life, at present parlor maid to the Establishment, who will introduce her peculiar and original "Leary Dance": BESSIE SANSON. *Benjamin Buttontop*, Manager of an unlicensed Theatre, at present under a cloud. Who will dance his own Burlesque Polka, and sing with Clara Staunton: FRED VOKES. *Sampson Biffles*, footman to the College, formerly a super in a third-class theatre: FAWDON VOKES.

1875.18

AROUND THE WORLD IN EIGHTY DAYS

A Grand Realistic and Spectacular Drama in Six Acts, 11 Scenes. Adapted by Messrs. Pillet and Connelly from Jules Verne's novel "Le Tour du Monde en Quatre Vingt Jours." Music by E. Harrison. Whole produced under the immediate supervision of Robert Johnston. Scenery by R. E. Farren, Philip W. Goatcher, J. H. Fisher. Novel and intricate machinery by Sherwood and assistants. Costumes by H. J. Eaves. Produced by Augustin Daly. Opened 16 August 1875 at the Grand Opera House and closed 28 August 1875 after 14 performances.[8]

CAST: *John Archibald*, an American: JOSEPH WHEELOCK. *Mr. Phileas Fogg*, who makes the bet: R. D'ORSAY OGDEN. *Jean Passe-Partout*, his Servant: LOUIS J. MESTAYER. *John Fix*, a smart detective: J. J. WALLACE. *Andrew Stuart*, an Engineer: G. F. Elliott. *Walter Ralph*, Director of Bank of England: H. Lewis. *Sir Philip Phelps*, a Banker: R. W. Percy. *Thomas Bulkley*, a Brewer: J. Owen. *Samuel Fallenton*, a Banker: F. Mack. *Mr. Obadiah*, a pompous Calcutta magistrate: JOHN WALSH. *Mr. McWhitely*, an old '49er: C. L. Leon. *Bill Miles*, Keeper of the Station in the Wilderness: R. F. Miles. *De Loosely*, an excitable young stock broker: F. Percival. *Mr. Blivens*, English Consular Agent at Suez: G. Clarke. *Djelmar*, Foster-brother to Aouda and Ayeesha: H. Moore. *Captain Andrew Speedy*, Master of Steamer *Henrietta*: CHARLES CLAIRE. *Servant* in Club House of Eccentrics: D. Waters. *Lieutenant of Dragoons*: HENRY LEWIS. *Aouda*, Widow of the Rajah: MARION SACKETT. *Ayeesha*, Sister of Aouda: HATTIE ARNOLD. *Nancy*, Sweetheart of Passe Partout: MAY GALLAGHER. *One Hundred Auxiliaries. Priests, Armed Guards, Fakirs, Dervishes, Hindoos, Amazons, Indians, Dismounted Dragoons, Passengers, etc.*

Act 1, Scene 1: Grand Saloon in the "Eccentric Club House." *Scene 2*: Wharf of the Steamship Canal at Suez.

Act 2, Scene 1: An East Indian Bungalow. *Scene 2*: The Pagoda of Pillrajii. *Scene 3*: An Oriental Hotel at Calcutta.

Act 3, Scene 1: Chinese Festival, Hong Kong. *Scene 2*: The Merchant's Exchange, San Francisco.

Act 4, Scene 1: Kearney Station on the Pacific Railroad. *Scene 2*: Giant's Stairway, a Weird and Picturesque Ravine in the Rocky Mountains.

Act 5, Scene 1: Cabin of the Steamer *"Henrietta." Scene 2*: The Upper Deck of the Steamer *"Henrietta."*

Act 6: Room in a Hotel at Liverpool.

[8]Programs do not identify ballets, specialities or musical numbers, apart from a Grand Amazon March, and the Chinese Festival (Act 3). Billed on title page but not in cast list: Theodore Hamilton, R. Johnston.

1875.19

BOULOTTE!

A Grand Folie Musicale in Three Acts, 4 Scenes. Adapted from the French opera-bouffe "Barbe-bleu" by Henri Meilhac and Ludovic Halévy. Music by Jacques Offenbach, arranged by Frederic Stanislaus. Stage manager, G. H. MacDermott. Scenic illustrations by Matt Morgan. Mechanical appliances and appointments by F. Dorrington. Costumes by Samuel May. Conductor, Frederic Stanislaus. Produced by Alexander Henderson and Samuel Colville's English Comic Opera Company. Opened 19 August 1875 at Wallack's Theatre and closed 1 September 1875 after 14 performances.

CAST: *Boulotte*: JULIA MATHEWS. *Fleurette*, afterwards the Princess Hermia: ROSE KEENE. *Queen Clementina*: MARGUERITE SELVI. *Waiterini*, the Queen's Favorite Page: Millie Cook. *Blue Beard's Wives (5)*: *Heloise*: Rose Temple [Keene]. *Eleonore*: Maud Egerton. *Rosalinde*: Marie Antoine. *Blanche*: Kate Villiers. *Isaure*: Agnes Villiers. *King Bobeche*: G. H. MacDERMOTT. *Popolani*: HAYDN CORRI. *Count D'Intheway*: L. DELORME. *Alvarez*: Harry Collier. *Count (Oscar) Crambo*: JOHN HOGAN. *General Notary*: John Harvey. *Prince Sapphire*: WILLIAM FORRESTER. *Blue Beard*: ALBERT BRENNIR. *Chorus of Courtiers, Guards, etc.*

Act 1: Cottages of Fleurette and Sapphire, with Mountain View.

Act 2: Reception Chamber in the Palace of King Bobeche.

Act 3, Scene 1: Dungeon in Bluebeard's Castle. *Scene 2*: Garden of King Bobeche.

ACT 1

"I and You, Lovers True" (Duet)
R. Keene, W. Forrester

"We lack not Village Maids" (Ballad)
J. Mathews

"To the Public Square Repairing" (Chorus)
Ensemble

"List to the Orders so stern" (Proclamation)
H. Corri

"Your Name Proclaim" (Chorus)
Ensemble

"Shall I Give mine" (Recitative)/

"Just look at all those precious Hussies" (Ballad)
J. Mathews

"'Tis Boulotte" (Recitative and Chorus)
Ensemble

"Mount within this Palanquin" (Solo and Chorus)
J. Hogan, Chorus

"The Legend of Blue Beard" (Song and Chorus)
A. Brennir

"All Honor Praise" (Finale)
Ensemble

ACT 2

"Not Devotion, but Promotion" (Chorus)
Ensemble

"As a Courtier would Please" (Song)
J. Hogan

Buffo Song
G. H. MacDermott

Chanson de Fortunio
L. Delorme

"You Take an Angel" (Rondo)
M. Selvi

"My Shepherd See" (Quartette)
R. Keene, M. Selvi, W. Forrester, G. H. MacDermott

"Rataplan, Rataplan" (Quartette)
R. Keene, M. Selvi, W. Forrester, G. H. MacDermott

"See here the Happy Couple" (Finale)
Ensemble

ACT 3

"Behold the Tomb" (Song)
A. Brennir

"Your Eyes on Yonder Tomb" (Duet)
J. Mathews, A. Brennir

"Oh, dear!" (Trio)
J. Mathews, A. Brennir, H. Corri
"All hail to Thee!" (Concerted Piece and Valse)
Five Wives
"One, two, three" (Nuptial Chorus)/
"Hymenœa, Hymenœa" (Chorus)
Ensemble
"We've just arrived" (Gypsey Chorus)
"Possessors of a Magic Art" (Valse)
J. Mathews
"Splendid Thought!" (Finale)
Ensemble

1875.20 THE PRINCESS OF TREBIZONDE!

A Revival of the Opera bouffe in Three Acts[9]. (Original French libretto by Charles Nuitter and Étienne Tréfeu.) Music by Jacques Offenbach. Produced under the direction of Harry Allen. Scenery by Matt Morgan. Costumes by A. J. Eaves. Musical director, Charles Christrup. Produced by Robinson's English Opera Bouffe Company. Opened 23 August 1875 at Robinson Hall and closed 4 September 1875 after 14 performances.

CAST: *Prince Cassimer*: HARRY ALLEN. *Cabriolo*: GEORGE ATKINS. *Tremolini*: Walter H. Woodfield. *Sparadrap*: C. W. Butler. *Lottery Manager*: GEORGE E. MERRILL. *Chief of the Hunter*: E. O. Jepson. *Zanetta*: Nellie Larkelle. *Prince Raphael*: CLARA FISHER. *Regina*: VENIE CLANCY. *Paola*: Nellie Allen. *Broccoli*: Annie Mortimer. *Ricciardo*: Alice Kemp. *Flaminio*: Julia Wilson. *Francerco*: Sadie Getchell. *First Page*: Emily St. Clair. *Second Page*: M. Delmar. *Pages, Peasants, Lords, Hunters, Soldiers, etc.*

1875.21 AROUND THE WORLD

The Porte Saint Martin version of the Musical Extravaganza in One Act, 18 Scenes. Based on the French adaptation of Jules' Verne's Jules Verne's novel "Le Tour du Monde en Quatre Vingt Jours," as adapted by Adolphe d'Ennery. Music composed and arranged by Jean-Jacques de Debillemont. Scenic designs by Mons. Poisson, Nezel, Robecchi, Cornil, adapted by Mons. Camille Weinschenk. Costumes by Chalain; properties by Hallée; statuary by Dagoni. Grand Ballets by Mons. Buisseret. Orchestra under the direction of Signor Conterno. Choruses by Mons. Selington. Entire spectacle produced by and under the personal supervision of Messrs. Imre and Bolossy Kiralfy, and Camille Weinschenk. Produced by the Kiralfys. Opened 28 August 1875 at the Academy of Music and closed 9 October 1875 after 43 performances.

CAST: *Aouda*, an East Indian Princess: MINNIE CONWAY. *Nemea*, her sister: DORA GOLDTHWAITE. *Nakahira*, with song, "Aouda's Slave": KATE FRASER FOX. *Betsy*: Kate Brevort. *Idali*, a Maisy Woman: Francis Browne. *Companions of Nakahira (3)*: *Olga*: Carrie Mott. *Giza*: Agnes Mapleton. *Daora*: Gertrude Lavine. *Snake Charmers (4)*: *Batona*: Addie Veron. *Cadoga*: Hattie Burnham. *Badoga*: Lulu Pierson. *Bala*: Adelaide Cook.

Phineas Fogg, a member of the Eccentric Club: OWEN MARLOWE. *Myles O'Pake*, an ex-Senator from New York: J. [Alexander] FITZGERALD. *Fix*, an English detective: JOHN W. JENNINGS. *Jean François Passepartout*, a French valet: HARRY RAINFORTH. *Mr. Blunt*, the Calcutta Magistrate: S. B. Villa. *Phil Tracy*: C. Huebner. *Arthur Maybur*: Fred WIlliams. *Jack Rivers*: E. T. Chapman. *Shafter*: E. Pierce. *Captain Collins*: R. Osmond. *Chief of the Brahmins*: Mr. Walton. *A Scout*: J. E. Stewart. *John Jones*: R. S. Wade. *Sir Roger Shendryn*: E. S. Tarr. *Black Bill*: F. Scallon. *Governor of Suez*: D. Leason. *A Parsee*: J. Mackay. *Railroad Conductor*: J. Varian. *Engineer*: A. J. Peck. *Boatswain*: S. J. Gregory. *Coal-heaver*: F. H. Robinson. *Waiter*: W. Barmore. *Station Master*: G. Hamilton. *Barkeeper*: J. Bartlett. *Auxiliaries, Brahmins, Priests, Punka Wallahs, Soldiers, Hindoos, Arabs, Egyptians, Malayans, Road Agents, Indians, Passengers, Policemen, Sailors, Members of the London Eccentric Club, Snake Charmers and Bayadere.*

Ballet: Mlles. PELLETIER (Premiere Danseuse Assoluta) , ROSETTI; KIRALFY SISTERS (Haniola, Emilie, Katie); Mons. ARNOLD KIRALFY, Secondas, Coryphées, Corps de Ballet.

Scene 1: A Club-Room in London. *Scene 2*: The Arrival at Suez; The Suez Canal. *Scene 3*: Off for the East Indies; An Interior of a Hindoo Bungalow. *Scene 4*: The Necropolis; The Great Religious Festival of the Suttee; A Marvelous Beauty. *Scene 5*: The Great European Hotel in Calcutta. *Scene 6*: Terrific Cave of Serpents. *Scene 7*: Garden of Nakahira's Palace in Borneo. *Scene 8*: Union Pacific Depot in San Francisco. *Scene 9*: On the Pacific Railroad. *Scene 10*: The Giant's Stairway in the Rocky Mountains. *Scene 11*: Grand Saloon of the Steamer *Henrietta*. *Scene 12*: The Steamer on the Ocean. *Scene 13*: Terrific Explosion! Loss of the *Henrietta*. *Scene 14*: A Waif on the Sea. *Scene 15*: The Lights of Liverpool. *Scene 16*: Liverpool by Day. *Scene 17*: L. & N. W. Hotel, Liverpool. *Scene 18*: The Eccentric Club, London.

BALLETS, SPECIALTIES
Grand Funeral Pageant (Scene 4)
Fête of the Snake Charmers (Scene 7)
Introduction of the Startling Reptile Dances (Scene 7)
The Revels of the Eccentrics (Scene 18)

1875.22 THE GRAND DUCHESS!

The Mexican Juvenile Opera Company in a Revival of the Opéra-bouffe in Three Acts, in French[10]. Libretto ("La Grande-Duchesse de Gérolstein") by Henri Meilhac and Ludovic Halévy. Music by Jacques Offenbach. Produced by the Mexican Juvenile Opera Company. Musical director, Eduardo Unda y Moron. Pablo Unda y Moron, Hijo & Co., Proprietors. Opened 30 August 1875 at Daly's Fifth Avenue Theatre and closed 4 September 1875 after 7 performances; returned 1-6 November 1875 to the Lyceum Theatre for 5 additional performances in repertory; returned 11-13 November 1875 to the Stadt-Theater for 2 additional performances.[11]

CAST: *Grand Duchess of Gérolstein*: Nina CARMEN U. Y MORON. *Wanda*: Nina GUADALUPE U. Y MORON. *Fritz*, a Soldier: Nino ESTEVEN MORON. *General Boum*: Nino GABRIEL U. Y MORON. *Baron Puck*: Nino ROSARIO SANDOVAL. *Prince Paul*: Nino T. DeJESUS CASTELLAN. *Nepomuc*: Nino Francisco Martinez. *Baron Grog*: Nino AURELIO RODRIGUEZ.

Maids of Honor: *Olga*: Nina Carmen Lobato. *Inez*: Nina Emilia Mayorga. *Charlotta*: Nina Soledad Mugica. *Amelia*: Nina Josepha Mugica. *Soldiers of the Grand Duchess' Army, Vivandieres, Ladies of the Court, etc.*

1875.23 THE GRAND DUCHESS OF GÉROLSTEIN

A Revival of the Opéra-bouffe in Three Acts, 4 Scenes[12] Original French libretto by Henri Meilhac and Ludovic Halévy. Music by Jacques Offenbach. Stage manager, G. H. MacDermott. Musical director, Frederic Stanislaus. Produced by Alexander Henderson and Samuel Colville's English Comic Opera Company. Opened 2 September 1875 at Wallack's Theatre and closed 11 September 1875 after 11 performances.

CAST: *The Grand Duchess of Gérolstein*: JULIA MATHEWS. *Wanda*, a country girl: ROSE TEMPLE. *Fritz*: ALBERT BRENNIR. *General Boum*: G. H. MacDERMOTT. *Prince Paul*: WILLIAM FORRESTER. *Baron Puck*: JOHN HOGAN. *Baron Grog*: Mons. L. Delorme. *Nepomuc*: Harry Collier. *Valet-de-Chambre*: Millie Cook. *Marquise de Laroche*: Polly Smallwood. *Vivandieres (5)*: *Marie*: Rose Selvi. *Babette*: Rose Keene. *Fanchette*: Maude Egerton. *Blanche*: Bessie Temple. *Françoise*: Marie Antoine. *Maids of Honor (4)*: *Eza*: Kate Villiers. *Amelia*: Agnes Villiers. *Olga*: Josie Intropodi. *Charlotte*: Angela Griffiths. *Lords and Ladies of the Court, Maids of Honor, Pages, Ushers, Soldiers, Vivandières, Country Girls, etc.*

Act 1: The Camp.

Act 2: The Palace.

Act 3, Scene 1: The Striped Chamber. *Scene 2*: The Camp.

---

[9]Adaptation uncredited; previously produced in a different English adaptation for Lydia Thompson 11 September 1871 at Wallach's Theatre for 7 performances.

[10]First produced in New York in French 24 September 1867 at the Théâtre Français for 156 performances, and in English 17 June 1868 at the New York Theatre. For Synopsis of Scenes and Musical Numbers, see original 1867 production. Between Acts 2 and 3, Senorita Soledad Unda y Moon, Prima Donna, 15 years old, will sing the Carnival of Venice, with variations.

[11]No credits for stage director, musical director, scenery or costumes in programs.

[12]First produced in New York in French 24 September 1867 at the Théâtre Français for 156 performances, and in English 17 June 1868 at the New York Theatre. For Synopsis of Scenes and Musical Numbers, see original 1868 production.

1875.24 ROBINSON CRUSOE

The Mexican Juvenile Opera Company in a brilliant and jocular opera in Three Acts, in Spanish. (Original Spanish libretto by Jose F. Godoy and Rafael Garcia Santisteban.) Music by Francisco A. Barbieri. Musical director, Eduardo Unda y Moron. Pablo Unda y Moron, Hijo & Co., Proprietors. Opened 6 September 1875 at Daly's Fifth Avenue Theatre and closed 11 September 1875 after 7 performances.[13]

CAST: *Miss Leona*: CARMEN UNDA y MORON. *La Reina Ananas*, Caribe Queen: ROSARIO SANDOVAL. *Guayaba*, Indian Caribe: GUADALUPE U. y MORON. *Colibri*: Emelia Mayorga. *Robinson (Crusoe)*: J. de CASTELAN. *Matatias*: GABRIEL U. y MORON. *Tiburcio*, Sea Captain: ESTEVAN MORON. *A Servant*: Miguel Sandoval. *Ambron*, Grand Sacerdote: Julian Lobato. *Domingo*, Negro: Francisco Martinez. *Un Loro*: Aurelio Rodriguez. *Choristers, Money Brokers, Dancers, Gentiles, Married People, Widows, Virgins, Caribees, Sailors, etc.*

Act 1: Voyage of Leona, Robinson and Matatias to the New World.

Act 2: Robinson obliged to marry the Caribee Queen.

Act 3: Reconciliation between Queen Ananas, Leona and Robinson.

1875.25 MADAME L'ARCHIDUC

An Opéra-bouffe in Three Acts[14], in French. Libretto by Albert Millaud. Music by Jacques Offenbach. Stage manager, Mons. E. Schmidt. Scenery by Hannibal W. Calyo. Costumes by Mons. Santella, Mme. Huchet. Musical director, Mons. Charles Van Ghele. Produced by Maurice Grau and C. A. Chizzola. Opened 6 September 1875 at the Lyceum Theatre, closing 25 September 1875 (matinee) after 20 performances; returned 26 October 1875 to the Lyceum Theatre for 1 additional performance.

CAST: *Marietta*: Mlle. CORALIE GEOFFROY. *Fortunato*: Mlle. FLORENCE DUPARC. *La Comtesse*: Mlle. MARIE NARDYNN. *Giacometta*: Mlle. Sophie Gherzi. *Giletti*: Mons. deQUERCY. *L'Archiduc (Ernest)*: Mons. DUPLAN. *Le Comte*: Mons. ROGER. *Conspirators (4)*: *Pontefiascone*: Mons. Darcy. *Frangipano*: Mons. Castel. *Bonaventuro*: Mons. Ludovic. *Bonardo*: Mons. Valter. *Ricardo*: Mons Benedick. *L'Hotelier*: Mons. Davalis. *Piano-dolce*: Mons. Adorcy. *Andantino*: Mons. Gerard. *Chi-lo-sa*: Mons. Leclerc. *Tutti-Frutti*: Mons. Kremer. *Pages, Domestiques, Femmes de Chambre, Dames Seigneurs, Dragons Femmes, Dragons Hommes, Paysannes*: Chorus of 50.

Act 1: The Brigand's Repose.

Act 2: The Great Hall at Castle Barilogano.

Act 3: Pavilion in the Archducal Gardens.

ACT 1[15]

Quatuor Bouffe des Inconnus (S.A.D.E.)
Les Quatre Inconnus

Choeur (Voici que l'heure solennelle)
Mlles. C. Geoffroy, S. Gherzy, Messrs. deQuercy, Davalis, Choeur

Couplets des Mariés (Pour nous marier à l'Église)
Mlle. C. Geoffroy, Mons. deQuercy

Couplets du voyage de noce (Où je vais? J n'en savons rien)
Mlle. C. Geoffroy

Complainte des Tabliers (Nous somm's tous de la mêm' famille)
Choeur

Quatuor (Ne pensons qu'à nous ma chérie)
Mlles. C. Geoffroy, M. Nardynn, Messrs. de Quercy, Roger

Couplets (Pardonnez-nous, monsieur, madame)
Mlle. C. Geoffroy

Strette (Elle a raison!)
Mlles. C. Geoffroy, M. Nardynn, Messrs. de Quercy, Roger

Chanson du petit capitaine (Qui je sais)
Mlle. F. Duparc

Duetto Bouffe Anglais (Oh! ce rosbeff very fine)
Mlle. F. Nardynn, Mons. Roger

Choeur des Dragons (Nous sommes le dragoni)
Mlles. C. Geoffroy, M. Nardynn, F. Duparc, Messrs. deQuercy, Roger, Benedick, Choeur

Scène (En route!)
Messrs. Benedick, deQuercy, Mlles. F. Duparc, C. Geoffroy

Couplets du Petit Bonhomme (Vous, officier)
Mlle. C. Geoffroy

Scène Finale (Allons, voyons, monsieur le Comte)
Tous

ACT 2

Choeur (Dans la salles des ancêtres)
Mlle. C. Geoffroy, Messrs. deQuercy, Benedick, Choeur

Duetto des rires (Si tu savais comme t'es drôle)
Mlle. C. Geoffroy, Mons. deQuercy

Rondeau (Allons, voyons je sais comprendre)
Mlle. F. Duparc

Sextuor de l'Alphabet (S.A.D.E.)
Mlle. C. Geoffroy, Mons. deQuercy, Les Quatre Inconnus

Choeur (Voici le Duc!)
Mlles. C. Geoffroy, Messrs. deQuercy, Duplan, Benedick, Adorcy, Gerard, Leclerc, Kremer, Choeur

Couplets d l'Original (Original! original!)
Mons. Duplan

Ronde Villageoise (C'est le soir on s'prend, on s'regarde)
Mlles. C. Geoffroy, F. Duparc, Mons. Duplan

Final Choeur et Scène (C'est la sonnette Ducale)
Tous, Choeur

Couplets (Tais-toi! Tais-toi!)
Mlle. C. Geoffroy

Scène Finale (Je veux lui faire un beau sort)
Mlle. C. Geoffroy, Messrs. deQuercy, Duplan, Choeur

ACT 3

Choeur des Patrouilles (Sous l'uniforme)
Mons. Duplan, Mlle. F. Duparc, Choeur

Chanson du Brigadier (C'est un sort privé d'allegresse)
Mons. Duplan, Mlle. F. Duparc

Choeur (Quel est ce bruit)

Couplets (Ce qu'il voulait?)
Mlle. C. Geoffroy

Polka de l'Arrestation (Pas de scandale ici)
Mons. Duplan, Mlles. F. Duparc, C. Geoffroy

Couplets de la Déclaration (Je sais que vous avez, madame)
Mlle. F. Duparc

Duo (Que voulez-vous dire?)
Mlles. C. Geoffroy, F. Duparc

Couplets "Pas ça" (Le Duc avec largesse)
Mlle. C. Geoffroy

Finale (Je ne sais plus Comtesse)
Mlles. C. Geoffroy, M. Nardynn, F. Duparc, Messrs. deQuercy, Duplan, Roger, Choeur

1875.26 GIROFLÉ-GIROFLA

A Revival of the Opéra-bouffe in Three Acts[16] Original French libretto by Albert Vanloo and Eugene Leterrier. Music by Charles Lecocq. Stage manager, G. H. MacDermott. Musical director, Frederic Stanislaus. Produced

[13]Musical numbers not listed in programs; no published vocal score found.
[14]French language premiere in New York. Previously produced in New York in English 29 December 1874 at the Lyceum Theatre for 8 performances in repertory.
[15]Musical numbers not listed in programs. List prepared from published French piano vocal score (Choudens Père et fils, Paris, 1874).

[16]First produced in New York in French 4 February 1875 at the Park Theatre; in English 19 May 1875 at Robinson Hall for 61 performances. For Synopsis of Scenes and Musical Numbers, see original May 1875 production.

by Alexander Henderson and Samuel Colville's English Comic Opera Company. Opened 13 September 1875 at Wallack's Theatre and closed 18 September 1875 after 7 performances.

CAST: *Giroflé, Girofla*, Twin Daughters of Bolero and Aurore: JULIA MATHEWS. *Aurore*, wife of Don Bolero: MARGUERITE SELVI. *Don Bolero d'Alcarazas*, Governor of a Spanish Province: G. H. MacDERMOTT. *Marasquin*, betrothed to Giroflé: WILLIAM FORRESTER. *Mourzouk*, Chief of the Moors, betrothed to Girofla: ALBERT BRENNIR. *Paquita*, Attendant on Giroflé and Girofla: ROSE TEMPLE. *Pedro*, a Page, in love with Paquita: ROSE KEENE. *Cousins to Giroflé, Girofla (4)*: *Fernande*: Millie Cook. *Guzman*: Agnes Villiers. *Gomez*: Marie Antoine. *Carlos*: Isobel Lewis. *The Uncle*: L. Delorme. *The Pirate Captain*: John Hogan. *The Notary*: Harry Collier. *The Groomsman*: Mr. DeSmith. *The Godfather*: Mr. Quine. *The Godmother*: Bessie Temple. *Moors, Pirates, Guests, Bridesmaids, etc.*

1875.27 LES DEUX AVEUGLES/ LA ROSE DE SAINT FLOUR

A Triple Bill of Opéra Bouffe, Comedy and Vaudeville[17], in French. Stage manager, Mons. E. Schmidt. Scenery by Hannibal W. Calyo. Costumes by Mons. Santella, Mme. Huchet. Musical director, Mons. Charles Van Ghele. Produced by Maurice Grau and C. A. Chizzola. Opened and closed 25 September 1875 at the Lyceum Theatre for 1 performance.

ACT 1

LES DEUX AVEUGLES, a Revival of the Laughable Farce (Bouffonerie musicale) in One Act[18], in French. Libretto by Jules Moinaux. Music by Jacques Offenbach.

CAST: *Patachon, Giraffier*: Messrs. DUPLAN and DARCY.

ACT 2

MME. BERTRAND & MLLE. RATON, an Amusing Comedy Vaudeville in One Act, in French. CAST: Mons. SCHMIDT, Mlles. LUCIE FAYE and FLORENCE DUPARC.

ACT 3

LA ROSE DE SAINT FLOUR, a Revival of the Opéra Bouffe (Operette) in One Act[19], in French. Libretto by Michel Carré. Music by Jacques Offenbach.

CAST: *Chapaillou, Marcachu*: Messrs. DARCY, CASTEL. *Pierrette*: Mlle. JULIE HOSDEZ.

1875.28 LA FILLE DE MADAME ANGOT

A Revival of the Opéra-comique in Three Acts[20], in French. Libretto by Clairville, Paul Siraudin and Victor Koning. Music by Charles Lecocq. Stage manager, Mons. E. Schmidt. Scenery by Hannibal W. Calyo. Costumes by Mons. Santella, Mme. Huchet. Musical director, Mons. Charles Van Ghele. Produced by Maurice Grau and C. A. Chizzola. Opened 27 September 1875 at the Lyceum Theatre and closed 5 October 1875 after 9 performances.

CAST: *Clairette*: Mlle. CORALIE GEOFFROY. *Mlle. Lange*: Mlle. MARIE NARDYNN. *Amaranthe*: Mlle. LUCIE FAYE. *Javotte*: Mme. Sophie Gherzy. *Cydalise*: Mlle. Emma Deriberpres. *Mlle. Delaney*: Mlle. Lucier. *Hersilie*: Mlle. Marie Vandamme. *Babet*: Mlle. Virginie Nelcy. *Therese*: Mlle. Marie Vandalet. *Herbelin*: Mlle. Jeanne Hartmann. *Ange Pitou*: Mons. de QUERCY. *Larivaaudière*: Mons. CASTEL. *Pomponnet*: Mons. DARCY. *Trénitz*: Mons. VALTER. *Louchard*: Mons. DUPLAN. *Cadet*: Mons. Benedick. *Buteux*: Mons. Ludovic. *Guillaume*: Mons. Gerard. *Un Incroyable*: Mons. Davalis. *Un Officier*: Mons. Julien. *Un Cabaretier*: Mons. Adorcy. (*Dance Specialty*: Mons. Grazzini.)

1875.29 GIROLFÉ-GIROFLA

A Revival of the Opéra-bouffe in Three Acts[21], in French. Libretto by Albert Vanloo and Eugene Leterrier. Stage manager, Mons. E. Schmidt. Scenery by Hannibal W. Calyo. Costumes by Mons. Santella, Mme. Huchet. Musical director, Mons. Charles Van Ghele. Produced by Maurice Grau and C. A. Chizzola. Opened 6 October 1875 at the Lyceum Theatre and closed 16 October 1875 (matinee) after 11 performances.

CAST: *Giroflé, Girofla*: Mlle. CORALIE GEOFFROY. *Pedro*: Mlle. FLORENCE DUPARC. *Paquita*: Mlle. JULIE HOSDEZ. *Aurore*: Mlle. KID. *Les Petites Cousins (8)*: *Guzman*: Mlle. Marie Vandamme. *Fernand*: Mlle. Marie Julien. *Almanazar*: Mlle. Emma Deriberprés. *Antonio*: Mlle. Sarah Noé. *Baquero*: Mlle. Hortense Gomer. *Gomez*: Mlle. Florence. *Rodriguez*: Mlle. Virginie Nelcy. *Martinez*: Mlle. Felicie Seygaud. *Marasquin*: Mons. LUDOVIC. *Mourzouk*: Mons. ROGER. *Bolero*: Mons. DUPLAN. *Chef des Pirates*: Mons. VALTER. *Le Parrain*: Mons. Adorcy. *Un Danseur*: Mons. Grazzini. *Le Notaire*: Mons. Gerard. *Le Percepteur*: Mons. Kremer. *L'Oncle d'Heriage*: Mons. Traisse. *La Marraine*: Mlle. Sophie Gherzi.

1875.30 LE CANARD À TROIS BECS!

An Opéra-bouffe in Three Acts, in French. (The Wonderful Duck) (Libretto by Jules Moineaux. Music by Emil Jonas.) Stage manager, Mons. E. Schmidt. Scenery by Hannibal W. Calyo. Costumes by Mons. Santella, Mme. Huchet. Musical director, Mons. Charles van Ghele. Produced by Maurice Grau and C. A. Chizzola. Opened 16 October 1875 at the Lyceum Theatre and closed 23 October 1875 after 7 performances.

CAST: *Marguerite*, the Captain's wife: Mlle. CORALIE GEOFFROY. *Barbe*, the Captain's servant: Mlle. FLORENCDE DUPARC. *Madelaine*, the Captain's Daughter: Mlle. JULIE HOSDEZ. *Sophronie*, the Captain's Sister: Mlle. LUCIE FAYE. *Spaniello*, a Young Spaniard: Mons. de QUERCY. *Van Ostebal*, a Sea Captain: Mons. ROGER. *Van Bonntrouch*, Burgomaster: Mons. DUPLAN. *Tromp Tonpif*, under the pseudonym of Souriant, secretary to the Burgomaster: Mons. DARCY. *Moulangauffre*, an Inn Keeper: Mons. Castel. *Chutentos*, a Young Spaniard: Mons. VALTER. *Pasmotto*, a Young Spaniard: Mons. DAVALIS. *Pilot*, a Student of the Captain's: Mons. Ludovic. *Sailors, Fishermen, Fishwomen, Populace, Buers and Sellers, Fishmongers, Soldiers, etc.*

Act 1: Un petit port auprès d'Ostende. Au loin la mer.

Act 2: Chez le Capitaine.

Act 3: Une Kermesse flamande.

ACT 1[22]

Choeur (Voyez le joli poisson frais)
Pêcheurs, pêcheuses, marchands, acheteurs
Scene (C'est lui, j'en suis sûre)
Mlles. Duparc, Geoffroy
Trio (Encore un mot, mes camaarades/Les Castiliens sont tous les frères)
Messrs. de Quercy, Davalis, Valter
Couplets (A quinze ans, j'avais conscience)
Mlle. Faye
Duetto (Non, non, belle dame)
Mons. de Quercy, Mlle. Geoffroy
Duo (Van Ostebal est un marin, un malin)
Messrs. Roger, Duplan
Trio (Je vais la voir et lui parler)
Messrs. de Quercy, Davalis, Valter
Finale (Hourra! hourra! gloire au capitaine)
Messrs. Roger, Duplan, Choeur

---

[17]No program found for this production; reviews do not indicate which roles Messrs. Duplan and Darcy played.

[18]First produced in New York in French 26 August 1857 at the Metropolitan Music Hall in repertory. For Synopsis of Scenes and Musical Numbers, see original 1857 production.

[19]First produced in New York in French 14 February 1863 at the Théâtre Français in repertory. For Synopsis of Scenes and Musical Numbers, see original 1863 production.

[20]First produced in New York in French 25 August 1873 at the Broadway Theatre. For Synopsis of Scenes and Musical Numbers, see original 1873 production. At the beginning of Act 3, a highly characteristic national republican dance "La Fricasse" will be performed by Mlle. Vandamme, Mons. Grazzini and the whole company.

[21]First produced in New York 4 February 1875 at the Park Theatre for (46) performances in repertory. For Synopsis of Scenes and Musical Numbers, see original 1875 production.

[22]Musical numbers not listed in programs. List prepared from published French libretto (Calmann Lévy, Paris, 1887), nouvelle edition.

ACT 2

Scene (Ma ceinture de flanelle)
Mons. Roger, Choeur des femmes

Scene (J'ai pu, mais non pas sans peine)
Mons. Darcy

Nocturne (Allons, plus de bavardage)
Mons. Roger, Choeur

Couplets (Ça me démange et m'épouvante)
Mlle. Geoffroy

Sérénade (Pour composer une sérénade)
Messrs. Davalis, de Quercy, Valter

Choeur (Trois bandits ont cachés ici)
Choeur

Duo (C'est comme un aimant qui m'attire)
Mlle. Geoffroy, Mons. de Quercy

Finale (Les voilà! les voilà!)
Tous

ACT 3

Choeur et refrain (C'est aujourd'hui fête)
Mons. Roger, Choeur\

Air (Du prince, sitôt le signal)
Mons. de Quercy, Trois Espagnoles

Duo (Vous êtes belle, je suis jaloux)
Mons. Roger, Mlle. Geoffroy

Quatuor (Avez-vous quelque arme illicite?)
Messrs. Roger, de Quercy, Davalis, Valter

Finale (Le canard l'a bien passée)
Mlle. Geoffroy, Tous

1875.31 ROBINSON CRUSOE, His Man Friday, Monkey, and the King of Caribee Islands

A Comical Extravaganza in One Act, 5 Scenes[23], preceded by an Olio. Scenery by R. L. Weed, Matt Morgan. Machinery, Nelse Waldron. Musical director, David Braham. Produced by Josh Hart. Opened 18 October 1875 at the Eagle Theatre and closed 30 October 1875 after 16 performances.

Olio: Germanisms, by Larry Tooley. John Wild's new interlude 'My Wife and Mother-in-Law,' with John Wild, James F. Crossin, J. A. Graver, Marie Gorenflo, Marie Stewart, Fanny Birch. Serio-Comic Songs by Jennie Hughes. Schoolcraft & Coes in their original sketch, Musical Academy. A. W. Sawyer in a grand aria from La Sonnambula. Mr. & Mrs. Whittington, Musical and Vocal Artists, and Master Newman, musical prodigy, age 7; Walters & Morton, Monarchs of Song and Dance. Commodore Nutt in his character songs and dances. Harry Kernell in his Irish Songs and Stories; Great Garnellas in Parlor Gymnastics. Edna Markley in her Beautiful Ballads. Camp Meeting Echoes, with Messrs. Schoolcraft, Coes, Walters, Morton and Schwicardi; Jolly Nash, England's greatest comique.

ROBINSON CRUSOE CAST: *Robinson Crusoe*, everybody's hero: Miss H. L. FRANKLIN. *Captain Will Atkins*, Smuggler, Pirate, etc.: WELSH EDWARDS. *Old Daddy Pigtail*, Tobacconist and Peasant: James F. Crossin. *Ben Bunting, Billy Bowline*, old salts: J. Bradley, A. Clark. *Cutpurse, Gongeye*, low creatures: A. Louis, D. Wall. *Pretty Jenny Pigtail*, the Pride of Hull: JENNIE HUGHES. (*Nautical Specialty*: ELLA WESNER.) *King Tyranny*, a real King: ALICE EVERETT. *Liberty*, so seldom seen: Angela Griffith. *Man Friday*, his original character: JAMES S. MAFFITT. *Monkey*: Little Mac. *The Dog*: Master Terrier. *The Cat*: Master Whiskers. *The Goat*: Master Kid. *The Parrott*: Master Cockatoo. *King Hoop-de-doodle-do*, King of the Caribee Islands: GEORGE H. COES. *Hokee Pokee, Wankee Fum*, Vagabond cannibals: C. Walters, M. Morton. *Picalillie*, the King's favorite Squaw: LUKE SCHOOLCRAFT.

Scene 1: Seaport of Hull. (Weed.) *Scene 2*: Cell of Tyranny. (Weed.) *Scene 3*: Island of Juan Fernandez. (Morgan.) *Scene 4*: Sea Shore of Juan Fernandez. (Morgan.) *Scene 5*: Crusoe's Hut. (Morgan.)

MUSICAL NUMBERS

Nautical Song and Dance (Scene 1)
E. Wesner

Song (Scene 3)
H. L. Franklin, Little Mac, Masters Terrier, Whiskers, Kid, Cockatoo

Cannibal Song and Dance (Scene 4)
G. H. Coes

Finale (Scene 5)

[23]Authorship of the extravaganza uncredited.

1875.32 HUMPTY DUMPTY IN EVERY CLIME

A Grand Holiday Trick Pantomime in Three Acts, 14 Scenes. (Play by George L. Fox.) Music composed or adapted by Giuseppe Operti. Scenery by William Voegtlin and Matt Morgan. Properties, appointments and mechanical effects by William Vail and Robert J. Cutler. Produced by George L. Fox. Opened 25 October 1875 at Booth's Theatre and closed 27 November 1875 after 41 performances.

CAST: *Immortals*: *Pluto*, King of Hades: THOMAS CHAPMAN. *Grumpio*, Pluto's Right Bower: HARRY MORGAN. *Cheribeseo*, Pluto's Left Bower: GEORGE SHIELDS. *Scarlet Imp*, a regular Devil: GEORGE TOPACK. *Brilliant*, the "Morning Star": Miss MATTIE TEMPLE. *Saltpetre, Blue Peter, Blue Blazes, Sulphur, Chain Lightning, Heat Lightning, Green Flame, Red Flame, Blue Flame, White Flame, Everybody's Flame, Choristers, Devils, Imps, Fiends and Spirits.*

Mortals: *Humpty Dumpty*, the original and only, in a new sphere: GEORGE L. FOX. *Old One Two*, a regular wormwood: ROBERT FRASER. *Tommy Tucker*, the indispensable: CHARLES W. RAVEL. *Little Goody Two Shoes*, the Captivating: LOUSIE BOSHELL. *Henry Augustus Upright*, the afflicted: PETER KYNOCK. *Captain Standin* of the Force: Mr. P. Woodward. *Monkey*, a perfect ape: George Topack. *Mr. Ladady*: George Germon. *Mrs. Doserem*: Ella Whittredge. *Mrs. Takem*: Sophie Ravel. *Policemen, Villagers, Gens D'Armes, Citizens.*

Specialties: Little Todd (Germanic Wonder on a column of gold), Mlle. Lucia and the Orrin Brothers (acrobats, gymnasts); Kynock and Smith (roller skaters); Edward Charles Dunbar (singer).

Act 1, Scene 1: The Abode of Pluto. *Scene 2*: Humpty Dumpty Village. *Scene 3*: The Rocky Bound Coast. *Scene 4*: Germany: The Village Inn and Post Office. *Scene 5*: A Familiar Street. Opticians and Umbrella Factory. *Scene 6*: Congress Hall, Saratoga. Rear entrance. *Scene 7*: Across the Continent, in the snow.

Act 2: Humpty's Wonders from Every Clime.

Act 3, Scene 1: Public Square, Drug Store and Residence. *Scene 2*: London, England. Confectionary and Music Store. *Scene 3*: Paris. Boarding Houses. *Scene 4*: Philadelphia. Mysterious Chamber. *Scene 5*: Hut and Wood, somewhere at night. *Scene 6*: Centennial Celebration of Our Beloved Country.

ACT 1

Scene 2

The Village Dance

Whispering Chorus

Grand Transformation
Clown: G. L. Fox. *Pantaloon*: R. Fraser. *Harlequin*: C. W. Ravel. *Columbine*: L. Boshell.

ACT 2

Humpty's Wonders from Every Clime: (Specialties)
Mlle. Lucia and the Orrin Brothers in Triple Parterre, Olympian and Calisthenic Exposition.
Messrs. Kynock and Smith in their wondrous Skatorial Exercises, illustrative of the Artist and Awkward Novice on ice.
Little Todd, the Germanic Wonder in his gymnastic performance on the Column of Gold. (Tutor, Mr. Charles Crosby)
Edward Charles Dunbar (English Vocalist and Milanese Minstrel)
Miss Louise Boshell in her Gymnast Act
Los Dos Payosos (Acrobats)

ACT 3

Scene 6

Centennial Celebration of Our Beloved Country

Up in the Clouds, Old Father Time; The Old State House, Philadelphia; Independence Hall; Independence Bell; Allegorical Tableau and Centennial Offering. Grand Striking and Picturesque Representations: Father of Our Country, America, Home of the Free!

1875.33 LE PETIT FAUST!

A Revival of the Opéra-bouffe in Three Acts[24] in French. Libretto by Hector Crémieux and Adolphe Jaime. Music by Hervé. Stage manager, Mons. E.

[24]First produced in New York in English 29 August 1870 at Kelly & Leon's; in French 26 September 1870 at the Grand Opera House. For Synopsis of Scenes and Musical Numbers, see September 1870 production. In Act 3, Mlle. Geoffroy will sing the Waltz from "Heloise and Abelard" which she created in Paris.

Schmidt. Scenery by Hannibal W. Calyo. Costumes by Mons. Santella, Mme. Huchet. Musical director, Mons. Charles van Ghele. Produced by Maurice Grau and C. A. Chizzola. Opened and closed 29 October 1875 at the Lyceum Theatre for 1 performance.

CAST: *Marguerite*: Mlle. CORALIE GEOFFROY. *Méphisto*: Mlle. MARIE NARDYNN. *Lisette*: Mlle. JULIE HOSDEZ. *Aglae*: Mlle. Sophie Gherzi. *Clorinde*: Mlle. Sophie. *Lisbel*: Mlle. Vaudelet. *Frantz*: Mlle. Julien. *Altmayer*: Mlle. Alphonsine. *Agnes*: Mlle. Cureau. *Brander*: Mlle. Nelcy. *Charlotte*: Mlle. Angelbert. *Lischen*: Mlle. Louise. *Fritz*: Mlle. Hortense. *Wagner*: Mlle. Noé. *Faust*: Mons. deQUERCY. *Valentin*: Mons. ROGER. *Le Cocher*: Mons. DUPLAN. *Le Pion*: Mons. Darcy. *The Anglo Saxon*: Mons. Ludovic. *Soldats, Etudiants, Viellards, Diables, Diablesses.*

1875.34 THE IRISH HEIRESS

A Musical Farce in One Act, accompanied by an olio. Adapted[25] from the play "Perfection, or The Lady of Munster" by Thomas Haynes Bayley. Machinist, Nelse Waldron. Musical director, David Braham. Produced by Josh Hart. Opened 1 November 1875 at the Eagle Theatre and closed 6 November 1875 after 8 performances.

Olio: 'Well, Good Day,' a laughable sketch, characters by Schoolcraft & Coes. Song and Dance by James Bradley. Favorite Songs by Edna Markley. John Wild's laughable farce, 'Port Wine vs. Jealousy,' with John Wild, James F. Crossin, and Marie Gorenflo. Master Barney in character songs and changes. Australian Musical Cabinet, performed by Messrs. Wallace and Leathwood. Irish Comicalities by Harry Kernell.

THE IRISH HEIRESS CAST: *Kate O'Brien*, with songs: JULIA MATHEWS. *Sir Lawrence Paragon*: WELSH EDWARDS. *Charles Paragon*: J. F. Croissin. *Sam*, Valet to Charles: JOHN WILD. *Footman*: J. Mason. *Susan*, maid to Miss O'Brien: Lizzie Edwards.

Olio: Miss Louise Franklin will sing "The Milk Maid's Marriage." Ambition, the laughable local sketch, with Sam Rickey, George H. Coes, John Wild, Master Barney, Luke Schoolcraft. John Jolly Nash in his unequalled Laughing Songs. Selections by Braham's Orchestra. The Laughable Pantomime, 'Bibo and Babbette,' with James S. Maffitt, W. H. Bartholomew, Marie Gorenflo, Luke Schoolcraft, John Wild.

1875.35 TRIAL BY JURY

A Dramatic Cantata in One Act, accompanied by an olio. Libretto by William S. Gilbert. Music by Arthur Sullivan. Stage director, Welsh Edwards. Conductor of orchestra, David Braham. Produced by Josh Hart. Opened 15 November 1875 at the Eagle Theatre and closed 20 November 1875 after 8 performances.

Olio: Did She Go, or Was She Led Astray?, a Burlesque, with George H. Coes, John Wild, Sam Rickey, George K. Fortescue, Florence Newman, Marie Gorenflo, Marie Stewart, Miss Griffith, James F. Crossin, James Bradley, Mr. G. Lewis. Crossley & Elder in their wonderful Field Sports. Rickey & Barney's laughable interlude, Our Boyhood Days!; Louise Franklin (songs). Following TRIAL BY JURY: Ethiopian Echoes, Luke Schoolcraft; Character Songs and Changes, Ella Wesner; Dress Rehearsal, or Wild's Old Man!, a laughable sketch by Sam Rickey, with Messrs. Rickey, Wild, Barney, Edwards, etc.

TRIAL BY JURY CAST: *The Learned Judge*: G. H. MacDERMOTT. *Counsel for the Plaintiff*: G. H. COES. *Foreman of the Court*: J. Danvers. *The Defendant*: W. FORRESTER. *Usher of the Court*: J. Hogan. *The Plaintiff*: ROSE KEENE. *Bridesmaids*: Julia Hogan, Ladies of the Chorus. *Gentlemen of the Jury*: Messrs. Quinn, Demilt, Gentlemen of the Chorus. (Chorus of 50).

Scene: A Court of Justice.

MUSICAL NUMBERS[26]

"Hark, the hour of ten is sounding"
Chorus

"When first my old, old love I knew" (Song)
W. Forrester

"All hail great judge"
Chorus

"When I, good friends, was called to the bar" (Song)
G. H. MacDermott, Chorus

"Swear thou the jury" (Recitative)
G. H. Coes, J. Hogan

"Where is the plaintiff?" (Recitative)
G. H. Coes, J. Hogan

"Comes the broken flower" (Chorus)
Bridesmaids

"O'er the season vernal" (Solo)
R. Keene

"Oh, never, never, never"
G. H. MacDermott

"May it please you, my lud" (Recitative and aria)
G. H. Coes, All

"That she is reeling"
G. H. MacDermott, J. Danvers, R. Keene, All

"Oh, gentlemen, listen, I pray" (Song)
W. Forrester, Bridesmaids

"A nice dilemma we have here" (Quartette)
G. H. MacDermott, G. H. Coes, W. Forrester, R. Keene

"I love him—I love him" (Duet)
R. Keene, W. Forrester

"The question, gentlemen" (Recitative)
G. H. MacDermott, G. H. Coes, All

"Oh, joy unbounded" (Finale and Grand Transformation Scene)
All

1875.36 KIM-KA!, or, The Adventures of an Aeronaut

An Oriental Pantomime in One Act[27], accompanied by an olio. Stage director, Welsh Edwards. Scenery by Matt Morgan. Conductor of orchestra, David Braham. Produced by Josh Hart. Opened 29 November 1875 at the Eagle Theatre and closed 4 December 1875 after 8 performances.

Olio: Dr. Cureall, or the Coal Heavers Revenge, a laughable farce, with Welsh Edwards, John Wild, James Bradley, Luke Schoolcraft, C. E. Walters. Songs and Dances, James Bradley. George H. Coes in his artistic banjo solos and songs. Editors Troubles, a laughable local interlude, with James F. Crossin, Harry Kernell, John Wild, Larry Tooley, James Bradley, Luke Schoolcraft. Ella Wesner in her unequalled character songs and changes. Jenny Lind, a laughable musical farce, with George H. Coes, Welsh Edwards, John Wild, James F. Crossin, James Bradley, Mr. Schwicardi, T. Williams, and Julia Mathews, as Miss Jennie Leatherlungs, alias Lind. Miss Mathews will introduce choice selections from her favorite operas and a comic duet with Mr. Wild. G. H. MacDermott in a new collection of his original character comic songs. The Murphy Musketeers, a Irish sketch, with Harry Kernell and James Bradley. Selected ballads by Louise Franklin. Walters and Morton in their unequalled songs and dances.

KIM-KA! CAST: *Ventilaw*, an English aeronaut: W. H. BARTHOLOMEW. *Kim-Ka*, the Emperor of China: WELSH EDWARDS. *Koblean-Kang*, Grand Mandarin: LUKE SCHOOLCRAFT. *San-ta-loo*, Grand Astrologer: JAMES F. CROSSIN. *Ya-tu-shon*, Grand Executioner: George H. Coes. *Attendants on the Emperor (4)*: *Moon-she*: Mr. Schwicardi. *Wang-lee*: John Wild. *Tang-yang*: C. E. Walters. *Sang-chu*: J. W. Morton. *Ko-ket*, the Princess: MARIE GORENFLO. *Te-ling*, her attendant: Miss Everett. *Mandarins, Dancers, Coolies, Ladies of the Court, etc.*

1875.37 THE DEAD SHOT!/ FROM ST. LOUIS TO NEW ORLEANS!

A Musical Farce in One Act, and an Ethiopian Sketch in One Act, accompanied by an olio. Musical director, David Braham. Produced by Josh Hart. Opened 6 December 1875 at the Eagle Theatre; THE DEAD SHOT closed 11 December 1875 after 8 performances, returned 20-25 December 1875 for an additional 8 performances; FROM ST. LOUIS TO NEW ORLEANS closed 25 December 1875 after 24 performances.

---

[25]Adaptation uncredited.

[26]Musical numbers not listed in programs. List prepared from published English piano vocal score (Chappell & Co., London, 1875, 1898).

[27]Authorship uncredited in programs.

Olio: School for Husbands, a laughable farce with James F. Crossin, Marie Gorenflo, John Wild, Hannah Birch. Songs and Dance, James Bradley. George H. Coes in his artistic Banjo Solos and Songs. Charles White's laughable Negro sketch, Who Departed First?, with Charles White, Luke Schoolcraft, Larry Tooley, and Welsh Edwards. Athletic Sports by Messrs. Crossley and Elder. Irishisms by Kernell and Bradley.

THE DEAD SHOT CAST: *Captain Cannon*: WELSH EDWARDS. *Williams*, his friend: James Bradley. *Mr. Hector Timid*, G. H. MacDERMOTT. *Mr. Wiseman*: JOHN WILD. *Frederick Thornton*: James F. Crossin. *Louisa*, Niece to Captain Cannon: JULIA MATHEWS. *Chatter*, her maid: Millie Cook. *Police Officers*: Company.

Olio: Germanisms, with Larry Tooley. Rickey & Barney in their Musical Sketch, Mike the Drummer Boy. Favorite Ballads: Louisa Franklin. The Great Laughing Comique, John Jolly Nash. Medley Music, Braham's Orchestra.

FROM ST. LOUIS TO NEW ORLEANS CAST: *Malcolm Bloodgood*: CHARLES WHITE. *Ezra Litchfield*: LUKE SCHOOLCRAFT. *Lambert Harkway*: JOHN WILD. *Isom Gunsby*: HARRY KERNELL. *Alf Treadwell*: GEORGE H. COES. *Doremus Hemmingway*: C. E. Walters. *Abe Dumbleton*: J. W. Morton. *Mealio Gardner*: James Bradley. *Barclay Pitts*: Larry Tooley. *Thadeus Clawson*: Mr. Schwicardi. *Rufus Pinckney*: Mr. Edwards. *Hank Isleton*: John Slocum. *Rupert Dodge*: James Graft. *Jake Darrelsmith*: James F. Crossin. *Auxiliaries*: 50. Featuring New and Old Time Songs, Dances, Hymns, Sayings, etc. making this the cream of fun and laughter. Concluding with the Burning Steamboat, in which will be introduced Mr. Hart's great original fire effects. In which will be introduced a new and beautiful panorama, painted by R. L. Weed, representing the Ohio and Mississippi Rivers, depicting life on board a River Steamer, and all the peculiarities of life in the South: Mississippi; St. Louis; Kaskaskia River; Memphis Sunset; Jackson, Missouri; Burning Steamer; Flood on Mississippi; Vicksburg; Bayou below Vicksburg; Mississippi Plantation Scene; Natchez under the Hill; Bayou Sara; Baton Rouge; New Orleans.

MUSICAL NUMBERS

"Emancipation Day"
Fifty Voices
(*Music by* David Braham. *Lyrics by* G. L. Stout.)

1875.38 GIROFLÉ-GIROFLA

A Revival of the Comic Opera, revised into One Act by G. H. MacDermott. Music by Charles Lecocq. (Original French libretto by Albert Vanloo and Eugene Leterrier.) Program accompanied by a vaudeville olio and the Ethiopian sketch, FROM ST. LOUIS TO NEW ORLEANS. Musical director, David Braham. Produced by Josh Hart. Opened 13 December 1875 at the Eagle Theatre and closed 18 December 1875 after 8 performances.

GIROFLÉ-GIROFLA CAST: *Giroflé, Girofla*, twin daughters of Bolero and Aurore: JULIA MATHEWS. *Aurore*, wife of Don Bolero: G. A. Mortimer. *Don Bolero d'Alcarazas*, Governor of a Spanish Province: G. M. MacDERMOTT. *Marasquin*, betrothed by Giroflé: LOUISE FRANKLIN. *Mourzouk*, Chief of the Moors, betrothed to Girofla: GEORGE H. COES. *Paquita*, Attendant of Giroflé and Girofla: Millie Cook. *Pedro*, a Page in love with Paquita: Marie Gorenflo. *Pirates, Moors, Cousins, Guests, Bridesmaids, Pages, etc.*

Olio: Harry Kernell in his original Irish Comicalities. One Night in a Bar-room!, a laughable interlude, with John Wild, Larry Tooley, Luke Schoolcraft, James Bradley, D. L. Harris, Charles White, James F. Crossin, Mr. Schwicardi. John Jolly Nash in a collection of his original songs. Which is Which, a negro sketch with John Wild, Luke Schoolcraft and James F. Crossin. Larry Tooley in his Irishisms. Selected music by Braham's orchestra, followed by FROM ST. LOUIS TO NEW ORLEANS.

1875.39 NIMBLE NIP!, or, Ogre Ugliphiz, Fairy Silvereyes & the Princess with the Strawberry Mark

A Holiday Pantomime in Two Acts, 11 Scenes, preceded by an Olio. (Play by John F. Poole.) Every scene, costume, appointment and effect entirely new and elegant. Musical director, Fred W. Zaulig. Produced by John F. Poole. Opened 20 December 1875 at the Olympic Theatre; reconstructed 10 January 1876; closed 29 January 1876 after 48 performances.[28]

Olio[29]: George S. Knight's laughable sketch, Weston, the Walkist, with G. S. Knight, G. W. H. Griffin, G. W. Reed, William West, W. B. Cahill, W. Marrin, Miss Thorton. Irish Sketches with Messrs. Murphy and Morton. Messrs. Johnson and Bruno in Acrobatic Songs and Dances. Three A.M., sketch with John Hart, G. W. H. Griffin, Julia Coventry, W. Marrin. Henrietta Mollenhauer in beautiful ballads and operatic selections. Messrs. Harper and Stansill in songs and dances. George S. Knight in new Dutch songs and recitations.

NIMBLE NIP CAST: *Prince Sweet-as-Sugar*, deep in love and trouble: SOPHIE WORRELL. *Princess Ever-so-fair*, with the Strawberry Mark: IRENE WORRELL. *Fairy Silvereyes*, the very queen of Fairies: EMMELINE YOUNG. *King Grumblegrowl*, the high-tempered monarch: G. W. H. GRIFFITH. *Ogre Ugliphiz*, a terrible wretch: E. D. GOODING. *Ramparagous*, a heartless vagabond: John Queen. *Blunderbore*, a souless ruffian: William West. *Boisterous*, a mild-mannered monster: John Gilbert. *Troublesome*, a gentle savage: S. Holdsworth. *Greatpaw*, a quiet villain: Wash Norton. *Fairy Fiorretta*: Addie Farwell. *Fairy Maydew*: Kitty Parker. *Fairy Violet*: Pearl Thornton. *Fairy Daisy*: Nelly Calvert. *Fairy Damask*: Kate Hasserly. *Fairy Mignonette*: Miss E. Roberts. *The Princess Leanandscraggi*: G W. Reed. *Our Army and Navy*: 80 Beautiful Young Ladies, led by the accomplished comedienne Alice Bennett. *Full Drum Corps*. *Drum Solo*: EVA SINCLAIR. 160 Auxiliaries.

Nimble Nip, the Clown: BLAND HOLT. *Pantaloon*: W. B. CAHILL. *Jack Harlequin*: Master MARTIN. *Columbine*: IDA GREENFIELD.

Act 1, Scene 1: Palace of King Grumblegrowl. *Scene 2*: Fairy Landscape. *Scene 3*: Dungeon beneath Grumblegrowl Castle. *Scene 4*: Palace Gardens, with fountain of real water. *Scene 5*: Road to Middletown. *Scene 6*: The Garden of Roses. *Scene 7*: Green Grotto.

Act 2, Scene 1: Up and down street. *Scene 2*: On board the "*Mary Jane*." *Scene 3*: A well-known street. *Scene 4*: Gorgeous Transformation Scene. The Aerial Palace of Fairy Silvereyes.

BALLETS, SPECIALTIES, MUSICAL NUMBERS

An uproarious chorus (Act 1, Scene 1)

Grand fairy musical outbreak and chorus (Act 1, Scene 2)

"Dancing the Trallaloo" (Duet)(Act 1, Scene 4)
S. Worrell, I. Worrell

Our Army and Navy in song, march, and military evolutions (Act 1, Scene 6)

Combination and concentration of mirth, music, jokes, jumps, laughter, leaps, activity, antics, Murder! (Act 2, Scene 1)

1875.40 HARLEQUIN! DEMON STATUE, The Enchanted Pills and Magic Apple Tree; or High Diddle Diddle, the Cat's in the Fiddle, the Cow Jumped Over the Moon!

An English Burlesque Harlequinade (Pantomime) in Two Acts, 12 Scenes[30]. Play by G. H. MacDermott. Music by David Braham. Scenery by Matt Morgan. Machinery and effects by Nelse Waldron, R. L. Weed. Costumes by Margaret Devoe. Entire production under the immediate supervision of Josh Hart. Musical director, David Braham. Produced by Josh Hart. Opened 27 December 1875 at the Eagle Theatre and closed 22 January 1876 after 32 performances.

CAST: *Immortals*: *The Demon of the Statue*, an Original Author, otherwise Scissors and Paste: JAMES F. CROSSIN. *First State Vampire*: Mr. Scissors. *Second State Vampire*: Mr. Paste. *Third State Vampire*: Mr. Gum. *Fourth Stage Vampire*: Mr. Cheap Literature. *The Statue*: The —. *The Fairy Fanciful*: Miss A. Griffiths.

Mortals: *Maciconli the First*, King of Gourmond Land, and Principal Gourmond, Rabbid for Rabbit Stew, which gets him into more stews than one: G. M. MacDERMOTT. *Baron Firstfiddle*, Prime Minister and chief administer to the King's appetite, he being 'appy and tight all the time: James Bradley. *Count Courteous*, Valet de Sham, all sham and of very little vallea (ice) value: George Lewis. *Prince Bluepoint, Prince Saddlerock, Prince Chowder*, three queer fish who get much baiting, each a suit-or (for) Princess Eglantine's hand, but not handsome enough to suit her: John Wild, Larry Tooley, Louisa Franklin. *Demetrius*, a fish-or boy, equally at home as both, in love

[28]Authorship uncredited in programs; no credits for scenery, costumes, stage director, etc.

[29]Olio changed weekly.

[30]Reconstructed 10 January 1876 with a new and original Irish sketch, 'The O'Hoolihans,' the first appearance (John Wild's burlesque) of the Clodoche Troupe, and the re-appearance of Ella Wesner and the laughable sketch of 'The Regular Army O!'

with the Princess, she says "I love him": JENNIE HUGHES. *Electric*, sort of jack on wires, up to every eletrick upon the Telegraph Board: Hannah Birch. *Princess Eglantine*, her father's daughter, 'apply spared from a fruitless search for a husband: MILLIE COOK. *Spirits—potent and impotent, Guards, Black-guards, Courtiers, Catchers, etc.*

Harlequinade Characters: *Clown*: GRIMALDI ADAMS. *Pantaloon*: W. BARTHOLOMEW. *Harlequin*: HARRY HUNTER. *Columbine*: MARIE GORENFLO. *Post master*: Mr. Nipum. *Bobby Grabem*, a policeman: James Bradley. *Mrs. Mackerel*, a fishwoman: Mrs. Lewis. *Mr. Blowhard*: Mr. Jones. *Widow Twankey*: Miss Nesbitt. *Paddy malone*: Larry Tooley. *Cheap John*, a vender of tins: Mr. Punch. *Samuel Brown*, dealer in old clothes: Mr. (G. L.) Stout. *William Baker*, the Mutton Pie Man: Mr. Blake. *Mr. Cat*, the Minstrel: Master Sargent. *Olango*: John Wild. *Master Mason*: James F. Crossin. *First Degree*: J. Brown. *Second Degree*: G. L. Stout. *Mr. Ketchum, Mr. Cheathum*, stock brokers: Messrs. Cash, Pelf. *Peter Explosion*: Mr. James. *Mr. Hardup*: R. F. Kerns. *Bobby*, a policeman: James Bradley. *Mr. Straightlace*: J. T. Smith. *Mr. Morter*, a hod carrier: Billy Brick. *Colonel (of Miniature Regiment)*: JENNIE HUGHES. *Specialties*: (Harry) Kernell & (James) Bradley; The Phenomenal Girards (Julian, Emil, Lewis).

Act 1, Scene 1: Home of the Modern Drama. *Scene 2*: The Royal Harbor and View of the Sea. *Scene 3*: Principal Street in Gourmond Land. *Scene 4*: The Dark valley of the Demon Statue. *Scene 5*: Gourmondize Hall in the Royal Palace. *Scene 6*: The Royal Orchard and Magic Apple Tree.

Act 2, Scene 1: Street. *Scene 2*: Post Office and Dry Goods Store. *Scene 3*: Trip. Harlequin and Columbine. *Scene 4*: Masonic Lodge and Stock Brokers. *Scene 5*: Pyrotechnics. *Scene 6*: Dark Cavern. (Transformation by Matt Morgan.)

SPECIALTIES[31]

Grand Magic Dance (Act 1, Scene 5)

Transformation of Characters in Harlequinade (Act 1, Scene 6)
G. Adams, W. Bartholomew, H. Hunter, M. Gorneflo

The Irish Policemen (Act 2, Scene 1)
H. Kernell, J. Bradley

Dance (Act 2, Scene 2)
H. Hunter, M. Gorenflo

Carnival de Diablerie (Legmania)(Act 2, Scene 3)
The Girards

Poses (Act 2, Scene 4)
H. Hunter, M. Gorenflo

Dance (Act 2, Scene 5)
H. Hunter, M. Gorenflo

Grand Parade of Miniature Regiment (Act 2, Scene 5)

Song and Chorus (Act 2, Scene 5)
J. Hughes, Chorus

Germanisms (Act 2, Scene 5)
L. Tooley

The Four Seasons (Transformation) (Act 2, Scene 6)

Grand Finale (Act 2, Scene 6)

ROSEMI-SHELL!,

1876.01 or, My Daughter! Oh, My Daughter!

An Emotional, Sensational, Nonsensical, Incidental, Dramatical, Musical, and contemporaneously Farcical what-you-may-call-it (Burlesque[32]) in One Act, preceded by an olio. Play by Sydney Rosenfeld. Music by David Braham. Scenery by Matt Morgan and R. L. Weed. Musical director, David Braham. Produced by Josh Hart. Opened 24 January 1876 at the Eagle Theatre and closed 5 February 1876 after 16 performances; returned 6 March 1876 to the Eagle Theatre and closed 11 March 1876 after an additional 8 performances. Total: 24 performances.

Olio: 'Dutch Shoemaker,' a laughable German sketch, with Larry Tooley, James Bradley, James F. Crossin, G. L. Stout, Hannah Birch. Favorite Ballads by Louisa Franklin. The Langlois Brothers, Egyptian Jugglers. 'The Laborers,' an original sketch written and performed by Harry Kernell and James Bradley. A. W. Sawyer, the Copophonian artist, in a grand aria from 'La Sonnambula.' 'Temperance Home,' a sketch by John Wild, with John Wild, Harry Kernell, Larry Tooley, James F. Crossin, James Bradley. Gorman and Romer, German specialty artists, in their act, 'Love und fun.' Medley music, Braham's orchestra.

ROSEMI-SHELL CAST: *Count de Fern-y*, the necessary Thorne to every Rose, a gallant Mister but a victim to Ey-tinge of cruel Mystery: LARRY TOOLEY. *Baron de Best-Fille*, a Roué, who gets his best fill of life before the play begins, but who has cause to rouet before it is over: JAMES F. CROSSIN. *Piermi-Shell*, a miserly barkeeper, very much of a villain in fact, as you will find out if you stay in long enough and live to see it, one of the deepest die: G. H. MacDERMOTT. *Mule-in-Hay*, with a cold in the head, called the sneezer, because that's sneezer way to call him; Piermi's servant: JOHN WILD. *Baroness de Morriss and Essex*, Prefect of the Seine, perfectly insane, who gets into a Parcelle of difficulties from managing too many Stages at once: James Bradley. *Andrew*, the nice little fellow for cent, who likes "Spoon," but not the bitter dose that often comes with it: Louise Franklin. *Baroness de Best-Fille*, supposed to be married to the Baron, and retired from the humdrum of life, though why 'f she's the Baron's wife, shouldn't live with him, is almost a con-humdrum: MARIE GORENFLO. *Rosemi-Shell*, the wife of the husband and the mother of the daughter, who suffers with conflicting emotions and the New Densarti System, though the last is a noodle sort of system to be suffering with, and enough to MacKaye man swear: GEORGE K. FORTESCUE. *Susie*, the daughter, oh, the daughter, who clings to her love with constant and un-Varian devotion: MILLIE COOK. *Supers, White-Guards and Black-Guards.*

MUSICAL NUMBERS

"Don't You Think I'm Blind!"

"Original Sneezing Song"

"Rumpty-Foozle Schnoots" (Chorus)

THE PIQUE FAMILY!,

1876.02 a Play on the Da-ly

A Travesti on Augustin Daly's drama "Pique" with new music, songs and dances, in One Act.[33] Travesti by Sydney Rosenfeld. Music incidental to the burlesque, and adapted to the author's original burlesque songs, has been composed, arranged and selected by Fred Perkins. Acting manager, Charles Villers. Scenery by Matt Morgan, Charles Graham. Vocal director, Vincent Hogan. Musical director, Fred Perkins. Stage mechanisms by L. Guernsey. Produced by Matt Morgan. Opened 13 March 1876 at the Lyceum Theatre and closed 25 March 1876 after 16 performances.

CAST: *Matthew Spanish*, from Massachusetts, who is full of Yankee notions: W. A. ROUSE. *Captain Arthur Harkins Spanish*, of the Pique family: CHARLES VILLERS. *Doctor Gastric*, juicedly useful (if you only knew it): WALTER LENNOX. *Rainbow Blessing*, who loves too many entirely: EVA WEST. *Jimmy Loose, Johnny Droo*, the Boy Gallants: MINNIE PALMER, FLORENCE ELLIS. *Inflation Jim*, a Tramping Scamp: VINCENT HOGAN. *Padding*, a ditto: James Danvers. *Phanny Dazzlingport* of the Pique family: Harry Josephs. *Widow Lucille*, whose English is more broken than her heart: Miss A. ESTELLE. *Mary Spanish*, a sentimental maid: Nellie Boyd. *Aunt Dollymount*, a nice old lady: H. W. Ellis. *Wretch*, the Waif: Julia Hogan. *Mother Merriles*: Mr. G. C. Randolph. *Charley Spanish*, the little Pique: Admiral Dot.

And the Grand Transformation Scene, Columbia's Court, by Matt Morgan.

1876.03 HUMPTY DUMPTY

A Revival of the Pantomime in Three Acts, 18 Scenes[34]. Music, original and selected, by Fred W. Zaulig. Scenery by Joseph A. De La Harpe and Richard S. Smith. Intricate machinery by James Tait. Properties and appointments by Joseph Arnold, Charles Sellers, Robert Cutler. Costumes by Annie Trimble. Ballets composed and arranged by Mons. Julien Martinetti and Mlle. Adele Buimi. Musical director, Fred W. Zaulig. Produced by John F. Poole. Opened 17 April 1876 at the Olympic Theatre and closed 8 July 1876 after 96 performances.

CAST: *Clown*: ROBERT FRASER. *Pantaloon*: Mons. MARTINETTI. *Harlequin*: GEORGE TOPACK. *Columbine*: Mlle. (Zela) BARETTA. *Burlesque*: EMMELINE YOUNG. *Sulphura*, the fire sprite: Master MARTIN. *Romance*: Addie Farwell. *Ballet*: Ida Devere. *The Four Quarters of the World*: *Europe*: Pearl Thonton. *Asia*: Marie Farrall. *Africa*: Mr. W. Marrin. *America*: Emily Herbert. *New Jersey*, somewhere about

[31]Musical numbers not listed in programs.

[32]Inspired by the play 'Rose Michel' adapted from the French of Ernest Blum by J. Steele MacKaye.

[33]Preceded by two one act farces, Morton's "Topknot's Dilemmas," and "The Wrong Man," and an olio.

[34]Although billed as a revival of the production which opened 10 March 1868 at the Olympic Theatre, with "every scene, every effect, every trick" duplicated, its author, George L. Fox is nowhere credited, and the preponderance of all-new settings and specialties suggests this HUMPTY DUMPTY was indeed a very different production.

the four quarters: Harry Phillips. *Ill News*, a fast traveler: Master Speed. *Good News*, the slowest of all: Master Welkum. *Burlesque's Supporters (4)*: *Lightfoot*: Mary Bond. *Breakdown*: Mlle. (Ina) Baptiste. *Quickstep*: Ida Lind. *Fandango*: Hattie Strudell. *Dr. Nitrous Oxide Gas Cureall*, a quack physician: J. C. Franklin. *Blowquick*, his valet: Mr. Ready. *Napkin*, a waiter: Mr. Bartell [W. H. Brittell]. *Upton Tactic*, a sergeant—a great disciplinarian: S. Holdsworth. *Penny Gaff*, proprietor of a peep show: Floyd Lee. *Peeler Copp*, a policeman: G. H. Griffin. *Gutter Snipe*, a ragpicker: A. Solvent. *Second Edition*, a Newsboy: Master White. *Gnome Cobbler*: Master Tony Logan. *Burden*, a porter: Mr. Anderson. *Paste Bucket*, a bill poster: Mr. Stick. *Kosschesnutz*, a prosperous lager beer saloon keeper: Mr. Allweight. *Miss Elegance Custom*, a fashionable young lady: Miss Gay. *Liza Laffenhausen*, a Dutch girl: Miss Lockwood. *Cora Shade*, (colored) hot corn woman: Miss Thomas. *Nymphalia*, Queen of the Nixies, or River Fairies: Mlle. Flora. *Pipula*, her elfin chief: Mlle. Rupert.

Berlin Ballet Troupe: Mlles. Ida DeVere, Zela Baretta, Agnes Eltra, Marie Higginson, Adele Buimi, Marie Honneaux, Ina Baptiste, Lottie Horton, Emily Herbert, Mary Blake, Maggie Blake, Agnes Seeley, Mary Kavanagh, Katie Waring, Nettie Pickards, Josephine Strudel, Amy Krohm, Ida Lind, Heralda Haslem, Millie Flora, Bertha Ruppert, Gussie Lockwood, Katie Simmons. *Specialties*: JAMES McDONALD (Skate dance), MIDGET McDONALD (Character Songs), LITTLE TODD (Column of Gold), W. J. MILLS (Lightning Changes and Songs).

Act 1, Scene 1: Retreat of Romance by Moonlight. *Scene 2*: Farm of Plenty at Sunrise. *Scene 3*: Mother Goose's Cerulean Cave. *Scene 4*: Gorgeous Grotto. (Smith.) *Scene 5*: Mazarine Maze. (De La Harpe.) *Scene 6*: Fairies' Retreat. (Smith.) *Scene 7*: Blue Bell Lane Post Office. (De La Harpe.) *Scene 8*: Housetops by Night. (De La Harpe.)

Act 2, Scene 1: Gardens of Versailles. (De La Harpe.) *Scene 2*: Sailors' Boarding House and Jewelry Store. (De La Harpe.) *Scene 3*: Draped Parlor. (De La Harpe.) *Scene 4*: Neapolitan Market Square. (De La Harpe.)

Act 3, Scene 1: Palace Garden. (De La Harpe.) *Scene 2*: English Drapery. (De La Harpe.) *Scene 3*: Graphic Club Billiard Room. (De La Harpe.) *Scene 4*: Exterior of Olympic Theatre. (De La Harpe.) *Scene 5*: Our Nation's Certificate. (De La Harpe.) *Scene 6*: Centennial Tableau—1776 and 1876. (Smith.)

ACT 1

Coral Ballet (Scene 6)
(*Composed and arranged by* Mons. Martinetti and Mlle. Adele Buimi.)

Naiad Groupings
Mlles. A. Buimi, Baretta, Corps de Ballet

Entrée Dansante
Mlles. Buimi, Baretta

Grand Entrée
Mlle. Devere

Adagio
Mlles. Devere, Buimi, Baretta, Coryphées, Corps de Ballet

Allegro
Coryphées, Cops de Ballet

Quartette
Mlles. Rupert, Baptiste, Strudell, Krohm

First Variation
Mlle. Baretta

Grand Variation
Mlle. Buimi

Solo
Mlle. Devere

Finale
Entire Ballet

ACT 2

James McDonald in his Champion Pedestal Skate Dance (Scene 1)

Midget McDonald in her choice character songs (Scene 3)

Neapolitan Ballet (Scene 4)

Tarantula
Coryphées, Corps de Ballet

Napolitaine
Mlles. Devere, Buimi

Pas des Sameurs
Coryphées, Corps de Ballet

Salorella
Mlle. Devere

Coda and Finale
Mlles. Devere, Buimi, Coryphées, Corps de Ballet

ACT 3

The German Wonder, Little Todd, in his performance on the Column of Gold (Scene 1)

W. J. Mills, Metamorphosic Artist, in his Lightning Changes and Songs (Scene 2)

1876.04 HIS GRACE, THE DUKE!

A Petite Comedie Musicale in One Act, preceded by an olio[35]. (Libretto by Edwin Kelly and Francis Leon, music by Giuseppe Verdi.) Director of amusements, Edwin Kelly. Orchestra under the direction of J. B. Vogel. Produced by (Edwin) Kelly and (Francis) Leon's Minstrels and Burlesque Opera Troupe. Opened 1 May 1876 at Kelly & Leon's (23rd Street Opera House) and closed 20 May 1876 after 21 performances; returned 26 February-2 March, 10 March 1877 to Kelly & Leon's for an additional 7 performances.

Olio: "Aunt Susie" (comic), John Morton. "Old Log Cabin in the Dell" (ballad), Edwin Kelly. "Giroflé-Girofla" Selections, Company. "Man of Many Names" (comic), Edwin Lester. "Gathering Shells on the Seashore" (ballad), J. H. Surridge. The Skidmores, Messrs. Lester, Walters, Morton, Martin and Company. Queen of Trumps, Wen Die Schwalben, Pot Pourri with The Only [Francis] Leon. Our Boys! with J. H. Surridge, Japanese Tommy, W. Ball. "My sweetheart when a boy" (ballad), Charles H. Gordon. Now here come the Monarchs, Walters & Morton in their songs and dances.

CAST: *Mr. Theophilus Nubbs*, a Theatrical Manager, victim of circumstances, willing to be right, but too weak to withstand temptation: EDWIN KELLY. *Ginger*, a servant, brave as a lion, deeply in love, a perfect Sallymander: Dave Wilson. *Miss Louise Charington*, a lady of ambitious tendencies, would like to be a Duchess, which is so unlike the generality of the fair citizens of this Republic, who despise rank; there never having been an instance of an American lady marrying for position or money: THE ONLY [Francis] LEON. *Miss Cora Moulton*, an ambitious young lady, but unlike the generality of American girls, is very willing to ally herself to a member of the bloated European aristocracy, not that money is an object, but a congenial companionship, my dear: J. H. Surridge. *Sally*, a waiting maid, stage struck, and anxious for an introduction to the footlights, notwithstanding the depravity of their surroundings, such is life: Edwin Lester. *Policeman*: Johnny Martin. *Patrolman*: Japanese Tommy. *Mons. Dumm*: Billy Props.

1876.05 THE GRAND DUTCH S

A Revival of the Burlesque of Offenbach's Opera Bouffe in One Act, preceded by an olio[36]. (Libretto by Edwin Kelly and Francis Leon. Music by Jacques Offenbach.) Director of amusements, Edwin Kelly. Orchestra under the direction of Frank Bowles. Produced by (Edwin) Kelly and (Francis) Leon's Minstrels and Burlesque Opera Troupe. Opened 22 May 1876 at Kelly & Leon's (23rd Street Opera House) and closed 10 June 1876 after 21 performances.

Olio: "Whisper Yes or No, Love" (ballad), Edwin Kelly. "Pull Down the Blinds" (comic), Edwin Lester. "Giroflé-Girofla" Selections, Company. "Me and Martha Ann" (comic), Lew Benedict. "Voice of the Mountain Land" (ballad), C. H. Gordon. The Skidmores, Messrs. Lester, Benedict, Walters, Morton and Company. Japanese Tommy as the Prima Donna. Lazy Dick! with Edwin Lester, Lew Benedict, William Ball, Walters & Morton's grand specialty entitled 'Zophelia.' Philosophical remarks by Lew Benedict

THE GRAND DUTCH S CAST: *General Boum*, supposed to be the originator of the Dutch Gap Canal and other successful military stratagems: EDWIN KELLY. *Fritz*, a full private and a big fool: J. H. Surridge. *Prince Paul* (and Virginia), a graduate of Yellow Covered Literature College, always waiting to marry the Duchess: Edwin Lester. *Nip and Tuck*, City Messenger of the Grand Army, very much flurried and in great haste: John Morton. *Baron Puck*, a special ambassador von Deutchland, our Vaderland, a statesman in hard luck, anxious to obtain the democratic nomination for the hand of his mistress: Charley Walters. *Baron Grog*, and her likes it. Proprietor of a matrimonial Alliance Agency, and dealer in mouth harmonicans: Lew Benedict. *Flowers of the Amry, willing to rough it (vocally) but must have things right (4)*: *Captain Fat*: William Ball. *Lieutenant McLean*: C. R. Clinton. *Corporal Canfruit*: Albert Welling. *Private Pickles*: John F. Charleston. *Papa's Sword*. A necessity of the Opera: ——. *Grand Duchess*, a fascinating young lady of war-like proclivities, much attached to her army: THE ONLY [Francis] LEON. *Wanda*, a wanderer from South America, a bashful young milliner good on Cadenzas, but not much on a long run: John Martin.

[35]Olio cast and content changed weekly.

[36]Olio cast and content changed weekly.

Page, torn from no book in particular, ut Bound to wait on the Grand Duchess: Japanese Tommy. *Ushers, Soldiers, Vivandiers, etc.*

1876.06

THE FAIR ONE WITH THE BLONDE WIG

A Revival of the Burlesque Extravaganza in One Act[37]. [Selected music from all the popular operas.] Stage director, James Barnes. Produced by George Wood. Opened 22 May 1876 at Wood's Museum and closed 27 May 1876 after 8 performances.

CAST: *Graceful*, Maid of Honor: ADAH RICHMOND. *Leander*, the Rightful Heir: LIZZIE KELSEY. *Princess Fair One*: Mr. HARRY ALLEN. *Queen*: Miss NELLIE ALLEN. *Huckabac*: A. H. Sheldon. *Hon. Sambo*: Harry Stewart. *Fairy Queen*: Nellie Sandford. *Marquise*: Violet Campbell. *Count Palaver*: Mamie French. *Envoy*: Marion Sackett. *Pedro*: Mr. Christie Miller. *Von Slasher*: Mr. R. J. Lewis. *Von Smasher*: Mr. E. Sheppard. *Von Krasher*: Mr. J. Mitchell.

MUSICAL NUMBERS

"Prince Leander is His Name" (Solo and Chorus)

"Le Venal Servile Train" (from BARBE BLEUE)
(*Music by* Jacques Offenbach.)

"Indian Drum"

"Hush! Hush!" (Solo and Concerted Piece)

Song (new)
A. H. Sheldon

Song (new)
L. Kelsey

Medley (new)
A. Richmond

"Happy Little Briggs" (Song and Dance)

"Would I Were a Bird" (Duett)
A. Richmond, L. Kelsey

"We Met by Chance" (Song)
H. Allen

Duet from NORMA [Fetch the Cat?]
A. Richmond, H. Allen
(*Music by* Vincenzo Bellini.)

"Don't Tell My Father" (Song)
A. Richmond

Finale (from MONSIEUR CHOUFFLEURI)
(*Music by* Jacques Offenbach.)

[37]First produced in New York in a longer two-act version 16 May 1870 at the Olympic Theatre for 32 performances. This one act version was preceded by a one act comedy Bamboozling with a different cast.

1876–1877 SEASON

Lotta Crabtree in MUSETTE
Billy Rose Theatre Collection, New York Public Library for the Performing Arts

1876–1877 SEASON

NORMA; or, Titiens in a Minstrel Band/ THE TWO OFF-UNS

1876.07

An Original Operetta in One Act, 2 Scenes, preceded by an Olio, and followed by a Burlesque (The Two Off-Uns). Libretto and music by Edwin Kelly and Francis Leon. Orchestra conducted by J. B. Vogel. Director of amusements, Edwin Kelly. Produced by (Edwin) Kelly & (Francis) Leon's Minstrels and Burlesque Opera Troupe. Opened 12 June 1876 at Kelly & Leon's (23rd Street Opera House) and closed 24 June 1876 after 14 performances.

Olio[1]: "Yes, we all will be there," Lew Benedict; "Messenger Swallow" (ballad), Edwin Kelly; "Les Cents Vierges" Selection (*Music by* Charles Lecocq.), Company; "Coaching to Pelham" (comic), Edwin Lester; "The Dew is on the Flower" (ballad), C. H. Gordon; The Skidmores; In and Out with Edwin Lester, Japanese Tommy and William Ball; Philosophical Remarks by Lew Benedict.

NORMA CAST: *Mr. Micvacker*: W. BALL. *Impressario Stagosh*: C. R. Clinton.
Characters in the Operetta (8): *Norma*: A la Titiens [FRANCIS LEON]. *Pollie*: Signor Kellini [EDWIN KELLY]. *Flavio*: Signor Lesterini [EDWIN LESTER]. *Orevoso*: Signor Ballirna [WILLIAM BALL]. *First Druid*: Signor Guckenimi. *Second Druid*: Signor Mugnheno. *Third Druid*: Signor Londorini. *Other Druid*: Signoras, etc.

Walters & Morton in New Songs and Dances.

THE TWO OFF-UNS[2] (a Burlesque of 'The Two Orphans,' Hart Jackson's adaptation of Eugène Cormon and Adolphe d'Ennery's 'Les Deux Orphelines.').

CAST: *Chevalier Maurice de Vaudrey*: C. R. Clinton. *Count de Liniers*, Minister of Police: William Ball. *Jacques Frochard*, an Outlaw: EDWIN KELLY. *Pierre Frochard*, the Cripple, his brother: J. Morton. *Officer of the Guard*: C. Walters. *Martin*, Citizen of Paris: C. H. Gordon. *Louise, Henrietta*, Orphans: JAPANESE TOMMY, EDWIN LESTER. *La Frochard*, Mother of Pierre and Jacques: Lew Benedict. *Soldiers, Guards, etc.*

THE BELLES OF THE KITCHEN/ A BUNCH OF BERRIES/ FUN IN A FOG

1876.08

The Vokes Family in a revival of their original, musical, saltatorial, operatic, tragical comical extravaganza in One Act[3], preceded by an elegant comedietta, The Post Boy. Season opened 19 June 1876 at the Union Square Theatre and closed 8 July 1876 after 21 performances. Replacing THE BELLES OF THE KITCHEN after 7 performances, A BUNCH OF BERRIES, a farcical extravaganza in One Act by E. L. Blanchard[4], opened 26 June 1876, preceded by The Post Boy, and closed 1 July 1876 after 7 performances. Beginning 3-4, 7-8 July 1876 FUN IN A FOG[5] returned to the repertory for 5 performances, THE BELLES OF THE KITCHEN returned 5-6 July 1876 for 2 performances, with NAN, THE GOOD FOR NOTHING.

THE BELLES OF THE KITCHEN CAST: *Lucinda Scrubbs*, a lady's maid with "airs and graces:" JESSIE VOKES. *Mary*, a house-maid of "aristocratic inclinations," with Song, Dance and Duet: VICTORIA VOKES. *Barbara*, a kitchen-maid, "the incarnation of fun," full of mirth, merriment and mischief: BESSIE SANSON. *Timethus Gibbs*, a doctor's assistant, and chief bottle-washer, with song, dance and legs ad libitum: FERD VOKES. *Wiggins*, a barber, with Wigs, Jigs, a Waltz and Dance, and trouble with Barbara: FAWDON VOKES.

A BUNCH OF BERRIES CAST: *Sir Gilbert Gooseberry* owner of Hollybush Hall: John Moore. *William Gooseberry*, his son, familiarly called Bill Berry: FAWDON VOKES. *Lord Strawberry*, on a visit: FREDERICK VOKES. *Lady Raspberry*, Sir Gilbert's sister: Miss Sargent. *Sir Gilbert's nieces (3)*: *May Berry*: VICTORIA VOKES. *Rose Berry*: ROSINA VOKES. *Hilda Berry*: JESSIE VOKES. *John Thomas*, servant to Sir Gilbert: I. Daveau. *Harris*, a policeman: E. Chapman.

FUN IN A FOG CAST: *Percival Posthethwaite*, travelling in America: FRED VOKES. *Dan*, his valet, in fear of Indian scalping: FAWDON VOKES. *Ella Hamilton*: JESSIE VOKES. *Grace*, the American joker: VICTORIA VOKES. *Janet*, the willing help: ROSINA VOKES.

FROW-FROW

1876.09

A Revival of the Burlesque in Five Acts[6], suggested by Augustin Daly's society drama 'Frou-Frou;" preceded by an Olio. Burlesque by Tom Donnelly. New and original music by Professor Vogel. Scenery by Simmonds. Produced by Edwin Kelly & Francis Leon. Opened 26 June 1876 at Kelly and Leon's Minstrels and closed 15 July 1876 after 21? performances.

Olio[7]: Comic Nursery Rhymes, Lew Benedict; "Summer Sweets Shall Bloom Again," Edwin Kelly; Offenbach's Burlesque Polka (arranged by Prof. Vogel), the Company; "Coaching to Pelham" (comic song), Edwin Lester; "My Heart Remains with Thee" (ballad), C. H. Gordon; "We, Us and Our Sweethearts" (Finale), Edwin Kelly, Lew Benedict, Edwin Lester, Walters, Morton and Company; Cider vs. Vinegar (sketch), with W. Ball, J. H. Surridge, Japanese Tommy; Ballad, C. H. Gordon; The Squeak Family, with Messrs. Kelly, Surridge, Clinton and Ball; He's Sure to Come (sketch), with Lew Benedict and Edwin Lester, with banjo accompaniment; Walters and Morton (monarchs of song and dance), Walters and Morton.

CAST: *Henry Sartorys* EDWIN KELLY. *Brigard*: W. Ball. *Comte DeValreas*: J. H. Surridge. *Baron DeCambri*: Edwin Lester. *Gilberte*: The Only [FRANCIS] LEON. *Louise*, her sister: Lew Benedict. *Baronne DeCambri*: C. R. Clinton. *Angelique*: Mr. Gordon. *Georgie*: JAPANESE TOMMY.

Act 1: The Home at Les Chamerettes. Love.

Act 2: Paris. Private Theatricals. Marriage.

Act 3: Home in Paris. Separation.

Act 4: Venice. Desertion.

Act 5: Paris

THE ISLAND OF BACHELORS!

1876.10

A Romantic Operetta in One Act, preceded by an Olio[8]. (Original French libretto "Les Cent Vierges" in Three Acts by Clairville, Henri Chivot and Alfred Duru.) Adaptation by Edwin Kelly and Francis Leon (based on Robert Reece's English version). Music by Charles Lecocq. Director of amusements, Edwin Kelly. Orchestra under the direction of Professor Vogel. Produced by (Edwin) Kelly & (Francis) Leon's Minstrels and Burlesque Opera Troupe. Opened 17 July 1876 at Kelly & Leon's (23rd Street Opera House) and closed 12 August 1876 after 28 performances; returned 5-9 March 1877 to Kelly & Leon's for 5 additional performances.

Olio: "Comic Nursery Rhymes," Lew Benedict; "Summer Sweets Shall Bloom Again" (ballad), Edwin Kelly; Offenbach's Burlesque Polka, arranged by Professor Vogel, Company; "Coaching to Pelham" (comic), Edwin Lester; "My Heart Remains with Thee" (ballad), C. H. Gordon; "We, Us and Our Sweethearts" (finale) Messrs. Kelly, Benedict, Lester, Japanese Tommy and Company.

THE ISLAND OF BACHELORS CAST: *Sir Jonathan Pluperson*, Governor of the Island: EDWIN KELLY. *Briddidick*, his Secretary: Lew Benedict. *Anatole Quillenbois*, shipwrecked: Edwin Lester. *Mons. Poulardot*, the same: C. R. Clinton. *Bitter*, a Colonist: William Ball. *Emma*, wife of Poulardot: J. H. Surridge. *Eglantine*, a new arrival: Japanese Tommy. *Gabrielle*, wife of Anatole: THE ONLY [Francis] LEON. *Colonists, Sailors, etc.*

Scene: An Island in the Pacific.

---

[1]Olio cast and content changed weekly.
[2]Played a return engagement 9-20 October 1876 at Kelly and Leon's Minstrels.
[3]THE BELLES OF THE KITCHEN was first produced in New York 15 April 1872 at the Union Square Theatre for 49 performances. For Synopses of Scenes and Musical Numbers, see original 1872 productions.
[4]Reviewers commented that an opening chorus, a chorus of fairies, a chorus of shepherdesses, a grotesque dance by Fred Vokes, an operatic selection by Fred and Victoria Vokes, and an amateur pantomime of 'Twelfth Night" were prominently featured.
[5]First produced in New York 11 August 1873 at the Union Square Theatre for 30 performances. For Synopsis of Scenes and Musical Numbers, see original 1873 production.

[6]First produced in New York 18 April 1870 at Kelly and Leon's Minstrels.
[7]Program for the week ending 8 July 1876.
[8]Olio cast and content changed weekly.

MUSICAL NUMBERS

Chorus of Colonists
Omnes [All]

"Let's Fly to Meet Our Wives" (Trio)
E. Kelly, L. Benedict, W. Ball

"I Have a Romantic Head" (Solo)
F. Leon

"Silence" (Quartette)
F. Leon, J. H. Surridge, E. Lester, C. R. Clinton

"Kind Conqueror" (Solo)
F. Leon

"Ring a Ding Dong" (Chorus)
Omnes [All]

1876.11 MONS. CHOUFLEURI AT HOME!

A Comic Opera in One Act, preceded by an Olio[9]. (Original French libretto to 'Monsieur Choufleuri Restera Chez Lui Le (24 Janvier 1833)" by Duc de Morny, et al.) Adaptation by Edwin Kelly and Francis Leon. Music by Jacques Offenbach (and Mons. de St. Rémy [Morny]). Orchestra under the direction of Professor Vogel. Director of amusements, Edwin Kelly. Produced by (Edwin) Kelly & (Francis) Leon's Minstrels and Burlesque Troupe. Opened 14 August 1876 at Kelly & Leon's (23rd Street Opera House) and closed 1 September 1876 after (17) performances.

Olio: "Speak, Only Speak" (ballad), J. H. Surridge; "Har de News" (comic) Lew Benedict; "Billy Nubbs, the Poet" (burlesque) Edwin Kelly; "I Love My Love" (ballad, *Music by* Carlo Pinsuti.), C. H. Gordon; "Young Fella, You're Too Fresh" (comic) C. H. Gordon; "Soldiers to the Front" (finale, Music selected from "Geneviève de Brabant"), Messrs. Kelly, Benedict, McAndrews, Japanese Tommy, Lester and Company; "Kissing in the Rain," Master Benny Grinnell; Our Boys! with Messrs. Surridge, Japanese Tommy, Ball; Ballad selected by C. H. Gordon; Lew Benedict's Philosophical Remarks.

MONSIEUR CHOUFLEURI CAST: *Monsieur Choufleuri*, a retired merchant: EDWIN KELLY. *Peterman*: J. W. McAndrews. *Baron Balandard*: Arthur Lake. *Herr Regular Busterino*: William Ball. *Chrysodule Babylas*, an artist: EDWIN LESTER. *Baroness Balandard*: J. H. Surridge. *Ernestine Choufleuri*: THE ONLY [Francis] LEON.

Characters in the Burlesque Opera: *Sontag*: FRANCIS LEON. *Tamburini*: EDWIN KELLY. *Rubini*: EDWIN LESTER.

MUSIC OF THE OPERA

"Pedro the Muleteer" (Duet)
F. Leon, E. Lester

"Tis Babylas" (Recitative and Trio)
F. Leon, E. Lester, E. Kelly

"Il Mio Caro" (Recitative, Trio and Chorus)
E. Kelly, E. Lester, F. Leon, Guests

"The Enchanted Guitar" (Finale and Chorus)
Omnes [All]

1876.12 SARDANAPALUS

A Romantic Play in Four Acts. Play by Lord Byron. Incidental music selected from great composers by Charles Calvert. Production supervised by Charles Calvert. Scenery by William Telbin and Walter Hann, of London, from illustrations to "Layard's Ancient Nineveh." Costumes designed by Alfred Thompson, of London. Lighting by John Witherspoon. Simulated conflagration by Randle, pyrotechnist to the Queen of England. Grand choruses under the direction of Professor C. N. Pyke. Produced by Henry Jarrett and Harry Palmer. Opened 14 August 1876 at Booth's Theatre and closed 30 November 1876 after 113 performances.

CAST: *Sardanapalus*, King of Assyria: F. C. BANGS. *Salemenes*, the King's brother-in-law: LOUIS ALDRICH. *Arbaces*, the Mede who aspired to the throne: E. K. COLLIER. *Beleses*, a Chaldean and Soothsayer: HENRY A WEAVER. *Assyrian Officers of the Palace (5)*: *Altada*: Harry Hogan. *Pania*: Edwin F. Knowles. *Sfero*: B. L. Matlock. *Zanes*: A. H. Forrest. *Balea*: A. Jacques. *Herald*: H. N. Wilson. *Zarina*: DORA GOLDTHWAITE. *Myrrha* an Ionian Female Slave, and the favorite of Sardanapalus: AGNES BOOTH. *Ballet*: Signor ERNESTO MASCAGNO, Mlle. MALVINA BARTOLETTI (Première Danseuse Assoluta); Mlles. Palladino, Mascarini, Stickel, Besesti, Parmegiani; Corps de Ballet. *Guards, Attendants, Chaldean Priests, Medes, Spearmen, Nobles, Musicians, Standard Bearers, Dancing Girls, Incense Bearers, etc.*

Act 1: The Royal Palace from the Banks of the Tigris.

Act 2: The Summer Palace. The Grand Assyrian Festival.

Act 3: The Hall of Nimrod. The Festival Continued.

Act 4: The Dream of Hades.

BALLETS

Grand Assyrian Festival (Act 2)
Mlle. Bartoletti, E. Mascagno, Grand Italian Ballet

Grand Tableau (Act 3)

Grand Opening Introduction
Corps de Ballet

Ballabile of the Orgia
Entire Ballet

Pas de Six
Mlle. Bartoletti; Signor Mascagno; Mlles. Palladino, Mascarini, Stickel, Besesti

Pas de Huit
Signor Mascagno, Mlle. Parmegiani, 6 Second principals

Grand Festival March
Entire Grand Ballet

Pas de Quatre
Mlles. Palladino, Mascarini, Stickel, Besesti

Grand Pas de Deux
Mlle. Bartoletti, Signor Mascagno

Grand Finale "Bacchanalia"
Entire Grand Ballet

1876.13 IXION!, or, The Man at the Wheel

A Revival of the Great Musical Burlesque in One Act, 6 Scenes[10], rewritten, reconstructed, reconcocted, renewed, renovated, adapted, localized and generally ventilated expressly for Josh Hart's Eagle Theatre, preceded by the Eagle Minstrels and a laughable comedy (Lost at Long Branch). New music by Henry Wannemacher. Stage manager, G. L. Stout. Produced with new scenery by R. Smith. Machinery by Nelse Waldron. Properties by J. Graft. Conductor of orchestra, Henry Wannemacher. Produced by Josh Hart. Opened 21 August 1876 at the Eagle Theatre and closed 2 September 1876 after 16 performances.

The Eagle Minstrels CAST: Dave Reed, J. J. Kelly, John Wild, H. G. Richmond.

Lost at Long Branch CAST: A. H. Sheldon, Marie LeBrun, and cast of "Ixion" below.

IXION CAST: *Ixion*, an ex-King in distress, invited "by Jupiter" to visit the skies "by Jove" and taken up "by Mercury," "by Jingo": JENNIE BEAUCLERC. *Mercury*, Jove's Messenger and Celestial Telegraph Boy: JULIA BEAUCLERC. *Jupiter*, King of Olympus, a Musical Monarch: NELLIE SANFORD. *Venus*, the Goddess of Beauty, a lady-like Goddess: LIZZIE KELSEY. *Cupid*, Son of Venus, dressed a little more than the Cupids we usually see on Valentines: MAUD BRANSCOMBE. *Apollo*, Jupiter's Private Secretary: ANNIE JOHNSON. *Juno*, Queen of the Gods, Jupiter's better half, a perfect lady in every respect: MARIE GORENFLO. *Ganymede*, the original "Active Boy," special messenger and man of all work: JOHN WILD. *Minerva*, a strong-minded female, defender of women's rights and woman's wrongs: Mr. A. H. SHELDON. *Mars*, God of War: Harry Richmond. *Bacchus*, Head Centre of the Celestial Whiskey Ring: JAMES BRADLEY. *Tonofmarrowbones, Prosperous, Paddlesoakers*, three diabolical conspirators from the 14th Ward: Messrs. D. A. Kelly, G. L. Stout, D. Smith. *Calliope*: A. Griffith. *Melpomene*: Julia Brown. *Polhymnia*: Jane Edwards. *Mortals, Greeks, Grecians, and other Greenhorns*: Much Enlightened Supernumeraries.

Scene 1: Doric Temple. *Scene 2*: Bacchus' Saloon in the Skies. *Scene 3*: Juno's Reception Hall. *Scene 4*: Sun Office. *Scene 5*: Among the Clouds. *Scene 6*: The Golden Showers.

MUSICAL NUMBERS, SPECIALTIES

"Branigan's March" (Finale)

[9]Olio cast and content changed weekly.

[10]The original New York Production of F. C. Burnand's burlesque IXION!, or, The Man at the Wheel, was produced 28 September 1868 at Wood's Museum.

1876.14

SIR DAN O'PALLAS, Chief of the Assyrian Jim Jams

A Burlesque (of Byron's romantic play 'Sardanapalus') in One Act, preceded by an Olio[11]. Adaptation by Edwin Kelly and Francis Leon. Orchestra under the direction of Professor Vogel. Director of amusements, Edwin Kelly. Produced by (Edwin) Kelly & (Francis) Leon's Minstrels and Burlesque Troupe. Opened 2 September 1876 at Kelly & Leon's (23rd Street Opera House) and closed 7 October 1876 after 32 performances.[12]

Olio: "Gathering Shells (by the Seashore)" (ballad), J. H. Surridge; "Bye and Bye" (comic), Lew Benedict; Billy Nubbs, the poet [Edwin Kelly]; "Voice of the Mountain Land" (ballad), C. H. Gordon; "Voice of the Mountain Land," C. H. Gordon; "Perhaps She's on the Railway" (comic), Edwin Lester; Finale (Selection from THE BRIGANDS), Messrs. McAndrews, Japanese Tommy, C. R. Clinton, Watson, etc.; Miss Romp as the Young Hyena, THE ONLY [Francis] LEON; Songs and Dances with George Watson; Two Men Behind Bars, by Bret Hart, with Messrs. McAndrews, Surridge, Lester and Ball; Ballad by C. H. Gordon; Lew Benedict's Philosophical Remarks.

SIR DAN O'PALLAS CAST: *Sir Dan O'Pallas*, Chief of the Assyrian Jim Jams, a combination of Hercules and Adonis in form and a blending of Lohengrin and Gambrinus in appearance, who believes in Powers' Greek Slave, and goes back upon his gorgeously Semeramidian Queen, and is a bully boy generally: EDWIN KELLY. *Salami*, of the ancients, not at all like the modern sausage, but a brother-in-law who must be provided for: C. H. Gordon. *Sore-Ina*, very sore upon Sir Dan's martial obliquity: William Ball. *Ah-Brace-Up*, a very medium Mede, with an eye to the nomination for King: C. Tilton. *Myrrha*, a sweet scented young lady, and a copy of the original Greek Slave invented by Mr. Powers, who has captivated Sir Dan and introduced domestic broils into the O'Pallas household, which eventually ends at the stake: THE ONLY [Francis] LEON. *Ballet*: Mlle. Leon Bartlett-Pear-O, aided by Signor Mus-go-yu-no, imported actresses and coryphées.

1876.15

A YOUNG RIP VAN WINKLE

A Burlesque in One Act, 7 Scenes, preceded by a Comedy[13] and vaudeville olio. Play by R. Reece. Stage manager, G. L. Stout. New music. Scenery, Richard Smith. Machinery, Nelse Waldron. Director of music, Henry Wannemacher. Produced by Josh Hart. Opened 11 September 1876 at the Eagle Theatre and closed 16 September 1876 after 8 performances.

Olio: H. G. Richmond in his amusing songs, sayings and doings. Bone Solo and Song, Dave Reed. Kate Castleton in her selection of serio-comic songs. Richmond's laughable sketch, 'Modern School, or McGilligan's Benefit,' with H. Richmond and J. Wild. Wash Norton in his inimitable vocalizations and instrumental solos. Pat Rooney, in his Irish Songs and Dances, and new song "Mike McNally, the Democrat." Operatic selections by the Eagle orchestra under the direction of Henry Wannemacher.

A YOUNG RIP VAN WINKLE CAST: *Rip Van Winkle, Jr.*: JENNIE BEAUCLERC. *Derrick*: A. H. SHELDON. *Nick Wedder*: JOHN WILD. *Hendrick*: Lizzie Kelsey. *Rory*: MARIE GORENFLO. *Stein*: Saidie Martinot. *Cockles*: James Bradley. *Gretchen*: Carrie Jamieson. *Martha*: Angeline Griffith. *Agatha*: Nellie Sanford. *Mrs. Wedder*: Miss Johnson. *Mrs. Cockles*: Annie Waite. *Meenie Van Winkle*: MAUD BRANSCOMBE.

Scenes 1 and 2: The Village of Falling Waters. *Scene 3*: The Interior of Rip's Cottage. *Scene 4*: On the way to the Catskill Mountains. *Scene 5-7*: The Catskill Mountains.

MUSICAL NUMBERS

Opening Chorus (Quartet) (Scene 1)

Song and Chorus (Scene 1)
J. Beauclerc, Characters

Trio (Scene 1)
J. Beauclerc, A. H. Sheldon, J. Wild

Solo, Dance and Chorus (Scene 1)
J. Beauclerc, Characters

Duo (Scene 2)
L. Kelsey, M. Branscombe

"The Two Obadiahs" (Scene 5)
J. Beauclerc, Members of the Hen-Pecked Club

Song (Scene 6)
J. Beauclerc

Song and Chorus (Scene 7)
J. Beauclerc, Chorus

1876.16

BABA!

A Spectacular Extravaganza in a Prologue, Three Acts, 12 Scenes[14]. Play by John A. Mack. Produced under the personal supervision of Bensen Sherwood. Stage manager, George F. DeVere. Tricks and transformations by Bensen Sherwood. Marches by Max Maretzek. Ballets composed and arranged by A. Blandowski. Scenery by John A. Thompson, B. B. Hughes. Musical director, Max Maretzek. Proprietor, John McCoole; Charles E. Arnold, manager. Opened 18 September 1876 at Niblo's Garden and closed 9 December 1876 after 85 performances.

CAST- MORTALS: *Amoret*, a romantic young tailor, with a soul above buttons, and a yearning for the aesthetic; who, after refusing Schaiba-Bou a suit of clothes, gives him perfect fits and closes his suit in another quarter: ELIZA WEATHERSBY. *Abdoul Kerym*, Grand Pasha of the Province of Angora, Brother to the Moon, and Papa of Two Daughters, the which he loveth passing well: VINING BOWERS. *Bou-Schaiba*, the Grand Vizier, a Magician, who is not liked despite his many charms, and whose spells are not obeyed to the letter: JOHN W. JENNINGS. *Schaiba-Bou*, his son, who cuts in to wed Princess Gulnare, and is much cut up by being cut out by Amoret: J. EDWIN IRVING. *Baba*, his adopted brother and Fidus Achates. Baba is also a tailor, but gives up sewing tears for sewing wild oats, and having, by falling in love, fallen in prison, stars fate in the face and "sees life": WILLIAM H. CRANE. *Moustapha*, the Obese, whose life is onkneesy one from his inability to rise in the ranks: W. E. MARSTON. *Tiptim*, the nictatious. The original Tiptim, the wink: JAMES DANVERS. *Mezrour*, Captain of the Watch—therefore knows what's o'clock: Harry Taylor. *Ganem*, the keeper of the Bazaar: Samuel Glenn. *Oglou*, an attendant in the bath: Mr. Jones. *Ramazan*, Bou-Schaiba's servant: Mr. Cathcart. *Chikoree*, known in the coffee trade: Mr. Roos. *Blakdes*, an apothecary, who like his drugs, is well shaken: Mr. Caldwell. *Gulnare*, the daughter of the Pasha, who has beauty and sense, but no love; and who, on finding the Keeper of her heart, bestows upon him her hand: JENNIE WEATHERSBY. *Phrosine*, her twin sister, who has beauty and love, but no sense, characteristics which render her exceedingly attractive and eventually win her a husband: EMMA STOCKMAN. *Lelia*, head splasher in the bath: Pearl Eytinge. *Fetnah*, head dasher in the bath: Ellen Dupuy. *Ladies and Gentlemen of the Court, Guards, Soldiers, Street vendors, Slaves, etc.*

IMMORTALS: *Damriel*, King of the Genii, yet the slave of Nerea: VINCENT HOGAN. *Danasch*, an affrite who believes in taking his turn: JEAN RAVEL. *Famivo*, the Genii of the Flame—in fact, a living coal: A. R. Brooks. *Gapowa*, the giant heavy porter—one to look up to: —. *Nerea*, the Queen of the Fairies. The Custodian of Hearts and Sovereign of the Lake of Cygnets: JULIA JOURDAN. *The Fairies who watch over the Princess (5)*: *Cynia*: Miss Rivers. *Emeraldina*: Rose May. *Coralina*: Nellie Devere. *Nuphar*: Emma Lewis. *Anemone*: —. *Ballet*: Mlles. ELIZABETH and HELEN MENZELLI (Premiere Danseuses), Mlles. Antonino, Ida DeVere, Malvina.

Prologue: Royal Observatory and Laboratory.

Act 1, Scene 1: Interior of Amoret's Tailor Shop. *Scene 2*: The Royal Bath. (Thompson.) *Scene 3*: A Prison. *Scene 4*: A Rocky Pass. *Scene 5*: The Silver, Gold and Emerald Grottos.

Act 2, Scene 1: A Street in Turkey. *Scene 2*: The Field of Mushrooms. (Hughes.) *Scene 3*: The Royal Salle à Manger. Instantaneous change to a Magnificent Sailing Ship on the Open Sea to the Abode of the Fairies. (Thompson.)

Act 3, Scene 1: Ultima Thule. The Lake of Enchanted Cygnets. *Scene 2*: Amoret and Baba at home. Palace in Ruins. *Scene 3*: A melancholy pair. Arrival of Royal Party. Amoret's Reward. Happiness and Hilarity. *Scene 4*: Grand Transformation Scene. The Revels of the Roses being a realization of the Feasts of Floralia.

BALLETS AND SPECIALTIES

The Grand Procession preceding the Pasha (Prologue)

Song (Original by M. Maretzek.)(Act 1, Scene 1)
E. Weathersby

"Azrael, I Am Thine" (Duet)(Act 1, Scene 1)
W. H. Crane, E. Weathersby

---

[11] Olio cast and content changed weekly.

[12] No specialties or musical numbers listed, except for the Snow Shovellers' Ballet with F. Leon.

[13] A Female Bluebeard CAST: A. H. Sheldon, James F. Crossin, D. A. Kelly, D. Smith, Marion Fisk, Nellie Sanford, Saidie Martinot.

[14] Production revised from Twelve to Nine Scenes after opening, some roles eliminated or recast.

Grand Oriental Ballet (Act 1, Scene 2, added after opening)

Les Odalisques de Serail (Act 1, Scene 2, added after opening)

Ballad (Original by M. Maretzek, added after opening)
J. Ravel

Les Amours des Diables (Ballet)(Act 1, Scene 5, added after opening)
Mlles. E and H. Minzelli, I. DeVere, Malvina, Coryphées and Corps de Ballet

Adagio
Principals, Coryphées

Solo
Mlle. Malvina

La Favorita
I. DeVere

Pas Seul
Mlle. Antonino

La Fascination, Pas de Deux
Mlles. E. and H. Minzelli

Apotheose
Principals, Coryphées, Corps de Ballet

Grand Oriental Amazon March (Act 2, Scene 1, added after opening)

Quintette (Original by Maretzek.)(Act 3, Scene 1, added after opening)

Grand Transformation Scene (Act 3, Scene 4)

1876.17 LA FILLE DE MADAME ANGOT

A Revival of the Opéra-comique in Three Acts[15], subititled 'Madame Angot's Child.' (Original French libretto by Clairville, Paul Siraudin and Victor Koning.) Music by Charles Lecocq. Stage director and musical director, Jesse Williams. Produced by Alice Oates Opera Company (Samuel Colville, Manager). Opened 18 September 1876 at the Grand Opera House and closed 23 September 1876 after 5 performances in repertory; returned 12 March 1877 to the Lyceum Theatre and closed 14 March 1877 after 4 performances in repertory.[16]

CAST: *Clairette*, the Child of the Market: Mrs. JAMES A. OATES [Alice Oates]. *Mme. Lange*: ROSE TEMPLE[17]. *Amaranthe*: Mrs. HARRY [Julia] CHAPMAN. *Cydalise*: Venie Clancy. *Hersilie*: Tracy White[18] *Javotte*: Gussie Winner. *Therese*: Bessie Temple. *Manon*: Ella Caldwell. *Pomponnet*: CHARLES H. DREW. *Ange Pitou*: HENRI LAURENT. *Larivaudière*: JOHN HOWSON. *Louchard*: JAMES H. JONES. *Trenitz*: A. W. MAFLIN. *Guillaume*: Ed. Horan. *Buteaux*: R. H. Nichols. *Captain of the Guard*: H. Amberg. *Leroux*: L. DeSmith. *Conspirators*: Messrs. Cotta, Van Dam, Bahrer, Watson, Merritt, Thompson, Arbuckle, Neilson, etc. *Hussars, Conspirators, Gendarmes, Citizens, Market People, etc.*

1876.18 THE PRINCESS OF TRÉBIZONDE!

A Revival of the Opéra-bouffe in Three Acts[19]. (Original French libretto by Charles Nuitter and Étienne Trefeu.) English adaptation by J. Cheever Goodwin. Music by Jacques Offenbach. Stage director and musical director, Jesse Williams. Produced by the Alice Oates Opera Company (Samuel Colville, Manager). Opened 21 September 1876 at the Grand Opera House and closed 22 September 1876 after 2 performances in repertory; returned 17 March 1877 to the Lyceum Theatre for 1 performance in repertory.

CAST: The Prince's Family: *Prince Raphaël*, the Young Prince: ALICE OATES [Mrs. James A. Oates]. *Prince Casimir*, his Father: HENRI LAURENT. *Sparadrap*: JAMES H. JONES.

The Showman's Family: *Cabriolo*, the Showman: JOHN HOWSON. *Trémolini*, the Clown: CHARLES H. DREW. *Zanetta*, the Princess: ROSE TEMPLE[20]. *Régina*, the Daughter of Cabriolo: VENIE CLANCY[21]. *Paola*, Sister to Cabriolo: Mrs. HARRY [Julia] CHAPMAN. *Loto*, Lottery Director: R. H. Nichols. *Richardo, Brocolio*, Courtiers: Ed. Horan, R. H. Nichols.

The Palace Guard: *Captain of the Watch*: Tracy White[22]. *Lieutenant*: Ella Caldwell. *The Mountebanks, Lottery Tickets, Operatic Acrobats, Plate Spinner, Wax Figures*: Misses Venie Clancy, Gussie Winner, Bessie Temple, Susie Parker, etc. *Spade Dance*: A. W. Maflin. *Specialty, The Tyrolean Warblers*: Gussie Winner, Annie Winner, Carrie Winner.

1876.19 DOWN BROADWAY, or, the Miniature "69th"

The Famous Local Extravaganza in One Act, 6 Scenes, preceded by an Olio. Play by Edward Harrigan. Music by David Braham. Scenery by R. L. Weed. Stage manager, J. Adams Graver. Costumer, Miss Kate Devoy. Musical director, David Braham. Produced by (Edward) Harrigan and (Tony) Hart. Opened 25 September 1876 at the Theatre Comique and closed 30 September 1876 after 8 performances[23].

Olio: That Rascal Tom!, a favorite farce with Billy Barry, G. W. H. Griffin, Sam Holdsworth, Alfred Beverly, Miss Fanny L. Burt, Miss Hannah Birch. Miss Eloise Allen, the favorite vocalist in popular songs. The Italian Ballet Master, (Edward) Harrigan's new act, with Edward Harrigan (as Signor Bartiletto, Morris Grady), Tony Hart (as Honora Grady), and Larry Tooley (as Mortimer Cheeseborough, an actor). Billy Carter will evolve from his banjo the history of his love for "Duck-Foot-Sue." Quilter and Goldrich, the great comedians in ordinary conversations. Frank Lewis, America's greatest motto vocalist in his original songs "Hurrah for the Minstrel Band," "Many Things That Ought Not to Be," and his great local song of "Telegrams, the Actor's Great Ball," etc.

Billy Barry's Centennial Marksmen, or the International Rifle Match, by the four picked teams: *The Mulligan Guards (4)*: *Captain Hussey* with song: E. Harrigan. *MCAroon*: Mr. Graver. *O'Pake*: Mr., Bradley. *O' Slaugherty*: Mr. Moore. *The Queen's Invincibles (4)*, from Canada: *Catain Viscount Sir Henry Wainwright, K. B.*, with song: T. Hart. *Mr. Jenks*: Mr. Bruno. *Mr. Windsor*: B. Carter. *Mr. Bowbell*: Mr. Beverly. *The Skidmores (4)*: *Captain Turnbull*, with song: B. Barry. *Laurence*: Mr. Holdsworth. *Mr. Grayson*: Mr. Hall. *Mr. Simpson*: Mr. Griffin. *Mr. Kernan*: Mr. Burt. *The Ginger Blues (7)*: *Captain Primrose*: B. Gray. *High Privates*, with song: Messrs. Hansel, O'Brien, Burk, Morgan, Fay. *Philip Steinmetz*, Purveyor and Umpire: L. Tooley.

Miss Alice Bennett, the American Nightingale in a choice selection of songs. Johnson and Bruno, Acrobatic and Contortion Song & Dance Artists and Master Linguists in the original specialties.

DOWN BROADWAY CAST: *Roger McElvine*, from Buffalo: EDWARD HARRIGAN. *Colonel of the 69th*: TONY HART. *Shine 'em up*: TONY HART. *Halfred Freeman*: TONY HART. *Jimmy Lush*: Larry Tooley. *Clog Dancer*: Mr. Bradley. *Ballad Singer*: Alfred Beverly. *Clubs*, a policeman: J. A. Graver. *Nerves*: G. W. H. Griffin. *Ethiopian Singer and Dancer*: Billy Barry. *Jim Stryker, Dick Swivel*, draymen: Messrs. M. T. Moore, W. T. Fielding. *Miss Cheerily*: Miss Alice Bennett. *Miss Morton*: Miss Hannah Birch. *Veteran Guard* with song; Messrs. Johnson, Bruno, Billy Barry, Billy Gray. *The Bummers* with song: G. W. H. Griffin, Sam Holdsworth, H. J. Burt, G. W. Hall.

Scene 1: View of Grand Central Depot. *Scene 2*: Statue of Washington, Union Square. *Scene 3*: Broadway and Houston Street. *Scene 4*: Interior of Harry Hill's. *Scene 5*: Interior of New Court House. *Scene 6*: Castle Garden ad the Battery.

MUSICAL NUMBERS, SPECIALTIES

"The Bummers" (Song and Chorus)(Scene 2)

"The Veteran Guard" (Specialty)(Scene 3)
E. Harrigan

Old Time Song and Dance (Scene 4)
B. Barry

J. T. Ryan as the Ballad Singer (Scene 4)

Grand Challenge Dance between the Lancashire Pet and Jimmy Lush (Scene 4)

"Sweet America" (Song)(Scene 5)
Messrs. Kelly, Ryan

---

[15]First produced in New York in French 25 August 1873 at the Broadway Theatre; in English 16 November 1874 at the Lyceum Theatre. For Synopsis of Scenes and Musical Numbers, see original 1874 production.

[16]English adaptation uncredited; no credits for scenery or costumes in programs.

[17]For return engagement, Mme. Lange was played by EME ROSEAU.

[18]For return engagement, Hersilie was played by Susie Parker.

[19]First produced in New York in English 11 September 1871 at Wallack's Theatre for 7 performances. For Synopsis of Scenes and Musical Numbers, see original 1871 production.

[20]For return engagement, Zanetta was played by EME ROSEAU.

[21]For return engagement, Régina was played by ROSE TEMPLE.

[22]For return engagement, Captain of the Watch was played by Susie Winner.

[23]Revived 5 November 1877 for 8 performances at the Theatre Comique.

Grand Chorus by the Mud-Brigade (Scene 5)
Appearance of the celebrated Italian Brass Band (Scene 5)
Grand March and Drill of the famous Miniature 69th Regiment (Scene 6)

1876.20

GIROFLÉ-GIROFLA

A Revival of the Opéra-bouffe in Three Acts[24], in French. (Libretto by Albert Vanloo and Eugène Leterrier.) Music by Charles Lecocq. Chorus and orchestra under the direction of Charles Van Ghele. Produced by Mlle. Aimée's French Opéra Bouffe Company. Opened 25 September 1876 at the Lyceum Theatre and closed 30 September 1876 (matinee) after 3 performances in repertory.

CAST: *Giroflé, Girofla*: Mlle. MARIE AIMÉE. *Aurore*: Mlle. Kid. *Pedro*: Mlle. FLORENCE DUPARC. *Paquita*: Mlle. BLANCHE GUEYMARD. *Marasquin*: Mons. RAULT. *Don Boléro*: Mons. DUPLAN. *Mourzouk*: Mons. REINE. *Chief of the Pirates*: Mons. Davalis. *Le Parran*: Mons. Salvator. *Le Danseur*: Mons. Perrin. *Le Notaire*: Mons. Bageard. *Le Precepteur*: Mons. Gerard. *Le Garçon d'Honneur*: Mons. Edward. *L'Oncle*: Mons. Leclerc. *Guzman*: Mme. Blanc. *Fernand*: Mlle. Niel. *Almanazar*: Mlle. Pezzulo.

1876.21

GIROFLÉ-GIROFLA!!

A Revival of the Opéra-bouffe in Three Acts[25]. (Original French libretto by Albert Vanloo and Eugène Leterrier.) English libretto by J. Cheever Goodwin. Music by Charles Lecocq. Stage director and musical director, Jesse Williams. Produced by the Alice Oates Opera Company (Samuel Colville, Manager). Opened 25 September 1876 at the Grand Opera House and closed 30 September 1876 after (4) performances; returned 15, 17 (matinee) March 1877 to the Lyceum Theatre for 2 additional performances.[26]

CAST: *Girolflé, Girofla*: ALICE OATES [Mrs. James A. Oates]. *Marasquin*, a young banker, suitor to Giroflé: CHARLES H. DREW. *Boléro D'Alcorazas*, a Spanish Grandee: JOHN HOWSON[27]. *Mourzouk*, a Moor, suitor to Girofla: GUSTAVUS F. HALL[28]. *Aurore*, wife to Bolero: Mrs. HARRY [Julia] CHAPMAN. *Paquita*: ROSE TEMPLE. *Pedro*: HENRI LAURENT. *Pirate Chief*: A. W. Maflin. *Matamoras*: James H. Jones[29]. *The Notary*: Ed Horan[30]. *Bridesman*: H. Amberg. *Tax Gatherer*: C. Bamer. *The Uncle*: C. Decker. *The Godfather*: H. Nichols. *The Godmother*: Bessie Turner. *The Danseuse*: A. W. Maflin. *The Pirates*: H. Nichols, G. Cotta, L. DeSmith, John Merritt, C. Decker. *The Ladies in Waiting*: Susie Parker, Annie Caldwell. *The Cousins*: Gussie Winner, Carrie Clancy, Susie Parker, Venie Clancy, Ella Caldwell, Tracy White, Annie Winner.

1876.22

JOSHUA WHITCOMB

A Burletta of Fun in One Act, preceeded by an Olio. Play by Denman Thompson. Scenic artist, David Smith. Produced by Josh Hart. Opened 25 September 1876 at the Eagle Theatre and closed 7 October 1876 after 16 performances; returned 6 November 1876 to Tony Pastor's Theatre and closed 25 November 1876 after an additional 21 performances; returned 15 January 1877 to Tony Pastor's Theatre and closed 27 January 1877 after an additional 14 performances; returned 30 July 1877 to Wood's Theatre and closed 11 August 1877 after 16 performances.[31] Total: 67 performances.

Olio: 'Sarah's Young Man,' a laughable farce, with A. H. Sheldon, J. F. Crossin, Carrie Jamieson, D. A. Kelly, Marion Fiske, Marie Gorenflo. Dave Reed in his Negro Comicalities. Jennie Hughes in a selection of new songs. Richmond's original Border Sketch, 'Sitting Bull,' with John Wild, Harry Richmond, D. A. Kelly. Irish Songs by Pat Rooney. Seri-Comic songs by Kate Castleton. The Great International Burlesque Shooting Match, with the American Team: John Wild, Dave Reed, J. Kelly, D. Holbrook, J. A. Swartz, L. Schwicardi, Harry Richmond, and the Irish Team, James Bradley, Pat Rooney, A. H. Sheldon, D. A. Kelly. Irish Songs, Dances and Sketches by Murphy & Morton. Selections by the Eagle Orchestra under the direction of Henry Wannemacher.

JOSHUA WHITCOMB CAST: *Uncle Josh*, an old Jackson Democrat: DENMAN THOMPSON. *John Martin*: James F. Crossin. *Bill Johnson*: D. A. Kelly. *Nellie Primrose*: Jennie Hughes. *Tot*: JULIA WILSON. *Frederick Dolby*: James Bradley. *Barrows*: J. J. Kelly. *Susie Cornell*: Marie Gorenflo. *Mrs. Johnson*: Annie Johnston.

1876.23

LIFE

A Comedy of City Types; a Novelty in Four Phases (Acts) and a Transformation. Play by Augustin Daly, adapted from several Parisian sources. Scenery by J. Roberts, Faucitt and Charles W. Witham. Mechanicals by Thomas Kelly. Properties by Robert Cutler. Wardrobe by Mme. Finchette. Lighting by J. C. Scollan. Musical director, James C. Kenny. Produced by Augustin Daly. Opened 27 September 1876 at Daly's Fifth Avenue Theatre and closed 18 November 1876 after 54 performances.

CAST: Characters of Reality: *Schuyler Samples*, type of the unwise, who roam, but do not soar: CHARLES F. COGHLAN. *Pony Mutuel*, a lively practitioner, whose tale may be told to the Marines: JAMES LEWIS. *Mr. Lynn Lessurely*, whose life was "rounded by a sleep": CHARLES FISHER. *Frank Dodge*, with a new way to win a widow: MAURICE BARRYMORE. *Harry Gresham*, otherwise "Osprey": George Parkes. *Nosen Pokiss*, "Confidential": W. DAVIDGE. *Mrs. Masham Mallory*, with a widow's Mite of a Million, and one Little Dog: AMY FAWSITT. *Mrs. Brown Boston*, with an Eye: Mrs. G. H. GILBERT. *Ethel*, type of the confiding: EMILY RIGL. *Mrs. Gresham*, type of the Injured: GEORGIANA DREW. *Mary Ann*, Cook and Conspirator: Mary Wells. *Capitola Aurora*, the Despoiled of Name: Sydney Cowell. *Jenny*, the Inventive: Helen Dingeon.

Characters of Fairyland: *Mr. Chumley Clever*, the Shakespearian revivalist-type of his kind: JOHN BROUGHAM. *Signor Oleri*, Maitre de Ballet, expressly imported for this type of occasion: Frank Bennett. *Traditi*, Interpreter Extraordinary: J. H. Ring. *Lord Loomax*: J. Deveau. *Dash*, Stage Manager of the great Shakespearian Temple: W. Beekman. *Signorina Guissipina Samiti*, otherwise Miss Josephine Smith: Miss DuSauld. *Miss Brightstairs*: Miss Wood. *Specialties*, Act 3, The Snow Ballet: *Spirit of the Sun*: Mlle. MARIE BONFANTI. *Spirit of the Snow*: AUGUSTA SOHLKE.

Act 1: Library in the Residence of Schuyler Samples, Esq. (Faucitt.)

Act 2: The Japanese Room of Mrs. Masham Mallory's Suite in "The Devonshire." (Witham.)

Act 3, Scene 1: Signorina Samiti's Parlors at "The Devonshire." (Faucitt.) *Scene 2*: The Shakespeare Theatre. *Scene 3*: A Glimpse at the audience from behind the Footlights. (Witham.) *Scenes 4 and 5*: The Snow Ballet and a glimpse of Fairyland. (Roberts.)

Act 4: Schuyler's Home. The morning after.

1876.24

LA GRANDE DUCHESSE DE GÉROLSTEIN

A Revival of the Opéra-comique in Three Acts[32], in French. (Libretto by Henri Meilhac and Ludovic Halévy.) Music by Jacques Offenbach. Chorus and orchestra under the direction of Charles Van Ghele. Produced by Marie Aimée's French Opera Bouffe Company. Opened and closed 27 September 1876 at the Lyceum Theatre after 1 performance; returned under the auspices of Maurice Grau 6 March 1877 to the Eagle Theatre for 1 performance[33].

CAST: *La Grande-Duchesse de Gérolstein*: Mlle. MARIE AIMÉE. *Fritz*: Mons. RAOULT. *Prince Paul*: Mons. BRANCIARD. *Baron Puck*: Mons. J. MEZIÈRES.

[24]First produced in New York in French 4 February 1875 at the Park Theatre. For Synopsis of Scenes and Musical Numbers, see original February 1875 production.
[25]First produced in New York in French 4 February 1875 at the Park Theatre; in English 19 May 1875 at Robinson Hall for 61 performances. For Synopsis of Scenes and Musical Numbers, see original May 1875 production.
[26]No credits in programs for scenery or costumes.
[27]For return engagement, Bolero D'Alcorazas played by JAMES H. JONES.
[28]For return engagement Mourzouk played by JOHN HOWSON.
[29]For return engagement, Matamoras played by Ed. Horan.
[30]For return engagement, The Notary played by W. Harris.
[31]No musical numbers listed in programs from the Eagle Theatre; later productions list interpolations.
[32]First produced in New York in French 24 September 1867 at the Théâtre Français for 156 performances. For Synopsis of Scenes and Musical Numbers, see original 1867 production.
[33]No program available for the Lyceum engagement; cast is for the Eagle Theatre engagement.

Baron Grog: Mons. RUIZ. *General Boum*: Mons. REINE. *Baron Grog*: Mons. RUIZ. *Nepomuc*: Mons. Benedick. *Wanda*: Mlle. BLANCHE GUEYMARD. *Iza*: Mlle. Marthe. *Amelia*: Mlle. Sophie Gherzi. *Charlotte*: Mlle. Niel. *Olga*: Mlle. Marie Vandamme. *Soldiers, Maids of Honor, etc.*

1876.25 LA PÉRICHOLE

A Revival of the Opéra-bouffe in Three Acts[34], in French. (Libretto by Ludovic Halévy and Henri Meilhac, based on "Le Carosse du Saint-Sacrament" by Prosper Merimée.) Music by Jacques Offenbach. Chorus and orchestra under the direction of Charles Van Ghele. Produced by Marie Aimée's French Opéra Bouffe Company. Opened and closed 28 September 1876 at the Lyceum Theatre after 1 performance.

CAST: *La Périchole*: Mlle. MARIE AIMÉE. *Piquillo*: Mons. RAOULT. *Don Andrès de Ribeira*: Mons. REINE. *Le Compte de Panatellas*: Mons. J. MEZIÈRES. *Don Pedro de Hinoyosa*: Mons. DUPLAN. *Tarapote*: Mons. RUIZ. *Un Vieux Prisonnier*: Mons. Benedick. *First Notary*: Mons. Leclere. *Second Notary*: Mons. Davalis. *Un Geolier*: Mons. Girard. *Cousins (3)*: *Guadalena*: Mlle. BLANCHE GUEYMARD. *Berginella*: Mlle. Letellier. *Mastrilla*: Mlle. Sophie Gherzi. *Maids of Honor (4)*: *Ninetta*: Mlle. Marie Vandamme. *Brambilla*: Mlle. Niel. *Frasquinella*: Mlle. Lecourt. *Manuelita*: Mlle. Marthe.

1876.26 LA FILLE DE MADAME ANGOT

A Revival of the Opéra-comique in Three Acts[35], in French. (Libretto by Clairville, Paul Siraudin and Victor Koning.) Music by Charles Lecocq. Chorus and orchestra under the direction of C. Van Ghele. Produced by Marie Aimée's French Opéra Bouffe Company. Opened and closed 29 September 1876 at the Lyceum Theatre after 1 performance; returned 25 October 1876 to the Academy of Music for 1 performance; returned 2 February 1877 under the auspices of Maurice Grau to the Eagle Theatre and closed 9 March 1877 after 4 performances in repertory.[36]

CAST: *Clairette*: Mlle. (MARIE) AIMÉE. *Ange Pitou*: Mons. RAOULT. *Pomponnet*: Mons. BRANCIARD. *Larivaudière*: Mons. REINE. *Trenitz*: Mons. Theophile. *Louchard*: Mons. RUIZ. *Cadet*: Mons. Benedick. *Butaux*: Mons. Girard. *Guillaume*: Mons. Perin. *Un Officier*: Mons. Davalis. *Un Incroyable*: Mons. Eugene. *Mlle. Lange*: Mlle. BLANCHE GUEYMARD. *Amaranthe*: Mlle. Adele Desirée. *Javotte*: Mlle. Mlle. Branciard. *Cydalise*: Mlle. Marie Vandamme. *Hersilie*: Mlle. Marthe. *Delaunay*: Mlle. Clara. *Therese*: Mlle. Sophie Gherzi. *Herbelin*: Mlle. Niel. *Babet*: Mlle. Marie. *Manon*: Mlle. Mathilde.

1876.27 THE GRANDE DUCHESS

A Revival of the Opéra-comique in Three Acts[37]. (Original French libretto to "La Grande Duchesse de Gérolstein" by Henri Meilhac and Ludovic Halévy.) Music by Jacques Offenbach. Stage director and musical director, Jesse Williams. Produced by the Alice Oates Opera Company (Samuel Colville, Manager). Opened and closed 29 September 1876 at the Grand Opera House after 1 performance in repertory.[38]

CAST: *La Grande-Duchesse de Gérolstein*: ALICE OATES [Mrs. James A. Oates]. *Wanda*: ROSE TEMPLE. *Fritz*, a Soldier: CHARLES H. DREW. *General Boum*: JOHN HOWSON. *Prince Paul*: HENRI LAURENT. *Baron Puck*: J. H. JONES. *Nepomuc*: A. W. MAFLIN. *Baron Grog*: ED. W. HORAN. *Maids of Honor (4)*: *Olga*: Tracy White. *Iza*: Bessie Temple. *Charlotte*: Venie Clancy. *Amelia*: Susie Winner. *Soldiers of the Grand Duchess' Army, Vivandières, Ladies of the Court, etc.*

1876.28 LA TIMBALE D'ARGENT

A Revival of the Opéra-bouffe (The Silver Cup) in Three Acts[39], in French. Libretto by Adolphe Jaime and Jules Noriac. Music by Léon Vasseur. Chorus and orchestra under the direction of Charles Van Ghele. Produced by Marie Aimée's French Opéra Bouffe Company. Opened and closed 30 September 1876 at the Lyceum Theatre after 1 performance; returned 21 March 1877 under the auspices of Maurice Grau to the Eagle Theatre and closed 22 March 1877 after 2 additional performances in repertory.

CAST: *Raab*: Mons. DUPLAN. *Pruth*: Mons. J. MEZIÈRES. *Barnabe*: Mons. Benedict. *Wilhem*: Mons. Perin. *Valter*: Mons. Salvator. *Gerome*: Mons. Davalis. *Tritz*: Mons. Gerard. *Molda*: Mlle. MARIE AIMÉE. *Müller*: Mlle. BLANCHE GUEYMARD. *Fichtel*: Mlle. FLORENCE DUPARC. *Gaben*: Mlle. Sophie Gherzi. *Mme. Barnabe*: Mlle. Valbelle. *Paola*: Mlle. Blanc. *Agath*: Mlle. Niel. *Marza*: Mlle. Noe. *Anich*: Mlle. Pezzuolo.

1876.29 SARDINE-APPLES!, King of Ninnyvah & Astoria, L.I.

A Burlesque in One Act, 7 Scenes, preceded by an olio. Play by A. H. Sheldon[40]. Incidental music selected from great composers by Henry Wannemacher. Scenery painted by Richard S. Smith and John Hillyard. Costumes by G. L. Stout. Regalia by LeBlanc Graner. Machinist, Nelse Wadron. Conductor of orchestra, Henry Wannemacher. Produced by Josh Hart. Opened 9 October 1876 at the Eagle Theatre and closed 14 October 1876 after 8 performances; returned 6 November 1876 to the Eagle Theatre and closed 25 November 1876 after an additional 24 performances. Total: 32 performances.

Olio: 'Port Wine vs. Jealousy,' John Wild's laughable sketch, with John Wild, Marie Gorenflo, James F. Crossin. Irish Songs and Dance with Murphy & Morton. Harry Richmond in his original songs and sayings (Ethiopian). Serio-Comic songs, Jennie Hughes. "Who's dat Knockin' on the Outside Gade?,' a character sketch by J. F. Sheridan, performed by James W. Mack and J. F. Sheridan. Irish songs and sayings, James Bradley. Song and Dance, Dave Reed.

SARDINE-APPLES CAST: *Sardine-Apples*, a King who "bangs" his subjects about: A. H. SHELDON. *Salamander*, the King's Brother-in-Law: JENNIE BEAUCLERC. *Pania*, see Ladies' fashions of 1876: LIZZIE KELSEY. *Esculapius*, the Cupbearer, a remarkably lively youth: JOHN WILD. *Arbaces*, the Mede who aspired to the throne: JULIA BEAUCLERC. *Beleses*, the author of "Lend Me a Dollar:" GEORGE K. FORTESCUE. *Maria*, an Iron Female Slave: Maud Branscombe. *Zarina*, the Queen beats the King: JENNIE HUGHES. *Altada*: Harry Richmond. *Sfero*: James Bradley. *Zanes*: J. Kelly. *Balea*: Dave Reed. *Guards, Goats, Organ Grinders, Insensible Boors, Dancing Girls, New York Fire Department, &c., &c., &c.*

Maccaroney Ballet Troupe: Messrs. Wild, Bradley, Richmond, Reed, Sheridan, Mack, Murphy, Morton (Star Premiers).

Scene1: Royal Palace from the Banks of the Tigris. *Scene 2*: Our Egyptian Curtain. *Scene 3*: The Royal Summer House. *Scene 4*: That same Egyptian Curtain once more. *Scene 5*: The Hall of Ramrod. *Scene 6*: The same old Egyptian Curtain. *Scene 7*: The Palace. The Conflagration! (by Fisher). Destruction of Astoria, L.I.

MUSICAL NUMBERS, SPECIALTIES

Scene 1

"Cider, Sweet Cider" (Concerted Music and Promenade)

Scene 2

Duett

Beauclerc Sisters

---

[34] First produced in New York in French 4 January 1869 at Pike Opera House for 35 performances. For Synopsis of Scenes and Musical Numbers, see original 1869 production. The new revised version in Three Acts, Four Scenes, premiered in New York 15 February 1877 under the auspices of Maurice Grau at the Eagle Theatre for 4 additional performances. See detail at that date below.

[35] First produced in New York in French 25 August 1873 at the Broadway Theatre in repertory. For Synopsis of Scenes and Musical Numbers, see original 1873 production.

[36] No program available for the Lyceum engagement; cast is for the Eagle Theatre engagement.

[37] First produced in New York in French 24 September 1867 at the Théâtre Français for 156 performances, and in English 17 June 1868 at the New York Theatre. For Synopsis of Scenes and Musical Numbers, see original 1868 production.

[38] No credits in programs for English adaptation, scenery or costumes.

[39] First produced in New York in French 24 August 1874 at the Lyceum Theatre. For Synopsis of Scenes and Musical Numbers, see original 1874 production.

[40] Inspired by the success of the romantic play by Lord Byron, SARDANAPALUS.

Scene 5
  Grand Astoria, L.I. Festival
    Maccaroney Ballet Troupe
  Comic Duets
    J. Wild, J. Hughes
  Crazy Quartet
    Messrs. Bradley, Richmond, Sheldon, Wild
  LaManola in Burlesque
    Misses Julia Beauclerc, Kelsey, Castleton, Gorenflo
  "Sweet Love Arise!"
    Jennie Beauclerc
Scene 6
  Solo and Chorus (All Aboard for Pelham)
Scene 7
  Conflagration! Babcock's Fire Extinguishers.

1876.30

CHING-CHOW-HI!

A Revival of the Opera Bouffe in One Act[41], preceded by an Olio[42]. (Libretto by William Brough, with music adapted Thomas German Reed. Adapted from the French Chinoiserie musicale "Ba-ta-clan," libretto by Ludovic Halévy.) Music by Jacques Offenbach. Musical director, W. Blakeney. Director of amusements, Edwin Kelly. Produced by (Edwin) Kelly & (Francis) Leon's Minstrels and Burlesque Opera Troupe. Opened 21 October 1876 at Kelly & Leon's (23rd Street Opera House) and closed 2 December 1876 after 43 performances.

Olio: "The Old Log Cabin in the Dell," Edwin Kelly (ballad); Brannigan's Band," Edwin Lester (comic); "Only a Dream of Home," George Leslie (ballad); "A 'licious Meal," James Quinn (comic); "Soldiers to the Front" (from GENEVIEVE DE BRABANT) Messrs. Kelly, Quinn, McAndrews, Japanese Tommy, Lester, Company (finale); "Kissing in the Starlight," The Only [Francis] Leon; The Watermelon Man, J. W. McAndrews; 'The Black Cupids!" (musical sketch) with Edwin Lester and J. W. Morton; The Haunted House, Sam Price; Stump Oratory—Reform, James Quinn.

CHING CHOW HI CAST: *Ching-Chow-Hi*, Emperor of China: EDWIN KELLY. *Ko-Ko-Ri-Ko*, Captain of the Emperor's Guard: J. H. Surridge. *Ke-Ki-Ka-Ko*, Chinese Mandarin: Edwin Lester. *Hi-Ki-Ki-Hi*, A Conspirator: George Leslie. *Ko-Fe-Hi-Ki*, Standard Bearer: William Ball. *Conspirators and Members of the Legislature (4)*: *Hi-Pe-Kin*: C. R. Clinton. *Hi-Fo-Fum-Ki*: F. Howard. *Wang-Chang*: George Watson. *Cheu-Chou Dec*: J. F. Jones. *Fe An-Nich-Ton*, Princess in the suit of Ching-Chang-Hi: THE ONLY [Francis] LEON.

Jugglers from the Japanese Court at Jeddo: *Ski-Hi*: J. W. McAndrews. *O-Mi*: J. W. Morton. *Mi-Hi*: James Quinn. *Wi-So*: Japanese Tommy. *O-Doo*: Sam Price. *Ow-So*: Johnny Martin.

MUSICAL NUMBERS
  "O Picture Charming" (Duet)
    F. Leon, E. Lester
  "If You Me as You Say" (Duet)
    F. Leon, E. Lester
  "O Fenihan" (Chorus)
    E. Kelly, Conspirators
  "I am, I am American" (Trio)
    E. Kelly, E. Lester, F. Leon
  "Killee Kekikako" (Chorus)
    G. Leslie, W. Ball, Conspirators

1876.31

LA JOLIE PARFUMEUSE

A Revival of the Opéra-comique in Three Acts[43], in French. Libretto by Hector Crémieux and Ernest Blum. Music by Jacques Offenbach. Chorus and orchestra under the direction of Charles Van Ghele. Produced by Marie Aimée's French Opéra Bouffe Company (Maurice Grau, Manager). Opened 23 October 1876 at the Academy of Music and closed 25 October 1876 after 4 performances; returned 29 January 1877 to the Eagle Theatre under the auspices of Maurice Grau and closed 15 March 1877 after (6) performances in repertory.[44]

CAST: *Rose Michon*: Mlle. (MARIE) AIMÉE. *Bavolet*: Mlle. Florence Duparc. *Clorinde*: Mme. Chain. *La Julienne*: Mme. Dranciard. *Arthemise*: Mlle. Sophie Guerzi. *Madelon*: Mme. Levaux. *Justine*: Mlle. Niel. *Lise*: Mlle. Salvator. *Poirot*: Mons. Brannerd. *La Cocardière*: Mons. Berrar. *Germain*: Mons. Perin. *First Client*: Mons. Davalis. *Second Client*: Mons. Leclere. *Grand Chorus*.

1876.32

MUSETTE; or, The Secret of Guilde Court

A Drama in Three Acts. Play by Fred Marsden. Produced under the immediate supervision of E. A. Locke. Orchestra under the direction of William Withers. Produced by Henry E. Abbey. Opened 27 November 1876 at the Park Theatre and closed 16 December 1876 after 22 performances.

CAST: *Musette*, Little Bright Eyes: LOTTA (CRABTREE). *Sir Hugh Tracy*, "The Mad Knight": J. W. CARROLL. *Adalante*, an ex-Gypsy Chief: P. A. ANDERSON. *William A. Bokus*, (Billy) a Bud about to Blossom: THOMAS WHIFFEN. *Squire Bokus*, who believes in his wife: THOMAS E. MORRIS. *Timothy Titus*, somewhat uncertain and decidedly unpleasant: Belvil Ryan. *Philip D'Arcy*, a man of fair words: W. J. Cogswell. *Maud*, an exotic among wild flowers: Annie Edmondson. *Angela D'Arcy*, a firm believer in herself: Sara Stevens. *Selina Bokus*, with whom duty is law: Mrs. D. B. Vanderen.

Act 1: The Home of the Gypsies.

Act 2: Rainbow Falls.

Act 3: Parlor in Redmond Hall.

MUSICAL NUMBERS[45]
  "Forget Me Not"
  "Sweet Bye and Bye"
  "The Old Log Cabin in the Dell"
  "Fancy Little Step"
  "Pull Back"
  "Home Below and Heaven Above"
  "Tit, Tat, Toe"
  "Plantation Dance"

1876.33

GALATEA, or, The Black Sculptor

A Comic Opera Burlesque in One Act, preceded by an Olio[46]. (Original German libretto by 'Poly Henrion.') Adaptation by Edwin Kelly and Francis Leon. Music by Franz von Suppé. Musical director, W. Blakeney. Director of amusements, Edwin Kelly. Produced by (Edwin) Kelly & (Francis) Leon's Minstrels and Burlesque Opera Troupe. Opened 4 December 1876 at Kelly & Leon's Opera House and closed 23 December 1876 after 22 performances.

Olio: "Mother, the Angels," J. H. Surridge (ballad). She am Far Away," Sam Price (comic). "Tell Me Darling," C. R. Clinton (ballad). "The Man of Many Names," Edwin Lester (comic). "Darkey at the Play," Messrs. Kelly, Lester, Price, Company (finale). Mlle. Bagatelle, an amateur, The Only [Francis] Leon, with imitations of Di Murska, Aimée, and a dizzy serio-comic singer, introducing "Queen of Trumps." Flewy, Flewy, William Courtright. A Five Cent Shave and a Schooner, with Messrs. Surridge, Price and Japanese Tommy. Jonah and the Whale, William Courtright.

---

41 First produced in New York as CHING CHOW HIGH 28 March 1870 at Kelly & Leon's Minstrels for 32 performances in 2 engagements.
42 Olio cast and content changed weekly.
43 First produced in New York in French 31 March 1875 at the Lyceum Theatre in repertory. For Synopsis of Scenes and Musical Numbers, see original 1875 production.

44 Mlle. Aimée interpolated "Pretty as a Picture," Music by Brigham Bishop, Lyrics by George Cooper, which was then replaced on 15 March 1877 by the Swell Song (in English) "Hildebrandt Montrose," Music by David Braham, Lyrics by Edward Harrigan.
45 All performed by Lotta with her banjo.
46 Olio cast and content changed weekly.

GALATEA CAST: *Galatea*: THE ONLY [Francis] LEON. *Mydas*, a wealthy merchant of Cyprus: EDWIN KELLY. *Pygmalion*, a Sculptor: J. H. Surridge. *Ganymede*, a Slave: Edwin Lester. *High Priests in the Temple of Venus*: William Ball, C. R. Clinton. *Bacchus*: (Japanese) Tommy. *Pilgrims, etc.*: Company.

1876.34 THE BLACK CROOK!!

A Revival of the Grand and Original Spectacular Drama (Musical Extravaganza) in Four Acts, 11 Scenes[47]. Play by Charles M. Barras. (Music by Thomas Baker, others.) Produced by Messrs. John F. Poole and T. L. Donnelly. Opened 18 December 1876 at the Grand Opera House and closed 30 December 1876 after 16 performances.

CAST: *Rudolphe*, a poor artiste: MARK BATES. *Hertzog*, surnamed The Black Crook: E. J. MACK. *Greppo*, his drudge, with songs: LOUIS HARRISON. *Count Wolfenstein*: SHIRLEY FRANCE. *Von Puffengruntz*, the Count's Steward: HUDSON LISTON. *Dragonfin*: J. C. FRANKLIN. *Zamiel*: GEORGE MORRIS. *Wolfgar*, a Gypsy Ruffian: H. Victor. *Bruno*, his companion: J. P. Carr. *Skudawelp*: H. D. Fisher. *Stieklebach*: H. D. Emon. *Amina*, betrothed to Rudolphe: PHOSA McALLISTER. *Dame Barbara*, her foster mother: Miss G. Howard. *Stalacta*, Queen of the Golden Realm, with songs: LULU JORDAN. *Carline*, with songs: Theresa Wood. *Rosetta*: Ida Lee. *Ballet*: Mlles. GIUSEPPINA MORLACCHI, Antonino, Cora Adriana, Malvino, Minnie Holt, Anna Zervira, 24 Coryphées, Ballet of 60. *Specialties*: SAWYER FAMILY (Scotch Hand-Bell Ringers and Crystal Goblet Players), Messrs. Crossley and Elder (Caledonian Athletes), Messrs. Kynock and Smith (skaters).

Act 1, Scene 1: A Valley at the foot of the Hartz Mountains. *Scene 2*: A Woody Pass. *Scene 3*: Laboratory of the Black Crook. *Scene 4*: An Apartment in the Castle of Wolfenstein. *Scene 5*: A Wild Glen in the heart of the Brocken.

Act 2, Scene 1: Subterranean Vault in the Castle of Wolfenstein. *Scene 2*: Lobby in the Castle of Wolfenstein. *Scene 3*: A wild pass in the Hartz Mountains. *Scene 4*: The Grotto of Stalacta.

Act 3: A Moorish Palace. Beautiful Prismatic Fountains of real water, in which will appear great specialty artists.

Act 4: Grand Transformation Scene, the Fairies' Retreat in the Bower of Ferns!

BALLETS, SPECIALTIES

Bridal Festival Dance (Grand Ballet)(Act 1, Scene 1)
Corps de Ballet

Pas de Fleurs
Mlles. Adriana, Antonino, Corps de Ballet

Grand Incantation Scene, introducing many weird and startling effects (Act 1, Scene 5)

Song (Act 2, Scene 4)
L. Jordan

"Smile Thy Sweetest Smile" (Ballad)
L. Jordan

Palm Ballad
Mlle. Morlacchi, Coryphées, Corps de Ballet

The Carnival de Venice and Minuet Dance (Set in 1776) (Act 3)
Mlles. Morlacchi, Antonino, Adriana, Malvino, M. Holt, A. Zervira

Specialties: (Act 3)

Sawyer Family; Crossley & Elder; Kynock & Smith.

Song and Dance (Act 3)
T. Wood

Songs and Dance (Act 3)
L. Harrison

Grand March of the Amazons (Act 3)

Grand Transformation Scene: Fairies' Retreat in the Bower of Ferns (Act 4)

[47]First produced in New York 12 September 1866 at Niblo's Garden for 475 performances.

1876.35 LITTLE NELL AND THE MARCHIONESS

A Revival of the Melodrama in Four Acts, 14 Scenes.[48] Suggested by an episode in "The Old Curiosity Shop" by Charles Dickens, adapted by John Brougham. Scenery by Messrs. Heinemann and Fassit. Produced under the immediate direction of E. A. Locke. Produced by Henry E. Abbey. Opened 18 December 1876 at the Park Theatre and closed 6 January 1877 after 22 performances.

CAST: *Little Nell*: LOTTA (CRABTREE). *The Marchioness*: LOTTA (CRABTREE). *Dick Swiveller*: W. H. CRANE. *Grandfather Trent*: J. W. CARROLL. *Sampson Brass*: HAROLD FORSBERG. *Daniel Quilp*: P. A. ANDERSON. *Ned Trent*: W. J. COGSWELL. *Mr. Slum*: W. J. COGSWELL. *Corkey Jack*: C. W. Butler. *Reuben Kadger*: H. Crolins. *Foxey Joe*: R. L. Jaurs. *Higgins*: Mr. Allen. *Burton*: F. S. Meredith. *Abdallah*: H. L. Jones. *Showman*: M. Johnson. *Mrs. Quilp*: Helen Deland. *Sally Brass*: Mrs. D. B. VANDEREN. *Mrs. Jarley*: Madame Michels. *Mrs. Jiniwin*: Jennie Fisher. *Mrs. Simmons*: Miss. C. Rosine. *Mrs. George*: Emily Maynard. *Sybil*, a Gipsy: Mary Mosely. *Gingerbread Woman*: Sarah Long. *Peasants, Showmen, Mountebanks, Thimble Riggers, etc. Specialties*: Messrs. Runnels, Murray and Clifford, The Kings of the Carpet, in their Challenge Act. Corkey Jack's Band of Real Negro Serenaders.

Act 1, Scene 1: The Home of Quilp. *Scene 2*: Street in London. (New; Heinemann.) *Scene 3*: Room in Samson Brass' House.

Act 2, Scene 1: The Old Curiosity Shop. (New; Fassit.) *Scene 2*: Room in Brass' House. *Scene 3*: The Old Curiosity Shop.

Act 3, Scene 1: Streets in London. *Scene 2*: Dick Swiveller's Apartment. (New; Fassit.) *Scene 3*: The Road to Highgate. *Scene 4*: The Fair at Highgate. (New; Heinemann.)

Act 4, Scene 1: Room in Brass' House. (New.) *Scene 2*: Quilp's House. *Scene 3*: Swiveller's Wedding. *Scene 4*: The Grave of Little Nell, and the Apotheosis of Innocence.

SPECIALTIES

Banjo Solo (Act 1, Scene 3)
Lotta

Specialties (Act 3, Scene 4)
Messrs. Runnels, Murray and Clifford; Corkey Jack's Band of Real Negro Serenaders

Lotta's Unrivalled Clog Dance (Act 3, Scene 4)
Lotta

1876.36 AZURINE, or, A Voyage to the Earth

A Lyric Fairy Spectacle in Four Acts, 10 Scenes. Entire spectacle by and under the personal direction of the Kiralfy Brothers. Music by Fred Perkins. Scenery by Mons. Froumont Robecchi, of Paris. Machinery and mechanical effects by Arthur Wright. Costumes by Chalains of Paris, and C. Buck. Produced by the Kiralfy Brothers (Imre, Bolossy). Opened 25 December 1876 at Niblo's Garden and closed 20 January 1877 after 28 performances.

CAST: *Spirits of the Air*: *Azurine*: FLORENCE ELLIS. *Eolin*: MARION FISKE. *Queen of the Genii*: ADA MELBOURNE. *Aquillonet*: W. H. LYTELL. *King of the Genii*: W. P. SHELDON.

Mortals: *Mathias*: H. M. ELLIS. *Pierre*: W. H. FITZGERALD. *Lucette*: ELLA MORTIMER. *Dame Martha*: Miss Whitney. *Lady of the Lake*: Minnie Gray. *Other characters by the Company. Sylphs, Sylphides, Naiads, Willis, Gnomes, Demons, Goblins, etc.*

Ballet: Mlles. JOSEPHINE deROSA, ANAIS LETOURNIER, MARIE GAUGAIN, ARNOLD KIRALFY[49]. *Secondas*: Mlles. Schrotter, Holt, Hearn, Thomas. Corps de Ballet.

Act 1, Scene 1: The Aerial Palace in the Land of Clouds. *Scene 2*: Pierre's Rustic Home.

Act 2, Scene 1: Village Square. *Scene 2*: Wood by Sunset. *Scene 3*: The Haunted Glen.

Act 3, Scene 1: Border of the Lake. *Scene 2*: Aquarium.

Act 4, Scene 1: The Hermit's Retreat. *Scene 2*: Palace of the Gnomes in the Center of the Earth. *Scene 3*: Golden Terrace.

[48]First produced in New York 14 August 1867 at Wallack's Theatre for 26 performances. For Synopsis of Scenes and Musical Numbers, see original 1867 production.

[49]Joined the production at the beginning of the third week of the run.

BALLETS
Grand Ballet Villageois (De Villageurs)(Act 2, Scene 1)
Mlle. Letourneur, Secondas, Corps de Ballet
Divertissements des Naiads (Under the Sea)(Act 3, Scene 2)
Mlles. DeRosa, Letourneur, Gaugain, Corps de Danseuses
Dance of the Gnomes (Act 4, Scene 2)

1876.37 ARAMINTA'S WEDDING

A Realistic Ethiopian Burletta in One Act, 3 Scenes, preceded by an Olio[50]. Written by William Courtright. Musical director, Frank Bowles. Director of amusements, Edwin Kelly. Produced by (Edwin) Kelly & (Francis) Leon's Minstrels. Opened 25 December 1876 at Kelly & Leon's Opera House and closed 30 December 1876 after 8 performances.

Olio: "Where's That Cat?" (comic), Sam Price. "Essie Dear" (ballad), C. R. Clinton. "Don't Wake the Baby" (comic), Edwin Lester. "Silvery Stars" (ballad), J. H. Surridge. "The Darkey at the Play" (finale), Edwin Kelly, Company. The Girl in Advance of the Times, by The Only [Francis] Leon. Flewy, Flewy, William Courtright. Sausage à la Santa Claus, with Messrs. Lester, Price, Japanese Tommy, Clinton, Ball, Henning. Soap [monologue], William Courtright. A Chip of the Old Block, with Messrs. Surridge, Kelly, Price, Leon.

ARAMINTA'S WEDDING CAST: *Deacon Barnrake*: WILLIAM COURTRIGHT. *Simon Barnrake*: Japanese Tommy. *Rev. Dr. Julius X. Widemouth*: EDWIN KELLY. *Jackson Doolittle*: William Ball. *Hiram Masterson*: Fred Howard. *Glover Phil*: Edwin Lester. *Mrs. Barnrake*: Sam Price. *Jane Lovely*: C. H. Henning. *Cloe Davis*:" W. B. Hill. *Araminta Barnrake*: J. J. SURRIDGE. *Zeke Anderson*: C. R. Clinton. *Luke Farbough*: S. B. Rice.

1877.01 SANTA CLAUS; or, Harlequin Bob Cratchet and Ding Dong Dell!

A Grand Holiday Pantomime in Two Acts, 15 Scenes. Adapted from Charles Dickens' "A Christmas Carol." Music by Henry Wannemacher. Scenery by Charles Graham and Richard Smith, (Ben Day). Machinery, tricks and effects by Nelse Waldron. Musical director, Henry Wannemacher. Produced by Josh Hart. Opened 1 January 1877 (matinee) at the Eagle Theatre and closed 20 January 1877 after 25 performances.

CAST: Mortals: *Ebeneezer Scrooge*, the Miser: ROBERT JOHNSTON. *Bob Cratchet*, his clerk: JOHN WILD. *Big Dan*: James Bradley. *Frank Freeheart*: J. F. Crossen. *Mr. Cheerly*: G. L. Stout. *Tiny Tim*: Master Willie. *Mrs. Cratchet*: Carrie Jamieson. *Belinda Cratchet*: Angeline Griffith. *Dark Sam*: L. Lewis. *Mr. Heartly*: Dave Reed. *Ellen Freeheart*: Annie Johnson. *Martha Cratchet*: Sadie Martineau. *Jane Cratchet*: Mary Bird. *Children, etc.*

Immortals: *Santa Claus*, the Children's Friend: D. A. KELLY. *Fairy Christmas*: Lizzie Kelsey. *Fairy Dazzle*: Miss Johnson. *Fairy True*: Agnes Waite. *Fairy Bright*: Miss Sadie (Martineau). *Fairy Gay*: Miss Angeline (Griffith).

Pantomime: *Clown*: A. H. SHELDON. *Pantaloon*: L. LEWIS. *Harlequin*: YOUNG AMERICA. *Columbine*: MARIE GORENFLO. *Fairies, Demons, Laborers, Drawfs, Curiosities, etc.*

Mortals: *Mungo*, the Monkey and Sprite: Master Martin. *Gimp*, the lame Policeman: James Bradley. *Golightly*, the active Man: J. F. Crossin. *Gurney Morra*, the curious Individual: JOHN WILD. *Mr. Southern*, the Page Teller: Harry Richmond. *McDonald*, the Boss Mason: Dave Reed. *Mr. Soyer*, the Fat Steward: G. L. Stout. *Pat Mack*, the Author: Dave Holbrooke. *The Female Sampson*: George Lewis. *Negro Dwarf*: Mr. Brown. *Scullery Maid*: Miss Johnson. *Arabella Shortcake*, the Bride: Miss Martineau. *Ann Turner*: Miss Bird. *Trulla Lallah*, the Baker's Wife: Miss Griffith. *Letty Maybird*, the Village Beauty: MINNIE VAIL. *Tilly Sweetener*, the town talker: Miss Jamieson. (*Specialties*: JAMES W. McKEE, JENNIE HUGHES.)

Act 1, Scene 1: In the Clouds. The Night before Christmas. The Star of Bethlehem. (Graham, Day.) *Scene 2*: The Counting House of Ebeneezer Scrooge. *Scene 3*: A City View. (Smith.) *Scene 4*: Bob Cratchet's Christmas Party. *Scene 5*: A Street. In the future. *Scene 6*: The Village Church at Christmas Eve. (Graham.) *Scene 7*: In the clouds. *Scene 8*: The Miser's home. *Scene 9*: The Crystal Grotto. (Graham.)

Act 2, Scene 1: View of the Eagle Theatre. (Smith.) *Scene 2*: The Fairy Farm of Fancy. (Smith.) *Scene 3*: The Union Dime Savings Bank. (Smith.) *Scene 4*: The Unfinished House. (Smith.) *Scene 5*: A Street in New York. *Scene 6*: The Abode of Misery. (Smith.)

MUSICAL NUMBERS, SPECIALTIES
Christmas Carol (*Organ Music composed by* Max Maretzek.)
Jolly Dance (Act 1, Scene 4)
Grand Transformation Scene (Act 1, Scene 8)
Comic Songs (Act 1, Scene 9)
J. W. McKee
Laughable Duets (Act 2, Scene 1)
J. Hughes, J. Wild
The Celebrated Eagle Laugh Makers in their Dizzy Quartette
Messrs. Wild, Richmond, Sheldon, Bradley
The Seasons (Beautiful transformation, Act 2, Scene 6)

1877.02 ZIP, or Point Lynde Light

A Drama in Four Acts.[51] Play by Fred Marsden. Produced under the immediate direction of E. A. Locke. Orchestra under the direction of William Withers. Produced by Henry E. Abbey. Opened 8 January 1877 at the Park Theatre and closed 13 January 1877 after 7 performances.

CAST: *Zip*: LOTTA (CRABTREE). *Philosophy Jack*: E. A. LOCKE. *Julkes Galetti*: P. A. Anderson. *Anthony Weltomot*: J. W. Carroll. *Father Phelps*: Thomas E. Morris. *Sir William Elkton*: W. J. Coggswell. *Hon. Chauncey Elmore*: W. Ramsey. *Mrs. Elkton*: Kate Meek. *Fanny*: Helen Deland. *Amanda Lovelace*: Mrs. D. B. Vanderen. *Old Judith*: F. Stover.

Act 1: Point Lynde Light. Isle of Angelsea.

Act 2: Elkton Grange.

Act 3: Drawing Room at Elkton Grange.

Act 4: No. 3 Crypt Row.

MUSICAL NUMBERS[52]
"Fishes and Crabs"
L. Crabtree, E. A. Locke
Banjo Solo
L. Crabtree
Operatic Medley
L. Crabtree, E. A. Locke
French Song, with accompaniment
L. Crabtree

1877.03 THE POLICE FORCE

A Local Operatic Terpsichorean Burletta in One Act, accompanied by an Olio. Director of amusements, Edwin Kelly. Produced by (Edwin) Kelly & (Francis) Leon's Minstrels and Burlesque Opera Troupe. Opened 15 January 1877 at Kelly & Leon's Opera House and closed 27 January 1877 after 14 performances[53].

Olio: Stuttering John; Giroflé-Girofla (selection); Billy Courtright; Rose of St. Flour (selection); Topics of the Day; Tricks on Dad; The Woodsawyer; Lew Benedict.

CAST: *The Unknown*: FRANCIS LEON. *Captain Bullseye*: EDWIN KELLY. 20 Policemen in Full Uniform. Thrilling Incidents of Police Life. Police Trials and Troubles. Moonlight Police Coterie.

1877.04 AROUND THE WORLD IN EIGHTY DAYS

A Revival of the Porte Saint Martin version of the Musical Extravaganza in a Prologue and Five Acts, 18 Scenes[54]. Based on the French adaptation of

[50]Olio cast and content changed weekly.

[51]Authorship uncredited.

[52]Song list prepared from a Boston program of April 1875.

[53]No program found.

[54]First produced in New York 28 August 1875 at the Academy of Music for 43 performances.

Jules Verne's novel "Le Tour du Monde en Quatre Vingt Jours," as adapted by Adolphe d'Ennery. Music composed and arranged by Jean-Jacques de Debillemont. Scenic designs by Robecchi, Fromont, Nezel, Philip Goatcher. Costumes by Chalain, Mlle. Gervais, Lorain; accessories by Charles Halle. Armors and jewels by Granger & Kennedy. Steam effects by J. Paxson. Mechanical effects by William McMurray. Staged by the Kiralfys (Imre, Bolossy). Produced by the Kiralfy Brothers. Opened 22 January 1877 at Niblo's Garden and closed 10 March 1877 after 50 performances.

CAST: *Aouda*, an Indian Princess: IMOGENE VANDYKE. *Nemea*, her sister: CLARA MILTON. *Nakahira*, Aouda's Slave: FLORENCE ELLIS. *Betsy*: Blanche Mortimer. *Phineas Fogg*, a member of the Eccentric Club: H. S. DUFFIELD. *Myles O'Pake*, an ex-Senator from New York: G. C. CHARLES. *John Fix*, an English Detective: J. J. WALLACE. *Passepartout*, a French valet: W. H. LYTELL. *Mr. Blunt*, a Calcutta Magistrate: W. H. FITZGERALD. *Sir Roger Shendryn*: C. Charles. *Arthur Mayburn*: J. Rudolph. *Phillip Jones, M.P.*: Harry Mortimer. *Governor of Suez*: R. T. French. *Chief of the Brahmins*: Harry D. Clifton. *Captain Phil Tracy*: V. Trat. *Jack Rivers*: G. T. James. *A Parsee*: J. Taylor. *Captain Collins*: C. H. Barton. *Railroad Conductor*: P. W. Slater. *Railroad Engineer*: C. Bowers. *Boatswain*: T. Williams. *Barkeeper*: G. Hanna. *Scout*: H. W. Tomlinson.

Ballet: Mlles. ADELE BONI, MAURI, JOSEPHINE DeROSA, MARIE GAUGAIN; Mons. ARNOLD KIRALFY, Terpsichorean Ensemble of 250.

Prologue, Scene 1: A Club Room in London. The Wager of Half a Million. Hurried Departure.

Act 1, Scene 1: The arrival at Suez. View of Suez Canal. *Scene 2*: Off for the East Indies. *Scene 3*: A Interior of a Hindoo Bungalow. *Scene 4*: The Necropolis. The great Religious Festival of the Suttee. Grand Funeral Pageant. The Victim. The Rescue. Thrilling Denouement.

Act 2, Scene 1: The European Hotel in Calcutta. *Scene 2*: Nakahira's Palace. Borneo.

Act 3, Scene 1: A Saloon at San Francisco. *Scene 2*: On the Pacific Railroad. The Train attacked by Road Agents. *Scene 3*: The Rocky Mountains.

Act 4, Scene 1: Saloon on the Steamer *"Henrietta." Scene 2*: The Steamer on the Ocean. *Scene 3*: Terrific Explosion. Loss of the *"Henrietta." Scene 4*: A Waif on the Sea. *Scene 5*: Lights of Liverpool. *Scene 6*: Liverpool, Day and Night.

Act 5, Scene 1: L. & N. W. Hotel, Liverpool. *Scene 2*: The Eccentric Club Palace, London. Result of the Wager.

BALLETS, SPECIALTIES

Grand Funeral Pageant (Act 1, Scene 4)

Grand Ballet (Act 2, Scene 2)

Mlles. DeRosa, Boni, Mauri, Gaugain, Mons. Kiralfy, Corps de Ballet

Nautical Echoes (Act 4, Scene 2)

Orphée Quartet

The Revels of the Eccentrics! (Act 5, Scene 2)

1877.05 THE ENCHANTED CAT

A Metamorphosiological Operetta in One Act, preceded by an Olio[55]. (Original French "La Chatte metamorphosée en femme") Libretto by Eugène Scribe[56]. Music by Jacques Offenbach. Musical director, W. Blakeney. Director of amusements, Edwin Kelly. Produced by (Edwin) Kelly & (Francis) Leon's Minstrels and Burlesque Opera Troupe. Opened 29 January 1877 at Kelly & Leon's Opera House and closed 17 February 1877 after 21 performances; returned 10 March 1877 to Kelly & Leon's for 2 additional performances.

Olio: "I'm So Lonely" (ballad), C. R. Clinton. "The German 5th" (comic), Edwin Lester. "Speak, Only Speak" (ballad), J. H. Surridge. "Bye! Bye! On our Journey" (comic), Lew Benedict. "Giroflé-Girofla" Selections, Edwin Kelly, Company. "Hail to the Chief," Chorus. "Flower of Innocence," Edwin Kelly. "Dearest Papa, I'm Girofla," C. R. Clinton. Drinking Song, J. H. Surridge. Pirate Chorus, William Ball, Company. "Brannigan's Band," Kelly & Leon's Minstrels. The Woodsawyer and Stuttering John, William Courtright. Charleston Girls, J. W. McAndrews, Edwin Lester. "Colored Jubilee Singers," Messrs. Courtright, Ball, Clinton, Howard. Topics of the Day, Lew Benedict.

[55]Olio cast and content changed weekly

[56]English adaptation, presumably by Kelly & Leon, uncredited in programs.

THE ENCHANTED CAT CAST: *Walter Thule*, a student and a misanthrope: EDWIN KELLY. *John Moritz*, alias Rambo Sambo: Edwin Lester. *An Indian Juggler*: Edwin Lester. *Martha*, Walter's housekeeper: J. H. Surridge. *Minnie Greshen*: THE ONLY [Francis] LEON. *The White Cat*: THE ONLY [Francis] LEON. *The Magnificent Angola*: Puss.

1877.06 7 FIFTH AVENUE

A Local Play in Five Acts, 8 Scenes. Play by George Fawcett Rowe. Scenery by Charles S. Getz, George Heister, John Thompson. Produced by Henry Jarrett and Harry Palmer. Opened 5 February 1877 at Booth's Theatre and closed 10 March 1877 after 35 performances.[57]

CAST: *Richard Blake*, an American: GEORGE RIGNOLD. *Simon Schuyler*, President of the Hudson Iron Company: JAMES H. TAYLOR. *Hon. Graham Liddisdale*, an Englishman, betrothed to Olivia: F. B. WARDE. *Colonel Mark Anthony Smart*: Vining Bowers. *Exodus Gerome*, a Wall Street broker: ATKINS LAWRENCE. *Richard Blogg*, Superintendant of the Hudson Iron Works: E. K. Collier. *Jem Maggs*, a Convict: H. A. Weaver. *Horatio Nelson*, colored servant of the Schuylers: JOHN WILD. *Hiram Shortey*, "Boss of all the bill-posters": CHARLES T. PARSLOE, JR. *Jacob Schnitz*, his assistant: GEORGE S. KNIGHT. *Larry Doolahan*, of Ballywhack: J. A. Meade. *Sergeant Mulligan*, of the Recruiting Service: Joseph A. Wilkes. *Mr. Jutkins*: James Fox. *Mr. Porter*: Andrew Barrett. *Olivia*, only daughter of Simon Schuyler: MAUDE GRANGER. *Mrs. Smythe*: ANNIE DELAND. *Cleopatra*, her daughter: KATE GIRARD. *Aunty*, an old Negress, mother to Horatio Nelson: Kate Singleton. *Marie Antoinette*: Marion Sackett.

Act 1: Saloon of the Steamer *Marseilles* on the banks of Newfoundland, September 1862. (Getz). The collision at sea.

Act 2, Scene 1: Wall Street. January, 1863. (Thompson.) *Scene 2*: Mrs. Smythe's home. *Scene 3*: Directors' Room of the Hudson Dock and Iron Company. A meeting of Shareholders.

Act 3, Scene 1: U.S. Recruiting Quarters on the Bowery. (Thompson.) *Scene 2*: The Works on the Hudson River. (Heister) Launch of the Iron-Clad.

Act 4: Fifth Avenue by night. (Heister.) Murder of Mr. Schuyler, the capitalist.

Act 5: A Mansion on Fifth Avenue. (Heister.) The riots of 1863.

1877.07 MARTON, LA JOLIE BOUQUETIÈRE

A Musical Comedy (English Operatic Comedy) in Four Acts, adapted from the French. Orchestra under the direction of A. Rossner. Manager, Joseph B. Ayres. Opened 5 February 1877 at the New Broadway Theatre and closed 10 February 1877 after 8 performances.[58]

CAST: *Marton*: Miss LOUISE LEIGHTON. *Mademoselle de Volange*: FLORENCE STORER. *Javotte*: Mrs. SYLVESTER POST. *Chevalier de Bellerive*: E. MACK. *Marquis de Volange*: G. W. Wessells. *Baron Troptard*: Tom Owens. *Count St. Cyr*: : A. H. Forrest. *Isidore Farine*: Charles Webster. *Dubois*: B. Anderson. *Ravannes*: G. R. Sprague. *Preval*: William Mason. *Servant*: Mr. Rathburn. *Gen D'Armes, Marketwomen, etc.*

1877.08 LA VIE PARISIENNE

A Revival of the Opéra-bouffe in Four Acts[59], in French. Libretto by Henri Meilhac and Ludovic Halévy. Music by Jacques Offenbach. Musical director, Mr. Hepps. Stage director, Charles Darcy. Produced by Maurice Grau. Opened 31 January-1 February 1877 at the Eagle Theatre; returned 10, 24 March 1877 for a total of 4 performances in repertory.[60]

[57]Musical numbers and specialties not listed in programs. Mentioned in reviews were:

Comic Songs and Dances (Act 4)

C. T. Parsloe, Jr., G. S. Knight

[58]Programs provide no details of authorship, design credits, direction, scenes or musical numbers.

[59]First produced in New York in French 29 March 1869 at the Théâtre Français for 11 performances. For Synopsis of Scenes and Musical Numbers, see original 1869 production.

[60]Mlle. Aimée will introduce a new English song and dance "Pretty Peggy."

CAST: *Gabrielle*: Mlle. (MARIE) AIMÉE. *Le Baron de Gondremarck*: Mons. DUPLAN. *Le Bresilien*: Mons. Branciart. *Frick*: Mons. Branciart. *Prosper*: Mons. Branciart. *Bobinet*: Mons. J. MEZIÈRES. *Raoul de Gardefeu*: Mons. RAOULT. *Alfred*: Mons. Perin. *Urbain*: Mons. Ruiz. *Joseph*: Mons. Davolis. *Alphonse*: Mons. Girard. *Gontran*: Mons. Theophile. *Un Employé*: Mons. Leclere. *Métella*: Mlle. BLANCHE GUEYMARD. *Pauline*: Mlle. FLORENCE DUPARC. *La Baronne de Gondremarck*: Mlle. SOPHIE GHERZI. *Leonie*: Mlle. Marie Vandamme. *Louise*: Mlle. Niel. *Clara*: Mlle. Clara. *Caroline*: Mlle. Joly. *Julie*: Mlle. Seygaud. *Augustine*: Mlle. Esthere. *Charlotte*: Mlle. Mathilde. *Albertine*: Mlle. Angele.

1877.09 LA PETITE MARIÉE!

A Opéra-bouffe in Three Acts, in French. Libretto by Eugène Leterrier and Albert Vanloo. Music by Charles Lecocq. Musical director, Mr. Hepps. Stage manager, Charles Darcy. Produced by Maurice Grau. Opened 6 February 1877 at the Eagle Theatre and closed 16 March 1877 after 9 performances in repertory.

CAST: *Graziella*: Mlle. MARIE AIMÉE. *Le Podestat Rodolpho*: Mons. W. REINE. *San Carlo*: Mons. RAOULT. *Raphaël de Montefiasco*: Mons. DUPLAN. *Casteldémoli*: Mons. J. MEZIÈRES. *Beppo*: Mons. RUIZ. *Un Muet*: Mons. Davalis. *Un Inconnu*: Mons. Girard. *Lucrézia*: Mlle. ADÈLE DESIRÉE. *Théobaldo*: Mlle. LETELLIER. *Béatrix*: Mlle. MATHE. *Une Inconnu*: Mlle. Sophie Gherzi.

Act 1: The courtyard of an inn in a small village near Bergamo.

Act 2: At Bergamo. The park of the palace.

Act 3: A veranda leading to the apartments in the palace.

ACT 1[61]

Choeur des Voyageurs (Mangeons vite, buvons vite)
Mlle. Mathe, Messrs. Raoult, Ruiz, Choeur

Choeur des Postillons (Hop! hop! gentils postillons)
Six Postillons

Chanson de l'étrier (Depuis plus de cent cinquante ans)
Mlle. Mathe, Messrs. Raoult, Ruiz, Choeur

Duo et couplets (Mon cher mari, c'est votre femme)
Mlle. Aimée, Mons. Raoult

Trio (Si vous n'aviez pas été si gentille)
Mlle. Aimée, Messrs. Raoult, J. Mezières

Quintetto (Voici l'instant)
Mlle. Aimée, Messrs. Raoult, Duplan, J. Mezières, Davalis

Valse de la crevache (Mon amour, mon idole)
Mlle. Adèle-Desirée

Rondeau (Le jour où tu te marieras)
W. Reine

Finale:
Choeur (Due chacun coure et se presse)
Sextuor (De terreur, de surprise)
Mlles. Aimée, Adele-Désirée, Letellier,
Messrs. Raoult, Duplan, J. Mezières, W. Reine, Choeur
Final (La voiture de Monseigneur)
Tous

ACT 2

Choeur (A midi our le quart)
Mlle. Letellier, Choeur

Réception des dignitaires (Salut aux nouveaux dignitaires)
Mlle. Aimée, Letellier, Messrs. Duplan, J. Mezières, Choeur

Couplets de l'Épée (Ce n'est pas, camarade)
Mlle. Letellier, Les Pages

Couplets du Jour et de la Nuit (Le jour, vois-tu bien)
Mlle. Aimée, Mons. W. Reine

Duo des Giffles (Ah! ce souvenir m'exaspére)
Mlle. Adele-Desirée, Mons. Duplan

Duo de la Lecture (Donnez-moi votre main)
Mlle. Aimée, Mons. W. Reine

Le Rossignol (Fabliau)(Or donc, en Romagne vivait)
Mlle. Aimée, Mons. W. Reine

Duo (Tu partiras)
Mlle. Aimée, Mons. Raoult

Couplets de l'enlèvement (Vraiment j'en ris d'avance)
Mlle. Aimée, Mons. Raoult

Ronde de nuit (Quand la nuit commence)
Mlle. Letellier, Mons. W. Reine, Les Pages

Scène du duel (Capitaine, le sabre au vent)
Messrs. Duplan, W. Reine

Ensemble (Je suis la sienne)
Tous

Ronde de la Petite Mariée (Dans la bonne société)
Mlle. Aimée, W. Reine

ACT 3

Introduction, La Diane (Plan! rataplan, c'est la tambour)
Messrs. Raoult, Duplan, Choeur

Quatuor (Couplets)(Dans la chambrette solitaire)
Mlles. Aimée, Adele-Desirée, Messrs. Duplan, J. Mezières

Couplets du Podestat (Vraiment, est-ce là la mine)
W. Reine

Couplets de Reproches (Pour vous sauvez)
Mlle. Aimée

Duo des Larmes (Tu pleures, Graziella)
Mlle. Aimée, Mons. Raoult

Couplet final (Enfin mon bonheur est complet)
Tous

1877.10 LA PÉRICHOLE

A Revival (new version) of the Opéra-bouffe in Three Acts, 4 Scenes[62], in French. Libretto by Ludovic Halévy and Henri Meilhac, based on "Le Carosse du Saint-Sacrament" by Prosper Merimée. Music by Jacques Offenbach. Musical director, Mr. Hepps. Stage director, Charles Darcy. Produced by Maurice Grau. Opened 15 February 1877 at the Eagle Theatre; season closed 31 March 1877 after 4 performances in repertory.

CAST: *La Périchole*: Mlle. MARIE AIMÉE. *Piquillo*: Mons. RAOULT. *Don Andrès de Ribeira*: Mons. REINE. *Le Compte de Panatellas*: Mons. J. MEZIÈRES. *Don Pedro de Hinoyosa*: Mons. DUPLAN. *Tarapote*: Mons. RUIZ. *Un Vieux Prisonnier*: Mons. Benedick. *First Notary*: Mons. Leclere. *Second Notary*: Mons. Davalis. *Un Geolier*: Mons. Girard. *Cousins (3)*: *Guadalena*: Mlle. BLANCHE GUEYMARD. *Berginella*: Mlle. Letellier. *Mastrilla*: Mlle. Sophie Gherzi. *Maids of Honor (4)*: *Ninetta*: Mlle. Marie Vandamme. *Brambilla*: Mlle. Niel. *Frasquinella*: Mlle. Lecourt. *Manuelita*: Mlle. Marthe.

Act 1: Public Square in Lima. (Lima, sur la place publique, devant le cabaret des Trois Cousines.)

Act 2: The Palace. (Le palais du Vice-Roi.)

Act 3, Scene 1: A Dungeon. (Un cachot.) *Scene 2*: Public Square in Lima. (Le même qu'au premier acte.)

ACT 1[63]

Choeur (Du Vice-Roi, c'est aujourd'hui la fête)
Mlles. B. Gueymard, Letellier, S. Gherzi, Choeur

Chanson du Trois Cousines (Promptes à servir la pratique)
Mlles. B. Gueymard, Letellier, S. Gherzi

Reprise du choeur (Ah! qu'on y fait gaiement glou glou)
Mlles. B. Gueymard, Letellier, S. Gherzi, Mons. Duplan, Choeur

Choeur (C'est lui, c'est notre vice-roi)
Choeur

Couplets de l'Incognito (Sans en rien souffler à personne)
Mons. Reine

[61]Musical numbers not listed in programs. List prepared from published French piano vocal score (C. Joubert, Paris, 1873). French –English libretto also published by Metropolitan Printing for Maurice Grau.

[62]New York premiere of the "expanded" new version in Four Scenes. First produced in New York in French in its earlier version 4 January 1869 at Pike Opera House for 35 performances. The original authors expanded Act 3 into two new scenes with added musical numbers.

[63]Musical numbers not listed in programs. List prepared from published French piano vocal score (Brandus & Cie., Paris, 1874).

Marche Indienne et Entrée des chanteurs
Mlle. Aimée, Mons. Raoult
Complainte: L'Espagnol et la jeune Indienne (Le conquérant dit à la jeune Indienne)
Mlle. Aimée, Mons. Raoult
Séguidille: Le muletier et la jeune personne (Vous a-t-on dit souvent)
Mlle. Aimée, Mons. Raoult
Choeur des saltimbanques (Levez-vous et prenez vos rangs)
Choeur
Le Lettre de la Périchole (O mon cher amant, je te jure)
Mlle. Aimée
Mélodrame
Choeur et Duetto des notaires (Holà, hé! holà! de là-bas)
Mlles. B. Gueymard, Letellier, S. Gherzi, Choeur
Griserie-Ariette (Ah! quel diner je viens de faire)
Mlle. Aimée, Choeur
Duetto de mariage (Je dois vous prévenir, Madame)
Mlles. Aimée, B. Gueymard, Letellier, S. Gherzi, Messrs. Raoult, J. Mezières, Reine, Duplan, Choeur
Final et Marche des palanquins (Qu'on se hâte et qu'on les marie)
Mlles. B. Gueymard, Letellier, S. Gherzi, Messrs. J. Mezières, Reine, Duplan, Leclere, Davalis, Choeur

ACT 2
Chanson des Dames de la cour (Cher seigneur, revenez à vous)
Mlles. Marthe, Lecourt, Niel, M. Vandamme, Dames de la Cour
Cancans-Couplets (On vante partout son sourire)
Mlles. Marthe, Lecourt, Niel, M. Vandamme, Dames de la Cour
Choeur des seigneurs (Quel marché de bassesse)
Tenors, basses
Couplets: Les femmes il n'y a qu'ça (Et là, maintenant que nous sommes seuls)
Messrs. Raoult, J. Mezières, Duplan
Choeur de la présentation (Nous allons donc voir un mari)
Mlle. Aimée, Messrs. Raoult, J. Mezières, Reine, Duplan, Francis, Choeur
Couplets: Ah! que les hommes sont bêtes (Que veulent dire ces colères?)
Mlle. Aimée
Rondo de bravoure (Écoute, ô Roi, je te présente)
Mons. Raoult
Galop d l'Arrestation (Sautez dessus! sautez dessus!)
Mons. Reine, Choeur
Ronde des maris . . . ré (Conduisez-le, bons courtisans)
Mons. Reine, Choeur, Tous

ACT 3
Scene 1
Couplets-Boléro (Les maris courbaient la tête)
Pedro, Raoult, J. Mezières, Choeur
Air (On me proposait d'être infame)
Raoult
Mélodrame
Duo (Dans ces couloirs obscurs)
Mlle. Aimée, Raoult
Couplets de l'Aveu (Tu n'es pas beau, tu n'es pas riche)
Mlle. Aimée
Trio du Joli Geôlier (Je suis le plus joli geôlier)
Mlle. Aimée, Raoult, Reine
Trio de la Prison (Roi pas plus haut qu'une botte)
Mlle. Aimée, Raoult, Reine
Mélodrame
Finale (Je t'adore si je suis folle)
Mlle. Aimée, Raoult
Scene 2
Choeur des Patrouilles (En avant, en avant! soldats!)
Duplan
Ariette-Valse des Trois Cousines (Pauvres gens, où sont-ils?)
3 Cousines
Ensemble (Les bandits sont partis)
Duplan, J. Mezières, 3 Cousines
Mélodrame
Complainte des Amoureux (Écoutez, peupl' d'Amérique)
Mlle. Aimée, Raoult
Finale (Tous deux, au temps de peine et de misère)
Mlle. Aimée, Mons. Raoult, Choeur

1877.11 GIROFLÉ-GIROFLA

A Revival of the Opéra-bouffe in Three Acts[64], in French. Libretto by Albert Vanloo and Eugène Leterrier. Music by Charles Lecocq. Musical director, Mr. Hepps. Stage director, Charles Darcy. Produced by Maurice Grau. Opened 23 February 1877 at the Eagle Theatre and closed 10 (matinee) March 1877 after 4 performances in repertory.

CAST: *Giroflé, Girofla*: Mlle. MARIE AIMÉE. *Aurore*: Mlle. BRANCIART[65]. *Pedro*: Mlle. Letellier. *Paquita*: Mlle. Blanche Gueymard. *Marasquin*: Mons. RAOULT. *Bolero*: Mons. Duplan. *Mourzouk*: Mons. REINE. *Chief of the Pirates*: Mons. Ruiz. *Le Parrain*: Mons. Benedick. *Le Danseur*: Mons. Perrin. *Le Notaire*: Mons. Bageard. *Le Precepteur*: Mons. Gerard. *Le Garçon d'honneur*: Mons. Davalis. *L'oncle*: Mons. Leclere. *Gusman*: Mlle. Marie Vandamme. *Fernand*: Mlle. Niel. *La Marraine*: Mlle. Gherzi.

1877.12 LES DRAGONS DE VILLARS

A Revival of the Opéra-comique (The Hermit's Bell) in Three Acts, in French[66]. Libretto by Lockroy [Joseph Simon] and Eugène Cormon. Music by Aimé Maillart. Stage manager, Charles Darcy. Scenery by Charles Graham. Musical director, Mr. Hepps. Produced by Maurice Grau. Opened 24 February 1877 at the Academy of Music for 1 performance; returned 9 March 1877 at the Eagle Theatre for 1 performance.

CAST: *Sylvain*: Mons. RAOULT. *Belamy*: Mons. REINE. *Thibaut*: Mons. DUPLAN. *Un Pasteur*: Mons. Ruiz. *Un Dragon*: Mons. Davalis. *Rose Friquet*: Mlle. MARIE AIMÉE. *Georgette*: Mlle. FLORENCE DUPARC.

1877.13 LA BOULANGÈRE A DES ÉCUS

An Opéra Bouffe (The Rich Bakeress) in Three Acts, in French. Libretto by Henri Meilhac and Ludovic Halévy. Music by Jacques Offenbach. Musical director, Mr. Hepps. Stage manager, Charles Darcy. Produced by Maurice Grau. Opened 26 February 1877 at the Eagle Theatre and closed 3 March 1877 (matinee) after 5 performances in repertory.

CAST: *Margot*: Mlle. MARIE AIMÉE. *Bernadille*: Mons. RAOULT. *Le Commissaire de Police*: Mons. REINE. *Coquebert*: Mons. BRANCIART. *Flammèche*: Mons. DUPLAN. *Délicat*: Mons. J. MEZIÈRES. *A Financier*: Mons. Benedick. *A Thief*: Mons. Theophile. *Jacquot*: Mons. Perain. *Toinon*: Mlle. FLORENCE DUPARC. *Madame de Parabère*: Mlle. Sophie Gherzi. *Madame de Fabran*: Mlle. Angele. *Madame de Phalaris*: Mlle. Esther. *Ravannes*, Page to the Duc d'Orleans: Mlle. LETELLIER. *Pages of Duc d'Orleans*: Mlles. Branciart, Marthe, Vandamme, Niel, Mathilde, Seygaud, Perrin. *A Grisette*: Mlle. Joly. *Bakeresses, Soldiers of the Watch, Exempts, etc.*

Scene: Paris in 1718.

---

[64]First produced in New York in French 4 February 1875 at the Park Theatre. For Synopsis of Scenes and Musical Numbers, see original 1875 production. An English language interpolation was added for the tour:
"Hildebrandt Montrose" (Swell Song)
M. Aimée
(*Music by* David Braham. *Lyrics by* Edward Harrigan.)

[65]Mlle. Branciart was a last minute replacement for Mlle. Adele Desirée who later assumed the role.

[66]First produced in New York in French 10 May 1869 at the Grand Opera House

ACT 1[67]

Scène et Couplets (Sur cette solitaire)
Mlle. Letellier

Duo (Ainsi te voilà?)
Mlle. Duparc, Mons. Raoult

Choeur de la halle (Sous les pilliers de la halle)
Les 4 Marchandes, Mouches

Couplets (Le beau temps que la Régence)
Mons. Reine

Choeur (Ah! qu'elle est fière)
Choeur

Couplets (Lorsque j'étais fill' de boutique)
Mlle. Aimée

Romance (Ce qu'j'ai, tu le demandes)
Mlle. Duparc

Final (Encor un gueux qu'on va pincer)
Mlles. Aimée, Duparc, Messrs. Raoult, Reine, Duplan, Mezières, Choeur

ACT 2

Choeur et Scène (Avec politesse)
Mlles. Aimée, Letellier, Pages, Grisettes

Ronde de Manon Frelu (Savez-vous l'histoire)
Mlle. Aimée

Couplets des Fariniers (Les fariniers, les charbonniers)
Mlle. Aimée, Messrs. Raoult, Duplan, J. Mezières

Morceau d'Ensemble (Nous voici tous!)
Mlle. Aimée, Messrs. Raoult, Reine, Duplan, Mezières, Branciart, Choeur

Couplets (Un homme d'un vrai mèrite)
Mlle. Aimée, Messrs. Raoult, Branciart

Final (Gardienne de l'honneur des femmes/Nous sommes ici trois cents femelles)
Mlle. Aimée, Duparc, Messrs. Raoult, Reine, Duplan, J. Mezières, Branciart, Choeur

ACT 3

Choeur de soldats (Vive le beau jeu de la drogue!)
Choeur

Scène des pages (C'est toi qui dit qu'on nous arrête)
Mlle. Letellier, les Pages

Couplets (Je sais qu'on n'trouvait pas en France)
Mlles. Duparc, Letellier, les Pages

Couplets (Jusqu'aux bords remplissons nos verres)
Mlle. Gherzy

Couplets (Eh bien! J'l'ai vu c'fameux régent) Mlle. Aimée

Final (Si vous vouliez êtr' bien aimables)
Mlles. Duparc, Aimée, Gherzy, Messrs. Raoult, Reine, Duplan, J. Mezières, Branciart, Chœur

1877.14 LA BELLE HÉLÈNE

A Revival of the Opéra-bouffe in Three Acts[68], in French. Libretto by Henri Meilhac and Ludovic Halévy. Music by Jacques Offenbach. Musical director, Mr. Hepps. Stage manager, Charles Darcy. Produced by Maurice Grau. Opened 12 March 1877 at the Eagle Theatre and closed 17 March 1877 (matinee) after 4 performances in repertory.

CAST: *Hélène*, Queen of Sparta: Mlle. MARIE AIMÉE. *Orestes*, Son of Agamemnon: Mlle. FLORENCE DUPARC. *Bacchis*, attendant on Hélène: Mlle. Blanche Gueymard. *Leona, Parthenis*, Women of Corinth: Mlles. Letellier, Marthe. *Paris*, Son of King Priam: Mons. Raoult. *Menelaus*, King of Sparta: Mons. DUPLAN. *Agamemnon*, King of Greece: Mons. REINE. *Calchas*, Grand Augur of Jupiter: Mons. J. MEZIÈRES. *Achille*, King of Phtiotis: Mons. Branciart. *Ajax I*, King of Salamine: Mons. Benedic. *Ajax II*, King of Locria: Mons. Theophele. *Philocome*, Servant to Calchas: Mons. Ruiz. *Euthecles*, Blacksmith: Mons. Gerard. *Guests, Slaves, the Populace, etc.*

1877.15 A TRIP TO THE MOON

A Comic Spectacular Extravaganza in Four Acts, 15 Scenes. Revised and adapted to the American stage (by J. J. Wallace, Esq.) from Henry Leigh's English version of "Le Voyage dans de Lune" adapted from the French of Jules Verne. Music by Jacques Offenbach. Scenery by Fromont and Robecchi, of Paris; W. P. Goatcher and J. Johnson, New York. Costumes by Mme Constant, of Paris; Miss Lorraine, Mme. Berg, Messrs. Jacobi, Bloom Brothers. Accessories and general paraphernalia by Charles Halle, of Paris; Messrs. Cutler and Kelly, New York. Optical effects by John Weatherspoon. Steam effects by Messrs. Paxson Brothers. Leader of orchestra, Fred Perkins. Entire production produced under the direction of the Kiralfys. (Imre, Bolossy). Opened 14 March 1877 at Booth's Theatre and closed 24 March 1877 after 12 performances.

CAST: *King Pin*: W. FITZGERALD. *Microscope*, the Wisdom of the States: W. H. LYTELL. *Kosmos*, King of the Lunar Regions: GEORGE C. CHARLES. *Cactus*, his Prime Minister, with points enough to hang an idea on: JOHN HERNE. *Clerks of the Weather (3)*, who have things their own way, whether or no: *Focus*: William Otway. *Quadrant*: H. Clifton. *Rectangle*: W. D. Brown. *Inhabitants of the Moon (3)*: *Speroid*: Alonzo Mortimer. *Apogee*: B. F. Sandford. *Gnomon*: Samuel Rogers. *Colossus*, the Guard who guards the King's only child: CHARLES FISHER. *Fido, Hector*, two guards who guard the Guard that guards the King's only child: R. Staples, Andrew Boyd. *Four Guards*, who guard the guards who guard the guard who guards the King's only child: *Vigo, Diago, Boro, Noro*: Messrs. O'Neill, Sherwood, Vincent, Davey. *Prince Caprice*, the Heir Apparent: VENIE CLANCY. *Princess Fantasy*, the King's only child: FLORENCE ELLIS. *Popette*, Queen of the Moon: BLANCHE MORTIMER. *Companions of Princess Fantasy (8)*: *Flamma*: Miss Glover. *Adja*: Miss Griffiths. *Microma*: Miss King. *Stella*: Miss Forest. *Phebe*: Miss Davenport. *Sidera*: Miss Wallace. *Nebulena*: Miss Poole. *Hyperba*: Miss Fiske. *Asphodel*, nurse to the King's only child: JENNIE HUGHES. *Courtiers, Mechanics at the Forge, Peasants, Citizens, Astronomers, Inhabitants of the Moon, Lunar Guards, Judges, Clerks, Jurymen.*

Ballet: Mlles. JOSEPHINE DeROSA, PALLADINO, MAURI, MASCARINA, MARIE GAUGAIN (Premières), ARNOLD KIRALFY (Grotesque Dancer), Coryphées, Corps de Ballet.

Act 1, Scene 1: The Garden of King Pin. *Scene 2*: The Observatory. *Scene 3*: The Royal Forge. (Fromont.) *Scene 4*: The Monster Gun.

Act 2, Scene 1: A City on the Moon. (Goatcher.) *Scene 2*: The Glass Palace of King Kosmos. (Robecchi.) *Scene 3*: The Mystic Park. *Scene 4*: Garden of the Lunar King. (Fromont and Johnson.)

Act 3, Scene 1: Apartments of the Princess Fantasy. *Scene 2*: Market-Place in the City of the Moon. *Scene 3*: The Regions of Snow.

Act 4, Scene 1: The Lunar Tribunal. *Scene 2*: The Crater. *Scene 3*: Eruption of the Volcano. *Scene 4*: The Silver City. Departure of the Flying Ship on a Voyage to the Earth.

BALLETS

Grand Ballet des Chimères (Act 2, Scene 4)
Mlles. DeRosa, Gaugain, Mauri, Mascarini, Grand Corps de Ballet
(*Composed and arranged by* Signor Mascagno, from La Scala, Milan.)

Grand Ballet de Neige (Act 3, Scene 3)
Mlle. Palladino, A. Kiralfy, Premières, Coryphées, Corps de Ballet

1877.16 LA JOLIE PARFUMEUSE!

A Revival of the Opéra-comique (The Pretty Perfumer) in Three Acts[69]. Original French libretto by Hector Crémieux and Ernest Blum. Music by Jacques Offenbach. Stage director and musical director, Jesse Williams. Produced by the Alice Oates Opera Company (Samuel Colville, Manager). Opened and closed 16 March 1877 at the Lyceum Theatre after 1 performance in repertory.[70]

CAST: *Rose Michon*, the Pretty Perfumer: ALICE OATES. *Clorinde*, Cocardière's wife: EME ROSEAU. *Julienne*: Mrs. JULIA CHAPMAN. *Justine*: Ella Caldwell. *Lise*:

---

[67]Musical numbers not listed in programs. List prepared from published French piano vocal score (Cho.udens, Père et Fils, Paris, 1875, Deuxieme edition). Mlle. Aimée also interpolated "La Paloma" (Spanish Song)

[68]First produced in New York 26 March 1868 at the Théâtre Français for 37 performances. For Synopsis of Scenes and Musical Numbers, see original 1868 production.

[69]English language premiere; adaptation uncredited. Previously produced in New York in French 31 March 1875 at the Lyceum Theatre.

[70]English adaptation uncredited; scenery and costumes uncredited in programs.

Rose Temple. *Arthemise*: Susie Winner. *Bavolet*, the bridegroom: CHARLES H. DREW. *Poirot*, his friend: HENRI LAURENT. *La Cocardière*, a grand gentleman: JOHN HOWSON. *Belfort*, a gardener: J. H. Jones. *Germain*, Cocardière's valet: A. W. Maflin. *Gaspard*: L. DeSmith. *Jean*: R. H. Nichols. *First Customer*: C. N. Decker. *Second Customer*: Ed. Horan. *Third Customer*: H. Amberg.

1877.17 MME. L'ARCHIDUC

A Revival of the Opéra-comique in Three Acts[71], in French. Libretto by Albert Millaud. Music by Jacques Offenbach. Musical director, Mr. Hepps. Stage manager, Charles Darby. Produced by Maurice Grau. Opened 19 March 1877 at the Eagle Theatre and closed 20 March 1877 after 2 performances in repertory.

CAST: *Marietta*: Mlle. MARIE AIMÉE. *Giletti*: *Comte*: *Comtesse*: *Archiduc Ernest*: Mons. DUPLAN. *Riccardo*: *Captain Fortunato*: Mons. DUPARC.

1877.18 LES DEMOISELLES DE MME. ANGOT

A Vaudeville (Opera) in One Act, in French[72]. (Libretto by Armand Jallais.) Musical director, Mr. Predigam. Stage manager, Charles Darcy. Produced by Maurice Grau. Opened and closed 23 March 1877 at the Eagle Theatre after 1 performance[73].

CAST: Mlle.FLORENCE DUPARC and Full Company.

1877.19 LA BELLE-POULE

An Opéra-bouffe (Opérette) in Three Acts, in French. Libretto by Hector Crémieux and Albert de Saint-Albin. Music by Hervé. Scenery by Charles Graham. Musical director, Mr. Predigam. Stage manager, Charles Darcy. Produced by Maurice Grau. Opened 27 March 1877 at the Eagle Theatre and closed 31 March 1877 after 3 performances in repertory.

CAST: *Poulette*: Mlle. MARIE AIMÉE. *Marchioness of Montembreche*: Mlle. ADELE DESIRÉE. *Foedora*: Mlle. BLANCHE GUEYMARD. *Amaranthe*: Mlle. Letellier. *Petit Pierre*: Mlle. Branciart. *A Peasant*: Mlle. Sophie Gherzi. *Thérèse*: Mlle. Marie Vandamme. *Noemie*: Mlle. Seygaud. *Babet*: Mlle. Angele. *Jacqueline*: Mlle. Marthe. *Poulet*: Mons. RAOULT. *Baron de Champignole*: Mons. REINE. *Jean Marcou*: Mons. DUPLAN. *Chevalier d'Aigrefille*: Mons. BRANCIART. *Les Maitres (4)*: *Professor of Music*: Mons. Ruiz. *Professor of French*: Mons. Perin. *Professor of Dancing*: Mons. Theophile. *Professor of Drawing*: Mons. Adorci. *Vincent*, a peasant: Mons. Benedic. *The Notary*: Mons. Benedic. *The Town Crier*: Mons. Girard. *Lafleur*, a valet: Mons. Perin. *Jasmin*: Mons. Davalis. *The Inn-Keeper*: Mons. Jolivet. *A Peasant*: Mons. Carpin. *Male and Female Peasants, Valets, Soubrettes, Guests, etc.*

Act 1: La grande place du village de Camarsac, aux environs de Bordeaux.

Act 2: Chez le baron de La Champignole

Act 3: Un salon chez la Marquise.

ACT 1[74]

Choeur (C'est la fête de Camarsac)

Chanson (Oui, j'suis l'coq du village)
Mons. Duplan, Choeur

Quatuor de chasse (Taratantarere! Taratantara!)
Messrs. Reine, Branciart, Mlles. Gueymard, Letellier

Couplets (Y'a des gens qui n'ont pas de chance)
Mons. Raoult

Choeur (Ohé! les amis!)
Mons. Raoult, Paysans, Mlle. M. Aimée

Duetto (Ne te mets pas martel en tête)
Mlle. Gueymard, Mons. Raoult

Romance (Tu lui diras que j'veux d'venir un homme)
Mons. Raoult

Choeur (Accourez, jeunes fillettes)
Choeur, Les Jeunes Filles, Les Valets, Les Professeurs, Les Paysans

Leçon (Au moulin de ma tante)
Mlles. Vandamme, Seygaud

Chanson du dragon (Savez-vous c'que c'est qu'un dragon du roi!)
Mlle. M. Aimée

La Lettre (Ma Belle Poul', faut que j'técrive)
Mons. Raoult

Finale (Baron, baron! quelle nouvelle!)

ACT 2

Choeur (Préparons, disposons tout pour cette fête)
Choeur, Les Soubrettes, Messrs. Perin, Reine

Rondeau (Je les reconnais au parfum)
Mons. Reine

Couplets (Salut à vous!—C'est moi, Baron!)
Mlle. Adele-Désirée

Valse (A la fête exquise)
Mlle. Gueymard

Choeur (La belle Polonaise)

Chanson Bordelaise (Au cun d'un boi)
M. Aimée, Choeur

Choeur (Salut au noble Espagnol)

Tyrolienne (Ie souis oun prince de Tolède!)[Je suis un Prince de Tolède]
Mons. Raoult, Choeur

Choeur (Ah? quel événement tragique)

Chanson (Madame, tout doit vous sourire)
Mlle. M. Aimée

Choeur (Quel vacarme on vient d'entendre!)

Finale (Quel bon tour! Quelle anecdote)

ACT 3

Introduction (On attend chez Mademoiselle)
Mons. Perin, Les Maitres

Chanson (Bonjour, messieurs, avancez-vous!)
Mlle. Adele-Désirée, Les Maitres

Menuet (Do, re, mi, sol, do, fa)
Mlle. M. Aimée

Duetto (J'm'suis laissé dir que l'Espagne)
Mlle. M. Aimée, Mons. Raoult

Couplets (Ce que tu fis en quittant ta Poulette)
Mlle. Gueymard

Choeur (Chère marquise, la famille)

Chanson (Le deux juin mil sept cent septante)
Mlle. M. Aimée

Couplet au Public (Je m'suis laissé dir que l'usage)
Mlle. M. Aimée, Chœur

1877.20 THE WONDER CHILD, or, The Follies of Earth, Air and Sea

A Genuine Novelty (Musical Spectacle) in Two Acts. Play by C. L. Graves. Music by George Loesch. Scenery by Henry E. Hoyt. Musical director, George Loesch. Produced by Joseph B. Ayres. Opened 30 April 1877 at the New Broadway Theatre and closed 16 May 1877 after 20 performances.

CAST: *Count Cleverboy*, the Wonder Child: STELLA BONIFACE. *Amanalina Woolstock*: FLORENCE LEVEAN. *Sculina Woolstock*: JENNIE GAWGER. *Birdina Woolstock*: ADELAIDE M. KEMBLE. *Princess Hildegarde*: Mlle. ELSE. *Baroness Woolstock*: Mrs. (Annie) YEAMANS. *Baron Woolstock*: JACQUES KRUGER. *Goodman*: THOMAS CHAPMAN. *Prince Bruino*: EDWARD CHAPMAN. *Prince Eaglino*: LEWIS [Louis] HARRISON. *Prince Dolphino*: Charles Howard. *Anglebrook*: Master EUNICE.

Harlequinade: *Clown*: JACQUES KRUGER. *Pantaloon*: THOMAS CHAPMAN. *Harlequin*: Master EUNICE. *Columbine*, with grand pas: Mlle. ELSE.

---

[71]First produced in New York in English 29 December 1874 at the Lyceum Theatre; in French 6 September 1875 at the Lyceum Theatre. For Synopsis of Scenes and Musical Numbers, see original 1875 production. No program found.

[72]Followed by the first two acts of LA BOULANGÈRE A DES ÉCUS.

[73]No program found.

[74]Musical numbers not listed in programs. List prepared from published French-English libretto from Aimée's Opéra Bouffe Company (Metropolitan Printing, New York, 1877).

Bears, Eagles, Dolphins, Monkeys, Mermaids, Frogs, Butterflies, Owls, Bats, Cranes, Cockles, Herons, Parrots, Magpies, Ravens, Swallows, Doves, Beetles, Guards, Banner-Bearers, Policemen, Ladies, Gentlemen, Hackmen, etc.

Scene: The Black Forest in Old Helvetia and the neighboring kingdom of Gallia, over a hundred years ago.

MUSICAL NUMBERS[75]

"Wonder Child Medley"
T. Chapman

"I See in Fear you Palpitate" (Solo)
E. Chapman

"To sell my Daughter to a Bird" (Duet)
J. Kruger, L. Harrison

"I'm a long-tailed Fish" (Solo)
C. Howard

"It's hard to lose a Meal" (Quartette)
S. Boniface, E. Chapman, J. Kruger, A. Yeamans

"It's follow my Leader" (Trio)
F. Levean, J. Gawger, A. M. Kemble

"Viva Count Woolstock"
S. Boniface, Solo and Grand Chorus

"Cheer up, my Sisters Dear" (Solo)
S. Boniface

"Trudging through the Wet and Dirt"
Invisible Chorus

"Softly Sleep" (a Lullaby Song)
F. Levean

"Brother Dear" (Trio)
S. Boniface, F. Levean, E. Chapman

"'Tis shameful thus to treat you" (Concerted Piece)
F. Levean, A. M. Kemble, J. Gawger, S. Boniface, E. Chapman, L. Harrison, C. Howard

"All Nature Rejoices"
Grand Chorus

[75]Musical numbers listed in separate program insert with plot synopsis, translated from the Armenian by Professor Hildergarde. Second week program included musical contents from the pantomime: "Romanga," "Wedding Bells," Tambourine Dance, "Let Me Dream Again," and "Les Ramaux" by Fauré.

1877–1878 SEASON

Lydia Thompson in ROBINSON CRUSOE (Photo: Mora)
Museum of the City of New York, Gift of J. D. Barton, 39.538.23

1877–1878 SEASON

EVANGELINE, or, The Belle of Acadia

1877.21

A Revival of the Musical Extravaganza in Three Acts[1]. Libretto by J. Cheever Goodwin. Music by Edward E. Rice. Scenery by J. Roberts, Charles W. Witham. Mechanism by Thomas Kelly. Properties and appointments by Robert Cutler. Lighting by J. C. Scollan. Orchestra under the direction of A. Rossner. Produced under the stage direction of Edward E. Rice. Produced by Augustin Daly. Opened 4 June 1877 at Daly's Fifth Avenue Theatre and closed 28 July 1877 after 56 performances.

CAST: *Gabriel*, our hero, a fascinating and perambulating young lover—in point of fact a roaming romeo: ELIZA WEATHERSBY. *LeBlanc*, a lawyer of the shyest shyster stamp, with a will and a way equally dark: NAT C. GOODWIN, JR. *The Lone Fisherman*, a patient and singularly taciturn toiler of the sea, with a natural tendency to hook whatever comes within his reach: HARRY HUNTER. *Captain Dietrich*, a Dutch mercenary in the British ranks, who shows no mercy, being a mercynary cuss: GEORGE S. KNIGHT. *Basil*, Evangeline's sire, whose vacillating mind is divided between the rental of her prospective husband and his own parental affection: M. C. DALY. *King Boorioboola*, royal proprietor of the Mid-African diamond fields, who, not being able to hear anything near, occupies an ear-trumpet: EDWIN S. TARR. *The Policeman*, sometimes called a Peeler, possibly because he was never known to heed an appeal a prisoner might make: Richard Golden. *Hans Wagner*, a spiritual corporal, with undue corporeal proportions: C. ROSENE. *The Jailor*, never without his key, vocal or instrumental, consequently always on the qui vive: Percy Vining. *Grab, Runemin*, a couple of the King's copper-colored Copps: H. R. Kropp, W. H. Singleton. *Ringbolt, Redshake*, a brace of conscientious deserters, who left their ship simply because they couldn't take it away with them: Messrs. RICHARD GOLDEN, HENRY E. DIXEY. *Lo*, the Poor Indian, the lowest and lonest savage of them all: James Nolan. *The Headsman*, not a mimic of stupid people, but very clever at taking off blockheads: S. M. Crane. *The Conductor*, though given to much punching, better acquainted with the P.R.R. than the P.R.: HENRY E. DIXEY. *Evangeline*, our heroine, a creature of impulse and an impetuous pet, pursued through love's impatient prompting by Gabriel, and with a view to edacious contingencies—by a whale: LIZZIE HARROLD. *Catherine*, the very mildest type of ante-nuptial mother-in-law—but wait: HARRY JOSEPHS. *Eulalie*, Evangeline's confidante, confidently hoping for women's rights: LIZZIE WEBSTER. *Queen Boorioboola Gha*, the King's much better adviser and supervisor of his whole conduct: Blanche Greene. *The Heifer*: Messrs. RICHARD GOLDEN, HENRY E. DIXEY. (*Sailors, Soldiers, Arcadian Peasants, Slaves, etc.*)

BLUE BEARD

1877.22

A Revival of the Burlesque in One Act[2]. Play rewritten and reconstructed by Henry B. Farnie. Stage manager, Willie Edouin. Scenery by Joseph Clare, Thomas Weston, J. Johnson, H. Isherwood. Appointments by F. Dorrington. Costumer, Mrs. Wilson. Musical director, Michael Connelly. Produced by the Lydia Thompson Company (Alexander Henderson, Proprietor; Samuel Colville, Manager). Opened 18 August 1877 at Wallack's Theatre and closed 25 August 1877 after 8 performances; season closed 29 September 1877.

CAST: *Selim*: LYDIA THOMPSON. *Blue Beard*: FREDERICK MARSHALL. *Corporal Zoug Zoug*, afterwards the Heathen Chinee: WILLIE EDOUIN. *Ibrahim*: Horatio Saker. *Fatima*: ALICE BURVILLE. *O'Shacabac*: ELLA CHAPMAN. *Hassan*: Marie Williams. *Sister Anne*: Lina Merville. *Fez*: Emily Duncan. *Zaid*: Kate Everleigh. *Beda*: Marion Elmore. *Pages, Peasants, etc.*: Misses Grey, Deacon, Lee Temple; Messrs. Amberg, Bohrer, Harper.

Act 1, Scene 1: Market-place in the Village of Latakia. (Clare.) *Scene 2*: The Zig-Zag Path to Castle Blue Beard. (Clare.)

Act 2, Scene 1: Grand Saloon in Blue Beard's Palace. (Weston, Johnson.) *Scene 2*: Portals of the Blue Chamber. (Isherwood.) *Scene 3*: Look-out Towers of Castle Blue Beard. (Weston.)

ACT 1
Scene 1
"Water Cold and Melons Rare" (Chorus of Peasants, Market People)
"Hail, Mighty Bashaw" (Grand Chorus)
Imposing Entrée of Blue Beard
"That's the Kind of Turk I Am" (Song and Chorus)
F. Marshall, Characters
"My Fatima, My Selim" (Duet)
L. Thompson, A. Burville
"Beat the Drum" (Chorus)
Scene 2
Duet and Dance
L. Thompson, W. Edouin
"Dreaming by Night" (Chorus of Pages)
"The Silver Moon is Winking" (Finale/Song, Chorus and Dance)

ACT 2
Scene 1
"Pool" (Song and Chorus)
M. Williams, Pages
"The Nightingale" (Song)
A. Burville
"Phillipopolis" (Song and Chorus)
L. Thompson, Characters
Duet, Chorus, Dance
L. Thompson, A. Burville, Characters
Scene 2
Song and Dance, with Banjo Accompaniment
E. Chapman
"Guide Me, Guide Me" (Duet)
L. Thompson, A. Burville
"Till We Meet Again" (Concerted Piece)
L. Thompson, Characters
Scene 3
"See see, this Stupid Key" (Song and Chorus)
Grand Finale
All the characters

OXYGEN!, or, Gas in Burlesque Metre

1877.23

A Burlesque in Two Acts, 3 Scenes. Play by Robert Reece and Henry B. Farnie. (Based on the opéra-bouffe "Dr. Ox" adapted from Jules Verne's novel of the same name.) Music by Jacques Offenbach, others as selected by Michael Connelly. Stage manager, Willie Edouin. Scenery by Joseph Clare, Thomas Weston and J. Johnston. Costumes by Mrs. Wilson, designed by Lydia Thompson. Appointments by F. Dorrington. Musical director, Michael Connolly. Produced by the Lydia Thompson Company (Alexander Henderson, Proprietor; Manager, Samuel Colville). Opened 27 August 1877 at Wallack's Theatre and closed 11 September 1877 after 16 performances; season closed 29 September 1877; returned 15 (matinee) December 1877 to the Eagle Theatre and closed 22 December 1877 after 9 additional performances[3]. Total: 25 performances.

CAST: *Prince Fritz* of Vergamen, on a reading tour with his tutor: LYDIA THOMPSON. *Hanserl, Otto*, his fellow students: Emily Duncan, Marie Williams. *Doctor Ox*, Professor of Chemistry at Göttingen: HORATIO SAKER. *Van Tricasse*, Burgomaster of Keekendone: FREDERICK MARSHALL. *Niclausse*, Leader of the Council: William Forrester. *Franz*, his son, betrothed to Suzel: WILLIE EDOUIN. *Tarantula*, Manager of the Opera House, Keekendone: ELLA CHAPMAN. *Van Blazen*, herald from Virgamen: KATE EVERLEIGH. *Clerk to the Council*: H. Amberg. *Suzel*, the Burgomaster's daughter: ALICE BURVILLE. *Lottchen, Gretelien*, her friends: LINA MERVILLE, MARION ELMORE. *Hermance*, her Gouvernante: ALICE ATHERTON. *Citizens, Citizenesses, Councillors, Pages, Students, etc.*

Act 1: Public Square and Town Hall of Keekendone. (Clare.)

Act 2, Scene 1: Laboratory of Dr. Ox. (Weston, Johnson.) *Scene 2*: Banqueting Room in the Town Hall. (Clare.)

---

[1]First produced in New York 27 July 1874 at Niblo's Garden for 16 performances. For Synopsis of Scenes and Musical Numbers, see original 1874 production.

[2]Preceded by a comedietta "Orange Blossoms" by J. P. Wooler Beginning 20 August 1877, Orange Blossoms was dropped, and BLUE BEARD expanded to Two Acts. Scene and song list reflects the two act version; cast list remained unchanged.

[3]Principal cast changes for the return: *Prince Fritz*: MARIE WILLIAMS. *Suzel*: EME ROSEAU.

ACT 1

"The Council Wise are coming here" (Chorus of Keekendoners)

"Not a Word, Sir!" (Concerted Piece)
E. Chapman, F. Marshall, W. Edouin, W. Forrester, Chorus

"We never smile, we never play" (Concerted Piece)
Keekendone Maidens, Virgamen Students

"We're all noddin'" (Duet)
L. Thompson, A. Burville

"My Oxygen" (Song and Chorus)
H. Saker, Students

Song and Dance
E. Chapman

"Let us now, with tranquil joy" (Finale)
All the characters

ACT 2
Scene 1

"Swell Song"[4] (Song)
L. Thompson

"All is prepared, the Gas is on" (Solo and Chorus)
L. Thompson, Students

Scene 2

"You're Another" (Concerted Piece)
F. Marshall, W. Forrester, Burghers

"Awfully Awful" (Trio)
A. Atherton, F. Marshall, W. Forrester

Dutch Trio and Wooden Dance
L. Thompson, E. Chapman, W. Edouin

"I am Complete" (Solo)
A. Burville

"A toast, a toast" (Concerted Piece) and Grand Finale

1877.24

OLD LAVENDER

A Moral Drama in Three Acts, 11 Scenes[5]. Play (and lyrics) by Edward Harrigan. Incidental music by David Braham. (Staged by Edward Harrigan.) Scenery by R. L. Weed. Costumes by Kittie Devoe. Properties by G. W. Burnton. Mechanical effects by James Gifford[6] Musical director, David Braham. Produced by Edward Harrigan and Tony Hart. Opened 3 September 1877 at the Theatre Comique and closed 8 September after 8 performances; returned 22 April 1878 to the Theatre Comique and closed 27 April 1878 after 8 additional performances; returned 26 August 1878 to the Theatre Comique and closed 31 August 1878 after an additional 8 performances. Total: 24 performances.[7]

CAST: *George Coggswell*, afterwards Old Lavender: EDWARD HARRIGAN. *Dick*, the Rat: TONY HART. *Paul Cassin*: Frank A. Blackburn. *Philip Coggswell*: F. CHIPPENDALE. *John Filbert*: T. F. Egberts. *Smoke*: BILLY GRAY. *Danvers*: Harry Stuart. *Captain McKenna*: Ed Burt. *Dan Driscoll*: H. A. Lee. *Pop Jones*: G. W. H. Griffin. *Jack Dingle*: Harry Marsh. *Servant*: John Kline. *Laura Coggswell*: ANNIE MACK. *Sallie Stacy*: MILLIE SACKETT. *Mrs. Crawford*: ANNIE YEAMANS.

CAST for April return: *George Coggswell*, afterwards Old Lavender: EDWARD HARRIGAN. *Dick*, the Rat, a Waif: TONY HART. *Paul Cassin*: O. H. Barr. *Philip Coggswell*: WELSH EDWARDS. *John Filbert*: James F. Crossen. *Smoke*: J. H. BURNETT. *Pop Jones*: Alfred Beverly. *Captain McKenna*: Ed Burt. *Dan Driscoll*: John Mealey. *Danvers*: G. W. H. Griffin. *Jack Dingle*: Michael Bradley. *Servant*: Michael Bradley. *Laura Coggswell*: ELIZA GLASSFORD. *Sally Stacy*: NELLIE JONES. *Mrs. Crawford*: ANNIE YEAMANS.

CAST for August return: *George Coggswell*, afterwards Old Lavender: EDWARD HARRIGAN. *Dick*, the Rat, a Waif: TONY HART. *Philip Coggswell*, a Banker: WELSH EDWARDS. *Paul Cassin*: Ed Burt. *John Filbert*: Harry A. Fisher. *Smoke*, a Negro dog speculator: JOHN H. BURNETT. *Pop Jones*, Proprietor of a Cafe: Billy Gray. *Danvers*, Clerk in Coggswell's Bank: Michael Bradley. *Captain McKenna* of the Police: J. F. Shields. *Servant*: George Brewster. *Laura Coggswell*: ELIZA GLASSFORD. *Mother Crawford*: ANNIE YEAMANS. *Sally Stacy*: JENNIE YEAMANS.

Act 1, Scene 1: Parlour in a New York Hotel. *Scene 2*: Wall Street. *Scene 3*: The Banking House of Philip Coggswell.

Act 2, Scene 1: Three years later. The Brooklyn Ferry by Night. Old Pop Jones' Coffee and Cake Saloon. *Scene 2*: The Albany Boat Pier. *Scene 3*: The Home of Old Lavender and the Rat.

Act 3. Scene 1: The Stranger's Rest. *Scene 2*: River front. *Scene 3*: The Interview—Citizen to Citizen. Man to Man. *Scene 4*: Wall Street. *Scene 5*: Final Scene of the Drama. The Robbery.

SPECIALTY

College Days, an original vocal characterization (Act 2, Scene 3)
E. Harrigan

1877.25

ROBINSON CRUSOE

A Burlesque in Two Acts, 6 Scenes. Play by Henry B. Farnie. (Music, original and selected, by Michael Connolly. Suggested by the novel of the same name by Daniel Defoe.) Stage manager, Willie Edouin. Scenery by Joseph Clare, Thomas Weston and J. Johnston. Appointments by F. Dorrington. Costumes by Mrs. Wilson. Musical director, Michael Connolly. Produced by the Lydia Thompson Company (Alexander Henderson, Proprietor; Manager, Samuel Colville.). Opened 12 September 1877 at Wallack's Theatre and closed 29 September 1877 after 19 performances; returned 12-20 November, 10-14 December 1877 to the Eagle Theatre for 14 additional performances. Total: 33 performances.

CAST: *Robinson Crusoe*: LYDIA THOMPSON. *Jim Cox*: FREDERICK MARSHALL. *Polly Hopkins*: ALICE BURVILLE. *Angelica*: ELLA CHAPMAN.

Pirates: *Will Atkins*: H. Saker. *Gig*: Marie Williams. *Binnacle*: Kate Everleigh. *Dib*: Rose Leighton. *Tib*: Bessie Temple. *Slider*: Lavinia Hogan. *Kapstan*: Miss C. Foster. *Ropeyarn*: Ada Lee. *Tarr*: Annie Winner. *Pitch*: Susie Winner. *Rosin*: Jennie White. *Oh-Kum*: Addie Deacon.

Indians: *Friday*: WILLIE EDOUIN. *Queen Ylang-Ylang*: ALICE ATHERTON. *Jesso*, her page: MARION ELMORE. *Wai-ho*: W. Forrester. *O-pop-o-nax*: Emily Duncan. *O-wy-o-wy*: J. Peck. *Latitat*: H. Amberg. *The Two Obadiahs*: Bohrer and Decker.

Act 1: Seaport at Hull. (Clare.)

Act 2, Scene 1: Sacred Grove of the Indians. (Johnston.) *Scene 2*: Tropical Island and Crusoe's Detached Villa. *Scene 3*: The Mystic Grove. *Scene 4*: The Jungle. (Johnston, Weston.) *Scene 5*: The Bay of Palms. (Johnston.)

ACT 1

"A Sale, a Sale" (Opening Chorus of Villagers, Jew Peddlers)

"Oh, what a row" (Concerted Piece)
L. Thompson, F. Marshall, M. Williams, E. Chapman

"My Love Serves in a Candy Shop" (Song and Chorus)
M. Williams, Pirates

"Punch in the Presence of the Passengaire" (Song and Chorus)
H. Saker, Pirates

Mixed Conspirators' Chorus
L. Thompson, F. Marshall

"Pretty Polly Hopkins" (Quartette à la Marionette)
L. Thompson, A. Burville, F. Marshall, E. Chapman

"Farewell Forever" (Quartette)
L. Thompson, A. Burville, F. Marshall, E. Chapman

"The Bird That Came in Spring" (Solo)
A. Burville

"All's Said, the Anchor's Weighed" (Finale)
All the Characters

ACT 2
Scene 1

"Kickapoo"Quartette
A. Atherton, E. Duncan, W. Forrester, M. Elmore

"Keep It Dark" (Concerted Piece)
H. Saker, M. Williams, A. Burville, E. Chapman, Pirates

"Some Girls Do" (Song and Dance)
E. Chapman

"Hail to Thee, Great Chief!" (Grand Chorus of Indians)

[4]Replaced during the run by "On the Strict Q.T," sung by Lydia Thompson.

[5]Previously presented as the final "end-piece" to program of variety and burlesque, as OLD LAVENDER WATER, or, Round the Docks, in One Act, Seven Scenes, 16-30 April 1877 at the Theatre Comique for 16 performances.

[6]For April return, credited to J. J. O'Reilly.

[7]No musical numbers listed in program. In Act 2, Scene 3, Messrs. Harrigan and Hart will render their original vocal characterization, "College Days." For August 1878 engagement, a new song performed by Edward Harrigan was added to Act 3, Scene 1: "Old 49."

Scene 2
Double Song and Dance
"Phillipopolis" (Song and Chorus)
L. Thompson, Characters
"Rum, Rum, Give Us Rum" (Chorus of Indians)
"Jeremiah, Blow the Fire" (Song and Chorus)
L. Thompson, Indians
"Through the Jungles Strong" (Grand Ensemble)
All the Characters
Scene 5
"Oh, Woman Is a Madcap" (Concerted Piece)
A. Burville, E. Chapman, H. Saker, Pirates
The Trial
Grand Finale (Robinson Crusoe thanks you kindly)
All the characters

1877.26 LA PETITE MARIÉE

A Revival of the Opéra-comique in Three Acts[8], in French. Libretto by Eugène Leterrier and Albert Vanloo. Music by Charles Lecocq. Stage manager, Charles Darcy. Costumes by Landolff, of Paris. Leader of orchestra, Charles Almeras. Produced by Marie Aimée's French Opéra Bouffe Company; presented by James C. Duff. Opened 12 September 1877 at Booth's Theatre and closed 15 September 1877 after 3 performances in repertory.

CAST: *Graziella*: Mlle. MARIE AIMÉE. *Lucrézia*: Mlle. ADELE DÉSIRÉE. *Teobaldo*: Mlle. BLANCHE GUEYMARD. *Beatrix*: Mlle. FLORENCE DUPARC. *San Carlo*: Mons. MOLLARD. *Il Podestate*: Mons. JOUARD. *Montefiascone*: Mons. DUPLAN. *Castel Demoli*: Mons. J. MEZIÈRES. *Beppo*: Mons. CASTEL. *A Dumb Man*: Mons. Davalis. *An Unknown Man*: Mons. Gerard. *An Unknown Woman*: Mlle. Sophie Gherzi.

1877.27 LA FILLE DE MADAME ANGOT

A Revival of the Opéra-comique in Three Acts[9], in French. Libretto by Clairville, Paul Siraudin and Victor Koning. Music by Charles Lecocq. Stage manager, Charles Darcy. Leader of orchestra, Charles Almeras. Produced by Marie Aimée's French Opera Bouffe Company; presented by James C. Duff. Opened 14 September 1877 at Booth's Theatre; season closed 29 September 1877 after 4 performances in repertory; returned 25 October 1877 to the Broadway Theatre for 1 performance; returned 5 December 1877 to Booth's Theatre for 1 performance in repertory; returned 9, 23-24 May 1878 to the Park Theatre for 3 performances; season closed 25 May 1878.

CAST[10]: *Clairette*: Mlle. MARIE AIMÉE. *Mlle. Lange*: Mlle. MARTAL. *Amaranthe*: Mlle. Adele Désirée. *Javotte*: Mlle. Adriene. *Cydalise*: Mlle. Duplessis. *Hersilie*: Mlle. Marie Vandamme. *Delaunay*: Mlle. Alphonsine. *Therese*: Mlle. Sophie Gherzi. *Herbelin*: Mlle. Seygaud. *Babet*: Mlle. Joly. *Ange Pitou*: Mons. MOLLARD. *Pomponnet*: Mons. LEGROS. *Larivaudière*: Mons. JOUARD. *Trenitz*: Mons. Hayme. *Louchard*: Mons. DUPLAN. *Cadet*: Mons. Davalis. *Buteux*: Mons. Girard. *Guillaume*: Mons. Mauriez. *Un Officier*: Mons. Jolivet. *Un Incroyable*: Mons. Salvator.

1877.28 STRUCK OIL

An American Drama in Three Acts, 9 Scenes[11]. Play by Samuel W. Smith. Scenery by Richard Marston. Opened 17 September 1877 at the Union Square Theatre and closed 27 October 1877 after 42 performances; returned 11-23 February 1878 to the Grand Opera House for an additional 16 performances; returned 15-21 April 1878 to the Grand Opera House for an additional 8 performances. Total this season: 66 performances.

CAST: *John Stofel*, a Pennsylvania Dutchman: J. C. WILLIAMSON. *Eben Skinner*, the Deacon: H. A. WEAVER. *Sergeant Flynn*, afterward Judge: J. G. SULLIVAN. *Doctor Pearson*: J. G. Peakes. *Corporal Sharp*: SOL SMITH. *Captain Becks*, Officer of the Day: J. W. Thorpe. *Billy Patterson*, a young Hoodlum: Master Kilday. *Pete Rowley*: WH. W. Wilkes. *Sheriff*: Lysander Thompson. *Lizzie Stofel*, daughter of John Stofel: MAGGIE MOORE [Mrs. J. C. Williamson]. *Susan Stofel*, her stepmother: Mrs. SOL SMITH.

Act 1, Scene 1: Interior of John Stofel's house and shop. *Scene 2*: A country landscape.

Act 2, Scene 1: A room in John Stofel's house. *Scene 2*: A Camp on the Banks of the River opposite Pittsburgh, with a view of the city at night. *Scene 3*: A Country Landscape. *Scene 4*: The Guard Room of the Volunteers' Camp.

Act 3, Scene 1: Oilsburg, with its Oil Wells, Derricks, etc. *Scene 2*: A Street in Oilsburg. *Scene 3*: John Stofel's Old House.

MUSICAL NUMBERS[12]
"Don't Make Me Laugh"
(*Music and Lyrics by* G. W. Hunt.)
"Pretty Wilhelmina"
(*Music and Lyrics by* G. W. Hunt.)
"Shoener Charley"
"Lizzie's Farewell"

1877.29 LA JOLIE PARFUMEUSE

A Revival of the Opéra-comique in Three Acts[13], in French. Libretto by Hector Crémieux and Ernest Blum. Music by Jacques Offenbach. Stage manager, Charles Darcy. Leader of orchestra, Charles Almeras. Produced by Marie Aimée's French Opéra Bouffe Company (Maurice Grau, Manager). Opened 17 September 1877 at Booth's Theatre and closed 29 September 1877 after 5 performances in repertory; returned 20 October 1877 to the Broadway Theatre for 1 additional performance; returned 20 December 1877 to the Lyceum Theatre for 1 additional performance; returned 8 May 1878 at the Park Theatrefor 1 additional performance; returned 7 June 1878 to Booth's Theatre for 1 additional performance. Total: 9 performances.

CAST[14]:*Rose Michon*: Mlle. MARIE AIMÉE. *Bavolet*: Mlle. FLORENCE DUPARC. *Clorinde*: Mlle. Blanche Gueymard. *La Julienne*: Mlle. Adele Désirée. *Arthemise*: Mlle. Sophie Guerzi. *Madelon*: Mlle. Adrienne. *Justine*: Mlle. Marie Vandamme. *Lise*: Mlle. Leygand. *Poirot*: Mons. Mollard. *La Cocardière*: Mons. Castel. *Germain*: Mons. Gerard. *First Waiter*: Mons. Davalis. *Second Waiter*: Mons. Jolivet.

1877.30 LA BELLE HÉLÈNE

A Revival of the Opéra-bouffe in Three Acts[15], in French. Libretto by Henri Meilhac and Ludovic Halévy. Music by Jacques Offenbach. Stage manager, Charles Darcy. Leader of orchestra, Charles Almeras. Produced by Marie

---

[8]First produced in New York 6 February 1877 at the Eagle Theatre for 9 performances in repertory. For Synopsis of Scenes and Musical Numbers, see original 1877 production.
[9]First produced in New York in French 25 August 1873 at the Broadway Theatre. For Synopsis of Scenes and Musical Numbers, see original 1873 production.
[10]Cast list prepared from Park Theatre engagement; no programs found for the earlier engagements.
[11]Added to the evening as a curtain raiser beginning 20 October, was 'The Chinese Question,' a sketch by Clay M. Greene. CAST: *Billy*, a Chinese butcher: J. C. WILLIAMSON. *Kitty McShane*, a domestic: MAGGIE MOORE. *Sam Se Le*, a Chinese girl: MAGGIE MOORE. *Mr. Freewill*, a philanthropist: H. A. WEAVER. *Fred Contrast*: J. G. SULLIVAN. *Harry Clarkson*: J. G. Peakes. *Mrs. Freewill*: Mrs. Sol Smith. *Nelly Freewill*: Clara Rainford. Maggie Moore sang her song "Larry Malone." On tour, the play was advertised with a subtitle: Struck Oil!, or The Pennsylvania German. On tour, Maggie Moore also sang two additional songs by G. W. Hunt: "Sweeter Than Marmalade" and "Nice Young Man," replacing "Shoener Charley" and " Lizzie's Farewell."
[12]All musical numbers performed by Maggie Moore, not necessarily in performance order.
[13]First produced in New York in French 31 March 1875 at the Lyceum Theatre. For Synopsis of Scenes and Musical Numbers, see original 1875 production.
[14]Cast list prepared from Park Theatre engagement; no program found for earlier engagements.
[15]First produced in New York in French 26 March 1868 at the Théâtre Français for 37 performances. For Synopsis of Scenes and Musical Numbers, see original 1868 production.

Aimée's French Opéra Bouffe Company (Maurice Grau, Manager). Opened 21 September 1877 at Booth's Theatre and closed 27 September 1877 after 4 performances in repertory; returned 29 October 1877 to the Broadway Theatre for 1 additional performance; returned 22 May 1878 to the Park Theatre for 1 performance.

CAST: *Hélène*, Queen of Sparta: Mlle. MARIE AIMÉE. *Orestes*, Son of Agamemnon: Mlle. FLORENCE DUPARC. *Parthoenis, Leona*, Women of Corinth: Mlles. Blanche Gueymard, Sophie Gherzi. *Bacchis*, attendant on Hélène: Mlle. Marie Vandamme. *Paris*, Son of King Priam: Mons. MOLLARD. *Ménelas*, King of Sparta: Mons. DUPLAN. *Agamemnon*, King of Greece: Mons. JOUARD. *Calchas*, Grand Augur of Jupiter: Mons. J. MEZIÈRES. *Achille*, King of Phtiotis: Mons. Legros. *Ajax I*, King of Salamine: Mons. Hayme. *Ajax II*, King of Locria: Mons. Salvator. *Philocome*, Servant to Calchas: Mons. Adorcy. *Euthecles*, Blacksmith: Mons. Gerard. *Guests, Slaves, the Populace, etc.*

1877.31 LA BOULANGÈRE A DES ÉCUS

A Revival of the Opéra Bouffe (The Rich Bakeress) in Three Acts, in French[16]. Libretto by Henri Meilhac and Ludovic Halévy. Music by Jacques Offenbach. Stage manager, Charles Darcy. Leader of orchestra, Charles Almeras. Produced by Marie Aimée's French Opéra Bouffe Company (Maurice Grau, Manager). Opened 24 September 1877 at Booth's Theatre and closed 26 September 1877 after 3 performances in repertory.[17]

French Opéra Bouffe Company included Mlles. MARIE AIMÉE, BERTHE MARIO, FLORENCE DUPARC, Blanche Gueymard, Adele Désirée, Sophie Gherzi, Marie Vandamme, Mlles. Duplessis, Adrienne; Messrs. MOLLARD, JOUARD, DUPLAN, J. MEZIÈRES, Legros, Castel, Hayne, Davalis. Chorus of 36. Orchestra of 25.

1877.32 LA MARJOLAINE

An Opéra-comique in Three Acts, in French[18]. Libretto by Albert Vanloo and Eugène Leterrier. Music by Charles Lecocq. Stage manager, Charles Darcy. Scenery by Messrs. Arrigoni and De La Harpe. Costumes by Landolff & Millet (Paris). Properties and accessories by Halle (Paris). Leader of orchestra, Charles Almeras. Produced by Marie Aimée's French Opéra Bouffe Company (Maurice Grau, Manager). Opened 1 October 1877 at the Broadway Theatre and closed 13 October 1877 after 14 performances; returned 26 October, 2 November 1877 to the Broadway Theatre for 2 additional performances; returned 3 December 1877 to Booth's Theatre for 2 performances in repertory; returned 21 December 1877 to the Lyceum Theatre for 1 performance; returned 3-4 May 1878 to the Park Theatre for 3 performances; returned 5 June 1878 to Booth's Theatre for 1 additional performance. Total this season: 23 performances.

CAST: *La Marjolaine*: Mlle. MARIE AIMÉE. *Aveline*: Mlle. FLORENCE DUPARC. *Petrus*: Mlle. Marie Vandamme. *Karl*: Mlle. De LaFontaine. *Christian*: Mlle. Duplessis. *Robert*: Mlle. Alphonsine. *Christophe*: Mlle. Mollard. *Franz*: Mlle. Julien. *A Maiden*: Mme. Salvator. *Gudule*: Mlle. Sophie Gherzi. *A Peasant Woman*: Mlle. Joly. *Palamède Van Der Boom*: Mons. J. MEZIÈRES. *Annibal de L'Estrapade*: Mons. JOUARD. *Frickel*: Mons. MOLLARD. *Péterschop*: Mons. DUPLAN. *D'Escoublac*: Mons. SALVATOR. *Schaerbeck*: Mons. HAYME. *A Town Crier*: Mons. Girard. *Two Aldermen, Peasant Men and Women, Servants, etc.*

Act 1: A Public Square in Brussels. Flanders, Sixteenth century.

Act 2: The Home of Van Der Boom.

Act 3: (A villa) At Boisfort, near Brussels.

ACT 1[19]

"Bourgeoises et bourgeois" (Choeur de Bourgeois)

"Mes amis, ju vous remercie" (Entrée de Burgomaster)

"Baissant les yeux modestement" (Choeur des jeunes filles)

"Jeunes, filles, selon l'usage" (Couplets de la Médaille)

"Vois-tu, j'ai le coeur trop sensible" (Couplets d'Aveline)
Mlle. F. Duparc

"Pendant que vous dormiez encore" (Rondeau des Blés)
Mlle. M. Aimée

"Dix est un chiffre rond" (Couplets de Palamède)
Mons. J. Mezières

"Ah! comme il était détraqué!" (Air du Carillon)
Mlle. F. Duparc, Messrs. Mollard, Duplan

"Je ne suis plus la Marjolaine" (Duo des Adieux)
Mlle. M. Aimée, Mons. Mollard

"Ils sont ici!" (Morceau d'ensemble)/

"Nous sommes consternées" (Choeur des maris)
Mlle. F. Duparc, Mons. Duplan, Chorus

"Il est précis, il est concis" (Chant de guerre)
Messrs. Salvator, Hayme, Jouard, Sopranos

"Permets qu'ici je te présente" (Présentation)/

"L'aventure est surprenante" (Ensemble)/

"Accourons tous, dépêchons-nous!" (Choeur)/

"Elle a la médaille" (Final)
Principals, Chorus

ACT 2

"Ah! compére, le gai festin!" (Choeur dans la coulisse)
Chorus

"Allons! venez çà, la fillette!" (Duo)
Mlle. F. Duparc, Mons. Mollard

Morceau d'Ensemble
Messrs. J. Mezières, Salvator, Hayme, Jouard, Chorus

"Magu'lonne allant à la fontaine" (Chanson de Maguelonne)
Mlle. M. Aimée

"Monsieur, monsieur, je vous en prie!" (Duo de la déclaration)
Mlle. M. Aimée, Mons. Jouard

"Voice l'heure du couvre-feu" (Ensemble du couvre-feu)
Mlle. M. Aimée, Chorus

"Je sens se fermer ma paupière" (Trio du deshabillée)
Mlles. M. Aimée, F. Duparc, Mons. Jouard

"Un mari semblable mérite" (Couplets de la vengeance)
Mlle. M. Aimée, Mons. Mollard

"A l'heure où s'unissent tremblants" (Couplets de l'invraisemblance)
Mons. Jouard

"Ciel! quel spectacle imprévu!" (Choeur)/

"Monsieur, comment êtes-vous chez ma femme" (Scène)

"Ah! vraiment! mon pauvre mari!" (Couplets du rire)
Principals, Chorus

ACT 3

"La nouveau propriétaire" (Choeur)/

"Ohé! ohé! les camarades!" (Choeurs des jeunes gens)
Mons. Jouard, Chorus

"Avril ramène les beaux jours" (Couplets du printemps)
Mons. Jouard

"C'est mon livret" (Ensemble et couplets du signalement)
Messrs. J. Mezières, Hayme, Salvator, Duplan, Jouard, Sopranos

"Il me grondait, il me brusquait" (Couplets des regrets)
Mlle. F. Duparc

"Coucous! coucous!" (Couplets des coucous)

Mlle. M. Aimée, Mons. Mollard, Chorus

"Ah! plaignez la misère" (Complainte)
Mlle. M. Aimée

"Et pourtant, quel rêve enchanteur" (Duo)
Mlle. M. Aimée, Mons. Jouard

"Avant de nous mettre en ménage" (Final)
Mlle. M. Aimée, Chorus

1877.33 GIROFLÉ-GIROFLA

A Revival of the Opéra-bouffe in Three Acts[20], in French. Libretto by Albert Vanloo and Eugène Leterrier. Music by Charles Lecocq. Stage manager,

[16]First produced in New York 26 February 1877 at the Eagle Theatre for 5 performances in repertory. For Synopsis of Scenes and Musical Numbers, see original 1877 production.

[17]No program found.

[18]Produced and published in France as an opéra bouffe.

[19]Musical numbers not listed in programs. List prepared from published French piano vocal score (Brandus & Cie., Paris, 1877).

[20]First produced in New York in French 4 February 1875 at the Park Theatre for (46) performances in repertory. For Synopsis of Scenes and Musical Numbers, see original 1875 production.

Charles Darcy. Leader of orchestra, Charles Almeras. Produced by Marie Aimée's French Opéra Bouffe Company (Maurice Grau, Manager). Opened 15 October 1877 at the Broadway Theatre; season closed 3 November 1877 after 4 performances in repertory; returned 6 December 1877 to Booth's Theatre for 1 additional performance in repertory; returned 7 May 1878 to the Park Theatre for 1 performance, 10 June 1878 to Booth's Theatre for 1 additional performance. Total: (10) performances.

CAST: *Giroflé, Girofla*: Mlle. MARIE AIMÉE. *Aurore*: Mlle. ADELE DÉSIRÉE. *Pedro*: Mlle. FLORENCE DUPARC. *Paquita*: Mlle. BLANCHE GUEYMARD. *Marasquin*: Mlle. BERTHE MARIO. *Don Boléro*: Mons. DUPLAN. *Mourzouk*: Mons. JOUARD. *Chief of the Pirates*: Mons. DeSmith. *Le Parrain*: Mons. Salvator. *Le Danseur*: Mons. Hayme. *Le Notaire*: Mons. Bageard. *Le Precepteur*: Mons. Gerard. *Le Garçon d'Honneur*: Mons. Davalis. *L'Oncle*: Mons. Mauriez. *Gusman*: Mons. Vandamme. *Fernand*: Mons. Alphonsine. *Almanazar*: Mons. Gherzi. *Pirates, Moors, Peasants, Cousins, Lords, Followers, etc.*

1877.34 LA GRANDE-DUCHESSE DE GÉROLSTEIN

A Revival of the Opéra-comique in Three Acts[21] , in French. Libretto by Henri Meilhac and Ludovic Halévy. Music by Jacques Offenbach. Stage manager, Charles Darcy. Leader of orchestra, Charles Almeras. Produced by Marie Aimée's French Opéra Bouffe Company (Maurice Grau, Manager). Opened 16 October 1877 at the Broadway Theatre; season closed 3 November 1877 after (4) performances in repertory; returned 16 May 1878 to the Park Theatre for 1 additional performance.

CAST: *La Grande-Duchesse de Gérolstein*: Mlle. MARIE AIMÉE. *Fritz*: Mons. MOLLARD. *General Boum*: Mons. JOUARD. *Baron Puck*: Mons. J. MEZIÈRES. *Prince Paul*: Mons. LEGROS. *Baron Grog*: Mons. SALVATOR. *Nepomuc*: Mons. Hayme. *Wanda*: Mlle. BLANCHE GUEYMARD. *Iza*: Mlle. Duplessis. *Olga*: Mlle. Sophie Gherzi. *Charlotte*: Mlle. Marie Vandamme. *Noemi*: Mlle. Alphonsine. *Soldiers, Maids of Honor, etc.*

1877.35 THE BOHEMIAN GIRL

A Revival of the Light Opera in Three Acts[22]. Libretto by Alfred Bunn, after Jules-Henri Vernoy de Saint-Georges' ballet-pantomime "The Gypsy." Music by Michael William Balfe. Director, C. D. Hess. Costumes and appointments by Millett, Paris. Conductor, Signor Giuseppe Operti. Produced by the C. D. Hess Opera Company. Opened 19 October 1877 at the Fifth Avenue Theatre and closed 30 October 1877 after 5 performances in repertory.

CAST: *Arline*: EMELIE MELVILLE. *The Gipsy Queen*: ZELDA SEGUIN. *Buda*: Mrs. C. B. Buch. *Thaddeus*: WILLIAM CASTLE. *Count Arnheim*: Henry Peakes. *Devilshoof*: EDWARD SEGUIN. *Florestein*: Tom Whiffen. *Captain of the Guard*: Frank Tams. *Full Chorus.*

1877.36 THE CHIMES OF NORMANDY

An Opéra-comique in Three Acts. (Original French libretto 'Les Cloches de Corneville' by Clairville and Charles Gabet.) English adaptation by Myron A. Cooney. Music by Robert Planquette. Director, C. D. Hess. Costumes and appointments by Millett, Paris. Conductor, Signor Giuseppe Operti. Produced by the C. D. Hess Opera Company. Opened 22 October 1877 at the Fifth Avenue Theatre and closed 10 November 1878 after 16 performances in repertory.[23]

CAST: *Mignonette*, a Waif: EMILIE MELVILLE. *Germaine*, the Lost Heiress: ZELDA SEGUIN. *Gertrude*, an inveterate gossip: Louise Searle. *The Marquis de Villeroi*, an exile: WILLIAM CASTLE. *Gaspard*, a miser: CHARLES MORTON. *Robin More*, an unlucky lover: C. H. Turner. *The Sheriff*: EDWIN SEGUIN. *The Notary*: J. J. Benitz.

MUSICAL NUMBERS[24]

"Song of the Cabin Boy"
"Now If You Listen to My Story"
"A Charming Little Maiden"
"One Day I Caught a Fish"
"How Can I Thoughts Express"
"I'm in a Pretty Pickle"
"Let's Shut Our Eyes"
"We Must Never Let Our Hearts"
"Knights of Old"
"Legend of the Bells"
"Of All the Fruits"
"In Your Haunted Castle"
"I Am a Rover of the Sea"
"They Say That Pretty Jennie"
"When I Am by His Side"

1877.37 LE PETIT FAUST

A Revival of the Opéra-bouffe in Three Acts[25], in French. Libretto by Hector Crémieux and Adolphe Jaime. Music by Hervé. Stage manager, Charles Darcy. Leader of orchestra, Charles Almeras. Produced by Marie Aimée's French Opéra Bouffe Company (Maurice Grau, Manager). Opened 22 October 1877 at the Broadway Theatre closed 27 October 1877 after 4 performances in repertory.

CAST: *Marguerite*: Mlle. MARIE AIMÉE. *Méphisto*: Mlle. BERTHE MARIO. *Faust*: Mons. MOLLARD. *Valentine*: Mons. J. MEZIÈRES. *A Coachman*: Mons. Duplan. *A Schoolmaster*: Mons. Hayme. *An Anglo-Saxon*: Mons. Salvator.

Female Pupils (8): *Lisette*: Mlle. Blanche Gueymard. *Aglae*: Mlle. Sophie Gherzi. *Clorinde*: Mlle. Marie Vandamme. *Frosch*: Mlle. Salvator. *Charlotte*: Mlle. Jouard. *Lischen*: Mlle. Duplesis. *Dorothée*: Mlle. Julien. *Agnes*: Mlle. Joly. *Male Pupils (6)*: *Siebel*: Mlle. LaFontaine. *Franz*: Mlle. Mollard. *Fritz*: Mlle. Louise. *Wagner*: Mlle. Julien. *Altmayer*: Mlle. Seygaud. *Brander*: Mlle. Alphonsine. *Soldiers, Students, Old Men and Women, Anglo-Saxons, Russians, Male and Female Demons.*

1877.38 BARBE BLEUE

A Revival of the Opéra-bouffe in Four Acts[26], in French. Libretto by Henri Meilhac and Ludovic Halévy. Music by Jacques Offenbach. Stage manager, Charles Darcy. Leader of orchestra, Charles Almeras. Produced by Marie Aimée's French Opéra Bouffe Company (Maurice Grau, Manager). Opened 31 October 1877 at the Broadway Theatre and closed 3 November 1877 after 3 performances in repertory; returned 7 December 1877 to Booth's Theatre for 1 performance in repertory; returned 20 May 1878 to the Park Theatre for 1 performance. Total: (5) performances.

CAST *Boulotte*: Mlle. MARIE AIMÉE. *Queen Clémentine*: Mlle. ADELE DÉSIRÉE. *Princess Hermia*: Mlle. FLORENCE DUPARC. *Heloise*: Mlle. Duplessis. *Rosalinde*: Mlle. Joly. *Isaure*: Mlle. Sophie Gherzi. *Blanche*: Mlle. Alphonsine. *Leonore*: Mlle. LaFontaine. *A Peasant Girl*: Mlle. Marie Vandamme. *Blue Beard*: Mons. MOLLARD. *King Bobèche*: Mons. DUPLAN. *Poplani*: Mons. J. MEZIÈRES. *Count Oscar*: Mons. JOUARD. *Prince Saphir*: Mons. LEGROS. *A Notary*: Mons. Salvator. *Alvarez*: Mons. Hayme. *Lords, Ladies, Pages, Guards at the Court of King Bobèche, Men-at-Arm of Blue Beard, Peasants, etc.*

1877.39 PIFF-PAFF!, or, The Magic Armory

A Fairy Musical Extravaganza in Two Acts, 5 Scenes. Libretto by Henry B. Farnie, after (the French 'Le Grand Duc de Matapa') of Clairville and Gastineau. Stage manager, Willie Edouin. Scenery by Charles Graham. Machinery by Nelse Waldron. Costumes designed by Lydia Thompson. Music arranged by Michael Connolly. Produced by Lydia Thompson. Opened 21 November 1877 at the Eagle Theatre and closed 8 December 1877 after 20 performances.

---

[21]First produced in New York in French 24 September 1867 at the Théâtre Français for 156 performances. For Synopsis of Scenes and Musical Numbers, see original 1867 production.

[22]First produced in New York 25 November 1844 at the Park Theatre for 17 performances in repertory. For Synopsis of Scenes and Musical Numbers, see original 1844 production.

[23]Musical numbers not listed in programs; this adaptation not published.

[24]Musical numbers not listed in programs. List prepared from published vocal selection with lyrics by Myron A. Cooney (Ditson & Co., Boston, n.d.) for the Hess Opera Company; not necessarily in performance order.

[25]First produced in New York in English 29 August 1870 at Kelly & Leon's; in French 26 September 1870 at the Grand Opera House. For Synopsis of Scenes and Musical Numbers, see original 1870 production.

[26]First produced in New York in French 13 July 1868 at Niblo's Garden for 81 performances. For Synopsis of Scenes and Musical Numbers, see original 1868 production.

CAST: *King Grammercie XXXVII*, Impecunious Sovereign: FREDERICK MARSHALL. *Cattivo*, his Generalissimo: W. H. LEIGH (W. H. Denny). *The Army of Grammercie (4)*: *Sir Ratcliffe*: Theodore Bohrer. *Sir Hayne*: W. H. Harper. *Sir De Broadway*: H. Ambergh. *Sir De Bowery*: L. deSmith. *Oldest Inhabitant*: Harry Harkaway. *Cherub*, Buttons of Prince Glamour: WILLIE EDOUIN. *Haunt-Vol*, Chief Falconer: Marie Williams. *Houp-La*: Emily Duncan. *Banjeau*, Court Minstrel: Ella Chapman. *Jaconde*: ALICE BURVILLE. *Prince Glamour*, Heir Apparent of Grammercie: LYDIA THOMPSON. *Queen Folichonne*, Grammercie's Second Wife: ALICE ATHERTON. *Finette, Minette*, the Princesses, her daughters: LINA MERVILLE, KATE EVERLEIGH. *Parfait Amour*, Pet Page: ADA LEE *Jaconde*, a Goatherdess: Alice Burville. *Hortense*, Wife of Cattivo: Marion Elmore. *Pages and Maids of Honour*: Misses Ida Lee, Annie Deacon, Clara Grey, Lavinia Hogan, Rose Leyton, Mary McLeod, Celia Pearson, Bessie Temple, Smith, Caldwell, McCullough, Swan, Howe, Gerentes, Yoster, Clark, Boyd, Lam, etc.

Act 1, Scene 1: The Old Castle of Grammercie. *Scene 2*: Refectory of Castle Grammercie.

Act 2, Scene 1: Vaults of the Magic Armory. *Scene 2*: Ivy Nooks. *Scene 3*: The Royal Bleaching Grounds.

ACT 1
Scene 1
"Low sighs the night wind" (Quartette)
M. Williams, E. Duncan, L. Merville, K. Everleigh
"They All Do It" (Song and Chorus)
F. Marshall, Company
"The Patronymic Name of Smith" (Song)
L. Thompson
"Simplete" (Song)
A. Burville
"Unto the Castle Gates I'll Guide You" (Duet)
L. Thompson, A. Burville
"Times up to now, to the gate" (Finale)
Principals, Chorus
Scene 2
"Pink Dominos" (Song)
L. Thompson
Laughing Duet
L. Thompson, W. Edouin
"Like a Turk" (Song and Chorus/Finale)
Principals, Chorus
ACT 2
Scene 1
"Oh, we titti, titti tremble" (Chorus)
"(Oh), Naughty, Naughty!" (Song)
A. Atherton
"Hail! Our Royal Master"
"Legend of the Genii" (Song and Chorus)
L. Thompson, Company
"P.T.O." (Concerted Piece)
Principals, Chorus
"All Alone I Stand Against the Lot"
L. Thompson, A. Burville, Company
Sensational Dance within a Circle of Fire
E. Chapman
Scene 2
"Maid of My Soul" (Patrol Chorus)
Scene 3
"Wash Tub Chorus"
Finale—Laugh at all our fun

1877.40 LES CENT VIERGES

A Revival of the Opérette in Three Acts[27], in French. Libretto by Clairville, Henri Chivot and Alfred Duru. Music by Charles Lecocq. Stage manager, Charles Darcy. Leader of orchestra, Charles Almeras. Produced by Marie Aimée's French Opéra Bouffe Company (Maurice Grau, Manager). Opened 4 December 1877 at Booth's Theatre for 2 performances in repertory; returned 22 December 1877 (matinee) to the Lyceum Theatre for 1 additional performance; returned 17 May 1878 to the Park Theatre in repertory. Total: (5) performances.

CAST: *Gabrielle*: Mlle. MARIE AIMÉE. *Eglantine*: Mlle. FLORENCE DUPARC. *Fanny*: Mlle. BLANCHE GUEYMARD. *Dolores*: Mlle. Marie Vandamme. *Parquerette*: Mons. Joly. *Betley*: Mlle. Duplessis. *Paola*: Mlle. Sophie Gherzi. *Le Duc Anatole de Quillenbois*: Mons. MOLLARD. *Sir Jonathan Pluperson*: Mons. DUPLAN. *Poulardot*: Mons. Castel. *Briddidick*: Mons. J. MEZIÈRES. *Crockley*: Mons. Hayme. *Colson*: Mons. Hayme. *Captain Thomson*: Mons. Legros. *A Constable*: Mons. Davalis. *Bitten*: Mons. Davalis. *Briton*: Mons. Davalis.

1877.41 LA REINE INDIGO

An Opéra-bouffe in Three Acts, 4 Scenes, in French. Libretto by Victor Wilder and Adolphe Jaime (adapted from the Viennese operette 'Indigo und die vierzig Räuber' by 'Maximilian Steiner'). Music by Johann Strauss. Stage manager, Charles Darcy. Scenery by Hannibal Calyo. Costumes by Landolff, of Paris. Leader of orchestra, Charles Almeras. Produced by Marie Aimée's French Opéra Bouffe Company (Maurice Grau, Manager). Opened 14 December 1877 at the Lyceum Theatre; season closed 22 December 1877 after 5 performances; returned 4 June 1878 to Booth's Theatre for 1 additional performance. Total: 6 performances.

CAST: *Fantasca*, the favorite Sultana of the late King Indigo: Mlle. MARIE AIMÉE. *Janio*, Court Jester to the late King Indigo: Mlle. BERTHE MARIO. *Montadada the First*, Widow of King Indigo (La Reine Indigo): Mlle. ADELE DÉSIRÉE. *Romadour*, Chief of the Eunuchs: Mons. JOUARD. *Babazouk*, a Merchant: Mons. Legros. *Mysouf*, General-in-Chief: Mons. CASTEL. *A Slave Dealer*: Mons. Girard. *An Eunuch*: Mons. Hayme. *Banana*: Mlle. Marie Vandamme. *Piastrella*: Mlle. Duplessis. *Zobeide*: Mlle. Mollard. *Farniente*: Mlle. Joly. *Venusia*: LaFontaine. *Boulibelle*: Mlle. Sophie Gherzi. *Tulipa*: Mlle. Alphonsine. *Chryseis*: Mlle. Julien. *Inmates of the Harem, Eunuchs, Peasants, Cooks, Ministers of the Court, Soldiers, Sailors, etc.*

Act 1: Interior of the Sultan's Harem in Turkey.

Act 2, Scene 1: A Palace worthy of 1001 Nights. *Scene 2*: The Ruins of Mosaire.

Act 3: A Bazaar by the Seaside.

ACT 1[28]
Introduction:
Choeur des Bayadères (Sous ses platanes)
Marche orientale et reprise du choeur
Couplets du Turc (Le Turc est d'une espèce à part)
Mlle. Aimée
Ronde du marchand des quatre saisons (Dès le jour avec son âne)
Mons. Legros
Chanson d l'anier (La chouse peut sembler profonde)
Mons. Legros
Air (Mon coeur est bien malade)
Mlle. Mario
Terzetto-Valse (Quel sombre et noir présage)
Mlles. M. Aimée, B. Mario, Mons. Jouard
Choeur (Salut à vous, o Reine incomparable!)
Finale:
Entrée des Almées
Choeur (O Reine illustre)
Scène (Vous m'avez outragée)
Mlle. A. Desirée
Ariette (Pauvres femmes)
Mlle. M. Aimée
Scène finale (Tout ça c'est bon)

ACT 2
Scene 1
Introduction:
Choeur (La nuit est tiède)
Couplets du voltigeur d'amour (Cavalier modèle)
Mlle. M. Aimée
Marche et choeur (Un palanquin est un meuble agréable)

[27]First produced in New York in French 23 December 1872 at the Olympic Theatre for 8 performances in repertory. For Synopsis of Scenes and Musical Numbers, see original 1872 production.

[28]Musical numbers not listed in programs. List prepared from published French piano vocal score (Heugel & Cie., Paris, 1875).

Couplets du merle blanc (L'Hymen, dit-on)
Mlle. M. Aimée
Duo (O chaste ivresse d'amour)
Mlles. M. Aimée, B. Mario
Choeur des soldats (Du silence!)
Scene 2
Bacchanale:
Choeur et solo (O joie ineffable)
Valse-Brindisi (O flamme enivrante!)
Mlle. M. Aimée
Récitative (Holà! qu'on serve mon en-cas)
Couplets (Ce matin, sottement)
Mlle. A. Desirée
Finale:
Récitative et berceuse (Dormez tous deux)
Scène du trésor (Frappe dur)
Stretta (Sonne, sonne!)
ACT 3
Introduction:
Choeur du marché (Tin! tin! tin!)
Air de Babazouk (Holà! Petites gens)
Mons. Legros
Choeur (Beaux galants)
yrolienne (Youp, la! pourquoi, bel amoreux)
Mlle. M. Aimée
Choeur (Danube d'azur) (Valse)
Couplet de la malle (Philosphe par goût)
Mlle. A. Desirée
Finale (Vive, vive la Reine!)

1877.42 LA PÉRICHOLE

A Revival of the Opéra-bouffe (new version) in Three Acts[29], in French. Libretto by Ludovic Halévy and Henri Meilhac, based on "Le Carosse du Saint-Sacrament" by Prosper Merimée. Music by Jacques Offenbach. Stage manager, Charles Darcy. Leader of orchestra, Charles Almeras. Produced by Marie Aimée's French Opéra Bouffe Company (Maurice Grau, Manager). Opened 22 December 1877 at the Lyceum Theatre for 1 performance in repertory.

CAST: *La Périchole*: Mlle. MARIE AIMÉE. *Piquillo*: Mons. MOLLARD. *Don Andrès de Ribeira*: Mons. JOUARD. *Le Compte de Panatellas*: Mons. J. MEZIÈRES. *Don Pedro*: Mons. DUPLAN. *Tarapote*: Mons. CASTEL. *Un Vieux Prisonnier*: Mons. Hayme. *First Notary*: Mons. Jolivet. *Second Notary*: Mons. Davalis. *Un Geolier*: Mons. Girard. *Cousins (3)*: *Guadalena*: Mlle. BLANCHE GUEYMARD. *Berginella*: Mlle. FLORENCE DUPARC. *Mastrilla*: Mlle. Sophie Gherzi. *Maids of Honor (4)*: *Ninetta*: Mlle. LaFontaine. *Brambilla*: Mlle. Alphonsine. *Frasquinella*: Mlle. Duplessis. *Manuelita*: Mlle. Marie Vandamme.

1877.43 BABES IN THE WOOD, or, Who Killed Cock Robin?

A Grand Comic Christmas Pantomime in Two Acts, 9 Scenes. The Comic Business (libretto) by Willie Edouin and William Gill. Music composed and directed by Charles Christop. The whole produced under the personal supervision of Willie Edouin. Scenery by Charles Graham. Machinery by Nelse Waldron. Costumes designed by Lydia Thompson. Produced by Lydia Thompson. Opened 24 December 1877 at the Eagle Theatre and closed 12 January 1878 after 25 performances; returned 28 January 1878 to the Grand Opera House and closed 9 February 1878 after 16 additional performances. Total this season: 41 performances.

CAST(Immortals): *Queen of Songbirds*, a charming note from Childhood's Operatic Score: EME ROSEAU. *Queen of Tragedy*, a Relic of by-gone Dismalities; in fact, 'the Dolour of our Daddie": ROSA LEYTON (Rose Leighton). *Cock Robin, Jenny Wren, Cock Sparrow, Parson Rook, and other Feathered Songsters of the Grove.*

(Mortals): *Sir Rowland Macassar*, the Cruel Uncle, Dark, Gloomy and Manfred-y: J. H. JONES. *Sir Roderick, Sir Rupert*, Dashing Young Swells, "All of the Olden Time": Rose Temple, Ada Lee. *Tommy, Sally*, The Dear Babes, Sweet Infants, who took the First Prize at the Baby Show: WILLIE EDOUIN, MARION ELMORE. *A Bad Man*, to all appearance a villain, but who eventually—but no matter!: MARIE WILLIAMS. *A Very Bad Man*, so deeply dyed in villainy that—well, you can't imagine!: WILLIAM GILL. *Lady Macassar*, Sir Rowland's Aimer and a Better Half: ALICE ATHERTON. *Miss Jones*, the Nursery Governess: LINA MERVILLE. *The Family Physician*, LL.D., M.R.C.S., P.Q.R.S.T., and A.S.S.: KATE EVERLEIGH. *Four Consulting M.D.s*: Messrs. Bohrer, DeSmith, Harper, Amberg. *Fitz-Flummery*, Sir Rowland's Valet: Lavinia Hogan. *Huntsmen, Pages, Guests, Attendants*: A powerful corps of well-trained and appropriately attired ladies and gentlemen. (*A Distinguished Foreigner*, better known as the Educated Donkey: A. W. MAFLIN.)

(The Harlequinade): *Pantaloon*: WILLIAM GILL. *Clown*, his son: WILLIE EDOUIN. *Harlequin*: A. W. MAFFLIN. *Harlequina*: MARIE WILLIAMS. *Columbine*: LINA MERVILLE. *Policeman*: J. H. Jones.

Act 1, Scene 1: Court Yard of Macassar Hall. *Scene 2*: Chamber in Sir Rowland's House. *Scene 3*: The School Room at Macassar. *Scene 4*: The Wood. *Scene 5*: Chamber in Macassar Hall. *Scene 6*: The Grove of the Song Birds.

Act 2, Scene 1: Police Station and Cobbler's. *Scene 2*: Fish Market and Rooms to Let. *Scene 3*: Cave of Despair. Transformation of the Zones.

ACT 1
Scene 1
"Grand Hunting Chorus"
R. Temple, A. Lee, Retainers
"Two Bad Men Are We" (Duet)
M. Williams, W. Gill
"The Game What They're At" (The Game That We're At)(Quartette and Chorus)
J. H. Jones, A. Atherton, M. Williams, W. Gill
Scene 2
"The Little Don of Spain" (Song)
K. Everleigh
Scene 3
"We Are Merry Little Kids" (Duet)
W. Edouin, M. Elmore
"More Like Their Dad Every Day" (Duet and Chorus)
J. H. Jones, A. Atherton
"Johnny Morgan" (Played the Organ)(Quartette and Full Chorus)
M. Williams, W. Gill, J. H. Jones, A. Atherton
"Good-bye Darling!" (Concerted Piece)
All characters, full chorus
Scene 4
"Echo Song"
E. Roseau
"The Same Old Game" (Trio)
W. Edouin, W. Gill, A. W. Mafflin
"Song of Conundrums" (Quartette)
W. Edouin, M. Elmore, M. Williams, W. Gill
Scene 5
"We've Been Called In" (Quartette)
Four Physicians
"Grease with Cash"
J. H. Jones, M. Williams
"The Man in the Moon Was Looking" (Song and Full Chorus)
A. Atherton, Physicians
Scene 6
"Queen of the Song Birds" (Appropriate Song)
Finale from "La Fille de Mme. Angot"
E. Roseau, Full Chorus
(*Music by* Charles Lecocq.)
ACT 2
Scene 1
Harlequinade
Scene 2
Hornpipe
A. W. Mafflin, L. Merville
Scene 3
Transformation of the Zones

[29]This revised three-act version first produced in New York 15 February 1877 at the Eagle Theatre in repertory for 4 performances. For Synopsis of Scenes and Musical Numbers, see previous 1877 production.

1878.01

A CELEBRATED HARD CASE

A Burlesque (of the play "A Celebrated Case" by Adolphe Cormon and Eugene D'Ennery) in One Act, 6 Scenes, preceded by an Olio. Play (and lyrics) by Edward Harrigan. Music by David Braham. Scenic artist, R. L. Weed. Produced by Edward Harrigan and Tony Hart. Opened 18 March 1878 at the Theatre Comique and closed 13 April 1878 after 32 performances; returned "with new music" 2 September 1878 to the Theatre Comique and closed 7 September 1878 after an additional 8 performances. Total: 40 performances.

Olio: John Wild in his sketch 'We Can't Agree' with J. Shay, J. F. Crossen and M. Bradley; Will H. Morton (Refined Comic); Billy Noonan and Alice Bateman in their Combat Clog; Quilter and Goldrich in their eccentric songs and dances; Robert Nickle, world renowned prestidigitateur; Ida Morris (serio-comic vocalist); Avery and LaRue (horizontal bar performance); Kitty O'Neil (jig dancer); Fields and Hoey in their sketch, Waiting for the Train; Harry Bennett (Irish songs and sayings).

A CELEBRATED HARD CASE CAST: *John Rainhard*, a bold militia boy who never fought at Fontenoy: EDWARD HARRIGAN. *Adri-Anna Rainhard*, the little Martha Washington who never told a lie for fear of a libel suit: TONY HART. *Sergeant Billy O'Rourke*, the original Billy, who greased his brogues. This characterization will be rendered without a shil-lah-la: JOHN WILD. *Count de Overshoes*, over all the troopers, a darling, afterwards "if you set it out," a duke, left one: BILLY GRAY. *Lather*, the hard case from Kalamazoo. The Democratic Party cannot reform him. An unprecedented crooked bloke: James F. Crossin. *Sunday-Gaul*, from Hicks' ball alley, Hoboken. A ball tosser no matter about the mixer: Michael Bradley. *No Count Ra-all*, a notorious masher. Lived long before his side-slugging Irish Comedians tormented us: Ed Burt. *Josephus*, the first orange blossom, the Duke's pedal brightener: Johnny Shay. *Madelaine Rainhard*, wife of John Rainhard. She has had many a jealous kick with John, but Allah be praised, she makes her last kick in the first scene of this monstrosity: ANNIE MACK. *Duchess de Overshoes*. This part would be played in broken Dutch, but as all the Dutch Comedians are broke, of course, we change it: NELLIE JONES. *Cannon Knees*, a schoolteacher on the war path. No reduction in salaries for the advancement of the ignorant head: ANNIE YEAMANS. *Valentine de Mooney*, a real descendant of the O'Mooney's, the girl from whom Adrianna gets her chewing gum: Marie Gorenflo. *Corporal U.S.*, 'tis not for us to speak: Jennie Lester. *Our Vivandière*, promoter of the Excise Law. The only beared beauty well: George Griffin. *Martha*, an Umbrella fairy: Susie Byrne. *Louise*, a parasol tinker: Clara Devoy. *Annette*, a tenement darling: Josie Devoy. *Bums, Tramps, Cracksmen, Fly Blokes*: Distinguished 14th Warders.

Scene 1: Home of John and Madelaine Rainhard. *Scene 2*: A Street. *Scene 3*: The Camp at Hoboken after Battle. *Scene 4*: The Park and Garden of the Duke de Overshoes. *Scene 5*: A Saloon. *Scene 6*: Another saloon not closed. Transformation to the City of Churches.

MUSICAL NUMBERS

"Our Irish Grenadiers" (Scene 2)
J. Wild, E. Harrigan, the Gallant 69th

"The Isle de Blackwell" (Scene 4)
E. Harrigan

1878.02

EVANGELINE, or, The Belle of Acadia

Rice's Extravaganza Combination in a Revival of the American Opera Bouffe Extravaganza in Three Acts[30]. Text by J. Cheever Goodwin. Original music by Edward E. Rice. Stage manager, Edwin S. Tarr. Musical director, A. W. Hoffman. Produced by Edward E. Rice. Opened 18 March 1878 at the Grand Opera House and closed 30 March 1878 after 16 performances.[31]

CAST: *Evangeline*, our heroine, a creature of impulse and an impetuous pet, pursued through love's impatient prompting by Gabriel, and with a view to edacious contingencies—by a whale: FLORENCE ELLIS. *Catherine*, the very mildest type of ante-nuptial mother-in-law—but wait: HARRY JOSEPHS. *Eulalie*, Evangeline's confidante, confidently hoping for women's rights: LIZZIE McCALL. *Queen Boorioboola Gha*, the King's much better adviser and supervisor of his whole conduct: Cora Stratton. *Mary Ann*, Evangeline's waiting maid: Hattie Richardson. *Gabriel*, our hero, a fascinating and perambulating young lover—in point of fact a roaming romeo: LIZZIE WEBSTER. *LeBlanc*, a lawyer of the shyest shyster stamp, with a will and a way equally dark: SOL SMITH RUSSELL. *Captain Dietrich*, a Dutch mercenary in the British ranks, who shows no mercy, being a mercynary cuss: GEORGE S. KNIGHT. *The Lone Fisherman*, a patient and singularly taciturn toiler of the sea, with a natural tendency to hook whatever comes within his reach: HARRY HUNTER. *Bazil*, Evangeline's sire, whose vacillating mind is divided between the rental of her prospective husband and his own parental affection: EDWIN S. TARR. *King Boorioboola*, royal proprietor of the Mid-African diamond fields, who, not being able to hear anything near, occupies an ear-trumpet: EDWIN S. TARR. *Hans Wagner*, a spiritual corporal with undue corporeal proportions: CHARLES ROSINE. *The Jailor*, never without his key, vocal or instrumental, consequently always on the qui vive: Horace Frail. *Grab, Runemin*, a couple of the King's copper-colored Copps: R. Voss, Jr., William Bullock. *Ringbolt, Deadshake*, a brace of conscientious deserters, who left their ship simply because they couldn't take it away with them: Mills Hall, A. Metzger. *The Policeman*, called by some a Peeler, possibly because he was never known to heed an appeal a prisoner might make: Harry [Henry] E. Dixey. *Lo*, the Poor Indian, the lowest and lonest savage of them all: H. M. Morse. *The Headsman*, not a mimic of stupid people, but very clever at taking off blockheads: George H. Ulmer. *The Conductor*, though given to much punching, better acquainted with the P.R.R. than the P.R.: Flora Lee. *The Heifer*, specially imported from Cowes: __. *Fishermen, Sailors, Soldiers, Arcadian Peasants, Africans, etc.*

ACT 1

"We Must be Off" (Opening Chorus)

"One moment, pray" (Recitative)

"There's a man" (Song)
L. Webster

"The Power of Gold" (Song)
S. S. Russell

"Thinking, love, of thee" (Ballad)
F. Ellis

"Into the water we go" (Bathing Trio)
F. Ellis, L. McCall, H. Josephs

"She's saved! She's saved!" (Choral)

"Sweet Evangeline"(Song and Dance)
L. Webster

"Sammy Smug" (Ballad)
S. S. Russell, Chorus

"Golden Chains" (Duet)
F. Ellis, L. Webster

Dance of the B.M.W.H.

"The Farming Man" (Ditty)
S. S. Russell

"In us you see" (Soldiers' Chorus and Septette)

"He Says I Must Go"(Grand Finale)

Evangeline Polka and Last Farewell Waltzes

ACT 2

"Hickery Hackery, Jim Jam" (Chorus of Natives)

"I'm in lofe" (Dutch Song)
G. S. Knight

"We are off to seek for Eva" (Comic Duet)
S. S. Russell, H. Josephs

"Sweet the song of birds" (Song and Dance)
L. Webster

Combat Music

"Twelve o'clock and all is well" (Chant of Watchmen)

"Prowling 'round the diamond fields" (Policeman's Narrative)

Royal Palace March

"King Polimeniche" (Song)
L. Webster, Chorus

"Come to the heart that is thine" (Romanza)
F. Ellis

"Where are thou now, my beloved" (Romanza)
F. Ellis

"In memory of this day" (Concerted)

"She's Acquitted, (He's Outwitted)" (Finale)

Evangeline Waltzes; Evangeline Polka Mazurka

ACT 3

"Fie, Upon you! Fie!" (Kissing Song)
F. Ellis

[30]First produced in New York 27 July 1874 at Niblo's Garden for 16 performances. For Synopsis of Scenes and Musical Numbers, see original 1874 production.

[31]No credits in programs for scenery, costumes.

"Go not, happy Day" (Duet)
F. Ellis, L. Webster
Vocal March
"(The) Six Miserable Ruffians" (Sextette)
"Does she love me?" (Song and Dance)
L. Webster
"My best beloved" (Song)
F. Ellis
Incidental Music
"Good night to one and all" (Grand Finale)
Evangeline March

1878.03

THE BOHEMIAN GIRL

A Revival of the Romantic Opera in Four Acts[32]. Libretto by Alfred Bunn. Music by Michael William Balfe. Stage manager, James A. Padgett. Musical director, William G. Dietrich. Produced by Ruben's Grand English Opera Company (L. M. Rubens, Proprietor). Opened 1 April 1878 at the Grand Opera House and closed 13 April 1878 after 12 performances in repertory[33].

CAST: *Count Arnheim*: VINCENT HOGAN. *Thaddeus*: CHARLES LANG. *Florestein*: THOMAS WHIFFIN. *Devilshoof*: STANLEY FELCH. *Captain of the Guard*: D. Lacy. *Arline*: SALLIE REBER. *Gipsey Queen*: ADELAIDE RANDALL. *Buda*: Carrie Burton. *Nobles, Soldiers, Gipsies, Retainers, Peasants, etc. Ballet*: Mlles. AUGUSTA (SOHLKE), HELENE MENZELLI, ADÈLE PAGLIERE.

1878.04

THE NEW FRITZ, OUR COUSIN GERMAN

A German Dialect Comedy in Four Acts. Play, music and lyrics by Joseph K. Emmet. Scenery by Charles Graham. Musical director, Ernest Neyer. Produced by Joseph K. Emmet. Opened 22 April 1878 at the Standard Theatre; amended version introduced 27 May 1878; "London version" opened 24 June 1878; production closed 29 June 1878 after 70 performances.

CAST: *Fritz*, his original character: JOSEPH K. EMMET. *Colonel Crafton*, a Refined Villain: J. H. ROWE. *Henry Schultz*, an actor: G. H. JORDAN. *Elias Grim*, a Lawyer: W. F. OWENS. *Abrams*, a Prize Fighter: W. W. Allen. *Snow*, Servant to Colonel Crafton: WILL H. BRAY. *Judge of the Court*: R. Allen. *Clerk of the Court*: E. B. Holmes. *Noodles*, a Fop: H. Fuller. *Jenkins*, a Policeman: T. J. Walker. *Katherina Schultz*: MINNIE PALMER. *Carline*, a German Peasant: Kate Pickman. *Louisa Crafton*, Colonel Crafton's Adopted Daughter: EMMA LORAINE. *Julia Crafton*, Colonel Crafton's daughter: Miss H. Douglas. *Madame Kline*: Annie Douglas. *Marie*: Little Minnie. *Little Schneider*: Master Willie.

Act 1: On the Rhine. Fritz in Germany.

Act 2: Fritz in America.

Act 3: Fritz in Trouble.

Act 4: Fritz the Happy Miller.

MUSICAL NUMBERS[34]
"Oh! He Hit Me in the Nose"
"Meet Me at the Garden Gate"
"Wake Out"
"The Brother's Lullaby" (with Guitar)
"Sauer Kraut Receipt" (with Banjo)
"She Fainted Away in My Arms"
"Climb Up, Climb Up! or the Mountain Guide"[35]
"Schneider, How You Vas? Do You Love Me?"
"Oh! Don't You Tickle Me"
Five Variations on "Home Sweet Home"

1878.05

NIA-FOR-LI-CA, In the Halls of Montezuma

A Glorious Ridiculosity (Musical Spectacle) in Three Acts. Play by Elliott Dawn. Stage manager, J. H. Browne. Musical director, Charles Puerner. Produced by Messrs. Gardner & Bache. Opened 22 April 1878 at Niblo's Garden and closed 27 April 1878 after 8 performances.

CAST Aztecs: *Wen Kroy*, High Muck-e-muck of the Aztecs, he spared the rod and spoiled the child: JAMES VINCENT. *Hot-o-scotch-o*, Muck-e-muck and Chancellor, left the green isle twixt two days, but struck a soft thing: WILLIAM B. CAHILL. *Cher-ri-boun-si*, Muck-e-muck and stick-in-the-mud, left Baden-Baden because beer slates run out: CHARLES STURGES. *Sto-no-fen-si*, Chamberlain and Confidential advisor: Miss AGGIE WOOD. *Sau-si-par-ril-la*, Chief of the Cops and Bribe-taker: MABEL STANLEY.

Teh-ua-na-cas: *Ti-na-cin-cin*, Chief of the Teh-ua-na-cas, but rather seedy at present: JAMES HAVILAND. *Go-ca-chi*, Prince of the Teh-ua-na-cas, he's got it bad: BELLE HOWITT. *Bet-on-himm*, Muck-e-muck of the Teh-ua-na-cas, but now under a cloud: FRANK TANNEHILL. (*Tom-n-Jer-ri*: BEATRICE STRAFFORD).

Aztecs: *Nia-for-li-ca*, the Princess, rather stuck-up; you'll know the rest after you see the play: LILLIAN CLEEVES CLARK. *Kra-si-ja-ne*, advisor to Nia-For-Li-Ca, but alas! a female Iago: J. F. SHERIDAN. *Toh-in-ka-li-ta*, amid-in-waiting, with a peacock feather duster: JENNIE YEAMANS. *Ta-va-shal-la*, spouse to Bet-on-him, but oh! what a talkative magpie: E. W. MARSTON. *Specialty*: THE GREAT LORELLAS (Champion High Kickers of the World).

Medicine Men: *Gu-mel-ast-ick*: W. G. RAYNEIR. *O-po-deld-ock*: J. E. INCE. *Par-ri-go-rick*: A. SIEGRIST. *Ju-ju-pas-ter*: L. KLINE.

Priestesses of the Sun: *Tra-la-la*: Miss Dalton. *Tre-le-le*: Miss Yeamans. *Tri-li-li*: Miss Grey. *Tro-lo-lo*: Miss Celeste. *Tru-lu-lu*: Miss Mordaunt. *Hha-ha*: Miss Smith. *Hhe-he-he*: Miss Day. *Hhi-hi-hi*: Miss Richards. *Hho-ho-ho*: Miss Dillon. *Hhu-hu-hu*: Miss Martin.

Hunters of the Chase: *Qa-qa*: Master Atkinson. *Qe-qe*: Master Smith. *Qi-qi*: Master Berckman. *Qo-qo*: Master Showell. *Qu-qu*: Master Budworth. *Xa-xa*: Master Tarrell. *Xe-xe*: Master McCarthy. *Xi-xi*: Master Martin. *Xo-xo*: Master Simm. *Xu-xu*: Master Devbert,

Slaves: *Sa-sy-bratee*: Mr. Holbrook. *Ug-li-brutee*: Mr. Gorman. *Lay-si-thing*: Mr. Ryan. *Me-ann-fel-la*: Mr. Gorman.

Temple of the Sun: *High Priest*: J. W. Pyke. *Low Priest*: S. J. Wallis. *Idols*: *Tes-cat-li-po-ca* (God of God and Evil), *To-no-ti-uh* (God of the Sun), *Quit-zi-coatl* (God of War).

Act 1: Life among the Aztecs. Evening.

Act 2: Priestesses of the Sun. Midnight.

Act 3: In the Guard House. Morning.

ACT 1
(Slaves') Specialty
Messrs. Holbrook, Ryan, Gorman Brothers
Grand Entry of Muck-e-Muck, Hot-o-scotch-o, Cher-ri-boun-si, Medicine Men, Retainers
Solemn Medicine Dance
Horrible Conditions; Enigmas 1, 2, 3; Musical Finale

ACT 2
Coconut Dance
Ten little Aztec Midgets
Kra-si-ja-ne's Lament
(J. F. Sheridan)
"Carrie Lee" (Ballad)
J. Vincent, J. F. Sheridan
Medley
J. F. Sheridan
"Po-lo-ma"
J. Yeamans

[32]First produced in New York 25 November 1844 at the Park Theatre for 17 performances in repertory. For Synopsis of Scenes and Musical Numbers, see original 1844 production.

[33]Alternate principal singers included LOUISE OLIVER, ISADORA MARTINEZ, A. E. STODDARD, ANNA GRANGER DOW, Miss J. Montgomery. No credits in programs for scenery or costumes.

[34]All musical numbers written, composed and sung by J. K. Emmet. During Acts 2 and 3, the orchestra will play Emmet's Lullaby, with Clarionette, Violin, Flute and Cornet variations. For the reconstruction, Emmet added the following songs: "Who Wants Some Milika?" (Don't You Want Some Milika?), "I Was a Deutscher Swell," "Don't I Love My Lena," and later "Dot's Her Up in de Window."

[35]Introducing the only genuine Silver Drum in the World, presented to Mr. Emmet by his St. Louis friends.

"Adieu"
L. C. Clark, J. Vincent
Melodious Finale

ACT 3
Hunters' Chorus
Ten little Aztec Warriors
Council Chambers (Clas-sick Quartette)
The Great Lorellas
The Temple of the Sun
Priestly Songs and Ceremonies
Grand Harmonious Finale

1878.06

LA VIE PARISIENNE

A Revival of the Opéra-bouffe in Four Acts[36], in French. Libretto by Henri Meilhac and Ludovic Halévy. Music by Jacques Offenbach. Stage manager, Charles Darcy. Leader of orchestra, Charles Almeras. Produced by Marie Aimée's French Opéra Bouffe Company. Opened 6 May 1878 at the Park Theatre in repertory; season closed 25 May 1878.

CAST: *Gabrielle*: Mlle. MARIE AIMEE. *Métella*: Mlle. BLANCHE GUEYMARD. *Pauline*: Mlle. FLORENCE DUPARC. *La Baronne de Gondremarck*: Mlle. SOPHIE GHERZI. *Le Baron de Gondremarck*: Mons. DUPLAN. *A Brazilian*: Mons. Mollard. *Frick*: Mons. Mollard. *Prosper*: Mons. Mollard. *Bobinet*: Mons. J. MEZIÈRES. *Raoul de Gardefeu*: Mons. LEGROS. *Urbain*: Mons. Castel. *Alfred*: Mons. Hayme. *Joseph*: Mons. Davalis. *Alphonse*: Mons. Gerard. *Gontran*: Mons. Salvator.

1878.07

LA PÉRICHOLE

A Revival of the Opéra-bouffe (new version) in Three Acts[37], in French. Libretto by Ludovic Halévy and Henri Meilhac, based on "Le Carosse du Saint-Sacrament" by Prosper Merimée. Music by Jacques Offenbach. Stage manager, Charles Darcy. Leader of orchestra, Charles Almeras. Produced by Marie Aimée's French Opéra Bouffe Company. Opened 10 May 1878 at the Park Theatre and closed 25 May 1878 (matinee) after 2 performances in repertory[38].

CAST: *La Périchole*: Mlle. MARIE AIMÉE. *Piquillo*: Mons. MOLLARD. *Don Andrès de Ribeira*: Mons. JOUARD. *Le Compte de Panatellas*: Mons. J. MEZIÈRES. *Don Pedro*: Mons. DUPLAN. *Tarapote*: Mons. CASTEL. *Un Vieux Prisonnier*: Mons. Hayme. *First Notary*: Mons. Jolivet. *Second Notary*: Mons. Davalis. *Un Geolier*: Mons. Girard. *Cousins (3)*: *Guadalena*: Mlle. BLANCHE GUEYMARD. *Berginella*: Mlle. FLORENCE DUPARC. *Mastrilla*: Mlle. Sophie Gherzi. *Maids of Honor (4)*: *Ninetta*: Mlle. LaFontaine. *Brambilla*: Mlle. Alphonsine. *Frasquinella*: Mlle. Duplessis. *Manuelita*: Mlle. MarieVandamme.

1878.08

LES CLOCHES DE CORNEVILLE

An Opéra-comique in Three Acts, 4 Scenes, in French[39]. Libretto by Clairville and Charles Gabet. Music by Robert Planquette. Stage manager, Charles Darcy. Leader of orchestra, Charles Almeras. Produced by Marie Aimée's French Opéra Bouffe Company. Opened 13 May 1878 at the Park Theatre and closed 25 May 1878 after 6 performances in repertory; re-opened 3 June 1878 at Booth's Theatre and closed 8 June 1878 after an additional 3 performances in repertory. Total: 9 performances.

[36]First produced in New York in French 29 March 1869 at the Théâtre Français for 11 performances. For Synopsis of Scenes and Musical Numbers, see original 1869 production.
[37]First produced in New York in French in its original two-act version 4 January 1869 at Pike Opera House for 35 performances; in its new three-act version 15 February 1877 at the Eagle Theatre for 4 performances in repertory. For Synopsis of Scenes and Musical Numbers, see 1877 production.
[38]Old version presented 23 December 1877 at the Lyceum Theatre with Mlle. Aimée for 1 performance this season.
[39]French language premiere in New York. Previously produced in New York in English 22 October 1877 at the Fifth Avenue Theatre for 16 performances

CAST: *Serpolette*: Mlle. MARIE AIMÉE. *Germaine*: Mlle. ISAYE MARTAL. *Manette*: Mlle. Sophie Gherzi. *Jeanne*: Mlle. Alphonsine. *Gertrude*: Mlle. Marie Vandamme. *Suzanne*: *Catherine*: Mlle. LaFontaine. *Marguerite*: Mlle. Duplessy. *Gaspard*: Mons. J. MEZIÈRES. *The Marquis*, Henri: Mons. JOUARD. *Grénicheux*: Mons. MOLLARD. *The Mayor*: Mons. DUPLAN. *A Notary*: Mons. Castel. *Cachalot*: Mons. F. Mauriez. *Grippardin*: Mons. Hayme. *Fouinard*: Mons. Salvator. *Peasants, Sailors, Drivers, Servants, etc.*

The action takes place during the reign of Louis XIV.

Act 1: Marché de Corneville.

Act 2: Une salle du château de Corneville.

Act 3: Un parc avec statues et bosquets.

ACT 1[40]
Scene 1
"C'est le marché de Corneville" (Choeur)
"On dit, sans contredit" (Chanson des on dit)
Mlle. M. Aimée
"Dans ma mystérieuse histoire" (Rondeau)
Mlle. M. Aimée
"Va petite Mousse" (Chanson du Mousse)
Mons. Mollard
"Même sans consulter mon coeur" (Duo)
Mlle. I. Martal, Mons. Mollard
"Nous avons hélas! Perdu d'excellents maîtres" (Chanson des cloches)
Mlle. I. Martal
"J'ai fait trois fois le tour du Monde" (Rondeau-valse)
Mons. Jouard
"C'est affreux, odieux" (Choeur)
Scene 2
Vieille Chanson (Entr'acte)
"Je ne sais comment faire" (Couplets)
Mons. Mollard
"Sur le marché de Corneville" (Choeur)
"Vous qui voulez des servantes" (Chanson des servantes
Mlle. M. Aimée
"Jeune fille dis-moi ton nom" (Finale)
Mons. Jouard

ACT 2
"A la lueur de ces flambeaux" (Choeur)
"Ne parlez pas de mon courage" (Air)
Mlle. I. Martal
"Fermons les yeux" (Trio)
Mlle. M. Aimée, Messrs. Mollard, Duplan
"Pristi, sapristi" (Chanson)
Mlle. M. Aimée
"J'avais perdu la tête et ma perruque" (Chanson)
Mons. Duplan
"Sous des armures à leur taille" (Chanson et choeur)
Mons. Jouard
"Vicomtesse et marquise" (Ensemble et couplets)
Mlle. M. Aimée
"C'est elle et son destin la guide" (Duo)
Mons. Duplan, I. Martal
"Quand on lui propose une affaire" (Chanson des oui ou non)
Mlle. I. Martal
"Gloire au valeureux Grénicheux" (Choeur et quintette)
Mlles. M. Aimée, I. Martal, Messrs. Mollard, Jouard, Duplan, Tenors, Basses
"C'est là, c'est là qu'est la richesse" (Finale et couplets)
Mons. Mezières

ACT 3
"Enfin, nous voilà transportées" (Chanson des gueux)
Mons. Mezières

[40]Musical numbers not listed in programs. List prepared from published French piano vocal score (C. Joubert, Paris, 1877, 1892).

'Regardez donc quel équipage" (Choeur)

"Oui, c'est moi, c'est Serpolette" (Chanson)
Mlle. M. Aimée

"La pomme est un fruit plein de sève" (Chanson du cidre)
Mlle. M. Aimée

"Je regardais en l'air" (Rondeau)
Mons. Mollard

"Une servante qui m'importe" (Romance et Duo)
Mlle. I. Martal, Mons. Jouard

"Pour le tresor que tu nous abandonnes" (Finale)

1878.09

LES DRAGONS DE VILLARS

A Revival of the Opéra-comique (The Hermit's Bell) in Three Acts, in French[41]. Libretto by Lockroy [Joseph Simon] and Eugène Cormon. Music by Aimé Maillart. Stage manager, Charles Darcy. Leader of orchestra, Charles Almeras. Produced by Marie Aimée's French Opéra Bouffe Company. Opened 18 May 1878 at the Park Theatre for 1 performance in repertory; season closed 25 May 1878.

CAST: *Rose Friquet*: Mlle. MARIE AIMÉE. *Georgette*: Mlle. FLORENCE DUPARC. *Sylvain*: Mons. MOLLARD. *Belamy*: Mons. JOUARD. *Thibaut*: Mons. DUPLAN. *Un Pasteur*: Mons. Castel. *Un Dragon*: Mons. Davalis. *Male and Female Peasants, Soldiers, etc.*

1878.10

HUMPTY DUMPTY'S DREAM

The Original Trick Pantomime in Two Acts, preceded by a Drama in One Act, The Miser. Music by Frank Peterschen. Scenery by Plaisted, Signor Arigoni, and John Thompson. Costumes by H. Seymour. Properties by E. C. Coss. Effects by D. Mackenzie. Opened 21 May 1878 at the Fifth Avenue Theatre and closed 15 June 1878 after 31 performances.[42]

ACT 1

THE MISER, an adaptation of Charles Dickens' "A Christmas Carol" in One Act

CAST: *Ebeneezer Scrooge*: JACQUES KRUGER. *Bob Cratchet*: WILLIAM HENDERSON. *Frank Freeheart*: Earle Stirling. *Mr. Cheerly*: J. Donnelly. *Santa Claus*: William Stout. *Fairy Christmas*: Jennie Warde.

Scenes: The Star of Bethlehem; The Illuminated Church; The Miser's Home; The Farm of Plenty; Grotto of Neptune; The Housetops; The Revolving Tower.

ACTS 2 and 3

HUMPTY DUMPTY'S DREAM, the Original Trick Pantomime by G. L. Fox and Robert Fraser.

CAST: *Humpty Dumpty and Clown*: ROBERT FRASER. *Old One-Two and Pantaloon*: J. C. FRANKLIN. *Tommy Tucker and Harlequin*: J. W. SANDFORD. *The Monkey and Sprite*: Willie Gaylord. *Goody Two Shoes and Columbine*: Mlle. ELISE.

Scenes: The Four Seasons: Spring (Plaisted), Summer (Arigoni), Autumn (Arigoni), Winter (Thompson.).

[41]First produced in New York 10 May 1869 at the Fifth Avenue Theatre for 15 performances in repertory. For Synopsis of Scenes and Musical Numbers, see original 1869 production.

[42]No further detail with regard to stage director, musical director or musical numbers in programs.

1878–1879 SEASON

Alice Oates in LE PETIT DUC (Photo: Dana)
Billy Rose Theatre Collection, New York Public Library for the Performing Arts

1878–1879 SEASON

1878.11 JOSHUA WHITCOMB

A (Revised Version of the) Comedy Drama in Three Acts[1]. Play by Denman Thompson. Stage manager, D. Nourse. Musical director, J. M. Navoni. Produced by Denman Thompson. Opened 2 September 1878 at the Lyceum Theatre and closed 30 November 1878 after 93 performances.[2]

CAST: *Uncle Josh*: DENMAN THOMPSON. *Tot*, a crossing sweeper: JULIA WILSON. *John Martin*, a lover of horse racing and theatres: EUGENE O. JEPSON. *Nellie Primrose*, a Boston belle: Clara Cary. *Frederick Dolby*, the young Englishman: Walter Gale. *Cy. Prime*, nigh on to eighty: HARRY WILSON. *Susie Martin*, with a mania for marriage: Helen Just. *Roundy*, a boot black: IGNACIO MARTINETTI. *Reuben Whitcomb*, Joshua's son: Charles Peters. *Aunt Matilda*, Joshua's sister: Mrs. D. Nourse. *Bill Johnson*, a loafer, just as bad as they make 'em: J. F. Ward. *Mrs. Johnson*, Tot's mother: Mrs. Owen Marlowe. *Amantha Bartlett*, one of the neighbor's gals: May Nelson. *Mr. Burroughs*, a model policeman: Frank W. Irving. *Aunt Martha*: Effie Wild.

Act 1: Boston

Act 2: Birthday Party.

Act 3: Joshua's New England home.

MUSICAL NUMBERS[3]

"Twinkle, Twinkle, Little Stars"
J. Wilson, I. Martinetti
(*Music and Lyrics by* Fred Macevoy.)

"Goodbye Annie Darling"
(*Music and Lyrics by* Fred Macevoy.)

"The Tot's Lullaby"
(*Music by* Walter Gale. *Lyrics by* Denman Thompson.)

1878.12 NEW FRITZ! OUR COUSIN GERMAN

A (Revised Version of the) German Dialect Comedy in Four Acts[4]. Play, music and lyrics by Joseph K. Emmet. Musical director, Ernest Neyer. Produced by Joseph K. Emmet. Opened 16 September 1878 at the Grand Opera House and closed 21 September 1878 after 7 performances; returned 14 October 1878 to the Standard Theatre and closed 8 November 1878 after 28 additional performances.[5] Total: 35 performances.

CAST: *Fritz*, his original character: JOSEPH K. EMMET. *Elias Grimm*, a Lawyer: MATT B. SNYDER. *Colonel Crafton*, a Refined Villain: D. R. YOUNG. *Abrams*, a Prize Fighter: W. W. Allen. *Snow*, Servant to Colonel Crafton: WILL H. BRAY. *Old Schneider*, a Jailor: William Haley. *Judge of the Court*: Martin J. Cody. *Clerk of the Court*: J. F. Wilkes. *Noodles*, a Fop, Son of Elias Grimm: Oliver Doud. *Jenkins*, a Policeman: Milton Byron. *Katherina*, in love with Fritz: LIBBIE KLINE. *Louisa Crafton*, Adopted Daughter of Colonel Crafton: ROSE GRAHAM. *Julia Crafton*, Colonel Crafton's Sister-in-law: MATTIE EARLE. *Lena*, Fritz's sister: Little Georgia. *Little Schneider*: Little Georgia.

Act 1: On the Rhine. Fritz in Germany.

Act 2: Fritz in America.

Act 3: Fritz in Trouble.

Act 4: Fritz the Happy Prisoner.

MUSICAL NUMBERS[6]

"Oh! He Hit Me in De Nose"
"Meet Me at the Garden Gate"
"The Brother's Lullaby" (with Guitar)
"Sauer Kraut Receipt" (with Banjo)
"She Fainted Away in My Arms"
"Climb Up, Climb Up! or the Mountain Guide"[7]
"Schneider, How You Was?"
"Dot's Her Up in De Window"
"Oh! Don't You Tickle Me"
Five Variations on "Home Sweet Home"

1878.13 THE MULLIGAN GUARD PIC-NIC

A Dramatic Sketch in One Act, 5 Scenes[8] preceded by an Olio. Play (and lyrics) by Edward Harrigan. Music by David Braham. Staged by Edward Harrigan. Scenery by R. L. Weed. Musical director, David Braham. Produced by Edward Harrigan and Tony Hart. Opened 23 September 1878 at the Theatre Comique and closed 26 October 1878 after 40 performances.

Olio: Billy Gray in the laughable sketch, Married in the Dark, with H. A. Fisher, E. Burt, A. Yeamans, N. Jones; Lulu Francis in an original medley arr. by Dave Braham; J. C. Carroll (Southern ventriloquist); John Wild in the farce, The Closed Up Verdict, with Messrs. Edwards, Wild, Gray, Fisher, Burt, Master Heusel, Mart. M. O'Brien; Clara Moore (vocalist); Robert Nickle (as Robert Le Diable); Harry Woodson (songs and impersonations); Campbell & Burke (Limerick Lads in Irish character changes); Tommy Turner (comic banjoist).

CAST: *Conrad McShane*, an M.P. with a day off: EDWARD HARRIGAN. *Daniel Mulligan*, who was drowned at Coney Island, another of mysteries: TONY HART. *Carlas McAllister*, a suitor in pursuit of the widow: JOHN WILD. *Tom Fagan*, a heeler from the Fourth Ward: BILLY GRAY. *Gipsy Jack*, the rover: Ed Burt. *Mat O'Brien*, the Band Leader: HARRY FISHER. *Jack Crogan*: John Mealey. *Captain Hussey* of the Guard: Michael Bradley. *Dunfries*, Committee Man: John McCullough. *Officer Smith*: A. Weston. *Captain Barton*: Welsh Edwards. *Mrs. Daniel Mulligan*, a buxom widow, but don't like the Weeds: ANNIE YEAMANS. *Mrs. McGinty*: EMILY YEAMANS. *Mary Ann Maguire*: Nellie Jones.

Scene 1: Mulligan's Flat. *Scene 2*: The Street. *Scene 3*: The Pier. *Scene 4*: The Grove. *Scene 5*: The Barge by Moonlight.

MUSICAL NUMBERS

"The Casey Social Club" (Casey's Social Club)(Scene 4)
E. Harrigan, J. Wild, and their 2 Queens

"Such an Education Has My Mary Ann" (Sweet Mary Ann)(Scene 5)
E. Harrigan

1878.14 LA CIGALE

A Wild Farcical Conceit in Three Acts. Original French play by Henri Meilhac and Ludovic Halévy. Adapted by Olive Logan. Stage manager, Ed Marble. Scenery by George Heister. Properties by George Henry. Mechanism by Hamilton Weaver. Produced by Lotta (Crabtree). Opened 26 October 1878 at the Park Theatre and closed 21 November 1878 after 23 performances.[9]

CAST: *La Cigale*, afterwards known as Lelio De Latour: LOTTA (CRABTREE). *Marignan*, an Artist: FREDERICK ROBINSON. *Michu*, his companion: F. BENNETT. *Count de Hoppe*: JAMES DUNN. *Edgar*, Viscount de Hoppe: CLEMENT BAINBRIDGE. *Carcasonne*, Manager and Clown of the Imperial Circus: ED MARBLE. *Bi Bi*, Hercules of the Imperial Circus: H. B. Bradley. *Filoche*, Lightning Calculator of the Imperial Circus: FRED PERCY. *Mons. Duclore*: W. H. Wallis. *Tourlot*, Landlord: J. P. Cooke. *Legs*: Master Cooke. *Servant* to the Countess: Mr. Parker. *Peter*: Mr. White. *Countess de Latour*: Mrs. Charles Poole. *Adele*, a Parisian Coquette, afterwards a Model: Agnes Proctor. *No. 6*: Miss Cameron. *No. 7*: Miss Doyle.

[1]Premiere of the longer version; previously produced in a shorter one-act version 3 April 1875 at the Globe Theatre for 16 performances.
[2]No musical numbers listed in programs.
[3]No musical numbers listed in programs. List prepared from music published to coincide with the production.
[4]First produced in New York 22 April 1878 at the Standard Theatre for 70 performances. For Synopsis of Scenes and Musical Numbers, see original 1878 production.
[5]No credits in programs for the new scenery, properties and mechanical effects; costumes uncredited.
[6]All musical numbers written, composed and sung by J. K. Emmet. During Acts 2 and 3, the orchestra will play Emmet's Lullaby with Clarionette, Violin, Flute and Cornet variations.
[7]Introducing the only genuine Silver Drum in the World, presented to Mr. Emmet by his St. Louis friends.
[8]This may be regarded as "Volume One" in the Mulligan Guard series.
[9]During the play Miss Lotta will introduce the following: A Banjo Solo; Opera Bouffe, Pot Pourri; La Cigale, and Carcasonne; Circus; The New La Cigale (written especially for Miss Lotta) by Ed Marble.

Act 1: An Old Inn at Fontainebleau.

Act 2: The Chateau De Latour.

Act 3: Marignan's Studio.

1878.15 OTTO, a German

A Local Musical Comedy Drama in Four Acts. Play by Frederick Marsden. Scenery by Joseph De La Harpe. Costumes by H. J. Eaves. Musical director, A. Rossner. Produced by George S. Knight. Opened 4 November 1878 at the Broadway Theatre and closed 7 December 1878 after 40 performances.[10]

CAST: *Otto Rutger*, a German: GEORGE S. KNIGHT. *Lizette*, Queen of Hearts: Mrs. GEORGE S. KNIGHT [Sophie Worrell]. *Gottleib Muller*, a rich brewer: W. M. Ward. *Dick Freely*, whose name indicates his character: John A. Mackay. *Casper Becks*, an importation of doubtful value: C. T. Nicholls. *Benjamin Freely*, a "Business Man, Sir": Matthew Holmes. *Adolph Morton*, more youthful than verdant: Walter Bronson. *Old Bill*, Guardian Spirit of the Brewery: W. H. Portello. *Christine*, enjoying love's young dream: Eva G. Barker. *Mrs. Freely*, who likes to have her say: D. B. Van Deren.

Act 1: Adrift. Hoboken, New Jersey.

Act 2: At Anchor.

Act 3: Storms.

Act 4: In Safe Harbor.

SPECIALTIES

Mandolin Solo; Harmonica Solo (Act 1)
G. S. Knight
"Der Wasserfall" (Act 2)
Mr. & Mrs. G. S. Knight
"One auf of de Boys"; "The Mule" (Act 2)
G. S. Knight
"Dot Leetle Baby Mine" (new) (Act 2)
G. S. Knight
(*Music and Lyrics by* Mark Quencher.)
The Water Mill; The Famous Fit Scene (Act 3)
G. S. Knight
Popular Ballads (Act 4)
Mrs. G. S. Knight

1878.16 THE BELLS OF CORNEVILLE!

An Opéra-comique in Three Acts, 4 Scenes[11]. French libretto to 'Les Cloches de Corneville' by Clairville and Charles Gabet. Music by Robert Planquette. Musical director, Antoine Reiff. Produced by the Tracy Titus Opera Company (Tracy Titus, Jonathan R. Rogers, Directors). Opened 11 November 1878 at the St. James Theatre and closed 30 November 1878 after 21 performances.

CAST: *Serpolette*: CATHERINE LEWIS. *Germaine*: LAURA JOYCE. *Annette*: EMMA METTLER. *Gertrude*: Laura Clancey. *The Marquis*: EUGENE CLARKE. *Gaspard*: HENRY PEAKES. *Grénicheux*: CHARLES F. LANGE. *Bailie*: M. W. FISKE. *Notary*: C. Roache.

ACT 1
Scene 1
"All who for servants" (Chorus)
C. Lewis, L. Joyce, L. Clancey, E. Mettler, Chorus
"They say" (Air and Chorus)
"Scandal-monger" (Recitative and coda)
"I may be princess" (Rondo)
C. Lewis
"On billow rocking" (Barcarolle)
C. F. Lange
"'Twas but an impulse" (Duet)
L. Joyce, C. F. Lange
"Legend of the bells" (Solo and Chorus)
L. Joyce, Chorus
"With joy my heart" (Valse rondo)
E. Clarke
"Such conduct is quite sad" (Ensemble)
Scene 2
Old Song (Entr'acte)
"Tho' they may not pursue me" (Couplets)
C. F. Lange
"Come, farmer small" (Chorus)
"Than us you will not find better" (Chorus of Manservants)
"Who are drivers lacking" (Chorus of Coachmen)
"Who are wanting maidens able" (Chorus of Maidservants)
"Tell me, girl" (Finale)

ACT 2
"Let our torches" (Concerted number)
L. Joyce, E. Clarke, Chorus
"By his side" (Air)
L. Joyce
"I'll shut my eyes" (Trio)
C. Lewis, C. F. Lange, M. W. Fiske
"Not a ghost at all" (Song)
C. Lewis
"Oh dear! Oh dear!" (Buffo Song)
M. W. Fiske
"Silent Heroes" (Recitative, Air and Chorus)
E. Clarke, C. Lewis, L. Joyce, C. F. Lange, Chorus
"What's she saying" (Ensemble and Couplet)
E. Clarke, C. Lewis, L. Joyce, C. F. Lange, Chorus
"'Tis she! A happy fate" (Duet)
L. Joyce, E. Clarke
"As he's looking somewhat pale" (Chorus and Quintette)
C. Lewis, L. Joyce, C. F. Lange, E. Clarke, M. W. Fiske, Chorus
"Love, Honour, Happiness" (Finale)
H. Peakes, C. F. Lange

ACT 3
"Aye, aye, aye" (Song of the Beggars)
H. Peakes
"There she goes with horses prancing" (Chorus and Song)
C. Lewis, C. F. Lange, Chorus
"The Cider Song" (Song and Chorus)
C. Lewis, Chorus
"That night I'll ne'er forget" (Song)
C. F. Lange
"My Lord! My Lord!" (Duet)
L. Joyce, E. Clarke
"Old man, I pardon thee" (Finale)
Principals, Chorus
"There's magic music" (Love the Minstrel)(Song and Chorus)

1878.17 THE LORGAIRE

An Irish Drama in a Prologue and Three Acts, 9 Scenes[12]. Play (and lyrics) by Edward Harrigan. Music by David Braham. Staged by Edward Harrigan.

[10]No credits in programs for scenery, costumes, stage direction or musical direction.

[11]First produced in New York in English in an adaptation by M. A. Cooney as THE CHIMES OF NORMANDY 22 October 1877 at the Fifth Avenue Theatre for 16 performances. English adaptation uncredited for this production; most likely a variation on the standard English and American performing edition, by H. B. Farnie and Robert Reece (English piano vocal score, Joseph Williams, London, 1878). In Act 3, Catherine Lewis interpolated the famous Drinking Song from GIROFLÉ/GIROFLA.

[12]An earlier and shorter version of THE LORGAIRE, or, The Murder at the Black Rock in One Act, 5 Scenes, was presented by Harrigan & Hart the weeek of 18 February 1878 at the Theatre Comique for 8 performances. For this new production, no songs were listed in programs. All known published songs from THE LORGAIRE were copyrighted for the 1889 revival.

Scenic artist, Thomas R. Weston. Costumes by Kate Devoy. Properties by James Hynes. Machinery by Robert Cutler. Calcium Lights by Richard Doyle. Musical director, David Braham. Produced by Edward Harrigan and Tony Hart. Opened 25 November 1878 at the Theatre Comique and closed 21 December 1878 after 32 performances.[13]

CAST: Prologue: *Colonel Francis Travers*: Edward Burt. *Colonel Robert Elliot*: W. H. Wilder. *Sergeant John Talbot*: Harry A. Fisher. *Robert Elliot*, Captain's child: Little Blanche Edwards. *Nano*, a Sepoy: J. Fitzsimmons. *Corporal*: John Mealey.

CAST: *The Lorgaire*, a Detective: EDWARD HARRIGAN. *Terry Mullahey*, a Fisherman: TONY HART. *Squire Felix Ryan*: Welsh Edwards. *Dennis Slattery*: Harry Fisher. *Sir Robert Elliot*: W. H. Wilder. *Robert Ryan*: T. F. Meagher. *Lieutenant Francis Travers*: Edward Burt. *Barney Malone*: Billy Gray. *Paudgeen Clancy*: John Wild. *Dan McCarty*: Michael Bradley. *Brian Lanagan*: John Shay. *Danny Dumphy*: Emil Heusel. *Black McGowan*: J. Fitzsimmons. *Sergeant*: John Mealey. *Shelah Slattery*: Annie Mack. *Norah Mullahey*: Lizzie Rich. *Kitty Mahone*: Angela Griffiths. *Molly Mahone*: Lizzie Edwards. *Widow Mullahey*: ANNIE YEAMANS. *Mrs. Grogan*: John F. Sheridan.

Prologue: The Town of Pondicherry. Period of the Indian Mutiny. View of Bengal Bay.

Act 1: County Galway, Ireland. Fifteen years later. Claddah, Ireland. The Fisherman's Home. View of "Lough Corrib."

Act 2, Scene 1: Apartment of Square Ryan's. *Scene 2*: The Barracks. *Scene 3*: The Christening Party at Schoolmaster Mahone's Cottage.

Act 3, Scene 1: The Hedge School, by night. *Scene 2*: The Barracks. *Scene 3*: Barns, View of Lough Corrib by Moonlight. The Parish Church. *Scene 4*: A Country Road. *Scene 5*: Hall at the Barracks.

1878.18

GIROFLÉ-GIROFLA!

A Revival of the Opéra-bouffe in Three Acts[14], in French. Libretto by Albert Vanloo and Eugène Leterrier. Music by Charles Lecocq. Musical director, Charles Schiller. Produced by the Bouffes Parisiennes (Durand & Co., Directors). Opened 2 December 1878 at the St. James Theatre and closed 7 December 1878 after 7 performances.[15]

CAST: *Giroflé, Girofla*: Mlle. ZELIE WEIL. *Aurore*: Mlle. BLONDELET. *Bolero*: Mons. JUIGNET. *Marasquin*: Mons. DORIA. *Mourzouk*: Mons. MIALLET. *Pedro*: Mlle. Letellier. *Paquita*: Mlle. Vandame. *The Cousins*: Mlles. Pezzuolo, Estephe, Henriette, Segaud.

1878.19

EVANGELINE, or The Belle of Acadia

A Revival of the Opera Bouffe Extravaganza in Three Acts[16]. Libretto by J. Cheever Goodwin. Music by Edward E. Rice. Musical director, J. C. Mullaly. Produced by John Stetson's Opera Bouffe Company. Opened 16 December 1878 at Booth's Theatre and closed 4 January 1879 after 24 performances.

CAST: *Gabriel*, our hero, a fascinating and perambulating youth lover, in point of fact a roaming Romeo: NELLIE LARKELLE. *Evangeline*, our heroine, a creature of impulse and an impetuous pet, pursued through love's impatient prompting by Gabriel, and with a view to audacious contingencies by a whale: CLARA FISHER. *Eulalie*, Evangeline's confidante, confidently hoping for Women's Rights: EUGENIA PAUL. *LeBlanc*, a lawyer of the shyest shyster stamp, with a will and a way equally dark: THOMAS WHIFFEN. *Captain Dietrich*, a Dutch necessary in the British ranks, who shows no mercy, being a mercy-nary cuss: LARRY TOOLEY. *The Lone Fisherman*, a patient and similarly taciturn toiler of the sea, with a natural tendency to hook whatever comes within his reach: JAMES S. MAFFIT. *Catherine*, the very mildest type of anti-nuptial Mother in Law: HARRY JOSEPHS. *Queen Boorioloboola Gha*, the King's much better advisor of his whole conduct: Emma Lorraine. *Mary Ann*, Evangeline's waiting maid: Flora Lee. *Basil*, Evangeline's sire, whose vacillating mind is divided between the rental of her prospective husband and his on parental affection: EDWIN S. TARR. *King Boorioloboola Gha*, Royal Proprietor of the Mid-African Diamond Fields, who, not being able to hear anything near occupies an ear trumpet: E. T. Sinclair. *Hans Wagner*, a spiritual corporal, with undue corporeal proportions: E. A. LOCKE. *The Jailer*, never without his key, vocal or instrumental, consequently always on the qui vive: N. D. Jones. *Grab, Runemin*, a couple of the King's copper-colored "Copps": A. V. Hauten, S. P. Norman. *Ringbolt, Deadshake*, a brace of conscientious deserters: Stuart H. Johns, George H. Connor. *The Policeman*, called by some a peeler, possibly because he was never known to heed any appeal a prisoner might make, locus a non, and all that sort of thing: J. H. Stuart. *Lo*, the Indian, the lowest and the lowest savage of them all: Byron George. *The Headsman*, not a mimic of stupid people, but very clever at taking off blockheads: R. S. Mitchell. *The Conductor*, though given to much punching, better acquainted with the P.R.R. than the P.R.: Annie Lee. *The Heifer*, specially imported from Cowes: Daly Brothers. *Specialty, Act 2*: GUS WILLIAMS (German songs and recitations).

1878.20

BABES IN THE WOOD & THE GOOD LITTLE FAIRY BIRDS; or, Who Killed Cock Robin?

A Pantomime Burlesque Extravaganza in Two Acts, 6 Scenes. Gathered from H. J. Byron's burlesque, several sources of authorship compensated for, re-written, revised and re-constructed by William Gill. Music selected, arranged and composed by Henry Sator. Stage manager, William Gill. Musical director, Henry Sator. Produced by Colville Opera Burlesque Company (Samuel Colville, Proprietor). Opened 23 December 1878 at the Park Theatre and closed 8 January 1879 after 19 performances.[17]

CAST: *Falcontrina*, Sir Rowland's only child, she's BUT A MAID, but has a voice like PATTI: EME ROSEAU. *Tommy, Sally*, Sweet infants, delightful toddlekins, who took the first prize at the baby Show: CHARLES H. DREW, MARION ELMORE. *Prince Prettyphellow*, anxious for the "resumption of specie payment," on the part of Sir Rowland, and who eventually squares accounts by accepting a Fair lender in lieu thereof: LINA MERVILLE. *Sir Rowland Macassar*, the cruel uncle, dark, gloomy and man-fred-y: WILLIAM B. CAHILL. *Lady Macassar*, Sir Rowland's AIDER and a BETTER half: ELEANOR DEERING. *A Bad Man*, a villain to all appearance, but who eventually—but no matter: MARIE WILLIAMS. *A Very Bad Man*, so deeply dyed in gore well you can't imagine: WILLIAM GILL. *Sir Rupert*, aid de-camp to the Prince: ADA LEE. *Miss Jones*, the Governess: A. W. MAFLIN. *The Family Physician*, LL. D.M.R.S.P.Q.R.S.T. and likewise A.S.S.: KATE EVERLEIGH. *Oppo Dilldock*, Esq., Sir Rowland's own physician: A. W. MAFLIN. *The Four Cures*: *A. Bolus*, Esq., M.D.: Mr. Bohrer. *B. Pod Oplyline*, Esq., M.D.: Mr. Amberg. *C. Cath. Arides*, Esq., M.D.: Mr. DeSmith. *D. Aqua Pura*, Esq., M.D.: Mr. Harper. *Fitz Flummery*, Confidential Valet: Annie Deacon. *Subjects of Courts—Cock Robin, Jenny Wren, Cock Sparrow, Rook Larks, Linnets, Huntsmen, Pages, Guests, Attendants, etc.* (*The Educated Donkey*: A. W. MAFLIN.)

Act 1, Scene 1: The courtyard of Sir Rowland's ruined castle. *Scene 2*: Corridor in the Castle. *Scene 3*: The school-room.

Act 2, Scene 1: A country lane. *Scene 2*: Chamber in the Macassar Castle. *Scene 3*: The Bird grove.

ACT 1
Scene 1
"The Bugle Horn" (Grand Chorus)
Retainers
"It Is Two Bad Men We Are" (Duet)
M. Williams, W. Gill
"Your Orders Shall Be Obeyed" (Finale)
W. B. Cahill, E. Deering, M. Williams, W. Gill, K. Everleigh, Full Chorus
Scene 2
"I'm Doctor Puff" (Doctor's Soliloquy)
K. Everleigh
Selected Aria
E. Roseau
"Villain Am I" (Duet and Grotesque Dance)
M. Williams, W. Gill
Scene 3
"Happy Little Kids" (Duet)
C. H. Drew, M. Elmore

[13]No musical numbers listed in program except Act 2, Scene 3, in which Messrs. Hayle and Pickert, Neil Conway, John Allen, John F. Sheridan, John Shay, Michael Bradley, assisted by two Irish Pipers, Kerrigan and Egan, perform characteristic Reel and Jig Dances. The reviewer for the New York Clipper remarked that the opening scene of Act 3 included a familiar variety sketch "School" done into Irish. Later revivals included more Harrigan and Braham musical numbers.

[14]First produced in New York in English 19 May 1875 at Robinson Hall for 61 performances. For Synopsis of Scenes and Musical Numbers, see original 1875 production. English adaptation uncredited.

[15]No program found.

[16]First produced in New York 27 July 1874 at Niblo's Garden for 16 performances. For Synopsis of Scenes and Musical Numbers, see original 1874 production.

[17]Scenery and costumes uncredited.

"When a Little Farm We Keep" (Duet)
E. Roseau, C. H. Drew
"Come hither scholars all!" (Grand concerted piece)
Principals, Chorus
"They are going" (Finale)
E. Roseau, Full Company

ACT 2
Scene 1
"Same Old Game" (Trio)
C. H. Drew, W. Gill, A. W. Maflin
"Like a Turk" (Quartette and Dance)
C. H. Drew, M. Elmore, M. Williams, W. Gill
Scene 2
"Grease with Cash" (Duet)
W. B. Cahill, M. Williams
"The Man in the Moon Has Gone to Rest" (Solo and Full Chorus)
E. Deering, Attendants
Scene 3
"Who Killed Cock Robin?"
Birds
Vocal selections
E. Roseau
"Joy, oh, what Rapture!" (Finale)
E. Roseau, Full Chorus

1878.21 MANHATTAN BEACH, or, Love Among the Breakers

An Operatic Lark in Two Escapades (Acts)[18]. Words by Charles Barnard. Music by Edward R. Mollenhauer. Stage manager, J. L. Vincent. Scenic artist, J. S. Schell. Musical director, Edward R. Mollenhauer. Produced by Minnie Cummings. Opened 23 December 1878 at Miss Minnie Cummings' Drawing Room Theatre and closed 28 December 1878 after 8 performances.

CAST: *Mr. Gay*: RUSSELL G. GLOVER. *Mr. Truelove*: THOMAS BARTLEMANN. *Mr. Faithful*: JULIAN FRANSISCO. *Mrs. Gay*: KATE GOODALL. *Mrs. Faithful*: VERNONA JARBEAU. *Mrs. Truelove*: MIRA LUCAS. And a Full Orchestra and Bathing Chorus.

1878.22 MONSIEUR JACQUES

A Revival of the Musical Piece in One Act (followed by a 'The Irish Emigrant,' a comic drama in Two Acts, by John Brougham). Play by Morris Barnett[19]. Music by Frederick Clay. Scenic artist, J. S. Schell. Produced by Minnie Cummings. Opened 30 December 1878 at Miss Minnie Cummings' Drawing Room Theatre and closed 31 December 1878 after 2 performances.

MONSIEUR JACQUES CAST: *Mr. Sequence*: Alf Blanchard. *Monsieur Jacques*: FRANK DREW. *Vivid*: A. Glosford. *Antonio*: John Wood. *Nina*: May Reywood.

THE IRISH EMIGRANT CAST: *Mr. Granite*, a wealthy merchant: Charles Dade. *Sterling*, an old clerk: James Woodworth. *Tom Bobalink*, a truckman: Henry F. Reed. *O'Bryan*, an Irish emigramt: FRANK DREW. *Henry Travers*: Edwin Carr. *Williams*: Edger Strong. *Polly Bobalink*: A. Sanger. *Miss Grimgriskin*: Grace Denger. *Mary Travers*: Louisa Beaudet.

1879.01 EVANGELINE

A Revival of the Musical Extravaganza in Three Acts[20]. (Libretto by J. Cheever Goodwin.) Music by Edward E. Rice. Musical director, Harry S. Braham. Produced by Edward E. Rice. Opened 6 January 1879 at the Lyceum Theatre and closed 22 January 1879 after 17 performances.[21]

CAST: *Evangeline*, our heroine, a creature of impulse and an impetuous pet, pursued through love's impatient prompting by Gabriel, and with a view to audacious contingencies by a whale: VENIE CLANCY. *Catherine*, the mildest type of anti-nuptial Mother in Law: GEORGE K. FORTESCUE. *Eulalie*, Evangeline's confidante, confidently hoping for Women's Rights: ROSE LEIGHTON. *Queen Booriolooboola Gha*, the King's much better advisor and supervisor of his whole conduct: Nellie Wood. *Mary Ann*, Evangeline's waiting maid: Marion Tracy. *Gabriel*, our hero, a fascinating and perambulating lover, in point of fact a roaming Romeo: LIZZIE WEBSTER. *LeBlanc*, a lawyer of the shyest shyster stamp, with a will and a way equally dark: WILLIAM FORRESTER. *Captain Dietrich*, a Dutch mercenary in the British ranks, who shows no mercy, being a mercy-nary cuss: CHARLES ROSENE. *The Lone Fisherman*, a patient and similarly taciturn toiler of the sea, with natural tendencies to hook whatever comes within his reach: HARRY HUNTER. *Bazil*, Evangeline's sire, whose vacillating mind is divided between the rental of her prospective husband and his own parental affection: WILLIAM STEVENS. *The Policeman*, called by some a peeler, possibly because he was never known to heed any appeal a prisoner might make, locus a non, and all that sort of thing: RICHARD GOLDEN. *Hans Wagner*, a spiritual corporal, with undue corporeal proportions: S. Crane. *The Jailer*, never without his key, vocal or instrumental, consequently always on the qui vive: Horace Frail. *Grab, Runemin*, a couple of the King's copper-colored "Copps": John Kropp, William Bullock. *Ringboldt, Deadshake*, a brace of conscientious deserters: W. H. Singleton, S. R. Morse. *King Booriolooboola Gha*, Royal Proprietor of the Mid-African Diamond Fields, who, not being able to hear anything near, occupies an ear trumpet: James Vincent. *Lo*, the Poor Indian, the lowest and the lowest savage of them all: H. M. Morse. *The Headsman*, not a mimic of stupid people, but very clever at taking off blockheads: G. H. Ulmar. *The Conductor*, though given to much punching, better acquainted with the P.R.R. than the P.R.: Marie Pallardis. *The Heifer*, specially imported from Cowes: — (Messrs. Cohen & Turner). *Fishermen, Sailors, Soldiers, Arcadians, Peasants, Africans, etc.*

1879.02 BABA!

A Revival of the Grand Oriental and Pantomimic Spectacle in a Prologue and Four Acts[22]. (Original play by John A. Mack.) Rewritten and revised by Maurice Pike. Acting manager, Maurice Pike. Scenic artists, Hannibal Calyo, assistants. Ballet arranged by Mons. Baptistan. Leader of orchestra, G. P. Barnard. Produced by F. W. Hofele. Opened 6 January 1879 at the Bowery Theatre and closed 25 January 1879 after 24 performances.

CAST: Mortals: *Amoret*, a romantic young tailor, with a soul above buttons, and a yearning for the aesthetic; who, after refusing Schaiba-Bou a suit of clothes, gives him perfect fits and closes his suit in another quarter, with songs: ETHEL LYNTON. *Baba*, his adopted brother and Fidus Achates. Baba is also a tailor, but gives up sewing tears for sewing wild oats, and having, by falling in love, fallen in prison: F. M. WILLS. *Abdul Kerym*, Grand Pasha of the Province of Angora, Brother to the Moon, and Papa of Two Daughters, and which he loveth passing well: CHARLES FOSTER. *Bou-Schaiba*, the Grand Vizier. A Magician, who is not liked despite his many charms, and whose spells are not obeyed to the letter: J. P. WINTER. *Schaiba-Bou*, his son, who cuts in to wed Princess Gulnare, and is much cut up by being cut out by Amoret: MAURICE PIKE. *Mustapha*, the Obese, whose life is onkneesy one from his inability to rise in the ranks: W. B. MURRAY. *Tiptim*, the nictatious. The original Tiptim, the wink: H. PRIOR. *Mazrour*, Captain of the Watch—therefore knows what's o'clock: Neil Gray. *Ouglu*, an attendant in the bath, the slave of the ring: G. Jones. *Ramazan*, Bou-Schaiba's servant, who like most of his class is blown up, with song: G. Andrews. *Gulnare*, the daughter of the Pasha, who has beauty and sense, but no love; and who, on finding the Keeper of her heart, bestows upon him her hand: ETHEL ALLEN. *Phrosine*, her twin sister, who has beauty and love, but no sense, characteristics which render her exceedingly attractive and eventually win her a husband, with a new medley written by D. Braham: MILLIE SCAKETT. *Lelia*, head splasher in the bath: Miss Condon. *Fetnah*, head dasher in the bath: Miss Louise Fox. (*Ladies and Gentlemen of the Court, Guards, Soldiers, Street vendors, Slaves, etc.*)

Immortals: *Damriel*, King of the Genii, yet the slave of Nerea: E. F. BARRY. *Danasch*, an affrite who believes in taking his turn: J. BIGLIN. *Gapowa*, the giant heavy porter—one to look up to: Mons. Behin. *Nerea*, the Queen of the Fairies. The Custodian of Hearts and Sovereign of the Lake of Cygnets: KATE GLASSFORD. *The Fairies who watch over the Princesses (5)*: *Cynia*: Miss Edmonson. *Emeraldina*: Kate Mason. *Coralina*: Ada Foster. *Nuphar*: Miss Jones. *Anemone*: Miss Grey. *Amazons, Fairies, Gnomes, Pixies, Demons, etc.*

---

[18]The scheduled curtain-raiser, a farce In and Out of Place!, was not performed, due to illness of its star Minnie Cummings. Frank Drew and Sol Smith were also featured.

[19]Authorship uncredited in programs. In its original form variously billed as melodrama, musical drama or musical burletta, MONSIEUR JACQUES was previously presented in New York in 1837 and numerous times thereafter in weekly or nightly engagements. For synopsis of Scenes and Musical Numbers, see 18 December 1854 production above.

[20]First produced in New York 27 July 1874 at Niblo's Garden for 16 performances. For Synopsis of Scenes and Musical Numbers, see original 1874 production.

[21]No credits in program for stage director (presumably Edward E. Rice), scenery or costumes. Musical numbers not listed in programs. Specialties:
"Idyl" (Act 1, by permission of John Braham.)
L. Webster
"The Heifer Dance" (a Delicious Absurdity)(Act 1)
Messr. Cohen, Turner

[22]First produced in New York 18 September 1876 at Niblo's Garden for 85 performances. For Synopsis of Scenes and Musical Numbers, see original 1876 production.

Ballet: *Premières*: Mlles. BETTY REMMELSBERG (Première Danseuse), Amelia Baptistan, Bertha Ruperth, Annie Daisey, Lizzie Reed. *Coryphées*: Mlles. Alice Richards, Emma Weston, Louisa Griffiths, Frankie Clemens. *Secondas*: Mlles. Selina Robinson, Lizzie Clarence, Annie Atkins, Sophie Ravel.

1879.03 ROBINSON CRUSOE

A Revival of the Burlesque in Two Acts, 6 Scenes[23]. (Play by Henry B. Farnie. Suggested by the novel of the same name by Daniel Defoe.) Stage manager, William Gill. Musical director, Henry Sator. Produced by Colville Opera Burlesque Company (Samuel Colville, Proprietor). Opened 9 January 1879 at the Park Theatre and closed 18 January 1879 after 11 performances.

CAST: *Robinson Crusoe*: MARIE WILLIAMS. *Tim Cox*: C. H. DREW. *Polly Hopkins*: EME ROSEAU. *Angelica*: LINA MERVILLE. *Will Atkins*: A. W. Maflin. *Gig*: Kate Everleigh.

Pirates: *Binnacle*: Ada Lee. *Dib*: Lizzie Wilson. *Tib*: Susie Winner. *Slider*: Elsie Dean. *Kapstan*: Annie Winner. *Ropeyarn*: Jennie Clark. *Tarr*: Mary Winner. *Pitch*: Clara White. *Rosin*: C. Foster. *Oh-Kum*: Nancy Tarbut.

Indians: *Friday*: WILLIAM GILL. *Princess Ylang-Ylang*: ELEANOR DEERING. *Jes-so*, her page: MARION ELMORE. *Way-ho*: WILLIAM B. CAHILL. *O-pap-o-nah*: Annie Deacan. *O-wy-o-wy*: W. H. Harpur. *Latitat*: H. Amberg. *Two Obadiahs*: Messrs. Francis and DeSmith. *Papoose*: La Petite Cary Elberts.

ACT 1

"A Sale! A Sale!" (Opening Chorus of Villagers, Jew Peddlers, etc.)

"O what a Row" (Concerted Piece)
M. Williams, C. H. Drew, K. Everleigh, L. Merville

"Love Serves in a Candy Store" (Song and Chorus)
K. Everleigh, Pirates

Mixed Conspirators' Chorus
M. Williams, C. H. Drew

"Pertty Polly Hopkins" (Quartette à la Marionette)
M. Williams, E. Roseau, C. H. Drew, L. Merville

"Farewell Forever" (Quartette)
M. Williams, E. Roseau, C. H. Drew, L. Merville

"Musical Introduction" (Solo)
E. Roseau

"All Said the Anchor's Weighed" (Finale)
All the characters

ACT 2

Scene 1

"Kickaboo" (Concerted Piece)

Quartette
E. Deering, A. Deacon, W. B. Cahill, M. Elmore

"Keep it Dark" (Concerted Piece)
A. W. Maflin, K. Everleigh, E. Roseau, L. Merville, Pirates

"Hail to Thee, Great Chief" (Grand Chorus of Indians)

Scene 2

"Laughing Song" (Double Song and Dance)
M. Williams, W. Gill

"Lovers' Talk" (Song and Chorus)
M. Williams, Characters

"Rum, Rum, Give Us Rum" (Chorus of Indians)

"Jeremiah, Blow the Fire" (Song and Chorus)
M. Williams, Indians

"Through the Jungles Strong" (Grand Ensemble)
All the characters

Scene 5

"Musical Introduction"
E. Roseau

Concerted Piece
E. Roseau, L. Merville, A. W. Maflin, Pirates

"Robinson Crusoe Thanks You Kindly" (Grand Finale)
All the characters

[23]First produced in New York 12 September 1877 at Wallack's Theatre for 19 performances; returned 12-20 November, 10-14 December 1877 to the Eagle Theatre for 14 additional performances. For Synopsis of Scenes, see original 1877 production.

1879.04 THE MULLIGAN GUARD BALL!

A Local Comic Drama in One Act, 7 Scenes[24], preceded by an Olio[25]. Play (and lyrics) by Edward Harrigan. Music by David Braham. Staged by Edward Harrigan. Scenic artist, Thomas R. Weston. Machinist, Robert Cutler. Properties, James Hynes. Musical director, David Braham. Produced by (Edward) Harrigan and (Tony) Hart. Opened 13 January 1879 at the Theatre Comique and closed 24 May 1879 after 152 performances.

Olio: Billy Gray in the Ethiopian sketch Almost a Marriage with Messrs. Fisher, Burt, Misses Yeamans, Jones; Emma Hoffman (vocalist); Kittie O'Neil (jig and reel dance); John Wild and John Shay in a sketch, The Gripsack, or, A Fool's Errand, with H. A. Fisher; Jennie Morgan (the American Linnet); The Snow Brothers (athletic performance with hats, dogs); Messrs. Goss and Fox, the Komical Kullurd Karacter Kmedians in an Ethiopian act, Komic Nigger Fun.

CAST: *Dan Mulligan*: EDWARD HARRIGAN. *Tommy Mulligan*, his son: TONY HART. *Sam Primrose*, Barber, Captain of the Skidmore Guards: JOHN WILD. *Palestine Puter*, Chaplain of the Skids: BILLY GRAY. *Gustavus Lochmuller*: HARRY A. FISHER. *Gustavus Lochmuller, Jr.*: EMIL HEUSEL. *Phil Garlic*: Ed Burt. *Walsingham McSweeny*: Michael Bradley. *Schnip Schneider*: John Mealey. *Ambrosial Rosenfelt*: Joseph Fitzsimmons. *Bridget Lochmuller*: Annie Mack. *Katy Lochmuller*: Nellie Jones. *Cordelia Mulligan*: MRS. ANNIE YEAMANS. *Maggie Murphy*: Lizzie Edwards. *Eunice Snow*: Nellie Boyd. *Anastasia Appledorn*: Tillie Nichols. *Caroline Williams*: Johnny Shay.

Mulligan Guards: *Tommy Gilmartin*: A. Melton. *Mickey Freely*: Frank Powers. *Dick Sheridan*: Billy West. *Phil Hurley*: B. Holy. *Abraham Purcel*: M. Forest. *O'Donovan Clancey*: B. Arnold. *Alonzo Brady*: G. Brown. *Timmy Flynn*: Frank Osgood.

Skidmore Guards: *Ferguson Clinton*: Ed Goss. *Pamerston Duby*: Jim Fox. *Sunrise Mitchell*: John Queen. *Mountchesington Grubb*: B. Overack. *Herman Gulliver*: Sam Smith. *Socrates Perkins*: H. Felton. *Nero Naylor*: Joe Buckley. *Sylvester Sampson*: Frank Nelson. *Musicians, Invited Guests, Colored and White Senators, Distinguished Ladies and Gentlemen of Celtic and African Origin, and a carefully selected Auxiliary Force.*

Scene 1: The Mulligans at Home. *Scene 2*: Local Street. *Scene 3*: Barber Shop. *Scene 4*: Street. *Scene 5*: The Ball Room. *Scene 6*: Street. *Scene 7*: Interior of Mulligan's Cottage.

MUSICAL NUMBERS

"The Skidmore's Fancy Ball" (Scene 4)
J. Wild, B. Gray, Skidmores

"The Babies in Our Block" (Scene 5)
E. Harrigan

"The Hall-Way Door" (Scene 7)
E. Harrigan

1879.05 H.M.S. PINAFORE, or, The Lass That Loved a Sailor

A Comic Opera in Two Acts. Libretto by William S. Gilbert. Music by Arthur Sullivan. Costumes by T. W. Lanouette. Setting by J. S. Schell. Musical director, Charles Schiller. Produced by James C. Duff[26]. Opened 15 January 1879 at the Standard Theatre, re-constructed[27] 14 April 1879 and closed 14 June 1879 after 175 performances[28].

CAST: *The Rt. Hon. Sir Joseph Porter, K.C.B.*, First Lord of the Admiralty: THOMAS WHIFFEN. *Captain Corcoran*, Commanding *H.M.S. Pinafore*: EUGENE CLARKE. *Ralph Rackstraw*, Able Seaman: HENRI LAURENT. *Dick Deadeye*, Able Seaman: WILLIAM DAVIDGE. *Bill Bobstay*, Boatswain: Charles Makin. *Bob Becket*,

[24]This may regarded as "Volume Two" in the Mulligan Guard series.

[25]Accompanying the customary variety or olio, Harrigan offered a short burlesque, The Great In-Toe Natural Walking Match, for the week of 24 March 1879. CAST: *Peg Bunion*: JOHN WILD. *Judge Steerer*: BILLY GRAY. *Charley Row-well*: John Shay. *Dan O'Lear-eye*: John Queen. *Dear Charley Hairy-man*: Ed Burt. *Ennis Killen*: Billy West. *Major Botts*: HARRY A. FISHER.

[26]Beginning 26 May 1879 William Henderson assumed management of the production from James C. Duff.

[27]New and beautiful scenery, costumes, enlarged chorus, etc.

[28]Stage direction uncredited. Stage manager, H. W. Montgomery. The production was preceded by a curtain-raiser, My Uncle's Will, featuring May Davenport, W. Davidge, and B. T. Ringgold; beginning 17 March 1879, this was replaced by Comical Countess, featuring May Davenport, H. W. Montgomery and William Davidge. This was succeeded 14 April 1879 by COX AND BOX; for detail, see its entry at this date below.

Carpenter's Mate: H. J. Burt. *Tom Tucker*, Midshipmite: Master Henry. *Tom Bowlin*: J. Wilmot. *Josephine*, the Captain's Daughter: EVA MILLS. *Little Buttercup*, Mrs. Cripps, a Portsmouth Bumboat woman: BLANCHE GALTON. *Hebe*, Sir Joseph's First Cousin: VERNONA JARBEAU. *First Lord's Sisters, His Cousins and His Aunts; Sailors, etc.*

Scene: Deck of the *H.M.S. Pinafore*, off Portsmouth, England.

Act 1: Noon.

Act 2: Moonlight.

ACT 1[29]

"We sail the ocean blue" (Opening Chorus)

"I'm called little Buttercup" (Recitative and Song)
B. Galton

Recitative
B. Galton, C. Makin

"The Nightingale sigh'd for the moon's bright ray" (Scena)
H. Laurent, Chorus

"A maiden fair to see" (Aria)
H. Laurent, Chorus

"I am the Captain of the Pinafore" (Recitative, Song and Chorus)
E. Clarke, Men's Chorus

Recitative
B. Galton, E. Clarke

"Sorry her lot" (Song)
E. Mills

"Over the bright blue sea Comes Sir Joseph Porter, K. C. B."
(Chorus of Women, behind the Scenes) Women's Chorus

"We sail the ocean blue" (Chorus of Sailors)
Men's Chorus

"I am the monarch of the sea"
T. Whiffen, V. Jarbeau, C. Makin, Chorus

"When I was a lad" (Song)
T. Whiffen, Chorus

Exit for Ladies

"A British tar is a soaring soul" (Trio and Chorus)
H. Laurent, C. Makin, H. J. Burt

"Refrain, audacious tar, your suit from pressing" (Duet)
E. Mills, H. Laurent

"Can I survive this overbearing?" (Finale)
Principals, Chorus

ACT 2

"Fair moon, to thee I sing!" (Song)
E. Clarke

"Things are seldom what they seem" (Duet)
B. Galton, E. Clarke

"The hours creep on apace" (Scena)
E. Mills

"Never mind the why or wherefore" (Trio)
E. Mills, E. Clarke, T. Whiffen

"The merry maiden and the tar" (Duet)
E. Clarke, W. Davidge

"Carefully on tiptoe stealing" (Soli and Chorus)
W. Davidge, E. Clarke, E. Mills, H. Laurent, V. Jarbeau, T. Whiffen, Men's Chorus

"Farewell, my own, Light of my life, farewell!" (Octette and Chorus)
H. Laurent, E. Mills, T. Whiffen, V. Jarbeau, W. Davidge, C. Makin, H. J. Burt, B. Galton, Chorus

"A many years ago, when I was young and charming" (Legend)
B. Galton, Chorus

"Oh joy, oh rapture unforseen!" (Finale)
Principals, Chorus

[29]Musical numbers not listed in programs. List prepared from published English vocal score (Metzler & Co, Ltd., London 1878, 1887).

H.M.S. PINAFORE,

1879.06 or, The Lass That Loved a Sailor

A Comic Opera in Two Acts[30]. Libretto by William S. Gilbert. Music by Arthur Sullivan. Scenery by De La Harpe and Crane. Orchestra under the direction of Harry Braham. Produced by Rice's Opera Bouffe Extravaganza Combination (Edward E. Rice, Manager). Opened 23 January 1879 at the Lyceum Theatre and closed 15 February 1879 after 25 performances.[31]

CAST: *The Rt. Hon. Sir Joseph Porter*, K.C.B., First Lord of the Admiralty: WILLIAM FORRESTER. *Captain Corcoran*, commanding the *H.M.S. Pinafore*: JOHN VINCENT. *Ralph Rackstraw*, Able Seaman: LIZZIE WEBSTER. *Dick Deadeye*, Able Seaman: Henry Hunter. *Bill Bobstay*, Boatswain: Richard Golden. *Tom Tucker*, Midshipmite: Little Jessie Fortescue. *Josephine*, the Captain's Daughter: VENIE G. CLANCY. *Little Buttercup*, a Portsmouth Bumboat Woman: GEORGE K. FORTESCUE. *Hebe*, Sir Joseph's First Cousin: ROSE LEIGHTON. (*Specialty*: Mons. Cohen & Turner.) *First Lord's Sisters, His Cousins, His Aunts, Sailors*: Full Chorus.

H.M.S. PINAFORE,

1879.07 or, The Lass That Loved a Sailor

A Comic Opera in Two Acts[32]. Libretto by William S. Gilbert. Music by Arthur Sullivan. Cast, chorus and orchestra under the direction of Max Maretzek. Costumes by Mr. Schwencke. Scenery by Mr. L. W. Seavey. Produced by D. H. Harkins. Opened 10 February 1879 at the Fifth Avenue Theatre and closed 8 March 1879 after 32 performances; re-opened 7 April 1879 at the Fifth Avenue Theatre and closed 19 April 1879 after 16 additional performances. Total: 48 performances.

CAST: *Josephine*, the Captain's daughter: BLANCHE CORELLI. *Little Buttercup*, a Portsmouth Bumboat Woman: KATE GURNEY. *Hebe*, Sir Joseph's First Cousin: IDA FOY. *Sir Joseph Porter*, K.C.B., First Lord of the Admiralty: JAMES H. BURNETT. *Captain Corcoran*, commanding the *H.M.S. Pinafore*: J. G. PEAKES. *Ralph Rackstraw*, able seaman: HENRY LAURENT. *Dick Deadeye*, able seaman: James Harten. *Bill Bobstay*, Boatswain: Arthur Van Houten. *Bob Becket*, Captain's mate: Peter Chrystal. *Tom Tucker*, Midshipmite: Master Louis. *Tom Bowlin*: Mr. Henry. *First Lord's Sisters, His Cousins and His Aunts*: Helen Mortimer and Ladies of the Corps de Ballet. *Sailors*: Chorus.

[30]A rival to the production at the Standard. First produced in New York 15 January 1879 at the Standard Theatre for 175 performances. For Synopsis of Scenes and Musical Numbers, see entry above. Specialties:

"William Was a Gay Young Sailor"
L. Webster

"Jack is Every Inch a Sailor"
V. G. Clancy

Flag Hornpipe
Messrs. Cohen & Turner

Burlesque Hornpipe
H. Hunter, R. Golden

[31]No credits for stage director or costumes. Stage manager, James Vincent. In response to poor reviews, the show was entirely recast beginning 3 February 1879: *The Rt. Hon. Sir Joseph Porter*: FRANK DREW. *Captain Corcoran*: J. M. BROWN. *Ralph Rackstraw*: ANTOINETTE SANGER. *Dick Deadeye*: F. K. Howard. *Bill*: Alfred Holland. *Bob Bobstay*: Mr. Cellier. *Josephine*: EUGENIE PAUL. *Little Buttercup*: ESTELLE MORTIMER. *Hebe*: SARA LASCELLES. *Sailors, Relatives, Marines, etc.* Orchestra under the direction of F. V. Jones. Rice's name no longer appears as producer, now billed as 'Lyceum Pinafore Company.' Gone were the previous interpolations, with one added:

"Here Take My Heart"
E. Paul, A. Sanger
(*Music by* F. V. Jones. *Lyrics by* Bartley Campbell.)

[32]A rival production to the original at the Standard Theatre. First produced in New York 15 January 1879 at the Standard Theatre for 175 performances. For Synopsis of Scenes and Musical Numbers, see entry above. H.M.S. PINAFORE was preceded by a curtain-raiser, "A Kiss in the Dark" which was succeeded two weeks later by a revival of TRIAL BY JURY; see entry at 24 February 1879 below.

H.M.S. PINAFORE,

1879.08 or, The Lass That Loved a Sailor!

A Nautical Comic Opera in Two Acts[33] Libretto by William S. Gilbert. Music by Arthur Sullivan. Stage manager, Frank A. Tannehill. Setting by George Hineman. Musical director, Charles Puerner. Produced by Edward F. Starin. Opened 10 February 1879 at Niblo's Garden and closed 15 February 1879 after 8 performances.

CAST: *The Right Hon. Sir Joseph Porter*, K.C.B., First Lord of the Admiralty: SOL SMITH. *Captain Corcoran*, commanding the *H.M.S. Pinafore*: H. R. HUMPHRIES. *Ralph Rackstraw*, Able Seaman: L. DIGBY. *Bill Bobstay*, Boatswain: Harry Chapman. *Dick Deadeye*, Able Seaman: A. B. BARKER. *Tom Tucker*, Midshipmite: Master Ralph Nautilus. *Josephine*, the Captain's daughter: LESITTA ELLAIN [LISETTA ELLANI]. *Little Buttercup*, a Portsmouth Bum Boat Woman: GRACE CLARE. *Hebe*, Sir Joseph's First Cousin: EMMA METTLAR. *Marines, Sailors, Seamen*: Numerous Auxiliaries.

1879.09 HIS-MUD-SCOW PINAFORE

A Musical Burlesque (of Gilbert and Sulivan's H.M.S. PINAFORE) in One Act, preceded by an Olio. Libretto by Add Ryman. Music arranged by W. S. Mullaly. Scenic effects by Charles Graham. Costumes by Mr. Ives. Mechanical effects by Nelse Waldron. Produced by the San Francisco Minstrels. Opened 10 February 1879 at San Francisco Minstrels' Hall and closed 10 May 1879 after 92 performances.[34]

Olio: "The King's Highway" (bass song), H. W. Frillman. "Bonnie Sweet Bessie" (ballad), William Raymond. "My Baby" (comic ditty), Charles Backus. "Sweet Little Rose of the Laa" (new ballad), D. S. Wambold. "So Awfully Thin" (comic song), Billy Birch. "Nancy Lee" (ballad), J. G. Russell. Finale (from The Chimes of Normandy), San Francisco Minstrels Company. Uncle Abe and Sister Ruth (Johnson and Powers, grotesque song and dance artists), George Thatcher (excerpts). Hayle and Pickert (clog dancers).

CAST: *Sir Joseph Porter, B.F.U.*, bottled for use: ADD RYMAN. *Captain Corkonion*: JAMES JOHNSON. *Alf. Strawrack*: BILLY BIRCH. *Purser*: William Raymond. *One-Eyed Dick*: GEORGE POWERS. *Bob Stay*: George Thatcher. *Tom Tucket*: H. W. Frillman. *Josephine*: F. M. RICARDO. *Hebe*: CHARLES BACKUS. *Little Buttertub*: CHARLES STEVENS. *Sisters, Cousins, Aunts, Sailors, and Visiting Congressmen.*

1879.10 THE SORCERER

A Comic Opera in Two Acts[35]. Libretto by William S. Gilbert. Music by Arthur Sullivan. Musical director, J. A. Kinney. Produced by Chandos Fulton and George Edgar. Opened 21 February 1879 at the Broadway Theatre and closed 8 March 1879 after 20 performances.[36]

CAST: *Sir Mamaduke Pointdexter*, an elderly Baronet: FRANK BUDWORTH. *Alexis*, of the Grenadier Guards, his son: TOM BULLOCK. *Dr. Daly*, Vicar of Ploverleigh: W. H. CROMPTON. *Notary*: J. P. Swinburne. *John Wellington Wells*, of J. W. Wells & Co., Family Sorcerers: WILLIAM HORACE LINGARD. *Lady Sangazure*, a Lady of ancient lineage: ANNIE BOUDINOT. *Aline*, her daughter, betrothed to Alexis: MATILDA SCOTT. *Mrs. Partlett*, a Pew-Opener: Florence Wood. *Constance*, her daughter: Minnie Clive. *Chorus of Peasantry.*

Act 1: Grounds of Sir Marmaduke's Mansion. Present day.

Act 2: Market-place of Ploverleigh. A half an hour later.

ACT 1[37]

"Ring forth, ye bells" (Chorus)

Recitative (Constance, my daughter, why this strange depression?)
F. Wood, M. Clive

"When he is here" (Aria)
M. Clive

Recitative (The air is charged with amatory numbers)
W. H. Crompton

"Time was, when Love and I were well acquainted" (A Pale Young Curate)(Ballad)
W. H. Crompton

Recitative (Sir Marmaduke, my dear young friend) and minuet
F. Budworth, W. H. Crompton, T. Bullock

"With heart and with voice" (Chorus of Girls)

Recitative (My kindly friends, I thank you for this greeting)

"Happy young heart" (Aria)
M. Scott

Recitative (My child, I join these congratulations)
A. Boudinot

"With heart and with voice" (Chorus of Men)

"Welcome joy! Adieu to sadness!" (Duet)
A. Boudinot, F. Budworth

"All is prepared" (Ensemble)
M. Scott, T. Bullock, J. P. Swinburne, Chorus

"For love alone" (Ballad)
T. Bullock

"My name is John Wellington Wells" (Song)
W. H. Lingard

"Sprites of earth and air" (Incantation)
M. Scott, T. Bullock, W. H. Lingard, Chorus

"Now to the Banquet we press" (Finale)
Principals, Chorus

ACT 2

"'Tis Twelve, I think" (Trio and Chorus)
M. Scott, T. Bullock, W. H. Lingard

"Dear friends, take pity on my lot" (Ensemble)
M. Clive, J. P. Swinburne, M. Scott, T. Bullock, Chorus

"It is not love" (Ballad)
T. Bullock

"Such a wife to soothe his years" (Quintette)
M. Scott, F. Wood, T. Bullock, W. H. Crompton, F. Budworth

"Oh, I have wrought much evil with my spells!" (Hate Me!)(Recitative and Duet)
A. Boudinot, W. H. Lingard

"Alexis! Doubt me not my loved one!" (Recitative and Air)
M. Scott

"Engaged to So-and-so" (Song)
W. H. Crompton

"Oh, joyous boon! Oh, mad delight!" (Ensemble)
M. Scott, T. Bullock, W. H. Crompton, Chorus

Recitative (Prepare for sad surprises)
T. Bullock

"Or he or I must die" (Finale)
Principals, Chorus

1879.11 TRIAL BY JURY

A Revival of the Comic Opera in One Act[38], followed by H.M.S. PINAFORE. Libretto by William S. Gilbert. Music by Arthur Sullivan. Cast, chorus and orchestra under the direction of Max Maretzek. Costumes by Mr. Schwencke. Scenery by Mr. L. W. Seavey. Produced by D. H. Harkins. Opened 24 February 1879 at the Fifth Avenue Theatre, and closed 8 March 1879 after 16 performances; re-opened 7 April 1879 at the Fifth Avenue Theatre and closed 12 April 1879 after 8 additional performances. Total: 24 performances.

CAST: *The Learned Judge*: VINCENT HOGAN. *The Plaintiff*: BLANCHE CORELLI. *Counsel for the Plaintiff*: James Harten. *The Defendant*: HENRY LAURENT. *Foreman of the Jury*: J. H. Burnett. *Usher*: Arthur Van Houten. *Bridesmaids, Spectators, Gentlemen of the Jury, etc.*

---

[33]A rival production to the original at the Standard Theatre. First produced in New York 15 January 1879 at the Standard Theatre for 175 performances. For Synopsis of Scenes and Musical Numbers, see entry above. H.M.S. PINAFORE was preceded by a comedietta, Winning a Widow. CAST: *Sir Edward Ardent*, Bart: FRANK A. TANNEHILL. *Mrs. Chillingstone*, Widow: ANNIE WARD TIFFANY.

[34]No scenes or musical numbers listed in playbills, apart from the finale, "She's a Daisy."

[35]Preceded by a curtain-raiser, Rough Diamond, or, Cousin Joe's Visit.

[36]No credits in programs for stage director, scenery or costumes. No musical numbers listed in programs.

[37]Musical numbers not listed in programs. List prepared from published English vocal score (Metzler & Co., Ltd. London, 1877, 1884).

[38]First produced in New York 15 November 1875 at the Eagle Theatre for 8 performances. For Synopsis of Scenes and Musical Numbers, see original 1875 production.

1879.12

THE BLACK CROOK

A Revival of the Musical Extravaganza in Four Acts, 17 Scenes[39]. Play by Charles M. Barras. Music by Thomas Baker, etc. Production staged by the Kiralfy Brothers (Imre, Bolossy). Scenery by Ed. Simmons, William Voegtlin, Harley Merry, H. Tryon, J. Thompson, Robecchi of Paris, Sig. Ferario of Milan, others. Armors and jewels by Granger of Paris, and Kennedy, of London. Costumes by Miss Fisher, of London, and Lorraine, of New York. Mechanical effects by John Leo. Leader of orchestra, Charles Puerner. Produced by Edward F. Starin. Opened 5 March 1879 at Niblo's Garden and closed 3 May 1879 after 72 performances.

CAST: *Mortals*: *Rudolph*, a poor artist: WILLIAM A. SANDS. *Count Wolfenstein*: HARRY S. DUFFIELD. *Hertzog*, the Black Crook: J. F. PETERS. *Greppo*, his servant: JOHN WARD. *Von Puffingrantz*, the Count's steward: WILLIAM H. COLLINGS. *Bruno*, a ruffian: Charles Livingston. *Wolfgar*, a ruffian: John Hammond. *Caspar*, a peasant: Peter Toole. *Armena*, betrothed to Rudolph: Annie Ward Tiffany. *Carline*, Armena's maid: Marion Fiske. *Dame Barbara*, Armena's foster mother: Mrs. Harry Jordan. *Rosetta*, a peasant: Lillie Pearson. *Ladies, Lords, Villagers, Peasants, Pages.*

Immortals: *Stalacta*, Queen of the Golden Realm: BELLE HOWITT. *Dragonfin*, her faithful sprite: August Siegrist. *Zamiel*, the arch fiend: Charles Mason. *Skuldawelp*, familiar to Hertzog: R. C. Clifford. *Fairies, Water Sprites, Semons, Skeltons, Spectres.*

Ballet: Mlles. BONFANTI, DeROSA, PAGLIERI; Secondas, Coryphées, Corps de Ballet. *Specialties*: The Leotard Brothers, The Three Lorellas, The Miranda Sisters, The Ulm Sisters, Les Frères Langlois.

Act 1, Scene 1: Village. View of Castle Wolfenstein. (Merry.) *Scene 2*: A Woody Pass, Hartz Mountains. (Merry.) *Scene 3*: A Hall in Castle Wolfenstein. (Thompson.) *Scene 4*: Laboratory of the Crook. (Ferrario.) *Scene 5*: Wild Cross Path in a Glen of the Brocken. (Designed by J. Kiralfy, painted by Merry.)

Act 2, Scene 1: Subterranean Vaults. (Ferrario, painted by Simmons.) *Scene 2*: Gothic Chamber. (Simmons.); The Grotto of Stalacta. (Voegtlin.)

Act 3, Scene 1: The Palace of Lace. (Fromont, painted by Simmons.) *Scene 2*: A Hall in the Castle. *Scene 3*: Grand Staircase of the Illuminated Terrace. (I. Kiralfy, painted by Merry.)

Act 4, Scene 1: Gothic Hall. (Thompson.) *Scene 2*: Rocky Pass. (Merry.) *Scene 3*: Burning Forest. (Merry.) *Scene 4*: Wood. (Merry.) *Scene 5*: Pandemonium. (Merry.) *Scene 6*: Rocky Pass. (Merry.) *Scene 7*: Grand Transformation Scene, representing the Enchanted Home of the Fairies! (Robecchi, painted by Tryon.)

BALLETS AND SPECIALTIES

Village Festive Dance and Chorus (Act 1, Scene 1)
Coryphées

Waltz Song (Act 1, Scene 3)
M. Fiske

Beautiful Cascade of Real Water; The Demon Fight; The Walking Skeleton; The Incantations; Grand Tableaux Infernale (Act 1, Scene 5)

Song (Act 2, Scene 2)
B. Howitt

Grand Ballet Des Demons (Act 2, Scene 2)
(*Composed and arranged by* Mons. Kiralfy; *new music by* Jacques Offenbach.)

Entrée Diabolatain
Ladies of the Ballet

Entrée Diabolatain
Coryphées

Les Salamanders
Danseuses Secondas

Grand Entrées by the Premiere Assolutas
Mlles. DeRosa, Paglieri

Grand Adadie

Entermede Brillante
Coryphées

Variations d'Art
Premières

Finale Ensemble Internale
Entire Corps de Ballet

Tableaux of Armena's Bridal Festival (Act 3, Scene 1)

The Leotard Brothers (Acrobatic Act)(Act 3, Scene 1)

The Three Lorellas (Eccentric Dancers)(Act 3, Scene 1)

The Miranda Sisters (Aerial Feats)(Act 3, Scene 1)

Kiralfy's Celebrated Ballet of All Nations (Act 3, Scene 1)

Entrée, Tartars, Italie and Austria
Corps de Ballet

La Flora D'Espagna
Danseuses Secondas

Ensemble et Hongroise
Coryphées

L'Italie
Mlle. Paglieri

Dance de Normandie
Ladies of the Ballet

South American Dance
Corps de Ballet

L'Amerique
Mlle. De Rosa

Great Britain
Danseuses Secondas

Grand Finale, China, Japan, and all Nations
Entire Ballet Corps

The Ulm Sisters (Trios)(Act 3, Scene 2)

Les Frères Langlois (Marvels of the Nineteenth Century)(Act 3, Scene 2)

Duet (Act 3, Scene 2)
M. Fiske, J. Ward

Grand Manoeuvre D'Amazon
B. Howitt, 120 Ladies of the Ballet

[39]First produced in New York 12 September 1866 at Niblo's Garden for 475 performances. For Synopsis of Scenes and Musical Numbers, see original 1866 production.

1879.13

H.M.S. PINAFORE,
or, The Lass That Loved a Sailor

A Comic Opera in Two Acts[40]. Libretto by William S. Gilbert. Music by Arthur Sullivan. Orchestra under the direction of John Philip Sousa. Presented by John Gorman's Philadelphia Church Choir Company (Management, James H. Meade). Opened 10 March 1879 at the Broadway Theatre and closed 26 April 1879 after 55 performances; re-opened 12 May 1879 at the Broadway Theatre and closed 24 May 1879 after an additional 16 performances. Total: 71 performances.[41]

CAST: *The Rt. Hon. Sir Joseph Porter, K.C.B.*, First Lord of the Admiralty: LOUIS DeLANGE. *Captain Corcoran*, Commanding the *H.M.S. Pinafore*: G. B. SNYDER. *Ralph Rackstraw*, Able Seaman: G. S. STURGIS. *Dick Deadeye*, Able Seaman: F. W. Huff. *Bill Bobstay*, Boatswain: Joseph J. Knox. *Josephine*, the Captain's Daughter: EMMA HENRY. *Little Buttercup*, a Bumboat Woman: Miss A. V. RUTHERFORD. *Hebe*, Sir Joseph's First Cousin: Miss M. P. Stevenson. *First Lord's Sisters, his Cousins, his Aunts, Sailors, Marines, etc.*: Chorus of 40.

1879.14

THE SORCERER

A Comic Opera, in Two Acts[42]. Libretto by William S. Gilbert. Music by Arthur Sullivan. Orchestra under the direction of G. Weingarten. Produced by Edward H. Harvey's Comic Opera Company [F. Rullman, manager]. Opened 10 March 1879 at the Lyceum Theatre and closed 22 March 1879 (matinee) after 13 performances in repertory.

CAST: *Sir Mamaduke Pointdexter*, a baronet of the old school, K.C.B.: GEORGE GASTON. *Alexis*, his son, a young officer: J. GRAFF. *Dr. Daly*, rector of Ploverleigh: H. R. Humphries. *Notary*: Mr. Demorest. *Lady Sangazure*, of ancient lineage: Miss E. Howard. *John Wellington Wells*, of the firm of Wells & Co., family sorcerers: C. H. DUNCAN. *Aline*, her daughter, betrothed to Alexis: MARIE HARVEY. *Mrs. Partlett*. pew-opener: Nellie Mortimer. *Constance*, her daughter—a charity girl: Miss Hall. *Chorus.*

followed by

[40]A rival production to the original at the Standard. First produced in New York 15 January 1879 at the Standard Theatre for 175 performances. For Synopsis of Scenes and Musical Numbers, see entry above.
[41]Played a return engagement 10 November 1879 at the Broadway Opera House for 24 performances; see separate entry in following season.
[42]A rival production to the original at the Broadway. First produced in New York 21 February 1879 at the Broadway Theatre for 20 performances. For Synopsis of Scenes and Musical Numbers, see entry above.

H.M.S. PINAFORE,
or, The Lass That Loved a Sailor

A Comic Opera in Two Acts[43]. Libretto by William S. Gilbert. Music by Arthur Sullivan.

CAST: *Sir Joseph Porter*, K.C.B., First Lord of the Admiralty: GEORGE GASTON. *Captain Corcoran*, commanding the *H.M.S. Pinafore*: H. R. HUMPHRIES. *Ralph Rackstraw*, able seaman: W. HAYDON TILLA. *Dick Deadeye*, able seaman: S. P. Strini. *Bill Bobstay*, boatswain: Livingstone Kent. *Bob Becket*, carpenter's mate: Mr. Demorest. *Tom Tucker*, midshipmite: Master Watson. *Josephine*, the Captain's daughter: MARIA HARVEY. *Hebe*, Sir Joseph's first cousin: MAUDE BRANSCOMBE. *Little Buttercup*, a Portsmouth Bumboat woman: NELLIE MORTIMER. *Aunt to Sir Joseph*: Miss Howard. *Quartermaster*: C. H. Duncan. (*First Lord's Sisters, His Cousins and His Aunts*: Chorus.)

1879.15

THE LITTLE DUKE

A Comic Opera in Three Acts. Original French libretto to the opéra-comique "Le Petit Duc" by Henri Meilhac and Ludovic Halévy. (American adaptation by T. R. Sullivan and Fred Williams.) Music by Charles Lecocq. Stage manager, L. J. Vincent. Orchestra under the direction of Charles V. Schiller. Produced by James C. Duff. Opened 17 March 1879 at Booth's Theatre and closed 5 April 1879 after 24 performances.[44]

CAST: *Henri*, Duc de Parthenay: FLORENCE ELLIS. *Le Chevalier de Montlandry*, a Soldier: W. H. MacDONALD. *Frimousse*, tutor to the Duke: ED. CHAPMAN. *Officers of the Regiment of Parthenay (8)*: *De Navailles*: Henry Fraser. *De Montchevrier*: Edward Burton. *De Tanneville*: Victor Harman. *De Nancey*: C. H. Marcy. *De Champvaillant*: Wilfred Montrose. *De Merignac*: George Gibbons. *De Chargny*: Sidney Barnes. *De Ribeaumont*: R. McDonald. *Bernard de Retz*, Aide-de-Camp: Fred Goldthwaite. *Blanche*, Duchesse de Parthenay: LOUISE BEAUDET. *Diane*, Marquise de Lansac, Directress of the Convent School: Mme. MARIE BEAUMAN. *Mlle. de la Roche*: Helen Grayson. *Mlle. de Champ Rouge*: Rosa Wilson. *Mlle. St. Maur*: Emily Hinckley. *Governess*: Ethel Champneys. *First Page of Honor*: Forinda Telbin. *Second Page of Honor*: Clarissa Stark. *Third Page of Honor*: Henrietta Fischer. *First Maid of Honor*: Miss E. Tadolini. *Second Maid of Honor*: Josephine Corcoran. *Third Maid of Honor*: Lucille Espantoza. *Vivandieres*: Misses Ella Vincent, Carlotta Pezzuolo, Gussie Lang, Edwina Carlton. *Dragoons of the Parthenay Regiment, Trumpeters, Pensionnaires of the Convent at Luneville, Maids of Honor, Pages, Lords and Ladies of the Court de la Grande Monarque, etc.*

Act 1: A Magnificent Apartment in the Palace of Versailles. At the time of Louis XIV, about 1700.

Act 2: The School of the Noble Ladies of Luneville.

Act 3: The Camp.

ACT 1[45]

Opening Chorus (Ladies young and courtiers old)
Chorus

"The Pages Song" (Since you laugh at a sighing lover)
Pages, Maids of Honor

"The Scholar and Soldier" (Duet)
E. Chapman, W. H. MacDonald

"The Wedding Ring Song" (Here come the youthful bride and groom)
Chorus

"The Wedding Ring Song" (Of our childish rapture jealous)
F. Ellis

Ballet and Chorus (Gavotte)(See the youthful pair advancing)
Chorus

"True Love" (Duet)
F. Ellis, L. Beaudet

"Love Lost and Found" (Song)
F. Ellis

Chorus of Pages (Poor little man)
Pages

Chorus of Officers (Our colonel, see!)
Chorus

ACT 2

"The Singing Lesson"
M. Beauman, H. Grayson, R. Wilson, E. Hinckley

Solfeggio
M. Beauman, H. Grayson, R. Wilson, E. Hinckley, Pupils

"The Compact" (Ensemble)
L. Beaudet, Young Ladies, W. H. MacDonald, Trumpeters

Song (I am not here to menace you)
W. H. MacDonald, M. Beauman

"To Arms!" (Ensemble)
W. H. MacDonald, L. Beaudet, Chorus

"Song of the Peasant"
F. Ellis

"The Bold Brigade" (Air with Chorus)
F. Ellis, M. Beauman, Young Ladies

"The Idyl" (Duet)
F. Ellis, E. Chapman

"Song of the Adieu" (Chorus of Soldiers)
Dragoons, Young Ladies

"Song of the Adieu" (Song)
F. Ellis, W. H. MacDonald, M. Beauman, Young Ladies

Finale (If victorious you return)
Young Ladies, Soldiers

ACT 3

"Drinking Chorus"
G. Gibbons, V. Harman, F. Goldthwaite, Officers, Soldiers, Vivandières

"Song of the Little Hunchback"
W. H. MacDonald

"Lament of Villagers" (Heaven help us!)
Chorus

"Victory" (Song and Chorus)
F. Ellis, Chorus

"The Word" (Ensemble)
F. ellis, W. H. MacDonald, Officers

"The Fortune of War" (Duet)
L. Beaudet, F. Ellis

"Song of the Sword" (Finale)
F. Ellis

1879.16

H.M.S. PINAFORE,
or, The Lass That Loved a Sailor

A Comic Opera in Two Acts[46]. Libretto by William S. Gilbert. Music by Arthur Sullivan. Produced by the Harvey Company. Opened 17 March 1879 at the Olympic Theatre and closed 26 March 1879 after 11 performances.

CAST: *Sir Joseph Porter*: W. C. CROSBY. *Captain Corcoran*: J. L. DOUGLAS. *Ralph Rackstraw*: E. J. Atkinson. *Dick Deadeye*: W. H. Lytell. *Bill Bobstay*: Mr. C. Demarest. *Bob Beckett*: R. Brower. *Tom Tucker*: W. D. Peck. *Josephine*: MATILDA SCOTT. *Hebe*: Alice Fitzgerald. *Buttercup*: DORA STEWART.

1879.17

H.M.S. PINAFORE

A Comic Opera in Two Acts[47], in German. Libretto by William S. Gilbert. Music by Arthur Sullivan. Entire production staged by Adolph Neuendorff. Orchestra under the direction of Max Maretzek. Produced by Adolph

[43]A rival production to the original at the Standard Theatre. First produced in New York 15 January 1879 at the Standard Theatre for 175 performances. For Synopsis of Scenes and Musical Numbers, see entry above.

[44]No credits in programs for stage direction, scenery or costumes.

[45]Musical numbers not listed in programs. List prepared from published piano vocal score (Oliver Ditson & Co., Boston, 1879).

[46]No program found for this production. A rival production to the original at the Standard Theatre. First produced in New York 15 January 1879 at the Standard Theatre for 175 performances. For Synopsis of Scenes and Musical Numbers, see entry above. Preceded by a comedietta, The Gaythornes, with Dickie Lingard; for the second week of the run (3 nights), Gilbert & Sullivan's THE SORCERER replaced The Gaythornes with the following cast: Misses Marie Harvey, Nellie Mortimer, Louise Leighton, Maude Branscombe, Messrs. W. Hayden Tilla, H. R. Humphries, Livingston Kent, C. Demarest, J. Graaf, G. Gaston, C. H. Duncan, S. P. Strini, with 24 in Chorus, as per listing in the New York Herald.

[47]German language premiere, preceded by a curtain-raiser, Hector. A rival production to the original at the Standard Theatre. First produced in New York in English 15 January 1879 at the Standard Theatre for 175 performances. For Synopsis of Scenes and Musical Numbers, see entry above.

Neuendorff. Opened 22 March 1879 at the Germania Theater and closed 11 April 1879 after (14) performances in repertory.

CAST: *Sir Joseph Porter*, K.C.B., First Lord of the Admiralty: Herr WILL. *Captain Corcoran*, commanding the *H.M.S. Pinafore*: Herr RANK. *Ralph Rackstraw*, able seaman: Herr BOWMANN. *Dick Scheelauge*, able seaman: Herr Reinhold Bojock. *Bill Bobstay*, Boatswain: Herr Kummer. *Bob Becket*, Captain's mate: Herr Hopf. *Tom Tucker*, Midshipmite: Herr Max Hopf. *Josephine*, the Captain's daughter: Frl. KUSTER. *Mrs. Cripps*, (genannt Butterblum) a Portsmouth Bumboat Woman: Frl. SCHMITZ. *Hebe*, Sir Joseph's First Cousin: Frl. KUHSE. *First Lord's Sisters, His Cousins and His Aunts.*

1879.18 LE PETIT DUC

An Opéra-comique in Three Acts[48]. Original French libretto to "Le Petit Duc" by Henri Meilhac and Ludovic Halévy. English adaptation by Saville Rowe [B. C. Stephenson] and Bolton Rowe [Clement Scott]. Music by Charles Lecocq. Stage manager, James A. Meade. Musical director, George Purdy. Produced by Alice Oates English Comic Opera Company (R.E.J. Miles, Director). Opened 31 March 1879 at Haverly's Lyceum Theatre and closed 5 April 1879 after 8 performances.

CAST: *Le Duc Raoul de Parthenay*: ALICE OATES. *La Duchesse Blanche de Parthenay*: LULU STEVENS. *Directress of the Convent School*: JAMES A. MEADE. *The Governess*: Agnes Halleck. *Mlle. de la Roche Tonnere*: Pauline Hall. *Mlle. de Champlatre*: Ada Dow. *Mlle. de St. Animone*: Alice Townsend. *First Maid of Honor*: Emma Duchateau. *Second Maid of Honor*: Miss J. St. Clair. *Third Maid of Honor*: Kate Ashton. *Fourth Maid of Honor*: Josie Knight. *Vivandiere*: Albertina Hall. *Manon*, a Drummer: Jennie Tanner. *(Chevalier) De Montlandry*: EDWARD CONNELL. *Frimousse*, the Tutor: JAMES G. TAYLOR. *Bernard*, the Duke's attendant: R. E. GRAHAM. *De Nevailles*: J. C. McLaughlin. *De Montchevrier*: Mills Hall. *De Tenneville*: C. N. Decker. *De Champvallier*: Ed. Horan. *De Marignac*: George Rugby. *De Nancois*: A. Gradwell. *De Fontgrivard*: George Clare. *De Savois*: W. F. Holmes. *Roger*, First Page: Alice Townsend. *Henri*, Second Page: Hattie Richardson. *Gerard*, Third Page: Bessie Temple. *Jules*, Fourth Page: Pauline Hall. *Pages, Maids of Honor, Noble Ladies of Luneville, Pensionnaires, Vivandiers, Soldiers, Villagers.*

1879.19 LE PETIT DUC

An Opéra-comique in Three Acts[49], in French. Libretto by Henri Meilhac and Ludovic Halévy. Music by Charles Lecocq. Director of the stage, Charles Darcy. Costumes by Messrs. Landolff and Millet, Paris. Director of the orchestra, Charles Almeras. Produced by Maurice Grau's French Opéra Bouffe Company. Opened 12 April 1879 at Booth's Theatre and closed 23 April 1879 after 11 performances; re-opened 5 May 1879 at the Park Theatre and closed 10 May 1879 after 7 additional performances.

CAST: *Raoul, Le Duc de Parthenay*: Mlle. MARIE AIMÉE. *De Montlandry*: Mons. JOUARD. *Frimousse*: Mons. DUPUIS. *Bernard*: Mons. SALVATOR. *De Navailles*: Mons. Hayme. *De Montchevrier*: Mons. Vinchon. *De Tanneville*: Mons. Jolivet. *De Champvallon*: Mons. Saleon. *De Merignac*: Mons. Gavant. *De Nancy*: Mons. Terrancle. *Diane de Chateau Lansac*, La Directrice: Mlle. RAPHAEL. *Diane, La Duchesse de Parthenay*: Mlle. LOUISE BEAUDET. *Roger*: Mlle. Vallot. *Gerard*: Mlle. Armand. *Julien*: Mlle. Amelie. *Gontran*: Mlle. Sylla. *Henri*: Mlle. Louise Duparc. *Gaston*: Mlle. Canonge. *Hélène*: Mlle. Estradere. *Mlle. de la Roche-Tonnere*: Mlle. Leroy. *Mlle. de Champlatre*: Mlle. Berthe. *Mlle. Sainte-Anemone*: Mlle. Vallot. *Margot*: Mlle. Amelie. *Manon*: Mlle. Estradere. *Premiere Sous Maitresse*: Mlle. Sylla. *Deuxieme Sous Maitresse*: Mlle. Marguerite. *Ninon*: Mlle. Salvator. *Ninette*: Mlle. Deblinde. *Marion*: Mlle. Ruffino. *Mariette*: Mlle. Seygaud. *Dragoons, Trumpeters, Pensionnaires of the Convent at Luneville, Maids of Honor, Pages, Lords and Ladies of the Court, etc.*

Act 1: The "Oeuil de Boeuf" at the Palace of Versailles. Beginning of the eighteenth century.

Act 2: A Ladies' Seminary at Luneville.

Act 3: An Encampment.

ACT 1[50]

Voici l'heure et dans un instant (Choeur d'introduction)
  Choeur
Notre coeur soupire (Entrée des pages)/
Puisqu'avec de la politesse (Couplets)/
Voyez-vous ça (Strette)
  Les Pages
Voici l'heure et dans un instant (Choeur d'introduction, reprise)
  Choeur
Le savant part tenant un livre (Duo)
  Messrs. Dupuis, Jouard
Voici venir les doux époux (Choeur)
  Mlle. Aimée, Choeur
Enfin nous voici, ma petite (Couplets)
  Mlle. Aimée
Et maintenant selon l'usage (Choeur)
  Mlles. Aimée, Raphael, Les Pages, Choeur
Ballet (Gavotte)
  Choeur
Entendez-vous là-bas (Ensemble)
  Les Pages, Les Demoiselles
C'est pourtant bien doux (Duo)
  Mlles. Aimée, L. Beaudet
La petite femme part d'un pas discret (Couplets)
  Mlle. Aimée
Il a l'oreille basse (Petit Choeur)
  Les Pages
Mon colonel, mon colonel (Choeur des officiers)
  Mons. Jouard, Choeur
Eh bien, alors, sonnez le boute-selle (Le Bout-selle)
  Mlle. Aimée, Mons. Jouard, Les Pages, Les Officiers
Quoi partir au milieu d'un bal (Choeur des femmes)
  Mlle. Aimée, Les Femmes
Que la trompette sonne (Final)
  Tous

ACT 2

L'amour seul est le bien suprême (La leçon de chant)
  Mlle. Raphael, Pensionnaires
Les voici les parlementaires (Ensemble)
  Mlles. Beaudet, Raphael, Mons. Jouard, Les Pesnionnaires, Les Parlementaires
Vous menacer (Couplets de Montlandry)
  Mons. Jouard, Mlle. Raphael
La guerre . . . la guerre (Morceau d'ensemble)
  Mlles. Beaudet, Raphael, Messrs. Dupuis, Jouard, Les Pensionnaires, Les Parlementaires
Mes bell's madam' écoutez-ça (Rondeau de la paysanne)
  Mlle. Aimée
Ils ont c'qui nomment des sabres tach's (Air avec choeur)
  Mlles. Aimée, Raphael, Les Pensionnaires
C'est une idylle (Duo de l'idyll)
  Mlle. Aimée, Mons. Dupuis
A sac! A sac, la ville est prise (Choeur des dragons)
  Mlles. Aimée, Raphael, Mons. Jouard, Les Pensionnaires, Les Dragons
Hélas, elle a raison (Couplets du départ)
  Mlles. Aimée, Beaudet, Mons. Jouard, Les Pensionnaires
Revenez vainqueurs (Ensemble)
  Mons. Jouard, Les Dragons, Les Pensionnaires
Allons, ne parlez pas ainsi (Final)
  Tous
Non! Je ne me battrai pas (Strette)
  Mlle. Aimée, Les Dragons, Les Pensionnaires

ACT 3

Tambours et trompettes (Introduction)
  Mons. Jouard, Un Officier, Choeur
Il était un petit bossu (Chanson du petit bossu)
  Mons. Jouard
Ah mon Dieu! Que deviendrons-nous (Lamento)
  Les Femmes, Les Marmitons, Les Cuisiniers
Victoire! Victoire! (Choeur)
  Choeur
La guerre c'est donc ça (Couplets)
  Mlle. Aimée
Pas de femmes, pas de femmes (Ensemble du mot d'ordre)
  Mlle. Aimée, Mons. Jouard, Officiers

---

[48]First produced in New York in a different English translation 17 March 1879 at Booth's Theatre for 24 performances.
[49]French language premiere in New York. Previously produced in New York in English 17 March 1879 at Booth's Theatre for 24 performances.
[50]Musical numbers not listed in program. List prepared from published French piano vocal score (Brandus et Cie., Paris, 1878).

Décidément, mon cher mari (Duo)
Mlles. Aimée, L. Beaudet, Choeur
Te souvient-il, ô ma duchesse (Couplets)
Mlles. Aimée, L. Beaudet
Prende garde, tais-toi (Ensemble de la tente)
Mlles. Aimée, L. Beaudet
Mon épée, ah! l'ordre est sévère (Couplets de l'épée)
Mlle. Aimée
Ma femme n'est pas rassurée (Couplets Final)
Mlle. Aimée, Tous

1879.20 THE ROSE OF AUVERGNE

A Revival of the Comic Opera in One Act[51]. (Original French libretto to "La Rose de Saint-Flour" by Michel Carré. English adaptation by Henry B. Farnie.) Music by Jacques Offenbach. Orchestra under the direction of Max Maretzek. Produced by D. H. Harkins. Opened 14 April 1879 at the Fifth Avenue Theatre (on a double bill preceding H.M.S. PINAFORE, replacing TRIAL BY JURY) and closed 19 April 1879 after 7 performances.[52]

CAST: *Fleurette*, Belle of the Village (landlady of a village cabaret): ROSE CHAPPELLE. *Pierre*, a Blacksmith: W. H. HAMILTON. *Alphonse*, a Shoemaker: A. H. BELL.

1879.21 COX AND BOX, or, The Long-Lost Brothers

A Musical Triumviretta in One Act, 17 Tableaux[53] (preceding H.M.S. PINAFORE). Libretto by Francis C. Burnand. Music by Arthur Sullivan. Orchestra under the direction of Mr. Dietrich. Produced by James C. Duff. Opened 14 April 1879 at the Standard Theatre and closed 24 May 1879 after 48 performances.[54]

CAST: *James John Cox*, a Journeyman Hatter: HART CONWAY. *John James Box*, a Journeyman Printer: THOMAS WHIFFEN. *Sergeant Bouncer*, Late of the Dampshire Yeomanry, with military reminiscences: CHARLES MAKIN.

Scene: Bouncer's Room.

MUSICAL NUMBERS[55]
"Rataplan" (Yes, yes, in those merry days)(Bouncer's Song)
C. Makin
"Stay, Bouncer, Stay" (Duet)
H. Conway, C. Makin
"Hush-a-bye, Bacon" (A Lullaby)
T. Whiffen
"My Master Is Punctual" (Song and Dance)
H. Conway
"Who are you, Sir?" (Trio)
H. Conway, T. Whiffen, C. Makin
"The Buttercup" (Duet, Serenade)
H. Conway, T. Whiffen
"Three years ago" (Romance)
T. Whiffen
"Sixes" (Gambling Duet)
H. Conway, T. Whiffen
"My hand upon it" (Finale)

[51]Previously produced in New York in this adaptation 19 July 1875 at Robinson Hall for 28 performances. Also produced in New York in its original French 14 February 1863 at the Théâtre Français 14 February 1863; and in other English language versions, including TOO MANY COOKS.
[52]No credits in programs for director, scenery or costumes. Maretzek is included on the presumption that he conducted both H.M.S. PINAFORE and THE ROSE OF AUVERGNE.
[53]Editor's note: COX AND BOX was reportedly produced in America as early as 13 August or 1 December 1875. I could find no indication or specific record of a prior New York presentation.
[54]No credits in programs for scenery or costumes.
[55]Musical numbers not listed in programs. List prepared from published English piano vocal score (T H Lacy, London, 1873).

1879.22 FATINITZA

An Operette in Three Acts, in German. Libretto by F. Zell and Richard Genée. Based on the libretto to "La Circassienne" by Eugène Scribe. Music by Franz von Suppé. Produced by Adolph Neuendorff. Opened 14 April 1879 at the Germania Theatre and closed 30 April 1879 after (14) performances in repertory.

CAST: *Count (Timofey Gavrilovitch) Kantschukoff*, Russian General: Herr FRANOSCH. *Princess Lydia (Imanova)*, his niece: Frl. KUSTER. *Izzet Pasha*, Governor of the Turkish Fortress at Rustchuk: Herr WILL. *Captain Wasili (Staravieff)*: Herr Kummer. *Lieutenant Osip (Safonoff)*: Herr Wolkenstein. *Cadets (8)*: *Iwan*: Frl. Umlauf. *Nikifor*: Frl. Keller. *Fedor*: Frl. Romanus. *Dimitri*: Frl. Wagner. *Wasili*: Frl. Castalloo. *Michailow*: Frl. Schlag. *Casimir*: Frl. Hecken. *Gregor*: Frl. Delgmann. *Vladimir Samoiloff (Fatinitza)*: Frl. KUHSE. *Julian Hardy*, Special War Correspondent of the "New York Herald": Herr RANK. *Steipann*, a Sergeant: Herr Bowmann. *Hassan Bey*, Leader of a Squad of Bashi-Bazouks: Herr Hopf. *Izzet Pasha's Wives (4)*: *Nursidah*: Frl. WERNER. *Zuleika*: ?. *Diona*: ?. *Besika*: ?. *Mustapha*, Guardian of the Harem: ?. *Vuika*, a Bulgarian: ?. *Hanna*, his wife: ?.

Act 1: At the Outposts in the Russian camp on the lower Danube. Winter.

Act 2: The Harem Room of Izzet Pasha in the fortress of Rustchuk.

Act 3: In the Summer Palace of General Kantschukoff at Odessa.

ACT 1[56]
Halt, wer da? (Introduction and Air)
Guard, Herr Bowmann, Cadets
Wutki, Wutki (Entrance of the Sutlers)
Vuika, Cadets and Soldiers
Erwache frei von allem Kummer (Chorus of Cadets)
Cadets and Soldiers
Warum musstet Ihr mich wecken? (Dream Song)
Frl. Kuhse
Was gibt's da? (Reporter's Song)
Herr Bowmann, Herr Rank, Cossacks, Soldiers
Abner desswegen (Exit of the Cadets)
Herr Rank, Cadets
Himmel, Bombem, Element! (Thousand Fifes and Drums)(Aria)
Herr Franosch
Woll enden Glauben (If she, with true heart)
Frl. Kuhse, Herr Franosch
Lecht deer Schneeseso weil (When in robes of white)(Quartet)
Frl. Kuster, Herr Rank, Frl. Kuhse, Herr Franosch
Theurer Oheim, länger konnt ich siedem (Sleighing Song)
Frl. Kuster, Herr Franosch
Eine Zuflucht winket der (There's a cloister near the field)(Quartet)
Herr Franosch, Frl. Kuster, Frl. Kuhse, Herr Rank
Nur kein Geschrei (Now up, away!) (Finale)
Chorus of Bashi-Bazouks

ACT 2
Den Gebieter zu entzücken (Toilet Chorus)
Frl. Werner, Besika, Donia, Suleika, Chorus of Slaves
Reformen thun Noth beider türkschen Nation
(When sick men are failing)
Herr Will
Ein bissel auf-freischen (He'll order waking)(Exit)
Herr Will, Frl. Werner, Besika, Diona, Suleika, Slaves
Mein Herz es zagt (I Fear to think)(Duet)
Frl. Kuster, Frl. Kuhse
Nun denn, so wisst (Is it a man?)(Sextet)
Frl. Kuhse, Frl. Kuster, Frl. Werner, Besika, Diona, Suleika
Jeder Trinker ist anfangs nüchtern (Every author is at beginning)(Kismet Duet)
Herr Will, Herr Rank
Silberglöckchen (Bell so silvery)(Bell Sextet)
Frl. Werner, Herr Rank, Herr Will, Diona, Suleika, Besika
Zwei Russen, des Spass ist gar nicht schlecht (The Karagois)
(Turkish Shadow Play)(Finale)

[56]Musical numbers not listed in programs. List prepared from published piano vocal score, text in English, (original) German and Italian (Oliver Ditson & Co., Boston, 1879).

ACT 3

Glockenklänge künden (Bell Song)
Frl. Kuster

Um Fatinitza's Spur zu finden ('Tis now three months)(Duet)
Herr Rank, Herr Franosch

Dich wider zu she'n (To this loving heart)(Trio)
Frl. Kuhse, Frl. Kuster, Herr Rank

Jubelsang ertönder Fremden (Praise and honors high)(Chorus and Finale)

1879.23 GIROFLÉ-GIROFLA

A Revival of the Opéra-comique in Three Acts[57]. Original French libretto by Albert Vanloo and Eugène Leterrier. Music by Charles Lecocq. Stage manager, J. A. Meade. Musical director and conductor, George Purdy. Produced by Alice Oates' English Comic Opera Company (R. E. J. Miles, director). Opened 14 April 1879 at Haverly's Lyceum Theatre and closed 19 April 1879 after 7 performances.[58]

CAST: *Giroflé, Girofla*: ALICE OATES. *Maresquin*, a young banker, suitor to Giroflé: E. D. BEVERLY. *Bolero D'Alcazaras*, a Spanish Grandee: JAMES G. TAYLOR. *Mourzouk*, a Moor, a suitor to Girofla: EDWARD CONNELL. *Paquita*: LULU STEVENS. *Aurora*, Wife of Bolero: AGNES HALLECK. *Pedro*: Joseph C. McLaughlin. *Pirate Chief*: R. E Graham. *Metamoros*: Edward Horan. *Notary*: H. Edwards. *Uncle*: C. N. Decker. *Taxgatherer*: Mills Hall. *Godfather*: George Clare. *Dancing Master*: Alex Gradwell. *Bridesman*: George Rugby. *Bridesmaids*: Misses D. Adai, J. Tanner. *Pirates*: Messrs. Hall, Decker, Harris, Clare, Gradwell, Rugby, Bowman, Horan, Leclerc, Kremer, Holmes. *Cousins (6)*: *Fernande*: Alice Townsend. *Julia*: Hattie Richardson. *Armande*: Bessie Temple. *Estevan*: Pauline Hall. *Guzman*: Emma Duchateau. *Carlo*: Albertina Hall. *Fishermen, Sailors, Villagers, etc.*

1879.24 LES CLOCHES DE CORNEVILLE

A Revival of the Opéra-comique in Three Acts[59]. (Original French libretto to 'Les Cloches de Corneville' by Clairville and Charles Gabet.) Music by Robert Planquette. Stage manager, J. A. Meade. Musical director and conductor, George Purdy. Produced by Alice Oates' English Comic Opera Company (R. E. J. Miles, director). Opened and closed 16 April 1879 (matinee) at Haverly's Lyceum Theatre after 1 performance.

CAST: *Serpolette*: ALICE OATES. *Germaine*: LULU STEVENS. *Marette*: ADA DOW. *Gertrude*: PAULINE HALL. *Suzanne*: HATTIE RICHARDSON. *Catherine*: Jennie Tanner. *Marguerite*: Inez Sexton. *Jeanne*: BESSIE TEMPLE. *Le Marquis*: EDWARD CONNELL. *Jean Grénicheux*: RICHARD BEVERLY. *The Baillie*: JAMES G. TAYLOR. *Notary*: R. E. Graham. *Christophe*: Alice Townshend. *Cachalot*: Mills Hall. *Gripardin*: Edward Horan. *Fouinard*: George Rugby. *Gaspard*, a miser: JAMES A. MEADE. *Full Chorus.*

1879.25 FATINITZA!

An Operette in Three Acts. (Original German libretto by F. Zell and Richard Genée. Based on the libretto to "La Circassienne" by Eugène Scribe.) English adaptation by Henry S. Leigh. Music by Franz von Suppé. Scenery by Charles W. Witham, J. Johnson. Costumes by Mr. Schwencke. Musical director, E. Hassa. Produced by D. H. Harkins. Opened 22 April 1879[60] at the Fifth Avenue Theatre and closed 31 May 1879 after 41 performances.

CAST: *Vladimir, Fatinitza*, a Young Russian lieutenant: JEANNIE WINSTON. *Princess Lydia*, Niece of the Count: SALLIE REBER. *Count Timofey Kantschakoff*, a Russian General: W. H. HAMILTON. *Izzet Pasha*, Governor of Turkish Fort Isaksha: VINCENT HOGAN. *Wasili*, Captain of Russian Infantry: L. F. Massen. *Osipp*, Lieutenant: Myron Calice. *Steipan*, Sergeant: JAMES HARTON. *Julian*, a Special Newspaper Correspondent: W. A. MORGAN. *Hassan Bey*, Leader of Bashi Bazouks: G. V. DeMorest. *Russian Cadets (4)*: *Ivan*: Rose Chappelle. *Nikophor*: Edith Everlie. *Feodor*: Pearl Everlie. *Demitri*: Jennie Maynard. *Izzet Pasha's Wives (4)*: *Nourmahal*: MARIE SOMERVILLE. *Zuleika*: JOSEPHINE ZINGSHEIM. *Diona*: ROSE CHAPPELLE. *Beseika*: MAY SYLVIE. *Massaldsha*, a Fortune Teller: E. B. Holmes. *Mustapha*, Guard of the Harem: F. Tannehill. *Winka*, a Bulgarian spy: C. F. Shattuck. *Hanna*, his Wife: L. E. Stone. *Adjutant*: James McArtney.

Characters in the Karagois: *Jussuf*: A. K. Osborn. *Surema*, his daughter: Mary Richardson. *Ben Jirmin*, his slave: F. Goodwin. *Niridah, Fatima*, two old gossips: Fannie Williams, Clara Maitland. *Achmet*, Keeper of Menagerie: John Humphrey.

Russian Soldiers, Bashi Bazouks, Cosscks, Moorish Women, Nubian Slaves, Russian Serfs, Sleigh Drivers, etc.

Act 1: Russian Encampment on the Danube.

Act 2: The Harem of Izzet Pasha.

Act 3: Reception Room in the General's Mansion at Odessa.

ACT 1[61]

Introduction (Awake! You sluggards all, arise!)
J. Harton, Guards

Ensemble (These monkey tricks I will not bear)
J. Harton, Cadets

Chorus (Arise, awake, most sound of sleepers)
Cadets, Soldiers

Romance (Lost is the dream that bound me)
J. Winston

Ensemble (Who is here? A spy—a spy!)
J. Harton, W. A. Morgan, Chorus

Song (With my notebook in my hnad)
W. A. Morgan

Ensemble (All the reporters hail me their master)
W. A. Morgan, J. Harton, L. F. Massen, P. Everlie, R. Chappelle, M. Calice, Chorus

Song (Thunder! Lightning! Who goes there?)
W. H. Hamilton

Duettino (Can'st thou unyielding see me before thee?)
J. Winston, W. H. Hamilton

Chorus (Snow, snow, high and low)
Chorus

Quartette (Dearest uncle, pray excuse me)
S. Reber, W. H. Hamilton, J. Winston, W. A. Morgan

Chorus (Let not one word or sound be heard)
Chorus

Finale (All your strength we laugh to scorn)
S. Reber, J. Winston, Chorus

ACT 2

Toilet Chorus (Washing, dressing, brushing, combing)
Izzet Pasha's Wives

Song (I pine but for progress, reform is my dream)
V. Hogan

Duet (New doubts, new fears, within my heart contend)
J. Winston, S. Reber

Sextette ('Tis well; then learn that this young Russian—is myself)
J. Winston, Izzet Pasha's Wives

Duettino (We are simply what fortune pleases)
V. Hogan, W. A. Morgan

Sextette (Silver tinklings, ringing brightly)
W. A. Morgan, V. Hogan, Izzet Pasha's Wives

The Karagois
Ensemble (Free, free from our foes at last)

S. Reber, Izzet Pasha's Wives,
W. A. Hamilton, J. Harton, W. A. Morgan, Russian, Turks

ACT 3

Air (Chime, ye bells—abroad your gleeful voices flinging)
S. Reber

Trio (Again, love, we meet)
J. Winston, S. Reber, W. A. Morgan

Chorus (Joy, joy, joy to the bride)
All, Chorus

---

[57]First produced in New York in French 4 February 1875 at the Park Theatre for (46) performances in repertory; in English 19 May 1875 at Robinson Hall for 61 performances. For Synopsis of Scenes and Musical Numbers, see May 1875 production

[58]English libretto uncredited; scenery and costumes uncredited.

[59]First produced in New York in English as THE CHIMES OF NORMANDY 22 October 1877 at the Fifth Avenue Theatre for 16 performances in repertory. For Synopsis of Scenes and Musical Numbers, see original 1877 production. English adaptation, scenery, costumes uncredited in programs.

[60]English language premiere; previously produced in New York in German 14 April 1879 at the Germania Theatre. See entry above for detail. No libretto or score found for Henry S. Leigh's adaptation.

[61]Musical numbers not listed in programs. List prepared from published libretto (Richardson & Foos, New York, 1879).

1879.26

LA MARJOLAINE

A Revival of the Opérette in Three Acts[62], in French. Libretto by Albert Vanloo and Eugène Leterrier. Music by Charles Lecocq. Stage managers, Messrs. J. Mezières, Salvator. Musical director, Charles Almeras. Produced by Maurice Grau's French Opera Boffe Company. Opened 24 April 1879 at Booth's Theatre and closed 26 April 1879 after 4 performances; returned 28 May 1879 to the Park Theatre for 1 additional performance[63].

CAST: *Marjolaine*: Mme. MARIE AIMÉE. *Aveline*: Mlle. Beaudet. *Petrus*: Mlle. Armand. *Karl*: Mlle. Vallot. *Christian*: Mlle. Estradere. *Robert*: Mlle. Amelie. *Christophe*: Mlle. Sylla. *Frantz*: Mlle. Florence Duparc. *Gudule*: Mlle. Leroy. *A Peasant*: Mlle. Deblinde. *A Maiden*: Mlle. Salvator. *Baron Palamède*: Mons. J. MEZIÈRES. *Annibal*: Messrs. JOUARD. *Frickel*: Mons. JUTEAU. *Peterschop*: Messrs. DUPLAN. *D'Escoublac*: Mons. DUPUIS. *Schaerbeck*: Mons. Hayme. *Le Bourgmestre*: Mons. Vinchon. *Two Aldermen*: Messrs. Gavaut, Passerard. *A Town Crier*: Mons. Terrancle. *Peasants, Men and Women Servants, etc.*

1879.27

LES CLOCHES DE CORNEVILLE

A Revival of the Opéra-comique in Three Acts[64], in French. Libretto by Clairville and Charles Gabet. Music by Charles Planquette. Director of the stage, Charles Darcy. Director of orchestra, Charles Almeras. Produced by Maurice Grau's French Opera Bouffe Company. Opened 28 April 1879 at Booth's Theatre and closed 3 May 1879 after 7 performances; returned 26 May 1879 to the Park Theatre for 1 additional performance.

CAST: *Serpolette*: Mlle. MARIE AIMÉE. *Germaine*: Mme. CÉCILE GREGOIRE. *Gaspard*: Mons. J. MEZIÈRES. *Henri de Corneville*: Mons. JOUARD. *Grenicheux*: Mons. JUTEAU. *Bailiff*: Mons. DUPLAN. *Manette*: Mlle. Canonge. *Jeanne*: Mlle. Vallot. *Gertrude*: Mlle. Sylla. *Suzanne*: Mlle. Estradere. *Catherine*: Mlle. Armand. *Marguerite*: Mlle. Deblinde. *The Notary*: Mons. Vinchon. *Cachalot*: Mons. F. Mauriez. *Gripparein*: Mons. Hayme. *Fouinard*: Mons. Dupuis. *Peasants, Male and Female Guard Champetre, Sailors, Cabin Boys, Cochmen, Maid Servants, Domestics, etc.*: Chorus of 60.

1879.28

H.M.S. PINAFORE, or, The Lass That Loved a Sailor

An All-Colored Opera Troupe in the Comic Opera in Two Acts[65]. Libretto by William S. Gilbert. Music by Arthur Sullivan. Scenery by E. H. Chase. Opened 28 April 1879 at the Globe Theatre and closed 10 May 1879 after 16 performances.[66]

CAST[67]:*Josephine*, the Captain's Daughter: ANNIE C. WILLIAMS. *Little Buttercup*, a Bumboat Woman: LOUISA ASBURY. *Hebe*, Sir Joseph's First Cousin: Maggie Jones. *The Rt. Hon. Sir Joseph Porter, K.C.B.*, First Lord of the Admiralty: CHARLES A. [Adam] ASBURY. *Captain Corcoran*, Commanding the *H.M.S. Pinafore*: WILLIAM MORRIS. *Ralph Rackstraw*, Able Seaman: Albert Games. *Dick Deadeye*, Able Seaman: George W. Hawkins. *Bill Bobstay*, Boatswain: E. Brown. *Tom Tucker*, Midshipmite: A. Slow. *Bob Becket*, Boatswain's Mate: J. A. Duval. *Sergeant of Marines*: W. H. H. Davis. *First Lord's Sisters, his Cousins, his Aunts, Sailors, Marines, etc.*: Full Chorus of 50.

[62]First produced in New York 1 October 1877 at the Park Theatre for 22 performances in repertory. For Synopsis of Scenes and Musical Numbers, see original 1877 production.

[63]No program found for New York engagement of this production; cast list prepared from a Boston tour dated 4 June 1879.

[64]First produced in New York in English 22 October 1877 at the Fifth Avenue Theatre as THE CHIMES OF NORMANDY. In French 13 May 1878 at the Park Theatre for 6 performances in repertory; for Synopsis of Scenes and Musical Numbers, see 1878 production.

[65]A rival to the production at the Standard; management declared "this is no burlesque" and that the production arrived direct from 60 performances at the Academy of Music, Philadelphia. First produced in New York 15 January 1879 at the Standard Theatre for 175 performances. For Synopsis of Scenes and Musical Numbers, see entry above.

[66]No credits in the program or on posters with regard to stage director, producer or musical director.

[67]Production posters announce a different cast: *Captain Corcoran*: ALBERT GAMES. *Ralph Rackstraw*: FRANK DAVIS. *Tom Tucker*: W. Wilton. *Bob Becket*: G. Keller. *Sergeant of Marines*: J. Davis.

1879.29

H.M.S. PINAFORE, or, The Lass That Loved a Sailor

A Comic Opera in Two Acts[68]. Libretto by William S. Gilbert. Music by Arthur Sullivan. Produced by Ford's Miniature Pinafore Company (Philadelphia); presented by Lester Wallack. Opened 5 May 1879 at Wallack's Theatre and closed 31 May 1879 after 24 performances.

CAST: *Sir Joseph Porter*: HARRY DAVENPORT. *Ralph Rackstraw*: Miss JENNIE. *Captain Corcoran*: J. B. SMITH. *Dick Deadeye*: F. W. HAEDRICK. *Bill Bobstay*: R. Schmidt. *Bob Becket*: C. Minchin. *Midshipmite*: Baby Goodman. *Tom Bowline*: Harry Wagner. *First Marine*: B. C. Anderson. *Josephine*: NELLIE EVEREST. *Buttercup*: DOLLIE WILLIAMS. *Hebe*: LILLIE PARSLOW. *First Aunt*: Ida Gallagher.

1879.30

H.M.S. PINAFORE, or, The Lass That Loved a Sailor

A Comic Opera in Two Acts[69]. Libretto by William S. Gilbert. Music by Arthur Sullivan. Children's company produced under the direction of Mr. Caryl Florio. Produced by J. H. Haverly's Grand English Opera Company. Opened 12 May 1879 at Haverly's Lyceum Theatre; Adult company[70]closed 7 June 1879 after 28 performances; Children's company[71] closed 5 July 1879 after 57 performances.

ADULT CAST: *Ralph Rackstraw*: WILLIAM CASTLE. *Captain Corcoran*: C. H. TURNER. *Sir Joseph Porter*: J. G. TAYLOR. *Dick Deadeye*: Henry Peakes. *Boatswain*: Ellis Ryse. *Josephine*: ANNIS MONTAGUE. *Buttercup*: LAURA JOYCE. *Hebe*: ADELAIDE RANDALL.

CHILDREN'S CAST: *Ralph Rackstraw*: Master OTTO NEWMAN. *Captain Corcoran*: Master WILLIE AHLSTRON. *Sir Joseph Porter*: Master ALFRED KLEIN. *Dick Deadeye*: Master ARTHUR DUNN. *Boatswain*: Master Pierre. *Boatswain's Mate*: Master William. *Josephine*: Miss JENNIE DUNN. *Buttercup*: Miss FRANKIE BISHOP. *Hebe*: Miss DAISY MURDOCH. *Cast of 101 Children.*

1879.31

MME. FAVART

An Opéra-comique in Three Acts, in French. Libretto by Henri Chivot and Alfred Duru. Music by Jacques Offenbach. Director of the stage, Charles Darcy. Director of the orchestra, Charles Almeras. Produced by Maurice Grau's French Opéra Bouffe Company. Opened 12 May 1879 at the Park Theatre and closed 29 May 1879 after 14 performances in repertory.

CAST: *Mme. (Justine) Favart*: Mlle. MARIE AIMÉE. *Suzanne*: Mlle. RAPHAEL. *Jolicoeur*: Mlle. Vallot. *Sans-Quartier*: Mlle. Sylla. *Larissolle*: Mlle. Amelie. *Babet*: Mlle. Armand. *Jeanneton*: Mlle. Estradere. *Charles Favart*: Mons. JOUARD. *(Marquis) De Pontsablé*: Mons. J. MEZIÈRES. *Hector de Boispréau*: Mons. JUTEAU. *(Le Major) Cotignac*: Mons. DUPLAN. *Biscotin*: Mons. Dupuis. *(Le Sergent) Larose*: Mons. Vinchon. *Travelers, Invited Guests, Soldiers, Officers, Fifers and Cantinieres, Cooks, Upholsters, Inn Waiters, and the characters in "La Chercheuse d'Espret."*: Chorus of 60.

Act 1: At Arras.

Act 2: At Douai.

Act 3: The Encampment at Maréchal Saxe.

ACT 1[72]

Introduction (Enfin le coche est arrivé)
Mons. Dupuis, Choeur

Trio (C'est lui! Ah! quel plaisir!)
Mlle. Raphael, Messrs. Juteau, Duplan

Couplets (Un soir nous nous rencontrâmes)
Mlle. Raphael

Couplets (Dans une cave obscure)
Mons. Jouard

[68]A rival production to the original at the Standard Theatre. First produced in New York 15 January 1879 at the Standard Theatre for 175 performances. For Synopsis of Scenes and Musical Numbers, see entry above.

[69]A rival production to the original at the Standard Theatre. First produced in New York 15 January 1879 at the Standard Theatre for 175 performances. For Synopsis of Scenes and Musical Numbers, see entry above.

[70]Performed Monday to Saturday evenings and Saturday matinees.

[71]Performed Monday to Friday matinees, and a Saturday 11AM matinee; after the Adult Company closed the Children's Company assumed a traditional eight performance week.

[72]Musical numbers not listed in programs. List prepared from published French piano vocal score (Choudens, Paris, 1878).

Choeur et Scène (Allons, vite à table)
Mlle. Aimée, Messrs. Juteau, Duplan
Couplets (Prenant mon air les plus bénin)
Mlle. Aimée
Ensemble, Ronde et Choeur (À l'auberge de Biscotin)
Mlle. Aimée, Messrs. Vinchon, Dupuis
Trio de l'Enlèvement (Adieu Suzanne)
Mlle. Raphael, Messrs. Juteau, Jouard
Ensemble (Pour la lieutenance)
Mlle. Aimée, Raphael, Messrs. Juteau, Jouard, Duplan, Vinchon, Choeur
Couplets (Mon p'tit papa je t'en supplie)
Mlle. Raphael
Strette (Va donc, va pour le mariage)
Tous

ACT 2
Romance (Suzanne est aujourd'hui ma femme)
Mons. Juteau
Chanson de l'échaudé (Quand du four on le retire)
Mons. Jouard
Choeur (Hommage à Monseigneur)
Mons. J. Mezières, Choeur
Couplets des Aïeux
Mons. J. Mezières
Quatuor (Ah! c'est affreux!)
Mlles. Aimée, Raphael, Messrs. Juteau, Jouard
Ensemble de la Sonnette (Marquis, grâce à votre richesse)
Mlle. Aimée, Messrs. J. Mezières, Jouard, Choeur
Menuet et Rondeau de la Vieille (Je passe sur mon enfance)
Mlle. Aimée
Final (La fureur le transporte)
Mlle. Aimée, Raphael, Messrs. Juteau, Jouard, Duplan, Choeur

ACT 3
Introduction (Nous avons gagné la victoire)
Petites Fifres, Vivandières, Trompettes
Romance (Quand il cherche dans sa cervelle)
Mons. Jouard
Choeur et Tyrolienne (Allons sans plus attendre)
Mlle. Aimée, Messrs. Juteau, Vinchon
Couplets (Le peril que court ma vertu)
Mlle. Raphael, Mons. Juteau
Air (J'entrai dans la royale tente)
Mlle. Aimée
Choeur et Duo (Favart! l'heure s'avance!)
Mlle. Aimée, Mons. Jouard
Choeur (Vive Favard!)
Choeur
Final (De Favard cett'femme d'esprit)
Mlle. Aimée, Chœur

1879.32 THE BROOK

Salsbury's Troubadours in a Laughable and Musical Extravaganza (Farce Comedy) in One Act.[73] Play by Nate Salsbury. Music selected, arranged and conducted by Frank Maeder. Scenery by Gaspard Maeder. Produced by Nate Salsbury. Opened 12 May 1879 at the San Francisco Minstrels' Hall and closed 21 June 1879 after 42 performances.

CAST: *Tracy Thornton*: NATE SALSBURY. *A Turtle*: Himself. *Percy Montrose*: JOHN WEBSTER. *One Fish-Pole*: And Line. *Festus Heavysides*: JOHN GOURLAY. *Two Bottles*: Uncorked. *Rose Dimplecheek*: NELLIE McHENRY. *A Boat*: Property Man. *Blanche Sylvester*: HELENE DINGEON. *Lunch Basket*: Quartette. *Umbrellas*: Well Spread.

Scene: Pic-Nic grounds for a dinner in the woods.

MUSICAL NUMBERS, SPECIALTIES[74]
I Was with Grant [recitation]
N. Salsbury
The Tramp [recitation]
N. Salsbury
"Love, Love, Beautiful Love"
J. Gourlay
"Dorkins' Night" (anon.)
J. Gourlay
Tipsy Duet
N. McHenry, H. Dingeon
"The Kiss"
N. McHenry
"Pretty as a Picture"
N. McHenry
(*Music by* Brigham Bishop. *Lyrics by* George Cooper.)
Operatic Selections
H. Dingeon

[73]Preceded by a curtain raiser, Husband in Clover.
[74]No musical numbers were listed in programs; list prepared from published, reviews, clippings, etc. Not in performance order.

1879.33 BABES IN THE WOOD, or, Who Killed Cock Robin?

Rice's Surprise Party in a Revival of the Musical and Pantomimic Extravaganza in Two Acts[75] Play by Willie Edouin, brushed up for the American public by Louis Harrison. Stage manager, Willie Edouin. Musical director, Henry Sator. Produced by Edward E. Rice, Manager. Opened 19 May 1879 at the Union Square Theatre and closed 24 May 1879 after 7 performances.

CAST: *The Bad Man*, a mysterious creature who is up to villainy of every shade and kind, but who eventually proves to be by no means as black as he is painted: ALICE ATHERTON. *The Very Bad Man*, a heavier villain by several pounds of deeper dye, and who finally dies in combat dire: W. A. MESTAYER. *Sir Rowland Macassar*, the remorseless "uncle" in whose care his elder brother has left his pledges: LOUIS HARRISON. *Dr. Fitzflummery*, an M.D. deah boy, quite M. T. headed, you know: JENNIE CALEF. *Prince Pretty Fellow*, who comes to collect his bond in cash, but gets it in the flesh nearest his heart: LINA MERVILLE. *Sir Rupert*, a court-eous young court-ier from the Prince's court: FLORENCE BAKER. (*Sir Filbert Hazelnut*: AMY GORDON.) *The Family Physician*, no well regulated family should be without him: HENRY E. DIXEY. *Golightly Carrywell*, Lady Macassar's pet page, in fact page 1, or one page in a hundred: Jessie Calef. *Tommy, Sally*, the Original Babes: WILLIE EDOUIN, MARION ELMORE. *Falcontrina*, the little birds love her, so does Prince Prettyfellow, and in fact all the other fellows: Louise Searle. *Lady Macassar*, Sir Rowland's Aide, and a better half, who, although she allows him no will of her own, assists him in appropriating her brother's: MARION SINGER. *Miss Jones*, Schoolm'm, and consequently a Martyr: Emma Burgess. *Four Consulting Physicians, more terpsichorean than musical*: *Dr. Bigfee*: Andrew Metzger. *Dr. Littlepill*: D. P. Steele. *Dr. Callagain*: Donald Harold. *Dr. Overpaid*: E. B. Morse. *Attendants, Huntsmen, Pages of Natural History, etc.*

The Sad, Tearful, Touching and Beautiful Episode of "Who Killed Cock Robin?": *Jenny Wren*: May Edouin (aged 3 1/2). *Cock Robin*: Flora Walsh (aged 6). *The Sparrow*: Carrie Wood (aged 7). *The Rook*: Lizzie Ayers (aged 9). *The Linnet*: Little Tot (aged 4). *The Policeman*: Miss Daisy Edouin (aged 2 1/2).

1879.34 LA JOLIE PARFUMEUSE

A Revival of the Opéra-comique in Three Acts[76], in French. Libretto by Hector Crémieux and Ernest Blum. Music by Jacques Offenbach. Stage managers, Messrs. J. Mezières and Salvator. Director of orchestra, Charles Almeras. Produced by Maurice Grau's French Opera Bouffe Company. Opened 22 May 1879 at the Park Theatre and closed 24 May 1879 after 3 performances in repertory.

CAST: *Rose Michon*: Mlle. MARIE AIMÉE. *Bavolet*: Mlle. RAPHAEL. *Clorinde*: Mlle. Armand. *La Julienne*: Mlle. Sylla. *Madelon*: Mlle. Vallot. *Justine*: Mlle. Amelie. *Lise*: Mlle. Estradere. *Poirot*: Mons. JUTEAU. *La Cocardière*: Mons. DUPLAN. *Germain*: Mons. Vinchon. *Two Waiters*: Mons. Hayme, Jolivet. *Waiters, Blind Musicians, Maids of Honor, Chambermaids, etc.*: Chorus of 60.

1879.35 HORRORS, or, The Marajah of Zogobad

Rice's Surprise Party in a Musical Extravaganza in Two Acts, 6 Scenes. Play by William Gill. Lyrics by Louis Harrison. Stage manager, Willie Edouin[77]. Musical director, Henry Sator. Produced by Edward E. Rice. Opened

[75]First produced in New York 24 December 1877 at the Eagle Theatre and Grand Opera House for 41 performances. For Synopsis of Scenes see original 1877 production.
[76]First produced in New York in French 31 March 1875 at the Lyceum Theatre in repertory. For Synopsis of Scenes and Musical Numbers, see original 1875 production.

28 May 1879 at the Union Square Theatre and closed 5 July 1879 after 41 performances.[78]

CAST: *Hamsetjee Bumstejee*, always in the arms of Morpheus. A Snorer from Snorersville, but wine works wonders: WILLIE EDOUIN. *Rumsetjee Bumsetjee*, a Parsee astrologer, ambitious to be the power behind the throne, and gets THROWN out of the town: WILLIAM A. MESTAYER. *Rajah Zog*, of Hibernian descent, full of majesty, gout, fond of hearing from the planets, tries to PLANIT so the prince will marry the princess: HENRY E. DIXEY. *Prince Achmet*, his son, who has to travel six months by act of parliament. The ACT-MET with his approval: LINA MERVILLE. *Zozo*, Court Jester, who thinks that position is everything, in fact, a regular IMP-osition: LOUIS HARRISON. *Begum D'Lite*, Princess of Bombay, DELIGHTFUL young lady, the Prince choose her not, she'll be-gum d'lite to the last: LOUISE SEARLE. *Zaidee*, a simple maiden, but sometimes they know a thing or two. An adorer of the prince: MARION ELMORE. *La Jolie Housekeepaire*, proprietress of a hotel in Ceylon. She sets her SEAL on the hearts of all her boarders: MARION SINGER. *Zizzis*, chief of the Princess' followers, who thinks that love is an eternal transport—so is a canal boat: FLORENCE I. BAKER. *Zohi, Zolo*, SCIONS of a noble house, SIGHING to rove with the Prince: EUGENIA PAUL, JENNIE CALEF. *Captain Darling*, of the American gunboat *Pensacola*: Emma Burgess. *What's in a name? Wait til you hear them (4)*: *Punjaeb Tong*: A. Stockmeyer. *Calcut Gong*: Edwin Nichols. *Saka Zeke*: D. P. Steele. *Biff Alalong*: Ed. Aiken. *French Manipulators of succulent hash (3)*: *Fricasseed Françoise*: E. R. Morse. *Alamode Jean*: Andrew Metzgar. *Fillet de Cocardasse*: Donald Harold. *Four nice clean tars, shiver the cabin boy's teeth (4)*: *Hallyard Zephyr*: Ida Glover. *Silver Foam*: Lizzie Dana. *Crested Wavelet*: Edith Loring. *Headland Breaker*: Jessie Calef. *Attendants on the Princess*: Rose Dana, Amy Gordon. *Court of the Rajah, Attendants on the Prince, Tum-tum beaters, Jungle Kakers, Nautch Girls, Sailors, Jugglers, Waiters, Snake Charmers, Star gazers in profusion.*

Act 1, Scene 1: Grand Courtyard of the Rajah's Palace. *Scene 2*: Corridor in the Rajah's Palace. *Scene 3*: On Board the Prince's Yacht.

Act 2, Scene 1: French Cafe in Ceylon. *Scene 2*: Exterior of La Jolie's Cafe. *Scene 3*: Temple of the Idol Swog.

ACT 1
Scene 1
Opening Chorus
"Oh, This Gout!" (Song and Chorus)
H. E. Dixey, Attendants
"How nice 't would be" (duet)
A. Atherton, M. Elmore
"He snores like a thunder storm" (Chorus)
Attendants
"Power behind the throne" (Song with Dance)
W. A. Mestayer
(*Music by* Edward E. Rice.)
"My Card" (Concerted)
L. Searle, Principals, Attendants
Introduction to Finale
"Good-by, Achmet" (Finale)
L. Merville, Principals, Attendants
Scene 2
"Baggage Smashers" (Solo and Chorus)
F. I. Baker, Attendants
"Across the Sands"[79] (Vocal Selection)
L. Searle
"He never can dance any more" (Duet)
H. E. Dixey, L. Harrison
Scene 3
"We're all afloat" (Chorus and Solo)
A. Atherton
"The Stowaway" (Solo and Chorus)
M. Elmore, Sailors
(*Music by* Woolson Morse. *Lyrics by* Dexter Smith.)
"Pipe all hands" (Concerted)
Characters, Sailors

ACT 2[80]
Scene 1
"The Bill of Fare"
M. Singer, Waiters
"Come and have some luncheon" (Chorus)
Characters, Waiters
"I really don't know, do you?"[81] (Song)
A. Atherton
Grand Pas de Deux
W. Edouin, W. A. Mestayer
Vocal Selection
M. Singer
"Horrors" (Bacchanalian Chorus)
A. Atherton, M. Elmore, E. Paul, J. Calef
Trio of Billiardists
"Now he's going away" (Song)
M. Elmore
(*Music and Lyrics by* Edward E. Rice.)
"On the Sly" (Card Quartette)
Grand Chorus of Horrors
Scene 2
"Oh, what a day we've had" (Solo and Chorus)
A. Atherton, Characters
Song
E. Paul
(*Music by* John J. Braham. *Lyrics by* Louis Harrison.)
Chorus
Scene 3
Characteristic Chorus of Tum-Tum Wallah
Grand Finale

1879.36 LES BRIGANDS

A Revival of the Opéra-bouffe in Three Acts[82], in French. Libretto by Henri Meilhac and Ludovic Halévy. Music by Jacques Offenbach. Stage managers, Messrs. J. Mezières and Salvator. Director of orchestra, Charles Almeras. Produced by Maurice Grau's French Opera Bouffe Company. Opened 30 May 1879 at the Park Theatre and closed 31 May 1879 after 3 performances in repertory.

CAST: *Fiorella*: Mlle. MARIE AIMÉE. *Fragoletto*, a Young Farmer: Mlle. RAPHAEL. *The Princess of Granada*: Mlle. BEAUDET. *Falsacappa*: Mons. JUTEAU. *Pietro*, his Lieutenant: Mons. DUPLAN. *Antonio*, Secretary to the Duke of Mantua: Mons. J. MEZIÈRES. *The Captain of the Carabineers*: Mons. JOUARD. *The Duke of Mantua*: Mlle. Armand. *Brigands (3)*: *Carmagnola*: Mons. Poyard. *Barbavano*: : Mons. Hayme. *Domino*: Mlle. Vallot. *Baron de Campotasso*, Esquire to the Duke: Mons. Dupuis. *Count Gloria-Cassis*, Chamerlain to the Princess: Mons. Vinchon. *Tutor to the Princess*: Mons. Terrancle. *Adolphe de Valladolid*: Mlle. Amelie. *Pipo*, an innkeeper: Mons. Salvator. *Zerlina*: Mlle. Deblinde. *Fiametta*: Mlle. Estradère. *Bianca*: Mlle. Berthe. *Cincinella*: Mlle. L. Duparc. *The Duchess*: Mlle. Sylla. *The Marquise*: Mlle. Salvator. *Pipa*: Mlle. Marguerite. *Pipetta*: Mlle. Louise. *A Courier*: Mlle. Mauries. *A Sheriff*: Mlle. Jolivet. *Brigands, Carabineers, Peasants, Pages, Lords and Ladies of the Court of Mantua, Pages and Ladies of the Court of Granada*: Chorus of 60.

---

[77]Boston programs prior to New York read "written for and produced under the immediate direction of Willie Edouin."

[78]No credits in program for composer, scenery or costumes.

[79]Interpolated for subsequent tour:
"Sweetest Flower of All"
E. Paul (Princess Begum)
(*Music and Lyrics by* C. E. Pratt.)
Then later replaced by:
"Clara"
A. Atherton

[80]Added for subsequent tour, following finale:
"At Sunrise" (March)
(*Music by* Edward E. Rice.)

[81]Replaced during subsequent tour by:
"(The) Babies on Our Block" (from THE MULLIGAN GUARD BALL)
A. Atherton
(*Music by* David Braham. *Lyrics by* Edward Harrigan.)

[82]First produced in New York in French 14 November 1870 at the Grand Opera House in repertory. For Synopsis of Scenes and Musical Numbers, see original 1870 production. In this revival, Mlle. Aimée will introduce "La Malaguena", a new song by Jacques Offenbach, and the beautiful Spanish song "La Paloma."

1879–1880 SEASON

Nat C. Goodwin and Eliza Weathersby in HOBBIES (1880)
Museum of the City of New York, Gift of Miss Helen Weathersby, 44.112.8

1879–1880 SEASON

THE MULLIGAN GUARD'S CHOWDER

1879.37

A Local Comedy in One Act, 6 Scenes[1], preceded by an Olio. Play (and lyrics) by Edward Harrigan. Music by David Braham. Staged by Edward Harrigan. Scenic artist, Charles W. Witham. Costumes, Annie Howard. Musical director, David Braham. Produced by Edward Harrigan and Tony Hart. Opened 11 August 1879 at the Theatre Comique and closed 15 November 1879 after 112 performances[2].

Olio: Mr. Johnny Shaw in the laughable Ethiopian sketch, Tickle Me Under the Chin, with Ed Burt, Harry Fisher, Mary Bird; Clara Moore (cantatrice) in her celebrated character songs "I'm Sixty-Two" and "Scotch Lassie"; Messrs. Goss and Fox (comedians) in an act called Julianna Johnson; Edwin Barry (great motto vocalist); John Wild and Billy Gray in the screaming and significant oddity "C.O.D.," with Harry Fisher.

CAST: *Dan Mulligan*: EDWARD HARRIGAN. *Tommy Mulligan*: TONY HART. *Mrs. Welcome Allup*: TONY HART. *Captain Simpson Primrose*: JOHN WILD. *Rev. Palestine Puter*: WILLIAM GRAY. *Young Dublin*: JOHN QUEEN. *Gustavus Lochmuller*: HARRY FISHER. *Walsingham McSweeny*: MICHAEL BRADLEY. *Snuff McIntosh*: Edward Burt. *Mr. Hershaw*: John Shay. *Mr. Hog-Eye*, a Chinaman: William West. *James Jarme*, Undertaker: James Fox. *Danny Daly*: James McCullough. *Conrad Swartz*: Eugene Rorke. *Painter Green*: Mr. Sullivan. *August Lardgreas*: Edwin Barry. *Cordelia Mulligan*: Mrs. ANNIE YEAMANS. *Bridget Lochmuller*: ANNIE MACK. *Katy Mulligan*: JENNIE YEAMANS. *Mrs. Gilmartin*: Mary Bird. *Full Moon Mourners, Mulligan Guard and all assistants in the joyous hilarity furnished from the Theatre Comique Auxiliary Corps.*

The Skidmore Guard, comprised of the following great exponents of the humorous African: *Captain Sim Primrose*: John Wild. *Chaplain Ferguson Clinton*: John Shay. *Palmerston Duby*: Michael Foley. *Sunrise Mitchell*: Charles Sheffer. *Chastine Nayler*: Edward Goss. *Sylvester Sampson*: James Fox. *Alexander Hopkins*: William West. *Herman Gulliver*: James Tierney. *Morgan Monroe*: Timothy Cronin. *Ralph Rackstraw*: Joseph Buckley. *Hiram Henshaw*: John Mealey. *Leon Seldom*: Thomas Ray. *Adam Brewster*: Eugene Rorke. *Murat Honeywood*: James Fitzsimmons.

Scene 1: A Hot Night in Mulligan Alley. *Scene 2*: Mulligan Court and McSweeny's Ball Alley by night. *Scene 3*: Mulligan Alley. *Scene 4*: Interior of Mrs. Allup's Lodgings. *Scene 5*: A street in the Metropolis. Decoration Day. *Scene 6*: The Jersey Beach. The Chowder Ground.

MUSICAL NUMBERS

"The Little Widow Dunn" (Scene 2)
E. Harrigan

"The Skids Are Out Today" (Scene 5)
Skidmore Guard

"Oh, Girly-Girly" (Scene 6)
E. Harrigan

THE MAGIC SLIPPER!

1879.38

A Chastely Beautiful Burlesque Extravaganza in Two Acts, 10 Scenes. Adapted by William T. Gill expressly for the company from the fairy tale of Cinderella (of Charles Perrault). (Stage direction by Charles Colville.) Musical director, Jesse Williams. Produced by the Colville Opera Burlesque Company (Samuel Colville, director). Opened 25 August 1879 at Haverly's Lyceum Theatre and closed 15 September 1879 after 24 performances; returned 3 May 1880 to the Grand Opera House and closed 8 May 1880 after an additional 8 performances[2]. Total this season: 32 performances.

CAST: *Immortals*: *Elfina the First*, Monarch of the Old Fairy Land, special patron of the Shepherds and their Lasses; Cinderella's Godmama: ROSE LEIGHTON. *Miss Harebell, Miss Honeydew*, Chief Members of the Privy Council: ANNIE DEACON, ALICE WRIGHT. *Members of the Fairy Board of Health, Sunshine Bureau Committee on Sweet Scents, Societies for the Spread of Light and Air among Humans, etc. (10)*: *Daffydowndilla*: Susie Winner. *Primrosa*: Bessie Temple. *Violetta*: Elsie Dean. *Daisyana*: Louisa Loring. *Cloverina*: Mary Winner. *Sweetcornia*: Laura Adams. *Wheatina*: Nita Gerald. *Heartseasa*: Annie Winner. *Roseleafa*: Theresa Lamborn.

Mortals: *Cinderella de Boulevard*, a young lady of domestic habits, who, although she has polished her sisters shoes for years, eventually takes the SHINE out of them (the sisters, not the shoes): EME ROSEAU. *Prince Hilderbrandio Poppetti*, a young gentleman of fortune and leisure on the look out for a wife. Ah! Oh, no! his *own*, of course. An extremely *moral* Prince: ALICE HASTINGS. *Hightoni*, his confidential valet, one who ought to be a South American Republican, he is so anxious to overturn existing governments: ELLA CHAPMAN. *Penotype*, the Prince's secretary. A young gentleman who acts as personal Policeman, being always *taken* up himself: ADA LEE. *Swagger*, Hightoni's second-in-command. A young aspirant for civic honors; a capital *ward runner*, who ward run a long way to secure a fat appointment: CARRIE McHENRY. *Baron de Boulevard*, who, although a politician is, strange to say, in a state brokedness: ED CHAPMAN. *Seraph*, his trusty servitor. A *page*, whose *volume* of soul is encased in buttons, and who desires to turn over a new *leaf*: ROLAND REED. *Clorinda, Thisbe*, the Baron's first and second darlings; two bashful *virgins, vergin* on the forties: R. E. GRAHAM, FANNIE WRIGHT. *Petitoe*, the Prince's dancing master. One who can piroquette and *chassez* (we chassee so): A. W. MAFLIN. *The Prince's Four Horsemen*: *Tara*: H. Amberg. *Tarata*: Horace Frail. *Taratarta*: Frank Pamentel. *Tarataratarr*: L. DeSmith. *Cockade*, a Coachman: (La Petite) Carrie Eberts. *Plush, Caloes*, Two Footmen: Masters Charles, Hunt. (*Specialty*, German Dialect: CHARLES A. GARDNER.[4])

Act 1, Scene 1: Fairy Lake in the Grove of Ferns. *Scene 2*: Another part of the Forest. *Scene 3*: A Baronial Ball. *Scene 4*: A Baronial Kitchen. *Scene 5*: Another Baronial Hall.

Act 2, Scene 1: Garden and Exterior of Baron's Hall. *Scene 2*: Another Baronial Hall. *Scene 3*: The Kitchen again. *Scene 4*: The Gardens of the Palace. *Scene 5*: The Ball Room at the Palace.

ACT 1

Scene 1

"The Morning Sun Comes Peeping" (Opening Chorus)

"Wait for the Little Fairy" (Song)
A. Hastings

Duet
A. Hastings, R. Leighton, Chorus

Scene 2

"Here, see, we come" (Hunting Chorus)

"My own little Pearl" (Concerted Piece)
A. Hastings, Ella Chapman, A. Lee, Shepherdesses

Scene 3

A Baronial Ball, Seraph Lamentation and Song

"Who'd Be a Baron?" (Trio)
Ed Chapman, R. Reed, A. W. Maflin

Scene 4

"Cinderella" (Ballad)
E. Roseau

"The Praises of Cupid" (Duet)
E. Roseau, A. Hastings

Scene 5

"Hail to thee, Great Prince" (Chorus)

"I am thy Daughter" (Grand Final)
E. Roseau, all the characters

ACT 2

Scene 1

"La Primavera"
E. Roseau

"Love shall guide me" (Operatic Duet)
E. Roseau, R. E. Graham

Scene 2

"More or less" (Trio)
Ed Chapman, R. E. Graham, F. Wright

"Unfortunate Baron and I" (Duet)
Ed Chapman, R. Reed

Scene 3

"Eye's delight" (Chorus)
E. Roseau, Chorus

Scene 4

"The Lum Tum Proper Caper" (Duet)
Ella Chapman, R. E. Graham

"The Watchman's Chorus" (Quartet)

Scene 5

Waltz Chorus

---

[1]Billed as "Volume the Third" in Mulligan Guards series.

[2]In October 1879, The In-Toe-Natural Walking Match (Specialty) feauring John Wild was added.

[3]Cast changes in principal roles for the return engagement: *Elfina the First*: ANNIE DEACON. *Miss Harebell*: EMMA CARSON. *Cinderella de Boulevard*: BLANCHE CHAPMAN. *Prince Hilderbrandio Poppetti*: KATE EVERLEIGH. *Thisbe*: Rose Leighton.

[4]Specialty added for the Grand Opera House engagement only.

Slipper Chorus
Grand Final
Full strength of cast

1879.39 LE PETIT DUC

A Revival of the Opéra-comique in Three Acts[5], in French. Libretto by Henri Meilhac and Ludovic Halévy. Music by Charles Lecocq. Stage manager, Mons. Mezières. Musical director, Charles Almeras. Produced by Maurice Grau's French Opera Company. Opened 1 September 1879 at the Fifth Avenue Theatre and closed 10 September 1879 after 2 performances in repertory; returned 22-23 March 1880 to the Fifth Avenue for 2 additional performances. Total: 4 performances.

CAST: *Le Duc de Parthenay*: Mme. MARIE AIMÉE. *De Montlandry*: Mons. JOUARD. *Frimousse*: Mons. DUPLAN. *Bernard*: Mons. Dupuis. *De Navailles*: Mons. Hayme. *De Montchevrier*: Mons. Vinchon. *De Tanneville*: Mons. Jolivet. *De Champvallon*: Mons. Borel. *De Merignac*: Mons. Gavant. *De Mancey*: Mons. Terrancle. *Diane de Chateau Lausac*: Mlle. Raphael. *La Duchesse de Parthenay*: Mlle. BEAUDET. *Roger*: Mlle. Sylla. *Gerard*: Mlle. Armand. *Julien*: Mlle. Amèlie. *Gontran*: Mlle. Louise Duparc. *Henri*: Mlle. Debray. *Gaston*: Mlle. Estephe. *Helene*: Mlle. Estradere. *Mlle. de la Roche Tonnerre, Mlle. de Champlatre, Mlle. de St. Anemone*: Mlles. Gouthure, Berthe, Bazin. *Margot*: Mlle. Louise. *Manon*: Mlle. Estradere. *Premiere Sous Maitresse*: Mlle. Sylla. *Deuxieme Sous Maitresse*: Mlle. Marguerite. *Ninon*: Mlle. Blanche. *Ninete*: Mlle. Berthe. *Marion*: Mlle. Ruffino. *Mariette*: Mlle. Seygand. *Dragoons, Trumpeters, Pensionnaires of the Convent at Luneville, Maids of Honor, Pages, Lords, Ladies of the Court, etc.*

1879.40 LES CLOCHES DE CORNEVILLE

A Revival of the Opéra-comique in Three Acts, 4 Scenes[6], in French. Libretto by Clairville and Charles Gabet. Music by Robert Planquette. Stage manager, Mons. Mezières. Musical director, Charles Almeras. Produced by Maurice Grau's French Opera Company. Opened 2 September 1879 at the Fifth Avenue Theatre and closed 12 September 1879 after 2 performances in repertory; returned 24 November 1879 to Booth's Theatre and closed 13 December 1879 after 5 additional performances; returned 10 March 1880 to the Fifth Avenue Theatre for 1 additional performance; returned 24 May 1880 to the Academy of Music for 1 additional performance. Total: 9 performances.

CAST: *Serpolette*: Mlle. MARIE AIMÉE[7]. *Germaine*: Mlle. CECILE GRÉGOIRE. *Gaspard*: Mons. J. Mezières. *Henri de Corneville*: Mons. JOUARD. *Grénicheux*: Mons. JUTEAU. *The Bailiff*: Mons. DUPLAN. *The Notary*: Mons. Vinchon. *Cachalat*: Mons. F. Mauriez. *Grippardin*: Mons. Haymes. *Fouinard*: Mons. Dupuis. *Manette*: Mlle. Marguerite. *Jeanne*: Mlle. Berthe. *Gertrude*: Mlle. Sylla. *Suzanne*: Mlle. Estradere. *Catherine*: Mlle. L. Duparc. *Marguerite*: Mlle. Gouthiere. *Peasants, Sailors, Coachmen, Servants, etc.*

Act 1: Marché de Corneville. (Corneville Market.)

Act 2: Une salle du château de Corneville. (A hall in the Chateau of Corneville.)

Act 3: Un parc avec statues et bosquets. (A park with statues and shrubbery.)

ACT 1[8]
- Opening Chorus (C'est le marché de Corneville . . .)
  Chorus
- Chanson (On dit, charmante Jeanne . . .)
  M. Aimée, All
- Bacchanale (Oui, nous devons faire taire . . .)
  M. Aimée, All
- Silence! Un semblable tapage . . .
  Messrs. Vinchon, Haymes, Dupuis, All
- Rondo (Dans ma mystérieuse histoire. .)
  M. Aimée
- Fantasie (Va, petit mousse . . .)
  Mons. Juteau
- Duet (Même sans consulter mon coeur. .)
  Mlle. Grégoire, Mons. Juteau
- Legende des Cloches (Nous avons, hélas! perdu d'excellents maîtres. .)
  Mlle. Grégoire, All
- Grand air (J'ai fait trois fois le tour du monde)
  Mons. Jouard
- Chorus (C'est affreux! Odieux!)
  Principals, Chorus
- Couplets (Je ne sais comment faire . . .)
  Mons. Juteau
- Marche Villageoise (Sur le marché de Corneville. .)
  Chorus
- Couplets (Vous qui voulez des servantes. .)
  M. Aimée, All
- Finale
  Principals, Chorus

ACT 2
- Opening Chorus (À la lueur de ces flambeaux. .)
  Mlle. Grégoire, Mons. Jouard, Chorus
- Trio (Fermons les yeux!)
  Messrs. Juteau, Duplan, Mlle. Aimée
- Couplets (Pristi! Sapristi! montons-nous la tête!)
  Mlle. Aimée, All
- Couplets (J'avais perdu la tête et ma perruque. .)
  Mons. Duplan
- Chant et Couplets (Non, vous le voyez, mes aïeux. .)
  Mons. Jouard, Chorus
- Petit Morceau (Que dit-elle? C'est moi. .)
  Mlle. Aimée, Mons. Jouard, All
- Duo et Couplets (C'est elle! et son destin la guide. .)
  Mons. Jouard, Mlle. Grégoire
- Morceau d'ensemble (Gloire au valeureux Grenicheux. .)
  Chorus, Messrs. Duplan, Jouard, Mlles. Grégoire, Aimée
- Duo and Couplets (C'est là, c'est là qu'est la richesse. .)
  Messrs. Mezières, Jouard
- Chorus et Finale (Oh! c'est l'enfer!)
  Mons. J. Mezières, Chorus

ACT 3
- Recitatif et Chanson (Enfin nous voilà transportés. .)
  Mons. J. Mezières
- Petit Morceau avec Couplet (Regardez donc quel équipage. .)
  Chorus, Mlle. Aimée, Mons. Juteau
- Chanson (Oui, c'est moi, c'est Serpolette. .)
  Mlle. Aimée, Chorus
- Ronde et Refrain (Le pomme est un fruit plein de sève . . .)
  Mlle. Aimée
- Rondeau (Je regardais en l'air . . .)
  Mons. Juteau
- Duo et Romance (Ah! monseigneur, à peine je respire . . .)
  Mlle. Grégoire, Mons. Jouard
- Finale, Air des Cloches
  Principals, Chorus

1879.41 LA PETIT MARIÉE

A Revival of the Opéra-comique in Three Acts, in French[9]. Libretto by Eugéne Leterrier and Albert Vanloo. Music by Charles Lecocq. Stage manager, Mons. J. Mezières. Musical director, Charles Almeras. Produced by Maurice Grau's French Opera Company. Opened 3 September 1879 at the Fifth Avenue Theatre for 1 performance in repertory.

CAST: *Graziella*: Mlle. MARIE AIMÉE. *Lucrézia*: Mlle. DELORME. *Theobaldo*: Mlle. Raphael. *Beatrice*: Mlle. Beaudet. *An Unknown Woman*: Mlle. Sylla. *The Podestate*: Mons. JOUARD. *San Carlo*: Mons. JUTEAU. *Montefiasco*: Mons. POYARD. *Castel Demoli*: Mons. J. Mezières. *Beppo*: Mons. Dupuis. *A Dumb Man*: Mons. Jolivet. *An Unknown Man*: Mons. Girard.

---

[5]Previously presented in New York in English 17 March 1879 at Booth's Theatre, and in French 12 April 1879 at Booth's Theatre for 18 performances in repertory. For Synopsis of Scenes and Musical Numbers, see original French production in 1878-1879 season.

[6]Previously presented in New York as THE CHIMES OF NORMANDY in English 22 October 1877 at the Fifth Avenue Theatre for 16 performances, and in French 13 May 1878 at the Park Theatre for 6 performances, returning to the Booth Theatre 3 June 1878 for an additional 3 performances.

[7]For return engagement at Booth's Theatre, Mlle. Paola Marié assumed the role of Serpolette. On tour the role was played by Mlle. Cecile Grégoire.

[8]Musical numbers not listed in programs. List prepared from published libretto for Maurice Grau's Company.

[9]Originally produced in New York in French 6 February 1877 at the Eagle Theatre for 9 performances in repertory. For Synopsis of Scenes and Musical Numbers, see original 1877 production.

1879.42

ENCHANTMENT

A Grand Operatic Spectacle in Four Acts, 20 Scenes. Music composed and arranged by Charles Puerner. Entire production, mis en scène, beautiful ballets under the personal direction and supervision of Imre and Bolossy Kiralfy. Scenery by William Voegtlin. Costumes designed by Grevin of Paris and Colonel Thompson of London. Orchestra conducted by Charles Puerner. Produced by the Kiralfys (Imre, Bolossy). Opened 4 September 1879 at Niblo's Garden and closed 13 December 1879 after 120 performances.

CAST: *Andre*, a young fisherman in love with Angeline: C. J. CAMPBELL. *The King*, the jolly King, who follows Andre in his travels: S. A. HEMPLE. *Duke Don Lodas*, betrothed to the Princess Angeline: GEORGE R. EDESON. *Peter*, Squire to the Duke: WILLIAM DAVIDGE, JR. *Casmagon*, the Notary, who gets roasted: MATTHEW HOLMES. *Maclow*, the Beggar of the Mountain: OTIS A. SKINNER. *Sambra*, companion to Arbra: Samuel Brown. *Count Bolone*, Minister of War: Thomas Francis Meagher. *Paul*: J. P. Jones. *Showman*: W. T. Sharon. *The Ape*: Young America. *Ephemeral*, Captain of the Ephemeral Guard: Homer Matthews. *Ephemerals (3)*: *Patemas*, who raises a family in twelve hours: S. O. Adams. *The Young Man*: B. Samuels. *The Son*: M. F. Thomas. *Waiter*: John Williams. *Princess Angeline*, the King's only daughter, in love with Andre: ROSE LEE. *Madelon*, in attendance on the Princess: AMY LEE. *Serpolette*, wife to Paul: EUGENIE NICHOLSON. *Therese*, the Cloth Merchant: Nina Everson. *Page to the King*: Maggie S. Tenant. *Arbra*, the Sorcerer: J. B. STUDLEY.

IMMORTALS: *Fairy Brilliantine*: JESSIE GREVILLE. *Fairy of Malice*: Bessie Hunter. *Fairies of the Magic Bush (6)*: *Argitta*: Annie Bufort. *Dorime*: Pearl Everlie. *Myrra*: Edith Everlie. *Zarilla*: Jenie Clark. *Eureka*: Mary Moore. *Semiras*: Carrie Lester. *Ladies, Soldiers, Demons, Villagers, Ghosts, Ephemerals, Egyptians, Shepherds, Chorus.*

Ballet: Mlles. CATARINA CASATI, (Adele) CORNALBA, EUGENIE CAPELINI, ADELE ZALLIO, AIDA CAMIS, LEONILDE ORTORI (Premières); Mlles. R. Capelini, Pasta and Ciappa (Secondes); Corps of Coryphées. *Specialty artists*: Les Vantoches Vallotte (Human automatons), Molva (graceful gymnast), La Troupe Rajade (comic eccentrics), Occarinistes (ocarina players).

Act 1, Scene 1: A City in the South of France. *Scene 2*: Andre's Home. *Scene 3*: The Devil's Gulf. *Scene 4*: Boudoir of the Princess. *Scene 5*: Garden of the King.

Act 2, Scene 1: The Mountain Inn. *Scene 2*: The Old Graveyard. *Scene 3*: The Blue Monkey Inn. *Scene 4*: The Plain of Windmills. *Scene 5*: Illuminated Venice.

Act 3, Scene 1: The Isle of a Day. *Scene 2*: The Magic Bush. *Scene 3*: Landscape. *Scene 4*: Castle of Lord Barrabille. *Scene 5*: Egyptian Palace and Tower of Babel.

Act 4, Scene 1: Chorus, Return of the King and Andre. *Scene 2*: Fantastic Landscape. *Scene 3*: The Enchanter's Palace. *Scene 4*: The Grotto. *Scene 5*: Apotheosis.

ACT 1
Scene 1
Market Chorus
Fisher's Song
C. J. Campbell
Arrival of the Princess (Chorus)
Departure of the Princess (Chorus)
"Adieu" (Chorus)
Scene 2
Song
C. J. Campbell
Scene 4
Love Duet
C. J. Campbell, R. Lee
Scene 5
"Tis Time" (Quartette)

ACT 2
Scene 2
The Duel; Dance of Death
Scene 3
The Wedding Procession
"Bom, Bom, Bom" (Quartette)
Scene 4
The Village Festival: Fleurs de Village (Grand Ballet)
Dance des Bergères
Secondas and Corps de Ballet
Entrée Dansante
Mlles. Cornalba, Capelini
Variation
Mlle. Cornalba
Fleurs de Village
Principal Secondas, Corps de Ballet
Great European Specialties
Molva (Great Russian Gymnast)
La Troupe Rajade (Orchestre Militaire)
Herbert Brothers (Acrobatic Feats)
Jack Its-chy Troupe (Feats of Jugglery, etc.)
Scene 5
Fête de Gondolières
Grand Carnival Evolution
Secondes, Entire Corps de Ballet

ACT 3
Scene 1
Chorus
Scene 2
Song
J. Greville
Septette and Chorus
Scene 4
Don Lodas the Somnabulist
Scene 5
Andre's Dream
Les Favorites de Babel au las Sphinx Misterieux (Grand Ballet)
Danse les Favorites et Nubiens
Secondas and Corps de Ballet
Danse des Sphinx Rouges
Mlles. Zallio, Ortori
Entree
Mlle. Camis
Jeune Egyptien
Mlle. E. Capelini
Grand Entrée Dansante
Mlle. Casati
Les Sphinx Noir
Secondas and Coryphees
Variation
Mlle. Ortori
Variation Animée
Mlle. Camis
Variation Vivacé
Mlle. A. Zallio
Variation de Force
Mlle. E. Capelini
Grand Variation
Mlle. Casati
Grand Adagio
Premières, Secondas, Coryphées, Corps de Ballet

ACT 4
Scene 1
Duet
C. J. Campbell, R. Lee
Scene 2
The Duel
Scene 4
Grand Septette
Scene 5
Grand Tableau

1879.43

MADAME FAVART

A Revival of the Opéra-comique in Three Acts[10], in French. Libretto by Henri Chivot and Alfred Duru. Music by Jacques Offenbach. Stage managers, Messrs. Mezières, Salvator. Musical director, Charles Almeras. Produced by Maurice Grau's French Opera Company. Opened 4 September 1879 at the Fifth Avenue Theatre and closed 11 September 1879

[10]Originally presented in New York 12 May 1879 at the Park Theatre for 14 performances in repertory. For Synopiss of Scenes and Musical Numbers, see original 1879 production.

after 2 performances in repertory; returned 15-18 March 1880 to the Fifth Avenue for 2 additional performances.

CAST: *Justine Favart*: Mlle. MARIE AIMÉE. *Suzanne*: Mlle. RAPHAEL. *Jolicoeur*: Mlle. Vallot. *Sans-Quartier*: Mlle. Sylla. *Larisolle*: Mlle. Amèlie. *Babet*: Mlle. Armand. *Jeanetton*: Mlle. Estradere. *Charles Favart*: Mons. JOUARD. *Marquis de Pontsablé*: Mons. J. Mezières. *Hector de Boispréau*: Mons. JUTEAU. *Cotignac*: Mons. DUPLAN. *Biscotin*: Mons. Dupuis. *Larose*: Mons. Vinchon.

1879.44 LA MARJOLAINE

A Revival of the Opérette in Three Acts[11], in French. Libretto by Alfred Vanloo and Eugène Leterrier. Music by Charles Lecocq. Stage managers, Messrs. Mezières, Salvator. Musical director, Charles Almeras. Produced by Maurice Grau. Opened 5 September 1879 at the Fifth Avenue Theatre for 1 performance; returned 17-20 March 1880 to the Fifth Avenue for 2 additional performances.

CAST: *Marjolaine*: Mme. MARIE AIMÉE. *Aveline*: Mlle. Beaudet. *Petrus*: Mlle. Armand. *Karl*: Mlle. Vallot. *Christian*: Mlle. Estradere. *Robert*: Mlle. Amèlie. *Christophe*: Mlle. Sylla. *Frantz*: Mlle. LOUISE DUPARC. *Gudule*: Mlle. Leroy. *A Peasant*: Mlle. Deblinde. *A Maiden*: Mlle. Salvator. *Baron Palamede*: Mons. J. Mezières. *Annibal*: Mons. JOUARD. *Frickel*: Mons. JUTEAU. *Peterschop*: Mons. DUPLAN. *D'Escoublac*: Mons. DUPUIS. *Schaerbeck*: Mons. Hayme. *Le Bourgmestre*: Mons. Vinchon. *Two Aldermen*: Messrs. Gavaut, Passerard. *A Town Crier*: Mons. Terrancle. *Peasants, Men and Women Servants, etc.*

1879.45 LA BOULANGÈRE A DES ÉCUS

A Revival of the Opéra Bouffe (Opérette) in Three Acts[12], in French. Libretto by Henri Meilhac and Ludovic Halévy. Music by Jacques Offenbach. Stage manager, Mons. J. Mezières. Musical director, Charles Almeras. Produced by Maurice Grau's French Opera Company. Opened 6 September 1879 at the Fifth Avenue Theatre for 1 performance in repertory.

CAST: *Margot*: Mlle. MARIE AIMÉE. *Toinon*: Mlle. GRÉGOIRE. *Ravanne*: Mlle. RAPHAEL. *Bemadille*: Mons. JUTEAU. *Le Commissaire*: Mons. JOUARD. *Coquebert*: Mons. POYARD. *Délicat*: Mons. J. Mezières. *Hammèche*: Mons. DUPLAN. *Pacot*: Mons. Hayme. *Un Financier*: Mons. Dupuis. *Un Voleur*: Mons. Marchand. *Capitaine des Gardes*: Mons. Jolivet. *Un Sergeant*: Mons. Girard. *Mme. de Parabere*: Mlle. Estradere. *Mme. de Sabran*: Mlle. Berthe. *Mme. De Phalaris*: Mlle. Ruffino. *Four Pages*: Mlles. Armand, Sylla, Duparc, Amèlie. *Dames, Seigneurs, Paysants, Domestiques, Boulangers et Boulangeres, Marmitons, etc.*

1879.46 LA JOLIE PARFUMEUSE

A Revival of the Opéra-comique in Three Acts[13], in French. Libretto by Hector Crémieux and Ernest Blum. Music by Jacques Offenbach. Produced by Maurice Grau. Opened 8 September 1879 at the Fifth Avenue Theatre for 1 performance in repertory.

CAST: *Rose Michon*, la jolie parfumeuse: Mme. MARIE AIMÉE. *La Cocardière*: *Clorinde*: *Bavolet*:

Company also included Messrs. JUTEAU, JOUARD, POYARD, MEZIÈRES, DUPLAN, Dupuis, Marchand, Jolivet, Girard. Mlles. GRÉGOIRE, RAPHAEL, Estradere, Berthe, Ruffino, Armand, Sylla, Duparc, Amèlie.

1879.47 LES BRIGANDS

A Revival of the Opéra-bouffe in Three Acts[14], in French. Libretto by Henri Meilhac and Ludovic Halévy. Music by Jacques Offenbach. Stage manager, Mons. J. Mezières. Musical director, Charles Almeras. Produced by Maurice Grau's French Opera Company. Opened 9 September 1879 at the Fifth Avenue Theatre and closed 13 September 1879 after 2 performances in repertory; returned 30 October 1879 to the Fifth Avenue Theatre and closed 8 November 1879 after 5 additional performances.[15] Total: 7 performances.

CAST: *Fiorella*: Mlle. MARIE AIMÉE. *Fragoletto*, a young farmer: Mlle. RAPHAEL. *The Princess of Granada*: Mlle. BEAUDET. *Falsacappa*: Mons. JUTEAU. *Pietro*, his lieutenant: Mons. DUPLAN. *Antonio*, Secretary to the Duke of Mantua: Mons. J. Mezières. *The Captain of Carabineers*: Mons. JOUARD. *The Duke of Mantua*: Mlle. Armand. *Carmagnola, Barbavano, Domino*, Brigands: Messrs. Poyard, Hayme, Jolivet. *Baron de Campotasso*: Mons. Dupuis. *Count Gloria-Cassis*: Mons. Vinchon. *Tutor to the Princess*: Mons. Terrancle. *Adolphe de Vallodolid*: Mlle. Amèlie. *Pipo*, an Innkeeper: Mons. Salvator. *Zerlina*: Mlle. Deblinde. *Fiametta*: Mlle. Estradere. *Bianca*: Mlle. Berthe. *Cincinella*: Mlle. L. Duparc. *The Duchess*: Mlle. Sylla. *The Marquis*: Mlle. Salvator. *Pipa*: Mlle. Marguerite. *Pipetta*: Mlle. Louise. *A Courier*: Mlle. Mauriez. *A Sheriff*: Mlle. Jolivet. *Brigands, Carabineers, Peasants, Pages, Lords and Ladies of the Court of Mantua; Pages and Ladies of the Court of Granada.*

1879.48 LA FILLE DE MADAME ANGOT

A Revival of the Opéra-comique in Three Acts[16], in French. Libretto by Clairville, Paul Siraudin and Victor Koning. Music by Charles Lecocq. Stage manager, Mons. J. Mezières. Musical director, Charles Almeras. Produced by Maurice Grau's French Opera Company. Opened 15 September 1879 at the Fifth Avenue Theatre and closed 1 October 1879 after 11 performances in repertory; returned 3 December 1879 to Booth's Theatre for 1 additional performance; returned 8 March 1880 to the Fifth Avenue Theatre 1 additional performance; returned 19 May 1880 to the Academy of Music for 1 additional performance. Total: 14 performances.

CAST: *Clairette*: Mlle. PAOLA MARIÉ. *Mlle. Lange*: Mlle. ANGÈLE. *Amaranthe*: Mlle. DELORME. *Javotte*: Mlle. Sylla. *Therese*: Mlle. Berthe. *Manon*: Mlle. Armand. *Babet*: Mlle. Duparc. *Cydalise*: Mlle. Sylla. *Delaunay*: Mlle. Estradere. *Herbelin*: Mlle. J. Debray. *Hersilie*: Mlle. A. Bazin. *Pomponnet*: Mons. JUTEAU. *Larivaudière*: Mons. JOUARD. *Louchard*: Mons. DUPLAN. *Trenitz*: Mons. VILANO. *Cadet*: Mons. Terrancle. *Guillaume*: Mons. Dupuis. *Buteux*: Mons. Mauriez. *Un Incroyable*: Mons. Terbel. *Un Officier*: Mons. Terbel. *Un Garçon*: Mons. Moreau. *Ange Pitou*: Mons. VICTOR CAPOUL.

1879.49 GIROFLÉ-GIROFLA

A Revival of the Opéra-bouffe in Three Acts[17], in French. Libretto by Albert Vanloo and Eugène Leterrier. Music by Charles Lecocq. Stage manager, Mons. Bouvard. Musical director, Charles Almeras. Produced by Maurice Grau's French Opera Company. Opened 15 September 1879 at the Fifth Avenue Theatre and closed 11 October 1879 after 11 performances in repertory; returned 5 December 1879 to Booth's Theatre for 1 additional performance; returned 13 March 1880 (matinee) to the Fifth Avenue Theatre for 1 additional performance; returned 5 May 1880 to the Academy of Music for 1 additional performance. Total: 14 performances.

CAST: *Giroflé, Girofla*: Mlle. PAOLA MARIÉ. *Pedro*: Mlle. ANGÈLE. *Aurore*: Mlle. DELORME. *Paquita*: Mlle. BEAUDET. *Gusmand*: Mlle. Amèlie. *Fernand*: Mlle. Seygand. *Almanzor*: Mlle. Estradere. *Nino*: Mlle. A. Bouvard. *Bolero*: Mons. DUPLAN. *Mourzouk*: Mons. JOUARD. *Chief of the Pirates*: Mons. Terrancle. *Godfather*: Mons. Dupuis. *A Dancer*: Mons. Gavant. *A Notary*: Mons. Gerard. *A Preceptor*: Mons. Thuillart. *An Uncle*: Mons. Borel. *Page*: Mons. Mauriez. *Marasquin*: Mons. VICTOR CAPOUL. *Cousins of the Bride, Men and Women of the Palace, Bridesmaids, Pages, Pirates and Moors attendant upon Mourzouk.*

1879.50 NEWPORT, or, The Swimmer, the Singer and the Cypher/ LOVE'S YOUNG DREAM

A Double Bill of a Farcical Comedy in Three Acts, preceded by a Comedietta in One Act. Directed by Augustin Daly, assisted by Fred

---

[11]Originally produced in New York 1 October 1877 at the Broadway Theatre for 23 performances in its first season. For Synopsis of Scenes and Musical Numbers, see original 1877 production.

[12]Originally presented in New York 26 February 1877 at the Eagle Theatre for 5 performances in repertory. For Synopsis of Scenes and Musical Numbers, see original 1877 production.

[13]Originally produced in New York in French 31 March 1875 at the Lyceum Theatre. For Synopsis of Scenes and Musical Numbers, see original 1875 production.

[14]Originally produced in New York 14 November 1870 at the Grand Opera House. For Synopsis of Scenes and Musical Numbers, see original 1870 production.

[16]Mlle. Aimée will introduce a new song by Offenbach "La Malaguena," and a Spanish song "La Paloma."

[16]Originally presented in New York in French 25 August 1873 at the Broadway Theatre. For Synopsis of Scenes and Musical Numbers, see original 1873 production.

[17]Originally produced in New York in French 4 February 1875 at the Park Theatre. For Synopsis of Scenes and Musical Numbers, see original 1875 production.

Williams and John Moore. Musical director, Edward Mollenhauer. Produced by Augustin Daly. Opened 17 September 1879 at Daly's Theatre and closed 29 September 1879 after (13) performances.

ACT 1

LOVE'S YOUNG DREAM, a Comedietta in One Act. Play by Joseph Francis. Music, original and selected, by Edward Mollenhauer. Scenery by Louis Duflocq.

CAST: *Jotham Dibble, Esq*: CHARLES FISHER. *Florence*, his daughter: May Fielding. *Nelly Beers, Jack Beers*, a dissolved partnership: ADA REHAN, GEORGE PARKES. *Fred Schemerhorn*: HARRY LACY. *Nap*, Waiter at the Superior Suphur Spring Pavilion: E. P. Wilks.

ACT 2

NEWPORT, or, The Swimmer, the Singer and the Cypher. A Farcical Comedy in Three Acts. Play by an American writer residing abroad[18]. Music by Charles Lecocq, DeBrille, Meyer Lutz and Edward Mollenhauer. Lyrics by Fred Williams. Scenery by James Roberts.

CAST: *Hon. Peter Porter*, U.S. Ambassador to Rome, on a "home leave": CHARLES LECLERCQ. *Hon. U. B. Blode*, late Consul at Hotlands: William Davidge. *Ben Boulgate*, the Champion Swimmer of the Universe, etc, etc.: HART CONWAY. *Captain Chickering*, of the Brooklyn Twenty-Second, just landed, from Canada: GEORGE PARKES. *Tom Sanderson*, a master bather, with an overmastering secret: JOHN DREW. *Captain Blackwell*, a Swell of the Beach, with a yacht to sell: F. Iredale. *Crutch Reynolds*, another—without the yacht: Walter Edmunds. *Undo*, Porter's private secretary: Frank Bennett. *Toggs*, Porter's Marine Tiger: Maggie Barnes. *Midget*, a Middy on Blackwell's yacht: Laura Thorpe. *Thompson*, Clerk at the Grand Flummery: E. Sterling. *Ginger*, Bell Boy at the Flummery: E. P. Wilks. *Officer*: P. Hunting. *Bathers, Promenaders, Guests, Arrivals*: Misses Sidney Nelson, Sara Lascelles, Emma Wharton, Isabelle Everson, Emma Turner, Lillie Stuart, Dora Knowlton, Ida Bruce, A. Lovell, E. Hinckley, Fanny McNeil, Grace Logan, Ella Remetze, Malvina; Mons. Sterling, Watson, Solomons, Murphy, Smith, Walshe, Hunting, Burnham, Laurence, Newborough, Edwards. *The Hon. Mrs. Peter Porter*, formerly of the Grand Comic Opera: CATHERINE LEWIS. *Widow Warboys*: Mrs. Charles Poole. *Miss Belle Blode*: Georgine Flagg. *Casette*, the Hon. Mrs. Peter Porter's maid: Annie Wakeman. *Swells of the Beach (3)*: *Miss Alexander Byrdde*: Estelle Clayton. *Miss Eugenia Fysshe*: May Bowers. *Miss Vicoria Cattelle*: Blanche Weaver.

Act 1: The Beach at Newport.

Act 2: A Yacht off Newport.

Act 3: The Grand Flummery Hotel in Newport.

ACT 1

Opening Chorus of Bathers
Company

"I Am the Champion Swimmer" (Song)
H. Conway

"The Continong" (Song)
H. Conway

"The Truth" (Song)
C. Lewis

"The Ambassador's Wooing" (Song)
C. Lewis

ACT 2

"Crutch and Toothpick" (Song)
C. Lewis

"Lalla Rookh" (Song)
C. Lewis

"Who Loves Must Dare" (Duet)
C. Lewis, H. Conway

ACT 3

Chorus of Porters, Waiters, and Guests
Company

"The Muddle Puddle Brakeman" (Song)
H. Conway

"Twixt You and Me" (Song)
C. Lewis

Finale
C. Lewis, H. Conway, Company

[18]Unidentified in programs, Olive Logan Sykes. The New York Times reviewer observed that the play was an uncredited adaptation of the French farce "Niniche."

1879.51

LA PÉRICHOLE

A Revival of the Opéra-bouffe in Three Acts, 4 Scenes[19], in French. Libretto by Ludovic Halévy and Henri Meilhac, based on "La Carosse du Saint-Sacrament" by Prosper Merimée. Music by Jacques Offenbach. Stage manager, Mons. Bouvard. Musical director, Charles Almeras. Produced by Maurice Grau's French Opera Company. Opened 24 September 1879 at the Fifth Avenue Theatre and closed 3 November 1879 after 8 performances in repertory; returned 13 March 1880 to the Fifth Avenue Theatre for 1 additional performance. Total: 9 performances.

CAST: *La Périchole*, a Street Singer: Mlle. PAOLA MARIÉ. *Guadalena*: Mlle. GRÉGOIRE. *Berginella*: Mlle. RAPHAEL. *Mastrilla*: Mlle. BEAUDET. *Manuelita*: Mlle. Armand. *Frasquinella*: Mlle. Sylla. *Brambilla*: Mlle. Estradere. *Ninetta*: Mlle. Bouvard. *Don Andrès de Ribeira*, Viceroy of Peru: Mons. JOUARD. *Don Pedro de Hinoyosa*, Governor of Lima: Mons. DUPLAN. *Count Panatellas*, First Gentleman of the Bedchamber: Mons. J. Mezières. *The Marquis of Tarapote*: Mons. VILANO. *An Old Prisoner*: Mons. POYARD. *Two Notaries*: Messrs. Gerard, Terbel. *A Jailor*: Mons. Gavant. *Piquillo*: Mons. VICTOR CAPOUL. *Notaries, Soldiers, Courtiers, Indians, Peasants, Guards, Pages, Servants*.

1879.52

BRIC-À-BRAC

An Entertainment in Two Acts, consisting of a Domestic Sketch followed by "Bric-à-Brac Reception." Conceived by J. C. Padgett and Jed Bassett. Musical director, Fred Intropodi. Opened 29 September 1879 at Wood's Broadway Theatre and closed 18 October 1879 after 24 performances.

ACT 1

Love and Rain, a Domestic Sketch.[20]

CAST: *Captain Charles Lumley*: J. C. PADGETT. *Lady Jane*: Miss B. NORTON *Andrew*, her servant: JED BASSETT.

Oscar N. Newell (Piano Solo: Gottschalk's fantasie on IL TROVATORE)

ACT 2

BRIC-À-BRAC RECEPTION. Miss Bluebottle begs the pleasure of your company at her residence this evening, and desires you to appear in a costume representing your favorite piece of bric-à-brac.

CAST: *Miss Blue Jug*: Miss C. Daniels. *Miss Chinaware*: Miss B. NORTON. *Mr. Stone Jug*: JED BASSETT. *Mr. Brown Jug*: J. C. PADGETT. *Hon. Bardwell Slote*, an imitation of W. J. Florence: J. C. PADGETT. *Miss Keziah Wrinkle*, the maiden who is sighing for someone to love: JED BASSETT. *A Sad Man*, full of tears: J. C. PADGETT. *Bobby Tubbs*: JED BASSETT. *Little Sally Waters*: Miss B. NORTON. *Specialty*: Miss Cora Daniels, in her original rendition of "Genevieve."

SPECIALTIES[21]

They are coming

"Sleigh-Bell Quartette" from FATINITZA
(*Music by* Franz von Suppé.)

Arrival of the Bric-à-Brac

A royal welcome

A loud call for Caesar's Saucer; the Saucer discussed

Let Mirth and Music rule the hour

"Song of the Saucer"

That's good

Chorus and March

Miss Yelloware becomes upper-attic

High C

Mr. Teakettle getting warmed up commences to sing

My Grandfather's Clock wound up for a month

That's good

A crash in Crockery

[19]This revised version was first produced in New York in French 15 February 1877 at the Eagle Theatre for 4 performances. This production has varying extant theatre programs, some of which read Three Acts, Four Scenes, and others which read Four Acts. For Synopsis of scenes and Musical Numbers, see 1877 revival.

[20]On 6 October 1879 this was replaced for the rest of the run by A Conjugal Lesson, a Domestic Sketch: CAST: *Mr. Simon Lullaby*: J. C. PADGETT. *Mrs. Simon Lullaby*: Miss B. NORTON.

[21]Reviewers remarked upon the variety of the program, ranging from Solos from Grand Operas to "Little Sally Waters," recitations from "Roger and I" to "Mary's Little Lamb," instrumental music from piano to banjo.

A Sensation
Mr. Brown Jug retires to replenish
More arrivals
Hon. Bardwell Slote, M.C., and H.O.G. (Highly Honorable Gentleman)
Miss Keziah Wrinkle, who is sighing for someone to love
Miss Daniels and her guitar ["Genevieve"]
Bobby Tubbs, who speaks a piece and goes to pieces
Little Sally Waters and the little farm she keeps
Animated China-Man; no likee Pi! Pi!
'Tis I, Gimlet, the Lame
Despatch from the Emperor of Japan
The Bric-à-Brac is resolved to accept his hospitality
En route
We will marry as soon as we can
Quartette
Grand Finale

1879.53

HOBBIES

Weathersby-Goodwin Froliques in a Humorous Fantasy (A Farce Comedy and a Burlesque) in Two Acts[22]. Play by Ben E. Woolf. Stage manager, Charles Bowser. Musical director, John Eller. Produced by Nat C. Goodwin. Opened 6 October 1879 at Haverly's Lyceum Theatre and closed 1 November 1879 after 32 performances. Returned 26 April 1880 to the Standard Theatre and closed 22 May 1880 after 28 additional performances.[23] Total: 60 performances.

CAST: Characters in the Comedy: *Minnie Clover*: ELIZA WEATHERSBY. *Professor Pygmalin Whiffles*, Piggy for short: NAT C. GOODWIN. *Miss Constance*, with songs: VENIE CLANCY. *Miss Euphemia Bang*: JENNIE WEATHERSBY[24]. *Major Garroway Bang*: Charles Bowser. *Arthur Doveleigh*: Raymond Holmes.

Characters in the Burlesque: *The Prince*: ELIZA WEATHERBSY. *The Princess*: VENIE CLANCY. *The Count*: Raymond Holmes. *The Villain*: NAT C. GOODWIN. *The Fairy*: JENNIE WEATHERSBY. *The Audience*: Charles Bowser.

MUSICAL NUMBERS, SPECIALTIES[25]
"Crutch and Toothpick" (from NEWPORT)
E. Weathersby

1879.54

ACROSS THE ATLANTIC

A Startling and Sensational Drama in Four Acts. Play by John W. Ransone. Produced by Ferdinand W. Hofele. Opened 13 October 1879 at the Olympic Theatre and closed 18 October 1879 after 8 performances.[26]

CAST: *Horace Durand*, a young actor: JOHN W. RANSONE. *Horace Blue*, a colored servant: JOHN W. RANSONE. *Jacob Chan*, a German guide: JOHN W. RANSONE. *Miles O'Flinn*, an Irishman coachman: JOHN W. RANSONE. *Louise*, a Bavarian girl: Mrs. JOHN W. RANSONE. *Katarina*, waiting maid to Emma Livingston, with songs: Mrs. JOHN W. RANSONE. *Augustus Chanpan*, alias Count St. Arnand: FRANK A. TANNEHILL. *Francis Black*, attorney at law: Walter Fessler. *George Livingston*, a rich Banker: CHARLES FOSTER. *General St. Arnand*, a French General: De Loss King. *General von Shonborn*, a Prussian General: J. R. Lewis. *Sergeant LaRue* of the French Army: C. Henry. *Sergeant Vochtel* of the Prussian Army: T. Atkins. *Detective Stone*: D. F. Hartnett. *Officer*: E. J. Phalon. *Boy*: S. G. DeForrest. *Emma Livingston*, the Banker's Daughter: HELENE ADDELL. *Mrs. Livingston*: Mrs. W. G. JONES. *French and Prussian Soldiers, Passengers, etc.*

Act 1: New York City.

Act 2: Paris, Switzerland and Germany during the Franco-Prussian War.

Act 3: French Army at Sedan.

Act 4: Sedan in possession of the Prussians.

SPECIALTIES
"I Can't Make It Out, Can You?"
"Yawcup Heinrich Risender von Dunner und Blitzen Bub"
"My Grandfather's Muhle"
"The Song of the Greutli Mountain"
I'ave got a sour heart [sketch]
Mr. & Mrs. J. W. Ransone
Dance at the Foot of the Hill

1879.55

BARBE BLEUE

A Revival of the Opéra-bouffe in Three Acts[27], in French. Libretto by Henri Meilhac and Ludovic Halèvy. Music by Jacques Offenbach. Stage manager, Mons. Bouvard. Musical director, Charles Almeras. Produced by Maurice Grau's French Opera Company. Opened 13 October 1879 at the Fifth Avenue Theatre and closed 5 November 1879 after 7 performances in repertory.

CAST: *Boulotte*: Mlle. PAOLA MARIÉ. *Princess Hermia*: Mlle. GRÉGOIRE. *Queen Clémentine*: Mme. DELORME. *Heloise*: Mlle. Armand. *Eleonore*: Mlle. Estradere. *Isaure*: Mlle. Bouvard. *Rosalinde*: Mlle. Esteve. *Blanche*: Mlle. Louise. *Dorothée*: Mlle. Seygaud. *Pages*: Mlles. Alphonsine, Ruffino. *Popolani*: Mons. JOUARD. *Count Oscar*: Mons. J. Mezières. *King Bobèche*: Mons. DUPLAN. *Prince Saphir*: Mons. POYARD. *Alvarez*: Mons. Gerard. *A Notary*: Mons. Mauriez. *Barbe-Bleue*: Mons. VICTOR CAPOUL.

1879.56

WIVES

A Novel and Picturesque Comedy in Five Acts. Play by Bronson Howard, based on Moliere's "L'École des Femmes" and "L'École des Maris." Music by Edward Mollenhauer. Lyrics by Fred Williams. (Stage direction by Augustin Daly.) Scenery by James Roberts and Louis Duflocq. Costumes by Eaves. (Musical direction, Edward Mollenhauer.) Produced by Augustin Daly. Opened 18 October 1879 at Daly's Theatre and closed 28 November 1879 after 42 performances.

CAST: *Arnolphe*, Marquis de Fontenoy, also known as Monsieur La Souche, who has a special recipe for "making a wife": CHARLES FISHER. *Scanarelle la Marre*, the guardian, jointly with Ariste, of Isabelle and Leonora, also having a pet recipe for "wife making": WILLIAM DAVIDGE. *The Vicomte Ariste*, his brother: GEORGE MORTON. *Chrisalde*, a mutual friend of the period: JOHN DREW. *Horace de Chateauroux*, the one ingredient overlooked in the good Arnolphe's recipe: HARRY LACY. *Captain Fiermonte*, of the King's Musketeers: George Parkes. *Dorval*, the cunning valet who helped to spoil Scanarelle's recipe: Hart Conway. *Alain*, in Arnolphe's service: Charles Leclercq. *Jean Jacques*, of Scanarelle's household: F. Bennett. *Captain Ballander*, of the Night Watch: W. Edmunds. *The Commissary*: Mr. Hunting. *The Notary*: Mr. Sterling. *Men of the Night Watch*, Men of the Chorus: Messrs. E. M. Smith, Walsh, Watson, Newborough, Edwards, Lawrence, Sterling, Meriden, Murphy, Solomon, Burnham, etc.

Agnes, the simple one: CATHERINE LEWIS. *Isabelle de Nesle*, the deep one: ADA REHAN. *Leonora de Nesle*, the artless one: MARGARET LANNER *Lisette*, the confidential one: Maggie Harold. *Georgette*, the deaf one: Sydney Nelson. *Musketeers, Ladies of the Chorus*: Misses Sara Lascelles, Ellie Stuart, Gussie Lang, Mlle. Malvenna, Emma Turner, Blanche Weaver, Isabelle Everson, Fanny McNeill, Dora Knowlton, Ella Remetze, Grace Logan, Emma Hinckley, Miss Maxwell.

The action takes place in Paris during the reign of Louis XIV and Cardinal Mazarin, in but a few hours.

Act 1: Scanarelle's residence in the Faubourg, St. Germain. Four o'clock. (Roberts.)

Act 2: The La-Souche Villa. Faubourg, St. Marguerite. Five o'clock. (Roberts.)

Act 3: At Scanarelle's, as before. Six o'clock. (Roberts.)

Act 4: A Square in old Paris, near the old Cathedral. Seven o'clock. (Duflocq.)

Act 5: Scanarelle's. Nine o'clock. (Roberts.)

MUSICAL NUMBERS[28]
"I'm Such a Little Fool"
C. Lewis
"Carefully on Tiptoe Stealing" (from THE CONSPIRATORS)
(*Music by* Charles Lecocq, adapted by E. Mollenhauer.)

---

[22]Preceded by a curtain-raiser, Romance under Difficulties, which was dropped after the opening; HOBBIES then constituted the entire evening's entertainment.

[23]No credits in programs for scenery or costumes. Specialties, musical numbers not listed; Nat C. Goodwin will interpolate imitations of the following stellar lights: Edwin Booth, Lawrence Barrett, Charles Fechter, John T. Raymond, Joseph Jefferson, Stuart Robson, Frank Mayo, many others.

[24]For the return engagement at the Standard, Susie Parker assumed the roles of Miss Euphemia Bang and the Fairy.

[25]Musical numbers, specialties not listed in programs.

[26]No credits for authorship of songs, stage director, scenery or costumes. Ransone was billed as the great California dialect comedian and vocalist.

[27]Originally produced in New York in French 13 July 1868 at Niblo's Garden for 102 performance in two engagements. For Synopsis of Scenes and Musical Numbers, see original 1868 production.

[28]Musical numbers not listed in programs. List prepared from published reviews.[32]

1879.57

DIE FLEDERMAUS

A Comic Operette in Three Acts, in German. (Original Viennese libretto by Richard Genée and Carl Haffner, based on "Le Réveillon" by Henri Meilhac and Ludovic Halévy.) Music by Johann Strauss. Produced by Gustav Amberg. Opened 18 October 1879 at the Thalia Theatre and closed 25 (matinee) October 1879 after 7 performances in repertory.

CAST: *Gabriel von Eisenstein*, a Wealthy Banker: Herr SCHNELLE. *Rosalinde*, Eisenstein's wife: MATHILDE COTTRELLY. *Franke*, Director of the Prison: Herr LUBE. *Prince Orlofsky*: Frl. AHL. *Alfred*: Herr Lenoir. *Dr. Falke*, the Family Physician: Herr FRITZE. *Dr. Blind*, an Attorney: Herr Rohbeck. *Adèle*, her Servant: Frl. FIEBACH. *Ida*, a Coryphee: Frl. KRAFFT. *Ramison*: Herr Wagner. *Frosch*, a Jailer: Herr Adolfi. *Ali Bey*, an Egyptian: Herr Schneider.

1879.58

TRIAL BY JURY/ H.M.S. PINAFORE, or, The Lass That Loved a Sailor

A Double Bill Revival of the Comic Operas in Two Acts[29]. Librettos by William S. Gilbert. Music by Arthur Sullivan. Musical director, Ernest Neyer. Presented by William Henderson. Opened 20 October 1879 at the Standard Theatre and closed 15 November 1879 after 33 performances.[30]

TRIAL BY JURY CAST: *Plaintiff*: VERNONA JARBEAU. *Judge*: F. A. PALMENTAL. *Defendant*: H. R. HUMPHRIES. *Counsel for Plaintiff*: W. A. PAUL. *Usher*: ALFRED HOLLAND. *Foreman of Jury*: A. H. Pelham. *Bridesmaids, Spectators, etc.*

H. M. S. PINAFORE CAST: *The Rt. Hon. Sir Joseph Porter, K.C.B.*, First Lord of the Admiralty: THOMAS H. WHIFFEN. *Ralph Rackstraw*, Able Seaman: ALONZO HATCH. *Captain Corcoran*, Commanding the *H.M.S. Pinafore*: WALLACE MACREERY. *Dick Deadeye*, Able Seaman: F. A. PALMENTAL. *Bill Bobstay*, Boatswain: Alfred Holland. *Tom Bowline*, Boatswain's Mate: A. H. Pelham. *Midshipmite*: Master Tony. *Josephine*, the Captain's Daughter: EVA MILLS. *Little Buttercup*, a Portsmouth Bumboat Woman: ESTELLE MORTIMER. *Hebe*, Sir Joseph's First Cousin: VERNONA JARBEAU. *First Lord's Sisters, his Cousins, his Aunts, Sailors, Marines, etc.*

1879.59

H.M.S. PINAFORE, or, The Lass That Loved a Sailor

The Miniature Operetta Company Revival of the Comic Opera in Two Acts[31]. Libretto by William S. Gilbert. Music by Arthur Sullivan. Stage manager, Jonathan H. Burnett. Musical director, F. Intropodi. Presented by the Miniature Operetta Company (W. Clarence Elmendorf, Proprietor and Manager). Opened 20 October 1879 at Wood's Broadway Theatre and closed 25 October 1879 after 8 performances.

CAST: *Josephine*, the Captain's Daughter: LILLIAN C. REYNOLDS. *Little Buttercup*, a Bumboat Woman: MAUD ELMENDORF. *Cousin Hebe*, Sir Joseph's First Cousin: Inez DeLeon. *The Rt. Hon. Sir Joseph Porter, K.C.B.*, First Lord of the Admiralty: IRENE PERRY. *Captain Corcoran*, Commanding the *H.M.S. Pinafore*: JERRY CAMMEYER. *Ralph Rackstraw*, Able Seaman: Master LeVERNE ENNIS. *Dick Deadeye*, Able Seaman: Richard Oakley. *Bill Bobstay*, Bo'sun's Mate: Charles Wilson. *Bob Beckett*, Carpenter's Mate: John Moore. *Tommy Tucker*, Midshipman: La Petite Annie McDonald. *First Officer, H.M.S. Pinafore*: Master Allie Elmendorf. *First Lord's Sisters, his Cousins, his Aunts, Sailors, Marines, etc.*)

1879.60

LE PETIT FAUST

A Revival of the Opéra-bouffe in Three Acts[32], in French. Libretto by Hector Crémieux and Adolphe Jaime. Music by Hervé. Stage manager, Mons. Bouvard. Musical director, Charles Almeras. Produced by Maurice Grau's French Opera Company. Opened 20 October 1879 at the Fifth Avenue Theatre and closed 22 October 1879 after 3 performances in repertory.

CAST: *Marguerite*: Mlle. PAOLA MARIÉ. *Lisette*: Mlle. BEAUDET. *Aglae*: Mlle. Estradere. *Clorinde*: Mlle. Esteve. *Charlotte*: Mlle. Bouvard. *Dorothée*: Mlle. Berthe. *Agnes*: Mlle. Alphonsine. *Siebel*: Mlle. Bazin. *Frantz*: Mlle. Armand. *Wagner*: Mlle. Vandamme. *Fritz*: Mlle. Duparc. *(Doctor) Faust*: Mons. JUTEAU. *Valentin*: Mons. VILANO. *A Coachman*: Mons. DUPLAN. *Un Pion*: Mons. Terbel. *Anglo-Saxon*: Mons. Gerard. *Méphisto*: Mlle. ANGÈLE. *Soldiers, Students, Old Men, Anglo Saxons, Russians, Male and Female Demons, etc.*

1879.61

LA GRANDE-DUCHESSE DE GÉROLSTEIN

A Revival of the Opéra-bouffe in Three Acts[33], in French. Libretto by Henri Meilhac and Ludovic Halévy. Music by Jacques Offenbach. Stage manager, Mons. Bouvard. Musical director, Charles Almeras. Produced by Maurice Grau's French Opera Company. Opened 23 October 1879 at the Fifth Avenue Theatre and closed 7 November 1879 after 7 performances in repertory; returned 11 December 1879 to Booth's Theatre for 1 additional performance; returned 12 March 1880 to the Fifth Avenue Theatre for 1 additional performance. Total: 9 performances.

CAST: *La Grande-Duchesse*: Mlle. PAOLA MARIÉ. *Wanda*: Mlle. ANGÈLE. *Isa*: Mlle. Armand. *Amèlie*: Mlle. Bazin. *Olga*: Mlle. Bouvard. *Charlotte*: Mlle. Estradere. *Prince Paul*: Mons. POYARD. *Baron Puck*: Mons. J. Mezières. *General Boum*: Mons. JOUARD. *Baron Grog*: Mons. Dupuis. *Nepomuc*: Mons. Gavant. *Fritz*: VICTOR CAPOUL. *Lords and Ladies of the Court, Maids of Honor, Pages, Ushers, Soldiers, Vivandières, Country Girls.*

1879.62

DER SEECADET

A Comic Opera in Three Acts, (Der Seekadett) in German. (Libretto by F. Zell, adapted fom 'Le Capitaine Charlotte' by Jean-François Bayard and Philippe Dumanoir.) Music by Richard Genée. Produced by Gustav Amberg. Opened 27 October 1879 at the Thalia Theatre and closed 10 March 1880 in repertory.

CAST: *Marie Franziska*: Fraulein FIEBACH. *Don Domingos*: Herr LUBE. *Donna Antonia*: Frau LUBE. *Lambert*: Herr SCHNELLE. *Fanchette*: Fraulein MATHILDE COTTRELLY. *Dom Januario*: Herr GUSTAV ADOLFI. *Rodriguez*: Herr PULS.

Officiere: *Franzesco*: Herr Loë. *Joaquino*: Herr Rohbeck. *Norberto*: Herr Wagner. *Cesario*: Herr Weinacht. *Ricardo*: Herr Schliemann. *Dom Silvio*: Herr Lenoir. *Dom Contreras*: Herr Kreutzberg. *Dom Ruiz*: Herr Pege. *Arthuro*: Herr Rothschild. *Dom Philippo*: Herr Herz. *Umberto*: Herr Wilke. *Dom Lu*: Herr Menges.

Seecadeten: *Diego*: Fraulein Ahl. *Antonio*: Fraulein Schlag. *José*: Fraulein Spitzner. *Frederigo*: Fraulein Camara. *Agosto*: Fraulein Grothusen. *Bernardino*: Fraulein Bischoff. *Henriques*: Fraulein Barre. *Sebastiano*: Fraulein Weiss. *Gomez*: Fraulein Grünewald. *Carlos*: Fraulein Dombi. *Gonzales*: Frau Arnold. *Bonifacio*: Frau Telle.

Mungo: Herr Schmitz. *Pages*: Frauleins Petri, Libussa. *Heralds*: Herren Markovitz, Seidl.

1879.63

FRITZ IN IRELAND, or, The Bell-ringer of the Rhine and the Love of the Shamrock

A Romantic Comedy (Irish Melodrama) in a Prologue and Three Acts. Play by William Carleton. Music (and lyrics) by Joseph K. Emmet. Scenery by George Heister, H. E. Hoyt. Original scenic and mechanical effects by Hamilton Weaver. Produced by Joseph K. Emmet. Opened 3 November 1879 at the Park Theatre and closed 27 December 1879 after 56 performances; played a return engagement 8 March 1880 at the Grand Opera House, closing 3 April 1880 after an additional 30 performances. Total this season: 86 performances.

CAST: *Fritz Schultz*: JOSEPH K. EMMET. *Lawyer Priggins*: JOHN MACKAY. *Baron Hertford*, alias Splodger, Lawyer Priggins' Jackall: J. H. RENNIE. *Captain Hercules O'Doud*: WILLIAM CARLETON. *Splodger*, Lawyer Priggins' Jackal: J. H. RENNIE. *Lord Seaton*: W. CHRISTIE MILLER. *Charles Seaton*: Oliver Doud. *Thomas Goldfinger*, Man Servant: J. H. Ryan. *Patrick Blackeye*, an Irish Negro: J. O. Burk. *Master Herbert*, nephew of Baron Hertfort: Little Annie Rennie. *Louisa Hertfort*: Emily Baker. *Lady Amelia*: LENORE BIGELOW. *Madame Schultz*, afterwards

---

[29]H.M.S. PINAFORE originally presented in New York 15 January 1879 at the Standard Theatre for 175 performances. For Synopsis of Scenes and Musical Numbers, see original 1879 production. TRIAL BY JURY was first produced in New York 15 November 1875 at the Eagle Theatre for 8 performances. For Synopsis of Scenes and Musical Numbers, see original 1875 production.

[30]No credits in programs for stage director; stage manager, W. A. Paul. No credits for scenery or costumes.

[31]Originally presented in New York 15 January 1879 at the Standard Theatre for 175 performances. For Synopsis of Scenes and Musical Numbers, see original 1879 production. This production's novelty was its cast of juveniles.

[32]First presented in New York in English 29 August 1870 at Kelly and Leon's, and in French 26 September 1870 at the Grand Opera House. For Synopsis of Scenes and Musical Numbers, see original September 1870 production.

[36]First presented in New York 24 September 1867 at the Theatre Français for 156 performances in repertory. For Synopsis of Scenes and Musical Numbers, see original 1867 production.

Madame Marrall: Mrs. Louisa Watson. *Judy Callahan*, maid servant: Tillie McHenry. *Lena Schultz*: Little Annie Rennie.

Prologue: Castle Clock, on the Rhine, Germany. (Heister.)

Act 1: Old Ruins adjoining Baron Hertfort's Estate. (Hoyt.)

Act 2: Oak Chamber, Baron Hertfort's Mansion. (Heister.)

Act 3: Baron Hertfort's Garden and Mansion. (Hoyt.)

MUSICAL NUMBERS[34]

"The Bells Are Ringing" (with Chuch Bells)
"The Swell"
"(Emmet's) Cuckoo Song"
"(The) Love of the Shamrock"
"Wilheinderick Strauss"
"The Brother's Lullaby" (Emmet's Lullaby)
"I Know What Love Is"

1879.64 THE TOURISTS IN A PULLMAN PALACE CAR

A Nonsensical and Musical Play in Three Acts. Play by William A. Mestayer. Stage director, William A. Mestayer. Director of orchestra, Fred Perkins. Produced by J. H. Haverly, in association with John P. Smith. Opened 3 November 1879 at Haverly's Lyceum Theatre and closed 15 November 1879 after 16 performances; returned 5 January 1880 to Haverly's Lyceum Theatre and closed 7 February 1880 after 48 additional performances. Total: 64 performances[35].

CAST: *Miss Baby*, the Pet. A Gushing Damsel, not too gushing, but just gush enough: ROSA COOKE. *Miss Isabella*, her sister, a Quiet Damsel, not too quiet, but just quiet enough: ETHEL LYNTON. *Miss Pamela*, their Aunt, not too old a maid, but just old enough: JENETTE [Jennie] REIFFARTH. *Marie*, their maid, a Fresh Damsel, not too fresh, but just fresh enough: MAY LIVINGSTON. *T. Henry Slum*, a disciple of Banting, but just anti-Fat enough: W. A. MESTAYER. *Sir Henry Cashmere*, a Nob, not too much nob, but just, etc.: JAMES BARTON. *Luigi Contadini*, the Detective. Not too much Detective, but just, etc.: AUGUSTUS J. BRUNO. *Jacob Kraus*, a Special. Not too special, etc.: Will H. Bray. *Louis Touchet*, a Butler. Not too much, etc.: J. N. Long. *Male and female passengers*. Not too much Male and Female, but just a little Neuter.

ACT 2 and 3: *Richard Morgye*: WILLIAM A. MESTAYER. *Faro Jack*: WILLIAM A. MESTAYER. *The Western Guerilla*: WILLIAM A. MESTAYER. *T. Henry Slum*: WILLIAM A. MESTAYER. *Admiral McGuinness*: AUGUSTUS J. BRUNO. *The Conductor*: AUGUSTUS J. BRUNO. *The Book-Agent*: AUGUSTUS J. BRUNO. *John Chinaman*: AUGUSTUS J. BRUNO. *The Bear*: AUGUSTUS J. BRUNO. *The French Valet*: J. N. Long. *Drawing-Room Car Porter*: Will H. Bray. *Sir Henry Cashmere*: JAMES BARTON. *The Gushing Maiden*: ROSA COOKE. *German Peasant Girl*: JENETTE REIFFARTH. *Mrs. Honorable Flimsy*: ETHEL LYNTON. *Telegraph Boy*: MAY LIVINGSTON.

Act 1: Newport.

Act 2: The Interior of a Pullman Palace Car.

Act 3: Pullman Palace Sleeping Car.

ACT 1

Serenade from COX AND BOX
(*Music by* Arthur Sullivan. *Lyrics by* F. C. Burnand.)

ACT 2

Railroad Galop
"Nursery Rhymes"
"Poor Cock Robin"
"The North Wind Doth Blow"
Luncheon Chorus from THE CHIMES OF NORMANDY
(*Music by* Robert Planquette.)
"Let All Obey" (Valet's Song)
"The Drinking Song"
Scene from H.M.S. PINAFORE
(*Music by* Arthur Sullivan. *Lyrics by* William S. Gilbert.)
"The Bell Trio"
"Tom Big Bay" (Porter's Song)
"The Chinaman"
"My Old Kentucky Home"
(*Music and Lyrics by* Stephen Foster.)
"The Telegraph Boy"
(*Music by* David Braham. *Lyrics by* William A. Mestayer.)
"Der Wasserfall" (German emigrant)
Selection from IL TROVATORE
(*Music by* Giuseppe Verdi.)
"The Skids Are Out Today" (from THE MULLIGAN GUARDS' CHOWDER)
(*Music by* Dave Braham. *Lyrics by* Edward Harrigan.)

ACT 3

"Jubilee Melodies"
"In the Morning by the Bright Light"
(*Music and Lyrics by* James Bland.)
"How Vas Dot Poodle"
General Finale:
"Forward to Do or Die" (from FATINITZA)
(*Music by* Franz von Suppé.)
The End of the Route

1879.65 FATINITZA

A Revival of the Operette in Three Acts[36]. Libretto by F. Zell and Richard Genée. Based on the libretto to "La Circassienne" by Eugène Scribe. English adaptation by Henry S. Leigh. Music by Franz von Suppé. Musical director, J. Q. Hoyt, Jr. Produced by Ferdinand W. Hofele. Opened 10 November 1879 at the Olympic Theatre and closed 15 November 1879 after 8 performances.[37]

CAST: *Valdimir, Fatinitza*, a young Russian lieutenant: RECA MURRELLI. *Princess Lydia*, Niece of the Count: FREDERIKA ROKOHL. *Count Timofey Kantschakoff*, Russian General: A. FRANOSCH. *Izzet Pasha*, Governor of the Turkish Fort Isaksha: ARTHUR VAN HOUTEN. *Wasili*, Captain of Russian Infantry: L. N. Guyon. *Osipp*, Lieutenant: Clinton Stevens. *Steipann*, Sergeant: Louis Lencioni. *Julian*, a Special Newspaper Correspondent: George S. Weeks. *Hassan Bey*, Leader of the Bashi Bazouks: GEORGE CALDWELL. *Russian Cadets (4)*: *Ivan*: May Sylvie. *Nikophor*: Minnie Hartman. *Feodor*: Sara Browning. *Demitri*: Lizette Wilson. *Izzet Pasha's Wives (4)*: *Nourmahal*: Pauline Hartman. *Zuleika*: Ida Casteldo. *Diona*: Clara Imfrey. *Beseika*: Edna Browning. *Massaldsha*, a Fortune Teller: Ezra Lyon. *Mustapha*, Guard of the Harem: Izidore Kline. *Winka*, a Bulgarian spy: W. D. Willis. *Hanna*, his wife: Miss Jackson. *Adjutant*: H. Williams.

Characters in The Karagois: *Jessuf*: A. Osborn. *Surema*, his Daughter: May Livingston. *Benjamin*, his Slave: F. Goodwin. *Niridah, Fatima*, two old gossips: Clara Williams, Amie Maitland. *Achmet*, Keeper of Menagerie: John Humphrey.

Russian Soldiers, Bashi Bazouks, Cossacks, Moorish Women, Nubian Slaves, Russian Serfs, Sleigh Drivers, etc.

1879.66 H.M.S. PINAFORE, or, The Lass That Loved a Sailor

A Return Engagement of Gorman's Philadelphia Church Choir Company in a Revival of the Comic Opera in Two Acts[38]. Libretto by William

---

[34]Musical numbers "and others" performed by J. K. Emmet, not in performance order. In the second month of the run, the following were addded:

"Oh, Don't You Tickle Me"

"She Fainted Away in My Arms"

Dot Toy Harmonic, upon which he will play five variations on "Home, Sweet Home"

For the return engagement, these were dropped. Added was: "The Mountain Guide" Cast changes for the return: *Lawyer Priggins*: W. W. ALLEN. *Captain Hercules O'Dowd*: M. B. SNYDER. *Charles Seaton*: Clarke Earle. *Louisa Hertford*: Kate Blancke. *Lady Amelia*: FANNIE FRANCES. *Madame Schultz*: Rose Graham. *Lena Schultz*: Little Georgie Snyder.

[35]No credits in programs for scenery or costumes. Played a return engagement 23 August 1880 at the Fifth Avenue Theatre for 32 performances. See entry in 1880-1881 season.

[36]Originally presented in New York in English 22 April 1879 at the Fifth Avenue Theatre for 41 performances. For Synopsis of Scenes and Musical Numbers, see original April 1879 production.

[37]No credits in program for scenery or costumes.

[38]First presented in New York 15 January 1879 at the Standard Theatre for 175 performances. For Synopsis of Scenes and Musical Numbers, see original 1879 production. Gorman's Philadelphia Church Choir Company previously presented H.M.S. PINAFORE 10 March 1879 at the Broadway Theatre in two engagements for 72 performances. Sousa in his autobiography "Marching Along" indicated that Dick Deadeye interpolated a song by Malloy, to the displeasure of Sullivan.

S. Gilbert. Music by Arthur Sullivan. Under the musical direction of John Phillip Sousa. Presented by John Gorman's Philadelphia Church Choir Company (Management, James H. Meade). Opened 10 November 1879 at the Broadway Opera House and closed 29 November 1879 after 24 performances.

CAST: *The Rt. Hon. Sir Joseph Porter, K.C.B.*, First Lord of the Admiralty: LOUIS DeLANGE. *Captain Corcoran*, Commanding the *H.M.S. Pinafore*: A. N. PALMER. *Ralph Rackstraw*, Able Seaman: M. F. DONOVAN. *Dick Deadeye*, Able Seaman: G. T. R. Knorr. *Bill Bobstay*, Boatswain: Joseph J. Knox. *Bob Beckett*, Boatswain's Mate: S. Snyder. *Tom Tucker*, midshipman: Master Howard Kohler. *Tom Bowline*: Mr. Woods. *Josephine*, the Captain's Daughter: EMMA HENRY. *Little Buttercup*, a Bumboat Woman: Miss A. V. RUTHERFORD. *Hebe*, Sir Joseph's First Cousin: Elida Cannon. *Sir Joseph's First Aunt*: Mrs. S. Beatty. *First Lord's Sisters, his Cousins, his Aunts, Sailors, Marines, etc.*: Chorus of 40.

1879.67 FATINITZA!

A Revival of the Comic Opera in Three Acts. (Original Viennese libretto to the operette by F. Zell and Richard Genée. Adapted from a libretto to "La Circassienne" by Eugène Scribe. Music by Franz von Suppé.) Chorus and orchestra under the direction of Ernest Neyer. Produced by William Henderson. Opened 17 November 1879 at the Standard Theatre and closed 10 December 1879 after 32 performances.[39]

CAST: *Valdimir, Fatinitza*, a young Russian lieutenant: VERNONA JARBEAU. *Princess Lydia*, Niece of the Count: FREDERIKA ROKOHL. *Count Timofey Kantschakoff*, Russian General: A. FRANOSCH. *Izzet Pasha*, Governor of the Turkish Fort Isaksha: ARTHUR VAN HOUTEN. *Wasili*, Captain of Russian Infantry: L. N. Guyon. *Osipp*, Lieutenant: Clinton Stevens. *Steipann*, Sergeant: Louis Lencioni. *Julian*, a Special Newspaper Correspondent: George S. Weeks. *Hassan Bey*, Leader of the Bashi Bazouks: GEORGE CALDWELL. *Russian Cadets (4)*: *Ivan*: Laura James. *Nikophor*: Minnie Hartman. *Feodor*: Sara Browning. *Demitri*: Lizette Wilson. *Izzet Pasha's Wives (4)*: *Nourmahal*: Pauline Hartman. *Zuleika*: Ida Casteldo. *Diona*: Clara Imfrey. *Beseika*: May Sylvie. *Massaldsha*, a Fortune Teller: Ezra Lyon. *Mustapha*, Guard of the Harem: Izidore Kline. *Winka*, a Bulgarian spy: George Moss. *Hanna*, his wife: Miss Jackson. *Adjutant*: H. Williams.

Characters in The Karagois: *Jessuf*: A. Osborn. *Surema*, his Daughter: Edna Browning. *Benjamin*, his Slave: F. Goodwin. *Niridah, Fatima*, two old gossips: Clara Williams, Amie Maitland. *Achmet*, Keeper of Menagerie: John Humphrey.

Russian Soldiers, Bashi Bazouks, Cossacks, Moorish Women, Nubian Slaves, Russian Serfs, Sleigh Drivers, etc.

Act 1: Russian Encampment on the Danube.

Act 2: The Harem of Izzet Pasha.

Act 3: Reception Room in the General's Mansion at Odessa.

1879.68 THE MULLIGAN GUARD'S CHRISTMAS

A Local Comedy in One Act, 6 Scenes[40], preceded by an Olio. Play (and lyrics) by Edward Harrigan. Music by David Braham. Produced under the supervision of Welsh Edwards. Scenic artist, Charles W. Witham. Costumer, Annie Howard. Machinist, Robert Cutler. Properties, Robert Pullar. Gas effects, Richard Doyle. Musical direction, David Braham. Produced by Edward Harrigan and Tony Hart. Opened 17 November 1879 at the Theatre Comique and closed 14 February 1880 after 104 performances.

Olio: John Wild and Billy Gray as The Rival Artists. Jennie Morgan (the American Linnet[41]). Goss and Fox in their act, You'll Miss Me When I'm Gone. Edwin Barry with new and popular melodies.

CAST: *Dan Mulligan*: EDWARD HARRIGAN. *Mrs. Welcome Allup*: TONY HART. *Captain Simpson Primrose*: JOHN WILD. *Rev. Palestine Puter*: WILLIAM GRAY. *Planxty McFudd*: WELSH EDWARDS. *Macauley Jangles*: Edward Burt. *Gustavus Lochmuller*: HARRY A. FISHER. *Young Dublin*: JOHN QUEEN. *Orlando Tucker*: William West. *Reverend Ferguson Clinton*: Charles Schafer. *Walsingham McSweeny*: MICHAEL BRADLEY. *Paddy Campbell*: John Mealey. *Gustavus Lochmuller, Jr.*: Master Husel. *Sheriff*: Charles Walton. *Engineer*: John W. Dickens. *Mr. Binnacle*: Edward Barry. *Bridget Lochmuller*: ANNIE MACK. *Cordelia Mulligan*: MRS. ANNIE YEAMANS. *Diana McFudd*: MARIE GORENFLO. *Rosy McFudd*: Mary Bird. *Ellen McFudd*: Belle Mordaunt. *Guests, Musicians, Policemen, Hackmen, Waiters*: Auxiliary Corps.

Scene 1: Centre Market and Harry Jennings' Dog Emporium. *Scene 2*: Kitchen in Dan Mulligan's Tenement Brick. Christmas Eve. *Scene 3*: Interior of the Grand Central Depot. *Scene 4*: Spuyten Duyvel Creek, with view of the Hudson River and the Snow-Mantled Cliffs of Manhattan Island. Christmas Day. *Scene 5*: Hallway in Dan Mulligan's Tenement Brick. Christmas Night. *Scene 6*: The Dining Apartment in Dan Mulligan's Tenement Brick. Christmas Night.

MUSICAL NUMBERS[42]

"The Sweet Kentucky Rose" (Scene 2)
T. Hart

"The Pitcher of Beer" (Scene 2)
E. Harrigan

"The Mulligan Braves" (Song and Dance)(Scene 2)
Mulligan Guard

"The Skids Are on Review" (March and Chorus)(Scene 3)
Skidmore Guard

"Tu-ri-ad-i-lum, or Santa Claus Has Come" (Song)(Scene 6)
E. Harrigan

1879.69 LA BELLE HÉLÈNE

A Revival of the Opéra-bouffe in Three Acts[43], in French. Libretto by Henri Meilhac and Ludovic Halévy. Music by Jacques Offenbach. Stage manager, Mons. Bouvard. Musical director, Charles Almeras. Produced by Maurice Grau's French Opera Company. Opened 26 November 1879 at Booth's Theatre and closed 12 December 1879 after 6 performances in repertory; returned 11 March 1880 at the Fifth Avenue Theatre for 1 performance.

CAST: *Hélène*: Mlle. PAOLA MARIÉ. *Orestes*: Mlle. ANGÈLE. *Parthenis*: Mlle. Raphael. *Levena*: Mlle. Bouvard. *Bacchis*: Mlle. Armand. *Ménélas*: Mons. DUPLAN. *Agamemnon*: Mons. JOUARD. *Calchas*: Mons. J. Mezières. *Achille*: Mons. Poyard. *Ajax I*: Mons. Vilano. *Ajax II*: Mons. Gerard. *Philocome*: Mons. Dupuis. *Euthycles*: Mons. Terrancle. *Paris*: Mons. VICTOR CAPOUL.

1879.70 H.M.S. PINAFORE, or, The Lass That Loved a Sailor

A Revival of the Comic Opera in Two Acts[44]. Libretto by William S. Gilbert. Music by Arthur Sullivan. Directed by William S. Gilbert. Musical director, Alfred Cellier. Presented by D'Oyly Carte Opera Company. Opened 1 December 1879 at the Fifth Avenue Theatre and closed 27 December 1879 after 28 performances.

CAST: *The Rt. Hon. Sir Joseph Porter, K.C.B.*, First Lord of the Admiralty: J. H. RYLEY. *Captain Corcoran*, Commanding the *H.M.S. Pinafore*: SIGNOR BROCOLINI [John Clark]. *Ralph Rackstraw*, Able Seaman: HUGH TALBOT. *Dick Deadeye*, Able Seaman: FURNEAUX COOK. *Bill Bobstay*, Bo'sun's Mate: Fred Clifton. *Bob Beckett*, Carpenter's Mate: Mr. Cuthbert. *Josephine*, the Captain's Daughter: BLANCHE ROOSEVELT [Miss Conreid]. *Little Buttercup*, a Portsmouth Bumboat Woman: ALICE BARNETT. *Hebe*, Sir Joseph's First Cousin: Jessie Bond. *First Lord's Sisters, his Cousins, his Aunts, Sailors, Marines, etc.*

1879.71 PRINCESS TOTO

An English Comic Opera in Three Acts. Libretto by William S. Gilbert. Music by Frederic Clay. Stage manager, W. A. Paul. Musical director, Ernest Neyer. Produced by William Henderson. Opened 13 December 1879 at the Standard Theatre and closed 3 January 1880 after 25 performances.

CAST: *Princess Toto*, King Portico's daughter: LEONORA BRAHAM. *Jelly*, her attendant: VERNONA JARBEAU. *Follette, Divine*, Ladies of the Court: Misses Lawrence,

---

[39]No credits in programs for stage direction, English adaptation of the libretto, scenery or costumes. With the exception of Mlle. Murrelli and a few other minor players, this is largely the same cast that appeared the previous week at the Olympic, for which the English libretto was credited to Henry S. Leigh.

[40]Billed as "Volume the Fourth" in Mulligan Guard series.

[41]Introduced a new Harrigan-Braham song during the run, "The Little Green Leaf in Our Bible."

[42]Program in the final week included the following additional musical numbers in the overture:"Beauty of Limerick," "Paddy Campbell's Sleigh Ride" and Finale—Xylophone Solo.

[43]Originally presented in New York in French 26 March 1868 at the French Theatre for 37 performances. For Synopsis of Scenes and Musical Numbers, see original 1868 production.

[44]Originally presented in New York 15 January 1879 at the Standard Theatre for 175 performances. For Synopsis of Scenes and Musical Numbers, see original 1879 production.

Shandley. *King Portico*: H. W. MONTGOMERY. *Zapeter*, his Prime Minister: WILLIAM HAMILTON. *Jamilek*, his Foreign Secretary: William A. Paul. *Prince Doro*, betrothed to Toto: H. C. CAMPBELL. *Prince Caramel*, betrothed to Toto: OLIVER W. WREN. *Count Floss, Baron Jacquier*, Courtiers: Alfred Holland, H. R. Humphries. *Prisoner*: J. A. Oliver.

Time: Never.

Act 1: Pavilion in King Portico's Palace.

Act 2: The Brigand's Haunt.

Act 3: A Tropical Island.

ACT 1[45]

Chorus of Courtiers (This is a court in which you'll find)
Chorus
Song (Oh! bride of mine)
H. C. Campbell
Bridesmaids' Chorus (Of our opinions to impart)
Female Chorus
Song (Like an arrow from its quiver)
L. Braham
Quintet (Come let us haste)
L. Braham, V. Jarbeau, H. C. Campbell, W. Hamilton, H. W. Montgomery
Trio (With Princely state)
H. R. Humphries, A. Holland, O. W. Wren
Quartet (My hand upon it, 'tis agreed)
O. W. Wren, H. R. Humphris, A. Holland, W. Hamilton
Vocal Waltz (Banish sorrow, till tomorrow)
L. Braham
Duet (Oh! tell me now, by plighted vow)
L. Braham, H. C. Campbell
Finale (A hat and bright little feather)
L. Braham, Chorus

ACT 2

Chorus of Brigands (Cheer up old man)
Chorus
Song (The world of dreams)
L. Braham
Couplets (At last I shall marry my own)
L. Braham, V. Jarbeau, A. Holland, O. W. Wren, Chorus
Song (There are Brigands in every station)
H. C. Campbell
Trio (So take my hand it is agreed)
L. Braham, H. C. Campbell, O. W. Wren
Duet (My own, own love)
L. Braham, H. C. Campbell
Trio and Dance of Red Indians (With skip and hop)
H. W. Montgomery, W. Hamilton, W. A. Paul
Finale (Away, away) L. Braham, V. Jarbeau,
W. A. Paul, W. Hamilton, H. W. Montgomery, Chorus

ACT 3

Chorus and Dance of Red Indians (Bang the merry tom, tom)
Chorus
Song and Chorus (The Pig with the Roman nose)
L. Braham
Barcarolle (When you're afloat)
V. Jarbeau, Quintet
Song (I am a foolish little maid)
L. Braham
Finale (So pardon pray)
L. Braham

THE PIRATES OF PENZANCE, or, The Slave of Duty

1879.72

A Comic Opera in Two Acts· Libretto by William S. Gilbert. Music by Arthur Sullivan. Produced under the personal direction of William S. Gilbert and Arthur Sullivan. Scenery by John A. Thompson. Costume designs by Faustin. Musical director, Alfred Cellier. Produced by D'Oyly Carte Opera Company. Opened 31 December 1879 at the Fifth Avenue Theatre and closed 6 March 1880 after 70 performances; re-opened 17 May 1880 at the Fifth Avenue Theatre and closed 5 June 1880 after 21 performances. Total: 91 performances.[46]

CAST: *Richard*, a Pirate Chief: SIGNOR BROCOLINI [John Clark]. *Samuel*, his Lieutenant: Furneaux Cook. *Frederic*, the Pirate Apprentice: HUGH TALBOT[47]. *Major General Stanley*: J. H. RYLEY. *Edward*, a Sergeant of Police: FRED CLIFTON. *Mabel, Kate, Edith, Isabel*, General Stanley's Daughters: BLANCHE ROOSEVELT[48], ROSINA BRANDRAM, JESSIE BOND, Miss Barlow. *Ruth*, a Pirate Maid-of-all-work: ALICE BARNETT. *General Stanley's Daughters, Pirates, Policemen, etc.*

Act 1: A Rocky Sea-shore on the Coast of Cornwall, England.

Act 2: A Ruined Chapel on General Stanley's Estate (by Moonlight).

ACT 1[49]

"Pour, Oh Pour the Pirate Sherry" (Opening Chorus and Solo)
F. Cook, Pirates
"When Fred'ric Was a Little Lad" (Song)
A. Barnett
"Oh, Better Far to Live and Die" (Song)
Sig. Brocolini, Pirates
"Oh, False One, You Have Deceived Me!" (Recitative)
A. Barnett, H. Talbot
"Climbing Over Rocky Mountain" (Chorus of Girls)
Daughters
"Stop, Ladies, Pray!" (Recitative)
J. Bond, R. Brandram, H. Talbot, Daughters
"Oh, Is There Not One Maiden Breast" (Aria)
H. Talbot, Daughters
"Poor Wand'ring One" (Air)
B. Roosevelt, Daughters
"What Ought We to Do? Gentle sisters, say!"
J. Bond, R. Brandram, Daughters
"How Beautifully Blue the Sky" (Duet)
B. Roosevelt, H. Talbot, Daughters
"Stay, We Must Not Lose Our Senses" (Recitative)
F. Talbot, Daughters, Pirates
"Hold, Monsters!" (Recitative)
B. Roosevelt, J. H. Ryley, F. Cook, Daughters, Pirates
"I Am the Very Modern Model of a Modern Major-General" (Song)
J. H. Ryley, Ensemble
"Oh! Men of Dark and Dismal Fate" (Finale)
Principals, Ensemble

ACT 2

"Oh! Dry the Glist'ning Tear" (Opening Chorus)
B. Roosevelt, Daughters
"Then, Frederic, let your escort lion-hearted" (Recitative)
H. Talbot, J. H. Ryley
"When the Foreman Bares His Steel" (Chorus, with Solos)
F. Clifton, B. Roosevelt, J. Bond, Police, Daughters
"Now for the Pirates' Lair!" (Recitative)
H. Talbot
"When First You Left Our Pirate Fold" (Trio)
A. Barnett, H. Talbot, Sig. Brocolini
"Away, Away! My Heart's on Fire" (Trio)
A. Barnett, Sig. Brocolini, H. Talbot
"All Is Prepared" (Recitative and Duet)
B. Roosevelt, H. Talbot
"Stay Fred'ric, Stay!" (Duet)
B. Roosevelt, H. Talbot
"Yes, I Am Brave" (Recitative)
H. Talbot

[45]Musical numbers not listed in programs. List prepared from published English piano vocal score (Metzler & Co., London, 1876).

[46]The total of 154 performances, widely quoted and disseminated elsewhere, includes Brooklyn and other touring performance dates of this original company outside New York under D'Oyly Carte's auspices.

[47]For the return engagement Frederic was played by WALLACE MACREERY.

[48]For the return engagement Mabel was played by SALLIE REBER.

[49]Musical numbers not listed in programs. List prepared from published English piano vocal score (Chappell & Co., London, 1880).

"Though in body and in mind"
F. Clifton
"When a Felon's Not Engaged in His Employment" (Song)
F. Clifton, Police
"A Rollicking Band of Pirates We" (Solo)
Pirates, F. Clifton, Police
"With Cat-Like Tread, Upon Our Prey We Steal" (Solo)
Pirates, Police, F. Cook
"Hush, Hush! Not a Word!" (Recitative)
H. Talbot, Pirates, Police, J. H. Ryley
"Sighing Softly to the River"
J. H. Ryley, Sig. Brocolini, Police, Pirates, Ensemble
Finale
B. Roosevelt, Ensemble

1880.01 FIRST LIFE GUARDS AT BRIGHTON

A Comic Military Opera (F.L.G.) in Three Acts. Libretto and music by John Stewart Crossy [J. C. Stewart]. Stage manager, Jerry Taylor. Acting manager, Frank C. Stewart. Scenery by George Heilge. Costumes by A. R. Vanhorn. Machinery by Frank H. Smith. Properties by Frank Garrett. Musical director, Antoine Reiff, Jr. Produced by J. S. Crossy's American Comic Opera Company (J. S. Crossy, Manager). Opened 5 January 1880 at the Broadway Opera House and closed 17 January 1880 after 16 performances.[50]

CAST: *Catain Sir Charles Courtland*: EUGENE CLARK. *Colonel Edward Preston*: HARRY ALLEN. *Lieutenant Walter Dashwood*: EDWARD CONNELL. *Doctor Lovejoy*: CHARLES F. LANG. *Jeremiah Quill*: W. HOWARD SEYMOUR. *Major Armstrong*: CHARLES FOSTER. *Sir T. Tichborne*: JERRY TAYLOR. *Sergeant F.L.G.*: W. H. MOYER. *Messenger*: Mr. T. Wilson. *Miss Lillie Gooding*: FLORENCE ELLIS. *Miss Emily Gooding*: LAURA JOYCE. *Miss Armstrong*: ELMA DELARO. *Mrs. Julia Armstrong*: Mrs. M. A. Sainger. *Betsy Jane*: Hattie Arnold. *Citizens, Life Guards, Boat Club, etc*: Full Chorus of 40.

Act 1: St. George's Pier, London.

Act 2: Beach at Brighton.

Act 3: Law of the Royal Hotel, Brighton.

1880.02 EVANGELINE AND THE LONE FISHERMAN

A Revival of the American Opera Bouffe Extravaganza in Three Acts[51]. (Book and lyrics by J. Cheever Goodwin.) Music by Edward E. Rice. Scenery by Ed. Simmons. Musical director, George Purdy. Produced by Edward E. Rice. Opened 5 January 1880 at the Standard Theatre and closed 17 January 1880 after 14 performances; re-opened 24 May 1880 at Niblo's Garden and closed 5 June 1880 after an additional 16 performances. Total: 30 performances.[52]

CAST: *Evangeline*, our heroine, a creature of impulse and an impetuous pet, pursued through love's impatient prompting by Gabriel, and with a view to audacious contingencies by a whale: VERNONA JARBEAU. *Gabriel*, our hero, a fascinating and perambulating youth lover, in point of fact a roaming Romeo: LOUISE SEARLE. *Catherine*, the very mildest type of anti-nuptial Mother in Law: GEORGE K. FORTESCUE. *Eulalie*, Evangeline's confidante, confidently hoping for Women's Rights: ROSE DANA. *Mary Ann*, Evangeline's waiting maid: Lavinia Bennett. *Basil*, Evangeline's sire, whose vacillating mind is divided between the rental of her prospective husband and his on parental affection: EDWIN S. TARR. *LeBlanc*, a lawyer of the shyest shyster stamp, with a will and a way equally dark: RICHARD GOLDEN. *The Lone Fisherman*, a patient and similarly taciturn toiler of the sea, with a natural tendency to hook whatever comes within his reach: HARRY HUNTER. *Captain Dietrich*, a Dutch necessary in the British ranks, who shows no mercy, being a mercy-nary cuss: CHARLES ROSINE. *Hans Wagner*, a spiritual corporal, with undue corporeal proportions: H. M. Morse. *King Boorioloboola Gha*, Royal Proprietor of the Mid-African Diamond Fields, who, not being able to hear anything near occupies an ear trumpet: E. T. Sinclair. *Queen Boorioloboola Gha*, the King's much better advisor of his whole conduct: M. A. Palladis. *The Policeman*, called by some a peeler, possibly because he was never known to heed any appeal a prisoner might make, locus a non, and all that sort of thing: Frederick Turner. *The Headsman*, not a mimic of stupid people, but very clever at taking off blockheads: John Kropp. *The Jailer*, never without his key, vocal or instrumental, consequently always on the qui vive: J. A. Hennessey. *Lo*, the Indian, the lowest and the lowest savage of them all: George Ulmer. *The Deserters*: Messrs. George Cohen, F. Turner. *Conductor*: Rose Warren.

Act 1: Arcadia.

Act 2: Africa.

Act 3: Arizona and Arcadia.

1880.03 MADAME ANGOT'S DAUGHTER

A Revival of the Opéra-comique in Three Acts[53]. Original French libretto to "La Fille de Madame Angot" by Clairville, Paul Siraudin and Victor Koning. Music by Charles Lecocq. Stage manager, Jerry Taylor. Acting manager, Frank C. Stewart. Costumes by A. R. Vanhorn. Properties by Frank Garrett. Musical director, Antoine Reiff, Jr. Produced by J. S. Crossy's American Comic Opera Company (John Stewart Crossy [J. C. Stewart], Manager). Opened 19 January 1880 at the Broadway Opera House and closed 31 January 1880 after 16 performances.[54]

CAST: *Ange Pitou*, a poet: EUGENE CLARK, CHARLES F. LANG. *Larvandière*, lover of Mlle. Lange: EDWARD CONNELL. *Pomponnet*, barber and hair dresser: HARRY ALLEN. *Louchard*, police spy: W. Howard Seymour. *Trenitz*, leader of conspirators: W. Howard Seymour. *Clairette Angot*, daughter of the market: FLORENCE ELLIS, HATTIE ARNOLD. *Mlle. Lange*, an actress: LAURA JOYCE, ELMA DELARO. *Amaranthe*: Mrs. M. A. Sainger. *Hersilie*, attendant to Mlle. Lange: Katie Griffiths. *Mlle. Delaunay, Oydalise*, Merveilleuses: Mrs. K. Buck, Jessie Robinson. *Market Women (5)*: *Babet*: J. Jenkle. *Javotte*: Ada Hamilton. *Manon*: Marie Coleman. *Therese*: Marie Billings. *Herbelin*: Clara Wisham. *Soldiers, Conspirators, Citizens, Market People, etc.*: Chorus of 40.

1880.04 THE ROYAL MIDDY

A Musical Comedy in Three Acts. Libretto by Fred Williams, adapted from the Viennese operette "Der Seekadet,"[55] libretto by F. Zell (from 'Le Capitaine Charlotte' by Jean-François Bayard and Philippe Dumanoir.) Music by Richard Genée. Music adapted and augmented by Edward Mollenhauer. Produced under the stage direction of Augustin Daly. Scenery by James Roberts, Louis Duflocq. Costumes by J. H. Eaves. Mechanical effects by James Tait. Accesories by Robert Cutler and R. W. Williams. Marches and Evolutions by Mlle. Malvina. Musical director, Edward Mollenhauer. Produced by Augustin Daly. Opened 28 January 1880 at Daly's Theatre and closed 1 May 1880 after 84 performances in repertory.

CAST: *Don Lamberto*, Governor of the Royal Naval Academy, Rear Admiral of the Portuguese Navy, formerly a poor lieutenant in the German army, secretly married to the Queen: ALONZO HATCH. *Don Januario Paraguassa Calobrio*, Marquis of Itapicuro and Papagayo Pernambuco, the wealthiest of five Brazilian brothers, all Millionaires: HART CONWAY. *Don Domingos Domingos de Barros*, Master of Court Ceremonies, very short sighted and very jealous: CHARLES LECLERCQ. *Captain Norberto*, Master of Fencing at the Royal Naval Academy—"the very butcher of a silk button": CHARLES FISHER. *Francesco, Joaquino*, Officers of the Queen's Guard: Walter Edmunds, E. M. Smith. *Mungo*, Confidential valet and receiver of cast-off diamonds to Don Januario, dusky but docile: FRANK BENNETT. *Rodriguez*, an attendant on the Governor, a Portuguese exquisite: Mr. Sterling. *Royal Middies and Pupils of the Naval Academy at Lisbon (7)*: *Diego*: Estelle Clayton. *Sebastino*: Georgine Flagg. *Julio*: May Bowers. *Giovannio*: Blanche Weaver. *Paulo*: Isabelle Evesson. *Enrico*: Nellie Howard. *Carlo*: Sara Lascelles. *Jago*: Lillie Vinton. *Maria Francesca*, Queen of Portugal, secretly married to Don Lamberto; devoted, but doubtful; generous, but jealous: MAY FIELDING. *Fanchette*, a wandering Zingara, who "reads in the stars and tells fortunes by cards," later transformed into the Royal Middy: CATHERINE LEWIS. *Donna Antonina*, Wife of Don Domingos, confidant of the Queen's secret, and perpetual torment of her short-sighted husband: ADA REHAN.

---

[50]Musical numbers not listed in program, except the interpolation:
"Lo! Hear the gentle Lark"
F. Ellis
(*Music and Lyrics by* Henry Bishop.)

[51]First produced in New York as EVANGELINE, or The Belle of Arcadia 27 July 1874 at Niblo's Garden for 14 performances. For Synopsis of Scenes and Musical Numbers, see original 1874 production.

[52]No credits in program for stage director, presumably Edward E. Rice. E. S. Tarr billed as stage manager. No credits for costumes. Musical numbers not listed in programs. During Act 1, the amusing conceit, The Heifer Dance will be presented by George Cohen and F. Turner.

[53]First produced in New York in English 16 November 1874 at the Lyceum Theatre for 16 performances.

[54]English adaptation, scenery uncredited.

[55]DER SEE ADET was previously presented in German in New York 27 October 1879 at the Thalia theatre in repertory.

Act 1: An Interior of the Governor's Palace at Lisbon, with view of the Harbor in the distance.

Act 2: The Esplanade in front of the Royal Naval Academy, with Marine View in the distance.

Act 3: Staircase and Apartment in the Royal Palace.

ACT 1

"To our Governor we sing" (Opening Chorus)
Chorus

"To thee my Queen" (Concerted Piece)
A. Hatch

"Again enfolded within thine arms" (Duet)
A. Hatch, M. Fielding

"The Mask" (Waltz Rondo)
M. Fielding

"My name is Fanchette" (Airetta)
C. Lewis

"Have you forgot" (Duet)
A. Hatch, C. Lewis

"I am Don Januario" (Bolero)
H. Conway

"All we seem to agree" (Whispering Quartette)
A. Hatch, H. Conway, C. Lewis, A. Rehan

"Through the night" (Duet)
H. Conway, C. Lewis

Finale (Concerted piece for Fanchette)
M. Fielding, A. Rehan, A. Hatch, H. Conway, C. Leclercq, Chorus

Introducing the Song of the Royal Middies: "Of all the fine fellows that sail on the sea."

ACT 2

"When ashore" (Chorus of Middies)/

"I am so sick" (Fanchette's song)
(C. Lewis)

"This hateful uniform"[56] (Song)
C. Lewis

"To our flag!" (Concerted Piece)
C. Lewis, M. Fielding, A. Rehan, A. Hatch, H. Conway, C. Leclercq, Chorus

"Sword in hand, man to man" (Quintette)
C. Lewis, A. Hatch, C. Leclercq, H. Conway, C. Fisher

"The Queen's Game of Chess" (Finale—Concerted)
Company

ACT 3

"Dom Mauritio" (Chorus of Citizens)
Chorus

"Who is the woman" (Song)
C. Lewis

"In woman's heart alone" (Duet)
C. Lewis, M. Fielding

Retrospective (Finale)
Company

1880.05 PRINCESS CARPILLONA, or, The Kings of the Golden Valley

A Burlesque Extravaganza in Two Acts, 11 Scenes, arranged by R. B. Caverly. Stage manager, John E. Henshaw. Musical director, J. C. Kenny. Produced by Caverly's Great English Folly Company (R. B. Caverly, Manager). Opened 2 February 1880 at the Broadway Opera House and closed 5 February 1880 after 4 performances.

CAST[57]: *Periwigulus*, the proud King of Rumantica: JAMES A. STURGES. *Brutus*, the Crooked, Prince Royal and Generalissimo of the Forces: J. H. STUART. *Perfidius*, Private Secretary to and Confidant of the Prince: IDA MORRIS. *Corin*: MAY TEN BROECK. *Placid*, the easy, Ex-King of the Peaceful island, dethroned by a distant relation, whose name has not transpired, and living *incog.* and in clover, in the verdant valley, under the name of Sublimus: JOHN E. HENSHAW. *Queen Dominanta*, his wife, a pattern of domesticity, sharing her husband's fortunes, under the name of Pastora: EMILY MAYNARD. *Chloe, Phillis*, their daughters: Alice Wallace, Jennie Don. *The Princess Carpillona*: LULU RICHMOND. *Genaro*, the King's Minstrel: LOUISE DEMPSEY. *Dandelina*: Capitola Forrest. *Amazonia*, the Fairy: Nita Gerald. *Aqua Marina*: CECILE ROMAINE. *Coralina* [Carolina]: Carrie Fuller. *Manola*, an Officer of the Royal Guard: Laura Bennett. *Nino*, Court Jester: Florence Delmaning. *Perseus*, Lord Chamberlain: Josie Richmond. *"What Is It?"*: The Unknown. *Soldiers, Ambassadors, Lords, Ladies of the Court, etc*: The Company. *Specialties*: The Three Brazziers.

Act 1, Scene 1: Part of Rantipolis, the Capital City of the Island of Rumantica. The Conqueror's return. *Scene 2*: Interior of a royal pavilion in the palace gardens. Carpillona's captivity. *Scene 3*: Brink of a precipice. Brutus meets with an accident. *Scene 4*: Somebody does something. *Scene 5*: The Golden Valley and Cottage of Sublimus. The disguised King and Queen receive a visitor. *Scene 6*: Willon Glen on the verdant valley. Amazonia as a magician. *Scene 7*: Seaweed Hall, the home of Aqua Marina.

Act 2, Scene 1: Riverside in the Golden Valley. A little spooning. Golden chains. *Scene 2*: A forest on the border of the valley. The charm broken and the recapture of Carpillona. *Scene 3*: Council Chamber of the King Periwigulus. Trial and doom of the prisoners. An advocate of cremation. *Scene 4*: Public Place before the palace, with preparations for the execution of Carpillona and Corin. Denouncement of the Prince. Apropos. Arrival of the protecting powers and dazzling prospect of a triumphant termination of the troubles of two Kings. Grand Finale.

BALLETS AND SPECIALTIES

Grand Carnival (Act 1, Scene 7)
The world renowned 3 Brazziers in their inimitable and astonishing performances.

Capitola Forest and Laura Bennett in their beautiful skipping-rope specialty.

John E. Henshaw in his great specialties.

The Richmond Sisters , Lady Song and Dance Artists, in their change act.

Miss Ida Morris, Queen of all Serio-Comic Vocalists.

Caverly's California Quartette.

Grand Chorus
Entire Company

1880.06 HORRORS

Rice's Surprise Party in a Revival of the Musical Extravaganza in Two Acts, 6 Scenes[58]. Play by William Gill. (Lyrics by Louis Harrison.) Stage director, Willie Edouin. Musical director, Henry Sator. Produced by Edward E. Rice. Opened 2 February 1880 at the Standard Theatre and closed 21 February 1880 after 21 performances; returned 19-20 March 1880 to the Standard Theatre for 3 additional performances. Total: 24 performances.[59]

CAST: *Hamsetjee Bumstejee*, always in the arms of Morpheus. A Snorer from Snorersville, but wine works wonders: WILLIE EDOUIN. *Rumsetjee Bumsetjee*, a Parsee astrologer, ambitious to be the power behind the throne, and gets THROWN out of the town: GEORGE W. HOWARD. *Rajah Zog*, of Hibernian descent, full of majesty, gout, fond of hearing from the planets, tries to PLANIT so the prince will marry the princess: HENRY E. DIXEY. *Prince Achmet*, his son, who has to travel six months by act of parliament. The ACT-MET with his approval: ALICE ATHERTON. *Tragedee*, Court Jester, who thinks that position is everything, in fact, a regular IMP-osition: LOUIS HARRISON. *Captain Beauforall*, the ladies' pet: LINA MERVILLE. *Zohi, Zolo*, SCIONS of a noble house, SIGHING to rove with the Prince: FLORENCE I. BAKER, JENNIE CALEF. *Zizzis*, chief of the Princess' followers, who thinks that love is an eternal transport—so is a canal boat: PAULINE HALL. *Captain Darling*, of the American gunboat *Pensacola*: Emma Burgess. *What's in a name? Wait til you hear them (4)*: *Punjaeb Tong*: Henry Kramer. *Calcut Gong*: Edwin Nichols. *Saka Zeke*: D. P. Steele. *Biff Alalong*: Ed. Aiken. *French Manipulators of succulent hash (3)*: *Fricasseed Françoise*: E. R. Morse. *Alamode Jean*: Andrew Metzgar. *Fillet de Cocardasse*: Donald Harold. *Billy Bowline*, a nice little tar: Rose Wilson. *Four nice clean tars, shiver the cabin boy's teeth (4)*: *Hallyard Zephyr*: Carrie Perkins. *Silver Foam*: Carrie Vinal. *Crested Wavelet*: Jessie Calef. *Headland Breaker*: Emma Duchateau. *Begum D'Lite*, Princess of Bombay, DELIGHTFUL young lady, the Prince choose her not, she'll be-gum d'lite to the last: NELLIE BEAUMONT. *Zaidee*, a simple maiden, but sometimes they know a thing or two. An adorer of the prince: MARION ELMORE. *La Jolie Housekeepaire*, proprietress of a hotel in Ceylon. She sets her SEAL on the hearts of all her boarders: MARION SINGER. *Attendants on the Princess*: Lizzie Dana, Edith Smith. *Court of the Rajah, Attendants on the Prince, Tum-tum beaters, Jungle Kakers, Nautch Girls, Sailors, Jugglers, Waiters, Snake Charmers, Star gazers in profusion.*

---

[56]Dropped early in the run, but restored for subsequent tour.

[57]Alternate programs list a different CAST: *Chloe*: Capitola Forrest. *Dandelina*: Lillian Doane. *Aqua Marina*: Josie Richmond. *Manola*: Blanche Raymond. *Perseus*: Cecile Romaine.

[58]First produced in New York as HORRORS, or The Marajah of Zogobad, 28 May 1879 at the Union Square Theare for 41 performances. For Synopsis of Scenes and Musical Numbers, see original 1879 production.

[59]Musical numbers not listed in program, except:

"A Ray of Sunlight" (Act 1)
M. Elmore, L. Merville
(*Music and Lyrics by* Edward E. Rice.)

1880.07

HUMPTY DUMPTY

The Great Trick Pantomime in Four Acts, 11 Scenes. Stage director, James S. Maffitt. Musical director, Henry Wannemacher. Scenery by Henry E. Hoyt, Gaspard Maeder, George Heister, Schell, LaMoss, John A. Thompson. Produced by Henry E. Abbey and Mr. Hickey. Opened 3 February 1880 at Abbey's Booth's Theatre and closed 24 March 1880 after 64 performances.

CAST IN THE PROLOGUE: *Genius of the Drama*: Hattie O'Neill. *Muse of Comedy*: Ella Whittredge. *Muse of Tragedy*: Marie Longley. *Eileen*: Little Belle Wharton. *Spirit of Pantomime*: Louis Snow. *Hamlet*: Frank Crane. *Stalacta*: Kate Francis. *Mephisto*: Blanche Franklin. *Ballet*: Bertha Rupert. *Poor Pillicoddy*: Henry Flohr. *Sir Joseph Porter*: Frank Crane. *Gabriel*: Carrie Williams. *Buffalo Bill*: W. Carpenter. *Little Red Riding Hood*: Little Hattie. *Mother Hubbard*: Little Alice. *Jack and Jill*: Little Johnnie and Jennie. *Little Bo-Peep*: Little Carrie. *Young H.D.*: Master Willie. *Children, etc.*

CAST IN THE PANTOMIME: *Humpty Dumpty, Sr.*: JAMES S. MAFFITT. *Humpty Dumpty, Jr.*: ROBERT FRASER. *Old One-Two*, Buckle my shoe, who finds his anger bootless: W. H. BARTHOLOMEW. *Old Three-Four*, Shut the door, who will find his own gait: N. D. JONES. *Reddy*, a policeman, Broadway squad: Robert Butler. *Grouty-Gritz*, the Canton Burgomaster: A. S. Mathews. *Kwill Pen*, his secretary in chief: FRANK CRANE. *Tommy Tucker*, who sang for his supper: J. F. Raymond. *Bobby Shaftoe*, who went to sea: Elizabeth Menzelli. *Little Goody Two Shoes*, known to those whom Mother Goose uses: Pauline Barretta. *Little Miss Muffet*, who sat on a tuffet: Kate Francis. *Korn Shock*, the jolly miller: A. Carpenter.

The Miller's Men who can sing or handle a stave: *Cyrus Chaff*: A. Dam. *Reuben Rye*: W. Comley. *Felix Fodder*: G. Lansing. *Stephen Stubble*: J. McGraw. *Benjamin Bran*: B. Smith. *Matthew Maize*: Edward Moses.

The Merry Lads and Lasses of the Village: *Tom and Timothy*: Misses Rupert and Gray. *Peter and Paul*: Misses Baptistan and Kate Francis. *Jonathan, Jacob*: Misses Crone and Reeves. *Samuel, Saul*: Misses Lizzie and Maggie Francis. *Mary and Martha*: Misses Lizzie and Jenny Timony. *Polly and Peg*: Nellie Gray and Barbour. *Josephine, Jessie*: Misses Mowbray and Felton. *Molly and Meg*: Misses Carrie LaForne and Hawkins.

The Alpine Shepherds who live by hook and by crook: *Francis Fleece*: T. Ryan. *Walter Wool*: W. Richardson. *Charles Crook*: G. Foos. *William Wether*: J. Hatzel. *Edward Ewe*: H. Humphreys. *Lionel Lamb*: C. Collins. *Peasants, Villagers, Vine Dressers, etc.*

Specialties: BROTHERS VALJEAN (jugglers/trained pigeons), FRED LEVANTINE (equilibrist), SNOW BROTHERS (acrobats), THE SPANISH STUDENTS (15 on guitar, mandolin, violin). *Ballet*: Mons. BAPTISTAN, Mlles. Marie Bonfanti, Menzelli; Berretta; Elise Scott, Coryphées.

Act 1, Scene 1: Vale of Tempe, Thessaly. (Hoyt and Maeder.) *Scene 2*: The Vineyards of Verzenay. (Hoyt and Maeder.) *Scene 3*: The Grotto of Terpsichore. (Heister.)

Act 2, Scene 1: New York Elevated Railroad. (Schell.) *Scene 2*: The Enchanted Wood of Mystery. (Schell.) *Scene 3*: The Moder Parisian Bakery. (Schell.) *Scene 4*: Barbier et Perruquier et Hotel de McMullen. (LaMoss.) *Scene 5*: Tailors vs. Dress Makers. (LaMoss.) *Scene 6*: The Rocky Dell and Fete Champetre. (Hoyt and Maeder.)

Act 3: Mansion Spaniola. (Thompson.)

Act 4: Transformation Scene.

ACT 1

Scene 2

"Wine of Verzenay" (Vintage Chorus)

"Click Clack goes the Mill!"
Jolly Millers

"Come, let's all be merry!"
Alpine Shepherds, Vine Dressers

Valley of (Piper Heidsieck) Champagne (Grand Ballet Divertissement and Characteristic Tableau)
Clowns: J. S. Maffitt, R. Fraser. *Pantaloons*: W. H. Bartholomew, N. D. Jones. *Harlequins*: J. Raymonde, J. W. Sanford. *Columbines*: P. Barretta, Mlle. Elise. *Sprites*: Messrs. Louis and Eddie Snow.

Scene 3

The Festival of the Vine: Pas de Pomona (Captivating Ballet Divertissement and Tableau originated and presented by Mons. Baptistan, J. Raymonde.)

ACT 2

Scene 6

Grand Ball La Frolic:
Brothers Valjean; Fred F. Levantine; Snow Brothers; Ballet.

ACT 3

The Spanish Students

ACT 4

Grand Transformation Scene: Humpty Dumpty's Valentine!!

1880.08

THE BLACK CROOK

A Revival of the Musical Extravaganza in Four Acts, 11 Scenes[60]. (Play by Charles M. Barras.) Music by Charles Puerner. Scenery by (Harley) Merry & Simmonds. Machinery by John Leo. Mechanical effects by A. Newman. Illuminations by Emmet Davidson. Leader of orchestra, Charles Puerner. Production (under the stage direction) of the Kiralfy Brothers (Imre, Bolossy). Produced by E. G. Gilmore. Opened 16 February 1880 at Niblo's Garden and closed 28 February 1880 after 17 performances.

CAST: Mortals: *Hertzog*, Sur-named the Black Crook: J. F. PETERS[61]. *Rudolph*, a Poor Artist: C. G. CRAIG[62]. *Count Wolfenstein*: WILLIS H. PAGE. *Greppo*, his servant: I. DAVIDSON. *Von Puffengruntz*: JAMES DUNN. *Bruno, Wolfgar*, Ruffians: Peter Toole, W. F. Nagle. *Caspar*, a Peasant: John Grace. *Amina*, betrothed to Rudolph: SADIE BIGELOW. *Dame Barbara*, Armina's Foster-Mother: Mrs. W. BRUTONE. *Carline*, Armina's Maid: LAURA DEMPSEY. *Rosetta*, a Peasant: Lillie Pearson.

Immortals: *Stalacta*, Queen of the Golden Realm: NELLIE LARKELL. *Dragonfin*, her Faithful Sprite: ARNOLD KIRALFY. *Zamiel*, the Arch-Fiend: JOHN ATWELL. *Skudawelp*, familiar to Hertzog: A. Phillips. *Red Glare*: J. Riley. *Specialties*: THE THREE RENALDOS (eccentric dancers), THE HERBERT BROTHERS, CARLING (the boy caricaturist), the Ulm Sisters. *Ballet*: Mlles. DeROSA, ADELE CORNALBA, CASSATI, CAPPELINI, ZALLIO; Mons. ARNOLD KIRALFY; Volanti.

Act 1, Scene 1: View of the Castle Wolfenstein. Village. *Scene 2*: A Woody Pass. Hartz Mountains. *Scene 3*: A Hall in Castle Wolfenstein. *Scene 4*: Laboratory of the Crook. *Scene 5*: Wild Cross Path in the Glen of the Brocken.

Act 2, Scene 1: Subterranean Vaults. Vision of the Count and Armina. *Scene 2*: Gothic Chamber. The Grotto of Stalacta.

Act 3, Scene 1: The Palace of Lace. *Scene 2*: A Hall in the Castle. *Scene 3*: Grand Staircase of the Illuminated Terrace.

Act 4: Gothic Hall. Rocky Pass. Burning Forest. Wood. Pandemonium. Transformation, representing the Home of the Fairies.

ACT 1

Scene 1

Festive Dance and Chorus
Coryphées

Scene 3

Song
L. Dempsey

Scene 5

Cascade of Real Water; The Demon Fight; The Walking Skeleton; The Incantations; Grand Tableau Infernale

ACT 2

Scene 2

Song
N. Larkell

Scene 3

Grand Blue Ballet

Les Escharpes
Volanti

Entre
Mlles. Casati, Cornalba

Grand Adagio
Mlles. Cornalba, Casati, Cappelini, Zallio, Corps de Ballet

Variations
Mlle. Zallio

Solo
Mlle. Cappelini

Pas Seul
Mlle. Cornalba

Grand Variations
Mlle. Casati

Fnale Ensemble
Entire Corps de Ballet, Premieres, Secondas

[60]First produced in New York 12 September 1866 at Niblo's Garden for 475 performances.
[61]After opening night, this role was assumed by C. G. CRAIG.
[62]After opening night, this role was assumed by FRANK NORCROSS.

ACT 3

Scene 1

Tableau of Armina's Bridal Festival

The Three Rinaldos

The Herbert Brothers

Grand Ballet of All Nations

Entre

Tartaric, Italic and Austrian Corps de Ballet

La Flora d'Espagna

Danseuse Secondas

Ensemble et Hongrois

Coryphées

Dance Normandy

Ladies of the Ballet

La France

Mlle. Zallio

South America

Mons. Kiralfy

Great Britain

Secondes Danseuses

America

Mlle. DeRosa

Grand Finale (China, Japan, All Nations)

Entire Corps de Ballet

The celebrated Infant Chinese and Japanese Combination (Eccentric Pantomime)

Scene 2

Master Carling in his Lightning Sketches

Scene 3

Grand Manoeuvre D'Amazon; The Combat; Tableau

ACT 4

Transformation, representing the Home of the Fairies

1880.09 THE MULLIGAN GUARD'S SURPRISE

A Local Comedy in One Act, 7 Scenes[63], preceded by an Olio. Play (and lyrics) by Edward Harrigan. Music by David Braham. (Staged by Edward Harrigan.) Produced under the supervision of Welsh Edwards. Scenery by Charles W. Witham. Costumer, Annie Howard. Mechanical effects by Robert Cutler. Properties by Robert Puller. Musical director, David Braham. Produced by Edward Harrigan and Tony Hart. Opened 16 February 1880 at the Theatre Comique and closed 15 May 1880 after 104 performances.

Olio: John Wild and Billy Gray in Brothers in Misfortune, with H. A. Fisher; Jennie Morgan (the American Linnet).

CAST: *Dan Mulligan*: EDWARD HARRIGAN. *Mrs. Rebecca Allup*: TONY HART. *Captain Simpson Primrose*: JOHN WILD. *Rev. Palestine Puter*: WILLIAM GRAY. *Planxty McFudd*: WELSH EDWARDS. *Gustavus Lochmuller*: HARRY A. FISHER. *Dick Dublin*: John Queen. *Mrs. Dublin*: John Queen. *Walsingham McSweeny*: MICHAEL BRADLEY. *Roger Dunleavy*: Edward Burt. *Dr. Algernon Winterbottom*: Edward Goss. *Ichabod Carpe*: William West. *Mrs. Ichabod Carpe*: Joe Buckley. *Lorenzo Islip*: T. Cronin. *Adelaide Cream*: J. Tierney. *Mercy Parsons*: J. Fox. *Gus Lochmuller, Jr.*: Master Husel .*Officer New*: John McCullough. *Carolne Melrose*: Charles Sheffer. *Wallabout Melrose*: M. Foley. *Con Murphy*: P. Coffee. *Cordelia Mulligan*: Mrs. ANNIE YEAMANS. *Bridget Lochmuller*: ANNIE MACK. *Katy Mulligan*: JENNIE YEAMANS. *Diana McFudd*: MARIE GORENFLO. *Rosy McFudd*: Belle Mordaunt. *Ellen McFudd*: Emily Yeamans. *Jennie Lanty*: Mary Bird.

Scene 1: Interior of Mulligan's Mansion. *Scene 2*: Mulligan Alley. *Scene 3*: Attic in Mulligan's Tenement. *Scene 4*: Mulligan Alley. *Scene 5*: The Wedding Party. *Scene 6*: Hallway in Mulligan's Tenement. *Scene 7*: The Surprise.

MUSICAL NUMBERS

"Linger Not, Darling" (Song and Chorus)(Scene 1)

A. Yeamans, A. Mack

"I'll Wear the Trousers, Oh!" (Song)(Scene 1)

E. Harrigan

"The Full Moons" (Full Moon Union)(Scene 2)

W. Gray, J. Wild

"Oh! Hark, Baby, Hark" (Song)(Scene 4)

T. Hart

"Dat Citron Wedding Cake" (Scene 4)

"Never Take the Horseshoe from the Door" (Scene 7)

E. Harrigan, Company

"Whist! the Bogie Man" (Scene 7)

E. Harrigan, Company

[63]Billed as "Volume the Fifth" in Mulligan Guards series.

1880.10 HIAWATHA

An American Operatic Extravaganza (Burlesque) in Two Acts, 7 Scenes. Libretto by Nathaniel Childs. (Suggested by the poem by Henry Wadsworth Longfellow.) Entire original music by Edward E. Rice. Stage director, Willie Edouin. Settings by William T. Voegtlin. Costumes by J. H. Eaves. Musical director, Henry Sator. Produced by Rice's Surprise Party (Edward E. Rice, Proprietor and Manager). Opened 21 February 1880 at the Standard Theatre and closed 18 March 1880 after 17 performances in repertory.

CAST: *Hiawatha*, an Indian chief. All lisping young ladies say He-aw-wath-a, charming fellow: ALICE ATHERTON. *William Penn Brown*, commonly known as Penn, a United States commissioner, who has penn-etrated the forest, not for-est but for plunder: WILLIE EDOUIN. *Remus Brown*, *Romulus Smith*, Siamese twin-like conspirators. Tools of Penn, but who go in t'win themselves: LOUIS HARRISON, HENRY E. DIXEY. *Mr. Lo*, formerly a poor Indian, now well off. With his wife, much of the Locomotive of the plot: GEORGE W. HOWARD. *Yenadizzi*, a beautiful, dashing young Indian of the period, in love with this Lo's daughter: LINA MERVILLE. *District Telegraph Boy*: Jennie Calef. *Honey Dew*, *Hazel Dell*, young warriors, attendants on Hiawatha: PAULINE HALL, NELLIE BEAUMONT. *Old Man Afraid-of-His-Whisky*, Mr. Lo's father: D. P. Steele. *Dr. Sawbones Landis*: Donald Harold. *Scar-Face Charley*: Andrew Metzger. *Sweet Face William*: E. H. Aiken. *Minnehaha*, the fairest Indian girl of the tribe, beloved by all. Everyone is expected to be tickled by her name: MARION SINGER. *Mrs. Lo*, wife of Lo, nee Miss High: MARION ELMORE. *Sally Bohee*, servant in the family of Lo: Florence Baker. *Adjunct conspirators who add junk to their plunder, Indians of all colors, Indianesses of all shades.*

Act 1, Scene 1: Valley of Bubbling Waters. *Scene 2*: Half mile from same. *Scene 3*: Moonlight in the valley.

Act 2, Scene 1: Lovers' Lane. *Scene 2*: Winter at the Waters. *Scene 3*: A Villainous Wood. *Scene 4*: Throne Hut of the Lo Tribe.

ACT 1[64]

Scene 1

"The Sun Arises" (Opening Chorus)

"A Marriageable Daughter" (Duet)

G. W. Howard, M. Elmore

"Behold in Me" (Song)

A. Atherton

"Bubble, Bubble" (Song)

M. Singer

"Good-bye for a Little While" (Finale)

M. Singer, A. Atherton, Quartette

Scene 2

"Conspirators Three" (Trio)

W. Edouin, L. Harrison, H. E. Dixey

Scene 3

"Lovely Night" (Song and Dance)

L. Merville

"Wedding Bells" (Song Introduced)

"That's What Puzzles the Quaker"

A. Atherton

Burlesque Serenade (10 different popular melodies played at the same time)

All the characters

Ah! Never More Sadly! Now Away" (Finale)

M. Singer, Chorus, A. Atherton

Hiawatha Mazourka (Orchestra directed by the composer)

ACT 2

Scene 1

"Pretty Little Boys" (Trio)

F. I. Baker, P. Hall, N. Beaumont

Scene 2

"Indians Never Lie" (Double Quartette)

M. Singer, A. Atherton

[64]The program notes that in addition to the musical numbers listed there are 20 pieces of incidental music.

"Tea and Toast and Kisses" (Duet)
A. Atherton, M. Singer
"It Was Many Years Ago" (Song and Dance)
M. Elmore
"Hail! Hail!" (Chorus)
Ensemble
"Yah! Yoh! Yum!" (Quartette)
W. Edouin, H. E. Dixey, L. Harrison, L. Merville
Scene 3
Song with Dance
W. Edouin, H. E. Dixey, L. Harrison, Ensemble
Scene 4
"The Shooters"
Chorus
"Speed My Arrow" (Song and Chorus)
L. Merville
"God of Love" (Duet and Chorus)
A. Atherton, M. Singer, Ensemble
"He's Won! He's Won! Good Night" (Grand Finale, Solo and Chorus)
M. Singer, A. Atherton, Chorus

THE BROOK,
1880.11 or, A Jolly Day at the Picnic

A Revival of the Laughable and Musical Extravaganza (Farce Comedy) in One Act[65]. Farce by Nate Salsbury. Music selected and arranged by Frank Maeder. Musial director, Frank Maeder. Produced by Salsbury's Troubadours (Charles J. Crouse, Business Manager). Opened 23 February 1880 at Haverly's Lyceum Theatre and closed 13 March 1880 after 24 perfomances. Re-opened 3 May 1880 at Daly's Theatre and closed 29 May 1880 after 32 additional performances. Total: 56 performances.

CAST (CROSS PURPOSES): *Colonel Croker*: NATE SALSBURY. *Dudley Croker*: JOHN WEBSTER. *Jack Crawley*: JOHN GOURLAY. *Aurora Blythe*: NELLIE McHENRY. *Carolie Blythe*: HELENE DINGEON.

CAST (THE BROOK): *Tracy Thornton*: NATE SALSBURY. *A Turtle*: Himself. *Percy Montrose*: JOHN WEBSTER. *One Fish-Pole*: And Line. *Festus Heavysides*: JOHN GOURLAY. *Two Bottles*: Uncorked. *Rose Dimplecheek*: NELLIE McHENRY. *A Boat*: Property Man. *Blanche Sylvester*: HELENE DINGEON. *Lunch Basket*: Quartette. *Umbrellas*: Well Spread.

H.M.S. PINAFORE,
1880.12 or, The Lass That Loved a Sailor

A Revival of the Comic Opera in Two Acts[66]. Libretto by William S. Gilbert. Music by Arthur Sullivan. Produced by the Ideals [Boston Ideal Opera Company], (Messrs. Tompkins and Hill, Managers). Opened 1 March 1880 at Niblo's Garden and closed 20 March 1880 after 21 performances.[67]

CAST: *The Rt. Hon. Sir Joseph Porter, K.C.B.*, First Lord of the Admiralty: HENRY CLAY BARNABEE. *Captain Corcoran*, Commanding the *H.M.S. Pinafore*: MYRON W. WHITNEY. *Ralph Rackstraw*, Able Seaman: W. H. FESSENDEN. *Dick Deadeye*, Able Seaman: GEORGE FROTHINGHAM. *Bill Bobstay*, Boatswain: Gus Kammerlee. *Bob Beckett*, Carpenter's Mate: J. A. Montgomery. *The Ancient Mariner*: H. F. Dixie [Henry F. Dixey]. *Tom Tucker*, Midshipmite: La Petite Lillian. *Josephine*, the Captain's Daughter: MARY BEEBE. *Little Buttercup*: ADELAIDE PHILLIPPS. *Hebe*, Sir Joseph's First Cousin: Adelaide Detchon. *First Lord's Sisters, his Cousins, his Aunts, Sailors, Marines, etc.*

ROBINSON CRUSOE, ESQ.
1880.13 AND HIS MAN FRIDAY

A Burlesque in One Act, 5 Scenes. (Adaptation by Edward E. Rice.) Suggested by the novel of the same name by Daniel Defoe. Stage director, Willie Edouin. Musical director, Henry Sator. Produced by Edward E. Rice. Opened 8 March 1880 at the Standard Theatre and closed 17 March 1880 (matinee) after 10 performances.[68]

CAST: *Robinson Crusoe, Esq.*, a youthful but daring adventurer: LINA MERVILLE. *Man Friday*, he is so pale they call him Friday, week: WILLIE EDOUIN. *James Cox*, a Tragedian who refuses to be crushed: GEORGE W. HOWARD. *Will Atkins*, a vicious kidnapping mariner, who steals Polly, with designs of marrying her: LOUIS HARRISON. *Billy Bowline*, his second in command and abbetor in villainy, for villainy abettor could not be found: MARION ELMORE. *Binacle*, another vicious mariner: NELLIE BEAUMONT. *Old Daddy Alltalk*, Auctioneer: Donald Harold. *Atkin's Crew (5)*: *Billy Buntling*: Jessie Calef. *Harry Mainsail*: Pauline Hall. *Jimmy Pitch*: Emma Duchateau. *Jack Tarr*: Carrie Vinal. *Charley Hatch*: Estella Lowell. *Solomon Isaacs, Isaac Solomon*, when there is an auction near, the auctioneer is sure to see them: D. P. Steele, E. Nichols. *Polly Peerkins*, Crusoe's sweetheart—f.b.f.—flirtatious but faithful: FLORENCE I. BAKER. *Jelly Jones*, her confidante, with a soft spot in her heart for Jim Cox: MARION SINGER. *Ylang Ylang*, the Indian Queen in search of a husband, hard to satisfy, finds each candidate better than the last: MARIA DAVIS. *Mille-Fleurs*, attendant on the Queen: Rose Wilson. *Whatdoyeusoy*, the Medicine Man, The Queen's Prime Minister and Adviser: HENRY E. DIXEY. *Iguesso*, a lively young Italian: Jennie Calef. *Hyacinthus*, an Indian Swell, who after style of swells of the present day, seeks to wed a fortune and a queen: FLORENCE I. BAKER. *Huebuck, Talktonge*, Indian Brave: E. R. Morse, Andrew Metzgar. *Indians, Peasants, Sailors, Pirates, Sepoys, Seagulls, etc.*

Act 1, Scene 1: The Seaport of Hull, England. *Scene 2*: The Mystic Grove of the Oracle. *Scene 3*: Crusoe's Island Home. *Scene 4*: The Jungle. *Scene 5*: Pirate's Retreat. Happy Denouement and Finale.

1880.14 LE PRÉ AUX CLERCS

An Opéra comique in Three Acts, in French. Libretto by François-Antoine Eugène de Planard. Music by Louis Joseph Ferdinand Hérold. Musical director, Charles Almeras. Produced by Maurice Grau. Opened 16 March 1880 at the Fifth Avenue Theatre and closed 19 March 1880 after 2 performances in repertory; returned 8 April 1880 to the Fifth Avenue Theatre for 1 additional performance; returned 4 May 1880 to the Academy of Music for 1 additional performance.

CAST: *Isabelle de Béarn*: Mlle. LEROUX-BOUVARD. *Marguerite de Valois*, La Reine de Navarre: Mlle. ANGÈLE. *Nicette*: Mlle. GRÉGOIRE. *A Maid Of Honor*: Mlle. A. Bouvard. *Marquis de Mergy*: VICTOR CAPOUL. *Comte de Comminges*: Mons. BOUVARD. *Cantarelli*: Mons. POYARD. *Girot*: Mons. JOUARD. *Un Brigadier*: Mons. Terrancle. *An Exempt*: Mons. Gerard. *An Usher*: Mons. F. Mauriez. *Courtesans, Mignons, Guards, Peasants, etc.*: Chorus of 60.

Act 1: The Guest's Hall of an Inn in the environs of Paris. 1582, under the reign of Henry III.

Act 2: An apartment in Louvre.

Act 3: A wedding festival at the Pré aux Clercs.

ACT 1[69]
Introduction (Ah quel beau jour de fête)
Mlle. Grégoire, Mons. Jouard, Choeur
Duo (Les rendez-vous de noble compagnie)
Mlle. Grégoire, Mons. Jouard
Air (Ce soir j'arrive donc)
V. Capoul
Morceau d'ensemble (Allons, allons dressons la table)
Mlle. Grégoire, Messrs. Capoul, Poyard, Jouard, Choeur
Finale (À la Navarre à ses montagnes)
Tous
Romance (Souvenir du jeune age)
Mlle. Leroux-Bouvard

ACT 2
Air (Jours de mon enfance)
Mlle. Leroux-Bouvard
Trio (Vous me disiez sans cesse)
Mlles. Angèle, Leroux-Bouvard, Poyard
Mascarade (Ah quel plaisir)
Tous
Petit Air (Ah Monsieur de grace)
Mlle. Grégoire
Finale (Tous est dit, du silence)
Tous

[65]Preceded by a curtain-raiser, Cross Purposes. First produced 12 May 1879 at the San Francisco Minstrels' Hall for 42 performances. For Synopsis of Scenes and Musical Numbers, see original 1879 production. Reviewers remarked that the production was much the same as before, with only minor variations in the incidental music.

[66]First produced in New York 15 January 1879 at the Standard Theatre for 175 performances. For Synopsis of Scenes and Musical Number, see original 1879 production.

[67]No credits in programs for stage director, musical director, scenery or costumes.

[68]Musical numbers not listed in programs.

[69]Musical numbers not listed in programs. List prepared from published French piano vocal score (Brandus et Cie., Paris, 185?).

ACT 3

Morceau d'ensemble (Que j'aime ces ombrages)
Mlle. Grégoire, Choeur

Ronde (À la fleur du bel age)
Mlle. Grégoire

Trio (C'en est fait le ciel même)
Mlles. Angèle, Leroux-Bouvard, Mons. V. Capoul

Finale (Je frémis. Qu'est-ce donc qui l'étonne)
Tous

Quatuor (L'heure vous appelle)
Mlles. Angèle, Leroux-Bouvard, Grégoire, Mons. Jouard

1880.15

BEADLE'S PIRATES FOR TEN CENTS

A Musical Burlesque (of Gilbert & Sullivan's "The Pirates of Penzance") in One Act, 3 Scenes, preceded by an Olio. Libretto by Add Ryman. Music by W. S. Mullaly. Musical director, W. S. Mullaly. Produced by the San Francisco Minstrels. Opened 22 March 1880 at the San Francisco Opera House and closed 24 April 1880 after 35 performances.[70]

Olio: "Mariner's Daughter" (bass song), H. W. Frillman; "Only a Rose from Mother's Grave" (ballad), W. Raymond; "Always Chewing Gum" (comic ditty), Charles Backus; "The Fisherman and His Child" (ballad), T. B. Dixon; "Billy's Request" (Comic Song), Billy Birch; "When the Moon with Glory Brightens" (ballad), J. G. Russell; Finale ("The Turkish Patrol," and "The Skids Are Out Today," Music by David Braham, Lyrics by Edward Harrigan), San Francisco Minstrels. [Interval] Edwin French (banjo artist with original songs); The Flat Boat Ball!, with Johnson and Powers; "Grandpapa's Pants", George Thatcher.

CAST: *Richard Dick*, foreman of the Pirates: ADD RYMAN. *Bob*, an apprentice: JAMES JOHNSON. *Bad Uns (5)*: *Sam*: J. B. Dixon. *Fred*: J. G. Russell. *Pete*: Charles Stevens. *Bill*: H. W. Frillman. *Nick*: William Raymond. *Captain of Police*, precinct unknown: BILLY BIRCH. *Members of the Locust Club (4)*: *Georgie*: George Powers. *Clarence*: Edwin French. *Leonard*: Charles Gibbons. *Gussie*: J. Martin. *General Stanley*, a veteran Home Guard: GEORGE THATCHER. *Mabel*, one of his daughters: F. M. RICARDO. *Fairy*, an ethereal beauty: CHARLES BACKUS. *Pirates, Policemen, Daughters, etc.*

Scene 1: A Rocky Beach. *Scene 2*: Corridor of General Stanley's Palace. *Scene 3*: Sleeping Apartment of General Stanley's Daughters.

1880.16

LA PETITE MUETTE

An Opéra Comique (The Little Dumb Girl) in Three Acts, in French. Libretto by Paul Ferrier. Music by Gaston Serpette. Stage manager, Mons. Bouvard. Musical director, Charles Almeras. Produced by Maurice Grau's French Opera Company. Opened 24 March 1880 at the Fifth Avenue Theatre and closed 27 March 1880 after 5 performances.

CAST: *Mercedès*: Mlle. PAOLA MARIÉ. *Casilda*: Mlle. ANGÈLE. *La Duchess*, Dona Séraphina: Mlle. Armand. *Rosita*: Mlle. A. Bouvard. *Paquita*: Mlle. Estradere. *Inasille*: Mlle. Berhe. *Juliano*: Mlle. L. Duparc. *Piquillo*: Mlle. Esteve. *Don Henrique*: Mons. JUTEAU. *Don José d'Albatros*: Mons. DUPLAN. *Camomillas*, le docteur: Mons. J. Mezières. *Pédrille*: Mons. POYARD. *Annibal*: Mons. TERBEL. *Antonio*: Mons. Terrancle. *Barnabé*: Mons. Gerard. *Domingo*: Mons. Mauriez. *Don Gil Perellos*: Mons. VILANO. *Don Rafael d'Estrella*: Mons. VICTOR CAPOUL.

Act 1: Devant le château de Don Jose d'Albatros.

Act 2: Dans une hôtellerie.

Act 3: Dans les jardins d'Aranjuez.

ACT 1[71]

Choeur et Couplets de Casilda (Preux vétérans)
Mlle. Angèle, Mons. Terbel, Choeur

Couplets de Don José (Je suis un Hidalgo)
Mons. Duplan, Choeur

Choeur de sortie (Portez armes)

Choeur et Couplets du docteur (Le voici, c'est lui-même)
Mons. J. Mezières, Choeur

Choeur de sortie (Non, tous ses confrères)

Duetto de la présentation (Mademoiselle, elle!)
Messrs. Duplan, F. Mezieres

Romance de Raphael (Oui, je vous aime)
Mons. Capoul

Trio à deux voix (Lisez, nous sommes en famille)
Messrs. Capoul, Duplan

Choeur, Habanera et Final (Son Excellence franchit le seuil)
Messrs. Capoul, Duplan, Terbel, Vilano, Mlle. Angèle, Choeur

ACT 2

Choeur et Couplets de Don Henrique (Buvons pour égayer nos veilles)
Mons. Juteau, Choeur

Chanson Militaire (Dans le régiment qui nous quitte)
Messrs. Juteau, Poyard, Mlle. Bouvard, Coryphées, Choeur

Ensemble (Calmez cet effroi)
Messrs. Capoul, Juteau, Choeur

Duo et Couplets (Raphaël! Mercedès!)
Mons. Capoul, Mlle. P. Marié

Trio et Couplets de Mercedès (Parlez! Parlez!)
Mlle. P. Marié, Messrs. Capoul, J. Mezières

Choeur, Valse Chantée et Final (Le boute-selle nous appelle)
Messrs. Capoul, Juteau, Choeur

ACT 3

Aubade (Réveillez-vous, belle endormie)
Mons. Capoul

Musique de scène

Terzetto (Bravo, marquis!)
Messrs. Capoul, Duplan, J. Mezières

Sextuor (Éloignons le mari)
Messrs. Capoul, Duplan, J. Mezières, Duplan, Vilano, Mlle. Paola-Marie

Le Lecture, Complainte et Chanson (Il faut à la literature)
Mlles. P. Marié, Armand, Messrs. Juteau, Vilano, Choeur

Couplet final (Oui je parle)
Messrs. Capoul, Duplan, J. Mezières, Juteau, Mlle. P. Marié, Chœur

1880.17

THE LITTLE DETECTIVE, or, Woman's Curiosity

A Revival of the Melodrama in Three Acts, 8 Scenes[72]. Scenery by George Heister, Henry E. Hoyt. Produced by Henry E. Abbey. Opened 29 March 1880 at Abbey's Park Theatre and closed 24 April 1880 after 13 performances in repertory.

CAST: *Florence Langton*, with song: LOTTA (CRABTREE). *Grizzle Guttridge*: LOTTA (CRABTREE). *Mrs. Gamage*, an old nurse: LOTTA (CRABTREE). *Harry Rackett*: LOTTA (CRABTREE). *Barney O'Brien*, with new Irish Medley and Shillalah Jig: LOTTA (CRABTREE). *Gaunse-ash-nee-joseph-e-ne-cli-te-lager-lodovica*, a Dutch girl with a Tyrolean songs: LOTTA (CRABTREE).

Roderick Tracy, a Detective: P. AUG. ANDERSON. *Barry Mallison*, the Robber: CLEMENT BAINBRIDGE. *Sir Gervaise Langton*, father of Florence: W. H. WALLIS. *Ludovic Stuyvesant*, a German Sharper and Swindler: ED MARBLE. *Phoebus Rockaway*, his associate: Fred Percy. *Stephen Hardcliffe*, former accomplice of Barry Mallison: H. B. Bradley. *Captain Gustave*, a Policeman: C. W. Parker. *Dozer, Nab*, watchmen: P. Cooke, G. White. *Madame Ritzdorf*: Mrs. George C. Boniface. *Stella*: Julia Hanchett. *Una*: Lulu Jordan.

Act 1: Evening at Baden-Baden. (Heister.)

Act 2, Scene 1: Garden at Baden-Baden. (Hoyt.) *Scene 2*: Lane near the Mansion. (Hoyt.) *Scene 3*: Boat-house on the Lake. (Hoyt.)

Act 3, Scene 1: Street in London. (Heister.) *Scene 2*: Thieves' Den in London. (Heister.) *Scene 3*: Street in London. (Heister.) *Scene 4*: Ruined Castle.

MUSICAL NUMBERS SPECIALTIES

"You Needn't Tell Your Mother" (Act 1)
Lotta

Irish Medley and Irish Jig (Act 2)
Lotta

Original Potpourri of Popular Melodies (Act 3, Scene 1)
Lotta

German Tyrolean Song (Act 3, Scene 2)
Lotta

[70]Musical numbers not listed in programs.

[71]Musical numbers not listed in programs. List prepared from published French piano vocal score (Félix Mackar, Paris, 1877)

[72]First produced in New York 18 September 1871 at Booth's Theatre for 7 performances.

1880.18

AGES AGO and CHARITY BEGINS AT HOME/ THE SPECTRE KNIGHT

Opera di Camera in a Double Bill of Operettas.[73] Orchestra under the direction of the composers. Scenic artist, John A. Thompson. Costumes, J. H. Eaves. Opera di Camera Management, Mr. and Mrs. German Reed. Opened 31 March 1880 at the Bijou Opera House and closed 22 May 1880 after 60 performances.

AGES AGO; A Musical Legend. An Operetta in One Act. Libretto by William S. Gilbert. Music by Frederic Clay.

CHARACTERS in the Play: *Rosa*, Sir Ebeneezer's niece: MARIE NELLINI. *Mrs. (Maggie) McMotherly*: MARIE BEAUMAN. *Mr. Columbus Hebblethwaite*: WILLIAM COURTNEY. *Sir Ebenezer Tare*, of the firm of Tare and Tret, Alderman and Tallow Chandler: DIGBY V. BELL. *The Steward*: WILLIAM HERBERT.

PICTURES in the Legend: *Lady Maud (de Bohun)*, painted by Leonardo da Vinci, 1472. Died, 1473: MARIE NELLINI. *Sir Aubrey [Cecil] Blount*, painted by Michelangelo, 1560. Died, 1579: WILLIAM COURTNEY. *Lord Carnaby Poppytop*, painted by Sir Godfrey Kneller, 1713. Died, 1720: DIGBY V. BELL. *Dame Cherry Maybud*, painted by Sir Joshua Reynolds, 1785. Died, 1786: MARIE BEAUMAN. *Mr. Brown*, painted by —. Died —: WILLIAM HERBERT.

Scene: Picture Gallery in the Glen-Cockaleekie Castle.

MUSICAL NUMBERS[74]

Recitative (Ha! what was that?)
D. V. Bell, M. Nellini
Aria (Columbus, dear)
M. Nellini, D. V. Bell, M. Beauman, W. Courtney
Couplets and Quintet (It does perplex, annoy and vex)
W. Courtney, M. Nellini,
Quartet (We fly to fields of fancy)
M. Beauman, W. Courtney, D. V. Bell, W. Herbert
Recitative (I breathe! I live!)
M. Nellini
Song (Moments so fleeting)
M. Nellini
Song (So please you, Sir)("Would you know that maiden fair")
M. Nellini
Duet (In pity tell, oh lady mine!)
W. Courtney, M. Nellini
Trio (I stand on my authority)
M. Nellini, W. Courtney, D. V. Bell
Duet (At twenty-three, Lord Carnaby)
D. V. Bell, M. Beauman
Quintet ('Tis done, the spell is broken)
M. Nellini, M. Beauman, W. Courtney, D. V. Bell, W. Herbert
Finale (The subject drop)
All

CHARITY BEGINS AT HOME. A Merry Operetta in One Act. Libretto by Bolton Rowe [B. C. Stephenson]. Music by Alfred Cellier.

CAST: *Susan (Bumpus)*: CARRIE BURTON. *Mrs. Bumpus*: MARIE BEAUMAN. *(Aloysius) Gorringe*: WILLIAM COURTNEY. *Mr. Bumpus*: WILLIAM HERBERT. *Joe (Bumpus)*: DIGBY V. BELL.

MUSICAL NUMBERS[75]

"The Photograph" (Duet)
W. Courtney, C. Burton
"The Pump" (Song)
C. Burton
"The Beadle" (Song and Duet)
W. Herbert, W. Courtney
"The Charity Box"
D. V. Bell
"The Fisherwoman's Song"
M. Beauman
Duet (You lazy, idle vagabond)
W. Herbert, M. Beauman
Duet (Oh! Beadle-dum! Oh! Beadle-dee!)
W. Courtney, W. Herbert
"Multiplication Duet" (Twice one are two)
C. Burton, W. Courtney
"Twinkle, Twinkle" (Quartet)
C. Burton, M. Beauman, D. V. Bell, W. Herbert
Finale (Be seated, pray)
All

THE SPECTRE KNIGHT; or, A Romance of Other Days. A Fanciful Operetta in One Act. Libretto by James Albery. Music by Alfred Cellier. Produced under the direction of J. G. Saville. Scenery by Gill Sherwood and John A. Thompson.

CAST: *The Grand Duke*, banished at the age of 40: WILLIAM HERBERT. *His Lord Chamberlain*, banished at the age of 35: WILLIAM COURTNEY. *His Steward*, banished at the age of 35: Frank Pearson. *Her Grace's First Lady-in-Waiting*, banished at the age of—: MARIE BEAUMAN. *Her Grace's Second Lady-in-Waiting*, banished at the age of—: ANNETTE FAVER. *Viola*, a maiden, banished at the age of 1, from which the ages of the other characters may be guessed—not mentioned: CARRIE BURTON. *Ghost*, The Spectre Knight, an imposter, buried A.D. 1294: DIGBY V. BELL. *Otho*, another Grand Duke, a young one, where they are plentiful, banished at the age of 7: DIGBY V. BELL. *His other Grace's First Page*: Lillie Shandley. *His other Grace's Second Page*: Eugenie Maynard. *His other Grace's Third Page*: Ruby Thornton. *His other Grace's Fourth Page*: Ethel Kyle.

Scene: A Haunted Glen. *Time*: The Educated will perceive; the uneducated will not require to know.

"MUSICAL NUMBERS[76]

"What letters have you brought?" (Recitative)
W. Courtney, W. Herbert
"Your Grace, I am an eligible Count" (Duo)
W. Courtney, W. Herbert
"You may talk" (Quartet)
M. Beauman, A. Faver, W. Courtney, W. Herbert
"Said Cupid to me" (Song)
D. V. Bell
"I am free" (Vocal Waltz)
C. Burton
"Pardon me, madam" (Recitative and Trio)
D. V. Bell, C. Burton, M. Beauman
"The little goldfinch in her nest" (Duet)
C. Burton, D. V. Bell
"You should not be long alone" (Replica of duet)
C. Burton, D. V. Bell
"Fill up and let us drink" (Recitative and Quartet)
C. Burton, M. Beauman, W. Courtney, W. Herbert
"Too whit, too whoo" (Round)
C. Burton, M. Beauman, W. Courtney, W. Herbert
Entrance of the Spectre
"I only mix with Ghosts well-known" (Song of the Spectre)(Song with refrain)
D. V. Bell, W. Herbert, C. Burton, M. Beauman, A. Faver, W. Courtney
"I am here" (Scena)
C. Burton, M. Beauman, A. Faver, W. Courtney, W. Herbert, D. V. Bell, Pages
Banquet Music
"I Love Them All" (I have been taught) (Song)
C. Burton
Finale (He has come to our doing)
A. Faver, M. Beauman, W. Courtney, W. Herbert
"Joy go with the festive glass"
C. Burton, M. Beauman, W. Courtney, W. Herbert

[73]On 17 May 1880 AGES AGO was replaced by THE SPECTRE NIGHT for the last week of the run.

[74]Musical numbers do not appear in programs. List prepared from published libretto and vocal score (Gilbert Before Sullivan, ed. by Jane W. Stedman, University of Chicago Press, 1967). Included in the vocal score are the following which do not appear in the libretto (preceding the first recitative above):

Trio (Good bye, good bye)
M. Nellini, M. Beauman, W. Herbert
Duet (When nature sleeps)
M. Nellini, M. Beauman
Song (Eh! What is that ye say)
M. Beauman

[75]Musical numbers not listed in programs. List prepared from published English piano vocal score (Joseph Williams, London, 1897).

[76]Musical numbers not listed in programs. List prepared from published English piano vocal score (Metzler & Co., London, 1878).

1880.19 EYES AND EARS IN LONDON

A Musical Monologue in Two Acts. (Program devised by Kate Field.) Manager, Thomas C. Lombard. Opened 9 April 1880 at Chickering Hall and closed 24 April 1880 after 4 performances in repertory.

CAST: KATE FIELD. *At the piano*: Frank Gilder.

ACT 1[77]

Rhapsodie, No. 6 (Franz Liszt) (Piano Solo)[78]
F. Gilder
Going up in a Balloon—Arrival in London—Seeing through a fog darkly—Rain.
"O, Lovely Umbrella" (Song)
(K. Field)
(*Music by* George Grossmith, Jr. *Lyrics by* Kate Field.)
Impudent and Facetious Cabmen—Our First Parents—The Zoological Gardens.
"The Zoo"[79] (Song)
(K. Field)
(*Music by* George Grossmith, Jr. *Lyrics by* Kate Field.)
Madame Tussaud's Wax-works.—Wax *versus* Humanity—A Ballad Concert[80]— The Season—The Horse—Conversations at Dinner Parties.
"Did You Ever?" (Song)
(K. Field.)
(*Music by* Aneusto Bendelari. *Lyrics by* Kate Field.)
"Mamma, What Shall I Do?" (Song)
(K. Field)
(*Music by* George Grossmith, Jr. *Lyrics by* Kate Field.)
Going to Receptions—Madame Sotto Voce's Original Ballad:
"The Silent Song"
(K. Field)
(*Composed by* George Grossmith, Jr.)
The Aesthetic Young Lady—A New Reading of Macbeth—Sensations among the upper classes.
"Spanish Muleteer Song"
(K. Field)
(*Music and lyrics by* H. Millard.)
Battle Cry of Freedom (Grand Caprice de Concert)
F. Gilder
(*Music by* Louis Gottschalk.)

ACT 2

English Grievance against Americans—Yankee Twang—The Langauge of Hee-Haws—Speech of a City Swell—Miss Nightingale's Appearance:
"Twickenham Ferry" (Song)
(K. Field)
(*Music and lyrics by* Theo. Marzials.)
Wandering through Whitechapel—Cheap Jack Auction—Going to the Theatre—Pantomime.
"Oh, You Ridiculous Man" (Song)
(K. Field)
(*Music and Lyrics by* P. Shuter.)
Visiting the Opera—Sleeping Beauties.
"Burlesque of Italian Opera"
(K. Field)
(*Music by* George Grossmith, Jr. *Lyrics by* Kate Field.)
Recitative by Prima Donna—Serenade by Tenor—Duet by Prima Donna and Tenor—Death of Prima Donna—Grand Chorus and Finale

[77]For the final performance, Miss Field was joined by the *English Glee Club*: Henrietta Beebe (soprano), Anna Bulkley Hills (contralto), A. D. Woodrufe (tenor), G. E. Aiken (bass), A. H. Pease. In addition to "When the Bee Sucks," they closed Act 1 with "How Sweet the Moonlight" (*Music by* H. Leslie.), opened Act 2 with "Ye Spotted Snakes" (*Music* by R. J. S. Stevens.), and closed the evening with "Hark! the Lark!" (*Music by* Dr. Cooke.).

[78]Replaced for the final performance by:
"Where the Bee Sucks (there lurk I)" (from THE TEMPEST)English Glee Club
(*Music by* Thomas Arne. *Lyrics by* Willaim Shakespeare.)

[79]Replaced for the final performance by:
"Where the Bee Sucks (there lurk I)" (from THE TEMPEST)
English Glee Club
(*Music by* Thomas Arne. *Lyrics by* William Shakespeare.)

[80]Added to the program for the final performance at this spot:
French Laughing Song
(K. Field)

1880.20 BOCCACCIO

An Operette in Three Acts, in German. Libretto by F. Zell and Richard Genée. Music by Franz Von Suppé. Opened 23 April 1880 at the Thalia Theatre and closed 17 May 1880 after 15 performances in repertory.

CAST: *Giovanni Boccaccio*: Frl. MATHILDE COTTRELLY. *Prinz von Palermo*: Herr SCHNELLE. *Fiametta*: Frl. Ahl. *Scalza*: Herr Schmitz. *Beatrice*: Frl. META. *Lambertuccio*: Herr ADOLFI. *Petronella*: Frau HORN. *Lotteringhi*: Herr LUBE. *Isabella*: Frau LUBE. *Gewürzkräner*: Herr Adolfi. *Fassbinder*: Herr Lube. *Leonetto*: Herr Lenoir. *Barbier*: Herr Schmitz.

(*Scene*: The action is set in fourteenth century Florence.)

ACT 1[81]

Introduction (Heut' am Tag' des Patrons von Florenz)
Ausrufer und Streitscene (Neu'ste Novellen aus den besten Quellen)
Ständchen und Duellscene (Holde Schöne, hör' diese Töne)
Lied des Boccaccio (Ich sehe einen jungen mann dort stehn)
Duettino (Die Glokken läuten hell und rein)
Lied (Hab' ich nurdeine Liebe)
Gang aus der Kirche
Duett (Ein armer Blinder flehet um Erbarmen)
Finale (Ehrsame Bürgerder Stadt, o bedenkt)

ACT 2

Serenade (Ein Stern zu sein, wie würd'es mich beglükken)
Fassbinder Lied (Tag-täg-lich zankt mein Weib)
Abgang (Tra-la-la-la)
Brief-Terzett (Wie pocht mein Herz so ungestüm)
Melodram
Couplet (Eine Frau darf wohl bedacht manche)
Cretin Lied (So oft man mich mach Neuem fragt)
Finale II (Benützen wir den Augenblick)

ACT 3

Introduction (Erfrischende Quellen sind seine Novellen)
Abgang (Immer zu undici, dodici, tredici)
Couplet (Um des Fürsten Zorn zu meiden)
Duettino (Mia bella fiorentina disprezzi lamor)
Septett (Ihr Toren, ihr wollt' hassen mich)
Finale III (Ihr Herren und Damen!)

1880.21 JOSHUA WHITCOMB

A Return Engagement of the Comedy Drama in Three Acts[82]. Play by Denman Thompson. Scenery by George Heister. Produced by Denman Thompson. Opened 26 April 1880 at Abbey's Park Theatre and closed 12 June 1880 after 49 performances.

CAST: *Uncle Josh*, an old Jackson Democrat: DENMAN THOMPSON. *Roundy*, a boot black: IGNACIO MARTINETTI. *John Martin*, a lover of horse racing and theatres: Eugene O. Jepson. *Frederick Dolby*, a young Englishman: Walter Gale. *Cy. Prime*, nigh on eighty: George A. Beane. *Bill Johnson*, a loafer: R. Benson. *Reuben*, son of Uncle Josh: FRED W. PETERS. *Mr. Burroughs*, a model policeman: G. Adams. *Mr. Foster*, sheriff of the county: D. Nourse. *Tot*, a crossing sweeper: JULIA WILSON. *Nellie Primrose*, a Boston belle: Isabelle Coe. *Susan Martin*, with a mania for marriage: Virginia Bray. *Mrs. Johnson*, Tot's mother: Edna Weeden. *Aunt Matilda*, Joshua's sister: Mrs. D. Nourse. *Amantha Bartlett*, one of the neighbor's gals: Blanche Vaughn. *Aunt Martha*: Miss E. Rogers.

MUSICAL NUMBERS, SPECIALTIES

"Tot's Lullaby" (Act 1) J. Wilson
(*Lyrics by* Walter Gale.)

[81]Musical numbers not listed in programs. List prepared from published German piano vocal score (Aug. Cranz, Leipzig, Bruxelles, n.d.)

[82]First produced in a one-act form 3 April 1875 at the Eagle Theatre; in its three-act form 2 September 1878 at the Lyceum Theatre for 93 performances. For Synopsis of Scenes and Musical Numbers, see original 1878 production.

1880.22 LE POSTILLION DE LONGJUMEAU

A Revival of the Opéra-comique in Three Acts[83], in French. Libretto by Adolphe de Leuven and Léon Lévy Brunswick. Music by Adolphe Adam. Stage manager, Mons. Bouvard. Musical director, Charles Almeras. Produced by Maurice Grau's French Opera Company. Opened 6 May 1880 at the Academy of Music and closed 8 May 1880 (matinee) after 2 performances in repertory.

CAST: *(Pierre) Chapelou*, a postillion: Mons. VICTOR CAPOUL. *Le Marquis de Corcy*: Mons. DUPLAN. *Biju*, a cart maker: Mons. JOUARD. *Madeleine*, Chapelou's wife: Mlle. LEROUX-BOUVARD. *Mme. de Latour*: Mlle. LEROUX-BOUVARD. *Messsr. de Saint-Phar*, First tenor at the academy: Mons. DUPLAN. *Alcindor*, singer at the academy: Mons. JOUARD. *Rose*, waiting maid: Mlle. A. Bouvard.

1880.23 LA PRINCESSE DE TRÉBIZONDE

A Revival of the Opéra-bouffe in Three Acts[84], in French. Libretto by Charles Nuitter and Étienne Tréfeu. Music by Jacques Offenbach. Stage manager, Mons. Bouvard. Musical director, Charles Almeras. Produced by Maurice Grau's French Opera Company. Opened 7 May 1880 at the Academy of Music and closed 8 May 1880 after 2 performances in repertory.

CAST: *Régina*: Mlle. PAOLA MARIÉ. *Prince Raphaël*: Mlle. ANGÈLE. *Prince Casimir*: Mons. POYARD. *Cabriolo*: Mons. JOUARD. *Trémolini*: Mons. JUTEAU. *Sparadrap*: Mons. VILANO. *La Directeur de la Loterie*: Mons. Terrancle. *Zanetta*: Mlle. GRÉGOIRE. *Paola*: Mlle. Delorme. *Riccardi*: Mlle Armand. *Flaminio*: Mlle. Bouvard. *Brocoli*: Mlle. Duparc. *Francesca*: Mlle. Vandamme. *Finochini*: Mlle. Berthe. *Pages, Chasseurs, Saltimbanques, Paysannes, Paysans, etc.*

1880.24 ILL TREATED IL TROVATORE!, or, The Mother, The Maiden and The Musicianer

An Original Burlesque, founded on the famous but confusing opera of that name, in Two Acts, 6 Scenes[85]. (Play by H. J. Byron.) Produced by the Colville Opera Burlesque Company. (Samuel Colville, Proprietor). Opened 10 May 1880 at the Grand Opera House and closed 15 May 1880 after 8 performances.

CAST: *Manrico*, a wandering minstrel, a real good fellow, though a true-bad-doer: EME ROSEAU. *Count di Luna*: ROLAND REED. *Fernando*, his creature: KATE EVERLEGH. *First Guard*: H. Amberg. *Second Guard*: Horace Frail. *Third Guard*: Mr. Adair. *Fourth Guard*: L. DeSmith. *Kinchen*, a Gypsy thief, lent for the occasion from the "Flowers of the Forest": ED CHAPMAN. *Cospetto*, and dizzy and dissipated Romaney: A. W. MAFLIN. *Ruiz*, not half a bad sort of fella, don't you know: ADA LEE. *Leonora*, a ward of DiLuna's, evidently awarded to Manrico: ELLA CHAPMAN. *Azucena*, an elderly Gypsy party, with a great deal on her mind: R. E. GRAHAM. (*Specialty*, German Dialect: CHARLES A. GARDNER.)

Schoolgirls at the Finishing Academy of Madame Catalina Grimalkina: *Mira Antoinetta Wilkins*: CARRIE McHENRY. *Paquita Mercedes Aldabella*: ANNIE DEACON. *Isabella*: Bessie Temple. *Frasquita*: Louisa Loring. *Briglia*: Theresa Lamborn. *Parthia*: Elsie Dean. *Priscilla*: Emma Carson. *Dorcas*: Genie Jones. *Annetta Lisa*: Alice Wright. *Madame Catalina Grimalkina*, Governess: Mrs. WILLIAM FORRESTER. *Inez*, Leonora's confidential and very tired tire woman: ROSE LEIGHTON. *Gypsies, Guards and Attendants.*

Act 1, Scene 1: Wing and Gardens of Chateau "DiLuna." *Scene 2*: Ruins at Biscay.

Act 2, Scene 1: The Exterior of a Finishing Academy. *Scene 2*: The Camp. *Scene 3*: Landscape. *Scene 4*: A Prison.

ACT 1
Scene 1
"Here at our post" (Opening Chorus)
"The late Count had a Brace of Sons" (Song)
K. Everleigh
"Gaily the Troubadour" (Song)
Ella Chapman
"Oh my Heart with Love is beating" (Duet)
Ella Chapman, R. Leighton
Arrival of the handsome Troubadour, Manrico, to serenade his Lady Fayre
Serenade
E. Roseau
The Count di Luna, in his capacity of guardian to Leonora, watches and waits for the amorous Troubadour
"Il Balen" (Song)
R. Reed
In the darkness of night, Leonora mistakes DiLuna for her lover, the Troubadour, and felin(e)ly expresses her pleasure in a CATchy duet
"Cats" (Duet)
R. Reed, Ella Chapman
"Wait Till I Get on My Robes" (Quartette)
Scene 2
"Anvil" (Chorus)
Company
"Stride La Vampa" (Scena)
R. E. Graham
Song
R. E. Graham
"Excelsior" (Finale)
E. Roseau, Company

ACT 2
Scene 1
"Impecuniosity" (Song)
Schoolgirls
A pedantic schoolmistress and her pretty pupils
"It's nice to be somebody's love" (Song)
Ella Chapman, Schoolgirls
The Count comes to school, and unexpectedly en*count*ers Manrico, who with the aid of the schoolgirls and *count*less umbrellas, nearly sends him to his last ac*count*.
"Beware my hate" (Concerted Piece)
E. Roseau, R. Reed, etc.
"The Whippoorwill" (Song)
E. Roseau
"Vivre Contende" (Concerted Piece)
E. Roseau, R. Reed, Chorus
Scene 2
Marching Song and Chorus
C. A. Gardner, Full Chorus
"Tramp o'er Moss and Fen" (Song and Chorus)
Scene 3
Song
C. A. Gardner
Hunting Song and ChorusK. Everleigh, Guards
Scene 4
"Ah, che la morte" (Solo)
E. Roseau
"Marche du Diable" (Concerted Piece)
Grand Finale
Company

1880.25 MINNIE PALMER'S BOARDING SCHOOL

A Comedy in One Act. Play by Mr. Clifford. Music and lyrics by William J. Scanlan. Incidental music composed and arranged by Christian Krause. Stage manager, George C. Davenport. Decorator, D. Grover Stockley. Leader of orchestra, Christian Krause. Produced by E. H. Gouge. Opened 14 May 1880 at the San Francisco Opera House and closed 31 May 1880 after 18 performances.

CAST: *Jessie Fairlove*, a Spoiled Child: MINNIE PALMER. *Samantha Smith*, Assistant Teacher at Alpha Academy, a maiden lady of advanced years, in search for a husband, with an eye to the profession: Emma Jones. *Mrs. Fairlove*, Jessie's Mamma, a young widow, President of S.F.P.O.C.T.C.: W. S. Harkins. *Jennie*, who thinks herself somebody, but belongs to nobody: Emma Libby. *David Doodle*, a Servant and Searcher after knowledge: WILLIAM J. SCANLAN. *Professor Jeremiah Gimcrack*, D.D.M.D.,

---

[83]First produced in New York in French 30 March 1840 at the Park Theatre.

[84]First produced in New York in English 11 September 1871 at Wallack's Theatre; in French 10 September 1874 at the Lyceum Theatre. For Synopsis of Scenes and Musical Numbers, see 1874 production.

[85]First produced in New York 8 February 1864 at the Olympic Theatre. Suggested by IL TROVATORE, Music by Giuseppe Verdi

M.A., Principal of Alpha Academy, the instructor and target of the shooting ideas of youth in general, and Jessie Fairlove in particular, a bachelor of arts, but not an artful bachelor: John E. Ince. *Harry Hamilton*, in love with Jessie, a young gentleman of means, by no means a mean young gentleman: GEORGE C. DAVENPORT. *Sylvester Sylvanus Squab*: GEORGE C. DAVENPORT. *Captain Bumshell*, a man of firearms: GEORGE C. DAVENPORT. *Simon Bumshell*, with recitation original with himself: GEORGE C. DAVENPORT. *Alphian Graduates, young shooting ideas, beginners and enders in knowledge*: Messrs. Supers, Misses Numeraries.

MUSICAL NUMBERS[86]

"Der Wasserfall"
"Don't You Tickle Me"
"True Love" (Duet)
Medley (*Music and Lyrics by* William J. Scanlan.)
M. Palmer
"She Taught Me to Play the Piano"
"Please Take My Arm"
"Mary, Get the Supper"
"Boarding School"
"Clarence Levere"
"Vivi Garibaldi"
"I Love Music"
"McDonnell's Ould Tin Roof"

1880.26 BOCCACCIO

An Operette in Three Acts[87]. Original Viennese libretto by F. Zell and Richard Genée. Music by Franz Von Suppé. Stage manager, Vincent Hogan. Musical director, Gustave A. Kerker. Produced by H. B. Mahn's Comic Opera Company. Opened 17 May 1880 at the Union Square Theatre and closed 12 June 1880 after 28 performances.

CAST: *(Giovanni) Boccaccio*, a Novelist and Poet: JEANNIE WINSTON. *Fiametta*, in love with him: ALICE HOSMER. *Pietro*, Prince of Palermo: W. A. MORGAN. *Scalza*, a Barber: VINCENT HOGAN. *Beatrice*, his daughter: HATTIE RICHARDSON. *Lambertuccio*, a Grocer: A. H. BELL. *Peronella*, his maiden sister: FANNIE PRESTIGE. *Lotteringhi*, a Cooper: FRED DIXON. *Isabella*, his wife: MARIE SOMERVILLE. *The Unknown*: W. A. Hudson. *Leonetto*, a friend to Boccaccio: BERTHA FOY.

Students (7): *Tofano*: Annie Winner. *Chichibio*: Clara Douglass. *Guido*: Mary Winner. *Rinieri*: Anna Callaway. *Cisti*: Bessie Jackson. *Federico*: Henrietta May. *Giotto*: May Clark.

Major Domo to the Duke: Mills Hall. *Donna Sancofiore*: Miss Vance. *Eliza, Marietta*, her daughters: Grace Wynne, Grace Clark. *Donna Nona Pulci*: Agnes Wynne. *Her Children (3)*: *Augustina*: Miss Vincent. *Elena*: Miss Prestige. *Angelica*: Miss Conroy. *Book Peddler*: Mills Hall.

Coopers (6): *Alberto*: H. Depew. *Gerbino*: Mr. Bernard. *Gindotto*: Mr. Barnes. *Ricciardo*: M. F. Manning. *Feodora*: Mr. Swicardi. *Nostogio*: H. Thomas. *Fresco*: H. Dale. *Checco*: F. Condit. *Beggars (3)*: *Giacometto*: Mr. Stein. *Tita Nana*: H. Newman. *Anselmo*: J. Fischer. *Fillappa*: May Booth. *Oretta*: Miss Beringer. *Viollanta*: Miss Buck. *People, Monks, Nuns, Soldiers, Children, etc.*

Act 1: Church of Santa Maria Novella, and Square in Florence. Gala Day.

Act 2: View of Florence from Casina Valley. House of Lambertucchio and Lotteringhi.

Act 3: Gardens and Palace of the Duke of Tuscany.

ACT 1[88]

Introduction (Rich and poor, old and young)
F. Condit, Beggars
Chorus (Golden sunlight, balmy air)
B. Foy, Beggars
Students' Chorus (Beautiful roses, this view discloses)
Students
Song (The latest novels of the best authors)
[Canvasser], Chorus
Chorus (Long live Boccaccio)
Chorus
Serenade (Lovely charmer, hear these sounds)
V. Hogan
Solo (Heavens, what a task!)
H. Richardson
Song/Quartet (They are coming—they are fighting)
V. Hogan, B. Foy, J. Winston, H. Richardson
Chorus (Though swords are clashing and whirling)
V. Hogan, Chorus
Song with Chorus (I see a gay young fellow standing nigh)
J. Winston, B. Foy, Students
Duettino (Listen to the bells' sweet chime)
A. Hosmer, F. Prestige
Romanza (If I have but affection)
A. Hosmer
Solo (I have had a great ambition since I reached a man's condition)
W. A. Morgan
Reprise (Listen to the bells' sweet chime)
Chorus
Duetto (A poor blind man implores your aid)
J. Winston, A. Hosmer
Finale (Worthy citizens of the town, remember well)
All

ACT 2

Introduction (The girl of my heart's a treasure)
B. Foy, Students
Serenade (To be a star would be my highest bliss)
J. Winston, W. A. Morgan, B. Foy
Cooper's Song (My wife has a scolding tongue)
F. Dixon
Terzetto (My heart beats quite tempestuously)
A. Hosmer M. Somerville, F. Prestige
Solo (Young maidens must beware)
M. Somerville
Cretin Song (When they ask me for the news)
J. Winston
Ensemble (Let us improve the moment dear)
J. Winston, A. Hosmer, A. H. Bell
Ensemble (Oh, I am happy, oh!)
W. A. Morgan, F. Dixon, A. H. Bell, A. Hosmer, M. Somerville, J. Winston
Entrance of the Unknown (Hear me! Leave off! 'Tis not me!)
W. A. Hudson, F. Dixon, V. Hogan, A. Hosmer, M. Somerville, H. Richardson, F. Prestige, Chorus
Waltz and Finale (Blissful tidings, reassuring)
A. Hosmer, All

ACT 3

Opening Chorus (Refreshing fountains)
Chorus
Brindisi (See the goblet flash and sparkle!)
W. A. Morgan, Chorus
Duettino (Mia bella fiorentina)
J. Winston, A. Hosmer
Sextetto (Ye foolish men, your grudge and spite)
J. Winston, F. Dixon, A. H. Bell, V. Hogan, H. Richardson, M. Somerville
Finale (Wit, truth and humor)
J. Winston, All

1880.27 LA VIE PARISIENNE

A Revival of the Opéra-bouffe in Four Acts[89], in French. Libretto by Henri Meilhac and Ludovic Halévy. Music by Jacques Offenbach. Stage manager, Mons. Bouvard. Musical director, Charles Almeras. Produced by Maurice Grau's French Opera Company. Opened 17 May 1880 at the Academy of Music and closed 18 May 1880 after 2 performances in repertory.

CAST: *Le Baron*: Mons. DUPLAN. *Un Bresilien*: Mons. JUTEAU. *Frix*: Mons. JUTEAU. *Prosper*: Mons. JUTEAU. *Bobinet*: Mons. J. Mezières. *Raoul*: Mons. POYARD.

---

[86]Not in performance order. All songs, apart from "Der Wasserfall," "Don't You Tickle Me," "True Love" and Minnie Palmer's Medley composed by William J. Scanlan and sung by him. Additional published musical numbers not in programs ("Jessie, The Belle of the School," "Song of the Boarding School," "Torment of the Boarding School," and "True Love") were credited to Art Henshaw (music) and George Jackson (lyrics).

[87]English language premiere. Previously produced in New York in the original German, 23 April 1880 at the Thalia. See previous listing for detail.

[88]Musical numbers not listed in programs. List prepared from published libretto by H. B. Mahn's Comic Opera Co. "performed for the first time in the English language at the Chestnut Street Theatre, Philadelphia, 5 April 1880." English adaptation uncredited.

[89]First produced in New York in French 29 March 1869 at the Theatre Françcais for 11 performances. For Synopsis of Scenes and Musical Numbers, see original 1869 production.

Alfred: Mons. VILANO. *Urbain*: Mons. VILANO. *Joseph*: Mons. Gerard. *Alphonse*: Mons. Curlier. *Gontran*: Mons. Terbel .*Un Employé*: MONS. Leclerc. *Gabrielle*: Mlle. PAOLA MARIÉ. *Métella*: Mlle. RAPHAEL. *Pauline*: Mlle. ANGÈLE. *La Baronne*: Mlle. GRÉGOIRE. *Léonie*: Mlle. Armand. *Louise*: Mlle. Bouvard. *Clara*: Mlle. Berthe. *Caroline*: Mlle. Duparc. *Charlotte*: Mlle. Van Damme. *Albertine*: Mlle. Estéve.

1880.28

LE POMME D'API/ LES CHEVALIERS DU PINCE-NEZ

A Double Bill of an Opérette and an Comédie-Vaudeville, in French. Stage manager, Mons. Bouvard. Musical director, Charles Almeras. Produced by Maurice Grau's French Opera Company. Opened 20 May 1880 at the Academy of Music for 1 performance.

CAST: Mlles. PAOLA MARIÉ, GRÉGOIRE, ANGÈLE, RAPHAEL. Messrs. JOUARD, J. MEZIÈRES, DUPLAN, JUTEAU, POYARD, VILANO.

LE POMME D'API. An Opérette in One Act. Libretto by Ludovic Halévy and William Busnach. Music by Jacques Offenbach.

CAST: *Catherine*, le pomme d'api: Mlle. GRÉGOIRE. *Gustave*, Nephew to Rabastens: Mlle. RAPHAEL. *Amilcar Rabastens*: Mons. DUPLAN.

Scene: Paris, 1873.

MUSICAL NUMBERS[90]

Couplets (L'employé m'a dit: de quel âge)
Mons. Duplan
Romance (Mon oncle ne vous fâchez pas)
Mlle. Raphael
Couplets (Bonjour monsieur je suis la bonne)
Mlle. Grégoire
Trio (Va donc, chercher le gril!)
Mlles. Raphael, Grégoire, Mons. Duplan
Duo (C'est un dimanche, un matin)
Mlle. Grégoire, Mlle. Raphael
Trio (À table! À table!)
Mlles. Raphael, Grégoire, Mons. Duplan
Chanson (Versez, versez)
Mlle. Raphael
Rondeau (J'en prendrai un, deux, trois)
Mlle. Grégoire
Romance (Consultez votre coeur)
Mlle. Raphael
Finale (J'en prendrai un, deux, trois)
Mlles. Raphael, Grégoire, Mons. Duplan

LES CHEVALIERS DU PINCE-NEZ. A comédie-vaudeville in Two Acts (by P Deslandes, Eugene Grangé and Lambert Thiboust).

CAST: *Chabannais*: Mons. J. Mezières. *Champrose*: Mons. POYARD. *Bec de Lievre*: Mons. DUPLAN. *Varoquet*: Mons. VILANO. *Beaucanard*: Mons. Henriot. *St. Gobin*: Mons. Carlier. *Fauvette*: Mlle. ANGÈLE. *Paul Joubert*: Mlle. Grégoire. *Mme. Aurelie Gaillard*: Mlle. Delorme. *Cecile*: Mlle. Armand. *Zoe*: Mlle. Berthe. *Mimi*: Mlle. Duparc. *Garçon de Restaurant*: Mlle. Leclerc.

1880.28

LA CAMARGO

An Opéra-comique in Three Acts, in French. Libretto by Albert Vanloo and Eugène Leterrier. Music by Charles Lecocq. Stage manager, Mons. Bouvard. Musical director, Charles Almeras. Produced by Maurice Grau's French Opera Company. Opened 21 May 1880 at the Academy of Music and closed 22 May 1880 after 3 performances in repertory.

CAST: *La Camargo*: Mlle. PAOLA MARIÉ. *Juana de Rio-Negro*: Mlle. ANGÈLE. *Colombe*: Mlle. GRÉGOIRE. *Écureuil*: Mlle. RAPHAEL. *Fil-en-Quatre*: Mlle. Vandamme. *Francine*: Mlle. Armand. *Flora*: Mlle. Berthe. *An Organ Grinder*: Mlle. Bazin. *A Macaroon Seller*: Mlle. Bazin. *Cydalise*: Mlle. A. Bouvard. *A Flower Girl*: Mlle. —. *Rosita*: Mlle. Esteve. *Clorinde*: Mlle. Estradere. *Ramponneau*: Mons. Terbel. *A Magician*: Mons. Marchand. *A Crier*: Mons. Marchand. *Louis Mandrin* (Valjoly): Mons. JOUARD. *Marquis de Pontcalé*: Mons. J. MEZIÈRES. *Saturnin*: Mons. JUTEAU. *The Philosopher*: Mons. DUPLAN. *Tournevis*: Mons. POYARD. *Peruchot*: Mons. VILANO. *Rossignol*: Mons. Terrancle. *Taquet*: Mons. DUPUIS. *Des Vieilles-Haudriettes*: Mons. Leclerc. *De la Glaciere*: Mons. F. Maurier. *Des Lions-Saint-Paul*: Mons. Gavant. *De la Huchette*: Mons. P. Maurier. *De la Grange Batelière*: Mons. Borel. *A Captain*: Mons. Girard. *A Tipstaff*: Mons. —. *Opera Dancers and Danseuses, Brigands, Soldiers, Country Gentlemen and Country Women, Ramponneau's Servants.*

Act 1: The Greenroom of the Opera. Eighteenth century.

Act 2: The Robbers' Castle.

Act 3: The Cabaret.

ACT 1[91]

Choeur (Que les Ris et les Jeux)
Choeur des Abonnés (à nos petites chattes)
Couplets (Mes aïeux, j'en ai la mémoire)
Messrs. Borel, Leclerc, Gavant, Maurier, Choeur
Chanson (Partout on me fête)
Mlle. P. Marié, Choeur
Couplets (Savez-vous auprès des femmes)
Mons. J. Mezières
Madrigal (Je comprendrais fort pen)
Mons. Jouard
Rêve (Je dormais . . . tout dans le nature)
Mlle. Angèle, Choeur
Rondeau (Si vous savez, mes chers amis)
Mlle. P. Marié
Chanson (Je vous ai dit mon ignorance)
Mons. Juteau
Quintette (L'écureuil!)
Mlles. Vandamme, Raphael, Mons. Poyard, Choeur
Finale (Oh! ciel! oh! ciel!)
Mlle. P. Marié, Mons. J. Mezières, Tous
Reprise de l'ensemble (Ah! c'est trop d'audace!)

ACT 2

Choeur (Ah! qu'il est doux pour des voleurs)
Messrs. Poyard, Terrancle, Duplan, Choeur
Ronde (Ils sont trente ou quarante)
Mlles. Raphael, Vandamme, Choeur
Rondeau (Ah! soyez distingués)
Mons. Jouard
Choeur des Prisonnières (Les yeux tout de larmes noyés)
Chanson (Presque toujours une cousine)
Mlle. Grégoire
Chanson (Laissez-moi, monsieur le voleur)
Mlle. P. Marié
Reprise du refrain du rondeauChoeur
Ballet-Pastorale (Voici d'abord une bergère)
Mlle. P. Marié
Duo (Ce serait une vie heureuse)
Mlle. P. Marié, Mons. Jouard, Choeur
Couplets (Certes, lorsque l'on n'aime pas)
Mlle. P. Marié, Mons. Jouard, Choeur
Finale/Choeur des Brigands (Ah! la bonne fortune!)
Mlles. Vandamme, Grégoire, P. Marié, Messrs. Vilano, Jouard, Choeur
Ensemble (Voyez ce regard fatidique)
Messrs. Jouard, J. Mezières, Mlle. Angèle, Choeur

ACT 3

Choeur (Chez Ramponneau)
Ariette (Jusqu'à là cour)
Mlle. Vandamme
Chanson (Le roi s'est dit: puis-je mourir)
Mlle. P. Marié, Mons. J. Mezières, Choeur
Ensemble (La police, la justice)
Messrs. Jouard, J. Mezières, Choeur
Duo (Étais-je bête)
Mons. Juteau, Mlle. Grégoire
Quintette (A la tienne, Etienne!)
Messrs. Poyard, Terbel, Terrancle, Duplan, Mlle. Vandamme
Duetto de Javotte et Margotte
Mlles. P. Marié, Angèle
Chanson de la Marmotte en vie
Mlle. P. Marié, Tous
Couplet Final (J' dois quéqu' chose à Javotte)
Mlle. P. Marié, Tous

---

[90]Musical numbers not listed in programs. List prepared from published French piano vocal score (Choudens, Paris, 1873).

[91]Musical numbers not listed in program. List prepared from French/English libretto published for Maurice Grau's Opera Company (New York, 1880).

1880–1881 SEASON

Harrigan and Hart (Undated)
Museum of the City of New York, Gift of William J. Hanley, 34.404.15

1880–1881 SEASON

1880.30

TRIFLES

The Jolly Mariners in a Musical Burletta in Two Acts. (Produced by Angie Schott). Opened 3 June 1880 at Haverly's 14th Street Theatre and closed 12 June 1880 after (12) performances.[1]

CAST: Miss Massie Gregson: ANGIE SCHOTT. Mrs. DeLorme: Jessie Greville. Mr. Brown De Brown: Sydney Smith. Captain Fairmount: Andrew Waldron. McGorlin Norton: Charles Wilson. Monkey: Master A. James.

Scene: Near a hotel at the seashore.

1880.31

THE SEA CADET or, The Very Merry Mariner

A Comic Opera in Three Acts[2]. Libretto by Sydney Rosenfeld. (Adapted from German operette "Der Seekadett," libretto by F. Zell, adapted fom 'Le Capitaine Charlotte' by Jean-François Bayard and Philippe Dumanoir.) Music by Richard Genée. Musical director, Giuseppe Operti. Produced by Edward E. Rice and Jacob Nunnemacher. Opened 7 June 1880 at the Fifth Avenue Theatre and closed 12 June 1880 after 7 performances.

CAST: Fanchette, the Soubrette, afterwards the Merry Mariner: BLANCHE CHAPMAN. Marie, Queen of Portugal: Henrietta Sennach. Donna Antonia, the Queen's Confidante: Marion Bernard. Dom Lamberto, Governor of the Province, and secretly married to the Queen: Eugene Clarke. Dom Januario (de Sonza-Silva e Pernambuco), the richest and handsomest of five brothers: HERBERT R. Archer. Dom Domingos (Boros de Barros), the jealous, near-sighted master of ceremonies: Matthew Holmes. Mungo, the Expressive Slave: Arthur Van Houten. Captain Norberto: W. L. Van Dorn. Brebantio: Emily Lascelles. Julio: Fanny Miller. Francesco, Jacquino, Officers: Edward Burton, W. H. Newborough. Roderigos, Servant: Clinton Stevens.

Pupils of the Naval Academy: *Diego*: Rose Regenti. *Sebastino*: Clotilda Operti. *Giovamo*: Emma Santley. *Paulo*: Florence Burton. *Enricho*: Maud Waldemere. *Carlo*: Gracie Sherwood. *Iago*: Lottie Derretta. *Antonio*: Blanche Andorci. *Claudio*: Madeline Andorci. *Cassio*: Louisa Maurel.

Maids of Honor to the Queen: *Donna Carlina*: Fannie Howe. *Donna Louisa*: Clara Howe.

1880.32

OUR GOBLINS, or, Fun on the Rhine in Germany

A Musical Extravaganza in Two Acts. Play by William Gill. Music arranged and partly composed by George Loesch. Produced by William C. Mitchell's Pleasure Party. Opened 14 June 1880 at Haverly's 14th Street Theatre and closed 10 July 1880 after 32 performances[3].

CAST IN THE PLEASURE PARTY: *Benjamin Franklin Cobb* of Chicago: WILLIAM GILL. *Octavius Longfellow Warbler* of Boston: AUGUSTUS J. BRUNO. *Alfred Comstock Silvermine* of Leadville: FRANCIS WILSON. *Mrs. B. F. Cobb*, Cobb's (much) better half: ELEANOR DEERING. *Miss Tillie St. Aubyn*, travelling with the Cobb Family: AMY GORDON.

CAST: in the Nightmare: *Ludovico*, a Returned Wanderer; unwillingly precipitated into a sea of gore, by a gentleman strongly resembling B. F. Cobb: WILLIAM GILL. *Baron Adolph von Schwartztruden*, a villainous Peer, with whom murder was a pastime and robbery a mere bagatelle, by a gentleman strongly resembling A. C. Silvermine: FRANCIS WILSON. *Franz*, a Minstrel of the Period. Melodious yet moody. Love sick yet loony, by a gentleman strongly resembling O. L. Warbler: AUGUSTUS J. BRUNO. *Countess Agatha von Smithers*, a Wicked Lady, a mixture of Lady Macbeth, Bartley Campbell's Galley Slave, Mary Sanderson, and a dose of Vinegar Bitters. By a lady strongly resembling Mrs. B. F. Cobb: ELEANOR DEERING. *Wilhelmina*, a persecuted maiden, Modestly mild, and mellifluously given to melodiously meandering, by a lady strongly resembling Tillie St. Aubyn: AMY GORDON.

Act 1: A Ruined Castle on the right-hand bank of the Rhine—as you ascend the river.

Act 2: As before, but renovated.

ACT 1
- "Dollar of Our Daddies!" (Trio)
  - A. Gordon, F. Wilson, A. J. Bruno
- "Satchel and Umbrella Club"
  - Pleasure Party
- "The Twilight Coterie" (Chorus and Dance)
  - Pleasure Party
- French Ballad
  - A. J. Bruno
- "Frightened Chorus"
  - Pleasure Party
- "Carnival de Venise" (Florid Outburst)
  - A. Gordon
- New and original medley, comprising selections from THE CHIMES OF NORMANDY, H.M.S. PINAFORE, Dave Braham, Negro Concertism, Modern Hymnscores, and Frog Opera
  - Pleasure Party
- "Music in the Air" (Finale)
  - Invisible Chorus

ACT 2
- Love Ballad
  - A. Gordon (Wilhelmina)
- "Spare the Stranger" (Trio)
  - A. Gordon (Wilhelmina), W. Gill, F. Wilson (Silvermine)
- Duet and Dance
  - F. Wilson (Silvermine), W. Gill (Ludovico)
- Double Song (of Revenge) and Dance (of Fiendish Malignity)
  - F. Wilson (Silvermine), A. J. Bruno (Warbler)
- "The Enchanted Guitar" (Duet)
  - A. Gordon (Wilhelmina), W. Gill (Ludovico)
- Concerted Piece by the Happy Family
- "Another Wide River to Cross"
  - E. Deering (Countess), Chorus
- "Farewell, Gents" (Quartette)
  - E. Deering (Countess), W. Gill (Ludovico), A. C. Silvermine (Baron), A. J. Bruno (Franz)
- "Laughing Chorus" (Grand Finale)
  - Pleasure Party

1880.33

RAINBOW REVELS

A Medley of Mirth, Music, Mischief and Mimicry (a Revue) in Two Acts. Written expressly for the Stewarts. Presented by the Stewarts (Richard, Nellie, Maggie, Docy). Opened 26 July 1880 at Haverly's 14th Street Theatre and closed 4 August 1880 after 12 performances.[4]

CAST: *Calebs Bushkin*, Esq. of Liberty Hall, Victoria; a retired actor Ditto Ditto disguised in —: RICHARD STEWART. *Toby Tottlepot*, a deaf gardener: RICHARD STEWART. *Mansieur Alphonse Napoleon Robespierre Patapon*, a Son of La Belle France: RICHARD STEWART. *Herr Hans von Schloggenbochs*, a German Huntsman: RICHARD STEWART. *Barney O'Hoolagan*, a swate persuadin' rogue: RICHARD STEWART. *Miss Amy Buskin*: DOCY STEWART. *Madame Struttini Vocibella*, Star Tragedienne and Prima Donna: DOCY STEWART. *Sally Moppet*, a lump of Yorkshire pudding: DOCY STEWART. *Norah Murphy*, a jewel from the Emerald Isle: DOCY STEWART. *Princess Stella*, a lady of many loves: DOCY STEWART. *Miss Beatrix Buskin*: MAGGIE STEWART. *Sophonisba Sereleaf*, a guisher of 40: MAGGIE STEWART. *Flirtina Fiyaway*, a dasher of 20: MAGGIE STEWART. *Jessie Mactavish*, Scotch (this'll do): MAGGIE STEWART. *Prince Powderpuff*, a Terpsichorean Hero of Extravaganza: MAGGIE STEWART. *Miss Constance Buskin*: NELLIE STEWART. *Billy Tops*, a pretty page: NELLIE STEWART. *Tasma Darlington*, an Australian Belle: NELLIE STEWART. *The Hon. Percy Fitz Daddleton*, the latest thing (out of a bandbox): NELLIE STEWART. *Lotta Schmidt*, from der Vaterland (mit ein Lied): NELLIE STEWART. *Prince Pettipet*, another Terpsichorean Hero, and Powderpuff's Rival: NELLIE STEWART.

ACT 1
- Operatic Quartette from LUCIA DI LAMMERMOOR
  - Company (C. Buskin,Nieces)
  - (*Music by* Gaetano Donizetti.)

[1]No program available. Details from reviews.

[2]Previously produced in the original German as DER SEECADET 27 October 1879 at the Thalia Theatre. DER SEECADET also formed the basis that same season for Augustin Daly's English language adaptation as THE ROYAL MIDDY.

[3]No credits for scenery, costumes of musical director. Re-opened in a reconstructed three-act version 28 March 1881 at the 14th Street Theatre for an additional 16 performances. See entry later in this season.

[4]The remainder of the week's engagement 5-7 August 1880 consisted of a varied program by the Stewarts (Australian artists in their American debut), Up the River! (an operetta), Act 2 of Rainbow Revels, an Operatic selection, and If! or, an Old Gem Reset (a Burlesque).

Imitations of Celebrated Actors: Charles Kean, Joseph Jefferson, John Drew, Henry Irving
R. Stewart
Comic English Medley Duet
N. Stewart, M. Stewart (Billy, Miss Sereleaf)
Operatic Scena "Ernani Involami" (from ERNANI)
D. Stewart (Mme. Vocibella)
(*Music by* Giuseppi Verdi.)
"See How It Sparkles" (Song from GIROFLÉ-GIROFLA)
N. Stewart (Tasma Darlington)
(*Music by* Charles Lecocq.)
Yorkshire Song
D. Stewart (Sally Moppet)
Grand Operatic Quartette[5]
(Entire Company)

ACT 2
A Dear Little Visitor from Germany, mit Song and Clog Dance
N. Stewart (Lotta Schmidt)
Opéra-Bouffe Duet
"Caller Herring" (Ballad)
M. Stewart (Jessie McTavish)
The Beggar's Opera. History Repeats Itself. Look at that Now!
Grand Irish Medley Duet
R. Stewart, D. Stewart (Barney O'Hoolagan, Norah Murphy)
Guitar Song
N. Stewart
"When the Clock Is Striking Eight" (Terpsichorean Duet)
M. Stewart, N. Stewart
Denouement and Grand Terpsichorean Finale to the Rainbow Revels

1880.34 THE GRIM GOBLIN

A Grand Pantomimic Burlesque Extravaganza in Two Acts. Play by George Conquest and H. Spry[6]. Music arranged by Oscar Barrett. Stage director, W. R. Floyd. Scenery by Joseph Clare. Costumes by George Flannery. Mechanical appliances by F. Dorrington. Musical conductor, Herman Brode. Produced by the George Conquest Pantomime and Burlesque Company. Opened 5 August 1880 at Wallack's Theatre and closed 11 September 1880 after 40 performances[7].

CAST: (*Gigantic Bat, Gnarled Oak, Monster Spider-Crab, a Dwarf, a Demon Head and a Sprite*: GEORGE CONQUEST.[8]) *Hic-Hac-Hoc*, the Grim Goblin: GEORGE CONQUEST, JR. *Prince Pigmy*, the Dwarf: GEORGE CONQUEST, JR. *Nix*, the Demon Head: GEORGE CONQUEST, JR. *Rokoko*, the Rock Fiend: GEORGE CONQUEST, JR. *The Vampire Bat*: GEORGE CONQUEST, JR. *Boohbeigh*, the 1,000,000th King of Noodledum: M. W. FISKE. *The Widow Grizzlegrief*: HARRY ALLEN. *Hopeful, Gobble, Guzzle*, the Widow's only Sons: MAUDE STAFFORD, A. W. MAFLIN, ED CHAPMAN. *Tallbones*, a gentleman of high standing: W. H. Manley. *Waspino*, a swell demon: Lillian Lancaster. *Fairy Honeydew*, Queen of all the Bees: Mlle. ETHERIA. *Princess Melodia*: LAURA CONQUEST. *Shakeigh Shank*, Lord Chamberlain: R. M. NICHOLS. *Body Guard of the Queen Bee (4)*: *Venomio*: H. Ricketts. *Poisano*: G. Ricketts. *Agonus*: W. Elliott. *Stingono*: E. Havens. *Pages attached to King Boobbeigh's Court (6)*: *Beppo*: Elsie Deane. *Peppo*: Bessie Temple. *Leppo*: Alice Wright. *Zeppo*: Louise Loring. *Sancho*: Susie Parker. *Pedro*: Sophie Hummel.

Other Pages: Misses L. Pierson, Emily Herbert, A. Caldwell, F. Caldwell, L. Carrington, B. Howard, C. Bowles, M. Stirling, A. Ruble, L. Ruble, M. Deering, Annie Dayton. *Lords and Guards*: Messrs. H. Amberg, L. Desmith, J. Hobbs, V. Hawley, H. Fraser, J. C. Taylor, H. Randall, J. C. Cooper, W. Montrose, F. C. Cooper, J. B. McDonald, J. H. Cann, K. E. Rosene, P. Trolyum. *Courtiers, Attendants, Demons, etc.*

Act 1, Scene 1: The Mountain Hut. *Scene 2*: Road to the City of Noodledum. *Scene 3*:

Act 2: The Cobweb Cave of the Grim Goblin.

[5]At the conclusion of Act 1, the New Act Drop, painted by William Voegtlin, will be displayed representing Laga Maggiora in Switzerland

[6]Elsewhere in the program authorship is credited to George Conquest and Henry Pettitt.

[7]Suspended performances 6-7 August 1880 due to the injury of George Conquest, resuming 9 August 1880.

[8]The acknowledged star of the show does not appear in the program's cast list; his specialties, in which he was accompanied by his son, are enumerated inside the program's plot synopsis.

ACT 1[9]
Scene 3
The Demon Head; Grand Ensemble
All the characters

ACT 2
The Vampire Bat; The Great European Sensation of the Flying Fairy and the Wonderful Phantom Flight.

1880.35 FUN ON THE BRISTOL, or A Night on the Sound

A Musical Comedy Oddity in Three Acts. (Play by George Fawcett Rowe. Music by Verdi, Donizetti, Bizet, Offenbach, Lecocq, etc.) Stage director, John F. Sheridan. Scenery (Act 2) painted by John A. Thompson. Vocal director, Henry Saville. Orchestral conductor, George Loesch. Produced by Henry C. Jarrett and Edward E. Rice. Opened 9 August 1880 at Haverly's 14th Street Theatre and closed 28 August 1880 after 24 performances. Reopened 11 April 1881 at Haverly's 14th Street Theatre and closed 30 April 1881 after 24 additional performances. Total: 48 performances.

CAST: *Mrs. O'Brien*, from Tipperary. A gushing two-times widow, and a candidate for a third term: JOHN F. SHERIDAN. *Dora*, her daughter by McAllister. A maiden fair to see: KATE CASTLETON. *Norah*, her daughter by O'Brien. Fresh as the rosy morn: Agnes Hallock. *Bella*, lady's maid. A brunette: MARION FISKE [O'BRIEN]. *Captain Cranberry*, of Newport, a retired Old Salt. Cease, Rude Boreas: Henry Saville. *Tom Cranberry*, his son, a model youth. He never told his love: FRANK TANNEHILL, JR. *Dick Sparks*, Nothing if not gallant: Myron Calice. *Count Menaggio*, Professor of Music. With a villa on the Lake of Nogo: MARK SMITH. *Pinkerton Hawkshaw*, who sticks to his friends. Blood is thicker than water: George Topack. *Jerry Thompson*, waiter on the *Bristol*. "Happily, for I am black"—Othello: William Courtwright. *Jerry Thompson, Jr.*, the very image of his father: Master Linden.

LIST OF PASSENGERS (Act 2): *Widow O'Brien*: JOHN F. SHERIDAN. *Captain Starch*: JOHN F. SHERIDAN. *Sergeant Giesbecker*: JOHN F. SHERIDAN. *Moses Levy*, a Hebrew Turk: JOHN F. SHERIDAN. *Dora McAllister*: KATE CASTLETON. *Romeo Rattlepate*, a Swell: KATE CASTLETON. *Mlle. Aimee-lia*, Opera Bouffe: KATE CASTLETON. *Belle Thompson*: MARION FISKE. *The Black Nightingale*: MARION FISKE. *Chloe*, a Black Turk-y: MARION FISKE. *Jerry*, Steward on the Bristol: William Courtwright. *Flewey*, an Exoduster: William Courtwright. *Captain (Hardly Ever) Gilbert*: William Courtwright. *Private Thompson*, a Black Turk: William Courtwright. *Thomas Cranberry*: FRANK TANNEHILL, JR. *Sullivan*, Jack of Clubs: FRANK TANNEHILL, JR. *Pinkey Crouse*, a French Turk: FRANK TANNEHILL, JR. *Pinkerton Hawkshaw*: Augustus J. Bruno. *James Overshoe*: Augustus J. Bruno. *Doctor Tanner*: Augustus J. Bruno. *Nora O'Bree-on* (O'Brien): Agnes Hallock. *Nilsson-na*, Prima Donna: Agnes Hallock. *Vladimir*, a Russian Turk-ees: Agnes Hallock. *Captain Cranberry*: Henry Saville. *Signor Belch-alini*, H. M. Opera: Henry Saville. *Jacob Grouse*, a German Turk: Henry Saville. *Capoul Sparks*: Myron Calice. *Campan-out-a*, H. M. Opera: Myron Calice. *Herr Ludwig*, a Dutch Turk: Myron Calice. *Count Menaggio*: MARK SMITH. *Torreador Carmen*, a Bull-y: MARK SMITH. *Pedro*, an Italian Turk: MARK SMITH. *Humpty*, a Clown: George Topack. *Dumpty*, a Clown: William Moore. *Passenger Agent*: William Hughes.

Act 1: Home of the Widow O'Brien on Fifth Avenue. New York, 1879.

Act 2: On Board the *Bristol*. (Thompson.)

Act 3: A Night on the Sound.

ACT 2[10]
Grand Musical Dramatic, Operatic, Terpsichorean and Nonsensical Divertissement
Potpourri Chorus. Flewey, the Exoduster
(W. Courtwright)
Toreador in the Bull-Fighter's Song (from CARMEN)
(M. Smith)
(*Music by* Georges Bizet.)
James Overshoe in Specialties, including
(A. J. Bruno)
"The (Second Degree) Full Moon Union" (from THE MULLIGAN GUARD PIC-NIC)
(*Music by* David Braham. *Lyrics by* Edward Harrigan.)

[9]Specialties, not musical numbers, listed in programs. One reviewer remarked on the song:
"La de da"
L. Lancaster

[10]Also included Grand Operatic Hash: The Pie-Rats of Penns-Ants, or, The Cruel Pa-Pe and Parnell-Sky Lover.

Captain Starch and Mlle. Aiméelia in a Little Flirtation
(J. J. Sheridan, K. Castleton)
The Black Nightingale
(M. Fiske)
Italian, French and Irish Operatic Quartette
Two English Swells of the Period
(K. Castleton, ?)
The Bristol Domestic Band in their novel 'Turkish Reveille'

ACT 3
Unravelling of the Mystery. The Widow in Hot Water. General Denouement.

1880.36 THE MULLIGAN GUARD PIC-NIC

A Local Comedy in One Act, 8 Scenes (Volume First of the Mulligan Series, reconstructed, revised and rewritten and entitled Volume Sixth[11]). Play (and lyrics) by Edward Harrigan. Music by David Braham. Produced under the supervision of Edward Harrigan. Scenery by Charles W. Witham. Mechanical effects by Robert Cutler. Musical director, David Braham. Produced by (Edward) Harrigan and (Tony) Hart. Opened 9 August 1880 at the Theatre Comique and closed 20 November 1880 after 120 performances.

CAST: *Dan Mulligan*: EDWARD HARRIGAN. *Rebecca Allup*: TONY HART. *Lemons*: JOHN WILD. *Tommy Fagin*: WILLIAM GRAY. *Gustavus Lochmuller*: HARRY FISHER. *Roderick O'Dwyer*: Ed Burt. *August Bimble*: Harry Sinclair. *Walsingham McSweeny*: M. Bradley. *Captain Primrose*: James Fox. *Rev. Ferguson Clinton*: Ed Goss. *Theophilus Grasp*: William West. *Mrs. Dublin*: John Queen. *Judge Cohog*: Robert Hall. *Gipsy Jack*: M. Foley. *Farmer Armyworm*: Jos. Buckley. *Hezekiah Sift*: James Tierney. *Mr. A. Blotter*, a clerk: James Fitzsimmons. *Gussy Lochmuller*: Emil Husel. *Mrs. Bridget Lochmuller*: ANNIE MACK. *Cordelia Mulligan*: Mrs. ANNIE YEAMANS. *Jennie Lantry*: Mary Bird. *Delia Darcy*: Belle Mordaunt. *Phoebe Casey*: Emily Yeamans. *Full Moons, Excursions, etc. by Auxiliaries.*

Scene 1: Exterior of Dan Mulligan's Brick and O'Dwyer's Tailor Shop. *Scene 2*: Apartments in Mulligan's Brick. *Scene 3*: Pier and Shipping. *Scene 4*: Pleasure Grove. *Scene 5*: Road to the Court House. *Scene 6*: Squire Cohog's Grocery and Court House. *Scene 7*: The Roadway. *Scene 8*: Deck of the Barge.

MUSICAL NUMBERS
Scene 2
"Roderick O'Dwyer"
"All Aboard for the M.G. P."
Scene 3
"Second Degree Full Moon Union" in lodge regalia, will be paraded under the command of *Blazing Meteor*: E. Goss. *Milky Way*: J. Fox.
Scene 4
"Mary Kelly's Beau"
E. Harrigan
"Locked Out After Nine" (Song and Quadrille)
Scene 8
"Sandy-Haired Mary in Our Area"
E. Harrigan, Company

1880.37 EDGEWOOD FOLKS

A Pastoral Comedy-Drama in Four Acts. Play by J. E. Brown. Incidental music by George Bowron. Stage director, J. W. Lanergan. Scenery by Henry E. Hoyt, Philip Goatcher, John A. Thompson, J. Johnson and Plaisted. Mechanical effects and properties by Hamilton Weaver and George Henry. Produced by Henry E. Abbey. Opened 23 August 1880 at Abbey's New Park Theatre and closed 18 September 1880 after 28 performances.[12]

CAST: *Tom Dilloway*, in which character he will introduce several of his famous Songs and Specialties: SOL SMITH RUSSELL. *Reverend Arthur Melville*: Charles Rockwell. *Ferguson*: J. W. Lanergan. *Fitz-Altamont*: B. T. Ringgold. *Deacon Absolom Hardewick*: Sol Smith. *Fosdick Skinner*: Walter Lennox, Sr. *J. Adolphus Gilson*: William Warmington. *Mr. Springton*: Harry Davis. *Wilson*: Z. Williamson. *Faith Hardewick*: Carrie McHenry. *Phoebe Jane Hardewick*, half sister to Melville: Mrs. Sol Smith. *Annie Dilloway*: MATTIE EARLE. *Hulda Hardewick*: Nellie Taylor. *Matilda Bates*: Jennie Wharton. *Little Sylvia*: Little Belle Wharton.

Scene: Edgewood, Connecticut, and New York City. The present day.

Act 1: Picnic at Edgewood. The Parson's Legacy.

Act 2: The Miner's Story. The Family Bible and its Secrets.

Act 3: Return to Edgewood. The Missing Link.

Act 4: Tom's Stratagem. The Will. Wedding Bells.

SPECIALTIES[13]
"Sophia! Phia! Phia!"
"Billy and Furgie"
"I'm Getting a Big Boy Now"
"The Girl That I Admire"
"Miss Brady's Piano Fortay"
"Hulda's Flirtation Episode"
"Yummie, Yum, Yum"
"The Elopement"
"The Counterfeit Deacon"
"The Deacon Says So, Too"

1880.38 THE TOURISTS IN A PULLMAN PALACE CAR

A Return Engagement of the Nonsensical and Musical Play in Three Acts[14]. Play by William A. Mestayer. Musical director, W. L. Bowron. Produced by J. P. Smith and William A. Mestayer. Opened 23 August 1880 at Haverly's Fifth Avenue Theatre and closed 18 September 1880 after 32 performances; re-opened 21 February 1881 at Niblo's Garden and closed 7 March 1881 after an additional 16 performances.[15]

CAST: *Miss Baby*, the Pet. A Gushing Damsel, not too gushing, but just gush enough: CARRIE SWAIN. *Miss Isabella*, her sister, a Quiet Damsel, not too quiet, but just quiet enough: LOUISE PAULLIN. *Miss Pamela*, their Aunt, not too old a maid, but just old enough: JEANNETTE [Jennie] REIFFARTH. *Marie*, their maid, a Fresh Damsel, not too fresh, but just fresh enough: ALICE HUTCHINGS. *T. Henry Slum*, a disciple of Banting, but just anti-Fat enough: WILLIAM A. MESTAYER. *Sir Henry Cashmere*, a Nob, not too much nob, but just, etc.: J. N. LONG. *James Winkerton*, the Detective. Not too much Detective, but just, etc.: T. Wilmot Eckert. *Rich*, a footman. Not too much Footman, but just etc.: Samuel Swain. *George Flamer*, a Special. Not too special, etc.: Will H. Bray. *Hans*, a Butler. Not too much, etc.: Henry Watson. *Male and female passengers*. Not too much Male and Female, but just a little Neuter.

ACT 2 and 3: *T. Henry Slum*: WILLIAM A. MESTAYER. *George Thespis*, clean gone on the legitimate: WILLIAM A. MESTAYER. *Sir Henry Cashmere*: J. N. LONG. *Hon. Augustus Bilk*: J. N. LONG. *The Conductor*: Henry Watson. *The German Immigrant*: Henry Watson. *The Rocky Mountain Bear*: Henry Watson. *Porter of P.P.C.*: Will. H. Bray. *Sam Portfolio*, an aspiring military man: Samuel Swain. *Detective in Disguise*: T. Wilmot Eckert. *Isabella*: LOUISE PAULLIN. *Eurydice*: LOUISE PAULLIN. *Baby*: CARRIE SWAIN. *Serio-Comic Singer*: CARRIE SWAIN. *Aunt Pamelia*: JEANNETTE REIFFARTH. *German Peasant Girl*: JEANNETTE REIFFARTH. *Marie*: Alice Hutchings.

ACT 2
"Cock Robin" (original with The Tourists)
"Tourists' March" (original with the Tourists)
Drinking Chorus (with Bell Accompaniment)
"Dark-Eyed Eloise" (original with the Tourists)
(*Music and Lyrics by* Will H. Bray.)
"Our Choir" (original with The Tourists)
"Lah De Dah"/"My Caty Dear"
W. A. Mestayer

[11]A revised and expanded version of the earlier MULLIGAN GUARD PIC-NIC presented in 1878. Preceded by a changing program of short farces by Edward Harrigan, variously titled Doctor Tanner Outdone, My Wife and My Mother-in-Law, and Happy Family, etc.
[12]Played a return engagement 6 February 1882 at the Windsor Theatre for 8 performances.

[12]Played a return engagement 6 February 1882 at the Windsor Theatre for 8 performances.
[13]Sol Smith Russell's specialties not listed in New York programs. List prepared from an undated touring program.
[14]First produced in New York 3 November 1879 at Haverly's Lyceum Theatre for 16 performances; re-opened 5 January 1880 at Haverly's Lyceum Theatre for 48 additional performances. For Synopsis of Scenes, see original 1879 production.
[15]No credits in programs for stage direction, scenery or costumes.

"La Colossa" (Spanish Song)
L. Paullin
"Yodel" (German Song)
J. Reiffarth
"Lauderbocken"
H. Watson
Comic Songs
C. Swain
"Tourists' Parade" (especially arranged for The Tourists)

ACT 3
Tower Scene from IL TROVATORE
L. Paullin, T. W. Eckert
(*Music by* Giuseppe Verdi.)
"'Tis Time to Say Good Night" (Quartette)
L. Paullin, J. Reiffarth, J. N. Long, T. W. Eckert
The Tourists' Cabin Songs (original with The Tourists)
LA FILLE DU TAMBOUR-MAJOR [Selection]
Music by Jacques Offenbach.)

1880.39 FRITZ IN IRELAND, or, The Bell-Ringer of the Rhine and The Love of the Shamrock!

A Revival of the Drama in a Prologue and Three Acts[16]. Play by William Carleton. Produced by Joseph K. Emmet. Opened 23 August 1880 at the Grand Opera House and closed 3 September 1880 after 12 performances[17]; re-opened 28 March 1881 at the Grand Opera House and closed 16 April 1881 after 21 additional performances. Total: 33 performances.

CAST: *Fritz Schultz*: JOSEPH K. EMMET. *Lawyer Priggins*: W. W. ALLEN. *Baron Hertford*, alias Splodger, Lawyer Priggins' Jackall: J. H. RENNIE. *Captain Hercules O'Dowd*: M. B. Snyder. *Lord Seaton*: W. CHRISTIE MILLER. *Charles Seaton*: Oliver Doud. *Thomas Goldfinger*, Man Servant: J. H. Ryan. *Patrick Blackeye*, an Irish Negro: J. O. Burk. *Master Herbert*, Nephew of Baron Hertford: Little Anna Rennie. *Lena Schultz*: Little Anna Rennie. *Louise Hertford*: Katie Blancke. *Lady Amelia*: FANNIE FRANCES. *Madame Schultz*, afterwards Madame Marroll: Rose Graham. *Judy Callahan*, Maid Servant: Tillie McHenry. *Lena Schultz*: Little Georgie Snyder. *Biddy O'Flanagan*: Tillie McHenry.

MUSICAL NUMBERS[18]
"The Bells Are Ringing"
"The Swell"
"The Cuckoo Song"
"The Shamrock"
"Wilheindrick Strauss"
"The Mountain Guide"
"The Brother's Lullaby"
"I Know What Love Is"
And other songs

1880.40 The New EVANGELINE

A Revised Version of the Extravaganza in Two Acts, 10 Scenes[19]. Libretto by J. Cheever Goodwin, revised by John J. McNally. Music by Edward E. Rice. Stage manager, Charles Groves. Musical director, George Purdy. Produced by Rice's New Extravaganza Combination (Edward E. Rice, Proprietor). Opened 30 August 1880 at Haverly's 14th Street Theatre and closed 11 September 1880 after 16 performances; re-opened 23 May 1881 at the Grand Opera House and closed 28 May 1881 after an additional 8 performances.[20]

CAST: *Evangeline*, a Neophyte of Love, who gets several lovers near fighting for fighting for her. In love with Gabriel: VERNONA JARBEAU. *Gabriel*, a youth who has proved a good One (Goodwin), has lived for years on Rice; has known his brougham (John); has had the Woolf(e) (B.E.) at his door: and who now comes to make an alibi (McNally by, John J.), in love with Evangeline LOUISE SEARLE. *Catherine*, Gabriel's mother. Younger than she was four years ago; for years don't count with her. Desires to be wife to LeBlanc; wife she don't it won't be her fault: GEORGE K. FORTESQUE. *Eulalie*, maid to and for Evangeline; who does many fellows shun because she loves Felician: ROSE DANA. *Felician*, a reporter, as per usual, truthful, underworked and overpaid. Devoted his his natio (imagination). In love with Eulalie: JENNIE CALEF. *LeBlanc*, in a new suit which is suited to him, since he won it in a suit with the tailor who sew it. As usual, the key-note of the play and an O.K. notary: ED. CHAPMAN. *Peter Papyrus*, LeBlanc's clerk, a man full of spirit(s), whose duties are onerous, but who will still honor us: CHARLES GROVES. *Captain Dietrich*, not of the militia, and consequently not so malicious as he seems: J. W. RANSONE. *Bazil*, father of Evangeline, who thinks he has received base ill-treatment: MAX FIGMAN. *King Boorioboola Gha*, who reigns (rains) in a storm, as usual: MAX FIGMAN. *Lone Fisherman*, sighing for the infinite and fishing for the finite. Can be seen on any fine night: HARRY HUNTER. *Hans Wagner*, Dutch, but dutiful: PAULINE HALL. *Policeman*, a man of heart, who plays clubs: George A. Schiller. *Jailer*, though not a politician much given to bolts: Annie Summerville. *Carry News*, a gossip who goes sipping tea and teasing friends: Jessie Calef. *Floraletta*, pretty and useful, i.e. pretty useful: Ella Winner.

Five who have been shipped because they are in good voice: *Abbernergezza*: H. M. Morse. *Hellosqueezer*: Horace Frail. *Knockemendways*: Gertie Geery. *First Fisherman*: Maude Turner. *Second Fisherman*: Nora Sigerman. *Fishermen, Soldiers, Pages, etc. Grand Chorus of 16 Young Ladies.*

Act 1, Scene 1: Interior of Bazil's Cottage by the Sea. *Scene 2*: The love of a reporter for a fair maid. *Scene 3*: Office of LeBlanc, the Notary. *Scene 4*: Peter Papyrus has a slight attack of James Preserves. *Scene 5*: Bazil's Cottage.

Act 2, Scene 1: The Diamond Fields of Africa. *Scene 2*: In Jail. *Scene 3*: The Court of Boorioboola Gha. *Scene 4*: A Lane in Acadia. *Scene 5*: The return home.

ACT 1[21]
"Can you wonder that I am afraid?" (Song)
C. Groves
Incidental for sailors
"He's captivated me" (Song)
L. Searle
"How I love my Vangie dear" (Peter's Lament)
C. Groves
"Our hearts are light and free" (Chorus and May-Pole Dance)

ACT 2
"Clink Clank" (Chorus of Natives)
Evangeline's Entrance Music
"A Lone, Deserted Maiden" (Song)
V. Jarbeau
"Bo-bo-ho-bohoho-bohohoho" (Crying Chorus)
E. Chapman, C. Groves, G. K. Fortesque, J. W. Ransome
"I Love a Young Man Dearly" (Song)
R. Dana

1880.41 AROUND THE WORLD IN EIGHTY DAYS

A Revival of the Grand Spectacular Combination in Five Acts, a Prologue and 13 Scenes[22]. Based on the French adaptation of Jules Verne's novel "Le Tour du Monde en Quatre-vingt Jours," as adapted by Adolphe D'Ennery. Production (conceived, staged and) produced by and under the personal supervision of Imre and Bolossy Kiralfy. Opened 30 August 1880 at Niblo's Garden and closed 2 October 1880 after 40 performances.[23]

---

[16]Originally produced in New York 3 November 1879 at the Park Theatre for 56 performances. For Synopsis of Scenes and Musical Numbers, see original 1879 production.

[17]Emmet did not perform Wednesday matinees, at which time his company performed another play, Our Mother in Law. FRITZ IN IRELAND closed prematurely following Emmet's arrest for drunkenness.

[18]All songs and dances introduced by J. K. Emmet.

[19]First produced in New York 27 July 1874 at Niblo's Garden for 14 performances. For Synopsis of Scenes and Musical Numbers, see original 1874 production.

[20]Stage direction uncredited in New York programs; in Boston tryout Willie Edouin is credited. Scenery and costumes uncredited. For return engagement, the following cast changes among the principals: *Evangeline*: ROSE DANA. *Eulalie*: JESSIE CALEF. *Captain Dietrich*: MAX FIGMAN. *Bazil, King Boorioboola Gha*: HORACE FRAIL. *Lone Fisherman*: GEORGE A. SCHILLER.

[21]Program listed only new songs composed by Rice for EVANGELINE. "Many of the favorite musical numbers of the old EVANGELINE have been retained in the new production." Also performed:
The Beautiful Heifer Dance
Messrs. Cohen & Turner

[22]First produced in New York 28 September 1875 at the Academy of Music for 43 performances.

[23]This production boasted all new costumes and scenery (from uncredited European designers), and two novel and beautiful ballets: "Homage à la

CAST: *Aouda*, an East Indian Princess: HELEN TRACY. *Nemea*, her sister: CARLOTTA EVELYN. *Bessie*: ALICE G. SHERWOOD. *Nakahira*, Aouda's slave: Louisa Dempsey. *Phineas Fogg*, Member of the Eccentric Club: HARRY MEREDITH. *Miles O'Pake*, an ex-Senator from New York: ED. J. BUCKLEY. *Fix*, an English detective, Scotland Yard: RUSSELL BASSETT. *Jean François Passepartout*, French valet: E. A. LOCKE. *Mr. Blunt*, a Calcutta magistrate: E. S. TARR. *Sir Roger Shewdryn*: L. F. Rand. *Arthur Mayburn*: Charles Bland. *Foster Jones*: A. H. Denham. *Governor of Suez*: L. M. Morton. *Shafter*: P. Henry. *Boatswain*: R. P. Langdon. *Engineer*: Theo. Leutze. *An Aged Parsee*: Henry Kramer. *Brahmin Chief*: J. M. Ford. *Phil Tracy*: F. Farrar. *Jack Rivers*: Barty Allen. *Conductor*: F. H. Bingham. *Engineer*: J. Wakefield. *Chief Scout*: R. M. Turner. *Adzub Ahan*, King of Borneo: ED. M. PIERCE. *Waiter*: Robert Porter. *Station Master*: A. Redmond. *Barkeeper*: G. H. Meagher. *Captain Collins*: P. F. Williams. *Ballet*: Mlles. DeROSA, CORNALBA, Mons. ARNOLD KIRALFY, Corps of Secondes, Danseuses and Coryphées. *Brahmins, Priests, Punka Wallahs, Dobez Wallahs, Soldiers, Hindoos, Arabs, Egyptians, Malayans, Road Agents, Passengers, Policemen, Sailors, Members of the London Eccentric Club, Snake Charmers and Bayaderes.*

DREAMS;

1880.42 or, Fun in a Photograph Gallery

A (Musical Comedy) Conceit in Two Acts. Play by Nathaniel Childs and Willie Edouin. (Music by W. J. Rostetter, Woolson Morse, Edward E. Rice, Harry Braham. Lyrics by Dexter Smith, Nat Childs, John J. McNally, F. T. Robinson.) Stage manager, Jacques Kruger. Musical director, W. J. Rostetter. Produced by Willie Edouin and Frank W. Sanger. Opened 30 August 1880 at the Bijou Theatre and closed 9 October 1880 after 42 performances.

CAST: Act 1: *John Antonio Binks*, a retired Farmer, age 70: WILLIE EDOUIN. *Thomas Binks*, his son, aged 46: JACQUES KRUGER. *Fred Binks, Harold Binks*, Thomas' sons, aged 22 and 26: FRANK W. SANGER, GEORGE LeCLAIRE. *Bob Bibbitty*, Office Boy to the Binks: JAMES T. POWERS. *Ruby Binks*, Johns' wife, age 65: ALICE ATHERTON. *Kitty Binks*, her niece: JULIA EDOUIN. *Grace Binks*, Thomas' second wife: LOTTA BELTON. *Maud Binks*, Fred's wife: IDA SHAPLEIGH.

Act 2: *John Antonia Binks*, age 21: WILLIE EDOUIN. *Ralph Haberson*, a Villain: WILLIE EDOUIN. — —, *a Tramp*[24]: WILLIE EDOUIN. *Pickleback Grabiball*, the photographer: JACQUES KRUGER. *Charlie Dunno*, Swell: JACQUES KRUGER. *Otis Verydizzy*: FRANK W. SANGER. *Jack Shivermytimbers*: FRANK W. SANGER. *Chip Cheeky*: JAMES T. POWERS. *Policeman 128*: JAMES T. POWERS. *Porter*: Walter Williamson. *Ruby Chillington*, age 19: ALICE ATHERTON. *Mary*, the Child of Misfortune: ALICE ATHERTON. *Flower Girl*: ALICE ATHERTON. *The City Swell*: ALICE ATHERTON. *Violet Parachute*: LOTTA BELTON. *Max Stinger*, Opera Tenor: Lotta Belton. *Lillie Succotash*, with Songs: IDA SHAPELEIGH. *Hortense*, French maid: ANNETTA Du MARÉ.

Act 1: At Home. John and Ruby's Parlor.

Act 2: Abroad. The Photograph Gallery.

MUSICAL NUMBERS[25]

"Serenade"
L. Belton, I. Shapleigh, J. Kruger, J. T. Powers
(*Lyrics by* Dexter Smith.)

"My Son John"
A. Atherton, Chorus

"Rainbow"
(*Lyrics by* Dexter Smith.)

Quartette from ROMEO AND JULIET
A. Atherton, I. Shapleigh, L. Belton, G. LeClaire

"Come into the Garden, Maud"
L. Belton

"Jane, My Pretty Jane"

"Lardy Da"
A. Atherton
(*Music by* Vincent Davies. *Lyrics by* E. V. Page.)

Operatic Medley

"The Cat's in Our Back Yard"
J. T. Powers, Chorus
(*Music by* W. J. Rostetter. *Lyrics by* Nathaniel Childs.)

"Sparks"

"Flower Girl" (Who'll Buy?)
A. Atherton
(*Music by* Woolson Morse. *Lyrics by* F. T. Robinson.)

"A. O. H. March"
A. Atherton, L. Belton, A. DuMaré, F. W. Sanger, G. LeClaire, J. T. Powers
(*Music by* Woolson Morse. *Lyrics by* John J. McNally.)

"Dream On"
I. Shapleigh, Chorus
(*Music and Lyrics by* Woolson Morse.)

"Bees Among the Clover"
(*Music and Lyrics by* Edward E. Rice.)

"All the World's a Stage"
A. Atherton, J. T. Powers
(*Music and Lyrics by* Edward E. Rice.)

"Photograph Duet"
I. Shapleigh, J. Kruger
(*Music by* Edward E. Rice. *Lyrics by* Nathaniel Childs.)

CARMEN,

1880.43 or, Soldiers and Seville-ians

M. B. Leavitt's Grand English Operatic Burlesque Company in a Burlesque in Two Acts. Written by Frank W. Green. Music composed and selected from the most popular repertoires by Frank Musgrave. Scenery by William Voegtlin. Grand Transformation by Professor Hughes, of London. Stage manager, James A. Meade. Maitre de ballet, Signor Novissimo. Musical director, Frank Musgrave. Produced by M. B. Leavitt (Sole Proprietor and Manager). Opened 13 September 1880 at Haverly's 14th Street Theatre and closed 2 October 1880 after 24 performances.

CAST: *Carmen*, pretty Gypsy, who takes to making cigars and love, the end of which is smoke: SELINA DOLARO.

Soldiers: *Don José*, a Brigadier, to his Brigade-DEAR, but to his Carmen CHEAP: MARIE WILLIAMS. *Zuniger*, Captain of the Brigade, who has often to be kept in check: FANNIE WENTWORTH. *Morales*, his Lieutenant, who has LEFT AN AUNT to join the corps, and whose MORALS are MOR-A-LESS dubious: DAISY RAMSDEN. *Pasquillo*, Captain of the Cadets: Alma Stanley. *Fernandez*: Minnie Marshall. *Juan*: Camille D'Elmar. *Spanish Soldiers (10)*, who have left their PAS to follow MARS, but in their usual HAUNTS are fond of GRAND-PAS: *Xeres*: Lillie French. *Amontillado*: Clara Maybel. *Figarello*: Grace Leaver. *Elvirez*: Marie Clifton. *Maraschino*: Maude St. Clair. *Farfan*: Annie Dunscombe. *Frasquin*: Nellie Grahame. *Manuel*: Kate Goodwin. *Carlos*: Emily Farneau. *Pedro*: Nellie Davis. *A Mad Bull*: Messrs. Tonner and Lynch.

Seville-Ians: *Michaela*, a blighted flower—her motto "L'HOMME PROPOSE," but unfortunately L'HOMME WON'T PROPOSE: (Mr.) MAT ROBSON. *Juanita* (It wouldn't be hard to find YOU A NEATER), *Camilla* (after whose cigars people often become ILLER), Cigar Girls: Adelaide Praeger, Laurie Trevor. *Frasquita, Mercedes*, Gypsy girls whose charms drive you to becoming GYPSY MANIACS: Minnie Leigh, Florence Beaufort. *Escamillo*, the Toreador, a regular bully boy, famed for BULLION and BULLY-IN: JAMES A. MEADE. *Gomez*, his brother, a gay young boy, who is COWED by his BULLY brother: Lizzie Mulholland. *Dancairo, Remendado*, Gypsy Smugglers, who in a double sense DO their DUTIES: J. W. Bradbury, Frank Hinde. *Sancho*, Landlord of the "Sitting Bull" Tavern, who isn't fond of STANDING AROUND: C. H. Spiller. *Orange Girls, Soldiers, Cigar Girls, Seville and Uncivil Citizens, Smugglers, Gypsies, Picadors, Matadors, etc.*: a Charming Corps of Coryphées.

Act 1, Scene 1: The Great Square of Seville. *Scene 2*: Exterior of the Seville Prison. *Scene 3*: The "Sitting Bull" Tavern.

Act 2, Scene 1: The Smugglers' Retreat in the Rocks. *Scene 2*: Exterior of the Bull Ring. *Scene 3*: The Grand Arena.

Beautées," Act 2, Scene 2: by Mlles. DeRosa, Cornalba, Mons. Arnold Kiralfy, and Ballet of 150 Ladies. Grand Ballet of "Bric-a-Brac," Act 5, Scene 2. Credits from the Kiralfy's previous AROUND THE WORLD: Music composed and arranged by Mons. Debillemont. Scenic designs by Poisson, Negel, Robecchi, Cornil, adapted by Mons. Camille Weinehenk. Costumes by Chalain; properties by Hallée; statuary by Dagoni. Orchestra under the direction of Charles Puerner.

[24]Earlier programs prior to New York identify this character as Hon. George Fitzsimmons, a Tramp; later touring programs identify this character as Mlle. Berino Micheleno.

[25]Not in performance order. Every engagement of this show on tour and in revival featured many different songs: For the Boston tour in January 1881, added were: "Dotting the I," "Hee Haw Brigade," "The Gay Photographer," "Sarah B," "Little Stockings by the Fire" (*Music and Lyrics by* Cheever Goodwin and J. L. Gilbert.), "Stella Confidanti," "Goodbye, Sweetheart, Goodbye," "Christmas Fairies," "Stars Shine Over Us," "Naviganti," "Hang the Mulligan Banner Up" (*Music by* David Braham. *Lyrics by* Edward Harrigan.), "Nightingale's Trill," and "The Robin." By 1885, the tour was performed in three acts as a farce comedy, with no songs listed in programs.

ACT 1
Scene 1
Soldiers on their rounds on the Square. The blighted, blushing flower who likes to *be lushing*. The Missing Lover and the Promising Corps. Hessian Cadets' Drill. Arrival of Don José. Carmen *carmences* her flirtation. The interview in which Michaela tries to *hint a few* facts. Carmen arrested. Don José's Temptation! Hesitation! Desperation! Determination! Insubordination and Incarceration!
Scene 2
Before consigning Don José to prison *bars*, his comrades try several *staves*, in musical *keys*, to stave off sorrow. The blighted flower transplanted. Trio of Triumph. "Spanish Song" by Carmen.
Scene 3
The Espagnola Ballet. Guitars, Cigars and Cognac. A performance on the Zither which is *ethereal*. Entry of the terrible Toreadors. Carmen's love at First Sight. The pretty *Belle* with two strings to her *Beau*. Flirtation! Invitation! Trepidation! Intimidation! Acceptation! Osculation! Altercation! Exultation! and Striking Situation!
ACT 2
Scene 1
Smugglers and Jugulars. Broken Bonds of Love's Fetters. A midnight encounter. Mutual recrimination. The Tale of a Tub. "Tubby, or not Tubby." The rivals meet. Howls! Scowls and Growls! The challenge accepted. Don José tries to *smother* his love for *his mother*, have *some other* object of affection. Departure for the fray.
Scene 2
Foemen and Showmen. Picadors (ready to pick a quarrel) and Matadors (not to be confused with doormats). Michaela and Carmen take the *veil*, and the rivals make love without *avail*. Carmen *apprises* them her hand is *a prize* to be fought for. Adjournment to the Bull Ring.
Scene 3
Characteristic Ballet of Picadors, Toreadors and Matadors (whom each adores). Carmen chosen Queen of the Revels. The terrific Bull-Fight. Death of the Bull, and defeat of the Bully. Furious Finale and delightful Denouement.

1880.44 LA FILLE DU TAMBOUR-MAJOR

An Opéra-comique in Three Acts, 4 Scenes, in French. Libretto by Henri Chivot and Alfred Duru. Music by Jacques Offenbach. Produced under the direction of V. Merle. Scenery by Hannibal W. Calyo. Costumes by Mr. Landolff, Paris, and Mme. Moreau. Musical director, Charles Almeras. Produced by Maurice Grau's French Opera Company. Opened 13 September 1880 at the Standard Theatre and closed 2 October 1880 after 21 performances; returned 18-19 October 1880 to the Standard Theatre for 2 additional performances.

CAST: *Stella*: Mlle. PAOLA MARIÉ. *Claudine*: Mlle. MARY ALBERT. *La Duchesse della Volta*: Mme. Delorme. *La Prieure* (Prioress): Mlle. Choquet. *Francesca*: Mme. Vallot. *Lorenza*: Mme. Malvina. *Lucrezia*: Mme. Estradère. *Monthabor* (Drum Major): Mons. DUPLAN. *Lieutenant Robert*: Mons. CLEMENT NIGRI. *Le Duc della Volta*: Mons. J. MEZIÈRES. *Griolet* (Drummer): Mons. F. TAUFFENBERGER. *Marquis Bambini*: Mons. Poyard. *Clampas*: Mons. Vilano. *Gregorio*: Mons. Millet. *Sergeant Morin*: Mons. Vinchon. *Zerbinelli*: Mons. Carlier. *Del Ponto*: Mons. Perret. *A Sergeant*: Mons. Emile. *Solders, Nuns, Pensionnaires, Lords, Ladies, Peasants, Brigands*.

The action is laid in Italy in the year 1800.

Act 1: Gardens of the Convent at Biella.

Act 2: Salon at the Palazza Della Volta, at Novarre.

Act 3, Scene 1: Hotel du Lion d'Or, at Milan. *Scene 2*: Public Place in Milan. Grand Entry of the French Army.

ACT 1[26]
Introduction:
Choeur des Pensionnaires (Reçois sainte madone)
Mmes. Malvina, P. Marié, Choquet
Chanson du fruit défendu (Prenez les grappes empourprées)
P. Marié
Choeur et couplets (Par un chaleur aussi forte)
Messrs. F. Tauffenberger, C. Nigri, Duplan, Choeur
Chanson de l'âne (Ce n'est pas un âne ordinaire)
Mlle. M. Albert, Messrs. F. Tauffenberger, C. Nigri, Duplan, Choeur
Ensemble (De grâce ayez pitié de moi!)
P. Marié, Messrs. F. Tauffenberger, C. Nigri, Duplan, Choeur
Couplets du tailleur (Tout en tirant mon aiguille)
Mons. F. Tauffenberger
Scène de la table:
Choeur (Puisque le couvert est mis)
P. Marié, Messrs. C. Nigri, Duplan, Choeur
Couplets (Depuis longtemps l'Italie)
P. Marié
Légende (Il était une grand' princesse)
Mlle. M. Albert, Mons. F. Tauffenberger
Final:
Ensemble (Messieurs les militaires)
Choeur
Couplets (Pour recevoir un régiment)
P. Marié
Final (Allons dépèchons et partons)
ACT 2
Couplets (Examinez ma figure)
Mme. Delorme
Rondeau (Ah! vraiment je le déclar')
P. Marié
Quatuor du billet de logement (C'est un billet de logement)
Messrs. F. Tauffenberger, J. Mèzieres, C. Nigri, Duplan
Couplets (Eh bien! en voila des manières)
Mlle. M. Albert
Valse et ensemble (Dansons et Valsons)
Mme. Delorme, Messrs. J. Mèzieres, Duplan, Choeur
Duo (Tenez j'aurai de la franchise)
P. Marié, Mons. C. Nigri
Couplets de l'uniforme (Le voilà ce bel uniforme)
Mons. F. Tauffenberger
Final:
Choeur (Par devant monsieur le notaire)
Chanson de la Fille du Tambour-Major (Que m'importe un titre éclatant)
P. Marié
ACT 3
Scene 1
Choeur et scène:
Choeur et scène (Chut! Il faut de la prudence)
Mlle. M. Albert, Messrs. C. Nigri, Vilano
Tarantelle (Nous étions à Novarre)
Choeur
Gigue (Je sais le p'tit cocher)
P. Marié, Messrs. F. Tauffenberger, J. Mèzieres, Duplan
Quatuor (Oui, ce sont vos amis)
P. Marié, Messrs. F. Tauffenberger, C. Nigri, Duplan
Duo de la confession (l'autre jour contre toute attente)
Mme. Delorme, Mons. Duplan
Scene 2
Final (Un mariage s'apprête)

1880.45 THE PIRATES OF PENZANCE, or, The Slave of Duty

The Boston Ideal Opera Company in a Revival of the Comic Opera in Two Acts[27]. Libretto by William Gilbert. Music by Arthur Sullivan. Stage director, J. H. Ryley. Musical director, F. Stanislaus. Produced by the Boston Ideal Opera Company. Opened 13 September 1880 at Booth's Theatre and closed 25 September 1880 after 14 performances.[28]

[26]Musical numbers not listed in programs. List prepared from published French piano vocal score (Choudens, Père et fils, Paris, 1879).

[27]First presented in New York 31 December 1879 at the Fifth Avenue Theatre for a total of 91 performances in two engagements. For Synopsis of Scenes and Musical Numbers, see original 1879 production
[28]No credits in programs for scenery or costumes.

CAST: *Richard*, a Pirate chief: MYRON W. WHITNEY. *Samuel*, his Lieutenant: W. H. MacDonald. *Frederic*, the Pirate Apprentice: TOM KARL. *Major General Stanley*, of the British Army: HENRY CLAY BARNABEE. *Edward*, a Sergeant of Police: GEORGE FROTHINGHAM. *Mabel, Edith, Kate, Isabel*, General Stanley's Daughters: MARY BEEBE, CLARA MERIVALE, LIZZIE BURTON, Agnes Mitchell. *Ruth*, Piratical 'Maid-of-all-work': ADELAIDE PHILLIPPS. *Chorus of Pirates, Police and General Stanley's Daughters.*

1880.46 THE SULTAN OF MOCHA

A Comic Opera in Three Acts. Music by Alfred Cellier. Director of music, Alfred Cellier. Stage manager, William Hamilton. Orchestra under the direction of Henry Tissington. Produced by the Blanche Roosevelt Comic Opera Company (John A. McCaull, Proprietor). Opened 14 September 1880 at the Union Square Theatre and closed 25 September 1880 after 13 performances.[29]

CAST: *H. H. The Seyd Shallah*, Sultan of Mocha: WILLIAM HAMILTON. *"Admiral" Sneak*: FRED DIXON. *Captain Flint*: HARRY ALLEN. *Peter*: EUGENE CLARKE. *Lord Chamberlain*: MILLS HALL. *Chief Scribe*: G. W. REYNOLDS. *Grand Vizier*: G. B. SNYDER. *Frank*: A. Barker. *Blackwall Bill*: J. Attwood. *Greenwich Pensioners (6)*: *Daniel Deadlight*: T. Cuthbert. *Bob Duckett*: L. Sanford. *Bosen Bill*: W. Merton. *Davy Jones*: Tom Bowling. *Hatchway Jim*: E. Reece. *Dolly*: LEONORA BRAHAM. *Isidora, Eureka*, Sultanas: CARRIE REYNOLDS, L. FEITNER. *Lucy*: Ivy Lepel. *Moggy*: Pearl Everleigh. *Sarah*: Clare Lester. *Jenny*: Emma Guthrie. *Greenwich People, Pensioners, Watchmen, Slaves, Sailors, Corsairs, Guards, Odalisques, etc.*

Act 1: Greenwich Palace, and River from the Park.

Act 2: The Market-place at Mocha.

Act 3, Scene 1: A Cavern on the Seashore. *Scene 2*: Interior of the Sultan's Palace.

ACT 1[30]

"Here's Three Times Three" (Opening Chorus and Hornpipe)

"Let the Lords of Legislation" (Song)
L. Braham

"The Letter" (Ballad)
L. Braham

"He is Returning" (Solo and Chorus)
L. Braham, Chorus

"The Telescope" (Song)
F. Dixon

"How now, what's the row" (Trio and Chorus)

"'Twas sad when I and Dolly parted" (Ballad)
E. Clarke

"The Island that dares to be free" (Wooden Leg Chorus of Pensioners)

"The Lass that waits for Peter" (Toast)
E. Clarke

"Pipes and Grog" (Song)
E. Clarke

"We'll Sail Away with Peter" (Chorus and Finale)

ACT 2

"I Love the Ocean" (Song)
F. Dixon

"Now tremble, you traitor" (Duo and Chorus)

"O Caspian" (Chorus of Slaves)

"Woman's Rights" (Song)
L. Braham

"Sultan Am I" (Procession and Song)
W. Hamilton

"Come buy, come buy" (Song)
H. Allen

"Sweet Hannah or Alice" (Duo and Chorus)

"You'd better stay at Mocha" (Chorus and Finale)

ACT 3

Scene 1

"A Sailor's Love" (Chorus by the crew)

"I Really Am So Sleepy" (Yawning Song)
E. Clarke

"Close, thou gentle sleep" (Slumber Song)
L. Braham

Scene 2

"From Chambers. ." (Chorus of Odalisques)

"It's very perplexing" (Trio)
W. Hamilton, L. Feitner, C. Reynolds

"Unrequited love" (Ballad)
W. Hamilton

"My boat is on the shore" (Barcarolle)
E. Clarke, L. Braham

"We are sober, we are ready" (We'll sail away with Peter)(Chorus and Finale)

1880.47 LAWN TENNIS

A Peculiarity (Farce Comedy) in Two Acts, including an Act 2 operatina "D'Jakh and D'Jill." Libretto and score by Ben E. Woolf. Stage manager, John Howson. Scenery by J. S. Schell, Philip W. Goatcher. Musical director, Jesse Williams. Produced by the W. J. Comley-James Barton Company. Opened 20 September 1880 at Abbey's Park Theatre and closed 2 October 1880 after 14 performances; re-opened 22 November 1880 at the Bijou Opera House and closed 22 December 1880 after 28 additional performances.[31]

CAST: *Cornwallis Algernon Prout*, recently arrived and recently married: JOHN HOWSON. *Alfred Puddifoot*, a dramatist who has come to nature for a plot: DIGBY V. BELL. *Captain Dowton*, an energetic Englishman: JAMES BARTON. *George Farleigh*, willing to be tamed: J. C. Armand. *Datchett*, a foreign servant: F. W. Lennox. *Mrs. Cornwallis Algernon Prout*: Hetty Tracy. *Bella Stanley*, a racket: LILLIAN BROOKS-BELL. *Cicely Ray*, another racket: MARIE JANSEN. *Laura Doll*, another racket in embryo: Adelaide Carleton[32]. *Mrs. Doll*, a whole set of rackets: Mrs. J. H. Rowe (Georgie Dickson).

Act 2, D'Jakh and D'Jill: *The King (Stupidenko XIV)*: JOHN HOWSON. *Don Guzman*: DIGBY V. BELL. *The Seneschal*: JAMES BARTON. *D'Jakh*, (Don Guzman's son): J. C. ARMAND. *D'Jill*, (the King's daughter): LILLIAN BROOKS-BELL. *The Abigail*: MARIE JANSEN. *Page*: W. Lennox.

Act 1: Lawn Tennis. (Schell.)

Act 2: Interior of the Man-Tamers' Club. (Goatcher.)

ACT 2

"Take That and That" (Duet)
J. Howson, D. V. Bell

"Of the Dignified Position" (Recitative and Song)
J. Howson

"Go, Tyrant, Go"/"Oh, Love" (Recitative and Aria)
D. V. Bell

"Ah, Father, how d'ye do?" (Duettino)
J. C. Armand, D. V. Bell

"Sweet Maiden" (Aria)
J. C. Armand

"I Love You" (Duet)
J. C. Armand, L. Brooks-Bell

"Ah, D'Jakh and D'Jill" (Scene)
J. Barton

"He's Turning Ninety-Four" (Trio)
J. C. Armand, L. Brooks-Bell, J. Barton

"Where Are You Going?" (Terzetto)
J. C. Armand, L. Brooks-Bell, J. Barton

"There's Nothing But Annoyance" (Song)
J. Howson

"The Cause of This Confusion" (Quartette)
J. Howson, M. Jansen, D. V. Bell, J. Barton

"D'Jakh and D'Jill" (Air and Quartette)
J. Howson, M. Jansen, D. V. Bell, J. Barton

"But ah, a Dreadful Thought" (Scene)
J. Howson

---

[29]Stage direction scenery, costumes uncredited. Libretto uncredited; in his Encyclopedia of Musical Theatre (Blackwell, 1994), Kurt Gänzl credits Albert Jarret and others for the original English libretto. He also credits John McCaull with staging the New York production.

[30]Musical numbers not listed in programs. List prepared from London program, Royal St. James Theatre.

[31]For return engagement, the production was revised into 3 Acts. A new Act was inserted between Acts 1 and 2, set in a Room in Mrs. Doll's House. The rehearsal of the Operatina.

[32]Replaced by Nellie Dickson for return engagement.

"'Tis Not on Hills" (Air and Quartette)
J. Howson, M. Jansen, D. V. Bell, J. Barton
"D'Jakh and I" (Air and Sextette)
J. C. Armand, L. Brooks-Bell, J. Howson, M. Jansen, D. V. Bell, J. Barton
"Dear Papa" (Air and Chorus)
L. Brooks-Bell, Characters
"Pooh Pooh" (Finale)
All the Characters

1880.48 FATINITZA!

A Revival of the Comic Opera in Three Acts[33]. (Original Viennese libretto to the operette by F. Zell and Richard Genée, based on the libretto to "La Circassienne" by Eugène Scribe.) Music by Franz von Suppé. Original orchestrations by Franz von Suppé. Musical director, Samuel L. Studley. Produced by the Boston Ideal Opera Company. Opened 27 September 1880 at Booth's Theatre and closed 6 October 1880 after 10 performances.[34]

CAST: *Vladimir* a young Russian Lieutenant, afterwards disguised as Fatinitza: ADELAIDE PHILLIPPS. *Princess Lydia Imanovna*, Niece of the Count: MARIE STONE. *Count Timofey Kantchukoff*, a Russian General: MYRON W. WHITNEY. *Izzet Pacha*, Governor of the Turkish Fort: HENRY CLAY BARNABEE. *Julian Hardy*, a Special Newspaper Correspondent: TOM KARL. *Russian Officers (3): Captain Vasil*: W. W. Tuttle. *Lieutenant Osip*: Gus Kammerlee. *Sergeant Steipann*: George Frothingham. *Russian Cadets (4): Dimitri*: Lizzie Burton. *Ivan*: May Calef. *Nikiphar*: Emma Tuttle. *Fedor*: Zephie Dinsmore. *Izzet Pasha's Wives (4): Zuleika*: H. A. Brown. *Diona*: Zephie Dinsmore. *Besika*: Stella Hatch. *Nursidah*: May Calef. *Marsaldshi*, a Fortune Teller: LIZZIE BURTON. *Mustapha*, the Guardian of the Harem: Henry F. Dixey. *Hassan Bey*, Leader of the Bashi-Bazouks: Gus Kammerlee. *Vuika*, a Bulgarian spy: A. J. Hubbard. *Cadets, Russian Soldiers, Bashi-Bazouks, Cossacks, Moorish Women, Slaves, Slave-Drivers, etc.*

Characters in the Karagois: *Jessuf*; *Surema*, his daughter; *Ben Jemin*, his slave; *Wiridah, Fatima*, two old gossips; *Ashmet*, keeper of the Menagerie: Several Slaves of the Harem.

1880.49 LA FILLE DU TAMBOUR MAJOR

An Opéra-Bouffe in Three Acts, 5 Scenes[35] Original French libretto by Henri Chivot and Alfred Duru. Music by Jacques Offenbach. Stage manager, James A. Meade. Maitre de ballet, Signor Novissimo. Musical director, Frank Musgrave. Produced by M. B. Leavitt English Opera Burlesque Company. Opened 4 October 1880 at Haverly's 14th Street Theatre and closed 9 October 1880 after 8 performances.

CAST: *Stella*: SELINA DOLARO. *La Duchesse della Volta*: ALMA STANLEY. *Claudine*: Fannie Wentworth. *The Abbess*: Adelaide Praeger. *Lorenza*: Allie Ollyeth. *Monthabor*, the Tambour Major: JAMES A. MEADE. *Captain Robert*: LEWIS FINKE. *Griolet*, the drummer: MARIE WILLIAMS. *Le Duc della Volta*: MAT ROBSON. *Le Marquis Bambini*: J. W. Bradbury. *Clampas*: Frank Hinde. *Gregorio*: H. C. Spiller. *Gabriel*: Laurie Trevor. *Henri*: Camille D'Elmar. *Raone*: Louise Leighton. *Violetta*: Daisy Ramsden. *Blanca*: Minnie Marshall. *Teresa*: Ethel Champness. *Lackey*: L. D'Smith. *Sergeant*: G. W. Percival. *Peasant*: C. T. McDonald. *Soldiers, Nuns, Pensionnaires, Lords, Ladies, Peasants, Brigands.*

Act 1: Gardens of the Convent at Biella.

Act 2: Salon at the Palazza della Volta Palace, at Novarre.

Act 3, Scene 1: Hotel du Lion d'Or, at Milan. *Scene 2*: Public Place in Milan. *Scene 3*: Grand Entry of the French Army.

1880.50 LES CLOCHES DE CORNEVILLE

A Revival of the Opéra-comique in Three Acts, 4 Scenes, in French[36]. Libretto by Clairville and Charles Gabet. Music by Robert Planquette. Stage manager, V. Merle. Musical director, Charles Almeras. Produced by Maurice Grau's French Opera Company. Opened 4 October 1880 at the Standard Theatre and closed 20 October 1880 after 5 performances in repertory.

CAST: *Serpolette*: Mlle. PAOLA MARIÉ. *Germaine*: Mlle. PAULINE MERLE. *Manette*: Mme. Armand. *Jeanne*: Mme. Vallot. *Gertrude*: Mme. Malvina. *Suzanne*: Mme. Estradere. *Catherine*: Mme. Duparc. *Marguerite*: Mme. Amélie. *Gaspard*, the Miser: Mons. J. MEZIÈRES. *The Marquis*: Mons. CLEMENT NIGRI. *Grenicheux*: Mons. F. TAUFFENBERGER. *Le Bailli*: Mons. DUPLAN. *Le Tabellion*: Mons. Terrancle. *Cacholot*: Mons. Carlier. *Grippardin*: Mons. Marchand. *Fouinard*: Mons. Perret. *Peasants, Sailors, Coachmen, Servants, etc.*

1880.51 OTTO, a German

A Revival of the Local Comedy in Four Acts[37]. Play by Frederick Marsden. Musical director, James Morrison. Produced by George S. Knight (William F. Robertson, Manager). Opened 4 October 1880 at the Grand Opera House and closed 16 October 1880 after 16 performances.[38]

CAST: *Otto Rutger*, a German: GEORGE S. KNIGHT. *Lizette*, Queen of Hearts: Mrs. GEORGE S. KNIGHT [Sophie Worrell]. *Gottleib Miller*, a rich brewer: W. H. Collings. *Dick Freely*, whose name indicates his character: Harry Pierson. *Casper Becks*, an importation of doubtful value: A. Lindsay. *Benjamin Freely*, a "Business Man, Sir": Robert Brower. *Adolph Morton*, more youthful than verdant: Walter Bronson. *Old Bill*, Guardan Spirit of the Brewery: C. F. Herbert. *Christine*, enjoying love's young dream: Irene Worrell. *Mrs. Freely*, who likes to have her say: D. B. Van Deren.

ACT 1
"Trembling Lips" (new song)
Mrs. G. S. Knight
Mandolin Solo
G. S. Knight
Harmonica Solo
G. S. Knight

ACT 2
"Becky Miller" (new song)
G. S. Knight
"Clang of the Wooden Shoe" (Song)
Mrs. G. S. Knight
Parodies on well-known poems
G. S. Knight
"Der Wasserfall" (Tyrolean Duet)
Mr. & Mrs. G. S. Knight

ACT 3
"The Water Mill"
G. S. Knight

ACT 4
"Good Night" (Ballad)
Mrs. G. S. Knight

1880.52 LE PETIT DUC

A Revival of the Opéra-comique in Three Acts, in French[39]. Libretto by Henri Meilhac and Ludovic Halévy. Music by Charles Lecocq. Stage manager, V. Merle. Musical director, Charles Almeras. Produced by Maurice Grau's French Opera Company. Opened 5 October 1880 at the Standard Theatre and closed 9 October 1880 after 3 performances in repertory.

CAST: *Le Duc de Parthenay*: Mlle. PAOLA MARIÉ. *Diane de Château-Lausac*: Mlle. DELORME. *La Duchesse de Parthenay*: Mlle. PAULINE MERLE. *De Montlandry*: Mons. NIGRI. *Frimousse*: Mons. DUPLAN. *Bernard*: Mons. Terrancle. *De Navailles*: Mons. Millet. *De Montchevrier*: Mons. Perret. *De Tanneville*: Mons. Leclerc. *De Champvallon*: Mons. Perret. *De Merrignac*: Mons. Marchand. *Le Mancey*: Mons. Saleon. *Roger*: Mlle. Vallot. *Gerard*: Mlle. Armand. *Julien*: Mlle. Amelie. *Gontran*:

[33]First produced in New York in English 22 April 1879 at the Fifth Avenue Theatre for 41 performances. For Synopsis of Scenes and Musical Numbers, see original 1879 production.
[34]English adaptation uncredited; no credits in programs for scenery or costumes.
[35]English language premiere, adaptation uncredited. Henry B. Farnie's adaptation was previously produced in London, but there is no indication whether it was used in New York. First produced in New York in French 13 September 1880 at Haverly's 14th Street Theatre for 23 performances in repertory. Scenery and costumes uncredited.
[36]First produced in New York in French 24 November 1879 at Booth's Theatre for in repertory. For Synopsis of Scenes and Musical Numbers, see original 1879 production.
[37]First produced in New York 4 November 1878 at the Broadway Theatre for 15 performances.
[38]No credits in programs for scenery, costumes, stage direction.
[39]First produced in New York in French 12 April 1879 at Booth's Theatre for 18 performances in two engagements. For Synopsis of Scenes and Musical Numbers, see original 1879 production.

Mlle. Louise Duparc. *Henri*: Mlle. Malvina. *Gaston*: Mlle. Blainville. *Helene*: Mlle. Estradere. *Mlle. de la Roche Tonnere*: Mlle. Vallot. *Mlle. De Champlatre*: Mlle. Berthe. *Mlle. de St. Anemone*: Mlle. Bazin. *Margot*: Mlle. Louise. *Manon*: Mlle. Estradere. *Premiere sous Maitresse*: Mlle. Choquet. *Duexieme sous Maitresse*: Mlle. Marguerite. *Ninon*: Mlle. Blanche. *Ninette*: Mlle. Berthe. *Marion*: Mlle. Ruffino. *Mariette*: Mlle. Seygaud. *Dragoons, Trumpeters, Pensionnaires, of the Convent at Luneveille, Maids of Honor, Pages, Lords, Ladies of the Court.*

H. M. S. PINAFORE,

1880.53 or, The Lass That Loved a Sailor

The Boston Opera Company in a Revival of the Comic Opera in Two Acts[40]. Libretto by William Gilbert. Music by Arthur Sullivan. Musical director, Samuel L. Studley. Produced by the Boston Opera Company. Opened 7 October 1880 at Booth's Theatre and closed 9 October 1880 after 4 performances[41].

CAST: *The Right Hon. Sir Joseph Porter, K.C.B.*, First Lord of the Admiralty: HENRY CLAY BARNABEE. *Captain Corcoran*, commanding *H.M.S. Pinafore*: M. W. WHITNEY. *Ralph Rackstraw*, Able Seaman: TOM KARL. *Dick Deadeye*, Able Seaman: GEORGE FROTHINGHAM. *Bill Bowstay*, Boatswain's Mate: Gus Kammerlee. *Bob Becket*, Carpenter's Mate: W. W. Tuttle. *Ancient Mariner*: Henry F. Dixey. *Tom Tucker*, Midshipmite: Little Lillian. *Josephine*, the captain's Daughter: MARIE STONE. *Hebe*, Sir Joseph's First Cousin: MAY CALEF. *Little Buttercup*, a Portsmouth Bumboat Woman: ADELAIDE PHILLIPPS. *First Lord's Sisters, Cousins and Aunts*: Mrs. Ada B. Mullen, Ladies of the Chorus.

DESERET,

1880.54 or, The Saint's Difficulties

An American Comic Opera in Three Acts. Libretto by W. A. Croffut. Music by Dudley Buck. Stage manager, Eugene F. Eberle. Scenery by William Voegtlin. Costumes by H. J. Eaves. Conducted by Charles Schiller. Produced by the Dudley Buck Opera Company. Opened 11 October 1880 at Haverly's 14th Street Theatre and closed 23 October 1880 after 16 performances.

CAST: *Rosamond*, the one fair daughter of Elder Montgomery, of the Church of the Latter Day Saints: JULIA POLK. *Arabella*, a regimental laundress, the Pet of the army, the Sylph of the Plain: BELLE COLE. *Sally*, wife No. 1 of Elder Scram: Kate French. *Major Clemm*, of the 27th U.S. Cavalry, stationed near Salt Lake City: Charles F. Lang. *Joseph Jessup*, a rascally Indian Agent: W. G. Cogswell. *Elder Scram*, a very much married Mormon Saint: J. Evarde. *Lieutenant Montgomery*, of the 27th U.S. Cavalry, brother of Rosamond: W. D. Marks. *Setting Hen*, Chief of the Arrapahoes: Eugene F. Eberle. *Corporal Riley*: H. A. Stuart. *Wives, Indians and Soldiers*: Chorus of 60.

Act 1: Camp of the 27th Regiment, U.S. Cavalry, near Salt Lake City. The Council.

Act 2: Reception Room in the house of Elder Scram, at Salt Lake City. The Party.

Act 3: Another part of the Camp at night. The Elopement.

MUSICAL NUMBERS[42]

"Escaped, aye, free at last"
"Frowning castles (by the Gliding Rhine)"
"I'm cheerful and happy"
"Now I'll get a wife"
"The Serenade"
"Through the woods"
"Where can my gallant brother be"

CINDERELLA,

1880.55 or, The Little Glass Slipper

A Pictorial and Melodious arrangement of the fairy tale (by Charles Perrault). Adaptation by Henry C. Jarrett. Music by Gioacchino Rossini, Felix Mendelssohn, others, suggested by Max Maretzek. Staged by Henry C. Jarrett. Scenery by Henry E. Hoyt. Costumes by Mons. and Mme. Alias of London, and Eaves. Musical director, Anthony Reiff. Produced by Henry C. Jarrett (William H. Morton, Manager). Opened 12 October 1880 at Booth's Theatre and closed 6 November 1880 after 32 performances.

CAST: *Prince Paragon*: CATHERINE LEWIS. *Cinderella*: ANNIE SHAFFER. *Clorinda, Thisbe*, the proud sisters: ELMA DELARO, JENNIE HUGHES. *The Fairy Queen*, Cinderella's Godmother: Little KATIE SEYMOUR. *Baron Pompilino*, Cinderella's father: William H. Seymour. *Count Alidoro*, Tutor to the Prince: Edward Connell. *Dandini*, the Prince's Valet: MARK SMITH. *Pedro*, Cinderella's humble friend: James Vincent. *Colin, Dazzle*, Pages to the Prince: Ethel Delmont, Rosa Cortland. *Court favorites (4)*: *Count Primrose*: William Lloyd. *Lord Daisy*: Charles Bright. *Sir William Rocket*: Leonard Saville. *Viscount Dash*: Arthur German. *Specialties*: LIZZIE SIMMS (Sensational Transformation Danseuse[43]), Messrs. TOPACK & MOORE (Celebrated Folly Gymnasts, as proxies for Humpty and Dumpty). *Ladies of the Court, Guards, Hunters, Servitors*: Corps of Auxiliaries.

MUSICAL NUMBERS[44]

Drinking Song (from GIROFLÉ-GIROFLA)
C. Lewis
(*Music by* Charles Lecocq.)
"Morning, It's Sweets Flinging"
"Now With a Grief No Longer Bending"
"Once a King There Chanced to Be"
"Swift as the Flash"

1880.56 GIROFLE-GIROFLA

A Revival of the Opéra-bouffe in Three Acts[45], in French. Libretto by Albert Vanloo and Eugène Leterrier. Music by Charles Lecocq. Stage manager, Mons. Bouvard. Musical director, Charles Almeras. Produced by Maurice Grau's French Opera Company. Opened 13 October 1880 at the Standard Theatre and closed 15 October 1880 after 3 performances in repertory.

CAST: *Giroflé, Girofla*: Mlle. PAOLA MARIÉ. *Pedro*: Mlle. ANGÈLE. *Aurore*: Mlle. DELORME. *Paquita*: Mlle. BEAUDET. *Gusmand*: Mlle. Amelie. *Fernand*: Mlle. Seygand. *Almanzor*: Mlle. Estradere. *Nino*: Mlle. A. Bouvard. *Bolero*: Mons. DUPLAN. *Mourzouk*: Mons. JOUARD. *Chief of the Pirates*: Mons. Terrancle. *Godfather*: Mons. Dupuis. *A Dancer*: Mons. Gavant. *A Notary*: Mons. Gerard. *A Preceptor*: Mons. Thuillart. *An Uncle*: Mons. Borel. *Page*: Mons. Mauriez. *Marasquin*: Mons. VICTOR CAPOUL. *Cousins of the Bride, Men and Women of the Palace, Bridesmaids, Pages, Pirates and Moors attendant upon Mourzouk.*

1880.57 BOCCACCIO

A Return Engagement of the Operette in Three Acts[46]. Original Viennese libretto by F. Zell and Richard Genée. Music by Franz von Suppé. Produced by H. B. Mahn's English Opera Company. Opened 18 October 1880 at the Grand Opera House and closed 4 November 1880 after 21 performances[47].

CAST: *(Giovanni) Boccaccio*, a Novelist and Poet: JEANNIE WINSTON. *Fiametta*, Lambertuccio's adopted daughter: FRANCESCA GUTHRIE. *Leonetto*, his friend, a student: W. MORGAN. *Pietro*, Prince of Palermo: CHARLES STARELLE. *Lotteringhi*, a Cooper: ELLIS RYSE. *Isabella*, Lotteringhi's wife: MARIE SUMMERVILLE. *Lambertuccio*, a Grocer: A. H. BELL. *Peronella*, Lambertuccio's sister: ROSE LEIGHTON. *Scalza*, a Barber: VINCENT HOGAN. *Beatrice*, Scalza's daughter: SOPHIE HUMMEL. *Fattelli*, a Bookseller: ARTHUR VAN HOUTEN. *Checco*, a Beggar: Sidney Barnes. *Fresco*, the Cooper's Apprentice: Harry Dall. *The Unknown*: Arthur Van Houten. *Major Domo of the Duke*: H. Arthur.

Lotteringhi's Journeymen (12): *Alberto*: H. Depew. *Ricciardo*: H. Newman. *Gerbino*: Sidney Barnes. *Feodore*: A. Swicarde. *Guidotto*: H. Dixon. *Nostogio*: F. Manning. *Beppo*:

---

[40]First presented in New York 15 January 1879 at the Standard Theatre for 175 performances. For Synopsis of Scenes and Musical Numbers, see original 1879 production.
[41]No credits in programs for stage direction, scenery or costumes.
[42]Musical numbers not listed in programs. List prepared from published piano vocal gems (William A. Pond, New York, 1880).
[43]Musical numbers not listed in New York program. List prepared from Boston tryout of August 1879.
[44]Miss Simms will positively make 10 distinct changes of costume while performing different dances characteristic of foreign nations in the unprecedented time of ten minutes, two seconds only elapsing between each change: Swiss, Irish, French, Welch, Alsatian, Hungarian, Spanish, Scotch, Chinese, English.
[45]Originally produced in New York in French 4 February 1875 at the Park Theatre. For Synopsis of Scenes and Musical Numbers, see original 1875 production.
[46]First produced in New York in German 23 April 1880 at the Thalia for 15 performances; in English 15 May 1880 at the Union Square Theatre for 28 performances. For Synopsis of Scenes and Musical Numbers, see original 1880 production.
[47]For the last 2 days of the run (5-6 November) FATINITZA replaced BOCCACCIO.

H. Fairchild. *Irsi*: Walter Allen. *Alani*: Joseph Hans. *Gomio*: S. Battle. *Ferzo*: A. McKirby. *Cherzi*: J. Waite. *Students (8)*: *Tofano*: May Booth. *Chichibio*: Clara Douglass. *Guido*: Grace Clark. *Cisti*: May Clark. *Federico*: Anna Calloway. *Giotto*: Ella Caldwell. *Rinieri*: Dora Feitner. *Lanto*: Aida Hamilton. *Beggars (3)*: *Chiacometto*: J. Hobbs. *Anselmo*: Henry Newman. *Tito*: H. Depew. *Lambertuccio's Servants (3)*: *Filippa*: Maud Allison. *Orietta*: May Booth. *Violanta*: Eugenia Dankeert. *Donna Joncofiere*: H. Dalton. *Eliza*, Donna Joncofiere's servant girl: Abbie Nicholson. *Chorus of 50.*

180.58

BABIOLE

A Pastoral Opéra Bouffe in Three Acts, in French. Libretto to the opérette villageoise by Clairville and Octave Gastineau. Music by (François Anatole) Laurent de Rillé. Stage manager, V. Merle. Musical director, Charles Alteras. Produced by Maurice Grau's French Opera Company. Opened 21 October 1880 at the Standard Theatre and closed 23 October 1880 after 4 performances.[48]

CAST: *Babiole*: Mlle. PAOLA MARIÉ. *Madeleine*, wife of Romarin: Mlle. MARY ALBERT. *Arabelle*: Mlle. MERLE. *Georgette*: Mlle. Vallot. *Estelle*: Mlle. Estradere. *Jeanne*: Mlle. Armand. *Babet*: Mlle. Malvina. *Monseigneur de Mirabelle*: Mons. J. MEZIÈRES. *The Bailiff*: Mons. Duplan. *Carcassol*: Mons. CLEMENT NIGRI. *Alain*, the gardener: Mons. F. TAUFFENBERGER. *Romarin*, the Miller: Mons. VINCHON. *Mourmelon*: Mons. Vilano. *Male and Female Peasants, Forest Keepers, Fiddlers, Village Guards.*

MUSICAL NUMBERS
- "Un p'tit ferme, un p'tit jardinet"
  - F. Tauffenberger
- "Rondeau de la sorcellerie"
  - P. Marié
- "Couplets de charme"
  - P. Marié

1880.59

REVELS, or Bon-Ton George, Jr.

Rice's Surprise Party in a Grand Comic Musical Extravaganza in Two Acts, 6 Scenes. Play by John J. McNally and Dexter Smith. Original and selected music by Henry Sator. (Production staged by Edward E. Rice.) Stage manager, John Mackay. Director of specialties, Henry E. Dixey. Musical director, Henry Sator. Produced by Edward E. Rice. Opened 25 October 1880 at Haverly's 14th Street Theatre and closed 27 November 1880 after 41 performances.

CAST: *Bon-Ton George, Jr.*, called St. George, tho' he is ain't a saint at all, in love with Maryanthus, beloved by her; also, the Princess and the Witch Kabylla, a dashing but troublesome lad: TOPSY VENN. *Rufus*, his half brother, who does not have half enough love for George, sine he affects love to Maryanthus: LINA MERVILLE. *Sir Ramsgate Bramblewig*, formerly a Pork Butcher of England, now Major Domo to a minor King; guardian of Maryanthus, and father of George and Rufus: GEORGE W. HOWARD. *Maryanthus*, Bramblewig's ward, a charming girl, in love with George: VICTORIA REYNOLDS. *Isis*, Bramblewig's maid, stupid but jolly, in love with Calapat: MARION ELMORE. *Dame Barbara*, an ancient Dame of middle age, who copies modern manners: EMMA BURGESS. *Calapat*, her son, very much a masher, who has a great deal of trouble because he is "such a dorg," in love with everybody generally, but Isis in particular: JOHN GOURLAY. *Scarbrand*, a Brute-Trainer, whose only friend is a sagacious turtle: JOHN A. MACKAY. *King of Egypt*, A. Gripper by name, and a gripper by nature, in love with Dame Barbara: DONALD HAROLD. *Professor Inkijab*, in truth a follower of the King: HENRY E. DIXEY. *Princess Alfreda*, Daughter of A. Gripper, who says little, but is talked of a great deal: MABEL MITCHELL. *Uarda*, her waiting-maid, waiting on the Princess and for Calapat: Venie Bennett. *King's Herald*: CARRIE E. PERKINS. *Hypatia*, a Fortune-Teller: MARION SINGER. *Kabylla*, a Wicked Witch, who tries to ruin George: MARION SINGER. *Sprite*, her aid: William Elliott. *Three knights who disport for three days*: *St. Andrew* of Scotland: Rose Wilson. *St. Erin*, of Ireland: Ada Lee. *St. Denis*, of France: May Livingstone. *Cleo, Ina*, two of the King's pages: May Smith, Blanche Cameron. *John Malithorn*, Postman: August Kramer. *Catch M, Grabem, Clubem, Shootem*, four hearts forever on the beat, four heads with nothing in 'em: Messrs. Steele, Morse, Aiken, Kramer. *Water Turtle and a Fiery Dragon*: William Elliott. *Knights, Squires,*

ACT 1[49]
Scene 1
- "Let Us Gaily Sing" (Opening Chorus)
- Duet
  - T. Venn, M. Reynolds
- "Oh, George!" (Trio)
  - T. Venn, E. Burgess, G. W. Howard
- Postman's Chorus
  - Principals, Chorus
- Fan Fan Waltz
  - Principals, Chorus

Scene 2
- "Nothing's Too Bad for Me" (Ruffian's Song)
  - J. A. Mackay
- "Don't lose your temper" (Trio)
  - M. Elmore, V. Bennett, J. Gourlay

Scene 3
- "See the mighty dragon comes"
  - Chorus
- "Mainly a Clogging Main" (Concerted)
- "Old, old age" (Duet)
  - V. Reynolds, M. Singer (Hypatia)
- Grand Finale
  - T. Venn, Chorus

CT 2
Scene 1
- Song
  - V. Reynolds
- "Oh, Barbara"
  - E. Burgess, J. Gourlay, D. Harold
- "We quake, we shake" (Chorus of Kings)

Scene 2
- "Policemen" (Song and Chorus)
  - J. Gourlay, Characters
- "Strolling in the Woodland"
  - T. Venn
  - (*Music and Lyrics by* Edward E. Rice.)
- Song

Scene 3
- Opening March and Entrance of Characters
- Card Chorus and Scene—Euchre!
- "The Sword Quadrille"
  - T. Venn, L. Merville, Knights
- Grand Finale (St. George Victorious)

1880.60

LA PÉRICHOLE

A Revival of the Opéra-bouffe in Three Acts, 4 Scenes, in French[50]. Libretto by Ludovic Halévy and Henri Meilhac. Music by Jacques Offenbach. Stage manager, V. Merle. Musical director, Charles Almeras. Produced by Maurice Grau's French Opera Company. Opened 25 October 1880 at the Standard Theatre and closed 26 October 1880 after 2 performances in repertory.

CAST: *La Périchole*, a street singer: Mlle. PAOLA MARIÉ. *Guadalena*: Mlle. Vallot. *Berginella*: Mlle. Malvina. *Mastrilla*: Mlle. Choquet. *Manuelita*: Mlle. Armand. *Frasquinella*: Mlle. Berthe. *Brambilla*: Mlle. Estradere. *Ninetta*: Mlle. Blauville. *Don Andrès de Ribeira*, Viceroy of Peru: Mons. VILANO. *Don Pedro of Hinoyosa*, Governor of Lima: Mons. DUPLAN. *Count Panatellas*, First Gentleman of the Bed-Chamber: Mons. J. MEZIÈRES. *The Marquis of Tarapote*: Mons. Vinchon. *An Old Prisoner*: Mons. Poyard. *Two Notaries*: Messrs. Gerard, Perret. *A Jailor*: Mons. Millet. *Piquillo*: Mons. CLEMENT NIGRI.

1880.61

PRINZ METHUSALEM

A Comic Opera (Operette) in Three Acts, in German. Libretto by Karl Treumann, adapted from a French libretto by Victor van Wilder and Alfred

[48]Musical numbers not listed in programs.

[49]Musical numbers not listed in programs. Apart from the first interpolation given, the list of songs prepared from published vocal selections (Ferrett, New York, 1880).

[50]First produced in New York in French in a two-act version 4 January 1869 at Pike's Opera House for 35 performances. Expanded three-act version in French introduced to New York 15 February 1877; for Synopsis of Scenes and Musical Numbers, see entry at that date.

Delacour. Music by Johann Strauss. (Stage director), Dr. Lube. Costumen, Herr Buchheister. Kapellmeister, Heinrich Greiner. Eigenthümer (proprietor), Wilhelm Kramer. Direction, Mathilde Cottrelly. Opened 29 October 1880 at the Thalia Theatre and closed 3 January 1881 in repertory.

CAST: *Prinz Methusalem*, of Riccarac: Frl. MARIE KÖNIG. *Sigismund, Fürst von [Duke of] Trocadero*: Herr GUSTAV ADOLFI. *Pulcinella*: Frl. KUSTER. *Marquis Carbonazzi*: Herr BOJOCK. *Count Vulcanio*, Lord Chamberlain: Herr. PULS. *Herzog Cyprian [Duke] of Riccarac*: Herr LUBE. *Sophistika [Sphisteira]*, his wife: Frl. LUBE. *Trombonius*, the composer: Herr SCHNELLE.

1880.62 FATINITZA

A Revival of the Comic Opera in Three Acts[51]. Original Viennese libretto to the operette by F. Zell and Richard Genée, based on the libretto to "La Circassienne" by Eugène Scribe.) Music by Franz von Suppé. Stage manager, Vincent Hogan. Musical director, Gustave A. Kerker. Produced by H. B. Mahn's English Comic Opera Company. Opened 5 November 1880 at the Grand Opera House and closed 6 November 1880 after 3 performances.[52]

CAST: *Vladimir*, a young Russian lieutenant, afterwards disguised as Fatinitza: JEANNIE WINSTON. *Princess Lydia (Imanovna)*, Niece of the Count: SALLIE REBER. *Count Timofey Kantchukoff*, a Russia General: ELLIS RYSE. *Izzet Pasha*, Governor of the Turkish Fort: VINCENT HOGAN. *Russian Officers (3)*: *Wasili*, Captain of Russian Infantry: Arthur Bell. *Osipp*, Lieutenant: M. Calice. *Steipann*, Sergeant: Arthur Van Houten. *Julian (Hardy)*, a Special Newspaper Correspondent: W. A. MORGAN. *Hassan Bey*, Leader of the Bashi-Bazouks: Fletcher Manning. *Russian Cadets (3)*: *Nikophor*: Clara Douglas. *Feodor*: Grace Clarke. *Demitri*: May Clarke. *Izzet Pasha's Wives (4)*: *Nourmahal*: Miss Somerville. *Zuleika*: Rose Leighton. *Diona*: Janet Edmondson. *Beseika*: Annie Callaway. *Massaldsha*, a Fortune Teller: May Booth. *Mustapha*, the Guard of the Harem: A. H. BELL. *Winka*, a Bulgarian spy: Sidney Barnes. *Hanna*, his wife: Mrs. Ellis Ryse. *Adjutant*: H. Dale. *Jeesuf*: Fletcher Manning. *Surema*, his daughter: Clara Dixon. *Ben Jimin*, his slave: H. Dale. *Niridah*, an Old Gossip: H. Depew. *Fatima*, an Old Gossip: J. Hobbs. *Achmet*, Keeper of Menagerie: J. Hans. *Russian Soldiers, Bashi Bazouks, Cossacks, Moorish Women, Nubian Slaves, Russian Serfs, Sleigh Drivers, etc.*

1880.63 ENCHANTMENT

A Revised Version of the Beautiful Fairy Spectacle in Four Acts, 16 Scenes[53]. Music composed and arranged by Charles Puerner. Entire production, mis en scène, beautiful ballets under the personal direction and supervision of Imre and Bolossy Kiralfy. Scenery by William Voegtlin. Costumes designed by Grévin of Paris and Colonel Alfred Thompson of London. Orchestra conducted by Charles Puerner. Produced by the Kiralfys (Imre, Bolossy). Opened 15 November 1880 at Haverly's Niblo's Garden Theatre and closed 4 December 1880 after 25 performances.

CAST: *André*, a poor fisherman: HENRI LAURENT. *The Governor*: FELIX MORRIS. *Don Lodas*, the Hunchback in love with Angeline: WILLIAM DAVIDGE, JR. *Peter*, his Lackey: Joseph M. Humphrey. *Arbra*, the Sorcerer: B. W. TURNER. *Count Bohn*, Minister of War: Thomas Francis Meagher. *Malcolm*, the Old Man of the Mountain: William H. Bokee. *Paternas*: L. A. Eastman. *Ephemeral*: B. H. Williamson. *Sweetheart*, an Ape: Young America. *An Ephemeral Soldier*: P. J. Toole. *Angeline*, the Governor's daughter, in love with Andre: BLANCHE CORELLI. *Rayeuse*, the Sorceress: ADELAIDE CHERIE. *Madelon*, a fish seller: JENNIE YEAMANS. *Rosette*, a cloth merchant: Kate Goodwin. *Eglantine*, Paternas' bride: Ada Boyle. *Serpolette*: Etta Clark. *Fairy Brilliantine*: Miss REYNOLDS. *Fairies of the Magic Bush (7)*: *Agitta*: Pearl Everleigh. *Bellina*: Edith Everleigh. *Myrra*: Clute Howard. *Zarilla*: Georgie Knowlton. *Eureka*: Millie Cooper. *Semiros*: Clara Moore. *Donina*: Susie Kirwin. *Lords, Ladies, Soldiers, Guard Ephemerai, Demons, Spirits, Sorcerers, Fairies.*

Ballet: Mlles. ADELE CORNALBA, EUGENE CAPPELINI, CAMIS; Corps of 100 Danseuses. *Specialties*: The Herbert Brothers, the Comical Staircase Band, the Russian Athletes, Awata Katsnoshin (the Japanese Prince).

Act 1, Scene 1: Market Place. *Scene 2*: Andre's Home. *Scene 3*: The Governor's Garden.

Act 2, Scene 1: The Land of Ephemerals. *Scene 2*: Mountain Path. *Scene 3*: The Devil's Path. *Scene 4*: The Blue Monkey Inn. *Scene 5*: The Plain of Windmills. *Scene 6*: Gondola Fete.

Act 3, Scene 1: The Mystic Hotel. *Scene 2*: Moonlight Cemetery. *Scene 3*: The Magic Bush. *Scene 4*: The Corridor of Babilon. *Scene 5*: The Sacrifice.

Act 4, Scene 1: The Palace of Enchantment. *Scene 2*: Grand Apotheosis.

BALLETS[54]

Grand Ballet (Act 2, Scene 5)
Mlles. Cornalba, Cappelini, Camis, Corps de Ballet

Specialties
Staircase Band; Russian Athletes in their Great Ladder Act; The Devene Family; Herbert Brothers.

Grand Ballet de Gondolieres (Act 2, Scene 6)
Corps de Ballet

Les Favorites de Babel (Act 3, Scene 4)
Mlles. Cornalba, Cappelini, Camis

1880.64 THE MULLIGAN GUARD'S NOMINEE

A Comic Play in One Act, 9 Scenes[55]. Play (and lyrics) by Edward Harrigan. Music by David Braham. Produced under the immediate supervision of Edward Harrigan. Scenic artist, Charles W. Witham. Properties, Robert Puller. Machinist, Robert Cutler. Gas effects, Richard Doyle. Musical director, David Braham. Produced by Edward Harrigan and Tony Hart. Opened 22 November 1880 at the Theatre Comique and closed 19 February 1881 after 104 performances.

CAST: *Dan Mulligan*: EDWARD HARRIGAN. *Rebecca Allup*: TONY HART. *Captain Simpson Primrose*: JOHN WILD. *Reverend Palestine Puter*: William Gray. *Gustavus Lochmuller*: HARRY FISHER. *Snuff McIntosh*: Ed Burt. *Humphrey Down*: Ed Burt. *Caroline Melrose*: James Tierney. *Wetmore Cinders*: William West. *Oliver Bullwinkle*: Edwin Barry. *August Bimble*: Harry Sinclair. *Walsingham McSweeny*: Michael Bradley. *Mrs. Honora Dublin*: John Queen. *Major Dandeline Douglas*: M. Foley. *Dick Dublin*: Fred Queen. *Tip Moloney*: Eugene Rourke. *Carl Robecker*: Robert Hall. *William Cromwell*: John Mealey. *Officer Sudden*: J. McCullough. *Officer Soon*: Joseph Buckley. *Officer Stop*: John Coffee. *Pedro Giovanna*: James Fitzsimmons. *Gus Lochmuller, Jr.*: Master Emil Husel. *Bridget Lochmuller*: ANNIE MACK. *Cordelia Mulligan*: ANNIE YEAMANS. *Diana McFudd*: EMILY YEAMANS. *Lucretia Crowley*: Mary Bird. *Henrietta Dempsey*: Belle Mordaunt. *Annetta McSorley*: Susie Byron. *Arabella Higgins*: Nellie Aldine. *Margery McNabb*: Nellie Walton. *Hackmen, Policemen, Mulligan Constituents, etc.*: Auxiliary Corps.

Skidmore Guard, Regimental Roll: JOHN WILD, WILLIAM GRAY, Edward Goss, James Fox, Michael Foley, George Merritt, John Oberist, W. Merritt, Joseph Buckley, James Fitzsimmons, John Coffee, Fred Queen, John McCullough, John Mealey, Thomas Ray.

Scene 1: Exterior of Cunard Wharf and West Street. *Scene 2*: City Hall Park and Adjacent Building. *Scene 3*: The "Wee Drop" Saloon and back parlor. *Scene 4*: Exterior of Puter & Co., Bankers, and Primrose's Barber Shop. *Scene 5*: Interior of Washington Hall. *Scene 6*: A Local Street. *Scene 7*: The Junction. Polling Booth. Place of Election. *Scene 8*: Albany Boat Pier. *Scene 9*: Main Cabin of the Albany Boat.

MUSICAL NUMBERS

"Canada I Oh" (Scene 3)
(Ladies of the F.N.A.[56])

"Down in Gossip Row" (Scene 3)
(Ladies of the F.N.A.)

"Hang the Mulligan Banner Up" (Scene 3)
(Mulligan's Supporters)

"Mulligan's Promises" (Scene 5)
E. Harrigan

"The Skidmore Masquerade" (Scene 5)

"The Skids Are Out Tonight" (Scene 7)
Skidmore Guards

"A Nightcap" (Scene 9)

1880.65 PRINCE ACHMET!

Rice's Surprise Party in a reconstructed version of the Musical Extravaganza "Horrors"[57] in Two Acts. New music selected and arranged by Henry Sator. Produced by Edward E. Rice. Opened 29 November 1880 at Haverly's 14th Street Theatre and closed 11 December 1880 after 16 performances.

---

[51]First produced in New York in English 22 April 1879 at the Fifth Avenue Theatre for 41 performances. For Synopsis of Scenes and Musical Numbers, see original 1879 production.

[52]English adaptation uncredited. No credits in programs for stage director, scenery or costumes.

[53]First presented in New York 4 September 1879 at Niblo's Garden for 120 performances.

[54]Ballets, not musical numbers, listed in programs. Critics remarked that Henri Laurent and Blanche Corelli performed songs.

[55]Billed as Volume 7th of the Mulligan Guards Series.

[56]At first known as the Fenian National Association, but later revealed as the Florence Nightingale Association.

[57]HORRORS, or the Marajah of Zogobad, was first produced in New York 28 May 1879 at the Union Square for 41 performances; Edward E. Rice was credited then as author, Louis Harrison with lyrics.

CAST: *Hamsetjee Bumsetjee*, always in the arms of Morpheus. A Snorer from Snorerville, but wine works wonder: JOHN GOURLAY. *Rumstejee Bumsetjee*, a Parsee Astrologer, ambitious to be the power behind the throne, and gets thrown out of the town: GEORGE W. HOWARD. *Rajah Zog*, of Hibernian descent, full of majesty, gout, fond of hearing from the planets, tries to planet so that the Prince will marry the Princess: HENRY E. DIXEY. *Prince Achmet*, his son, who has to travel six months by act of Parliament. The Actmet with his approval: TOPSY VENN. *Tragedee*, Court Jester, who thinks position is everything, in fact a regular imposition: JOHN A. MACKAY. *Captain Beauforall*, the ladies' pet: LENA MERVILLE. *Zohi, Zolo*, scions of the noble house, who are sighing to rove with the Prince: VICTORIA REYNOLDS, ADA LEE. *Zizzis*, chief of the Princess' followers, who thinks that love is an eternal transport—so is a canal boat: CARRIE PERKINS. *Captain Darling*, of the American gunboat *"Pensacola"*: EMMA BURGESS. *Merrypate, Makelaugh*, silent but useful: May Livingston. *What's in a name? Wait till you hear them (5): Punjaeb Tong*: William Smith. *Calcut Tong*: Andrew Metzger. *Saka Zeke*: D. P. Steele. *Biff Alalong*: Ed Aiken. *French manipulators of succulent hash (3): Fricaseed Françoise*: E. R. Morse. *Alamode Jean*: August Kremer. *Fille de Cocardesse*: Donald Harold. *Billy Bowline*, a nice little tar: Emma Duchateau. *Four nice clean tars, shiver the cabin boy's back teeth, etc.*: *Hallyard Zephyr*: Blanche Seymour. *Silver Foam*: May Smith. *Crested Wavelet*: Mabel Mitchell. *Headland Breaker*: Lulu Campbell. *Begum D'Lite*, Princess of Bombay, delightful young lady, though the Prince chose her not, she'll be-gum d'lite to the last: VENIE BENNETT. *Zaidee*, a simple maiden, but sometimes they know a thing or two. An adorer of the Prince: MARION ELMORE. *La Jolie Housekeepaire*, proprietress of a hotel in Ceylon. She sets her seal on all the hearts of her boarders: MARION SINGER. *Attendants on the Princess*: Violet Ulpah, Frances Lum. *Court of the Rajah, Attendants on the Prince, Tum-tum Beaters, Jungle Kakers, Nautch Girls, Sailors, Jugglers, Waiters, Snake Charmers, Star-Gazers in profusion.*

MUSICAL NUMBERS[58]

"The Lum-Tum Capah" (Act 1, Scene 2)
T. Venn

1880.66

NISIDA

A Comic Opera in Three Acts, in German. Original French libretto to the comic operette "Nisida" by F. Zell and Moritz West. Music by Richard Genée. Regie (Stage director), Dr. Lube. Costumes, Herr Buchheister. Conductor, Heinrich Greiner. Eigenthümer (proprietor), Wilhelm Kramer. Direction, Mathilde Cottrelly. Opened 7 December 1880 at the Thalia Theatre and closed 1 January 1881 in repertory.

CAST: *Nisida*: Fraulein MATHILDE COTTRELLY. *Don Leonida Balestro*, Corregidor of Havana: Herr GUSTAV ADOLFI. *Donna Miguela*, his sister: Frau LUBE. *Donna Mercedes* de Carrragui: Frau MARIE KÖNIG. *Don Montiel de Carragui*, her brother: Herr SCHNELLE. *Don Rodrigo Sandoval*: Herr F. Lenoir. *Don Graciano de Anteladados*: Herr O. Meyer. *Barnacle*, Impressario aus Madrid: Herr LUBE. *Rinaldo, Rinaldini*, Theateragenten: Herren Schnitz, Vosod. *Mariano*: Herr Danser. *Carmen*, Cafetière: Fraulein Raberg. *Spartaco*: Herr F. Varena. *Luna*: Herr Puls. *Cardinal, Banalon*: Herren Albrecht, Wagner. *Barda*, Zimmermadchen in der "Albergo grande': Frl. Hartmann. *Bepta, Encarnacion*, Mädchen aus dem Wolfe: Frau Lentz, Fraulein Camara. *Zeitungsjunge(4)*: *Erister*: Frau Tell. *Zweiter*: Fraulein Grünewald. *Dritter*: Fraulein Wiener II. *Bierter*: Fraulein Schlag II. *Scrite, Zivette*: Frauleins Winer I, Schlag II.

Act 1: Almeda (in der Rhede von Havana) mit der "Albergo grande."

Act 2: Tropischer Garten der "Albergo grande" mit dem "Spielsaton."

Act 3: Landgutt der Carriguio nahe Havana am See. Tropische Vegetation.

ACT 1[59]

- Introduction
- Trio
- Song with Chorus
- Quartet and Couplets
- Quintet
- Entrée of Nisida
- Duet
- Finale

ACT 2

- Introduction
- Couplets
- Sextet
- Duet
- Duet with Chorus
- Finale Act 2

ACT 3

- Introduction (Romance and Chorus)
- Barcarole/Duet
- Waltz Quartett
- Couplets
- Finale

1880.67

HIAWATHA!

A long way after Longfellow

Rice's Surprise Party in a Revival of the Operatic Burlesque in Two Acts[60]. Libretto by Nathaniel Childs. Music by Edward E. Rice. Stage manager, John A. Mackay. Scenery by William Voegtlin. Musical director, Henry Sator. Produced by Edward E. Rice. Opened 13 December 1880 at Haverly's 14th Street Theatre and closed 25 December 1880 after 16 performances.

CAST: *Hiawatha*, an Indian Chief. All lisping young ladies say HE AH-WATH a charming fellow: TOPSY VENN. *William Penn Brown*, commonly known as Penn, a United States Commissioner, who has PENN-ETRATED the forest, not FOR-REST, but for plunder: JOHN A. MACKAY. *Romulus Smith, Remus Brown*, Siamese twin-like conspirators, Tools of Penn, but who go in t'win themselves: HENRY E. DIXEY, JOHN GOURLAY. *Mr. Lo*, formerly a poor Indian, now well-off. With his wife, much of a Lo-Co-motive of the plot: GEORGE W. HOWARD. *Yenadizzi*, a beautiful dashing young Indian of the period, in love with this Lo's daughter: LENA MERVILLE. *District Telegraph Boy*: ROSE WILSON. *Honeydew, Hazel Dell*, Young warriors, attendants on Hiawatha: CARRIE E. PERKINS, LAVINIA BENNETT. *Old Man Afraid of His Whiskey*, Mr. Lo's Father: Donald Harold. *Scar-Face Charley*: Andrew Metzger. *Sweet-Face William*: Edward Aiken. *Minnehaha*, the fairest Indian girl of the tribe, beloved by all. Everyone is expected to be tickled by her name: MARION SINGER. *Mrs. Lo*, wife of Mr. Lo—*nee* Miss High: MARION ELMORE. *Sally Bohee*, servant in the family of Lo: VICTORIA REYNOLDS. *Adjunct conspirators who ADD JUNK to their plunder; Indians of all colors; Indianesses of all shades; also live and dead animals in profusion.*

1880.68

HUMPTY DUMPTY

A Revival of the Pantomime Extravaganza in Three Acts[61]. Scenery by Henry E. Hoyt and Gaspard Maeder. Musical director, Julius Peters. Produced by Henry E. Abbey's Mammoth Pantomimic Organization (S. M. Hickey, Proprietor and Manager). Opened 20 December 1880 at Niblo's Garden and closed 8 January 1881 after 24 performances.

CAST (Prologue): *Genius of the Drama*: Marie Langler. *Muse of Comedy*: BELLE GABRIELLE. *Spirit of Pantomime*: ALBERT MARTINETTI. *Tragedy*: C. Kompe. *Burlesque*: Bertha Kline. *Opera*: Angie Soulke. *Spectacle*: Carrie Folsom. *Melodrama*: J. Tiernan. *Farce*: J. H. Greene.

CAST (Pantomime): *Old One-Two*, Buckle My Shoe: W. JULIAN MARTINETTI. *Old Three-Four*, Open the Door: JOSEPH LEON. *Tommy Tucker*: ALBERT MARTINETTI. *Tommy Tucker, No. 2*: J. F. RAYMOND. *Little Goody Twoshoes*: PAULINE MARTINETTI. *Little Goody Twoshoes, No. 2*: BELLE GABRIELLE. *Grouty-Gritz*, the Village Burgomaster: John Mullen. *Quill Pen*, his clerk: J. Tiernan. *The Jolly Millers (4)*: *Korn Shook*: William Jones. *Cyrus Chaff*: H. L. Simpson. *Reuben Rye*: J. Thompson. *Felix Fodder*: W. A. Allen. *The Village Lasses (4)*: *Abigail Allspice*: Miss Kline. *Rachel Racket*: Miss Folsom. *Mary Maydew*: Miss Jarbea. *Susan Sweetapple*: Miss Soulke.

Transformation of Characters: *Clowns (2)*: *Humpty Dumpty, Sr.*: JAMES S. MAFFITT. *Humpty Dumpty, Jr.*: ROBERT FRASER. *Pantaloons*: J. MARTINETTI, JOSEPH LEON. *Harlequins*: ALBERT MARTINETTI, J. F. RAYMOND. *Columbines*: PAULINE MARTINETTI, BELLE GABRIELLE.

Specialties, Act 2: THE MARTINETTI FAMILY, ALBERT VALJEAN (Egyptian Juggler and Balancer, Trained Pigeons). BELLE GABRIELLE (Chrystalonicon), the Troupe Davine (Mlles. ALZA, Letta, Magerald; W. M. Davine), the Rajade Troupe, the Tyrolean Warblers.

Act 1, Scene 1: Vale of Temple, Thessaly. *Scene 2*: Tyrolean Village. Hotel McMullen and Barbier; Butcher vs. Baker.

Act 2: The Rocky Dell. Dark and Dismal Day. A Sudden Transformation; Grand Carnival of Sensations.

Act 3, Scene 1: Milliners and Tailors. *Scene 2*: Model Bakery. *Scene 3*: Dry Goods and Umbrella Store. *Scene 4*: Marvelous Exhibition of the Mechanical and Scenic Art. The Great Transformation Scene, entitled Humpty Dumpty's Valentine. (Hoyt and Maeder.)

---

[58]Musical numbers not listed in programs.

[59]Songs not listed in programs. List prepared from piano reduction of the score (Boosey & Hawkes, London, n.d.).

[60]First produced in New York 21 February 1880 at the Standard Theatre for 17 performances in repertory. For Synopsis of Scenes and Musical Numbers, see original 1880 production.

[61]First produced 3 February 1880 at Abbey's Booth Theatre for 64 performances. For Synopsis of Scenes and Musical Numbers, see original 1880 production.

1880.69

OLIVETTE

An Opéra-comique in Three Acts. Original French libretto to the opérette 'Les Noces d'Olivette' by Henri Chivot and Alfred Duru. English adaptation by Henry B. Farnie. Music by Edmond Audran. Stage manager, John Howson. Scenery by John A. Thompson, Charles W. Witham. Costumes designs by the author, executed by Emma Berg. Musical director, Jesse Williams. Produced by the (W. J.) Comley-(James) Barton Company, by arrangement with Richard D'Oyly Carte. Opened 25 December 1880 at the Bijou Opera House, moved 31 January 1881 to the Fifth Avenue Theatre and closed 26 February 1881 after 68 performances. Re-opened 18 April 1881 at the Fifth Avenue Theatre and closed 14 May 1881 after 40 additional performances. Total: 108 performances.

CAST: *Captain de Merrimac*, of the Man o' War *"Cormorant"*: JOHN HOWSON. *Valentine*, Officer of the Rousillon Guards, his nephew: J. C. ARMAND. *Duc des Ifs*, cousin and heir presumptive to the Countess: JAMES BARTON. *Coquelicot*, his foster brother and henchman: DIGBY V. BELL. *Marvejol*, local pluralist, Seneschal to the Countess and Maire of Perpignan: W. J. COGSWELL. *Postiche*, another pluralist, barber and inn-keeper at Perpignan: F. L. Lennox. *Boussole*: F. Henry. *Loup de Mer*: T. A. Marriott. *Olivette*, daughter of the Seneschal Marvejol: CATHERINE LEWIS. *Bathelde*, Countess of Rousillon, in love with Valentine: HETTY TRACY. *Veloutine*, the Seneschal's housekeeper: MARIE JANSEN. *Moustique*, the Captain's boy on board the *"Cormorant:"*: Helen Stuart. *Jayoux, Fallesamour*, Pages of the Countess: Kate French, Ellen Vincent. *Mlle. de Montjoye, Mlle. de Lenori*, Ladies of the Countess' Suite: Misses Millie Boston, Lizzie Paur. *Caton*, maid of the Main-Brace Tavern: Bessie Temple. *Courtiers and Nobles*: Messrs. Hanselman, Ridgeway, Schwicardi, Randal *Citizens, Wedding Guests and Sailors*: Misses Osborne, May, Saukevert, Watson, Hilliges, Pomroy. *Soldiers of the Guard, Pages, etc.*

The action passes at Perpignan, in the centre of Rousillon, on the shore of the Mediterranean, under Louis XIII.

Act 1: The Seneschal's House at Perpignan. Shore of the Mediterranean. (Thompson.)

Act 2: Ballroom of the Palace of Rousillon. (Witham.)

Act 3: Interior of the Main-Brace Tavern. The *"Cormorant"* at Anchor. (Thompson.)

ACT 1[62]

"Just Fancy What Is Said" (Gossip Chorus)
Chorus
"Timid and Graceful" (Air)
W. J. Cogswell, Chorus
"The Convent Slept" (Song)
C. Lewis
"The Yacht and the Brig" (Marine Madrigal)
C. Lewis, J. C. Armand, J. Howson, J. W. Cogswell, Sopranos
"First Love" (Valse-Song)
H. Tracy
"O Woman's Fickle!" (Song)
H. Tracy
"Bob Up Serenely!" (Couplets)
J. Barton
"Darling, Good Night!" (Serenade)
J. C. Armand
Concerted Piece (Your partisans, brave soldiers, handle)
C. Lewis, M. Jansen, J. C. Armand, J. Barton, W. J. Cogswell, Chorus[63]
"Speak, Sir Captain!" (Finale) (Scene)
Tutti e Coro
"O, My Father!" (Sob Song)
C. Lewis
Marriage Bells Chorus
Tutti e Coro

ACT 2

"Soon the Bride" (Chorus)
Chorus
"The Matron of an Hour" (Air)
C. Lewis
"It Is He" (Quintette)
H. Tracy, C. Lewis, J. C. Armand, J. Barton, W. J. Cogswell
"Wayward Woman" (Air)
H. Tracy
"What? She Your Wife!" (Duet)
J. C. Armand, J. Howson
"Not Wife, Nor Maid" (Song)
C. Lewis
"I Love My Love So Well!" (Song and Refrain à due)
H. Tracy, C. Lewis
"What Joy in Honey-Mooning" (Finale)
Tutti e Coro
"The Farandol"
H. Tracy

ACT 3

"Jamaica Rum!" (Chorus and Song)
Midshipmen, Chorus
"Jamaica Rum" (A Grog-orian Chant)
Midshipmam [L'Ecureuil]
"Nearest and Dearest" (Romance)
H. Tracy
"The Torpedo and the Whale" (In the North Sea lived a Whale)(Legend)
C. Lewis, Chorus
Exit of Sailors (The fishing being loaded)
"Where Balmy Garlic Scents the Air" (Bolero)
J. Howson
"No, No!—'Tis You!" (Laughing Quartette)
C. Lewis, J. C. Armand, J. Howson, J. Barton
Marche Militaire
"All Is Ended" (Chorus Finale)
Tutti e Coro

[62]Musical numbers not listed in programs. List prepared from published piano vocal score (William A. Pond, New York, 1881); score carries the additional credit "dialogue and stage business adapted for America by Henry W. Montgomery."
[63]All musical scores assign a bass singing role named Lonfuseau to this song, but no such character name appears in theatre programs or published score cast list.

1880.70

BABES IN THE WOOD, or, Who Killed Cock Robin?

Rice's Surprise Party in a Revival of the Operatic Musical Extravaganza (Pantomime) in Two Acts[64]. Play by Willie Edouin, brushed up for the American public by Louis Harrison. Musical director, Henry Sator. Produced by Edward E. Rice. Opened 27 December 1880 at Haverly's 14th Street Theatre and closed 1 January 1881 after 8 performances.[65]

CAST: *The Bad Man*, a mysterious creature who is up to villainy of every shade and kind, but who eventually proves to be by no means as black as he is painted: TOPSY VENN. *The Very Bad Man*, a heavier villain, by several pounds of deeper DYE, and who finally DIES in combat DIRE: DONALD HAROLD. *Takeit Sneak*, a pick-up of unconsidered trifles: HENRY E. DIXEY. *Sir Rowland Maccassar*, the remorseless "uncle," in whose care his elder brother has left his pledges: GEORGE W. HOWARD. *Dr. Fitzflummery*, an M.D., deah boy, quite M.T.-headed, you know: VICTORIA REYNOLDS. *Prince Pretty-Fellow*, who comes to collect his bond in cash, but gets it in the flesh nearest his heart: CARRIE E. PERKINS. *Sir Rupert*, a COURTeous young COURTier from the Prince's COURT: VENIE G. BENNETT. *The Family Physician*: Edward Aiken. *Golightly Carrywell*, Lady Maccassar's pet page, in fact page 1, or one page in a hundred: EMMA DUCHATEAU. *Tommy, Sally*, The Babes: JOHN GOURLAY, MARION ELMORE. *Falcontrina*, the little birds love her, so does Prince Pretty-fellow, and in fact all the other fellows: MARION SINGER. *Lady Maccassar*, Sir Rowland's AIDE, and a better half, who, although she allows him no will of his own, assists him in appropriating his brother's: JOHN A. MACKAY. *Miss Jones*, Schoolm'am, and consequently a martyr: EMMA BURGESS. *Four Consulting Physicians*, more Terpsichorean than Medical: *Dr. Bigfee*: Andrew Metzger. *Dr. Littlepill*: Henry Kramer. *Dr. Callagain*: Edward Morse. *Dr. Overpaid*: David P. Steele. *Attendants, Huntsmen, Pages of Natural History, etc.*

Introducing the sad, tearful, touching and beautiful episode of Who Killed Cock Robin: *Jenny Wren*: Miss Daisy Deene. *Cock Robin*: Miss Flora Walsh. *The Sparrow*: Little Flora. *The Rook*: Miss Lizzie Ayers. *The Linnet*: Little Tot. *The Policeman*: Miss Glennie Slocum.

[64]This adaptation first presented in New York 24 December 1877 at the Eagle Theatre and Grand Opera House for 42 performances. For Synopsis of Scenes and Musical Numbers, see original 1877 production.
[65]No additional credits in program with regard to authorship, scenery, costumes, stage direction, etc.

1881.01

THE BROOK

Salsbury's Troubadours in a Revival of the Laughable and Musical Extravaganza entirely re-arranged and compiled into Two Acts[66]. (Play by Nate Salsbury. Music selected, arranged by Frank Maeder.) Acting manager, Frank Maeder. Musical director, C. E. Borgman. Produced by Nate Salsbury. Opened 3 January 1881 at Haverly's 14th Street Theatre and closed 15 January 1881 after 16 performances.[67]

CAST: (Act 1): *Colonel Montrose*: NATE SALSBURY. *Percy Montrose*: JOHN WEBSTER. *Members of the Opera House Company (3)*: *Festus Heavysides*: C. A. STEDMAN. *Rose Dimplecheek*: NELLIE McHENRY. *Blanche Sylvester*: RAY SAMUELS.

Act 2: *Tracy Thornton*: NATE SALSBURY. *A Turtle*: Himself. *Percy Montrose*: JOHN WEBSTER. *One Fish-Pole*: And Line. *Festus Heavysides*: C. A. STEDMAN. *Two Bottles*: Uncorked. *Rose Dimplecheek*: NELLIE McHENRY. *A Boat*: property Man. *Blanche Sylvester*: RAY SAMUELS. *Lunch Basket*: Quartette. *Umbrellas*: Well Spread.

Act 1: Introductory. Conservatory at Montrose Villa. Evening of a Grand Reception given in honor of the Colonel's professional guests.

Act 2: Depicts the Pleasures of a Jolly Picnic.

1881.02

BLACK VENUS

A Spectacle in Five Acts. Based on a Parisian Spectacle by Adolphe Belot. Music by Charles Puerner. Scenery by Harley Merry and William Voegtlin; Messrs. Robecchi and Carpeza of Paris; Concordi in Rome; Reicher in Berlin. Costumes, armors and accessories executed in Paris. Stage machinery by John Leo, Rufus Williams. Illuminations by Emmet Davidson. Ballet music by celebrated European composers. Entire production produced by and under the management and direction of Imre and Bolossy Kiralfy. Opened 12 January 1881 at Niblo's Garden and closed 19 February 1881 after 45 performances.

CAST: *Baroness de Guéran*: GABRIELLE DuSAULD. *Miss Beatrix Poles*, an American traveler: FANNY SIMMONS. *Brenda*: BELLE MELVILLE. *M. de Morin*: HARRY DALTON. *Dr. Delange*: J. H. HOWLAND. *Perriers*: Alfred Horton. *Baron de Guéran*: D. R. YOUNG. *Joseph*, a Valet: W. H. LYTELL. *Julie*: Annie Lee. *Mr. Lex*, Civil Justice at Khartoum: E. S. TARR. *Rodar*, Captain of Nile Steamer: C. J. Toole. *Walenda*, the Black Venus: EMMA WILMOT. *King Monza*, an African Potentate: R. M. HENRY. *Nassar*, a Guide: HARRY MEREDITH. *Ali Bembe*, an Egyptian slave: A. H. Denham. *Mazourka*, an African guide: S. M. Burton. *Ameri*, an attentive Amazon: Flora Lee. *Ballet*: Mlles. DeROSA, CORNALBA. Mons. ARNOLD KIRALFY (Grotesque Dancer). *Sailors, Slaves, Palanquin Bearers, Forters, Maskers, Egyptian Soldiers, Guards, Traders, Zulus, Nyamos, Nyams, Momboutous, Zembis, Africans, Amazons, Caravan Drivers, Attendants, etc.*

Act 1: Boudoir of Mme. de Guéran in Paris, with a view of the new Grand Opera House. The City of Cairo in Egypt. The River Nile. The Slave Vessel on the Nile. The Vessel on Fire. The Rescue.

Act 2: Khartoum. The Desert. Grand African Caravan. The Rising of the Sun. The Burning Sand Storm Of The Desert.

Act 3: Palace of King Monza. Grand Cortege. Interior of the Palace of Venus.

Act 4: Temple of Black Venus.

Act 5: The Blue Mountains in Central Africa. Battle of the Amazons. The Rescue and Tableau Finale.

BALLETS

Grand Ballet Des Masques (Act 1)
Corps de Ballet
Characteristic Dance on the Deck of Slave Ship (Act 1)
Grand African Caravan (500 Performers and 50 live animals[68])(Act 2)
Grand Ballet Des Enclaves (Act 4)
Mlles. DeRosa, Cornalba; Mons. A. Kiralfy, Ballet of 150
Battle of the Amazons (introducing 40 Lady Riders)(Act 5)

[66]First produced in a one-act version 12 May 1879 at San Francisco Minstrel's Hall for 42 performances.
[67]No additional credits in program with regard to authorship, musical numbers, specialties, scenery or costumes.
[68]Camels, Dromedaries, Zebras, Sacred Cows, Oxen, Donkeys, Goats, Hounds.

1881.03

OLIVETTE

An Opéra-comique in Three Acts[69]. Original French libretto to the opérette 'Les Noces d'Olivette' by Henri Chivot and Alfred Duru. American adaptation by a distinguished American writer. Music by Edmond Audran. Stage manager, H. W. Montgomery. Dance in Act 2 arranged by Henry Montgomery. Scenery by Henry E. Hoyt, Philip W. Goatcher. Costumes made from the original French designs by H. J. Eaves. Chorus and orchestra under the direction of C. von Schiller. Produced by James C. Duff. Opened 17 January 1881 at Abbey's Park Theatre and closed 5 February 1881 after 21 performances.

CAST: *Captain de Merrimac*, of the Man-of-War *"Cormorant"*: ED MARBLE. *Valentin*, Officer in the Rousillon Guards, his nephew: CHARLES LANG. *Marvejol*, Seneschal to the Countess of Rousillon, and Maire of Perpignan: EDWARD CONNELL. *Postiche*, Barber and Innkeeper: Henry Dixon. *Duc des Ifs*, Cousin and heir-presumptive of the Countess of Rousillon: HARRY COURTAINE. *Coquelicot*, his foster-brother and valet: William Davidge, Jr. *Bathilde*, Countess of Rousillon: JULIA POLK. *Olivette*, Daughter of the Seneschal: MARIE CONRON. *Veloutine*, Maid of Olivette: SARA LASCELLES. *Cansterre, De Joyeux, Follesamours*, Pages of the Countess: Misses Browning, Holland, Grousseau. *Piou-Piou*: Miss Marco Stuart. *La Baronne de Verptre*: Lizzie Newman. *Mlles. De Cernay, De Montjoie, De Lenoir*, Maids of Honour: Misses E. Champneys, Sherwood, DeVere. *Coralie*: Louise Fox. *Jeanne*: Cora Cassade. *Suzanne*: Helen Griffiths. *Moustique*, Merrimac's Cabin-boy: Sophie Hummel. *L'Ecureuil, Mistigris, Lartimon*, Midshipmen on board the *"Cormorant"*: Misses Ruby Thorton, Richards; Mons. Henry Hayes. *Boussole, Loup-de-Mer*, Sailors: Messrs. J. Pelham, Randall. *Catou, Nichette, Bleuette*, Maids at the "Main-brace Tavern": Misses M. Kirk, Carrington, Annie Gardner. *Nobles of the Court of Rousillon, the Watch of Perpignan, Citizens, Gossips, Wedding Guests, Sailors, etc.*

Act 1: The Seneschal's House at Perpignan. Shore of the Mediterranean. (Hoyt.)

Act 2: Ball-room in the Palace of Rousillon. (Goatcher.)

Act 3: Interior of the Main-brace Tavern. The Cormorant at Anchor. (Goatcher.)

1881.04

ZANINA, or The Rover of Cambaye

A Musical Comedy in Three Acts[70]. Original French libretto to the comic operette "Nisida" by F. Zell and Moritz West. English adaptation by Augustin Daly. Music by Richard Genée. An original East Indian interlude by Harry W. French. Several musical numbers by E. Mollenhauer, words of the songs by Fred Williams. Scenery by James Roberts and Hughson Hawley. Mechanical effects by James Tait. Elegant native and national costumes by J. H. Eaves. Lighting and lightning effects by John Weatherspoon. Produced by Augustin Daly. Opened 17 January 1881 at Daly's Theatre and closed 12 February 1881 after 32 performances.

CAST: Natives: *His Oriental Excellency Booma Poota*, Governor of Cambaye, an Eastern Majesty of boundless rapacity: DIGBY BELL. *Montiel*, his nephew, a buccaneer out of business—on the outlook for a new war, and a new warrant: JOHN BRAND. *Moro Khan*, the Goveror's Valkeel or Secretary; a knave in cafe au lait: J. Macdonough. *Allabad*, occasionally Pilot, sometimes Pirate, always irate: William Paul Bown. *Morok*, a Malay: Mr. Roberts. *Panalon*, another: Mr. Lawrence. *Nuna*, "Light of the Eastern Skies," the Governor's niece and the ex-pirate's sister—much like the rest of her sex in other sections of the globe: MAY FIELDING. *Meada*, her aunt—with three millions in her own right and no takers in sight: MAY SYLVIE. *Muttra*, a native, with European tendencies but with the universal craving for rupees: ADA REHAN. *Nauchida*, mistress of the Royal Gardens and of the Governor's secret for making Official Tea: MAGGIE HARROLD. *Natives, Peddlers, Newsboys, English Residents, Members of the Bombay Squad, etc.*: Misses Evesson, Howard, Flagg, Featherstone, Montgomery, Pening, Donaldson, 30 others. *Captain Trafalgar*, lately stationed at Gibraltar, now transferred to the Indian contingent, with a contingent transference of affection;—also the connecting link the foregoing and the following: HARRY LACY.

Distinguished Foreign Arrivals: *Lumlini Strakoschino Barnaco*, of Madrid; Impressario extraordinary for the universe: JAMES LEWIS. *Simmondsino Rinaldo*, Operatic Agent, Musical Manager, Merchant in Theatres, etc: CHARLES LECLERCQ. *Frenchinini Rinaldini*, his hated rival but constant companion: E. P. WILKS. *Africanus*, Proprietor of the celebrated Senegambian Mastodonions, forty strong, count 'em: THOMAS HENGLER. *Luna*, his mate: Mr. Delamanning. *The Band*: Messrs. Beekman, Sterling, Bennett, Murpy, Welling; Misses Vaughn, Kirkland, Shandley, Clary, etc. *Signorina (Delamanna) Zanina*, the Impressario's niece, a runaway herself; she comes to Cambaye in search of a runaway and is searched for in vain: LAURA JOYCE. *Wedding Guests*, Act 3: Misses Vinton, Hinchley, K. Dennin, S. Williams, Brooks, Seymour, C. Flagg, Galliand.

[69]A rival to the original production; first produced in New York in English 25 December 1880 at the Bijou Opera House for 63 performances. No songs listed in programs.
[70]First produced in New York in German 7 December 1880 at the Thalia Theatre for 4 weeks in repertory.

Act 1: The Chat at Cambaye. (Hawley.)
Act 2: The Imperial Bungalow on the Delhi Road. (Roberts.)
Act 3: The Shore opposite the Taj Mahal, with Nuna's Pavilion. (Roberts.)

ACT 1

Introduction—"See the Steamer"
W. P. Bown, M. Harold, Chorus
"Evening News!"
Chorus of Newsboys
"New Palm Wine!"
Chorus of Peddlers
"Why did we Madrid forsaking" (Trio)
J. Lewis, C. Lerclerq, E. P. Wilks
"All the news of all the nations"
Chorus
"I Am the great impressario" (Trio)
J. Lewis, C. Lerclerq, E. P. Wilks
"The Rover of Cambaye" (Song and Chorus)
J. Brand, Corsairs
"Noontide sunshine, warm and glowing" (Quartette)
M. Fielding, M. Silvie, H. Lacy, D. Bell
"This morning bright and early" (Couplets)
D. Bell
Quintette
M. Fielding, M. Silvie, J. Brand, H. Lacy, D. Bell
"I'm a cherry sweet to taste" (Song)
L. Joyce
"Smoking is clearly annoying" (Smoking Duet)
L. Joyce, D. Bell
Finale, Act 1
"Uli, ali ola, e!" (Concerted piece)
T. Hengler, Senegambians
"Gaze on her portrait" (Air)
J. Lewis
"Massa, here be Zanina" (Concerted Piece)
L. Joyce, J. Brand, M. Fielding, M. Silvie, J. Lewis, D. Bell, T. Hengler, Chorus
"This insult rude" (Andante)
L. Joyce, J. Brand, M. Fielding, M. Silvie, J. Lewis, D. Bell, Chorus
"In cities vast of Hindostan" (March of the Cambaye Police)
"Good Night!" (Boléro)
L. Joyce, Characters, Chorus

ACT 2[71]

"In the tromba" (Concerted Piece)
J. Brand, Corsairs
"Love Is Made of Smiles and Tears" (Song)
H. Lacy
"Three Million Rupees!" (Sextette)
L. Joyce, M. Silvie, J. Lewis, D. Bell, C. Lerclerq, E. P. Wilks
"The stars that hear our solemn vow" (Duet)
L. Joyce, J. Brand
"A supper in the open air" (Concerted Piece)
L. Joyce, H. Lacy, Corsairs
Nautch Dancers and Jugglers
"Love with doubt can never dwell" (Cavatina)
M. Fielding
Finale, Act 2
"Let shouts of triumph loud ascending"
Chorus

[71]Incidental to Act 2 will be given an East Indian Divertissement, in which will participate the Tribe of Hindoo Natives expressly imported to this country for this play:
Knife Throwing and Bird Shooting
Ballaya, Sr.
Growing rice from grains of sand, transforming a rag baby into Pigeons, and the Indian Basket Trick
Immam, assisted by Ballaya, Jr.
The Nautch
Boorie Bai, Sahebjan, Wazier, Oomdah, Alibunda
The Music on the Sitar and Tum-Tum by Khojoolalla and Sabrung.

"Niece, what do you here?" (Concerted Piece)
L. Joyce, J. Lewis, Chorus
"The Cazik's land the Spaniard saw" (Song of the Cazik)
L. Joyce, Chorus
"Hold! I say!" (Concerted Piece)
L. Joyce, J. Lewis, D. Bell, J. Brand, C. Leclerq, E. P. Wilks, Chorus
"Have mercy, heaven, it is the hurricane!"
Chorus

ACT 3

"Let the music sound" (Concerted Piece)
Wedding Chorus
"Ching a ring a ring"
Chorus of Senegambians
"Fragrant as their perfume" (Air and Round)
M. Fielding, Native Ladies
"Laughter, mirth and music gay"
General Chorus
"Partners henceforth you and I" (Duet)
C. Leclerq, E. P. Wilks
"Most potent, grave and reverend Dervish" (Duet)
D. Bell, J. Lewis
"Lightly o'er the rippling stream" (Barcarole)
L. Joyce, J. Brand
Finale
"Registered our marriage vow" (Andante)
L. Joyce
"The earth is green and fair to see" (Waltz Quartette)
L. Joyce, M. Fielding, J. Brand, H. Lacy
"Open sea, bright rolling sea"
Chorus

1881.05 THE CHIMES OF NORMANDY

A Revival of the Comic Opera in Four Acts[72]. French libretto to the opéra-comique 'Les Cloches de Corneville' by Clairville and Charles Gabet. Music by Robert Planquette. Stage and chorus director, Arthur W. Tams. Musical director, Signor Tomasi. Produced by the Emma Abbott Grand English Opera Company. Opened 24 January 1881 at the Fifth Avenue Theatre and closed 29 January (matinee) 1881 after 2 performances in repertory.[73]

CAST: *Mignonette*, a Waif: JULIE ROSEWALD. *Germaine*: CLARA POOLE. *Gertrude*, a Gossip: THERESE MARCEY. *Robin Moore*, a Fisherman: PAULINE MAUREL. *Gaspard*, a Miser: HENRY C. PEAKES. *Sheriff*: ARTHUR W. TAMS. *Notary*: William Connell. *Marquis Villeroi*, a Rover: WILLIAM CASTLE. *Grand Chorus*.

1881.06 THE PIE-RATS OF PENN-YANN

A Burlesque of Gilbert and Sullivan's "The Pirates of Penzance" in One Act, 3 Scenes, preceded by an Olio. Libretto by Tony Pastor. Scenic effects by Edward Simmons. Costumes by W. Dazian. Musical arrangements by H. T. Dyring. Produced by Tony Pastor. Opened 7 February 1881 at Tony Pastor's Music Hall and closed 5 March 1881 after 28 performances.

Olio: The New Man, with Dan Collyer, Frank Girard, Jennie Christie, Miss J. Crolius; Miss Bessie Grey (ballads); Samuel Holdsworth (character ballads); Reynolds & Walling in Dot Turnpike Gate; Florence Merton (farm ballads, home songs); A Terrible Shock, with Dan Collyer, Frank Girard, W. Lester, P. Allen, Jennie Christie; Tony Pastor's Comic Rhymes; Ferguson & Mack (Irish debators, with songs and dance); Bonnie Runnells (Dutch creations).

CAST: *Little Freddy*, a Pretty Boy—indentured as a prowler, he aspires to become an operatic howler, and reaching manhood he becomes a growler: FLORA IRWIN. *Peter*, King of the Prowlers. A gentleman who hesitates not at appropriating other people's goods believing it an appropriate capah!: W. D. MARKS. *Richard*, his Viceroy. A prowler who deserves to emulate the late respectable Captain Kyd, in levying tribute on the commerce of the Hudson and its tributaries: SAMUEL HOLDSWORTH.

[72]First produced in New York in English 22 October 1877 at the Fifth Avenue Theatre for 16 performances in repertory. For Synopsis of Scenes and Musical Numbers, see 1877 production.
[73]English adaptation uncredited; this version presented in 4 Acts. No credits in programs for scenery, costumes.

Brigadier Stanislaus, of the German brigade, who having made a fortune in Limburger, thinks it quite the cheese to run a brewery on the Hudson: JOHN MORRIS. *Teddy Quinn*, from the Fourth Precinct, raised to the rank of Sergeant and in command of the River Squad, "one of the finest police in the world": FRANK GIRARD. *Roundsman 9,706*, a bold policeman of the Broadway squad, but rather too careful of the dye on his mustache to die in discharge of his duty: WILLIAM LESTER. *Maria*, formerly called Mabel, but for the sake of novelty changed to the former. A loving heart with deep concern for the loneliness of little Freddy: LILLIAN RUSSELL. *Ruthie*, Poor thing! a prowler girl of more winters than summers. Sweet on little Freddy but too conscientious to tell the truth: MAY IRWIN. *Katie*, the younger Miss Stanislaus, very saucy, very pert, and a young lady who is sure to be heard in a crowd: FLORENCE MERTON. *Mary, Isabelle*, Sisters to Maria: Misses Gray, Vining.

The Finest Police in the World: Our corps of comedians headed by FERGUSON and MACK, (William) LESTER and ALLEN, Barney Reynolds and Dave Walling, DAN COLLYER, etc. *The Prowlers of Penn-Yann*: Messrs. Atwood, Cuthbert, Hall, Hastie, Wynne, Delmonte, Randel, Holland, Reynolds, Gillespie, Dunstan, Bellany, Brown, Hadfield. *The Daughters of Stanislaus*: Misses Wyman, Intropodi, Grey, Wills, Vining, Cook, Wilson, Remar, Stark, Newman, Crolius, Rignold, Marcy, Madden, Phillips, Denwood, Collister, Andrews, others.

Scene 1: Rocky Pass near Penn Yann. Home of the Pirates. *Scene 2*: Street in Penn Yann. Policemen's Chorus. *Scene 3*: The Ancestral Home of Stanislaus.

MUSICAL NUMBERS[74]

Scene 1

"Pour oh pour the Prowler's whiskey" (Opening)
[Samuel, Chorus]

"When Freddy was a little boy" (Song)
[Ruth]

"Oh better for to live and die" (Song)
[King]

"Hopping over muddy crossings" (Chorus)
[Girls]

"Let us freely have our pleasure" (Song and Chorus)
[Kate]

"Oh is there not one little maid" (Song)
[Fred]

"Now there's that horrid Milly Jones" (Chorus)
[Girls]

"Ladies, by your invasion" (Chorus)
[Prowlers]

Scene 2

"When the loafer shies his fist" (Song)
[Sergeant]

"Oh, ye sentinels of order" (Song)
[Maria]

"When you first left our prowler gang" (The Paradox)
[Ruth]

"Policeman Song"/

"Where the pocketbook expert is not a snatching" (Roundsman's Song and Chorus)

Scene 3

"A happy go lucky lot are we" (Chorus)
[Prowlers]

"For in pleasing the public he" (Song)

1881.07

BILLEE TAYLOR,
or, The Reward of Virtue

A Nautical Comic Opera in Two Acts. Libretto by Henry Pottinger Stephens. Music by Edward Solomon. Produced under the stage direction of Charles Harris. Scenery designs by Henry Emden. Costumes designed by George Pilotell. Musical director, Alfred Cellier; conductor, Ernest Neyer. Produced by Richard D'Oyly Carte and Edward E. Rice. Opened 19 February 1881 at the Standard Theatre and closed 31 May 1881 after 104 performances; re-opened 6 June 1881 at Niblo's Garden[75] and closed 18 June 1881 after 16 additional performances. Total: 120 performances.

CAST: *Captain, The Hon. Felix Flapper*, R. N. of the *H.M.S . Thunderbolt*: J. H. RYLEY. *Sir Mincing Lane*, a self-made man: W. H. SEYMOUR. *Ben Barnacle*, Bosun of the *H. M. S Thunderbolt*: A. W. F. McCOLLIN. *Christopher Crab*, a villainous school-master: WILLIAM HAMILTON. *Billee Taylor*, a virtuous gardener: ARNOLD BREEDON. *Arabella Lane*, Sir Mincing Lane's daughter: ALICE BURVILLE. *Susan*, a village maiden: Madeleine Lucette. *Eliza Dabsey*, Phoebe's aunt: NELLIE MORTIMER. *Phoebe Farleigh*, another village maiden: CARRIE BURTON. *Charity Girls, Peasants, Sailors, Soldiers, Villagers*: Chorus of 60. *Dance specialties*: French Twin Sisters, T. M. Hengler, Major Burke. With Misses Hilliger, Maynard, Fox, Lawrence, Hall, Delaro, Harrison, Sherwood, Hummell, Cooper.

Act 1: A Village Garden on the shore of Southampton Water.

Act 2: Portsmouth Harbor. —*H.M.S. Thunderbomb* at Anchor.

ACT 1[76]

"To-day, To-day" (Chorus of Peasants)

"The Virtuous Gardener" (Ballad)
A. Breedon

"Ifs and Ans" (Duet)
A. Burville, A. Breedon

"We Stick to Our Letters" (Chorus of Charity Girls)
10 Charity Girls

"Peerless Phoebe" (Song)
M. Lucette

"The Two Rivers" (Barcarolle)(Yesterday and Tomorrow)
C. Burton, M. Lucette

"The Self-Made Knight" (Song)
W. H. Seymour

"The Guileless Orphan" (Song)(The Wilful Girl)
C. Burton

"Revenge, Revenge!" (Trio)
A. Burville, J. H. Ryley, W. Hamilton

"The Gallant Thunderbomb" (Sailors' Chorus)

"All on Account of Eliza" (Song)
A. W. F. McCollin

"Hark! the merry marriage bells!" (Wedding Chorus)

Finale ('Tis hard by fate thus to be parted)

ACT 2

"Back Again" (Opening Chorus)
Sailors, Women

Ballet Music

Black Cook's Dance

"The Poor Wicked Man" (Song)
W. Hamilton

"The Ballad of the Billow"
A. Burville

"The Faithful Crew" (Chorus)
C. Burton, Chorus

"In Days Gone By" (Duet and Chorus)
A. Breedon, C. Burton, Chorus

"Trim Little Phoebe" (Trio)
J. H. Ryley, C. Burton, M. Lucette

"With Fife and Drum" (Chorus)

"Richard Carr" (Concerted Piece and Song)
A. W. F. McCollin, W. H. Seymour, C. Burton, J. H. Ryley

"Love, Love, Love" (Song)
W. H. Seymour

"See Here, my Lads" (Concerted Piece)
A. W. F. McCollin, Sailors

"I am No Man" (Concerted Piece)
C. Burton, A. Burville, A. Breedon, J. H. Ryley, Chorus

Quarrelling Duet (Not very long ago I lov'd)
C. Burton, A. Burville

Grand Finale (This is a statement most untoward)

---

[74]Musical numbers not listed in programs. List prepared from an incomplete prompt book/script published in "Tony Pastor presents Afterpieces from the Vaudeville Stage," by Susan Kattwinkel. (Greenwood Press, Westport, Connecticut, 1998).

[75]Return engagement presented under the auspices of Edward E. Rice's Original Opera Comique Company. Major cast changes: *Sir Mincing Lane*: H. A. CRIPPS. *Billee Taylor*: EUGENE CLARK. *Arabella Lane*: VERNONA JARBEAU. *Susan*: Rose Chappelle. Musical director, Napier Lothian.

[76]Musical numbers not listed in programs. List prepared from published American libretto (S. T. Gordon & Son, New York, 1880) and English libretto (Joseph Williams, London, 1880).

1881.08

HOBBIES

N. C. Goodwin's Froliques in a Revival of the Humorous Fantasy in Two Acts[77]. Play by Ben E. Woolf. Produced by Nat C. Goodwin (Management, John E. Warner). Opened 21 February 1881 at Haverly's 14th Street Theatre and closed 7 March 1881 after 16 performances.[78]

CAST: Characters in the Comedy: *Professor Pygmalin Whiffles*, Piggy for short: NAT C. GOODWIN. *Minnie Clover*, with songs: DAISY RAMSDEN. *Miss Euphemia Bang*, with songs: JENNIE WEATHERSBY. *Miss Constance Bang*, with songs: ELMA DELARO. *Major Garroway Bang*: Charles Bowser. *Arthur Doveleigh*: Frank E. Lamb.

Characters in the Travesty: *The Villain*: NAT C. GOODWIN. *The Prince*, with songs: DAISY RAMSDEN. *The Princess*, with songs: ELMA DELARO. *The Fairy*: JENNIE WEATHERSBY. *The Audience*: Charles Bowser. *The Count*: Frank E. Lamb.

1881.09

MULLIGAN'S SILVER WEDDING

A Local (Comic) Play in One Act, 9 Scenes[79]. Play (and lyrics) by Edward Harrigan. Music by David Braham. Produced under the immediate supervision of Edward Harrigan. Scenery by Charles W. Witham. Mechanical effects by Robert Cutler. Properties by Robert Puller. Lights by Richard Doyle. Musical director, David Braham. Produced by Edward Harrigan and Tony Hart. Opened 21 February 1881 at the Theatre Comique and closed 30 April 1881 after 80 performances.

CAST: (The Guests): *Alderman Daniel Mulligan*: EDWARD HARRIGAN. *Dennis Mulligan*: TONY HAT. *Captain Simpson Primrose*: JOHN WILD. *Reverend Palestine Puter*: WILLIAM GREY. *Gustavus Lochmuller*: HARRY FISHER. *Edgar DeAngelles*: Edward Burt. *Washington Irving Crumbs*: M. Drew. *Caroline Melrose*: James Tierney. *Walsingham McSweeny*: Michael Bradley. *Timothy Heaves*: Edward Goss. *Mr. Hog Eye*: William West. *Jolly Johnson*: Edwin Barry. *Crabs*: George Merritt. *Satelite Fresco*: Michael Foley. *Luminary Soot*: John Oberist. *Shepherd of the Fold*: James Fox. *Gussy Lochmuller*: (Master) Emil Husel. *Brien McQuirk*: James Fitzsimmons. *Doctor McGinn*: Robert Hall. *Officer Late*: James O'Rourke. *Honora Dublin*: John Queen. *Clorinda Perkins*: ANNIE MACK. *Cordelia Mulligan*: Mrs. ANNIE YEAMANS. *Winsome Winnie*: EMILY YEAMANS. *Celia Quigly*: Mary Bird. *Edith McGarrigan*: Belle Mordaunt. *Camille O'Hara*: Susie Byron. *Carlo*: Never-Take-the-Whip. *John Murphy*, Trainer: Morgan Benson. *Mulligan's Constituency and Weddingites*: Our Auxiliary Corps.

Scene 1: Interior of Alderman Mulligan's House. *Scene 2*: Exterior of Primrose and Puter's Restaurant. *Scene 3*: Criterion Concert Hall. *Scene 4*: Exterior of McSweeny's Hay Loft and Stable. *Scene 5*: The Hay Loft. *Scene 6*: Exterior of McSweeny's Hay Loft and Stable. *Scene 7*: Mulligan Alley. *Scene 8*: Hallway in Alderman Mulligan's House. *Scene 9*: Apartments in Alderman's Mulligan's House.

MUSICAL NUMBERS[80]

Scene 1

"The Castaways"
T. Hart

Scene 3

"Don't You Miss the Train, Boys"
E. Barry

"The Mirror's the Cause of It All"
E. Barry

"John Reilly's Always Dry"
E. Harrigan

"South Fifth Avenue"
Messrs. Wild, Gray, Goss, Fox, Tierney, Queen, West, Husel

Scene 4

"(The) Third Degree Full Moon Union"
Fiery Mountain: W. Gray. *Lunar Crater*: J. Wild. *Satellites*: Messrs. E. Goss, J. Fox, W. West, J. Fitzsimmons, M. Foley, J. Oberist, J. McCullough, John Coffee, Fred Queen, G. Merritt, W. Merritt, J. O'Rourke, Thomas Ray.

Scene 9

"Wheel the Baby Out"
E. Harrigan

1881.10

JOSHUA WHITCOMB

A Revival of the Melodrama in Three Acts[81]. Play by Denman Thompson. Produced by Denman Thompson. Opened 28 February 1881 at the Grand Opera House and closed 12 March 1881 after 16 performances.

CAST: *Uncle Josh*, an old Jackson Democrat: DENMAN THOMPSON. *Roundy*, a Street Arab: IGNACIO MARTINETTI. *John Martin*, a lover of horse racing and theatres: Eugene O. Jepson. *Frederick Dolby*, a young Englishman: Walter Gale. *Cy. Prime*, nigh on eighty: George A. Beane. *Bill Johnson*, a loafer: Robert Benson. *Reuben*, son of Uncle Josh: FRED W. PETERS. *Mr. Burroughs*, a model policeman: G. Adams. *Mr. Foster*, sheriff of the county: Daniel Nourse. *Tot*, a crossing sweeper: JULIA WILSON. *Nellie Primrose*, a Boston belle: Isabelle Coe. *Susan Martin*, with a mania for marriage: Alice Logan. *Mrs. Johnson*, Tot's mother: Blanch Robertson. *Aunt Matilda*, Josh's sister: Mrs. Daniel Nourse. *Amantha Bartlett*, a neighbor's gal: Miss F. Roberts. *Aunt Martha*: Miss E. Rogers.

Act 1: Uncle Josh's arrival in Boston

Act 2: Uncle Josh at the birthday party.

Act 3: Uncle Josh's New England home.

MUSICAL NUMBERS

"Tot's Lullaby" (Act 1)
J. Wilson
(*Music by* Walter Gale. *Lyrics by* Denman Thompson.)

"In the Bright Sunlight" (Act 3)
J. Wilson, I. Martinetti
(*Music by* Ferd. Von Olker. *Lyrics by* William R. Watts.)

"You'll Surely Have to Guess" (Xylophone Song and Dance)
J. Wilson, I. Martinetti

1881.11

CINDERELLA AT SCHOOL

A Musical Comedy in Two Acts, 6 Scenes. Book, music and lyrics by Henry Woolson Morse. Based on the play "School" by T. W. Robertson. Produced under the direction of Fred Williams. Groupings and dances by Mme. Malvina. Scenic artist, James Roberts. Costumes by Lanouette. Musical director, Edward R. Mollenhauer. Produced by Augustin Daly. Opened 5 March 1881 at Daly's Theatre and closed 30 April 1881 after 65 performances.

CAST: *Arthur Bicycle*, a perambulating Deity of the upper-crust, with distinguished connections: HARRY LACY. *Jack Polo*, of the Meadow Brook Hunt, Stroke-oar of Harvard in the race of '80: JOHN BRAND. *Lord Lawntennys*, a relic of other days and other lands, ona visit to his long-lost nephew, and on a search for a long-lost niece: CHARLES LECLERCQ. *Professor Kindergarten*, Principal of the Papyrus Seminary for Young Ladies, at Laurelton: PAUL BOWN. *Syntax*, Tutor, the Professor's head-usher and husher: JAMES LEWIS. *Jenkinson*, Attendant on Lord Lawntennys: E. P. Wilks. *Members of the Meadow Brook Hunt, also of Columbia Crew and Harvard*: Messrs. F. Macdonough, J. Lawrence, H. Roberts, N. Burnham, C. Milton, T. D. Murphy, Saleon, Harman, Perring, Hamilton, Palmer, Campbell.

Niobe Marsh, a charity pupil at Kindergarten's, the Cendrillon of the School: MAY FIELDING. *Merope Mallow*, a young lady from Brazil, the richest girl in her class and comparatively ignorant, but superlatively "smart": LAURA JOYCE. *Psyche Persimmons*, the sleepiest girl in the Seminary: ADA REHAN. *Miss Zenobia Tropics*, head teacher at the Papyrus, a firm believer in bone-formin: MRS. G. H. GILBERT. *Miss Globes*, her assistant: Agnes Perring.

The Rest of the School Girls: *Chloris Slatepencil*, who lisps: NELLIE HOWARD. *Circe Slatepencil*, who giggles: GEORGINE FLAGG. *Lotis Slatepencil*, who sighs: Sally Williams. *Penelope Slatepencil*, who eats: M. Kirkland. *Pansy Pickle*, who knows everything: Blanche Vaughn. *Primrose Pickle*, who knows nothing: Lillie Vinton. *Sally Chalk*, who pouts: Virginia Brooke. *Carrie Mell, Marian Glassy*, two very sweet girls: Emma Hinckley, K. Morris. *Daisy Dimple*, a simple little thing: Miss Jasper. *Virginia Creeper*, an insinuating thing: Clara Flagg. *Fragrant Pupils (7)*: *Rhoda Dendron*: E. Denin. *Minnie Nett*: G. Denin. *Ollie Ander*: L. Perring. *Amy Rylis*: Miss Trevalyan. *Ann Emony*: G. Malmane. *Jessie Meen*: E. Featherstone. *Marie Gold*: F. Stirling. *Very learned girls (3)*: *Etty Mollogy*: Miss Shandley. *Ada Verb*: Miss Yates. *Prosa Dee*: Miss Byant.

Act 1, Scene 1: A Forest glade at the change of a leaf. *Scene 2*: Another part of the forest. *Scene 3*: The School Room.

---

[77]First produced in New York 6 October 1879 at Haverly's Lyceum Theatre for 32 performances, returning 26 April 1880 to the Standard Theatre for an additional 28 performances. For Synopsis of Scenes and Musical Numbers, see original 1879 production.

[78]Scenery and costumes uncredited. Musical numbers not listed in programs; Nat C. Goodwin will interpolate imitations of Henry Irving (new), John McCullough (new), Stuart Robson, John T. Raymond, Joseph Jefferson, E. A. Sothern (new), Lawrence Barrett, Frank Mayo, and the London comic singer in the latest English sensation song, "You're always sure to catch 'em with the P'st, P'st, P'st" originally sung by him in America.

[79]Blled as Volume 8th of the Mulligan Series.

[80]Also performed: Xylophone SoloE. King

[81]First produced in a one-act form 3 April 1875 at the Eagle Theatre; in its three-act form 2 September 1878 at the Lyceum Theatre for 93 performances. For Synopsis of Scenes and Musical Numbers, see original 1878 production.

Act 2, Scene 1: Exterior of Papyrus' Seminary by moonlight. *Scene 2*: Merope receives a letter from Jack and reads it. *Scene 3*: The Boat Race.

ACT 1
Scene 1
"Green Are the Waving Branches" (Opening Chorus)
Schoolgirls
"Poor Cinderella" (Song and Chorus)(The Story of Cinderella)
M. Fielding, Schoolgirls
"What Is Love?" (Song)(The Origin of Love)
P. Bown
"The Cause of Civilization" (Song)
P. Bown, Young Ladies
"You Are an Orphan" (Duet)
M. Fielding, J. Lewis
"The Morning Mist Spread O'er the Mead" (Hunting Song and Chorus)
J. Brand, Huntsmen
"Oh! No Regular Wife" (Song and Chorus)
J. Brand, Huntsmen
"Pretty Little Shoe" (Song and Chorus)
H. Lacy
"Come, My Pretty Maiden" (Quartet)
L. Joyce, M. Fielding, J. Brand, H. Lacy
Scene 2
Calisthenic Exercise and Chorus
Schoolgirls
Scene 3
"Why Am I So Sad To-day?" (Song)
M. Fielding
Excuse Song and Chorus ("Oh, please, my dear Miss Tropics!")
A. Rehan, L. Joyce, G. Flagg, N. Howard, S. Williams, J. Lewis, Schoolgirls
"My Dear Young Ladies" (Song and Chorus) C. Leclerq, Schoolgirls
Selection from "The Raven"
J. Lewis
Elocution Class
S. Williams, G. Flagg, N. Howard, A. Rehan
"Upon Paul's Steeple" (Double Quartet)
Medley from Mother Goose's Melodies
M. Fielding, L. Joyce
"To Educate These Young Ladies" (Song)
P. Bown
Finale
Principals, Chorus

ACT 2
Scene 1
"Hark! to the Sunset Gun" (Opening Chorus)
Schoolgirls
"The Linnet in the Tree" (Song)
M. Fielding
"Tis Love Has Caused All Mortal Trouble" (Concerted Piece)
P. Bown, J. Lewis, L. Joyce, Schoolgirls
"Did You Ever Hear Such Topics?" (Chorus)
Schoolgirls
"Fairest Maiden" (Duet)
J. Lewis, A. Rehan
"I'm Sure to Astonish You All" (Song)
L. Joyce
"I Kiss My hand to Thee" (Song)
J. Brand
Duet and Chorus ("Swing with Me")
J. Brand, L. Joyce, Schoolgirls
"Courting in the Moonlight" (Song)
J. Lewis
"A Cotton Cloth Ghost" (Concerted Piece)
J. Lewis, P. Bown, G. H. Gilbert, M. Fielding, L. Joyce, Schoolgirls
"Farewell" (Concerted Piece)
M. Fielding, Schoolgirls
Scene 2
"I've Got a Letter from My Jack" (Song)(Jack's Letter)
L. Joyce
Scene 3
"Hurrah! they come" (Concerted Piece)
Schoolgirls, College Boys, L. Joyce, J. Brand, Full Chorus
"Columbia Won the Race To-day" (Song)
J. Brand, Chorus
Finale
Principals, Chorus

1881.12 OILY VET, or The Wilful Maid and the Sad Sea Dog

A Burlesque of Edmond Audran's opéra-comique "Olivette" in One Act, 4 Scenes, preceded by an Olio. Adaptation written for Tony Pastor with all the original music. Produced by Tony Pastor. Opened 7 March 1881 at Tony Pastor's Theatre and closed 2 April 1881 after 28 performances.

CAST: *Valentine*, a young officer of the guard, a very nice Valentine, only one in a box: FLORA IRWIN. *Duke of Ifs and Buts*, a conundrum, whom the Countess gives up: SIGNOR OLMI. *Captain Merry Mac*, a veteran of the sea, called Oily Vet, probably because he likes his oil: JOHN MORRIS. *Marjeral*, the mayor, an easy-going old horse: GEORGE W. PALMER. *Ko-Ko*, a servant, the amendment of a good constitution: DAN COLLYER. *Matelot*: FRANK GIRARD. *Olivette*, a graceful stopper and a thoroughbred: LILLIAN RUSSELL. *The Countess*, a lady who doesn't know her own mind: MAY IRWIN. *Velveteen*, her companion: BESSIE GRAY. *Peasants, Sailors, Villagers, Pages, etc.*

Scene 1: A Village Street. The home of Olivette. *Scene 2*: A Ball room. *Scene 3*: A Road near the Seaside. *Scene 4*: The Coast. Merry Mac's Ship.

MUSICAL NUMBERS
Scene 1
Grand Chorus of Villagers
"The School Girls Slept" (Song)
L. Russell
"The Power of Love" (Waltz Song)
M. Irwin
"Darling Good Night" (Serenade)
F. Irwin
Grand Ensemble and Chorus
"Sob Song"
L. Russell
The Bridal Procession
"Hymen's Engineer" (Grand Chorus)
Company
Scene 2
"Bolero" (Song)
J. Morris
"Bob Up Serenely" (Song)
S. Olmi
"What Joy in Honeymooning" (Grand Farandole)
Company
Scene 3
"Shoemaker Rum" (Grand Chorus of Sailors)
Scene 4
"The Mud Scow and the Whale" (Song)
L. Russell
Grand Farandole and Truly, Artistic but Funny Finale

1881.13 THE BLACK CROOK

A Revival of the Extravaganza in Four Acts, 16 Scenes[82]. Scenery by Harley Merry, Recantini of Paris, Ed. Simmond, Magnani. Produced under the stage direction of the Kiralfy Brothers (Imre, Bolossy). Opened 7 March 1881 at Niblo's Garden and closed 9 April 1881 after 40 performances.[83]

[82]First produced in New York 12 September 1866 at Niblo's Garden for 475 performances.
[83]Musical director uncredited. Authorship uncredited in all programs; original credits: Book by Charles M. Barras. Music composed and selected by Thomas Baker, Louis Baer, A. W. Hoffman.

CAST: *Mortals*: *Hertzog*, the Black Crook: J. F. PETERS. *Count Wolfenstein*: R. M. BURTON. *Rudolph*, a poor artist: WILLIAM ADRIAN. *Von Puffengruntz*, the Count's Chamberlain: EDWIN S. TARR. *Greppo*, a henchman: W. H. LYTELL. *Wulfgar*: W. R. Taylor. *Bruno*: C. Schmitlein. *Caspar*: R. J. Toole. *Amina*, a village maiden: BELLE MELVILLE. *Dame Barbara*: FANNIE SIMMONS. *Carline*: Louise Dempsey. *Rosetta*: Flora Lee. *Guards, Attendants, Servitors, Villagers, etc.*

Immortals: *Stalacta*, the Fairy Queen: PAULINE MARKHAM. *Attendant Fairies (6)*: *Coraline*: Julia Fenton. *Dewdrop*: Affie Hearne. *Diamantine*: Lizzie Brandt. *Brilliantine*: Nellie Weston. *Sapphirine*: Lizzie Timmoney. *Pearline*: Rosina Thomas.

Sprites: *Dragonfin*: YOUNG AMERICA. *Bristleup*: Leonardo Ruppel.

Demons: *Zamiel*: A. H. DENHAM. *Skudelwhelp*: CHARLES BLESSER. *Redglare*: M. Franklin. *Blueblaze*: Jacob Shene. *Sulphureno*: W. Newman. *Ashgash*: J. Smith.

Ballet: Mlles. DeROSA, CAPPELINI; Corps de Ballet. *Specialties*: The Herbert Brothers (Acrobats); Professor Davis (Ventriloquist).

1881.14 OLIVETTE

A Revival of the Opéra-comique in Three Acts[84]. Original French libretto to the opérette 'Les Noces d'Olivette' by Henri Chivot and Alfred Duru. American adaptation by Leander P. Richardson. Music by Edmond Audran. Produced under the personal supervision of C. D. Hess. Scenery by Philip Goatcher (Acts 1, 3), Charles W. Witham (Act 2). Costumes by (Henry) Dazian. Musical director, Antonio DeNovellis. Produced by the Acme Olivette Company. Opened 19 March 1881 at the Bijou Opera House and closed 16 April 1881 after 29 performances.

CAST: *Valentine*, Officer of the Rousillon Guards: WILLIAM T. CARLETON. *Captain de Merrimac*, of the Man o' War *"Cormorant"*: HENRY PEAKES. *Duc des Ifs*, cousin and heir presumptive to the Countess: J. H. JARVIS. *Coquelicot*, his foster brother and henchman: JAMES PEAKES. *Marvejol*, local pluralist, Seneschal to the Countess and Maire of Perpignon: GEORGE OLMI. *Boussole*: Mr. Graham. *Loup de Mer*: Mr. Bennett. *Olivette*, daughter of the Seneschal Marvejol: SELINA DOLARO. *Bathilde*, Countess of Rousillon, in love with Valentine: FANNY WENTWORTH. *Veloutine*, the Seneschal's housekeeper: Belle Girard. *Moustique*, Captain's boy on board the *Cormorant*: Nellie Clifton. *Jayouf, Fallesamour*, Pages of the Countess: Henrietta Irving, Miss Cauldwell. *Mlle. de Mont Oye, Mlle. de Lenoir*, Ladies of the Countess' Suite: Misses L. Gardner, A. Gardner. *Courtiers and Nobles*: Messrs. Parker, Reed, Fazer. *Citizens, Wedding Guests and Sailors*: Misses Harmon, Hall, Merrian, Browning, Vance, Hartman. *Soldiers of the Guard, Pages, etc.*

1881.15 VOYAGERS IN SOUTHERN SEAS, or The Children of Captain Grant

The Boston Theatre Company in a Grand Romantic and Spectacular Drama in One Act, 13 Scenes. Play by Jules Verne and Adolphe D'Ennery[85]. (Based on Jules Verne's "The Children of Captain Grant.") Music by Mons. Debillement, of the Porte St. Martin Theatre, Paris. Produced under the immediate direction of Eugene Tompkins. Ballet produced under the direction of Bibeyran Mamert. Scenery by Charles S. Getz. Stage architecture by W. P. Prescott. Costumes by Annie Endress. Properties by J. B. Sullivan. Light effects by George Sevey. Musical director, H. J. Widmer. Produced by the Boston Theatre Company (Messrs. Eugene Tompkins and Hill, Managers). Opened 21 March 1881 at Booth's Theatre and closed 16 April 1881 after 32 performances.

CAST: *Captain Grant*, Commander of the *"Britannia"*: FRANK WESTON. *Paganel*, a French savant: Leslie Allen. *Bob*, a sailor: D. J. Maguinnis. *Ayrton*, Mate of the *"Britannia"*: Mark M. Price. *Lord Glenarvon*, owner of the *"Duncan"*: OTIS SKINNER. *Thalcave*, a Patagonian: George R. Parks. *Burck*: M. J. Jordan. *Mulray*: John T. Craven. *Captain Wilson*, Commander of the *"Duncan"*: H. A. CRIPPS. *Dick, Forster*, Sailors of the *"Britannia"*: A. E. Chase, E. Y. Backus. *Guide*, in the Antuco Pass: D. R. Moss. *Hotel Keeper*, in Valparaiso: Arthur Moulton. *Lady Arabella*, Aunt to Lord Glenarvon: Mrs. M. A. PENNOYER. *Children of Captain Grant (3)*; *James Grant*: Rachel Noah. *Mary Grant*: Mary Tucker. *Robert Grant*: Master Harry Woodruff. *Elmina*: Charlene Weidman. *Ballet Specialties*: Mlles. MARIE BONFANTI, ERNESTINE BOSSI, Gigia Ripamoti, Leonilde de Sante, Mauree Marechal, Michela Nappa, (Secondas), 50 Coryphées; ARIEL, the Flying Wonder.

Scene 1: Balker Island. The Wreck. *Scene 2*: Scotland. Glenarvon Castle. *Scene 3*: The Yacht. The "Duncan." *Scene 4*: South America. The Antuco Pass. The Earthquake. *Scene 5*: Balker Island. Abandoned. *Scene 6*: A Posada at Valparaiso. *Scene 7*: The Gold Fetes at Valparaiso. *Scene 8*: An Australian Forest. *Scene 9*: The Mouth of the Murray. *Scene 10*: The Whale. *Scenes 11, 12, 13*: Balker Island. The Rescue. The Open Sea. The Aurora Borealis.

BALLETS AND SPECIALTIES

Ballet (Scene 7)
Mlles. Bonfanti, Bossi, Secondas, Coryphées

Ariel! (Scene7)

1881.16 OUR GOBLINS; or, Fun on the Rhine

An Entirely Reconstructed Version of the Musical Extravaganza in Three Acts[86]. Play by William Gill. Music arranged and the greater part of it composed expressly for the Goblins by Fred. Perkins. Produced by William C. Mitchell's Pleasure Party. Opened 28 March 1881 at the 14th Street Theatre and closed 9 April 1881 after 16 performances.[87]

CAST IN THE PLEASURE PARTY: *Benjamin Franklin Cobb*: WILLIAM GILL. *Mrs. B. F. Cobb*, his better half: ELEANOR DEERING. *Major Eaton Waffles*, Mrs. Cobb's father, formerly of the army of the Potomac: J. M. NORCROSS. *Alfred Comstock Silvermine*, a mining speculator, on a visit to the Cobbs, afterwards a fellow voyager with them to Europe: FRANCIS WILSON. *Octavius Longfellow Warbler*, a dabbler to the muses, also soon to be on the "continong": WILLIAM FORRESTER. *Tillie St. Aubyn, Clarissa St. Aubyn*, sisters, both delighted with the idea of the amateur performance and the European trip: EMMA CARSON, MIRA V. BARRIE.

During Act 1, occurs the rehearsal of Warbler's play, 'Society in a Nutshell:' *Strebelow Duval*, a society husband: A C. Silvermine [F. Wilson]. *Mrs. Strebelow*, a society wife: Mrs. Cobb [E. Deering]. *A Heavy Father*: B. F. Cobb [W. Gill]. *A Dutiful Child*: Tillie St. Aubyn [E. Carson]. *A Basso Profundo*: Major Waffles [J. M. Norcross]. *A Pretty Waitress*: Clarissa St. Aubyn [M. V. Barrie]. *Stage Manager*: O. L. Warbler [W. Forrester].

CAST in Act 3: *Ludovico*, a frightened goblin, by a gentleman strongly resembling B. F. Cobb: WILLIAM GILL. *Countess Agatha von Smithers*, a tragic goblin, by a lady strongly resembling Mrs. B. F. Cobb: ELEANOR DEERING. *Baron von Schwartzbruden*, a gory goblin, by a gentleman strongly resembling A. C. Silvermine: FRANCIS WILSON. *Franz*, a musical goblin, by a gentleman strongly resembling O. L. Warbler: WILLIAM FORRESTER. *Wilhelmina*, an unsophisticated goblin, by a lady strongly resembling Tillie St. Aubyn: EMMA CARSON. *Sigismunda*, an attendant goblin, by a lady closely resembling Clarissa St. Aubyn: MIRA V. BARRIE. *Hildebrand*, a warder goblin, by a gentleman closely resembling Major Waffles: J. M. NORCROSS.

Act 1: The Cobb's Rural Retreat, America. The Cobb family and their friends are about to depart for a trip to Europe. Previous to going they contemplate giving a garden party to their friends, and an Amateur Theatrical Performance; the latter they rehearse during the Act.

Act 2: View of a ruined castle on the Rhine, Germany. We find the party in Germany, visiting an old ruined castle, and Cobb, after drinking some wine, goes to sleep, and in:

Act 3: The Castle in its original form, Dreamland. The characters mentioned in the legend are embodied and in his nightmare Cobb is terribly frightened by the creatures of his imagination, and when he wakes up he finds it to be all a dream.

ACT 1

"Such a Bore" (Duet)
W. Forrester, E. Carson
(*Music by* Fred A. Perkins.)

"All on Account of Eliza" (Song)(from BILLEE TAYLOR)
W. Gill, Chorus
(*Music by* Edward Solomon. *Lyrics by* Henry Pottinger Stephens.)

"(The) Torpedo and the Whale" (Song and Chorus)(from OLIVETTE)
W. Forrester, Company
(*Music by* Edmund Audran.)

Bass Solo
J. M. Norcross

"Merry Bells" (Duet)
E. Crason, M. V. Barrie

"A Philosophic Song and Dance"
F. Wilson

Medley Finale
Company

[84]A rival production to the original which was first produced in New York in English 25 December 1880 at the Bijou Opera House for 63 performances. Note the different translation.

[85]English language adaptation uncredited.

[86]First produced in New York 14 June 1880 at Haverly's 14th Street Theatre for 32 performances.

[87]No credits for scenery, costumes or musical director.

ACT 2

"Dollar of Our Daddies!" (Concertelle)
Company

"We Dance the Fancy Dances" (Song and General Dance)
W. Gill, Company

Frightened Chorus
Company

"What a Dreadful Tale" (Chorus)
Company

Ballad (selected)
E. Carson

"Love Is Lord" (Song and Chorus)
W. Forrester, Company

"Invisible Chorus" (Finale)
Goblins

ACT 3

Love Ballad
E. Carson

"Harm Him Not" (Quartette)
F. Wilson, E. Carson, W. Gill, J. M. Norcross

"Haughty Baron, I" (Duet)
W. Gill, F. Wilson

"The Secret" (Trio)
E. Carson, M. V. Barrie, J. M. Norcross

"Those Cats" (Duet)
W. Forrester, E. Carson

"The Magic Guitar" (Duet)
E. Carson, W. Forrester

"Farewell, Gents" (Quartette)
W. Gill, E. Deering, F. Wilson, W. Forrester

"A Laughing Farewell" (Finale)
Company

1881.17 BILLY THE TAILOR, or A Stitch in Time Saves a Patch

An Original Burletta of the comic opera ("Billee Taylor, or The Reward of Virtue"[88]) in One Act, preceded by an Olio. Conductor, Gustave Reuter. Produced by the Rentz-Santley Novelty Company (M. B. Leavitt, Proprietor). Opened 11 April 1881 at Tony Pastor's Theatre and closed 16 April 1881 after 8 performances.

CAST: *Billy the Tailor*, a young men trying to press his suit: CAPITOLA FORREST. *Sir Mince Meat Lane*, the Bonanza King of Sandy Hook: CHARLES WHITING. *Captain Flip Flapper*, the Commander of the *Thunderbomb*: MABEL SANTLEY. *Ben Barnstable*, ye ancient mariner: JOHN E. HENSHAW. *Christopher Soft Shell Crab*, an unfortunate villain and country schoolmaster: JAMES VINCENT. *Tom Brace, Davy Jones*, Sailors of the Press Gang: Peter Goldrich, Dick Quilter. *Phoebe*, a guileless orphan: ROSA LEE. *Susan*, her schoolmate: MAY TEN BROECK. *Arabella Mince Meat Lane*, a young lady dying for a husband: LULU MORTIMER. *Sailors, Villagers, Charity Girls, etc.*

SCENERY, EVENTS, SONGS

His Royal Nibbs' Inn. View of Anywhere.

"To-day, To-day" (Chorus)

The Charity Girls. The Self-Made Knight. The Tailor's Goose.

"Revenge, Revenge" (Trio)

The Gallant Thunderbomb.

"The Torpedo and the Whale"

"All on Account of Eliza"

Jamaica Rum

"Love, Love" (Solo and Chorus)

The Faithful Crew

[88]BILLEE TAYLOR opened 19 February 1881 at the Standard Theatre for 101 performances. Music by Edward Solomon, libretto by Henry Pottinger Stephens.

1881.18 LITTLE NELL AND THE MARCHIONESS

A Revival of the Melodrama in Four Acts[89]. Suggested by an episode in "The Old Curiosity Shop" by Charles Dickens, adapted by John Brougham. Scenery by Philip H. Goatcher. Mechanical effects and properties by Hamilton Weaver, George Henry. Produced by Lotta Crabtree (John W. Carroll, Representative and Manager). Opened 11 April 1881 at Abbey's Park Theatre and closed 23 April 1881 after 14 performances.

CAST: *Little Nell*: LOTTA (CRABTREE). *The Marchioness*: LOTTA (CRABTREE). *Old Grandfather Trent*: W. H. WALLIS. *Dick Swiveller*: C. H. BRADSHAW. *Daniel Quilp*: P. AUGUSTUS ANDERSON. *Sampson Brass*: H. B. BRADLEY. *Ned Trent*: FRED PERCY. *Corkey Jack*: George Walmsley. *Mr. Slum*: W. Allen. *Reuben Kadger*: C. Parker. *Foxey Joe*: J. Miller. *Higgins*: Jesse K. Hines, Jr. *Burton*: F. C. Lever. *Showman*: J. Smith. *Abdallah*: C. Hammond. *Mrs. Quilp*: Lulu Jordan. *Mrs. Jarley*: Mrs. George C. Boniface. *Sally Brass*: JULIA HANCHETT. *Mrs. Giniwin*: Mrs. Elizabeth Andrews. *Mrs. Simmons*: Miss M. Morgan. *Mrs. George*: Mrs. C. Swain. (*Villagers, Morris Dancers, Guests, Showmen, Minstrels, etc.*)

1881.19 PENN'S AUNTS AMONG THE PIRATES, AND HOW THEY GOT THERE

A Musical Burlesque of the comic opera ("The Pirates of Penzance, or The Slave of Duty"[90]) in One Act, preceded by an Olio. Conductor, Gustave Reuter. Produced by the Rentz-Santley Novelty Company (M. B. Leavitt, Proprietor). Opened 18 April 1881 at Tony Pastor's Theatre and closed 23 April 1881 after 8 performances.

CAST: *Richard*, a very piratical cuss: MAY TEN BROECK. *Sammy*, his able and willing lieutenant: Capitola Forrest. *Whiffer Snapper*: LAURA BENNETT. *Frederick*, a love-sick pirate: ROSA LEE. *William H.M.S. Gilbert*, the author of the "Pirates": JOHN E. HENSHAW. *Arthur Pinafore Sullivan*, the composer of the "Pirates": PETER GOLDRICH. *The Major General*: LEW BENEDICT. *Captain of Police*: Dick Quilter. *Ruth*, the nurse, a reconstructed Buttercup: MABEL SANTLEY. *Mabel*, the heroine: LULU MORTIMER.

Pen's Aunts: *Driscella*: Fanny Florence. *Jemmima*: Annie Whiting. *Sophy*: Capitola Forest. *Martha*: Laura Bennett. *Mary*: Lottie Bordeaux. *Rosa*: Grace Leaver. *Jane*: Maud St. Clair. *Lucy*: Marie Clifton. *Pirates, Policemen, Managers, and others.*

Scene: Somewhere, Nowhere, Everywhere.

1881.20 THE BELLES OF THE KITCHEN

The Vokes Family in a revival of their original, musical, saltatorial, operatic, tragical comical extravaganza in One Act[91], preceded by a comedy, Cousin Joe. Produced by John Stetson. Opened 2 May 1881 at the Union Square Theatre and closed 21 May 1881 after 21 performances. Replacing THE BELLES OF THE KITCHEN, a revival of THE WRONG MAN IN THE RIGHT PLACE opened 23 May 1881, preceded by Cousin Joe, and closed 28 May 1881 after 7 performances. THE BELLES OF THE KITCHEN and COUSIN JOE played a week's return engagement 19 December 1881 at Booth's Theatre for 7 additional performances.

COUSIN JOE CAST: *Margery*: VICTORIA VOKES. *Lady Plato*: JESSIE VOKES. *Cousin Joe*: FRED VOKES. *Sir William Evergreen*: A. Cowper. *Lord Plato*: J. H. Howland. *Captain Blenheim*: E. H. Warren-Wright.

THE BELLES OF THE KITCHEN CAST: *Lucinda Scrubbs*, a lady's maid with "airs and graces:" JESSIE VOKES. *Mary*, a house-maid of "aristocratic inclinations," with Song, Dance and Duet: VICTORIA VOKES. *Barbara*, a kitchen-maid, "the

[89]First produced in New York 14 August 1867 at Wallack's Theatre for 26 performances. For Synopsis of Scenes and Musical Numbers, see original 1867 production.

[90]THE PIRATES OF PENZANCE opened 31 December 1879 at the Fifth Avenue Theatre for 91 performances in two engagements. Music by Arthur Sullivan, libretto by William S. Gilbert.

[91]THE BELLES OF THE KITCHEN was first produced in New York 15 April 1872 at the Union Square Theatre for 49 performances. In the final week, 23-28 May 1881, the Vokes Family substituted their laughable sketch, THE WRONG MAN IN THE RIGHT PLACE, with all the original songs, duet and dances. THE WRONG MAN IN THE RIGHT PLACE was first produced in New York 27 May 1872 at the Union Square Theatre for 6 performances.

incarnation of fun," full of mirth, merriment and mischief: BESSIE SANSON. *Timethus Gibbs*, a doctor's assistant, and chief bottle-washer, with song, dance and legs ad libitum: FERD VOKES. *Wiggins*, a barber, with Wigs, Jigs, a Waltz and Dance, and trouble with Barbara: FAWDON VOKES.

THE WRONG MAN IN THE RIGHT PLACE CAST: *Emily Merton*, Niece to the Proprietress of a Young Ladies College near London: JESSIE VOKES. *Clara Staunton*, a Romantic Young Lady, remaining at the college during vacation. Who will sing with Benjamin Buttontop an Operatic Duet: VICTORIA VOKES. *Sarah Jane*, a Young Person desirous of improving her position in life, at present parlor maid to the Establishment, who will introduce her peculiar and original "Leary Dance": BESSIE SANSON. *Benjamin Buttontop*, Manager of an unlicensed Theatre, at present under a cloud. Who will dance his own Burlesque Polka, and sing with Clara Staunton: FRED VOKES. *Sampson Biffles*, footman to the College, formerly a super in a third-class theatre: FAWDON VOKES.

1881.21 THE MASCOTTE

An Opéra-comique in Three Acts. Original French libretto by Henri Chivot and Alfred Duru. Music by Edmond Audran. Stage manager, Napier Lothian, Jr. Scenery by William Voegtlin. Costumes by J. H. Eaves. Musical director, Frank Howson. Produced by the Wilbur Opera Company (A. L. Wilbur, Proprietor and manager). Opened 5 May 1881 at the Bijou Opera House and closed 13 August 1881 after 108 performances.[92]

CAST: *Lorenzo XIV*, Prince of Piombino: HARRY BROWN. *Frederick*, Prince of Pisa: J. E. CONLY. *Pippo*, a Shepherd: JOHN BRAND. *Rocco*, a Farmer: W. PAUL BOWN. *Sergeant Parafonte*: G. M. PALMER. *Matteo*, Innkeeper: J. T. CRAVEN. *Court Physician*: Ed Morris. *Bettina*, "The Mascotte": EMMA HOWSON[93]. *Fiametta*, daughter of Prince Lorenzo: LILLIE WEST.

Francesca, Antonia, Peasants: Bessie Germon, Susie Kirwin. *Paola, Pietro*, Peasant Boys: Georgie Lincoln, Edith Everley. *Pages (10)*: *Angelo*: Ella Caldwell. *Luigi*: Kate Livingstone. *Marco*: Ellen Vincent. *Carlo*: Maude Russell. *Paulo*: Pearl Everley. *Tito*: Marquita Blanco. *Beppo*: Ella Campbell. *Delto*: Ella Moore. *Alphonso*: Isadore May. *Ferdinand*: Maude Forrest. *Peasants, Ladies and Gentlemen of the Court, Maids of Honor, Soldiers.*

Act 1: Vineyard and Farm at Piombino.

Act 2: Interior of Prince Lorenzo's Palace.

Act 3: Inn near Pisa.

MUSICAL NUMBERS[94]

"The Gobble Duet"

1881.22 LA MASCOTTE

An Opéra-comique in Three Acts[95]. Original French libretto by Henri Chivot and Alfred Duru. Music by Edmond Audran. Scenery by Philip W. Goatcher, Henry E. Hoyt, T. Weston. (Stage direction by I. W. Norcross, Jr.) Musical director, H. J. Widmer. Produced by the Grayson-Norcross Opera Company. Opened 9 May 1881 at Abbey's Park Theatre and closed 28 May 1881 after 21 performances.

CAST: *Bettina*, the "Mascot": HELEN E. H. CARTER. *Pippo*, a Shepherd: SETH M. CRANE. *Lorenzo XVII*, Prince of Piombino: SYDNEY SMITH. *Fiametta*: LIZZIE HARROLD. *Frederic*, Prince of Pisa (Act 1): HELEN GRAYSON. *Tilla*: W. Haydon. *Frederic* (Acts 2, 3): W. HAYDON. *Rocco*, a Farmer: WILLIAM ALLEN. *Parafanti*, Sergeant: CHARLES J. ROSS. *Matheo*, Inn-Keeper: JAMES E. MILLER. *Physician*: Ed Morris. *Pages to the King (6)*: *Carlo*: Lina Lorraine. *Marco*: Florence Durant. *Angelo*: Ethel M. Bird. *Luigi*: May Shackford. *Paolo*: Annie Nicholson. *Pluto*: Tilly Parker. *Paola*: Cora Crane. *Antonio*: Hattie King. *Francesca*: Nellie Hall. *Peasants, Lords and Ladies of the Court, Servants, etc.*

Act 1: Rocco's Farm in Piombino, Italy, where the peasants are celebrating the vintage festival. Fifteenth century. (Goatcher.)

Act 2: A Grand Fête at the Grand Ducal Palace at Piombino. (Hoyt.)

Act 3: The Large Hall of an Italian Inn in the Duchy of Pisa. (Weston.)

ACT 1[96]

Introduction and Opening Chorus (Now the vintage time is over)
Three Peasant Girls, Chorus

"Drinking Song" (Our good wine cures melancholy)
Three Peasant Girls, Chorus

"Legend of the Mascots" (Ballad)
S. M. Crane, Chorus

"Now the Vintage Time"
Chorus

"Come, Now, My Beauty" (Song and Chorus)
H. H. Carter, Tenors, Basses

"Don't Come Too Near"
H. H. Carter, Tenors, Basses

Entering Chorus (When the gay sport)
H. H. Carter, L. Harrold, H. Grayson, S. Smith, W. Allen, Chorus

"Wise Men in All Ages" (Presage Song)
S. Smith, H. Grayson, W. Allen, Chorus

"When the Gay Sport" (Exit)
Chorus

"This Country Lad" (Couplet)
L. Harrold

"That Peculiar Charm" (Song)
L. Harrold, H. Grayson

"When I Behold"[97] (Duet)
H. H. Carter, S. M. Crane

Scenic Music

Finale (Chorus)
H. H. Carter, L. Harrold, H. Grayson, S. M. Crane, S. Smith, W. Allen, Chorus

Coaching Chorus (Come, let us now be off quick as a bird!)
H. H. Carter, Principals, Chorus

ACT 2

"O, What Beauty!" (Chorus)
Pages

"Excuse My Boldness" (Couplets of the Pages)
Pages

"From Thy Presence"
First and Second Sopranos

Ah, Let Me Be!" (Entrance)
H. H. Carter, S. Smith

"Now, Of My Village" (Couplets of the Countess)
H. H. Carter

"What a Charming, Bright Display"
S. M. Crane, Chorus

Air of Saltarelle (All hail to you, my lords!)
[Saltarelle]

"Knowest Thou Those Robes?" (Duet)
H. H. Carter, S. M. Crane

"From Courtiers as They Pass" (Couplets)
W. Haydon

"To Hunt the Stag" (Couplets)
S. Smith

Finale
All the characters, Chorus

"One Day, a Captain Bold" (Song)
H. H. Carter, W. Haydon, L. Harrold, S. Smith, S. M. Crane, Chorus

ACT 3

Chorus of Soldiers of Pisan Army
C. J. Ross, J. E. Miller, Tenors, Basses

Entrance of the Prince
W. Haydon

"Song of the Drum"
W. Haydon, Tenors, Basses

---

[92]English adaptation uncredited; no credits for costumes in programs. A revival with a different cast under different management returned as LA MASCOTTE to the Bijou 5 September 1881. See separate entry in that season.

[93]Succeeded for return engagement by Selina Dolaro.

[94]Musical numbers not listed in programs.

[95]A rival production to that at the Bijou Opera House, originating in Boston. Although the English adaptation is uncredited in programs, the published vocal score credits the English translation and adaptation of words to music by Theodore T. Barker, and dialogue and stage direction to I. W. Norcross, Jr. A rival translation by Louis C. Elson , dialogue and stage direction by J. W. Norris, was also published by White, Smith & Co., Boston, 1881. It too claims to be the Grayson-Norcross production.

[96]Musical numbers not listed in programs. List prepared from published American piano vocal score (Oliver Ditson Co., Boston, 1881).

[97]In the original French the Duo des Dindons, also popularly known as The Gobble Duet.

Entrance of the Refugees
S. Smith, W. Allen, C. J. Ross, L. Harrold
"The Orang-Outgang Song"
L. Harrold, Chorus
Entrance of the Wedding Party
"I Near the Goal" (Ariette)
L. Harrold, W. Haydon, S. M. Crane, S. Smith, Chorus
"How Is This, Pippo?" (Quartette)
H. H. Carter, S. M. Crane, S. Smith, W. Allen
"Ah, With Wrath" (Ensemble)
H. H. Carter, S. M. Crane, S. Smith, W. Allen
"Pray, Tell Me Why?" (Finale)
All the characters, chorus

1881.23 PHOTOS!

The Harrisons and their Matchless Company in a Musical Eccentricity in Two Acts. Play by B. E. Woolfe. Produced by the Harrisons (Management, Martin W. Hanley) Opened 9 May 1881 at the Grand Opera House and closed 14 May 1881 after 8 performances.[98]

CAST: *Act 1*: *Lottie Gwinne*, seeking the emotional: ALICE HARRISON. *Clara Harleigh*, seeking sunny smiles and a rich husband: CARRIE DANIELS. *Milly*, seeking a dime novel hero: Therese Wood. *Marston Moore*, seeking a row: LOUIS HARRISON. *Belvidere Potter*, seeking a responsive heart: R. E. GRAHAM. *Mr. Buchner*, seeking a family group, smiling: W. H. Thompson. *Mr. Brindle*, seeking captive maidens, with the "Curse of Gonsalo": Harry Warren.

Sitters in Act 2: *Mlle. Leontine*, serio-comic singer: ALICE HARRISON. *Livia*, a Roman Vestal: ALICE HARRISON. *Marchmont Carruthers*: LOUIS HARRISON. *Otto*, a German reporter: LOUIS HARRISON. *Dionysius*, Emperor of Rome: LOUIS HARRISON. *Fritz*, our Cousin German: R. E. GRAHAM. *Sarah Bernhardt*: R. E. GRAHAM. *Brutus*, Rome's hardest hitter: R. E. GRAHAM. *Clara Harleigh*, introducing contralto song and guitar solo: CARRIE DANIELS. *Mlle. Adagio*: Therese Wood. *Chinius*, a Roman Warrior: Harry Warren. *Mr. Skye*: Jay Hunt. *Negatives, Positives, Cabinets*: Company.

1881.24 CASTLES IN SPAIN

A Grand Musical Spectacular Drollery in Three Acts, 18 Scenes, combining all the features of Opera Bouffe and Grand Spectacle.[99] Play by Arturo Cuyás. Music selected from the best numbers of the most popular Spanish Comic Operas (by Francisco Asenjo Barbieri, Joaquin Gaztambide y Garbayo, Emilio Arrieta y Correra, Cristóbal Oudrid y Segura, Ricardo Caballero y Martínez); incidental music for the play and ballet by Juan Goula. Ballet master, Signor Giovanni Lepri. Ballet music composed by Ricardo Moragas. Chorus trained by F. de Rialp. Scenery by F. Soler. Costumes by Bloom and Dazian. Leader of orchestra, Charles Puerner. Produced under the supervision of E. S. Tarr. Produced by Alberto Bernis. Opened 9 May 1881 at Niblo's Garden and closed 14 May 1881 after 8 performances.

CAST: *Mother Gafas*, a bewitching Witch, afterwards transformed into the Queen of Beauty, *Donna Rodriguez*, a Duenna, and *Spiritina*, a Vivandiere: PAULINE MARKHAM. *Clara, Lucinda*, daughters of Sergeant Granada: AMY LEE, LOUISE PAULLIN. *Monica*, their "proverbial" aunt: Mrs. OWEN MARLOWE. *Henrique, Lorenzo*, Fellow Students: HART CONWAY, W. H. FITZGERALD. *Don Candido Estupendo*, Marquis of Carabobo: HARRY H. PRATT. *Sergeant Granada*, who was in Flanders: JAMES C. DUNN. *Ricardo, Eduardo*, the Twins, nephews to the Marquis: W. J. Shea, J. R. Gildersleeve. *Carbon*, Business Manager for the Infernal Palace: Eugene F. Eberle. *Counsellor Verba*: Eugene F. Eberle. *Grifo*, his Infernal Majesty: Robert Brower. *Dr. Plasta*: Robert Brower. *Sinecure*, an Abbe: E. M. Porter. *Fermin*, a Student: L. Davis. *Pages of the Marquis' Household (4)*: *Folio*: Kate Ethel. *Quarto*: A. Featherstone. *Octavo*: A. Montague. *Blank*: C. Maurel. *Ballet Specialties*: Mlle. AMALIA LEPRI (Première Danseuse Assoluta), Mlle. LEONILDA ORTORI. *Students, Pages, Servants, Soldiers, Wizards, Witchs, Vivandieres, Dwarfs, Demons, Trumpeters, Nymphs, Watteau Shepherds, Birds, Monkeys, Frogs, Parrots, etc.*

Act 1, Scene 1: View of the Housetops in Madrid by Moonlight. *Scene 2*: An attic room; the dwelling of Sergeant Grenada. *Scene 3*: The Enchanted Cave: The Witches' Abode. *Scene 4*: A Street in the Suburbs by Moonlight. *Scene 5*: The Infernal Palace.

Act 2, Scene 1: An Apartment in Carabobo's Castle. *Scene 2*: Entrance to a Spanish Village. *Scene 3*: The Gardens of Carabobo's Mansion. *Scene 4*: An Encampment of Austrian Soldiers. *Scene 5*: Exterior view of Carabobo's Castle by Moonlight. Capture of Carabobo's Castle by a grotesque army of "harmless creatures." *Scene 6*: Tableau Finale. Attack and Explosion. The Castle in Flames!

Act 3, Scene 1: A Cellar in Carabobo's Castle. *Scene 2*: A Gothic Hall. *Scene 3*: The Enchanted Vault. *Scene 4*: Autumn. *Scene 5*: Winter. *Scene 6*: Spring. *Scene 7*: Summer. Grand Apotheosis and Transformation Scene.

ACT 1
Scene 1
Enrique's Serenade to Clara
H. Conway
(*Music by* Francisco Asenjo Barbieri.)
Scene 2
Clara's Song
A. Lee
(*Music by* Cristóbal Oudrid y Segura.)
Scene 3
The Three Visions: "Castles in the Air" (Chorus)
P. Markham, Witches
(*Music by* Joaquin Gaztambide y Garbayo.)
Scene 4
Duet
A. Lee, L. Paullin
(*Music by* Francisco Asenjo Barbieri.)
Scene 5
Grand Demon Ballet and Triumphal March of the Infernal Legion

ACT 2
Scene 1
Invocation Chorus
(*Music by* F. de Rialp.)
Drinking Song
H. Conway, W. H. Fitzgerald, Chorus
(*Music by* Emilio Arrieta y Correra.)
Scene 2
Students' Chorus
(*Music by* Cristóbal Oudrid y Segura.)
Scene 3
Duet
W. H. Fitzgerald, L. Paullin
(*Music by* Francisco Asenjo Barbieri.)
Ballet: Minuet of the Kiss (Louis XV Style)
Scene 4
Spiritina's Song
Chorus of Soldiers and Vivandieres
(*Music by* Francisco Asenjo Barbieri.)
Smoking Chorus
P. Markham, Vivandières
(*Music by* Ricardo Caballero y Martínez.)

ACT 3
Scene 3
Grand Transformation of the Four Seasons (Ballet)
Scene 4
Autumn: Pastoral Waltz
Mlle. A. Lepri, Corps de Ballet
Scene 5
Winter: Youth and Old Age (Comic Ballet)
Hungarian Polka
March of Cossacks
Pas à Trois
Scene 6
Spring: Pas of Two Canary Birds
Mlles. A. Lepri, Ortori
Ballet of Birds and Frogs
Corps de Ballet

[98]No credits in programs for stage director, scenery, costumes, or musical director. Specialties (songs, dances, imitations) were introduced in Act 2; though not individually listed in programs, the Boston programs referred to Alice Harrison's imitations of Clara Morris, Maggie Mitchell, and Mlle. Aimée in "La Périchole." J. K. Emmet and Lawrence Barrett were also imitated by Messrs. Harrison or Graham.

[99]The zarzuela CASTLES IN SPAIN that has had a run of 400 nights in Barcelona, 250 in Madrid, 90 in Havana and 114 in Mexico City, formed the inspiration for this production which boasts a new and original American libretto and a musical score assembled from other zarzuelas.

Scene 7
Summer: Grand Apotheosis and Transformation Scene

1881.25 DONNA JUANITA

A Comic Opera in Three Acts. Original Viennese libretto by F. Zell and Richard Genée. Music by Franz von Suppé. Stage manager, Vincent Hogan. Musical director, Gustave A. Kerker. Produced by H. B. Mahn's Comic Opera Company. Opened 16 May 1881 at the Fifth Avenue Theatre and closed 4 June 1881 after 21 performances.[100]

CAST: *René Dufaure*, French Cadet: JENNIE WINSTON. *Donna Juanita*: JENNIE WINSTON. *Petrita*: JANET EDMONDSTON. *Gaston Dufaure*, in love with Petrita: WALLACE MACREERY. *Donna Olympia*: ROSE LEIGHTON. *Don Pomponio*, Alcalde of San Sebastian and husband of Donna Olympia: ELLIS RYSE. *Colonel Douglas*, English Commandant of San Sebastian: ARTHUR H. BELL. *Don Riego*, Notary and Public Writer: W. A. MORGAN. *Gil Polo*, Keeper of Posada: VINCENT HOGAN. *Marco*: Marie Somerville. *Picador*: Arthur Van Houten. *Dolores*: May Booth. *Aguador*: Joseph Hans. *Tepa*: Clara Douglas. *Fitzroy*: Harry Dale. *Duplan*: S. Battle.

Students: *Rajos*: May Clark. *Pedro*: Anna Callaway. *Leon*: Martha Campbell. *Gomez*: Grace Clark. *Alonzo*: Kate Low. *Jose*: Sallie Wynne. *Francisco*: J. Vincent.

Lady Conspirators: *Donna Mercedes*: Clara Douglas. *Donna Rosaura*: May Clark. *Donna Ersilia*: Grace Clark. *Donna Laura*: May Booth. *Donna Pepita*: Dora Feitner. *Donna Encarnacion*: Marie Beauman. *Donna Anna*: Jeanne Vincent. *Donna Isabella*: Mrs. Ellis Ryse. *Donna Marietta*: Anna Callaway. *Donna Inez*: Clara Dixon. *Donna Zerlina*: M. Campbell. *Donna Elvira*: Kate Low. *Scotch and French Soldiers, Nobles, Peasants, Singing Boys, etc.*

Act 1: Plaza in San Sebastian.

Act 2: Interior of Don Pomponio's Palace.

Act 3: Fort in San Sebastian.

ACT 1[101]

Introduction and Chorus (Hip, hooray!)
V. Hogan, Chorus
"In the Wine of Our Country" (Song and Chorus)
J. Edmondston, V. Hogan, Chorus
"France in arms for war" (Romance with Chorus)
W. Macreery, J. Edmondston, V. Hogan, Chorus
"Behold! He comes!" (Concerted Piece with song)
W. A. Morgan, Chorus
"Ça ira" (Exit)
W. A. Morgan, Chorus
"Folks do not much like me here" (Comic Duet)
E. Ryse, A. H. Bell
"When I was young" (Couplets)
R. Leighton
"Can they not leave us alone" (Quintet)
J. Edmondston, R. Leighton, W. Macreery, W. A. Morgan, E. Ryse
"René's Song"
J. Winston
Finale (Concerted Piece and Grand Ensemble)
Principals, Chorus

ACT 2

"May the saints above" (Introduction and Chorus)
W. A. Morgan, E. Ryse, A. H. Bell, M. Somerville, Chorus of Students
"A Spaniard Was My Fond Papa" (Rondo)
J. Winston, W. A. Morgan, E. Ryse, A. H. Bell
"The Conspiracy Scene" (Concerted Piece)
J. Winston, R. Leighton, E. Ryse, A. H. Bell, Conspirators, Chorus of Ladies
"Had nature only granted" (Duettino)
J. Winston, E. Ryse
"Could I ever be false?" (Romance and Terzetto)
J. Edmondston, J. Winston, W. Macreery
"With dance, with song" (Finale Chorus)
Principals, Chorus

ACT 3

"They require not words" (Duetto Mauresco)
J. Edmondston, W. Macreery
"Come, dear, we will chase" (Children's Duet)
J. Winston, A. H. Bell
"Now, trumpeters, commence" (Chorus and Ensemble)
Principals, Chorus

---

[100]English language librettist, stage director, scenery, costumes uncredited in programs. Very likely the English translation by Henry S. Leigh was used.

[101]Musical numbers not listed in programs. List prepared from published English piano vocal score, lyrics by Henry S. Leigh (J. Williams, London, 1880); very possibly Leigh's adaptation was not used, or else substantially revised without credit for New York, as the critics scorned the nameless librettist's work.

1881–1882 SEASON

Catherine Lewis (Photo: Houseworth)
Billy Rose Theatre Collection, New York Public Library for the Performing Arts

1881–1882 SEASON

1881.26 ELFINS AND MERMAIDS

A Serio-Comic Opera in Two Acts. Libretto and music by Charles Brown. Musical director, Ernest Neyer. Produced by Charles Brown. Opened 4 June 1881 at the Standard Theatre and closed 14 June 1881 after 10 performances.[1]

CAST: *The Admiral*, the Right Hon. Lord Viscount Adelle Lee, K.C.B., commanding *H.M.S. Victory*. A brave, noble and gallant officer, for zeal and valor loved by all who knew him: HAYDON TILLA. *The Earl of Tudor*, Midshipman: J. BEAUMONT. *Sir Charles Crownly*, Staff Commander: L. M. FLORIN. *And a full crew of British sailors.*

Italian Pirates: *Count Navi*, Chief of Pirates, known as Admiral Clueline. A terrible conspirator and ex-official of the Italian government: J. A. FUREY. *Count Izia*, a rich Italian who has given up high life and estate to join the pirates. In ardent love with Mari: J. PHILLIPS. *Count Devoli*, part owner of many ships; known as Anchor Jack: H. H. Howard. *Signor Cabal Cubalo*, known as Tom Bowline, a romantic pilot and fisherman of Naples Bay. Married to Mari: H. R. HUMPHRIES. *Countess Arena*, wife of Navi: BELLA FLOYD. *Viscountess Mari Lee*, wife to Tom Bowline. Being beautiful, causes the rivalry and jealousy between Isia, Devoli and her husband BELLE COLE. *Goldwave*, child to Mari: Lottie Ince. *And a full crew of Pirates.*

Act 1: Upper Deck of the Red Rock Wave. Sea view near Naples, Italy, at night.

Act 2: Same view. The Pirates' Red Rock Haunt. A Coast and Light-House at night.

1881.27 CINDERELLA AT SCHOOL

A Revival of the Musical Comedy in Two Acts, 6 Scenes[2]. Book, music and lyrics by Henry Woolson Morse. Based on the play "School" by T. W. Robertson. Scenery by James Roberts. Costumes by Lanouette. Orchestrations by Edward Mollenhauer. Produced by Edward E. Rice and Nat C. Goodwin, Jr. Opened 9 August 1881 at Daly's Theatre and closed 3 September 1881 after 32 performances; returned 3 November 1881 to Daly's Theatre and closed 9 November 1881 after 8 additional performances. Total: 40 performances.

CAST: *Arthur Bicycle*, a perambulating Deity of the upper-crust, with distinguished connections: HARRY MACDONOUGH. *Jack Polo*, of the Meadow Brook Hunt, Stroke-oar of Harvard in the race of '80: DIGBY BELL. *Lord Lawntennys*, a relic of other days and other lands, on a visit to his long-lost nephew, and on a search for a long-lost niece: CHARLES LECLERCQ. *Professor Kindergarten*, Principal of the Papyrus Seminary for Young Ladies, at Laurelton: H. ROBERTS. *Syntax*, Tutor, the Professor's head-usher and husher: JAMES LEWIS. *Jenkinson*, Attendant on Lord Lawntennys: W. H. Beekman. *Members of the Meadow Brook Hunt, also of Columbia Crew and Harvard*: Messrs. N. S. Burnham, C. Milton, Saleon, Harman, Perring, Hamilton, others.

Niobe Marsh, the Cendrillon of the School: MAY FIELDING. *Merope Mallow*, a young lady from Brazil: LAURA JOYCE. *Psyche Persimmons*, the sleepiest girl in the Seminary: ADA REHAN. *Zenobia Tropics*, head teacher at the Papyrus: Mrs. A. PERRING. *Miss Globes*, her assistant: B. Weaver.

Chloris Slatepencil, who lisps: Nelly Howard. *Circe Slatepencil*, who giggles: Isabel Evesson. *Lotis Slatepencil*, who sighs: Sally Williams. *Penelope Slatepencil*, who eats: Miss Hopcraft. *Pancy Pickle*, who knows everything: Emily Denin. *Primrose Pickle*, who knows nothing: Miss Cleor. *Sally Chalk*, who pouts: Lillie Lee. *Carrie Mall, Marian Glassy*, two very sweet girls: Emma Hinckley, Alice Moore. *Daisy Dimple*, a simple little thing: Josie Nagle. *Virginia Creeper*, an insinuating thing: Helen Hewett. *Fragrant Pupils (5)*: *Rhode Dendron*: Miss Parkhurst. *Minni Nett*: Miss K. Denin. *Olie Ander*: Miss L. Perring. *Jessie Meen*: Miss Morris. *Marie Gold*: G. Malmane.

1881.28 SMIFF

A Spectacular Musical Comedy in Three Acts, 7 Scenes. Play by George Fawcett Rowe. Music composed, selected and arranged by Frank Musgrave. Scenery by Hughson Hawley, William F. Voegtlin, John A. Thompson, Seymour Parker. Machinery by Benson Sherwood and William Vail. Costumes by S. W. Laurey; Reimer of Milan. Orchestra under the direction of W. L. Bowron. Produced by J. H. Haverly. Opened 22 August 1881 at Haverly's Fifth Avenue Theatre and closed 3 September 1881 after 16 performances.

CAST: The Smiff Family: *Philander Smiff*, Impressario and Eccentric Comedian: GEORGE FAWCETT ROWE. *Albert Smiff, Thaddeus Smiff*, his sons: JAMES COOPER, J. E. NAGLE, JR. *Daphne Smiff*, Leading Lady: LOUISE BALFE. *Laurelia Smiff*, Æsthetic Juvenile: ALMA STUART STANLEY. *Mimosa Smiff*, Soubrette: KATE GURNEY.

John Gennesee, of Virginia City, Nevada: GEORGE C. DAVENPORT. *Alonzo Brown*, of Manchester, England: CHARLES S. DICKSON. *Jasen Pegrim*, a Professor of Legerdemain: Murry Woods. *Miss Cadwallader*, a Cook's Excursionist: Mary Stuart. *Pipes*: Harry Reeves. *Parsons*: A. Henderson. *And numerous auxiliaries.*

Characters in the Legend: *Psyche*: LOUISE BALFE. *Cupid*: KATE GURNEY. *Venus*: ALMA STUART STANLEY. *King Pompos*: JAMES COOPER. *Rumfisina*: J. E. NAGLE, JR. *Zephyr*: GEORGE FAWCETT ROWE. *The Graces (3)*: *Euphrosyne*: Kate Ethel. *Aglaia*: Mary Keene. *Thalia*: Julia Montague.

Act 1, Scene 1: The Stage Door of the Theatre Royal, Snughampton. *Scene 2*: The Stage of the Theatre. Full Dress Rehearsal of the Classic Legend of Psyche. *Scene 3*: A Mountain in Kyllene. *Scene 4*: Cupid's Palace. *Scene 5*: Transformation, and departure of the Smiff Family for New York on the transatlantic steamship, *"Swei Lager."*

Act 2: Deck of the steamship *"Swei Lager."* (Dutch Line) Terrible catastrophe in mid-ocean.

Act 3: A Desert Island. Night. Happy Revelation!

MUSICAL NUMBERS[3]

Kiss Song
L. Balfe

Sextet (Act 2)

1881.29 THE MAJOR

A Local Comedy in Four Acts, 8 Scenes. Play (and lyrics) by Edward Harrigan. Music by David Braham. Staged by Edward Harrigan. Settings by Robert Cutler, Charles W. Witham. Musical director, David Braham. Produced by (Edward) Harrigan and (Tony) Hart. Opened 29 August 1881 at the Theatre Comique and closed 7 January 1882 after 152 performances.

CAST: *Major Gilfeather*: EDWARD HARRIGAN. *Enry Iggins*: TONY HART. *Phineas Bottlegreen*: JOHN WILD. *Caleb Jenkins*: WILLIAM GRAY. *Granville Bright*: EDWARD BURT. *Mr. Spotem*: HARRY FISHER. *Percival Popp*: M. F. Drew. *John Murphy*: John Queen. *Phadrig Murphy*: M. Bradley. *Mr. Dip*: James Tierney. *Mr. Grab*: Edward Goss. *Mr. Pry*: Thomas Ray. *Steward*: M. Foley. *Henry Huxley*: W. Merritt. *Mr. Sole*: Fred Queen. *Mr. Welt*: George Merritt. *Ephraim Shroud*: William West. *Mr. Plaid*: Robert Hall. *Clara Jenkins*: JAMES FOX. *Aunty Green*: John Oberist. *Burnside Ruffle*: Emil Heusel. *Slip Runner*: Morgan Benson. *Policemen*: Messrs. Rourke, McCullough. *Arabella Pinch*: ANNIE MACK. *Miranda Briggs*: ANNIE YEAMANS. *Henrietta*: GERTIE GRANVILLE. *Amelia Bright*: Marie Gorenflo. *Bridget Murphy*: Mary Bird.

Act 1, Scene 1: The Dock of the Inman Line. (Witham.) *Scene 2*: Exterior of Miranda Biggs' Boarding House. (Witham.) *Scene 3*: Parlor at Mrs. Biggs' Boarding House. (Witham.)

Act 2, Scene 1: View of Exchange Office and Photograph Gallery. (Witham.) *Scene 2*: Interior and exterior of Caleb Jenkins' Exchange Office. (Cutler and Witham.)

Act 3, Scene 1: Corridor of Police (Witham.) Station. *Scene 2*: Housetop by night, showing the interior of Percival Popp's Firework Factory, and exterior of same. (Witham[4].)

Act 4: Coney Island by Moonlight. (Cutler and Witham.)

---

[1]No credits in programs for scenery or costume designs; stage direction is presumably by the author-producer; musical numbers not listed in programs.

[2]First produced in New York 5 March 1881 at Daly's Theatre for 65 performances. For Synopsis of Scenes and Musical Numbers, see original 1881 production. Direction uncredited; most likely the original direction by Fred Williams and dances by Mme. Malvina from the previous production were retained in part, re-staged by Edward E. Rice. For this revival the following were added:

"To Our Leafy Haunts We Go" (Chorus) (replaced "The Cause of Civilization")
Schoolgirls

"Corn Beef Hashed" (Song) (replaced "To Educate These Young Ladies")
H. Roberts (Kindergarten)

"Maiden Fair Awake to Me" (added Act 2, Scene 1, before "Courting in the Moonlight")
J. Lewis

"Oh! dear—Oh! dear!" (added Act 2, Scene 1, before "Cotton Cloth Ghost")
Schoolgirls

"Upon Paul's Steeple" (later dropped)

[3]No musical numbers listed in programs.

[4]Mechanical effects of this scene designed, constructed and perfected by our Master Machinist, Robert Cutler.

MUSICAL NUMBERS

"Major Gilfeather"
E. Harrigan, Chorus

"Clara Jenkins' Tea"

"Miranda, When We Are Made One"
E. Harrigan, A. Yeamans

"The Veteran Guard Cadets"
Madrigal Boys

Medley, Darky Chorus

1881.30 MICHAEL STROGOFF

A Drama in Three Acts[5], preceded by a farce and a sketch. (Original French play by Adolphe d'Ennery adapted from the novel 'Michel Strogoff' by Jules Verne.) Dramatized expressly for this theatre. Director of amusements, Charles L. Farwell. Scenic artist, Larry Smith. Musical director, G. P. Barnard. Produced by Jacob Aberle. Opened 29 August 1881 at Aberle's Theatre and closed 10 September 1881 after 18 performances.

CAST: *Michael Strogoff*, the Courier: CHARLES L. FARWELL. *Czar of Russsia*: George W. Johnson. *Harry Blount*, an English reporter: L. W. Barker. *Alcide Josivet*, a French reporter: H. L. Bascombe. *Ivan Ogareff*: ALF A. WALLACE. *Grand Duke*: J. W. George. *General Kissoff*, Chief of Police: E. Doran. *The Emir*: Max Miller. *Wassili Feodor*: M. McCormick. *Postmaster*: D. Edwards. *Tartar Officer*: G. Levanion. *Telegraph Operator*: E. Delmonte. *General Vearnoff*: C. Grey. *Nadia*: MAMIE WALLACE. *Marfa (Strogoff)*: ADDIE FARWELL. *Sangarre*: MARTHA MILLER.
(*Ballet*: Mlles. GASPARRO (Premiere), May Henning, Annie Atkens, Josephine Walby, Corps de Ballet. *Specialties*: Messrs. Levaion and McCormack, Athletic exercises; Hercules and His Cannon Balls, by J. Conklin; Brass Band, Drum Corps.)

Act 1: The Czar of Russia. Entrance of the Courier. His mission and departure. The Reporters. Naida and Michael. On the steamer. The Gypsies. Ivan Ogareff, the traitor. Imposing Tableau.

Act 2: The Post House. The blow. The distant battle. The telegraph. Descent of the Tartars. Grand Tableau. Marfa, the Mother of Michael. The denial. The festivities. Marfa denies her son. The punishment of the Knout. The terrible ordeal by fire. Imposing tableau.

Act 3: The reporters. Michael and Naida. The Russian Soldiers. The Grand Duke's Residence. The false Courier. An unexpected event. Death of the Traitor. The Battle of Irkutsk.

SPECIALTIES

Grand Ballet—Tarantella (Act 1)
Corps de Ballet
Premier: Mlle. Gasparro. And Misses M. Henning, A. Atkens, J. Walby.

Grand March of the Tartar Army (Act 2)

Athletic Exercises (Act 2)
Messrs. Levaion, McCormack

Grand Ballet (Act 2)

The Wonderful Hercules and His Cannon Balls (Specialty)(Act 3)
J. Conklin

Full Brass Band and Drum Corps (Act 3)

The Battle of Irkutsk (Act 3)

1881.31 MICHAEL STROGOFF

A Dramatic Pageant (Melodrama) in Five Acts, 10 Scenes. Original French play by Adolphe d'Ennery adapted from the novel 'Michel Strogoff' by Jules Verne. English adaptation by Henry J. Byron. Orchestra and music under the direction of Charles Puerner. Produced under the stage direction of Thomas B. MacDonough. Scenery by William F. Voegtlin, Hughson Hawley, Gaspard Maeder, George Heister. Costumes designed by Mons. Thomas of Paris. Mechanical effects by John Denham and J. Leo. Properties by E. R. Morse and C. Blessing. Orchestra under the direction of William Withers. Produced by Samuel Colville, J. H. Haverly and E. G. Gilmore. Opened 31 August 1881 at Booth's Theatre and closed 1 October 1881 after 37 performances; moved 3 October 1881 to Haverly's Niblo's Garden and closed 5 November 1881 after 40 additional performances. Total: 77 performances[6].

CAST: *Michael Strogoff* of the Imperial Messengers: F. C. BANGS. *Ivan Ogareff*, a disgraced Russian officer: J. N. GOTTHOLD. *Governor of Moscow*: A. D. Billings. *General Kiezoff*: John Swinbourne. *Richard Hunt*, New York correspondent: Isadore Davidson. *John Philpot*, London correspondent: Felix Morris. *Feofar*, Emir of Bokhara: George Robinson. *Chief of Police*: Delancey Barclay. *Innkeeper*: George Bowson. *Passport Agent*: Charles Torrence. *Telegraph Clerk*: T. F. Atkins. *Tartar Chief*: Z. Tailraf. *Aide-de-Camp* to Governor of Moscow: Walter Eytinge. *High Priest*: W. H. Pope. *Officer*: George Copin. *First Traveler*: Harry Cope. *Second Traveler*: William Tate. *First Fugitive*: Thomas Barton. *A Bohemian*: Andrew Mahone. *The Grand Duke*: Frank Beresford. *General Verouzoff*: John Bright. *Wassili Fedor*: John T. Burke. *Aide-de-Camp*: Theodore Townshend. *Marfa Strogoff*: ELIZA L. BATES. *Sangarre*, a Gypsy woman: FLORENCE ROBINSON. *Nadia Fedor*: RACHEL SANGER. *Fugitives, Travelers, Tartars, Gypsies, etc.*

Prologue, Scene 1: Michel Strogoff's Mission. Ante-room in the Palace of the Governor of Moscow. (Heister.) *Scene 2*: Illuminated Fête at Moscow. (Maeder.)

Act 1: Post-House on the Frontier. (Hawley.) Ivan Ogareff's Treachery.

Act 2, Scene 1: Telegraph Office. Mother and Son. *Scene 2*: Battlefield at Kolyvan. (Voegtlin.)

Act 3, Scene 1: Ivan Ogareff's Tent. *Scene 2*: Tartar Camp. (Voegtlin.) Michel Strogoff's Doom.

Act 4, Scene 1: The Banks of the Angora. (Maeder.) *Scene 2*: Partial Destruction of Irkutsk. (Voegtlin.)

Act 5: Ante-Room of the Grand Duke's Palace. The 24th of September. (Hawley.)

BALLETS

Incidental Ballet (Prologue, Scene 2)
Mlle. LaBella, (Corps de Ballet)

Grand Procession; Reception of Feofar, Emir of Bokhara;

Incidental Ballet (Act 3, Scene 2)

1881.32 MICHAEL STROGOFF

A Spectacular Melodrama in Five Acts, 11 Scenes[7]. Original French play by Adolphe d'Ennery adapted from the novel 'Michel Strogoff' by Jules Verne. (Adapted for the American stage by A. R. Cazauran.) Music by Franz von Suppé. Stage manager, George Edeson. Scenery by Bertoza, of Venice; J. Mazzanovich; Ed. Simmonds; Kautizky, of Vienna; Magnani, of Florence; Carpezat, of the Grand Opera House, Paris; Robecchi, of Paris; Lutzkmeyer, of Darmstadt; Habelman, of Berlin; Bricohi, of Vienna. Costumes by Dombrovsky, of Imperial Theatre, Moscow. Musical director, F. W. Zauling. Entire spectacle produced by and under the personal direction and supervision of Imre and Bolossy Kiralfy. Opened 3 September 1881 at the Academy of Music and closed 17 September 1881 after 17 performances.[8]

CAST: *Michael Strogoff*, Courier of the Czar: WILLIAM RIGNOLD. *Ivan Ogareff*, an exiled officer: CHARLES CHAPPELLE. *The Czar of Russia*: Harry Gwynette. *Feofar*, Khan of Bokhara: George Harmon. *The Grand Duke*: F. Munroe. *Ezekiah Sharp*, American War Correspondent: George R. Edeson. *Harry Blunt*, English War Correspondent: A. Thomas. *Dr. Wassili Fedor*, an exile: S. Morton. *General Kissoff*: H. Montgomery. *Dombroosky, Muravieff*: A. H. Denham, J. Cox. *Telegraph Operator*: J. W. Bankson. *Weadimir*, an Innkeeper: L. Steele. *A Tartar Lancer*: W. B. Johns. *Tartar Officer*: C. Thomas. *First Corporal*: Lysander Thompson. *Second Corporal*: F. Barton. *Chief Executioner*: Sig. Sebastian. *High Priest*: D. H. Adams. *Boatman*: E. Bronson. *Driver*: F. Williamson. *Nadia*, the Exile's Daughter: ELLIE WILTON. *Sangara*, a Gypsy: ADA NELSON. *Marfa Strogoff*: Mrs. J. L. CARHART. (*Premiere Danseuse Assoluta*: Mlle. BAZZANO. *Grotesque Dancer*: Mons. ARNOLD KIRALFY. Coryphées, Corps de Ballet.) *Nobles, Tartars, Soldiers, Market People, Jugglers, Populace, Gypsies, etc.*

Act 1: The Fete at the new Palace. *Scene 1*: The Czar's Apartment. (Bertoza.) *Scene 2*: The Fair of Nijni-Novgorod. (J. Mazzanovich.)

Act 2, Scene 1: The Post House. (J. Mazzanovich.) *Scene 2*: The Telegraph Station at Tomsk. (Simmonds.) *Scene 3*: After the Bombardment. (Kautizky.)

---

[5]The first of three concurrent rival adaptations of the Jules Verne novel.
[6]This production, a rival to the Kiralfy version at the Academy of Music, had previously played the Adelphi Theatre, London. Later played a return engagement under the longer title, MICHAEL STROGOFF, The Relief of Irkutsk, 19 January 1885 at the Grand Opera House for an additional 8 performances, under the management of Charles L. Andrews; 28 September 1885 at Henry C. Miner's Peoples Theatre for an additional 8 performances, under the longer title MICHAEL STROGOFF, The Courier of the Czar, again under the auspices and direction of Charles L. Andrews.
[7]A rival production to the adaptation presented 31 August 1881 at Booth's Theatre and Niblo's Garden for 77 performances.
[8]This production, a rival to the Henry J. Byron version at Booth's Theatre, subsequently toured with the longer title MICHAEL STROGOFF; or, The Czar's Courier.

Act 3, Scene 1: Tent of Ogareff. (Magnani.) *Scene 2*: Camp of Feofar Khan. (Carpezat.)

Act 4, Scene 1: Banks of the Angara. Panorama of the Angara River. (Robecchi.)

Act 5, Scene 1: The Fortifications. (Lutzkmeyer.) *Scene 2*: Interior of the Duke's Palace. (Habelman.) *Scene 3*: The Palace at Irkutsk. (Briochi.)

BALLETS

Grand Gypsy Ballet (Act 1, Scene 2)
Mlle. Bazzano, Mons. A. Kiralfy, Coryphées, 60 Corps de Ballet

The Imperial Dragoons (Act 1, Scene 2)

Grand Triumphal Finale (Act 1, Scene 2)

Grand Tartar Ballet, 'Les Favorites de l'Emir' (Act 3, Scene 2)
Mlle. Bazzano, Mons. A. Kiralfy, Coryphées, Grand Corps de Ballet

Imposing Finale (Act 5, Scene 3)

1881.33 LA MASCOTTE

A Revival of the Opéra-comique in Three Acts[9]. Libretto by Henri Chivot and Alfred Duru. Music by Edmond Audran. Produced by the Wilbur Opera Company. Opened 5 September 1881 at the Fifth Avenue Theatre and closed 17 September 1881 after 16 performances.

CAST: *Lorenzo XIV*, Prince of Piombino: HARRY BROWN. *Frederick*, Prince of Pisa: J. E. CONLY. *Pippo*, a Shepherd: W. BISHOP. *Rocco*, a Farmer: ED CHAPMAN. *Sergeant Parafonte*: G. M. PALMER. *Matteo*, Innkeeper: J. T. CRAVEN. *Court Physician*: Ed Morris. *Bettina*, "The Mascotte": LOUISE SEARLE. *Fiametta*, daughter of Prince Lorenzo: LILLIE WEST.

1881.34 LA MASCOTTE

A Revival of the Opéra-comique in Three Acts[10]. Libretto by Henri Chivot and Alfred Duru. Music by Edmond Audran. Musical director, Jesse Williams. A. J. DeFossez, Manager. Produced by the Audran Opera Company. Opened 5 September 1881 at the Bijou Opera House and closed 27 October 1881 after 60 performances.

CAST: *Lorenzo XIV*, Prince of Piombino: GEORGE W. DENHAM. *Frederick*, Prince of Pisa: ALONZO HATCH. *Pippo*, a Shepherd: LITHGOW JAMES. *Rocco*, a Farmer: JOSEPH S. GREENSFELDER. *Antonia*: Emma Duchateau. *Francesca*: Bessie Temple. *Bettina*, "The Mascotte": SELINA DOLARO. *Fiametta*, daughter of Prince Lorenzo: BLANCHE CHAPMAN.

1881.35 LE VOYAGE EN SUISSE

The Hanlon-Lees Company in a Parisian "Absurdity" in Three Acts, 5 Tableaux. Adapted into English by Henry Pettitt from the French by Messrs. Bluhm and Toche. Music composed and selected by Herr Carl Meyder (London) and Harry Widmer (New York). Scenery by Henry Hoyt. Costumes by G. H. Stinchcombe (London); Lanouette (New York). Machinist, A. Filler. Chorus master, D. Baron. Musical director, Harry Widmer. Produced by Henry E. Abbey. Opened 12 September 1881 at Abbey's Park Theatre, moved 28 November 1881 to the Metropolitan Alacazar, moved 19 December 1881 to Niblo's Garden and closed 31 December 1881 after 118 performances.[11]

CAST: *Captain Patrick Maguire*, a retired officer: T. H. GLENNY. *Frank Maguire*, his son: NELSON DECKER. *Dwindledown*, an adventurer: W. S. PENLEY. *John, Bob*, Model Servants: WILLIAM HANLON-LEES, FREDERICK HANLON-LEES. *The Captain's Nephews (3)*: *Ned*: EDWARD HANLON-LEES. *Harry*: GEORGE HANLON-LEES. *Jack*: ALFRED HANLON-LEES. *Henri D'Escargot*, an artist: FRANCIS G. WYATT. *Crevasse*, a Continental Hotel Keeper: Percy Meynall. *Peter Porter*, an Innkeeper: J. Berri. *Tipp*, a Waiter: R. Jones. *Juliette*, the Village Beauty: Miss A. RANDOLPH. *Marie*, a Parisian: Daisy England. *Other Village Beauties (5)*: *Euphrasia*: Miss E. Kean. *Anastasia*: Miss Gonzales. *Ambrosina*: Lillian Taylor. *Alice*: Miss Merritt. *Adelaide*: Miss Barton. *Guests, Passengers, Waiters, etc*: Messrs. Crook, Zais, Allen, Mason, Baron, Whitwell, Marks, Harton; Misses Paton, Harland, Holland, Vina, Gonzales, Florence Isaacs.

Act 1: The Marriage. The Interruption. The Plot. The Start.

Act 2: The Swiss Sleeping Car. The Honeymoon. The Chase. The Accident. The Last Resource. The Explosion.

Act 3: At the Righi-Kulm Hotel. The Conspirators. The Strange Guests. The Divorce. The Wreck of the Hotel.

1881.36 MME. FAVART

An Opéra-comique in Three Acts[12]. Libretto by Henri Chivot and Alfred Duru. Music by Jacques Offenbach. English libretto by Henry B. Farnie. Produced under the direction of Charles Harris. Scenery by James A. Thompson. Mechanical effects by Benson Sherwood and William Vail. Costumes designs by Pilotell. Musical director, Alfred Cellier. Produced by the W. J. Comley-James Barton Opera Company, by arrangement with R. D'Oyly Carte. Opened 19 September 1881 at Haverly's Fifth Avenue Theatre and closed 1 October 1881 after 14 performances; re-opened 23 January 1882 at Haverly's Fifth Avenue Theatre and closed 4 February 1882 after an additional 13 performances. Total: 27 performances.

CAST: *Mme. Favart*, an actress: CATHERINE LEWIS. *Charles Favart*, Dramatic Author, afterwards Manager Theatre Comique: FREDERICK LESLIE. *Major Cotignac*: WILLIAM HAMILTON[13]. *Suzanne*, his daughter: MARIE JANSEN. *Hector de Boispreau*, afterward Lieutenant of Police, in love with Suzanne: J. C. ARMAND[14]. *Biscotin*, Inkeeper of the "Grand Monarch": RICHARD GOLDEN[15]. *Officer*: Mr. Wilkinson. *Pierre, Nicholas*, waiters: Jennie Boyd, Alice Cooper. *Officers of Marquis de Ponstable (4)*: *Canssouci*: Maud Beaumont. *Joli-Coeur*: Eme Lascelles. *Fracasse*: Minnie DeRue. *Vertpre*: Lulu Carter. *Marquis de Ponstable*: JOHN HOWSON. *Travelers, Soldiers, Officers, Courtiers, Ladies of the Court, Vivandières, Martial Band, and a large Corps of Auxiliaries.*

Act 1: Inn of "Grand Monarque" at Arras.

Act 2: Saloon in the House of Hector de Boispreau at Donal.

Act 3: Camp of the Maréchal Saxe.

ACT 1[16]

"The Coach Has Come" (Chorus)
R. Golden, Waiters, Chorus

"'Tis He!" (Trio and Air)
M. Jansen, J. C. Armand, W. Hamilton

"Calendar of Bacchus" (Song)
F. Leslie

Chorus, Air and Scene (Now for the dinner, now to table!)
C. Lewis, J. C. Armand, W. Hamilton, Chorus

"Ave! My Mother" (Air)
C. Lewis

Ensemble, Rondo and Chorus (After marching all the long day)
C. Lewis, Mr. Wilkinson, R. Golden, Servants, Chorus of Soldiers

"Farewell, Suzanne" (Trio)
M. Jansen, J. C. Armand, F. Leslie

Finale—Chorus, Air, Strette

Chorus (Now the coach is waiting for that old Cotignac)
W. Hamilton, J. C. Armand, M. Jansen, C. Lewis, Chorus

Air (No! You will never make us part!)
M. Jansen

Strette (This match, since down my throat you bang it)
W. Hamilton

Finale

ACT 2

"The Debutante" (Song and Chorus)
M. Jansen, Chorus

"The Two Eves" (Romance)
J. C. Armand

"Puff" (Bouffe Song)
F. Leslie

---

[9] First produced in New York in English as THE MASCOT 5 May 1881 at the Bijou Theatre for 108 performances. For Synopsis of Scenes and Musical Numbers, see original 1881 production.

[10] First produced in New York in English as THE MASCOT 5 May 1881 at the Bijou Theatre for 108 performances. For Synopsis of Scenes and Musical Numbers, see original 1881 production.

[11] Musical numbers and specialties not listed in programs.

[12] English language premiere. First produced in New York in French 12 May 1879 at the Park Theatre for 14 performances.

[13] For return engagement, H. A. Cripps played Major Cotiganc.

[14] For return engagement, C. J. Campbell played Hector de Boispreau.

[15] For return engagement, Fred H. Frear played Biscotin.

[16] Musical numbers not listed in programs. List prepared from published libretto (Oliver Ditson & Co., Boston, 1881).

"The Ladies' Pet" (Chorus and Air)
J. Howson, Chorus
Quartet (Ah, 'tis too bad!)
C. Lewis, M. Jansen, J. C. Armand, F. Leslie
Duo, Scene and Bell Chorus (Conjure up not a glitt'ring vision)
C. Lewis, J. Howson, Chorus
"An Old Woman's Dream" (Vocal Minuet)
C. Lewis
"Something's Wrong" (Chorus)
Chorus
Finale (Tutti and Chorus)(Now then, my Marshal Saxe!)
C. Lewis, M. Jansen, J. C. Armand, J. Howson, F. Leslie, Chorus

ACT 3
"Right! Left!" (Drill Chorus)
Vivandières
(*Music by* Alfred Cellier.)
"I Faint! I Die!" (Chorus and Duo)
M. Jansen, F. Leslie
Chorus and Tyrolienne (See up the hill ascending)
J. C. Armand, C. Lewis, Chorus
Air ('Tis not in number perillies)
M. Jansen, J. C. Armand
Duet and Chorus (Yes, be brave, if but for a moment!)
C. Lewis, F. Leslie
"One Loving Kiss!" (Duo)
C. Lewis, F. Leslie
"Brava! Well Done!" (Chorus)
Chorus
Finale (Now, all is over, lover meet lover)
Principals, Chorus

PATIENCE, or, Bunthorne's Bride

1881.37

A Comic Opera in Two Acts. Libretto by William S. Gilbert. Music by Arthur Sullivan. Produced under the stage direction of Charles Harris. Scenery by J. Mazzanovich. Costumes by Miss Fisher, from designs by W. S. Gilbert. Conducted by W. P. Halton. Produced by Richard D'Oyly Carte Opera Comique Company (Helen Lenoir, Manager). Opened 22 September 1881 at the Standard Theatre until 4 March 1882; performed 4 performances weekly[17] from 6-25 March 1882; re-opened at the Standard Theatre 19-24 June 1882. Total: 177 performances.

CAST: *Archibald Grosvenor*, an Idyllic Poet: JAMES BARTON. *Officers of the Dragoon Guards (3): Colonel Calverly*: WILLIAM T. CARLETON. *Major Murgatroyd*: ARTHUR WILKINSON. *Lieutenant the Duke of Dunstable*: LYN CADWALLADR (Cadwaladyr). *Mr. Bunthorne's Solicitor*: William White. *Reginald Bunthorne*, a Fleshly Poet: J. H. RYLEY. *Chorus of Dragoon Guards*.

Rapturous Maidens (4): *Lady Angela*: ALICE BURVILLE. *Lady Saphir*: Rose Chappelle. *Lady Ella*: Jenny Stone. *Lady Jane*: Augusta Roche. *Patience*, a Dairy Maid: CARRIE BURTON. *Chorus of Rapturous Maidens*.

Act 1: Exterior of Castle Bunthorne.

Act 2: A Glade.

ACT 1[18]
"Twenty Lovesick maidens We" (Chorus of maidens)
"Love Feeds on Hope" (Solo)
A. Burville
"Go, Breaking Heart" (Solo)
J. Stone
"Still Brooding on their Mad Infatuation" (Recitative)
C. Burton
"I Cannot Tell what this Love may be" (Song)
C. Burton
"The Soldiers of our Queen" (Chorus of Dragoons)
"If You Want a Receipt for that Popular Mystery" (Solo)
W. T. Carleton
"In a Doleful Train" (Chorus)
A. Burville, J. Stone, J. H. Ryley
"Now is this not Ridiculous?" (Chorus)
Dragoons
"Mystic Poet, hear our prayer" (Solo)
A. Burville
"Though my book I Seem to Scan" (Solo)
J. H. Ryley
"Though so Excellently Wise" (Solo)
R. Chappelle
Oh, Hollow! Hollow! Hollow! (Recitation)
J. H. Ryley
"When First I Put This Uniform On" (Song)
W. T. Carleton
"Am I Alone?" (Recitative)/
"If You're Anxious for to Shine" (Song)
J. H. Ryley
"Long Years Ago" (Duet)
C. Burton, A. Burville
"Prithee, Pretty Maiden, Willow, Willow, Waly" (Duet)
C. Burton, J. Barton
"Let the Merry Cymbals Sound" (Chorus)(Finale)
"Now Tell Us We Pray You" (Chorus)
Dragoons
"Your Maiden Hearts" (Solo)
L. Cadwalladr
"If There be Pardon in your Heart" (Solo)
C. Burton
"True Love Must be Single-Hearted" (Duet)
C. Burton, J. H. Ryley
"I Hear the Soft Note of the Echoing Voice" (Sextette)
J. Stone, R. Chappelle, A. Burville, L. Cadwalladyr, A. Wilkinson, W. T. Carleton

ACT 2
"Sad Is that Woman's Lot" (Recitative)/
"Silvered Is the raven Hair" (Song)
A. Roche
"Turn, oh Turn in this Direction" (Chorus of Maidens)
"A Magnet Hung in a Hard-ware Shop" (Song)
J. Barton
"Love Is a Plaintive Song" (Song)
C. Burton
"So Got to Him and Say to Him" (Duet)
A. Roche, J. H. Ryley
"It's Clear that Medieval Art" (Trio)
L. Cadwalladyr, A. Wilkinson, W. T. Carleton
"If Saphir I Choose to Marry" (Quintette)
A. Burville, R. Chappelle, L. Cadwalladyr, A. Wilkinson, W. T. Carleton
"When I Go out of Doors" (Duet) J. H. Ryley, J. Barton
"I'm a Waterloo-House Young Man" (Chorus of Maidens and Grosvenor)
J. Barton, Maidens
"After much Debate Internal" (Finale)
Principals, Chorus

OLIVETTE!

1881.38

A Revival of the Opérette in Three Acts[19]. Libretto by Henri Chivot and Alfred Duru. English adaptation by Henry B. Farnie. Music by Edmond Audran. Stage director, John Howson. (Scenery by John A. Thompson, Charles W. Witham.) Musical director, Alfred Cellier. Produced by the Comley-Barton Opera Company, by arrangement with Richard D'Oyly Carte[20]. Opened 10 October 1881 at the Metropolitan Casino and closed 29

[17]Thursday, Friday, Saturday matinee and evening.
[18]Musical numbers not listed in programs. List prepared from published English piano vocal score (Chappell & Co., London, 1881).

[19]First produced in English in New York 25 December 1880 at the Bijou Opera House for 63 performances. For Synopsis of Scenes and Musical Numbers, see original 1880 production.
[20]Apart from the principals Catherine Lewis and John Howson, the production was fully recast and re-staged for its later engagements.

October 1881 after 21 performances; returned 9 January 1882 to the Fifth Avenue Theatre and closed 21 January 1882 after 14 performances; reopened 15-18 March 1882 at the Fifth Avenue Theatre for 5 additional performances in repertory. Total: 39 performances.

CAST: *Olivette*, daughter of the Seneschal Marvejol: CATHERINE LEWIS. *Bathilde*, Countess of Rousillon (in love with Valentine): DORA WILEY[21]. *Veloutine*, Maid of Olivette: ANNIE RANDOLPH[22]. *Pages of the Countess (3)*: *Cansterre*: J. Grousseaux. *De Joyeu*: A. Newman. *Follesamour*: L. Champnes. *Maids of Honor (3)*: *Mlle. DeCernay*: H. Griffiths. *Mlle. de Montjoie*: M. Sherwood. *Mlle. de Lenoir*: L. Fuller. *Midshipmen on board the "Cormorant" (3)*: *L'Ecureuil*: Miss M. Carrington. *Mistigris*: Miss M. Gardner. *Lartimon*: Miss L. Kirk. *Sailors (2)*: *Boussole*: Miss Amy Wallace. *Loup de Mer*: Miss Nellie Rong. *Maids at the Main-Brace Tavern (3)*: *Caton*: Miss Henriette Varey. *Nichette*: Miss Allie Lane. *Bleuette*: Miss Sophie Gonzales. *Moustique*, the Captain's boy on board the "*Cormorant*:": Eme Lascelles. *Valentin*, Officer of the Rousillon Guards, nephew to DeMerrimac: J. P. PAXTON. *Marvejol*, Seneschal to the Countess of Rousillon: GUSTAVUS HALL. *Duc des Ifs*, heir presumptive of the Countess of Rousillon: GEORGE GASTON. *Coquelicot*, his foster brother and valet: CHARLES BUTLER. *Captain DeMerrimac*, of the Man o' War "*Cormorant*": JOHN HOWSON. *Courtiers, Nobles, Citizens, Wedding Guests and Sailors, Soldiers of the Guard, Pages, etc.*

CAST for Fifth Avenue return: *Olivette*, daughter of the Seneschal Marvejol: CATHERINE LEWIS. *Bathilde*, Countess of Rousillon, in love with Valentine: MARIE JANSEN. *Veloutine*, the Seneschal's housekeeper: JENNIE BOYD. *Moustique*, the Captain's boy on board the "*Cormorant*:": Emma Lascelles. *Pages of the Countess (4)*: *Jayoux*: Minnie DeRue. *Fallesamour*: Lou Carter. *Antoine*: Nellie Wisdom. *Pelisse*: Annetta Hall. *Mlle. de Montjoyes, Mlle. de Lenoir*, Ladies of the Countess' Suite: Misses Marshton, Lacey. *Caton*, maid of the Main-Brace Tavern: Miss Henderson. *Captain de Merrimac*, of the Man o' War "*Cormorant*": JOHN HOWSON. *Valentin*, Officer of the Rousillon Guards, his nephew: J. C. ARMAND. *Coquelicot*, his foster brother and henchman: F. H. FREAR. *Marvejol*, local pluralist, Seneschal to the Countess and Maire of Perpignan: H. A. CRIPPS. *Piou Piou*, a villager: Dolly Chase. *Boussole*: W. J. Thomas. *Loup de Mer*: Mr. Hatter. *Courtiers, Nobles, Citizens, Wedding Guests and Sailors, Soldiers of the Guard, Pages, etc.*

1881.39 HUMPTY-DUMPTY

Nick Roberts' European Specialties and Clown Minstrels in an Extravaganza in Three Acts, a Prologue and 19 Scenes[23]. Stage manager, Arthur Hernandez. Musical director, H. T. Dyring. Produced by Nick Roberts. Opened 10 October 1881 at Tony Pastor's New 14th Street Theatre and closed 22 October 1881 after (16) performances.

CAST (Prologue): *His Majesty, Pluto*, King of Hades: Tillie Van Buren. *The Demon Page*: Sadie Monroe. *Fairy Queen*: Emily Lulu. *His Majesty's Green Imp*: Dick Reno. *Red Imp*: Frederick Warner.

CAST (Humpty-Dumpty): *Interlocutor*: ARTHUR HERNANDEZ. *Tambos*: JOHN C. HARRINGTON, JOHN H. BYRNE. *Bones*: ANDY McKEE, WILLIAM HARRINGTON. *Three Clowns*: GRIMALDI, DROMIO, PEDRO. *Old One-Two*, Pantaloon: ARTHUR HERNANDEZ. *Tommy Tucker*, Harlequin: EDWIN FRITZ. *Goody Two Shoes*, Columbine: LOUISE DeLUISI. *Handy Spanky*: A. A. Harris. *Leddy*, a cop: Albert Bellamy. *Granny*: F. Hildebrand. *Minnie Nickle*: Miss Reggan. *Hattie Patty*: Emma LeClaire. *Fairy Brilliant*: Mlle. (Emily) Lulu. *Jocko*, a monkey: Harry S. Lyons.

Specialties: Belle Clifton, Onofri Brothers (Achille, Fortune, Oreste, Charles); Clipper Quartette (Bob McIntire, F. T. Ward, G. F. Campbell, F. A. Howard).

Prologue: Hades.

Act 1, Scene 1: The Abode of Pluto. *Scene 2*: Nick Roberts' U.S. Minstrels.

Acts 2 and 3: Humpty Dumpty.

ACT 1

Interlocutor; Tambo and Bones

Overture
U.S. Minstrels

Opening Chorus (original)
Clipper Quartette

"Dublin Bay"
F. A. Howard
(*Music by* George Barker. *Lyrics by* Mrs. Crawford.)

Comic Ditty
A. McKee

"Sally in Our Alley"
R. McIntyre
(Traditional. *Music setting by* Henry Carey.)

Comic Refrain
J. C. Harrington

"The Blue Alsatian Mountains"
P. DeLeo
(*Music by* Michael Maybrick [Stephen Adams]. *Lyrics by* Claribel.)

Finale (Telephone)
Company

ACT 2

Scene 1
Village and Farmers, Clowns; Tommy Tucker and Good Two Shoes. Grotesque and Acrobatic Exercises. Andy McKee. Arrival of Fop. Skirmishes with the monkey. The pursuit begins and capture seems near at hand, when the gracious Fairy interferes and we start on our glorious Harlequinade.

Scene 2
Grimaldi, Police and Newspapers.

Scene 3
Harrington Brothers (Acrobatic Song and Dance)

Scene 4
Tillie Van Buren (Xylophone solo)

Scene 5
Clown. Pantaloon and Ladies' Seminary. Cornice Wall, Doors and Darkey Waiters.

Scene 6
Grimaldi and Pantaloon shaking dice

Scene 7
Onofri Brothers (French locomotive specialty)

ACT 3

Scene 1
Horizontal Bar
D. Reno, F. Clifton, Grimaldi

Scene 2
Paul DeLeo (Greatest Male Soprano)

Scene 3
Fireworks
Clown, A. Hernandez

Scene 4
Original Rifle Song and Dance (Double Skipping Rope)
B. Clinton, L. DeLuisi

Scene 5
Grimaldi, Pantaloon and Police killing time

Scene 6
Onofri Brothers (Pantomimic Scene "Do, Mi, Sol, Do")

Scene 7
Grimaldi and the Galvanic Battery

Scene 8
Protean Specialties, including "Balmoral" Clipper Quartette
(Classic Music, Laughing Songs, Flute Imitations, Warbles, Plantation Shouts)

Scene 9
Dark Scene

Scene 10
Grand Acrobatic Tableaux

1881.40 THE SNAKE CHARMER

A Comic Opera in Three Acts, 4 Scenes. Original French libretto to the Opéra-bouffe ('Le Grand Mogol') by Henri Chivot. Music by Edmond Audran. Produced under the stage direction of Jesse Williams. Scenery by Hughson Hawley, Charles Graham and Mons. Rehctaog. Produced by the Audran Opera Comique Company (A J. Defossez, Manager). Opened 29 October 1881 at the Bijou Opera House and closed 17 December 1881 after 50 performances; by arrangement with John A. McCaull, Manager, re-

[21]Succeeded by MARIE JANSEN for the Fifth Avenue engagement.
[22]Succeeded by JENNIE BOYD for the Fifth Avenue engagement.
[23]First produced 3 February 1880 at Abbey's Booth Theatre for 64 performances. For Synopsis of Scenes and Musical Numbers, see original 1880 production.

opened 14 August 1882 at the Bijou Opera House, moved 28 August 1882 to the Metropolitan Alcazar and closed 2 September 1882 after 18 additional performances. Total: 68 performances.[24]

CAST: *Prince Mignapour*, the Great Mogul: SELINA DOLARO. *Nicobar*, Grand Vizier: GEORGE W. DENHAM. *Astrakan*: JOSEPH S. GREENSFELDER. *Tao Tsin*, a Chinese juggler: FRED W. LENNOX. *Grand Brahma*: Mr. Cardoza. *Officer of the Prince*: C. Tucker. *D'Jemma*, the Snake Charmer: LILLIAN RUSSELL[25]. *Princess Bengaline*: BLANCHE CHAPMAN. *A Slave*: Miss Greenville. *First Vender*: Bessie Temple. *Second Vender*: Laura Duchateau. *Third Vender*: Kate Livingston. *Ministers*: W. P. Hampshire, J. C. Smith, J. Reicards, E. Peringh, M. Walker. *Couriers*: W. L. Taylor, E. D. Grant, T. S. Guise, A. Schcardi, E. O. Fisher.

Act 1: Street Scene in Delhi. (Hawley.)

Act 2, Scene 1: Jardin de Rose. *Scene 2*: Palace of the Great Mogul. (Graham.)

Act 3: Astrakan's Bazaar. (Rehctaog.)

MUSICAL NUMBERS[26]

Duet
L. Russell, J. S. Greensfelder

Prince's Love Song
S. Dolaro

Astrakan's Philosophical Song (Act 3)
J. S. Greensfelder

Finale Act 2

French Café Chantant Song (Act 3)
S. Dolaro

1881.41 LES CLOCHES DE CORNEVILLE

A Revival of the Comic Opera in Three Acts, 5 Scenes[27]. Original French libretto by Clairville and Charles Gabet. English adaptation by Henry B. Farnie. Music by Robert Planquette. Produced under the direct supervision of James C. Scanlan. Scenery by John A. Thompson, Henry E. Hoyt, William Voegtlin. Costumes by (Henry) Dazian. Mechanical effects by Benson Sherwood, Hamilton Weaver. Orchestra under the direction of Henry J. Widmer. Produced by E. R. Gilmore. Opened 31 October 1881 at the Metropolitan Casino and closed 26 November 1881 after 29 performances.

CAST: *Serpolette*: KATE MUNROE. *Germaine*: HELEN DINGEON. *Manette*: ROSE WILSON. *Village Maidens (7)*: *Catherine*: M. Sommerville. *Jeannie*: Miss DeNoel. *Nannette*: Miss L. Shandley. *Susanne*: Miss Lubin. *Gertrude*: Miss Rossner. *Marguerite*: Miss Langley. *Rose*: Miss Champneys. *Henri*, Marquis de Corneville: EDWARD CONNELL. *Gaspard*, the Miser: WILLIAM H. SEYMOUR. *The Bailie*: WELSH EDWARDS. *Grenicheux*, the Fisherman: CHARLES J. CAMPBELL. *Gobo*: Richard Golden. *Christophe*: Pauline Hall. *Peasants, Sailors, etc.*

Act 1, Scene 1: Cliffs on the Sea-shore near Corneville. *Scene 2*: Outside the Village. *Scene 3*: The Market Place in Corneville. (Thompson.)

Act 2: A Chamber in the Chateau. (Hoyt.)

Act 3: Orchard in the Grounds of the Chateau. (Voegtlin.)

ACT 1[28]

Scene 1

Chorus (All who for servants are enquiring)
Chorus

Gossip Couplets (They say the Bailie asked Germaine)
K. Munroe, Misses Rossner, DeNoel, L. Shandley, Lubin, Girls

Couplets (They say that Jeanne, sheep-tending)
K. Munroe, Maidens, Chorus

Recitative (What means this noisy bawling)
R. Golden

Rondo (I may be Princess)
K. Munroe

Barcarolle (On billow rocking, at tempest mocking)
C. J. Campbell

Duet ('Twas but an impulse)
H. Dingeon, C. J. Campbell

"Legend of the Bells"
H. Dingeon, Chorus

Valse Rondo (To me no stranger, hardship or danger)
E. Connell

Finale (Such conduct is quite sad)
W. H. Seymour, K. Munroe, H. Dingeon, Chorus

Scene 3

Couplets (Tho' they may not pursue me)
C. J. Campbell, Chorus

Valse Song (That night I ne'er forget)
C. J. Campbell

Finale (Come, farmer small or with big rental)
Chorus

Chorus of Manservants (Than us you'll not find better)

Chorus of Coachmen (Who are drivers lacking?)

Chorus of Maidservants (Who are wanting maidens able?)

Finale [continued](Tell me, girl, what may be your name?)
Principals, Chorus

ACT 2

Concerted Number (Let our torches light up the gloom)
H. Dingeon, E. Connell, Chorus of Sailors

Air (By his side)
H. Dingeon

Song (I'll shut my eyes)
K. Munroe, C. J. Campbell, W. Edwards

Song (Not a ghost, at all!)
K. Munroe

Buffo Song (Oh dear! Oh dear!)
W. Edwards

Recitative, Air and Chorus (Nay! no phantom they)
E. Connell

Ensemble and Couplets (What's she saying?)
K. Munroe, E. Connell

Duo ('Tis she! A happy fate has brought her)
H. Dingeon, E. Connell

Chorus and Quintette (As he's looking somewhat pale)
C. J. Campbell, Chorus

Finale (Love, honor, happiness, moon of honey)
Principals, Chorus

"Legend of the Bells" (reprise)

ACT 3

Ballad (Oh! the brave days will come back)(Song of the Beggars)
W. H. Seymour

Chorus and Couplets (There she goes with horses prancing)
K. Munroe, C. J. Campbell, Chorus

Couplets (Tho' no more plain Serpolette)
K. Munroe, Chorus

"The Cider Song" (Song and Chorus)
K. Munroe, Chorus

Duo (My lord, my lord, my silly heart is beating)
H. Dingeon, E. Connell

Finale (Old man, I pardon thee with pleasure)
E. Connell, Principals, Chorus

1881.42 DONNA JUANITA!

A Return Engagement of the Comic Opera in Three Acts[29]. Libretto by F. Zell and Richard Genée. Music by Franz von Suppé. Director, H. B.

[24] English adaptation uncredited in programs, reviews.
[25] The role of D'Jemma was played by LILLY POST for the return engagement.
[26] Musical numbers not listed in programs. List prepared from published reviews, no score or libretto found.
[27] First produced in New York in English as THE CHIMES OF NORMANDY 22 October 1877 at the Fifth Avenue Theatre for 16 performances.
[28] Musical numbers not listed in programs. List prepared from published English vocal score and libretto (Joseph Williams, London, 1878, ca). English libretto bears Robert Reece's name as co-author, which billing does not appear in American programs.

[29] First produced in New York 16 May 1881 at the Fifth Avenue Theatre for 24 performances. For synopsis of Scenes and Musical Numbers, see original May 1881 production.

Mahn. Stage manager, Vincent Hogan. Musical conductor, Gustave A. Kerker. Produced by H. B. Mahn's Comic Opera Company. Opened 7 November 1881 at Niblo's Garden and closed 12 November 1881 after 9 performances.[30]

CAST: *René Dufaure*, French Cadet: FLORA BARRY. *Donna Juanita*: FLORA BARRY. *Petrita*: RENIE REIGNARD. *Gaston Dufaure*, a French prisoner, in love with Petrita: PERCY J. COOPER. *Donna Olympia*: ROSE LEIGHTON. *Don Pomponio*, Alcalde of San Sebastian and husband of Donna Olympia: ELLIS RYSE. *Colonel Douglas*, English Commandant of San Sebastian: FRED DIXON. *Don Riego*, Notary and Public Writer: Arthur Van Houten. *Gil Polo*, Keeper of Posada: Vincent Hogan. *Marco*: Marie Reynolds. *Picador*: Sidney Barnes. *Dolores*: May Booth. *Aguador*: Joseph Otley. *Tepa*: Clara Douglas. *Fitzroy*: Harry Dale. *Duplan*: S. Battle.

Students: *Rajos*: Dixie Chapman. *Pedro*: Anna Callaway. *Leon*: Martha Campbell. *Gomez*: Rose Parker. *Alonzo*: Miss Van Dusen. *Jose*: Miss Miller. *Francisco*: J. Vincent.

Lady Conspirators: *Donna Mercedes*: C. Douglas. *Donna Rosaura*: Rose Parker. *Donna Ersilia*: Miss Miller. *Donna Laura*: May Booth. *Donna Pepita*: Dora Feitner. *Donna Encarnacion*: Marie Beaumont. *Donna Anna*: Jeanne Vincent. *Donna Isabella*: Mrs. Ellis Ryse. *Donna Marietta*: Anna Callaway. *Donna Inez*: Clara Dixon. *Donna Zerlina*: M. Campbell. *Donna Elvira*: Dixie Chapman. *Scotch and French Soldiers, Nobles, Peasants, Singing Boys, etc.*: Chorus of 70.

PATIENCE, or, Bunthorne's Bride

1881.43

A Satire on the Æsthetic Craze (Comic Opera) in Two Acts[31]. Libretto by William S. Gilbert. Music by Arthur Sullivan. Stage manager, A. W. F. McCollin. Scenery by Joseph Clare. Stage mechanisms by John Denham. Properties by E. R. Morse. Gas effects by John Thompson. Æsthetic costumes by Schwencke. Modern costumes by Eaves. Director of music, Joseph A. Kuhn. Produced by Edward E. Rice's Opera Comique Company. Opened 14 November 1881 at Booth's Theatre and closed 26 November 1881 after 15 performances; re-opened under the aegis of the Boston Comic Opera Company 22 March 1882 at Booth's Theatre for 1 additional performance.

CAST: *Reginald Bunthorne*, a Fleshly Poet: A. W. F. McCOLLIN. *Archibald Grosvenor*, an Idyllic Poet: EUGENE CLARKE. *Officers of the Dragoon Guards (3)*: *Colonel Calverly*: GUSTAVUS F. HALL. *Major Murgatroyd*: GEORGE A. SCHILLER. *Lieutenant the Duke of Dunstable*: HENRI LAURENT. *Mr. Bunthorne's Solicitor*: Thomas Sage. *Rapturous Maidens (4)*: *Lady Angela*: VERNONA JARBEAU. *Lady Saphir*: IRENE PERRY. *Lady Ella*: FANNIE HALL. *Lady Jane*: ROSA COOKE. *Patience*, a Village Milk Maid: ROSE TEMPLE. *Chorus of Dragoon Guards, Rapturous Maidens*.

BOCCACCIO!

1881.44

A Return Engagement of the Operette in Three Acts[32]. Original Viennese libretto by F. Zell and Richard Genée. Music by Franz von Suppé. Director, H. B. Mahn. Stage manager, Vincent Hogan. Musical conductor, Gustave A. Kerker. Produced by H. B. Mahn's Comic Opera Company. Opened 14 November 1881 at Niblo's Garden and closed 16 November 1881 after 4 performances.[33]

CAST: *Boccaccio*, a novelist and poet: FLORA BARRY. *Leonetta*, his friend, a student: ROSE LEIGHTON. *Flametta*, Lambertuccio's adopted daughter: RENIE REIGNARD. *Pietro*, Prince of Palermo: PERCY J. COOPER. *Lotteringhi*, a cooper: ELLIS RYSE. *Isabella*, Lotteringhi's wife: ARIE REYNOLDS. *Lambertuccio*, a grocer: FRED DIXON. *Peronella*, Lambertuccios' sister: Mrs. ELLIS RYSE. *Scalza*, a barber: VINCENT HOGAN. *Beatrice*, Scalza's daughter: MARTHA CAMPBELL. *Fatelli*, a bookseller: *Checo*, a beggar: Sidney Barnes. *Eresco*, the cooper's apprentice: *The Unknown*: Henry Van Houten. *Major Domo of the Duke*: H. Arthur.

Lotteringhi's Journeymen (12): *Alberto*: H. Depew. *Riccairdo*: Mr. Kettle. *Gerbino*: Sidney Barnes. *Feodore*: A. Swicarde. *Guidotto*: H. Dixon. *Nostogio*: F. Manning. *Beppo*: H. Fairchild. *Irsi*: Walter Allen. *Alani*: James Otley. *Gomio*: S. Battle. *Ferzo*: Alonzo Stone. *Cherzi*: J. Waite. *Students (8)*: *Tofano*: Mattie Campbell. *Guido*: Miss Van Dusen. *Federico*: Anna Calloway. *Rinieri*: Dora Feitner. *Chicibio*: Claa Douglass. *Cisti*: Dixie Chapman. *Giotto*: Rose Parker. *Lanto*: Aida Hamilton. *Beggars (3)*: *Chiacometto*: J. Hobbs. *Anselmo*: Henry Newman. *Tito*: H. Depew. *Lambertuccio's Servants (3)*: *Filippa*: Miss Miller. *Orietta*: May Booth. *Violanta*: Clara Dixon. *Donna Joncofiere*: Miss Mark. *Eliza*, Donna Joncofiere's servant girl: Abbie Nicholson. *Chorus of 70*.

THE MASCOT

1881.45

A Revival of the Opéra-comique in Three Acts[34]. Original French libretto by Henri Chivot and Alfred Duru. Music by Edmond Audran. Director, H. B. Mahn. Stage manager, Vincent Hogan. Musical conductor, Gustave A. Kerker. Produced by H. B. Mahn's Comic Opera Company. Opened 17 November 1881 at Niblo's Garden and closed 19 November 1881 after 4 performances.[35]

CAST: *Bettina*, The Mascot: ROSE LEIGHTON. *Lorenzo*, Prince of Piombino: ELLIS RYSE. *Fiametta*, his daughter: MARIE REYNOLDS. *Pippo*, a Shepherd: VINCENT HOGAN. *Frederick*, the Prince of Pisa: PERCY F. COOPER. *Rocco*, a Farmer: ARTHUR VAN HOUTEN. *Pages of Lorenzo (4)*: *Angelo*: May Booth. *Luigi*: Mattie Campbell. *Paolo*: Clara Douglass. *Carlo*: Rose Parker. *Parafante*, Sergeant: John Hobbs. *Matheo*: S. Fairchild. *Doctor*: Harry Dale. *Peasant*: Sidney Barnes. *Soldier*: S. Battle. *Grand Chorus*.

MADAME FAVART

1881.46

A Revival of the Opéra-comique in Three Acts, in French[36]. Libretto by Henri Chivot and Alfred Duru. Music by Jacques Offenbach. Stage manager, Mons. V. Merle. Musical directors, M. de Lestrac, A. Gravenstein. Produced by Maurice Grau's French Opera Company. Opened 28 November 1881 at Abbey's Park Theatre for 1 performance in repertory.

CAST: *Mme. Favart*: Mlle. PAOLA MARIÉ. *Favart*: Mons. CLEMENT NIGRI. *Marquis de Ponstable*: Mons. J. MEZIÈRES. *Major Cotignac*: Mons. A. Poyard. *Hector*: Mons. F. Tauffenberger. *Biscotin*: Mons. Boscotin. *Suzanne*: Mlle. Cecile Grégoire. *Pierre*: ? *Nicholas*: ? *Sans-Quartier*: M. Malvina. *Joli-Coeur*: Mlle. Vallot. *Fracasse*: *Vespre*:

FUN ON THE BRISTOL!, or, A Night on Long Island Sound

1881.47

A Revival of the Musical Comedy Oddity in Three Acts[37]. (Play revised by George Fawcett Rowe. Music by (Giuseppe) Verdi, (Gaetano) Donizetti, (Georges) Bizet, (Jacques) Offenbach, (Charles) Lecocq, etc. Stage director, John F. Sheridan. Scenery (Act 2) painted by John A. Thompson.) Musical director, Christian Krause. Produced by Henry C. Jarrett and Edward E. Rice. Opened 28 November 1881 at Haverly's 14th Street Theatre and closed 3 December 1881 after 8 performances.

CAST: *Widow O'Brien*, his great original creation: JOHN F. SHERIDAN. *Dora*, her daughter by McAllister: CARRIE DANIELS. *Norah*, her daughter by O'Brien: KATE FOLEY. *Bella Thompson*: MARION FISKE. *Count Menaggio*: HARRY DeLORME. *Thomas Cranberry*: FRANK TANNEHILL, JR. *Captain Cranberry*: RICHARD WALDON. *Richard Sparks*: Will A. Paul. *Jerry Thompson*: George Richards. *Pinkerton Haukshaw*: William Hughes.

ACT 2

Grand Musical Olio, introducing the following entirely original Novelties:

Potpourri Chorus: Gems from THE PIRATES OF PENZANCE, OLIVETTE, LA MASCOTTE and PATIENCE.

---

[30]English adaptation ("as translated solely for this company") uncredited. No credits for scenery or costumes.

[31]A rival production of the Comic Opera whose first authorized D'Oyly Carte production was presented in New York 22 September 1881 at the Standard Theatre for 177 performances. For Synopsis of Scenes and Musical Numbers, see detail of earlier production.

[32]First produced in New York in German 23 April 1880 at the Thalia Theatre for 15 performances; in English 15 May 1880 at the Union Square Theatre for 28 performances.

[33]English adaptation uncredited ("as translated solely for this company"). No credits for scenery or costumes.

[34]First produced in New York 5 May 1881 at the Bijou Opera House for 108 performances. For Synopsis of Scenes and Musical Numbers, see original 1881 production.

[35]English adaptation uncredited. No credits for scenery or costumes.

[36]First produced in New York in French 12 May 1879 at the Park Theatre for 14 performances in repertory. For Synopsis of Scenes and Musical Numbers, see original 1879 production.

[37]First produced in New York 9 August 1880 at Haverly's 14th Street Theatre for 24 performances; returned 11 April 1881 to Haverly's 14th Street Theatre for 24 additional performances. For Synopsis of Scenes, see original 1880 production.

"Mary's Gone wid' a Coon"
G. Richards
Guitar Solo
C. Daniels
Song and Hornpipe
K. Foley
Burlesque and Operatic Scene: IL TROVATORE
(*Music by* Giuseppe Verdi.)
Leonora: M. Fiske. *Azucena*: C. Daniels. *Manrico*: H. DeLorme. *Count DeLuna*: R. Waldon. *Ruez*: F. Tannehill, Jr. *Farrando*: W. E. Paul. *François*: G. Richards.
John F. Sheridan as the Serio-Comic Songstress
Jimmy Riddle Band
Company
Turkish Reveille (John F. Sheridan as The Jew)

1881.48 LA MASCOTTE

An Opéra-comique in Three Acts, in French[38]. Libretto by Henri Chivot and Alfred Duru. Music by Edmond Audran. Stage manager, Mons. V. Merle. Musical directors, M. de Lestrac, A. Gravenstein. Produced by Maurice Grau's French Opera Company. Opened 30 November 1881 at Abbey's Park Theatre and closed 3 December 1881 (matinee) after 2 performances in repertory; re-opened 24 April 1882 at the Fifth Avenue Theatre and closed 29 April 1882 after 2 additional performances in repertory.

CAST: *Bettina*: Mlle. PAOLA MARIÉ. *Laurent XVII*, Prince of Piombino: Mons. J. MEZIÈRES. *Pippo*, Shepherd: Mons. CLEMENT NIGRI. *Prince Frittellini*: Mons. F. TAUFFENBERGER. *Rocco*, Farmer: Mons. E. DUPLAN. *Matheo*, Innkeeper: Mons. G. MUSSY. *Sergeant Parafante*: Mons. Dupin. *Fiametta*, Daughter of Laurent: Mlle. JULIE LENTZ. *Pages (5)*: *Carlo*: Mlle. Vallot. *Marco*: Mlle. Malvina. *Angelo*: Ruffino. *Luidgi*: Duparc. *Beppo*: Merly. *Paola*: Vandamme. *Francesca, Antonia*, Peasant Girls: Mlles. Dupin, Vernet. (*Members of the Italian Comedy Company, Four Maids of Honor, a Doctor, Lords and Ladies of Court, Soldiers and Peasants.*)

Act 1: La Cour de la ferme de Rocco.

Act 2: Une Salle du Palais du Grand-Duc, à Piombino.

Act 3: Une Hostellerie Italienne dans le Duché de Pise.

ACT 1[39]
Introduction, Choeur (Le vendage se termine)
Choeur
Couplets du vin doux (Il fait fuir l'humeur morose)
3 Paysannes
Ballade (Un jour, le diable, ivre d'orgueil)(Légende des mascottes)
C. Nigri, Choeur
Entrée (Allons, la belle)
P. Marié, Choeur
Couplets de Bettina (N'avancez pas ou je tape)
P. Marié
Choeur (On aime à voir après la chasse)
Choeur
Couplets des présages (Les gens sensés et sages)
J. Mezières
Couplets (Ah! qu'il est beau)
J. Lentz
Couplets du "Je ne sais quoi" (D'un athlète, ou d'un villageois)
J. Lentz, F. Tauffenberger
Duetto (Je sens lorsque j t'aperçois)(Duo des dindons)
P. Marié, C. Nigri
Final (On sonne! On sonne!)
Mlles. P. Marié, J. Lentz, Messrs. Tauffenberger, C. Nigri, J. Mezières, E. Duplan, Choeur

ACT 2
Choeur (Qu'elle est belle)
Les Pages
Couplets des pages (Excusez mon audace extrême)
Les Pages
Entrée (Ah! laissez-moi)
P. Marié, J. Mezières
Couplets de le Comtesse (Que je regrette mon village)
P. Marié
Choeur (Ah! quel spectacle charmant)
Choeur
Air de Saltarello (Salut à vous! seigneur!)
C. Nigri [Saltarello]
Duetto (Sais-tu que ces beaux habits-là)
P. Marié, C. Nigri
Couplets (Des courtisans qui passeront)
F. Tauffenberger
Couplets (Chasser le cerf au son du cor)
J. Mezières
Final (C'est la futur de la princesse)
Tous, Choeur
Chanson du Capitaine (Un jour un brave capitaine)
P. Marié

ACT 3
Choeur des Soldats (Verse, verse, verse à boire)
Messrs. Dupin, Mussy, Choeur
Entrée du Prince (Très bien? bonjour! soldats!)
F. Tauffenberger
Couplets du Tambour (De nos pas marquant la cadence)
F. Tauffenberger
Entrée des Chanteurs Ambulants (Ne troublez pas brave gens)
Mons. Dupin
Chanson de l'orang–outang (Le grand singe d'Amerique)
J. Lentz
Entrée de la noce
Ariette (Je touche au but)
J. Lentz, F. Tauffenberger, C. Nigri, J. Mezières, Choeur
Quatuor (Quoi, Pippo quand je vous rclaime)
C. Nigri, J. Mezières, P. Marié, J. Lentz
Final (Eh! pourquoi donc crier ainsi)
Tous, Chœur

1881.49 LA FILLE DE MADAME ANGOT

A Revival of the Opéra-comique in Three Acts, in French[40]. Libretto by Paul Ferrier and Jules Prével. Music by Charles Lecocq. Stage manager, Mons. V. Merle. Musical directors, Messrs. de Lestrac, A. Gravenstein. Produced by Maurice Grau's French Opera Company. Opened 1 December 1881 at Abbey's Park Theatre for 1 performance in repertory; returned 12 May 1882 to the Fifth Avenue Theatre for 1 additional performance in repertory.

CAST: *Clairette*: Mlle. PAOLA MARIÉ. *Mlle. Lange*: Mlle. HELENE LEROUX. *Amaranthe*: Mlle. F. DELORME. *Larivandiere*: Mons. J. MEZIÈRES. *Ange Pitou*: Mons. Joseph Mauras. *Pomponnet*: Mons. A. Poyard. *Louchard*: Mons. E. DUPLAN.

1881.50 LES MOUSQUETAIRES AU COUVENT

An Opéra-comique in Three Acts, in French. Libretto by Paul Ferrier and Jules Prével (based on the comédie-vaudeville 'Le Habit ne fait pas le moine' by Saint-Hilaire and Duport). Music by Louis Varney; (additional music by Achille Mansour). Stage director, Mons. V. Merle. Musical directors, Messrs. de Lestrac, A. Gravenstein. Produced by Maurice Grau's French Opera Company. Opened 2 December 1881 at Abbey's Park Theatre for 1 performance in repertory; returned 25 April 1882 to the Fifth Avenue Theatre for 1 additional performance in repertory.

---

[38]New York premiere in French. Previously produced in New York in English 5 May 1881 at the Bijou Opera House for 108 performances.
[39]Musical numbers not listed in programs. List prepared from published French piano vocal score (Choudens, J. Tallandier editeur, Paris, n.d.).

[40]First produced in New York in French 25 August 1873 at Daly's Broadway Theatre in repertory. For Synopsis of Scenes and Musical Numbers, see original 1873 production.

CAST: *Simone*: Mlle. PAOLA MARIÉ. *Marie (de Pontcourlay)*: Mlle. JULIE LENTZ. *Louise*: Mlle. PAULINE MERLE. *Mother Superior (La Supérieure)*: Mlle. F. DELORME. *Brissac*: Mons. CLEMENT NIGRI. *Gontran*: Mons. F. TAUFFENBERGER. *(Abbé) Bridaine*: Mons. E. DUPLAN. *Le Gouverneur*: Mons. A. POYARD. *Soeur Opportune*: Mlle. Vandamme. *Blanche*: Mlle. Vallot. *Isabelle*: Mlle. Duparc. *Agathe*: Mlle. Malvina. *Jacqueline*: Mlle. Vernet. *Rigobert*: Mons. DUPIN. *Pichard*: Mons. Perret. *Farin*: Mons. Terrancle. *Langlois*: Mons. Carlier. *Un Moine*: Mons. Merly. *Un Moine*: Mons. Charson.

Act 1: Une cour de l'hotellerie de Pichard: Au Mousquetaires gris.

Act 2: Une salle d'étude au couvent des Ursulines.

Act 3: Une cour attenant au couvent.

ACT 1[41]

Choeur (Sans nous chercher querelle)
Choeur

Couplets des marchandes (Étrennez-moi, voici des roses)
Mons. Dupin, Les Marchandes, Choeur

Choeur (Que ces mousquetaires)
P. Marié, Mons. Dupin, Choeur

Ronde du beau Mousquetaire (S'il est un joli régiment)
P. Marié

Chanson de Bridaine (Eh! oui c'est moi l'abbé Bridaine)
E. Duplan

Trio (Parle! explique-toi!)
F. Tauffenberger, C. Nigri, E. Duplan

Choeur (C'est un jour de fête)
Choeur

Villanelle (Quel plaisir c'est à la brune)
P. Marié

Choeur en Sourdine (Maudit soit le gouverneur)
P. Marié, A. Poyard, E. Duplan, Choeur

Choeur (Le gouverneur nous fit largesse)
P. Marié, E. Duplan, Choeur

Chanson Villageoise (Dans le village on dansera)
P. Marié

Prière (Le front dans la poussière)
P. Marié

Couplets (Nous venons de la Palestine)
F. Tauffenberger, C. Nigri

Final (Dans le village on dansera)

ACT 2

Choeur (Il faut mes soeurs qu'on rivalise)
Mlle. Vaudamme, J. Lentz, P. Merle, Mlle. Malvina, Les Pensionnaires

Dictée (Donc Rebecca sa cruche pleine)
Mlle. Vaudamme

Scène (Que dites-vous de mon idée)
Mlles. Malvina, Vallot, Duparc, J. Lentz, Les Pensionnaires

Romance (Mon Dieu de mon âme incertaine)
J. Lentz

Couplets des Pensionnaires (Mon père je m'accuse)
Mlles. Malvina, Vallot, Duparc, J. Lentz, Les Pensionnaires

Morceau d'ensemble (Je voudrais qu'approchant sans crainte)
J. Lentz, P. Merle, F. Delorme, Mlle. Vaudamme, F. Tauffenberger, C. Nigri, Les Pensionnaires

Rondeau de la petite Curieuse (Curieuse! curieuse!)
P. Merle

Romance (Il serait vrai! Ce fut un songe)
F. Tauffenberger

Choeur, scène (De la cloche qui nous appelle)
Les Personnages, Pennsionnaires

Couplets de Brissac (L'amour n'est pas quoiqu'on en dise)
C. Nigri

Final (Juste ciel quel affreux scandale)

ACT 3

Choeur (dans la coulisse)(Sous les grands murs du vieux couvent)

Choeur des Pensionnaires (Deux à deux posément)
Mlle. Vaudamme, Les Pensionnaires

Couplets de Simone (A la porte des révérends)
P. Marié

Duetto (Il faut fuir, le danger nous presse)
J. Lentz, F. Tauffenberger

Quintetto de l'échelle (Prenons l'échelle)
P. Marie, J. Lentz, P. Merle, F. Tauffenberger, C. Nigri

Final (dans le village on dansera)

1881.51

LES CLOCHES DE CORNEVILLE

A Revival of the Opéra-comique in Four Acts, in French[42]. Libretto by Clairville and Charles Gabet. Music by Robert Planquette. Stage director, Mons. V. Merle. Musical directors, Messrs. de Lestrac, A. Gravenstein. Produced by Maurice Grau's French Opera Company. Opened 5 December 1881 at Abbey's Park Theatre for 1 performance in repertory.

CAST: *Serpolette*: Mlle. PAOLA MARIÉ. *Germaine*: MLLE. JULIE LENTZ. *Manette*: Mlle. Vaudamme. *Jeanne*: Mlle. Vallot. *Gertrude*: Mlle. Duparc. *Suzanne*: Mlle Malvina. *Catherine*: Mlle. Valle. *Marguerite*: Mlle. Dupin. *Gaspard*: Mons. J. MEZIÈRES. *The Marquis*: Mons. V. Dangon. *Grenicheux*: Mons. CLEMENT NIGRI. *The Bailiff*: Mons. E. DUPLAN. *Cachalot*: Mons. G. Mussy. *Grippardi*: Mons. Terrancle. *Fouinard*: Mons. Perret. *Peasants, Male and Female; Guard-Champetre, Sailors, Coachmen, Maid-servants, Domestics, etc.*

1881.52

FRITZ IN IRELAND, or, The Bell-ringer of the Rhine and the Love of the Shamrock

A Revival of the Play (with Music) in a Prologue and Three Acts[43]. Play "entirely rewritten" by William Carleton. Music (and lyrics) by Joseph K. Emmet. Produced by Joseph K. Emmet (George W. Wilton, Manager). Opened 5 December 1881 at Haverly's 14th Street Thatre and closed 24 December 1881 after 21 performances; re-opened 2 January 1882 at Niblo's Garden and closed 7 January 1882 after 7 additional performances; re-opened 1 May 1882 at the Grand Opera House for an additional 7 performances. Total: 35 performances.

CAST: *Fritz Schultz*: JOSEPH K. EMMET. *Lawyer Priggins*: De LOS KING. *Baron Hertford*, alias Splodger, Lawyer Priggins' jackal: W. STANDISH. *Captain Hercules O'Dowd*: H. C. ALBAUGH. *Lord Seaton*: W. CHRISTIE MILLER. *Charles Seaton*: W. J. Donnelly. *Thomas Goldfinger*, a man-servant, the great O'Neil: J. H. Ryan. *Patrick Blackeye*, an Irish Negro: W. J. Donnelly. *Master Herbert*, a nephew of Baron Hertford: Little Annie Smith. *Lady Amelia*: MISS VANDENHOFF. *Louisa Hertford*: Kate Blancke. *Mme. Schultz*, afterwards Mme. Marroll: Jennie Harold. *Judy Callahan*, maid-servant: Pollie Poland. *Lena Schultz*: Little Annie Smith.

1881.53

LES NOCES D'OLIVETTE

An Opéra Comique in Three Acts, in French[44]. Libretto by Henri Chivot and Alfred Duru. Music by Edmond Audran. Stage director, Mons. V. Merle. Musical directors, Messrs. de Lestrac, A. Gravenstein. Produced by Maurice Grau's French Opera Company. Opened 6 December 1881 at Abbey's Park Theatre for 1 performance in repertory; returned 5 May 1882 to the Fifth Avenue Theatre for 1 additional performance in repertory.

CAST: *Olivette*: Mlle. PAOLA MARIÉ. *Le Duc des Ifs*: Mons. J. MEZIÈRES. *De Merrimac* [Mérimac], Captain of a Vessel: Mons. CLEMENT NIGRI. *Valentin*, his nephew, an Officer: Mons. F. TAUFFENBERGER. *Marvejol*, Seneschal of Perpignan:

[41]Musical numbers not listed in programs. List prepared from published French piano vocal score (Choudens Père et Fils, Paris, 1880).

[42]First produced in New York in English 22 October 1877 at the Fifth Avenue Theatre for 16 performances. First produced in New York in French 13 May 1878 at the Park Theatre for 6 performances in repertory. For Synopsis of Scenes and Musical Numbers, see original 1878 production.

[43]Originally produced in New York 3 November 1879 at the Park Theatre for 86 performances in two engagements.

[44]French language premiere in New York. First produced in New York in English 25 December 1880 at the Bijou Opera House for 68 performances, followed by a return engagement 18 April 1881 at the Fifth Avenue Theatre for 40 performances.

Mons. A. POYARD. *Lonfuseau*, Intendant to Duc des Ifs: Mons. G. Mussy. *Lartimon*, First Boatswain: Mons. Charson. *Barabssou*, Innkeeper: Mons. Millet. *Bathilde*, Countess de Roussillon: Mlle. JULIE LENTZ. *Ourika*, a Mulatto servant of Marvejol: Mlle. PAULINE MERLE. *Moustique*, Cabin Boy: Mlle. Vallot. *L'Écureil*, Cabin Boy: Mlle. Malvina. *Mistigris*, Cabin Boy: Mlle. Vandamme. *A Servant*: Mlle. Dupin. *Lords and Ladies of the Court, Soldiers, Sailors, Servants, etc.*

La scène se passe dans le comté de Rousillon, vers la fin de règne de Louis XIII.

Act 1: Le Théâtre représente une place publique à Perpignan. A droite, la maison du sénéchal Marvejol avec un balcon practicable peu élevé; à gauche, une auberge portant des mots BARBASSOU, AUBERGISTE ET PERRUQUIER.

Act 2: Une salle à Paris coupés dans le palais de la comtesse de Rousillon.

Act 3: Le Théâtre représente une grande salle d'auberge.

ACT 1[45]

Choeur (Vous savez ce qu'on dit)
Couplets (Mon Olivette)
A. Poyard
Couplets des grilles (Quand il s'était avec adresse)
P. Marié
Madrigal maritime (Vous serez la gente corvette)
P. Marié, P. Merle, C. Nigri, A. Poyard
Choeur (Vive la Comtesse)
Air (Pays du gai soleil)
J. Lentz
Couplets (Vous êtes, dit-on)
J. Lentz
Couplets du Plongeon (Lorsque d'une femme)
J. Mezières
Sérénade (Ce doux et charmant)
F. Tauffenberger
Morceau d'ensemble (Ah! quel forfait épouvantable)
Choeur-Nocturne (Voice l'heure)
Final (Approchez, mon cher capitaine)
Couplets (O mon père)
P. Marié

ACT 2

Rondeau des noces (Se marier avec un vieux)
P. Marié
Quintette (Le voici, le voici!)
J. Lentz, P. Marié, F. Tauffenberger, J. Mezières, A. Poyard
Déclaration de Valentin (Sur votre front)
F. Tauffenberger
Couplets des aveux (Souvent dans la cour du palais)
J. Lentz
Duetto des deux maris (Quoi! votre femme avez-vous dit)
F. Tauffenberger, C. Nigri
Couplets des dédommagements (Ah! nous sommes bien malheureux!)
P. Marié, F. Tauffenberger
Romance (Comme une soeur)
J. Lentz
Final (Dans le parc pour la fête)
Farandole (Sous la tonnelle)
J. Lentz, P. Marié
Scène de l'arrestation (Chantez, dansez)

ACT 3

Choeur (Avant d'quitter l'rivage)
Chanson du vin de Rousillon (Il force à boire)
Mlles. Malvina, Vallot, Vaudamme
Ariette (Des caprices du jeu)
J. Lentz
Choeur (Voilà notre capitaine)
Chanson du mousse (Mes amis qu'il était beau)
P. Marié
Bolero (Nous nous rendions à Perpgnan)
J. Mezières
Quatuor des rires (Qu'entends-je Olivette)
P. Marié, F. Tauffenberger, C. Nigri, J. Mezières
Final (Pardonnez-nous!)

[45]Musical numbers not listed in programs. List prepared from published French piano vocal score (Choudens, Paris, 1879).

1881.54 LA FILLE DU TAMBOUR-MAJOR

A Revival of the Opéra-comique in Three Acts, 4 Scenes, in French[46]. Libretto by Henri Chivot and Alfred Duru. Music by Jacques Offenbach. Stage director, Mons. V. Merle. Musical directors, Messrs. de Lestrac, A. Gravenstein. Produced by Maurice Grau's French Opera Company. Opened 7 December 1881 at Abbey's Park Theatre for 1 performance in repertory; returned 28 April 1882 to the Fifth Avenue Theatre for 1 additional performance in repertory.

CAST: *Stella*: Mlle. PAOLA MARIÉ. *Claudine*: Mlle. JULIE LENTZ. *La Duchesse della Volta*: Mme. F. Delorme. *La Prieure*, Prioress: Mlle. Van Damme. *Francesca*: Mme. Vallot. *Lorenza*: Mlle. Malvina. *Lucretia*: Mlle. Florence Duparc. *Monthabor*, Drum Major: Mons. E. DUPLAN. *Robert*, Lieutenant: Mons. CLEMENT NIGRI. *Le Duc della Volta*: Mons. J. MEZIÈRES. *Griolet*, Drummer: Mons. F. TAUFFENBERGER. *Marquis Bambini*: Mons. A. Poyard. *Ciampas*: Mons. Mussy. *Gregorio*: Mons. Millet. *Sergeant Morin*: Mons. Terrancle. *Zerbinelli*: Mons. Carlier. *Del Ponto*: Mons. Perret. *A Sergeant*: Mons. Emile. *Soldiers, Nuns, Pensionnaires, Lords, Ladies, Peasants, Brigands.* Military Band on the Stage.

1881.55 PATIENTS; or, Bunion-Salve's Bride!

A Burlesque (of Gilbert and Sullivan's "Patience") in One Act, preceded by an Olio. Libretto by Frank Dumont. Music by W. S. Mullaly. Musical director, W. S. Mullaly. Produced by the San Francisco Minstrels. Opened 12 December 1881 at the San Francisco Opera House and closed 15 April 1882 after 128 performances.[47]

Olio: "Boccaccio Overture" by Franz von Suppé, arranged by W. S. Mullaly, Boy Choristers and Vocal Sextette. "Norah Acushla" (song and chorus), H. W. Roe. "Will You Love Me When I am Bald" (comic ditty), Charles Backus. "Mother's Good Night" (ballad), Stanley Grey. "The Yeoman's Wedding Song" (bass song), H. W. Frillman. "Idioms of the Day" (comic song), Billy Birch. "Glory or the Grave" (ballad), L. Braham. "The Yorktown Celebration" (Finale, *Music by* W. S. Mullaly, *Lyrics by* Frank Dumont), San Francisco Minstrels. [Interval] The Great Ricardo in his new song "Too Utterly Utter, or, The Æsthetic Girl." Susan's Serenade! by the grotesque eccentrics Johnson and Powers. Bob Slavin in Pathetic Ditties and Humorous Parodies. Harry Kennedy (premier ventriloquist), with song "An Old-Fashioned Photograph of Mother." Edwin French with new banjo solos, songs and anecdotes, including "Lauterbach."

CAST: *Bunion (Corn) Salve*, a very stout poet: BILLY BIRCH. *Archy-the Bald-Headed Governor*, a lean and slender poet: BOB SLAVIN. *Hunter's Point Dragoons (3): Colonel Cavalryboots*: A. C. MORELAND. *Major Purgatory*: JAMES JOHNSON. *Lieutenant Duke de Liverystable*: H. W. FRILLMAN. *Gay and Festive Dragoons of the Passing Regiment (5): Private Bottle*: L. Braham. *Private Office*: H. W. Roe. *Private Conversation*: Edwin French. *Private Caucas*: H. Wyatt. *Private Reception*: Mr. McManus. *Patients*, (on a monument) an Orange County "Pure Milk" Milkmaid, with winning Whays: CHARLES BACKUS. *Æsthetic Maidens (5): Lady Angel Licked Her*: F. M. RICARDO. *Lady Crazy Jane*: Stanley Grey. *The "Lady's Fire"*: George Powers. *Lady Umbrella*: FRANK DUMONT. *Hungry Love Sick Maidens*: The Madrigal Boys.

1881.56 OLIVETTE

A Revival of the Comic Opera in Three Acts[48]. Libretto by Henri Chivot and Alfred Duru. Music by Edmond Audran. Musical director and stage manager, Jesse Williams. Produced by the Audran Opera Comique

[46]First produced in New York in French 13 September 1880 at the Standard Theatre for 23 performances in repertory. For Synopsis of Scenes and Musical Numbers, see original 1880 production. No program found for this engagement.

[47]No credits in program for stage director, scenery or costumes. Program note: The Burlesque terminates with a solemn warning to Æsthetic Poets—and it will haunt you in your dreams. Note: Antiquarians will observe that the Archaic and Mythological instruments used in the Opera—viz. Pandean Pipes, Mandolins, Timbals, Aeolian Harps, Lutes, "Liars" &c. are copied from rare and Mediaeval Engravings and Statuary, now in the possession of the adaptor; and from William Birch's Art Collection rescued from Morrell's Warehouse.

[48]First produced in English in New York 25 December 1880 at the Bijou Opera House for 63 performances. For Synopsis of Scenes and Musical Numbers, see original 1880 production.

Company (A. J. Defossez, Manager). Opened 19 December 1881 at the Bijou Opera House and closed 26 December 1881 after 10 performances.[49]

CAST: *Olivette*, daughter of the Seneschal Marvejol: SELINA DOLARO. *Bathilde*, Countess of Rousillon, in love with Valentine: LILLIAN RUSSELL. *Veloutine*, the Seneschal's housekeeper: EMMA DUCHATEAU. *Moustique*: Kate Livingstone. *Duc des Ifs*, Cousin and Heir Presumptive to the Countess: RAYMOND HOLMES. *Captain de Merrimac*, of the Man o' War *"Cormorant"*: JOSEPH S. GREENSFELDER. *Valentine*, officer of the Rousillon Guards, his nephew: W. F. HAMPSHIRE. *Coquelicot*, foster-brother and henchman to the Duc des Ifs: FRED W. LENNOX. *Marvejol*, local pluralist, Seneschal to the Countess and Maire of Perpignan: E. S. Grant.

PATIENCE, or Bunthorne's Bride

1881.57

Gilbert & Sullivan's Æsthetic Opera Craze in Two Acts[50]. Libretto by William S. Gilbert. Music by Arthur Sullivan. Produced under the direct supervision of James C. Scanlan. Scenery by William Voegtlin. Costumes by (Henry) Dazian. Orchestra under the direction of Salvator Guerra. Produced by Haverly's Opera Company (J. H. Haverly, Proprietor). Opened 19 December 1881 at the (Metropolitan) Casino and closed 31 December 1881 after 15 performances; returned 6 February 1882 to Haverly's 14th Street Theatre and closed 15 February 1882 after 10 performances.[51] Total: 25 performances.

CAST: *Reginald Bunthorne*, a fleshly poet: WILLIAM H. SEYMOUR. *Archibald Grosvenor*, an idyllic poet: C. M. PYKE[52]. (*Officers of the Dragoon Guards*, 3): *Colonel Calverley*: JAMES F. DALTON[53]. *Major Murgatroyd*: HENRI LEAROCK[54]. *Lieutenant*, Duke of Dunstable: ALONZO HATCH. *Bunthorne's Solicitor*: Mr. Bentley. *Rapturous Maidens (4)*: *Lady Angela*: Louise Manfred. *Lady Saphir*: PAULINE HALL. *Lady Ella*: Rose Wilson. *Lady Jane*: Gertrude Orme. *Patience*: DORA WILEY[55]. *Mammoth Double Chorus of Dragoons and Rapturous Maidens.*

MULDOON'S PICNIC!

1882.01

Barry & Fay with their own Comedy Company in their original creation (Farce Comedy) in Two Acts, 4 Scenes, preceded by an Olio. Play by Billy Barry and Hugh Fay. Leader of orchestra, C. N. Edwards. Produced by Billy Barry and Hugh Fay (William Harris, Management). Opened 9 January 1882 at Niblo's Garden and closed 28 January 1882 after 24 performances.[56]

CAST: *Olio*: The Electric Three (John Callan, Morris Haley, James Callan; vocalists, dancers and comedians), The Garnellas (Dick, Bob; acrobats), Billy Barry (songs, sayings, recitations), The St. Felix Sisters (Charlotte, Henrietta, Clementine; singing specialties), John J. Fields and Frank Hanson (Musical comedians, instruments), Villion Troupe (Mlle. Elese, Sig. Mondoza, W. Villion (Bicycle Equestrians).

CAST: *Play*: *Michael Muldoon*: HUGH FAY. *Michael Mulcahy*: BILLY BARRY. *The Reverend Mr. Tracy*: John Fields. *Jack Mayflower*: John Callan. *Tim McCormick*: Morris Haley. *Mr. Flynn*: Bob Garnella. *Mr. Smith*: James Callan. *Mrs. Muldoon*: Laura Phillip. *Miss Gertrude Muldoon*: Clementine St. Felix. *Mitty*: Henrietta St. Felix. *Jenny*: Little Violet.

Act 1: Muldoon's Home.

Act 2, Scene 1: Muldoon and Mulcahy on Skates. *Scene 2*: The Donkey Ride to the Picnic. *Scene 3*: The Picnic Grounds, introducing Muldoon and Mulcahy's Great Three-Handed Reel.

SQUATTER SOVEREIGNTY

1882.02

A Comic Play in Three Acts. Play (and lyrics) by Edward Harrigan. Music by David Braham. Staged by Edward Harrigan. Settings by Charles W. Witham. Musical director, David Braham. Produced by Messrs. (Edward) Harrigan and (Tony) Hart. Opened 9 January 1882 at the Theatre Comique and closed 3 June 1882 after 170 performances.

CAST: *Felix McIntyre*, an Astronomer: EDWARD HARRIGAN. *Widow Nolan*: TONY HART. *Darius Dauber*: JOHN WILD. *Salem Sheerer*: WILLIAM GRAY. *Captain Ferdinand Kline*: HARRY FISHER. *Charles Parker*: EDWARD BURT. *George Parker*: M. F. Drew. *Terence McIntyre*: M. Bradley. *Denny Maguire*: John Queen. *Fred Kline*: James Tierney. *Tommy Darcy*: GEORGE MERRITT. *Jimmy Casey*: Edward Goss. *Horatio McIntyre*: William West. *Wellington McIntyre*: James Fox. *Pedro Donetti*: John Oberist. *Paddy Duffy*: EUGENE ROURKE. *Miss Bella Parker*: ANNIE MACK. *Josephine Jumble*: ANNIE YEAMANS. *Nellie Nolan*: GERTIE GRANVILLE. *Miss Emily Parker*: Marie Gorenflo. *Kitty Maguire*: Mary Bird. *Katrina Swartz*: Susie Byron. *Louisa Kringle*: Emily Yeamans. *Lena Stucke*: Lizzie Finn. *McIntyres and Maguires represented by* Messrs. M. Foley, Fred Queen, J. McCullough, G. L. Stout, William Merritt, Thomas Ray, Robert Hall, Emil Husel, J. Coffee, J. Fitzsimmons. *Xylophone Solo*: Ed King.

Act 1: Widow Nolan's Shanty. The Match.

Act 2: Drawing Room in Captain Kline's Mansion. The Brimstone.

Act 3: View of Shantytown by Moonlight. Ignition.

MUSICAL NUMBERS[57]

"The McIntyres"

"The Maguires"

"Widow Nolan's Goat"
T. Hart

"Miss Brady's Pianoforte" (Piano Fortay)

"The Forlorn Old Maid" (Duet)

"Paddy Duffy's Cart"
G. Merritt

DREAMS, or, Fun in a Photograph Gallery

1882.03

A Revival of the Quaint and Queer Musical Conceit (Farce Comedy) in Two Acts[58]. Play by Nathaniel Childs and Willie Edouin. Musical director, George Purdy. Produced by Willie Edouin and Frank W. Sanger (Manager). Opened 16 January 1882 at the Bijou Theatre and closed 28 January 1882 after 14 performances; re-opened 22 May 1882 at the Grand Opera House and closed 31 May 1882 after an additional 9 performances. Total: 23 performances.[59]

CAST: Act 1: *John Antonio Binks*, a retired Farmer, age 70: WILLIE EDOUIN. *Thomas Binks*, his son, aged 46: JOHN A. MACKAY. *Fred Binks*, Thomas' son, aged 22: W. SMITH. *Bob Bibbitty*, Office Boy to the Binks: JAMES T. POWERS. *Ruby Binks*, Johns' wife, age 65: ALICE ATHERTON. *Kitty Binks*, her niece: MARION ELMORE. *Grace Binks*, Thomas' second wife: LOTTA BELTON. *Maud Binks*, Fred's wife: CARLOTA PARKER. *Hattie*, her sister: SYLVIA GERRISH. *Ada*, Thomas' second wife's sister: Reca Murrilli.

Act 2: *John Antonio Binks*, aged 21: WILLIE EDOUIN. *Mrs. Chillington*: WILLIE EDOUIN. *Pickleback Grabiball*, the photographer: JOHN A. MACKAY. *Charles*: W. Smith. *Chip Cheeky*: JAMES T. POWERS. *Policeman 128*: JAMES T. POWERS. *Porter*: F. B. White. *Ruby Chillington*, aged 19: ALICE ATHERTON. *The City Swell*: ALICE ATHERTON. *Meg Binks*, our sister: MARION ELMORE. *Lillie Succotash*: CARLOTTA PARKER. *Mrs. Chillington*: LOTTA BELTON. *Violet Parachute*, with Songs: LOTTA BELTON. *Polly*, House Maid: Sylvia Gerrish. *Lillian*, with songs: Reca Murrilli.

---

[49]Scenery and costumes not credited in programs. English adaptation uncredited.

[50]A rival production to the first authorized D'Oyly Carte production, presented in New York 22 September 1881 at the Standard Theatre for 177 performances. For Synopsis of Scenes and Musical Numbers, see detail above.

[51]No credits in program for stage direction.

[52]Succeeded 9 February 1882 by Signor BROCCOLINI.

[53]Succeeded for 14th Street engagement by LEITHGOW JAMES.

[54]Succeeded for 14th Street engagement by RICHARD GOLDEN.

[55]Succeeded for 14th Street engagement by EMMA HOWSON.

[56]No credits for scenery, costumes, stage director. Played a return engagement 8-20 January 1883 at Tony Pastor's New 14th Street Theatre for 16 performances; again 26 March 1883 at Tony Pastor's New 14th Street Theatre for 8 performances, always preceded by an Olio.

[57]Not necessarily in performance order.

[58]First produced in New York 30 August 1880 at the Bijou Opera House for 42 performances. For Synopsis of Scenes, see original 1880 production.

[59]No credits in program for scenery, costumes or stage direction. Program noted Alice Atherton's picture frame, a new and ingenious mechanical revolving scene, worked in full view of the audience with life-like pictures of Joseph K. Emmet, Mary Anderson and Joseph Jefferson.

1882.04

PATIENCE, or, The Stage-Struck Maidens

A Burlesque[60] in Three Scenes, preceded by an Olio. (Burlesque by Fred Intropodi.) All the original music (by Arthur Sullivan). Scenery by Ed Simmons. Costumes by George E. Hayden. Chorus under the direction of Signor Intropodi. Orchestra conducted by Adolph Nichols. Produced by Tony Pastor. Opened 23 January 1882 at Tony Pastor's Music Hall and closed 18 March 1882 after 64 performances.

OLIO[61]: Bryant and (Gus H.) Saville, Philosophers of Music and Comedy in "The Cornet Band"; the Star Grotesques (Charles V. Seamon, Edward Girard, T. E. Somers, William Girard) in an arrangement of Negro Comicalities, Burlesque Ballets, etc.; Alice Reeves in a program of ballads; A Little Misunderstanding, sketch with Dan Collyer, Frank Girard, Ed Girard, Jennie Christie; Tony Pastor's Selection of Comic Muse; Fanny Beane and Charles Gilday (Songs and Dances); William Carroll (Songs, Stories, Witticisms).

CAST: *Patience*, the maid with the milking pail: LILLIAN RUSSELL. *Ben-Thorne*, sweetly sweet, neatly neat, charmingly charming as a leading man: JACQUES KRUGER. *Lady Jane Jemima*, a saucily saucy maid: MAY IRWIN. *Grosvenor*, prettily pretty: Flora Irwin. *Lady Angelina*, pertily pert: Flora M. Pike. *Lady Ella*, elegantly elegant: Bessie Gray. *Lady Saphir*, languishingly languid: Alice Reeves. *Colonel Calverly*, dashingly dashing: Frank Girard. *The Major*, martially martial: Vincent Aubrin. *The Duke*, courtingly courtly: James Bernard. *The Solicitor*, pleadingly pleading: Dan Collyer. *Maidens*, strikingly struck: Susie Russell, Adele Everleigh, Bessie Vining, Jennie Grey, Clara Primrose, Lilly Johnson, Marie Wyman, Eva Donell, Lucy Barrington, Nellie Puroy, Jennie Winfred, Clara Bellville, Louise King, Louise Montclaire, Belle Huestis. *Dragoons*, lovingly love-sick: Messrs. Girard, Bernard, Aubrin, Jerome, Somers, Atwood, Cooper, Hastie, Hall, E. Girard, Wynne, Ridgeway, Cameron, Seamon, Bowman, Williams, Jones, Eveleen, Melville, Montjoy, Bemis.

Act 1: Exterior of the Old Castle. Discover of rapturous maidens, madly and devotedly in love with Ben-Thorne, Manager and Actor. Patience enters—He discloses his love for her—chance for the Dragoons, but horror! Reappearance of Walter Archibald, a young juvenile actor—Rapturous maidens transfer their affections.

Act 2: On the Road to the Forest Glade. Rapturous maidens still following their Walter Archibald. The story of the "Clothier and the Gentile."

Act 3: A Forest Glade. Lady Jane disconsolate. Patience has peculiar ideas of love. Ben-Thorne and Lady Jemima arrange a plot, but no matter. Discarded by rapturous maidens. Grand Finale.

1882.05

L'AFRIQUE

A Comic Opera in Two Acts. Libretto and music by Wayman C. McCreery. Musical director and stage manager, Jesse Williams. Scenic effects by Hughson Hawley. Costumes by Bloom. Produced by the Bijou Comic Opera Company (John A. McCaull, Proprietor and Manager). Opened 30 January 1882 at the Bijou Opera House and closed 18 February 1882 after 21 performances.

CAST: *Captain Fitzhugh Montague Jones*: FRED W. LENNOX. *Lieutenant Geoffry Plantagenet Hamilton DeBracy*: PHILIP BRANSON. *Sergeant Tops*: JOSEPH S. GREENSFELDER. *Mynheer Arent Van Zwickenboot*: HARRY STANDISH. *Mynheer Pietrus Zayderhausen*: E. S. GRANT. *Corporal Hops*: J. S. PERCIVAL. *Georgiana Montague Jones*, daughter of the Captain: MARIE GLOVER. *Alice*, her maid: LIZZIE KEILER. *Soldiers, Dutch Boers, English Girls*: Chorus of 40.

Time: Just before the outbreak of the Zulu War. The action occupies one day.

Act 1: Fort Robinson, on the border of the Transvaal.

Act 2: Van Zwickenboot's Residence, three miles from Fort Robinson.

1882.06

MANOLA!, or, Blonde and Brunette

A Comic Opera in Three Acts. Original French libretto to the opéra-bouffe 'La Jour et la Nuit' by Albert Vanloo and Eugène Leterrier. English adaptation by Henry B. Farnie. Music by Charles Lecocq. Produced under the personal direction of James Barton. Scenery by Burkey, George Heister and Burridge. Ladies' dresses by Godchaux et Cie; men's costumes by (Henry) Dazian. Maitre de ballet, Marc Herbert. Musical director, Alfred Cellier. Produced by the (W. J.) Comley-(James) Barton Opera Company. Opened 6 February 1882 at the Fifth Avenue Theatre and closed 11 February 1882 after 7 performances; re-opened 13-14 March 1882 at the Fifth Avenue Theatre for 2 additional performances.

CAST: *Manola*, a Creole girl, betrothed to Miguel: CATHERINE LEWIS. *Prince Calabazas*, Prince of Villa Viciosa: JOHN HOWSON. *Don Brasiero*, Baron de Tras-os-Montés: FREDERICK LESLIE. *Beatrice*, Contessa d'Asti Spumante, betrothed to Brasiero: MARIE JANSEN. *Sanchita*, Landlady of the "Lovers Rest" Posada: Rose Chappelle. *Miguel*, Equerry to Don Brasiero: C. J. CAMPBELL. *Pablo*, Servant and Bravo to Don Calabazas: F. H. Frear. *Tessa*, Maid to Beatrix: Emma Lascelles. *Christoval*: G. Paxton. *A Soldier*: Mr. Harold. (*Dance Specialty*: Mlle. Elise.) *Pages, Maids of Honor, Peasants, Dancing Girls, etc.*

Act 1: Hall in Palace of Don Brasiero. (Burkey.)

Act 2: Garden Terrace at Don Brasiero's. (Heister.)

Act 3: Sanchita's Inn. "The True Lovers' Rest." (Burridge.)

MUSICAL NUMBERS[62]

"Little God of Love"

Bolero (Act 3)
Mlle. Elise

1882.07

FATINITZA

A Revival of the Comic Opera in Three Acts[63]. (Original Viennese libretto to the operette by F. Zell and Richard Genée, based on the libretto to "La Circassienne" by Eugène Scribe.) Music by Franz von Suppé. Musical director, Samuel L. Studley. Produced by the Boston Ideal Opera Company (Miss E. H. Ober, Proprietor and Manager). Opened 6 February 1882 at Booth's Theatre and closed 18 February 1882 after 3 performances in repertory.[64]

CAST: *Vladimir*, a young Russian lieutenant, afterwards disguised as Fatinitza: MATHILDE PHILLIPPS. *Princess Lydia Imanovna*, Niece of the Count: MARIE STONE. *Count Timofey Kantchukoff*, a Russia General: MYRON W. WHITNEY. *Izzet Pasha*, Governor of the Turkish Fort: W. H. MacDONALD. *Julian Hardy*, a Special Newspaper Correspondent: TOM KARL. *Russian Officers (3)*: *Count Vasil*: J. A. Laughrin. *Lieutenant Osip*: Gus Kammerlee. *Sergeant Steipann*: George Frothingham. *Russian Cadets (3)*: *Dimitri*: Lizzie Burton. *Ivan*: May Calef. *Nikophor*: Miss Reed. *Izzet Pasha's Wives (4)*: *Zuleika*: Marie Coleman. *Diona*: Zephie Dinsmore. *Besika*: Hattie Brown. *Nursidah*: May Calef. *Marsaldshi*, a Fortune Teller: Lizzie Burton. *Mustapha*, the Guardian of the Harem: A. G. Nichols. *Hassan Bey*, Leader of the Bashi-Bazouks: G. Kammerlee. *Vuika*, a Bulgarian spy: A. J. Hubbard.

1882.08

THE CHIMES OF NORMANDY

A Revival of the Comic Opera in Three Acts[65]. Libretto to the French opéra-comique 'Les Cloches de Corneville' by Clairville and Charles Gabet. Music by Robert Planquette. Musical director, Samuel L. Studley. Produced by the Boston Ideal Opera Company (Miss E. H. Ober, Proprietor and Manager). Opened 7 February 1882 at Booth's Theatre for 1 performance in repertory.[66]

CAST: *Serpolette*, the Good-For-Nothing: MARIE STONE. *Germaine*, the Lost Marchioness: GERALDINE ULMAR. *Gertrude*: Zephie Dinsmore. *Jeanne*: MAY

---

[60]Suggested by William S. Gilbert and Arthur Sullivan's comic opera.

[61]The Olio changed weekly; this is the program for the opening week. The Olio was replaced 5 March 1882 by a comic entertainment by Denman Thompson entitled CASTLE GARDEN; the following week it was succeeded by a burlesque, OUR CLAUDE DUVAL, or The Female Highwaymen.

[62]Musical numbers not listed in programs. List prepared from published reviews; no score found.

[63]First produced in New York in English 22 April 1879 at the Fifth Avenue Theatre for 41 performances. For Synopsis of Scenes and Musical Numbers, see original 1879 production.

[64]English adaptation uncredited. No credits in programs for stage director, scenery or costumes.

[65]First produced in New York in English 22 October 1877 at the Fifth Avenue Theatre for 16 performances. For Synopsis of Scenes and Musical Numbers, see 1877 production.

[66]English adaptation uncredited. No credits in programs for stage director, scenery or costumes.

CALEF. *Manette*: LIZZIE BURTON. *Suzanne*: MARIE COLEMAN. *Henri*, Marquis of Corneville: TOM KARL. *Jean Grenicheux*, a Fisherman: W. H. FESSENDEN. *Gaspard*, a Miser: MYRON W. WHITNEY. *The Bailli*: W. H. MacDONALD. *The Notary*, Le Tabellion: GEORGE FROTHINGHAM. *Villagers, Attendants of the Marquis.*

1882.09

LA MASCOT

A Revival of the Comic Opera in Three Acts[67]. Libretto to the opéra-comique 'La Mascotte' by Henri Chivot and Alfred Duru. Music by Edmond Audran. Musical director, Samuel L. Studley. Produced by the Boston Ideal Opera Company (Miss E. H. Ober, Proprietor and Manager). Opened 9 February 1882 at Booth's Theatre and closed 17 February 1882 after 2 performances in repertory.[68]

CAST: *Bettina*, the Mascot: GERALDINE ULMAR. *Fiametta*, Daughter of Lorenzo: LIZZIE BURTON. *Pippo*, a Shepherd: W. H. MacDONALD. *Lorenzo XVII*, Prince of Piombino: HENRY CLAY BARNABEE. *Rocco*, a Farmer: GEORGE FROTHINGHAM. *Frederick*, Prince of Pisa: W. H. FESSENDEN. *Parafanti*, Sergeant: J. A. Loughrin. *Matheo*, Innkeeper: Gus Kammerlee. *Physician*: Joseph H. Sturgess. *Pages of the King (6)*: *Carlo*: Marie Coleman. *Marco*: Zephie Dinsmore. *Angelo*: Florence Reed. *Luegi*: May Calef. *Paolo*: Hattie Brown. *Pluto*: Carrie Kammerlee.

1882.10

THE PIRATES OF PENZANCE, or, The Slave of Duty

A Return Engagement of the Revival of the Comic Opera in Two Acts[69]. Libretto by William S. Gilbert. Music by Arthur Sullivan. Musical director, Samuel L. Studley. Produced by the Boston Ideal Opera Company (Miss E. H. Ober, Proprietor and Manager). Opened 10 February 1882 at Booth's Theatre and closed 14 February 1882 after 2 performances in repertory.[70]

CAST: *Richard*, a Pirate Chief: MYRON W. WHITNEY. *Samuel*, his Lieutenant: W. H. MacDonald. *Frederic*, a Pirate Apprentice: TOM KARL. *Major General Stanley*, of the British Army: HENRY CLAY BARNABEE. *Edward*, Sergeant of Police: GEORGE FROTHINGHAM. *Mabel, Edith, Kate, Isabel*, General Stanley's Daughters: MARIE STONE, ZEPHIE DINSMORE, LIZZIE BURTON, May Calef. *Ruth*, Pirate Maid-of-all-work: MATHILDE PHILLIPPS. (*Chorus of Pirates, Police and General Stanley's Daughters.*)

1882.11

OLIVETTE!

A Revival of the Comic Opera in Three Acts[71]. Original French libretto (Les Noces d'Olivette) by Henri Chivot and Alfred Duru. Music by Edmond Audran. Musical director, Samuel L. Studley. Produced by the Boston Ideal Opera Company (Miss E. H. Ober, Proprietor and Manager). Opened 11 February 1882 (matinee) at Booth's Theatre and closed 16 February 1882 after 2 performances in repertory.[72]

CAST: *Captain De Merrimac*, Commander of "The Cormorant": W. H. MacDONALD. *Valentine*, Officer of the Rousillon Guards: TOM KARL. *Duc des Ifs*, Cousin and Heir to the Countess: HENRY CLAY BARNABEE. *Coquelicot*, his Foster Brother: GEORGE FROTHINGHAM. *Marvejol*, Mayor of Perpignan: Gus Kammerlee. *Olivette*: MARIE STONE. *The Countess of Rousillon*: GERALDINE ULMAR. *Veloutine*: Lizzie Burton. *Moustique*, Captain's Boy: May Calef. *Innkeeper*: A. J. Hubbard. *Mistigris*, a Mariner: A. E. Nichols. *Lartimon*: Mr. Johnson. *Courtiers, Officers, Sailors, Soldiers, Servants, Guards, Pages, etc.*

[67]First produced in New York in English as THE MASCOT 5 May 1881 at the Bijou Theatre for 108 performances. For Synopsis of Scenes and Musical Numbers, see original 1881 production.

[68]No credits in program for English libretto, stage director, scenery or costumes designs.

[69]First presented in New York 31 December 1879 at the Fifth Avenue Theatre for a total of 91 performances in two engagements. For Synopsis of Scenes and Musical Numbers, see original 1879 production. The Boston Ideal Opera Company previously presented THE PIRATES OF PENZANCE 13 September 1880 at Booth's Theatre for 14 performances.

[70]No credits in program for stage director, scenery or costumes designs.

[71]First produced in English in New York 25 December 1880 at the Bijou Opera House for 63 performances. For Synopsis of Scenes and Musical Numbers, see original 1880 production.

[72]No credits in program for English libretto, stage director, scenery or costumes designs.

1882.12

H.M.S. PINAFORE, or, The Lass That Loved a Sailor

A Revival of the Comic Opera in Two Acts[73]. Libretto by William S. Gilbert. Music by Arthur Sullivan. Musical director, Samuel L. Studley. Produced by the Boston Ideal Opera Company (Miss E. H. Ober, Proprietor and Manager). Opened 11 February 1882 at Booth's Theatre and closed 18 February 1882 after 2 performances in repertory.[74]

CAST: *The Right Honorable Sir Joseph Porter, K.C.B.*, First Lord of the Admiralty: HENRY CLAY BARNABEE. *Captain Corcoran*: MYRON W. WHITNEY. *Ralph Rackstraw*: TOM KARL *Dick Deadeye*, Able Seaman: GEORGE FROTHINGHAM. *Bill Bobstay*, Boatswain: Gus Kammerlee. *Tom Tucker*: Fred Pattison. *Josephine*: MARIE STONE. *Hebe*: MAY CALEF. *Buttercup*: AADELAIDE PHILLIPS. *First Lord's Sisters, Cousins and Aunts.*

1882.13

THE BOHEMIAN GIRL

A Revival of the Romantic Opera in Four Acts[75]. Libretto by Alfred Bunn. Music by Michael Balfe. Musical director, Samuel L. Studley. Produced by the Boston Ideal Opera Company (Miss E. H. Ober, Proprietor and Manager) Opened 15 February 1882 at Booth's Theatre for 1 performance in repertory.[76]

CAST: *Count Arnheim*, Governor of Presburg: MYRON W. WHITNEY. *Arline*: MARIE STONE. *Thaddeus*, a prescribed Pole: TOM KARL. *Devilshoof*: W. H. MacDONALD. *Florestein*: HENRY CLAY BARNABEE. *Gipsey Queen*: Lizzie Burton. *Buda*: Emma Tuttle. *First Gipsey*: J A. Montgomery. *Captain of the Guard*: Gus Kammerlee. *Gipsies, Peasants, Lords, Ladies.*

1882.14

THE MASCOT!

A (Rival Production of the) Comic Opera in Three Acts[77]. Libretto to the French opéra-comique 'La Mascotte' by Henri Chivot and Alfred Duru. (English adaptation by I. W. Norcross.) Music by Edmond Audran. Conductor, Hans Kreissig. Produced by Haverly's Opera Company. Opened 16 February 1882 at Haverly's 14th Street Theatre and closed 18 February 1882 after 4 performances; returned 8 May 1882 to the Germania Theatre under the auspices of I. W. Norcross and closed 24 June 1882 after ?49 additional performances[78].

CAST: *Bettina*, the Mascot: EMMA HOWSON. *Lorenzo XVII*, Prince of Piombino: J. W. NORCROSS, JR. *Frederic*, the Prince of Pisa: ALONZO HATCH. *Rocco*, a Farmer: RICHARD GOLDEN. *Pippo*, a Shepherd: J. F. DALTON. *Fiametta*, Daughter of Lorenzo XVII: PAULINE HALL.

CAST for return engagement: *Bettina*, the Mascot: DORA WILEY. *Pippo*, a Shepherd: W. T. CARLETON. *Lorenzo XVII*, Prince of Piombino: JAMES STURGES. *Rocco*, a Farmer: RICHARD GOLDEN. *Frederic*, the Prince of Pisa: HENRY MOULTEN *Fiametta*, Daughter of Lorenzo XVII: PAULINE HALL. *Mattheo*, Innkeeper: W. M. Cameron. *Parofante*, Sergeant: W. F. Rochester.

Pages to the King (12): *Angelo*: Alice Arlington. *Marco*: Jennie Elbon. *Luigi*: Sophie Hummel. *Bippo*: Clara Wisdom. *Paola*: Alice Reeves. *Antonio*: Lizzie Miller. *Paris*: Nellie DeVere. *Rolla*: Ida Barry. *Caesar*: Lizzie Shandley. *Paola*: Carrie Wing. *Augustus*: Annie Whitcomb. *Romeo*: Gracie Sherwood. *Francesca, Paolina*, Village Girls: Ida Lester, Minnie Boston. *Pages, Ladies and Gentlemen of the Court, Soldiers, Peasants, etc. Ballet*, Bouquet Ballet, Act 2: Mlle. ADELE CORNALBA, Mlles. Barretti, Ortori, Mons. Novissimo.

[73]First produced in New York 15 January 1879 at the Standard Theatre for 175 performances. For Synopsis of Scenes and Musical Numbers, see original 1879 production.

[74]No program found; Boston Ideal Opera Company list prepared from its other repertory.

[75]First produced in New York 25 November 1844 at the Park Theatre for 17 performances in repertory. For Synopsis of Scenes and Musical Numbers, see original 1844 production.

[76]No program found; Boston Ideal Opera Company list prepared from its other repertory.

[77]First produced in New York in English as THE MASCOT 5 May 1881 at the Bijou Theatre for 108 performances. For Synopsis of Scenes and Musical Numbers, see original 1881 production.

[78]No program found for first engagement.

1882.15

THE ROYAL MIDDY

A Revival of the Opera Comique (Musical Comedy) in Three Acts[79]. (Adapted into English by Fred Williams from the Viennese operette "Der Seekadett," libretto by F. Zell, from 'Le Capitaine Charlotte' by Jean-François Bayard and Philippe Dumanoir. Music by Richard Genée; music adapted and augmented by Edward Mollenhauer.) Presented under the supervision of Al Henderson. Musical director and stage manager, Jesse Williams. Produced by the Emilie Melville Opera Company (Messrs. Locke and Blanchette, Proprietors and Managers). Opened 20 February 1882 at the Bijou Opera House and closed 25 (matinee) February 1882 after 7 performances.

CAST: *Fanchette*, a Parisian soubrette, afterwards a Royal Middy: EMILIE MELVILLE. *Don Januario de Pernambuco de Pumariega*, a rich Brazilian: TOM CASSELLI. *Mungo*, his colored servant: FRED W. LENNOX. *Maria Francesca*, Queen of Portugal: LILLIE POST. *Don Lamberto de Queronda*, Admiral of the Fleet: WALLACE MACREERY. *Don Domingos*, Master of Ceremonies: Al Henderson. *Donna Antonina*, his wife: ELMA DELARO. *Don Norberto*, Officer of the Marine Academy: Charles Dungan. *Don Rodriguez, Don Henriquez*, Officers: R. Valerga, F. Howard. *Royal Middys (8)*: *Diego*: Tillie Valerga. *Ruiz*: Sitara Butler. *Gomez*: Isabel Maslin. *Henriquez*: Kittie Ayers. *Gilpelo*: Hattie Swift. *Manuel*: Annie Caldwell. *Jose*: Kate Livingston. *Hendere*: Julia Coyle. *Albuquerque*, Secretary: J. T. Sherwood.

1882.16

APAJUNE, or, The Water Sprite

A Comic Opera in Three Acts[80]. Original Viennese libretto, 'Apajune, Der Wassermann' by F. Zell and Richard Genée. Music by Carl Millöcker. Musical director and stage manager, Jesse Williams. Produced by the Emilie Melville Opera Company and the Bijou Opera House Company (John A. McCaull, Proprietor and Manager). Opened 25 February 1882 at the Bijou Opera House and closed 11 March 1882 after 15 performances.[81]

CAST: *Natalitza*, "the Pearl of Totroceni": EMILIE MELVILLE. *Princess Heloise*, Prutschesko's wife, formerly a Parisian hotel-keeper: ELMA DELARO. *Ilinka*, his niece, in love with Manol Nitchano: LILLIE POST. *Prince (Alamir) Prutchesko*, a Roumanian Bovar: WILLIAM GILBERT. *Marco*, a young peasant: TOM CASSELLI. *Captain Manolla Nitchano*, Captain of the Roumanian Hussars: FRED LENNOX. *Yosa*, a sergeant in Nitchano's regiment: J. S. GREENSFELDER. *Alexandri*, Steward of the Prince's Roumanian Estates: Charles W. Dungan. *Ivan*: W. H. Stanley. *Jacob*, the tavern-keeper: Harry Standish. *Milhaelo*, the village provost: E. S. Grant. *Dobroi, Katinka*, Natalitza's parents: D. J. Sherwood, Miss T. Valerga. *Dominick, Lesette*, servants: F. Howard, Miss Andrews. *Peasants, Gypsies, Servants, etc.*

Act 1: Exterior in Roumania.

Act 2: Reception Room in the Palace of Prince Prutschesko.

Act 3: Apajune's Grotto.

1882.17

CLAUDE DUVAL, or, Love and Larceny

A Romantic Comic Opera in Three Acts. Libretto by Henry Pottinger Stephens. Music by Edward Solomon. Produced under the stage management of Charles Harris. Scenery by Arthur Voegtlin, Hughson Hawley. Costume designs by Pilotell. Conductor, P. W. Halton Produced by Richard D'Oyly Carte's Opera Company (Helen Lenoir, Manager). Opened 6 March 1882 at the Standard Theatre and closed 29 April 1882 after 53 performances[82].

CAST: *Claude Duval*, known as Sir Harry Villebois: WILLIAM T. CARLETON. *Charles Lorrimore*, an adherent of Lord Clarendon: LYN CADWALLADR (Cadwaladyr). *Sir Whiffle Whaffle*, an old beau: ARTHUR WILKINSON. *Martin McGruder*, an English Squire: WILLIAM HAMILTON. *Captain Harleigh*, Coldstream Guards: J. A. FUREY. *Boscatt*, of Duval's Band: F. Dixon. *Blood-Red Bill*, Lieutenant of Duval's Band: J. H. RYLEY. *Constance, Rose*, McGruder's nieces: CARRIE BURTON, Marie Hunter. *Mrs. Betty*, McGruder's Sister: JENNIE HUGHES. *Dolly*: Victoria Reynolds.

Flower Girls: Clara Allen, Alice Arlington, Ethel Champneys, Annie Dayton, Marie DeNoel, Nellie DeVere, Sophie Hummel, Marie Langdon, Eugenie Maynard, Agnes Merrill, Lizzie Miller, Lillie Shandley, Grace Sherwood, Belle Urquhart, Lillie Walters, Clara Wisdom. *Highwaymen, Peasants, Village Maidens, Soldiers, Pages, Guests, etc.*

Act 1: Newmarket Heath. England, 1670. (Voegtlin.)[83]

Act 2: The Village Green of Milden. (Voegtlin.)

Act 3: The Great Hall of Milden Manor. (Hawley.)

ACT 1[84]

"Hurrah! for the gipsy tent" (Opening Chorus of Disguised Highwaymen)
"Maidens we" (Chorus of Village Girls)
"Fortune Telling" (Solo)
J. H. Ryley
"Yesterday and to-day" (Romance)
L. Cadwalladr
"Mum's the word" (Concerted Piece)
J. H. Ryley, Chorus
"King of the King's highway" (Song)
W. T. Carleton
"What days were those!" (Duet)
W. T. Carleton, L. Cadwalladr
"We are quaking" (Trio)
W. Hamilton, C. Burton, J. Hughes
Finale

ACT 2

"When our work is done" (Chorus of Villagers)
"Over the Barley Mow" (Chorus of Flower Gatherers)
"The Willow and the Lily" (Ballad)
C. Burton
"Claude Duval" (Recitative and Song)
W. T. Carleton
"On a crust and a handful of pease" (Quartet)
C. Burton, J. Hughes, W. Hamilton, W. T. Carleton
"In Normandy" (Duet)
C. Burton, L. Cadwalladr
"Silence! Silence!" (Chorus and Solo)
J. H. Ryley, Highwaymen
"The Ornamental Baronet" (Song)
A. Wilkinson
"Steady, keep together" (The March of the Coldstream Guards)
"The Soldier knows no other law" (Solo)
J. A. Furey
Finale

ACT 3

"It is quite a consolation" (Chorus of Disguised Highwaymen)
"William's sure to be right" (Song)
J. H. Ryley
"The Unprotected Spinster" (Romance)
J. Hughes
"Leave me, leave me" (Duet)
C. Burton, L. Cadwalladr
"Welcome to Knight and Maiden" (Masque and Dance)
Finale

1882.18

THE JOLLY BACHELORS!

An Operatic Absurdity in Two Acts. Libretto by John A. Stevens. Music by Edward I. Darling. Stage manager, A. H. Bell. Costumes by Roemer and Sons. Musical director, Fred Zaulig. Produced by the John A. Stevens' Comic Opera Company (E. B. Vosburgh, Manager). Opened 13 March 1882 at the Windsor Theatre and closed 18 March 1882 after 8 performances.[85]

[79]First produced in New York 28 January 1880 at Daly's Theatre for 84 performances. For Synopsis of Scenes and Musical Numbers, see original 1880 production.
[80]Previously produced in German 13-28 January 1882 at the Thalia Theatre. Musical numbers not listed in programs.
[81]English adaptation uncredited. Scenery, costumes uncredited in programs.
[82]For the first three weeks of its run, CLAUDE DUVAL alternated with PATIENCE for 4 performances each weekly.

[83]The final tableau of Act 1 is a reproduction of the famous picture, W. P. Frith, R. A., of a lady dancing a "Coranto" on the Heath with Claude Duval as the condition of her release.
[84]Musical numbers not listed in programs. List prepared from published piano vocal score (J. M. Stoddart, Philadelphia, 1882).
[85]No credits in program for stage director, scenery.

CAST: *Prince Cosmo*: JENNIE WINSTON. *Princess Floria*: AMY GORDON. *Dr. Aquarella Dodo*: LEONORA BRADLEY. *Dot*: CARRIE WILLIAMS. *King Myops*: F. M. HOWARD. *Pascarel*: W. A. MORGAN. *Racabac*: A. H. BELL. *Von Teufel*: J. C. Kline. *Basil*: F. Cutter. *Court Messenger*: Charles H. Kimball. *Herald*: W. C. Montrose.

Maidens: Misses Grace Clark, May Clark, Alice Bohnie, Ella Carman, Anna Carman, Mary Maxwell, Rose Sanger, Belle Harcourt, Lillian Drew, Sadie Lane, Emma Edwards, Dolly Delroy, Georgie Elder, Jennie C. Clark, Clara Earle, Fannie Miller, Netta Harrington, Eva Featherston, Jennie Elbon. *Bachelors*: Messrs. W. E. Cabott, J. H. Smiley, J. C. Pardy, E. Cutter, W. A. Barnes, W. C. Doughlass, F. Binkhurst, L. T. Hooey, W. H. Stuart, Charles H. Jones, L. L. Kalduff, John G. Pike, C. H. Hopper, J. C. Cady, E. C. Cobin, W. Taylor. *Courtiers, Attendants, etc.*

Act 1: Palace of King Myops.

Act 2: The Jolly Bachelors. Two years later.

ACT 1

Opening Chorus
"Only a Hundred Years Old"
"Free As the Lark" (Aria)
"Don't Call Her Old"
"From Our Sovereign's Wide Dominions"
"He Is the Prince"
Drinking Song
"Here We Come with Rhythmic Measure"
"Women's Will"
Gavotte
Finale

ACT 2

Opening Chorus
"Let Us Laugh, Let Us Sing"
"Step Lightly, Speak Softly"
"The Jolly Maidens"
"The Forest Trees"
"Witches Wailing"
"I Told You So"
Lullaby (Solo and Chorus)
"To Dwell Beside Us Evermore"
"Young Cupid"
"Anchored in the Bounding Sea"
"Pull Up"
"Hanging, Hanging, Hanging"
Finale

THE PIRATES OF PENZANCE, or, The Slave of Duty

1882.19

A Revival of the Comic Opera in Two Acts[86]. Libretto by William S. Gilbert. Music by Arthur Sullivan. Stage direction, Harry Standish. Scenery by Schaeffer. Costumes by Eaves. Musical director and stage manager, Jesse Williams. Produced by the the Bijou Opera House Company (John A. McCaull, Proprietor and Manager)[87]. Opened 13 March 1882 at the Bijou Opera House and closed 1 April 1882 after 21 performances.

CAST: *Richard*, a pirate chief: JOSEPH GREENSFELDER. *Samuel*, his lieutenant: FRED W. LENNOX. *Frederick*, a pirate apprentice: WALLACE MACREERY. *Major General Stanley*, of the British Army: WILLIAM GILBERT. *Edward*, a Sergeant of Police: Tom Casselli. *General Stanley's Daughters (4)*: *Mabel*: BLANCHE ROOSEVELT. *Edith*: Susie Winner. *Kate*: TILLIE VALERGO. *Isabel*: Kate Ayres. *Ruth*, a piratical maid-of-all-work: JULIE deRUYTHER. *General Stanley's Daughters, Pirates, Policemen, etc.*

[86]First presented in New York 31 December 1879 at the Fifth Avenue Theatre for a total of 91 performances in two engagements. For Synopsis of Scenes and Musical Numbers, see original 1879 production.
[87]Producer uncredited in programs.

BILLEE TAYLOR, or, The Lass Who Loved a Sailor

1882.20

A Burlesque in Three Scenes, preceded by an Olio. Burlesque by Fred Intropodi. Suggested by the comic opera of the same name by Henry Pottinger Stephens and Edward Solomon. (All the music from the original.) Orchestra conducted by Adolph Nicholls. Produced by Tony Pastor. Opened 20 March 1882 at Tony Pastor's Music Hall and closed 8 April 1882 after (24) performances.

OLIO: Fun at School, or, Sallie Smithers in Trouble. A Comedy Creation of Intense Amusement. *Sally Smithers*: MAY IRWIN. *Amos Sourpring*: JACQUES KRUGER. *Charley Whiting*: Frank Girard. *Harry Laurence*: Frank Wyatt. *Fred Pyne*: W. Ryle. *Henry Hoppinger Hopkins*: Dan Collyer. *Barney*: Fred Cooper. *Jennie Roberts*: Jennie Christie. *Nettie Dash*: Susie Russell. *Tillie Orville*: Flora M. Pike. And Eva Barrington, Ena Donnell, Edna McDonald, Tilly Johnson, Julia Irving, Cara Primrose.

Tony Pastor's Comic Album; Mlle. Baretta in her sketch, The Scholar's Return, assisted by Frank Girard; Miss Lillie Western (Double Banjos); E. C. Dunbar (Italian Piffiari) in his Toreador Song, and "Pretty as a Violet."

CAST: *Phoebe*, beloved by William, Barnacle, and Lobster: LILLIAN RUSSELL. *Captain Barnacle* of the Police Boat: JACQUES KRUGER. *William*, the most virtuous and conscientious tailor in the business: FLORA IRWIN. *Sir Wellington Lance*, Commander in Chief of the Armies: FRANK GIRARD. *Chris Lobster*, the Schoolmaster: Vincent Aubrin. *Eliza*, Barnacle's old flame: Jennie Christie. *Bella*, daughter of Sir Wellington: Flora M. Pike. *Susanna*, a Poorhouse Matron: Bessie Gray. (*Dance Specialty*: Mlle. BARRETTA.) *Charity Girls*: Misses Susie Russell, Alice Reeves, Beebe Vining, Jennie Grey, Clara Primrose, Eva Barrington, Lilly Johnson, Ena Donnell, Edna McDonald, Jennie Arlington, Julia Irving, Annie Wyman, Belle Eustis, Mamie Barry. *Sailors of the "Thunderbomb"*: Messrs. Bernard, Jerome, Daly, Atwood, Cooper, Hastie, Hall, McCarty, Wynne, Ridgeway, Williams, Jones, Buckley, Melville, Montjoy. Chorus of 100.

Act 1: Landscape. The Home of Lobster.

Act 2: Roadside.

Act 3: The Deck of the *"Thunderbomb."*

ACT 1

"When the countryman has a day to himself" (Song and Chorus)
V. Aubrin, Chorus
"The Virtuous Tailor" (Ballad)
F. Irwin
"Ifs and Ands" (Duet)
F. M. Pike, L. Irwin
"Peerless Phoebe" (Grand Chorus)
Charity Girls
"The Two Rivers" (Duet)
L. Russell, B. Grey
"The Self-made Knight" (Song)
F. Girard
"All on Account of Eliza" (Romance)
J. Kruger
Wedding Chorus
Company
Concerted Finale
L. Russell, F. Irwin, J. Kruger, Company

ACT 2

"The Gallant Thunderbomb" (Sailors' Chorus)
Sailors
Sailor's Hornpipe (Dance)
Mlle. Barretta
Soldiers' Chorus with fife and drum
Soldiers

ACT 3

"The Faithful Crew" (Song)
L. Russell, Chorus
"In days gone by" (Duet)
F. Irwin, L. Russell, Company
"Trim Little Phoebe" (Trio)
J. Kruger, L. Russell, B. Grey
"Love, Love, Love" (Song)
F. Girard
Grand Finale (All on Account of Eliza)
All the characters

THE PIRATES OF PENZANCE,

1882.21 or, The Slave of Duty

A Revival of the Comic Opera in Two Acts[88]. Libretto by William S. Gilbert. Music by Arthur Sullivan. Produced by the Boston Comic Opera Company (John Stetson, Proprietor). Opened 20 March 1882 at Booth's Theatre and closed 24 March 1882 after 4 performances in repertory.

CAST: *Mabel*: GERTRUDE FRANKLIN. *Ruth*: ROSA COOKE. *Kate*: ROSA DANA. *Edith*: Fannie Hall. *Isabel*: Mollie Fuller. *Richard*: SIGNOR BROCOLINI. *Samuel*: J. E. NASH. *Frederic*: HENRI LAURENT. *The Policeman*: William Hamilton. *The Major General*: A. W. F. McCOLLIN.

H.M.S. PINAFORE,

1882.22 or, The Lass That Loved a Sailor

A Revival of the Comic Opera in Two Acts[89]. Libretto by William S. Gilbert. Music by Arthur Sullivan. Produced by the Boston Comic Opera Company (John Stetson, Proprietor). Opened 25 March 1882 (matinee) at Booth's Theatre and closed 25 March 1882 (evening) 1882 after 2 performances in repertory.

CAST: *The Rt. Hon. Sir Joseph Porter, K.C.B.*, First Lord of the Admiralty: ?. *Captain Corcoran*, Commander of the *H.M.S. Pinafore*: ?. *Ralph Rackstraw*, Able Seaman: H. MORSELLE. *Dick Deadeye*, Able Seaman: ?. *Bill Bobstay*, Boatswain: ?. *Bob Becket*: ?. *Tom Tucker*: ?. *Sergeant of Marines*: ?. *Josephine*, the Captain's Daughter: GERTRUDE FRANKLIN. *Hebe*, Sir Joseph's First Cousin: Vernona Jarbeau. *Little Buttercup*, Mrs. Cripps, a Portsmouth bum-boat woman: ROSA COOKE.

BILLEE TAYLOR,

1882.23 or, The Reward of Virtue

A Revival of the Comic Opera in Two Acts[90]. Libretto by Henry Pottinger Stephens. Music by Edward Solomon. Stage manager, A. W. F. McCollin. Scenery by Joseph Clair. Costumes by George E. Hayden. Musical director, J. C. Mullaly. Produced by the Boston Comic Opera Company (John Stetson, Proprietor). Opened 27 March 1882 at the Booth's Theatre and closed 1 April 1882 after 7 performances.

CAST: *Captain, the Hon. Felix Flapper*, R.N., of *H.M.S. Thunderbomb*: A.W.F. McCOLLIN. *Sir Mincing Lane*, a Self-made man: JAMES A. GILBERT. *Sambo*, the Cook: T. M. Hengler. *Ben Barnacle*, a Bo'sun of *H.M.S. Thunderbomb*: WILLIAM HAMILTON. *Christopher Crab*, a Villainous Schoolmaster: SIGNOR BROCOLINI. *Billee Taylor*, a Virtuous Gardener: HENRI LAURENT. *Arabella Lane*, Sir Mincing Lane's daughter: VERNONA JARBEAU. *Susan*, a Charity Girl: Fannie Hall. *Eliza Dabsey*, Phoebe's Aunt: ROSA COOKE. *Phoebe Farleigh*, a Village Maiden: HATTIE MOORE. *Charity Girls (10*: Misses Fuller, Cameron, Lawrence, Hotchkiss, Knight, McSorley, Gould, Harrison, Booth, Citti. *Specialties*: Major Burke (Musket Drill), La Verde Sisters (Double Sailor's Hornpipe). *Peasants, Soldiers, Sailors, Villagers, Pretty Charity Girls, etc.*

1882.24 GREEN-ROOM FUN

Salsbury's Troubadours in a Musical Novelty in Three Acts. Play by Bronson Howard. Acting manager, Frank Maeder. Musical conductor, Charles E. Borgman. Proprietors, Nate Salsbury, John Webster and Frank Maeder. Opened 10 April 1882 at Booth's Theatre and closed 15 April 1882 after 7 performances.[91]

CAST: *Captain Henry Opdyke*, U.S.A., on leave and off duty: JOHN WEBSTER. *Eagle of the Craig*: Captain Henry Opdyke [John Webster]. *The Reverend Ernest Duckworth*, on duty without his leave: JOHN GOURLAY. *The Earl of Kensington*: Rev. Ernest Duckworth [John Gourlay]. *Mr. Booth McC. Forrest*, a heavy tragedian lightly treated: NATE SALSBURY. *The "Old Chief" War Cloud*: Booth McC. Forrest [Nate Salsbury]. *Miss Kittie Plumpet*, a born actress, with a special line and a man on the end of it: NELLIE McHENRY. *The Indian Princess*: Kittie Plumpet [Nellie McHenry]. *Mrs. Camilla Westlake*: RAY SAMUELS. *The Marchioness of Belgravia*: Mrs. Camilla Westlake [Ray Samuels]. (*Coryphées*[92], Church Choir Ballet, by three ladies of the congregation volunteering for The Benefit for Little Cannibals: Amelia Thinn, Amelia Medeyum, Amelia Phatt.)

Act 1: Rehearsal at home. Learning their parts. Costumes. Two pairs of lovers. Pulpit and stage. Art and flirtation. A Double Lovers' Quarrel.

Act 2: Rehearsal on the stage. The War of the Tuning Fiends. Two Jealous Women. Troubles of a Stage Manager A Death Scene and A Dying War Whoop. A change of lovers.

Act 3: Green Room of the Theatre during a performance. Amateur Anxiety and Professional Woes. Amateur Costumes and Amateur Properties. Haps and Mishaps of Amateur Acting. The Church Choir Ballet. The War Whoop. Love Triumphant over Art.

1882.25 THE MASCOT

A Revival of the Comic Opera in Three Acts[93]. French libretto to the opéra-comique 'La Mascotte' by Henri Chivot and Alfred Duru. Music by Edmond Audran. Stage manager, J. H. Rennie. Conductor, G. B. Snyder. Produced by J. H. Rennie. Opened 10 April 1882 at Tony Pastor's New 14th Street Theatre and closed 5 May 1882 after 27 performances; returned 2-3 June 1882 for 3 additional performances.[94]

CAST: *Bettina*, the Mascot: FANNY WENTWORTH. *Frederic*, Prince of Pisa: Helen Grayson. *Fiametta*, daughter of Lorenzo XVII: Maggie Duggan. *Paola*: Bessie Grey. *Pippo*, a Shepherd: J. A. MONTGOMERY. *Lorenzo XVII*, Prince of Piombino: J. H. RENNIE. *Rocco*, a Farmer: WILLIAM J. STANTON. *Parafante*, Sergeant: Vincent Aubrin. *Matheo*, Inn-keeper: Frank Wyatt. *The Doctor*: Fred Cooper.

Peasants, Lords and Ladies of Court, Soldiers, etc.: Messrs. Joseph Jerome, Fred. Cooper, Frank Wyatt, William Ridgeway, William Ryle, James McCarthy, Dudley, Myers, Atwood, S. M. Hall, William H. Hastie, William Cameron, Daly, Joseph Buckley, James Nichols. Misses Beebe Vining, Eva Barrington, Jennie Grey, Ena Donnell, Laura Johnson, Emma Clavelle, Eugenie Dankworth, May Clark, Anna Wyman, Alice Reeves, Clara Primrose, Eda McDonald, Gussie Rosner, Mary Hall, Vincent, Hall, DeGey, Nicholson, Lascelles, Lambert.

Act 1: The Farm of Rocco.

Act 2: The Grand Ducal Palace of Piombino.

Act 3: The Inn of Matheo.

MUSICAL NUMBERS

"The Song of the Mascot"
Grand Finale (Act 1)
Gobble Duet and Chorus
Exciting Finale and Tableau (Act 2)
"The Captain Bold" (Song)
"The Orang Outang" (Dance)
M. Duggan
"The Song of the Mascot" (reprise)
Grand Sensational Finale (Act 3)

GIROUETTE,

1882.26 or, The Weathercock

A Musical Comedy in Three Acts. Libretto adapted from the French opérette "La Giroulette" by Henri Bocage and Émile Hémery. American adaptation by Fred Williams and Robert Stoepel. Music by Auguste Coedès. Produced under the personal direction of Augustin Daly. Dances by Mlle. Malvina. Scenery by James Roberts. Mechanical effects by James Tait.

---

[88]First presented in New York 31 December 1879 at the Fifth Avenue Theatre for a total of 91 performances in two engagements. For Synopsis of Scenes and Musical Numbers, see original 1879 production.

[89]First produced in New York 15 January 1879 at the Standard Theatre for 175 performances. For Synopsis of Scenes and Musical Numbers, see original 1879 production. No program for this engagement.

[90]First opened in New York 19 February 1881 at the Standard Theatre for 101 performances; re-opened 6 June 1881 for an additional 16 performances. Total: 117 performances. For Synopsis of Scenes and Musical Numbers, see original 1881 production.

[91]Played return engagements 4 September 1882 to the Windsor Theatre for 7 performances; 9 April 1883 at the Standard Theatre for 28 performances; 10 September 1883 at the Grand Opera House for 8 performances.

[92]Added for return engagements.

[93]First produced in New York in English as THE MASCOT 5 May 1881 at the Bijou Theatre for 108 performances. For Synopsis of Scenes and Musical Numbers, see original 1881 production.

[94]English adaptation uncredited. No credits for scenery or costumes.

Properties by Charles Mulhern. Costumes by H. J. Eaves. Produced by Augustin Daly. Opened 13 April 1882 at Daly's Theatre and closed 20 May 1882 after 44 performances.[95]

CAST: *Baron Pepin de Birmenstorff*, sometimes known as Pepin the Little, and often as Pepin the Weathercock: WILLIAM GILBERT. *Captain Colardo*, deaf—but devoted—the slave of discipline, and Commander-in-Chief of the valiant forces of Birmenstorff: E. P. WILKS. *The True Eustache*, a lively young foreigner from Seville, who never having felt the Thunderbolt of Love, while seeking it beneath the tender glances of the Fair Fredérique whom he comes to wed, feels it in the lightning flash of sucy Suzanne's absorbing orbs: SIGNOR MONTEGRIFFO. *The False Eustache*, otherwise known to fable and his friends as Hildebert de Brindisi, while trolling for Carp, carp-tures the heart of the Fair Fredérique by his trolls and trills: HARRY MACDONOUGH. *Princess Frédérique*, Pepin's daughter, his sole and lonely one, the fair and festive cause of "IT" all, but as the swells end swell, and all are quite satisfied with their different bargains,—why: Love's labor's not lost, strayed or stolen this time: MAY FIELDING. *Suzanne the Saucy*, Fredérique's amid and confidential companion, so confidential in fact as often to be mistaken for her mistress: FRANCESCA GUTHRIE. *Pélagie the Proud*, the aesthetic aunt of the true-blue young man, and otherwise true and blue by times: MARIE WILLIAMS. *Lieutenant Dragonette*, chief in command of the Princess' Virginal Vanguard. Quite willing, however, to be reduced to the married ranks at the earliest opportunity: AGNES PERRING. *Corporal Lucette*, of the same capricious corps, with similar sentiments surreptitiously sounded: ISABEL EVESSON.

Maidenly Members of the Virginal Guard, who afterwards assist Hildebert to mystify Pepin (8): *Olga*: Miss Bryant. *Nadeje*: Laura Perring. *Briska*: Alice Moore. *Sacha*: E. Thornton. *Naida*: Miss Moulton. *Ednidge*: Miss Urquhart. *Cassolette*: Miss Yewell. *Katinka*: Miss Whitcomb. *Other members of the same corps by* Misses Stewart, Raymone, Cavanaugh, Verne, Everett, Cameron, Thomas, Cite, Miller, Hazelton, Brandon, Castaldo, Bryant, Bentley, Pixley, Ashton, Sandmeyer. *Amidas*, the missing equerry of the true Eustache: H. ROBERTS. *Ricardo, Raoul, Gaston, Oscar, Emile, Ernest, Carolus*, friends and companions of Hildebert: Messrs. Harmon, Saleon, Carman, Milton, Hamilton, Hopper, Wronski, Barry. *Pepin's Guard*: Messrs. Scheeckle, Lauguebach, Loe, Stultz, Gross, Bolze, Lehman, Roberts. *Dance Specialty*, Pas de Seville in Act 1: Signoras La Bella, La Gosse.

Act 1: The Little Bridge over the Danube, near the Orange Groves of Pepin the Little. The Weathercock is set in motion!

Act 2: The Ancestral Hall of the Pepins of Birmenstorff. Three Eustaches enter the field.

Act 3: The Old Mill Prison in the Valley of Windmills. The True and the False change places.

MUSICAL NUMBERS[96]

The Weathercock Chorus

Eustache's Rondeau (I have arrived from Seville)
S. Montegriffo

Chorus of Virginal Female Guards

Bellringers' Specialty

1882.27

PHOTOS

A Revival of the Musical Eccentricity in Two Acts[97]. Play by B. E. Woolfe. Stage manager, Murray Woods. Conductor, Chapin Lucy. Produced by the Harrisons (Louis, Alice) under the management of M. W. Hanley. Opened 17 April 1882 at the Bijou Opera House and closed 29 April 1882 after 14 performances.

CAST: *Act 1*: *Lottie Gwinne*, seeking the emotional: ALICE HARRISON. *Clara Harleigh*, seeking sunny smiles and a rich husband: Alice Hosmer. *Milly*, seeking a dime novel hero: Therese Wood. *Marston Moore*, seeking a row: LOUIS HARRISON. *Belvidere Potter*, seeking a responsive heart: George W. Howard. *Mr. Buchner*, seeking a family group, smiling: W. H. Thompson. *Brindle*, seeking captive maidens, with the "Curse of Gonsalo": Harry Warren.

Sitters in Act 2: *Mlle. Leontine*, serio-comic singer: ALICE HARRISON. *Livia*, a Roman Vestal: ALICE HARRISON. *Marchmont Carruthers*: LOUIS HARRISON. *Otto*, a German reporter: LOUIS HARRISON. *Dionysius*, Emperor of Rome: LOUIS HARRISON. *Rip Van Winkle*: George W. Howard. *Con*, the Shaughraun: George W. Howard. *Brutus*, Rome's hardest hitter: George W. Howard. *Sarah Bernhardt*: Harry Warren. *Chiunius*, a Roman Warrior: Harry Warren. *Clara Harley*, introducing songs: Alice Hosmer. *Milly*: Therese Wood. *Mr. Sky*, seeking to find out what it is all about: Murray Woods. *Negatives, Positives, Cabinets*: Company.

1882.28

ALL AT SEA

A Musical Comedy in Three Acts. Play by George H. Jessup. Scenery by Voegtlin. Produced by the San Francisco Minstrels (Billy Burch, Charles Backus, Managers). Opened 17 April 1882 at the San Francisco Minstrels' Opera House and closed 3 June 1882 after 56 performances.[98]

CAST: *Dr. Pillen*, Surgeon of S. S.: A. W. MAFLIN. *Hon. Rufus O'Connor*, an ex-Congressman: W. W. ALLEN. *Charles Sutherland*, a Gallant Officer: GEOFFREY TYRRELL. *Harry Vinton*, a wealthy New Yorker: W. P. HAMPSHIRE. *Peter Van Schaak*, an Adventurer: C. W. Allison. *Levy*, always looking for business: Frank Bush. *Lucy Pillen*, sweetly sentimental, but Wild, (Oscar): KATE CASTLETON. *Kate O'Connor*, a Lass who loves a Sailor—alas!: AGNES HALLOCK. *May Blackburn*, not at all too too: EMMA DUCHATEAU. *Miss Skinner*, a maiden lady—her first sea voyage: LOU THROPP. *Passengers, Sailors, Stewards, etc.*

Act 1: Deck of Steamship, with view of Queenstown Harbor.

Act 2: Interior of Grand Saloon of Steamship.

Act 3: Grand Saloon Illuminated.

MUSICAL NUMBERS, SPECIALTIES

Invisible Chorus
Company

Trio from MANOLA
K. Castleton, A. Hallock, G. Tyrrell
(*Music by* Charles Lecocq.)

Duet from DON PASQUALE[99]
A. Hallock, G. Tyrrell
(*Music by* Gaetano Donizetti.)

Grand Medley—Selections from all the late operas
Company

"My Sweetheart, when I Was a Boy"[100]
W. P. Hampshire

"Good Young Man That Died"
K. Castleton

Romeo and Juliet (Operatic Scena)
Romeo: A. Hallock. *Juliet*: K. Castleton. *Capulet*: C. W. Allison. *Nurse*: A. W. Maflin.

"Because of Thee"
G. Tyrell

"Awfully Awful" (Trio)
L. Thropp, W. W. Allen, A. W. Maflin

"Echo Song"
A. Hallock

"The Four Doctors"
W. W. Allen, A. W. Maflin, W. P. Hampshire, C. W. Allison

"For Goodness Sake Don't Say I Told You"
K. Castleton

Hebrew Eccentricities
F. Bush

1882.29

LES DRAGONS DE VILLARS

A Revival of the Opéra-comique in Three Acts, in French[101]. Libretto by Lockroy [Joseph Simon] and Eugène Cormon. Music by Aimé Maillart. Stage manager, V. Merle. Musical directors, Mons. De Lestrac, A. Gravenstein. Produced by Maurice Grau's French Opera Company. Opened 27 April 1882 at Haverly's Fifth Avenue Theatre for 1 performance in repertory.

CAST: *Rose Friquet*: Mme. ANAIS PRIVAT. *Georgette*: Mlle. CECILE GRÉGOIRE. *Sylvain*: Mons. JOSEPH MAURAS. *Sergeant Bellamy*: Mons. MAUGE. *Thibaut*:

---

[95]Musical director not identified in programs, nor in reviews.

[96]Musical numbers not listed in programs; no published score found for this translation; list prepared from published reviews.

[97]First produced in New York 9 May 1881 at the Grand Opera House for 8 performances.

[98]Stage direction, musical director, costumes design uncredited in programs.

[99]Replaced during the run by Duet from GENEVIEVE DE BRABANT.

[100]Replaced during the run by:
"Hush" (Trio)
K. Castleton, A. Hallock, A. W. Maflin

[101]First produced in New York in French 10 May 1869 at the Union Square Theatre in repertory. For Synopsis of Scenes and Musical Numbers, see original 1869 production.

Mons. E. DUPLAN. *Un Pasteur*: Mons. G. Mussy. *Un Dragon*: Mons. Richard. *Un Lieutenant de Dragons*: Mons. Merly. *Une Jeune Fille*: Mlle. Vallot. *Dragons, Paysans.*

1882.30 LE JOUR ET LA NUIT

An Opéra-bouffe in Three Acts, in French[102]. Libretto by Albert Vanloo and Eugène Leterrier. Music by Charles Lecocq. Stage manager, V. Merle. Musical directors, Messrs. DeLestrac and A. Gravenstein. Produced by Maurice Grau's French Opera Company. Opened 1 May 1882 at Haverly's Fifth Avenue Theatre and closed 6 May 1882 (matinee) after 3 performances in repertory.

CAST: *Manola*: Mlle. PAOLA MARIÉ. *Béatrix*: Mlle. CECILE GRÉGOIRE. *Sanchette*: Mlle. Vallot. *Prince Picrates de Calabazas*: Mons. J. MEZIÈRES. *Don Brasiero de Tras os Montes*: Mons. E. DUPLAN. *Miguel*: Mons. CLEMENT NIGRI. *Don Degomez*: Mons. G. Mussy. *Cristobal*: Mons. A. Poyard. *Remaining characters (Hommes et Femmes du Chateau, Alguazils, Cornettes, Étudiants, Grisettes) by* Mlles. Malvina, Dupin, Vandamme, Duparc, DeLestrac, Merly, Ruffino, Goldstein. Messrs. Perrit, Musso, Merle.

The scenes take place in Portugal in the seventeenth century.

Act 1: Une grande salle du châteeau de Don Brasiero.

Act 2: Un parc chez Doin Brasiero.

Act 3: La cour d'une hôtellerie.

ACT 1[103]

Introduction

Choeur (Nous attendons le seigneur intendant)
C. Nigri, Les Cornettes

Scène (Un intendant, la chose est sure)

Couplets (Seigneur, je sais broder)

Romance (Sous le regard de deux grands yeux)
C. Nigri

Couplets (Mon cher ami, sache bien qu'ici-bas)
E. Duplan

Couplets (Comme l'oiseau qui fuit effarouché)
P. Marié

Couplets (Les femmes! ne m'en parlez pas)
J. Mezières

Ensemble (A notre nouvelle maîtresse)
P. Marié, C. Nigri, J. Mezières, Les Femmes

Scène (A mon tour de me présenter)
J. Mezières, C. Nigri, P. Marié

Air (Eh bien, oui! je suis la baronne)
P. Marié

Duetto (Tirons-nous!)
P. Marié, C. Nigri

Couplets (Certainement, c'est bien charmant)
C. Grégoire

Final

Prière (O grand saint Michel!)
P. Marié, C. Grégoire, C. Nigri

Choeur et Scène (La nuit enchanteresse)
P. Marié, C. Grégoire, J. Mezières, E. Duplan, Choeur

Ballade de la lune (O mon épouse! o mon trésor)
E. Duplan, P. Marié, C. Grégoire

ACT 2

Romance (Laisse-moi rallumer, ma belle)
C. Nigri

Sérenade bouffe (En toute circonstance)
Les Cornettes

Sortie (Tels sont les voeux que nous formons)
Tutti

Couplets (Voyez! Elle est charmante)
P. Marié

Chanson du Romarin (Ma mère m'a dit: <Va-t-au jardin>)
P. Marié

Chanson du Fourniment (Y avait un' fois un militaire)
P. Marié

Chanson Duetto du Rossignol et de la Fauvette (Un rossignol rencontre une fauvette)
P. Marié, C. Grégoire

Choeur (Puisqu'il parait que le grand prince)
Choeur

Ensemble (O moment suprême!)
P. Marié, C. Grégoire, C. Nigri, J. Mezières

Couplets du Portugais (Les Portugais sont toujours gai)
J. Mezières

Ensemble du Parasol (Qu'on m'apporte mon parasol)
P. Marié, C. Grégoire, C. Nigri, E. Duplan, J. Mezières

Mélodie (J'ai vu le jour dans le pays)
P. Marié

Scène (Vous savez charmer les serpents)
J. Mezières

Chanson Indienne (Le serpent dort sur la mousse)
P. Marié

Sortie (Maïa maïa hio)
P. Marié

Couplets Duetto (Adieu-donc, prince charmant)
P. Marié, C. Nigri

Musique du scène

Final (On appelle!)
P. Marié, C. Grégoire, C. Nigri, E. Duplan, J. Mezières, G. Mussy

ACT 3

Introduction

Choeur (Ohé, l'hotelière!)
Mlle. Vallot, A. Poyard, Les Grisettes, Étudiants

Boléro (En Portugal, les Portugaises)

Couplets de l'hotelière (Mon cabaret, entre nous je m'en vante)
Mlle. Vallot

Sortie (Alza, alla!)
Étudiants

Couplets (Je passais un jour dans la rue)
E. Duplan

Duetto (Nous sommes deux amoreux)
P. Marié, C. Nigri

Air de muletier (Si je mène pa le chemin)
P. Marié

Quatuor (C'était la demoiselle de compagnie)
P. Marié, C. Grégoire, C. Nigri, E. Duplan

Couplets (Il est deux choses ici-bas)
P. Marié, C. Grégoire, C. Nigri, E. Duplan

Choeur (C'est un courrier!)
Tous les personnages

Couplet Final (Messieurs, on attend votre arrêt)
P. Marié

1882.31 LA MASCOTTE

A Revival of the Opéra-comique in Three Acts[104]. Libretto by Henri Chivot and Alfred Duru. Music by Edmond Audran. Musical director, W. E. Taylor. Produced by the C. D. Hess Acme Opera Company. Opened 1 May 1882 at the Standard Theatre and closed 13 May 1882 after 10 performances in repertory.[105]

CAST: *Bettina*, the Mascotte: ADELAIDE RANDALL. *Lorenzo*, Prince of Piombino: HENRY PEAKES. *Pippo*, the Shepherd: MARK SMITH. *Frederic*, the Prince of Pisa: ALFRED WILKIE. *Rocco*, the Farmer: JAMES PEAKES. *Court Physician*: Herber Jones. *Sergeant Parafonte*: W. W. Cornell. *Matteo*: Henri Leone [Leoni]. *Francesca*: Josie Renner. *Paola*: Blanche Adorci. *Planquette, Audran*, Pages: Kate Griffiths, Kate Bauer. *Fiametta*: EMMA ELSNER.

---

[102]French language premiere in New York. Previously produced in New York in English as MANOLA, etc.

[103]Musical numbers not listed in programs. List prepared from published French piano vocal score (C. Joubert, Paris, 1881).

[104]First produced in New York in English as THE MASCOT 5 May 1881 at the Bijou Theatre for 108 performances. For Synopsis of Scenes and Musical Numbers, see original 1881 production.

[105]English adaptation uncredited. Stage direction, scenery and costumes uncredited in programs.

1882.32

OLIVETTE

A Revival of the Opérette in Three Acts[106]. Original French libretto to 'Les Noces d'Olivette' by Henri Chivot and Alfred Duru. Music by Edmond Audran. Directed by J. H. Rennie. Costumes by Eaves. Produced by J. H. Rennie. Opened 6 May 1882 at Tony Pastor's New 14th Street Theatre and closed 20 May 1882 after 17 performances.[107]

CAST: *Valentine*, Officer of the Rosillon Guards: HENRI LAURENT. *Captain De Merrimac*, of the Man o' War *"Cormorant"*: JAMES STURGIS. *Duke des Ifs*, Cousin and Heir presumptive to the Countess: HARRY DeLORME. *Coquelicot*, his foster brother and henchman: W. J. STANTON. *Marvejol*, local pluralist, Seneschal to the Countess: W. GILLOW. *Boussole*: Mr. Buckingham. *Loup de Mere*: Mr. Pratt. *Olivette*, Daughter of the Seneschal Marvejol: FANNY WENTWORTH. *Bathilde*, Countess of Rousillon, in love with Valentine: MARION LAMBERT. *Veloutine*, the Seneschal's housekeeper: Maggie Duggan. *Moustique*, Captain's boy on board the "Cormorant": Gussie Rossner. *Jayoux*, *Fallesamour*, Pages of the Countess: Misses A. Hall, E. Vincent. *Mlle. de Mont Oye*, *Mlle. De Lenoir*, Ladies of the Countess' Suite: Miss Dankworth, Allen. *Levant*: R. G. Charles. *Courtiers and Nobles*: Ladies and Gentlemen of the Chorus. *Citizens, Wedding Guests and Sailors, Soldiers of the Guard, Pages, etc.*

1882.33

THE WIDOW

A Comic Opera in Three Acts. Libretto by Frank H. Nelson. Music by Calixe Lavelle [Calixa Lavallée]. Musical director, W. E. Taylor. Produced by the C. D. Hess Acme Opera Company. Opened 8 May 1882 at the Standard Theatre and closed 10 May 1882 after 3 performances.

CAST: *Donna Paquita*, the Widow: ZELDA SEGUIN WALLACE. *Adèle*, Marchioness Beauseant: EMMA PRESSY. *Nanine*, niece of Duc de Trop: ADELAIDE RANDALL. *Marquis (Peyrolles) Beauséant*, alias M. Guiboulard: MARK SMITH. *Passepoil*, a domestic: James G. Peakes. *Duc de Trop*, Nanine's Uncle and Guardian: HERBERT JONES. *Count Frederick*, Brother of the Duc: H. F. FAIRWEATHER. *Marcel (Dubois)*, in love with Nanine: WILLIAM CASTLE. (*Gaspar Minard*, in love with Lizette: ??. *Lizette Grizzell*, in love with Gaspar: ??. *Madame Grizzell*, Proprietress of the Chateau at Narbonne: ??. *Seigneurs, Peasants, etc.*)

Act 1: The Chateau of the Duc de Trop.

Acts 2 and 3: The Chateau of Count Frederic, near Bordeaux.

ACT 1[108]

"The Rocks and Hills"
W. Castle, Chorus
"Oh! Trust My Love" (Duet)
W. Castle, A. Randall
"I Am Loved"
W. Castle
"Happy and Free"
Z. S. Wallace, Chorus
"They Always Do"
Z. S. Wallace, H. Jones
"I Am Not Fancy Free" (Duet)
Z. S. Wallace, A. Randall
"The Marquis Is a Good Old Soul" (Duet)
Z. S. Wallace, A. Randall
"'Tis Joy to Meet"
(Gaspar, Lizette, Chorus)
"The Patient Angler"
(Gaspar, Chorus)
"Let Me on That Finger" (Duet)
(Lizette, Gaspar)
"I'm Too Delicate to Work"
J. G. Peakes
"My Love" (Duet)
M. Smith, E. Pressy
"Farewell For Ever"
Z. S. Wallace, M. Smith, J. G. Peakes
"Oh! Why Did He Come"
J. G. Peakes
Finale (I'd Like to see you safe away)(Concerted)
Principals, Chorus
Chorus
"All Nature's gay"

ACT 2

"Laughing Chorus" (That such thing could occur)
(Lizette, Chorus)
"Single I Will Never Be"
(Lizette)
"In Your Heart Is There No Palpitation?" (Duet)
(Lizette, Gaspar)
"All on Account of the Widow"
M. Smith
"You Will Forgive" (Trio)
A. Randall, M. Smith, H. Jones
"I'll Ne'er Forget" (Quartet)
(Lizette, Madame, Gaspar), M. Smith
"If a Woman Is Curious"
E. Pressy
Finale (Concerted)(Come friends, the sports are glorious ones)
E. Pressy, M. Smith, H. Jones, Chorus

ACT 3

"Smiling Hope" A. Randall
"Hark! Love, 'Tis I" (Trio)
A. Randall, (Madame), W. Castle
"When a Man is Married"
E. Pressy, M. Smith, Chorus
"Oh! Pray Don't Speak So Loud"
E. Pressy, M. Smith, Chorus
"'Tis Very Awkward" (Quartet)
(Lizette, Madame, Gaspar), E. Pressy, afterwards M. Smith, J. G. Peakes
"Sighing Song" (Duet)(Ah! you have never felt love's dart)
Z. S. Wallace, H. Jones
"No One Here" (Trio)
E. Pressy, (Gaspar), M. Smith
"Can I Believe My Eyes" (Concerted)
Chorus
"I Have a Husband"
E. Pressy, Female Chorus
"This Lady Was Your Wife" (Dialogue)
A. Randall, Principals, Chorus

1882.34

CINDERELLA AT SCHOOL

Rice's Surprise Party in a Revival of the Musical Comedy in Two Acts, 6 Scenes[109]. Book, music and lyrics by Henry Woolson Morse. Based on the play "School" by T. W. Robertson. Musical director, Joseph A. Kuhn. Produced by Edward E. Rice. Opened 8 May 1882 at Booth's Theatre and closed 20 May 1882 after 15 performances.[110]

CAST: *Dr. Syntax*, Tutor, the Professor's head usher and husher: HENRY E. DIXEY. *Arthur Bicycle*, a Trambulating Deity of the Upper Crust, with distinguished foreign connections: EUGENE CLARKE. *Jack Polo* of the Meadow Brook Hunt, stroke-oar of the "Harvard" in the race of '80: W. H. WEST. *Lord Lawntennys*, a relic of other days and other lands, on a visit to his long-lost nephew, and on a search for his long-lost

[106]First produced in New York 25 December 1880 at the Bijou Opera House for 88 performances in two engagements. For Synopsis of Scenes and Musical Numbers, see original 1880 production.

[107]English adaptation uncredited. No credits in programs for scenery, music direction.

[108]Musical numbers not listed in programs. List prepared from (an earlier) published vocal score (J.M. Russell, Boston, 1881). Score and script were revised for its New York production; the character of Count Frederick was added, and Gaspar, Lizette, and Madame Grizzelle do not appear in the cast list.

[109]First produced in New York 5 March 1881 at Daly's Theatre for 65 performances; and again 9 August 1881 for an additional 32 performances. For Synopsis of Scenes and Musical Numbers, see original 1881 production.

[110]No credits in program for scenery or costumes. No credits for stage direction; R. Hamilton Nicholls billed as stage manager, Edward E. Rice as proprietor and manager.

niece: GEORGE A. SCHILLER. *Professor Kindergarten*, Principal of the Papyrus Seminary for Young Ladies at Laurelton: EDWIN AIKEN. *Jenkinson*, attendant on Lord Lawntennys: Charles B. Kelley. Messrs. Metzgar, Howe, Howard, Cappa, Sage, Innes, Watterson, West, Galloway, Kelley.

Niobe Marsh, a charity pupil at Kindergarten's Seminary; the Cendrillon of the School: TOPSY VENN. *Merope Mallow*, a young lady from Brazil; the richest girl in her class, and comparatively ignorant, but superlatively "smart": IRENE PERRY. *Psyche Persimmon*, the sleepiest girl in the Seminary: NELLIE J. PRESCOTT. *Circe Slatepencil*, who giggles: Jennie Calef. *Penelope Slatepencil*, who eats: Lulu Campbell. *Pansy Pickle*, who knows everything: A. Wynn. *Chloris Slatepencil*, who lisps: Nelly Howard. *Zenobia Tropics*, head teacher at the Papyrus, and a firm believer in bone-forming: GEORGE K. FORTESCUE. *Miss Globes*, her assistant: Annie Grinnell.

The Rest of the School Girls: *Lotis Slatepencil*, who sighs: Hindie Harrison. *Primrose Pickle*, who knows nothing: Addie Innis. *Carrie Mall*, *Marian Glassy*, two very sweet girls: Annie Wells, Minnie Hall. *Daisy Dimple*, a simple little thing: Alice Hyde. *Virginia Creeper*, an insinuating thing: Grace Emerson. *Fragrant Pupils (6)*: *Rhoda Dendron*: Grace Allen. *Minni Nett*: Clara Howell. *Ollie Ander*: Flora Pike. *Amy Rylis*: Dolly Denver. *Anny Money*: Emma Cole. *Jessie Meen*: Clara Brown.

1882.35 LA PÉRICHOLE

A Revival of the Opèra-bouffe in Three Acts, in French[111]. Libretto by Ludovic Halévy and Henri Meilhac. Music by Jacques Offenbach. Stage manager, V. Merle. Musical directors, Messrs. De Lestrac and A. Gravenstein. Produced by Maurice Grau's French Opera Company. Opened 10 May 1882 at Haverly's Fifth Avenue Theatre for 1 performance in repertory.

CAST: *La Périchole*: Mlle. PAOLA MARIÉ. *Mastrilla*: Mlle. Vallot. *Guadalena*: Mlle. Vandamme. *Berginella*: Mlle. Malvina. *Mannelita*: Mlle. Dupin. *Frasquinella*: Mlle. Seygand. *Brambilla*: Mlle. Duparc. *Ninetta*: Mlle. Ruffino. *Piquillo*: Mons. CLEMENT NIGRI. *The Viceroy*, (Andrès de Ribeira): Mons. G. MUSSY. *Don Pedro*: Mons. E. DUPLAN. *Panatella*: Mons. J. MEZIÈRES. *A Prisoner*: Mons. A. Poyard. *Tarapote*: Mons. Chasson. *Two Notaries*: Messrs. Perret, Marchand. *A Jailer*: Mons. Millet.

1882.36 THE CHIMES OF NORMANDY

A Revival of the Opéra-comique in Three Acts[112]. French libretto to 'Les Cloches de Corneville' by Clairville and Charles Gabet. Music by Robert Planquette. Musical director, W. E. Taylor. Produced by the C. D. Hess Acme Opera Company. Opened 13 May 1882 at the Standard Theatre and closed 3 June 1882 after 12 performances in repertory.[113]

CAST: *Germaine*: ZELDA SEGUIN WALLACE. *Mignonette*: ADELAIDE RANDALL. *Marquis of Villeroi*: MARK SMITH. *Robin More*: ALFRED WILKIE. *Gaspard*, the Miser: MYRON W. WHITNEY. *Sheriff of Villeroi*: James G. Peakes. *Notary*: Herbert Jones. *Gertrude*: JOSIE RENNER. *Manette*: Annie Hartman. *Susanne*: Miss Adorci. *Nannie*: Lizzie Newnan. *Marie*: Miss Bauer. *Lizette*: Miss Eissung.

1882.37 OLIVETTE

A Revival of the Opérette in Three Acts[114]. Original French libretto to 'Les Noces d'Olivette' by Henri Chivot and Alfred Duru. Music by Edmond Audran. Musical director, W. E. Taylor. Produced by the C.D. Hess Acme Opera Company. Opened 22 May 1882 at the Standard Theatre and closed 24 May 1882 after 3 performances in repertory.

CAST: *Captain de Merrimac*, of the Man o' War *"Cormorant"*: HENRY PEAKES. *Vallentine*, Officer of the Rousillon Guards: MARK SMITH. *Duke des Ifs*, Cousin and Heir Presumptive to the Countess: W. JAMES. *Coquelicot*, his foster brother and henchman: JAMES G. PEAKES. *Marvejol*, Local Pluralist, Seneschal to the Countess, and Maire of Perpignan: H. F. FAIRWEATHER. *Bathilde*, the Countess of Rousillon, in love with Valentine: ADELAIDE RANDALL. *Olivette*, daughter of the Seneschal Marvejol: FANNY WENTWORTH. *Mostique*, Captain's boy aboard the *"Cormorant"*: JOSIE RENNER. *Valentine*, the Seneschal's housekeeper: Miss Adorci. *Joyaux*, *Fallesamour*, Pages of the Countess: Misses Griffith and Bauer. *Mlle. De Mont Oye*, *Mlle. De Lenoire*, Ladies of the Countess' Suite: Misses Zeigsheim, Feitner. *Courtiers and Nobles*: Messrs. Randall, Christy, Reed, Frazer, etc. *Citizens*, *Wedding Guests and Sailors*: Misses Harman, Merrian, Browning, Vance, Hartman. *Soldiers of the Guards*, *Pages, etc*

1882.38 PATIENCE, or, Bunthorne's Bride

A Revival of the Comic Opera in Two Acts[115]. Libretto by William S. Gilbert. Music by Arthur Sullivan. Stage director, W. J. Stanton. Scenery by Simmons. Costumes by Eaves. Musical director, Carlos Torriani. Produced by the J. H. Rennie Opera Comique Company. Opened 22 May 1882 at Tony Pastor's New 14th Street Theatre and closed 1 June 1882 after (13) performances.

CAST: *Reginald Bunthorne*, a Fleshly Poet: J. H. RENNIE. *Archibald Grosvenor*, an Idyllic Poet: ALMA STUART STANLEY. *Lieutenant the Duke of Dunstable*: HARRY PEPPER. *Officers of the Dragoon Guards (3)*: *Colonel Calverly*: W. T. GILLOW. *Major Murgatroyd*: W. J. STANTON. *Bunthorne's Solicitor*: Mr. Buckingham. *Rapturous Maidens (4)*: *Lady Angela*: MAY HILL. *Lady Saphir*: Marion Lambert. *Lady Ella*: Bessie Grey. *Lady Jane*: Maggie Duggan. *Patience*, a Dairy Maid: FANNY WENTWORTH. *Chorus of Dragoon Guards (20)*, *Rapturous Maidens (20)*.

1882.39 DREAMS! or, Binks' Photograph Gallery

A Revival of the (Musical Comedy) Conceit in Two Acts. Play by Nathaniel Childs and Willie Edouin. Musical director, George Purdy. Produced by Willie Edouin and Frank W. Sanger. Opened 23 May 1882 at the Grand Opera House and closed 31 May 1882 after 12 performances[116].

CAST: Act 1: *John Antonio Binks*, a retired Farmer, age 70: WILLIE EDOUIN. *Thomas Binks*, his son, aged 46: MAX FIGMAN. *Fred Binks*, Thomas' son, aged 22: W. Smith. *Bob Bibbitty*, Office Boy to the Binks: JAMES T. POWERS. *Ruby Binks*, Johns' wife, age 65: ALICE ATHERTON. *Grace Binks*, Thomas' second wife: LOTTA BELTON. *Maud Binks*, Fred's wife: Sylvia Gerrish. *Kitty Binks*, her niece: DAISY RAMSDEN. *Hattie Binks*: ALICE HOSMER. *Rose*: Mamie Rogers.

Act 2: *John Antonie Binks*, age 21, photographer: WILLIE EDOUIN. *Ralph Haberson*, a Villain, photographer: WILLIE EDOUIN. *Augustus Henfield*: MAX FIGMAN. *Jack Shivermytimbers*, a Sailor: MAX FIGMAN. *Charles*: W. Smith. *Chip Cheeky*: JAMES T. POWERS. *Policeman 128*: JAMES T. POWERS. *Porter*: Walter Williamson. *Ruby Chillington*, age 19: ALICE ATHERTON. *Mary*, the Child of Misfortune: ALICE ATHERTON. *The City Swell*: ALICE ATHERTON. *Meg Henfield*: Daisy Ramsden. *Violet Parachute*, with Songs: LOTTA BELTON. *Mrs. Chillington*: LOTTA BELTON. *Polly*, Housemaid: Sylvia Gerrish. *Lillie Succotash*: ALICE HOSMER. *Maud Wellington*: Mamie Rogers.

Act 1: At Home. John and Ruby's Parlor.

Act 2: Abroad. The Photograph Gallery.

ACT 1[117]

Serenade (new) from THE MUSKETEERS
(*Music by* Louis Varney.)

"Once Again" (Song)
(*Music by* Arthur Sullivan. *Lyrics by* Lionel H. Lewin.)

"Ave Maria" (Trio)

"The Cat's in Our Back Yard"
(*Music by* W. J. Rostetter. *Lyrics by* Nathaniel Childs.)

"Farandole" (from OLIVETTE)
(*Music by* Edmund Audran.)

"Little Stockings by the Fire"

"Over the Garden Wall"
(*Music by* C. D. Fox. *Lyrics by* Harry Hunter.)

---

[111]First produced in New York in French in a two-act version 4 January 1869 at Pike's Opera House for 35 performances.

[112]First produced in New York in English 22 October 1877 at the Fifth Avenue Theatre for 16 performances in repertory. For Synopsis of Scenes and Musical Numbers, see 1877 production.

[113] English adaptation uncredited. No credits for stage direction, scenery or costumes in programs.

[114]First produced in New York 25 December 1880 at the Bijou Opera House for 63 performances. For Synopsis of Scenes and Musical Numbers, see original 1880 production.

[115]First produced in New York 22 September 1881 at the Standard Theatre for 177 performances. For Synopsis of Scenes and Musical Numbers, see original production. Interpolated for this revival is a duet between Fanny Wentworth and Alma Stuart Stanley in Act 2. Music by W. W. Furst.

[116]First produced in New York in an earlier version 30 August 1880 at the Bijou Theatre for 42 performances. No credits in programs for stage director, stage manager, scenery, costumes.

[117]Every engagement of this show on tour and in revival featured many different songs. By 1885, the tour was performed in three acts as a farce comedy, with no songs listed in programs.

"The Gay Photographer" [Minstrel Song]
"A. O. H. March"
(*Music by* Woolson Morse. *Lyrics by* John J. McNally.)
"Veteran Guard Cadets"
"Paddy Duffy's Cart" (from SQUATTER SOVEREIGNTY)
(*Music by* David Braham. *Lyrics by* Edward Harrigan.)
Duet from PATIENCE
(*Music by* Arthur Sullivan. *Lyrics by* William S. Gilbert.)
"All for Joy" (Finale)

ACT 2
March from APAJUNE
(*Music by* Carl Millöcker.)
"Miss Brady's Piano Fortay" (from SQUATTER SOVEREIGNTY)
(*Music by* David Braham. *Lyrics by* Edward Harrigan.)
"Silly Billy" (Latest London Success)
"Arthur and Martha" [Minstrel Song]
(*Music and Lyrics by* Arthur Lloyd.)
"Oh! Osca, Dear! Oh! Osca, Dear"
"A Lancashire Lass"
"A la Français"
"Clara Jenkins' Tea" (from THE MAJOR)
(*Music by* David Braham. *Lyrics by* Edward Harrigan.)
"Pretty Lips"

H.M.S. PINAFORE,

1882.40 or, The Lass That Loved a Sailor

A Revival of the Comic Opera in Two Acts[118]. Libretto by William S. Gilbert. Music by Arthur Sullivan. Musical director, W. E. Taylor. Produced by the C. D. Hess Acme Opera Company. Opened 25 May 1882 at the Standard Theatre and closed 1 June 1882 after 7 performances in repertory.[119]

CAST: *The Rt. Hon. Sir Joseph Porter, K.C.B.*, First Lord of the Admiralty: MARK SMITH. *Ralph Rackstraw*, Able Seaman: ALFRED WILKIE. *Captain Corcoran*, Commander of the *H.M.S. Pinafore*: JAMES G. PEAKES. *Dick Deadeye*, Able Seaman: HENRY C. PEAKES. *Bill Bobstay*, Boatswain: Henri Leone [Leoni]. *Boatswain's Mate*: J. Reed. *Midshipmite*: Master Joseph N. Motte. *Josephine*, the Captain's Daughter: ADELAIDE RANDALL. *Buttercup*, (Mrs. Cripps, a Portsmouth bum-boat woman): EMMA ELSNER. *Hebe*, Sir Joseph's First Cousin: Emma Hagger.

[118]First produced in New York 15 January 1879 at the Standard Theatre for 175 performances. For Synopsis of Scenes and Musical Numbers, see original 1879 production.
[119]No credits in programs for stage direction, scenery or costumes.

1882–1883 SEASON

Alice Atherton in A BUNCH OF KEYS (Photo: Scholl)
Billy Rose Theatre Collection, New York Public Library for the Performing Arts

1882–1883 SEASON

1882.41 VENUS

A Musical and Political Fairy Extravaganza in Two Acts, preceded by an Olio. (Based on the burlesque "The Happy Land" by William S. Gilbert and Gilbert a'Beckett, adapted from William S. Gilbert's "The Wicked World") Music by Thomas Hindley. Scenery by Mr. Burcky. Produced by J. H. Rennie. Opened 5 June 1882 at Tony Pastor's New 14th Street Theatre and closed 17 June 1882 after (16) performances.

Olio: Jumbo, A Trick Elephant, a Burlesque in One Act, suggested by P. T. Barnum's recent importation of an elephant.

VENUS CAST: Fairy Inhabitants Of Venus: *Daisy*, the flower of the flock: FANNIE WENTWORTH. *Morning Glory*, Queen of the fairies: ALMA STUART STANLEY. *Nux Vomica*, an aged fairy: Maggie Duggan. *Heartsease*, a sleepy fairy: Kate Gurney. *Tulip*, an innocent fairy: Annie Dayton. *Violet*, a democratic fairy: Florence Gillette. *Pansey*, a sweet fairy: E. Gardner. *Primrose*, a prim fairy: Lizzie Primrose. *Heliotrope, Jasmine, Honey Suckle, and Chorus of Fairies.*

Male Fairies: *Cereus*, supposed to be 2,000 years old: J. H. RENNIE. *Poppy*, supposed to be 2,000 years old: WILLIAM N. GRIFFITH. *Narcissus*, supposed to be 2,000 years old: W. J. STANTON.

Mortals: *Hon. Roscoe Conlin*, representing New York: J. H. RENNIE. *Hon. James G. Braine*, representing Maine: WILLIAM N. GRIFFITH. *General Malone*, readjuster: W. J. STANTON. *The Man in the Moon*: W. J. STANTON.

Act 1: Venus by Daylight.

Act 2: Venus by Moonlight.

1882.42 PATIENCE, or Bunthorne's Bride

A Revival of the Comic Opera in Two Acts[1]. Libretto by William S. Gilbert. Music by Arthur Sullivan. Stage manager, John E. Nash. Musical director, Signor Guerra[2]. Produced by the McCaull Opera Company (John A. McCaull, Proprietor and Manager). Opened 5 June 1882 at the Bijou Opera House and closed 29 July 1882 after 56 performances; re-opened 9 September 1882 at the Bijou Opera House and closed 7 October 1882 after 28 additional performances.[3] Total: 84 performances.

CAST: *Reginald Bunthorne*, a Fleshly Poet: EDWARD P. TEMPLE. *Archibald Grosvenor*, an Idyllic Poet: HARRY ST. MAUR. *Colonel Calverly*: John E. Nash. *Lieutenant The Duke of Dunstable*: HARRY PEPPER. *Major Murgatroyd*: William Gillow. *The Solicitor*: William Ridgeway. *Patience*, a Dairy Maid: LILLIAN RUSSELL. *Rapturous Maidens (4)*: *Lady Jane*: AUGUSTA ROCHE. *Lady Angela*: MARION LAMBERT. *Lady Saphir*: EMILY LAWRENCE. *Lady Ella*: Miss G. Bowler. *Chorus of Dragoon Guards, Rapturous Maidens.*

CAST for return engagement: *Patience*, a Dairy Maid: LILLIAN RUSSELL. *Rapturous Maidens (4)*: *Lady Jane*: LAURA JOYCE. *Lady Angela*: LILY POST. *Lady Saphir*: Emie Weathersby. *Lady Ella*: Victoria Reynolds. *Reginald Bunthorne*, a Fleshly Poet: JOHN HOWSON. *Archibald Grosvenor*, an Idyllic Poet: DIGBY BELL. *Officers of the Dragoon Guards (3)*: *Colonel Calverly*: JOSEPH S. GREENSFELDER. *Lieutenant the Duke of Dunstable*: CHARLES J. CAMPBELL. *Major Murgatroyd*: GEORGE GASTON. *The Solicitor*: Harry Standish. *Chorus of Dragoon Guards, Rapturous Maidens.*

1882.43 PLIGHTED BY MOONLIGHT

An Operette in One Act, accompanied by a program of ballet. (Original French libretto "Le Mariage aux Lanternes"[4] by Michel Carré and Léon Blum.) Music by Jacques Offenbach. Stage manager, Mons. Paul Juignet. Orchestra under the direction of Antonio DeNovellis. Produced by J. Fred Zimmerman. Opened 19 June 1882 at the Metropolitan Alcazar and closed 3 July 1882 after 15 performances.[5]

ACT 1

Nachtschatten (Waltz)(*Music by* Johann Strauss.)/

Fashion (Polka)(Music by Johann Strauss.)/

Tarantella (Grand Ballet)(Music by Daniel François Esprit Auber.)
Ida Ross, Emma Ross, Corps de Ballet of 30

ACT 2

PLIGHTED BY MOONLIGHT.

CAST: *Pierre*: Signor MONTEGRIFFO. *Lisa*: ADELAIDE RANDAll. *Catherine*: Fannie Wentworth. *Fanchette*: Rosa Cooke.

ACT 3

Grand Ballet (*Music by* Ballet Master Signor G. Lepri.)
Signorina Amalia Lepri (Prima Ballerina Assoluta),
Ida Ross, Emma Ross, Full Corps de Ballet

Blondine (March)(*Music by* Rudolf Bial.)/

Lustschwärmer (Waltz)(*Music by* Johann Strauss.)/

Donaustrand (Galop)(*Music by* Johann Strauss.)
(Ballet Company)

1882.44 THE TWO MEDALLIONS!

A Musical Comedy in Three Acts. Book, music and lyrics by Frederick Miller. Opened 19 June 1882 at Tony Pastor's New 14th Street Theatre and closed 24 June 1882 after 8 performances.

CAST: *The Two Medallions*: *Ilene*, a fugitive from the Gipsies: AMY LEE. *Pinkette*, the Squire's pet: EMMA CLAVELLE. *Clotilde Calebson*, "must wedded be on or before her twenty-first birthday": Sara Lascelles. *Tableaux Matilde*, her giddy sister: Mary Stuart. *Penobscot Quincy Butts*, the Village Squire: HARRY A. SMITH. *Professor J. Phineous Billings*, Editor of the bi-weekly Bazoo: C. B. HAWKINS. *Clarence Barnes*, the Squire's annual visitor, in search of the Two Medallions: T. J. HAWKINS. *Spooks*, the Squire's servant: Jonathan H. Burnett.

A terrible gory affair transpires in Act 2 of which the following are the Dramatis Personae: *Princess Louise*: AMY LEE. *Prince Roderic*: AMY LEE. *Countess Adrienne*: Sara Lascelles. *Mathusalem Josie*: Mary Stuart. *Harry Elwood*: T. J. Hawkins. *The Royal Guard*: Jonathan H. Burnett.

ACT 1

Opening Chorus

"Ding, Dong, Ding" (Chorus of School Children)

"I'm the only one that's left of all the Family"

"A grand mistake"

"The Pledge"

"Why, then, should I"—

"I am Ilene"

"A Brother new"

ACT 2

"A little cry"

"Dream song"

"Kiss and make it up"

"I love as none can tell"

"Policeman's song"

"A little Empress"

"Can you tell me?"

ACT 3

"In wine that sparkles"

"Oh! Such a night"

"All the guns in town"

---

[1]First produced in New York 22 September 1881 at the Standard Theatre for 177 performances. For Synopsis of Scenes and Musical Numbers, see original 1881 production.

[2]For the return engagement, the musical director was C. F. Wernig.

[3]Scenery and costumes uncredited. For the return engagement, Jesse Williams was billed as Director of Amusements, and C. F. Wernig as Leader of Orchestra. Concurrent with the return engagement, the Boston Miniature Ideal Opera Company presented daily matinees of PATIENCE with a cast of juveniles under the stage direction of James Scanlan, musical direction of John Braham.

[4]Previously presented in New York in German 18 March 1860 at the Stadttheater, in French 6 February 1864 at the Théâtre Français/Niblo's Saloon, and in English as MARRIED BY LANTERNS 31 August 1868 at Wood's Museum.

[5]English adaptation uncredited. No credits for scenery or lighting.

"Bye-O-Bye"
"Hearts we oft love best"
"Meadow on the Squire's farm"
"The Trumpet's call"

1882.45 THE MERRY WAR

A Comic Opera in Three Acts[6]. Original Viennese libretto ('Der lustige Krieg') by F. Zell and Richard Genée, based on the libretto to the opéra-comique 'Les Dames capitaines' by Mélesville. American adaptation by J. W. Norcross, Jr. Music by Johann Strauss. Produced under the immediate supervision of I. W. Norcross. Costumes by Messrs. P. Godchaux, Eaves and Joseph Buchheister. Musical director, Ernst Catenhusen. Produced by the I. W. Norcross Opera Company. Opened 27 June 1882 at the Germania Theatre and closed 22 July 1882 after 27 performances; moved 29 July 1882 to the Metropolitan Alcazar and closed 18 August 1882 after an additional 21 performances; returned 2 October 1882 to Haverly's 14th Street Theatre and closed 14 October 1882 after 16 perfomances; returned 21 May 1883 to the Cosmopolitan Theatre and closed 2 June 1883 after an additional 14 performances. Total this season: 78 performances.

CAST: *Umberto Spinola*: WILLIAM T. CARLETON. *Artemesia*, Princess of Malaspina, wife of the prince of Massa-Carrara: BELLE COLE. *Marquis Fillippo Sebastiani*, nephew to the Princess: RICHARD GOLDEN. *Balthasar Groot*, a tulip planter from Haarlem: GUSTAV ADOLFI. *Elsa*, wife of Balthasar Groot: LOUISE PAULLIN. *Young noblemen in the service of the Genoese Republic (3)*: *Riccardo Surrazza*: C. H. Jones. *Carlo Spuizzi*: F. H. Hunt. *Fortunato Franchetti*: W. H. Ross. *Colonel Von Scheelen*, colonel in the service of the Duc of Limburg: W. H. Myer. *Biffi, Gini*, sergeants in the Genoese service: Misses Rose Wilson, Mr. William Cunnard. *Court Ladies of the Princess (6)*: *Theresa*: Miss Arlington. *Camilla*: Miss Elbon. *Giovannina*: Miss Lincoln. *Agnese*: Miss Power. *Bettina*: Miss Hummel. *Francesca*: Miss Shandley. *Violetta*, widowed Countess of Lomellina, cousin to Artemesia: DORA WILEY. *Chorus of Officers, Soldiers, Servants, etc.*

Ballet Divertissement: Act 3, "The Japanese Ballet': Mlles. ADELE CORNALBA, BARRETTI, CURILLO, Full Corps de Ballet.

Act 1: Camp of the Genoese Army. Early in the eighteenth century.

Act 2: The Neutral Castle of Malaspina.

Act 3: (Interior of Castle at) Massa.

MUSICAL NUMBERS[7]

"The Easiest Way's Always the Best"
"There's Not a Drop of Blood"
W. T. Carleton
"We Came All the Way from Holland"
"The Weal and Woe"
D. Wiley
"Hear Me! Hear Me!"
D. Wiley, W. T. Carleton
"Very Nice Conduct"
G. Adolfi, L. Paullin
"Romanza"
(*Music by* Ernst Catenhusen.)
"Now Darker Falls the Night"
D. Wiley, W. T. Carleton
"War-Song"
B. Cole
(*Music by* Ernst Catenhusen.)
"Two Months Have Passed"
G. Adolfi

1882.46 VACATION DAY/ THE DOCTOR OF ALCANTARA

A Triple Bill of a Saynète, a Comic Opera and a Ballet. Orchestra under the direction of Antonio DeNovellis. Produced by J. Fred Zimmerman. Opened 4 July 1882 at the Metropolitan Alcazar and closed 28 July 1882 after (22) performances.

ACT 1

VACATION DAY. A Saynète in One Act[8], in which Signora Vanoni will sing in Italian, French, English and Spanish.

CAST: *Polycarpe Grosmenu*: PAUL JUIGNET. *Mary*, a maid: Rose Marion. *Gabrielle*: MARIA VANONI.

ACT 2

THE DOCTOR OF ALCANTARA. A Revival of the Comic Opera in Two Acts[9]. Libretto and music by Julius Eichberg.

CAST: *Carlos*: Signor MONTEGRIFFO. *Don Pomposo*: ELLIS RYSE. *Baltahasar*: Harry Allen. *Dr. Paracelsus*: VINCENT HOGAN. *Isabella*, Paracelsus' daughter: ADELAIDE RANDALL. *Inez*, his maid: Fanny Wentworth. *Donna Lucrezia*, his wife: ROSA COOKE.

ACT 3

SYLVIA, a Ballet d'action. Music by Leo Delibes. Ballet master, Signor Lepri. Dresses and scenery by John A. Thompson.

CAST: Signora (AMALIA) LEPRI, Misses Ida and Emma Ross, Maggie Summerfield, Leontine, Weston, Richards, Marchal, Baretta, Ida Francis, Gray, Kate Francis, Haslam, Ashton, Rupert, Phillis, Allyn, Rosa, Griffiths, Dale, Bohner, Plews, Atkins, etc.

1882.47 OLIVETTE

A Revival of the Opérette in Three Acts.[10] Original French libretto ('Les Noces d'Olivette') by Henri Chivot and Alfred Duru. Music by Edmund Audran. Opened 31 July 1882 at the Bijou Opera House and closed 12 August 1882 after 14 performances.

CAST: *Olivette*: SELINA DOLARO. *Countess Bathilde de Rousillon*: LILLY POST. *Merimac*: JOSEPH S. GREENSFELDER. *Coquelicot*: FRED H. FREAR. *Veloutine*: VICTORIA REYNOLDS. *Valentine*: CHARLES J. CAMPBELL. *Duc des Ifs*: GEORGE GASTON. And Chorus.

1882.48 PATIENCE, or Bunthorne's Bride

A Revival of the Comic Opera in Two Acts[11]. Libretto by William S. Gilbert. Music by Arthur Sullivan. Produced under the stage direction of James C. Scanlan. Scenery by John Mazzanovich. Stage mechanism by F. Dorrington. Properties by E. Siedle. Gas and calcium effects by J. F. Driscoll. Musical director, John Braham. Produced by (John) Braham and (James) Scanlan's Boston Miniature Ideal Opera Company. Opened 31 July 1882 at Wallack's Theatre and closed 7 September 1882 after 40 performances.[12]

CAST: *Reginald Bunthorne*, a Fleshly Poet: Master ARTHUR DUNN. *Archibald Grosvenor*, an Idyllic Poet: Master HARRY HAMBLIN. *Mr. Bunthorne's Solicitor*: Master JACK JACOBS. *Colonel Calvalry*, Officer of Dragoons: Master AUGUSTUS COLLINS. *Major Murgatroyd*, Officer of Dragoons: Master FRANK KEEFE. *Lieutenant, the Duke of Dunstable*, Officer of Dragoons: Master GEORGE MORGAN. *Rapturous Maidens (4)*: *The Lady Angela*: Miss MARGUERITE FISH. *The Lady Saphir*: LILLIAN CALEF. *The Lady Ella*: Miss MINNIE CONNOR. *The Lady Jane*: Miss IDA MÜLLE. *Patience*, a Dairy Maid: Miss JENNIE DUNN. *Chorus of Rapturous Maidens, Officers of Dragoons.*

1882.49 THE MASCOT

A Revival of the Opéra-comique in Three Acts[13]. (Original French libretto by Henri Chivot and Alfred Duru.) English libretto by J. W. Norcross, Jr.

[6]First New York production in English; previously produced in New York in German 15 March 1882 at the Thalia Theatre.
[7]Musical numbers not listed in programs. List prepared from published piano vocal selections (Norcross Opera Company, New York, 1882).
[8]Authorship uncredited.
[9]First produced in New York 28 May 1866 at the Théâtre Français in repertory. For Synopsis of Scenes and Musical Numbers, see original 1866 production.
[10]First presented in New York 25 December 1880 at the Bijou Opera House for 63 performances. For Synopsis of Scenes and Musical Numbers, see original 1880 production. English adaptation not credited in programs.
[11]First produced in New York 22 September 1881 at the Standard Theatre for 177 performances. For Synopsis of Scenes and Musical Numbers, see original 1881 production.
[12]A novelty production produced with a cast of juveniles.
[13]First produced in New York 5 May 1881 at the Bijou Opera House for 168 performances in two engagements. For Synopsis of Scenes and Musical Numbers, see original 1881 production.

Music by Edmond Audran. Stage manager, Charles T. Parr. Ballet arranged by Signor G. Lepri. Produced by Vin Haurie. Opened 19 August 1882 at the Metropolitan Alcazar and closed 26 August 1882 after 7 performances.

CAST: *Bettina*, The Mascot: ADAH RICHMOND. *Lorenzo XVII*, Prince of Piombino: A. W. MAFLIN. *Fiametta*, his daughter: PAULINE HALL. *Frederick*, the Prince of Pisa: ROBERT NELSON. *Pippo*, a Shepherd: CHARLES DUNGAN. *Rocco*, a Farmer: W. H. COMPTON. *Matteo*: William Gillow. *Sergeant*: Charles Barker. *Pages of Lorenzo (8)*: *Angelo*: Mollie Powen. *Mario*: Jennei Elbon. *Paola*: Carrie Wing. *Luigi*: Clara Douglass. *Beppo*: Annie Reeves. *Antonio*: Annie Elbon. *Rene*: Nellei Irving. *Paris*: Jennie Loton. *Francesca*: Ida Lester. *Paolina*: Minnie Boston. *Servants, Peasants, Soldiers, Lords and Ladies, etc.*

Incidental to Act 2, a Grand Floral Divertissement, expressly composed for the occasion by Signor G. Lepri, will be performed with Mlle. Marietta Bonfanti, Mlle. Amalia Lepri, Complete Alcazar Corps de Ballet.

1882.50 THE BLACKBIRD

A Romantic Historical Picturesque Irish Drama in Five Acts. Play by George L. Stout. Staged under the supervision of Edward Harrigan. Scenery by Charles W. Witham. Musical director, David Braham. Produced by (Edward) Harrigan and (Tony) Hart. Opened 26 August 1882 at the Theatre Comique and closed 21 October 1882 after 65 performances.

CAST: *Redmund Darcy*, Colonel in Stuart's Army: DeWOLF HOPPER. *Private Goslin*: JOHN WILD. *Peery Dunleavy*, a Process Server: Harry A. Fisher. *Fighting Fitzpatrick*, a Fiddler: John Queen. *Pierre Dupont*, a French smuggler: Frank Budworth. *Bartle Donovan*: William Scallan. *Ned Malone*: WILLIAM WEST. *Orderly Jones*: J. A. LEWIS. *Father James*, a Fugitive Priest: Henry Ward. *Lord Clanricard*: H. Johnston. *Tim Lanigan*: James Fitzsimmons. *Jones Neville*, Major in the Army of George II: Mark M. Price. *Sergeant Saltpeter*: William Gray. *Captain Chester*: M. F. Drew. *Dancing Dugan*: M. Bradley. *Barney Sullivan*: GEORGE MERRITT. *Randal Brady*: WILLIAM MERRITT. *Paddy Leach*: JOHN G. SPARKS. *Gregory Roach*: JOSEPH M. SPARKS. *Terence Finnigan*: James McCullough. *Andy Houlihan*: Charles Coffey. *Larry Lynch*: W. Atkins. *Con O'Carolan*, a Piper: EDWARD HARRIGAN. *Maurteen Mahr*, an Idiot Boy: TONY HART. *Lady Helen*, Darcy's wife: Mattie Earle. *Mona Mahr*, her foster sister: GERTIE GRANVILLE. *Biddy Doyle*, Landlady of Sea-Gull's Nest: Annie D. Ware. *Peggy Reilly*: Annie Scanlan. *Mollie Rourke*: Ada Farwell. *Mary Doolen*: Susie Byron. *Kitty Mahr*: Sadie Morris. *Onah Flaherty*: Lizzie Finn. *Gracie Noonan*: Bertha Wild. *Bedelia Gilhooley*: Jessie West. *Delia Hafferty*: Annie Hall. *Nellie Dooley*: Annie Langdon. *Betsey Malone*: Mary Langdon. *Soldiers, Smugglers, Peasants, Children, Keeners, etc.*

Act 1: The Sea-Gull's Nest, Coast of Galway. (ca. 1714)

Act 2: Interior of Darcy Castle.

Act 3: Exterior and Interior of Nancy Mahr's Cabin.

Act 4: The Devil's Pool and Waterfall by Moonlight.

Act 5: The Prison and Round Tower of Castle Dusnas-Caugh. The Storm and Escape.

MUSICAL NUMBERS[14]

"The Mountain Dew"
E. Harrigan
(*Music by* David Braham. *Lyrics by* Edward Harrigan.)

"The Trooper's the Pride of the Ladies"
W. Merritt
(*Music by* David Braham. *Lyrics by* Edward Harrigan.)

"The Blackbird" (song of Jacobite period)

"Johnny Cope" (song of Jacobite period)

1882.51 BILLEE TAYLOR

A Revival of the Comic Opera in Two Acts[15]. Libretto by Henry Pottinger Stephens. Music by Edward Solomon. Stage manager, Arthur Leclerc. Musical director, Alexander Spencer. Scenery by (William F.) Voegtlin. Costumes by (Henry) Dazian. Produced by the McCaull Opera Company (John A. McCaull, Proprietor and Manager), by arrangement with James C. Scanlan. Opened 28 August 1882 at the Bijou Opera House and closed 8 September 1882 after 12 performances.

CAST: *Phoebe Farleigh*: CARRIE BURTON. *Arabella Lane*: EME WEATHERSBY. *Susan*: Amy Harvey. *Eliza Dabsey*: JENNIE HUGHES. *Billee Taylor*: CHARLES J. CAMPBELL. *Captain Felix Flapper*: EDWARD CHAPMAN. *Christopher Crab*: EDWARD CONNELL. *Sir Mincing Lane*: ALBERT HENDERSON. *Ben Barnacle*: GEORGE A. SCHILLER.

1882.52 OLIVETTE

A Revival of the Comic Opera in Three Acts[16]. Libretto by Henri Chivot and Alfred Duru. Music by Edmond Audran. Stage manager, Harry Standish. Ballet master, Signor G. Lepri. Musical director, Charles F. Wernig. Bijou Opera House Company (by arrangement with John A. McCaull) presented by Vin Haurie. Opened 4 September 1882 at the Metropolitan Alcazar and closed 16 September 1882 after 12 performances.

CAST: *Olivette*, daughter of the Seneschal Marvejol: SELINA DOLARO. *Bathilde*, Countess of Rousillon, in love with Valentine: LILY POST. *Veloutine*, the Seneschal's housekeeper: EMMA GUTHRIE. *Moustique*: Kitty Ayres. *Captain de Merrimac*, of the Man o' War *"Cormorant"*: JOSEPH S. GREENSFELDER. *Valentin*, officer of the Rousillon Guards, his nephew: J. TAYLOR. *Duc des Ifs*, Cousin and Heir Presumptive to the Countess: GEORGE GASTON. *Coquelicot*, foster-brother and henchman to the Duc des Ifs: HARRY STANDISH. *Marvejol*, local pluralist, Seneschal to the Countess and Maire of Perpignan: E. S. Grant. *Ballet*: Mlles. (MARIA) BONFANTI, (AMALIA) LEPRI, Full Corps de Ballet.

1882.53 MME. L'ARCHIDUC

A Revival of the Opéra-comique in Three Acts, in French[17]. Libretto by Albert Millaud. Music by Jacques Offenbach. Stage director, Charles Darcy. Costumes, Mme. Moreau. Musical director, Mons. Lagye. Produced by Maurice Grau's French Opera Company. Opened 11 September 1882 at the Fifth Avenue Theatre and closed 16 September 1882 after 7 performances; returned 13 October 1882 to the Bijou Opera House for 1 additional performance, and 19 March 1883 to the Casino Theatre for 1 additional performance.

CAST: *Marietta*: Mme. LOUISE THÉO. *Fortunato*: Mme. BUISSON. *The Countess*: Mme. DORSAY. *Giacometta*: Mme. VALLOT. *The Archduke Ernest*: Mons. DUPLAN. *Giletti*: Mons. NOE. *The Count*: Mons. HUGUET. *The Duke of Pontefiascone*: Mons. Grivel. *The Marquis of Frangipano, The Count of Bonaventura, Bonardo*, conspirators: Messrs. Mussy, Salvator, Terrancle. *Ricardo*: Mons. Vinchon. *An Innkeeper*: Mons. Julien Ber. *Piandolce*: Mons. Millet. *Beppino*: Mons. Norbert. Chorus of 60.

1882.54 THE BEAUTIFUL GALATEA/ TRIAL BY JURY

A Double Bill of a Comic Opera in One Act, and a Revival of Gilbert & Sullivan's extremely laughable musical absurdity (Dramatic Cantata) in One Act. Produced under the immediate supervision of I. W. Norcross. Opened 14 September 1882 at Tony Pastor's New 14th Street Theatre and closed 16 September 1882 after (4) performances.

ACT 1

THE BEAUTIFUL GALATEA. A Comic Opera in One Act[18]. Original German libretto 'Die schöne Galathée' by Poly Henrion.[19] Music by Franz von Suppé. Incidental to the opera will be given a Grand Ballet Divertissement introducing Mlle. Ortori, supported by a full Corps de Ballet.

CAST: *Galatea*, a Statue: PAULINE CANISSA. *Pygmalion*, a Sculptor: FRANK G. CAUFFMAN. *Midas*, an art enthusiast: FRED FREAR. *Ganymede*, an Apprentice: PAULINE HALL. *Chorus of Youths and Maidens of Cyprus.*

---

[14]Not necessarily in performance order. Incidental music of the play, also the overtures to each act, are composed of Irish and Scottish airs, the bulk of them being Jacobite Songs of the year 1746, carefully selected and arranged by David Braham.

[15]First opened in New York 19 February 1881 at the Standard Theatre for 101 performances; re-opened 6 June 1881 to Niblo's Garden for an additional 16 performances. Total: 117 performances. For Synopsis of Scenes and Musical Numbers, see original 1881 production.

[16]First produced in English in New York 25 December 1880 at the Bijou Opera House for 63 performances. For Synopsis of Scenes and Musical Numbers, see original 1880 production.

[17]First produced in New York in French 6 September 1875 at the Lyceum Theatre for 21 performances in repertory. For Synopsis of Scenes and Musical Numbers, see original 1881 production.

[18]English language premiere in New York; adaptation uncredited in programs. No credits for scenery, costumes, musical direction.

[19]Pen name for Leopold Karl Dietmar Kohn von Kohlnegg.

ACT 2

TRIAL BY JURY. A Revival of the Dramatic Cantata in One Act.[20] Libretto by William S. Gilbert. Music by Arthur Sullivan.

CAST: *Plaintiff*: PAULINE CANISSA. *Defendant*: ED PAXTON. *Judge*: FRED FREAR. *Usher*: ARTHUR VAN HOUTEN. *Counsel*: A. G. CARTER. *Clerk*: Arthur Harold. *Foreman of the Court*: Mr. Paulett. *Jury, Witnesses, etc.*

1882.55 LA JOLIE PARFUMEUSE

A Revival of the Opéra-comique in Three Acts, in French[21]. Libretto by Hector Crémieux and Ernest Blum. Music by Jacques Offenbach. Stage director, Charles Darcy. Costumes, Mme. Moreau. Musical director, Mons. Lagye. Produced by Maurice Grau's French Opera Company. Opened 18 September 1882 at the Fifth Avenue Theatre and closed 23 September 1882 after 6 performances; re-opened 9 October 1882 at the Bijou Theatre for 2 additional performances in repertory, 18 October 1882 at the Fifth Avenue Theatre for 3 additional performances in repertory, 17 March-10 April 1883 at the Casino Theatre for 4 additional performances in repertory, 21 May 1883 at Daly's Theatre for 1 additional performance.

CAST: *Rose Michon*: Mme. LOUISE THÉO. *Bavolet*: Mme. BETTY. *Clorinde*: Mme. MOREL. *La Julienne*: Mme. VANDAMME. *Arthemise*: Mme. VALLOT. *Madelon*: Mme. Caro. *La Cocardière*: Mons. DUPLAN. *Poirot*: Mons. Grivel. *Germain*: Mons. Noe. *Justine*: Mme. Delavigne. *Lise*: Mme. Delournay. *A Soubrette*: Mme. Adrienne. *Waiters*: Messrs. Vinchon, Nys, Gerard, Norbert. Chorus of 60.

1882.56 MY SWEETHEART

An Elastic Musical Comedy in Three Acts. Play by William Gill. Produced by the John R. Rogers Comedy Company. Opened 18 September 1882 at Haverly's 14th Street Theatre and closed 23 September 1882 after 8 performances.[22]

CAST: *Tony (Faust)*, with songs, etc.: R. E. GRAHAM. *Joe Shotwell*, a broken-down old sport—"you know me": T. J. HAWKINS. *Dr. Oliver*, a true friend: John Sutton. *Harold Bartlett*, a gambler: John Gilbert. *Dudley Harcourt*, too too: L. R. WILLARD. *Old Hatzel*, a Wealthy Farmer: T. J. HAWKINS. *Mrs. Fleeter*, an Adventuress: Maggie Arlington. *Mrs. Hatzel*, the Farmer's Loving Wife: Mrs. Louise Morse. *Tina*, the farmer's daughter with songs, dances, etc.: MINNIE PALMER.

Act 1: A happy home in the country. (Hatzel's Farm in the Mountains of Pennsylvania.)

Act 2: A palace in the city. (Tony's Palatial Residence in New York.)

Act 3: Return to the old farm. (Home again.)

1882.59 BREAKING THE SPELL

An Operetta (Comic Opera) in One Act (accompanied by a program of ballets). (Based on the légende bretonne 'Le Violoneux' with French libretto by Eugène Mestépès and Émile Chevalet. English libretto by Henry B. Farnie.) Music by Jacques Offenbach. Ballets arranged by Signor G. Lepri. Orchestra leader, Herr K. Christrup. Produced by Vin Haurie. Opened 25 September 1882 at the Metropolitan Alcazar and closed 7 October 1882 after 162 performances.

ACT 1

BREAKING THE SPELL CAST: *Old Matthew*, a Chelsea pensioner: J. H. POULETT. *Peter Bloom*, a Gardener: PAUL VERNON. *Jennie Wood*, Maid of the Inn: FANNY WENTWORTH.

Scene: A garden adjoining a Tavern on the Thames, near Chelsea Hospital, London.

MUSICAL NUMBERS[23]

"Jenny Is False" (Romance)
P. Vernon

"Oh How Happy We Shall Be" (Duet)
P. Vernon, F. Wentworth

"My Heart is Ever Gay" (Song)
J. H. Poulett

"Hark! 'Tis the Bugle!" (Duet)
F. Wentworthy, J. H. Poulett

"Am I Awake" (Duet)
F. Wentworth, P. Vernon

Scene (My father's writing)
F. Wentworth, P. Vernon, J. H. Poulett

"In My Youth" (Finale)
F. Wentworth, P. Vernon, J. H. Poulett

ACT 2

Grand Ballet Fantastique, "Le Styx"
Ariel, the Flying Dancer; the Girards
Premiere: Mlle. Amalia Lepri. *Seconda*: Mlle. F. Pasta. And the Full Alcazar Corps de Ballet.

ACT 3

Trio (Ballet), "Styrienne"
Mme. M. Martens, Miss S. Van Huyck, Mr. M. A. Martens

Aesthetic Minuet
The Girards (Julian, Marius, Jacques, George)

Solo
Miss S. Van Huyck

Duo, "Des Chats"
Mme. M. Martens, Mr. A. Martens

Alice Again (sketch)
John Gourlay

Floral Ballet
Premiere: Mlle. Amalia Lepri. *Seconda*: Mlle. Adele Camais. And the Full Alcazar Corps de Coryphées.

1882.57 DONNA JUANITA

A Revival of the Comic Opera in Three Acts[24] Original Viennese libretto by F. Zell and Richard Genée. American adaptation by Fred Dixon. Music by Franz von Suppé. Stage manager, Fred Dixon. Musical director, William Eaton Brown. Conductor, Herr K. Christrup. Produced by the Boston English Opera Company (William E. White, W. A. Edwards, Managers). Opened 25 September 1882 at Tony Pastor's 14th Street Theatre, moved 9 October 1882 to the Alcazar and closed 21 October 1882 after 28 performances.

CAST: *René Dufar*, the Spy, afterwards disguised as Donna Juanita: ROSE BEAUDET. *Petrita*, betrothed to Gaston: HATTIE STARR. *Donna Olympia*, wife of the Alcalde: ANNIE CALLOWAY. *Marco*, Student: Tillie Parker. *Paquita*, a Titana: Clara Dixon. *Gaston Dufar*, a French soldier on parole: PERCY COOPER. *Don Pomponio*, Alcalde of the city: ELLIS RYSE. *Colonel Douglass*, English Commander: J. W. ARMSTRONG. *Riego*, Notary and Letter Writer: ARTHUR VAN HOUTEN. *Gil Polo*, the innkeeper: J. C. Montgomery. *Picador*: Walter Allen. *Diego*, a traitor: C. St. Aubyn. *Chorus of Students, Monks, Children, etc.*

Incidental to Act 3, a new and original ballet, Nymph of the Forest, arranged by Signor Novissimo, will be performed by Mlles. MARIE BONFANTI (Première Assoluta), Adele Camais (Seconda), F. Pasta, 30 Coryphées, Full Corps de Ballet.

1882.58 LES CLOCHES DE CORNEVILLE

A Revival of the Opéra-comique in Three Acts, 4 Scenes, in French[25]. Libretto by Clairville and Charles Gabet. Music by Robert Planquette.

---

[20]First produced in New York 15 November 1875 at the Eagle Theatre for 8 performances. For Synopsis of Scenes and Musical Numbers, see original 1875 production.

[21]First produced in New York in French 31 March 1875 at the Lyceum Theatre; in English as THE PRETTY PERFUMER 5 October 1876 at the Brooklyn Theatre. For Synopsis of Scenes and Musical Numbers, see original 1875 production. Théo interpolated her song "Piouit" according to critics.

[22]Programs list no musical numbers. Critics remarked upon interpolated music, songs, dances, her shy entrance solo, a cuckoo duet with Tony, a love duet, a lullabye duet, a stirring Tyrolienne.

[23]No musical numbers listed in programs; list of scenes and musical numbers prepared from published English piano vocal score (Metzler & Co., London, 1870?).

[24]Previously produced in New York in English 16 May 1881 at the Fifth Avenue Theatre for 24 performances in an uncredited English version.

[25]First produced in New York in French 5 October 1880 at the Standard Theatre for 5 performances in repertory; in English as THE CHIMES OF

Stage director, Charles Darcy. Costumes, Mme. Moreau. Musical director, Mons. Lagye. Produced by Maurice Grau's New French Opera Company. Opened 25 September 1882 at the Fifth Avenue Theatre and closed 27 September 1882 after 3 performances; re-opened 10 October 1882 at the Bijou Opera House for 1 additional performance, 21 (matinee) October 1882 at the Fifth Avenue Theatre for 1 additional performance, 20 March-12 April 1883 at the Casino Theatre for 3 additional performances in repertory.

CAST: *Serpolette*: Mme. LOUISE THÉO. *Germaine*: Mme. DORSAY. *Gaspard*: Mons. J. MEZIÈRES. *The Marquis*: Mons. NOE. *Grenicheux*: Mons. GRIVEL. *The Bailiff*: Mons. DUPLAN. *Remaining characters by* Mmes. Vallot, Adrienne, Moreau, Caro, Delournay, Delavigne, Berthe, Messrs. Mussy, Salvator, Vinchon, Julien Ber. Chorus of 60.

1882.60 MANTEAUX NOIRS

A Comic Opera in Three Acts[26]. Libretto by Walter Parke and Harry Paulton, adapted from the libretto to the opera "Giralda, ou La Nouvelle Psyche" by Eugène Scribe[27]. Music by Procida Bucalossi. Produced under the stage direction of Charles Harris. Scenery by John Mazzanovich, John A. Thompson and Philip Goatcher. Costumes by Wilhelm. Director of music, Alfred Cellier. Produced by Richard D'Oyly Carte's Opera Company (Helen Lenoir, Manager). Opened 26 September 1882 at the Standard Theatre and closed 27 October 1882 after 36 performances.

CAST: *Don Luis de Rosamonte*, an Officer: WILLIAM T. CARLETON. *Don José (de Manilla)*, Grand Chamberlain (secretly married to Donna Clorinda): ARTHUR WILKINSON. *Dromez*, the miller: RICHARD MANSFIELD. *Nicholas*, a Farmer: W. Gillow. *Manuel*, a Tailor: William White. *Palomez*, Astronomer Royal: J. A. Furey. *Don Philip of Aragon*, King Consort: J. H. RYLEY. *Isabel*, Queen of Castile: FANNY EDWARDES. *Clorinda (de Lorenzana)*, the Queen's Attendant: Joan Rivers. *Gomez*, the Queen's Page: Billie Barlow. *Lazarillo*, a Tailor's Boy: Mina Rowley. *Girola*, the Belle of Valados: SELINA DOLARO. *Peasant Boys (2)*: *Pedro*: Miss Lynne. *Samson*: Miss Vickers. *Peasant Girls (4)*: *Anna*: Miss Allen. *Maria*: Miss Florence. *Teresa*: Miss Langley. *Inez*: Miss Forster. *Rosina, Beatrix*, Maids of Honor: Misses Hummel, Weddle. *First Bridesmaid*: Miss Rousby. *Guzman*, a Page: Miss Wisdom. *The Queen's Pages*: Misses Sherwood, Shandley.

Act 1: The Village of Valodos. Twilight. (Mazzanovich.)

Act 2: Interior of the Mill. Darkness. (Thompson.)

Act 3: The Palace at Santiago. Light. (Goatcher.)

ACT 1[28]

"Joy to the lover" (Wedding Chorus)

"Who can it be?" (Scene)

"Of the Court a Magnate am I" (Aria)
A. Wilkinson

"Yes, of Spain a staunch Grandee" (Chorus)

"Joy to the lover" (Chorus and Scene)
S. Dolaro, Chorus

"Six months ago" (Rondo)
S. Dolaro

"I never could, like some girls, smile" (Song)
S. Dolaro

"There's naught so uncertain" (Song)
R. Mansfield

"Aid me, Cupid" (Song)
W. T. Carleton

"It is my duty" (Duet)
S. Dolaro, R. Mansfield

"Viva! viva! Gracious Queen" (Chorus)

"Good people, gladly" (Recitative)
F. Edwardes

"How blest must be this country life" (Duet)
F. Edwardes, J. H. Ryley, Chorus

"Away! Away!" (Finale)
Principals, Chorus

ACT 2

"Safe to the bridal home!" (Chorus)

"The heart sighs ever to be free" (Ballad); Melodrame
S. Dolaro

"Love is never blind!" (Duet)
S. Dolaro, W. T. Carleton

"I sing Love's dulcet lay" (Serenade)
J. H. Ryley, A. Wilkinson

"Hush! hush! hush!" (Whispering Quartette)
S. Dolaro, W. T. Carleton, J. H. Ryley, A. Wilkinson

"Search the mill!" (Finale)
Principals, Chorus

ACT 3

"Love and pleasure" (Introduction and Chorus)

"Powers of Goodness" (Concerted Piece)
F. Edwardes, A. Wilkinson, Chorus

"In Spain our love and sweet romances" (Song)
F. Edwardes

"Say, girl, are you the Miller's bride" (Concerted Piece)
S. Dolaro, F. Edwardes, W. T. Carleton, J. H. Ryley, Chorus

"Anita is sad" (Fandango)
S. Dolaro

"False, false woman" (Duet)
S. Dolaro, W. T. Carleton

"Here ends all artifice and guile" (Finale)
Principals, Chorus

1882.61 LA MASCOTTE

An Opéra-comique in Three Acts, in French[29]. Libretto by Henri Chivot and Alfred Duru. Music by Edmond Audran. Stage director, Charles Darcy. Costumes, Mme. Moreau. Musical director, Mons. A. Lagye. Produced by Maurice Grau's French Opera Company. Opened 28 September 1882 at the Fifth Avenue Theatre and closed 30 September 1882 after 4 performances; re-opened 11 October 1882 at the Bijou Opera House for 1 additional performance, 3-14 (matinee) April 1883 at the Casino Theatre for 4 additional performances in repertory.

CAST: *Bettina*, La Mascotte: Mme. LOUISE THÉO. *Fiametta*: Mme. BETTY. *Laurent XVII*: Mons. J. MEZIÈRES. *Pippo*: Mons. HUGUET. *Fritellini*: Mons. NOE CADEAU. *Rocco*: Mons. DUPLAN. *Matheo*: Mons. MUSSY. *A Sergeant*: Mons. David. *Remaining characters by* Mmes. Vallot, Adrienne, Moreau, Delavigne, Caro, Vandamme. Chorus of 60.

1882.62 AROUND THE WORLD IN EIGHTY DAYS

A Revival of the Musical Extravaganza in Five Acts[30] Based on the French adaptation of Jules Verne's novel "Le Tour du Monde en Quatre Vingt Jours," as adapted by Adolphe d'Ennery. Music composed and arranged by Jean-Jacques de Debillemont. Scenic designs by Poisson, Negel, Robecchi, Cornil, adapted by Mons. Camille Weinehenk. Costumes by Chalain; properties by Hallée; statuary by Dagoni. Staged by the Kiralfys (Imre, Bolossy). Produced by the Kiralfys. Opened 2 October 1882 at Niblo's Garden and closed 21 October 1882 after 25? performances; re-opened a return engagement 16 April 1883 at Haverly's 14th Street Theatre and closed 28 April 1883 after 16? additional performances.

NORMANDY 22 October 1877 at the Fifth Avenue Theatre for 16 performances in repertory.

[26]Subtitled BLACK CLOAKS.

[27]The original music to the opera by Adolphe Adam was not used.

[28]Musical numbers not listed in programs. List prepared from published English piano vocal score (J. B. Cramer & Co., London, 1882).
Interpolated for the American production:
Ballad
W. T. Carleton
(*Music by* Alfred Cellier. *Lyrics by* J. R. Planche.)

[29]Previously produced in New York in English as THE MASCOT 5 May 1881 at the Bijou Theatre for 168 performances in two engagements.

[30]First produced in New York 28 August 1875 at the Academy of Music for 43 performances.

CAST: *Aouda*: CORA TANNER. *Nemea*: ROSE WILSON. *Bessie*: BLANCHE MORTIMER. *Nakahira*: JOSIE LOANE. *Idali*: Francis Browne. *Olga*: Carrie Mott. *Giza*: Agnes Mapleton. *Daora*: Gertrude Lavine. *Phileas Fogg*: W. F. CLIFTON. *Miles O'Pake*: FRANK KILDAY. *Fix*: J. J. WALLACE. *Passepartout*: GEOGE R. EDESON. *Mr. Blunt*: J. L. Mason. *Sir Roger Shewdryn*: Edward Barry. *Arthur Mayburn*: L. Morton. *Foster Jones*: J. Wakefield. *Governor of Suez*: Frank Richmond. *Shafter*: W. Porter. *Boatswain*: P. Williams. *Engineer*: C. Runyon. *Aged Parsee*: M. S. Johns. *Brahman Chief*: A. H. Denham. *Phil Tracy*: W. Holliman. *Jack Rivers*: W. Smithline. *Conductor*: H. Rogers. *Engineer*: P. Taylor. *King of Borneo*: James Van Pelt. *Chief Scout*: P. Toole. *Station Master*: J. Mahmed. *Waiter*: C. Notelzah. *Barkeeper*: J. A. Cook. *Captain Collins*: W. S. Hurd. *Specialties*: Mlle. Theodora de Gillert, Mlle. Turri, Mons. ARNOLD KIRALFY.

1882.63 THE VICAR OF BRAY

An English Comic Opera in Two Acts. Libretto by Sydney Grundy. Music by Edward Solomon. Produced under the personal supervision of Edward Solomon. Stage manager H. A. Cripps. Scenery by John A. Thompson. Costumes by (Henry) Dazian. Musical director, Edward Solomon. Produced by James Barton. Opened 2 October 1882 at the Fifth Avenue Theatre and closed 7 October 1882 after 7 performances.

CAST: *Reverend William Barlow*, Vicar of Bray: HARRY ALLEN. *Reverend Henry Sandford*, his curate: LYN CADWALLADAR [Llewellyn Cadwalladr]. *Thomas Merton*, Esq., of Bray Manor: GEORGE OLMI. *Mr. Bedford Rowe*, a Confidential Family Solicitor: HARRY BROWN. *Dorothy*, the Vicar's Daughter: MARIE JANSEN. *Mrs. Merton*, widow of the late Thomas Merton, of Jamaica: JENNIE HUGHES. *Nelly Bly*, of the Theatre Royal, Bray: EDITH BLAND. *Students of Divinity, Ladies of the Ballet, Teachers, Huntsmen, Jockeys.*

Act 1: Low Church. The Village Green.

Act 2: High Church. The Vicarage Grounds.

ACT 1[31]

"Hooray! hooray!" (Chorus of Children)
"To a slow and stately measure" (Chorus of Lady Teachers)
"O, why is my love" (Song)
M. Jansen
"All the bold" (Exit Chorus of Teachers)
"On, Students, on!" (Chorus of Students; Solo)
Chorus, L. Cadwalladar
"As good as he ought to be" (Song)
L. Cadwalladar
"Hail to the Vicar!" (Ensemble and Entrance of Vicar)
D. Jansen, L. Cadwalladar, H. Allen, Chorus
"The Rev. Mr. Barlow" (Song)
H. Allen
"Bow, Students, bow!" (Chorus)
Children, Teachers, Students
"I'm as sharp as a ferret" (Song)
H. Brown
"Good morning, dear Vicar" (Exit)
H. Brown, Children, Teachers, Students
"Has anyone seen the Pytchley Pack?" (Entrance of Mrs. Merton)
J. Hughes
"Now if you'll excuse me" (Trio)
H. Brown, H. Allen, J. Hughes
"The shy widow" (Duet)
H. Allen, J. Hughes
"Tell me true, love" (Duet)
L. Cadwalladar, M. Jansen
"Jolly, jolly huntsmen!" (Chorus of Huntsmen)
"Our chorus is somewhat peculiar" (Solo)
G. Olmi
"Please to make way for us" (Chorus)
Corps de Ballet
Dance
E. Bland
"O, shocking sight" (Ensemble)
Teachers
"Back! Students, back!" (Finale)

ACT 2

"Listen to the merry bells" (Chorus of Teachers)
"What is life?" (Concerted Piece)
Student, Teachers, H. Allen
"The Jackson case" (Song and Chorus)
H. Allen, Students
"The Wily Widower" (Duet)
H. Allen, J. Hughes
"You ask me why" (Solo)
J. Hughes
"Come back to me" (Duet)
M. Jansen, L. Cadwalladar
"Propriety, prisms and prunes" (Duet)
M. Jansen, L. Cadwalladar
"Just a word" (Trio)
L. Cadwalladar, G. Olmi, M. Jansen
Entrance
E. Bland, Corps de Ballet
Pas de Cinq (Dance)/Exit of Vicar, Corps de Ballet
"Confidential family solicitor" (Concerted Piece)
G. Olmi, H. Brown, Huntsmen
"We no longer gyrate" (Chorus)
Corps de Ballet
"See, see, we saw!" (Concerted Piece)
Teachers, Students, Huntsmen, Ballet
"Lucky little boys and girls" (Chorus of Children)
"Lady Fair" (Wedding Chorus)
"O William, sweet William" (Finale)

INTERPOLATIONS

"The Silver Line" (from LORD BATEMAN)
M. Jansen
(Lyrics by Henry Pottinger Stephens.)
"The Red Rose and the White" (from LORD BATEMAN)
G. Olmi
(Lyrics by Henry Pottinger Stephens.)

1882.64 THE BOHEMIAN GIRL

A Revival of the Romantic Opera in Four Acts, 6 Scenes[32]. Libretto by Alfred Bunn. Music by Michael William Balfe. Musical director, Signor Antonio DeNovellis. Produced by the Strakosch English Opera Company. Opened 2 October 1882 at the Grand Opera House in repertory; season closed 7 October 1882 after (3) performances in repertory.

CAST: *Count Arnheim*, Governor of Presburg: GEORGE SWEET. *Thaddeus*, a proscribed Pole: Signor J. PERUGINI. *Florestan*, nephew of the Count: Fred Dixon. *Devilshoof*, Chief of the Gypsies: EDWARD CONNELL. *Queen of the Gypsies*: Mrs. ZELDA SEGUIN WALLACE. *Captain of the Guard*: Arthur Bowers. *Buda*, Arline's attendant: ?. *Arline*: KATHARINE VON ARNHEIM. *Gypsies, Soldiers, Citziens, Lords and Ladies.*

1882.65 FATINITZA

A Revival of the Comic Opera in Three Acts[33]. (Original Viennese libretto to the operette by F. Zell and Richard Genée, based on the libretto to "La Circassienne" by Eugène Scribe.) Music by Franz von Suppé. Musical director, Signor Antonio DeNovellis. Produced by the Strakosch English

[31]Musical numbers not listed in programs. List prepared from published English piano vocal score (Joseph Williams, London, 1882), only interpolations noted in programs.

[32]First produced in New York 25 November 1844 at the Park Theatre for 17 performances in repertory. For Synopsis of Scenes and Musical Numbers, see original 1844 production. Interpolated for this revival:
"Bliss Forever Past"
Mrs. Z. S. Wallace
(Music and Lyrics by Michael William Balfe.)

[33]First produced in New York in English 22 April 1879 at the Fifth Avenue Theatre for 41 performances. For Synopsis of Scenes and Musical Numbers, see original 1879 production.

Opera Company. Opened 3 October 1882 (matinee) at the Grand Opera House in repertory; season closed 7 October 1882 after (2) performances in repertory.

CAST: *Vladimir* a young Russian Lieutenant, afterwards disguised as Fatinitza: Mrs. ZELDA SEGUIN WALLACE. *Princess Lydia Imanovna*, Niece of the Count: LETITIA FRISCH. *Count Timofey Kantchukoff*, a Russian General: EDWARD CONNELL. *Izzet Pacha*, Goveror of the Turkish Fort: VINCENT HOGAN. *Julian Hardy*, a Special Newspaper Correspondent: TOM KARL. *Russian Officers (3)*: *Captain Vasil*: Mr. Manara. *Lieutenant Osip*: H. Manrico. *Sergeant Steipann*: Willet Seaman. *Mustapha*, the Guardian of the Harem: Mr. Jourgans. *Cadets, Russian Soldiers, Bashi-Bazouks, Cossacks, Moorish Women, Slaves, Slave-Drivers, etc.*

Characters in the Karagois: *Jessuf*; *Surema*, his daughter; *Ben Jemin*, his slave; *Wiridah*, *Fatima*, two old gossips; *Ashmet*, keeper of the Menagerie: Several Slaves of the Harem.

1882.66 BILLEE TAYLOR

A Revival of the Nautical Comic Opera in Two Acts[34]. Libretto by Henry Pottinger Stephens. Music by Edward Solomon. Stage manager, H. A. Cripps. Produced under the personal supervision of Messrs. Stephens and Solomon. Produced under the management of James Barton. Opened 9 October 1882 at the Fifth Avenue Theatre and closed 14 October 1882 after 7 performances.[35]

CAST: *Captain, the Honorable Felix Flapper*, R. N. of H. M.'s *"Thunderbomb"*: W. H. SEYMOUR. *Sir Mincing Lane*, Knight: H. A. CRIPPS. *Billee Taylor*: HARRY DeLORME. *Ben Barnacle*: HARRY BROWN. *Christopher Crab*: SIGNOR BROCCOLINI. *Phoebe Fairleigh*: MARIE JANSEN. *Arabella Lane*: VERNONA JARBEAU. *Eliza Dabsey*: JENNIE HUGHES. *Susan*: ROSE CHAPELLE. *Specialty*: THE GIRARDS (Aesthetic Quadrille, Act 2). *Charity Girls, Soldiers, Sailors, etc.*

1882.67 LA TIMBALE D'ARGENT

A Revival of the Opéra-bouffe in Three Acts, in French.[36] Libretto by Adolphe Jaime and Jules Noriac. Music by Léon Vasseur. Stage manager, C. H. Darcy. Musical director, Mons. A. Lagye. Produced by Maurice Grau's French Opera Company. Opened 12 October 1882 at the Bijou Opera House and closed 14 (matinee) October 1882 after 2 performances in repertory; re-opened 23 October 1882 at the Fifth Avenue Theatre for 1 additional performance, 21-24 March 1883 at the Casino Theatre for 2 additional performances in repertory[37].

CAST: *Molda*: Mme. LOUISE THÉO. *Muller*: Mlle. BETTY. *Fichtel*: Mlle. BUISSON. *Mme. Barnabe*: Mlle. Vallot. *Gaben*: Mlle. Vandamme. *Pola*: Mlle. Adrienne. *Agathe*: Mlle. Caro. *Marza [Maya]*: Mlle. Delournay. *Raab*: Mons. DUPLAN. *Pruth*: Mons. J. MEZIÈRES. *Barnabe*: Mons. Vinchon. *Wilhelm*: Mons. Girard. *Walter*: Mons. Terrancle. *Gerome*: Mons. Ber. *Fritz*: Mons. Norbert. Chorus of 60.

1882.68 TROMPETTE

An Operetta in Three Acts, in German. (Original French[38]) Libretto by Henri Meilhac and Ludovic Halévy. Music by Charles Lecocq. Costumes by Charles Buchheister. Produced by Amberg's German Operetta Company (Adolf Neuendorff, Proprietor and Manager). Opened 13 October 1882 at the Germania Theatre in repertory.

CAST: *The Countess Cameroni*, Trompette: MARIE GEISTINGER. *Leaders of the Fronde (6)*: *The Duke*: Herr FRANZ MEYER. *The Duchess*: Frl. Schatz. *The Marquise*: Frl. Mellner. *The Baron*: Herr Schmidt. *The Baroness*: Frl. Beil. *The Vicomtesse*: Frl. Ehrlich. *Filoufine*, Intendant of the Count Cameroni: Herr Junker. *Officers of the Royal Army (7)*: *Manicamp*: Herr SCHÜTZ. *Invigne*: Herr Düring. *D'Estilly*: Herr Lenoir. *Perpignasse*: Herr Friedrich. *Montcarel*: Herr Wichert. *Chateaubrun*: Herr Mühlbauer. *Pont-Aubray*: Herr Herr Metsch. *Boisvillette*, Officer in the service of the Fronde: Herr SCHULTZE. *Taboureau*, tavern-keeper: Herr (Adolf) LINK. *Jacqueline*, his wife: Frl. SEEBOLD. *Bernard*, butcher: Herr SCHMITZ. *Madelon*, his wife: Frau HAUBRICH. *First Solo Violinist* of the King: Frl. Rudolfi. *Violinists of the King (6)*: *Jean*: Frl. Rother. *Jacques*: Frl. Clermont. *Charles*: Frl. Speranska. *Baptiste*: Frl. Kövesy. *Paul*: Frl. Reinecke. *Gaston*: Frl. Zugbaum. *A Sergeant*: Herr Beck. *A Stage Driver*: Herr Dehorn. *A Citizen*: Herr Prätorius. *A Bailiff*: Herr Malz. *A Servant*: Herr Paffhausen. *Soldiers of the Royal Army, Soldiers of the Fronde, Citizens of Paris, Wives of Citizens, Wedding Guests, Servants, Bailiffs.*

Act 1: Near Paris. 1652.

Act 2: In Paris.

Act 3: In the residence of Count Cameroni.

1882.69 FRIEND AND FOE

A Comedy in Five Acts. Play by Bartley Campbell. Music and Lyrics by William J. Scanlan. Stage director, Robert Johnston. Costumes by S. W. Laureys. Mechanical effects by W. Winnie. Musical director, Fred White. Produced by W. H. Power. Opened 16 October 1882 at the Windsor Theatre and closed 21 October 1882 after 8 performances.[39]

CAST: *Carrol Moore*: WILLIAM J. SCANLAN. *Quentin LaFont*: R. C. White. *Ambrose*: C. B. Hawkins. *Pierre Fontaine*: J. R. McCann. *Captain Rolfman*: P. Shelley. *Burkhan*, a Jailor: A. L. McCrany. *Gounod*: A. J. Spellman. *Corp. Manheim*: G. A. Foster. *Andrea Fontaine*: Florine Arnold. *Annette*: Annie Franklin. *Madam Bullville*: Sadie Radcliffe. *Cecile*: Blanche Whitney. *Soldiers, Peasants, etc.*

Act 1: The Choice.

Act 2: The Irish Volunteer.

Act 3: Arrest of the Patriot Spy.

Act 4: The Rescue.

Act 5: The Shamrock and the Lilly.

MUSICAL NUMBERS[40]

"I Love Music"
(W. J. Scanlan)
"The Poor Irish Minstrel"
(W. J. Scanlan)
"Moonlight at Killarney"
(W. J. Scanlan)
"Irish Potheen"
(W. J. Scanlan)
"Over the Mountain"
(W. J. Scanlan)
"Mrs. Reagan's Party" (Mrs. Reilly's Party)
(W. J. Scanlan)
"Peek-a-Boo"
(W. J. Scanlan)

1882.70 THE SORCERER

A Revival of the Comic Opera in Two Acts[41]. Libretto by William S. Gilbert. Music by Arthur Sullivan. Director of amusements, Jesse Williams. Scenery by (George W.) Dayton and (Harley) Merry. Costumes by (Henry) Dazian and P. Godchaux et Cie. Produced by the McCaull Opera Company (John A. McCaull). Opened 17 October 1882 at the Bijou Opera House and closed 6 January 1883 after 87 performances; re-opened 17 April 1883 at the Casino Theatre and closed 4 May 1883 after 21 additional performances. Total: 108 performances.

[34]First produced in New York 19 February 1881 at the Standard Theatre for 101 performances. For Synopsis of Scenes and Musical Numbers, see original 1881 production.

[35]Scenery, costumes and musical director uncredited in programs.

[36]First produced in New York in French 20 September 1876 at the Lyceum Theatre for 1 performance in repertory. For Synopsis of Scenes and Musical Numbers, see original 1876 production.

[37]The Fifth Avenue Theatre program notes that Mme. Théo will introduce two new chansonettes: "Bras dessus, bras dessous" and "Ne me chatouillez pas." The Casino program notes that Mme. Theo will introduce for the first time in New York the famous "Chanson du Colonel" from LA FEMME À PAPA.

[38]First produced in France as La Petite Mademoiselle, and in Germany as Die Feinden des Cardinals. German adaptation uncredited in program.

[39]No credits in programs for scenery.

[40]Added for subsequent tour: Scanlan's "Rose Song," "Bye, Bye, Baby, Bye, Bye," "My Nellie's Blue Eyes." Also published, and likely interpolated: "There's Always a Seat in the Parlor for You." "If I Catch That Man That Taught Her to Dance," "McDonnell's Old Tin Roof," "McCormack the Washer," "Rock Dat Ship."

[41]First produced 21 February 1879 at the Broadway Theatre for 20 performances. For Synopsis of Scene s and Musical Numbers, see original 1879 production.

CAST: *Aline*: LILLIAN RUSSELL. *Lady Sangazure*: LAURA JOYCE. *Constance*: MADELINE LUCETTE. *Mrs. Partlett*: JULIE de RUYTHER. *John Wellington Wells*: JOHN HOWSON. *Dr. Daly*: DIGBY BELL. *Sir Marmaduke*: GEORGE OLMI. *Alexis*: CHARLES J. CAMPBELL. *Notary*: George A. Schiller. *Buttons*: A. W. MAFLIN.

1882.71 THE QUEEN'S LACE HANDKERCHIEF

An Operetta in Three Acts. Original Viennese operette libretto ('Das Spitzentuch der Königin') by Bohrmann-Riegen[42] and Richard Genée. American adaptation by James Frenor. Music by Johann Strauss. Produced under the stage direction of Jesse Williams. Scenery by Harley Merry and Mr. Lippincott. Costumes by P. Godchaux et Cie. Orchestra under the direction of Ernst Catenhusen. Produced the McCaull Opera Comique Company (John A. McCaull, Proprietor and Manager), by arrangement with Townshend Percy. Opened 21 October 1882 at the Casino Theatre and closed 28 October 1882 after 8 performances; re-opened 30 December 1882 at the Casino Theatre and closed 10 March 1883 after an additional ??72 performances; re-opened 11 June 1883 at the Casino Theatre and closed 7 July 1883 after ?28 additional performances. Total: 113? performances.

CAST: *The King of Portugal*: LOUISE PAULLIN. *The Queen*: LILY POST. *Donna Irene*, the Queen's confidante: MATHILDE COTTRELLY. *Marquise of Villa Real*: JENNIE REIFFARTH. *Cervantes*, Poet: Signor PERUGINI. *Count Villalobos Rodriguez*: JOSEPH S. GREENSFELDER. *Don Sancho De Avellaneda y Villapinguedones*, Tutor to the King: GEORGE GASTON[43]. *Don Quixote*: JAY TAYLOR. *Marquis de la Marechal Villareal*, Minister of War: HARRY STANDISH. *Ministers (5)*: *Duke of Ferria*: Mr. McCREERY. *Count San Gregorio*: Mr. Dowd. *Count Lemos*: Mr. Ross. *Don Diego de Parades*: Mr. W. Taylor. *Brazilian Ambassador*: Mr. E. Horan. *Dancing Master*: Mr. Lellman. *Master of Ceremonies*: Mr. Kaufman. *Warden*: Mr. Tibbets. *Antonio*, Innkeeper of the Sierra Suazo: Mr. E. Aiken. *Officer of the King*: Annie Caldwell. *First Lady in Waiting*: Annette Hall. *Second Lady in Waiting*: Eme Duchateau. *Third Lady in Waiting*: Maud Haslam. *Chorus of 70*.

Act 1: The Royal Palace at Lisbon. (Merry.)

Act 2: Coronation Chamber in the Palace of the King of Portugal. (Lippincott.)

Act 3: Mountain Scene in Sierras. (Merry.)

ACT 1[44]
- Opening (I am the King's tutor)
  G. Gaston
- Romance and Duet
  L. Post, M. Cottrelly
- "Truffle Song"
  L. Paullin
- Duet
  G. Gaston, J. Taylor
- Finale

ACT 2
- Scene and Couplet
- Doctors Scene
- Cervantes Solo
  Signor Perugini
- Trio from CLAUDE DUVAL
  H. Standish, J. Taylor, G. Gaston
  (*Music by* Edward Solomon. *Lyrics by* Henry Pottinger Stephens.)
- Finale

ACT 3
- Couplet
  G. Gaston
- Finale

1882.72 OLIVETTE

A Revival of the Opérette in Three Acts.[45] Original French libretto ('Les Noces d'Olivette') by Henri Chivot and Alfred Duru. Music by Edmund Audran. Stage manager, Arthur LeClerq. Orchestra under the direction of Carl Christrup. Manager, A. R. Samuels. Opened 23 October 1882 at the Alcazar and closed 4 November 1882 after 14 performances.

CAST: *Olivette*: CATHERINE LEWIS. *Countess of Rousillon*: FANNY WENTWORTH. *Veloutine*: HATTIE DOLARO. *Moustique*: Alice Arlington. *Captain de Merrimac*: M. W. FISKE. *Valentine*: Harry DeLorme. *Duc des Ifs*: FRED DIXON. *Coquelicot*: J. E. Nash. *Marvejol*: A. Henderson. *L'Ecuriel*: S. A. L. Bentley. *Sailors, Villagers, etc.*

1882.73 LE VOYAGE EN CHINE

A Revival of the Opéra-comique in Three Acts, in French.[46] Libretto by Eugène Labiche and Alfred Delacour. Music by François Bazin. Stage manager, Charles Darcy. Musical director, Mons. A. Lagye. Produced by Maurice Grau's French Opera Company. Opened 24 October 1882 at the Fifth Avenue Theatre for 1 performance.

CAST: *Henri de Kernoisan*: Mons. N. MAIRE. *M. Pompéry*: Mons. Dangon. *Aledor de Rosenville*: Mons. Ducos. *Maurice Fréval*: Mons. NOE. *Bonneteau*: Mons. J. MEZIÈRES. *Martial*: Mons. Vinchon. *Marie (Pompéry)*: Mlle. ANAIS PRIVAT. *Caroline*: Mme. Thal. *Berthe Pompéry*: Mme. DORSAY.

1882.74 MORDECAI LYONS

A Local Play in Three Acts, a Prologue and 5 Scenes. Play (and lyrics) by Edward Harrigan. Music by David Braham. Staged by Edward Harrigan. Scenery by Charles W. Witham. Musical director, David Braham. Produced by (Edward) Harrigan and (Tony) Hart. Opened 26 October 1882 at the Theatre Comique and closed 25 November 1882 after 36 performances.

CAST (Prologue): *Confidence Bob*: JOHN WILD. *Dad Bailey*: William Gray. *Jack Hastings*: HARRY FISHER. *Dr. Rchard Carroll*: M. F. Drew. *Boy*: Master Guion. *Officers*: Joseph Sparks, M. Foley, John Sparks. *Alice Hastings*: Mattie Earle. *Esther Lyons*, a Child: Little Katie Scallan. *Mordecai Lyons*: EDWARD HARRIGAN. *Leon Mendoza*: TONY HART.

(Act 1): *Charles Chester*: Mark Price. *Confidence Bob*: JOHN WILD. *Dad Bailey* (with Song): William Gray. *Jack Hastings*: HARRY FISHER. *Palmeston Bunker*: Edward Burt. *D'Arcy Livingston*: John Queen. *Sydney Withers*: M. F. Drew. *Orion Speed*: M. Bradley. *Mr. Lullaby*: WILLIAM WEST. *Stephen Radcliffe*: William Scallan. *Warren*, a Servant: Charles Coffey. *Jimmy Reilly* (with Song): GEORGE MERRITT. *Barnaby Guy* (with Song): William H. Merritt. *Filkins*: James Fitzsimmons. *Littleton Spence*: J. McCullough. *Addison Adze*: W. Atkins. *Mordecai Lyons*: EDWARD HARRIGAN. *Leon Mendoza*: TONY HART. *Mlle. Esther*: Anna Mack Berlein. *Miss Downing*: Mattie Earle. *Mary Radcliffe*: GERTIE GRANVILLE. *Elizabeth Radcliffe*: Ada Farwell. *Mrs. Scallop*: Susan Byron. *Kittie*, a Maid: Sadie Morris. *Flower Girl*: Annie Langdon.

Prologue: Mordecai Lyons' Old Clothes Shop and Loan Office.

Act 1: The Radcliffe Villa on the Hudson. Eighteen years later. The Convict.

Act 2, Scene 1: The "Victoria Shades." The interior of an English chop-house. The "Free and Easy.' *Scene 2*: Theatre Alley. *Scene 3*: Dressing-Room in Theatre. The Curse.

Act 3: Interior of Radcliffe Mansion. Five months later. The Wedding.

MUSICAL NUMBERS[47]
- "Mordecai Lyons"
- "Cash, Cash, Cash"
- "The Old Bowery Pit"
- "She Lives on Murray Hill"
- "When the Clock in the Tower (Station) Strikes Twelve"

---

[42]Heinrich Bohrmann and Julius von St. Albino Nigri (whose pen name was Riegen) wrote the first version of the libretto.

[43]For return engagement in December 1882, Francis Wilson succeeded George Gaston as Don Sancho.

[44]Musical numbers not listed in programs. List prepared from production prompt book.

[45]First presented in New York 25 December 1880 at the Bijou Opera House for 63 performances. For Synopsis of Scenes and Musical Numbers, see original 1880 production. Adaptation uncredited.

[46]First produced in New York 11 January 1875 at the Park Theatre for (11) performances in repertory. For Synopsis of Scenes and Musical Numbers, see original 1875 production.

[47]Not necessarily in performance order.

1882.75 RIP VAN WINKLE

A Romantic Opera in Three Acts, 5 Scenes. Libretto by H. B. Farnie, (Henri Meilhac and Philippe Gille), revised by Dion Bouciault. (Based on Washington Irving's 'Rip Van Winkle' and 'The Legend of Sleepy Hollow.') Music by Robert Planquette. Stage under the direction of Charles Harris. Scenery by George W Dayton. Costumes designed by Wilhelm. Mechanical effects by Fillery. Music under the direction of Alfred Cellier. Produced by Richard D'Oyly Carte's Opera Company (Helen Lenoir, Manager). Opened 28 October 1882 at the Standard Theatre and closed 23 November 1882 after 28 performances.

CAST: *Rip Van Winkle*: WILLIAM T. CARLETON. *Nick Vedder,* Landlord of the George III Inn: RICHARD MANSFIELD. *Knickerbocker*, Village Schoolmaster: W. H. SEYMOUR. *Derrick Van Slous*, the Village Lawyer: ARTHUR ROUSEBY. *Captain Rowley* of the Grenadiers: ARTHUR WILKINSON. *Tom Tit*, an Officer: Billie Barlow. *Peter Van Dunk*, the Burgomaster: J. H. RYLEY. *Gretchen*, Rip Van Winkle's wife: SALLIE REBER. *Little Alice*, Rip's daughter: THEODORA LINDA daCOSTA. *Little Hans*, Nephew of Derrick: Maggie Gonzales. *Little Jan Vedder*, Katrina's brother: Pollie Gillow. *Sara*: Mina Rowley. *Jacintha*: Alice Gresham. *Minnie*: Ida Weddle. *Katrina*, Vedder's daughter: SELINA DOLARO. *Dan*: Clara Wisdom. *Hermann*: Ada Vickars.

The Goblin Crew of Hendrik Hudson: *Hendrik Hudson*, the Phantom Captain: ARTHUR ROUSBY. *First Lieutenant*: LLEWELLYN CADWALLADR [Lyn Cadwallader]. *Second Lieutenant*: W. Gillow. *The Goblin Dwarf*: William White. *Third Lieutenant*: Lillie Shandley. *Fourth Lieutenant*: Billie Barlow. *Fifth Lieutenant*: Alice Gresham.

Act 3: *Alice Van Winkle*, Daughter of Rip, the little child of Act 1: SALLIE REBER. *Jan Vedder*, Proprietor of the George Washington Hotel, the little Jan of Act 1: RICHARD MANSFIELD. *Lieutenant Van Slous* of the U.S. Frigate Constitution, the little Hans of Act 1: L. LLEWELLYN CADWALLADR [Lyn Cadwallader].

Act 1: Sleepy Hollow on the Hudson.

Act 2, Scene 1: Tangled Brake in the Kaatskills. *Scene 2*: The Haunted Glen in the Kaatskills.

Act 3, Scene 1: The Haunted Glen after Twenty Years. *Scene 2*: Wide Awakeville on the Hudson.

ACT 1[48]

"Far and Near" (Chorus)/
"On this Solemnity" (Scene)/
"Sweet Sir" (Couplets)
S. Reber, J. H. Ryley, S. Delaro, R. Mansfield, Chorus
"Yes, No and Nothing at all" (Rondo)
S. Delaro, Chorus
Exit of Peasants
Chorus
"Oh! Where's my Girl?"
W. T. Carleton
"Where Floweth the Wild Mohawk River" (Canoe Song for 2 Voices)
S. Reber, W. T. Carleton
"Can't you See?" (Chorus of Cowards)
"Oh! Beware!" (Legend of the Kaatskils)
S. Reber, Chorus
"Ere the Marriage Contract" (Trio)/
W. T. Carleton, M. Gonzales, T. L. daCosta
"These Little Heads (Now Golden)" (Air)
W. T. Carleton, Children
"Where Is the Woman?" (Song)
A. Rouseby
"The Village Well" (Truth in the Well)(Rondo)
S. Delaro, Chorus
"When I Come Back" (Finale, Act 1)
Principals, Chorus

ACT 2
Scene 1
"By the Thicket" (Lantern Chorus)
"Now the Twilight Shadows" (Ballad)
S. Reber, S. Delaro, Chorus
"The Night Is Dark" (Patrol Chorus)
Chorus
"Van Vattel's Vengeance" (Song)
J. H. Ryley, Chorus
"Now Won't You Come? (Trio)
S. Reber, W. T. Carleton, A. Rouseby
"Echo Song"
W. T. Carleton, Chorus
Scene 2
"The Phantoms" (Scene and Chorus)
"Blow high, blow low!" (Sea Song)
A. Rouseby, W. T. Carleton, Chorus
"On the Grassy Banks of Scheldt" (Nine-pins Song and Chorus)
W. Gillow, Chorus
"My Pipe!" (Serenade)
L. Cadwalladyr, Chorus
"May you Live and Prosper!" (Drinking Song)
W. T. Carleton, Chorus
"Slumber, Mortal!" (Sestett & Chorus, Finale Act 2)
Principals, Chorus

ACT 3
"Woodcutters' Chorus"
"Whatsoever may be won" (Election Chorus)
"Ladies Cannot sit in Congress" (Couplets and Ensemble)
S. Delaro, Chorus
"True Love from o'er the Sea" (The Letter Song)
T. L. DaCosta
"Rock'd upon the Billow!" (Hammock Song and Chorus)
L. Cadwalladyr, Chorus
"Truth in the Well" (Song)
W. T. Carleton
"I Know you not!" (Trio)
T. L. DaCosta, L. Cadwalladyr, W. T. Carleton
"Some Say"
Chorus
Finale
Principals, Chorus

1882.76 THE TOURISTS IN A PULLMAN PALACE CAR

A Revised Version of the Nonsensical and Musical Play in Three Acts[49]. Play by William A. Mestayer. Stage manager, J. N. Long. Director of orchestra, Max Horter. Manager, H. W. Brown. Opened 6 November 1882 at the Alcazar and closed 11 November 1882 after 7 performances; returned 11-16 June 1883 to the Cosmopolitan Theatre for an additional 7 performances. Total: 14 performances.

CAST: *Miss Baby*, (the Pet) a Gushing Damsel, not too gushing, but just gush enough: THERESA VAUGHN. *Miss Isabella*, her sister, a Quiet Damsel, not too quiet, but just quiet enough: LIZZIE OTT. *Miss Pamela*, their Aunt, an old maid—not too old a maid, but just old enough: ELLA HATTON. *Marie*, their maid, a Fresh Damsel, not too fresh, but just fresh enough: ELSA BROSI. *T. Henry Slum*, a disciple of Banting—not too much banting, but just anti-Fat enough: WILLIAM A. MESTAYER. *Sir Henry Cashmere*, a Nob, not too much nob, but just, etc.: J. N. LONG. *Jacob Krause*, the Detective. Not too much Detective, but just, etc.: CHARLES STURGES. *Solomon Goldsteine*, a Special—not too Special, etc.: HARRY CLARKE. *Hobbs*, a Butler. Not too much, etc.: THOMAS A. DALY. (*Male and female passengers*. Not too much Male and Female, but just a little Neuter.)

ACT 2 and 3: *T. Henry Slum*: W. A. MESTAYER. *Faro Jack*: W. A. MESTAYER. *Louis*, French Butler: J. N. LONG. *Sir Henry Cashmere*: J. N. LONG. *Hon. Augustus Bilk*: Harry Clarke. *Conductor*: CHARLES STURGESS. *Porter of the Pullman Palace Car*: THOMAS A. DALY. *Book-Agent*: JOE OTT. *Miss Baby*: THERESA VAUGHN. *German Emigrant*: THERESA VAUGHN. *Marie*: ELSA BROSI. *Aunt Pamela*: ELLA HATTON. *Isabel*: LIZZIE OTT. (*Quartette*: Messrs. Long, Clarke; Misses Vaughn and Brosi.)

---

[48]Musical numbers not listed in programs. List prepared from published English piano vocal score (Chappell & Co., London, 1882), which does not reflect alterations and interpolations to the score for the American production.

[49]First produced in New York in two engagements 3 November 1879 and 5 January 1880 at Haverly's Lyceum Theatre for a total of 64 performances. For Synopsis of Scenes, see original 1879 production.

ACT 1[50]
"Shirt Song"
W. A. Mestayer, Chorus
ACT 2
"Who Killed Cock Robin?"/
"How Can I Leave Thee?"/
"A Little More Cider"
Quartette
Vocal Eccentricities
T. A. Daly
German Medley
T. Vaughn
Aunt Pamela's "Discords"/
"Songs of the Times"
"Cats on the Garden Wall"
T. A. Daly, C. Sturgess
"Echoes from Germany"
H. Clarke
Book-Agent's Harmonica
J. Ott
The Tourist Grenadiers (Specialty)
ACT 3
"Sweet and Low"/"Steal Away"
Quartette
Ethiopian melodies
T. A. Daly, Chorus
Finale: Selection from THE MASCOTTE

1882.77

THE BLACK CROOK

A Revival of the Extravaganza in Four Acts, Sixteen Scenes[51]. (Book by Charles M. Barras. Music composed and selected by Thomas Baker, Louis Baer, A. W. Hoffman.) Produced under the personal supervision of Imre and Bolossy Kiralfy. Produced by Imre and Bolossy Kiralfy. Opened 13 November 1882 at Haverly's 14th Street Theatre and closed 2 December 1882 after 24 performances; returned 14 May 1883 to the Grand Opera and closed 19 May 1883 after an additional 8 performances.

CAST: *Mortals*: *Hertzog*, surnamed the Black Crook, alchemist and sorcerer: JAMES F. PETERS. *Count Wolfenstein*: W. F. WALLIS. *Rudolph*, a poor artist: WILL A. SANDS. *Greppo*, a Henchman (with song): ARTHUR MOULTON. *Von Puffengruntz*, the Count's Chamberlain: WELSH EDWARDS. *Wulfgar*: Leonard Ruppel. *Bruno*: W. Ronaldo. *Armina*, a village Maiden: Fannie Desmond. *Dame Barbara*: Florence Vincent. *Carline*: Neila Smart. *Rosetta*: Mlle. Leontine.

Immortals: *Stalacta*, the Fairy Queen (with songs): NELLIE LARKELLE.

Attendant Fairies: *Caraline*: Nellie Sexton. *Dewdrop*: Kate Wilson. *Diamantine*: Polly Higginson. *Brilliantine*: Nellie Weston. *Sapphitine*: Jennie Timmony. *Pearline*: Ella Dunbar.

Sprities: *Dragonfin*: Young America. *Bristleup*: R. Leonardo.

Demons: *Zamiel*: Frank Richmond. *Skuldewelf*: Charles Blesser. *Redglare*: Philip Dow. *Blueblaze*: John Fisher. *Sulphurino*: J. J. Henry. *Ashgash*: David W. Smith.

Ballet: Mlles. DeROSA, ASTEGGIANO. *European Specialties*: The Great Garnellas (Bob and Dick, the Acrobatic Wonders), Duncan (ventriloquist), Les Trois Incroyables (grotesque eccentricities), Martens Family (Tyrolean Warblers).

BALLETS AND MUSICAL NUMBERS
Festive Dance by Coryphées (Act 1, Scene 1)
The Live Skeleton; Grand Tableau Infernale (Act 1, Scene 5)
"Stalacta" (Song) (Act 2, Scene 2)
Grand Stalacta Ballet (Act 2, Scene 2)
Mlles. DeRosa, Asteggiano, Corps de Ballet
Entrée des Syrenes; Entrée Mlle. Asteggiano; Variations, Mlle. DeRosa; Finale.
European Specialities; Grand Ballet of All Nations (Act 3, Scene 1)
Entrée de Nations; Grand Pas de Champagne, "Goldlack" by Secondas Danseuses; Original Arabian Dance, "The Odalisque" by Mlle. Asteggiano; Csardas by Secondas; U.S. America, Mlle. DeRosa; Les Britons, Corps de Ballet; Pas de Matelot, Coryphées; Finale Brilliante, Entire Coryphées and Corps de Ballet.
Duncan (Ventriloquist);"Cat Duet" (Act 4, Scene 1)
Martens Family
Grand Amazonian March (Act 4, Scene 2)
N. Larkelle, Corps de Ballet
Grand Finale Apotheosis (Act 5, Scene 5)

1882.78

IOLANTHE,
or, The Peer and The Peri

A Fairy (Comic) Opera in Two Acts. Libretto by William S. Gilbert. Music by Arthur Sullivan. Stage under the direction of Charles Harris. Scenery by George W. Dayton & Son. Peers' costumes made by Frank Smith & Co., London; fairies' costumes by Alias, London. Musical director, Alfred Cellier[52]. Produced by Richard D'Oyly Carte's Opera Company (Helen Lenoir, Manager). Opened 25 November 1882 at the Standard Theatre, closing 24 February 1883 after 89 performances; re-opened under the stage direction of James Barton 5 March 1883 at the Fifth Avenue Theatre and closed 17 March 1883 after 16 additional performances. Total: 105 performances.

CAST: *Strephon*: WILLIAM T. CARLETON. *Lord Mount Ararat*: ARTHUR WILKINSON. *Lord Tolloller*: LLEWELLYN CADWALLADR [Lyn Cadwaladr]. *Private Willis* (a Sentry): Lithgow James. *The Trainbearer*: William White. *The Lord Chancellor*: J. H. RYLEY. *Chorus of Peers*.

Iolanthe: MARIE JANSEN. *The Fairy Queen*: AUGUSTA ROCHE. *Celia*: MINA ROWLEY. *Leila*: KATE FORSTER. *Fleta*: Billie Barlow. *Phyllis*: SALLIE REBER. *Chorus of Fairies*.

Act 1: An Arcadian landscape. Between 1700 and 1882.

Act 2: The Palace Yard, Westminster.

ACT 1[53]
Opening Chorus of Fairies, Soli ("Tripping hither, tripping thither")
M. Rowley, K. Forster
Invocation ("Iolanthe! From thy dark exile thou art summoned")
A. Roche, M. Jansen, M. Rowley, K. Forster, Chorus of Fairies
Entrance of Strephon: Solo ("Good morrow, good mother")
W. T. Carleton, Chorus of Fairies
Exit of Fairies: Solo ("Fare thee well, attractive stranger")
A. Roche, Chorus of Fairies
Entrance of Phyllis: Soli ("Good morrow, good lover!")
S. Reber, W. T. Carleton
Duet ("None shall part us from each other")
S. Reber, W. T. Carleton
Entrance and March of Peers ("Loudly let the trumpet bray")
Tenors, Basses
Entrance of Lord Chancellor: Song ("The law is the true embodiment")
J. H. Ryley, Chorus of Peers
Trio and Chorus of Peers ("My well-loved lord and guardian dear")
S. Reber, L. Cadwalladr, A. Wilkinson

[50]Added for return engagement:
"Locomotive Gallop"
(*Music by* Max Horter.)
"Tourists' March"
(*Music by* Max Horter.)
"Must we then part forever?"
Quartet
"The Lover and the Bird"
Ella Caldwell [Miss Isabella]
"Songs of the Porter"
W. H. Bray [Hobbs]
"Peek-a-Boo"
T. Vaughn, J. Ott
"Conductor's Comicalities"
C. Sturges
"Spanish Song"
Anetta Zelma [Marie]

[51]First produced in New York 12 September 1866 at Niblo's Garden for 475 performances.

[52]Henry J. Widmer was musical director for the Fifth Avenue Theatre engagement.

[53]Musical numbers not listed in programs. List prepared from published English piano vocal score (Chappell & Co., Ltd., 1882).

Recitative ("Nay, tempt me not")
S. Reber
Chorus of Peers and Song ("Spurn not the nobly born")
L. Cadwalladr, Chorus
"Lords, it may not be!"
S. Reber, L. Cadwalladr, A. Wilkinson, W. T. Carleton, J. H. Ryley, Chorus of Peers
Song ("When I went to the Bar as a very young man")
J. H. Ryley
Finale Act 1 ("When darkly looms the day")
S. Reber, M. Jansen, A. Roche, K. Forster, M. Rowley, W. T. Carleton, L. Cadwalldr, A. Wilkinson, J. H. Ryley, Chorus of Fairies and Peers

ACT 2
Song ("When all night long a chap remains")
L. James
Chorus of Fairies and Peers ("Strephon's a member of Parliament!")
Chorus
Song ("When Britain truly ruled the waves")
A. Wilkinson, Chorus
Duet ("In vain you plead to us, Don't go!")
K. Forster, M. Rowley, Chorus of Fairies, A. Wilkinson, L. Cadwalladr
Song ("Oh, foolish fay")
A. Roche, Chorus of Fairies
Quartette ("Tho' p'raps I may incur your blame")
S. Reber, L. Cadwalladr, A. Wilkinson, L. James
Recitative and Song ("Love, unrequited, robs me of my rest")
J. H. Ryley
Trio ("He who shies at such a prize")
L. Cadwalladr, A. Wilkinson, J. H. Ryley
Recitative and Song ("My Bill has now been read a second time")
W. T. Carleton
Duet ("If we're weak enough to tarry")
S. Reber, W. T. Carleton
Recitative and Ballad ("My lord, a suppliant at your feet I kneel")
M. Jansen
Recitative ("It may not be—for so the fates decide!")
M. Jansen, A. Roche, J. H. Ryley, Fairies
Finale Act 2 ("Soon as we may, off and away!")
S. Reber, M. Jansen, A. Roche, K. Forster, M. Rowley, L. Cadwalldr, A. Wilkinson, W. T. Carleton, J. H. Ryley, Chorus of Fairies and Peers

1882.79 McSORLEY'S INFLATION

A Local Comedy in Three Acts, 4 Scenes. Play (and lyrics) by Edward Harrigan. Music by David Braham. Staged by Edward Harrigan. Scenery by Charles W. Witham. Mechanical effects by William McMurray. Properties by Robert Puller. Musical director, David Braham. Produced by (Edward) Harrigan and (Tony) Hart. Opened 27 November 1882 at the Theatre Comique and closed 31 March 1883 after 141 performances.

CAST: *Peter McSorley*: EDWARD HARRIGAN. *Bridget McSorley*: TONY HART. *Rufus Rhubarb*: JOHN WILD. *Major Wabble*: James Fox. *Coroner Slab*: Edward Burt. *August Funke*: Harry A. Fisher. *Lavinia Donovan*: John Queen. *John Killaleen*: John Queen. *Deputy Brush*: M. F. Drew. *Tim Sullivan*: M. Bradley. *Senator Lightning*: WILLIAM WEST. *Catherine McAlarney*: JOSEPH SPARKS. *Rosey O'Brien*: JOHN SPARKS. *Tom Tough*: M. Foley. *Sid Baker*: G. L. Stout. *Caleb Nocake*: William Merritt. *Sam Goodacre*: George Merritt. *Clerk of the Market*: William Scallan. *Carl Funke*: Charles Coffey. *Hung Lung*: J. McCullough. *Jamesey*: Master Guion. *Mary McKeon*: Anna Mack Berlein. *Annie Dempsey*: GERTIE GRANVILLE. *Mrs. Bagley*: Annie D. Ware. *Sister Prudence*: Susie Byron. *Sister Seldon*: Ada Farwell. *Newsboys, Policemen, Citizens, Delegates, Butchers, Hucksters.*

The Charleston Blues, Act 3: *Captain*: J. Wild. *Sergeant*: J. Fox. *Privates*: W. West, J. Queen, W. Merritt, M. F. Drew, G. Merritt, Joseph Sparks, John Sparks, J. McCullough, C. Coffey, J. Fitzsimmons, D. Christie, R. Snyder, M. Benson.

Act 1: The Home of the McSorley's. "The Swell."

Act 2, Scene 1: The Coroner's Office and August Funke's Beer Tunnel. *Scene 2*: McNally's Flats. The Colored Convention. "The Expansion."

Act 3: Washington Market on Saturday Night.

MUSICAL NUMBERS
"Songs for the People"
"I Never Drink Behind the Bar"
"The Market on Saturday Night" (Act 1)
T. Hart, Female Friends
"The Old Feather Bed" (Act 2)
T. Hart, Female Friends
"McNally's Row of Flats"
"The Salvation Army, O!" (Act 3)
J. Wild, Salvation Army Band (5)
"The Charleston Blues" (Act 3)
J. Wild, the Charleston Blues
Xylophone Solo
E. King

1882.80 THE ELECTRIC SPARK

A Comic Opera in Three Acts. Libretto by Charles F. Pidgin. Music by Charles D. Blake. Musical director, H. Braham. Produced by Atkinson's Jolities (Charles Atkinson, Proprietor and Manager). Opened 27 November 1882 at the Alcazar and closed 9 December 1882 after 15 performances.

CAST: *John Senior Bull*, an old toy maker, much inclined to magic, electricity, fits of passion, very absent-minded, but who tries to "remember to remember": HARRY BROWN. *John Junior Bull*, his only son, very boyish, very smart in his own opinion, very handsome, very sympathetic, "too bad, poor thing!" very much in love with Sally: FRANK DANIELS. *Tom Bright*, his only nephew, very lazy, in his uncle's opinion, very hungry, very fond of dancing, much in love with Daisy: ALEX M. BELL. *Daisy Dane*, the village belle, very young, very smart, very bright, very much in love with Tom: AMY LEE. *Sarah Ann Smiles*, Mr. Bull's housekeeper, very impudent, "I say, I say, of course," very coquettish, very fond of dress, very sure she will get a rich husband: JENNIE YEAMANS. *Prince Mephisto*, his Satanic Majesty on a lark, very powerful, very diabolic, very hospitable, very shrewd: Tom Bright [Alex M. Bell]. *Miss Fortune*, very cute, very cunning, very much inclined to raise a rumpus, very successful in doing so: Daisy Dane [Amy Lee]. *The Tyrolean Peasant Boy*, very petite, piquant, pretty, precocious: Sarah Smiles [Jennie Yeamans].

1882.81 IRISH ARISTOCRACY

A Farce Comedy in Three Acts. Play by William Carleton. Management, S. M. Hickey. Opened and closed 30 November 1882 at the Academy of Music after 2 performances.[54]

CAST: *Michael Muldoon*: HUGH FAY. *Michael Mulcahey*: WILLIAM BARRY. *O'Roger Mulcahey*, just landed: John T. Sullivan. *Peter Belcher*, a practical joker: THOMAS F. BRENNAN. *John Mandamus*, attorney at law: THOMAS Q. SEABROOKE. *Charley Riddle*, a doctor: CHARLES BARTON. *Mrs. Muldoon*: Mrs. JENNIE FISHER. *Miss Honore Muldoon*: MARY LEECE. *Phebe Plympkins*: MYRA GOODWIN. *Little Jennie Muldoon*: Little Jessie Storey.

Acts 1 and 2: Home of Muldoon.

Act 3: The Picnic.

1882.82 JOSHUA WHITCOMB

A (Revised Version of the) Comedy Drama in Four Acts[55]. Play by Denman Thompson. Produced by Denman Thompson. Opened 18 December 1882 at Haverly's 14th Street Theatre and closed 30 December 1882 after 14 performances; returned 12 February 1883 to the Grand Opera House and closed 17 February 1883 after an additional 7 performances.[56]

---

[54]Program note: Introducing The Celebrated Trick Donkey, Danger; Muldoon and Mulcahey on Wheels; the famous Three-handed Reel. Reviewers remarked that the play was a re-working of "Muldoon's Picnic."

[55]Premiere of a longer four-act version; previously produced in a shorter one-act version 3 April 1875 at the Globe Theatre for 16 performances, and in a three-act version 2 September 1878 at the Lyceum Theatre for 93 performances. Songs added during subsequent tour:
"The Little Stars Won't Tell"
J. Wilson, I. Martinetti
"Moonlight Shadows"
J. Wilson, I. Martinetti
"When Pansies Droop and Die"
J. Wilson
"My Jack Is a Sailor"
J. Wilson

[56]No programs found for this engagement; cast list prepared from September 1883 tour. No musical numbers listed in programs.

CAST: *Uncle Josh*, an old Jackson democrat: DENMAN THOMPSON. . *Roundy*, a boot black: IGNACIO MARTINETTI. *John Martin*, a lover of horse racing and theatres: MYRON CALICE. *Frederick Dolby*, a young Englishman: Walter Gale. *Cy. Prime*, nigh on to eighty: George A. Beane. *Bill Johnson*, a loafer, just as bad as they make 'em: R. Benson. *Reuben Whitcomb*, Joshua's son: Eugene Van Dusen. *Mr. Burroughs*, a model policeman: G. Adams. *Tot*, a crossing sweeper: JULIA WILSON. *Nellie Primrose*, a Boston belle: Isabelle Coe. *Susie Martin*, with a mania for marriage: Edith Murilla. *Mrs. Johnson*, Tot's mother: Edna Weedon. *Aunt Matilda*, Joshua's sister: Mrs. D. Nourse. *Amantha Bartlett*, one of the neighbor's gals: F. Roberts.

Act 1: Uncle Josh's Arrival in Boston.

Act 2: Uncle Josh at Birthday Party.

Act 3: Uncle Josh at the Drunkard's Home.

Act 4: Joshua's New England Home.

1883.01

FRITZ AMONG THE GYPSIES

A German Dialect Comedy in Three Acts. Play by Joseph K. Emmet. Stage manager, William C. Miller. Produced by Joseph K. Emmet (George W. Wilton, Manager). Opened 1 January 1883 at Haverly's (14th Street) Theatre and closed 10 February 1883 after 42 performances.[57]

CAST: *Fritz*, in search of a brother: JOSEPH K. EMMET. *Aron Melchior*, Chief of a Gypsy Tribe: WILLIAM C. [Christie] MILLER. *Chevalier Rockley*, the Mysterious Visitor: CHARLES SUTTON. *Bruno*, one of a neighboring tribe: Charles Abbott. *Mike Finnegan*, a detective: Joseph P. Wade. *Jenkins*, an English comique: J. O'Rourke. *Adolphus Snow*, an Ethiopian: W. J. Donnelly. *Zillah*, Pearl of the Gypsy Tribe: GEORGIA TYLER. *Linda*, a Yankee girl: JENNIE CHRISTIE. *Blissa*, a Gypsy Fortune Teller: Lizzie Scanlan. *Klina*, a Foundling: Little Peggie Miller. *Little Schneider*: Little Peggie Miller.

MUSICAL NUMBERS[58]

"Bells Are Ringing"
"Don't You Wish You Had"
"Emmet's Cuckoo Song"
"Emmet's Sweel Song"
"Kiss Me or Darling Baby Come"
"The Love of the Shamrock""Sweet Violets"
"Wake Out"
"I Know What Love Is"
"Wilheindrick Strauss"

1883.02

MULDOON'S PICNIC

A Revival of the Irish Play (Farce Comedy) in One Act, 3 Scenes[59], preceded by an Olio. Produced by Tony Pastor. Opened 8 January 1883 at Tony Pastor's 14th Street Theatre and closed 20 January 1883 after 16 performances; re-opened 26 March 1883 at Tony Pastor's 14th Street Theatre and closed 31 March 1883 after 8 additional performances.

Olio CAST: The Ordeys (Karoly, Augusta), The Kernells, Nimmie Kent, Flora Pike, Florence Bell; May and Flora Irwin, Jacques Kruger in a musical sketch, Opera Mad; or, Trovatore Ill-treated in the kitchen; John E. Henshaw, May Ten Broeck in their original musical travesty, Deception!

CAST: *Michael Muldoon*: HARRY KERNELL. *Dennis Mulcahey*: DAN COLLYER. *Tim O'Brien*: John Kernell. *Charles Lovelace*: Frank Budworth. *Reverend Mr. Brown*: Frank Girard. *Policeman*: Joseph Buckley. *Cornelius Donahue*: John H. Henshaw. *Roger O'Malley*: Tommy Granger. *Clarence McSweeney*: Rich Coleman. *Oscar Cassidy*: Eddy Joyce. *Mrs. Muldoon*: JENNIE SATTERLEE. *Mrs. O'Brien*: FLORA IRWIN. *Ella Muldoon*: May Irwin. *Jennie Muldoon*: Camilla Bennett. *Mrs. Montrose*: Beebe Vining. *Mrs. O'Malley*: Florence Bell. (*Policemen, Ministers, Picnickers in abundance.*)

Scene 1: The Home of Muldoon. *Scene 2*: Going to the Picnic. *Scene 3*: The Picnic. (Wait for the Finale, the great Three-Handed Reel.)

[57]No credits for stage direction, scenery, costumes, musical direction in programs. Musical numbers not listed in programs. List prepared from published piano vocal gems (Joseph A. Church, NY).

[58]Musical numbers not listed in programs. List prepared from published piano vocal gems (Church).

[59]First produced in New York 9 January 1882 at Niblo's Garden for 24 performances. Authorship uncredited for this production; no other credits in program.

1883.03

HIGH AND LENGTHY, or The Steer and the Peri

A Burlesque of Gilbert and Sullivan's "Iolanthe" in Two Acts, accompanied by an Olio. Produced by Birch, Hamilton and Backus' San Francisco Minstrels. Opened 8 January 1883 at the San Francisco Opera House and closed 20 January 1883 after 14 performances.

CAST: *Lord Chancellor*: WILLIAM HAMILTON. *Iolanthe*: DESDEMONA BIRCH. *Syphon*: BILLY SWEATNAM. *The Fairy Queen*: CHARLES SALVINI BACKUS. *Oil of Nary a Rat*: BOB SLAVIN. *Blushing and Beautiful Fairy Creatures*: Ricardo and the Madrigal Boys.

1883.04

VIRGINIA; or, Ringing the Changes

A Comic Opera (Operatic Extravaganza) in Two Acts. Libretto by Henry Pottinger Stephens. Music by Edward Solomon. Scenery by Mr. (Walter) Burridge. Costumes by (Henry) Dazian and P. Godchaux. Director of amusements, Jesse Williams. Produced by McCaull Opera Company (John McCaull, Proprietor and Manager), by arrangement with Messrs. Brooks and Dickson. Opened 9 January 1883 at the Bijou Opera House and closed 14 February 1883 after 37 performances.

CAST: *Nicholas de Ville*, a mysterious personage: JOHN HOWSON. *Paul Plantagenet*, a Gamekeeper, (in love with Virginia): CHARLES J. CAMPBELL. *Robinson Brown Jones*, a railway guard: GEORGE OLMI. *Samuel Nubbles*, a "Navvy": DIGBY BELL. *Signor Macaroni*, a prominent photographer: A. W. MAFLIN. *Lady Magnolia*, a Landed Proprietress: EMIE WEATHERSBY. *Virginia Somerset*, a Goose Girl: LUCY COUCH. *Mrs. Cowslip*, a Farmeress: LAURA JOYCE. *Amy*, the Grocer's Daughter: Emma Guthrie. *Alice*, the Butcher's Daughter: Victoria Reynolds. *Mildred*, the Bookseller's Daughter: Nelly Howard. (*Peasants, Milkmaids, Navvies, Butchers, etc.*)

Time: The Impossible Present.

Act 1: The Farm on the Cliff.

Act 2: The Town of Clifton-Super-Mare.

ACT 1[60]

"Merry May" (Opening Chorus)
Villagers
"Mrs. Cowslip's Lament" (Just one and twenty years ago)
L. Joyce
"The Family Foundling" (Quartette)
G. Olmi, E. Guthrie, V. Reynolds, N. Howard
Recitative and "The Red Rover" (Song)
J. Howson
"Cock-a-doodle-do" (Chorus of Milkmaids)
Entrance and Song (Oh, what a scamper I've had on the lea!)
L. Couch, Milkmaids
"Boys, Boys, Boys" (Chorus of Younger Sons)
"Lady Magnolia" (Song)
E. Weathersby, L. Couch, Younger Sons
"Grandmother Told Me So" (Song)
L. Couch
"The Ring Makes the World Go Round" (Quintet)
L. Couch, E. Weathersby, G. Olmi, C. J. Campbell, J. Howson
"Love's Seasons" (Waltz Quartet)
L. Couch, E. Weathersby, C. J. Campbell, G. Olmi
"Frollicking" (Duet)
L. Joyce, J. Howson
"The Jolly Pioneer" (Chorus of Navvies)
"Which My Sally Didn't Love Me True" (Song)
D. Bell, Chorus
Concerted Piece (Spare our village, men of toil)
Maidens, Navvies
Finale (To the church away)
Principals, Chorus

ACT 2

Chorus of Fishwives (Honest seaside folk are we)
Boatmen, Visitors

[60]Musical numbers not listed in programs. List prepared from American piano vocal score (William A. Pond, New York, 1883).

Scotch Soliloquy (O woman, like the wanton breeze)
C. J. Campbell
"The Model Lodging House Keeper" (Song)
L. Joyce
Chorus of Bathers (Oh, for a plunge in the briny)
L. Couch, Chorus
"Swells of the Ocean"
Chorus of Boys
"A Professional Beauty" (Duet)
L. Couch, J. Howson
"Polyglot Trio" (English spoken. .)
J. Howson, L. Joyce, D. Bell
De Ville's Love Song (When I came from below)
J. Howson
"Paul and Magnolia" (Duet)
C. J. Campbell, E. Weathersby
Chorus of Photographers (Painters use the brush and pencil)
Chorus
"The British Peer" (Song)
G. Olmi, L. Couch
"The Two Lives" (Ballad)
L. Couch
"Does It Catch On?" (Duet)
J. Howson, D. Bell
"The Spell Is O'er" (Finale)
Principals, Chorus
"The Homesick Loon"

1883.05

M'LISS, Child of the Sierras

A Play (with Songs, Dances and Medleys) in Four Acts. (Stage manager, M. C. Daly. Musical director, G. P. Bernard.) Opened 29 January 1883 at the Grand Opera House and closed 3 February 1883 after 8 performances.[61]

CAST: *M'Liss*, The Waif of the Mountains: ANNIE PIXLEY. *Yuba Bill*: GEORGE C. BONIFACE. *John Gray*: CHARLES MAUBURY. *Judge Beeswinger*: M. C. DALY. *Juan Walters*: A. Z. Chipman. *Templeton Fake*: Donald Harold. *Old Smith*: William Johnson. *Jack Brown*: William Schroeder. *Sacramento Dan*: C. H. Harmer. *Mrs. Smith*: Emma Cliefden. *Clytie Morpher*: Blanche Moulton.

Act 1: The Plot. The Abduction Foiled.

Act 2: The Assassination. The Accusation by M'Liss.

Act 3: The Trial. The Lynchers Defeated. The Escape of Gray.

Act 4: Mountain Home changed to City Parlor. Marriage of M'Liss. Five years later.

1883.06

THE BLACK VENUS!

A Revival of the Romantic and Picturesque Spectacle in a Prologue and Five Acts, 14 Scenes[62]. (Play by Adolph Belot.) New music arranged by Charles Christrup. Stage management under the direction of George R. Edeson. Scenery by Magnani, Robecchi and Recantini of Paris, Milan and Florence; Harley Merry of New York; Walter Burridge and Thomas Neville. Costumes by Mme. Gervais, Mons. Landolf of Paris; Misses Loraine, Rowleigh and Hefferan of New York. Machinery and mechanical effects by William Crane, George Doyle. Armor accessories by William Schmidtlein, A. Newman. Properties and appointments by Charles Blesser. Gas effects by Emmett Davidson. Produced by the Kiralfy Brothers (Imre, Bolossy). Opened 5 February 1883 at Niblo's Garden and closed 24 February 1883 after 25 performances.

CAST: *Baron de Gueran*, an explorer: J. AL. SAWTELLE. *Arthur Layton*, an American traveler: FRANK KILDAY. *Joseph LaRue*, his servant: GEORGE EDESON. *Nassar*, an African guide: J. J. Wallace. *Ali Bembe*, the slaver of the Nile: Edwin Barry. *Monza*, King of the Momboutous: L. J. Martin. *Al Raschid*, Judge of Khartoum: Joseph L. Mason. *Hassan*, a follower of Nassar: A. H. Denham. *Mons. Perriers*, an African explorer: H. A. Mahned. *Dr. de Lange*, a Frenchman: L. Josephs. *Omar*, an old slaver: R. B. Bouchier. *Acbar*, *Ivan*, Donkey Merchants: D. Henry, P. Toole. *Augustin*, a Domestic: B. S. Boxer. *Walinda*, called by the Momboutous "The Black Venus": KATE PELL. *Baroness de Gueran*, a devoted wife: ADELAIDE CHERIS. *Blanche Brevan*, a young French girl: Bella Sawyer. *Miss Beatrix Poles*, an English traveler: Jennie Weathersby. *Aika*, an attendant on Black Venus: Tillie Antonio. *Julie*, the Baroness' waiting maid: A. Tillson. *Amazons, Momboutous, Nyam-Nyams, Salvers, Slaves, Palanquin Bearers, Camel Drivers, Egyptian Soldiers, Ambassadors, Lion Hunters, Sailors, Nubians, etc.*

Ballet: Mlles. THEODORA DeGILLERT, TURRI, CAPPELINI. Corps de Ballet of 100 Danseuses.

Prologue: Paris. Apartments in the Mansion of Mme. DeGueran. Farewell to France.

Act 1: Cairo, Egypt. *Scene 1*: The European Hotel at Cairo. Story of the Black Venus. *Scene 2*: Interior of an African Kraal. *Scene 3*: Panorama of the Nile. The Nile Steamer. *Scene 4*: The River Nile. The Slave Ship. The Burning of the Slave Ship.

Act 2: Africa. *Scene 1*: Public square at Khartoum. *Scene 2*: Interior of Hotel at Khartoum. (Recantini.) *Scene 3*: The Mountains of Walinda. The Black Venus. The Lion Chase. Sudden appearance of the Amazon Warriors of Walinda.

Act 3: The Caravan. *Scene 1*: Tropical Forest. (Harley Merry.) *Scene 2*: The Caravan, introducing Camels, Zebras, Horses, Goats, Nubian Slaves and Bearers. The Sand Storm.

Act 4: The Momboutous. *Scene 1*: Exterior of King Monza's Palace. The American and the guide. *Scene 2*: The Palace of Monzo.

Act 5: The Walinda's. *Scene 1*: Reception Departments of the Black Venus. *Scene 2*: The Palace of the Black Venus. The Lions of the Desert. Death of the Black Venus.

BALLETS
Characteristic Dance (Act 2, Scene 1)
Coryphées, Corps de Ballet
Grand Nubian Ballet (Act 4, Scene 2)
Mlles. T. DeGillert, Turri, Cappelini
Dance des Momboutous
Entrees
Mlles. Turri, Cappelini
La Favorite
Mlle. DeGillert
Pas de huit des Cloches
8 Secondes Danseuses
Grand Adagio
Variation
Premières Danseuses
Finale Brilliant
Entire Corps de Ballet

1883.07

ZARA!

A Comedy (with Musical Selections and Dances) in Three Acts. Play by Fred Marsden. (Stage manager, M. C. Daly. Musical director, G. P. Bernard.) Opened 5 February 1883 at the Grand Opera House and closed 10 February 1883 after 8 performances.

CAST: *Zara*, pure as the Lilies, (of gypsy blood): ANNIE PIXLEY. *Archibald Severn*, whose motto is fidelity: GEORGE C. BONIFACE. *Ross Drake*, a long time in the shadow: CHARLES MAUBURY. *Sir Godfrey Moslyn*, too ready to believe in others: M. C. DALY. *Essic Launceford*, who plays for great stakes: A. Z. CHIPMAN. *Jasper Severn*, with a longing for more: W. T. JOHNSON. *Erasmus Pope*, with a poetic weakness: Donald Harold. *William Growel*, silent and faithful: William Schroeder. *Grace Vane*, brought up in a bad school: EMMA CLIEFDEN. *Mrs. Elden*, an exotic well preserved: Blanche Moulton.

Act 1: The Old Lodge Gate. The Defense.

Act 2: The Old Hall at Moslyn. The Discovery.

Act 3: The Grounds of the Manor. The Exposure.

MUSICAL NUMBERS
"The Switzer's Home"
A. Pixley
"Pretty as a Picture"
A. Pixley
"I'll Meet You, Dan"
A. Pixley
"The Huntsman's Home"
A. Pixley
"The White Cockade"
A. Pixley

---

[61]No musical numbers listed in programs; program note: Miss Pixley will introduce Choice Selections of Songs, Dances and Medleys.

[62]First produced in New York in a different version by the Kiralfy Brothers 12 January 1881 at Niblo's Garden for 45 performances.

1883.08 COUNTESS DUBARRY

A Comic Opera in Three Acts, in German. Viennese libretto ('Gräfin Dubarry') by F. Zell and Richard Genée. 'Music by Karl Millöcker. Stage director, Herman Conreid. Scenery by Namszynowsky. Costumes by Buchheister. Conductor, Gustave Kerker. Manager, Carl Herrmann, for the Thalia Theatre Opera Company. Opened 12 February 1883 at the Fifth Avenue Theatre and closed 17 February 1883 after 7 performances; returned as GRÄFIN DUBARRY 31 March-6 April 1883 to the Thalia Theatre for 4 additional performances in repertory.[63]

CAST: *Jeanne*, the Countess Dubarry: Frl. RABERG. *Duc D'Aiguillon*: Herr HERNBERG. *Vicomte de Navailles*: Herr ADOLFI. *Jean*, Count Dubarry: Herr MENDEL. *Meaupou*: Herr Blohm. *Madame de Mailly*: Frl. Ruthenberg. *Madame de Sable*: Frl. Brosi. *Madame de Mirresoix*: Frl. Weilzenboeck. *Countess d'Egmont*: Frl. Michaels. *Baroness de Vigoreux*: Frl. Erdmann. *Mademoiselle de Lajardie*: Frl. Pegel. *Madame de Gruau*: Frl. Meyer. *Vicomtesse de Waldeck*: Frl. Meyer. *Marquise de Surville*: Frl. Eisner. *M. Desprez*, Royal Councillor: Herr Silbernagel. *M. De Mergy*: Herr Jericho. *M. De Meaulion*: Herr Hoffmann. *M. De Varingville*: Herr Salzer. *Leonard*, hairdresser: Herr A. KLEIN. *Lucette*, his wife: Frl. HECHT. *Criquet*, his apprentice: Frl. Weizenbock. *First Mask*: Frau Voigt. *Second Mask*: Frl. Klozinsky. *Third Mask*: Frau Peisser. *Fourth Mask*: Frl. Schliemann. *Servants, Heralds, Guards, Hunters, and People.*

Act 1: Leonard's shop in Paris. 1775.

Acts 2 and 3: Castle of Lucienne.

1883.09 FRITZ IN IRELAND, or,The Bell Ringer of the Rhine and the Love of the Shamrock

A Characteristic Irish Drama in Three Acts. (Play by Joseph K. Emmet.) Produced by Joseph K. Emmet (George W. Wilton, Manager.) Opened 12 February 1883 at the Cosmopolitan Theatre and closed 24 February 1883 after 15 performances.[64]

CAST: *Fritz Schultz*: JOSEPH K. EMMET. *Lawyer Priggins*: H. M. Wilson. *Baron Hertfort*, alias Splodger: Charles Abbott. *Captain Hercules O'Dowd*: F. C. Huebner. *Lord Seaton*: William C. Miller. *Charles Seaton*: Martin Cody. *Thomas Goldfinger*, (the great O'Neil) a man servant: Joseph P. Wade. *Patrick Blackeye*, an Irish Negro: W. J. Donnelly. *Master Herbert*, a nephew of Baron Hertfort: Little Peggy Miller. *Lady Amelia*: Georgia Tyler. *Louise Hertfort*: Kate Blancke. *Madame Schultz*: Lizzie Scanlan. *Judy Callahan*, maid servant: Jennie Christie. *Little Lena Schultz*: Little Peggy Miller.

1883.10 HEART AND HAND

An Opéra Comique in Three Acts. Original French libretto to the opérette ('Le Coeur et la main') by Charles Nuitter and Alexandre Beaumont. Music by Charles Lecocq. Produced under the stage direction of Jesse Williams. Costumes by Emma Berg. Produced by the McCaull Opera Company (John A. McCaull, Proprietor and Manager). Opened 15 February 1883 at the Bijou Opera House and closed 3 March 1883 after 19 performances.[65]

CAST: *The King of Aragon*: JOHN HOWSON. *Don Gaetan*: DIGBY BELL. *Don Mosquitos*: GEORGE OLMI. *Morales*: CHARLES J. CAMPBELL. *Bal De Mero*: GEORGE A. SCHILLER. *Officers*: Ed S. Grant, Eugene Harvey, Frank Howard. *Micaëla*: MARIANNE CONWAY. *(Donna) Scolastica*: LAURA JOYCE. *Josepha*: EMIE WEATHERSBY. *Anita*: Mamie Siegfried. *Dolores*: Edith Brandon.

Act 1: Grounds of the Castle of the King of Aragon.

Act 2: Interior of the Palace.

Act 3: Camp.

1883.11 FATINITZA!

A Revival of the Comic Opera in Three Acts[66] (Original Viennese libretto to the operette by F. Zell and Richard Genée, based on the libretto to "La Circassienne" by Eugène Scribe.) Music by Franz von Suppé. Musical director, Samuel L. Studley. Produced by the Boston Ideal Opera Company. (Miss E. H. Ober, Proprietor and Manager). Opened 19 February 1883 at the Fifth Avenue Theatre in repertory; season closed 3 March 1883 after (2) performances in repertory.[67]

CAST: *Vladimir* a young Russian Lieutenant, afterwards disguised as Fatinitza: MATHILDE PHILLIPPS. *Princess Lydia Imanovna*, Niece of the Count: MARIE STONE. *Izzet Pacha*, Governor of the Turkish Fort: HENRY CLAY BARNABEE. *Ivan*: Florence Reede. *Russian Officers (3)*: *Captain Vasil*: J. A. Loughrin. *Lieutenant Osip*: F. J. Macarthy. *Sergeant Steipann*: George Frothingham. *Hassan Bey*, Leader of the Bashi-Bazouks: J. Macarthy. *Count Timofey Kantchukoff*, a Russian General: MYRON W. WHITNEY. *Julian Hardy*, a Special Newspaper Correspondent: TOM KARL. *Dimitri*, a Russian Cadet: Lizzie Burton. *Izzet Pasha's Wives (4)*: *Zuleika*: Hattie A. Brown. *Diona*: Fannie Rice. *Besika*: Zephie Dinsmore. *Nursidah*: Kate Davis. *Marsaldshi*, a Fortune Teller: LIZZIE BURTON. *Mustapha*, the Guardian of the Harem: A. E. Nichols. *Vuika*, a Bulgarian spy: A. J. Hubbard. *Cadets, Russian Soldiers, Bashi-Bazouks, Cossacks, Moorish Women, Slaves, Slave-Drivers, etc.*

Characters in the Karagois: *Jessuf*; *Surema*, his daughter; *Ben Jemin*, his slave; *Wiridah, Fatima*, two old gossips; *Ashmet*, keeper of the Menagerie: Several Slaves of the Harem.

1883.12 THE MUSKETEERS

An Opéra-comique in Two Acts[68]. Original French libretto ('Les Mousquetaires au Couvent') by Paul Ferrier and Jules Prével (based on the comédie-vaudeville 'Le Habit ne fait pas le moine' by Saint-Hilaire and Duport). Music by Louis Varney; (additional music by Achille Mansour). Musical director, Samuel L. Studley. Produced by the Boston Ideal Opera Company (Miss E. H. Ober, Proprietor and Manager). Opened 20 February 1883 at the Fifth Avenue Theatre in repertory; season closed 3 March 1883 after (2) performances in repertory.

CAST: *Narcisse de Brissac*, Captain in the Red Musketeers: W. H. MacDONALD. *Gontran de Solanges*, his comrade: TOM KARL. *Abbé Bridaine*, ex-tutor of Gontran, visitor to Convent: GEORGE FROTHINGHAM. *Governor of Touraine*, Count de Pontcourlay: F. J. MACARTHY. *Rigobert*, Sergeant in the Red Musketeers: J. A. Loughrin. *Pichard*, Landlord of the Inn "The Grey Musketeers": J. H. Sturgiss. *Fracasse, Patatras*, Conspirators against the Cardinal, disguised as Monks: A. J. Hubbard, W. H. Eichman. *Langlois, Farin*, Citizens: J. E. Miller, A. E. Nichols..

Simone, Waitress at Pichard's Inn: MARIE STONE. *Marie de Pontcourlay*, Niece of the Governor: GERALDINE ULMAR. *Louise*, her sister: LIZZIE BURTON. *Superior of the Ursuline Convent*: HATTIE A. BROWN. *Sister Opportune*: Kate Davis. *Claudine, Jacqueline*, Flower and Sweet-stuff Girls: Zephie Dinsmore, Florence Reed. *Isabel*: May Shackford. *Clorinda*: Marie Coleman. *Clarissa*: Zephie Dinsmore. *Agatha*: Florence Reed.

ACT 1[69]

"We're Men of War"
J. A. Loughrin, Chorus

"Of New Pluckt Roses" (Couplets)
Z. Dinsmore, F. Reed

"How They Treat Us" (Chorus and Scene)
M. Stone, Chorus

"The Grey Musketeers" (Song)
M. Stone, Chorus

"Good Morning" (Chorus)

"A Woman and a Sword" (Song)
W. H. MacDonald

"Own Up!" (Trio)
T. Karl, W. H. MacDonald, G. Frothingham

"Squeak Goes the Fiddle" (Chorus)

"When the Simple Peasant" (Villanelle)
M. Stone

"You'll Have to Stop That Row!" (Scene and Chorus)
J. H. Sturgiss, M. Stone

[63]Musical numbers not listed in programs.

[64]No credits in programs for stage director, scenery, costumes or musical director. According to the reviewers, Joseph K. Emmet performed his customary musical specialties.

[65]American adaptation uncredited. No credits for scenery, musical direction, most likely Jesse Williams. No musical numbers listed in programs.

[66]First produced in New York in English 22 April 1879 at the Fifth Avenue Theatre for 41 performances. For Synopsis of Scenes and Musical Numbers, see original 1879 production.

[67]English adaptation uncredited; no credits in programs for scenery or costumes.

[68]English language premiere. Previously produced in French in New York 2 December 1881 at Abbey's Park Theatre, returning 25 April 1882 to the Fifth Avenue Theatre, for 2 performances in repertory.

[69]Musical numbers not listed in programs. List prepared from the American Acting edition, translated by Dexter Smith (Oliver Ditson, Boston, 1881).

"Chorus of Welcome"
M. Stone, Chorus
"Oh That We Might Fly" (Duet)
G. Ulmar, T. Karl
Finale:
"Landlord, Fill Up!"
All, Chorus
"Should Robin at My Window" (Song)
M. Stone
"Near Them" (Chorale)
M. Stone, Chorus
"Chartreuse Monks" (duet)
T. Karl, W. H. MacDonald, Chorus
"Oh, How My Heart!" (Strette)
M. Stone, Chorus
ACT 2
"The Ologies" (Opening Chorus)
H. A. Brown, Pupils
"Let Us Confess Our Faults" (Scene)
Pupils
"By Night and Day" (Romance)
G. Ulmar
"O Father, We Regret" (Two-Part Song)
Pupils
"Draw Near" (Ensemble)
G. Ulmar, L. Burton, H. A. Brown, K. Davis, T. Karl, W. H. MacDonald, Pupils
"Two and Two" (Two Part Song)
Pupils
"The Captive and the Bird" (Ballad)
W. H. MacDonald
"Ye Summer Birds" (Valse Song)
G. Ulmar
"My Dream of Love" (Romance)
T. Karl
"Now to Hear the Pilgrims Preaching" (Chorus and Scene)
W. H. MacDonald, T. Karl, Chorus
"Love's Not a Science" (Couplets)
W. H. MacDonald
"We Must Admit" (Strette)
G. Ulmar, L. Burton, Chorus
"With Us Darling" (Finale)
T. Karl, All, Chorus

1883.13

LA MASCOT

A Revival of the Opéra-comique in Three Acts[70]. Original French libretto by Henri Chivot and Alfred Duru. Music by Edmond Audran. Musical director, Samuel L. Studley. Produced by the Boston Ideal Opera Company (Miss E. H. Ober, Proprietor and Manager). Opened 22 February 1883 (matinee) at the Fifth Avenue Theatre in repertory; season closed 3 March 1883 after (4) performances in repertory.

CAST: *Bettina*, the Mascot: GERALDINE ULMAR. *Fiametta*, Daughter of Lorenzo: LIZZIE BURTON. *Pippo*, a Shepherd: TOM CARL. *Lorenzo XVII*, Prince of Piombino: HENRY CLAY BARNABEE. *Rocco*, a Farmer: GEORGE FROTHINGHAM. *Frederick*, Prince of Pisa: HERNDON MORSELL. *Parafanti*, Sergeant: J. A. Loughrin. *Matheo*, an Innkeeper: J. E. Miller. *Physician*: J. H. Sturgiss. *Pages to the King (6)*: *Carlo*: Marie Coleman. *Marco*: Zephie Dinsmore. *Angelo*: Hattie Brown. *Luegi*: May Shackford. *Paolo*: Florence Reed. *Pluto*: Carrie Endicott. *(Hunters, Peasants, Soldiers, Villagers, etc.)*

1883.14

THE PIRATES OF PENZANCE, or, The Slave of Duty

A Revival of the Comic Opera in Two Acts[71]. Libretto by William S. Gilbert. Music by Arthur Sullivan. Musical director, Samuel L. Studley. Produced by the Boston Ideal Opera Company (Miss E. H. Ober, Proprietor and Manager). Opened 22 February 1883 at the Fifth Avenue Theatre; season closed 3 March 1883 after (3) performances in repertory.[72]

CAST: *Richard*, a Pirate Chief: MYRON W. WHITNEY. *Samuel*, his Lieutenant: A. J. HUBBARD. *Frederic*, a Pirate Apprentice: HERNDON MORSELL. *Major General Stanley*, of the British Army: HENRY CLAY BARNABEE. *Edward*, Sergeant of Police: GEORGE FROTHINGHAM. *Mabel, Kate, Edith, Isabel*, General Stanley's Daughters: MARIE STONE, LIZZIE BURTON, ZEPHIE DINSMORE, Hattie A. Browne. *Ruth*, Piratical Maid-of-all-work: MATHILDE PHILLIPPS. *(Chorus of Pirates, Police and General Stanley's Daughters.)*

1883.15

PATIENCE, or, Bunthorne's Bride

A Revival of the Comic Opera in Two Acts[73]. Libretto by William S. Gilbert. Music by Arthur Sullivan. Musical director, Samuel L. Studley. Produced by the Boston Ideal Opera Company (Miss E. H. Ober, Proprietor and Manager). Opened 23 February 1883 at the Fifth Avenue Theatre in repertory; season closed 3 March 1883 after (4) performances in repertory.

CAST: *Reginald Bunthorne*, a Fleshly Poet: HENRY CLAY BARNABEE. *Archibald Grosvenor*, an Idyllic Poet: TOM KARL. *Officers of Dragoon Guards (3)*: *Colonel Calverley*: F. G. Cauffman. *Major Murgatroyd*: George Frothingham. *Lieutenant Duke of Dunstable*: Herndon Morsell. *Mr. Bunthorne's Solicitor*: J. H. Sturgiss. *Rapturous Maidens (4)*: *Lady Angela*: Lizzie Burton. *Lady Saphir*: Hattie A. Brown. *Lady Ella*: Fannie Rice. *Lady Jane*: MATHILDE PHILLIPS. *Patience*, a Village Milkmaid: MARIE STONE. *Chorus of Officers of Dragoon Guards, Rapturous Maidens.*

1883.16

MICAËLA

A Comic Opera in Three Acts. Original French libretto to the opérette ('Le Coeur et la Main') by Charles Nuitter and Alexandre Beaumont. Music by Charles Lecocq. Costumes by W. Dazian & Sons. Scenery by George W. Dayton & Son. Musical director, Charles Schiller. Produced under the direction of James C. Duff. Opened 26 February 1883 at the Standard Theatre and closed 16 March 1883 after 20 performances; returned under the title HEART AND HAND 23 August 1883 to Daly's Theatre and closed 15 September 1883 after 24 additional performances[74]. Total: 44 performances.

CAST: *The King of Aragonia*: J. H. RYLEY. *Don Gaetan*, Duke of Madera: GEORGE SWEET. *Morales*: WALLACE McCREERY. *Don Mosquitos*: H. W. MONTGOMERY. *Baldomero*: M. Lee. *Captain Barros*: John Vernon. *Lieutenant Moros*: John Compton. *Court Ladies, Courtiers, Bombardiers and Guards. Princess Micaëla*: MARIE CONRON. *Donna Scholastica*: Mrs. FRED WILLIAMS. *Josefa*: VERNONA JARBEAU. *Pages (5)*: *Ascania*: Miss Waldemere. *Pascual*: Miss Sherwood. *Lazaro*: Miss Wyman. *Jose*: Miss Irving. *Pablo*: Miss Coles. *Peasant Girls (5)*: *Anita*: Miss Jacques. *Pepa*: Miss Maynard. *Dolores*: Sophie Hummel. *Inez*: Miss A. Dayton. *Pekita*: Miss L. Shandley. *Brides, Pages, Peasants, etc.*

Act 1: The Royal Park.

Act 2: Grand Saloon in the Palace.

Act 3: General Quarters at Court.

1883.17

RIFLEMEN AT VASSAR, N. G., S. N. Y.

A Burlesque in 3 Scenes, preceded by an Olio. Suggested by Louis Varney's comic opera "Les Trois Mousquetaires." Burlesque by Fred Intropodi. Musical director, Adolph Nicholls. Produced by Tony Pastor. Opened 26 February 1883 at Tony Pastor's New 14th Street Theatre and closed 10 March 1883 after 16 performances.

---

[70]First produced in New York in English as THE MASCOT 5 May 1881 at the Bijou Theatre for 168 performances in two engagements. For Synopsis of Scenes and Musical Numbers, see orginal 1881 production. English adaptation uncredited in programs.

[71]First presented in New York 31 December 1879 at the Fifth Avenue Theatre for a total of 91 performances in two engagements. For Synopsis of Scenes and Musical Numbers, see original 1879 production.

[72]No credits in program for stage director, scenery or costumes designs.

[73]First presented in New York 22 September 1881 at the Standard Theatre for 177 performances. For Synopsis of Scenes and Musical Numbers, see original 1881 production.

[74]American adaptation uncredited. For the return engagement, scenery was credited to Roberts; A. Tomasi succeeded Schiller as musical director; cast changes among the principals included *Baldomero*: J. Loe; *Captain*: Vincent Kent; *Lieutenant*: J. Dungan; *Donna Scholastica*: ROSA COOK; *Josepha*: LOUISE PAULLIN. Musical numbers not listed in programs. Ballet specialty in Act 3:

Picturesque Hungarian Ballet (arranged by Signor Novissimo)

Olio: Heathen Chinese Labor!, A sketch with with songs, dances, specialties, with Frank Budworth, Frank Girard, Joseph Buckley, Flora M. Pike, Bebe Vining, Florence Bell. Rosa Linden (Ballads). Emma Alfredo (gymnast), assisted by James Alfredo. Tony Pastor's Merry Musings. Charles E. Ellis and Clara Moore (German Sketch Artists). The Four Musical Kings (Wood, Beasley, Weston Brothers).

CAST: *Maud*: ZOIE MARQUISINI. *Captain Slash*, a Captain of the National Guard: FLORA IRWIN. *Professor Algebra*: JACQUES KRUGER. *Colonel Brisket*, commanding the 114th Regiment, National Guard, State of New York: J. H. STUART. *Mlle. Williames*, Principal of Ladies' Seminary: MAY IRWIN. *Susanna*, a waiting maid: FLORA M. PIKE. *Clarinda*: Florence D. Kellogg. *Louise*: Bebe Vining. *Marianne*: Florence Bell. *Governor Groveland*: Frank Girard. *Sergeant Remington*: Frank Budworth. *Mr. Mulvaney*, an innkeeper: C. T. Parr. *The Stalwart Brothers*: Charles T. Ellis, Joseph Buckley. *Soldiers of the National Guard*: Messrs. Hastie, Kenworth, Perring, Atwood, Parr, Foudray, Holland, Myers, Gaunt, Jerome, Powers, Taylor. *Pupils of Vasser Seminary*: Misses Florence D. Kellogg, Florence Bell, Egli, Newman, C. Newman, Atkinson, Freeth, St. Clair, Clifton, Lester, Butler.

Act 1: A Village Fête (on the Hudson).

Act 2: A Country Lane.

Act 3: The School Room of Vassar Seminary.

1883.18 THE DIME NOVEL

A Musical Comedy in Two Acts. Comedy by Archibald Clavering Gunter. Music by Jesse Williams. Produced under the direction of Archibald Clavering Gunter. Produced by John A. McCaull. Opened 5 March 1883 at the Bijou Opera House and closed 10 March 1883 after 7 performances.[75]

CAST: *Tom Hilton*, alias Captain Kidd, Junior, a good boy, who, inspired by the dime novel, becomes a bad pirate, for two days is the terror of New Rochelle: W. J. FERGUSON. *Bill Higgins*, his boatswain who has also read dime novels: GEORGE A. SCHILLER. *Harold Morton*, his midshipman: NELLIE HOWARD. *Barry O'Burke*, Mrs. Lawrence's Irish servant, who emigrated to escape the famine: J. H. STUART. *Adolphus Suckling*, D.D., Headmaster of Suckling Academy: GEORGE GASTON. *Bleary*, the boss tramp of New Rochelle: T. Hilton. *Lillian Lawrence*, who wishes to become a pirate bride: LOUISE PAULLIN. *Mrs. Agnes Lawrence*, Lillian's mother: JULIE deRUYTHER. *Millicent Lawrence*, Lillian's aunt: Virginia Fairfax. *Susan Fielding*, a practical girl: Emma Guthrie. *Myra Martin*, a piratical chit: Josie Dell. *Schoolboys who would like to be pirates, Girls who have read dime novels, etc.*

Act 1: Garden of Mrs. Lawrence's Summer Villa. Afternoon.

Act 2: Hen Island. Next morning.

1883.19 THE MASCOT

A Burlesque in 3 Scenes, preceded by an Olio. (Inspired by the opéra-comique "La Mascotte", libretto by Henri Chivot and Alfred Duru. Music by Edmond Audran.) Musical director, Adolph Nicholls. Produced by Tony Pastor. Opened 12 March 1883 at Tony Pastor's New 14th Street Theatre and closed 17 March 1883 after 8 performances.[76]

Olio: Smoked Out, a sketch with Joseph Buckley, Frank Girard, Frank Budworth, Florence Bell, P. B. Gaunt, W. Atwood. Florence D. Kellogg (ballads). John and Louisa Till (The Royal Marionettes). Tony Pastor's Comic Songs. Kelly and O'Brien (Grotesque and versatile comedians, acrobatic dancers, with their novelty 'Insanity'). Wheatley and Traynor (the Dublin Boys, song and dance) including "The Honor and Glory of Ireland," "The Brothers Malone," "Two Old Irish Gentlemen," "The Two Harvestmen," and Wheatley's Trial Dance.

CAST: *Lorenzo XXXLIV*, Prince of New Jersey: JACQUES KRUGER. *Pippo*, a pretty Shepherd: FLORA IRWIN. *Bettina*, a turkey tender (the Mascot): MAY IRWIN. *Fiametta*, the daughter of Lorenzo: FLORENCE D. KELLOGG. *Frederick*, Prince of Long Island: FLORENCE BELL. *Rocco*, an unfortunate farmer: FRANK BUDWORTH. *Matheo*, an innkeeper: Frank Girard. *The Sergeant*: C. T. Parr. *Dr. Schenck*: Charles Atwood. *The Minister*: T. H. Kenworth. *Pages (6)*: *Angelo*: Bebe Vining. *Luigi*: Jennie Bardine. *Carlo*: Claudia Pauli. *Angelo*: Blanche Pauli. *Marco*: Jennie St. Clair. *Antoine*: Miss Newman.

Peasants, Hunters, Ladies and Gentlemen of the Court, etc.: Misses Wally Egli, Claudia Pauli, Clara Newman, Julia Freeth, Tilly Clifton, Maud Butler, Priscilla Newman, Blanche Pauli, Ella Atkinson, Jennie St. Clair, Ida Lester, Jennie Buckley. Messrs. William Hastie, T. H. Kenworth, Ernest Perring, P. B. Gaunt, J. M. Jerome, Ed. M. Powers, Charles Atwood, Charles T. Parr, Oscar Holland, Eugene Myers, Walter L. Taylor, Thomas Bowden.

Scene 1: The Farm of Rocco. *Scene 2*: The Grand Ducal Palace of Piombino. *Scene 3*: The Inn of Matheo.

[75]No credits in programs for costumes, scenery, musical direction, most likely Jesse Williams.

[76]Authorship of the burlesque uncredited, but most likely Fred Intropodi, author of all Tony Pastor's other successful burlesques.

1883.20 FRITZ IN ENGLAND AND IRELAND

A Characteristic Drama in a Prologue and Three Acts. (Play by Joseph K. Emmet.) Produced by Joseph K. Emmet (George W. Wilton, Manager.) Opened 12 March 1883 at Niblo's Garden and closed 24 March 1883 after 14 performances.[77]

CAST (Prologue): *Fritz*: JOSEPH K. EMMET. *Lawyer Priggins*: H. M. Wilson. *Bruno*: Charles Abbott. *Aaron Melchior*: H. Weston. *Zillah*: Georgia Tyler. *Blissa*: Lizzie Scanlan. *Klina*: Little Laura Bell. *Gypsies*: Company.

CAST (Play): *Fritz*: JOSEPH K. EMMET. *Lord Seaton*: A. Constantine. *Captain O'Doud*: Martin J. Cody. *Lawyer Priggins*: H. M. Wilson. *Splodger*: Charles Abbott. *Charles Seaton*: Harry Paddock. *Patrick Black*: W. J. Donnelly. *Thomas Goldfinger*: Joseph P. Wade. *Master Herbert*: Little Laura Bell. *Lady Louisa*: Georgia Tyler. *Lady Amelia*: Lizzie Scanlan. *Judy Callahan*: Nellie Lingard. *Aaron Melchior*: H. Weston.

Prologue: England.

Acts 1, 2, 3: Ireland.

MUSICAL NUMBERS[78]

"Sounds from Home"
J. K. Emmet

"Ringing the Chimes"
J. K. Emmet

"Lullaby"
J. K. Emmet

1883.21 H.M.S. PINAFORE, or, The Lass That Loved a Sailor

A Revival of the Comic Opera in Two Acts[79]. Libretto by William S. Gilbert. Music by Arthur Sullivan. Directed by James C. Duff. Scenery by George W. Dayton. Musical director, Charles Schiller. Presented by James C. Duff. Opened 17 March 1883 at the Standard Theatre and closed 24 March 1883 after 8 performances.

CAST: *The Rt. Hon. Sir Joseph Porter, K.C.B.*, First Lord of the Admiralty: J. H. RYLEY. *Captain Corcoran*, Commanding the *H.M.S. Pinafore*: W. H. HAMILTON. *Ralph Rackstraw*, Able Seaman: WALLACE MACREERY. *Dick Deadeye*, Able Seaman: J. H. STUART. *Boatswain*: Alexander Henderson. *Midshipmite*: Master Montgomery. *Josephine*, the Captain's Daughter: MARIE CONRON. *Hebe*, Sir Joseph's First Cousin: VERNONA JARBEAU. *Little Buttercup*, a Portsmouth Bumboat Woman: JULIE deRUYTHER. *First Lord's Sisters, his Cousins, his Aunts, Sailors, Marines, etc.*

1883.22 THE MASCOT

A Revival of the Opéra-comique in Three Acts[80]. Original French libretto by Henri Chivot and Alfred Duru. Music by Edmond Audran. Entire production under the immediate supervision of Henry E. Dixey. Musical director, J. C. Mullaby. Produced by John Stetson. Opened 19 March 1883 at the Fifth Avenue Theatre and closed 24 March 1883 after 7 performances.

CAST: *Lorenzo XVII*, Prince of Piombino: HENRY E. DIXEY. *Pippo*, a Shepherd: EUGENE CLARKE. *Frederick*, Prince of Pisa: ALONZO HATCH. *Rocco*, a Farmer: WILLIAM PAUL BOWN. *Matteo*, Innkeeper: Frank Flake. *Parafanti*, Sergeant: Mills Hall. *Court Physician*: Ham Nichols. *Fiametta*, Daughter of Lorenzo: HATTIE RICHARDSON. *Bettina*, the Mascot: LETITIA FRISCH.

Pages to the Prince (6): *Carlo*: Louisa Bickford. *Marco*: Laura Thomas. *Angelo*: Flora Echard. *Luigi*: Lillie Hunt. *Paolo*: Edith Sweet. *Fluto*: J. S. Strong. *Peasants, Soldiers, Lords, Ladies of the Court, etc.*

[77]No other credits in program for stage direction, scenery, costumes, musical direction.

[78]Not necessarily in performance order; also included were Emmet's most popular songs and characteristic dances.

[79]Originally presented in New York 15 January 1879 at the Standard Theatre for 175 performances. For Synopsis of Scenes and Musical Numbers, see original 1879 production.

[80]First produced in New York in English as THE MASCOT 5 May 1881 at the Bijou Theatre for 168 performances in two engagements. For Synopsis of Scenes and Musical Numbers, see original 1881 production.

BILLEE TAYLOR,

1883.23 or, The Lass Who Loved a Sailor

A Revival of the Burlesque in 3 Scenes[81], preceded by an Olio. (Burlesque by Fred Intropodi. Inspired by the nautical comic opera with libretto by Henry Pottinger Stephens, music by Edward Solomon. All the music from the original.) Musical director, Adolph Nicholls. Produced by Tony Pastor. Opened 19 March 1883 at Tony Pastor's New 14th Street Theatre and closed 24 March 1883 after 8 performances.

Olio: A Woman of Few Words, sketch with Joe Buckley, Frank Girard, Florence Bell, Bebe Vining; Harry Mack (equilibrist), Florence D. Kellogg (songs); Fred Hallen and Enid Hart in Over the Stile!, opera in miniature form; Dan Collyer's sketch, A Doctor for an Hour!, with Dan Collyer, J. Buckley, Frank Girard, Frank Budworth; Tony Pastor's Comic Muse; Lester and Allen (Negro imitations).

CAST: *Phoebe*, beloved by William, Barnacle, and Lobster: ROSE TEMPLE. *Captain Barnacle* of the Police Boat: JACQUES KRUGER. *William*, the most virtuous and conscientious tailor in the business: FLORA IRWIN. *Sir Wellington Lance*, Commander in Chief of the Armies: FRANK GIRARD. *Chris Lobster*, the Schoolmaster: FRANK BUDWORTH. *Eliza*, Barnacle's old flame: ENID HART. *Bella*, daughter of Sir Wellington: FLORENCE KELLOGG. *Susanna*, a Poorhouse Matron: BEBE VINING. (*Dance Specialty*: Mlle. BARRETTA.) *Charity Girls*: Misses Bell, Butler, Pauli, Clifton, Lester, St. Clair, Freeth, Egli, Atkinson, Watson, Grey, Vining, Pauli, Bartine. *Sailors of the "Thunderbomb"*: Messrs. Parr, Holland, Kenworthy, Taylor, Myers, Powers, Hastie, Jerome, Gaunt, Johnson.

PATIENCE,

1883.24 or, Bunthorne's Bride

A Revival of the Comic Opera in Two Acts[82]. Libretto by William S. Gilbert. Music by Arthur Sullivan. Produced under the stage direction of James Barton. Musical director, Ernest Neyer. Opened 26 March 1883 at the Standard Theatre and closed 7 April 1883 after 14 performances.[83]

CAST: *Reginald Bunthorne*, a Fleshly Poet: J. H. RYLEY. *Archibald Grosvenor*, an Idyllic Poet: James Barton. *Officers of Dragoon Guards (3)*: *Colonel Calverly*: W. H. Hamilton. *Major Murgatroyd*: George Gaston. *Lieutenant Duke of Dunstable*: W. P. Hampshire. *Mr. Bunthorne's Solicitor*: William White. *Rapturous Maidens (4)*: *Lady Jane*: AUGUSTA ROCHE. *Angela*: Hattie Anderson. *Saphir*: Helen Lowell. *Ella*: Ruby Rogers. *Patience*, a Village Milkmaid: MARIE JANSEN. *Chorus of Officers of Dragoon Guards, Rapturous Maidens.*

1883.25 OLIVETTE

A Revival of the Comic Opera in Three Act.[84] Original French libretto to the opérette 'Les Noces d'Olivette' by Henri Chivot and Alfred Duru. Music by Edmond Audran. Stage manager, John E. Nash. Costumes by A. Schwenke. Musical director, George Towle. Produced by the Catherine Lewis Comic Opera Company (Oscar L. Arfwedson, Manager). Opened 26 March 1883 at the Fifth Avenue Theatre and closed 28 March 1883 after 6 performances in repertory.

CAST: *Olivette*: CATHERINE LEWIS. *The Countess*: ALICE VINCENT. *Moustique*: Mary Stanford. *Veloutine*: EME LASCELLES. *Captain de Merrimac*: JOSEPH S. GREENSFELDER. *Valentine*: HENRI LAURENT. *Coquelicot*: FRED LENNOX. *The Duke des Ifs*: T. V. RICKETTS. *Marvejol*: JOHN E. NASH. *Peasants, Soldiers, Courtiers, etc.*

A BUNCH OF KEYS,

1883.26 or, The Hotel

A Satire on Hotels (Farce Comedy) in Three Acts. Play by Charles H. Hoyt and Willie Edouin. Musical director, Watty Hydes. Produced by the San Francisco Minstrels "Sparks" Company (Frank W. Sanger, Manager). Opened 26 March 1883 at the San Francisco Opera House and closed 23 June 1883 after 104 performances.

CAST: *Teddy Keys*, a wild rosebud with accompanying thorns: ALICE ATHERTON. *Rose Keys*, her eldest sister; also of the rose variety, but full-blown, and rather of the Prim-rose order: CARRIE GODFREY. *May Keys*, also a sister of Teddy, the Third and last of the Bunch of Keys: ANNA BREVOOR. *Dolly Dobbs*, a regular domestic—that is, she breaks no crockery: Marietta Nash. *Matilda Jenkins*, searching for her lost one: Genie Holtzmeyer. *Gilly Spooner*, a rural masher, engaged to Rose: JULIAN MITCHELL. *Jonas Grimes*, a brakeman who is one of nature's noblemen—this is the author's ideal of a perfect man. Watch him: JAMES T. POWERS. *Tom Harding*, May's lover: C. B. Stevens. *Sam Foss*, looking for a job, and gets one: Harry Delorme. *Littleton Snaggs*, Esq., a legal gentleman, who knows as much of running a hotel as a good many in that business do: WILLIE EDOUIN.

Disguises assumed in Acts 2 and 3: *J. Frisk, Sr.*, a dealer in lightning rods: C. B. Stevens. *J. Rockford Smith*, a drummer: C. B. Stevens. *Colonel St. Clair Bray*, a politician: JULIAN MITCHELL. *Rose Keys*: JULIAN MITCHELL. *Miss Emma Poughkeepsie*, operatic artiste: CARRIE GODFREY. *Signorina Jersecite*, operatic artiste: ANNA BREVOOR. *Sergeant Lawrence Jenkins*, a drummer: ALICE ATHERTON. *Plug Muldoon*, a Maori: Harry Delorme.

Act 1: The will. Anxiety of the Keys Family. Arrival of Littleton Snaggs. Reading of the will. Concealment of the codicil. Snaggs opens the Grand View Hotel, as possession is nine points of the law. Teddy volunteers to assist, much to the disgust of the Keys family.

Act 2: The Hotel. Hotel opened. Enough provisions for a regiment. We must see the will. Let's try the safe. Teddy's desire to give a ball. Guests arrive. Opera singers, politicians, Lighting Rod Agent. Matilda's search. The proposal. Snaggs not drunk, but sleepy. The suicide.

Act 3: Hotel after a storm. More guests. Arrival of a supposed drummer. The plot exposed. Success of the Keys family. Recovery of the codicil. Arrival of the real drummer. The decision. Consternation of Snaggs. Matilda's victory.

MUSICAL NUMBERS

"Ocean Swell" (Chorus)
"All Aboard"
"Market on Saturday Night" (from THE McSORLEYS)
(*Music by* David Braham. *Lyrics by* Edward Harrigan.)
"Nothing of the Sort" (Song and Chorus)
"Old Cabin Home" (Hoodlum Trio)
"Arthur and Martha"
"I Won't Play with You Any More"
Duet from THE MASCOTTE
(*Music by* Edmond Audran.)
New Medley of Popular Songs
"Kulula"
"The Charleston Blues" (from THE McSORLEYS)
(*Music by* David Braham. *Lyrics by* Edward Harrigan.)
Trio and Chorus from IOLANTHE
(*Music by* Arthur Sullivan. *Lyrics by* William S. Gilbert.)

1883.27 LA PERICHOLE

A Revival of the Opéra-bouffe in Three Acts, in French.[85] Libretto by Ludovic Halévy and Henri Meilhac, based on "Le Carosse du Saint-Sacrament" by Prosper Mérimée. Music by Jacques Offenbach. Musical director, Mons. A. Lagye. Produced by Maurice Grau's French Opera Company. Opened 27 March 1883 at the Casino Theatre and closed 9 April 1883 after 3 performances in repertory.

CAST: *La Périchole*: Mme. LOUISE THÉO. *Guadalena*: Mlle. Morel. *Berginella*: Mlle. Buisson. *Mastrilla*: Mlle. Vallot. *Manuelita*: Mlle. Vandamme. *Frasquinella*: Mlle. Caro. *Brambilla*: Mlle. Salvator. *Ninetta*: Mlle. Adrienne. *Piquillo*: Mons. GRIVEL. *Don Andrès de Ribeira*: Mons. SALVATOR. *Panatellas*: Mons. J. MEZIÈRES. *Don Pedro*: Mons. DUPLAN. *Tarapote*: Mons. Vinchon. *Le Marques de Santarrau*: Mons. Ducos. *Un Notaire*: Mons. Gerard. *Un Giolier*: Mons. Millet.

1883.28 LA MARJOLAINE

A Revival of the Opérette in Three Acts, in French.[86] Libretto by Alfred Vanloo and Eugène Leterrier. Music by Charles Lecocq. Musical director, Mr. A. Lagye. Produced by Maurice Grau's French Opera Company. Opened 29 March 1883 at the Casino Theatre for 1 performance.

---

[81]First produced in New York 20 March 1882 at Tony Pastor's Music Hall for (24) performances. For Synopsis of Scenes and Musical Numbers, see 1883 production.

[82]First presented in New York 22 September 1881 at the Standard Theatre for 177 performances. For Synopsis of Scenes and Musical Numbers, see original 1881 production.

[83]Producer uncredited; scenery and costumes not credited in programs.

[84]First presented in New York 25 December 1880 at the Bijou Opera House for 63 performances. For Synopsis of Scenes and Musical Numbers, see original 1880 production. English adaptation uncredited in programs.

[85]First produced in New York in French 4 January 1869 at Pike's Opera House for 35 performances. For Synopsis of Scenes and Musical Numbers, see original 1869 production.

[86]First produced in New York in French 1 October 1877 at the Broadway Theatre for 22 performances in repertory during the season. For Synopsis of Scenes and Musical Numbers, see original 1877 production.

CAST: *La Marjolaine*: Mme. LOUISE THÉO. *Aveline*: Mlle. Buisson. *Palamede*: Mons. J. MEZIÈRES. *Annibal*: Mons. Huguet. *Frickel*: Mons. Noe Cadeau. *Peterschop*: Mons. DUPLAN. *Le Bourgmestre*: Mons. Vinchon. *D'Escoublac*: Mons. Salvator. *Schaerbeck*: Mons. Ducos. *Other characters by*: Mmes. Vallot, Vandamme, Caro, Duparc, Adrienne, Delournay, Salvator, Gatineau, Expert, Tamarelle, Messrs. Gerard, Norbert, Estiot.

1883.29 PRINCE CONTI

An Opéra-comique in Three Acts. Original French libretto ('Les Prés Saint-Gervais') by Victorien Sardou and Philippe Gille, based on Sardou's play of the same name.[87] Music by Charles Lecocq. Musical director, George Towle. Produced by the Catherine Lewis Comic Opera Company (Oscar L. Arfwedson, Manager). Opened 29 March 1883 at the Fifth Avenue Theatre and closed 30 March 1883 after 2 performances in repertory.

CAST: *Prince De Conti*: CATHERINE LEWIS. *La Rose*: HENRI LAURENT. *Harpin*: JOSEPH S. GREENSFELDER. *Nicole Van Haag*: FRED LENNOX. *Grégoire*: JOHN E. NASH. *La Terreur*: T. V. RICKETTS. *Sans Vergogne*: W. F. Wyckoff. *Landlord*: J. Galloway. *Maximilian*: F. St. Albyn. *Waiter*: May Stanford. *Friquette*: CONSTANCE F. LEWIS. *Madame Van Haag*: NELLIE MORTIMER. *Angélique*: EME LASCELLES. *Toinon*: ALICE VINCENT.

Schoolboys: Misses Lillie Boniface, Bertha Livingston, Rena Maginley, Cora Porter, Ada Clinton, Sadie Croghan. *Schoolmasters, Housewives, Soldiers, Grisettes*: Full Company.

Act 1: A Square in Paris. 1786.

Act 2: The Forest at Versailles.

Act 3: Another part of the Forest at Versailles.

1883.30 LA FILLE DE MADAME ANGOT

A Revival of the Opéra-comique in Three Acts, in French.[88] Libretto by Clairville, Paul Siraudin and Victor Koning. Music by Charles Lecocq. Musical director, Mr. A. Lagye. Produced by Maurice Grau's French Opera Company. Opened 2 April 1883 at the Casino Theatre and closed 13 April 1883 (matinee) after 4 performances in repertory; returned 15 May 1883 to Daly's Theatre for 1 additional performance.

CAST: *Clairette*: Mme. LOUISE THÉO. *Mlle. Lange* Mlle. LEROUX. *Amaranthe*: Mlle. Thal. *Hersilie*: Mlle. Buisson. *Cydalise*: Mlle. Vallot. *Delaunay*: Mlle. Caro. *Javotte*: Mlle. Delournay. *Therese*: Mlle. Gatineau. *Manon*: Mlle. Adrienne. *Babet*: Mlle. Salvador. *Herbelein*: Mlle. Berthe. *Ange Pitou*: VICTOR CAPOUL. *Pomponnet*: Mons. Grivel. *Larivandiere*: Mons. J. MEZIÈRES. *Louchard*: Mons. Duplan. *Treitz*: Mons. Ducos. *Cadet*: Mons. Mussy. *Guillaume*: Mons. Terrancle. *Buteux*: Mons. Vinchon. *Un Officier*: Mons. Girard. *Un Cabaratier*: Mons. Millet. *Incroyable*: Mons. Norbert.

1883.31 CINDERELLA AT SCHOOL

A Revival of the Musical Comedy in Two Acts, 6 Scenes[89]. Book, music and lyrics by Henry Woolson Morse. Based on the play "School" by T. W. Robertson. Produced under the supervision of Henry E. Dixey. Musical director, J. C. Mullally. Opened 2 April 1883 at the Fifth Avenue Theatre and closed 7 April 1883 after 7 performances.[90]

CAST: *Syntax*, Tutor, the Professor's head-usher and husher: HENRY E. DIXEY. *Arthur Bicycle*, a perambulating Deity of the upper-crust, with distinguished connections: EUGENE CLARKE. *Jack Polo*, of the Meadow Brook Hunt, Stroke-oar of Harvard in the race of '80: PAUL ARTHUR. *Lord Lawntennys*, a relic of other days and other lands, on a visit to his long-lost nephew, and on a search for a long-lost niece: FRANK REA. *Professor Kindergarten*, Principal of the Papyrus Seminary for Young Ladies, at Laurelton: W. P. BROWN. *Jenkinson*, Attendant on Lord Lawntennys: Hamilton Nichols. *Members of the Meadow Brook Hunt, also of Harvard and Yale Crews*: Messrs. Watterson, Perring, Attwood, Campbell, Drayton, Hall, Roland, Sullivan, Clark.

Psyche Persimmons, the sleepiest girl in the Seminary: VERNONA JARBEAU. *Merope Mallow*, a young lady from Brazil, the richest girl in her class and comparatively ignorant, but superlatively "smart": ROSE TEMPLE. *Niobe Marsh*, a charity pupil at Kindergarten's, the Cendrillon of the School: FRANCESCA GUTHRIE. *Chloris Slatepencil*, who lisps: LIZZIE THOMAS. *Sally Clark*, who pouts: Miss Wells. *Circe Slatepencil*, who giggles: Carrie Jackson. *Pancy Pickle*, who knows everything: Hindie Harrison. *Zenobia Tropics*, head teacher at the Papyrus, a firm believer in bone-forming: JENNIE HUGHES. *Miss Globes*, her assistant: Agnes Perring.

The Rest of the School Girls: *Lotis Slatepencil*, who sighs: Miss Ruby. *Penelope Slatepencil*, who eats: Kitty Wilson. *Primrose Pickle*, who knows nothing: Hattie Tracey. *Carrie Mall, Marian Glassy*, two very sweet girls: Misses Shandley, Wentworth. *Daisy Dimple*, a simple little thing: Miss Eckhardt. *Virginia Creeper*, an insinuating thing: Miss Newman. *Fragrant Pupils (6)*: *Rhoda Dendron*: Miss Bouia. *Minni Nett*: Miss Johnson. *Ollie Ander*: Miss Moore. *Amy Rylis*: Miss Atwood. *Anny Money*: Clara Brown. *Jessie Meen*: Marie Stewart. *Ada Verb, Pros Dee*, two very learned girls: Martha Golden, Lizzie Rochelle. (*Specialties*: *Solo on the Melophone and Zither*, School Scene: Adelaide Praeger. *Skipping-Rope Dance*: Katie Sharp.)

1883.32 THE MUDDY DAY

A Local Play in Three Acts, 4 Scenes. Play (and lyrics) by Edward Harrigan. Music composed and arranged by David Braham. Staged by Edward Harrigan. Scenery by Charles W. Witham. Mechanical effects by William McMurray. Properties and papier mache work by Robert Pullar. Costumes by Mrs. Jack. Produced by (Edward) Harrigan and (Tony) Hart. Opened 2 April 1883 at the Theatre Comique and closed 19 May 1883 after 56 performances.

CAST: *Captain Roger McNab*, of the *Muddy Day*: EDWARD HARRIGAN. *Mary Ann O'Leary*: TONY HART. *Jonas Highwater*: JOHN WILD. *Celia McCloud*: James Fox. *Jobson Fletcher*: Edward Burt. *Captain Herman Schoonover*: Harry A. Fisher. *Simcoe Fletcher*: M. F. Drew. *Gabe Jackson*: William West. *Hannah Jackson*: JOHN QUEEN. *Darby McFee*: JOHN QUEEN. *Reverend Barnacle Bloodroot*: William Barlow. *Rev. Islip Instep*: James Barlow. *Marcille Corrello*, First Mate of the *King William*: M. Bradley. *Cornelius O'Hochady*: M. Foley. *Erastus Ringworm*: Joseph Sparks. *Gilbert Rubberheel*: William Merritt. *Martha Oldsong*: John Sparks. *Mary Lampwick*: George Merritt. *Henry Schoonover*: Charles Coffey. *William Henry Pinkroot*: James Fitzsimons. *Phillip Mixture*: J. McCullough. *Rose Standish*: William O'Rourke. *Bartley Clearstarch*: G. L. Stout. *Trafalgar Quinlan*: J. Sullivan. *Wilford*: Master Guion. *Teddy*: Master Groneberg. *Ruth Fletcher*: Annie Mack Berlein. *Lydia O'Leary*: Sallie Williams. *Gertrude Watson*: Annie D. Ware. *Maggie Kline*: Ada Farwell. *Fanny May*: Marie Gorenflo. *Nellie Howard*: Bertha Wild. *Ellen Terry*: Kate Langdon. *Lolo Montez*: Annie Langdon. *Kittie Bowers*: Jessie West. *Mattie Fielding*: Sadie Morris. *Ethel Blair*: Annie Hall. *May Miner*: Lizzie Finn. *Lillian Lang*: Mrs. Scallan. (*Xylophone Specialty*: Ed King.)

Act 1: Kitchen in Ruth Fletcher's House.

Act 2, Scene 1: View of West Street. *Scene 2*: The Floating Bethel. Wharves and Shipping.

Act 3: Pier and Dump with a view of river and adjacent city by night.

MUSICAL NUMBERS

"The Golden Choir"
Company

"(On Board O') The Muddy Day"
E. Harrigan

"The Family Overhead"

"The Little Bunch o' Berries"
T. Hart

"Silly Boy"
M. F. Drew

"The Turnverein Cadets"
12 Cadets

Xylophone Solo
E. King

1883.33 GREEN-ROOM FUN!

Salsbury's Troubadors in the Musical Novelty in Three Acts. Play by Bronson Howard. Acting manager, Frank Maeder. Musical conductor, W. W. Furst. Produced by Salsbury's Troubadors (Charles J. Crouse, Business Agent). Opened 9 April 1883 at the Standard Theatre and closed 5 May 1883 after 29 performances.

CAST: *Mr. Booth McC. Forrest*, a heavy tragedian: NATE SALSBURY. *The "Old Chief" War Cloud*: NATE SALSBURY. *Miss Kitty Plumpet*, a Born Actress, with a Special Line, and a man on the end of it: NELLIE McHENRY. *The Indian Princess*: NELLIE McHENRY. *The Reverend Ernest Duckworth*, on duty without his leave: John Webster. *The Earl of Kensington*: John Webster. *Captain Henry Opdyke*, on leave and off duty: Lewis Baker. *Eagle of the Craig*: Lewis Baker. *The Prompter*: Fred A. Bowman. *Herr Shrickonghost*, the leader: W. W. Furst. *The Stage Carpenter*: G. W. Bouvier. *Mrs.*

[87]English language adaptation uncredited in programs.

[88]First produced in New York 25 August 1873 at Daly's Broadway Theatre in repertory. For Synopsis of Scenes and Musical Numbers, see original 1873 production.

[89]First produced in New York 5 March 1881 at Daly's Theatre for 65 performances. For Synopsis of Scenes and Musical Numbers, see original 1881 production.

[90]No credits in program for scenery, costumes or producer. Augustin Daly produced the original 1881 production.

Camilla Westlake, a model young widow, born like a poet, she can't be made: MARIE HUNTER. *The Marchioness of Belgravia*: MARIE HUNTER. *Coryphées*, the Church Choir Ballet by Three Ladies of the Congregation volunteering for the Benefit Little Cannibal: Amelia Thinn, Amelia Medeeyum, Amelia Phatt.

Act 1: Rehearsal at home. Learning their parts. Costumes. Two pairs of lovers. Pulpit and stage. Art and flirtation. A double lovers' quarrel.

Act 2: Rehearsals on the stage. The War of Tuning Fiends. Two jealous women. Troubles of a stage manager. A Death Scene and a Dying War-Whoop. A Change of Lovers.

Act 3: Green Room of the Theatre during the performance. Amateur Anxiety and Professional Woes. Amateur Costumes and Amateur Properties. Haps and Mishaps of Amateur Acting.

1883.34 LE GRAND CASIMIR

A Comédie-vaudeville (Opérette) in Three Acts, in French. Libretto by Jules Prével and Albert de Saint-Albin. Music by Charles Lecocq. Produced by Maurice Grau's French Opera Company. Opened 11 April 1883 at the Casino Theatre and closed 14 April 1883 after 2 performances in repertory; returned 18 May 1883 to Daly's Theatre for 1 additional performance in repertory. Total: 3 performances.

CAST: *Angélina*: Mme. LOUISE THÉO. *Casimir*: Mons. J. MEZIÈRES. *Sotherman*: Mons. GRIVEL. *Le Grand-Duc*: Mons. DUPLAN. *Gobson*: Mons. VINCHON. *Galetti*: Mons. Ducos. *Picasso*: Mons. Noe Cadeau. *Joseph*: Mons. Girard. *Pietro*: Baby Mauge. *Ninettta*: Mlle. BOISSON. *Pétronilla*: Mlle. Vallot. *Colomba*: Mlle. Caro. *Séraphina*: Mlle. Vandamme. *Lydia*: Mlle. Adrienne. (*Clowns, Écuyers, Écuyères, Habitants et Habitantes de Bastia.*)

Act 1: Le Cabinet Directorial d'un Cirque anglais.

Act 2: Un Carrefour à Bastia.

Act 3: L'Hôtel du Lion-d'Or à Bastia.

ACT 1[91]

Choeur d'Introduction (Que nous veut-on, l'on nous invite)
Choeur
Couplets (Clowns, écuyers, troupe modèle)
Mons. Vinchon, Choeur
Couplets de jongleur (Avec six boules je jonglais)
Mons. Vinchon
Couplets du chic et du chèque (Au chèque tu n'es pas sensible)
Mons. Duplan
Coupets du dompteur (J'ai dompté trois ours à la fois)
Mons. J. Mezières
Duo (Soit, auparavant que je meure)
Mme. L. Théo, Mons. J. Mezières
Final (Vive le Grand Casimir)
Mme. L. Théo, Messrs. J. Mezières, Grivel, Girard, Duplan, Vinchon, Choeur

ACT 2

Introduction et choeur (On célèbre le mariage)/
Couplets (Parti depuis deux ans)
4 Demoiselles d'honneur, Mons. Cadeau
Couplets (Tu seras toujours mon chéri)
Mlle. Boisson
Choeur des cloches (Allons, allons, dépêchons-nous)
Messrs. J. Mezières, Ducos
Polka du cheval/Musique de scène
Rondeau (Il le savait bien, le perfide)
Mme. L. Théo
Choeur (Voilà la noce qui revient)
Musique de scène
Couplets (Au fond de votre verre)
Mlle. Boisson, Mons. J. Mezières
Couplets de la pèche (Vous n'savez p'têt'pas comme on pêche)
Mons. J. Mezières
Final (Ah! le bon champagne qu'il nous a payé)
Mme. L. Théo, Mlle. Boisson,
Messrs. J. Mezières, Grivel, Girard, Duplan, Vinchon, Choeur

ACT 3

Rondo des 2 Pigeons (Deux Pigeons s'aimaient d'amour tendre)
Mme. L. Théo
Trio (Mais, vraiment, c'est à n'y pas croire)
Messrs. Grivel, Duplan, Ducos
Couplets (Comme on traite les bigames)
Couplet Final (Vous avez vu par quelles défaillances)

[91]Musical numbers not listed in programs. List prepared from published French piano vocal score (Brandus et Cie., Paris, 1879).

1883.35 DER PRINZ GEMAHL

An Operetta in Three Acts, in German. Libretto by Julius Hopp (and Heinrich Bohrmann-J. Riegen[92]). Music by Ludwig Engländer. Artistic director, Heinrich Conried. Orchestra under the direction of Gustave A. Kerker. Produced by the Thalia Theatre (Carl Herrmann, Manager). Opened 11 April 1883 at the Thalia Theatre and closed 24 April 1883 after 14 performances; returned as THE PRINCE CONSORT under the auspices of the Thalia Comic Opera Company 4 June 1883 to Wallack's Theatre and closed 16 June 1883 after 12 additional performances. Total: 26 performances[93].

CAST: *Helene*, reigning Princess of Lachenstein: Frl. RABERG. *Papischeff*, Minister of all Portfolios: Herr ADOLFI. *Eustachia*, his Sister: Frl. KÖNIG. *Hotteroto*, his Confidant: Herr LUBE. *Rosina*: Frl. HECHT. *Arthur*, Prince of Lohenstein: Herr HUBERT WILKE. *Evergreen (Immergrün)*, an Adventurer: Herr STEINBERGER. *Baron Mack*, Ambassador of Lohenstein: Herr Frölich. *Councillors (3)*: *Lollerfeld*: Herr Blohm. *Bightblue*: Herr Blohm. *Barmen*: Herr Sternheim.

Court Ladies (10): *Gertrude*: Frl. Stork. *Martha*: Frl. Michaelis. *Anna*: Frl. Meyer. *Rose*: Frl. Erdman. *Clara*: Frl. Lieb. *Josephine*: Frl. Nichols. *Ida*: Frl. Eisner. *Marie*: Frl. Pegel. *Susanne*: Frl. Weissner. *Louise*: Frl. Schlag. *Ladies of the Court, Ambassadors, Soldiers, Servants, etc.*

1883.36 CAD: THE TOMBOY

A Comedy Drama in Five Acts. Play by Leonard Grover. Produced by Carrie Swain (C. B. Palmer, Manager). Opened 23 April 1883 at Daly's Theatre and closed 5 May 1883 after 14 performances.[94]

CAST: *Cad*, the Tomboy: CARRIE SWAIN. *Cad*, the Song and Dance Artist: CARRIE SWAIN. *Cad*, the Telegraph Artist: CARRIE SWAIN. *Cad*, the Heiress: CARRIE SWAIN. *Emma*, an Adventuress: HANNAH SARGENT. *Mrs. Cobb*, Blind, but not uncared for: Alice Grey. *Fannie*: Ella Hunt *Matron of the Asylum*: Mabel Stone. *Robert Cobb*: C. J. Fyffe. *Henry Disbrow*: C. W. Sutton. *Grinshaw*, an Attorney: Sol Smith. *Tom Burns*, a Gas Fitter: Murray Woods. *Policeman*: James Bevans. *Doctor*: Fred Leavitt. *Guard*: E. J. McCullough. *Cabman*: Charles Whitney. *Tramp*: George Robinson.

1883.37 FORTUNIO AND HIS SEVEN GIFTED SERVANTS

An Operatic Extravaganza in One Act, 4 Scenes. Libretto adapted for American representation, from J. R. Planché ('Fortunio, or the Seven Gifted Servants'). Music by Francis T. S. Darley. Stage manager, William H. Fitzgerald. Scenery by (Walter) Burridge. Musical director, William J. Rostetter. Manager, C. H. Green. Opened 23 April 1883 at the Cosmopolitan Theatre and closed 5 May 1883 after 14 performances.

CAST: (*Three Daughters of Baron Dunover*): *Myrtina Dunover*, afterwards "Fortunio": ADELAIDE RANDALL. *Pertina Dunover*: Susie Singer. *Flirtina Dunover*: Rose Temple. *Herald of King Alfourite*: Hattie Starr. *The Fairy Favorable*: Jennie Prince. *Baron Dunover*: LITHGOW JAMES. *Princess Vindicta*, Sister of Alfourite: JENNIE REIFFERTH. *The Seven Gifted Servants*: *Lightfoot*: Hattie Starr. *Marksman*: Susie Singer. *Fine Ear*: Rose Temple. *Tippler*: Mr. Van Houten. *Gourmand*: Mr. Van Vechten. *Boisterer*: Mr. A. Collins. *Strongback*: Walter Allen. *King Alfourite*: WILLIAM H. FITZGERALD. *Florida*, companion of Vindicta: Miss M. Taylor. *Lady in Waiting*: Miss Earle. *Minister of State*: Samuel W. Keene. *The Dragon*: FRANZ WETTER. *Emperor Matapa*: LITHGOW JAMES. *Chamberlain*: S. W. Keene. *Princess Volante*,

[92]Otherwise known in Vienna as Julius Nigri von Saint-Albino.

[93]No program found for the Thalia engagement. Cast list prepared from Wallack's Theatre engagement and prior tour under the title THE PRINCE CONSORT. According to press reviews, Herren Klein, Meyer, Silbernagel were in the Thalia company.

[94]No credits in programs for director, scenery or costumes. During the evening, Miss Swain will introduce her famous Lullaby; critics also noted a waltz song, her celebrated medleys (a Negro Jubilee and a Tyrolean Air) and dances.

daughter of Matapa: BILLIE BARLOW. *Page to King*: Miss T. Hanlan. *Peasants, Courtiers, Soldiers of Matapa, Pages, Guards, Ladies in Attendance on Volante, Fairies*: Chorus of 60.

Scene 1: The outskirts of a Spanish Village. *Scene 2*: The Courtyard of (King) Alfourite's Palace. *Scene 3*: The Summer Camp of Matapa, with Race Course. *Scene 4*: The Palace of King Alfourite, with Illuminated Gardens. Transformation Scene. Appearance of the Fairy Favorable in her Chariot, drawn by Four and Twenty Golden Sheep.

MUSICAL NUMBERS[95]

Scene 1
- Opening Chorus (Behold the Herald of the King)
  H. Starr, Chorus
- Recitative and Song (What's to be done?)
  L. James
- Song (Of Old we're told the Amazons did fight)
  A. Randall, S. Singer, R. Temple
- Finale (Your servants, sir, in us you see)
  A Randall, Seven Servants

Scene 2
- Song (In the good old days 'twas bliss to be a King")
  W. H. Fitzgerald
- Quartette (Unaccompanied)
  A. Randall, J. Reiffarth, W. H. Fitzgerald, S. W. Keene
- Duet (From my station in life)
  A. Randall, J. Reiffarth
- Chorus of Peasants and Soldiers (Theterrible dragon is on his way!)
- Quartette (Come, Master Dragon, we're ready for you)
  A. Randall, R. Temple, Mr. Van Houten, W. Allen
- Entrance of the Dragon (Weary am I)
  F. Wetter
- (Battle and) Finale
  A. Randall, J. Reifferth, W. H. Fitzgerald, All

Scene 3
- Recitative (Now are we ready)
  L. James, Chorus
- Entrance of Fortunio
- Bread Chorus (The bread we bring)
  A. Randall, Chorus
- Exit of Matapa and His Court
- Recitative and Ballad (Yes! here am I in foreign land)
  A. Randall
- Entrance of Matapa, Violante and Court
- The Race (They're off! They're off!)
  L. James, A. Randall, S. Singer, S. W. Keene, Mr. Van Houten, R. Temple, Chorus
- Finale (Oh most unfortunate of days!)
  L. James, A. Randall, Servants, Chorus

Scene 4
- Song and Chorus (The Act it was a glorious thing)
  W. H. Fitzgerald, Chorus
- Duet and Final Chorus (How oft in truth a gracious deed)
  W. H. Fitzgerald, A. Randall, Servants, Chorus

1883.38

THE PRINCESS OF TREBIZONDE

A Revival of the Comic Opera in Three Acts[96]. Original French libretto to the opéra-bouffe 'La Princesse de Trébizonde' by Charles Nuitter and Étienne Tréfeu. English libretto by Charles Lamb Kenney. Music by Jacques Offenbach. Produced under the stage direction of Jesse Williams. Scenery by Messrs. Philip Goatcher, George W. Dayton, Farren. Costumes by Miss Berg. Produced by the McCaull Comic Opera Company (John A. McCaull, Proprietor and Manager). Opened 5 May 1883 at the Casino Theatre and closed 9 June 1883 after 36 performances

CAST: *Prince Raphael*, son of Casimir: LILLIAN RUSSELL. *Paola*, a female juggler: LAURA JOYCE. *Regina*, a tight-rope walker: MADELINE LUCETTE. *Zanetta*, a danseuse: EMMA CARSON. *Cabriolo*, leader of a troop of jugglers: JOHN HOWSON. *Tremolini*, clown: DIGBY BELL. *Prince Casimir*: GEORGE OLMI. *Skaradrap*, tutor of Raphael: A. W. MAFLIN. *Lottery Men*: E. S. Grant, Charles Howard. *Rocoli*: Miss Hanley. *Becardo*: Miss Weddle. *Flammis*: Miss Caldwell. *Francises*: Miss Allen. *Pages, Hunters, Courtiers, Peasants, etc.*

Act 1: Market Place. (Goatcher.)

Act 2: A Terrace in front of a Baronial Castle. (Dayton.)

Act 3: Salon in Prince Casimir's Palace. (Farren.)

1883.39

SATANELLA, or, the Power of Love

A Revival of the Comic Opera in Five Acts, 7 Scenes[97]. (Libretto by Edmund Falconer and Augustus Harris.) Music by Michael William Balfe. Stage manager James Barton. Scenery by Walter Burridge, George W. Dayton. Costumes by P. Godchaux (principals), Cole and Company, Schwencke and Mrs. Hill. Mechanical effects by A. Filler. Properties by Joseph Brabyn. Musical director, George E. Loesch. Produced by the Barton English Opera Company. Opened 9 May 1883 at the Standard Theatre and closed 19 May 1883 after 12 performances.

CAST: *Count Rupert*: GEORGE TRAVERNER. *Hortensius*: J. H. Stuart. *Karl*, tenant of the Castle: W. H. Hampshire. *The Vizier*: William White. *Fabian*: Helen Lowell. *Franz*: Sophie Hummel. *Bracaccio*, pirate leader: W. H. HAMILTON. *Arimanes*, the fiend: FRED BORNEMANN. *Satanella*, a female demon: ALICE MAY. *Lelia*, Count Rupert's foster-sister: MARIE JANSEN. *Stella*, engaged to Count Rupert: ROSE TEMPLE. *Dame Bertha*, Lelia's guardian: Lizzie Parr. *Ballet*: Mlle. ADELINA MATHIEU; Mlles. Louise Watson, Laura Rose, Kate Estcourt, Josephine Ciemietcka, Lizzie Leroy, Alice Richards. *Nobles, Male Retainers, Pirates, etc.*

Act 1: The Park of Count Rupert's Palace on a Fete Day. (Burridge.)

Act 2: A Tower in Old Brockenbourg. (Burridge.)

Act 3: A Sea Coast near Leila's Cottage. (Burridge, Dayton.)

Act 4, Scene 1: The Infernal Kingdom of Arimanes. (Dayton.) *Scene 2*: A Market Square in Tunis. (Burridge.)

Act 5, Scene 1: A room in Rupert's Castle. (Dayton.) *Scene 2*: Transformation. (Dayton.)

SPECIALTIES[98]
- Demon Ballet Divertissement (*Arranged by* Signor Novissimo. *Music by* George A. Loesch.)
  A. Mathieu, Ballet

1883.40

BOB

A Comedy Drama in Three Acts. Play by Fred Marsden. Produced under the stage direction of stage manager, Fred Percy. Scenery by E. H. Chase. Produced by Lotta Crabtree (J. A. Crabtree, Manager). Opened 14 May 1883 at the Fifth Avenue Theatre and closed 26 May 1883 after 14 performances[99].

CAST: *Bob*, a Wild Flower transplanted to a Conservatory: LOTTA (CRABTREE). *Wybert Romayne*, who believes the end justifies the means: JEROME STEVENS. *Lieutenant Frank Elden*, very brave and very susceptible: CLEMENT BAINBRIDGE. *Major Jasper Elden*, a brave warrior captured: W. H. WALLIS. *Professor Doremeso Sharp*, in perfect harmony with his calling: C. H. BRADSHAW. *M. Victor Delpuis*, an exile for good and sufficient reasons: RALPH DELMORE. *Janson Garnet*, who sinned and suffered: FRED PERCY. *Edna Garnet*, with an enduring faith: GERTRUDE JOHNSON. *Mrs. Major Elden*, the lamp of the household: LULU JORDAN. *Miss Plum*, a modern Lavonia: Mrs. SOL SMITH.

School Girls, Fair and Fancy Free (8); *Miss Selton*: Mary Brown. *Miss Ormund*: Minnie Hazel. *Miss Nobrain*: Ida Rosa. *Miss Phair*: Lulu Bradley. *Miss Rich*: Kittie Wallace. *Miss Duhl*: Maggie Moore. *Miss Phoolish*: Carrie Meadre. *Miss Morton*: Eva Frazier.

Act 1: Miss Plum's establishment at Cedar Cottage. Bob's denunciation.

Act 2: The Library at Garnet Oaks. Bob's discovery.

Act 3: The Grounds at Garnet Oaks. Bob's reward.

---

[95]Musical numbers not listed in programs. List prepared from published piano vocal score (J. M. Stoddart & Co., Philadelphia, 1883).

[96]First produced in New York 11 September 1871 at Wallack's Theatre for 7 performances. For Musical Numbers, see original 1871 production.

[97]First produced in New York in an earlier version 23 February 1863 at Niblo's Garden for (21) performances.

[98]Musical numbers not listed in programs.

[99]No credits in programs for composer, lyricist, musical director or costumes. Program notes that Lotta will introduce new songs and dances.

MUSICAL NUMBER[100]

"How Much Does the Baby Weigh?"
L Crabtree
(*Music and Lyrics by* Will Hays.)

1883.41 BOCCACCIO

A Revival of the Operette in Three Acts, in French[101]. (Original Viennese libretto by F. Zell and Richard Genée. French adaptation by Henri Chivot and Alfred Duru.) Music by Franz von Suppé. Musical director, Mons. A. Lagye. Produced by Maurice Grau's French Opera Company. Opened 14 May 1883 at Daly's Theatre and closed 19 May 1883 after 6 performances in repertory.

CAST: *Boccaccio*: Mme. LOUISE THÉO. *Prince Orlando*: Mons. GRIVEL. *Oandolfi*, a Gardener: Mons. DUPLAN. *Tromboli*, a Cooper: Mons. Mauge. *Quiquibio*, a Barber: M. Ducos. *Lelia*, friend to Boccaccio: Mlle. Betty. *Beppo*, Pedlar: Mons. Vinchon. *The Unknown*: Mons. Girard. *Cecco*, an Old Beggar: Mons. Giraud. *Captain of the Guards*: Mons. Terrancle. *A Citizen*: Mons. Emile. *Beatrice*: Mlle. THEROUX. *Peronella*, wife to Pandolfo: Mlle. Thal. *Zanetta*, wife to Quiquibio: Mlle. Dorsay. *Frisca*, wife to Tromboli: Mme. Vallot. *First Delle d'Honneur*: Mme. Buisson. *Second Delle D'Honneur*: Mme. Salvator. *Giotto*: Mlle. Vandamme. *Frederico*: Mlle. Delournay. *Tofano*: Mlle. Duparc. *Raphaele*: Mlle. Adrienne. *Students, Men and Women of the People, Lords and Ladies of the Court, Maids of Honor, Valets, Pages, etc.*

1883.42 POP

Rice's Surprise Party in a Highly Sensational Melo-Dramatic Operatic Comedy Melange (Summer Entertainment of Frivolity and Mirth, a Musical Comedy) in Three Acts, 7 Scenes[102]. (Play and music, original and selected, by Edward E. Rice.) Scenery by (George W.) Dayton & Sons. Properties by A. W. Stephens. Mechanical effects by H. Raymond. Gas effects by E. A. Kelly. Director of orchestra, Fred J. Eustis. Entire production under the personal supervision and direction of Edward E. Rice. (Produced by Edward E. Rice.) Opened 21 May 1883 at the Bijou Opera House, moved 9 July 1883 to Haverly's (14th Street) Theatre and closed 21 July 1883 after 76 performances; returned 19-24 November 1883 to the Fifth Avenue Theatre for 7 additional performances. Total: 83 performances.

CAST: *Adolphus Pop*, a dramatic author, whose works have not met with the recognition they deserve: JOHN A. MACKAY. *Anthony Belsize*, from Alabama, a wealthy Southerner, who is never in a hurry, who used to masquerade in female attire in his youth: GEORGE K. FORTESCUE. *Charles Page*, a rising young English attorney, very much in love with Belle: N. S. BURNHAM. *Jem Smart*, alias Asa Jebb, alias Colonel Flammer, dramatic agent, a doubtful character, who would be better if circumstances were different: W. T. Doyle. *Knous*, a German servant, who wrestles with the vernacular in a most remarkable manner: D. Gorman. *Spriggins*, a model office boy, or attorney's clerk, in the employ of Sharp & Lewis: Albert Murdock. *Bill Bishop*, a common fellow, who believes self-preservation the first law of nature: Edward Taylor. *Justice Barlow*, of the New York Police Court: James Mills. *Bags*, the Detective: H. L. Rattenberry. *Sophia Belsize*, Niece of Anthony Belsize, a perfect Southern beauty: KATE CASTLETON. *Belle Adams*, a daughter of Belsize by his first wife, an actress at the Theatre Royal: IRENE PERRY. *Adele Pop*, sister to Adolphus, a ballet dancer and vocalist at the Royal Alhambra: MAY STEMBLER. *Jeannette*, a French waiting maid, who loves when she loves: LILLIE GRUBB. *Telegraph Messenger*: Ida Smith. *Sailors, passengers on the steamship, etc.*

Act 1, Scene 1: Attorney's office in London. *Scene 2*: Street in London. *Scene 3*: Apartments of Adolphus Pop.

Act 2: Saloon of the Steamship *"Scythia."* Benefit entertainment for the Bulgarian Twins.

Act 3, Scene 1: Dramatic agent's office in New York. *Scene 2*: Union Square in New York. *Scene 3*: Police Court in New York.

ACT 2

Tyrolean Warblings
M. Stembler, L. Grubb, I. Smith

"For Goodness Sake, Don't Say I Told You"
K. Castleton
(*Music by* Maggie Duggan. *Lyrics by* Joe Bradford.)

Belle Adams' Specialties
I. Perry

"Sunflower and Lily" (Medley Duet)
K. Castleton, G. K. Fortescue

Scene from 'Pygmalion and Galatea'
Galatea: M. Stembler. *Pygmalion*: L. Grubb.

Burlesque Scene from 'Romeo and Juliet'
Romeo: H. L. Rattenberry. *Juliet*: K. Castleton. *Capulet*: N. S. Burnham. *Nurse*: D. Gorman.

Pop's Imitations!
J. A. Mackay

Grand Operatic Potpourri!
Introducing gems from popular operas of the day: OLIVETTE; (MADAME) L'ARCHIDUC; LA MASCOTTE; CARMEN; THE MERRY WAR; extracts of melody from several sources, including Harrigan & Hart's "Veteran Guard Cadets," "Major Gilfeather," "Is That Mr. Riley?," etc.

1883.43 CHEEK

A Comedy Drama in Four Acts. Play by Fred Marsden. Produced by Gustave A. Mortimer. Opened 28 May 1883 at Haverly's (14th Street) Theatre and closed 23 June 1883 after 32 performances.[103]

CAST: *Dick Smythe*, always ready to take the chances: ROLAND REED. *Colonel Walter Sandford*, one of the F.F.V.s: WELSH EDWARDS. *Ray Sandford*, who has turned over a new leaf: Frank Foster. *Albert Sandford*, who plays a dangerous game: Frank Losee. *James Atwell*, with literary aspirations: H. Reese Davies. *Moses*, free from bondage: Oliver Jenkins. *Policeman 303*, a novelty: A. T. McCart. *Walt Alton*, who has tried a little of everything: Oliver Jenkins. *Samuel*: R. I. Karby. *Nell*, can take care of herself: BLANCHE VAUGHAN. *Jane Atwell*, a somewhat homely character: Annie Mortimer. *Mrs. Abel Racket*, with an extended experience: Alice Hastings.

Act 1: The exterior of Atwell's cottage; Westmoreland view. Tableau—Confederates in crime.

Act 2: Interior of the Homestead; Tableau—Conscience awakened.

Act 3: Madison Square, New York, under the Electric Light. Tableau—Cheek conquers muscle.

Act 4: An Old Virginia Mansion. Tableau—Acting on the Square.

[100]Musical numbers not listed in programs. Listed prepared from published sheet music.

[101]French language premiere in New York; previously presented in German 23 April 1880 at the Thalia and in English 15 May 1880 at the Union Square Theatre.

[102]In second week of the run re-titled POP-POP; moved as POP! to Haverly's (14th Street) Theatre; re-opened at the Fifth Avenue Theatre as POP, or, The Fortunes of a Dramatic Author.

[103]No stage director, composer, lyricist, scenery or costume credits in programs. Tryout and touring programs note that Roland Reed introduced new songs and medleys, and Blanche Vaughn introduced a Medley with Roland Reed, and that Roland Reed introduced "I'm a Perfect New York Dude!," written expressly for him.

1883–1884 SEASON

Mathilde Cottrelly in THE BEGGAR STUDENT
Billy Rose Theatre Collection, New York Public Library for the Performing Arts

1883–1884 SEASON

1883.44

PRINCE METHUSALEM

A Comic Opera in Three Acts, 4 Scenes. (Original Viennese libretto 'Prinz Methusalem' by Karl Treumann, adapted from a libretto by Victor Wilder and Alfred Delacour.) English libretto by Leo Goldmark. Music by Johann Strauss. Stage director, M. Lube. Scenery by Charles Hueist. Costumes by Buchheister. Musical director, Ernst Catenhusen. Orchestrations by Johann Strauss. Produced under the direction of Ernst Catenhusen. Opened 25 June 1883 at the Cosmopolitan Theatre and closed 5 July 1883 after (12) performances.[1]

CAST: *Prince Methusalem*, Son of Cyprian: CATHERINE LEWIS. *Pulcinella*, Daughter of Sigismund: BELLE ROSE. *Sophistica*, Wife of Cyprian: Mme. Lube. *Cyprian*, Duke of Ricarac: J. H. RYLEY. *Sigismond*, Duke of Trocadero: GUSTAVE ADOLPHI. *Trombonius*, composer of the future: WILLIAM H. FITZGERALD. *Count Vulcanio*, Grand Chamberlain: WILLIAM HERBERT. *M. Feirstein, Mandelbaum*, Ambassadors from Ricarac: Messrs. M. Loe, Gross. *Spadi*, officer: BILLIE BARLOW. *Gasparo*, sergeant: Miss S. Hummel. *First Bravo*: Mr. Connell. *Second Bravo*: Mr. Taylor. *Third Bravo*: Mr. Hammond. *Fourth Bravo*: Mr. Wagner. *Night Watchman*: Mr. Lehmann. *Pages (4)*: *Carlo*: Lillie Shandley. *Pietro*: Eugenie Maynard. *Francisco*: Sadie Winner. *Enrico*: Carrie Parker. *Signora Ernesta, Signora Arabella*, Ladies of the Court: Lizzie Newman, Emma Palaccio.

Act 1: Garden in front of the castle of the reigning Duke of Trocadero.

Act 2, Scene 1: Street in Trocadero; the residence of Duke Sigismund. *Scene 2*: Castle of Sigismund.

Act 3: Street in Trocadero.

1883.45

PRINCE METHUSALEM

An Opera Comique in Three Acts, 4 Scenes. Original Viennese libretto ('Prinz Methusalem') by Karl Treumann, adapted from a libretto by Victor Wilder and Alfred Delacour. English libretto by Sydney Rosenfeld. Music by Johann Strauss. Produced under the stage direction of Jesse Williams. Scenery by Philip Goatcher. Costumes by Mme. Printz. Musical director, Professor Hill. Orchestrations by Johann Strauss. Produced by the McCaull Opera Comique Company (Rudolph Aronson and John A. McCaull). Opened 9 July 1883 at the Casino Theatre and closed 13 October 1883 after 102 performances.[2]

CAST: *Prince Methusalem*, Son of Cyprian: MATHILDE COTTRELLY. *Pulcinella*, Daughter of Sigismund: LILLY POST. *Sophistica*, Wife of Cyprian: JULIE de RUYTHER. *Spadi*: ROSE BEAUDET. *Sigismund*, Duke of Trocadero: FRANCIS WILSON. *Cyprian*, Duke of Ricarac: A. W. MAFLIN. *Trombonius*, composer of the future: JAY TAYLOR. *Count Vulcanio*, Grand Chamberlain: HARRY STANDISH. *Carbonazzi*: ELLIS RYSE. *Fairstein*: Mr. Kaufman. *Mandelbaum*: Mr. McCarthy. *First Bravo*: Mr. Schrader. *Second Bravo*: Mr. McDonough. *Third Bravo*: Mr. E. Grant. *Fourth Bravo*: Mr. Barbara. *Night Watchman*: Mr. Fay.

Act 1: Exterior of Duke Sigismund's Castle.

Act 2, Scene 1: Street in Trocadero. *Scene 2*: Breakfast-room of Duke Sigismund's Castle.

Act 3: The Market Place of Trocadero.

MUSICAL NUMBERS[3]

"The Dotlet on the 'i'"
F. Wilson

1883.46

THE MULLIGAN GUARD BALL

A Local Comedy in Two Acts, 7 Scenes[4]. Play (and lyrics) by Edward Harrigan. Music by David Braham. (Staged by Edward Harrigan.) Musical director, David Braham. Scenery by Charles W. Witham. Mechanical effects by William McMurray. Properties and Papier Mache work by Robert Puller. Produced by (Edward) Harrigan and (Tony) Hart. Opened 6 August 1883 at the Theatre Comique and closed 22 September 1883 after 56 performances.

CAST: *Dan Mulligan*: EDWARD HARRIGAN. *Tommy Mulligan*: TONY HART. *Captain Sim Primrose*: JOHN WILD. *Palestine Puter*: George H. Wood. *Ferguson Clinton*: JAMES FOX. *Gustavus Lochmuller*: HARRY A. FISHER. *Mrs. Honora Dublin*: JOHN QUEEN. *Walsingham McSweeney*: M. Bradley. *Gabe Go-off*: PETER C. GOLDRICH. *Mr. Edgeup*: RICHARD QUILTER. *Pizarro Push*: WILLIAM WEST. *Mr. Overocker*: Joseph Sparks. *Jackson McGee*: JAMES BARLOW. *Mr. Ceiling*: CHRISTIE MILLER. *Simpkin Dainty*: JOHN SPARKS. *Mr. Cloudy*: M. Foley. *Lafayette*: GEORGE MERRITT. *Carl Schroder*: George L. Stout. *Isaac Goldstein*: James Fitzsimmons. *Cassius O'Rourke*: Thomas Granger. *Bolivar McQuade*: Charles Coffey. *Mr. Shock*: William Merritt. *Washington Duplex*: J. McCullough. *Mr. Doolittle*: Emil Heusel. *Mr. Hardacre*: William A. Barlow. *Mr. Bimble*: J. Ward. *Gussie Lochmuller*: Master Guion. *Mrs. Mulligan*: Mrs. ANNIE YEAMANS. *Kitty Lochmuller*: Gertie Granville. *Mrs. Lochmuller*: Jennie Christie. *Cleopatra McSweeney*: Ada Farwell. *Maggie Kearney*: Lizzie Finn. *Miss Riley*: Sadie Morris. *Mary Mullen*: Annie Langdon. *Delia Murphy*: Kate Langdon. *Sallie Malloy*: Annie Hall.

Act 1: Preparations. *Scene 1*: The Home of the Mulligans. *Scene 2*: Catherine Street. *Scene 3*: Simpson Primrose's Barber Shop and Maggie Kearney's Hair Dressing Establishment.

Act 2: The Ball. *Scene 1*: View of Canal Street. *Scene 2*: Walsingham McSweeney's Wee Drop. *Scene 3*: View of Grand Street. *Scene 4*: The Harp and the Shamrock. The Mulligan Guard Ball.

MUSICAL NUMBERS

"Little Widow Dunn"

"Down in Gossip Row"

"The Skidmore Fancy Ball"

"The Pitcher of Beer"

"The Babies on Our Block"

"We're All Young Fellows, Bran New"

Solo and Variations for Xylophone
E. King

1883.47

THE DEVIL'S AUCTION, or, The Golden Branch

A Spectacular Extravaganza in Three Acts, 9 Scenes. Written by Gallagher, Gilmore and Gardner. Stage manager, Charles E. Fisher. Scenery by Harley Merry. Costumes by P. Godchaux & Co. Musical director, Francis Tamponi. Management of Charles H. Yale. Opened 18 August 1883 at the 14th Street Theatre and closed 1 September 1883 after 17 performances; returned 24 September 1883 to the Windsor Theatre and closed 29 September 1883 after an additional 8 performances.[5]

CAST: CHRISTIANS: *Toby*, a donkey, afterwards transformed into a man: JAMES S. MAFFITT. *Père Andoche*, an old Norman farmer: W. H. BARTHOLOMEW. *Barberouse*, a Necromancer, surnamed the Green Dwarf: Dore Davidson. *Carlos*, a poor shepherd: A. W. Decker. *Going Gone*, an Auctioneer: Charles E. Fisher. *Lavigne*, a Woodcutter: J. A. Throw. *Trezbien*, a Bailiff: J. C. Tiernan. *Normans (2)*: *Victor*: H. G. Gooding. *Adolph*: Frank Thompson. *Peasants (2)*: *Gustave*: J. C. Showles. *Alexander*: A. S. Franks. *Madeline*, Andoche's daughter: ANNIE BARCLAY. *Mère Cazotte*, A spinster: Nellie Heywood. *Janet*, a Milkmaid: Sallie Apt. *Nanine*, Lavigne's wife: Ella Sheldon. *Peasants, Villagers, etc.*

MONGOLIANS: *Kow-Wow-Shang*, Emperor of China, and Cousin to the Moon: W. H. BARTHOLOMEW. *Tsching-Sing*, Grand Mandarin: T. C. Thomas. *Koblang Kang*, an Astrologer: J. A. Throw. *Moon Shong*, a Soothsayer: William Edgerton. *Kao Peki*: Edward Lavine. *Kwang See*: George J. Knight. *Sang Koi*: J. Vincent. *Yen Yum*: Albert Leach. *Princess Pai Ping*: Amy Willaims. *Ko Ket*, her attendant: Kitty Wilson. *Children of the Moon, etc.*

MAHOMEDANS: *Kara Mustapha*, the Grand Caliph: C. W. Wheeler. *Muli*, a Cadi: Harry Williams. *Orasmin*: James Mason. *Khan of Tartary*: W. H. Allen. *Turks, Slaves of the Harem, etc.*

IMMORTALS: *Chrystaline*, the Fairy Protectress: KATE GIRARD. *Fairies, etc.*

INFERNALS: *Mephisto*, the Evil One: Walter Hubbell. *Chaos*, a Imp of Darkness: Albert Martinetti. *Demons, Gnomes, etc.*

Ballet: Mlle. ADELE CORNALBA (Star Première Danseuse Assoluta), Mlles. ASTEGANIO and ELISE (Premières); Mlles. Sallie Apt, Felicita Pasta, Kitty Wilson,

[1]A rival production to that produced at the Casino. Musical numbers not listed in program.

[2]A rival production to that produced at the Cosmopolitan.

[3]Musical numbers not listed in programs. This most famous number was published.

[4]Revised version of the play first produced in a shorter form in New York 13 January 1879 at the Theatre Comique for 152 performances.

[5]Played a return engagement 26 May 1884 at Henry C. Miner's People's Theatre for an additional 8 performances.

Lizzie Scheffer, Mellie Gray, Ada Laurent, Josephine Voos; Misses Sheldon, Pierson, Drew. The Grand English Ballet Troupe. *Specialties*: THE LORELLAS (Grotesque Artists).

Act 1, Scene 1: The Haunted Dell of Gigantic Mushrooms. *Scene 2*: Andoche Valley at Daybreak. *Scene 3*: The Ruined Castle. *Scene 4*: The Andoche Valley at Sunset.

Act 2, Scene 1: In Normandy. *Scene 2*: The Mysterious Chamber. *Scene 3*: The Flower Kingdom.

Act 3, Scene 1: Subterranean Cavern of Mammoth Reptiles. *Scene 2*: Out All Night, or the Sun on a Lark. (Merry.)

BALLETS AND SPECIALTIES

Pas de Villageois (Act 1, Scene 2)
Mlle. Eloise, Grand English Ballet Troupe

Grand Finale and Tableaux (Act 1, Scene 4)

Grand Chinese Festival; Chinese Grotesque Aerial Act; Grand Chinese Divertissement (Act 2 , Scene 4)
Mlles. Asteganio, Eloise, Coryphées, Corps de Ballet

Gambols in Impland (Act 3, Scene 1)
The Lorellas

Oriental Revels (Act 3, Scene 3)
Mlle. Cornalba

Grand Tournament Ballet (Act 3, Scene 3)
Misses Apt, Pasta, Wilson, Scheffer, Gray, Laurent, Voos

Grand Entrez (Act 3, Scene 3) A. Cornalba

The Grand Peacock Ballet (Act 3, Scene 3)
A. Cornalba, Mlle. Asteganio

Galop
Misses Sheldon, Pierson, Gray, Drew

Solo
Mlle. Asteganio

Excelsior Variation
Mlle. Cornalba

Grand Finale
Coryphées, Corps de Ballet

1883.48

EXCELSIOR

A Mimical Dramatic Ballet Spectacle in Three Acts, 10 Scenes. (Original Italian) Play by Luigi Manzotti. Original music by Romualdo Marenco. Staged by Imre and Bolossy Kiralfy. Reproducer of the ballet and first mimic artist, Ettore Coppini. Scenery painted by Henry E. Hoyt, Harley Merry and Ed. Roemer. Costumes designed by Draner and Cledat de Lavigerie of Paris, Wilhelm of London. Novel electrical effects by the Edison Electric Light Company, under the personal direction of W. F. Conner. Musical director, A. W. Hoffman. Produced by the Kiralfy Brothers (Imre, Bolossy). Opened 21 August 1883 at Niblo's Garden and closed 15 December 1883 after 135 performances.

CAST: *Light*: Mlle. NANI. *Darkness*: ETTORE COPPINI. *Civilization*: Miss (ALBERTINE) FLINDT. *Valentine*, a Boatman: Signor CONTI. *A Slave*: Signor Conti. *Papin*, the Inventor of the Steamboat: Signor FAROANE. *A Grand Arabian Nobleman*: Signor Borsa. *Volta*, the Electrician: Signor BRIGHENTI. *The Slave Merchant*: Signor BRIGHENTI. *An Italian Engineer*: Signor BRIGHENTI. *Fritz*, a Boatman: Signor Saraco. *A Chinaman*: Signor Saraco. *Chief of the Italian Miners*: Signor Saraco. *George*, a Tavern-keeper: JOHN HASLAM. *A Mexican*: JOHN HASLAM. *An Italian Miner*: JOHN HASLAM. *Guilliaum*: Signor FARDO. *A Grand Turk*: Signor FARDO. *A French Engineer*: Signor FARDO. *A Boatman*: Signor Roccini. *A Sub Engineeer of the French*: Signor Roccini. *A Brigand in the Desert*: Signor Roccini. *An Englishman*: Mons. Arnold. *Fanny*, Valentine's sweetheart: Signora BRAMBILLA. *Indian Danseuse*: Frl. Hofschuler. *An Arab Merchant's Daughter*: Signora CAPPELLINI. *La Cosmopolitaine*: Mlle. MILON. *Ballet*: Parisian Eden Theatre Ballet Company, Venetian Ballet Troupe. Mlles. FLINDT, MILON, NANI, Frl. HOFSCHUELER. Messrs. ARNOLD (Kiralfy), HASLAM, BALDI, SARACO, (Ettore) COPPINI, CONTI, BRIGHENTI.

Act 1, Scene 1: City in Ruins. (Roemer.) *Scene 2*: The Temple of Light and Progress. (Hoyt.)

Act 2, Scene 1: Village on the Banks of the Weser. (Hoyt.) *Scene 2*: Brooklyn Bridge. (Merry.) *Scene 3*: Interior of Oriental Kraal of Pasha. (Roemer.) *Scene 4*: The Desert. (Hoyt.) *Scene 5*: Grand Ballet of All Nations.

Act 3, Scene 1: Laboratory of Volta. (Roemer.) *Scene 2*: A Cosmopolitan Telegraph Headquarters. (Hoyt.) *Scene 3*: The Mont Cenis Tunnel. The Palace of Peace and Union.

BALLETS, SPECIALTIES[6]

La Renomée (Grand Divertissement)(Act 1, Scene 2)

La Civilization (Entrée by Miss Flindt)(Act 1, Scene 2)

La Renaissance (Act 1, Scene 2)
Corps de Ballet

Postillons (Act 2, Scene 1)
Corps de Ballet

Vision of Liberty (Act 2, Scene 3)

Grand Ballet of All Nations (Act 2, Scene 5)

La Cosmopolitaine
Mlle. Milon; Messrs. Arnold, Haslam, Baldi, Saraco

L'Almée
Frl. Hofschueler

Abolitan de L'Esclavage (Pas ensemble)
Mlles. Flindt, Nani; Signors. Coppini, Conti, Brighenti

Homage au Progresse
Entire Ballet Corps

Grand Ballet of Messenger Boys (Act 3, Scene 2)
Corps de Ballet, Frl. Hofschueler

La Concorde (Grand Balabile) (Act 3, Scene 2)
Mlle. Hofschueler, Tout le Corps de Ballet

Apotheosis, Crowning tableau of EXCELSIOR, or the Triumph of Light over Darkness, and the peaceful union of all nations (Act 3, Scene 2)

1883.49

ZENOBIA, Queen of Palmyra

A Grand Spectacular Lyric Drama in Four Acts, 5 Scenes. Libretto and music by S. G. Pratt. Produced under the personal directon of S. G. Pratt. Scenery by Richard S. Smith. Musical director, Antonio DeNovellis. Produced by Max Strakosch. Opened 21 August 1883 at the 23rd Street Theatre and closed 25 August 1883 after 5 performances.

CAST: *Zenobia*, the Queen of Palmyra: DORA HENNINGS. *Julia*, her daughter: ELLA WALLACE. *Sindarina*, her slave: Miss. L. Brosi. *Zabdas*, General of Zenobia's forces: E. CONNOLL. *Aurelian*, Emperor of Rome: A. MONTEGRIFFO. *Probus*, Officer of Roman Legion: Mr. Wade. *Longinus*, high priest: Mr. BORDEMAN. *Ghost of Odenatus*: Mr. Gardner. *Soldiers, Senators, Populace, etc.*: Chorus of 60.

Act 1: Before the great Temple of the Sun Palmyra. Zenobia in her chariot. Defeat. Defiance.

Act 2: Zenobia alone. The warning. The Slaves' attempt upon her life prevented. Fight. Betrayal.

Act 3: Aurelian before Palmyra. Zenobia and Julia's capture. Mutual love. Soldiers demand Zenobia's head. Tableau.

Act 4: *Scene 1*: I Prison in Rome. The Slaves ask forgiveness. Zabdas led to execution. Julia's and Aurelian's love. Longinus' ode to immortality. March to execution. *Scene 2*: Grand triumphal procession. Aurelian in his chariot. Zenobia in chains, Also Julia and Longinus. Populace demand pardon. The Emperor proclaims Julia his Empress and releases Zenobia and Longinus. Great joy!

1883.50

FROLICS OF A DAY

A Musical Farcical Absurdity in Three Acts, 5 Scenes. Produced by Frank Majilton. Opened 3 September 1883 at the 14th Street Theatre and closed 8 September 1883 after 8 performances.

---

[6]A piano reduction of the ballet score was published in Milan (G. Ricordi, 1881), presented in Six Acts (Parte), 11 Scenes (Quadro): Preludio. Parte I. Quadro 1: L'Oscurantismo. Quadro 2: La Luce. La Fama (Danza). Entrata della Civiltà. Il Risorgimento. (Gran Valzer e Galop). Parte II. Quadro 3. Il Primo Battelo a Vapore. In vincitore della regata (Polka). Sulle rive del Weser. (Mazurka). Quadro 4: Prodigi della invenzione. Parte III. Quadro 5. Il genio dell'elettricismo. Quadro 6: Effetti della elettricità. Parte IV.Quadro 7. Il Simun. Quadro 8. Il Canale di Suez. Danze della Cosmopolita. L'Indiana (Danza caratteristica). Adagio d'azione e passo a due. Omaggio a Lesseps (Danza caratteristica). Parte V. Quadro 9. L'ultima Mina. Il traforo del Cenisio. Quadro 10. Oscurantismo, Luce e gloria. Parte VI. Quadro 11. Apoteosi. Civilità, Progresso, Concordia. (Grand Scena finale). La Concordia. Quadriglia-Marcia della Nazioni. .

CAST: *Mr. Bartle Burke*, an auctioneer and solid man: THOMAS LISBOURNE. *Mr. Denby*, a lawyer: Ed Chapman. *Mr. Gewgaw*: GEORGE E. JAMES. *Gabriel Gadforth*, a Dyer and a Cleaner: HERBERT GRESHAM. *Mr. Fripps*: R. M. Roberts. *Cabman*: JOHN LISBOURNE. *Policeman*: FRANK MAJILTON. *Bertie Kelvin*: ETTIE WHYTE. *Mlle. Salprunelle*: Fanny Temple. *Mrs. Gadforth*: ANNETA HARRIS. *Miss Georgina Gewgaw*: ERNESTINE ARNNAM. *Miss Mary Chatterton*: CAROLINE MAJILTON.

Act 1, Scene 1: Old Frowsey's Drawing Room. Noon. *Scene 2*: On the road to the Haymarket. *Scene 3*: The Cigar Divan, Haymarket, Piccadilly, The Temptation.

Act 2: Cremorne.

Act 3: Old Frowsey's Drawing Room.

SPECIALTIES

Great Irish Show Song and Chorus (Act 2)

Great Irish Impersonations (Act 2)
T. Lisbourne

Celebrated Majilton Act (Act 2)
E. Whyte, J. Lisbourne, F. Majilton

1883.51 LA PRINCESSE DES CANARIES

An Opéra-bouffe in Three Acts, 4 Scenes, in French. Libretto by Henri Chivot and Alfred Duru. Music by Charles Lecocq. Acting manager, A. Durand. Stage manager, V. Merle. Musical director, A. Lagye. Produced by Maurice Grau's French Opera Company. Opened 10 September 1883 at the Fifth Avenue Theatre and closed 5 October 1883 after 15 performances in repertory; returned 10 January 1884 to Haverly's Comedy Theatre for 1 additional performance.

CAST: *Pépita*: Mlle. MARIE AIMÉE. *Inez (Inès)*: Mlle. ANGÈLE. *Catarina*: Mlle. DELORME. *First Gossip*: Mlle. Buisson. *Second Gossip*: Mlle. Vallot. *A Peasant*: Mlle. DeWitt. *A Cadet*: Mlle. Lescot. *General Pataquès*: Mons. J. MEZIÈRES. *General Bombardos*: Mons. DUPLAN. *Pédrille*, Innkeeper and Postmaster: Mons. CLEMENT NIGRI. *Inigo*, his cousin: Mons. LARY. *Guzman*, Prince of the Canaries: Mons. GUY. *Sergeant Cléophas*: Mons. DUCOS. *A Miller Boy*: Mons. Vinchon. *A Nobleman*: Mons. Trouvé. *Lords and Ladies of the Court, Toreadors, Peasants, Flower Girls, Populace, Soldiers, Servants, Sixteen Cadets (in Travesty)*.

The scene is set in Great Canary.

Act 1: A Village several leagues from Palmas, the capital of Great Canary.

Act 2: Chateau of Galagardos.

Act 3: Vestibule of the Arenas at Palmas.

ACT 1[7]

"Ah! Quel bon vin!" (Opening Chorus and Couplets)
Mons. C. Nigri, Chorus

"Ah! Ah! Ah! Ah! Pauvre Inigo" (Choeur des Commères)
Mons. Lary, Gossips

"Mon petit mari, Cheri, Tous les jours à toi je pense!"
Mlles. Angèle, M. Aimée, Mons. Duplan, Chorus

"De mon coeur vous êtes le maître" (Couplets)
Mlle. Angèle

"Pour elles, c'est un jour de fête" (Trio)
Messrs. Duplan, C. Nigri, Lary, Chorus

"Comm' tout's les femmes, je suis coquette" (Couplets)
Mlle. M. Aimée

"Plaisir délectable!" Finale Act 1 (Choeur des Villageois et Villageoises)
Messrs. C. Nigri, Lary, Chorus

ACT 2

"Marchons d'un air conquérant" (Opening Chorus)
Mons. Ducos, Cadets

"Si dans un beau jour de bataille" (Chanson Militaire)
Mons. Duplan

"Général, la corvée est faite!" (Quintette)
Mlles. Angèle, M. Aimée, Messrs. C. Nigri, Duplan, Lary

"Bonjour, Général Bombardos"
Messrs. J. Mezières, Duplan

"Nous avons vu sur notre routte Des Allemandes pleins de choucroûte"
(Chanson Anglaise) Mlles. M. Aimée, Angèle, Mons. Duplan

"Rataplan, Rataplan" (Choeur des Cadets)
Cadets

"Sans crainte et sans aucun danger" (Finale)
Principals, Chorus

ACT 3

"Nous voici tous un rendez-vous" (Opening Chorus)
Chorus

"Accourez à ma boutique!" (Chanson)
Messrs. Lary, C. Nigri

"Les fleurs que nous admirons" (Choeur des Bouquetières)
Mlle. Angèle, Chorus

"Qu'il est fier et splendide" (Chanson du Toréador)
Mlle. M. Aimée, Chorus

"Oui, nous triomphons" (Finale/Couplet au Publique)
Mlles. M. Aimée, Angèle, Chorus

[7]Musical numbers not listed in programs. List prepared from published libretto for Maurice Grau's Opera Company (Metropolitan Printing and Engraving, New York, 1883).

1883.52 THE MERRY DUCHESS

A (Sporting) Comic Opera in Two Acts. Libretto by George R. Sims. Music by Frederic Clay. Produced under the stage direction of Richard Barker. Scenery by George Heister and William F. Voegtlin. Costumes by W. Dazian & Sons. Musical director, Ernest Neyer. Produced by Messrs. Brooks & Dickson. Opened 13 September 1883 at the Standard Theatre and closed 20 October 1883 after 46 performances.

CAST: *Brabazon Sykes*: HARRY [Henry] E. DIXEY. *Freddy Bowman*: JOHN NASH. *Farmer Bowman*: Edward Connell. *Sir Lothbury Jones*: W. Forrester. *Captain Walker*: WALTER HAMPSHIRE. *Lord Johnie*: J. Watson. *Inspector Green*: W. Jones. *Alderman Gog*: W. Dohrman. *The Trainer*: G. Wilson. *The Duchess of Epsom Downs*: SELINA DOLARO. *Rowena*: LOUISE LESTER. *Doretha Bowman*: JEAN DELMAR. *Ethelfreda*: Sophie Hummel. *Sylvia*: Dickie Delano. *Jimmy*: Addie Davis. *Martin*: Fanny Knight. *Chloe*: Belle Urquhart. *Marion*: Eva Walton. *Hodge*: Annie Dayton. *Reapers, Peasants, Jockeys, Flower Girls, Tigers and Betting Men, Policemen, and all sorts and conditions of Men and Women*: Chorus of 80.

Act 1: The Cornfields of Muddleham—Harvest Time. (Heister.)

Act 2: Doncaster Race Course—Race Time. (Voegtlin.)

ACT 1[8]

Chorus of Reapers (Haste, the sun is shining)
Chorus

"The Captive Bird" (A maiden is like a bird that's free)
L. Lester

"Love's Messenger" (Take me a message, O bird of the sky)
W. Hampshire

Duet (Farewell darling)
W. Hampshire, J. Delmar

"The Tigers' Chorus" (Tigers are we)
Chorus

Entrance of the Duchess (Where is she?)
W. Forrester, S. Dolaro, Chorus

"The Song of the Merry Duchess" (A Duchess, I've an easy task)
S. Dolaro

"The Jockey's Song" (The sailors of England as lions are bold)
J. E. Nash

"Love's Memories" (Duet and Ensemble)
H. E. Dixey, L. Lester

Recitative (With honest pride my manly breast doth swell)
E. Connell

Song (We are constabulary)
W. Jones

Finale (I've done the deed)
Omnes

[8]Musical numbers not listed in programs; list prepared from published book of words (J. J. Little, New York, 1883).

Sextet and Chorus (Oh cruel day!)
S. Dolaro, L. Lester, E. Connell, W. Forrester, W. Hampshire, J. Delmar
Invocation to Damozel (O thou, within whose veins there flows)
Omnes

ACT 2
Opening Chorus (Any price, any price)
Betting Men
Chorus (We are here your colors twining)
Jockeys, Girls
Vocal Waltz (Love is a fairy, tricksome and airy)
S. Dolaro, J. Delmar, J. E. Nash, W. Hampshire
"A Spanish Love Song" (I'm the gay chatelaine)
L. Lester, H. E. Dixey, Old Chappies
Quintette (My jockey from his love they take)
S. Dolaro, J. Delmar, W. Hampshire, J. E. Nash, E. Connell
Duet (O sun shine out in splendor)
J. E. Nash, S. Dolaro
Finale (Sons of Britannia, the proud and the free)
Omnes
The Race (Hip, hip, hurrah! for Damozel)
Chorus

1883.53

THE MULLIGAN GUARD PIC-NIC

A Local Comedy in Two Acts [9]. Play (and lyrics) by Edward Harrigan. Music by David Braham. (Staged by Edward Harrigan.) Scenery by Charles W. Witham. Mechanical effects by William McMurray. Properties and Papier Mache work by Robert Puller. Director of music, David Braham. Produced by (Edward) Harrigan and (Tony) Hart. Opened 24 September 1883 at the Theatre Comique and closed 3 November 1883 after 48 performances.

CAST: *Dan Mulligan*: EDWARD HARRIGAN. *Rebecca Allup*: TONY HART. *Lemons*: JOHN WILD. *Palestine Puter*: George H. Wood. *Gustvaus Lochmuller*: HARRY A. FISHER. *Theophilus Grasp*: WILLIAM WEST. *Walsingham McSweeney*: M. BRADLEY. *Mrs. Honora Dublin*: JOHN QUEEN. *Tommy Fagan*: M. Foley. *August Bimble*: JOSEPH SPARKS. *Captain Primrose*: PETER C. GOLDRICH. *Gypsy Jack*: Richard Quilter. *Officer Reiley*: J. McCullough. *Roderick O'Dwyer*: CHRISTIE MILLER. *Squire Cohough*: GEORGE MERITT. *James Bigcrop*: George L. Stout. *Mr. Ringer*: James Fitzsimmons. *Washington Bancroft*: William A. Barlow. *Danny O'Rourke*: JOHN SPARKS. *Patsy McNabb*: James Barlow. *Sim Carter*: Charles Coffey. *Josiah Proudfoot*: Emil Heusel. *Zachariah Shed*: Thomas Granger. *Cordelia Mulligan*: MRS. ANNIE YEAMANS. *Jenny Langtry*: GERTIE GRANVILLE. *Bridget Lochmuller*: Jennie Christie. *Mary McCabe*: Ada Farwell. *Kitty Martin*: Marie Gorenflo. *Susie Malone*: Sadie Morris. *Harriet Littlepage*: Sadie Morris. *Jane Dorsey*: Annie Langdon. *Johanna Schwarz*: Mrs. W. Scallan. *Julia Kehoe*: Annie Hall. *Sarah Maguire*: Kate Langdon.

Act 1: The Morning of the Picnic. Anxiety.

Act 2: The Arrival of the Barge. The Departure. The Grove. A Little Trouble and the Usual Denouement.

MUSICAL NUMBERS
"Roderick O'Dwyer"
"All Aboard for the M.G.P."
"Sandy-Haired Mary in Our Area"
"The Second Degree Full Moon Union"
"Going Home with Nelly After Five"[10]
"Hurry, Little Children, Sunday Morning"[11] (Song and Dance)
M. Bradley, E. Heusel,
R. Quilter, P. C. Goldrich, W. Barlow, J. Barlow, Joseph Sparks, John Sparks
Xylophone Solo
E. King

[9]A revised version of the play first produced in New York in a shorter form 23 September 1878 at the Theatre Comique for 40 performances; revised into a longer one-act form 9 August 1880 at the Theatre Comique for 120 performances.
[10]Newly written for this revival.
[11]Newly written for this revival.

1883.54

LA MASCOTTE

A Revival of the Opéra-comique in Three Acts, in French[12]. Libretto by Henri Chivot and Alfred Duru. Music by Edmond Audran. Acting manager, A. Durand. Stage manager, V. Merle. Musical director, A. Lagye. Produced by Maurice Grau's French Opera Company. Opened 24 September 1883 at the Fifth Avenue Theatre and closed 29 September 1883 after 4 performances in repertory; returned 24 October 1883 at the Standard Theatre for 1 additional performance in repertory; returned 1 January 1884 to Haverly's Comedy Theatre for 1 additional performance.[13]

CAST: *Bettina*: Mlle. MARIE AIMÉE. *Fiametta*: Mlle. ANGÈLE. *(Le Roi) Laurent XVII*: Mons. J. MEZIÈRES. *Pippo*: Mons. CLEMENT NIGRI. *Fritellini*: Mons. LARY. *Rocco*: Mons. DUPLAN. *A Sergeant*: Mons. Vinchon. *Matheo*: Mons. Ducos. *Pages (4)*: *Carlo*: Mlle. Vallot. *Frederico*: Mlle. Buisson. *Angelo*: Mlle. Marie. *Lindgi*: Mlle. Zanette. *A Peasant*: Mons. Gèrard. *First Peasant Girl*: Mlle. Lescot. *Second Peasant Girl*: Mlle. Vandamme. *Third Peasant Girl*: Mlle. DeWitt.

1883.55

BOCCACCIO

An Opera Comique in Three Acts, in French[14]. Original Viennese libretto to the operette by F. Zell and Richard Genée. French adaptation by Henri Chivot and Alfred Duru. Music by Franz von Suppé. Acting manager, A. Durand. Stage manager, V. Merle. Musical director, A. Lagye. Produced by Maurice Grau's French Opera Company. Opened 25 September 1883 at the Fifth Avenue Theatre and closed 3 October 1883 after 4 performances in repertory; returned 2-26 January 1884 to Haverly's Comedy Theatre for 3 additional performances in repertory[15].

CAST: *Boccaccio*: Mlle. NIXAU. *Béatrice*: Mlle. ANGÈLE. *Zanetta*: Mlle. L. Astruc. *Peronelle*: Mlle. Delorme. *Frisca*: Mlle. Vallot. *A Maid of Honor*: Mlle. Buisson. *Giotto*: Mlle. Lescott. *Frederico*: Mlle. DeWitt. *Tofano*: Mlle. Delournay. *Raphaele*: Mlle. Vandamme. *Orlando*: Mons. Guy. *Lelio*: Mons. Lary. *Pandolfi*: Mons. Duplan. *Tromboli*: Mons. Clement Nigri. *Quiquibio*: Mons. Duclos. *A Book Peddler*: Mons. Vinchon. *Cecco*: Mons. Gerard. *A Citizen*: Mons. Millet. *Captain of the Guards*: Mons. Claudius. *The Unknown*: Mons. Antigua.

1883.56

Z-SELTZER!

A Burlesque in One Squirm and a Collapse, preceded by a minstrel program. Prepared and seasoned by Frank Dumont. Original and incidental music by W. S. Mullaly. New appointments by John A. Martin. Produced by Billy Birch's San Francisco Minstrels. Opened 1 October 1883 at the San Francisco Minstrels and closed 3 November 1883 after 28 performances.

CAST: *Progress*, the Queen of Light and Fairy land (a young fairy seeking a worldly knowledge): The Only (FRANCIS) LEON. *President Arthur* of Washington D.C.: GEORGE H. COES. *John Harmony Kelly* of New York: A. C. MORELAND. *Ben Butler* of Massachusetts: FRANK CUSHMAN. *Electricity*, the Giddy fairy: F. M. Ricardo. *Invention*, another foolish fairy: Frank Casey. *Flash*, an active sprite: M. Martin. *The Lilliputian Amazon*: J. M. Woods. *Fairies, Tall, Lean, Angular, Short and Fat.*

The Imported Ballet of Brunettes and Blondes, representing beautiful Coryphées from every Clime, and of every Shade and Color. The Premiere Assoluta from LaScala, Italy: *Mlle. Hoffschuler Leoni*: [the Only FRANCIS LEON]. *Mlle. Wilhemina Flindt Birchirini*: [BILLY BIRCH]. *Mlle. Guillaume Eau de Vie Smithi*: [William Smith]. *Mlle. Barberoni Baltimori Slavini*: [BOB SLAVIN]. *Mlle. Timothi Seedi Cronini*: [TIM CRONIN]. *Fraulein Jameserio Quincy Adamsi*: [James E. Adams]. *Mlle. Lucca Fromage Schoolcrafti*: [LUKE SCHOOLCRAFT]. *Mlle. Dan Bologna Waldroni*: [Dan Waldron]. *Mlle. Martin Singe Marytini*: [M. Martin]. *Mlle. Frank Dumonterio*: [FRANK DUMONT]. *Fraulein Franz Casi*: [FRANK CUSHMAN].

1883.57

LA FILLE DE MADAME ANGOT

A Revival of the Opéra-comique in Three Acts, in French[16]. Libretto by Clairville, Paul Siraudin and Victor Koning. Music by Charles Lecocq.

[12]French language premiere in New York. First produced in New York in English 5 May 1881 at the Bijou Theatre for 168 performances in two engagements.
[13]Cast list prepared from Standard Theatre engagement; cast unchanged for Haverly's Comedy Theatre.
[14]First produced in New York 23 April 1880 at the Thalia Theatre for 15 performances.
[15]For return engagement, Mlle. FOUQUET assumed the title role of Boccaccio.
[16]First produced in New York in French 25 August 1873 at Daly's Broadway Theatre in repertory. For Synopsis of Scenes and Musical Numbers, see original 1873 production.

Acting manager, A. Durand. Stage manager, V. Merle. Musical director, A. Lagye. Produced by Maurice Grau's French Opera Company. Opened 2 October 1883 at the Fifth Avenue Theatre and closed 4 October 1883 after 2 performances in repertory; returned 31 December 1883 to Haverly's Comedy Theatre for 1 additional performance.

CAST: *Clairette Angot*: Mlle. AIMÉE. *Mademoiselle Lange*: Mlle. ANGÈLE. *Amaranthe*: Mlle. Delorme. *Javotte*: Mlle. Gatinau. *Cydalise*: Mlle. Vallot. *Mlle. Delaunay*: Mlle. DeWitt. *Hersille*: Mlle. Buisson. *Babet*: Mlle. Delournay. *Manon*: Mlle. Vandamme. *Therese*: Mlle. Salvator. *Herbelin*: Mlle. Lescot. *Ange Pitou*: Mons. LARY. *Larivaudière*: Mons. J. MEZIÈRES. *Trénitz*: Mons. Ducos. *Pomponnet*: Mons. Guy. *Louchard*: Mons. DUPLAN. *Buteux*: Mons. Vinchon. *Guillaume*: Mons. Trouve. *Cadet*: Mons. Moreau. *Un Incroyable*: Mons. Perret. *Un Officer*: Mons. Gerard. *Un Cabaretier*: Mons. Millet.

1883.58 THE PRINCESS OF TRÉBIZONDE!

A Revival of the Opéra-comique in Three Acts[17]. Libretto by Charles Nuitter and Étienne Tréfeu. English libretto by Charles Lamb Kenney. Music by Jacques Offenbach. Produced under the stage direction of Professor Hill. Scenery by Messrs. Philip Goatcher, George W. Dayton and Harley Merry. Musical direction, Ernst Catenhusen. Produced by the McCaull Opera Company (John A. McCaull, Proprietor and Manager). Opened 15 October 1883 at the Casino Theatre and closed 27 October 1883 after 14 performances.

CAST: *Prince Casimir*: THOMAS GUISE. *Sparadrap*, Tutor of Raphael: A. W. MAFLIN. *Cabriolo*, Showman: ARTHUR BELL. *Tremolini*, Clown: FRANCIS WILSON. *Lottery Men*: Messrs. McCarthy, Kauffman and Taylor. *Prince Raphael*, Casimir's son: JEANNIE WINSTON. *Zanetta, Regina*, Cabriolo's daughter: EMMA CARSON, MARIE JANSEN. *Paola*, Strong Woman: JULIE deRUYTHER. *Rocoli*: Lillie Walters. *Becardo*: Miss Temple. *Flaminis*: Miss Thal. *Francisca*: Miss Clinton. *Pages, Hunters, Courtiers, Peasants, etc.*

Act 1: Market Place. (Goatcher.)

Act 2: A Terrace in front of a Baronial Castle. (Dayton.)

Act 3: Salon in Prince Casimir's Palace. (Merry.)

1883.59 LE COEUR ET LA MAIN

An Opera Comique in Three Acts, in French[18]. Libretto by Charles Nuitter and Alexandre Beaumont. Music by Charles Lecocq. Acting manager, A. Durand. Stage manager, V. Merle. New costumes, scenery and accessories. Musical director, A. Lagye. Produced by Maurice Grau's French Opera Company. Opened 22 October 1883 at the Standard Theatre and closed 27 (matinee) October 1883 after 3 performances in repertory; returned 11-19 January 1884 to Haverly's Comedy Theatre for 2 additional performances in repertory.

CAST: *(Princess) Micaëla of Aragon*: Mlle. JEANNE FOUQUET. *Josepha*: Mlle. Buisson. *(Doña) Scholastica*: Mlle. DELORME. *Anita*: Mlle. Vallot. *Inez*: Mlle. Lescot. *Pepita*: Mlle. Vandamme. *Dolorès*: Mlle. Daniel. *Pablo*: Mlle. DeWitt. *Ascanio*: Mlle. Estiot. *Pasquale*: Mlle. Delournay. *The King* (Le Roi): Mons. DUPLAN. *(Prince) Gaétan* (Duc de Madère): Mons. CLEMENT NIGRI. *Moralès*: Mons. LARY. *Mosquitos*: Mons. Guy. *Baldomero* (Brigadier des Gardes du Palais): Mons. VINCHON. *A Lieutenant*: Mons. Girard. *A Captain*: Mons. Antigua. *A Soldier*: Mons. Millet. *Mariées, Paysannes, Gardes, Dames*: Chorus of 40.

ACT 1[19]

Introduction (C'est demain le mariage)
Mlle. Buisson, Sopranos

Couplets (Au mariage des princesses)
Mlle. Buisson, Chorus

Choeur des gardes (C'est nous les gardes du palais)
Mons. Lary, Mons. Vinchon, Tenors, basses

Choeur (C'est l'heure de la promenade)
J. Fouquet, Mlle. Delorme, Pages, Maids of Honor

Mélodie (M'y voici; mais pourrai-je)
J. Fouquet, Sopranos

Couplets du Roi (Vlan! j'ai perdu mon gendre)
Mons. Duplan

Couplets à boire (Au soldat après la parade)
Mons. Lary, Tenors, Basses

Rondeau (Ah! que de mal on a)
J. Fouquet

Ronde (Ma fille, c'est un mari)
J. Fouquet, Sopranos

Romance et duo (Par toi, divine créature)
J. Fouquet, C. Nigri

Finale (Notre vigilance)
Mlle. Buisson, Mlle. Delorme, Mons. Duplan, C. Nigri, Mons. Guy, Chorus

Couplets (Je suis un prince un peu fantasque)
C. Nigri

Strette (On n'a jamais vu ça!)
Mons. Guy, Chorus

ACT 2

Introduction (La princesse qui nous marie)
Mlle. Buisson, Les Mariées, Les Pages

Chant nationale

Choeur de l'almanach de Gotha (Dans l'almanach de Gotha)
J. Fouquet, Mlles. Buisson, Delorme, Mons. Duplan, Chorus

Sextuor (Il me regarde à peine)
Mlles. J. Fouquet, Buisson, Mlle. Delorme, Messrs. Duplan, C. Nigri, Guy, Chorus

Dance (La vie cadence)
Chorus

Couplets du Casque (Y avait un jour dans l'infant'rie)
C. Nigri,
Mlles. J. Fouquet, Buisson, Delorme, Mons. Duplan

Choeur (Bientôt, à la cathédrale)
Mlles. Buisson, Delorme, Mons. Duplan, Chorus

Couplets (Ma Micaëla, ma chère)
Mons. Duplan, Mlle. Delorme

Mélodrame

Couplets (Au fond de l'alcôve blottie)
J. Fouquet

Couplets en duo (C'est là leur chambre nuptiale)
Mlle. Buisson, Mons. Lary

Grand Duo (Mon devoir ailleurs me rappelle)
J. Fouquet, C. Nigri

Boléro (Un soir Perez, le capitaine)
J. Fouquet, C. Nigri

ACT 3

Introduction (Il a l'épaulette)
Messs. Lary, Vinchon, Tenors, Basses

Couplets du novice (Près du couvent, dans la plaine)
J. Fouquet, Tenors, basses

Romance (Ah! j'enviais les hirondelles)
J. Fouquet

Ensemble (Le parlementaire a sur les yeux)
Messrs. Duplan, Guy, Officers

Choeur des paysannes (Ah! sir, exaucez nos prières)
Les Paysannes

Couplets (Ne craignez rien, les belles filles)
Mons. Duplan

Couplets (Depuis notre hymen)
C. Nigri

[17]First produced in New York in English 5 May 1883 at the Bijou Opera House for 36 performances. For Synopsis of Scenes and Musical Numbers, see original May 1883 production.
[18]French language premiere in New York. Previously produced in New York in two rival English adaptations: as HAND AND HEART 15 February 1883 at the Bijou Theatre for 19 performances; as MICAËLA 26 February 1883 at the Standard Theatre for 48 performances in two engagements.
[19]Musical Numbers and Scenes not listed in programs. List prepared from published French piano vocal score (Brandus & Cie., Paris, 1882).

Couplets des maris (Monsieur me croit infidèle)
Mlle. Buisson
Finale (Je suis princesse et votre épouse)
Tutti

1883.60 LES CLOCHES DE CORNEVILLE

A Revival of the Opéra-comique in Three Acts, in French[20]. Libretto by Clairville and Charles Gabet. Music by Robert Planquette. Acting manager, A. Durand. Stage manager, V. Merle. Musical director, A. Lagye. Produced by Maurice Grau's French Opera Company. Opened 23 October 1883 at the Standard Theatre and closed 27 October 1883 after 2 performances in repertory; returned 22 January 1884 to Haverly's Comedy Theatre for 1 additional performance[21].

CAST: *Serpolette*: Mlle. DORSAY. *Germaine*: Mlle. LESTUE. *Jeanne*: Mlle. Vallot. *Mariette*: Mlle. Buisson. *Gertrude*: Mlle. Lescot. *Susanne*: Mlle. DeWitt. *Catherine*: Mlle. Daniel. *Marguerita*: Mlle. Delournay. *Henri, the Marquis of Corneville*: Mons. CLEMENT NIGRI. *Grenicheux*: Mons. LARY. *Gaspard*: Mons. J. MEZIÈRES. *The Bailiff*: Mons. Duplan. *Le Tabellion*: Mons. Ducos. *Cachalot*: Mons. Vinchon. *Gripardin*: Mons. Gerard. *Tommard*: Mons. Mousot. *A Peasant*: Mons. Peret. Chorus of 40.

1883.61 LA JOLIE PARFUMEUSE

A Revival of the Opéra-comique in Three Acts, in French[22]. Libretto by Hector Crémieux and Ernest Blum. Music by Jacques Offenbach. Acting manager, A. Durand. Stage manager, V. Merle. Musical director, A. Lagye. Produced by Maurice Grau. Opened and closed 26 October 1883 at the Standard Theatre after 1 performance; returned 3-21 January 1884 to Haverly's Comedy Theatre for 6 additional performances in repertory.

CAST: *Rose Michon*: Mlle. MARIE AIMÉE. *Bavolet*: Mlle. ANGÈLE. *Clorinde*: Mlle. FOUQUET. *La Julienne*: Mlle. Delorme. *Arthemise*: Mlle. Vallot. *Madelon*: Mlle. Lescot. *La Cocardière*: Mons. DUPLAN. *Poirot*: Mons. LARY. *Germain*: Mons. Gérard. *Justine*: Mlle. DeWitt. *Lise*: Mlle. Delournay. *A Soubrette*: Mlle. Daniel. *Waiters*: Messrs. Vinchon, Nys. *Un Client*: Mons. Morel. *Second Client*: Mons. Antigua.

1883.62 THE BEGGAR STUDENT

A Comic Opera in Three Acts, 4 Scenes[23]. Original Viennese libretto to the operette ('Der Bettelstudent') by F. Zell and Richard Genée, based on 'Fernande" by Victorien Sardou and 'The Lady of Lyons' by Edward Bulwer-Lytton. (English adaptation by Emil Schwab.) Music by Carl Millöcker. Produced under the stage direction of Jesse Williams. Scenery by Harley Merry, William F. Voegtlin and Charles Huist. Costumes by Mme. Prinz and Mr. Karmstedt. Produced by the McCaull Opera Company (John A. McCaull, Proprietor and Manager). Opened 29 October 1883 at the Casino Theatre and closed 2 February 1884 after 110 performances.[24]

CAST: *Countess Palmatica*: ROSE LEIGHTON. *Her Daughters (2)*: *Laura*: BERTHA RICCI. *Bronislava*: MATHILDE COTTRELLY. *General Ollendorf*, Governor of Cracow: FREDERICK LESLIE. *Saxon Officers (6)*: *Lieutenant Poppenberg*: Master HARRY HAMBLIN. *Major Olzhoff*: HARRY STANDISH. *Lieutenant Wangenheim*: G. Furey. *Lieutenant Schweinitz*: L. M. Hall. *Captain Henrici*: A. Barbara. *Ensign Richtofen*: L. Schrader. *Cousins of Palmatica (2)*: *Bogomil*: HARRY MACDONOUGH. *Eva*, his wife: ROSE BEAUDET. *Janitsky*, a Polish noble: W. S. RISING. *Burgomaster*: F. Senger. *Enterich*, a jailor: ELLIS RYSE. *Puffke*, his assistant: A. D. Barker. *Sitzka*, an inn-keeper: George Pyke. *Onouphrie*, servant: J. B. Fischer. *Alexis*, a prisoner: Joseph Fahey. *Symon Symkovicz* (the Beggar Student): WILLIAM T. CARLETON.

Act 1, Scene 1: Courtyard of Military Prison at Cracow. *Scene 2*: Springtide Fair at Cracow.

Act 2: Grand Salon in the Palace of Countess Palmatica.

Act 3: Garden of the same.

ACT 1[25]
Introduction (Our husbands, alas! They've lock'd up in jail)
E. Ryse, A. D. Barker, Chorus
When with good cheer the festive board doth smile
Chorus
Ollendorf's Entrance (And they say toward ladies one should gallantly behave)
F. Leslie
Entrance Duo (The world to soaring genius ever quick recognition has refused!)
W. T. Carleton, W. S. Rising, Saxon Officers
Confounded cell, at last I leave thee!
W. T. Carleton, W. S. Rising, Saxon Officers
Chorus and Ensemble (Hurrah, hip, hurrah! the fair has begun)
Entrance Trio (Some little shopping really we ought to do)
B. Ricci, M. Cottrelly, R. Leighton, J. B. Fischer
Ensemble and Song (That is the Prince Wibicki with his Secretary there!)
L. Leslie, B. Ricci, M. Cottrelly, R. Leighton, R. Beaudet, W. T. Carleton, Saxon Officers
Finale (You love each other!)
Principals, Chorus

ACT 2
Trio (I at last have found a husband)
B. Ricci, M. Cottrelly, R. Leighton, J. B. Fischer
Duet (This kiss, sweet love, our union shall cement forevermore!)
M. Cottrelly, W. S. Rising
Duet (Shall I tell her? or keep silence?)
B. Ricci, W. T. Carleton
Ensemble (Most happy bride, for you life's skies are clearing!)
F. Leslie, W. T. Carleton, R. Leighton, W. S. Rising, Saxon Officers, Chorus
Couplet (One day I was perambulating along the Ganges)
F. Leslie
Topical verses (There in the chamber Polish they acted quite Mongolish)
F. Leslie
Finale (Wedding bells are sweetly ringing)
Principals, Chorus

ACT 3
Introduction (Shabby young hussy! penniless cheat!)
Chorus
Couplet (I'm penniless and outlawed too)
W. T. Carleton
Ensemble (Hush they come! See, there the fellow stands!)
R. Leighton, W. T. Carleton, F. Leslie, R. Beaudet, H. Macdonough, W. S. Rising, B. Ricci, M. Cottrelly, Saxon Officers
Final Chorus (The land is free, united we, a daring game brought luck and fame!)
W. T. Carleton, B. Ricci, M. Cottrelly, Principals, Chorus

1883.63 CORDELIA'S ASPIRATIONS

A Local Play in Three Acts, 5 Scenes. Play (and lyrics) by Edward Harrigan. Music by David Braham. Staged by Edward Harrigan. Scenery by Charles

[20]First produced in New York 22 October 1877 at the Fifth Avenue Theatre for 16 performances in repertory. For Synopsis of Scenes and Musical Numbers, see original 1877 production.

[21]For Haverly's Comedy Theatre return engagement, the following cast changes: *Serpolette*: Mlle. MARIE AIMÉE. *Germaine*: Mlle. ASTRUC.

[22]First produced in New York 31 March 1875 at the Lyceum Theatre in repertory. For Synopsis of Scenes and Musical Numbers, see original 1875 production. In Act 3, Mlle. Aimée will introduce her world-famous song and dance, "Pretty as a Picture." Cast unchanged for return engagement.

[23]English language premiere. First produced in New York in German 19 October-17 November 1883 at the Thalia Theatre. Musical director (Jesse Williams) uncredited in programs. Scenery credits appear only in programs for subsequent tour.

[24]Musical director uncredited in New York programs; subsequent tour credits Antonio DeNovellis.

[25]Musical numbers not listed in programs. List prepared from published piano vocal score (White, Smith & Co., Boston, 1883). Interpolated as per published sheet music:
"This Very Hour He Thinks of Me"
(*Music by* A. Nevendorff. *Lyrics by* Emil Schwab.)

W. Witham. Mechanical effects by William McMurray. Wardrobe by Mrs. Mary Jack. Musical director, David Braham. Produced by Messrs. (Edward) Harrigan and (Tony) Hart. Opened 5 November 1883 at the Theatre Comique and closed 5 April 1884 after 176 performances.

CAST: *Dan Mulligan*: EDWARD HARRIGAN. *Rebecca Allup*: TONY HART. *Palestine Puter*: George H. Wood. *Planxty McFudd*: HARRY FISHER. *Walsingham McSweeney*: M. Bradley. *Ridgeway*: W. Miller. *Gustavus Lochmuller*: JOSEPH SPARKS. *Cordelia Mulligan*: ANNIE YEAMANS. *Diana McFudd*: Gertie Granville. *Mrs. Lochmuller*: Jennie Christie. *Ellen McFudd*: Ada Farwell. *Rosey McFudd*: Annie Langdon. *Mrs. Diggins*: Annie Hall. *Mulvey*: M. Foley. *Mr. Bowser*: GEORGE MERRITT. *Dunbar*: William Merritt. *Clerk*: George L. Stout. *Simpson Primrose*: JOHN WILD. *Tommy*: Master Harry Guion. *Policeman*: J. McCullough. *Mrs. Brown*: Sadie Morris. *Mrs. Risley*: Marie Gorenflo. *Annetta*: Lizzie Finn. *Mrs. Buchheister*: Kate Langdon. *Mrs. Crumps*: Mrs. W. Scallan. *Jim Grace*: P. C. GOLDRICH. *Dangerfield*: WILLIAM WEST. *Clinton*: W. A. Barlow. *Topsy*: John Queen. *Billy Kersands*: JOHN SPARKS. *Cal Hicks*: RICHARD QUILTER. *Jim Bland*: James Barlow. *Sam Lucas*: Emil Heusel. *Joe Hardhead*: Charles Coffey. *Jay Weldon*: Thomas Granger. *Emigrants, Officials, Policemen, Hackmen, etc.*

Act 1, Scene 1: Castle Garden. *Scene 2*: Local Street. *Scene 3*: Mulligan's Home in Mulligan's Alley.

Act 2: The Mulligan Mansion on Murray Hill.

Act 3: Salle á Manger.

MUSICAL NUMBERS

"Just Across from Jersey"
"My Dad's Dinner Pail"
"Wear the Trousers Oh!"
"The Waiters (Chorus), or Two More to Come" (Waiters' Chorus)
"Samuel Johnson's (Colored) Cake Walk"

1883.64 LIEUTENANT HELENE OF THE GUARDS

A Romantic Comic Opera in Three Acts. Libretto by Ernst Gschmeidler. Music by Ernst Catenhusen. Produced under the personal supervision of James C. Scanlan and Ernst Catenhusen. Scenery by George W. Dayton. Costumes by H. J. Eaves and J. Buckheister. Musical director, Ernst Catenhusen. Produced by John Stetson, by arrangement with Edward E. Rice. Opened 12 November 1883 at the Fifth Avenue Theatre and closed 17 November 1883 after 7 performances.[26]

CAST: *Lieutenant Helene*, Countess de Vannes: AMY GORDON. *Clemence*, her maid: FANNY RICE. *Manuela*: JESSIE CALEF. *Teresa*: ANNIE WINNER. *Josephine*, the Innkeeper's wife: MARIE UART. *Charles de Valois*, Captain of the Guards: HUBERT WILKE. *His Lieutenant*: Charles Shackford. *An Officer*: Florence Bemister. *Barberon*, Maire of the Village: Felix J. Morris. *Domingo*, Robber Chief: W. A. Morgan. *Jose, Pablo*, two robbers: E. S. Grant, J. L. Slattery. *A Banker*: J. H. Finn. *Forgeout*, the schoolmaster: H. A. Amberg. *Munier*, the Innkeeper: GEORGE A. SCHILLER. *Gillaume*, a Rustic: Horace Frail. *Count de Vannes*, Father of Helene: J. Otley. *Fripperpon*, the Secretary: HENRY E. DIXEY. Leiboldt's Military Band will furnish the military music upon the stage. *Peasants, Soldiers, Bandits, Couriers, etc.*

Act 1: Small French village near the Spanish Frontier. 1759.

Act 2: Robbers' Cave and Ruined Cloister in Spain.

Act 3: Hall in the Count de Vannes' Castle.

1883.65 ORPHEUS AND EURYDICE

An Opéra-bouffe in Three Acts, 7 Scenes[27]. Original Viennese libretto to 'Orphée aux Enfers' by Hector Crémieux (and Ludovic Halévy). American adaptation by Max Freeman. Music by Jacques Offenbach. Entire production under the supervision of Max Freeman. Scenery by Lippincott; John Mazzanovich; Lafayette W. Seavey; Harley Merry. Costumes by P. Godchaux & Co., from designs by Alfred Thompson. Light effects by Edward A. Kelly. Musical director, Gustave Kerker. Produced by Rice's Opera Bouffe Company (Edward E. Rice, Proprietor). Opened 1 December 1883 at the Bijou Opera House and closed 15 March 1884 after 109 performances; re-opened 24 March 1884 at Niblo's Garden and closed 29 March 1884 after an additional 8 performances[28].

CAST: *Jupiter*, King and Father of Gods and Men: DIGBY BELL. *Aristeus*, a Shepherd: MAX FREEMAN. *Pluto*, King of the Lower World: MAX FREEMAN. *Orpheus*, famous for his skill in music: HARRY PEPPER. *Styx*, Porter in Hades: GEORGE C. BONIFACE, JR. *Eurydice*, Wife of Orpheus: MARIE VANONI. *Diana*, Goddess of the Chase: LAURA JOYCE BELL. *Cupid*, the Little God of Love: IDA MÜLLE. *Public Opinion*: AUGUSTA ROCHE. *Venus*, Goddess of Beauty: PAULINE HALL. *Juno*, Wife of Jupiter: AMELIA SUMMERVILLE. *Minerva*, Goddess of War and Wisdom: Genee Holtzmeyer. *Hebe*, Waitress in Olympus: Daisy Murdoch. *Fortuna*, Goddess of Good Luck: Jennie Prince. *Mercury*, Messenger of the Gods: Billie Barlow. *Mars*, God of War: H. F. Fairweather. *Vulcan*, God of Fire: E. S. Grant. *Bacchus*, God of Wine: Clara Davenport. *Æsculapius*, God of Medicine: Edward Aiken. *Apollo*, God of Music: Rita Carroll. *Janus*, Porter in Olympus: Andrew Metzger. *Hercules*, God of Strength: Henri Leone [Leoni]. *Cerberus*, Dog of Hades: Master Charles Coulter. *The Three Graces*, daughters of Jupiter and Eurynome: *Thalia*: Lizzie Tracy. *Aglaia*: Helen Lowell. *Euphrosyne*: Effie Edgerton. *The Nine Muses*, daughters of Jupiter and Mnenosyne: *Calliope*: Louise Martin. *Clio*: M. Thomas. *Euterpe*: Hattie Maynard. *Melpomene*: Alice Ames. *Erato*: Eva Young. *Polyhymnia*: Lulu Freeth. *Urania*: Minnie Flagg. *Terpsichore*: Lillie Glover. *Heba*: Kittie Ford. *The Three Furies, Danaides, Satyrs, Gods, Goddesses*: Chorus of 40.

Prologue and Act 1, Scene 1: Public Opinion. (Lippincott.) *Scene 2*: Landscape in the Suburbs of Thebes, showing Orpheus' Conservatory of Music and Aristeus' Manufactory of Honey. (Mazzanovich.)

Act 2, Scene 1: Tableau of the Gods sleeping on the Clouds. *Scene 2*: View of the Sun after a Lark. *Scene 3*: Olympus. (Seavey.)

Act 3, Scene 1: Plutus' Little Boudoir. *Scene 2*: Hades, with the River Styx. *Scene 3*: Apotheosis. (Merry.)

ACT 1[29]

Prologue, Scene 1

Prologue
A. Roche

Scene 2

Solo (Since love has set my heart a-dreaming)
M. Vanoni

Duet (Oui, mon ami)
H. Pepper, M. Vanoni

Recitative and Song (I am Aristeus, a shepherd of Arcadia)
M. Freeman [Aristeus]

Solo (O death, for thee I'm fondly sighing)
M. Vanoni

Duet (Come, it is honor that calls you)
M. Vanoni, H. Pepper

ACT 2

Scene 1

Chorus of Gods Sleeping (O blissfullness! O sleep, tho treasure)
Chorus

Chorus of Grumblers (Ron, ron, ron . . .)
Chorus

Entrance of Cupid (I'm Cupid, you see, god of love)
I. Mülle

Entrance of Venus (Venus am I, goddess of love)
P. Hall

Entrance of Jupiter (By Saturn, what's the matter here?)
D. Bell

Scenes 2 and 3

Solo (Where'er I rove, through forest and mountain)
L. J. Bell

---

[26]No musical numbers listed in programs.

[27]produced in New York in French 17 January 1867 at the Théâtre Français for 14 performances.

[28]Played a return engagement 27 October 1884 at the Grand Opera House, moving 3 November 1884 to the Fifth Avenue Theatre for an additional week.

[29]Musical numbers not listed in programs. List prepared from published libretto "adapted and produced under the stage direction of Max Freeman at the Bijou Opera House for the first time in English" (Edward E. Rice, New York, n.d.) Interpolation with does not appear in published text:

"In Other Respects" (new couplet)
(*Music by* Edward E. Rice. *Lyrics by* Sydney Rosenfeld.)

Scena (To arms! Ye gods and demigods!)
M. Freeman [Pluto], I. Mulle, L. J. Bell, P. Hall, All
Scena (To captivate the fair Almena)
L. J. Bell, P. Hall, G. Holtzmeyer, A. Summerville
Finale (To complain he now advances)
M. Freeman [Pluto], D. Bell, H. Pepper, A. Roche, Chorus

ACT 3
Scene 1
Song and Chorus (They tell me I'm too bashful by far)
M. Vanoni, Chorus
Duet (When I was monarch of Arcadia)
G. C. Boniface, M. Vanoni
Fly Duet (I thought I felt here on my shoulder a touch as light as insects' wing)
M. Vanoni, D. Bell
Scene 2
Chorus of Gods and Goddesses (Hurrah for Pluto's festive cheer)
Gods, Goddesses
Jupiter's Song and Chorus (Come, now, charming, beautiful Amaranthe)
D. Bell, M. Vanoni, Chorus
Scena (My wifey dear, I'm willing to believe)
H. Pepper, D. Bell, A. Roche, Chorus
Grand March of the Gods and Goddesses (I would really be furious)
D. Bell, A. Roche, Gods and Goddesses
Eurydice's Response (O Bacchus!)
M. Vanoni
Scene 3
Apotheosis and Grand Finale
C. Davenport, All

1883.66 THE PRINCESS OF MADAGASCAR

An Aboriginal Operetta in One Act, 3 Scenes, preceded by an Olio. Libretto, music, songs and elaborations by Joseph A. Gulick and A. C. Comstock, Jr. Arranged by James Gorman. Produced by Birch's San Francisco and Haverly's Mastodon Minstrels (J. H. Haverly, Director). Opened 3 December 1883 at Haverly's San Francisco Minstrel and Comedy Theatre and closed 22 December 1883 after 24 performances.

Olio: "Teresa" (Serenade), Walter Carpenter Hawkins; Bridget O'Donahue, by Billy Richardson; "White Wings" (*Music and Lyrics by* Joseph A. Gulick.), Thomas Campbell; "Tidings of Comfort and Joy", Billy Birch; "Baby Darling" (*Music and Lyrics by* Joseph A. Gulick and A. C. Comstock, Jr.), Joseph M. Woods; "When the Democrats Get In" (new, *Music and Lyrics by* Joseph A. Gulick and A. C. Comstock, Jr.), Hughey Dougherty; The Jockey Ball", Seamon and Girard; Jay Gould's Yacht (Great Nautical Finale), with A. C. Moreland, Hughey Dougherty, D. H. Thompson; [Interval] Bobby Newcomb (Song and Dance); Billy Richardson (British Demosthenes); Seamon and Girard (Two Dudes); Bob Slavin (Rhapsodical Ravings).

CAST: *Montefakir*, King of Madagascar: A. C. MORELAND. *Lallah Taffy*, his Prime Minister: HUGHEY DOUGHERTY. *Lucre Abscondo*, Chauncellor of the Exchequor: BOB SLAVIN. *Princess Kadee Aleek*, the Marble Heart: PAUL VERNON. *Prince Ding Dong*, from Fiddleland: BILLY RICHARDSON. *Jimblaino, Tildeno*, Wise men of Madagascar: Charles V. Seamon, Edward Girard. *Prince "Sing a Note Higher,"* in Love: Bobby Newcomb. *Courier* from the Emperor Dido: Charles Boning. *Master of the Throne Room*: D. H. Thompson. *The Three-Legged Pirate of Kamschatka*: Manning J. Collyer. *Friday*: G. Hogan. *Saturday*: Robert Hooley. *Singleout, Doubleout, Pickemout*, Three Salves, Bodyguards to the Princess: Messrs. H. Hogan, E. Murphy, Thomas LeMack. *Malagassy Nobles and Chiefs* (5): *Bilrice*: Mr. Campbell. *Oc Nomowac*: Mr. Wood. *Two Pairr*: Mr. Shattuck. *Anteup*: Mr. Winter. *Cases*: Mr. Holland.

Scene 1: The Forest of the Idols. *Scene 2*: The Council Chamber. *Scene 3*: The Royal Palace.

MUSICAL NUMBERS
"Malagassy War Song"
Hottentots
"Love Lurks Around unknown"
B. Richardson, P. Vernon
"Mind Your P's and Q's"
H. Dougherty
"The King's got four aces"
Courtiers, Slaves
"Hail to the Princess"
B. Newcomb, Grand Chorus
"The two wise men"
Astrologers

1883.67 ESTRELLA

A Comic Opera in Three Acts. Libretto by Walter Parke. Music by W. Luscombe Searelle. Produced under the stage direction of James C. Scanlan. Musical director, W. Luscombe Searelle. Produced by Edward E. Rice. Opened 11 December 1883 at the Standard Theatre and closed 13 December 1883 after 3 performances[30].

CAST: *Count Pomposo di Vesuvio*, a Venetian gentleman betrothed to Estrella: HUBERT WILKE. *Signor Lorenzo*, a young advocate, in love with Estrella: W. S. RISING. *The Doge of Venice*, a model of Justice and Dignity: EDWARD P. TEMPLE. *Phylloxera*, an impoverished wine-grower, father of Estrella: Horace Frail. *Giovanni Tommaso*, Major-Domo to the Court: GEORGE A. SCHILLER. *Estrella*, betrothed tot he Count, but in love with Lorenzo: AMY GORDON. *Tartarella*, mother to Estrella—a strong-minded woman: Jennie Hughes. *Brigetta*, companion to Estrella, in love with the Count: FANNY RICE. *Page to the Doge*: Kathleen Lynne. *Ninetta*: Polly Winner. *Violetta*: Emma Calef. *Henrietta*: Madeline Dixon. *Notary*: Mr. Slattery. *Chorus of Peasants, Soldiers, Wedding Guests, Moorish Pirates, Lawyers, etc.*

The action is set in Venice during the Renaissance.

MUSICAL NUMBERS[31]
"Listen to the Nightingale"
"The Kissing Duet"

1883.68 3 OF A KIND!

Nate Salsbury's Troubadours in a Farce Comedy in Three Acts. Play by Edward E. Kidder. Acting manager, Frank Maeder. Musical director, Theodore Bendix. Proprietors, (Nate) Salsbury, (John) Webster and (Frank) Maeder. Opened 31 December 1883 at the Third Avenue Theatre and closed 5 January 1884 after 7 performances; returned 4 February 1884 to the New Park Theatre and closed 16 February 1884 after an additional 16 performances.[32]

CAST: *Three of a Kind*: *Jack Potts*: NATE SALSBURY. *Bob Flush*: JOHN WEBSTER. *Phil Straight*: W. S. DABOLL. *Dollie Dashwood*, who should have been a boy: NELLIE McHENRY. *Dainty*, the farmer's adopted daughter: Josie Langley. *Priscilla Prism*, ancient, but gushing: Thomas E. Jackson. *Ezra Whittle* of the Happy Homestead Farm: Fred. Bowman. *Mr. Salvage Delaine*, a merchant: L. J. Loring. *Villagers, Maids, Widows and Guests.*

Act 1: The Happy Homestead Farm.—Country Board.

Act 2: The Farm House Parlor.—Country Amusements.

Act 3: The Franklin Flats.—Country Results.

1884.01 LA VIE PARISIENNE!

A Revival of the Opéra-bouffe in Four Acts, in French[33]. Libretto by Henri Meilhac and Ludovic Halévy. Music by Jacques Offenbach. Stage manager, Mons. V. Merle. Musical director, Mons. A Lagye. Produced by Maurice Grau. Opened 7 January 1884 at Haverly's Comedy Theatre and closed 17 January 1884 after 5 performances in repertory.

[30]Production closed due destruction of the theatre by fire 14 December 1883.
[31]Musical numbers not listed in programs.
[32]Scenery and costumes uncredited. "During the evening, many musical selections will be given of an original and catchy nature."
[33]First produced in New York in French 29 March 1869 at the Théâtre Français for 11 performances. For Synopsis of Scenes and Musical Numbers, see 1869 production.

CAST: *Gabrielle*: Mlle. MARIE AIMÉE. *Métella*: Mlle. JEANNE FOUQUET. *Pauline*: Mlle. ANGÈLE. *La Baronne* (Baroness de Gondremarck): Mlle. Vallot. *Leonie*: Mlle. DeWitt. *Clara*: Mlle. Lescot. *Caroline*: Mlle. Daniel. *Julie*: Mlle. Delournay. *Augustine*: Mlle. Gatineau. *Josepha*: Mlle. Salvator. *(Baron de) Gondremarck*: Mons. DUPLAN. *Un Bresilien*: Mons. Lary. *(Baron) de Frick*: Mons. Lary. *Prosper*: Mons. Lary. *Robinet*: Mons. J. MEZIÈRES. *Raoul de Gardefeu*: Mons. GUY. *Alfred*: Mons. Ducos. *Urbain*: Mons. Ducos. *Joseph*: Mons. Peret. *Alphonse*: Mons. Gèrard. *Gontran*: Mons. Salvator. *Un Employe*: Mons. Lamant. *Waiters, Masks, etc.*

1884.02

MADAME FAVART

A Revival of the Opéra-comique in Three Acts, in French[34]. Libretto by Henri Chivot and Alfred Duru. Music by Jacques Offenbach. Stage manager, Mons. V. Merle. Musical director, Mons. A Lagye. Produced by Maurice Grau. Opened 14 January 1884 at Haverly's Comedy Theatre and closed 19 January 1884 after 2 performances in repertory.

CAST: *Madame Favart*: Mlle. MARIE AIMÉE. *Suzanne*: Mlle. Buisson. *Premiere Servante*: Mlle. Vallot. *Deuxieme Servant*: Mlle. Vandamme. *Jolicoeur*: Mlle. Vallot. *Sans Quartier*: Mlle. DeWitt. *Larissolo*: Mlle. Lescot. *Favart*: Mons. CLEMENT NIGRI. *Pontsable*: Mons. J. MEZIÈRES. *Hector*: Mons. LARY. *Cottignac*: Mons. Ducos. *Biscotin*: Mons. Gèrard. *Le Sergent*: Mons. Vinchon. *Un Exempt*: Mons. Nys. *Le Tapissier*: Mons. Perret.

1884.03

OLIVETTE

A Revival of the Opéra-comique (Les Noces d'Olivette) in Three Acts, in French[35]. Libretto by Henri Chivot and Alfred Duru. Music by Edmond Audran. Stage manager, Mons. V. Merle. Musical director, Mons. A Lagye. Produced by Maurice Grau. Opened 18 January 1884 at Haverly's Comedy Theatre for 1 performance in repertory.[36]

CAST: *Olivette*: Mlle. MARIE AIMÉE. *La Comtesse*: Mlle. JEANNE FOUQUET. *Ourika*: Mlle. Buisson. *First Mousse*: Mlle. Lescot. *Second Mousse*: Mlle. DeWitt. *Third Mousse*: Mlle. Vandamme. *Valentin*: Mons. LARY. *DeMerrimac*: Mons. GUY. *Le Duc des Ifs*: Mons. J. MEZIÈRES. *Le Seneschal*: Mons. Ducos. *Longfuseau*: Mons. Gerard. *Quartier Maitre*: Mons. Vinchon. *Aubergiste*: Mons. Millet.

1884.04

UNSER FRITZ,
The Bohemian

A Drama in a Prologue and Three Acts. Play by Thomas Kean. Stage manager, Maurice Pike. Leader of orchestra, Frank Webb. Produced by Joseph K. Emmet. Opened 21 January 1884 at the 14th Street Theatre and closed 31? January 1884 after 11? performances.

CAST (Prologue): *Fritz*, the Bohemian: JOSEPH K. EMMET. *Tony Bougares*: MARTIN J. CODY. *Marie Clootz*: CLARA BAKER. *The Waif*: Baby Mamie Livesey.

CAST (Drama): *Fritz*, the Bohemian: JOSEPH K. EMMET. *Duke de Bessiers*: H. A. Moray. *Lord Philip de Chambroy*: GEORGE SPRAGUE. *Sig. Algorotti*, an organ grinder: Maurice Pike. *Tony Bougares*: MARTIN J. CODY. *Adolph Spinks*: Edward Rue. *Julius Caesar*: C. W. Swain. *Marie Clootz*: CLARA BAKER. *Fluerette*: Kate Blancke. *Duchess de Bessiers*: Lizzie Scanlon. *Julia Flyaway*: Kate French. *Little Katherina*: Emma Livesey.

Act 1: Fifteen years later.

1884.05

LA GRANDE DUCHESSE DE GÉROLSTEIN

A Revival of the Opéra-bouffe in Three Acts, in French[37]. Libretto by Henri Meilhac and Ludovic Halévy. Music by Jacques Offenbach. Stage manager, Mons. V. Merle. Musical director, Mons. A Lagye. Produced by Maurice Grau. Opened 23 January 1884 at Haverly's Comedy Theatre and closed 26 January 1884 after 3 performances in repertory.

CAST: *La Grande Duchesse de Gérolstein*: Mlle. MARIE AIMÉE. *Wanda*: Mlle. ANGÈLE. *Iza*: Mlle. Buisson. *Chalotte*: Mlle. Vallot. *Olga*: Mlle. DeWitt. *Amelie*: Mlle. Lescot. *Fritz*: Mons. LARY. *Baron Puck*: Mons. J. MEZIÈRES. *Prince Paul* (of Steis-Stein-Steis-Laper-Bottmoll-Schorstenburg): Mons. GUY. *General Boum*: Mons. Vinchon. *Nepomuc*: Mons. Ducos. *Baron Grog*: Mons. Salvator.

1884.06

WANTED, A PARTNER

A Burlesque on an actor's life (A Musical Absudity) in Three Acts, "Have I your eye?." Manager, James Barton. Stage manager, H. A. Cripps. Musical director, George P. Towle. Produced under the personal supervision of William A. Mestayer and James Barton. Opened 28 January 1884 at the Star Theatre and closed 9 February 1884 after 14 performances; re-opened 18 February 1884 at the New Park Theatre and closed 23 February 1884 after 7 additional performances. Total: 21 performances.[38]

CAST: *Colonel Vere de Vere Hix*, a Theatrical Manager and Agent: HARRY BLOODGOOD. *Macy Simpson Crawford Altman*, a Would-be Actor: ROBERT E. GRAHAM. *O'Donovan Steele*, an Irish, but downtrodden Comedian: JOHN GILBERT. *Eli D. Hugg*, Hix's factotum, with yearnings for the legitimate: JAMES B. RADCLIFFE. *Leander Thoroughbrace*, The Angel": Charles A. Stedman. *Signor Trampolini*, a Tenor: H. A. CRIPPS. *Oney Dangerfield*, nee John Green, a Comedian with an appreciation of the good things of this life: WILLIAM A. MESTAYER. *Winifred Wynne*, a Soubrette of the modern school: Kate Foley. *Mrs. Colonel Hix*, the White Sergeant—supposed to be in the country: Lisle Riddell. *Irene Trevelian*, an Aspirant: Sophie Hummel. *Clare St. Aubyn*, a Professional Beauty: Helen Lowell. *Dennis*, a Railroad gate keeper: John Gilbert. *Newsboy*: Sophie Hummel. *Pretty Jane*: Helen Lowell.

Act 1: Hix's office—The Angel.

Act 2: On the Stage—The Rehearsal.

Act 3: Railroad Depot—Stranded.

1884.07

FRITZ IN IRELAND

A Revival of the Irish Drama (Romantic Comedy) in a Prologue and Three Acts.[39] Play by William Carleton. Music composed by Joseph K. Emmet. Stage manager, Maurice Pike. Leader of orchestra, Frank Webb. Produced by Joseph K. Emmet. Opened 1? February 1884 at the 14th Street Theatre and closed 9 February 1884 after 10? performances; re-opened 31 March 1884 at Niblo's Garden and closed 5 April 1884 after 8 additional performances.

CAST (Prologue): *Fritz (Schultz)*: JOSEPH K. EMMET. *Baron Hertfort*: GEORGE R. SPRAGUE. *Lawyer Priggins*: MAURICE PIKE. *Madame Schultz*: Kate French. *Lena*: Little Emma Livesey.

CAST (Drama): *Fritz (Schultz)*: JOSEPH K. EMMET. *Captain (Hercules) O'Doud*: MARTIN J. CODY. *Lawyer Priggins*: MAURICE PIKE. *Charles Seaton*: Edward Rue. *Lord Seaton*: H. A. MOREY. *Thomas Goldfinger*: C. W. Swain. *Patrick Black*: William Schroeder. *Lady Amelia*: CLARA BAKER. *Lady Louisa (Hertfort)*: Kate Blancke. *Judy Callahan*: Lizzie Scanlon. *Madame Schultz*: Kate French. *Master Herbert*: Little Emma Livesey.

---

[34]First produced in New York in French 12 May 1879 at the Park Theatre for 14 performances. For Synopsis of Scenes and Musical Numbers, see original 1879 production.

[35]First produced in New York 25 December 1880 at the Bijou Theatre for 98 performances in two engagements. For Synopsis of Scenes and Musical Numbers, see original 1880 production.

[36]The 15 January 1884 performance of OLIVETTE was cancelled due to the illness of Mons. Lary, and LA PRINCESSE DES CANARIES was substituted; there are extant programs for both titles for this same date.

[37]First produced in New York in French 24 September 1867 at the Théâtre Français for 156 performances. For Synopsis of Scenes and Musical Numbers, see original 1867 production.

[38]No credits for costumes or scenery in programs. No musical numbers listed; J. B. Radcliffe performed the following specialties in Act 2: Character Sketches, the Hot Corn Man, the Cigar Song, Harmonica Solos, etc. Robert E. Graham gave imitations of J. K. Emmet and impersonations of Henry Irving.

[39]First produced in New York 3 November 1879 at the Park Theatre for 86 performances in two engagements. For Synopsis of Scenes and Musical Numbers, see original 1979 production.

1884.08

THE MERRY WAR

A Revival of the Operetta in Three Acts[40]. Original Viennese libretto to the operette ('Der lustige Krieg') by F. Zell and Richard Genée, based on the libretto to "Les Dames capitaines" by Mélesville. English libretto adapted by Sydney Rosenfeld. Music by Johann Strauss. Produced under the direction of Jesse Williams. Produced by McCaull Opera Comique Company (John A. McCaull, Proprietor). Opened 4 February 1884 at the Casino Theatre and closed 12 April 1884 after 69 performances.[41]

CAST: *Artemisia*, Princess of Malaspina, wife of the Prince of Massa Carrara: GERTRUDE ORME. *Violetta*, Widowed Countess of Lomellini, Cousin to Artemisia: LILLY POST. *Balthazar Groots*, a Tulip Planter from Holland: FREDERICK LESLIE. *Marquis Fillippo Sebastini*, Nephew to the Princess: Signor PERUGINI. *Elsa*, his wife: MATHILDE COTTRELLY. *Young Noblemen in the service of the Genoese Republic (3)*: *Riccardo Surrazo*: H. C. CRIPPS. *Carlo Spinzi*: C. T. PARR. *Fortunato Franchetti*: J. A. FUREY. *Colonel von Schleelen*, in the service of the Duke of Limberg: Emil Sanger. *Biffi*, *Gini*, Sergeants in the Genoese Service: A. D. Parker, C. M. Pyke. *Captain of the Guard*: ROSE BEAUDET. *Theresa*, cadet: Clara Wisdom. *Umberto Spinola*, a young Nobleman and General commanding the Genoese Army: WILLIAM T. CARLETON. *Court Ladies, Noblemen, Soldiers, etc.*

Time: Early part of the eighteenth century.

Act 1: Camp of the Genoese Army.

Act 2: Neutral Castle of Malaspina.

Act 3: Interior of Palace at Massa.

ACT 1

ACT 2

Romanza
W. T. Carleton
(*Music by* Ernst Catenhusen.)

ACT 3

"Triomphal" March
(*Music by* Rudolph Aronson.)

1884.09

PRINCESS IDA, or, Castle Adamant

A Comic Opera in a Prologue and Two Acts. A Respectful Operatic per-version of Alfred Lord Tennyson's poem "The Princess—A Medley." Libretto by William S. Gilbert. Music by Arthur Sullivan. Produced under the personal supervision of Frank Thornton. Company of artists organized by Edward E. Rice. Scenery designed by Joseph Clare, John Thompson. Costumes by P. Godchaux & Co. Mechanisms by Benson Sherwood. Appointments by N. Robb. Gas effects by J. Thompson. Orchestra under the direction of John Mullaly. Produced by John Stetson. Opened 11 February 1884 at the Fifth Avenue Theatre and closed 22 March 1884 after 48 performances.

CAST: *King Hildebrand*: SIGNOR C. BROCOLINI. *Hilarion*, King Hilarion's Son: WALLACE McCREERY. *His Friends (2)*: *Cyril*: W. S. RISING. *Florian*: CHARLES F. LANG. *Sons of King Gama (3)*: *Arac*: M. AINSLEY SCOTT. *Guron*: JAMES EARLY. *Scynthias*: E. J. CLONEY. *King Gama*: J. H. RYLEY. *Princess Ida*, Gama's Daughter: CORA S. TANNER. *Lady Psyche*, Professor at Princess Ida's College: FLORENCE BEMISTER. *Lady Blanche*, Professor at Princess Ida's College: GENEVIEVE REYNOLDS. *Melissa*, Lady Blanche's Daughter: HATTIE DOLARO. *Girl Graduates (3)*: *Sacharissa*: Eva Barrington. *Chloe*: Eily Coghlan. *Ada*: Clara Primrose. *Soldiers, Courtiers, Girl Graduates, Daughters of the Plough, etc.*

Prologue: Exterior of King Hildebrand's Palace. (Clare.)

Act 1: Gardens in Castle Adamant. (Clare.)

Act 2: Outerwalls and Courtyard of Castle Adamant. (Thompson.)

PROLOGUE[42]

Chorus and Solo ("Search throughout the panorama")
C. F. Lang, Chorus

Song ("Now harken to my strict command")
C. Brocolini, Chorus

Recitative and Song ("Today we meet, my baby bride and I")
W. McCreery

Chorus ("From the distant panorama")
Chorus

Trio ("We are warriors three")
M. A. Scott, J. Early, E. J. Cloney, Chorus

Song ("If you give me your attention")
J. H. Ryley

Finale ("P'raps if you address the lady most politely")

ACT 1

Chorus of Girls and Solos ("Towards the empyrean heights of every kind of love")
F. Bemister, H. Dolaro, E. Coghlan

Chorus of Girls ("Mighty maiden with a mission")
Chorus of Girls

Recitative and Aria ("Minerva! Minerva! Oh hear me")
C. S. Tanner

Song ("Come mighty Must!")
G. Reynolds

Trio ("Gently, gently, evidently, we are safe so far")
W. McCreery, W. S. Rising, C. F. Lang

Trio ("I am a maiden cold and stately")
W. McCreery, W. S. Rising, C. F. Lang

Quartette ("The world is but a broken toy")
C. S. Tanner, W. S. Rising, W. McCreery, C. F. Lang

Song ("A lady fair, of lineage high")
F. Bemister, W. McCreery, W. S. Rising, C. F. Lang

Quintet ("The woman of the wisest wit")
F. Bemister, H. Dolaro, W. McCreery, W. S. Rising, C. F. Lang

Duet ("Now wouldn't you like to rule the roost")
H. Dolaro, G. Reynolds

Chorus of Girls and Solos ("Merrily ring the luncheon bell!")
G. Reynolds, W. S. Rising

Song ("Would you know the kind of maid")
W. S. Rising

Finale ("Oh! Joy, our chief is sav'd")

ACT 2

Chorus and Solo ("Death to the invader!")
H. Dolaro

Song ("I built upon a rock")
C. S. Tanner

Song ("When-e'er I spoke sarcastic joke")
J. H. Ryley, Chorus of Girls

Chorus of Ladies and Soldiers ("When an anger spreads his wing")

Song ("This helmet, I suppose, was meant to ward off blows")
M. A. Scott, J. Early, E. J. Cloney, Chorus

Chorus during the fight ("This is our duty plain")
Chorus

Finale ("With joy abiding, Together gliding")

1884.10

ON THE YELLOWSTONE

A Grand Spectacular Drama in Five Acts, 6 Scenes, with realistic display of the gorgeous marvels of America's Great Wonderland! Music by Giuseppi Operti. Produced by Mary C. Blackburn. Opened 13 February 1884 at the Cosmopolitan Theatre and closed 23 February 1884 after 10 performances.

CAST: *Jumping Bear*: HARRY MITCHELL. *Kelly*: RANDOLPH MURRAY. *Alfred Higgins*: JAMES F. PETERS. *Rube*: Walter White., *Colonel*, Commanding Fort Sully: J. B. Brown. *Lieutenant*: John H. Browne. *Red Cloud*: Harold Russell. *Old Chief*: H. R. Brennan. *Crow Chief*: Lee Bates. *Wash Higgins*: L. Livingston. *Bill Higgins*: E. S. Piessert. *Indian Dancer*: Mons. LeStrange. *Fannie Kelly*: Lida H. Talbot. *Mrs. Higgins*, wife of Alfred: Madam IVAN MICHELLS. *Nancy Jane*, her daughter: MARY C. BLACKBURN. *Corps of more than 100 Auxiliaries.*

Act 1: Grotesque formation of the Grand Canyon of the Yellowstone.

Act 2: The Geyser Group.

[40]First produced in New York in German as DER LUSTIGE KRIEG 15 March 1882 at the Thalia for a season; first produced in a different English translation in New York 27 June 1882 at the Germania Theatre for 48 performances.

[41]Scenery, costumes and musical director uncredited.

[42]Musical numbers not listed in programs. List prepared from published English piano vocal score (Chappell & Co., London, 1884), which may not reflect songs dropped or interpolated.

Act 3: Falls and Rapids of the Yellowstone.

Act 4, Scene 1: Tall Grass Prairie. *Scene 2*: The Wyknips of the Crows.

Act 5: The Black Hills. Interior and Exterior of Fort Sully.

SPECIALTIES
- Grand War Dance (Act 2)
  - Corps de Ballet
- Indian Dance (Act 2)
  - Corps de Ballet, Mons. LeStrange
- Grand Finale (Act 5)

1884.11 RED LETTER NIGHTS!, or, Catching a Croesus

An Eccentric Comedy in Four Acts and a Kirmess'. Play by Augustin Daly, adapted from the German by Jacobson. New and original music by Jacobson, arranged by Henry Widmer. (Directed by Augustin Daly.) Dances under the direction of Mme. Malvina. Scenery by James Roberts (Acts 1-3). Musical director, Henry Widmer. Produced by Augustin Daly. Opened 12 March 1884 at Daly's Theatre and closed 19 April 1884 after 45 performances.

CAST: *Mr. Cornelius Poswog*, lately in "Lard": JAMES LEWIS. *Tom Crayon*, at present in "Oil" and "Colors": JOHN DREW. *Nick Rowsky*, a brother artist and member of the Tyle Club: WILLIAM GILBERT. *Pony Byron*, also of the Tyle: HELEN LEYTON. *Van Nickel*, an artist in "Charcoal and chalk": W. BEEKMAN. *Lord Muddlefud*, having invested his surplus in O.T., has come over to investigate and realize: CHARLES FISHER. *Reginald Muddlefud*, his nephew and heir: YORKE STEPHENS. *Lyncimachus Lightbody*, one of the vanguard of enterprising commerce: George Parkes. *Billy Badge* of the Fire Patrol: William Thompson. *Trap*, from the Sheriff's Office: J. Stapleton. *Mrs. Fidelia Poswog*, a woman of her word: Mrs. G. H. GILBERT. *Tony*, her daughter: ADA REHAN. *Ruby*, Tony's companion: May Fielding. *Mrs. Rhoda Dendron*, cousin to Tony, a widow in pursuit of No. 2: VIRGINIA DREHER. *Dobbie*, general help, and eaves-dropper-in-chief of the Poswog domicile: MAY IRWIN. *Tyroleans*: Misses Stokes, Cushman; Messrs. Sloane, Dorrichon. *Gypsies*: Misses Kasmer, Crissy, Gordon; Messrs. Fernand, Hamilton, etc.

The action takes place in New York, last year.

Act 1: Poswog's Parlors, in the Poswog Flat.

Act 2: Poswog's Parlors, in the Poswog Flat.

Act 3: Poswog's Parlors, in the Poswog Flat.

Act 4: Belmonico's during a Kermess.

Act 5: Poswog's Parlors, in the Poswog Flat.

MUSICAL NUMBERS[43]
- "No Discount on That"
  - J. Lewis
- "Grandpapa" (Duet)
  - J. Lewis, M. Fielding
- "I'm Only a Little Dutch Girl"
  - W. Gilbert
- "The Song of Modesty"
  - W. Gilbert
  - (*Lyrics by* Sydney Rosenfeld.)
- "The Kirmess Punch"
  - H. Leyton
- "A Mad Adventure"
  - M. Fielding
- "Echo's Answer"
  - M. Fielding
- "I'm a Gypsy Maid"
  - M. Fielding

1884.12 LA VIE!

An Operatic Burlesque in Three Acts. Original French libretto ('La Vie Parisienne') adapted into English by Henry B. Farnie. Music by Jacques Offenbach. Produced under the supervision of Max Freeman. Scenery by Harley Merry. Costly dresses by Henry Dazian. Novel mechanisms by Gale. Gas effects by Kelly. Orchestra under the direction of Gustave Kerker. Management of (Robert E. J.) Miles and Barton. Opened 18 March 1884 at the Bijou Opera House and closed 3 May 1884 after 50 performances.

CAST: *The Baron von Wiener Schnitzel*: RICHARD MANSFIELD. *Joe Tarradiddle*, Tout of Langham Hotel, afterward a gilded youth, and eventually Lord Mayor and Admiral of the Port of London: JACQUES KRUGER. *Delancy Splinterbarre*, Vice-President of the Four-in-Hand Club: NICK LONG. *Lord Guy Silverspoon*, Chum of Splinterbarre: CHARLES W. DUNGAN. *Snip*, Ticket Inspector, afterward Martin the Footman: SAMUEL REED. *Toby*, Snip's brother: GEORGE A. SCHILLER. *T. Arion Busch*, member of the Teutonic Singing Society: ALEXANDER M. BELL. *Knobsticker*, of the Strand Squad: Frank Howard. *Club-'Em*, model Policeman: Henry Rolland. *Mr. Muggins*, newly married: Arch. McDonnell. *Baby Green*: Percy Sage. *Jones*, the Butler: Joseph Silver. *Florence*, the maid, engaged to Joe, afterward Lady Mayoress: MARIE BOCKEL. *Gabrielle Strassbourg*, an Alsatian Glove Girl: FANNIE RICE. *Trixie*, of the Savoy: Ella Wallace. *Christine von Schnitzel*, the Baron's daughter: KATE DAVIS. *Lady Katherine Wyverne*, engaged to Silverspoon: Alice Vincent. *Housemaids, afterwards Duchesses (3)*: *Sue*: Kittie Cohen. *Mary*: Minnie Dilthy. *Bridget*: Maude Villar. *Taunton Tarrington*, of the Royal Thames Yacht Club: Carrie Drury. *Victor Emanuel*, Tiger to Splinterbarre: Odille Orme. *First Custom House Inspector*: Victorine Girard. *Second Custom House Inspector*: Minnie Flagg. *Lady Petty Coat Lane*: Mollie M. Power. *Wire*, Telegraph Operator: Marie Mulle. *Extra*, Newsboy: Bessie Carlton. *Miss Muggins*: Laura Burt. *Captain Fluker*: Carrie Donnelly. *Lord Sandown*: Eugenie Maynard. *Earl of Skye*: Maude Wentworth. *Lord Gamboyle*: Carrie Baldwin. *Lord Blunderville*: Lillie Shandley. *Viscount Fib*: Anna Dayton. *Baron Shandegall*: Grace Sherwood. *Chorus of 40*.

Act 1: The Railway Station at night.

Act 2: The Impromptu Hotel. Splinterbarre's chambers.

Act 3: The Illuminated Garden of the Wyverne Mansion.

ACT 1[44]
- Station Chorus (Employees are we all)
  - Chorus
- Rondo (The Lady's art)
  - A. Vincent
- Chorus (The Heavens low'r)
  - Chorus
- Scene (Trixie here)
  - E. Wallace, N. Long, P. Sage, C. W. Dungan, Chorus
- Duettino (Such brazen conduct)
  - C. W. Dungan, N. Long
- Song ("The Tout")
  - J. Kruger
  - (*Music by* Frank Musgrave. *Lyrics by* W. Pink)
- Trio (I'm a model Cicerone)
  - K. Davis, R. Mansfield, N. Long
- Song (Shall we e'er meet)
  - K. Davis
- Finale: Chorus (Guards and Porters)
  - Chorus
- Yacht Song (Long float)
  - C. Drury, Chorus
- Ensemble and Chorus (Here we come)
  - Principals, Chorus

ACT 2
- Song (Lost loves)
  - N. Long
- Duet (Bootmaker I)
  - F. Rice, A. M. Bell
- Exit (Tra la la)
  - F. Rice, A. M. Bell
- Romance (Our hearts will meet)
  - K. Davis
  - (*Music by* G. Jacobi.)
- Letter Rondo (Dear Gossip)
  - K. Davis
- Duet (You haunt a maiden)
  - K. Davis, J. Kruger

[43]Not in performance order.

[44]Musical numbers not listed in programs. List prepared from published English piano vocal score (Boosey & Co., London, 1883).

Baccarat Chorus (Short and long whist)
Chorus
Duet (The Baron as banker)
K. Davis, N. Long, R. Mansfield, Chorus
Table d'Hote Chorus (Here we come)
Chorus
Song ("The colonel's widow")
F. Rice, A. M. Bell, N. Long, R. Mansfield, Chorus
Song ("For thee, my love, for thee")
J. Kruger
(*Music by* Frank Musgrave. *Lyrics by* W. Pink)
Finale: Scene (Now ladies!)
A. M. Bell, N. Long, Chorus
Air and Chorus (Next to a band)
K. Davis, Chorus
Tyrolienne (Auf der Berliner Brück')
F. Rice

ACT 3
Housemaids' Chorus (Get all ready)
K. Cohen, M. Dilthy, M. Villar
Chorus (Let England old)
Chorus
Vocal Gavotte (Among the Lilies)
F. Rice
(*Music by* Alphons Czibulka.)
Chorus (The board is spread)/Polka Chantée
Principals, Chorus
Exit (All whirling)
Chorus
Scene (Baron! your health)/
Chorus and Waltz (He is tight)
Principals, Chorus
Finale (On! dance on)
Principals, Chorus

1884.13 DAN'S TRIBULATIONS

A Local Comedy in Three Acts, 5 Scenes. Play (and lyrics) by Edward Harrigan. Music by David Braham. Stage director, Edward Harrigan. Scenery by Charles W. Witham. Costumes by Mrs. Mary Jack. Musical director, David Braham. Produced by (Edward) Harrigan and (Tony) Hart. Opened 7 April 1884 at the Theatre Comique and closed 31 May 1884 after 64 performances.

CAST: *Dan Mulligan*: EDWARD HARRIGAN. *Rebecca Allup*: TONY HART. *Thomas Mulligan*: TONY HART. *Simpson Primrose*: JOHN WILD. *Palestine Puter*: GEORGE H. WOOD. *Walsingham McSweeney*: M. Bradley. *Gustave Lochmuller*: HARRY A. FISHER. *J. Johnson Fillup*: WILLIAM WEST. *Mr. Jeremiah Still*: WILLIAM MERRITT. *Mr. Hog Eye*, a laundryman: William West. *Mrs. Honora Dublin*: JOSEPH SPARKS. *Caroline Melrose*: James Barlow. *Mrs. Chanty Melrose*: William A. Barlow. *Officer Moran*: J. McCullough. *Officer Dornor*: George L. Stout. *Bradley*: Thomas Granger. *John Riley*: M. Foley. *John James Caughahawood*: RICHARD QUILTER. *Malichi McGovern*: P. C. GOLDRICH. *Constantine McGovern*: George Lewis. *Jeremiah McGonigal*: D. Christy. *John Quigley*: JOHN SPARKS. *John James Trainor*: Emil Heusel. *Peter Donagan*: J. Branigan. *Mr. Schwartz*: Charles Coffey. *Mr. Nolt*: GEORGE MERRITT. *Mr. Philensnyder*: Philip Engel. *Cordelia Mulligan*: ANNIE YEAMANS. *Bridget Lochmuller*: JENNIE CHRISTIE. *Kitty Mulligan*: Sadie Morris. *Mrs. Mallon*: Marie Gorenflo. *Mrs. Thompson*: Ada Farwell. *Clementine*: Kate Langdon. *School Girls (3)*: *Julia*: Annie Langdon. *Mary*: Lizzie Finn. *Sally*: Annie Hall. *Amanda*: Jennie Bageard. *Gussie*: Clara Scallan. *Mrs. Jenkins*: Mrs. W. Scallan.

Act 1: Mulligan Grocery and Liquor Store. Stop Thief.

Act 2, Scene 1: Mulligan Alley at Night. The Wedding Party. Conflagration. *Scene 2*: Continuation of the Alley, Smoke and Cinders. *Scene 3*: Rebecca Allup's Attic. Suicide.

Act 3: Parloir dans la maison de Madame Mulligan, Academie Française.

MUSICAL NUMBERS
"My Little Side Door"
"Coming Home from Meeting"
"The French Singing Lesson"
"Cobwebs on the Wall"
Xylophone Solo
Ed King

1884.14 FALKA

An Opéra-comique in Three Acts. Original French libretto ('Le Droit d'aînesse') by Eugene Leterrier and Albert Vanloo. English adaptation by H. B. Farnie. Music by Francis Chassaigne. Stage manager, Herbert A. Cripps. Scenery by John Thompson, Henry Hoyt and John Mazzanovich. Musical director, Ernst Catenhusen. Produced by the McCaull Opera Comique Company (John A. McCaull, Proprietor and Manager). Opened 14 April 1884 at the Casino Theatre and closed 2 August 1884 after 110 performances.

CAST: *Falka*, Niece of Folbach: BERTHA RICCI. *Edwige*, Sister of Boleslas: MATHILDE COTTRELLY. *Alexina de Kelkirsch*, a young heiress: Carrie Burton. *Minna*, her maid: Hattie Richardson. *Janotha*, Landlady of the Inn: JULIE deRUYTHER. *Von Folbach*, Military Governor of Montgratz: J. H. RYLEY. *Tancred*, Folbach's nephew, usher in a village school: FRANK TANNEHILL, JR. *Arthur*, Student, son of a rich Hungarian Farmer: HARRY MACDONOUGH. *Lay Brother Pelican*, Doorkeeper of the Convent: ALFRED KLEIN. *Konrad*, Captain of the Governor's Pages: BILLIE BARLOW. *Teckeli*, Sergeant of the Patrol: T. A. Guise. *Boboky*, Tzigan Scout: Leona Clark. *The Seneschal*: A. W. Maflin. *Boleslas*, Chief of the Tzigani: HUBERT WILKE. *Military Pages, Soldiers of the Watch, Maids of Honor, Tzigani.*

The action takes place in Hungary, middle of the eighteenth century.

Act 1: Exterior of the Inn, Montgratz. (Thompson.)

Act 2: Audience Hall of Folbach's Castle. (Hoyt.)

Act 3: Battlements of the Castle. (Mazzanovich.)

ACT 1[45]
"While all the town is sleeping" (Patrol Chorus)
B. Barlow, Soldiers
"Whatever's the row?" (Scene)
Soldiers, Citizens
"Governor Folback!" (Couplets)
J. H. Ryley, B. Barlow, Soldiers, Citizens
Melos (Patrol in Distance)
"I'm the Captain!" (Air and refrain)
M. Cottrelly, F. Tannehill, Jr., H. Wilke
"There was no ray of light!" (Nocturne)
M. Cottrelly
"For your indulgence" (Rondo Duet)
B. Ricci, H. Macdonough, J. deRuyther
"Now then! Hurry, scurry!" (Trio)
B. Ricci, H. Macdonough, J. deRuyther
"More new sensation" (Finale Act 1)

ACT 2
"Tap Tap!" (Chorus)
Maids of Honor
"P'raps you will excuse us stating" (Couplets)
H. Macdonough, Maids of Honor
"Now comes our chief" (Chorus)
"The boarding school girl" (Couplets)
B. Ricci, H. Macdonough, J. H. Ryley, A. Klein, Chorus
"Ah! Is she not a beauty?" (Exit Chorus)
Chorus
"La la la la" (Bohemian Chorus)
"Cradled upon the heather" (Air tzigane)
H. Wilke, M. Cottrelly, Chorus
"It was Tancred!" (Ensemble)
B. Ricci, M. Cottrelly, F. Tannehill, Jr., J. H. Ryley, H. Wilke, Chorus
"Cook'd" (Exit)
Chorus
"Oh joy! Oh rapture!" (Trio)
B. Ricci, M. Cottrelly, H. Wilke

[45]Musical numbers not listed in programs. List prepared from published piano vocal score (White-Smith Music Pub. Co., New York, 1884).

"His aspect's not so overpow'ring" (Quintet)
B. Ricci, M. Cottrelly, F. Tannehill, Jr., J. H. Ryley, H. Wilke
"What's this rumor?" (Finale Act 2)

ACT 3
"Rampart and bastion gray" (Bridal Chorus)
"Catchee Catchee" (Hungarian Rondo and Dance)
Chorus
"At even tide" (Romanza)
B. Ricci
"With a tear in our voice!" (Duet)
M. Cottrelly, H. Wilke
"Slumber! O sentinel" (Duo Berceuse)
B. Ricci, H. Macdonough
"There the bells go" (Bell Chorus)
Chorus
"Nunky, darling" (Trio)
B. Ricci, H. Macdonough, J. H. Ryley
"And now, a long goodbye!" (Finale Act 3)

1884.15 SKIPPED BY THE LIGHT OF THE MOON

A Humorous Creation (Farce Comedy) in Three Acts. Play by Louis Harrison and John Gourlay. Orchestra under the direction of T. Marwood. Presented by Sam Harrison, Management. Opened 14 April 1884 at the Fifth Avenue Theatre and closed 17 May 1884 after 35 performances.[46]

CAST: *Felix Crackle*: LOUIS HARRISON. *Obadiah Dingle*: JOHN GOURLAY. *James Warfield*: W. H. Collings. *Garnishee McIntyre*: Edward Morris. *Frank Pelham*: Douglass White. *John Sharpleigh*: W. D. Stone. *Thomas*: Charles Helmych. *Mrs. Felix Crackle*: Josie Batchelder. *Mrs. Obadiah Dingle*: Annie Wood. *Sarah*: Emma Schultz. *Millicent Warfield*: Josephine Bailey.

Act 1: Saratoga. They Arrive.

Act 2: Saratoga. They Skip.

Act 3: Taming a Shrew.

1884.16 A RAG BABY

A Farce Comedy in Three Acts[47]. Play by Charles H. Hoyt. Whole production under the direction of Charles H. Hoyt. Musical director, Harry Braham. Produced by the Rag Baby Comedy Company (Eugene Tompkins, Manager). Opened 14 April 1884 at Tony Pastor's New 14th Street Theatre and closed 3 May 1884 after 24 performances[48].

CAST: *Old Sport*, the local pride, a gentleman enamored of a sporting life: FRANK DANIELS. *Tony Jay, Esq.*, a rich young man: HARRY MILLS. *Patrick Finnigan* an average policeman: M. J. Gallagher. *Patrick Magillahoggarty*, pedestrian tourist: M. J. Gallagher. *Harry Younghusband*, a new father: H. J. Conor. *Michael Sheedy*, friend of P.M.: H. J. Conor. *Fred Barbour*, Pharmacist: H. J. Conor. *Dusty Bob*, ordinary tough: H. J. Conor. *Christian Berriel*, a wealthy undertaker: D. P. Steele. *St. Clair Flaherty*, friend of Sheedy: D. P. Steele. *Dennis O'Brien*, an Italian musician: D. P. Steele. *Darius Gaffield*, a married man: W H. Stedman. *Dr. Toombs*, tu doces, &c.: W H. Stedman. *Luigi Buoncompagni*, an Irish musician: W H. Stedman. *Venus Grout*, a rough diamond: JENNIE YEAMANS. *Clairette Fay*, belle of the boarding school: Rachel Booth. *Miss Pratt*, principal of the boarding school: Helen Reimer. *Mrs. Weatherbee*, a widow woman: Helen Reimer. *Mrs. Maginnis*, an Italian musician: Helen Reimer. *Lou Clarke*, one of Miss Pratt's trials: Addie Cumming. *Alice Berriel*, Christian's wife: Addie Cumming. *Jessie Richmond*, another trial: May Steele. *Mrs. Gaffield*, a better half: May Steele. *Handsome*, the homeliest dog alive: Himself.

Act 1: A Quiet Morning in the Country.

Act 2: A Quiet Morning in a Drug Store.

Act 3: A Quiet Evening in a Drug Store.

MUSICAL NUMBERS
"Keep Out of Finnegan's Way" (Song)
"Dancing in the Barn" (Song)
Trio from THE BEGGAR STUDENT
(*Music by* Carl Millöcker.)
Irish Reel
Rattle Song and Chorus
Medley, including airs from A TRIP TO AFRICA, THE BEGGAR STUDENT, PRINCESS IDA, PRINCE METHUSALEM, etc.
"South Fifth Avenue" (from MULLIGAN'S SILVER WEDDING)
(*Music by* David Braham. *Lyrics by* Edward Harrigan.)
Tramps Trio (Song and Dance)
"Tut, tut, tut!" (Character song from THE BEGGAR STUDENT)
(*Music by* Carl Millöcker.)
Medley of Popular Airs
Finale

1884.17 A GREAT SCHEME, Our Dime Museum

A Wild Farce in Three Acts. Play by Leonard Grover. Scenery by Harley Merry. Costumes by Eaves. Mechanical effects by Alex. Zanfretta. Produced by Gale and Spader. Opened 16 April 1884 at the New York Comedy Theatre and closed 19 April 1884 after 5 performances.

CAST: *Gerald Bunn Barkadoo*, Manager of the Thompkins Square Combination: LEONARD GROVER. *Vercingatorix Gasp*, Dramatic Editor, "Gripsack Bugle," Author of the Society Drama: EDWARD MARBLE. *Quality Jobick*, Artist of the Thompkins Square Combination: Marcus Moriarty. *Dittimus Ditt*, Proprietor of the Ditt House: Herbert Stacy. *Knockabout Wart*, Janitor of Sock's Opera House, Gripsack: John Russell. *Middleweight Chump*, the Faithful Partner: Alex Zanfretta. *Judge Tinplate Plug*, when the Court is in session: Alex Zanfretta. *Eager Charles*, willing to do anything to get home: James Russell. *The Plot*, as thin as he can possibly make himself up: Henry Zanfretta. *Fill Up, Git*, Two Necessary Evils: Folly Wallace, James Kensett. *Miss Maude Stride*, the distinguished Camille of Barkadoo's Thompkins Square Combination: LOUISE DEMPSEY. *Miss Genevieve Fluke*, the Original "Little Barefoot" (in Idaho) of the B. Thompkins Square Combination: Ada Byron. *Miss Tilly Fresh*, Dining-room girl of the Ditt House, who ekes out the cast in the Society Drama: Ida Bowdoin May. *Miss Peggy Fierce*, one of Bret Harte's waifs, bound to be an actress: DAISY RAMSDEN. *Miss Danger, Miss Excuseme*, Candidates for the Prize of Beauty: John Russell, James Russell. *Mrs. Retrousée*, Mother of the Prize of Beauty: Miss Henderson.

Act 1: Interior of Sock's Opera House, Gripsack, Idaho.

Act 2: Left wing of the Ditt House.—The Dime Museum.

Act 3: Cour d'Alaine Mountains.—The Hawbuck Mine.

1884.18 A NIGHT IN VENICE

A Comic Opera in Three Acts. Original German libretto (to the operette 'Eine Nacht in Venedig') by F. Zell and Richard Genée, based on "Le Château Trompette" by Jules Cormon and Michel Carré. Music by Johann Strauss. Ballet arranged by Mlle. Eugenia Cappallini. Scenery by James Roberts. Costumes by Mme. Loe; pigeon costumes designed by Messrs. P. Godchaux & Co. Orchestra and chorus under the direction of Anthony Reiff. Produced by James C. Duff. Opened 26 April 1884 at Daly's Theatre and closed 24 May 1884 after 33 performances.[49]

CAST: *Duke of Urbino*: WALTER TEMPLE. *Senators of Venice (3)*: *Bartholomeo Delacqua*: AUGUSTUS BRUNO. *Stefano Barbaruccio*: D. G. Longworth. *Georgia Testaccio*: E. P. Wilks. *Caramello*, the Court Barber: W. H. FITZGERALD. *Pappacoda*, a Maccaroni Cook: E. L. CONNELL. *Enrico Piselli*, Nephew of Delacqua: Master Walter Hampshire. *Centurio*, Page: Ida Bell. *Balbi*, Guard: Alexander Mair. *Annina*, a Fisher Girl, and foster sister to Barbara: LOUISE LESTER. *Ciboletta*, Delacqua's Cook: ROSA COOKE. *Barbara*: Alice Vincent. *Agricola, Constantia*, Senators' Wives: Marie Bauman, Maude Waldemere.

Act 1: An Open Square in Venice.

[46]No musical numbers listed in programs,
[47]Billed as something which perhaps satirizes the drug business and the sporting craze.
[48]Played return engagements; for details, see 16 August 1884 at the 14th Street Theatre in following season.
[49]Duff's new American translation uncredited in programs and reviews.

Act 2: Grand Apartment in the Duke's Palace.

Act 3: St. Mark's Place.

SPECIALTIES[50]

Twenty Pigeons of St. Marco
Ladies of the Chorus

Grand Pigeon Ballet

1884.19 IRISH ARISTOCRACY

Barry & Fay's Musical Comedy Company in a Revival of the Farce Comedy in Three Acts[51]. Play by William Carlton. Stage manager, Sidney Barnes. Orchestra leader, Charles Ayres. Produced by Barry & Fay's Comedy Company (W. H. McGiven, Manager). Opened 5 May 1884 at the 14th Street Theatre and closed 10 May 1884 after 8 performances; returned 26 May 1884 to the Grand Opera House and closed 31 May 1884 after an additional 9 performances. Total: 17 performances.[52]

CAST: *Michael Muldoon*: HUGH FAY. *Michael Mulcahey*: WILLIAM BARRY. *Peter Belcher*, a practical joker: T. F. BRENNEN. *John Mandamus*, Attorney at Law: CLARENCE HERITAGE. *Charles Riddle*, a doctor: SIDNEY BARNES. *O'Roger Mulcahey*, just landed: T. J. Grady. *Mrs. Muldoon*: MAGGIE FIELDING. *Honoria Muldoon*: EDITH AINSWORTH. *Phebe Plymkins* (Honoria's chum): EMILY DEVEREAUX. *Jennie Muldoon*: Little Jessie Storey.

1884.20 BLUE BEARD

A Revival of the Operatic Burlesque in Two Acts, 4 Scenes. Play by Henry B. Farnie[53], (freely revised by Max Freeman). Production under the personal supervision of Max Freeman. Orchestra conducted by Gustave Kerker. Produced by the Bijou Burlesque Company, Management of (Robert E. J.) Miles and Barton. Opened 6 May 1884 at the Bijou Opera House and closed 14 June 1884 after 42 performances.[54]

CAST: *Blue Beard*: JACQUES KRUGER. *Corporal Zoug Zoug*, afterwards the Heathen Chinee: ARTHUR W. TAMS. *Adonis*: CHARLES W. DUNGAN. *Ibrahim*: GEORGE A. SCHILLER. *Selim*: EMMA CARSON. *Fatima*: FANNY RICE. *O'Shacabac*: IRENE PERRY. *Hassan*: PAULINE HALL. *Sister Anne*: Genevieve Reynolds. *Beda*: Jessie Glassford. *Fez*: Mattie Ferguson. *Said*: Marie Mülle. *Zef*: Maggie Arlington. *Pages, Peasants, etc.*

Act 1, Scene 1: Market Place in the Village of Latakia. *Scene 2*: The Zig Zag Path to Castle Blue Beard.

Act 2, Scene 1: Grand Salon in Blue Beard's Palace. *Scene 2*: Portals of Blue Chamber and Look Out Towers of Castle Blue Beard.

1884.21 MADAM PIPER

A Musical Melange (American Opera) in Three Acts. Music composed and play concocted by Woolson Morse, assisted at times, in the stirring, by J. Cheever Goodwin. Stage director, Harry Edwards. Produced under the supervision of William A. Mestayer. Scenery by Philip Goatcher, George W. Dayton. Costumes by George E. Hayden. Mechanism by F. Dorrington. Properties by E Siedle. Gas effects by J. F. Driscoll. Musical director and conductor, Michael Connelly. Produced by Lester Wallack and William A. Mestayer. Opened 12 May 1884 at Wallack's Theatre and closed 16 June 1884 after 36 performances.[55]

CAST: *Madam Piper*, a widow by three husbands, to wit: Jack Spratt, Simon Simple and Peter Piper,—in search of a fourth. A woman not the same yesterday, today and forever, but blessed with a large family: ELMA DELARO. *Her Daughters*, Sweet Ps every one of them, with assorted eyes and complexions (18): *May Piper*, one of them, in love with Eugene, and the heroine of "Mary, Mary, Why So Contrary?": THERESA VAUGHN. *Gillian Piper*, another of them, who together with Jack, "climbed That Memorable Hill": ADELAIDE PRAEGER. *Dora Piper*, still another of them: Frankie Kemble. *Minnie Piper*, still more of them: Edna Courtney. *Cora Piper*, still s'more of them: Belle [Isabelle] Urquhart. *Milly Piper*, s'mother of them: Edith Mai. *Dolly Piper*: Belle Deering. *Winnie Piper*: Carrie Drury. *Susie Piper*: Edna Graham. *Lucy Piper*: Rita Carroll. *Bella Piper*: Grace Grover. *Polly Piper*: Mabel Stuart. *Tilly Piper*: Nellie Devere. *Stella Piper*: Josie Knight. *Katie Piper*: Maude Cavendish. *Sarah Piper*: Irene Hamilton. *Dizzie Piper*: Daisy Wood. *Fanny Piper*: Ada Clifton. *King Cole*, a monarch with a mystery, convivial, but every inch a king, also a jolly old soul: JOHN HOWSON. *B. Spratt*, Brother-in-law to Madam Piper. A bachelor by inclination and a victim of circumstances: WILLIAM A. MESTAYER. *Simon Simple*, also known as Simple Simon, Madam Piper's only son, and a very bad boy: Gracie Wilson. *Jack*, a student who doesn't burn, but pours over the midnight "Hoyle," fond of Jill: Harry Rattenberry. *Eugene*, another student, fond of his books and Mary: WILL S. RISING. *Shanks*, a lottery agent: George Froisart. *Captain Quick*, Commandant of King Cole's fort. Cut to the quick by the students: A. D. Barker. *Colonel Slow*, slow to take offense at the students: Joseph Sturges.

Men of Letters, Fond of Lamb (Charles) and Sweet Ps: *Mr. A*: Mr. Archer. *Mr. B*: Mr. Warner. *Mr. C*: Mr. Jerome. *Mr. D*: Mr. Blake. *Mr. E*: Mr. Nichols. *Mr. F*: Mr. Hughses. *Mr. G*: Mr. Francis. *Mr. H*: Mr. Edwards. *Mr. I*: Mr. Boice. *Mr J*: Mr. Kimball. *Mr. K*: Mr. Leadbury. *Mr. L*: Mr. Paxton. *Mr. M*: Mr. Hunt. *Mr. N*: Mr. DeSmidt. *Mr. O*: Mr. (Joseph) Ott. *Fiddlers (3)*: King Cole's Jolly Fiddlers. *Mary's Lamb, A Jug, Spratt's Rat, Shank's Donkey, Peasants, Servants, Pages, Soldiers, and many other characters too numerous to mention.*

Time: Anytime. *Plot*: Anything the author pleases. *Music*: Original, more or less.

Act 1: Nowhere. (Goatcher.)

Act 2: Elsewhere. (Goatcher.)

Act 3: Anywhere. (Dayton.)

1884.22 WELL-FED DORA

A Travesty of Victorien Sardou's "Fédora" in Two Acts, 6 Scenes. Play by Sydney Rosenfeld. Presented under the personal supervision of Sydney Rosenfeld. Costumes by P. Godchaux. Marches and dances arranged by A. W. Maflin. Musical director, Charles Puerner. Produced by George K. Fortesque (George W. Lederer, Manager). Opened 19 May 1884 at the Fifth Avenue Theatre and closed 31 May 1884 after 14 performances.

CAST: *The Princess Well-Fed Dora*: GEORGE K. FORTESCUE. *The Countess*: CARRIE GODFREY. *Helene*, Maid to the Princess: VENIE BURROUGHS. *Guests and Gossipers*: Misses Blanche Stone, Salome Stone, Polly Winner, Annie Winner, Lizzie Winner, Amy Wells, Virginia Wellington, Josie Gregory, Minnie Miller, Lucy Mitchell, Mary Runnells, Carrie Behr, Leila Blow, Gussie Shaler, Eva Shaler, Clotilde Operti, May Danforth, Katie Mertens. *Sirieux*: HETTY TRACY. *Desire*: Norma Wills. *Dimitri*: Hindie Harrison. *Messenger No. 1*: Salome Stone. *Messenegr No. 2*: Eva Shaler. *Loris Ipanoff*: EDWARD P. TEMPLE. *Gretch*, the Detective: FRANK M. WILLS. *Coachman*: George Kyle. *Lazinski*, the Flutist: F. K. Elyk. *Doctor*: George Strathmore. *Gretch's Henchmen (6)*: *Pierre*: Carl J. Alberti. *Antoine*: Charles St. Aubyn. *Robert*: Charles Raymond. *Gaspard*: Robert Wilson. *Guillaume*: Hannibal Smith. *Jacques*: Mark Lessiems.

Act 1, Scene 1: Vladimir's Home, Moscow. *Scene 2*: Ante Room at the Countess' in Paris. *Scene 3*: Parlors of the Countess.

Act 2, Scene 1: Fedora's Boudoir. *Scene 2*: Well-Fed Dora's Garden. *Scene 3*: Well-Fed Dora's Parlor.

ACT 1

Scene 2

The Gossipers' Chorus

"The Rose's Greeting"
C. Godfrey
(*Music by* Julius J. Lyons. *Lyrics by* Genie Holtzmeyer-Rosenfeld.)

[50]Musical numbers not listed in programs; no published libretto or score found for this translation.

[51]First produced in New York as IRISH ARISTOCRACY 30 November 1882 at the Academy of Music for 2 performances. For Synopsis of Scenes and Musical Numbers, see original 1882 production. New songs and dances were added for this revival.

[52]Specialties and Musical Numbers not listed in programs, which contain the note, "Wait for the Three Handed Reel."

[53]Inspired by the French opéra-bouffe BARBE-BLEUE by Henri Meilhac and Ludovic Halévy; Music by Jacques Offenbach. An earlier version of Farnie's burlesque featuring Lydia Thompson and her troupe was presented in New York 16 August 1871 at Wallack's Theatre for 30 performances.

[54]Scenery and costumes uncredited. Musical numbers not listed in programs.

[55]Musical numbers not listed in programs.

Scene 3
  The Nihilists' March
  Spirited Finale
ACT 2
Scene 1
  Conspirators' Chorus
  "It's All a Matter of Taste"
    G. K. Fortescue
Scene 2
  "Where Art Thou Now, My Lazinski?" (Burlesque Romanza)
  "It's a Very Good Scheme If It Works" (New topical song)
Scene 3
  Finale

1884.23 CAPTAIN MISHLER

A Play (Farce Comedy) in Three Acts, 6 Scenes. Play by Fred G. Maeder. Songs by Gus Williams. Produced under the personal direction of Fred G. Maeder. Scenery by Messrs. Charles Fox, William Schaeffer, Gaspard Maeder, Harley Merry. Management, John H. Robb. Opened 26 May 1884 at the New York Comedy Theatre and closed 28 June 1884 after 41 performances; returned 2-7 February 1885 to the Grand Opera House for 8 additional performances. Total: 49 performances.

CAST: *Captain Mishler* of the 84th Precinct: GUS WILLIAMS. *Edward Warker*: J. Newton Gotthold. *Frank Tracey*: Arthur Moulton. *Budd Bridle*: De Loss King. *Cromwell Holliday*: J. H. Armstrong. *"Mysterious Billy"*: W. T. Johnson. *Sergeant Hall*: J. G. Willett. *Roundsman Murry*: Arthur Showell. *Ida Tracey*: Isabel Waldron. *Grace Warker*: Josie Loane. *Violet Pillsbury*: Florence Vincent. *Emma Knight*: Emma Hagger. *Little Jeanette*: Little Olive Berkley.

Act 1: Home of Captain Mishler, near Fleetwood Park. (Vision of Murder at Fleetwood Park.) (Fox, Schaeffer and Maeder.)

Act 2, Scene 1: Head Quarters 84th Precinct Municipal Police, New York. *Scene 2*: Street in 84th Precinct. *Scene 3*: Parlor in Edward Warker's Mansion. (Merry.)

Act 3, Scene 1: The Home of Warker. *Scene 2*: Interior of Captain Mishler's Home. (Merry.)

MUSICAL NUMBERS
  "Pretty Little Dark Blue Eyes"
    G. Williams
  "Captain Mishler"
  "When I'm on Duty"
  "Knock at the Window To-night, Love"

1884–1885 SEASON

Henry E. Dixey in ADONIS (Photo: Sarony)
Billy Rose Theatre Collection, New York Public Library for the Performing Arts

1884–1885 SEASON

1884.24

97 OR 79

A Comedy in Five Acts. Play by Adolph Neuendorff. Opened 2 June 1884 at the Third Avenue Theatre and closed 7 June 1884 after 8 performances.[1]

CAST: *Dr. Pizarro McGuire*, Professor of Chemistry: BARRY FAY. *Patrick Flynn*, a Soldier Messenger of '97': WILLIAM BARRY. *Dr. Boniface Griswold*, Professor of Geometry: J. B. EVERHAM. *Euphrosne*, his wife: ANNIE DELAND. *Frederic White*, a Police Justice: Rudolph Strong. *Molly*, Professor McGuire's wife: Isabella Thornton. *Sarah Smythe*, Proprietress of a Laundry: Anita Harris. *Charles Wells*, Manufacturer of Soap: THOMAS Q. SEABROOKE. *Susan*, Laundry Girl: Elvie Seabrooke. *Billy Corrigan*, Soldier Messenger of '97': C. J. Burbage. *Cain, Abel*, Detectives: W. B. Murray, C. G. Ray. *Philander Peterson*, Crier of Judge White's Court: P. F. Backus. *Maria*, Justice White's Wife: Alice Roberts. *Annie*, Servant in McGuire Mansion: Emily Deveraux. *Tom*, Servant in the Griswold Mansion: Sidney Barnes.

Act 1: Trouble Opens.

Act 2: Vexacious Trouble.

Act 3: Serious Trouble.

Act 4: Trouble and Muddle.

Act 5: Trouble and Serenity.

1884.25

PENNY-ANTE, or, The Last of the Fairies

A Musical Burlesque in Three Acts. Text (book, lyrics) by Jeff S. Leerburger. Music by Fred J. Eustis. Scenery by Henry E. Hoyt. Costumes by Henry Dazian and Eaves. Musical director, Fred J. Eustis. Management, Jeff S. Leerburger. Opened 9 June 1884 at the 14th Street Theatre and closed 21 June 1884 after 16 performances.

CAST: Mortals: *Bonifacio Bias*, head clerk: JAMES STURGES. *Simon Cheat*, Dry Goods Merchant: AINSLEY SCOTT. *Francis Hoops*: FRED W. OAKLAND. *Captain Wiltush*, of the M.P. Force: ED MORRIS. *Will Laces*: C. Champney. *Jailer*: S. Charles. *Melinda Cheat*: Louise Searle. *Cleopatra Cramps*: JENNIE REIFFARTH. *Ida Skirts*: Grace Leslie. *Lilly Ruffles*: Hindie Harrison. *Jennie Frills*: Carrie Wallace.

Semi-Mortals: *Signor Penny-Ante*: CHARLES H. DREW. *Gin-Sling*, studying for the bar: Joe W. Harris. *Father Time*: Charles Sturges.

Immortals: *Fairy Queen*: CARRIE GODFREY. *Amicita*: IDA BELL. *Sirene*: Alice Butler. *Styline*: Eme Lascelles. *Fashionable Fairies (11)*: *Bonnetine*: Virginia Wellington. *Ribbonsine*: Stella Stewart. *Flora*: Bessie Ainsley. *Feather*: Juliet Duchateau. *Ornamentine*: Josie Gregory. *Lineine*: Bertha Livingstone. *Modistine*: Kate Hatfield. *Mantuine*: Louisa Hill. *Pearla*: Nettie Harrington. *Nympha*: Marie Grenville. *Rosette*: Lilly Grey. *Fairy Jewels (4)*: *Saphira*: Mabel Mortimer. *Rubina*: Clotilde Operti. *Topaze*: Nelly Rutgers. *Jacintha*: Maud Newson. *Chorus of Policemen, Convicts, Dry Goods Clerks, Saleswomen and Fairies.*

Act 1: Cheat, Skinnem & Co.'s Dry Goods Store.

Act 2: The City Prison.

Act 3: A hitherto undiscovered Fairy Grotto in Harlem.

MUSICAL NUMBER[2]

Policemen's Chorus

Waltz Song

Messenger Boys' Chorus

1884.26

THE CORNER GROCERY, or, The Bad Forgetful Boy

A Farce Comedy in Three Acts. Play by Dan Sully. Stage manager, Ed. M. Favor. Produced by Dan Sully. Opened 9 June 1884 at Tony Pastor's 14th Street Theatre and closed 9 August 1884 after 72 performances; returned 13 April 1885 to Tony Pastor's 14th Street Theatre and closed 31 May 1885 after 56 additional performances. Total: 128 performances[3].

CAST: *Michael Nolan* , the Upright Man: DAN SULLY. *Henry Budweiser*, Part Owner of the Corner Grocery: GEORGE A. BEAN, JR[4]. *Thomas Nolan*, the Clerk of the Corner Grocery: HARRY HEALEY[5]. *Lawyer Rapp*, Somewhat of a Detective: EDWARD M. FAVOR[6]. *Jimmy Nolan*, the Bad, Forgetful Boy: Master MALVEY. *Patrick Conroy*, "One of the Finest:" ALFRED C. FAVOR[7]. *Messenger, A.D.T.*, an Original: An Original[8]. *Jenny Burke*, Nolan's Ward: LOUISE A. FOX. *Mrs. Michael Nolan*, a Chip of the Old Block: FANNIE SANFORD.

Time: Present.

Act 1: The Corner Grocery. (Five Points, New York City.) Funny.

Act 2: Nolan's Home. Pathos and Fun.

Act 3: The Birthday Party. No end of fun.

MUSICAL NUMBERS, SPECIALTIES

"(Das) Wasserfall" (Song)
L. Fox, assisted by F. Sanford

Specialty
D. Sully

1884.27

THE NAIAD QUEEN!

A Revival of the Beautiful Fairy Spectacle Extravaganza in Four Acts, 5 Scenes. (Original play by W. E. Burton.) New and original music by George Barnard. Produced under the immediate direction of W. J. Fleming. Scenery by Arthur Voegtlin, Thomas Neville. Properties by James Jones. Mechanical effects by Levi Guernsey. Costumes by A. Roemer and Son. Ballets by Signor Novissimo. Calciums by McCaffrey, Murray and Wilson. Produced by George Wood, Manager. Opened 14 June 1884 at the Cosmopolitan Theatre and closed 21 June 1884 after 9 performances.

CAST: Immortals: *Lurline*: Nettie Abbott. *Idex*: Ella Granville. *Fluvia*: Hattie Birdsell. *Amphibio*: Julian Girard.

Mortals: *Rupert, the Fearnought*: T. DREW. *Schnapps*, his squire: J. F. PETERS. *Rupert's companions (5)*: *Rudolph*: C. Perring. *Rinaldo*: G. L. Livingston. *Manfredo*: S. Rand. *Albert*: Mr. Sanford. *Ronaldo*: Mr. Gifford. *Pilgrim*: Mr. Walcott. *Baron Lorchausen*: Mr. RUSSELL. *Lady Una of Lorchhausen*: FANNY GIRARD. *Mistress Bridget*: Mrs. Nelson Kneass. *Knights, Servants, Fairies, Water Demons, Amazons*: Ballet and Auxiliary Corps.

Ballet: Mlle. ADELE CORNALBA (Première Assoluta), Mlles. LAURA ROSE, ANNETTA FLECCIA (Premières), Signor NOVISSIMO, Mlles. Annie Gregory, Marie Hoby, Lena Univer, Annie Daisy (Secondas). *Coryphées*: Sarah Meehan, Katie Francis, Polly Egleson, Katie Fielding, Cassie Francis, May Mott, Helen Kellogg, Frances Baldwin, Florence Kellogg, Bertha Minerva, Amelia Duryea, Lillie Sheldon, Ella Atkinson, Mamie Jacobson; 50 Beautiful Young Ladies for the Amazonian Marches.

Act 1: Rupert's Castle; A Submarine Expedition; Romantic view of Lurlie Berg; Cavern under the Rhine; Bath of Beauty.

Act 2, Scene 1: Submarine Cavern. *Scene 2*: Stalactite Hall and Grotto.

Act 3: The Baron's Hall. The Storm. Grotto beneath the Rhine.

Act 4: Meeting of the Amazons. Combat. Grand Transformation Scene. Birth of the Butterflies. Revolving Suns. Blushing Lilies. Shower of Gold. Excelsior!

SPECIALTIES, BALLETS

Chorus of Knights (Act 1)

Invisible Fairy Chorus (Act 1)

Demons' Dance and Chorus (Act 2, Scene 1)

The Girards in Silent Moments (Act 2, Scene 2)

Grand Bouquet Ballet (Act 2, Scene 2)
Mlles. Fleccia, Rose, Corps de Ballet

Grand Startling Spirit Ballet (Act 3)
Mlle. Cornalba, Signor Novissimo, Corps de Ballet

---

[1]No musical numbers listed in programs; Barry and Fay performed their customary specialties.

[2] No song list in program; list prepared from reviews.

[3]THE CORNER GROCERY played an earlier New York engagement at a variety house for which no production details were found, 4-9 February 1884 at the Grand Central Theatre (formerly Aberle's on Eighth Street).

[4]For return engagement, the role of Henry Budweiser was played by HARRY MORRIS.

[5]For return engagement, the role of Thomas Nolan was played by C. J. BIRBECK.

[6] For return engagement, the role of Lawyer Rapp was played by JOHN ROBINSON.

[7]For return engagement, the role of Officer Conroy was played by MAURICE FLYNN.

[8]For return engagement, the role of the Messenger was played by Master Collins.

Amazons, Grand March and Tableau (Act 4)
Transformation Scene and Finale (Act 4)

1884.28 OLIVETTE

A Revival of the Opérette in Three Acts.[9] Original French libretto ('Les Noces d'Olivette') by Henri Chivot and Alfred Duru. Music by Edmund Audran. Stage manager, Max Figman. Costumes by A. Schwenke. Musical director, G. B. Snyder. Produced by the Blanche Corelli Opera Company (Jules Grau, Acting Manager). Opened 30 June 1884 at the Cosmopolitan Theatre and closed 5 July 1884 after 8 performances.

CAST: *Captain de Merrimac*: EDWARD L. CONNELL. *Valentine*: H. H. Waldo. *Marvejal*: H. Haskell. *Coquelicot*: MAX FIGMAN. *Posticho*, Inn-keeper and Barber: P. M. Lang. *Duc des Ifs*: WILLET SEAMAN. *Bathilde*, Countess of Rousillon: ELMA DELARO. *Velontin*: BEBE VINING. *Moustique*, Merrimac's Cabin Boy: May Steele. *Olivette*: BLANCHE CORELLI. *Peasants. Soldiers, Sailors, etc.*

1884.29 LA MASCOTTE

A Revival of the Comic Opera in Three Acts[10]. (Original French libretto to the Opéra-comique by Henri Chivot and Alfred Duru.) Music by Edmond Audran. Stage manager, Max Figman. Costumes by A. Schwenke. Musical director, G. B. Snyder. Produced by the Blanche Corelli Opera Company (Jules Grau, Acting Manager). Opened 7 July 1884 at the Cosmopolitan Theatre and closed 12 July 1884 after 7 performances.

CAST: *Lorenzo XVII*, Prince of Piombino: JAMES STURGES. *Pippo*, a Shepherd: WILLET SEAMAN. *Rocco*, a Farmer: MAX FIGMAN. *Doctor*: Charles Kemball. *Mattheo*: Charles Kimball. *Parafanto*: J. Callahan. *Frederick*, the Prince of Pisa: Miss EVA BARRINGTON. *Fiametta*, his daughter: BEBE VINING. *Carlo*: Lillie Aldrich. *Palo*: Janie Gray. *Angelo*: Dudie McGuire. *Marco*: Clara Wilson. *Francisca*: Sadie Kerby. *Bettina*, The Mascot: BLANCHE CORELLI. *Ladies, Courtiers, Peasants, Soldiers, etc.*

1884.30 H.M.S. PINAFORE

A Revival of the Comic Opera in Two Acts[11]. Libretto by William S. Gilbert. Music by Arthur Sullivan. Stage manager, George Gaston. Costumes by A. Schwenke. Musical director, Hans Kreissig. Produced by the Blanche Corelli Opera Company (Jules Grau, Acting Manager). Opened Opened 14 July 1884 at the Cosmopolitan Theatre and closed 19 July 1884 after 7 performances.

CAST: *The Rt. Hon. Sir Joseph Porter, K.C.B.*, First Lord of the Admiralty: GEORGE GASTON. *Captain Corcoran*, Commanding the *H.M.S. Pinafore*: EDWARD CONNELL. *Ralph Rackstraw*, Able Seaman: ALONZO HATCH. *Dick Deadeye*, Able Seaman: James Sturges. *Boatswain's Mate*: John Innes. *Bob Becket*, Carpenter's Mate: Charles Kimball. *Cousin Hebe*, Sir Joseph's First Cousin: Ella Caldwell. *Little Buttercup*, a Bumboat Woman: GENEVIEVE REYNOLDS. *Josephine*, the Captain's Daughter: BLANCHE CORELLI. *First Lord's Sisters, his Cousins, his Aunts, Sailors, Marines, etc.*

[9]First presented in New York 25 December 1880 at the Bijou Opera House for 63 performances. For Synopsis of Scenes and Musical Numbers, see original 1880 production. For this revival the following were added:

"'Tis I Alone Can Tell"
W. Seamon
(*Music by* Reigg.)
"Oh! Mama"
B. Corelli
(*Music by* Josti.)

[10]First produced in New York 5 May 1881 at the Bijou Opera House for 168 performances in two engagements. For Synopsis of Scenes and Musical Numbers, see original 1881 production.

[11]Originally presented in New York 15 January 1879 at the Standard Theatre for 175 performances. For Synopsis of Scenes and Musical Numbers, see original 1879 production.

1884.31 PATIENCE, or, Bunthorne's Bride

A Revival of the Comic Opera in Two Acts[12]. Libretto by William S. Gilbert. Music by Arthur Sullivan. Stage manager, George Gaston. Costumes by A. Schwenke. Musical director, Hans Kreissig. Produced by the Blanche Corelli Opera Company (Jules Grau, Acting Manager). Opened 21 July 1884 at the Cosmopolitan Theatre and closed 26 July 1884 after 6 performances.[13]

CAST: *Reginald Bunthorne*, a Fleshly Poet: Master GEORGE GASTON. *Archibald Grosvenor*, an Idyllic Poet: JOHN J. DUFF. *Colonel Calvalry*, Officer of Dragoons: CARLOS FLORENTINE. *Major Murgatroyd*, Officer of Dragoons: CHARLES KIMBALL. *Lieutenant, the Duke of Dunstable*, Officer of Dragoons: ALONZO HATCH. *Mr. Bunthorne's Solicitor*: J. Cammeyer. *Rapturous Maidens (4)*: *The Lady Angela*: ADA STANHOPE. *The Lady Saphir*: SOPHIE HUMMEL. *The Lady Ella*: BELLA NICHOLSON. *The Lady Jane*: GENEVIEVE REYNOLDS. *Patience*, a Dairy Maid: BLANCHE CORELLI. *Chorus of Rapturous Maidens, Dragoon Guards.*

1884.32 THE CHIMES OF NORMANDY

A Revival of the Opéra-comique in Three Acts, 5 Scenes[14]. Original French libretto (Les Cloches de Corneville) by Clairville and Charles Gabet. Music by Robert Planquette. Stage manager, Arthur W. Tams. Musical director, Gustave Kerker. Management, John Donnelly and Gustave Kerker. Opened 21 July 1884 at the Bijou Opera House and closed 30 August 1884 after 11 performances in repertory.

CAST: *Mignonette*, a Waif: ADELADIE RANDALL. *Germaine*, niece of Gaspard: ROSE LEIGHTON. *Robin More*, a Fisherman: ALFRED WILKIE. *Henri, the Marquis of Villeroi*: EDWARD CONNELL. *Gaspard*, a Miser: C. P. FLOCKTON. *The Sheriff of Villeroi*: ARTHUR W. TAMS. *Notary*: H. S. Dale. *Getrude*: Kate Hatfield. *Manette*: Josie Hanley. *Susanne*: Kate Hoyt. *Eloise*: Kenyon Tilton. *Peasants, Coachmen, Villagers, Servants, etc,*

1884.33 THE BOHEMIAN GIRL

A Revival of the Romantic Opera in Four Acts, 6 Scenes[15]. Libretto by Alfred Bunn . Music by Michael William Balfe. Stage manager, Arthur W. Tams. Musical director, Gustve Kerker. Management, John Donnelly and Gustave Kerker. Opened 28 July 1884 at the Bijou Opera House and closed 30 August 1884 after 18 performances in repertory.

CAST: *Count Arnheim*, Governor of Presburg: EURICO CAMPOBELLO. *Thaddeus*, a proscribed Pole: ALFRED WILKIE. *Florestan*, nephew of the Count: H. S. Dale. *Devilshoof*, Chief of the Gypsies: EDWARD CONNELL. *Queen of the Gypsies*: ROSE LEIGHTON. *Captain of the Guard*: L. R. Allison. *Buda*, Arline's attendant: Kate Hatfield. *Arline*: ADELAIDE RANDALL. *Gypsies, Soldiers, Citizens, Lords and Ladies.*

1884.34 THE LITTLE DUKE

A Revival of the Opéra-comique in Three Acts[16]. Original French libretto (Le Petit Duc) by Henri Meilhac and Ludovic Halévy. (New) English adaptation by H. C. Bunner and W. J. Henderson. Music by Charles Lecocq. Scenery by Henry Hoyt, Harley Merry and Joseph Clare. Costumes by Henry Dazian and Cerbi. Musical director, Antonio DeNovellis. Produced by McCaull Opera Comique Company (John A. McCaull). Opened 4 August 1884 at the Casino Theatre and closed 4 October 1884 after 63 performances.[17]

[12]First produced in New York 22 September 1881 at the Standard Theatre for 177 performances. For Synopsis of Scenes and Musical Numbers, see original 1881 production.

[13]A novelty production produced with a cast of juveniles.

[14]First produced in New York 22 October 1877 at the Fifth Avenue Theatre for 16 performances in repertory. For Synopsis of Scenes and Musical Numbers, see original 1877 production. English adaptation uncredited.

[15]First produced in New York 25 November 1844 at the Park Theatre. For Synopsis of Scenes and Musical Numbers, see original 1844 production.

[16]First produced in English in a different adaptation 17 March 1879 at Booth's Theatre for 24 performances.

[17]Stage director uncredited. Stage manager, H. A. Cripps. Musical numbers not listed in programs; neither libretto nor piano vocal score found for this translation.

CAST: *Henri*, Duc de Parthenay: GEORGINA VON JANUSCHOWSKY. *Blanche*, Duchess de Parthenay: AGNES FOLSOME. *Madam de Lausac*: Genevieve Reynolds. *Bernard*, Page to the Duc: Billie Barlow. *Pages (4)*: *Girard*: Florence Bell. *Robert*: Millie Vanberg. *Gustave*: Kate Ethel. *Adolph*: Mamie Broughton. *Governess*: Lillie Vinton. *Mlle. de la Roche*: Rosa Marion. *Mlle. du Vernay*: Annette Hall. *Mlle. Champvert*: Lillie Comee. *Mlle. L. Armande*: Ina Weddell. *Margot, Nanette*, Vivandières: C. Edgerton, L. Percy. *Le Chevalier de Montaland*: HUBERT WILKE. *Frimousse*, Tutor to the Duc: J. H. RYLEY. *Officers of the Regiment Parthenay (4)*: *De Merignac*: J. A. FUREY. *De Tanneville*: A. Barbera. *De Navailles*: C. Jones. *De Montcheurier*: L. M. Hall. *Dragoons, Trumpeters, Maids of Honor, Pages, Lord and Ladies of the Court de la Grande Monarque.*

Act 1: Palace of the Tuilleries. (Hoyt.)

Act 2: Academy of Madam de Lausac. (Merry.)

Act 3: Camp of the Regiment Parthenay. (Clare.)

1884.35 FRA DIAVOLO

A Revival of the Romantic Opera in Three Acts[18]. Original French libretto (to the Opéra-comique 'Fra Diavolo, or L'Hotellerie de Terracina') by Eugène Scribe. Music by Daniel Auber. Stage manager, Arthur W. Tams. Musical director, Gustve Kerker. Management, John Donnelly and Gustave Kerker. Opened 11 August 1884 at the Bijou Opera House and closed 16 August 1884 after 7 performances.

CAST: *Zerlina*: ADELAIDE RANDALL. *Fra Diavolo*: ALFRED WILKIE. *Lorenzo*: George Appleby. *Lord Allcash*: Paul Arthur. *Lady Allcash*: ROSE LEIGHTON. *Beppo, Giacomo*, Two Italian bandits: EDWARD CONNELL, ARTHUR W. TAMS. *Matteo*, Zerlina's father: Joseph Silvers. *Soldiers, Peasants, Bandits, etc.*

1884.36 LOVE IN YE DAYS OF CHARLES YE SECOND

An Operetta in One Act, accompanied by an Olio. Libretto by Bridgeman (based on the play "Tom Noddy's Secret" by Thomas Haynes Bayly.) Music by Bendall. Scenery by Harley Merry. Machinery by Nelson Waldron. Costumes by A. Roemer & Son. Musical director, William J. Rostetter. Produced by (Albert) Koster) and (John) Bial. Opened at Koster & Bial's Concert Hall 16 August 1884 and closed 29 August 1884 after 16 performances.

Olio: The Martens Trio (Tyrolean Songs); Lizzie Simms (Danseuse a Transformation); Laura Lee (sympathetic and artistic Ballad Singer); Wainratta (King of the Wire); The Martens in their comic sketch 'The Musical Automatons:' *Mr. Bric-à-Brac*, a Manager: Andrew Jacques. *Patrick McGuire*, a Showman: Fred Clifton.

LOVE IN YE DAYS OF CHARLES YE SECOND CAST: *Dr. Dilly Dally, D. D. D.*: FRED CLIFTON. *Peter Pentameter*: Signor IMANO. *Captain Ormond*: WALT HAMPSHIRE. *Mary*: LAURA LEE. *Gabriella*: SOPHIE HUMMEL.

Scene: England in the year 1651.

1884.37 A RAG BABY

A Revival of the Farce Comedy (which, perhaps, satirizes the Drug Business and the Sporting Craze) in Three Acts[19]. Play by Charles H. Hoyt. Produced under the direction of Charles H. Hoyt. Musical director, Harry Braham. Produced by the Rag Baby Comedy Company (Eugene Tompkins, Management). Opened 16 August 1884 at the 14th Street Theatre and closed 30 August 1884 after 17 performances; returned 13 April 1885 to the Grand Opera House for an additional 8 performances.[20]

CAST: *Old Sport*, a local pride, a gentleman enamored of a sporting life: FRANK DANIELS. *Tony Jay, Esq.*, a rich young man: CHARLES H. DREW. *Patrick Finnegan*, an average policeman: MARK SULLIVAN. *Patrick Magillahoggarty*, tough tramp: MARK SULLIVAN. *Fred Barbour*, pharmacist: H. J. Conor. *Harry Younghusband*, a new father: H. J. Conor. *Michael Sheedy*, dude tramp: H. J. Conor. *Dusty Bob*, ordinary tough: H. J. Conor. *Christian Berriel*, a wealthy undertaker: E. A. Osgood. *St. Clair Flaherty*, spectre tramp: E. A. Osgood. *Denis O'Brien*, an Italian musician: E. A. Osgood. *Darius Garfield*, a married man: W. H. Stedman. *Dr. Toombes, tu doces*, etc.: W. H. Stedman. *Luigi Buoncompagni*, an Irish musician: W. H. Stedman. *Venus Grout*, a rough diamond: BESSIE SANSON. *Clairette Fay*, belle of the boarding school: RILLIE DEAVES. *Miss Pratt*, principal of the boarding school: Helen Reimer. *Mrs. Weatherbee*, a widow woman: Helen Reimer. *Mrs. Maginnis*, an Italian musician: Helen Reimer. *Lou Clark*, one of Miss Clark's trials: Clara Lane. *Alice Berriel*, Christian's wife: Clara Lane. *Jessie Richmond*, another trial: Tina Jackson. *Mrs. Garfield*, a better half: Tina Jackson. *Handsome*, the homeliest dog alive: Himself.

Act 1: A quiet morning in the country.

Act 2: A quiet morning in a drug store.

Act 3: A quiet evening in a drug store.

ACT 1

"Dancing in the Barn"
(B. Sanson)

Trio from PRINCESS IDA
(R. Deaves, C. Lane, T. Jackson)
(*Music by* Arthur Sullivan. *Lyrics by* William S. Gilbert.)

Finale

ACT 2

"Rattle Chorus"
(*Music by* Arthur Thayer.)

Whistling duo

Hunting Song
(B. Sanson)

Grand Medley, including airs from PRINCE METHUSALEM, THE MERRY WAR, THE BEGGAR STUDENT, A TRIP TO AFRICA, BILLEE TAYLOR, THE SORCERER, PRINCESS IDA, etc.

"South Fifth Avenue" (from MULLIGAN'S SILVER WEDDING)
(*Music by* David Braham. *Lyrics by* Edward Harrigan.)

"The Song of the Little Sailor" (from FANTINE, Boston)[21]
(*Music by* Firmin Bernicat and André Messager. *Lyrics by* R. M. Field and B. E. Woolf.)

"The Shop Near by" (Trio, original)
(H. J. Conor, M. Sullivan, E. A. Osgood)

Waltz Song from THE MERRY WAR
(C. H. Drew)
(*Music by* Johann Strauss.)

ACT 3

"Going to the Market"[22] (Song)

"Tut, Tut" (Song and Chorus)

"'Twould Never Never Do"[23] (Topical Song)

"Beautiful Little Baby" (Finale)

1884.38 MARITANA

A Revival of the Romantic Opera in Four Acts[24]. (Libretto by Edward Fitzball. Based on the play "Don César de Bazan" by Adolphe d'Ennery and Philippe Dumanoir.) Music by Vincent Wallace. Stage manager, Arthur W. Tams. Musical director, Gustve Kerker. Management, John Donnelly and Gustave Kerker. Opened 18 August 1884 at the Bijou Opera House and closed 23 August 1884 after 7 performances.

---

[18]First produced in New York in English as THE DEVIL'S BROTHER 20 June 1833 at the Park Theatre. English adaptation uncredited for this revival.

[19]First produced in New York 14 April 1884 at Tony's Pastor 14th Street Theatre for 24 performances.

[20]Played a return engagement 1 March 1886 at the Grand Opera House.

[21]Another English language adaptation of FRANÇOIS LES BAS BLEUS, whose French version premiered in New York under the title FANCHON 29 September 1884; see detail below. FANTINE played Boston, not New York. Not to be confused with the later English language adaptation VICTOR, THE BLUE-STOCKING.

[22]May be "Going to Market," Music by Louis Diehl, Lyrics by Harold Wynn. Replaced for subsequent tour by:
"Some other evening will do just as well"
B. Sanson
(*Music by* Harry Braham. *Lyrics by* Charles H. Hoyt.)

[23]Replaced for subsequent tour by:
"Do I look any more like Sullivan?" (Character Song)

[24]First produced in New York 4 May 1848 at the Bowery Theatre. For Synopsis of Scenes and Musical Numbers, see original 1848 production.

CAST: *Maritana*: ADELAIDE RANDALL. *Don Caesar de Bazan*: ALFRED WILKIE. *Lazarillo*, a lad devoted to Don Caesar: ROSE LEIGHTON. *Charles II*, King of Spain: Paul Arthur. *Marquis di Montifiore*: Kate Hatfield. *Captain of the Guard*: Joseph Silvers. *Alcalde*: Harry Dale. *Don José*: EURICO CAMPOBELLO. *Toreadors, Soldiers, Peasants, etc.*

1884.39

SIEBA AND THE SEVEN RAVENS

A Romantic Spectacle in Four Acts, 12 Scenes. Original music by R. Marcuco. Dramatic music composed by Adolph Neuendorf. Ballets by Ettore Coppini. Scenery by Philip Goatcher, Charles Fox, William Schaeffer, Cav. Magnani. Costumes designed by Miss Fischer. Entire Grand Spectacle produced under the personal direction of the Kiralfy Brothers (Imre, Bolossy). Produced by the Kiralfy Brothers. Opened 18 August 1884 at the Star Theater and closed 18 October 1884 after 72 performances.

CAST: *Sieba*: ODETTE TYLER. *Puck*, a Spirit: VERNONA JARBEAU. *Sybilla*, a Maid in the Castle: Amy Lee. *Countess Ruperta*, Duchess of Dagomen: EMMIE WILMOT. *Savanta*, the Good Fairy: OLGA BRANDON. *Electra*, Queen of Dreamland: ETHEL BRANDON. *Theora*, a Court Attendant: Mrs. Selden Irwin. *Harold*, Prince of Helka: A. S. LIPMAN. *Nicodemus*: M. A. KENNEDY. *Cadmo*: John Jack. *Surtur*, the Evil Spirit: FRANK TANNEHILL, JR. *Chancellor*: Walter Eytinge. *Cuthbert*, a Warrior: O. H. Denham. *Martin*: Charles Sprague. *Sir Gilbert*: Harold Robinson. *Ladies, Maids, Esquires, Warriors, Knights, Retainers, Pages, Choristers, Attendants, Musicians, Guards, Executioners, Soliders, Servants, etc. Ballet*: Mlles. CARLOTTA BRIANZA, Millon, Locatelli; Signor Camerano.

Act 1, Scene 1: Fairy Land. (Goatcher.) *Scene 2*: Allegorical. (Fox.) *Scene 3*: The Forest in Winter. (Goatcher.) *Scene 4*: Nuptial Festal Scene.

Act 2, Scene 1: Courtyard of Harold's Castle, in Helka. (Schaeffer.) *Scene 2*: A Hall in the Castle. *Scene 3*: Storming of Prince Harold's Castle. (Schaeffer.)

Act 3: The Festal Hall of the Duchess of Dagomen. (Magnani.)

Act 4, Scene 1: The Encampment of the Duchess of Dagomen. (Schaeffer.) *Scene 2*: The Dungeon. (Fox.) *Scene 3*: Moonlight Ruins. (Magnani.) *Scene 4*: A Paradise of Roses.

ACT 1
- "Folks Think I Am So Good"
  - M. A. Kennedy
- Grand Pageantry Ballet
  - Corps de Ballet

ACT 2
- "All Young Girls Are Fond of Pleasure"
  - V. Jarbeau
- French and Spanish Song
  - V. Jarbeau
- "Ain't He Nice and Fat"
  - M. A. Kennedy
- "Spinning Waltz"
  - V. Jarbeau

ACT 3
- Grand Banquet Ballet

ACT 4
- "Plum Pudding"
  - V. Jarbeau, M. A. Kennedy

1884.40

THE SEVEN RAVENS

A Romantic Fairy Spectacle (7—Ravens—7) in Four Acts, 7 Scenes, combining drama, pantomime, opera and ballet. Original play by Emil Pohl. Translated from the German by G. P. Lathrop. Music by C. Lehnhardt and Ludwig Engländer[25]. Produced under the stage direction of Heinrich Conried. Ballets and marches by Luigi Mazzantini. Scenery by Otto Namczynowski (Berlin) and Harry Byrnes (New York). Character costumes designed by Franz Gaul (Vienna); ballet costumes designed by C. DeGrimm (New York). Electric jewels and paraphernalia by Inspector Rudolph (Vienna). Machinery and mechanical effects by William Crane. Properties and appointments by Charles Blesser. Orchestra directed by A. W. Hoffman. Produced by Messrs. John F. Poole and E. G. Gilmore. Opened 18 August 1884 at Niblo's Garden and closed 8 November 1884 after 96 performances.

CAST: *Count Walter*, of Felsenberg: GUSTAVUS LEVICK. *Gramsalbus*, a Hermit: J. W. PIGOTT. *Rotto*, a Cellarer: FRED LOTTO. *Rudeheart*, a Powerful Spirit: C. L. FARRELL. *Relskebert*, the Chancellor: J. Jewett. *Grinthorp*, a Retainer: J. Haslam. *Cuniber, Hans*, Bondmen: J. Murphy, Mr. MacDonald. *Sheriff of Pretsel*, a Vassal: Mr. Ledbury. *Fliesmund*, the Overseer: Mr. Hall. *Firedog*, Executioner: Mr. Holman. *Lovesoul*, the Good Spirit: PAULINE HALL. *Rosalind*, Sister to the Ravens: BLANCHE THORNE. *Edwina*, the Langradine: MATTIE EARLE. *Blandine*, her maid: CARRIE WALLACE. *Orte*, her waiting woman: MAUDE CLIFTON. *Fairy Womanhood*: EDNA COURTNEY. *Fairy Queen*: RUBY ST. QUENTIN. *Fairy Lightheart*: Celia Terry. *Kathe, Melitta*, Village Belles: Eme Lascelles, Ada Forbes. *Guards, Retainers, Huntsmen, Peasants, Fairies, Amazons, etc.* Grand Combined Corps de Ballet. *Principals*: Mlles. THEODORE deGILLERT, VA LUI, NINA CONTI, MIZL RIEDER, BETTI DAUBL, Pasti, Lontin, Signor LUIGI MAZZANTINI.

Act 1, Scene 1: Home of the Fairy Queen. *Scene 2*: Rosalind's retreat. Wood in Mid-Winter; transformation to Mid-Summer.

Act 2, Scene 1: Castle of Count Walter. *Scene 2*: Rosalind's Home. *Scene 3*: Castle Exterior. Grand Battle Scene.

Act 3: Prison of Rosalind with magic change to Bower of Roses.

Act 4: Wood. Preparation for the execution of Rosalind. Grand Tableau. The Seven Ravens Transformed.

ACT 1[26]
- Scene 2
- Snow Flake Ballet
  - Mlles. Lui, Rieder, Conti, Daubl, Pasti, Lontin, Coryphées and Corps de Ballet

ACT 2
- Scene 3
- Spinning Song
  - (*Music by* Ludwig Engländer.)
- Drinking Song
  - (*Music by* Ludwig Engländer.)

ACT 3
- The Flower Ballet
  - T. De Gillert, M. L. Mazzantini, Coryphées and Corps de Ballet

ACT 4
- Grand March of the Amazons

1884.41

INVESTIGATION

A Local Farcical Comedy in Three Acts. Play (and lyrics) by Edward Harrigan. Music by David Braham. (Staged by Edward Harrigan.) Scenery by Charles W. Witham. Mechanical effects by William McMurray. Properties by Robert Puller. Dresses by Mary Jack. Furniture by Messrs. Coogan Brothers. (Musical director, David Braham.) Produced by Edward Harrigan and Tony Hart. Opened 1 September 1884 at the Theatre Comique and closed 23 December 1884 after 131 performances.

CAST: *DeArcy Flynn*, a tenement house agent: EDWARD HARRIGAN. *Bernard McKenna*, in the Glue line: TONY HART. *Leander Tuck*, Stage Manager of the Theatre Comique: JOHN WILD. *Clarence Montgomery*: W. J. Dagnan. *Oscar Onderdonk, Ezra Wheatfield, Orion Overhoe*, Legislative Committee: M. BRADLEY, GEORGE MERRITT, HARRY FISHER. *Gaspard Pitkins*: James Fox. *Mrs. Hop Sing*: Charles Sturges. *Mr. Paul Werner*: H. Thompson. *Lorenzo Hogan*: JOHN SPARKS. *Hop Sing*, a Chinaman: WILLIAM WEST. *Mrs. Virginia Pitkins*: M. Foley. *Charles Gilder*: J. Hardman. *Esau Whitecow*: J. Davis. *Joe Warbles*: J. Lewis. *Alexis Canfruit*: B. Gaston. *Emma Duflop*: James Tierney. *Ruth Sinclair*: J. G. Brevarde. *Clara Carlsbad*: Charles Coffey. *Adelaide Foglip*: Emil Husel. *Mr. Garritville*: L. George. *The Rev. Jonah Woolgather*: W. Williams. *Mr. Savage*: J. McCullough. *Wilford Smily*: W. Merritt. *Joe Dognose*: G. L. Stout. *Royal Rubin*: Edward Murphy. *Policemen, Street Characters, etc. Mrs. Belinda Tuggs*: ANNIE YEAMANS. *Sarah Tuggs*: ANNIE LANGDON. *Julia Tuggs*: Sadie Morris. *Mrs. Onderdonk*: A. Scallon. *Mrs. Wheatfield*:

[25]Program credits notwithstanding, critics remarked upon the freely interpolated music of Verdi and Strauss, among others.

[26]Added to Act 1, Scene 2, following Snow Flake Ballet, during the run:
- Polka Comique
  - L. Mazzantini, B Daubl

Marie Gorenflo. *Mrs. Overhoe*: Ada Farwell. *Kate Milton*: Annie Hall. *Grace Darlington*: Kate Langdon. *Young Ladies of the Cooking School (7)*: *Eugenia Foster*: Lizzie Finn. *Georgina Danford*: Nellie Seymour. *Mercy Franklin*: Lillian Taylor. *Gussie Evans*: Jennie Bageard. *Emma Mardon*: Della Stillwell. *Louisa Ashton*: E. Dankworth. *Emelia Bandcroft*: Nellie Hoyt. *Edith Coupon*: EMILY YEAMANS. (*Romeo*: EDWARD HARRIGAN. *Juliet*: ANNIE YEAMANS.)

Act 1: Interior of Miss Julia Tugg's Cooking School.

Act 2: Branigan's Barracks in Mulberry Bend.

Act 3, Scene 1: A Street in New York. *Scene 2*: The Green Room of the Theatre Comique. *Scene 3*: Garden Scene, "Romeo and Juliet."

MUSICAL NUMBERS

"The Man That Knows It All"

"Plum Pudding"

"(There'll Be Lovers) As Long as the World Goes Round"

"The Boodle, (the Boodle for Me)"

"Hello, Babby" (Xylophone solo by Ed King)

1884.42 ADONIS

An Original Spectacular Burlesque Nightmare (Musical Spectacle) in Two Acts. A Perversion of Common Sense by William Gill. The Stage Business, etc. invented and produced under the personal direction of Henry E. Dixey[27]. Original music by John Eller and Edward E. Rice. Selected music 'cheerfully contributed by Beethoven, Audran, Suppé, Planquette, Offenbach, Strauss, Mozart, Haydn, Dave Braham, and many others too numerous to individualize.' Costumes by P. Godchaux & Co.; steel armor by H. Wadman. Stage under the direction of James C. Scanlan. Musical director, Henry Sator. Produced by Edward E. Rice. Opened 4 September 1884 at the Bijou Theatre and closed 17 April 1886 after 603 performances.

CAST: *Adonis*, an accomplished young gentleman, of undeniably good family, inasmuch as he can trace his ancestry back through the Genozoic, Mesozoic and Palaeozoic period, until he finds it resting on the Archaean Time. His family name, by the way, is "Marble": HENRY E. DIXEY. *Marquis de Baccarat*, a highly polished villain. It is well enough to describe his character, as no one would think it to look at him: HERBERT GRESHAM. *Bunion Turke*, father of Rosetta, an unblushing appropriator of the stock in trade of a well-known and worthy old histrionic miller: GEORGE HOWARD. *Talamea*, a Sculptress, who like most of her sex, is in love with her own creation: LILLIE GRUBB. *Artea*, a Goddess, Patroness of the fine arts. N.B.—The student will vainly search for this character in the Heathen, or any other mythology: CARRIE GODFREY. *Duchess of Area*, aesthetic to the verge of eccentricity, rich to the verge of Millionairism. Sentimental to the verge of gush: JENNIE REIFFARTH. *Four Daughters of the Duchess*, Professional Beauties: *Lady Nattie*: Bertie Fisch. *Lady Hattie*: Jennie Reeves. *Lady Mattie*: Ida Bell. *Lady Pattie*: Mollie Fuller. *Rosetta*, a simple village maiden, and the happy possessor of a clear conscience and a strong will: AMELIA SUMMERVILLE. *Gyles, Nyles, Myles Byles*, everyday rustics: Messrs. Amberg, Frail, Roberts, Kramer. *Gills, Bills, Sills, Tills*, homely rustics: Messrs. Watson, Gilson, and the Carroll Brothers. *The Plumed Knights*: Misses Gray, Miller, Blow, Davenport, Girard, Mertens, Runnells, Behr, Robinson, Cerbi, Shaler, Johnson, Vanosten, Metcalf, Cramer Morris, Mulle. *A Section of the British Army, The Duchess Tigers The Bric-a-Brac Guards.*

Act 1, Scene 1: Talamea's Studio in Athens. *Scene 2*: The humble but honest home of the Miller. *Scene 3*: Garden of the Duchess of Area's Mansion.

Act 2, Scene 1: A Country Village. *Scene 2*: The Enchanted Wood. *Scene 3*: Interior of a Country Store. *Scene 4*: Forest. *Scene 5*: The Mystic Home of the Goddess of Art.

ACT 1[28]

Scene 1

Opening Chorus

"The Invocation"

"We Are the Duchess' Daughters"
B. Fisch, J. Reeves, I. Bell, M. Fuller

Pedestal Clog Dance
H. E. Dixey

"It Is Alive"
Chorus

Scene 2

"I'm a Merry Little Mountain Maid"
A. Somerville

"Go, Basest Lord" (Trio)
A. Somerville, H. Gresham, G. Howard

Scene 3

The Bric-à-Brac Guards

March of the Oriental Servitors

Chorus of the Little Boy Grooms

"The Susceptible Statuette"
H. E. Dixey

"Words Without Tune"
Chorus

"Most Romantic Meeting" (Duet)
H. E. Dixey, A. Somerville

"He Would Away" (Grand Finale)
H. E. Dixey, all the characters

ACT 2[29]

Scene 1

"Oh, Yes, We Are the Chorus"
Chorus

Ballad ("The Wall Street Broker")
L. Grubb
(*Music by* Edward E. Rice. *Lyrics by* H. S. Hewitt.)

The Village Fete; The Opera Bouffers; The Queen's Lace Handkerchief; Olivette; The Merry War; Orpheus d'Enfers.

"The Blushing Bride'
Chorus

The Soldiers' Chorus

Scene 2

"Golden Chains" (Duet)
L. Grubb, C. Godfrey

"I Know My Rights"[30] (Duet)
A. Somerville, H. Gresham

Scene 3

"Take Me Down the Bay"
H. E. Dixey

"Girls Hide Away"
Chorus

"Whatever Has Become of Him?"[31]
Chorus

Scene 4

"The Its and the Whats" (Burlesque on Comic Opera Chorus)
The Duchess Tigers

Scene 5

Grand Finale

1884.43 MADAME BONIFACE

An Opéra-comique in Three Acts, in French. Libretto by Ernest Dupré and Charles Clairville. Music by Paul Lacôme. Stage manager, V. Merle. Musical director, A. Lagye. Produced by Maurice Grau's French Opéra Bouffe Company. Opened 8 September 1884 at Wallack's Theatre and closed 25 September 1884 after 8 performances in repertory; played a return engagement 10-18 April 1885 at the Star Theatre for 2 performances in repertory.

CAST: *Friquette (Boniface)*: Mme. LOUISE THÉO. *Isabelle*: Mlle. EUGÉNIE NORDALL. *Clorinde*: Mlle. VALLOT. *Cydalise*: Mlle. ASTRUC. *Boniface*: Mons. J.

---

[27]Later productions credited Henry E. Dixey and Edward E. Rice as co-authors.

[28]Added 19 March 1885 on the occasion of the 200th performance:
"I'm O'Donohue from Nowhere"
H. E. Dixey
(*Music by* Edward E. Rice. *Lyrics by* William Gill.)

[29]New song added early in the run to the end of Act 2, Scene 1:
"It's English, You Know" (Patter Song)
H. E. Dixey
(*Music by* Edward E. Rice. *Lyrics by* H. S. Hewitt.)
Some programs credit Henry E. Dixey with this song's lyrics.

[30]Dropped during the run

[31]Dropped during the run

MEZIÈRES. *Comte Annibal (de Tournedor)*: Mons. GAILLARD. *Fridolin*: Mons. GUY. *La Vieille Brèche*: Mons. DUPLAN. *Jacquot*: Mons. DUCOS. *Varoquet*: Mons. VINCHON. *Un Valet*: Mons. Perret. *Louison*: Mlle. Caro. *Jeanne*: Mlle. Gabrielle. *Catherine*: Mlle. L. Barrot. *Jacquotte*: Mlle. Vandamme. *Miette*: Mlle. Gatineau. *Lords (3)*: *Civric*: Mlle. G. Barrot. *Miraval*: Mlle. Dass. *Balville*: Mlle. Daniel. *Lavrillere*: Mlle. Estiot. *Claudine*, a Servant: Mlle. Marthe. *Brigitte*: Mlle. Berthe. *An Abbé*: Mlle. Tournyaire. *First Young Man*: Mlle. Blanche. *Second Young Man*: Mlle. Delina. *Third Young Man*: Mlle. Louise.

Act 1: La confiserie de Boniface. Paris, sous Louis XV.

Act 2: Un salon chez Annibal.

Act 3: La cour de la maison de Boniface.

ACT 1[32]

"A la boutiuque" (Introduction)
Mons. Ducos, Choeur
"Ce matin je quitte" (Air bouffe)
Mons. Duplan
"Comme la fleur qui brille" (Romance)
Mons. Gaillard
"Elle y venait" (Rondeau)
Mons. Guy
"Merci, mes chers amis" (Scène et couplets)
Mme. L. Théo, Choeur
"Pourquoi prendre ce front sévère" (Couplets)
Mme. Théo
"Faisons des cornets" (Trio)
Mme. L. Théo, Messrs. J. Mezières, Gaillard
"Comme nous passions sur la place" (Final)
"Adieu c'est dit je m'en vais en voyage" (Rondeau des adieux)
Mme. L. Théo

ACT 2

"Pour un joyeux repas" (Choeur d'introduction)
Choeur
"D'où te vient ce projet morose" (Couplets et ensemble)
Mlles. Vallot, Astruc, Mons. Guy
"Il ramène une belle" (Petit choeur de sortie)
Choeur
"Monsieur je suis à Boniface" (Couplets)
Mme. L. Theo
"Au calme plat" (Chanson)
Mons. Duplan
"Moi, si j'étais époux" (Couplets)
Mons. Gaillard
"Dès les premiers jours du monde" (Couplets et ensemble)
Mme. L. Théo, Mlle. E. Nordall, Mons. J. Mezières
"Ah! je vous aime à la folie" (Duo)
Mme. L. Théo, Mons. Gaillard
"Ah! quel souper délectable!" (Final)

ACT 3

"Come tous les matins à la confiserie" (Choeur)
Mons. Ducos, Choeur
"Pourquoi vous chagriner" (Terzettino et couplets)
Mme. L. Théo, Mlle. E. Nordall, Mons. Guy
"Ah! que tu connais peu les femmes" (Couplets-Menuet)
Mons. Gaillard
"Tu vas m'écouta" (Chanson Auvergnate)
Mme. L. Théo
"Comme nous passions sur la place" (Final)

1884.44 THE CORSICAN BROTHERS & CO., or, What London Laughs At

A Musical and Specialty Melange in Two Acts, 4 Scenes. Play by F. C. Burnand and H. P. Stephens[33]. Revised and arranged for American audiences by Edward J. Henley. Scenery by William Schaeffer, Charles Fox. Musical director, H. F. Ball. Produced by Moore and Holmes' Royal British Burlesque and Specialty Company (Kiralfy Brothers, Management). Opened 8 September 1884 at the New Park Theatre and closed 20 September 1884 after 16 performances.

CAST: *Louis Dei Franchi, Fabian Dei Franchi*, Of Course-I-Can Brothers: EDWARD J. HENELY. *Monsieur De Chateau Reynaud*: MARIE LOFTUS. *Monsieur Maynard*: EDMOND GRACE. *Griffo*: George LeClerq. *Orlando*: Frank Edgerton. *Coloma*: George W. Moore. *Judge*: Arthur Corney. *Madame Dei Franchi* from Corksica: PATRICK FEENEY. *Marie*: Miss Emmet. *Celestine*: Hughie Hughes. *Coralia*: Louise Moore. *Estelle*: Florence Kirby. *Emilie De Lesparre*: GRACE PEDLEY. *Specialties*: Miss Blanche (Queen of the rope), Madeline Rosa (ventriloquist), Craggs Family (acrobats).

Act 1: The Dei Franchi Chateau. (Schaeffer.)

Act 2, Scene 1: The Illuminated Gardens of the Chateau St. Fleurs, Paris. (Fox.) *Scene 2*: On the Road to Fontainebleau. *Scene 3*: The Forest of Fontainebleau. (Fox.)

ACT 2
Scene 1
European Specialties:
Marvelous Craggs Family of Acrobats
Miss Blanche, Queen of the Rope
Madeline Rosa (World's only Lady Ventriloquist)

1884.45 LA JOLIE PARFUMEUSE

A Revival of the Opéra-comique in Three Acts, in French[34]. Libretto by Hector Crémieux and Ernest Blum. Music by Jacques Offenbach. Stage manager, V. Merle. Musical director, A. Lagye. Produced by Maurice Grau's French Opéra Bouffe Company. Opened 15 September 1884 at Wallack's Theatre and closed 27 September 1884 after 6 performances in repertory; played a return performance 6 April 1885 at the Star Theatre[35].

CAST: *Rose Michon*: Mme. LOUISE THÉO. *Bavolet*: Mlle. CÉCILE LEFORT. *Clorinde*: Mlle. Eugénie Nordall. *La Julienne*: Mme. Delorme. *Withemise*: Mlle. Vallot. Lescot. *Madelon*: Mlle. Caro. *Justine*: Mlle. Gabrielle Barrot. *Lise*: Mlle. Dass. *A Soubrette*: Mlle. Daniel. *La Cocardière*: Mons. DUPLAN. *Poirot*: Mons. LARY. *Germain*: Mons. Girard. *Waiters*: Messrs. Vinchon, Nys, Perret, Estiot.

1884.46 MAMZELLE NITOUCHE

A Comic Vaudeville in Three Acts, 4 Scenes. Original French libretto to the comédie-vaudeville 'Mam'zelle Nitouche' by Henri Meilhac and Albert Millaud. Music by Hervé. Stage director, Frederick Percy. Musical director, Carl Von Schiller. Produced under the personal supervision of Lotta (Crabtree). Produced by Lotta (Crabtree; Business Manager, A. S. Pennoyer). Opened 15 September 1884 at Daly's Theatre and closed 4 October 1884 after 21 performances.[36]

CAST: *Denise de Flavigny*: LOTTA (CRABTREE). *Célestin*, Organist of the Convent: C. H. BRADSHAW. *Ferdinand Champlatreux*, a young officer: FREDERIC DARRELL. *The Major*, Count of Castle Gibus: R. J. DUSTAN. *Loriot*, Corporal of Dragoons: J. H. Stuart. *Gustave, Robert, ?*, Officers of Dragoons: Edgar F. Girard, H. R. Asten, E. C. Barnum. *First Soldier*: C. Harrie Hopper. *Second Soldier*: Charles Stevens. *Director of Pontarcy Theatre*: W. St. Clair. *Stage-Manager*: George Fredericks. *Call Boy*: A. Sharpe. *The Lady Superior*: Adelaide Eaton. *Janitress*: Alice Brown. *Corinne*, Opera Bouffe Artist at Pontarcy Theatre: Josie Shepherd. *Artists at the Pontarcy Theatre (3)*: *Sylvia*: Alice Brown. *Lydia*: Dollie Delroy. *Gimblette*: Bertha Livingstone. *Pupils, Soldiers, etc.*

Act 1: The School of Pontarcy Convent. Afternoon.

Act 2: Green Room of the Pontarcy Theatre. Evening.

Act 3, Scene 1: The Barrack Yard. Midnight. *Scene 2*: The School Room. Sunrise.

---

[32]Musical numbers not listed in programs. List prepared from published French piano vocal score (Enoch & Costallat, Paris, 1883).

[33]Original London production credited music to Meyer Lutz, uncredited for the American production. Musical numbers not listed in programs.

[34]First produced in New York 31 March 1875 at the Lyceum Theatre in repertory. For Synopsis of Scenes and Musical Numbers, see original 1875 production. Program notes: At Wallack's, Mme. Theo introduced her song hit "Pi-ouit;" at the Star, Mme. Théo introduced "Where Are You Going, My Pretty Maid?"

[35]For the Star Theatre engagement, cast changes: *Withemise*: Mlle. Lescot. *Justine*: Mlle. Vandamme.

[36]English adaptation uncredited. How much of Hervé's score remained is doubtful. Critics remarked upon a French song in Act 1 and an interpolated Japanese song in Act 2, both performed by Lotta.

1884.47

LA MASCOTTE

A Revival of the Opéra-comique in Three Acts, in French[37]. Libretto by Henri Chivot and Alfred Duru. Music by Edmond Audran. Stage manager, V. Merle. Musical director, A. Lagye. Produced by Maurice Grau's French Opéra Bouffe Company. Opened 18 September 1884 at Wallack's Theatre and closed 27 September 1884 after 5 performances in repertory; played a return engagement 7-16 April 1885 at the Star Theatre for 3 performances in repertory.

CAST: *Bettina*: Mme. LOUISE THÉO. *Fiametta*: Mlle. CÉCILE LEFORT. *Pages (5)*: *Angelo*: Mlle. Vallot. *Marco*: Mlle. Gabrielle. *Carlo*: Mlle. Caro. *Luidgi*: Mlle. Daniel. *Beppo*: Mlle. Barrot. *Peasant Girls (2)*: *Francesca*: Mlle. Vandamme. *Antonia*: Mlle. Marthe. *Laurent XVII*: Mons. J. MEZIÈRES. *Pippo*: Mons. GAILLARD. *Prince Fritellini*: Mons. LARY. *Rocco*: Mons. DUPLAN. *Sergeant Parafante*: Mons. Vinchon. *Matheo*: Mons. Ducos. *A Peasant*: Mons. Gerard. *First Soldier*: Mons. Perret. *Second Soldier*: Mons. Yalowicz.

1884.48

A PARLOR MATCH, or, Turning a Crank

Evans & Hoey's Meteors in a Tidal Wave of Merriment (Farce Comedy) in Three Acts. Play by Charles H. Hoyt. Musical director, F. J. Titus. Produced under the management of Harry Mann. Opened 22 September 1884 at Tony's Pastor's New 14th Street Theatre and closed 4 October 1884 after 16 performances[38]

CAST: *I. McCorker*, a literary man: CHARLES E. EVANS. *Old Hoss*, a collector for an auction room: WILLIAM HOEY. *Captain William Kidd*, a lineal descendant of the famous pirate: DANIEL HART. *Ephraim Bellomont*, his next door neighbor, and descendant of Governor Bellomont, who captured the pirate Kidd: FRANK J. CAMPBELL. *Algernon St. L. Smith*: FRANK J. CAMPBELL. *Ralph Bellomont*, his son: R. N. Dungan. *Harry Wilson*, a friend of the Kidds: R. N. Dungan. *Curtis Shadburne*, spiritualist: R. N. Dungan. *St. Clair Todd*, a Harvard student: Edward Werner. *McKee*, of Allon, M. P.: Edward Werner. *Bernard McNulty*, a laborer: Frank Ellis. *Giveadam Penny*, a laborer: Stoney Linton. *Innocent Kidd*, the Captain's angel child: JENNIE YEAMANS. *Lucille Kidd*, her sister: MATTIE FERGUSON. *Aline Kidd*, the eldest sister: Emelie Edwards. *Miss Jemima Corbin*, a lady afflicted with deafness: Emelie Edwards. *Mrs. Aurelia Kidd*, the Captain's better half: Edward Werner. *Miss Diana Todd*, a relative of the Kidds: Edward Werner. *Nannie*: Herself.

Act 1: Exterior of Captain Kidd's House.

Act 2: McCorker's Headquarters.

Act 3: Parlor in Captain Kidd's Home.

ACT 1

Chorus from the latest operatic success, FANTINE[39] (Boston)
(*Music by* Firmin Bernicat and André Messager. *Lyrics by* R. M. Field and B. E. Woolf.)

"The Man that knows it all" (Song, from INVESTIGATION)
(*Music by* David Braham. *Lyrics by* Edward Harrigan.)

ACT 2

Splinter Medley

"Hello, Babby" (Song and Dance, from INVESTIGATION)
(*Music by* David Braham. *Lyrics by* Edward Harrigan.)

"Pretty Pond Lillies" (Song)
(*Music and Lyrics by* Lillie Hall.)

"La Paloma" (Spanish Folk Song)
(*Music and Lyrics by* Sebastian Yradier.)

ACT 3

"Poor Little Me" (Song and Dance)

"A Parlor Match" Medley

1884.49

MADAME L'ARCHIDUC

A Revival of the Opéra-comique in Three Acts, in French[40]. Libretto by Albert Millaud. Music by Jacques Offenbach. Stage manager, V. Merle. Musical director, A. Lagye. Produced by Maurice Grau's French Opéra Bouffe Company. Opened 22 September 1884 at Wallack's Theatre and closed 26 September 1884 after 2 performances in repertory.

CAST: *Marietta*: Mlle. LOUISE THÉO. *Fortunato*: Mlle. CÉCILE LEFORT. *Comtesse*: Mlle. EUGÉNIE NORDALL. *Giacommetta*: Mlle. Vandamme. *Archiduc Ernest*: Mons. DUPLAN. *Giletti*: Mons. LARY. *Comte*: Mons. GAILLARD. *Pontefiasconne*: Mons. Guy. *Bonaventura*: Mons. Salvator. *Frangipanne*: Mons. Ducos. *Bonardo*: Mons. Yalowicz. *Ricardo*: Mons. Vinchon. *A Landlord*: Mons. Girard. *Piano-Dolce*: Mons. Estiot. *Beppino*: Mons. Nys.

1884.50

FANCHON

An Opéra-comique in Three Acts, in French. Libretto ("François les bas bleus") by Ernest Dubreuil, Paul Burani and Eugène Humbert. Music by Firmin Bernicat and André Messager. Stage manager, V. Merle. Musical director, A. Lagye. Produced by Maurice Grau's French Opéra Bouffe Company. Opened 29 September 1884 at Wallack's Theatre and closed 4 October 1884 after 7 performances in repertory.

CAST: *Fanchon*: Mlle. LOUISE THÉO. *The Comtesse de la Savonnière*: Mme. DELORME. *Melitza*: Mlle. Vallot. *Nicolet*: Mlle. Eugénie Nordall. *Manon*: Mlle. Gabrielle. *Juliette*: Mlle. Caro. *François Bernier* (François les bas bleus): Mons. GAILLARD. *The Marquis de Pontcornet*: Mons. J. MEZIÈRES. *The Chevalier de Lansac*: Mons. LARY. *Kirschwasser*: Mons. Guy. *Jasmin*: Mons. Ducos. *Gratinet*: Mons. Salvator. *Courtalin*: Mons. Vinchon. *A Valet*: Mons. Perret. *A Soldier*: Mons. Yalowicz. *A Citizen*: Mons. Estiot.

Act 1: Au Carrefour St. Eustache. Paris, 1789.

Act 2: Chez le Marquis de Pontcornet.

Act 3: Au Pont-Neuf.

ACT 1[41]

""Où donc est notre secrétaire?" (Introduction)
Mme. Delorme, Mlle. Nordall, Chorus

"Regardez la belle prestance" (Chanson Militaire)
Mons. Guy

"François! François!" (Entrée de François)

"C'est François, les bas-bleus" (Ronde)
Mons. Gaillard

"Voici la petite chanteuse" (Rondeau de Fanchon)
Mlle. L. Théo, Chorus

"Avec soin formez chaque lettre" (Duo de la leçon d'écriture)
Mons. Gaillard, L. Théo

"Ami François, c'est jour de fête" (Morceau d'ensemble)

"Y'avait un p'tit matelot" (Chanson du petit matelot)
Mlle. L. Théo

"Peuple français, le politique" (Final-Chanson politique)
Mons. Gaillard

ACT 2

"C'est un scandale épouvantable!" (Choeurs des domestiques)

"Oui, mes amis, et vous pouvez m'en croire" (Couplets de Jasmin)
Mons. Ducos

"Je suis perplexe" (Couplets)
Mons. J. Mezières

"J'aime la femme et je m'en vante" (Couplets de Lansac)
Mons. Lary

---

[37]First produced in New York in English 5 May 1881 at the Bijou Theatre for 200 performances in two engagements, and in French 30 November 1881 for at Abbey's Park and the Fifth Avenue Theatre for 4 performances in repertory. For Synopsis of Scenes and Musical Numbers, see original French 1881 production.

[38]No credits in program for stage director (Charles H. Hoyt), scenery or costumes. Played a return engagement 28 September 1885 at the Grand Opera House for 8 performances.

[39]Another English language adaptation of FRANÇOIS LES BAS BLEUS, whose French version premiered in New York under the title FANCHON 29 September 1884; see detail below. FANTINE played Boston, not New York. Not to be confused with the later English language adaptation VICTOR, THE BLUE-STOCKING.

[40]First produced in New York in English 29 December 1874 at the Lyceum Theatre. Presented in French 6 September 1875 at the Lyceum Theatre. For Synopsis of Scenes and Musical Numbers, see original 1875 production.

[41]Musical numbers not listed in programs. List prepared from published French piano vocal score, "François les bas bleus" (Enoch Frères & Costallat, Paris, 1883).

"Il faut laisser tour espérance" (Romance de François)
Mons. Gaillard
"Fanchon! ah! c'est toi que je revois" (Duo)
Mlle. L. Théo, Mons. Gaillard
"J'ai de la figure" (Rondeau de la comtesse)
Mme. Delorme
"Monsieur le Marquis, mon père" (Romance de Fanchon)
Mlle. L. Théo
"Place à la garde-suisse" (Final)
"Astique bien ton fourniment" (Chanson à Boire)
Mlle. L. Théo

ACT 3
"Sur le repos du populaire" (Introduction: patrouille et choeur)
Chorus
"À toi j'avais donné ma vie" (Romance)
Mons. Gaillard
"Je rafraîchis! Moi, j'enflamme!" (Duo du Cidre et du Café)
Mme. Delorme, Mons. J. Mezières
"C'est du limon" (Choeur du limon)
"On dit que le Parisien" (Chanson populaire)
Mlle. L. Théo
"Votre femme m'a dit 'je t'aime'!" (Arioso)
Mons. Gaillard
"La petite chanteuse" (Final)

SUPPLEMENT
"Oui, j'ai vu le ministre" (Trio)
Mme. Delorme, Messrs. J. Mezières, Lary

1884.51 THE BEGGAR STUDENT

A Revival of the Opera Comique (Comic Opera) in Three Acts, 4 Scenes[42]. (Original Viennese libretto to the operette 'Der Bettelstudent' by F. Zell and Richard Genée, based on "Fernande" by Victorien Sardou and "The Lady of Lyons" by Edward Bulwer-Lytton. English adaptation by Emil Schwab.) Music by Karl Millöcker. Stage manager, H. A. Cripps. Musical director, Signor Antonio DeNovellis. Produced by the McCaull Opera Company (John A. McCaull, Proprietor). Opened 6 October 1884 at the Casino Theater and closed 6 November 1884 after 28 performances.

CAST: *The Countess Palmatica*: LAURA JOYCE BELL. *Laura, Bronislava*, her daughters: LILLIE POST, MATHILDE COTTRELLY. *General Ollendorf*, Governor of Cracow: DIGBY BELL. *Symon Symonovicz*, the Beggar Student: MARK SMITH. *Janitzky*, a Polish noble: CHARLES H. CLARK. *Saxon Officers (5)*: *Lieutenant Poppenberg*: BILLIE BARLOW. *Major Olzhoff*: JAMES A. FUREY. *Captain Henrici*: L. M. Hall. *Ensign Richtofen*: A. Barbara. *Lieutenant Schweinitz*: L. Schraeder. *Cousins of Palmatica (2)*: *Bogumil*: Edward Cameron. *Eva*: Miss Ray Samuels. *Burgomaster*: Henry Plate. *Enterich*, a jailor: Emil Senger. *Puffke*, his assistant: C. Edwards. *Sitzka*, an inn-keeper: A. D. BARKER. *Onouphrie*, servant to the Countess: E. H. Van Vechten. *Polish Nobles, Pages, Students, Bridesmaids, Peasants, Children and Market-people, Hebrew Traders, Lancers, Soldiers.*

1884.52 BOCCACCIO

A Revival of the Operette in Three Acts, in French[43]. Original Viennese libretto by F. Zell and Richard Genée. French adaptation by Henri Chivot and Alfred Duru. Music by Franz von Suppé. Stage manager, V. Verle. Musical director, A. Lagye. Produced by Maurice Grau's French Opéra Bouffe Company. Opened 6 October 1884 at Wallack's Theatre and closed 7 October 1884 after 2 performances in repertory; played 3 return performances 13, 18 and 23 April 1885 at the Star Theatre. Total: 5 performances.

CAST: *(Giovanni) Boccaccio*: Mme. LOUISE THÉO. *Beatrice*: Mlle. CÉCILE LEFORT. *Zanette*: Mlle. Astruc. *Petronelle*: Mme. Delorme. *Frisca*: Mlle. Eugénie Nordall. *A Young Girl*: Mlle. Berthe. *A Lady of Honor*: Mlle. Vandamme. *Giotto*: Mlle. Caro. *Frederico*: Mlle. Dass. *Tofano*: Mlle. Vandamme. *Raphaele*: Mlle. Gabrielle Barrot. *Orlando*: Mons. Guy. *Lelio*: Mons. Lary. *Pandolfo*: Mons. Duplan. *Tromboli*: Mons. Gaillard. *Quiquibio*: Mons. Ducos. *A Book Peddler*: Mons. Vinchon. *Cecco*: Mons. Girard. *A Citizen*: Mons. Estiot. *The Captain of the Guards*: Mons. Claudius. *The Unknown*: Mons. Girard.

1884.53 MY SWEETHEART

A Revival of the Elastic Musical Comedy in Three Acts[44]. Play re-written and revised by William Gill. Music and costumes new. Stage manager, T. J. Hawkins. Musical director, R. E. Lawson. Produced by Samuel Colville. Opened 6 October 1884 at the 14th Street Theatre and closed 18 October 1884 after 14 performances; returned 27 April 1885 to the Union Square Theatre and closed 16 May 1885 after an additional 21 performances.[45]

CAST: *Tina*, just home from boarding school: MINNIE PALMER. *Tony (Faust)*, Tina's sweetheart: CHARLES ARNOLD. *Joe Shotwell*, a broken-down gambler: T. J. HAWKINS. *Dr. Oliver*, a retired physician: H. R. Davies. *Harold Bartlett*, an adventurer: Augustus Cook. *Dudley Harcourt*, an old English fop: LAWRANCE D'ORSAY. *Old Hatzel*, a wealthy farmer: John S. Walsh[46]. *Mrs. Fleeter*, an adventuress: Jennie Satterlee[47]. *Mrs. Hatzel*, the farmer's loving wife: Mrs. Mary Myers. *Little Gee Ge*, Tony's pet: Baby Wood.

1884.54 LA FILLE DE MADAME ANGOT

A Revival of the Opéra-comique in Three Acts, in French[48]. Libretto by Clairville, Paul Siraudin and Victor Koning. Music by Charles Lecocq. Stage manager, V. Merle. Musical director, A. Lagye. Produced by Maurice Grau's French Opéra Bouffe Company. Opened 8 October 1884 at Wallack's Theatre and closed 11 October 1884 after 3 performances in repertory; played a return performance 9 April 1885 at the Star Theatre.

CAST: *Clairette*: Mme. LOUISE THÉO. *Mlle. Lange*: Mlle. CÉCILE LEFORT. *Amaranthe*: Mme. Delorme. *Javotte*: Mlle. Gatineau. *Cydalise*: Mlle. Vallot. *Mlle. Delauny*: Mlle. Caro. *Hersilie*: Mlle. Vandamme. *Babet*: Mlle. Adorci. *Manon*: Mlle. Blanche. *Therese*: Mlle. Berthe. *Herbelein*: Mlle. G. Barrot. *Ange Pitou*: Mons. LARY. *Pomponnet*: Mons. GUY. *Larivaudière*: Mons. F. MEZIÈRES. *Louchard*: Mons. DUPLAN. *Trénitz*: Mons. Ducos. *Cadet*: Mons. Girard. *Buteux*: Mons. Vinchon. *Guillaume*: Mons. Sallard. *Un Incroyable*: Mons. Estiot. *An Officer*: Mons. Claudius. *An Innkeeper*: Mons. Perret.

1884.55 LA TIMBALE D'ARGENT

A Revival of the Opéra-bouffe in Three Acts, in French[49]. Libretto by Adolphe Jaime and Jules Noriac. Music by Léon Vasseur. Stage manager, V. Merle. Musical director, A. Lagye. Produced by Maurice Grau's French Opéra Bouffe Company. Opened 10 October 1884 at Wallack's Theatre and closed 11 October 1884 after 2 performances in repertory; played a return performance 11 April 1885 at the Star Theatre.[50]

---

[42]First produced in New York in English 29 October 1883 at the Casino Theatre for 107 performances. For Synopsis of Scenes and Musical Numbers, see original 1883 production.

[43]Previously produced in New York in German 23 April 1880 at the Thalia Theatre; in English 17 May 1880 at the Union Square Theatre for 28 performances. This production marked its French language premiere in New York

[44]First produced in New York 18 September 1882 at the Fourteenth Street Theatre for 8 performances. For Synopsis of Scenes, see original 1882 production.

[45]For return engagement, scenery was credited to Richard Halley; music (director), Henry Tissington; mechanism, G. B. Winne; properties, William Henry; lights, M. Kehoe. Additional role: *Tim O'Leary*: Eugene O'Rourke. Later played a return engagement 10 October 1887 at the 14th Street Theatre for 14 performances for which no program nor cast detail was found.

[46]For return engagement, Farmer Hatzell played by H. R. Davies.

[47]For return engagement, the role of Louisa Shotwell, nee Mrs. Fleeter, played by Mattie Earle.

[48]First produced in New York in French 25 August 1873 at the Daly's Broadway Theatre in repertory. For Synopsis of Scenes and Musical Numbers, see original 1873 production.

[49]First produced in New York in French 24 August 1874 at the Lyceum Theatre for 17 performances in repertory. For Synopsis of Scenes and Musical Numbers, see original 1874 production. Program note: In Act 2, Mme. Théo will sing two of her famous chansonettes

[50]For Star Theatre engagement, cast changes: *Mme. Barnabe*: Mlle. Lescot. *Petit Pierre*: Mlle. Adorci.

CAST: *Molda*: Mlle. LOUISE THÉO. *Müller*: Mlle. CÉCILE LEFORT. *Fichtel*: Mlle. Eugénie Nordall. *Mme. Barnabe*: Mlle. Vallot. *Agath*: Mlle. Caro. *Petit Pierre*: Mlle. Gabrielle. *Gaben*: Mlle. Vandamme. *Pola*: Mlle. Dass. *Marza*: Mlle. Gatineau. *Therese*: Mlle. Tournyaire. *Raab*: Mons. E. DUPLAN. *Pruth*: Mons. F. MEZIÈRES. *Barnabe*: Mons. E. Vinchon. *Wilhem*: Mons. Girard. *Walter*: Mons. Estiot. *Jerome*: Mons. Yalowicz. *Fritz*: Mons. Sallard.

1884.56 SKIPPED BY THE LIGHT OF THE MOON

A Revival of their Humorous Creation (Farce Comedy) in Three Acts[51]. Play by Louis Harrison and John Gourlay. Stage manager, James F. Tighe. Orchestra under the direction of Isador Vollman. Presented by Sam Harrison, Management. Opened 20 October 1884 at the 14th Street Theatre and closed 8 November 1884 after 24 performances; returned 1 December 1884 to the Grand Opera House for 8 additional performances, 12 January 1885 to Niblo's Garden for 8 additional performances, 13 April 1885 to People's Theatre for 8 additional perofrmances, and 25 May 1885 to the Grand Opera House for an additional 8 performances. Total: 56 performances.

CAST: *Felix Crackle*: LOUIS HARRISON. *Obadiah Dingle*: JOHN GOURLAY. *James Warfield*: W. H. Collings. *Garnishee McIntyre*: Edward Morris. *Frank Pelham*: Charles W. Sutton. *John Sharpleigh*: James F. Tighe. *Restauranteur*: Charles Helmych. *Sarah*: Emma Schultz. *Mrs. Obadiah Dingle*: Annie Wood. *Mrs. Felix Crackle*: Eleanor Lane. *Millicent Warfield*: Belle Dickson.

1884.57 NELL GWYNNE

An Opera Comique (Comic Opera) in Three Acts. Libretto by Henry B. Farnie (based on the play 'Rochester' by W. T. Moncrieff). Music by Robert Planquette. Scenery by John Mazzanovich, Henry E. Hoyt and Gaspard Maeder. Master machinist, G. P. Sherwood, Jr. Musical director, Antonio DeNovellis. Produced by the McCaull Opera Comique Company (John A. McCaull, Proprietor and Manager). Opened 8 November 1884 at the Casino Theatre and closed 13 December 1884 after 38 performances.[52]

CAST: *Actresses at the Kings Theatre (2)*: *Nell Gwynne*: MATHILDE COTTRELLY. *Lady Falbala*: MATHILDE COTTRELLY. *Joan*, Cook at the Dragon: MATHILDE COTTRELLY. *Zaphet*, a Gypsy: MATHILDE COTTRELLY. *Lady Clare*, Ward of the King: LAURA JOYCE BELL. *Jessamine*, Old Weasel's niece: IDA VALERGA. *Marjorie*, Weasel's servant: Irene Perry. *Mistess Prue*, *Mistress Sue*, villagers: Annette Hall. Millie Vanberg. *King Charles II*: CHARLES W. DUNGAN. *Buckingham*, Exile from Court: WILLIAM H. HAMILTON. *Rochester*, Landlord and waiter at the Dragon: JAY TAYLOR. *The Beadle*, the local authority: DIGBY BELL. *Weasel*, Village Usurer and Pawnbroker: J. H. RYLEY. *Peregrine*, Buckingham's page: Billie Barlow. *Falcon*, a Strolling Player: W. H. FESSENDEN. *Talbot*, Cousin to Lady Clare: Edward Cameron. *Hodge*, *Podge*, villagers: J. A. Furey, L. C. Shrader. *Villagers, Huntsmen, Nobles, Pages, Ladies of Court, etc.*

Act 1: Village on the Borders of the New Forest. (Mazzanovich.)

Act 2: Interior of Weasel's House, Rat Castle. (Hoyt.)

Act 3: The New Forest. (Maeder.)

ACT 1[53]

"No Heel-Taps" (Chorus)

"He Brings our Score" (Scene)

"To you Ladies" (Air and Chorus)
W. H. Hamilton, Chorus

"The British Waiter" (Duetto Bouffe)
J. Taylor, W. H. Hamilton

"Only an Orange Girl" (Rondo)
M. Cottrelly

"O Heart! My Lover's Near!" (Quartette)
I. Valerga, J. Taylor, W. H. Hamilton, J. H. Ryley

"Once upon a Time" (Song)
W. H. Hamilton

"O'er their Young Hearts" (Quartette)
M. Cottrelly, L. J. Bell, J. Taylor, W. H. Hamilton

"Clubs and Cudgels" (Chorus)

"'Tis I!" (Beadle's Song)
D, Bell, Chorus

Exit of Peasants

"Sweetheart, if Thou be Nigh!" (Serenade)
W. H. Fessenden

"O Surprise!" (Finale, Act 1)
Tutti e Coro

ACT 2

"About the Middle of the Week" (Pawn Chorus)

Exit of Peasants

"Rustic Rondo"
M. Cottrelly

"Tic, Tac" (Song of the Clock)
I. Valerga

"Maid of the Witching Eye" (Gipsy Duettino)
M. Cottrelly, L. J. Bell

"Now the Spell" (Sextuor)
M. Cottrelly, I. Valerga, L. J. Bell, J. Taylor, W. H. Hamilton, J. H. Ryley

"First Love" (Song)
M. Cottrelly

"The Dappled Fawn" (Duet)
I. Valerga, W. H. Fessenden

"Illusions!" (Song)
W. H. Hamilton

"Turn About" (Duetto)
W. H. Hamilton, J. Taylor

"What's Passing Here" (Finale, Act 2)
Tutti e Coro

ACT 3

"The Eager Hounds" (Hunting Chorus)

"The Broken Cavalier" (The Legend of Chelsea Hospital)
M. Cottrelly

Exit of the Hunting Party

"The Trysting Tree" (Romance)
W. H. Fessenden

"The Ball at Whitehall" (Scene and Air)/

"Green Sleeves" (Old Air)
M. Cottrelly

"Happy the Lot" (Idyll)
W. H. Ryley, D. Bell

"The Rendez-vous" (Quartette)
M. Cottrelly, L. J. Bell, J. Taylor, W. H. Hamilton

"Timid Bird" (Duettino)
I. Valerga, W. H. Fessenden

"Only an orange girl!" (Finale, Act 3)
Tutti e Coro

1884.58 FANTASMA, or, Funny Frolics in Fairyland

A Spectacular Pantomime in Three Acts, 9 Scenes. Invented, arranged and produced by the Hanlons, presented by their great Italian Pantomime Company. Scenery by John A. Thompson. Machinery and properties by Robert J. Cutler. Opened 10 November 1884 at the Fifth Avenue Theatre and closed 6 December 1884 after 32 performances; played a return engagement 20 April 1885 at Niblo's Garden, closing 2 May 1885 after an additional 16 performances. Total: 48 performances.

CAST: *Fantasma*, Fairy Queen, disguised as a witch: KATE DAVIS. *Zamaliel*, King of the Realm of Heads: NAT T. JONES. *Pico*, out of one trouble into another: LOUIS PIZZARELLO. *Cassander*, another of the same kind: ALLESSANDRO ANGIOLINI. *Arthur*, who loves Lena: GEROLAMO PASTORINI. *Lena*, who preferred one heart to many heads: ROSINA MASCHI. *Farmer Close*, father to Lena: LORENZO CATTANIO. *Farmer Happy*, father of Arthur: Pietro Mare. *Madge*, servant to Farmer Close: Mattie Temple. *Mother Goslin*, sister to Farmer Happy: Alice Newton. *Enasibus*,

[51]First produced in New York 14 April 1884 at the Fifth Avenue Theatre for 35 performances. For Synopsis of Scenes, see original 1884 production. Specialties and Musical Numbers not listed in programs.[5]

[2]Stage director uncredited; Stage manager, H. A. Cripps. No costume designer credited.

[53]Musical numbers not listed in programs. List prepared from published English piano vocal score (Metzler & Co., London, 1884).

Fantasma's dragon: P. Philippo. *Bruin*, a "sure enough" Bear: Philip Purcer. *Spirits attendant on Zamaliel (6)*: *Ichthyo*: Adolph Riccardi. *Blastus*: Henry Noresta. *Zazor*: Carlos Ravella. *Sychar*: Wilhelm Javello. *Zurile*: Oreste Bizzaroli. *Hakbar*: Rudolfo Carmina. *Frigido*, the Arctic Fiend: J. D. Nathaniel. *Goddess of Liberty*: Ruth Stetson. *Lichen*, an unhappy mother: Lizzie Vance. *Scrapestring*, a musician: J. T. McGovern. *Policeman*, the Finest: D. J. Natt. *Doughball*, a baker: H. George. *Dr. Lance*, "New School": Sig. Noresta. *Martingale*, a jockey: Sig. Ravello. *Nurse Girls (6)*: *Trotter*: Millie Croft. *Juniper*: Vinnie Carr. *Syruptu*: Annie Woodman. *Honeysuckle*: Berha Lovejoy. *Anise*: Fannie Maynard. *Cordelia*: Fannie Knight. *Lodging House Keepers (4)*: *Fidget*: Roxie Rudolfo. *Slatter*: Katrini Lorenzo. *Dustpan*: Phillipa Purcena. *Besom*: Marie Petro. *Peasants, Witches, Ghosts, Fairies, Servants, Tradespeoples, etc.*

Act 1, Scene 1: Beautiful Rustic Landscape. *Scene 2*: The Demon's Cabinet. *Scene 3*: Winter Scene.

Act 2, Scene 1: Castle exterior. *Scene 2*: Castle interior. *Scene 3*: Witch's laboratory. *Scene 4*: Realms of Heads.

Act 3: Grand Harlequinade. *Scene 1*: Rival Lodging Houses. *Scene 2*: Street.

ACT 1[54]

Scene 1
- Chorus of Harvesters

Scene 3
- Grand Allegorical Ballet

ACT 2

Scene 1
- Dance of the Owls

Scene 3
- "We Dance and Sing" (Witches' Chorus)

Scene 4
- Violin Solo, à la Paganinni
  L. Pizzarello
- "Hail to Our King!"/"Hail to Our Queen!"
  Chorus

ACT 3

Scene 2
- Specialties
  K. Davis

1884.59 ILL-FED-DORA

A Burlesque (of Victorien Sardou's 'Fedora', and Stanley Rosenfeld's burlesque 'Well-Fed Dora') in One Act[55], accompanied by an Olio. Costumes by (Henry) Dazian. Musical direction, Jesse Williams. Produced by (John) Koster and (Albert) Bial. Opened 23 November 1884 at Koster & Bial's Concert Hall and closed 26 December 1884 after (50) performances.

Olio: Fairy March from the forthcoming opera CULPRIT FAY, Music by Alden, Libretto by Judge Gedney; Orchestral Selections.

UNCLE JACK: *Uncle Jack*, singing master: FRANK CUSHMAN. *Uncle Horace*, ballet master: Vincent Hogan. *Vivian White*, their nephew: Harry Standish. *Carlotta*, costumer: The Only (FRANCIS) LEON. *La Norona*, Spanish Dancer: The Only FRANCIS) LEON. *Victorine Le Page*, French vocalist: The Only (FRANCIS) LEON. *Specialty*, Italian and French Song and Ballet Dance: L'Ariel.

LISCHEN AND FRITZCHEN Selections. (*Music by* Jacques Offenbach.) *Lischen*: LOUISE LESTER. *Fritzchen*: ALEX. BELL.

ILL-FED-DORA CAST: *Princess Ill-Fed-Dora, Malakoff* (the cough isn't serious though once very stout is now so thin (Banting treatment) that she is termed Ill-Fed-Dora): FRANCIS LEON. *Louis Rip-him-off-Attiloff*, very much off indeed: FRANK CUSHMAN. *Count Way-off*: Mr. Branscombe. *Countess Take-your-ear-off*: Mr. Russell. *Gretch*, a wretch on the ketch, in fact a detective: Miss Temple. *Ensemble by the Aristocracy*. *Scene*: Fed-Dora's Conservatoire in Paris.

THE SEVEN MAIDENS Selections. (Original Viennese libretto 'Zehn Mädchen und Kein Mann' by W. Friedrich [Wilhelm Friedrich Riese] based on the libretto 'Six demoiselles à marier' by Adolphe Jaime and Adolphe Choler. *Music by* Franz von Suppé.) *Major Bellmouse*: VINCENT HOGAN. *His Daughters (7)*: *Limmonia*, the Italian: LOUISE LESTER. *La Gascogne*, the French: ETTA BROOKS. *Alminia*, the Tyrolean, and *Maschinka*, the Bohemian: St. Felix Sisters. *Warsawa*, the Pole: Miss Henderson. *Hidalga*, the Castilian: Bessie Temple. *Danubia*, the Austrian: Louise Hill. *Agememnon Paris*: ALEX. BELL. *Sidonia*: Sophie Hummel.

1884.60 AN ADAMLESS EDEN/ THE ALSATIANS

A Double Bill of a Comic Opera Burlesque in Two Acts, preceded by an Operetta in One Act. Produced by Lila Clay's Music and Dramatic Company. Opened 24 November 1884 at the New York Comedy Theatre and closed 3 January 1885 after 42 performances.[56]

THE ALSATIANS[57]. An Operetta in One Act. Music by Jacques Offenbach. (Adapted from Lischen et Fritzchen, a conversation alsaciennne, original French libretto by Paul Boisselot.)

CAST: *Lischen* (Karlina): MARIE MULLE. *Frischen* Karl): TOPSY VENN.

AN ADAMLESS EDEN. A Comic Opera Burlesque in Two Acts. Libretto by Henry Savile Clark. Music by Walter Slaughter. Produced under the direction of Emma R. Steiner. Musical director, Julia deBetrand.

CAST: *Peter Popps, Esq.*, a "Masher" and a "Pilgrim": TOPSY VENN. *Mrs. Sophie Syntax*, Chairwoman of the School Board: PAULINE HALL. *Lady Mantrap*, the Chief Secretary: AMY AMES. *The Duchess of Breeks*, Viceroy of the Garden of Eden: MARIE E. SANGER. *Lady Dorothy Demmoreo*, Attorney General: E. Gertrude Gardiner. *Christine*, Maid to Duchess: Venie Burroughs. *Algy*, First Pilgrim: Venie Burroughs. *Regy*, Second Pilgrim: Georgy Gray. *Perjury Jones*, Superintendant of Police: Mabelle Stuart. *Lady Cockle Curlew*, Physician in ordinary: Sidney Haven. *Sarah Stamps*, Postmistress-General: Rita Carroll. *Sir Ruby Wallop*, Commander-in-Chief: Annette Nicholson. *Skimmery Hall*, School Board Tutor: Gertrude Citti. *Fred Blazer*, Special Correspondent: Emma Duchateau. *Lady Minever*: Marie St. Aubyn. *Lady Sable*: Constance Foy. *Lady Gales*: Elise Villiers. *Child of the School Board*: Georgie Gray.

Inhabitants of the Island: Misses Annette Nicholson, Nellie Arnoldi, Constance Foy, Bella Danvers, Florence Morrison, Kate McGregor, Helen Livingstone, Ada Chamberlain, Janet Foy, Alice Grey, Elise Villiers, Kate Ashford, Hilda Gresham, Blanche Montford.

Scene: The Fabled Island of Eden. *Time*: Any time.

Act 1: Palace of the Viceroy.

Act 2: Garden of the Palace.

MUSICAL NUMBERS[58]
- "Now ended in a Panic" (Opening Chorus)
  (Sopranos)
- "The way we live now" (Song)
  T. Venn
- "Love, be sure, finds out the way" (Duet)
  T. Venn, P. Hall
- "He's kiss'd me" (Trio)"
  T. Venn, M. E. Sanger, A. Ames
- "Sam and the Mormon" (Plantation Song and Dance)
  P. Hall
- "I hurl you defiance" (Duet of Defiance)
  P. Hall, E. G. Gardiner
- "I've a motion" (Political Chorus)
  M. E. Sanger, A. Ames, E. G. Gardiner, P. Hall, Chorus

[54]Musical numbers listed from Boston tour.

[55]Subtitled Two Screams and a Howl. Authorship uncredited, presumably by Francis Leon. Program note: The first act passes without notice in Petersburgh. The action of the play is in Paris and commences with the second act. The three acts condensed into one, will be played without once raising the fan till the end. The novel arrangement for effecting whatever change of scene may be required in sight of the audience has been duly patented by the inventor.

[56]Played return engagements (without the curtain raiser) 26 January 1885 and 1 June 1885 at the Third Avenue Theatre. Now billed as an "Opera de Camera."

[57]English language premiere, adaptation uncredited; on 18 December 1884 THE ALSATIANS was replaced by GANDOLFO!, an operetta in One Act by Charles Lecocq. French libretto by Henri Chivot and Alfred Duru adapted into English by Marius De Lazare. CAST: *Gandolfo*, Chief Magistrate of Florence: AMY AMES. *Sabrinardi*, an Adventurer: MARIE SANGER. *Angela*, Gandolfo's wife: MARIE MÜLLE. *Frisca*, Angela's maid: BÉBÉ VINING. *Amoroso*, a Young Musician: MAY STEMBLER.

"The Electric Waltz Song" sung by Miss May Stembler, written expressly for her by Fred Eustis.

[58]Musical numbers not listed in programs. List prepared from published English piano vocal score (Boosey & Co., London, 1881.) Two songs mentioned in reviews not found in published score: "It's All a Matter of Taste." "The Whistling March."

"An Adamless Eden" (Song)
M. E. Sanger, Chorus
"Love has won" (Quintette)
V. Burroughs, G. Gray, M. E. Sanger, A. Ames, T. Venn
Ballet of Postwomen (Just so. Yes dear)
Chorus
Finale (Now we've done, man has won)
Tutti

1884.61

CUPID!

A Spectacular Pantomimic Burlesque Extravaganza in Three Acts, 7 Scene[59]. Play by Lloyd Clarance[60]. Plot and arrangement by Cornelius R. Silbon. Music composed and arranged by Professor Braham. The whole produced under the direction of Cornelius R. Silbon. Dances arranged by Maggie Thompson. Mechanical and trick arrangements by Professor Elliott. Costumes by Alias, Burnett and Vokes. Produced by Tony Pastor. Opened 1 December 1884 at Tony Pastor's New 14th Street Theatre and closed 13 December 1884 after 16 performances.

CAST: *Old Darmstead*, good-hearted but in trouble: ALFRED WOOD. *Margo*, Witch of Great Renown: CORNELIUS R. SILBON. *Terror*, a Wicked Wolf: Mr. WILLIAM WIBBERLY. *Prince Forethought*, a young dasher, "up to the times": KATE VICTORIA. *Dandini*, Prince's companion: MAGGIE THOMPSON. *Arline*, the Old Man's Darling: HARRIET WOOD. *Spitefullina*, *Scratchitina*, sisters, old but in the Matrimonial Market: Messrs. AUGUSTUS VIRTO, VERNER CLARGES. *Cupid*, the God of Love: JULIA WOOD. *Little Nell*: ADA SILBON. *Tomkins*, *Simkins*, Flunkeys: Masters Alberto, Keen. *Mischievous Cat*: ED SILBON. *Imps, Demons, Peasantry of both sexes, Soldiers, Sailors, all the Crowned Heads of every European country, and prominent characters of the known world.*

Specialties: The 4 SILBONS (Edward, Walter, Kate, Cornelius), aerialists; The 6 ELLIOTTS (James, Thomas, Katie, Polly, Anna, Mattie), bicyclists and tricyclists; The WOOD Family (4: Harriette, Frances, Bella, Alfred), the English Nightingales; PROFESSOR ABT (Optical Illusions, Electric and Calcium Light Effects); VERNER CLARGES (Eccentric Comedian), AUGUSTUS VIRTO (Musical Genius), JAGENDORFER (Austrian Hercules), WILLIAM WIBBERLY (English Juggler), MENDOZA (Animal Impersonator), PRINCE EDGAR (High wire act), J. H. MOWBRIE (Equilibrist).

Act 1, Scene 1: In the Clouds. Darkness. Cupid's Birth. The Vision. The Fatal Shot. Struck in the Heart. *Scene 2*: Village Green. Old Darmstead troubled by his poverty. The Oppressive Sisters. Choosing the May-Queen. Bad news. Arline's Bravery. Arrival of Prince Forethought. He meets Arline. Cupid's Aim. Love at first sight. Now let the sports begin. The Prince's invitation to the Garden Party. *Scene 3*: In the Woods. The Wicked Wolf. Arline on her journey. In Danger. Cupid to the Rescue. *Scene 4*: Old Margo's Cottage. Arrival of the Wolf. His Disguise. Arline and Her Mission to Charity. Again in Danger. Cat vs. Wolf. Darmstead to the Rescue. Death of the Wolf.

Act 2, Scene 1: Arline lost in the Woods. Her Dream and Vision of the Future. Awakening. Was but a dream. Let me dream again. Arline deploring her friendless condition. Appearance of Margo. Instantaneous transformations. Arline's wishes realized. Her departure in a coach drawn by Bicycles fully equipped. Margo, the Witch, Transformed. The Silbons. Spectacular Electric Light Effects. *Scene 2*: Old Darmstead at home, annnoyed by his creditors. *Scene 3*: The Garden Party. Arrival of the Guests. "The Unknown." Twelve o'clock. Disappearance of the unknown. The Lost Slipper. Disappointment of the Sisters. Margo, the Witch successful. Triumph of Arline. The Betrothal. "Our happiness has been ordained above, and brought about by Cupid, God of Love."

ACT 1[61]
Scene 2
Prince Edgar on the Invisible Wire
W. Wibberly in his juggling feats
Julia and Frances Wood, "Me and My Old Man"
J. H. Mowbrie (Equilibrist)
Jargfendorfer, The Austrian Hercules (Feats of Strength)
The Elliotts (Whirling Phantoms)
The Silbons, Aerialists

ACT 2
Scene 1
Professor Abt and his wonderful Grecian Mystery, consisting of beautiful Art Pictures, Dissolving Chromotopes, Dancing Skeleton.
The Silbon's Beautiful Acrobatic Statue Entertainment
Scene 2
Vocal and Instrumental EntertainmentWood Family
Scene 3
The Elliotts, the Unicycles, Grand Quadrilles on Wheels

[59]Written expressly to exhibit the unequalled specialties of the 4 Silbons and the 6 Elliotts.
[60]Program misstates author's name as Lyodd Clarence.
[61]Among the musical numbers performed according to reviewers was "Wait til the Clouds Roll By."

1884.62

MAM'ZELLE

A Farcical Comedy in Three Acts, 6 Scenes. Play by George H. Jessop and William Gill. Stage manager, A. K. Feeley. Acting manager, Edgar Strakosch. Musical director, J. E. Nicol. Produced by the Aimée Comedy Company (Management, Maurice Grau.). Opened 15 December 1884 at the Fifth Avenue Theatre and closed 27 December 1884 after 14 performances in repertory[62].

CAST: *Toinette Jacotot*, a little French milliner known as Mam'zelle: Mlle. MARIE AIMÉE. *Fleur de Lis*, the Songbird of two continents: Mlle. MARIE AIMÉE. *T. Tarleton Tupper, Esq.*, a Husband who is snubbed: J. O. BARROWS. *Lionel Leslie*, a Bachelor who is worried: W. A. WHITECAR. *Bob Pritchard*, a Lawyer's Clerk who is also jealous: FRANK E. LAMB. *Colonel Hiram Poster*, a Manager who is prosperous: Newton Chisnell. *François*, a French American who is mysterious: Lester Victor. *Toppleby*, a Waiter who is ubiquitous: A. K. Feeley. *Thisway*, an Usher who is disgusted: J. A. Anderson. *O'Club*, a Policeman, who is "One of the Finest": Frank Roberts. *Mrs. Louisa Tupper*, a Wife who is Bored: LAURA WALLACE. *Mary*, a Domestic who is ambitious: CHARLINE WEIDMAN.

Act 1: Apartments in T. T. Tupper's House.

Act 2, Scene 1: Lobby of Poster's Café Chantant. *Scene 2*: Stage of the Café Chantant. *Scene 3*: End of the performance at Café Chantant. *Scene 4*: After the performance on the stage.

Act 3: Elegant Apartments in Fifth Avenue Hotel. Off to the Texas Ranch.

MUSICAL NUMBERS[63]
In Act 2, Scene 2, Aimée will render some of her most famous and world-renowned Chansonettes. Also "Lovely Angeline" (Song and dance expressly composed by Frank B. Converse) and conclude with her great specialty, "Pretty as a Picture," (Music by Brigham Bishop, Lyrics by George Cooper).

1884.63

PRINCE METHUSALEM

A Revival of the Opera Comique in Three Acts, 4 Scenes[64]. (Original Viennese libretto, 'Prinz Methusalem' by Karl Treumann, adapted from a libretto by Victor Wilder and Alfred Delacour.) English libretto adapted by Sydney Rosenfeld. Music by Johann Strauss. Scenery by Philip Goatcher. Musical director, Selli Simonson. Produced by the McCaull Opera Company (Joseph A. McCaull). Opened 15 December 1884 at the Casino Theatre and closed 10 January 1885 after 28 performances.[65]

CAST: *Prince Methusalem*, Son of Cyprian: BERTHA RICCI. *Pulcinella*, Daughter of Sigismund: ROSALBA BEECHER. *Sophistica*, Wife of Cyprian: ALICE MAY. *Spadi*: HELEN STANDISH. *Sigismund*, Duke of Trocadero: FRANCIS WILSON. *Cyprian*, Duke of Ricarac: A. W. MAFLIN. *Trombonius*, composer of the future: HUBERT WILKE. *Count Vulcanio*, Grand Chamberlain: ALFRED KLEIN. *Carbonazzi*: GEORGE BONIFACE, JR. *M. Fierstein*, *Mandelbaum*, Ambassadors from Ricarac: C. Kauffman, H. McDonough. *First Bravo*: L. C. Schrader. *Second Bravo*: E. H. Van Vechten. *Third Bravo*: A. M. Barbara. *Fourth Bravo*: E. Platti. *Night Watchman*: A. D. Barker. *The Little Colonel*: A. W. Maflin, Jr.

[62]Played return engagements 7 December 1885 at the Grand Opera House, 5 April 1886 and 21 March 1887 at the People's Theatre.
[63]Also performed by Mlle. Aimée during the national tour in this spot:
"Love at Sight"
M. Aimée
(*Music by* J. E. McNicol.)
[64]First produced in New York in English 9 July 1883 at the Casino Theatre for 102 performances. For Synopsis of Scenes and Musical Numbers, see 1883 Casino Theatre production.
[65]Stage director, costume design uncredited. Original stage direction by Jesse Williams, presumably restaged by the stage manager, A. W. Maflin. Original costumes by Mme. Printz

1884.64 A TRIP TO AFRICA

An Opéra Comique in Three Acts[66]. Original Viennese libretto to the operette, 'Die Afrikareise,' by Richard Genée and Moritz West. (Entire production under the personal direction of James C. Duff.). Music by Franz von Suppé. Scenery by Joseph Clare. Costume designs by Mme. Loe. Musical director, Adolf Nowak. Produced by James C. Duff. Opened 23 December 1884 at the Standard Theatre and closed 21 February 1885 after 62 performances.[67].

CAST: *Titania Fanfani*, a young heiress: EMMA SEEBOLD. *Tessa*, a Neapolitan milliner: MAE ST. JOHN. *Buccametta*, her mother: HATTIE NEFFLEN. *Sebie*, an Abyssinian slave: Miss ENGLANDER. *Antarsid*, Prince of the Maronites: A. L. KING. *Fanfani Pasha*: CHARLES STANLEY. *Miradillo*, a tourist: ALEXANDER KLEIN. *Pericles*, hotel keeper: JOHN E. NASH. *Nakid*, a Coptic in poison and perfumes: Fred Clifton. A *Muezzin*: R. S. Imano. *Hosh*, a slave: Ed. Sullivan. *First Sais*: C. L. Weels. *Second Sais*: William Gillon. A *Beggar*: M. Hughes. *Maronites, Hotel Servants, Guests of Fanfani Pasha, Slave Traders, Greek and Arabian People.*

Act 1: An open square at Cairo.

Act 2: Fanfani Pasha's Villa at Cairo.

Act 3: The Interior of Africa.

ACT 1[68]

Introduction (We're awaiting at our stands)
J. E. Nash, Miss Englander, Chorus

Tourist Song (Who's talking here about me?)
A. Klein, Miss Englander, J. E. Nash, Chorus

Appearance of the Muezzin (Now I have, the best I could, explained to you)
A. Klein, J. E. Nash, R. S. Imano, Chorus

Entrée of the Prince (Prince Antarsid now approaches)
A. L. King, C. L. Weels, W. Gillon, Maronites, Pages

Like winds that lightly
A. L. King

Titania's Entrance (O, what do I see!)
E. Seebold, Miss Englander, A. L. King, A. Klein, F. Clifton, J. E. Nash

Tho' we were strangers hitherto
E. Seebold

Quartette (Well, that's astounding surely)
E. Seebold, A. Klein, C. Stanley, J. E. Nash

Trio (Big beard visage flaming)
C. Stanley, M. St. John, H. Nefflen

Finale (Hoio! Hoio let music sound Holaro!)
Principals, Chorus

ACT 2

Introduction and Chorus of Slaves (Feasting, dancing mirth and revels gay)

Entrance of Fanfani (Kush! Kush! Kush!)
C. Stanley

Snuff Song (Aught to say against snuff taking)
C. Stanley
(*Arranged by* Adolph Neuendorff)

Flower Duet (A word of magic import)
E. Seebold, A. L. King

Ensemble (Let us stay here where we may hear)
E. Sebold, A. Klein, M. St. John, N. Nefflen, A. L. King, C. Stanley

"Spring-Tide" (Spring hath made a new appearance)
(*Music by* Adolph Neuendorff)

Duet (Ah I could not well conceal it)
M. St. John, A. Klein

Trio (I come just right)
C. Stanley, M. St. John, A. Klein

Finale (Beiram, the pleasant feast at last is here)
Principals, Chorus

ACT 3

Chorus (Now the morn anew is breaking)

Romance (What a dream)
A. L. King

Trio (Africa is full of danger)
E. Seebold, A. L. King, A. Klein

Entrance of the Bedouins (We Bedouins of the Nile)
Chorus

Finale (Mira Mira Fata Morgana)
Principals, Chorus

[66]Previously produced in New York in German 27 December 1883 at the Thalia Theatre.
[67]English version by Emil Schwab, (music) adapted and arranged for the American stage by Adolph Neuendorff The English adapters' names do not appear in New York programs; they are taken from a November 1884 Boston program, which producer James C. Duff credits as his inspiration for the New York production.
[68]Musical numbers not listed in programs. List prepared from published American piano vocal score (White Smith & Co., Boston, 1884), translated and adapted by Emil Schwab. Libretto adapted and arranged for the English stage by Ad. Neuendorff, published by George Wyatt, Boston, 1884. Interpolation as per published sheet music:
"Life"
(*Lyrics by* George Russell Jackson.)

1884.65 VASSAR GIRLS

A Musical Vaudeville in One Act, preceded by a vaudeville Olio. Vaudeville by (Francis) Leon and (Frank) Cushman. Musical direction, Jesse Williams. Produced by (John) Koster and (Albert) Bial. Opened 27 December 1884 at Koster & Bial's Concert Hall and closed 10 January 1885 after 16 performances.

Olio: Orchestral Selections; Pauline Harvey (Balladist). Vic's Coachman, a new Local and Musical Sketch. *Victoria—Whole—Scamp Kerosini*: The Only (FRANCIS) LEON. *Ernest Shilling—Coupe (nee wholeskamp)*: FRANK CUSHMAN. Synopsis: After the "BRIDLE" "I am no longer" Sir, Single. Affairs are "HALTERED"a "BIT." "Long may we rein." "Papa rejects us!" "Then he must be "BLINDER" than ever." This "SPURS" me on to fresh endeavor. Are there any "TRACES" of relenting? "No!" "I am dreaming, Sad-dle-y dreaming!" CAPITAL vs. LABOR.

Olio: The Caron Brothers, George and Alphons, as the Acrobatic Dudes; The St. Felix Sisters; Pauline Harvey (Balladist); Orchestral Selections.

VASSAR GIRLS CAST: *Mr. Theophilus Nubbs*, a Theatrical Manager, a victim of circumstances: FRANK CUSHMAN. *Ginger*, head-waiter at Vassar: George Caron. *Sally*, stage-struck help: Sally Caron. *Miss Cora Monten*, a pupil waiting to be a Dutchess: Bessie Temple. *Miss Sarah Cherrington*, a girl that's up to the times, gets her fine work in on the duke—her lady friend gets left—A real good-hearted girl—will give you anything—she don't want—generous to a fault: The Only (FRANCIS) LEON. *Chambermaids, Waiters, etc.*: Misses Louise Hill, Dora Miller, Sallie Clarens, Hattie White, Marie Darien, Cora Bonheur, etc.

MUSICAL NUMBERS

Vassar March
"Only This"
Duet from IL TROVATORE
"Vassar Waiters—Jubilee"
"Swim Out"
"Laughing Yodel"
"An American Toast by the Liberty Amazons"

1884.66 WE, US AND CO. AT MUD SPRINGS

A Whimsical Musical Absurdity (Farce Comedy) in Three Acts. Play by William A. Mestayer and Charles Barnard. Music by Frederick Eustis. Scenery by John Thompson. Musical director, Fred Eustis. Produced by William A. Mestayer and Theresa Vaughn (John H. Russell, Manager). Opened 29 December 1884 at the Fifth Avenue Theatre and closed 17 January 1885 after 24 performances; re-opened a return engagement 20 April 1885 at the Fifth Avenue Theatre and closed 16 May 1885 after 32 additional performances.[69] Total: 56 performances.

[69]Musical numbers not listed in programs. List prepared from published American piano vocal score (White Smith & Co., Boston, 1884), translated and adapted by Emil Schwab. Libretto adapted and arranged for the English stage by Ad. Neuendorff, published by George Wyatt, Boston, 1884. Interpolation as per published sheet music:
"Life"
(*Lyrics by* George Russell Jackson.)

CAST: *T. Willie Rockingham*, Athletic: WILLIAM A. MESTAYER. *Dr. Mulo Medicus*, Veterinary: Ezra F. Kendall. *Dr. Pulsiver*, Hydropath: W. F. Rochester. *Tammany K. O'Turk*, Political: Charles F. McCarthy. *Bedalia Macochintoddy*: Charles F. McCarthy. *Knox Dunlap*, Terpsichorean: Samuel Reed. *Kerfew Tolls*, Culchaw: Harry Amberg. *George Magillicuddy*, a Terror: Joseph Ott. *Melinda Magilicuddy*, an Heiress: THERESA VAUGHN. *Euphemia Coppergall*, an Affinity: Jennie Fisher. *Cylinder Cogwheel*, Operatic: Marie Bockel. *Bella Bustle*, a Reminder: Libbie Noxon. *Rosa Perfectus*, de trop: Belle Deering.

Act 1: Dr. Pulsiver's Office in New York.

Act 2: Mud Springs, Sunset. (Thompson.)

Act 3: The Revolving House.

1885.01 NANON

A Comic Opéra in Three Acts, in German[70]. Libretto ('Nanon, die Wirthin vom goldenene Lamm') by F. Zell, based on the play "Ninon, Nanon et Madame de Maintenon" by Emmanuel Théaulon, Armand d'Artois and Lesguillon. Music by Richard Genée. Produced under the stage direction of L. Ottomeyer. Musical director, Ed. Boelz. Produced by Gustav Amberg. Opened 2 January 1885 at the Thalia Theatre and closed 25 April 1885 after (56) performances in repertory.

CAST: *Nanon Patin*, The Hostess of the Golden Lamb: EMMY MEFFERT. *Ninon d'l'Enclos*: FRANZISKA RABERG. *Gaston*, Page to Ninon: Pavlowna Büchner. *Mme. de Maintenon*: HELENE DELIA. *Jacqueline*: Hulda Michaelis. *Mme. de Fulpert*: Charlotte Random. *Mlle. d'Armenonville*: Sophie Zanaufchek. *Mme. de Frontenac*: Johanna Schatz. *Comtesse d'Houlières*: Hermine Lorenz. *Thérèse*: Albertine Sabrich. *Lisette*: Marie Schlag. *Marion*: Duicha Beroni. *Marquis d'Aubigné*: FERDINAND SCHÜTZ. *Vicomte de Marsillac*, (Hector), Nephew of Marquis de Marsillac: EDUARD ELSBACH. *Abbé La Plâtre*: Bernard Rank. *Bombardini*, Drum-Major: Ernst Gschmeidler. *Sergeant*: Hermann Gerold. *Commissioner*: Heinrich Zilzer. *Notary*: Arthur Stoltzenberg. *Marquis de Marsillac*: MAX LUBE. *King Louis XIV*: OTTO MEYER. *Officers, Court Ladies and Gentlemen, Soldiers, Peasants, etc.*

Act 1: Inn of the Golden Lamb.

Act 2: Salon of Ninon d L'Enclos.

Act 3: Sanctuary of Mme. de Maintenon.

ACT 1[71]

"Bei Nanon ist nicht blos der herrlichste Wein" (Opening Chorus)
E. Meffert, Chorus

"Mein freundliches Wirtshaus umvankt ist's Weine" (Drinking Song)
E. Meffert

"Den Kopf jetzt in die Höh" (Song and Chorus)
E. Meffert, E. Elsbach, M. Lube, Chorus

"Einst mals hielt vor dieser Schenke" (Song)
E. Meffert, E. Elsbach, M. Lube

Aufmarsch der Trommler und Pfeifer und Minnelied

"Was ist denn heut wohl für ein Tag" (Song of the Minstrel)
F. Schütz

"Setzen den Fall wir nur" (Duet)
E. Meffert, F. Raberg

"Das war ein Trunk der uns behagte" (Quartet)
E. Meffert, F. Schütz, E. Elsbach, M. Lube

"Hier sind alle Anrevwandten" (Finale)
Chorus

"Sehan, Onkel Mathieu bringt ein Schweinchen"

ACT 2

"Bei Ninon sich einzuführen" (Opening Chorus)

"Was in Frankreich heut gefällt"
Gaston

"Treublich ich stets" (Song)
F. Raberg, P. Büchner, J. Schatz, H. Lorenz, B. Rank

"Was ist denn heut wohl für ein Tag" (Minnelied)
F. Schütz

"Tritt man bei Ninon an" (Song)
E. Elsbach

"Die Herren von Marseillac! Wilkommen meine Herrn!" (Sextet)
P. Büchner, F. Raberg, J. Schütz, H. Lorenz, E. Elsbach, M. Lube

"Grignan! Nanon! Ist's möglich?" (Duo)
E. Meffert, F. Schütz

"Und nun sagen Sie geschwind"
F. Schütz

"Jung an Jahrent" (Song)
E. Elsbach

"Bei Ninon sich amüsiven" (Finale)

Minuet

"Beim ersten Mal, wo er sich geschlagen" (Waltz)
F. Raberg

ACT 3

"Anna, zu Dir ist mein liebster Gang" (Introduction)
B. Rank

"Wenn ich auch Philosoph bin" (Couplets)
M. Lube

"Was ist denn heut wohl für ein Tag" (Trio)
F. Schütz, M. Lube, B. Rank

"Ich brauch keine Professoren" (Couplets)
E. Meffert

"Heil sei der Gräfin Delicat" (Finale)

1885.02 McALLISTER'S LEGACY

A Farcical Comedy in Three Acts. Play (and lyrics) by Edward Harrigan. Music by David Braham. (Staged by Edward Harrigan.) Scenery by Charles W. Witham. Mechanical effects by William McMurray. Properties by Robert Fuller. Dresses by Miss Mary Jack. Musical director, David Braham. Produced by (Edward) Harrigan and (Tony) Hart. Opened 5 January 1885 at the New Park Theatre, moved 2 March 1885 to the 14th Street Theatre, and closed 14 March 1885 after 80 performances.

CAST: *Doctor Patrick McAllister*: EDWARD HARRIGAN. *Molly McGouldrick*: TONY HART. *July Showers*: JOHN WILD. *Valentine Clancy*: HARRY FISHER. *Stephen Tewksbury*: M. Bradley. *Randolph Ruskin*: James Fox. *Frederick Bichonnet*: Charles Sturges. *Rhoda Ruskin*: James Tierney. *Standish Steadfast*: George Merritt. *Ellen Daly*: George Merritt. *Baldy O'Brien*: John Sparks. *Mr. Bubble*: John Murphy. *Mr. David Lerium*: G. L. Stout. *Richard McGouldrick*: W. J. Dagnan. *Beauregard Clayborne*: William West. *Dr. Dooley*: M. Foley. *Phadrig McIrnerny*: Thomas Ray. *Quigley McQuillan*: Charles Coffey. *Alex Blake*: E. Murphy. *Peter McAllarney*: James McCullough. *Doctor P. McAllister*: William Merritt. *Mrs. Helvetia Van Dusen*: ANNIE YEAMANS. *Tillie Van Dusen*: ANNA LANGDON. *Rosy Healy*: ADA FARWELL. *Sarah Gaffney*: A. Scallan. *Legatees*: Misses Sadie Morris, Kate Langdon, Annie Hall, Emily Yeamans, Marie Gorenflo, Lizzie Finn, Della Stilwell, Jennie Bageard. Messrs. Emil Husel, Edward Murphy, James Brevarde, Joseph Davis. *Stock Brokers, Communists, Policemen, etc.*

Act 1: View of the Interior of Molly McGouldrick's Farm House and Baldy O'Brien's Smithy.

Act 2, Scene 1: Waiting Room in the Van Dusen Mansion. *Scene 2*: Hallway in the Rookery in Africa, on Thompson Street. *Scene 3*: The Levee at the Colored Brokers. How Money Is Made by Millionaires.

Act 3: Interior of New York Stock Exchange. New Tennessee. A Warm Day from Trinity to teh Ferry.

MUSICAL NUMBERS

"Pat and His Little Brown Mare"

"Blow the Bellows, Blow"

"Mister Dooley's Geese"

"Molly"

"Oh My! How We Pose" (Xylophone solo by Ed King)

1885.03 OVER THE GARDEN WALL

A Comic Complication (Farce Comedy) in Three Acts, constructed for laughing purposes only. Play by Scott Marble and George S. Knight. Opened 5 January 1885 at Tony Pastor's 14th Street Theatre and closed 10 January 1885 after 8 performances; returned 23 March 1885 to the Fifth Avenue Theatre and closed 4 April 1885 after 16 performances; returned 18

---

[70]English language premiere in New York. First produced in New York in German 2 January 1885 at the Thalia Theatre for (56) performances in repertory.

[71]Musical numbers not listed in programs. List prepared from published German piano vocal score (White, Smith & Co., Boston).

May 1885 to Niblo's Garden for 8 additional performances.[72] Total: 32 performances.

CAST: The Following Persons are all in trouble: *J. Julius Snitz*, a Politician, Poet and Husband: GEORGE S. KNIGHT. *Julius Snitz, Jr.*, his nephew, specially engaged: R. E. GRAHAM. *Tom Tracy*, Snitz's friend: Seth M. Crane. *Moses Wrangle*, discoverer of "Wrangle's New Life for Infants": T. J. Jackson. *Our Own Bridget*, a servant: GEORGE W. MONROE. *Mrs. Betsy Snitz*, Wife of J. Julius: Therese Newcomb. *Rosa*, Wife of Julius, Jr.: Marion Fleming. *Nellie Wrangle*, daughter of Moses: MRS. GEORGE S. KNIGHT [Sophie Worrell].

Time: Suit yourself. *Place*: Anywhere, or thereabouts.

Act 1: Eventide. This side the Wall. Suspicion!

Act 2: Early Morn. Both sides the Wall. Accusation!

Act 3: That night. Same as Act 1. _______!

ACT 1

"The Gay Hussar"[73]
S. M. Crane

The Band
Quartet

The Kazoo
Quartet

Medley
Quartet

"The Man That Knows It All" (from INVESTIGATION)
G. S. Knight, S. M. Crane, H. Haskell
(*Music by* David Braham. *Lyrics by* Edward Horrigan.)

ACT 2

"My Pretty Baby"[74]
M. Fleming

"Caroline" (Carolina)
Mrs. G. S. Knight

"Oh, Maria" (Oh, Marie)
Mrs. G. S. Knight

"Dear Familiar Faces"
G. S. Knight, H. Haskell

"Not Much"
G. S. Knight, H. Haskell

"Far Away"
G. S. Knight

Parody
G. S. Knight

ACT 3[75]

"Eh! Did I Hear You"
G. W. Monroe

"Moonlight"
Mrs. G. S. Knight

Spanish Song
Mrs. G. S. Knight

"Tyrolean"
Mrs. G. S. Knight, S. M. Crane

"To Whit, To Who"
Quartet

Finale
Company

[72]Stage direction, music, scenery and costume design uncredited. By November 1886, a national tour of the show contained entirely new and different songs and specialties. See separate entry in 1886-87 season.

[73]Replaced for the Fifth Avenue Theatre engagement by:
"Baby's Smile"

[74]Replaced for the Fifth Avenue Theatre engagement by:
"Open Your Window"
(*Music and Lyrics by* R. E. Graham.)

[75]Added for the Fifth Avenue Theatre engagement to Act 3, following "To Whit, To Who":
"The Scapegoat"
S. M. Crane (Tom Tracy)

1885.04 A BOTTLE OF INK

Rice's Surprise Party in a Novel Entertainment (Farce Comedy) in Two Acts. Play by George H. Jessop and William Gill. Produced under the direction of John A. Mackay. Musical director, George W. Towle. Produced by Edward E. Rice. Opened 6 January 1885 at the New York Comedy Theatre and closed 25 January 1885 after 24 performances.

CAST: *Jefferson Jingo*, Editor of the Daily Prairie Blizzard, a Journal of Civilization: JOHN A. MACKAY. *Pie*, his Confidential Office Boy and Blotter: GEORGE A. SCHILLER. *Josiah Buttlebury*, an Ambitious Citizen: CHARLES L. HARRIS. *Hermann Zwugg*, not an Ambitious Citizen: JEFFERSON DeANGELIS. *Signor O'Relli*, Tenor in the Vere de Vere Organization: C. F. Lang. *Pete*, the Terror of Salt Canyon: N. S. Burnham. *Clara Vere de Vere*, Star of the Vere de Vere Organization: MAUDE BEVERLY. *Eliza Ann*, a Waif with a Mission: HATTIE STARR. *Mrs. Buttlebury*, Wife of Josiah: EDITH JENNESS. *Mrs. Zwugg*, Wife of Herman: Florence Conliffe. *Miss Flyaway*: Sadie Cortelyou. *Kitty*, Buttlebury's Daughter: IDA MÜLLE. (*Specialties*: J. P. Locke, Maud Miller.)

Act 1: Editorial Room of the "Prairie Blizzard," Prairie City.

Act 2: A Forest Scene in the Pairie City Theatre. The Rehearsal.

ACT 2

The Tyrolean Warblers
H. Starr, E. Jenness, S. Cortelyou

Marvelous Double Cornet Solo (Specialty)
J. P. Locke

Grand Scene from PRINCESS IDA, Vocal gems
(*Music by* Arthur Sullivan. *Lyrics by* William S. Gilbert.)
Princess Ida: H. Starr. *Psyche*: I. Mulle. *Melissa*: E. Jenness. *Prince Hilarian*: C. F. Lang. *Cyril*: J. DeAngelis. *Florian*: N. S. Burnham.

Reminiscences of Lecocq's charming opera, MADAME ANGOT
M. Beverly

Scene from PYGMALION AND GALATEA
Pygmalion: E. Jenness. *Galatea*: H. Starr.

Jefferson Jingo's Opportunity (Imitations of leading actors)
J. Mackay

"He Talks Like a Polly" (Latest sensation)
M. Beverly

Grand Scene from ORPHEUS AND EURYDICE
(*Music by* Jacques Offenbach.)
Jupiter: H. Starr. *Juno*: M. Miller. *Cupid*: I. Mulle. *Venus*: S. Cortelyou. *Mercury*: E. Jenness. *Hebe*: E. Jenness.

Operatic Potpurri Par Excellence
(Company)

1885.05 APAJUNE,
the Water Sprite

A Revival of the Comic Opera in Three Acts[76]. Original Viennese libretto, 'Apajune, Der Wassermann' by F. Zell and Richard Genée. English adaptation by Sydney Rosenfeld. Music by Carl Millöcker. Stage director, W. H. Daly. Scenery by Gaspard Maeder (Acts 1, 3), Henry E. Hoyt (Act 2). Costumes embroidered by Gantillon. Master machinist, G. P. Sherwood, Jr. Musical director, Selli Simonson. Produced by the McCaull Opera Company (John A. McCaull). Opened 12 January 1885 at the Casino Theatre and closed 21 February 1885 after 42 performances.

CAST: *Prince Alamir Prutschesko*, a Roumanian Bovar: FRANCIS WILSON. *Heloise*, his wife, formerly a Parisian hotel-keeper: MATHILDE COTTRELLY. *Ilinka*, his niece, in love with Manol Nitchano: Belle Archer. *Manol Nitchano*, Captain of the Roumanian Hussars: WILL S. RISING. *Marcu*, a young peasant: Jay Taylor. *Natalitza*, his bride, "the Pearl of Totroceni": LILLY POST. *Alexandri*, Steward of the Prince's Roumanian Estates: HERBERT ARCHER. *Joza*, a sergeant in Nitchano's regiment: Ellis Ryse. *Michaelo*, the village provost: A. M. Barbara. *Jacob*, the tavern-keeper: Emil Senger. *Dabroi, Katinka*, Natalitza's parents: L. A. Schrader, Miss Perring. *Carolinka*, a peasant girl: Kate Ethel. *Dominique, Louise*, servants at the Castle: A. H. Hall, Rose Marion. *Courier*: Florence Bell.

[76]First produced in New York 25 February 1882 at the Bijou Opera House for 15 performances. For Synopsis of Scenes, see original 1882 production. Musical numbers not listed in programs; no published libretto or score found.

1885.06

THE KINDERGARTEN

A Musical Comedy in Three Acts. Book, music and lyrics by Robert Griffin Morris. Musical director, C. F. Titus. Produced by Harry Williams. Opened 2 February 1885 at Leavitt and Pastor's Third Avenue Theatre and closed 7 February 1885 after 8 performances; returned 11 June 1885 to Poole's Theatre and closed 16 June 1885 after 10 additional performances.

CAST: *Philander Montmorenci St. Clair Dutchene*: STANLEY MACY. *Orlando Smythe*: . *The Grinder*: *The Sleepy Boy*: GEORGE BRUENiNG. *The Widow's Tiger*: GEORGE BRUENING. *Tommy Magee*: *Miranda Magee*: ADA DEAVES. *Ivy Magee*: RILLIE DEAVES. *Leonora Phosphates*: *Tilly Smythe*: *Sissy Racket*: . Principals also included LYDIA YEAMANS, JENNIE YEAMANS, J. W. CAFFREY, FANNY COHEN, MAUD LEITH, Eugene Wellington, D. L. Williams.

ACT 1[77]

"I'm So Sad"

"Dancing"

"Dorothy"

"Christmas Bells"

"Rafferty's Daughter Kate"

Medley
Company

ACT 2

"Solfeggio Company"

"Please to Put That Down"

"Orange Blossoms"

Spanish Dance

"Waiting for Charley"

"Eyes So Bright"

"Magnolia"

"Soldier Boy Canteen"

"Nellie's Blue Eyes"

"King of the Swells"

"The Little Pickaninny from Ole Varginny"
L. Yeamans

Medley
Company

ACT 3

"Widow Magee"

"Happiest Hours from the Twilight"

Song

"Sunset" (Duet)

"Let's All Obey"

"Minnie Gavotte"
Company

Finale

1885.07

THE DRUM-MAJOR'S DAUGHTER

An Opera Comique in Three Acts, 5 Scenes[78]. Original French libretto ('La Fille du Tambour-Major') by Henri Chivot and Alfred Duru. Music by Jacques Offenbach. Costumes designed by W. T. Carleton. Scenery by John A. Thompson. Conductor, Signor F. Intropodi. Produced by the Carleton English Opera Company (William T. Carleton, Proprietor). Opened 2 February 1885 at the 14th Street Theatre and closed 7 February 1885 after 8 performances.

CAST: *Stella*: DORA WILEY. *Griolet*, the Little Drummer: JESSIE BARTLETT DAVIS. *Claudine*: ROSE BEAUDET. *Monthabor*, the Drum Major: W. H. CLARK. *Duke Della Volta*: RICHARD GOLDEN. *Duchess Della Volta*: Clara Wisdom. *The Abbess*: JESIE BARTLETT DAVIS. *Bianca*: Emily Young. *Lorenza*: Miss Pettitt. *Marquis Bambini*: Frank Doud. *Clampas*: F. Risdale. *Sergeant*: Mr. Dixon. *Captain Robert*: WILLIAM T. CARLETON. *Soldiers, Nuns, Lords, Ladies, Brigands, Peasants.*

Act 1: Garden of the Convent at Biella. Italy, 1800.

Act 2: Salon at the Palazza Della Volta, at Novare.

Act 3, Scene 1: A Wooded Ravine. *Scene 2*: Interior of Inn. *Scene 3*: Public Place in Milan.

1885.08

IXION! or, The Man at the Wheel

A Revival of the Burlesque in Two Acts, 3 Scenes. (Original) Play by F. C. Burnand. Adaptation and lyrics by Sydney Rosenfeld. Music selected, composed and arranged by Michael Connelly. Whole production under the supervision of Townsend Percy. Scenery and costumes designed by Alfred Thompson. Dances arranged by Jefferson DeAngelis. Musical director, William J. Rostetter. Opened 4 February 1885 at the Comedy Theatre and closed 21 March 1885 after 53 performances.

CAST: *Ixion*: ALICE HARRISON. *Cupid*: KATE FOLEY. *Jupiter*: CARRIE GODFREY. *Juno*: GERTRUDE GARDNER. *Minerva*: HARRY BROWN. *Ganymede*: AMY AMES. *Apollo*: Kathleen Lynne. *Mercury*: Eva Barrington. *Mars*: BELLE URQUHART. *Diana*: BÉBÉ VINING. *Bacchus*: Beulah Sandford. *The Eagle*: Eleanor Ellis. *Clerk of the Weather*: Lizzie Bradley. *Senator Curz*: Sidney Haven. *Editor Shurtis*: Rita Chase. *Queen Dia*: Mabel DeBabian. *First Citizen*: Miss Thropp. *Second Citizen*: Fanny McNeil. *Third Citizen*: Mabel Bennett. *Venus*: PAULINE HALL.

Citizens, Gods and Goddesses: Misses Hall, Champness, Duchateau, Holzman, Elwood, Howard, Lonsdale, Pierson, Price, Etheal, Barton, Miles, Thompson, DeVielle, Wilson, Gilbert, Sullivan, Elton, Thropp, Belmore, Ennis, Truepenny, Hoffman, Hamilton, White

Act 1, Scene 1: A Wood in Thessaly. *Scene 2*: The Wine Vault of Bacchus (on Olympus). *Scene 3*: Reception Hall in the Palace of Juno.

Act 2, Scene 1: The Sun Fire Insurance Company's Office. *Scene 2*: Cupid's Chateau in Spain.

ACT 1

Opening Chorus

"Away Up in the Skies" (Duet)

"Bye and Bye"

"It's Different When You're Full" (Topical Song)

"Night in Venice" (Duet)
(*Music by* Luigi Arditti.)

"Mother Dooley's Geese" (from McALLISTER'S LEGACY)
(*Music by* Dave Braham. *Lyrics by* Edward Harrigan.)

"A Little Doll" (Song)

"Kitty"
(*Music by* Michael Connolly.)

"Hidden Music"
(*Music by* Julius J. Lyons.)

"'Tis I Alone Can Tell" (Song)

"Ixion March"
(*Music by* Julius J. Lyons.)

"Never a Law to Prevent It" (Topical Song)

Finale
(*Music by* Michael Connelly.)

ACT 2

"I'm a Chappie" (Song)

"Blow the Bellows" (from McALLISTER'S LEGACY)
(*Music by* Dave Braham. *Lyrics by* Edward Harrigan.)

"Nanon Waltz" (from NANON)
(*Music by* Richard Genée.)

"My Roundelay" (Spanish)

"Patter Song"
(*Music by* Julius J. Lyons.)

Gavotte from NANON
(*Music by* Richard Genée.)

Solo and Quartette
(*Music by* ? Yeu.)

The Horn, Apajune
(*Music by* ? Millor.)

[77]For subsequent tour, Robert Griffin Morris composed the following new songs: "Sweet Dudity," "Moleem Saboo," "Cootch Poor Waunee," "Learned Man," and "Hard to Please."

[78]First produced in New York in French 13 September 1880 at the Standard Theatre for 23 performances. English language premiere, adaptation uncredited. Possibly Henry B. Farnie's English version, revised, or without credit.

"Coo Song" (Solo)
(*Music by* Julius J. Lyons.)
"How We Pose" (from McALLISTER'S LEGACY)
(*Music by* Dave Braham. *Lyrics by* Edward Harrigan.)
"Amazon March"
"(It was) A Dream" (Song)(from ADONIS)
(*Music by* Alfred G. Robyn. *Lyrics by* Annie R. Noxon.)
Finale

1885.09 THE MASCOTTE

A Revival of the Opéra-comique in Three Acts[79]. Original French libretto by Henri Chivot and Alfred Duru. Music by Edmond Audran. Costumes designed by W. T. Carleton. Conductor, Signor F. Intropodi. Produced by the Carleton English Opera Company. (W. T. Carleton, Proprietor). Opened 9 February 1885 at the 14th Street Theatre and closed 21 February 1885 after 16 performances.

CAST: *Bettina*, the "Mascot": DORA WILEY. *Fiametta*: ROSE BEAUDET. *Angelo*: Clara Wisdom. *Pages to the King (4)*: *Unigi*: Miss Young. *Paolo*: Miss Bartlett. *Antonio*: Miss Schroeder. *Marco*: Miss Boyton. *Prince Lorenzo*: GUSTAVE ADOLPHI. *Rocco*, a Farmer: Richard Golden. *Prince Frederick*: Jessie Bartlett Davis. *Matteo*, Inn-Keeper: Ed Horan. *Sergeant*: Frank Risdale. *The Doctor*: Frank Doud. *Pippo*, a Shepherd: W. T. CARLETON. *Peasants, Courtiers, Soldiers, etc.*

1885.10 THREE OF A KIND

Nate Salsbury's Troubadours in a Return Engagement of the Farce Comedy in Three Acts[80]. Play by Edward E. Kidder. Acting manager, Frank Maeder. Musical director, W. Barter Johns. Opened 9 February 1885 at the Grand Opera House and closed 14 February 1885 after 8 performances; re-opened 23 March 1885 at Henry C. Miner's People's Theatre for an additional 8 performances.[81]

CAST: *Three of a Kind*: *Jack Potts*: NATE SALSBURY. *Bob Flush*: John Webster. *Phil Straight*: W. S. Daboll. *Dollie Dashwood*, who should have been a boy: NELLIE McHENRY. *Dainty*, the farmer's adopted daughter: Josie Langley. *Priscilla Prism*, ancient, but gushing: Thomas E. Jackson. *Ezra Whittle* of the Happy Homestead Farm: L. J. Loring. *Mr. Selvage Delaine*, a merchant: Fred. Bowman. *Villagers, Maids, Widows and Guests.*

1885.11 GASPARONE

A Comic Opera in Three Acts. Original Viennese libretto to the operette by F. Zell and Richard Genée. English adaptation by Sydney Rosenfeld. Music by Carl Millöcker. Scenery by Joseph Clare. Musical director, Adolf Nowak. Produced by James C. Duff. Opened 21 February 1885 at the Standard Theatre and closed 4 (matinee) April 1885 after 44 performances[82].

CAST: *Carlotta*, Countess of Santa Croce, a widow: MARIE CONRON, EMMA SEEBOLD. *Babolena Nasoni*, Podesta of Syracuse: RICHARD MANSFIELD. *Sindulfo*, his son: WILLIAM H. FITZGERALD. *Count Erminio*: HARRY HILLIARD. *Luigi*, his friend: John E. Nash. *Benozzo*, Innkeeper: ALEXANDER KLEIN. *Sora*, his wife: MAE ST. JOHN. *Zenobia*, Duenna to Carlotta: HATTIE NEFFLIN. *Marietta*, Waiting-maid to Carlotta: Alice Vincent. *Masaccio*, Smuggler, Benozzo's Uncle: CHARLES STANLEY. *Clerk of the Court*: William Gilmore. *Ruperto Corticelli*, General: William Gillow. *Guardino*, Lieutenant of Carbineers: C. L. Rosario. *Smugglers, Soldiers, Peasants, Milksellers, Gendarmes, Coastguards, Carbineers, Sailors*: Chorus of 50.

Act 1: Square of a Village located at the seashore in the neighborhood of Syracuse, in Sicily. 1820.

Act 2: Ancient chamber in the Castle of Santa Croce.

Act 3: Open Square in Syracuse, Sicily.

ACT 1[83]
Opening Chorus (Wihu! Wihu!)
C. Stanley, A. Klein, Chorus
Chorus and Song (When on the foe we're stealing)
R. Mansfield, Chorus
Scene (She's come, now tell us what's amiss?)
A. Klein, R. Mansfield, M. St. John, M. Conron, Chorus
Trio (Well, then, let us together go)
M. Conron, R. Mansfield, H. Nefflin
Duet (What joy is mine that still you're here)
M. Conron, H. Hilliard
Finale (Hear the noise from afar)
Principals, Chorus

ACT 2
Opening Chorus (Hark to the music, Estrella!)
Chorus
Song (And yet strange views of matrimony)
H. Nefflin
Chorus and Ensemble (The light of day at last is breaking)
M. Conron, R. Mansfield, H. Hilliard, H. Nefflin, Chorus
Duet (It is not right that you should doubt me)
A. Klein, M. St. John
Duet (O'er the sea fall the shadows of night)
M. Conron, H. Hilliard
Finale (Come in, come in, come all of you in)
Principals, Chorus

ACT 3
Opening Chorus (The bold Carbineers are now marching in)
Chorus
Waltz (Her lord and master, the man shall be)
A. Klein
Septet (Sir Magistrate!)
A. Klein, C. Stanley, R. Mansfield, M. St. John, H. Nefflin, H. Hilliard, M. Conron
Finale (Gasparone now makes reparation)
M. Conron, M. St. John

1885.12 PIERRETTE

An Operetta in One Act, accompanied by an Olio. Libretto adapted from a French comedietta by Mr. F. Williams. Music by Robert Stoepel. Musical director, Jesse Williams. Produced by (John) Koster and (Albert) Bial. Opened 2 March 1885 at Koster & Bial's Music Hall and closed 14 March 1885 after 16 performances.

Olio: (Henry) LeClair and (W. J.) Russell. The Tissots' Tableaux Vivantes. James P. Locke. Romale Brothers. Mlle. Adele. Alfredo and Cury.

CAST: *Pierrette*: Mme. MARIE VANONI. *Pompon*: VINCENT HOGAN.

MUSICAL NUMBERS
Galop-Song
Duet
Mme. Vanoni, V. Hogan

1885.13 THE PIRATES OF PENZANCE, or, The Slave of Duty

A Revival of the Comic Opera in Two Acts[84]. Libretto by William S. Gilbert. Music by Arthur Sullivan. Stage director, J. A. Furey. Musical director,

[79]English adaptation uncredited. First produced in New York 5 May 1881 at the Bijou Opera House for 200 performances in two engagements. For Synopsis of Scenes and Musical Numbers, see original 1881 production.
[80]First produced in New York 31 December 1883 at the Third Avenue Theatre for 8 performances; returned 4 February 1884 to the New Park Theatre for an additional 16 performances. For Synopsis of Scenes, see original 1883 production.
[81]Scenery and costumes uncredited. "During the evening, many musical selections will be given of an original and catchy nature."
[82]Also presented in its original German 21 February 1885 at the Thalia.
[83]Musical numbers not listed in programs. List prepared from published libretto (Hermann Bartsch, Typographer, New York, 1885). Also interpolated in Act 2, per programs:
Gavotte (from 1776, operette by L. Goldmark)
(*Music by* Ludwig Engländer.)
[84]First presented in New York 31 December 1879 at the Fifth Avenue Theatre for a total of 91 performances in two engagements. For Synopsis of Scenes and Musical Numbers, see original 1879 production.

Antonio DeNovellis. Produced by the McCaull Opera Comique Company (John A. McCaull, Proprietor and Manager), by special arrangement with Richard D'Oyly Carte. Opened 9 March 1885 at the Casino Theatre and closed 14 March 1885 after 7 performances.

CAST: *Richard*, a Pirate Chief: CHARLES W. DUNGAN. *Samuel*, his Lieutenant: J. A. Furey. *Frederic*, a Pirate Apprentice: GEORGE APPLEBY. *Major General Stanley* of the British Army: J. H. RYLEY. *Edward*, a Sergeant of Police: DIGBY BELL. *Mabel, Edith, Kate, Isabel*, General Stanley's Daughters: MARY BEEBE, KATE ETHEL, ROSE LEIGHTON, Ethel Clare. *Ruth*, Pirate Maid-of-all-work: LAURA JOYCE BELL. *Chorus of General Stanley's Daughters, Pirates and Policemen.*

1885.14 DIE FLEDERMAUS

A Comic Operette in Three Acts[85]. Original Viennese libretto by Richard Genée (and Carl Haffner), based on "Le Réveillon" by Henri Meilhac and Ludovic Halévy. (English adaptation by Sydney Rosenfeld.) Music by Johann Strauss. Stage director, W. H. Daly. Musical director, Signor Antonio DeNovellis. Scenery by Henry E. Hoyt. Stage machinist, G. P. Sherwood, Jr. Produced by the McCaull Opera Comique Company (John A. McCaull, Proprietor and Manager). Opened 16 March 1885 at the Casino Theatre and closed 25 April 1885 after 42 performances.

CAST: *Eisenstein*, a Wealthy Banker: MARK SMITH. *Franke*, Director of the Prison: DeWOLF HOPPER. *Dr. Falke*, the Family Physician: C. W. DUNGAN. *Prince Orloffsky*: IRENE PERRY. *Alfred*: Edwin Whitney. *Frosch*, a Jailer: Charles Plunkett. *Blind*, an Attorney: E. H. Van Veghten. *Joan*, Prince Orloffsky's Servant: A. W. Maflin. *Murry*, a Canadian: Joseph Fay. *Canconi*, an Italian: J. Cameron. *Adolphus*: W. J. Stavro. *Ali Bey*, an Egyptian: C. Kauffman. *Ramusin*: A. Gervaise. *Russian Waiters (4)*: Messrs. Childs, Taylor, Jones, O'Brien. *Rosalind*, Eisenstein's wife: ROSALBA BEECHER. *Adele*, her Servant: MATHILDE COTTRELLY. *Ida*, a Coryphée: IDA VALERGA. *Coryphées (10)*: *Mélanie*: Agnes Folsom. *Faustinne*: Minnie DeRue. *Felicita*: E. Graham. *Sidi*: Ida Mosher. *Natalie*: S. Uarda. *Mini*: F. Hazleton. *Sylvia*: G. Clark. *Irene*: N. Hamilton. *Sabine*: M. Echardt. *Hermine*: J. Pierce.

Act 1: Drawing-room in Eisenstein's home.

Act 2: Villa and Garden of Prince Orlofsky.

Act 3: Prison Inspector's Office.

1885.15 THE MAJOR

A Revised Version of the Local Comedy in Three Acts, 8 Scenes[86]. Play by Edward Harrigan. Music by David Braham. Staged by Edward Harrigan. Scenery by Charles W. Witham. Mechanical effects by A. D. Peck. Properties by Joseph D. Wray. Musical director, David Braham. Produced by Edward Harrigan. Opened 16 March 1885 at the 14th Street Theater and closed 18 April 1885 after 40 performances.

CAST: *Major Gilfeather*: EDWARD HARRIGAN. *Enry Iggins*: TONY HART. *Phineas Bottlegreen*: JOHN WILD. *Caleb Jenkins*: JAMES FOX. *John Murphy*: MICHAEL BRADLEY. *Percival Popp*: EDWARD BURT. *Granville Bright*: CHARLES STURGES. *Clara Jenkins*: JAMES TIERNEY. *Phadrig Murphy*: John Sparks. *Mr. Spotem*: HARRY FISHER. *Mr. Welt*: John Murphy. *Mr. Sole*: George Merritt. *Mr. Tape*: Thomas Ray. *Mr. Plaid*: Charles Coffey. *Conried Swartz*: Emil Heusel. *Mr. Clam*: James Brevarde. *Officer*: James McCullough. *Mr. Stoke*: George L. Stout. *Mr. (Ephraim) Shroud*: William West. *The Monkey*: Master Martin. *Minstrel boy*: Joe Davis. *Slip Runner*: Morgan Benson. *Miranda Biggs*: ANNIE YEAMANS. *Henrietta*: GERTIE GRANVILLE (HART). *Arabella Pinch*: JENNIE SATTERLEE. *Amelia Bright*: Sadie Morris. *Mrs. John Murphy*: Addie Farwell. *Mrs. Plum*: Marie Gorenflo. *Mrs. Brown*: Emily Yeamans. *Miss Dudlet*: Annie Langdon. *Miss Livingston*: Kate Langdon. *Miss Perkins*: Della Stilwell. *Sarah Ann Wilkins*: Annie Hall. *Rosie Haly*: Jennie Bageard. *Sailors, Custom House Officers, Policemen, Visitors, Negroes, Curiosities, etc.*

Act 1, Scene 1: Dock of the Guion Line of Steamships. *Scene 2*: Exterior of Mrs. Biggs' and Mrs. Plum's Boarding Houses. *Scene 3*: A Parlor in Mrs. Biggs' Boarding House.

Act 2, Scene 1: Exterior of Caleb Jenkins' Policy Shop and Percival Pop's Fireworks' Factory. *Scene 2*: Interior of the Policy Shop. *Scene 3*: Interior of the Tombs. *Scene 4*: Exterior of the Fireworks Factory.

Act 3: Coney Island at Night.

ACT 1[87]
Scene 2
"Major Gilfeather"
Scene 3
"Henrietta Pye" (Duet)
G. Granville, ?

ACT 2
Scene 2
"Clara Jenkins' Tea"
"4-11-44"

ACT 3
"I Really Can't Sit Down"

1885.16 H.M.S. PINAFORE, or, The Lass That Loved a Sailor

A Revival of the Comic Opera in Two Acts[88]. Libretto by William S. Gilbert. Music by Arthur Sullivan. Scenery by Joseph Clare. Directed by James C. Duff. Presented by James C. Duff. Opened 4 April 1885 at the Standard Theatre and closed 18 April 1885 after 15 performances.[89]

CAST: *The Rt. Hon. Sir Joseph Porter, K.C.B.*, First Lord of the Admiralty: THOMAS WHIFFEN[90]. *Captain Corcoran*, Commanding the *H.M.S. Pinafore*: JOHN E. McWADE. *Ralph Rackstraw*, Able Seaman: HARRY HILLIARD. *Dick Deadeye*, Able Seaman: CHARLES STANLEY. *Bill Bobstay*, Bo'sun's Mate: Fred Clifton. *Bob Beckett*, Carpenter's Mate: John E. Nash. *Tom Tucker*, Midshipmite: Master Henry. *Josephine*, the Captain's Daughter: MAE ST. JOHN. *Hebe*, Sir Joseph's First Cousin: Louise Melvin. *Little Buttercup*, a Portsmouth Bumboat Woman: ALICE BARNETT[91]. *First Lord's Sisters, his Cousins, his Aunts, Sailors, Marines, etc.*

1885.17 LE JOUR ET LA NUIT

A Revival of the Opéra-bouffe in Three Acts, in French[92]. Libretto by Albert Vanloo and Eugène Leterrier. Music by Charles Lecocq. Stage manager, Mons. V. Merle. Musical director, Mons. A. Lagye. Produced by Maurice Grau. Opened 8 April 1885 at the Star Theatre for 1 performance in repertory.

CAST: *Manola*: Mme. LOUISE THÉO. *Béatrice*: Mlle. CÉCILE LEFORT. *Sanchette*: Mlle. EUGÉNIE NORDALL. *Anita*: Mlle. Vandamme. *First Cornette*: Mlle. Vandamme. *Catarina*: Mlle. Lescot. *Third Cornette*: Mlle. Lescot. *Pepita*: Mlle. Gatineau. *Second Cornette*: Mlle. Gatineau. *Pablo*: Mlle. Caro. *Fourth Cornette*: Mlle. Caro. *Lizardo*: Mlle. Dass. *Paolo*: Mlle. Dass. *Antonio*: Mlle. Daniel. *Fifth Cornette*: Mlle. Daniel. *Juan*: Mlle. Vandamme. *Esperanza*: Mlle. Amiel. *Medina*: Mlle. Tournyaire. *Inez*: Mlle. Schlosser. *(Prince) Picrates de Calabazas*: Mons. J. MEZIÈRES. *Don Braseiro (de Tras os Montes)*: Mons. E. DUPLAN. *Miguel*: Mons. E. LARY. *Don Degomez*: Mons. G. GUY. *Christobal*: Mons. L. Ducos. *Un Soldat*: Mons. Yalowicz. *(Hommes et Femmes du Château, Alguazils, Étudiants, Grisettes, etc.)*

---

[85]English language premiere. Previously presented in New York in German at the Thalia Theater 18 October 1879 for 7 performances in repertory. Musical numbers not listed in programs; no libretto, musical scene or book of words found for this description.

[86]First produced in New York 29 August 1881 at the Theatre Comique for 152 performances. During the run, the second intermission was dropped, and the play presented in two acts.

[87]The following four numbers were newly written for this production: "Henrietta Pye," "That's an Old Gag with Me," "4-11-44," "I Really Can't Sit Down." Also performed, placement not indicated in programs: "Miranda, When We Are Made One," "That's an Old Gag with Me."

[88]Originally presented in New York 15 January 1879 at the Standard Theatre for 175 performances. For Synopsis of Scenes and Musical Numbers, see original 1879 production.

[89]No credits available for costumes or musical director.

[90]Whiffen played for the opening night, succeeded thereafter by J. H. RYLEY

[91]Barnett played for the opening night, succeeded thereafter by ELMA DELARO.

[92]Previously produced in New York in French 1 May 1882 at Haverly's Fifth Avenue Theatre for 3 performances in repertory. For Synopsis of Scenes and Musical Numbers, see original 1882 production.

1885.18 IXION, or, The Man at the Wheel

A Resurrection (Revival) of the Classic Burlesque in Two Acts.[93] (Play by F. C. Burnand.) Adapted by Henry LeClair. Musical director, Jesse Williams. Produced by (John) Koster and (Albert) Bial. Opened 13 April 1885 at Koster & Bial's Concert Hall and closed 16 May 1885 after 60 performances.[94]

Olio: The Martens Trio. French Troupe Davene. Henry LeClair and W. J. Russell in their protean comedy. A Practical Joke. Rosa Lee. Louise Murio. Dragon Troupe of Japanese.

CAST: *Ixion*: HENRY LeCLAIR. *Jupiter*: Miss MAY STANFORD. *Venus*: Miss LILLIE SHANDLEY. Powerful Cast and Grand Chorus.

1885.19 LES CLOCHES DE CORNEVILLE

A Revival of the Opéra-comique in Three Acts, in French[95]. Libretto by Clairville and Charles Gabet. Music by Robert Planquette. Stage manager, Mons. V. Merle. Musical director, Mons. A. Lagye. Produced by Maurice Grau. Opened 14 April 1885 at the Star Theatre and closed 17 April 1885 after 2 performances in repertory.

CAST: *Serpolette*: Mme. LOUISE THÉO. *Germaine*: Mlle. CÉCILE LEFORT. *Gaspard*: Mons. J. MEZIÈRES. Company included Mlles. Nordall, Delorme, Vandamme, Dass, Caro, Gatineau, Lescot, Daniel, Amiel, Tournyaire, Schlosser; Messrs. E. Duplan, E. Lary, G. Guy, Perret, Estiot, Gaillard, Ducos, Salvator, Perrot, Vinchon, Girard, Yalowicz. Chorus of 40.

1885.20 LA FILLE DU TAMBOUR-MAJOR

A Revival of the Opéra-comique in Three Acts, 4 Scenes, in French[96]. Libretto by Henri Chivot and Alfred Duru. Music by Jacques Offenbach. Stage manager, Mons. V. Merle. Musical director, Mons. A. Lagye. Produced by Maurice Grau. Opened 15 April 1885 at the Star Theatre and closed 18 April 1885 after 2 performances in repertory.

CAST: *Stella*: Mme. LOUISE THÉO. *Claudine*: Mlle CÉCILE LEFORT. *LA Duchesse*: Mme. Delorme. *La Superieur*: Mlle. Vandamme. *Lorenza*: Mlle. Dass. *Lucrezia*: Mlle. Caro. *Francesca*: Mlle. Gatineau. *Del Puente*: Mons. Perret. *Zerbinelli*: Mons. Estiot. *Monthabor*: Mons. DUPLAN. *Della Volta*: Mons. J. MEZIÉRES. *Griolet*: Mons. GUY. *Robert*: Mons. Gaillard. *Clampas*: Mons. Ducos. *Bambini*: Mons. Salvator. *Gregorio*: Mons. Perret. *Le Sergent*: Mons. Vinchon. *Un Domestique*: Mons. Girard. Magnificent Mis-en-scène, Military Band and 100 Auxiliaries.

1885.21 TWINS

An Eccentric Comedy in Three Acts. Play by Joseph Derrick. Scenes by Joseph Clare. Musical director, John Eller. Produced by Col. T. Allston Brown. Opened 20 April 1885 at the Standard Theatre and closed 2 May 1885 after 14 performances.

CAST: *The Twins*: *Dr. Titus Spinach*, Bishop of Banglepore: JOHN A. MACKAY. *Timothy Spinach*, Headwaiter, the Grand" Goatstile-on-Sea: JOHN A. MACKAY. *Amos Billings*, a retired merchant: CHARLES STANLEY. *Adolphus Billings*, his son: J. H. Browne. *Richards*, a butler: Fred Clifton. *The O'Haversack*: H. W. Montgomery. *Mr. Rollux*, Manager of the "Grand": J. E. Nash. *Rampunkah*, the Bishop's Hindoo Servant: Harry Holliday. *Mr. Arrack* old-fashioned guest: J. W. Piggott. *Mrs. Billings*: Louise Eldridge. *The Hon. Mrs. Grand*: Mrs. Harry Courtaine [Emma Grattan]. *Edith Gracely*: Olga Brandon. *Matilda Spinach*: HATTIE NEFFLEN. *Lydia Haversack*: AGNES THOMAS. *Waiters, Chambermaids, Guests, Servants, etc.*

Time: The present.

Act 1: Billings' Drawing Room. Dorchester Square. First day.

Act 2: Coffee Room and Terrace. The Grand, Goatstile. Second day.

Act 3: Billings' Drawing Room. Third day.

1885.22 CORDELIA'S ASPIRATIONS

A Revival of the Local Comedy in Three Acts, 5 Scenes[97]. Play by Edward Harrigan. Music by David Braham. Staged by Edward Harrigan. (Scenery by Charles W. Witham.) Musical director, David Braham. Produced by Edward Harrigan and Tony Hart. Opened 20 April 1885 at the 14th Street Theatre and closed 9 May 1885 after 24 performances.

CAST: *Dan Mulligan*: EDWARD HARRIGAN. *Rebecca Allup*: TONY HART. *Simpson Primrose*: JOHN WILD. *Palestine Puter*: JAMES FOX. *Planxty McFudd*: HARRY FISHER. *Walsingham McSweeney*: M. Bradley. *Gustavus Lochmuller*: CHARLES STURGES. *Ridgeway*: Edward Burt. *Mulvey*: Charles Coffey. *Dunbar*: John Murphy. *Mr. Bauser*: GEORGE MERRITT. *Clerk*: George L. Stout. *Tommy*: Master Charlie. *Policeman*: J. McCullough. *Cordelia Mulligan*: ANNIE YEAMANS. *Mrs. Lochmuller*: Jennie Satterlee. *Diana McFudd*: Sadie Morris. *Ellen McFudd*: Ada [Addie] Farwell. *Rosy McFudd*: Emily Yeamans. *Mrs. Brown*: Marie Gorenflo. *Mrs. Rieley*: Kate Langdon. *Mrs. Buchheister*: Annie Hall. *Mrs. Chump*: Della Stilwell. *Annette*: Jennie Bageard.

THE UNCLE TOM COMBINATION: *Jim Grace*: WILLIAM WEST. *Mr. Dangerfield*: JAMES BREVARDE. *Mr. Clinton*: Joe Davis. *Topsey*: Master Martin. *Billy Kersands*: Thomas Ray. *Cal Hicks*: EMIL HEUSEL. *Jim Bland*: Geoge Edwards. *Sam Lucas*: Philip Lipson. *Joe Hardhead*: George Lewis. *Jay Weldon*: A. Simmons. *Emigrants, Officals, Policemen, Hackmen, etc.*

1885.23 GIROFLÉ-GIROFLA

A Revival of the Opéra-comique in Three Acts, in French[98]. Libretto by Albert Vanloo and Eugène Leterrier. Music by Charles Lecocq. Stage manager, Mons. V. Merle. Musical director, Mons. A. Lagye. Produced by Maurice Grau's Famous French Opera Company. Opened 20 April 1885 at the Star Theatre and closed 25 April 1885 after 2 performances in repertory.

CAST: *Giroflé, Girofla*: Mme. LOUISE THÉO. *Pedro*: Mlle. ASTRUC. *Aurore*: Mlle. Delorme. *Paquita*: Mlle. Eugénie Nordall. *Gusmand*: Mlle. Vandamme. *Fernand*: Mlle. Dass. *The Godmother*: Mlle. Caro. *Don Dolero D'Arcarazas*: Mons. Duplan. *Marasquin*: Mons. Lary. *Maurzouk*: Mons. Gaillard. *The Pirate Chief*: Mons. Vinchon. *The Godfather*: Mons. Vinchon. *The Lawyer*: Mons. Perret. *The Preceptor*: Mons. Yalowicz. *The Uncle*: Mons. Girard. *A Dancer*: Mons. Amiel. *The Page*: Mons. Estiot.

1885.24 LA PETITE MARIÉE

A Revival of the Opéra-comique in Three Acts, in French[99]. Libretto by Eugéne Leterrier and Albert Vanloo. Music by Charles Lecocq. Stage manager, Mons. V. Merle. Musical director, Mons. A. Lagye. Produced by Maurice Grau's Famous French Opera Company. Opened 21 April 1885 at the Star Theatre for 1 performance in repertory.

CAST: *Graziella*: Mme. LOUISE THÉO. *Lucrézia*: Mme. Delorme. *Theobaldo*: Mme. Astruc. *Beatrice*: Mlle. E. Nordall. *An Unknown Woman*: Mlle. Marie Vandamme. *The Podestate (Podesta)*: Mons. GAILLARD. *San Carlo*: Mons. LARY. *Montefiasco*: Mons. J. MEZIÈRES. *Casteldemoli*: Mons. GUY. *Beppo*: Mons. Ducos. *A Mute*: Mons. Vinchon. *An Unknown*: Mons. Girard.

1885.25 LE GRAND CASIMIR

A Revival of the Opérette in Three Acts, in French[100]. Libretto by Jules Prével and Albert de Saint-Albin. Music by Charles Lecocq. Stage manager, Mons. V. Merle. Musical director, Mons. A. Lagye. Produced by Maurice

---

[93]Original version first produced in New York 28 September 1868 at Wood's Museum for 120 performances in 2 engagements.
[94]Production schedule reverted to a twice daily schedule.
[95]First produced in New York 22 October 1877 at the Fifth Avenue Theatre for 16 performances in repertory. For Synopsis of Scenes and Musical Numbers, see original 1877 production. No program found for this engagement.
[96]First produced in New York in French 13 September 1880 at the Standard Theatre for 23 performances. For Synopsis of Scenes and Musical Numbers, see original 1880 production.
[97]First produced in New York 5 November 1883 at the Theatre Comique for 176 performances. For Synopsis of Scenes and Musical Numbers, see original 1883 production.
[98]First produced in New York in French 4 February 1875 at the Park Theatre for (46) performances in repertory. For Synopsis of Scenes and Musical Numbers, see original 1875 production.
[99]First produced in New York in French 6 February 1877 at the Eagle Theatre for 9 performances in repertory. For Synopsis of Scenes and Musical Numbers, see original 1877 production.
[100]First produced in New York 11 April 1883 at the Casino and Daly's Theatres for 3 performances in repertory. For Synopsis of Scenes and Musical Numbers, see original 1883 production

Grau's Famous French Opera Company. Opened 22 April 1885 at the Star Theatre and closed 24 April 1885 after 2 performances in repertory.

CAST: *Angélina*: Mme. LOUISE THÉO. *Ninetta*: Mlle. E. NORDALL. *Petronilla*: Mlle. Lescot. *Colomba*: Mlle.Caro. *Seraphina*: Mlle. Marie Vandamme. *Lydia*: Mlle. Dass. *A Servant*: Mlle. Tournyaire. *Casimir*: Mons. J. MEZIÈRES. *Sothermann*: Mons. LARY. *Le Grand Duc*: Mons. DUPLAN. *Picasso*: Mons. GUY. *Gobson*: Mons. Vinchon. *Galetti*: Mons. Ducos. *Josephe*: Mons. Gerard. *Second Regisseur*: Mons. Estiot. *A Clown*: Mons. Amiel. *Antonio*: Mons. Estiot. *Pietro*: Mons. Nys.

POLLY, or, The Pet of the Regiment

1885.26

A Comic Opera in Two Acts, 3 Scenes. Libretto by James Mortimer. Music by Edward Solomon. Produced by the Gaiety Comic Opera Company (I. B. Rich, Proprietor; Edward E. Rice, Manager). Opened 27 April 1885 at the Casino Theatre and closed 20 June 1885 after 79 performances.

CAST: *Polly Pluckrose*, the Pet of the Regiment: LILLIAN RUSSELL. *Lady McAsser*, the General's Sister: ALICE BARNETT. *The General's Eight Fair Daughters*: *Eliza*: Florence Bemister. *Sarah*: Josie Hall. *Susan*: Emma Hanley. *Ann*: Agnes Folsom. *Jane*: Emma Schell. *Phoebe*: Annie Lukie. *Martha*: May Bardell. *Baby*: Lulu Campbell. *Private Mangle*, of the 200th Hussars: H. S. HILLIARD. *Sergeant Ripeclay*: E. H. AIKEN. *Eight Officers of the 200th Hussars*: *Ensign Daffodil*: Belle Urquhart. *Ensign Tatill*: Hindie Harrison. *Lieutenant Braznose*: Louise Gordon. *Lieutenant Hazen*: Carrie Andrews. *Adjutant Gonzales*: Rose Beaudet. *Captain Blink*: Rita Carroll. *Captain Braze*: Eily Kavanagh. *Major Drumhead*: Edith Cornish. *Colonel Percival Tussell*, commanding the 200th Hussars: JOHN T. McWADE. *Major-General Bangs*, C. B., commanding the 47th Division: J. H. RYLEY.

Act 1: Park adjoining Whitehall. Time is the present.

Act 2, Scene 1: The General's Tent. *Scene 2*: The Camp.

ACT 1[101]

Chorus of Soldiers (No life is so exciting)
(Chorus)
"I am Major General Bangs" (Song)
J. H. Ryley
Introduction to Chorus of Daughters (She's the sister of a General)
J. H. Ryley, Chorus
"The J. H. Ryley's Eight Fair Daughters" (Chorus)
Eight Daughters, Hussars
"I Was the Daughter" (Introduction and Song)
L. Russell
"Were I a Flower" (Recitative and Duet)
S. Hilliard, L. Russell
"Yes, That Is Love" (Ballad)
L. Russell
Recitative (Bewitching girl!)
J. H. Ryley, L. Russell
Quartette (Behold him kneeling)
L. Russell, H. S. Hilliard, J. T. McWade, J. H. Ryley
"The Discovery" (Concerted Piece)(Come hither, Miss or Madam—which are you?)
L. Russell, A. Barnett, J. H. Ryley, Chorus
"You mustn't marry" (Introduction and Song)
J. T. McWade, Chorus
Introduction and Finale (Polly, my own dear child)
Tutti

ACT 2

"The muffled cheer" (Opening Chorus)
J. H. Ryley, Soldiers
"I joined the Army" (Song)
J. H. Ryley
Introduction (Your noble sister, Sir)
J. T. McWade, J. H. Ryley, Chorus
"Dear Papa" (Chorus of Daughters)
Eight Daughters
Introduction (My dears, I don't know how to act)
J. H. Ryley, Chorus
"I was content" (Song)
L. Russell, Chorus
"In a Vale" (Duet)
J. H. Ryley, L. Russell
"Take these Slippers" (Presentation Chorus)
Eight Daughters
good-night, good-night" (Serenade Chorus)
Chorus
"What thrill is this?" (Ballad)
L. Russell
"Sad is my lot" (Recitative and Solo)
L. Russell, H. S. Hilliard
"Dear Mother England" (Patriotic Song)
Soloists, Full Chorus
Concerted Piece (A light breaks in upon me)
J. H. Ryley, H. S. Hilliard, L. Russell, Officers, Daughters, Soldiers (Chorus)
Finale (A telegram from town)
Tutti

[101]Musical numbers not listed in programs. List prepared from published English piano vocal score (E. Ascherberg & Co., London, 1894?). Interpolations not contained in published score:
Grand March of the 200th Hussars (Act 2)
Sword Drill, Musket Drill; Lance Practice; Duryee Zouaves' Fife and Drum Corps (Act 2)
"She Was a Cau-, She Was a Shun"
E. H. Aiken
"The Silver Line" (from LORD BATEMAN, London)
L. Russell
(*Lyrics by* Henry Pottinger Stephens.)

DER FELDPREDIGER

1885.27

An Operette in Three Acts, in German[102]. Libretto by Hugo Wittmann and Alois Wohlmuth, based on the story 'Der seltsame Brautgemach' by Friedrich Schilling. Music by Karl Millöcker. Staged under the direction of L. Ottomeyer. Musical director, Ed. Poelz. Produced by Gustave Amberg, Manager. Opened 1 May 1885 at the Thalia Theatre and 22 May 1885 after 16 performances in repertory.

CAST[103]: *Heidekrug*, burgomaster in Trautenfeld: MAX LUBE. *His Daughters (2)*: *Minna*: EMMA SEEBOLD. *Rosette*: FRANZISKA RABERG. *Hellwig*, Major of Hussars: EDUARD ELSBACH. *Kühnwald*, student: CONRAD JUNKER. *Piffkow*, town beadle: FERDINAND SCHÜTZ. *Barbara*, Housekeeper at Heidekrug's: ALBERTINE HABRICH. *Rieke*, servant: Minna Castelli. *General Blucher*: MAX PATEGG. *De Thorilliere*, French officer: O. Meyer. *v. Rubke*, a Prussian officer: H. Stolzenberg. *A Headman of Cossacks*: Franz v. Metsch. *Bliemchen*, an actor: Bernhard Rank. *Vestryman's Wife*: Ruscha Michaelis. *Quartermaster's Wife*: Therese Zugbaum. *Justice's Wife*: Lina Guttmann. *Custom Officer's Wife*: Marie Schlag. *County Gamekeeper's Wife*: Duschka Veroni. *Village Treasurer's Wife*: Felicita Spiranska. *Wife of the Chief Citizen*: Johanna Meyer. *Veterinary Surgeon's Wife*: Bertha Zugbaum. *A Rat Catcher*: Heinrich Zilzer. *An Invalid*: Franz Kloezinsky. *A Quack Doctor*: Adolf Reif. *A Colporteur*: Karl Hartmann. *A Scissor Grinder*: Hermann Gerold. *An Organ Grinder*: Hans Beck. *Frommsinn*, vestryman: Conrad Beck. *Treibein*, cobbler: Heinrich Habrich. *Kummelhold*, postmaster: Wilhelm Paffhausen. *Giersclund*, tax collector: Louis Pratorius. *Hausdarm*, tailor: Edward Hirsch. *Citizens and their Ladies of Trautenfled, Prussian Soldiers, German Lancers, French Soldiers, Cossacks, People.*

Scene: A German Frontier Town, 1812-1813.

ACT 1[104]

Introduction (Ach, wer an der Grenze wohnt)
F. Schütz, Chorus
Austrittslied (Ueber biden Jolianten)
M. Lube
Ensemble (Juchei, Juchei!)
M. Lube, F. Schütz, E. Elsbach, Chorus
Terzett [Trio] (Der Schelm, er foll uns nicht entrinen)
M. Lube, E. Elsbach, F. Schütz
Terzett [Trio] (Gröktes Unglüch für ein Mädchen)
E. Seebold, F. Raberg, M. Lube

[102]Concurrently produced in an English adaptation as THE BLACK HUSSAR 4 May 1885 at Wallack's Theatre.
[103]Cast list prepared from a 7 May 1885 Thalia program; character names, etc. from Thalia production on Chicago tour 15 June 1885.
[104]Song list prepared from German language libretto from the Thalia (Samifch & Goldmann, New York, 1885).

Finale (Schlagt auf bie Hauspostille)
Alle [All]

ACT 2

Chorus (Guten Morgen, Frau Kirchenwalterin!)
Chorus

Ensemble (Da fommt er ichon mit raichem Gang)
M. Lube, F. Schütz, Chorus

Duett (Endlich wieder eine Stunde)
E. Elsbach, E. Seebold

Ensemble (Zerstrent Euch hier in der Rahe)
E. Elsbach, C. Junker, All

Quartet (Zög nicht, mein Bolt erwach')
E. Elsbach, C. Junker, E. Seebold, F. Raberg

Finale (Ranonendonner, es zittert das Haus)
Alle [All]

Lied (Zwan wollte Ratja frei'n)
E. Seebold

ACT 3

Lied (Ach, endlich ist berughigt das Toben)
E. Seebold

Lied (Und're Mädchen mögen ichmachten)
F. Raberg

Walzer (Nur ein Traum)
F. Schütz, Chorus

Arie [Aria] (Ha, ha! Mir icheint, ich mittre Blut)
M. Lube

Schlussgefang (Der Freiheit Stimme rujet Dich)
E. Elsbach

1885.28 THE BLACK HUSSAR

An Opera Comique in Three Acts[105]. Original Viennese libretto to the operette ('Der Feldprediger') by Hugo Wittmann and Alois Wohlmuth, based on the story 'Der seltsame Brautgemach' by Friedrich Schilling. English adaptation by Sydney Rosenfeld. Music by Carl Millöcker. Stage manager, William H. Daly. Scenery by Philip Goatcher. Mechanism by F. Dorrington. Appointments by E. Siedle. Gas effects by J. F. Driscoll. Musical director, Antonio DeNovellis. Produced by McCaull Opera Comique Company (John A. McCaull, Proprietor). Opened 4 May 1885 at Wallack's Theatre and closed 15 August 1885 after 104 performances.

CAST: *Friedrich von Helbert*, Colonel of the Black Hussars, disguised as an Army Chaplain: MARK SMITH. *Hans von Waldmann*, Adjutant of the Black Hussars, disguised as a student: EDWIN W. HOFF. *Staff Officers of the Black Hussars (9): Major Rokow*: Zoe DeVielle. *Captain Plush*: Bessie Frazer. *Captain Bender*: Millie Vanberg. *Captain Woolf*: Rose Marion. *Lieut. Conrad*: Ida Mosher. *Lieut. Van Vleet*: Lizzie Sherwood. *Lieut. Duzenburg*: Dollie Chase. *Lieut. Konig*: Emily Seymour. *Lieut. Beyer*: Emma Muller. *Theophil Hackenback*, Magistrate of Trautenfeld: DeWOLF HOPPER. *Piffkow*, his Factotum, with numerous offices—Town Crier, Night Watchman, Barber, etc: DIGBY BELL. *Mefflin*, a Tragedian of the Meiniger Company, No. 14: A. W. MAFLIN. *François Thorilliere*, a Captain in the French Army: E. H. Van Veghten. *Rubke*, a Captain in the Prussian Army: J. A. Furey. *Wutki*, Hetman of the Cassocks: A. Barbara. *Citizens of Trautenfeld (5): Klappig*: L. M. Hall. *Rothmichael*: Charles Kauffman. *Birnbaum*: Percy O'Brien. *Knoedel*: Walter Taylor. *Schupsack*: Charles Jones. *Shadow*, a Black Hussar disguised as a a Pedlar: Carles O'Neil. *Bruck*, a Black Hussar disguised as a Scissors Grinder: A. D. Barker. *Eiken*, a Black Hussar disguised as a Beggar: Frank Howard. *Selchow*, a Black Hussar disguised as a Ratcatcher: L. C. Schrader. *Prittwitz*, a Black Hussar disguised as a Bookseller: H. W. Frazer. *Putnam*, a Black Hussar disguised as a Quack Doctor: Henry Platte. *Hackenback's Daughters (2): Minna*: LILLY POST. *Rosetta*: MARIE JANSEN. *Barbara*, an Orphan, Hackenback's Housekeeper: MATHILDE COTTRELLY. *Rieke*, a maid: Kate Ethel. *Mrs.*, the Wife of the Church Warden: Nellie Cox. *Mrs.*, the Wife of the King's Stable Keeper: Minnie Echard. *Mrs.*, the Wife of the State Reduction Cashier: Carrie Jackson. *Mrs.*, the Wife of the Custom House Officer: Annette Hall. *Mrs.*, the Wife of the Army Sutler: Gertie Clarke. *Mrs.*, the Wife of the Forest Gamekeeper: Millie Ray.

The action takes place in and near the town of Trautenfeld on the borders of Germany and Russia. 1812.

Act 1: The Grand Room in Magistrate Hackenback's House.

Act 2: The Public Square of Trautenfeld.

Act 3: In the forest near Trautenfeld.

ACT 1[106]

"We who dwell upon the border" (Opening Chorus of Citizens)
D. Bell, Chorus

"All night long I've weighed and sifted" (Magistrate's Song)
D. Hopper

"Hooray! hooray! Oh, happy Fate!" (Ensemble)
D. Hopper, D. Bell, M. Smith, Chorus

"That is his way"
Chorus

"We'll have his likeness in a minute" (Trio)
D. Hopper, M. Smith, D. Bell

"Of all fates poor maids pursuing" (Trio)
L. Post, M. Jansen, D. Hopper

"Let's take this book before us" (Finale)

ACT 2

"Ah, good morning; how's Mrs. Church warden to-day?" (Gossipers' Chorus)
Chorus

"See where he comes with noble stride" (Factotum's Narrative)
D. Bell, D. Hopper, Chorus

"You've won these trousers by your trouble"
D. Bell

"What a happy meeting this is" (Duet)
M. Smith, L. Post

"Disperse yourselves near by" (Conspirators' Chorus)
M. Smith, E. W. Hoff, Conspirators

"What mean these sounds of alarm and dismay" (Finale)

"Ivan loved his Katza well" (Russian Song)
L. Post, Chorus

ACT 3

"Oh, her Mamma" (Introduced Song)
M. Jansen

"Read the Answer in the Stars" (Trio)
D. Hopper, D. Bell, M. Cottrelly

"When love and peace are in such bonds united" (Finale)

1885.29 ARE YOU INSURED?

A Local Comedy in Three Acts[107]. Play by Edward Harrigan. Music by George F. Braham. (Staged by Edward Harrigan.) Musical director, George F. Braham. Produced by Martin W. Hanley. Opened 11 May 1885 at the 14th Street Theatre and closed 18 May 1885 after 8 performances.[108]

CAST: *Philander Dividend*, Agent for the Perpetual Insurance Company: CHARLES STANLEY. *Sarsfield Per-Annum*, Agent for the India Rubber Insurance Company: WILLIAM H. FITZGERALD. *Jerry Jangles, Raymond Shadow*, of the Jangles Combination: W. S. DABOLL, DAN COLLYER. *Charles Bitterroot*: GEORGE MERRITT. *Sheriff Roger Bouncer*: DAN HART. *Timothy Bitterroot*: JOSEPH SPARKS. *Hodge*, of Hodge's Hotel: Edward Eggleton. *Fanny Bouncer*: JENNIE YEAMANS. *Priscilla Bouncer*: Fanny Wentworth. *Dorcas Bouncer*: Sophie Hummel. *Charity Bouncer*: Fanny Daboll. *Caroline Bitterroot*: Annetta Zelna. *Miss Skaggs*: Jennie Bageard.

Act 1: A Village Post Office and Drug Store.

Act 2: Apartments of Timothy Bitterroot in Hodge's Hotel.

Act 3: The Laundry in Hodge's Hotel.

ACT 1

"The Actors Who've Seen Better Days"
W. S. Daboll, D. Collyer

105Previously presented in German 1 May 1885 at the Thalia.

106Musical numbers not listed in programs. List prepared from the authorized book of words (McCaull Opera Comique Company, New York, 1885). Other titles mentioned in reviews but not precisely found in the book of words: The Factotum's (Piffkow's) Patter Song, The Chaplain's Ode, The Sleeping Sextette, The Lovers' Quartette, The Hussar's War Song, The Song of Peace, The Burgomaster's Mock Battle Song, The Topical Trio. In advertisements: "I am a Man of Brains," "Julius Caesar" (Piffkow's Song).

107Also billed as Edward Harrigan's new and latest eccentricity.

108Scenery and costumes uncredited.

"Are You Insured?"
C. Stanley, W. H. Fitzgerald

ACT 2

"How the Birds Sing"
J. Yeamans

"Hodge's Country Dance"
J. M. Sparks, C. Stanley, W. H. Fitzgerald

"Naughty, Naughty Men"
F. Wentowrth, F. Daboll, S. Hummel, A. Zelna

ACT 3

"Pretty Little Laundry Girls"
F. Wentworth, F. Daboll, S. Hummel, A. Zelna

Favorite Specialty
J. Yeamans

"The Advertising Man"
D. Collyer

Tarantella (from GASPARONE)
F. Wentworth
(*Music by* Carl Millöcker.)

1885.30

FRA DIAVOLO

A Revival of the Opéra-comique in Three Acts[109]. Original French libretto by Eugène Scribe. Music by Daniel Auber. Stage manager, George W. Denham. Musical director, Gustave Kerker. Produced by the Ford-Wallace American-English Opera Company. Opened 18 May 1885 at the Fifth Avenue Theatre and closed 20 June 1885 after 10 performances in repertory.[110]

CAST: *Fra Diavolo*: GEORGE W. TRAVERNER. *Zerlina*: ALFA NORMAN. *Lorenzo*: Thomas A. Christy. *Beppo*: Henry Peakes. *Giacomo*: ALONZO STODDARD. *Matteo*: Louis [Luigi] Carlberg. *Lord Allcash*: JAMES G. PEAKES. *Officer*: L. H. MacNichol. *Guide*: Robert Stanley. *Francesco*: Henry Guise. *Lady Allcash*: ZELDA SEGUIN-(WALLACE).

1885.31

FIN-FIN, THE PRETTY BRIGAND

An Operetta in One Act, accompanied by an Olio. Written by Harry LeClair and W. J. Russell. Musical director, Jesse Williams. Produced by (John) Koster and (Albert) Bial. Opened 18 May 1885 at Koster & Bial's Concert Hall and closed 13 June 1885 after 48 performances.

Olio: Carl Rankin, Harry LeClair, Lizzie Simms, Adams & Casey, Helene Cortland.

CAST: ROSA LEE, LAURA BURT, GEORGIE PARKER, LILLIE SHANDLEY, May Standford, Julie Shandley, Carrie Gould, Edith Gray, Percy Irving, Leo Cole; Messrs. HARRY LeCLAIR, W. J. RUSSELL, Max Arnold.

MUSICAL NUMBERS[111]

"Dear Old English Chappies"
Misses L. Burt, C. Gould, E. Gray, L. Shandley

"So Wie Du" (new Waltz Song)
R. Lee

Sailor's Hornpipe
L. Cole

Policeman's Chorus

"The Poor Little Newsboy"
L. Burt

1885.32

THE BOHEMIAN GIRL

A Revival of the Romantic Opera in Four Acts[112]. Libretto by Alfred Bunn Music by Michael William Balfe. Stage manager, George W. Denham. Musical director, Gustave Kerker. Produced by the Ford-Wallace American-English Opera Company. Opened 25 May 1885 at the Fifth Avenue Theatre and closed 11 June 1885 after 10 performances in repertory.

CAST: *The Count Arnheim*: ALONZO STODDARD. *Arline*: ALFA NORMAN. *Thaddeus*: GEORGE W. TRAVERNER. *The Gypsy Queen*: ZELDA SEGUIN-(WALLACE)[113]. *Devilshoof*: HENRY PEAKES. *Florestan*: MAURICE CONNELL. *Buda*: Miss Mitchell.

---

[109]First produced in New York in English as THE DEVIL'S BROTHER 20 June 1833 at the Park Theatre.

[110]English adaptation uncredited. Interpolated for this revival, as per reviews:
"Let All Obey"
A. Stoddard

[111]No program found; song list prepared from advertisements in the New York Times and Herald. During the run a burlesque of THE BELLES OF THE KITCHEN was added.

[112]First produced in New York 25 November 1844 at the Park Theatre for 17 performances in repertory. For Synopsis of Scenes and Musical Numbers, see original 1844 production.

[113]Though Zelda Sequin was announced for and appeared in the role during the run, reviewers saw BERTHA FRICKE.

1885–1886 SEASON

Lotta Crabtree in MLLE. NITOUCHE
Billy Rose Theatre Collection, New York Public Library for the Performing Arts

1885–1886 SEASON

AROUND THE WORLD IN EIGHTY DAYS

1885.33

A Revival of the Brilliant Spectacle in Five Acts, 13 Scenes[1]. Based on the French adaptation of Jules Verne's novel "Le Tour du Monde en Quatre Vingt Jours," as adapted by Adolphe d'Ennery. Music composed and arranged by Jean-Jacques de Billemont. Scenic designs by Charles Fox and William Schaeffer; Magnini. Costumes by Chalain; properties by Hallée; statuary by Dagoni. Entire spectacle (conceived, staged and) produced under the personal direction of the Kiralfys (Imre, Bolossy). Produced by the Kiralfys. Opened 1 June 1885 at Niblo's Garden and closed 20 June 1885 after 24 performances.

CAST: *Aouda*, an East Indian Princess: HELEN TRACY. *Nemea*, her sister: ROSE WILSON. *Bessie*: Louise Allen. *Nakahira*, Aouda's slave: Ricca Allen. *Phileas Fogg*, Member of the Eccentric Club: CHARLES CHAPPELLE. *Miles O'Pake*, an ex-Senator from New York: E. J. BUCKLEY. *Fix*, an English detective, Scotland Yard: J. F. PETERS. *Jean François Passepartout*, French valet: GEORGE R. EDESON. *Mr. Blunt*, a Calcutta magistrate: W. H. BARTHOLOMEW. *Sir Roger Shewdryn*: William Howard. *Arthur Mayburn*: L. Morton. *Foster Jones*: J. Wakefield. *Governor of Suez*: F. E. Kille. *An Aged Parsee*: M. S. Johns. *Brahmin Chief*: A. H. Denham. *Phil Tracy*: W. Holliman. *Jack Rivers*: W. Eastman. *Conductor*: Frank Richmond. *Chief Scout*: P. Toole. *Dazum Ahan*, King of Borneo: James Van Pelt. *Barkeeper*: J. A. Cook. *Captain Collins*: William S. Hurd. *Ballet*: MLLE. DeRosa, Mons. ARNOLD KIRALFY, Corps of Secondes, Danseuses and Coryphées. *Brahmins, Priests, Punka Wallahs, Dobez Wallahs, Soldiers, Hindoos, Arabs, Egyptians, Malayans, Road Agents, Passengers, Policemen, Sailors, Members of the London Eccentric Club, Snake Charmers and Bayadères.*

PROLOGUE:
Club of the Eccentrics.

ACT 1, SCENE 1:
Suez, with a view of the Canal.
(Fox & Shaffer.)

Scene 2:
East Indian Bungalow.

Scene 2:
TheRoyal Mecropolis.
(Magnini.)

ACT 2, SCENE 1:
Hotel in Calcutta, with a view of the City.

Scene 2:
Palace in Borneo.

ACT 3, SCENE 1:
Saloon in San Francisco.

Scene 2:
Kearney Station on the Pennsylvania Railroad.

Scene 3:
The Giant's Stairway.

ACT 4, SCENE 1:
Saloon on the Steamer for Europe.

Scene 2:
Deck of the Steamer.

Scene 3:
Lights of Liverpool. View of the City by Day and Night.

ACT 5, SCENE 1:
Hotel Parlor in Liverpool.

Scene 2:
The New Eccentric Club.

A CAPITAL PRIZE

1885.35

A Farce Comedy in Three Acts. Play by Dan Sully. Produced by Tony Pastor. Opened 1 June 1885 at Tony Pastor's New 14th Street Theatre and closed 27 June 1885 after 32 performances.

CAST: *Fred Holtz*: HARRY MORRIS. *Major Teddy Kelly*: J. B. DYLLYN. *Giuseppe Macaroni*: J. B. DYLLYN. *Michael Soft*: W. M. Keough. *Cal. Q. Later*, gas man: Ed. Barnes. *General D. Livery*, letter carrier: Ed. Barnes. *A. Fee*, lawyer: Ed. Barnes. *Theo. Dolite*, a civil engineer: Ed. Barnes. *Officer Grab*: M. J. Sullivan. *Isickle*, an iceman: M. J. Sullivan. *Reuben Smart*: M. J. Sullivan. *Charley Raike*: Hugh Mack. *Uriah Lyre*: Hugh Mack. *Hannah Beasley*: P. Randalls. *Tug Trace*, a farmer: P. Randalls. *Phil A. Grower*, a beat: Maurice Flynn. *Adam Rake*, a farmer: Maurice Flynn. *M. T. Glass*, a speculator: Wash. Favor. *Happy Cal's Band*: THE OLYMPIA QUARTETTE. *Rosey Holtz*: Ada Melrose. *Mrs. Mary Holtz*: Mme. Defossez. *Birdie Loo*: Anna Boyd. *Mrs. Daisey Lipp*: Lena Cole.

Act 1: Beer Saloon of Fred Holtz.

Act 2: Lodging House of Fred Holtz.

Act 3: Farm House of Fred Holtz.

MUSICAL NUMBERS, SPECIALTIES
Capital Prize Medley (Act 1)
"The Italian" (Act 3) J. B. Dyllyn

PATIENCE, or, Bunthorne's Bride

1885.34

A Revival of the Comic Aesthetic Opera in Two Acts[2]. Libretto by William S. Gilbert. Music by Arthur Sullivan. Stage manager, Frank Deshon. Musical director, Carlo Toriani. Produced by Harris Opera Company. Opened 1 June 1885 (matinee) at the New Park Theatre and closed 2 June 1885 after 4 performances[3]

CAST: *Patience*, a Village Maiden: POLLY FAIRBAIRN. *Rapturous Maidens (4)*: *Lady Jane*: ABBIE NICHOLSON. *Lady Angela*: MAY DOUGLAS. *Lady Saphir*: MARIE KNOWLES. *Lady Ella*: Florence Lytell. *Reginald Bunthorne*, a Fleshly Poet: FRANK DESHON. *Archibald Grosvenor*, an Idyllic Poet: ROBERT S. NODINE, JR. *Colonel Calverly*: J. W. MacSweeny. *Lieutenant The Duke of Dunstable*: Charles Bigelow. *Major Murgatroyd*: Fred Palmer. *The Solicitor*: Thomas Dagnell. *Chorus of Dragoon Guards, Rapturous Maidens.*

LA MASCOTTE

1885.36

A Revival of the Comic Opera in Three Acts[4]. Music by Edmond Audran. Stage manager, Frank Deshon. Musical director, Carlo Toriani. Produced by Harris Opera Company. Opened 3 June 1885 (matinee) at the New Park Theatre and closed 6 June 1885 after 8 performances[5]

CAST: *Lorenzo XVII*, Prince of Piombino: FRANK DESHON. *Pippo*, a Shepherd: R. S. Nodine, Jr. *Rocco*, a Farmer: C. A. BIGELOW. *Frederic*, the Prince of Pisa: J. P. MacSWEENY.*Matteo*, an Innkeeper: Fred Palmer. *Sergeant*: James Lyman. *Bettina*, the Mascot: POLLY FAIRBAIRN. *Fiametta*, daughter of Lorenzo: MAY DOUGLAS. *Annette*, a village maiden: Jennie Schuman. *Lords, Ladies, Peasants.*

H.M.S. PINAFORE, or, The Lass That Loved a Sailor

1885.37

Revival of the Comic Opera in Two Acts[6]. Libretto by William S. Gilbert. Music by Arthur Sullivan. Stage manager, Frank Deshon. Musical director,

---

[1]First produced in New York 28 September 1875 at the Academy of Music for 43 performances. Advertised "Entirely New Scenery", and Two Novel and Beautiful Ballets. Those included "Homage à la Beautée" (Act 2, Scene 2) by Mlle DeRosa, Mons. Arnold and Ballet, introducing the grotesque Jersey Light Guard by Eight Seconda Danseuses. Including the Jersey Light Guard by 8 Seconda Danseuses. Act 5, Scene 2: Ballet of Bric-à-Brac. Musical numbers not listed in programs.

[2]First produced in New York 22 September 1881 at the Standard Theatre for 177 performances. For Synopsis of Scenes and Musical Numbers, see original 1881 production.

[3]Performed twice daily.

[4]First produced in New York in English as THE MASCOT 5 May 1881 at the Bijou Theatre for 168 performances in two engagements. For Synopsis of Scenes and Musical Numbers, see original 1881 production.

[5]Performed twice daily.

[6]Originally presented in New York 15 January 1879 at the Standard Theatre for 175 performances. For Synopsis of Scenes and Musical Numbers, see original 1879 production.

Carlo Toriani. Presented by Harris Opera Company. Opened 8 June 1885 at the New Park Theatre and closed 13 June 1885 after 6 performances (matinees only).

CAST: *The Rt. Hon. Sir Joseph Porter, K.C.B.*, First Lord of the Admiralty: C. A. BIGELOW. *Captain Corcoran*, Commanding the *H.M.S. Pinafore*: J. P. MacSWEENY. *Ralph Rackstraw*, Able Seaman: R. S. NODINE. *Dick Deadeye*, Able Seaman: T. J. O'BRYANT. *Boatswain*: Fred Palmer. *Josephine*, the Captain's Daughter: POLLY FAIRBAIRN. *Hebe*, Sir Joseph's First Cousin: May Douglas. *Little Buttercup*, a Portsmouth Bumboat Woman: ABBIE NICHOLSON. *Sailors, Marines, Sisters, Cousins, Aunts, etc.*

1885.38 THE CHIMES OF NORMANDY

A Revival of the Comic Opera in Three Acts [7]. Original French libretto (Les Cloches de Corneville) by Clairville and Charles Gabet. Music by Robert Planquette. Stage manager, Frank Deshon. Musical director, Carlo Toriani. Produced by Harris Opera Company. Opened 8 June 1885 at the New Park Theatre and closed 13 June 1885 after 6 performances[8].

CAST: *Gaspard*, a Miser: FRANK DESHON. *Henri*, Marquis de Corneville: J. P. McSWEENY. *Grenecheux*, a Fisherman: R. S. NODINE. *The Bailli*: Fred. Palmer. *The Notary*: C. A. Bigelow. *Serpolette*, the Mischief Masher of the Village: POLLY FAIRBAIRN. *Germaine*, the lost heiress: MAY DOUGLAS. *Nanette*: Jennie Schuman. *Peasants, Sailors, etc.*

1885.39 Burlesque of LA BELLE HÉLÈNE

A Burlesque (of Jacques Offenbach's opera comique) in Two Acts. Burlesque by Harry LeClair. Music selected and arranged by William J. Rostetter. Produced by (John) Koster and (Albert) Bial. Opened 15 June 1885 at Koster & Bial's Concert Hall and closed 29 August 1885 after (64) performances.[9]

Olio: Herbert Brothers (Gymnasts), Harry Le Clair (Protean Comic), Ella Wesner (the Captain), Lottie Elliott (Endurance dancer).

CAST: Messrs. HARRY LeCLAIR, George Wood, Max Arnold. Misses ROSA LEE, LIZZIE PAINE, GEORGIE PARKER, LAURA BURT, LILLIE SHANDLEY, M. Chase, Julie Shandley, May Hall, Louise Hill.

1885.40 BILLEE TAYLOR, or, the Reward of Virtue

A Revival of the Charming Operetta (Nautical Comic Opera) in Two Acts[10]. Libretto by Henry Pottinger Stephens. Music by Edward Solomon. Produced under the stage direction of James C. Scanlan. Scenery by Homer Emens. Costumes designed by Georges Pilotell[11]. Musical director, Edward Solomon. Produced by the Gaiety Comic Opera Company (Isaac B. Rich, Proprietor; Edward E. Rice, Manager). Opened 22 June 1885 at the Casino Theatre and closed 27 June 1885 after 7 performances.

CAST: *Captain, The Hon. Felix Flapper*, R. N. of the *H. M. S . Thunderbolt*: J. H. RYLEY. *Billee Taylor*, a virtuous gardener: H. S. HILLIARD. *Sir Mincing Lane*, a self-made man: EDWARD P. TEMPLE. *Christopher Crab*, a villainous school-master: JOHN E. McWADE. *Ben Barnacle*, Bo'sun of the *H. M. S Thunderbolt*: WILLIAM WHITE. *Arabella Lane*, Sir Mincing Lane's daughter: VERNONA JARBEAU. *Eliza Dabsey*, Phoebe's aunt: ALICE BARNETT. *Susan*, a village maiden: Josie Hall. *Phoebe Farleigh*, The Pet of the Village: LILLIAN RUSSELL. *Premiere Danseuse, Sailor's Hornpipe, Act 2*: Lizzie Sims. *Charity Girls, Peasants, Sailors, Soldiers, Villagers.*

[7]First produced in New York 22 October 1877 at the Fifth Avenue Theatre for 16 performances in repertory. For Synopsis of Scenes and Musical Numbers, see original 1877 production.

[8]Performed every evening while H.M.S. PINAFORE was performed at matinees.

[9]No program available.

[10]First produced in New York 19 February 1881 at the Standard Theatre for 101 performances; re-opened 6 June 1881 at Niblo's Garden for an additional 16 performances. Total: 117 performances. For Synopsis of Scenes and Musical Numbers, see original 1881 production.

[11]Costumes and effects from the original production.

1885.41 NANON, The Hostess of the Golden Lamb

An Opéra Comique in Three Acts[12]. Original Viennese libretto ('Nanon, die Wirthin vom goldenene Lamm') by F. Zell, based on the play "Ninon, Nanon et Madame de Maintenon" by Emmanuel Théaulon, Armand d'Artois and Lesguillon. Music by Richard Genée. American translation by Sydney Rosenfeld. Produced under the stage direction of Heinrich Conried. Scenery by John Mazzanovich, Henry Hoyt and Harley Merry. Costumes designed by C. de Grimm. Musical director, Jesse Williams. Produced by Rudolf Aronson. Opened 29 June 1885 at the Casino Theatre and closed 14 November 1885 after 152 performances.

CAST: *Nanon Patin*, The Hostess of the Golden Lamb: SADIE MARTINOT. *Ninon d'l'Enclos*: PAULINE HALL. *Gaston*, Page to Ninon: BILLIE BARLOW. *Mme. de Maintenon*: ALICE VINCENT. *Jacqueline*, Waitress: Agnes Folsom. *Mme. de Fulpert*: ROSE BEAUDET. *Mlle. d'Armenonville*: Carrie Andrews. *Mme. de Frontenac*: Florence Bell. *Comtesse d'Huilièries*: Adele Langdon. *Thérèse*, Aunt of Nanon: Marie Koenig. *Lisette*: Sadie Wells. *Marion*: Emma Hanley. *Marquis d'Aubigné*: W. T. CARLETON. *Vicomte de Marsillac*, Nephew of Marquis de Marsillac: W. H. FITZGERALD. *Abbé*: William Herbert. *Pierre*: Harry Standish. *Bombardini*, Drum-Major: Alexis Markham. *Sergeant*: G. T. Wade. *Commissioner*: C. L. Weeks. *Notary*: O. Heilig. *Marquis de Marsillac*: FRANCIS WILSON. *Louis XIV*: GUSTAVUS LEVICK. *Officers, Court Ladies and Gentlemen, Soldiers, Peasants, etc.*

Act 1: Inn of the Golden Lamb. (Mazzanovich.)

Act 2: Salon of Ninon d L'Enclos. (Hoyt.)

Act 3: Sanctuary of Mme. de Maintenon. (Merry.)

MUSICAL NUMBERS[13]

"Little Eva's Wish" (Open thy lattice)
(*Music by* John F. Huddart. *Lyrics by* Morris H. Warner.)

"I Am an Impressario"
F. Wilson

"It's Only a Question of Time"
W. H. Fitzgerald

"Anna in Rapture I Come to Thee"
W. T. Carleton

"Anna in Rapture I Come to Thee" (reprise)
W. T. Carleton

"Hidden Music"
P. Hall (*Music by* Julius J. Lyons.)

1885.42 FUNNY VALENTINES

A Musical Farce Comedy in Three Acts. Book, music and lyrics by J. H. Farrell. Produced under the personal supervision of W. J. Ferguson. Opened 13 July 1885 at Tony Pastor's Fourteenth Street Theatre and closed 18 July 1885 after 8 performances.

CAST: *Pennie Valentine*, sentimental—sometimes: EARLE REMINGTON. *Miss Dashington Blaize*, who flirts—now and then: ANNA BOYD. *Rosa*, who thoroughly understands the care of babies: ANNA BOYD. *Miss Gush*, President of the Women's Supremacy Society, who gushes occasionally: Lena W. Cole. *Maggie*, a French Nurse from—: Lena W. Cole. *Miss Thomasina Haughty*, who says nothing—but thinks a great deal: Kate Ferguson. *Jane*, an everyday nurse girl: Kate Ferguson. *Mrs. Hartz*, who resolves that her husband shall not elope: Dollie Warren. *Royal Valentine*, in a box: H. W. BRINKLEY. *Moses*, old 'Clo': H. W. BRINKLEY. *General Calendar*, a Bachelor Lawyer: Odell Williams. *Sidney Lightbody*, his Clerk—he tries to be English: J. Joseph Fields. *Our Grocer's Boy*: J. Joseph Fields. *Asa Hartz*, the Dentist—who flirts at all times: J. J. Leslie. *Our Butcher's Boy*: J. J. Leslie. *Mr. Blinks*: William E. Hines. *Officer O'Halley*, our Policeman: William E. Hines. *Regan*, the installment man, "and don't you forget it": William E. Hines. *Mr. Hans Molar*, the man who gets the gas: Myers Clarke. *J. Hilton Gold*, the Bank Cashier: D. Germaine. *Tommy Tongs*, our Iceman: D. Germaine. *A. Guy Valentine*, comic: J. H. FARRELL.

[12]English language premiere in New York. First produced in New York in German 2 January 1885 at the Thalia Theatre for (56) performances in repertory.

[13]Musical numbers not listed in programs. List prepared from published sheet music, reviews. No libretto, musical score or book of words found for this adaptation.

Act 1: A Race for a Fortune. We've all tried it.

Act 2: Our Own Kitchen. We all have it.

Act 3: Dr. Hartz' Dental parlor. We've all been there.

MUSICAL NUMBERS

"Sing, O Songster of the Night"
"Lovce is all Nonsense"
"The Companions for Me"
"Shout High"
"I Love That Girl"
"He Tries to Be English"
"Mamma's Little Joy"
"Officer O'Halley"
"The Household Brigade"
"'Phist. There, Baby"
"Patter, Patter, Went the Rain"

1885.43

THE MIKADO, or, The Town of Titipu

A Japanese Comic Opera in Two Acts[14]. Libretto by William S. Gilbert. Music by Arthur Sullivan. Directed by Sydney Rosenfeld. Costumes by Eaves. Orchestra directed by Fred Perkins. Produced by Sydney Rosenfeld (and Edward T. Abraham[15]). Opened and closed 20 July 1885 at the Union Square Theatre after 1 performance; re-opened 10 August 1885 under the auspices of Henry C. Miner at Henry Miner's People's Theatre, moved 17 August 1885 to the Union Square Theatre and closed 29 August 1885 after 21 performances. Total: 22 performances.

CAST: *The Mikado of Japan*: J. W. HERBERT[16]. *Nanki-Poo*, his son, disguised as a wandering minstrel, and in love with Yum-Yum: A. MONTEGRIFFO. *Ko-Ko*, Lord High Executioner of Titipu: ROLAND REED. *Pooh-Bah*, Lord High Everything Else: HERBERT ARCHER[17]. *Pish-Tush*, a Noble Lord: GEORGE H. BRODERICK. *Three Sisters, Wards of Ko-Ko*: *Yum-Yum*: ALICE HARRISON. *Pitti-Sing*: BELLE ARCHER[18]. *Peep-Bo*: LIZZIE QUIGLEY[19]. *Katisha*: EMMA MABELLA BAKER. *Chorus of School Girls, Nobles, and Coolies.*

1885.44

SCHEMING!

A Comedy (with Songs) in Three Acts. Play by Edwin R. Lang. Produced by Lang's Comedy Comiques. Opened 20 July 1885 at Tony Pastor's 14th Street Theatre and closed 25 July 1885 after 8 performances.

CAST: *Peagreen Pinkroot*, a drummer who has seen a great deal of the world and wants to see more—fresh, but not too fresh, but just fresh enough: EDWIN R. LANG. *Timothy Toddles*, a tramp: EDWIN R. LANG. *Jake*, a Dutch servant: EDWIN R. LANG. *Brown*, the Impostor: EDWIN R. LANG. *William Jason Smart*, another drummer—fresh, very fresh, too fresh, wants a waltz: Harry Mills. *Miss Kratzmeyer*, selling vegetables: Harry Mills. *Evening Breeze*, the Dude: Harry Mills. *Mons. Blatz*, the French Music teacher: Harry Mills. *Hiram Bland*, who is scheming to have his daughter marry his old friend Brown: E. B. FITZ. *Oliver Brown*, in search of his son: William A. Lang. *Ike*, a farm hand: William A. Lang. *Pete*, the coachman: William A. Lang. *Tomahawk*, an Indian: William A. Lang. *Josephine Bland*, Pa's pet daughter: Viola Rosa. *Katie*, a Dutch servant girl: Viola Rosa. *Prima Donna*: Viola Rosa. *Jennie Somers*, full of life and continually playing tricks on her uncle: ANNA BOYD. *Sarah Meena Jones*, from Maine, a woman of few words, and a member of the Salvation Army: ANNA BOYD. *Dolly*, maid of all work: KATHERINE WEBSTER.

Act 1: Scheming!

Act 2: More Scheming!

Act 3: Scheming at an End.

Note: Between the Second and Third Acts a wedding is supposed to have taken place, and Pinkroot signs his name as Brown, which causes much confusion and excitement.

MUSICAL NUMBERS, SPECIALTIES[20]

"Is Your Mama Well"
"Wild Flowers"
(*Music and Lyrics by* Lillie Hall.)
"Because I Don't Dress Like a Dude"
"Since the Street Cars Have Run on Broadway"
(*Music and Lyrics by* William Devere.)
"Hurry, Little Children"
(*Music by* David Braham. *Lyrics by* Edward Harrigan.)
"Only a Tramp"
E. R. Lang
(*Music and Lyrics by* Edwin R. Lang.)
"Wise Men Have in All Ages"
"English, By Jove"
(*Music and Lyrics by* Harry Mills.)
"A Rich Man's Son"
"In Laughing I Find I Grow Fat"
E. B. Fitz
(*Music and Lyrics by* E. B. Fitz.)
"Song of the Sailor" (from FANTINE, Boston)
(*Music by* Firmin Bernicat, completed by André Messager. *Lyrics by* B. E. Woolf and R. M. Field.)
"Ring Dat Golden Bell"
"Im walde en auf der heiday" (Dutch Song)
"Sally Brown"
LA FILLE DE MADAME ANGOT Selection
(*Music by* Charles Lecocq.)
"We've All Been Out on a Tear"
(*Music and Lyrics by* Edwin R. Lang.)
"Pledge Us, Do!"
Meg and I
(Poem by Con T. Murphy) (Act 1)
E. R. Lang
Musical Specialty (Act 2)
E. B. Fitz, K. Webster
"Essence of Old Virginia" (Act 2)
W. A. Lang

1885.45

CHATTER

A Musical Comedy in Three Acts[21]. Based on the original Viennese Posse mit Gesang "Die Näherin," (libretto by Ludwig Held and Eduard Jacobson[22]). Music by Carl Millöcker. Stage manager, Charles H. Jones. Scenery by Philip Goatcher. Mechanism by F. Dorrington. Appointments by E. Siedle. Gas effects by J. F. Driscoll. Musical director, Antonio DeNovellis. Produced by John McCaull. Opened 17 August 1885 at Wallack's Theatre and closed 12 September 1885 after 28 performances.[23]

CAST: *Jeremiah Hackett*, Esq. of Nyack: DeWOLF HOPPER. *Mrs. Jeremiah Hackett*, his wife: GENEVIEVE REYNOLDS. *Frederick Hackett*, their son: EDWIN HOFF. *Rose*, his wife: OLGA BRANDON. *Papa Cooper, Mamma Cooper*, Mrs. Hackett's parents: Thomas Wills, Hannah Miller. *Dennis*, servant at Hackett's: Charles Plunkett. *Coachman*: C. H. Jones. *Mary*, chambermaid: Kitty Wilson. *Mrs. Winter*, Chief of Employment Bureau: JENNIE REIFFARTH. *Ganymede Gurgle*, her musical assistant:

[14]This premiere production was unauthorized, and was closed by injunction. THE MIKADO was subsequently presented in its authorized production 19 August 1885 at the Fifth Avenue Theatre by Richard D'Oyly Carte for 250 performances. For Synopsis of Scenes and Musical Numbers, see 19 August 1885 production.

[15]According to the New York Times of 21 and 22 July 1885, Rosenfeld assigned his rights as producer to Edward T. Abraham.

[16]At the People's Theatre and Union Square, succeeded by CHARLES L. HARRIS.

[17]At the Union Square, succeeded by W. PAUL BOWN.

[18]At the Union Square, succeeded by HATTIE STARR.

[19]At the Union Square, succeeded by JESSIE QUIGLEY.

[20]Not in performance order.

[21]Previously produced in New York in German at the Thalia Theatre 8 April 1881.

[22]Jacobson adapted Held's Viennese libretto for its Munich and Berlin productions.

[23]English adaptation uncredited; reviewers attributed it to Sydney Rosenfeld. The critic for the New York Times remarked that approximately one quarter of the musical score was by Millöcker, the balance being comprised of potpourris by a dozen composers from Mozart to Offenbach.

HARRY MACDONOUGH. *Buntles*, her clerk: Mountjoy Walker. *Bill*, a street Arab: Gustave Frankel. *Veachy*, a wreck: L. M. Hall. *Bridget*, chambermaid, first floor, front: Kate Ethel. *Dolly*, chambermaid, second story, front: Annette Hall. *Nelly*, waitress: Clara Allen. *Kitty*, nurse: Louise Estore. *Lotti Greasmeyer*, the seamstress: MATHILDE COTTRELLY.

ACT 1:
Intelligence Office.

ACT 2:
The Home of the Hacketts, at Nyack.

ACT 3:
Fête Champetre at the Hacketts'.

ACT 1
"Where can we get a seamstress"
"A whole nickel! You have saved my life!"
"I don't like to talk much, but—"
M. Cottrelly
"Songs of Many Nations" (Duet)
M. Cottrelly, H. Macdonough

ACT 2
"Fill up on Champagne and pate de foie gras"
H. Macdonough
"Crying because I am so (hic) happy"
C. Plunkett
"Waiter's Song"/"Melancholy Tale of an Oyster"
"Die Gehemnisse des Teufels"
"Comes a Birdie Flying"
M. Cottrelly

ACT 3
"For All of Which My Son-in-Law Must Pay" (Topical song)
D. Hopper
"Read the Answer in the Stars" (Trio with new verses, from THE BLACK HUSSAR)
M. Cottrelly, H. Macdonough, D. Hopper
(*Music by* Carl Millöcker. *Lyrics by* Sydney Rosenfeld.)
Finale

1885.46

CLIO

A Spectacular Production in Five Acts. Play by Bartley Campbell. Original music composed, arranged and conducted by Giuseppe Operti. Stage director, George W. Herbert; produced under the personal supervision of Bartley Campbell. Ballets by Mamert Bibeyran. Scenery by D. B. Hughes, Gaspard Maeder, George Heineman. Costumes and armors by (Henry) Dazian & Son. Machinery and mechanical effects by William Crane, Nelson Waldron. Properties and appointments by Charles Blesser. Gas light effects by Davidson & Francis. Produced by Bartley Campbell and E. G. Gilmore. Opened 17 August 1885 at Niblo's Garden and closed 12 September 1885 after 32 performances.

CAST: *Lucia* (Clio): ADELE BELGARDE. *Didi*: Marion Elmore. *Countess Ellice*: May Newman. *Duchess de Montmarte*: MRS. CHARLES POOLE. *Fabian*, an Artist: FRANK LOSEE. *Count Giovannie*, a Roué with no faith in women: B. T. RINGGOLD. *Pietro*, a Model: Thomas H. Burns. *Paulo*, Lucia's father: Harry Rich. *Marquis Mattu*, an old Campaigner: Harold Forsburg. *Prince Zellar*, a Cairo merchant: Harry Carter. *King of France*: EDGAR L. DAVENPORT. *Philippaux*, a learned cook: Jay Hunt. *Alsazage*: F. W. Strong. *Spring*: Master Tommy Russell. *Premiere Assoluta* (Ballet): Mlle. ADÈLE CORNALBA. *Premiere Character Danseuse*: Mlle. ELOISE. *Chorus of 50 Ladies and Gentlemen; 50 Coryphées; 25 Children.*

Act 1: Plaza of St. Marks, Venice. (Hughes.)

Act 2: Fabian's Studio, Florence. (Maeder.)

Act 3: An apartment in the Villa of the Duchess de Montmarte. Florence. (Maeder.)

Act 4: The King's Palace, France. (Heineman.) Earthquake Scene.

Act 5: Fabian's Studio, Florence. (Maeder.)

ACT 1
Grand Fête Scene; Novel Venetian Ballet Mlle. Eloise, 50 Coryphées

ACT 4
The Revels; New and Characteristic Grecian Ballet
Mlles. Cornalba, Eloise, Coryphées, Corps de Ballet

1885.47

THE MIKADO, or, The Town of Titipu

A Japanese Comic Opera in Two Acts[24]. Libretto by William S. Gilbert. Music by Arthur Sullivan. Directed by Richard Barker. Scenery designed by Harley Merry, H. L. Reid. Wardrobe from original designs of the Savoy Theatre[25]. Mechanisms by J. H. Lundy. Orchestra directed by P. W. Halton. Produced by Richard D'Oyly Carte (John Stetson, manager). Opened 19 August 1885 at the Fifth Avenue Theatre, moved 1 February 1886 to the Standard Theatre, returned 1 March 1886 to the Fifth Avenue Theatre and closed 17 April 1886 after 250 performances.

CAST: *The Mikado of Japan*: F. FEDERICI. *Nanki-Poo*, his son, disguised as a wandering minstrel, and in love with Yum-Yum: COURTICE POUNDS. *Ko-Ko*, Lord High Executioner of Titipu: GEORGE THORNE. *Pooh-Bah*, Lord High Everything Else: F. BILLINGTON. *Pish-Tush*, a Noble Lord: G. BYRON BROWNE. *Three Sisters, Wards of Ko-Ko*: *Yum-Yum*: GERALDINE ULMAR. *Pitti-Sing*: KATE FORSTER. *Peep-Bo*: GERALDINE ST. MAUR. *Katisha*, an Elderly Lady, in love with Nanki-Poo: ELSIE CAMERON. *Chorus of School Girls, Nobles, Guards and Coolies.*

Act 1: Court-yard of Ko-Ko's official residence. (Merry.)

Act 2: Ko-Ko's Garden. (Reid.)

ACT 1[26]
"If you want to know who we are"
Chorus of Men
"A wand'ring minstrel I" (Song and Chorus)
C. Pounds
"Our great Mikado, virtuous man" (Song)
G. B. Browne, Chorus
"Young man, despair" (Song)
F. Billington, C. Pounds, G. B. Browne
"And have I journey'd for a month" (Recitative)
C. Pounds, F. Billington
"Behold the Lord High Executioner!" (Chorus with Solo)
G. Thorne, Chorus
"As some day it may happen" (Song)
G. Thorne, Chorus of Men
"Comes a train of little ladies"
Chorus of Girls
"Three little maids from school are we" (Trio)
G. Ulmar, K. Forster, G. St. Maur, Chorus of Girls
"So please you, sir" (Quartet and Chorus)
G. Ulmar, K. Forster, G. St. Maur, F. Billington
"Were you not to Ko-Ko plighted" (Duet)
G. Ulmar, C. Pounds
"I am so proud" (Trio)
G. Thorne, G. B. Browne, F. Billington
"With aspect stern and gloomy stride" (Finale)

ACT 2
"Braid the raven hair" (Solo)
K. Forster, Chorus of Girls
"The sun, whose rays are all a-blaze" (Song)
G. Ulmar
"Brightly dawns our wedding day" (Madrigal)
G. Ulmar, K. Forster, C. Pounds, G. B. Browne
"Here's a how-de-do" (Trio)
G. Ulmar, C. Pounds, G. Thorne
"Mi-ya-sa-ma, mi-ya-sa-ma" (Entrance of Mikado and Katisha)
"A more humane Mikado" (Song)
F. Federici, Chorus

[24]This was the authorized production; previously presented in New York in an unauthorized production 20 July 1885 at the Union Square Theatre for 1 performance, followed by engagements at Henry Miner's People's Theatre and the Union Square Theatre.
[25]Ladies dresses from Messrs. Liberty & Co. (London); gentlemen's dresses designed by Mr. Wilhelm, from Japanese authorities, executed by Auguste & Co. (London).
[26]Musical numbers not listed in programs. List prepared from published English vocal score (Chappell & Co., London, 1885).

"The criminal cried" (Trio and Chorus)
K. Forster, G. Thorne, F. Billington, Chorus
"See how the Fates their gifts allot" (Glee)
K. Forster, E. Cameron, F. Billington, F. Federici
"The flowers that bloom in the spring" (Duet)
C. Pounds, G. Thorne, with G. Ulmar, K. Forster, F. Billington
"Alone, and yet alive" (Recitative and Song)
E. Cameron
"On a tree by a river" (Song)
G. Thorne
"There is a beauty, in the bellow of the blast" (Duet)
E. Cameron, G. Thorne
"For he's gone and married Yum-Yum" (Finale)

THE MIKADO, or, The Town of Titipu

1885.48

The Japanese Comic Opera in Two Acts[27]. Libretto by William S. Gilbert. Music by Arthur Sullivan. Directed by James C. Duff. Scenery by Hughson Hawley (Act 1), Joseph Clare (Act 2). Costumes purchased from First Japanese Manufacturing & Trading Company, Messs. Vantine & Co., H. C. Parke. Orchestra directed by Anthony Reiff. Produced by James C. Duff. Opened 24 August 1885 at the Standard Theatre and closed 21 November 1885 after 91 performances[28].

CAST: *The Mikado of Japan*: WILLIAM H. HAMILTON. *Nanki-Poo*, his son, disguised as a wandering minstrel, and in love with Yum-Yum: HARRY S. HILLIARD. *Ko-Ko*, High Executioner: J. H. RYLEY. *Pooh-Bah*, Lord High Everything Else: THOMAS WHIFFEN. *Pish-Tush*, a Noble Lord: ALONZO E STODDARD. *Three Sisters*, Wards of Ko-Ko: *Yum-Yum*: VERNONA JARBEAU. *Pitti-Sing*: SALLIE WILLIAMS. *Peep-Bo*: CARRIE TUTEIN. *Katisha*, an elderly lady in love with Nanki-Poo: ZELDA SEGUIN. *Chorus of School Girls, Nobles, Guards and Coolies.*

OLD LAVENDER

1885.49

A Dramatic Picture of City Life (Local Play) in Four Acts, 6 Scenes[29]. Play (and lyrics) by Edward Harrigan. Music by David Braham. Staged by Edward Harrigan. Scenery by Charles W. Witham. Mechanical effects by William A. Vail. Properties by Joseph H. Logan. Dresses by Mrs. Mary Jack. Produced by Edward Harrigan. Opened 31 August 1885 at Harrigan's Park Theatre and closed 28 November 1885 after 100 performances.

CAST: *Old Lavender*: EDWARD HARRIGAN. *Smoke*, a Negro: JOHN WILD. *Dick*, the Rat: DAN COLLYER. *Martin Reilly*: M. J. Bradley. *John Filbert*: HARRY FISHER. *Paul Cassin*: H. A. Weaver, Jr. *Philip Coggswell*: E. A. EBERLE. *Mother Crawford*: ANNIE YEAMANS. *Laura Coggswell*: Stella Boniface. *Sally Stacy*: AMY LEE. *Zolia Brown*: GEORGE MERRITT. *Gideon Guile*: WILLIAM WEST. *Henry Mercer*: Richard Quilter. *Paudeen McGarrity*: John Sparks. *Silas Longmetre*: Arthur C. Moreland. *Jack Dingle*: PETER GOLDRICH. *Lascar Joe*: James Fox. *Morris Hopkins*: Rob Hooley. *Tom Darrow*: Joseph Davis. *Louis Donnette*: Charles Coffey. *Tom Rumnius*: Thomas Ray. *Silas Grenell*: W. Merritt. *Pop Jones*: G. L. Stout. *Policeman*: James McCullough. *Gideon Welthy*: J. A. Dewey. *Mrs. Heartsoul*: Ada Farwell. *Mrs. Guile*: Annie Langdon. *Ms. Stone*: Emily Yeamans. *Mrs. Mercer*: Kate Langdon. *Mrs. Grenell*: Delia Stillwell. *Mrs. Wilbur*: Annie Hall. *Mrs. Caldwell*: Julia Leonard. *Pages*: Masters Willie, George, Thomas, Charles. *Serenaders, Street Characters, Sailors, etc.*

ACT 1:
Interior of the Owl Club House. The Inauguration. The Clock in the Tower strikes Twelve.

ACT 2:
The Banking House of Philip Coggswell. The Forged Check.

ACT 3: The River Front (by Moonlight). Pop Jones' Coffee and Cakes. Midnight at the Ferry. Lavender's Home.

ACT 4, SCENE 1:
Interior of Mother Crawford's Sailor's Boarding House. The Stranger's Rest. Scene 2:
Wall Street looking to the river. Scene 3: Private Office of Philip Coggswell, Banker. The Jolly Old Owl.

MUSICAL NUMBERS
"Poverty's Tears Ebb and Flow"
"Extra, Extra"
"(The) Jolly Old Owls" (The Owl)
"Get Up, Jack; John, Sit Down"
"Sweetest Love"
"Please Put That Down"

BROTHER MAX

1885.50

A Musical Comedy Drama in a Prologue and Three Acts. Play by R. E. Graham. Musical director, W. B. Johns. Leader of orchestra, Fritz Gagel. Manager and Proprietor, George Heuer. Opened 31 August 1885 at Tony Pastor's Fourteenth Street Theatre and closed 5 September 1885 after 8 performances.

CAST (Prologue): *Norah*: BELLA VIVIAN. *Alma*: Lizzie Fletcher. *Mrs. Holtzman*: Mrs. F. A. Tannehill. *Walter Brooks*: J. M. COLVILLE. *John Ross*: George Nash. *Captain Stormboy*: Frank E. Jamison. *The Twins*: Two Babies. (The Play) *Max*, a happy Switzer: R. E. GRAHAM. *Walter Brooks*: J. M. COLVILLE. *John Ross*: George Nash. *Farmer Lantz*: WILLIAM MOORE. *Mrs. Holtzman*, Max's mother: Mrs. F. A. Tannehill. *Alma*, Max's sister: Lizzie Fletcher. *Little Walter, Little Alma*, Max's Pets: Little Adah, Little Alberta. *Norah*, Max's Sweetheart: BELLA VIVIAN. *Sailors, Base Ball Nines, etc.*

Prologue: America. Farewell!
"I go to win fortune for the angels of our homes and firesides." "He will never come back."

ACT 1:
Switzerland. Evening. The happy home. Prosperity and love. The promised land. The return. A ragpicker. "Norah's sweetheart from Ireland."

ACT 2:
"Five o'clock in the morning." Max's mistake. "She's crazy." "He's your brother, Walter Brooks." A mother's grief. "Vengeance belongs to me!" Face to face. "I'm safe." "Yah, safe to get hung." "That wretch is your husband." "Your life for hers!"

ACT 3:
America. On the Hudson. "If I can't have her love he shall not enjoy it." The base ball craze, I am de captain of de whole business. The dangerous gate. Base Ball vs. Love. A daughter of Erin. The coaxing duet. "I'll not let them kill my papa." "That's the end of Walter Brooks." Alma in anger. Max a Prisoner. Base Ball to the rescue. Little Walter as a hero. Max pops. "Scare me again." You have joined Germany and Ireland. He is the Captain of the Base Ball Nine.

MUSICAL NUMBERS[30]
"Promised Land"
"De Captain of De Base Ball Nine"
"Cradle Duet"
"Baby's Smile"
"Open Your Window"
"Graham's Laugh"
"Coaxing Duet"

[27]A rival production to those at the Fifth Avenue and Union Square Theatres. First presented in New York in an unauthorized production 10, 17-29 August 1885 at the Union Square Theatre and Henry Miner's People's Theatre for 22 performances. The authorized production opened 19 August 1885 at the Fifth Avenue Theatre under the auspices of Richard D'Oyly Carte for 250 performances. For Synopsis of Scenes and Musical Numbers, see 19 August 1885 D'Oyly Carte production.

[28]Played a return engagement 12 April 1886 at the Grand Opera House for 8 performances.

[29]Previous shorter versions of OLD LAVENDER were presented in New York for one week engagements 3 September 1877 at the Theatre Comique, 22 April 1878 at the Theatre Comique, and 26 August 1878 at the Theatre Comique for a total of 24 performances. This new and final version was expanded to full length with six new songs added.

[30]During the play, Mr. Graham, assisted by Miss Vivian, will sing the following new and original songs and duets.

1885.51

NA-NON

A Burlesque (of Richard Genée's opera comique 'Nanon') in Two Acts[31]. Burlesque by Carl Hauser and J. L. Ford. Music selected and arranged by William J. Rostetter. Produced under the personal supervision of Harry LeClair. Produced by (John) Koster and (Albert) Bial. Opened 31 August 1885 at Koster & Bial's Concert Hall and closed 31 October 1885 after (72) performances.

CAST: *Na-Non*, the Hostess of the Golden Goose: HARRY LeCLAIR. *Ninon de Long-Clothes*, of the old Bleeker Street aristocracy: SOPHIE HUMMEL. *Lily the Page*, a bright one in the history of Ninon: LAURA BURT. *Mme. de Maniac*, a stately and erratic Lady with strong predilections for song and dance: GEORGIE PARKER. *Marquis O'Brien*, of the old Noblesse O'Blige: LIZZIE PAINE. *Signor Pastorini*, Dealer in Sasparilla and Theatrical Ideas, enamored to Ninon: W. J. RUSSELL. *The Abbe*, with an eye to the welfare of the tenderest lambs of his flock: GERALD GRIFFIN. *Consolidated Messenger Boy No. 999*, always on time: Lillie Shandley. *Gaily*, the troubadour: Herr Ignatz Conradi. *Jean Babtist Johnson*, Groom: Master O. Fellow. *McGinniss*, Policeman No. 4-11-44: Gerald Griffin.

Simple-minded peasants, relatives to Na-non): *Henry*: Miss Chamberlin. *Jacques*: Florence T. Morton. *Gustave*: Eva Barrington. *August*: Julie Shandley. *Clementina*: Lillie May Hall. *Mary*: Ethel Carrington. *Susan*: Ruby Carr.

ACT 1

Prologue
L. Burt

"Not much" (Song)
W. J. Russell

"The Swell with the Glass in His Eye" (Song)
L. Burt

"Smashed" (Song)
S. Hummel

"Read the answer in the Herald" (Comic Trio)
S. Hummel, L. Paine, W. J. Russell

"How we pose" (Character Song and Dance)
Entire Company

ACT 2

"Ohe Mama" (Song)
S. Hummel

"The pretty little Quaker" (Song)
L. Burt

Character Song with Imitations
W. J. Russell

Engagement extraordinary and first appearance of Mlle. Sarah Bernhardt
G. Parker

"Hi Jennie Ho Jennie Johnson" (Song and Dance)
G. Parker

"It's German dat's so" (New and original topical song)
H. LeClair

1885.52

DIE FLEDERMAUS

A Return Engagement of the Comic Operette in Three Acts[32]. Original Viennese libretto by Carl Haffner and Richard Genée, based on "Le Reveillon" by Henri Meilhac and Ludovic Halévy. Lyrics by Richard Genée. Music by Johann Strauss. Stage manager, A. W. Maflin. Musical director, Antonio DeNovellis. Scenery by Philip Goatcher. Mechanism by F. Dorrington. Appointments by E. Siedle. Gas effects by J. F. Driscoll. Produced by the McCaull Opera Company (John McCaull, Proprietor and Manager). Opened 14 September 1885 at Wallack's Theatre and closed 26 September 1885 after 14 performances[33].

CAST: *Eisenstein*, a Wealthy Banker: MARK SMITH. *Franke*, Director of the Prison: DeWOLF HOPPER. *Dr. Falke*, the Family Physician: C. W. DUNGAN. *Prince Orloffsky*: OLGA BRANDON. *Alfred*, a Tenor: Edwin Hoff. *Frosch*, a Jailer: Charles Plunkett. *Blind*, an Attorney: L. M. Hall. *Joan*, Prince Orloffsky's Servant: A. W. Maflin. *Murry*, a Canadian: Harry Brougham. *Canconi*, an Italian: L. A. Shrader. *Ali Bey*, an Egyptian: Charles Kauffman. *Ramusin*, a Japanese: H. W. Frazer. *Russian Waiters (4)*: Messrs. Jones, Taylor, Childs, Walker. *Rosalind*, Eisenstein's wife: ROSALBA BEECHER. *Adele*, her Servant: MATHILDE COTRELLY. *Ida*, a Coryphée: JENNIE PRINCE. *Coryphées (10)*: *Mélanie*: Kate Ethel. *Faustinne*: Kitty Wilson. *Felicita*: Gertrude Clarke. *Sidi*: Annette Hall. *Natalie*: Edith Edwards. *Mini*: Zoe DeVielle. *Sylvia*: Clara Allen. *Irene*: Ella Kelly. *Sabine*: Josephine Knapp. *Hermine*: Carrie Jackson.

1885.53

SHANE-NA-LAWN!

An Irish Play in Three Acts. Play by James C. Roach and J. Armory Knox (Texas Siftings). Music and lyrics by William J. Scanlan. Stage manager, G. W. Pike. Musical director, W. H. Brockway. Produced by Augustus Pitou. Opened 21 September 1885 at Henry C. Miner's People's Theatre and closed 26 September 1885 after 8 performances; returned 26 April 1886 at Niblo's Garden and closed 8 May 1886 after an additional 16 performances[34]. Total: 24 performances.

CAST: *Shane-na-Lawn*: WILLIAM J. SCANLAN. *John Power*: J. B. Turner. *Gerald Power*: Frank Ambrose. *Squire Redmond*: G. W. PIKE. *Harry Redmond*: W. K. Ogden. *Mat Kirwin*: Walter Fessler. *Ronald*: Gus Reynolds. *Buckley*: W. R. Webster. *Agent Dillon*: Albert Klein. *Captain Fitzgerald*: Walter Wallace. *Rose Redmond*: ETHEL BRANDON. *Peggy O'Moore*: MARION WARREN. *Mrs. Power*: Mrs. J. B. Turner. *Moll Shehough*: Louise Harris.

Scene: Ireland, 1790, under the Grattan Parliament, one of the happiest periods of Irish history.

SPECIALTIES, MUSICAL NUMBERS

Selection from William Makepeace Thackeray's 'Pendennis'
W. J. Scanlan

"The Low Backed Car"
W. J. Scanlan (*Music and Lyrics by* Samuel Lover.)

"Come Live in My Heart and Pay No Rent"[35]
W. J. Scanlan

"What's in a Kiss" (also in THE IRISH MINSTREL)
W. J. Scanlan

"My Nellie's Blue Eyes" (also in THE IRISH MINSTREL)
W. J. Scanlan

"Over the Mountain" (from FRIEND AND FOE)
W. J. Scanlan

"Scanlan's Rose Song" (also in THE IRISH MINSTREL)
W. J. Scanlan

"Come Along, My Darlin'"
W. J. Scanlan

"Peek-a-Boo" (from FRIEND AND FOE)
W. J. Scanlan

"Peggy O'Moore"
W. J. Scanlan

"Remember Boy, You're Irish"
W. J. Scanlan

1885.54

CAPTAIN OF THE QUEEN'S OWN

A Musical Comedy in Three Acts. Libretto by Laura Leclair Phillips. New music arranged by Ella Wesner. Musical director, Fred White. Opened 28 September 1885 at Tony Pastor's 14th Street Theatre and closed 10 October 1885 after 16 performances.

CAST: *Captain Septimus Symmetry*, of the "Queen's Own" on a lark in America, and very much sought after: ELLA WESNER[36]. *George Adolphus Smiggins*, an Inventor of no mean pretense: T. H. Glenney. *Harry Brown*, a man of good family, who has traveled and is fond of Petticoats: Will J. Mack. *Paul Johnson*, Politician—hoping to become Minister to France, etc.: Richard Lyle. *Buckie West*, a man for the emergency, who knows how to keep a hotel like clockwork, and has a charming way of detaining his

[31]Between Acts 1 and 2, a Grand Selection from THE MIKADO was presented: "Behold the High Executioner," "Braid the raven hair," "A Wandering Minstrel," "If Patriotic Sentiment is wanted, " "Song of the Sea," "Yeo-ho! heave-ho!," "The Flowers of Spring," "Brightly dawns our wedding day," "Three Little Maids from Scool," "For he's gone and married Yum-Yum," "With Laughging song and Merry Dance."

[32]First produced in New York in German 21 November 1874 at the Stadt Theater, and in English 15 March 1885 at the Casino Theatre for 42 performances. For Synopsis of Scenes and Musical Numbers, see March 1885 production.

[33]English adaptation uncredited.

[34]Played return engagements 6 September 1886 at Poole's Theatre for 32 performances, 14 March 1887 at the Grand Opera House for 8 performances, and 2 May 1887 at the People's Theatre for 8 performances.

[35]Interpolation; music and lyrics not by William Scanlan.

[36]Billed as the acknowledged male impersonator of Europe and America.

guests: ED. J. CONNELLEY. *Marie Duprez*, Circus Rider—nee Marie Adair: Virginia Ross. *Lucy*, daughter of the Innkeeper, and pretty sure of herself: Mamie Bernard. *Widw Belair*, relict of a retired coal merchant: CORA LYLE.

Act 1: Newport Beach.

Act 2: Hotel Scene.

Act 3: Elegant Boudoir. Former home of Marie Duprez.

MUSICAL NUMBERS

"The Captain" (Act 1)
E. Wesner

"I've Just Introduced Them"
E. Wesner

"A Kiss and a Squeeze in the Moonlight"
E. Wesner

"Don't Care That" (Quartet) (Act 2)

"Champagne" (Act 2)
E. Wesner

"John, the Gentlemen's Son"
E. Wesner

Love Song
E. Wesner

Mexican Song (Act 3)
E. Wesner

1885.55 M'LLE. NITOUCHE

A Revival of the Comic Vaudeville (Comédie-vaudeville) in Three Acts, 4 Scenes, in French[37]. Libretto by Henri Meilhac, Albert Millaud (and Ernest Blum). Music by Hervé. Stage manager, V. Merle. Musical director, Salvator Guerra. Produced by Maurice Grau. Opened 1 October 1885 at Wallack's Theatre and closed 14 October 1885 after 5 performances in repertory.

CAST: *Denise de Flavigny*, Mam'zelle Nitouche: Mme. ANNA JUDIC. *The Mother Superior*: Mme. DELORME. *Lyric Artists (4)*: *Corinne*: Mlle. VALLOT. *Sylvia*: Mlle. DeWitt. *Lydia*: Mlle. Caro. *Gimblette*: Mlle. Mirybel. *A Nun*: Mlle. Delest. *First Pupil*: Mlle. Ellen. *Second Pupil*: Mlle. Perrin. *Third Pupil*: Mlle. Andree. *Fourth Pupil*: Mlle. Jeanne Blanc. *Célestin*: Mons. MEZIÈRES. *Fernand de Champlatreaux*: Mons. COOPER. *The Major*, Count de Château Gibus: Mons. Ginet. *Loriot*: Mons. Germain. *The Manager*: Mons. Gregoire. *The Stage Manager*: Mons. Salvator. *Gustave*: Mons. Dupuis. *Robert*: Mons. Estiot. *A Dragon*: Mons. Vinchon.

1885.56 LILI

A Comédie-opérette in Three Acts, in French. Libretto by Albert Millaud, Alfred Hennequin (and Ernest Blum). Music by Hervé. Stage manager, V. Merle. Musical director, Salvator Guerra. Produced by Maurice Grau. Opened 5 October 1885 at Wallack's Theatre and closed 21 October 1885 after 4 performances in repertory[38].

CAST: *Amélie*: Mme. ANNA JUDIC. *Antonine*: Mme. ANNA JUDIC. *Mme. Bouzincourt*: Mme. DELORME. *Victorine*: Mlle. VALLOT. *Mme. de Vieuxbois*: Mlle. Delest. *Mme. Gransec*: Mlle. Caro. *Mme. Anderson*: Mlle. DeWitt. *(Antonin) Plinchard*: Mons. COOPER. *Le Baron de la Grange Batelière*: Mons. GERMAIN. *Le Vicomte de St. Hypothese*: Mons. MEZIÈRES. *Bonpain*: Mons. GREGOIRE. *René*: Mons. Dupuis. *Mons. Bouzincourt*: Mons. Ginet. *A Servant*: Mons. Estiot.

Act 1: (Garden of a villa in the environs of Paris.) 1842.

Act 2: (A Boudoir Parlor in the Chateau de la Grange-Batelière.) 1850.

Act 3: (Parlor and conservatory of the Baron's House.) Present day.

ACT 1[39]

"Démontrer que par A plus B" (Couplets)
Mons. Gregoire

"J'suis plein d'égards pou la beauté" (Couplets)
Mons. Cooper

"Tout jeune encore" (Couplets)
Mons. Mezières

"En ce temps, digne de mémoire" (Couplets)
A. Judic [Amélie]

"Celui que j'aime est un pioupiou" (Triolets)
A. Judic [Amélie]

"Des petites filles, j'en sais" (Couplets)
A. Judic [Amélie]

ACT 2

"Tout est bien conclu" (Rondeau)
Mons. Germain

"Voilà le plus clair de l'affair" (Duettino)
Messrs. Cooper, Germain

"Ah! Combien de fois, l'âme émue" (Duo)
Mons. Cooper, A. Judic [Amélie]

"Histoire de Théréson, la belle Provençale" (Chanson)
A. Judic [Amélie]

ACT 3

"En bonne mère de famille" (Couplet)
A. Judic [Amélie]

"Oui, si grand'mère entend poursuivre" (Couplet)
A. Judic [Antonine]

"Je serais fier, jeune fille" (Couplet)
Mons. Cooper

"Je vais revoir cette Amélie" (Couplet)
Mons. Cooper

"De ma refraichir la mémoire" (Couplets)
A. Judic [Amélie]

"Vous ne pouvez la regarder sans rire" (Duo et Couplets)
Mons. Cooper, A. Judic [Amélie]

"Ce n'est pas tout ça brrr!" (Couplet Final)
Mons. Cooper, A. Judic [Antonine

1885.57 LA FEMME à PAPA

A Musical Comedy (Vaudeville) in Three Acts, in French. Libretto by Alfred Hennequin and Albert Millaud. Music by Hervé. Stage manager, V. Merle. Musical director, Salvator Guerra. Produced by Maurice Grau. Opened 6 October 1885 at Wallack's Theatre and closed 17 October (matinee) 1885 after 5 performances in repertory; played return performances 2 March 1886 and 13 April 1886 at the Star Theatre.[40]

CAST: *Anna*: Mme. ANNA JUDIC. *Coralie*: Mlle. VALLOT. *Cora*: Mlle. Mirybel. *Lucienne*: Mlle. Delest. *Gabrielle*: Mlle. DeWitt. *Leona*: Mlle. Caro. *An Errand Boy*: Mlle. Perrin. *Mariette*: Mlle. Andrée. *Jacquinette*: Mlle. Jeanne Blanc. *Toinon*: Mlle. TOURNYAIRE. *Florestan de la Bonnardière*: Mons. GREGOIRE. *Aristide*: Mons. GREGOIRE. *Le Prince de Chypre*: Mons. Cooper. *Bodin-Bridet*: Mons. MEZIÈRES. *Tob*: Mons. Germain. *The Head Waiter*: Mons. Dupuis. *Pacard*: Mons. Vinchon. *A Sheriff*: Mons. Estiot. *A Servant*: Mlle. Vandamme.

Act 1: Courtyard of a Model Farm.

Act 2: Public Parlor of "The Golden Lion" Hotel.

Act 3:Parlor in the House of Bodin-Bridet.

ACT 1[41]

"Ça! . . . que rien ne nous interrompe!"
(Petit Choeur)

"Oui, touchez-là mon cher élève" (Couplets)
Mons. Gregoire [Aristide]

"La journée est bonne et gaie" (Petit Choeur)
[who sang last number?]

"Les Inséparables" (Maman m'a dit . . .) (Couplets)
A. Judic

"Le devoir d'une femme honnête" (Air nouveau)
A. Judic

"Les Parisiennes" (Les femmes seront toujours reines) (Rondeau)
A. Judic

[37] Produced in France as MAM'ZELLE NITOUCHE.

[38] Settings and costumes uncredited. No musical numbers appear in the program.

[39] Musical numbers not listed in programs. List prepared from 'The Judic Edition' French libretto published by F. Rullman, New York, 1885, with English translation.

[40] Stage direction, costumes and scenery uncredited.

[41] Musical numbers not listed in programs. List prepared from 'The Judic Edition' French libretto published by F. Rullman, New York, 1885, with English translation.

ACT 2

"Chaud, chaud, pour la fête du prince" (Petit Choeur)

"C'est un grave professeur" (Couplets)
Mons. Gregoire [Florestan]

"Le Pensionnaire" (Lorsque j'étais pensionnaire) (Rondeau)
A. Judic

"Le jeune Alfred aimait avec droiture" (Romance)
A. Judic

"Chanson de Colonel" (Tambours, clairons, musique en tête) (Ronde)
A. Judic

"Le Champagne" (C'est bon l'champagn'!) (Couplets)
A. Judic

ACT 3

"Souvenez-vous" (Couplet)
A. Judic, Mons. Gregoire [Aristide]

"À la bonne heure, on vous voit mieux" (Duo)
A. Judic, Mons. Gregoire [Aristide]

"Oui, j'suis heureux!" (Couplet Final)
A. Judic, Mons. Gregoire [Aristide]

1885.58

EVANGELINE!

Rice's Star Burlesque Company in a Revised Version of the Musical Extravaganza in Three Acts, 10 Scenes[42]. Libretto by J. Cheever Goodwin. Music by Edward E. Rice. Staged by Edward E. Rice. Musical director, Gustavus Kerker. Produced by Edward E. Rice. Opened 7 October 1885 at the 14th Street Theatre and closed 1 May 1886 after 252 performances[43].

CAST: *Evangeline*, the heroine of an enduring affection which very nearly proves her ruin: IRENE VERONA. *Eulalie*, her confidante—confidently hoping for women's rights: MOLLIE FULLER. *Catherine*, Gabriel's aunt, an antidote for melancholy—"Love's young dream becomes a nightmare": GEORGE K. FORTESCUE. *Mary Anne*, Eva's maid: Carrie Wallace. *Marie, Rose*, in Eva suite—two sweet to need description: May Danforth, May Steele. *Elaine*, a waif, in love: Annie Lukie. *The Queen*, the King's consort (though from the play it would appear she never cons aught but her fingers): Mamie Taylor. *LeBlanc*, the notary,—although notary coroner, in quest of somebody, and led to believe that there's a good deal in a name: JOHN A. MACKAY. *Gabriel*, Eva's worshipper: FAY TEMPLETON. *Felician*, Eulalie's sweetheart: Josie Hall. *The Lone Fisherman*, a mystery: JAMES MAFFITT. *Captain Dietrich* of the Queen's own, familiar with hard-tack and "Hardies Tactics": GEORGE A. SCHILLER. *King Boorioboola Gha*, a sufferin' sovereign: FRED H. FREER. *Benedict*, the blacksmith, who believes black myths until convinced to the contrary by his daughter Eva: EDWIN S. TARR. *Basil*, Gabriel's pa: J. H. Finn. *Hans Wagner*, corporal, but fond of the spiritual: D. P. Steele. *Chief of Police*, a "peeler": Edward Morris. (*The Jailor*, who keeps the keys: W. H. Kohnie.[44]) *Lo*, the Poor Indian: David P. Steele. *The Headsman*, a mimic, very clever at taking off blockheads: Robert Wade. *Fritz Hubert, Rudolph Maurice*, Captain Dietrich's aides, and an adorable pair: AMELIA SUMMERVILLE, KATE UART. *Unambebe*, Captain of the Amazons: Hindie Harrison. *The Heifer*, two of a kine-d: Messrs. Turner, West. *The Six Miserable Ruffians.*

Act 1: Acadia. *Scene 1*: Exterior view of Benedict's house, and a bird's eye view of the sea bird's-eye (d) beside. *Scene 2*: A Lane. *Scene 3*: Benedict's Kitchen.

Act 2: Africa. *Scene 1*: The Diamond Fields. *Scene 2*: The back yard of Boorioboola Gha's Palace. *Scene 3*: The Prison. *Scene 4*: The Palace and Public Square.

Act 3, Scene 1: Arizona. The Forest's edge. *Scene 2*: An Autumn Acadian by-way. *Scene 3*: Acadia. Benedict's house, with a view of the sea. Turned Japanese.

ACT 1

"We Must Be Off" (Opening Chorus)

"One Moment, Pray" (Recitative)
F. Templeton

"There's a Man" (Song)
F. Templeton, Chorus

"I'm a Fascinating Notary" (Song)
J. A. Mackay

"Thinking, Love, of Thee" (Ballad)
I. Verona

"Into the Water We Go" (Bathing Quintette)
I. Verona, M. Fuller, G. K. Fortescue, M. Steele, M. Danforth

"She's Saved! She's Saved!" (Choral)

"My Love and I"[45] (Song and Dance)
F. Templeton

"Sammy Smug" (Descriptive Song)
J. A. Mackay, Chorus

"My Heart"[46] (Ballad)
I. Verona

"Golden Chains"[47] (Duet)
I. Verona, F. Templeton

Entrance Music of the Shepherds and Shepherdesses[48]

Dance Music of the Beautiful Milk White Heifer

"I Hope It Won't Happen Again"[49] (Ditty)
J. A. Mackay

"In Us You See" (Soldiers' Chorus and Septette)

"He Says She Must Go"(Finale)

ACT 2

"Clink! Clank!"[50] (Miners' Chorus)

"We Are Off (to Seek for Eva)" (Duet)
G. K. Fortescue, J. A. Mackay

"My Thoughts Are Far Away"[51] (Ballad)
I. Verona

"Let's Quietly Steal Away"[52] (A Musical Trifle)

"Sweet the Song of Birds" (Duet)
F. Templeton, I. Verona

"I Like It, Don't You?" (Topical Song)
F. Templeton

"Twelve O'Clock, and All Is Well" (Chant)

"Prowling 'Round the Diamond Fields" (Policeman's Narrative)

Romanza[53]
I. Verona

March of the Royal Amazons[54]

"She's Acquitted, (He's Outwitted)" (Finale)

ACT 3

"Fie Upon You! Fie!" (Kissing Song)
I. Verona

"(We Are the) Six Miserable Ruffians"[55] (Sextette)

"Does She Love Me?" (Song and Dance)
F. Templeton

"O Gabriel, My Best Beloved" (Song)
I. Verona

"Goodnight to One and All" (Finale)

"Homeward Bound" (March)

1885.59

NINICHE

A Musical Comedy (Vaudeville-opérette) in Three Acts, in French[56]. Libretto by Alfred Hennequin, Albert Millaud, (Émile Najac). Music by

[42]First presented in New York 27 July 1874 at Niblo's Garden for 14 performances.
[43]Design of scenery and costumes uncredited.
[44]Character added to cast list in the second month of the run.

[45]Newly composed for this revival.
[46]Newly composed for this revival.
[47]Dropped after opening.
[48]Newly composed for this revival.
[49]Newly composed for this revival.
[50]Newly composed for this revival.
[51]Newly composed for this revival.
[52]Newly composed for this revival.
[53]Newly composed for this revival.
[54]Newly composed for this revival.
[55]First time performed in New York.
[56]English adaptations preceded the French NINICHE to New York, both without the Boullard score: MANHATTAN BEACH, or Down Among the Breakers, 23 December 1878, Minnie Curry's Drawing Room Theatre, 5 performances. NEWPORT, or The Swimmer, the Singer and the Cypher, 15 September 1879, Daly's, 12 performances.

Marius Boullard. Stage manager, Mons. V. Merle. Musical director, Salvator Guerra. Produced by Maurice Grau. Opened 9 October 1885 at Wallack's Theatre and closed 24 October 1885 after 3 performances in repertory; played a return performance 8 April 1886 at the Star Theatre[57].

CAST: *Niniche*, now the Countess Corniska: Mme. ANNA JUDIC. *Widow Sillery*: Mme. DELORME. *Georgina*: Mlle. DeWitt. *Annette*: Mlle. Andrée. *Errand Boy*: Mlle. Ellen. *Amanda*: Mlle. Olga. *Castagnette*: Mlle. Mirybell. *Cora*: Mlle. Caro. *Juliette*: Mlle. Jeanne Blanc. *A Fisherwoman*: Mlle. Perrin. *Grégoire*, Bather: Mons. COOPER. *Count Corniski*, a Diplomat: Mons. MEZIÈRES. *Anatole de Beaupersil*: Mons. GERMAIN. *Narcisse*, Head Waiter at the Casino: Mons. Dupuis. *Baptiste*, Waiter: Mons. Dupuis. *Dupiton*: Mons. Paul Ginet. *Desablettes*, Count's Secretary: Mons. GREGOIRE. *A Gentleman*: Mons. Vinchon. *A Servant at Baths*: Mons. Perret. *A Valet*: Mons. Estiot. *A Sheriff*: Mons. Girard. *Travelers, Male and Female, Bathers, Fishermen, Women.*

Act 1: The Beach at Trouville. Present day.

Act 2: An Elegantly Panelled Parlor in the house of Niniche in Paris.

Act 3: Entrance of the New Hotel.

ACT 1[58]

"Sur la plage allons prendre l'air" (Choeur et reprise)

"Si j'avais suivi les voeux de mon père" (Couplets)
Mons. Cooper

"En frissonnant, je me hasarde . . . " (Couplets)
A. Judic

"C'est, je vous le jure, toute une aventure" (Rondeau)
A. Judic

"Je n'ai plus rine du ton de la cocotte" (Air des Scythes)
A. Judic

ACT 2

"En revenant, après six mois" (Couplets) (Air de Renaudin de Caen)
A. Judic

"C'était la petite Niniche!" (Avec ce costume, Anatole) (Couplets)
A. Judic

"Si vous connaissez la comtesse" (Duettino)
Mons. Cooper, A. Judic

ACT 3

"Je viens de chez le commissaire" (Couplets)
A. Judic

"Certes! . . . monsieur doit plaire aux dames!" (Couplets)
Mons. Cooper

"Une fois seule avec le comte" (Couplet) (Air de Favart)
A. Judic. Mons. Cooper

"Voici la minut' deelicate. ." (Couplet au Public)
Mons. Cooper, A. Judic

1885.60 LE GRAND CASIMIR

A Revival of the Opera bouffe (Opérette-vaudeville) in Three Acts, in French[59]. Libretto by Jules Prével, Albert de Saint-Albin, (Edmond Gondinet). Music by Charles Lecocq. Musical director, Salvator Guerra. Produced by Maurice Grau. Opened 15 October 1885 at Wallack's Theatre and closed 16 October 1885 after 2 performances in repertory.[60]

CAST: *Angélina*: Mme. ANNA JUDIC. *Ninetta*: ALICE RAYMOND. *Petronilla*: Mlle. Caro. *Colomba*: Mlle. DeWitt. *Lydia*: Mlle. Delest. *Siraphina*: Mlle. Mirybel. *Casimir*: Mons. MEZIÈRES. *Le Grand Duc*: Mons. GREGOIRE. *Sotherman*: JOSÉ DUPUIS. *Picasso*: Mons. Germain. *Galetti*: Mons. Ginet. *Gobson*: Mons. Vinchon. *Joseph*: Mons. Girard. *Second Stage Manager*: Mons. Estiot. *A Clown*: Mons. Yalowicz.

1885.61 LA MASCOTTE

A Revival of the Opéra-comique in Three Acts, in French[61]. Libretto by Henri Chivot and Alfred Duru. Music by Edmond Audran. Musical director, M. Salvator Guerra. Produced by Maurice Grau. Opened and closed 23 October 1885 at Wallack's Theatre after 1 performance in repertory; played 2 return performances 5 March 1886 and 9 April 1886 at the Star Theatre.

CAST: *Bettina*: Mme. ANNA JUDIC. *Fiametta*: Mlle. RAYMONDE. *Laurent XVII*: Mons. MEZIÈRES. *Pippo*: Mons. GAILLARD. *Prince Fritellini*: Mons. COOPER. *Rocco*: Mons. GERMAIN. *Matheo*: JOSÉ DUPUIS. *Sergeant Parafante*: Mons. Vinchon. *Pages (5)*: *Carlo*: Mlle. Vallot. *Marco*: Mlle. Andrée. *Angelo*: Mlle. Caro. *Luigi*: Mlle. Perrin. *Beppo*: Mlle. Vandamme. *Peasant Girls (3)*: *Paola*: Mlle. Delest. *Francesca*: Mlle. Mirybel. *Antonia*: Mlle. DeWitt.

1885.62 ANOTHER MIKADO

A Burlesque (of Gilbert and Sullivan's comic opera) in Two Acts. Burlesque by Carl Hauser and J. L. Ford. Music by Arthur Sullivan. Costumes by C. de Grimm. Produced by (John) Koster and (Albert) Bial. Opened 2 November 1885 at Koster & Bial's Concert Hall and closed 20 February 1886 after (128) performances.[62]

CAST: *Yanki-Sam*, Mikado of City-Pooh: WILLIAM PAUL BOWN. *Viky-Shaw*, Queen of Britti-Pooh: MURRY WOODS. *Langtry Pooh*: LOUISE LESTER. *The Lord High Kockey-Lorum*: FRED WARREN. *Wards of Kockey-Lorum (3)*: *Yum-Yum*, First Ward: LAURA BURT. *Pity Sing*, Second Ward: SOPHIE HUMMEL. *Peek-a-Booh*, Third Ward: LOUISE FOX. *Mlle. Ki-Ki-Pooh*, Danseuse: GEORGIE PARKER. *Freddy-Pooh*, a youth of Britti-Pooh: CARRIE GOULD. (Full Chorus.) *Specialties*: Japanese Mitsutas (acrobats), the Lentons.

1885.63 AMORITA

An Opéra-Comique in Three Acts. Original Viennese libretto (to the operette 'Pfingsten in Florenz') by Richard Genée and Julius Riegen. American adaptation by Sydney Rosenfeld and George Goldmark. Music by Alfons Czibulka. Produced under the stage direction of Heinrich Conried. Scenery by Henry E. Hoyt and Gaspard Maeder. Music director, Jesse Williams. Produced by Rudolph Aronson. Opened 16 November 1885 at the Casino Theatre and closed 13 February 1886 after 91 performances.

CAST: *Fra Bombarda*, Dictator of the Republic of France: FRANK CELLI. *Aldo Castrucci*, Furrier and Councilor: FRANCIS WILSON. *Sparacani*, Corporation Attorney: W. H. FITZGERALD. *Lorenzi*, Physician to the Duke of Medici: HARRY STANDISH. *Fra Bombarda's Followers (2)*: *Count Asinelli*: ALFRED KLEIN. *Morro*: James Furry. *Basta* Jailor: C. L. Weeks. *Geronimo*, Jeweler and Councilor: G. F. Wade. *Al-Den-Danger*, Ambassador from Morocco: O. Heilig. *Umberto*, Bell ringer: Charles T. Parr. *Paolo*: Georgie Dennan. *Councilmen (3)*: *Competi*: O. Lehman. *Castarao*: C. Tibbets. *Luchesi*: Hugo Fritsch. *Angelo Malanotti*, a sculptor: PAULINE HALL. *Amorita*, Castrucci's daughter: MADELINE LUCETTE. *Perpetua*, Castrucci's wife: GEORGIE DICKSON. *Peppina*: BILLIE BARLOW. *Cechina*: Agnes Folsom. *Fortebraccio* Captain of the Dictator's body guard: ROSE BEAUDET. *Beppo*, Apprentice to Castrucci: Emma Hanley. *Female Slaves from Fez (6)*: *Aldurah*: Lizzie Miller. *Fatma*: Dolly Delroy. *Tetna*: Florence Bell. *Zuleika*: Adelaide Langdon. *Nelly*: Annie Dayton. *Anda*: Evelyn Granville. *Edmondo, Antonio*, Two Young Artists: Carrie Andrews, Victoria Schilling. *Francisco, Camillo*, Pages to Fra Bombarda: Eugenie Maynard, Millie Ray. *Artists, Soldiers, Pages, Moorish Boys, Flower Girls, Citizens, etc.*

Act 1: Square in Florence.

Act 2: Fra Bombarda's Conservatory.

Act 3: Pavilion in Fra Bombarda's Garden.

ACT 1[63]

"Peace still smiling, trade is booming" (Introduction)
Chorus

"Though, banished still I dare" (Song)
P. Hall, Chorus

[57]Cast and credits from April engagement at the Star; no credits for scenery or costumes.

[58]Musical numbers not listed in programs. List prepared from 'The Judic Edition' French libretto published by F. Rullman, New York, 1885, with English translation.

[59]First produced in New York in French 22 April 1885 at the Star Theatre for 2 performances. For Synopsis of Scenes and Musical Numbers, see original 1885 production. Later adapted into English as THE LION TAMER, 30 December 1891, Broadway, 130 performances.

[60]Stage director uncredted; stage manager, V. Merle. Scenery and costume design uncredited.

[61]First produced in New York in English 5 May 1881 at the Bijou Theatre for 168 performances in 2 engagements. In French 30 November 1881 at Abbey's Park Theatre for 2 performances in repertory. For Synopsis of Scenes and Musical Numbers in French, see 1881 French production.

[62]According to reviewers, favorite songs from other Gilbert and Sullivan comic operas were interpolated; no program available.

[63]Musical numbers not listed in programs. List prepared from published libretto (Hermann Bartsch, Printer, New York, 1885.)

"We are vassals, guard our sov'reigns castles" (Soldiers' Chorus)
R. Beaudet, Chorus
"Father-in-law, son-in-law!" (Duet)
F. Wilson, W. H. Fitzgerald
"Round me still the bells are ringing" (Aria)
M. Lucette
"Not quite alone! You here!" (Duet)
P. Hall, M. Lucette
"What has happened? What's the matter?" (Finale).
F. Celli, G. Dickson, F. Wilson, W. H. Fitzgerald, M. Lucette, R. Beaudet, P. Hall, Chorus

ACT 2
"Pass round the wine cup, your glasses be clinking!" (Bachanale)
F. Celli, F. Wilson, W. H. Fitzgerald, Chorus
"Some men, they say, are born to rule" (Ballad)
F. Celli
"The beauty of nature the poets portray" (Song)
F. Wilson
"I know his condition" (Duet)
P. Hall, F. Wilson
"A happy sain, across the plain. ." (Song)
W. H. Fitzgerald
"Loudly I'd like to rejoice" (Waltz)
P. Hall
"We'll be married, indeed!" (Trio)
M. Lucette, F. Wilson, P. Hall
"Welcome the strangers!" (Finale)
F. Celli, O. Heilig, F. Celli, G. Dickson, F. Wilson, W. H. Fitzgerald, Chorus

ACT 3
"How sweet in his sleep" (Aria and Duet)
M. Lucette, F. Celli
"I have often stopped and wondered" (Song)
F. Wilson
"Thou weenst thy angel she would be—"
(Chorus of Artists)
"Blest Whitsuntide" (Finale)
P. Hall, M. Lucette, All

1885.64 THE SKATING RINK

A Burlesque Absurdity (Farce Comedy) in Three Acts. Play by Robert Griffin Morris. Musical director, P. J. Oehl. Produced by Frank W. Sanger. Opened 23 November 1885 at the Standard Theatre and closed 5 December 1885 after 15 performances; re-opened 18 January 1886 at the Grand Opera House for an additional 8 performances, 8 February 1886 at the Grand Opera House for an additional 8 performances, 7 March 1886 at Henry C. Miner's Peoples Theatre for an additional 8 performances. Total this season: 39 performances.[64]

CAST: *Ronald Delaine*, a "dream in flesh and blood and startling clothing; effusively verbose, yet speculative." The kind of man who opens a rink: NAT C. GOODWIN. *Miss Waxdoll*: NAT C. GOODWIN. *Patrick McCune*, in search of his daughter: NAT C. GOODWIN. *Camille*, from the Lyceum School of Dramatic Art: NAT C. GOODWIN. *Erasmus Carter*, with sweeping assertions: JAMES B. RADCLIFFE. *Timothy Tubbs*, Amelia's doting dad: HENRY V. DONNELLY. *Mickey Bubbage*, lecturer and thumper: Edward F. Goodwin. *Philander McShane*, Professor of the gliding art: MAJOR NEWELL. *Ignis Fatus*, king of the rollers: Charles Fletcher. *Hither and Thither*, a roller who gathers no Moss: William Fletcher. *Tenacity*: A. Puppe. *Clarence O'Dear*, only a butterfly: FRANK E. MORSE. *Miss Amelia Tubbs*, looking for a fate: DAISY MURDOCH. *Sallie Tubbs*, Amelia's maiden aunt: MARIETTA UART. *Matilda Squibbs*, Amelia's friend: HELEN LOWELL. *Miss Franchita Beauharnais*, queen of the rink: Lillian Fletcher. *Phoebe*: HATTIE SCHELL. *Mr. Wall Street Bull*: P. Mache. *Mr. Wall Street Bull*: P. Mache. *Villagers, Skaters, etc.* (*Imperial Quartette*: F. H. Kenworthy, first tenor; W. Ridgeway, second tenor; J. L. Guilmette, first basso; W. H. Hatter, second basso.)

Act 1: Tubb's Cottage at the Seaside.

Act 2: The Saurian Rink. 10 A.M. Practice skating.

Act 3: The Saurian Rink. Night. Grand Carnival.

[64]Stage direction, scenery and costumes not credited. Acting manager, G. W. Floyd. Stage manager, Henry V. Donnelly.

MUSICAL NUMBERS[65]
"Gentle Faces" (Quartette)
N. C. Goodwin, D. Murdoch, H. Lowell, J. B. Radcliffe
"Far Far Away"
N. C. Goodwin, D. Murdoch, H. Lowell
"The Skating Rink"
Company
"See Saw" (Duet)
D. Murdoch, N. C. Goodwin
Grand Medley
Company
Selections Imperial Quartette
"Since Maggie Learned to Skate"
N. C. Goodwin

1885.65 THE RATCATCHER, or, The Pied Piper of Hamelin

A Grand Lyric and Dramatic Spectacle in Four Acts, 10 Scenes. Based on the great Vienna success (inspired by Pied Piper legend). Music by Selli Simonson. Entire production under the personal direction of the Kiralfy Brothers. Scenery by Robecchi and Carpizal of Paris, of Paris; Magnani of Milan; Perera of Madrid; and Ed. Roemer. Costumes designed by the Kiralfy Brothers, executed by Mons. and Mme. Machiner and mechanical effects by Frank Smith and W. Crane. Properties and accessories by Charles Blesser. Gas effects and electric lighting by Charles Blesser. Musical director, W. W. Hoffmann. Produced by the Kiralfy Brothers (Imre, Bolossy). Opened 30 November 1885 at Niblo's Garden and closed 23 January 1886 after 65 performances.

CAST: *Hans von Kronold*, Burgomaster: J. F. HAGAN. *Walter Burghardt*: J. DeBevoise. *Simpliciton Rumple*: JAY HUNT. *Fresch*, a Tailor: ARTHUR TAMS. *Philip Strong*, Blacksmith: Walter Owen. *Waxman*, Cobbler: James Otley. *Leechke*: C. Latour. *Hippel*: J. Murphy. *John Fresch*, Tailor's Son: Mamie Ryan. *Hilda von Kronold*, the Burgomaster's Daughter: JULIA STUART. *Martha*, the Nurse: Mrs. G. C. GERMON. *Tina*, Innkeeper's Niece: ANNIE BOYD. *Dora*: L. Newman. *Louise*: Miss Vinton. *Hostess*: Lillian Ainsleigh. *Roderick Bitter*: Henri Leoni. *John Sauer*: G. Pullman. *Lupin*: F. W. Baldwin. *Seltzers*: H. Williams. *Kleine*: Henry Koch. *Powderstein*: N. Parnie. *Peter*: Master John Oakley. *Nettie*: CLARA LIND. *Bertha*: Leona Clark. *Celia*: Emily Beaumont. *Gracie*: Miss Knowlton. *Singold*, the Piper: HUBERT WILKE. *Premiere Danseuse*: Mlle. LA BRUJERE.

Act 1, Scene 1: Council Chamber in Hamelin. *Scene 2*: A Suburb of the Town.

Act 2, Scene 1: Interior of the Inn. *Scene 2*: The Burgomaster's Garden. *Scene 3*: Outside the Town Gate. *Scene 4*: The Market Place. *Scene 5*: The River Banks.

Act 3: Court House and Square.

Act 4, Scene 1: Exterior of the Church. *Scene 2*: The Koppelburg.

ACT 1
Scene 1
"The Plague of Rats"
(Chorus of Populace)
"I Am a Minstrel Gay"
H. Wilke
Scene 2
"My Name Is Singold" (Song of the Child Charmer)
H. Wilke
"I Capture Every Heart" (Waltz Song)

ACT 2
Scene 1
Drinking Chorus of Burghers
"Czardas" (Hungarian national Song)
"A Lesson in Magic Arts" (Comic Duo)[66]
H. Wilke, J. Hunt

[65]Program note: The Specialties introduced in THE SKATING RINK are entirely original with Mr. N. C. Goodwin.
[66]Replaced for subsequent tour by:
"It's Just as Transparent as Glass" (Song)
J. Hunt.

Scene 2
  The Festival Village Beauties
  Dance of the Villagers
  Variations
    Mlle. La Brujere
  Gavotte Dansante 8 Secondas
  Valse Pictures and Floral
    Mlle. La Brujere, Secondas, Corps de Ballet
Scene 3
  Singold's "Love Song"[67]
    H. Wilke
Scene 4
  "Stupid Mankind" (Song)
    A. Boyd
Scene 5
  Singold's "Charm Song"
    H. Wilke
  Singold's Midnight Incantation
    H. Wilke
  The Procession of Rats

ACT 3
  Tableau: Procession of the Trades (after Hans Markert's historic picture)
  Grand Festival Ballet
  Sports of the Revellers (Eccentric Salutation)
  The Mountebank's Frolics
  The Genius of Joy (Variation)
    Mlle. La Brujere
  Novel Musical Dance
  Pedal Chimes (Variation)
  The Lures of Mirth
    Mlle. La Brujere
  Grand Finale

ACT 4
Scene 1
  Children of Hamelin lured away by the revengeful minstrel
Scene 2
  Grand Tableau (Finale)

1885.66 THE GRIP

A Comedy in Three Acts, 4 Scenes. Play by Edward Harrigan. Music by David Braham. Staged by Edward Harrigan. Scenery by Charles W. Witham. Mechanical effects by William A. Vail. Properties by Joseph H. Logan. Gas effects by James Garbit. Musical director, David Braham. Produced by Edward Harrigan. Opened 30 November 1885 at Harrigan's Park Theatre and closed 13 February 1886 after 88 performances.

CAST: *Patrick Reilly*: EDWARD HARRIGAN. *Captain Erasmus Pebble*: JOHN WILD. *Catherine O'Hollerhan*: DAN COLLYER. *Handsome Grogan*: M. J. BRADLEY. *Colonel Patrick Reilly*: HARRY FISHER. *John Clancy*, his son: HENRY WEAVER, JR. *Roland Pebble*: PETER GOLDRICH. *Lucinda Pebble*: James Fox. *Jay Evarts Spread*: Arthur C. Moreland. *Rosco Walker*: WILLIAM WEST. *Tom Walker*: GEORGE MERRITT. *Lysander Hartley*: Richard Quilter. *Myles O'Brady*: JOHN SPARKS. *Captain Phil Clancy*: George L. Stout. *Tim Mahone*: Joseph Sparks. *Tom Tit*: Charles Coffey. *C. F. Clinger*: James McCullough. *Jeems McArdle*: Thomas Ray. *Member for Annex District*: William Merritt. *Gash*: Robert Snyder. *Rosanna Reilly*: ANNIE YEAMANS. *Rosalind Reilly*: STELLA BONIFACE. *Carrie Hollerhan*: AMY LEE. *Tuteress*: Ada Farwell. *Hattie Montgomery*: Annie Langdon. *Kate Singleton*: Kate Langdon. *Nancy*: Emily Yeamans. *Venie DeLarne*: Adele Stillwell. *Ella DeCamp*: Annie Hall. *Josephine Golder*: Ray Bristoe. *Adelaide Berry*: Annie Lander. *Minnie Rexford*: Georgie Hawley. *Boatmen, Strikers, Aldermen and numerous local characters.*

Act 1: Cooperstown Seminary with view of Morris and Essex Canal.

Act 2, Scene 1: Exterior of Widow O'Hollerhan's home. *Scene 2*: Drawing room at Colonel Reilly's.

Act 3: Garden of Reilly Mansion, with view of Widow O'Hollerhan's home.

MUSICAL NUMBERS
  "A Soldier Boy's Canteen" (Act 1)
    E. Harrigan
  "Oh! Dat Low Bridge"
  "No Wealth Without Labor"[68]
  "School Days, School Days"
  "The Aldermanic Board"
  "Grogan, the Masher"

1885.67 THE BLACK HUSSAR

A Revival of the Operetta in Three Acts[69]. Original Viennese libretto ('Der Feldprediger') by Hugo Wittmann and Alois Wohlmuth. English adaptation by Sydney Rosenfeld. Music by Carl Millöcker. Musical director, Antonio DeNovellis. Produced by McCaull Opera Company (John A. McCaull). Opened 7 December 1885 at the Star Theatre and closed 2 January 1886 after 28 performances.

CAST: *Friedrich von Helbert*, Colonel of the Black Hussars, disguised as an Army Chaplain: MARK SMITH. *Hans von Waldmann*, Adjutant of the Black Hussars, disguised as a student: EDWIN W. HOFF. *Staff Officers of the Black Hussars (9): Major Rokow*: Zoe DeVielle. *Captain Plush*: Bessie Frazer. *Captain Bender*: V. Lovelock. *Captain Woolf*: Ella Knapp. *Lieut. Conrad*: Grace Hollingsworth. *Lieut. Van Vleet*: Ella Kelly. *Lieut. Duzenburg*: Carrie Mitchell. *Lieut. Konig*: Gertie Clarke. *Lieut. Beyer*: Ida Bartelle. *Theophil Hackenback*, Magistrate of Trautenfeld: DeWOLF HOPPER. *Piffkow*, his Factotum, with numerous offices—Town Crier, Night Watchman, Barber, etc: GEORGE BONIFACE, JR. *Mefflin*, a Tragedian of the Meiniger Company, No. 14: A. W. MAFLIN. *François Thorilliere*, a Captain in the French Army: L. M. Hall. *Rubke*, a Captain in the Prussian Army: Mountjoy Walker. *Wutki*, Hetman of the Cassocks: A. Maina. *Citizens of Trautenfeld (5): Klappig*: Charles Carlyle. *Rothmichael*: James Armstrong. *Birnbaum*: L. Granitzer. *Knoedel*: Lindsay Morison. *Schupsack*: Charles Jones. *Shadow*, a Black Hussar disguised as a Pedlar: F. Handsue. *Bruck*, a Black Hussar disguised as a Scissors Grinder: L. Tesio. *Eiken*, a Black Hussar disguised as a Beggar: Henry Brougham. *Selchow*, a Black Hussar disguised as a Ratcatcher: L. C. Shrader. *Prittwitz*, a Black Hussar disguised as a Bookseller: H. W. Frazer. *Putnam*, a Black Hussar disguised as a Quack Doctor: G. F. Hasbrook. *Hackenback's Daughters (2): Minna*: LILLY POST. *Rosetta*: MARIE JANSEN. *Barbara*, an Orphan, Hackenback's Housekeeper: MATHILDE COTTRELLY. *Rieke*, a maid: Kate Ethel. *Mrs.*, the Wife of the Church Warden: Nellie Jennings. *Mrs.*, the Wife of the King's Stable Keeper: Mary Frank. *Mrs.*, the Wife of the State Reduction Cashier: Carrie Jackson. *Mrs.*, the Wife of the Custom House Officer: Rita Shrader. *Mrs.*, the Wife of the Army Sutler: Ida Sitgreaves. *Mrs.*, the Wife of the Forest Gamekeeper: Shila Uarda.

1885.68 M'LLE. NITOUCHE

A Return Engagement of the (Comic Vaudeville) Comédie-vaudeville in Three Acts, 4 Scenes[70]. Original French libretto ('Mam'zelle Nitouche') by Henri Meilhac, Albert Millaud (and Ernest Blum). Music by Hervé. Musical director, W. Eaton Brown. Produced by Lotta (George Zebold, Manager). Opened 14 December 1885 at the Standard Theatre and closed 19 December 1885 after 7 performances.

CAST: *Denise de Flavigny*: LOTTA (CRABTREE). *Nitouche*, Kin Yai Me, a Japanese Princess: LOTTA (CRABTREE). *A Drummer Boy*: LOTTA (CRABTREE). *Célestin*, Organist of the Convent: C. H. BRADSHAW. *Ferdinand Champlatreux*, Young Officer: FRANK CARLYLE. *The Major*, Count of Castle Gibus: J. H. STUART. *Loriot, Robert*, Officers of Dragoons: James A. Mahoney, H. R. Asten. *First Soldier*: Frank W. Parker. *Second Soldier*: Charles Foster. *Director of the Pontarcy Theatre*: Bert Coote. *Stage Manager*: George Fredericks. *Call Boy*: A. Sharpe. *The Lady Superior*: Adelaide Eaton. *Corinne*, Opera Bouffe Artist, Pontarcy Theatre: Emma Hinckley. *The Janitress*: M. Brown. *Artists at the Pomarcy Theatre (3): Sylvia*. Elsie Gerome. *Lydia*: Josie Shepherd. *Gimbelette*: Alice Lovette. *Pupils, Soldiers, etc.*

---

[67]Late in subsequent tour, replaced by:
  "Forget-me-not" (Song)
    H. Wilke.

[68]Dropped shortly after opening.

[69]First produced in New York 4 May 1885 at Wallack's Theatre for 104 performances. For Synopsis of Scenes and Musical Numbers, see original May 1885 production. Staging uncredited.

[70]Produced in France as MAM'ZELLE NITOUCHE. First produced in New York in English by Lotta 15 September 1884 at Daly's Theatre for 21 performances. For Synopsis of Scenes and Musical Numbers, see 1884 production.

1885.69

OH! WHAT A NIGHT

A (Farce) Comedy in Three Acts. Play by George Hoey. Songs (music) by Gus Williams. (Lyrics by J. P. Skelly.) Musical director, A. Lohmann. Produced under the management of John H. Robb. Opened 28 December 1885 at the Grand Opera House and closed 2 January 1886 after 9 performances.[71]

CAST: *Major Herman Pottgeiser*: GUS WILLIAMS. *Howard Laing*: C. F. TINGAY. *Alexander Gridley*: C. E. Lothian. *Henry Hobbs*, of Dover Street, London: De Loss King. *Anatole*, Celeste's coachman: A. W. Showell. *Stephens*, Howard Laing's valet: C. E. Collins. *Celeste Vavasour*, a Burlesque Actress: TOPSY VENN. *Angeline Gridley*, Alexander Gridley's wife: Josie Loane. *Mrs. Pottgeiser*: Florence Vincent. *Betsey*: Anita Harris.

Act 1: Howard Laing's Bachelor Apartments, before dark.

Act 2: Alexander Gridley's Apartments, Crown Prince Flats, Second Floor, right hand side, after dark.

Act 3: Celeste's Apartments, Crown Prince Flats, Second Floor, left hand side, "The Wee Sma' Hours."

MUSICAL NUMBERS

"Just Plain Jim"

"England, and Home, Sweet Home"

"Try and Be Home When the Clock Strikes Nine" (Mind and Be Home . . .)

"She's the Image of Her Mother in a Thousand Different Ways"

"What Can I Tell Her"

"Oh, What a Night!"

"A Lock of Hair" (recitation)
G. Williams

1885.70

WRINKLES

Watson and McDowell's Company of Comedians in a Musical Absurdity in Two Acts. Opened 28 December 1885 at the Harlem Theatre Comique and closed 2 January 1886 after 9 performances.

CAST: *Rudolph Geudelmeyer*, a man of many troubles: HARRY WATSON. *Orlando Sniffins*, Geudelmeyer's evil genius: ALFRED McDOWELL. *Louis Delcroix*, a young man who adores the fair sex: M. J. THOMAS. *Postman*: W. R. Green. *Policeman*: James Powell. *Rosy Geudelmeyer*, , jealous of her husband, but inclined to flirt a little upon her own account: ALICE WATSON. *Maggie McDermott*, a lady who finds the disadvantage of having two strings to her bow: ANNETTE ZELNA. *Sallie*, a domestic: Mollie Vinton.

[Act 1 where?]

Act 2: The Masquerade: *King William, Clown, Koko*: HARRY WATSON. *Mlle. Bonfanti; Count Kill-Em-Quick; Pooh Bah*: ALFRED McDOWELL. *The Unknown; French Gallant*: M. J. THOMAS. *Yum Yum; Pinkie Kraus; Spanish Zingara*: ALICE WATSON. *Nora McShane; Pitti-Sing; Spanish Zingara*: ANNETTE ZELNA. *Shepherdess; Peep-Bo*: Mollie Vinton.

Act 1: Drawing room of Geuedelmeyer's house.

Act 2: Hall in Geudelmeyer's house.

ACT 2

"Der Wasserfall" (Contralto Song)

"Lauterbach" (Duet)

Tyrolienne Medley

"Read the Answer in the Stars" (Quartette)(from THE BLACK HUSSAR)
(*Music by* Carl Millöcker. *Lyrics by* Sydney Rosenfeld.)

"Three Little Maids from School" (from THE MIKADO)
(*Music by* Arthur Sullivan. *Lyrics by* William S. Gilbert.)

"Drinking Song" (Baritone solo, from THE BEGGAR STUDENT)
(*Music by* Carl Millöcker.)

Grand Finale (from LA PÉRICHOLE)
(*Music by* Jacques Offenbach.)

[71]Stage director, scenery and costumes uncredited. Stage manager, De Loss King. Played return engagements 1 November 1886 at the Grand Opera House for 9 performances, 6 December 1886 at the People's Theatre for 8 performances.

1886.01

CRAZY PATCH

A Farcical Comedy in Three Acts. (Play by Archibald Clavering Gunter.) Constructed for laughing purposes only. Stage director, J. N. Long. Musical director, Frank Pallmer. Produced by Kate Castleton (Harry Phillips, Management). Opened 18 January 1886 at the Standard Theatre and closed 30 January 1886 after 14 performances.[72]

CAST: *Sybilla Tubbs*, just from Boarding School, and very bashful: KATE CASTLETON. *Sarah Tubbs*, of advanced years, still a spinster, but swears she will be a widow before she dies: Esther Williams. *Three Awfully Jolly Nice Girls: Mignonette DeVigne*: Willie Royston. *Chrysanthemum Chandos*: Courtney Haviland. *Hyacinthe Granville*: Elsie Graham. *Lucy Levins*, the Domestic of Caterpilla Villa, who loves Tubbianni of the Tivoli: Ada Gilman. *Jupiter Tubbs*, retired Merchant, turned Viticulturist, with a hatred for bugs and birds: L. R. STOCKWELL. *Dr. Arthur Sullivan*, he believes in magnetism of the eye: J. N. Long. *Arthur Mirvins Tubbs*, a reformed dude, of musical ideas, Tubbs' nephew; in his profession known as Tubbianni, the Tenor of the Tivoli: WILLIE ROYSTON. *William Smith*, who imagines himself to be Sullivan, the Boston fighter: John D. Gilbert. *Felix McGlue*, a most reliable policeman: EDDIE GIRARD.

The action takes place at Caterpilla Villa, Napa, California.

Act 1: Morning. Funny.

Act 2: Noon. Funnier.

Act 3: Night. Funniest.

1886.02

JACK-IN-THE-BOX

An English Melodrama in Four Acts, 11 Scenes[73]. Play by George R. Sims and Clement Scott. Music by W. C. Levey. Produced under the direction of J. M. Glover. Scenic display by Richard Marston. Musical director, Walter Hyde. Produced by Frank L. Gardner. Opened 8 February 1886 at the Union Square Theatre and closed 6 March 1886 after 32 performances.

CAST: *Jack Merryweather*, called Jack-in-the-Box: CARRIE SWAIN. *Mr. Richard Moreland*, a rich Australian: C. W. BARRY. *Edward Moreland*, alias DeVere, his son: WALTER BENTLEY. *Boy Carlton*, his nephew: F. McCULLOUGH ROSS. *Carlo Toroni*, an Italian padrone: RALPH DELMORE. *George Bolton*, a friend of Carlton's: Paul Thomas. *Professor O'Sullivan*, an ex-showman: HUGH FAY. *Police Sergeant Williams* of Scotland Yard: Thad. Shine. *Beppo, Tonio*, Italians at Torni's: Harold Russell, Newton Dana. *Rocco*, an Italian boy: Little Mamie. *Milly de Vere*, Edward Moreland's daughter: BLANCHE THORNE. *Mrs. Merryweather* of the old original: JULIA BRUTONE. *Catarina*, Beppo's sweetheart: Adelaide Arthur. (*Ballet Specialty*, Act 3: Mr. E. Fry [Eddie Foy].) *Italians, Country People, Policemen, Show People, etc.*:

Act 1, Scene 1: Roy Carlton's Rooms. *Scene 2*: A Street near the Strand. *Scene 3*: The Show Folks' Home.

Act 2, Scene 1: Roy Carlton's Rooms. *Scene 2*: A Street. *Scene 3*: At Toroni's.

Act 3, Scene 1: "The Red Lion," near Croydon. *Scene 2*: A Lane near "The Red Lion." *Scene 3*: Croydon Fair.

Act 4, Scene 1: Exterior of "The Red Lion." *Scene 2*: Interior of "The Red Lion."

ACT 1

Scene 2

"You and I"
C. Swain, H. Fay (*Music and Lyrics by* Claribel. [Mrs. Charles Barnard].)

ACT 2

Scene 2

"Head-Over Heels"
C. Swain

Scene 3

"Sweet Italy"
C. Swain

ACT 3

Scene 3

"The Showman"
C. Swain

[72]Musical numbers not listed in New York programs. Program note: Gems from the latest operatic successes introduced, and Miss Castleton's latest success, "I've Never Done Anything Since." Programs from subsequent tours reflect a constantly changing list of specialties.

[73]Billed in England as a Musical Variety Drama.

"From a Trip to the Moon"
Italian Burlesque Ballet
Mr. E. Fry [Foy]

1886.03 THE LEATHER PATCH

A Local Comedy in Three Acts, 7 Scenes. Play (and lyrics) by Edward Harrigan. Music by David Braham. Staged by Edward Harrigan. Scenery by Charles W. Witham. Mechanism by William Vail. Properties by Joseph Logan. Gas effects by Samuel Garbitt. Musical director, David Braham. Produced by Edward Harrigan. Opened 15 February 1886 at Harrigan's Park Theatre and closed 1 May 1886 after 88 performances.

CAST: *Jeremiah McCarthy*, undertaker: EDWARD HARRIGAN. *Jefferson Putnam*: JOHN WILD. *Caroline Hyer*: DAN COLLYER. *Airy McCafferty*: M. J. Bradley. *Linda Corncover*: James Fox. *Judge Herman Doebler*: HARRY FISHER. *Counselor Delancy Wriggle*: A. C. Moreland. *Levy Hyer*: PETER GOLDRICH. *Jemmy*, the Kid: Richard Quilter. *Dennis McCarthy*: GEORGE MERRITT. *Dr. Noah Corncover*: WILLIAM WEST. *Moses Cohen*: JOSEPH SPARKS. *Roderick McQuade*: JOHN SPARKS. *Joseph Levy*: Philip Engels. *Aaron Levy*: James McCullough. *Geoghen*, a hearse driver: Charles Coffey. *Mr. Doublerow*: Thomas Ray. *Thomas Conroy*: George L. Stout. *Roby McKeene*: J. Davis. *Officer Dunlap*: William Merritt. *Sailor*: Robert Snyder. *Parsley Allsnow*: Edward Murphy. *Madeline McCarthy*: ANNIE YEAMANS. *Libby O'Dooley*: AMY LEE. *Mrs. O'Dooley*: NELLA WETHERILL. *Mrs. Cronan*: Ada Farwell. *Nellie Conroy*: Annie Langdon. *Rachel Cohen*: Emily Yeamans. *Jennie Crimmons*: Kate Langdon. *Wedding Guests (6)*: *Jennie*: Miss Moulton. *Kitty*: Adele Stillwell. *Mamie*: Annie Hall. *Julie*: Annie Lander. *Zachie*: Ray Bristoe. *Lizzie*: May Trompton. The Ensemble made up from the Auxiliary Corps.

Act 1, Scene 1: The Back Office of Jeremiah McCarthy's Undertaker Shop. The Will and Codicil. *Scene 2*: Exterior of Jeremiah McCarthy's Undertaker Shop and Stable. Resurrection of "The Leather Patch." *Scene 3*: The Home of the McCarthy's, Christmas Eve. On the track of "The Leather Patch."*Act 2, Scene 1*: Christmas Morning in the Hallway of a Rookery. The Wake of Levy Hyer. Still Pursuing "The Leather Patch." *Scene 2*: A view of Paradise Park and its Purlieus. On the way to the Undertaker's Masquerade Ball. A Touch of Nature and Visions of "The Leather Patch." *Scene 3*: Grand View of Baxter Street. Consternation over "The Leather Patch."*Act 3*: Sitting Room in Judge Doebler's House. The Triple Marriage. Joy and Happiness brought about by "The Leather Patch."

MUSICAL NUMBERS
"Denny Grady's Hack" (Act 1, Scene 1)
E. Harrigan
"It Showered Again" (Act 1, Scene 3)
E. Harrigan
"Baxter Avenue" (Act 2, Scene 3)
Joseph Sparks
"Put on Your Bridal Veil" (Act 3)
Colored Wedding Party

1886.04 THE GYPSY BARON

A Comic Opera in Three Acts. Original Viennese libretto ('Der Zigeuerbaron') by Ignaz Schnitzer, based on the story 'Saffi' by Mór Jókai. American adaptation by Sydney Rosenfeld. Music by Johann Strauss. Scenery by Henry E. Hoyt, T. S. Plaisted. Costumes designed by Mme. Loe. Produced under the stage direction of Heinrich Conried. Musical director, Jesse Williams. Produced by Rudolph Aronson. Opened 15 February 1886 at the Casino Theatre and closed 8 May 1886 after 86 performances.[74]

CAST: *Sándor Barinkay*: WILLIAM CASTLE. *Kalman Zsupán*: FRANCIS WILSON. *Count Carnero*: WILLIAM H. FITZGERALD. *Jozsy*: ALFRED KLEIN. *Count Homonay*: Ph. Moore. *Pali*: E. Hegeman. *Ferko*: J. A. Furey. *Michaly*: J. Tibbetts. *Sáffi*: PAULINE HALL. *Czipra*: MAE ST. JOHN. *Arsena*: Letitia Fritch. *Mirabella*: Georgie Dickson. *Ottokar*: BILLIE BARLOW. *Bunko*: Victoria Schilling. *Sidi*: Agnes Folsom. *Ilka*: Rose Beaudet. *Katinka*: Emma Hanley. *Musicians, Students, Soldiers, Gypsies, etc.*

Act 1: A Gypsy Encampment. (Plaisted.)

Act 2: Ruins near the River Temes. (Hoyt.)

Act 3: Public Square in Vienna. (Plaisted.)

ACT 1[75]
Opening Chorus (A sailor he can never be . . .)
Barcarole, B. Barlow, M. St. John
Entrance Song (In early years an orphan I)
W. Castle, Chorus
Ensemble (Who knocks at my modest door?)
M. St. John, W. Castle, W. H. Fitzgerald, P. Hall, F. Wilson
Ensemble (The gallant comes to woo)
Chorus, L. Fritch, W. Castle, F. Wilson, W. H. Fitzgerald, G. Dickson, Girls
Gypsy Song (The gypsy tribe, though poor is noted)
P. Hall
Finale
B. Barlow, L. Fritch, W. Castle, P. Hall, M. St. John, G. Dickson, Gypsies, Chorus

ACT 2
Opening (A guardian, I)
M. St. John, W. Castle, P. Hall
Treasure Waltz (Ah, in a dream by me beholden)
P. Hall, W. Castle, M. St. John, Gypsy Chorus
Duet (Who made us one?)
Barikay, Chorus, P. Hall
Recruiting Song (Place thy willing hand in mine)
P. Moore, Chorus
Czardas (Let all rejoice who now combine)
P. Moore, Chorus
Finale
All
Ensemble
L. Fritch, G. Dickson, M. St. John, W. Castle, P. Moore, B. Barlow, F. Wilson, W. H. Fitzgerald

ACT 3
Opening (Let's rejoice, let's rejoice)
Gypsy Chorus
People, W. H. Fitzgerald, L. Fritch, F. Wilson, B. Barlow
March Song (From the Tajo's strand)
F. Wilson, Chorus, Soldiers' Chorus
Final Chorus
W. Castle, Chorus

1886.05 THREE OF A KIND

Nate Salsbury's Troubadours in a Revival of the Farce Comedy in Three Acts[76]. Play by Edward E. Kidder. Acting manager, Frank Maeder. Musical director, Charles E. Borgman. Opened 15 February 1886 at the Grand Opera House and closed 20 February 1886 after 8 performances.[77]

CAST: *Three of a Kind*: *Jack Potts*: NATE SALSBURY. *Bob Flush*: John Webster. *Phil Straight*: W. S. Daboll. *Dollie Dashwood*, who should have been a boy: NELLIE McHENRY. *Dainty*, the farmer's adopted daughter: Josie Langley. *Priscilla Prism*, ancient, but gushing: Thomas E. Jackson. *Ezra Whittle* of the Happy Homestead Farm: L. J. Loring. *Mr. Selvage Delaine*, a merchant: Fred. Bowman. *Villagers, Maids, Widows and Guests.*

1886.06 A TOY PISTOL

A Farce Comedy in Two Acts. Play by William Gill. Produced under the direction of Charles Frohman. Scenery by Ludovic Seavey. Properties by Thomas Gosmen. Produced by Charles Frohman. Opened 20 February 1886 at the Comedy Theater and closed 3 April 1886 after 41 performances[78].

CAST: *Isaac Roost*, editor of *The Toy Pistol*: TONY HART. *Pie*, his assistant: J. B. MACKIE. *The Veteran*: F. R. JACKSON. *Greeley*: JOHN RICE. *Rossa O'Donovan*:

---

[74]Played return engagements the following season 22 November 1886 at the Grand Opera House for 8 performances and 2 May 1887 to Harrigan's Park Theatre for 8 performances. Cast included Laura Bellini, Harry DeLorme, Signor Taglieri, Gustavus Hall, Jacques Kruger, Marion Singer, Lydia O'Neill, Jennie Reiffarth.

[75]Musical numbers not listed in program; list prepared from published libretto.

[76]First produced in New York 9 February 1885 at the Grand Opera House for 8 performances, returning 23 March 1885 to Henry Miner's People's Theatre 23 March 1885 for an additional 8 performances. For Synopsis of Scenes, see original 1885 production.

[77]Scenery and costumes uncredited. "During the evening, many musical selections will be given of an original and chatty nature."

JOHN RICE. (*A Milesian Mikado*: TONY HART.) *Ernest Seeker*: D. G. Longworth. *J. Lancelot Hustler*: D. G. Longworth. *Primrose Path*: D. G. Longworth. *Miss Dora Mi Solfar*: ANNIE ADAMS. *Miss Colorado*: Mattie Ferguson. *Miss Juliet*: Mattie Ferguson. *Miss Chatter*: Bertie Amberg. *Gracie*: Eva Granville. *Messenger Boy*: Vera Wilson. *Puck*: Bijou Fernandez. *Subtly New*: LENA MERVILLE. *The Swell*: LENA MERVILLE.

Act 1: Office of The Toy Pistol.

Act 2: Interior of the New York and China Tea Company's Store, Harlem.

MUSICAL NUMBERS[79]
"Collar Cuffs"
"I Give It Up"

1886.07 Burlesque of LA PRINCESS DE TRÉBIZONDE

A Burlesque (of Jacques Offenbach's opera comique) in Two Acts, preceded by an Olio. Burlesque by Carl Hauser and J. L. Ford. Music intact, by Jacques Offenbach. Costumes by Baron C. deGrimm. Stage manager, William Paul Bown. Produced by (John) Koster and (Albert) Bial. Opened 22 February 1886 at Koster & Bial's Concert Hall and closed 27 March 1886 after 60 performances.[80]

Olio: Ed. Clarence, Jessie Warner, Alice Grevain, the Dare Brothers (Athletes).

CAST: *Cabriolo*, the retired circus manager: WILLIAM PAUL BOWN. *Prince Raphael*: LOUISE LESTER. *Regina*, the tight rope dancer: LAURA BURT. *Lanetta*: Sophie Hummel. *Paola*: Jessie Warner. *Tremolini*, the clown: FRED WARREN. *Gitana*, the gypsy: GEORGIE PARKER. *Sparadrop*: HAROLD MORRIS. Cast also included Agnes Earle, Ed. Clarence.

1886.08 LA GRANDE-DUCHESSE DE GÉROLSTEIN

A Revival of the Opéra-bouffe in Three Acts[81], in French. Libretto by Henri Meilhac and Ludovic Halévy. Music by Jacques Offenbach. Stage manager, Mons. V. Merle. Musical director, Salvator Guerra. Produced by Maurice Grau. Opened 3 March 1886 at the Star Theatre and closed 6 March 1886 after 2 performances in repertory.

CAST: *La Grande-Duchesse de Gérolstein*: Mme. ANNA JUDIC. *Wanda*: Mlle. Raymonde. *Iza*: Mlle. DeWitt. *Amelia*: Mlle. Myribel. *Olga*: Mlle. Deleste. *Charlotte*: Mlle. Caro. *Fritz*: Mons. MINART. *Prince Paul*: Mons. COOPER. *Baron Puck*: Mons. J. MEZIÈRES. *General Boum*: Mons. GINET. *Baron Grog*: Mons. GREGOIRE. *Nepomuc*: Mons. Dupuis. *Lords and Ladies of the Court, Maids of Honor, Pages, Ushers, Soldiers, Vivandières, Country Girls, etc.*

1886.09 LA COSAQUE

A Vaudeville Operette (Comédie-vaudeville) in Three Acts, in French. Libretto by Henri Meilhac and Albert Millaud. Music by Hervé. Stage manager, Mons. V. Merle. Musical director, Salvator Guerra. Produced by Maurice Grau. Opened 4 March 1886 at the Star Theatre and closed 10 April 1886 after 2 performances in repertory.[82]

CAST: *Princesse (Anna Semionowna Makinskoff)*: Mme. ANNA JUDIC. *Phémie*: Mlle. Raymond. *Mme. Dupontin*: Mlle. DELORME. *Mavroucha*: Mlle. Mirybel. *Malvina*: Mlle. Perrin. *Mme. Saint Flemard*: Mlle. Caro. *Albertine*: Mlle. Jeanne Blanc.. *Angelina*: Mlle. DeWitt. *Jeanne*: Mlle. Andrée. *Louise*: Mlle. Tournyaire. *Catcha*: Mlle. Vandamme. *Jules Primitif*: Mons. COOPER. *Prince Grégoire*: Mons. PAUL GINET. *Prince Fédor*: Mons. GERMAIN. *Prince Cyrille*: Mons. GREGOIRE. *Notary*: Mons. Vinchon. *Pierre Strogoff*: Mons. Dupuis. *Stephane*: Mons. Estiot. *Edouard*: Mons. Perret. *Alexandre*, a Moujik: Mons. Girard. *A Servant*: Mons. Yalowicz. *Vassals, Moujiks, Customers, Saleswomen, etc.*

Act 1: (The Machinskoff Palace at) St. Petersburgh. Present day.

Act 2: (Madame Dupotin's Store.) Paris.

Act 3: (A richly furnished salon.) Paris.

ACT 1[83]
"Vous pouvez, mon cher ami" (Duettino)
Messrs. Germain, Cooper
"Hurrah! Hurrah! Pour la Princesse" (Choeur)
"La Légende de Marfa" (La Petite Cosaque du Don)
A. Judic
"Je suis une femme accomplie" (Rondeau)
A. Judic
"La Cosaque, un peu braque" (Couplets)
A. Judic
"Le conseil de familie ici se réunit" (Terzettino)
Messrs. Gregoire, Ginet, Germain
"Quand je pénétrai dans la cage" (Couplets de la Patte)
A. Judic

ACT 2
"Riez, riez, j'en suis heureuse" (Couplets)
A. Judic
"J'amasse à l'abri des hasards" (Couplet)
Mons. Cooper
"Selon le client qui s'avance" (Couplet)
A. Judic
"Auprès de vous c'est autre chose" (Duettino)
Mons. Cooper, A. Judic
Couplets de Colinette
Mons. Cooper
Réponse de la Bergère au Berger
A. Judic
"Dans mon pays on cont' l'histoire" (Chansonette)
A. Judic

ACT 3
"Quelle noce singulière" (Choeur)
"Mon Dieu, mesdames, j'étais prête" (Couplets du coiffeur)
A. Judic
"Tu ne comprends donc rien de rien" (Déclaration)
A. Judic
"Allons, il faut en français" (Couplet Final)
Mons. Cooper, A. Judic, All

1886.10 THE IVY LEAF

W. H. Powers' Company in a Picturesque Irish Drama in Five Acts, 6 Scenes. (Play by Con. T. Murphy.) Incidental music arranged by Prof. Spiel. Scenic and mechanical effects by R. J. Cutler. Costumes by A. Roemer & Son. Produced by W. H. Power. Opened 8 March 1886 at Niblo's Garden and closed 13 March 1886 after 8 performances.[84]

CAST: *Murty Keerigan*, a true-hearted Irish lad: J. P. SULLIVAN. *Gerald Daly*, a young officer: F. E. Dunbar. *Robert Nolan*, in love with Colice's fortune: W. H. POWER. *Dennis Donovan*, his henchman: GRATTAN PHILLIPS. *Darby Flynn*: Dan McCarthy. *Captain Cannon* of the military police: F. H. Cobb. *Barney O'Leary*: H. C. Henry. *Teddy*, the Piper: B. Delaney. *Martin Hughes*: Edwin Carr. *Dan O'Connor*: Charles Goodwin. *Colice O'Brien*, an heiress: MAY WOOLCOTT. *Maureen Deelish*, a true Irish colleen: DELIA POWER. *Mrs. Deelish*: Lizzie Williams. *Katie McIntyre*: Kitty Coleman. *Norine O'Brien*, sister to Colice: Little Mabel. *Peasants, Military, Police, etc.*

Act 1: Home of Mrs. Deelish.

Act 2, Scene 1: Exterior of same. *Scene 2*: The Eagle's Crag.

Act 3: Lakes of Killarney, from Kenmare Road.

Act 4: The Ivy Tower.

Act 5: The Ivy Leaf.

---

[78]Played a return engagement 3 May 1886 at the People's Theatre for 8 performances.

[79]No musical numbers listed in programs. During Act 2 Tony Hart impersonated an Italian, a young Hebrew, an Irish woman, and a Chinaman.

[80]No program found for this production.

[81]Previously presented in New York in French 24 September 1867 at the French Theatre for 156 performances. For Synopsis of Scenes and Musical Numbers, see original 1867 production.

[82]Cast from April engagement at the Star; no credits for scenery or costumes in programs.

[83]Musical numbers not listed in programs. List prepared from 'The Judic Edition' French libretto published by F. Rullman, New York, 1885, with English translation.

[84]Played a subsequent week's engagement 29 March 1886 at the New Windsor Theatre for 8 performances.

MUSICAL NUMBERS[85]

"Mother's Plaid Shawl"
(*Music and Lyrics by* John T. Kelly.)

"The Huckster"
(*Music and Lyrics by* Barney Fagan.)

1886.11 WE, US AND CO.

A Return Engagement of the Musical Absurdity (Farce Comedy) in Three Acts[86]. Play by William A. Mestayer (and Charles Barnard). Musical director, Max Horter. Produced by William A. Mestayer and Theresa Vaughn. Opened 8 March 1886 at the Standard Avenue Theatre, moved 15 March 1886 to Henry C. Miner's People's Theatre and closed 20 March 1886 after 14 performances; returned 10 May 1886 to Henry C. Miner's People's Theatre for an additional 8 performances[87].

CAST: *T. Willie Rockingham*, Athletic: WILLIAM A. MESTAYER. *Dr. Mulo Medicus*, Veterinary: Ezra F. Kendall. *Knox Dunlap*, Terpsichorean: Gus Bruno. *Dr. Pulsiver*, Hydropath: Robert Evans. *Kerfew Tolls*, Culchaw: Harry Amberg. *George Magillicuddy*, a Terror: Joseph Ott. *August Glotzheimer*, Political: Jefferson DeAngelis. *Lena Bimpleback*, Domestic: Jefferson DeAngelis. *Melinda Magillicuddy*, an Heiress: THERESA VAUGHN. *Cylinder Cogwheel*, Operatic: Hattie Richardson. *Euphemia Coppergall*, an Affinity: Mary Gray. *Rosa Perfectus*, de trop: Belle Stokes. *Bella Bustle*, a Reminder: Ada Deaves. (*Specialties*: The Ideal Quartette [between Acts 2 and 3]; the little German Band on the new instrument, Vocophone, original with W. A. Mestayer.)

MUSICAL NUMBERS

"Will He Ever Return to Me?" (Contralto ballad)
T. Vaughn (*Music and Lyrics by* Professor Max Horter.)

Burlesque of Italian Opera
W. A. Mestayer, T. Vaughn

"One, Two, Three" Three Little Maids; Parody on "Tit Willow" (from THE MIKADO)
C. B. Hawkins

"I'm a Hustler Just the Same"
W. A. Mestayer

1886.12 THE MIKADO, or, The Town of Titipu

A Revival of the Comic Opera in Two Acts[88]. Libretto by William S. Gilbert. Music by Arthur Sullivan. Scenery by George Seavy (Act 1), Joseph Clare (Act 2). Orchestra directed by Clarence West. Produced by John Templeton. Opened 15 March 1886 at Niblo's Garden and closed 27 March 1886 after 16 performances.[89]

CAST: *The Mikado of Japan*: CHARLES L. HARRIS. *Nanki-Poo*: JAY TAYLOR. *Ko-Ko*: WILLIAM H. SEYMOUR. *Pooh-Bah*: GEORGE BRODERICK. *Pish-Tush*: WILLIAM GUIBERSON. *Three Sisters, Wards of Ko-Ko*: *Yum-Yum*: LUCILLE MEREDITH. *Pitti-Sing*: HATTIE STARR. *Peep-Bo*: SELINA ROUGH. *Katisha*: EMMA MABELLA BAKER. *Chorus of School Girls, Nobles, Guards and Coolies.*

1886.13 JOSHUA WHITCOMB

A Revival of the Melodrama in Four Acts[90]. Play by Denman Thompson. Produced by Denman Thompson. Opened 15 March 1886 at the Grand Opera House and closed 20 March 1886 after 7 performances.

CAST: *Uncle Josh*, an old Jackson Democrat: DENMAN THOMPSON. *Roundy*, a Bootblack: IGNACIO MARTINETTI. *John Martin*, a lover of horse racing and theatres: George E. Robinson. *Frederick Dolby*, a young Englishman: Walter Gale. *Cy. Prime*, nigh on to eighty: George A. Beane. *Bill Johnson*, a loafer as bad as they make 'em: Robert Benson. *Reuben*, son of Uncle Josh: EUGENE VAN DUSEN. *Mr. Burroughs*, a model policeman: Charles Adams. *Mr. Foster*, sheriff of the county: Daniel Nourse. *Tot*, a crossing sweeper: EDITH MURILLA. *Nellie Primrose*, a Boston belle: Annie Thompson. *Susan Martin*, with a mania for marriage: Alice Logan. *Mrs. Johnson*, Tot's mother: Edna Weedon. *Aunt Matilda*, Joshua's sister: Mrs. Daniel Nourse. *Amantha Bartlett*, one of the neighbor's gals: Miss Louise Roos.

1886.14 PEPITA, or, The Girl with the Glass Eyes

A Comic Opera in Three Acts. Libretto by Alfred Thompson. Music by Edward Solomon. Produced under the personal direction of Alfred Thompson and Edward Solomon. Ballet arranged by Signor Novissimo. Scenery by (Arthur) Voegtlin. Costumes by Alfred Thompson. Conductor, Edward Solomon. Produced by J. M. Hill. Opened 16 March 1886 at the Union Square Theater and closed 22 May 1886 after 80 performances.

CAST: *Professor Pongo*, Doctor of Sciences: JACQUES KRUGER. *Don Giavolo*, Governor of Scaliwaxico: FRED CLIFTON. *Don Pablo*, his son and heir: CHAUNCEY OLCOTT. *Don Juan*, his inevitable friend: George Wilkinson. *Curaso*, valet to Pablo: FRED SOLOMON. *Donna Carmansuita*, Directress of Seminary for Young Ladies: ALMA STUART STANLEY. *Pasquela*, a forward pupil: Lizzie Hughes. *Maraquita*, an advanced idem: Carrie Jackson. *Chiquita*, a prominent ditto: Cora Striker. *Juana*, a lady in waiting: Julia Wilson. *Pepita*, Professor Pongo's Daughter: LILLIAN RUSSELL. *The Duennas*, assistant teachers: __. *The Young Ladies of Donna C.'s Seminary*: __. *Students, Guests, Waiters, Automata, etc. Coryphees*: Mlles. Pasta, S. Watson, Forster Atkins.

The action takes place in the city of Scaliwaxico. *Time*: High Old. *Period*: Uncertain.

Act 1: The Students' Frolic. Before Professor Pongo's House in Scaliwaxico.

Act 2: The Professor's Prodigy. Interior of Pongo's Sanctum.

Act 3: The Governor's Fete. Don Diavolo's Palace.

1886.15 THE LITTLE TYCOON

An American-Japanese Comic Opera in Two Acts. Words (libretto) and music by Willard Spenser. All under the direction William H. Daly. Musical director, Fred. Perkins. Produced by The Temple Theatre Comic Opera Company (George C. Brotherton, Proprietor and Manager). Opened 29 March 1886 at the Standard Theatre, moved 19 April 1886 to the Fifth Avenue Theatre and closed 26 June 1886 after 91 performances.[91]

CAST: *General Knickerbocker*, one of the old-time Knickerbockers: R. E. GRAHAM. *Alvin Barry*, a young Wall Street broker, afterwards the Great Tycoon of Japan: W. S. RISING. *Rufus Ready*. Alvin's college friend, afterward Gull-Gull, Interpreter to the Great Tycoon: R. N. DUNBAR. *Lord Dolphin*, Suitor for the hand of Violet: ED. H. VAN VEGHTEN. *Teddy*, Lord Dolphin's valet: JOSEPH MEALEY. *Custom House Officers*: J. W. Daniels, John Banner. *Montgomery*, General Knickerbocker's footman: Frank Darcy. *Violet*, General Knickerbocker's daughter, afterward the Little Tycoon: CARRIE M. DIETRICK. *Dolly Dimple*. Violet's school friend: NETTA GUION. *Miss Hurricane*. Chaperone to Tourist Maidens: ELMA DELARO.

Tourist Maidens, Tourists, Hobgoblins, Brigands, etc., etc.: *Ladies of the Chorus*: Misses Ruth Rich, Carrie Neilson, Minnie Leighton, Katie LaValle, Georgie Rush, Florence Ford, Lola Martin, Florence Sack, Katie Millard, Amy Vernon, Jessie Terry, Blanche Howard, Alma Varry, Katherine Lingard, Mable Royston, Jennie Auretian, Nellie Cox, Marie Hart. *Gentlemen of the Chorus*: Messrs. Stockett, White, Everett, Fox, Ramsdell, Schmidt, Johnston, Eising, Moore, Lennen, Goodall, Munroe, Ryder, Chapin, N. Pearce, Gus App, George App, Theo. Rodeau.

Act 1: The Deck of the Steamship *"Electric."*

Act 2: House and Grounds of General Knickerbocker.

ACT 1[92]

"On the Sea" (Opening Chorus)
E. Delaro, N. Guion, R. N. Dunbar, Chorus

[85]No songs listed in programs. Musical numbers are later interpolations, as indicated from published sheet music.

[86]First produced in New York 29 December 1884 at the Fifth Avenue Theatre for 24 performances; 20 April 1885 at the Fifth Avenue Theatre for 32 additional performances. For Synopsis of Scenes and Musical Numbers, see original 1884 production.

[87]Played return engagements 14 February 1887 at Henry Miner's People's Theatre for 8 performances, and 14 March 1887 at the Windsor Theatre for an additional 8 performances.

[88]First presented in New York 20 July, 10-29 August 1885 at the Union Square and People's Theatres for 22 performances. First authorized production presented 19 August 1885 at the Fifth Avenue Theatre by Richard D'Oyly Carte for 250 performances. For Synopsis of Scenes and Musical Numbers, see 19 August 1885 D'Oyly Carte production.

[89]Stage direction, costumes uncredited. Billed "with most of the principal artists who first produced the Opera in New York."

[90]First produced in a one-act form 3 April 1875 at the Eagle Theatre; in its three-act form 2 September 1878 at the Lyceum Theatre for 93 performances, and in its four-act form 18 December 1882 at Haverly's 14th Street Theatre for 14 performances. For Synopsis of Scenes, see original 1882 production.

[91]Scenery and costumes uncredited.

[92]Musical numbers not listed in programs. List prepared from published vocal score (1882, by the author), revised according to published book of words (1886). Added in mid-May as per the New York Clipper: "Once Was Enough for Him" (Topical Song) R. E. Graham.

"We'll Watch for the (Blowing) Whale"
R. N. Dunbar, Chorus
"As You See Them"
E. Delaro, N. Guion, Chorus
"Doomed as I Am to Marry a Lord" (Solo)
C. M. Dietrick, Chorus
"Oh, It is Such an Unheard-of Proceeding (to Marry Her to a Lord)"
R. N. Dunbar
"For We're Immensely High-Toned"
R. N. Dunbar, College Students
"We've a Scheme" (Solo)
C. M. Dietrick, Chorus
"Love Comes Like a Summer Sigh"[93]
C. M. Dietrick, Ensemble
"To Song and Dance"
R. E. Graham, Chorus
"Now When I Was a Boy"
R. E. Graham, Chorus
"Heel and Toe We Always Go"
E. H. Van Veghten, J. Mealey
"The Fatal Step"
R. N. Dunbar, Chorus of Maidens and College Students
"Dark Though My Fate May Be" (Soli and Duo)
C. M. Dietrick, W. S. Rising
Hobgoblin Dance and Chorus (Ha! Ha! Ha! Ha! Ha! We've come)
"Love Reigns!" (Soli and Duo)
C. M. Dietrick, W. S. Rising
"Och, thin! "(Valet's Song and Dance)
J. Mealey
"Oh, Don't You See How?" (Solo)
R. E. Graham, Chorus
"A Lament"
(Soli and Ensemble)
"Oh Why This Apprehension?" (Finale Act 1)
C. E. Dietrick, E. Delaro, N. Guion, W. S. Rising, R. E. Graham, R. N. Dunbar, J. Mealey, Chorus

ACT 2
"Sad Heart of Mine" (Song)
C. E. Dietrick
"To See Thee" (Duo)
C. E. Dietrick, W. S. Rising
"Ah, Destiny!" (O, Destiny) (Soli and Trio)
C. E. Dietrick, W. S. Rising, R. E. Graham
"Oh, You Incense, You Madden Me!"
C. E. Dietrick, W. S. Rising, R. E. Graham, R. N. Dunbar, Brigands
"Checkmated We"
R. N. Dunbar, W. S. Rising, Chorus
"Tell Me, Daisy" (Song)
C. E. Dietrick
"Yes, We've All Seen Sham"
N. Guion, Japanese Maidens
"Speak Low, Walls Have Ears"
E. Delaro, N. Guion, Tourist-Maidens
"Tycoon March" (Entrance of the Great Tycoon and Suite)
"Sham, Great Tycoon"
Japanese Chorus
"The Cats on Our Back Fence"
R. E. Graham, Chorus
"An American Always Pans Out" (Song)
R. N. Dunbar, Chorus
"Yes, I'll Be the Little Tycoon" (Finale)
C. E. Dietrick, E. Delaro, N. Guion, W. S. Rising, R. E. Graham, R. N. Dunbar, J. Mealey, Ensemble

1886.16 THE BLACK CROOK

A Revival of the Extravaganza in Four Acts, 16 Tableaux[94]. (Book by Charles M. Barras. Music composed and selected by Thomas Baker, Louis Baer, A. W. Hoffman.) Produced under the stage direction of Kiralfy Brothers (Imre, Bolossy). Scenery by Robecchi and Carpezat of Paris; Magnani of Florence; Messrs. Forrest, Seabury, W. T. Porter, Harley Merry, George Bell, of New York. Costumes by Miss Fisher of London; Mme. Gervass of Paris; Misses Alena and Picino. Mechanical effects by M. Alexander and W. H. Crane. Musical director, A. W. Hoffman. Produced by the Kiralfy Brothers. Opened 29 March 1886 at Niblo's Garden and closed 24 April 1886 after 32 performances[95]

CAST: MORTALS: *Hertzog*, the Black Crook: J. F. PETERS. *Count Wolfenstein*: JOHN DeGEZ. *Rudolph*, a poor artist: W. F. CLIFTON. *Von Puffenkrantz*, the Count's Chamberlain: W. H. BARTHOLOMEW. *Greppo*, a henchman: J. F. WARD. *Wolfgar*: J. Anderson. *Bruno*: F. Star. *Amina*, a village maiden: OLGA BRANDON. *Dame Barbara*: Mrs. SELDEN IRWIN. *Carline*: Louise Allen. *Guards, Attendants, Servitors, Villagers, etc.*

IMMORTALS: *Stalacta*, the Fairy Queen: ROSE WATSON. *Dragonfin*: August Siegrist.

DEMONS: *Zamiel*: A. H. Denham. *Skudelwhelp*: M. Blesser.

Principal Dancers: Mlle. DeROSA (Star Danseuse); Mons. ARNOLD (Grotesque Dancer), Mlle. CAMMIS. *Specialties*: Mons. and Mlle. TISSOT, THE MIGNANI FAMILY, HERBERT BROTHERS (Star Gymnasts). Corps de Ballet.

1886.17 H.M.S. PINAFORE, or, The Lass That Loved a Sailor

A Revival of the Comic Operas in Two Acts[96]. Libretto by William S. Gilbert. Music by Arthur Sullivan. New scenery and dresses. Stage Manager, Press Eldridge. Produced by (John) Koster and (Albert) Bial. Opened 29 March 1886 at Koster & Bial's Music Hall and closed 1 May 1886 after (60) performances.

CAST: *The Right Hon. Sir Joseph Porter, K.C.B.*, First Lord of the Admiralty: PRESS ELDRIDGE. *Captain Corcoran*, commanding *H.M.S. Pinafore*: VINCENT HOGAN. *Ralph Rackstraw*, Able Seaman: GERALD COVENTRY. *Dick Deadeye*, Able Seaman: FRED WARREN. *Josephine*, the Captain's Daughter: LOUISE LESTER. *Hebe*, Sir Joseph's First Cousin: GEORGIE PARKER. *Little Buttercup*, a Portsmouth Bumboat Woman: JENNIE LUDLOW. *First Lord's Sisters, Cousins and Aunts*: Full Chorus. Company also included E. Howard Danforth, Charles Danforth, Robert Fisher, C. Shattuck, Edward Carr.

1886.18 LA BELLE HÉLÈNE

A Revival of the Opéra-bouffe in Three Acts, in French[97]. Libretto by Henri Meilhac and Ludovic Halévy. Music by Jacques Offenbach. Stage manager, Mons. V. Merle. Musical director, Salvatore Guerra. Produced by Maurice Grau. Opened 5 April 1886 at the Star Theatre and closed 10 April 1886 after 2 performances in repertory.

CAST: *Hélène*: ANNA JUDIC. *Orestes*: Mlle. Raymonde. *Parthaenia*: Mlle. DeWitt. *Loena*: Mlle. Caro. *Bacchis*: Mlle. Mirybel. *Paris*, Prince of Troy: Mons. MINART. *Agamemnon*: Mons. PAUL GINET. *Mélélas*, King of Sparta: Mons. GERMAIN. *Calchas*: Mons. MEZIÈRES. *Achilles*: Mons. Vinchon. *Ajax I*: Mons. JOSÉ DUPUIS. *Ajax II*: Mons. GREGOIRE. *Philocome*: Mons. Estiot. *Euthycles*: Mons. Vinchon. *A Slave*: Mons. Perret.

1886.19 LA ROUSSOTTE

A Vaudeville Operetta (Comédie-vaudeville) in Three Acts and a Prologue, in French. Libretto by Henri Meilhac, Ludovic Halévy and Albert Millaud. Music by Marius Boullard (and Hervé, Charles Lecocq). Stage manager, Mons. V. Merle. Musical director, Salvatore Guerra. Produced by Maurice Grau. Opened and closed 6 April 1886 at the Star Theatre after 1 performance in repertory.[98]

---

[93]Also known as The Little Tycoon Waltz.

[94]First produced in New York 12 September 1866 at Niblo's Garden for 475 performances.

[95]Played a return engagement 17 May 1886 at the Grand Opera House for 8 performances.

[96]H.M.S. PINAFORE was originally presented in New York 15 January 1879 at the Standard Theatre for 175 performances. Beginning 25 April 1886 selections from TRIAL BY JURY were also presented. For Synopsis of Scenes and Musical Numbers, see original 1879 production. No program found for this production.

[97]First produced in New York in French 26 March 1868 at the Théâtre Français for 37 performances. For Synopsis of Scenes and Musical Numbers, see original 1868 production.

[98]No program available.

CAST: *La Rousotte, (Anne-Marie)*: Mme. ANNA JUDIC. *Madame de Saint-Excédant*: Mlle. DELORME. *Adèle*: Mlle. DeWitt. *Madame Victor*: Mlle. Mirybel. *Héloïse*: Mlle. Caro. *Marie*: Mlle. DeWitt. *Cécile*: Mlle. Perrin. *Médard*: Mons. COOPER. *(Comte) Dubois-Toupet*: Mons. J. MEZIÈRES. *Gigonnet*: Mons. GREGOIRE. *Montflambert*: Mons. Germain. *Edouard*: Mons. Dupuis. *Un Criado*: Mons. Perret. *Un Senor*: Mons. Estiot.

PROLOGUE[99]

"Sont ils gentils ces petits mioches" (Couplets)
[Savarin] (*Music by* Charles Lecocq.)

"Ainsi que vient l'argent" (Couplets)
Mons. J. Mezières (*Music by* Charles Lecocq.)

"C'est aujourd'hui qu'la gross' Germaine" (Ronde)
A. Judic [Anne-Marie], Mons. J. Mezières (*Music by* Charles Lecocq.)

ACT 1

"Le souvenir de cette jeune fille" (Couplets)
J. Dupuis (*Music by* Charles Lecocq.)

"Attendez je m'rappell' maint'nant" (Couplets)
A. Judic [La Roussotte] (*Music by* Charles Lecocq.)

"Pour les compter, mes amoureux" (Couplets)
A. Judic [La Roussotte] (*Music by* Marius Boullard.)

"N'fait's pas ça! J'suis très bonn' fille" (Couplets)
A. Judic [La Roussotte] (*Music by* Marius Boullard.)

ACT 2

"Un peu d'silence. O n'est pas sourd" (Couplets)
A. Judic [La Roussotte] (*Music by* Marius Boullard.)

"J' n'ai pas d'ancêtr's dans ma famille" (Pi.ouit)
A. Judic [La Roussotte] (*Music by* Hervé.)

"Sans Médard je ne pourrais vivre" (Couplets et Trio Bouffe)
A. Judic [La Roussotte], Messrs. J. Dupuis, J. Mezières (*Music by* Charles Lecocq.)

ACT 3

"Maint'nant j'ai pris le bel usage" (L'Amazone)
A. Judic [La Roussotte] (*Music by* Hervé.)

"En ma qualité de poëte" (Couplet Final)
J. Dupuis, A. Judic [La Roussotte] (*Music by* Hervé.)

1886.20 LA PÉRICHOLE

A Revival of the Opéra-bouffe in Four Acts, in French[100]. Libretto by Ludovic Halévy and Henri Meilhac, based on Prosper Merimée novel "Le Carosse du Saint-Sacrement." Music by Jacques Offenbach. Stage manager, Mons. V. Merle. Musical director, Salvatore Guerra. Produced by Maurice Grau. Opened 7 April 1886 at the Star Theatre and closed 17 April 1886 after 2 performances in repertory.

CAST: *La Périchole*: Mme. ANNA JUDIC. *Berginella*: Mlle. DeWitt. *Guadalena*: Mlle. Mirybel. *Mastrilla*: Mlle. Delest. *Manuelita*: Mlle. Caro. *Frasquinella*: Mlle. Olga. *Ninetta*: Mlle. DeWitt. *Brambilla*: Mlle. Vandamme. *Piquillo*: Mons. JOSÉ DUPUIS. *Don Andrès de Ribeira*: Mons. GREGOIRE. *El Conde de Panatellas*: Mons. J. MEZIÈRES. *Don Pedro*: Mons. Germain. *Un Prisonero Viejo*: Mons. Ginet. *Tarapotte*: Mons. Vinchon. *Un Carcelero*: Mons. Estiot. *Notarios*: Messrs. Girard, Perret.

1886.21 LA VIE PARISIENNE

A Revival of the Opéra-bouffe in Four Acts, in French[101]. Libretto by Henri Meilhac and Ludovic Halévy. Music by Jacques Offenbach. Stage manager, Mons. V. Merle. Musical director, Salvatore Guerra. Produced by Maurice Grau. Opened and closed 12 April 1886 at the Star Theatre after 1 performance in repertory.

CAST: *Gabrielle*: Mme. ANNA JUDIC. *Pauline*: Mlle. Raymond. *Métella*: Mlle. MIRYBEL. *Baroness de Gondremark*: Mlle. DeWitt. *Leonie*: Mlle. Cécile Gregoire. *Louise*: Mlle. Delest. *Clara*: Mlle. Caro. *Caroline*: Mlle. Perrin. *Julie*: Mlle. Tournyaire. *Augustine*: Mlle. Andrée. *Albertine*: Mlle. Marie. *Baron de Gondremark*: Mons. GINET. *Un Bresilien*: Mons. Minart. *Frik*: Mons. Minart. *Prosper*: Mons. Minat. *Bobinet*: Mons. J. MEZIÈRES. *Bavul de Gardefeu*: Mons. COOPER. *Alfred*: Mons. Germain. *Urbain*: Mons. Germain. *Joseph*: Mons. Peret. *Alphonse*: Mons. Girard. *Gontran*: Mons. Dupuis. *Un Employe*: Mons. Estiot.

1886.22 LA JOLIE PARFUMEUSE

A Revival of the Opéra-comique in Three Acts[102], in French. Libretto by Hector Crémieux and Ernest Blum. Music by Jacques Offenbach. Stage manager, Mons. V. Merle. Musical director, Salvatore Guerra. Produced by Maurice Grau. Opened and closed 17 April 1886 at the Star Theatre after 1 performancel in repertory.

CAST: *Rose Michon*: Mme. ANNA JUDIC. *Bavolet*: Mlle. Raymond. *La Julienne*: Mlle. Delorme. *Clorinde*: Mlle. Myribel. *Lise*: Mlle. DeWitt. *Justine*: Mlle. Vandamme. *Arthemise*: Mlle. Deleste. *Madelon*: Mlle. Caro. *Poirot*: Mons. Poirot. *La Cocardière*: Mons. GREGOIRE. *Germain*: Mons. Girard. *First Waiter*: Mons. Vinchon. *Second Waiter*: Mons. Estiot.

1886.23 IRISH ARISTOCRACY

Barry & Fay's Company in a Revival of the Farce Comedy in Three Acts[103]. (Play by William Carleton.) Opened 19 April 1886 at the Standard Theatre and closed 1 May 1886 after 16 performances; returned 31 May 1886 to the People's Theatre and closed 5 June 1886 after an additional 8 performances. Total: 24 performances.[104]

CAST: *Michael Muldoon*: HUGH FAY. *Michael Mulcahey*: WILLIAM BARRY. Company also included Daniel Lacy, William Lackaye, Jeppe Delano, C. J. Newton, Maggie Gallagher, Florence Worth, Fannnie Delano, Little Vevie.

1886.24 ARCADIA

An Extravagansic Burlesque in Two Acts, 8 Scenes. Libretto by William Gill. Music composed and selected by John J. Braham. Staged by William Gill. Scenery by J. S. Schell and Harley Merry. Costumes designed by Helen Leslie. Mechanism by Peter Henderson. Properties by Joseph Sullivan. Electric effects by James McElroy. Musical director, John J. Braham. Produced by (Robert E. J.) Miles and Barton. Opened 26 April 1886 at the Bijou Theatre and closed 15 May 1886 after 21 performances.[105]

CAST: *Tom, Tom*, the Piper's son, an attractive if somewhat larcenous young rascal: LIZZIE ST. QUINTIN. *Trumpetta*, Queen of the War Fairies, a susceptible monarch: HATTIE DELARO. *Bulbul*, the Nightingale, Trumpetta's daughter: HATTIE RICHARDSON. *Little Sallie Waters*, who possesses a remarkable penchant for "playing with the children in the sun," to say nothing of her other numerous peculiarities: ADA BOSHELL. *Captain Clubber*, a member in good standing of some of our best clubs: FLORENCE THROPP. *Lootella*, Trumpetta's aid-de-camp: Maud Goodwin. *The Piper's Wife*, Tomtom's mother, who has seen much better days, and who once had a strong Scotch accent, which was unfortunately lost on the "*Oregon*," and for diver's reasons not recovered: ALICE HOSMER. *Pogowog*, the warrior-magician, a bad egg, under the yolk of Trumpetta: GEORGE RICHARDS. *Justice Bluffy*, of the Empsty-Empsth Judicial Court: JOHN W. RANSONE. *Pogowog's Minions (4)*: *Blow*: F. F. Ward. *Bluster*: R. MacIntyre. *Chinn*: George Campbell. *Baktork*: Albert Hart. *Clerk of the Court*: J. Andrews. *The Piper*, Tomtom's father, who may, perhaps, mention incidentally his connection with the late lamented Duke of Argyll: WILLIAM GILL. *Police, a Mephistophelian Band, War Fairies, Cowboys, Geographical Quarters, etc.*

Act 1, Scene 1: Courtyard of the Warrior-Magician. *Scene 2*: Garden of Trumpetta's Fairy Palace. *Scene 3*: The Miserable Home of the Piper. *Scene 4*: Courtyard of the Empsty-Empsth Judicial Court.

Act 2, Scene 1: A Cell in the Penitentiary. *Scene 2*: Mephistopheles' Country Seat. *Scene 3*: Trumpetta's Garden. *Scene 4*: The Hall of Science.

---

[99]Musical numbers not listed in programs. List prepared from published French piano vocal score (C. Jouber, Paris, 1881?).

[100]First produced in New York 4 January 1869 at Pike's Opera House. For Synopsis of Scenes and Musical Numbers, see original 1869 production.

[101]First produced in New York in French 29 March 1869 at the Théâtre Français for 11 performances. For Synopsis of Scenes and Musical Numbers, see original 1869 production.

[102]First produced in New York in French 31 March 1875 at the Lyceum Theatre in repertory. For Synopsis of Scenes and Musical Numbers, see original 1875 production.

[103]First produced in New York as IRISH ARISTOCRACY 30 November 1882 at the Academy of Music for 2 performances. For Synopsis of Scenes, see original 1882 production. New songs and dances were added for this revival.

[104]No program found for this engagement.

[105]A revised version of ARCADIA played a return engagement 30 January-11 February 1888 at the Third Avenue Theatre for 18 performances, featuring Corinne as Tomtom.

ACT 1
Scene 1
"Victoria, Victoria"
Chorus
"Not a Drummer" (Song)
L. St. Quintin, Chorus
"Little Sallie Waters" (Song)
A. Boshell, Chorus
Scene 2
Song
H. Richardson
"Perhaps I Don't" (Trio)
G. Richards, L. St. Quintin, H. Richardson
Quartette 'Olla Podrida'
Duet ("Send Me a Tender Token")
H. Richardson, L. St. Quintin
Sword Dance
G. Richards
Finale
Scene 3
"I Once Was Wealthy" (Song)
A. Hosmer
"I Sang This Song" (Song)
W. Gill
Doleful Dance of Two
Scene 4
Grand Finale

ACT 2
Scene 2
Laughing Quartette
Scene 3
Song
H. Delaro
"Hic-hiccough Hic-hiccough" (Affecting Ballad)
W. Gill, A. Hosmer (*Music by* Arthur Sullivan, after "Willow Tit-willow" from THE MIKADO.)
Dialect Specialties
Scene 4
Ballad L.
St. Quintin
Sentimental Trio
Grand Finale

1886.25 THE MIKADO, or, The Town of Titipu

A Revival of the Comic Opera in Two Acts[106]. Libretto by William S. Gilbert. Music by Arthur Sullivan. Stage directed by F. A. Leon. Orchestra directed by John C. Mullaly. Produced by John Stetson, by arrangement with Richard D'Oyly Carte. Opened 26 April 1886 at the Metropolitan Opera House and closed 8 May 1886 after 16 performances.[107]

CAST: *The Mikado of Japan*: N. S. BURNHAM. *Nanki-Poo*, his son, disguised as a wandering minstrel, in love with Yum-Yum: ROY STAINTON. *Ko-Ko*, Lord High Executioner of Titipu: J. W. HERBERT. *Pooh-Bah*, Lord High Everything Else: Signor BROCCOLINI. *Pish-Tush*, a Noble Lord: GEORGE OLMI. *Three Sisters, Wards of Ko-Ko*: *Yum-Yum*: MARY BEEBE. *Pitti-Sing*: AGNES STONE. *Peep-Bo*: MAMIE CERBI. *Katisha*, an Elderly Lady, in love with Nanki-Poo: ALICE CARLE. *School Girls, Nobles, Guards and Coolies*: Mammoth Chorus of 200.

[106]First presented in New York 20 July 1885, 17-29 August 1885 at the Union Square and Henry Miner's People's Theatres for 24 performances. Presented 19 August 1885 at the Fifth Avenue Theatre by Richard D'Oyly Carte for 250 performances. For Synopsis of Scenes and Musical Numbers, see original 1885 production.

[107]Stage direction, scenery and costumes uncredited. Wardrobe from original designs of the Savoy Theatre, London; stage manager, W. H. Conly.

1886.26 DON CAESAR

An Opéra-comique in Three Acts. Original German libretto (to the comic operette 'Don Cesar') by Otto Walther, adapted from the French play 'Don César de Bazan' by Adolphe d'Ennery and Philippe Dumanoir. American adaptation by William von Sachs, Jr. Music by Rudolf Dellinger. Scenery by Philip W. Goatcher, W. H. Day. Mechanism by F. Dorrington. Appointments by C. Seidle. Gas effects by J. F. Driscoll. Musical director, Signor Antonio DeNovellis. Produced by the McCaull Opera Comique Company (John A. McCaull, Proprietor and Manager). Opened 3 May 1886 at Wallack's Theatre and closed 28 May 1886 after 26 performances.[108]

CAST: *Don Caesar*, Count of Irum and Garoffa: Signor PERUGINI. *King Carlos II*: EDWIN W. HOFF. *Don Fernandez De Mirabillas*, Prime Minister: CHARLES W. DUNGAN. *Don Ranudo Onofrio De Colibrados* Royal Archivist: DeWOLF HOPPER. *Donna Uracca*, his wife: GENEVIEVE REYNOLDS. *Maritana*: BERTHA RICCI. *Falconers of the Queen* (9): *Pueblo Escudiro*: MATHILDE COTTRELLY. *Sancho*: Zoe DeVielle. *Juan*: Agnes Bowen. *Pedro*: Ida Bartelle. *Jose*: Grace Hollingsworth. *Manuel*: Josie [Josephine] Knapp. *Federigo*: Grace Seavey. *Lorenzo*: Emma Muller. *Eugenio*: Therese Casaboni. *Martinez*, a captain: *The Alcalde*: Charles H. Jones. *Alerta*, a soldier: MOUNTJOY WALKER. *Men and women of the people, peasants, soldiers, fishermen, pages, hunting suites, etc.*

Act 1: A street in Madrid. (Goatcher.)

Act 2: The Prison. (Day.)

Act 3: A castle in the neighborhood of Madrid. (Day.)

1886.27 PRINCE KARL

A Comedy in Four Acts. Play by Archibald Clavering Gunter. Original and selected music by George Purdy. Produced under the direction of William Seymour. Scenery by E. LaMoss. Mechanical effects by Matt Graham. Costumes by Sarah Ormond. Gas and calcium effects by John Witherell. Produced by R. M. Field. Opened 3 May 1886 at the Madison Square Theater and closed 14 August 1886 after 122 performances; returned 21 February 1887 to the Union Square Theatre and closed 12 March 1887 after an additional 21 performances; returned 30 May 1887 to the Madison Square Theatre and closed 9 July 1887 after an additional 42 performances. Total: 185 performances.

CAST: *Karl von Arhmien*, Prince of the German Empire, Baron Holstein, Duke of Hesse-Dunderber, etc.: RICHARD MANSFIELD. *Spartan Spotts*, ex-bankrupt on his last speculation: CHARLES KENT. *J. Cool Dragon*, a Chicago lawyer, in pursuit of the German heir: William Seymour. *Howard Algernon Briggs*, an American crudity: A. R. Whytal. *Markey Davis*, late of England, proprietor of the Hotel Bellevue, Coblentz: James Nolan. *Gustavus*, waiter at the same: H. P. Whittemore. *Sylvio Salvolio*, an Italian brigand, "the terror of the mountain": C. E. Boardman. *Giuseppe*, his lieutenant: G. B. Bates. *Pippo di Monti*, Captain of Gendarmes: E. E. Rose. *Mrs. Daphne Dabury Lowell*, an American mother-in-law: Mrs. J. R. VINCENT. *Mrs. Florence Armin Lowell*, the heiress-widow: MAIDA CRAIGEN. *Miss Alicia Lowell*, a product of Vassar College: HELEN DAYNE. *Waiters, Porters, German Policemen, Brigands and Gendarmes.*

Act 1: Office and Corridor of a Hotel near Coblentz, with a view of the Rhine.

Act 2: The Same. Next morning.

Act 3: Hall in the Old Castle of Karlshop. One week later.

Act 4: The Ruined Chalet by the Mountain Road in Italy. The Haunt of the Brigands. One day later.

1886.28 A TIN SOLDIER

A Farce Comedy in Three Acts. Play by Charles H. Hoyt. Staged by Charles H. Hoyt. Musical director, Charles Zimmerman. Produced by (Charles H.) Hoyt and (Charles H.) Thomas. Opened 3 May 1886 at the Standard Theatre and closed 3 July 1886 after 63 performances.[109]

CAST: *Rats*, a perfect little gentleman: JAMES T. POWERS. *Vilas Canby*, "The Professor," a practical plumber: GEORGE BONIFACE, JR. *Brooklyn Bridge*, a gentleman of high position: Paul Arthur. *Trip Walker*, a mail carrier: James H. Dyer. *Il Conte di Luna*, Italian art connoisseur: James H. Dyer. *Col. I. B. Boosey*, hero of Gettysburg: James H. Dyer. *Colonel Wood B. Fuller*, hero of Gettysburg: Gus Hennessy. *Wright Handy*, Bridge's partner: Gus Hennessy. *Lyon Waite*, meat merchant:

[108]Stage direction and costume design uncredited. No musical numbers listed in programs, no libretto, book of words or musical score found for this production.

[109]No credits for scenery or costume design.

W. Gilmore. *Rob Graves*, business man: W. S. Taylor. *Steele Coffin*, Secretary of Tarring and Feathering Committee: W. Jordan. *Violet Hughes*, a domestic earthquake: AMY AMES. *Patsy*, a young thing: Marion Elmore. *Victoria Bridge*, a bride of six weeks: Isabelle Coe. *Carrie Story*, who lives with Mrs. Hogg, next door: Flora Walsh. *Mrs. Fulton Ferry*, mother-in-law of Brooklyn Bridge: Julia Elmore. *Nora Marks*, a domestic: Fannie Batchelder. *Tarring and Feathering Committee, etc.*

Act 1: Dining-room of Bridge's house. A pleasant morning at home.

Act 2: Kitchen of Bridge's house. A pleasant day at home.

Act 3: Backyard of Bridge's house. A restful evening at home.

ACT 1[110]

"A Little Tin Soldier"

Bewitching Gavotte

ACT 2

"You'll Get There" (Topical Song)
(G. Boniface) (*Music and Lyrics by* Charles H. Hoyt.)

"The Tough" (Song and Dance)
(J. T. Powers)

Illustrations of Jugglery, and other things that Rats saw and variety show

"Where can he be?" (Song)
(A. Ames)

"Faust Waltz" (composed expressly by Charles Gounod for another purpose)

"Dancing mad" (Serenade)

ACT 3

"For all of which I mean that Bridge shall pay" (Song)

"The Monkey Monk" (Grand Medley)

"Swinging on a Gospel Gate" (Plantation Song)

Terpsichorean Duo
(*Music by* Charles Zimmerman.)

Finale

1886.29 PIN-A-4/TRIAL BY JURY

A Double Bill of a Burlesque of H.M.S. Pinafore and a Revival of the Comic Opera, in Two Acts[111]. Original libretto by William S. Gilbert. Original music by Arthur Sullivan. Stage Manager, Press Eldridge. Produced by (John) Koster and (Albert) Bial. Opened 3 May 1886 at Koster & Bial's Music Hall and closed 8 May 1886 after 8 performances.

CAST: FRED WARREN, PRESS ELDRIDGE, C. F. RAYMOND, E. HOWARD DANFORTH, CHARLES SHATTUCK, ROSA LEE, LOU SANDFORD, LILLIE SHANDLEY, Full Chorus. *Specialties*: Muehlman Trio, Sharpley and West (Swiss Song Birds).

1886.30 ERMINIE

A Comic Opera in Three Acts. Libretto by Harry Paulton and Claxson Bellamy. Based on the melodrama ('L'Auberge des Adrets' by Benjamin Antier, Saint-Amand and Paulyanthe, adapted into English as) 'Robert Macaire.' Music by Edward Jakobowski. Staged by Edward Paulton. Scenery designed by Henry E. Hoyt, T. S. Plaisted. Costumes by Dazian and Mme. Loe. Musical director, Jesse Williams. Produced by Rudolf Aronson. Opened 10 May 1886 at the Casino Theatre and closed 2 October 1886 after 150 performances; re-opened 15 November 1886 at the Casino Theatre and closed 17 September 1887 after an additional 362 performances. Total: 512 performances[112].

CAST: *Erminie*: PAULINE HALL. *Cerise*: MARION MANOLA. *Princess de Gramponeur*: Jennie Weathersby. *Javotte*: Agnes Folsom. *Marie*: Victoria Schilling. *Delaunay*, a Young Officer: ROSE BEAUDET. *Cadeaux, Ravennes*, Two Thieves: FRANCIS WILSON, W. S. DABOLL. *Marquis de Ponvert*: Carl Irving. *Eugene Marcel*, the Marquis' Secretary: Henry Pepper. *Chevalier de Brabazon*, Marquis' guest: MAX FREEMAN. *Dufois*, Landlord of the Lion d'Or: Murray Woods. *Simon*, Waiter at the Lion d'Or: A. W. Maflin. *Viscomte de Brissac*: C. L. Weeks. *Sergeant*: E. Furry.

Act 1: Inn at Ponvert. (Hoyt.)

Act 2: The Pink Ball-room. (Hoyt.)

Act 3: Corridor and Staircase. (Plaisted.)

ACT 1[113]

Opening Chorus (Around in a whirl, we skip, dance and twirl)
Chorus

"Vive le C. Irving" (Chorus and Ensemble)
C. Irving, P. Hall, M. Manola, V. Schilling, Chorus

"When Love Is Young" (Song and Chorus)
P. Hall

"Past and Future" (Duet)
P. Hall, H. Pepper

Entrance of Soldiers and Chorus (All for glory the soldier's life)
Soldiers

"A Soldier's Life" (Song)
C. Irving

"(Downy) Jail-Birds of a Feather" (Thieves' Duet)
F. Wilson, W. S. Daboll

"At Midnight on My Pillow Lying" (Dream Song)
P. Hall

Concerted Piece (The blissful pleasure I profess)
P. Hall, M. Manola, H. Pepper, W. S. Daboll, F. Wilson, C. Irving, M. Freeman

Finale (Away to the chateau)
Principals, Chorus

ACT 2

Opening Chorus (Here on lord and lady waiting)
V. Schilling, Chorus

"Woman's Dress" (Song)
V. Schilling

"Darkest the Hour" (Song)
H. Pepper

Chorus and Song of Joy (Joy attend on Erminie)
P. Hall, Chorus

"The Sighing Swain" (Song)
P. Hall

"What the Dicky Birds Say" (Song and Whistling Chorus)
F. Wilson

"Join in Pleasure" (Vocal Gavotte)
Chorus

"Lullabye" (Dear Mother, in Dreams I See Her)
P. Hall

ACT 3

Supper Chorus (Come to supper, let's repair)
Chorus

"Good Night" (Concerted Piece)
P. Hall, V. Schilling, M. Manola, A. Folsom, H. Pepper, C. Irving, W. S. Daboll, F. Wilson, Chorus

Finale (Should we gain your favors)
P. Hall, Principals, Chorus

ADDITIONAL MUSICAL NUMBERS, INTERPOLATIONS

"We're a Philanthropic Couple"

"See Thee and Forget Thee! Never!"[114]
(*Music and Lyrics by* Henry Hallam)

"To Erminie" (Caryll)
Henry Hallam

"The Love Bird"
Isabelle Urquhart (*Music and Lyrics by* Frederic Solomon.)

"When Love Is Asleep"
Isabelle Urquhart (*Music and Lyrics by* Frederic Solomon.)

"Jeannette" (Hiller)
Nettie Henry

---

[110]Added for subsequent tour:
"(We Are Very Wide Awake), The Moon and I" (Song to the Moon)
(Burlesque on THE MIKADO). A. Ames.

[111]H.M.S. PINAFORE was originally presented in New York 15 January 1879 at the Standard Theatre for 175 performances. At some matinees TRIAL BY JURY was originally produced in New York 15 November 1875 at the Eagle Theatre for 8 performances. For Synopsis of Scenes and Musical Numbers, see original productions.

[112]Played a return engagement 16 January 1888 at the Casino Theatre for an additional 136 performances. Total for all 3 engagements: 648 performances.

[113]Musical numbers not listed in programs. List prepared from published American piano vocal score (White-Smith Publishing Company, New York, 1886). Interpolations from reviews, published sheet music, etc.

[114]Authorship uncredited in music published by Richard Saalfield.

IXION,
1886.31 or, The Man at the Wheel

A Reconstructed Version of the Burlesque in Two Acts[115]. (Original version by F. C. Burnand.) Stage manager, Press Eldridge. Produced by (John) Koster and (Albert) Bial. Opened 10 May 1886 at Koster & Bial's Concert Hall and closed 30 July 1886 after (87) performances.

CAST: *Ixion*: AGNES EARLE. *Giblet*: PRESS ELDRIDGE. *Queen Dia*: LOU SANFORD. *Juno*: LOU SANFORD. *Jupiter*: ROSA LEE. *Venus*: LILLIE SHANDLEY. *Cupid*: LAURA BURT. *Minerva*: ELLA WESNER. *Apollo*: GEORGIE GREGORY. *Mercury*: Eva Barrington. *Ganymede*: FRED WARREN. *Bacchus*: F. J. CARINI. *Mars*: CHARLES SHATTUCK. *Diana*: Georgie Tyrell. *Vesta*: Ada Chamberlain. *Ceres*: Lottie Church. *Hercules*: CARL STARCK. *Hebe*: Carrie Danley. *Clerk of the Weather*: Annie Evelyne. *Popopo*: Miss Durando.

1886.32 OXYGEN

A Revised Version of the Burlesque Extravaganza in Two Acts, 5 Scenes[116]. Libretto by (H. B. Farnie and) Robert Reece, adjusted to a new metre by William Gill. Music composed and selected by John J. Braham and Gustave A. Kerker. Stage director, Frederic Darrell. Costumes devised by Lydia Thompson. Musical director, William Withers. Produced by (Robert E. J.) Miles and Barton's Bijou Burlesque Company. Opened 17 May 1886 at the 14th Street Theatre and closed 29 May 1886 after 16 performances.

CAST: *Prince Fritz*, who unlike most German princes, desires to marry for love: LYDIA THOMPSON. *Suzel*, who wants a hero and get him: ADDIE CORA REED. *Franz* of the genius "Lout" a young man with a sweet tooth: RICHARD F. CARROLL. *Hermance*, a giddy young thing: LILLIE ALLISTON. *Niclausse*, President of the Board of Aldermen: ALEXANDER CLARK. *Otto*, a young student on a lark: Ruth Stetson. *Hansel*, another young student on a similar lark: Leila Farrell. *Lottchen, Gretchen*, two types of Flemish beauty: Virgie Graves, Marian Langdon. *The Burgomaster*, in other words, the Mayor of Keekendone: LOUIS DeLANGE. *Tarantula*, an impressario in hard luck: Daisy Ramsden. *Dr. Ox*, a scientist who invents something and wishes he hadn't: FREDERIC DARRELL. *Envoy* who blows his own trumpet: Annie Sutherland. *Clerk of the Court*: Lucy Escott. *Specialists*: Davenport Brothers, Smith and Rowland. *Primrose Quartette*: Messrs. Gibbons, Dietz, Barrett, Kavanagh. *Maids of Keekendone*: Messrs. Gibbons, Dietz: Misses Mears, McIntyre, Linwood, Langdon, Hamlin, Escott, Barrett. *Students*: Misses Davenport, Wentworth, Carlington, Elliott, Conron, Cameron, Dean. *Warriors, Aldermen, American Opera, etc.*

Act 1: City Hall Square in the Flemish town of Keekendone.

Act 2, Scene 1: Dr. Ox's Laboratory. *Scene 2*: Banquet Hall in the Town House. *Scene 3*: A Street in Keekendone. *Scene 4*: A Park in Keekendone.

ACT 1[117]

Opening Chorus
Students (*Music by* John J. Braham.)
"Acrobatic, Operatic Quartette"
(*Music by* John J. Braham.)
"Monastery Bells"
Chorus
Duet
L. Thompson, A. C. Reed
"On to the Hall" (Song)
F. Darrell, Chorus (*Music by* John J. Braham.)
Grand Finale (including the original Mandolina Gavotte)
L. Thompson, Chorus

ACT 2
Scene 1

Opening Chorus
Students (*Music by* John J. Braham.)
"The Metre That Measures the Gas" (Song)
F. Darrell
"It's Cockney, by Jove" (Song of the Day)
L. Thompson
"Two Little Tramps from Jail" (after THE MIKADO)
"Now to Free the Gas Boys" (Song)
L. Thompson, Chorus of Students (*Music by* John J. Braham.)

Scene 2

"The Pair of Dudinettes" (Trio)
(*Music by* John J. Braham.)
Spanish Trio and Dance
R. Stetson, L. Farrell, A. Sutherland
Ballad (Selected)
A. C. Reed
"Pretty as a Butterfly" (Oratorio)
D. Ramsden
"McGinty at the Rink"
L. Thompson
Song and Dance
Smith and Rowland
Mid-air musings
Davenport Brothers
Grand War Chorus
Duet
L. Thompson, A. C. Reed

Scene 3

Topical nursery trio

Scene 4

Grand march and phantom fight of the warriors
Plantation hymns and marvelous acrobatism
Grand Finale

1886.33 THE CROWING HEN

An Opéra-comique in Three Acts. Original French libretto ("Serment d'amour") by Maurice Ordonneau. Music by Edmond Audran. (English adaptation by Mrs. Mary Bella Beale Brainerd.) Musical director, Signor Antonio DeNovellis. (Staged by John A. McCaull.) Produced by McCaull Opera Comique Company (John A. McCaull, Proprietor and Manager). Opened 29 May 1886 at Wallack's Theatre and closed 10 July 1886 after 43 performances.[118]

CAST: *La Marquise de la Haute Garenne*: MATHILDE COTTRELLY. *Count de Flavignac*: SIGNOR PERUGINI. *Gavaudan*, Major Domo: DeWOLF HOPPER. *Grivolin*, Innkeeper: HERNDON MORSELL. *Martial*, Gamekeeper: CHARLES H. JONES. *Rosetta*, his daughter: BERTHA RICCI. *Marion*: Celie Ellis. *Javotte*: Josie [Josephine] Knapp. *Francine*: Kate Ethel. *Jeannette*: Bessie Cleveland. *Bel-Azur*, Captain of the Police: A. Maina. *Clerks (6)*: *Lancelot*: Zoe deVielle. *Marcelin*: Ida Bartelle. *Theodule*: Grace Seavey. *Andre*: Agnes Bowen. *Jean*: Emma Muller. *Pierre*: Rita Shrader. *Peasants, Officers, Soldiers, Citizens.*

Act 1: The Park of the Castle.

Act 2: The Crowing Hen.

Act 3: Interior of the Castle.

MUSICAL NUMBERS[119]

"Tou-la-ou" Song
"Jean la Princette"
"The Way It's Done"
(*Music and Lyrics by* H.S. Hewett.)

1886.34 THE BRIDAL TRAP

A Comic Opera in Three Acts. Original French libretto to the opéra-comique ("Serment d'Amour") by Maurice Ordonneau. Music by Edmond Audran. American adaptation by Sydney Rosenfeld. Stage director, James Scanlan. Scenery by Harley Merry, LaMaas. Costumes designed by Helen Leslie. Mechanical effects by William Gale. Musical director, S. Simonson.

---

[115]First produced in New York 28 September 1868 at Wood's Museum & Metropolitan Theatre for 120 performances in 2 engagements.

[116]First produced in New York as OXYGEN, or Gas in a Burlesque Meter, 27 August 1877 at Wallack's Theatre for 16 performances. For Synopsis of Scenes and Musical Numbers, see original 1877 production.

[117]First week's program announces that the second week beginning 24 May will have new features, new songs, new dances and new specialties.

[118]Author of English adaptation uncredited; stage director, settings and costumes uncredited in programs.

[119]Musical numbers not listed in programs. No libretto, book of words or musical score found for this production. List prepared from reviews, etc.

Produced by (Robert E. J.) Miles and Barton. Opened 31 May 1886 at the Bijou Opera House and closed 26 June 1886 after 28 performances.

CAST: *Foutelard*, the Steward: ROLAND REED. *The Count*: FRANCIS GAILLARD. *Grivolin*: HARRY MILLS. *Martial*: E. S. Grant. *Bel-Azur*: Paul Vernon. *Rosette*: LAURA CLEMENT. *Marion*: JENNIE PRINCE. *The Marquise*: AUGUSTA ROCHE. *Notaries (8)*: *Marcelin*: Eugene Nicholson. *Lanncelot*: Ida Van Osten. *Theodule*: May Sanford. *Baptiste*: Daisy Temple. *Edmond*: Madge Perry. *Fabian*: Lulu Tonteine. *Adolphe*: Addie Lee. *Hyacinth*: Helen Schuler. *Javotte, Francine*, Peasants: Maud Leicester, Lizzie Winner.

Act 1: Chateau and Park of the Marquise. (Merry.) "The Rustic Heroine."

Act 2: The Tavern of the "Golden Horse" at Orleans. One year later. (LaMaas.) "The Steward's Enterprise."

Act 3: Salon in the Chateau of the Marquise. One week later. (Merry.) "The trap is set and sprung."

ACT 1[120]

Opening Chorus (Let these sturdy old woods awaken)
Chorus

Marion's Lament (Once, fickle boy, you wooed me)
J. Prince

Rustic Song (Merrily! Verily! Oh!)
Chorus, F. Gaillard, L. Clement

Couplets (No! Indeed you are not the wife)
H. Mills

Waltz Duet (Love's Vow)
L. Clement, F. Gaillard

The Steward's Song (I seek not for rank)
R. Reed

Melody (Who shall be bold when love arrives?)
L. Clement

Comic Trio (Tear out your heart)
L. Clement, A. Roche, R. Reed

Finale (You have heard what they said)
Ensemble

ACT 2

Tavern Chorus (Here is the spot where dull cannot enter)
Chorus, Notaries, J. Prince

Chorus (See there the hostess of this place)
Notaries, Chorus

Ariette (How proud I ought to feel)
L. Clement

Song (The pleasure of doubt)
J. Prince, Notaries

Idylle (Daphnis through the bowers strayed)
A. Roche, R. Reed

Soldiers' Chorus (What ho, bring us some wine, good host)
Chorus

Song of the Regiment (Now gaily gather for good cheer)
F. Gaillard, Chorus

Cook's Song (We have a way of cooking things)
R. Reed

Ensemble and Duet of the Robin and the Nightingale(What is this?)
Chorus, F. Gaillard, L. Clement

Finale (Now is the hour of our promised festivity)
Ensemble

ACT 3

Toilet Chorus (Robed in the garb that suits th'occasion)
L. Clement, Sopranos

Romance and Rondeau (Now shall the fields be in beauty beholden)
F. Gaillard, L. Clement

Trio (What do you say?)
L. Clement, J. Prince, F. Gaillard

Bridal Chorus (Now to the chapel we repair)
Sopranos, H. Mills, A. Roche, J. Prince

Duet (Oh, I don't think I can, sir)
L. Clement, R. Reed

Finale
Ensemble

[120]Musical numbers not listed in programs; list prepared from published piano vocal score (Willis-Woodward, New York, 1886). Also interpolated:
"Accent Song"
R. Reed
(*Music and Lyrics by* Sydney Rosenfeld.)

1886.35 A SOAP BUBBLE

A (Farce) Comedy in Three Acts. Play by Montgomery Phister. Produced by P. F. Baker and T. J. Farron. Opened 31 May 1886 at the New Windsor Theater and closed 5 June 1886 after 8 performances.[121]

CAST: *B. Wiley Dodge*, a Philanthropic Detective who never detetcts: P. F. BAKER. *V. Ray Silent*, a Barber, a descendant of William the Silent: P. F. BAKER. *Aunt Jemima*, tanned by the sun: P. F. BAKER. *V. L. Chops*, a Barb(e)rous Butcher with a scheme of his own: T. J. FARRON. *Strawberry Girl*: T. J. FARRON. *Guy Cheat'em*, the skylarking lover of Dodge's fair daughter: W. T. Dobson. *Mr. D. Sharp*, a Policeman, why named is not known: H. W. Rich. *Spoonbill*, a sort of blank: H. W. Rich. *Captain Dismal*, a man with a voice who follows the sea: E. H. Mack. *Billy the Bull*, who challenges the world, and wants to be shaved in his own Be-l-lud: E. H. Mack. *A Sponge*, well-known and easily recognized without a description: J. A. Ryan. *First Baldhead, Second Baldhead, Third Baldhead*, a modest trio: Harry Rawlins, James Ryan, S. Short. *La La Dodge*, a cute little Dodge, not belied by her name: Gracie Emmet. *Lucy Dodge*, a practically fascinating Dodge, much sought after by the Dodgers: GERTRUDE CITTI. *Bridget McHash*, an ideal domestic, not given to beaux: KATIE SHIELDS.

Act 1: B. Wiley Dodge's Villa.

Act 2: The mysterious barber shop at Long Branch.

Act 3: Seaside villa.

ACT 1

"McCarthy"
T. J. Farron

"Swim Out"
H. W. Rich

"Papa's Baby Girl"
P. F. Baker

Operatic Chorus
P. F. Baker, T. J. Farron, Company

ACT 2

"Wooden Shoe Song" and Dance
P. F. Baker (*Music by* P. F. Baker.)

"Corporal Mulcahey" (Swell Song and Chorus)
T. J. Farron, Company

"Little Coquette"
P. F. Baker, G. Emmet (*Music by* P. F. Baker.)

ACT 3

"Aunt Jemima" (Negro Song)
P. F. Baker

Medley Selections by the Inimitable Chris & Lena Quartette
P. F. Baker, E. H. Mack, H. W. Rich, W. T. Dobson

"I'm Shy" and Celtic Imitations
G. Emmet

Finale Medley Chorus
P. F. Baker, T. J. Farron, Company (*Music compiled by* P. F. Baker.)

[121]No credits in program for stage director, scenery, costumes or musical director.

1886–1887 SEASON

Tony Hart in DONNYBROOK (his last photograph)
Museum of the City of New York, Gift of the New York Public Library

1886–1887 SEASON

1886.36

THE MAID OF BELLEVILLE

An Operette in Three Acts. (Original Viennese libretto, 'Die Jungfrau von Belleville,' by F. Zell and Richard Genée, based on the novel 'La Pucelle de Belleville' and its stage adaptation 'Agnès de Belleville' by Paul de Kock and the Cogniard Brothers. American adaptation by Richard Stahl.) Music by Carl Millöcker. Produced under the direction of George W. Lederer. Musical director, Richard Stahl. Produced by George W. Lederer. Opened 24 June 1886 at the Star Theatre and closed 7 July 1886 after 14 performances.[1]

CAST: *Miss Javotte Bergamotte*, Virginie's aunt: ALICE HARRISON. *Virginie*: ROBERTA CRAWFORD. *Adrienne*, Virginie's half-sister: LAURETTA MILLARD. *Émile Montreaux*, a young student: HATTIE GRINNELL. *Babette*, a maid: Emma DuChateau. *Godibert*, a Sergeant in the Army: HERBERT ARCHER. *Troupeau*, a retired lamp manufacturer: FRANK DAVID. *Baron Archibald de Châteaurien*: SAMUEL REED. *Doudoux*, a Student: CHARLES COOTE. *Veaudore, Tir*, Troupeau's friends and neighbors: BEN F. GRINNELL, JAMES LEAHY. *Karl*, a Servant: W. Webb. *Grisettes, Citizens and their Wives, Firemen, etc.*: Misses Willard, Escott, Barton, Winner, Barrett, Cameron, Jackson, Carlington, Arnold, Grunwald Sisters, Wood Sisters, Holmes, Lester, DuChateau, Granville, Varnett, Perceval, O'Brien, Milliard, Willeye, Sevard, Brown, Gray, Bronson, Baird, Gregori, Burroughs, Williams. Messrs. Schwartz, Adams, Dixon, Enfield, Burkhardt, Hughes, Stobel, McGill, Webb, Mead, Daggett, Moore, Watson, Davis, Hoyt, Priest, Hostetter, Leahy, Burns, Starr, Bransombe, Shattuck, Binger.

Act 1: Troupeau's Villa at Belleville, a suburb of Paris.

Act 2: Parlors in Troupeau's Villa.

Act 3: Troupeau's New Palace.

1886.37

FALKA

A Revival of the Comic Opera in Three Acts[2]. Original French libretto to the opérette ('Le Droit d'aînesse') by Eugène Leterrier and Albert Vanloo. English adaptation by Henry B. Farnie. Music by Francis Chassaigne. Stage manager, Herbert A. Cripps. Scenery by John Thompson, Henry E. Hoyt and J. Mazzanovich. Musical director, Antonio DeNovellis. Produced by the McCaull Opera Comique Company (John A. McCaull, Proprietor and Manager). Opened 12 July 1886 at Wallack's Theatre, closing 17 July 1886, re-opened 2 August 1886 at Wallach's Theatre and closed 28 August 1886 after 35 performances.[3]

CAST: *Falka*, Niece of Folbach: BERTHA RICCI. *Edwige*, Sister of Boleslas: ANNIE MEYERS. *Alexina de Felkirsch*, a young heiress: JOSIE [Josephine] KNAPP. *Minna*, her maid: CLARA ALLEN. *Janotha*, Landlady of the Inn: KATE ETHEL. *Von Folbach*, Military Governor of Montgratz: DeWOLF HOPPER. *Boleslas*, Chief of the Tzigani: HUBERT WILKE. *Tancred*, Folbach's nephew, usher in a village school: GEORGE C. BONIFACE, JR. *Arthur*, Student, son of a rich Hungarian Farmer: HARRY MACDONOUGH. *Lay Brother Pelican*, Doorkeeper of the Convent: ALFRED KLEIN. *Konrad*, Captain of the Governor's Pages: ELSIE DURAND. *Tekeli*, Sergeant of the Patrol: W. J. McLaughlin. *Boboky*, Tzigan Scout: Leona Clark. *The Seneschal*: Herbert A. Cripps. *Military Pages, Soldiers of the Watch, Maids of Honor, Tzigani.*

1886.38

VENUS AND ADONIS

A Burlesque in Two Acts[4]. Produced by (John) Koster and (Albert) Bial. Opened 31 July 1886 (matinee), reconstructed 6 September 1886 and closed 9 October 1886 after (80) performances.

CAST: *Venus*: ROSA LEE. *Adonis*: LOUISE DEMPSEY. *Cactus*: PRESS ELDRIDGE. *Vaseline*: FRED WARREN. *Theodorine*: ELLA WESNER. *Dividicus*: CHARLES F. SHATTUCK. *Captain Bullock*: Miss Phillips. *Colonel Bantam*: ADA CHAMBERLAIN. *A. D. T. Boy*: Ida Waters. Full Chorus.

1886.39

SOLDIERS AND SWEETHEARTS

A Musical Comedy in Three Acts. Libretto by Susie Russell and Owen Westford. Music by George Schleiffarth. Entire production under the direction of W. H. Daly. Drill-master, Major Burk. Scenery by Harley Merry. Costumes by H. Bucheister. Musical director, Fred Intropodi. Produced by E. B. Ludlow and Sam Harrison. Opened 16 August 1886 at the Bijou Theatre and closed 4 September 1886 after 21 performances.

CAST: *Major Ashley*: CHARLES OVERTON. *Lieutenant Ashley*, his son: FREDERICK DARRELL. *Corporal Flint*, the major's orderly: CHARLES ALLISON. *Daffy Downs*, the Lieutenant's orderly: HENRY V. DONNELLY. *Sergeant Dancker* of the Guard House: HENRY LEONI. *Private Sloane* of the 14th Regiment: W. H. Ryno. *John Smiedt*, keeper of the Retreat: THOMAS WELCH. *Jonacus Jaggs, Esq.*, an impessario: OWEN WESTFORD. *Marie Bartlett*: SYLVIA GERRISH. *Maggie Smith*, her friend: LOUISE EDGAR. *Mlle. Legrande Foudre*, a prima donna: RAGNA LINNE. *Nan McGilder*, a rustic: SUSIE RUSSELL. *Nan's followers (4)*: *Katie Ray*: Ada May Drew. *Hattie Clay*: Leona Ross. *Phoebe Day*: Agnese Holk. *Sadie May*: Lulu Hesse. *Soldiers, Choristers, Villagers, etc.*

Act 1: Skirmishing.

Act 2: In Action.

Act 3: The Victory.

MUSICAL NUMBERS[5]

"Keep Your Eye on It"
O. Westford (*Lyrics by* Harry B. Smith.)

1886.40

THE MAID AND THE MOONSHINER

A Comic Opera in Three Acts. Libretto by Charles H. Hoyt. Music by Edward Solomon. Staged by Charles H. Hoyt, assisted by Julian Mitchell. Scenery by Joseph Clare, Hughson Hawley. Costumes designed by Messrs. James McCreery & Co., N. May, Smith Manufacturing Company. Orchestra conducted by Edward Solomon. Produced by James C. Duff. Opened 16 August 1886 at the Standard Theatre and closed 28 August 1886 after 15 performances.

CAST: *Bourbon Miller*, the leader of a band of Moonshiners: JOHN E. BRAND. *Upton O. Dodge*, his lieutenant, a gentleman of extremely practical and unsentimental turn of mind: TONY HART. *Colonel Randolph Roanoke Peyton*, an old-school Virginia gentleman—victim of a family tradition: JAMES RADCLIFFE. *Captain Bryton Beach*, U.S.A., sought by everybody: JOSEPH ARMAND. *Captain Monmouth Parke*, his most dangerous rival: GEORGE WILKINSON. *Captain Ivan Suwarrow*, unpopular with Parke or Beach: A. L. NICHOLLS. *Captain Fahrbach*, knows nothing of Parke or Beach: Franklin Boudinot. *Pomp*, not even a circumstance since the war: John Hogan. *Reverend Mr. R. Thayer*, a development of the present times: Fred Solomon. *Virginia*, the favorite child of the old Virginian: LILLIAN RUSSELL. *Miss Honora Lee*, Peyton's sister—a widow, cursed with beauty and fortune: ELMA DELARO. *Peyton's Tribulations (3)*: *Leonora*: Carrie Tutein. *Marguerite*: Annie Leslie. *Violetta*: Queenie Vassar. *Moonshiners, Virginia's Cousins, Negro Jockeys, etc.*

Act 1: A Steamboat Landing on the James River. Morning. (Clare.)

Act 2: The Exterior and Garden of the Peyton Mansion. Night. (Hawley.)

Act 3: A Glen in the Blue Ridge Mountains, and Cave with the Distillery of the Moonshiners. Daybreak. (Clare.)

ACT 1[6]

"We merrily sing, the praise we sing" (Opening Chorus)
Moonshiners

"Sweet spirit hear my prayer" (Solo)
J. E. Brand

"Dear Captain, hear me speak" (Song)
T. Hart, Chorus

"We very much regret to state" (Chorus of colored jockeys)

"Why should I fear because she chose to roam" (Song)
J. Armand

---

[1]Scenery, costumes, and English adaptation uncredited in programs. No song list in programs; according to reviewers, two topical song interpolations by Richard Stahl were added, one for Alice Harrison, the other for Roberta Crawford.

[2]First produced in New York 4 April 1884 at the Casino Theatre for 110 performances. For Synopsis of Scenes and Musical Numbers, see original 1884 production.

[3]Stage direction, costumes uncredited.

[4]No program found for this production.

[5]Musical numbers not listed in programs.

[6]Musical numbers not listed in programs. List prepared from published book of words, McBreen, printers, 1886.

"Rolling home! Rolling home!" (Chorus of Young Ladies)
"Taken on a foreign tour" (Song)
L. Russell
Finale Act 1:
"Rejoice, rejoice with me" (Trio)
L. Russell, J. Armand, E. Delaro
Recitative (Heaven be praised)
L. Russell, J. Armand
"When fortune parts" (Waltz Duet)
L. Russell, J. Armand
Recitative
J. E. Brand, T. Hart, J. Armand, J. Radcliffe, All
"A college is an institute of wonderful utility" (Song)
T. Hart, Moonshiners
Recitative
Colored Jockeys
"Hurrah for the sound of the dog's cheery bark" (Ensemble)
All

ACT 2[7]
"We do not wish to be abused" (Opening Chorus)
Young Ladies
"Oh, strange delusion! Oh, wild confusion!" (Trio)
C. Tutein, A. Leslie, Q. Vassar
"A woman's heart is like a dove" (Song)
L. Russell
"Sad is her lot whom fate selects" (Recitative and Aria)
E. Delaro
"When the lovely queen of the night" (Chorus)
Moonshiners
Recitative
J. E. Brand, T. Hart, Chorus
"The deed I am about to do" (Solo)
J. E. Brand, Chorus
"Oh, light, both beauteous and reliable" (Serenade to a Dark Lantern)
T. Hart
"When the silver moon is beaming" (Recitative and Serenade)
Four Officers, Four Girls
"But for a little while we part" (Octette)
Four Officers, Four Girls
"You sometimes think a thing divine" (Song)
T. Hart
"Colonel Peyton is my name" (Song)
J. Radcliffe
Finale, Act 2: "The learned man in public is a man of intellect" (Chorus of Moonshiners)
Recitative
L. Russell, J. Radcliffe, E. Delaro, Moonshiners, Girls
"When the merry fiddler's tune we hear" (Solo)
L. Russell, All
"Oh! let me go, you naughty man" (Grand Chorus)
Moonshiners, Girls
"I wouldn't in the least object"
J. Radcliffe, All

ACT 3
"Do you suppose we could wed?" (Solo)
L. Russell, J. E. Brand, Moonshiners, Chorus
"If you wish to become that delectable creature" (Song)
F. Solomon, Girls
"The Flag of Truce" (Hurrah for the Milk White Flag) (Song and Chorus)
T. Hart, Chorus
"Our situation's truly most absurd" (Prayer)
L. Russell, Chorus
Finale, Act 3: "Come and listen now to what I have to say" (A bold, bad moonshiner am I) (Song)
T. Hart, Chorus
Reprises
Principals, Chorus
"For tho' we've been so long about it" (Grand Chorus)
L. Russell, All

[7]Added after opening to Act 2: "Love" (Waltz Song). L. Russell.

1886.41 AROUND THE WORLD IN EIGHTY DAYS

A Revival of the Musical Extravaganza in Five Acts[8]. Based on the French adaptation of Jules Verne's novel "Le Tour du Monde en Quatre Vingt Jours," as adapted by Adolph d'Ennery. Music composed and arranged by Jean-Jacques de Billemont. Scenic designs by Poisson, Negel, Robecchi, Cornil, adapted by Mons. Camille Weinehenk. Costumes by Chalain; properties by Hallée; statuary by Dagoni. Staged by the Kiralfy Brothers (Imre, Bolossy). Produced by the Kiralfys. Opened 21 August 1886 at Niblo's Garden and closed 11 September 1886 after 25 performances[9]

CAST: *Aouda*: BEATRICE LIEB. *Phileas Fogg*: JOSEPH SLAYTER. *Passepartout*: ARTHUR MOULTON. *O'Pake*: HENRY W. MITCHELL. *Fix*: CLAUDE BROOKE. *Mr. Obadiah*, a pompous Calcutta magistrate: W. H. BARTHOLOMEW. *Arthur Mayburn*: ED MORTIMER. *Foster Jones*: J. WAKEFIELD. *Nakahira*: RICCA ALLEN. *Ballet Specialty*: CLARA QUALITZ, ARNOLD KIRALFY, Mlle. VIVIAN.

1886.42 INVESTIGATION

A Revival of the Local (Farcical) Comedy in Three Acts[10]. Play (and lyrics) by Edward Harrigan. Music by David Braham. Staged by Edward Harrigan. Scenery by Charles W. Witham. Mechanical effects by William Vail. Properties by Joseph Logan. Gas effects by John Whalen. Musical director, David Braham. Produced by Edward Harrigan. Opened 23 August 1886 at Harrigan's Park Theatre and closed 9 October 1886 after 56 performances.

CAST: *D'Arcy Flynn*: EDWARD HARRIGAN. *Leander Tuck*: JOHN WILD. *Lorenzo Hogan*: DAN COLLYER. *Oscar Onderdonk*: M. J. BRADLEY. *Orion Overhoe*: HARRY FISHER. *Ezra Wheatfield*: GEORGE MERRITT. *Bernard McKenna*: JOHN SPARKS. *Gaspard Pitkins*: Richard Quilter. *Canby Canfruit*: Peter Goldrich. *Mrs. Hop-Sing*: Charles Sturges. *Philip Werner*: Charles Sturges. *Mr. Hop-Sing*: WILLIAM WEST. *Miss Duflop*: Joseph Sparks. *Clarence Montgomery*: Charles Coffey. *Tramp*: George L. Stout. *Emma Sinclair*: Harry Guion, Jr. *Adelaide Foglip*: James G. Brevarde. *Barkeeper*: James G. Brevarde. *Mr Whitecow*: Edward Murphy. *Mr. Willie Wabble*: T. Holland. *Charles Gilder*: Joseph Davis. *Mr. Smiley*: William Merritt. *Mr. Savage*: James McCullough. *Aunt Hannah*: Thomas Ray. *Gaspard Pitkins, Jr.*: Master Alfred Waite. *Hiram Snow*: Robert Snyder. *Belinda Tuggs*: ANNIE YEAMANS. *Sarah Tuggs*: AMY LEE. *Julia Tuggs*: Annie Langdon. *Mrs. Hogan*: Nellie Wetherell. *Mrs. Onderdonk*: EMILY YEAMANS. *Maid*: EMILY YEAMANS. *Mrs. Overhoe*: Nellie Collins. *Mrs. Wheatfield*: Grace DeWitt. *Hattie Roberts*: Kate Langdon. *Martha Fielding*: ANNIE HALL. *Cooking School Girls*: Misses Young, Nellie Russell, Hastings, Miss Hargrave, Ivy Schuyler.

1886.43 JOSEPHINE SOLD BY HER SISTERS

An Opéra-bouffe in Three Acts. Original French libretto ('Joséphine vendue par ses soeurs') by Paul Ferrier and Fabrice Carré. American adaptation by William von Sachs. Music by Victor Roger. Musical director, Antonio DeNovellis. Orchestrations by Victor Roger. Produced by the McCaull Opera Comique Company (John A. McCaull, Proprietor and Manager). Opened 30 August 1886 at Wallack's Theatre and closed 9 October 1886 after 42 performances.[11]

CAST: *Josephine*: LOUISE PARKER. *Benjamine*: MATHILDE COTTRELLY. *Mother Jacob*: EMILY SOLDENE. *Rebecca*: Josie [Josephine] Knapp. *Leah*: Emma Miller. *Rachel*: Clara Allen. *Hagar*: Dolly Delroy. *Simeoune*: Grace Seavey. *Sarah*: Carrie Nott. *Deborah*: Annette Hall. *Judith*: Grace Filkins. *Dinah*: May Grosvenor. *Esther*: May Yohe. *Fatima*: Zoe DeVielle. *Zeleika*: Agnes Bowen. *Montosol*: EUGENE OUDIN. *Potiphar Bey*: HERNDON MORSELL. *Alfred Pharaoh Pasha*: DeWOLF HOPPER. *Mourzouf*: Hamilton Adams. *Postman*: Charles H. Jones. *Citizens, Servants and Janissaries*.

Act 1: Janitress' Lodge and Yard of an Apartment House in Paris. Present day.

Act 2: The Harem of Alfred Pharaoh Pasha in Cairo.

Act 3: Salon of Alfred Pharaoh in Paris.

[8]First produced in New York 28 September 1875 at the Academy of Music for 43 performances.
[9]Also played a return engagement 13 December 1886 at the Grand Opera House for 8 performances.
[10]First produced 1 September 1884 at the Theatre Comique for 131 performances. For Synopsis of Scenes and Musical Numbers, see original 1884 production. For this revival, "The Man That Knows It All" was dropped, and a new song was added: "On Union Square."
[11]Stage direction, costumes uncredited.

MUSICAL NUMBERS[12]

Opening Chorus

"Love Song of Montosol" (Baritone)(Act 1)
E. Oudin

Song (Act 1)
L. Parker

"The Pyramids" (Tenor)(Act 2)

1886.44 SHANE NA LAWN

A Revival of the Irish Play in Three Acts[13]. Play by James C. Roach and J. Armory Knox (Texas Siftings). Music and lyrics by William J. Scanlan. Staged by Augustus Pitou. Scenery by Joseph Clare. Costumes designed by J. McNiven, manufactured by W. Dazian. Musical director, W. H. Brockway. Produced by Augustus Pitou. Opened 6 September 1886 at Poole's Theatre and closed 2 October 1886 after 32 performances, returned 14 March 1887 to the Grand Opera House for 8 performances, and 2 May 1887 to the People's Theatre for 8 performances. Total this season: 48 performances.

CAST: *Shane-na-Lawn*: WILLIAM J. SCANLAN. *John Power*: J. B. Turner. *Gerald Power*: George W. Deyo. *Squire Redmond*: SIDNEY R. ELLIS. *Harry Redmond*: Charles Dade. *Mat Kirwin*: George W. Barnum. *Ronald*: Gus Reynolds. *Buckley*: C. R. Webster. *Agent Dillon*: Albert Morrell. *Captain Fitzgerald*: H. L. Cleveland. *Rose Redmond*: (Miss) Lillie Lee. *Peggy O'Moore*: MARION WARREN. *Mrs. Power*: Mrs. W. G. Jones. *Moll Shehouge*: Mrs. J. B. Turner.

SPECIALTIES, MUSICAL NUMBERS

Scanlan's selection from Thackeray's 'Pendennis'
W. J. Scanlan

"The Low Backed Car"
W. J. Scanlan (*Music and Lyrics by* Samuel Lover.)

"Scanlan's Rose Song"
W. J. Scanlan
"Remember Boy, You're Irish"
W. J. Scanlan

"Come Along, My Darlin'"
W. J. Scanlan

"Peggy O'Moore"
W. J. Scanlan

"Why Paddy Is Always Poor"
W. J. Scanlan

"Gathering the Myrtle with Mary"
W. J. Scanlan

"Peek-a-Boo"
W. J. Scanlan

1886.45 LITTLE JACK SHEPPARD

A Melo-dramatic Operatic Burlesque in Three Acts, 10 Scenes. Libretto by William Yardley and Henry Pottinger Stephens[14]. Music selected and arranged by W. Meyer Lutz, with original contributions by Gustave A. Kerker, W. Meyer Lutz, Florian Pascal, R. Corney Grain, Arthur Cecil, Hamilton Clarke, Henry J. Leslie, Alfred Cellier. Produced under the personal supervision of William Yardley and Nat C. Goodwin. Dances arranged by Paul Veron. Scenery by Harley Merry. Costumes by A. Chasemore. Musical director, Gustave A. Kerker. Produced by (Robert E. J.) Miles and Barton's Bijou Burlesque Company. Opened 13 September 1886 at the Bijou Opera House and closed 10 December 1886 after 101 performances; re-opened 25 April 1887 at the Bijou Opera House and closed 30 April 1887 after 8 additional performances. Total: 109 performances.

CAST: *Jonathan Wild*: NAT C. GOODWIN. *Blueskin*: C. B. BISHOP. *Sir Roland Trenchard*: E. F. Goodwin. *Kneebone*: Frank Currier. *(Abraham) Mendez*: F. T. Ward. *Mr. Wood*: A. Hart. *Marvel*: Robert McIntyre. *Quilt Arnold*: George F. Campbell. *Little Jack Sheppard*: LOIE FULLER. *Thames Darrell*: ROSE LEIGHTON. *Winifred Wood*: ADDIE CORA REED. *Mrs. Sheppard*: Jennie Weathersby. *Polly Stanmore*: Lelia Farrell. *Edgewood Bess*: Helen Sedgwick. *Kitty Kettleby*: Mabel Morris. *Captain Cuff*: Ida Van Osten. *Ireton*: Maude Leicester. *Shotbolt*: Maude Waldemere. *Little Gog*: Lillie Craig. *Little Magog*: Mabel Craig. And the famous Clipper Quartette.

Blueboys: Georgie Lincoln, Louise Escott, Minnie Escott, Adelaide Lee, Barbara Eyre. *Dairymaids and Peasants*: Lulu Tutein, Sadie Calhoun, Ray Seemon, Bessie Seemon, Flora Echard, Daisy Temple. *Janissaries*: Lulu Hesse, Madge Perry, Nora Bagaley, Louise Weldon, Marie Harriott, Laura Wood. *Soldiers, Yokels, Minters, Attendants, etc.*

Act 1: Dollis Hill Farm.

Act 2, Scene 1: "Crown and Sovereign." Cave of Harmony in the Old Mint (Southwark). *Scene 2*: Old London Bridge.

Act 3, Scene 1: The Condemned Cell in Newgate. *Scene 2*: Wild's Room in Newgate. *Scene 3*: The Cells (Newgate). *Scene 4*: The Lower Leads (Newgate). *Scene 5*: View of Old London from Newgate Roof. *Scene 6*: Willesden Green.

ACT 1[15]

Opening Chorus
(*Music by* W. Meyer Lutz.)

"Yokels' Chorus"
(*Music by* Corney Grain.)

"If You Take Into Your Head" (Duet)
(*Music by* Florian Pascal.)
"Winifred Wood" (Solo)
A. C. Reed (*Music by* Florian Pascal.)

"There Once Was a Time" (Solo)
R. Leighton (*Music by* Alfred Cellier.)

"A Fairy Tale" (Duet)
(*Music by* Hamilton Clarke.)

"Keep the Ball A-Rolling"
(Quintet) (*Music by* W. Meyer Lutz.)

Chorus and March of the Janissaries
(*Music by* Florian Pascal.)

"Jonathan Wild" (I'm Jonathan Oscar Wild)(Song)
N. C. Goodwin (*Music by* Arthur Cecil.)

"Jack's (Keeps 'Em All) Alive-O" (Song)
L. Fuller (*Music by* W. Meyer Lutz.)

"True Blue" (Song)
C. B. Bishop (*Music by* W. Meyer Lutz.)

"Ri-fol" (Song)
(*Music by* W. Meyer Lutz.)

Quartette (Air to "Kissing Bridge")
By Michael Watson, arranged by W. Meyer Lutz.)

Mayday Chorus, Morris Dance, Finale
(*Music by* Alfred Cellier.)

ACT 2

Opening Chorus
(*Music by* Hamilton Clarke.)

"You Mustn't Believe All You Hear" (Song)
L. Fuller (*Music by* W. Meyer Lutz.)

"Think What Might Have Been" (Duo)
(*Music by* W. Meyer Lutz.)

"The Silver Star" (Song)
R. Leighton (*Music by* Florian Pascal.)

"Leave the Whole Business to Me" (Trio)
R. Leighton, A. C. Reed, C. B. Bishop (*Music by* W. Meyer Lutz.)

"Botany Bay" (Old Air) (Arranged by W. Meyer Lutz.)
C. B. Bishop

Finale
(*Music by* W. Meyer Lutz.)

ACT 3

"All Nations" (Polyglot Duo)
L. Fuller, N. C. Goodwin (*Music by* W. Meyer Lutz.)

[12]Musical numbers not listed in programs. List prepared from published piano selection.

[13]First produced in New York 21 September 1885 at Henry C. Miner's People's Theatre for 8 performances; returned 26 April 1886 at Niblo's Garden for an additional 16 performances. Total: 24 performances. For Synopsis of Scenes, see original 1885 production.

[14]Inspired by the novel by Harrison Ainsworth.

[15]Musical numbers not listed in programs. List prepared from published English vocal score "as performed at Gaiety Theatre, London" (Richard A. Saalfield, New York, 1886), which may not reflect interpolations and alterations for the American production. Also performed: "That's All," N. C. Goodwin (*Music and Lyrics by* William Yardley and Henry Pottinger Stephens).

"Farewell"
(*Music by* W. Meyer Lutz.)
Wedding Chorus
(*Music by* Florian Pascal.)

1886.46 OUR IRISH VISITORS

A Revival of the New and Original Absurdity (Farce Comedy) in Three Acts.[16] Play by Thomas E Murray and Mark Murphy. Musical director, Louis F. Boos. Produced by J. M. Hill. Opened 13 September 1886 at the Third Avenue Theatre and closed 18 September 1886 after 8 performances; returned 22 November 1886 to the Third Avenue Theatre and closed 27 November 1886 after an additional 8 performances [17]

CAST: *Colonel Gilhooly*, a Bogus Lord: THOMAS E. MURRAY. *Jerry McGinnis*, the Alderman: MARK MURPHY. *Dorothy*: KATE FOLEY.

1886.47 ADONIS

A Revival of the Gill & Dixey's Fascinating Burlesque Nightmare in Two Acts, 6 Scenes[18]. Libretto (revised) by Edward E. Rice and William Gill. (Original music by Edward E. Rice. Selected music cheerfully contributed by Beethoven, Audran, von Suppé, Planquette, Offenbach, Strauss, Mozart, Haydn, David Braham, John Eller, Henry Sator, and many others too numerous to individualize.') Musical director, Henry Sator. Produced by Edward E. Rice and Henry E. Dixey. Opened 20 September 1886 at the Fifth Avenue Theatre and closed 2 October 1886 after 16 performances.

CAST: *Adonis*, an accomplished young gentleman, of undeniably good family, inasmuch as he can trace his ancestry back through the Genozoic, Mesozoic and Palaeozoic period, until he finds it resting on the Archaean Time. His family name, by the way, is "Marble": HENRY E. DIXEY. *Marquis de Baccarat*, a highly polished villain. It is well to describe his character: HERBERT GRESHAM. *Bunion Turke*, father of Rosetta (a burlesque on the crusty old fathers of melodrama) who turns his daughter out-of-doors upon the least provocation: GEORGE H. HOWARD. *Talmea*, a sculptress, who, like most of her sex, is in love with her own creation: LILLIE GRUBB. *Artea*, a goddess, Patroness of the Fine Arts. N.B. The student will vainly search for this character in the Heathen or any other Mythology: ALICE ARNOLD. *Duchess of Area*, aesthetic to the verge of eccentricity, rich to the verge of millionairism, sentimental to the verge of gush: ANNIE ALLISTON. *Daughters of the Duchess, Professional Beauties (4)*: *Lady Mattie*: Ida Bell. *Lady Nattie*: Carrie Behr. *Lady Hattie*: Emma Hanley. *Lady Pattie*: Mollie Fuller. *Rosetta*, a simple village maiden, the happy possessor of a clear conscience, and a strong will: AMELIA SUMMERVILLE. *Gyles, Nyles, Myles, Byles*, ordinary every-day rustics: Messrs. Metzger, Frail, Roberts, Aiken. *Gills, Bills, Sills, Tills*, homely rustics (who will perform a circus), The Little Four: Messrs. Watson, Gilson, Carroll Brothers. *The Plumed Knights*: Misses Marion Giroux, Carrie Andrews, Jennie Bell, Clara Davenport, Edith Merrill, Emma Calef, Lizzie Clark, Emma Mulle, Grace Sherwood, Addie Langton, Annie Winner, Rita Carroll, Minnie Miller, Lottie Hanley, Adele Iverson, Georgie Lincoln.

Act 1, Scene 1: Talamea's Studio in Athens. *Scene 2*: The Humble but Honest Home of the Miller. *Scene 3*: Garden of the Duchess of Area's Mansion.

Act 2, Scene 1: A Country Village. *Scene 2*: The Enchanted Wood. *Scene 3*: The Barber's Shop and Notion Store.

ACT 1
Scene 1
"The Invocation" (Opening Chorus)
"We Are the Duchess' Daughters" (Quartette)
I. Bell, C. Behr, E. Hanley, M. Fuller
Pedestal Clog Dance
H. E. Dixey
"It's Alive"
Chorus

Scene 2
"I'm a Merry Little Mountain Maid"
A. Summerville
Trio
A. Summerville, H. Gresham, G. W. Howard

Scene 3
The Bric-à-Brac Guards and March of the Oriental Servitors
Chorus of the Little Boy Grooms
"The Susceptible Statuette" (Song)
H. E. Dixey
"Most Romantic Meeting" (Duet and Dance)
H. E. Dixey, A. Summerville
"He Would Away" (Grand Finale)
H. E. Dixey, Entire Company

ACT 2
Scene 1
"Oh Yes, We Are the Chorus"
Chorus
Ballad
L. Grubb
The Village Fête: The Serpent and the Dove; The Opera Bouffers; The Model Venuses; The Jolly Tars; The Robinson Crusoes and the Little Men Fridays; The Merry Wars.
"The Blushing Bride" (Chorus)
H. E. Dixey, A. Summerville

Scene 3
Grand Finale

1886.48 MAM'ZELLE

A Revival of the Farcical Comedy in Three Acts, 6 Scenes[19]. Play by George H. Jessop and William Gill. Stage manager, Thomas H. Burns. Musical director, Theodore Bendix. Produced by the Aimée Comedy Company (Management, Morris Simmonds and T. Allston Brown.). Opened 20 September 1886 at the Union Square Theatre and closed 2 October 1886 after 11 performances in repertory.[20]

CAST: *Toinette Jacotot*: Mlle. MARIE AIMÉE. *Fleur de Lis*: Mlle. MARIE AIMÉE. *T. Tarleton Tupper*: THOMAS H. BURNS. *Lionel Leslie*: A. DEL CAMPO. *Bob Pritchard*: JOHN MARBLE. *Colonel Hiram Poster*: Newton Chisnell. *François*: Lester Victor. *Topplebey*: Collin Verrey. *Taisway*: W. L. Browning. *O'Club*: J. Charles. *Mrs. Louisa Tupper*: CLARA BAKER. *Mary*: JENNIE WILLIAMS.

MUSICAL NUMBERS

Aimée appears in English, French and Spanish songs. During each act selections will be made from the following: "Fairly Caught," "Estudiantinas," "Creep into Bed, Baby," "Rip, Rip," "Les Canards Tyroliens;" her great successes "Chicken Pie" and "Pretty as a Picture."

1886.49 MARITA

A Musical Comedy in Three Acts, 4 Scenes. Original French libretto by Victorien Sardou. English adaptation by Barton Hill. Original music, songs and duets by Theodore Bendix. Stage manager, Thomas H. Burns. Scenery by George Heinemann. Musical director, Theodore Bendix. Produced by the Aimée Comedy Company (Management, Morris Simmonds and T. Allston Brown.). Opened 28 September 1886 at the Union Square Theatre and closed 30 September 1886 after 3 performances in repertory.

CAST: *The Count Strozzi*: SAMUEL MOSELEY[21]. *Frederick D'Avril*: A. DEL CAMPO. *His Friends (3)*: *Musardin*: THOMAS H. BURNS. *Canovard*: JOHN MARBLE. *Valentine*: E. A. Ketchum. *Comete*: Lester Victor. *Father Tidman*: NEWTON CHISNELL. *Mathois, Christian*: Graham J. Henderson, Charles Edeson. *Vergaz*: Collin Varrey. *Marcassoni*: L. W. Browning. *Marita*: Mlle. MARIE AIMÉE.

---

16 A smaller production played earlier New York area engagements 18 January 1886 at the Third Avenue Theatre, 17 May 1886 at the People's Theatre.

17 No programs found for the Third Avenue Theatre engagements. Returned 6 June 1887 to the Union Square Theatre for 35 performances; for details, see entry in 1887-1888 season.

18 First produced in New York 4 September 1884 at the Bijou Theatre for 603 performances. For Synopsis of Scenes and Musical Numbers, see original 1884 production.

19 First produced in New York 15 December 1884 at the Fifth Avenue Theatre for 14 performances. For Synopsis of Scenes, see original 1884 production.

20 No credits in programs for scenery or costumes.

21 Reviewers claimed to have seen Lester Victor covering for an ailing Samuel Moseley.

Elena di Strozzi: Clara Baker. *Madam Tidman*: Emma Skerrett. *Charlotte, Denise*: Fannie Nash, Jennie Williams. *Jost, Didi, Nellie, Katie, Loulen*: *Rosette*: Ada Laurent. *Angelique*: Elsie Robb. *Armette*: Belle Stapleton. *Students, Swiss and Italian Peasants, Masquers, Pifferari, etc.*

Act 1: Lausanne, Switzerland. The Home of Father Tidman.

Act 2: Tivoli, near Rome. The Sybil's Temple.

Act 3, Scene 1: The Studio. Rome. *Scene 2*: Mountain of Lausanne.

ACT 1

"Mountain Melodies"
M. Aimée

"Dear Grandpapa" (Children's Song)

ACT 2

"Song of the Brunette"

"Quanta bella la campagna"

"The Song of Sorrento"
M. Aimée

ACT 3

"The Lament of the Frogs"

"To arms! To arms!" (Chorus)
Students

1886.50 THE COMMODORE

A Comic Opera in Three Acts. Original French libretto to the opérette ("La Créole") by Albert Millaud. English adaptation by Henry B. Farnie, Robert Reece. Music by Jacques Offenbach. Stage manager, E. T. Steyne. Scenery by Henry E. Hoyt, T. S. Plainsted. Costumes by Georges Pilotell and Charles Alias. Conducted by Michael Connolly. Produced by the Earl of Lonsdale [Hugh Cecil Lowther] for the Violet Cameron Comic Opera Company. Opened 4 October 1886 at the Casino Theatre and closed 23 October 1886 after 21 performances.

CAST: *The Commodore*, Cruising in the English channel: LIONEL BROUGH. *Maître Garble, Maître Babble*, two notaries learned in the law: SIDNEY BROUGH, EDWARD MARSHALL. *Sabord*, Bo'sun of the Flag Ship: Clyde Howard. *Beaupré*, Quartermaster: H. TOMKINS. *Frontignac*, a young lawyer: JOHN BARNUM. *Captain René* of the Mousquetaires Rouge: VIOLET CAMERON. *Antoinette*, Daughter of the Commodore: EDITH BRANDON. *Zoe*, a creole from Guadaloupe: CONSTANCE LOSEBY. *Berthe, Lolotte*, Maids at the Inn: Frances Lytton, Nelly Woodford. *Yagarita*, Zoe's maid: G. Austin. *Pierre*, Gardener at the Villa: B. Burrows. *Paul*, Cabin Boy: Evelyn Vaye. *Yvonne*, Antoinette's maid: Violet Dashwood. *Christopher*: Julie Couteur. *Yeaune*: Lillie Russell. *Hornpipe (Dance Specialty, Act 3)*: Alice Lethbridge.

Act 1: In Port.

Act 2: A Villa.

Act 3: On Board the (French) Man-o'-War.

ACT 1[22]

"Anchored in the Roadstead" (Chorus and Solo)
H. Tomkins, Chorus

"First Love" (Song)
E. Brandon

"The Capitaine René" (Chorus)
Chorus

"O France, beloved France!" (Song)
V. Cameron

"Up Helm!" (Trio)
E. Brandon, V. Cameron, L. Brough

"So shy" (Song)
J. Barnum

"The Commodore's to mate his daughter" (Finale)
Principals, Chorus

"Come, dearest Girl" (Song) V. Cameron

"The Anchor's Weigh'd" (Finale)
Principals, Chorus

ACT 2

"Lover's Talk" (Song)
V. Cameron

"I welcome you" (Scene and Air)
C. Loseby, E. Brandon, V. Cameron, L. Brough

"Make love to me" (Duet)
C. Loseby, J. Barnum

"You have no right" (Duet)
C. Loseby, V. Cameron

"Certain are we" (Chorus)
Chorus

"The simple days of long ago" (Notaries' Duet)
S. Brough, E. Marshall

"Whom do I Love" (Finale)
Principals, Chorus

ACT 3

"I guard the lonely deck for thee" (Sleep Song)
V. Cameron

"Vengeance"/"Let us swear" (Sestette)
C. Loseby, E. Brandon, V. Cameron, J. Barnum, S. Brough, E. Marshall

"We're the lads!" (Capstan Chorus)
H. Tomkins, Chorus

Hornpipe Specialty
E. Vaye

"The Commodore is fast asleep" (Quatuor)
C. Loseby, E. Brandon, V. Cameron, J. Barnum

Entrance of Crew (Melodrame)

"Thanks, Commodore" (Finale)
Principals, Chorus

1886.51 THE IRISH MINSTREL

A Modern Irish Play in Three Acts. Play by Fred Marston. Music and lyrics by William J. Scanlan. Stage manager, Sidney R. Ellis. Musical director, W. H. Brockway. Produced by Augustus Pitou. Opened 4 October 1886 at Poole's Theatre and closed 9 October 1886 after 8 performances.

CAST: *Larry O'Flynn*, the Irish Minstrel: WILLIAM J. SCANLAN. *Robert Wynbert*, who wants his own way: SIDNEY R. ELLIS. *Matt Dougan*, who never permits trifles to annoy him: GUS REYNOLDS. *Morris Cregan*, with an honest pride in his name: J. B. TURNER. *Dan Cregan*, who yields to temptation: George W. Deyo. *Nellie Cregan*, a true-hearted colleen: LILLIAN LEE. *Maggie McKay*, "Glad she's alive:" MARION WARREN. *Mrs. Bridget McKay*, "a dacent widdy": Mrs. J. B. Turner.

Act 1: The Exterior of Morris Gregan's Cottage. The Refusal.

Act 2: The Cregan Kitchen. On the brink.

Act 3: Grounds of Craig-na-doyle. An Unexpected Savior.

SPECIALTIES, MUSICAL NUMBERS

Selection of William Makepeace Thackeray's "Pendennis"
W. J. Scanlan

"Over the Mountain"
W. J. Scanlan

"The Poor Irish Minstrel"
W. J. Scanlan

"What's in a Kiss"
W. J. Scanlan

"Scanlan's Rose Song"
W. J. Scanlan

"Bye-Bye, Baby, Bye-Bye"
W. J. Scanlan

"Something for the Babies"
W. J. Scanlan

"My Nellie's Blue Eyes"
W. J. Scanlan

"Peek-a-Boo"
W. J. Scanlan

[22]Musical numbers not listed in programs. List prepared from published English piano vocal score "as presented at the Royal Avenue Theatre [London]" (Richard A. Saalfield, New York, 1886), which may not reflect interpolations and alterations for the American production.

1886.52 THE O'REAGANS

An Original Local Comedy in Three Acts, 7 Scenes. Play by Edward Harrigan. Music by David Braham. Staged by Edward Harrigan. Dancing under the supervision of M. J. Bradley. Military manoeuvres by Edward Murphy. Scenery by Charles W. Witham. Costumes by Mrs. Mary Jack. Mechanical work by William Vail. Gas effects by John Whalen. Musical director, David Braham. Produced by Edward Harrigan. Opened 11 October 1886 at Harrigan's Park Theatre and closed 29 January 1887 after 128 performances.

CAST: *Bernard O'Reagan*: EDWARD HARRIGAN. *Silas Cohog*: JOHN WILD. *Lulu Cohog*: DAN COLLYER. *Darrell Kilhealy*: M. J. BRADLEY. *Herman Krouse*: HARRY FISHER. *Paddy Kelso*: JOHN SPARKS. *Charley Dreams*: George Merritt. *Ludlow Filkins*: Peter Goldrich. *Stevie McAleer*: Richard Quilter. *Rif Bloomfield*: William West. *Earnest Stuke*: JOSEPH SPARKS. *Bernard O'Reagan, M.P.*: JOSEPH SPARKS. *Bill Scarley*: Charles Sturges. *Alphonse Rochefort*: Charles Sturges. *Emery Sarms*: James McCullough. *Eels*, a tramp: G. L. Stout. *Hop Yet*: Joseph Davis. *Claude Montrose*: Joseph Davis. *Aaron Rosenstein*: Charles Coffey. *Hannah Skiver*: Thomas Weber. *Marigold Tangles*: Harry Guion, Jr. *Saunders Silkheel*: James G. Brevarde. *Sergeant Duster*: Edward Murphy. *Laudice Bushyhead*: Tim Holland. *Ambulance Surgeon*: William Merritt. *Roscoe Skiver*: Master Alfred Waite. *Centre Market*, a Tramp: Robert Snyder. A *New Coon*: Eggie Fortie. *Officer Perkins*: Harry Crawford. *Bedalia McNeirney*: ANNIE YEAMANS. *Mrs. Hop Yet*, solo on Chinese fiddle: ANNIE YEAMANS. *Kate McNeirney*: AMY LEE. *An Unfortunate*: Annie Langdon. *Kate*, a Ballet Girl: Annie Langdon. *Mrs. Kehoe*: Nellie Wetherell. *Mrs. Sylvie Dreams*: Emily Yeamans. *Mrs Chow-Chow*: Emily Yeamans.

Chorus of the Gilded Zephyr Burlesque Troupe: *Emma*: Kate Langdon. *Julia*: Annie Hall. *Bertha*: Florence Hasting. *Sophia*: Grace Waite. *Mamie*: Lulu Leach. *Lillian*: Pearl Randall. *Constance*: Lillian Leach. *Maude*: Lottie Hirsch. *Policemen, Tenants, Longshoremen, etc.*: The Company.

Act 1, Scene 1: The Locker by Bernard O'Reagan. The Arrival. *Scene 2*: Exterior of Bedalia McNeirney's Boarding House. A Bat Around Town. The Bribery. *Scene 3*: Parlors of the Boarding House. The Loss of Ireland's Money. The Blackmail. The Elopement. A Delegation. Refreshments and Broken Glass.

Act 2: Gilligan's Court by Night. A Landslide of Mongolians. Chinese Girls on a Lark. Kilhealey's Clean Sweep.

Act 3, Scene 1: Sheepshead Bay, with a View of Toni Dougan's Hotel, the Creek and Coney Island. The Boat-race and Clam-bake. Auction Pools under Difficulties, Missionary and Pugilist. Pink Eye's Victory. *Scene 2*: Exterior of the Cunard Wharf. The Widow Granna and Widow McNeirney. *Scene 3*: Cunard Dock and Steamer. The Gilded Zephyr Burlesque Troupe. Ireland Gets Her Own. The Cousins. Home Rule Forever. Arrival of the U.S. Black Marines." Bon voyage.

MUSICAL NUMBERS[23]

"Mulberry Springs" (Act 1, Scene 1)
"The Little Hedge School" (Act 1, Scene 3)
"Strolling on the Sands" (Act 3, Scene 1)
"(When) The Trumpet in the Cornfield Blows" (Act 3, Scene 1)
"The U.S. Black Marines" (Act 3, Scene 3)

1886.53 CAPT. JACK SHEPPARD

A Burlesque in Three Acts. Libretto by Carl Hauser and Vincent Hogan. (Inspired by Little Jack Sheppard.) Music by William J. Rostetter. Produced under the direction of Vincent Hogan. Produced by (John) Koster and (Albert) Bial. Opened 11 October 1886 at Koster & Bial's Concert Hall and closed 5 February 1887 after 135 performances[24].

CAST: *Captain Jack Sheppard*, Leader of Whyo Gang: ELLA WESNER. *East River Bess*, his Sweetheart: ANNA BOYD. *Jonathan Wild*, a Detective: JAMES B. RADCLIFFE. *Mendez*, his assistant: Gustav Adolfi. . *Sir Rowland*, a Canadian exile: Charles F. Shattuck. *Coonskin*, Jack's lieutenant: Vincent Hogan. *Polly*, his Sweetheart: Lillie LaVerde. *Brooklyn Barrel*, Jack's friend: Miss Chip Howard. *Winny Wood*, his Sweetheart: Fannie McNeil. *Mrs. Sheppard*, Jack's Mother: Annie Anderson.

Members of the Whyo Gang, Bootblacks and Anarchists Lillie Shandley, Regina Ennelli, Ethel Kemp, Ida Walters, Clara Warren, Marie Cammeyer, Annie Walters, C. H. Nutt, Sadie Curtis, Annie Gates, Nellie Waters, Birdie Gray, Lillie Pearce, Polly Hall, Lillie Morrison. (*Specialties*: Mlle. DORST, Mons. ORESTE, Danseurs Excentriques from the Eden Theatre, Paris; The Vanishing Lady.)

ACT 1[25]

Opening Chorus
Company
"You forward hussey"
A. Boyd
"If you take into your head"
A. Anderson, C. Shattuck
"They call me the Belle"
F. McNiel
"A fairy tale" (Duet)
C. Howard, F. McNiel
"Keep the Ball a-rolling" (Quintet)
C. Howard, F. McNiel, V. Hogan, C. Shattuck
"Anarchists and bootblacks"
Chorus
"Oh, what a world this is"
G. Adolfi
"That terrible Jonathan Oscar Wild"
J. B. Radcliffe
"I am Captain Jack"
E. Wesner
"See how they glare"
Chorus
Finale
Company

ACT 2

Serenade
Whyo Gang
"My heart is broke"
G. Adolfi
Compulsory Jig
J. B. Radcliffe
"Silver Star"
C. Howard
Champagne Song
E. Wesner
Song and Dance
L. LaVerde
Hornpipe
L. LaVerde
"It's awfully nice"
A. Boyd
"Nix my dolly"
E. Wesner
Soprano Solo
R. Elleni
"Botany Bay"
V. Hogan, Chorus
"Reel," Black Sal and Dusty Bob
Company
Rufus Penstock and his Cigar (Song)/Harmonica Solo
J. B. Radcliffe

[23]Added to Act 2 after opening: "Who Cooks the Bake."

[24]In late November CAPT. JACK SHEPPARD began playing a twice daily performance schedule.

[25]At the 50th performance 24 November 1886, the following changes were interpolated into the production:

"It's All Very Fine and Large,"
E. Wesner
"His Heart Was True to Poll" (Act 2)
A. Boyd
"He's English and So Sweet" (Song and Dance)(Act 2)
L. LaVerde
"The Dickie Birds"
V. Hogan
"La Contenta" (Soprano Solo)(Act 2)
R. Ennelli
"Forbidden Music" (Act 2)
C. Howard
"Foaming Beer" (Song)(Act 2)
C. F. Shattuck.
(*Music and Lyrics by* Paul Steinhagen.)

Danse Eccentrique
Mlle. Dorst, Mons. Oreste
Reception of Nations (Danse): Royal March (Spain); La Marseillaise (France); National Anthem (Mexico); Watch on the Rhine (Germany); God Save the Queen (England); Star Spangled Banner (America)

ACT 3
The Vanishing Lady (The instantaneous disappearance of a Lady in full sight of the audience; introduced by James B. Radcliffe.)
Mlle. Dorst and Mons. Oreste
"Leave the Whole Business to Me"
E. Wesner, A. Boyd, V. Hogan
"The Moon is full"
G. Adolfi
"Song of all Nations"
J. B. Radcliffe, C. Howard
Grand Finale
Company

1886.54 KENILWORTH

A Musical Extravaganza in Three Acts, 6 Scenes. Play by Robert Reece and Henry B. Farnie (suggested by Sir Walter Scott's novel). Music selected from Franz von Suppé, Tosti, Felix Keston, Jacques Offenbach, Johann Strauss, Olivier Métra, Edmond Audran and Carl Millöcker. Stage manager, E. T. Steyne. Scenery by Henry E. Hoyt, Messrs. Parker, Chidley and Johnson. Costumes by Mons. and Mme. (Charles) Alias, after designs by Mons. (Lucien) Besche. Conductor, Michael Connelly. Produced by the Earl of Lonsdale [Hugh Cecil Lowther]. Opened 25 October 1886 at the Casino Theatre and closed 13 November 1886 after 21 performances.[26]

CAST: *Dudley*, Earl of Leicester, an ambitious noble who married Amy Robsart, aspires to Prince Consort—but there we will correct him and history too before we are done: VIOLET CAMERON. *Sir Walter Raleigh*, Poet, Traveler and Statesman, to whom England owes the Pipe and the Potatoe—the tube and the tuber. He will use his mantle as cloak—but we should not anticipate: CONSTANCE LOSEBY. *The Earl of Sussex*, Leicester's Rival for the Queen's favor. His politics are, but we shall see: JULIE COUTEUR. *Amy Robsart*, Countess of Leicester, married before the Registrar with the usual result of such bridals: EDITH BRANDON. *Janet Foster*, Amy's confidential. She accompanies her mistress to Kenilworth, disguised as—but that would be anticipating: ALICE LETHBRIDGE. *Queen Elizabeth*, a virginal arrangement in Tudoresque. The giddiest little silly that ever set a Court by the ears. She will nearly fall into the trap prepared for the others, and will probably, but, hush, "No scandal about Queen Elizabeth, I hope:" John Barnum. *Tony Foster*, Seneschal at Cumnor Hall. A most objectionable person, according to his daughter, Janet—and she ought to know: SIDNEY BROUGH. *Giles Gosling*, Tapster at the "Beare Inn," Cumnor: Mr. Tomkins. *Wayland Smith*, Cheap Jack, and itinerant Showman: Henry Lytton. *Mike Lambourne*, Cut-throat in Varney's pay, afterwards reformed, and a member of the force: Edward Marshall. *Sir Richard Varney*, Master of the Horse to Leicester. Secretly in love with Amy. An amalgam of all that's villainous in nature and an "amoosing cuss" withal: LIONEL BROUGH. *Pages, Ladies of the Tabouret, Ladies in waiting, Sailors on the Royal Yacht, Huntresses, Village Lads and Lasses, Falconers, etc.*

Act 1, Scene 1: Ye Beare Inn at Cumnor. *Scene 2*: Amy's Room in Cumnor Hall. *Scene 3*: Old Greenwiche! Ye Shippe and Ye Palace.

Act 2: Pleasaunce at Kenilworth.

Act 3, Scene 1: Mervin's Bower in Kenilworth Castle. *Scene 2*: The Western Turret by the Moat. (Change to Lantern Fête in the Gardens of Kenilworth.)

1886.55 THE MIKADO, or, The Town of Titipu

A Revival of the Comic Opera in Two Acts[27]. Libretto by William S. Gilbert. Music by Arthur Sullivan. Chorus and orchestra directed by John Braham. Produced by John Stetson, by arrangement with Richard D'Oyly Carte. Opened 1 November 1886 at the Fifth Avenue Theatre and closed 20 November 1886 after 21 performances.[28]

CAST: *The Mikado of Japan*: N. S. BURNHAM. *Nanki-Poo*, his son, disguised as a wandering minstrel, in love with Yum-Yum: COURTICE POUNDS. *Ko-Ko*, Lord High Executioner of Titipu: J. W. HERBERT. *Pooh-Bah*, Lord High Everything Else: Signor BROCCOLINI. *Pish-Tush*, a Noble Lord: JOSEPH C. FAY. *Three Sisters, Wards of Ko-Ko*: *Yum-Yum*: GERALDINE ULMER. *Pitti-Sing*: AGNES STONE. *Peep-Bo*: EDITH JENNESSE. *Katisha*, an Elderly Lady, in love with Nanki-Poo: ALICE CARLE. *Chorus of School Girls, Nobles, Guards and Coolies.*

1886.56 KARL, THE PEDDLER

A Farce Comedy in Four Acts. Play by Con T. Murphy. New songs, new dances, new music by Gustave H. Kline. Musical director, Gustave H. Kline. Produced by Phil H. Irving. Opened 15 November 1886 at Hart's Theatre Comique, Harlem and closed 20 November 1886 after 7 performances; returned 25 April 1887 to Tony Pastor's 14th Street Theatre and closed 30 April 1887 after 8 additional performances.[29]

CAST: *Karl*, the Peddler: CHARLES A. GARDNER. *Erastus Tibbs*: ROBERT V. FERGUSON. Company also included Walter Lawrence, David B. Young, Thomas F., Fitzgerald, Robert McNair; Misses Eva Byron, Marion May, Emily Kean.

1886.57 PRINCESS IDA, or, Castle Adamant

A Revival of the Comic Opera in Two Acts and a Prologue[30]. Libretto by William S. Gilbert. A Respectful Operatic per-version of Alfred Lord Tennyson's poem "The Princess—A Medley." Music by Arthur Sullivan. Chorus and orchestra under the direction of John Braham. Produced by John Stetson, by arrangement with R. D'Oyly Carte. Opened 22 November 1886 at the Fifth Avenue Theatre and closed 11 December 1886 after 22 performances.[31]

CAST (in order of appearance): *King Hildebrand*: Signor BROCCOLINI. *Hilarion*, His Son: COURTICE POUNDS. *His Friends (2)*: *Cyril*: PHIL BRANSON. *Florian*: STUART HAROLD. *King Gama*: J. W. HERBERT. *Sons of King Gams (3)*: *Arac*: Joseph C. Fay. *Guron*: N. S. Burnham. *Scynthius*: V. Holland. *Princess Ida*, Gama's Daughter: GERALDINE ULMAR. *Lady Blanche*, Professor at Princess Ida's College: ALICE CARLE. *Melissa*, Lady Blanche's Daughter: AGNES STONE. *Lady Psyche*, Professor of Humanities: HELEN LAMONT. *Girl Graduates (3)*: *Sacharissa*: Edith Jennesse. *Chloe*: Miss Branson. *Ada*: Miss McCann. *Soldiers, Courtiers, Girl Graduates, Daughters of the Plough, etc.*

1886.58 MY AUNT BRIDGET

A Farce Comedy in Three Acts[32]. Play by Scott Marble. Produced by Robert D. Monroe. Opened 6 December 1886 at the Poole's Theatre and closed 11 December 1886 after 8 performances; returned 11 April 1887 to the Thrid Avenue Theatre for an additional 8 performances, and 16 May 1887 to Tony Pastor's Theatre for 8 additional performances. Total: 24 performances.

CAST: *Bridget McVeigh*: GEORGE W. MONROE. *P. Alton McVeigh*: JOHN C. RICE. *Jack Treyser*: E. J. Ratcliffe. *Joe Nervy*: W. H. Leary. *Tompkins Blazor*: F. W. Holland. *Dora Blazor*: Minnie Richardson. *Polly Glyder*: Josie DeVoy. *Abby Shrinker*: Mrs. E. M. Post. *Nellie Ryder*: Polly Carey.

MUSICAL NUMBERS, SPECIALTIES
"Eh, Did I Hear You?"
G. W. Monroe

---

[26]KENILWORTH's previous English production was billed as a new Fairy Burlesque Extravaganza. It was produced under the direction of author Henry B. Farnie; inasmuch as no stage director is credited with the American production, very likely the author's original staging was adapted for the American tour, for which Miss Violet Cameron repeated her starring role. No musical numbers listed in programs.

[27]First presented in New York 20 July 1885, 17-29 August 1885 at the Union Square and Henry Miner's People's Theatres for 22 performances. Presented 19 August 1885 at the Fifth Avenue Theatre by Richard D'Oyly Carte for 250 performances. For Synopsis of Scenes and Musical Numbers, see original 1885 production.

[28]Stage direction, scenery and costumes uncredited. Wardrobe from original designs of the Savoy Theatre, London; stage manager, W. H. Conly.

[29]No program found for this production; previously produced 11 May 1885 at the Third Avenue Theatre. One song, "Karl's New Lullaby" with music by Gustave Kline and lyrics by Charles A. Gardner.

[30]Originally produced in New York 11 February 1884 at the Fifth Avenue Theatre for 42 performances. For Synopsis of Scenes and Musical Numbers, see original 1884 production.

[31]Stage direction, scenery and costumes uncredited. Wardrobe from original designs of the Savoy Theatre, London; stage manager, W. H. Conly.

[32]A sequel to the successful play "Over the Garden Wall" by Scott Marble, first produced in New York 23 March 1885 at the Fifth Avenue Theatre.

1886.59 TURNED UP/THOSE BELLS

A Double Bill of a Farce Comedy (Turned Up) in Three Acts, preceded by a Burlesque of Mr. Henry Irving (Those Bells) in One Act. Farce Comedy by Mark Melford. Burlesque by Sydney Rosenfeld. Music by Gustave A. Kerker. Scenery by Harley Merry. Musical director, Gustave A. Kerker. Produced by Nat C. Goodwin, supported by (Robert E. J.) Miles & Barton's Bijou Burlesque and Comedy Company[33]. Opened 11 December 1886 at the Bijou Opera House and closed 22 January 1887 after 49 performances.

CAST ("Those Bells"): *Mathias Irving*: NAT C. GOODWIN. *Annette*, his daughter: MABEL MORRIS. *Father Watler*: Ed. F. Goodwin. *Christian*: LELIA FARRELL. *Sozzel*: Carrie Wallace. *Mesmerist*: A. Sleep. *Judge*: M. Partial. *Solomon Lescynski*: H. E. Brew. *Catherine*, Mathias wife: HARRY DeWITT. *Villagers, Peasants, etc.*: Chorus.

MUSICAL NUMBERS

"It's Original with Me"
N. C. Goodwin

CAST ("Turned Up"): *Carraway Bones, Esq.*, Undertaker and General Dealer: NAT C. GOODWIN. *Captain Medway* of the "*Petrel*": C. B. Bishop. *George Medway*, his only son: Robert Hilliard. *General Baltic*: Harry Bradley. *Mr. Nod Steddam*, a Briefless Barrister: Charles Coote. *Old Lobb*, Ferryman: H. C. Dewitt. *Inspector Nibble*: Otto Wilkins. *Ephraim*: Little Mabel Craig. *Sabina Medway*, George's sister: LOIE FULLER. *Ada Baltic*: Lelia Farrell. *Mrs. Medway*: LILLIE ALLISTON. *Cleopatra*: ROSE LEIGHTON. *Mrs. Pannall*, Housekeeper at Richmond Ferry: JENNIE WEATHERSBY.

Act 1: Breeze.

Act 2: Storm.

Act 3: Hurricane.

1886.60 DONNYBROOK!

A Romantic Musical Comedy-Drama in Four Acts, 8 Scenes. Play by H. Wayne Ellis. Musical director, Fred. White. Produced by Charles Seymour. Opened 13 December 1886 at the Henry C. Miner's People's Theatre and closed 18 December 1886 after 8 performances.[34]

CAST: *Tather Jack Walsh*, a broth of a boy: RICHARD F. CARROLL. *Tim Bradley, Dempsey Tim*: P. E. Smith. *Kelly*, Landlord of "The Three Shamrocks": E. W. Howland. *Captain Lawrence Daly* of the 14th Light Dragoons: Edgar Crossman. *Shiel Dempsey*, a Lawyer and an Agent; Edwin Browne. *Squire Murphy*, "as foine a specimen of an elderly gentleman as ye'll find in a day's walk": J. F. Hagan. *Corney Kelly*, "an ould retainer who tries to keep up appearances for the honor of the family: W. Paul Bown. *Miss Margaret Flannigan*, Kate's Governess and Companion: Annie Deland. *Kate O'Grady*, Con's sister, bright-eyed bonny Kate: BELLE STOKES. *Nelly Brady*, "the darlin' colleen that I'd like to spend a life with, Vide Con's sentiments: CARRIE TUTEIN. *Con O'Grady*, "Master Con," a whole souled, bright young gentleman, fond of his dogs, gun and horses, proud of his sister, with a soft spot in his heart for sweet Nellie Brady: TONY HART.

Act 1: The old Manor House by the lake.

Act 2: Donnybrook Fair.

Act 3, Scene 1: The Rock by the lake in the Vale of Avoca. *Scene 2*: Con's return from hunting. Kate's abduction. *Scene 3*: The Island in the Lake of Avoca.

Act 4, Scene 1: Interior of the old Manor House. *Scene 2*: The entrance to the cellars. *Scene 3*: The Picture Gallery.

ACT 2

New and Original Songs: "Nelly Brady," "Irish Brigade," "Queen of the Flowers," "Lovely Nell," "The Blarney," "Mrs. Higgins' Parlor Floor"
T. Hart

Songs and Dances ("When the Hawthorne Buds Are Springing")
C. Tutein

Famous Specialties
R. F. Carroll

Musical Gems
A. L. Sutherland

The Great Irish Cuckoos
Smith and Howland

Wonderful Gymnasts
Messrs. O'Brien and Leslie

Irish Bagpiper
Eddie Joyce

Irish Four-handed Reel
Entire Company

1886.61 PAT'S WARDROBE

A Farce Comedy in Three Acts. Stage director, James Vincent. Presented by the Pat Rooney Comedy Company (Fred Wilson, Manager). Opened 20 December 1886 at the Poole's Theatre and closed 25 December 1886 after 8 performances.[35]

CAST: *Pat O'Hoolihan*: PAT ROONEY. *Lionel Eustach*: JAMES VINCENT. *Mr. Paragon*: W. H. Hatter. *Mrs. Paragon*: Mrs. (PAT) ROONEY. *Mrs. Crocker*: EMMA HOWARD. *Christopher*: Little KATIE ROONEY. *Twilight Quartette.*

Act 1: Honeymoon over. Tired and weary.

Act 2: A new order of things generally.

Act 3: Blue blood nobility abroad.

MUSICAL NUMBERS, SPECIALTIES

Specialties
P. Rooney

Vocal Specialties
Twilight Quartette

1886.62 OVER THE GARDEN WALL

A Revival of the Popular Musical Comedy Success in Three Acts[36]. Proprietress, Mrs. George S. Knight. Opened 27 December 1886 at the 14th Street Theatre and closed 8 January 1887 after 16 performances.[37]

CAST: *J. Julius Snitz*, Politican, Poet and Husband: GEORGE S. KNIGHT. *Julius Snitz, Jr.*, his nephew: EDWIN FOY. *Tom Tracy*, Snitz's friend and advisor: Edwin P. Temple. *Moses Wrangle*, a dangerous man, discoverer of "Wrangle's Infant Food": Charles Frew. *Frigid Bill*, the Ice Man: Frank Pruyn. *Our Own Bridget*, a prize domestic: JAMES QUINN. *Rosa*, Wife of Julius, Jr.: Minnie Dupree. *Violet, Lilly, Pinkey*, Wrangle's Infantry: Clementine St. Felix, Charlotte St. Felix, Henrietta St. Felix. *Mrs. Betsy Snitz*, (Wife of J. Julius): Nellie Sanford. *Nellie Wrangle*, daughter of Moses: MRS. GEORGE S. KNIGHT [Sophie Worrell].

Time: Suit yourself. *Place*: Anywhere, or thereabouts.

Act 1: Eventide. This side of the Wall. Suspicion!

Act 2: Early Morn. Both sides the Wall. Accusation!

Act 3: That night inside the Wall_______!

ACT 1

"Three Little Giggling Girls"
St. Felix Sisters (Three Girls) (*Music by* Theodore Bendix.)

"Wrangle's Infantry" (March)
Mrs. G. S. Knight, Three Girls

Medley and Laughing Song
G. S. Knight, Mrs. G. S. Knight, Three Girls, M. Dupree, E. P. Temple, E. Foy

"Gentlemen, Do Not Fight" (Finale)
Company (*Music by* Theodore Bendix.)

---

[33]Program note: TURNED UP is the sole property of Willie Edouin and is produced by arrangement with Frank W. Sanger, under the direction of Charles Groves.

[34]Stage director, scenery and costume designs uncredited.

[35]No program found for this engagement. A Proctor's Theatre, Brooklyn program dated 12 March 1888 includes vocal gems from comic operas, 'pretty little songs' and the following original songs:

New Original March
K. Rooney (*Music by* Fred Perkins. *Lyrics by* Fred Wilson.)

"Let Her Go, Gallagher" (Rooney's latest)
P. Rooney

"A Quiet Little Home,"
W. H. Hatter.

[36]First produced in New York, billed as a Comic Complication (Farce Comedy), 5 January 1885 at Tony Pastor's 14th Street Theatre for 8 performances; returned 23 March 1885 to the Fifth Avenue Theatre for 16 performances; returned 18 May 1885 to Niblo's Garden for 8 additional performances. This revival also played a prior New York area engagement 27 September-2 October 1886 at the Windsor Theatre as part of its ongoing tour. Authorship of this revised version uncredited; previous production credited to Scott Marble and George S. Knight.

[37]No other credits in programs for stage director, scenery, costumes, musical direction or authorship of songs.

ACT 2

Songs, Burlesque Imitations and Dances
E. Foy

"Wild Flowers and Buttonhole Bouquet"
Mrs. G. S. Knight, Three Girls (*Music by* C. T. Ellis.)

"To-morrow" (Song and Dance)
Mrs. G. S. Knight (*Music by* Theodore Bendix.)

"As Usual"
G. S. Knight, E. P. Temple (*Music by* George S. Knight.)

"Far Away" (G. S. Knight)
(*Music by* George S. Knight.)

ACT 3

"To Whit, To Whoo"/Septette from THE SPECTRE KNIGHT
(*Music by* Alfred Cellier.)
Mrs. G. S. Knight, E. P. Temple, G. S. Knight, Three Girls

"Moonlight" (Waltz)(Song and Dance)
Mrs. G. S. Knight

Serenade and Cat Trio
G. S. Knight, Three Girls

"That'll Be Nice"
J. Quinn (*Music by* George S. Knight.)

Specialty of Trios, Songs, Dances
St. Felix Sisters

Specialty of Eccentric Character Songs, and Pas Seul à la Bonfanti
E. Foy

"Happiness" (Finale)
Company (*Music by* George S. Knight.)

1887.01 EVANGELINE, or, The Belle of Acadia

A Revival of the Musical Extravaganza in Three Acts[38]. Libretto by J. Cheever Goodwin. Suggested by Longfellow's poem. Music by Edward E. Rice. Staged by Edward E. Rice. Produced by Edward E. Rice. Opened 3 January 1887 at Niblo's Garden and closed 8 January 1887 after 8 performances[39].

CAST: *Evangeline*, the heroine of an enduring affection which very nearly proves her ruin: MAY STEMBLER. *Catherine*, Gabriel's aunt, an antidote for melancholy—"Love's young dream becomes a nightmare": GEORGE K. FORTESCUE. *Ferdinand*: Hindle Harrison. *LeBlanc*, the notary,—although notary coroner, in quest of somebody, and led to believe that there's a good deal in a name: GEORGE A. SCHILLER. *Gabriel*, Eva's worshipper: IRENE VERONA. *Felician*, Eulalie's sweetheart: Hindle Harrison. *The Lone Fisherman*, a mystery: JAMES S. MAFFITT. *Captain Dietrich* of the Queen's own, familiar with hard-tack and "Hardies Tactics": DANIEL MASON. *Chief of Police*, a peeler—so-called because he was never known to heed any appeal a prisoner might make: Edward Morris. *The Heifer*, two of a kine-d: Messrs. Charles Udell, James W. Reynolds. *The Miserable Ruffians (6)*: *Scarfaced Willie*: W. H. Mack. *Wild West Jake*: Charles Udell. *Man Not Afraid of His Shadow*: James W. Reynolds. *Roaring Pete*: S. W. Wade. *Three Finger Jack*: Benjamin J. Miles. *Little Willie Buffalo*: Fred Turner.

1887.02 THE OLD HOMESTEAD

A Continuation of Joshua Whitcomb (Rural Melodrama) in Four Acts. Play by Denman Thompson and George W. Ryer. Incidental music by Double Quartette. Settings by Homer Emens, Hughson Hawley. (Staged by Denman Thompson.) Produced under the personal supervision of J. W. Rosenquest, Manager. Produced by Denman Thompson. Opened 10 January 1887 at the Fourteenth Street Theatre and closed 4 June 1887 after 155 performances.

CAST [in order of appearance]: *Joshua Whitcomb*: DENMAN THOMPSON. *Cy Prime*: GEORGE A. BEANE. *Happy Jack*: WALTER GALE. *Eb. Ganzey*: J. L. MORGAN. *Frank Hopkins*: ALFRED T. SWARTZ. *John Freeman*: FRANK THOMPSON. *Aunt Matilda Whitcomb*: LOUISA MORSE. *Rickety Ann*: ANNIE THOMPSON. *Annie Hopkins*: Virginia Marlow. *Nellie Freeman*: Lillian Stone. *Maggie O'Flaherty*: Minnie Luckstone. *Henry "Redhead Hank" Hopkins*: WALTER LENNOX, SR. *Judge Patterson*: Gus Kammerlee. *François Fogarty*: Frank Mara. *Mrs. Henry Hopkins*: C. E. Knowles. *Miss Ida Hopkins*: Linda Cleveir. *Miss Nellie Patterson*: Annie Thompson. *Jack Hazzard*: Walter Gale. *Reuben Whitcomb*: T. D. FRAWLEY. *Hoboken Terror*: J. L. Morgan. *One of the Finest*: John B. Atwell. *U.S. Letter Carrier*: Charles R. Farrar. *Seth Perkins*: Walter Lennox, Sr. *Len Holbrook*: C. M. Richardson. *Pat Clancy*: Frank Mara. *Mrs. Murdock*: Mrs. Owen Marlow.

Act 1: Homestead Farm of the Whitcombs' at Swanzey, New Hampshire. (Emens.)

Act 2: Parlors in the Hopkins' Mansion, New York City. (Hawley.)

Act 3: Grace Church at Night, Broadway near 10th Street, New York City. (Hawley.)

Act 4: Kitchen in the Old Homestead. (Emens.)

MUSICAL NUMBERS[40]

Quartette (Act 1)
A. T. Swartz, V. Ackerly, C. Kruger, G. Kammerlee

Music (Act 2)
L. Cleveir, G. Kammerlee, Quartette

Incidental Music (Act 3)
Double Quartette

Incidental Music (Act 4)
Quartette

"The Old Oaken Bucket"
(*Music and Lyrics by* Kiallmark and Woodworth.)

"The Old Red Cradle"
(*Music by* J. L. Gilbert. *Lyrics by* A. J. Grannis.)

"Marguerite"
(*Music and Lyrics by* Charles A. White.)

"Rock-a-Bye Baby"
(*Music and Lyrics by* Effie I. Canning.)

"Irene Lorraine"
(*Music and Lyrics by* W. A. Keller.)

"Let's Make a Little Home for the Old Folks"
(*Music and Lyrics by* A. Wheeler.)

"When Mother Puts the Little Ones to Bed"
(*Music and Lyrics by* A. Wheeler.)

"Singing to Baby This Sweet Lullaby"
(*Music and Lyrics by* A. McNeal.)

"Nearer My God to Thee"
(*Music and Lyrics by* Mason and Adams.)

1887.03 THE BLACK CROOK

A Revival of the Extravaganza in Four Acts, Sixteen Scenes[41]. (Book by Charles M. Barras. Music composed and selected by Thomas Baker, Louis Baer, A. W. Hoffman.) Entire production under the stage direction of Messrs. Imre and Bolossy Kiralfy. Scenery by Harley Merry, Mr. Porter, George Bell, Robecchi of Paris, Magnani, Forrest Seabury. Ballets by Imre Kiralfy. Musical director, A. W. Hoffman. Produced by Imre and Bolossy Kiralfy. Opened 17 January 1887 at the Niblo's Garden and closed 19 February 1887 after 40 performances; re-opened 11 April 1887 at Niblo's Garden and closed 30 April 1887 after 24 additional performances[42]

CAST: MORTALS: *Hertzog*, the Black Crook: J. B. ROBERTS. *Count Wolfenstein*: J. DeGEZ. *Rudolph*, a poor artist: JOSEPH SLAYTOR. *Von Puffenkrantz*, the Count's Chamberlain: W. H. BARTHOLOMEW. *Greppo*, a henchman: ARTHUR MOULTON. *Wolfgar*: L. Rubel. *Bruno*: F. Starr. *Amina*, a village maiden: LOUISE ALLEN. *Dame Barbara*: Mrs. Irwin. *Carline*: Rose Chessneam. *Guards, Attendants, Servitors, Villagers, etc.*

IMMORTALS: *Stalacta*, Fairy Queen: HETTIE GRENNELL. *Dragonfin*: Mr. Siegrist.

DEMONS: *Zamiel*: A. H. Denham. *Skudelwhelp*: Charles M. Blesser.

Principal Dancers: Mons. ARNOLD, Mlle. CLARA QUALITZ, Mlles. DeRosa, Newman. *Specialties*: The Siegrist Brothers (acrobats), the Mignani Family (musical street pavers), D'Alvini (juggler).

---

[38] First produced in New York 27 July 1874 at the Niblo's Garden for 14 performances. For Synopsis of Scenes and Musical Numbers, see original 1874 production. No program available. Reviewers remarked upon the following: "Kiss Me, Sweet" (Song and Dance), I. Verona; "I Like It" (Topical Song), I. Verona; Acrobatic Song and Dance, Miserable Ruffians.

[39] Also played a return engagement 25 April 1887 at the Grand Opera House for 8 performances.

[40] The first four numbers as they appear in programs. All additional titles taken from published sheet music represent individual specialties introduced during the New York run, subsequent tour and revivals. Not in performance order.

[41] First produced in New York 12 September 1866 at Niblo's Garden for 475 performances.

[42] Played a return engagement 23 May 1887 at the Grand Opera House for 8 performances.

1887.04 INDIANA

An Opera Comique in Three Acts. Libretto by Henry B. Farnie, based on a French vaudeville. Music by Edmond Audran. Stage manager, Herbert A. Cripps. Scenery by Joseph Clare. Stage mechanism, Neil McGiehan. Musical director, Herman Perlet. Produced by the McCaull Opera Comique Company (John A. McCaull, Proprietor and Manager). Opened 17 January 1887 at the Star Theatre and closed 5 February 1887 after 21 performances; re-opened 11 July 1887 at Wallack's Theatre and closed 23 July 1887 after 14 additional performances. Total: 35 performances.

CAST: *Indiana Grayfaunt*: LILY POST. *Lady Prue*: LAURA JOYCE BELL. *Nan*: ANNIE MEYERS. *Maud*: Adine Drew. *Matt o' the Mill*: DIGBY BELL. *Lord Dayrell*: GEORGE OLMI. *Philip Jervaux*: EDWIN W. HOFF. *Sir Mulberry Mullet*: ELLIS RYSE. *Peter*: Herbert A. Cripps. *Annette*: Ida Eissing. *Captain Hazzard*: Bessie Fairbairn. *Madge*: Cécile Eissing. *Folliet*: C. Blanchard. *Cosmo*: G. Hollingsworth. *Giles*: W. F. McLaughlin. *First Keeper*: A. Maina. *First Lackey*: C. Daly. *Winifred*: Belle Jennings. *Belle*: Tolie Pettit. *Eben*: Grace Ward. *Dickon*: Belle Cavis.

Act 1: The Mill at the Ford.

Act 2: At Dayrell Place.

Act 3: Interior of the Mill.

ACT 1[43]

"To-day we'll dance" (Chorus)
Chorus

"When logs on the ingle" (Mill Song)
Chorus

"It is time" (Scene)
W. F. McLaughlin, C. Eissing, A. Meyers

"'Tis a gossip too" (Exit)
A. Meyers, Chorus

"Seek the woman" (Bouffe Song)
E. Ryse, Chorus

"Bah! he must think me" (Duet)
D. Bell, G. Olmi

"Poor young thing" (Air)
G. Olmi

"I see his game" (Stretti)
D. Bell, G. Olmi

"Ah! you have not far" (Exit)
G. Olmi

"The Ferry boat" (Melodrame)

"Why in wild quest" (Recitative)
L. Post

"Love will guide" (Valse)
L. Post

"Ah! let us see" (Quintette)
L. Post, A. Meyers, C. Eissing, D. Bell, W. F. McLaughlin

Entrance of Peasants

"The change is done" (Recitative and Scene)
L. Post, A. Meyers, C. Eissing, D. Bell, Chorus

"Before Lord Dayrell" (Scene)
E. H. Hoff

"Love will guide" (Ensemble)
L. Post, Principals, Chorus

ACT 2

"Pray excuse me" (Yawning Chorus)
Chorus

"Skirts are fuller" (Letter-bag Ensemble)
Chorus

"Watch always at thy lattice" (Canzonet)
G. Olmi

"In no sweet frame of mind" (Ensemble)
Chorus

"How well you look" (Scene)
G. Olmi, L. J. Bell, L. Post

"Jasper's jacket" (Rustic ditty)
L. Post, Chorus

"There are Bet and Bell" (Refrain/Exit)
Chorus

The Dancing Lesson
L. J. Bell, D. Bell

"I must go" (Scene)
G. Olmi, L. J. Bell, E. W. Hoff, D. Bell

"Till on my venture bold" (Ensemble)
L. Post, E. W. Hoff, D. Bell, G. Olmi, Maud, L. J. Bell

"The aforesaid Lord Dayrell" (Scene) (The Lease Duet)
L. Post, E. W. Hoff

"There, at the dreamy hour" (Ensemble)
L. Post, E. W. Hoff

"Good-night" (Valse)
G. Olmi, Chorus

"My quests no earthly use" (Scene and Recitative)
L. Post, G. Olmi, L. J. Bell

"Stay, oh stay" (Morceau d'Ensemble)
L. Post, L. J. Bell, E. W. Hoff, G. Olmi, Chorus

"My Lords and Ladies" (Coda Finale)
L. Post, E. W. Hoff, G. Olmi, Chorus

ACT 3

"Hark the trill" (Aubade)
A. Meyers, Sopranos

"Alas! how quickly" (Air)
A. Meyers, Sopranos

"O sunny south" (Air)
L. Post

"Lowly the lass" (Song)
G. Olmi

"Here by the ford we'll wait" (Chorus)
Chorus

"Open the shutters wide" (Song and Chorus)
A. Meyers, Chorus

"How break my word" (Duet)
L. Post, E. W. Hoff

"All complication now is ended" (Finale)
Principals, Chorus

INTERPOLATION

"The Plain Potatoe" (Fable)
D. Bell (*Music by* John Crook.)

[43]Musical numbers not listed in programs. List prepared from published English libretto (Boosey and Co., London and New York, 1886).

1887.05 THE KINDERGARDEN

A (Revised Version of the) Musical Farce Comedy in Three Acts[44]. Play by Robert Griffin Morris. Costumes by M. Herrmann. Musical director, Charles Van Leer. Produced by Robert Mack. Opened 17 January 1887 at Poole's Theatre and closed 5 February 1887 after 24 performances; returned 3 May 1887 to Dockstader's Theatre and closed 18 June 1887 after 55 additional performances. Total: 79 performances.[45]

CAST: *Philander Montmorenci St. Clair Duchesne*, a gentleman of doubtful education and in embarrassing circumstances, yet alive to the main chance at anybody's expense: STANLEY MACY. *Orlando Smythe*, a dude, but not the millionaire he looks: BENJAMIN F. GRINNELL. *The Grinder*, Philander's shadow, afterwards the Widow's sunshine: Fred S. Sanford. *Tommy Magee*, the Widow's son and the town's terror: E. A. Archer. *Georgie Goodson*, the Widow's "Tiger," and a daisy: GEORGE BRUENING. *Widow Magee*, supposed to be Irish and wealthy: FRED MENDOZA. *Ivy Magee*, the Widow's romantic daughter, a Vassar exotic and living only to elope: LAURA DINSMORE. *Ivy's Three Disgraces*: *Leonora Phosphates*: Blanche Seymour. *Tilly Smythe*: Rheta Mann. *Sissy Racket*: Clara Lloyd. *Invisible others, One Set Tree with Falling Leaves, Cigar Sign, Seltzer Bottle, Chairs, etc.*

Dockstader's CAST: *Philander Montmorenci St. Clair Duchesne*: BENJAMIN GRINNELL. *Orlando Smythe*: HARRY BOOKER. *The Grinder*: Fred S. Sanford. *The Sleepy Boy, or the Widow's Tiger*: GEORGE BRUENING. *Tommy Magee*: Harry Cottrell. *Georgie Goodson*: Tommy McShane. *Tormented Sweet Willie*: Charley

[44]First produced in New York as THE KINDERGARTEN 2 February 1885 at the Third Avenue Theatre for 8 performances; returned 11 June 1885 to Poole's Theatre for 10 additional performances. For Synopsis of Scenes and Musical Numbers, see original 1885 production.

[45]Played a return engagement 11 June 1888 at Poole's Theatre for 8 performances.

McShane. *Widow Magee*: FRED MENDOZA. *Ivy Magee*: RHETA MANN. *The Three Disgraces*: *Leonora Phosphates*: Minnie Geoffreys. *Tilly Smythe*: Nellie Bowers. *Sissy Racket*: Blanche Seymour.

Act 1: Necessity the Mother of Invention. Organizing the Kindergarden. "Have I your ear?"

Act 2: Three months later. The Kindergarden in operation. "She is with me."

Act 3: The Elopement. The Kindergarden fulfills its mission. "'Tis but a Summer's joke."

ACT 1

"As You See Us, So Are We" (from THE LITTLE TYCOON)
Misses L. Dinsmore, B. Seymour, R. Mann, C. Lloyd (*Music and Lyrics by* Willard Spencer.)

"The Fatal Step" (from THE LITTLE TYCOON)
E. A. Archer, B. F. Grinnell, Company (*Music and Lyrics by* Willard Spencer.)

"Sweet Heather Bells"
Company (*Music by* Frank Howard.)

"The High-Toned Lady from Over the Sea"
F. Mendoza (*Music by* James Conroy.)

Medley

ACT 2

"Solfeggio" (from THE LITTLE DUKE)
Company (*Music by* Hervé.)

"Please to Put That Down" (from OLD LAVENDER)
C. Lloyd (*Music by* David Braham. *Lyrics by* Edward Harrigan.)

"The Sassiest Girl in Town"
R. Mann (*Music by* Edward Solomon.)

"The Bridal Veil" (from THE LEATHER PATCH)
Company (*Music by* David Braham. *Lyrics by* Edward Harrigan.)

"Waiting for Charlie" F. Mendoza

Solea (Spanish Dance)
L. Dinsmore (*Music by* Luigi R. Logheder.)

"A Soldier Boy's Canteen" (from THE GRIP)
Company (*Music by* David Braham. *Lyrics by* Edward Harrigan.)

"My Nellie's Blue Eyes"
B. Seymour

"Sweet Dudidity"
C. Lloyd, B. F. Grinnell (*Music by* Robert Griffin Morris.)

Medley

ACT 3

"Widow Magee"
F. Mendoza (*Music by* Robert Griffin Morris.)

"Come to the Green Wood"
C. Lloyd (*Music by* Charles Van Leer.)

"I'm Just as Young as I Used to Be"
G. Bruening

"How Dear to Me" (Duet)
N. Bowers, E. A. Archer

"It Wouldn't Surprise Me at All"
B. F. Grinnell (*Music by* Frank David.)

"Let's All Obey"
F. S. Sanford

Minuet
Company

1887.06

THE MASCOT

A Revival of the Opéra-comique in Three Acts[46]. Original French libretto ('La Mascotte') by Henri Chivot and Alfred Duru. Music by Edmond Audran. Scenery by Harley Merry. Music under the direction of Gustave A. Kerker. Produced by (Robert E. J.) Miles & Barton's Bijou Opera Comique Company. Opened 24 January 1887 at the Bijou Opera House and closed 26 February 1887 after 35 performances; returned 24 March 1887 and closed 26 March 1887 after 4 additional performances. Total: 39 performances.[47]

CAST: *Prince Lorenzo*: NAT C. GOODWIN. *Bettina*, the Mascot: LILLIE GRUBB. *Fiametta*, daughter of Lorenzo XVII: LELIA FARRELL. *Frederic*, Prince of Pisa: FLORA IRWIN. *Rocco*, a Farmer: C. B. BISHOP. *Pippo*: STUART HAROLD. *The Doctor*: E. F. Goodwin. *Parafante*, Sergeant: William Barnes. *Matheo*, Inn keeper: Harry C. DeWitt. *Antonia*: Pony Stevens. *Paolo*: Lucy Escott. *Francesco*: Ida Van Osten. *Angelo*: Carrie Wallace. *Luigi*: Georgie Lincoln. *First Officer*: William Haswell. *Second Officer*: Otto Wilkins. *Peasant*: Robert Vance.

Act 1: Italian Farm Yard.

Act 2: Room in the Palace of the Grand Duke of Piombino.

Act 3: Hall of an Italian Inn, in the Duchy of Pisa.

1887.07

McNOONEY'S VISIT

A Play in Three Acts, 4 Scenes. Play (and lyrics) by Edward Harrigan. Music by David Braham. Staged by Edward Harrigan. Dancing under the supervision of M. J. Bradley. Scenery by Charles W. Witham. Mechanical effects by William Vail. Costumes by Mary Jack. Musical director, David Braham. Produced by Edward Harrigan. Opened 31 January 1887 at Harrigan's Park Theatre and closed 16 April 1887 after 88 performances.

CAST: *Martin M'Nooney*: EDWARD HARRIGAN. *Ely Umstead*: JOHN WILD. *Clara Grizzle*: DAN COLLYER. *Lionel Mellow*: M. J. BRADLEY. *Judge Halzweiser*: HARRY FISHER. *Mary McQuirk*: JOHN SPARKS. *Henry Mellow*: George Merritt. *Melissa Umstead*: PETER GOLDRICH. *Ferdinand Skully*: RICHARD QUILTER. *Caesar Grizzle*: William West. *A Lunatic*: William West. *Pedro Giovanna*: JOSEPH SPARKS. *Solomon McQuirk*: JOSEPH SPARKS. *Singleton Slinger*: JOSEPH SPARKS. *Dexter Twigem*: Charles Sturges. *Keeper*: James McCullough. *Inspector Byrnes*: James McCullough. *Doctor Gargle*: G. L. Stout. *Adam Beausant*: G. L. Stout. *Fergus Clincher*: Charles Coffey. *Herbert Hopper*: Joseph Davis. *Car Driver*: James G. Brevarde. *Court Officer*: Edward Murphy. *Truckman*: Frank Sparks. *Officer*: T. Holland. *Sport*: William Merritt. *Clerk*: Harry Guion, Jr. *Street Gamin*: Master Alfred Waite. *Amos Sparrowbones*: John H. Decker. *Norah Gilmartin*, a widow: ANNIE YEAMANS. *Adele Spoonful*: AMY LEE. *Mary Mellow*: ANNA LANGDON. *Doctor Hilaria Spoonful*: Nellie Wetherill. *Rosy Daisy*: EMILY YEAMANS. *Norah McGovern*: EMILY YEAMANS. *President Good Samaritans*: KATE LANGDON. *Mrs. McNeily*: Annie Hall. *Good Samaritans*: Florence Hastings, Lulu Leach, Lillian Leach, Nell Fullerton, Minnie Richards, Grace Randall. *Squatters, Convicts, Skeptics, Guests, etc.*

Act 1: The Welcome Hour Nursery.Goats' Milk for the Babies.

Act 2: Interior of the Tombs. The Special Sessions. Exterior of the tombs.

Act 3: Reception Room of Dr. Spoonful. Massage, treatment.

MUSICAL NUMBERS

"Ho! Mollie Grogan" (Act 1)

"The Black Maria, O!" (Act 2)

"The Toboggan Slide" (Act 3)

1887.08

THE HUMMING BIRD

Nate Salsbury and His Troubadours in a Farce Comedy in Three Acts. Play by Fred Williams and George Stout. Musical conductor, Charles E. Borgman. Produced by Salsbury's Troubadours. Opened 7 February 1887 at the Star Theatre and closed 26 February 1887 after 23 performances[48].

CAST: *Mr. Joseph Brass*, Actor and Manager: NATE SALSBURY. *Mr. Augustus Honeymoon*, Oyster Packer: GEORGE BACKUS. *Mr. Robert Rackett*, an Artist: JOHN WEBSTER. *Jerry McLaughlin*, Policeman and Janitor: F. B. Blair. *The "Tramp"*: F. Bowman. *Sally Styles*, a Stage-struck Lady's Maid: NELLIE McHENRY. *Mrs. Fanny Honeymoon*: Leonora Bradley. *Mrs. Matilda Fullalove*, a young widow: Marie Bockel. *Biddy*: Emma Gilbert.

The action takes place in New York City at the present day.

Act 1: Central Park, near Statue of Shakespeare.

Act 2: Honeymoon's Home.

Act 3: Rackett's Studio.

ACT 1

The Herald Advertisement; What came of it; Humming Bird; Mignonette; Thespis and Daisy.

ACT 2

The Rackett Club Dinner; Uncle Baggin-dollar, from Cincinnati; Entangled; Kicked out.

---

[46]First produced in New York in English 5 May 1881 at the Bijou Opera House for 168 performances in 2 engagements. For Synopsis of Scenes and Musical Numbers, see original 1881 production.

[47]English adaptation and stage direction uncredited; stage manager, Paul Vernon.

[48]In revised form, played a return engagement 23 September 1887 at the Bijou Theatre for 27 performances; see entry in following season.

ACT 3
Mr. X. Y. Z.; Who owns the lace scarf?; The Knot Unties; The Humming Bird hums again; Then "Who is Uncle Baggin-dollar?"; Light at Last; "Then, take me, Clifford."

1887.09

PA

A Home Comedy in Three Acts. Play by Cal Wallace. Stage director, Frederick Percy Marsh. Musical director, C. Van Etten. Produced by Sol Smith Russell. Opened 14 February 1887 at the Standard Theatre and closed 19 February 1887 after 7 performances.[49]

CAST: *Perkimen Guinney*, "Pa": SOL SMITH RUSSELL. *Raymond Dawsey*, a believer in the doctrine of Metempsychosis: Fred Percy Marsh. *A. Sparticus Hubbs*, a musical monomaniac: Frank Lawton. *Sydney Bumpps*, a medical student in embryo: Fred P. Ham. *Captain Startle*, U.S.N., the demon: ALBERT H. WARREN. *Mrs. Hal Rymer*, the wife of a jealous old man: Mattie Ferguson. *Pa's Daughters (3): Hope*, my eldest daughter: VIRGINIA NELSON. *Sybil*, married but divorced: EMILY BANCKER. *Beatrice*, called Bee, Pa's childish prattler: EMMA HAGGER.

Act 1: Pa's Home.

Act 2: Pa's Garden.

Act 3: The Elopement.

1887.10

RUDDYGORE, or, The Witch's Curse

A Supernatural Opera in Two Acts. Libretto by William S. Gilbert. Music by Arthur Sullivan. Staged by Richard Barker. Scenery by H. L. Reid, Hughson Hawley. Costumes by Wilhelm, Messrs. Cater & Company, Mme. Leon. Musical director, P. W. Halton. Produced by D'Oyly Carte Opera Company. Opened 21 February 1887 at the Fifth Avenue Theatre and closed 9 April 1887 after 53 performances.

CAST: *Mortals: Robin Oakapple*, a Young Farmer: GEORGE THORNE. *Richard Dauntless*, his Foster-Brother, a Man-o'-Wars Man: COURTICE POUNDS. *Sir Despard Murgatroyd* of Ruddygore, a Wicked Baronet: FRED BILLINGTON. *Old Adam Goodheart*, Robin's Faithful Servant: Leo Kloss. *Rose Maybud*, a Village Maiden: GERALDINE ULMAR. *Mad Margaret*: KATE FORSTER. *Dame Hannah*, Rose's Aunt: ELSIE CAMERON. *Professional Bridesmaids (2): Zorah*: AÏDA JENOURE. *Ruth*: Miss MURRAY.

Ghosts: Sir Rupert Murgatroyd, the First Baronet: Mr. Winterbottom. *Sir Jasper Murgatroyd*, the Third Baronet: Mr. Poole. *Sir Lionel Murgatroyd*, the Sixth Baronet: Mr. Roche. *Sir Conrad Murgatroyd*, the Twelfth Baronet: Mr. James. *Sir Desmond Murgatroyd*, the Sixteenth Baronet: Mr. Jeffrey. *Sir Gilbert Murgatroyd*, the Eighteenth Baronet: Mr. Brand. *Sir Mervyn Murgatroyd*, the Twentieth Baronet: Mr. Huntley. *Sir F. Federici Murgatroyd*, the Twenty-First Baronet: F. FEDERICI. *Chorus of Officers, Ancestors, Professional Bridesmaids, Bucks, Blades.*

The action takes place early in the present century.

Act 1: The Fishing Village of Rederring in Cornwall. (Reid.)

Act 2: Picture Gallery in Ruddygore Castle. (Hawley.)

ACT 1[50]
"Fair is Rose as bright May day" (Chorus of Bridesmaids)
A. Jenoure, Bridesmaids
"Sir Rupert Murgatroyd His leisure and his riches" (Song and Chorus)
E. Cameron, Chorus
"If somebody there chanced to be" (Song)
G. Ulmar
"I know a youth who loves a little maid" (Duet)
G. Ulmar, G. Thorne
"From the briny seas comes young Richard" (Chorus of Bridesmaids) "I shipped, d'ye see, in a revenue sloop" (Song)
C. Pounds
Hornpipe
"My boy, you may take it from me" (Song)
G. Thorne
"The battle's roar is over, O my love!" (Duet)
G. Ulmar, C. Pounds
"If well his suit is sped" (Entrance of Bridesmaids)
"In sailing o'er life's ocean wide" (Trio)
G. Ulmar, C. Pounds, G. Thorne
"Cheerily carols the lark Over the cot" (Recitative and Aria)
K. Forster
"Welcome gentry"
Chorus
"O why am I moody and sad?" (Song and Chorus)
F. Billington
"You understand? I think I do" (Duet)
C. Pounds, F. Billington
"Hail the bride of seventeen summers" (Finale)

ACT 2
"I once was as meek as a newborn lamb" (Duet)
G. Thorne, L. Kloss
"Happily coupled are we, you see" (Duet and Chorus)
G. Ulmar, C. Pounds
"In bygone days I had thy love" (Song)
G. Ulmar, Chorus of Bridesmaids
"Painted emblems of a race" (Chorus of Ancestors)
G. Thorne, F. Federici, Chorus
"When the night wind howls in the chimney cowls" (Song)
F. Federici, Chorus
"He yields! He yields!" (Chorus)
"Away, remorse! Compunction, hence!" (Recitative and Song)
G. Thorne
"I once was a very abandon'd person" (Duet)
K. Forster, F. Billington
"My eyes are fully open to my awful situation" (Trio)
K. Forster, G. Thorne, F. Billington
Melodrame
"There grew a little flower 'neath a great oak tree" (Song)
E. Cameron, F. Federici
"When a man has been a naughty Baronet" (Finale)

1887.11

FRITZ, OUR COUSIN GERMAN

A (Reconstructed Version of the) Great Specialty of the German Emigrant (Drama) in Four Acts, 9 Scenes[51]. Play by Charles Gayler, (reconstructed by Joseph K. Emmet). Produced by Joseph K. Emmet. Opened 21 February 1887 at the Standard Theatre and closed 2 April 1887 after 42 performances.[52]

CAST: In Holland: *Fritz*, Hungarian Gypsy by adoption: JOSEPH K. EMMET. *Henry Norton*, an artist: C. D. Bennett. *Karl Winkleman*, a gypsy: M. J. Cody. *Peter Finnecum*: William Yerance. *Katarina*: HELEN SEDGWICK. *Little Heinrick*: Baby Wood. *Little Louisa*: Baby Spencer. *Little Mena*: Little Lillian.

In America: *Fritz*, an immigrant: JOSEPH K. EMMET. *Henry Norton*, an artist: C. D. Bennett. *Karl Winkleman*, an immigrant: M. J. Cody. *Peter Finnecum*: William Yerance. *Noodle*: J. S. Brinsley. *Cadge*, a New York rough: Albert Klein. *Sloper*, a New York rough: J. C. Cannon. *Snow*, a colored servant: W. C. Utter. *Judge of Court*: M. Downs. *Clerk of Court*: H. Raymond. *Katarina*, an emigrant: HELEN SEDGWICK. *Miss Blanche Gould*: Clara Simpson. *Mrs. Susan Gould*: Mary Lawrence. *Moppy*: Julia Langdon. *Judy*: Lizzie Winner. *Mrs. O'Shane*: Alice Spencer. *Lilly Schneider*: Baby Spencer. *Little Libbie O*: Baby Lillian. *Little Tillie*: Baby Wood. *Policeman*: Frank Conners.

Act 1: Fritz's Basket Shop in Holland.

Act 2, Scene 1: Castle Garden, New York. *Scene 2*: Woodsdown. *Scene 3*: Antechamber, Woodsdown. *Scene 4*: A garret.

Act 3, Scene 1: The house of mystery, New York. *Scene 2*: Antechamber, Woodsdown. *Scene 3*: A court room.

Act 4: The millwheel, home of Fritz.

[49]No credits in program for costumes; no musical numbers listed. A program note states that the specialties, incidental music and comic songs were expressly written for this production.

[50]Musical numbers not listed in programs. List prepared from English piano vocal score (Chappell & Co., London, 1887; William A. Pond & Co, New York, 1887.)

[51]First produced in New York 11 July 1870 at Niblo's Garden for 63 performances.

[52]No credits in program for staging, scenery costumes, musical director, or musical numbers. Subsequent tour credits Fred E. Butters as musical director for J. K. Emmet. Played a return engagement 9 January 1888 at Henry C. Miner's People's Theatre for 14 performances.

1887.12

LORRAINE

An Opera Comique in Three Acts. Original German libretto by Oscar Walther. English adaptation by William J. Henderson. Music by Rudolph Dellinger. Scenery painted by Joseph Clare. Stage mechanism by Neil McGieghan. Musical director, Adolf Neuendorff. Produced by McCaull Opera Comique Company (Joseph A. McCaull, Proprietor). Opened 28 February 1887 at the Star Theatre and closed 12 March 1887 after 14 performances.[53]

CAST: *Lorraine*: Signor PERUGINI. *Louis XIV*, King of France: GEORGE OLMI. *Gaspard de Chateauvieux*, a Nobleman of High Degree: DeWOLF HOPPER. *D'Effiat*, Director of the Royal Amusements: HARRY STANDISH. *Ollivier de la Tour*: MATHILDE COTTRELLY. *Pierre*, Lorraine's foster-father: HERNDON MORSELL. *Pages to the King (8)*: *Henri*: Gertie Clark. *Jerome*: Florence Willey. *Gervais*: Clara Allen. *Victor*: Ida Bartelle. *Francois*: Grace Seavey. *Achille*: Minnie Echard. *Eugene*: Bessie Calloway. *Alphonso*: May Yohe. *Courtiers (4)*: *Le Bleu*: Charles Jones. *St. Trompe*: George Carlisle. *De la Sancierra*: Carlo Russo. *De Pantecat*: Antonio Amadeo. *An Old Man*: Lindsay Morrison. *Captain of the King's Guards*: Angel M. Barbara. *Madeline*, niece to Gaspard: GERTRUDE GRISWOLD. *Oudarde*, Gaspard's wife: EMILY SOLDENE. *Louise la Vallière*, Favorite of the King: JOSEPHINE KNAPP. *Pages, Falconers, Hunting Suites, Soldiers, Courtiers, Lords and Ladies.*

Act 1: Park of King Lois XIV's Hunting Castle.

Act 2: Audience Hall in Castle.

Act 3: King's Ante-chamber in Castle.

ACT 1[54]

"Now hurrah! Now hurrah!" (Opening Chorus)
M. Cottrelly, Chorus

"From out the darkness of the ages" (Solo)
G. Olmi

"Over hill, over dale, and by mountain" (Ballade)
M. Cottrelly

"Blue blood is what we keep alive on" (Terzetto)
D. Hopper, G. Griswold, E. Soldene

"All in the gentle time of Spring" (Love Song)
G. Griswold

"Now to my lord and king" (Entrée and Papa Song)
Signor Perugini

Finale
Signor Perugini, E. Soldene, G. Griswold, E. Soldene, H. Morsell, Chorus

"A Wanderer upon the land and sea" (Provence Song)
Signor Perugini

ACT 2

"When all around in slumber lies" (Introduction and Chorus)
Soldiers

"Now across and beyond the deep" (Morning Song)
M. Cottrelly

"Oh, strange indeed is this our parting" (Duet)
Signor Perugini, G. Griswold

"When I was a childish prattler" (Kiss Song)
E. Soldene

"Now our King's command fulfilling" (Ensemble)
Chorus

"Now according to our ancient custom" (Drinking Song)
M. Cottrelly

"Waltz away! Happy day!" (Finale)
Signor Perugini, G. Griswold, M. Cottrelly, H. Standish, Chorus

"A Wanderer upon the land and sea" (Provence song/reprise)
Signor Perugini

ACT 3

"Oh, silent night, thy light and shadows" (Opening)
Signor Perugini, Chorus

"Adieu, Lorraine, this day is full of sorrow" (Pierre's Adieux)
H. Morsell, G. Griswold, Chorus

Finale
Signor Perugini, G. Griswold, Chorus

[53]Stage direction and costume design uncredited. Stage manager, E. T. Steyne.
[54]Musical numbers not listed in programs. List prepared from published book of lyrics (J. L. Regan Printing Co., Chicago, Illinois, 1886).

1887.13

THE SKATING RINK

A Revival of the Burlesque Absurdity (Farce Comedy) in Three Acts[55]. Play by Robert Griffin Morris. (Music by Gustave A. Kerker, others.) Produced under the direct supervision of Frank W. Sanger. Scenery by Harley Merry. Musical director, Gustave A. Kerker. Stage mechanism by George W. Gale. Gas effects by Edward A. Kelly. Produced by Nat C. Goodwin and Frank W. Sanger. Opened 28 February 1887 at the Bijou Opera House and closed 23 March 1887 after 24 performances.

CAST: *Ronald Delaine*, a "dream in flesh and blood and startling clothing; effusively verbose, yet speculative." The kind of man who opens a rink: NAT C. GOODWIN. *Miss Waxdoll*: NAT C. GOODWIN. *Patrick McCune*, in search of his daughter: NAT C. GOODWIN. *Camille*, from the Lyceum School of Dramatic Art: NAT C. GOODWIN. *Erasmus Carter*, with sweeping assertions: JOHN W. RANSONE. *Timothy Tubbs*, Amelia's doting dad: Charles B. Bishop. *Mickey Barbage*, lecturer and thumper: Edward F. Goodwin. *Philander McShane*, Professor of the gliding art: JOHN CANFIELD. *Ignus Fatus*, king of the rollers: Charles Fletcher. *Hither and Thither*, a roller who gathers no Moss: William Fletcher. *Tenacity*: A. Puppe. *Clarence O'Dear*, only a butterfly: H. DeWITT. *Miss Amelia Tubbs*, looking for a fate: LILLIE GRUBB. *Phoebe*: LOIE FULLER. *Sallie Tubbs*, Amelia's maiden aunt: LILLIE ALLISTON. *Matilda Squibbs*, Amelia's friend: JENNIE REEVES. *Miss Franchita Beauharnais*, queen of the rink: Lillian Fletcher. *Mr. Wall Street Bull*: P. Mache. *Villagers, Skaters, etc.*

ACT 1

"Bathing Chorus"
(*Music by* Gustave A. Kerker.)

"Gentle Faces"

"Next" (Topical Song)
(*Music by* Gustave A. Kerker. *Lyrics by* Sydney Rosenfeld.)

"A Roller Rink"

ACT 2

Gliding Chorus

Waltz Song

Song and Dance

"Folly" (Song and Dance)

"See-Saw" (Duet)

Finale

Grand Medley

ACT 3

Grand March

Swell Song

"Since Maggie Learned to Skate" (Song and Chorus)

Trio

"Go Away"
(*Music by* Gustave A. Kerker.)

Grand Finale

1887.14

BIG PONY,
The Gentlemanly Savage

An American Comic Opera in Three Acts. Play by Andrew Carpenter Wheeler (Nym Crinkle). Music by Edward I. Darling. Production under the supervision of William H. Daly. Scenery by Harley Merry. Orchestration and musical direction by Gustave A. Kerker. Produced by Nat C. Goodwin (C. W. Durant, Proprietor). Opened 31 March 1887 at the Bijou Theatre and closed 23 April 1887 after 25 performances.[56]

CAST: *Big Pony*, Chief of the Umbilicas: NAT C. GOODWIN. *Don Filibusto*, the Spanish father: C. B. Bishop. *Sig. Sancho Mendingo*, the Castilian bridegroom: Stuart Harold. *Lieutenant Arlington*, U.S.A.: Henry Moulton. *Sergeant O'Glory*, U.S.A.: E. W. Leon. *Sancho's retainers (4)*: *Polecat Pete*: Edward F. Goodwin. *Mustang Mike*: H. C. DeWitt. *Gopher Joe*: Robert Vance. *Billy the Stag*: Otto Wilkins. *Senorita Inez*, the Don's daughter: LILLIE GRUBB. *Senorita Marie*, her cousin: LOIE FULLER. *Sagastina*, the duenna: Estelle Mortimer. Indians in the Choir: *Oo-ka-how-ya-gah*, the cloud bitter of the Umbilicas: Dolly Delroy. *Un-ka-ki-yi*, the slough swallower of the sunset land: Madge Perry. Squaws: *So-ro-sis-si*, the lone sage bush of the wash out: J. Laurence. *In-ki-tink-i-mink*, the

[55]First produced in New York 23 November 1885 at the Standard Theatre for 14 performances. For Synopsis of Scenes, see original 1885 production.
[56]Musical numbers not listed in programs.

sap of the sugar maple: H. Dye. *Indians, Cowboys, Mexicans, Monks, Spanish Girls, Squaws, Bucks, Soldiers, etc.*

Act 1: A Mexican Vintage of the estate of Don Filibusto.

Act 2: Big Pony's Camp in a canyon.

Act 3: Spanish Monastery and Court.

1887.15 A TRIP TO AFRICA

A Revival of the Opéra Comique in Three Acts[57]. Original Viennese libretto to the operette ('Die Afrikareise') by Richard Genée and Moritz West. Music by Franz von Suppé. Entire production under the personal direction of James C. Duff. Scenery by Henry Clare. Musical director, J. S. Hiller. Produced by James C. Duff. Opened 11 April 1887 at the Standard Theatre and closed 14 May 1887 after 28 performances.[58]

CAST: *Titania Fanfani*: LILLIAN RUSSELL. *Fanfani Pasha*, her uncle: J. H. RYLEY. *Antarsid*, Prince of the Mironites: EUGENE OUDIN. *Miradello*, a European traveler: CHARLES W. DUNGAN. *Pericles*, hotel keeper: John E. Nash. *Sibil*, a slave: Bessie Cleveland. *Hosh*, hotel servant: James E. Fox. *Tessa*, a French milliner: MADELINE LUCETTE. *Buccametta*, her mother: ZELDA SEGUIN. *Nakid*, a Koptic Dealer in poisons and perfumes: J. E. Weisner. *A Muezzin*: Franklin Boudinot. *A Mironite*: Edward E. Webb. *First Sais*: Arthur Underwood. *Second Sais*: A. E. McDowell. *Chorus of Citizens, Mironites, Bedouins, Persian Women, etc*: Chorus of 50.

Act 1: A Public Square in Cairo.

Act 2: Fanfani's Gardens, on the Banks of the Nile.

Act 3: An Oasis in the great Desert, Africa.

1887.16 CORDELIA'S ASPIRATIONS

A Revival of the Play (with Music) in Three Acts, 5 Scenes[59]. Play (and lyrics) by Edward Harrigan. Music by David Braham. Staged by Edward Harrigan. Scenery by Charles W. Witham. Mechanical effects by William Vail. Properties by Louis Filber. Wardrbe by Mrs. Mary Jack. Dancing under the supervision of M. J. Bradley. Musical director, David Braham. Produced by Edward Harrigan. Opened 18 April 1887 at Harrigan's Park Theatre and closed 30 April 1887 after 16 performances.

CAST: *Dan Mulligan*: EDWARD HARRIGAN. *Simpson Primrose*: JOHN WILD. *Rebecca Allup*: DAN COLLYER. *Palestine Puter*: PETER GOLDRICH. *Planxty McFudd*: HARRY A. FISHER. *Walsingham McSweeney*: M. J. BRADLEY. *Gustavus Lochmuller*: JOSEPH SPARKS. *Ridgeway*: Charles Sturgis. *Mulvey*: Charles Coffey. *Mr. Bowser*: GEORGE MERRITT. *Clerk*: George L. Stout. *Tommy*: Master Harry Guion. *Policeman*: J. McCullough. *Cordelia Mulligan*: ANNIE YEAMANS. *Diana McFudd*: AMY LEE. *Mrs. Lochmuller*: NELLIE WETHERELL. *Ellen McFudd*: Ada Farwell. *Rosey McFudd*: Annie Langdon. *Mrs. Buchheister*: Kate Langdon. *Mrs. Diggins*: Annie Hall. *Mrs. Brown*: Lulu Leach. *Mrs. Risley*: Lillian Leach. *Mrs. Crumps*: Florence Hastings. *Annetta*: Minnie Richards. *Mrs Hiram Slocum*: Nell Fullerton. *Miss Snowflake*: Grace Randall.

The Uncle Tom Combination: *Jim Grace*: Peter Goldrich. *Mr. Dangerfield*: William West. *Mr. Clinton*: E. Murphy. *Topsy*: Joe Davis. *Billy Kersands*: John G. Sparks. *Cal Hicks*: RICHARD QUILTER. *Jim Bland*: Charles Sullivan. *Sam Lucas*: Robert Gordon. *Joe Hardhead*: Charles Coffey. *Jay Weldon*: J. Decker. *Emigrants, Officials, Policemen, Hackmen, etc.*

1887.17 THE DEACON'S DAUGHTER

A Comedy Drama (with Songs) in Four Acts. Play by A. C. Gunter. Stage director, M. C. Daly. Produced by Annie Pixley (Archie Mackenzie, Agent). Opened 25 April 1887 at the Union Square Theatre and closed 4 June 1887 after 43 performances.

CAST: *Ruth Homewebb*, "Nom de Theatre," Mabel Hawthorne, the leading juvenile at the Criterion Theatre: ANNIE PIXLEY. *Isaiah Jubal Homewebb*, of Pautukset, Connecticut, "The Deacon": M. C. DALY. *Charley Lawton*, a young New York business man: George Backus. *Irving de Vere Chillington*, a club man with artistic tendencies. The star of amateur theatricals: W. G. Reynier. *Signor Malatesta Tomkins*, a painter of the Impressionists' school: ED. TEMPLE. *Squire Hiram Slimbergast*, who goes to the theatres in New York: Robert Fisher. *Amadie*, Signor Tomkins' assistant: P. Redmond. *Mrs. Rachel Homewebb*, the Deacon's Wife: Annie Douglass. *Mrs. Dashington Brown*, a Society Conundrum: Annie Barclay. *Mary O'Dougherty*, Ruth's maid: Irene Avenal.

Act 1: Parlor in Mabel Hawthorne's Flat, New York. The home of the actress.

Act 2: Three months elapse. Farmyard at the Homewebb Place. The home of the deacon.

Act 3: Four weeks later. Signor Tomkins' Photograph Gallery, New York. The page's dilemma.

Act 4: The same day, 11 P.M. Mabel Hawthorne's Flat. The Deacon's Daughter.

MUSICAL NUMBERS, SPECIALTIES

New Songs, Medleys
A. Pixley

"Wash Tub Song"
A. Pixley (*Music by* Edgar Selden.)

1887.18 THE BLACK HUSSAR

A Revival of the Opera Comique in Three Acts[60]. Original Viennese libretto ('Der Feldprediger') by Hugo Wittmann and Alois Wohlmuth, based on the story 'Der seltsame Brautgemach' by Friedrich Schilling. English adaptation by Sydney Rosenfeld. Music by Carl Millöcker. Musical director, Antonio DeNovellis. Produced by McCaull Opera Company (John A. McCaull). Opened 7 May 1887 at Wallack's Theatre and closed 30 May 1887 after 24 performances.

CAST: *Friedrich von Helbert*, Colonel of the Black Hussars, disguised as an Army Chaplain: HUBERT WILKE. *Hans von Waldmann*, Adjutant of the Black Hussars, disguised as a student: EDWIN W. HOFF. *Staff Officers of the Black Hussars (9)*: *Major Rokow*: Grace Seavey. *Captain Plush*: Florence Hicley. *Captain Bender*: Emma Muller. *Captain Woolf*: Alice Hamilton. *Lieut. Conrad*: Bessie Calloway. *Lieut. Van Vleet*: Tillie Frank. *Lieut. Duzenburg*: Zoe DeVielle. *Lieut. Konig*: Minnie Echart. *Lieut. Beyer*: Ida Bartelle. *Theophil Hackenback*, Magistrate of Trautenfeld: DeWOLF HOPPER. *Piffkow*, his Factotum, with numerous offices—Town Crier, Night Watchman, Barber, etc: JEFFERSON DeANGELIS. *Mefflin*, a Tragedian of the Meiniger Company, No. 14: ALFRED KLEIN. *François Thorilliere*, a Captain in the French Army: Carl Irving. *Rubke*, a Captain in the Prussian Army: Charles H. Jones. *Wutki*, Hetman of the Cassocks: A. Barbara. *Citizens of Trautenfeld (5)*: *Klappig*: Carlo Russo. *Rothmichael*: F. Hedlung. *Birnbaum*: D. Hasselberg. *Knoedel*: Carl Formes. *Schupsack*: George Carlyle. *Shadow*, a Black Hussar disguised as a Pedlar: L. Tesio. *Bruck*, a Black Hussar disguised as a Scissors Grinder: Louis Shrader. *Eiken*, a Black Hussar disguised as a Beggar: A. Amadao. *Selchow*, a Black Hussar disguised as a Ratcatcher: K. Peiser. *Prittwitz*, a Black Hussar disguised as a Bookseller: M. Maina. *Putnam*, a Black Hussar disguised as a Quack Doctor: S. R. Hardie. *Hackenback's Daughters (2)*: *Minna*: MARION MANOLA. *Rosetta*: CELIE ELLIS. *Barbara*, an Orphan, Hackenback's Housekeeper: MATHILDE COTTRELLY. *Rieke*, a maid: Clara Allen. *Mrs.*, the Wife of the Church Warden: Rita Shrader. *Mrs.*, the Wife of the King's Stable Keeper: Susie Cox. *Mrs.*, the Wife of the State Reduction Cashier: Mae Valette. *Mrs.*, the Wife of the Custom House Officer: Annette Hall. *Mrs.*, the Wife of the Army Sutler: Lucie Pixley. *Mrs.*, the Wife of the Forest Gamekeeper: Annie Peiser.

1887.19 THE PYRAMID

A Comic Opera in Two Acts, 3 Scenes. Libretto by Charles Puerner and Caryl Florio[61]. Music by Charles Puerner. Chorus and orchestra under the direction of Charles Puerner. Scenery by Gaspard Maeder and William Schaeffer; William F. Voegtlin. Costumes by Miss Eller and F. Roemer.

[57]First produced in New York 23 December 1884 at the Standard Theatre for 62 performances. For Synopsis of Scenes and Musical Numbers, see original 1884 production. For this revival, the following was interpolated into Act 3: Arabesque Song, L. Russell (*Music by* J. S. Hiller.).

[58]English version by Emil Schwab, adapted and arranged for the English stage by Adolph Neuendorff. The English adapters' names do not appear in New York programs; they are taken from a November 1884 Boston program, which producer James C. Duff credits as his inspiration for the New York production.

[59]First produced in New York 5 November 1883 at the Theatre Comique for 176 performances. For Synopsis of Scenes and Musical Numbers, see original 1883 production.

[60]First produced in New York in German 1 May 1885 at the Thalia Theatre, and in English 4 May 1885 at Wallack's Theatre for 104 performances. For Synopsis of Scenes and Musical Numbers, see original 1885 production. Stage direction not credited, presumably the work of the author Sydney Rosenfeld, original stage manager William H. Daly and John A. McCaull, producer.

[61]The reviewer in the Clipper remarked that the libretto was drawn from a recent popular novel and Gerstaecker's short story "Germelshausen."

Opened 16 May 1887 at the Star Theatre and closed 11 June 1887 after 28 performances.[62]

CAST: Mortals: *Albert Leroy, William Dodge*, American Tourists: HARRY HILLIARD, PAUL ARTHUR. *Abdul*, an Egyptian Guide: C. Witt. *Donkey Drivers and Guides.*
Mummies: *Ramses XXVII*, King of Egypt: FRANK DAVID. *Rhea*, his daughter: ADDIE CORA REED. *Tai*, her companion: HELEN STANDISH. *Hatasu*, an elderly maiden: ROSA COOKE. *Sabako*, a High Priest: ELLIS RYSE. *Memphis*, Keeper of the Vaults: Herbert D. Chesley. *Companions of Rhea, Courtiers, Warriors, Guards.*

Act 1, Scene 1: Exterior of a Pyramid. *Scene 2*: Interior of a Pyramid.

Act 2: Moonlight Scene on the Nile.

ACT 1[63]

Chorus of Guides and Donkey Drivers (We are sons of Egypt's soil)
Chorus

Introduction and Chorus of Guards (From our sleep of ages waken'd)
H. D. Chesley, Chorus

Chorus of Girls (Laughing tripping full of glee)

Recitatif and Air (O light! O life! What joy to breathe once more!)
A. C. Reed

Song (Centuries ago When I in youth gay morning)
A. C. Reed

Chorus, Entrance of King (Lowly homage pay!)

Song (By nature I'm a tyrant)
F. David

Ensemble (Bring them forth!)
Chorus

Duet (When two fond hearts together beating)
A. C. Reed, H. Hilliard

Trio (The pains this loving heart doth know)
R. Cooke, E. Ryse, P. Arthur

Finale (From the temple rites returning)
Principals, Chorus

ACT 2

Chorus of Girls (Softly flow, o royal Nile!)

Song (O lovely night, how fair and how serene!)
H. Hilliard

Song (When moments are so few, and life so brief)
A. C. Reed

Madrigal (Love knows naught of age or youth)
A. C. Reed, R. Cooke, H. Hilliard, P. Arthur

Solo ('Tis proper to be very shy)
H. Standish, Chorus of Girls

Song (A tiger was crouched in his lair)
E. Ryse

Duet (What is fame, and what is glory)
E. Ryse, F. David

Sextette (Ah how perplexing is the case!)
A. C. Reed, R. Cooke, H. Hilliard, E. Ryse, P. Arthur, F. David

Song (Within these walls of solitude)
F. David

Duet (Although I'm no more fresh and green)
R. Cooke, F. David

Finale
Principals, Chorus

1887.20

GASPARONE

A Revival of the Comic Opera in Three Acts[64]. Original Viennese libretto to the operette by F. Zell and Richard Genée. English adaptation by Sydney Rosenfeld. Music by Carl Millöcker. Produced by James C. Duff. Opened 16 May 1887 at the Standard Theatre and closed 28 May 1887 after 14 performances.

CAST: *Carlotta*, Countess of Santa Croce, a widow LILLIAN RUSSELL. *Babolena Nasoni*, Podesta of Syracuse: J. H. RYLEY. *Sindulfo*, his son: E. W. WEBB. *Count Erminio*: EUGENE OUDIN. *Luigi*, his friend: John E. Nash. *Benozzo*, Innkeeper: F. GAILLARD. *Sora*, his wife: MADELEINE LUCETTE. *Zenobia*, Duenna to Carlotta: ZELDA SEGUIN. *Masaccio*, Smuggler, Benozzo's Uncle: Frank Boudinot. *Smugglers, Soldiers, Peasants, Milksellers, Gendarmes, Coastguards, Carbineers, Sailors*: Chorus of 50.

1887.21

IOLANTHE, or, The Peer and the Peri

A Revival of the Comic Opera in Two Acts[65]. Libretto by William S. Gilbert. Music by Arthur Sullivan. Entire production under the personal direction of James C. Duff. Orchestra directed by J. S. Hiller. Produced by James C. Duff . Opened 30 May 1887 at the Standard Theatre and closed 11 June 1887 after 14 performances.[66]

CAST: *Phyllis*: LILLIAN RUSSELL. *Iolanthe*: FLORENCE BEMISTER. *The Fairy Queen*: ZELDA SEGUIN. *Celia*: Bessie Cleveland. *Strephon*: C. W. DUNGAN. *The Earl of Mount Ararat*: HARRY ALLEN. *The Earl Tolloller*: GEORGE S. APPLEBY. *Private Willis*: FRANK BOUDINOT. *The Lord Chancellor*: J. H. RYLEY. (*Dukes, Marquises, Earls, Viscounts, Barons and Fairies*: Chorus of 50.)

1887.22

FALKA

A Return Engagement of the Opérette in Three Acts[67]. Original French libretto ('Le Droit d'aînesse') by Eugene Leterrier and Albert Vanloo. English adaptation by H. B. Farnie. Music by Francis Chassaigne. Produced by the McCaull Opera Company. Opened 31 May 1887 at Wallack's Theatre and closed 11 June 1887 after 14 performances.[68]

CAST: *Falka*, Niece of Folbach: MARION MANOLA. *Edwige*, Sister of Boleslas: MATHILDE COTTRELLY. *Alexina de Felkirsch*, a young heiress: CELIE ELLIS. *Von Folbach*, Military Governor of Montgratz: DeWOLF HOPPER. *Boleslas*, Chief of the Tzigani: HUBERT WILKE. *Tancred*, Folbach's nephew, usher in a village school: JEFFERSON DeANGELIS. *Arthur*, Student, son of a rich Hungarian Farmer: HARRY MACDONOUGH. *Lay Brother Pelican*, Doorkeeper of the Convent: ALFRED KLEIN.

[62]Producer and stage director uncredited; stage manager, E. S. Grant.
[63]Musical numbers not listed in programs. List prepared from published vocal score (Fuenkenstein & Puerner, 1887).

[64]First presented in New York in German 21 February 1885 at the Thalia Theatre, and in English 21 February 1885 at the Standard Theatre for 44 performances. For Synopsis of Scenes and Musical Numbers, see original 1885 English language production.
[65]First presented in New York 25 November 1882 at the Standard Theatre for 105 performances. For Synopsis of Scenes and Musical Numbers, see original 1882 production.
[66]Scenery and costumes uncredited.
[67]First produced in New York 14 April 1884 at the Casino Theatre for 110 performances. Also produced this season 12 July 1886 at Wallack's Theatre in two engagements for 35 performances. For Synopsis of Scenes and Musical Numbers, see original 1884 production.
[68]No New York program found for this engagement; minimal detail from the New York Dramatic Mirror.

1887–1888 SEASON

Lillian Russell in THE QUEEN'S MATE (Photo: Falk)
Billy Rose Theatre Collection, New York Public Library for the Performing Arts

1887–1888 SEASON

1887.23 OUR IRISH VISITORS

A Revival of the New and Original Absurdity (Farce Comedy) in Three Acts.[1] Play by Thomas E. Murray and Mark Murphy. Musical director, Louis F. Boos. Produced by J. M. Hill. Opened 6 June 1887 at the Union Square Theatre and closed 9 July 1887 after 35 performances.

CAST: *Colonel Gilhooly*, a Bogus Lord: THOMAS E. MURRAY. *Jerry McGinnis*, the Alderman: MARK MURPHY. *Sammy Tupper*: CHARLES W. YOUNG. *Yank Salem*: CHARLES W. YOUNG. *Fritz Kepner*: JAMES REILLY. *Dorothy*: ANNIE LEWIS. *Mrs. McGinnis*: Mrs. Helena Hardenburg. *Arabella*: Miss PERCY LORRAIN. *Mrs. Gilhooly*: Miss ADDIE BOOS. *Bruno*: The Bear. (*Cecilian Quartette*, Specialty: Will Walling, Arthur Cook, William Ridgeway, Harry W. Roe. *Specialty*: George Wiegand.)

Act 1: Arrival of the Visitors. The fun commences. A circus passes the farm. The Colonel and the Alderman decide to take in the circus. The bear coming this way. Tableau of consternation.

Act 2: Trouble on the farm. Nothing to eat. No place to sleep. The visitors on a strike. Dorothy to the rescue. "A dance! A dance!" Dorothy in vocal selections. Mlle. Samson's Female Ballet Troupe. More trouble on the farm. Arabella in select ballads. War to the knife. Gilhooly makes love to the Alderman's wife. The discovery. The duel. Murder! Thieves! Robbers! Fire! Tableau of Horrors.

Act 3: The Vistors go on a pic-nic. The last day of the season. Fritz has a dream. Gilhooly and McGinnis row a boat race. Sam in eccentricities. Mrs. Gilhooly in a cornet solo. Fritz in German dialect effusions. Vocal Selections and Artistic Singing by the Renowned "Cecilian Quartette." The fun interrupted by a fight. Peace at last.

MUSICAL SPECIALTIES[2]

Medley of Irish Melodies, arranged by L. F. Boos

Medley: "I'm Awaiting My Love's Return," "I Had Fifteen Dollars in My Inside Pocket," "Clara Nolan's Ball," "Cricket on the Hearth," with xylophone solo performed by Louis Nusbaum.

Selections from ERMINIE
G. Wiegand (*Music by* Edward Jakobowski.)

San Francisco March (*Music by* Carter.)

Vocal Selections (Act 2)
A. Lewis

Ballads (Act 2)
P. Lorain

Cornet Solo (Act 3)
A. Boos

"List to the Birds"
Company (*Music by* Charles E. Verner.)

Selections (Act 3)
Cecilian Quartette

1887.24 JACQUETTE

A Comic Opera in Three Acts. Libretto by J. Cheever Goodwin. Based on the French "La Béarnaise" by Eugène Leterrier and Albert Vanloo. Music by André Messager. Produced by the McCaull Opera Company (John A. McCaull, Proprietor and Manager). Opened 13 June 1887 at Wallack's Theatre and closed 2 July 1887 after 21 performances.

CAST: *The Duke of Parma*: ALFRED KLEIN. *Countess Bianca*: MARION MANOLA. *Chevalier Pomponio*: DeWOLF HOPPER. *Captain Perpignac*: HUBERT WILKE. *Grabosson*: CARL IRVING. *Jacquette*: MATHILDE COTTRELLY. *Bettina*: Celie Ellis. *Girafo*: JEFFERSON DeANGELIS. *The Cadet*: HARRY MACDONOUGH. *Carlo*: Grace Seavey. *Landlady*: Annetta Hall. *Achille*: Louise Cox. *Lorenzo*: Tillie Frank. *Amilcharel*: Leona Clarke. *Ascandio*: Rose Murallo. *Officer*: Louis Shrader.

MUSICAL NUMBERS[3]

Mandolin Serenade Topical Song
D. Hopper

Lullaby (Act 2)
M. Cottrelly

1887.25 H.M.S. PINAFORE, or, The Lass That Loved a Sailor

A Revival of the Comic Opera in Two Acts[4]. Libretto by William S. Gilbert. Music by Arthur Sullivan. Produced under the stage direction of James C. Scanlan Scenery by Philip Goatcher. Musical director, G. B. Snyder. Presented by Messrs. Hayden, Dickson and Roberts. Opened 13 June 1887 at Madison Square Garden and closed 18 June 1887 after 12 performances.[5]

CAST: *The Rt. Hon. Sir Joseph Porter, K.C.B.*, First Lord of the Admiralty: CHARLES COOTE. *Captain Corcoran*, Commanding the *H.M.S. Pinafore*: GUSTAVUS HALL. *Ralph Rackstraw*, Able Seaman: HARRY HILLIARD. *Dick Deadeye*, Able Seaman: HENRY C. PEAKES. *Bill Bobstay*, Bo'sun's Mate: John Clark. *The Silent Marine*: Robert Fraser. *Tom Tucker*, Midshipmite: Little Lottie. *Josephine*, the Captain's Daughter: EMMA HENRY. *Hebe*, Sir Joseph's First Cousin: Sylvia Gerrish. *Little Buttercup*, a Portsmouth Bumboat Woman: DELL KELLOGG. *First Lord's Sisters, his Cousins, his Aunts, Sailors, Marines, etc.*

1887.26 THE BEGGAR STUDENT

A Revival of the Comic Opera in Three Acts, 4 Scenes[6]. Original Viennese libretto ('Der Bettelstudent') by F. Zell and Richard Genée, based on "Fernande" by Victorien Sardou and "The Lady of Lyons" by Edward Bulwer-Lytton. (English adaptation by Emil Schwab.) Music by Karl Millöcker. Stage manager, Herbert A. Cripps. Musical director, Adolph Nowak. Produced by the McCaull Opera Comique Company (John A. McCaull, Proprietor and Manager). Opened 25 July 1887 at Wallack's Theatre and closed 20 August 1887 after 28 performances.

CAST: *Symon (Symkovicz)*, the beggar student: HUBERT WILKE. *Janitska*, his companion: EDWIN HOFF. *General Ollendorf*, Commander of the Fortress of Cracow: DeWOLF HOPPER. *Enterich*, a jailor: HERBERT A. CRIPPS. *Laura*: MARION MANOLA. *Bronislava*, her sister: ANNIE MYERS. *Countess Palmatica*, Mother of Laura and Bronislava: LAURA JOYCE-BELL. *Eva*, Cousin of the Countess: Josephine Knapp. *Ensign Poppenberg*: Sadie Wells. *Bogomil*: Mountjoy Walker. *Onofrie*, servant: Lindsay Morrison. *Inn Keeper*: George Pyke. *Officers (4)*: *Henrici*: A. Barbara. *Holtzberg*: Louis Shrader. *Steinwitz*: George Carlyle. *Conradi*: F. Hedlund.

1887.27 LAGARDÈRE; or, the Hunchback of Paris

A Grand Romantic and Spectacular Drama in Four Acts and a Prologue, 13 Scenes. Based on the French play "Le Bossu" by Ancient Bourgeois and Paul Feval[7]. Entire production designed and produced under the personal direction of Imre Kiralfy. Scenery by Cav. S. Magnani of Parma; Harley Merry of New York; Robecchi and Amable of Paris. Costumes designed by Wilhelm of London. Director of Ballet, Signor Ettore Coppini. Musical director, A. W. Hoffman. Produced by Imre Kiralfy. Opened 17 August 1887 at Niblo's Garden and closed 15 October 1887 after 70 performances.

---

[1]A smaller production played earlier New York area engagements 18 January 1886 at the Third Avenue Theatre, 17 May 1886 at the People's Theatre, 13 September 1886 at the Third Avenue Theatre.
[2]Not in performance order.

[3]Musical numbers not listed in programs, no libretto or score found.
[4]Originally presented in New York 15 January 1879 at the Standard Theatre for 175 performances. For Synopsis of Scenes and Musical Numbers, see original 1879 production.
[5]Performed twice daily with rotating casts. The vast size of the auditorium permitted a full scale English man o' war surrounded by real water.
[6]First produced in New York in German 19 October 1883 at the Thalia Theatre, and in English 29 October 1883 at the Casino Theatre for 107 performances. For Synopsis of Scenes and Musical Numbers, see original 1883 production.
[7]Previously adapted into English as "The Duke's Motto" by John Brougham August 1870 at Niblo's Garden.

CAST: *Henri d'Lagardère*, Captain in the King's Chasseurs à Cheval: MAURICE BARRYMORE. *Henriquez*, an Armorer of Sagovia: MAURICE BARRYMORE. *Aesop*, the Hunchback: MAURICE BARRYMORE. *Duc de Gonzague*, an Italian noble of French descent: JOSEPH SLAYTOR. *Marquis de Chaverny*, his relative: MAURICE DREW. *Philippe d'Orleans*, Regent of France: G. F. NASH. *Duc de Nevers*, cousin to Gonzague: F. Osborne. *Comte de Navaille*: W. H. BARTHOLOMEW. *Peyrolles*: ROBERT A. FISCHER. *Gentlemen of the Sword (7)*: *Cocardasse*: Harold Forsberg. *Passepoil*: W. H. LYTELL. *Staupitz*: John DeGez. *Jouel*: L. Rubel. *Saldagne*: F. Maxwell. *Pinto*: E. Davidson. *Facuza*: John Manning. *Nathaniel*, Chief of the Gypsy Tribe: J. Murray. *Breant*, Usher to the Regent: T. Deuvil. *Tonio*, an Armorer's Apprentice: N. S. Florence. *Notary*: P. Hughes. *Blanche de Caylus*, secretly married to Duc de Nevers, afterwards wife to Gonzague: HELEN TRACY. *Blanche de Nevers*, her daughter: MARIE FLOYD. *Pepita*, a Gypsy girl: HELEN SEDGWICK. *Martine*, hostess of Auberge: M. Beebe. *Page de Duc de Nevers*: Ray Allen. *Angelique*: J. Dutton. *Madelaine*: Ella Atkinson. *Noblemen, Courtiers, Guards, Gypsies, Pages, Bravos, Valets, & Ballet Specialty*: Mlle. CLARA QUALITZ, Monsieur ARNOLD (KIRALFY), The Great Grotesque Dancer.

Prologue, Scene 1: Interior of an Inn on the Spanish Frontier. (Magnani.) *Scene 2*: Ruins near the Castle of Caylus by Moonlight. (Magnani.) *Scene 3*: The Foss of the Chateau Caylus. (Robecchi and Amable.) *Act 1, Scene 1*: Armorer's Workshop in Segovia. (Magnani.) *Scene 2*: Rocky Pass. (Merry.)*Act 2, Scene 1*: Boudoir in the Palace of Gonzague. (Magnani.) *Scene 2*: The Oratory of the Princess. (Mignani.) *Act 3, Scene 1*: The Little House in the Rue de Chantre. (Mignani.) *Scene 2*: Grand Hall in the Royal Palace. *Scene 3*: The Regent's Fête. (Robecchi and Amable.) *Act 4, Scene 1*: Bridge de la Conferance, old Paris and the Seine by moonlight. (Robecchi and Amable.) *Scene 2*: Antechamber in Gonzague's Palace. (Mignani.) *Scene 3*: Hale in Gonzague's Palace. (Mignani.).

ACT 1
Scene 2
Gypsy Revels
Mlle. C. Qualitz, Mlle. Neuman, Corps de Ballet (Grand Ballet Divertissement composed by Signor Manzotti and produced by Signor Ettore Coppini.)

ACT 3
Scene 3
The Seven Ages (Grand Character Ballet invented, designed and arranged by Imre Kiralfy.)
Infants and Children: Corps de Ballet. *Whining School*: Coryphées. *Lovers*: Eight Secondes Danseuses. *Soldiers*: Corps de Ballet, led by C. Qualitz. *Justice*: Four Secondes. *The Slipper'd Pantaloon*: C. Qualitz, Mons. Arnold. *The Old Age*.
Grand Finale
Entire Ballet Corps

1887.28 BELLMAN

An Operette in Three Acts[8]. Original Viennese libretto by Moritz West and Ludwig Held. English adaptation by J. Cheever Goodwin and William von Sachs. Music by Franz von Suppé. Stage manager, Herbert A. Cripps. Musical director, Adolph Nowak. Scenery by Philip Goatcher and Joseph Clare.[9] Produced by the McCaull Opera Comique Company (John A. McCaull, Proprietor and Manager). Opened 22 August 1887 at Wallack's Theatre and closed 8 October 1887 after 49 performances.[10]

CAST: *Carl Bellman*, Poet: HUBERT WILKE. *Niels Elvegaard*, Herring Dealer: DeWOLF HOPPER. *Gunpowder Manufacturers (2)*: *Otto Funk*: HARRY MACDONOUGH. *Clausen Stein*: JEFFERSON DeANGELIS. *Leaders of the "Caps" (3)*: *Colonel Kolmodin*: CHARLES W. DUNGAN. *Count Blasedruff*: Herbert A. Cripps. *Major Bjorn*: Carl Irving. *Leaders of the "Hats" (3)*: *Puckel*: Grace Seavey. *Killgren*: Florence Willey. *Kulkus*: Tillie Frank. *Burgomaster*: A. Barbara. *Notary*: Lindsay Morison. *Lasse, Goren*, Laplanders (2): Charles H. Jones, Louis Shrader. *Countess Ulla*, the King's Betrothed: MARION MANOLA. *Tronda*, Wife of Elvegaard: LAURA JOYCE-BELL. *Karin*, her daughter: JOSEPHINE KNAPP. *Lutte*, a Laplander: Tolie Pettit. *Pages, Officers, Fishermen, Laplanders, etc.*

Act 1: Street in Stockholm. (Goatcher.)

Act 2: Cave on the borders of the North Sea. (Goatcher.)

Act 3: Hunting Castle on Lake Mälar. (Clare.)

1887.29 A HOLE IN THE GROUND

A Farce Comedy in Three Acts. Play by Charles H. Hoyt. (Music and Lyrics by Charles Zimmerman.) Stage manager, Julian Mitchell. Scenery by Hughson Hawley and Homer F. Emens. Musical director, Charles Zimmerman. Produced by (Charles H.) Hoyt and (Charles H.) Thomas. Opened 12 September 1887 at the 14th Street Theatre and closed 8 October 1887 after 32 performances[11].

CAST: *A Capitalist*: WILLIAM MACK. *A Romantic Young Man*: OTIS HARLAN. *A Stranger*: GEORGE RICHARDS. *A Commercial Tourist*: Alf M. Hampton. *A Second Commercial Tourist*: WILLIAM Mack. *A Station Agent*: FRANK LAWTON. *A Roper-in for Centropolis Hotel*: Alf M. Hampton. *A Roper-in for Grand Union Hotel*: WILLIAM MACK. *A Boy*, anxious to be a R.R. Man: W. H. Jordan. *A League Base Ball Umpire*: JULIAN MITCHELL. *Tailor-Made Girls*: Dudie Douglass, Fannie Stevens, Irene Hernandez. *A Deaf Lady*: Alice Walsh. *A Young Mother*: Helen Leslie. *A Telegraphic Operator*: NANNETTE COMSTOCK. *A Brat*: Daisy Hall. *A Tarrier*: Helen Leslie. *A Second Tarrier*: Alice Walsh. *A Third Tarrier*: Daisy Hall. *The Lady of the Lunch Counter*: FLORA WALSH.

Act 1: Exterior of the Railway Station.

Act 2: Interior of the Railway Station.

Act 3: Same as Act 2.

ACT 1
"The Solid Citizens"
(*Music and Lyrics by* Charles Zimmerman.)
"Fiji Serenade"
Trio from RUDDYGORE
(*Music by* Arthur Sullivan. *Lyrics by* William S. Gilbert.)
"Tailor Made"
(*Music and Lyrics by* Charles Zimmerman.)

ACT 2
"The Traveling Man"
(*Music and Lyrics by* Charles Zimmerman.)
"The Railroad Guide"
(*Poetry by* Charles Hoyt, set to his own misinterpretation of Charles Gounod.)
Medley
(Arranged by C. Zimmerman.)
"(The Great) Ballyhooly (Blue Ribbon Army)" (from MONTE CRISTO, JR., London)
A. Walsh, H. Leslie, D. Hall
(*Music and Lyrics by* Robert Martin.)

ACT 3
"Signal Lights"
(*Music and Lyrics by* Charles Zimmerman.)
Incidental music by Charles Zimmerman

1887.30 THE WILY WEST

A Burlesque (Musical Comedy) in Two Acts. Play by Fred J. Havner, being a satire on Buffalo Bill's Wild West Show. Produced by Fred J. Havner. Opened 12 September 1887 at Harrigan's Park Theatre and closed 1 October 1887 after 24 performances.

CAST: *Arizona Mike*: JOHN T. KELLY. *Willie Golden*, a floorwalker at Macy's: A. J. [Gus] BRUNO. *Nanita*, the Indian maiden: ANNIE WILLIAMS. *Lulu Diamond*: ?. With RUTH DARYL, Blanche Howard, The BURKE BROTHERS, THE DELMANNING BROTHERS.

Act 1: Macy's Store

Act 2: The Wily West.

Act 3: The Wily West.

MUSICAL NUMBERS, SPECIALTIES[12]
Song and Dance Specialty
Delmanning Brothers
Wild West Parade (Finale, Act 1)

[8]May previously have been produced in New York in German in 1887 at the Thalia Theatre.
[9]Storm, Lightning and Cloud Effect in Act 2 by William G. Bent, F. Brewer, Brooklyn Calcium Light Company.
[10]Musical numbers not listed in programs, no libretto or score found.

[11]Scenery and costumes uncredited. Played return engagements 28 November 1887 at the People's Theatre for 8 performances; 7 May 1888 at the Grand Opera House for 8 performances.
[12]No program found; list of musical numbers from reviews, not in performance order.

Delmanning Brothers, Burke Brothers

Songs

A. Williams

Irish Dialect

J. T. Kelly

Negro Act

1887.31 A CIRCUS IN TOWN

Rice's Surprise Party in a Musical and Farcical Comedy in Two Acts. Play by Edward Holst and Woolson Morse, adapted from the Danish. Music composed, selected and arranged by Richard Stahl. Musical director, Richard Stahl. Produced by Edward E. Rice and Henry E. Dixey. Opened 12 September 1887 at the Bijou Opera House and closed 20 September 1887 after 9 performances.

CAST: *Victor Magillicuddy*, who loves and is deceived: JOHN A. MACKAY. *Signor Furioso*, Proprietor of the great Parisian Hippodrome and London Menagerie: W. H. HAMILTON. *Phillip*, a youth of the period: PAUL ARTHUR. *Felix Featherly*, his dude friend: EDWARD GERVAISE. *Old Sleuth*, Private Detective—Motto "We never sleep.": W.C. MANDEVILLE. *Young Sleuth*, Private Detective—Motto "We never sleep": THOMAS LEWIS. *M'lle. Ritta*, Equestrienne Artiste and Queen of the Circus: ADAH RICHMOND. *M'lle. Patrice*, The Empress of the Air: HATTIE DELARO. *Zulu*, the Mermaid who thinks a good deal: Grace Wilson. *Zozo*, the Ceiling Walker, who stutters outrageously: Emma Hanley. *Zampa*, the wonderful flying-trapeze artist, who giggles interminably: JOSIE HALL. *Bridget Motmorenci*, an overworked domestic. A descendant of a line of Kings: RICHARD GOLDEN. *Postman*: Vic Davenport. *Policeman*: E. H. Taylor. *Porter*: Charles Allen. *A Peddler*: Lew Davenport. *A Messenger Boy*: Blanche Chester.

MUSICAL NUMBERS[13]

"When the Glasses Clink" (Drinking Chorus)

"When the Tambourine Is Playing" (Duet)

"Strolling by the Bay" (Song and Dance)

"Flowers ne'er Fading" (Waltz Song)

Musical Medley

"In Jaunty Suits" (Jockey Chorus)

"The Latest Style" (Dude Chorus)

Grand Finale

"When Roses Fade and Die"

(*Music and Lyrics by* Richard Golden.) Piano Solo composed and arranged by Josie Hall

The Davenport Brothers in their Sports of the Arena

1887.32 THE ARABIAN NIGHTS, or, Aladdin's Wonderful Lamp

A Spectacular Burlesque in Three Acts and a Prologue, 7 Scenes[14]. Play by Alfred Thompson. Designed by Alfred Thompson. Scenery by Messrs. Noxon, Albert and Toomey. Costumes by (Henry) Dazian. Ballets directed by Rose Beckett. Musical director, Anthony Reiff. Produced by the Imperial Burlesque Company (David Henderson & Co., Proprietors and Managers). Opened 12 September 1887 at the Standard Theatre and closed 29 October 1887 after 56 performances; re-opened 5 December 1887 at the Academy of Music and closed 24 December 1887 after an additional 24 performances[15]. Total: 80 performances.

CAST: Prologue: *The Caliph Haroun-al-Raschid*: GEORGE CLARE. *The Sultana Scheherazade*: Helen Harrington. *The Magician*: J. H. RYLEY. *Spirit of the Lamp*: Miss Cogan. *Spirit of the Ring*: Miss Pierrepont.

The Drama: *Ski-Hi*, Emperor of Mongolia: FRANK W. HOLLAND. *Princess Balroubadora*, his daughter: CELIE ELLIS. *Tickiky-Nokra*, Grand Vizier: TOM MARTIN. *Chow-Chow*, Magician: J. H. RYLEY. *Klub-Lubba*, Inspector of Police: E. J. CONNELLY. *Kickapoo*, Chow-Chow's Valet: LENA MERVILLE. *Aladdin*, the Hero of the Play: LOIE FULLER. *The Widow Totsicum*, his mother: LILLIE ALLISTON. *Fol-Dol*, her Maid-of-All-Work: Jennie Elliston. *Zal-Am-Bo*, Aladdin's Comrade: ZOE DeVIELLE. *Tambo-Rina*, Lady of Honor: Agnes Burke. *Genie of the Lamp*: Miss Cogan.

Aladdin's Comrades and Pages of the Imperial Court (6): *Fal-Lala*: Rose Franks. *Ni-See*: Rose Wilson. *Lum-Tum*: Linda Barnett. *Chid-Dee*: Linda Linnet. *Loot-Lee*: Miss Chamberlayne. *Tip-Top*: Marie Austin. *Principal Danseuses, Danseur*: ADELE CORNALBA, Mlles. Vivian, Dorst; Mons. Oreste.

Prologue: The Caliph's Alcove.

Act 1, Scene 1: The City of Boodleboo. *Scene 2*: The Dismal Swamp. *Scene 3*: The Crypt of Crimson Crystals.

Act 2, Scene 1: The Widow's Humble Shanty. *Scene 2*: Perpendicular Panorama. *Scene 3*: The Peerless Palace of Parti-Colored Parasols.

Act 3: Exterior of Aladdin's Palace.

PROLOGUE

Chorus of Odalisques; The Telephone Call; A Chestnut; Three Chestnuts; Chow-Chow, the Magician; The Album; Appearance of Aladdin; Chorus.

ACT 1

Scene 1

Chorus of Market People; Enter Aladdin and His Six Companions

"Base Ball"[16] (Song)

L. Fuller, Chorus

Cat Chorus, Magician, Kickapoo, Klub-Lubba, Market People; The Proclamation; The Emperor and the Peerless Princess.

"I'm the Princess" (Song)

C. Ellis, Chorus

A Man in the Bath; Grand Chorus and Finale

Scene 2

Owl's Dance; Terrified Trio; The Magic Tripod; Open Sesame; The Veil of Vapor, or Steam Curtain.

Scene 3

Love Ballad

L. Fuller

Love and Folly

(Grand Divertissement arranged by Miss Rose Beckett)

Dance of Demons; Mashers and Follies; The Treasurers.

Tartar Dance

Mlle. Dorst, Mons. Oreste

ACT 2[17]

Scene 1

"Listen to My Love, Dolly" (Trio)

S. Williams, L. Merville, E. J. Connelly

The Widow and the Magician

Grand Medley and Grotesque Dance

J. H. Rylcy, L. Alliston

Burlesque Pugilism; Magical Change to a Persian Boudoir; A Feast in a Shanty; Sheriffs Become Chairs; The Messenger to England; Return of the Wanderer.

"I'm the Best If I Know, Says the Queen"[18] (Topical Duet)

J. H. Ryley, E. J. Connelly

All of to the Palace.

Scene 2

Cocktail Chorus; Kind Regards.

Scene 3

Song C. Ellis

Aladdin's Triumph; Entrance

Barbaric Ballet

Nautch Dance

Slaves of the Sun (Solo)

A. Cornalba

---

[13]Not necessarily in performance order. Messrs. Holst and Morse attempted to have their names withdrawn from production credits, inasmuch as they had no say in the production or musical numbers.

[14]Inspired by the collection of tales "The Thousand and One Nights" published in English by Edward William Lane. Stage director uncredited.

[15]Played a return engagement 19 December 1887 at the People's Theatre for 8 performances.

[16]Replaced during the run by "Polo" (Song)L. Fuller, Chorus.

[17]Added to Act 2, end of Scene 1 for subsequent tour: "But He Doesn't Know Everything Yet" (Trio), Helen Harrington (Aladdin), William Gill (Klub-Lubba), L. Merville.

[18]Dropped during the run.

Bee Dance
Mlle. Vivian
Prismatic Beauties (Excelsior Variation)
A. Cornalba
Cerulean Seraphs
"The Dolls' Quadrille"
Mlles. Dorst, M. Vivian, L. Merville, Mons. Oreste
Entrance Ensemble

ACT 3
Pages' Serenade ("It Is Not Always May")
R. Franks, Chorus (*Music by* Anthony Reiff.)
Duet
L. Fuller, C. Ellis
Trio
L. Alliston, C. Ellis, R. Franks
Chow-Chow's Disguise
"The Light of Other Days" (Patter Song)
Rapid Transit to Aladdin's Yacht, *Volunteer*
Nautical Ballet
Cutlass Drill; Hornpipe
Chow-Chow's Torpedo Attack; Arrival of the Caliph's Yacht; The Lamp Restored; Grand Chorus.
Grand Transformation Scene
The Coral Caves; The Bridal Veil; The Home of the Lamp.

1887.33 THE MARQUIS

An Operetta in Three Acts. Original French libretto to the Opéra-comique ('Jeanne, Jeannette and Jeanneton') by Clairville and Alfred Delacour. English libretto by Robert Reece, revised for America by Max Freeman. Music by Paul Lacôme. Stage director, Max Freeman. Scenery by Henry E. Hoyt. Costumes by (Henry) Dazian, after designs by Georges Pilotell. Director of music, John J. Braham. Produced by Rudolph Aronson. Opened 19 September 1887 at the Casino Theatre and closed 3 December 1887 after 77 performances.

CAST: *Marie*: BERTHA RICCI. *Mae*: ISABELLE URQUHART. *Jacquette*: SYLVIA GERRISH. *Clorinde*: Rose Wilson. *Florine*: Estelle Morris. *D'Auberval*: Rose Ricci. *Franchette*: Lucy Rivers. *Marion*: LILLIAN GRUBB. *Marquis de Noce*: MARK SMITH. *Prince de Soubise*: COURTICE POUNDS. *LaGrenade*, Sergeant: MAX FREEMAN. *Bailiff*: Arthur W. Tams. *Notary*: Edgar Smith. *Chevalier de Rochefoucauld*: HENRY LEONI. *Courier of Comtesse duBarry*: C. L. Weeks. *Briolet* (the Baker): JAMES T. POWERS.

Act 1, Scene 1: At the Diligence Office, 1760. *Scene 2*: The Cadran Bleu Tavern. Five years later.

Act 2: Boudoir of the Ballerina.

Act 3: At Trianon, with the Illuminated Gardens of Versailles.

MUSICAL NUMBERS[19]
"Compact" (Trio)
I. Urquhart, B. Ricci, L. Grubb
"With Bumpers, Friends, Fill Every Glass" (Drinking Chorus and Cook's Recitative)
J. T. Powers, Chorus
"Not Long Ago" (Chorus and Song of the Sad Lover)
L. Grubb
"As You See, I am One of the Army" (Bouquet Song)
M. Smith
"No! Fate, Why Be Defying?" (Waltz Duet)
L. Grubb, M. Smith
"Like Many Girls" (Song of the Beau)
B. Ricci
"To Sunlight, Love and Song" (Grand Valse) (Duo and Chorus)
C. Pounds, I. Urquhart, Chorus

[19]Musical numbers not listed in programs. List prepared from published piano vocal selection (Richard A. Saalfield, New York, 1887).

1887.34 THE HUMMING BIRD

A Return Engagement of the Musical Comedy in Three Acts[20]. Play by Fred Williams and George Stout. Musical conductor, Selli Simonson. Produced by Salsbury's Troubadours (Frank Maeder, Manager). Opened 23 September 1887 at the Bijou Opera House and closed 15 October 1887 after 27 performances.[21]

CAST: *Mr. Augustus Honeymoon*, an Oyster Packer, the Humming Bird: JOHN WEBSTER. *Mr. Joseph Brass*, Actor and Speculator: FRANK B. BLAIR. *Mr. Robert Rackett*, the Painter of Portraits: LOUIS N. GLOVER. *Jerry McLaughlin*, Policeman and Janitor, one of the "auld sod": Felix Haney. *James*, the customary footman: T. Watkins. *Mr. H. Nibbs*, the Tramp: G. W. Bouvier. *Sally Styles*, the Stage-struck Lady's Maid: NELLIE McHENRY. *Mrs. Fanny Honeymoon*, the much-abused wife: Louise Searle. *Mrs. Matilda Fullalove*, a young widow: ETHEL CORLETTE.

1887.35 LE GRAND MOGOL

An Opéra-bouffe in Three Acts, 4 Scenes, in French[22]. Libretto by Henri Chivot and Alfred Duru. Music by Edmond Audran. Stage manager, Mons. Merle. Costumes by Landolff of Paris. Musical director, Mons. Martin. Produced by Maurice Grau (A. Durand, Manager). Opened 26 September 1887 at the Star Theatre and closed 5 October 1887 after 6 performances in repertory.

CAST: *Irma*: Mlle. JULIA BENNATI. *Princess Bengaline*: Mlle. EUGÉNIE NORDALL. *A Merchant*: Mlle. Caroli. *Kioumy*: Mlle. Tournyaire. *Prince Mignapour*: Mons. GUERNOY. *Nicobar*: Mons. J. MEZIÈRES. *Joquelet*: Mons. MARIS. *Captain Crakson*: Mons. Tony. *The Grand Brahmane*: Mons. Vinchon. *Madras*: Mons. Delafosse. *An Officer*: Mons. Blatsche. *A Merchant*: Mons. Schulte. *Lords and Ladies, Guards of the Palace, etc.*

ACT 1[23]
"Allons! Et point de paresse!" (Choeur)
"Mon nom est Joquelet" (Air)
Mons. Maris
"Je ne veux pas de vous" (Couplets)
Mlle. J. Bennati
"Si le prince m'a-t-on conté" (Légende du Collier Noir)
Mlle. J. Bennati
"Place à Bengaline!" (Choeur)
"J'aime l'éclat des cours" (Couplets)
Mlle. E. Nordall
"Je voudrais rèvèler à la nature" (Duetto)
Mlle. E. Nordall, Mons. Guernoy
"Si j'étais un petit serpent" (Romance)
Mons. Guernoy
"Pour voir Irma" (Final)
"Allons, petit serpent" (Chanson du Kiri-Kiribi)
Mlle. J. Bennati

ACT 2
Scene 1
"Si le prince se marie" (Trio bouffe)
Mlle. E. Nordall, Messrs. Tony, Mezières
"Qu'on me laisse agir à mon gré" (Couplets)
Mlle. E. Nordall
"Dans ce beau palais de Delhi" (Duetto)
Mlle. J. Bennati, Mons. Mari
"Un antique et fort viel adage" Couplets du chou et de la rose)
Mons. Guernoy
"Nous sommes prêtresses d'Indra" (Choeur)

[20]First produced in New York 7 February 1887 at the Star Theatre for 21 performances, billed as a Farce Comedy. For Synopsis of Scenes, see original production. Reviewers remarked that the musical specialties were all different, and a marked improvement over the first engagement.
[21]Costumes and scenery uncredited.
[22]Previously produced in New York in an English adaptation as "The Snake Charmer" 29 October 1881 for 64 performances in two engagements.
[23]Musical numbers not listed in programs. List prepared from published French piano vocal score (Choudens Père et fils, Paris, 1884).

"L'indolente panthère" (Chanson indoue)
Mlle. E. Nordall
"Sur l'ordre de sa hautesse" (Choeur)
"Dans nos guinguettes de Paris" (Couplets du vin de suresne)
Mlle. J. Bennati
"Le jour vient de finir" (Final)

Scene 2
"Gardiens du palais" (Choeur)
"Au moment de te marier" (Couplets des conseils)
Mons. Mari
"Silence! le voici" (Final)

ACT 3
"Après les pénibles voyages" (Choeur des voyageurs)
"Petite soeur il faut sécher tes larmes" (Mélodie)
Mons. Mari
"Par tour le pays je chemine" (Chanson)
Mons. Guernoy
"O ma maîtresse bien aimée" (Duo)
Mlle. J. Bennati, Mons. Guernoy
"A la femme en naissent" (Couplets)
Mlle. Nordall
"Ah! Pour moi quelle heureuse chance" (Quatuor)
Mlle. J. Bennati, Mons. Guernoy, Messrs. Tony, Maris
"D'ou vient un pareil tapage" (Final)

SUPPLEMENT
Ballet des jongleurs (Valse et final)

1887.36 SERMENT D'AMOUR

An Opéra-bouffe in Three Acts, in French[24]. Libretto by Maurice Ordonneau. Music by Edmond Audran. Stage manager, Mons. Merle. Costumes by Landolff of Paris. Musical director, Mons. Martin. Produced by Maurice Grau (A. Durand, Manager). Opened 29 September 1887 at the Star Theatre and closed 8 October 1887 after 3 performances in repertory.

CAST: *Rosette*: Mlle. MARY PIRARD. *La Marquise*: Mlle. ROSINA STANI. *Marion*: Mlle. EUGÉNIE NORDALL. *Javotte*: Mlle. Caroli. *Francine*: Mlle. Tournyaire. *Lancelot*: Mlle. Sebert. *Marcelin*: Mlle. Caroli. *Theodule*: Mlle. Dermond. *Andre*: Mlle. Guillaume. *Gavaudan*: Mons. J. MEZIÈRES. *Le Compte*: Mons. MARIS. *Grivolin*: Mons. STEPHEN. *Martial*: Mons. Sablon. *Bel Azur*: Mons. Vinchon. *Un Officier*: Mons. Blatche. *Un Bourgeois*: Mons. Delafosse. *Peasants, Officers, Soldiers.*

ACT 1[25]
"De la vieille forêt discrète" (Introduction)
Chorus
"Toi, qui me trouvais autrefois" (Couplets des reproches)
Mlle. E. Nordall
"Vive Monseigneur! (Choeur et scènes)
"Trois joli's fillettes" ("Holà, vertinguette!!) (Chanson de Vertinguette)
M. Pirard
"Mam'zell' non, vous n'et's pas parfaite" (Couplets de Grivolin)
Mons. Stephen
"Quand par les verts chemins" (Duo du Serment d'Amour)
M. Pirard, Mons. Maris
"Je veux, c'est là ma seule loi" (Couplets d l'intendant)
Mons. J. Mezières
"Il parlait d'une voix si tendre" (Mélodie)
M. Pirard
"Il faut savoir broyer son coeur" (Trio Bouffe)
M. Pirard, R. Stani, Mon. J. Mezières
"Vous savez ce qu'on dit?" (Final)

ACT 2
"Le cabaret le meilleur de la ville" (Choeur de l'hôtellerie)
"C'est aujord'hui Dimanche" (Couplets des petits clercs et de Marion)
Mlle. E. Nordall, Chorus
"Voici Madame Grivolin" (Choeur)
"J'entre comme une reine" (Ariette)
M. Pirard
"Vous êtes surpris, mes amis" (Couplets du beau mari)
Mlle. Nordall
"Holà! maître hôtelier" (Choeur)
"Nous voici dans la bonne ville d'Orleans" (Couplets militaires)
Mons. Maris
"Pour plaire, en nos ragoûts" (Couplets de la cuisine)
Mons. J. Mezières
"Qu'ai-je vu?" (Ensemble)
"Un rossignol dans un buisson" (Duo de la fauvette et du rossignol)
M. Pirard, Mons. Maris
"Daphnis se lamente" (Idylle)
R. Stani, Mons. Stephen
"Il est plus de midi" (Final)

ACT 3
"Quand on termine la toilette" (Choeur de la toilette)
"Par les chemins ombreux" (Rondeau et romance)
M. Pirard, Mons. Maris
"Qu'as-tu dit?" (Trio)
M. Pirard, Mlle. E. Nordall, Mons. Mari
"Pour la chapelle qu'on s'apprête" (Choeur de la chapelle)
"Eh quoi! Vous si sévère" (Duetto)
M. Pirard, Mons. J. Mezières
"Nous revenons de la chapelle" (Final)

1887.37 LA FILLE DE MADAME ANGOT

A Revival of the Opéra-comique in Three Acts, in French[26]. Libretto by Clairville, Paul Siraudin and Victor Koning. Music by Charles Lecocq. Stage manager, Mons. Merle. Costumes by Landolff of Paris. Musical director, Mons. Martin. Produced by Maurice Grau (A. Durand, Manager). Opened 3 October 1887 at the Star Theatre and closed 12 October 1887 after 5 performances in repertory.

CAST: *Mlle. Lange*: Mlle. JULIA BENNATI. *Clairette*: Mlle. MARY PIRARD. *Ange Pitou*: Mons. GUERNOY. *Pomponnet*: Mons. Stephen. *La Rivaudiere*: Mons. Tony. *Louchard*: Mons. Sablon. *Trenitz*: Mons. Desclos. *Cadet*: Mons. Duchateau. *Buteau*: Mons. Vinchon. *Guillaume*: Mons. Delafosse. *Un Incroyable*: Mons. Schulte. *Un Officier*: Mons. Brassine. *Amaranthe*: Mlle. Stani. *Javotte*: Mlle. L. Uzzini. *Cydalise*: Mlle. Caroly. *Mlle. Delaunay*: Mlle. Dermont. *Hersilie*: Mlle. Sibert. *Babet*: Mlle. Dass. *Therese*: Mlle. Tournyaire. *Herbelin*: Mlle. Vandamme.

1887.38 LA MASCOTTE

A Revival of the Opéra-comique in Three Acts, in French[27]. Libretto by Henri Chivot and Alfred Duru. Music by Edmond Audran. Stage manager, M. Merle. Costumes by Landolff of Paris. Musical director, Mons. Martin. Produced by Maurice Grau (A. Durand, Manager). Opened 6 October 1887 at the Star Theatre and closed 11 October 1887 after 3 performances in repertory.

CAST: *Bettina*: Mlle. JULIA BENNATI. *Fiametta*: Mlle. EUGÉNIE NORDALL. *Angelo*: Mlle. Sibert. *Marco*: Mlle. Caroly. *Carlo*: Mlle. Dermont. *Luidgi*: Mlle. Dass. *Paola*: Mlle. Caroly. *Francesca*: Mlle. Guillaume. *Antonia*: Mlle. Vandamme. *(Le Roi) Laurent XVII*: Mons. J. MEZIÉRES. *Pippo*: Mons. MARIS. *Fritelline*: Mons. GUERNOY. *Rocco*: Mons. TONY. *Le Sergent*: Mons. Vinchon. *Matheo*: Mons. Sablon. *Un Paysan*: Mons. Schulte. *Premier Soldat*: Mons. Blatche. *Deuxieme Soldat*: Mons. Tonda.

---

[24]Billed as an opéra comique in France.
[25]Musical numbers not listed in programs. List prepared from published French piano vocal score (Choudens Père et fils, Paris, 1886).

[26]First produced in New York in French 25 August 1873 at the Broadway Theatre in repertory. For Synopsis of Scenes and Musical Numbers, see original 1873 production.
[27]First produced in New York in French 24 September 1883 at the Fifth Avenue Theatre for 6 performances in repertory. For Synopsis of Scenes and Musical Numbers, see original 1883 production. No program found for this revival.

1887.39 THE LEATHER PATCH

A Revival of the Comedy in Three Acts, 7 Scenes[28]. Play (and lyrics) by Edward Harrigan. Music by David Braham. Staged by Edward Harrigan. Dancing under the supervision of M. J. Bradley. Scenery by Charles W. Witham. Mechanism by William Vail. Properties by Louis Filber. Gas effects by William Whallen. Musical director, David Braham. Produced by Edward Harrigan. Opened 10 October 1887 at Harrigan's Park Theatre and closed 5 November 1887 after 32 performances.

CAST: *Jeremiah McCarthy*, undertaker: EDWARD HARRIGAN. *Jefferson Putnam*: JOHN WILD. *Caroline Hyer*: DAN COLLYER. *Airy McCafferty*: M. J. Bradley. *Linda Corncover*: JOSEPH SPARKS. *Judge Herman Doebler*: HARRY FISHER. *Counselor Delancy Wriggle*: Charles Sturges. *Levy Hyer*: Peter Goldrich. *Jimmy*, the Kid: RICHARD QUILTER. *Dennis McCarthy*: George Merritt. *Dr. Noah Corncover*: William West. *Moses Cohen*, with song: JOSEPH SPARKS. *Roderick McQuade*: JOHN SPARKS. *Joseph Levy*: Mr. Decker. *Aaron Levy*: James McCullough. *Mr. Doublerow*: James McCullough *Geoghen*, a hearse driver: Charles Coffey. *Officer Dunlap*: Charles Coffey. *Sailor*: Mr. Burke. *Thomas Conroy*: George L. Stout. *Soldier*: Robert Snyder. *Parsley Allsnow*: Mr. Burke. *Madeline McCarthy*: ANNIE YEAMANS. *Libby O'Dooley*: AMY LEE. *Mrs. O'Dooley*: Emily Yeamans. *Rachel Cohen*: Emily Yeamans. *Nellie Conroy*: Annie Langdon. *Jennie Crimmons*: Kate Langdon. *Wedding Guests (6)*: *Jennie*: Minnie Richards. *Kitty*: Adele Fielding. *Mamie*: Annie Landor. *Julie*: Annie Spencer. *Zachie*: Ray Johnson. *Lizzie*: May Trompton. The Ensemble made up from the Auxiliary Corps.

1887.40 MY SWEETHEART/ THE RING AND THE KEEPER

A Double Bill of a Musical Comedy preceded by an Operetta, each in One Act. Stage manager, R. A. Roberts. Musical director, Samuel Waas. Produced by Minnie Palmer (C. D. Hess, Personal direction). Opened 10 October 1887 at the 14th Street Theatre and closed 22 October 1884 after 14 performances.

THE RING AND THE KEEPER An Operetta by J. P. Wooler; music by Montgomery. CAST: *Lady Constance*, in the disguise of her maid, afterwards her page: MINNIE PALMER. *Sir Philip Aylmer*, disguised as a gamekeeper: R. A. ROBERTS.

MY SWEETHEART A Revised Version of the Musical Comedy by William Gill[29], CAST: *Tina*, a Prospective Heiress (her original creation): MINNIE PALMER. *Tony Faust*, a Prospective Heir: R. A. ROBERTS. *Joe Shotwell*, a Broken-Down Sport (his original character): T. J. HAWKINS. *Dudley Harcourt*, a Dude: THOMAS WEBBER. *Dr. Oliver*, a Friend: Hal. Clarendon. *Farmer Hatzell*, not in love with work: Ben. Hendricks. *George Washington Snow*, a Servant: C. W. Allison. *Miss Louisa Fleeter*, an Adventuress: Carrie Reynolds. *Mrs. Hatzel*, the Farmer's Loving Wife: Jane Gray. *Papa's Baby Boy*: Himself. *Daisy Hatzell*: Miss Ida.

1887.41 FATINITZA

A Revival of the Opéra-comique in Three Acts, in French[30]. (Original Viennese libretto by F. Zell and Richard Genée, based on the libretto to 'La Circassienne' by Eugène Scribe. French adaptation by Alfred Delacour and Victor Wilder.) Music by Franz von Suppé. Stage manager, M. Merle. Costumes by Landolff of Paris. Musical director, M. Martin. Produced by Maurice Grau (A. Durand, Manager). Opened 14 October 1887 at the Star Theatre and closed 15 October 1887 after 3 performances in repertory.

CAST: *Wladimir (Fatinitza)*: Mlle. JULIA BENNATI. *Lydia*: Mlle. EUGÉNIE NORDALL. *La Massalja*: Mlle. Stani. *Dimitri*: Mlle. Aiguillon. *Ivan*: Mlle. Caroli. *Fedor*: Mlle. Vandamme. *Nikifor*: Mlle. Dass. *Nursidah*: Mlle. Sebert. *Zuleika*: Mlle. Caroli. *Diona*: Mlle. Dermond. *Bezika*: Mlle. Uzzini. *Julien Dubois*: Mons. GUERNOY. *Tchitchatcheff*: Mons. J. MEZIÉRES. *Izzet Pacha*: Mons. Tony. *Steipna*: Mons. Stephen. *Mustapha*: Mons. Declos. *Wasil Andrenowitz*: Mons. Sablon. *Osip Waseilowitch*: Mons. Blatche. *An Adjutant*: Mons. Delafosse. *Wuika*: Mons. Vinchon.

1887.42 THE OLD HOMESTEAD

A Return Engagement of the Rural Melodrama in Four Acts[31]. Play by Denman Thompson and George W. Ryer. Settings by Gaspard Maeder and William Schaeffer. Produced by Denman Thompson. Opened 17 October 1887 at Niblo's Garden, closing 12 November 1887 after 32 performances; moved 21 November 1887 to the 14th Street Theatre and closed 24 December 1887 after an additional 40 performances. Total: 72 performances.[32]

CAST [in order of appearance]: *Joshua Whitcomb*: DENMAN THOMPSON. *Cy Prime*: GEORGE A. BEANE. *Happy Jack*: WALTER GALE. *Eb. Ganzey*: J. L. MORGAN. *Frank Hopkins*: CHAUNCEY OLCOTT. *John Freeman*: FRANK THOMPSON. *Aunt Matilda Whitcomb*: LOUISA MORSE. *Rickety Ann*: ANNIE THOMPSON. *Miss Annie Hopkins*: Lillian Stone. *Miss Nellie Freeman*: May Jimenez. *Maggie O'Flaherty*: Minnie Luckstone. *Henry Hopkins*: Walter Lennox, Sr. *Judge Patterson*: Gus Kammerlee. *Francois Fogarty*: Frank Mara. *Mrs. Henry Hopkins*: Venie Thompson. *Miss Annie Hopkins*: Lillian Stone. *Miss Nellie Patterson*: Annie Thompson. *Jack Hazzard*: Walter Gale. *Reuben Whitcomb*: Harry Earle. *Hoboken Terror*: J. L. Morgan. *One of the Finest*: Tom Law. *U.S. Letter Carrier*: Charles R. Farrar. *Len Holbrook*: C. M. Richardson. *Pat Clancy*: Frank Mara. *Mrs. Murdock*: Venie Thompson.

1887.43 THE CORSAIR

A Spectacular Byronical, Operatic Burlesque or Opera-bouffe in Three Acts. Libretto adapted from the early English and other sources[33] (by Edward E. Rice). Music by Edward E. Rice and John J. Braham. Invented by and produced under the direction of Henry E. Dixey. Scenery by John A. Thompson and H. L. Reid. Costumes designed by Carrie E. Perkins. Musical director, Gustave A. Kerker. Produced by Edward E. Rice and Henry E. Dixey. Opened 18 October 1887 at the Bijou Theatre and closed 17 March 1888 after 180 performances[34].

CAST: *Conrad the Corsair*, familiarly known as "The Scourge of the Seas," ironical and Byronical: ANNIE SUMMERVILLE. *Birbanto*, his second in command, but very far from being anything in orders: FRANK DAVID. *Seyd Pacha*, a Turk, in fact, a turbaned Turk: Signor J. C. BROCCOLINI. *Syng Smaul*, the Pacha's Major Domo, Footman, Horseman and Drago(on) Man: GEORGE A. SCHILLER. *Yussuf*, a renegade Slave Dealer with a job lot of Circassian beauties; Sir, cash in and take your choice: Edward Morris. *Hassan*, a boatswain and a base'un: Carrie Behr. *Ganem*, Captain of the Pacha's guard: KATE UART. *Ali*, *Ahmed*, his lieutenants: Jennie Bartine, Maud Waldermere. *Bachsheesh*, *Mustapha*, two corsairs who put on no fine airs: David P. Steele, Harry Mahoney. *Medora*, the original Maid of Athens, niece and ward of Yussuf; not the first pledge entrusted to an uncle: LOUISE MONTAGUE. *Gulnare*, the Pacha's favorite, the reigning beauty, though she's knowing: CLARA LANE. *Zuliema*, ex-favorite, ex-asperated, a light of other days, a little faded: ROSA COOKE. *Fatima*, *Bebe*, attendants of the Pacha: May Danforth, Lila Blow. *Animah*, *Fetnab*, *Zobeide*, Belles of the Harem, though not of the harem-scare'em sort: Ida Howell, Ruth Stetson, Blanche Eden. *Leilah*, the little fawn, *Otoldi*, *Ualda*, *Serena*, Dancing Slaves: Ameah Glovina, Florence Baker, May Steele, Lillie Howard. *The Mule Fling*, a whimsical bit of nonsense: Messrs. George Cohen, Fred Turner. *Slaves*, *Odalisques and Almas*: Misses Eva Shaler, May Hanley, Polly Winner, Estelle Clinton, Maude Emerson, Anna L. Jackson, Emily Beaumont, Cora Weigund, Myra Smith, Xesia Cortlandt, Laura Curtis, Nellie Osborne, Annie Winn, Alice Osborne, Kitty Ford, Dixie Chapman, Addie Lee, Florence Latebe, Blanche Thornton, Evelyn Astor. *Corsairs and Guards*: Messrs. Frank Baldwin, Charles Templeton, Dan Good, F. L. Hill, A. Gradwell, Harry Mahoney, Louis McGowan, Leo Lawrence, Harry Roberts, Gus Kremer, Otto Heilig, James H. Innes.

Act 1, Scene 1: Market Place in Stamboul and Oriental Slave Bazaar. (Thompson.) *Scene 2*: On the Beach. (Thompson.) *Scene 3*: On board the "*Rove of the Seas.*" (Reid.)

[28]First produced in New York 15 February 1886 at the Park Theatre for 88 performances. For Synopsis of Scenes and Musical Numbers, see original 1886 production.

[29]First produced in New York 18 September 1882 at the Fourteenth Street Theatre for 8 performances. For Synopsis of Scenes, see original 1882 production.

[30]French language premiere in New York. Previously produced in New York in German 14 April 1879 at the Germania Theatre for in repertory.

[31]First produced in New York 10 January 1887 at the 14th Street Theatre for 155 performances. For Synopsis of Scenes, see original 1887 production.

[32]Stage director, costumes uncredited. No musical numbers listed in programs.

[33]Suggested by Lord Alfred Byron's poem. In early February 1888 the Clipper announces that Louis Harrison is rewriting and reconstructing the production.

[34]Played a return engagement 25 March 1889 at the Grand Opera House for 8 performances.

Act 2, Scene 1: Pirate grotto by the seashore. (Reid.) *Scene 2*: A street in Stamboul. (Reid.) *Scene 3*: The Beautiful Gardens of the Pacha. (Thompson.)

Act 3, Scene 1: The Harem and the Luxurious Home of the Pacha. (Reid.) *Scene 2*: Another Street in Stamboul. (Thompson.) *Scene 3*: Bird's eye view of Stamboul by moonlight. The Palace of Pearl. (Thompson.)

ACT 1

"Corsairs Bold" (Opening Chorus)

"I'm a dashing pirate"[35] (Solo and Chorus)
A. Summerville, Chorus

"Buckets of Gore" (Song with Dance)
F. David

"Who would be beautiful to be sold?" (Chorus of Slaves, Solo)
E. Morris, Chorus

Turkish march

"Birds in the bush" (Duet)
A. Summerville, L. Montague

"He's afraid! Must dissemble" (Concerted Finale of Scene)

"Let's scuttle" (Duet song and dance) E. Morris, F. David

"Sailing Away o'er the deep blue sea"[36]
Sailors' Chorus

"Oh, now nice" (Barcarolle)
L. Montague

"Sparkling Champagne" (Song and Chorus)
F. David

"Take heed, beware" (Finale)

ACT 2

"When in the west the day is declining" (Waltz Song)
L. Montague

"Rosy morn"[37] (Song with dance)
A. Summerville, L. Montague

"Upon the sea" (Eccentric Chorus, Solo)
F. David, Chorus

Grand March of the Amazons

Opening waltz to Scene 3[38]

"They say that I am growing wrinkled" (Ballad and Waltz)
R. Cooke

"Beware you saucy minx" (Dagger Song)
L. Montague

"Bright wine and love" (Drinking Song)
A. Summerville

"On guard, strike hard"
Chorus

"Up, Corsairs, have at them" (Concerted Finale)

ACT 3

Vocal Waltz and Opening of the Scene[39]

"Fear not, my love"[40] (Romanza)
L. Montague

"The old love"[41] (Ballad)
J. C. Broccolini

"It doesn't agree with me" (Topical Song)
F. David

"Once upon a time" (Song)
C. Lane

"The Moonlight Kiss" (Musical Morceau, Octette)

"Yes, she is a darling" (Duet)
A. Summerville, L. Montague

The Mule Fling

Grand Transformation and Finale

[35]Composed expressly for this presentation.
[36]Composed expressly for this presentation.
[37]Composed expressly for this presentation.
[38]Composed expressly for this presentation.
[39]Composed expressly for this presentation.
[40]Composed expressly for this presentation.
[41]Composed expressly for this presentation.

1887.44

DOROTHY

A Comic Opera in Three Acts[42]. Libretto by B. C. Stephenson. Music by Alfred Cellier. Ballets arranged by Rose Beckett. Scenery by Walter Burridge, Hughson Hawley, Homer Emens. Costumes designed by Mme. Martens. Director of music, Antonio DeNovellis. Produced by James C. Duff, by arrangement with Henry J. Leslie. Opened 5 November 1887 at the Standard Theatre and closed 17/24? December 1887 after 43 performances[43].

CAST: *Squire Bantam*: WILLIAM HAMILTON. *Geoffrey Wilder*: EUGENE OUDIN. *Harry Sherwood*: JOHN E. BRAND. *John Tuppitt*: F. Boudinot. *Lurcher*: HARRY PAULTON. *Tom Strutt*: J. E. Nash. *Dorothy Bantam*: LILLIAN RUSSELL. *Lydia Hawthorne*: AGNES STONE. *Mrs. Privett*: ROSE LEIGHTON. *Phyllis (Tuppitt)*: MARIE HALTON. *Chorus of Hop-Pickers, Peasants, Guests, Bridesmaids, etc*: Chorus of 50.

The action takes place in the county of Kent, (England), 1740.

Act 1: The Hop Gardens. (Burridge.)

Act 2: Chanticleer Hall. (Hawley.)

Act 3: The Round Coppice. (Emens.)

ACT 1[44]

"Lads and lasses round about the hop pole trip" (Chorus and Ballet)
M. Halton, J. E. Nash, F. Boudinot, Chorus

"Be wise in time, O Phyllis mine" (Song and Trio)
L. Russell, A. Stone, M. Halton

"We're sorry to delay you" (Quartet)
L. Russell, A. Stone, E. Oudin, J. E. Brand

"With such a dainty dame none can compare" (Ballad)
E. Oudin

"A father's joy and pride they are" (Quintet)
L. Russell, A. Stone, E. Oudin, J. E. Brand, F. Boudinot

"I am the Sheriff's faithful man" (Song and Trio)
H. Paulton, E. Oudin, J. E. Brand

"You swear to be good and true" (Quartet)
L. Russell, A. Stone, E. Oudin, J. E. Brand

"Under the pump" (Chorus with Solo)
Chorus, H. Paulton

"Now take your seats at table spread" (Finale)
Principals, Chorus

ACT 2[45]

Introduction and Country Dance

"Though born a man of high degree" (Song)
E. Oudin, Chorus

Entrance Dorothy and Lydia

Graceful Dance

"Contentment I give you" (Song)
W. Hamilton

"To bed so soon, Good night" (Septet and Chorus)
L. Russell, A. Stone, E. Oudin, J. E. Brand, H. Paulton, W. Hamilton

"One moment pray" (Recitative and Quartet)
L. Russell, A. Stone, E. Oudin, J. E. Brand

"I stand at your threshold sighing" (Song)
J. E. Brand

"Are you sure . . . " (trio)
E. Oudin, J. E. Brand, W. Hamilton

[42]Originally billed in London as a comedy opera. No stage director credited.
[43]Played a return engagement 16 April 1888 at the Grand Opera House for 8 performances.
[44]Musical numbers not listed in programs. List prepared from published English piano vocal score (Chappell & Co, London, 1886).
[45]Interpolated by Stephenson and Cellier in the third week of the London run and performed in New York, per C. Hayden Coffin's autobiography (Hayden Coffin's Book, Alston Rivers Ltd., London, 1930): "Queen of My Heart," E. Oudin. "It was introduced into the second act in the baronial hall, sung as a serenade outside Miss Dorothy's door, when the rest of the household were supposed to have retired for the night."

"What noise was that" (Chorus)
L. Russell, A. Stone, E. Oudin, J. E. Brand, W. Hamilton, H. Paulton
"Hark forward! Hark forward! Away!" (Finale)
Principals, Chorus

ACT 3
Ballet
"Dancing is not what it used to be" (Old Woman's Chorus)
Chorus
"The time has come" (Ballad)
M. Halton
"What joy untold" (Septet and Chorus)
M. Halton, J. E. Nash, F. Boudinot, Chorus
"You swear to be good and true" (Finale)
Principals, Chorus

1887.45 CORDELIA'S ASPIRATIONS

A Return Engagement of the Comedy in Three Acts[46]. Play (and lyrics) by Edward Harrigan. Music by David Braham. Staged by Edward Harrigan. Musical director, David Braham. Produced by Edward Harrigan. Opened 7 November 1887 at Harrigan's Park Theatre and closed 19 November 1887 after 16 performances.

CAST: *Dan Mulligan*: EDWARD HARRIGAN. *Rebecca Allup*: DAN COLLYER. *Palestine Puter*: Peter Goldrich. *Planxty McFudd*: HARRY A. FISHER. *Walsingham McSweeney*: M. J. Bradley. *Ridgeway*: Charles Sturgis. *Gustavus Lochmuller*: JOSEPH SPARKS. *Cordelia Mulligan*: ANNIE YEAMANS. *Diana McFudd*: Amy Lee. *Mrs. Lochmuller*: Mamie Richards. *Ellen McFudd*: Annie Langdon. *Rosey McFudd*: Emily Yeamans. *Mrs. Diggins*: Miss Leslie. *Mulvey*: Charles Coffey. *Mr. Bowser*: George Merritt. *Dunbar*: William Merritt. *Clerk*: George L. Stout. *Simpson Primrose*: JOHN WILD. *Tommy*: Master John Burke. *Policeman*: J. McCullough. *Mrs. Brown*: Gertie Tuttle. *Mrs. Risley*: Mattie Winn. *Annetta*: Fannie Knight. *Mrs. Buchheister*: Kate Langdon. *Mrs. Crumps*: Emma Leslie.

The Uncle Tom Combination: *Jim Grace*: Peter Goldrich. *Mr. Dangerfield*: William West. *Mr. Clinton*: John Burke. *Topsy*: John Sparks. *Billy Kersands*: Joe Williamson. *Cal Hicks*: RICHARD QUILTER. *Jim Bland*: Dan Burke. *Sam Lucas*: Robert Gordon. *Joe Hardhead*: Charles Coffey. *Jay Weldon*: Jay Decker. *Emigrants, Officials, Policemen, Hackmen, etc.*

1887.46 THE DEACON'S DAUGHTER

A Revival of the Musical Comedy (Comedy-Drama) in Four Acts[47]. Play by A. C. Gunter. Stage manager, M. C. Daly. Musical director, Frank Webber. Produced by Annie Pixley (Smiley Walker, Business Manager). Opened 7 November 1887 at the Grand Opera House and closed 12 November 1887 after 8 performances; returned 23 January 1888 at the 14th Street Theatre and closed 28 January 1888 after 8 performances.[48]

CAST: *Ruth Homewebb*, "Nom de Theatre," Mabel Hawthorne, the leading juvenile at the Criterion Theatre: ANNIE PIXLEY. *Isaiah Jubal Homewebb*, of Pautukset, Connecticut, "The Deacon": M. C. DALY. *Charley Lawton*, a young New York business man: W. C. Reynier. *Irving DeVere Chillington*, a club man with artistic tendencies. The star of amateur theatricals: Frederic Sackett. *Signor Malatesta Tomkins*, a painter of the Impressionists' school: R. J. DUSTAN. *Squire Hiram Slimbergast*, who goes to theatres in New York: Daniel Gilfether. *Amadie*, Signor Tomkins' assistant: W. F. Macnichol. *Mrs. Rachel Homewebb*, the Deacon's Wife: Annie Douglass. *Mrs. Dashington Browne*, a Society Conundrum: Annie Barclay. *Mary O'Dougherty*, Ruth's maid: May Thompson.

[46]First produced in New York 5 November 1883 at the Theatre Comique for 176 performances. For Synopsis of Scenes and Musical Numbers, see original 1883 production.
[47]First produced in New York 25 April 1887 at the Union Square Theatre for 43 performances. For Synopsis of Scenes and Musical Numbers, see original 1887 production.
[48]Cast list prepared from 14th Street Theatre engagement. Also played for one week each 13 February 1888 at the Windsor Theatre, 19 November 1888 at the Grand Opera House, 24 December 1888 at the Star Theatre, 11 February 1889 at the Windsor Theatre.

1887.47 THE BEGUM

A Hindoo Comic Opera in Two Acts. Libretto by Harry B. Smith. Music by Reginald DeKoven. Stage manager, H. A. Cripps. Scenery by Joseph Clare. Costumes designed under the personal supervision of Mathilde Cottrelly. Mechanism by Niel MacGiehan. Orchestra under the direction of Adolph Nowak. Produced by the McCaull Opera Company (John A. McCaull, Proprietor and Manager). Opened 21 November 1887 at the Fifth Avenue Theatre and closed 10 December 1887 after 22 performances.[49]

CAST: *The Begum of Oude*, a monarch matrimonially inclined: MATHILDE COTTRELLY. *Howja-Dhu*, her Prime Minister: DeWOLF HOPPER. *Pooteh-Wehl*, his son: EDWIN HOFF. *Klahm-Chowdee*, a Private Soldier: HUBERT WILKE. *Myhnt-Jhuleep*, the Court Astrologer: DIGBY BELL. *Aminah*, his daughter: MARION MANOLA. *Jhust-Naut*, the Court Jester: JEFFERSON DeANGELIS. *Asch-Khart*, an officer in the royal household: HARRY MACDONOUGH. *Naomouna*, a fortune teller: LAURA JOYCE BELL. *Damayanti*, a Nautch dancer: ANNIE MEYERS. *Nieces of the Begum (4)*: *Tafeh*: Josephine Knapp. *Kahra-Mel*: Nina Bertini. *Nougat*: Grace Seavey. *Bon Bon*: Paula Franko. *Chorus of Nautch Girls, Officers of the Army of Oude*.

The action takes place in Northern India.

Act 1: The Begum's Palace, interior.

Act 2: On the banks of the Ganges.

MUSICAL NUMBERS[50]
Song (When war began I said)
D. Hopper, Chorus
Duet (What though I be attired in warlike raiment)
D. Hopper, D. Bell
Romanza (Love is pain or love is pleasure)
E. Hoff
Duet (I love! At last I've met my fate)
M. Manola, E. Hoff
Snake Charmer's Song (Amid the moss the cobra lies)
M. Manola
Ballad ('Tis the old, old story)
M. Manola
Duet (In the carnage of a scrimmage)
J. DeAngelis, H. MacDonough
Quartette (We think, and minds salubrious)
A. Meyers, L. J. Bell, D. Bell, D. Hopper
"Hear ye the birds"
"Do you remember?"

1887.48 PETE

A Domestic Drama of the South in Four Acts. Play (and lyrics) by Edward Harrigan[51]. Music by David Braham. Staged by Edward Harrigan. Dancing under the supervision of M. J. Bradley. Scenery by Charles W. Witham. Mechanical effects by William Vail. Gas effects by John Whalen. Musical director, David Braham. Produced by Edward Harrigan. Opened 22 November 1887 at Harrigan's Park Theatre and closed 21 April 1888 after 175 performances.

CAST: *Pete*: EDWARD HARRIGAN. *Gaspar Randolph*: JOHN WILD. *Vi'let*: DAN COLLYER. *Dr. Clifford*: Frank E. Aiken. *Victor Lemaire*: HARRY A. FISHER. *Colonel Coolidge*: Marcus Moriarty. *Emanuel Shadrach*: William West. *Alderman Brannigan*: JOSEPH SPARKS. *Squire Bainbridge*: George Merritt. *B. Jabez Bender*: Charles Sturges. *Major Steel*: George L. Stout. *Whyland Whipple*: JOHN SPARKS. *Hampton Bailey*: Peter Goldrich. *Ruth Callowfoot*: RICHARD QUILTER. *Sunset Freckles*: Michael J. Bradley. *Mate*: James McCullough. *Auntie Charlotte*: Dan Burke. *Enos Clinker*: James Burke. *Sampson Flyhigh*: Joseph Williamson. *Rasmus*: Robert Gordon. *Susie Rivers*: John Decker. *Laz Fisheye*: Robert Snyder. *The Blossom Quartette*: Messrs. Francis, Spearman, Dickson, Rennie. *Mary Duffy*: ANNIE YEAMANS. *Marie Coolidge*: Esther Williams. *Winnie Coburg*: Amy Lee. *Mary Morgan*: Lavinia Shannon. *Mirandy*: Annie Wilson. *Little May*: Katie Patterson.

[49]Musical numbers not listed in programs.
[50]Musical numbers not listed in programs. List prepared from published piano vocal gems (J. M. Armstrong Co, Philadelphia, 1887); last two titles published by Stern.
[51]According to the Clipper, this play was suggested by an earlier sketch by Harrigan called 'Slavery Days' (1876).

Guests of Blossom Lady Hotel: Annie Langdon, Emily Yeamans, Minnie Richards, Kate Langdon, Emma Leslie, Fanny Knight, Mattie Winn, Gertie Tuthill.

Act 1: Parlor of the Coolidge Homestead. The Wedding Day and Morn of Jubilee. The first shot at Sumter. "Remember Gentl'm, 'y conduct belong to dis plantation." Dixie's Land"

Act 2: Blossom Landing on the St. John's River, Florida. Twelve years later. Sundown. Old Pete and Little May. A story of the War.

Act 3: The Old Mill at Bush Creek by Moonlight. Camp meeting. The rescue.

Act 4: Exterior of the Coolidge Homestead. The Sale. Douncement.

MUSICAL NUMBERS

"The Bridal March"

"Massa's Wedding Night"

"Heigh Ho! Lingo Sally"

"The Old Barn Floor"

"The Stonewall Jackson"

"Slavery's Passed Away"

"Haul de Woodpile Down" (Howl the Woodpile Down)

"The Old Black Crow"

"Where the Sweet Magnolia Grows" (When the Sweet Magnolia Grows)

"Let Us Wander in the Orange Grove To-night" (As We Wander Through the Orange Grove)

1887.49

SHE

A Weird Romance in Three Acts, 5 Scenes. Play by William Gillette. Based on H. Rider Haggard's novel of the same name. Music by William W. Furst. Scenery by William Schaeffer and Gaspard Maeder; Hughson Hawley and Homer Emens. Costumes by Henry Dazian. Mechanical effects by Thomas Gossman. Musical director, William W. Furst. Produced under the stage direction of Ben Teal. Produced by William Gillette and Al Hayman. Opened 29 November 1887 at Niblo's Garden and closed 24 December 1887 after 31 performances[52].

CAST: *Horace Holly*: F. F. MACKAY. *Leo Vincey*: WILTON LACKAYE. *Martin Brown*: Charles Bowser. *Job*: Howard Coveney. *Abdallah*: George D Fawcett. *Mohammed*: F. Barnes. *Billali*: H. W. Frillman. *Simbali*: E. Waters. *First Sentinel*: F. Clare. *Ayesha, "She"*: LAURA CLEMENT. *Ustane*: LOIE FULLER. *Dillyesha*: Fanny Addison. *Attendant*: Mollie Brown. *Arab Sailors, Male and Female Amhaggar, Guards, Mutes, Attendants, etc.*

Act 1, Scene 1: Deck of an Arab Dhow. The Head of the Ethiopian. (Schaeffer & Maeder.) *Scene 2*: Great Cave of the Amhaggar. Dance of the Hot Pot. (Schaeffer & Maeder.)

Act 2: The Underground Palace of She. (Hawley & Emens.)

Act 3, Scene 1: Chasm of the Rocking Stone. (Hawley & Emens.) *Scene 2*: Cave of the Fire of Life. (Hawley & Emens.)

1887.50

MADELON

An Opéra-comique in Three Acts. Original French libretto ('La Petite Mademoiselle') by Henri Meilhac and Ludovic Halévy. Music by Charles Lecocq. English adaptation by Max Freeman. Scenery by Henry E. Hoyt. Costumes by Mme. Loe and assistants. Stage director, Max Freeman. Director of music, John J. Braham. Produced by Rudolph Aronson. Opened 5 December 1887 at the Casino Theatre and closed 14 January 1888 after 42 performances.[53]

CAST: *Trompette*, wife of Tabouureau: BERTHA RICCI. *Pompanon*, the Tripiere: ISABELLE URQUHART. *Jomine*: SYLVIA GERRISH. *The Viscountess*: Rose Wilson. *Hernandez*, Leader of the Royal Violinists: Lucy Rivers. *The Baroness*: Rose Ricci. *The Duchess*: Florence Barry. *Madelon*, Princess de Cameroni: LILLIAN GRUBB. *Babette*, Barmaid of the Inn: LILLIAN GRUBB. *Rabicamp*, Officer in the Royal Army: MARK SMITH. *Lamkin*, Sausage Chopper: MARK SMITH. *Jolivett*, Officer in the service of the Fronde: COURTICE POUNDS. *Filoufin*, Steward in the Chateau Cameroni: Arthur W. Tams. *Bernard*, Pompanon's husband: EDGAR SMITH. *Laroche*, Chief Detective: Frank J. Rich. *Montcavrel*: Henry Leoni. *Moineau*, Sergeant: James Horan. *Rodolphe*, Chimney Sweep: Henry Price. *Officers in the King's Army (4)*: *Seoigny*: Charles Knapp. *Penpigny*: C. L. Weeks. *Pont d'Aubray*: George W. Faust. *Chateaubrun*: R. K. Dashiel. *Taboureau*, Keeper of the Inn, "The Golden Pineapple": JAMES T. POWERS. *Fisher Boys of the Seine, Picardy Peasants, Vivandiers, Royal Violinists, Soldiers, Citizens and Courtiers.*

Act 1: Camp of the Royal Army before Paris, 1652.

Act 2: Paris by Day and Night.

Act 3: The Chateau of the Prince Cameroni, near Paris.

MUSICAL NUMBERS[54]

"On to Paris"

Sabot Dance (Act 2)

Fisherboys of the Seine, Picardy Girls

The King's Violinists will perform 'Amaryllis' by Louis XIII. (Act 3)

1887.51

OUR JENNIE

A Farce Comedy in Three Acts. Play by Clay M. Greene. Management, C. W. Roberts. Opened 26 December 1887 at the People's Theatre and closed 31 December 1887 after 8 performances[55].

CAST: *Larry Fogarty*, a washerwoman's son: JOHN T. BURKE. *James Walton*, the husband: J. J. MACREADY. *Jinks*, later Henry: J. W. SUMMERS. *Willie Wilkie*, a dude: Collin Varry. *Frank Farr*, the son: Fred M. Mayer. *Bridget Fogarty*: Emily Stowe. *Mrs. Farr*, the mother: ADELAIDE EATON. *Our Jennie*: JENNIE YEAMANS.

MUSICAL NUMBERS, SPECIALTIES

Songs, Dances, Banjo Solos

J. Yeamans

1887.52

TURNED UP

A Revival of the Farce Comedy in Three Acts[56] by Mark Melford. (Staged by Nat C. Goodwin.) Produced by Nat C. Goodwin (George W. Floyd, Management)[57]. Opened 26 December 1887 at the Grand Opera House and closed 31 December 1887 after 9 performances; returned 13 February 1888 to the 14th Street Theatre for 16 performances, 12 March 1888 to the People's Theatre for 8 performances, 30 April 1888 to the Grand Opera House for 8 performances. Total: 41 performances.

LEND ME FIVE SHILLINGS A farce in One Act.

CAST: *Golightly*: NAT C. GOODWIN. *Spruce*: J. B. Mason. *Captain Phobbs*: T. H. Burns. *Moreland*: : E. F. Goodwin. *Sam*: Charles Coote. *Mrs. Major Phobbs*: Esther Lyons. *Mrs. Captain Phobbs*: Lucy Escott. *Walters*: Frank Morse.

TURNED UP

CAST: *Caraway Jones, Esq.*, Undertaker and General Dealer: NAT C. GOODWIN. *George Medway*: J. B. Mason. *Nod Steddam*: Charles Coote. *Captain Medway*: T. H. Burns. *General Baltic*: E. F. Goodwin. *Old Lobb*: Frank Morse. *Ephraim*: Little May Richards. *Sabina Medway*: Maud Haslam. *Ada Baltic*: Lucy Escott. *Mrs. Medway*: Marian Erle. *Cleopatra*: Weevie Vivien. *Mrs. Pannall*: Estelle Mortimer.

1888.01

MAZULM, THE NIGHT OWL

Imre Kiralfy's Grand and Colossal Revival of the Famous Pantomime in Three Acts, 14 Scenes.[58] Rewritten and arranged expressly for him by Mons. Jerome Ravel. Staged by Imre Kiralfy. Scenery by H. L. Reid, Robecchi and Amable of Paris. Produced by Imre Kiralfy. Opened 9 January 1888 at the Academy of Music and closed 10 March 1888 after 72 performances.

---

52 Played a return engagement 24 December 1887 at the People's Theatre for an additional 9 performances.

53 Previously produced in New York in German only as TROMPETTE, 13 October 1882 at the Germania Theatre in repertory.

54 Musical numbers not listed in programs; no libretto or score found.

55 No program found; reviewers remarked upon the number of musical specialties performed by J. Yeamans.

56 TURNED UP was preceded by a curtain-raiser, Lend Me Five Shillings. TURNED UP was first produced in New York 11 December 1886 at the Bijou Theatre for 49 performances. For Synopsis of Scenes and Musical Numbers, see original 1886 production. Program credits and cast from April 1888 Grand Opera House engagement.

57 Program note: TURNED UP is the property of Willie Edouin, and is produced by arrangement with Frank W. Sanger, Esq.

58 First produced in an earlier form as MAZULME THE NIGHT OWL! 18 October 1842 at Niblo's Garden.

CAST: *Mazulm*, the night owl and Genius of the Mystic Tomb: A. H. DENHAM. *Chevalier Bariano*, a Dissipated Gallant: W. H. BARTHOLOMEW. *Emile*, a young peasant in love with Julia: ALBERT MARTINETTI. *Maclou*, servant to Bariano: Monsieur Gavant. *The Great Chief*: L. S. Robertson. *Rox Hi*, Grand Vizier: Peter Boniface. *Colengne*, an M. D.: August Siegrist. *Moler*, a Charlatan: Robert W. Borston. *Colin*, a Miller's Man: L. Rubel. *Carmaso*, a Surgeon: J. Hamilton. *Commissaries of Police*: William Eunice. *Joints*, a Grand Carver: Henri Dutton. *Mariana*, a poor peasant: Mlle. NEWMAN. *Julia*, her daughter: LOUISE ALLEN. *Spirits of Purity*, a Guide: Hattie Grinnell. *Male and female Peasants, Nuns, Spirits, Skeletons, Fishermen and their wives, Market Women, Merchants, Turkish and Japanese Guards, Travelers, Seafaring Men, Turkish and Japanese Ladies, Amazons, Porters, Demons, Cupids, Nymphs and Fairies.*

Characters of Harlequinade: *Clown*: TOMMY DARE. *Harlequin*: ALBERT MARTINETTI. *Policeman*: WILLIAM EUNICE. *Pantaloon*: W. H. BARTHOLOMEW. *Columbine*: LOUISE ALLEN.

(*Ballet*: Mlle. CLARA QUALITZ, Mons. ARNOLD KIRALFY, Mlle. CLARA NEWMAN, Secondas, Corps de Ballet. *Specialties*: BRAATZ BROTHES, VAIDIS SISTERS, Mlle. FRANZIONI, DARE BROTHERS.)

Act 1, Scene 1: A Rustic Interior. (Reid.) *Scene 2*: A Mystic Tomb, in a Romantic Glen by Moonlight. (Robecchi and Amable.) *Scene 3*: Bariano's Palace. (Robecchi and Amable.)

Act 2, Scene 1: A Friendly Inn. *Scene 2*: A Market in Constantinople. *Scene 3*: The Bosphorous. *Scene 4*: Braatz Brothers. *Scene 5*: The Japanese Garden. (Reid.)

Act 3, Scene 1: The Palace of Jewels. (Robecchi and Amable.) *Scene 2*: A Street. *Scene 3*: A Bedroom in a Hotel. *Scene 4*: Pawnbroker and Baker Shops. *Scene 5*: Mystic Cave. *Scene 6*: Wonderland Opened. Mazulm's abode of Enchantment. (Robecchi and Amable.)

ACT 1

Scene 1

The dying mother! Julia, her daughter, and her lover, Emile. Persecution of the Baron Bariano. An attempt to entangle Julia in the meshes! The Spirit of Purity watches over her.

Scene 2

The Abode of the Night Owl. By the Mother's Grave! The Pall Bearers. A Deadly Bargain! The fair Julia carried off. Emile's despair. The invocation. The Night Owl! Appearance of Mazulm! The tombs burst and heave out their tenants! A Ghastly Procession! The Spirit Guide and the Magic Branch.

Scene 3

The Ball and Festival in Progress. Bariano and Maclou, his faithful "creature!" The Night Owl's Talisman. Purity reappears and reassures the suffering Maiden. The Villain Petrified. Great escape of Emile. Ballet of Sports (*Invented and arranged by* Imre Kiralfy.)

1. Horse Racing
   Coryphées
2. Lawn Tennis
   8 Secondas
3. Fishing Sport
   Mlles. Qualitz, Newman
4. Old Sports
   MM. Arnold
5. BaseBall Dance
   Corps de Ballet
6. Rowing Dance
   Secondas
7. Tobogganing, Polo and Grand Finale
   Entire Grand Ballet Corps

ACT 2

Scene 1

A Friendly Inn.

Scene 2

The famous Dare Brothers in the Eccentric Bar Act. The live Elephant Boulanger. Maclou steals the eggs. A novel Detective Agency and Hatching Machine! General Melee. Escape to the Sea Coast. Magic change to the sea.

Scene 3

The steamer at anchor! On to Japan! The Escape! An Age of Reason! Purity the Faithful Guide. Maclou and his practical knowledge of Ship Building. A Lesson for our Navy! A Dynamitic Explosion and most infernal machine.

Scene 4

Musical Acrobatic Performance
Braatz Brothers

Scene 5

March and Festival in Progress. The Chief's Protection. The Big Fish is Carved. Sudden appearance of Bariano! The story of Jonah and the Whale outdone! Maclou's Mangled Remains restored by a new and Magical Elixir of Life.

Japanese Paradise Ballet
Mlle. Franzioni

Most gorgeous and resplendent in every detail. Spirited Tableau and trick change to a Fortification.

Between Acts 2 and 3 the Vaidis Sisters. The most accomplished and daring of female aerialists appear in a series of the most perilous mid-air performances ever enacted!

ACT 3

Scene 1

A scene of wonderful magnificence and startling effect, in which is introduced the Grand Metallic March of the Amazons. The entire Ballet costumed in Glittering Steel, Shining Gold, Pure Silver, Copper—a most wonderful and weird effect. Purity the Brightest of all Jewels. Transformation for Harlequinade Tableau.

Scene 2

A Street.

Scene 3

A Bedroom in a Hotel.

Scene 4

Pawnbroker and Baker Shops.

Scene 5

The Last Leaf. Emile calls upon Mazulm. Sudden appearance of the Night Owl. "Receive the just penalty of your wickedness." Bariano and Maclou consigned to the tender mercies of Eblis for Eternity. Change to a Realm of Bliss.

Scene 6

Nymphs, Sylphs and Fairies. Purity has saved Julia. A Happy Ending.

1888.02

ERMINIE

A Revival of the Operetta (Comic Opera) in Three Acts[59]. Libretto by Harry Paulton, (Claxson Bellamy). (Based on the French melodrama "L'Auberge des Adrets" and its sequel "Robert Macaire" by Benjamin Antier, Saint-Amand and Paulyanthe.) Music by Edward Jakobowski. Scenery by Henry E. Hoyt (Act 2). Costumes by Georges Pilotell. Musical director, Jesse Williams. Produced by Rudolph Aronson. Opened 16 January 1888 at the Casino Theatre and closed 12 May 1888 after 117 performances.[60]

CAST: *Erminie*: PAULINE HALL. *Javotte*: MARIE JANSEN. *Cerise*: KITTY CHEATHAM. *Princess de Gramponeur*: LOUISE SYLVESTER. *Marie*: Georgie Dennin. *Delaunay*, a Young Officer: SADIE KIRBY. *Cadeaux, Ravennes*, Two Thieves: FRANCIS WILSON, WILLIAM S. DABOLL. *Eugene Marcel*, the Marquis' secretary: Henry Hallam. *Chevalier de Brabazon*, Marquis' Guest: CHARLES PLUNKETT. *Marquis de Pontvert*: GEORGE OLMI. *Dufois*, Landlord of the Lion d'Or: Murry Woods. *Simon*, Waiter at the Lion d'Or: A. W. Maflin. *Vicomte de Brissac*: B. F. Joslyn. *Sergeant*: J. A. Furey. *(Flower Girls, Soldiers, Peasants, Clowns, Lords and Ladies, etc.)*

1888.03

CHECK 44, or, Tobogganing

A Satirical, Lyrical, Diaphanous Lampoon (Farce Comedy) in Three Acts. Play by William A. Mestayer. Musical director, Max Horter. Produced by William A. Mestayer and Theresa Vaughn (John B. Slocum, Management). Opened 16 January 1888 at the Star Theatre; moved 13 February 1888 to Niblo's Garden and closed 18 February 1888 after 36 performances.[61]

CAST: *Garnet Plum Smith*, the Cashier: WILLIAM A. MESTAYER. *Antonio Smitherini*, operatic: BERNARD DYLLYN. *Sophocles Kersmith*, paying teller: JOSEPH

[59]Originally produced in New York 10 May 1886 at the Casino Theatre for 571 performances. For Synopsis of Scenes and Musical Numbers, see original 1886 production. A new song interpolated for this production, as per published sheet music: "This Afternoon at Four," M. Jansen (*Music and Lyrics arranged by* Max Freeman.).
[60]Stage direction uncredited. Assistant stage manager, A. W. Maflin.
[61]Stage direction, scenery and costumes uncredited.

A. OTT. *Eben Goldsmith*, a Hayseed: SOL AIKEN. *Jackson Smiff*, Acrobatic: ROBERT GARNELLA. *Cordial Smiff*, Gymnastic: RICHARD GARNELLA. *Regen O. Smythe*, an Officer: W. H. Sloan. *McKee Locksmith*, a Tramp: William Ball. *Miss Wayback Creamlaid Smith*, an Antique: Mary Gray. *Toady Goldsmith*, not out yet: Marion Russell. *Sarah Blacksmith*, a Settler: Beatrice Tait. *Julie LaSmythe*, a Maid: Lillian Hamilton. *Belle Smith*, a Maid: Annie Jackson. *Persia Goldsmith*, an Heiress: THERESA VAUGHN.

Act 1: Money Bank.

Act 2: Snow Bank.

Act 3: Sand Bank.

ACT 1

Burlesque Italian Opera
B. Dyllyn

Duet from LA PÉRICHOLE
T. Vaughn, W. A. Mestayer (*Music by* Jacques Offenbach.)

Concerted Finale

ACT 2

"It's Something You've Got to Get Used To" (Topical Song)
W. A. Mestayer, J. A. Ott

Ballad
T. Vaughn

Selections
B. Dyllyn

Toboggan Chorus
Company

Clodoche Quadrille
The Garnellas, J. A. Ott, W. H. Sloan

ACT 3

Duet
T. Vaughn, W. A. Mestayer

Song and Dance
L. Hamilton

Acrobatic Act
The Garnellas

Finale
Company

1888.04 LITTLE PUCK

A Farce Comedy in Three Acts. Play by Archibald C. Gunther, Fred G. Maeder, Robert Fraser and Howard P. Taylor. Based on the story "Vice Versa and Fallen Idol" by F. Anstey. Stage director, Robert Fraser. Musical director, William Withers. Proprietor, Frank Daniels (Management, Samuel P. Cox). Opened 16 January 1888 at the 14th Street Theatre, moved 23 January 1888 to the Theatre Comique (Harlem) and closed 28 January 1888 after 16 performances; returned 13 February 1888 to the People's Theatre for an additional 8 performances[62]. Total: 24 performances.

CAST: *Peckingham Giltedge*, a matter-of-fact stock broker: FRANK DANIELS. *Billy Giltedge*, a young American hopeful, his wayward son: CHARLES W. SWAIN. *Dr. Hercules Savage*, the severe master and mentor of Savage Academy for young gentlemen: GEORGE WOODWARD. *Jinks Hoodoo, Esq.*, brother-in-law to Giltedge. A curse to everybody, including himself. Proprietor of Hoodoo's Dime Museum: HARRY MACK. *Sluggers*, Butler of Giltedge: ROBERT FRASER. *Abe Striker*, The Bully of Savage Academy: George Mayo. *Charley Blocker*, The Boy: Frank Barlow. *Harry Shivers*, who has seen spirits: William LaMont. *Simeon Moseback*, of Moseback, Wildcat & Co., Bankers, Wall Street: W. G. Gilmore. *Professor Liverjamb*, Dancing Master at Savage Academy: William White.

Clara Giltedge, Billy's Sister: RILLIE DEAVES. *Tabitha Tittleback*, Housekeeper to Giltedge: Louise K. Quinten. *Miss Ticklesham*, Schoolmistress: Florence Rowe. *Mrs. Simeon Moseback*: Mary Challoniet. *A Demon*: Master Martner. *Minnie Titters*: Hattie Delaro. *Victoria*: Nellie Seymour. *Lucy Langton*: May Granville. *Seraphina*: Bertie Damon. *Violet Severance*: May Grosvenor. *Violetta*: Jennie Stetson. *Miranda Savage*, Dr. Savage's Daughter, in love with Billy: BESSIE SANSON. *Imps, School Boys, School Girls, etc.*

Act 1: A Room in Peckingham Giltedge's House.

Act 2: A Play Ground. Exterior of Dr. Savage's Academy.

Act 3: A Parlor in Peckingham Giltedge's House.

[62]Played return engagements 15 October 1888 at the People's Theatre and 11 February 1889 at the Theatre Comique, Harlem. Musical numbers not listed in programs; for Synopsis of Musical Numbers, see October 1888 production.

1888.05 C.O.D.

A Musical Comedy in Three Acts. (Play by Stanley Macy.) Stage manager, Barney McDonough. Musical director, Henry P. Smith. Sole Proprietor, James W. Mace. Opened 16 January 1888 at Poole's Theatre and closed 21 January 1888 after 10 performances.

CAST (Acts 1 and 2): *C. Oliver Dates*, a theatrical manager out of luck: STANLEY MACY. *Dennis Fogarty*, an Exile from Erin, and Express porter who went to act: GUS BRUNO. *Hector Waybill*, express agent, storekeeper, post master, and hotel keeper, gone on the show business: BARNEY McDONOUGH. *Walker Palmdays*, the old man of the Co., who dates back to the elder Booth: GUS FRANKEL. *Cipher Dotlet*, an Eight Avenue Drug Clerk en route: EMIL HEUSEL. *Long John*, son of Waybill, the only messenger boy left in town: GEORGIE BREUNING. *Cousin Sam*, hotel porter who understands his business: E. A. Archer. *Eve Adams*, our charming soubrette: BESSIE CLARK. *Rose Rattle*, our Society Artist, who wants to elevate everything: EMILY NORTHROP. *Carry Gripsack*, not in love with amateurs: Tillie McHenry. *Kittie Waybill*, sister of Long John, afterwards a real pro: MARIE CAHILL. *Brakesmen, Express Messengers, etc.*

CAST (Act 3): *Basso Profunnyo*, who will sing: C. Oliver Dates [STANLEY MACY]. *The Mighty Pascha*, who makes you tremble when he smiles: Walker Palmdays [Gus Frankel]. *The Great Begorra Begum*, an Irish Turk: Dennis Fogarty [GUS BRUNO]. *Windy Whiskers*, in love with the princess: Hector Waybill [BARNEY McDONOUGH]. *Creamy Tartar*, cause of the interstate R. R. law: Long John [GEORGIE BREUNING]. *Cleanthis*, a Turkey heart-breaker: Cipher Dotlet [EMIL HEUSEL]. *Messala Ring Up*, a Turkey-ish warble: Cousin Sam [E. A. Archer]. *Inas*, the pet of the pyramids: Eve Adams [BESSIE CLARK]. *Majarien*, the princess of the isle: Rose Rattle [EMILY NORTHROP]. *Nyda*, favorite of the Pascha: Carry Gripsack [Tillie McHenry]. *Tirza*, the Oriental nightingale: Kittie Waybill [MARIE CAHILL]. *Guards, Attendants, Slaves, etc.*

Act 1: Depot, Express Office and Store at Jonahville. Day before Christmas.

Act 2: R. R. Hotel Jonahville. Christmas Eve.

Act 3: Stage of Town Hall, Painted Post. C.O.D. Company giving full performance of the burlesque of "The Princess of the Isle," a romance of the Orient. Christmas Night.

ACT 1

"How can they resist me"
"Expressman's Chorus"
"She Can't Lick Me"
"Love's Answer"
"Crying Quartette"
"Queen of may" (Song and Dance)
"Electric Dolls"

ACT 2

"Doll's Lullaby"
"These Amateurs Make Me Sick"
"Brakeman's Chorus"
"Jamie Dear"
"Purple Pansies" (Song and Dance)
Quartette
"Christmas Bells"

ACT 3

"Domino Chorus"
"I am the Pascha"
"Night Birds Cooing"
"The Old Love, and the new"
"Yum, Yum"
"Twilight" (Song and Dance)
"The Song that reached my heart"
C.O.D. Medley

1888.06 ARCADIA

A Revival of the Operatic, Extravaganzic Burlesque in Two Acts, 9 Scenes. Play by William Gill. Original music composed and selected by John J. Braham. Costumes by Mme. Schwinke. Musical director, Fred A. Rothstein. Produced by Corinne (Jennie Kimball, Manager). Opened 30 January 1888 at the Third Avenue Theatre and closed 18 February 1888 after 24 performances; moved 27 February 1888 to Dockstader's Theatre and closed 31 March 1888 after an additional 40 performances; returned 18 June 1888 to the Thalia Theatre and closed 23 June 1888 after an additional 8 performances. Total: 72 performances.

CAST: *Tomtom*, the Piper's Son, an attractive, if somewhat larcenous young rascal: CORINNE. *Trumpetta*, Queen of the War Fairies, a susceptible monarch: JENNIE

KIMBALL. *Bulbul*, the Nightingale, Trumpetta's daughter: FRANCESCA REDDING. *Little Sallie Waters*, who possesses a remarkable penchant for "playing with children in the sun" to say nothing of her other numerous peculiarities: CHARLES FOSTELLE. *Lootella*, Trumpetta's aide-de-camp: Pauline Sanderson. *The Piper's Wife*, Tomtom's mother, who has seen much better days: Dorris Studleigh. *The Little Sergeant*: Virginia Kimball. *Pogowog*, the Warrior Musician, a bad egg, under the yoke of Trumpetta: James Sturges. *The Piper*, Tomtom's father, who may, perhaps, mention incidentally his connection with the late lamented Duke of Argyle: Newton Chisnell. *Justice Bluffy*, of the Empsty-Emptsh Judicial Court: Harry Woodbury. *Captain Clubber*, a member in good standing of some of our best clubs: Clarence Duffy.

Pogowog's Minions (4): *Blow*: R. E. Callahan. *Bluster*: J. F. Callahan. *Chinn*: W. P. Bryant. *Baktork*: W. H. Brown. *Acrobatic Villains (6)*: *Breakneck Jack*: William Ward. *Wild West Jake*: Edward Turner. *Buffalo Bill*: Mell Dyer. *Pawnee Joe*: Charles Wood. *Texas Jim*: C. Evans. *Utah Tom*: John Daly. *Clerk of the Court*: Frank Conway. *Bag Piper*, a genuine Scotch: George Murray. *Boliver*, Baby Elephant: Parker Twin Brothers. *The Funny Owl*: Hubbard Knowles. *Bunny*, the little pig: Himself. *Dancing Girl*, Spana Gitana: Mlle. Carlos. *First Officer*, Gold: (Miss) Bulbul. *Second Officer*, Silver: Mittie Atherton. *Third Officer*, Garnet: Louise Hastings. *Fourth Officer*, Green: Lillie Snow. *Fifth Officer*, Black: Edith Crawford. *Sixth Officer*, Blue: (Miss) Lootella. *(Corinne Ideal Quartette), School Girls, Police, Mephistophelian Band, War Fairies, Cowboys, etc.*

Act 1, Scene 1: Courtyard of the Warrior Magician. *Scene 2*: Garden of Trumpetta's Fairy Palace. *Scene 3*: The miserable house of the Piper. *Scene 4*: Court-room at Empty-Emptsh Judicial Court.

Act 2, Scene 1: A Cell in the Penitentiary. *Scene 2*: Mephistopheles' country seat. *Scene 3*: Trumpetta's agitation. *Scene 4*: The Kindergarten. *Scene 5*: Grand Transformation to Trumpetta's Garden.

ACT 1[63]

Scene 1

"Victoria, Victoria"
Chorus

"Not a Drummer" (Song)
Corinne, Chorus

"Little Sallie Waters" (Song)
C. Fostelle, Chorus

Scene 2

Song
F. Redding

"Perhaps I Don't" (Trio)
J. Sturgess, Corinne, F. Redding

Olla Podrida (Quartette, selected):

Duet
F. Redding, Corinne

Dance of Pogowog

Finale (selected)

Scene 3

"I Sang This Song" (Song)
N. Chisnell

Policemen's Chorus and Eccentric Drill

Scene 4

"Lovely Angeline" (Song and Dance)
Corinne

Grand Finale

ACT 2

Scene 1

"Where Art Thou Now, My Beloved" (Song)
Corinne

Scene 2

Ballet Dance

The Corinne Ideal Quartette

The Dancing Elephant

Scene 3

"Oh, So Happy!" (Affecting Ballad)
N. Chisnell, D. Studleigh

"It Is Awful Nice, But It Is Awkward" (Topical Song)
Corinne

Scene 4

Beautiful Gavotte

"Little Peach in an Orchard Grew" (Song)
Corinne

"Nursery Rhymes" (Quartette)

Scene 5

Royal Amazon March

Grand Finale

1888.07 VICTOR, THE BLUE STOCKING

A Light Opera in Three Acts[64]. Adapted from the French opéra-comique "François les bas bleus," libretto by Ernest Dubreuil, Paul Burani and Eugène Humbert. Music by Firmin Bernicat and André Messager. Stage manager, Fred Williams. Musical director, George Loesch. Produced by the Boston Ideal Opera Company (W. H. Foster, Manager). Opened 6 February 1888 at the Fifth Avenue Theatre and closed 11 February 1888 (matinee) after 4 performances in repertory; played a return engagement during the week of 20 February 1888 at Niblo's Garden for 7 additional performances. Total: 11 performances.

CAST: *Victor Delmar* (a letter-writer): HARRY L. RATTENBERRY. *Marquis de Palsambleu* (an absurd old aristocrat): CLEMENT BAINBRIDGE. *Mons. de Florac* (Fanchette's cousin): FRITZ WILLIAMS. *Sergeant Gruyère*: JOSEPH C. MIRON. *Bertrand*: George E. Holmes. *Friquet*: Louise Edgar. *Auguste* (Palsambleu's butler): Frank Hanshue. *Celestine*, Countess de la Bonbonière, the Marquis' sister (the Fortune Teller): HARRIET AVERY. *Ulrica*: HELEN D. CAMPBELL. *Fanchette*, a street singer: ZÉLIE deLUSSAN. *Citziens, Grisettes, Servants, Guests, Soldiers.*

Act 1: The square of St. Eustace, Paris, church in background. 1789.

Act 2: Handsome antechamber at Palsambleu's.

Act 3: An open square, Paris. An Inn, a Guard-house.

ACT 1[65]

"Impatiently we long have waited" (Opening Chorus)
L. Edgar, H. Avery, Grisettes

"I may say without boasting or blowing" (Song)
J. C. Miron, Chorus

"Your pardon, friends, I crave" (Song and Chorus)
H. L. Rattenberry, Chorus

"Love is a charm that binds me" (Song)
F. Williams

"I've songs of every style and fashion" (Song)
Z. deLussan, Chorus

"Now with care you must form every letter" (Duet)
H. L. Rattenberry, Z. deLussan

"Each Frenchman is surely aware" (Political Song)
C. Bainbridge

"Behold us gathered here to-day" (Anniversary Song)
J. C. Miron, G. E. Holmes, Soldiers, Chorus

"There was a little sailor lad" (Song)
Z. deLussan, Chorus

"Why is this past believing?" (Trio)
H. D. Campbell, Z. deLussan, H. Avery

"Of course each Frenchman is aware" (Finale)
Principals, Chorus

ACT 2

"Servants are we, master is he" (Opening Chorus)
F. Hanshue, Servants

"'Tis most perplexing" (Song)
C. Bainbridge

"There was a little sailor lad" (reprise)
H. Avery, C. Bainbridge, Z. deLussan

"My father! can it be?" (Quartet)
Z. deLussan, H. Avery, H. D. Campbell, C. Bainbridge

"'Tis she! Mystery stranger" (Quartet)
F. Williams, Z. deLussan, C. Bainbridge, H. Avery

"The last farewell must now be spoken" (Duet)
H. L. Rattenberry, Z. deLussan, Chorus

"We're the guard, so you'd best make way for us" (Finale)
Principals, Chorus

[63]Also performed by Corinne according to programs: "The Great Scotch Sword Dance" and "I Like It" (Topical Song).

[64]Previously produced in New York in French 29 September 1884 at Wallack's Theatre in repertory. English adaptation uncredited.

[65]Musical numbers not listed in programs. List prepared from published libretto (Boston Ideals; Alfred Mudge & Son, printers, Boston, 1885).

"What would a soldier do" (Valse)
Z. deLussan, Chorus

ACT 3

"Early and late, with soldierly gait" (Opening Chorus)
Guards, Chorus

"Though I'm but a little fifer now" (Song)
L. Edgar, Chorus

"Thou to whom my heart was given" (Song)
H. L. Rattenberry

"Oh, Paris town's the spot for me" (Song with Dance)
Z. deLussan, Chorus

"By fortune I've been treated" (Finale)
Z. deLussan, Chorus, All

1888.08 MAGGIE, THE MIDGET

A Melodrama in Four Acts. Play by Fred Williams. Music by David Braham. Produced under the direction of William L. Lykens. Dances by Arthur Novissimo. Musical director, Otto Vogler. Produced by Maggie Mitchell. Opened 12 March 1888 at the 14th Street Theatre and closed 24 March 1888 after 16 performances.

CAST: *Margaret St. George*: MAGGIE MITCHELL. *Hon. Captain Jack Falconer*: CHARLES ABBOTT. *Augustus Blackstone Gunn*, Counsellor-at-Law: James T. Galloway. *Lycurgus Potts*, a Magistrate: R. F. McClannin. *Richard Ashburn*: Frank Doud. *Ishmael Akbar*, a Spanish Gypsy: EARLE STIRLING. *Pedro*, a Landlord: Dodson Lomax. *James Jenkins*, a Footman: George W. Neville. *Nicholas Demdyke*, a Game Keeper: T. Smith. *Street Boys of St. Jean de Luz (4)*: *Jack Aspel*: Tom Leonard. *Antoine*: Harry Martin. *Lopez*: (Mr.) Phyllys Forest. *Max*: John Butler. *Jose*, a Courier: Charles Martin. *Claire Gordon*: Elmira Strong. *Mrs. Godfrey St. George*: Lillian Andrews. *Mrs. Glorvina Potts*: Marion P. Clifton. *Marcella*, Hostess: Eliza S. Hudson. *Miss Alice Charlotte*: Annie Chase. *Miss Mary Neville*: Annie Friese. *Miss Stella Norton*: Georgie Houser. *Guests, Game Keepers, Servants*.

Act 1: The Basque Country at the foot of the Pyrenées.

Act 2: Mt. St. George.

Act 3: Same as Act 2.

Act 4: Same as Act 3, evening of the same day.

ACT 1

Chorus and Fandango
Muleteers, Gitanos

Bull Fighters' Dance
M. Mitchell, E. Stirling

ACT 2

Tarantella
M. Mitchell, E. Stirling

1888.09 THE PEARL OF PEKIN

A Chinese and English Comic Opera in Three Acts[66]. Libretto by Charles Alfred Byrne. (Adapted from the French opéra-bouffe, 'Fleur de thé,' libretto by Alfred Duru and Henri Chivot. Music by Charles Lecocq.) Music by Gustave Kerker and Charles Lecocq. Staged by Edward E. Rice. Scenery by Edward G. Unitt & King. Costumes designed by Carrie E. Perkins. Chorus and orchestra under the direction of Gustavus A. Kerker. Produced by Edward E. Rice and Henry E. Dixey. Opened 19 March 1888 at the Bijou Theatre and closed 26 May 1888 after 80 performances.

CAST: *Pearl of Pekin*, daughter of Tyfoo and a simple Chinese maiden: ALICE JOHNSON. *Finnette*, wife of Petit Pierre and a vivandière: IRENE VERONA. *Four charming French waiting maids*: *Pierrette*: Clairette Vanderbilt.. *Angelique*: Carrie Behr. *Pepine*: Grace Wilson. *Fantine*: Bertie Fisch. *Petit Pierre*, a dashing young quarter-master of the French Navy, stationed on board "La Victoria," whose wife has opened a restaurant in Pekin as a side speculation: PHILIP BRANSON. *Sosoriki*, a Japanese of some distinction, Chief of the Imperial Tigers, and with still higher aspirations: JOSEPH W. HERBERT. *Paul Mathot*, Boatswain of "La Victoria," useful if not ornamental: Herbert Charter. *Sing High*, a Chinese attendant: John C. Leach. *Tyfoo*, Mandarin and Governor of Pekin, who frequently remarks That "He is as knowing as a Sphinx": LOUIS HARRISON. Chinese Band, High Kee (leader). *French Sailors, Chinese men and women, Mandarins, Officers of the State, ad infinitum*.

Act 1: French Inn at Pekin, with a view of the city in the distance. China, 1861.

Act 2: Royal Apartments in the Governor's Palace.

Act 3: The Blue Kiosk, overlooking the Conservatory and Gardens of the Palace.

MUSICAL NUMBERS[67]

Sailors' Chorus (Where ever we roam o'er the seas) (Act 1)
(*Music by* Gustave Kerker.)

"He Loved Her Tender" (Act 2)
J. W. Herbert

"A Pretty Maid"

"I Was Born in Tokio"
J. W. Herbert

"(We Are) Four Little Tchin-Tchin Girls"[68]
G. Wilson, C. Behr, B. Fisch, C. Vanderbilt (*Music by* Gustave Kerker.)

"Bad as They Are, We Love These Men"

"I Love My Old Love Still"
A. Johnson (*Music by* Gustave Kerker.)

"Pearl of Pekin" (Love, let the wine of life now course through thy veins)

Waltz Song (Finale Act 2)
(*Music by* Gustave Kerker.)

Juggling Song (Now that Pearl of Pekin's married)
J. W. Herbert (*Music by* Gustave Kerker.)

"What a Subject to Paint on a Fan"[69] (Trio) (Act 2)
A. Johnson, J. W. Herbert, I. Verona (*Music by* Gustave Kerker.)

"I Hope It Won't Happen Again"[70]
L. Harrison (*Music by* Edward Rice. *Lyrics by* Louis Harrison.)

"Signor McStinger"
L. Harrison (*Music by* R. T. Whitman.)

1888.10 DOLORES

A Historical Drama (Parisian Spectacle) in Six Acts, 10 Scenes. Based on Victorien Sardou's "La Patrie." Entire spectacle staged by Bolossy Kiralfy. Ballets composed and arranged by Bolossy Kiralfy. Scenery by Messrs. Magnani, Ferario, Ryan, J. Cheret, Porter. Produced by Bolossy Kiralfy. Opened 2 April 1888 at Niblo's Garden and closed 14 April 1888 after 16 performances[71].

CAST: *Count de Rysoor*: NEWTON GOTTHOLD. *Karloo*: JOHN MALONE. *Duke of Alva*: J. H. FITZPATRICK. *La Tremouille*: W. F. BLAND. *Noircarmes*: W. H. Wallis. *Jonas*: MAX FIGMAN. *Vargas*: Edward See. *Captain Rincon*: Frederick DeVere. *Miguel*: Charles Gotthold. *Ensign*: W. A. Somers. *Delrio*: A. C. Moore. *Pedro*: F. A. Montrose. *Galena*: Austin Forbes. *Cornellis*: J. Roberts. *Bakerseel*: G. Norton. *Domingo*: W. Winter. *Cortadilia*: John Haslam. *Charles*, the Headsman: A. Stockbridge. *Raffaella*: CHARLOTTE DEAN. *Sarah Matthesson*: RICCA ALLEN. *Gudule*: Annie Dunbar. *Joshua Keppenstock*: Annie Barrett. *Dolores*: ELEANOR CAREY. *Principal Danseuses*: Mlles. FRANCESCINA PARIS, CECILIA NICODE. *Ballet*: The Konroths (Helena, Henrietta), Mlles. Rosch, Haslam, Dunbar, Bannister, Young, Louise, Folugi.

Act 1: The Old Butchers' Market at Brussels. (Magnani.)

Act 2: Count de Rysoor's Home. (Magnani.)

Act 3: The Duke of Alva's Cabinet. (Magnani.)

Act 4, Scene 1: The Corridor in the Palace. (Ferario.) *Scene 2*: The Duke of Alva's Grand Fete. (Ryan.)

Act 5: "Hotel de Ville" at Brussels. (Cheret.)

Act 6, Scene 1: Ante-room of the "Torture Chamber." (Magnani.) *Scene 2*: The City of Brussels. The Procession. (Porter.) *Scene 3*: The Home of Rysoor. (Magnani.) *Scene 4*: The Great Square. "The Burning Stake." (Porter.)

ACT 1

The Wild Gypsies (Bolossy Kiralfy's Creation)

Entrance of the Tziganes
Corps de Ballet

Characteristic Pas
C. Nicode

Entrée
F. Paris

---

[66]First produced in New York in French as 'Fleur de thé' 1 February 1869 at the Theatre Français. This adaptation first presented in New York in English 19 March 1888 at the Bijou for 70 performances. For Synopsis of Scenes and Musical Numbers, see 1888 production.

[67]Musical numbers listed in programs. Only Kerker's songs listed in programs; list also prepared from published vocal gems (T. B. Harms, Inc., New York, 1888), excepting "A Pretty Maid."

[68]Also known as "We Are Four Little Ching Chang Girls" in programs.

[69]Also known as "Painting the Town" in programs.

[70]Added in April 1888.

[71]Played a return engagement 21 May 1888 at the Grand Opera House for 8 performances.

Pas de Huit Hongrois
The Konroths, Mlles. Rosch, Haslam, Allen, Dunbar, Bannister, Young
Solo
F. Paris
The Wild Gypsies
Grand Ensemble, Corps de Ballet

ACT 4
Scene 2
Dresdina (Grand Ballet Divertissement)
(*Music by* G. Jacobi.)
Ceramic Slow Valse
Corps de Ballet
The Coquettes
Mlles. L. Ricca, R. Allen, Konroth, Haslam, Dunbar, Folugi, Bannister
Pas de Deux
Mlles. Rosch, Konroth
Andante
Groups of Caryatids
Intermede
Mlles. Rosch, Konroth
Grand Solo Variation
F. Paris
Grand Dresdina Finale

1888.11 MONTE CRISTO, JR.

An Operatic Burlesque Melo-Drama in Three Acts, 6 Scenes. Adapted (from the London version[72]), arranged and produced under the immediate supervision of Mrs. Jennie Kimball. Original music by Meyer Lutz, Ivan Caryll, and Tito Mattei, arranged by Fred A. Rothstein. Ballets, incidental dances and marches arranged by Mme. Augusta Sohlke. Scenery by George Dayton and Rene Geraud. Costumes designed by Mme. Schwenke. Musical director, Fred A. Rothstein. Produced by Corinne (Jennie Kimball, Sole Manager). Opened 2 April 1888 at Dockstader's Theatre and closed 21 April 1888 after 24 performances.[73]

CAST: *Edmond Dantes*, a young sailor, afterwards *The Count of Monte Cristo*: CORINNE. *Nortier*, conspirator and criminal investigator: HARRY BROWN. *De Villefort*, his son, the prefect of police: JAMES STURGES. *Fernand*, a Catalan fisherman, afterwards Count de Morcef: ELSIE GEROME. *Mercedes*, betrothed to Dantes: FRANCESCA REDDING. *Mariette*, a lively young person: DORIS STUDLEIGH. *Carconte*, a charming hag, wife to Caderousse: Ethel Stanley. *Babette, Victorine*, interesting features of the neighborhood: Annie Osterman, Virginia Kimball. *Valentine*: Mittie Atherton. *Albert*: Sadie Spencer. *Captain of Hussars*: Pauline Sanderson. *Captain of Guard*: Kirk Towns. *Boatswain*: Louise Tyler. *Clarette*: Rose Stewart. *Danglars*, a supercilious super-cargo: Harry Woodbury. *Caderousse*, tailor and toper: Newton Chisnell. *Morel*, a ship-owner, with views on insurance: Frank Hayden. *Old Dantes*, Edmond's father, afflicted with Caderousse's complaint: Frank Conway. *Professional Guides (4)*: *Barney*: James Parker. *Danny*: Charles Parker. *Toby*: Dick Callahan. *Fagan*: James Callahan. (*Premiere Danseur*: CHARLES FOSTELLE.) *Peasants, landsmen, sailors, dancing girls, hussars, guards, gendarmes, etc.*

Act 1: The Harbor at Marseilles.

Act 2, Scene 1: The Chateau d'If. *Scene 2*: Cave on the Island of Monte Cristo, Jr. *Scene 3*: The Jewels.

Act 3, Scene 1: The Auberge of the Pont du Gard. *Scene 2*: The Salon in Paris.

ACT 1[74]
Chorus of Peasants and Fishermen; the Dancing Girls
"Cupid's Dart" (Song)[75]
(*Music by* Ivan Caryll.)
"(They) All Love Jack" (Song) (from LITTLE JACK SHEPPARD)
Corinne
"Je Suis (Un Grand) Detective" (Song) (from MONTE CRISTO, JR., London)
H. Brown (*Music by* W. Meyer Lutz.)
Duet
H. Brown, J. Sturges
March of the Bridesmaids

ACT 2
Scene 1
Patrol March by Gendarmes
"77 and 83" (Duet)[76] (from MONTE CRISTO, JR., London)
Corinne, H. Brown (*Music by* W. Meyer Lutz.)
Scene 2
English Music Hall Medley
Corinne
"The Dashing Cavaliers" (March and Chorus)
"Four Professional Guides" (Song and Dance) (from MONTE CRISTO, JR., London)
(*Music by* W. Meyer Lutz.)
Minuet
"The Great Ballyhooly (Blue Ribbon Army)" (Song) (from MONTE CRISTO JR., London)
J. Sturges, Company (*Music and Lyrics by* Robert Martin.)
"(Which My) Sally Didn't Love Me True" (Song) (from VIRGINIA, or Ringing the Changes)
H. Brown (*Music by* Edward Solomon. *Lyrics by* H. Pottinger Stephens.)
Medley

ACT 3
Scene 1
"(I'm) A Jolly Little Chap (All Round)" (Song) (from MONTE CRISTO, JR., London)
Corinne (*Music and Lyrics by* Robert Martin.)
Scene 2
Sappho Ballet
C. Fostelle, Ballet
Finale

1888.12 THE IRISH MINSTREL

A Revival of the Domestic Irish Drama in Three Acts[77]. Play by Fred Marston. Music and lyrics by William J. Scanlan. (Staged by Augustus Pitou.) Musical director, George Loesch. Produced by Augustus Pitou. Opened 16 April 1888 at Henry Miner's People's Theatre and closed 21 April 1888 after 8 performances.

CAST: *Larry O'Flynn*, the Irish Minstrel: WILLIAM J. SCANLAN. *Morris Cregan*, with an honest pride in his name: J. B. TURNER. *Dan Cregan*, who yields to temptation: Hardee Kirkland. *Robert Wynbert*, who wants his own way: J. O. LeBRASSE. *Matt Dougan*, who never permits trifles to annoy him: THADDEUS SHINE. *Nellie Cregan*, a true-hearted colleen: KATE BLANCKE. *Maggie McKay*, in love with Rory: Kitty O'Shea. *Mrs. Bridget McKay*, "a dacent widdy": Millie Sackett.

MUSICAL NUMBERS
During the evening, Mr. Scanlan will sing the favorite Irish song, "The Low Back'd Car," and also the following new and original songs of his own composition: "The Irish Minstrel," "What's in a Kiss," "Irish Potheen," "Bye, Bye, Baby, Bye, Bye," "My Nellie's Blue Eyes," "Scanlan's Rose Song," "Something for the Babies" (a companion piece to his great creation, "Peek-a-Boo")

1888.13 EVANGELINE

A Revival of the Musical Extravaganza in Three Acts[78]. Libretto by J. Cheever Goodwin. Music by Edward E. Rice. Stage manager, James Otley.

---

[72]Original London production was credited to 'Richard Henry,' (R. W. Butler and H. Chance Newton), with music by W. Meyer Lutz, Ivan Caryll, Hamilton Clarke, G. W. Hunt, Henry J. Leslie and Robert Martin. A rival American production was produced the following season 17 November 1888 at the Standard Theatre for 32 performances.

[73]Played a return engagement 1-15 October 1888 at H. R. Jacobs' Third Avenue Theatre for 16 additional performances. Program note: The famous song "Dear Heart" sung by Corinne at every performance.

[74]New York programs listed only the specialties: Hungarian Polka by Corinne; Vienna Ballet Troupe in Character Danses; Storm Galop by Charles Fostelle; Selections by the Corinne Ideal Quartette. List of musical numbers taken from subsequent Boston tour.

[75]Revised version of "Cupid Caught Me" from the London production MONTE CRISTO, JR.

[76]Revised version of "77 and 93" from the London production of MONTE CRISTO, JR.

[77]First produced in New York 4 October 1886 at Poole's Theatre for 8 performances. For Synopsis of Scenes and Musical Numbers, see original 1886 production.

[78]First produced in New York 27 July 1874 at Niblo's Garden for 16 performances. For Synopsis of Scenes, see original 1874 production.

Musical director, William Rostetter. Produced by W. W. Tillotson. Opened 16 April 1888 at Niblo's Garden and closed 21 April after 8 performances.[79]

CAST: *Evangeline*, (Eva) the heroine of an enduring affection which very nearly proves her ruin: BESSIE TANNEHILL. *Gabriel*, a good singer, so that if you were a shipper you would rate him as good in voice: ANNA BOYD. *Eulalie*, her confidante—confidently hoping for women's rights: HATTIE WATERS. *Catherine*, Gabriel's aunt, an antidote for melancholy—"Love's young dream becomes a nightmare": GEORGE K. FORTESCUE. *Ferdinand*: Addie Wade. *Mary Anne*, Eva's maid, ready to marry anybody, until Wagner has made her acquaintance: Lottie Glover. *Marie, Rose*, in Eva suite—two sweet to need description: Caprice Van Lissa, Lillian Cleaver. *LeBlanc*, the notary,—although notary coroner, in quest of somebody, and led to believe that there's a good deal in a name: RICHARD GOLDEN. *Felician*, Eulalie's sweetheart: Minnie Varrell. *The Lone Fisherman*, a mystery, though from his name it would appear he is a Mr. M: JAMES F. MAFFIT. *Captain Dietrich* of the Queen's own, familiar with hard-tack and "Hardees Tic-tacs": BARNEY REYNOLDS. *King Boorioboola Gha*, a sufferin' sovereign: James Otley. *Basil*, the blacksmith, whose bearing will be noted as much below par: W. RIDGWAY. *Hans Wagner*, corporal, but fond of the spiritual: Ben J. Miles. *Chief of Police*, a "peeler": Sherman Wade. *The Jailer*, who keeps the keys and is always on the qui-vive: Harry Keyes. *Lo*, the lo-west and lo-nest savage of them all: James Finn. *The Headsman*, a mimic, very clever at taking off blockheads: C. Sharp. *Fritz Hubert, Rudolph Maurice*, Captain Dietrich's aides: Olive Russell, Lillie Watkins. *The Heifer*, two of a kind: Charles E. Udell, Ben J. Miles. *The Miserable Ruffians (4): Hank Frail*, eat much discord: W. S. Wade. *Carlo*, the Lion Tamer: Joseph McKinley. *Wizard Mike*, the Terror of Wizard Oil: Charles E. Udell. *Reddy Dick*, the Terror of Blue Gulch: A. H. Clarke. *Villagers, Fishermen, Amazons, Diamond Diggers, etc.*

ACT 1

"We Must Be Off" (Opening Chorus)

"One Moment, Pray" (recitative)

"There's a Man" (Song)
A. Boyd

"Thinking Love of Thee" (Ballad)
B. Tannehill

"I Am a Fascinating Notary"
R. Golden

"Into the Water We Go" (Bathing Quintette)
B. Tannehill, H. Waters, G. K. Fortescue, L. Cleaver, C. Van Lissa

"She's Saved! She's Saved!" (Chorale)

"Kiss Me Sweet or My Love and I" (Song and Dance)
A. Boyd

"Sammy Smug" (Descriptive Song)
R. Golden, Chorus

"My Heart" (Ballad)
B. Tannehill

"Golden Chains" (Duet)
B. Tannehill, A. Boyd

Entrance Music of the Shepherd and Shepherdesses

"Sweet Evangeline" (Wedding Minuet)

Dance of the Beautiful Heifer

"In Us You See" (Soldiers' Chorus and Sextette)

"He Says She Must Go" (Grand Finale)

ACT 2

"Clink! Clank!" (Miners' Chorus)

"We Are Off to See Eva" (Duet)
R. Golden, G. K. Fortescue

"Let's Quietly Steal Away" (Musical Trifle)

"I Think So—Don't You?" (Topical Song)

"I Am in Love with a Sweet Little Girl" (Song)
B. Reynolds

"Sweet the Song of Birds" (Duet)
A. Boyd, B. Tannehill

"Twelve O'Clock and All Is Well" (Chant)

"Prowling 'Round the Diamond Fields" (Policeman's Narrative)

"Come to Me Quickly, My Darling" (Romanza)
B. Tannehill

March of the Royal Amazons

"She's Acquitted" (Finale)

ACT 3

"We Are Four Miserable Ruffians" (Quartette)
W. S. Wade, J. McKinley, C. E. Udell, A. H. Clarke

"Laughing Eyes of Blue" (Song and Dance)
A. Boyd

"My Best Beloved" (Song)
B. Tannehill

"Goodnight to One and All" (Grand Finale)

"Homeward Bound"

1888.14 OLD LAVENDER

A Revival of the Dramatic Picture of City Life in Three Acts, 6 Scenes[80]. Play (and lyrics) by Edward Harrigan. Music by David Braham. Staged by Edward Harrigan. Scenery by Charles W. Witham. Mechanical effects by Williamson. Gas effects by John Whalen. Properties by Louis Filber. Produced by Edward Harrigan. Opened 23 April 1888 at Harrigan's Park Theatre and closed 5 May 1888 after 16 performances.

CAST: *Old Lavender*: EDWARD HARRIGAN. *Smoke*, a Negro: JOHN WILD. *Dick*, the Rat: DAN COLLYER. *Philip Coggswell*: Frank E. Aiken. *Paul Cassin*: HARRY A. FISHER. *John Filbert*: CHARLES COFFEY. *Dick Jingle*: PETER GOLDRICH. *Martin Reilly*: Charles Sturges. *Mr. Zolia Brown*: George Merritt. *Gideon Guile*: JOSEPH SPARKS. *Silas Longmetre*: William West. *Henry Mercer*: Richard Quilter. *John Stone*: Dan Burke. *Lascar Joe*: James Burke. *Pop Jones*: George L. Stout. *Mother Crawford*: ANNIE YEAMANS. *Laura Coggswell*: Esther Williams. *Sally Stacy*: AMY LEE. *Nellie Slocum*: Annie Langdon. *Ms. Stone*: Emily Yeamans. *Mrs. Goslow*: Minnie Richards. *Mrs. Mercer*: Kate Langdon. *Miss Keepcool*: Minnie Patterson. *Martha Hollis*: Emma Leslie. *Page*: Master John Hernon. *Serenaders, Street Characters, Sailors, etc.*

1888.15 AMANUENSIS

A Double Bill of a Comedy and an Extravaganza in Two Acts. Play and songs by John Lynd. Music original and arranged by Ellis Brooks. Stage director, George R. Edeson. Scenery by Homer F. Emens (Act 2). Musical director, Louis J. Cornu. Produced by Lou Dockstader and Maurice Grau (Manager, Al Bradshaw). Opened 23 April 1888 at Dockstader's Theatre and closed 28 April 1888 after 8 performances.

Act 1: Lawyer's office.

Act 2: Roof of the lawyer's building.

ACT 1: Comedy

CAST: *Mudill Paitt*: GEORGE R. EDESON. *Dan Debow*: Tony Farrell. *Cowden Skaird*: Maurice F. Drew. *Abel Skinner*: William Paul Bown. *Joe Kerr*: Master Will E. Burton. *Vera Sweet*: MABEL STERLING. *Trollie Laher*: JENNIE LELAND. *Soprania Noyes*: Louise Sanford. *Altoa Voss*: MATTIE FERGUSON. *Scrubbie McClean*: EMMA MADDERN.

ACT 2: Extravaganza

"Dark Lantern Flashes"
W. E. Burton, J. Leland

"Love and Law" (A logical ballad)
L. Sanford

"The Clothesline on the Roof" (A plaint in brogue)
E. Maddern

"Only an Eclipse of Love" (A moonlit melody)
M. Sterling

"Weather Probabilities" (A vocal sarcasm)
W. P. Bown

"The Girl and the Gum Tree" (A bit of natural history)
M. Ferguson

"Romeo and Juliet in 1888" (An old dialogue with a modern air)
T. Farrell, M. Sterling

"When Broadway and the Bowery Meet" (A Composition of Theatrical Flotsam and Jetsam)
T. Farrell, J. Leland

The Gallery Boy (A diversity in dialect)
M. F. Drew

[79]Stage director, scenery and costumes uncredited.

[80]First produced in New York 3 September 1877 at the Theatre Comique for 24 performances in 3 engagements. New and revised version presented 31 August 1885 at Harrigan's Park Theatre for 100 performances. For Synopsis of Scenes and Musical Numbers see original 1885 production.

"McAllister's Four Hundred" (A Social exposition)
M. F. Drew, L. Sanford
"I Will Return, My Love" (A sentimental expression)
M. Ferguson
"Plucking Out the Notes" (A banjo solo)
J. Leland
"Where the Willow makes a Shade" (A story of a veteran)
W. P. Bown
"A Gentlemen from Ireland" (Who has brought his voice and feet along)
M. F. Drew
"Topical Lines and Nursery Rhymes" (A tune, a pantomime, and a news epitome)
Messrs. G. R. Edeson, W. P Bown, W. E. Burton, M. F. Drew; Misses L. Sanford, M. Ferguson, E. Maddern, J. Leland, M. Sterling
"Now and Then" (Something that sounds current and looks a hundred years ago)
Company

1888.16 UPSIDE DOWN

A Grand Chef d'Oeuvre (Farce Comedy) in Three Acts[81]. Play by Thomas A. Daly and John J. McNally. Produced by (Isaac B.) Rich and (William) Harris. Opened 23 April 1888 at Niblo's Garden and closed 28 April 1888 after 8 performances.

CAST: *Miss Tellie Graff*, pretty, pert and peculiar: LIZZIE DERIOUS DALY. *Miss Grace Fullgal*, also and likewise: GRACE SHERWOOD. *Miss Ann Thrope*, a maiden lady, timid, modest, retiring: MARION FISKE. *Miss Etta Share*, a maid with lots of ginger: MARIE CARLYLE. *Otto Gowell, Will Getthere*, two lively young men who would rather travel with a circus than go to college: THOMAS A. DALY, DANIEL DALY. *Professor Phonny Graff*, an inventor: AARON WOODHULL. *I. McCrank*, on whom the Professor experiments: George W. Derious. *Ben Dover*, a regular circus cove: Frank Livingston. *Dan Drough*, a stable boy: Charles H. Phillips. *Mr. S. Cape*, a constable: George Taggart.

Act 2: *Ancient Chestnut*, the clown: THOMAS A. DALY. *Whiskers*: DANIEL DAY. *Ring Master*: Aaron Woodhull. *The Gorilla*: George W. Derious. *Mons. Trocity*: Frank Livingston. *Bill Board*: Charles H. Phillips. *Mlle. Geriflie*: LIZZIE DERIOUS DALY. *Miss Present*: GRACE SHERWOOD. *Tutie Frutie*: MARIE CARLYLE. *Miss Conversation*: MARION FISKE. *Specialties*: Lenton Brothers (Act 2); Banjo, the celebrated trick elephant.

Act 1: Everything "Upside Down"—Home of Professor Phonny Graff.

Act 2: Everything "Wrong Side Out"—Interior of Circus Tent.

Act 3: Everything "Right Side Up"—On the Professor's Lawn.

1888.17 NATURAL GAS

A Farce Comedy (Musical Farce) in Three Acts. Constructed for Laughing Purposes Only. Play by H. Grattan Donnelly. Stage director, John Craven. Musical director, Fred. Perkins. Produced by (Henry V.) Donnelly, (Eddie) Girard and (John H.) Russell. Opened 1 May 1888 at the Fifth Avenue Theatre and closed 16 June 1888 after 42 performances.[82]

CAST: *Christopher Bluff*: HENRY V. DONNELLY. *Whirlem O'Rourke*: EDDIE GIRARD. *Nois E. Howell*: John T. Craven. *Ginger Whipsaw*: Frank Cushman. *Jobson Doodle*: Guy Henessey. *Kitty Malone*: AMY AMES. *Jimpsy*: JENNIE YEAMANS. *Daisy*: Katherine Howe. *Jeanette*: MAY YOHE. *Flossie*: Kate Allen. *Tillie*: Jessie Oyler. *Galatea*: Frankie Franklyn. *Marion*: Fanny Johnson. *Clara*: Marie Hormby.

Act 1: Christopher Bluff's Gas Exchange.

Act 2: The Malone Mansion.

Act 3: The Lawn Tennis Party.

MUSICAL NUMBERS[83]
Selections from THE GYSPY BARON, ERMINIE, INDIANA, DON CESAR, BELLMAN, RUDDYGORE, THE FAMOUS TRIO, SUMMER SEASON, LORRAINE, etc.

[81]No credits in programs for stage direction, scenery, costumes or music, none found in reviews.
[82]Scenery, costumes uncredited.
[83]No musical numbers listed in New York programs; tryout and touring programs included the following note with regard to interpolations.

1888.18 THE QUEEN'S MATE

A Comic Opera in Three Acts, 4 Scenes. Original French libretto (to the opéra-bouffe 'La Princesse des Canaries') by Henri Chivot and Alfred Duru. Music by Charles Lecocq. English adaptation by Harry Paulton and Mostyn Tedde. Scenery by Henry E. Hoyt, Harley Merry. Costumes from designs by Mme. Martens and Assistant. Musical director, Antonio DeNovellis. Produced by the James C. Duff Comic Opera Company. Opened 2 May 1888 at the Broadway Theatre, closing 30 June 1888; re-opened 13 August 1888[84] at the Broadway Theatre and closed 8 September 1888 after 82 performances; returned 7 January 1889 at the Standard Theatre and closed 26 January 1889 after 21 performances. Total: 103 performances.

CAST: *Two Foster Sisters*: *Anita*, wife of Inigo: CAMILLE D'ARVILLE. *Inez*, wife of Pedrillo: LILLIAN RUSSELL. *Guzman*, Prince of Canary Islands: Harry W. Emett. *Pedrillo*, inn keeper: FREDERIC DARRELL. *Inigo*, husband of Anita: HARRY PAULTON. *Bombardos, Pataques*, rival generals: W. H. CLARK, J. H. RYLEY. *Topaz*, a Toreador: S. Russell Childs. *Hans*, sentinel: Frederick Clifton. *Catarina*: ROSE LEIGHTON. *Gomez*, sergeant: HATTIE DELARO. *Juan*, Miller's Man: J. E. Stille. *Chorus of Peasants, Courtiers, Cadets, Toreadors, etc.*

Act 1: Interior of Pedrillo's Post House in the Canary Islands. (Hoyt.)

Act 2: Hall in the Chateau of Galogardos. (Merry.)

Act 3, Scene 1: The Market Place of Palmas. *Scene 2*: The Lace Palace. (A Fantasia by Hoyt.)

ACT 1[85]
"Capital, excellent, heart-warming wine!" (Chorus of Peasants)
F. Darrell, Chorus
"Never a moment left for leisure" (Song)
F. Darrell, Chorus
"Poor Little Man" (Song)
H. Paulton, Village Girls
"Bring the Brightest of Faces" (Duet and Chorus)
C. D'Arville, L. Russell, W. H. Clark, H. Paulton, F. Darrell
"That Is All You Will Know" (Romance)
L. Russell
"Bing! Bang! Boom" (Trio)
W. H. Clark, F. Darrell, H. Paulton
"Perfect punctuality, a virtue rare" (Finale)
F. Darrell, H. Paulton, L. Russell, C. D'Arville, Chorus
"In a village once lived a maiden" (The Bolero)
C. D'Arville
Finale

ACT 2
"Shoulder to Shoulder" (Chorus and Song)
H. Delaro, Chorus
"In time of peace a man engages" (Song)
W. H. Clark, Chorus
"Your orders have been observed, sir" (Quintet)
L. Russell, F. Darrell, C. D'Arville, W. H. Clark, H. Paulton
"Disguise defies a husband's eyes" (Ensemble)
C. D'Arville, L. Russell, W. H. Clark, F. Darrell, W. H. Clark
"The news is most surprising" (Chorus)
Chorus
"My excellent friend, Bombardos" (Duet)
J. H. Ryley, W. H. Clark
"Vivandière's Duet" (We are not demure or shy)
L. Russell, C. D'Arville
"Far away from hostile spying" (Finale)
W. H. Clark, H. Paulton, F. Darrell, C. D'Arville, Chorus
"When as sovereign here I reign" (Song)
C. D'Arville, Chorus
Finale

[84]Major cast changes for the return engagement included: *Anita*: LILLIAN RUSSELL. *Inez*: AGNES STONE. *Guzman*: Fred Clifton. *Pedrillo*: Edward Lowe. *Gomez*: IDA VAN OSTEN. *Juan*: HENRI LEONI. For January 1889 return engagement, cast included LILLY POST, MARIE HALTON, HATTIE DELARO, HARRY PAULTON, RICHARD GOLDEN, Edward Lowe, Fred Clifton, William McLaughlin.
[85]Musical numbers not listed in programs; list prepared from published book of words (New York, 1888), wherein the character of Anita is named Pepita.

ACT 3

"We hasten to the rendezvous" (Opening Chorus)
W. H. Clark, Chorus

"My Peasant Home" (Song)
C. D'Arville

"Buy my nuts! They're all hot" (Duet)
H. Paulton, F. Darrell

"Fairest of earth's attire" (Chorus of Flower Girls)
Chorus

"Toreadors, I see you're ready" (Toreador March and Song)
C. D'Arville, All

Grand March of the Knights of San Jago

"Loud your voices raise" (Finale)
C. D'Arville, All

1888.19 THE LADY OR THE TIGER?

A Comic Opera in Three Acts. Libretto by Sydney Rosenfeld. Based on the short story of the same name by Frank R. Stockton. Music by Julius J. Lyons and Adolph Nowak. Stage manager, H. A. Cripps. Settings by Philip Goatcher. Costumes designed by Mme. Mathilde Cottrelly and Matt Morgan. Lighting effects, J. F. Driscoll. Musical director, Adolph Nowak. Produced by McCaull Opera Company (John A. McCaull, Proprietor and Manager). Opened 7 May 1888 at the Wallack's Theatre and closed 30 June 1888 after 56 performances.

CAST: *Pausanias*, King of Sparta: DeWOLF HOPPER. *Menander*, His Prophet: JEFFERSON DeANGELIS. *Theotychides*, His General: FRANCIS GAILLARD. *The Five Ephori*, or Chief Magistrates of Sparta: Alfred Klein, George W. Kyle, Louis Shrader, C. H. Jones, Lindsay Morison. *The Young Athenian Princes*: Grace Seavey, Clare Childs, Emma Miller, Tillie Frank, Florence Willy, Marie Van Doonick, Bessie Callaway, Gertie Jones, Imogen Johnson, Lou Edgar. *Lamachus*, a Soldier in love with the King's Daughter: EUGENE OUDIN. *Irene*, the King's Daughter: CATERINA MARCO. *Hilaria*, Her Confidante: MADELEINE LUCETTE. *Daroona*, a Persian Captive: MAUD WILSON. *Polyxena*, an Elderly Athenian Maiden: MATHILDE COTTRELLY. *Chorus of Spartan Soldiers and Citizens, Grecian Delegates.*

The action takes place in Sparta, 479 B.C.

Act 1: Courtyard of the King's Palace, overlooking the city of Sparta.

Act 2: Interior of the Palace, overlooking the Gardens.

Act 3: The Arena.

MUSICAL NUMBERS[86]

"Who Shall the Convict Be?"
"His Life Hangs on a Chance"
"If You Ask Me the Reason"
"When from His Couch Uprising"
March of the Epori
"I Love Thee, Adore Thee"
"Oh, It is Indeed a Blessing"
"Quite Instinctively"
"By a Small Refining Touch"
"And That Chap We Select"
"A Smuggler or a Juggler"
"'Tis a Very Ticklish Question"
"'Tis for a Land of Roses"
"Oh, This is Most Ecstatical"
"Sing Hop-de-doodle-doo"
"My Fatal Choice Shall Sever"
Dance
"You Will Pardon Me for Wishing"
"Yes or No"
"Do Not Hurry, Do Not Worry"
"Ah, When You've Decided"
"You're on Very Good Terms with Yourself"
"Into the Arena" (March)

1888.20 NADJY

A Comic Opera in Three Acts. (Original French libretto to the opérette 'Les Noces improvisées' by Armand Liorat and Albert Fonteny.) (American) Libretto by Alfred Murray. Music by Francis Chassaigne. Produced under the stage direction of Richard Barker. Incidental ballet under the direction Mamert Bibeyran. Scenery by Henry E. Hoyt, Richard Marston. Costumes designed by Besche, Mme. Loe, (Henry) Dazian. Director of music, Jesse Williams. Produced by Rudolph Aronson (in association with Alfred Hays?). Opened 14 May 1888 at the Casino Theatre and closed 13 October 1888 after 154 performances.

CAST: *Nadjy*, Premiere Danseuse of the Grand Opera House, Vienna: MARIE JANSEN. *Princess Etelka*, Ward of Emperor of Austria: ISABELLE URQUHART. *Angelia*, Wife of Faragas: JENNIE WEATHERSBY. *Rakoczy*, a Hungarian patriot: MARK SMITH. *Count de Rosen*, Nephew of Margrave of Bobrumkorff: HENRY HALLAM. *Margrave of Bobrumkorff*: FRED SOLOMON. *Konrad* an Austrian Officer: KATE UART. *The Mayor*: ARTHUR W. TAMS. *Ladislas*: A. W. Maflin. *Hilderbrand*: J. A. Furey. *De Launey*: SYLVIA GERRISH. *Irma*: GEORGIE DENNIN. *Rosières (6)*: *Mimosa*: FLORENCE MELLIN. *Orezza*: Nellie Buckley. *Guiletta*: V. deLacy. *Carnetta*: Eugenie Maynard. *Julie*: Edith Mai. *Katrina*: May Chester. *Faragas*, Friend and Follower of Rakoczy: JAMES T. POWERS.

Act 1: The Garden of the Margrave of Bobrumkorff's Chateau, near Vienna. (Hoyt.)

Act 2: Reception Room in the Margrave of Bobrumkorff's Chateau. (Hoyt.)

Act 3: Street in the Town of Pesth, Hungary. (Marston.)

MUSICAL NUMBERS[87]

"It All Depends" (Topical Song)
J. T. Powers

"Raise a Shout of Joy"

Exit Chorus (Fill each class and let it pass)
F. Mellin, H. Hallam, A. W. Maflin, Chorus

"Lightly, Lightly" (Boat Song)
I. Urquhart, J. Weathersby, M. Smith, F. Mellin, Maids of Honor

"The Poor Married Man"
F. Mellin

"At the Signal to Battle" (Patriotic Song)

"Invocation to Venus"
F. Solomon

"Go"

Czardas

"A Woman's Lot"
M. Jansen

"We are the Deities"

"Long the Crowds"

1888.21 TOWN LOTS, or A Paper City

A Farce Comedy in Three Acts. Play by Herbert Hall Winslow. Produced [staged] by Charles E. Rice. H. H. Winslow and H. H. Windsor, Proprietors. Opened 28 May 1888 at the Bijou Opera House and closed 2 June 1888 after 8 performances.[88]

CAST: *Culpepper Meek*: JACQUES KRUGER. *Jerry Judkins*: Charles Burke. *Dr. Surekill*: John Saunders. *McManus McIntosh*: John Saunders. *Bow E. Knife*: John Saunders. *Hezekiah Newcomb*: Al. J. Schlicht. *Colonel Thunderbolt*: Al. J. Schlicht. *Elder Saintly*: Al. J. Schlicht. *Peter Petrowsky*: E. A. Burton. *The Genius*: Charles A. Saville. *Hon. Con Solidate*: A. M. Thatcher. *Mr. Fifthavenue*: T. E. Ballinger. *Joe Blizzard*: Master Thomas Maguire. *Tip Flipper*: Master Thomas Maguire. *Diana Myte*: Hattie Weems. *Texas Tommy*: Hattie Weems. *Betty Collar*: Jean Delmar. *Mrs. Feather Duster*: Louise Dempsey. *Mrs. Fifthavenue*: Louise Dempsey. *Mlle. Cadenza*: Gypsy Tattersall. *Irene*: Claire Harley. *Gladys*: Lizzie Winner. *Violet*: Caprice Van Lissa.

---

[86]Musical numbers not listed in programs. List prepared from published libretto (F. V. Strauss, New York, 1888) and published potpourri (Willis Woodward Co, New York, 1888). May not be in performance order.

[87]Musical numbers not listed in programs. List prepared from published piano vocal gems (R. A. Saalfield, New York, 1888) and piano selection (Carl Fischer, New York, 1888). Not in performance order.

[88]No program available.

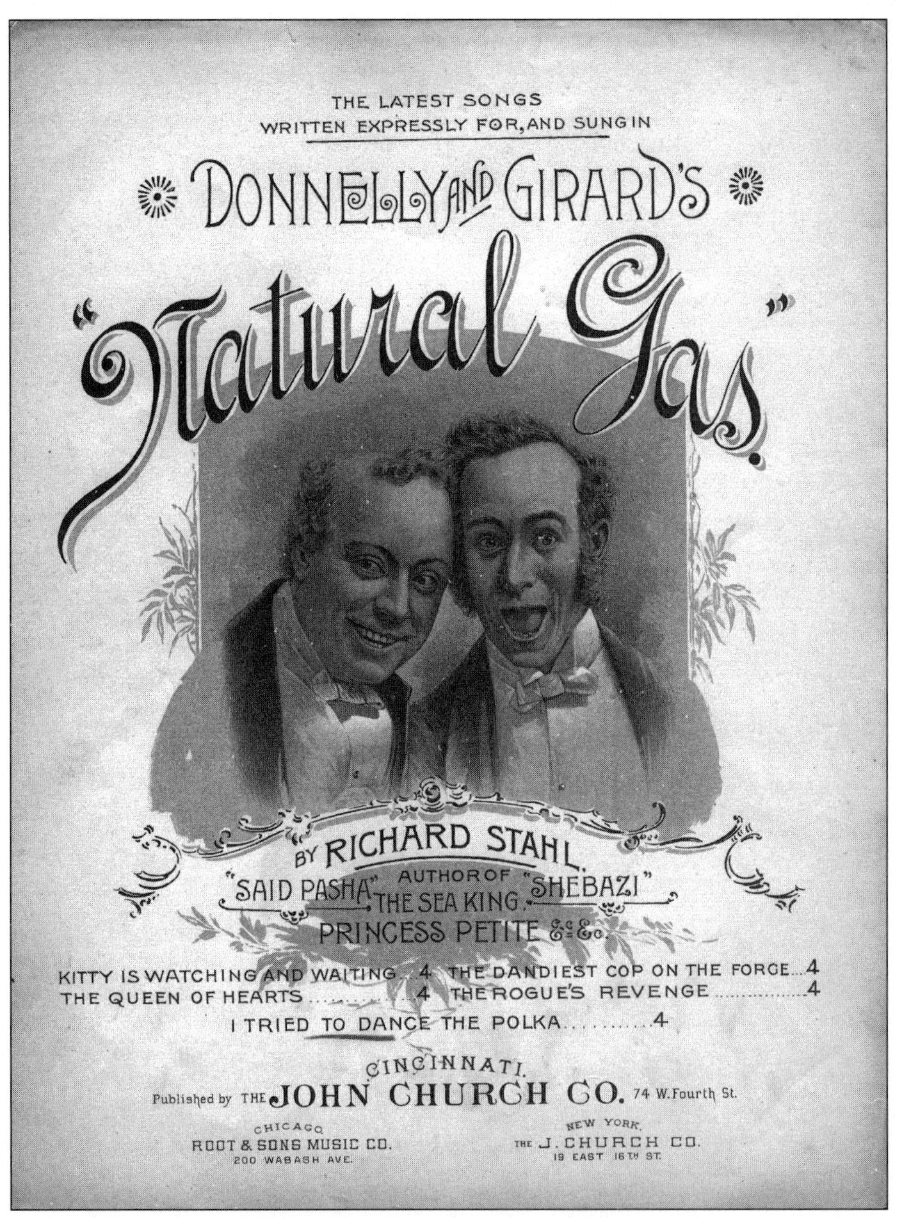

Sheet music for Donnelly and Girard's NATURAL GAS
Richard C. Norton

1888–1889 SEASON

1888.22 PRINCE METHUSALEM

A Revival of the Comic Opera in Three Acts, 4 Scenes[1]. Original Viennese libretto ('Prinz Methusalem') by Karl Treumann, adapted from a libretto by Victor Wilder and Alfred Delacour. English adaptation by Sydney Rosenfeld. Music by Johann Strauss. Stage manager, H. A. Cripps. Produced by the McCaull Opera Company (John A. McCaull, Proprietor). Opened 16 July 1888 at Wallack's Theatre and closed 18 August 1888 after 35 performances.

CAST: *Prince Methusalem*, son of Cyprian: MARION MANOLA. *Pulcinella*, daughter of Sigismund: ANNIE MEYERS. *Sophistica*, wife of Cyprian: MARIE A. SANGER. *The Tiger*: Master Freddie DeAngelis. *Sigismund*, Duke of Trocadero: DeWOLF HOPPER. *Cyrprian*, Duke of Ricarac: JEFFERSON DeANGELIS. *Trombonius*, Composer of the future: John J. Raffael. *Carbonazzi*, Grand Chamberlain: Lindsay Morrison. *Count Vulcanio*, Major Domo: ALFRED KLEIN. *Mandelbaum, Feuerstein*, Ambassadors from Ricarac: H. A. Cripps, Fred. Hedlund. *Spadi*, Officer: Josephine Knapp. *Gasaparo*, sergeant: Grace Seavey. *First Bravo*: Louis Shrader. *Second Bravo*: Ernest deHorn. *Third Bravo*: Charles H. Jones. *Fourth Bravo*: Angel Barbara. *Night Watchman*: Antonio Amadeo. *Pages (4)*: *Carlo*: Clare Childs. *Pietro*: Lou Edgar. *Francisco*: Tolie Pettit. *Enrico*: Belle Braham. *Ambassadors, Ladies of the Court, etc.*

1888.23 MATHIAS SANDORF

A Monster Spectacular Production in Four Acts, 14 Scenes[2]. Play by William Maurens and Paul Busnach from the story by Jules Verne. Entire production staged and ballets arranged by Bolossy Kiralfy. Scenery by T. E. Ryan; Magnini; Gaspard Maeder and William Schaeffer; Carpezzat and Levastre; Amable and Gardy. Produced by Bolossy Kiralfy. Opened 18 August 1888 at Niblo's Garden and closed 13 October 1888 after 66 performances.

CAST: *Count Mathias Sandorf*: J. M. COLVILLE. *Etienne Bathory*: W. S. HARKINS. *Pierre Bathory*: W. S. Harkins. *Sarcany*: Robert Neil. *Silas Torenthal*: W. H. WALLIS. *Zirone*: W. Richardson. *Cape Matifou*: Frederick DeVere. *Poite Pescade*: Edward S. Seay. *Count Zathmar*: J. HAUGHTON. *Francisca*: F. Carlton. *Sergeant*: A. Van de Werker. *Mitzie Torenthal*: LILA VANE. *Mme. Bathory*: Cecile Rush. *Pepita*: Louise Allen. *Bathilda*: Ray Allen. *Annetta*: Annie Dunbar. *Pierre*: Gertrude Magill. *Rena*: Constance Wallace. *Clown Specialty*: BROTHERS ALEXANDROW (Russian Musical Clowns). *Ballet*: Mlle. FRANCESCA PARIS, Mlle. CECILIA NICODE; Mons. BELLAC, Mlle. AOUDA (Parisian Equilibrists). *Corps de Ballet*: Mlles. Louise Allen, R. Allen, Bannister, Konroth, Redmond, Young, Rosch, Prager, Konroth, Haslam, Dunbar, Falugi, Kully, Heom.

Act 1, Scene 1: Suburbs of Trieste. (Ryan.) *Scene 2*: Count Sandorf's Library. Three weeks later. (Magnini.) *Scene 3*: Prison in Fortress at Pisano. (Maeder and Schaeffer.) *Scene 4*: Exterior of Fortress at Pisano. (Maeder and Schaeffer.) *Scene 5*: The Torrent, Falls of the Troiba. (Maeder and Schaeffer.)

Act 2, Scene 1: Reception Room of Banker Torenthal at Pargusa. (Magnini.) *Scene 2*: Grand Fair at Ragusa. (Maeder and Schaeffer.) *Scene 3*: Ballet Specialty.

Act 3, Scene 1: Cabin of the "*Savarena*." (Maeder and Schaeffer.) *Scene 2*: Spnaish Mountain Posada. (Carpezat and Levastre.)

Act 4, Scene 1: Island of Anekirta. (Maeder and Schaeffer.) *Scene 2*: A street in Tetuan. (Maeder and Schaeffer.) *Scene 3*: House of Maskadem. (Maeder and Schaeffer.) *Scene 4*: Public Square of Tetuan, Morocco. (Amable and Gardy.)

ACT 2
Scene 2
Specialty[3]
The Brothers Alexandrow
The Automaton Dance
Hamlet Irving: Mlle. R. Allen. *Adonis Dixey*: Mlle. L. Allen. *La Tosca Bernhardt*: Mlle. Nicode. *Helen Grazebrok Langtry*: Mlle. Rosch.
Scene 3
America (National and Military Ballet)
Mlles. F. Paris, C. Nicode, Corps de Ballet
Indian Dance
Corps de Ballet
Cowboy Dance
Mlles. Paris, Nicode
Plantation Dances
Mlles. Nicode, L. Allen, R. Allen, Bannister, Konroth, Redmond, Young
Entrance of the Sons of America
America (Solo)
Mlle. Paris
Our Navy
Mlles. Rosch, Prager, Konroth, Haslam, Dunbar, Falugi, Kully, Heom
Seventh Regiment
Fife and Drum
Our Heroes, the Spirit of 1776
Uncle Sam Jr.'s Walk
Grand Finale
Entire Corps de Ballet
ACT 3
Scene 4
The Fête of the Storks (Grand Oriental Ballet)
Mlles. Paris, Cappellini; Mlles. Rosch, Konroth, Corps of Secondas, Coryphées
Valse Mauresque
Danse des Clochettes
Adagio
Variation
Mlles. Rosch, Konroth
Entrée
Mlle Cappelini
Variation
Mlle. Paris
Grand Finale and Fête of the Storks

1888.24 LORRAINE

A Revival of the Opéra-comique in Three Acts[4]. Original German libretto by Oscar Walther. American adaptation by William J. Henderson. Music by Rudolph Dellinger. Production under the personal supervision of Mathilde Cottrelly. Musical director, Adolph Nowak. Produced by McCaull Opera Company (John A. McCaull, Proprietor). Opened 20 August 1888 at Wallack's Theatre and closed 1 September 1888 after 14 performances.[5]

CAST: *Lorraine*: EUGENE OUDIN. *Louis XIV*, King of France: CHARLES W. DUNGAN. *Gaspard de Chateauvieux*, a Nobleman of High Degree: DeWOLF HOPPER. *D'Effiat*, Director of the Royal Amusements: JEFFERSON DeANGELIS. *Ollivier de la Tour*: ANNIE MYERS. *Pierre*, Lorraine's foster-father: HERBERT A. CRIPPS. *Pages to the King (8)*: *Henri*: Grace Seavey. *Jerome*: Emma Miller. *Geyais*: Marie Van Doonik. *Victor*: Florence Willey. *Francois*: Gertie Clarke. *Achille*: Pauline Jonsen. *Eugene*: Lou Edgar. *Alphonso*: Tolie Pettit. *Courtiers (4)*: *Le Bleu*: Louis Shrader. *St. Trompe*: Fred. Hedlund. *De la Sancierra*: Harry Myers. *De Pantecat*: Carl Formes. *An Old Man*: Lindsay Morison. *Captain of the King's Guards*: Angel Barbara. *Madeline*, niece to Gaspard: MARION MANOLA. *Oudarde*, Gaspard's wife: ALICE GAILLARD. *Louise la Vallière*, Favorite of the King: JOSEPHINE KNAPP. *Pages, Falconers, Hunting Suites, Soldiers, Courtiers, Lords and Ladies.*

1888.25 THE OLD HOMESTEAD

A Return Engagement of the Rural Melodrama in Four Acts[6]. Play by Denman Thompson and George W. Ryer. (Staged by Denman Thompson.) Settings by Paul Philippoteaux (Act 1), Philip Goatcher (Acts 2, 3, 4). Musical director, Anthony Reiff. Produced by Denman Thompson. Opened 30 August 1888 at the Academy of Music and closed 1 June 1889 after 277 performances.[7]

CAST [in order of appearance]: *Joshua Whitcomb*: DENMAN THOMPSON. *Cy Prime*: GEORGE A. BEANE. *Happy Jack*: WALTER GALE. *Frank Hopkins*: CHAUNCEY OLCOTT. *Eb. Ganzey*: J. L. MORGAN. *John Freeman*: FRANK THOMPSON. *Aunt Matilda Whitcomb*: LOUISA MORSE. *Rickety Ann*: ANNIE

---

[1]1First produced in New York 26 June 1883 at the Metropolitan Theatre, 9 July 1883 at the Casino Theatre for 102 performances. For Synopsis of Scenes and Musical numbers, see original 1883 production.
[2]Billed as the Grand Parisian success.
[3]Specialty included the Blondin Donkey, dropped after the opening.

[4]First produced in New York 28 February 1887 at the Star Theatre for 16 performances. For Synopsis of Scenes and Musical Numbers, see original 1887 production.
[5]Scenery and costumes uncredited; previous production under auspices of John A. McCaull had scenery painted by Joseph Clare, presumably reused for this engagement.
[6]First produced in New York 10 January 1887 at the 14th Street Theatre for 155 performances. For Synopsis of Scenes, see original 1887 production.
[7]Stage director, costume designer uncredited; no musical numbers listed in programs.

THOMPSON. *Miss Annie Hopkins*: Venie Thompson. *Miss Nellie Freeman*: Lillian Stone. *Maggie O'Flaherty*: Minnie Luckstone. *The Old Homestead Double Quartette*: Messrs. [Chauncey] OLCOTT, EARLE, AKERLEY, BAKER, MYERS, KREUGER, (Gus) KAMMERLEE, (Tom) LAW. *Henry Hopkins*: Walter Lennox, Sr. *Judge Patterson*: Gus Kammerlee. *Francois Fogarty*: Frank Mara. *Mrs. Henry Hopkins*: Rosa Cook. *Miss Annie Hopkins*: Venie Thompson. *Miss Nellie Patterson*: Annie Thompson. *Miss Cora Patterson*: Irene Comstock. *Jack Hazzard*: Walter Gale. *Reuben Whitcomb*: Harry Earle. *Hoboken Terror*: J. L. Morgan. *The Dude*: Frank Thompson. *One of the Finest*: Tom Law. *U.S. Letter Carrier*: C. M. Richardson. *Mrs. Maguire*: Rosa Cook. *Len Holbrook, Warren Ellis*, Country Fiddlers: C. M. Richardson, P. Redmond. *Pat Clancy*: Frank Mara. *Mrs. Murdock*: Marie Kimball. *The Three Stratton Gals*: Minnie Luckstone, Lillian Stone, Miss Baker.

MUSICAL NUMBERS[8]

"The Palms" (Act 3)
C. Olcott, Old Homestead Choir (*Music by* Jean Baptiste Faure.)

"The Dream of Long Ago" (Waltz Song)
C. Olcott (*Music by* Charles Kreuger. *Lyrics by* Chauncey Olcott.)

1888.26

BOCCACCIO

A Revival of the Operette in Three Acts[9]. Original Viennese libretto by F. Zell and Richard Genée. English adaptation by Harry B. Smith. Music by Franz von Suppé. Production under the personal supervision of Mathilde Cottrelly. Musical director, Adolph Nowak. Produced by McCaull Opera Company (John A. McCaull, Proprietor). Opened 3 September 1888 at Wallack's Theatre and closed 6 October 1888 after 35 performances; re-opened a return engagement 11 March 1889 at Palmer's Theatre and closed 30 March 1889 after 21 additional performances. Total this season: 56 performances.[10]

CAST: *Boccaccio*: MARION MANOLA. *Fiametta*: LAURA MOORE. *Peronella*: LAURA JOYCE BELL. *Isabella*: ANNIE MYERS. *Beatrice*: JOSEPHINE KNAPP. *Phillippa*: Tolie Pettit[11]. *Prince Pietro*: CHARLES W. DUNGAN. *Leonetto*: Edmund Stanley. *Lambertuccio*: DeWOLF HOPPER. *Lotteringhi*: DIGBY BELL. *Scalza*: JEFFERSON DeANGELIS. *Fresco*: John J. Raffael. *Checco*: Angel Barbara. *The Duke*: C. H. Jones. *The Book Seller*: Louis Shrader. *The Major Domo*: Lindsay Morison. *Students (8)*: *Tofano*: Grace Seavey. *Chicibo*: Clare Childs. *Gardo*: Dora Feitner. *Cisti*: Florence Willey. *Fedrico*: Marie Van Doonik. *Grotto*: Tillie Frank. *Rineri*: Emma Miller. *Engardo*: Gertie Clarke.

1888.27

WADDY GOOGAN

A Local Play in Three Acts, 7 Scenes. Play (and lyrics) by Edward Harrigan. Music by David Braham. Staged by Edward Harrigan. Scenery by Charles W. Witham. Properties by William H. Brown. Mechanism by William Vail. Gas effects by John Whalen. Musical director, David Braham. Produced by Edward Harrigan. Opened 3 September 1888 at Harrigan's Park Theatre and closed 8 December 1888 after 112 performances.

CAST: *Waddy Googan*: EDWARD HARRIGAN. *Joe Cornello*: EDWARD HARRIGAN. *Roland Ringgold*: FRANK E. AIKEN. *Carlo Donnetto*: HARRY FISHER. *Philip Goble*: JOSEPH SPARKS. *Antonio Ronzani*: Marcus Moriarty. *Charles Ringgold*: Fred W. Peters. *Sampson Whybert*: George Merritt. *Mr. Frisbie*: George Merritt. *Shang Wilkins*: CHARLES STURGES. *Police Captain*: Peter Goldrich. *Reuben Douglas*, Skipper: Peter Goldrich. *Skimmy Schemahorn*: William West. *Humphrey Bannister*: Harry E. Chase. *Jack Googan*: Charles Coffey. *Arthur Wiggins*: Daniel Burke. *Syd Morris*: George Middleton. *Nicolo*: James Burke. *Bill Lincoln*: R. E. Callahan. *Beppo*: C. F. Noble. *Thorndyke*: J. F. Callahan. *Mr. Welling*: C. B. Bryant. *Pedro*: James McCullough. *Doorman*: George L. Stout. *Phillipo*: John Decker. *Paul*: Joseph Williamson. *Jimmy*: Master John Hernon. *Louis*: Robert Snyder. *Mrs. Mary Googan*: ANNIE YEAMANS. *Mother Donnetto*: ESTHER WILLIAMS. *Bianca Gillano*: ANNE O'NEILL. *Mrs. Madiline Sylvester*: Marion Lester. *Miss Mabel Sylvester*: Margie Graves. *Miss Bella Sylvester*: Ida Ward. *Mrs Frisbie*: Emily Yeamans. *Daisy Deane*: May Gordon. *Mother Rosa*: Miss Richards. *Maude Rogers*: Maria Roberts. *Lillie*: Gertie Tuthill. *Jennie*: Lulla Tuthill. *Kitty Winks*: Lizzie Leone. *Nellie Bly*: Kate Tams. *Mabel Harrison*: Rita Brunton. *Lottie Riggs*: May Carlisle. *Miss Martha Slasher*: Laura Lyons. *Annie Boget*: Etta Lyons.

Act 1: Ship-Yard at Red Hook.

Act 2, Scene 1: The Home of Roland Ringgold. *Scene 2*: The Bowery at Night. *Scene 3*: The Willow Garden and Café.

Act 3: Under the Dump on the River Front. *Scene 2*: Old Spring Street. *Scene 3*: Police Station.

ACT 1
"Old Boss Barry"

ACT 2
"Isabelle St. Clair"
"Where the Sparrows and Chippies Parade"

ACT 3
"Italian Joe"
"The Midnight Squad"

1888.28

STRUCK GAS

A Musical Comedy (Farce Comedy) in Three Acts. Play by Frank Tannehill, Jr. Produced by Charles A. Watkins. Opened 3 September (matinee) 1888 at Miner's People's Theatre and closed 8 September 1888 after 9 performances.[12]

CAST: *Billy Butters*, an ex-Minstrel: T. J. CRONIN. *Roger Wellington*, of Wellington Farm: MARK DENNISON. *Frederick Wilding*, a Speculator: W. C. ROBYNS. *Asa Spriggins*, Attorney-at-law: H. C. DeWitt. *Drake, Duck*, two tramps: Harry Lamson, Ira T. Moore. *Grace Rollins*, an unfortunate: Emma Gilbert. *Mrs. Million*, a lodging housekeeper: Adrienne Mitchell. *Nan*, (Wellington's daughter): CARRIE TUTEIN. (*Specialty*: HARRY PEPPER.)

Act 1: Wellington Farm, near Pittsburgh, Pennsylvania.

Act 2: Nan's Laundry, Bleecker Street, New York.

Act 3: Back to the Farm.

MUSICAL NUMBERS[13]

Chestnut Medley (Act 1)
C. Tutein, H. Pepper

"Haul the Woodpile Down" (Act 1)
C. Tutein, Company

Nan's Plighting (Duet and Dance) (Act 2)
C. Tutein, H. Pepper

"Shot! Shot! Shot!" (Act 2)
C. Tutein, Company

"Tit for Tat" (Song and Dance) (Act 2)
C. Tutein

"Pretty Maid Milking Her Cow"

"Believe Me"

"Hawthorne Buds" (Ballad) (Act 3)
C. Tutein

1888.29

ZIG-ZAG

A Musical Farce Comedy in Three Acts. Play by Frank Tannehill, Jr. and Von Brunck. Stage manager, Fred E. Queen. Dances arranged by Fred E. Queen. Musical director, Francis E. Reiter. Produced by W. W. Tillotson's Comedy Company. Opened 1 October 1888 at the Star Theatre and closed 13 October 1888 after 16 performances; re-opened return engagements 18 February 1889 at the Bijou Theatre and closed 2 March 1889 after 17 additional performances, and 29 April 1889 at Niblo's Garden, closing 11 May 1889 after 20 additional performances. Total this season: 53 performances.[14]

---

[8]Musical numbers not listed in programs. List prepared from published sheet music, reviews; for additional music numbers, see original 1887 production.

[9]First produced in New York in German 23 April 1880 at the Thalia Theatre, and in English 15 May 1880 at the Union Square Theatre for 28 performances.

[10]No credits for scenery or costume design.

[11]Replaced by Lucy Pixley for return engagement.

[12]Played a return engagement 2 September 1889 at Tony Pastor's Theatre for an additional 16 performances.

[13]New York program lists songs, but doesn't identify which scenes they were performed in. Kansas City tour program dated 1 November 1888 offers detail, as above. Harry Pepper performed his specialty ballads between Act 2 and 3, with stereopticon effects:

"Farewell, Marguerite"/"Pictures of Home"/"Sally in Our Alley"
H. Pepper

"How Does the Idea Strike You?" (added for tour)
H. Pepper.

The Kansas City program from 1 November 1888 lists him performing duets with Carrie Tutein throughout the performance. Toured in subsequent seasons with Frank and Bessie Tannehill performing their own specialties.

[14]For its return engagements, the title of ZIG-ZAG was de-hyphenated, and an exclamation point added, ZIG ZAG! At the Bijou and Niblo's Garden,

CAST: Act 1: *Flirt*, the Incorrigible: ANNA BOYD. *Rene Staley*, the Chum: ALICE E. JOHNSON[15]. *Mrs. Hopper*, the Subduer: KITTIE HILL[16]. *Jaggs Green*, the Apprentice: SAMUEL REED. *Bertie Staley*, the Lover: JOSEPH OTT. *A. Edw. Evermont*, the Author: FRED E. QUEEN. *Mr. Hopper*, the Subdued: ALFRED C. WHELAN. *K. Greese*, the Agent: GEORGE KYLE. *Willie Brood, Charlie Brooks*, the Dashaway Brothers: Charles Wayne, James Tierney. *Brave Mann*, the Policeman: Henry Thomas. *Rose-Bouche*: Evelyn Temple. *Lily-Valley*: Winnie Deane. *Helia-Trope*: Hope Curtis. *Geranium-Leaf*: Dorothy Neville. *Pansy-Blossom*: Estella Hoyt. *Autumn-Fern*: Lucy Mitchell.

Acts 2 and 3: *Nadjy*: ANNA BOYD. *Mme. Judica*: ANNA BOYD. *Clarence Lightfoot*: ANNA BOYD. *Mme. Early Rose*: ALICE E. JOHNSON. *Mrs. Maidenblush*: KITTIE HILL. *Balcazo*, the tenor: JOSEPH OTT. *Pedro*: FRED E. QUEEN. *Roaring Bill*: ALFRED C. WHELAN. *Lucifer Lucky*: Charles Wayne. *Charlie Palior*: James Tierney. *Sing Sing*: GEORGE KYLE. *Sweeney McCafferty*: GEORGE KYLE.

MYTHOLOGY: *Apollo*: ANNA BOYD. *Venus*: ALICE E. JOHNSON. *Mercury*: Winnie Deane. *Jupiter*: Estella Hoyt. *Vulcan*: Hope Curtis. *Juno*: Lucy Mitchell. *Diana*: Dorothy Neville. *Ceres*: Evelyn Temple. *Turkish Maidens, Opera Buffers, etc.*

Act 1: Mr. Hopper's Residence, New York. The Runaways.

Act 2: Hopper's Turkish Boudoir, New York. The Chase.

Act 3: Hopper's Turkish Boudoir, New York. The Capture.

1888.30 ON THE FRONTIER

A Grand Melo-Dramatic Spectacle in Five Acts. Play by Annie Lewis Johnson. Stage manager, Harry S. Healey. Musical director, Professor Marco. Management, Will P. Webster. Opened 1 October 1888 at Windsor Theatre and closed 6 October 1888 after 8 performances.

CAST: *Jack Osborne*, a Mountain Hero: JAMES M. HARDIE. *Bluffflower*, Princess of the Hassaha Tribe: SARA VON LEER. *Bill Morley*, a renegade: D. L. Lacy. *Colonel Austin*, of the U.S. Army: H. S. Healey. *M. M. Patrick O'Dare*, a reporter: W. H. LEARY. *Hans Vanwinkle*, keeper of mine ranch: EMILE HEUSEL. *War Eagle*, an Indian Chief: Claude Marco. *Mrs. Osborne*, Jack's mother: Miss T. C. Clinton. *Jim*, Jack's friend: Kate Medinger. *Deadwood Kate*: FLORENCE FRENCH. *Rose Austin*, the Colonel's daughter: BEATRICE CONSTANCE. *Nonga*, a medicine woman: ——. *Miners, Soldiers, a Band of Genuine Indians.*

Act 1: Jack's Home. Departure of the Soldiers.

Act 2: The Attack on the Settlement.

Act 3: The Battle.

Act 4: The Stake. The Rescue.

Act 5: Fight to the death, your life or mine.

ACT 1

"Fiji Mick"
W. H. Leary (*Music and Lyrics by* J. E. Nicol.)

ACT 2

Song
B. Constance

"Gallagher, Let Her Go" (Song)
W. H. Leary (*Music and Lyrics by* Barney McDonough and H. F. Smith.)

Song
F. French

"The German Swell" (introducing Wing Dancing)
E. Heusel

Quartette, (Sweet and Low)
J. M. Hardie, K. Medinger, C. Marco, F. French

ACT 3

Song and Chorus
J. M. Hardie, Company

Burlesque Drill (introducing original march song)
W. H. Leary, E. Heusel, F. French (*Music and Lyrics by* Barney McDonough and H. F. Smith.)

"Happiest Hours of Twilight" (Song and Dance)
W. H. Leary, E. Heusel, F. French (*Music and Lyrics by* Stanley Macy.)

1888.31 ONE OF THE OLD STOCK

A Drama of New England Life in Four Acts, 9 Scenes. Play by Charles L. Davis. Orchestra under the direction of Charles F. Kauffman. Sole proprietor and manager, Charles L. Davis. Opened 15 October 1888 at the Windsor Theatre and closed 20 October 1888 after 8 performances.

CAST: *Uncle Alvin Joslin*, an Old Vermont Farmer: CHARLES L. DAVIS. *Hiram Hawver*, a hop and grain buyer: DANIEL JARRETT. *Toby Tightpenny*, a miserly old money-lender: CHARLES A. STEDMAN. *Patrick Kilpatrick*, an Irish boy with American ideas: William Robinson. *Sheriff Barker*: ARTHUR COOKE. *Policeman 44*: William Dixon. *Henry*, a dude, in love with Bessie: James Leahey. *Theodore Allen*, a New England rustic: Robert Lewis. *Flash*, a young man who aspires to be a second Gould: William Robinson. *Robert Daws*, an old family servant: James W. Morton. *John Ashes*: John W. Clark. *Seth Skidmore*, who plays the fiddle for all the doings: L. W. Bradstreet. *Eli Whitfield*, town constable: Philip Plummer. *Obediah Westbrook*, town deacon: Lester Collins. *Vic Dietz*, an accomplice of Hiram Hawver: William F. Noremac. *Bessie Joslin*, Uncle Alvin's daughter, a wayward girl: RAY BRISCOE. *Clorinda Joslin*, Uncle Alvin's better half, who wants things her own way, and has 'em: CONNIE THOMPSON. *Sarah Way*, a study for ancient history; age unknown: KITTIE MASTERS. *The Boston Quartet*: Arthur Cook, Charles Dickson, John W. Clark, William Leahey. (*Specialty*: Edward Kirwin.)

Act 1: The Alvin Joslin Homestead in Vermont near Burlington. Laughable Sidesplitting tableaux.

Act 2, Scene 1: Hiram Hawver's Office in Burlington, Vermont. *Scene 2*: Street in Burlington, Vermont. *Scene 3*: Woods on Alvin Joslin's Farm. *Scene 4*: Punktown Station. *Scene 5*: Uncle Alvin's Home.

Act 3: Hiram Hawver's beautiful mansion on Fifth Avenue, New York. The Reception. Father and daughter reunited. The arrest of Hawver.

Act 4, Scene 1: Toby compelled to witness the robbery. *Scene 2*: Sheriff's Sale of the old Homestead. The Sale interrupted. Grand Glorification.

MUSICAL NUMBERS, SPECIALTIES

Selection (Acts 1 and 3)
The Boston Quartet

Sleigh Bells Specialty (Act 2)
E. Kirwin

Popular ballads
A. Cooke

Country Dance (Act 4)

1888.32 A BRASS MONKEY

A Satire on Superstition (Farce Comedy) in Three Acts. Play by Charles H. Hoyt. (Staged by Charles H. Hoyt.) Musical director, Charles Zimmerman. Produced by (Charles H.) Hoyt and (Charles W.) Thomas. Opened 15 October 1888 at the Bijou Opera House and closed 4 January 1889 after 104 performances.[17]

CAST: *Jonah*, a victim of superstition and about everything else: CHARLES REED. *Doolittle Work*, a graduate of a business college: ALF M. HAMPTON. *Dodge Work*, a revengeful man: TIM MURPHY. *August Frost*, just a little too previous: George A. Beane, Jr. *Maddern Sinn*, Administrator of the Work Estate: WILLIAM F. MACK. *The Royal Bengal Tiger* of the Southern Mines, avenger of a sister's wrongs: M. Heckert. *Savage Hogg*, a man who wants his rights: GEORGE A. BEANE, JR. *Badger*, his particular friend: OTIS HARLAN. *Frisco Fog*, appears late in the day: James Horan. *Mr. Barnes of New York, Mr. Potter of Texas*, two well-known dealers: OTIS HARLAN, WILLIAM F. MACK. *Fowle Ball*, not a great hit: Frank Baldwin. *The Mascot*, a terror to hard luck: Handsome. *Birdie*, Jonah's wife, the special correspondent of the Society Gazette: ALICE WALSH. *Cousins of the Works (3)*: *Edith Grace*: Hattie Walters. *Hope Grace*: Marie Bell. *Charity Grace*: Fannie McIntire. *Mrs. Hogg*, an old man's darling: Alice Evans. *Mrs. Badger*, her particular friend: May Montford. *Virginia Bright, Ruby Royal*, girls of the ——: Marie Zahn, Josephine Zahn. *Baggage*, Jonah's daughter's child, but meddlesome: FLORA WALSH. *Citizens, Auction Buyers, Ragtag and Bobtail of Society.*

Act 1: A Dining-room in the basement of the house of the late Patch Work. Friday, the 13th.

Act 2: The Auction Rooms of the late Patch Work. Some other unlucky day.

Act 3: Same.

ACT 1[18]

"The Good Die Young" (Trio)

---

the show's musical director was W. H. Nelson. Musical numbers and specialties not listed in programs.

[15]At the Bijou, played by GERTIE HOYT; at Niblo's Garden, played by Marie Bockell.

[16]At the Bijou and Niblo's Garden, played by Alice Vane.

[17]Scenery and costumes uncredited.

[18]Opening night reviewers also commented on the song "When You Come to Think of It" (C. Reed). Interpolations for the subsequent tour included

"My Delight" (Song)

"Out on a Racket"
(*Music by* Percy Gaunt)

"Papa's Baby" (Song)

ACT 2

"Summer Resort" (four ladies to one gentleman) (German)

"Grab" (Song)

"Drill, Ye Tarriers, Drill" (Trio)

(*Music and Lyrics by* Thomas Casey.)

Lullaby, Medley

ACT 3

Medley

"Auction Sale" (arranged by Zimmerman)

1888.33 PENELOPE

A Burlesque in Three Acts. Libretto by Henry Pottinger Stephens. Music by Edward Solomon. Produced under the direction of Jay Rial. Scenery by D. B. Hughes. Costumes by Mme. and Mons. Alias. Musical conductor, William Robinson. Produced by Lydia Thompson and Her Own Grand English Burlesque Company (M. B. Leavitt, Manager). Opened 15 October 1888 at the Star Theatre and closed 20 October 1888 after 8 performances.

CAST: *Ulysses*, King of Ithaca: LYDIA THOMPSON. *Tektos*, Head of the Police: LOUIS KELLEHER. *Cymon*, Ulysses' devoted servant: J. Belton Radcliffe. *Icarius*, King of Sparta: Charles Horace Kenney. *Glaucus*, Prime Minister: Harry Starr. *Agrippe*, Ulysses' sleuth-hound: Master Fritz James. *Glyke, Daphne*: Florence Brandon, Ella Carrington. *Waiter*: Beattie Howe. *Suitors of Penelope (5)*: *Arctos*: May Bell Raymond. *Endymion*: Minnie Sannon. *Hamax*: Rose Newham. *Carthos*: Ada May. *Philander*: Marie Williams. *Nevera*, Penelope's nurse: Lillie Alliston. *Penelope*, Icarus' daughter: AIDA JENOURE. *Calypso*, Queen of the Island: FLORENCE BANKHARDT. *Capella, Corales*, Her Attendants: Florence Brandon, Ella Carrington. *Hermes*, Ulysses' Lieutenant: CHRISTINE BLESSING. *Cupid*: MILLIE MARION. *Peasants, Sailors, Sirens, etc.*: Brenda Harper, Lottie Watson, Louise Watson, Adelaide Hamilton, Beaumont Sisters, Misses Constantine, Ward, Nelson, Steinberg, Full Chorus.

Act 1: Exterior of Palace. Sparta.

Act 2: The Island of Calypso.

Act 3: The Palace. Ithaca.

SPECIALTIES, MUSICAL NUMBERS[19]

"Here lies an actor" (Pathetic ballad)

F. James

Five minutes with J. Belton Radcliffe

Eccentric Dance

R. Newham

The refined character mimics, The Pylades

1888.34 LITTLE PUCK

A Return Engagement of the Farce Comedy in Three Acts[20]. Play by Archibald C. Gunther, Fred G. Maeder, Robert Fraser and Howard P. Taylor. Based on the story "Vice Versa and Fallen Idol" by F. Anstey. Stage director, Robert Fraser. Musical director, William Withers. Proprietor, Frank Daniels (Management, Samuel P. Cox). Opened 15 October 1888 at the People's Theatre and closed 22 October 1888 after 8 performances; returned 11 February 1889 to the Theatre Comique, Harlem, for an additional 7 performances. Total: 15 performances.

CAST: *Peckingham Giltedge*, a matter-of-fact stock broker: FRANK DANIELS. *Billy Giltedge*, a young American hopeful, his wayward son: IGNACIO MARTINETTI. *Dr. Hercules Savage*, the severe master and mentor of Savage Academy for young gentlemen: HARRY COURTAINE. *Jinks Hoodoo, Esq.*, brother-in-law to Giltedge. A curse to everybody, including himself. Proprietor of Hoodoo's Dime Museum: HARRY CONOR. *Abe Striker*, The Bully of Savage Academy: HARRY CONOR. *Sluggers*, Butler of Giltedge: JOHN E. INCE. *Charley Blocker*, The Boy: William White. *Professor Liverjamb*, Dancing Master at Savage Academy: William White. *Harry Shivers*, who has seen spirits: Harry Mack. *Simeon Mossback*, of Mossback, Wildcat & Co., Bankers, Wall Street: Harry Mack.

Clara Giltedge, Billy's Sister: MARIE DONELLE. *Tibitha Tittleback*, Housekeeper to Giltedge: Marie Hilton. *Miss Ticklesham*, Schoolmistress: Marie Hilton. *Mrs. Simeon Mossback*: Mamie Curtis. *Minnie Titters*: Emma Hanley. *Mlle. Seraphina*: Emma Hanley. *Lucy Langton*: Jennie Stetson. *Mlle. Violetta*: Jennie Stetson. *Violet Severance*: Leona Clarke. *Mlle. Victoria*: Leona Clarke. *Miranda Savage*, Dr. Savage's Daughter, in love with Billy: BESSIE SANSON. *School Boys, School Girls, etc.*

ACT 1

"Do You Think the Test, Sir?"

Chorus

"You Swear to Be Good and True" (Duet)(from DOROTHY)

(*Music by* Alfred Cellier. *Lyrics by* B. C. Stephenson.)

"You Understand" (Duet and Dance)

"Meet Me Again" (Solo)

"Signs, Omens and Predictions" (Duet)

"Drill, Ye Tarriers, Drill!" (with all the vigor possible)

(*Music and Lyrics by* Thomas Casey.)

The Mystic Organ Grinder

ACT 2

"Fe-Fi-Fo-Fum" (Chorus and Dance)

Burlesque Chorus and Dance of Greeting to Dancing Master

Minuet à la "Little Puck" (with calcium effects)

Entire Company

"In the Morning When Day Is Born"

"The Midnight Squad" (from WADDY GOOGAN)

(*Music by* David Braham. *Lyrics by* Edward Harrigan.)

"List to the Wood-Dove Wooing"

"Swinging, Swinging"

"Sister Mary"

"Down in My Heart"

"Has Anyone Seen My Mary Ann" (the latest London success)

The Mystic Organ Grinder again

"Isabella St. Clair" (from WADDY GOOGAN)

(*Music by* David Braham. *Lyrics by* Edward Harrigan.)

"He's a Rider" (Finale)

ACT 3

"Razzle-Dazzle" (Solo and Chorus)

"Old Potts and Young Potts"

"Old Boss Harry" (Chorus)(from WADDY GOOGAN)

(*Music by* David Braham. *Lyrics by* Edward Harrigan.)

The Beautiful "L'Incroyable" Quintette, with calcium effects

"We Boys and We Girls"

"Don't Flirt"

"My Soldier Boy"

"With Banners Waving"

"Pretty Bird"

Quintette Dance

"Fischerine du Kleinere"

Four Little Coryphées

The Mystic Organ Grinder once more

"The Midnight Squad" (Finale)

Entire Company

The Idol, "Little Puck's" power at an end

1888.35 THE YEOMEN OF THE GUARD, or, The Merryman and His Maid

A Comic Opera in Two Acts. Libretto by William S. Gilbert. Music by Arthur Sullivan. Produced under the direction of Richard Barker. Scenery by Thomas Weston. Costumes by (Henry) Dazian, Mme. Loe. Director of music, Jesse Williams. Produced by Rudolph Aronson, by arrangement with the D'Oyly Carte Opera Company. Opened 17 October 1888 at the Casino Theatre and closed 19 January 1889 after 100 performances.

CAST: *Sir Richard Cholmondeley*, Lieutenant of the Tower: GEORGE BRODERICK. *Colonel Fairfax*, under sentence of death: HENRY HALLAM. *Sergeant Meryll* of the Yeomen of the Guard: GEORGE OLMI. *Leonard Meryll*, his son: Charles Renwick. *Jack Point*, a Strolling Jester: J. H. RYLEY. *Wilfred Shadbolt*, Head

---

"Wild Man of Borneo"

(Music by W. T. Barton)

Proverbs Medley, including the famous "Razzle-Dazzle" Trio

(Music by W. T. Barton)

"Are You On?"

(Music by Percy Gaunt)

"McGee's Backyard"

(*Music by* Charles Zimmerman. *Lyrics by* Charles Hoyt.)

[19]Not listed in programs; list prepared from reviews.

[20]First produced in New York 16 January 1888 at the 14th Street Theatre, 23 January 1888 at the Harlem Opera House, 13 February 1888 at the People's Theatre, for a total of 24 performances. For Synopsis of Scenes, see original 1888 production.

Jailor of the Tower and Assistant Tormentor: FRED SOLOMON. *The Headsman*: H. Adams. *First Yeoman*: G. Carlyle. *Second Yeoman*: J. Priest. *Third Yeoman*: M. J. Thomas. *Fourth Yeoman*: L. Roach. *First Citizen*: Edgar Smith. *Second Citizen*: Stanley Starr. *Elsie Maynard*, a Strolling Singer: BERTHA RICCI. *Phoebe Meryll*, Sergeant Meryll's Daughter: SYLVIA GERRISH. *Dame Carruthers*, Housekeeper to the Tower: ISABELLE URQUHART. *Kate*, her niece: KATE UART. *Chorus of Yeomen of the Guard, Gentlemen, Citizens, etc.*

Act 1: Tower Green, London. Sixteenth century.

Act 2: The same. Two days later, by moonlight.

ACT 1[21]

"When a maiden loves she sits and sighs" (Introduction and Song)
S. Gerrish

"Tower Warders, under orders" (Double Chorus)
People and Warders

"This is the autumn of our life"
Solo Warder

"When our gallant Norman foes" (Song with Chorus)
I. Urquhart, Warders

"Alas! I waver to and fro" (Trio)
S. Gerrish, C. Renwick, G. Olmi

"Is life a boon?" (Song)
H. Hallam

"Here's a man of jollity" (Entrance of Crowd, Elsie and Point)
Chorus

"I have a song to sing, O!" (Duet)
B. Ricci, J. H. Ryley

"How say you, maiden, will you wed?" (Trio)
B. Ricci, J. H. Ryley, G. Broderick

"I've jibe and joke and quip and crank" (Song)
J. H. Ryley

"'Tis done! I am a bride!" (Recitative and Song)
B. Ricci

"Were I thy bride" (Song)
S. Gerrish

"Oh, Sergeant Meryll, is it true—" (Finale)

ACT 2

"Night has spread her pall once more" (Chorus)
Chorus

"Warders are ye?" (Solo)
I. Urquhart

"Oh! a private buffoon is a lighthearted loon" (Song)
J. H. Ryley

"Hereupon we're both agreed" (Duet)
J. H. Ryley, F. Solomon

"Free from his fetters grim" (Ballad)
H. Hallam

"Strange adventure!" (Quartet)
K. Uart, I. Urquhart, H. Hallam, G. Olmi

"Hark! What was that, sir?" (Scene)
B. Ricci, S. Gerrish, I. Urquhart, H. Hallam, F. Solomon, J. H. Ryley, G. Broderick, G. Olmi, Chorus

"A man who would woo a fair maid" (Trio)
B. Ricci, S. Gerrish, H. Hallam

"When a wooer goes a-wooing" (Quartet)
B. Ricci, S. Gerrish, H. Hallam, J. H. Ryley

"Rapture! Rapture!" (Duet)
I. Urquhart, G. Olmi

"Comes the pretty young bride" (Finale)

1888.36 ADONIS

A Revival of the Beautiful Burlesque Dream (Musical Comedy) in Two Acts, 6 Scenes[22]. (Libretto by Edward E. Rice and William B. Gill. Original music by Edward E. Rice. Selected music 'cheerfully contributed by Beethoven, Audran, von Suppé, Planquete, Offenbach, Strauss, Mozart, Haydn, David Braham, John Eller, Henry Sator, and many others too numerous to individualize.' Stage director, Herbert Gresham. Musical director, Selli Simonson. Produced by (Edward E.) Rice and (Henry E.) Dixey's Adonis Company. Opened 12 November 1888 at the Star Theatre and closed 24 November 1888 after 16 performances[23].

CAST: *Adonis*, an accomplished young gentleman, of undeniably good family, inasmuch as he can trace his ancestry back through the Genozoic, Mesozoic and Paleozoic period, until he finds in resting on the Archaen time. His family name, by the way, is "Marble." He is also a work of art, and the Chevalier de Mauprat; Henry Irving, with song; Clementina, a country girl with recitations suiting the action to the word, and ballet dance; Clito, à la Wilson Barrett; Adolphus Fitzflummery, a model dry goods clerk; Isaac, a wandering Jew merchant; Sam Small, a tough barber; The Statue: HENRY E. DIXEY. *Marquis de Baccarat*, a highly polished villain. It is well to describe his character, as no one would think it to look at him: HERBERT GRESHAM. *Bunion Turke*, father of Rosetta, an unblushing appropriator of the stock in trade of a well-known and worthy old histrionic miller: George W. Howard. *Rosetta*, his daughter, a simple village maiden, the happy possessor of a clear conscience, a strong will: CARRIE E. PERKINS. *Talmea*, a sculptress, who, like most of her sex, is in love with her own creation: IDA BELL. *Duchess of Area*, aesthetic to the verge of eccentricity, rich to the verge of millionairism, sentimental to the verge of gush: ANNIE ALLISTON. *Artea*, a goddess, Patroness of the Fine Arts: LILA KAVANAGH. *Daughters of the Duchess, Professional Beauties (4)*: *Lady Mattie*: Geraldine McCann. *Lady Nattie*: Lulu Tabor. *Lady Hattie*: Marion Giroux. *Lady Pattie*: Minnie Miller. *Gills, Bills, Sills, Tills*, homely rustics (who will perform a circus): Gilson, Alexander, Carroll Brothers. *Gyles, Nyles, Myles, Byles*, ordinary every-day rustics (the original Clipper Quartette): Messrs. McIntyre, Campbell, Don, Heywood. *Plumed Knights*, impersonated by the following bright bevy of Youth and Grace: Misses Bertha Holden, Arline Athens, Annie Winner, Mignon Arington, Emma Calef, May Hanley, Jessie Holden, Ida Peltzer, Edith Merrill, Rita Gough, Emma Mule, Marion Wells, Ella Rock, May Peltzer, Evelyn Blow, Bonnie Wells, Rita Carroll, Nora Kiernan. *The Typical Policemen*: Masters Gilbert Gregory, Walter Long, James Kiernan, Thomas Kiernan, Ernest Murdock, James Carroll.

Act 1, Scene 1: Talamea's Studio in Athens. *Scene 2*: The humble but honest home of the Miller. *Scene 3*: Garden of the Duchess of Area's Mansion.

Act 2, Scene 1: A Country Village. *Scene 2*: Chestnut Avenue. *Scene 3*: Interior of a Country Store.

ACT 1

Scene 1

Opening Chorus

"The Invocation"

"We Are the Duchess' Daughters" (Quartette)
G. McCann, L. Tabor, M. Giroux, M. Miller

Pedestal Clog Dance
H. E. Dixey

"It's Alive"
Chorus

Scene 2

"I'm a Merry Little Mountain Maid"
C. E. Perkins

Trio
C. E. Perkins, H. Gresham, G. W. Howard

Scene 3

The Bric-à-Brac Guards and March of the Oriental Servitors

Chorus of the Little Boy Grooms

"The Susceptible Statuette"
H. E. Dixey

"Most Romantic Meeting" (Duet and Dance)
H. E. Dixey, C. E. Perkins

"He Would Away" (Grand Finale)
H. E. Dixey, all the characters

ACT 2

Adonis Waltz

Scene 1

"Oh yes, we are the Chorus"
Chorus

"The Serpent and the Dove" (Ballad)
I. Bell

"It's English, You Know"
H. E. Dixey

Recitations and Pas Seul

[21]Musical numbers not listed in programs. List prepared from published piano vocal score (Chappell & Co., London, 1888, and William Pond Co., New York.), libretto and recordings.

[22]First produced in New York 4 September 1884 at the Bijou Theatre for 603 performances. For Synopsis of Scenes and Musical Numbers, see original 1884 production.

[23]Scenery and costumes uncredited. Played a return engagement 6 May 1889 at the Grand Opera House for 16 performances.

"The Blushing Bride"
Chorus
"He's Safe" (Recitative)
Scene 3
Grand Finale
Adonis Quick-Step

1888.37 SHE

A Revival of the Weird Romance in Four Acts, 5 Scenes.[24] Play by William Gillette. Based on H. Rider Haggard's novel of the same name. Music by William Furst. Scenery by William Schaeffer, Gaspard Maeder, Hughson Hawley and Homer Emens. Musical director, E. A. Wolf. Produced under the stage direction of Al Hayman. Produced by Al Hayman. Opened 12 November 1888 at the 14th Street Theatre and closed 24 November 1888 after 16 performances.

CAST: *Horace Holly*: MATT SNYDER. *Leo Vincey*: WILLIAM S. HARKINS. *Martin Brown*: Charles Bowser. *Job*: George Parkhurst. *Abdalla*: George Heisey. *Mohammed*: W.S. Barnes. *Billali*: H. W. Frillman. *Simbali*: E. Waters. *First Sentinel*: F. Schoester. *Ayesha, "She"*: LAURA CLEMENT. *Ustane*: TELLULA EVANS. *Dillyesha*: Fanny Snyder. *Attendant*: Mollie Brown. *Arab Sailors, Male and Female Amhaggar, Guards, Mutes, Attendants, etc.*

Act 1, Scene 1: Deck of an Arab Dhow. *Scene 2*: The Head of the Ethiopian.

Act 2: Great Cave of the Amhaggar. Dance of the Hot Pot. (Schaeffer & Maeder.)

Act 3: The Underground Palace of She. (Hawley & Emens.)

Act 4, Scene 1: Chasm of the Rocking Stone. (Hawley & Emens.) *Scene 2*: Cave of the Fire of Life. (Hawley & Emens.)

1888.38 MONTE CRISTO, JR.

George Edwardes' London Gaiety Theatre Burlesque Company in a Burlesque in Three Acts, 6 Scenes. Libretto by Richard Henry [Richard W. Butler, Henry Chance Newton]. Music by W. Meyer Lutz, Ivan Caryll, Hamilton Clarke, G. W. Hunt, Henry J. Leslie. Produced [staged] by Charles Harris. Corps de ballet under the direction of Fred Storey. Scenery by William Beverley, W. Perkins, E. G. Banks, William Telbin. Costumes by Percy Anderson. Musical director, Lovell Phillips, Meyer Lutz. Produced by Gaiety Company (George Edwardes, Proprietor). Opened 15 November 1888 at the Standard Theatre and closed 15 December 1888 after 32 performances; re-opened a return engagement 30 May 1889 at the Standard Theatre and closed 1 June 1889 after 4 additional performances. Total: 36 performances.

CAST: *Edmond Dantes*: NELLY [Nellie] FARREN. *Noirtier*: FREDERICK LESLIE. *Mercedes*: MARION HOOD. *Fernand*: FANNY MARRIOTT. *Mariette*: LETTY LIND. *Victorine*: SYLVIA GREY. *Albert*: Jenny Dawson. *Carconte*: Linda Verner. *De Villefort*: CHARLES DANBY. *Morel*: FRED STOREY. *Danglars*: Charles Medwin. *Caderousse*: Alfred Balfour.

Ensemble: Misses Gregory, Henderson, Bond, Ryder, Akers, Langton, Belton, Connaught, Holmes, Roe, Bennett, Summerville, Chapman, Manton, Lily McIntyre, Rollitt, Russell, Moore, Payne, Hilyar, M. McIntyre, Harrington, L. Davis, A. Davis, E. Raynor, Balsh, Barrister, Payne, Josephs, A. Errington, B. Errington, C. Jenkins, Holland, O. Russell, K. Douglas, Defossec, Harrington, B. Whittaker L. Claire, Wentworth, Collins, Morton, Ogden, Beger, Bell, Wells, George, Bedle, Van Buren, Wadeson, Walters, Riversdale, Douglas. Messrs. Nichol, Steolcenberg, Walker, Gross, Silvers, Palmer, Stirling, Johnson, Ridgway, Stern, Roe, Duffhues.

Act 1: The Harbour Marseilles. (Beverley.)

Act 2, Scene 1: Chateau d'If. *Scene 2*: Cave of the Island of Monte Cristo. *Scene 3*: The Jewels. (All by Perkins.)

Act 3, Scene 1: The Auberge du Port du Garde. (Banks.) *Scene 2*: Salon in Paris. (Telbin.)

ACT 1[25]
Chorus (On the Shores of the Mediterranean)
(*Music by* Ivan Caryll.)
Vocal Waltz ("Cupid Caught Me")
M. Hood
(*Music by* Ivan Caryll.)
Sailors Chorus
(*Music by* W. Meyer Lutz.)
Dance à la Hornpipe
Graceful Dance
Wedding Chorus (Tempo di polka)
(*Music by* Henry J. Leslie.)
"Je suis un grand detective" (Recitative and Song)
F. Leslie
(*Music by* W. Meyer Lutz.)
Melus (Recognition)
(*Music by* W. Meyer Lutz.)
Duet ("The Respectable Son and His Awful Dad")
C. Danby, F. Leslie
(*Music by* G. W. Hunt.)
Finale Act 1
(*Music by* W. Meyer Lutz.)
ACT 2
Patrol Chorus
(*Music by* W. Meyer Lutz.)
Melus à la Trovatore
(*Music by* W. Meyer Lutz.)
Duet ("77 & 93")
N. Farren, F. Leslie
(*Music by* W. Meyer Lutz.)
Melus (The Leap)
The Sack Scene
Storm
(*Music by* Ivan Caryll.)
The Guides' Quartet
(*Music by* W. Meyer Lutz.)
Chorus of Explorers
(*Music by* W. Meyer Lutz.)
Ballyhooly ("The Ballyhooly Blue Ribbon Army") (Song)
C. Danby
(*Music by* Robert Martin.)
Soli & Chorus (On a picnic if you're going)
(*Music by* Robert Martin.)
Finale Act 2 (From this hour)
(*Music by* W. Meyer Lutz.)
ACT 3
Chorus and March (The Patrol)
(*Music by* Ivan Caryll.)
Song "(I'm) a Jolly Little Chap All Round"
N. Farren
(*Music by* Robert Martin.)
Imitation Song
(*Music by* W. Meyer Lutz.)
Sestett & Galop
(*Music by* W. Meyer Lutz.)
Chorus (By Fernand we're invited)
(*Music by* Hamilton Clarke.)
Mashers' Chorus
(*Music by* Ivan Caryll.)
March
(*Music by* Hamilton Clarke.)
Mazurka and Finale
(*Music by* Hamilton Clarke.)

1888.39 THE CRYSTAL SLIPPER, or, Prince Prettiwitz and Little Cinderella

A Spectacular Extravaganza in a Prologue and Four Acts. Libretto by Harry B. Smith, adapted from the English by Alfred Thompson. (Based on the Cinderella story by Charles Perrault.) Music by Fred J. Eustis. Maitre de ballet, Arthur Novissimo. Musical director, Fred J. Eustis. Produced by John W. Norton & Co., Proprietors. Opened 26 November 1888 at the Star Theatre and closed 22 December 1888 after 33 performances.

CAST: *Baron Anthracite*: R. E. GRAHAM. *Yosemite*, the Baron's valet: EDWIN [Eddie] FOY. *Count Twobetter*: Tom Martin. *Tweedledum, Tweedledee*, Court Flunkies: James E. Sullivan, Harry Kelly. *Cinderella*: MARGUERITE FISH. *Prince Pollydore von Prettiwitz*: MAMIE CERBI. *Mardi Gras*, the Prince's buffoon: DAISY RAMSDEN. *Fairy Graciosa*: HOMIE WELDON. *Angostura, Florodefuma*, the two wicked sisters: CHARLES WELDON, TOPSY VENN. *Captain Riffraff*, of the

[24]First produced in New York 29 November 1887 at Niblo's Garden for 31 performances.
[25]Musical numbers not listed in programs. List prepared from published English pianoforte score (C. Jeffreys, London, 1886), which does not reflect alterations and interpolations made for the American production. Not in published score: "I Like It, I Do," F. Marriott; "Tis a Glorious Thing to Plot,"C. Danby, N. Farren.

Guards: Maude Waldemere. *Tip-Top*, Chief of the Pages: Babette Rodney. *"She"*: Ida Haggard. *Court Pages (6)*: *Flick*: Ada Chamberlaine. *Flock*: Lulu Hesse. *Tric*: Rose Franck. *Trac*: Olive Lynne. *Piff*: Lillian LeMont. *Paff*: Beatrice Mooney. *Hostess of the "Golden Pretzel"*: Edith Hoyt. *Thomas Cat*: Master Eddie Rategan. *Lischen*: Mabel Morris. *Gretchen*: Addie Inness. *Rosa*: Belle Bowles. *Theresa*: Minnie Murray. *Indian Queen*: Mary James. (*Specialty*: LITTLE TICH (Harry Relph). *Principal Danseuses*: Mlle. CLARA QUALITZ, Mlle, Madelaine Morando, Mlle. Clara Neumann. *Corps de Ballet*: Lea Mazone, Laurie Brooks, Louise Griffith, Louis Ronaldo, Josephine Leon, Ida Maccari, Alice Woodbury, Grace Woodbury, Mlles. Quick, Manzoni, Nelsons, Griffith, Gautier, Gueringhelli, Emilie, Reamer, Summerfield, Montain.) *Townspeople, Courtiers, Guards, Showmen, Acrobats, Running Footmen, Coachmen, Ladies of Honor, Suitors, Fairies, Amazons, Demons.*

Prologue: The Catacombs.

Act 1: Grand Square in the City of Pretzelstadt.

Act 2, Scene 1: Baronial Kitchen in Anthracite Castle. *Scene 2*: Elizabethan Gardens of the Castle. *Scene 3*: A Glimpse of Fairyland.

Act 3, Scene 1: Peristyle of the Palace of Polydore of Prettiwitz. *Scene 2*: The Prince's Ball in the Court Conservatories in Polydore's Palace.

Act 4: The Throne Room in the Palace.

PROLOGUE[26]

Subterranean Revels

Song and Dance
I. Haggard, Demon Crabs

ACT 1

Parade of the Pretzelstadt Musketeers

"A Fool Is My Brother" (Jester's Song)
(*Music by* Fred Eustis. *Lyrics by* Alfred Thompson.)

"We Are a Daisy Family" (Quartette)
R. E. Graham, C. Warren, T. Venn, E. Foy

"A Cent for This and a Cent for That" (A Cent-a-piece)(Duet)
M. Fish, E. Foy
(*Music by* Hervé. *Lyrics by* Fred Eustis.)

"Zing Boom" (Song)
M. Fish, Chorus

"I Am a Prince" (Arrival of Prince and Suite)
M. Cerbi
(*Music and lyrics by* Fred Eustis.)

Maypole Dance
8 Folly Dancers

Finale

ACT 2

Scene 1

"When the Wheel Goes Round" (Song)
M. Fish, E. Foy, E. Rategan

"Baron's Song"
R. E. Graham

Trio
R. E. Graham, C. Warren, T. Venn

"Once a Prince there chanced to be, who to marry had a mind"
M. Fish

"You shall be present at the Prince's Ball"
H. Weldon

Irish Reel

Scene 2

Song
M. Fish

Song
M. Cerbi

Scene 3

The Mother Goose Rhymes Divertissement

Buttercups and Daisies
Corps de Ballet

Four and Twenty Blackbirds
Corps de Ballet

Jack and Jill, Funny and Quick
L. Mazone

Little Boy Blue
L. Brooks

Little Bo Peep and Her Sheep
Mlle. Morando

A Frog he would a wooing go
Mlle. Qualitz, L. Ronaldo

Finale, Galop
Mlle. Qualitz, Mlle. C Neumann, Mlle. M. Morando, Corps de Ballet

ACT 3

Scene 1

"Merrily We Trip the Dainty Measure"
D. Ramsden, B. Rodney, M. Waldemere, Pages

"How to Receive an Invited Guest" (The Flunkies' Rehearsal)

"Nothing Like Us"
J. E. Sullivan, H. Kelly

Scene 2

"Whispered Love"

Court Gavotte
(*Music by* Fred Eustis.)

Grand Banquet Ballet
Preceded by a Procession embodying a sumptuous service of Royal Plate in Gold and Silver. Triumphal Entry of Knives, Forks and Spoons. Gorgeous devices in cups, flagons, épergnés. Princely plates and dainty dishes. Menus printed on satin. A delicious dessert. Menu: Oysters on the Half Shell, Ice Cream, Cherry and Pistache, Lemon and Chocolate (Mlles. Manzoni, Quick, Brooks, Avanzini, Nelsons, Griffith, Gautier, Gureinghelli); Champagne Sec (Mlles. J. Leon, I. Maccari, A. Woodbury, Emilie, Reamer, Summerfield, Montain, G. Woodbury), Dolls' Quadrille (8 Principal Dancers, including Little Tich)
Chartreuse (Mlle. C.), Qualitz; *Café Noir* (Mlle. M. Morando).

ACT 4

"Lorraine Serenade" (from LORRAINE)
Solo and Chorus (*Music by* Rudolph Dellinger. *English Lyrics by* William J. Henderson.)

"Because My Mother Told Me So" (Duet)

"I Went with Him" (Duet)

"The Dudes and the Slipper" (Duet)

Little Tich, the Diminutive Grotesque (Specialty)

"The Voodoo Venus"/"Big Shoe Act"

Transcendental Transformation: The Halls of Time; The Fair Wishbone; The Wedding Presents; Cinderella's Clock; Realms of the Revolving Hours; Finale

1888.40 THE LORGAIRE!

A (Revised Version of the) Irish Drama in Three Acts, 7 Scenes[27]. Play (and lyrics) by Edward Harrigan. Music by David Braham. Produced under the immediate supervision of [staged by] Edward Harrigan. Scenery by Charles W. Witham. Mechanical effects by William Vail. Gas effects by John Whalen. Musical director, David Braham. Produced by Edward Harrigan. Opened 10 December 1888 at Harrigan's Park Theatre and closed 30 January 1889 after 60 performances.[28]

CAST: *The Lorgaire*: EDWARD HARRIGAN. *Sir Robert Elliott*: Frank E. Aiken. *Dennis Slattery*: HARRY FISHER. *Felix Ryan*: G. L. Stout. *Dan Garrity*: JOSEPH SPARKS. *Phil Gillespie*: JOSEPH SPARKS. *Terry Mullahey*: FRED W. PETERS. *Robert Ryan*: Marcus Moriarty. *Barney Mahone*: George Merritt. *Paudeen*: William West. *Corney Driscoll*: Charles Sturges. *Humphy Bill*: PETER GOLDRICH. *Dionysius Nugent*: Charles Coffey. *Blind Peter*: Daniel Burke. *Lame Jimmy*: James Burke. *Connaughty*, the Piper: J. T. Callahan. *Phadrig*: R. E. Callahan. *Sergeant Haley*: James Rennie. *The Poet*: C. B. Bryant. *Coast Guardsman*: James McCullough. *Bundy Dorrigan*: J. Decker. *The Lame Tramper*: Joseph Williamson. *Lanty Lanagan*: W. Brennan. *Rauney Duffey*: Robert Snyder. *The Wee Bite*: Master John Hernon. *Cornelius Agrippa*: Master Willy Leary. *Nancy Nugent*: ANNIE YEAMANS. *Norah Mullahey*: Anne O'Neill. *Sheelah*: Louise Sylvester. *Widow Mullahey*: Marion Lester. *Ellen Dooney*: Ida Ward. *Biddy McCarthy*: Emily Yeamans. *Mollie Driscoll*: May Gordon. *Mrs. Mahone*: Mamie Richards. *Mary Keenan*: Marian Roberts. *Sally of the Bay*: Gertie Tuttle. *Yall Margrate*: Lulla Tuttle. *Kate O'Donahue*: Lizzie Leone. *Miss Mary Clancy*: Kate Tams. *Mary Meehan*: May Carlisle. *Baggemy Mag*: Laura Lyons. *Whispering Lize*: Etta Lyons. *Coast Guards, Peasants, Distillers, Milk Maids, Fishermen.*

Act 1: The Fishing Village of Kilcogan.The Arrival of the Lorgaire. The Secret Mission. The Snake-head Chain and Coin. The Beggars' Gathering. A Crime and its Consequence.

[26]Added to the production 12 December 1888: "We May Have to Come to It Yet" R. E. Graham (Music and Lyrics by Thomas E. Powers).

[27]First produced in New York in an earlier short version 25 November 1878 at the Theatre Comique for 32 performances.

[28]Costumes uncredited.

Act 2, Scene 1: Interior of the Manor House. The Hedge Schoolmaster. Knowledge and Feathers. Monsieur la Contrabandiste. The Will and Marriage Record. *Scene 2*: The Cell of the Castle. A Friend Indeed to a Friend in Need. The Story of a Brogue. *Scene 3*: The Castle Peak and Sea-Gull's Cliff. The Beggars Rest. A Leap for Life.

Act 3, Scene 1: The Hedge School. The Connie Soogah. The Christening Party. Gab and Garrulity. The Betrayal and Arrest. *Scene 2*: The Repose of the Leprechaun. *Scene 3*: The Parish Church. The Crock of Gold. The Marriage Register. A Struggle to the Death. A Crime Unveiled. Happy Denouement.

MUSICAL NUMBERS

"Listen to the Anvil" (Opening Chorus)

"Dolly, My Crumpled Horn Cow"

"I'm a Terror to All" (Duet)

"La Plus Belle France"

"(Oh,) My Molly Is Waiting for Me"

"The Beggars"

"Paddy and His Sweet Poteen"

"The Snoring Song"

Also the following beautiful airs adapted from ancient Irish melodies: "Sheelah, Weave the Spell"; "The Fair-Haired Boy"; "Bells of Shandon"

1888.41 MISS ESMERALDA

George Edwardes' London Gaiety Theatre Burlesque Company in a Melodramatic Burlesque of Victor Hugo's "Notre Dame de Paris" in Two Acts, 5 Scenes[29]. Adaptation by A. C. Torr [Fred Leslie] and Horace Mills. Original music by Meyer Lutz and Robert Martin. Produced (under the stage direction of) Walter Raynham. Grand ballets arranged by Fred Storey. Scenery by W. Beverly, T. E. Ryan, W. Telbin. Augmented orchestra and military stage band under the direction of Lovell Phillips. Produced by the Nellie Farren Burlesque Company (George Edwardes, Proprietor). Opened 17 December 1888 at the Standard Theatre and closed 5 January 1889 after 24 performances; re-opened a return engagement 25 February 1889 at the Standard Theatre and closed 23 March 1889 after 31 additional performances; re-opened a return engagement (in repertory with MONTE CRISTO, JR.) 27 May 1889 at the Standard Theatre and closed 29 May 1889 after 4 additional performances. Total: 59 performances.

CAST: *Captain Phoebus*, a dashing officer of the period: NELLIE FARREN. *Claude Frollo*, a monk of the deepest dye: FRED LESLIE. *Esmeralda*, a young lady whose charms simply defy description: MARION HOOD. *Fleur-de-Lis*, very apt to lose her temper: LETTY LIND. *Lafitte*, a friend of Esmeralda: Sylvia Grey. *Ernest*, a friend of Phoebus: Fanny Marriott. *Mme. Gondalaurier*: Linda Verner. *Zillah*, a gypsy girl: May Russell. *Corporal Gringoire*, a gallant son of Mars: CHARLES DANBY. *Quasimodo*, the hunchback of Notre Dame: FRED STOREY. *Judge*: ALFRED BALFOUR. *Clopin*, Gypsy King: Charles Medwin.

Ensemble: Misses Henderson, Bond, Ryder, Akers, Langton, Belton, Connaught, Holmes, Roe, Summerville, Chapman, Lily McIntyre, Rollitt, Russell, Moore, Hilyar, M. McIntyre, Harrington, L. Davis, A. Davis, E. Raynor, Balsh, Barrister, Payne, Josephs, A. Errington, B. Errington, C. Jenkins, Holland, Russell, K. Douglas, Harington, B. Whittaker, L. Claire, Wentworth, Collins, Morton, Ogden, Beger, Bell, George, Bedle, Van Buren, Wadeson, Walters, Riversdale, Douglas. Messrs. Nichol, Walker, Gross, Silvers, Palmer, Johnston, Stern, Duffhues.

Act 1: Marketplace in Paris, with a view of Notre Dame. (Beverly.)

Act 2, Scene 1: Prison Yard. (Ryan.) *Scene 2*: View of Paris. (Telbin.) *Scene 3*: Session Court. (Telbin.) *Scene 4*: Jardin de Paris. (Ryan.)

MUSICAL NUMBERS[30]

"The Romany Rye"
C. Medwin

"I've Always Been Bad Since I Was a Lad"
F. Leslie

"The Dashing Little Soldier"
F. Leslie

"Sweet the Breath of Summer Roses"
M. Hood

"Well, I Said So"
F. Storey, F. Leslie (*Music and Lyrics by* F. Bowyer.)

"Killaloe"
F. Leslie (*Music and Lyrics by* Robert Martin.)

1888.42 PAT'S NEW WARDROBE

A Revised Version of the Farce Comedy in Three Acts, 5 Scenes[31]. Stage manager, James Vincent. Musical director, Thomas H. Gaggs. Presented by the Pat Rooney Comedy Company "Asana Banad" (Fred Wilson, Manager). Opened 17 December 1888 at the Third Avenue Theatre and closed 22 December 1888 after 9 performances.

CAST: *Pat O'Hoolihan*: PAT ROONEY. *Lionel Eustach*: JAMES VINCENT. *Mr. Paragon*: W. H. HATTER. *Mr. Collard*: Harry Ernest. *Crullers*: HARRY WOODSON. *Mr. Wild*: W. Wentworth. *Teddy*: I. Pieri. *George*: R. J. Graham. *Mrs. Paragon*: LAURA BENNETT. *Mrs. Crocker*: Emma Howard. *Christopher*: Little KATIE ROONEY. *Quaker City Quartet*: Messrs. Woodson, Ernest, Pieri and Graham.

MUSICAL NUMBERS, SPECIALTIES

(Vocal) Gavotte from ERMINIE (Act 1, Scene 2)
W. H. Hatter, L. Bennett, K. Rooney, H. Woodson
(*Music by* Edward Jakobowski. *Lyrics by* Claxson Bellamy and Harry Paulton.)

"Naughty Girl" (Act 1, Scene 3)
K. Rooney

"The Yodel" (Act 2)
K. Rooney

"Hear Them Bells" (Act 2)
H. Woodson

Grand Medley Chorus of Popular Airs (Act 2)
Quartette, Full Company

Musical Specialties (Act 3)
L. Bennett

Song (Act 3)
W. H. Hatter

Vocalizations, Imitations, Warbles, Echoes, Refrains
Quaker City Quartet

"Hello, Maginnis"
P. Rooney

Waltz Song
P. Rooney

"Nobody Knows"
K. Rooney

Imitations (of her father, etc.)
K. Rooney

Flirtation (an original aesthetic sketch)
P. Rooney, K. Rooney

1888.43 HE, SHE, HIM AND HER

A Pantomimical (Farce) Comedy in Three Acts. Play by Charles P. Brown. Musical director, J. Clarence West. Acting manager, Joseph W. Keeler. Sole proprietors, C. R. Gardiner and George H. Adams. Opened 17 December 1888 at the People's Theatre and closed 22 December 1888 after 8 performances.

CAST: *Toby Periwinkle*, a country lad: GEORGE H. ADAMS. *Moses Perwienkle*, owner of the farm: William Dixon. *Hans Fulfulgis*: SAM BERNARD. *Bobby White*, with a red apple: Will Mayo. *Steven Gaynor*, a man of the world: W. H. Murphy. *Julian Fitspots*, seeking seclusion: Signor Nardini. *Dave Grogan*, looking for a job: Thomas O'Brien. *Jim Barnes*, a tramp of the period: W. S. Belknap. *Mr. Waller*, a mysterious stranger: Charles Adams. *George Carp*, a natural kicker: Charles Hagan. *Avery Hill*, deaf and dumb: Andy Morris. *Robert Edwards*, bearer of good news: Fred Shear. *The Demon*, from below: Pete Crofut. *Tootsie Brant*, a fortunate waif: TOMA HANLON. *Mrs. Murry Hill*, has her laugh with her: Alida Perreault. *Claire Kingdon*, the pretty boarder: Carrie Francois. *Kate Alden*, a poor relation: Blanche Nicholls. *Mary Marden*, fond of flirting: Oliver Tremaine. *Grace*, hunting a beau: Ray Gillette. *Ella*, who expects a letter: Annie Martel. *Blanche*, who hates the men: Ada Marvin. *Ethel*, a whistler: Hattie Ballard.

Time: Anytime.

Place: Anywhere.

[29]In London, subtitled The Monkey and the Monk.

[30]Musical numbers not listed in American programs. English piano vocal score published by C. Jeffreys, London, 1888. List prepared from reviews, English programs.

[31]Authorship uncredited. First produced in an earlier version as PAT'S WARDROBE in New York 20 December 1886 at Poole's Theatre for 8 performances.

Argument: Suit yourself.

Plot: None.

MUSICAL NUMBERS, SPECIALTIES

"Lawn Tennis" (Opening)
Chorus

"Love's Dream" (Farm Trio)

Mixed Quartette

Irish Specialty

Our "Sis" Song

Sextette Song and Dance

"The Last Rose of Summer"

Male Quartette

Grand Medley Finale (Act 2)

"Oh, Ah!"

Sam Bernard's Specialty

Female Quartette

Vocal Gavotte

Grand Musical Finale

1888.44 A TIN SOLDIER

A Revival of the Farce Comedy in Three Acts[32]. Play by Charles H. Hoyt. Produced under the personal direction of Charles H. Hoyt. Musical director, Percy Gaunt. Produced by (Charles H.) Hoyt and (Charles W.) Thomas (Management, Frank McKee). Opened 24 December 1888 at the 14th Street Theatre and closed 5 January 1889 after 18 performances.[33]

CAST: *Rats*, a perfect little gentleman: EUGENE CANFIELD. *Vilas Canby*, "The Professor," a practical plumber: JESSE JENKINS. *Brooklyn Bridge*, a gentleman of high position: CHARLES F. RAYMOND. *Col. I. B. Boosey*, hero of Gettysburg: WILLIAM CARLETON. *Wright Handy*, Bridge's partner: WILLIAM CARLETON. *Il Conte di Luna*, Italian art connoisseur: Daniel Kelley. *Colonel Wood B. Fuller*, hero of Gettysburg: Daniel Kelley. *Trip Walker*, a mail carrier: Daniel Kelley. *Steele Coffin*, Secretary of Tarring and Feathering Committee: W. Jordan. *Violet Hughes*, a domestic earthquake: KATE DAVIS. *Victoria Bridge*, a bride of six weeks: Isabelle Coe. *Patsy*, a young thing: MARIE CAHILL. *Carrie Story*, who lives with Mrs. Hogg, next door: DOLLIE KLINE. *Mrs. Fulton Ferry*, mother-in-law of Brooklyn Bridge: Bessie Grey. *Nora Marks*, a domestic: Bessie Grey. *May Ketchum*, a whistling girl: Alice Hodgdon. *Rob Graves*, business man: Mike Kelly. *Tarring and Feathering Committee, etc.*

ACT 1

Irish Reel

ACT 2

"Do You Think So?" (Topical Song)
(*Music and Lyrics by* Charles H. Hoyt.)

"The Lion Tamer" (Song and Dance)
(*Music by* Percy Gaunt.)

Illustration of what Rats saw at the Circus, "Once in a While" and Imitations

"Faust" Waltz (composed by Charles Gounod expressly for another purpose)

"Dancing Mad"

"March of the Plumbers"
(*Music by* Percy Gaunt.)

ACT 3

"Generosity"
(*Music and Lyrics by* Charles H. Hoyt.)

Grand Potpourri, introducing "Jockey Chorus," "Dandy," "Last Night," "Too Fresh."

Waltz Song

Cornet Imitations

"Busy Bees"
(arranged by Percy Gaunt)

[32]First produced in New York 3 May 1886 at the Standard Theatre for 63 performances. For Synopsis of Scenes, see original 1886 production.

[33]No credits for scenery or costume design.

1888.45 THE KITTY

A Farce Comedy in Three Acts[34]. Play by Charles Alfred Byrne. Produced under the stage direction of William A. Mestayer. Musical director, Prof. Fleischer. Produced by J. P. Smith. Opened 31 December 1888 at Dockstader's Theatre and closed 12 January 1889 after 17 performances.

CAST: *Tariff Bill*, a typical New York ward politician of the old school, but a thoroughbred from way back: WILLIAM A. MESTAYER. *Dennis Mudd*, an amalgamated teutonic Yankee Celt, not ashamed of Old Ireland, but naturalized for political reasons: W. J. RUSSELL. *Hi Prince*, a full-fledged Reuben: CHARLES KIRKE. *Antonie*, a Delmonico waiter: CHARLES KIRKE. *Hop Lung*, a Celestial domestic: CHARLES KIRKE. *Jay Montgomery Mudd*, a stage door statue who loves the sensitive plant of the Casino: Harry E. Pike. *Singleton Sway*, the oldest inhabitant: Harry Deaves. *Cinch Spinach, Dupree Dodge*, two hayseeds with asparagus trimmings: JOHN WEST, M. GALLAGHER. *His Oysters*, by a real Shrewsbury: Charles Johnson. *Kitty O'Mulligan*, a centennial maiden of Irish proclivities, sister-in-law of Dennis, and possessor of the champion face: MARY GRAY. *Sally Mudd*, a country girl of the suburban type: Belle La Verde. *May, Rose, Daisy*, just out: Celia Valmer, Viola Randall, Ida Hazelton. *Arabella*, (a sensitive plant from the New York Casino. The rival of the nightingale, the dudelet's joy and a general heart annihilator): THERESA VAUGHN.

Act 1: Post office and grocery store of Mudd, at Reubenville, New Jeresy.

Act 2: (Delmonico's) Restaurant, New York City.

Act 3: Swago Matrimonial Agency in New York City.

ACT 1

"The Jays"
C. Kirke, M. Gallagher, J. West

Operatic Burlesque
T. Vaughn, W. Mestayer

March
Company

Kerosene Evolutions
M. Gallagher, J. West

Medley—Finale
Company

ACT 2

"My Last Thoughts" (Waltz)
T. Vaughn (*Music by* Richard Stahl.)

Parodies
M. Gallagher, J. West

The German Yodelers
T. Vaughn, C. Valmer

ACT 3

The "Nadjy" Dance
W. Mestayer, W. J. Russell, M. Gray (*Music by* Francis Chassaigne.)

Topical Song
W. J. Russell

Chinese Characteristics
C. Kirke

Finale
Laughing Chorus

1889.01 THE PEARL OF PEKIN

A Return Engagement of the Opéra-bouffe in Three Acts[35]. (Based on the original French 'Fleur de thé,' libretto by Alfred Duru and Henri Chivot. Music by Charles Lecocq.) Music by Gustave Kerker and Charles Lecocq. Scenery by Messrs. Edward G. Unitt and King. Costumes by Carrie E. Perkins. Musical director, Gustave Kerker. Chinese band, High Kee (Leader). Produced under the supervision of Edward E. Rice, assisted by Gustave Kerker and Charles Alfred Byrne. Produced by Edward E. Rice and Henry E. Dixey. Opened 7 January 1889 at the Bijou Opera House, moved 28 January 1889 to the Standard Theatre and closed 23 February 1889 after 56 performances. Total including first engagement: 136 performances.

[34]Billed as "A Cat-aleptic Cachinatious Con-cat-enacting Cataract of Mirth, in Three Meows and a Psht."

[35]First produced in New York in French as 'Fleur de thé' 1 February 1869 at the Theatre Français. This adaptation first presented in New York in English 19 March 1888 at the Bijou for 70 performances. For Synopsis of Scenes and Musical Numbers, see 1888 production.

CAST: *Pearl of Pekin,* daughter of Tyfoo and a simple Chinese maiden: BELLE THORNE. *Finette,* wife of Petit Pierre and a vivandière: IRENE VERONA. *Four charming French waiting maids: Fantine*: Bertie Fisch. *Pierrette*: Clarette Vanderbilt. *Angelique*: Carrie Behr. *Pepine*: Edith Cole. *Petit Pierre,* a dashing young quartermaster of the French Navy, stationed on board "La Victoria," whose wife has opened a restaurant in Pekin as a side speculation: PHILIP BRANSON. *Sosoriki,* a Japanese of some distinction, Chief of the Imperial Tigers, and with still higher aspirations: JOSEPH W. HERBERT. *Paul Mathot,* Boatswain of "La Victoria," useful if not ornamental: Edward Webb. *Sing High,* a Chinese attendant: John C. Leach.

Sailors and Chinese Boys (8): Jocrisse: May Hanley. *Henry*: Ida Orme. *Jacque*: Nettie Harrington. *Victor*: Dollie Delroy. *Hugo*: Annie Seabury. *Eugene*: Dora Percival. *Gustave*: Flora Wragland. *Auguste*: Minnie Dreher. *Henchmen*: Messrs. Pipley, Durham, Hill, Dorgan.

Tyfoo, Mandarin and Governor of Pekin, who frequently remarks That "He is as knowing as a Sphinx": LOUIS HARRISON. (*Chinese Band,* High Kee, leader.) *French Sailors, Chinese Giants, men and women, Mandarins, Officers of the State, ad infinitum.*

ADDITIONAL MUSICAL INTERPOLATIONS[36]

"Chop Sticks" (Chinese Song and Dance) (Act 2)
"If I Were a Bird" (Trio) (Act 2)
J. W. Herbert, B. Thorne, I. Verona
Entr'acte and Opening (Act 3)
Madrigal (Quartette for mixed voices) (Act 3)
Finale (Act 3)
"The Lady Picking Mulberries" (Act 3)[37]
B. Thorne (*Music and Lyrics by* Edgar S. Kelley.)
"When Ching-a-Lung Hit High (Act 3)[38]
L. Harrison (*Music and Lyrics by* Louis Harrison.)

1889.02 FANTASMA

A New Version of the Spectacular Pantomime in Three Acts, 13 Scenes[39]. Invented, arranged and produced by the Hanlons. Scenery painted by William Schaeffer, Gaspard Maeder and Homer Emens. Costumes by Dazian and Schovenke. Musical director, George L. Tracy. Opened 14 January 1889 at the 14th Street Theatre and closed 19 January 1889 after 8 performances.

CAST: *Farmer Close,* father to Lena: WILLIAM HANLON. *Fantasma,* Fairy Queen, disguised as witch: LAURA BURT. *Zamaliel,* King of the Realm of Heads: CHARLES H. RIEGEL. *Pico,* the faithful, always in trouble: FRANCOIS X. ZELTNER. *Lena,* in love with Arthur: IDA MAUSSEY. *Arthur,* devoted to Lena: J. H. SMILEY. *Hagwrath,* an imp, Zamaliel's right bower: Royal Roche. *Serena,* Fantasma's fairy assistant: Rose M. Forte. *Madge,* a milkmaid: Rose M. Forte. *Spirits attendant on Zamaliel (4): Balios*: Edward Murphy. *Hazzard*: T. J. McGrane. *Ichthyo*: Joseph Smiley. *Zazar*: L. Morris. *Spikes*: J. Murphy. *Enasebus,* Fantasma's dragon: C. Launcelot. *Xanthos*: C. Turnour. *Pico, Jr.,* with song: Little Tootsey. *Prophetess,* with song: Mattie Lee. *Fischia*: May Belmont. *Dahlia*: Lily Van Cliff. *Camelia*: Nellie Cameron. *Cupid*: Little Tootsey. *Lover at the gate* with song: A. C. Orcutt. *Boniface*: William Garrene. *Landlady*: A. Roccordi. *Hunter*: J. C. Morton. *Peddler*: Arthur Lowrey. *Peasants, Witches, Ghosts, Mermaids, Bears, Skeletons, Tradespeoples, etc.*

Act 1, Scene 1: The Hag's Retreat. *Scene 2*: The Village Home of Lena. *Scene 3*: The Ruined Abbey. *Scene 4*: The Skeleton Pass. *Scene 5*: The Mysteries of the Deep, 20,000 Leagues under the sea.

Act 2, Scene 1: Castle Exterior. *Scene 2*: The Haunted Dormitory. *Scene 3*: The Witches' Laboratory.

Act 3, Scene 1: The Labyrinth of the Doomed. *Scene 2*: Serena searching for Pico. *Scene 3*: Fantasma finds a place of shelter for Lena. *Scene 4*: Campaign Speech for Women's Rights. *Scene 5*: The Vulcan Volcano.

ACT 1
Scene 1
Weird Dance of the Witches
Scene 5
The Mermaids' Revels

ACT 2
Scene 1
The Phantom Minuet
Scene 3
"My Wooing"
M. Lee, A. C. Orcutt
"The Pilot's Daughter"
M. Lee, A. C. Orcutt

ACT 3
Scene 5
Grand Transformation to Fantasma's Realm

1889.03 MYLES AROON

An Irish Comedy Drama in Four Acts, 8 Scenes. Play by George H. Jessop and Horace Townsend. Music and lyrics by William J. Scanlan. (Staged by Augustus Pitou.) Musical director, F. Loesch. Produced by Augustus Pitou. Opened 21 January 1889 at the 14th Street Theatre and closed 2 February 1889 after 16 performances[40].

CAST: *Myles Aroon*: WILLIAM J. SCANLAN. *Squire Raymond Thurston*: Charles Mason. *Mike Carney*: Thaddeus Shine. *Gerald Fosdyke*: Edward R. Marsden. *Pat Phelan*: Robert McNair. *Joe Upton*: Charles R. Dade. *Dennis*: ALBERT MORRELL. *Lady Glover*: STELLA TEUTON. *Maggie Farrell*: MATTIE FERGUSON. *Mrs. Farrell*: Millie Sackett. *Lucy O'Shea*: Mary Warner. *Annie O'Connor*: Lucy Waters. *Nora*: Stella Maris. *Katie*: Charlotte Ray. *Mother Bet*: LAURA WILSON. *Nellie Glover*: Little Gertie Boswell.

Act 1: Conservatory at Castle Crevagh.

Act 2, Scene 1: Fair Green of Crevagh. *Scene 2*: A Path in the Woods. *Scene 3*: The Glen of the Good People.

Act 3, Scene 1: Interior of Mrs. Farrell's Cottage. *Scene 2*: A path in the woods. *Scene 3*: Lisbeg, Mother Bet's Hovel on the mountain side.

Act 4: Garden of Lady Glover's Home.

MUSICAL NUMBERS[41]

"Scanlan's Swing Song"
"You and I, Love" (from SHANE-NA-LAWN)
"My Maggie"
"Live, My Love, Oh, Live"
"Moonlight at Killarney" (from FRIEND AND FOE)
"Peek-a-Boo" (from FRIEND AND FOE)

1889.04 NADJY

A Return Engagement of the Comic Opera in Three Acts[42]. (Original French libretto to the opérette 'Les Noces improvisées' by Armand Liorat and Albert Fonteny.) (American) Libretto by Alfred Murray. Music by Francis Chassaigne. Produced under the stage direction of Richard Barker. Incidental ballet under the direction H. Fletcher Rivers. Scenery by Henry E. Hoyt, Richard Marston. Costumes designed by Besche, Mme. Loe, (Henry) Dazian. Director of music, Jesse Williams. Produced by Rudolph Aronson (by arrangement with Alfred Hays). Opened 21 January 1889 at the Casino Theatre and closed 8 May 1889 after 108 performances. Total including first engagement: 262 performances.

CAST: *Princess Etelka,* Ward of Emperor of Austria: LILLIAN RUSSELL. *Nadjy,* Premiere Danseuse of the Grand Opera House, Vienna: FANNY RICE. *Angelia,* Wife of Faragas: ELMA DELARO. *Rakoczy,* a Hungarian patriot: JOHN E. BRAND. *Count de Rosen,* Nephew of Margrave of Bobrumkorff: HENRY HALLAM. *Margrave of Bobrumkorff*: FREDERIC SOLOMON. *Konrad* an Austrian Officer: SYLVIA GERRISH. *Ladislas*: Laura Russell. *The Mayor*: EDGAR SMITH. *Hilderbrand*: H. Adams. *De Launey*: BLANCHE ROBERTS. *Katinka*: ZELMA RAWLSTON. *Irma*:

[36]For Synopsis of Scenes and Musical Numbers, see original 1888 production. Additional interpolations listed in programs from the Bijou and Standard Theatre engagements and subsequent tour are hereby listed.
[37]Added for Standard Theatre engagement.
[38]Added for second week of Standard Theatre engagement.
[39]First version of FANTASMA, or Funny Frolics in Fairyland produced in New York 10 November 1884 at the Fifth Avenue Theatre for 32 performances; played a return engagement 20 April 1885 at Niblo's Garden for an additional 16 performances.

[40]Scenery and costumes uncredited.
[41]Not in performance order.
[42]First produced 14 May 1888 at the Casino Theatre for 154 performances. For Synopsis of Scenes and Musical Numbers, see original 1888 production. Produced in London as NADGY.

EMMA LAWRENCE. *Rosieres (6)*: *Mimosa*: Florence Melin. *Orezza*: Fanny Adams. *Guiletta*: Ina Weddell. *Carnetta*: Madge Perry. *Julie*: Edith Mai. *Katrina*: Marguerite Rutledge. *Faragas*, Friend and Follower of Rakoczy: JAMES T. POWERS.

1889.05

RUNNING WILD

A Musical Farce Comedy in Three Acts[43]. Book, music and lyrics by Charles T. Vincent and Kenneth Lee. Stage director, T. B. Butler. Musical director, Fred. Neidermeyer. Produced by E. M. Kayne. Opened 21 January 1889 at the Star Theatre and closed 26 January 1889 after 8 performances.[44]

CAST: *D'Oily Float*: JOHN WILD. *Joe King*, the man who's running wild: JOHN WILD. *Barry Cassidy*, the artist who paints Ireland green: CHARLES H. BRADSHAW. *Daniel Dogge*, the Guardian in love with his ward: F. M. KENDRICK. *Ignatius Malone*, the Butler that is always "on deck": T. B. BUTLER. *The Gentleman* who removes the ashes: Harry Brinsley. *Cardamon Moxie*, who treads the high seas: Theo. M. Brown. *Dollie*, the miss that's running wild: GERTRUDE FORT. *The Lady* that does the cleaning: (Miss) ST. GEORGE HUSSEY. *Penelope Podd*, the maiden all forlorn: Adele Bray. *Dora, Flora*, the girls that always agree: Lottie Hyde, May Sheriden. *The Teacher* that dispenses the music: Lena Haswell. *The Girl* who never frowns: JULIE MACKEY. *The Young Lady* that never scorns: ADA JONES. *The Little Miss* that always smiles: Millie Sheriden.

Act 1: Lawn of Dogge's House. "Good morning!"

Act 2: Parlors of Dogge's House. "Good evening!"

Act 3: Barry Cassidy's Studio. "Good gracious!"

MUSICAL NUMBERS

"Queen of the Belles"
G. Fort

"Daunt yer know?" (Duet)
G. Fort, J. Wild

"Just a Little Sunshine" (Trio)
G. Fort, J. Mackey, A. Jones, L. Hyde, May Sheriden, L. Haswell

"Cry, Baby, Cry"
A. Jones

Medley
Company

"Bid Me Goodbye and Go"
J. Mackey

Phantom Quadrille
T. B. Butler

Trio Lullabye
G. Fort, J. Mackey, A. Jones

Selection from A TRIP TO AFRICA
Misses Hyde, May and Millie Sheriden, L. Haswell (*Music by* Franz von Suppé.)

Chorus from THE QUEEN'S LACE HANDKERCHIEF (*Music by* Johann Strauss.)

"Mary Ann Malone"
S. G. Hussey

"Where Did You Get That Hat?"
J. Wild (*Music and Lyrics by* Joseph J. Sullivan.)

1889.06

NATURAL GAS

A Return Engagement of the Farce Comedy in Three Acts[45]. Constructed for Laughing Purposes Only. Play by H. Grattan Donnelly. Musical director, John Holding. Produced by John H. Russell. Opened 28 January 1889 at the Bijou Theatre and closed 16 February 1889 after 24 performances.[46]

CAST: *Christopher Bluff*: HENRY V. DONNELLY. *Whirlem O'Rourke*: EDDIE GIRARD. *Nois E. Howell*: Mark Sullivan. *Ginger Whipsaw*: Ben Collins. *Jobson Doodle*: S. W. Keene. *Bobby*: Joseph Jackson. *Kitty Malone*: JENNIE SATTERLEE. *Jimpsy*: LENA MERVILLE. *Daisy*: Ethel Corlette. *Jeannette*: MAY YOHE. *Flossie*: Fanny Johnston. *Tillie*: Marie Hornby. *Galatea*: Lea Raymond. *Helen*: Mamie Sherwood.

1889.07

PETE

A Revival of the Domestic Drama of the South in Four Acts[47]. Play (and lyrics) by Edward Harrigan. Music by David Braham. Staged by Edward Harrigan. Scenery by Charles W. Witham. Mechanical effects by William Vail. Gas effects by John Whalen. Director of music, David Braham. Produced by Edward Harrigan. Opened 31 January 1889 at Harrigan's Park Theatre and closed 2 March 1889 after 44 performances.

CAST: *Pete*: EDWARD HARRIGAN. *Alderman Brannigan*: EDWARD HARRIGAN. *Gaspar Randolph*: DANIEL BURKE. *Vi'let*: JOSEPH SPARKS. *Dr. Joseph Clifford*: Charles Coffey. *Victor Lemaire*: Harry A. Fisher. *Emanuel Shadrach*: William West. *Squire Bainbridge*: George Merritt. *Colonel Randolph Coolidge*: Charles Sturges. *B. Jabez Bender*: Charles Sturges. *Major Steel*: George L. Stout. *Whyland Whipple*: James Rennie. *Hampton Bailey*: Peter Goldrich. *Mate*: James McCullough. *Auntie Charlotte*: James Burke. *Enos Clinker*: Harry Guion. *Sampson Flyhigh*: Joseph Williamson. *Rasmus*: Master John Hernon. *Susie Rivers*: W. Brenan. *Laz Fisheye*: Robert Snyder. *Mary Duffy*: ANNIE YEAMANS. *Marie Coolidge*: Anne O'Neill. *Winnie Coburg*: Ida Ward. *Mirandy*: J. Decker. *Little May*: Katie Patterson.

Guests of Blossom Landing Hotel: Misses Emily Yeamans, Mamie Richards, Lulla Tutthil, Kate Tams, Lizzie Leone, Marian Roberts, May Carlisle, Gertie Tutthil.

1889.08

THE WATER QUEEN

A Fairy Spectacle in Four Acts, 9 Scenes. Entire spectacle, novel effects, ballets composed and arranged under the personal direction of Bolossy Kiralfy.[48] Music specially selected and composed by Georges Jacobi. Scenery by Mons. Carpezat; Gaspard Maeder and William Schaeffer; Harley Merry; Magnini of Milan; T. E. Ryan of London. Costumes by Alias of London; Quattrocchi of New York. Properties by Fawcett Robinson; Croce of the Eden Theatre, Paris. Produced by Bolossy Kiralfy. Opened 11 February 1889 at Niblo's Garden and closed 2 March 1889 after 25 performances.

CAST: *Sir Egbert*, "The Bold": FRED DeVERE. *Ernest*, Sir Egbert's Servant: ED SEE. *Draco*, the Evil Spirit: W. H. WALLIS. *Porthos*, "A Poor Devil": WILLIAM RICHARDSON. *Albert*, a Trooper: Al Vanderhoef. *First Sprite*: Jno. Haslam. *The Water Queen*: HATTIE GRINNELL. *Ida*, a Nymph of the Rhine: HELEN SEDGWICK. *Lady Elsa*, the Lady of the Manor: RICCA ALLEN. *Gretchen*, Ernest's Earthly Lover: ANNA ALLEN. (*Specialties*: Herbert Brothers, Alex Androw Brothers. *Ballet*: Mlles. NICODE, KONRADT, PARIS, ROSCH; Mons. CAPPELLINI, Coryphées, Corps de Ballet.) *Villagers, Knights, Water Nymphs, Sprites, Gnomes, Soldiers, Amazons, Demons, etc.*

Act 1, Scene 1: A Town near the Rhine. *Scene 2*: Rustic Interior. (Schaefer.) *Scene 3*: The Enchanted Forest. (Maeder & Schaeffer.)

Act 2, Scene 1: Sub-marine Cave. (Merry.) *Scene 2*: Realms of the Water Queen.

Act 3: The Golden Palace. (Magnini.)

Act 4, Scene 1: Hall of the Rendezvous. (Magnini.) *Scene 2*: Moonlight Ruins. (Ryan.) *Scene 3*: Grand Transformation. (Maeder & Schaeffer.)

ACT 1

Scene 1

Rustic and Floral Divertissement
Mlle. Nicode, Roach, Coryphées

Scene 2

Duet
A. Allen, E. See

ACT 2

Scene 1

Song and Dance
H. Sedgewick

Chorus of Nymphs

[43]Billed as an "Explosion of Smothered Fun."

[44]Scenery and costumes uncredited, Played a return engagement 2 December 1889 at the Comedy Theatre for 8 performances.

[45]First produced in New York 1 May 1888 at the Fifth Avenue Theatre for 42 performances. For Synopsis of Scenes and Musical Numbers, see original 1888 production. Also performed 8 November 1888 at the Grand Opera House for 8 performances.

[46]Stage direction, scenery and costumes uncredited.

[47]First produced in New York 22 November 1887 at Harrigan's Park Theatre for 175 performances. For Synopsis of Scenes and Musical Numbers, see original 1887 production.

[48]For subsequent tour, authorship of the spectacle was credited to Robert Griffin Morris. The cast, scenery and specialties were vastly revised.

Scene 2
Song
H. Grinnell
"A Kiss" (Chorus of the Fairies)
Grand Stalactite Ballet
Evolution of the Corps de Ballet
Entrée Cappellini
Coquette
Mlle. Paris
Grand Adagio Animo
Piccicato
Mlles. Rosch, Konradt
Finale Brilliante
Entire Corps de Ballet
ACT 3
Betrothal Festival
Chorus of Pages
Gymnastic Evolutions
Herbert Brothers
Grand Ballet Bal Masqué
Entrée and Minuet
Corps de Ballet
Hongrois
Mlles. Nicode, Konradt
Travestie Encroyable
Eight Coryphées
Pierettes
Eight Secondas
Characteristic Dance
Mlle. Paris; Cappellini
Bonheur
Our police
Grand Finale Ensemble
Entire Corps de Ballet
ACT 4
Scene 1
Specialty
Alex Androw Brothers
Manoeuvres of the Amazons
Scene 3
The Four Seasons—Grand Transformations

1889.09

LATER ON

A Farce Comedy in Three Acts. Play by H. Grattan Donnelly. Songs by (Fred) Hallen and (Joe) Hart. Musical director, Harry Saxton. Produced by Fred Hallen and Joe Hart (Harry Hine, Management). Opened 11 February 1889 at the Star Street Theatre and closed 16 February 1889 after 8 performances.[49]

CAST: *Pansy Weed*, a wild flower with funds and fun: GEORGIE PARKER. *Rose Seed*, an American girl, with wit and manners: HILDA THOMAS. *Patchoula Seed*, fair and hopeful, with a literary turn: FLORA ZANFRETTA. *Tillie Tipps*, with an eye to the main chance: LILLIE MAEHL. *Mollie Waits*, because she can't help it: DODDIE MORTON. *Four very noisy girls*: *Bertie Cartridge*: Jeanette Bageard. *Susie Caps*: Virginia Earl. *Venie Powder*: Frankie Raymond. *Gracie Shot*: Miss Graham. *Bandana Clutch*, a sheriff with ambition and indigestion: JOHN T. KELLY. *Hayes Seed*, who is bound to have a title in the family: BERNARD DYLLYN. *Mr. Blossom*: W. P. GUIBERSON. *Mildmay Smiles*, a student in hard luck: W. P. GUIBERSON. *Jack Plunger*: FRED HALLEN. *Jolly Todd*, a book-maker from Sheepshead Bay: JOE HART.

The action takes place here, there or anywhere, at the present time.
Act 1: Seaview Hotel.
Act 2: Seeds' Villa.
Act 3: The Seeds, Thursday at home.

ACT 1
Quarreling Duet
L. Maehl, D. Morton
"Dear Old Pals"
F. Hallen, J. Hart
"Fairy Step"
G. Parker
Eccentric Dance
J. Hart
Grand Musical Finale
Company
ACT 2
Toys, Laughter and Dances
J. T. Kelly
Lively Antics
G. Parker
"Return" (Quartette)
H. Thomas, L. Maehl, B. Dyllyn, W. P. Guiberson
"Later On" (Duet)
F. Hallen, J. Hart
Song (Character and Descriptive)
B. Dyllyn
ACT 3
"Love's Match Test" (Quartette)
H. Thomas, L. Maehl, B. Dyllyn, W. P. Guiberson
"Two Enemies" (Duet)
J. T. Kelly, B. Dyllyn
"I Went With Him"
F. Hallen, J. Hart
Terpsichorean
F. Hallen
Trio Song and Dance
F. Hallen, J. Hart, G. Parker
Banjo Solo
J. Hart
"We Hope to See You Again Later On"
Company

1889.10

SAID PASHA

A Comic Opera in Three Acts. Libretto by Scott Marble and Richard Stahl. Music by Richard Stahl. Stage director, Edwin Stevens. Production under the personal direction of Richard Stahl. Scenery by W. J. Fetters & Son. Costumes by Mme. Smith & Co., San Francisco. Produced by the California Opera Company (San Francisco; John Kreling Brothers, Proprietor and manager). Opened 25 February 1889 at the Star Theatre and closed 9 March 1889 after 16 performances; re-opened a return engagement 15 April 1889 at Niblo's Garden and closed 27 April 1889 after 16 additional performances. Total: 32 performances.[50]

CAST [in order of appearance]: *Said Pasha*, a Turkish diplomat, hence a Turkish mat, about to visit India: FRANCIS GAILLARD. *Hassen Bey*, officer of the Turkish patrol (this patrol in the time of peace was set to music): R. N. DUNBAR[51]. *Hadad*, an Englishman by birth, a sailor by occupation, a liar by profession, and a tramp by force of circumstances: EDWIN STEVENS. *Nockey*, his companion—"Why?": STANLEY FELCH. *Toubebad*, sergeant of guards: M. L. Alsop. *Serena*, the Pasha's daughter, in love with Hassen Bey, also in disguise as "Lemel," a sailor of the crew: HELENE DINGEON. *Terano*, a Mexican nobleman, in search of an ideal woman, whom he discovered in a dream (not on earth): HUBERT WILKE[52]. *Turkish Soldiers, Sons of Pasha, Ladies of the Harem, Mexicans, etc. Rajah*, the commander of Misfit Indians: JOSEPH GREENSFELDER. *His Officers of Government (3)*: *Ali Musfid*: G. Cassidy. *Musfid Ali*: J. Jones. *Plain Musfid*: R. F. Adams. *Alti*, the Ideal Queen: CARRIE

[49]No credits in program for scenery, costumes, stage director or musical director. Stage manager [director], Joe Hart. Played a return engagement 23 September 1889 at the 14th Street Theatre for 8 performances; a Second Edition played 11 February 1891 at the 14th Street Theatre; frequent revisions, national tours and new editions followed as late as 19 November 1894 when Hallen and Hart played the American Theatre for 1 week. Numerous musical numbers by Joseph Hart were published and credited to the production, presumably later interpolations: "The Irish Poker Club," "Keep Those Golden Gates Open," "Maggie," "We're Glad to Hear the News," "Teddy," "So Did I," "Comrades."

[50]No credits in program for musical director, presumably under the direction of the composer. Revised into two acts for the Niblo's Garden engagement; Act 2 reset in the Rajah's Palace, India.
[51]Succeeded by STUART HAROLD for Niblo's Garden engagement.
[52]Succeeded by CHARLES TURNER for Niblo's Garden engagement.

GODFREY. *Balah Sojah*: ALICE GAILLARD. *Semer, Punga*, the Queen's attendants: Lizzie Saenger, Mollie Bradshaw. *Indians, Natives, Slaves, etc.*

Act 1: Constantinople.

Act 2: The Village of Altara, India.

ACT 1[53]

"Let the loud glasses cling!" (Opening Chorus and Solo)
R. N. Dunbar, Chorus

"Two birdies with their feathers" (Entrè and Duet)
E. Stevens, S. Felch

"Our great pasha" (Entrè Song and Chorus)
F. Gaillard, Chorus

"I'm a nobleman of Mexico" (Entrè song)
H. Wilke

"We are the darlings" (Entrè of ladies)
Ladies' Chorus

"They are beautiful" (Waltz song and chorus)
H. Wilke, H. Dingeon, F. Gaillard, R. N. Dunbar, Chorus

"If you want to know the secret" (Song and chorus)
F. Gaillard

"Oh! Deep within my inmost heart" (Song)
H. Dingeon

"Now watch me, while I try to win this lady fair" (Song and Chorus)
E. Stevens, H. Dingeon

"My love is like the lily fair" (Romanze)
R. N. Dunbar

"Now away we will go" (Finale Act 1)
F. Gaillard, R. N. Dunbar, H. Wilke, H. Dingeon, E. Stevens, Chorus

ACT 2

"Maidens we, young, blithe and merry" (Introduction and Opening Chorus)
Chorus

"I will not weep or vainly sigh" (Solo)
C. Godfrey

"What strange sounds I hear?" (Ensemble and chorus)
E. Stevens, C. Godfrey, F. Gaillard, H. Dingeon, R. N. Dunbar, H. Wilke, Chorus

"At last we are alone" (Duet)
H. Wilke, C. Godfrey

"Life seems only sunshine" (Quintett)
E. Stevens, H. Dingeon, C. Godfrey, H. Wilke, F. Gaillard

"Love is a queer thing" (Song)
A. Gaillard

"You shall be rich and powerful" (Duet)
A. Gaillard, S. Felch

"If some other sweetheart" (Kissing duet)
H. Dingeon, R. N. Dunbar

"Now let begin" (Chorus and Gavotte)
Chorus

"He's found his ideal" (Finale Act 2)
Omnes

1889.11 THE O'REAGANS

A Revival of the Local Comedy in Three Acts, 7 Scenes[54]. Play (and lyrics) by Edward Harrigan. Music by David Braham. (Staged by Edward Harrigan.) Scenery by Charles W. Witham. Gas effects by John Whalen. Musical director, David Braham. Produced by Edward Harrigan. Opened 4 March 1889 at Harrigan's Park Theatre and closed 20 March 1889 after 20 performances.[55]

CAST: *Bernard O'Reagan*: EDWARD HARRIGAN. *Paddy Kelso*: JOHN SPARKS. *Silas Cohog*: PETER GOLDRICH. *Darrell Kilhealy*: George Merritt. *Herman Krause*: Harry Fisher. *Charley Dreams*: Daniel Burke. *Rif Bloomfield*: William West. *Bernard O'Reagan*, M.P.: CHARLES COFFEY. *Alphonse Rochfort*: Charles Sturges. *Bill Scarley*: Charles Sturges. *Policeman*: G. L. Stout. *Lulu Cohog*: JOHN DECKER. *Mr. Sarms*: James McCullough. *Ludlow Filkins*: James Rennie. *Earnest Strike*: Joseph Williamson. *Centre Market*: Robert Snyder. *Hop-Yet*: Harry Guion. *Saunders Silkheel*: James Burke. *Chow Chow*: John Hernon. *Thomas Farrell*: John Brennan. *Hiram Slocum*: William Young. *Bedalia McNeirney*: ANNIE YEAMANS. *Mrs. Hop Yet*, solo on Chinese fiddle: ANNIE YEAMANS. *Kate McNeirney*: ANNE O'NEILL. *Kate*, a Ballet Girl: Annie Langdon. *Mrs. Sylvie Dreams*: Emily Yeamans. *Emma A*: Minnie Richards. *Julia*: Kate Tams. *Bertha*: Lizzie Leone. *Sophia*: Marion Roberts. *Mamie*: Gertie Tuthill. *Lillian*: Lula Tuthill. *Constance*: May Carlisle. *Policemen, Tenants, Longshoremen, etc*

1889.12 A MIDNIGHT BELL

A Sketch (Rural Comedy) in Four Acts. Play by Charles H. Hoyt. (Staged by Charles H. Hoyt.) Stage manager, Will Carleton. Scenery by Homer F. Emens. Musical director, Percy Gaunt. Produced by Charles H. Hoyt and Charles Thomas. Opened 5 March 1889 at the Bijou Theatre and closed 1 July 1889 after 136 performances.

CAST: *The Clergyman*, the Rev. John Bradbury: R. J. Dillon. *The Selectman*, Lemuel Tidd, Deacon, Sheriff, etc.: THOMAS Q. SEABROOKE. *The City Lawyer*, Napier Keene: Frank Lane. *The Bank Cashier*, Stephen Labaree: William Humphrey. *The Bank Teller*, Ned Olcott: Hart Conway. *The Bank President*, T. J. Olcott: T. J. Herndon. *The Country Boy*, Martin Tripp: Eugene Canfield. *The Village Doctor*, Hiram Wing: Jesse Jenkins. *The Village Fiddler*, Ezekiel Slover: PERCY GAUNT. *The Tenor of the Choir*, Job Saxt: William Bennett. *The Schoolm'am*, Nora Fairford: Isabelle Coe. *The Minister's Sister*, Dot Bradbury: MAUDE ADAMS. *The Old Maid*, Miss Lizzie Grout: Annie Adams. *The Widow*, Abigail Grey: Marie Uart. *The Soprano of the Choir*, Nellie Bowen: ELVIA CROX. *The Village Maiden*, Annie Grey: Beth Bedford. *The Help*, Tildy Frost: Bessie Weyl. *The Village Pet*: Little Dot Clarendon. *School Children and Villagers.*

Act 1: Dining Room at Squire Olcott's.

Act 2: The School House and the Slide.

Act 3: The Sewing Society at Miss Lizzie's.

Act 4: The Choir Rehearsal in the Church Gallery.

ACT 2

The Children's Songs: "Lightly Row," "Hear Dem Bells," "Cricket on the Hearth"

ACT 3

The Grace Church Quartette

"When Pop Was a Little Boy Like Me"
E. Canfield (*Music by* Percy Gaunt.)

The Village Dance

ACT 4

The Choir Rehearsal

1889.13 EVANGELINE

A Revival of the Musical Extravaganza in Three Acts, 10 Scenes[56]. Libretto by J. Cheever Goodwin. Music by Edward E. Rice. Staged by Edward E. Rice. Scenery by John A. Thompson and H. L. Reed. Mechancal effects by Frank J. Bassett. Costumes designed by Carrie E. Perkins. Musical director, Max Hirschfield. Produced by Rice's Great American Burlesque Company (Edward E. Rice, Proprietor). Opened 11 March 1889 at the Star Theatre and closed 23 March 1889 after 16 performances.

CAST: ACADIANS: *Evangeline*, the heroine of an enduring affection which very nearly proves her ruin: IRENE VERONA. *Eulalie*, her confidante—confidently hoping for women's rights: Lila Blow. *Catherine*, Gabriel's aunt, an antidote for melancholy—"Love's young dream becomes a nightmare": GEORGE K. FORTESQUE. *Marie, Rose*, on Eva's suite—two sweet to need description: Lillian Cleaver, Caprice Van Lissa. *Elaine*, a waif, very much in love: LOTTIE GLOVER. *Gabriel*, a dashing young country laddie who thinks Evangeline just too sweet to live: FRANKIE KEMBLE. *LeBlanc*, a cunning notary, who believes that there's a good deal in a name: GEORGE A. SCHILLER. *Basil*, the blacksmith, father of Evangeline: EDWIN S. TARR. *Felician*, Eulalie's adorer, a vivacious young party who is simply nervous: Cora Tinnie. *The Heifer*: George Cohen, James Reynolds. *Shepherds, Shepherdesses, Peasants, etc.*

THE QUEEN'S OWN: *Captain Dietrich* of the Queen's own, familiar with hard-tack and "Hardies Tactics": RICHARD O'GORMAN. *Hans Wagner*, corporal, but fond of the spiritual: W. H. MACK. *Fritz, Maurice*, Captain Dietrich's aides and abettors: Maud Emerson, Helen Marlborough. *Sodiers of the Army*.

AFRICANS: *King Boorioboola Gha*, a suffering sovereign: EDWIN S. TARR. *His Chief of Police*, a "peeler," so-called because he was never known to heed any appeal a

[53]Musical numbers not listed in programs. List prepared from published piano vocal score (White, Smith and Co., New York, 1889). Additional song interpolated: "My Sweet and Pretty May."

[54]First produced in New York as McNOONEY'S VISIT 11 October 1886 at Harrigan's Park Theatre for 128 performances. For Synopsis of Scenes and Musical Numbers, see original 1886 production. For this revival, "Grogan, the Masher" replaced the song "The Little Hedge School" in Act 1, Scene 3.

[55]Costumes uncredited.

[56]First produced in New York 27 July 1874 at Niblo's Garden for 16 performances. For Synopsis of Scenes and Musical Numbers, see original 1874 production. Musical numbers not listed in this revival program.

prisoner might make: Sherman Wade. *His Headsman*, very clever at taking off heads: James Finn. *Unambebe*, Captain of the Amazons: Mae Branson. *Policemen, Amazonian Guards, etc.*

ARIZONA PETS: *Lo*, the poor Indian: J. H. Finn. *Six Merry but Miserable Ruffians*: *Ahthere Charley*: S. W. Wade. *Arizona Abraham*: W. H. Mack. *Rosemary Tom*: James Reynolds. *Little Ten Willie*: George Cohen. *Tight Pants Teddy*: Charles Udell. *Scar Faced Jo Jo*: Benjamin Miles.

The Lone Fisherman, the original: JAMES F. MAFFIT. *The Ricesque Quartette*: Messrs. McKinley, Udell, Finn, Kremer. *Premiere de Ballet*, the Little Fawn: AMELIA GLOVER.

1889.14

THE IRISH MINSTREL

A Revival of the Domestic Irish Drama in Three Acts[57]. Play by Fred Marsden. (Music and lyrics by William J. Scanlan. Staged by Augustus Pitou. Musical director, George Loesch.) Produced by Augustus Pitou. Opened 18 March 1889 at the Grand Opera House and closed 23 March 1889 after 9 performances.

CAST: *Larry O'Lynn*, the Irish Minstrel: WILLIAM J. SCANLAN. *Morris Cregan*, with an honest pride in his name: ROBERT McNAIR. *Dan Cregan*, who yields to temptation: Edward R. Marsden. *Robert Wynbert*, who wants his own way: J. O. LeBrasse. *Matt Dongan*, who never permits trifles to annoy him: THADDEUS SHINE. *Nellie Cregan*, a true-hearted colleen: MATTIE FERGUSON. *Maggie McKay*, in love with Rory: IRENE AVENALL. *Mrs. Bridget McKay*, "a dacent widdy": Millie Sackett.

1889.15

4-11-44

"McNooney's Visit," Revised (version of the local play) and Re-Christened in Three Acts, 5 Scenes[58]. Play (and lyrics) by Edward Harrigan. Music by David Braham. Musical director, David Braham. (Staged by Edward Harrigan.) Produced by Edward Harrigan. Opened 21 March 1889 at Harrigan's Park Theatre and closed 6 April 1889 after 20 performances.

CAST: *Martin McNooney*: EDWARD HARRIGAN. *Ely Ulmsted*: PETER GOLDRICH. *Mary McQuirk*: JOSEPH SPARKS. *Judge Halzweiser*: HARRY FISHER. *Lionel Mellow*: Dan Burke. *Henry Mellow*: George Merritt. *Clara Grizzle*: John Decker. *Melissa Unstead*: James Burke. *Caleb Jenkins*: William West. *A Lunatic*: William West. *Dexter Twigem*: Charles Sturges. *Keeper*: James H. McCullough. *Doctor Gargle*: George L. Stout. *Adam Bausant*: George L. Stout. *Fergus Clincher*: Charles Coffey. *Sandy Sniffles*: Harry Guion, Jr. *Court Officer*: Joseph Williamson. *Licorice Jimmy*: John Brennan. *Enos Roper*: John Herndon. *Rufus Boneset*: Robert Snyder. *Nora Gilmartin*: ANNIE YEAMANS. *Adele Spoonful*: Annie O'Neil. *Mary Mellow*: Ida Ward. *Rosa Daisey*: Emily Yeamans. *Nora McGovern*: EMILY YEAMANS. *Dr. Hilaria Spoonful*: K. TAMS. *Good Samaritans*: Minnie Richards, Lizzie Leone, Marion Roberts, Gertie Tuthill, Lula Tuthill, Mary Carlisle.

Act 1: The Welcome Home Nursery Goats Milk for Babies.

Act 2, Scene 1: The Policy Shop. *Scene 2*: The Cells of the Tombs. *Scene 3*: Interior of the Special Sessions.

Act 3: Reception Room of Dr. Spoonful.

MUSICAL NUMBERS

"Ho! Mollie Grogan"
"4-11-44"

1889.16

ERMINIE

A Revival of the Comic Opera in Three Acts[59]. Libretto by Harry Paulton (and Claxson Bellamy). Based on the melodrama ('L'Auberge des Adrets' by Benjamin Antier, Saint-Amand and Paulyanthe, adapted into English as 'Robert Macaire.') Music by Edward Jakobowski. Scenery designed by Henry E. Hoyt, T. S. Plaisted. Costumes by (Henry) Dazian and Mme. Loe. Director of music, John J. Braham. Produced by Rudolph Aronson's Comic Opera Company (Rudolf Aronson, director). Opened 1 April 1889 at Niblo's Garden and closed 6 April 1889 after 8 performances.[60]

CAST: *Erminie*: ADDIE CORA REED. *Cerise*: ISABELLE URQUHART. *Javotte*: Katie Gilbert. *Princess de Gramponneur*: RUTH ROSE. *Marie*: Marie Glover. *Captain Delaunay*, a young officer: Edgeworth Starritt. *Cadeaux, Ravennes*, two thieves: J. H. RYLEY, MARK SMITH. *Eugene Marcel*, the Marquis' secretary: Charles J. Campbell. *Chevalier de Brabazon*, Marquis' guest: RICHARD CUMMINGS. *Marquis de Pontvert*: GEORGE H. BRODERICK. *Dufois*, Landlord of the Lion d'Or: Ellis Ryse. *Simon*, waiter at the Lion d'Or: Charles Lang. *Vicomte de Brissac*: C. F. Weeks. *Sergeant*: Henri Leoni.

1889.17

THE MAY QUEEN

An Operetta in Three Acts, 4 Scenes. Original Viennese libretto (to the operette "Der Glücksritter") by Richard Genée, Wilhelm Mannstädt, Bruno Zappert.[61] Music by Alfons Czibulka. Production under the supervision of Mathilde Cottrelly. Musical director, Adolph Nowak. Produced by the McCaull Opera Company (John A. McCaull, Proprietor and Manager). Opened 1 April 1889 at Palmer's Theatre and closed 7 May 1889 after 37 performances.[62]

CAST: *The Queen*: HARRIET AVERY. *Lady Beatrice Hamilton*, niece of Lord Middleditch: MARION MANOLA. *Roxana*, her governess: LAURA JOYCE BELL. *Nancy*, confidante of Lady Beatrice: ANNIE MYERS. *Harry MacDonald*: EUGENE OUDIN. *Toby*, his servant: DIGBY BELL. *Lord Middleditch*, Lord Mayor of London: DeWOLF HOPPER. *Giles, Styles*, his servants: JEFFERSON DeANGELIS, John J. Raffael. *Duke of Montrose*, an adherent of the King: CHARLES W. DUNGAN. *Lieutenant Wilmore*: Edmund Stanley. *Young women of the people (4)*: *Ellen*: Josephine Knapp. *Lydia*: Louise Edgar. *Betty*: Florence Willey. *Rose*: Lucy Pixley. *Populace, Soldiers, Court Ladies, Nobles, Pages, etc.*

Act 1: A Square in London. 1660.

Act 2, Scene 1: Room in Lord Middleditch's House. *Scene 2*: Apartment of State.

Act 3: Royal Apartment in Palace at Whitehall.

MUSICAL NUMBERS[63]

Snow Song
A. Myers
Gavotte
King's Victory Song (Female Quartette) (Act 3)
"The May Queen"

1889.17

THE GRIP

A Revival of the Comedy in Three Acts[64]. Play (and lyrics) by Edward Harrigan. Music by David Braham. (Staged by Edward Harrigan.) Scenery by Charles W. Witham. Mechanical effects by William Vail. Gas effects by John Whalen. Musical director, David Braham. Produced by Edward Harrigan. Opened 8 April 1889 at Harrigan's Park Theatre and closed 13 April 1889 after 8 performances.

CAST: *Patrick Reilly*: EDWARD HARRIGAN. *Colonel Reilly*: HARRY FISHER. *Ellen Hoolihan*: JOSEPH SPARKS. *Larry Delaney*: William West. *John Clancy, Jr.*: Charles Coffey. *John Clancy, Sr.*: George L. Stout. *Mail Man*: Charles Sturges. *Roger Quigley*: George Merritt. *Anthony Lorrigan*: Dan Burke. *Peter Gaffney*: James Burke. *Roland Pebble*: Peter Goldrich. *Smiley McQuinlan*: Harry Guion, Jr. *Ellen Daily*: John Decker. *Peter McInerney*: John Williams. *Michael Meehan*: Mr. McCullough. *Conrad Sullivan*: Robert Snydon. *James Donovan*: John Hernan. *Rosanna Reilly*: ANNIE YEAMANS. *Rosalind Reilly*: Annie O'Neill. *Kate Quigley*: Ida Ward. *Maid*: Emily Yeamans. *School Girls*: Misses K. Tams, Minnie Richards, Lizzie Leone, Marion Roberts, Gertie Tuthill, Lula Tuthill, Mary Carlisle.

Act 1: The Canteen. On the Morris and Essex Canal.

Act 2: Drawing Room at Colonel Reilly's. Evening.

Act 3: Drawing Room at Colonel Reilly's. Morning.

MUSICAL NUMBERS[65]

"(A) Soldier Boy's Canteen"
"School Days! School Days!"
"I Really Can't Sit Down"
"Mister Dooley's Geese"

[57]First produced in New York 16 April 1888 at the Henry Miner's People's Theatre for 8 performances. For Synopsis of Scenes and Musical Numbers, see original 1888 production.

[58]McNOONEY'S VISIT was first produced in New York 31 January 1887 at Harrigan's Park Theatre for 88 performances.

[59]This was a touring company making a one week stop. First produced in New York 10 May 1886 at the Casino Theatre for 648 performances in a series of three engagements. For Synopsis of Scenes and Musical Numbers, see original 1886 production.

[60]Direction uncredited. Original direction by Edward Paulton, restaged by stage manager Arthur W. Tams.

[61]English adaptation uncredited, aided by DeWolf Hopper.

[62]Stage direction, scenery and costumes uncredited. Herbert A. Cripps, stage manager.

[63]Musical numbers not listed in programs.

[64]First produced in New York 30 November 1885 at Harrigan's Park Theatre for 88 performances. For Synopsis of Scenes and Musical Numbers, see original 1885 production.

[65]Not necessarily in performance order.

1889.19

DOVETTA

A Comic Opera in Three Acts. Libretto by Betsey Banker and Charles Raynaud. Music by Mrs. E. Marcy Raymond. Produced under the stage direction of H. W. Dodd. Dances invented by Rose Beckett. Scenery by Thomas R. Weston & King. Costumes by Eaves Costume Company. Musical director, Julian Edwards. Opened 22 April 1889 at the Standard Theatre and closed 4 May 1889 after 12 performances.[66]

CAST: *Papalahonta*, Chief of the Mikromikrahs, an Indian tribe of Arizona: HARRY BROWN. *Broken Arrow*, His Squaw: EMILY SOLDENE. *Rainbow*, an Indian Brave: JOSEPH LYNDE. *Dovetta*, Daughter of a Former Chief: FATIMAH DIARD. *Muskrat*, an Indian, a Victim of "Pale Face" Beverages: FRED MATTHEWS. *Brambleton*, United States Commissioner: Frank David. *Florrie Brambleton*, his Sister: ROSE LEIGHTON. *Robert Brambleton*, his Son: WILL S. RISING. *Clubby, Brommy*, Officers of Brambleton's Volunteer Corps: Hattie Delaro (Barnes), Ruby Stuart. *Servants, A Volunteer Corps of Ex-Detectives, Indians, Mexicans, Ballet, etc.*

Act 1: Exterior of Brambleton's Residence in Washington, D.C.

Act 2: An Indian Reservation in Arizona.

Act 3: Exterior of a Picturesque Pagoda in New Mexico.

1889.20

UNCLE JOE, or, Fritz In A Madhouse

A Natural Drama in Four Acts. Play by Joseph K. Emmet. (Staged by Joseph K. Emmet.) Scenery by Philip Goatcher and John H. Young. Musical director, Frank Webbe. Produced by Joseph K. Emmet. Opened 22 April 1889 at the 14th Street Theatre and closed 15 June 1889 after 64 performances.[67]

CAST: *Uncle Joe Parker*: EDMOND D. LYONS. *Richard Parker*: C. D. BENNETT. *Baron von Woelfenstein*: HAROLD HARTSELL. *Charles O'Reilly*: J. Cody. *Hon. Bob Penley*: R. N. Hickman. *Montague Drury*: Frank H. Dayton. *Dr. Mickett*: A. R. Adams. *Burrows*: G. R. Montgomery. *Brown*: H. W. Brinkley. *First Keeper of the Insane Asylum*: C. St. Aubuyne. *Second Keeper of the Insane Asylum*: J. S. Davis. *Johnie Johns*: W. C. Utter. *Collie Parker*: LOUISE BALF. *Mrs. Joe Parker*: ETHEL GREYBROOK. *Lady Grace Howard*: Mary A. Penfield. *Mrs. Chumbley*: Alice Mansfield. *Maria Snattus*: Marie Carlyle. *Laura Withus*: Mary A. Penfield. *Flora*: Alice Spencer. *The Plant*: Baby Spencer. *Fritz von Wolfenstein*: JOSEPH K. EMMET.

Act 1: The Grange. The country seat of Uncle Joe Parker, with a distant view of the harbor of Melbourne, Australia.

Act 2: Richard Parker's chambers, Melbourne, Australia.

Act 3: Mrs. Mickett's boarding house.

Act 4: Ranch of Fritz.

MUSICAL NUMBERS

During the play Mr. Emmet will introduce new songs[68], assisted by the Eagle Quartette, with banjo, guitar, drum, church-bells, and full chorus, also the celebrated St. Bernard dog Plinlimmon, the largest and handsomest dog in the world, for which Mr. Emmet paid $5,000,000—the highest price ever paid for a dog.

1889.21

THE BLACK CROOK

A Revival of the Extravaganza in Five Acts, 16 Scenes[69]. (Book by Charles M. Barras. Music composed and selected by Thomas Baker, Louis Baer, A. W. Hoffman.) Entire spectacle produced under the stage direction of Imre Kiralfy. Scenery by Robecchi & Amable of Paris. Costumes by Landolff of Paris; Miss Fisher of London. Produced by Imre Kiralfy. Opened 29 April 1889 at the Standard Theatre and closed 11 May 1889 after 14 performances.

CAST: MORTALS: *Hertzog*, the Black Crook: J. F. PETERS. *Count Wolfenstein*: HENRY MAYNARD. *Rudolphe*, a poor artist: JOSEPH SLAYTOR. *Von Puffengruntz*, the Count's chamberlain: W. H. BARTHOLOMEW. *Greppo*, a henchman: FRANK LESTER. *Wolfgar*: L. Rubie. *Bruno*: F. Starr. *Amina*, a village maiden: LOUISE ALLEN. *Dame Barbara*: EMILY SOLDENE. *Carline*: RAY ALLEN. *Rosette*: Minnie Holden. *Guards, Attendants, Servitors, Villagers, etc.*

IMMORTALS: *Stalacta*, Queen of the Fairies: ROSE WATSON. *Dragonfin*: ALBERT MARTINETTE.

DEMONS: *Zamiel*: E. J. Lean. *Skudelwhelp*: Charles M. Blesser.

Principal Dancers: Mlle. LILE; Mons. ARNOLD. *Specialties*: DARE BROTHERS (Comical gymnasts), BIBB & BOBB (Musical eccentrics), THE TISSOTS (Living pictures, cat serenade).

Act 1, Scene 1: Village. (Merry.) *Scene 2*: Wood. *Scene 3*: Hall and Castle. *Scene 4*: Laboratory of the Crook. (Magnani.) *Scene 5*: The Devils in the Brocken. (Porter.)

Act 2, Scene 1: The Subterranean Vaults. (Magnani.) *Scene 2*: Interior of the Castle. *Scene 3*: The Realms of Stalacta.

Act 3:Palace. (Magnani.)

Act 4, Scene 1: The Tissots. *Scene 2*: Bibb & Bobb. *Scene 3*: Terrace.

Act 5, Scene 1: Gothic Hall. *Scene 2*: Ruins of the Castle. *Scene 3*: Rocky Pass. The Burning of the Forest. *Scene 4*: Pandemonium. (Robecchi.)

ACT 1[70]

Scene 1

- Festive Dance
  - Coryphées

Scene 5

- The Incantation
- Live Skeletons
- Grand Tableau Infernale

ACT 2

Scene 3

- Stalacta Revels
  - Mlle. Lile, Grand Ballet Corps

ACT 3

- The Sporting Ballet
- Jockey Dance
  - 8 Coryphées
- Lawn Tennis
  - 8 Secondas
- Fishing
  - Premiers
- Old Sport
  - Mons. Arnold
- Baseball
  - 8 Secondas
- Boating
  - 8 Secondas
- Tobogganing; Grand Finale
  - Entire Corps de Ballet

ACT 4

Scene 1

- The Tissots (Specialty)

Scene 2

- Bibb & Bobb (Specialty)

Scene 3

- Amazonian Manoeuvre
  - R. Watson, Company

ACT 5

Scene 5

- Grand Apotheosis. The Garden of Beauty. The Dawn of Love.

1889.22

CLOVER

A Comic Opera in Three Acts and a Prologue. Original Viennese libretto (to the operette 'Die Jagd nach dem Glück'[71]) by Richard Genée and Bruno Zappert. Music by Franz von Suppé. English adaptation by Harry B. Smith. Produced under the supervision of Mathilde Cottrelly. Musical director, Adolph Nowak. Produced by the McCaull Opera Company (John A. McCaull, Proprietor and manager). Opened 8 May 1889 at Palmer's Theatre and closed 5 October 1889 after 173 performances.[72]

CAST: Prologue: *Count Willfried*: CHARLES W. DUNGAN. *Stella*, his daughter: MARION MANOLA. *Rudolf*, his adopted son: EUGENE OUDIN. *Casimir*, Rudolf's

---

[66]Played weekday matinees only in its second week, alongside THE BLACK CROOK in the evenings. Producer uncredited.

[67]Played return engagements 11 November 1889 at the Grand Opera House for 8 performances; 29 December 1890 at the Grand Opera House for 8 performances.

[68]Songs, old and new, per published reviews, included "Sleep, Baby, Sleep" (Emmet's Lullaby) and "Laughing Jack."

[69]First produced in New York 12 September 1866 at Niblo's Garden for 475 performances.

[70]Programs list only ballets and specialties, not songs.

[71]Literally "The Chase After Luck."

[72]Scenery and costumes uncredited; for subsequent tour, 'new' scenery credited to Charles W. Witham.

servant: DeWOLF HOPPER. *Fanny*, Stella's foster sister: ANNIE MYERS. *Dr. Track*: Lindsay Morison. *Florine*, a danseuse: CARRIE BURTON. *Rosetta*, her friend: JOSEPHINE KNAPP. *Marquis de Rocheferieres*: George Wade. *Abbe Daudin*: Louis Schrader. *Lieutenant Kilborg*, in the service of the King of Sweden: CHARLES W. DUNGAN. *Four Vagabonds*: *Robert*: JEFFERSON DeANGELIS. *Bertram*: HERBERT A. CRIPPS. *Martial*: EDMUND STANLEY. *Pascal*: CHARLES MYERS. *Don Cristoval D'Olivarez*: JEFFERSON DeANGELIS. *Senora Petronella*, his sister: MATHILDE COTTRELLY. *Country Folk, Ballet Girls, Cavaliers, Fisher Girls, Masqueraders, Gondoliers.*

Prologue: Bavaria.

Act 1: Paris.

Act 2: Sweden.

Act 3: Venice.

MUSICAL NUMBERS[73]

"Dream Song" (The gay songs and love songs of yearning)
M. Manola

"Yodel Song" (Girls of fourteen declare)
A. Myers

"Fair Goddess, Fortune" (Duett)
M. Manola, E. Oudin

"In My Dreams"
E. Oudin

"A Loving Husband"
M. Cottrelly, J. DeAngelis

"Gondola Song" (I greet you all, my jolly crew!)
M. Manola, Sopranos

"What Is This Old Crow Seeking?"
A. Myers, D. Hopper

"Stella" (Romanza)
(*Lyrics by* Monroe H. Rosenfeld.)

"(But there are) Things 'tis better not to dwell on"
(*Lyrics by* Sydney Rosenfeld.)

1889.23

THE BRIGANDS

An Operetta in Three Acts[74]. (New) English libretto by William S. Gilbert[75]. (Adapted from the French opéra-bouffe "Les Brigands," with libretto by Henri Meilhac and Ludovic Halévy.) Music by Jacques Offenbach. Produced under the stage direction of Max Freeman. Incidental ballet under the direction of Mons. Mamert Bibeyran. Scenery by Henry E. Hoyt. Costumes by (Henry) Dazian and Mme. Loe. Director of music, Gustave Kerker. Produced by Rudolph Aronson. Opened 9 May 1889 at the Casino Theatre and closed 14 September 1889 after 113 performances.

CAST: *Fiorella*, the Brigand's daughter: LILLIAN RUSSELL. *Fragoletto*, a young farmer: FANNY RICE. *Princess of Grenada*: ISABELLE URQUHART. *Adolph de Valladolid*, her favorite page: Sylvia Gerrish. *Falsacappa*, the Brigand Chief: EDWIN STEVENS. *Pietro*, his lieutenant: FREDERIC SOLOMON. *Joseph Antonio*, Financier to the Duke of Mantua: HENRY E. WALTON. *Duke of Mantua*: HENRY HALLAM. *Count of Gloria Cassis*, Chamberlain to the Princess: JOHN E. BRAND. *Captain of Carabineers*: RICHARD F. CARROLL. *Baron of Campotasso*, Master of Ceremonies to the Duke: GEORGE OLMI. *Brigands (5)*: *Domino*: ARTHUR W. TAMS. *Carmagnola*: A. W. MAFLIN. *Barbavano*: EDGAR SMITH. *Cecco*: HENRY LEONI. *Beppo*: Charles Renwick. *The Preceptor*: J. A. Furey. *Pipo*, Innkeeper: Fred Hall. *Italian Peasant Girls (4)*: *Fiametta*: Anna O'Keefe. *Bianca*: Georgie Dennin. *Zerlina*: Edith Edwards. *Cincinella*: Edgeworth Starritt. *Pipo's Daughters (4)*: *Pipa*: Delia Stacey. *Pipetta*: Laura Russell. *Pepita*: Gertie Silverthorn. *Petipa*: Emma Lawrence. (*Chorus of Brigands, Peasants, etc.*)

Act 1: Mountain Pass, Calabria.

Act 2: Wayside Inn. (Pipo's Posada)

Act 3: The Lavender Salon in Duke of Mantua's Castle.

ACT 1[76]

Opening Chorus of Brigands (Two by two, or three by three)
A. W. Tams, E. Smith, A. W. Maflin, H. Leoni, C. Renwick, Chorus (*Music by* Gustave Kerker.)

Recitative (This is the road to wisdom true)
A. O'Keefe, E. Edwards, E.Stevens

Entrance of Falscapappa ('Tis I, Falsacappa')
E. Stevens, Chorus

Entrance of Fiorella (A hat and a bright little feather)
Lillian Russell

Chorus and Ensemble (We've seized this very little chap)
Lillian Russell, F. Rice, A. W. Tams, E. Stevens, Chorus

Fragoletto's Song (When you on my cottage employed/You may pillage ...)
F. Rice
(*Music by* Gustave Kerker.)

Rondeau (Take the turning on the right, sir)
Lillian Russell, Chorus

Chorus and Song (Falscappa, behold my booty)
F. Rice, Chorus

Finale Act 1 (Come sing, and turn about gaily)
Principals, (Brigands') Chorus
(*Music by* Gustave Kerker.)

March of the Caribineers (We are mighty Caribineers)
Caribineers

ACT 2

Opening Chorus (Gaily does our furnace roar)
F. Hall, D. Stacey, Laura Russell, Cooks

Entrance of Brigands (Spare a roll—a penny thing)
F. Solomon, F. Rice, E. Stevens, Lillian Russell, A. W. Tams, A. W. Maflin, Brigands

Kiss Duet (Ha, la! ho, la! good notary)
L. Russell, F. Rice, Chorus
(*Music by* Gustave Kerker.)

Song (Walk in-walk in-walk in, I pray you!)
E. Stevens, F. Rice, F. Solomon, Chorus

Entrance of Baron (For men, whose province is cooking)
G. Olmi, R. F. Carroll, Caribineers, Brigands

Song (I represent the army)
R. F. Carroll, G. Olmi, Chorus

Chorus of Brigands (In you go, come, bustle)
Brigands

Entrance of Princess (Granada, Spain's most favoured city)
I. Urquhart, J. E. Brand, J. A. Furey, S. Gerrish, Chorus

Song (Indeed, I cannot tell you clearly)
Lillian Russell

Chorus of Brigands reprise (In you go, come, bustle)
Brigands

Finale Act 2 (We, without pomp or martial show)
Principals, Chorus
(*Music by* Gustave Kerker.)

ACT 3

Opening Chorus (Aurora appears—we'll hail Aurora)

Song (A prince there was, whose beauty)
H. Hallam, Chorus

Treasurer's Song (Oh, woman, in thy soft caresses)
H. E. Walton

Chorus (Here comes the Princess)
E. Stevens, F. Solomon, Lillian Russell, F. Rice, H. Hallam, Brigands, Lords and Ladies

---

[73]Musical numbers not listed in programs; not in performance order. List, first 7 titles, prepared from published piano vocal gems (Oliver Ditson Company, Boston, 1889). Vocal gems are copyrighted by John A. McCaull, but do not identify Harry B. Smith as lyricist.

[74]First produced in New York in French 14 November 1870 at the Grand Opera House.

[75]Several critics remarked that Gilbert's earlier work had been revised by Max Freeman or Edgar Smith without credit.

[76]Musical numbers not listed in programs. List prepared from earlier published English libretto (Boosey & Co., London, 1871) which does not reflect uncredited revisions for this American production. Musical interpolations by musical director Gustave Kerker indicated above; also included:

"I Got It" (Topical Song)
(Music by Gustave Kerker.)

Published vocal gems from the Casino production (only authorized edition, William A. Pond, New York, 1889) include the following

"Song of the Chief" (Entrance of Falsacappa)

"Take the Turning on the Right, Sir"

"Falsacappa Behold My Booty"

"Fiorella" (Dancing, singing, Dance and folly)

Chorus of Brigands ("The creaking top-boots are cracking")

"Walk in, walk in"

"We Are the End of Such as This"

"Grenada, Spain's Most Favored City"

"Indeed I Cannot"

Chorus ("This is unexpected")
Principals, Chorus.

Finale Act 3 (Some folk are true Spaniards by birth)
Spaniards, Carabineers
Ensemble ('Tis Fiorella, you know her)
Lillian Russell, F. Rice, Principals, Chorus

1889.24 THE OOLAH

A Comic Opera in Three Acts[77]. Original French libretto (to the opérette 'La Jolie Persane') by Eugène Leterrier and Albert Vanloo. English adaptation by Sydney Rosenfeld. Music by Charles Lecocq. Produced under the direction of Richard Barker. Scenery by Philip Goatcher and John H. Young. Costumes by W. Dazian & Company. Mechanical effects by Messrs. Fillott and Wynne. Properties and elaborations by William Henry. Gas and electrical effects by James Stewart. Director of the orchestra, Signor Antonio DeNovelllis. Produced by Francis Wilson and Company (A. H. Canby, Manager). Opened 13 May 1889 at the Broadway Theatre and closed 12 October 1889 after 156 performances.

CAST: *Hoolahgoolah*, the Oolah: FRANCIS WILSON. *The Prince of Eriven*: HUBERT WILKE. *Akhalzakek*, a wealthy merchant: CHARLES PLUNKETT. *Nedjef*, his son-in-law: THOMAS PERSSE. *The Cadi*: HARRY MACDONOUGH. *The Ooolah's Friends (5)*: *The Fig Dealer*: Benjamin F. Joslyn. *The Barber*: Carlo Segelini. *The Tailor*: W. Carr. *The Watchman*: Henry Hoffman. *The Baker*: H. Ledbury. *Darinoora*, daughter of Akhalzakek: LAURA MOORE. *Bampoora*, betrothed to the Oolah: ELMA DELARO. *Altoora*: IDA FITZHUGH. *Shimrana*: Ida Eissing. *Velis*: Josie Winner. *Tourouloupi*, the Cadi's wife: MARIE JANSEN. *Dignitaries, Merchants, Water-carriers, Dancing Girls, Tradespeople, Peasants, Slaves, etc.*

Act 1: Public place in a Persian village near Teheran. The Oolah's abode.

Act 2: Interior of Akhalzakek's residence.

Act 3: Public Bazaar in Teheran.

ACT 1[78]
Introduction (Let's array, let's array, for this glad holiday)
Chorus
"The Cadi's Song" (Peaches with a bloom delicious)
H. Macdonough
Exit (Hiding, hiding)
Chorus
"The Oolah's Entrance Song" (When married folks fall out and part)
F. Wilson (*Music by* W. W. Lowitz.)
Ballad (When I was but a gentle child)
L. Moore
March and Entrance of the Prince (Air, Scene and Cadi's Song)
H. Wilke, H. Macdonough
Couplets (Behold Velis a charming creature)
H. Macdonough, J. Winner, H. Wilke, Chorus
Duet and Romance (Take back the gifts that came from you)
L. Moore, T. Persse
Finale (In good time, Cadi, you appear)
L. Moore, H. Wilke, E. Delaro, T. Persse, H. Macdonough, F. Wilson, C. Plunkett

ACT 2
Introduction, Bridesmaids' Chorus (Where can they be)
I. Eissing, Sopranos
Chorus (Here collectedly, unexpectedly)
Chorus
"Be Good!"
M. Jansen (*Music by* David Braham.)
"Nobody Knows"
(*Music by* S. Barnes.)
Chorus (All hail! All Hail!)
Persian Song (As to the sun whose splendor bright)
L. Moore
Exit
Chorus
Ensemble (Here is the wine, the wedding wine)
Principals, Chorus
Air (Here, in the calm of night)
H. Wilke
Finale (Scene, Chorus, Scene)
Principals, Chorus
"Song of the Somnambulist"
F. Wilson
Scene, Stretta
Principals, Chorus

ACT 3
Introduction (Ah! the Prince. Fate is propitious)
F. Wilson, Chorus
Waltz Song (Here is brocade with silver fretwork)
H. Wilke
Duet (Madame, it grieves me much to curb you)
L. Moore, F. Wilson
Duet (Though by a strange caprice of fate)
L. Moore, T. Persse
Quartette (My Darinoora, heart's delight)
L. Moore, E. Delaro, F. Wilson, C. Plunkett
Trio (When you long have been suspected)
F. Wilson, M. Jansen, E. Delaro
Finale (Drinking Act[79])

[77]Illustrating the Complexities of Persia's Marriage Laws.
[78]Musical numbers not listed in programs. List prepared from published vocal score (R. A. Saalfield, New York, 1889). Added after opening:
"Nobody Knows" (Topical song including burlesque of Letty Lind dances)
F. Wilson
"Count Me Out"
M. Jansen.

[79]Act 3 Finale/Drinking Act does not in published vocal score, but was described in newspaper reviews.

1889.25 PAT'S NEW WARDROBE

A Return Engagement of the Screaming Musical Farcical Comedy in Three Acts, 5 Scenes[80]. Musical director, James Vincent. Produced by The Rooney Comedy Company (R. J. Graham, Manager; Pat Rooney, Proprietor). Opened 20 May 1889 at Niblo's Garden and closed 25 May 1889 after 8 performances.

CAST: *Pat O'Hoolihan*: PAT ROONEY. *Lionel Eustach*: James Vincent. *Mr. Paragon*: W. H. Hatter. *Mr. Collard*: Harry Ernest. *Crullers*: W. S. Laird. *Mr. Wild*: W. Eunice. *Teddy*: J. Pieri. *George*: R. J. Graham. *Mrs. Paragon*: Josie Rooney. *Mrs. Crocker*: Emma Howard. *Christopher*: KATIE ROONEY.

ACT 1
Scene 2
(Vocal) Gavotte from ERMINIE
W. H. Hatter, J. Rooney, K. Rooney, W. S. Laird (*Music by* Edward Jakobowski. *Lyrics by* Claxson Bellamy and Harry Paulton.)
Scene 3
"Naughty Girl" (by permission of Julia Wilson)
K. Rooney

ACT 2
"The Yodel" (Song)
K. Rooney
"Hear Them Bells" (Song)
W. S. Laird
Grand Medley Chorus of Popular Airs
Quartette, Full Company

ACT 3
"Quiet Little Home"
W. H. Hatter
New Original Songs, including "Hello, Maginnis" and Waltz Song
P. Rooney
Original Song, "Nobody Knows," Imitations of her father
K. Rooney
Quaker City Quartette
Messrs. Laird, Ernest, Pieri, Graham
Vocalizations, Imitations, Warbles, Echoes, Refrains
Flute and Guitar Serenade; Ocarina Solo
"The Blue Bells of Scotland" with variations
Flirtation! (an original aesthetic sketch)
P. Rooney, K. Rooney, Company

[80]Previously presented 17 December 1888 at the Third Avenue Theatre for 8 performances, being a revised version of the play PAT'S WARDROBE presented 20 December 1886 at Poole's Theatre for 8 performances.

1889–1890 SEASON

Marie Cahill in MCKENNA'S FLIRTATION (Photo: Conly)
Billy Rose Theatre Collection, New York Public Library for the Performing Arts

1889–1890 SEASON

1889.26 ARDRIELL

A Comic Opera in Two Acts[1]. Libretto and music by J. Adahm [J. A. Norris]. (Adapted from the opéra-comique "La Poupée de Nuremberg," libretto by Adolphe de Leuven and Arthur de Beauplan. Music by Adolphe Adam.) Produced under the stage direction of Lillian Brown Norris. Scenery by Philip Goatcher and John H. Young. Costumes by Eaves Costume Company. Musical director, Frederic Intropodi. Produced by J. A. Norris and Lillian Brown Morris. Opened 3 June 1889 at the Union Square Theatre and closed 8 June 1889 after 7 performances.

CAST: *Urastras Shacky*, an old toy-maker—crazed on the subject of marriage: CHARLES THEODORE. *Cherub Uber*, his son—a boorish boy, in love with Manthie: WALTER PERKINS. *Major Grabb*, a U.S. Army officer—long lost brother of Urastras: JAMES CLARENCE HARVEY. *Neil*, son of the Major—much abused by Urastras, to whom he is apprenticed, and in love with Ardriell: ROY STAINTON. *Dolph, Gerro*, foremen of toymakers: T.S. Guise, M. deM. Woodcock. *Marthie*, a kitchen maid—in love with Cherub: May Leyton. *Leone, Sybil*, chums of Ardriell: Annie Lippincott, Helen Fiske. *Ardriell*, a pretty milliner—in love with Neil: LOUISE PAULLIN. *Chorus of Toy-makers, (Men) Masqueraders, Villagers, etc.*

Act 1, Scene 1: Large conservatory connecting Shacky's house with workshop. *Scene 2*: Fancy Ball Room.

Act 2: Best room in Shacky's house.

ACT 1[2]
Scene 1
- Opening Chorus of Men (We are toiling here throughout the day)
  Chorus
- Solo (But tell me you, what secret there)
  T. S. Guise
- Solo (I can't see Why it is that I, By young men so am slighted)
  M. Leyton
- Trio (To bother me is quite too bad)
  M. Leyton, W. Perkins, C. Theodore
- Recitative and Duet (Now sir, you get to bed!)
  C. Theodore, R. Stainton
- Recitative and Solo (Now gallant fellows, one and all)
  J. C. Harvey, Chorus
- Recitative and Duet (Hold!—is this the way)
  C. Theodore, J. C. Harvey, Chorus
- Solo (For months I've known, My son, my own)
  C. Theodore
- Solo (The Almanac does nothing lack)
  C. Theodore
- Duet (As women we, you must agree)
  M. Leyton, C. Theodore
- Solo (A charming girl my heart possesses)
  R. Stainton
- Duet (So here I find at last you)
  L. Paullin, R. Stainton
- Duet (Goodbye, sweet heart, I'll soon return to thee)
  L. Paullin, R. Stainton

Scene 2
- Finale (Merrily here let us appear)
  Principals, Chorus

ACT 2
- Solo (Shadows deep the night is stealing)
  M. Leyton
- Quintet (You dear papa will show to you This girl he has made)
  C. Theodore, W. Perkins, M. Leyton, R. Stainton, L. Paullin
- Incantation Trio (Your hands now both of you in mine must place)
  R. Stainton, C. Theodore, W. Perkins
- Waltz (Where am I?)
  L. Paullin, M. Leyton, R. Stainton, C. Theodore, W. Perkins
- Quintet (Now for supper we are ready)
  L. Paullin, M. Leyton, R. Stainton, C. Theodore, W. Perkins
- Trio (Great heaven! This is fine!)
  C. Theodore, W. Perkins, L. Paullin
- Quartet (With empty hands, On the lonely sands)
  L. Paullin, R. Stainton, W. Perkins, C. Theodore
- Dance
  W. Perkins
- Solo and Refrain (What's all this row? This big pow-wow?)
  W. Perkins, Chorus
- Conspirators' Chorus (Now then our courage screw)
  C. Theodore, W. Perkins, Toy-makers
- Solo and Quartet (If you will listen sir, to me)
  L. Paullin, R. Stainton, M. Leyton, W. Perkins
- Chorus (Merrily here, Let us appear!)
  H. Fiske, A. Lippincott, J. C. Harvey, M. deM. Woodcock, T. S. Guise, Villagers
- Finale (Our wooing's done)
  Principals, Chorus

1889.27 LOVELY GALATEA/ THE DRESS REHEARSAL

An Operetta in One Act, preceded by a Vaudeville and a Musical Extravaganza.(Produced by (John) Koster and (Albert) Bial. Opened 3 June 1889 at Koster & Bial's Concert Hall and closed 15 June 1889 after (18) performances[3].

THE DRESS REHEARSAL

CAST: HILDA THOMAS, HARRY SEFTON, MAMIE BARNARD, LILLY SHANDLEY, JOSIE GREGORY, MAY SHANNON, SALLY HANDROW, JENNIE JOYCE, others.

LOVELY GALATEA Original German libretto by Poly Henrion [Leopold K. Dittmar Kohl von Kohlenegg].) Music by Franz von Suppé.

CAST: *Galatea*: HILDA THOMAS. *Gannymede*: JENNIE JOYCE. *Midas*: GUSTAV ADOLPHI. *Pygmalion*: W. E. NANKIVILLE.

1889.28 THE BOHEMIAN GIRL

A Revival of the Light Opera in Three Acts, 6 Scenes[4]. Libretto by Alfred Bunn, after Jules-Henri Vernoy de Saint-Georges' ballet-pantomime "The Gypsy." Music by Michael William Balfe. Musical director, Paul Steindorff. Produced by the English Opera Company (James W. Morrissey, Director). Opened 10 June 1889 at the Grand Opera House and closed 15 June 1889 after 7 performances.

CAST: *Arline*: PAULINE L'ALLEMAND. *The Gipsy Queen*: ATHALIE CLAIRE. *Thaddeus*: FARNK BAXTER. *Count Arnheim*: G. Tagliapietra. *Devilshoof*: EDWARD CONNELL. *Florestein*: William Kammerer. *Buda*: Miss A. Brand. *Officer*: H. McPherson. *Soldiers, Gypsies, Retainers and Peasants*: Chorus of 60.

Act 1: The Grounds of Arnheim Castle.

Act 2, Scene 1: A Street in Presburg. (Twelve years later.) *Scene 2*: Woods near Presburg. *Scene 3*: Public Square, Presburg. *Scene 4*: Hall of Justice.

Act 3: Arline's boudoir.

[1]Critics remarked that ARDRIELL was in fact a revised version of THE ELECTRICAL DOLL toured in 1880-1881 by Atkinson's Jollities.
[2]Musical numbers not listed in programs. List prepared from published piano vocal score (La Redo Music, Inc., Chicago, 1888.) J. Adahm Norris thanks Stanley Felch for valuable assistance in the libretto.

[3]No program found for this production.
[4]First produced in New York 25 November 1844 at the Park Theatre for 17 performances in repertory. For Synopsis of Musical Numbers, see original 1844 production.

1889.29 THE CHIMES OF NORMANDY

A Revival of the Opéra-comique in Three Acts, 4 Scenes[5]. French libretto to 'Les Cloches de Corneville' by Clairville and Charles Gabet. Music by Robert Planquette. Musical director, Paul Steindorff. Produced by the English Opera Company (James W. Morrissey, Director). Opened 17 June 1889 at the Grand Opera House and closed 22 June 1889 after 7 performances.

CAST: *Serpolette*, the good-for-nothing: LOIE FULLER. *Germaine*, the lost Marchioness: ATHALIE CLAIRE. *Gertrude*: Marie Kellogg. *Jeanne*: Marie Meyer. *Nanette*: Annie Bell. *Suzanne*: Belle Muni. *Henri*, Marquis of Corneville: EDWARD CONNELL. *Jean Grénicheux*, a fisherman: FRANK BAXTER. *Gaspard*: HARRY BROWN. *Bailiff*: R. A. Bresee. *Notary*: H. Ashlin. *Villagers, Attendants of the Marquis*: Chorus of 60.

1889.30 MONTE CRISTO, JR.

A Burlesque in One Act, accompanied by an Olio. (Libretto and music by Frederic Solomon.) Director of music, William J. Rostetter. Produced by (John) Koster and (Albert). Bial. Opened 24 June 1889 (matinee) at Koster & Bial's Concert Hall and closed 14 September 1889 after (108) performances.[6]

Olio: Austin Sisters, Aerial Wonders, Kellar Phenomenon.

CAST: *Teddy Dantes*, afterwards Monte Cristo: MAY HOWARD. *Not-here*, a Detective: George Murphy. *Piano-forte*, his son: Charles H. Stanley. *Catamouse*, Innkeeper: W. A. McCORMICK. *Cartoone*, his wife: JOHN MARION. *More-beer*: Charles H. Stanley. *Mercedes*: Connie Leslie. *Firebrande*: Jennie Joyce. *Dangler*: Lillie Shandley. *Captain Blanger*: JOSIE GREGORY. *Peasants, Sailors, etc.*

1889.31 THE WHITE ELEPHANT

A Musical Comedy in Three Acts. Libretto by John Fowler. Music selected, arranged and composed by J. Clarence West. Produced under the director of the author, John Fowler. Stage direction, E. A. Locke. Musical director, J. Clarence West. Produced by Frank L. Goodwin and Cud Given. Opened 15 July 1889 at the Bijou Theatre and closed 26 July 1889 after 14 performances.

CAST: *Hezikiah Sultry*, the apple of his mother's eye—true, a green one, but otherwise fresh: HARRY C. CLARKE. *Timothy Tottles*, an elder, old enough to know better. A pillar of the church and a prop of other things called sacred: E. A. LOCKE. *Frank Risk*, an Elephantine Speculator. A man of destiny: GUY NICHOLS. *Getsome, Takesome*, two gentlemen well-versed in the true inwardness of elephants, but hardly naturalists: ALF HAMPTON, LEE HARRISON. *A Sporting Man*: LEE HARRISON. *A Seedy Man*: ALF HAMPTON. *Ruby*, an all-round terror, but decidedly interesting: GEORGIE PARKER. *Geraldine Risk*, a wifely consideration: BESSIE CLEVELAND. *Mrs. Sultry*, a mother-in-law. Need more be said?: Frances Arline. *Maud, Bell, Alice*, of the sweet seventeen brigade: Carrie Francois, Olive Tremaine, Miss Potter. *Indispensable Adjuncts*: Misses Muni, Smith, Howard, Ansel, Walton, Perreault, Chase.

MUSICAL NUMBERS

Opening Chorus
(*Music by* Richard Stahl.)
"Have You Seen the Elephant?" (Song)
"I Don't See Where It Comes In" (Song)
H. C. Clarke
"I Would If I Could, But I Can't" (Song)
"Jakey Schmidt" (Specialty)
G. Parker

[5]First produced in New York in English in an adaptation by M. A. Cooney as THE CHIMES OF NORMANDY 22 October 1877 at the Fifth Avenue Theatre for 16 performances. English adaptation uncredited for this production; most likely a variation on the standard English and American performing edition, by Henry B. Farnie and Robert Reece (published score, Joseph Williams, London, 1878).

[6]Performed 9 times weekly. Late in the run Jennie Joyce (replacement) as Teddy Dantes introduced J. K. Thomas's beautiful ballad, "The Day when you'll forget me."

1889.32 THE BANDITTI, or, Lamb'd in Corsica

A Burlesque of "The Brigands"[7] in One Act, accompanied by an Olio. Libretto and music by Fred Solomon. Director of music, William J. Rostetter. Produced by (John) Koster and (Albert) Bial. Opened 5 August 1889 at Koster and Bial's Music Hall and closed 14 September 1889 after 54 performances[8].

CAST: MAY HOWARD, CONNIE LESLIE, JENNIE JOYCE, GEORGE MURPHY, JOHN MARION.

1889.33 ANTIOPE

A Ballet Spectacle in Three Acts, 6 Scenes. Music by Georges Jacobi. Scenery by T. E. Ryan. Staged and produced by Bolossy Kiralfy. Opened 17 August 1889 at Niblo's Garden and closed 28 September 1889 after 57 performances.

CAST: *Kamarina*, Queen of Athenians: ANNIE RUSSELL. *Antiope*, her sister: MAUDE DICKSON. *Delta*, Attendant of the Queen: ALICE GILBERT. *Concord*, a friendly fairy: ROSE RIDGWAY. *Melisa, Helena*, Ladies of the Queen's Court: ADA DARE, RENA CAPRI. *Prince Tesio*, of Illyria: HERMAN WALDO. *Mopsus*, military attendant of the Prince: JOSEPH HALLIWELL. *Discord*, a jolly evil spirit: HARRY DICKSON. *Soldiers, Slaves, Amazons, Dancers, etc. Ballet*: CARMENCITA, Signor and Signora Pialras, Mlle. FRANCESCINA PARIS, Yank Hoe and Mlle. Omene (Japanese Fantasist and Illusionist).

The time and place are imaginary.

Act 1, Scene 1: Ruins by Night. Discord rejoicing. Entrance Concord. *Scene 2*: Reception Festival Hall.

Act 2, Scene 1: Specialties. *Scene 2*: The Queen's Camp.

Act 3, Scene 1: Tent of Prince Tesio. *Scene 2*: Triumphal Procession into the City of Athens.

ACT 1

Scene 2
Pas-de-Lyres
Eight Secondas
"Dawn of Love" (Song)
M. Dickson
"Mashing Eyes" (Song)
J. Halliwell
Grand Ballet Divertissement
Entrance of the Corps de Ballet
Solo
H. Konradt
Grand Entrée
Mlle. Paris
Grotesque Specialty
A. Kiralfy
Egyptian Girls
Mlle. Nicode, M. Konradt
Gallop
Mlle. Paris
Finale Brilliant
Entire Ballet Corps

ACT 2
Scene 1
Yank Hoe and Mlle. Omene (Specialty)
Song
J. Halliwell

[7]LES BRIGANDS, an opéra-bouffe in Three Acts. Libretto by Henri Meilhac and Ludovic Halévy. Music by Jacques Offenbach. Current English language version with libretto by William S. Gilbert.

[8]No program available, cast detail from the Dramatic Mirror and Clipper. THE BANDITTI and MONTE CRISTO, JR. were performed on the same program; 9 performances/week.

Gavotte
A. Gilbert
Song
H. Waldo
Scene 2
"The Oath, Glory of War" (Song)
A. Russell
Adagio and Grand March Dansante
Corps de Ballet
ACT 3
Scene 1
The Tissots
Concord rejoicing (dance)
R. Ridgway
The Queen, a prisoner of war (Trio)
M. Dickson, A. Russell, H. Waldo
Duet and dance
A. Gilbert, J. Halliwell
Scene 2
Triumphal Procession into City of Athens
Carmencita
Les Prouettes (a) Entrance of the boys; (b) Pas de quatre; (c) Stephanie Gavotte.
Specialty
The Pialras
Variation
Mlle Paris
Our Police
Juvenile Ballet
Grand Finale: Triumph of Antiope

1889.34 BRIC-À-BRAC

A Musical Comedy Extravaganza (Farce Comedy) in Three Acts. Play (and lyrics) by Frank Tannehill, Jr. Produced under the direction of Frank Tannehill, Jr. Dances arranged by Alfred M. Hampton. Scenery by Edward Simmons. Costumes by Mme. Holland. Musical conductor, Theodore A. Metz. Produced by James Jay Brady. Opened 17 August 1889 at Tony Pastor's Theatre and closed 31 August 1889 after 15 performances.

CAST: *Jee Gold*, a billionaire: TOM MARTIN. *Old Bear*, of Wall Street: FRANK W. HOLLAND. *Jovial Jolly*, an Inventor: E. B. FITZ. *Committee of Honesty (4)*: *Europe Sage*: C. B. Hawkins. *Asia Turnip*: Harry C. Stanley. *Africa Melon*: Harry C. Dietz. *America Smith*: JOHN P. SAVAGE. *Terry Hall*, Emperor of the Dudes: ALFRED M. HAMPTON. *Myrtle Gold*, Jee's Daughter: MAUDE GIROUX. *Mrs. Jee Gold*: KATHERINE WEBSTER. *Camille*, a Servant: Charles B. Phillips. *Pattie Oyster*: Vera Bedell. *Consomme*: Leila Holland. *Hashey*: Hope Curtis. *Sweetbread*: Lottie Hyde. *Vermouth*: Caprice Van Lissa. *Noodles*: May Stuart. *Rampant Rage*: Tom Martin. *Herr Mostly*: Frank W. Holland. *Meyerbeer Wagner*: Frank W. Holland. *Agents for Barnum*: Frank W. Holland, E. B. Fitz. *Nugget Joe*: E. B. Fitz. *Jugular Knockout*: E. B. FITZ. *Professor Go-On*: Alfred M. Hampton. *The Tyrant Emperor*: Alfred M. Hampton. *The Greek Slave*: MAUDE GIROUX. *Scarlatina*: KATHERINE WEBSTER. *It*: KATHERINE WEBSTER. *Members of the Ideal Cooking School, Anarchists, Greek Soldiers and Dancing Girls, African Maidens, etc.*

Act 1: Home of Jee Gold, New York City.

Act 2: Philanthropy Hall, New York City. (A lapse of four years.)

Act 3: An unexplored portion of Africa.

ACT 1
"The Cooking School"
(*Music and Lyrics by* Frank Tannehill, Jr. and Henry J. Sayers.)
"When We Are Married" (Duet)
M. Giroux, A. M. Hampton
(*Music and Lyrics by* Frank Tannehill, Jr. and Isidore Witmark.)
ACT 2
Grand Medley Entire Company
(*Music and Lyrics by* Everybody.)
"Soldiers of the Tyrant Emperor" (March Song)
(*Music and Lyrics by* Frank Tannehill, Jr. and Henry J. Sayers.)
Greek Dance
(*Music by* Theodore A. Metz.)
"I'm a Devil" (Song)
(*Music and Lyrics by* Frank Tannehill, Jr. and Theodore A. Metz.)
"Oh, Mighty King" (Solo)
(*Music and Lyrics by* Frank Tannehill, Jr. and Albert Krause.)
Octette (from MARTHA)
(*Music by* Friedrich von Flotow.)
"They Are Beautiful" (Waltz Song and Chorus)
(*Music and Lyrics by* Richard Stahl.)
ACT 3
Gavotte (from THE MAY QUEEN)
(*Music by* Alfons Czibulka.)
"It" (Song)
(*Music and Lyrics by* Frank Tannehill, Jr. and Theodore A. Metz.)
Clarinet Solo
H. C. Stanley
Instrumental Delights
K. Webster, Invisible Spirits
"It Was a Dream" (Song)
M. Giroux
"That's All" (Song)/Imitations of Nat Goodwin, George Knight and James Powers, etc.
A. M. Hampton

1889.35 (HERRMANN'S) TRANSATLANTIQUE VAUDEVILLES

A Specialty Entertainment (Vaudeville Revue) in Two Acts. Orchestra under the direction of William Lloyd Bowron. Produced by Professor A. Herrmann. Opened 17 August 1889 at the Bijou Theatre and closed 7 September 1889 after 25 performances.

CAST: HARRY PEPPER, CARRIE TUTEIN, THE ATHOLS, EUNICE VANCE, HERR THOLEN, KATIE SEYMOUR, LE PETITE FREDDY, LES FRÈRES TACCHI, GAIETY DANSEUSES from London (Rose Newham, Minnie Talbot, Kittie Talbot, Daisy Lynton), MONS. TREWEY, GUS WILLIAMS, THE MARVELOUS PINAUD FAMILY.

ACT 1
The Singing Master
H. Pepper, C. Tutein
The Spider and the Fly (Contortionist Specialty)
The Athols
Eunice Vance (Vocalist)
Quaker Song; Topical Song
Herr Tholen and genuine singing poodle 'Boulager' (Musical Clown)
Dainty Katie Seymour (Skirt Dancer)
Les Frères Tacchi (Musical mimicry, with bell accompaniment)
ACT 2
Pas de Quatre
4 Gaiety Danseuses
Le Petit Freddy (Child Phenomenon)
Mons. Trewey (Novelties and Shadow Pictures)
Gus Williams (Monologue and Song)
The Pinauds (Pantomimists)

1889.36 PAOLA, or, The First of the Vendettas

A Satirical Operetta (Comic Opera) in Two Acts. Libretto by Harry Paulton and Mostyn Tedde [Edward A. Paulton]. Music by Edward Jakobowski. Staged by John Nash. Scenery by Philip Goatcher and John H. Young, Charles Graham. Costumes designed by Mme. Martens. Conductor, Julian Edwards. Produced by J. C. Duff Opera Company (James C. Duff, Proprietor). Opened 26 August 1889 at the Fifth Avenue Theatre and closed 5 October 1889 after 42 performances.

CAST: BARONIS: *Braggadocio*, tallow-chandler. In the mountains only, "Black Bart": WILLIAM McLAUGHLIN. *Griffo*, his shopman and lieutenant, "Our own idiot": FRED CLIFTON. *Guglielmo*, beggar and bandit: A. M. HOLBROOK. *Sapolio*, a poor, invertebrate nephew to uphold a precious responsibility: HARRY PAULTON. *Paola*, his sister. "As near as Corsica can get to the Arcadian shepherdess": LENORE SNYDER. *150 Loving Kinsmen*: Ladies and Gentlemen of the Chorus.

CAROLIS: *Margarine*, "She has been a fine woman in her day": FANNY EDWARDS. *Gruello*, her faithful attendant. "The family wet blanket": Clem Herschell. *Lucien*, Margarine's son, "Who loves, alas! where only he should hate": CHAUNCEY OLCOTT. *Poor Relations*, "A small heap of bricks, the noble ruins of an ancient house": Gentlemen of the Chorus.

NEUTRALS: *Chilina*, a rich connection of Margarine's, "Talking of angels, what's the matter with Chilina?": LOUISE BEAUDET. *Gazzi*, an officer. "The child of the horse-marine": Catherine McLean. *Martino*, a sailor. "The son of the bounding main": Lillian Hawthorne. *Anna*: Annie Cameron. *Maria*: Carrie Boelen. *Clari*: Mittie Atherton. *Bruno*: H. Clarke. *Pietro*: E. Williams. *Bonano*: F. Hartberg. *Soldiers, Sailors, Beggars, Townspeople, etc.*: Chorus of 60.

Act 1: A seaport town in Corsica. The reopening of the Vendetta. (Goatcher & Young.)

Act 2: In the Mountains. The Last of the First of the Vendettas. (Graham.)

MUSICAL NUMBERS[9]

"It Isn't on That We Rely"
L. Beaudet, Chorus

"Native Glens" (Duet)
C. Olcott, L. Snyder

"On the Beach" (Duet)
L. Beaudet, H. Paulton

"The Knife" (Trio)
H. Paulton, F. Clifton, W. McLaughlin

"I Am Perfect" (Solo)
L. Snyder

"In This, My Native Land" (Topical Song)
H. Paulton

"Please Yourself" (Duet)
H. Paulton, L. Beaudet

Serenade (In the argent light of the summer moon)
C. Olcott

"Poor Relations"
Chorus

Sextette (Act 2)

1889.37 McKENNA'S FLIRTATION

A Farce Comedy in Three Acts. (Play by Edgar Selden.) Scenery by Joseph De La Harpe and C. W. Valentine. Produced by William M. Dunlevy. Opened 2 September 1889 at the New Park Theatre and closed 30 November 1889 after 107 performances.[10]

CAST: *Michael Ryan*, a retired milkman: HUGH FAY. *Timothy McKenna*, a contractor: WILLIAM BARRY. *Timothy McKenna*, his son, in love with Mary Ellen: CHARLES LAMB. *Greenleaf Blackstone Kent*, a Shyster Lawyer: ARTHUR C. MORELAND. *Willet Chase*, a Society chappie, Don't you know: J. A. WHEELOCK. *Patrick McGurk*, Hod-carrier and general workman: CHARLES STURGES. *Mrs. O'Donald*, who keeps a beer saloon: James J. Murray. *Policeman McCarthy*, one of the finest: James J. Murray. *Pan Handle Mike*, who looks tough: R. E. McAllister. *Mrs. Mary Ellen Ryan*, a victim of circumstances: MARION A. EARLE. *Mary Ellen Ryan*, in love with Tim: MARIE CAHILL. *Anastasia McGovern*, McKenna's sister-in-law and housekeeper: Adele Bray. *The Four Lilacs*: *Nellie Cary*: Saidee McDonald. *Maggie Cases*: Nettie Lowrie. *Sadie Monahan*: Vernie Henshaw. *Kattie Fagan*: Lena Wood. *Susan G. O'Brien*: Minnie Leighton. *Lillie Daly*: Mabel Morris.

Act 1: McKenna's Flats on the Rocks in Harlem. The Flirtation.

Act 2: Reception Room in Ryan's Mansion. The Challenge.

Act 3: Picnic Park on the East River. The Duel.

MUSICAL NUMBERS[11]

"When Our Dinner Hour Comes' Round"

"(My Little) Tot's High Chair"

"You'll Never Know a Mother's Love Again"

"Katie's Sweet Heart"

"On the Harlem When the Moon Shines Bright"

"The Typical Mashers"

1889.38 THE FAIRIES' WELL

A Romantic Irish Drama in Four Acts, 7 Scenes. (Play by Con T. Murphy)[12] Produced under the personal stage direction of Dion Boucicault. Musical director, Professor Paul MacSwiney. Produced by W. H. Powers' Company. Opened 9 September 1889 at the 14th Street Theatre and closed 21 September 1889 after 16 performances.

CAST: *Larry Dee*, Tracy Farrell's whipper-in: CARROLL JOHNSON. *Andy Coogan*, Farrell's gamekeeper: John F. Ward. *Dan Carmody*, Mona's uncle: CHARLES FREW. *Mark Condon*, on Condon's Height: ALFRED FREMONT. *Tracy Farrell* of Farrell Court: A. J. MULLER. *Jonah Kelly*, from the mines: P. Toohey. *Patsey*, the Piper: John McLaughlin. *Eunice Beresford* of Beresford House: FLORENCE HAMILTON. *Mona Carmody*: DAISY TEMPLE. *Marry Ellen Brody*: Fanny Osborne. *Nellie Carmody*: Little Zella. *Clara O'Grady, Alice O'Grady, Jennie O'Grady, Kitty O'Grady*: Little Gertie, Nellie, Amy, Rosie. *Ladies, Gentlemen, Peasants, etc.*

Act 1, Scene 1: Exterior of Carmody's Home. *Scene 2*: Farrell's Pool.

Act 2: Hallow E'en at Beresford House.

Act 3: The Fairies' Well on Condon Heights.

Act 4, Scene 1: Beresford Hall. *Scene 2*: Farrell's Lane. *Scene 3*: The duel in Farrell's Park.

MUSICAL NUMBERS[13]

"I Sing of Eyes That Are Dearer to Me"
D. Temple

"There's a Legend That Is Famous"
D. Temple

1889.39 NATURAL GAS

A Revised Version of the Farce Comedy in Three Acts[14]. Constructed for Laughing Purposes Only. Play by H. Grattan Donnelly. Musical director, Fred Perkins. Produced by (Henry V.) Donnelly and (Eddie) Girard. Opened 9 September 1889 at the Bijou Theatre and closed 21 September 1889 after 16 performances; re-opened 31 March 1890 at the Fifth Avenue Theatre and closed 26 April 1890 after an additional 28 performances[15]. Total: 44 performances.

CAST: *Christopher Bluff*: HENRY V. DONNELLY. *Whirlem O'Rourke*: EDDIE GIRARD. *Nois E. Howell*: Mark Sullivan. *Ginger Whipsaw*: PETE MACK. *Jobson Doodle*: Herbert Sackett. *Kitty Malone*: JENNIE SATTERLEE. *Jimpsy*: RACHEL BOOTH. *Daisy*: Katherine Howe. *Flossie*: Kate Allen. *Katrina*: Fannie Johnston. *Tillie*: Joie Sutherland. *Gracie*: Lillian Barr.

ACT 1[16]

"The Night Maloney Landed in New York"
E. Girard

[9]Musical numbers not listed in programs. First eight songs contained in published piano vocal selection (William A. Pond, New York, 1889); last two titles from reviews.

[10]No credits in program for costumes or musical director.

[11]Additional songs performed on subsequent tour: "My Loved One," "The Proper Thing, You Know."

[12]Authorship of the play uncredited in programs. Based upon the Irish legend "If maid would her future husband see, On All Hallow E'en, 'tween twelve and three, Let her go alone, if the moon is bright, and look in the well on Condon's Height." New scenery, costumes uncredited.

[13]Musical numbers not listed in programs. List prepared from reviews.

[14]First produced in New York 1 May 1888 at the Fifth Avenue Theatre for 42 performances. For Synopsis of Scenes, see original 1888 production.

[15]Played an additional New York area engagement 5 May 1890 at the Grand Opera House for 8 performances.

[16]New York programs contained no list of musical numbers; touring programs between the New York engagements included this list, as performed by the same New York cast. A later interpolation, as per published sheet music (1890): "Only a Woman's Heart" Mary Howard (*Music and Lyrics by* Charles Graham).

Grand Finale Medley
Entire Company

ACT 2

"Oh, What Joy"
L. Barr

"When the Tide Comes In"[16]
K. Howe

"The Great Summer Season"
H. V. Donnelly, E. Girard

Finale

ACT 3

The Great Whistling Trio
H. V. Donnelly, E. Girard, J. Sutherland

Grand Medley: "Sweetheart," "Play Ball," "Ching Chang," "The Gooda Monk"

"Hail to Kit Maloney" (Finale)

1889.40

THE DRUM MAJOR

A Military Operetta in Three Acts, 4 Scenes[18]. English translation and adaptation by Max Freeman and Edgar Smith. (Adapted from the French opéra-comique "La Fille du tambour-major," libretto by Henri Chivot and Alfred Duru.) Music by Jacques Offenbach. Produced under the stage direction of Jesse Williams. Incidental ballet and marches under the direction of H. Fletcher Rivers. Scenery by Henry E. Hoyt, Andrew J. Hoyt, T. S. Plaisted, W. J. Mansz. Costumes by Mme. Loe. Director of music, Jesse Williams. Produced by Rudolph Aronson. Opened 16 September 1889 at the Casino Theatre and closed 19 November 1889 after 64 performances.

CAST: *Stella*, Daughter of the Drum-Major: PAULINE HALL. *Claudine*, Cantineer: MARIE HALTON. *Duchess Della Volta*: EVA DAVENPORT. *The Abbess*: Sylvia Gerrish. *Drummer Boy*: Florence Bell. *Francesca*: Georgie Dennin. *Lorenzo*: Blanche Roberts. *Gravolet*, Drummer: JAMES T. POWERS. *Monthabor*, the Drum-Major: EDWIN STEVENS. *Robert*: JOHN E. BRAND. *Duke Della Volta*: N. S. BURNHAM. *Marquis Bambini*: CHARLES CAMPBELL. *Gregorio*, Gardener: A. W. MAFLIN. *Clampas*: Edgar Smith. *Sergeant*: Frank Ridsdale. *Notary*: George R. White.

Act 1: Convent and grounds at Biella.

Act 2: Salon of the Duke Della Volta.

Act 3, Scene 1: Room in the Inn of the Lion d'Or. *Scene 2*: Street in Milan.

MUSICAL NUMBERS[19]

"Forbidden Fruit" (Couplets)
P. Hall, Chorus

"Honor and Glory" (Air)
J. E. Brand

"Italia! Land of Song" (Song)
P. Hall

"One, Two!" (Song)
M. Halton

"Stella" (Vocal Waltz and Scene)
E. Davenport, N. S. Burnham, C. Campbell, E. Stevens, Chorus

"It Must Be Now" (Duet)
P. Hall, J. E. Brand

"When Soldiers Marched" (Air)
P. Hall

"The Little Jehu!" (Song)
P. Hall

"Lo, The Notaries" (Finale)
Principals, Chorus

1889.41

LATER ON

A Return Engagement of the Musical Farce Comedy in Three Acts[20]. Play by H. Grattan Donnelly. (Songs by Fred Hallen and Joseph Hart.) Musical director, Frederick Gagel. Produced by Fred Hallen & Joseph Hart (Harry Hine, Management). Opened 23 September 1889 at the 14th Street Theatre and closed 28 September 1889 after 8 performances.

CAST: *Pansy Weed*, a wild flower with funds and fun: ANNIE LEWIS. *Rose Seed*, an American girl, with wit and manners: MOLLIE FULLER. *Mollie Waits*, because she can't help it: JOSEPHINE HALL. *Patchoula Seed*, fair and hopeful, with a literary turn: FLORA ZANFRETTA. *Tillie Tips*, with an eye to the main chance: Lillie Maehl. *Four very noisy girls*: *Susie Caps*: Virginia Earl. *Bertie Cartridge*: Jeanette Bageard. *Venie Powder*: Josie Sadler. *Gracie Shot*: Camille Cleveland. *Bandana Clutch*, a sheriff with ambition and indigestion: JOHN T. KELLY. *Hays Seed*, a retired army officer who is bound to have a title in the family: Robert Broderick. *Midmay Smiles*, a student in hard luck: C. T. Vincent. *Jack Plunger*, a better on the horses: FRED HALLEN. *Jolly Todd*, a bookmaker from Sheepshead Bay: JOE [Joseph] HART.

ACT 1

"Dear Old Pals" (Medley)

"Good-Bye, My Darling"
F. Hallen, J. Hart

"My Little Red Umbrella" (Fairy footsteps)
A. Lewis

Dancing Grotesque
J. Hart, A. Lewis

Bathing Song and Dance Finale (Medley)
J. Hart, F. Hallen, A. Lewis, Company

ACT 2

Character Songs
J. T. Kelly

"Love Match Test"
V. Earl, Company

"Who's That a-Calling" (Negro Hymn)
A. Lewis, Company

"Friskie Linda" (Serenade)

ACT 3

"The Two Enemies" (Duet)
J. T. Kelly, R. Broderick

"So Did I"
F. Hallen, J. Hart

Duet and Dance
F. Hallen, M. Fuller

"Wedding Bells" (Gavotte)

"We Hope to See You Later On"
F. Hallen, J. Hart, Company

1889.42

FAUST ON TIME

A Burlesque (of the opera Faust by Charles Gounod) in One Act, accompanied by an Olio[21]. Libretto, music and lyrics by Frederick Solomon. Produced by (John) Koster and (Albert) Bial. Opened 23 September 1889 at Koster & Bial's Concert Hall and closed 5 October 1889 after 18 performances.

Olio: Eldora (the demon juggler), Lester and Allen and Jules Keller in the sketch, Sim's Dempsey's Visit to Paris.

CAST: LOUISE DEMPSEY, JENNIE JOYCE, CONNIE ELSIE, JOHN W. RANSOME, ALLIE GILBERT, HELEN CONKLIN, Chorus.

MUSICAL NUMBERS

Ballet from NADJY
(*Music by* Francis Chassaigne)

---

[17]For return engagement at the Fifth Avenue Theatre, Mayme Kelso assumed the role of Daisy, and this song was replaced by "Cherie" (Mayme Kelso).

[18]A new English adaptation prepared for the Casino; previously produced in French in New York 13 September 1880 at the Standard Theatre for 23 performances, and 4 October 1880 at the 14th Street Theatre for 8 performances in a different English adaptation.

[19]Musical numbers not listed in programs. List prepared from published piano vocal selections (William A. Pond, New York, 1889).

[20]First produced in New York 11 February 1889 at the Star Theatre for 8 performances. For Synopsis of Scenes and Musical Numbers, see original February 1889 production. A Second Edition played 11 February 1891 at the 14th Street Theatre; frequent revisions, national tours and new editions followed as late as 19 November 1894 when Hallen and Hart played the American Theatre for 1 week.

[21]No program found for this production.

"Father Victory March"
Soldiers
Selections from the opera FAUST
(*Music by* Charles Gounod.)(Finale)

1889.43

THE OLD HOMESTEAD

A Return Engagement of the Rural Melodrama in Four Acts[22]. Play by Denman Thompson and George W. Ryer. (Staged by Denman Thompson.) Settings by Homer Emens (Act 1), Hughson Hawley (Act 3). Produced by Denman Thompson. Opened 26 September 1889 at the Academy of Music and closed 10 May 1890 after 255 performances.[23]

CAST [in order of appearance]: *Joshua Whitcomb*: DENMAN THOMPSON. *Cy Prime*: GEORGE A. BEANE. *Happy Jack*: WALTER GALE. *Frank Hopkins*: JAMES NORRIE. *Eb. Ganzey*: J. L. MORGAN. *John Freeman*: FRANK THOMPSON. *Aunt Matilda Whitcomb*: LOUISA MORSE. *Rickety Ann*: ANNIE THOMPSON. *Miss Annie Hopkins*: VENIE THOMPSON. *Miss Nellie Freeman*: LILLIAN STONE. *Maggie O'Flaherty*: MINNIE LUCKSTONE. *The Old Homestead Double Quartette*: Messrs. Barnard, Harry Earle, Akerley, Baker, Myers, Kruger, Gus Kammerlee, Tom Law. *Henry Hopkins*: Walter Lenox, Sr. *Judge Patterson*: Gus Kammerlee. *Francois Fogarty*: Frank Mara. *Mrs. Henry Hopkins*: Rosa Cook. *Miss Nellie Patterson*: Annie Thompson. *Reuben Whitcomb*: Harry Earle. *Hoboken Terror*: J. L. Morgan. *The Dude*: Frank Thompson. *One of the Finest*: Tom Law. *U.S. Letter Carrier*: C. M. Richardson. *Mrs. Maguire*: Rosa Cook. *Len Holbrook, Warren Ellis*, Country Fiddlers: C. M. Richardson, P. Redmond. *Pat Clancy*: Frank Mara. *Mrs. Murdock*: Marie Kimball. *The Three Stratton Gals*: Minnie Luckstone, Lillian Stone, Miss Baker.

ACT 3
"The Palms"
F. F. Bernard, Old Homestead Choir
(*Music by* Jean Baptiste Faure.)

1889.44

THE PEARL OF PEKIN

A Return Engagement of the Chinese and English Comic Opera in Three Acts[24]. Libretto by Charles Alfred Byrne. (Adapted from the French opéra-bouffe, 'Fleur de thé,' libretto by Alfred Duru and Henri Chivot. Music by Charles Lecocq.) Music by Gustave Kerker and Charles Lecocq. Staged by Edward E. Rice. Scenery by Edward G. Unitt & King. Costumes designed by Carrie E. Perkins. Musical director, Herman Perlet. Produced by Edward E. Rice and Henry E. Dixey. Opened 30 September 1889 at Niblo's Garden and closed 5 October 1889 at Niblo's Garden after 8 performances.

CAST: *Pearl of Pekin*, daughter of Tyfoo and a simple Chinese maiden: AIDA JENOURE. *Finnette*, wife of Petit Pierre and a vivandière: BERTHA FISCH. *Four charming French waiting maids*: *Pierrette*: Hattie Starr. *Angelique*: Hattie Delaro Barnes. *Pepine*: Florence Davis. *Fantine*: Amy Gardner. *Petit Pierre*, a dashing young quarter-master of the French Navy, stationed on board *"La Victoria,"* whose wife has opened a restaurant in Pekin as a side speculation: EDWARD WEBB. *Sosoriki*, a Japanese of some distinction, Chief of the Imperial Tigers, and with still higher aspirations: GILBERT CLAYTON. *Paul Mathot*, Boatswain of *"La Victoria,"* useful if not ornamental: F. L. Hill. *Sing High*, a Chinese attendant: John C. Leach. *Tyfoo*, Mandarin and Governor of Pekin, who frequently remarks That "He is as knowing as a Sphinx": LOUIS HARRISON. (*Chinese Band*, High Kee, leader.) *French Sailors, Chinese men and women, Mandarins, Officers of the State, ad infinitum.*

[22]First produced in New York 10 January 1887 at the 14th Street Theatre for 155 performances. For Synopsis of Scenes, see original 1887 production. Scenery for Acts 2 and 4 are new.

[23]Stage director, costume designer uncredited. No musical numbers listed in programs.

[24]First produced in New York 19 March 1888 at the Bijou for 80 performances, with a return engagement 7 January 1889 at the Bijou and Standard Theatres for an additional 56 performances. For Synopsis of Scenes and Musical Numbers, see both 1888 and 1889 productions.

1889.45

ZIG-ZAG

A Return Engagement of the Musical Farce Comedy in Three Acts[25]. Play by Frank Tannehill, Jr. and Von Brunck. Musical director, W. H. Nelson. Produced by W. W. Tillotson. Opened 30 September 1889 at the 14th Street Theatre and closed 5 October 1889 after 8 performances.

CAST: *Flirt*, the Incorrigible: ANNA BOYD. *Rene Staley*, the Chum: MARIE BOECKELL. *Mrs. Hopper*, the Subduer: ALICE VANE. *Jaggs Green*, the Apprentice: SAMUEL REED. *Bertie Staley*, the Lover: CON MALVEY. *A. Edw. Evermont*, the Author: Charles W. Meyer. *Mr. Hopper*, the Subdued: ALFRED C. WHELAN. *K. Greese*, the Agent: GEORGE KYLE. *Charlie Brooks, Willie Brood*, the Dashaway Brothers: Frank Fisher, George Clark. *Rose Bouche*: Evelyn Temple. *Geranium Leaf*: Mita Stanley. *Pansy Blossom*: Dot Neville. *Autumn Fern*: Lucy Mitchell. *Signora Judica*: ANNA BOYD. *Clarence Lightfoot*: ANNA BOYD. *Mme. Early Rose*: MARIE BOECKELL. *Mrs. Maidenblush*: ALICE VANE. *Balbazo*, the Tenor: Con Malvey. *Roaring Bill*: ALFRED C. WHELAN. *Lucifer Lucky*: Frank Fisher. *Charlie Pallor*: George Clark. *Sing Sing*: George Kyle.

MYTHOLOGY: *Apollo*: ANNA BOYD. *Venus*: MARIE BOECKELL. *Mercury*: Dot Neville. *Hebe*: Meta Stanley. *Helios*: Evelyn Temple. *Minerva*: Lucy Mitchell. *Turkish maidens, Opera Buffers, etc.*

1889.46

THE SEVEN AGES

A Kaleidoscopic Representation (Musical Extravaganza) in Two Acts, 8 Scenes. Libretto by William Gill and Henry E. Dixey. Music by Edward E. Rice. Produced under the personal direction of Henry E. Dixey. Costumes, scenery and appointments designed by Harley Merry, Walter Burridge. Orchestra under the direction of John J. Braham. Produced by Edward E. Rice. Opened 7 October 1889 at the Standard Theatre and closed 15 February 1890 after 152 performances.

CAST: *Bertie Van Loo*, a graduate of Columbia, possessed of wealth in plenty, health in abundance and blood of the deepest Cerulean tinge: HENRY E. DIXEY. *His Aristocratic Sisters (4)*: *Dolly*: Geraldine McCann. *Clara*: Marion Geroux. *Imogene*: Minnie Miller. *Edith*: Ella Rock. *Myra Van Twiller*, Bertie's Chere Amee: MARIE WILLIAMS. *Tripp*, a servant: E. H. Aiken. *Shakespeare* (rather bronzed): GEORGE W. HOWARD. *Avonia*, she will tell you who she is: ELAINE EILLSON. *Baby Van Loo*, the infant mewling in its perambulator: HENRY E. DIXEY. *Carolus Van Loo*, the baby's uncle: GEORGE W. HOWARD. *Nicholas Van Knicker*, a schoolmaster: GEORGE A. SCHILLER. *Susannah*, in the employ of Master Van Wart: Lila Blow. *Zuzette*, in the employ of Master Van Loo: Cora Tinnie. *Citizens, Emigrants, Perambulator Girls*. *Albertus Van Loo*, the schoolboy with the shining morning face: HENRY E. DIXEY. *Jacob Van Wart*, a scholar: HERBERT GRESHAM. *Her Companions (4)*: *Barbara*: Geraldine McCann. *Barbette*: Marion Giroux. *Gretchen*: Minnie Miller. *Barbette*: Marion Giroux. *Katrine*: Ella Rock. *Bertie Van Loo*, the lover sighing like a furnace: HENRY E. DIXEY. *Best Men (4)*: *Derrick*: Lila Blow. *Elliot*: Cora Tinnie. *Seymour*: Edith Merrill. *Derrick*: Eileen Kar. *Courtiers, Guests, Mohawks*. *Colonel Van Loo*, the soldier seeking the bubble—Reputation: HENRY E. DIXEY. *Major Van Koff* of van Loo's regiment: GEORGE W. HOWARD. *Jacob Van Wart*, a Tory traitor: HERBERT GRESHAM. *Officers in the Continental Army (4)*: *Captain Van Tassel*: Minnie Miller. *Lieutenant Ten Eyck*: Geraldine McCann. *Lieutenant Vanderwater*: Marion Giroux. *Lieutenant van Slote*: Ella Rock. *Martha*: Lila Blow. *Dorothy*: Cora Tinnie. *Continental and British Troops, Indians, Citizens, Drum and Fife Corps*. *Judge Van Loo*, the justice with eyes severe and beard of formal cut: HENRY E. DIXEY. *Van Mulligan*, court officer: GEORGE A. SCHILLER. *Van Blow*, District Attorney: D. L. Don. *Van Biff*, a desperate character: George Gilson. *Leonidas Van Stryker*, a reputable citizen: George Campbell. *Senator Van Grabb*, an upright statesman: George Campbell. *Adolph*, Van Loo's chef: C. B. Ward. *Valentine Blogsberry*, comedian and manager of a burlesque and comic opera company: Edward Aiken. *Violetta Vivian*, a leading burlesquer: Cora Tinnie. *Mistress Longgabble*, an injured wife: Geraldine McCann. *Marah Petrouva Eugalista Novogorodovitch*: Emma Jones Ince. *Court Loungers, Lawyers, etc.* *Grandfather Van Loo*, the lean and slippered pantaloon: HENRY E. DIXEY. *Admiral Barnacle*, one of the old boys: GEORGE W. HOWARD. *General Van Tromp*, another: HERBERT GRESHAM. *Master Van Duzen*, another: GEORGE A. SCHILLER. *Susannah*, a lady's maid: Lila Blow. *Phoebe*, a child: Mabel Pollock. *Baby Van Loo*, an infant: Pinkie Blossom. *Marquette*: Cora Tinnie. *Servants and Old Boys.*

Introduction: Disposition of the Players; Introduction. Library in the Van Loo Mansion. Present Day. (Merry.)

[25]First produced 1 October 1888 at the Star Theatre for 16 performances, returned 2 March 1889 to the Bijou Theatre for 17 additional performances, and 29 April 1889 to Niblo's Garden for an additional 20 performances. For Synopsis of Scenes and Musical Numbers, see original 1888 production.

Act 1, Scene 1: The Infant. Battery Park in young New York. 1740. (Burridge.) *Scene 2*: The Schoolboy. Playground of the van Knicker Academy. 1750. (Burridge.) *Scene 3*: The Lover. Ball Room and Conservatory of the Van Loo Mansion. 1765. (Burridge.)

Act 2, Scene 1: The Soldier. The Common in young New York. 1775. (Burridge.) *Scene 2*: The Justice. The Van Stuyvesant Police Court. (Merry.) *Scene 3*: The Pantaloon. The Van Loo Library. 1830. (Merry.) *Scene 4*: The Oblivionist. Exit of Grandfather van Loo and Return of Bertie from a flight of the imagination. "We are such stuff as dreams are made on, and our little life is rounded with sleep."

ACT 1

Chorus of Emigrants, Italian, German and Hibernians

Chorus of Perambulator Girls

Skipping Rope Chorus

"I'm a Harum Scarum Boy" (Song)
H. E. Dixey

Introduction to Ball Room Scene

"Here's My Ticket" (Chorus of Guests)

"When We Chance to Meet" (Duet)
H. E. Dixey, M. Williams

"In Fashions Ring" (Deportment Song)

"Welcome the Bridegroom" (Wedding Chorus)

"Saved by the One She Loves" (Gavotte and Finale)

ACT 2

"With Caution Tread" (Eccentric Chorus)

"The Reason Why" (Song)
M. Williams

"Grand March of Continentals

Military Song and Chorus

Court Officers' Song

"Hail to the Judge" (Chorus)

Entrance of the Comic Opera Company

The Judges' Comic Opera and Finale to scene

"Understand Don't You See, don't you know" (Topical Song)

"Hush Little Girl Don't Cry" (Ballad)
(*Music and Lyrics by* Edward E. Rice.)

"Off We Go" (Finale)

1889.47

SPIDER AND FLY

A Spectacular Burlesque Pantomime Extravaganza in a Prologue and Three Acts, 8 Scenes. Authors, Robert Fraser and William Gill. Produced under the personal stage direction of Robert Fraser. Musical director, Frederic W. Zaulig. Produced by M. B. Leavitt. Opened 7 October 1889 at the Theatre Comique (Harlem), moved 14 October 1889 to the Windsor Theatre and closed 19 October 1889 after 16 performances.[26]

CAST: *Progressa*, the Queen of the Modern Fairies: BESSIE CLEVELAND. *Beautina*, her prime minister: HILDA THOMAS. *Anarchis*, the promoter of a mistaken theory: PAULINE MARKHAM. *Ignorance, Idleness*, co-laborers in the field of Barbarism: ADA DARE, LOUISE ALLEN. *Knowledge, Industry*, co-workers in the area of civilization: Marguerite Wood, Lulu Reddan. *Gloriana Sand*, the grocer's wife: Kitty Hill. *Dorothy*, her daughter: Mlle. Dorst. *Boblink*, a sleepy messenger: Ray Allen. *Cordelia*, head engineer of the Pie Department: LOUISE ALLEN. *Irish Woman*: Evelyn Gray. *Colored Woman*: Clemontine Johnson. *Fairy Cook*: Mamie Hall. *Spider*, an Industrious Youth: JAMES R. ADAMS. *Fly*, an Idle Boy: THOMAS DARE. *Sands*, a grocer: Carl Anderson. *Twirletti*, Dancing Master and Owner of a Gymnasium: Monsieur Oreste. *McGinty*, a policeman: SAMUEL J. RYAN. *Lord Spooner*, a noble British peer, a suitor for the hand of Dorothy: P. H. Thurber. *Jake Hessian*: August Siegrist. *Young High Son, High Young Son*: Frank and John Lenton (Brothers and Gymnasts). *Railroad Door-keeper*: James Buckley. *A Russian*: D. S. Wolf. *A Swell*: J. C. Tiernan.

Prologue: The wreck of the good ship *"Prosperity."* The Fairy Newport. The Haunts of Ignorance and Idleness. Magical change to the Center of Civilization. Adoption of Spider and Fly.

Act 1, Scene 1: Exterior of Sand's Grocery Store. *Scene 2*: Interior of Sand's Grocery Store.

Act 2, Scene 1: A Street in New York. *Scene 2*: The Berkley Gymnasium.

Act 3, Scene 1: A Ball Room. *Scene 2*: Exterior of the Ball Room. *Scene 3*: Jones' Wood in a Snow Storm. *Scene 4*: Suggestion for the Columbus Fair.

PROLOGUE

Ballet of the Nations

ACT 1

Scene 2

Ballad
B. Cleveland

The Gaiety Dance
L. Allen

ACT 2

Scene 2

Calesthenic Exercises

The great horizontal bar contest by the invincible Dares

Descriptive Ballads
H. Thomas

Spider on the stilts
J. R. Adams

ACT 3

Scene 1

"The Masquerade Ball"
Chorus

The Railroad Ballet

Scene 4

Grand Transformation

Gorgeous March of Civilization's Troops

1889.48

MYLES AROON

A Return Engagement of the Irish Comedy Drama in Four Acts, 8 Scenes[27]. Play by George Jessop and Horace Townshend. Music and lyrics by William J. Scanlan. Scenery by William Schaeffer and Gaspard Maeder, Charles W. Witham. Musical director, George Loesch. Produced by Augustus Pitou. Opened 11 November 1889 at the Star Theatre and closed 7 December 1889 after 32 performances; re-opened a return engagement 27 January 1890 at the 14th Street Theatre and closed 1 February 1890 after 8 additional performances[28]. Total: 40 performances.

CAST: *Myles Aroon*: WILLIAM J. SCANLAN. *Squire Raymond Thurston*: Charles Mason. *Mike Carney*: Thaddeus Shine. *Gerald Fosdyke*: Edward R. Mawson. *Pat Phelan*: Robert McNair. *Joe Upton*: J. O. LeBrasse. *Barney*, the piper: William Murphy. *Dennis* (introducing Irish Jig): WILLIAM McGONIGLE. *Lady Glover*: HELEN WEATHERSBY. *Maggie Farrell*: MATTIE FERGUSON. *Mrs. Farrell*: Millie Sackett. *Lucy O'Shea*: Mary Warner. *Annie O'Connor*: Lucy Waters. *Nora*: Dora Vinton. *Katie*: Cecil Wallace. *Mother Bet*: LAURA WEBSTER. *Nellie Glover*: Constance Wallace.

1889.49

ERMINIE

A Revival of the Comic Opera in Three Acts[29]. Libretto by Harry Paulton (and Claxson Bellamy). Based on the melodrama ('L'Auberge des Adrets' by Benjamin Antier, Saint-Amand and Paulyanthe, adapted into English as) 'Robert Macaire.' Music by Edward Jakobowski. Produced under the direction of Jesse Williams. Scenery designed by Henry E. Hoyt (Acts 1, 2), T. S. Plaisted (Act 3). Costumes by Georges Pilotell. Musical director, Jesse Williams. Produced by Rudolph Aronson. Opened 20 November 1889 at the Casino Theatre and closed 4 January 1890 after 53 performances.

[26]No credits for scenery or costumes. A touring production, which played a return engagement 4-9 May 1891 at the Windsor Theatre for 8 performances.

[27]First produced in New York 21 January 1889 at the 14th Street Theatre for 16 performances. For Synopsis of Scenes and Musical Numbers, see original January 1889 production.

[28]Played a return engagement 17 March 1890 at the Grand Opera House for 8 performances.

[29]First produced in New York 10 May 1886 at the Casino Theatre for 648 performances in a series of three engagements. For Synopsis of Scenes and Musical Numbers, see original 1886 production.

CAST: *Erminie*: PAULINE HALL. *Javotte*: GEORGIE DENNIN. *Cerise Marcel*, Erminie's companion: Blanche Roberts. *Princess de Gramponeur*: EVA DAVENPORT. *Delaunay*, a Young Officer: Sylvia Gerrish. *Marie*: Emma Lawrence. *Sergeant*: Florence Bell. *Cadeaux, Ravennes*, Two Thieves: JAMES T. POWERS, EDWIN STEVENS. *Eugene Marcel*, the Marquis' Secretary: CHARLES J. CAMPBELL. *Marquis de Pomvert*: JOHN E. BRAND. *Chevalier de Brabazon*, Marquis' Guest: N. S. Burnham. *Simon*, Waiter at the Lion d'Or: A. W. Maflin. *Dufois*, Landlord of the Lion d'Or: Ellis Ryse. *Vicomte de Brissac*: Frank Ridsdale. *Benedict*: E. B. Knight. (*Flower Girls, Soldiers, Peasants, Clowns, Lords and Ladies, etc.*)

1889.50 KAJANKA

A Christmas Pantomime (Parisian Spectacle) in Three Acts, 9 Scenes. Libretto by George D. Melville. Music by Sidney H. Horner. (Production staged by George D. Melville.) Scenery by Joseph D. Clare. Costumes by Mrs. George D. Melville. Musical director, Sidney H. Horner. Produced by the Miller Brothers (Manager, Ben Stern). Opened 2 December 1889 at Niblo's Garden and closed 11 January 1890 after 48 performances; reopened a return engagement 24 March 1890 at Niblo's Garden and closed 5 April 1890 after 16 additional performances. Total: 64 performances[30].

CAST: THE IMMORTALS: *Electra*, Nature's Good Fairy Queen: MAY STEMBLER. *Beelzebub*, Her Satanic Majesty: RICCA ALLEN. *Zamello*, Son of Beelzebub: WILLIAM RUGE. *Beelzebub's Daughters (6)*: *Zamo*: Jennie Millard. *Bellalo*: Luella Dewey. *Malo*: Susie Mace. *Impia*: Laura Gray. *Damonio*: Ruby Moor. *Furio*: Josie Foster.

MORTALS: *Charo Hicty*, High Priest of the Jains: FRED WARREN. *Tongo Runga*, High Priest of the Brahm: Walter Owen. *Priests of the Brahm (4)*: *Jad Yani*: John Rixford. *Kat Lanh*: Lew Snow. *Yat Borah*: William Siegrist. *Zap Longi*: Elmer Krumbine.

PANTOMIMIC CHARACTERS: *Harlequin*: Alice Warren. *Columbine*: Olga Unnever. *Pantaloon*: FRED WARREN. *Clown*: GEORGE D. MELVILLE. *The Papillon Dancers*: Misses Rose and Alice Batchelder, Nellie Sennett, Edith Macklin. *The Comique French Acrobats*: The Donazettis (6). *The Wonderful Transformation Dancer* in 7 distinct character dances: EDITH CRASKE. *Hindoo Peasants, Nautch Girls, Studentes of the Gynmasium, Fairies, Cherubs, etc.*

Act 1, Scene 1: Beelzebub's Cave. *Scene 2*: The Idol Room of the Jainish Temple. *Scene 3*: Exterior of the Jainish Temple by moonlight.

Act 2, Scene 1: Ruins of the Brahmin Temple. *Scene 2*: The Fairy Grotto. *Scene 3*: The Floral Bower.

Act 3, Scene 1: Room on the sixth floor. *Scene 2*: The earthquake. *Scene 3*: Electra's home.

ACT 1
Scene 1
Descent of the Imp. Startling appearance of Electra. Her triumph over Beelzebub. The sentence of Zamello to the Idol, Kajanka. Transformation.
Scene 2
The banishment of Beelzebub. Quarrel of the sects. Entrance of the Hindoo worshippers. Destruction of the Idol by Zamello. Consternation of sects. Zamello's power. Transformation.
Scene 3
Entrance of Brahm. Destruction of Livia and Brahm by Kajanka. Tableau.

ACT 2
Scene 1
Electra's scheme to release Zamello. Triumphant March of Kajanka. Runga's subjugation. Kajanka destroyed by lightning. Zamello's deliverance. Electra's discomfiture. Transformation.
Scene 2
The Fairy Papillon Dancers. All for fun. Transformation.
Scene 3
Grand Floral March. Miss Edith Craske in transformation dances. The Sisters Batchelder, Nellie Sennett and Edith Macklin in a medley of the latest English songs. The French acrobats, 6 Onofris. Grand Finale.

ACT 3
Scene 1
"Where have I been?" The clown's amusement. A mysterious candle. "What funny beds." "He's under the table." "Where is he now?" The Clown cut in two. Electra protects her own. Beelzebub foiled in her attempt to recover the Talisman. Transformation.
Scene 2
Beelzebub's brief triumph.
Scene 3
(Finale)

[30]Played a return engagement 28 April 1890 at the Grand Opera House for 8 performances.

1889.51 IRISH ARISTOCRACY

A Revival of the Farce Comedy in Three Acts[31]. (Play by William Carleton.) Scenery by Joseph De La Harpe, C. W. Valentine. Stage mechanism by T. H. Femistre. Accessories by H. A. Weeber. Gas effects by J. Curtis. Orchestra under the direction of Emil O. Wolff. Management, William M. Dunleavy. Produced by William Barry and Barry Fay. Opened 2 December 1889 at the Park Theatre and closed 30 December 1889 after 33 performances.

CAST: *Michael Muldoon*: HUGH FAY. *Michael Mulcahey*: WILLIAM BARRY. *John Mandamus*, a young lawyer: CHARLES ROSS. *Peter Belcher*, a practical joker: CHARLES STURGES. *Charlie Riddle*, an aspiring M.D.: CHARLES LAMB. *O'Roger*: James J. Murray. *Harry Johnson*: Henry W. Wentz. *George Washington July*: Charles R. Wright. *Berrie Harkinson*: Frank N. Elmer. *Walter Skin*: Joseph A. Kavanagh. *Mrs. Muldoon*: KATE DAVIS. *Phoebe Plimkins*, Honora's chum: MABEL FENTON. *Jennie* Muldoon: Little Annie Lloyd. *Clara Nolan*: NETTIE LOWRIE. *Mamie Smith*: May Jordan. *Nellie Brady*: Cora Hubon. *Benlah Brown*: Bessie Osterman. *Dorothy Johsnon*: Sadie McDonald. *Ray Hastings*: Lottie Mortimer. *Honora Muldoon*: JENNIE YEAMANS. (*Specialty*: THE PRIMROSE QUARTETTE.)

Act 1: Kitchen in Muldoon's Home.

Act 2: Reception Room in Muldoon's Home.

Act 3: Picnic Park in the suburbs of the Metropolis.

SPECIALTIES, MUSICAL NUMBERS
Incidental to the play new songs, dances and medleys will be introduced and the meritorious Primrose Quartette will appear.
Famous Three Handed Reel (Act 3)

1889.52 THE TALLAPOOSA

A Naval Comic Opera in One Act, preceded by a Minstrel Olio[32]. Freely adapted from the German "Mannshaft au Bord." Produced by Lew Dockstader. Opened 3 December 1889 at Dockstader's Theatre and closed 4 December 1889 after 2 performances.

CAST: *Captain Rural*, of Indiana: LEW DOCKSTADER. *Sidney Oakum*, Midshipman on the *Tallapoosa*: JAY TAYLOR. *Doctor Capicum*: GEORGE MARION. *Barney Ketchum*, Politician: LUKE SCHOOLCRAFT. *Aphonia*, Rural's wife: EMMA MABELLA BAKER. *Otto*: James A. Leahy. *Frank*, Cabin Boy: Edith Mason. *Emily*, Ketchum's daughter: Nora Vernon. *Mrs. O'Grady*: Selina Rough. *Mrs. Flynn*: Marie Glove. *Mrs. Burns*: Annie Gross. *Midshipman*: Edward Sloman. *Dance Specialty*: Violet Newham. *Sailors, Marines, Roustabouts*: Grand Chorus of 50.

1889.53 YOUNG DON JUAN

A Burlesque (of the opera, Don Giovanni, by Wolfgang Amadeus Mozart.) in One Act, accompanied by an Olio. Burlesque by Frederick Solomon. Costumes by Mme. Van Axte. Produced by (John) Koster and (Albert) Bial. Opened 9 December 1889 at Koster & Bial's Concert Hall and closed 4 January 1890 after 36 performances.

Olio: Alexandroff Brothers; Sebastian Miller; Washburn Sisters; Thomas O'Brien; Laura Lee; Theodore Hoch; Sicilian Quartet; 'Our Army and Navy.

CAST: *Don Juan*: REGINA EMELLI. *Masetto*: JENNIE JOYCE. *Ottavio*: JOSIE GREGORY. *Leporello*: JAMES B. RADCLIFFE. *Scorcher*: Paul Saville. *Elowa*: John Marion. *Pedro*: Henry Moulton. *Anna*: Helen Conklin. *Serlina*: Lillie LaVerde. *Carma*: Minnie Mackay. *First Gendarme*: Lillie Shandley. *Second Gendarme*: May Shannon. *Third Gendarme*: Georgie Mortimer.

[31]First produced in New York as IRISH ARISTOCRACY AT MULDOON'S PICNIC 30 November 1882 at the Academy of Music for 2 performances. For Synopsis of Scenes and Musical Numbers, see original 1882 production. New songs and dances were added for this revival.
[32]In a departure from house policy, both the minstrel olio and comic opera were performed in whiteface.

1889.54

FAUST UP TO DATE

George Edwardes' London Gaiety Theatre Company in a Musical Burlesque in Two Acts, 3 Scenes[33]. Libretto by George R. Sims and Henry Pettitt. Music by Meyer Lutz. Produced under the stage direction of Walter Raynham. Scenery by T. E. Ryan, William Telbin. Musical director, Lovell Phillips. Produced by Henry E. Abbey and Maurice Grau. Opened 10 December 1889 at the Broadway Theatre and closed 18 January 1890 after 43 performances; re-opened 21 April 1890[34] at the Broadway Theatre and closed 3 May 1890 after 14 additional performances. Total: 57 performances.

CAST: *Mephistopheles*: E. J. LONNEN. *Valentine*: CHARLES DANBY. *Old Faust*: E. VACOTTI. *Lord Chancellor*: E. H. HASLEM. *Schelzer*: Elsie Everett. *(Young) Faust*: ADDIE CONYERS. *Siebel*: KATIE BARRY. *Donnner*: Nellie Langton. *Wagner*: Maude Stone. *Blitzen*: Gertrude Hillyar. *Katrina*: Edith Rayner. *Lisa*: Florence Levey. *Elsa*: Lillian Price. *Hilda*: Maude Wilmot. *Lieschen*: Estelle Rowe. *Vivandière*: Mary Stuart. *Schwank*: Miss Rutherford. *Martha*: MARIA JONES. *Waitresses*: Ada Bellore, Josie Wilcox, Gertrude Capel. *Marguerite*: GRACE PEDLEY. *Crowd, Chorus, Waiters*: (Misses Florence Levey, Lillian Price, Edith Rayner, Maude Wilmot, Estelle Rowe, Mary Stuart, Ada Bellore, Josie Wilcox.)

Act 1, Scene 1: The Paris Exhibition. (Ryan.) *Scene 2*: The Garden. (Ryan.)

Act 2: Nuremburg Square, Nuremburg. (Telbin.)

ACT 1[35]

Tarantella
Chorus
"I'm a simple little maid" (Song)
G. Pedley
"Come along, old fellow" (Duet)
E. J. Lonnen, A. Conyers
"Sing and Dance"
Chorus
"Good-bye, true love" (Duet)
A. Conyers, G. Pedley
"I shall have 'em" (Song)
E. J. Lonnen
"The Waxworks Show"
Chorus
"I wooed my love" (Song)
K. Berry
Serenade (Prithee pretty maiden)(Song)
A. Conyers
Jewel Song (What a charming bracelet! What a pretty ring!)(Song)
G. Pedley
"I'm afraid there is somebody looking" (Duet)
M. Jones, E. J. Lonnen
(*Music by* Edward Solomon.)
Bell Quintet (Ding-a-ring, a-ding, ding ding!)
G. Pedley, M. Jones, A. Conyers, E. J. Lonnen, K. Berry
Finale—"I cannot part with thee"
Principals, Chorus

ACT 2

Scandal Chorus (Come now haste to the well)
Chorus
Pas de Quatre (Skirt Dance)
(L. Price, F. Levey, M. Wilmot, E. Rayner)
"The Dawn of Love" (Song)
G. Pedley
"Up to Date" (Song)
A. Conyers
(*Music and Lyrics by* Frederick Bowyer.)
"I raise an objection to that" (Duet)
E. J. Lonnen, E. H. Haslem
(*Lyrics by* Robert J. Martin.)
"The Soldiers Return"
Chorus
"A Soldier Born" (Song)
C. Danby
"'Ave a Glass, won't yer?" (Cockney Costermonger Song)
E. J. Lonnen
(*Lyrics by* Albert Chevalier.)
"Oh! Marguerite, my darling" (Serenade Duet)
A. Conyers, E. J. Lonnen
The Fight (Dance on the Corsican Brothers Ghost Melody)
"Hurry Up" (Valentine's death)
Chorus
Valse de Quatre (Dance)
"He knew it!" (Song)
C. Danby
(*Music by* Charles Ingle. *Lyrics by* Albert Chevalier.)
"For You" (Incidental song)
(*Music by* Sidney Smith. *Lyrics by* Arthur Chapman.)
Finale (I cannot part with you; I shall have 'em; A Soldier Born)

[33]Inspired by Charles Gounod's opera FAUST.
[34]Critics remarked upon new songs and comedy interpolations.
[35]Musical numbers not listed in programs. List prepared from published vocal score (William A. Pond & Co., New York, 1889). Additional interpolations not in published piano vocal score: "Enniscorthy" (*Music and Lyrics by* Robert J. Martin); "Don't Know,"C. Danby (*Music and Lyrics by* Frederic Solomon, arranged by W. T. Francis.)

1890.01

THE BRIGANDS

A Revival of the Operetta in Three Acts in English[36]. English libretto by William S. Gilbert. (Adapted from the French opéra-comique 'Les Brigands,' libretto by Henri Meilhac and Ludovic Halévy.) Music by Jacques Offenbach. Produced under the stage direction of Max Freeman. Incidental ballet under the direction of Mons. Mamert Bibeyran. Scenery by Richard Marston (Acts 1, 2), Henry E. Hoyt (Act 3). Costumes by (Henry) Dazian and Mme. Loe. Director of music, Gustave Kerker. Produced by Rudolph Aronson. Opened 6 January 1890 at the Casino Theatre and closed 22 February 1890 after 49 performances.

CAST: *Fiorella*, the Brigand's daughter: LILLIAN RUSSELL. *Fragoletto*, a Young Farmer: ANNA O'KEEFE. *Princess of Grenada*: ISABELLE URQUHART. *Adolph de Valladolid*, her favorite page: Laura Russell. *Brigands (3)*: *Pietro*: FRED SOLOMON. *Falsacappa*: GEORGE OLMI. *Antonio*: ARTHUR W. TAMS. *The Duke of Mantua*: HENRY HALLAM. *Joseph Antonio*, Treasurer to the Duke of Mantua: Max Lube. *Captain of Carabineers*: RICHARD F. CARROLL. *Count of Gloria Cassis*, Chamberlain to the Princess: HENRI LEONI. *Baron of Campotasso*, Master of Ceremonies to the Duke: CHARLES PRIEST. *Brigands (4)*: *Carmagnola*: Charles Renwick. *Barbavano*: Edgar Smith. *Cecco*: L. Hall. *Beppo*: Henry Vogel. *The Preceptor*: J. A. Furey. *Pipo*, Innkeeper: Edgeworth Starritt. *Italian Peasant Girls (3)*: *Fiametta*: DELIA STACEY. *Bianca*: SYLVIA THORNE. *Zerlina*: Drew Donaldson. *Pipo's Daughters (5)*: *Pipa*: Nellie Douglas. *Pipetta*: Eva Johns. *Pepita*: May Grosvenor. *Petipa*: Florence Wilson. *Petipetta*: Clara Randall.

1890.02

THE GONDOLIERS, or, The King of Barataria

A Comic Opera in Two Acts. Libretto by William S. Gilbert. Music by Arthur Sullivan. Scenery by Hawes Craven. Costumes by Percy Anderson. Directed by F. A. Leon. Musical director, Jesse Williams. Produced by A. M. Palmer and (Richard) D'Oyly Carte. Opened 7 January 1890 at the Park Theatre, closing 13 February 1890; moved 18 February 1890 to Palmer's Theatre and closed 19 April 1890 after a total of 103 performances.

CAST[37]: *The Duke of Plaza-Toro*, a Grandee of Spain: GEORGE TEMPLE. *Luiz*, his attendant: ARTHUR MARCEL. *Don Alhambra Del Bolero*, The Grand Inquisitor:

[36]This adaptation first presented in New York 9 May 1889 at the Casino Theatre for 113 performances. For Synopsis of Scenes and Musical Numbers, see original 1889 production.
[37]Richard D'Oyly Carte rehearsed a new cast which succeeded the original at the time of the transfer to Palmer's Theatre, as follows: CAST: *The Duke of Plaza-Toro*, a Grandee of Spain: FRANK DAVID. *Luiz*, his attendant: Mr. (Helier) LeMAISTRE. *Don Alhambra Del Bolero*, The Grand Inquisitor: FREDERIC BILLINGTON. *Marco Palmieri, Giuseppe Palmieri, Francesco, Antonio, Giorgio*, Venetian Gondoliers: RICHARD CLARKE, RICHARD TEMPLE, Messrs. Boole, O. J. Rowlands, Albert Kavanagh. *Annibale*: Percy Charles. *The Duchess of Plaza Del Toro*: KATE TALBY. *Casilda*, Her Daughter: NORAH PHYLLIS. *Gianetta, Tessa, Fiametta, Vittoria, Giulia*, Contadine: ESTHER PALISSER, MARY

JOHN A. MUIR. *Marco Palmieri, Giuseppe Palmieri, Antonio, Francesco, Giorgio,* Venetian Gondoliers: RICHARD CLARKE, RUTLAND BARRINGTON, Messrs. (Helier) LeMaistre, McCarthy, A. Lee. *Annibale*: Percy Charles. *The Duchess of Plaza Del Toro*: KATE TALBY. *Casilda*, Her Daughter: AGNES McFARLAND. *Gianetta, Tessa, Fiametta, Vittoria, Giulia*, Contadine: ESTHER PALLISER, MARY DUGGAN, Misses A. Watts, Sadger, Pyne. *Inez*, the King's Foster-Mother: Miss (Marie) Rochefort. *Chorus of Gondoliers, Contadine, Men-at-Arms, Heralds and Pages.*

Act 1: The Piazetta, Venice. 1750.

Act 2: Pavilion in the Palace of Barataria. Three months later.

ACT 1[38]

Chorus of Contadine (with Solos) ("List and Learn")
Gondoliers, Messrs. McCarthy, R. Clarke, R. Barrington
Entrance of Duke, Duchess, Casilda, Luiz ("From the sunny Spanish shore")
G. Temple, K. Talby, A. McFarland, A. Marcel
Song ("In enterprise of martial kind")
G. Temple
Recitative and Duet ("O rapture, when alone together")
A. McFarland, A. Marcel
Duet ("There was a Time")
A. McFarland, A. Marcel
Song ("I stole the Prince")
J. A. Muir, A. McFarland, J. A. Muir, G. Temple, K. Talby, A. McFarland, A. Marcel
Recitative "But, bless my heart"
A. McFarland, J. A. Muir
Quintet ("Try we life long")
G. Temple, K. Talby, A. McFarland, A. Marcel, J. A. Muir
Chorus ("Bridegroom and bride")
Chorus
Solo ("When a merry maiden marries")
M. Duggan
Finale—Song ("Kind sir, you cannot have the heart")
E. Palliser
Quartet ("Then one of us")
R. Clarke, R. Barrington, E. Palliser, M. Duggan

ACT 2

Chorus of Men ("Of happiness the very pith")
Chorus of Men, R. Clarke, R. Barrington
Song ("Rising early in the morning")
R. Barrington, Chorus
Song ("Take a pair of sparkling eyes")
R. Clarke
Scena, Chorus of Girls, Quartet, Duet and Chorus ("Here we are at the risk")
E. Palliser, M. Duggan, Misses A. Watts, Sadger
Chorus and Dance ("Dance a Cachucha")
Song ("There lived a king, as I've been told")
J. A. Muir, R. Clarke, R. Barrington
Quartet ("In a contemplative fashion")
R. Clarke, R. Barrington, E. Palliser, M. Duggan
Chorus of Men ("With ducal pomp")
Chorus, G. Temple, K. Dalby
Song ("On the day I was wedded")
K. Dalby
Recitative and Duet ("To help unhappy commoners"/ "Small Titles and Orders")
G. Temple, K. Dalby
Gavotte ("I am a courtier grave and serious")
G. Temple, K. Dalby, A. McFarland, R. Clarke, R. Barrington
Quintet ("Here is a case unprecedented")
Finale ("Now let the royal lieges")
R. Clarke, R. Barrington, A. McFarland, E. Palliser, M. Duggan, Chorus

BLUEBEARD, JR.,
1890.03 or, Fatima and the Fairy

A Spectacular Extravaganza in Four Acts, 12 Scenes and a Prologue. Libretto by Clay M. Greene. Music by Fred J. Eustis, Richard Maddern and John Braham. Produced under the direction of Richard Barker. Ballets arranged by Mamert Bibeyran. Scenery painted by William Voegtlin, Ernest Albert, Henry M. Hoyt, Charles Fox. Costumes designed by Arthur Chasemore, William Voegtlin. Musical director, Fred J. Eustis. Produced by the Ideal Extravaganza Company (John W. Norton & Company, Proprietor). Opened 13 January 1890 at Niblo's Garden and closed 15 February 1890 after 40 performances.

CAST: Prologue: *Palmydaze*, the King of Chestnuts: FRANK B. BLAIR. *Spring Violet*, the genius of novelty: EDITH MURILLA. *Zara*, the genius of true love: KATE UART.
Play: *Ben Ali Barbazuli*, formerly known as Bluebeard: FRANK B. BLAIR. *O'Mahdi Benzini*, Fatima's fond parent: EDWIN [Eddie] FOY. *Selim*, a Persian officer, Fatima's best young man: ALICE JOHNSTON. *Selim's brother officers (6)*: *Mustapha*: Babette Rodney. *Abdallah*: Mattie Hornby. *Yusef*: Jennie Reeves. *Ibrahim*: Rose Franck. *Fadallah*: Josie Lynne. *Molek*: Bessie Pope. *Selim's Gaurds (6)*: *Carmini*: Hattie Kuley. *E. Hida*: Bessie Lynch. *Seyd*: Lena Manzone. *Orasmin*: Hilda Maccari. *Memel*: Florence Floring. *Baba*: Carrie Johnston. *Asta Gazonda, Asta Gazoo*, two chiefs of police: Lee Harrison, J. E. Sullivan. *Mufti*, valet to Bluebeard: ARTHUR DUNN. *Fatima*, Mrs. Bluebeard No. 8: EDITH MURILLA. *Ayesha*, a full-blown Oriental rose: TOPSY VENN. *Zara*, the genius of true love: KATE UART. *Suleima*, a village maiden: Homie Weldon. *Soldiers, Dancers, Sailors, Nautch Girls, Negroes, Children and Peasants. Ballet Specialties*: Mlle. CLARA QUALITZ, Madelaine Morondo, William Martini.

Prologue: The gloomy grotto of the King of Chestnuts. (Voegtlin.)

Act 1: Grand Square in Constantinopolis, on the banks of the Phosphorus. (Voegtlin.)

Act 2, Scene 1: Selim's Sumptuous Salon in the Regimental Barracks. (Albert.) *Scene 2*: The Glittering Grotto of Fantastic Fancy. (Voegtlin.)

Act 3, Scene 1: Street in Constantinopolis. (Albert.) *Scene 2*: Entrance to Bluebeard's Palace. (Albert.) *Scene 3*: Gold Terrace in Bluebeard's Palace. (Albert.)

Act 4, Scene 1: Blue Room in the Castle. (Albert.) *Scene 2*: The Battlements of the Castle. (Voegtlin.) *Scene 3*: Interior of the Tower. (Fox.) *Scene 4*: Grand Battle Tableaux—triumph of Selim and death of Bluebeard. *Scene 5*: Room in the Castle. (Fox.) *Scene 6*: Grand Transformation Scene. Truth and Light. (Albert.)

ACT 1[39]

Opening Chorus of Picknickers, Boatmen, Water Carriers, etc.
"When the Cat's Away the Mice Will Play" (Song and Chorus)
E. Murilla, Chorus
"Drop a Nickel in the Slot" (Song)(Put a Nickel in the Slot)
E. Foy
(*Music by* Richard Maddern. *Lyrics by* Clay Greene.)
"The Army So Grand" (Song)
A. Johnson
"An Oriental Swell"
F. B. Blair, Chorus
"I Will Be His Wife" (Grand Closing Chorus)

ACT 2[40]

Scene 1

"(Like) June Skies" (Song and Chorus)
A. Johnson, Guards
(*Music by* John Braham. *Lyrics by* John F. Harley.)

DUGGAN, Mattie Geoffrey, Cora Tinnie, Miss A. Watts. *Inez*, The King's Foster-Mother: Rose Leighton. *Chorus of Gondoliers, Contadine, Men-at-Arms, Heralds and Pages.*

[38]Musical numbers not listed in programs. List prepared from published English piano vocal score (Chappell & Co., Ltd., 1889).

[39]Songs and specialties changed during the run. A later review remarked upon the song "Listen to My Tale of Woe."

[40]Added after opening to the beginning of Act 2, Scene 1:
"Little Annie Rooney" (Song)
E. Foy
(*Music and Lyrics by* Michael Nolan.)
"What Is This Vision I See?" (Duet)(from Act 4)
E. Murilla, T. Venn, Beheaded Wives.

"The Little Peach" (Duet)
E. Murilla, A. Dunn

Scene 2

Grand Ballet Divertissement

Dance of the Grasshoppers: "Karoo-Karoo, how do ye do" [Chorus]
(*Music by* Walter Slaughter.)

The Children's Heroes: Jack the Giant-Killer; Puss in Boots, Cinderella, etc.

The Old Woman Who lived in a Shoe and Her Children

White Moths

Lady Bugs

The Firefly
M. Morondo

The Barn Yard Fowls

The Ostrich
C. Qualitz

The Harlequin Butterflies The Hawk
W. Martini

Grand Finale
Entire Corps de Ballet

ACT 3

Scene 1

"Sweet One, Ta Ta" (Flirtation Chorus)

"Of Course I Never Carry Tales" (Duet and Chorus)

"Ghostly Vengeance, We Invoke Thee"

"The Hebrew Fancy Ball"[41]
L. Harrison, J. E. Sullivan

"We're Perfection Odalisque"
Chorus

"Be Brave and Wait, I Will Release You"

Grand Wedding March

Scene 2

"When Johnny Gets His Gun" (Trio)
E. Foy, A. Dunn, E. Williams
(*Music and Lyrics by* Charles Warren.)

Scene 3

Sumptuous Wedding Pageant

Persian Military March
A. Johnson, Amazons, Officers

The Light of Asia

Girls of the Ganges

Snake Charmers

A Hindu Hourie
M. Morondo

Nautch Dancers

Queen of the Nautch
C. Qualitz

Grand Finale
Entire Corps de Ballet

ACT 4

Scene 1

"He's on the Police Force Now"[42] (Song)
E. Foy
(*Music by* Richard Maddern. *Lyrics by* William Jerome.)

"Little Lord Fauntleroy" (Specialty)
(*Music and Lyrics by* Fred J. Eustis)

"What is This Vision I See?" (Duet and Chorus)
E. Murila, E. Williams, Beheaded Wives

"Take Them Both to Death"

Scene 2

Executioner's Chorus

[41]Dropped after opening.

[42]A parody set to the music of "He's in the Asylum Now." William Jerome later wrote a parody of the song "Annie Rooney" which Foy performed in his specialty spot.

Scene 3

"Your Time Has Come"

Scene 5

"Hand to Hand, Heart to Heart"
A. Johnson

Scene 6

Grand Transformation Scene

Darkness; Fable; Progress; Music and Poetry; Light and Beauty

1890.04 A MIDNIGHT BELL

A Revival of the Sketch (Rural Comedy) in Four Acts[43]. Play by Charles H. Hoyt. (Staged by Charles H. Hoyt.) Stage manager, Will Carleton. Scenery by Homer F. Emens. Musical director, Harry Luckstone. Produced by Charles H. Hoyt and Charles Thomas. Opened 13 January 1890 at the Bijou Theatre and closed 8 February 1890 after 32 performances.

CAST: *The Clergyman*, the Rev. John Bradbury: RICHARD J. DILLON. *The Selectman*, Lemuel Tidd, Deacon, Sheriff, etc.: GEORGE RICHARDS. *The City Lawyer*, Napier Keene: Frank Lane. *The Bank Cashier*, Stephen Labaree: J. W. Hague. *The Bank Teller*, Ned Olcott: George H. Trader. *The Bank President*, T. J. Olcott: Thomas J. Herndon. *The Country Boy*, Martin Tripp: Eugene Canfield. *The Village Doctor*, Hiram Wing: H. J. Hirschberg. *The Village Fiddler*, Ezekiel Slover: HARRY LUCKSTONE. *The Schoolm'am*, Nora Fairford: Fanny McIntyre. *The Minister's Sister*, Dot Bradbury: MAUDE ADAMS. *The Old Maid*, Miss Lizzie Grout: Annie Adams. *The Widow*, Abigail Grey: Marie Uart. *The Soprano of the Choir*, Nellie Bowen: SALLIE STEMBLER. *The Village Maiden*, Annie Grey: Helen Mowat. *The Help*, Hannah: Laura Ayers. *The Village Pet*: Little Dot Clarendon. *School Children and Villagers.*

1890.05 PRINCE LAVENDER'S RECEPTION

A Terpsichorean and Musical Divertissement (a Burlesque of Arthur Wing Pinero's play 'Sweet Lavender') in One Act, accompanied by a Olio. Burlesque by Fred Solomon. Produced by (John) Koster and (Albert) Bial. Opened 20 January 1890 at Koster & Bial's Concert Hall and closed 15 February 1890 after 36 performances.[44]

Olio: Braatz Brothers. M. Alfredo and his mysterious globe. Donaldson Brothers. F. W. Dale. Al Reeves.

CAST: *Prince Lavender*: JENNIE JOYCE. With MAY SHANNON, JOSIE GREGORY, MAMIE BARNARD, LILLIE SHANDLEY.

1890.06 SHANE-NA-LAWN

A Revival of the Irish Comedy Drama in Three Acts.[45] Play by James C. Roach and J. Armory Know (Texas Siftings). Music and lyrics by William J. Scanlan. Stage manager, J. O. LeBrasse. Musical director, George Loesch. Produced by Augustus Pitou. Opened 3 February 1890 at the 14th Street Theatre and closed 8 February 1890 after 8 performances.

CAST: *Shane-na-Lawn*: WILLIAM J. SCANLAN. *John Power*: Robert McNair. *Gerald Power*: Edward R. Mawson. *Squire Redmond*: J. O. LaBRASSE. *Harry Redmond*: Charles Dade. *Mat Kirwin*: Charles Mason. *Ronald*: Thaddeus Shine. *Buckley*: C. R. Webster. *Agent Dillon*: Albert Morrell. *Captain Fitzgerald*: H. L. Waters. *Rose Redmond*: HELEN WEATHERSBY. *Peggy O'Moore*: MATTIE FERGUSON. *Mrs. Power*: Millie Sackett. *Moll Shehouge*: Laura Wilson.

SPECIALTY, MUSICAL NUMBERS

Selection from William Makepeace Thackeray's 'Pendennis'
W. J. Scanlan

[43]First produced in New York 5 March 1889 at the Bijou Theatre for 136 performances. For Synopsis of Scenes and Musical Numbers, see original 1889 production.

[44]No program available.

[45]First produced in New York 21 September 1885 at Niblo's Garden, returning 26 April 1886 to Niblo's Garden for a total of 24 performances. For Synopsis of Scenes, see original 1885 production.

"The Low Backed Car"
W. J. Scanlan
(*Music and Lyrics by* Samuel Lover.)
"Give Paddy but a Chance and He'll Show You What He's Made Of"
W. J. Scanlan
"Peggy O'Moore"
W. J. Scanlan
"Scanlan's Rose Song"
W. J. Scanlan
"Gathering the Myrtle with Mary"
W. J. Scanlan
"Peek-a-Boo"
W. J. Scanlan

1890.07 THE CITY DIRECTORY

A Musical Absurdity (Farce Comedy) in Three Acts. Constructed for Laughing Purposes Only. Play by Paul M. Potter. Music by W. S. Mullaly. (Scenery) Painted by F. Dangerfield. Musical director, W. S. Mullaly. Produced by John H. Russell for Russell's Comedians. Opened 10 February 1890 at the Bijou Theatre and closed 21 June 1890 after 154 performances[46].

CAST: *John Smith*, a detective: CHARLIE REED. *John Smith*, a capitalist: JOHN W. JENNINGS. *John Smith*, an athlete: ALF HAMPTON. *John Smith*, a ballet-master: IGNACIO MARTINETTI. *John Smith*, an actor: WILLIAM COLLIER. *John Smith*, a bunco-steerer: WILLIAM F. MACK. *John Smith*, a messenger boy: JOSEPH JACKSON. *John Smith*, an elevator boy: JOSIE SADLER. *Mrs. John Smith*, Minerva Flats: Helen Reimer. *Mlle Nanon*, prima donna: MARGUERITE FISH. *Laura, Dora, Cora*, Rosebuds: Maud Wilson, Sadie Kirby, Ollie Archmere. *Little Fawn*, premiere danseuse Gaiety: AMELIA GLOVER.

Act 1: Minerva Flats, New York.

Act 2: Green-Room, Gaiety Theatre. Amateur Night.

Act 3: Re-union Smith Family, Smithville, New York.

MUSICAL NUMBERS, SPECIALTIES[47]
"Since Casey Runs the Flat"
C. Reid
(*Music and Lyrics by* B. H. Janssen.)
"Since Maggie Learned to Sing"
C. Reid
(*Music and Lyrics by* B. H. Janssen.)
"He Ain't in It"
C. Reid
(*Music and Lyrics by* Philip Hastings.)
"Guess Again"
Introduction of Old Timers, the Chestnut Medley[48] (Act 3)

1890.08 THE KING'S FOOL

A Romantic Opera in Three Acts. Original Viennese libretto ('Der Hofnarr') by Hugo Wittmann and Julius Bauer. English adaptation by John P. Jackson. Music by Adolf Müller. Directed by Heinrich Conried. Scenery designed by Heinrich Conreid, painted by Joseph Clare. Costumes after original designs by Franz Gaul, by Henry Dazian. Musical director, Paul Steindorff. Electric and water effects by William J. Blackburn. Produced by Conreid's Comic Opera Company. Opened 17 February 1890 at Niblo's Garden and closed 1 March 1890 after 16 performances.

CAST: *Philip*, King of Navarre: J. P. McGOVERN. *Prince Julius*, his nephew: HELEN BERTRAM. *Yvonne*, Felisa's Foster Sister: DELLA FOX. *Felisa D'Amores*: ADA GLASCA. *Corisanda*, Countess of Pompignan: JENNIE REIFFARTH. *The Prothonotary*: Charles F. Lang. *Carillon*, Court Jester: JOSEPH W. HERBERT. *The Chancellor*: Arthur Earle. *The Legate*: M. L. Amber. *Count Rivarol*, Colonel: J. ALDRICH LIBBEY. *Archibald de Zarnoso*, Lieutenant of Lansquenets: FERRIS HARTMAN. *A Watchmaster*: H. Hilton. *Officer*: Kate Trayer. *Nieces of Countess (16)*: *Jeanne de Pompignan*: Louise Hilliard. *Blanche de Pompignan*: Emily Bell. *Marguerite de Beaulieu*: Molly Hilliard. *Marie D'Etcherverry*: Ada Walker. *Agnes D'Ellisagaray*: Nellie Barstow. *Celine de Beaumont*: Lulu Nichols. *Madeline D'Ustaritl*: Mabel Nichols. *Clarie de Grammout*: Clara Lavine. *Jeanne de Chavigny*: Belle Zarth. *Bertha De Autrelal*: Jessie Ralph. *Clarisse de Rochefort*: Fannie Haywood. *Antonie de Fermosa*: Bertha Dowling. *Olympia de Clairville*: Alice Western. *Elvire D'Artigny*: Florence Collis. *Alphonsine D'Abest*: Lillie Madison. *Clotilde de Marlborough*: Annie Sanford. *First Lansquenet*: E. Eckhardt. *Second Lansquenet*: A. Lynam. *Third Lansquenet*: Frank Pruette. *Antonio*, gardener: C. Stubel. *Algidius*, doorkeeper: F. Cohn. *Female Fencer*: Helen Engelhart. *Lansquenets, Country Folks, Vivandières, Fencing Girls, Courtiers, Pages, Peoples, etc.*

The action takes place at the beginning of the sixteenth century.

Act 1: The Castle at Salveterra, Spain.

Act 2: The Camp at Pampeluna.

Act 3: Royal Garden of the Castle at Pau in the Pyrenées.

MUSICAL NUMBERS[49]
"Fair Columbia"
(*Lyrics by* Heinrich Conreid and B. F. Roeder.)
"These Words No Shakespeare Wrote"
(*Lyrics by* Heinrich Conreid and B. F. Roeder.)

1890.09 THE CHANDELIERS, or, Venice in New York

A Burlesque (of Gilbert & Sullivan's 'The Gondoliers') in One Act, accompanied by an Olio. Libretto and music (adaptation) by Frederick Solomon. Produced by (John) Koster and (Albert) Bial. Opened 17 February 1890 at Koster & Bial's Concert Hall and closed 22 February 1890 after 9 performances.

Olio: CARMENCITA; The American Four; the Sisters Coulson; C. W. Littlefield; Harry LaRose; Satsuma.

CAST: *Prince Lutz*: JENNIE JOYCE. *Don Alhambra Palace*: JOSIE GREGORY. *Duke Plates and Sorcers*: PAUL SAVILLE. *Marks Baptisto*, First Chandelier: J. B. RADCLIFFE. *Tomaso*, Second Chandelier: JOHN MARION. *Casilda*: LILLY SHANDLEY. *Tessie*: VERA BEDDELL. *Jenny*: Meda Mitchell. *Inez* Mamie Barnard. *Fiametta*: May Shannon. *Julia*: Irene Rice. *The Notary*: Maude Russell.

1890.10 LITTLE PUCK

A Return Engagement of the Farce Comedy in Three Acts[50]. Play by Archibald C. Gunther[51]. Based on the story "Vice Versa and Fallen Idol" by F. Anstey. Proprietor, Frank Daniels (Management, Samuel P. Cox). Opened 24 February 1890 at the New Park Theatre and closed 5 April 1890 after 42 performances.

CAST: *Peckingham Giltedge*, a matter-of-fact stock broker: FRANK DANIELS. *Billy Giltedge*, a young American hopeful, his wayward son: ARTHUR E. MOULTON. *Dr. Hercules Savage*, the severe master and mentor of Savage Academy for young gentlemen: ROBERT EVANS. *Jinks Hoodoo, Esq.*, brother-in-law to Giltedge. A curse to everybody, including himself. Proprietor of Hoodoo's Dime Museum: HARRY CONOR. *Abe Striker*, The Bully of Savage Academy: HARRY CONOR. *Sluggers*,

[46]The production was "rejuvenated" for its 100th performance 7 May 1890. No credits given for the director or costume designer. Production played a return engagement 6 October 1890 at the Bijou Theatre for an additional 32 performances; for cast detail, see entry in following season.
[47]Musical numbers not listed in programs. List prepared from published sheet music, reviews, etc.
[48]Replaced during the run by the Smithville Gems, including numbers from Gilbert & Sullivan's latest opera, THE GONDOLIERS by permission of R. D'Oyly Carte.

[49]Musical numbers not listed in programs; no libretto or piano vocal score found.
[50]First produced in New York 16 January 1888 at the 14th Street Theatre, 23 January 1888 at the Harlem Opera House, 13 February 1888 at the People's Theatre, for a total of 24 performances; returned 15 October 1888 to the People's Theatre, and 11 February 1889 to the Theatre Comique, Harlem, for an additional 15 performances. Musical numbers not listed in programs. For Synopsis of Scenes, see original January 1888 production; for Synopsis of Musical Numbers, see 15 October 1888 production.
[51]Previous productions assign joint authorship also to Fred G. Maeder, Robert Fraser and Howard P. Taylor.

Butler of Giltedge: BURT HAVERLY. *Luigi Banoni*, Italian fruit vendor: BURT HAVERLY. *Charley Blocker*, The Boy: William White. *Professor Liverjamb*, Dancing Master at Savage Academy: William White. *Harry Shivers*, who has seen spirits: W. H. Stedman. *Simeon Mossback*, of Mossback, Wildcat & Co., Bankers, Wall Street: W. H. Stedman.

Miranda Savage, Dr. Savage's Daughter, in love with Billy: BESSIE SANSON. *Clara Giltedge*, Billy's Sister: LOUISE EISSING EMBREE. *Tabitha Tittleback*, Housekeeper to Giltedge: Marie Hilton. *Miss Ticklesham*, Schoolmistress: Marie Hilton. *Mrs. Simeon Mossback*: Lillian Walters. *Minnie Titters*: Annetta Zelta. *Mlle. Seraphina*: Mamie Curtis. *Lucy Langdon*: Mary Stuart. *Mlle. Violetta*: Jennie Stetson Bryan. *Violet Severance*: Emilie Beaumont. *Mlle. Victoria*: Rose Chesneau.

Scholars in Dr. Savage's Academy (5): *Rozie*: Thomas Kiernan. *Soxie*: James Carroll. *Moxie*: Gilbert Gregory. *Nosey*: James Kiernan. *Freckles*: Walter Long. *School Boys, School Girls, etc.*

1890.11 THE GRAND DUCHESS

A Revival of the Opéra-bouffe in Three Acts, 4 Scenes[52]. (Original French) Libretto ('La Grande-Duchesse de Gérolstein') by Henri Meilhac and Ludovic Halévy. English adaptation by Charles L. Kenney and Edgar Smith. Music by Jacques Offenbach. Produced under the stage direction of Max Freeman[53]. Ballet master, Mons. Mamert Bibeyran. Scenery by Philip Goatcher and John H. Young, T. H. Plaisted. Costume designs by C. DeGrimm. Director of music, Gustave Kerker. Produced by Rudolph Aronson. Opened 25 February 1890 at the Casino Theatre and closed 31 May 1890 after 100 performances.

CAST: *Grand Duchess*: LILLIAN RUSSELL. *Wanda*: FANNY RICE. *Iza*: ISABELLE URQUHART. *Olga*: Anna O'Keefe. *Amèlie*: Delia Stacey. *Charlotte*: Laura Russell. *Melanie*: Frew Donaldson. *Celestine*: SYLVIA THORNE. *General Boum*: FREDERIC SOLOMON. *Fritz*: HENRY HALLAM. *Baron Puck*: RICHARD F. CARROLL. *Prince Paul*: Max Lube. *Baron Grog*: Arthur W. Tams. *Nepomuc*: George Olmi. *Adjutant*: Henry Leoni. *Majors (4)*: *Nick*: Charles Renwick. *Dick*: J. A. Furey. *Mick*: Charles Priest. *Slick*: George R. White. *Notary*: M. J. Thomas.

Act 1: Encampment in Winter. (Goatcher & Young.)

Act 2: Salon of the Grand Duchess. (Plaisted.)

Act 3, Scene 1: Boudoir. (Goatcher & Young.) *Scene 2*: Encampment in Summer. (Goatcher & Young.)

MUSICAL NUMBERS[54]

Waltz Song (Round in circles flying, twirl ye, maidens free)

"Piff, Paff Pouf" (Never balked, never hesitating)
F. Solomon, H. Hallam

Rondo (Oh! I dote on the military)
H. Hallam, R. F. Carroll, F. Solomon, Chorus

Military Chorus (The drums all rattle)
Chorus

"To wed the fairest of Princesses" (Duet)
Lillian Russell, ?

Letter Song (I plac'd o'er my heart the portrait you gave me when we parted)
I. Urquhart, A. O'Keefe, D. Stacey, Laura Russell

"The sabre of my sire" (Song)
Lillian Russell, F. Rice, H. Hallam, R. F. Carroll, M. Lube, G. Olmi, Chorus

Finale (We'll quarter him this very nice)
Omnes

Drinking Song (There liv'd in times now long gone by)
R. F. Carroll, M. Lube, F. Solomon, G. Olmi, I. Urquhart, A. T. Tams. Chorus

[52]First produced in New York in French 24 September 1867 at the Théâtre Français for 156 performances, and in English 17 June 1868 at the New York Theatre. This adaptation was newly written for the Casino Theatre.
[53]In April 1890, Max Freeman's name was replaced in programs as stage director by Ernest Salvator, then later by Arthur W. Tams.
[54]Musical numbers not listed in programs. List prepared from published piano vocal gems, "the only authorized edition as performed at the Casino), New York), published by William A. Pond & Co., New York, 1890). Not in performance order.

1890.12 MY AUNT BRIDGET

A Revival of the Most Laughable of Singing and Dancing Farce Comedies in Three Acts[55]. Play by Scott Marble. Stage director, W. Andrew Mack. Musical director, Joseph Nicol. Produced by the "My Aunt Bridget" Company (Robert B. Monroe, Manager.) Opened 17 March 1890 at the 14th Street Theatre and closed 29 March 1890 after 16 performances; re-opened 28 April 1890 at the 14th Street Theatre and closed 3 May 1890 after 8 performances[56].

CAST: *Bridget McVeigh*, who arrived in the Spring, "Oh! by Gosh": GEORGE W. MONROE. *P. Alton McVeigh*, depending on his aunt. "Stay where you are!": JOHN C. RICE. *Jack Treyser*, Alton's college chum and diplomist: LOUIS MONICO. *Joe Nervey*, a New York collar button vender: W. A. MACK. *Tompkins Blazer*, a coal dealer, glad of it: BERNARD DYLLYN. *Dora Blazer*, Alton's jealous sweetheart: CATHERINE LINYARD. *Miss Decimer Recimer*, one of the "400," who wants to elevate the stage: KATE DAVIS. *Nellie Rider*, Dora's friend. "W-w-wait a minute": NELLIE ROSEBUD. *Kitty Blazor*: Brownie Wells. *Bonnie Annie Laurie*: Minnie Carleton. *Lila Butte*: Dora Pearl. *Rob Roy*: James Cavanaugh. *A. Ringer*: Royce Alton. *Polly Glyder*, who wants to *h'act h'out on the stoige*: LENA MERVILLE.

ACT 1[57]

Hunting Song
C. Linyard, B. Wells, N. Rosebud

"Skipped by the Light of the Moon" (Song and Dance)
J. C. Rice, L. Merville

"Good Ship Spring"
G. W. Monroe

ACT 2

"Sally in Our Alley"
W. A. Mack
(*Music and Lyrics by* Henry Carey.)

B. Dyllyn in his well-known character songs

Sextette
C. Linyard, K. Davis, B. Byllyn, W. A. Mack, L. Monico, J. Cavanagh

Quartette
C. Linyard, K. Davis, B. Dyllyn, L. Monico

"Come with Us" (Grand Medley)
Company, Chorus

"You Should Hear Her Whistling"
L. Merville

"Charlie Brown" (a smoking song)
W. A. Mack

"Once in a While" (contralto solo)
K. Davis

"Gaily, Gaily, Gaily"
Company

La Directoire
L. Merville, N. Rosebud, B. Wells

"Love's Old Sweet Song"
C. Linyard

Quartette
B. Dyllyn, W. A. Mack, L. Monico, J. Cavanagh (Selection from) THE QUEEN'S LACE HANDKERCHIEF C. Linyard, K. Davis, Company
(*Music by* Johann Strauss.)

Wing and Character Dances
J. C. Rice, L. Merville, N. Rosebud

ACT 3

"Eh, Did I Hear You?"
G. W. Monroe
(*Music and Lyrics by* Barney Fagan.)

Miss Kate Davis in her celebrated character impersonations

"Have settled their troubles at last" (Finale)
G. W. Monroe, J. C. Rice, Company

[55]Previously produced in New York 6 December 1886 at John Thompson's Eighth Street Theatre.
[56]Settings, costumes uncredited. Acts 1, 2 and 3 not specified in program, apart from list of specialties.
[57]Pursuant to published sheet music, the following was interpolated during the tour: "Nora Maguire," W. A. Mack (*Music and Lyrics by* Thomas LeMack).

1890.13 OUR BELLE HÉLÈNE

An Original Absurdity in One Act, accompanied by an Olio. Abstracted and condensed from Jacques Offenbach's operas by Frederic Solomon. Director of music, William J. Rostetter. Produced by (John) Koster & (Albert) Bial. Opened 31 March 1890 at Koster & Bial's Concert Hall and closed 3 May 1890 after 45 performances.

Olio: The Pialras (athletes). Florence (juvenile vocalist).

CAST: *Helen*, Queen of Sparta: JENNIE VALMORE. *Calchas*, High priest and tutor: George Murphy. *Paris*, the son of King Priam: JENNIE JOYCE. *Orestes*, the Son of a Gun: JOSIE GREGORY. *Menelaus*, Helen's Husband: Fred Warren. *Bachis*, Helen's maid: May Shannon. *Loena*, known as Shorty: Minnie Mackay. *Philocome*, Grand Usher of the Gods: Mamie Barnard. *Ajax I, Ajax II*, two holy terrors: Ida Chamberlain, Dolly Clark. *Achilles*, the Masher: Irene Rice. *Agamemnon*, Orestes' Papa: MADGE LESSING. *Dance Espagnole* (Specialty): CARMENCITA. *Kings, Slaves, Goddesses, Gods, etc.*

1890.14 THE MIKADO, or, The Town of Titipu

A Revival of the Comic Opera in Two Acts[58]. Libretto by William S. Gilbert. Music by Arthur Sullivan. Stage direction of John Nash. Scenery by Ernest Albert. Musical director, Julian Edwards. Produced by the J. C. Duff Comic Opera Company (James C. Duff, Proprietor). Opened 31 March 1890 at the Broadway Theatre and closed 5 April 1890 after 7 performances.[59]

CAST: *The Mikado of Japan*: MARK SMITH. *Nanki-Poo*: CHARLES O. BASSETT. *Ko-Ko*: DIGBY BELL. *Pooh-Bah*: WILLIAM McLAUGHLIN. *Pish-Tush*: JOSEPH C. FAY. *Three Sisters, Wards of Ko-Ko*: *Yum-Yum*: LILLY POST. *Pitti-Sing*: LOUISE BEAUDET. *Peep-Bo*: LEONA CLARKE. *Katisha*: LAURA JOYCE BELL. *School Girls, Nobles, Guards and Coolies*: Chorus of 75.

1890.15 THE PIRATES OF PENZANCE, or, The Slave of Duty

A Revival of the Comic Opera in Two Acts[60]. Libretto by William S. Gilbert. Music by Arthur Sullivan. Stage director, John E. Nash. Musical director, Julian Edwards. Produced by the J. C. Duff Comic Opera Company (James C. Duff, Proprietor). Opened 14 April 1890 at the Broadway Theatre and closed 19 April 1890 after 7 performances.[61]

CAST: *Richard*, a Pirate Chief: WILLIAM McLAUGHLIN. *Samuel*, his Lieutenant: FRANK PEARSON. *Frederic*, a Pirate Apprentice: CHARLES O. BASSETT. *Major-General Stanley* of the British Army: MARK SMITH. *Edward*, a Sergeant of Police: DIGBY BELL. *General Stanley's Daughters (4)*: *Mabel*: LILLY POST. *Kate*: MAUD McINTYRE. *Edith*: GERTRUDE SEARS. *Isabel*: Carrie Boelen. *Ruth*, a Piratical "Maid-of-all-work": LAURA JOYCE BELL. *Chorus of Pirates, Police and General Stanley's Daughters.*

1890.16 CASTLES IN THE AIR

A Comic Opera in Three Acts. Libretto by Charles Alfred Byrne. (Based on Cervantes' "Los dos habladores.") Music by Gustave Kerker. (Produced) Under the stage direction of Max Freeman. Scenery by Joseph Clare. Costumes designed by Thomas J. McIlvaine. Director of music, Adolph Nowak. Presented by the DeWolf Hopper Opéra Bouffe Company (Charles E. Locke, J. Charles Davis, Management; B. D. Stevens, Director). Opened 5 May 1890 at the Broadway Theatre and closed 16 August 1890 after 106 performances.

CAST: *Filacoudre*, the Judge: DeWOLF HOPPER. *Repetito*, his clerk: ALFRED KLEIN. *Cabolastro*, a wealthy citizen: THOMAS Q. SEABROOKE. *Jocrisse*, a young officer: Edmund Stanley. *Chief of Police*: Lindsay Morrison. *Pierre*, a barber: George Wade. *Bul-Bul*, a young nobleman out at elbows: MARION MANOLA. *Blanche*, daughter of Cabolastro: DELLA FOX. *Angelique*, his wife: ROSE LEIGHTON. *Louise*, his niece, betrothed to Jocrisse: Elvia Crox. *Victorine*, a glover: Anna O'Keefe. *Stephanie*, a perfume vendor: Lilly Fox. *Desirée*, a jeweler: Louise Edgar. *Glovers, Perfumers, Barbers, Cobblers, Police, Boys, Vendors, Idlers, Attendants.*

The action takes place on the Island of Martinique, W.1, any time the audience may choose to imagine.

Act 1: Public Square at St. Pierre, Martinique.

Act 2: House of Cabolastro.

Act 3: Gardens of House.

MUSICAL NUMBERS[62]

"The Wedding Bell" (Song)
D. Fox

"We Look, and Smile, and Bow, Just So"
Women's Chorus

"The Young Man Athletic" (Duet)
D. Fox, D. Hopper

"The Cricket"
M. Manola, D. Fox, R. Leighton, E. Crox, E. Stanley, T. Q. Seabrooke

"Just Us Two" (Duet)
D. Fox, M. Manola

"Castles in the Air" (Finale Act 1)

"What in the World Could Compare to This?" (Duettino)
R. Leighton, D. Hopper

"You Can Always Explain Things Away"
D. Hopper

"If 'Tis a Dream?"
M. Manola
(*Music and Lyrics by* Marion Manola.)

"This Little Pig Went to Market"
D. Hopper
(*Lyrics by* J. Cheever Goodwin.)

"Who Is Right?"

1890.17 AROUND THE WORLD IN 80 DAYS!

A Revival of the Spectacular Comedy in Five Acts, a Prologue and 13 Scenes[63]. Based on the French adaptation of Jules Verne's novel "Le Tour du Monde en Quatre Vingt Jours," as adapted by Adolphe d'Ennery. Music by Jean-Jacques de Billemont. Scenery by G. Magnani, Arthur Grenus, Harley Merry, Joseph Claire, Alf. John. Costumes by Mons. Landolff of Paris; Mme. Torrès of New York. Conceived, staged under the personal direction of, and produced by Imre and Bolossy Kiralfy. Opened 5 May 1890 at Niblo's Garden and closed 24 May 1890 after 24 performances.

CAST: *Aouda*, an East Indian Princess: DOROTHY ROSSMORE. *Nemea*, her sister: MARGUERITE ST. JOHN. *Bessie*: Ella Salisbury. *Nakahira*, Aouda's slave: Bella Wilson. *Phileas Fogg*, Member of the Eccentric Club: W. F. CLIFTON. *Miles O'Pake*, an ex-Senator from New York: MAURICE DREW. *Fix*, an English detective, Scotland Yard: J. J. WALLACE. *Jean François Passepartout*, French valet: W. H. LYTELL. *Mr. Blunt*, a Calcutta magistrate: W. H. Bartholomew. *Sir Roger Shewdryn*: William Howard. *Arthur Mayburn*: L. Morton. *Foster Jones*: J. Wakefield. *Governor of Suez*: William Renous. *An Aged Parsee*: M. S. Johns. *Brahmin Chief*: William Stewart. *Phil Tracy*: W. Wallace. *Jack Rivers*: J. Montague. *Conductor*: L. Rubel. *Chief Scout*: Fred Cole. *Dazum Ahan*, King of Borneo: James Van Pelt. *Barkeeper*: John Manning.

[58]First presented in New York 20 July, 10-29 August 1885 at the Union Square and People's Theatres for 22 performances. First authorized production presented 19 August 1885 at the Fifth Avenue Theatre by Richard D'Oyly Carte for 250 performances. For Synopsis of Scenes and Musical Numbers, see 19 August 1885 D'Oyly Carte production.
[59]Costume design uncredited.
[60]First presented in New York 31 December 1879 at the Fifth Avenue Theatre for a total of 91 performances in two engagements. For Synopsis of Scenes and Musical Numbers, see original 1879 production.
[61]Scenery and costumes uncredited.

[62]Musical numbers not listed in programs. First seven titles contained in published piano vocal selection (T. B. Harms & Co., New York, 1890); additional titles from reviews, recordings, published sheet music.
[63]This adaptation first produced in New York 28 August 1875 at the Academy of Music for 43 performances.

Captain Collins: William S. Hurd. *Premiere Danseuse Assoluta*: Mlle. PARIS. Corps of 100 Dancers. *Brahmins, Priests, Punka Wallahs, Dobez Wallahs, Soldiers, Hindoos, Arabs, Egyptians, Malayans, Road Agents, Passengers, Policemen, Sailors, Members of the London Eccentric Club, Snake Charmers and Bayadères.*

Prologue: Club of the Eccentrics.

Act 1, Scene 1: Suez, with a view of the Canal. (Grenus.) *Scene 2*: East Indian Bungalow. *Scene 3*: The Royal Mecropolis. (Magnani, A. John.)

Act 2, Scene 1: Hotel in Calcutta, with a view of the City. *Scene 2*: A Garden in Tokio. (Merry.)

Act 3, Scene 1: A Room in San Francisco. *Scene 2*: Kearney Station on the Pennsylvania Railroad. *Scene 3*: The Giant's Stairway.

Act 4, Scene 1: Saloon on the Steamer for Europe. *Scene 2*: Deck of the Steamer. *Scene 3*: Lights of Liverpool. View of the City by Day and Night.

Act 5, Scene 1: Hotel Parlor in Liverpool. *Scene 2*: The Palace of the New Eccentric Club. (Magnani.)

PROLOGUE

A wager of half a million.

ACT 1

Arrival of the Steamer "Magnolia." A Chase for $20,000. Purchase of an Elephant. Fix in a Fix. Funeral Pageant. The Rajah's Wife. "Down on your knees." To the rescue.

ACT 2

The Discriminating Judge. Grand Festive March. Entrance of Nakahira at Borneo. Introducing the Great Salambo's, the Electro Dynamitic Wonders of the age. The sensation of all Europe. The Great Mikado Ballet (by Imre Kiralfy.)

ACT 3

The Attack by the Road Agents. Another day lost. The Ladies Prisoners. "Only one shot will save the ladies." Thrilling Tableau.

ACT 4

Fogg, the Captain. I will give a whole year's wages. Full Three-Master at Sea. "If I don't reach Liverpool to-night, I'm a Lost Man. " Breaking up of the Ship. The Explosion. The Wreck. Liverpool.

ACT 5

I have lost my bet, but not my honor. No; it is Sunday, not Monday—yet in time. Eccentric Musical Dance, Secondas Danseuse. The last stroke of the hour. He has lost. No! I am here, Gentlemen. Grand Finale.

H.M.S. PINAFORE,

1890.18 or, The Lass That Loved a Sailor

A Revival of the Comic Opera in Two Acts[64]. Libretto by William S. Gilbert. Music by Arthur Sullivan. Stage manager, John E. Nash. Chorus and orchestra directed by Julian Edwards. Presented by J. C. Duff Comic Opera Company (James C. Duff, Proprietor). Opened 12 May 1890 at the Academy of Music and closed 31 May 1890 after 24 performances.

CAST: *The Rt. Hon. Sir Joseph Porter, K.C.B.*, First Lord of the Admiralty: DIGBY BELL. *Captain Corcoran*, Commanding the *H.M.S. Pinafore*: W. H. CLARKE. *Ralph Rackstraw*, Able Seaman: CHAUNCEY OLCOTT. *Dick Deadeye*, Able Seaman: FRANK PEARSON. *Bill Bobstay*, Bo'sun: W. H. McLaughlin. *Josephine*, the Captain's Daughter: GERTRUDE SEARS. *Hebe*, Sir Joseph's First Cousin: Katie Gilbert. *Little Buttercup*, a Portsmouth Bumboat Woman: LAURA JOYCE BELL. *First Lord's Sisters, his Cousins, his Aunts, Sailors, Marines, etc.*: Cast of 200.

[64]First presented in New York 15 January 1879 at the Standard Theatre for 175 performances. For Synopsis of Scenes and Musical Numbers, see original 1879 production.

1890–1891 SEASON

James T. Powers in A STRAIGHT TIP (Photo: Falk, Undated)
Museum of the City of New York, Gift of Mrs. James T. Powers, 46.246.204

1890–1891 SEASON

1890.19 THE BRAZILIAN

A Comic Opera in Three Acts. Libretto by Max Pemberton and Edgar Smith[1]. Music by Francis Chassaigne. Stage director, Ernest Salvator. Maitre de ballet, Mons. Mamert Bibeyran. Scenery by Matt Morgan, John H. Young. Costumes designed by Besche. Director of music, Gustave Kerker. Produced by Rudolph Aronson. Opened 2 June 1890 at the Casino Theatre and closed 13 August 1890 after 73 performances.

CAST: *Babette*: MARIE HALTON. *Manuela*: EDITH AINSWORTH. *Chiquita*: GRACE GOLDEN. *Flora*: Eva Johns. *Rosa*: Delia Stacey. *Fonseca*: Florence Bell. *Fernandes*: Drew Donaldson. *Emilia*: Laura Russell. *Don Inigo*: GEORGE OLMI. *Don Ramòa*: John Brand. *Daniel*: FREDERIC SOLOMON. *Herr Kirchwasser*: RICHARD F. CARROLL. *Gonçalvez*: HENRY HALLAM. *Antonio*: ARTHUR W. TAMS. *Rodrigues*: HENRY LEONI. *Diogo*: Max Lube. *First Sentry*: A. W. Maflin. *Second Sentry*: Stanley Starr. *Jailer*: M. J. Thomas. *Swordsman*: Frank Ridsdale. *Aide-de-Camp*: Charles Renwick. *A Bandit*: J. A. Furey.

Act 1: Public Square in Brazilian Town. (Morgan.)

Act 2: Mountain Pass. (Young.)

Act 3: Don Inigo's Fortress. (Morgan.)

MUSICAL NUMBERS[2]

"To Thee We Cry"
E. Ainsworth
"Seguedilla" ('Tis the Seguedilla that's enchanting)
Bolero (We will dance as the sprite of the morn)
M. Halton
"Castagnette Song"
"Berceuse" (Though brigand by birth)
H. Hallam
"Cigarette Song" (Surely life has many troubles)
M. Halton
Waltz Song and Chorus (We'll speed on the dance, speed on, speed on!)

1890.20 THE MIKADO, or, The Town of Titipu

A Revival of the Comic Opera in Two Acts[3]. Libretto by William S. Gilbert. Music by Arthur Sullivan. Stage manager, John E. Nash. Scenery by Ernest Albert. Chorus and orchestra directed by Julian Edwards. Produced by J. C. Duff Comic Opera Company (James C. Duff, Proprietor). Opened 2 June 1890 at the Academy of Music and closed 7 June 1890 after 8 performances.

CAST: *The Mikado of Japan*: FRANK PEARSON. *Nanki-Poo*, his son, disguised as a wandering minstrel, in love with Yum-Yum: CHAUNCEY OLCOTT. *Ko-Ko*, Lord High Executioner of Titipu: DIGBY BELL. *Pooh-Bah*, Lord High Everything Else: WILLIAM MCLAUGHLIN. *Pish-Tush*, a Noble Lord: JOSEPH C. FAY. *Three Sisters, Wards of Ko-Ko*: *Yum-Yum*: GERTRUDE SEARS. *Pitti-Sing*: LEONA CLARKE. *Peep-Bo*: MAUDE MCINTYRE. *Katisha*, an Elderly Lady, in love with Nanki-Poo: LAURA JOYCE BELL. *Chorus of School Girls, Nobles, Guards and Coolies.*

1890.21 THE SEA KING

A Romantic Opera Comique in Three Acts. Libretto by Richard Stahl and Webster C. Fulton. Music by Richard Stahl. (Staged by William J. Gilmore). Scenery by Homer F. Emens, Gaspard Maeder and William Schaeffer. Costumes designed by Baron C. DeGrimm. Augmented chorus and orchestra under the direction of Carl Martens. Produced by William J. Gilmore Opera Company (Charles H. Yale, Management). Opened 23 June 1890 at Palmer's Theatre and closed 2 August 1890 after 42 performances.

CAST: *Don Bamboula*, Duke of Valencia, a grandee of Spain: EDWIN STEVENS. *Dolores*, his niece: ESTHER PALLISER. *Rosita*, a village beauty: ANNIE MEYERS. *Miguel*, Don Bamboula's favorite page: LENA MERVILLE. *Donna Olima*, an aged duenna: ELMA DELARO. *Don Pedrillo*: Thomas H. Persse. *Pedro*, Don Bamboula's secretary, and also one of the Royal Body Guard: JOSEPH C. MIRON. *Don Bamboula's Body Guard (2)*: *Palmo*: Charles H. Jones. *Pompo*: George W. Cerbi. *Village Maidens (8)*: *Marcella*: Tolie Pettit. *Aretta*: Cecile Eissing. *Nanetta*: Angela Tegalini. *Onita*: Eva Evans. *Pepita*: Lulu Farrance. *Carmencita*: May Eckhard. *Oreta*: Clara Allen. *Nanita*: Blanche Howard. *Angelo*, a falconer: H. Steiger. *Mateo's Lieutenants (3)*: *Marco*: Ed Everett. *Beppo*: E. B. Knight. *Romero*: H. D. Chase. *Pages (4)*: *Nico*: Olga Unnever. *Rico*: Ada Raymond. *Pico*: Lizzie Wilson. *Sico*: Beatrice Barkle. *Falconers (4)*: *Oratto*: Ida Eissing. *Marcetto*: Josie Knight. *Onoto*: Alma Desmond. *Macota*: Edgeworth Wallace. *Mateo de Quevedo*, the banished heir to the dukedom of Valencia, called "The Sea King": HUBERT WILKE. *Huntsmen, Falconers, Pages and Maids of Honor, Smugglers, the Sea King's Attendants, Soldiers, etc.*

Act 1: Ruins of an old Castle on the Spanish Coast. (Emens.)

Act 2: Grotto of the Sea King. (Maeder & Schaeffer.)

Act 3: Royal Palace in Spain. (Maeder & Schaeffer.)

MUSICAL NUMBERS[4]

"The Legend (of the Sea King)" (Act 1)
E. Palisser
"Hunting Song" (Hunting is a sport entrancing)(Act 1)
"I'm Not Very Pretty" (Solo)(Act 1)
E. Stevens
"I'll Wait My Love, for Thee" (Act 1)
Lullaby (The shades of night gather 'round us)
"Yes, Once Again" (Duet)
H. Wilke, E. Palisser
"He Who Fights (and Runs Away)" (Act 2)
J. C. Miron, Chorus
"Things Are Very Different Now" (Act 2)
E. Stevens
"I Hope I'll Know Better Next Time" (Act 2)
Finale

1890.22 LA FILLE DE MADAME ANGOT

A Bijou Edition (Burlesque) of the Comic Opera in One Act, accompanied by a Vaudeville Bill and a Pantomime "Die Puppenfee." Libretto by Frederic Solomon, adapted from the French original by Clairville, Siraudin and Koning. Music by Charles Lecocq. Director of music, William J. Rostetter. Produced by (John) Koster and (Albert) Bial. Opened 7 July 1890 at Koster & Bial's Concert Hall and closed 11 October 1890 after (126) performances.

CAST: *Larivaudiere*, Guvnor of the City: FRED WARREN. *Louchard*, his chief clerk: GUS WHEATMAN. *Ange Pitou*, a song writer: JENNIE JOYCE. *Pomponnet*, the Village Barber: JOSIE GREGORY. *Malle Lange*: Ada Chamberlain. *Clairette*, Madame Angot's daughter: MADGE LESSING. *Babette*: Nellie Hess. *Javotte*: Irene Rice. *Amaranthe*: Maude Harvey. *Trenitz*, an officer: Allie Vivian. *Fisher boys and girls, Officers, Conspirators, Market women, etc.*

1890.23 THE RED HUSSAR

A Comedy Opera in Three Acts. Libretto by Henry Pottinger Stephens. Music by Edward Solomon. Stage director, John E. Nash. Ballet arranged by Rose Beckett. Scenery by W. Perkins, A. Calcott, E. J. Banks[5]. Costumes by Mr. and Mme. Martens. Musical director, Julian Edwards. Produced by A. M. Palmer. Opened 5 August 1890 at Palmer's Theatre and closed 11 October 1890 after 78 performances[6].

---

[1]Edgar Smith revised William Lestoq and Max Pemberton's English version, adapted from a text by Henry B. Farnie.

[2]Musical numbers not listed in programs. List prepared from published piano vocal gems (William A. Pond Co., New York, 1890).

[3]First presented in New York 20 July, 10-29 August 1885 at the Union Square and People's Theatres for 22 performances. First authorized production presented 19 August 1885 at the Fifth Avenue Theatre by Richard D'Oyly Carte for 250 performances. For Synopsis of Scenes and Musical Numbers, see 19 August 1885 D'Oyly Carte production.

[4]Musical numbers not listed in programs. List prepared from published piano vocal gems, first six titles (T. B. Harms & Co., New York, 1890), and reviews.

[5]In London these same scenic designers were billed as W. Calcott, and E. G. Banks.

[6]Transferred 13 October 1890 to the Grand Opera House for an additional 8 performances. Subsequently toured with Marie Tempest and a new cast under the auspices of the J. C. Duff Opera Company, with new scenery by Charles W. Witham.

CAST: *Kitty Carroll* (who disguises herself as a Red Hussar): MARIE TEMPEST. *Barbara Bellasys*: ISABELLE URQUHART. *Mrs. Magpie*: Fanny Edwards. *Daisy*: Leona Clarke. *Ralph Rodney*: HERNDON MORSELL. *Sir Harry Leighton*: JAMES SAUVAGE. *Sir Middlesex Mashem*: J. W. HANDLEY. *Corporal Bundy*: WILLIAM GILBERT. *Mr. William Byles*: Joseph C. Fay. *Gaylord*: Melville Stewart. *Maybud*: Carl Hartberg. *Drummer Boy*: Master Willie Barbier. *Flemish Dance Specialty*, Act 2: Gussie Coogan, Anna Allen. *Villagers, Peasants, Soldiers, Drummer Boys, etc.*

Act 1: The "Crown," Lyndhurst. (Perkins.)

Act 2: The Camp Bruges, Flanders. (Calcott.)

Act 3: The Gardens of Avon Manor. (Banks.)

ACT 1[7]

"Merry England" (Opening Chorus)
"Why Don't You Join the Army?"
"In the Morning of the Year"
J. Sauvage
"When Life and I"
H. Morsell
"Two's Company" (Trio)
"The Glee Maiden" (Waltz Song)
M. Tempest
"Blake's Own"
"Sir Middlesex Mashem"
"A Whimsical Girl Was I"
M. Tempest
"The Maiden and the Cavalier" (Duet)
Finale Act 1

ACT 2

Opening Chorus
Sabot dance and solo
Girls exit
"My Castle in Spain" (Castles in Spain)
J. Sauvage
"Betty Martin"
"My Love Must be a Soldier"
Drummer boys' chorus
"Song of the Regiment"
M. Tempest
"Guides of the Night"
H. Morsell
"How d'ye do"
Finale act 2

ACT 3

"A Jubilee Today"
"Happy Little Bridesmaids"
Country Dance
"Only Dreams" (Waltz Song)
M. Tempest
"Variations"
W. Gilbert
"One Little Kiss"
Finale

1890.24 MME ANGOT

A Revival of the Comic Opera in Three Acts[8]. Original French libretto ('La Fille de Mme. Angot') by Clairville, Siraudin and Koning. English adaptation by H. J. Byron, adapted by Edgar Smith. Music by Charles Lecoq. Stage director, Ernest Salvador. Scenery by John H. Young, Henry E. Hoyt. Costumes designed by Chatinere. Director of music, Gustave Kerker. Produced by Rudolph Aronson. Opened 14 August 1890 at the Casino Theatre and closed 11 October 1890 after 60 performances.

CAST: *Clairette Angot*: MARIE HALTON. *Amaranthe*: EVA DAVENPORT. *Babet*: Grace Golden. *Hersilie*: Eva Johns. *Javotte*: Lizzie Leone. *Herbelin*: Drew Donaldson. *Mascarade*: Florence Bell. *Delange*: Madge Yorke. *Cydalise*: Nettie Black. *Larivaudière*: FRED SOLOMON. *Ange Pitou*: HENRY HALLAM. *Pomponnet*: Charles H. Drew. *Louchard*: Max Lube. *Trenitz*: A. W. Maflin. *Cadet*: M. J. Thomas. *Officer*: George Olmi. *Buteaux*: HENRI LEONI. *Guillaume*: ARTHUR TAMS. *Incroyable*: Charles Renwick. *Mlle. Lange*: CAMILLE D'ARVILLE.

Act 1: The Market of the Innocents, Paris 1793. (Young.)

Act 2: Mlle. Lange at Home. (Hoyt.)

Act 3: The Gardens of Calypso, near Paris. (Young.)

1890.25 KAJANKA

A Return Engagement of the Parisian Spectacle in Three Acts, 9 Scenes[9]. Libretto by George D. Melville. Music by Sidney H. Horner. (Production staged by George D. Melville.) Scenery by Joseph D. Clare. Costumes by Mrs. George D. Melville. Musical director, Sidney H. Horner. Produced by the Miller Brothers. Opened 16 August 1890 at Niblo's Garden and closed 30 August 1890 after 17 performances.

CAST: THE IMMORTALS: *Electra*, Nature's Good Fairy Queen: FLORENCE MORRISON. *Beelzebub*, Her Satanic Majesty: KATE BELLINGHAM. *Zamello*, Son of Beelzebub: WILLIAM RUGE. *Beelzebub's Daughters (6)*: *Zamo*: Nellie Sennett. *Bellalo*: Ada Menette. *Malo*: Ada Anson. *Impia*: Lula Don. *Damonio*: Dell Lincoln. *Furio*: Emma Don.

MORTALS: *Charo Hicti*, High Priest of the Jains: JOE ALLEN. *Tongo Runga*, High Priest of the Brahm: R. W. BRODERICK. *Priests of the Brahm (4)*: *Jad Yani*: Leon Boudray. *Kat Lanh*: John Rixford. *Yat Borah*: Alan Castor. *Zap Longi*: Hugh Coyle. *Clown*: CHARLES W. RAVEL. *The Mariposa Dancers*: Misses Nellie Sennett, Ada Menette, Ada Anson, the Sisters Don, the Sisters Lincoln. *The Comique French Acrobats*: The Marlanis (8), assisted by Charles W. Ravel. *The Wonderful Transformation Dancer*: Mlle. BERTOTTO. *Hindoo Peasants, Nautch Girls, Fairies, etc.*

1890.26 THE MERRY MONARCH

A Comic Opera in Comic Acts. Original French libretto ("L'Etoile"[10] [The Star of Fate] by Eugène Leterrier and Albert Vanloo. American adaptation by J. Cheever Goodwin. Music by Woolson Morse. Produced under the stage direction of Richard Barker. Ballet master, Professor Mamert Bibeyran. Scenery by Homer F. Emens, Henry E. Hoyt and T. S. Plaisted. Costumes designed by Percy Anderson. Orchestra under the direction of Antonio DeNovellis. Orchestration by John Philip Sousa. Produced by Francis Wilson and Company (A. H. Canby, Management). Opened 18 August 1890 at the Broadway Theatre and closed 4 October 1890 after 49 performances.

CAST: *King Anso IV*, the Merry Monarch: FRANCIS WILSON. *Sirocco*, the Royal Astrologer: Charles Plunkett. *Herrison*, Ambassador Extraordinary, etc. GILBERT CLAYTON. *Kedas*, Minister of Police: HARRY MACDONOUGH. *Tapioca*, Private Secretary to Herrison: WILLET SEAMAN. *High Chamberlain*: B. F. Joslyn. *Possamus, Hocacus*, Royal train-bearers: John Coleman, Jesse Henderson. *Lilita*, Princess Royal, betrothed to King Anso: LAURA MOORE. *Aloes*, Maid-in-waiting to the Princess: NETTIE LYFORD. *Oasis*, first maid of honor: CECILE EISSING. *Idra*, second Maid of Honor: Belle Hartz. *Lazuli*, a traveling peddler of parfumery: MARIE JANSEN. *Dignitaries, Civilians, Amazon Guards, Ladies of the Court, Dancing Girls and Pages, etc.*

Act 1: A Public Place in India, before Sirocco's Observatory. (Emens.)

Act 2: The Hall of the Statues, in King Anso's Palace. (Hoyt.)

Act 3: The Corridor of the Elephants in King Anso's Palace. (Hoyt, Plaisted.)

ACT 1[11]

Opening Chorus (Gaily, gaily, let us sing)
Chorus

---

[7]Musical numbers not listed in programs. List prepared from published English piano vocal score (Metzler, London, 1889), which necessarily does not reflect interpolations or alterations to the score for the American production. One song published in the New York Herald concurrent with the New York run:

"Fly, Little Song, to My Love"
M. Tempest

[8]First produced in New York in French 25 August 1873 at the Broadway Theatre in repertory. Produced in New York in English 16 November 1874 at the Lyceum Theatre for 16 performances in repertory; this adaptation was not previously produced in New York.

[9]Original production billed as a Christmas Pantomime. First produced in New York 2 December 1889 at Niblo's Garden for 64 performances in two engagements. For Synopsis of Scenes, see original 1889 production. For this revival, an untitled song for Beelzebub was added to Act 3, Scene 2.

[10]Original French score by Emmanuel Chabrier discarded. The American edition of the published score, however, credits Chabrier first before Morse.

[11]Musical numbers not listed in program; list prepared from published vocal score and book of song words (T. B. Harms, New York, 1890).

"Cash" (Quartette)
G. Clayton, L. Moore, N. Lyford, W. Seaman
"When I Was a Child of Three" (Ballad)
L. Moore, G. Clayton, N. Lyford, W. Seaman
"For Thy Dear Sake" (Duet)
N. Lyford, W. Seaman
"Vanity Drives Them All to Me" (Rondeau)
M. Jansen
"Star Song"
M. Jansen
"(I'm a) King with a Capital K" (Song)
F. Wilson
Ensemble (Believe me! you've done a most courageous thing)
Principals, Chorus
"The Fatal Chair" (Couplets)
F. Wilson, Chorus
Finale
F. Wilson, M. Jansen, All

ACT 2
"Pre-Eminently Handsome"
Female Chorus
"I Can't Imagine" (Song)
M. Jansen
Quintette (Yes, it is he!)
F. Wilson, C. Plunkett, M. Jansen, G. Clayton, W. Seaman
Chorus of Welcome (with joyful jubilation. .)
Ensemble (Take him away!)
L. Moore, N. Lyford, G. Clayton, H. Macdonough, W. Seaman, Mixed Chorus
"The Omniscient Ostrich" (The Birds Who Knows It All)(Ditty)
F. Wilson, Chorus
Resume of Finale
L. Moore, F. Wilson, Chorus

ACT 3
"Military Chorus" (Oh, the cymbals clash)
Chorus
"Sneezing Song" (Of all the minor ills. .)
M. Jansen
"Love Will Find the Way" (Song)
F. Wilson
"Turtle Dove Duet" (Though in idle jest she has spoken)
M. Jansen, L. Moore
"Love Is Blind" (Ballad)
L. Moore
"Wedding Bells Are Sweetly Ringing" (Wedding Chorus)
Chorus
Finale
M. Jansen, L. Moore, All

1890.27 HENDRIK HUDSON, or, The Discovery of Columbus

A Comic Opera Burlesque in Three Acts. Play by William Gill and Robert Fraser. Music from all sources arranged and partly composed by Fred. Perkins. Produced under the stage direction of William H. Daly. Scenery by Gaspard Maeder and William Schaffer. Costumes by Dazian from Parisian designs. Produced by William Lykens. Opened 18 August 1890 at the 14th Street Theatre and closed 30 August 1890 after 16 performances; re-opened a return engagement 27 October 1890 at the Park Theatre and closed 8 November 1890 after an additional 16 performances. Total: 32 performances.[12]

CAST: *Hendrik Hudson*, a mariner bold, discoverer of the North River and Columbus: FAY TEMPLETON. *Kill von Kull*, editor of the New Amsterdam Kicker: EDWIN STEVENS. *Miss Manhattan*, a wealthy Indian princess: TOMA HANLON. *Ysabel*, the Marquis' daughter, as haughty as her sire, if not more so: ALICE CARLE. *Abigail*, Hudson's English wife, a woman of the future: ESTELLE MORTIMER. *Fritz von Twinkle*, an exquisite leader of the 'Gilded Youths' of the period: Rose Newham. *Christopher Columbus*, discovers America and loses himself: EVA RANDOLPH. *Marquis Perfecto del Cabanes*, a haughty Spanish grandee: Alf C. Whelan. *McParlan*, *McCann* deputy sheriffs: Ed. Schnitz Edwards, Charles Kirke. *Gaff Ensign*, Hudson's lieutenant: Harry N. Dowley. *Emmelina*, the maid of the Inn: Florence Barry. *Hans*, landlord of the New Amsterdam, "Wein Handlung": John W. Lince. *Don Abbotoire*, Captain of the Guard: John W. Lince. *Speck*, a Ruralist: Charles McClelland. *Mina*, a female ditto: Marie Glover. *Juanita*, *Alicia*, Spanish Maidens: Nellie Russell, Elise Gilman. *Dutch Maids, Pages, Soldiers, Spanish Ladies*: Misses McClellan, Millard, Gilman, Prince, Russell, DeGrenier, Rice, Ray, Glover, Bond, Raymond, Heaton, Deane, Scanlan, Armstrong; Alvord, Marion, Cohen, Courtney, Thornton. Messrs. McClellan, McWade, Luice, Fawkner, W. Bennett, H. Bennett, Abbey, Smith, Dye, Henderson, Stephenson, Carlton, Cover, Conditt, Cammeyer.

Act 1: The Town of New Amsterdam.

Act 2: The Everglades, Florida.

Act 3: The Curio Hall of The Columbus Fair, New Amsterdam. Changing to a Peep at Niagara Falls.

MUSICAL NUMBERS[13]
"The Same Old Thing"
F. Templeton

1890.28 THE SEVEN SUABIANS

A Comic Opera in Three Acts. Libretto by Harry B. Smith. Adapted from the German Volksoper "Die sieben Schwaben" by Hugo Wittmann and Julius Bauer. Music by Carl Millöcker. Production under the supervision of Mathilde Cottrelly. Director of music, John S. Hiller. Scenery by Gaspard Maeder and William Schaeffer; Arthur Voegtlin. Produced by the McCaull Opera Company (John A. McCaull, Proprietor). Opened 1 September 1890 at Hammerstein's Harlem Opera House and closed 13 September 1890 after 14 performances.

CAST: *Count Otmar von Mansperg*: CHAUNCEY OLCOTT. *Johann Stickel*, Burgomaster of Stuttgart: HARRY RATTENBURY. *Katherine*, his daughter (Katchen): LILLY POST. *Emerenz*, a young widow, his niece: JOSEPHINE KNAPP. *Bombastus Theophrastus Paracelsus*, an astrologer, alchemist and magician: ROBERT F. COTTON. *Spatzle*, his famulus: WILLIAM BLAISDELL. *Hannele*, maid in the Burgomaster's house: ANNIE MEYERS. *Nicodemus Zopf*, *Erasmus Zungle*, Aldermen: Talbot Joyce, W. F. Rochester.

The Seven Suabians: *Allgauerle*: Charles Turner. *Gelbfussler*: Harry D. Chase. *Knoepfleschwab*: Jamerson Finney. *Spiegleschwab*: John E. Murphy. *Blitzschwab*: Georg Cerbi. *Nestleschwab*: Charles Meyers. *Seehaas*: Charles Jones.

Otmar's Friends: *Dietrich von Weissenberg*: Harry L. Conley. *Hans von Stauffen*: John E. Dudley. *Heinrich von Rothenfels*: James J. Rose. *Otto von Esslingen*: Felix Chene. *Ulrich von Oettingen*: John Braithwaite. *Bernard von Eschen*: H. R. Clark. *Wolf von Gutlingen*: John Richardson. *Ernst von Trautenfels*: C. W. Benham.

Black Grete: MATHILDE COTTRELLY. *Rosa, Barbara, Nannette*, maid servants: Jessie Corlette, Cora Henderson, Veronica Govers. *Heindl, Scheucher*: citizens: Otto Prince, John W. Lawrence. *Angsterle*, night-watchman: Harry Meyers. *Pilsener*, city clerk: Frank Boardman. *Curt von Bodenstein*, messenger of the Duke: Blanche Holt. *Soldiers, Citizens, Maid Servants, etc.*

Act 1: Public Square in Stuttgart. (Maeder & Schaeffer.)

Act 2: The Fire Sea. (Maeder & Schaeffer.)

Act 3: Council Chamber in City Hall (Voegtlin.)

ACT 1[14]
Romanza
L. Post
Song
A. Meyers, Chorus
Duet
A. Meyers, W. Blaisdell
Comic Song
R. F. Cotton
March Finale

ACT 2
Song
W. Blaisdell, Seven Suabians

[12]For return engagement under the auspices of the Henrik Hudson Burlesque Company (W. W. Tillotson), the following principal cast changes were made: *Hendrik Hudson*: ANNIE BOYD. *Kill Von Kull*: LOUIS HARRISON. *Miss Manhattan*: ADDIE CORA REED. *Ysabel*: KENYON BISHOP. *Fritz von Twinkle*: Elsie Gerome. *Marquis Perfecto Del Cabannas*: HARRY STANDISH. *Gaff Ensign*: Mack Charles *Alicia*: Sadie Dean. The show's subtitle was also dropped.

[13]Musical numbers not listed in programs.

[14]Musical numbers not listed in programs. List prepared from program synopsis.

Duet
C. Olcott, L. Post
Concerted Waltz Number
R. F. Cotton, Otmar's Friends
Finale ("Song of the Clock")

ACT 3
Comic Scene and Chorus
Burger Council
Card Duet
W. Blaisdell, A. Meyers
Trio
A. Meyers, L. Post, M. Cottrelly
Finale

1890.29 LATER ON

A Second Edition of the Musical Farce Comedy in Three Acts[15]. Play by H. Grattan Donnelly. (Music and lyrics by Joseph Hart.) Musical director, Frederick Gagel. Produced by Fred Hallen & Joseph Hart (Harry Hine, Management). Opened 1 September 1890 (matinee) at the New Park Theatre and closed 6 September 1890 after 8 performances; returned 14 February 1891 to the 14th Street Theatre and 26 February 1891 closed after 16 additional performances; returned 25 May 1891 to the 14th Street Theatre and closed 30 May 1891 after 8 additional performances.[16] Total: 32 performances.

CAST: *Pansy Weed*, a wild flower with funds and fun: ANNIE LEWIS. *Rose Seed*, an American girl, with wit and manners: MOLLIE FULLER. *Patchoula Seed*, fair and hopeful, with a literary turn: ADA SOMERS. *Mollie Waits*, because she can't help it: MILLIE PRICE. *Tillie Tips*, with an eye to the main chance: Blanche de Clairmont. *Four very noisy girls: Susie Caps*: Edith Merrill. *Bertie Cartridge*: Jennie Reynolds. *Venie Powder*: Sophie Vernon. *Gracie Shot*: Lillian Carmen. *Bandana Clutch*, a sheriff with ambition and indigestion: MARK MURPHY. *Hays Seed*, a retired army officer who is bound to have a title in the family: JOHN E. MCWADE. *Mildmay Smiles*, a student in hard luck: Harry Hilton. *Rufus Bass*, a gardener: Samuel P. Cutter. *Cyrus Stout*, a bartender: George O'Donnell. *Jack Plunger*: FRED HALLEN. *Jolly Todd*: JOE [Joseph] HART.

ACT 1[17]
"Dear Old Pals"
"Good-Bye, My Darling, Good-Bye"/
"They're After Us"
F. Hallen, J. Hart
"Fairy Footsteps"
"I Never Tell Tales Out of School"
Dancing Grotesque
J. Hart, A. Lewis
Bathing Song and Dance
4 Noisy Girls
"Three New Sports in Town" (Medley)
J. Hart, F. Hallen, A. Lewis, Company

ACT 2
"Sights on Broadway"
"Love's Match Test"
B. de Clairmont
"Oh', Dat Watermelon" (Negro Song)
A. Lewis
"Comrades"
J. E. McWade, Quartette
(*Music and Lyrics by* Felix McGlennon.)
Musical Bells and Bottles
Character Songs
M. Murphy
"Razzle Dazzle"
J. Reynolds, L. Carmen, S. Vernon
(*Music and Lyrics by* Willard Thompson.)
"Steady, Boys, (Steady)"
A. Somers
"Oh, My Gal" (Song and Dance)
F. Hallen, J. Hart, M. Fuller, M. Price
Mexican Serenade

ACT 3
"German Warble"
M. Price
"We'll Lash Him"
S. P. Cutter, G. O'Donnell
"Pictures of Home"
J. E. McWade, Quartette
Selections:
F. Hallen, J. Hart
"That Was Me"
"His Wake in the Morning"
"(Little) Annie Rooney"
(*Music and Lyrics by* Michael Nolan.)
"Talking Drummer"
"Behind the Scenes"
"(Then They) Winked the Other Eye"
"Steamboat Race" (Negro Hymn)
Duet and Dance
F. Hallen, M. Fuller
Drinking Song
F. Hallen, J. Hart
Kangaroo Dance
Sweet Robins Song
Gavotte
"We Hope to See You Later On"
F. Hallen, J. Hart, Company

1890.30 MY AUNT BRIDGET

A Revival of the Farce Comedy in Three Acts[18]. Play by Scott Marble. Produced by George W. Monroe and John C. Rice (Robert B. Monroe, Manager). Musical director, Joseph Nicol. Opened 8 September 1890 at the Bijou Theatre and closed 20 September 1890 after 16 performances; reopened 15 December 1890 at Niblo's Garden and closed 27 December 1890 after 17 additional performances. Total: 33 performances.[19]

CAST: *Bridget McVeigh*, who arrives in the Spring, "Oh! by Gosh": GEORGE W. MONROE. *P. Alton McVeigh*, depending on his aunt. "Stay where you are!": JOHN C. RICE. *Jack Treyser*, Alton's college chum and diplomist: CHARLES J. ROSS. *Joe Nervy*, a New York collar button vender: W. ANDREW MACK. *Tompkins Blazor*, a coal dealer, glad of it: FRANK W. HOLLAND. *Dora Blazor*, Alton's jealous sweetheart: CATHERINE LINYARD. *Miss Delcimer Recimer*, one of the "400," who wants to elevate the stage: MABEL FENTON. *Nellie Rider*, Dora's friend. "W-w-wait a minute": SADIE MCDONALD. *Kitty Blazor*: Flora Echard. *Bonnie Annie Laurie*: Minnie Carleton. *Lila Butte*: ADA JONES. *Rob Roy*: James Cavanaugh. *A Ringer*: W. Henry Whyte. *Polly Glyder*, who wants to *h'act h'out on the stoige*: NELLIE ROSEBUD.

ACT 1
Hunting Song
C. Linyard, S. McDonald, F. Echard, A. Jones
"Good Ship Spring"
G. W. Monroe

ACT 2
"Nora Maguire"
W. A. Mack
(*Music and Lyrics by* Thomas LeMack.)

[15]First produced in New York 11 February 1889 at the Star Theatre for 8 performances, and a return engagement 23 September 1889 at the 14th Street Theatre for 8 performances. Frequent revisions, national tours and new editions followed as late as 19 November 1894 when Hallen and Hart played the American Theatre for 1 week.
[16]Scenery, costumes and stage direction uncredited.
[17]Also interpolated during the run, as per published sheet music (1891) by Joseph Hart:
"The Irish Poker Club"
"The Irish Stew"

[18]First produced in New York 6 December 1886 at Poole's Theatre for 8 performances.
[19]Program detail from Niblo's Garden engagement.

Sextette from LUCIA DI LAMMERMOOR
C. Linyard, A. Jones, W. A. Mack, F W. Holland, W. H. Whyte, J. Cavanagh
(*Music by* Gaetano Donizetti.)
Grand Medley
Entire Company
"The Irish Jubilee"
G. W. Monroe
(*Music by* Charles B. Lawlor. *Lyrics by* James Thornton.)
"Then They Winked the Other Eye"
N. Rosebud
"Sweetheart, Goodbye"
W. H. Whyte
"Love Comes Like a Summer Sigh"/
"Steady, Boys, Steady"
C. Linyard, Chorus
Male Quartette
Messrs. Holland, Mack, Whyte, Cavanaugh
(Selection from) THE QUEEN'S LACE HANDKERCHIEF
Entire Company
(*Music by* Johann Strauss.)
Negro Song and Wing Dance
J. C. Rice, N. Rosebud, A. Jones

ACT 3
Character Dancing
J. C. Rice
"Eh, Did I Hear You?"
G. W. Monroe
(*Music and Lyrics by* Barney Fagan.)
"Comedy vs. Tragedy" (Travesty)
C. J. Ross, M. Fenton
Grand Chorus
Company

1890.31 THE PUPIL IN MAGIC

The Lilliputians in a Grand Spectacular Comedy-Drama (Der Zauberlehrling) with Chorus and Ballet in Four Acts, 9 Scenes, in German and English. Play by Robert Breitenbach. Music selected and arranged by Carl Josef. Stage management, choreographic arrangements, decorative designs by director Charles Rosenfeld. Choreographic part arranged by the Maitre de Ballet, Mr. Leoni. Scenery by Franz Komolossy, Franz Gruber. Costumes by Sophie Klein. Musical director, Mr. Christiani. Produced by Carl and Theodor Rosenfeld. Opened 15 September 1890 at Niblo's Garden and closed 18 October 1890 after 40 performances; moved 20 October 1890 to the Metropolitan Theatre and closed 25 October 1890 after 8 additional performances; opened a return engagement 22 December 1890 at the Park Theatre and closed 17 January 1891 after 41 additional performances. Total: 99 performances.[20]

CAST: *Friedrich Rademacher*, Mechanic and Automaton Manufacturer: Mr. Kahn. *Mrs. Wiese*, his sister: Mrs. Wilke. *Fritz*, her son: SELMA GORNER. *Andrew*, factotum at Rademacher's: Mr. Weinholtz. *Kampfhaha*, Landlord: Mr. Ferenz. *The Princess Lydia Farasoff*: MINCHEN BECKER. *Martha*, Ladies' Maid to the Princess: Miss Beste. *Ossip*, Servant to the Princess: Mr. Durand. *Automatons (7)*: *Weeping She*: IDA MAHR. *Smiling She*: BERTHA JAEGER. *The Old Tyrolese*: JOHANN WOLF. *A Tyrolese Woman*: TONI MEISTER. *A Young Tyrolese*: ADOLF ZINK. *A Trumpeter*: MAX WALTER. *A Velocipedist*: HERMAN RING. *Puck*, a Tricky Lover: FRANZ EBERT. *Titi, Fifi*, Dancers: IDA MAHR, BERTHA JAEGER. *Stutzl, Mariedl, Andredl*, Peasants: JOHANN WOLF, TONI MEISTER, ADOLF ZINK. *Chauvin, Loyal*, French Officers: MAX WALTER, HERMAN RING. *Lieutenant Westermann*, Traveler to the Arctic Region: Carl Schulz. *Germain*, valet: Mr. Cotta. *Jean*, servant: Mr. Marx. *Kallschall, Eizapfhen, Mrs. Klappe*, Esquimaux: Messrs. Truhauf, Reimer, Miss Schulz. *John, Jack*, sailors: Messrs. Steinmann, Schleicher. *Puffer*, Purser: Mr. Koch. *Ede*, Upholsterer: Mr. Denecke. *Reiter*, Painter: Mr. Wenig. *Pump*, Student: Mr. Jung. *Melanie*: Miss Tamm. *Valerie*: Miss Koehler. *Ella*: Miss Schluter. *Clara*: Miss Ferdely. *Emma*: Miss Czatkowska. *Laura*: Miss Van der Roehr. *Automatons, servants, Japanese, Ladies and Gentlemen of the corps de ballet, Esquimaux, excursionists, watchmen, bicyclists.*

The action takes place at the present time.

Act 1, Scene 1: The Workshop of the Automaton Manufacturer. Nuremberg. (Komolossy.) *Scene 2*: Nuptial Fairy Festivities. Nuremberg. (Komolossy.)

Act 2, Scene 1: The Magnificent Parlor of a Millionaire. Paris. (Gruber.) *Scene 2*: The Paris World Exhibition of 1889. The Eiffel Tower. (Gruber.)

Act 3, Scene 1: At the Arctic Pole. (Gruber.) *Scene 2*: A Fairy Palace. The Palace of Games. (Gruber.)

Act 4, Scene 1: The Wandering Wood. (Komolossy.) *Scene 2*: The Lake of the Woods. (Gruber.) *Scene 3*: The Workshop of the Automaton Manufacturer. Nuremberg. (Komolossy.)

ACT 1
The Night Revels of the Automata
Entire Corps de Ballet

Nuptial Dance of the Automata, blue and pink babies, clowns, harlequins, pantaloon, columbine, sprites, white and black cats, girls from the Spree-Woods, soldiers, storks and children in swathing clothes. The bridal march, children throwing flowers, church choir, priests, amazons, bridesmaids, court ladies, men bearing the canopy.

ACT 3
The Realm of the Games
Corps de Ballet
Gavotte of the Sylphées
16 Ladies of the Corps de Ballet
Entrance of the Plays: Domino, back-gammon, cards, skittles, billiards, chess, esquires.
The Cobolds of Gold.
Concert on the Musical Money Bags
Lilliputians
The Golden Shower
Grand Final Group

1890.32 A PARLOR MATCH

A Revival of the Farce Comedy, Edition De Luxe, in Three Acts[21]. Play by Charles H. Hoyt. Musical director, Marcus Meyer. Produced by Charles E. Evans and William Hoey (Direction, W. D. Mann.) Opened 15 September 1890 at the New Park Theatre and closed 25 October 1890 after 42 performances.

CAST: *I. McCorker*, a literary man: CHARLES EVANS. *Old Hoss*, a collector for an auction room: WILLIAM HOEY. *Captain William Kidd*, a lineal descendant of the famous pirate: JAMES T. GALLOWAY. *Ephraim Bellomont*, his next door neighbor, and descendant of Governor Bellomont, who captured the pirate Kidd: M. J. SULLIVAN. *Ralph Bellomont*, his son, in love with Lucille: E. C. Jobson. *Abel Lever*, a spiritualist: E. C. Jobson. *McKee*, of Allon, M. P.: Hugh Mack. *Alec. Tricity*: William Keough. *St. Clair Todd*, a Harvard student: Peter Randall. *Lucille Kidd*, in love with Ralph: MARIE LOUISE DAY. *Aline Kidd*, with a preference for Harvard: LILLIAN MARKHAM. *Mrs. Aurelia Kidd*, the Captain's better half: Grace Gayler Clark. *Friends of the Family (3)*: *May B. Knott*: Adele Levey. *Ouida Dunnett*: Carlotta Levey. *Lotta Payne*: May Lillian Levey. *Innocent Kidd*, her papa's angel child: CLARA THROPP.

ACT 1
"Il Sogno" (The Dream)
M. L. Day
"Sing Cheerily, My Hearty (A, Yo, Heave Ho)"
C. Thropp, Company

ACT 2
"A Parlor Match Medley"-An Olla Podrida of the latest music, Imported and Domestic
Company
Instrumental Solos
W. Hoey
"Espanita" (A Spanish Love Song)
C. Thropp, M. L. Day
"Our Navy" (A Nautical Sketch)
Olympia Quartette
Specialty
Sisters Levey
Danse Du Diable
Company

[20]Played a return engagement 4 September-3 October 1891 at the Thalia Theatre for 36 performances.

[21]First produced in New York 22 September 1884 at Tony Pastor's for 16 performances. Subsequently revived and revised for many editions presented both on tour and in New York. For a Synopsis of Scenes, see original 1884 production.

ACT 3

"Perfect Little Gentlemen"
The Seance Seekers

"They're After Me"
W. Hoey
(*Music by* William Hoey. *Lyrics by* Frank Scott.)

Mandolin Trio
Sisters Levey

Finale
Company

1890.33

PAUL JONES

An Opéra Comique in Three Acts. Original French libretto ("Surcouf") by Heni Chivot and Alfred Duru. English adaptation by Henry B. Farnie. Music by Robert Planquette. Produced under the stage direction of Alfred J. Caldicott and Albert James. Dances arranged by John D'Auban. Scenery by John H. Young. Costumes by Mons. and Mme. Auguste, from designs by Mons. Clédat de la Vigerie Bianchini (Paris) and Mons. Lucien Besche (London). Musical director, Alfred J. Caldicott. Produced by Marcus R. Mayer and Charles J. Abud. Opened 6 October 1890 at the Broadway Theatre and closed 8 November 1890 after 35 performances.

CAST: *Paul Jones*, the national hero: AGNES HUTTINGTON. *Rufino de Martinez*, a Spanish naval officer: KARL MORA. *Bicoquet*, a St. Malo Ship Chandler: ERIC THORNE. *Don Trocadero*, Spanish Governor of the Island Estrella: Hervé d'Egville. *Kestral*, Skipper of a Yankee Privateer: Winslow Walters. *Bouillabaisse*, old smuggler: HALLEN MOSTYN. *Petit Pierre*, Fisher Lad at St. Malo: ALBERT JAMES. *First Lieutenant*: George Preston. *Chopinette*, wife of Bouillabaisse: FANNY WENTWORTH. *Malaguena*, Niece of Don Trocadero: MILLIE MARSDEN. *Yvonne*, Niece of Bicoquet: MARGUERITE VAN BREYDEL. *Fishermen, Privateersmen, Spanish and American man-o'-Warsmen, Lasses of St. Malo, Watteau Boys and Girls, Ladies of the Chateau, Spanish Officers, Pages, Creoles, etc.*

Act 1: Harbor of St. Malo, France.

Act 2: Chateau of Kerbignac-on-the-Bay.

Act 3: The Governor's Palace at the Island of Estrella, near the Mosquito shore.

ACT 1[22]

"Come! Shop There!" (Chorus)
F. Wentworth, Chorus

"Heave Ho!" (Trio)
A. Huntington, A. James, H. Mostyn

"The Lee Shore" (Romance)
A. Huntington

"Maidens of St. Malo" (Chorus)
M. Van Breydel, Chorus
"Well, girls!" (Scene)
"The Merman's Cave" (Air)

"A Little Bird on Weary Wing" (Duet)
M. Van Breydel, A. Huntington

Finale (So your boats and your nets)

ACT 2

"Capitan! Ola!"
K. Mora, Chorus
"You're welcome, friends" (Solo)
"Lull'd by waves" (Serenade)

"The Shipping News" (Duet)
E. Thorne, M. Van Breydell

"He Look'd at My Sabots"
F. Wentworth

"Before the Altar (Now I'm Kneeling)" (Romance)
M. Van Breydell

"True to my troth" (Morceau d'Ensemble)

"Ever and Ever Mine" (Romance)
A. Huntington

"For lack of gold" (Duet)
M. Van Breydel, A. Huntington

"The Lassies!" (Stave)
H. Mostyn

Finale, Act 2 (They say the pirate. .)

ACT 3

"Open the Council" (Air bouffe)
H. D'Egville, Chorus
"Viva! Viva! Trocadero" (Exit)

"O'er Ocean Gleaming" (Trio)
M. Van Breydel, M. Marsden, F. Wentworth

"Till the Light Fades" (Chorus and Scene)
M. Van Breydel, M. Marsden, etc.

"It Cannot Be!" (Duo Berceuse)
M. Van Breydel, A. Huntington
"On my heart" (Duo)

"King of the Mosquitos" (Chorus)
"Ah-wah-ik-to-mani" (Indian Song)
A. James
"P'raps he will shock us" (Exit)
Chorus

"Arrest Him" (Scene and Melos)
A. Huntington, M. Van Breydel, Chorus

Finale, Act 3 (The oracle is now fulfill'd)

1890.34

THE CITY DIRECTORY

A Return Engagement of the Musical Absurdity (Farce Comedy) in Three Acts[23]. Play by Paul M. Potter. Music by W. S. Mullaly. Scenery by F. Dangerfield. Musical director, ??. Produced by John H. Russell for Russell's Comedians. Opened 6 October 1890 at the Bijou Theatre and closed 1 November 1890 after 32 performances[24].

CAST: *Mr. John Smith*, a detective: CHARLIE REED. *Mr. John Smith*, Stage Manager Gaiety: WILLIAM COLLIER. *Mr. John Smith*, Ballet Master Gaiety: IGNACIO MARTINETTI. *Mr. John Smith*, a bunco-steerer: WILLIAM F. MACK. *Mr. John Smith*, a capitalist: BURT HAVERLY. *Mr. John Smith*, an athlete from Kalamazoo: CHARLES V. SEAMON. *Mr. John Smith*, an elevator boy: ALF HAMPTON. *Mr. John Smith*, Young America: JOSIE SADLER. *Mr. John Smith*, a Messenger Boy: Joseph Jackson. *Mrs. John Smith*, Minerva Flats: FLORA IRWIN. *Miss Ruth Smith*, Prima Donna Gaiety: MAY IRWIN. *Mlle Nanon*, Prima Donna: ALICE HARRISON. *Misses Laura Smith, Dora Smith, Cora Smith*, rosebuds: Rosa France, Bessie Cleveland, Mayme Kelso. *Jennie*, Mrs. Smith's maid: Lillian Rivers. *Little Fawn*, premiere danseuse Gaiety: AMELIA GLOVER.

1890.39

POOR JONATHAN

A Comedy Opera in Three Acts. Adapted from the original German (operette 'Der arme Jonathan', libretto) by Hugo Wittmann and Julius Bauer (based on the French comedy 'Les Deux Anglais' by P-F Merville). English translation by John P. Jackson and Ralph A. Weill. Music by Carl Millöcker. Produced under the stage direction of Heinrich Conreid. Scenery by H. L. Reid, John H. Young. Costumes by Baron C. DeGrimm. Director of music, Gustave Kerker. Produced by Rudolph Aronson and John McCaull. Opened 14 October 1890 at the Casino Theatre and closed 6 May 1891 after 208 performances.

CAST: *Harriet*: LILLIAN RUSSELL. *Molly*: FANNY RICE. *Students at the Women's Medical College (3)*: *Miss Big*: EVA DAVENPORT. *Miss Grant*: GRACE GOLDEN. *Miss Hunt*: Rose Wilson. *Arabella*, Count Nowalsky's sister: SYLVIA THORNE. *Tobias Quickly*, an Impressario: EDWIN STEVENS. *Rubygold*, a wealthy American: HARRY MACDONOUGH. *Catalucci*, a Composer: CHARLES CAMPBELL. *Professor Dryander*: A. W. Tams. *François*, Steward at Rubygold's: MAX FIGMAN. *Count Nowalsky*: Edgar Smith. *Brostologne*: James Maas. *Lawyer Holmes*: H. Holbrook. *Jonathan Tripp*: JEFFERSON DEANGELIS. *Servants, Female Students, Guests, Visitors at Monte Carlo, Members of the Diplomatic Corps, U.S. Army and Navy Officers, West Point Cadets.*

Act 1: Rubygold's Residence in New York. (Reid.)

Act 2: Monte Carlo. (Young.)

Act 3: West Point and view of the Hudson. (Young.)

[22]Musical numbers do not appear in programs. List prepared from published American piano vocal score (Charles D. Koppel, New York), 1890). English vocal score contains additional music not contained in American editions: all music in Act 2 beginning with "For lack of gold" and in Act 3 beginning with "King of Mosquitos".

[23]First presented in New York 10 February 1890 at the Bijou Theatre for 154 performances. For Synopsis of Scenes and Musical Numbers, see original February 1890 production.

[24]Director, designer of costumes uncredited.

MUSICAL NUMBERS[25]

"Wilt Thou My True Love Be?" (Thou'lt Be My Love)(Song)
L. Russell, C. Campbell, Chorus

Song of the Impressario ("Yes, 'Tis the Impressario")
E. Stevens

"As If But Yesterday" (Duet)
L. Russell, H. Macdonough

"Ah! We Hapless Prima Donnas" (Prima Donnas' Waltz Song)
L. Russell, C. Campbell, Chorus

Chorus of Graduates (Young Lady Students' Chorus)
E. Davenport, G. Golden, R. Wilson, Students

"When We Were Still Young" (Duet)
J. DeAngelis, F. Rice

"I am the Unfortunate Jonathan" (Song)
J. DeAngelis

"Ever Before Me"

"Alas! For Me"

"The National Guard" (Cadet Drill)
(*Music by* Rudolph Aronson.)

1890.35 BLUE JEANS

A Comedy-Drama in Four Acts, 8 Scenes. Play by Joseph Arthur. Music composed and arranged by W. S. Mullaly. Scenery by Homer F. Emens. Mechanical effects by J. B. DeBeauvais & Son; Edward Peck. Light effects by Richard Francis. Produced by J. Wesley Rosenquest & Joseph Arthur. Opened 6 October 1890 at the 14th Street Theatre and closed 7 March 1891 after 187 performances.

CAST: *Perry Bascom*: ROBERT HILLIARD. *Colonel Henry Clay Risener* of the Rising Sun: George D. Chaplin. *Ben Boone*: George Fawcett. *Jacob Tutewiler*: J. J. WALLACE. *Jim Tutewiler*: JACQUES KRUGER. *Isaac Hankins*: W. J. Wheeler. *Seth Igoe*: Ben Deane. *June*: JENNIE YEAMANS. *Sue Eudaly*: Judith Berolde. *Cindy Tutewiler*: Alice Leigh. *Samantha*: Marion Strickland. *Nell Tutewiler*: LAURA BURT. *Beleena Kicker*: LAURA BURT. *Bascom's Child*: Gracie Sherwood.[26]

The old Village Band, "Rising Sun Roarers," led by the Champion Drum-Major F. B. Berrian; Albert E. Caldwell, Director. *The Columbia Quartette*: Henry Molten (First tenor), Joseph Graham (Second tenor), James Leahy (First bass), Charles Odell (Second bass). And the Messrs. F. S. Winthrop, George L. Leeds, T. Walker, J. J. Marcy, Misses Annie E. Williams, Ada Chester, Bertha Dowling, Edith Raymond, Ida Wagner, Ida Francis.

The story of the play is laid in what is known as the "Bluejeans deestrict" in Indiana.

Act 1: Yard and Interior of Jacob Tutewiler's House, in the suburbs of Rising Sun, Indiana.

Act 2: Perry Bascom's Orchard. Two years later.

Act 3, Scene 1: Dining Room in Perry Bascom's House. Three months later. *Scene 2*: Exterior of Bascom's Mill. *Scene 3*: Interior of the Mill.

Act 4, Scene 1: Sitting room in Jacob Tutewiler's House. *Scene 2*: Corridor in the Poe House. *Scene 1*: Sitting room in Jacob Tutewiler's House.

MUSICAL NUMBERS[27]

Village Band of the "Rising Sun Roarers"

The Columbia Quartette

"Old Virginia Walkaround"

1890.36 THE OLD HOMESTEAD

A Revival of the Rural Melodrama in Four Acts[28]. Play by Denman Thompson and George W. Ryer. (Staged by Denman Thompson.) Scenic artist, Homer F. Emens. Proprietor and Manager, Denman Thompson. Opened 6 October 1890 at the Academy of Music and closed 10 January 1891; returned 26 January 1891 to the Academy of Music and closed 25 April 1891 after 216 performances.

CAST: Act 1: *Joshua Whitcomb*: DENMAN THOMPSON. *Cy Prime*: GEORGE A. BEANE. *Happy Jack*: WALTER GALE. *Frank Hopkins*: FRANK THOMPSON. *Eb. Ganzey*: J. L. MORGAN. *John Freeman*: FRANK KNAPP. *Aunt Matilda Whitcomb*, Joshua's sister: LOUISA MORSE. *Rickety Ann*: ANNIE THOMPSON. *Miss Annie Hopkins*: Lillian Stone. *Nellie Freeman*: Celia Baker. *Maggie O'Flaherty*: Minnie Luckstone. *The Old Homestead Double Quartette*: Messrs. NORRIE, EARLE, ACKERLEY, (STEPHEN) BAKER, MYERS, KRUGER, (GUS) KAMMERLEE, LAW. Act 2: *Henry Hopkins*: Walter Lenox Sr. *Judge Patterson*: Gus Kammerlee. *François Fogarty*: Frank Mara. *Mrs. Henry Hopkins*: Mrs. W. I. Kilpatrick. *Nellie Patterson*: Lena N. Jones. Act 3: *Jack Hazzard*: Walter Gale. *Reuben Whitcomb*, Joshua's son: Harry Earle. *Hoboken Terror*: J. L. Morgan. *One of the Finest*: Tom Law. *U. S. Letter Carrier*: C. M. Richardson. *Mrs. McGuire*: F. Mara. Act 4: *Seth Perkins*: Walter Lenox, Sr. . *Len Holbrook, Warren Ellis*, Country Fiddlers: C. M. Richardson, P. Redmond. *Pat Clancy*: Frank Mara. *Mrs. Murdock*: Marie Kimball. *The Three Stratton Gals*: Misses Luckstone, Stone, Baker. *Boys Choir of 24.*

SPECIALITIES

"The Palms" (Act 3)
F. F. Barnard, Old Homestead Choir
(*Music by* Jean Baptiste Faure.)

"Rock-a-Bye Baby" (Act 4)
M. Kimball, Old Homestead Quartette
(*Music and Lyrics by* Effie I. Canning.)

1890.37 SUZETTE

A Comic Opera in Three Acts. Libretto based on the French ('Le Voyage de Suzette'[29]) by Mons. Henri Chivot and Alfred Duru. Music by Oscar Weil. Scenery by Joseph Clare. Produced by the Minnie Palmer Opera Company. Presented by Messrs. (Charles E.) Locke and (J. Charles) Davis. Opened 11 October 1890 at Herrmann's Theatre and closed 6 November 1890 after 26 performances.

CAST: *Marquis of Tollebranch*: CHARLES S. DICKSON. *Marchioness*: BERTHA RICCI. *Captain Vieubec*: A. W. F. MacCOLLIN. *Domingo*, Vieubec's servant: T. J. Cronin. *Jouarde*, an Inn-keeper: GEORGE LAURI. *Renée*, his son: HARRY HILLIARD. *Jeanne*: Ray Walton. *Michel's Pilot*: W. J. D. Prince. *De Frontignac*: Florence Myatt. *Marigny*: Lillian Martinez. *Hubert*: Kate Uart. *Suzette*, Jouarde's foster-daughter: MINNIE PALMER. (*Fishermen and women, servants, ladies and gentlemen, officers of the King, Dragoons, etc.*)

Act 1: A small fishing port of Normandy. Time of Louis XV.

Act 2: Interior of a chateau.

Act 3: Interior of Jouarde's Inn.

ACT 1[30]

"We're jolly good fishermen" (Solo and Chorus)
G. Lauri, Chorus

"Like a dream" (Song)
H. Hilliard

"When a little girl" (Song)
M. Palmer

"I'm not so very clear" (Duet)
M. Palmer, H. Hilliard

"Oh! My wig!" (Ensemble and Chorus)
M. Palmer, A. W. F. MacCollin, T. J. Cronin, Chorus

"At last!" (Duet)
[Diane, Octave]

"If we are really lovers" (Quartet)
M. Palmer, [Diane], H. Hilliard, [Octave]

"Never yet": (Ensemble and Chorus)
G. Lauri, A. W. F. MacCollin, M. Palmer, Chorus

"A sad mistake" (Finale)
M. Palmer, [Diane, Octave], Tenors, Basses

ACT 2

"Every effort" (Chorus)
Chorus

---

[25] Musical numbers not listed in programs; list prepared from published piano vocal selection (William A. Pond, New York, 1890) and libretto (H. J. Wehman, New York, 1890).

[26] Character added to programs after opening night.

[27] Musical numbers not listed in programs Note: A hugely popular song inspired by the play, but not performed in BLUE JEANS:

"The Picture That Is Turned to the Wall"
(*Music and Lyrics by* Charles Graham.)

[28] First produced in New York 10 January 1887 at the 14th Street Theatre for 155 performances. For Synopsis of Scenes, see original 1887 production. This revival boasted a new set for Act 4 and a reinforced choir.

[29] Original French score by Léon Vasseur was evidently discarded.

[30] Musical numbers not listed in programs. List prepared from published vocal score (Oliver Ditson Co, Boston, 1889). The characters of Diane and Octave appear in the published vocal score but not the program cast list.

"'Tis clear" (Chorus and Ensemble)
M. Palmer, [Octave], Chorus
"But yesterday" (Song)
[Diane]
"Ah, now" (Duet)
M. Palmer, H. Hilliard
"Most noble lord" (Chorus)
M. Palmer, [Diane, Octave], Chorus
"What the dickens" (Trio)
[Diane], A. W. F. MacCollin, [Octave]
"I should call" (Duo and Scene)
M. Palmer, Octave, H. Hilliard, Male Chorus
"Where can he be" (Duet and Finale)
M. Palmer, [Diane]. A. W. F. MacCollin, T. J. Cronin, Chorus

ACT 3
"Why so frightened?" (Duet)
M. Palmer, H. Hilliard
"We are on hand" (Chorus and Ensemble)
M. Plamer, H. Hilliard, [Octave], Chorus
"The jolly dragoons" (Chorus)
Chorus
"To the charge"
[Diane], Chorus
"Good manners" (Song)
M. Palmer
"Now to the feast" (Chorus)
Chorus
Finale
Principals, Chorus

1890.38 THE DUMB GIRL OF SEVILLA

An Original Burletta in One Act, accompanied by a Vaudeville Bill. Libretto by Frederic Solomon. Director of music, William J. Rostetter. Produced by (John) Koster and (Albert) Bial. Opened 13 October 1890 at Koster & Bial's Concert Hall and closed 8 November 1890 after 36 performances.

CAST: *Dumb Girl of Sevilla*: CARMENCITA. *Fabio Garcia*, Captain of the Brigands: JENNIE JOYCE. *Lopez*, his lieutenant: JOSIE GREGORY. *Scipio*, Fabio's Factotum: FRED WARREN. *Caduga*, his wife: ADA CHAMBERLAIN. *Catalina*, their daughter: MADGE LESSING. *Pedrilla*, her brother: Louise Miller. *Leonora*, waiting maid to Caduga: Dolly Clark. *Spada*, the dumb girl's father: Gus Wheatman. *Robbers, Peasants, etc.*

During the burlesque, Carmencita will introduce "La Sevilla" and "El Bolero."

1890.40 CLAUDIUS NERO

A Historical Dramatic Pageant in Four Acts, 7 Scenes. Adapted from Ernest Eckstein's historical romance 'Nero.' Dramatization by Max Freeman. Staged by Max Freeman. Ballets by Professor Mamert Bibeyran. Scenic artists, Joseph Clare, Leon Mohn, Maeder & Schaeffer. Costumes constructed by Charles E. Locke. Lions trained by "Professor" Darling[31]. Musical director, Karl Broschi. Proprietors and managers, Charles E. Locke and (J. Charles) Davis. Opened 21 October 1890 at Niblo's Garden and closed 13 December 1890 after 62 performances.

CAST: *Claudius Nero*, Imperator: WILTON LACKAYE. *Agrippina*, his empress mother: ALICE FISCHER. *Nicodemus*, Roman Knight, a Nazarene: GEORGE HEATH. *Acte*, his ward: CARRIE TURNER. *Artemidorus*, a young Nazarene: WILLARD NEWELL. *Tigellinus*, Prefect of Praetorians: Byron Douglas. *Poppaea Sabina*, Nero's betrothed: BLANCHE WEAVER. *Acceronia*, Agrippina's confidante: Henrietta Lander. *Lupus*, a Roman Gamin: ROSE BEAUDET. *Seneca*, Prime Minister: James Lackaye. *Lollario*, Chief of the Chatti: Franz Reinau. *Glodiana*, Agrippina's maid: Frances Herbert. *Galba*, Nero's successor: Frederick Daily. *Cyrus*, an Egyptian magician: George White. *Ben-Habi*, Juggler: James Kearney. *Citizens and Knights of Rome (6)*: *Sempronius*: W. T. Donnelly. *Vitellius*: Francis Purey. *Mutius*: J. W. Massey. *Quintus*: C. W. Hery. *Fabius*: James L. Weer. *Centurion*: Charles Miller. *Nazarenes (6)*: *Herodia*: Maud Grafton. *Chloe*: Anita Rothe. *Lallia*: Leslie Fursman. *Manapia*: Minnie Parker. *Chrysa*: Marie Feretti. *Barbilla*: Pauline Davidson. *Senators, Clients, Praetorians, Lictors, Heralds, Gauls, Chatti, Sarmatians, Syrians, Sicambri, Moors, Greeks, Britons, Egyptians, Jugglers, Grecian Actors, Priests of Isis, Priestesses of Vesta, Consuls, Tribunes, Augustans, Patricians, Prisoners, Persians, Hindoos, Gladiators, Puppet Players, Rope Dancers, Musicians, Nazarenes, Hebrews, Danseuses, Female Slavaes, Roman Women. Dance Specialties*: Mlles. Theodore de Gillert, Señorita Rosita, Nano Deasy, Bartoletti.

The action takes place in Rome and Alba from 59 to 68 A.D.

Act 1: Atrium—A Coutyard near the Campus Martius, Rome.

Act 2, Scene 1: Acte's apartment in Nicodemus' Villa, Rome. *Scene 2*: A Public Square near Evander's Temple, Rome.

Act 3, Scene 1: The Villa of the Empress Agrippina, Alba. *Scene 2*: Public Place near the Tower of Maecenas, with view of the city, Rome.

Act 4: On the Roman Campagna, a short distance from Rome.

ACT 1
Entrance of Nero and Agrippina
Combat de Danse
Female Gladiators, Jugglers, T. deGillert, Corps de Ballet
L'Amour Triomphant (Grand Ballet)
N. Deasy, Bartoletti, Corps de Ballet

ACT 2
Octet of male voices and French horns
Grand Ballet Divertissement
Mlles. T. deGillert, Rosita, N. Deasy, Bartoletti, Corps de Ballet

ACT 3
The song of Claudiana
The sonnet to Lion

ACT 4
Apotheosis

[31]Trained lions presented by Mr. Darling between Acts 2 and 3.

1890.41 A TEXAS STEER, or, Money Makes the Mare Go

A Farce Comedy in a Prologue and Three Acts. Play by Charles H. Hoyt. (Staged by Charles H. Hoyt.) Musical director, William Lloyd Bowron. Produced by Charles H. Hoyt. Opened 10 November 1890 at the Bijou Theatre and closed 24 January 1891 after 88 performances.

CAST: *Maverick Brander*, a Texas cattle king: TIM MURPHY. *Captain Fairleigh Bright*, U.S.A.: W. S. HARKINS. *Messrs. Yell, Bragg and Blow*, glorious products of Texas: Charles Stanley, William Cullington, Raymond Finlay. *Brassey Gall, Esq.*, member of "The Third House": Newton Chisnell. *Colonel Pepper*, a retired army officer: James F. Horan. *Christopher Columbus, Jr.*, a colored statesman: Will H. Bray. *Knott Initt*, Brander's private secretary: Julian Mitchell. *Othello Moore*, a private waiter at the Arlington: Barry Maxwell. *Lieutenant Greene*, U.S.A.: James F. Horan. *Sergeant-at-Arms*: C. L. Warren. *Anatole*, a valet: Newton Chisnell. *G. Whitaker Bellows*, a senator: Fred Sidney. *Green Goodhead*, a judge: John Deady. *Press Button*, an artist: Fred Sidney. *Crab, Mink*, field hands: John Deady, Olney Griffin. *Inspector Slowboy*, of the Washington police: John Deady. *Mrs. Brander*, the cattle king's wife: ALICE WALSH. *Mrs. Major Campbell*, whose husband is stationed in Texas: Alice King Livingstone. *Dixie Style*, an orphan from Indiana: Georgie Lake. *Bossy*, Brander's pet: FLORA WALSH. *Street Band, Waiters, Indians, Greasers, and general riff-raff of a Frontier town.* The American Quartette will supply Southern melodies.

Prologue: The Dooryard of Mr. Brander's Home. The Congressman-elect. Texas.

Act 1: Private Reception Room at the Arlington, Washington. The Congressman arrives at the Capitol.

Act 2: Ante-room and Dining-room of Mr. Brander's apartments at the Arlington. The Congressman investigated.

Act 3: Mr. Brander's Parlors. The Congressman Indorsed.

1890.42 THE CLEMENCEAU CASE

A Travesty[32] in One Act, 3 Scenes, accompanied by a Vaudeville Bill. Libretto and music by Frederic Solomon. Scenery by Ink & Pasteboard. Director of music, William J. Rostetter. Produced by (John) Koster and (Albert) Bial. Opened 10 November 1890 at Koster & Bial's Concert Hall and closed 13 December 1890 after (45) performances.

Vaudeville: MARIE LLOYD, CARMENCITA.

[32]Burlesque of the play of the same name, whose American adaptation by William Fleron was based on Armand D'Artois "L'Affaire Clemenceau" from the Alexandre Dumas, fils, novel.

CAST: *Iza*: JENNIE JOYCE. *Pierre Clemenceau*: JOSIE GREGORY. *Constantin Ratz*, a young officer: MADGE LESSING. *Count Serge Goinoff*: MAMIE BERNARD. *Georgina*: Lou Miller. *Cosette*: Dolly Clark. *Loisette*: Irene Rice. *Countess Donebrownasker*: Geoge Topack. *Monsieur Ratz*: George Steele. *Masqueraders, Guests, Pages, etc. (Specialty*: CARMENCITA.)

The action takes place in Paris.

During the burlesque, Carmencita will introduce "Santiago" (Valse Española). Vocal accompaniment composed and arranged by William J. Rostetter.

1890.43

PIPPINS

A Burlesque in Three Acts, 9 Scenes. Libretto by J. Cheever Goodwin[33]. Music by John J. Braham and Frederic Gagel. Produced under the stage direction of Richard Barker. Maitre de ballet, Mlle. Rose Beckett. Scenery by John H. Young, Ludwig W. Seavey, and H. L. Reid. Costumes designed by Baron C. DeGrimm. Music director, John J. Braham. Produced by W. B. Barton. Opened 26 November 1890 at the Broadway Theatre and closed 6 December 1890 after 13 performances.

CAST: *Atalanta*, Wayward Daughter of King Schoenus: AMELIA SUMMERVILLE. *Nyce, Daphne, Chloe*, Abused Maids of Honor at Schoenus' Court: Connie Delmore, Marie Carlyle, Marion Abbot. *Mississarrus*, Loving but not tender: Estelle Mortimer. *Ladies of the Court, Huntresses, etc. King Schoenus*, Father and Slave of Atalanta: ALEXANDER CLARK. *Narcissus, Hyacinthus*, Gilded Youth of the Period: ADA DARE, Helene Beatice. *Thraso*, Athletic Tutor to Hippomones: E. SNITZ EDWARDS. *Cupid*, You all know him: FANNIE WARD. *Hippomenes*, Young and Romantic: KATHERINE B. HOWE. *Paidagogus*: Louis De Lange. *Ballet, Hunters, Courtiers, Lords and Attendants*: Chorus of 50.

The action takes place 2000 years B.C. at Scyros.

Act 1, Scene 1: King Schoenus' Ante-Chamber. (Young.) *Scene 2*: Ante-Chamber in Hippomenes' Palace. (Seavey.) *Scene 3*: King Schoenus' Hunting Grounds. (Young.)

Act 2, Scene 1: Gymnasium of Hippomenes. (Reid.) *Scene 2*: Ante-room of King Schoenus' Ball Room. (Seavey.) *Scene 3*: King Schoenus' Ball Room. (Reid.)

Act 3, Scene 1: Palace Garden of King Schoenus. (Young.) *Scene 2*: Country road and landscape. (Seavey.) *Scene 3*: Scyros Race Course. (Seavey.)

ACT 1[34]

Hunters' Chorus; Laughing Chorus; Fortune Telling Song; Finale

ACT 2

Drinking Song; Sea Song (Nantasket Down the Bay); Finale

ACT 3

Serenade; Good-night (Duet); Mock Serenade; Finale

1890.44

SHIP AHOY!

An American Opera in Thee Acts. Libretto by H. Grattan Donnelly. Music by Fred Miller, Jr. Stage production directed by I. W. Norcross, Jr. Scenery and costmes designed by William H. Day. Orchestra under the direction of Fred Miller, Jr. Management, Arthur Miller. (Produced by I. W. Norcross, Jr.) Opened 8 December 1890 at the Standard Theatre and closed 10 January 1891 after 36 performances. Re-opened a return engagement 18 May 1891 at the Standard Theatre and closed 30 May 1891 after 14 additional performances. Total: 50 performances.

CAST: *Commodore Columbus Cook*, commanding U.S.S. "*Cuckoo*": EDWARD M. FAVOR. *Colonel Mapleson Mulberry*, Manager of the Oriole Opera Company: TOM RICKETTS. *Lieutenant Lollypop*, Executive Officer of the "*Cuckoo*": WALTER H. FORD. *Ensign Toddles*, a sweet young thing from Annapolis: NEWTON BROWN, JR. *Barnacle Duff*, Seaman of the U.S.S. "*Cuckoo*": Charles W. Allison. *Simpson Christy*, Property man of the Oriole Opera Company: Snitz Edwards. *Captain of the Marines*: Dora Webb. *Lieutenant of the Marines*: Ida Marsh. *Midshipman*: May Ford. *Mlle. Auburni Ernani*, the American Prima Donna: BERTHA RICCI. *Mlle. Georgia Carolina*, the Prima Donna Contralto from the Grand Opera House, Paris, Kentucky: EDITH SINCLAIR. *Mlle. Lulu Lalla*, an ambitious debutante: CARRIE TUTEIN. *Brunetta*: Ida Marsh. *Ladies of the Chorus, Sailors, Marines, Cadets, etc*

Act 1: The Isle of Palms. Today.

Act 2: Quarter-deck of the "*Cuckoo*."

Act 3: Reception Hall, Hygeia Hotel, Old Point Comfort. Chesapeake Bay.—Fortress Monroe in the distance.—Arrival of the "White Squadron."

ACT 1[35]

Opening Chorus (Bears the deep blue sea a sail?)
C. Tutein, Chorus

Colonel's Song (I was born at an early day in life)
T. Ricketts, Chorus

Song (We gaze day by day o'er the deep ocean foam)
Chorus

Duet (Far o'er the waste of stormy ocean)
B. Ricci, E. Sinclair

Song (How dare you think)
B. Ricci, T. Ricketts, E. Sinclair

Operatic Scene-Operatic Queens
B. Ricci, C. Tutein, E. Sinclair

Grand chorus (A sail! A sail! A Sail! A sail!)
Everyone

Song for Chorus (Sisters, sisters, we will stand together!)
Chorus

Rowers' Chorus (Now bend to your oars)
Solo, Mens' Chorus

Song for the Girls (Sailors, sailors, we are twenty maidens lonely)
Womens' Chorus

Lollypop's Song (I am Lieutenant Lollypop)
W. H. Ford, Chorus

Song (Hold, sir, hold!)
C. Tutein

Chorus of Ladies (We laugh, ho, ho)

Quartette (We are rescued, behold)
B. Ricci, E. Sinclair, N. Brown, Jr., W. H. Ford

Finale Act 1 ("The Flag of the Union")
Everybody

ACT 2

Opening Chorus (Oh sometimes I'm bound for Liverpool)
Sailors

Grand Chorus (Oh it's homeward bound and safe and sound)
Chorus

Commodore's Song ("Of all great men of history")
E. M. Favor, Chorus

Chorus (Hurrah, hurrah, we're homeward bound)
Everybody

Song (To tell thee of my proud career)
B. Ricci, E. Sinclair, C. Tutein, Chorus

Colonel's Song (Did that ever occur to you?)
T. Ricketts

Colonel and Commodore's Drinking Song (Fill high the flowing bowl)
E. M. Favor, T. Ricketts, Chorus

Trio (When fall the silvery moonbeams bright)

Finale Act 2 (I've sailed the world around and round)

ACT 3

Opening March
Cadets

Chorus' Song (We are members of that dandy corps)
Chorus

Song and Chorus (Over many a mile of stormy sea)
Chorus

Trio ("We respect the uniform")
T. Ricketts, N. Brown, Jr., W. H. Ford

Song and Dance (If you want to marry an elegant man)
T. Ricketts, C. Tutein

Lollypop's Ballad ("The lad of My Love")
W. H. Ford

---

[33]May be an uncredited adaptation of the English burlesque ATALANTA, produced 17 November 1888 at the Strand, London.

[34]No songs in New York programs. Titles taken from 1877 Boston production.

[35]Musical numbers not listed in programs. List prepared from an undated production manuscript on deposit at New York Public Library for the Performing Arts; performance revisions and interpolations may have been made in variation from the manuscript.

Ernani's Song ("When a maiden's of pure affection)
B. Ricci
Carolina's Song ("A Woman's Love)
E. Sinclair
Toddles' Song ("This is a practical age")
N. Brown, Jr.
Duet (Farewell, dear love)
B. Ricci, E. Sinclair
Song/Quadrille (In our hearts now at last we true happiness feel)
B. Ricci, W. H. Ford, E. Sinclair, N. Brown, Jr.
Concluding Chorus (Tell far and wide the story)
Everybody

O'NERO, or, The Lady of Lions

1890.45

A Roaring Burlesque in One Act[36], accompanied by a Vaudeville Bill. Libretto by Frederic Solomon. Director of music, William J. Rostetter. Produced by (John) Koster and (Albert) Bial. Opened 22 December 1890 at Koster & Bial's Concert Hall and closed 28 March 1891 after (126) performances.

CAST: O'Nero, Emperor of Rome: FANNIE DOSWELL. *Tickleanus*, his friend: JOSIE GREGORY. *Titus Chromo*, a Lictor: George Steele. *Cholycles, Narcissus, Lageritus*, Roman Swells: Grace Stacey, Pearl Leroux, Maggie Steinewald. *Agrippina*, the Emperor's Mother: George Topack. *Poppea*, the Emperor's bride: MAY SHANNON. *Actie*, a flower girl: MADGE LESSING. *Niblo*, a dog: Himself. *Romans, Flower Girls, Lions, Slaves.*

THE PIRATES OF PENZANCE, or, The Slave of Duty

1890.46

A Revival of the Comic Opera in Two Acts[37]. Libretto by William S. Gilbert. Music by Arthur Sullivan. Stage director, John E. Nash. Musical director, Julian Edwards. Produced by the J. C. Duff Comic Opera Company. Opened 22 December 1890 at the Broadway Theatre and closed 24 December 1890 after 3 performances in repertory.

CAST: *The Pirate King*: WILLIAM J. MCLAUGHLIN. *Samuel*, a Pirate Lieutenant: JOSEPH C. FAY. *Frederic*, a Pirate Apprentice: CHARLES O. BASSETT. *Major-General Stanley* of the British Army: A.W.F. McCOLLIN. *Sergeant*, Metropolitan Police: FRED CLIFTON. *General Stanley's Daughters (4)*: *Mabel*: LILLY POST. *Edith*: MINNIE DERUE. *Kate*: BERTHA LEHMAN. *Isabel*: CORNELIA BASSETT. *Ruth*, a Piratical "Maid-of-all-work": GRACE ATHERTON. *Chorus of Pirates, Police and General Stanley's Daughters.*

PATIENCE, or, Bunthorne's Bride

1890.47

A Revival of the Comic Opera in Two Acts[38]. Libretto by William S. Gilbert. Music by Arthur Sullivan. Stage director, John E. Nash. Musical director, Julian Edwards. Produced by the J. C. Duff Comic Opera Company. Opened 25 December 1890 at the Broadway Theatre and closed 27 December 1890 after 4 performances in repertory.[39]

CAST: *Reginald Bunthorne*, a fleshly poet: A. W. F. McCOLLIN. *Archibald Grosvenor*, an Idylic poet: CLEMENT BAINBRIDGE. *Officers of the Dragoon Guards (3)*: *Colonel Calverley*: WILLIAM J. MCLAUGHLIN. *Major Murgatroyd*: JOSEPH C. FAY. *Lieutenant, The Duke of Dunstable*: J. E. STILLE. *Bunthorne's Solicitor*: J. Moore. *Aesthetic Maidens (4)*: *Lady Angela*: MINNIE DERUE. *Lady Saphir*: Cornelia Bassett. *Lady Ella*: Annie Cameron. *Lady Jane*: FANNIE EDWARDS. *Patience*: LILLY POST. *Rapturous Maidens, Heavy Dragoons.*

[36]Inspired by the production of CLAUDIUS NERO, 21 October 1890 at Niblo's Garden.
[37]First presented in New York 31 December 1879 at the Fifth Avenue Theatre for a total of 91 performances in two engagements. For Synopsis of Scenes and Musical Numbers, see original 1879 production.
[38]First presented in New York 22 September 1881 at the Standard Theatre for 177 performances. For Synopsis of Scenes and Musical Numbers, see original 1881 production.
[39]Scenery and costumes uncredited.

IOLANTHE, or, The Peer and the Peri

1890.48

A Revival of the Comic Opera in Two Acts[40]. Libretto by William S. Gilbert. Music by Arthur Sullivan. Stage director, John E. Nash. Musical director, Julian Edwards. Produced by the J. C. Duff Comic Opera Company. Opened 29 December 1890 at the Broadway Theatre and closed 3 January 1891 after 7 performances in repertory.[41]

CAST: *The Lord Chancellor*: A.W.F. McCOLLIN. *Earl of Mountararat*: JOSEPH C. FAY. *Earl Tolloller*: J. E. STILLE. *Private Willis*: WILLIAM J. MCLAUGHLIN. *Strephon*, an Arcadian Shepherd: CLEMENT BAINBRIDGE. *Train Bearer*: J. Moore. *Queen of the Fairies*: FANNIE EDWARDS. *Iolanthe*, a Fairy, Strephon's Mother: CORNELIA BASSETT. *Fairies (3)*: *Celia*: Minnie DeRue. *Leila*: Lillian Hawthorne. *Fleta*: Annie Cameron. *Phyllis*, an Arcadian Shepherdess and Ward in Chancery: LENORE SNYDER. *Chorus of Dukes, Marquises, Earls, Viscounts, Barons and Fairies.*

REILLY AND THE 400

1890.49

A Comedy in Three Acts, 5 Scenes. Play (and lyrics) by Edward Harrigan. Music by David Braham. Staged by Edward Harrigan. Scenery by D. Frank Dodge. Mechanical work by Robert J. Cutler. Electrical effects by John Whalen. Musical director, David Braham. Produced by Edward Harrigan. Opened 29 December 1890 at Harrigan's Theatre and closed 20 June 1891 after 202 performances.

CAST: *Wiley Reilly*: EDWARD HARRIGAN. *Salvator Magnus*: JOHN WILD. *Lizzie Calhoun*: JOSEPH SPARKS. *Commodore Tobytow*: JAMES RADCLIFFE. *Herman Schmelze*: HARRY FISHER. *Jerome Jailers*: George Merritt. *Ned Reilly*: HARRY DAVENPORT. *Percy Oggles*: Fred Peters. *Mrs. Jackson*: Charles T. White. *Cream Cooler*: Peter Goldrich. *Hippolite Duval*: Richard Quilter. *Milkman*: Richard Quilter. *Valentine McClinchy*: Dan Burke. *Bessie Bowlow*: John Decker. *That's What*: James Burke. *Jimmy the Con*: William West. *Roundsman Moran*: James McCullough. *Iceman*: James Rennie. *Butcher*: Alfred Waite. *James McGouldrick*: John Walsh. *Dionysius Dorrigan*: Charles Coffey. *Slattery*: Edwin Murphy. *Ignatius McCune*: Edward Gordon. *August Shutzer*: Joseph Williamson. *Emil Shutzer*: Master Tony. *Lavine Gale*: . *Emiline Gale*: ISABELLE ARCHER. *Maggie Murphy*: EMMA POLLOCK. *Kittie Lynch*: ADA LEWIS. *Maryann Dooley*: ANNIE YEAMANS.
Guests: Daisy Andrews, Lorraine Dreux, Margery Teel, Miss Martinez, Fannie Batchelder.

Act 1: Pawn Office of Uncle Reilly.

Act 2, Scene 1: 'Tween Decks on the "Lee Shore." *Scene 2*: Hester Street at Night. *Scene 3*: Casey's Hall.

Act 3: The Saloon Deck on the "Lee Shore."

ACT 1
"The Jolly Commodore"
"Uncle Reilly"

ACT 2
Scene 1
"Jim Jam Sailor Superfine"
(*Dance arranged by* Dan Burke.)
"I've Come Home to Stay"
Scene 3
"Maggie Murphy's Home"
E. Pollock, Chorus
"Taking in the Town"

ACT 3
"The (Great) Four Hundred"

THE BABES IN THE WOOD, Robin Hood and His Merry, Merry Men, and Harlequin, Who Killed Cock Robin?

1890.50

A Pantomime in Three Acts, 9 Scenes. New version of the old story retold by E. L. Blanchard. Music by Walter Slaughter, Alfred Cellier, Edward

[40]First presented in New York 25 November 1882 at the Standard Theatre for 105 performances. For Synopsis of Scenes and Musical Numbers, see original 1882 production.
[41]Scenery and costume design uncredited.

Solomon, H. J. Leslie, Ivan Caryll, Edward Jones. Scenery by Messrs. Telbin, T. E. Ryes, W. Perkins, E. J. Banks (all of London), Herr Kautsky (Vienna), John Buss, Albert of Chicago. Ballets designed and produced by A. Betrand. Costumes by Messrs. Auguste & Cie, Misses Fisher, Mons. and Mme. Alias, Mme. Maertens. Musical director, Edward Jones. Stage manager, Napier Lothian, Jr. Produced under the direction of Henry J. Leslie and J. C. Duff. Produced by E. G. Gilmore. Opened 30 December 1890 at Niblo's Garden and closed 7 February 1891 after 48 performances.

CAST: *Robin Hood*: AÏDA JENOURE. *Maid Marion*, Governess to the Babes: LOUISE BEAUDET. *Toxophila*: Barbara Allen. *Robin Hood's Merry, Merry Men (11)*: *Will Scarlet*: Ruth Davenport. *Little John*: Phoebe D'Alroy. *Large William*: Kate Bowen. *Allen-a-Dale*: Inez Murray. *Weak in the Head*: Millicent Burke. *Nick o' the Wood*: Minnie Clifford. *Draw the Bow*: Blanche Leslie. *Sling the Hatchet*: Lena Travers. *Strong in the Arm*: Laura Wyndham. *Will o' the Wisp*: Helen Dunbar. *Jack o' Lantern*: Dorothy Hyem. *Robin Redbreast*: Edith Craske. *Wren*: Rose Sutherland. *Sparrow*: Lillie Fording. *Principal Foresters*: Emily Clark, Violet Clark. *Eglantine*, Queen of the Fairies: Elaine Ellison. *Cissy and Bertie*, Babes in the Wood: GEORGE K. FORTESCUE, WILLIAM A. MESTAYER. *The Baron*, the wicked uncle: JOSEPH W. HERBERT. *The Baroness*: Frances Lyon. *James*, their factotum: George H. Browne. *The Robbers*: J. R. Costello, S. Healey. *Friar Tuck*: Henry W. Dodd. *Clown*: S. Healey. *Pantaloon*: J. R. Costello. *Pantaloon*: J. G. Vanana. *Columbine*: Edith Craske. *Premiere Assoluta*: Mlle. ADELE CORNALBA. *Premieres*: Edith Craske, V. Chitten, C. Chitten. *Secondes*: Mesdames Gorman, Cogan, Manzoni, Picco, Avanzini, Mousset, Quick, Hoope.

Act 1, Scene 1: A moonlit glen. "Who killed Cock Robin?" (Kautsky.) *Scene 2*: A garret. (Buss.) *Scene 3*: In the King's hideout?. (Ryes.)

Act 2, Scene 1: The Nursery. (Perkins.) *Scene 2*: Grand panorama of Sherwood Forest. *Scene 3*: Insect Island. (Telbin.)

Act 3, Scene 1: Conservatory of the Baronial Mansion. (Banks.) *Scene 2*: The Baronial Ball-room. (Telbin.) *Scene 3*: A Street. (Buss.)

ACT 1
Scene 3
Ballet of Nymphs and Rabbits

ACT 2
Scene 1
The Housemaid's Dance
Scene 3
Grand Procession and Ballet of International Insects

ACt 3
Scene 2
Grand Procession and Tableaux representing characters in Shakespeare's plays of Hamlet, Othello, Richard III, Macbeth, Merchant of Venice, and A Midsummer Night's Dream. Original and Descriptive music by Alfred Cellier.
Scene 3
The Harlequinade
Clown: S. Healey. *Harlequin*: L. G. Vanara. *Pantaloon*: J. R. Costello. *Columbine*: E. Craske.

1891.01 AN IRISHMAN'S LOVE

An Irish Drama with Music in Five Acts. Play by William McGrath. (Music by Reginald Barrett.) Proprietor and manager, J. H. Lester & Co. Opened 12 January 1891 at the H. R. Jacobs' Third Avenue Theatre and closed 17 January 1891 after 8 performances.[42]

CAST: *Teddy Brannigan*: PATRICK MILES. *Dennis O'Day*: FRANK DAVIS. *Squire Avery*: PERCY KINGSLEY. *Shamus Webb*: H. H. Horton. *Arthur Henley*: W. H. Prendergast. *Eileen O'Donnell*: Lida Holden Lester. *Rosie Magee*: Blanche Boyer. With Young Ireland, J. W. Flood, Maurice Holden, Little Dot Clarendon.

MUSICAL NUMBERS
"An Irishman's Love"
"Rosie Asthore"
(*Lyrics by* Percy Kingsley.)
"Irish Eyes of Blue"
(*Music and Lyrics? by* ? Wheeler.)

1891.02 THE DAZZLER

A Musical Farce Comedy in Three Acts. Book, music and lyrics by Thomas Addison. Direction, Cosgrove and Grant. Musical director, William H. Way. Produced by Lydia Thompson (Ernest Hutchinson, Manager). Opened 19 January 1891 at the Park Theatre and closed 24 January 1891 after 8 performances; re-opened 2 February 1891 at the Standard Theatre and closed 21 February 1891 after 24 additional performances; re-opened 13 April 1891 at Niblo's Garden and closed 18 April 1891 after 8 additional performances[43].Total: 40 performances.

CAST: *Ezekiel Pipes*, a modest man: JOE A. OTT. *Tannhauser Bock*, a retired brewer: MAX MILLER. *Mulligan*, of Bally Mulligan, an Irish king: THOMAS J. GRADY. *Viscount Haricot de Mutton*, no duplicate: R. S. Nodine, Jr. *Jones*: Sherman Wade. *Smashem*, a crank: Sherman Wade. *Iceman*, chilly: Alfred Grant. *Reub Yank*, nobody's child: B. Bedell. *Juliane*, a curiosity: Jessie Hatcher. *Angele*, up to date: Annie Carter. *Kate, Carrie, Edith, Alice, Florrie*, Chameleons: Alice Brigham, Susie Mace, Lilly Madison, Bessie Huntington, Margaret Sloan. *Charlie Plunker*: BLANCHE ARKWRIGHT. *Kitty Starlight*, a revelation. An actress who shuns the public gaze: LYDIA THOMPSON.

Act 1: Staten Island, New York. The present summer.

Act 2: A Restaurant. The same evening.

Act 3, Scene 1: Tonsorial Apartment. *Scene 2*: Ball room. Night, almost 12.

MUSICAL NUMBERS[44]
During the action of the comedy, Lydia Thompson and her company of comedians will introduce New Music, Songs, Dances, Specialties, Medleys, comprising over 50 numbers.
"Hauled Back Again!" (Haul Me Back Again) (Act 3)
J. A. Ott
(*Music by* Fannie Beane. *Lyrics by* Sloan and Burnham.)
"He Never Came Back"
(*Music and Lyrics by* William Jerome)

1891.03 A STRAIGHT TIP

A (Musical) Farce Comedy in Three Acts. Play by John J. McNally. Music by Richard Stahl and (lyrics by) Edgar Smith. Produced under the direction of Frank Tannehill, Jr. Musical director, John Mullaly. Produced by (Isaac B.) Rich and (William) Harris. Opened 26 January 1891 at the Park Theatre and closed 16 May 1891 after 123 performances.[45]

CAST: *Dick Dasher*, something of a masher, who longs to be a hero, in love with Kitty: JAMES T. POWERS. *Dennis Dolan*, an Irishman, rich in brogue, heart and pocket: JOHN SPARKS. *Kitty Dolan*, his pretty daughter, with a taste for sports: EMMA HANLEY. *Bedelia Dolan*, a sister of Dennis, with aristocratic notions: EMILY STOWE. *Abner Hawkins*, of Bangor, Maine, in love with Bedelia: RICHARD GORMAN. *Jack Potsand Poole*, a gambler who tries to play hearts: PETER F. DAILEY. *A. Hardupp Beerbohn*, a non-commissioned surveyor, otherwise a tramp: F. T. WARD. *Howland Taire*, an actor, in hard luck: Albert Hart. *A. Taltout*, well-known on the race track: Albert Hart. *Daisy Dazzle*, who wants to star: Delia Stacy. *Several pleasing and delightful necessities (3)*: *Cora Cashmere*: Eloise Mortimer. *Violet Velours*: Lilla Linden. *Belle Delaine*: Maggie Garrett. *Bunco and Three Card Monte Men (3)*: *Bill Katchon*: John P. Curran. *Jim Fleese*: Howard Graham. *Lank Lean*: Oscar Schoening. *Fresh every hour, but none the worse for it (2)*: *Cherry Bonbon*: Polly Winner. *Mignon Marshmallow*: Dane DeVamper. (*Carmencita*: JAMES T. POWERS.)
The action takes place here and now, for instance.

Act 1: Dolan's Summer Hotel.

Act 2: The Race Track.

Act 3: Garden of Dolan's Hotel.

ACT 1
Four stage-struck Maidens[46]

---

[42]No program available.

[43]No credits for costumes or scenery in programs, nor any list of musical numbers. Played a return engagement 11 May 1891 at the Grand Opera House for 8 performances. Interpolated as per publiushed sheet music:
"A Letter to His Dad"
James F. McDonald
(*Music by* Isidor Witmark. *Lyrics by* William Collier.)

[44]A later tour under the auspices of Cosgrove & Grant featured Kate Castleton in the leading role. Musical score varied substantially from the New York engagement.

[45]Scenery and costumes uncredited.

[46]Replaced late in the run by:
"Simple Little Flirts" (Trio)
E. Mortimer, L. Linden, Hope Curtis [Belle Delaine]
(*Music by* F. T. Ward.)

Dick Dasher—Pantomime: the stage-door masher, lady dressing for street, the messenger boy, the seven ages of a cane.

J. T. Powers

Medley: Original and selected music

ACT 2[47]

Grand Medley[48]

Melange

"Troubles with Love"

P. F. Dailey

"The Song That Broke My Heart'

Dick Dasher

J. T. Powers

"Something After This Style"

"The Four Beauties" (Butterfly Dance)[49]

J. T. Powers, Girls

(*Music by* Richard Stahl. *Costumes designed by* James T. Powers.)

ACT 3

"The Gay Cavalier"

E. Hanley

Dick Dasher—his travesty burlesque of the latest craze, "Carmencita"

J. T. Powers

Famous Original Clipper Quartette in one of their unique mélanges

1891.04 THE FAKIR

A Three-Act Derrick (Farce Comedy in Three Acts). Play by Paul M. Potter and Harry L. Hamlin. Music, all new, composed and arranged by Charles E. Bergman. Stage director, John T. Craven. Produced by Hamlin's Farce Comedy Company (William A. McConnell, Management). Opened 2 March 1891 at the Standard Theatre and closed 7 March 1891 after 7 performances.[50]

CAST: *Seth Boker*, a retired fakir: MARK SULLIVAN. *Mrs. Boker*: HELEN REIMER. *Patty Boker*, the Fakir's daughter: ROSA FRANCE. *Jack Gassaway*, a man of leisure: LESLIE EDMUNDS. *Rosa Vandeyblunk*: JEANNETTE ST. HENRY. *Charity Banks*, who cherishes ambition: LIZZIE DERIOUS DALY. *Ell Quick*, a child of nature: Max Arnold. *Larry Ludlow*: John Gilroy. *Colonel Lexington*, a managerial speculator: Alf Hampton. *Members of the Whirlygig Burlesque Company (4)*: *Fay Follibud*: Katherine B. Howe. *Nydia*: Lillian Markham. *Daphne*: Mollie Sherwood. *Chloe*: Dudie Tracy.

Act 1: Boker's Cottage, Springville.

Act 2: Green Room, Folly Theatre, New York.

Act 3: Boker's Residence.

1891.05 THE PRODIGAL SON

A Pantomime in Three Acts. French libretto [without words] to 'L'Enfant Prodigue' by Michel Carré, Jr. Music by André Wormser. Directed by Augustin Daly. Conducted by Henry Widmer. Produced by Augustin Daly. Opened 3 March 1891 at Daly's Theatre and closed 7 March 1891 after 7 performances.

CAST: *Phrynette*: ADELAIDE PRINCE. *Baron*: SIDNEY HERBERT. *Pierrot Junior*: ADA REHAN. *Pierrot Senior*: CHARLES LECLERCQ. *Mme. Pierrot*: Mrs. G. H. GILBERT. *Virginie*: ISABEL IRVING. *The Senegambian Footman*: WILFRED BUCKLAND.

Act 1: Pierrot's Home.

Act 2: Phrynette's Boudoir, Paris.

Act 3: Again the Home of Pierrot.

1891.06 MYLES AROON

A Revival of the Irish Comedy Drama in Four Acts, 8 Scenes[51]. Play by George H. Jessop and Horace Townsend. (Staged by Augustus Pitou.) Scenery by Schaffer and Maeder; Charles Witham. Musical director, George Loesch. Produced by Augustus Pitou. Opened 9 March 1891 at the 14th Street Theatre and closed 14 March 1891 after 8 performances[52].

CAST: *Myles Aroon*: W. J. SCANLAN. *Squire Raymond Thurston*: Charles Mason. *Mike Carney*: THADDEUS SHINE. *Gerald Fosdyke*: Hardee Kirkland. *Pat Phelan*: Robert McNair. *Joe Upton*: J. O. LeBrasse. *Lady Glover*: STELLA TEUTON. *Maggie Farrell*: MATTIE FERGUSON. *Mrs. Farrell*: MILLIE SACKETT. *Lucy O'Shea*: Mary Warner. *Annie O'Connor*: Lucy Waters. *Nora*: Dora Vinton. *Katie*: Cecil Wallace. *Mother Bet*: Laura Webster. *Nellie Glover*: Constance Wallace.

1891.07 THE IRISH MINSTREL

A Revival of the Domestic Irish Drama in Three Acts[53]. Play by Fred Marsden. Music and lyrics by William J. Scanlan. (Staged by Augustus Pitou.) Musical director, George Loesch. Produced by Augustus Pitou. Opened 16 March 1891 at the 14th Street Theatre and closed 21 March 1891 after 8 performances.[54]

CAST: *Larry O'Lynn*: WILLIAM J. SCANLAN. *Morris Cregan*: ROBERT MCNAIR. *Dan Cregan*: Hardee Kirkland. *Robert Wynbert*: J. O. LeBrasse. *Mat Dougan*: THADDEUS SHINE. *Nellie Cregan*: MATTIE FERGUSON. *Maggie McKay*: Cecil Wallace. *Mrs. Bridget McKay*: Millie Sackett.

MUSICAL NUMBERS

"My Nellie's Blue Eyes"

W. J. Scanlan

"What's in a Kiss?"

W. J. Scanlan

"Over the Mountain" (from *FRIEND AND FOE*)

W. J. Scanlan

"I Love Music"

W. J. Scanlan

Scanlan's Famous "Rose Song"

W. J. Scanlan

"Peek-a-Boo" (from *FRIEND AND FOE*)

W. J. Scanlan

1891.08 McKENNA'S FLIRTATION

A Revival of the Farce Comedy in Three Acts.[55] (Play by Edgar Selden.) Musical director, Fred Schneider. Produced by Louis S. Goullaud and William L. Malley, Managers for Barry & Fay. Opened 16 March 1891 at the Niblo's Garden and closed 28 March 1891 after 16 performances.[56]

CAST: *Michael Ryan*, a retired milkman: FRANK J. KEENAN[57]. *Timothy McKenna*, a contractor: WILLIAM BARRY. *Timothy McKenna*, his son, in love with Mary Ellen: Charles Lamb. *Greenleaf Blackstone Kent*, a Shyster Lawyer: CHARLES STURGES. *Willet Chase*, a Society chappie, Don't you know: J. A. Wheelock. *Patrick McQuirk*, a hod-carrier and general workman: Samuel Clark. *Mrs. O'Donnell*, who keeps a beer saloon: JAMES J. MURRAY. *Policeman McCarthy*, one of the finest: James J. Murray. *Pan Handle Mike*, who looks tough: R. E. McAllister. *Mrs. Mary Ellen Ryan*, a victim of circumstances: Florence Ashbrooke. *Mary Ellen Ryan*, in love with Tim: DUDDIE DOUGLAS. *Anastasia McGovern*, McKenna's sister-in-law and housekeeper: R. E. Stevens. *The Three Lilacs*: *Mamie Fogarty*: Bessie Osterman. *Maggie Casey*: Lydia Barry. *Sadie Monahan*: Daisy Mayer.

---

[47]Added to Act 2 during the run (after "Troubles with Love":
"Down on the Farm"

[48]Replaced late in the run by:
"O'Reilly's Kettledrum"
(*Music by* John Philip Sousa.)

[49]Late in the run the Butterfly Dance was replaced by a Twilight Dance, music by F. T. Ward.

[50]No credits in program for stage, director, scenery or costume design; no musical numbers listed.

[51]First produced in New York 21 January 1889 at the 14th Street Theatre for 16 performances. For Synopsis of Scenes and Musical Numbers, see original 1889 production.

[52]Played return engagements 20 April 1891 at the Grand Opera House for 8 performances, 27 April 1891 at Harry Miner's People's Theatre for 8 performances. Costumes uncredited. For this revival, "Moonlight at Killarney" was dropped.

[53]First produced in New York 16 April 1888 at the Harry Miner's People's Theatre for 8 performances. For Synopsis of Scenes and Musical Numbers, see original 1888 production.

[54]Scenes, costume and scenic designs uncredited.

[55]First produced in New York 2 September 1889 at the New Park Theatre for 107 performances. For Synopsis of Scenes and Musical Numbers, see original 1889 production. Song added for this revival: "Leisure Hours."

[56]No credits in program for stage director, costumes or scenery.

[57]Keenan was a temporary replacement for the ailing Hugh Fay.

1891.09

U AND I

George W. Lederer's Comic Players in a Musical Satire in Three Acts. Play, music and lyrics by Edgar Smith and Richard Carroll. Acting manager, W. F. Falk. Musical diector, Paul Schindler. Proprietor and manager, George W. Lederer. Opened 23 March 1891 at the Standard Theatre and closed 2 May 1891 after 42 performances.[58]

CAST: *Professor John Ungerblotz*, a victim of circumstances and mixed drinks: GUS WILLIAMS. *O'Donovan Innes*, of Haverstraw, New York, who visits the Metropolis to see life, and sees enough to last him forever: JOHN T. KELLY. *Oliver Twist Haphazard*, a janitor, the despotic ruler of the Sitting Bull Flats: Charles Wayne. *Adam Clubber*, a policeman, whose ideas of keeping the peace is to keep at a distance from all disturbances: HARRY KELLY. *Percy Van Astor*, American by birth, but British by adoption: Charles F. Walton. *Another Johnny*: Seymour G. Hess. *Mlle. Vermicelli*, a comic opera deity worshipped by the "Johnnies": GERTRUDE ZELLA. *Babette*, Mlle. Vernicelli's maid, called Babette because it is tonier than Bridget: Florrie West. *Mrs. Ungerblotz*, the Professor's wife, whose temporary absence from home is the cause of all the trouble: ROSE LEIGHTON. *Comic Opera Sylphs*. Erratic as persons in their sphere of ussefulness usually are (7): *Maud S*: Anna Caldwell. *Bella B*: Josie Fairbank. *Carrie G*: Florence Carlisle. *Gracie M*: Ida Fairbank. *Jennie R*: Zelma Rawlston. *Alice K*: Agnes Sherwood. *Mollie M*: Florence Franton.

The action takes place at Sitting Bull Flats, right now.

Act 1: Parlor in Mlle. Vernicelli's apartments.

Act 2: Dining room in Prof. Ungerblotz's apartments, one flat higher.

Act 3: The Garden Party of the Roof.

MUSICAL NUMBERS, SPECIALTIES

Kissing Song
G. Zella

1891.10

ADAM'S TEMPTATION, or, Birds of Paradise

An Original Extravaganza in One Act, accompanied by a Vaudeville Bill. Libretto by Frederic Solomon. Director of music, William J. Rostetter. Produced by (John) Koster and (Albert) Bial. Opened 30 March 1891 at Koster & Bial's Concert Hall and closed 27 June 1891 after (100) performances.

VAUDEVILLE: Jutan; the Glinseretti Troupe; Daniel F. Hart; The Sternheims; the Weston Brothers.

CAST: *Adam Gilly*, the youth who never saw a girl: JENNIE JOYCE. *Eve Mumpwug*, the girl who never saw a youth: MADGE LESSING. *Tom Binnacle*, First Lieutenant, U.S.N.: JOSIE GREGORY. *Captain Noodleheimer, U.S.S. Dolphin*: PAUL SAVILLE. *Pat O'Hooligan*, Boatswain: Morris Weston. *Martha Mumpwug*, Eve's mother: May Shannon. *Squire Gilly*, her brother: Sam Weston. *Lilly*: Grace Stacy. *Flower Girls, Sailors, Amazons, etc.* (*Specialty*: CARMENCITA.)

1891.11

WANG

A Operatic Burletta (Comic Opera) in Two Acts. Libretto by J. Cheever Goodwin. Music by Woolson Morse. Produced under the stage direction of H. A. Cripps. Scenery by John H. Young. Costumes designed by Alfred Thompson. Orchestra under the direction of J. S. Hiller. Produced by DeWolf Hopper Opera Company (B. D. Stevens, Manager). Opened 4 May 1891 at the Broadway Theatre and closed 3 October 1891 after 151 performances.

CAST: *Wang*, the Regent of Siam: DeWOLF HOPPER. *Colonel Fracasse*, Military Instructor of Siamese troops: SAMUEL REED. *Jean Boucher*, Lieutenant of French troops: EDMUND STANLEY. *Pepat*, Keeper of the Royal Elephant: ALFRED KLEIN. *Chow-Sury*, inn-keeper: GEORGE WADE. *Panompin*, a Cambodian envoy: LOUIS SHRADER. *High Priest*: Camm Mauvel. *La Veuve Frimousse*, widow of the late French Consul at Pechaburi: MARION SINGER. *Marie*, her step-daughter, adored by Mataya: JEANETTE ST. HENRY. *Gillette*, her eldest daughter, beloved by Jean: ANNA O'KEEFE. *Nannette*, another daughter: HELEN BERESFORD. *More daughters (7)*: *Coralie*: Louise Edgar. *Delphine*: May Levinge. *Fleurette*: Dorothy Maddern. *Julie*: Ida Laclaire. *Babbette*: Maude Conway. *Rosalie*: Dolly Chase. *Chevette*: Ada Miller. *M.D.S.—242*: Agnes Reiley. *Mataya*, the Crown Prince of Siam: DELLA FOX. *Guards, Courtiers, French Officers and Sailors, Siamese Troops, Pages and Cambodians.*

Act 1: Public Landing on River Menam, at Pechaburi.

Act 2: Throne Room of Royal Palace at Bangkok.

[58]Scenery and costumes uncredited.

ACT 1[59]

Opening Chorus (Gaily o'er the bounding billows)
"Sailors' Chorus" (Yeo ho! lads, yeo ho!)

Trio (So give us the night. .)
D. Fox, E. Stanley, S. Reed

"A Pretty Girl" (A Summer's Night)
D. Fox

Song (Of all the awkward squads . . .)
S. Reed

"Where Are You Going My Pretty Maid? (Duet)
J. St. Henry, D. Fox

"Mary! Mary! Why so contrary?" (Concerted Number)
A. O'Keefe, Girls

Entrance of the Regent Wang
Chorus

"The (Eminent) Regent Wang"
D. Hopper, Chorus

Duet (If you love me as I love you. .)
D. Hopper, M. Singer

Soldiers' Chorus (Hush! hark! What do we hear?)
Chorus

Finale (Allow me to remark in this connection. .)
Principals, Chorus
"To Be a Lone Widow"
M. Singer
"Are Then the Vows So Lately Spoken"
J. St. Henry

ACT 2

"We've Been Shopping" (Opening Chorus)

"Every Rose Must Have Its Thorn"

"Ask the Man in the Moon"
D. Hopper, D. Fox, S. Reed

Song (When You Meet a Royal Highness)
C. Mauvel, Chorus of Girls

"Baby! Baby! Dance My Darling Baby!"

Chorus of Burmese Envoys (Sharper than the serpent's fang. .)
D. Hopper, E. Stanley, Chorus

"More Dear to Me"

"The Man With a Elephant on His Hands" (Song)
D. Hopper

"Coronation March" (Finale)

1891.12

APOLLO, or, The Oracle of Delphi

A Burlesque Operetta in Three Acts. (Original German) Libretto (Das Orakel) by Ignatz Schnitzer. American translation and adaptation by Helen F. Tretbar and Edgar Smith. Music by Joseph Hellmesberger, Jr. Produced under the direction of Heinrich Conried. Settings by Henry E. Hoyt. Costumes by Mme. Loe. Orchestra under the direction of Gustave Kerker. Produced by Rudolph Aronson. Opened 7 May 1891 at the Casino Theatre and closed 11 July 1891 after 65 performances.

CAST: *Pythia*: LILLIAN RUSSELL. *Parisina, Lerina*, Damsels of Corinth: LOUISE BEAUDET, GRACE GOLDEN. *Harpia*: EVA DAVENPORT. *Virgins of the Temple (6)*: *Polydora*: Sylvia Thorne. *Thisbe*: Villa Knox. *Erycia*: Madge Yorke. *Cermione*: Rose Wilson. *Olympia*: Florence Bell. *Doris*: Carrie Boelen. *Dioskuros*, Guardian of the Temple: EDWIN STEVENS. *Helios*, a Young Athenian: FERDINAND SCHÜTZ. *Young Fops (3)*: *Glaukos*: HARRY MACDONOUGH. *Mermeros*: MAX FIGMAN. *Dimoklos*: EDGAR SMITH. *Tiamis*, Friend of Helios: Charles Renwick. *Nausikles*, Merchant of Leopos: James Maas. *Agrion*, Host in Delphi: M. Conrad. *A Herald*: Otto Weyl. *Adrastos*, Apollo's High Priest at Delphi: FEFFERSON DeANGELIS.

Act 1: The Castilian Spring at Delphi.

Act 2: In the Temple of Apollo.

Act 3: The Terrace leading to the Temple.

[59]Musical numbers not listed in programs. List prepared from published libretto. Additional songs not found in the libretto include: "Welcome Madame Frimouse" (Chorus of Welcome), "Get on Board" and "No Matter What Others May Say" (Trio).

1891.13

THE TAR AND THE TARTAR

A Comic Opera in Three Acts. Libretto by Harry B. Smith. Music by Adam Itzel, Jr. Produced under the stage direction of Napier Lothian, Jr. Scenery designed by Joseph Clare. Costumes from designs by Baron C. DeGrimm, made by Henry Dazian. Musical direction, Adam Itzel, Jr. Produced by Harry Askin. Opened 11 May 1891 at Palmer's Theatre and closed 5 September 1891 after 122 performances.

CAST: *Muley Hassan*, a sailor shipwrecked near the coast of Morocco: DIGBY BELL. *Farina*, a Circassian professional beauty: HELEN BERTRAM. *Alpaca*, a Tartar, formerly wife of Muley Hassan, now Queen of the Sultan's harem: LAURA JOYCE BELL. *Taffeta*, companion to Farina: ANNIE MEYERS. *Khartoon*, master of the revels and royal purveyor of amusements: W. F. ROCHESTER. *Pajama*, the court physician: FRED FREAR. *Yussuf*, servant to Cardamon: Charles Meyer. *Lambrekin*, a lady of the harem: JOSEPHINE KNAPP. *Moket*, Sultan of Morocco: Charles H. Jones. *Tolu*, a village girl: Grace Hamilton. *Odeliska*: Carrie Noyes. *Cardamon*, a Bedouin chief: HUBERT WILKE. *Chorus of Fishermen, Villagers, Wives of the Sultan, Pages of the Sultan, Guards, etc.*

Act 1: The Sea-coast near the city of Morocco.

Act 2: Court-yard of the Sultan's Palace.

Act 3: Rose Garden of the Seraglio.

MUSICAL NUMBERS[60]

"The Rocket and the Stick"
(Solo and Chorus)

Serenade (Sultan, oh, cease thy slumber)
(Solo and Female Chorus)

"Three Letters"[61]
(Solo)
(*Lyrics by* Sydney Rosenfeld.)

"Pygmalion and Galatea"
(Solo and Chorus)

"Itzel's Lullaby" (Hush thee, hush thee, baby dear)
(Solo)

"I Want a Situation"
(Solo and Chorus)

"Nothing Is Like It Used to Be"
(Solo and Chorus)

"My Fair Gitana"
(Solo)

"My Faithful Heart"
(Solo and Chorus)

"Oh! What a Difference in the Morning"
D. Bell
(*Music by* Felix McGlennon. *Lyrics by* Crapo.)

1891.14

AUNT BRIDGET'S BABY

Monroe's Celebrities in a Musical Farce-Comedy in Three Acts[62](Play by George W. Monroe.) Costumes designed by Baron C. DeGrimm. Musical director, Watty Hydes. (Produced) Under the management of Robert B. Monroe. Opened 18 May 1891 at the Bijou Theatre and closed 13 June 1891 after 32 performances.[63]

CAST: *Bridget McVeigh*, an Irish lady of wealth, ambitious for knowledge: GEORGE W. MONROE. *Owen McFee*, the supposed boodler, in love with Bridget: ED HEFFERMAN. *Shadow Pinchem*, an amateur detective, "always there": Thomas LeMack. *Captain Astoroid*, one of the eight hundred: FRANK W. HOLLAND. *Dudley Astoroid*, his adopted son: J. ALDRICH LIBBEY. *Bruce Ashton*, his nephew: W. ANDREW MACK. *Billy*, Spliters' sweetheart: Frank Casey. *Jonas Dobbins*, the "Bosun": J. P. McSweeney. *'Enry Joplin*, from the "h'other side": J. H. Cavanaugh. *Davy Jones*: Royce Alton. *The Stowaways*: Messrs. Heffernan, Mack and LeMack. *Calis Thenics*, teacher of vocal and physical culture: KATE DAVIS. *Seta LaMont*, teacher of dancing for the Baby: CHARLOTTE BURBY. *Sophie, Eloise*, college girls, home on a vacation, and to get married: CATHERINE GERALD, ADA DARE. *Annette de Dong*, a regular French maid: Sadie McDonald. *Splinters*, "Aunt Bridget's Baby": NELLIE ROSEBUD. *Specialty*: Castilian (Lady) Troubadours.

Act 1: Bridget's house at Long Branch, exterior.

Act 2: Asteroid's Yacht.

Act 3: Bridget's house at Long Brach, interior.

ACT 1[64]

"The Pilot"[65]
W. A. Mack, J. A. Libbey

"Oh, What a Sad History" (Duet)
G. W. Monroe, N. Rosebud

Sand Jig
N. Rosebud

"The World's Fair"
T. LeMack

Operatic Finale
G. W. Monroe, E. Hefferman, Company

ACT 2

Mandolin Selections by our mermaids of melody
Castilian Troubadors

"Good-by, Bridgy"
G. W. Monroe

"Boys Together"[66](Always Together)
W. A. Mack
(*Music by* W. A. Mack. *Lyrics by* Thomas LeMack.)

Grand Medley:[67]
"The Tar's Song" (Male Quartette)
W. A. Mack, J. H. Cavanaugh, J. A. Libbey, F. W. Holland
"The Minstrel Man"
G. W. Monroe Company
"The (Wedding of the) Lily and the Rose" (Song and Dance)
N. Rosebud, W. A. Mack, T. LeMack
(*Music and Lyrics by* Thomas LeMack.)

"Once in a While"
K. Davis

"Our Hebrew Uncles"
Stowaways

"The Longshoreman"
J. P. McSweeney

"The Italian Band"
Stowaways

"The Fairy Bells"
F. Casey

"Oblige the Ladies"
N. Rosebud

"Katie Connor"
Company

"The Big, Black Coon"
Stowaways

60Musical numbers not listed in programs. List prepared from published piano vocal selection (Hitchcock and McCargo Publishing Co., Ltd., New York, 1891).

61Program note: Author acknowledges his indebtedness to Mr. Sydney Rosefeld for this song.

62A sequel to "My Aunt Bridget" by George W. Monroe.

63Stage direction, scenery uncredited. Subsequently toured, in a form revised and reconstructed by Scott Marble, with a different musical score.

64Added after opening to Act 1, before the Finale:
"The Broadway Butterflies"
(*Lyrics by* Matt Woodward.)

65Replaced by "Dreams" (Quartette) for subsequent tour.

66Replaced after opening by:
"The Picture That Is Turned Towards the Wall"
W. A. Mack
Replaced for subsequent tour by:
"Zarita"
J. A. Libbey

67Added to the Medley for tour:
"The Nasty Way He Sez It" (Imitation of Albert Chevalier)
N. Rosebud
"Paddy, Wait Awhile"
Kate Thomas (Calis Thenics)
"A Job Lot"
G. W. Monroe

Grand Finale
N. Rosebud, E. Hefferman, T. LeMack, W. A. Mack, Company

ACT 3[68]

Songs
K. Davis

"I'll Give You Three Chances to Guess"
G. W. Monroe
(*Music and Lyrics by* Thomas LeMack.)

"The Bugler"[69]
J. A. Libbey

Wedding Chorus
Company

Finale
G. W. Monroe, Company

1891.15 A KNOTTY AFFAIR

A Farce Comedy in Three Acts, 4 Scenes. Play by Herbert Hall Winslow. Original music by William P. Brown. Scenery by Harley Merry. Costumes by Baron C. DeGrimm. Musical director, William P. Brown. Produced by John C. Rice (Management, E. J. Nugent). Opened 18 May 1891 at the Park Theatre and closed 30 May 1891 after 16 performances.[70]

CAST: *Jay Proctor Knott*, which is not his name: JOHN C. RICE. *Wilhelm Van Keuren*, who assumed the name for reasons of his own: CHARLES J. ROSS. *Benjamin Franklin Sniggs*, who yearns to be a sporting editor: GUS FRANKEL. *Don Roderigo Aguila de Lopez*, a Portuguese nobleman: GEORGE W. BARNUM. *Squire Jabeg Fielding*, postmaster of Boomville: Joseph J. Riley. *Silas Caw*, candidate for sheriff: John Griffin. *Silas Caw, Jr.*: Edward Lang. *Jackson Jones*, a man of action: James C. Cherrye. *Detective Smart*: George Gaskin. *Sadie Fielding*, in love with the editor: HELEN LOWELL. *Kitty Carleton*, the editor's unwelcome ward: SALLY COHEN. *Madge Morrison*, with a breach of promise suit: MATTIE EARLE. *Dora Fielding*, Sadie's sister: PATTI STONE. *Leonora*, with a missing husband: Florence Barry. *Dudu De Forest*: ADA JONES. *Marguerite Montmorency*: Nellie Ransom. *Clementine St. Clew*: Grace Chase. *Blossom*, with a dance: BESSIE CLAYTON. (*Specialty*: Ross and Fenton.)

Act 1: Exterior of Jay Proctor Knott's residence. Tying the knot.

Act 2: Two apartments in the Sunset Flats, New York City. The Tug of War.

Act 3, Scene 1: An ante-room adjoining the Kirmess Hall. *Scene 2*: Grand Hall of the Kirmess. The knot untied.

ACT 2[71]

The Music Lesson
J. C. Rice, S. Cohen

His Latest Local Ditty
G. Frankel

"The Cobbler"[72]
A. Jones

What He Heard on a Street Car
C. J. Ross

"Thy Dear Eyes"
P. Stone

ACT 3
Scene 2

Little Blossom (The Beautiful Minuet)

Inimitable Dances[73]
J. C. Rice

"Antony and Cleopatra" (original burlesque)
C. J. Ross, A. Jones

("A Picture of Mother") Manhasset Quartette
Messrs. Riley, E. Lang, J. C. Cherrye, G. Gaskin
(*Music by* H. Peck. *Lyrics by* P. A. Collins.)

Grand Finale

---

[68]For subsequent tour, the first 3 songs in Act 3 were replaced by:
"The Floorwalker"
N. Rosebud
"Said Aaron to Moses" (Duet)
G. W. Monroe, E. Hefferman
The Quaker City Quartette

[69]placed after opening by:
"Heart of My Heart" (Story of the Rose)
J. A. Libbey
(*Music and Lyrics by* Andrew Mack.)

[70]Stage director not credited in programs.

[71]Added for subsequent tour to close Act 2:
"The Wine Song"
Company

[72]Replaced for subsequent tour by:
"The Picture That Is Turned Toward the Wall"
A. Jones
(*Music and Lyrics by* Charles Graham.)
"Sweet Marie"
A. Jones
(*Music and Lyrics by* Raymon Moore.)

[73]Replaced for subsequent tour by:
"Love, I Will Be True" (Song and Dance)
J. C. Rice, R. J. Jones, S. Cohen, M. Florence

1891–1892 SEASON

Henry Clay Barnabee as the Sheriff of Nottingham in ROBIN HOOD
(Photo: Falk, Undated)
Museum of the City of New York, Gift of Mrs. McCorsky Butt, 33.94.141

1891–1892 SEASON

1891.16 YE OLDEN TIMES

A Burlesque Operetta in One Act, accompanied by a Vaudeville Bill. [Libretto by Frederic Solomon.] Produced [staged] by Gus Bruno. Director of music, William J. Rostetter. Presented by (John) Koster & (Albert) Bial. Opened 29 June 1891 at Koster & Bial's Concert Hall and closed ?8 August 1891 after ?54 performances.

CAST: *Yorick Choplet Hamelet*, a Jester just for fun: GUS BRUNO. *Sir Hatrack*, Lord of Manor: Alf. Wood. *Toostrong*, Tramp: Major JOHN WEST. *Metoo*, Tramp: Colonel MATT GALLAGHER. *Prince Dandyline*, nothing but money: Mildred Stacey. *Wildrose*, a tame flower: MADGE LESSING. *Musthavetherent*—a Landlady: May Shannon. *Mash*, a Miller: Gertie Sharpeley. *Dance Specialty*: CARMENCITA. *Peasants, Courtiers, Huntsmen, etc.*

MUSICAL NUMBERS

Opening Chorus

Song
M. Lessing

"Lively Girl's Inn"
Courtiers, Huntsmen

Tramps' Story and Song
J. West, M. Gallagher

Mayday Revels

Gavotte; Hallelujah Girls
G. Bruno, Company

1891.17 THE GRAND DUCHESS

A Revival of the Opéra-bouffe in Three Acts[1] Original French libretto ('La Grande-Duchesse de Gérolstein') by Henri Meilhac and Ludovic Halévy. English translation and adaptation by Charles L. Kenney and Edgar Smith. Music by Jacques Offenbach. Stage director, Max Freeman. Scenery by Philip Goatcher and John H. Young (Acts 1, 3), T. H. Plaisted (Act 2). Costumes by Mme. Loe. Director of music, Gustave Kerker. Produced by Rudolf Aronson. Opened 13 July 1891 at the Casino Theatre and closed 22 August 1891 after 36 performances.

CAST: *Grand Duchess*: LILLIAN RUSSELL. *Wanda*: GRACE GOLDEN. *Olga*: Villa Knox. *Iza*: Eva Davenport. *Amèlie*: Sylvia Thorne. *Charlotte*: Madge Yorke. *Melanie*: Nettie Black. *Celestine*: Mabel Potter. *General Boum*: EDWIN STEVENS. *Fritz*: FERDINAND SCHUETZ. *Baron Puck*: JEFFERSON DEANGELIS. *Prince Paul*: HARRY MACDONOUGH. *Baron Grog*: EDGAR SMITH. *Nepomuc*: Max Figman. *Adjutant*: Charles Renwick. *Majors (4)*: *Nick*: Otto Weyl. *Dick*: M. Rosen. *Mick*: Charles Priest. *Slick*: George White. *Notary*: William Conrad.

1891.18 A HIGH ROLLER

Comstock's Company of Clever Comedians in a Farce Comedy in Two Acts. Play by T. Rosenfeld and Archibald Gordon. The whole created, invented, devised and arranged by Barney Fagan. Scenery by W. H. Day. Costumes designed by Baron C. DeGrimm. Mechanical effects by R. H. Mayland. Organization originated by Alex Comstock. Musical director, Gus Gebert. Produced by W. W. Randall & Dickson. Opened 3 August 1891 at the Bijou Theatre and closed 29 August 1891 after 32 performances[2].

CAST: *Eiffel Tower*: BARNEY FAGAN. *Manager Evergreen Swift*: Harry W. Emmett. *Doctor Bluffington Squills*: BARRY MAXWELL. *Captain Bulkhead*: Arthur C. Moreland. *Mr. Broadway Strand*: John Callan. *Grafton Rakeoff*: Frank H. White. *Master O. P. Side*: JESSIE VILLARS. *Potage*: Harry Ernest. *Poisson*: John Pieri. *Roti*: Richard J. Graham. *Legume*: Ed Hanson. *Marlinspike*: Mr. George-Jacquin. *Bobstay*: Herbert Zublin. *Figure Head*: Robert J. Gordon. *Mrs. Bluffington Squills*: Louise Sylvester. *Flora Vanwhynot*: Allie Gilbert. *Clara Vonwherefore*: Belle LaVerde. *Susie Bricabrac*: Lillian Melbourne. *Mrs. McBrannigan*: James Russell. *Mrs. Gilhooley*: John Russell. *First Mate*: Tillie Richardson. *Second Mate*: Jennie Lippman. *Third Mate*: Annie Conroy. *Fourth Mate*: Carrie Livingston. *Sara Cuse*: May Willie. *Maybe Init*: Etta Lyons. *Maybe Not*: Dorothy Drew. *Dolly Delsarte*: Madge Fleming. *Psyche Not*: Frankie Macmillan. *Polly Pullback*: Jeannette Rhea. *Laura Lowforehead*: Lillian Bishop. *Katie Did*: Lillie Vance. *Gussie Giggle*: Mabel Morris. *Belle Bangle*: Evelyn Matthews. *Annie Laurie*: Kitty Burgess. *Winnie White*: Celia Curtis. *Gertie Green*: Ray Walton. *Bella Black*: Dorothy DeLyle. *Accordion Pleats*: Griffin and Marks (tumblers). *Friends of Passengers, Deck Hands, Masqueraders, etc.*

ACT 1

"Goodbye Chorus"
Whole Company

Quaker City Quartette
H. Ernest, J. Pieri, R. J. Graham, E. Hanson
Imitations, Warbles, Refrains; Instrumental Selections on the Mandolin, Guitar, Flute, Ocarinas

"Moonlight Serenade"
Whole Company

"Doctor's Song"
B. Maxwell

"Sailors Chorus"
Officers: T. Richardson, J. Lippman, A. Conroy, C. Livingston. *Sailors*: M. WIllie, M. Moseley, E. Lyons, D. Drew, M. Fleming, F. Macmillan, J. Rhea, L. Bishop, L. Vance, E. Walker, M. Morris, E. Matthews, K. Burgess, C. Curtis, R. Walton, D. DeLyle.

ACT 2

Minuet
M. Willie, M. Moseley, E. Lyons, M. Fleming, F. Macmillan, L. Bishop, L. Vance, E. Walker, M. Morris, E. Matthews, D. Drew, J. Lippman, T. Richardson

Flirtation Song and Dance
B. Fagan, J. Callan, J. Russell, R. Gordon; B. LaVerde, L. Melbourne, A. Gilbert, D. Zublin

Danse Decolletée
R. Walton, C. Curtis, K. Burgess, J. Rhea

Miss Jessie Villars—Up to the times

O'Brien & Redding will amuse you

The Russell Brothers: Impersonations of Irish Female Characters
["One Word of Kindness"
(*Music and Lyrics by* Barney Fagan.)]

Grand Electrical Choreographic March
4 Officers, 16 Soldiers

Military Song and Dance[3]
B. Fagan, J. Callan, J. Russell, R. Gordon; B. LaVerde, L. Melbourne, A. Gilbert, D. Zublin

Medley Finale
B. Fagan, Entire Company

1891.19 DCK WHTNGTON!! AND HIS CAT

A Burlesque in One Act, accompanied by a Vaudeville Bill. Libretto by Frederic Solomon. Director of music, Carl Stix. Produced by (John) Koster & (Albert) Bial. Opened 10 August 1891 at Koster and Bial's Concert Hall and closed 17 October 1891 after (?99) performances.

CAST: *Dick Whittington*: JENNIE JOYCE. *Alderman Fitzwarren*: GUS BRUNO, JR. *Alice*, his daughter: MADGE LESSING. *Simon Sappy*, Fitzwarren's cashier: GUS BRUNO. *Prince Rodentzville*: JOSIE GREGORY. *Mme. Fitzwarren*: May Shannon. *Violet*, her maid: Ray Vernon. *Apprentice*: Maud Harvey. *Apprentices, Work Girls, Guards, etc.*

At the close of the Burlesque will be introduced The Reception of All Nations: France, England, Germany, America.

---

[1]This adaptation first produced in New York 25 February 1890 at the Casino Theatre for 100 performances. For Synopsis of Scenes and Musical Number, see original 1890 production.

[2]The production was revised, rewritten and recast for subsequent tour. Two songs were added to the program:

"Katie"
B. Fagan
(*Music and Lyrics by* Barney Fagan.)

"Don't Get into the Habit of It"
John B. Gilbert

[3]The New York Times' reviewer referred to this as the TAR AND TARTAR Chorus.

1891.20
CAPTAIN KARL!

A Grand Romantic Comedy in Three Acts, 5 Scenes. Play by Charles A. Gardner. Music (and lyrics) by Gustave H. Kline. Musical director, Gustave H. Kline. Produced by Charles A. Gardner (Management, Sidney R. Ellis). Opened 22 August 1891 at the Grand Opera House and closed 29 August 1891 after 9 performances.[4]

CAST: *Karl*, the Vine Grower, afterwards Captain Karl: CHARLES A. GARDNER[5]. *Rudolph Bandler*, Lawyer to the Baroness: OGDEN STEVENS. *Adolphus Sigismund*, an Eccentric: ROBERT V. FERGUSON. *Father Baptist*, a Village Priest: William H. Leyden. *Bruno*, a Young Baron: HENRY KINGSLEY. *Klinger*: Ignace Conradi. *Rudloph*: Royce Alton. *Katz*: Frank Grauss. *Boatman*: Alexander Johnstone. *Gertrude*, an Orphan: EVA BYRON. *The Baroness*, Step-Mother to Bruno: MARION MAY. *Wilhelmina*, Gertrude's companion: NELLIE WALTERS. *Little Otto*: Little Hazel Regan. *Christina*: Carrie Grauss. *Margerat*: Bertie Alton.

Act 1: Home of the Vintage Workers.

Act 2: The Vineyards.

Act 3, Scene 1: Karl's Hut. *Scene 2*: A Village Road. *Scene 3*: The Rectory.

MUSICAL NUMBERS[6]

"Invitation to the Wedding"
"Language of Flowers"
"Captain Karl's March"
"Bubble Song"
"Love Is Divine"
"Sweet Land Tyrol"
"Close Those Tired Eyes" (Cradle Song)
"The Lilac"
Fatherland Tyrol Quartette Selections (Act 3)
Carrie Grauss (soprano), Ignace Conradi (tenor robusto), Rose Mirzl (alto), Frank Grauss (basso).

1891.21
FLEURETTE

An Operetta-Comedy from the French in Three Acts. Libretto by Mrs. Charles A. Doremus and Edgar Smith. Music by Emma R. Steiner. Entire production under the personal direction of Emma R. Steiner. Dances arranged by Rose Newham. Scenery by John H. Young. Costumes designed by Thomas McIlvaine. Orchestra under the direction of Emma R. Steiner. Management, F. M. McCloy. Opened 24 August 1891 at the Standard Theatre and closed 5 September 1891 after 14 performances.

CAST: *Fleurette*: MAMIE SCOTT. *The Duchess*: MARIE LOUISE DAY. *Victorine*: BÉBÉ VINING. *Madame Pumpernickel*: MARIE SANGER. *Fanchette*: ROSE NEWHAM. *Dinorah*: ROSE BEAUDET. *Mlle Duval*: Adelaide Banks. *Lady Cyrille*: Vesta Dora Hastings. *Mlle. Blanche*: Dorothy Bessinger. *Collordeau*: EDWARD M. FAVOR. *Marcel*, a count disguised as a student: EDWARD WEBB. *The Baron*, engaged to the Duchess: FRED BORNEMANN. *Caesar*, corporal of Home Guards: Thomas Guise. *Lucien, Edouard*, Students, friends of Marcel: Herr Borodkin, Gustavus Rival. *A Dude*: Harry Sherwood. *A Tough*: A. L. Lyons. *An Alsacian*: A. Hartberg. *Flower Girls, Citizens, Soldiers, Swells, etc.*

Flower Girls: Misses Williams, Linnette, Maher, Pauline Edwards, Florence Hastings, Gervaise, Hawthorne, Burns, Kelly, DuBois, Fairhurst, Morris. *Students*: Messrs. Kilduff, Bassi, Lyon, Rodeau, Von Buren, Van Houten, Reel, Williams, Blake, Riopelle, Loutrell, Brady.

The action takes place in a town in France.

Act 1: A Street near the Market Place.

Act 2: The Students' Ball.

MUSICAL NUMBERS

Eccentric Dance
R. Newham
"I'd Like to Be Somebody's Baby"
(*Lyrics by* Matt. C. Woodward.)

1891.22
INDIGO

A Spectacular Operetta in Three Acts, 4 Scenes[7]. Libretto ('Indigo und die vierzig Räuber') by Maximilian Steiner. American translation and adaptation by Max Freeman and Edgar Smith. Music by Johann Strauss. Scenery by John H. Young, Henry E. Hoyt and William J. Manz. Costumes by Mme. Loe and Assistants. Director of music, Gustave Kerker. Produced under the direction of Max Freeman. Produced by Rudolph Aronson. Opened 25 August 1891 at the Casino Theatre and closed 3 October 1891 after 41/50Aronson bio performances[8].

CAST: *Fantasca*: PAULINE L'ALLEMAND. *Toffana*: LOUISE BEAUDET. *Radamanta*: EVA DAVENPORT. *Banana*: Villa Knox. *Zuliema*: Madge Yorke. *Tutti Frutti*: Mabel Potter. *Marmalade*: Nettie Black. *Vanilla*: Bertie Florence. *Dodo*: Minnie Renwood. *Cada*: Carrie Boelen. *Indigo*: EDWIN STEVENS. *Janio*: FERDINAND SCHÜTZ. *Romadour*: HARRY MACDONOUGH. *Hanki-Panki*: MAX FIGMAN. *Arrabi Jabes*: A. W. Tams. *Falsetto*: William Conradi. *Soprano*: George Mackenzie. *Ali Baba*: JEFFERSON DEANGELIS. (*Eight Bajadères, Chorus*).

Act 1: Gardens in the Royal Harem. (Young.)

Act 2, Scene 1: The Ruins of Mosara. *Scene 2*: The Interior of the Caves of Forty Thieves. (Hoyt.)

Act 3: Slave Mart and Bazaar on the Indigonian Islands. (Manz.)

MUSICAL NUMBERS[9]

"The Gods with Old Jupiter"
P. L'Allemand, Bajadères, Chorus
"This Spray of Maiden Hair"
F. Schütz
"Every Day with My Big Donkey"
J. DeAngelis, Chorus
"I Put Mankind in But Two Classes" (Song and Chorus)
J. DeAngelis, Chorus
"Is This Enchanted Ground?"
P. L'Allemand, F. Schütz, H. Macdonough
"On Soft Banks of Flowers Reposing"
P. L'Allemand

1891.23
THE KHEDIVE

A Comic Opera in Three Acts, 4 Scenes. Written by Louis Blake, Harry B. Edwards and Miah Blake. Entire production under the management and personal direction of Harry B. Edwards. Costumer, Minnie Woodruff. Leader of the orchestra, Albert Krausse. Produced by the Imperial Opera Company. Opened 27 August 1891 at Niblo's Garden and closed 5 September 1891 after 12 performances.

CAST: *The Khedive (of Turkey)*: FERRIS HARTMAN. *Psamtick*, his private secretary: W. F. ROCHESTER. *Cyrus*, Commander of the Army: WALLACE MACRERY. *Ormoo*, his lieutenant: Joseph Durel. *The Sultan*: John J. Raffael. *Malta*, a high priest: Harry McDowell. *Luner See*, the Sultan's prime thinker: Himself. *Janina*: LOTTA GILMAN. *Mareeta*: Bettina Gerard. *Samarantha*: AUGUSTA ROCHE. *Sultan's Wives (4)*: *Haydee*: Rita Mann. *Sappho*: Ollie Walters. *Charmian*: Lilla Walcott. *Fadia*: Winnie Marshall. *Peasants, Villagers, Soldiers, Arabs, Wives*.

Act 1, Scene 1: The Khedive's Palace, exterior. Egyptian. *Scene 2*: The Khedive's Palace, Interior. Egyptian.

Act 2: An Oasis in the Desert. Egyptian.

Act 3: The Sultan's Palace, Garden of Roses. Turkish.

MUSICAL NUMBERS[10]

"Hail to Cyrus"
(*Music by* Louis Blake.)
Solo
W. Macrery
Buffo Waltz
(*Music by* Louis Blake.)
Tenor Solo ("My love will always be the same")
(*Music by* Louis Blake.)
Quartette ("Love is quite a serious matter!")
(*Music by* Miah Blake.)

[4]No credits in program for stage director, scenery or costume design.
[5]Billed as the Jolly German Dialect Comedian and Sweet Singer.
[6]All numbers, apart from Quartette, sung by Charles R. Gardner.
[7]English language premiere. Previously produced in New York in German 12 April 1875 at the Germania Theatre.

[8]Subsequently toured in a shortened two act form, preceded by Mascagni's opera 'Cavalleria Rusticana.'
[9]Musical numbers not listed in programs. List prepared from published piano vocal gems (William A. Pond & Co., New York, 1891).
[10]Musical numbers not listed in programs. List prepared from published piano selection (Philip Werlein, New Orleans, Louisiana, 1892), except last duet named in reviews.

Mezzo Solo ("Love divine")
(*Music by* Harry B. Edwards.)
Comic Song ("My Mem-ory-andum Book")
(*Music by* Miah Blake.)
Solo and Chorus ("Gentle maidens, do not fear us!")
(*Music by* Miah Blake.)
Soprano Solo ("Ask the Sphinx!")
(*Music by* Louis Blake.)
Chorus ("Gaily the bells are ringing")
(*Music by* Louis Blake.)
The Prayer. Solo and Chorus
(*Music by* Louis Blake.)
Scene between Sultan and Wives (My sweethearts all, good evening!)
J. J. Raffael, Wives
(*Music by* Louis Blake.)
"Thomas and Maria" (Cat Song)
(*Music by* Miah Blake.)
Grand March from "The Khedive"
(*Music by* Louis Blake.)
Duet (*Arranged by* P. F. Campiglio)(Act 3)
F. Hartman, A. Roche

1891.24

8 BELLS

A Nautical Pantomimic Comedy (Acrobatic Pantomime) in Three Acts, 4 Scenes[11]. Written and invented by John F. Byrne. (Based on the farce "To Paris and Back for £5" by J. Maddison Morton.) Music arranged by A. E. Herwig. Mechanical effects invented by John F. Byrne. Produced by Primrose & West's Comedy Company. Opened 7 September 1891 at the Union Square Theatre and closed 19 September 1891 after 16 performances; returned 21 November 1892 to the Grand Opera House and closed 26 November 1892 after an additional 9 performances.

CAST: *Charles Fitzgerald*, in love with Rose O'Connor: PERCY KINGSLEY. *Major O'Connor*, Retired Officer: C. F. HERBERT. *Lieuteant Spike* of the Royal Marines: George W. Kerr. *Grabb*, Detective of Scotland Yard: E. A. Kerr. *Mr. Bonné*, a French gentleman: Howard Powers. *Station Agent*, London and Northwestern Railway of England: TOM BROWNE. *Officer of Steamer "Havre"*: GEORGE MORTIMER. *Sammy Smuggs*, an old salt: J. D. McCabe. *Friends of Charles (4)*: *Harry Mainard*: K. A. Edwards. *Frank Golight*: M. D. Johnson. *Mr. Sothern*: Philip Howard. *Mr. Bowers*: K. W. Gregory. *Rose O'Connor*, the Major's Daughter: JESSIE VILLARS. *Friends of Rose (3)*: *Kate Florence*: Lizzie Hight. *Lucy Starlight*: Dora Branscombe. *Annie Gray*: Edith Hoyt. *Favette*, Bonné's Daughter: Hortense Dean. *Nancy*, servant to O'Connor: Mrs. HELENE BYRNE. *Tabatha*, Housekeeper to O'Connor: B. F. THOMAS.

The Bells: *Henry*, Servant to O'Connor: JOHN F. BYRNE. *Daniel McGozzle*, in love with the ladies but not with his name: JOHN F. BYRNE. *Mons. LeTour*, an artist: JOHN F. BYRNE. *John*, servant to O'Connor: JAMES BYRNE. *James*, Servant to O'Connor: MATTHEW BYRNE. *Fowler*, Servant at O'Connor's house: ANDREW BYRNE. *Waiter*, at the London Dock: ANDREW BYRNE. *Steward*, on board Steamer "*Havre*": ANDREW BYRNE. *Citizens, Travelers, etc.*

Act 1: Home of the O'Connors. By moonlight.

Act 2, Scene 1: The railway depot and steamship dock. *Scene 2*: Adjoining staterooms aboard the steamer "*Havre*".

Act 3: Safe on the French coast.

MUSICAL NUMBERS
Electric Quartette (Act 2)
Messrs. Powers, E. A. Kerr, McCabe, G. W. Kerr
The King of the Whistlers (Specialty)(Act 3)
T. Browne
"Blow, Blow, Softly Blow" (Nautical Song and Chorus)
(*Music by* Carl von Wegern. *Lyrics by* C. F. Herbert)

1891.25

REILLY AND THE 400

A Revival of the Comedy in Three Acts, 5 Scenes[12]. Play (and lyrics) by Edward Harrigan. Music by David Braham. Staged by Edward Harrigan. Scenery by D. Frank Dodge. Mechanical work by Robert J. Cutler. Electrical effects by John Whalen. Musical director, David Braham. Produced by Edward Harrigan. Opened 14 September 1891 at Harrigan's Theatre and closed 9 December 1891 after 100 performances. Re-opened 18 April 1892 at Harrigan's Theatre and closed 7 May 1892 after 24 additional performances. Total: 124 performances.

CAST: *Wiley Reilly*: EDWARD HARRIGAN. *Salvator Magnus*: JOHN WILD. *Lizzie Calhoun*: JOSEPH SPARKS. *Commodore Toby Tow*: JAMES RADCLIFFE. *Herman Schmeltz*: HARRY FISHER. *Jerome Jajjers*: George Merritt. *Ned Reilly*: HARRY DAVENPORT. *Percy Oggles*: Fred Peters. *Hippolite Duval*: Richard Quilter. *Valentine McClinchy*: Dan Burke. *Bessie Bowlow*: John Decker. *That's What*: James Burke. *Jimmy the Con*: William West. *Roundsman Moran*: James McCullough. *Iceman*: James Rennie. *Butcher*: Willis Pickert. *James McGouldrick*: John Walsh. *Dionysius Dorrigan*: Charles Sturges. *Slattery*: John Mayon. *Ignatius McCune*: Edward Gorman. *August Shutzer*: Joseph Williamson. *Fireman*: Joseph Healy. *Hyram Doolittle*: George Secor. *Emil Shutzer*: Master Tony. *Lavine Gale*: HATTIE MOORE. *Emiline Gale*: EVELYN POLLOCK. *Maggie Murphy*: EMMA POLLOCK. *Kittie Lynch*: ADA LEWIS. *Miss Murray Hill*: Emily Yeamans. *Miss Van Tassel*: FANNIE BATCHELDER. *Maryann Dooley*: ANNIE YEAMANS.

Guests: Daisy Andrews, Josie Knight, Margery Teel, Miss Thornton, Miss Buckley, Martha Franklin, Miss St. Clair.

1891.26

BOYS AND GIRLS

A Farce Comedy in Three Acts. Play by John J. McNally. Produced under the stage direction of Julian Mitchell. Produced by (Isaac B.) Rich & (William) Harris. Opened 21 September 1891 at the Park Theatre and closed 3 October 1891 after 16 performances.[13]

CAST: *Professor Theo. Sofi*: JOSEPH MITCHELL. *Arthur Sofi*, his son: IGNACIO MARTINETTI. *Mollie Fyer*, his niece: FLORA IRWIN. *Mme. Alert*: MAY IRWIN. *Frank Asnew*, her stepson: Frank Shepherd. *Lotta Goode*, her niece: Sadie Kirby. *Jacob Goldenfeld*: JAMES A. STURGIS. *Isaac Goldenfeld*, his son: William B. Wood. *Willie Liftwell*, a walking agent: Mr. Julian.[14] *May B. Wurz*: Blanche Howard. *Annie Howe*: Laura J. Russell. *Maida Coup*: Nellie Victoria Parker. *Bill Bolter*: JOSEPH MITCHELL. *Andrew Nales*: Harry Leopold. *Berry U. Dacent*: JAMES A. STURGIS. *Tom, Dick, Harry, Robinson, Smith*: THE LEOPOLD BROTHERS (John, Willie, Frederick, Joseph, Master Lewis)[15].

Act 1: Two adjacent back yards.

Act 2: A cheap restaurant.

Act 3: The backyards.

SPECIALTIES, MUSICAL NUMBERS
"Oh, What Difference in the Morning!" (At Night! At Night!)
M. Irwin
(*Music and Lyrics by* Norton Atkins. *Additional verses, and arranged by* Isidore Witmark.)
"Comrades"
(*Music and Lyrics by* Felix McGlennon.)
"Maggie Murphy's Home" (from *REILLY AND THE 400*)
(*Music by* David Braham. *Lyrics by* Edward Harrigan.)
Sabot Dance
M. Irwin
Song
S. Kirby

1891.27

THE CADI

A Comedy in Three Acts. Play by Bill Nye. Music by (David) Braham. Stage director, Charles T. Parsloe[16]. Scenery by (Arthur) Voegtlin. Mechancial effects by Raymond. (Musical director, David Braham.) Produced by Thomas Q. Seabrooke and Bill Nye Comedy Company. Opened 21 September 1891 at the Union Square Theatre and closed 19 December 1891 after 104 performances[17].

---

[11]For subsequent tour, the play was subtitled 'The Misfortunes of McGozzle.'
[12]First produced in New York 29 December 1890 at Harrigan's Theatre for 202 performances. For Synopsis of Scenes and Musical Numbers, see original 1890 production. For subsequent tour, "Taking in the Town" was replaced by:
"Take a Day Off, Mary Ann"

[13]Incomplete program did not include scenes, songs or specialties, the list of which was prepared from reviews. Re-opened in revised form as THE NEW BOYS AND GIRLS 22 February 1892 at the Park Theatre for 16 additional performances. See separate entry below.
[14]Most likely director Julian Mitchell.
[15]The Leopold Brothers did not appear in the return engagement.
[16]During the run, Adolph Bernard succeeded Parlsoe as billed stage director.
[17]Costumes and musical direction uncredited.

CAST: *The Cadi*, Frontier Editor, Postmaster, Justice of the Peace: THOMAS Q. SEABROOKE. *Lieutenant George Packenham*, Cavalry Officer, on detached service: EUGENE MOORE. *Silent Sage Hen*, late of the Siwash Tribe: R. J. Dustan. *Taylor Wellington*, wild young son of a good Irish family: Francis Neilson. *Hop Long*, Laundryman, Grub Staker, and an Amateur Burglar: CHARLES T. PARSLOE. *Arnold J. Constable*, an Officer of the Court: Jay Wilson. *Croupy Daggett*, Grammatical Boy, who knows more than he looks to: MINNIE DUPREE. *Arietta Kilgore*, Postmistress, Dressmaker and a Telegraph Operator: Lizzie Hudson Collier. *Dora Stanley*, a young English girl: Ruth Carpenter. *Helen French*, the Schoolmistress: JENNIE GOLDTHWAITE. *Miners, Cow Boys, and Unique Quartette.*

Act 1: Owl Creek, Wyoming. Court Room and Post Office. Morning.

Act 2: Owl Creek, Wyoming. Post Office and Court Room. Afternoon.

Act 3: New York City. Drawing-Room in the house of Percy B. S. Goble, Fifth Avenue.

MUSICAL NUMBERS, SPECIALTIES

"The Prodigal Son"
T. Q. Seabrooke
(*Music arranged* by Josephine Gro. *Lyrics by* Bill Nye.)

1891.28

MAVOURNEEN

A Comedy Drama in Four Acts, 7 Scenes. Play by George H. Jessop and Horace Townsend. Songs by William J. Scanlan. Entire production under the personal supervision of Augustus Pitou. Settings by Homer F. Emens, H. L. Reid, John H. Young. Costumes designed by H. A. Ogden. Original dramatic music by George Loesch. Minuette and Irish Reel arranged by Luke Martin. Musical director, George Loesch. Produced by Augustus Pitou. Opened 28 September 1891 at the 14th Street Theater and closed 25 December 1891 after 104 performances.

CAST: *Terence Dwyer*: WILLIAM J. SCANLAN. *John Dwyer*: FRANK BURBECK. *Captain Marchmont*: Frazer Coulter. *Abbe Maloney*: Charles M. Collins. *Mark*: John Findlay. *Shamus Corrigan*: Thaddeus Shine. *Colonel*: Frank Peters. *Cusack*: J. O. LeBrasse. *Club Porter*: George Orth. *Lady Caroline Dwyer*: Helen Tracey. *Lady May Tyrrell*: Nanette Comstock. *Mrs. Dwyer*: Emma Maddern Stevens. *Kate Morris*: GRACE THORNE. *Helen Dwyer*: Tiny Burton. *Georgie Dwyer*: Little DOT CLARENDON. *Susie Morris*: Ray Maskell. *Kitty Morris*: Little Dot Clarendon. *Peasants, Guests, Officers, Chair-Bearers and Link-Boys.*

The play is set in Ireland from 1774 to 1784.

Act 1, Scene 1: The Dwyer homestead in Innishshannon. (Emens.) *Scene 2*: An old ruin in the Dunn Mountains (Emens.)

Act 2: John Dwyer's home in Dublin. (Reid.)

Act 3, Scene 1: Daly's club-house and the Parliament building. Ten years later. (Young.) *Scene 2*: A Street in Dublin. (Young.) *Scene 3*: Kate Morris' poor home. (Reid.)

Act 4: John Dwyer's home in Dublin. (Reid.)

MUSICAL NUMBERS

"(Plain) Molly O!"
(W. J. Scanlan)

"Mrs. Reilly's Party"
(W. J. Scanlan)

"(Story of) The Auld Countrie"
(W. J. Scanlan)

"Bye-bye, Baby, Bye-bye"
(W. J. Scanlan)

"The (Little) Christmas Tree"
(W. J. Scanlan)

"(My) Mavourneen"
(W. J. Scanlan)
(*Lyrics by* Bartley Campbell.)

1891.29

ROBIN HOOD

A Comic Opera in Three Acts. Libretto by Harry B. Smith. Music by Reginald DeKoven. Produced under the stage direction of Jerome Sykes. Dances by Signor Romeo. Scenery by Ernest Albert. Costumes designed by Catherine F. Seidle. Orchestra under the direction of Samuel L. Studley. Produced by the Bostonians (Tom Karl, W. H. MacDonald, Henry Clay Barnabee, Managers and Proprietors). Opened 28 September 1891 at the Standard Theatre and closed 31 October 1891 after 35 performances; re-opened 16 May 1892 at the Garden Theatre and closed 25 June 1892 after 42 performances. Total: 77 performances.

CAST: *Robert of Huntington*, afterwards Robin Hood: TOM KARL, Edwin W. Hoff (alt.). *Sheriff of Nottingham*: HENRY CLAY BARNABEE. *Outlaws (4)*: *Little John*: W. H. MacDONALD. *Will Scarlet*: EUGENE COWLES. *Friar Tuck*: GEORGE FROTHINGHAM. *Alan-a-Dale*: JESSIE BARTLETT DAVIS, Flora Finlayson (alt.). *Sir Guy of Gisborne*, Ward of the Sheriff: PETER LANG. *Lady Marian Fitzwalter*, a ward of the Crown, afterwards Maid Marian: CAROLINE HAMILTON, Lea Van Dyke (alt.). *Dame Durden*, a widow: JOSEPHINE BARTLETT. *Annabel*, her daughter: LEA VAN DYKE, Maud Ulmer (alt.). *Villagers, Milkmaids, Outlaws, King's Foresters, Archers, Pedlars, etc.*

The action takes place in England at the time of Richard I.

Act 1: Market Square, Nottingham.

Act 2: Sherwood Forest.

Act 3: Courtyard of the Sheriff's house in Nottingham.

ACT 1

Introduction and Opening Chorus
J. B. Davis, W. H. MacDonald, E. Cowles, L. Van Dyke, Chorus

"Auctioneer's Song"
L. Van Dyke, J. B. Davis, W. H. MacDonald, E. Cowles, G. Frothingham, Chorus

"Milkmaids' Song"
L Van Dyke, J. B. Davis, Milkmaids

Entrance of Robin Hood ("Come the Bowmen in Lincoln Green")
L. Van Dyke, J. Bartlett, J. B. Davis, T. Karl, Archers, Milkmaids, Chorus

"I Came as a Cavalier"
C. Hamilton

Duet ("Come Dream So Bright")
C. Hamilton, T. Karl

Song ("I Am the Sheriff of Nottingham")
P. Lang, H. C. Barnabee, Chorus

Trio (When a peer makes love to a damsel fair. .)
H. C. Barnabee, P. Lang, C. Hamilton

Finale
Principals, Chorus

ACT 2

Opening Chorus (Oh cheerily soundeth the hunter's horn)
J. B. Davis, W. H. MacDonald, E. Cowles

"(Song of) Brown October Ale"
W. H. MacDonald, Male Chorus

"Oh, Promise Me"
J. B. Davis
(*Lyrics by* Clement Scott.)

"The Tinkers' Song"
P. Lang, H. C. Barnabee, Tinkers

Sextette, Round and Scene (Oh, see the lambkins play)
T. Karl, P. Lang, H. C. Barnabee, W. H. MacDonald, G. Frothingham, E. Cowles

"Forest Song" (Ye Birds in Azure Winging)
C. Hamilton

Serenade, Duet and Scene
T. Karl, C. Hamilton, J. B. Davis, E. Cowles

Finale
Principals, Chorus

ACT 3

"The Armorer's Song"
E. Cowles

"When a Maiden Weds" (Song)
L. Van Dyke

"The Legend of the Chimes" (Song)
J. B. Davis, Chorus

Duet ("Love, Now We Nevermore Will Part")
C. Hamilton, T. Karl

Quintette (When life seems made of pains and pangs)
L. Van Dyke, J. Bartlett, P. Lang, H. C. Barnabee, G. Frothingham

Country Dance
Chorus

Finale
Principals, Chorus

1891.30

THE TYROLEAN

A Comic Opera in Two Acts. Original (Viennese) libretto[18] "Der Vogelhändler" by Ludwig Held and Moritz West. American adaptation by Helen F. Tretbar. Music by Carl Zeller. Produced under the stage direction of Heinrich Conried. Scenery by Henry E. Hoyt. Costumes by Mme. Loe. Director of music, Gustave Kerker. Produced by Rudolf Aronson. Opened 5 October 1891 at the Casino Theatre and closed 9 January 1892 after 100 performances; returned 11-13 February 1892 to the Casino Theatre for 3 additional performances.[19] Total: 103 performances.

CAST: *Adam*, a bird dealer: MARIE TEMPEST. *Christel*, Postmistress: ANNIE MEYERS. *Princess Marie*: ANNA MANTELL. *Countess Adelaide*: Jennie Reiffarth. *Countess Minnie*: Carrie Boelen. *Hennie*, a waitress: Eva Johns. *Toni, Sopp*, Tyroleans: Madge Yorke, Bertie Florence. *Guinea*, Courtier: Drew Donaldson. *Baron Weps*: FREDERIC SOLOMON. *Count Stanislaus*: RICHIE LING. *Bailiff*: Henri Leoni. *Worm, Tipple*, Professors: HARRY MACDONOUGH, JEFFERSON DEANGELIS. *The Tyrolean Quartet*: Pepi Ramersdorf (Soprano), Nandl Hofe (Alto), Anton Reiner (Tenor), Carl Hofer (Basso).

The action takes place in a Village on the Rhine in the Tyrol in 1800.

Act 1: At the Hunting Pavilion.

Act 2: In the Palace of the Prince.

MUSICAL NUMBERS[20]

"Nightingale Song"[21] (When my sire was twenty years)
M. Tempest

"I am Little Christel"
A. Meyers

1891.31

THE MERRY MONARCH

A Return Engagement of the Operetta in Three Acts[22]. Original French libretto 'L'Etoile'[23] [The Star of Fate] by Eugène Leterrier and Albert Vanloo. American adaptation by J. Cheever Goodwin. Music by Woolson Morse. Originally produced under the stage direction of Richard Barker. Ballet master, Professor Mamert Bibeyran. Scenery by Homer F. Emens, Henry E. Hoyt and T. S. Plaisted. Costumes designed by Percy Anderson. Orchestra under the direction of Signor Antonio DeNovellis. Orchestration by John Philip Sousa. Produced by Francis Wilson and Company. Opened 5 October 1891 at the Broadway Theatre and closed 26 December 1891 after 84 performances.

CAST: *King Anso IV*, the Merry Monarch: FRANCIS WILSON. *Sirocco*, the Royal Astrologer: CHARLES PLUNKETT. *Herrison*, Ambassador Extraordinary, etc. GILBERT CLAYTON. *Kedas*, Minister of Police: FRED LENNOX. *Tapioca*, Private Secretary to Herrison: WILIIAM STEIGER. *High Chamberlain*: B. F. Joslyn. *Possamus, Hocacus*, Royal train-bearers: John Coleman, Jesse Henderson. *Lilita*, Princess Royal, betrothed to King Anso: LAURA MOORE. *Aloes*, Maid-in-waiting to the Princess: NETTIE LYFORD. *Oasis*, first maid of honor: CECILE EISSING. *Idra*, second Maid of Honor: Belle Hartz. *Lazuli*, a traveling peddler of parfumery: MARIE JANSEN. *Dignitaries, Civilians, Amazon Guards, Ladies of the Court, Dancing Girls and Pages, etc.*

1891.32

TUXEDO

A Musical Farce in Two Acts. Book, music and lyrics by Ed Marble. Staged by Julian Mitchell. Musical director, Frederick Gagel. Produced by George Thatcher's Minstrels, allied with (Isaac B.) Rich & (William) Harris's Comedy Company (Henry J. Sayers, Manager). Opened 5 October 1891 at the New Park Theatre and closed 31 October 1891 after 32 performances. Re-opened 7 March 1892 at the Park Theatre and closed 19 March 1892 after an additional 16 performances. Total: 48 performances.[24]

CAST: *Sidney Vincent*, history unknown: RAYMON MOORE. *Gregory Gabble*, a retired auctioneer, twice married: ED MARBLE. *Jackson Park*, a typical Chicago man: EUGENE O'ROURKE. *Lord Chulmondley Charingcross*, pedigree: JOHN A. COLEMAN. *Red McGee, Plunkett T. Plunkett*, Song and Dance artists: HUGHEY DOUGHERTY, C. EDGAR FOREMAN. *Cy Wilcox* from Pigeon Centre, New Jersey, with impediment: H. W. Frillman. *Zeb Wattles*, Mildred's uncle, similarly afflicted (Slim Jim): George W. Dukelan. *Michael*, the butler: Andrew J. Powers. *John*, the footman: James H. Powers. *James*, a coachman: William J. Powers. *Mildred*, the auctioneer's daughter: IRENE MURPHY. *Mrs. Gregory Gabble*, No. 2, Mildred's very obliging mama: Agnes Hallock. *Thisbee Euydice Pemberson*, from Boston, a devotee of "Browning": IDA FITZHUGH. *Sadie Newett*, one of the Four Hundred: Blanche Hayden. *Lillie Sawett*, her chum: Grace Hamilton. *Fannie*, the usual necessary French maid: Mamie Gilroy. *George Thatcher*: GEORGE THATCHER. (*Specialties*: TOM LEWIS, RICHARD J. JOSE, GEORGE W. LEWIS.)

Jesters: George Thatcher, Hughey Dougherty, George Lewis, Andrew J. Powers, William J. Powers, James H. Powers. *Questers*: Ed Marble, Eugene O'Rourke, H. W. Frillman.

Act 1: The Gabble Villa at Tuxedo.

Act 2: George Thatcher's Minstrels. On the lawn at Tuxedo, for Sweet Charity's Sake.

ACT 1

"You and I" (Ballad)
R. Moore
(*Music and Lyrics by* Raymon Moore.)

"Cupid" (Song and Dance)
J. A. Coleman, M. Gilroy

General Potpourri
Introduction, Robin Hood
Ensemble
"They Notice It So, You Know"
J. A. Coleman
"She Married a Minstrel"[25]
A. Hallock, Chorus
"Chicago's Great World's Fair"
E. O'Rourke, Company
"Come Down, Mrs. Flynn"
H. Dougherty, C. E. Foreman, Chorus
"The Charmer"[26]
I. Fitzhugh
"Cavalleria Rusticana"
T. Lewis, Chorus
"Tuxedo Girls" ("Ta-ra-ra-Boom-de-ré")
Girls
(*Music and Lyrics by* Henry J. Sayers.)

The Soul-Stirring Drama, The Fatal Cabinet, or The Mad Lover's Revenge, with a Blood-Curtling Denouement.

ACT 2[27]

George Thatcher's Minstrels

---

[18]Literally "The Bird-Seller." Based on the French comedy "Ce qui deviennent les roses" by Charles Varin and de Biéville.

[19]Performed with the opera "Cavalleria Rusticana" by Pietro Mascagni as a curtain-raiser until 5 December 1891

[20]Musican numbers not listed in programs; no libretto or vocal score found for this adaptation.

[21]A rival version of the Nightingale Song with lyrics by Grace Carleton was also published, claiming to have been sung by Marie Tempest. Another version with lyrics by George Cooper was also published.

[22]First produced in New York 18 August 1890 at the Broadway Theatre for 49 performances. For Synopsis of Scenes and Musical Numbers, see original 1890 production.

[23]Original French score by Emmanuel Chabrier discarded.

[24]No credits in programs for costumes or scenery.

[25]Dropped for subsequent tour.

[26]Replaced for subsequent tour by:
The Pirates of Penzance (Selection)
I. Fitzhugh
(*Music by* Arthur Sullivan. *Lyrics by* William S. Gilbert.)

[27]For subsequent tour, "The Picture That Is Turned to the Wall," "No Room for Me," "The Modern Beau Brummel," and "Baby's Asleep, Cradle's Gone" were dropped and replaced by:
"Tied to Mother's Apron Strings"
R. Moore
"Comical Ditty"
H. Dougherty
"The Lone Grace"
R. J. Jose

Additional interpolations during the run or on tour, as per published sheet music:
"Can't-Yer-Koon-Jine?"
(*Music arranged by* Adam Itzel. *Lyrics by* Edward Marble.)
"Grace Conroy"
R. Moore
(*Music and Lyrics by* Michael Nolan.)
"In May"
R. Moore
(*Music and Lyrics by* Edwin M. Stern.)
"Katie and Tom, or, Love's Helping Hand"
R. Moore
(*Music and Lyrics by* Henry J. Sayers.)

Quartette (Selected)
R. J. Jose, R. Moore, T. Lewis, H. W. Frillman
Advent of George Thatcher and Hughey Dougherty
"Mistakes Are Apt to Happen"
G. Thatcher
"The Bell Buoy"
H. W. Frillman
"The Picture That Is Turned to the Wall"
R. Moore
(*Music and Lyrics by* Charles Graham.)
"No Room for Me"
H. Dougherty
"The Modern Beau Brummel"
J. A. Coleman
"Baby's Asleep, (Cradle's Gone)"
R. J. Jose
Terminating with Presidential Possibilities
President Benjamin Harrison: H. Dougherty. *Hon. Grover Cleveland*: C. E. Foreman.
Stemming the tide. Telephone communications.
George Thatcher's Famous Monologue
The Story of Faust and Marguerite
(Composed and produced under the personal direction of George W. Lewis.) *The Fausts*: The Powers Brothers. *The Marguerites*: Misses Gilroy, Hayden, Hamilton. *Mephistopheles*: G. W. Lewis.
Parade of the Minstrels: Homeward Bound (A Farewell Greeting to Old Favorites and New Friends)

1891.33 THE DWARF'S WEDDING AT THE COURT OF PETER THE GREAT

The Lilliputians in a Musical Comedy (Operetta)[Die Zwergenhochzeit] in Four Acts, in German and English. Libretto by Hans Gross. Music by Emil Christiani and Victor Holländer. Arranged by director, Carl Rosenfeld. Master of ballet, Mr. Leoni. Scenery painted by F. Komlossy. Costumes by Sophie Klein, Berlin; Mr. Rotter, Hamburg. Leader of the orchestra, Emil Christiani. Produced by Carl and Theodor Rosenfeld. Opened 6 October 1891 at the Thalia Theatre and closed 7 November 1891 after 40 performances[28].

CAST: THE LILLIPUTIANS: *The Czar*: Mr. Durand. *The Bishop*: Mr. Cotta. *The Master of Police*: Mr. Wilke. *The Master of the Palace*: Mr. Bechtel. *Illuscha*, General Advisor and Plenipotentiary of the Emperor: SELMA GOERNER. *Don Lopez de Santiganos*, the Emperor's favorite: JOHN WOLF. *Eulalia*, his wife: Mrs. Tietze. *Anna, Clara*, their daughters: MINCHEN BECKER, BERTHA JAEGER. *Bogdanoff*, supervisor in the Goldmines: Mr. Dittebrandt. *Hessely*, a young free colonist: MAX WALTER. *Popoff*, a slave: Mr. Kahn. *Children of Popoff (5)*: *Sonja*: IDA MAHR. *Ivan*: TONI MEISTER. *Ossip*: HERMAN RING. *Alexei*: ADOLF ZINK. *Peter*: FRANZ EBERT. *First Chamberlain*: Mr. Wichert. *Second Chamberlain*: Mr. Lueck. *The Courier of the Court*: Mr. Brand. *First Watchman*: Mr. Steinmann. *First Man*: Mr. Albert. *First Woman*: Miss Schlueter. *The Assistant Supervisor*: Mr. Reimer. *First Pandur*: Mr. Ferenz. *First Crier*: Mr. Koch. *Amazons, Soldiers, Priests, Ladies and Gentlemen of the Court, Slaves.*

Act 1: In the Goldmines of Siberia.

Act 2: The Engagement in the Emperor's Palace.

Act 3: The Life for the Czar.

Act 4: Recalled to Life.

SPECIALTIES
March of the Amazons (Act 1)
Russian National Dance (Act 2)
Duo Dance
F. Ebert, A. Zink

1891.34 BEAUTIFUL STARS

A Spectacular Romance in Four Acts and a Prologue, 16 Scenes. Libretto by William H. Day. Music by Charles Puerner. Staged by William H. Day, John B. Day. Entire production, scenery, costumes, properties and effects designed by William H. Day and John B. Day. Ballets composed and produced under the direction of Prof. Mamert Bibeyran. Opened 12 October 1891 at Niblo's Garden and closed 17 October 1891 after 8 performances.

CAST of Prologue: *The King*: TULLY MARSHALL. *Queen Blondine*: HORTENSE VAN ZILE. *Children* of the King: The Babes. *Nephew* of Queen Blondine: Stella Livingstone. *The Dowager Queen*: KATHERINE M. PIKE. *Feintise*, her waiting maid: Cecile Rush. *Rousette*, Sister to Queen Blondine: IDA RUSH. *A Fairy Queen*: NINA FARRINGTON. *Corsair*, a wicked but soft-hearted pirate: HARRY C. STANLEY. *Corsine*, thinks her husband is wicked, and to please him, is wicked herself: MADGE CARR. *First Pirate*: Daniel Chandon. *Officers, Heralds, Pirates, etc. etc.*

CAST of the Play: *Princess Belle Etoile*: RUTH MATTHIESSEN. *Cheri*: John Malone. *Petit Soleil, Herreaux*, Twin brothers of Belle Etoile: Guenn Coye, Jean Coye. *The King*: TULLY MARSHALL. *Queen Blondine*: HORTENSE VAN ZILE. *The Dowager Queen*: KATHERINE M. PIKE. *Feintise*, her waiting maid: Cecile Rush. *Rousette*, Sister to Queen Blondine: IDA RUSH. *A Fairy Queen*: NINA FARRINGTON. *An Officer*: Edith Carss. *Corsair*, reformed, but wicked: HARRY C. STANLEY. *Corsine*, thinks Corsair reformed, but fears he is growing miserly: MADGE CARR. *The Captain*: Daniel Chandon. *Officers, Retainers, Noblemen, Soldiers, Servants, Reformed Pirates, Guests, Fairies, Imps, Sailors, etc, etc.*

Prologue, Scene 1: A Castle by the Sea. *Scene 2*: The Open Sea. *Scene 3*: The Pirates' Lair.

Act 1: Corsair Home. Seventeen years later.

Act 2, Scene 1: Palace Grounds overlooking the Beautiful City. *Scene 2*: Corridor of the Palace. *Scene 3*: A Room within the Palace. *Scene 4*: The Home of the Fairies of the Rose.

Act 3, Scene 1: The Luminous Forest. *Scene 2*: The Palace Grounds. *Scene 3*: The Rocky Cavern. *Scene 4*: The Palace Grounds. *Scene 5*: A Mountain Top. *Scene 6*: The Palace of Enchantment.

Act 4, Scene 1: The Audience Chamber. *Scene 2*: The Grand Salon.

ACT 2
Scene 1
The Review of the King's Body Guards
Scene 3
Love Conquers All (Grand Ballet)

ACT 3
Scene 1
The Fairies of the Rabbit Warren (Ballet)
Scene 3
Ballet of the Imps of the Dragon
Scene 6
Ballet of the Birds of Enchantment

ACT 4
Scene 2
The Procession of the Feast
The Bridesmaids' Dance
The Vision—Beautiful Star

1891.35 CARMEN UP TOO LATE, or, The Bold Toreador

A Burlesque in One Act, accompanied by a Vaudeville Bill. Libretto by Fred Solomon. Director of music, William J. Rostetter. Produced by (John) Koster & (Albert) Bial. Opened 19 October 1891 at Koster and Bial's Concert Hall and closed 2 January 1892 after 100 performances.

CAST: *Carmen*: MADGE LESSING. *Alphonse*: JOSIE GREGORY. *Captain Zuniga*: GUS BRUNO. *Michaila*: Dolly Clark. *Frasquita*: Vera Bedell. *Castanetta*: Allie Vivian. *Inez*: May Shannon. *Escamillo*, the Toreador: JENNIE JOYCE. *Cigarette girls and boys, Soldiers, etc.*

Incidental to the Burlesque, Spanish Ballet by the Lelia Rossi Ballet Troupe: Sequedille, Habanera, Bolero, Cachucha, Zapateato.

1891.36 LA CIGALE

An Opéra Comique in Three Acts. Original French libretto[29] (La Cigale et la Fourmi) by Henri Chivot and Alfred Duru. English adaptation by F. C.

[28]Played a subsequent New York area engagement 23 November 1891 at the Harlem Opera House for 8 performances.

[29]Suggested by La Fontaine's fable of The Grasshopper and the Ant.

Burnand[30]. Music by Edmond Audran. Additional music by Ivan Caryll. Produced under the stage direction of Richard Barker. Scenery by Henry Hoyt, Benson Sherwood, Harley Merry, W. C. Smock. Musical director, Jesse Williams. Produced by Lillian Russell Opera Comique Company (T. Henry French, Proprietor and Manager). Opened 26 October 1891 at the Garden Theatre and closed 13 February 1892 after 112 performances.

CAST: *Marton* (The Grasshopper, La Cigale): LILLIAN RUSSELL. *Chevalier Franz de Bernheim*: CARL STREITMANN. *William*: ARTHUR RYLEY. *Vincent Knapps*: G. TAGLIAPIETRA. *Duke of Fayensberg*: CHARLES DUNGAN. *The Cavalier*: Charles Alexander. *Curfew Watch*: J. Dore. *Mendicant*: James G. Peakes. *Matthew Vanderkoopen*, Landlord of the Golden Lamb, Bruges; Uncle to Marton and Charlotte: LOUIS HARRISON. *Charlotte* (The Ant, La Fourmi): ATTALIE CLAIRE. *Rosina*: Sylvia Thorne. *Dancers at the Opera* (6): *Marietta*: Lena Lorraine. *Juliette Grisenbach*: M. McGill. *Alizia*: Ray Allen. *Zitanella*: Florence Franton. *Tamburina*: Florence Carlisle. *Cecilia*: Nellie Weston. *Francoise*: Cecelia Curtis. *Leila*: Fernande Auber. *La Frivolini*: Ethel Ross-Selwick. *Camille Dubarri*: Fanny Johnston. *Catherine*: Marion Welles. *Duchess of Fayensberg*: Suzanne Leonard. *Marina*: Mabel Potter.

Peasants, Courtiers, Wedding Guests: Misses Louise Auber, Maude Manning, René Ferrers, Hetta Baudet, Annie Seaberry, Emily Lisle, Rose James, Jessie Fahnestock, Louise Clarke, Georgia Bell, Teckla Morton, Estelle Allen, Lucy Williams, Dora Scott, Helen Rutledge, Adele Doré, Ione Dunham, Vera Thorpe, Beatrice Tiffany, Martha Habelman. Messrs. C. Atwood, W. Gervais, A. Bassi, H. K. Clarke, E. Ellyson, W. I. Henshaw, George Palmer, Charles Roux, B. F. Vail, William Scholz, Dean Dora, W. R. Benham, George Lawrence, Pelham Morton, Otto Heilig, Charles Griffin.

Act 1: The Old Home (near Bruges). (Hoyt, Sherwood.)

Act 2: Fair and Market Place at Bruges, one year later. (Merry, Smock.)

Act 3: Interior of the Ducal Palace. (Hoyt, Sherwood.)

ACT 1[31]

"The weddings' done, these two are one" (Opening Chorus)
(*Lyrics by* Gilbert à Beckett.)

"Hey boys! gay boys, shout hurrah!) Children's Chorus
(*Music by* Ivan Caryll.)

"The Golden Harvester" (Song)
A. Claire
(*Lyrics by* Gilbert à Beckett.)

Quartet (Strings)
(*Music by* Ivan Caryll.)

"The Merry Cricket" (Song)
L. Russell
(*Lyrics by* F. C. Burnand and Gilbert à Beckett.)

"The Bashful Suitor" (Duet)
L. Russell, G. Tagliapietra

"Bird Voices" (Song)
G. Tagliapietra

"Tragedy and Comedy" (Song)
L. Russell
(*Lyrics by* Gilbert à Beckett.)

"Too Late"
C. Streitman
(*Music by* Ivan Caryll.)

"Picnic" (At a picnic we are so jolly)(Chorus)

"Dance and Sing!" (Chorus and Dance)
(*Music by* Ivan Caryll.)

"One Day Margot, or Three to One" (Song)
L. Russell

Finale: "Farewell"
(*Music by* Edmund Audran and Ivan Caryll.)

"La Gloria"
L. Russell, A. Claire, C. Streitman, L. Harrison, G. Tagliapietra, A. Ryley, Chorus
(*Music by* Ivan Caryll.)

ACT 2

"Bells for our fête are ringing" (Market Chorus)
(*Lyrics by* Gilbert à Beckett.)

"Trifle Not with Love" (Song)
C. Streitman
(*Music by* Ivan Caryll.)

"Hearts are full of joy and gladness" (Concerted Piece)
L. Russell, C. Dungan, Chorus
(*Lyrics by* Gilbert à Beckett.)

"Mother Dear" (Gavotte Song)
L. Russell
(*Lyrics by* Gilbert à Beckett.)

"Petit Noël" (Duet)
L. Russell, A. Claire
(*Lyrics by* Gilbert à Beckett.)

"Too little foresight you are showing" (Quartett)
L. Russell, A. Claire, G. Tagliapietra, A. Ryley
(*Lyrics by* Gilbert à Beckett.)

"Doubt Not" (Duet)
L. Russell, C. Streitman
(*Lyrics by* Gilbert à Beckett.)

"Excuse me, La Diva, for I pray" (Trio)
L. Russell, C. Streitman, C. Dungan
(*Music by* Ivan Caryll.)

Finale (Early the fête, the children wait)
L. Russell, A. Claire, G. Tagliapietra, A. Ryley, L. Harrison
(*Music by* Ivan Caryll.)

ACT 3

"Dance and let all in these halls be gay" (Passepied)
(*Music by* Ivan Caryll.)

Gavotte
(*Music by* Lila Clay.)

"List to me" (Song)
C. Streitman

"The Grasshopper and the Butterfly" (Concerted Piece and Song)
L. Russell, A. Claire, C. Streitman, A. Ryley, L. Harrison
(*Lyrics by* Gilbert à Beckett.)

"My dear old home of bygone years" (Dream)
(*Music by* Edmund Audran and Ivan Caryll.)

"Santa Claus" (Chorus)
(*Music by* Ivan Caryll.)

Finale (Oh, day of joy of summer bloom)

INTERPOLATIONS[32]

"A Summer Song"
L. Russell
(*Music by* T. Pearsall Thorne. *Lyrics by* Gilbert Burgess.)

"Golden Dream" (Gavotte)
L. Russell
(*Music by* Jesse Williams. *Lyrics by* J. Cheever Goodwin.)

1891.37 HOSS AND HOSS

The Funniest of all Farcical Entertainments (a Farce Comedy) in Three Acts. Play by the company (Charlie Reed, William Collier). (Original songs and music by Frank Pallma, Charlie Reed, William Collier, Arthur E. Moulton, J. Sherrie Mathews and Harry Bulger, others.) Musical director, ?. Produced by W. G. Smythe. Opened 2 November 1891 at the Park Theatre and closed 28 November 1891 after 32 performances.[33]

CAST: *Lawyer Charlie Hoss*, one of the best lawyers in his office: CHARLIE REED. *Judge Willis Hoss*, who owns the bench: WILLIE COLLIER. *Birdie Hoss*, the Judge's son: Arthur Moulton. *Hank Thanks*, the Sheriff, don't bother him: James E. Gentry. *Jack Rose*, a daisy: M. L. Herbert. *Henry Chalk*, a Milkman: Thomas D. Daly. *Wilfred Chops*, a Butcher: J. R. Murchie. *Graham Bread*, a Baker: J. C. Cheviot. *Dedric Heat*, an Iceman: Frank Conway. *Bill Bowser*, from Sioux City: Daniel Brasill. *Messenger*: Joseph McGuire. *Sybil Cerves*, the cause of the trouble: LOUISE ALLEN. *Celia Cliquot*, "La Belle France": MAY A. YOHE. *Sue Brette*, Birdie's "Best": Rosa France. *Charlotte Russe*, a Wild Flower: Adele Farrington. *Mrs. Lobelia Hoss*, the Judge's wife: HELEN REIMER. *Polly Hoss, Hobby Hoss*, the Judge's daughters: Clara Lamont, Helena Collier. *Annie Rooney*, "Did you ring sir?": LILLIAN RAMSDEN. *Jurors, Musicians, Undertakers, and other waiters.*

---

[30]In a program note, Burnand (as librettist) graciously thanks Mr. Gilbert à Beckett for his assistance in setting new words to old music. The published score credits Gilbert à Beckett with lyrics and concerted pieces.

[31]Musical numbers not listed in programs. List prepared from published English piano vocal score (Hopwood & Crew, Ltd., London 1890), which may not reflect alterations and interpolations for the American production. List of interpolations prepared from published sheet music, reviews, etc.

[32]Musical numbers not listed in programs; list prepared from published vocal selection (Audran, Caryll) and interpolations from published sheet music.

[33]No credits in programs for scenery, costumes or musical director.

Act 1: The Judge's Home, Saugerties, New York.

Act 2: The Country Court. The Lawyer and the Judge.

Act 3: "Café Hoss and Hoss," New York.

MUSICAL NUMBERS

"The Nightingale" (from *THE TYROLEAN*)
M. Yohe
(*Music by* Carl Zeller.)

"Annie Laurie"

"Take a Day Off, Mary Ann" (from *THE LAST OF THE HOGANS*)
L. Ramsden
(*Music by* David Braham. *Lyrics by* Edward Harrigan.)

Quartet from *RIGOLETTO*
(*Music by* Giuseppe Verdi.)

Kangaroo Dance

Travesty Burlesque of Spanish dancing à la Carmencita

1891.38

MISS HELYETT

An Operatic Comedy in Three Acts. Original French libretto by Maxime Boucheron. Arranged and re-written by David Belasco[34]. Music by Edmond Audran. Lyrics by Fred Lyster. Under the direction of E. D. Price; produced under the personal direction of David Belasco. Dances arranged by Professor Mamert Bibeyran. Scenes painted by Edward G. Unitt. Costumes designed by Captain Alfred Thompson. Director of music, William Furst. Produced by Charles Frohman[35]. Opened 3 November 1891 at the Star Theatre, moved 11 January 1892 to the Standard Theatre and closed 13 February 1892 after 116 performances.

CAST: *Paul Grahame*, a young American artist who has studied in Paris and Italy: MARK SMITH. *Todder Bunnythorne*, too rich to think: M. A. Kennedy. *Obadiah Smithson*, a Quaker: HARRY HARWOOD. *Admiral Terence O'Shaughnessy* of the "Cork Naval Reserve": GEORGE W. TRAVERNER. *Jacques Baccarel*, a French artist, friend of Paul: J. W. Herbert. *Max Culmbacher*, taking a holiday abroad: N. S. Burnham. *Mr. Mac Gilly* on his wedding tour: Edgar [Atchison] Ely. *Professor Bonnefoy*, a dancing master from Paris: Gilbert Sarony. *La Señora Carmen Rimbomba Della Torquemada*, Spanish to the backbone: KATE DAVIS. *Manuela*, her daughter: LAURA CLEMENT. *Mrs. Max Culmbacher*, on her eleventh trip abroad: Adelaide Emerson. *Mrs. McGilly*, a bride of sixteen: Lillian Elmore. *La Stella*, premiere danseuse assoluta from the Eden Theatre, Paris: Henrietta Rich. *Pascal, Carlos*, guides: Lotta Nicol, Mollie Sherwood. *Doing the Grand Tour (7)*: *Molly*: Nina Lejeune. *Polly*: Juno Burbank. *Dolly*: Grace Wallace. *Rolly*: Rollie Parkin. *Milly*: Beatrice Tait. *Tilly*: Aida Courtney. *Nelly*: Nannie Morse. *Miss Helyett*, Daughter of Smithson, born in Verity Village, Pennsylvania: MRS. LOUISE LESLIE CARTER.

The action takes place at the Hotel del Norte, on the Spanish slope of the Pyrenées at the present time.

Act 1: The Adventure of a Young Quakeress. Afternoon.

Act 2: In search of "The Man of the Mountain." The next evening.

Act 3: The Real and the Ideal. The following day.

ACT 1

"Ta-ra-ra Boom-de-ay!"[36]
(*Music by* Henry J. Sayers.)

ACT 2

ACT 3

1891.39

A TRIP TO CHINATOWN

Idyll of San Francisco (Farce Comedy or Musical Trifle) in Three Acts. Book and lyrics by Charles H. Hoyt. Music composed and arranged by Percy Gaunt. Staged by Julian Mitchell. Musical director, Percy Gaunt. Produced by Charles H. Hoyt and Charles H. Thomas. Opened 9 November 1891 at the Madison Square Theatre and closed 7 August 1893 after 657 performances.[37]

CAST: *Welland Strong*, a man with one foot in the grave: HARRY CONOR. *Ben Gay*, a wealthy San Francisco bachelor, of the Union Club: GEORGE A. BEANE, JR. *Tony Gay*, his niece: LILLIAN BARR. *Rashleigh Gay*, nephew of Ben Gay: Lloyd Wilson. *Willie Grow*, proposed at the Bohemian Club: Blanche Arkwright. *Norman Blood*, chum of Rashleigh: Arthur Pacie. *Noah Heep*, waiter at "The Riche" Restaurant: HARRY GILFOIL. *Hoffman Price*, manager of Cliff House: Frank E. Morse. *Slavin Payne*, a servant of Ben Gay: HARRY GILFOIL. *Turner Swift*, who runs the ice-crusher: W. D. Lewis. *Isabella Dame*, friend of the Gays: Geraldine McCann. *Professional Dancers (2)*: *Cora Fay*: Maggie Daly [Margaret Vokes]. *May Wing*: Lucy Daly. *Flirt*, Mrs. Guyer's maid: Ollie Archmere. *Mrs. Guyer*, a widow from Chicago, not too strenuous on culture, but makes up for it in "biff": ANNA BOYD.

Act 1: Reception room in house of Ben Gay.

Act 2: "The Riche" Restaurant.

Act 3: Piazza of Cliff House, looking towards the Seal Rocks.

ACT 1[38]

"The (Pretty Young) Widow"
(*Music by* Percy Gaunt. *Lyrics by* Charles H. Hoyt.)

"Push Dem Clouds Away"[39] (African Cantata)
(*Music and Lyrics by* Percy Gaunt.)

"Reuben and Cynthia" (Reuben, Reuben, I've Been Thinking)
H. Conor, A. Boyd
(*Music and Lyrics by* Percy Gaunt.)

"Crisp Young Chaperone"
(*Music and Lyrics by* W. Barton.)

"Out for a Racket"
(*Music and Lyrics by* Percy Gaunt.)

ACT 2

Burlesque of Italian Opera (arranged by P. Gaunt)
Trio

Medley including "The Cat Came Back," "After the Ball," "Reuben and Cynthia," "It Was a Dream," "Georgie"
(arranged by Percy Gaunt)

Whistling Extraordinary

"The Waiting Maid"
(*Music and Lyrics by* Percy Gaunt.)

ACT 3[40]

"(On) The Bowery"
H. Conor
(*Music by* Percy Gaunt. *Lyrics by* Charles H. Hoyt.)

---

[34]The adaptation for the London production which preceded this American production was credited to F. C. Burnand.

[35]For subsequent tour, only David Belasco's name appears in programs as producer and director.

[36]Published sheet music credits Angelo Asher with the music, and Richard Norton with the lyrics; Sayers' popular song was claimed by many, rewritten and adapted by many publishers without regard to copyright.

[37]No credits in programs for scenery or costumes. This production played the Theatre Comique in Harlem for 1 week a year earlier on tour 17 November 1890 for 8 performances with the same cast, excepting: *Tony Gay*: HILDA THOMAS. *Rashleigh Gay*: Ed. S. Metcalfe. *Willie Grow*: Irene Murphy. *Count de Rien*: Louis Finiger. *Hoffman Price*: James E. Morse. *Fowle Kerr*: John C. Leach. *Isabelle Dame*: Mattie Hornby.

[38]Added to the show during its run:

Serpentine (Butterfly) Dance (added 29 February 1892)
Loie Fuller

Added to the show during its tour:

"After the Ball"
J. Aldrich Libby
(*Music and Lyrics by* Charles K. Harris.)

"You Gave Me Your Love" (I Love You, My Darling Wife)
J. P. Witmark
(*Music by* Minnie Belle. *Lyrics by* David Marion.)

[39]Replaced late in the run by:

"Love Me Little, Love Me Long" (A Senegambian Pastorale)(African Cantata)
(*Music and Lyrics by* Percy Gaunt.)

[40]An all-new Act 3 was introduced 1 May 1893. Added were a Toe Dance and Flower Dance. "On the Bowery" was retained.

1891.40 THE HUSTLER

A Musical Farce (Comedy) in Three Acts. Play by Lew [Lewis] Rosen. Musical director, George Bowron. Produced by Thomas H. Davis and William T. Keough. Opened 23 November 1891 at the Bijou Theatre and closed 5 December 1891 after 16 performances. Re-opened 29 February 1892 at Niblo's Garden and closed 5 March 1892 after 8 additional performances. Total: 24 performances[41].

CAST: *Con McFadden*, "The Hustler," an individual with a plethora of airy, fairy schemes for making millions: "I'll let you in and figure it out for you!": JOHN KERNELL. *Anheuser Busch*, a German capitalist, worth anywhere from $2,000,000 to ninety-eight dollars: BARNEY REYNOLDS. *Anna Danta*, mistress of the Cambridge Flats: GUS MILLS. *Cooler Smith*, "I have a letter from my mother": William Gould. *"Bud,"* a grocer's boy, who will work if the family suits him: "no objections to boarding": Eddie Readway [EDD REDDWAY]. *Faraway Jones*, "Have you seen Eckles?": Leonard Somers. *Three Merry Troubadours*: *Tommy Tenner*: Milo Knill. *Arthur Altow*: Harry Leighton. *Lower Base*: Mack Menter. *Pussy Winks*, McFadden's quiet niece: MOLLIE THOMPSON. *Susie Miller*, an album fiend: ZELMA RAWLSTON. *Chickey New*—"my pa said": Mamie Conway. *The young lady contingent (4)*: *Violet*: Rose Laporte. *Daisy*: Virginia Lampert. *Rose*: Hilda Laporte. *Lily*: Nellie Burt. *Spanish Dance Specialty*: MLLE. LEONILDA STACCIONE. *Hustler Quartette*: Harry Leighton (alto), Milo Knill (tenor), Leonard Somers (baritone), Mack Menter (basso).

Act 1: Cambridge Flats, New York.

Act 2: A Summer Establishment at Lenox.

Act 3: Cambridge Flats.

ACT 1[42]
- Vocal and Terpsichorean Melange, with a Cart-Wheel Accompaniment
  M. Thompson
- Dashing Equestriennes
  Misses Thompson, Rawlston, Harris, Laporte Sisters, R. France
- "Do You Catch the Idea" (with Pantomimic Illustrations)
  J. Kernell, B. Reynolds
- Medley of Popular Melodies
  G. Mills

ACT 2
- Songs, Tyrolean Warblings and Imitations
  B. Reynolds
- Parisian Duster Dance
  Mlle. L. Staccione
- "I Don't Know"
- Grand Medley

ACT 3
- Spanish Dance
  M. Staccione
- Specialty
  The Hustler Quartette
- John Kernell's latest offerings:
  "How Hogan Paid His Rent"
  "The Picture That is Turned to the Wall"
  (*Music and Lyrics by* Charles Graham.)
- "The Hustler Has Won" (Grand Finale)

1891.41 CINDERELLA

A Spectacular Pantomime Extravaganza in Three Acts, 9 Scenes. New version of the old story (by Charles Perrault) re-told, re-written and produced by Henry John Leslie. Original music composed by Alfred Cellier, Edward Solomon, Ivan Caryll, Henry John Leslie. Maitresse de ballet, Sign. Vincenzina Chitten. Scenery by W. Telbin, T. E. Ryan, W. Perkins, Ernest Albert; William Schaffer and Gaspard Maeder. Costumes executed by Mad Auguste & Co., Alias and Miss Fisher; Felix and Landolph; Mme. Maerins. Musical director, A. W. Hoffman. Produced by E. G. Gilmore, Eugene Tompkins. Opened 24 November 1891 at the Academy of Music and closed 26 December 1891 after 40 performances.

CAST: *Cinderella*: FANNY WARD. *Duke of Chappies*: NINA FARRINGTON. *The Insect Queen*: NINAN FARRINGTON. *Earl of Dudes*: Norma Cole. *Chauncy Baron of Stone-Broke*: CHARLES BURKE. *Belva*, Baroness of Stone-Broke: LILLIE ALLISTON. *Tottina Ann, Gloriana Jane, Prunella Gaitors*, Sisters of Cinderella: Edwin H. Carroll, Fred Mendoza, Katherine Pyke. *Jeames I, Jeames II, Thomas I, Thomas II*, Flunkies (Adonis Four): George B. Gilson, Robert Watson, Mathew Carroll, James A. Carroll. *Fairy Queen Ladybird*: JENNIE REEVES. *Her Attendants*: Mabel Knowles, Marie Williams. *Spirit of the Age*: Marie Leyton. *Quicksilver*: Lillian DeWolf. *Page to the Prince*: Georgie Brighton. *Sergeant Samson*: Master Willie Barbier. *Clown*: George D. Melville. *Pantaloon*: William Burke. *Harlequin*: Augustus Sohlke. *Sprite*: W. Lowe. *Policeman*: J. J. Geary. *Columbine*: Edith Craske. *Prince Charming*: BERTHA RICCI. Ballet: *Première Assoluta*: Mlle. PARIS. *Premieres*: Mmes. V. and C. Chitten. *Special Dancers*: Mmes. Minnie Gorman, the Barrison Sisters, Rose Newham. *Secondes*: Mmes. Hearn, Brinck, Camis, Strauss, Leyton.

Act 1, Scene 1: Cloudland. *Scene 2*: Cinderella's kitchen. *Scene 3*: In the Prince's deer forest.

Act 2, Scene 1: The pantry bewitched. *Scene 2*: A path through the woods. *Scene 3*: Insect Island.

Act 3, Scene 1: The Conservatory of the Prince's Palace. *Scene 2*: The Royal Ball Room. *Scene 3*: Gorgeous Transformation, "The Supremacy of the Sun."

ACT 1[43]
Scene 2
- Cook's Dance
- Sisters' Duet

Scene 3
- Grand Ballet of Nymphs and Rabbits

ACT 2
Scene 1
- The Housemaid's Dance
- The Four Flunkies

Scene 3
- Grand Procession and Ballet of International Insects

ACT 3
Scene 2
- Grand Fancy Dress Ball
- The Comical Harlequinade
  G. D. Melville, W. Burke, A. Sohlke, W. Lowe, J. J. Geary, E. Craske

Scene 3
- The Supremacy of the Sun (Grand Transformation Scene)
  Spirit of Snow; Ice Bound; Home of the North Wind; The Summer Idyll; The Radiant Realm of the Sun God.

1891.42 THE GOSSOON

An Irish Comedy Drama in Four Acts. Play by Edward E. Kidder. (Music and lyrics by B. H. Janssen.) Scenery by Mohn & Becker. Opened 30 November 1891 at the People's Theatre and closed 5 December 1891 after 9 performances[44].

CAST: *Clancy O'Connell*, a young Irish squire, called "The Gossoon": CARROLL JOHNSON. *Gordon Keene*, an English adventurer, assuming the name of Percival Kirke: MART E. HEISEY. *Dandy Darragh*, an old Dublin beau: Thomas J. Dempsey. *Bernard Malley*, a young farmer: Harry Fenwick. *Cullen*, a ne'er-do-well: W. D. Stone. *Rody Dugan*, a creature of circumstance: Hugh J. Ward. *Rose O'Connell*, the pride of the place: LIDA MCMILLEN. *Annabel Grey*, an Irish-American: Annie Schindle. *Pansey Peters*, a London waiting-maid: G. A. Mortimer. *Peasants, Fiddlers, Village Girls, etc.*

Act 1: Rody's Cabin, with a view of the Lakes of Killarney. Summer.

Act 2, Scene 1: The open country. Moonlight. Same evening. *Scene 2*: Interior of Clancy's House. Midnight. *Scene 3*: The Hunting Lodge.

Act 3: The Lakes of Killarney in Winter. Three months later.

Act 4: Room in Clancy's house.

---

[41]Director, designers of costumes and scenery uncredited.

[42]Musical numbers not listed in New York programs. List prepared from subsequent Brooklyn tour engagement.

[43]Also performed in the production:
"Nightingale Waltz Song" (from *THE TYROLEAN*)
(*Music by* Carl Zeller.)

[44]Producer, stage director, costumes, musical director uncredited. Played a return engagement 31 October 1892 at the Grand Opera House for 8 performances.

MUSICAL NUMBERS
"The Irish Are True"
C. Johnson
"Sweet Annabel"
C. Johnson
"Merry Wedding Bells" (Ring, Merry Bells)
C. Johnson

1891.43 THE NEW CITY DIRECTORY

Russell's New Comedians in a New Edition of the Farce Comedy in Three Acts[45]. Libretto by Paul M. Potter, reconstructed by Louis Harrison. Musical interruptions by W. S. Mullaly. (Staged by Louis Harrison.) New scenery by Homer F. Emens. Produced by the Bijou Theatre Company (John H. Russell, J. Wesley Rosenquest, Proprietors and Managers). Opened 7 December 1891 at the Bijou Theatre and closed 20 February 1892 after 88 performances.[46]

CAST (The New Canvassers): *John Smith*, detective: WILLIS P. SWEATNAM. *John Smith*, stage manager: DAN DALY. *John Smith*, banker: Burt Haverly. *John Smith*, German actor: CHARLES SEAMAN. *John Smith*, janitor and call boy, Gaiety: LUKE SCHOOLCRAFT. *John Smith*, advance agent: JOSEPH C.. MIRON. *John Smith, Jr.*: JULIUS P. WITMARK. *John Smith*, dude: DAVID WARFIELD. *John Smith*, messenger: Joseph Jackson. *Mrs. John Smith*: Lillie Eldridge. *Nanon Smith*, of the Gaiety: BESSIE CLEVELAND. *Rosebuds (3)*: *Laura Smith*: Mayme Kelso. *Flora Smith*: Kate Uart. *Dora Smith*: Marion Weller. *Little Fawn*, the American dancer: Amelia Glover.

Act 1: Music Room, Minerva Flats.

Act 2: The Green Room, Gaiety Theatre.

Act 3: The Camp Meeting and Clambake, Smith's Island, Great South Bay.

MUSICAL NUMBERS, SPECIALTIES[47]
"Street Bands"
"Always Together"
J. P. Witmark
(*Music and Lyrics by* Thomas LeMack.)
"He Was a Pal of Mine!"
J. P. Witmark
(*Music by* Isidor Witmark. *Lyrics by* M. J. Cavanagh.)

1891.44 A NIGHT AT THE CIRCUS

A Circo-Comedy in Three Acts[48]. Play by H. Grattan Donnelly. Musical director, W. H. Nelson. Produced by Nellie McHenry (John Webster, Proprietor). Opened 21 December 1891 at the Park Theatre and closed 26 December 1891 after 9 performances; re-opened 21 March 1892 at the Bijou Theatre for 32 additional performances. Total: 41 performances[49].

CAST: Acts 1 and 2: *Archibald Banger* of Friske and Banger: JOHN WEBSTER. *Nicholas Friske*, one of the (old) boys: BEN LODGE. *Signor Bonanza*, Manager of the Imperial Circus: J. H. BRADBURY. *Pinkerton Kopp*, a private detective: W. H. MACK. *Kicker*, an ambitious office boy: JOHN GILROY. *Dixey Weed*: Ben F. Grinnell. *Bill Sticker*: H. B. Barnum. *Calliope Friske*, with an eye on everybody: GENEVIEVE REYNOLDS. *Belvidere Banger*, a jealous wife: HELEN HARRINGTON. *Remi Riter*, a Hammond operator: MARGARET MACDONALD. *Bud Manhattan*, a New York debutante: ALICE MAY. *Oriole Ogontz*, a Philadelphia Venus: HELEN BYRON. *Ida Vassar*, a Boston beauty: Henrietta Byron. *Socrates*, a Tiger: Tiddle de Wink. *Twin Sisters (2)*: *Mlle. Electra*, queen of the arena: NELLIE MCHENRY. *Mlle. Madeleine Milan*, a visiting governess: NELLIE MCHENRY.

Act 3: *The Ring Master*: J. H. BRADBURY. *Rusty*: JOHN GILROY. *Snifty*: W. H. MACK. *Pete Jenkins*, comic singer: JOHN WEBSTER. *The Wild Man of Borneo*: Nicholas Friske [Ben Lodge]. *Cannonball Tosser*: Ben F. Grinell. *Shouter*: H. B. Barnum. *Calliope Friske*, with an eye on everybody: GENEVIEVE REYNOLDS. *Belvidere Banger*, a jealous wife: HELEN HARRINGTON. *Empress of the Air*: Margaret MacDonald. *Bounding Jockey*: Alice May. *The Duettists*: Margaret MacDonald. *The Danseuses*: (4). The *Equine Beauty*: Cupid. *Socrates*, a tiger: Snowball. *Queen of the Arena*: NELLIE MCHENRY. *Nancy Brown*: NELLIE MCHENRY. *Mlle. Malan*: NELLIE MCHENRY.

Act 1: Law Office of Friske & Banger.

Act 2: A Temperance Hotel.

Act 3: Dressing Tent of the Great Imperial Circus.

1891.45 THE LAST OF THE HOGANS

A Local Play (Musical Farce) in Three Acts, 4 Scenes. Play (and lyrics) by Edward Harrigan. Music by David Braham. (Staged by Edward Harrigan.) Dancing under the supervision of Dan Burke. Scenery by D. Frank Dodge. Musical director, David Braham. Produced by Edward Harrigan. Opened 22 December 1891 at Harrigan's Theatre and closed 16 April 1892 after 160 performances.[50]

CAST: *Judge Dominick McKeever*: EDWARD HARRIGAN. *Esaw Coldstream*: JOHN WILD. *Angelina Gibson*: JOSEPH SPARKS. *Alonzo Trimmins*: James Radcliffe. *Conrad Dinkelhart*: HARRY FISHER. *Aged Prophet*: George Merritt. *Hughey Hogan*: George Merritt. *Bernard McGinly*: Charles Coffey. *Eliza Kingfoot*: Charles Coffey. *Harry Merryfield*: Fred W. Peters. *Annie Hogan*: Charles F. McCarthy. *Marcus McGinly*: John Decker. *Mug Mullen*: Richard Quilter. *Jack Nagley*: Charles Sturges. *Elder Culpepper*: George J. Secor. *Deacon Bloodroot*: John Rennie. *Rufe Ringworm*: William West. *The Parson*: Dan Burke. *Polo Jim*: John Walsh. *Shad Licorice*: James McCullough. *Stuff Mattress*: James Burke. *Sid Cowlick*: Joseph Williamson. *Stag Stivers*: Willis Pickert. *Plush Plunkett*: John Mayon. *Weep Walley*: Edward Murphy. *Angelina Appplegate*: HATTIE MOORE. *Addie Hogan*: EMMA POLLOCK. *Mary Ann Brennan*: ADA LEWIS. *Susie Somerset*: FANNIE BATCHELDER. *Daisy Dimple*: Marguerite Teale. *Kitty Hogan*: Annie Buckley. *Matilda Merryfield*: ANNIE YEAMANS. *Special Engagement, Box Act*: THE DAVENPORT BROTHERS.

The Hogans: Messrs. Edward Gorman, Joseph Healy, John Brennan, Robert Snyder, Dennis Davis, John Hernan, Tim Young. Misses Pauline Edwards, Josie Knight, Martha Franklin, Daisy Sinclair, Katie Paterson.

Act 1: Judge McKeever's Apartments.

Act 2: Down by the River Side.

Act 3: The Gull Club House.

MUSICAL NUMBERS
"The Last of the Hogans"
"Hats Off to Me"
"Old Neighborhood"
"Knights of the Mystic Star"
"On De Rainbow Road" (The Rainbow Road)
"Take a Day Off, Mary Ann"
"Danny By My Side"

1891.46 YON YONSON

A Farcical Drama in Three Acts. Play by Gus Heege. Scenery by Joseph Hart. Acting manager, John E. Hogarty. Musical director, Vincent Eldon. Produced by Jacob Litt. Opened 28 December 1891 at the Park Theatre and closed 23 January 1892 after 33 performances[51].

CAST: *Yon Yonson*, a Swede from Yimtown, Nord Dakota: GUS [Augustus] HEEGE. *Amos Jennings*, of the firm of Jennings & Co.: H. D. Byers. *John T. Holloway*, his manager: Harold Hartsell. *Gerald Harcourt*, an English tourist: Franclyn Hurleigh. *Roly*, Harcourt's nephew: Master Frankie Jones. *Vanderbilt Botts*, a real estate boomer: J. W. Davenport. *Wendell Phillips Simpson*, a footman: J. W. Davenport. *Hankins*, Engineer of the Saw Mill: William Barrie. *Mister McSorley*, a station agent: Frederick Hicks. *Mr. Wheeze*, a hypochondriac: VINCENT ELDON. *Grace Jennings*, adopted daughter of Amos Jennings: HELENE LOWELL. *Mrs Laflin*, proprietress, Rush City Junction Hotel: SADIE CONNELLY. *Jennie Morris*: ANNIE LEWIS. (*Lumbermen's Quartette*, Specialty: Frederick Hicks, Vincent Eldon, C. W. Clark, A. L. Mann.)

---

[45]First produced in New York 10 February 1890 at the Bijou Theatre for 152 performances.
[46]Director and costume design uncredited.
[47]Added during the run:
"John and Mary"
"When de Reszke Strikes High C"
(*Music and Lyrics by* Louis Harrison.)
[48]Billed as "The Blazing Sun of the Farce-Comedy Sky" and Jolly Nellie McHenry and Her Greatest Show on Earth illustrating the soul-tickling, laugh-inspiring Circo-Comedy.
[49]Played a return engagement 2 May 1892 at the Grand Opera House for 8 performances. Act 3 Circus characters not included in original New York program, but were taken from subsequent tour program credits.

[50]Costumes uncredited.
[51]Played a return engagement 7 March 1892 at the Grand Opera House for 8 performances.

Act 1: N. P. Junction R. R. Hotel.

Act 2: The Lumber Camp and Log Jam.

Act 3: Reception Room, Hotel LaFayette, Lake Minnetonka, Minnseota.

SPECIALTIES, MUSICAL NUMBERS[52]

Comic Pantomime from *UNCLE TOM'S CABIN* (Act 1)

Lumbermen's Quartette (Act 2)
F. Hicks, V. Eldon, C. W. Clark, A. L. Mann

Irish Jig Specialty
S. Connelly

"Take a Day Off, Mary Ann" (from *THE LAST OF THE HOGANS*)
A. Lewis
(*Music by* David Braham. *Lyrics by* Edward Harrigan.)

1891.47 THE LION TAMER

A Comic Opera in Two Acts, 3 Scenes. English libretto by J. Cheever Goodwin. Based on the French opérette "Le Grand Casimir"[53] by Jules Prével and Albert de Saint-Albin. Music by Richard Stahl. Produced under the stage direction of Richard Barker. Ballet master, Professor Mamert Bibeyran. Scenery by John H. Young, Richard Marston. Costumes designed by Percy Anderson. Orchestrations by John Philip Sousa. Produced by the Francis Wilson Comic Opera Company (A. H. Canby, Manager). Opened 30 December 1891 at the Broadway Theatre and closed 7 May 1892 after 130 performances.

CAST: *Casimir*, the Lion Tamer: FRANCIS WILSON. *The Grand Duke*, Angelina's admirer: CHARLES PLUNKETT. *Sotherman*, Juggler and Equilibrist: GILBERT CLAYTON. *Gobson*, Ringmaster: FRED LENNOX. *Count di Verdigris*, Corsican Conspirator: SETH M. CRANE. *Picasso*, Lieutenant of Dragoons: WILLIAM PRUETTE. *Marquis di Chianti*, Nephew of Count Verdigris: WILLIAM STEIGER. *Joseph*, Casimir's attendant: John E. Dudley. *Baptista*, a waiter: B. F. Joslyn. *Selim, Hassam*, Bounding Brothers of Barbary: Masters John Coleman, Jesse Henderson. *Lucia*, Daughter of Count Verdigris: LAURA MOORE. *Nina*, her waiting maid: Nettie Lyford. *Colombia*, a Peasant: Cecile Eissing. *Angelina*, Casimir's wife, an Equestrienne: MARIE JANSEN. *Clowns, Acrobats, Riders, Grooms, Conspirators, Peasants, etc.*

Act 1: Marseilles. Dressing Tent of the Circus. (Young.)

Act 2, Scene 1: Chapel of Court Verdigris, Corsica. *Scene 2*: Public Square, Bastia, Corsica. (Marston.)

ACT 1[54]

Opening Chorus (What can be the explanation)
F. Lennox, Chorus

"Love's Rosy Dream" (I love her so)
G. Clayton

"Song of the Circus" (When brooks have burst their icy chains/ Houp la!)
M. Jansen

"The Bounding Brothers of Barbarry"
F. Wilson, J. Coleman, J. Henderson, Chorus

Chorus (Hail! All hail! The peerless Casimir)

"The Lion Tamer" (Song)
F. Wilson

"Casimir and Angeline" (Duet)
F. Wilson, M. Jansen

Finale (Oh! Bearing so daring!)
J. E. Dudley, G. Clayton, M. Jansen, Chorus

ACT 2

Scene 1

Chorus of Conspirators (There can not be the slightest doubt)
S. M. Crane, W. Steiger, Chorus

"Where Are Thou, Illustrious Stranger" (Aria)
L. Moore

Oath of Conspiration (In this consecrated place)
S. M. Crane

Finale, Scene 1 (Hold! Touch not a hair of that beloved head)
L. Moore, S. M. Crane, F. Wilson, W. Steiger, Chorus

Scene 2

Bridal Chorus (Double Quartette)(Never falter! to the altar)
F. Wilson, Double Quartette

Chorus (Fill your glasses, Lords and lasses!)

"The Life of a Bold Dragoon" (Song)
W. Pruette, Chorus

"The Isle of Lillipotu" (Song)
F. Wilson

"Widow's Weeds" (Song)
M. Jansen

Ensemble (The Stirrup cup, we've copiously coiffed)
S. M. Crane, F. Wilson, Chorus

Concerted Number (Surround these men)
W. Pruette, W. Steiger, S. M. Crane, L. Moore, Conspirators, Chorus

Finale (If you'll swear to hereafter do better)
Principals, Chorus

1892.01 BLUE JEANS

A Revival of the Comedy-Drama in Four Acts, 8 Scenes[55]. Play by Joseph Arthur. Music composed and arranged by W. S. Mullaly. Scenery by Homer F. Emens. Mechanical effects by J. B. DeBeauvais & Son; Edward Peck. Light effects by Richard Francis. Produced by J. Wesley Rosenquest & Joseph Arthur. Opened 4 January 1892 at the 14th Street Theatre and closed 9 April 1892 after 107 performances.

CAST: *Perry Bascom*: ROBERT HILLIARD. *Colonel Henry Clay Risener* of the Rising Sun: George D. Chaplin. *Ben Boone*: Andrew Robson. *Jacob Tutewiler*: J. J. WALLACE. *Jim Tutewiler*: Charles D. Udell. *Isaac Hankins*: W. J. Wheeler. *Seth Igoe*: Joseph Graham. *June*: JENNIE YEAMANS. *Sue Eudaly*: Judith Berolde. *Samanthe Hankins*: Marion Strickland. *Cindy Tutewiler*: Mrs. Charles Edmonds. *Nell Tutewiler*: CELIE ELLIS. *Beleena Kicker*: CELIE ELLIS. *Bascom's Child*: Little Mary Morrison.

The Old Village Band, "Rising Sun Roarers," led by Drum-Major Malloy; O. F. McCormick, Director. *The Columbia Quartette*: Wakefield Reed (First tenor), Joseph Graham (Second tenor), James Leahy (First bass), Louis Casavant (Second bass).

1892.02 JOAN OF ARC, or, The Merry Maid of Orleans

A Burlesque in One Act, accompanied by a Vaudeville Bill. (Inpsired by the play by Victorien Sardou.) Libretto and music by Frederic Solomon. Director of music, Michael Schlig. Produced by (John) Koster & (Albert) Bial. Opened 4 January 1892 at Koster & Bial's Concert Hall and closed 5 March 1892 after 81 performances.[56]

CAST: *Joan of Arc*: JENNIE JOYCE. *Princess Marie*: MADGE LESSING. *Talbot*, Earl of Shrewsbury: Agnes Evans. *Lionel*, his Aide de Camp: Dollie Clark. *Duchess Isabelle*: May Shannon. *King Charles VII*: James T. Kelly. *Phillip of Burgundy*: Sol Mirandoli. *Jeanette*: Vera Bedell. *Pierre*: Irene Rice. *Jacques*: Clara Primrose. *Villagers, Wine-growers, Amazons, etc.*

Scene: A French village, outside Orleans.

---

[52]Not listed in programs.

[53]Charles Lecocq's original French score was discarded for an all-new American score by Richard Stahl. The original French version was previously presented in New York 22 April 1885 at the Star Theatre for 2 performances in repertory.

[54]Musical numbers not listed in programs. List prepared from published piano vocal selection and book of words (T. B. Harms, New York, 1891). Song published in vocal selection, but not in book of words: "Oh, Tonio!"

[55]First produced in New York 6 October 1890 at the 14th Street Theatre for 187 performances. For Synopsis of Scenes and Musical Numbers, see original 1890 production.

[56]The "Nightingale Song" sung by kind permission of Rudolph Aronson.

1892.03

NANON, the Hostess of the Golden Lamb

A Revival of the Comic Opera in Three Acts[57]. Original Viennese libretto by F. Zell, (based on the the play 'Ninon, Nanon et Madame de Maintenon' by Emmanuel Théaulon, Armand d'Artois and Lesguillon). American adaptation by Sydney Rosenfeld. Music by Richard Genée. Staged by Heinrich Conried. Scenery by Henry E. Hoyt. Costumes by Mme. Loe. Orchestra conducted by Gustave Kerker. Produced by Rudolph Aronson. Opened 12 January 1892 at the Casino Theatre and closed 13 February 1892 after 34 performances.

CAST: *Nanon Patin*, Hostess of "The Golden Lamb": MARIE TEMPEST. *Ninon de l'Enclos*: DREW DONALDSON. *Gaston*, Page to Ninon: GRACE GOLDEN. *Mme. de Maintenon*: EVA DAVENPORT. *Jacquelin*, Waitress: Sylvia Thorne. *Mme. de Fulpert*: Helene Beatrice. *Mlle. d'Armonville*: Ottilie Reiffarth. *Comtesse Houlières*: Carrie Noyes. *Mme. de Frontenac*: Madge Yorke. *Baptiste*: Elison Campbell. *Thérèse*, Aunt of Nanon: May Hanley. *Marquis de Marsillac*: EDWIN STEVENS. *Marquis d'Aubigne*: FERDINAND SCHUETZ. *Hector, Vicomte de Marseillac*: MAX FIGMAN. *Pierre*: Edward Elkas. *Bombardini*, Drum-Major: William Conrad. *Sergeant*: Otto Weyl. *Commissioner*: J. T. Dalton. *King Louis XIV*: JAMES MAAS. *Abbé*: Frederic Solomon.

1892.04

EVANGELINE

A Revival of the Comic Opera Extravaganza in Three Acts, 8 Scenes[58]. (Libretto by J. Cheever Goodwin.) Music by Edward E. Rice. Conductor of orchestra, Frank Barry. C. H. Smith, Manager, presented with the Boston Theatre Production Cast. Opened 18 January 1892 at Niblo's Garden and closed 30 January 1892 after 16 performances; returned 28 March 1892 to Niblo's Garden and closed 2 April 1892 after 8 additional performances. Total: 24 performances.[59]

CAST: *Gabriel*, "Our Hero," a fascinating and perambulating young lover—in point of fact, a roaming Romeo: HILDA THOMAS. *Evangeline*, "Our Heroine," a creature of impulse and impetuous pet, pursued through love's impatient promptings by Gabriel, and with a view to edacious contingencies—by a Whale: RUTH DAVENPORT. *The Lone Fisherman*, the original, who created the part 17 years ago, ubiquitous in movements, with a natural tendency to hook whatever comes within reach: JAMES F. MAFFIT. *Catherine*, the very mildest type of anti-nuptial mother-in-law—but wait: RICHARD HARLOW. *Eulalie*, Evangeline's confidante, confidently hoping for women's rights: ESTELLE CLINTON. *Felican*, Eulalie's adorer, a vivacious young party who is simply nervous: SADIE STEPHENS. *LeBlanc*, a lawyer of the shyest shyster stamp, with a will and a way equally dark: GEORGE A. SCHILLER. *Captain Dietrich*, a Dutch mercenary in the British ranks, who shows no mercy, being a mercy-nary genius: HARRY WEST. *Rose, Marie*, In Eva's suite, too sweet to need description: Annie Wynne, Sophie Sigel. *Mary Ann*, Eva's maid: Elma Winton. *Elaine*, a waif, in love: Annie Nillson. *Fritz, Maurice*, Captain Dietrich's aides and abettors: Grace Tabor, Ethel Langdon. *Rudolph*, Marie's admirer: Helen Smith. *Hubert*, friend of Rose: Ella Rock. *Benedict*, Evangeline's sire, whose vacillating mind is divided between the rental of her protective husband and his own parallel affections: EDWIN S. TARR. *King Boorioboola Gha*, royal proprietor of the mid-African diamond fields: Tom Reilly. *Hans Wagner*, a spiritual corporal: Ben J. Miles. *The Jailor*, never without his key, vocal or instrumental, consequently on the qui vive: G. Clarke. *Grab, Runewin*, a couple of the King's copper-colored "Copps": Ed Stone, Mr. Pelham. *Dead Hake, Ringbolt*, a brace of conscientious deserters who left their ship simply because they could not take it with them: Mr. Braham, Mr. Morris. *Policeman*, called by some a peeler, possibly because he never was known to heed an appeal a prisoner might take: Bernard J. Reilley. *Lo*, the poor Indian, the lo-est and the lo-nest savage of them all: Louis deSchmidt. *The Headsman*, not a mimic of stupid people, but very clever at taking off blockheads: Fred Bailey. *The Heifer*: Specially imported from Cowes: James A. Reynolds, E. T. Kelly. *Queen Boorioboola Gha*, the King's much better adviser and supervisor of his whole conduct: Clara Whitney. *The Merry but Miserable Ruffians (4)*: *Ah-There Charlie*: Henry Campbell. *Arizona Abraham*: James Reynolds. *Rosemary Tom*: Harry Bullock. *Little Ten Willie*: Anson Wade. *Frank Myers, Lon McCullough*, soldiers from the ships: David McHugh, Ed. Collins.*Shepherdesses, Fishermen, Soldiers, Acadians, Peasants, Africans*.

Act 1,Scene 1: Exterior view of Benedict's house, and a bird's eye view of the sea. *Scene 2*: A Lane. *Scene 3*: Benedict's Kitchen.

Act 2: Africa. *Scene 1*: The diamond fields. *Scene 2*: The back part of Boorioboola Gha's Palace on a cold day.

Act 3: Arizona and Acadia. *Scene 1*: The Forest's edge. *Scene 2*: An autumn Acadian byway. *Scene 3*: Acadia. Benedict's home, with a view of the sea.

1892.05

A STRAIGHT TIP

A Revival of the Racing Comedy in Three Acts[60]. Play by John J. McNally. Produced under the stage direction of Julian Mitchell. Musical director, Louis Miller. Produced by (Isaac B.) Rich & (William) Harris. Opened 25 January 1892 at the Park Theatre and closed 20 February 1892 after 32 performances.[61]

CAST: *Dick Dasher*, something of a masher, who longs to be a hero, in love with Kitty: JAMES T. POWERS. *Dennis Dolan*, an Irishman, rich in brogue, heart and pocket: JOHN SPARKS. *Kitty Dolan*, his pretty daughter, with a taste for sports: EMMA HANLEY. *Bedelia Dolan*, a sister of Dennis, with aristocratic notions: JENNIE SATTERLEE. *Abner Hawkins*, of Bangor, Maine, in love with Bedelia: RICHARD GORMAN. *Jack Potsand Poole*, a gambler who tries to play hearts: PETER F. DAILEY. *A. Hardupp Beerbohn*, a non-commissioned surveyor, otherwise a tramp: F. T. WARD. *Howland Taire*, an actor, in hard luck: Albert Hart. *A. Taltout*, well-known on the race track: Albert Hart. *Daisy Dazzle*, who wants to star: DELIA STACY. *Several pleasing and delightful necessities (3)*: *Cora Cashmere*: Eloise Mortimer. *Violet Velours*: Leona Ambrose. *Belle Delaine*: Rose Figman. *Bunco and Three Card Monte Men (3)*: *Bill Katchon*: John P. Curran. *Jim Fleese*: Howard Graham. *Lank Lean*: Oscar Schoening. *Lead P. Cinch*, a 100 to 1 shot: Colonel Ole Folks. (*Carmencita*: JAMES T. POWERS.)

ACT 1

"The Little Racket"

Dick Dasher's Pantomime Imitations: The Stage-Door Masher, Lady dressing for the street, the Dry Goods Clerk
J. T. Powers

Potpourri: "French March;" "Jolly Boys;" "Sweet Sixteen" Waltz; "Hoopla;" "The Book-maker;" "That Band Did Play."

ACT 2

Grand Medley

"It Takes a Girl to Do It Every Time"

"Comrades"
(*Music and Lyrics by* Felix McGlennon.)/

"Mary and John"
P. F. Dailey
(*Latter day words for both songs by* William Jerome.)

Songs
W. T. Powers

Twilight Song and DanceLadies
(*Music by* Richard Stahl. *Costumes designed by* James T. Powers.)

ACT 3

Travesty Burlesque of Spanish dancing à la Carmencita
J. T. Powers

Famous Original Clipper Quartette in one of their unique mélanges

1892.06

AUNT BRIDGET'S BABY

A Return Engagement of Monroe's Celebrities in the Musical Farce-Comedy in Three Acts[62]. (Play by George W. Monroe.) Musical director, C.

[57]First produced in New York in English 29 June 1885 at the Casino Theatre for 152 performances. For Synopsis of Scenes and Musical Numbers, see original 1885 production.

[58]First produced in New York 27 June 1874 at Niblo's Garden for 14 performances. For Synopsis of Scenes and Musical Numbers, see original 1874 production.

[59]Program includes no credits, for stage director, scenery or costume design; no musical numbers listed.

[60]First produced in New York 26 January 1891 at the New Park Theatre for 123 performances. For Synopsis of Scenes, see original 1891 production.

[61]Scenery and costumes uncredited. The original score by Richard Stahl and Edgar Smith is no longer credited, and appears to have been replaced by interpolations. Played a return engagement 18 April 1892 at the Grand Opera House for 8 performances.

[62]Billed as a Steeplechase of Fun and Music; a sequel to "My Aunt Bridget" by George W. Monroe. First produced in New York 18 May 1891 at the Bijou Theatre for 32 performances. For Synopsis of Scenes, see original 1891 production.

W. Reinhart. (Produced) Under the management of Robert B. Monroe. Opened 25 January 1892 at the Union Square Theatre and closed 30 January 1892 after 7 performances.[63]

CAST: *Bridget McVeigh*, an Irish lady of wealth, ambitious for knowledge: GEORGE W. MONROE. *Owen McFee*, the supposed boodler, in love with Bridget: WALTER JONES. *Shadow Pinchem*, an amateur detective, "always there": Tote Ducrow. *Captain Astoroid*, one of the eight hundred: FRANK W. HOLLAND. *Dudley Astoroid*, his adopted son: JOHN PIERI. *Bruce Ashton*, his nephew: Bert St. John. *Billy*, Splinters' sweetheart: Herbert Zublin. *Jonas Dobbins*, the "Bo'sun": Edward Hanson. *Ferdinand*, Bridget's body servant: R. J. Graham. *Henry*: Harry Ernest. *Davy Jones*: Royce Alton. *The Stowaways*: Messrs. Jones, Ducrow, Holland. *Splinters*, "Aunt Bridget's Baby": NELLIE ROSEBUD. *Eloise, Sophia*, college girls, home on a vacation, and to get married: ELVIA CROX, CATHERINE GERALD. *Calis Thenics*, teacher of vocal and physical culture: KATE ALMA. *Seta LaMonte*, teacher of dancing: May Jordan. *Annette DeDong*, a regular French maid: Daisy Zublin. *Specialty*: Castilian (Lady) Troubadours.

ACT 1

"Dreams" (Quartette)
E. Crox, C. Gerald, B. St. John, J. Pieri

Sand Jig
N. Rosebud

Buck Dance
M. Jordan

Finale
G. W. Monroe, W. Jones, Company

ACT 2

Mandolin Selections by our mermaids of melody
Castilian Troubadors

"Good-by, Bridgy"
G. W. Monroe

"I Would Tarry"
E. Crox

Grand Medley:

"(The Wedding of) The Lily and the Rose" (Song and Dance)
N. Rosebud, D. Zublin, T. Ducrow, H. Zublin
(*Music* by Andrew Mack. *Lyrics by* Thomas LeMack.)

"Paddy, Wait Awhile"
K. Alma

"The Italian Band"
Stowaways

"The Cuckoo Club"
N. Rosebud

"Our Hebrew Uncles"
Stowaways

"The Man-o'-Wars Man"
F. Casey

"Oblige the Ladies"
E. Hanson

"In the Gloaming"
G. W. Monroe

"The Big, Black Coon"
Stowaways

Grand Finale
N. Rosebud, W. Jones, F. W. Holland, T. Ducrow, D. Zublin, M. Jordan, Company

ACT 3

"The Floorwalker"
N. Rosebud

Quartette
J. Pieri, H. Ernest, E. Hanson, R. J. Graham

Wedding Chorus
Company

Finale
G. W. Monroe, Company

[63]Stage direction, scenery and costumes uncredited. Subsequently toured, in a form revised and reconstructed by Scott Marble, with a different musical score.

1892.07 UNCLE CELESTIN

A Vaudeville (Opéra-bouffe) in Three Acts. Original French libretto ("L'Oncle Célestin") by Maurice Ordonneau and Henri Kéroul. Music by Edmond Audran. English translation by Georges Millet. Lyrics by Fred Lyster. Stage director, Heinrich Conreid. Scenery by Henry E. Hoyt. Costumes by Mme. Loe and assistants. Director of music, Gustave Kerker. Produced by Rudolph Aronson. Opened 15 February 1892 at the Casino Theatre and closed 16 April 1892 after 60 performances.

CAST: *Pontaillac*: JEFFERSON DEANGELIS. *Pamela*, his wife: JENNIE REIFFARTH. *Clementina*, their daughter: ANNIE MEYERS. *Gustave de Parmessol*: SYLVIA GERRISH. *Moreau*, Gardener: HENRY LEONI. *Count Accasias*: Harry MacDonough. *Countess Accasias*: Jennie Weathersby. *Gotran*, Viscount Accasias: Maurice Abbey. *Ratinet, Sr.*, lawyer: Alfred Holbrook. *Ratinet, Jr.*, lawyer: George H. Mackenzie. *Mme. de Bellefountain*: Villa Knox. *Madelon*: Clara Coudray. *Narcisse*, valet: A. W. Maflin. *Postman*: J. A. Furey. *Boat Captain*: H. W. Carbon. *Travelling Circus Company (6)*: *Tight Rope Walker*: Lizzie Leoni. *Acrobat*: Hailton Adams. *Danseuse*: Minnie Renwood. *Columbine*: Carrie Neilson. *Fat Woman*: Kate Powers. *Pierrot*: Madge Perry. (*Dance Specialty*: LOIE FULLER. *The American Bird Warbler*: Mabel Stephenson. *Herr Rederpowski*, Pianist: George H. Mackenzie.) *Ensemble*: Misses Coudray, Dubois, Hodgson, Holbrook, Leon, Lyons, Mead, Randolph, Senac, Weddell.

Act 1: Drawing-room of the Pontaillacs, Faubourg St. Germain, Paris.

Act 2: Summer resort, Stewed Rabbit Inn, on the River Seine, near Paris.

Act 3: Conservatory at the Pontaillacs. Paris.

MUSICAL NUMBERS, SPECIALTIES[64]

"Good Wine Needs No Bush" (Chorus)

"Clementina's Ditty" (Fast under lock and key)
A. Meyers

"Normandy" (Duet and Chorus)
A. Meyers, S. Gerrish

"Des Acacias" (Trio)

Chorus (Now begins the trouble)

Letter Song (He said, alone I have been living)
A. Meyers

Serpentine Dance
L. Fuller, Ensemble

1892.08 CAPTAIN THERESE

A Comic Opera in Three Acts. Book by Alexandre Bisson and F. C. Burnand. Music by Robert Planquette. Lyrics by F. C. Burnand and Gilbert a'Beckett. Arranged for the American production by Louis Harrison. Produced under the stage direction of Max Freeman. Scenery by John H. Young. Costumes by Alias. Musical director, Herman Perlet. Produced by Agnes Huntington and Her Opera Company (Marcus R. Mayer, Ben Stern, Directors). Opened 15 February 1892 at the Union Square Theatre for 1 performance; re-opened 20 February 1892 at the Union Square Theatre and closed 28 February 1892 after 11 performances.

CAST: *Thérèse* (Captain Thérèse): AGNES HUNTINGTON. *Herminie*, a canoness: MILLIE MARSDEN. *Marcellaine*, a waiting maid: EFFIE CHAPUY. *Claudine*, a servant maid: Vinnie Cassell. *Chambermaid*: Annetta May. *Tancrède*, Vicomte de la Touche: ERIC THORNE. *Phillip*, a French captain: CLINTON ELDER. *Duvet*, a notary: Albert James. *Marquis de Vardeuil*, Colonel, First Lorraine Dragoons: Scott Russell. *Colonel Sombrero* of the Spanish contingent: HALLEN MOSTYN. *Sergeant La Tulipe*: Sid Reeves. *Of the French Army (2)*: *Vadeboncoeur*: John W. Smiley. *Boulignac*: J. Hart. *Campastro* of the Spanish contingent: J. Wyn Nichols. *Major de la Confrière* of the French Army: Karl Mora. *An Orderly*: Joseph Severo. *Domestics, Peasants, French and Spanish Soldiers, etc.*

The action takes place in Dijon, France, in the late seventeenth century.

Act 1: The Chateau and Park of the Marquis de Veudeuil.

Act 2: The Camp at Vellars.

Act 3: Room in the Auberge near the camp.

[64]Musical numbers (except Serpentine Dance) not listed in programs. List prepared from published piano vocal gems (William A. Pond, New York, 1892).

ACT 1[65]

Opening Chorus/

"The Three Lovers" (Marceline's Song)
E. Chapuy, Chorus
(*Lyrics by* F. C. Burnand.)

"A Soldier's Life" (Song)
E. Thorne
(*Lyrics by* Gilbert à Beckett.)

"The Pensionnaire's Song"
A. Huntington
(*Lyrics by* Gilbert à Beckett.)

"The Gypsy and the Solicitor, or the Lawyer's Fortune" (Quintette)
E. Chapuy, V. Cassell, S. Russell, A. James, J. W. Smiley, J. Hart
(*Lyrics by* F. C. Burnand.)

"Thérèse" (Song)
C. Elder
(*Lyrics by* F. C. Burnand.)

"In Days Sweet and Olden" (Duet)
C. Elder, A. Huntington
(*Lyrics by* Gilbert à Beckett.)

"The Song of Captain Thérèse" (Rataplan)
K. Mora, M. Marsden, A. James, A. Huntington
(*Lyrics by* F. C. Burnand.)

"The Morning Galop" (Song)
A. Huntington
(*Lyrics by* Gilbert à Beckett.)

Chorus of Recruits (Joyous dashing gay and free)
(*Lyrics by* Gilbert à Beckett.)

Finale
A. Huntington, M. Marsden, Chorus
(*Lyrics by* Gilbert à Beckett.)

ACT 2

Opening Chorus (Generous wine, dear girls to meet us)

Ensemble (Not wise for you to stay here long)
J. Hart, E. Chapuy, E. Thorne, Chorus
(*Lyrics by* F. C. Burnand.)

"The Song of the Butterfly"
E. Chapuy, E. Thorne
(*Lyrics by* F. C. Burnand.)

"Song of the Great Commander" (Song and Chorus)
H. Mostyn
(*Lyrics by* F. C. Burnand.)

Trio (What a terrible day!)
M. Marsden, A. Huntington, A. James
(*Lyrics by* F. C. Burnand.)

"The Lawyer and the Lady's Maid" (Duet)
E. Chapuy, A. James
(*Lyrics by* F. C. Burnand.)

Mazurka

Finale/
"The Trumpet Call"
C. Elder, Principals, Chorus
(*Lyrics by* Gilbert à Beckett.)

ACT 3

Opening Chorus (When the battle is over)/

Herminie's Song (But there are those at home)
Soldiers, Peasant Girls, M. Marsden
(*Lyrics by* F. C. Burnand.)

"His Only Love" (Song)
A. Huntington
(*Lyrics by* Gilbert à Beckett.)

"True Love" (Duet)
C. Elder, A. Huntington
(*Lyrics by* F. C. Burnand.)

"The Pardon" (Duet)
C. Elder, E. Thorne

Duo
M. Marsden, A. Huntington

Quintette
C. Elder, H. Mostyn, M. Marsden, A. Huntington, A. James

The Court Martial (This tribunal severe)
M. Marsden, A. Huntington, C. Elder, E. Chapuy, A. James, E. Thorne
(*Lyrics by* F. C. Burnand.)

"To-morrow!" (Song)
E. Thorne, C. Elder, H. Mostyn
(*Lyrics by* F. C. Burnand.)

Entry of Guests
(*Lyrics by* F. C. Burnand.)

"Rataplan" (Finale)
A. Huntington, Principals, Chorus

1892.09 THE NEW BOYS AND GIRLS

A Musical Farce in Three Acts[66]. Play by John J. McNally. Produced under the stage direction of Julian Mitchell. Musical director, John C. Sorg. Produced by the (Isaac B.) Rich & (William) Harris Company. Opened 22 February 1892 at the Park Theatre and closed 5 March 1892 after 16 performances.[67]

CAST: *Willet Work*, who has peculiar ideas of fun: GEORGE F. MARION. *Bury U. Decent*, poet and undertaker: GEORGE F. MARION. *William Tyre*, a painter of still life, from Zanesville: OTIS HARLAN. *Otto Work*: IGNACIO MARTINETTI. *Françoise Café*: IGNACIO MARTINETTI. *Bennet Work*: WILLIAM B. WOOD. *Herr Aix Handel*: WILLIAM B. WOOD. *Taylor Hede*, a tailor: James A. Sturgis. *Hammond Aigs*, a cook: James A. Sturgis. *Frank Asnew*, Theatrical manager: Frank Shepherd. *Bill Bowl*,a waiter: Joseph Mitchell. *Beefsteak John*, his assistant: Thomas Parker. *Mme. Alert*, a fashionable dressmaker: MAY IRWIN. *Kitty*, a waitergirl: MAY IRWIN. *Priscilla Sharp*: MAY IRWIN. *Molly Fyer*, a nice: FLORA IRWIN. *Hannorah Harrigan*: FLORA IRWIN. *Lotta Goode*: Sadie Kirby. *May B. Wurz*: Laura J. Russell. *Maida Coupe*: Blanche M. Howard. *Annie Howe*: Nellie V. Parker.

Act 1: Madame Alert's Fashionable Dressmaking Establishment, Boston. "The arrival of the Joker."

Act 2: The Overlook Restaurant, St. Botolph Street, Boston. "The joke progressing."

Act 3: Madame Alert's Drawing Room. The next morning. "Vengeance overtakes the Joker."

ACT 3

Boys and Girls Musicale:
Septette
G. Marion, Wood & Shepherd, Boys and Girls Trio, Irwin Sisters
"The Columbia March"
Misses Kirby, Howard, Russell, Parker
Willie Tyre's Escape from Guttenberg

1892.10 PAUL JONES

A Revival of the Opéra-comique in Three Acts[68]. Original French libretto ("Surcouf") by Henri Chivot and Alfred Duru. English adaptation by H. B. Farnie. Music by Robert Planquette. Stage director, Albert James. Dances arranged by John D'Auban. Scenery by John H. Young. Costumes by Mons.

---

[65]Musical numbers not listed in programs. List prepared from published English piano vocal score (Hopwood & Crew, London, 1890), which necessarily does not reflect the alterations by Louis Harrison and interpolations for the American production. Interpolations included:

"Regret" (Cowen interpolation)
A. Huntington

"Transmogrification"
M. Marsden

"Only for Thee" (Duet)
E. Thorne, A. Huntington

"Your Captain, sir, I represent"
A. Huntington

[66]A revised version of the farce comedy (BOYS & GIRLS) which played 21 September 1891 at the New Park Theatre for 16 performances. No musical numbers in programs.

[67]No credits in programs for scenery or costumes.

[68]First produced in New York 6 October 1890 at the Boadway Theatre for 35 performances. For Synopsis of Scenes and Musical Numbers, see original 1890 production.

and Mme. Alias; Mme. Auguste. Musical director, Herman Perlet. Produced by Agnes Huntington and Her Opera Company (Direction of Marcus R. Mayer, Benedict Stern.) Opened 29 February 1892 at the Union Square Theatre and closed 5 March 1892 after 7 performances.

CAST: *Paul Jones*, the national hero: AGNES HUNTINGTON. *Rufino de Martinez*, a Spanish naval officer: CLINTON ELDER. *Bicoquet*, a St. Malo Ship Chandler: SCOTT RUSSELL. *Don Trocadero*, Spanish Governor of the Island Estrella: Eric Thorne. *Kestral*, Skipper of a Yankee Privateer: J. Wyn Nickoles. *Bouillabaisse*, old smuggler: HALLEN MOSTYN. *Petit Pierre*, Fisher Lad at St. Malo: ALBERT JAMES. *First Lieutenant*: George Pyke. *Chopinette*, wife of Bouillabaisse: VINNIE CASSELL. *Malaguena*, Niece of Don Trocadero: MILLIE MARSDEN. *Yvonne*, Niece of Bicoquet: EFFIE CHAPUY. *Fishermen, Privateersmen, Spanish and American man-o'-Warsmen, Lasses of St. Malo, Watteau Boys and Girls, Ladies of the Chatezu, Spanish Officers, Pages, Creoles, etc.*

1892.11 THE PEARL OF PEKIN

A Revival of the Comic Chinese and English Opera in Three Acts[69]. (Original French libretto, 'Fleur de thé,' by Alfred Duru and Henri Chivot. Music by Charles Lecocq.) Libretto by Charles Alfred Byrne. Music by Gustave Kerker and Charles Lecocq. Acting manager, George Dunlap. Musical and stage director, Max Knauer. Produced by Edward Stevens. Opened 7 March 1892 at Niblo's Garden and closed 12 March 1892 after 8 performances.

CAST: *Finette*, wife of Petit Pierre, a vivandiere: IRENE VERONA. *Pearl of Pekin*, daughter of Tyfoo, a simple Chinese maiden: IDA STEMBELR. *Four charming French waiting maids*: *Pierette*: Ray Semon. *Angelique*: Nina Ainscoe. *Pepine*: Stella Madison. *Fantine*: Minnie Rogers. *Petit Pierre*, a dashing young quarter-master of the French navy, stationed on La Victoria, whose wife has opened a restaurant in Pekin as a side speculation: EDWARD WEBB. *So So Ri Ki*, a Japanese of some distinction, Chief of the Royal Tigers, and with still higher aspirations: OSCAR GIRARD. *Paul Mathot*, boatswain of La Victoria, useful if not ornamental: Mr. Hethert. *Sing High*, a Chinese attendant à la Hermann: Jno. Williams. *Tyfoo*, Mandarin and Governor of Pekin, who frequently remarks that he is as knowing as a Sphinx: EDWIN CHAPMAN. *The Hyperion Quartette*, interpolations, Act 1: Charles Van Dyne (first tenor), Frank Kenworthy (second tenor), J. H. Roberts (first bass), Charles Hall (second bass).

1892.12 FRITZ IN IRELAND

A Revival of the Play with Music in Three Acts and a Prologue[70]. (Play by William Carleton.) Musical director, Frank Webbe. Produced by Joseph K. Emmet. Opened 7 March 1892 at the Standard Theatre and closed 19 March 1892 after 16 performances[71].

CAST: The Prologue: *Lawyer Priggins*: George H. Rexford. *Baron Hertford*: George Rogers. *Madam Shultz*: E. Wright. *Lena Schultz*: Baby Spencer. *Honest*: Master Charles Halvorsen. *Henne*: Master Frankie Fair. *Meenie*: Baby Henriques. *Fritz*: JOSEPH K. EMMET.

The Play: *Captain O'Dowd*: Vernon Ramsdell. *Lawyer Priggins*: George H. Rexford. *Lord Seaton*: Sidney Price. *Splodger*: George Rogers. *Thomas Goldfinger*: Charles M. McDonald. *Charles Seaton*: Horace Sparks. *Patrick Black*: W. C. Utter. *Master Herbert*: Baby Spencer. *Lady Amelia*: HELEN SEDGWICK. *Judy Callahan*: Miss Lytton. *Lady Louisa*: Laura Howe. *Old Hag*: Alice Spencer. *Fritz*: JOSEPH K. EMMET. *Herald Quartette*: Messrs. Andrada, Ebert, Silver, Rogers, and Kerrigan, the Poet.

1892.13 FRA DIAVOLO

A Travestie in One Act, 3 Scenes, accompanied by a Vaudeville Bill. (Inpsired by the comic opera by Auber.) Libretto and music by Frederic Solomon. Director of music, Michael Schlig. Produced by (John) Koster & (Albert) Bial. Opened 7 March 1892 at Koster & Bial's Concert Hall and closed 28 May 1892 after 108 performances.

CAST: *Fra Diavolo*: JENNIE JOYCE. *Zerlina*: MADGE LESSING. *Lorenzo*: Agnes Evans. *Lord Allsmash*: Irene Rice. *Lady Allsmash*: May Shannon. *Matteo*: Gertie Sharpeley. *Antonio*: Vera Bedell. *Francesco*: Dollie Clark. *Giacomo*: Sol. Mirandoli. *Beppo*: James T. Kelly.

Scene 1: A Village in Italy. *Scene 2*: Zerlina's Bed Room. *Scene 3*: Outside the "Jolly Brigands."

1892.14 THE FORESTERS

A Poetic Comedy in Four Acts, 5 Scenes. Play (and lyrics) by Alfred Tennyson. Music for the ballads and choruses composed by Arthur Sullivan. Staged by Augustin Daly?. Incidental music by Henry Widmer. Dances arranged by Herr Marwig. Scenery from sketches of Sherwood Forest by James W. Whymple, painted by Henry E. Hoyt, Bruce Smith, John H. Young, Lafayette W. Seavey. Mechanical effects devised by James Tait. Electrical effects by John Walsh. Costumes designed by Graham Robertson. Produced by Augustin Daly. Opened 17 March 1892 at Daly's Theatre and closed 23 April 1892 after 43 performances.

CAST: *Richard Coeur de Lion*: GEORGE CLARKE. *Prince John*: John Craig. *Robin Hood*: JOHN DREW. *Sir Richard Lea*: Charles Wheatleigh. *In the interest of Prince John (4)*: *The Abbot*: Thomas Bridgeland. *Sheriff*: Charles Leclercq. *Judiciary*: William Gilbert. *Mercenary*: Wildred Buckland. *Waller Lea*, Son of Sir Richard: Ralph Nisbet. *Followers of Robin Hood (5)*: *Little John*: HERBERT GRESHAM. *Friar Tuck*: EUGENE JEPSON. *Will Scarlet*: HOBART BOSWORTH. *Old Much*: Tyrone Power. *Young Scarlet*: Lloyd Daubigny. *First Friar*: George Lesoir. *First Beggar*: William Sampson. *First Retainer*: Tyrone Power. *Kate*, Attendant on Marian: KITTY CHEATAM. *Old Woman*: May Sylvie. *Titania*, Queen of the Fairies: Percy Haswell. *First Fairy*: Miss Massoni. *Maid Marian*: ADA REHAN. (*Dance Specialty*, Act 1: A. Saraband.)

Attendants on Marian: Misses Linthicum, Celeste, Eaton, Shotwell. *Fairies*: Misses Florence Conron, Lula Smith, Belle Wharton, Olive Barry, Tennye Poole, Bryton, Thebault, Deacon, Dean, Hall, Long, Kalisba. *Foresters*: Messrs. Lindau, Sifson, Sullivan, Lascelles, Hill, Marks, Singer, Paxton, Boult, Mora. *Retainers, Foresters, Beggars, Fairies, etc.*

Act 1, Scene 1: Terrace at Sir Richard's. *Scene 2*: Hall at Robin Hood's. (Seavey.)

Act 2: Sherwood Forest. (Smith.)

Act 3: The Fairy Glen in the Forest. (Hoyt.)

Act 4: The Heart of the Forest. (Young.)

ACT 1
- "Love Flew in at the Window"
  A. Rehan
- "The Lady and the Maid"
  K. Cheatam
- "Long Live Richard"
  Chorus
- "To Sleep"
  Chorus

ACT 2
- "There Is No Land (Like England)"
  H. Bosworth, Chorus

ACT 3
- "Queen of the Woods"
  H. Bosworth, Chorus
- "The Bee Buzz'd"
  K. Cheatam
- "The Fairies"
  P. Haswell, Miss Massoni, Chorus

ACT 4
- Finale

1892.15 U & I

A Revival of the Musical Satire in Three Acts.[72] (Play, music and lyrics by Edgar Smith and Richard Carroll.) Management, Harry W. Semon.

[69]First produced in New York in French as 'Fleur de thé' 1 February 1869 at the Theatre Français. This adaptation first presented in New York in English 19 March 1888 at the Bijou for 70 performances. For Synopsis of Scenes and Musical Numbers, see 1888 production.

[70]First produced in New York 3 November 1879 at the Park Theatre for 56 performances. For Synopsis of Scenes and Musical Numbers, see original 1879 production.

[71]Played an earlier New York area engagement 4 January 1892 at the Grand Opera House for 8 performances.

[72]First produced in New York as U AND I 23 March 1891 at the Standard Theatre for 42 performances. Authors, director, scenery and costumes, musical director uncredited.

Opened 21 March 1892 at Niblo's Garden and closed 26 March 1892 after 8 performances.

CAST: *O'Donovan Innes*, of Haverstraw, New York, who visits the Metropolis to see life, and sees enough to last him forever: TIM CRONIN. *Professor John Ungerblotz*, a victim of circumstances and mixed drinks, with a Platte Deutsche dialect: GUS BRUNO. *Oliver Twist Haphazard*, a janitor, the despotic ruler of the Sitting Bull Flats: Samuel Curry. *Adam Clubber*, a policeman, whose ideas of keeping the peace is to keep at a distance from all disturbances: FRANK GARDNER. *Percy Van Astor*, American by birth, but British by adoption: WILL GARDNER. *Herr Gustave Von Full Up on Beer*, the rival of all foreign pianists: Harry Standish. *Mlle. Vermicelli*, a comic opera deity worshipped by the "Johnnies": STELLA STUART. *Babette*, Mlle. Vermicelli's maid, called Babette because it is tonier than Bridget: Ada Melrose. *Mrs. Ungerblotz*, the Professor's wife, whose temporary absence from home is the cause of all the trouble: CALLIE T. GARDNER. *Comic Opera Sylphs*. Erratic as persons in their sphere of usefulness usually are (7): *Bella*: Anna L. Kinnir. *Maud*: Mai Stuart. *Carrie*: Marie Nelson. *Gracie*: Nettie Nelson. *Fannie*: Emma Wells. *Mabel*: Grace Gaily. *Kitty*: Kitty Beck.

1892.16 THE CHILD OF FORTUNE

A Comic Opera in Three Acts. (Original) Libretto (to the Viennese operette "Das Sonntagskind") by Hugo Wittmann and Julius Bauer. American adaptation by Helen F. Tretbar. Music by Carl Millöcker. Produced under the stage direction of Heinrich Conried. Scenery by Henry E. Hoyt. Costume designs by Mme. Loe. Director of music, Gustave Kerker. Produced by Rudolf Aronson. Opened 18 April 1892 at the Casino Theatre and closed 14 June 1892 after 63 performances.

CAST: *Lady Sylvia Rockhill*: LILLY POST. *Betty Pornell*, called Droll: ANNIE MEYERS. *Mistress Tyras*: JENNIE REIFFARTH. *Bopp*: Clara Coudray. *Miss Annie*: Mabel Potter. *Page*: Nina Farrington. *Officers (3)*: *Sir Edgar*: CHARLES BASSETT. *Sir Lothair*: WILLIAM PRUETTE. *Sir Hannibal*: HENRY LEONI. *Ralph Butterfield*, a Stock Broker: HARRY MACDONOUGH. *Sheriff Plunkett*: George Mackenzie. *Superintendent Warren*: Maurice Abbey. *Mr. Pudding*: William Conrad. *The Count*: A. W. Maflin. *Bob*, the Jailer: James A. Furey. *Tristan Florival*: JEFFERSON DEANGELIS.

The action takes place in Scotland at the present time.

Act 1: Grand Hall in the Castle Rockhill.

Act 2: Garden of the Castle.

Act 3: Debtors' Prison at Dunkirk.

MUSICAL NUMBERS[73]

"Photographer, Am I"
J. DeAngelis

"My Widow's Weed"
L. Post

"Pleasure A Bounding"
L. Post, A. Meyers, C. Bassett, W. Pruette, H. Leoni

"What a Rival Threatens"
C. Bassett, W. Pruette, H. Leoni

"My Child Let Us Suppose"
J. DeAngelis, A. Meyers

"Three Magic Sisters"
L. Post, H. Macdonough

"To-day I've Won a Treasure"
J. DeAngelis, A. Meyers, L. Post, W. Pruette, H. Leoni, H. Macdonough

1892.17 POLLY MIDDLES

A Fantastic Operetta in Two Acts, 4 Scenes. Libretto by Archibald Clavering Gunter. Music by W. W. Lowitz. Produced under the direction of Richard Barker. Scenery by Henry E. Hoyt. Costumes by Dazian. Orchestration by W. W. Lowitz and Charles Puerner. Produced by the Annie Pixley Company (Nat Roth, Manager). Opened 18 April 1892 at the 14th Street Theatre and closed 21 May 1892 after 35 performances.[74]

CAST: *Moderns of the Ninteenth Century*: *Polly Middles*, soubrette at the Drury Lane Theatre: ANNIE PIXLEY. *Mark Antony Dobbs*, an ex-American army contractor and salvationist: GEORGE C. BONIFACE, JR. *The Earl of Poverty-Towers*, an Irish aristocrat: WILLIAM P. GUIBERSON. *The Hon. Cecil Howard*, V. C., Captain in the Coldstream Guards: CHARLES J. CAMPBELL. *Lady Herr Max von Settenbach*, a German savant: Charles Allison. *Hamlet Malvolio Brown*, the leading heavy at the Drury Lane Theatre: ALFRED C. WHEELAN. *Guides to Pompeii (4)*: *Giuseppe*: J. B. Simpson. *Tuscanni*: G. Krimer. *Lombardi*: J. W. Smiley. *Bimbini*: J. A. Thompson. *Cornelia Poverty-Towers*, daughter of Lord Poverty-Towers: YOLANDE WALLACE. *Amy Battledown*, who knows everything—just in speaking parts: LUCY COOTE. *Lady Melinda Battledown*,a matron of the British drama: ROSA COOKE. *Italian Lazzaroni, Beggar Boys and Peasant Girls.*.

Romans of the First Century: *Paula*, a slave girl of Pompeii: ANNIE PIXLEY. *Marcus Antonius Dobonius*, a freedman, army contractor for javelins, pillae, etc., to the Roman government: GEORGE C. BONIFACE, JR. *M. Crasas Pansa*, a Patrician with estates in Hibernia—Ædile of Pompeii: WILLIAM P. GUIBERSON. *L. Cecillus Dudonius*, a Roman swell, Centurion of the Praetorian Guards: CHARLES J. CAMPBELL. *Maximus Sentuoris*, a Roman Auger of Pompeii: Charles Allison. *Horatius Brumpus*, an ignoble British slave, Nomenclator to Dubonius: ALFRED C. WHEELAN. *Sestio*, a slave dealer: J. B. Simpson. *Cornelia*, daughter of Pansa, a Patrician maiden: YOLANDE WALLACE. *Chloris*, an ignoble Anglican, slave to Dubonius: ROSA COOKE. *Lesbia*, a society maiden of Pompeii: ROSA COOKE. *Roman Citizens, Praetorian Guards, Slaves, Dancing Girls, etc. of A.D. 77.*

Act 1, Scene 1: The runs of Pompeii, A.D. 1877. *Scene 2*: Pompeii in the Reign of Vespatian, A.D. 77.

Act 2, Scene 1: The fête of Dobonius at the Villa of Pansa, 23 August, A.D. 79. *Scene 2*: The ruins of Pompeii.

1892.18 A PARLOR MATCH, Up to Now

A Revival of the Farce Comedy in Three Acts[75]. Play by Charles H. Hoyt. Musical director, Watty Hydes. Produced by Charles E. Evans and William Hoey (Management, W. D. Mann.) Opened 18 April 1892 to Harry Miner's People's Theatre and closed 23 April 1892 after 8 performances.

CAST: *I. McCorker*, a literary man: CHARLES EVANS. *Old Hoss*, a collector for an auction room: WILLIAM HOEY. *Captain William Kidd*, a lineal descendant of the famous pirate: JAMES T. GALLOWAY. *Ephraim Bellomont*, his next door neighbor, and descendant of Goveror Bellomont, who captured the pirate Kidd: THOMAS LEMACK. *Ralph Bellomont*, his son, in love with Lucille: Frank E. Struvy. *Abel Lever*, a spiritualist: Frank E. Struvy. *McKee*, of Allon, M. P.: Joseph A. Weber. *Asa High*, A sporty gentleman: Charles H. Prince. *St. Clair Todd*, a Harvard student: James Y. Glisson. *Lucille Kidd*, in love with Ralph: LILLIAN ELMA. *Aline Kidd*, with a preference for Harvard: LILLIAN MARKHAM. *Mrs. Aurelia Kidd*, the Captain's better half: Eva Randolph. *Friends of the Family (3)*: *Gladys Riche*: Adele Levey. *Gladys Knott*: May Levey. *Vesta Bule*: Lotta Levey. *Innocent Kidd*, her papa's angel child: MINNIE FRENCH. (*Quartette*: Messrs. Glisson, Struvy, Prince, Weber.)

ACT 1[76]

Song
L. Elma

"Sing Cheerily, My Hearty"
M. French, Company

ACT 2

"A Parlor Match Medley"-An Olla Podrida of the latest music, Imported and Domestic
Company

Instrumental Solos
W. Hoey

"Dancing Up to Date"
M. French

"Tar's Song" etc.
Quartette

Specialties
Sisters Levey

New Finale Materialization of the World's Fair Characters
Entire Company

[73]Musical numbers not listed in programs. List prepared from published vocal gems (William A. Pond & Co., New York, 1892).

[74]No musical numbers listed in programs; no libretto or musical score found.

[75]First produced in New York 22 September 1884 at Tony Pastor's 14th Street Theatre for 16 performances. Subsequently revived and revised for many editions presented both on tour and in New York. For a Synopsis of Scenes, see original 1884 production.

[76]Later interpolated on tour in 1893, as per published sheet music:

"The Story Is Always the Same"
Cheridah Simpson
(*Music by* Charles J. Orth. *Lyrics by* Alfred B. Shanz.)

ACT 3
"Perfect Little Gentlemen"
The Seance Seekers
"A Job Lot"
W. Hoey
Mandolin Trio
Sisters Levey
"Good Luck Comes to Those Who Wait" (Finale)
Company

1892.19 A JOLLY SURPRISE

A Musical Comedy in Three Acts. Play by Arthur Wallack. Staged and produced under the personal direction of Jesse Williams. Costumes by M. Herman. Musical director, Watty Hydes. Produced by Fanny Rice (George W. Purdy, Manager). Opened 18 April 1892 at the Bijou Theater and closed 14 May 1892 after 32 performances[77].

CAST: *David Bradbur*, once free, but now tied to the apron strings: CHARLES H. BRADSHAW. *Charles Carol*, once tied to the apron strings, but now free: ROBERT VERNON. *A. Jay*, hustler, author, actor, manager: JOHN W. RANSONE. *Robert*, a coachman: CHARLES LAWLER. *Hot Scotch, Jay Blinks, Sheridan Stride*, Gentlemen of the Comedy Company: J. THORNTON, R. W. GUISE, D. G. Luckman. *Patsy*, elevator boy: John Donahue. *Mrs. Ten Eyck*, a mother-in-law: MRS. SOL SMITH. *Lucy Bradbur*, a young wife: EVA TURNER. *Mary*, maid to Lucy: Nellie Hawthorne. *Tilly Ray, Lilly Gay, Milly Fay*, Ladies of the Comedy Company: Effie Chamberlain, Hattie Nelson, Nelse Chamberlain. *Carle*, a faithful friend: Himself. *Kitty*, maid to Violet: Becky Haight. *Violet Carol*, known as Violet Gray: FANNY RICE.

Characters in 'Gal-a-tea-a Up to Date: *Gal-a-tea-a*, the beautiful statue: FANNY RICE. *Pygmaleon*, master in the art of sculpting: CHARLES LAWLER. *Ganymede*, Hot Scotch, the beautiful Greek boy: J. THORNTON. *Midas*, an enterprising broker: JOHN W. RANSONE. *Symondes*, a merchant: R. W. Guise.

Act 1: Room in Mr. Bradbur's Home. Morning. "What is home without a mother-in-law?"

Act 2: Room in Violet's flat. Evening. Stage struck. A surprise.

Act 3: Mrs. Ten Eyck's residence in Long Branch. "Several surprises. All's well that ends well."

ACT 1[78]
"It Takes a Girl to Do It (Every Time)"
F. Rice

ACT 2
"Ma Says, Why So Shy" (Trio)
N. Hawthorne, E. Chamberlain, N. Chamberlain
Character Songs
J. W. Ransone
"Good Bye"
F. Rice
Diametic Imitations
J. W. Ransone
Character sketch: "Swinging in the Lane"/"Sophia"
F. Rice
Dance
B. Haigt, J. Donahue
Scene from the opera *RUDDYGORE*
Rose" F. Rice. *Robin*: R. W. Guise.
Character songs with quick changes
C. Lawler, J. Thornton
"Two Tramps"; "The Cook and the Bobby"; "Scenes in New York"
Drinking song from the opera *DONNA JUANITA*
F. Rice, Company
Finale

ACT 3
"Coin' Thro' the Dye"
J. Thornton
"The Awakening of Galatea" (Quintet)
F. Rice, C. Lawler, J. W. Ransone, J. Thornton, R. W. Guise
"The Ship Went Sailing" (Quartet)
C. Lawler, J. W. Ransone, J. Thornton, R. W. Guise

[77]Scenery uncredited; composer(s) and lyricist(s) not credited.
[78]No musical numbers in New York programs. List prepared from subsequent tour.

1892.20 JUPITER, or, The King and the Cobbler

A Comic Opera in Two Acts. Libretto by Harry B. Smith. Music by Julian Edwards. Produced under the stage direction of Napier Lothian, Jr. Scenery designed by Homer Emens. Costumes by Henry Dazian, from designs by Alfred Thompson. Conducted by Julian Edwards. Produced by the Digby Bell Opera Company (Henry Askin, Thomas W. Prior, Management). Opened 2 May 1892 at Palmer's Theatre and closed 9 July 1892 after 72? performances.

CAST: *Dentatus*, a Roman Patrician: H. M. IMANO. *Grampus*, a slave dealer: FRED CLIFTON. *Pyrrhus*, his clerk: Charles Meyers. *Octopus*, a Centurion: C. H. Jones. *Patricius Malonius*, Chief of Police: J. Waddington. *Marcus Coonius*, Attendant on Jupiter: E. Forrest Jones. *Publius*: H. W. Ravenscroft. *Caius*: Mr. Chase. *Julius*: Mr. Evans. *Pandora*: LAURA JOYCE BELL. *Sergius*, a Charioteer: JOSEPHINE KNAPP. *Juno*, Queen to Jupiter: HILDA HOLLINS. *Claudia*, betrothed to Spurius: MAUD HOLLINS. *Lucilla*, a slave: SYLVIA THORNE. *Ganymede*: TRIXIE FRIGANZA. *Narcissus*: Miss Fairbanks. *Venus*: Miss Boyd. *Terpsichore*: Ella Ringquist. *Thalia*: Louise Segalini. *Euterpe*: Florine Murray. *Diana*: Florence Chase. *Cupid*: Miss MacDonald. *Jupiter*, King of Olympus: DIGBY BELL. *Spurius Cassius*, a cobbler: DIGBY BELL. *Chorus of Citizens, Guards, Cobblers, Gods and Goddesses.*

Act 1: A Square in Rome. (The Appian Way.)

Act 2: Mount Olympus.

ACT 1[79]
"Happy day, thrice happy day" (Introduction)
M. Hollins, Children, Chorus
"Do you sigh for fame and glory"
M. Hollins
"Slave Sale"
F. Clifton, E. F. Jones, H. M. Imano, S. Thorne, J. Knapp, Chorus
"Chariot Race Song" ('Tis in the amphitheatre.)
J. Knapp
Entrance of Jupiter (Welcome, welcome, wealthy stranger)
"Life Is Such a Stupid Bore" (Trio)
M. Hollins, L. J. Bell, H. M. Imano
"'Twere vain to tell"
Entrance of D. Bell
"The Cobbler's Song"
Finale (Consent and do whatever they demand)("You May Soar and Search")

ACT 2
Opening Chorus and Solo (The deities who here abide)
Chorus
"I Call Aloud for Thee"
H. Hollins
Chorus of Muses (Clash, and clang ye cymbals loud!)
"Fly Fast, Fond Dove" (Song)
J. Knapp
"Love Is Lost" (Duet)
J. Knapp, S. Thorne
"Sailing to the Moon" (Trio)
M. Hollins, L. J. Bell, H. M. Imano
"I Pray Thee Hear Me" (Duet)
D. Bell, L. J. Bell
"A Very Old Gag, But It Went" (Song)
D. Bell
"Come Draw Nigh" (Chorus of Conspirators)
"Who shall be King?" (Ensemble)
H. M. Imano, J. Knapp, S. Thorne, Chorus
"He's no king" (Ensemble)
L. J. Bell, D. Bell, H. M. Imano
Finale (With a tap, tap, tap)

[79]Musical numbers not listed in programs. List prepared from later published vocal score (J. Church Co., Cincinnati, 1893). Also sung, but not in vocal score: "I'll Make a Law to Stop It," "I'll Wait for Thee."

1892.21

STARLIGHT

A Musical Farce Comedy in Three Acts. Play by Fred D. Maeder and Robert Frazer. Stage under the personal direction of Vernona Jarbeau. Conductor of music, Charles E. Candee, Jr. Management, Jeff. D. Bernstein. Opened 2 May 1892 at the New Park Theatre and closed 7 May 1892 after 8 performances.[80]

CAST: *Quackleton Quaver*, a musical crank and dealer in sheet music, anxious to become a manager: ROSS SHOW. *Old Muddlebrain*, the boss crank: CHARLES KIRKE. *Harold Marker*, an artist with a true artist's appreciation of the beautiful: W. H. GUNNING. *Michali Bralligani*, (Mickey Brallgant), a political exile: Budd Ross. *Munzio Flammetti*, the red brigand, but has a voice and a weakenss for Starlight: WILLIAM SELLERY. *Swipes*, a tough: WILLIAM SELLERY. *Italian Companions of Starlight (6)*: *Raphael*: Tillie Richardson. *Anita*: Annie Martell. *Francesca*: Ella Conroy. *Paoli*: Grace Galey. *Marie*: Lillian Wooton. *Jeanetto*: Kate Schollenberg. *Mrs. Highflyer Lionhunter*, a society gusher: RITA SELBY. *Miss Lucy Raffle*, a sweet young thing, a niece of Muddlebrain: CARRIE LIVINGSTON. *Miss Foxy Millbanke*: Kate Schollenberg. *Miss Draytone Borrower*: Lillian Wooton. *Bertie, Maud*, her nieces: Annie Martell, Tillie Richardson. *Carlotta*, known to her companions as "Starlight": VERNONA JARBEAU.

Act 1: Italy, at the spur of Vesuvius. The Mountain Home of "Starlight."

Act 2: Irvington on the Hudson, the fashionable home of Mrs. Lionhunter. The reception in honor of Starlight.

Act 3: Quaver's Music Store, preparing for rehearsal of his opera.

MUSICAL NUMBERS[81]

"Tarantella" (from *GASPARONE*)
(*Music by* Franz von Suppé.)
"Where Are You Going, My Pretty Maid" (imitation of Mme. Theo)
"Will You Come Out and Play?"
"The Nigger and the Bee"
"Sligo"
"That's Enough, Don't You Think?"
(*Music and Lyrics by* Vernona Jarbeau.)
Celebrated Spanish Songs

1892.22

WANG

A Revival of the Comic Opera (Operatic Burletta) in Two Acts[82]. Libretto by J. Cheever Goodwin. Music by Woolson Morse. Production under the stage direction of H. A. Cripps. Scenery by John H. Young. Costumes desiged by Alfred Thompson. Musical director, J. S. Hiller. Produced by the DeWolf Hopper Opera Comany (B. D. Stevens, Manager). Opened 9 May 1892 at the Broadway Theatre and closed 4 June 1892 after 28 performances.

CAST: *Wang*, the Regent of Siam: DeWOLF HOPPER. *Colonel Fracasse*, Military Instructor of Siamese troops: SAMUEL REED. *Jean Boucher*, Lieutenant of French troops: EDMUND STANLEY. *Pepat*, Keeper of the Royal Elephant: ALFRED KLEIN. *Chow-Sury*, inn-keeper: GEORGE WADE. *Panompin*, a Cambodian envoy: LOUIS SCHRADER. *Papanti*, Professor of Etiquette: Camm Mauvel. *Kurachi*, a waiter: M. J. Hollihan. *La Veuve Frimousse*, widow of the late French Consul at Pechaburi: MARION SINGER. *Marie*, her step-daughter, adored by Mataya: JEANETTE ST. HENRY. *Gillette*, her eldest daughter, beloved by Jean: ANNA O'KEEFE. *More daughters (8)*: *Nannette*: Helen Beresford. *Coralie*: Jennie Clifton. *Delphine*: Emily Beaumont. *Fleurette*: Margaret Wood. *Julie*: Ida Lecaire. *Babbette*: Louise Conway. *Rosalie*: Dolly Chase. *Chevette*: Nellie Douglass. *M. D. S.—242*: AGNES REILEY. *Mataya*, the Crown Prince of Siam: DELLA FOX. *Guards, Courtiers, French Officers and Sailors, Siamese Troops, Pages and Cambodians.*

1892.23

SPORT McALLISTER, One Of The 400

A Farce Comedy in Three Acts. Play by Charles T. Vincent. Directed by William A. Brady. Produced by Robert Gaylor. Opened 16 May 1892 at the Bijou Theatre and closed 11 June 1892 after 32 performances[83].

CAST: *Jeremiah McAllister*, better known as "Sport McAllister," an Irish Gentleman of sporting proclivities: ROBERT GAYLOR. *Dennis McGinty*, his rival in matters pertaining to politics: J. P. CARROLL. *John McAllister*, Sport's son, an amateur actor: HUGH MACK. *Percy Devere*, Sport's stepson: PETER RANDALL. *Chauncey Ryskes*, representative of the Hard Creek Insurance Company: Charles W. Young. *Patsey Slow*, one of the lower ten: M. J. Sullivan. *Servis Time*, a cook: M. J. Sullivan. *Representatives of the Foreign Vote (4)*: *T. Jefferson Cinch*: George E. Dodge. *Peter Hinkle*: William Keough. *Francois Boulanger*: Harry McDargh. *Guessippe Spaghetti*: H. E. Darce. *Policeman Sands*: WILLIAM KEOUGH. *Tilda*, a maid of all work: GEORGIE PARKER. *Genevieve McGinty*, an ambitious amateur actress: CAMILLE CLEVELAND. *Mrs. McAllister*, Sport's wife: MAY GAYLOR. *Minnie Chester*, a friend of the family: Irene Hernandez. *Neighbors of McAllister (4)*: *Sadie Brady*: Bessie Gilbert. *Katie Murphy*: Elsie von Rosen. *Sallie McCarthy*: Belle LaVerde. *Minie Martin*: Ada Montrose.

Act 1: Jeremiah McAllister's home.

Act 2: Behind the scenes at Hinkle's Lyceum Theatre.

Act 3: Private gymnasium in McAllister's house.

ACT 2[84]

"Tailor Made Girls"
G. Parker, C. Cleveland, others
Song-selected
C. Cleveland
Mixed Dance
R. Gaylor, G. Parker
"The Peruvian Gal-a-loo"
Company
Cornet Solo
B. Gilbert
The Olympia Quartette
Messrs. Keough, Sullivan, Mack, Randall
"El Mexicana" (Dance)
G. Parker
Unique Specialties
R. Gaylor

ACT 3

Finale

1892.24

ELYSIUM

A Lyric Comedy in Three Acts. Play by William Fleron. (Based on Marie Urchard's novel "My Uncle Barbassou.") Music by Jesse Williams. Lyrics by Pearl Eytinge. Staged by William Fleron. Scenery by Homer Emens (exterior), Arnold, Constable & Co. (interior). Costumes by Adame Adolphus. Conductor of orchestra, Mr. Davis. Opened 16 May 1892 at Herrmann's Theatre and closed 11 June 1892 after 28 performances.[85]

CAST: *Andre de Peyrade*: CLEMENTS BAINBRIDGE. *Beaujoli*: MAX FIGMAN. *Barbassou*: A. W. F. McCOLLIN. *Madame Barbassou*: PEARL EYTINGE. *Herbert Brooks*: Alexis (Markham) Gisiko. *Pierre*: Lionel Lawrence. *Gems of the Orient (10)*: *Koochi*: Jennie Goldthwaite. *Havira*: Maggie Deane. *Nazli*: Lillie Linden. *Zourah*: Rose Figman. *Lolah*: Cora Harris. *Fatimah*: Eva Taylor. *Selmah*: Dora Percival. *Zuleikah*: Rita Emerson. *Idalla*: René Ferris. *Katinka*: Maud Fenton. *Marie*, a maid: Lillie Madison. *Mlle. Pansy*: Dorothy Drew. *Koota-Koota Dance*, Act 2: Avita. *French Songstress*: Mle. Ottilie.

Act 1: Afternoon and evening at Barbassou's country seat in the South of France. Present.

Act 2: The following day in "Elysium."

Act 3: A bijou residence in Paris (Faubourg, St. Germain), owned, but not occupied, by Barbassou.

MUSICAL NUMBERS[86]

"Papa's Little Girl"
M. Deane
Cat Duet and Chorus

---

[80]No credits for scenery or costumes in programs.
[81]Vocals by Vernona Jarbeau, not necessarily in performance order.
[82]First produced 4 May 1891 at the Broadway Theatre for 150 performances. For Synopsis of Scenes and Musical Numbers, see original 1891 production.
[83]Scenery and costume designers, musical director uncredited.

[84]Pursuant to published sheet music, the following was interpolated on tour:
"One Word of Kindness" (also in A HIGH ROLLER)
Beatrice Norman
(*Music and Lyrics by* Barney Fagan.)
[85]No producer credited in programs; Charles Frohman leased the theatre for the season, but his name does not appear for this final production of the season.
[86]Musical numbers not listed in programs.

M. Deane, J. Goldthwaite

1892.25 THE ROBBER OF THE RHINE

A Romantic Comic Opera in Two Acts, 4 Scenes. Libretto by Maurice Barrymore. Music by Charles Puerner. Produced under the direction of Richard Barker. Dancing master, Mons. Mamert Bibeyran. Scenery by Hughson Hawley and William Schaefer. Costumes designed by Percy Anderson. Orchestra directed by Charles Puerner. Produced by Thomas H. Pratt's Comic Opera Organization. Opened 28 May 1892 at Harry Miner's Fifth Avenue Theatre and closed 2 July 1892 after 36 performances.[87]

CAST: *Waldemar,* the Robber of the Rhine: C. HAYDEN COFFIN. *Cunigonde,* the Brigandess: MARIE DRESSLER. *Flip,* the Brigand Vivandière: EDITH KENWARD. *Brigands (5)*: *Klootz*: Henry C. Peakes. *Kaspar*: Ross David. *Schpoof*: Wilder Pease. *Schweip*: Glyn Bigge. *Schplitz*: J. A. Day. *Baron Otto Piffleseltzer,* an Exquisite: J. H. RYLEY. *La Comtesse Terrine de Foie Gras,* his Aunt: CECILIA POLLOCK. *The Abbé Seraphin,* his Chaplain: EDWARD TEMPLE. *Dr. Hyacinth,* his Physician: George M. Herbert. *Oscar,* his Jester: John Ince. *Alphonse, Arthur, Hypolite, Armand, Georges, Lewis,* his retinue: [unidentified]. *The Rhinegrave von Bumsterhausen,* a great personage: WILLIAM F. OWEN. *Frommesel,* Court Chaplain: Sydney Price. *Dr. Pulver von Seidlitz,* Court Physician: HENRY J. BAGGE. *Agatha, Ursula, Derothea, Susa, Elsa, Edina,* Bridesmaids: [unidentified]. *The Gräfin Hildegarde,* the Rhinegrave's Daughter: MARION MANOLA-MASON. *Townspeople, Citizens, Peasants, Soldiers, etc.*

The action takes place in the Middle Ages along the Rhine.

Act 1, Scene 1: The Brigands' Lair. (Hawley.) *Intermezzo*: Hildegarde's Tourelle. (Hawley.) *Scene 2*: Market Place of Bumsterhausen. (Hawley.)

Act 2: Antechamber in Rhinegrave Castle. (Schaefer.)

1892.26 POCAHONTAS, Up to Date

A Burlesque in One Act, preceded by an Olio. Libretto and music by Harry LeClair. Director of music, William J. Rostetter. Produced by (John) Koster and (Albert) Bial. Opened 30 May 1892 at Koster & Bial's Concert Hall and closed 3 September 1892 after 126 performances.[88]

OLIO: Dufour and Hartley (French duettists) including the Paris Folly Dance; The Brothers Borani in 'The Disappearing Demons'; CARMENCITA in new dances; the Spanish Students; Joseph Natus, Samuel Dearing.

CAST: *Captain John Smith,* a man in search of land and beauty: DOROTHY DENNING. *Pocahontas,* the gentle Indian Princess: MADGE LESSING. *King Powahatan,* the cruel father, one of the F.F.V.: CHRISTINE BLESSING. *William, John,* two of Smith's sailors: Maggie O'Keefe, Belle Rosen. *Great Chief*: Allie Vivian. *Captain Jack*: Maud Harvey. *Manitoba John*: Maud Tempest. *Sergeant at Arms*: Gertie Sharpeley. *Little Indian Squaws (4)*: *Laughing Water*: Grace Langdon. *White Wing*: Irene Rice. *Gowanga*: Dolly Clark. *Asaleta*: Marie Carr. *Dr. O'Callahan*: James T. Kelly. *Lula Backnumber*: Harry LeClair. *Indians, Squaws, Papooses, Schoolgirls, etc.*

[87]Musical numbers not listed in programs; no libretto or musical score found.

[88]No musical numbers listed in programs.

1892–1893 SEASON

May Irwin (Photo: Thors)
Billy Rose Theatre Collection, New York Public Library for the Performing Arts

1892–1893 SEASON

1892.27

KING KALIKO

A Comic Opera in Three Acts. Libretto by Frank Dupree. Music by Frederic Solomon. Production under the stage direction of Jesse Williams and Martin Hayden. Scenery by William Schaffer & Loritz. Costumes by Mme. Thompson, from sketches by Frank Dupree. Musical director, Jesse Williams. Produced under the direction of Frank Dupree and George Witherspoon. Opened 7 June 1892 at the Broadway Theatre and closed 18 June 1892 after 13 performances.

CAST: *His Majesty King Kalico*, Sovereign of the Sandwich Islands: EDWIN STEVENS. *His Excellency Gideon Graball*, the Power behind the Throne: WILLIAM BLAISDELL. *Phineas Clip, Esq.*, a Yankee traveler: R. L. Scott. *Lieutenant Edward Hawley*, of the U.S.S. *"Lackawana"*: ARTHUR PACIE. *Lieutenant George C. Wexford Smythe*. Military Attaché of the British Legation: Bernard Lester. *General Kanoa*, Commander in Chief of the King's army: Sol. Mirandoli. *Hon. Oahu Testa*, President of the House of Lords: F. C. Palmer. *Prof. P. Christopher Jones*, leading light of the opposition party: Frank Brinkhurst. *Tai Fong Su*, a rich Chinese merchant of Honolulu: Robert Magee. *Colonel Pilipo Nuuana*, Lord Chamberlain of the Royal Household: Agnes Paul. *Members of Parliament (4)*: *Hon. Palani Po*: J. F. Dalton. *Hon. Ahilapalapa*: Thomas Hibbart. *Hon. Kealakeakua*: J. G. Cosgrave. *Hon. Molokini*: William Evans. *Yulee*, God-daughter of the King: NINA BERTINI. *Leila*, her friend and companion: CLARA LAVINE. *H.R.H. Princess Hokuokalani*, Cousin to the King: EVA DAVENPORT. (*Specialty, Act 2*, "The Coconut Dance": Messrs. Ducro, Martinetti, Fulton Brothers, Turnour, Rolfe.)

Friends of Yulee and Leila (8): *Hinano*: Sallie Maddern. *Kealo*: Vera Thorpe. *Wela*: Juliette Marco. *Lehua*: Eugeneie Maynard. *Malia*: Katie Glover. *Lauhala*: Dorothy Sherrod. *Kukui*: Adelaide Russell. *Waiala*: Rilla Barton. *Onomea, Waikiki*, Heralds: Nella Navaro, Lida Lear. *Legislators, Conspirators, Courtiers, Soldiers, Sailors, Pages, Natives, Chinese, Ladies of Honor, Kahili Bearers, Spearmen, etc.*

Act 1: Grounds of Parliament Building, Honolulu.

Act 2: The Palace Gardens.

Act 3: Throne Room of Iolani Palace.

MUSICAL NUMBERS[1]

"Love's Fragile Flower" (Waltz Ballad)

"Love Is a Tyrant"
A. Pacie

The Coconut Dance
Messrs. Ducro, Martinetti, Fulton Brothers, Tumour, Rolfe

1892.28

THE VICE ADMIRAL

A Nautical Comic Opera in Three Acts[2]. Original Viennese libretto (to the operette "Der Viceadmiral") by F. Zell and Richard Genée. English translation by John P. Jackson. Music by Carl Millöcker. Stage director, I. W. Norcross, Jr. Scenery painted by Henry Hoyt. Costumes by Mme. Loe. Director of music, Paul Steindorff. Produced by Rudolph Aronson. Opened 18 June 1892 at the Casino Theatre and closed 10 September 1892 after 73 performances.[3]

CAST: *Sybyllina*: ANNIE MEYERS. *Gilda*: VILLA KNOX. *Serafina*: EMMA HANLEY. *Donna Candida De Quesada*: JENNIE REIFFARTH. *Don Carambolo*: Mabel Potter. *Marquis Henry De Villeneuve*, Vice-Admiral: CHARLES BASSETT. *Don Mirabolante*, a Spanish Grandee: HARRY MACDONOUGH. *Don Narcisso*: Maurice Abbey. *Don Deodado*: A. W. Holbrook. *Lieutenant Manrique*: HENRY LEONI. *Lieutenant Lovell*: George Mackenzie. *Punto*, a Sailor: JEFFERSON DeANGELIS.

Act 1: Conservatory at Don Mirabolante's.

Act 2: Reception Hall at Don Mirabolante's.

Act 3: Quarter-Deck of the French Man-of-War, *"Guadaloupe."*

[1]Musical numbers not listed in programs.
[2]First produced in New York in German 24 October 1889 at the Terrace Garden Amberg Theatre.
[3]Musical numbers not listed in programs.

1892.29

SINBAD, or The Maid of Balsora

A Spectacular Extravaganza in Four Acts, 9 Scenes. (Book and lyrics by Harry B. Smith[4].) Music written and arranged by W. H. Batchelor. Produced under the direction of Richard Barker. Ballets arranged by Mamert Bibeyran. Scenery designed by Fred Dangerfield, W. T. Voegtlin. Costumes by Baron C. DeGrimm, William Dazian and Sarah Bolwell. Electrical effects by Martin Kruger. Musical director, Jesse Williams. Produced by the American Extravaganza Company (David Henderson, Manager). Opened 27 June 1892 at the Garden Theatre and closed 8 October 1892 after 105 performances.

CAST: *Sinbad*, a Dashing Young 'Prentice: LOUISE MONTAGUE. *Count Maledetto Spaghetti*, a Nobleman from foreign shores: SPENCER GRACEY. *Ninetta*, Sibad's' sweetheart: EFFIE CHAPUY. *Snarleyow*, a Villain who woos and tries to wed Ninetta: W. F. MACK. *Fresco*, the Idle Apprentice who blossoms into a Cannibal King: JOHN D. GILBERT. *Old Man of the Sea*: EDD READWAY [REDDWAY]. *Angelo*: Ida Bell. *Rafael*: HATTIE DELARO [BARNES]. *Nicolo*, father of Ninetta: DAN HART. *Maraschina*, who wins the Count: JENNIE WEATHERSBY. *Fiametta*, in love with Angelo: HARRIET WILLIAMS. *Zerlina*, in love with Rafael: Xenia Carlstedt. *Salamagundi*, Snarleyow's Lieutenant: JESSIE VILLERS. *Cupid*, the Guardian Fairy: Fanny Ward. *Tuesday, Wednesday*, Ethiopian slaves: Messrs. C. Crawford, E. Crawford. *Neapolitan Typewriters (6)*: *Perdita*: Louise Auber. *Anita*: *Rosita*: Jessie Fahnestock. *Pepita*: Hope Curtis. *Rosita*: Dora Scott. *Zepita*: Annie Pelham. *Marguerita*: Evangeline West. *Sinbad's Fellow 'Prentices (6)*: *Marco*: Miss Scott. *Giovanni*: Miss Gibbs. *Tito*: Miss Devere. *Luigi*: Miss Debow. *Sancho*: Miss Connelly. *Alessandro*: Miss MacDonald. *Smugglers Bold (6)*: *Orlando*: Gertrude Rutledge. *Malvolio*: Ida Bartelle. *Pedro*: Estelle Allyn. *Orsino*: Emmie V. Dixon. *Dromio*: Edith Merrill. *Roderigo*: Edith Ellison. *Persians, Savages, Negroes, etc.*

Flower Girls: Misses Henrietta Konrath, Nanon Dacy, Serina Schwartz, Martha Morris, Florence Carlisle, Bertha Wasserman. *Fisher Boys*: Misses Mollie McGill, Helen Konrath, Nellie Weston, Wilhelmina Oelka, Cecilia Curtis, Louise Freeman.

Act 1: The Port of Balsora at daybreak. (Dangerfield.)

Act 2, Scene 1: The Deck of the Roc. (Voegtlin.) *Scene 2*: The Depths of the Ocean. (Dangerfield.)

Act 3, Scene 1: A Tropical Isle. (Dangerfield.) *Scene 2*: In the Jungle. (Dangerfield.) *Scene 3*: The Valley of the Diamonds. (Dangerfield.)

Act 4, Scene 1: The Palace of Sinbad. (Dangerfield.) *Scene 2*: On the Road to the Chapel. *Scene 3*: Transformation. (Dangerfield.)

ACT 1[5]

Dance of Flowers
Flower Girls, Fisher Boys

"I Haven't Got It Now"
D. Hart

Entrance and Song
I. Bell, H. D. Barnes, Misses Devere, Debow, Scott, Gibbs, 'Prentices

"Tick-a-Tack-a-Tack" (Chorus of Typewriters)

"Clang Clang" (Duet and Chorus)
L. Montague, E. Chapuy

"He Couldn't Wink His Eye"
J. D. Gilbert

"I Declare I Must Win Him" (Raffle Chorus)

"Do You Catch On" (Song)
S. Gracey

Chorus of Smugglers

"I'm a Rover of the Sea" (Song)
W. F. Mack

Operatic Finale

ACT 2

Scene 1

"We're on the Sea" (Barcarolle)

[4]Smith's name appears in all tryout programs; in New York the libretto was uncredited.
[5]Added during the run to Act 1, after "Chorus of Typewriters":
"I Want To Be Somebody's Baby" (Song)
J. Weathersby
The published vocal selection (1890) also included two songs not in New York program list, "In a Minute" and "Lullaby of the Waves" which may be the same as "That's What the Wild Waves Are Saying."

"Bay of Biscay" (Hornpipe)
"Swearing Chorus"
"True as Steel"
L. Montague, Chorus
"That's What the Wild Waves Are Saying" (Quartette)
S. Gracey, J. D. Gilbert, W. F. Mack, J. Weathersbee
"The Night-in-Jail"[6] (Song)
J. D. Gilbert
"I'm Seventeen Today" (Song)
E. Chapuy
Scene 2
Tableau

ACT 3
Scene 1
Entrance of Pygmies (Danse L'Africaine)
"The Bogie Man" (Song)
W. F. Mack, Pygmies
"Money, Beautiful Money" (Song)
Entire Company
Burlesque Statue Clog
J. D. Gilbert, C. Crawford, E. Crawford
Scene 2
"Oh When I Meet Her in the Fountain" (Trio)
J. D. Gilbert, C. Crawford, E. Crawford
"The Bottom of the Sea" (Song and Dance)
E. Readway
Scene 3
"A Winter's Carnival" (Grand Ballet)
Dance Classique
Signorina Paris
Ballet Ensemble
Night
E. Craske
Winter
S. Paris
Grand Ensemble and Harlequinade
Grand Finale
Icicles and Snowflakes: Misses Deen, Welch, Sinclair, Annie Bouen, Middleton, Radcliffe, Becks, Nellson, Brant, Gobs, Gayer, Adams, Brant, James, Hughs, Smith, Scott, Gibbs, DeVer, Debow, Connelly, J. Connelly, Cookson, Bradshaw, Sailor, Scanlon, Foster, Mortimer, Clafery. *Sleighers*: Misses Holga Univer, Millie Barnard, Millie Lorello, Annie Hill, Addie Rivers, Lottie Hyde. *Tobogganeers*: Miss Helene Konrath, Henrietta Korath, Wilhelmina Oelka, Selma Schwartz, *Skaters*: Misses Nora Dacy, Mollie McGill, Nellie Weston, Florence Carlisle, Bertha Wasserman, Cecile Curtis.

ACT 4
Scene 1
"Modern Drama"
J. D. Gilbert, J. Weathersby
Smugglers' Chorus
Grand Wedding Cavalcade
Wedding Chorus ("Wedding Bells")
Grand Operatic Ensemble
Scene 2
Medley
Scene 3
Transformation "The Fleeting Seasons"

1892.30 THE MASCOT

A Revival of the Opéra-Comique in Three Acts[7]. Original French libretto ("La Mascotte") by Henri Chivot and Alfred Duru. Music by Edmond Audran. Produced under the stage direction of Napier Lothian, Jr. Costumes by George E. Hayden and Mme. Randolph. Orchestra under the direction of Julian Edwards. Produced by Henry E. Dixey's Opera Company (Management, Harry Askin). Opened 18 July 1892 at Palmer's Theatre and closed 27 August 1892 after 42 performances.

CAST: *Bettina*, the Mascot: CAMILLE D'ARVILLE. *Fiametta*, daughter of Lorenzo: YOLANDE WALLACE. *Pippo*, a shepherd: WILLIAM PRUETTE. *Rocco*,a farmer: FRED LENNOX. *Frederic*, Prince of Pisa: HILDA HOLLINS. *Antonio*, with dance: Ella Ringquist. *Matheo*, an innkeeper: Charles Jones. *Giuseppe*, a peasant: Florence Willey. *Paola*: Agnes Blake. *Angelo, Luigi*, Heralds: Trixie Friganza, Maud McIntyre. *Lorenzo XVII*, Prince of Piombino: HENRY E. DIXEY. *Peasants, Pages, Lords and Ladies, Soldiers, etc.*

Act 1: Rocco's farm. The vintage festival.

Act 2: Palace at Piombino.

Act 3: Italian Inn. Duchy of Pisa.

1892.31 FATHERLAND

A Tyrolean Play in Four Acts. Play by Charles A. Gardner. Music by Gustave H. Klne. (Lyrics by M. May.) Scenery by Sydney Chidley. Produced under the management of Sidney R. Ellis. Opened 1 August 1892 at the Union Square Theatre and closed 13 August 1892 after 16 performances.[8]

CAST: *Herman Leopold*, a guide: CHARLES A. GARDNER. *Henry Stanford*, from America: HENRY LEE. *Digby Barnes*, an artist: ROBERT V. FERGUSON. *Hans Veeder*, "once a young man": BARNEY REYNOLDS. *Otto Wolfe*, a smuggler: W. H. Turner. *Guides (4)*: *Rudolph*: Ignace Conradi. *Ludwig*: Frank Grauss. *Mat*: Carl Hofer. *Cris*: George Metz. *Rhoda Stanford*, a widow: EMMA VADERS. *Dorothea*, Herman's sister: MARION DAY. *Charlotte Wagner*, Rhoda's sister: Ethel Grey. *Little Meenie*: Baby Parker. *Peasant Girls (4)*: *Rosa*: Mirzl Meister. *Lena*: Olga Schweitzer. *Gretchen*: Carrie Grauss. *Wilhelma*: Ettie Green. And the Tyrolean Singers (Act 4).

Act 1: The Heart of the Tyrol.

Act 2: Herman's Home.

Act 3: The Man-Hunt.

Act 4: A Saengerfest in Munich.

MUSICAL NUMBERS[9]
"Gesundheit"
"Chamois Hunter"
"Pretty Bobolink"
"Bubble Song"
"German Swell"
"The Lilac"
"Alpine"
"Echo"
"Spinning Wheel"
"Bacchus' Choruses"

1892.32 A VILLAGE WEDDING

A Grande Scène Bouffe ('Une Noce Villagéoise') in One Act (accompanied by a Vaudeville Bill and the Burlesque 'Pocohontas Up-to-Date'). Libretto by Blondelet Vergeron[10]. Music by Edouard Deransart. Director of music, William J. Rostetter. Produced by (John) Koster & (Albert) Bial. Opened 8 August 1892 at Koster & Bial's Concert Hall and closed 29 October 1892 after (108) performances.

CAST: *Joseph Cornu*, the Bridegroom: Mons. DUFOUR. *Joli Coeur*, the Best Man: MADGE LESSING. *Denicheux*, Village Constable: JAMES J. KELLY. *Boulafoin*, Major's Deputy: CHRISTINE BLESSING. *Lolotte*, the Bride: DOROTHY DENNING. *Clairette*, a Peasant Girl: Mlle HARTLEY. *Mme. Gregoire*, Innkeeper: Dolly Clark. *Peasant Girls (4)*: *Manon*: Irene Rice. *Louisette*: Maud Harvey. *Marguerite*: Ray Vernon. *Susanne*: Marie Carr. *Peasants, Villagers, etc.*

[6]Replaced during the run by:
"The Three Scamps"
J. D. Gilbert, D. Hart, W. F. Mack

[7]English adaptation uncredited. First performed in English in New York 5 May 1881 at the Bijou Theatre for 168 performances in 2 engagements.

[8]Stage direction, costumes and musical direction uncredited.

[9]Not in performance order. Gardner sang all the songs, assisted by the Company on the last four.

[10]Most likely an adaptation of "Une Rose Villagéoise," libretto by Charles Blondelet and C. Saclé, music by Edouard Deransart.

1892.33

WANG

A Revival of the Comic Opera (Operatic Burletta) in Two Acts[11]. Libretto by J. Cheever Goodwin. Music by Woolson Morse. Production under the stage direction of H. A. Cripps. Scenery by John H. Young. Costume designs by Alfred Thompson. Musical director, J. S. Hiller. Produced by the DeWolf Hopper Opera Company (B. D. Stevens, Manager). Opened 15 August 1892 at the Broadway Theatre and closed 15 October 1892; re-opened 14 November 1892 at the Broadway Theatre and closed 19 November 1892 after a total of 70 performances.

CAST: *Wang*, the Regent of Siam: DeWOLF HOPPER. *Colonel Fracase*, Military Instructor of Siamese troops: SAMUEL REED. *Jean Boucher*, Lieutenant of French troops: EDMUND STANLEY. *Pepat*, keeper of the Royal Elephant: ALFRED KLEIN. *Pepanti*, Professor of Etiquette: Camm Mauvel. *High Priest*: G. Colletti. *Chow-Sury*, Inn-Keeper at Pechaburi: J. A. Parks. *Panompin*, a Cambodian envoy: Louis Shrader. *Kurachi*, a waiter: M. J. Houlihan. *La Veuve Frimousse*, Widow of the late French Consul at Pechaburi: MARION SINGER. *Marie*, her step-daughter, adored by Mataya: MARIE MILLARD. *Gillette*, her eldest daughter, beloved by Jean: ANNA O'KEEFE. *More Daughters (8)*: *Nannette*: Helen Beresford. *Coralie*: Eugenie Maynard. *Delphine*: Eva Swinburne. *Fleurette*: Margaret Wood. *Julie*: Ida Leclaire. *Babbette*: Louise Conway. *Rosalie*: Anna Hook. *Chevette*: Grace Weldon. *M.D.S.—242*: Agnes Reiley. *Mataya*, the Crown Prince of Siam: DELLA FOX. *Guards, Courtiers, French Officers and Sailors, Siamese Troops, Pages, Slaves and Cambodians.*

1892.34

THE KID

A Sparkling Musical Comedy in Three Acts, 4 Scenes. Book, music and lyrics by Henry White and Laurent Howard. Scenery by L. W. Seavey. Costumes by Paul Vernon. Properties of John Elfers. Musical director, Anthony J. Gray. Opened 22 August 1892 at the Columbus Theatre and closed 27 August 1892 after 8 performances; returned 26 September 1892 to the Windsor Theatre and closed 1 October 1892 after an additional 8 performances.[12] Total: 16 performances.

CAST: *Ebenezer Newrich*, rich but unpretentious: ED CHRISSIE. *Samuel Baxter*, a condescending servant: Edward J. Begley. *Swipes*, a gentleman from the Bowery: James R. Murray. *Billy Rustle*: James F. Callahan. *Tommy Drummer*, an advance agent: George E. Crump. *Irving Barret Smith*: Howard Graham. *A Phonograph Bearer*: Henry Mason. *A Guide at Niagara*: B. Porter. *Mrs. Maria Newrich*, who never does things by halves: KATE FRANCIS. *Evangline*, her youngest kid: DOTTIE PINE. *Emily*, her eldest, with two beaux to her string: GERTRUDE FORT.

Ladies of the Royal Burlesque Company (4): *Miss St. George*: Lena Bruce. *Miss St. John*: Emma Carr. *Miss St. Felix*: Lou Skillman. *Miss St. Dennis*: Carrie Richardson. *Specialty*: The Kid Quartette. *Telephone Girls, Passengers, etc.*

Act 1: The Fashionable Residence of Mr. Newrich. "Telephone"

Act 2: The Elevated Railroad Station, Third Avenue and 28th Street.

Act 3, Scene 1: Corridors of Hotel at Niagara. *Scene 2*: Niagara Falls by moonlight.

1892.35

AROUND THE WORLD IN EIGHTY DAYS

A Revival of the Extravaganza in Two Acts[13]. Based on the French adaptation of Jules Verne's novel "Le Tour du Monde en Quatre Vingt Jours," as adapted by Michael d'Ennery. Music composed and arranged by Mons. Debillemont. Produced by W. J. Fleming. Opened 27 August 1892 at Niblo's Garden and closed 3 September 1892 after 9 performances.[14]

CAST: *Phileas Fogg*: SYDNEY PRICE. *Passepartout*, his servant: GEORGE M. KIDDER. *John Archibald*, the American: W. J. FLEMING. *Mr. Fix*, the detective: FRANK PETERS. *Members (of the) Eccentric Club (5)*: *Andrew Stuart*: C. A. Williams. *Walter Ralph*: J. W. Walsh. *Sir Phil Phelps*: C. A. Leach. *Thomas Bulkley*: S. Halpern. *Samuel Fallintine*: A. W. Collier. *Servant*: J. Cochran. *Mr. Blivens*: H. Minnick. *Djelnar*: C. Rich. *High Priest*: W. P. Kitts. *Mr. Obediah*, a Calcutta magistrate: A. G. Harris. *Oyster Puff*: C. A. Cochran. *Barkeeper*: W. Jordan. *Bill Mills*: C. Clark. *Tom*: L. Bogart. *Conductor*: G. Edwards. *Captain Speedy*: K. P. Williams. *Lieutenant*: H. Samis. *Indian Chief*: W. A. Cattell. *Mate*: W. Ayres. *Engineer*: W. Brown. *Messenger*: J. Cochran. *Aouda* the Rajah's widow: LIZZIE R. RICHELLE. *Ayesha*, her sister: MINNIE C. REES. *Nancy*, Passepartout's sweetheart: IRENE GURNETT.

1892.36

THE NEW CITY DIRECTORY

A Refurbished Production of the Musical Absurdity in Three Acts[15]. Fifth Season. Libretto by Paul M. Potter. Music by W. S. Mullaly and Alexander Haig. '92 and '93 edition by Louis Harrison. Produced by N.Y. Bijou Theatre Company for Russell's Comedians. Opened 27 August 1892 at the Grand Opera House and closed 3 September 1892 after 9 performances.

CAST (The New Canvassers): *John Smith*, Stage Manager of the Gaiety: DAN DALY. *John Smith*, Janitor and Call Boy, Gaiety: LUKE SCHOOLCRAFT. *John Smith*, Detective: WILLIAM CAMERON. *John Smith*, Baker: ADD RYMAN. *John Smith*, Athlete: TYRONE POWER. *John Smith*, Advance Agent: JOSEPH C. MIRON. *John Smith Jr.*: JULIUS WITMARK. *John Smith*, Messenger: JOSEPH JACKSON. *Nanon Smith*, of the Gaiety: LYDIA YEAMANS-TITUS. *Mrs. John Smith*, Minerva Flats: MARGARET FITZPATRICK. *Misses Laura Smith, Dora Smith, Cora Smith*, rosebuds: Bessie Cleveland, Ethel Ormond, Nellie Parker. *Premiere Danseuse*: AMELIA GLOVER.

SPECIALTIES[16]

Baby Song
L. Yeamans-Titus

"Sally in Our Alley"
L. Yeamans-Titus
(*Music and Lyrics by* Henry Carey.)

1892.37

PATIENCE, or, Bunthorne's Bride

A Revival of the Comic Opera in Two Acts[17]. Libretto by William S. Gilbert. Music by Arthur Sullivan. Scenery by Richard Marston. Musical director, Herman Brode. Produced by Henry E. Dixey's Opera Company (Harry Askin, Management). Opened 30 August 1892 at Palmer's Theatre and closed 10 September 1892 after 13 performances.[18]

CAST: *Reginald Bunthorne*: HENRY E. DIXEY. *Archibald Grosvenor*: WALTER BROWN. *Officers of the Dragoon Guards (3)*: *Colonel Calverley*: W. J. McLAUGHLIN. *Major Murgatroyd*: FRED LENNOX. *Lieutenant, The Duke of Dunstable*: HAROLD BLAKE. *Patience*, a milkmaid: LEONORE SNYDER. *Rapturous Maidens (4)*: *The Lady Jane*: FANNIE EDWARDS. *The Lady Angela*: YOLANDE WALLACE. *The Lady Ella*: MAUD HOLLINS. *The Lady Saphir*: Trixie Friganza. *Chorus of Maidens and Dragoon Guards.*

1892.38

THE BLACK CROOK

A Revival of the Musical Extravaganza in Four Acts, 16 Scenes[19]. Libretto by Charles M. Barras. Music composed and selected by Thomas Baker, A. W. Hoffmann. Ballets composed by M. A. Bertrand; Act 2 Ballet music by M. Jacobi. Scenery by Charles S. Getz, Homer F. Emens, Harley Merry, J. S. Getz, John W. Sommer. Costumes designed by Howell, Russell and Wilhelm of London; Alfredo Edel of Paris. Production under the stage direction of Lawrence McCarty. Musical director, A. Bertrand. Produced by Eugene Tompkins. Opened 1 September 1892 at the Academy of Music and closed 20 May 1893 after 306 performances.

---

[11]First produced 4 May 1891 at the Broadway Theatre for 151 performances. For Synopsis of Scenes and Musical Numbers, see original 1891 production.

[12]No New York program available; detail from the Clipper, Dramatic Mirror, etc. Ladies of the Royal Burlesque Company taken from a Chicago program dated November 1892.

[13]This version first presented in New York 28 August 1875 at the Academy of Music for 43 performances.

[14]No program available; detail from the Clipper, Dramatic Mirror, etc.

[15]First produced in New York 10 February 1890 at the Bijou Theatre for 154 performances, and 6 October 1890 at the Biju for a return engagement of 32 performances. Total: 186 performances.

[16]Musical numbers not listed in programs. List prepared from published reviews.

[17]First presented in New York 22 September 1881 at the Standard Theatre for 177 performances. For Synopsis of Scenes and Musical Numbers, see original 1881 production.

[18]No credits in programs for stage director or costume design.

[19]First produced in New York 12 September 1866 at Niblo's Garden for 475 performances.

CAST: *Count Wolfenstein*: GEORGE K. ROBINSON. *Rudolphe*, a poor artist: NESTER LENNON. *von Puffengruntz*, the Count's steward: W. H. BARTHOLOMEW. *Hertzog*, the Black Crook, alchemist and sorcerer: S. E. SPRINGER. *Greppo*, his drudge: Sam Collins. *Dragonfin*: James Marba. *Zamiel*, the arch-fiend: Russell Hunting. *Caspar*, a villager: George Smith. *Skudelwhelp*, familiar to Hertzog: E. H. Griffith. *Redglare*, the recording demon: Willard Lee. *Bruno*, a gipsy ruffian: J. J. Gerry. *Wolfgar*, his companion: Sylvester Warren. *Stalacta*, the queen of the Golden Realm: ELISE GRAY. *Amina*, betrothed to Rudolphe: GERTRUDE WOOD. *Dame Barbara*, her foster mother: Mrs. Seldon Irwin. *Carline*: Sadie McDonald. *Rosetta*: Mabel Vine. *Dancers*: Mlle. ZOLE TORNAGHI (Premiere Danseuse Assoluta), Nicola Guerra (Premier Danseur), Mlles. Amalia Maveroffer, Marie Rizzi. *Specialties*: Kins-Ners (French equilibrist), Fielding (Juggler), The Paquelino Brothers (Head-balancers), FRENCH QUADRILLE DANCERS.

Act 1, Scene 1: A Valley at the Foot of Hartz Mountains. (Emens). *Scene 2*: A Rocky Pass. (Getz.) *Scene 3*: An apartment in the Castle of Wolfenstein. (Emens.) *Scene 4*: Laboratory of the Black Crook. (Sommer.) *Scene 5*: A Wild Glen in the Heart of the Brocken. (C. S. Getz, assisted by J. S. Getz, J. Sommer.)

Act 2, Scene 1: Subterranean Vault in the Castle of Wolfenstein. (J. S. Getz.) *Scene 2*: Lobby in the Castle of Wolfenstein. (Emens.) *Scene 3*: The Grotto of Stalacta. (Merry.)

Act 3, Scene 1: Apartment in the Castle of Wolfenstein. (Emens.) *Scene 2*: Illuminated Golden Terrace of the Castle of Wolfenstein. (Getz, assisted by J. S. Getz, J. Sommer.)

Act 4, Scene 1: Lobby in the castle of Wolfenstein. (Emens.) *Scene 2*: A Wood. (Getz.) *Scene 3*: Pandemonium. (Getz.) *Scene 4*: Dazzling Transformation Scene. (C. S. Getz, assisted by J. S. Getz, J. Sommer.)

ACT 1[20]
Scene 1
Bergères and Postillons
Danse Rustique
Coryphées
Scene 3
Song
S. MacDonald
ACT 2
Scene 3
Grand Ballet of Gems
Z. Tornaghi, N. Guerra, A. Maveroffer, M. Rizzi
Grand Adagio
Variations by Rizzi, Maveroffer, Guerra, Tornaghi; Waltz; Galop; Finale
(*Costumes designed by* Howell Russell.)
ACT 3
Scene 2
Fielding, the Marvel
Ballet (Popular Airs, originated by Lawrence McCarty, executed under the direction of A. Bertrand.) "Mary Green," "Hi-Diddly-Hi-Ti;" "Oh, What a Difference," "Ta-ra-ra-boom-de-ay;" "The Bowery;" "Maggie Murphy's Home."
French Quadrille Dancers from the Casino de Paris: La Sirene, Serpentine, Eglantine, Dynamite.
Grand March of the Amazons
ACT 4
Scene 4
The Realms of Stalacta

1892.39

12 P.M.

A Musical Comedy in Two Acts. Presented by Frank Williams' Company. Opened 5 September 1892 at the Bijou Theatre and closed 17 September 1892 after 16 performances.[21]

CAST: *Ezra Bancroft*, the craft uncle, "A borrower, not a thief:" DANIEL J. HART. *Charlie Column*, reporter on the New York "Roaster:" ALF HAMPTON. *Baron Goodbluff, Count Indebt*, Damaged European Goods: Ned Munroe, W. S. K. Mack. *Swift*, a slow butler: Richard Hunt. *Frances Bancroft*, who would like to be a baroness: ADELE RENO. *Jessie Bancroft*, delighted at the prospect of being a Countess: BELLE LEVERDE. *Edna Vandergould*, with great expectations: Helen Murray. *Nurse* to Baby Jack: Marie McGinty. *Jacqueline* (Jack for short), like other people's children: JENNIE YEAMANS.

Act 1: Sitting-room at the Bancroft House. Cornwall on Hudson. Charles Column solves a mystery. Bancroft a "spiritualist for revenue only." Music and a cup of coffee.

Act 2: Uncle Ezra's "Den." His troubles begin at "12 P.M." "Do others, or they'll do unto you."

1892.40

IOLANTHE, or The Peer and the Peri

A Revival of the Comic Opera in Two Acts[22]. Libretto by William S. Gilbert. Music by Arthur Sullivan. Produced under the stage direction of John Nash. Scenery by Richard Marston. Costumes by Mme. Schwenka, Mme. Radolph. Orchestra under the direction of Adolph Liesegang. Produced by Henry E. Dixey's Opera Company (Harry Askin, Management). Opened 12 September 1892 at Palmer's Theatre and closed 24 September 1892 after 14 performances.

CAST: *The Lord Chancellor*: HENRY E. DIXEY. *Earl of Mount Ararat*: FRED LENNOX. *Earl of Tolloller*: HAROLD BLAKE. *Private Willis* of the Grenadier Guards: WILLIAM J. MCLAUGHLIN. *Strephon*, an Arcadian Shepherd: WALTER BROWNE. *The Train Bearer*: Master Henry E. Dixey, Jr. *Queen of the Fairies*: FLORA FINLAYSON. *Iolanthe*, a Fairy, Strephon's Mother: YOLANDE WALLACE. *Fairies (3)*: *Celia*: Trixie Friganza. *Leila*: Lillian Hawthorne. *Fleta*: Lola Hawthorne. *Phyllis*, an Arcadian Shepherdess and Ward in Chancery: LEONORE SNYDER. *Chorus of Dukes, Marquises, Earls, Viscounts, Barons and Fairies.*

1892.41

ROBIN HOOD

A Burletta in One Act, 3 Scenes, accompanied by an Olio and "A Village Wedding."[23] Libretto and music adapted by Frederic Solomon. Director of music, William J. Rostetter. Produced by (John) Koster & (Albert) Bial. Opened 12 September 1892 at Koster & Bial's Concert Hall and closed 29 October 1892 after (63) performances.

Olio: Marie Vanoni (comedienne); Mason and Rallston (comedians); Frank Clayton (eccentric musician); Amann (European mimic).

CAST: *Robin Hood*: DOROTHY DENNING. *Sir Gilbert*: RAY VERNAN. *Allan-a-Dale*: CHRISTINE BLESSING. *Richard I*: IRENE RICE. *Will Scarlet*: GERTIE SHARPELEY. *Little John*: HUGH MYDLETON. *Geti*: JAMES T. KELLY. *Friar Tuck*: SOL MIRANDOLI. *Maid Marion*: MADGE LESSING. *Claribelle*: MARIE CARR. *Dame Durden*: DOLLY CLARKE.

SPECIALTIES, MUSICAL NUMBERS[24]
Bow and Arrow Dance
M. Lessing

1892.42

PURITANIA, or The Earl and the Maid of Salem

A Romantic Opera in Two Acts, 5 Scenes. Book by C.M.S. McLellan. Music by Edgar Stillman Kelley. Produced under the stage direction of Frederic Solomon. Scenery painted by Charles W. Witham. Costumes designed by Baron C. DeGrimm. Musical director, Ad Neuendorff. Produced by the Pauline Hall Opera Company (George B. McLellan, Director). Opened 19 September 1892 at H. C. Miner's Fifth Avenue Theatre and closed 5 November 1892 after 55 performances.

CAST: *Vivian George Trevelyan*, Earl of Barrenlands: PAULINE HALL. *Elizabeth*, the maid of Salem: LOUISE BEAUDET. *Abigail*, a woman hater: EVA DAVENPORT. *Jonathan Blaze*, Chief Justice of the Salem Court: JACQUES KRUGER. *Charles II*, King of England: JOHN BRAND. *Killsin Burgess*, a conspirator from habit: HARRY MCDONOUGH. *The Lord Chamberlain*: Arthur E. Miller. *Skimmilk Softly*, Chief of the Practical Explosionists: W. Marriott. *Paul*, a young villager of Salem: Irene Verona. *Smith*, the Witch Finder General: FREDERIC SOLOMON. *Puritans, Villagers, Colonists, Soldiers, Sailors, Judges, Courtiers, Pages, Officers, Conspirators, Maids of Honor, etc.*

Act 1: Salem, Massachusetts. 1665.

Act 2, Scene 1: A subterranean chamber in the palace of King Charles II, of England, Whitehall. *Scene 2*: Throne room in the palace.

[20]Programs list only ballets and specialties, not all musical numbers.
[21]Programs contain no mention of author, director, designers, musical director, or musical numbers.

[22]First presented in New York 25 November 1882 at the Standard Theatre for 105 performances. For Synopsis of Scenes and Musical Numbers, see original 1882 production.
[23]For detail, see entry above at 8 August 1892.
[24]No program available. Reviewers remarked upon 22 original musical numbers.

ACT 1[25]

"Hail to Everything Under the Sun" (Opening Chorus)

Contralto Song
E. Davenport

Chorus of Judges

"A Maiden's Art"
L. Beaudet

"She Says She's Possessed"
Chorus

Entrance Song of Vivian

"Love Is a Pretty Bubble" (Duet)
P. Hall, L. Beaudet

"Dip to Him Several Times"
Chorus

"A Rare Anomaly"
F. Solomon

"Test Song"
F. Solomon

"The Tiger of Tangaree" (Solo)
P. Hall

"Farewell" (Finale)

ACT 2

Scene 1

Introduction—Prelude to Conspirator's Scene

"For That's What Nobody Knows" (Solo)
H. MacDonough

"A Little Puff of Powder" (Chorus of Conspirators)

"Spirit of the Night" (Song)
H. MacDonough, Chorus

Scene 2

"Come, Youth and Beauty" (Grand Chorus)

"All Honor to Charles, Our King" (Chorus of Cavaliers)

"I Am the King" (Solo)
J. Brand

"Greeting to the King" (Solo)
P. Hall

"What an Interesting Vision?"
Chorus

"My Mother Said 'Don't'"
L. Beaudet

"He Loves—She Loves"
Chorus

"There Once Was a Witch" (Trio)

Response
P. Hall, L. Beaudet, Chorus

"Tell Us, Mutilated Strangers" (Quartet, Minuet Movement)
F. Solomon, E. Davenport, J. Kruger, H. MacDonough

"Finale

1892.43 CANDY

The Lilliputians in a Great American Spectacular Musical Comedy in Four Acts, 6 Scenes, in German and English. Play (and lyrics) by Robert Breitenbach. Music selected and arranged by Carl Joseph. Stage management, choreographic arrangement, decorative designs, dresses and elaborate properties by director Carl Rosenfeld. Produced under the direction of Carl and Theodore Rosenfeld. Opened 19 September 1892 at the Union Square Theatre and closed 10 December 1892 after 96 performances.

CAST[26]: *Sam Nollendorf*, a New York Millionaire: Mr. Kahn. *Kitty*, his daughter: MINCHEN BECKER. *Lyon Davis*, a rich farmer: MAX WALTER. *Wilhelm Mueller*, formerly a Theatrical Hair Dresser in Berlin, now a Messenger Boy: SELMA GOERNER. *Tom Klapps*, a bootblack: FRANZ EBERT. *Xandle*, a newsboy: ADOLPH ZINK. *Lori*, his sister: BERTHA JAEGER. *Ada Pfannenkuchen*, a Chansonette singer: IDA MAHR. *Rev. Binocle*: HERMANN RING. *Rosine*, his wife: TONI MEISTER. *Prince Ole Hugh Ham*, ruler of an exotic empire: Mr. Lueck. *King Kahira*: Mr. Streiman. *Princess Kilula*, his daughter: Miss Koehler. *Lycolos*, master of ceremonies at the Court of King Kahira: Mr. Durand. *Buffekaris*, high priest at the Court of King Kahira: Mr. Bechtel. *Rosila, Jezzonsa*, Court Ladies of Princess Kilula: Misses Lange, Maurer. *Colonel Meyers*: Mr. Schneegans. *Miss Meyers*: Miss Schlueter. *Anna*, niece of Mr. Nollendorf: Miss Werner. *Jean*, servant at Nollendorf's: Mr. Wilke. *Clara*, chambermaid at Nollendorf's: Miss Schultz. *Klinghammer*, plumber: Mr. Brown. *Jack, Pat*, servants: Messrs. Mueller, Joseph. *Impressario Sloman*: Mr. Dehneke. *A Policeman*: Mr. Waechter. *Captain Johnson*: Mr. Kuhn. *Tom, Dick, Harry*, pirates: Messrs. Steimann, Fruehauf, Wohlmuth. *Amazons, Servants, Courtiers and Court Ladies of the Prince, Guests at Nollendorf's Ball, Sailors, Crew of the Steamer "Microscope," etc.*

Act 1, Scene 1: The Music Parlor of a New York Millionaire. *Scene 2*: The Candy Palace.

Act 2: The Midget Club Room.

Act 3: The Deck of the Steamer *"Microscope."*

Act 4, Scene 1: The Desert Island, (Kitchiwah). *Scene 2*: The Bower of Roses[27].

ACT 1[28]

The Dancing Candies
Entrance of Chocolate Drops, Sugar Sticks, Rock Drops, Glass, Satin Bonbons, Male and Female Trick Bonbons, Burnt Almonds, German Cake Vendors, Plums, etc.

Episode by all the Lilliputians
Polka of Roosters, Hens, Chickens; The Duel of the Roosters; The Funeral; The Second Wedding; Final Galop.

The Fruits: Grapes, Bananas, Pineapples, Pears, Apples, Oranges, Pumpkins, etc.

The Electrical Candy Paradise (Closing Tableau)

ACT 2

March of the Amazons

Finale Quodlibet

ACT 3

Ballabile of the Sailors—The Quadrille of All Nations by all the Lilliputians
England, Ireland, Germany, the United States of America.

Finale, Can-Can.
The Lilliputians' Band

ACT 4

Princess Kilula's Festival of Flowers
Flower Waltz, Marguerites, Lillies, Carnations; The Awakening of the Flowers; The Great Flower Concert by all the Lilliputians.

Grand Finale Tableau. Eberts Butterfly Voyage.

1892.44 SQUATTER SOVEREIGNTY

A Revival of the Local Play in Three Acts[29]. Play by Edward Harrigan. Music by David Braham. (Staged by Edward Harrigan.) Scenery by D. Frank Dodge. Mechanical effects, Daniel S. Purnell. Electrical effects, John Whalen. Musical direction, David Braham. Produced by Edward Harrigan. Opened 19 September 1892 at Harrigan's Theatre and closed 26 November 1893 after 80 performances[30].

CAST: *Felix McIntyre*, Astronomer: EDWARD HARRIGAN. *Darius Dauber*: JOHN WILD. *Salem Sheerer*: DAN COLLYER. *Paddy Duffy*: JOSEPH SPARKS. *Denny McGuire*: CHARLES F. McCARTHY. *Captain Ferdinand Kline*: HARRY FISHER. *Terence McIntyre*: Dan Burke. *Fred Kline*: Fred Peters. *Tommy* with song: George Merritt. *Jimmy Casey*: William West. *Doctor Charles Parker*: Edward Gorman. *Herman Swartz*: Emil Husel. *Pedro Donetto*: James Burke. *Josephine Jumble*: Hattie Moore. *Nelly Nolan*: EMMA POLLOCK. *Louisa Kringle*: ADA LEWIS. *Maria Parker*: FANNIE BATCHELDER. *Bella Parker*: Annie Buckley. *Katrine Schultz*: Marie Gorenflo. *Lena Stueke*: Margery Teal. *Lulu Gratz*: Daisy St. Clair. *Widow Nolan*: ANNIE YEAMANS.

The McIntyres: Richard Quilter, Charles Coffey, Charles Sturges, Edward Gorman, James McCullough, Edward Murphy, William West, Dan Burke. *The Maguires*: John Decker, Willis Pickert, T. Young, John Walsh, John Mayon, John Brennan, Dave Braham, Jr.

---

[25]Interpolation also published: "There's No Such Thing as Pain" (*Music by* Adolph Nevendorff. *Lyrics by* C. M. S. McLellan.)

[26]"The Lilliputian actors' names appear in capital letters.

[27]During the run, scene revised as The Island of White Blossoms.

[28]Program lists only ballet specialties, not songs. One reviewer spoke of the song:

"That Is Love"
I. Mahr

[29]First produced in New York 9 January 1882 at the Theatre Comique for 170 performances. For Synopsis of Scenes and Musical Numbers, see original 1882 production. For this production, "The Forlorn Old Maid" was dropped.

[30]Costumes uncredited.

1892.45 A PARLOR MATCH

A Revival of the Farce Comedy in Three Acts[31]. Play by Charles H. Hoyt. Musical director, Will P. Brown. Produced by (Charles) Evans and (William) Hoey. Opened 19 September 1892 at the Bijou Theatre and closed 29 October 1892 after 48 performances[32].

CAST: *I. McCorker*, a literary man: CHARLES EVANS. *Old Hoss*, collector for an auction room: WILLIAM HOEY. *Captain William Kidd*, a lineal descendant of the famous pirate: JAMES T. GALLOWAY. *Ephraim Bellomont*, his next door neighbor, and descendant of Governor Bellomont, who captured the pirate Kidd: M. J. SULLIVAN. *Ralph Bellomont*, his son, in love with Lucille: Frank E. Struvy. *McKee*, of Allon, M. P.: Hugh Mack. *Asa High*, A sport: William Keough. *Wagner Carr*, a sleeper: R. W. Guise. *St. Clair Todd*, a Harvard student: Peter Randall. *Euphonia Allon*, the Captain's maiden sister-in-law: Lillie Alliston. *Lucille Kidd*, in love with Ralph: MADGE YORKE. *Aline Kidd*, with a preference for Harvard: LILLIAN MARKHAM. *Friends of the Family (5)*: *Vesta Bule*: Helen Douglas. *Gladys Riche*: Effie Chamberlain. *Marie Quick*: Myra Davis. *Lida Little*: Florence Wilson. *Nora Marks*: Leona Amrose. *Innocent Kidd*, her papa's angel child: MINNIE FRENCH. (*Olympia Quartette*: M. J. Sullivan, Hugh Mack, William Keogh, Peter Randall.)

ACT 1
"Oh Promise Me"[33] (from ROBIN HOOD)
M. Yorke
(*Music by* Reginald DeKoven. *Lyrics by* Clement Scott.)
"Sing Cheerily, My Hearty"[34]
M. French, Company

ACT 2
"A Parlor Match Medley"[35] An *Olla Podrida* of the latest music, Imported and Domestic
C. E. Evans, W. Hoey, M. French, M. Yorke, L. Markham, Company
Instrumental Solos
W. Hoey
"Constancy" (Club Trio)
E. Chamberlain, M. Davis, L. Amrose
Military Drill and Medley
Olympia Quartette
"Dancing Up to Date"
M. French
"The World's Fair"[36] (Finale)
Company

ACT 3
"Perfect Little Gentlemen"
The Seance Seekers
"(I Am) Not the Only One"[37]
W. Hoey
(*Music by* John Mayhew. *Lyrics by* Matt Woodward and William Jerome.)
Finale
Company

1892.46 THE SORCERER

A Revival of the Comic Opera in Two Acts[38]. Libretto by William S. Gilbert. Music by Arthur Sullivan. Orchestra under the direction of Julian Edwards. Musical director, Adolph Liesegang. Produced by Henry E. Dixey's Opera Company (Harry Askin, Management). Opened 26 September 1892 at Palmer's Theatre and closed 1 October 1892 (matinee) after 6 performances.[39]

CAST: *Sir Marmaduke Pointdextre*, an elderly Baronet: WILLOIAM MCLAUGHLIN. *Alexis*, of the Grenadier Guards, his son: HAROLD BLAKE. *Doctor Daly*, Vicar of Ploverleigh, specially engaged: FRED LENNOX. *John Wellington Wells*, of J. Wells & Co., Family Sorcerers: HENRY E. DIXEY. *Notary*: J. Vance. *Page*: Master Henry E. Dixey, Jr. *Lady Sangerzare*, a lady of ancient lineage: FLORA FINLAYSON. *Aline*, her daughter, betrothed to Alexis: LENORE SNYDER. *Mrs. Partlett*, a pew opener: Fanny Edwards. *Constance*, her daughter: YOLANDE WALLACE.

---

[31]Billed as Series 9 of A PARLOR MATCH. Originally produced in New York 22 September 1884 at Tony Pastor's for a 2 week run. Subsequently revived and revised for many editions presented both on tour and in New York. For a Synopsis of Scenes, see original 1884 production. For this revival, the following new song was interpolated:
"The Man Who Broke the Bank at Monte Carlo"
W. Hoey
(*Music and Lyrics by* Fred Gilbert.)
[32]Direction, settings and costumes uncredited.
[33]Replaced during the run by:
"Language of Flowers"
M. Yorke, F. E. Struvy
Which was later replaced by:
"Hello" (Duet)
M. Yorke, F. E. Struvy
[34]Replaced during the run by:
"And the Verdict Was"
C. E. Evans, Company
"Sailor Chorus"
Company
[35]Late in the run, the Series 10 Medley was identified as follows:
"Daisy Bell"
Chorus
(*Music and Lyrics by* Harry Dacre.)
"Oh, My Lodgings"
C. E. Evans, Company
"Doubting Love"
L. Markham
"Little Johnny Duggan"
C. E. Evans, Company
"The Garrison Ball"
M. Yorke, Company
"Monte Carlo Boys"
W. Hoey, Company
"Tell Me, Honey" (Finale)
C. E. Evans, W. Hoey, M. French, Company
[36]Replaced late in the run by "Midway Plaisance":
Sailor's Hornpipe (from England)
M. French
"Estelle-Por La Femme de Narcisse" (from France)
Cheridah Simpson (Lucille)
"Tyrolean Duet" (from Germany)
P. Randall, G. Metzger (Aline)
"(The) Gondoliers' Serenade" (from Italy)
M. J. Sullivan, W. Keogh, P. Randall
Dancers (from Russia)
The DeForeests
Song and Chorus (from Japan)
Stella Bonheur (Vesta)
"The Harp That Once Thro" (from Ireland)
H. Mack
"The Pipes" (from Scotland)
W. Hoey
"La Cruche Casse" (from Spain)
Sisters Merrilees
"Uncle Sam and Columbia" (from America)
J. T. Galloway, L. Alliston
Finale (Chorus of Popular Airs)
[37]Other sources credit this song to Fred Gilbert (music) and George Vickers (lyrics). Replaced late in the run by:
"They All Take After Me"
W. Hoey
(*Music and Lyrics by* Fred Gilbert.)
Replaced during subsequent tour by:
"Oh That We Two Were Maying"
C. Simpson, Augusta Klous (Aline)
[38]First presented in New York 21 February 1879 at the Broadway Theatre for 20 performances. For Synopsis of Scenes and Musical Numbers, see original 1879 production.
[37]The week's final performance consisted of a benefit with selections from *THE SORCERER*, *PATIENCE* and *THE MASCOT*.
[40]First presented in New York 15 November 1875 at the Eagle Theatre for 8 performances. For Synopsis of Scenes and Musical Numbers, see original 1875 production.

preceded by:

TRIAL BY JURY,
or, Love and Duty

A Revival of the Comic Opera in One Act[40]. Libretto by William S. Gilbert. Music by Arthur Sullivan.

CAST: *The Judge*: FRED CLAYTON. *Plaintiff*: YOLANDE WALLACE. *Counsel for the Plaintiff*: FRED LENNOX. *The Defendant*: HAROLD BLAKE. *Foreman of the Jury*: J. GILLOW. *Usher*: WILLIAM MCLAUGHLIN.

1892.47 THE LADY OR THE TIGER

A Revival of the Comic Opera in Two Acts, 3 Scenes[41]. Libretto by Sydney Rosenfeld. Music by Julius J. Lyons. Production under the stage direction of H A. Cripps. Director of music and conductor, J. S. Hiller. Produced by the DeWolf Hopper Opera Company. Opened 17 October 1892 at the Broadway Theatre and closed 12 November 1892 after 28 performances.

CAST: *Pausanias*, Regent of Sparta: DeWOLF HOPPER. *Menander*, His Prophet: JEFFERSON DeANGELIS. *Lamachus*, a Soldier in love with the King's Daughter: EDMUND STANLEY. *Theotychides*, A General: SAMUEL REED. *Irene*, Daughter of Pausanias: ANNA O'KEEFE, MARIE MILLARD (alt.). *Polyxena*, an Elderly Athenian Maiden: MARION SINGER. *Darouna*, a Persian Captive: IDA NAMARO. *The Five Ephori*, or Chief Magistrates of Sparta: Alfred Klein, Camm Mauvel, Louis Shrader, Will Jones, John A. Parks. *The Young Athenian Princes*: Ottilie Reiffarth, Helen Wright, Mollie Hilliard, Matte Stevens, Ella Flint, Emma Allien, Eva Swinburne, Margarite Wood, Pauline Johnson. *Hilaria*, Confidante of Irene: DELLA FOX. *Spartans, Soldiers, Athenians, Princes, Ladies, etc.*

1892.48 MRS O'BRIEN, ESQUIRE

A Farce Comedy in Three Acts. Play by John F. Sheridan. Produced by John F. Sheridan. Opened 31 October 1892 at the Bijou Theatre and closed 12 November 1892 after 16 performances.

CAST: *Bridget O'Brien, Esq.*: JOHN F. SHERIDAN. *Nora*: GRACE WHITEFORD. *Dora Sparks*: FANNY LIDDIARD. *Mrs. Henry Sparks*: EFFIE GERMON. *Rose*: Ida Orme. *Richard Sparks*: WILL R. BERNARD. *Major Tillen*: Alfred James. *Benjamin Brewster*: GEORGE SINCLAIR. *Charlie Bleeter*: Percy O'Blein. *Peter Dunn*: Ralph Post. *Fritz*: Julius Erickson. *Alfonso*: Sam Marion.

1892.49 BLUEBEARD/THE RENDEZVOUS

A Double Bill of a burlesque and a comic opera, accompanied by an Olio. Director of music, William J. Rostetter. Produced by (John) Koster & (Albert) Bial. Opened 31 October 1892 at Koster & Bial's Concert Hall and closed 31 December 1892 after (82) performances.

ACT I

BLUEBEARD, a Bijou Edition (Burlesque) of 'Barbe-Bleue' in One Act, 3 Scenes. (Libretto and musical adaptation) Arranged by Frederic Solomon. Music by Jacques Offenbach.

CAST: *Blue Beard*: FREDERIC SOLOMON. *Fatima*, his seventh wife: MADGE LESSING. *Selim*, Fatima's rejected suitor: Victoria Walters. *Hassan*, Blue Beard's Chamberlain: JENNIE ST. CLAIR. *Abdallah*, Fatima's Papa: CHARLES R. BURROUGHS. *Sister Anne*: CHRISTINE BLESSING. *Mustaphina*, Blue Beard's housekeeper: MARIE CARR. *Blue Beard's favorite Maids-in-Waiting (4)*: *Heloise*: Maude Harvey. *Eleonore*: Lillian Bishop. *Isaure*: Jessie Banks. *Hermia*: Anita Austin. *Abdul Bey*: Belle Taylor. *Abon Emir*: Gertie Sharpeley. *Slaves, Wives, Bazooks, Guards, etc.*

Scene 1: Outside the Town Hall. Bagdad. *Scene 2*: Exterior of the Blue Chamber. *Scene 3*: The Turret of Blue Beard's Castle.

ACT 2

THE RENDEZVOUS, a comic opera in One Act. Libretto by Melieres. Music by Jacques Offenbach.

CAST: *Jean Jacquot* of the Imperial Hussars: FREDERIC SOLOMON. *Jacques Jaspin* of the French Navy: CHRISTINE BLESSING. *Marie Michors*, in love with Jean: MADGE LESSING. *Mina Mignot*, in love with Jacques: Victoria Walters. *Lenoir*, Gendarme: Belle Taylor. *Jeanne*, Mistress of the Café: Maude Harvey. *Grisettes (5)*: *Cecile*: Jennie St. Clair. *Suzanne*: Gertie Sharpeley. *Polly*: Marie Carr. *Eugenie*: Lillian Bishop. *Jeannette*: Anita Austin.

Scene: The Tivoli Gardens. Present time.

1892.50 TUXEDO

A Revival of the Vaudeville in Two Acts[42]. Play, (music and lyrics) by Ed Marble. Musical director, Dox Cruger. Produced by Thatcher's Minstrels and (Isaac B.) Rich and (William) Harris' Comedy Company (Management, W. H. A. Cronkhite). Opened 7 November 1892 at the Park Theatre and closed 19 November 1892 after 18 performances.

CAST: *Sidney Vincent*, history unknown: RAYMON MOORE. *Gregory Gable*, a retired auctioneer: JAY QUIGLEY. *Jackson Park*, a typical Chicago man: BURT SHEPARD. *Lord Chulmondley Charingcross*: JOHN A. COLEMAN. *Red McGee, Plunket T. Plunket*, Song and Dance artists: HUGHEY DOUGHERTY, GEORGE W. LEWIS. *Cy Wilcox* from Pigeon Centre, New Jersey: H. W. Frillman. *Zeb Wattles*, Mildred's uncle (Slim Jim): George W. Dukelan. *Thisbee Euydice Pemberton*, of Boston: IDA FITZHUGH. *Sadie Newett*, one of the Four Hundred: Blanche Hayden. *Sadie Newett's friend*: Laura Mulick. *Lillie Sawitt*, from St. Louis: Grace Hamilton. *Mildred's Spanish Maid*: Mamie Lolo Yberri. *George Thatcher*: GEORGE THATCHER. (*Specialties*: TOM LEWIS, RICHARD J. JOSE, GEORGE W. LEWIS.)

1892.51 ROBIN HOOD

A Revival of the Comic Opera in Three Acts[43]. Libretto by Harry B. Smith. Music by Reginald DeKoven. Produced by the Bostonians (Henry Clay Barnabee, Tom Karl, W. H. MacDonald, Managers and Proprietors). Opened 7 November 1892 at the Garden Theatre and closed 24 December 1892 after 49 performances; returned 22 May 1893 to the Garden Theatre and closed 1 July 1893 after an additional 42 performances. Total: 91 performances.

CAST: *Sheriff of Nottingham*: HENRY CLAY BARNABEE. *Robin Hood*: TOM KARL. *Little John*: W. H. MacDONALD. *Will Scarlet*: EUGENE COWLES. *Allan-a-Dale*: JESSIE BARTLETT DAVIS. *Friar Tuck*: GEORGE FROTHINGHAM. *Guy of Gisborne*: Peter Lang. *Maid Marian*: CAMILLE D'ARVILLE. *Dame Durden*: JOSEPHINE BARTLETT. *Annabel*: BERTHA WALTZINGER.

1892.52 THE FENCING MASTER

An Opéra Comique in Three Acts. Libretto by Harry B. Smith. Music by Reginald DeKoven. Produced under the stage direction of Max Freeman. Scenery by H. L. Ried and William Schaeffer; Ernest Gros. Costumes designed by Alfred Thompson. Musical director, Gustave Kerker. Produced by J. M. Hill's Opera Company. Opened 14 November 1892 at the Casino Theatre and closed 25 February 1893 after 120 performances; returned 11 December 1893 to Daly's Theatre and closed 23 December 1893 after 14 additional performances[44]. Total: 136 performances.

CAST: *Francesca*, Torquato's daughter, brought up as a boy: MARIE TEMPEST. *Torquato*, Fencing Master of the Milanese Court: WILLIAM BRODERICK. *Pasquino*, Private Astrologer to the Duke: JEROME SYKES. *Galeazzo Visconti*, the Duke of Milan: CHARLES HOPPER. *Count Guido Malespina*: F. MICHELENA. *Filippa*, the Duke's ward: GRACE GOLDEN. *The Marchesa di Goldoni*: MRS. (LOUISE) PEMBERTON-HINCKS. *Theresa*, daughter of a Milanese money lender: BESSIE CLEVELAND. *Pietro*, an innkeeper: Agnes Sherwood. *Michaele Steno*, Doge of Venice: HENRY LEONI. *Rinaldo*, Captain of the Doge's guards: J. A. Furey. *A Gondolier*: George Mackenzie. *Fortunio*, rightful heir to the ducal throne: HUBERT WILKE. *Students in Torquato's Academy*: Misses Jeanette Perie, Vera Jerome, Julie Senac, Wellington, Chase, Bartlett, Clayborn, Fenton, Pelham, Marion.

---

[41]First produced in New York 7 May 1888 at Wallack's Theatre for 56 performances. For Synopsis of Scenes and Musical Numbers, see original 1888 production. For this production, the question mark following the show's title was dropped; Acts 2 and 3 were combined as Act 2, Scenes 1 and 2. Adolph Nowak's name was no longer listed as co-composer. Settings and costumes uncredited.

[42]First produced in New York 5 October 1891 at the Park Theatre for 32 performances. For Synopsis of Scenes and Musical Numbers, see original 1891 production.

[43]First produced in New York 28 September 1891 at the Standard Theatre for 77 performances in two engagements. For Synopsis of Scenes and Musical Numbers, see original 1891 production.

[44]Return engagement CAST: *Francesca*: LILLY POST, Laura Schirmer Mapleson (alt.) Additional principals included Thea Dorre, Gerald Gerome, Frederic Solomon, W. H. Frederick, Dot Connolly, Marian Langdon, A. M. Holbrook, W. West, Norman & Pease. Also played a return engagement 22 January 1894 at the Grand Opera House for 8 performances under the auspices of Fred C. Whitney; produced restaged by Al M. Holbrook.

The action takes place in Italy in the first quarter of the fifteenth century.

Act 1: Milan.

Act 2: The Piazetta, Venice.

Act 3: The Marchesa's Villa near Venice.

ACT 1[45]

Opening Chorus and Tarantella (Under thy window I wait)
F. Michelena, L. Pemberton-Hicks, Watchmen, Chorus

Duet, Gavotte and Chorus (Oh listen! And in verse I will relate)
B. Cleveland, J. Sykes

"The Life of a Rover" (Song)
H. Wilke

Scene, Ensemble and Entrance Song (What noise is that)
Students, F. Michelena, W. Broderick

Chorus (When a student goes to the wars, my lads)
M. Tempest, Students, F. Michelena, W. Broderick

Habanera and Quintet (True love is a gem so fair and rare)
L. Pemberton-Hicks, M. Tempest, G. Golden, F. Michelena, H. Wilke

Waltz Quintet (Lady fair, I must decline)
L. Pemberton-Hicks, M. Tempest, G. Golden, F. Michelena, H. Wilke

Chorus and Entrance (See in pomp the Duke appears)
Chorus, C. Hopper, J. Sykes

Chorus (I play all games of chance)
C. Hopper, J. Sykes, Money-lenders

Finale Act 1 (Now the ducal wedding fête)

ACT 2

Opening Chorus (O-hè! O-hè!)
Gondoliers, Citizens

Barcarolle (Loveliest Night)
B. Cleveland, F. Michelena

"Marinesca" (Quintet)(Oh! Come my love, the stars are bright)
G. Golden, M. Tempest, L. Pemberton-Hicks, C. Hopper, H. Wilke

"Ev'ry Knight Must Have a Star" (Song)
H. Wilke

Serenade (Singing a serenade is no light task)
C. Hopper, A. Sherwood, J. Sykes, B. Cleveland, Chorus

Solo and Chorus (We are miscreant bravos bold)
W. Broderick, Bravos

"The Nightingale and the Rose" (Song)
M. Tempest

Duet (Ah, yes, I love thee)
M. Tempest, H. Wilke

March and Chorus (See! in pomp and pride)
Chorus

Finale Act 2 (Bucentoro draws near)

ACT 3

Carnival Scene and Chorus (Ho-la! To the fête!)
G. Golden, Chorus

Duet and Chorus (We are very poor musicians)
C. Hopper, J. Sykes, Bravos

Serenade (Wild bird that singeth)
L. Pemberton-Hicks, Cavaliers

Aubade ("Will-o'-the Wisp" Song)
M. Tempest

Duet (Dwells an image in my heart)
M. Tempest, H. Wilke

Finale Act 3 (I will return to thee)

1892.53 FUN ON THE BRISTOL

A Revival of the Farce Comedy in Two Acts. Play by John F. Sheridan. Produced by Frank Sanger's Company. Opened 14 November 1892 at the Bijou Theatre and closed 3 December 1892 after 24 performances.

CAST: *Widow O'Brien*: JOHN F. SHERIDAN. *Nora O'Breeon*: Gracie Whiteford. *Dora McAllister*: Fanny Liddiard. *Bella Thompson*: Archie Hunter. *Captain Cranberry*: Alfred James. *Tommy Canberry*: Percy O'Blein. *Dick Sparks*: Will R. Bernard. *John Waffles*: George Sinclair. *Jerry Thompson, Pete Brown*, Stewards on Bristol: Sam Marion, Ralph Post. *Hawkshaw Pinkerton*: Julius Errickson. *Captain Somers*: Charles Manners. *Specialties*: Mons. Geram (Eccentric French Dancer), Mlle. Blanche Siegrist, C. B. Ward (Tenor vocalist), Misses Levigne and Hartz, Messrs. Marion and Post (Grotesque Dancers and Comedians).

1892.54 THE MULLIGAN GUARDS' BALL

A Revival of the Local Play in Three Acts, 8 Scenes[46]. Play (and lyrics) by Edward Harrigan. Music by David Braham. (Staged by Edward Harrigan.) Scenery by D. Frank Dodge. Mechanical effects by Daniel S. Purnell. Electric effects by John Whalen. Musical director, David Braham. Produced by Edward Harrigan. Opened 30 November 1892 at Harrigan's Theatre and closed 18 March 1893 after 126 performances.

CAST: *Dan Mulligan*: EDWARD HARRIGAN. *Simpson Primrose*: JOHN WILD. *Tommy Mulligan*: DAN COLLYER. *Pizarro Push*: JOSEPH SPARKS. *Gustavus Lochmuller*: HARRY FISHER. *Walsingham McSweeney*: Charles Coffey. *Reverend Palestine Puter*: William West. *Honora Dublin*: Charles McCarthy. *Ferguson Clinton*: Charles Sturgis. *Brigham Slopover*: George Merritt. *Gardiner Garlic*: Fred Peters. *Jimmy Sullivan*: Dan Burke. *Roderick O'Dwyer*: John Decker. *August Bimble*: Emil Huesel. *Podgy Delany*: Richard Quilter. *Lafayette*: John Mayon. *Tramp*: James Burke. *Policeman*: James McCullough. *Morris Goldstein*: Dave Braham, Jr. *Teddy Gallagher*: Willis Pickert. *Barney Driscoll*: Edward Murphy. *Bud Bloomer*: John Walsh. *Wooley Moon*: T. Young. *Sid Chambers*: John Brennan. *Lipsie Warren*: Michael Kearney. *Duck McGlum*: John Flynn. *Gussie Lochmuller*: Master Mooney. *Bridget Lochmuller*: HATTIE MOORE. *Maggie Kearney*: EMMA POLLOCK. *Kitty Lochmuller*: ADA LEWIS. *Cleopatra McSweeney*: FANNIE BATCHELDER. *Annie Riley*: Annie Buckley. *Cora Casey*: Marie Gorenflo. *Susie Sopus*: Daisy St. Clair. *Mary O'Brien*: Pauline Edwards. *Cordelia Mulligan*: ANNIE YEAMANS.

Act 1, Scene 1: Home of Dan Mulligan. *Scene 2*: A Local Street. Familiar Friends. *Scene 3*: Primrose's Barber Shop.

Act 2, Scene 1: McSweeney's Wee Drop Saloon. *Scene 2*: A Local Street. On to the Hop. *Scene 3*: The Mulligan Guards' Ball. Stand from under.

Act 3, Scene 1: Hallway at Mulligan's. *Scene 2*: Home of Dan Mulligan. The Silver Wedding. Turk.

ACT 1

"The Pitcher of Beer"

"Nellie After Five"

ACT 2

"Down in Gossip Row"

"The Little Widow Dunn"

"The Skidmore Fancy Ball"

"Babies on Our Block"

ACT 3

"Our Front Stoop"

1892.55 THE ISLE OF CHAMPAGNE

A Comic Opera in Three Acts, 5 Scenes. Libretto by Charles Alfred Byrne and Louis Harrison. Music by William W. Furst. Ballet divertissement arranged by Prof. Mamert Bibeyran. Scenery by Henry E. Hoyt. Costumes designed by Captain Alfred Thompson. Director of music, Paul Steindorff. Produced by Thomas Q. Seabrooke Grand Comic Opera Company (Charles MacGeachy, Management). Opened 5 December 1892 at the Manhattan Opera House and closed 21 January 1893 after 50 performances[47].

CAST: *King Pommery Sec'nd*, Ruler of the Isle: THOMAS Q. SEABROOKE. *Apollinaris Frappé*, his Prime Minister: WALTER ALLEN. *Prince Kissingen*, his son: Robert Dunbar. *Moet, Chandon*, his Army: LEE HARRISON, CLARENCE HARVEY. *Conspirators (3)*: *Marquis Mumm*: David Torrence. *Baron Heidsic*: Karl Formes, Jr. *Duc Monopole*[48]: Frank Soule. *Sam Binnacle*, Shipwrecked sailor of New Bedford, Massachusetts: EUGENE O'ROURKE. *Priscilla*, a New England maiden: MINNIE LANDES. *Abigail Peck*, her aunt, also of New Bedford, Massachusetts: ALICE HOSMER. *Diana*, the Belle of the Isle: ELVIA CROX. *Diana's companions (4)*: *Brigitte*: Florence Willey. *Artea*: Beatrice Hamilton. *Sophie*: Alma Desmond.

---

[45]Musical numbers not listed in programs. List prepared from published piano vocal score (G. Schirmer, New York, 1892, 1893).

[46]First produced in New York 13 January 1879 at the Theatre Comique for 152 performances. For Synopsis of Scenes and Musical Numbers, see original 1879 production.

[47]Stage direction uncredited; staged under the general management of Harry Standish.

[48]Role later renamed Bouche Sec.

Charmantine: Kate Ethel. *Pages in the Champagne Palace (3)*: *Chic*: Dora Allen. *Petite*: Sadie Dean. *Jolie*: Mae Stuart. *Premiere Danseuse*: Mlle. CLARA QUALITZ. *Archers, Citizens, Citizenesses, Cherry Girls, Cobweb Girls, Flower Girls, Ladies and Gentlemen of the Court of Champgane, Sailors, Doctors, etc.*

The action takes place on the Isle of Champagne; Longitude, 120 West; Latitude, 22 South.

Act 1: Exterior of the Champagne Palace.

Act 2, Scene 1: Hall of Ancestors. *Scene 2*: Hall of Cobwebs.

Act 3, Scene 1: The Royal Mausoleum. *Scene 2*: The Merry Shore.

MUSICAL NUMBERS[49]

"The Spider and the Fly" (Duet)
T. Q. Seabrooke, E. Crox
"The Cobweb Waltz Song"
"We're the Light Brigade" (Comic Duo with Dance)
"O, Fly Sweet Bird" (Waltz Song)
M. Landes
"Old King Mumm Could Make Things Hum"
T. Q. Seabrooke
"There's a Land in the Silvery Shimmery Moon"
"Song of All Nations, or She Had to Decline"
"Love at First Sight" (Duet)
"I'm a King with a Crown"
"The North Pole"
E. O'Rourke, Chorus
"Oh Dream of Life" (Duet)
E. Gregori, J. F. Sheehan, Chorus
"O'er Hill and Dale" (Sabot Dance)
"I'm Pommery Second the King"
T. Q. Seabrooke, S. Collins, J. H. Gilroy, Tenors
"No Mercy He Need Expect"
"Here's to Old Champagne" (Finale, Act 3)
T. Q. Seabrooke, Chorus

1892.56 A SOCIETY FAD

Russell's Comedians in an Eccentric Farce in Three Acts. Constructed for Laughing Purposes Only. Play by John G. Wilson. Music arranged by Gustave Kerker and Alex. Haig. Scenery by Homer F. Emens. Musical director, Alex Haig. Produced by Russell's Comedians (Albert Riddle, Manager). Opened 5 December 1892 at the Bijou Theatre and closed 25 February 1893 after 96 performances.[50]

CAST: *Lord Francis O'Farrell*, of the Grenadier Guards: TYRONE POWER. *Job Matchbang*, a wealthy American: JOHN JENNINGS. *Hamilton Jefferson*, a young American: JULIUS WITMARK. *Wiggins*, Lord Francis' valet: DAN DALY. *Hickory Jackson*, servant at Matchbang's: Luke Schoolcraft. *Alec McDuffer*, a private detective: WILLIAM CAMERON. *Dan Shadow*, his assistant: JOSEPH C. MIRON. *Sickels*: Joseph Jackson. *Mrs. Maria Matchbang*: MARGARET FITZPATRICK. *Margaret*, her daughter: NELLIE PARKER. *Vestalia*, from Kansas: LYDIA YEAMANS-TITUS. *Luella Snowdon*, from Boston: KATE UART. *Bella Livingstone*, from New York: ETHEL ORMONDE. *Dance Specialty*, Act 2: AMELIA GLOVER.

Act 1: Drawing-room at Matchbang's.

Act 2: The Roof Garden.

Act 3: Reception Room and Conservatory at Matchbang's.

1892.57 IF I WERE YOU

A Domestic Comedy in Three Acts[51]. Play by William Young. Stage director, Stanislaus Stange. Scenery by Charles W. Witham. Musical director, Carlo Torriani. Produced the Manola-Mason Company (Direction, Wesley Sisson). Opened 20 December 1892 at Hermann's Theatre and closed 6 January 1893 after 25 performances.

CAST: *Sir Timothy Carew*, of Fernymead: HERBERT ARCHER. *Major Fyvie* of the Highlanders: ROBERT MCWADE. *Lieutenant Beauchamp* of the "Skelton Brigade": JUNIUS BRUTUS BOOTH. *Jack Charteris*, just from the Antipodes: JOHN MASON. *Thomas*, a footman: Charles Adams. *Mrs. Primrose*, widow, still highly eligible: ANNIE M. CLARKE. *Doris Carew*, Sir Timothy's niece: MARION MANOLA (-MASON). *Philopoena*, Mrs. Primrose's daughter: Hattie E. Schell. *Susan*, a housemaid: Mabel Torrey.

The action takes place at the present time at Fernymead, a quiet English neighborhood.

Act 1: Mrs. Primrose's Drawing Room.

Act 2: Love's Lane, Fernymead.

Act 3: Drawing Room at Sir Timothy's.

MUSICAL NUMBERS[52]

Duet ("If I Were You")
M. Manola, J. Mason
(*Music by* Julian Edwards.)

1892.58 MISS BLYTHE OF DULUTH

A Comedy-Drama in Three Acts. Play (and lyrics) by William B. Gill. Music by Harry Braham. Musical director, D. S. Godfrey. Produced by Annie Pixley. Opened 26 December 1892 at the Grand Opera House and closed 31 December 1892 after 8 performances[53].

CAST: *Bessie Blythe*, Miss Blythe of Duluth: ANNIE PIXLEY. *Ida Barkley*, her married sister: LULU KLEIN. *Lady Astley*, Sir Talbot's wife: GENEVIEVE BEAMAN. *Miss Letitia*, Barkley's sister: Anna Douglass. *John Barkley*, a leather manufacturer: FREDERIC SACKETT. *Abner Bryce*, a young man from the West: HARRY B. BELL. *Sir Talbot Astley*, Agent of an English syndicate: FRED J. BUTLER. *Ruggles*, an imported butler: Joseph Brennan.

Act 1: Room in Barkley's Villa. Ozonia-by-the-Sea. Morning.

Act 2: The same. Evening.

Act 3: Exterior of Ozonia Hotel. The next day.

MUSICAL NUMBERS

"The Roof Garden"
A. Pixley
"The College Drill"
A. Pixley
"The Pixley Medley"
A. Pixley

1892.59 SUPERBA

A Unique Mechanical and Pantomime Spectacle in Three Acts, 13 Scenes. Invented and arranged by the Hanlon Brothers. Music composed, adapted and arranged by Max Frehrmann. Scenes by Ernest Albert, Grover and Walter Burridge, (George Heinemann; John A. Thompson). Costumes by Dazian. Produced under the supervision of the Hanlon Brothers. Opened 26 December 1892 at the 14th Street Theatre and closed 7 January 1893 after 16 performances.

CAST: *Superba*, a Righteous Queen, the Guardian of True Love: LOUISE DEMPSEY. *Wallalia*, a Wicked Queen, tributary to King Malign: ALMA STRONG. *Sylvia*, a Maiden, gentle, sweet and fair: KATE CHESLEY. *Leander*, a Lover, resolute, bold and true: MAUD MIDGELEY. *Pierrot*, active, pale and dumb: WILLIAM SCHRODE. *Mora*, foster sister of Sylvia: Ada Melrose. *Barty*, fond of mischief and Mora: Louis Peters. *Brigitta*, old but active: John Schrode. *King Malign*, a winged Demon: JOSEPH HARVEY. *Wallalia's Wicked Imps (4)*: *Hazareth*: Henry Schrode. *Zampa*: A. Roccardi. *Sacatrapas*: George Schrode. *Nimble*: R. Neville. *First Soldier*: J. Phillipi. *Second Soldier*: A. Phillipi. *Surgeon*: A. Carlous. *Suberba's Fairy Assistants (6)*: *Sanora*: Alma Russell. *Dahlia*: F. C. Clarke. *Camelia*: Alice Tack. *Stolacta*: Edith Curtis. *Zephyra*: Louisa Vercellesi. *Fuchsia*: Clara Vercellesi. *Acrobatic Specialties*: THE FOUR SCHRODE BROTHERS (William, John, Henry, George). *Fairies, Imps, Sprites, Peasants, Servants, Bull-fighters, Cowboys, etc.*

Act 1, Scene 1: Home of Sylvia. *Scene 2*: The Magic Garden. *Scene 3*: Arsenal and grand square near Prince Leander's Palace. (Heinemann.) *Scene 4*: Leander in pursuit of Sylvia. *Scene 5*: Chasm of the charmed rock.

Act 2, Scene 1: Abbey of the Echoes. *Scene 2*: The flowery lane. *Scene 3*: Enchanting transformation.

Act 3, Scene 1: Forest scene. *Scene 2*: Dentistry à la Pierrot. *Scene 3*: Wallalia's Studio. (Thompson.) *Scene 4*: Superba's retaliation. *Scene 5*: Grand Transformation.

---

[49]Musical numbers not listed in programs. List prepared from published vocal selection. (Witmark, New York, 1892). One interpolation:

"The Prodigal Son"
(*Music by* Josephine Gro. *Lyrics by* Bill Nye.)

[50]No costume designer or musical numbers listed in programs.

[51]Preceded by a curtain-raiser, The Army Surgeon, by Stanislaus Stange.

[52]Other specialties and interpolations not listed in programs.

[53]Direction, scenic and costume design uncredited.

ACT 1[54]

Scene 1

Wallalia's plot to separate the lovers. Superba plans to defeat the wicked queen. Sylvia abducted.

Scene 2

Pierrot finds it hard to write a letter. Barty's jealousy of Pierrot leads to amusing results.

Scene 3

Grotesque Dance

Phillipi Troupe

The wedding procession interrupted. Syvlia spirited away. Comic scene. Pierrot endeavors to pass the sentries. The dandy soldier. The educated horse. The skilled surgeon.

Scene 4

Leader in pursuit of Sylvia. Barty and Mora assist in the search. Sylvia consigned to a fairy tomb. Superba states the condition by which Leander may regain his love. The King's summons to Wallalia. Leander rescues Sylvia with Superba's charm, but loses her and finds himself in Wallalia's power. Leander rejects with scorn Wallalia's proffered love. Wallalia's rage. Leander given to the lions. Superba to the rescue. Mora and Barty get a scare. Pierrot and the lions. Recapture of Leander. Doomed to a fearful fate. The Mystery of the Charmed Rock.

ACT 2

Scene 1

Procession of monks. Superba announces the voyage on the sea of roses. Pierrot's encounter with the monks. He samples a cask of wine and likes the sample. The enchanted candies. Sylvia's aeriel flight. Pierrot, the donkey and the balloon.

Serpentine Dance (*Arranged by* Mme. Eloise Kruger.)

A. Melrose, assisted by Misses Clark, Curtis, L. Vercellesi, C. Vercellesi

Pierrot invited to the Fairy Ball. Arranges his toilet before the Magic Mirror. The bull fight tableaux.

Scene 2

Pierrot presents Mora with a bouquet. The opening flowers.

Song

A. Melrose

Scene 3

The Fairy Vessel on a Sea of Roses.

ACT 3

Scene 1

Leander despairs. He scorns Wallalia's proffered love. Naught but death! "Hold, rash fool, not death but happiness is near!" Barty and the Five Senses. Pierrot's adventures with the crocodile. The cowboy chase.

Acrobatic Act

Schrode Brothers

Scene 2

Song

L. Dempsey

Scene 3

Pierrot's visit in search of the key. The mysterious bench. The artist dismembered. Pursuit of Pierrot.

Scene 4

Suberba's retaliation. Overthrow of Wallalia. Reunion of the lovers.

Scene 5

The Wealth of the World and the Genius of America: The Landing of Columbus; Washington crossing the Delaware; American Genius (Fulton, Franklin, Morse, Edison); Emancipation; Europe; Asia; Africa; America; World's Fair Groups.

[54]On subsequent tour, the following were interpolated into the score, as per published sheet music:

"The Christmas Ball"

Julia Mackey

(*Music and Lyrics by* E. A. Warren.)

"Cash!"

Rosie Sutherland

(*Music by* Harry F. Carson. *Lyrics by* Arthur J. Lamb.)

1892.60 LA CIGALE

A Revival of the Opéra-Comique in Three Acts[55]. English libretto by F. C. Burnand[56]. Based on the French original (La Cigale et La Fourmi) by Henri Chivot and Alfred Duru. Music by Edmond Audran. Additional music by Ivan Caryll. Produced under the stage direction of Richard Barker. Scenery by Henry Hoyt, Benson Sherwood, Harley Merry, W. C. Smock. Musical director, Jesse Williams. Produced by Lillian Russell Opera Comique Company (T. Henry French, Proprietor and Manager). Opened 26 December 1892 at the Garden Theatre and closed 7 January 1893 after 14 performances.

CAST: *Marton* (The Grasshopper, La Cigale): LILLIAN RUSSELL. *Chevalier Franz de Bernheim*: C. HAYDEN COFFIN. *William*: JOHN E. DUDLEY. *Vincent Knapps*: W. T. CARLETON. *Duke of Fayensberg*: Charles Dungan. *Cavalier*: Charles Roux. *Curfew Watch*: Jean Dore. *Mendicant*: James G. Peakes. *Matthew Vanderkoopen*, Landlord of the Golden Lamb, Bruges; Uncle to Marton and Charlotte: LOUIS HARRISON. *Charlotte*: Laura Clement. *Rosina*: Teckla Morton. *Marietta*: Martha Habelman. *Dancers at the Opera (6)*: *Juliette Grisenbach*: Miss M. McGill. *Aliza*: Florence Carlisle. *Zitanella*: Ella Sharman. *Tamburina*: Miss Cuthbert. *Cecilia*: Nellie Weston. *Francoise*: Nanne DeVere. *Leila*: Agnes Blake. *La Frivolini*: Florence Franton. *Camille DuBarri*: Fanny Johnson. *Catherine*: Marion Welles. *Duchess of Fayensberg*: ADA DARE. *Marina*: Maude Manning. *Peasants, Courtiers, Wedding Guests, etc.*

1893.01 ORPHEUS/ THE MILLER'S DAUGHTER

A Double Bill of a Burlesque and an Opéra-bouffe, accompanied by a Vaudeville Bill. Director of music, William J. Rostetter. Produced by (John) Koster & (Albert) Bial. Opened 2 January 1893 at Koster & Bial's Concert Hall and closed 11 February 1893 after 54 performances.

ORPHEUS, a Bijou Edition (Burlesque) of 'Orphée aux Enfers' in One Act, 3 Scenes. (Libretto and musical adaptation) Arranged by Frederic Solomon. Music by Jacques Offenbach.

CAST: *Orpheus*, a poor musician: FREDERIC SOLOMON. *Eurydice*, his wife: MADGE LESSING. *Adonis*, Orpheus' friend: DOROTHY DENNING. *Pluto*, the Hustler: Victoria Walters. *Jupiter*, by Jove: Charles T. Burroughs. *Juno*, his wife: CHRISTINE BLESSING. *Public Opinion*: Marie Carr. *Mars*, God of War: Carrie Appleton. *Mercury*, a messenger boy: Irene Rice. *Diana*, Goddess of the Chase: Jennie St. Clair. *Venus*, Goddess of Love: Helen Delafield. *Cupid*, Son of Venus: Mae Powers. *Hercules*, Son of Jupiter: Kate Davis. *Bacchus*, God of Wine: Maggie O'Keefe. *Minerva*, Goddess of Wisdom: Jessie Banks. *Hebe*, Goddess of Youth: Anita Austin. *Morpheus*, God of Sleep: Gertie Sharpley. *Hymen*, God of Marriage: Mabel Blair. *Thalia*, Muse of Comedy: Ruth Ward. *Fortima*, Goddess of Fortune: Maude Harvey. *Students, Gods, Goddesses, etc.*

Scene 1: A Cornfield near Orpheus' House. *Scene 2*: Jupiter's Temple. *Scene 3*: Outside Hades.

THE MILLER'S DAUGHTER, an Opéra-bouffe in One Act. Libretto by Théodore Barrière. Music by Léo Delibes.

CAST: *Pierre*, a country bumpkin: FREDERIC SOLOMON. *Nanette*, the miller's daughter: MADGE LESSING. *Rudolphe*, her father: Charles T. Burroughs. *Valentine*, Drum Major: Jennie St. Clair. *Dagobert*, Captain of the Guard: CHRISTINE BLESSING. *Drummers, Millers, etc.*

Scene: A Village near Lille, France. 1802.

1893.02 THE MOUNTEBANKS

A Comic Opera in Two Acts. Libretto by William S. Gilbert. Music by Alfred Cellier[57]. Entire production under the personal supervision of Richard

[55]First produced in New York 26 October 1891 at the Garden Theatre for 112 performances. For Synopsis of Scenes and Musical Numbers, see original 1891 production. In his autobiography (Hayden Coffin's Book, Alston Rivers Ltd., London, 1930), C. Hayden Coffin states that the following new song was interpolated for him in the London production of LA CIGALE 21 May 1891:

"Look with Thine Eyes in Mine, Love"

C. H. Coffin

(*Music by* Ivan Caryll. *Lyrics by* Fred Weatherly.)

Whether Carl Streittman performed it in October 1891 is doubtful; Coffin certainly performed it in NYC.

[56]In a program note, Burnand graciously thanks Mr. Gilbert à Beckett for his assistance in setting new words to old music.

[57]The musical score was completed upon Cellier's death by the London production's musical director, Ivan Caryll.

Barker. Dances arranged by Mamert Bibeyran. Scenery painted by Joseph Claire. Costumes designed by Percy Anderson. Musical director, Charles Puerner. Produced by the Lillian Russell Opera Comique Company (T. Henry French, Proprietor and Manager). Opened 11 January 1893 at the Garden Theatre and closed 27 February 1893 after 47 performances.

CAST: *Alfredo*, a young peasant loved by Ultrice, but in love with Teresa: C. HAYDEN COFFIN. *Pietro*, proprietor of a troupe of Mountebanks: W. T. CARLETON. *Bartolo*, Pietro's clown: LOUIS HARRISON. *Arrostino Annegate*, Captain of the Tamorras, a secret society: CHARLES DUNGAN. *Giorgio Raviolo, Luigi Spaghetti*, Members of his band: John Dudley, Charles Roux. *Risotto*, one of the Tamorras, just married to Minestra: HENRY HALLAM. *Elvino Di Pasta*, an innkeeper: GEORGE BRODERICK. *Beppo*: Russell Malcolm. *Giuseppe*: A. Bassi. *Ultrice*, in love with and detested by Alfredo: MABELLA BAKER. *Nita*, a dancing girl: Laura Clement. *Minestra*, Risotto's bride: ADA DARE. *Teresa*, a village beauty, loved by Alfredo, but in love with herself: LILLIAN RUSSELL. *Tamorras, Monks, Village Girls, etc.*

The action takes place early in the nineteenth century.

Act 1: Exterior of Elvino's Inn, in a picturesque Sicilian pass. Morning.

Act 2: Exterior of a Dominican Monastery. Moonlight.

ACT 1[58]

"The Chaunt of the Monks"
Chorus
Chorus of Girls ("Come, all ye maidens")
Duet ("If you please")
H. Hallam, A. Dare
Chorus of Girls ("Only think, a Duke and Duchess")
Song/Solo and Chorus ("High Jerry Ho!")
J. Dudley, Chorus
Recitative ("Teresa, Little Word")
Song (Bedecked in Fashion Trim")
C. H. Coffin
Ballad ("It's My Opinion")
L. Russell
Quartette ("Upon my word, Miss")
M. Baker, L. Russell, C. H. Coffin, G. Broderick
Quartette ("Fair maid take pity")
C. H. Coffin, M. Baker, L. Russell, G. Broderick
Soli and Chorus of Girls ("Tabor and Drum")
Song and Trio ("Those days of old")
L. Clement, L. Harrison, W. T. Carleton
Recititative ("Oh, luck unequalled")
M. Baker
Song ("I'm only joking")
L. Russell
Finale ("Come and Take Your Places All")

ACT 2

Duet ("I'd be a young girl if I could")
A. Dare, H. Hallam
Recitative and Song ("All alone in my eerie")
L. Russell
Duet ("If I can catch this jolly Jack-Patch")
L. Russell, A. Dare
Duet ("If our action's stiff and crude")
L. Harrison, L. Clement
Trio ("Where gentlemen are eaten up with jealousy")
L. Harrison, L. Clement, W. T. Carleton
Soli and Chorus ("Time there was when earthly joy")
Chorus
Song ("When your clothes from your hat to your socks")
W. T. Carleton
Soli and Chorus ("The Duke and Duchess hither wend their way")
C. Dungan, C. H. Coffin, Chorus
Song ("Where's my duck-a-deary?")
L. Russell
Duet, Recitative and Trio ("In days gone by")
C. H. Coffin, L. Russell, M. Baker
Scena and Song ("An hour? Nay, nay")
M. Baker
Soli and Chorus ("Oh, please you not to go away")
Chorus
Finale ("Hope lived, and free from fear, Love sang her roundelay")

1893.03 FRIEND FRITZ

A Play (with Music) in Three Acts. Play and lyrics by Stanislaus Stange. Adapted from the French novel "L'Ami Fritz" by Émile Erckmann and Alexandre Chatrian. Original and characteristic score by Julian Edwards. Scenery by Lafayette W. Seavey. Entire stage production under the sole direction of Mons. Marius. Produced by the Manola-Mason Company (Mason Brothers, directors). Opened 26 January 1893 at Herrmann's Theatre and closed 25 February 1893 after 36 performances.

CAST: *Fritz Kobus*, landed proprietor: JOHN MASON. *David Sichel*, rabbi: Robert McWade. *Frederic*, land surveyor: Seth M. Crane. *Hanezo*, tax collector: Edward P. Temple. *Christel*, Kobus' tenant, Suzel's father: Edward McWade. *Of Messanges Farm (5)*: *Pierre*: Charles Moore. *Antoine*: James L. Dickerson. *Gaspard*: W. H. Ekmirg. *Jean*: George Stansfield. *Katherine*, Kobus' housekeeper: Georgie Dickson. *Lisbeth*, waiting woman: Hattie E. Schell. *Louise, Marie*, peasant girls: Mabel Torrey, D. K. Graham. *Suzel*: MARION MANOLA.

The action takes place at the present time in Alsace.

Act 1: Fritz Kobus' home in Clairfontaine. A bachelor's birthday. "Would I had been born oftener."

Act 2: Messanges Farm. Suzel, "She took the fruit thereof . . . and he did eat."

Act 3: Fritz Kobus' home in Clairefontaine. A universal duty. "She became his wife . . . and he loved her."

MUSICAL NUMBERS[59]

"The Heart That Loves"
"I Would Not If I Could"
"Snow-King's Death"
"Bachelor's Song"
"Nobody Knows"
"Song of the Wedding Ring"
"I'll Follow the Rule"

1893.04 LA FILLE DE MME. ANGOT/ THE REHEARSAL

A Double Bill of a Burlesque and an Operetta, accompanied by a Vaudeville Bill. Director of music, William J. Rostetter. Produced by (John) Koster & (Albert) Bial. Opened 13 February 1893 at Koster & Bial's Concert Hall and closed 15 April 1893 after 54 performances.

LA FILLE DE MME. ANGOT, a Bijou Edition (Burlesque) in One Act, 3 Scenes. (Libretto and musical adaptation) Arranged by Frederic Solomon. Music by Charles Lecocq.

CAST: *Clairette*: MADGE LESSING. *Lange*: CHRISTINE BLESSING. *Amaranthe*: Jennie St. Clair. *Babette*: Ruth Ward. *Javotte*: May Appleton. *Cosette*: Crissie Carlyle. *Ange Pitou*: Irene Verona. *Pomponet*: Marie Carr. *Louchard*: Charles R. Burroughs. *Trenitz*: DOROTHY DENNING. *Lari Naudierre*: FREDERIC SOLOMON. *Fishwives, Courtiers, Conspirators, Dancers and Hussars, etc.*

Scene 1: Market Place, Rue des Rivoli, Paris. 1800. *Scene 2*: Reception Room in Lange's Chateau. *Scene 3*: Jardin de Calypso.

THE REHEARSAL, a new edition[60] of the Operetta in One Act. Libretto by H. B. Farnie.

CAST: *Horatio Parnassus*, author and stage manager: FREDERIC SOLOMON. *Augustus Fitzmoonshine*, Manager: CHARLES R. BURROUGHS. *Miss Carrie D'away*, Prima Donna: MADGE LESSING. *Dollie Siggleton*, Principal Boy: Irene Verona. *Tottie Pomeroy*, Soubrette: Marie Carr. *Tinie Tidbit*, Soubrette: Jennie St. Clair. *Mollie Splitzentini*, Contralto Assoluta: CHRISTINE BLESSING. *Other Soubrettes, Prima Donnas, Sopranos, Leading Ladies, Misleading Ladies, Kickers, etc.*

Scene: The present.

Incidental to the presentation, the following will be introduced:

---

[58]Musical numbers not listed in programs. List prepared from published piano vocal score and libretto (Chappell & Co., London, 1892), which does not reflect cuts and interpolations for the American production.

[59]Musical numbers not listed in programs. List prepared from published vocal selection, not in performance order.

[60]An earlier edition of the operetta appeared 13-18 February 1893 at Koster & Bial's.

Sextette (from LES HUGUENOTS, *Music by* Giacomo Meyerbeer.)
Grand Chorale (from FAUST, *Music by* Charles Gounod.)
"The Children's Home" (*Music by* Frederick Cowen.)

1893.05

THE BASOCHE, or, King of the Students

An Opéra-Comique in Three Acts. English libretto by Madeleine Lucette Ryley, from the French original ("La Basoche") by Albert Carré. Music by André Messager. Scenery by Ernest Gros, Arthur Voegtlin. Costumes by Mmes. Loe and Freslinger, after designs by Chatinere, Paris. Musical director, Gustave Kerker. Produced by the Duff Opera Company (James C. Duff, Proprietor). Opened 27 February 1893 at the Casino Theatre and closed 11 March 1893 after 14 performances.

CAST: *His Majesty Louis XII* of France: WILLIAM H. HAMILTON. *Le Duc de Longueville*: J. H. RYLEY. *Student Members of the Basoche* (3): *Clément Marot*, a poet: CHARLES BASSETT. *L'Eveille*, his friend: JOHN J. RAFFAEL. *Roland*: HENRI LEONI. *Master Guillot*, Landlord of "The Pewter Platter": MAURICE ABBEY. *The Chancellor of "The Basoche"*: Bowman Ralston. *The Equerry of the King*: William Castleman. *Jacquet*, Guillot's servant: Charles E. Skerritt. *A Royal Page*: Mary Sears. *The Watchman*: Edward Regas. *Marie d'Angleterre*, wife of Louis XII, and sister to Henry VIII of England: HELEN BERTRAM. *Jeanette*: Millie Atherton. *Clarice*: Bert Lehman. *Colette*, a peasant: JULIETTE CORDON. (*Dance Specialty*: Gussie Cogan.)

Act 1: Street scene in Paris, 1534. (Gros.)

Act 2: Interior of The Pewter Platter Inn. (Voegtlin.)

Act 3: Grand Salon in Palace of Louis XII. (Voegtlin.)

MUSICAL NUMBERS, SPECIALTIES[61]

Characteristic Hungarian Dance (*Arranged by* Miss Beckett.)(Act 2)
G. Cogan

1893.06

A MAD BARGAIN

A Farce Comedy (Musical Comedy) in Three Acts. Play by John J. McNally and Julian Mitchell. Entire production under the personal supervision of Julian Mitchell. Scenery by John Thompson. Musical director, Herman Berl. Produced by (Isaac B.) Rich and (William) Harris' Comedy Company. Opened 27 February 1893 at the Bijou Theatre and closed 11 March 1893 after 16 performances; re-opened 1 May 1893 at the Star Theatre and closed 6 May 1893 after 8 additional performances. Total: 24 performances.

CAST: *Arthur Jones*, as fresh as a daisy: JAMES T. POWERS. *Albert Jones*, his cousin: PETER F. DAILEY. *Andrew Jones*, no relation: Frank Howard. *John Robinson*, a bill collector: W. W. Allen. *Timothy Tracy*, a dramatist: C. P. Morrison. *David Davitt*, a constable: Frank M. Kendrick. *Dr. Adlai Still*, Chief of the Nervine Hospital: RICHARD CARLE. *Al Butts*, a connoisseur: Frank Howard. *Worthington*, Arthur Jones' valet: RICHARD CARLE. *Williams*, a butler: Frank Author. *Bill Litt*, a postman: John Frees. *Rose Robinson*, in love with Arthur: Rachel Booth. *Mrs. Timothy Tracy*, retired but sentimental: Louise Sylvester. *Mrs. John Robinson*, nice though frivolous: Delia Stacey. *Helen Brown*, a visiting relative: Delle Jackson. *Isabella Robinson*, the janitor's daughter: Miss Forrest. *Camilla Montague*, the Autocrat of the Flat: ROSA COOK.

Act 1: Home of Mrs. John Robinson.

Act 2: Apartments of Arthur Jones in Consolation Flats.

Act 3: Home of Mrs. John Robinson.

ACT 1

Medley

Illuminated Burlesque of the Serpentine Dance
J. T. Powers

ACT 2

Pantomime Song and Dance
J. T. Powers

"Flirting at the Ball"

Song
D. Jackson

Miss Forest's Latest Terpsichorean Efforts

ACT 3

Latter Day Parodies
P. F. Dailey

[61]Musical numbers not listed in programs. Only published English adaptation of THE BASOCHE is the British edition, with libretto by Sir August Harris, lyrics by Eugene Oudin (Chappell, 1891).

1893.07

GIROFLÉ-GIROFLA

A Revival of the Opera Comique in Three Acts[62]. New adaptation by M. C. Woodward, assisted in certain scenes by J. Cheever Goodwin. Music by Charles Lecocq. Entire production under the personal supervision of Richard Barker. Dances arranged by Mamert Bibeyran. Scenery by Henry E. Hoyt, Richard Marsden, Joseph Clare. Costumes designed by Percy Anderson. Musical director, Charles Puerner. Produced by the Lillian Russell Opera Comique Company (T. H. French, Proprietor and Manager). Opened 3 March 1893 at the Garden Theatre and closed 1 April 1893 after 35 performances.

CAST: *Giroflé*: LILLIAN RUSSELL. *Girofla*: LILLIAN RUSSELL. *Paquita*: LAURA CLEMENT. *Aurore*: ROSE LEIGHTON. *Marasquin*: C. HAYDEN COFFIN. *Mourzouk*: WILLIAM T. CARLETON. *Pedro*: HENRY HALLAM. *Bolero*: LOUIS HARRISON. *Pirate Chief*: Charles Roux. *Matamoras*: E. L. Fulton. *Fernande*: Ada Dare. *Guzman*: Fanny Johnston. *Pages*: Minnie Washburn, Ada Courtney, Annie Lester, Amy Wade. *Cousins*: Lottie King, Martha Habelman, Lucy Williams, Jessie King, Gertrude Rutledge, Edith Miller, Teckla Morton. *Godmother*: Marion Wells. *Godfather*: Pelham Morton. *Notary*: C. Atwood. *Clerk*: A. Bassi. *Groomsman*: C. Alexander. *Uncle*: Jean Doré. *Premiere Danseuse*: FLORENCE FRANTON. *Ballet*: Florence Carlisle, May Cuthbert, Mollie Weston, Carrie Street, Mollie McGill, Nannie DeVere, Sadie Sherwood, Emily Kunze, Frances Baldwin, Leonora Ruize, Elise Stoeckhe, May Mott. *Pirates, Moores, Sailors, Peasants*.

Act 1: Gardens of the Palace of Bolero. (Hoyt.)

Act 2: A Moorish Salon. (Marston.)

Act 3: Pavilion of the Bolero's Palace. (Clare.)

1893.08

HOSS AND HOSS

A Revival of the Funniest of all Farcical Entertainments (Farce Comedy) in Three Acts[63]. Play by the company (Charlie Reed, William Collier). (Original songs and music by Frank Pallma, Charlie Reed, William Collier, Arthur E. Moulton, J. Sherrie Mathews and Harry Bulger, others.) Musical director, John C. Sorg. Produced by W. G. Smythe. Opened 13 March 1893 at the Bijou Theatre and closed 8 April 1893 after 32 performances[64].

CAST: *Judge Willis Hoss*, who owns the bench: WILLIE COLLIER. *Lawyer Charlie Hoss*, one of the best lawyers in his office: MARK SULLIVAN. *Birdie Hoss*, the Judge's son: ARTHUR MOULTON. *Napoleon Roquefort*, an interruption: IGNACIO MARTINETTI. *Hank Thanks*, the Sheriff, don't bother him: James E. Gentry. *Walter Wangle*, born in Newark—glad of it: Daniel Baker. *Jack Rose*, a daisy from Tuffton: M. L. Heckert. *Henry Chalk*, a Milkman: Thomas D. Daly. *Wilfred Chops*, a Butcher: J. R. Murchie. *Graham Bread*, a Baker: David Andrada. *Dedric Heat*, an Iceman: Daniel Baker. *Sigfried Rette* a juror: Thomas D. Daly. *Mel Mushon*, so is he: J. R. Murchie. *Fizz Ginsel*, another: David Andrada. *O. K. Wood*, same case: Daniel Baker. *Bill Bowser*, from Kickville: Daniel Brasill. *Messenger*: C. J. Clark. *Sybil Cerves*, the cause of the trouble: LOUISE ALLEN. *Sue Brette*, Birdie's "Best": ADELE FARRINGTON. *Celia Cliquot*, a sparkler: HELENA COLLIER. *Lobelia Hoss*, the Judge's wife: HELEN REIMER. *Polly Hoss, Hobby Hoss*, the Judge's daughters: MARIE CELESTE, KITTY COLLIER. *Annie Rooney*, "Did you ring sir?": HELENA COLLIER. *Minnie Ha Ha*: Helen Reimer. *Jurors, Musicians, and other waiters*.

1893.09

THE GONDOLIERS, or, The King of Barataria

A Revival of the Comic Opera in Two Acts[65]. Libretto by William S. Gilbert. Music by Arthur Sullivan. Musical director, Gustave Kerker. Produced by the J. C. Duff Opera Company (James C. Duff, Proprietor). Opened 16 March 1893 at the Casino Theatre and closed 1 April 1893 after 18 performances[66].

[62]First produced in New York in French 4 February 1875 at the Park Theatre for (46) performances in repertory, and in English 19 May 1875 at Robinson Hall for 61 performances.

[63]Previously played in New York 2 November 1891 at the Park Theatre for 32 performances. For Synopsis of Scenes, see original 1891 production. Interpolated for this revival, as per published sheet music:
"Two Little Girls in Blue" (previously introduced in A TRIP TO CHINATOWN)
D. J. Andrada
(*Music and Lyrics by* Charles Graham.)

[64]Stage director, scenery and costumes uncredited.

[65]Originally presented in New York 7 January 1890 at Park Theatre for 103 performances. For Synopsis of Scenes and Musical Numbers, see original 1890 production.

[66]Stage direction, scenery and costumes uncredited.

CAST: *The Duke of Plaza-Toro*, a Grandee of Spain: J. H. RYLEY. *Luiz*, His Attendant: HENRI LEONI. *Don Alhambra Del Bolero*, the Grand Inquisitor: W. H. HAMILTON. *Venetian Gondoliers (6)*: *Marco Palmieri*: CHARLES BASSETT. *Giuseppe Palmieri*: JOHN J. RAFFAEL. *Antonio*: WILLIAM CASTLEMAN. *Giorgio*: Charles Miller. *Annibale*: Charles Holly. *Francesco*: O. Simonson. *The Duchess of Plaza-Toro*: GRACE ATHERTON. *Casilda*, Her Daughter: VILLA KNOX. *Five Contadine*: *Gianetta*: HELEN BERTRAM. *Tessa*: Effie Chapuy. *Fiametta*: Millie Atherton. *Vittoria*: Bert Lehman. *Giulia*: Bessie Knox. *Inez*, the King's Foster Mother: Mary Sears.

1893.10 CORDELIA'S ASPIRATIONS

A Revival of the Comedy (with Songs) in Three Acts[67]. Play (revised) by Edward Harrigan. Music by David Braham. Musical director, David Braham. Produced by Edward Harrigan. Opened 20 March 1893 at Harrigan's Theatre and closed 29 April 1893 after 48 performances.

CAST: *Dan Mulligan*: EDWARD HARRIGAN. *Simpson Primrose*: JOHN WILD. *Rebecca Clinton*: DAN COLLYER. *Gus Lochmuller*: JOSEPH SPARKS. *Plaxty McFudd*: HARRY FISHER. *Walsingham McSweeney*: Charles Coffey. *Palestine Puter*: William West. *Honora Dublin*: Charles McCarthy. *Theodore Chamboudet*: Charles Sturgis. *Robert Ridgeway*: George Merritt. *Hoke Buckheister*: Fred Peters. *Junkman*: Dave Braham, Jr. *Bridget Lochmuller*: HATTIE MOORE. *Diana McFudd*: EMMA POLLOCK. *Ellen McFudd*: ADA LEWIS. *Rosy McFudd*: FANNIE BATCHELDER. *Mrs. Rosy Geegan*: Annie Buckley. *Mrs. Riley*: Marie Gorenflo. *Mrs. Lopes*: Daisy St. Clair. *Mrs. O'Brien*: PAULINE EDWARDS. *Mrs. Corncure*: Renie Egan. *Mrs. Plattenia*: Lillie Flynn. *Mamie Reilly*: Little Annie Kehoe. *Cordelia Mulligan*: Mrs. ANNIE YEAMANS.

Uncle Tom Combination: Dan Burke, Emil Huesel, John Mayon, James McCullough, Edward Murphy, T. Young, Michael Kearney, John Decker, Richard Quilter, James Burke, Willis Pickert, John Walsh, John Brenann, John Flynn, Alfred Waite.

Act 1: Home of Dan Mulligan.

Act 2: The Mulligan Mansion. The Reception.

Act 3: The First Breakfast at the Mansion.

ACT 1

"The Uncle Tom Combination"

"Just Across from Jersey"

"Good Bye Old Friends"

"My Dad's Dinner Pail"

ACT 2

"The Waiters' Chorus"

"Sam Johnson's Cake Walk"

"Whiskey, You're the Devil"
(J. Wild)

ACT 3

"Mulligan's Lament"

"I'll Wear the Trousers, Oh!"

"Ho! For Mulligan Alley"

1893.11 THE POET AND THE PUPPETS

A Travesty by Charles Brookfield in One Act, 4 Scenes. (Suggested by Oscar Wilde's play "Lady Windermere's Fan.") Preceded by "His Wedding Day,"[68] a farce in One Act by Herbert Graham. Produced by Charles Frohman. Opened 3 April 1893 at the Garden Theatre and closed 20 May 1893 after 49 performances.

CAST (The Prologue): *Oscar O'Flaherty Wilde*, a Poet: HENRY MILLER. *A Fairy*: MAY IRWIN. *A Bard*: Harry Mills. *An Author*: Thomas Reilly. *A Realist*: Henry Woodruff. *An Author-Manager*: MAX FIGMAN. *A Dramatist*: Harry Brown.

(The Play) *Lord Windermere*: R. A. ROBERTS. *Lord Gonebusters*: Harry Brown. *Lord Pentonville*: HENRY LILFORD. *Hon. Gwynne Bennett*: Henry Woodruff. *Sir Charles Stillwater*: Hawley Webb. *Hamlet*: MAX FIGMAN. *Spirit of Arbitration*: Harry Mills. *Parker*: Fred Strong. *Lady Windermere*: Elaine Eilson. *Mrs. Earlybird*: Alice Johnson. *Ophelia*: MAY IRWIN. *Miss Yesmama*: MAY ROBSON. *Guests, Servants, etc.*

Scene 1: The Poet's Study. *Scene 2*: Lady Windermere's Ball-room. *Scene 3*: Lord Pentonville's Smoking-room. *Scene 4*: At Lady Windermere's ?.

MUSICAL NUMBERS

"Daddy Wouldn't Buy Me a Bowwow"
M. Irwin
(*Music and Lyrics by* Joseph Tabrar.)

Three-Legged Dance
M. Robson

1893.12 FRITZ IN A MAD HOUSE

A Revival of the Natural Drama (with Music) in Four Acts[69]. Play by Joseph K. Emmet, revised by J. K. Emmet, Jr. Produced by J. K. Emmet. Opened 3 April 1893 at the Grand Opera House and closed 8 April 1893 after 8 performances[70].

CAST: *Uncle Joe Parker*: HUDSON LISTON. *Richard Parker*: HARRY COFFIN. *Baron von Wolfenstein*: GEORGE MIDDLETON. *Collie Parker*: EMILY LYTTON. *Mrs. Parker*: FLORENCE FOSTER. *Burrows*: Hugh Hilton. *Lady Grace Howard*: Marie Rogers. *Laura Myrtle*: Annie M. Ware. *Flora*: Mamie Donnelly. *Snatters*: Florence Germaina. *The Plant*: Baby Sinott Spencer. *Fritz von Wolfenstein*: J. K. EMMET, JR.

1893.13 ADONIS

A Revival of the Famous Burlesque (Musical Comedy) in Two Acts[71]. Libretto rewritten), music and lyrics by Edward E. Rice and William Gill. Musical director, Henry Sator. Produced by Henry E. Dixey (Messrs. Stempson and Burbank, Managers). Opened 8 April 1893 at the Casino Theatre and closed 1 July 1893 after 85 performances[72].

CAST: *Adonis*, an accomplished young gentleman, of undeniably good family, whose name, by the way, is "Marble"; *Henry Irving*, who acts; *Clementine*, who recites; *Clito*, who weds; *Paderewski*, who plays; *Gussie*, a dry goods clerk who sells; *Quinine*, a drug store clerk who drugs; *Jimmie*, a barber who shaves; *Dee Zinskey*, old clothes man; *Stamp*, the postmaster who posts: HENRY E. DIXEY. *Marquis de Baccarat*, a highly polished villain. It is well to describe his character: JOHN C. BUCKSTONE. *Bunion Turke*, father of Rosetta, an unblushing appropriator of the stock in trade of a well-known and worthy old histrionic miller: Odell Williams. *Talmea*, a sculptress, who, like most of her sex, is in love with her own creation: LOUISE MONTAGUE. *Artea*, a goddess, Patroness of the Fine Arts: HELEN MONTFORD. *Duchess of Area*, aesthetic to the verge of eccentricity, rich to the verge of millionairism, sentimental to the verge of gush: KATE DAVIS. *Daughters of the Duchess, Professional Beauties (4)*: *Lady Nattie*: Fannie Ward. *Lady Hattie*: Mabel Montgomery. *Lady Mattie*: Nina Farrington. *Lady Pattie*: Brownie Wells. *Rosetta*, a simple village maiden, the happy possessor of a clear conscience, a strong will and a soprano voice: AMELIA SUMMERVILLE. *Gyles, Nyles, Myles, Byles*, ordinary every-day rustics: Messrs. Gorman, Barrett, Huntley, Collyer. *Timmins*: Edwin H. Aiken. *Miss Doolitte*: Fannie Ward. *Poor Blind Man*: James Alexander. *Mr. Nervine*, who believes in shaving himself: Matt Alexander. *Oriental Menials, Caucasian Menials, Guards, Villagers with the Good Old-Time Chorus.*

1893.14 A TEXAS STEER, or Money Makes the Mare Go

A Revival of the Farce Comedy in Three Acts and a Prologue[73]. Play by Charles H. Hoyt. Stage director, Julian Mitchell. Scenery by Homer F. Emens and Arthur Voegtlin. Produced by Charles H. Hoyt and Charles H. Thomas. Opened 10 April 1893 at the Bijou Theatre and closed 3 June 1893 after 56 performances[74].

CAST: *Maverick Brander*, a Texas Cattle King: TIM MURPHY. *Captain Fairleigh Bright*, U.S.A.: JOHN MARSHALL. *Messrs. Yell, Brag and Blow*, Members of the Farmers' Alliance: Charles Stanley, James Horan, C. L. Warren. *Brassy Gall, Esq.*,

[67]First produced in New York 5 November 1883 at the Theatre Comique for 176 performances.

[68]Previously presented in a four act version on tour; replaced after two nights by the short play "Frédéric Lemaitre" by Clyde Fitch.

[69]First produced in New York 22 April 1889 at the 14th Street Theatre as UNCLE JOE, or Fritz in a Madhouse for 64 performances. For Synopsis of Scenes, see original 1889 production.

[70]Also played a return engagement 26 February 1894 at the American Theatre for 8 performances.

[71]First produced in New York 4 September 1884 at the Bijou Theatre for 603 performances. For Synopsis of Scenes and Musical Numbers, see original 1884 production.

[72]Stage direction, scenery and costumes uncredited.

[73]First produced in New York 10 November 1890 at the Bijou Theatre for 88 performances. For Synopsis of Scenes and Musical Numbers, see original 1890 production.

[74]Played a return engagement 19 June 1893 at the Grand Opera House for 8 performances.

member of the Third House: Newton Chisnell. *Colonel Pepper*, a retired army officer: James Horan. *Christopher Columbus, Jr.*, a colored statesman: Will H. Bray. *Knott Initt*, Brander's private secretary: Sumner Clark. *Othello Moore*, a private waiter at the Arlington: John T. Craven. *Lieutenant Greene*, U.S.A.: Sumner Clark. *Sergeant at Arms*: John Deady. *Anatole*, a valet: Newton Chisnell. *G. Whittaker Bellows*, a senator: Robert McIntyre. *Green Woodhead*, a judge: George A. Grace. *Low Dodge*, an artist: Charles Bradford. *Crab, Mink*, Field Hands: Edw. Corbin, George Jennings. *Sam*, Row Boy, Arlington Hotel: Olney Griffin. *Mrs. Brander*, the cattle king's wife: Alice Walsh. *Mrs. Major Campbell*, whose husband is stationed in Texas: Florence Stevens. *Dixie Style*, an orphan from Indiana: Alice Evans. *Bossy*, Brander's pet: MAMIE GILROY. *Street Band, Indians, Greasers, and general riff-raff of a frontier town, etc.* The Madison Square Theatre Quartette will supply Southern Melodies.

1893.15

REILLY AND THE 400

A Revival of the Local Play in Three Acts, 5 Scenes[75]. Play by Edward Harrigan. Music by David Braham. (Staged by Edward Harrigan.) Scenery by D. Frank Dodge. Electrical effects by John Whalen. Musical director, David Braham. Produced by Edward Harrigan. Opened 1 May 1893 at Harrigan's Theatre and closed 13 May 1893 after 16 performances.[76]

CAST: *Wiley Reilly*: EDWARD HARRIGAN. *Salvator Magnus*: JOHN WILD. *Lizzie Calhoun*: JOSEPH SPARKS. *Commodore Toby Tow*: JAMES RADCLIFFE. *Herman Smeltz*: HARRY FISHER. *Lems Leggers*: George Merritt. *Ned Reilly*: CHARLES COFFEY. *Percy Oggles*: Fred Peters. *Hippolite Duval*: Richard Quilter. *Valentine McClinchy*: Dan Burke. *Bessie Bowlow*: John Decker. *That's What*: James Burke. *Jimmy the Con*: William West. *Roundsman Moran*: James McCullough. *Iceman*: Charles Sturges. *Butcher*: Willis Pickert. *James McGouldrick*: Charles F. McCarthy. *Dionysius Dorrigan*: John Walsh. *Slattery*: John Mayon. *Ignatius McCune*: Alfred Waite. *August Shutzer*: Joseph Williamson. *Corporal Jimmy*: Ed Murphy. *Fireman*: Mr. Kearney. *Emil Shutzer*: Master Mooney. *Lavine Gale*: HATTIE MOORE. *Maggie Murphy*: EMMA POLLOCK. *Kittie Lynch*: ADA LEWIS. *Miss Murray Hill*: Emily Yeamans. *Emiline Gale*: FANNY BATCHELDER. *Miss Van Tassel*: Annie Buckley. *Maryann Dooley*: ANNIE YEAMANS.

Guests: Lillie Flynn, Rennie Egan, Miss St. Clair, Miss Edwards, Marie Gorenflo.

1893.16

PANJANDRUM

An Original Olla-Podrida (Musical Fantasy) in Two Acts, 4 Scenes. Libretto by J. Cheever Goodwin. Music by Woolson Morse. Production under the stage direction of H. A. Cripps. Scenery by Ernest M. Gros. Costumes by Alfred Thompson. Director of Music and Conductor, J. S. Hiller. Produced by the DeWolf Hopper Company (B. D. Stevens, Manager). Opened 1 May 1893 at the Broadway Theatre; Second Edition opened 28 June 1893 and closed 30 September 1893 after 154 performances.

CAST: *Pedro* (later imposter Panjandrum): DeWOLF HOPPER. *Luiz*: Edmund Stanley. *Rotomago*: Samuel Reed. *Don José*: ALFRED KLEIN. *Rosolio*: Louis Schrader. *Bobo*: Camm Mauvel. *Manuel*: John A. Parks. *Alcalde*: John A. Parks. *Donna Inez*: Jeannette St. Henry. *Indra*: Anna O'Keefe. *Donna Maria*: MARION SINGER. *Piko*: Agnes Reilly. *Ysabel*: Helen Beresford. *Paquita*: DELLA FOX. *Spanish Ladies, Peasants, Natives, Alguazils, Narranjeros, Bandilleros, Chulos, Picadores, Matadores, Priests, Priestesses, Guards, Sailors, Soldiers, etc.*

Act 1: Exterior of the Plaza del Toros, Subaya, Philippine Islands.

Act 2, Scene 1: Quay at Manilla. Isle of Luzon. *Scene 2*: In the Jungle. Borneo. *Scene 3*: Courtyard of the Palace, and Temple of the Sun, at Kutching, Isle of Borneo.

MUSICAL NUMBERS[77]

"A Sad Predicament"
"A Perfect Wreck"
"Ay De Mi"
"Fakirs from Fakirsville"
"Love Song of the Espada"
"Sunshine After Rain"
"The Old, Old Story"
"What Would You Say?"
"When Two Hearts Love" (Duet)
"Love Is Not for a Daytime"

[75]First produced in New York 29 December 1890 at Harrigan's Theatre for 202 performances. For Synopsis of Scenes and Musical Numbers, see original 1890 production.
[76]Costumes uncredited.
[77]Musical numbers not listed in programs. List prepared from published piano vocal selections (T. B. Harms, Inc., New York, 1893).

1893.17

1492, Up to Date or Very Near It

Rice's Surprise Party in a Musical Extravaganza in Three Acts, 9 Scenes. Libretto by R. A. Barnet. Music by Carl Pflueger[78]. Entire production under the personal supervision and direction of Edward E. Rice. Scenery designed by Richard Marston, Hugh L. Reid, John L. Thompson, Mark Lawson, Frank Rafter. Costumes designed by Alfred Thompson. Musical director, Herman Perlet. Produced by Edward E. Rice. Opened 15 May 1893 at Palmer's Theatre and closed 1 July 1893 for summer holiday; re-opened 26 August 1893 at Palmer's Theatre; Second Edition opened 5 February 1894 at the Garden Theatre; revised version opened 27 August 1894[79] at the Garden Theatre for 52 performances; production closed 13 October 1894 after a total of 452 performances.

CAST: *Ferdinand of Aragon*, King of Spain: WALTER JONES. *Charley Tatters*, a fringe on the edge of the crust of society: WALTER JONES. *Alonzo de Quintanilla*, royal treasurer: EDWARD M. FAVOR. *Don Juan*, the King's son, aged four: W. H. Sloan. *Felix*, of the tribe of coppers: W. H. Sloan. *Captain Martin Pinzon, Don Pedro Margerite*, Conspirators of the old-fashioned type: CHARLES F. WALTON, JOHN C. SLAVIN. *Charles VIII*, King of France: Louis de Smith. *Don Ferdinand Allegro*: Yolande Wallace. *Adolphus Fitznoodle*, a regular chappie, up-to-date: YOLANDE WALLACE. *Maid Mabel*, a sailor lassie: YOLANDE WALLACE. *Maid Marion*, a sailor lassie: Eileen Karl. *The Royal Herald*: Eileen Karl. *Ward Knickerbocker*, cacique of the 400: C. J. Alden. *Jim Confidence*, of the tribe of buncoes: C. J. Alden. *Bob*, a New York newsboy: James Lee. *Erasmus*, a vender of maize: Frederic Howard. *Isabella of Castille*, Queen of Spain: RICHARD HARLOW. *Fraülein*, a German waif: THERESA VAUGHN. *Infanta Joanna*, in love with Columbus: THERESA VAUGHN. *Infanta Catalina*, her sister: HATTIE WILLIAMS. *Mary Ann Kehoe* of the Royal Household of the new world: EDITH SINCLAIR. *Chistopher Columbus*: MARK SMITH. (*Specialty*: JAMES F. HOEY.) *Courtiers, Ladies, Peasants, Students, Ballet, Amazons, Newsboys, Moors, Sailors, Bull Fighters, Soldiers, Pages, Standard Bearers, etc.*

Casino Girls: Misses Ida Fairbanks, Annie Winner, Belle Sherwood, Josie Fairbanks, Hattie Williams, Edith Burbank. *Spanish Ballet*: Misses Emma Marsh, Nina Walsh, Mamie Forbes, Josie Fairbanks, Caudi Revere, Annie Winner, Clara Palmer, Ida Fairbanks. *Sensational Fantastic Toe Danseuse*: Mabel Clark. *"Kick and Boom the Hurrah" Dudes*: Misses Kittie Burton, Dora Webb, Kittie Connors, May Leclair, Mabel Waite, Carrie Siden. *"Serpentine" Dancers*: Misses Emma Marsh, Nina Walsh, Ida Fairbanks, Josie Fairbanks. *"Chef" Ballet*: Misses Emma Marsh, Nina Walsh, Caudi Revere, Pearl Bellford, Mamie Forbes, Jessie Haynes. *Female Chorus*: Misses Dora Webb, Kitty Hurton, Lizzie Scanlon, Mabel Waite, Edith Burbank, Annie Weimer, Josie Fairbanks, Ida Fairbanks, Belle Sherwood, Hattie Williams, Kittie Connors, Bertie Dyer, Clara Palmer, Jessie Haines, Helen Marlborough, Emma Marsh, Nina Walsh, Mamie Forbes, Caudi Revere, Carrie Siden, May Leclair, S. Romain, Emma Mulle, Pearl Belford, Dolly Theobold, Hattie Hall, Bella Lorella, Madge Wagner, Patty Moore, Molly Thompson, Sally Randal, Helen Smith, Carrie Noyes, Ida Rock. *Male Chorus*: Messrs. Edward Thomas, Louis deSmidt, George Wright, Paul Bracket, G. W. Kranich, S. H. Dudley, Frederick Howard, James Lee, George Gradwell, Ray Gaul, George Grant, J. P. Savage, Joseph Flaherty. *Newsboys*: Masters James Lee, Gilbert Gregory, Thomas Maguire, Fred Earwood, Isador Balty, Ray Gaul, S. S. Goldman, Willie Torpey, Pedro Sisson, Dolly Theobold.

Act 1: Throne Chamber in the King's Palace. (Marston.) *Act Drop*: Exterior of the World's Fair. (Reid.)

Act 2, Scene 1: On the Ocean. *Scene 2*: Vision. The Discovery of America, 1492. *Scene 3*: The Progress of Enlightenment. (Thompson.) *Scene 4*: The Real Discovery of Columbus. (Thompson.) *Scene 5*: The Statue of Liberty, New York Harbor. (Lawson.) *Scene 6*: Columbus returns to Earth. Discovery of Madison Square, 1892. (Marston.) *Act Drop*: Entrance to the World's Fair. (Reid.)

Act 3, Scene 1: Royal Kitchen in the Palace. (Thompson.) *Scene 2*: Spanish Palace up to date. (Lawson.) Changing to the new electrical scene, The Ideal Home of Columbus. (Rafter.)

ACT 1[80]

[78]Program note by Edward E. Rice: With the consent of the author and composer, I have introduced some popular music of the day, a morceau by Rubinstein, three numbers by Mr. Perlet, and a few of my own, also a Grand Finale to the second act, "Our National Song," written expressly for me by Adam Itzel, Jr. of Baltimore. I make this explanation in order that Mr. Pfleuger may not be accused of plagiarism.
[79]See separate entry in 1893-1894 season.
[80]Musical numbers not listed in programs. List prepared from published vocal score. During the run, a number of new specialties were introduced. Between Acts 2 and 3 in Queen Isabella's Art Gallery, the Kilyani Troupe exhibited a series of Living Pictures. Interpolations during the run included:

"Yew-re-liar-ity" (Burlesque Yodel Song)
W. Jones
(*Music by* George B. Seevers. *Lyrics by* Charles House.)

"Give us cash! Give us cash!" (Opening Chorus)
"TheTreasurer's Song" (*Arranged from Genée by* Carl Pflueger.)
E. M. Favor, Chorus
Duet (I'll be faithful for evermore)
T. Vaughn, M. Smith
"The King's Song"
W. Jones, Chorus
Processional and "The Queen's Song"
R. Harlow, Chorus
Spanish Dance (*Music by* Aberano Colon.)
Finale

ACT 2
Columbus' Vision (Toss'd and shaken by the billows of the deep)
M. Smith, Chorus
Chorus of Newsboys (Herald, Tribune and Times . . .)
Newsboys
Conspirator's Music
Casino Girl's Chorus (We are careless chorus maidens)
Chorus
Finale

ACT 3
Barcarolle (*Arranged from a Spanish Air by* Carl Pflueger.)
Vocal March (Return of Columbus)
Amazonen March (Spanish)
Ballet Music (Ensemble, Solo, Finale)
Finale ("Wait till we see the sweet bye and bye"; "The Hen and the China Egg")

1893.18 ROBIN HOOD

A Revival of the Light Opera in Three Acts[81]. Libretto by Harry B. Smith. Music by Reginald DeKoven. Produced by the Bostonians (Henry Clay Barnabee, Tom Karl and W. H. MacDonald, Proprietors and Managers). Opened 22 May 1893 at the Garden Theatre, closing 27 May 1893; re-opened 5 June 1893 and closed 1 July 1893 after 35 performances.

CAST: *Sheriff of Nottingham*: HENRY CLAY BARNABEE. *Robin Hood*: EDWIN W. HOFF. *Little John*: W. H. MacDONALD. *Will Scarlet*: EUGENE COWLES. *Allan-a-Dale*: FLORA FINLAYSON. *Friar Tuck*: GEORGE FROTHINGHAM. *Guy of Gisborne*: Peter Lang. *Maid Marian*: CAMILLE D'ARVILLE. *Dame Durden*: JOSEPHINE BARTLETT. *Annabel*: BERTHA WALTZINGER.

1893.19 THE KNICKERBOCKERS

A Comic Opera in Three Acts. Libretto by Harry B. Smith. Suggested by Washington Irving's "Knickerbocker's History of New York." Music by Reginald DeKoven. Produced under the direction of John E. Nash. Scenery by Richard Marston. Costumes designed by Catherine Siedle. Musical director, Samuel L. Studley. Produced by the Bostonians (Henry Clay Barnabee, Tom Karl and W. H. MacDonald, Proprietors and Managers). Opened 29 May 1893 at the Garden Theatre and closed 3 June 1893 after 7 performances.

CAST: *William the Testy*, the Governor of New Amsterdam: HENRY CLAY BARNABEE. *Miles Bradford*, a Puritan Captain: W. H. MacDONALD. *Hendrick*, Son of the Burgomaster Schermerhorn: EDWIN W. HOFF. *Antony Van Corlear*, the Governor's Trumpeter: EUGENE COWLES. *Burgomaster Schermerhorn*: GEORGE FROTHINGHAM. *Captain Van Wart*, a Dutch Sailor, afterwards a citizen of New Amsterdam: Peter Lang. *Katrina*, the Governor's daughter: CAMILLE D'ARVILLE. *Priscilla*, a Puritan damsel: JESSIE BARTLETT DAVIS. *Dame Kieft*, the Governor's Wife: JOSEPHINE BARTLETT. *Barbara*, a village girl: Lillian Hawthorne. *Burghers, Sailors, Soldiers, Puritans, etc.*

Act 1: Market Place in New Amsterdam.

Act 2: The Governor's Garden in the Bowerie.

Act 3: The Dutch Camp on the Hudson.

MUSICAL NUMBERS
"Song of the Flint and Steel"
"Name the Day"
"A Puritan Damsel"
"Upon Our Little Farm"
"Hans Rap" (#4)(Solo and Men's Chorus)
"If You and I Should Meet"
"If There Is a Lad"
"Sing Your Merriest Songs" (Solo, Chorus)(#7)
"A Maiden Vexed" (The Spinning Song)(#8)
C. D'Arville
"I Have a Swain in the Army"
"Hasten, Time" (#10)(Quartette)
"An Overworked Trumpeter"
"I Have a Pipe"
"Way to the Knife"
"Only in Dreams" (#14)
E. W. Hoff
"Sleep You Pretty Creatures"
"Twelve Hours a Day"
"Do You Sigh for Love or Glory?" (#17)
C. D'Arville
"Here's a Song to the Flag" (#18)
"The Song of the Cuckoo Clock"

1893.20 THE ISLE OF CHAMPAGNE

A Return Engagement of the Comic Opera in Three Acts, 5 Scenes[82]. Libretto by Charles Alfred Byrne and Louis Harrison. Music by W. W. Furst. Scenery by Henry E. Hoyt. Costumes designed by Catherine Siedle. Musical director, Paul Steindorff. Produced by the Thomas Q. Seabrooke Opera Company (George W. Lederer, Director). Opened 29 May 1893 at the H. C. Miner's Fifth Avenue Theatre and closed 8 July 1893 after ?48 performances.

CAST: *King Pommery Sec'nd*, Ruler of the Isle: THOMAS Q. SEABROOKE. *Apollinaris Frappé*, his Prime Minister: WALTER ALLEN. *Prince Kissingen*, his son: JOSEPH F. SHEEHAN. *Moet, Chandon*, his army: Samuel Collins, John H. Gilroy. *Conspirators (3)*: *Marquis Mumm*: Lon Allyn. *Baron Heidsic*: Karl Formes, Jr. *Duc Bouche*: Arthur C. Carlton. *Sam Binnacle*, shipwrecked sailor of New Bedford, Massachusetts: EUGENE O'ROURKE. *Priscilla*, a New England maiden: ELSA GREGORI. *Abigail Peck*, her aunt, also of New Bedford, Massachusetts: Alice Leigh. *Diana*, the belle of the Isle: ELVIA CROX. *Diana's companions (4)*: *Brigitte*: ADELE RITCHIE. *Artea*: Tennye Poole. *Sophie*: Helen Gilmore. *Charmantine*: Florence Willey. *Pages in the Champagne Palace (3)*: *Chic*: Dora Allen. *Petite*: Sadie Dean. *Jolie*: Marie George. *Premier Danseuse*: Concettina Chitten. *Archers, Citizens, Citizenesses, Cherry Girls, Cobweb Girls, Flower Girls, Ladies and Gentlemen of the Court of Champgane, Sailors, Doctors, etc.*

"The Mandolin Serenade"
(*Music by* Richard Stahl.)
"My Little Star"
"Isabella"
R. Harlow (from Chicago run)
"Chappies"
Y. Wallace
(*Music and Lyrics by* Edward E. Rice.)
"Jenny Kissed Me"
(*Music by* Mercy Bateman. *Lyrics by* Leigh Hunt.)

[81]First produced in New York 28 September 1891 at the Standard Theatre for 77 performances in two engagements. For Synopsis of Scenes and Musical Numbers, see original 1891 production.

[82]First produced in New York 5 December 1892 at the Manhattan Opera House for 56 performances. For Synopsis of Scenes and Musical Numbers, see original production earlier in this season.

1893–1894 SEASON

Lulu Glaser (Photo: Falk)

Billy Rose Theatre Collection, New York Public Library for the Performing Arts

1893–1894 SEASON

1893.21 THE TALISMAN

An Opéra-comique in Three Acts, 4 Scenes, in English. (Original French) Libretto ("Le Talisman") by Adolphe d'Ennery and Paul Burani. Translated from the French by A. R. Schade. Music by Robert Planquette. Staged by Max Freeman. Scenery by Arthur Voegtlin; Ryan of London. Musical director, Gustave Kerker. Produced by Oscar Hammerstein. Opened 21 June 1893 at the Manhattan Opera House and closed 8 July 1893 after 19 performances.

CAST: *Louis XV*: MAX FREEMAN. *Chevalier de Valpinçon*: J. ALDRICH LIBBEY. *Georges de la Garde*: Robert Dunbar. *Nicolas*: RICHARD F. CARROLL. *Marquis de Chavanes*: Ellis Ryse. *Colonel*: Edgar Smith. *La Popelinière*, Commissary-General: Propert Carleton. *An Officer*: William Eberle. *Master of the Royal Household*: Frank Hodges. *Michelette*: BIANCA LESCAUT. *Renée de Chavannes*: MARGUERITE LAMAR. *Maids of Honor (4)*: *Athenais*: Lulu Hesse. *Solanges*: Cheridah Simpson. *Henriette*: Harriet Williams. *Louise*: Genevieve Hill. *Leocadie*: Alice Butler. *Ballet Specialty*: CLARA QUALITZ.) *Peasants, Ladies and Gentlemen of the Court, Pages, Outriders, Officers and Soldiers, Dancers, male and female.*

The action takes place in France in 1760.

Act 1, Scene 1: Interior of the Castle of Georges de la Garde. (Voegtlin.) *Scene 2*: Military Encampment at Berry. (Voegtlin.)

Act 2: The Palace of Versailles. (Ryan.)

Act 3: The Gardens at Versailles. (Voegtlin.)

BALLETS, SPECIALTIES[2a]

"Versailles" (Grand Ballet arranged by Katti Lanner; *music by* Leopold Wengell.)

C. Qualitz, Corps de Ballet

Spring (Childhood); Summer (Youth); Autumn (Middle Age); Winter (Old Age); Flora's Maidens; Zephyrs; Bacchantes; Pompletta (an original historical and mythological terpsichorean novelty.)

1893.22 LA BELLE HÉLÈNE/ THE ADMIRAL

A Double Bill of a Travestie and an Operetta[1], accompanied by a Vaudeville Bill. Director of music, William J. Rostetter. Produced by (John) Koster & (Albert) Bial. Opened 19 June 1893 at Koster & Bial's Concert Hall and closed 26 August 1893 after (90) performances.

LA BELLE HÉLÈNE[2], a Travestie (Burlesque) of the Opéra-bouffe in One Act, 3 Scenes. (Libretto and musical adaptation) Abridged by Frederic Solomon. Music by Jacques Offenbach.

CAST: *Calchas*, Helen's Guardian: FREDERIC SOLOMON. *Cymbeline*, his deserted wife: CHRISTINE BLESSING. *Helen*, Queen of Troy: RUTH DAVENPORT. *Paris*, her lover: IRENE VERONA. *Agememnon*, King of Greece: CHARLES R. BURROUGHS. *Orestes*, his son: DOROTHY DENNING. *Bacchis*, in love with Orestes: Jennie St. Clair. *King Achilles*, the Myrmidon: Marie Carr. *Philcomes*, Calchas' attendant: Jessie Banks. *Parthenis, Leonea*, Ladies of title: Anita Austin, Clara Schlee. *King Menelaus*, Helen's husband: SOL. MIRAND. *Guards, Slaves, the Populace, etc.*

The action takes place in Sparta during the age of fable, preceding the Trojan war.

Scene 1: Outside Calchas' Temple. *Scene 2*: Helen's Boudoir. *Scene 3*: A pleasure garden.

Incidental to the travestie, Mr. Frederic Solomon will sing a new descriptive song entitled "The Abbe's Dream."

[1]For the first two weeks of its run, LA BELLE HÉLÈNE was accompanied by PAUL'S DILEMMA, before yielding the stage to THE ADMIRAL.
[2]On 14 August 1893 for the final two weeks, LA BELLE HÉLÈNE was replaced by a return engagement of ORPHEUS.
[2a]Musical numbers not listed in programs; no libretto or musical score found for this adaptation.

THE ADMIRAL, a Nautical Operetta in One Act. Libretto by (Hugh) Morton. Music by Frederic Solomon. Opened 26 June 1893 at Koster & Bial's.

CAST: *General Brooks*, U.S. Army: CHARLES R. BURROUGHS. *The General's Daughters (9)*: *Amina*: RUTH DAVENPORT. *Sadie*: Anita Austin. *Pollie*: Flora Williams. *Rita*: Anna Ott. *Bertha*: Maggie O'Keefe. *Georgina*: Mollie Gayler. *Nettie*: Lillian Bishop. *Tottie*: Mae Powers. *Lydia*: Crissie Carlyle. *Admiral William Atkins*, H. M. Navy: SOL. MIRAND. *British Sailors (4)*: *Bill Bowsprit*: Clara Schlee. *Jack Binnacle*: Grace Langdon. *Tom Marlinspike*: Jessie Banks. *Ned Mainstay*: May Appleton. *Ensign Miles*, U.S. Army: Eugenia St. Clair.

Scene: General Brooks' country house, Sheepshead Bay.

1893.23 THE BLACK CROOK

A Revival of the Extravaganza in Four Acts, Sixteen Scenes[3]. Book by Charles M. Barras. Music composed and selected by Thomas Baker, Louis Baer, A. W. Hoffman. Produced under the stage direction of Lawrence McCarty. Scenery by Charles S. Getz, Homer F. Emens, Ernest Albert and Walter Burridge, J. S. Getz, J. S. Clare, John W. Sommer. Costumes designed by Howell, Russell and Wilhelm of London; Edel of Paris. Ballet music, Act 2, composed by M. Jacobi. Ballets by Mons. A. Bertrand. Produced by Eugene Tompkins. Opened 14 August 1893 at the Academy of Music and closed 23 September 1893 after 48 performances.

CAST: *Hertzog*, surnamed the Black Crook, alchemist and sorcerer: GEORGE MORTON. *Greppo*, his drudge: THOMAS O'BRIEN. *Rudolphe*, a poor artist: NESTOR LENNON. *Count Wolfenstein*: SYLVESTER WARREN. *Von Puffengruntz*, Wolfenstein's steward: A. C. DELTWYN. *Dragonfin*: Prince Pharoah. *Zamiel*, the arch-fiend: E. D. Goodwin. *Caspar*, a villager: George Smith. *Skudelwhelp*, familiar to Hertzog: E. H. Griffith. *Redglare*, the recording demon: Frank McCabe. *Bruno*, a gypsy ruffian: J. J. Gerry. *Wolfgar*, his companion: George Allen. *Stalacta*, the Queen of the Golden Realm: GRACE TABOR. *Amina*, betrothed to Rudolphe: Clara Havel. *Dame Barbara*, her foster mother: Kate Montrose. *Rosetta*: Ada Minetti. *Carline*: Louise Montrose. *Premiere Danseuse Assoluta*: Mlle. LEONELDA STACCIONI. *Premier Danseur*: Signor [Alfredo] BIANCIFIORI. *Premiere Danseuse*: Mlle. EMILIA BARTOLETTI. *Specialties*: Dagmar, Decelle (Danish singers and warblers), French Quadrille Dancers from the Casino, Paris.

Act 1, Scene 1: A Valley at the foot of the Hartz Mountains. (Emens.) *Scene 2*: A Rocky pass. (Getz.) *Scene 3*: An apartment in the Castle of Wolfenstein. (Emens.) *Scene 4*: Laboratory of the Black Crook. (Sommer.) *Scene 5*: A Wild Glen in the Heart of the Brocken. (Albert and Burridge.)

Act 2, Scene 1: Subterranean Vault in the Castle of Wolfenstein. (Clarke.) *Scene 2*: Lobby in the Castle of Wolfenstein. (Emens.) *Scene 3*: The Grotto of Stalacta. (Albert & Burridge.)

Act 3, Scene 1: Apartment in the Castle of Wolfenstein. (Emens.) *Scene 2*: Illuminated Golden Terrace of the Castle of Wolfenstein. (Getz.)

Act 4, Scene 1: Lobby in the Grace Palace of Wolfenstein. (Emens.) *Scene 2*: A Wood. (Getz.) *Scene 3*: Pandemonium. (Getz.) *Scene 4*: Introduction to Transformation. *Scene 5*: The Brilliant Transformation. (Albert & Burridge.)

ACT 1

Scene 1

Danse Rustique

Coryphées

Scene 3

Song

L. Montrose

Scene 5

Grand Incantation Scene

ACT 2

Scene 3

Grand Ballet of the Birth of the Rainbow

Mlles. Staccioni, Bortoletti; M. Biancifiori

(*Costumes designed by* Howard Russell.)

Grand Adagio; Variation (Bortoletti); Variation (Biancifiori); Variation (Staccioni); Waltz; Gallop and Finale.

[3]First produced in New York 12 September 1866 at Niblo's Garden for 475 performances.

ACT 3

Scene 1

Specialty

L. Montrose, T. O'Brien

Scene 3

Ballet of Popular Airs (Originated by Lawrence McCarty, executed under the direction of A. Bertrand): "Hi-Diddley-Hi-Ti" (Music by George LeBrunn), "Oh, What a Difference (in the Morning)" (Music by Felix McGlennon), "After the Ball" (Music by Charles K. Harris), "The Bowery" (Music by Percy Gaunt), "Maggie Murphy" (Music by David Braham), "Ta-ra-ra-boom-de-ay" (Music by Henry Sayers).

Mardo, the Marvel

The French Quadrille Dancers from the Casino, Paris. (Under the direction of La Sirene, the creator of "fin-de-siecle" dancing in America.)

La Sirene; Rayon de Soleil; Lys d'Argent; Rayon d'Or.

Grand March of the Amazons

ACT 4

Scene 2

Song

T. O'Brien

Scene 4

Cobweb Dance

Mlle. Bartoletti, Coryphées

Scene 5

The Brilliant Transformation Scene 'Life', as illustrated in the Seven Ages of Man

1893.24 ROBERT GRAU'S AMERICAN CELEBRITIES

An Appropriate Drawing Room Entertainment[4] in Three Acts. Musical director, Baxter Johns. Produced by Robert Grau (and Loie Fuller). Opened 16 August 1893 at the Garden Theatre and closed 2 September 1893 after 19 performances.

CAST: LOIE FULLER, OLGA BRANDON, FLORENCE LEVY, ISABELLE URQUHART, ALICE J. SHAW, CARRIE DANIELS, MAE BRUCE, FLORENCE THROPP, GUY STANDING, John E. Kellerd, Paul Arthur, Charles Diehl.

SPECIALTIES, MUSICAL NUMBERS[5]

A Morning Call, a sketch with Guy Standing, Isabelle Urquhart.

Mae Bruce (vocal selections)

Carrie Daniels (banjo)

The Visit[6], an emotional comedy translated from the Danish of E. Brandes, by William Archer. With Olga Brandon, John E. Kellerd, Paul Arthur, Charles Diehl.

Alice Shaw (the whistler, "Chacone" and "Il Bacio")

Loie Fuller in six dances[7].

Florence Thropp (vocal selections)

Florence Levy (dance selections)

1893.25 L'ENFANT PRODIGUE

A Revival of the Musical Play without Words (a Pantomime) in Three Acts[8]. French libretto by Michel Carré, Jr. Music by André Wormser. Directed by Ariel Barney. Pianist, Aimé Lachaume. Dresses by Redfern, of Paris. Produced by Edwin Cleary's French Company, by arrangement with Augustin Daly. Opened 21 August 1893 at Daly's Theatre and closed 7 October 1893 after 49 performances.

CAST: *Pierrot Junior*: Mlle. PILAR MORIN. *Pierrot Senior*: Mons. COURTES. *Phrynette*: Mlle. REINE ROY. *Le Baron*: Mons. DALLEN. *Mme. Pierrot*: Mme. EUGÉNIE BADE. *Servant*: WILFRED BUCKLAND.

1893.26 A NIGHT AT THE CIRCUS

A Revival of the Circo-Comedy in Three Acts[9]. Play by H. Grattan Donnelly. Opened 26 August 1893 at the Park Theatre and closed 9 September 1893 after 17 performances.

CAST: Acts 1 and 2: *Archibald Bager* of Friske and Banger: BENJAMIN F. GRINNELL. *Nichola Friske*, one of the (old) boys: Harry Booker. *Signor Bonanza*, Manager of the Imperial Circus: J. H. Bradbury. *Pinkerton Kopp*, a private detective: John Donahue. *Kicker*, an ambitious office boy: Robert Watson. *Dixey Weed*: Will West. *Bill Sticker*: William Allen. *Calliope Friske*, with an eye on everybody: Beatrice Hamilton. *Belvidere Banger*, a jealous wife: Helen Gliddon. *Remi Riter*, a Hammond operator: Eunice Rennie. *Bud Manhattan*, a New York debutante: Venie DeWitt. *Oriole Ogontz*, a Philadelphia Venus: Josephine Fenton. *Ida Vassar*, a Boston beauty: Josie DeWitt. *Socrates*, a Tiger: Snowball. *Twin Sisters (2)*: *Mlle. Electra*, queen of the arena: NELLIE McHENRY. *Mlle. Madeline Milan*, a visiting governess: NELLIE McHENRY.

Act 3: *The Ring Master*: J. H. Bradbury. *Rusty*: Robert Watson. *Snifty*: John Donahue. *Pete Jenkins*, comic singer: Benjamin F. Grinell. *The Wild Man of Borneo*: Harry Booker. *Cannonball Tosser*: Will West. *Shouter*: William Allen. *Calliope Friske*, with an eye on everybody: Beatrice Hamilton. *Belvidere Banger*, a jealous wife: Helen Gliddon. *Empress of the Air*: Margaret MacDonald. *Bounding Jockey*: Eunice Rennie. *Bounding Jockey*: Venie DeWitt. *The Equine Beauty*: Cupid. *Socrates*, a tiger: Snowball. *Queen of the Arena*: NELLIE MCHENRY. *Nancy Brown*: NELLIE MCHENRY. *Mlle. Milan*: NELLIE MCHENRY.

1893.27 DAN'S TRIBULATIONS

A Revival of the Farcical Comedy in Three Acts, 5 Scenes[10]. Play by Edward Harrigan. Music by David Braham. (Production staged by Edward Harrigan.) Dancing arranged by Dan Burke. Scenery by D. Frank Dodge. Music director, David Braham. Produced by Edward Harrigan. Opened 28 August 1893 at Harrigan's Theatre and closed 7 October 1893 after 48 performances.

CAST: *Dan Mulligan*: EDWARD HARRIGAN. *Simpson Primrose*: JOHN WILD. *Rebecca Allup*: JOSEPH SPARKS. *Reverend Palestine Puter*: James Radcliffe. *Gustavus Lochmuller*: Harry A. Fisher. *August Bimble*: George Merritt. *John Quigley*: Charles F. McCarthy. *Honorah Dublin*: Charles F. McCarthy. *Tommy Fagan*: James McCullough. *Timothy Fillup*: Charles Sturges. *Roderick O'Dwyer*: Edward J. Mack. *Caroline Melrose*: John Decker. *Horace Nichols*: Richard Quilter. *Boss Brady*: Dan Burke. *Tom Mulligan*: Edward W. Hume. *Hog Eye*, a Chinaman: William West. *Walsingham McSweeney*: Charles Coffey. *Mr. Still*: M. Kearney. *Hiram Heaves*: Dave Braham, Jr. *Policeman*: T. Young. *Boy*: Master Mooney. *Brady's Gang*: James Burke, Joseph Williamson, Edward Murphy, John Mayon, Willis Pickert, John Flynn, George D. Davis, Edward Gorman, John Brennan. *Mrs. Bridget Lochmuller*: HATTIE MOORE. *Katie McGloin*: EMMA POLLOCK. *Julia*: FANNIE BATCHELDER. *Kittie Mulligan*: PAULA EDWARDS. *Ella*: Marjorie Teal. *Jennie*: Daisy Sinclair. *Surprise Party Guests*: Lillie Flynn, Rene Eagan, Mildred St. Pierre, Miss Gorenflo, Lillian Menzies. *Cordelia Mulligan*: ANNIE YEAMANS.

Act 1: Dan Mulligan's Grocery and Bar.

Act 2, Scene 1: Mulligan's Alley. *Scene 2*: Exterior of Mulligan's Grocery and Lochmuller's Butcher Shop. *Scene 3*: The Attic. The Funeral.

Act 3: Dan Mulligan's Home.

[4]Billed as having been "organised in Europe."

[5]No program found; list not in performance order. Little more than a vaudeville ollapodrida in the words of the critics, the performance varied during the course of its three-week run. Added for the final week were Signor Tagliapietra and Josephine Turner in solo turns and a duet, "I Live and Love," and also The Regent Quartette.

[6]Dropped after the opening.

[7]Including her Butterfly Ballet from *A TRIP TO CHINATOWN*, and a dance with stereopticon views of George Washington, Grover Cleveland, and Cupid and the Moon projected onto her skirt.

[8]First produced in New York 3 March 1891 at Daly's Theatre for 7 performances, under the title *THE PRODIGUAL SON*.

[9]First produced in New York 21 December 1891 at the Park Theatre for 8 performances, returned 21 March 1892 to the Bijou Theatre for 32 performances. For Synopsis of Scenes and Musical Numbers, see original 1891 production. Interpolated for this revival, as per published sheet music:

"Yew-ra-liar-ity" (introduced in 1492)

(*Music by* George Seevers. *Lyrics by* Charles House.)

[10]First produced in New York 7 April 1884 at the Theatre Comique for 64 performances.

MUSICAL NUMBERS
"The Little Bunch of Berries" (Act 1)
"The Little Side Door" (Act 1)
"The Full Moon Union, 1st Degree!" (Act 2, Scene 1)
"Hurry Little Children, Sunday Morn!" (Act 2, Scene 1)
"Roderick O'Dwyer!"

1893.28 THE CITY DIRECTORY

Russell's Comedians in a Revival of the Musical Entertainment in Two Acts[11]. Constructed for Laughing Purposes Only. (Original libretto by Paul M. Potter. Music by W. S. Mullaly.) This edition compiled by Louis Harrison. Musical director, Alex. Haig. Produced by Russell's Comedians (Albert Riddle, Manager). Opened 5 September 1893 at the Bijou Theatre and closed 30 September 1893 after 31 performances.[12]

CAST: *Delsarte Bacon Smith*, a Promoter: WILLIS P. SWEATNAM. *Bulwer Darwin Smith*, a Dramatic Author: JAMES THORNTON. *Rudolph O'Gorman Smith*, a Thespian Artist: WILLIAM CAMERON. *The Denver Coffee Cooler*, a Pugilist: WILLIAM F. MACK. *Friday Smith*, a Janitor: William B. Wood. *Patient Smith*: WILLIAM CAMERON. *The Baroness Smith* of Coney Island: MATHILDE COTTRELLY. *Olga Smith*: Nellie Parker. *Ray Smith*: KATE UART. *Attilie Smith*: *Dance Specialty*, Act 2: AMELIA GLOVER.

Act 1: The Promoter's Office.

Act 2: The Stage of the Gaiety. Rehearsal of the Burlesque of "Faust and Marguerite" and the Vaudeville Entertainment.

1893.29 A TRIP TO MARS

The Lilliputians in a Spectacular Play (with Music) in Four Acts, 12 Scenes, in German and English. Play by Robert Breitenbach. Music composed and arranged by Fritz Krause. Production and ballets directed by Carl Rosenfeld. Ballets rehearsed by Signor Luca Resta. Scenery and costumes designed by Carl Rosenfeld. Produced by Carl and Theodor Rosenfeld. Opened 8 September 1893 at Niblo's Theatre and closed 4 November 1893 after 68 performances; re-opened a return engagement 25 December 1893 at Niblo's Garden and closed 30 December 1893 after an additional 10 performances. Total: 78 performances.

CAST: *Professor Heddison*, inventor of the mystic cabinet: Mr. Kahn. *Spaetzle, Sr.*, proprietor of a brewery: Mr. Wilke. *Jimmie Spaetzle*, his son (Mr. Burck): FRANZ EBERT. *Lelia*, variety actress: BERTHA JAEGER. *Short*, detective and reporter (Mr. Felix): ADOLF ZINK. *Miss O'Connor* (Miss Schlueter): IDA MAHR. *Mr. Dixon* (Mr. Axien): MAX WALTER. *Mr. Baring* (Mr. Lindner): CHRISTIAN PONS. *A policeman* (Mr. Marquard): LUDWIG MERKEL. *McDonald*, director of the observatory: Mr. Lueck. *Charlotte*, servant girl: Miss Koehler. *First Policeman*: Mr. Durand. *Second Policeman*: Mr. Steimann. *First Spectator*: Mr. Geber. *Second Spectator*: Mr. Waldorf. *Telephone Girl*: Miss Koerber. *Mumpitz XIX*, King of United States of North Marsika: HERMAN RING. *Marsa*, his daughter: ELISE LAU. *Mircuncula*, his mother-in-law: TONI MEISTER. *Melos, Macros*, slaves: Messrs. Schultz, Mueller. *First Courtier*: Mr. Berger. *Second Courtier*: Mr. Fruehauf. *First Herold*: Mr. Hellman. *Second Herold*: Mr. Bender. *Roller-skater*: LUDWIG MERKEL. *A stove*: Mr. Felix. *Slaves, Marsellites, Astronomers, Servants, Audience*.

Act 1, Scene 1: Auditorium of Professor Heddison. *Scene 2*: The Observatory. *Scene 3*: Machinery Hall.

Act 2, Scene 1: The New Herald Building, Broadway and 35th Street. *Scene 2*: In the Clouds. *Scene 3*: The Trip to Mars. "The Flying Heads."

Act 3, Scene 1: The Blue Grotto on Mars. *Scene 2*: In front of the Palace on Mars.

Act 4, Scene 1: Landscape in Spring on Mars. *Scene 2*: Winter's Approach on Mars. *Scene 3*: On the Dome of the World Building. *Scene 4*: The Mammoth Christmas Tree,

ACT 1
The Magic Cabinet. People of normal size will be changed into dwarfs in view of the audience. This illusion is an invention of Manager Carl Rosenfeld.

ACT 2
The Flying Heads. The Heads of the Lilliputians, provided only with wings, will swing unsupported in air towards Mars in full view of the audience. This illusion is an invention of Manger Carl Rosenfeld, and created an immense sensation in Europe several years ago.

ACT 3
The Water Falls. The March of the Characteristic Boots. The Lilliputian Chariot drawn by the four smallest black ponies.

ACT 4
The Return of the Lilliputians from Mars to Earth. The Mammoth Christmas Tree.

1893.30 THE RISING GENERATION

A Comedy (with Songs) in Three Acts and a Prologue. Play by William Gill. Music by Emil O. Wolff. Entire production under the supervision of William Gill and William Barry. Dancing under the supervision of Messrs. Manning and Davis. Scenery by De La Harpe and Wash Valentine. Musical director, Emil O. Wolff. Produced by William L. Malley and ? Lamb. Opened 11 September 1893 at the Park Theatre and closed 30 September 1893 after 24 performances.

CAST: Prologue: *Martin McShayne*, an aqueduct employee: WILLIAM BARRY. *Dionysius O'Hara*, tutor to Van Tyke's children: James H. Manning. *Elwood Van Tyke*, Esq., a wealthy merchant: SAMUEL M. FORREST. *John Connolly*, a shady lawyer: Richard F. Sullivan. *Tommy McShayne*, one of the Rising Generation, age 14: Harry M. Welch. *Ferdie Van Tyke*, another, age 14: James Carroll. *Bolivar*, one of the Growler Gang: David Ballantine. *Elsie Connolly*, another of the Rising Generation, age 12: EVA SCOTT. *Elinor Van Tyke*, another, age 12: VALLIE EGAR. *Johanna McShayne*, Martin's fair sister: ANNIE MACK-BERLIEN.

Acts 1 and2: *Hon. Martin McShayne*, aqueduct contractor and State Senator: WILLIAM BARRY. *Professor Dionysius O'Hara*, Principal of the O'Hara College: James H. Manning. *Thomas J. McShayne*, attorney-at-law: Henry Brinsley. *Elwood Van Tyke*, merchant: SAMUEL M. FORREST. *Richard Allison*, his private secretary: Minert H. Linderman. *Ferdinand Van Tyke*, a spendthrift: Harry W. Fenwick. *John Connolly*, shadier than ever: Richard F. Sullivan. *Officer Roach*, of the First Precinct: Richard F. Sullivan. *Buck Moran*, one of the boys: Joseph Davis. *Michael Angelo*, a peanut connoisseur: Eugene C. Rogers. *Verdi Mascagni*, an impressario: J. Carroll. *Weary Watkins*, a shaker: Charles Barrie. *Elinor Van Tyke*, a society belle: LILLIE B. LINDEMAN. *Elsie Connolly*, as good as gold: LYDIA BARRY. *Darlings of Society (6)*: *Gustavus McNulty*: Joseph Davis. *Percival O'Toole*: J. Carroll. *Algernon Moriarty*: Harry Welch. *Flossie McTaggert*: Eva Butler. *Mamie Golden*: Louise Valentine. *Allie O'Reilly*: Cora O'Neill. *Johanna McShayne*, fairer than ever: ANNIE MACK-BERLIEN. *Workmen, Guests, Musicians, Growler Gang, etc.*

Prologue: Upper Fifth Avenue, New York. The Merchant's Mansion and the Workingman's Shanty. Harlem. 1882.

Act 1, Scene 1: Street in Harlem. *Scene 2*: McShayne's Den, showing a portion of the old shanty, and a part of the new mansion. (Ten years later.)

Act 2: A Portion of Battery Park, New York, affording a view of the Refuge on State Street. A part of the barge office. The Statue of Liberty and the Elevated Road by night. (Two years later.)

Act 3: McShayne's Den. The Christening. "The way a Harlem baby should go to be Christened."

MUSICAL NUMBERS[13]
"Sing Me Those Pretty Songs Again"
Quartette
(*Music and Lyrics by* Harry Kennedy.)

[11]A revised version of the success *THE CITY DIRECTORY* which opened 10 February 1890 at the Bijou for 152 performances. Also advertised as *THE WORLD'S FAIR CITY DIRECTORY*.

[12]No credits in programs for stage director, costume or scenery designer; no musical numbers listed. Reviewers remarked that James Thornton and other principals performed songs and specialties they were known for.

[13]Added for subsequent tour:
"Maggie Mooney" (Song and Chorus)(from THE FLAMS)
J. H. Manning
(*Music and Lyrics by* James Thornton.)

"Two Little Girls in Blue"[14] (from *A TRIP TO CHINATOWN*)
L. Barry
(*Music and Lyrics by* Charles Graham.)
"Darlings of Society" (Song and Dance)
Misses Butler, Valentine, O'Neill, Messrs. Davis, Welch, Carroll
(*Music by* Emil Wolff. *Lyrics by* William Gill.)
"It's the Custom in Ireland"
C. Barry, Company
"We Have Presents for the Baby"
Entire Company
(*Music and Lyrics by* Isadore Witmark.)
"After the Wedding"
(*Music and Lyrics by* Wendell Tennant.)
"Hot Tamale Alley"
(*Music by* George M. Cohan. *Lyrics by* May Irwin.)

1893.31 A TEMPERANCE TOWN

A Farce Comedy in Four Acts, 5 Scenes. Play by Charles H. Hoyt. Staged by Charles H. Hoyt. Scenery designed by Arthur Voegtlin. Produced by (Charles) Hoyt and (Charles W.) Thomas' Company. Opened 18 September 1893 at the Madison Square Theatre and closed 6 January 1894 after 125 performances[15].

CAST: *Ernest Hardman*, the village clergyman: RICHARD H. DILLON. *Launcelot Jones*, known as "Mink," the town drunkard: GEORGE RICHARDS. *St. Julien Jones*, his son, usually called "Bingo": EUGENE CANFIELD. *Squire Belcher*, the leader of the county bar: WILLIAM CULLINGTON. *Kneeland Pray*, who runs the drug store: JOSEPH FRANKAU. *John Worth*, who had money left him, and is spending it: W. H. Currie. *Frank Hardman*, a Montana mining king: FRANK RUSSELL. *Fred Oakhurst*, the town rum-seller: E. F. NAGLE. *Dr. Caldwell Sawyer*, the town physician: Frank A. Lyon. *Uncle Joe Viall*, the oldest man in town: George Ober. *William Russell*, one of the rum crowd: F. Russell. *Wes Perry*, another of the rum crowd: Herman A. Sheldon. *Judge Graham Doe* of the Circuit Court: George Ober. *One of the Crossman children*: Mabel Earle. *Learned Sprigg*, a lawyer from Boston: Herman A. Sheldon. *Sheriff*: Madison Corey. *Tinker Hull*, the organist: Charles Adams. *Will Peake*, the hired spy of the "Ramrods": Harry Luckstone. *Ruth Hardman*, the clergyman's daughter: CAROLINE MISKEL. *Patience Hardman*, his wife: Laura Ayers. *Roxana*, his niece and household aid: Dallas Tyler. *Arabella*, Judge Doe's daughter: Lulu Tabor. *Mary Jane Jones*, who was fool enough to marry "Mink": MARIE UART. *Villagers, Court Officals, etc.*

The action takes place in a village in Vermont, somewhere about Thanksgiving Day, 1882.

Act 1: Backyard of the Parsonage. "The Temperance Crowd."

Act 2: Fred Oakhurst's Saloon. "The Rum Crowd."

Act 3, Scene 1: Dining Room at the Parsonage. "The Thanksgiving Dinner." *Scene 2*: Outside the Church. "The Thanksgiving Sermon."

Act 4: Interior of the Court House. "The Trial of the Rumseller."

MUSICAL NUMBERS[16]

"When Pop Was a Little Boy Like Me" (Song and Dance)(Act 2)
E. Canfield
"I'm Just as Young as I Used to Be" (Song and Dance)(Act 3, Scene 1)
G. Ober
"They Called Her Lovely Mary, the Lily of the West" (Act 3, Scene 2)
G. Richards

1893.32 THE RAINMAKER OF SYRIA, or, The Woman King

A Comic Opera in Two Acts[17]. Libretto by Sydney Rosenfeld. Music by Rudolph Aronson. Oriental dances and marches directed by H. Fletcher Rivers. Scenery by Ernest Gros, H. L. Reid. Costumes designed by Percy Anderson. Musical director, Gustave Kerker. Produced by H. W. Roseborn. Opened 25 September 1893 at the Casino Theatre and closed 14 October 1893 after 21 performances[18].

CAST: *Hatshepu*, Ruler of Egypt: BERTHA RICCI. *Thesaurus*, King of the Ruten: HARRY DAVENPORT. *Nitocris*, a vestal, his daughter: KATE DAVIS. *Saklip*, his calendar maker: CHARLES HOPPER. *Amosis*, a young wonder-worker: MARK SMITH. *Salatis*, a fellow student of Amosis: FANNIE WARD. *Pupils of the Magi*: Ada Mansfield, Beatrice Leslie, Rose Ricci, Jeannette Perie. *Watercarrier*: Sophie Holt. *Officers in Hatshepu's Army*: Nina Farrington, Florence Bell. *Oldest Inhabitant*: Melvin Hye. *Page*: Georgie Dennin. *Herald*: Annie Delevan. *Courtier*: Maud Fenton. *Nefru-Ari*, the dancing girl: Florence Franton.

Act 1: Public Square in Syria. (Gros.)

Act 2: Chamber in the Palace of King Thesaurus. (Reid.)

1893.33 COMRADES

Hyde's Comedians in a (Musical) Comedy in Three Acts. Play by William J. Berry and Edward Corbett. Musical director, Professor Miller. Produced by James Hyde. Opened 2 October 1893 at the Park Theatre and closed 14 October 1893 after 16 performances.

CAST: *J. Fakir Delsarte*, of no means, but resources illimitable: HENRI LYNN. *Jack Derby*, a Bookmaker: JAMES ALLISON. *Killarney*, whose inclination runs to theatricals: GEORGE A. BOOKER. *Reginald*, a dark understudy for Delsarte: JOHNNIE RAY. *Mr. Bull*, Broker, simply introduced: EDWARD HANSON. *Mr. Bear*, to tell the story: JOHN PIERI. *Hans*, a farmer: Harry Ernest. *Bryan Boru*, among other things, a private detective: Richard Graham. *Mrs. Bull, Mrs. Bear*, we know our husbands: EMMA RAY, DOROTHY PARKHURST. *Pupils of Delsarte (6)*: *Polly*: Lucy Allison. *Lolly*: Mabel Narbis. *Jolly*: Cora Vail. *Folly*: Belle Barclay. *Dolly*: Sadie Raymond. *Mrs. Young Blood*, an incident: Alida Perrault. *Mollie Merry*, a Protegee of Mrs. Bull and Mrs. Bear: HELENE MORA[19]. *Specialty*: ANNABELLE. (*Specialties*: Booker & Narbis, The Allisons, Quaker City Quartette.)

Act 1: Delsarte's Studio, New York City.

Act 2: Ocean Grove. Tour of the Grand Consolidated Hamlet.

Act 3: Interior of the Hotel Topaz on the Hudson.

MUSICAL NUMBERS

Butterfly, Serpentine and Sun Dances (Specialty, Act 2)
Anabelle
"Always Mind Your Sister, Jennie"
H. Mora
(*Music and Lyrics by* Charles Graham.)
Specialties by Helene Mora, Johnnie Ray, Booker and Narbis, the Allisons, and the Quaker City Quartette.

1893.34 THE GOLDEN WEDDING

A Patchwork of Nonsense and Melody (Musical Farce Comedy) in Three Acts, 4 Scenes. Play, music and lyrics by Fred Miller, Jr. Musical director, Louis Miller. Manager, Arthur Miller. Opened 2 October 1893 at the Bijou Theatre and closed 14 October 1893 after 16 performances.[20]

CAST: *Penobscot Franklin Blythe*, the Judge, the last lineal descendant of his family: ROBERT EVANS. *Sir Thomas Topack*, on his first visit to America: DAN DALY. *Philip Fairfield*, of Fairfield & Son, Boston: Walter Vanderlip. *Tippecanoe Tappington Boliver*, the new editor of "The Blazor": Charles A. Burke. *O'Fly*, the handy man at the villa: D. L. DON. *Janette*, the Judge's daughter: VIOLA FORTESCUE. *Robert*, a wandering sailor lad: FLORENCE DUNBAR. *Foxey*, the boat house girl: ELSIE ADAIR. *Mrs. Charlotte Comstock*, the widow, the Judge's sister: GRACE VAUGHN. *Mrs. Camelia Blythe*, the Judge's wife: LIZZIE DuROY. *Mrs. Blythe's Nieces (6)*: *Miss Josephine Calebson*: Evelyn Hamilton. *Miss Eugenia Calebson*: Lizzie Sanger. *Miss Victoria Calebson*: Marian LeRoy. *Miss Amelia Calebson*: Frances Olcott. *Miss Estelle Calebson*: Estelle Allen. *Miss Esther Calebson*: Bessie Field. *Mr. Floyd*: George F.

[14]Replaced during subsequent tour by: "I Love My Love in the Springtime" (from THE PASSING SHOW, 1894) L. Barry (*Music by* Ludwig Engländer.)
[15]Costumes design, musical director uncredted. Musical numbers not listed in programs.
[16]Musical numbers not listed in programs. List prepared from published playscript contained in 'Dramas from the American Theatre 1762-1909,' Richard Moody, editor. World Publishing Company, Cleveland, 1966, as previously published in America's Lost Plays, Vol. IX, by permission of Barrett H. Clark.
[17]On 9 October 1893 the title was changed to *THE WOMAN KING, or The Rainmaker of Syria*. Subsequently toured as *THE WOMAN KING, or the Royal Prize*.

[18]Stage direction uncredited; musical numbers not listed in programs; no libretto or musical score found.
[19]Advertised as the initial starring tour of the unrivaled female baritone and comedienne.
[20]No stage director, scenery or costume designer, nor musical numbers listed in programs.

Campbell. *Mr. Dobbs*: W. S. Laird. *Mr. Field*: George S. Trimble. *Mr. Darby*: Wakefield Reed.

At the conclusion of Act 2, Burlesque rehearsal of Mrs. Comstock's tragedy, THE GORILLAS, for the benefit of the Blytheville Mutual Admiration Society: *Queen Salamanca*: GEORGE FORTESCUE. *The Villain*: DAN DALY. *Princess Cynthiana*: VIOLA FORTESCUE. *Prince Pietro*: GRACE VAUGHN. *Duke of Vincennes*: Evelyn Hamilton. *Count Billeano*: Charles A. Burke. *Oli Olio*: D. L. DON. *The Army*: Messrs. G. F. Campbell, W. S. Laird, G. S. Trimble, W. Reed; Misses E. Hamilton, L. Sanger, M. LeRoy, F. Olcott, E. Allen, B. Field. And the Clipper Quartette.

Act 1: Blythe Villa. Morning.

Act 2, Scene 1: Garden, Blythe Villa. Afternoon. *Scene 2*: Drawing-room at Mrs. Comstock's.

Act 3: Evening of the "Golden Wedding" of Mr. and Mrs. Blythe, two years later.

1893.35 ERMINIE

A Revival of the Comic Opera in Three Acts[21]. Libretto by Harry Paulton (and Claxson Bellamy). Based on the melodrama (L'Auberge des Adrets by Benjamin Antier, Saint-Amand and Paulyanthe, adapted into English as) Robert Macaire. Music by Edward Jakobowski. Staged by Richard Barker. Scenery designed by Homer F. Emens (Act 1), Richard Marston (Acts 2, 3). Musical director, Signor Antonio DeNovellis. Produced by Francis Wilson (Management of A. H. Canby). Opened 3 October 1893 at the Broadway Theatre and closed 16 December 1893 after 77 performances.[22]

CAST: *Cadeaux*: FRANCIS WILSON[23]. *Ravennes* (Ravvy): WILLIAM BRODERICK. *Marquis de Pontvert*, Father of Erminie: John McWade. *Eugene Marcel*, Secretary to the Marquis: Harold C. Blake. *Chevalier de Brabazon*, Guest of the Marquis: EDWARD P. TEMPLE. *Captain Delauney*, a young officer: BESSIE CLEVELAND. *Dufois*, Landlord of the Lion d'Or: H. A. Cassidy *Simon*, Waiter at the Lion d'Or: Edmund Lawrence. *Vicomte de Brissac*: Propert Carleton. *Sergeant*: William Steiger. *Benedicte*, a servant to the Marquis: E. B. Knight. *Erminie de Pontvert*: AMANDA FABRIS. *Javotte*: LULU GLASER. *Cerise Marcel*, Sister to Eugene: Cécile Eissung. *Princess de Gramponeur*: JENNIE WEATHERSBY[24]. *Marie*, a peasant: Christie MacDonald. *Guests, Peasants, Soldiers, Servants, Characters at the Fair, etc.*

1893.36 THE WOOLEN STOCKING

A Play in Three Acts, 5 Scenes. Play by Edward Harrigan. Music by David Braham. (Produced under the stage direction of Edward Harrigan.) Dancing under the supervision of Dan Burke. Produced by Edward Harrigan. Opened 9 October 1893 at Harrigan's Theatre and closed 16 December 1893 after 81 performances[25]. Re-opened a return engagement in revised form[26] 19 February 1894 at Harrigan's Theatre and closed 24 February 1894 after an additional 8 performances. Total: 89 performances.

CAST: *Larry McLarney*, a Boss Stevedore: EDWARD HARRIGAN. *Cool Clinker*: JOHN WILD. *Colonel August Hoffmeyer*: JOSEPH SPARKS. *Isidore Rosenstein*: James Radcliffe. *Cornelius Callahan*: HARRY FISHER. *Old Pop Geoghan*: GEORGE MERRITT. *Paddy Dempsey*: EDWARD MACK. *Bob Slivers*: Charles Sturges. *Mary Doyle*: CHARLES F. McCARTHY. *Judge Phineas Fennessy*: Charles Coffey. *Dick Calahan*: Harry W. Wright. *Birdsall Birdseye*: William West. *Sisseretta Sicamore*: John Decker. *Al. Huggins*: Richard Quilter. *John McFadden*: Dan Burke. *Hardie Sicamore*: James McCullough. *Delancy Lonsdale*: Edward W. Hume. *Conrad Getz*: Joseph Williamson. *Timmeen*: David Braham, Jr. *Dr. Gillim O'Gill*: John Mayon. *Officer McKenzie*: Michael Kearney. *Dennis McCue*: Edward Murphy. *Mr. Jowowsky*: Edward Gorman. *Coal Shoveler*: James Burke. *Hester Street Vendors*: Willis Pickert, John Flynn, George D. Davis, T. Young, John Brennan, Master Mooney. *Albertina Lovegood*: HATTIE MOORE. *Nellie Dempsey*: EMMA POLLOCK. *Lena Hoffmeyer*: FANNIE BATCHELDER. *Henrietta Wolfenstein*: Marjorie Teal. *Rachel Wolfenstein*: Mildred St. Pierre. *Jennie*: Irene Eagan. *Mrs. Livingstein*: Marie Gorenflo. *Lilly Mendoza*: Paula Edwards. *Rosy Rosenkratz*: Daisy St. Clair. *Julia Hockheimer*: Lillian Menzies. *Esther Lavinsky*: Lillie Flynn. *Widow Honora Hickey*: ANNIE YEAMANS.

Act 1: Hickey's Hotel on the river front, Monday, Decoration Day.

Act 2, Scene 1: Hoffmeyer's Hotel and Concert Garden, Wednesday evening. *Scene 2*: Larry McLarney's Stable. Friday evening. *Scene 3*: Hester Street. The Jewish Colony.

Act 3: Parlors at Mrs. Lovegood's, Wednesday evening. The Welcome Home Party.

ACT 1
- "Little Daughter Nell"
- "Sergeant Hickey of the G.A.R."

ACT 2

Scene 1
- "The Sunny Side of Thompson Street"
- "Way Down Town"
- "Il Bacio" (with interruptions)
  H. Moore
- Unexpected Finale

Scene 2
- "Pessimism in the Ate"

Scene 3
- "Callahan's Gang"
- "They Never Tell All What They Know"

ACT 3
- (Finale)

1893.37 STARLIGHT

A Return Engagement of the Musical Farce Comedy in Three Acts[27]. Play by Fred D. Maeder and Robert Frazer. Staged under the personal direction of Vernona Jarbeau. Costumes by Miss Mooney. Conductor of music, Fred Hylands. Management, Jeff. D. Bernstein. Opened 23 October 1893 at the Park Theatre and closed 4 November 1893 after 16 performances.[28]

CAST: *Quackleton Quaver*, a musical crank and dealer in sheet music, anxious to become a manager: ROSS SNOW. *Old Muddlebrain*, the boss crank: ED SANDFORD. *Harold Marker*, an artist with a true artist's appreciation of the beautiful: FAMES F. MACDONALD. *Michali Bralligan*, a tramp from America: GUS PIXLEY. *Munzio Flammetti*, the red brigand, but has a voice and a weakness for Starlight: WILLIAM SELLERY. *Swipes*, a tough: WILLIAM SELLERY. *Italian Companions of Starlight (5)*: *Raphael*: Cora Strong. *Anita*: Hattie Wells. *Francesca*: Lella Collins. *Paoli*: Tillie Haines. *Madeline*: Alice Pixley. *Mrs. Highflyer Lionhunter*, a society gusher: MAY BAKER. *Miss Lucy Raffle*, a sweet young thing, a niece of Muddlebrain: BEATRICE NORMAN. *Mrs. Lionhunter's Guests (4)*: *Bertie*: Lella Collins. *Maud*: Cora Strong. *Rose*: Alice Pixley. *Beatrice*: Tillie Haines *Kittie*, Mrs. Highflyer Lionhunter's maid: Hattie Wells. *Carlotta*, known to her companions as "Starlight": VERNONA JARBEAU.

MUSICAL NUMBERS[29]
- "Farewell to Italy"
- "I May Be This"
- "Pinouit"
- "Where Are You Going, My Pretty Maid?" (Imitation of Mme. Theo)
- "What Do I Care?"
- "The Nigger and the Bee"
- "Parthenia Took a Fancy to a Coon"
  V. Jarbeau
  (*Music and Lyrics by* Bob Cole.)

---

[21]First produced in New York 10 May 1886 at the Casino Theatre for 648 performances in a series of three engagements. For Synopsis of Scenes and Musical Numbers, see original 1886 production. For this production, E. Jakobowski composed a "New Erminie Walltz" to be performed as the Entr'acte before Act 3. Published selections by Jakobowski and Paulton from the *NEW ERMINIE* included: "Baa Baa," "Joys of the Rustic Dance," "New Erminie Waltz Song," "Darkest the Hour," "What the Dickeybirds Say," "Downy Jail Birds of a Feather," "Lullaby."

[22]Costumes uncredited.

[23]Recreating his original role.

[24]Recreating her original role.

[25]Direction, scenery and costumes uncredited.

[26]On the basis of a Philadelphia tour program, the revised production dropped Act 2, Scenes 2-3.

[27]First produced in New York 2 May 1892 at the New Park Theatre and closed 7 May 1892 after 8 performances. For Synopsis of Scenes, see original 1892 production.

[28]No credits for scenery in programs.

[29]All vocals by Vernona Jarbeau, not necessarily in performance order.

"The Story of a Kiss"
Imitation of Albert Chevalier's Coster-Monger Songs
Spanish Songs

1893.38 FRITZ IN PROSPERITY

A Play in Four Acts, 6 Scenes. Play by Sydney Rosenfeld. Stage manager, Charles Steadman. Musical director, Edward Weber. Produced by Joseph K. Emmet (Jr.). Opened 23 October 1893 at the Grand Opera House and closed 28 October 1893 after 8 performances.[30]

CAST: *Roger Silverstone*, Attorney-at-Law, professional politician, and wire puller at large: Charles Bowser. *Guy Furniss*, Member of Congress: B. R. Graham. *Mr. Samuel Van Horne*, Eastern Financier: J. W. Hague. *Bradley Van Horne*, his son: Eugene B. Sanger. *Bill Folger*, a disreputable citizen: Charles Stedman. *Dennis Murphy*, foreman: William Malloy. *Grace Van Horne*, daughter of Samuel Van Horne: Emily Lytton. *Letitia Burden*, her Aunt: Blanche Weaver. *Mrs. Cobb*, Fritz's housekeeper: Fanny Denham Rouse. *Kota*, her daughter: Edith Evelyn. *Bibs*, a child: Little Juliette de Grignan. *Schneider*: Baby Spencer Sinott. *Fritz Glauber*: JOSEPH K. EMMET (JR.). *Workingmen, Women and Children.*

The action takes place in South Dakota in 1893.

Act 1: Fritz's Shooting Box, in two tableaux.

Act 2: Interior of Fritz's home.

Act 3, *Scene 1*: The Valley, with a view of the Dam. *Scene 2*: Another view of the Dam. *Scene 3*: The Flood.

Act 4: The Van Horne Parlors at the Pierre Hotel.

1893.39 PRINCESS NICOTINE

An Opera Comique in Three Acts, 4 Scenes. Libretto by Charles Alfred Byrne and Louis Harrison. (Adapted from the novel "The Cocked Hat" by Pedro A. de Alarcon.) Music by William Furst. Produced under the direction of Richard Barker. Ballet arranged by Signor [Augusto] Francioli; Pickaninny Dance arranged by Lucy Daly. Scenery designed by D. Frank Dodge, Richard Marston, Harley Merry. Costumes designed by Catherine Siedle. Musical director, Gustave Kerker. Produced by the Lillian Russell Opera Comique Organization (George W. Lederer, Thomas Canary, Proprietors and Directors). Opened 25 October 1893 at the Casino Theatre and closed 27 January 1894 after 98 performances.

CAST: *Rosa*, the Princess Nicotine: LILLIAN RUSSELL. *Chicos*, a tobacco planter: Perry Averill. *Don Pedro*, the local governor: DIGBY BELL. *Cabana*, first Algualzil: GILBERT CLAYTON. *Novo Mundo*, second Alguazil: DAN COLLYER. *Bishop*: James Peakes. *Alcalde*, Police Magistrate: T. J. Cronin. *Watchman*: L. H. Ducker. *Catalina*, a plantation waif: LUCY DALY. *The Duchess*, wife of Don Pedro: MARIE DRESSLER. *Gomez*, Page to the Duchess: Madeleine Shirley. *Chica*: May Duryea. *Manuela*: Lila Blow. *Chiquita*: Blanche Sherwood. *Pepita*: Marie Celeste. *Drummer Boy*: Georgie Dennin. *Nurse*: Grace Wallace Belasco. *Fifer*: Florence Bell. (*Premiere Danseuse*: Florence Franton.) *Planters, Attendants, Cigarette Girls, Burros, Matadors, Picadors, Torreadors, Banderillos, Plantation Pickaninnies, Ladies and Gentlemen of the Court.*

The action is set in Cuba.

Act 1: A Tobacco plantation in the Vuelta Abajo District. (Dodge.)

Act 2: A Tobacco Planter's Hacienda. (Marston.)

Act 3, *Scene 1*: Street of Cuidad Real. *Scene 2*: Gardens of the Governor. (Merry.)

MUSICAL NUMBERS[30a]

"Airy, Fairy Lillian"
(*Music by* Maurice Levi. *Lyrics by* Tony Raymond.)
"When I Sing My High Cs"
"Princess Nicotine"
Cuban Bull Fight Ballet (Arranged by Signor Augusto Francioli)
F. Franton, Ballet

[30]No stage director, musical director, scenery or costume designers named in programs. No musical numbers listed.

[30a]Musical numbers not listed in programs. No libretto or musical score found.

1893.40 THE ALGERIAN

A Comedy Opera in Three Acts. Libretto by Glen MacDonough[31]. Music by Reginald DeKoven. Produced under the stage direction of Ben Teal. Conductor of orchestra, Louis F. Cornu. Opened 26 October 1893 at the Garden Theatre, moved 27 November 1893 to Daly's Theatre and closed 9 December 1893 after 47 performances[32].

CAST: *Celeste*, Countess de Monvel: MARIE TEMPEST. *Colonel Paul Lagrange*, Commandant at Algiers, pro tem: JULIUS STEIGER. *Macquart*, his aide: A. H. Wagner. *Suzette*, known as 'Baya, the Star of the Orient': ADELE RITCHIE. *Claire*, otherwise known as 'Shefilaire, the Pearl of the Faithful': Bertha Bayliss. *Marie*, otherwise known as "Natilyah, the Lily of the East': Rose Figman. *Joan*, otherwise known as 'Aouda, the Beloved of the Prophet': Nellie Braggins. *Tartarin of Tarascon*: FRANK DAVID. *Prince Gregory*, President of the 'Society for the Preservation of the Picturesque East': JOSEPH HERBERT. *Mitaine*, proprietor of 'Mitaine's Mastadon Menagerie': Ben Lodge. *Seffi*, Tartarin's attendant: James S. Maffitt. *Hassan*, Muezzin at the Mosque El Tebo: Frederick Kelly. *Dancing Girl*: Nanette Lascelles. *Spahis, Chasseurs and Algerians.*

The action takes place at the present time in Algiers.

Act 1: A Landing-Place at Algiers.

Act 2: The Harem of the late Muley Abdallah.

Act 3: The Garden of the Commandant.

ACT 1

Opening Chorus
Quintet (Who will the princess be)
J. Herbert, Girls
"Breton Boat Song"
M. Tempest, Chorus
"One Day a Little Maid" (Chanson)
M. Tempest, Chorus
"The Weather Vane" (Song)
M. Tempest
"Tartarin, the Terrible" (Song)
F. David, Chorus
"When Baya's Raven Tresses" (Love Test)
J. Steger
Finale (Act 1)

ACT 2

"Algerian Serenade"
J. Steger
"Oh, Rash Muezzin!" (Duet)
M. Tempest, J. Steger
"In Old Villanelle" (Chanson)
A. Ritchie
"Tartarin Now Comes" (Chorus and Duet)
F. David, J. Herbert
"Lightly, Lightly, in the Shifting Shadows"
A. Ritchie, Chorus
"Tambourine Song"
M. Tempest, Girls
"Sitting, the Lute A-Striking" (Song)
F. David, Chorus
Nubian Dance
"March of the Watch" (Scene and Chorus)
F. Kelly, A. H. Wagner, J. Steger, F. David, M. Tempest, A. Ricthie, Chorus
Finale (Act 2)

ACT 3

"The Reveille" (Opening Chorus)
A. H. Wagner, Soldiers
"Castles in Spain" (Duet)
M. Tempest, J. Steger

[31]Program note: The story of the Opera, though radically different from the story of the book, was suggested by an incident in Alphonse Daudet's novel "Tartarin of Tarascon."

[32]Producer, scenery and costume designers not identified in New York program. Tryout presented under the management of J. M. Hill. Played a return engagement 26 March 1894 at the American Theatre for 1 week.

Trio (Sing ho!)
M. Tempest, J. Steger, F. David
"And Now as Colonel" (Couplets)
M. Tempest, Chorus
Finale (Act 3)

1893.41 THE KOH-I-NOOR

A Comic Opera in One Act, 3 Scenes, preceded and followed by a vaudeville program. Libretto and music by Oscar Hammerstein[33]. Produced by John Koster, Albert Bial and Oscar Hammerstein. Opened 30 October 1893 at Koster & Bial's Music Hall and closed 25 November 1893 after 28 performances.

VAUDEVILLE: Florence Thropp (Comedienne); Evans and Luxmore (Musical Eccentrics); Mons. and Mme. Del-Mely (Duettists Eccentrique); Ada Reeve (Comedienne).

THE KOH-I-NOOR CAST: *Lord Belgrave*: CHARLES RENWICK. *Duke Piff*, his uncle: Joseph Thomas. *Kohn*, a diamond dealer: N. S. Burnham. *Minzesheimer*, clerk to Kohn: B. Currier. *Shakespeare*, prison keeper: J. H. Roberts. *Smike, Smoke*, Knights of the Jimmy: Harry Stanley, George Knowles. *Fipp, Fopp*, hackmen: B. Mitchell, R. Davids. *Clarkson*, footman: F. Webb. *Maria*, ladies' maid: Emma Ralston. *Lady Dunham*: RUTH DAVENPORT. *Duchess Mink*: ALICE BUTLER. *August Querker*, composer and organ grinder to her Majesty, the Queen of England: F. O'Neill. *Citizens, Peasants, Bakers, Tradesmen, etc.*: Chorus.

Scene 1: Cheapside, London. *Scene 2*: Highgate, London. *Scene 3*: Old Bailey, London.

MUSICAL NUMBERS
"It Might Have Been" (Duet, Scene 3)
C. Renwick, R. Davenport

VAUDEVILLE (Following the opera): Mlle. Paquerette (French Eccentrique); The Glinserettis (Acrobats); Harriet Vernon (Burlesque Artist).

"Versailles," a Grand Ballet Divertissement. Spring (Childhood); Summer (Youth); Autumn (Middle Age); Winter (Old Age). Flora's Maidens, Zephyrs, Bacchantes: C. Newman, A. Bassignani, L. Bassignani, M. Strauss, V. Bors, T. Witt. An original historical and mythological terpsichorean novelty "Pompeletta" arranged and introduced by Clara Qualitz. Costumes created and devised and jewelled by herself. Music by William W. Furst. Minuet de la Coeur—Valse, Ensemble; Grand Adagio; The Vision; Bacchanale Finale.

1893.42 DELMONICO'S AT SIX

A Farce Comedy in Three Acts. Play by Glen MacDonough. Produced under the stage direction of Ben Teal. Musical director, E. Buzzell. Produced by C. B. Jefferson, (Marc) Klaw and (Abraham L.) Erlanger. Opened 6 November 1893 at the Bijou Theatre and closed 18 November 1893 after 16 performances; returned 26 March 1894 at the Bijou and closed 7 April 1894 after an additional 16 performances. Total: 32 performances.[34].

CAST: *Trixie Hazelmere*, the Queen of the Vaudevilles: MARIE JANSEN. *Hamilton Clark, M.D.*, her suitor: FRANK TANNEHILL, JR. *Alphonse*, alias Count de Toi, a waiter at Delmonico's: IGNACIO MARTINETTI. *Captain Frank Holland* of the Fourth Cavalry: WILLIAM NORRIS. *Montague MacPounders*, the "Modern Sampson": Charles Mason. *G. Benson*, from the Central Office: Frederick W. Peters. *Mrs. Hamilton Clark*: MAY MERRICK. *Jessie Clark*, her stepdaughter: Hope Ross. *Estelle*, the Pearl of Parlor Maids: Bessie Lackey.

The action takes place today in New York.

Act 1: The Home of Hamilton Clark. Sowing the Cyclone.

Act 2: A Dining-room at Delmonico's. Threatening weather.

Act 3: Trixie Hazelmere's Apartment. Reaping the Blizzard.

MUSICAL NUMBERS[35]
"Be Good" (from *THE OOLAH*)
M. Jansen
(*Music by* John J. Braham. *Lyrics by* J. Cheever Goodwin.)
"Oh Mamma (Buy Me That)"
M. Jansen
(*Music and Lyrics by* Al Himan.)

1893.43 PLAYMATES

A Musical Comedy in Three Acts. Book, music and lyrics by W. R. Seeley. Produced under the direction of Paul C. Blum. Musical director, William Reynolds. Proprietors, Bessie Bonehill, William R. Seeley. Opened 13 November 1893 at the Park Theatre, and closed 25 November 1893 after 16 performances; re-opened 13 January 1894 at Niblo's Garden and closed 18 January 1894 after an additional 8 performances.[36]

CAST: *Gussie Crotchett*, cashier: W. R. SEELEY. *Lord Bluffwell*: CHARLES JEROME. *Sir Doolittle*: WILLIAM JEROME. *William Frogdon*, head of the firm of Frogdon & Co.: JAMES CHERRY[37]. *Captain Mainbrace*: Kirwin West. *Professor Pattiwisky*, music teacher: Sig. A. BORELLI. *Charles*, clerk: George Brengle. *Alice Frogdon*, William Frogdon's daughter: MINNIE THURGATE. *Eliza Frogdon*, William Frogdon's maiden sister: ANNETTE ZELNA. *Pets of the Store (3)*: *Rosie*: Estella Sanders. *Hattie*: Minerva Adams. *Violet*: Minnie Poore. *Lottie Sample*: Melytha Adams. *Jack Wellington*, cashier: BESSIE BONEHILL.

Act 1: Interior of Frogdon's store, New York.

Act 2: A wharf. Ocean steamer about to sail for England. The storm. The wreck. Saved.

Act 3: Drawing room of Frogdon's house. Alice's birthday party.

ACT 1
"Three Little Chaps"
B. Bonehill
Quarreling Duet
B. Bonehill, M. Thurgate
"Dinkey Arno"
M. Thurgate, M. Adams
Mandolin Solo
Finale
B. Bonehill, Company

ACT 2
Parodies by Jeromes
C. Jerome, W. Jerome
"Playmates"
B. Bonehill
Instrumental Duets
W. R. Seeley, K. West
"Jolly Jack with Hornpipe"
B. Bonehill
Medley
Entire Company

ACT 3[38]
Minuette
B. Bonehill, M. Thurgate, M. Poore, M. Adams
"Buttercups and Daisies"
B. Bonehill
Specialties
A. Borelli, C. Jerome, W. Jerome, A. Zelna, M. Thurgate
Piano Specialty
A. Borelli
Imitation of the World's Fair Soloist
A. Zelna
Grand Finale
Company

[33]Program note: "Produced without change of music or text, exactly as written during the 48 hours of seclusion as stipulated in the wager."
[34]Scenery and costumes uncredited.
[35]For return engagement, M. Jansen sang the following two songs:
"Hook and Eye"
M. Jansen
(*Music and Lyrics by* Joseph Hart.)
"The Vivandiere"
M. Jansen
(*Music and Lyrics by* Joseph Hart.)
[36]No credits given for scenery or costume design.
[37]Succeeded by William H. Maxwell for return engagement.
[38]Added to Act 3 for return engagement:
"Marguerite"
M. Thurgate

1893.44

KING RENÉ'S DAUGHTER/ PHILÉMON AND BAUCIS

A Double Bill of Comic Operas. Opened 22 November 1893 at Herrmann's Theatre and closed 2 December 1893 after 15 performances.

PHILÉMON AND BAUCIS, an Opéra Comique in Two Acts. Libretto by Jules Barbier and Michel Carré. Music by Charles Gounod.

CAST: *Jupiter*: WILLIAM McLAUGHLIN. *Vulcan*: WILLIAM PRUETTE. *Philemon*: CHARLES BASSETT. *Baucis*: LENORE SNYDER.

followed by

KING RENÉ'S DAUGHTER, a Lyric Drama in One Act.[39] Founded upon Henrik Herz's famous (Danish) play of the same name, (adapted into English by Edmund Phipps). Music by Julian Edwards. Costumes designed by Mme. Leo.

CAST: *King René*, Count of Provence (bass): WILLIAM PRUETTE. *Iolanthe*, his daughter (soprano): ELEANOR MAYO. *Count Tristan of Vaudemont* (tenor): CHARLES BASSETT. *Sir Geoffrey of Orange* (baritone): H. M. RAVENSCROFT. *Sir Almeric* (tenor): W. H. Faucherard. *Ebn Jahia*, a Moorish Physician (bass): Joseph Fay. *Bertrand* (bass): Charles Miller. *Martha*, his wife (mezzo soprano): Minnie De Reu. (*Count Tristan's followers.*)

The action takes place in Provence, in a valley of Vaucluse and lasts from afternoon to sunset. The period is the middle fo the Fifteenth Century.

1893.45

AMERICA

A Grand Historical, Allegorical Ballet Spectacle in a Prologue, Three Acts, 16 Scenes. Entire spectacle designed, (conceived) and produced by Imre Kiralfy. Music by Angelo Venanzi. Scenery painted by Amable and Gardy, Rube and Chaperon, Fromont and Lemeunier of Paris, and Mr. Witham of Boston. Costumes and accessories designed by Alfred Edel. Musical director, Fred J. Eustis. Produced by Henry B. Abbey, John B. Schoeffel and Maurice Grau. Opened 5 December 1893 at the Metropolitan Opera House and closed 27 January 1894 after 40 performances in repertory.[40]

CAST: *Bigotry*: ISABELLE URQUHART. *Liberty*: CARLOTTA GILMAN. *Progress*: CLARA BENTON. *Priscilla*: Mlle. STOCCHETTI. *Lillian*: Mlle. STOCCHETTI. *Isabella*: FLORINE MALCOLM. *Perseverance*: SPENCER GRACEY. *Columbus*: S. GORDON EDWARDS. *Washington*: S. GORDON EDWARDS. *Lincoln*: S. GORDON EDWARDS. *Premiere Danseuses Assoluta*: Mlles. STOCCHETTI, SANTORI. Corps de Ballet of 150. (*Specialties*: Sylvester Schaffer & Acrobatic Troupe.)

Prologue, Scene 1: Santa Fe. *Scene 2*: The Departure from Huelva. *Scene 3*: The Voyage of Discovery. *Scene 4*: San Salvador. *Scene 5*: Triumphal Return to Spain.

Act 1, Scene 1: The Plymouth Plantation, 1621. *Scene 2*: Merrymount, 1623.

Act 2, Scene 1: Washington Crossing the Delaware. *Scene 2*: The Surrender of Yorktown. *Scene 3*: Peace and the Triumph of Liberty. *Scene 4*: The Temple of Peace.

Act 3, Scene 1: The Palace of Progress. *Scene 2*: The Early Pioneers in the Far West. *Scene 3*: The Close of the War of Secession, 1865. *Scene 4*: Schaffer Troupe. *Scene 5*: The Triumph of Columbia.

PROLOGUE[41]
- Glorious Chant of Victory (Scene 1)
- Chorus of Women of Huelva (Scene 2)
- A Ballad (Oh! Judge not foolishly..) (Scene 2)
  - C. Benton
- The Mutineers; Joyful Hymn of Thanks (Scene 3)
- Songs of Exultation (Scene 4)
  - Crew
- Song (We salute thee, O finder of a World!) (Scene 4)
  - C. Benton
- Grand Processional Pageant (Glad April, with the gentle Western breeze)(Scene 5)
  - Entire Corps de Ballet, Grand Chorus, Corps of Auxiliaries

ACT 1
- Song (Scene 1)(Hail! Souls elect!)
  - C. Gilman
- The Maypole of Merrymount (Act 1, Scene 2)
  - Solo with variations
    - Mlle. Santori
  - Dance Characteristique
    - Mlle. Stocchett
  - May Song
  - May-pole Dance
  - Original Sensational Shooting Feats
    - S. Schaffer
  - Comic Eccentricities
    - Messrs. Basco, Roberts
- Grand Ballet of Merrymakers (Act 1, Scene 2)
- Grand Finale, Bacchanale Chorus and Dance

ACT 2
- The Temple of Peace (Scene 4)
  - Entrance of Peace, Liberty, Independence, Happiness, Love, Friendship, Kindness and Benevolence (Peace, fair goddess with white wings)
  - Entrance of Progress, Commerce, Industry, Wealth, Prosperity, Agriculture, and Invention (The arms that once were strong in strife)
  - Entrance of Civilization, Liberality, Generosity, Humanity, Toleration, Culture and Grace (As in the balmy air of morn)
  - Entrance of Education, Intellect, Knowledge, Reason, Judgement, Strength and Action (Still beauty has but little force)
  - Entrance of Fine Arts, Literature, Painting, Sculpture, Architecture, Poetry and Music (In art man finds relief from care)
  - Entrance of Science, Perseverance, Invention, Astronomy, Mathematics, Physics, Chemistry and Mechanism (Deep mysteries, once deemed forbidden)
- Grand Ballet of Arts and Sciences (Scene 4)
  - Mlles. Santori, Stocchetti, Entire Corps de Ballet

ACT 3
- Grand Ballet of American Inventions (Scene 1)
  - Franklin's Lightning Rod; Whitney's Cotton Gin; McCormick's Reaper; Hoe's Printing Press; Morse's Electric Telegraph; Howe's Sewing Machine; Yost's Typewriter; Bells' Telephone; Edison's Phonograph and Electric Light.
- Pioneers' Duet and Quintette (Scene 2) (Prospecting is such a jolly life)
- Chorus of Union Soldiers (Scene 3)
- Song (Behold the heroes of inexorable fate)(Scene 3)
  - C. Benton
- The Famous Schaffer Troupe in their original Marvelous Acrobatic Feats (Scene 4)
- Congregation of Nations, and Grand Cortege of the States and Territories of the Union (Scene 5)

1893.46

OLD LAVENDER

A Revival of the Local Play in Three Acts, 7 Scenes[42]. Play by Edward Harrigan. Music by David Braham. (Staged by Edward Harrigan.) Dancing under the supervision of Dan Burke. Scenery by D. Frank Dodge. Electric gas effects by John Whalen. Produced by Edward Harrigan. Opened 18 December 1893 at Harrigan's Theatre and closed 20 January 1894 after 40 performances.

CAST: *George Coggswell*, afterwards known as "Old Lavender": EDWARD HARRIGAN. *Smoke*: JOHN WILD. *Dick the Rat*: JOHN DECKER. *Martin Reilly*: JOSEPH SPARKS. *Philip Coggswell*: EDWARD MACK. *Paul Cassin*: John C. Dixon. *John Filbert*: HARRY FISHER. *Martin Brown*: JAMES RADCLIFFE. *Pop Jones*: GEORGE MERRITT. *Pedro Donnetto*: Dan Burke. *Jack Dingle*: Richard Quilter. *Serenaders and Sailors*: William West, Edward Gorman, Master Mooney, Edward W. Hume, James Williamson, Charles Sturges, James McCullough, Dave Braham, Jr. *Laura Coggswell*: ESTHER WILLIAMS. *Sally Stag*: EMMA POLLOCK. *Servia Cune*: Lillie Flynn. *Shop Girl*: Irene Eagan. *Mother Crawford*: ANNIE YEAMANS.

---

[39]No individual musical numbers listed in programs or published piano vocal score (John Church Co, Cincinnati, Ohio, 1893).

[40]Performed 5 performances weekly (Tuesday, Thursday, Saturday evenings, Wednesday and Friday matinees) in repertory with Metropolitan Opera House's own opera presentations.

[41]Published typescript from Chicago World's Fair production at the Auditorium Theatre 19 April 1893 provided additional detail not found in the New York program.

[42]First produced in New York 3 September 1877 at the Theatre Comique for 24 performances. For Synopsis of Scenes and Musical Numbers, see original 1877 production.

Act 1, Scene 1: Ante-room of the Owl Club. *Scene 2*: Vestibule of the Owl Club. *Scene 3*: Banking House of Philip Coggswell. The Discharge.

Act 2: Near the Ferry at Night.Old Lavender's Home.

Act 3, Scene 1: Mother Crawford's Sailor Boarding House. *Scene 2*: Wall Street. *Scene 3*: Private Office of Philip Coggswell, Banker. The Brothers.

ACT 1
Scene 1
"The Jolly Old Owls"
"When the Clock in the Tower Strikes Twelve"
Scene 2
"Please to Put That Down"

ACT 2
"Love, Love, Sweetest Love"
"Extra! Extra!"
"Poverty's Tears Ebb and Flow"

ACT 3
Scene 1
"Get Up Jack, John Sit Down"

1893.47 THE VOYAGE OF SUZETTE

A Spectacular Comedy in Three Acts, 10 Scenes. (American) Libretto by Alfred Byrne and Louis Harrison. Adapted from the French ("Le Voyage de Suzette") by Henri Chivot and Alfred Duru. Original music by Jesse Williams and Charles Puerner. Entire production under the personal supervision of Richard Barker. Ballets under the direction of Augusto Francioli. Scenery by Joseph Clare, William Hoover, John H. Young, H. L. Reid, Richard Marston. Costumes designed by Catherine Seidle and Captain Alfred Thompson. Produced by Henry T. French. Opened 23 December 1893 at the American Theatre and closed 20 January 1894 after 31 performances.[43]

CAST: *Blanchard*, a rich merchant: GEORGE C. BONIFACE. *André*, his son: NELSON WHEATCROFT. *Pinsonnet*, servant of André: J. W. Pigott. *Verduron*, schoolmaster: HARRY DAVENPORT. *Baldwin Butterfield*, an American patent medicine man: MAX FIGMAN. *Omar Pasha*, Chief of Smyrna Police: J. W. SHANNON. *Don Giraflor*, a Spanish noble: Vincent Sternroyd. *Corricopoulos*, Greek brigand: C. W. Dungan. *General Zephyris*, Governor of Athens: Joseph Adelman. *Caboul*, Steward of Pasha: Charles Atwood. *Don Carlos*, Friend of Giraflor: John E. Dudley. *Selim*, a favorite slave: Victor Millwood. *Demetrius*, a Brigand: Macy Harlan. *Kaleb, Jose, Hamed*, Envoys of Blanchard: C. P. Hanon, E. F. Stone, William Simpson. *Suzette*, daughter of Verduron: SADIE MARTINOT. *Cora*, freed slave: MAXINE ELLIOTT. *Paquita*, maid servant to Suzette: EUNICE VANCE. *Mrs. Butterfield*: Fannie Ward. *La Rosalba*, opera singer: Lee Lamar. *Zenobia*: Annie Errol Boyd. *Daphne*: Teckla Morton. *Gulnare*: Carrie Noyes. *Premiere Danseuse*: TERESINA MAGLIANI. *Ballet of Fifty*. (*Specialties*: THE PICCHIANI FAMILY, Mlle. ALCIDE CAPITAINE, BILLY BURKE, A. Siegrist, William Eunice, William Proctor, Florence Franton, Ray Allen.) *Persian Signors, Dignitaries, Slaves (Male and Female), Sailors, Spanish Men and Women, Albanians, Palikaris, Greek Dignitaries, Odalisques, Turkish Police.*

Act 1, Scene 1: Home of Blanchard the Rich, Persia. (Clare and Hoover.) *Scene 2*: Schoolroom of Verduron the Poor, Spain. (Clare and Hoover.) *Scene 3*: Port of Barcelona. (Young and Hoover.)

Act 2, Scene 1: Palace of Governor General Zephyris, Athens. (Clare and Hoover.) *Scene 2*: Tent of Corricopoulos, Greece. (Reid and Hoover.) *Scene 3*: The fête of the Brigands. (Marston and Hoover.)

Act 2, Scene 1: Palace of the Pasha, Smyrna. (Marston and Hoover.) *Scene 2*: Green Room of the Circus. (Clare and Hoover.) *Scene 3*: An Audience with the Pasha. (Reid and Hoover.) *Scene 4*: Realistic Circus Scene. (Clare and Hoover.)

ACT 1
Scene 3
Acrobatic Feats
Picchiani Family
Ballet of Fisher Boys and Fisher Maidens

[43]Producer, musical director uncredited.

ACT 2
Scene 3
The Ballet of the Four Seasons

ACT 3
Scene 2
Specialty (The Queen of the Air)
Mlle. A. Capitaine
Procession of 24 Trained Animals
Billy Burke, the well-known clown, will exhibit the wonderful comic elephant, Pantaloon.
An Old Time Comic Pantomime:
Clown: A. Siegrist. *Pantaloon*: M. Figman. *Policeman*: W. Eunice. *Butcher*: W. Proctor. *Harlequin*: F. Franton. *Columbine*: R. Allen.

1893.48 ROBIN HOOD

A Revival of the Comic Opera in Three Acts[44]. Libretto by Harry B. Smith. Music by Reginald DeKoven. Staged by John E. Nash. Scenery by Frank Marsden. Costumes designed by Mrs. Catherine Siedle. Musical director, Samuel L. Studley. Produced by the Bostonians (Henry Clay Barnabee, Tom Karl, W. H. MacDonald, Proprietors and Managers). Opened 25 December 1893 at the Broadway Theatre, closing 13 January 1894; re-opened 19 February 1894 and closed 17 March 1894 after 50 performances in repertory.

CAST: *Sheriff of Nottingham*: HENRY CLAY BARNABEE. *Robin Hood*: EDGAR TEMPLE. *Little John*: W. H. MacDONALD. *Will Scarlet*: EUGENE COWLES. *Alan-a-Dale*: JESSIE BARTLETT-DAVIS. *Friar Tuck*: GEORGE FROTHINGHAM. *Guy of Gisborne*: Peter Lang. *Maid Marian*: MARGARET REID. *Dame Durden*: JOSEPHINE BARTLETT. *Annabel*: Mena Cleary. *Forresters, Outlaws, Villagers, Nobles, Archers, Soldiers, Archers, etc.*

1893.49 A COUNTRY SPORT

A Farce Comedy in Three Acts. Play by John J. McNally. Produced under the stage direction of Frank Tannehill, Jr. Produced by (Isaac B.) Rich & (William) Harris. Opened 25 December 1893 at the Bijou Theatre and closed 24 March 1894 after 104 performances[45].

CAST: *Harry Hardy*, "A Country Sport": PETER F. DAILEY. *Con Connelly*, His Guardian: JOHN G. SPARKS. *B. Jabez Jorkins*, his other guardian: FRANK R. JACKSON. *E. Washington Strutt*, out for the stuff: RICHARD CARLE. *"Andy"* doing many things: Lillie Allyne. *Asa Clubbs*, the finest: Ed A. Begley. *Ben Tarline*, a fresh old salt: James F. Callahan. *Pat*, the Irishman: James F. Callahan. *Michael Cohen*, doing everybody: Roland Carter. *Watson*, just from the Fair: George S. Gates. *Margie McIntyre*, a quiet lady: ADA LEWIS. *Gladys Connelly*, daughter of 'Con': Agnes Paul. *Tilda Welworth*, who helps do nothing: GEORGIE LINGARD. *Mrs. Tom Thompson*, a widow: May Levigne. *Mrs. Sam Sampson*, another: Freda Depew. *Mrs. John Johnson*, still another: Kathleen G. Warren. *Olla Lone*: Angie Gaines. *Carrie Weight*: Lyda Darrell. *Elizabeth Alwright*, B.A., "P.O.P.C.": MAY IRWIN. *Yokels, city chaps, Bowery gents, members of her Majesty's service.*

Time: To-day, yesterday and to-morrow. Plot furnished on application by letter. Please enclose stamp.

Act 1: Jorkinsville, on the Hudson.

Act 2: On the Bowery.

Act 3: Home of Con Connelly, New York.

ACT 1
Medley (The latest of everything)

ACT 2
Happy school girls
Rehearsal for "the business."

[44]First produced in New York 28 September 1891 at the Standard Theatre for 35 performances, followed by a return engagement 16 May 1892 at the Garden Theatre for 42 performances. For Synopsis of Scenes and Musical Numbers, see original 1891 production.
[45]Played a return engagement 2 April 1894 at the American Theatre for 1 week.

Specialty (Andrew and Tilda)
L. Allyne, G. Lingard
The Professor in Scenes for the Vaudeville Club
Margie will waltz.
The Garden City Quartette
Grand Medley

ACT 3
"Mamie, Come and Kiss Your Honey Boy"
M. Irwin
(*Music and Lyrics by* May Irwin.)
Specialty
P. Dailey

1893.50

AFRICA

George Thatcher and His Company of Comedians in a Musical Comedy in Three Acts, 5 Scenes. Music by Randolph Cruger. Entire production under the personal stage direction of Napier Lothian, Jr. Scenery designed by John A. Thompson. Costumes by Henry Dazian. Orchestra under the direction of Randolph Cruger. Management, W. H. A. Cronkhite. Produced by (George) Thatcher, (Isaac B.) Rich and (William) Harris. Opened 25 December 1893 at the Star Theatre, closing 13 January 1894 after 21 performances; moved 15 January 1894 to the Park Theatre and closed 27 January 1894 after an 14 additional performances[46]. Total: 35 performances.

CAST: Acts 1 and 2: *Maurice Merrill*, with a mania for exploring Africa: John A. Coleman. *Matthew Miller* of the Mapledale Hunt Club: Charles H. Hopper. *Moses Merrill*, father of Maurice: Charles J. Stine. *Menander Mudge*, College Professor: H. W. Frillman. *Maggs, Miggs, Muggs*, College Chums of Maurice: R. J. José, Thomas Lewis, John Daly. *Menelaus McAllister*, servant of the modern school: William Vidocq. *Mike Milligan*, the favorite college professor: E. C. Jobson. *Marion Morton*, Moses' niece in love with Maurice: Hilda Hollins. *Mabel Merrill, Maude Merrill*: Helen and Henrietta Byron. *Millicent Merrill*, Moses' maiden sister, who adores college boys: Blanche Hayden. *Minerva Mudge*, the professor's daughter: Florence Raymond. *Melissa Maddox*, a house maid, also of the modern school: Madge Ellis. *Mark Mansfield*, a professional necessary of life: OTIS HARLAN. *Mr. Medikus*, a vender of Hair Restorative, who is mistaken for an expert on insanity: GEORGE THATCHER. *Members of the Mapledale Hunt Club, Grooms, Maids, etc.*

Act 3: *Maurice Merrill*, an explorer au fait: John A. Coleman. *African Explorers (11)*: *Matthew Miller*: Charles H. Hopper. *Moses Merrill*: Charles J. Stine. *Menander Mudge*: H. W. Frillman. *Muggs, Miggs*: R. J. Jose, Thomas Lewis. *Mike Milligan*: E. C. Jobson. *Mabel Merrill*: Helen Byron. *Maude Merrill*: Gertrude Reynolds. *Millicent Merrill*: Blanche Hayden. *Minerva Mudge*: Florence Raymond. *Melissa Maddox*: Madge Ellis.

Africans: *Mungo Jungo*, a Chief: C. B. Wheeler. *King Orizaba's Attendants (5)*: *Asbestos*: John Daly. *Bango*: Archie Baldwin. *Wango*: Will Heeley. *Tungo*: Arthur Daly. *Boolu*: Frank Heeley. *Ladies of the Court (6)*: *Gazzam*: William Vidocq. *Lummy Tummy*: Nellie Parkes. *Hummy Hummy*: Jennie Scot. *Tolulu*: Cecile Loraine. *Sky-Hy*: Maude Forbes. *Pooty-Petto*: Julia Raymond. *Queen Originoco*, Queen of Africa: Hilda Hollins. *Hunyadi*, Prime Minister to King Orizaba: OTIS HARLAN. *Orizaba*, King of Africa: GEORGE THATCHER. *Guards, Hottentots, Amazons, Attendants, etc.*

Act 1, Scene 1: Moses Merrill's Villa, Staten Island, New York. *Scene 2*: Library in Moses Merrill's Villa. *Scene 3*: The Club House and Grounds of Mapledale Hunt Club.

Act 2: Deck of the Steam Yacht "*Moses Merrill.*"

Act 3: African Jungle.

SPECIALTIES, MUSICAL NUMBERS[47]
"Ho! for Africa" (Benefit entertainment en route arranged by Mr. Medikus, contributed to by the Harvard Quartet)(Act 1)O. Harlan, J. A. Coleman, G. Reynolds, Company
Feast Dance of the African Chiefs (Act 3)
A. Baldwin, A. Daly, F. Heeley, W. Heeley, W. Vidocq, J. Daly
Also Marches, Tom-Tom instrumentalist, and the grand sacrificial scene.

[46]Libretto uncredited in New York programs; out-of-town tryout credits libretto by Clay M. Green and J. Cheever Goodwin.
[47]Only ballets and specialties listed in programs. Musical numbers from published sheet music.

"I Met Her at the Ball" (interpolation on tour)
R. J. José
(*Music and Lyrics by* D. L. White.)

1894.01

THE PUPIL IN MAGIC

A Revival of the Lilliputians in a Grand Spectacular Comedy-Drama ('Der Zauberlehrling') with Chorus and Ballet in Four Acts, 8 Scenes, in German[48]. Play by Robert Breitenbach. Music selected and arranged by Carl Josef. Stage management, choreographic arrangements, decorative designs by director Carl Rosenfeld. Choreographic part arranged by the Maitre de Ballet, Mr. Leoni. Scenery by Franz Komolossy, Franz Gruber. Costumes by Sophie Klein. Musical director, Mr. Christiani. Produced by Messrs. Rosenfeld Brothers (Carl, Theodor). Opened 1 January 1894 at Niblo's Garden and closed 6 January 1894 after 9 performances.

CAST: *Friedrich Rademacher*, Mechanic and Automaton Manufacturer: Mr. Kahn. *Mrs. Wiese*, his sister: Mrs. Koepler. *Fritz*, her son: ADOLF ZINK. *Andrew*, factotum at Rademacher's: Mr. Wilke. *Kampfhaha*, Landlord: Mr. Burk. *The Princess Lydia Farasoff*: MINCHEN BECKER. *Martha*, Ladies' Maid to the Princess: Miss Beste. *Ossip*, Servant to the Princess: Mr. Durand. *Automata (7)*: *Weeping She*: IDA MAHR. *Smiling She*: BERTHA JAEGER. *The Old Tyrolese*: JOHANN WOLF. *A Tyrolese Woman*: TONI MEISTER. *A Young Tyrolese*: Mr. Merkel. *A Trumpeter*: MAX WALTER. *A Velocipedist*: Christ. Pons. *Puck*, a Tricky Lover: FRANZ EBERT. *Titi, Fifi*, Dancers: IDA MAHR, BERTHA JAEGER. *Stutzl, Mariedl, Andredl*, Peasants: HERMAN RING, TONI MEISTER, Mr. Merkel. *Chauvin, Loyal*, French Officers: Max Walter, Mr. Pons. *Lieutenant Westermann*, Traveler to the Arctic Region: Mr. Lueck. *Germain*, valet: Mr. Cotta. *Jean*, servant: Mr. Marx. *Kallschall, Eizapfhen, Mrs. Klappe*, Esquimaux: Messrs. Truhauf, Reimer, Miss Schulz. *Puffer*, Purser: Mr. Koch. *Ede*, Upholsterer: Mr. Wilke. *Reiter*, Painter: Mr. Wenig. *Pump*, Student: Mr. Jung. *Melanie*: Miss Wilhelmy. *Ella*: Miss Schluter. *Clara*: Miss Ferdely. *Automatons, servants, Japanese, Ladies and Gentlemen of the corps de ballet, Esquimaux, excursionists, watchmen, bicyclists.*

1894.02

A TEXAS STEER, or, Money Makes the Mare Go

A Revival of the Farce Comedy in Three Acts[49]. Play by Charles H. Hoyt. Entire production under the personal direction of Charles H. Hoyt. Scenery by Arthur Voegtlin. Produced by Charles H. Hoyt (Frank McKee, Management) Opened 8 January 1894 at the Madison Square Theatre and closed 10 February 1894 after 35 performances[50].

CAST: *Maverick Brander*, a Texas cattle king: TIM MURPHY. *Captain Fairleigh Bright*: John Marshall. *Members Farmers' Alliance (3)*: *Major Yell*, lawyer: Mat Snyder. *Colonel Bragg*, faro banker: James F. Horan. *Colonel Blow*, bartender: C. L. Warren. *Brassy Gall*, , Esq., member of the Third House: Newton Chisnell. *Colonel K. N. Pepper*, a retired army officer: James Horan. *Christopher Columbus Jr. Fishback*, a colored statesman: Will H. Bray. *Knott Innitt*, Brander's private secretary: Sumner Clark. *Othello Moore*, a private waiter at the Arlington: John T. Craven. *Lieutenant Green*, U.S.A.: Sumner Clarke. *Sergeant at-Arms*: John Deady. *Anatole*, a valet: Newton Chisnell. *G. Whittaker Bellows*, a senator: Robert McIntyre. *Green Woodhead*, a judge: George A. Grace. *Lowe Dodge*, an artist: Charles Bradford. *Crab, Mink*, Field Hands: Edw. Corbin, George Jennings. *Sam*, row boy, Arlington Hotel: Olney Griffin. *Mrs. Brander*, the cattle king's wife: ROSE SNYDER. *Mrs. Major Campbell*, whose husband is stationed in Texas: Gertrude Perry. *Dixie Style*, an orphan from Indiana: Stella Kenny. *Bossy*, Brander's pet: ALICE EVANS. *Street Band, Waiters, Indians, Greasers and general riff-raff of a frontier town.*

1894.03

THE MAID OF PLYMOUTH

A Comic Opera in Two Acts. Libretto by Clay M. Greene. Based on the Longfellow's poem "The Courtship of Miles Standish." Music by Thomas

[48]First produced in New York 15 September 1890 at Niblo's Garden, the Metropolitan Opera House and the Park Theatre for a total of 91 performances. For Synopsis of Scenes and Specialties, see original 1890 production.
[49]First produced in New York 10 November 1890 at the Bijou Theatre for 88 performances. For Synopsis of Scenes and Musical Numbers, see original 1890 production.
[50]Costumes, musical direction uncredited. The Madison Square Theatre Quartette will supply Southern melodies.

Pearsall Thorne. Stage director, John E. Nash. Scenery by Frank Marsden. Costumes designed by Catherine Siedle. Musical director, Samuel L. Studley. Produced by the Bostonians (Henry Clay Barnabee, Tom Karl, W. H. MacDonald, Proprietors and Managers). Opened 15 January 1894 at the Broadway Theatre and closed 10 February 1894 after 28 performances.

CAST: *The Elder*, ecclesiastical custodian of the Pilgrim fathers: HENRY CLAY BARNABEE. *Miles Standish*, the Captain of Plymouth: EUGENE COWLES. *John Alden*, his Secretary and Friend: EDWIN W. HOFF. *Hobomok*, the faithful guide and interpreter. A purely theatrical idea of "Lo, the Poor Indian." Otherwise he is not an object of interest: GEORGE FROTHINGHAM. *Sir Loveshy Montague*, the first Puritan Masher, who can hardly be termed a fiction of history, since there must have been a first of his class: Mena Cleary. *Magistrate*: Peter Lang. *The Sergeant*, diminutive in stature, but mighty in valor: Harry Dale. *The Sentry*, not an extraordinary specimen as sentries go: Clement Herschel. *Priscilla (Alden)*, the Puritan maiden whose praises have been sung many a time by poet and historian: MARGARET REID. *Mascanoma*, a very much idealized specimen of the aboriginal maiden (Being likewise a historical license): JESSIE BARTLETT DAVIS. *Primrose*, a worldly young person, who arrived on the second voyage of the Mayflower. This is one of the numerous fictions of history: BERTHA WALTZINGER. *Dame Prudence*, a matronly Puritan: JOSEPHINE BARTLETT. *Soldiers, Puritans, Maidens and Sailors.*

Act 1: Plymouth, Massachusetts. 1623.

Act 2: Plymouth Harbor. Same date. Plymouth Rock in foreground.

MUSICAL NUMBERS[51]

"I'm a prim little Puritan maiden"
M. Reid

"'Twas Written So" (Duet)
M. Cleary, J. B. Davis

"If You're Fond of Purity"
E. Cowles, Chorus of Soldiers

"I dare not ask a kiss"
Ambassadors, Maidens

"Hand to Hand, Heart to Heart" (Gavotte)
Ambassadors, Maidens

"So Very Tender" (Trio)
E. Cowles, J. Bartlett, G. Frothingham

"Come to me, Sing to me" (Duet)
B. Walzinger, H. C. Barnabee

"Why don't you speak for yourself, John?"
M. Reid

"Because I Love You So"
J. B. Davis

"My love is all my life to me"

"Why must we always wait?"

1894.04

THE LEATHER PATCH

A Revival of the Comedy (with Music) in Three Acts, 7 Scenes[52]. Play by Edward Harrigan. Music by David Braham. (Staged by Edward Harrigan.) Scenery by D. Frank Dodge. (Orchestra under the direction of David Braham.) Produced by Edward Harrigan. Opened 22 January 1894 at Harrigan's Theatre and closed 17 February 1894 after 32 performances.[53]

CAST: *Jeremiah McCarthy*, undertaker: EDWARD HARRIGAN. *Jefferson Putnam*: JOHN WILD. *Caroline Hyer*: JOSEPH SPARKS. *Judge Herman Doebler*: HARRY FISHER. *Lawyer Wriggle*: James B. Radcliffe. *Moses Cohen*: James B. Radcliffe. *Rody McQuade*: Charles McCarthy. *Dennis McCarthy*: GEORGE MERRITT. *Linda Corncover*: John Decker. *Airy McCafferty*: Dan Burke. *Dr. Noah Corncover*: WILLIAM WEST. *Levy Hyer*: James McCullough. *Officer Dunlap*: Charles Coffey. *Thomas Conroy*: Edward Mack. *Jemmy*, the Kid: Michael Kearney. *Mr. Doublerow*: David Braham, Jr. *Sailor*: Edward Murphy. *Countryman*: Charles Sturges. *Mrs. O'Dooley*: Hattie Moore. *Libby O'Dooley*: FANNIE BATCHELDER. *Jennie Crimmons*: Lillian Flynn. *Madeline McCarthy*: ANNIE YEAMANS. *Hackmen and Mourners*: Messrs. Gorman, Williams, Mooney, Brennan, Young and Flynn.

[51]Not listed in programs. List prepared from published piano vocal selections (T. B. Harms, Inc., New York, 1894); last song title from reviews.
[52]First produced 15 February 1886 at the Park Theatre for 88 performances. For Synopsis of Scenes and Musical Numbers, see original 1886 production.
[53]Costumes uncredited.

1894.05

PRINCE KAM, or, A Trip to Venus

A Comic Opera in Two Acts, 7 Scenes. Libretto by Charles Alfred Byrne and Louis Harrison. Music by Gustave Kerker. Scenery designed by H. L. Reid, Frank Rafter. Costumes designed by Mme. Catherine Siedle. Musical director, Gustave Kerker. Produced by E. E. Rice for the Camille D'Arville Comic Opera Company. Opened 29 January 1894 at the Casino Theatre and closed 24 February 1894 after 28 performances.

CAST: *Prince Kam*, Poom's son and heir: CAMILLE D'ARVILLE. *Poom*, the Grand Llama of Thibet: HALLEN MOSTYN. *Jaundis*, Prince Equerry and Royal Astrologer: HARRY MACDONOUGH. *Ooo*, the Grand Electrician: Donald Quee, Jr. *Mars*, God of War: WILLIAM PRUETTE. *Cupid*, God of Love: LA REGALONCITA. *Abdul Mouriff*, a Slave Dealer: HENRY LEONI. *Zik-Zit*, Captain of the Town Guards: Follett Jocelyn. *Captain of the Guard*: Annie Sutherland. *Venus*, Goddess of Beauty: FANNIE JOHNSON. *Absurdaria*: Louise Sylvester. *Isis, Peep*, Patrician Girls: Trixie Friganza, Nellie Braggins. *Psyche*: Nellie Braggins. *Slaves (4)*: *Midge*: Elena Martinez. *Keblee*: Nina Ainscoe. *Badoura*: Stella Hoyt. *Scherezade*: Nannie Morse. *Wise Men (4)*: *Knowitall*: Albert Shean. *Canttellhim*: J. C. Marshall. *Yourhearme*: S. J. Curtis. *Itoldyouso*: M. P. Haynes.

Guards of Mars: Messrs. Clark, Nottingham, Moore, Bohnet, Holly, Cogley, Murphy, Irving, Ripley, Terry, Pullman, Lawrence. *Guards of Venus*: Misses Morse, Hamilton, Wade, Hoyt, Kendall, Jocelyn, Ainscoe, Williams, Palmer, Martinez, Lawrence, Holly, Ennis, Dreher, Shields, Bigger, Swift, Shepherd, Marsh. *Bell Chorus*: Misses Friganza, Hamilton, Swift, Holly, Martinez, Ainscoe, Jocelyn, Morse, Dreher, Hoyt, Johnson (Soloist). *Slave Dealers*: Messrs. Shean, Marshall, Curtis, Haynes. *Slave Attendants*: Misses Shepherd, Train, Ennis, Marsh. *Ballet des Enfants*: La Regaloncita, La Graciosa, La Preciosa.

Act 1, Scene 1: The Market Place in Thibet. (Reid.) *Scene 2*: Exterior of the Palace. (Reid.) *Scene 3*: The Palace Gardens. (Rafter.) *Scene 4*: The Electrical Laboratory. (Rafter.) *Act Drop*: The Transit of Venus. (Rafter.)

Act 2: On the Planet Mars. (Reid.) *Act Drop*: Venus and Mars. (Rafter.)

ACT 1

"Very Fond of Living"

"I've Traveled by Night and by Day"
C. D'Arville

"Please, Dear Master" (Slave Chorus)

"If the Sweetheart You Love Loves You"[54]
C. D'Arville

"I'm Chock Full of Electricity"
H. Mostyn

The Strangest Apparition

"Off We Go to Venus" (Madrigal)

"The Baggage Smashers"

"Man Is Such a Schemer from His Childhood" (Man Is a Deceiver)

Finale

ACT 2

Awakening of Venus; "None as graceful as are we"; Chorus of Girls

"I Am the God of War"
W. Pruette

"No No" (Duet)
W. Pruette, F. Johnston

The Arrival

"As We Peep at the Earth from the Sky"

"This Remarkable Hilarity"

"Fleeting" (Sextette)

Cupid's Dance

"A Little Nonsense" (Quartette)

"For You Have Twenty-Four" (Recitative Song and Septette)

Finale

[54]Also published under the variant title "When the Sweetheart You Love Is True," with lyrics by C. A. Byrne.

1894.06

THE RAINMAKERS

A Farcical Comedy in Three Acts. Play by Frank Dumont. Scenery by Arthur Voegtlin. Costumes designed by Baron DeGrimme. Electrical effects by J. Frank Eline. Musical direction, Fred Perkins. Produced by Henry V. Donnelly and Edward Girard. Opened 29 January 1894 at the Park Theatre and closed 24 February 1894 after 32 performances[55].

CAST: *Percival Airtight*, hotel clerk: HENRY V. DONNELLY. *Phelix Bottles*, hotel porter: EDDIE GIRARD. *Phoenix Spangel*, circus proprietor: CHARLES J. ROSS. *Giovania Deuce*, Italian inventor: BERNARD DYLLYN. *Valentine Butts*, head waiter: Edward Garvie. *Sim Sawdust*, butcher's boy; Frank O'Brien. *Sendum Upp*, justice of the peace: John F. Corrigan. *Plenty Horses* in the War Department: John Connelly. *Mrs. General Peiper Heidsieck*: MABEL FENTON. *Bolivar*: ANNIE MARTELL. *Precious dining-room girls (5)*: *Pearl*: Ida Rock. *Ruby*: Kate B. Allen. *Emerald*: Fannie Engle. *Turquoise*: Georgie Hawley. *Garnet*: Helen Smith.

Act 1: Hotel Chick, Bedford, Illinois.

Act 2: Spangle's farm, home of the Circus.

Act 3: The Conservatory of Roses.

ACT 1[56]

"Dining Room Girls" (Opening Chorus)

"The Hotel Porter"
E. Girard
(*Music and Lyrics by* Frank Dumont.)

"He Don't Know Where 'e Are"
H. V. Donnelly, E. Girard, C. J. Ross, B. Dyllyn, F. O'Brien

"Orange Blossoms"
M. Fenton, A. Martell, Dining-room girls
(*Music by* Richard Stahl. *Lyrics by* Frank Dumont.)

ACT 2

"Tally-Ho Girls in the Coaching Club"
A. Martell, Dining room girls
(*Music by* Fred Perkins. *Lyrics by* Edward Garvie.)

"The Game Sports"
H. V. Donnelly, E. Girard
(*Music and Lyrics by* Thomas LeMack.)

ACT 3

"When You Are Married"
E. Garvie

"The Whistling Dago"
A. Martell, H. V. Donnelly, E. Girard
(*Music and Lyrics by* Frank Dumont.)

Comedy vs. Tragedy (Travesty)
M. Fenton, C. J. Ross

"Characters in the Play"
B. Dyllyn

"Mamie, Come Kiss Your Honey Boy"[57] (from A COUNTRY SPORT)
H. V. Donnelly, E. Girard
(*Music and Lyrics by* May Irwin.)

"Gentleman of Leisure"
F. O'Brien

"The Electric Girls"
M. Fenton, A. Martell, Dining-room girls
(*Music by* Richard Stahl. *Lyrics by* Frank Dumont.)

"The Electric Boys"
H. V. Donnelly, E. Girard, C. J. Ross, B. Dyllyn
(*Music by* Richard Stahl. *Lyrics by* Frank Dumont.)

[55]Direction uncredited. Played a return engagement 9 April 1894 at the Columbus Theatre, Harlem, for an additional 8 performances. Later tours featured all different musical specialties.

[56]Musical numbers not listed in New York programs. List prepared from 5 March 1894 tour. Additional interpolation as per published sheet music:

"Yew-ra-liar-ity" (introduced in 1492)
(*Music by* George Seevers. *Lyrics by* Charles House.)

[57]Original with Donnelly and Girard.

1894.07

A TRIP TO CHINATOWN

A Revival of the Farce Comedy in Three Acts[58]. Play and lyrics by Charles H. Hoyt. Music composed and arranged by Percy Gaunt. Scenery by Arthur Voegtlin. Entire production under the personal direction of Charles H. Hoyt. Mechanical effects by Matt Lynch. Properties and accessories by George Henry. Produced by Charles H. Hoyt. Opened 12 February 1894 at the Madison Square Theatre and closed 31 March 1894 after 49 performances[59].

CAST: *Welland Strong*, a man with one foot in the grave: HARRY CONOR. *Ben Gay*, a wealthy San Francisco bachelor, of the Union Club: GEORGE A. BEANE, JR. *Of the Bohemian Club (2)*: *Rashleigh Gay*, nephew of Ben Gay: MARK SMITH. *Norman Blood*, chum of Rashleigh: JULIUS P. WITMARK. *Willie Grow*, proposed at the Bohemian Club: MARGUERITE MacDONALD. *Noah Heap*, waiter at "The Riche" restaurant: HARRY GILFOIL. *Hoffman Price*, manager of Cliff House: E. Soldene Powell. *Slavin Payne*, a servant of Ben Gay: HARRY GILFOIL. *Stillman*: William Morse. *Tony Gay*, niece of Ben Gay: EFFIE CHAPUY. *Isabelle Dame*, friend of the Gays: Sallie Maddern. *Premiere Danseuse*: Papinta. *Flirt*, Mrs. Guyer's maid: Nellie Rosebud. *Mrs. Guyer*, a widow from Chicago, not too strenuous on culture, but makes up for it in "biff": ANNA BOYD.

ACT 1[60]

"The Pretty Widow"
(*Music by* Percy Gaunt. *Lyrics by* Charles H. Hoyt.)

"Out for a Racket"
(*Music by* Percy Gaunt. *Lyrics by* Charles H. Hoyt.)

"Honey O" (African Cantata)
(*Music and Lyrics by* Percy Gaunt.)

"Crisp Young Chaperone" (The Chaperone)
(*Music by* W. Barton.)

ACT 2

Trio Burlesque of Italian Opera
(*Music arranged by* Percy Gaunt.)

Medley, including "I Fain Would Kiss," "Simply Friends," "Reuben and Cynthia," "Love's Dear Eyes," "Whistling Extraordinary," "Flirt."
(*Music arranged by* Percy Gaunt.)

ACT 3

Specialty
Papinta

"(On) the Bowery"
(*Music by* Percy Gaunt. *Lyrics by* Charles H. Hoyt.)

1894.08

THE OGALLALLAS

A Romantic Indian (Comic) Opera in Three Acts. Story (libretto) by Young E. Allison. Music by Henry Waller. Stage director, John E. Nash. Musical director, Samuel L. Studley. Scenery by Frank Marsden. Costumes designed by Mrs. Catherine Siedle. Musical director, Samuel L. Studley. Produced by the Bostonians (Henry Clay Barnabee, Tom Karl, W. H. MacDonald, Proprietors and Managers). Opened 12 February 1894 at the Broadway Theatre and closed 17 February 1894 after 7 performances.

CAST: *Captain Deadshot*, elsewhere known as Arthur Cambridge: EDGAR TEMPLE. *War Cloud*, Chief of the Ogallallas: W. H. MacDONALD. *Brig. General*

[58]First produced 9 November 1891 at the Madison Square Theatre for 657 performances. For Synopsis of Scenes and Musical Numbers, see original 1891 production.

[59]Played a return engagement 14 May 1894 at the 14th Street Theatre for 8 performances.

[60]Interpolated during the run and/or subsequent our, as per published sheet music:

"Two Little Girls in Blue"
Lloyd Wilson (then later J. Aldrich Libbey)
(*Music and Lyrics by* Charles Graham.)

"Do, Do, My Huckleberry, Do"
H. Conor
(*Music by* John Dillon. *Lyrics by* Harry Dillon.)

"Two Pictures" (Dear Parents' Faces)
J. P. Witmark
(*Music by* John W. Bratton. *Lyrics by* Walter H. Ford.)

Andover, U.S.A.: HENRY CLAY BARNABEE. *Cardenas*, a Mexican bandit, ally of War Cloud: EUGENE COWLES. *Mississinewa*, Chief Medicine Man of Ogallallas: GEORGE B. FROTHINGHAM. *General Meriden*, Commander U. S. Forces: W. A. Howland. *Wickliffe, Buckskin Joe*, Scouts: Harry Dixson, Clement Herschell. *Edith*, Daughter of General Meriden: BERTHA WALTZINGER. *Minnetoa*, an Indian Girl: LUCILLE SAUNDERS. *Mrs. Diana Scarborough*, a widow: Josephine Bartlett. *Kate*, companion of Edith: Lillian Hawthorne. *Cosita*, a Mexican Girl: Lola Hawthorne. *Scouts, Indians, Mexicans, Indian Maidens, Mexican Girls, Wives and Daughters of Offciers of Fort Columbia.*

Act 1: A Far Western Roadside. Morning.

Act 2: An Indian Encampment. Next morning.

Act 3: The Mexican Encampment. Same evening.

ACT 1[61]

Chorus of Scouts (The sun is over the mountain)
Chorus

Galloping Chorus of Scouts (Clink clank, clink clank)
Chorus

Entrance of Deadshot and Buckskin Joe

"Song of the Carabine" (Slender and fine, sweetheart of mine)
E. Temple

Chorus (But with the sun is shadow)
Chorus

"The Breath of May" (Waltz Song)
B. Waltzinger, Chorus

"Beware of Love" (Song)
H. C. Barnabee, Girls

"Be Not Alarmed" (Quartette and Chorus)
E. Temple, B. Waltzinger, H. C. Barnabee, L. Hawthorne

"Last of the Knights of Old" (Song and Ensemble)
E. Temple, Chorus

"War Song of the Ogallallas" (Song and Ensemble)
W. H. MacDonald, Chorus

ACT 2

Chorus of Indian Maidens (Pastorale)
Indian Maids

"Ah, 'Twas Love" (Recitative and Romance/Aria)
B. Waltzinger

"When I'm Near Thee" (Duet)
E. Temple, B. Waltzinger

"Love May Come Again" (Recitative and Aria)
L. Saunders

"Love Is a Story" (Quartette)
B. Waltzinger, E. Temple, L. Saunders, W. H. MacDonald

"Hiawatha Song" (Trio)
H. C. Barnabee, L. Hawthorne, G. B. Frothingham

"Chant of the Sun Feast" (Hail forever! Hail to the Sun!)
Medicine Men, Indians

Chorus of Mexicans (Hurrah! for a life's that's free)
Chorus

Scene (To my tent where I was resting)
E. Cowles, W. H. MacDonald, B. Waltzinger

"Mexican Serenade" (O, eyes like the brightest stars)
E. Cowles

Duel Scene (Renegade and dog!)
E. Temple, Indians, B. Waltzinger, E. Cowles

"Where the Lances Gleam" (Finale)
Chorus

ACT 3

"Care's the King of All" (Song)
E. Cowles, Chorus

Duet (Oh, now farewell, farewell!)
E. Temple, B. Waltzinger

"Like a Splendid Bird" (Trio)
B. Waltzinger, E. Temple, L. Saunders

"Indian Death Song" (And what is this life)
W. H. MacDonald

[61]Musical numbers not listed in programs; list prepared from published book of the opera (The Bostonians, 1893).

1894.09

ABOUT TOWN

Russell's Comedians illustrating a sketch of everyday life in Three Acts. Based on the German farce "Der Corner Grocer aus der Avenue A" by Adolph Philip. Music selected and arranged by Alexander Haig. Scenery by Fred Dangerfield. Costumes designed by Mme. Catherine Siedle. Musical director, Alexander Haig. Produced by Russell's Comedians (Albert Riddle, Manager). Opened 26 February 1894 at the Casino Theatre and closed 24 March 1894 after 28 performances[62].

CAST: *Rube Hayes*, the grocer who shouldn't have left the farm: DAN DALY. *Owen Slathers*, a barber: JACQUES KRUGER. *Willie Dew*, a bank clerk, with an affection for Rosetta: WILLIAM CAMERON. *Waldorf Metropole*: DAVID WARFIELD. *Houston Streete*, a heeler: WILLIAM F. MACK. *Pinky Hughes*, a servant whose politeness stops with his pay: WILLIS P. SWEATNAM. *Charlie Starter*: Charles V. Seamon. *I. N. Cog*, the legacy: Henri Laurent. *Gilbert Fees*, a detective: Thomas Wharton. *Policeman McGonnigle*: Joseph Jackson. *Katherine*, a landlady, who goes to her last name because she changes her last so frequently: JENNIE REIFFARTH. *Rosetta Slathers*, the barber's daughter, who elevates the family by way of the stage: ADA DARE. *Mrs. Olerichs*, the mother-in-law: Kate Lester. *Lucy Davis*, a waiting-maid, with an affection for the corner grocer: Madeline Lack. *Mrs. Magrueder*: MAYME KELSO. *Mrs. Metropole*: Harriet Sterling. *Ornaments of the stage, and friends of Rosetta (12)*: Madge Tompkins, Ella Wilson, Maude Beverly, Georgie Gordon, Flora Tate, Rosa Blye, Nellie Parker, Kate Uart, Maym Kelso, Julia Glover, Jessie Ralph, Amy Stewart. (*Dance Specialty*, Act 2: Amelia Glover.)

Act 1: Slathers' barber shop, Avenue A, (New York City). A year elapses during the action.

Act 2: Mrs. Olerich's Fifth Avenue Drawing -room. The musicale.

Act 3: Mrs. Olerich's summer residence at Lennox. The garden party.

ACT 1

"Come On, Come On" (Solo and Chorus)
Company

"Look at Me" (Solo and Chorus)
J. Reiffarth

"In the Same Old Place," "Casey's Dog," "It Will Be Mine" (Songs)
D. Daly

ACT 2

Eccentric Dance
M. Lack, D. Daly

Solo and Chorus
A. Dare, Ladies

Dances
J. Glover

"Could I," "Old Vienna" (Songs)
M. Kelso

Character Dances
W. Cameron

"Midway Paloma" (Song)
D. Daly

Imitations
D. Warfield

ACT 3

"Linger Longer, Lucy"
A. Dare, Ladies

Burlesque on "Linger Longer, Lucy"
D. Daly, W. Cameron, W. F. Mack, D. Warfield, C. V. Seaman, J. Jackson

"Sunshine Above" (Song)
N. Parker

"The Coontown Musketeers"
W. Sweatnam

[62]English adaptation uncredited in New York; prior to New York credited to H. Fulton. Direction likewise uncredited in New York; prior to New York credited by C. D. Marius.

"The Dooleys"
D. Daly, W. Cameron, C. V. Seaman
"Still Is the Night" (Song)
M. Kelso
"About Town" (Finale)

1894.10 FRITZ IN A MAD HOUSE

A Revival of the Play with Music in Four Acts[63]. Play by J. K. Emmet. Produced by Henry T. French. Opened 19 February 1894 at Henry Miner's People's Theatre, moved 26 February 1894 to the American Theatre and closed 3 March 1894 after 16 performances.[64]

CAST: *Baron von Wolfenstein*: Charles R. Steadman. *Fritz von Wolfenstein*, his son: J. K. EMMETT, JR. *Collie Parker*, in love with Fritz: EMILY LYTTON. *Joe Parker*, her uncle LOUIS GIESEL. *Mrs. Parker*, his wife: BLANCHE WEAVER. *Richard Parker*, their son: Willard Newell. *Burrows*: Simeon Walton. *Specialties*: MAGGIE CLINE, Baby Spencer Sinott.

1894.11 THE PRINCESS OF TRÉBIZONDE

A Revival of the Opéra-bouffe in Three Acts[65]. Original French libretto ("La Princesse de Trébizonde") by Charles Nuitter and Étienne Tréfeu. Adapted into English by Charles Lamb Kenney. Music by Jacques Offenbach. Production under the direction of Fred Solomon. Director of music and conductor, Max Hirschfeld. Produced by Pauline Hall Opera Company (George B. McLellan, Manager) Opened 5 March 1894 at Harrigan's Theatre and closed 31 March 1894 after 32 performances.

CAST: *Prince Raphael*: PAULINE HALL. *Tremolini*, a clown and Cabriolo's assistant: FRED SOLOMON. *Prince Cassimir*, Raphael's father: JOHN BRAND. *Sparodrop*, Raphael's tutor: JOHN RANSOME. *Thierry*, director of the Lottery: HARRY ROLLINS. *Monsieur Vert*, a Page: MARK ABORN. *Bricola, Ricardo*, pages to Casimir: Edna Andrews, Sallie Johnson. *Gendarme*: Sidney Durham. *Zanetta*, Cabriolo's Daughter: JOSEPHINE KNAPP. *Paola*, an equilibrist: EVA DAVENPORT. *Regina*, a tight rope dancer: JULIE RING. *Annette*, a circus rider: LILLIAN BISHOP. *Pierre*: G. V. Levine. *Gustave*: Helen Dunbar. *Cabriolo*, proprietor of a circus: RICHARD GOLDEN. *Villagers, acrobats, freaks, courters, pages and maids.*

Act 1: Public Square in Lisle, France. 1830.

Act 2: Count Cabriola's Castle.

Act 3: Palace of Prince Casimir.

1894.12 YON YONSON

A Revival of the Farcical Drama in Three Acts[66]. Play by Gus Heege. Scenery by Joseph Hart. Produced by Jacob Litt and Thomas H. Davis. Opened 12 March 1894 at the Park Theatre and closed 17 March 1894 after 8 performances.

CAST: *Yon Yonson*, a Swede from Yimtown, Nord Dakota: GUS [Augustus] HEEGE. *Amos Jennings*, of the firm of Jennings & Co.: J. C. HUFFMAN. *John T. Holloway*, his manager: Charles Mitchell. *Gerald Harcourt*, an English tourist: Clinton Maynard. *Roly*, Harcourt's nephew: Master Tommy Magiver. *Vanderbilt Botts*, a real estate boomer: Sidney Craver. *Wendell Phillips Simpson*, a footman: Sidney Craver. *Hankins*, Engineer of the Saw Mill: Jason Downs. *Mister McSorly*, a station agent: W. J. Corns. *Grace Jennings*: VICTORY BATEMAN. *Mrs Laaughlin*, proprietress of the Junction Hotel: SADIE CONNELLY. *Jennie Morris*: Merri Osborne. (*Lumbermen's Quartette*, Specialty: Sidney Craven (first tenor), Clinton Maynard (second tenor), Philip Rees (baritone), W. J. Corns (second bass).

[63]First produced in New York 22 April 1889 at the 14th Street Theatre for 64 performances. For Synopsis of Scenes and Musical Numbers, see original 1889 production.
[64]No program available. Maggie Cline sang her specialty "Patsy and the Horseshoe."
[65]First produced in New York in an English burlesque adaptation 11 September 1871 for 7 performances. No song list for this adaptation.
[66]First opened in New York 28 December 1891 at the Park Theatre for 33 performances. For Synopsis of Scenes, see original 1891 production.

1894.13 HENDRIK HUDSON, or, The Discovery of Columbus

A Revival of the Burlesque Opera-Bouffe in Three Acts, 5 Scenes[67]. Libretto by William Gill and Robert Frazer. Music arranged and compiled by Fred. Perkins and Watty Hydes. Scenery designed by J. J. Quinn. Costumes designed by Mme. Schwencke and Dazian. Musical director, Watty Hydes. Produced by the Kimball Opera-Comique Company (Mrs. Jennie Kimball, Manager). Opened 19 March 1894 at the 14th Street Theatre and closed 31 March 1894 after 16 performances.

CAST: *Hendrik Hudson*, a mariner bold, discoverer of the North River and Columbus: CORINNE. *Carmen*, a Spanish dancing coquette: CORINNE. *Kill von Kull*, a real estate agent, the first of his tribe: WILLARD SIMMS. *Miss Manhattan*, a wealthy Indian princess: ADDIE CORA REED. *Christopher Columbus*, discovers America and loses himself: GLADYS VIVIAN. *Gaff Ensign*, Hudson's lieutenant: Harry Dietz. *Abigail*, Hudson's English wife, a woman of the future: LULU NICHOLS. *Fritz von Twinkle*, an exquisite leader of the 'Gilded Youths' of the period: MABEL NICHOLS. *Marquis Perfecto Del Cebanos*, a haughty Spanish grandee: CHARLES ALLISON. *Ysabel*, the Marquis' daughter, as haughty as her sire, if not more so: FANNIE DECOSTA. *McCann, McParlin*, Deputy Sheriffs: Charles Kirke, Thomas J. Grady. *Emelina*, the maid of the Inn: Georgie Bush. *Hans*, landlord of the New Amsterdam, "Weise Handlung": Charles Gameron. *Don Abbotoire*, captain of the guards: William Brown. *Von Slick*, one of Kill von Kull's victims: Leslie Stowe. *Attendants of Ysabel (7)*: *Juanita*: Gertie Murray. *Lucretia*: Lillian Cooley. *Lima*: Allie Black. *Lizetta*: Edith Crawford. *Zittella*: Franc Madigan. *Bellettie*: Yetta Mittler. *Dancing Girls (7)*: *Esmerelda*: Lou Hastings. *Rosetta*: Minnie Murray. *Diero*: Lillian Stewart. *Muzette*: Laurel Vane. *Clairetta*: Cora Relyea. *Fleuretta*: Gertie Murray. *Santella*: Sophie Stewart. *Pedro, Juan*, Pages to Columbus: Irene Vaughn, Etta Storms. *Columbian Guards*: Messrs. Ed Mack, George Williams, Mell Dyer, F. Cohen, Fred Echort, D. Joslin, Frank Crane, John Leland, Frank Conway, J. C. Dean, J. Hines, Samuel Stewart, George Putnam, Charles Turner, H. Degraw. *Dutch Maids, Sailors, Spanish Noblemen, Pages, Tourists, Freaks, etc.*

The action takes place in Bowling Green in 1609.

Act 1: New Amsterdam (New York City.) An afternoon in Midway Plaisance.

Act 2: The Everglades of Florida.

Act 3, Scene 1: Electric Palace at World's Fair. *Scene 2*: Midway Plaisance. *Scene 3*: Egyptian Darkness.

ACT 1
An Afternoon in Midway Plaisance (Humoresque fantasie by Gustave Luders.)
Going to the Fair by the Illinois Central Train; The Chinese Temple and Theatre; In Old Vienna; The Persian Dancers; The German Village and Two Bands; In front of the Beauty Show; The Swiss Panorama and Alpine Horn; Cairo Street—the Egyptian Dancers, a procession; At Hagenbeck's, with the lions on horseback; Finale.

ACT 3
Scene 2
Spanish, Tambourine and Picture Songs and Dances
Corinne
Mandolin Serenades and Solos; "La Paloma" (Spanish Song)
Corinne
Imitation of 'What We See on the Stage'
W. Simms
Charming Tyrolean Serenades
H. Dietz
German Parody Medley "Und der Deutscher Lied"
C. Kirke, T. J. Grady
The Swell Colored Girls, or an Imitation of the Plantation Swells
Nichols Sisters
Scene 3
The Phantom Cuirassiers: Grand Electric Sword Combat Drill and March, headed by Gladys Vivian. (Arranged and produced by Barney Fagan.)
"Hail, Columbia, Happy Land" (Finale)

[67]First produced in New York 18 August 1890 at the 14th Street Theatre for 16 performances.

1894.14 GIROFLE-GIROFLA

A Revival of the Opéra-bouffe in Three Acts[68], in English. Original French libretto by Albert Vanloo and Eugène Leterrier. Music by Charles Lecocq. Cachuca Ballet arranged by Signor Augusto Francioli. Scenery by D. Frank Dodge, Henry E. Hoyt and Joseph Clare. Costumes designed by Mme. Thompson. Musical director, Julian Edwards. Produced under the stage direction of Max Freeman. Produced by the Lillian Russell Opera Comique Organization (George W. Lederer, Thomas Canary, Proprietors and Directors). Opened 26 March 1894 at the Casino Theatre and closed 28 April 1894 after 36 performances.

CAST: *Giroflé-Girofla*: LILLIAN RUSSELL. *Don Bolero D'Alcazaras*, her father: DIGBY BELL. *Aurora*, his wife: MARIE DRESSLER. *Marasquin*: Signor Perugini. *Mourzouk*, Chief of the Moors: WILLIAM PRUETTE. *Pedro*: Charles Campbell. *Paquita*: Lucy Daly. *Chief of the Pirates*: J. Dore. *The Notary*: Arthur Etherington. *The Uncle*: F. W. Regas. *The Village Clerk*: A. Bassi. *The Groomsman*: Charles E. Shober. *The Godfather*: J. A Furey. *The Godmother*: Estelle Allyn. *Cousins of Giroflé, Girofla (8)*: *Fernando*: Ada Dare. *Guzman*: Marie M. Tempest. *Almanzor*: Gertrude Rutledge. *Sarrago*: May Duryea. *Guadilli*: Georgie Dennin. *Alhambro*: Martha Habelman. *Perrano*: Tessie King. *Scocenzo*: Maud Ducker. (*Cachuca Ballet Specialty*, Act 2: Lillian Thurgate.) *Courtiers and Court Ladies, Bridesmaids, Pages, Moors and Pirates.*

Act 1: Don Bolero's Chateau by the sea. (Dodge.)

Act 2: Reception Hall in the Chateau-Mooresque. (Hoyt.)

Act 3: Glade near the Chateau. (Clare.)

1894.15 UTOPIA, LIMITED, or, The Flowers of Progress

A Comic Opera in Two Acts. Libretto by William S. Gilbert. Music by Arthur Sullivan. Prouced under the direction of Charles Harris. Scenery by H. L. Reid and C. D. McGiehan. Musical director, John Braham. Produced by the D'Oyly Carte Opera Company. Opened 26 March 1894 at the Broadway Theatre and closed 12 May 1894 after 55 performances.

CAST: *King Paramount I*, King of Utopia: J. J. DALLAS. *Scaphio, Phantis*, Judges of the Utopian Supreme Court: J. W. HOOPER, FRANK DANBY. *Tarara*, the Public Exploder: J. H. Poskitt. *Calynx*, the Utopian Vice-Chamberlain: Leslie Walker.

Imported Flowers of Progress: *Lord Dramaleigh*, a British Lord Chamberlain: FRANK BOOR. *Captain Fitzbattleaxe*, First Life Guards: CLINTON ELDER. *Captain Sir Edward Corcoran*, K.C.B. of the Royal Navy: MR. PETERKIN. *Mr. Goldbury*, a Company Promoter—afterwards Comptroller of the Utopian Household: JOHN COATES. *Sir Bailey Barre*, Q. C.: Eckford Smith. *Mr. Blushington* of the County Council: Buchanan Wake. *Princess Zara*, eldest daughter of King Paramount: ISABEL REDDICK. *Princesses Nekaya, Kalyba*, the Younger Sisters: Aileen Burke, Millicent Pyne. *Lady Sophy*, their English Gouvernante: KATE TALBY. *Salata, Melene, Phylla*, Utopian maidens: Alice Pennington, Edith Courtney, Maisie Turner.

Act 1: A Utopian Palm Grove.

Act 2: Throne Room in King Paramount's Palace. (Night.)

ACT 1[69]

"In lazy languor" (Opening Chorus)
A. Pennington, E. Courtney, M. Turner, Maidens
"The song of birds" (Solo)
M. Turner
"O make way for the wise men"
Chorus
"In every mental lore" (Duet)
J. W. Hooper, F. Danby
"Let all your doubts take wing" (Duet)
J. W. Hooper, F. Danby
"Quaff the nectar"
Chorus
"A King of autocratic power we" (Song)
J. J. Dallas
"Although of native maids the cream" (Duet)
A. Burke, M. Pyne
"Bold-faced ranger" (Song)
K. Talby
"First you're born" (Song)
J. J. Dallas, All
"Subjected to your heavenly gaze" (Duet)
J. J. Dallas, K. Talby
"Oh, maiden rich"
I. Reddick, C. Elder, Troopers, Chorus
"Ah! Gallant soldier" (Duet)
I. Reddick, C. Elder, Chorus
"It's understood, I think" (Quartette)
C. Elder, I. Reddick, J. W. Hooper, F. Danby
"Oh, admirable art!" (Duet)
I. Reddick, C. Elder, Chorus
"Although your royal summons to appear" (Finale)
J. J. Dallas, J. W. Hooper, J. H. Poskitt, F. Danby, I. Reddick, C. Elder, E. Smith, Chorus
"What these may be, Utopians all"
I. Reddick, F. Boor, B. Wake, Chorus
"A company Promoter this"
I. Reddick, J. Coates, Corcoran, F. Boor, E. Smith, B. Walker, J. J. Dallas, J. W. Hooper, F. Danby, J. H. Poskitt, Chorus
"Some seven men form an association"
J. Coates, J. J. Dallas, J. W. Hooper, F. Danby, J. H. Poskitt, C. Elder, I. Reddick, Chorus

ACT 2

"Oh, Zara!/"A tenor, all singers above"
C. Elder
"Words of love too loudly spoken" (Duet)
I. Reddick, C. Elder
"Society has quite forsaken" (Song)
J. J. Dallas, Chorus
Entrance of court
Drawing room music
"This ceremonial our wish displays" (Recitative)
J. J. Dallas
"Eagle high on cloudland soaring"
Chorus
"With fury deep we burn" (Duet)
J. W. Hooper, F. Danby
"If you think that when banded in unity" (Trio)
J. W. Hooper, F. Danby, J. J. Dallas
"With wily brain" (Trio)
J. W. Hooper, F. Danby, J. H. Poskitt, Chorus
"A wonderful joy our eyes to bless" (Song)
J. Coates
"Then I may sing and play?" (Quartette)
A. Burke, F. Boor, M. Pyne, J. Coates
"Oh, would some demon power"/"When but a maid" (Song)
K. Talby
"Ah, Lady Sophy"
J. J. Dallas, K. Talby
"Oh, the rapture unrestrained" (Duet)
K. Talby, J. J. Dallas
Graceful dance/Tarantella
"Upon our sea-girt land"
J. W. Hooper, F. Danby, J. H. Poskitt, Chorus
"There's a little group of isles" (Finale)
I. Reddick, J. J. Dallas, All

1894.16 THE DAZZLER

Cosgrove and Grant's Comedians in the Fourth Edition of the Comedy in Three Acts, 4 Scenes.[70] Direction, Cosgrove and Grant. Musical director,

[68]First produced in New York in French 4 February 1875 at the Park Theatre; in English 19 May 1875 at Robinson Hall. For Synopsis of Scenes and Musical Numbers, see original May 1875 production.
[69]Musical Numbers not listed in programs. List prepared from recordings and published score.

[70]First edition produced in New York 19 January 1891 at the Park Theatre for 8 performances; 2 February 1891 at the Standard Theatre for 24 additional performances; 13 April 1891 at Niblo's Garden for 8 additional performances

William H. Way. Produced by Cosgrove and Grant (H. E. Reed, Manager). Opened 26 March 1894 at the Park Theatre and closed 7 April 1894 after 16 performances.[71]

CAST: *Ezekiel Pipes*, a modest man: JOE A. OTT. *Tannhauser Bock*, a retired brewer: MAX MILLER. *Smashem Jones*, a conundrum: ALBERT HART. *Mulligan*, of Bally Mullgan, an Irish king, in search of Kitty Starlight: JOHN P. CURRAN. *Viscount Haricot de Mutton*, in love with Julienne: Howard Graham. *Algernon Fitzsimmons*, a wanderer: Frank T. Ward. *Julienne*, Bock's daughter: Jessie Hatcher. *Angele*, up to date: Annie Wilmuth-Curran. *Guests, Actresses, etc. (4)*: *Alice*: Grace Gayler. *Florrie*: Grace Rutter. *Katie*: Rose Krohe. *Carrie*: Dorothy Gray. *Kitty Starlight*, when at home; but at Staten Island, Mrs. Tony Twitters, a fascinating widow: ANNIE LEWIS.

Act 1: The beach at Staten Island, New York. The present summer.

Act 2: Main corridor, Sea Beach Hotel. The same evening.

Act 3, Scene 1: Temporary Tonsorial Apartment adjoining Ball-room. *Scene 2*: Ball room at Sea Beach Hotel. Almost midnight.

ACT 1
- Quartette
  - A. Lewis, J. Hatcher, H. Graham, F. T. Ward
- German Song and Dance
  - M. Miller
- "I Want a Nice Young Man" (Song)
  - A. Lewis
- Duet and Dance
  - A. Lewis, M. Miller
- "Sweet Marie" (Song)
  - J. P. Curran
- Medley (Serenade)
  - A. Lewis, Company

ACT 2
- "He Wore a Worried Look" (Comic Song)
  - J. A. Ott
- "My Alpine Home" (Song)
  - A. Wilmuth-Curran
- Creole Love Song, with Dance
  - A. Lewis
- Musical Comicalities
  - J. A. Ott, J. P. Curran
- Grand Ensemble:
  - "Washington Post March"
    - Company
  - Skirt and Spanish Dance
    - G. Gayler
  - Contralto Solo
    - D. Gray
  - Song and Dance
    - Five Comedians
  - Finale ("The Scotch Highlanders")
    - Company

ACT 3
- Specialties
  - Clipper Quartette
- Ensemble:
  - Marching Song
    - Ladies
  - Duet and Chorus, with Dance
    - A. Lewis, J. Hatcher, Ladies
  - "The Dazzler March"
    - J. Hatcher, Ladies
- Finale

1894.17 THE IDEA

Hallen & Hart in their latest comic success (Comic Play with Music) in Three Acts. Play by Herbert Hall Winslow and Joseph Hart. Music by W. T. Francis and Joseph Hart. Scenery by Arthur T. Voegtlin, John G. Buss. Costumes by J. Bloom and Mme. Schwenkee. Music director, W. T. Francis. Management, James Jay Brady. Opened 9 April 1894 at the Park Theatre and closed 28 April 1894 after 24 performances.[72]

CAST: *Peach Blow*, companion to Mrs. Howes, with the ideas of fun and mischief: FANNY BLOODGOOD. *Johnny Gett*, with racing and keno ideas: FANNY BLOODGOOD. *Mrs. Hoffman Howes*, with an idea how to keep a secret: MOLLIE FULLER. *Mrs. Nellie Dogood*, with ideas concerning a second husband: Marguerite LaMar. *May B. Quiet*, with good ideas of Johnny Gett: Carrie DeMar. *Miss Gedney Howes*, with archery ideas: Florence Holbrook. *Miss Victoria Howes*, with musical ideas: Edith Murray. *Miss Marlborough Howes*, with society ideas: Jennie Grovini. *Morton Howes*, the model son of Gilsey, with secret ideas of his own: J. ALDRICH LIBBY. *Gilsey Howes*, rich and retired, with ideas of reforming everybody and everything: CHARLES B. LAWLOR. *Carl Pretzel*, whose ideas are somewhat mixed: Al. Wilson. *Reed Wallpaper*, editor of "The Saturday Idea": Harry Hyde. *Saunders*, with Colored Ieas: Larry Dooley. *Wells Fargo*, "The Idea Express Company": Henry Reab. *Policeman 999*, with no ideas at all: Charles Kettler. *Hoffman Howes*, the youngest son of Gilsey Howes, with pronounced ideas of dress and honor: FREDERIK HALLEN. *Olean Bradford*, from the "Idea Oil Well," Pennsylvania, with several good ideas of his own: JOSEPH HART.

Act 1: Gilsey Howes' country residence, suburbs of New Orleans. (Voegtlin.)

Act 2, Scene 1: Gilsey Howes' office, New Orleans. (Voegtlin.) *Scene 2*: The Ideal Keno Club, New Orleans. (Voegtlin.)

Act 3: Parlor of Gilsey Howes' city residence, New Orleans. (Buss.)

ACT 1[73]
- "You Will Get It Bye and Bye"
  - F. Hallen, J. Hart, A. Wilson
- "She Would Be a Novelty"
  - J. Hart, F. Bloodgood
- "Love and Archery"
  - J. A. Libbey, M. Fuller
- "The Village Blacksmith"
  - H. Hyde, C. DeMar, F. Holbrook, E. Murray, J. Grovini
- "When the Man in the Moon Goes to Sleep"
  - F. Hallen, J. Hart, M. Fuller
- "Sweet Repose" (Sextette)
  - Company
- "The Fishing Maidens"
  - F. Bloodgood, C. DeMar
- "German Troubles"
  - A. Wilson
- "I Heard a Song"
  - E. Murray
- "Marvelous Dancing"
  - E. Murray, J. Grovini
- "I Love Her in Spite of All" (I Love You in Spite of All)
  - J. A. Libbey
  - (*Music and Lyrics by* Charles K. Harris.)
- "Move On"
  - L. Dooley
- "The Columbus Family" (Finale)
  - F. Hallen, J. Hart, F. Bloodgood, C. DeMar, Company

ACT 2
- "A Little Yellow Dog"/"The Ship I Love"
  - J. A. Libbey
- "The Pretty Typewriters"
  - C. DeMar, F. Holbrook, E. Murray, J. Grovini
- "Yes, in a Minute"

[71]No credits to the author, composer, lyricist, designers of costumes or settings. Thomas Addison was credited as author for the first edition in 1891.

[72]Stage direction uncredited.

[73]According to published vocal selection from *THE IDEA*, Joseph Hart also performed these songs he wrote: "That Was Me," "A Dream in the Old Arm-Chair," "I Have No Heart," and "It Still Belongs to Thee." Also performed/interpolated, as per published sheet music:
- "Then Say Good Bye!"
  - J. A. Libbey
  - (*Music and Lyrics by* Dennis Mackin.)

Parody of "Madeline and William"/
Parody of "Coaxey's Army"/
Parody of "Larboard Watch"/
Parody on "Sweet Marie"
F. Hallen, J. Hart
German Warbling
A. Wilson
"Gay Paree"/
"Dr. Jekyll and Mr. Hyde"
C. B. Lawlor
Finale
F. Hallen, J. Hart, Company

ACT 3
Burlesque, Opera—Negro Dance
L. Dooley
"Whisper Alone to Me"
M. LaMar
Spanish Tambourine Gavotte
C. DeMar, F. Holbrook, E. Murray, J. Grovini
"A Good Joke"
J. Hart, C. B. Lawlor
"Two Sides to a Story"
F. Hallen, J. Hart
"Marguerite"
F. Hallen, M. Fuller
Piano Agitations
J. Hart
"Nellie to Me Is a Queen" (Finale)
F. Hallen, J. Hart, Company

1894.18 CINDERELLA

A Fairy Extravaganza in Three Acts, 11 Scenes[74]. Book by Horace Lennard. Music by Oscar Barrett. Adapted from the French tale by Charles Perrault. Produced under the stage direction of Oscar Barrett. Scenery by H. Emden, Hawes Craven, J. Pritchard Barrett. Produced by Henry Abbey. Opened 23 April 1894 at the Abbey Theatre and closed 16 June 1894 after 64 performances.

CAST: Mortals: *Cinderella*: ELLALINE TERRISS. *Thisbe, Clorinda*, her half-sisters: SEYMOUR HICKS, FRED EASTMAN. *Baron Pumpolino*, her father: Harry Parker. *Baroness*, her step-mother: MINNIE INCH. *Pedro*, the Baron's servant: Reuben Inch. *Prince Felix*: KATE CHARD. *Dandini*, his valet: KATE BARRY. *Fernando*, his Equerry: Florrie Harmon. *Alidoro*, his tutor: S. B. Steele. *Dorothy*: Bertha Staunton. *Nancy*: L. Palmer. *Margery*: N. Herbert. *Diggory*: Carrie Forrest. *Oliver*: Miss Parker. *Ralph*: Nellie Gunn. *The Grand Chamberlain*: Deane Brand. *The Minister of War*: W. Bestic. *The Minister of Marine*: W. Jacobson. *The Minister of Finance*: C. Jacobson. *The Minister of Agriculture*: Mr. Carzley. *Roman Warrior*: Carrie Forrest. *Priestess*: Hilda Thorpe. *Romeo*: Catalina Gomez. *Juliet*: Florence LeClerq. *Tudor Lady*: Dora Rignold. *Tudor Gentleman*: E. Wigley. *The Black Cat*: D. Abrahams. *The Wood Pigeon, the Fox*, Premiere Danseuses: Misses Louie Loveday, Lottie Dickens.

Immortals: *The Sylph Coquette*: Victoria Inch. *The Fairy of the Slipper*: Nina Gillett. *The Fairy Potter*: Miss E. Clark. *The Fairy Weaver*: Cissie Chamberlain. *The Fairy Electrician*: Edwina Brooke. *The Fairy Brassfounder*: Miss. N. Clark. *Beauty*: Florence Leclercq. *Virtue*: Dora Rignold. *Patience*: Miss St. George. *Industry*: Hilda Thorpe. *The Fairy Godmother*: ELSIE IRVING. *Fairies, Woodmen, Fox Hunters, Halberdiers, Pages, etc.*

Act 1, Scene 1: The Factories of Fairyland. (Emden.) *Scene 2*: In the King's Wood—Autumn. (Craven.) *Scene 3*: At Baron Pumpolino's. (Barrett.) *Scene 4*: The Kitchen at the Baron's. (Emden.) *Scene 5*: The Fairy Boudoir. (Emden.)

Act 2, Scene 1: Near the Palace Gates. (Emden.) *Scene 2*: Grounds of the Royal Palace. Grand Bal Champetre. (Emden.) *Scene 3*: After the Ball. (Emden.) *Scene 4*: Back in the Kitchen. (Emden.) *Scene 5*: Terrace Outside the Palace. Apotheosis. (Emden.) *Scene 6*: The Bridal Bower. (Emden.)

[74]Billed "As played at Mr. Henry Irving's Lyceum Theatre, London."

1894.19 ADONIS, or, Ye Statue, Ye Miller, Ye Maiden, and Ye Lordly Villyain

A Revival of the Burlesque in Two Acts, more or less up to date[75]. (Libretto by William Gill and Henry E. Dixey[76]. Music by Edward E. Rice. Selected music 'cheerfully contributed by Beethoven, Audran, Suppé, Planquette, Offenbach, Strauss, Mozart, Haydn, Dave Braham, John Eller, Henry Sator, and many others too numerous to individualize.') Chorus and orchestra under the direction of Gustave Kerker. Produced by (Edward E.) Rice's Big Burlesque Company. Opened 7 May 1894 at Palmer's Theatre and closed 19 May 1894 after 14 performances.

CAST: *Adonis*, an accomplished young gentleman of undeniably good family, whose name, by the way, is Marble, and who, to avoid serious complications, is obliged during the action of the piece to assume the following disguises: HENRY E. DIXEY. *Henry Irving*, with song. "It's English, you know": HENRY E. DIXEY. *Pepita Petticoat*, with imitations of Carmencita, Paquerette, La Loie Fuller and the Gaiety Girl: HENRY E. DIXEY. *Wilson Barrett*, as Clito: HENRY E. DIXEY. *Gussie Gervaise*, a dry goods clerk who sells: HENRY E. DIXEY. *Quinine Quilt*, a druggist who drugs: HENRY E. DIXEY. *Moses Moss*, a clothing merchant who clothes: HENRY E. DIXEY. *Dempsy Brown*, a model barber who barbs: HENRY E. DIXEY. *Marquis de Baccaret*, a highly polished villain. It is well to describe his character, as no none would think it to look at him: ALEXANDER CLARK. *Bunion Turke*, father of Rosetta, an unblushing appropriator of the stock in trade of a well-known and worthy histrionic old miller: ED CHAPMAN. *Rosetta*, a simple village maiden, the happy possessor of a clear conscience and a strong will: CARRIE E. PERKINS. *Talamea*, a sculptress who, like most of her sex, is in love with her own creation: VILLA KNOX. *Artea*, a goddess, patroness of fine arts: Irene Vera. *Duchess of Area*, aesthetic to the verge of eccentricity, rich to the verge of millionairism, sentimental to the verge of gush: MATHILDE COTTRELLY. *Lady Nattie, Lady Hattie*, Daughters of the Duchess: Grace Rutter, Josie Ditt. *Lady Mattie, Lady Pattie*, Professional Beauties: Frankie Bailey, Belle Sherwood. *Gyles, Nyles, Myles, Byles* and other ordinary every-day rustics: Messrs. Westman, Bohanon, Rummel, Williams, Alexander, Murphy, Connors. *Timmins*: Gilbert Gregory. *Miss Doolittle*: Gussie Deane. *Gladys Needlework*: Marie Willis. *Susie Mangle*: Alice Parvin. *Poor Blind Man*: James Alexander. *Mr. Nervine*, who believes in shaving himself: Mat. Alexander. *Oriental Menials, Caucasian Menials, Guards, Villagers* with the old-time chorus selections by the Regent Quartette: Messrs. Bohanon, Williams, Westman, Rummel. *Old Fashioned Circus*: Alexander Brothres, Messrs. Connors, Murphy. *The Duchess Tigers*: Messrs. Carroll, Maguire, Gregory, Long, Douglas, Grant. *Happy Chorus*: Misses Drayton, Demar, Willis, Skillman, Winner, Parvin, Bigger, Train, Moreland, Deane, Taylor, Thompson, Thomas, Sterling, Haines, Birdwin, Stetson, Knight, Neville.

1894.20 MAVOURNEEN

A Revival of the Irish Melodrama in Four Acts, 7 Scenes[77]. Play by George H. Jessop and Horace Townsend. Music and lyrics by William J. Scanlan. (Staged by Augustus Pitou.) Scenery by Homer F. Emens, H. L. Reid, John Young. Costumes designed by Charles Hawthorne. Musical director, Albert Krausse. Produced by Augustus Pitou. Opened 7 May 1894 at the 14th Street Theatre and closed 26 May 1894 after 24 performances.[78]

CAST: *Terrence Dwyer*: CHAUNCEY OLCOTT. *John Dwyer*: Fred J. Butler. *Captain Marchmont*: Palmer Collins. *Abbe Maloney*: W. H. Burton. *Colonel*: O. Kane Hillis. *Shamus Corrigan*: George M. Brennan. *Mark*: George A. Wilson. *Cusack*: J. O. LeBrasse. *Club Porter*: William J. Jones. *Lady Caroline Dwyer*: Florence Robinson. *Lady May Tyrell*: BLANCHE RING. *Mrs. Dwyer*: Emma Stevens. *Kate Morris*: Ella Atkinson. *Helen Dwyer*: Little Dot Clarendon. *Georgie Dwyer*: Little Kennett Barnes *Susie Morris*: Gertie Boswell. *Kitty Morris*: Little Dot Clarendon. *Peasants, Guests, Officers, Chair Bearers and Link Boys.*

MUSICAL NUMBERS[79]

[75]First produced in New York 4 September 1884 at the Bijou Theatre for 603 performances. For Synopsis of Scenes and Musical Numbers, see original 1884 production.

[76]In its earliest productions, the libretto was credited to E. E. Rice and William Gill.

[77]First produced in New York 28 September 1891 at the 14th Street Theatre for 104 performances. For Synopsis of Scenes, see original 1891 production. Dropped from original production: "Mrs. Reilly's Party," "Bye-bye, Baby, Bye-bye."

[78]Also played 11-16 September 1893 at the Grand Opera House for 8 performances.

[79]All songs performed by Chauncey Olcott.

"Plain Molly O!" (Molly-O)

"Ring the Bells"[80]

"The (Little) Christmas Tree"

"The Auld Countrie" (The Story of the Ould Countre)

"She's Like the Violets Blue"[81]

"Mavourneen"[82]

1894.21 THE PASSING SHOW (1894)

A Topical Extravaganza [Musical Revue] in Three Acts, 5 Scenes. (Libretto) Written by Sydney Rosenfeld. Music composed and conducted by Ludwig Engländer. Marches and step dancing by Barney Fagan. Maitre de Ballet, Signor Augusto Francioli. Scenery painted by D. Frank Dodge. Costumes designed by Mme. Thompson. Produced by Thomas Canary and George W. Lederer. Opened 12 May 1894 at the Casino Theatre and closed 25 August 1894 after 121 performances[83].

CAST: *Fritz Ranger*, the detective, often disguised, but always: JEFFERSON DEANGELIS. *Laf Quickstep*, an enterprising amusement caterer and joy maker at large: JOHN E. HENSHAW. *Lord Brabazon*, in search of a daughter and other troubles: Paul Arthur. *Rosamond*, the singer, with an obscure history but transparent virtues: ADELE RITCHIE. *Lady Eastlake Chapel Barter Tanqueray Zicka, Stephanie*, Countess of Forget-Me-Not: Grace Filkins. *Weebit*, a bit of dancing sunshine, or words to that effect; for further particulars see small bills: LUCY DALY. *Chollie Keal*, an important shareholder in "The Dawdle Club": QUEENIE VASSAR. *Mme. Pinero*, of Amazon fame: MAY TEN BROECK. *Her Three Amazon Charges*: *Lady Tom-a-Line*: Madge Lessing. *Lady Dick-a-Line*: Lillian Thurgate. *Lady Harry-a-Line*: Belle Stewart. *The Judge*, a familiar comic opera personage: GEORGE A. SCHILLER. *Armand St. Julien Faversham Annesley*, a good young lover: WILLIAM CAMERON. *Messrs. Rowe, Rummel*, Attorney's and Counselors-at-Law: John Marr, Gus Pixley. *Hannele*, with visions: Mabel Stephenson. *Lord Callous*, a high-born nobleman: Seymour Hess. *District Attorney*: Seymour Hess. *Lady Beenthere*, a high-born lady: MAY TEN BROECK. *Members of the Dawdle Club*: Jessie Carlisle, Letta Meredith, Agnes Sherwood, Juno Burbank, Ella Wilson. *Schweinfleisch*, Sergeant of the Guard: Curt Newall. (*Specialties*: Minnie Thurgate, Seymour Hess, Lee Harrison, William Redstone, George F. Wade, Carl Formes, Mlle. Siberna. *Ensemble*: Sylvia Thorne, Clara Selten, Anna Weber, Cryssie Carlisle, Minnie Packard, Misses Präger, Furstner, Franko, Biazzi, Sisters Scudellari and Witt.)

Act 1: In the gardens of Howkumyeso.

Act 2, Scene 1: In the Drawing Room of the Dawdle Club. Vaudeville Entertainment. *Scene 2*: Street near Herald Square. *Scene 3*: On the stage of the Dawdle Club.

Act 3: The Palace of Justice, tempered with Mercy, etc.

ACT 1[84]

Wooden Shoe Ballet

"Old Before His Time"

ACT 2

Scene 1

Lucy Daly and the Casino Pickaninnies

["Leader of De Company B" (*Music and Lyrics by* Dave Reed, Jr.)

"Riding in the Heavenly Rowboat" (*Music and Lyrics by* Barney Fagan.)]

Mabel Stephenson (Specialty)

Hungarian Czardas Dance

M. Thurgate, L. Thurgate

Imitations of Ada Rehan and Rosina Vokes

G. Filkins

"Some Time Ago"

J. E. Henshaw

"The Fellow That Played the Drum"

J. E. Henshaw

Very Living Pictures:

Phryne before the Board; Adam and Eve after the fall was over; Venus at the Bath.

Scene 2

"Hot Tamales"

Q. Vassar, A. Sherwood, J. Carlisle, S. Thorne, C. Selten, A. Weber, C. Carlisle, E. Wilson, M. Packard

"Coxey's Army"

W. Cameron, G. A. Schiller, S. Hess, L. Harrison, J. Marr, G. Pixley

Unique Specialties

J. E. Henshaw, G. Pixley, M. Stephenson

Scene 3

"Round the Operas in Twenty Minutes" (Operatic and Choreographic Intermezzo, written and arranged for the Dawdle Club by Alfred Thompson. Music by Wagner, Verdi, Mozart, Bizet, Gounod, Leoncavallo, Mascagni, etc. arranged by Ludwig Engländer.)

M. Jean de Latchkey (as Tannhaüser): J. E. Henshaw. *M. Edouard de Latchkey* (as Mephisto):P. Arthur. *Mr. Colassalla* (as Escamillo): W. Redstone. *Sig. Buncona* (as Don José): J. Marr. *M. Rataplançon* (as Pagliacco): L. Harrison. *The Rival Fausts*: G. F. Wade, C. Formes. *Mme. Musicalvé* (as Carmen): G. Filkins. *Miss Summa Dreams* (as Marguerite): A. Ritchie. *Mme. Caramelba* (as Margarita): Mlle. Siberna. *Mme. Samebrick* (as Siebel): A. Sherwood. *Mme. Naughtica* (as Elsa): J. Carlisle. *Signor Shovelangro* (as Impressario): G. A. Schiller. *The Fencing Master*: M. Lessing. *The Tyrolean*: Q. Vassar. *Chorus from the Grand Opera, Paris; Covent Garden Theatre, London; Metropolitan Opera House, New York.*

"L'Enfant Prodigue" (Incidental Divertissement)

Baron Million (with gold and a hornpipe): M. Thurgate. *Pierrots*: Misses Präger, Furstner, Sisters Scudellari. *Phrynettes*: Misses Franko, Biazzi, Sisters Witt. Trained lions, tigers and bears borrowed from Hagenbeck's.

ACT 3

"The Phalanx of Phidias" (Grand Grecian March registered by Alfred Thompson and Barney Fagan.)

Captain: Miss Burbank. *Lieutenant*: Miss Meredith.

The Apotheosis of the Evening Star

[80]Added for this revival.

[81]Added for this revival.

[82]Added for this revival.

[83]Direction uncredited; presumably the joint work of Messrs. Rosenfeld and Lederer. Played return engagements 29 October 1894 at the Casino Theatre for 24 performances, and 31 August 1895 at the Grand Opera House for 8 performances.

[84]Added in third week of the run, Act 2, Scene 1, Vernona Jarbeau specialty: Specialty: "Pi-ouit" V. Jarbeau; "Where Are You Going, My Pretty Maid?" (Imitation of Mme. Théo) V. Jarbeau.

Programs listed only ballets and specialties. List of musical numbers prepared from programs, reviews, sheet music. Interpolated for tour and/or return engagements, as per published sheet music: "You Can't Play in Our Yard" (*Music by* H. W. Petrie. *Lyrics by* Philip Wingate.); "If This Be Love" Rosabel Morrison (*Music and Lyrics by* Edward J. Abram.); "Her Eyes Don't Shine Like Diamonds" (*Music and Lyrics by* Dave Marion.); "The Pretty (Young) Widow" (*Music and Lyrics by* Alberto Himan.); "I Love My Love in the Springtime" (*Music by* Ludwig Engländer. *Lyrics by* Sydney Rosenfeld.); "Onward, Onward"; "Sex Against Sex".

1894.22 TABASCO

A Comic Opera in Three Acts, 4 Scenes. Libretto by R. A. Barnet. Music by George W. Chadwick. Entire production under the direction of Monsieur C. D. Marius. Scenery by Henry E. Hoyt and Castel Bert and D. Frank Dodge. Musical director, Ludwig Engländer. Produced by the Thomas Q. Seabrooke Comic Opera Company (W. F. Falk, Manager). Opened 14 May 1894 at the Broadway Theatre and closed 23 June 1894 after 48 performances.

CAST: *Dennis O'Grady*, afterwards François, the Pasha's Chief Cook and Supervisor of the Kitchen: THOMAS Q. SEABROOKE. *Hot-Head-Ham-Pasha*, Bey of Tangiers: WALTER ALLEN. *Marco*, a Spanish trader: JOSEPH F. SHEEHAN. *Ben-Hid-Den*, Grand Vizier: OTIS HARLAN. *Exhausted Hawkins*: Robert E. Bell. *Dusty Rhodes*: Edgar Smith. *A-Sel*, the false slave: George W. Thomas. *The Bey's Body Guard (4)*: *General Mohammed*: G. Bardini. *Major-General Mahomad*: H. C. Davis. *Lieutenant-General Mahomad*: Arthur Concors. *Adjutant-General Mahomad*: Walter Arling. *Ambassador*: D. S. Loeb. *Attendant*: John Crane. *Ben-Abed-Ab-Der U Hassem*: William S. Lavine. *Fatima*, the beautiful slave: CATHERINE LINYARD. *Has-Been-A*, a third-term Harem's favorite: LILLIE ALLISTON. *Saa-Dee-Hassam*, Court Crier: Grace Vaughn. *Lola*, Marco's sister: ELVIA CROX. *Premiere Danseuse*: Mlle. Paris.

Act 1: Square and Quay at Tangiers.

Act 2, Scene 1: Ante Room, Bey's Palace. *Scene 2*: Street in Tangiers.

Act 3: The Bey's Palace, Tangiers.

ACT 1[85]

"Dawning, the Dawning, the Shadows westward Fall"
Chorus

Grand Vizier's Song (The markets lumps whenever I take hold)
O. Harlan

"(I Do Not Care) What Other People Say" (Pasha's Song and Chorus)
W. Allen

"Reading of the Mail"
Chorus

"François and Cooks" (Song and Chorus)
T. Q. Seabrooke, Chorus

"O Lovely Home" (Fatima's Song)
C. Linyard

"Gem of the Orient" (Ensemble)

"The Shamrock Blooms White" (François' Lament)
T. Q. Seabrooke

Finale

ACT 2

"A Beauty, My Boy, You Are, You Are"
Chorus

"Hush, Hush, Silent Be"
L. Alliston, Harem

Love Duet ("My Heart Again to Hope Begins")
C. Linyard, J. F. Sheehan

Bolero (Spanish)("In Barcelona Lived a Maid")
J. F. Sheehan, Quartet

Ditty (Irish)
T. Q. Seabrooke, Quartet

Rigaudin (French)
E. Cox, Quartet

Ballad (Plantation)(Oh, my honey, honey, love)
C. Linyard, Quartet

"Ho, Mariners, Ho" (Song and Chorus)

ACT 3

"Greet the Old Man with a Smile" (Entrance Song and Chorus)

"An Original Idea" (Pasha's Song)
W. Allen

March of the Pasha's Guard ("Tabasco March")

Dance of the Harem (Waltz)
Mlle. Paris, Ballet Ensemble

Finale

[85]Musical numbers by Chadwick and Barnet not listed in programs. List prepared from published vocal score to Boston tryout (B. F. Wood, 1894). Interpolations not in published piano vocal score, but listed in programs:

"Drum Major Jimmy"
(*Music by* Hubbard Smith.)

"O'Heigh!"
E. Crox
(*Music by* Ludwig Engländer.)

1894–1895 SEASON

Della Fox in THE LITTLE TROOPER (Photo: Falk)
Billy Rose Theatre Collection, New York Public Library for the Performing Arts

1894–1895 SEASON

THE MIKADO, or, The Town of Titipu

1894.23

A Revival of the Comic Opera in Two Acts[1]. Libretto by William S. Gilbert. Music by Arthur Sullivan. Scenery by Ernest Albert. Musical director, Selli Simonson. Produced by J. C. Duff's Opera Company. Opened 14 June 1894 at the Fifth Avenue Theatre and closed 1 September 1894 after 81 performances[2].

CAST: *The Mikado of Japan*: EDWIN STEVENS. *Nanki-Poo*, his son, disguised as a wandering minstrel in love with Yum-Yum: A. S. KINGSLEY. *Ko-Ko*, Lord High Executioner of Titipu: JOSEPH HERBERT. *Pooh-Bah*, Lord High Everything Else: MARK SMITH. *Pish-Tush*, a Noble Lord: H. W. Ravenscroft. *Yum-Yum, Pitti-Sing, Peep-Bo*, three sisters, wards of Ko-Ko: ELOISE MORGAN [Ollie Archmere], LILLIAN SWAIN, FLORENCE COOLEY. *Katisha*, an elderly lady in love with Nanki-Poo: DREW DONALDSON. *Chorus of School Girls, Nobles, Guards and Coolies.*

DR. SYNTAX

1894.24

A Comic Opera in Two Acts, 6 Scenes. Libretto by J. Cheever Goodwin. (Adapted from the musical 'Cinderella at School'[3] by the same authors, based on Thomas Robertson's play 'School.') Music by Woolson Morse. Production under the stage direction of Joseph Humphreys and H. A. Cripps. Settings by Ernest Gros. Costumes by Mme. Loe and C. A. Eaves. Director of music and conductor, John S. Hiller. Produced by DeWolf Hopper. Opened 23 June 1894 at the Broadway Theatre and closed 17 November 1894 after 169 performances[4].

CAST: *Dr. Syntax*: DeWOLF HOPPER. *Jack Alden*: CYRIL SCOTT. *Lord Lawntennis*: Alfred Klein. *Arthur Barrington*, his nephew: Edmund Stanley. *Professor Scowles*: Thomas Guise. *Bobs*: Louis Schrader. *Miss Zenobia Tropics*: ALICE HOSMER. *Merope Mallow*: EDNA WALLACE HOPPER. *Niobe Marsh*: BERTHA WALTZINGER. *Psyche Persimmons*: JENNIE GOLDTHWAITE. *Pansy Pickle*: Lillian Relma. *Sally Dimple*: Louise Campbell. *Circe Slatepencil*: Leonie Dueth. *School Girls, Gentlemen of the Hunt, Students, etc.*

Act 1, Scene 1: A Forest Glade. *Scene 2*: Another part of the forest. *Scene 3*: The School Room.

Act 2, Scene 1: Exterior of the Seminary. *Scene 2*: At the Seminary Gates. *Scene 3*: At the River Side.

MUSICAL NUMBERS[5]

"By Jove, It is a Pretty Little Slipper!"

"When the Kindly Night Has Come"

"Don't Be So Cruel, Ducky Dear!" (Duet)
D. Hopper, A. Hosmer

"Could'st Thou But Know" (Duet)
E. Stanley, B. Waltzinger

"Cinderella Song" (Oh, poor Cinderella was a maid forlorn)
B. Waltzinger, Chorus

"How Strangely Sweet!"

"The Farewell Song"

[1]First presented in New York 20 July, 10-29 August 1885 at the Union Square and People's Theatres for 22 performances. First authorized production presented 19 August 1885 at the Fifth Avenue Theatre by Richard D'Oyly Carte for 250 performances. For Synopsis of Scenes and Musical Numbers, see 19 August 1885 D'Oyly Carte production.
[2]Stage direction, costumes uncredited.
[3]First produced in New York 5 March 1881 at Daly's Theatre for 65 performances.
[4]Later played a return engagement 7 January 1895 at the Harlem Opera House for 8 performances.
[5]Musical numbers not listed in programs. List prepared from published piano vocal selections (T. B. Harms & Co., New York, 1894), not in performance order.

MISS INNOCENCE ABROAD

1894.25

A Comedy Farce in Three Acts. Adapted from the French by F. C. Philips and Charles Brookfield. Satirizing the English Matrimonial Bureau. Arranged for the American stage by Edward Paulton. Produced under the stage direction of Ben Teal. Produced by Fanny Rice. Opened 25 August 1894 at the Bijou Theatre and closed 22 September 1894 after 33 performances.

CAST: *Richard Bunbury*, alias Thomas Smith, anxious to marry someone who is "pretty, bright and cheery": GEORGE R. EDESON. *Reginald Foster*, alias Aubrey Plantagenet of the Guards, who would like to marry someone with money: CHARLES COOTE. *John Waring*, a man of wealth and horses, who thought he didn't want to marry, but changed his mind: MELVILLE STEWART. *Sir Herbert Tamworth*, who wants to marry a flower named Rose: Frank Jones. *Augustus Craven*, a man with a secret, who is very much married: WILLIAM HENDERSON. *Mrs. Col. St. Mirim*, Founder of the Elite Matrimonial Mart: ROSE BEAUDET. *Miss Pandora Box*, willing to marry, but not very particular: Gladys Greene. *Miss Hope Deferred*, anxious to marry—well—for instance: Nellie Jordan. *Rose Bunbury*, who wants to marry for love: Beckie Haight. *Mrs. Augustus Craven*, who runs the Millinery Shop and the Craven Family: Emily Wakeman. *Ada*: Carrie Birkle. *Molly Flower*, Innocence Abroad, fighting life's battles alone, but she hopes you won't think less of her for this: FANNY RICE.

Act 1: St. Mirim's Matrimonial Mart. Kersen Street, London.

Act 2: Bunbury's Home.

Act 3: Reception Room at St. Mirim's.

MUSICAL NUMBERS[6]

"It Takes a Girl to Do It, Every Time"
F. Rice

Impersonations of (Albert) Chevalier and Charlotte Collins
F. Rice

"For a Girl"
F. Rice

"Oh, Sophia" (or House-a-Fire)
F. Rice

1492, Up to Date or Very Near It

1894.26

A Return Engagement (Second Edition) of the Brilliant Historical Extravaganza in Three Acts, 5 Scenes[7]. Book and lyrics by R. A. Barnet. Music by Carl Pflueger. Whole production under the personal supervision and direction of Edward E. Rice. Scenery by Richard Marston, Frank Rafter, Adrian, Dean B. Conner, Mons. E. Artus. Costumes by Alfred Thompson. Musical director, Gustave Kerker. Produced by Edward E. Rice. Opened 27 August 1894 at the Garden Theatre and closed 13 October 1894 after 57 performances[8].

CAST: *Christopher Columbus*: JOHN PEACHEY. *Ferdinand of Aragon*, King of Spain: WALTER JONES. *Charley Tatters*, a fringe on the edge of the crust of society: WALTER JONES. *Alonzo de Quintanilla*, Royal Treasurer: EDWARD M. FAVOR. *Don Juan*, the King's son, aged four: WILL H. SLOAN. *Felix*, of the Tribe of Coppers: WILL H. SLOAN. *Captain Martin Pinzon, Don Pedro Marguerite*, Conspirators of the old-fashioned type: Charles F. Walton, John C. Slavin. *Charles VIII*, King of France: Louis DeSmith. *Adolphus Fitznoodle*, a regular chappie, up-to-date: YOLANDE WALLACE. *Maid Mabel*, a sailor-lassie: YOLANDE WALLACE. *Maid Marian*, a sailor-lassie: Eileen Karl. *The Royal Herald*: Eileen Karl. *Colonel of the Columbian Guard*: Eileen Karl. *Ward Knickerbocker*, Cacique of the 400: George Gans. *Jim Confidence*, of the Tribe of Buncoes: John H. Keefe. *Bob*, a New York newsboy: James Lee. *Reube Hayseed*, from Painted Post: John H. Keefe. *Erasmus*, A Vender of Maize: Frank Egan. *Isabella of Castille*, Queen of Spain: RICHARD HARLOW. *Fräulein*, a German waif: THERESA VAUGHN. *Infanta Joanna*, in love with Columbus: THERESA VAUGHN. *Infanta Catalina*, her sister: Mabelle Bouton. *Bridga de Murphy* of the Royal Household of the New World: EDITH SINCLAIR. *Courtiers,*

[6]Specialties and musical numbers not listed in programs. List prepared from contemporary press clippings.
[7]Originally produced for 3 consecutive engagements15 May 1893 at Palmer's Theatre, 26 August 1893 at Palmer's Theatre, and 5 February 1894 at the Garden Theatre for a total of 452 performances. For Musical Numbers, see original 1893 production.
[8]Later played a return engagement 19 November 1894 at the Harlem Opera House for 1 week.

Ladies, Peasants, Students, Ballet, Amazons, Newsboys, Moors, Sailors, Bull Fighters, Soldiers, Pages, Standard Bearers, etc: Chorus.

Twelve Daily Hints from Paris: Mabelle Bouton, Ida Fairbanks, Annie Winner, Gertie Clark, Josie Fairbanks, Susie Hale, Emma Marsh, Nina Walsh, Maud States, Violet Potter, Annie Lukie, Edith Burbank. *Spanish Ballet*: Nina Walsh, Emma Marsh, Josie Fairbanks, Annie Winner, Susie Hale, Gertrude Clark, Ida Fairbanks, Mamie Forbes. *Sensational Fantastic Toe Danseuse*: Mabel Clark. *Specialty*: La Regaloncita. *'Kick and Boom the Hurrah' Dudes*: Genevieve Hill, Jessie Fahnstock, Mabel Waite, Helen Smith, Gussie Dean, Carrie Sieden. *Chef Ballet*: Gertrude Clark, Edith Burbank, Emma Marsh, Annie Lukie, Violet Potter, Polly Winner. *Female Chorus*: Annie Lukie, Lizzie Scanlon, Edith Burbank, Annie Winner, Josie Fairbanks, Ida Fairbanks, Emma Marsh, Grace Belasco, Kittie Conners, Helen Marlborough, Geneieve Hill, Gertrude Corey, Mamie Forbes, Gertrude Clark, Mabel Waite, Susie Hale, Teckla Morton, Helen Smith, Edith Tutien, Dorothy Neville, Polly Winner, May Bradley, Carrie Sieden, Gussie Dean, Jessie Fahnstock, Maud States. *Male Chorus*: Edward Thomas, Frederick Howard, Paul Bracket, O. Schuster, Otto Heilig, James Lee, Edward Devoy, C. J. Baldwin, George Gans, J. P. Savage. *Newsboys*: Masters James Lee, Frank Egan, James Carroll, Edward Quinn, Frederick Howard, S. S. Goldman, John Quigley, Pedro Sisson, Mamie Forbes, Gertrude Clark, La Regaloncita, La Graciosa, La Preciosa.

Act 1: Throne Chamber in the King's Palace. (Marston.) *Act Drop*: The Vision of Columbus. (Rafter.)

Act 2, Introductory: The Voyage of Columbus. (Conner.) *Scene 1*: On the Ocean. (Adrian.) *Scene 2*: The landing at San Salvador and Discovery of New York Harbor. (Up to Date.) (Conner.) *Scene 3*: Discovery of Madison Square, 1894. (Marston.) *Act Drop*: The Triumph of Time. (Artus.)

Act 3, Scene 1: *Scene 2*: Spanish Palace Up-to-Date. (Rafter.) Changing to the new electrical scene, The Ideal Home of Columbus. (Rafter.)

SPECIALTIES[9]

"Ich Liebe Dich"
(*Music by* Edvard Grieg.)

1894.27 COON HOLLOW

A Romantic Comedy in Four Acts, 5 Scenes. Play by Charles E. Callahan. Leader of orchestra, Herbert Clarke. Produced by (Al) Caldwell & Reedy (Proprietors) Opened 27 August 1894 at the 14th Street Theatre and closed 8 September 1894 after 16 performances[10].

CAST: *Philip Maury*, a cotton planter: C. E. DUDLEY. *Jared Fuller, Ben Clark, Tom Eastman*, E. Pluribus Unum: Roydon Erlynne. *Ralph Markham*, Maury's nephew: L. F. MORRISON. *Diogenes Sharp*, a projector: GEORGE F. HALL. *Lem Stockwell*, a mountaineer: Lester Lonergan. *Uncle Bob White*, a dark citizen: George W. Nichols. *Ras*: William Bradley. *Chunks*: Louis Henry. *Chips*, a sprout: Marie Hensell. *Sophie Chalker*, Chips' twin sister: Marie Hensell. *Jean Beehymer*: LOUISE ARNOTT. *Clyde Horrod*, a mountain thistle: Floy Crowell. *Rosie White*, a Southern brunette: Ella Spencer. *Phoebe*: Alice Bushong. *Chloe*: Effie Smith. *Dido*: Lizzie Casselle. *Georgia*, a roadside violet: LOUISE HAMILTON.

Act 1: Sulphur Springs Retreat. The Burglar.

Act 2: Coon Hollow. The Bursted Dam.

Act 3, Scene 1: At Beehymer's. The Flight. *Scene 2*: The Steamboat Race.

Act 4: The Cotton Empress. The Tragedy.

MUSICAL NUMBERS[11]

"Goodness Gracious Children"
(*Music by* Otto M. Heinzman. *Lyrics by* Charles L. Halberstadt.)

"Come Back Sweetheart"
W. Bradley
(*Music and Lyrics by* James I. Horton.)

"Way Down Coon Hollow"
(*Music by* Hattie Starr. *Lyrics by* George Starr.)

1894.28 THE LITTLE TROOPER

A Vaudeville Operetta in Three Acts. Libretto by Clay M. Greene. (Based on a French Vaudeville opérette "Les 28 Jours de Clairette," libretto by H. Raymond and A. Mars, music by Victor Roger.) Music by William Furst. (*Lyrics by* J. Cheever Goodwin.) Produced under the direction of Richard Barker. Settings by Ernest Gros. Costumes by Dazian. Musical director, Adolph Bauer. Produced by the Della Fox Comic Opera Company (Nat Roth, Manager). Opened 30 August 1894 at the Casino Theatre and closed 27 October 1894 after 68 performances.

CAST: *Emile Duval*, Captain 13th Hussars: PAUL ARTHUR. *Gibard*, Lieutenant 13th Hussars: JEFFERSON DeANGELIS. *Michonnet*, Lieutenant 13th Hussars: CHARLES J. CAMPBELL. *Benoit*, Lieutenant 13th Hussars: ALF C. WHELAN. *Pepin*, Sergeant-Major 13th Hussars: Ed Knight. *Jules La Tour*, Colonel 13th Hussars: CHARLES DUNGAN. *Corporal*, 13th Hussars: John Dudley. *Mathilde Louvin*, proprietress of the Bon Marche: VILLA KNOX. *Octavie*, forewoman of the Bon Marche: EVA DAVENPORT. *Rosalie*, housemaid at Chateau Regnal: MARIE CELESTE. *Sales girls at Bon Marche (4) Virginie*: HATTIE WILLIAMS. *Coralie*: Eugenie Nicholson. *Ninette*: Crissie Carlyle. *Lady*: Violet Aubrey. *Clairette Duval*, Emile's wife: DELLA FOX. *Privates and Officers of the 13th Hussars, Peasants, Ladies and Gentlemen, Shop Girls and Saleswomen, etc.*

The action takes place in Paris and its suburbs in 1802.

Act 1: Milliner Department, Bon Marche.

Act 2: Barracks of the 13th Hussars.

Act 3: Chateau, near Montargis.

MUSICAL NUMBERS[12]

"Trot, Trot, Trot!" (Song of the Hussars)
D. Fox, Chorus
(*Music by* Victor Roger.)

"Jilted!"
V. Knox
(*Music by* Victor Roger.)

"The Freedom of the Press!" (Song)
M. Celeste
(*Music by* Victor Roger.)

"My first request I'll be confessing" (Act 2)
C. J. Campbell, E. Davenport, Chorus
(*Music by* William Furst. *Lyrics by* J. Cheever Goodwin.)

"Ah, Love, You Do Not Know!" (Duo)
V. Knox, P. Arthur
(*Music by* William Furst. *Lyrics by* J. Cheever Goodwin.)

"Fencing Song"
D. Knox
(*Music by* Victor Roger.)

"Pit Pat!"
(*Music by* Victor Roger.)

"The Colonel's the Man for Me!"
(*Music by* William Furst. *Lyrics by* J. Cheever Goodwin.)

"She Was a Daisy" (Song)
D. Fox
(*Lyrics by* J. Cheever Goodwin.)

"There's magic in a flashing eye"
J. DeAngelis

"The first I met was a young lieutenant"
D. Fox

"The Trooper's Song" (Daisy)
D. Fox

"I am Benoit" (Ensemble)

"He is a man" (Septette) (Act 3)

[9]Musical numbers not listed in programs. Between Acts 2 and 3, Queen Isabella's Art Gallery (Fourth Series of Original Living Pictures) will be exhibited by the Kilanyi Troupe.

[10]Stage direction, settings and costumes uncredited. No musical numbers listed in programs. Touring programs indicated Plantation Songs and Dances were given in Act 3, Scene 2; A troupe of Southern Serenaders, singers, dancers, etc. including the Coon Hollow Quartet, appeared in Act 4. Later played return engagements 16 December 1895 at the Columbus Theatre for 8 performances, 13 January 1896 at the People's Theatre for 8 performances, 20 April 1896 at the Grand Opera House for 8 performances, 10 May 1897 at the Columbus Theatre for 8 performances, and 11 October 1897 at the People's Theatre for 8 performances.

[11]Musical Numbers not listed in programs; not in performance order. List prepared from published sheet music, whose score changed during many years of touring.

[12]Musical numbers not listed in programs; not in performance order. List, first 9 titles, prepared from published piano vocal gems (T. B. Harms & Co., New York, 1894). Remaining titles from reviews, etc.

1894.29 THE DEVIL'S DEPUTY

A Comic Opera in Three Acts. Libretto by J. Cheever Goodwin. Music by Edward Jakobowski. Produced under the stage direction of Richard Barker. Settings by Richard Marston and Homer Emens. Costumes designed by Percy Anderson. Musical director, Ernest Catenhusen. Produced by Francis Wilson (Management of A. H. Canby). Opened 10 September 1894 at Abbey's Theatre and closed 3 November 1894 after 56 performances[13].

CAST: *Melissen*, an Inn-keeper: FRANCIS WILSON. *Lorenzo*, a singer from the Grand Opera: RHYS THOMAS. *General Karamatoff*, Chief of the Army of the Princess: J. C. MIRON. *Sergeant*: J. T. Chaillee. *Bartow*, Uncle to Elverine: W. A. Laverty. *Princess Mirane*: ADELE RITCHIE. *Elverine*, Melissen's sweetheart: LULU GLASER. *Bagatella*, Countess Karamatoff: MAUD BLISS. *Bob*, valet to Lorenzo: Christie MacDonald. *Mademoiselle Kobolt*: Amelia Gardner. *Peasants, Soldiers, Maids in Waiting, Grandmothers, Nurses, Doctors, etc.*

Act 1: Interior of a Mountain Inn, in Hesse. (Emens.)

Act 2: Palace Grounds of Princess Mirane, in France. (Marston.)

Act 3: Before the Palace of Princess Mirane. (Marston.)

ACT 1[14]

Grandmothers Quatrain (When husbands stay out late at night)

"The Cake Song" (Cakes there are of all descriptions)
L. Glaser, Chorus

"Storm Chorus" (The night is dark and growing darker)
L. Glaser, Chorus

Melissen's Entrance Song (Why in the world do you shake and shiver so?)
F. Wilson, Chorus

"The Song of the Devil" (While toiling up the mountain road)
F. Wilson, Chorus

Grandmothers' Quatrain (reprise)

"Wedded Life
F. Wilson, L. Glaser

Recitative and Duet (Here I am. Holy smoke!)
R. Thomas, F. Wilson

"Love Is a Chameleon!" (Song)

Soldiers' Chorus (With care profound)
J. C. Miron, Chorus

Finale (What ho! Within!)

ACT 2

Opening Chorus (Wrapped in tranquilizing slumber)

"Sweet Sixteen"

Duet (His eyes are black—I don't like black)
M. Bliss, A. Ritchie

"Babette!" (Stuttering Song)
F. Wilson

"Lady Mine!"
R. Thomas

"(He's) Mine, All Mine!" (Song)
L. Glaser, Chorus

Finale (Set the wedding bells a-ringing)

ACT 3

Opening Chorus (In a state of agitation)

"In the Days (When He Came Wooing)" (Duet)
L. Glaser, J. C. Miron

"Weave! Weave!"
Chorus

"O, Strange, Oh Sweet Surprise" (Trio)
R. Thomas, A. Ritchie, M. Bliss

Finale

[13]Later played a return engagement 29 April 1895 at the Harlem Opera House for 8 performances.

[14]Musical numbers not listed in programs. List prepared from published book of song words and piano vocal selections (T. B. Harms, New York, 1894). Interpolation not included in book of song words:

"If You Want a Kiss" (Duet)
F. Wilson, L. Glaser
(*Music and Lyrics by* Hubbard T. Smith.)

1894.30 HUMPTY DUMPTY UP TO DATE

The Lilliputians in a Grand Spectacular Extravaganza in Four Acts, 15 Scenes, in German and English. Play by Robert Breitenbach. Music composed and arranged by Max Gabriel and Charles B. Hoffmann. Scenery, decorations, costumes, stage management, choreographic arrangements and decorative designs by director Carl Rosenfeld. Musical director, A. Kuttner. Produced by Carl and Theodore Rosenfeld. Opened 11 September 1894 at the Fifth Avenue Theatre and closed 3 November 1894 after 64 performances[15].

CAST: *Schaumberg*, a wine merchant: H. Ehrendt. *Elise*, his daughter: BERTHA JAEGER. *Haenschen*, his nephew: F. Steimann. *Stefan, Klaus*, coopers: H. Oesfeld, H. Dehncke. *Patrick*, apprentice: LUDWIG MERKEL. *Klopfer*, blacksmith: G. Winter. *Josie*, his sister: J. Niemann. *Jimmy*, his apprentice: ADOLF ZINK. *Bellachini*, circus proprietor: A. Durand. *Preciosa, Carina*, members: IDA MAHR, TONI MEISTER. *Mrs. Knutsche*, hotel keeper: A. Koehler. *The Teacher*: P. Wilke. *A Police Officer*: F. Marquardt. *Jack, Jean*, servants: D. Mellini, M. Bauer. *Old Elise*: ELISE LAU. *Fairy Gloriosa*: ELISE LAU. *Riecke*, her daughter: SELMA GOERNER. *Pantaloon*: HERMANN RING. *Humpty Dumpty*: FRANZ EBERT. *The Giant Kaleb*: Kaleb. *Coopers, Servants, Spectators, Gypsies, etc.*

Act 1, Scene 1: Courtyard of a Wine Importer. *Scene 2*: A Wine Cellar. *Scene 3*: The Palace of Drinks.

Act 2, Scene 1: Roadway, with a Forge. *Scene 2*: A Country Stable. *Scene 3*: A Forest, Night and Morning.

Act 3, Scene 1: Bar-room in a Country Hotel. *Scene 2*: In the Clouds. *Scene 3*: The City of Diamonds. *Scene 4*: With the Giant. *Scene 5*: The Grotto of Diamonds.

Act 4, Scene 1: Amphitheatre. *Scene 2*: 1,001 Humpty Dumptys. *Scene 3*: In Front of a Cottage. *Scene 4*: Apotheosis—The Living Tulip.

ACT 1[16]

Scene 1

Opening Chorus (The cooper has a jolly trade..)

Solo (They call me the little witch . . .)
S. Goerner

Solo (Thou wouldst not listen to the woman's right . . .)
E. Lau

Duet (What does it mean, I now am small . . .)
H. Ring, F. Ebert

Scene 2

Trio (Trust in me, my honest friends . . .)
E. Lau, B. Jaeger, ?

Chorus of Ghosts (See here the black ghosts..)
Ghosts, F Ebert, H. Ring

Scene 3

The Ballet of Drinks

Chocolate, tea, coffee, beer, wine, whiskey, seltzers, Croton water, milk, champagne, The Mammoth Punchbowl. The Bowery Booze. The Lilliputians as the Spirits of Punch.

ACT 2

Scene 1

Solo (The happiest life in all the world . . .)
A. Zink

Ensemble
Chorus, I. Mahr, T. Meister, Artists

[15]Later played a return engagement 31 December 1894 at the Harlem Opera House for 8 performances.

[16]Musical numbers, excepting the ballets, do not appear in programs. Musical numbers taken from the published English libretto on sale at performances.

Scene 3

The Ballet of Flies

Hunters' Chorus (Halloh! Halloh! Halloh!)

ACT 3

Scene 2

Solo (I have saved those two once more. .)
E. Lau

Scene 5

The Ballet of Precious Stones and Metals

Gold, silver, copper, rubies, sapphires, emeralds, topazes, corals, pearls, diamonds. Finale, The Chimes. The Ribbon Surprise. All Lilliputians.

ACT 4

Scene 1

Solo (Heigho, the world is open to me. .)
S. Goerner

Scene 2

Ballet of Pierrots
1,001 Humpty Dumpties

Scene 3

Solo (Thou hast suffered and at repenting. .)
E. Lau

1894.31 MY AUNT BRIDGET

A Revival of the Refined Musical Farce Comedy in Three Acts[17]. Play by Scott Marble. Opened 17 September 1894 at the Third Avenue Theatre and closed 22 September 1894 after 9 performances; returned 18 March 1895 to Niblo's Garden and closed 23 March 1895 after 8 performances[18].

CAST: *Bridget McVeigh*, who arrives in the Spring, "Oh! by Gosh": GEORGE W. MONROE. *Alton McVeigh*, depending on his aunt: RAYMOND HITCHCOCK. *Jack Treyser*, Alton's college chum: THOMAS PEASLEY[19]. *Joe Nervey*, a New York collar button vender: Eddie Magee[20]. *Tompkins Blazer*, a coal dealer, glad of it: LINDSEY MORRISON[21]. *Boyce Alton*, always with us: David Swift[22]. *Dora Blazer*, Alton's jealous sweetheart: MAMIE RYAN. *Polly Glyder*, who wants to *hact hon* the stage: ALICE HANSON[23]. *Miss Recalmer*, one of the "400," who wants to elevate the stage: LIZZIE RICHMOND[24]. *Nellie Ryder*, W-w-wait a minute: ELLA FALK. *Blue Jeans*: Nellie Bland. *Lelle Butte*: Ella Murtha. *Peache Blow*: Susie Russell. *Gertie June*: Etna Ford. (*Specialties*: LISKA (Premiere Danseuse), Senorita Marie Goday.)

ACT 1

"And Her Golden Hair (Was Hanging Down Her Back)" (Song and Dance)
T. Peasley, A. Hanson
(*Music by* Felix McGlennon. *Lyrics by* Monroe H. Rosenfeld.)

Specialty
Liska

"Maiden's Sea Trip"[25] (Song and Chorus)
G. W. Monroe

ACT 2[26]

Grand Medley
Entire Company

"Aunt Bridget's" (Serenade)
Company

"Larry Mulligan" (Song)
T. Peasley
(*Music and Lyrics by* Dave Reed, Jr.)

"Till We Meet Again" (Duet)
(*Music by* Eben Howe Bailey. *Lyrics by* W. H. Putnam.)

"My Pearl's a Bowery Girl" (Song)
E. Magee
(*Music by* Andrew Mack. *Lyrics by* William Jerome.)

"Venetian Lullaby" (Song)
E. Falk

"Life's a Game of Cards" (Song)

"My Little Woman" (Bass Solo)
L. Morrison
(*Music and Lyrics by* George L. Osgood.)

"Vito" (Spanish Song and Dance)
M. Goday

"The Girl Who Leads the Fashions" (Song)
G. W. Monroe

"Cupid" (Song and Dance)
N. Bland

"Hallow'een" (Song with Dancing)
T. Peasley, L. Richmond

"Phoebe"
A. Hanson, Pickaninnies

ACT 3

"Ours Is a Happy (Little) Home"[27] (Song)
G. W. Monroe
(*Music by* Harry Randall. *Lyrics by* J. W. Sewell.)

Parodies
R. Hitchcock

"Roaming with Nora" (Song and Dance)
A. Hanson

Grand Finale
Entire Company

1894.32 STRUCK OIL

A Revival of the Comedy in Three Acts, 7 Scenes[28]. [Play by Samuel W. Smith.] (Songs by Al. H. Wilson, Andrew Mack.) Scenery by John H. Young. Musical director, Frank J. Webbe. Produced by Augustus Pitou. Opened 17 September 1894 at the 14th Street Theatre and closed 29 September 1894 after 16 performances; returned 29 October 1894 to the People's Theatre for 8 additional performances. Total: 24 performances.

---

[17]Previously produced in New York 6 December 1886 at John Thompson's Eighth Street Theatre and 28 April 1890 at the 14th Street Theatre for 1 week.

[18]Later played a return engagement 6 December 1895 at the Columbus Theatre for one week. A previous version played 6 December 1886 at John Thompson's Eighth Street Theatre.

[19]Succeeded by BEN F. GRINNELL for Niblo's engagement.

[20]Succeeded by Thomas J. Grady for Niblo's engagement.

[21]Succeeded by HARRY McDOWELL for Niblo's engagement.

[22]Succeeded by Milo J. Knill for Niblo's engagement.

[23]Succeeded by MABEL FLORENCE for Niblo's engagement.

[24]Succeeded by MAY DURYEA for Niblo's engagement.

[25]Replaced by the following for Niblo's engagement:

"The Husbands" (Song and Chorus)
G. W. Monroe

[26]Added to Act 2 for Niblo's engagement:

"You Can't Play in Our Yard" (Song and Quartette) (from *PASSING SHOW OF 1894*)
R. Hitchcock
(*Music by* H. W. Petrie. *Lyrics by* Philip Wingate.)

Dropped for Niblo's engagement: "Life's a Game of Cards," "Vito," "The Girl Who Leads the Fashions," Hallow'een."

[27]Replaced for Niblo's engagement by:

"Eh! Did I Hear You?" (Song)
G. W. Monroe
(*Music and Lyrics by* Barney Fagan.)

[28]Authorship of the play uncredited. Advertised with "New scenery, new costumes, new effects, new songs." First produced 17 September 1877 at the Union Square Theatre for 42 performances, plus 2 return engagements for an additional 24 performances.

CAST: *John Stofel*, the German shoemaker: AL. (Metz) H. WILSON. *Lizzie Stofel*, his daughter: JANE STUART. *Mrs. Susan Stofel*, his wife: EMMA M. STEVENS. *Eben Skinner*: WILLIAM HERBERT. *Flynn*: George M. Brennan. *Sharp*: Fred M. Lee. *William Pearson*: Milton Lipman. *Captain Becks*: Walter A. Snow. *Rowley*: R. J. Moye. *Sheriff*: Charles Watson. *Boy*: Clifford S. Moye.

Act 1: The Shoemaker's Home.

Act 2, Scene 1: A Room in John Stofel's House. *Scene 2*: The City of Pittsburgh. *Scene 3*: The Guard House.

Act 3, Scene 1: The Oil Regions. *Scene 2*: A Street in Oilsburgh. *Scene 3*: The Shoemaker's Home.

MUSICAL NUMBERS[29]

"Mit a Little English"
A. H. Wilson
(*Music and Lyrics by* A. H. Wilson.)

"My Old Dutch Pipe"
A. H. Wilson
(*Music and Lyrics by* A. H. Wilson.)

"L,-O,-V,-E, Dot Spells Love"
J. Stuart
(*Music and Lyrics by* Andrew Mack.)

"Dot Boy I Love"
J. Stuart
(*Music and Lyrics by* Andrew Mack.)

1894.33 A GAIETY GIRL

A Musical Comedy in Two Acts. Book by Owen Hall. Music by Sidney Jones. Lyrics by Harry Greenbank. Staged by George Edwardes. Settings by Hugh Logan Reid. Musical director, Granville Bantock. Produced by Augustin Daly. Opened 18 September 1894 at Daly's Theatre and closed 24 November 1894 after 81 performances[30].

CAST: *Charles Goldfield*: CHARLES RYLEY. *Major Barclay*: Fred Kaye. *Bobbie Rivers*: W. LOUIS BRADFIELD. *Harry Fitzwarren*: Arthur Hope. *Romney Farquhar*: Cecil Hope. *Sir Lewis Grey*: LEEDHAM BANTOCK. *Lance*: E. G. Woodhouse. *Auguste*: Fritz Rimma. *Rev. Montague Brierly*: HARRY MONKHOUSE. *Rose Brierly*: DECIMA MOORE. *Miss Gladys Stourton*: Sophie Elliott. *Alma Somerset*: BLANCHE MASSEY. *Cissy Verner*: Florence Lloyd. *Edytha*: Marie Yorke. *Ethel Hawthorne*: Grace Palotta. *Mina*, a French maid: JULIETTE NESVILLE. *Lady Virginia Forrest*: MAUD HOBSON. *Daisy*: Ethel Selwyn. *Lady Grey*: Mrs. Edmund Phelps. *Haidee Walton*: Cissy Fitzgerald. *Principal Dancers*: Maggie Crossland, Lucy Murray, May Lucas.

Act 1: The Cavalry Barracks at Winbridge.

Act 2: On the Riviera.

ACT 1[31]

"When a Masculine Stranger Goes By" (Opening Chorus)

"O Sing a Welcome" (Chorus)

"I'm a Judge of the Modern Society Sort" (Song)
L. Bantock

"Beneath the Skies" (Song)
C. Ryley

"Here Come the Ladies" (Chorus)

"To the Barracks We Have Come" (Concerted Piece)

"High-class Chaperone" (Song and Chorus)

"To the Barracks We Have Come" (reprise)

"Oh, My Daughter" (Duet)
D. Moore, H. Monkhouse

"When Once I Get Hold of a Good-looking He" (Trio)
M. Hobson, L. Bantock, H. Monkhouse

"Jimmy on the Chute"
H. Monkhouse
(*Music and Lyrics by* Harry Greenbank.)

"Private Tommy Atkins"
C. Ryley
(*Music by* S. Potter. *Lyrics by* Henry Hamilton.)

"To My Judicial Mind" (Finale)
Principals, Chorus

ACT 2

"Here on Sunlit Sands" (Opening Chorus)
"That Ladies Cannot Bathe" (Concerted Piece)
M. Yorke, S. Elliott, J. Neville, C. Fitzgerald

"It Seems to Me" (Song)
D. Moore, F. Lloyd, C. Fitzgerald

"Boys of the Household Brigade" (Trio)
W. L. Bradfield, A. Hope, C. Ryley
(*Lyrics by* Henry Hamilton.)

"When Your Pride Has Had a Tumble" (Song)
J. Neville

"When in Town" (Trio)
L. Bantock, H. Monkhouse, M. Hobson

"Stiboo, Stibee" (Duet)
W. L. Bradfield, D. Moore

"We're Awfully Anxious" (Trio)

Carnival Chorus

"Poor Pierrot" (Song)
W. L. Bradfield, Chorus

"Sunshine Above" (Song)
C. Ryley

"It Find It Really Better Far" (Finale)
L. Bantock, C. Ryley, H. Monkhouse, Chorus

1894.34 THE BLACK CROOK

A Revival of the Musical Extravaganza in Four Acts, 16 Scenes[32]. (Libretto by Charles M. Barras. Music composed and selected by Thomas Baker, A. W. Hoffmann.) Ballets composed by M. A. Bertrand; Act 2 Ballet music by M. Jacobi. Scenery by Charles S. Getz, Homer F. Emens, Harley Merry, J. S. Getz, John W. Sommer. Costumes designed by Howell, Russell and Wilhelm of London; Alfredo Edel of Paris. Production under the stage direction of Lawrence McCarty. Produced by Eugene Tompkins. Opened 24 September 1894 at the Grand Opera House and closed 6 October 1894 after 16 performances[33].

CAST: GEORGE MORTON, VIVIAN OSBORNE, SAM COLLINS, E. K. GOODWIN, RUSSELL HUNTING, GUSSIE COGAN, LETTA MEREDITH, ALLIE GILBERT, ELLA CRAVEN.

---

[29]Not in performance order.

[30]Also played return engagements 26 November 1894 at the Harlem Opera House for 8 performances, and 7 May 1895 at Daly's Theatre for 31 performances.

[31]No musical numbers listed in programs. List prepared from published English piano vocal score (Hopwood & Crew, London, 1893); vocal selections as published in America contained only "Private Tommy Atkins" (*Music by* S. Potter, *Lyrics by* Henry Hamilton), "I'm a Judge of the Modern Society Sort," "Beneath the Skies," "To the Barracks We Have Come," "Oh, My Daughter," "Jimmy on the Chute," "It Seems to Me," "Boys of the Household Brigade," "When Your Pride Has Had a Tumble," "Stiboo, Stibee," and "Sunshine Above."

[32]First produced in New York 12 September 1866 at Niblo's Garden for 475 performances. For Synopsis of Scenes and Musical Numbers, see original 1866 production; this revival was "substantially revised" from the original Among the interpolations, as per published sheet music:

"Another Little Coon in Town"
A. Gilbert, S. Collins
(*Music and Lyrics by* Joe Flynn.)

[33]Also played a return engagements 14 October 1895 at the Grand Opera House for 1 week, and 21 September 1896 at the 14th Street Theatre for 1 week.

1894.35 A TRIP TO CHINATOWN

A Revival of the Idyll of San Francisco (Farce Comedy or Musical Trifle) in Three Acts[34]. Play by Charles H. Hoyt. Music composed and arranged by Percy Gaunt. Staged by Julian Mitchell. Scenery by Arthur Voegtlin. Mechanical effects by Matt Lynch. Musical director, William Nelson. (Produced by Charles H. Hoyt.) Management, Frank McKee. Opened 24 September 1894 at the American Theatre and closed 6 October 1894 after 14 performances[35]

CAST: *Welland Strong*, a man with one foot in the grave: HARRY CONOR. *Ben Gay*, a wealthy San Francisco bachelor, of the Union Club: GEORGE A. BEANE, JR. *Of the Bohemian Club (2)*: *Rashleigh Gay*, nephew of Ben Gay: George Sinclair. *Norman Blood*, chum of Rashleigh: JULIUS P. WITMARK. *Willie Grow*, proposed at the Bohemian Club: Margaret McDonald. *Noah Heep*, writer at "The Riche" Restaurant: HARRY GILFOIL. *Hoffman Price*, manager of Cliff House: F. Waller. *Slavin Payne*, a servant of Ben Gay: HARRY GILFOIL. *Turner Swift*, who runs the ice-crusher: F. L. Beamish. *Stillman*: William Morse. *Tony Gay*, niece of Ben Gay: NELLIE VICTORIA PARKER. *Isabelle Dame*, friend of the Gays: Cora Tinnie. *Premiere Danseuse*: BESSIE CLAYTON. *Flirt*, Mrs. Guyer's maid: Sadie Kirby. *Mrs. Guyer*, a widow from Chicago, not too strenuous on culture, but makes up for it in "biff": GERALDINE McCANN.

ACT 1[36]

"The Pretty (Young) Widow" (from *THE PASSING SHOW 1894*)
(*Music and Lyrics by* Alberto Himan.)

"Out for a Racket"
(*Music and Lyrics by* Percy Gaunt.)

"Honey O'" (African Cantata)
(*Music and Lyrics by* Percy Gaunt.)

"Crisp Young Chaperone" (A Chaperone)
(*Music and Lyrics by* W. Barton.)

ACT 2

Burlesque of Italian Opera (arranged by Percy Gaunt)
Trio
Medley including "Naughty Sporty Boys," "The Girl Who Ran Away," "That Old First Love of Mine," "Her Eyes Don't Shine Like Diamonds," "Reuben and Cynthia," "I Said Good-Night and You Good-Bye," Whistling Extraordinary, "Won't You Be My Sweetheart" (arranged by Percy Gaunt).

ACT 3

Toe Dance and Pierrot Dance
B. Clayton

"(On) the Bowery"
H. Conor
(*Music by* Percy Gaunt. *Lyrics by* Charles H. Hoyt.)

[34]First produced in New York 8 December 1890 at the Harlem Opera House. Subsequently presented 9 November 1891 at the Madison Square Theatre for 657 performances. For Synopsis of Scenes and Musical Numbers, see 1891 production.

[35]This current season's revival also played a return engagement 28 January 1895 at the Columbus Theatre for 1 week, 8 April 1895 at the Grand Opera House for 1 week, and 6 May 1895 at the Columbus Theatre for 1 week; also the following season 16 March 1896 at the People's Theatre for 1 week.

[36]Addition song interpolated, as per published sheet music:
"Her Eyes Don't Shine Like Diamonds"
J. P. Witmark
(*Music and Lyrics by* David Marion.)
Additional song specialties introduced by Harry Conor, as per published sheet music:
"Put Me Off at Buffalo"
(*Music by* John Dillon. *Lyrics by* Harry Dillon.)
"Songs We Hear on the Stage"
(*Music by* John W. Bratton. *Lyrics by* Walter Ford.)
"He Picked It Up and Let It Drop"
(*Music and Lyrics by* Harry Conor.)
"She Was Right"
(*Music and Lyrics by* A. Powell.)
"When Enoch, He Knocked, She Knocked Enoch"
(*Music and Lyrics by* Charles Brighton.)
"Do, Do, My Huckleberry Do"
(*Music by* John Dillon. *Lyrics by* Harry Dillon.)

1894.36 THE IRISH ARTIST

A Comedy Drama in Four Acts, 7 Scenes. Play by Augustus Pitou and George H. Jessop. Songs by Chauncey Olcott. (Staged by Augustus Pitou.) Settings by John H. Young. Costumes by H. A. Ogden. Musical director, Albert Krausse. Produced by Augustus Pitou. Opened 1 October 1894 at the Fourteenth Street Theatre and closed 10 November 1894 after 48 performances[37].

CAST: *Maurice Cronin*: CHAUNCEY OLCOTT. *Sir Robert Dean*: DANIEL GILFETHER. *Edmund Dean*: Charles F. Gotthold. *Cormac Cronin*: Harry Meredith. *Father Denis Mahone*: J. W. HAGUE. *Jerry Sweeney*: Luke Martin. *Paddy Blake*: Clara Hunter. *Mike*: Frank Petters. *Gardner*: George Wallace. *Kate Mahone*: LOTTA LYNNE [Lotta Lincthicum]. *Lady Katherine Dean*: Etta Baker Martin. *The Widow Blake*: Effie Germon. *Maggie Cronin*: Ila Irvine. *Bridget Cronin*: Grace Burton. *Mary Dean*: Tiny Burton. *Villagers, Fishermen, Smugglers.*

The action takes place at Drim-na-Cor, County Wexford, Ireland, 1815.

Act 1: The Birthplace of Maurice Cronin.

Act 2, Scene 1: The Home of Father Mahone. *Scene 2*: Rocky Coast by Moonlight. *Scene 3*: Drim-na-Cor.

Act 3, Scene 1: The Widow Blake's House. *Scene 2*: The Smugglers' Cave.

Act 4: Dean's Grave, the Home of Sir Robert Dean.

MUSICAL NUMBERS[38]

"Katy Malone"

"Olcott's Irish Serenade"

"Look in My Heart"

"My Beautiful Irish Maid"

"Now as you see"

"Believe, me, if all those endearing young charms" (Traditional; *Lyrics by* Tom Moore)

1894.37 A MILK WHITE FLAG, and Its Battle-Scarred Followers on the Field of Mars and in the Court of Venus

Hoy'ts Contribution to Dramatic Literature (Musical Farce Comedy) in Three Acts. Play (and lyrics) by Charles H. Hoyt[39]. Music by Percy Gaunt. Staged by Julian Mitchell. Dances arranged by Frank Lawton. Scenery by Arthur Voegtlin. Musical director, Percy Gaunt. Produced by Hoyt and McKee's Comedy Company (Charles H. Hoyt, Frank McKee, Proprietors). Opened 8 October 1894 at Hoyt's Theatre and closed 23 February 1895 after 153 performances[40].

CAST: *The Colonel*, Christian Barriel, a retired coal merchant: CHARLES STANLEY. *The Major*, Paul Baring, a prominent life insurance man: LLOYD WILSON. *The Judge Advocate*, Howland Hooper, a well-known young lawyer: ARTHUR PACIE. *The Surgeon*, Mark Tombs, leading physician of the town: EDWARD GARVIE. *The Bandmaster*, Steele Ayres, who is also a popular music teacher: FRANK BALDWIN. *The Private*, Willing Singer, a hired man: Sam Weston. *The Dancing Master*, Gideon Foote, who also has a school for children: Frank Lawton. *The Lieutenant*, Phil Graves, also a prominent undertaker: John S. Marble. *Vivandiers,*

[37]Also played return engagements this season 19 November 1894 at the Columbus Theatre for 8 performances, 31 December 1894 at the People's Theatre for 8 performances, and 27 May 1895 at the American Theatre for 8 performances.

[38]All musical numbers written, composed and sung by Chauncey Olcott.

[39]Author's note on the title page: A Tribute to our Citizen Soldiers by one who would gladly join their ranks if he knew how to dance. The Field of Battle is not necessarily St. Alban's Vermont, or Harrisburg, Pennsylvania, but a town of that deliciously provincial character was in the author's thoughts as he wrote. Visitors from the West may imagine it's Zanesville, Ohio, or Oshkosh, Wisconsin.

[40]Also played return engagements 1 April 1895 at the Harlem Opera House for 8 performances, 13 January 1895 at the Grand Opera House for 8 performances, and 14 March 1898 at the Columbus Theatre for 8 performances.

A, B, C, D: Toma Hanlon, Lillian Markham, Rosa France, Etta Williamson. *The Standard Bearer*, Carrie Flagg: Marguerite Binford. (All the above belonging to and being a part of the Ransome Guards.) *The General*, Hurley Burleigh, an officer of the regular army and guest of the guards: Frank J. Keenan. *The Dear Departed*, Piggott Luce, a successful "promoter": George A. Beane. *"Wicked" Dodge*, spy of the Daly Blues: Lew Bloom. *The Orphan*, Pony Luce, daughter of the "promoter": AIMEE ANGELES. *The Particular Friend of the Bereaved Wife*, "Lize" Dugro: LILLIE DEAVES. *The Bereaved (Widow)*, who either is or isn't the promoter's wife: ISABELLE COE. *The Drum Corps*: Adele Archer (Captain), Zulah Williams, Cora Bolton, Lida Dexter. *The Messenger Boys*: Julia Raymond, Winona Shannon, Willie Norton, Frankie Wilson. *The Band*, all nice men: Fred W. Boardman, William Cushing, Ad Dorsch, E. P. Brown, J. F. Boardman, George Goddard, E. F. Balch, Paul Pfarr.

Act 1: Private quarters of the officers of the Ransome Guards.

Act 2: The Reception room at the house of Piggott Luce.

Act 3: Grand Hall of the Armory.

ACT 1[41]

"Swell Girls"

"Warriors Bold"

Medley: including "Monte Carlo"

"Dear Old Bells"[42]

"I Am a Highly Educated Man"[43]

"Say Au Revoir, Not Good-Bye"
(*Music and Lyrics by* Harry Kennedy.)

"Southern Revel"

"Without Him, What's the Band?" (Barton)

ACT 2

"Whistling Superlative"

"Wouldn't You Like to Fondle Little Baby?"[44]

"Come to Me, My Own"

"Fairest Flower Divine"[45]

ACT 3

"(It's) English As You See It on Broadway"[46]

"A Bouquet in Bloom"[47]

"Ransome Guards' Quick-step"

"Hail to the Daughter"

"Anthem of the Milk White Flag"

1894.38 LITTLE CHRISTOPHER COLUMBUS

A Burlesque Opera in Three Acts[48]. Libretto by George R. Sims and Cecil Raleigh. Music by Ivan Caryll and Gustave Kerker. Staged by Edward E. Rice, assisted by George Walton and Thomas Terriss. Settings by Hugh Logan Reid, Frank Rafter, Henry Heinman and Richard Marston. Costumes by Edel. Musical director, Gustave Kerker. Produced by Rice Burlesque Company (Edward E. Rice, Proprietor). Opened 15 October 1894 at the Garden Theatre, moved 20 May 1895 to Palmer's Theatre and closed 1 June 1895 after 264 performances[49].

[41]Added for subsequent tour: "Love Me for Old Love's Sake" (*Music by* Richard Stahl), "Baby Isn't Old Enough to Know" (Stahl), "Love's Serenade" (Stahl), "I'm a Lady, Yes I Am," (Stahl-Edward Garvie) "Songs of a Pilgrim," "Sweetest Story Ever Told". On tour, two years later, added were: "Don't Send Her Away," "Jusque La" and Dance Serenade, and "Sweetheart Love Ne'er Grows Old."
[42]Replaced during the run by: "I Went Home with Michael"
[43]Replaced during the run by: "Old Love Letters"
[44]Replaced during the run by: "The Orphan's Contribution"
[45]Replaced during the run by "Beauteous Queen."
[46]Placed during the run by "Don't You Trifle with Me, Honey."
[47]Replaced early in the run by: "Cheer Up, Cherries Are Ripe"
[48]Titled changed to LITTLE CHRISTOPHER 3 December 1894 and for subsequent tour.
[49]Later played return engagements 2 March 1896 at the Grand Opera House for 8 performances, and 9 March 1896 at the Harlem Opera House for 8 performances.

CAST: *Little Christopher Columbus*, a cabin boy: HELEN BERTRAM. *O'Hoolegan*, private detective: GEORGE WALTON. *Captain Joseph H. Slammer* of the S.S. *Choctaw*: Herman Blakemore. *The Mayor of Cadiz*: Edwin Chapman. *Diego*: John W. Wilson. *Don Juan* of the Spanish police: EDGAR TEMPLE. *Josh Hemingway*, from Slab Hollow, Vermont: James B. Gentry. *The Bey of Barataria*: ALEXANDER CLARKE. *The Grand Vizier of Barataria*: HENRI LEONI. *Head Turk*: Follett Jocelyn. *Officer of the Colombian Guard*: Charles B. Powell. *Baratarian Herald*: Irene Vera. *Spanish Officers (6)*: *Pedro*: Lucy Escott. *Lopez*: Tillie Richardson. *Manuel*: Frankie Bailey. *Roderigo*: Grace Belasco. *Sancho*: Helen Brackett. *Fernandez*: Madge Alphabet. *Cerisca, Anita*, Spanish Vivandieres: Annie Seaberry, Nettie Harrington. *The Second Mrs. Tanqueray Block* of Chicago: HARRY MACDONOUGH. *Guinivere Block*, her daughter: Yolande Wallace. *Pepita*, the Dancing Girl: Mabel Bouton. *Hannah, Imogene*, Captain Slammer's lively daughters: Nettie Lyford, Mabel Potter. *Mercedes*: Lila Blow. *Lola*: Josie Ditt. *Zuleika*, a Turkish dancer: Bertha Waring. *Two Waifs*: Sisters Abbott. *Miss Chrysanthemum*: Nina Ainscoe. *Spanish Soldiers, Fisher Lads, Flower Sellers and Street Vendors, American Sailors, Court Attendants, World's Fair Visitors from Every Nation.*

Lyric Theatre Dancing Girls: Misses May Gore, Molly Bonheur, Florence Linton, Marie Linton. *Flower Girls*: Misses Elena Martinez, Grace Gayler, Pauline Train, Bertha Dowling, Lela Williams, Nettie Burdwin, Mollie Gayler, Nina Ainscoe. *Sailor Boys*: Misses Kittie Shields, May Hamilton, Bertie Holly, Lula Ward, Loie Riccardi, Lenora Wilson, Neena de Rue, Mabel Le Clair. *Governor's Guard*: Misses Lillian Green, May Gill, Marjorie Wilburn, Ena Welch, Genevieve Hill, Lizzie Leoni, Catalina Gomez. *Fisher Boys*: Misses Louise Lehman, Anna Carman, Estelle Botsford, Lula Farrance, Hetta Beaudet, Julia Lee, Florence Raymond. *Male Chorus*: Messrs. James S. Murray, Malcolm E. Russell, Charles Van Dyne, Pierre Young, George C. Miller, F. W. Regas, H. Weitzer, Charles B. Powell, Charles M. Holly, William Gillow, Robert H. MacIntyre, Otto D. Lehman, George E. Merrill, William Howard, Ernest de Horn, Jean Dore.

Act 1: The Great Square of Cadiz, Anniversary of the Columbus Fetes. (Marston.)

Act 2: Throne Room of the Bey of Barataria. (Heinman.)

Act 3: In the Midway Plaisance of the World's Fair Columbian Exposition, Chicago. Looking westward or any way you like. (Reid, Rafter.)

ACT 1[50]

"Here in Cadiz" (Opening Chorus)
(*Music by* Ivan Caryll.)

"I Love, I Love Her So" (Song)
(*Music by* Gustave Kerker.)

"We Are Gay Young American Tars" (Chorus)
(*Music by* Gustave Kerker.)

"The Captain Bold" (Song)
(*Music by* Gustave Kerker.)

"The Land of Love" (Song)
(*Music by* Ivan Caryll.)

"For I'm O'Hooligan"
(*Music by* Gustave Kerker.)

"In an Unconventional Way" (Chorus)
(*Music by* Ivan Caryll.)

"Columbus Was a Famous Man" (Song)
(*Music by* Ivan Caryll.)

"The India Rubber Shoe" (Police Song and Chorus)
(*Music by* Ivan Caryll.)

"Lazily, Drowsily" (Siesta Song and Chorus)
(*Music by* Ivan Caryll.)

"If In Your Dreams"[51] (Duet)
(*Music by* Ivan Caryll.)

"Oh, Yes! Oh, Yes!" (Finale)
(*Music by* Ivan Caryll.)

[50]At the time of the transfer to Palmer's, the following had been interpolated, as per published sheet music:

"Poor Little Mary"
Bessie Bonehill
(*Music by* Maurice Levi. *Lyrics by* Walter H. Ford.)

By the time of the Grand Opera House return engagement in March 1896, the following had been added:

"Sweethearts" (*Music by* Herman Perlet.)

"Oh My Love" (*Music by* Ivan Caryll.).

[51]Dropped during the run.

ACT 2[52]

"Fates, Fates, Fates" (Opening Chorus)
(*Music by* Gustave Kerker.)

"The Law of Barataria" (Chorus)
(*Music by* Gustave Kerker.)

"I Love, I Adore Her" (Song)
(*Music by* Gustave Kerker.)

"Hail to the Bey" (Song and Recitative)
Barataria Quintette
(*Music by* Gustave Kerker.)

"The Sisters Giggle" (Duet)
(*Music by* Ivan Caryll.)

The Marionette Dance
(*Music by* Ivan Caryll.)

ACT 3

"Chorus of Foreigners"[53]
(*Music by* Ivan Caryll.)

"Nummy Num Num"[54] (Duet)
(*Music by* Ivan Caryll.)

"Rumpty Tumpty"[55] (Song)
(*Music by* Ivan Caryll.)

"Oh Honey, My Honey" (Plantation Song)
(*Music by* Ivan Caryll.)

Finale
(*Music by* Ivan Caryll and Gustave Kerker.)

1894.39

THE PACIFIC MAIL

A Comic Play (Farce Comedy with Songs) in Three Acts. Play by Paul M. Potter. Freely adapted from Tom Taylor's play "The Overland Route." Staged by Eugene W. Presbrey. Settings by Ernest Albert. Produced by William H. Crane Company (Joseph Brooks, Director) Opened 22 October 1894 at the Star Theatre and closed 1 December 1894 after 42 performances[56].

CAST: *Sylvanus Urban*, a citizen of the world: WILLIAM H. CRANE. *Mrs. Urban*, née Tippengray, wife of Sylvanus: Ffolliot Paget. *Captain Weatherby* of the S.S. *City of Pekin*: Orrin Johnson. *Colin Croft*, his first officer: Boyd Putnam. *Sir Barnaby Bruce*, an English diplomatist from Hong Kong: H. A. Weaver, Sr. *Ida Bruce*, his daughter: Anne O'Neill. *Mr. Winks*, his valet: G. V. DeVere. *Humphrey Cossett*, Lieutenant U.S.N.: Joseph Wheelock, Jr. *Lucilla Cossett*, his wife: Lizzie Hudson Collier. *Tom Cupper*, her page: B. Douglas Ryer. *Judge Yancey*, an America diplomatist from Pekin: George F. DeVere. *Amoret Yancey*, his daughter: Mary Saunders. *Mrs. Chiverley*, her maid: Ida Burrows. *Harvey Packlemerton*, in the tea business: H. A. Langdon. *Euphemia Packlemerton*, his wife: Kate Denin Wilson. *Milly*, her maid: Vallie Egar. *Major Fogarty*, a China free lance: Percy Brooke. *Montague Carlton*, a wandering Englishman: D. J. Fingleton. *Greenwich*, steward: William Lewers. *"Coolidge Brothers,"* gums and spices, Singapore: James O. Barrows. *Wah Hing*: Hal Clarendon. *Lew Chew*: G. W. Marburg.

Act 1: Cabin of the *City of Pekin*. How the new doctor came aboard.

Act 2: Deck of the *City of Pekin*. How the doctor was involved in grievous trouble.

Act 3: A coral reef in the Pacific. How the doctor saved all hands from the wreck.

1894.40

ROB ROY

A Romantic Comic Opera in Three Acts. Libretto by Harry B. Smith. Music by Reginald DeKoven. Produced under the direction of Max Freeman. Settings by Joseph Physioc, D. Frank Dodge and Henry E. Hoyt. Costumes by Catherine Siedle. Musical director, Antonio DeNovellis. Produced by Fred C. Whitney. Opened 29 October 1894 at the Herald Square Theatre and closed 23 March 1895 after 168 performances.

CAST: *Rob Roy MacGregor*, a Highland Chief: WILLIAM PRUETTE. *Janet*, daughter of the Mayor: JULIETTE CORDEN. *Prince Charles Edward Stuart*, called "The Young Pretender": BARRON BERTHALD. *Flora MacDonald*, heiress of a Chief of the Clan MacDonald, a partisan of the pretender: LIZZIE MacNICHOL. *Dugald MacWheeble*, Mayor of Perth: RICHARD F. CARROLL. *Lochiel*, a Highlander, otherwise Donald Cameron, of the Cameron Clan: WILLIAM H. McLAUGHLIN. *Captain Ralph Sheridan*, of King George's Grenadiers: Anna O'Keefe. *Sandy MacSherey*, town crier: Joseph Herbert. *Tammas McSorlie*, the Mayor's henchman: Harry Parker. *Lieutenant Cornwallis*, of King George's Grenadiers: Mitti Atherton. *Lieutenant Clinton*: Louise Crane. *Angus MacAllister*: Jeannette Perie. *Duncan Campbell*: Julie Senac. *Stuart MacPherson*: Frankie Leonard. *Donald MacAlpine*: Carrie Rieger. *Nelly*, bar-maid of "The Crown and Thistle": Anita Austin. *Highlanders, Lowland Townsmen, Watchmen, English Grenadiers, Drummer Boys, etc.*

Time: 1745.

Act 1: An open place before the house of the Mayor of Perth. (Physioc.)

Act 2: Rob Roy's retreat in the Highlands. (Dodge.)

Act 3: Exterior of Sterling Castle by moonlight, with English troops in the bivouac. (Hoyt.)

ACT 1[57]

Opening Scene and Ensemble
W. H. McLaughlin, H. Parker, Highlanders

"Who's for the Chase, My Bonnie Hearts" (Entrance and Song)
L. MacNichol, Chorus

"Then I Will Live Love for Thee" (Duet)
L. MacNichol, B. Berthald

"Ding Dong" (Town Crier's Song)
J. Herbert, Chorus

"We Come to the Sound of the Drum" (Song and Chorus)
A. O'Keefe, English Soldiers

"The White and the Red, Huzzah!" (Chorus of Highlanders)

"My Heart Is in the Highlands" (Song of Rob Roy)
R. F. Carroll, Servant

"My Name Is Where the Heather Blooms" (Scene and Duet)
W. Pruette, J. Corden

Finale

ACT 2

Introduction and Opening Scene
J. Corden, W. Pruette, Chorus

"The Merry Miller" (Song)
J. Corden, Chorus

Scene and Concerted Number
W. Pruette, W. H. McLaughlin, J. Corden, L. MacNichol, B. Berthald, Chorus

"Lay of the Cavalier"
B. Berthald, Chorus

"Song of the Ballad-mongers"
R. F. Carroll, H. Parker, Servants

"Come, Lairds o' the Highland" (Song)
W. Pruette, Chorus

"My True Love Is a Shepherdess" (Quintet and Chorus)
W. H. McLaughlin, R. F. Carroll, H. Parker, B. Berthald, W. Pruette, Chorus

"Dearest Heart of My Heart" (Romanza)
L. MacNichol

Finale

---

[52]Specialties are also interpolated in the second and third acts. In early February 1895, Bessie Bonehill assumed the role of Little Christopher with her own Act 2 specialty, "Buttercups and Daisies." These were later replaced by "Only One Girl in the World for Me," "Henrietta," and "In Harlem."

[53]Replaced at the end of the run by:

"On to Chicago" (Opening Chorus)
(*Music by* Gustave Kerker.)

[54]Dropped during the run.

[55]Dropped during the run.

[56]No musical numbers or specialties listed in programs. Also played return engagements 10 December 1894 at the Harlem Opera House for 4 performances in repertory; as FUN ON THE PACIFIC MAIL 28 March 1898 at the 14th Street Theatre for 8 performances.

[57]Musical numbers not listed in programs. List prepared from published piano vocal score (G. Schirmer, New York, 1894.

ACT 3

"Rising When the Dawn Is Gray" (Introduction and Chorus)
A. O'Keefe, Chorus

"Who Can Tell Where She Dwells?" (Chansonette and Duet)
B. Berthald, L. MacNichol

"Song of the Turnkey"
W. H. McLaughlin

"The Land of Romances" (Serenade)
R. F. Carroll, J. Herbert

"Rustic Song" (When the Lark is skyward)
W. Pruette, J. Corden, Chorus

Finale

1894.41 THE QUEEN OF BRILLIANTS

A Spectacular (Comic) Opera in Three Acts. American libretto by H. J. W. Dam, (revised from the English of Brandon Thomas). Adapted from the German of Theodore Taube and Isidor Fuchs. Music by Edward Jakobowski. Produced under the direction of Richard Barker. Settings by Hawes Craven, Joseph Harker and W. Perkins. Costumes by A. Comelli. Musical director, Paul Steindorff. Produced by Henry E. Abbey, John B. Schoeffel and Maurice Grau. Opened 7 November 1894 at Abbey's Theatre and closed 1 December 1894 after 29 performances.

CAST: *Florian Bauer*, a poor young architect from Vienna: HUBERT WILKE. *Della Fontana*, an Adventurer, Podesta of Borghovecchio, a Innkeeper, and Agent for Madame Engelstein's Matrimonial Agency, "The Temple of Hymen," at Vienna: DIGBY BELL. *Caprimonti (2)*: *Lucca Rabbiato*, an Itinerant Knife-Grinder: J. G. Taylor. *Grelotto*, Town Clerk of Borghovecchio: George Honey. *Colonel Victor Pulvereitzer* of the Imperial Guard: SIDNEY HOWARD. *Count Radaman Caprimonte*, Head of the Noble but Impecunious House of Caprimonte of Borghovecchio: Owen Westford. *Caprimonti (2)*: *Beppo*: Henry Parry. *Andrea*: George Mackenzie. *The Doctor*, Della Fontana's servant: Fowler Thatcher. *Fritz*, the Count's Servant: Wensley Thompson. *Don Garcia*, Client at Madame Engelstein's: Theo May. *Footman* at Madame Engelstein's: Spencer Kelly. A *Hackney Coachman*: James G. Peakes. *Head Gardener* at Betta's New Villa, Borghovecchio: George Fournier. *Madame Engelstein*, Proprietress of the celebrated Matrimonial Agency at Vienna, "The Temple of Hymen, " and Founder of the "Retreat of Peace" at Borghovecchio: LAURA JOYCE BELL. *Emma*, her daughter: Madge Greet. *Orsola*, Lucca' wife: Annie Meyers. *Mina*, the Serpent Charmer of Della Fontana's Troupe: Susanne Leonard. *Head Matron* at the "Retreat of Peace," Borghovecchio: Florence Doyne. *Betta*, also a Caprimonte, neglected and allowed to run wild, afterwards "Queen of Brilliants": LILLIAN RUSSELL. *Postillions, Citizens, Work-people, Fisher-boys and Girls, Matrons etc. at Borghovecchio, Clients, Engaged Couples, Servants, etc. at Madame Engelstein's, Soldiers, Gardeners, Acrobats, Clowns, Pages, Heralds, Footmen, Council, Students, etc.*

Act 1: Piazza at Borghovecchio. (Craven.)

Act 2: Madame Engelstein's "Temple of Hymen." (Harker.)

Act 3: Villa overlooking Harbour at Borghovecchio. (Perkins.)

MUSICAL NUMBERS[57a]

"Whisper, O Whisper Me, Soft in My Ears"
L. Russell

1894.42 THE BROWNIES

A Fairy Spectacle in Three Acts, 8 Scenes. Book (and lyrics) by Palmer Cox. (Based on his children's stories of the same name.) Music by Malcolm Douglas. Produced under the stage direction of Ben Teal. Ballets arranged by Charles Marwig. Settings by Charles Getz and J. W. Sommer. Costumes by Palmer Cox and Reginald Birch. Orchestrations and musical direction by Fred Perkins. Produced by C. B. Jefferson, (Marc) Klaw and (Abraham L.) Erlanger. Opened 12 November 1894 at the 14th Street Theatre and closed 2 February 1895 after 108 performances[58].

CAST: FAYS: *Queen Titania*, betrothed to Prince Florimel: MARY LOUISE DAY. *Dame Drusilda*, the Spinster Fairy: IDA MÜLLE. *Ladies in Waiting to the Queen (4)*: *Daffodil*: Maude Thompson. *Violet*: Louise Endicott. *Jasmine*: Georgie Denin. *Mignonette*: Florence Thornton. *Other Ladies in Waiting, Fairy Guards, Train Bearers, Attendants, etc.*

BROWNIES: *King Stanislaus*, Ruler of the Band: CHARLES H. DREW. *Prince Florimel*, heir apparent by adoption to the Brownie Throne: ALICE JOHNSON. *J. Chappie Goodforme*, leader of the Brownie 400: Eugene Sanger. *Count Ronaldo*, a Courtier: Grace Hamilton. *Inspector Clubbem*, the Brownie Police Department: Charles Hagan. *Tom Binnacle*, a Sailor tried and true: Frederick R. Runnells. *Reginald Mortarboard*, a University Man of Silence: A. W. MAFLIN. *King Stanislaus' International Standing Army (5)*: *Kraut von Bismarck*, German: Wallie Clark. *Sam Doodledoo*, American: Willis Pickert. *Paddy Whacker*, Irishman: Stephen Ferguson. *Li Lo*, Chinaman: Sydney Grant. *The Brownie Twins*: The Whippler Twins. *Ratovsky*, a Russian with a mission and a bomb: Tom Collins. *The German Band*: Snitz Edwards (leader), Messrs. Charles Drew, Fred Runnells, Wallie Clarke, G. F. Wright.

DEMONS: *Dragonfels*, an evil spirit: GEORGE L. BRODERICK. *Mangleplot*, prime minister: Frank Soule. *Beetlebore*:H. B. Meiggs. *Fatalfoe*: Frank Simons. *Mandrake*: William Brown. *Wolfinger*, Demon Usher: W. A. Kilrain. *Grouthead*: Joseph W. Smiley. *Boundingboor*: A. Seigrist. *Marvelous Demon Acrobats*: The (4) Famous Richards.

MYTHOLOGICAL CHARACTERS: *Euphrosyne*, Goddess of Mirth and Friend of the Brownies: Lee Lamar. *Neptune*, God of the Sea: W. A. Krone.

Act 1, Scene 1: Palace courtyard of Queen Titania in Festal Attire—Dual celebration of Titania's Wedding and Eve of May. *Scene 2*: Mountainous seacoast. *Scene 3*: The Open Sea with the Brownies adrift.

Act 2, Scene 1: The Enchanted Island of Dragonfel, with exterior view of Dragonfel's Castle. *Scene 2*: The Interior of Dragonfel's Castle. *Scene 3*: Earthquake with Volcanic Eruption.

Act 3, Scene 1: The Jeweled Mines of Dargonfel. *Scene 2*: A night in Brownieland, with Blossoming of the Moon Flower and Night-blooming Cereus.

MUSICAL NUMBERS, SPECIALTIES[59]

ACT 2

Scene 2

The Oriental Ballet of Beautiful Women (Act 2, Scene 2)
(*Music by* Fred Perkins.)

Newhouse & Waffle in "The Wandering Minstrels" (Act 2, Scene 2)

The World's Greatest Acrobats, the 4 Richards (Act 2, Scene 2)

The German Band (Act 2, Scene 2)

The Marvelous Flying Ballet (Act 3, Scene 2)

1894.43 A NIGHT AT THE CIRCUS

A Revival of the Circo-Comedy in Three Acts[60]. Play by H. Grattan Donnelly. Opened 19 November 1894 at Niblo's Garden and closed 24 November 1894 after 8 performances[61].

CAST: Acts 1 and 2: *Archibald Banger* of Friske and Banger: JOHN WEBSTER. *Nicholas Friske*, one of the (old) boys: Joe Dailey. *Signor Bonanza*, Manager of the Imperial Circus: J. H. Bradbury. *Pinkerton Kopp*, a private detective: Alf. Pearce. *Kicker*, an ambitious office boy: Billy Barry, Jr. *Dixey Weed*: Henry Zahner. *Bill Sticker*: H. B. Barnum. *Calliope Friske*, with an eye on everybody: Dorine Dymmock. *Belvidere Banger*, a jealous wife: Alice Pennoyer. *Remi Riter*, a Hammond operator: Jennie Jarboe. *Bud Manhattan*, a New York debutante: Rose Gautier. *Oriole Ogontz*, a Philadelphia Venus: May Taylor. *Ida Vassar*, a Boston beauty: Maud Taylor. *Socrates*, a Tiger: Snowball. *Twin Sisters (2)*: *Mlle. Electra*, queen of the arena: NELLIE McHENRY. *Mlle. Madeline Milan*, a visiting governess: NELLIE McHENRY.

Act 3: *The Ring Master*: J. H. Bradbury. *Rusty*: Billy Barry, Jr. *Snifty*: Alf. Pearce. *Pete Jenkins*, comic singer: JOHN WEBSTER. *The Wild Man of Borneo*: Joe Dailey. *Cannonball Tosser*: Henry Zahner. *Shouter*: H. B. Barnum. *Calliope Friske*, with an eye on everybody: Dorine Dymmock. *Belvidere Banger*, a jealous wife: Alice Pennoyer. *Empress of the Air*: Jennie Jarboe. *$10,000 Beauty*: Maud Taylor. *Bounding Jockey*: Rose Gautier. *The Equine Beauty*: Cupid. *Socrates*, a tiger: Snowball. *Queen of the Arena*: NELLIE McHENRY. *Nancy Brown*: NELLIE McHENRY. *Mlle. Malan*: NELLIE McHENRY.

[57a]No musical numbers listed in programs; no libretto or musical score found.

[58]Played a return engagement 19 April 1897 at the Grand Opera House for an additional 8 performances

[59]No musical numbers listed in programs; no libretto or musical score found. Mme. Nelson's Aerial Ballet added to the show 6 December 1894.

[60]Originally produced in New York 21 December 1891 at the Park Theatre for 9 performances; returned 21 March 1892 to the Bijou Theatre for an additional 32 performances.

[61]Later played return engagements 19 October 1896 at the Grand Opera House for 1 week, and 9 November 1896 at the Manhattan Theatre for 12 performances.

1894.44 THE SOUTH BEFORE THE WAR

A Picturesque Spectacle in One Act. Musical director, Professor Wagner. Produced by Whallen and Martell. Opened 19 November 1894 at the Bijou Theatre and closed 24 November 1894 after 8 performances[62].

CAST: *Old Eph Clawson*, with a family connection: CHARLES HOWARD. *Aunt Chloe*, mammy of them all: BILLY WILLIAMS. *Young Eph*: Fred Seville. *George Harrison*, a Planter: Mack Charles. *Miss Jennie Harrison*, the Planter's sister: Alice St. Clair. *Miss Irene Weller*, a visitor: Miss Josie Earl. *H. Stanley*, visitor at the Harrison Plantation: William Ferry. *George Edmonson*, a visitor: John Gardner. *Charles Baker*, a visitor: Sep Earl. *Squire Beck*: Joe Kelly. *Eliza*, the maid, with song: Eva Wooden. *Magnolia Blossom*: Pearl Woods. *Virginia Rosebud*: Pearl Woods. *Simpson Livermore*: Dashing Charlie. *Bob*, the Louisville wonder: H. Williams. *Zeke Blossom*, with song: Ed DeMoss. *The Lavenderville Trio*: Clark Brothers, George Moore. Grand Chorus of 50 Voices.

MUSICAL NUMBERS, SPECIALTIES[63]

Scene 1

Uncle Eph's Dream/Cotton Picking/Uncle Eph's Death

"(The) Days when I was young"
C. Howard

"Bile ole possum down"
C. Walker

"Slavery has passed away"
A. St. Claire

"Swanee River"
C. McClain

"Oaken Bucket"
H. Williams

"Climb up, children climb"
B. McLean

"Nancy Teel"

"Hard Times"

"Yellow Rose"

"Rosa Lee"

Scene 2

Grand Chorus of Fifty Voices

Scene 3

"Take Good Care of Mother" (Song)
Imperial Quartette

Scene 4

Kate Carter, the Dancing Wonder

Scene 5

"Wash Day on the Levee"
Beantown Comedy Quartette
Uncle Nat Fewclothes: Eugene Clark. *Aunt Nancy*, his wife: Charles Walker. *Simon Johnson*, the hot-corn man: Ben Hun. *George Washington*: George C. Moore.

Scene 6

Prize Buck and Wing Dancing
Katy Carter, Pearl Woods, Anna Scott, Lulu Cross, Lola Lanchmere, Grace Butner, Archie Kendall, Walter Esher, Annie Hubbard, Chattanoogas, Apes Doolittle, Japus Clark, Billy Caldwell.

Scene 7

Popular Selections
Lola Lanchmere (the Hawaiian Beauty)

Scene 8

Return to the Play, the Camp Meeting on Frog Island, introducing Ferry, the Frog, without an equal.
Deacon Sobersides, the man who runs the Camp Meeting, a free man: JAMES HALL. *Rev. Jonson Swiggs*, of Zion's Baptist Congregation: Charles Walker. *Zeke Blossom*, a real darkey: Billy McLean. *Brother Andrew Douglas*, of the government: Ben Hun. *Colonel Hezekiah Morocco*, of Ancient Africa: William Cottrell. *Ex-Chief Pluck* of Dahomey: Eugene Clark. *His Right Bower*: Dan Millar. *His Left Bower*: Henry C. Williams. *Brutus Jenkins*: Billy Farrell. *Salina Sassafras*, a Spanish type of beauty: Costella Chandler. *Georgianna Hessler*, from Old Virginia: Anna Hubbard. *Vine Hickleberry*, one of the F.F.V.'s: Katie Carter. *Anastasia Columbus*: Lola Lanchmere. *Bertie Mayflower*: Pearl Wood. *Clarissa Sweetbird*: Mrs. H. Williams. *Virgie Mountjoy*: Lulu Cross. *Chloe Mendoza*: Anna Scott. *Carrie Hipper*: Tichie Kendall. *Minor characters*.

Scene 9

The South Premier "3" Quartettes:
Buckingham Quartette; Dan Miller, Joe Chandler, H. Scott, Billy Caldwell.
Twilight Quartette: Joe Hodges, Billy Farrell, Lew Sheppard, A. D. Byrd
Standard Quartette: William Cottrell, Ed Demoss, H. C. Williams, R. L. Scott

Scene 10

Mammoth Cake Walk
100 Prize Cake Walkers

[62]Played two New York area engagements at the London Theatre, a variety house, for one week each, 27 March 1893 and 1 January 1894.
[63]No song list available with New York program. Musical numbers from Baltimore tryout November 1893.

1894.45 PRINCE ANANIAS

A Comic Opera in Two Acts. Libretto by Francis Neilson. Music by Victor Herbert. Produced under the stage direction of Jerome Sykes. Dances arranged by Signor Romeo. Settings by Ernest Albert. Costumes designed by Catherine F. Seidle. Musical director, Samuel L. Studley. Produced by the Bostonians (Henry Clay Barnabee, W. H. MacDonald, Proprietors). Opened 20 November 1894 at the Broadway Theatre and closed 12 January 1895 after 55 performances.

CAST: *Boniface*, King of Navarre: GEORGE B. FROTHINGHAM. *Cedric*, Duke d'Angers: William Castleman. *Killjoy*, Chamberlain to the King: Peter Lang. *Louis Biron*, (Prince Ananias) a vagabond poet and adventurer: W. H. MacDONALD. *George Le Grabbe*, an Outlaw: EUGENE COWLES. *La Fontaine*, manager of a band of strolling players: HENRY CLAY BARNABEE. *Eugene*, his assistant: JOSEPH SHEEHAN. *Jacques*, an innkeeper: James E. Miller. *Ivon*, a villager: Francis D. Boyle. *Felicie*, Countess of Pyrenées, sister to Killjoy: JOSEPHINE BARTLETT. *Mirabel*, daughter to Killjoy: MENA CLEARY. *Ninette*, a village belle: D. ELOISE MORGAN. *Idalia*, La Fontaine's leading lady: JESSIE BARTLETT DAVIS. *Lords, Ladies, Heralds, Pages, Halberdiers, Players, Villagers, Attendants, etc.*

Act 1: Exterior of an Inn.

Act 2: A Glade near the Palace of the King of Navarre.

ACT 1[64]

Introduction and Chorus

"Under an Oak" (Song)
E. Cowles

Lewis' Entrance (Chorus)

"Who Might You Be?" (Louis' song)
W. H. MacDonald

"It Needs No Poet" (Duet)
W. H. MacDonald, D. E. Morgan

Chorus
H. C. Barnabee, J. Sheehan, Players

"An Author-Manager Am I" (LaFontaine's song)
H. C. Barnabee

Scene and Chorus (When a maid applies for a part. .)
D. E. Morgan, H. C. Barnabee

"The Hamlet of Fancy" (Song)
J. B. Davis

"When I Was Born I Weighed Ten Stone" (Duet)
W. H. MacDonald, E. Cowles

"I Am No Queen" (Duet)
W. H. MacDonald, J. B. Davis

[64]Musical numbers not in programs. List prepared from published piano vocal score (E. Schuberth & Co., New York, 1894). Also performed as per published sheet music:
"The Time Will Come" (The Outlaw's Song)
E. Cowles
(*Music by* Eugene Cowles. *Lyrics by* Fred Dixon.)

Finale (Farewell provincial towns; Ah! He's a Prince)

ACT 2

"Amaryllis"
J. B. Davis, Chorus

"Ah! Cupid, Meddlesome Boy! Good bye!" (Song)
J. Sheehan

Duo (I thought it very easy to sit down and write a play)
J. Sheehan, H. C. Barnabee, Male Chorus

"Ah! List to Me" (Quintette)
D. E. Morgan, J. B. Davis, J. Sheehan, W. H. MacDonald, E. Cowles

"Love Ne'er Came Nigh" (Song)
E. Cowles

Quartette (Now Herodotus omits . . . .)
P. Lang, H. C. Barnabee, W. H. MacDonald, E. Cowles

"Titled Widows All Are We"
D. E. Morgan, Court Ladies

Entrance of the King

"A Regal Sadness Sits on Me" (Song)
G. B. Frothingham

"Love Is Spring" (Song)
J. B. Davis

Song (A large expansive smile)
W. H. MacDonald, Chorus

Finale

1894.46 THE FLAMS

A Musical Farce Comedy in Three Acts. Book, (new) music and lyrics by Harry Paulton and Edward Paulton. Stage director, H. S. Millward. Manager, W. D. Mann. Settings by Homer F. Emens. Musical director, William P. Brown. Produced by William F. Hoey. Opened 26 November 1894 at the Bijou Theatre and closed 22 December 1894 after 32 performances[65].

CAST: *Corilanus Flam*: JOHN C. RICE. *Jacob Van Kopf*: MATT C. WOODWARD. *Lally Darryl*: George W. Howard. *Minnington Muff*: Charles Renwick. *Lord Parapet*: John Cushman. *Duke of Dumblane*: Charles French, Jr. *Conrad*: George O'Donnell. *Baggage*: Charles Gardner. *Aunt Jane*: LILLIE ALLISTON. *Eva Van Kopf*: JESSIE MERRILEES. *Mamie Van Kopf*: CHERIDAH SIMPSON. *Miss Prunes*: Nina Norman. *Miss Quirk*: Rita Emerson. *Miss White*: Carrie Merrilees. *Miss Black*: Edith Merrilees. *Marmaduke Flam*: WILLIAM F. HOEY. (*Dance Specialty*: Master Willie Hersey.)

Act 1: Van Kopf's Drawing Room.

Act 2: Garden and Terrace at Van Kopf's Summer Villa.

Act 3: Reception Room in Van Kopf's House.

ACT 1

Piano Solo
C. Simpson

"Ours Is a Happy Little Home"
W. Hoey
(*Music by* Harry Randall. *Lyrics by* J. W. Sewell.)

ACT 2

Instrumental Solos
W. Hoey

"The Man Who Broke the Bank at Monte Carlo"
W. Hoey
(*Music and Lyrics by* Fred Gilbert.)

"The Naughty Continong"
Sisters Merrilees

"I Don't Want to Play in Your Yard"[66]
C. Simpson
(*Music by* H. W. Petrie. *Lyrics by* Philip Wingate.)

"Ah Me!" (Quinette)
G. W. Howard, C. Renwick, G. O'Donnell, C. Simpson, J. Merrilees
(*Music and Lyrics by* William P. Brown.)

Eccentric Dancing
Master W. Hersey

"(I'm a) Dandy Colored Coon" (The Dandy Coon)
W. Hoey, Company
(*Music by* George Le Brunn. *Lyrics by* Richard Norton.)

"Days of Long Ago"[67]
C. Renwick

Pas de Deux
J. C. Rice, C. Merrilees

"(Private) Tommy Atkins"
W. Hoey, Company
(*Music* by S. Potter. *Lyrics by* Henry Hamilton.)

ACT 3[68]

Boating Song
Company
(*Music and Lyrics by* William P. Brown.)

Love in All Dialects (*by* Matt. C. Woodward)
J. C. Rice

Bagpipe Solos
W. Hoey

Finale
Company

1894.47 JACINTA, or, The Maid of Manzanillo

A Mexican Comic Opera in Two Acts. Libretto by William H. Lepere. Music by Alfred G. Robyn. Produced under the stage direction of Max Freeman. Manzanillo Ballet arranged by Signor A. Francioli. Scenery by D. Frank Dodge. Costumes by Simpson, Crawford & Simpson. Musical director, Herman Perlet. Produced by the Louise Beaudet Opera Bouffe Company (Fred C. Whitney, Director). Opened 26 November 1894 at the Harry C. Miner's Fifth Avenue Theatre and closed 9 December 1894 after 15 performances.

CAST: *Jacinta*, loved by one too many: LOUISE BEAUDET. *Blanca*, daughter of Delgardo: CECILE EISSING. *Inez*, Jacinta's aunt: JENNIE REIFFARTH. *Delgardo*, Alcalde of Colima: EDWIN STEVENS. *Metepec*, censor of morals (not Delgardo's): Harry Brown. *Miguel*, a Captain of State Guards, in love with Blanca: STUART HAROLD. *Romaldo*, a townsman: W. S. Johns. *Panilla, Paloma*, fascinating girls: Aileen Burke, Marienne Convere. *Morrelos*, a naval commander, who is in love with Jacinta: SIGNOR PERUGINI [Jack Chatterton]. *Chorus of Guards, Sailors and Townspeople*.

Act 1: The Plaza of Manzanillo.

Act 2: The Garrison of Alcalde at Colima.

ACT 1[69]

"Viva! Let Us Treasure" (Opening Chorus)

"Our Ship Was as Taut as a Vessel Can Be"

---

[65]Later played return engagements 24 December 1894 at the Harlem Opera House for 8 performances, 4 February 1895 at the Grand Opera House for 8 performances, 4 March 1895 at the Columbus Theatre for 8 performances, and 25 March 1895 at the 14th Street Theatre for 8 performances.

[66]Replaced for subsequent tour by:
"For Ever and For Aye"
C. Simpson
(*Music and Lyrics by* Harry French.)

[67]Replaced for subsequent tour by:
"The Clang of the Forge"
John T. McGurn
(*Music and Lyrics by* Paul Rodney.)

[68]Program note: A series of Burlesque Living Pictures will be introduced in this act.

[69]Musical numbers not listed in programs. List prepared from St. Louis tryout dated May 1893.

"No More, No More to Part Forever" (Duet)
Entrance of Delgardo, Blanca, Metepec
"By Way of Explanation" (Trio)
"A Soldier Scarcely Ever Feels" (Duet)
"We Were Taught to Walk Demurely"
"Tell Him, Rose, That I'll Return" (Solo)
"Whist! Sweet Idle Moon" (Duet)
"Long Life with Crosses Few" (Finale)

ACT 2
"O Moonlight" (Female Chorus)
"Alas! How Sad My Fate" (Recitative and Solo)
"What, Ho! Guards Within"
"Near Him at Last" (Solo)
"Doubting Heart Thou Art To-day" (Solo)
"Ever Ready" (Chorus)
"Two Lovers Once Wooed the Same Maiden" (Recitative and Solo with Chorus)
"The Manzanillo" (Grand Dance)
"Love's a Most Exacting Master" (Trio)
"Morelos, Hail" (Finale)

1894.48 THE GRAND DUCHESS

A Revival of the Opera Bouffe in Three Acts, 4 Scenes[70]. English libretto by Charles Lamb Kenney and Edgar Smith. (Adapted from the original French by Henri Meilhac and Ludovic Halévy.) Music by Jacques Offenbach. Produced under the stage direction of Richard Barker. Scenic artist, Henry E. Hoyt. Costumes by Dazian. Musical director, Paul Steindorff. Produced by the Lillian Russell Comic Opera Company (Messrs. Henry E. Abbey, John B. Schoeffel and Maurice Grau, Managers). Opened 5 December 1894 at Abbey's Theatre and closed 22 December 1894 after 19 performances.

CAST: *Fritz*: HUBERT WILKE. *Baron Puck*: DIGBY BELL. *General Boum*: HALLEN MOSTYN. *Prince Paul*: Sidney Howard. *Baron Grog*: OWEN WESTFORD. *Népomuc*: George Honey. *Wanda*: Annie Myers. *Iza*: Susanne Leonard. *Olga*: Ada Dare. *The Grand Duchess*: LILLIAN RUSSELL. *Peasants, Soldiers, Vivandieres, Courtladies, Pages, Maids of Honor, Servants.*

1894.49 NOTORIETY

A Play with Songs in Three Acts, 5 Scenes. Play by Edward Harrigan. Music by David Braham. (Staged by Edward Harrigan.) Settings by D. Frank Dodge. Mechanical effects by Steve Simmons. Properties by Louis Filber. Electrical effects by John Whalen. (Musical director, David Braham.) Produced by Edward Harrigan. Opened 10 December 1894 at Harrigan's Theatre and closed 2 February 1895 after 64 performances.

CAST: *Barney Dolan* of Dolan's Road House: EDWARD HARRIGAN. *Mealy Moon*, Trainer of Pugilists: JOHN WILD. *Lida Bugbear*, France Medjum: JOSEPH SPARKS. *Frederick Hoffman*, millionaire: HARRY FISHER. *Carlos Cassidy*, Rent Collector: Charles F. McCarthy. *Paddy Malone*, Landscape gardener: George Merritt. *Ollie Montague*, from London: Harry Wright. *Dr. Charles Atwater*, known as Rainbow Charley: Edward Harrigan, Jr. *Barnum Brock*, of the Burnt Rag: William West. *Gilligan*, an Old Performer: Dan Burke. *Con Conover*, a nice con: Charles Coffey. *Linda Linseed*, Typewriter: DAVID BRAHAM, JR. *Marjary Humphreys*, from Sing Sing: James McCullough. *Leander Larkins*, Dramatic Coach: John Bennan. *Kinks*, of the Burnt Rag: James Burke. *Granny Doyle*, of Cherry Hill: John Mayon. *Horseshoer Mike*, an old neighbor: John Flynn. *Bat Kelly*, a Middle-weight: Ed Murphy. *Mr. Raynor*, Attorney: Edward Gorman. *Arimita Atwater* of the Mission: Hattie Moore. *Frankie Hoffman*, a girl up to date: QUEENIE VASSAR. *Bessie Dolan*, of Dolan's Road House: Emma Pollock. *Melancholy Mary*, of the Slums: Vivian Bernard. *Lillie Lulu*, Comic Opera favorite: Ray Briscoe. *Mamie Kelly*, of the Burnt Rag: Lillian Stewart. *Cora Conners*, of the Burnt Rag: Cora Marsh. *Lilly Looney*, of the Burnt Rag: Marger Teal. *Ida Simmons*, of the Burnt Rag: Miss Thomas. *Molly Malone*, dealer in junk, horses and stocks: ANNIE YEAMANS.

Act 1: Dolan's Road House.

Act 2, Scene 1: A Parlor at Hotel Brewster. The Tally Ho! *Scene 2*: Street in the 19th Precinct. *Scene 3*: The Burt Rag. Yale and Princeton painting the town.

Act 3: Lawn at the Malone Villa. Open air performance of "As You Like It."

ACT 1
"The Girl That's Up to Date"
(Q. Vassar)
"The Old Neighborhood"
(E. Harrigan)

ACT 2
Scene 1
"The Tally Ho (Song)"
Scene 3
"Melancholy Mary"
(V. Bernard)
"Out on a College Rah! Rah!"
(H. Wright)
"Up in the Tenderloin"

1894.50 THE SIDE SHOW

A Comedy in Three Acts. Play by George C. Jenks. Opened 17 December 1894 at Niblo's Garden and closed 22 December 1894 after 8 performances.[71]

CAST: *Grimes* (Grimesey, My Boy), a fly kid, with lots of fun on his hands: JAMES B. MACKIE. *Smiley Sharpe*, with the Pentucket Hotel on his hands: George H. Turner. *Pullemin Shooter*, with half the Side Show and a lot of kicking freaks on his hands: W. H. Trueheart. *Wright in the Push* with the other half of The Side Show and its troubles on his hands: Tony Kennedy. *Weary Walker*, with plenty of leisure and a perpetual thirst on his hands: Waldo Whipple. *Rural Sage*, with the dignity of the town on his hands: John T. Hanson. *Dora Spofford*, with all the work of the hotel on her hands: KITTIE GILMORE. *Four Maidens from Boston with an engagement in the Side Show on their hands*: *Eulalia*: Helen Russell. *Bettina*: LAURA ASHBY. *Meena*: Sadie Spencer. *Leila*: Maude Winston. *Penelope*, with a parachute leap and the plot of the play on her hands: LOUISE SANFORD. (*Circus Specialty*: Marba and Massord, world-famous acrobats and whirlwind dancers.) *Patrons of the Side Show, Guests of the Hotel, Freaks, Acrobats, Animals, Musicans, Drummers, Mashers, Jays, Tramps, Salvation Army, etc.*

Act 1: Office of Pentucket Hotel, Georgetown, Massachusetts. Arrival of guests, Side Show Fakirs, and Summer Boarders from Boston.

Act 2: Exterior of Circus and Side Show, showing the exterior of Pentucket Hotel. Balloon Ascension and Parachute Leap. A Regular Circus Day.

Act 3: Interior of Side Show. Freaks on a strike. Introducing regular legitimate circus acts, such as Equilibrists, Wire Walkers, and Burlesque Riding Act on the educated horse, "Sot."

ACT 1
"Billy Jones"
J. B. Mackie
"Somebody Loves Me"
K. Gilmore
(*Music and Lyrics by* Hattie Starr.)
"The Engagement Ring"
K. Gilmore

ACT 2
"The Side Show"
J. B. Mackie
Eccentric Yankee and Singing and Dancing Specialty
J. T. Hanson
"New March"
K. Gilmore, H. Russell, L. Ashby

[70]First produced in New York in French 24 September 1867 at the Théâtre Français for 156 performances in repertory. With Lillian Russell starred, this version was first performed in New York 25 February 1890 at the Casino Theatre for 100 performances. For Synopsis of Scenes and Musical Numbers, see 1890 production.

[71]No other credits in program.

Salvation Army Company

Knock-about Song and Dance
W. H. Trueheart, T. Kennedy

Doll Dance
Misses Sanford, Gilmore, Russell, Ashby

Medley
Company

Original Specialty
Misses Spencer, Winston

Specialty
N. Litchfield

ACT 3

"The Bowery Girls"
Misses Sanford, Gilmore, Russell, Ashby
(*Music by* Belle Stewart. *Lyrics by* William Jerome.)

Nix and Nixie (the two brainiest men in the world)

Centipede Dance
Misses Russell, Gilmore

Parodies
J. B. Mackie

Chang, the Chinese Giant
Messrs. Turner, Hanson

Buck and Wing Dancing
W. Whipple

The Great Equilibrist
L. Ashby

Specialty
L. Sanford

Burlesque Circus

Finale
Company

1894.51 McFADDEN'S ELOPEMENT

A Farce Comedy in Three Acts. Play by Frank Dumont. Produced by Thomas H. Davis and William T. Keough. Opened 31 December 1894 at Jacobs' (Third Avenue) Theatre and closed 5 January 1895 after 9 performances.[72]

CAST: *Con McFadden*, always looking for the best of it, but often getting the worst of it: JOHN KERNELL. *Colonel Willie Drew*, who has the misfortune to be McFadden's partner: PHIL PETERS. *Rush Hulick*, who can invent anything but an invention that will work: Dan Waldron. *Charles Dusenbory*, a promising young drug clerk: George F. Hall. *Richard Croker, Pat Sheedy*, tourists who travel when walking is good: Mort Emerson, Charles Emmonds. *Lawyer McTavish*, a product of rural circumstances: Seymour Rice. *Cinders*, a cuning young creature: Nettie Peters. *Tillie Hulick*, a romantic young creature: Emily Vivian. *Mabel Cash*, a young creature from the handkerchief counter: Clara Knott. *Martha Primrose*, who has seen several summers: Julia Emmonds. *Mrs. Rush Hulick*, the head of the Hulick family: Tillie Barnum.

Act 1: The Hulick Farm near New York.

Act 2: Colonel Willie Drew's Flat in New York.

Act 3: Hulick's New Country House and Miss Primrose's Female Seminary.

ACT 1

"I Was Talking in My Sleep"
M. Emerson, C. Emmonds

"Two Old Sports"
M. Emerson, C. Emmonds

"I Did"
M. Emerson, C. Emmonds

"And Her Golden Hair Was Hanging Down Her Back"
N. Peters
(*Music by* Felix McGlennon. *Lyrics by* Monroe H. Rosenfeld.)

A few melodies
J. Kernell, P. Peters

ACT 2

"The Summer Man"
G. F. Hall

Imitations
G. F. Hall

"The Girl I Would Have Left Behind"
D. Waldron

"The Magic Frame"
D. Waldron

"The Popular Airs"
Company

ACT 3

"Nothing Too Good for the Irish"
J. Kernell

"I'm Going to be a Conductor"
J. Kernell

"Round the Operas"
P. Peters, N. Peters

"It's a Good Thing, Push It Along"
Company

1894.52 THE OLD HOMESTEAD

A Revival of the Rural Melodrama in Four Acts[73]. Play by Denman Thompson and George W. Ryer. (Staged by Denman Thompson.) Scenic artist, Homer F. Emens. Musical director, H. Braham. Organist, Fred Rycroft. Manager, Frank Thompson. Opened 31 December 1894 at the Star Theatre and closed 27 April 1895 after 136 performances[74].

CAST: Act 1: *Joshua Whitcomb*: DENMAN THOMPSON. *Cy Prime*: WILL M. CRESSY *Happy Jack*: WALTER GALE. *Frank Hopkins*: WALTER BUBIER. *Eb. Ganzey*: J. L. MORGAN. *John Freeman*: FRANK KNAPP. *Aunt Matilda Whitcomb*, Joshua's sister: LOUISA MORSE. *Rickety Ann*: ANNIE THOMPSON. *Miss Annie Hopkins*: Lillian Stone. *Nellie Freeman*: Bertha M. Silsby. *Maggie O'Flaherty*: Minnie Luckstone. *The Old Homestead Double Quartette*: RICHARD J. JOSÉ, FRED RYCROFT, JOHN H. DAVIS, STEPHEN BAKER, THOMAS LEWIS, R. E. ROGERS, FRED CLARE, H. W. FRILLMAN. Act 2: *Henry Hopkins*: G. H. BARTON. *Judge Patterson*: H. W. Frillman. *François Fogarty*: Frank Mara. *Mrs. Henry Hopkins*: Annie Thompson. *Nellie Patterson*: Lena N. Jones. Act 3: *Jack Hazzard*: Walter Gale. *Reuben Whitcomb*, Joshua's son: THOMAS LEWIS. *Hoboken Terror*: J. L. Morgan. *One of the Finest*: R. E. Rogers. *U. S. Letter Carrier*: Frank Kanpp. *Mrs. McGuire*: Lizzie Farrell. Act 4: *Seth Perkins*: Charles H. Clark. *Len Holbrook, Warren Ellis*, Country Fiddlers: C. M. Richardson, P. Redmond. *Pat Clancy*: Frank Mara. *Mrs. Murdock*: Marie Kimball. *The Three Stratton Gals*: Misses Luckstone, Silsby, Farrell.

SPECIALTIES

Old Homestead Double Quartette (Act 1)

"The Midnight Fire Alarm" (Act 2)
H. W. Frillman

"The Psalms" (Act 3)
T. Clifford
(*Music by* Jean Baptiste Faure.)

"Day After Day" (Act 4)
R. J. José, Old Homestead Quartette
(*Music by* John St. George. *Lyrics by* Richard J. José.)

---

[72]No stage director, scenery, costumes or musical director credited.

[73]First produced in New York 10 January 1887 at the 14th Street Theatre for 155 performances. For Synopsis of Scenes, see original 1887 production.

[74]THE OLD HOMESTEAD was joined by Denman Thompson's "Songs Illustrated and Illuminated" for Wednesday matinees and Sunday matinees. THE OLD HOMESTEAD later played return engagements in New York 6 January 1897 at the Harlem Opera House for 1 week, 18 October 1897 at the Academy of Music for 40 performances, 15 August 1898 at the Academy of Music for 48 performances, 21 November 1898 at the Harlem Opera House for 1 week, and 27 March 1899 at the Academy of Music for 48 performances.

1895.01

ROBIN HOOD

A Revival of the Comic Opera in Three Acts[75]. Libretto by Harry B. Smith. Music by Reginald DeKoven. Produced under the stage direction of Jerome Sykes. Dances arranged by Signor Romeo. Scenery by Ernest Albert. Costumes designed by Catherine F. Seidle. Musical director, Samuel L. Studley. Produced by the Bostonians (Henry Clay Barnabee and W. H. MacDonald, Proprietors and Managers). Opened 10 January 1895 at the Broadway Theatre and closed 12 January 1895 after 4 performances[76].

CAST: *Sheriff of Nottingham*: HENRY CLAY BARNABEE. *Robin Hood*: JOSEPH SHEEHAN. *Little John*: CHARLES R. HAWLEY. *Will Scarlet*: EUGENE COWLES. *Alan-a-Dale*: JESSIE BARTLETT DAVIS. *Friar Tuck*: GEORGE FROTHINGHAM. *Guy of Gisborne*: Peter Lang. *Maid Marian*: CAROLINE HAMILTON. *Dame Durden*: JOSEPHINE BARTLETT. *Annabel*: Mena Cleary.

1895.02

A RUN ON THE BANK

A Farce Comedy in Three Acts. Play by Charles E. Blaney. Incidental music composed and arranged by Maurice Levi. Musical director, Maurice Levi. Tour directed (produced) by E. D. Stair. Opened 14 January 1895 at the Bijou Theatre and closed 19 January 1895 after 8 performances[77].

CAST: *Lord Percy Soakup, Baron Harold DeCanter*, Gentlemen of unlimited nerve and experience: "HAPPY" WARD, HARRY VOKES. *Bow Legs*, crooked by nature: HARRY CLAY BLANEY. *General Note Shaver*, a banker to bank on: Tony Williams. *Ready Money*, a bank runner: Sid DeGray. *His Most*, a dynamiter: Sid DeGray. *Willie Chase*, one of Pinkerton's best: Alfred Grant. *Coonie Acker*, a counterfeiter: Alfred Grant. *Con Man*, a gentleman of leisure: Charles Jerome. *Barley Corn*, a rustic: Joe Russell. *Bill Booze*, a bar fly: Joe Russell. *Eagle Eye*, a blind man: T. Wilmot Eckert. *Adam Shame*, a depositor: T. Wilmot Eckert. *Clubs R. Trumps*, a policeman: T. Wilmot Eckert. *Lager Hops*, a brewer: T. Wilmot Eckert. *Nera Man*, a female book agent: Gilberti Learock. *Estelle Shaver, Belle Shaver*, the Banker's daughters: MARGUERITE DALY VOKES, INEZ RAE. *Hasty Writer*, a private secretary: Clara Belle. *Sassy Moll*, a tough girl: MARGUERITE DALY VOKES. *Minnie Apolis, Carrie Romance, Grace Church*, friends of the family: Emma Berg, Starra Kimball, Daisy Dudley.

Act 1: Home of General Note Shaver in the suburbs.

Act 2: The Percy and Harold Bank.

Act 3: Parlor off of Ballroom in Palace Hotel, San Francisco.

ACT 1

"Tell Me, Ruby, Will You Be True"
Ladies

"Airy Fairy Lillian"
(*Music by* Maurice Levi. *Lyrics by* Tony Raymond.)/
"Poor Little Mary"/

"Her Eyes Don't Shine Like Diamonds" (from A TRIP TO CHINATOWN)
S. DeGray
(*Music and Lyrics by* David Marion.)

Original Specialty
H. C. Blaney

Parodies
C. Jerome

"Linger Longer Loo" (from *DON JUAN*, London)
(*Music by* Sidney Jones.)/

"Di, Di, Di" (from GO-BANG, London)
Ladies
(*Music by* F. Osmond Carr. *Lyrics by* Adrian Ross.)

"The Man That Stole My Luncheon"
Gentlemen

"Amateur Circus"
Company

ACT 2

"The Bulls and Bears"

ACT 3

Duets from Famous Operas and Popular Selections
T. W. Eckert, E. Berg

Specialty (Percy and Harold)
Ward and Vokes

Demon Dance
Misses Daly, Belle

Imitations
A. Grant

"Hush Yo' Business, Oh! Go On"
Ward and Vokes, Company

1895.03

OFF THE EARTH

A Fantastic Operatic Travesty in Three Acts, 5 Scenes. (Libretto) Written and composed by John D. Gilbert. Music arranged and ensemble music composed by Fred J. Eustis. Produced under the direction of Gerald Coventry. Dances arranged by Harry Barnes. Settings by Frank E. Gates and Edward A. Morange, (Ernest Albert). Costumes designed by Wilhelm, London. Dance music written by Harry Barnes. Musical director, Fred J. Eustis. Produced by the American Travesty Company (Alexander Davidson, Manager; George Bowles, Business Manager). Opened 21 January 1895 at the Harlem Opera House and closed 26 January 1895 after 8 performances.

CAST: *Prince Charles*, an up-to-date young man: LOUISE MONTAGUE. *Dimples*, with a fad: SADIE McDONALD. *Gavotte*, wants to be the heroine of a fairy tale: LILLIAN HAWTHORNE. *Luna*, queen of the moon: KATE UART. *Queen Dowager*: Lola Hawthorne. *Patience Waite*: Helen Douglas. *Annie Howe*: Edna Thornton. *Charity Hopp*: Vivian Rossiter. *Stag Party*, a merchant prince: H. W. TREDNICK. *Hart Burns*: Joseph Doner. *The Jailer*: Joseph Doner. *Pepperal*: Henry Carter. *Prime Minister Toadstool*: Henry Carter. *Polka Dot*: George C. Cheeney. *Eli Getz*: Charles Johnson. *Philip Tank*: William Morgan. *A Lion*: George Ali. *A Parrot*: Charles Beni. *Porter*: (Master) Charles Sweeney. *Cluster*: EDDIE FOY. *Coryphées*: Misses Mordecai, Doyle, Lennox, Hartley.

Act 1, Scene 1: The Bazaar of Wonders. (Albert.) *Scene 2*: Cloudland. (Gates and Morange.)

Act 2: The Fairy Forest of Phosphorescent Fughi. (Gates and Morange.)

Act 3, Scene 1: The Moon by Earth Light. (Gates and Morange.) *Scene 2*: Luna's Regal Palace. (Gates and Morange.)

ACT 1

"We Want Our Money Back"
Chorus

"India Rubber Shoes" (Chorus and Tableaux)
(from *LITTLE CHRISTOPHER COLUMBUS*)
(*Music by* Ivan Caryll.)

"Hither He Comes" (Chorus)

"La Favorita" (Song)
L. Montague

"Girl Wanted" (Song)
E. Foy

"Physical Culture Girls" (Song)
S. McDonald

"The Rainbow" (Song)
Lillian Hawthorne, Chorus

"Truscalina Brown" (Song)
E. Foy

Tableau

ACT 2

"Listen While I Tell You" (Recitative and Gavotte)
K. Uart, Fairies

"Still His Whiskers Grew" (Song)
E. Foy

"That Funny Feeling" (Song)
E. Foy

---

[75]Originally presented in New York 28 September 1891 at the Standard Theatre for 35 performances, returning that season to the Garden Theatres for 42 additional performances. For Synopsis of Scenes and Musical Numbers, see original 1891 production.

[76]This touring revival also played 25 May 1896 at the Harlem Opera House for 1 week.

[77]Also played return engagements 25 March 1895 at the Columbus Theatre for 8 performances, and 23 March 1896 at the Grand Opera House for 8 performances.

"I Spy Little Girl" (Song)
L. Montague

"(I Shall) Die, Die, Die" (Duet) (from *GO-BANG*, London)
E. Foy, S. McDonald
(*Music by* F. Osmond Carr. *Lyrics by* Adrian Ross.)

Grand Operatic Finale

ACT 3

"We're in Love with Dainty, Fair Gavotte" (Song)
Lunar Chappies

The Wiener Schnitzel Band

"They're Waiting for Me" (Song)
E. Foy

"La Frolique" (Grand fête scene and dance)

1895.04

THE 20TH CENTURY GIRL

A Burletta (Musical Comedy) in Three Acts. Libretto by Sydney Rosenfeld. Music by Ludwig Engländer. Produced under the stage direction of Richard Barker. Ballet master, Signor Francioli. Settings by D. Frank Dodge. Costumes designed by Catherine Siedle. Musical conductor, Selli Simonson. Produced by Thomas Canary and George W. Lederer. Opened 25 January 1895 at the Bijou Theatre and closed 23 February 1895 after 35 performances; re-opened in a revised version[78] 6 May 1895 at the Bijou Theatre and closed 11 May 1895 after 8 additional performances. Total: 43 performances[79].

CAST: *Mr. Michael MacNamara*, a man of vast political "inflooence"—in fact, a tower of strength: JOHN T. KELLY. *Nick Weddle*, his Managing Man, and most everything else: SIDNEY DREW. *Judson Dinglewort*, an American country gentleman: EDWIN STEVENS. *Paul Whiffletree*, his secretary: Archie Crawford. *Professor August Hermann Karl von Bilderbogen*: AL H. WILSON. *Geoffrey*, a college student: William Lavine. *Shrimps*, Dinglewort's valet: Harry Kelly. *Messenger*: Harry Kelly. *Newsboy*: Harry Kelly. *Ginger*: Samuel Fisher. *Percy Verance*, the Girl-Bachelor: HELEN DAUVRAY. *Seminary Girls (6)*: *Molly*: Minnie Landes. *Rose*: Edith Howe. *Grace*: Cissie Fitzgerald. *Ethel*: Nina Farrington. *Flo*: Helen Marlborough. *Bess*: Crissie Carlyle. *Mrs. Potts*, Principal of the aforesaid Seminay: JENNIE WEATHERSBY. *Students, Athletes, Members of the Country Club, Girl Bachelors, Cadets, Fairies, Citizens, etc.*

Act 1: The Dinglewort Lawn.

Act 2: Interior of the Dinglewort Mansion.

Act 3: River View of the above.

MUSICAL NUMBERS[80]

"The Play's the Thing"

"The Ambitious Magpie"

"Beyond the Seas"

"(Oh, Where Is) The Antidote"

"I Love You" (Duet)

"Words That Were Never Spoken"

"Pearl of the Heart"

"On Broadway"
H. Vauvray

"(Song of) The Twentieth Century Girl"

"MacNamara"

"Dorothy Drew"[81]
Conchita
(*Music by* Claude Perrier. *Lyrics by* Charles Willis.)

1895.05

THE MAJOR

A (Revised Version of the) Farce with Songs in Three Acts, 7 Scenes[82]. Play and lyrics by Edward Harrigan. Music by David Braham. Scenery designed by D. Frank Dodge. Produced by Edward Harrigan. Opened 9 February 1895 at Harrigan's Theatre and closed 9 March 1895 after 33 performances.

CAST: *Major Gilfeather*: EDWARD HARRIGAN. *Phineas Bottlegreen*: JOHN WILD. *Mike Gillespie*: JOSEPH SPARKS. *Herman Backheister*: HARRY A. FISHER. *Ellen Murphy*: Charles F. McCarthy. *Henry Higgins*: HARRY WRIGHT. *Percival Popp*: GEORGE MERRITT. *Granville Bright*: EDWARD HARRIGAN, JR. *Mr. Welt*: Charles Scott. *Harriet Jenkins*: Dave Braham, Jr. *Caleb Jenkins*: James McCullough. *Aunty Green*: James Burke. *Mr. Shroud*: William West. *Ellen Green*: John Mayon. *Mr. Grab*: John Flynn. *Spotem*: W. B. Gunning. *Mrs. Harriet Pinch*: Hattie Moore. *Henrietta*: Jessie Wyatt. *Amelia Bright*: Emma Pollock. *Stella Stone*: Lillian Stewart. *Miss Miranda Briggs*: ANNIE YEAMANS.

Act 1, Scene 1: Dock of the Cunard Line. *Scene 2*: Exterior of Boarding House. *Scene 3*: Parlor at Miss Biggs'.

Act 2, Scene 1: Jenkins' Policy Office, 4-11-44. *Scene 2*: Corridor and Cells of Prison. *Scene 3*: House Tops.

Act 3: Parlor at Miss Biggs'. Room six.

MUSICAL NUMBERS

"Major Gilfeather"

"I Really Can't Sit Down"

"Miranda, When We Are Made One"

"4-11-44"

1895.06

MADELEINE, or, The Magic Kiss

A Comic Opera in Three Acts. Libretto by Stanislaus Stange. Music by Julian Edwards. Produced under the stage direction of Max Freeman. Musical director, Julian Edwards. Produced by Camille D'Arville (Thomas Canary, George W. Lederer, Managers). Opened 25 February 1895 at the Bijou Theatre and closed 4 May 1895 after 80 performances[83].

CAST: *The Baron de Grimm*: AUBREY BOUCICAULT. *Dr. Gourmet*, his physician: George C. Boniface, Jr. *Frederi Ribeau*, an Alsatian artist: J. K. Murray. *Frederi*, the Baron's steward: H. M. Ravenscroft. *Jules*, his scribe: Henry A. Stanley. *Mary Doodle*, a Sextuple Widow: MARIE DRESSLER. *Margot*, *Vivette*, Dr. Gourmet's daughters: Hilda Hollins, Maud Hollins. *Madeleine*, the Baron's Ward: CAMILLE D'ARVILLE. *People of the Village of D'Amour.*

The action takes place in the Village of D'Amour, Normandy, on 15 June 1794.

Act 1: Gardens of the Chateau D'Amour. The Festival of Roses. The Baron's Hundredth Birthday. The Legend of Grimm. The Betrothal. The First Kiss.

Act 2: Main Hall of the Chateau D'Amour. The Second Kiss. The Marriage. The Third Kiss.

Act 3: Same as Act 1. The Legend Fulfilled.

MUSICAL NUMBERS[84]

"The Kiss of Love"

"Heart, Foolish Heart"

---

[78]Principal cast changes for the return engagement: *Judson Dingleowrth*: DAN DALY. *Private Hoolihan*, MacNamara's Guard (new character): CHRISTINE BLESSING. *Ginger*: Harry Standish. *Percy Verance*: MOLLY FULLER. *Mrs. Potts*: CHRISTINE BLESSING.

[79]This production was further revised into Two Acts starring Conchita, John T. Kelly, Harry Kelly, William Cameron, Thomas Lewis, Gus Williams, Maurice Evans and Georgia Hawley, and presented on tour under the auspices of Frederick Hallen. Musical director, Arthur C. Pell. It played New York area return engagements 20 May 1895 at the Harlem Opera House for 8 performances, 30 September 1895 at the Grand Opera House for 8 performances, and 30 December 1895 at the 14th Street Theatre for 8 performances.

[80]Musical numbers not listed in programs. List prepared from published piano vocal selections, not in performance order.

[81]Interpolation for return engagement.

[82]First produced in New York 29 August 1881 at the Theatre Comique for 152 performances. The cast list and song list indicate substantial changes to the original script were made; dropped from the original production were "Clara Jenkins' Tea" and "The Veteran Guards Cadets."

[83]Later played return engagements 6 May 1895 at the Harlem Opera House for 8 performances, and 6 June 1898 at the American Theatre for 8 performances.

[84]Musical numbers not listed in programs. List prepared from published piano vocal selections (John Church Co., Cincinnati, 1893), not in performance order.

"I Would Have Told Thee Long Ago"

"Song of the Husbands"

"Mary Had a Little Lamb"

"The Legend of Grimm"

"'Twas But a Dream"

"I Love You So"

"'Tis Sad to Love in Vain"

"Dickie and the Birdie"

"The Doctor and the Scribe"

"The Bridal Song"
Hollins Sisters, Chorus

"Serenade"

1895.07 THE GRAND VIZIER

An Operatic Burletta in Two Acts, 3 Scenes. Libretto by Edgar Smith. Music by Frederick Gagel. Staged by Edgar Smith. Musical director, Frank Pallma. Produced by Thomas Q. Seabrooke. Opened 4 March 1895 at the Harlem Opera House and closed 9 March 1895 after 8 performances.

CAST: *Dennis O'Grady*, a shipwrecked sailor masquerading as Monsieur Mouchoir, a French physician: THOMAS Q. SEABROOKE. *Hasabad Temper*, a hypochondriacal ruler: WALTER ALLEN. *Carlos*, an Italian trader: Albert Arling. *Rhubarb, Kamfor*, trained nurses attending Hasabad: Charles McDonald, Daniel Baker. *Tuffnut*, a slave dealer: Karl Formes, Jr. *Phatfellah, Haffed*, Members of Tunis' "finest": Arthur Carleton, Arthur Concors. *Sing Hi*: D. S. Loeb. *Amina*, an Algerian slave: FLORENCE NILLEY. *Bacnumba*, a harem veteran: CARRIE PERKINS. *Haidee*, of Hasabad's household: Hattie Moore. *Mirza, Gulnare, Badoura*, of the populace: Nanette Nixon, Madge Anderson, Dora Allen. *Trumpette*, a page: Aggie Vars. *Zobeide*: Kitty Powers. *Nela*, a breeze from Italy: IRENE MURPHY. *Populace, Guards, Sailors, Pages.*

Act 1: A Market Place at Tunis.

Act 2, Scene 1: The Palace Garden. *Scene 2*: The Blue Room in the Palace.

MUSICAL NUMBERS[85]

"Swim Out, O'Grady"
T. Q. Seabrooke

"Who Is Egen?"
T. Q. Seabrooke

1895.08 ALADDIN, JR.

American Extravaganza Company in the Spectacular Extravaganza in Four Acts. Book (and lyrics) by J. Cheever Goodwin. Music composed and arranged by W. H. Batchelor, W. F. Gloves and Jesse Williams. Produced under the direction of Richard Barker. Scenery and effects designed by Frederick Dangerfield. Costumes designed by Howell Russell. Ballets composed by Carlo Coppe and arranged by Filiberto Marchetti. Music of the ballet by Georgio Jacobi. Electrical effects by Martin Krueger and James Pennyfather. Musical director, Jesse Williams. Produced by David Henderson. Opened 8 April 1895 at the Broadway Theatre and closed 18 May 1895 after 48 performances.

CAST: *Aladdin, Jr.*, a scamp: ANNA BOYD. *Chee Kee*, Aladdin's sister: FRANKIE M. RAYMOND. *Badroulbadour*, Ki Yi's daughter: ALLENE CRATER. *Widow Bohea*, Aladdin's mother: ADA DEAVES. *Oolong*, son of the Vizier: Irene Verona. *Ki Yi*, Emperor of China: J. W. HERBERT. *Chow Chow*, his Vizier: John E. Cain. *Abanazar*, a magician: HENRY NORMAN. *Crambo*, Abanazar's apprentice: John J. Burke. *Pansy Mulcahy, Lilly Mulcahy*, Good Girls, the Widow's Assistants: Charles Turner, John E. Murphy. *Lucifer*, the Cat: DAVID ABRAHAMS. *Genii of the Lamp*, a nightmare: Albert Froom. *Tu Tee Fru Tee, Lee Tel Wee Lee*, Chinese swells: Misses L. Easton, Mary Thorne. *Da See Gur Lee, Poo See Wee Lo*, Chinese belles: Josie Shalders, Nellie Lynch. *Sprit of the Ring*, a dream: Bessie Pope. *Mandarins, Guards, Amazons, Swells, Fisher Boys and Girls, Flower Boys and Girls, Wise Men, Court Ladies, Carrier Boys, Dancing Girls, Musicians, Priests, High Officials, Maids of Honor, Street Arabs, Slaves, etc.*

[85]No New York program available; credits from the Clipper and Dramatic Mirror, song titles from reviews.

Act 1: Pekin: Grand Square, Exterior of the Royal Baths at Pekin.

Act 2, Scene 1: Echo Dell. Exterior of Mystic Cave. Moonlight. *Scene 2*: Interior of Cave. *Scene 3*: The Golden Glen and Resort of Silver Storks.

Act 3, Scene 1: Interior of Widow Bohea's Laundry. *Scene 2*: Gardens of the Imperial Palace.

Act 4, Scene 1: Egypt; Palace of Ebony and Gold on the Banks of the Nile. *Scene 2*: The Gates of the Great Walls of China.

ACT 1

Opening Chorus

"An Emperor's Lot" (Ki Yi's Entrance and Song)
J. W. Herbert

"Laundry Trio"
A. Deaves, C. Turner, J. E. Murphy

"The Rackety Boys Song"
A. Boyd

"A Magician of High Degree"
H. Norman

"Women, Wine and Song" (Septette and Concerted Number)
H. Norman, J. W. Herbert, J. E. Cain, A. Boyd, F. M. Raymond, I. Verona, A. Deaves

Entrance of Princess Badroulbadour

"Message of the Rose" (Duet)
A. Boyd, A. Crater

"I Must Away" (Dramatic and Concerted Finale)

ACT 2

Scene 1

"The Feast of Lanterns"

"Love Among the Freaks"
J. W. Herbert

"(Little) Alabama Coon"
F. M. Raymond
(*Music and Lyrics by* Hattie Starr.)

"I Don't Suppose You Have" (Song)
J. J. Burke

"The Ha Ha Song"
C. Turner, J. E. Muphy

Arrival of the Wizard and Aladdin

Scene 3

Grand Amber Ballet and Celestial Festival
Corps de Ballet

ACT 3

Scene 1

Medley Duet
J. J. Burke, A. Deaves

"Bow Down!"
Chorus

"I've Booked the Date" (Concerted Finale)

Scene 2

"The Way He Arranges His Face"
J. W. Herbert

"(I Am the) Beauteous Widow Bohea"
J. W. Herbert, J. E. Cain, A. Deaves

"I Didn't Think She'd Do It"
A. Boyd

Character Dance
C. Bartho

"Dorothy Flop"
N. Lynch, J. Shalders

"Infelice"
H. Norman

"Farewell, Fondest and Dearest" (Dramatic Finale)

ACT 4

Scene 1

"To and Fro"
F. M. Raymond, Chorus

"The Stars Alone Can Tell"
H. Norman, J. J. Burke, J. W. Herbert, J. E. Cain, A. Deaves
(*Music and Lyrics by* Jesse Williams.)

Abanazar's Barbaric Pageant

The Celebration of the Coming Nuptials

"Fill High! Drink Deep!" (Drinking Song)
H. Norman, Chorus

Scene 2

"Tricks of the Trade"
J. J. Burke

Finale

Transformation: The Birth of the Butterfly

1895.09

LA PÉRICHOLE

A Revival of the Opera Bouffe in Three Acts, 4 Scenes[86]. Libretto by Henri Meilhac and Ludovic Halévy. Music by Jacques Offenbach. Produced under the directon of Max Freeman. Scenery by Henry E. Hoyt. Costumes designed by Mme. Catherine Siedle. Orchestra and chorus under the direction of Paul Steindorff. Produced by Liillian Russell Opera Company (Henry E. Abbey, John B. Schoeffel and Maurice Grau, Directors). Opened 29 April 1895 at Abbey's Theatre and closed 18 May 1895 after 24 performances.

CAST: *Piquillo*, a street singer: RICHIE LING. *Don Andres*, Viceroy of Peru: FRED SOLOMON. *Don Pedro*, Goveror of Lima: William Blaisdell. *Le Marquis*, an old prisoner: Owen Westford. *Count Panatellas*, First Gentleman of the Bedchamber: George Honey. *The Jailer*: J. P. Canduit. *First Notary*: George Mackenzie. *Second Notary*: James Peakes. *Guadalena, Mastrilla, Berginella*, three cousins who keep a Cabaret or small inn: Misses Alice Reed, Laura Pardy, Clara Selten. *Ninetta, Brambilla, Frasquinella, Manuelita*, ladies of the court: Misses Ada Dare, Florence Doyle, Martha Habelman, Susie Leonard. *La Périchole*: LILLIAN RUSSELL. *Courtiers, Guards, Notaries, Servants, Pages, the people including Indians.*

Act 1: A public square in the city of Lima, (Peru).

Act 2: The Florentine Salon in the Palace of the Viceroy in view of the port.

Act 3, Scene 1: The prison of the recalcitrant husband beneath the palace. *Scene 2*: Street in Lima.

SPECIALTIES, INTERPOLATIONS[87]

Waltz Song (interpolation, Act 1)
L. Russell
(*Music by* L. Emil Bach.)

1895.10

A GAIETY GIRL

A Revival of the Musical Comedy in Two Acts[88]. Book by Owen Hall. Music by Sidney Jones. Lyrics by Harry Greenbank. Settings by Hugh Logan Reid. Musical director, George Purdy. Produced by Augustin Daly. Opened 7 May 1895 at Daly's Theatre and closed 1 June 1895 after 31 performances.

CAST: *Officers of the Life Guards (5)*: *Charles Goldfield*: LELAND H. LANGLEY. *Major Barclay*: W. J. Manning. *Bobbie Rivers*: BERT HASLEM. *Harry Fitzwarren*: Donald Hall. *Romney Farquhar*: James Frazer. *Sir Lewis Grey*, Judge of the Divorce Court: Percy Marshall. *Lance*, Goldfield's servant: Mr. Bradley. *Auguste*, bathing attendant: William P. Carleton. *Rev. Montague Brierly*, honorary physician of the Life Guards: W. H. Rawlins. *Miss Gladys Stourton*: Miss Beaugarde. *Girls of the Gaiety (5)*: *Alma Somerset*: ELENA FLOWERDEW. *Cissy Verner*: Margaret Fraser. *Haidee Walters*: Helen Fraser. *Ethel Hawthorne*: Ethel Craddock. *Mina*, maid to Lady Virginia: Nina Martino. *Rose Brierly*: Ethel Sydney. *Lady Virginia Forrest*: Winifred Dennis. *Society Ladies (3)*: *Lady Edytha Aldwyn*: Minnie Sadler. *Miss Gladys Stourton*: Miss Beaugarde. *Hon. Daisy Ormsbury*: Dolly Kirsch. *Lady Grey*: May Silvie. *Principal Dancers*: Margaret Fraser, Helen Fraser, Maud Percy.

[86]First produced in New York in French 4 January 1869 at Pike's Opera House for 35 performances. For this production the English adaptation was uncredited.

[87]Musical numbers not listed in programs.

[88]First produced in New York 18 September 1894 at Daly's Theatre for 81 performances. For Synopsis of Scenes and Musical Numbers, see entry earlier this season. No credits in programs for stage direction, presumably copied after George Edwardes' original.

1895.11

THE VIKING

A Spectacular Comic Opera in Two Acts. Book (and lyrics) by Estelle Clayton. Music by Edward Irving Darling. Scenery designed by Estelle Clayton, executed by Ernest Gros and Harry Raymond. Costumes by Mme. Thompson. Musical directors, Caryl Florio and Frederick Perkins. Orchestrated by Max Maretzek. Produced by Estelle Clayton (William L. Lykens, Business Manager). Opened 9 May 1895 at Palmer's Theatre and closed 18 May 1895 after 11 performances.

CAST: *King Igaliko the Great*, a Wise and Powerful Viking, the Father of Nothing but Boys: BURT HAVERLY. *Saga*, his soothsayer: GILBERT CLAYTON. *Prince Eric*, his son, a hardy Norseman: BERNARD DYLLYN. *His Good-for-Nothing Sons (3)*, the Pauper Princes: *Olaf*: CHARLES KIRKE. *Ivan*: WILLIAM MANDEVILLE. *Bjohnson Bjones*: HARRY DIETZ. *Lief Ericsson*, a rival Viking, the Father of Nothing but Girls: JNO. E. GREGORY. *Thora*, his daughter: GRACE REALS. *Saffa*, her sister, pretty mutineer: Clara Lipman. *Froda*, a little Norsemaid: Lillian Green. *Helga*, Foster Mother to the Viking's sons: ROSA COOKE. *Princess Njarda*, King Igaliko's niece: BEATRICE GOLDIE. *Chorus of Hardy Norsemen and Norsemaids, Subjects of the Viking; Court Ladies, Sailors, Vassals, Barbarians; Daughters of the Rival Norse King*: 100 Ladies and Gentlemen.

The action takes place about the year 1000.

Act 1: The frozen shore of Norway under the Midnight Sun.

Act 2: The great hall of the palace of King Igaliko.

ACT 1

Opening Chorus
L. Green, R. Cooke, G. Clayton, Chorus

Solo (A very wise man am I)
G. Clayton

Entrance of Princess Njarda
B. Goldie, Chorus

Solo
G. Clayton

Trio (Three pauper princes are we)
C. Kirke, H. Dietz, W. Mandeville, Chorus

Entrance of the Viking King
B. Haverly, Chorus

Trio (There's nothing new under the sun)
C. Kirke, H. Dietz, W. Mandeville, Chorus

Finale
Company

ACT 2

Drinking Song
C. Kirke, H. Dietz, W. Mandeville, Chorus

Solo (There once was a gallant Norseman)
B. Haverly, Chorus

Solo (So maiden fair, beware!)
B. Goldie

Sextette (Good-night! Good-night!)
B. Goldie, C. Lipman, G. Reals, B. Haverly, B. Dyllyn, G. Clayton

Solo and Chorus (You clamored for the rights of men)
G. Reals, C. Lipman, Chorus

Duet (Who cares for a woman's smile)
B. Dyllyn, G. Reals

Chorus (sh-sh-sh!)
C. Lipman, Sisters

Solo (False-hearted and perjured females)
J. E. Gregory, B. Dyllyn

Finale
J. E. Gregory, B. Dyllyn, B. Haverly, Chorus

Solo (O Fairest of nations)
G. Reals, Chorus
Grand Finale

1895.12

THE TZIGANE

A Russian Comic Opera in Three Acts. Libretto by Harry B. Smith. Music by Reginald DeKoven. Produced under the direction of Max Freeman. Settings by Henry E. Hoyt. Costumes by Mme. Caroline Siedle. Musical director, Paul Steindorff. Produced by the Lillian Russell Opera Company (Henry E. Abbey, John B. Schoeffel and Maurice Grau, Directors). Opened 16 May 1895 at Abbey's Theatre and closed 15 June 1895 after 36 performances.

CAST: *Vera*, a fortune-teller at the Fair of Nijnii Novgorod (The Tzigane): LILLIAN RUSSELL. *Maryska*, her rival, proprietress of a wine-booth at the fair: FLORA FINLAYSON. *Kazimir Androvitch*, an officer in love with Vera: HUBERT WILKE. *Vassili*, a serf: JEFFERSON DeANGELIS. *General Boguslav Schlemnitchkikoff*: FRED SOLOMON. *Count Guido Cesario*, Neapolitan Ambassador to Russia: JOSEPH HERBERT. *Ninetta*, a ballet dancer, admired by the Count: Clara Lane. *Sergius Suvaroff*, Governor of an estate near Novgorod, afterward a court official: Mr. McGurn. *Prascovia, a village girl*: CLARA SELDEN. *Lieutenant Vladimir*: Jeannette Perle. *Lieutenant Stanislaus*: Helen Beatrice. *Lieutenant Gregor*: Lotta Gale. *Lieutenant Ivan*: May Raymond. *Naryschkin*, Chief of the Russian Police: Mr. Adamini. *A Page*: Miss Foster. *Tartar, Chinese and Russian Merchants, Cossacks, Tzigani, Hussars, Village Children, Masqueraders, etc.*

The action takes place in Russia, during the invasion of Napoleon, 1812.

Act 1: The Great Fair at Nijni-Novogorod.

Act 2: An Ice Palace, Moscow. The Ambassadors' Ball.

Act 3, Scene 1: A Cossack Camp. *Scene 2*: A Russian village (in mid-winter).

ACT 1[89]

Opening Ensemble (From many a northern town we come)
Chorus

"Khorovod" (Dance Song)
F. Finlayson, Chorus

Cossack Song and Chorus
H. Wilke, Cossacks

Entrance of Vera

Fortune Telling Duet
L. Russell, H. Wilke

Chorus of Hussars and Solo
F. Solomon

Neapolitan Song (Duet)
J. Herbert Giulio, C. Lane

ACT 2

Torchlight Chorus

Boasting Duet
F. Solomon, J. DeAngelis, Chorus

Sleigh Bell Chorus; "Sleighing Song"
L. Russell, Chorus

"Pierrot and Columbine" (Chansonette)
L. Russell, F. Solomon, J. DeAngelis, C. Lane, F. Finlayson

"My Lady" (Ballad)
H. Wilke

Finale/Flag Song
L. Russell, Company

ACT 3

Opening Ensemble (Welcome, welcome)

"Tzigane Song"
F. Finlayson, J. Herbert, F. Solomon, Chorus

"Song of the Bugle"
L. Russell

Ensemble (Ah, thou art lost)
L. Russell, All

Semi-chorus of Children

Dancing Bear Song
F. Solomon, J. Herbert, F. Finlayson, C. Lane

Romance (The summer came and lived its golden day)
L. Russell

Finale

1895.13

LILY OF KILLARNEY, or, the Colleen Bawn

A Revival of the Romantic Opera in Three Acts, 7 Scenes[90]. Libretto by John Oxenford and Dion Boucicault. (Based on the play "The Colleen Bawn" by Dion Boucicault.) Music by Julius Benedict. Staged by Mr. Parry. Musical director, Mr. Van den Berg. Produced by Messrs. Parry and Van den Berg. Opened 27 May 1895 at the Grand Opera House and closed 1 June 1895 after 3 performances in repertory.

CAST: *Eily O'Connor*, the Colleen Bawn: HELEN BERTRAM. *Ann Chute*, the Heiress: EMMA SIEBERT. *Mrs. Cregan*, Hardress' Mother: KATE MICHELENA. *Sheelah Mann*: Katherine Griffiths. *Hardress Cregan*: CHARLES BASSETT. *Myles Na Coppaleen*: PAYNE CLARKE. *Father Tom*: Graham Reed. *Mr. Corrigan*: Harry Dodd. *O'Moore*, a Magistrate: F. W. Regas. *Hyland Craig*, a guest: George Martin. *Danny Mann*: WILLIAM T. CARLETON. *Bridesmaids, Corps de Ballet.*

1895.14

A YENUINE YENTLEMAN

A Play with songs in Four Acts. Play by Gus Heege. Music by Percy Gaunt. Scenery by John H. Young. Produced by Jacob Litt. Opened 27 May 1895 at the Bijou Theatre and closed 1 June 1895 after 8 performances[91].

CAST: *Sven Hanson*: GUS HEEGE. *Hon. H. Gordon Castle*: —. *Charles Nelson Baron Rosenkranz*: —. *Matt Hogan*: J. C. Huffman. *Tim Maguire*: —. *Roger*: —. *Mrs. Florence Nelson*: —. *Jessie Castle*: MERRI OSBORNE. *Mrs. Ruth*: —. *Mrs. Cordelia O'Grady*: SADIE CONNOLLY. *Sal Snifkins*: —.

Company also included Newton Chisnell, Ralph Stewart, Albert Bruning, G. Frankel, William T. Raymond, Sidney Craven, J. C. Huffman, Ambrose Miller, Bob Bradford, Frederick Peel, George M. Welty, Emma Field, Merri Osborne, Edith Marlowe, Sadie Connolly.

Act 1: On shipboard in Southampton Harbor.

Act 2: Coeur d'Alene county, Idaho.

Acts 3 and 4: Sven's Cabin.

MUSICAL NUMBERS, SPECIALTIES

Irish songs
S. Connolly

Darkey songs
M. Osborne

Swedish Dialect specialties
G. Heege

1895.15

HAMLET II

A Operatic Burlesque (of the Shakespeare tragedy) in Three Acts. Play by H. Grattan Donnelly. Music by Homer Tourjée. Entire production under the stage direction of James Barton Key. Scenery by Sydney Chidley, H. Logan Reid. Costumes designed by Mrs. Catherine Seidel. Electric light effects by Mayerhofer Company. Ballet divertissements arranged by Mme. Eloise Kruger. Musical direction, Jesse Williams. Produced by H. Grattan Donnelly and Homer Tourjée. Opened 27 May 1895 at the Herald Square Theatre and closed 7 June 1895 after 15 performances.[92]

[89]Musical numbers not listed in programs. List prepared from published libretto (Brooklyn Citizen Job Printing, Brooklyn, New York, 1895). Additional song titles listed in reviews, not found in published libretto: "Ballad of the Ring," "My Lad, 'Tis of Thee," "A Heart That Beats for Thee," "Cupid Is King" (Duet with L. Russell.).

[90]First produced in New York 1 January 1868 at the Academy of Music.

[91]No program available. A touring company also played return engagements in New York 25 November 1895 at the Columbus Theatre for 8 performances, and 1 March 1897 at the Columbus Theatre for 8 performances.

[92]No program available; song list prepared from published piano vocal selections (John A. Church, Cincinnati, 1895).

CAST: *Hamlet II*: EDWARD J. HENLEY. *King Claudius*: JOHN BUNNEY. *Polonius*: JACQUES KRUGER. *The Ghost*: GEORGE BRODERICK. *Horatio*: Drew Donaldson. *Laertes*: Helen Harrington. *Rosencrantz*: Adele Archer. *Guildenstern*: Sallie Randall. *Marcellus*: Laura Wainsford. *Bernardo*: Vera Beverly. *Osric*: Irene Bentley. *First Player*: Robert Mack. *Second Player*: George Meeker. *Captain of the Watch*: Mary Gibson. *First Grave-Digger*: Robert Mack. *Second Grave-Digger*: George Meeker. *Sylvia*: FLORENCE ELLIS. *Leonora*: Marie Edith Rice. *Queen Gertrude*: KATE DAVIS. *Ophelia*: CATHERINE LEWIS. *The Player Queen*: Elsie Sheridan. *Yorick's Skull*: Itself. *Ladies of the Court, Cadets, Drummers, Trumpeters, Royal Guards, Halberdiers, Courtiers, etc.*

Act 1: The Battlements of Elsinore. (Chidley.)

Act 2: Fete in the Royal Palace Gardens. (Chidley.)

Act 3: The Throne-Room of the Palace. (Reid.)

MUSICAL NUMBERS

"All in a Garden Fair"
"The Rose Will Bloom"
"To Be or Not to Be"
"Tell me Pretty Daisy"
"Although I Am of Princely Rank"
"What Is the Matter with Ham?"
Danish Cadets March
Elsinore Waltz

1895.16

A DAUGHTER OF THE REVOLUTION

A Historical Comic Opera in Three Acts[93]. Libretto by J. Cheever Goodwin. Music by Ludwig Engländer. Staged by Richard Barker. Dances arranged by Prof. A Francioli. Scenery designed by Fred Dangerfield[94]. Costumes designed by H. A. Ogden. Musical director, Ludwig Engländer. Produced by the Camille D'Arville Opera Company (Philip A. Shea, Manager). Opened 27 May 1895 at the Broadway Theatre and closed 29 June 1895 after 35 performances.[95]

CAST: *General Gottlieb Grumm*, Commander of the Hessian Forces: HALLEN MOSTYN. *Sergeant Carl Creamer*, attached to Hessian Headquarters: HARRY MACDONOUGH. *Arthur Lee*, Captain in Revolutionary Army: CLINTON ELDER. *General De'Heister*, Commander and Chief of Hessian Forces: HARRY STANLEY. *Ozis Brewster*, dealer in military supplies: Logan Paul. *George Washington*: Edward Knight. *First Soldier*: E. H. Turner. *Second Soldier*: J. B. Park. *Officer*: E. J. Williams. *Lady Margaret Grumm*, General's wife and better two-thirds: SIDNEY WORTH. *Molly Morgan*, laundress: Annie Lewis. *First Lady*: Mary Sears. *Second Lady*: Jessie Clark. *Marion Dunbar*, betrothed to Lee: CAMILLE D'ARVILLE. *Citizens of New York of both sexes, British and Hessian Military, Naval Officers and Privates, Colonial Dames, American Officers and Troops, Camp Followers, etc.*

The action takes place in the fall and winter of 1776.

Act 1: Bowling Green, New York City.

Act 2: Ball-room at General Grumm's residence in New York.

Act 3, Scene 1: Washington crossing the Delaware. *Scene 2*: British Camp at Trenton, New Jersey.

---

[93]This was a revised version of 1776 produced in New York 26 February 1884 at the Thalia Theatre, in German, to a libretto by Leo Goldmark.
[94]A second different opening night playbills credits William Hoover jointly as set designer.
[95]Musical numbers not listed in programs; no libretto or musical score found.

1895–1896 SEASON

DeWolf Hopper in EL CAPITAN (Photo: Falk)
Billy Rose Theatre Collection, New York Public Library for the Performing Arts

1895–1896 SEASON

1895.17 THRILBY

A Operatic Burlesque (of George duMaurier's 'Trilby' as adapted into play form by Paul M. Potter) in Two Acts, 3 Scenes[1]. Play (and lyrics) by Joseph W. Herbert. Music by Charles Puerner. Staged by R. H. Burnside. Settings by Joseph Physioc. Costumes by Eaves Costume Company. Musical director, W. T. Francis. Produced by the Garrick Burlesque Company (John P. Slocum, Manager). Opened 3 June 1895 at the Garrick Theatre and closed 13 July 1895 after 42 performances.

CAST: *Caramels*: R. F. COTTON. *Butter-Scotch*: E. D. LYONS. *Little Willie*: ADELE RITCHIE. *Spaghetti*: ALEXANDER CLARK. *Jocko*: Louis Wesley. *Mr. Faggot*: A. G. Andrews. *Goerge DuMaurier*: A. G. Andrews. *Ignatius McFadden*: MARK MURPHY. *Mr. Flaw*: WILLIS P. SWEATNAM. *Anita*: Fleurette. *The Zulu*: MARGARET McDONALD. *The Dodo*: Grace Rutter. *Thrilby*, à la Spaghetti: CARRIE E. PERKINS. *Mrs. McFadden*: FLORENCE IRWIN. *Mrs. Faggot*: Lillian Green.

Model Artists, Artists' Models etc.: Helen Hathaway, Hattie Crabtree, Adelaide Leeds, Kate Ward, Marie Wood, Lucy Smiles, Irene Bentley, Ollie Craig, Lillian Tulane, Beatrice Clements, Grace Scott, Julia Lovelace, Bessie Clayton, May Russell, Ella Kitson, May Lavigne, Teddie DuCoe, Alice Lorraine; Messrs. Underwood, Dorfman, Layborn, Powell, Carleton, Kilduff, Fuller, Vogel.

Act 1: Studio of the Three Privateers, in the Italian quarter of New York.

Act 2, Scene 1: Lobby of the Theatre des Gadzooks. Scene 2: Interior of the theatre.

ACT 1[2]

Opening Chorus
Students, Models

Song (I love a maid, I love her well)
A. Ritchie

Trio (There's only one girl in this world for me)
E. D. Lyons, A. Ritchie, R. F. Cotton

Song (Although she has posed/A popular heroine well-advertised)
C. E. Perkins

"The Marvels of Hypnotism" (Song)(We live in an age of rapidity)
A. Clark

"(Don't You Remember Sweet) Alice Ben Bolt"[3]
C. E. Perkins

"Has Anyone Seen Our Cat?" (Quartette)
C. E. Perkins, [Taffy], ??, ??

"The Brave Soldier Boy"
Chorus

Zulu's Song (There are some things in this wide world)
M. McDonald

Song and Chorus (In our quiet Quaker city)
A. G. Andrews, Chorus

Finale

ACT 2
Scene 1

"We Belong to the Johnny Brigade" (Song and Chorus)
A. G. Andrews, Chorus

"Ignatius McFadden's Debut" (Song and Chorus)
F. Irwin, Chorus

"Two Little Dolls" (Song)
A. Ritchie

"Othello and I Had a Cell" (Song)
F. Irwin

(Waltz from) "Der Obersteiger" (Don't Be Cross)(Song and Chorus)
A. Ritchie, Chorus
(*Music by* Carl Zeller.)

Finale (Ne'er did we such a rascal see)
A. Clark, Chorus

Scene 2

Opening Chorus (Oh Mr. Manager tell us of the play)
Chorus

New Defender Ballet
Misses G. Scott, B. Clayton, E. Kitson, M. Lavigne, A. Lorraine, M. Russell, J. Lovelace, T. DuCoe

Dance Eccentrique
E. Murray

Burlesque Hornpipe
L. Wesley

Negro Songs and Stories
W. P. Sweatnam

Specialty ("My Daughter Biddy McFadden")
M. Murphy

Finale:
"Although she has posed (reprise)
C. E. Perkins
"We live in an age of rapidity"(reprise)
A. Clark
"Othello and Mac have a cell" (reprise)
F. Irwin
"Der Obersteiger" (reprise)
A. Ritchie

[1]During the run a final scene to Act 2 was added for the production's 'Third Edition': *Scene* 3: New York Yacht-Club House, Newport.

[2]Musical numbers not listed in programs, only the ballet; list prepared from production typescript. Also published, but not in typescript: "La-La-La-La," (*Lyrics by* Joseph P. Herbert and Arthur Trevelyan.).

[3]Original lyrics from the poem by Thomas Dunn, set to music by Nelson Kneass, interpolated with success into the play "Trilby."

1895.18 THE MERRY WORLD

Second Annual Review of Contemporaneous Metropolitan Successes (A Musical Revue) in Three Acts, 8 Exhibits (Scenes)[4]. Libretto by Edgar Smith. Music by Nicholas Biddle. Produced under the stage direction of Edgar Smith. Director of music, Herman Perlet[5]. Produced by Thomas Canary and George W. Lederer. Opened 8 June 1895 at the Casino Theatre and closed 6 July 1895 after 29 performances; re-opened 12 August 1895 at the Casino Theatre and closed 21 September 1895 after 42 additional performances. Total: 71 performances[6].

CAST: CHARLES DICKSON, DAN DALY, LEE HARRISON, SAM FISHER, DAVID WARFIELD, LOUIS MANN, W. A. McCORMACK, AMELIA SUMMERVILLE, HATTIE MOORE, CHRISTINE BLESSING, R. A. ROBERTS, WILLARD SIMMS, W. WALLACE BLACK, RANDOLPH CURRY, VIRGINIA EARLE, SHERRIE MATTHEWS and HARRY BULGER, Belle Thorne, May Howard, Jeanette Bageard, Louis Granat, Robert G. Ingersoll, Charles Guyer, Henry Ernest, Julian Myers, Arthur Concors, May Howard, Florence Carlisle, Nanette Nixon, Martha Habelman, Emma Levy, H. A. Clark, May Donohue, Nelsy Chamberlain, Molly McGill, Misses O'Neil and Sutherland.

ACT 1[7]
Exhibit 1

The Dramatist's Den
Mephisto, an up-to-date devil: C. Dickson. *D. Boucicault Simpkins*, an impecunious playwright: D. Daly.

Exhibit 2

Herald Square at Night
Swipes, *Rabsy*, *The Canary*, newsboys: L. Harrison, S. Fisher, L. Granat. *Other Newsboys*: the real things.

Exhibit 3

Madame Sans Gêne[8], a bit of dramatic impertinence in Three Scenes,

[4]Also billed as "A Dramatic Pousse Café, intended to cheer you up after dinner, and containing a little of everything except plot." The 'First Annual Review' at the Casino was the previous year's THE PASSING SHOW. Sydney Rosenfeld withdrew prior to the opening, assigning Edgar Smith full credit.

[5]Musical director for the return engagement was Paul Schindler.

[6]Settings and costumes uncredited. Also played a return engagement in New York 18 November 1895 at the 14th Street Theatre for 8 performances.

[7]After the opening, the show was shortened. Matthews and Bulger departed, Act 3 was discarded altogether, and the Burlesque of Trilby was moved to Act 3.

[8]A burlesque of the French play by Victorien Sardou and Emile Moreau, Madame San Gêne.

in which the following ladies and gentlemen will take liberties with the characters opposite their names: *Napoleon*: R. A. Roberts. *De Neipperg*: D. Daly. *Fouché*: D. Warfield. *Lefebre*: L. Mann. *Dujour*: R. Curry. *Drummer Boy*: W. W. Black. *Aujourdhui*: W. A. McCormack. *Mme. Sans-Gêne*: A. Summerville. *Marie*: J. Bageard. *Queen of Naples*: H. Moore. *Princess Eliza*: C. Blessing. *Cabriolet*: N. Nixon. *Nestpas*: M. Habelman. *Madame Decollete*: E. Levy. *Hussars, Guards, Laundresses, Courtiers, etc*. Incidental to this Act, David Warfield will introduce his travesties (including the Othello of the elder Salvini); at the end of the Act, Charles Dickson will address the audience, à la Mr. (Richard) Mansfield.

Scene 1: Sans Gêne's Library. *Scene 2*: The Ministry of Police. *Scene 3*: Napoleon's Library.

ACT 2[9]

Exhibit 1

Around the Comic Operas

Dr. Syntax: R. A. Roberts. *Joey*: W. Simms. *Rob Roy*: C. Dickson. *Wang*: W. W. Black. *Landlord*: L. Harrison. *Francois*: W. A. McCormack. *Pierre*: R. Curry. *Vaseline*: V. Earle. *Madeleine*: B. Thorne. *Robin Hood*: M. Howard. *Cadenza*; J. Bageard. *Cavatina*: N. Nixon. *Long John*: M. Donohue. *Villagers, Soldiers, Robin Hood's Men, Little Troopers, Bridesmaids, etc*.

Incidental to this Exhibit, Charles Guyer will give his acrobatic tramp specialty, and Lizzie Daly will dance.

Exhibit 2

A Street, wherein Matthews and Bulger will present their specialty

Exhibit 3

A Burlesque of Paul Potter's masterpiece on DuMaurier's creation, Trilby, in Three Scenes:

Taffy: D. Daly. *The Laird*: D. Warfield. *Svengali*: L. Mann. *Zou Zou*: C. Dickson. *Rev. Mr. Braggart*: W. Simms. *Jocko*: L. Harrison. *Dodor*: W. W. Black. *Mr. Palmer*: W. A. McCormack. *Trilby*: A. Summerville. *Little Billee*: V. Earle. *Madame Vinard*: J. Bageard. *Mrs. Braggart*: C. Blessing. *Babette*: N. Chamberlain. *Julie*: M. McGill.

Scene 1: The Studio. *Scene 2*: The Foyer. *Scene 3*: The Concert.

Incidental to the Burlesque, Misses O'Neil and Sutherland will perform their acrobatic dancing; Lizzie Daly, Florence Carlisle, Willard Simms and Charles Guyer will dance in the garb of Salvationists; Dan Daly and Christine Blessing will execute a cyclonic dance.

ACT 3

Exhibit 1

A Dash of Tragedy in the shape of 'Antony and Cleopatra':

Cleopatra: M. Fenton. *Antony*: C. J. Ross. *Keplon*: L. Harrison.

Exhibit 2

De Peach Dinner, on the grounds of the Country Club

Mephisto: C. Dickson. *D. Boucicault Simpkins*: D. Daly. *Robert G. Ingersoll*: W. A. McCormack. *Chauncey M. Depew*: W. W. Black. *Grover Cleveland*: H. Ernest. *Benjamin H. Harrison*: J. Myers. *Clarence F. Lexow*: A. Concors.

Incidental to this Exhibit, Willard Simms offered his imitations, and May Howard led the 'Broadway Girls.'

1895.19 THE SPHINX

An Egyptian Comic Opera in Three Acts. Libretto by William Maynardier Browne. Music by Lewis S. Thompson. Produced under the direction of William Seymour. Settings by Charles W. Whitham. Costumes by Mme. Bryce-Gemmel. Orchestra directed by Julian Edwards. Produced by Harry Askin. Opened 8 July 1895 at the Casino Theatre and closed 10 August 1895 after 35 performances.

CAST: *Professor P. Papyrus*, A. M., Ph. D., etc. of Harvard: EDWIN STEVENS. *This*, of Memphis, a magician: WALTER ALLEN. *Neferkera*, Sheik of the Tribe of Zois: A. S. KINGSLEY. *Nectanebo*, a Bedouin noble: CARL HARTBERG. *Mr. Ptimmins*, Professor Papyrus' valet: Tallmadge Baldwin. *Pteecha*, Principal of a Ladies' Seminary: LAURA JOYCE BELL. *Shafra, Amasis*, her leading pupils: CHRISTIE MacDONALD, Myra Miles. *Tilly Ptolemy, Fanny Rameses*, other school-girls: Kate Trayer, Louise Poyneer. *Hathor*, the spirit of the Great Sphinx: MARIE MILLARD.

Bedouins of the Tribe of Zois: Frank Symons, Joseph Smiley, Alexander West, Robert Blake, Harry Blake, Edward Aiken, Frank Pruette, Robert E. Vance, H. W. Stonge, James F. Woods, Philip Robson, Edward Jordan, Howell Coombs, A. McKinley, Edward Frisby, Samuel Lewis, John S. Moore, Rafael Lazarus; Mabel Keith, Jennie Lewis, Kate Trayer, Alice Gilman, Kate Aubrey, Minnie Howard, Hulda Kause, Alice Marshall, Alice Beardsley, Mildred King, Amelia Gardner, Jennie Carrigan, Mamie Terriss, Katherine Poor, Maud Smith, Flora Gardner, Mildred Palmer, Maud Ulmer, Minnie Slavin.

The action takes place today in Egypt.

Act 1: Pteecha's Seminary, near Cairo.

Act 2: At the foot of the Great Sphinx.

Act 3: The Bedouin's Camp in the Oasis.

ACT 1[10]

Opening Chorus (Ten times five is fifteen. .)

Entrance of This (Pray, tell us if you can, sir. .)
C. MacDonald, Girls

This' Song (Oh, who I am, and what I am. .)
W. Allen

Song (Was there ever, do you think, such a silly. .)
L. J. Bell, Chorus

Entrance of Bedouins (Listen, what a glad surprise . . .)
C. MacDonald, Chorus

Recitative (Horror! This sacred and profane. .)
L. J. Bell, A. S. Kingsley

Bedouin Song (Oh a bedouin free is the life for me. .)
A. S. Kingsley

"Soft, Soft"
Chorus

"Hail! P. Papyrus"
L. J. Bell, Chorus

Song (Yes, I am known as Papyrus. .)
E. Stevens

Finale

ACT 2

Entrance of Chorus and Prayer to Hathor
T. Baldwin

Recitative (Impatient ones could ye no longer wait. .)
M. Millard, Chorus

Hathor's Song (What is this chant that holds me . . .)
M. Millard

Duet (A well-informed and well-bred male . . .)
M. Millard, E. Stevens

"Gustave Lorraine" (Quartette)
E. Stevens, A. S. Kingsley, T. Baldwin, W. Allen

Finale

ACT 3

Duet (Love, ah love)
M. Millard, E. Stevens

"Four Little Mice" (Quintette)
C. MacDonald, M. Miles, T. Baldwin, C. Hartberg

"(And) What Do You Think He Said?" (Song)
E. Stevens, Chorus

Finale

1895.20 DOROTHY

A Revival of the Comic Opera in Three Acts[11]. Libretto by B. C. Stephenson. Music by Alfred Cellier. Whole production under the direc-

---

[9]Added after opening to Act 2, preceding Around the Comic Operas:

Exhibit 1: Black America

Hodges, Larchmere and Grant, Canary & Lederer's Female and Male Pickaninnies

"Aunt Jemima's Big Pound Cake" (The Cake Walk Song)
Pickaninnies
(*Music and Lyrics by* John T. Kelly.)

Exhibit 2: A Street

The Broadway Girls, led by May Howard

Messrs. Matthews and Bulger will sing and talk to you

[10]Musical numbers not listed in programs. List prepared from published vocal score (Miles, & Thompson, Boston, 1895).

[11]Originally produced in New York 5 November 1887 at the Standard Theatre for 48 performances. For Synopsis of Scenes and Musical Numbers, see original 1887 production.

tion of Henry J. Leslie. Ballets arranged by Rose Beckett. Incidental dances by Claude Revere. Costumes by Auguste Co., London; Eaves Costume Co., New York. Musical director, Charles Puerner. (Produced by Henry J. Leslie.) Opened 8 August 1895 at the Standard Theatre and closed 31 August 1895 after 28 performances[12].

CAST: *Dorothy (Bantam)*: DOROTHY MORTON. *Lydia (Hawthorne)*: MAUD HOLLINS. *Phyllis*: Hilda Hollins. *Mrs. Privett*: Edith Sinclair. *Lady Betty*: Maud Courtenay. *Geoffrey Wilder*: CHARLES BASSETT. *Harry Sherwood*: DAVID TORRENCE. *Squire Bantam*: BASIL TETSON. *John Tupppitt*: Al. Holbrook. *Tom Strutt*: Henry Stanley. *Lurcher*: EDWARD M. FAVOR. Grand Chorus, Orchestra and Ballet of 100.

1895.21 KISMET, or, Two Tangled Turks

A Turkish Comic Opera (Musical Comedy) in Two Acts. Book (and lyrics) by Richard F. Carroll. Music by Gustave Kerker. Produced under the stage direction of Max Freeman. Settings by John Thompson, Frank E. Gates, Edward A. Morange. Costumes designed by Louis Meynell. Musical director, Selli Simonson. Produced by the Harry Askin Opera Company[13]. Opened 12 August 1895 at the Herald Square Theatre and closed 31 August 1895 after 24 performances.

CAST: *Kismet*, the Sultan of Turkey: LIZZIE MacNICHOL. *Chinchilla*, the Grand Vizier: HARRY DAVENPORT. *Dan De Lyon*, an Irish free lance: AUBREY BOUCICAULT. *Ovah*, the Moor: William Schuster. *Sum*, Dey of Algiers: Edward S. Wentworth. *The Muezzin*, the crier of prayers: William Schuster. *So-Jah*, the Aga of Janizaries: Helen Welch. *A-Jeeb, B-Jeebers*, attendants in charge of the harem: Edw. H. Carroll, Charles Whalen. *Absinthea*, the Sultan's favorite wife: Jeanette St. Henry. *Ramadamus*, the Sultana Valdé (the Sultan's Mother): ROSE LEIGHTON. *Odalisques (5)*: *Fat-Ma*: Agnes Daly. *Lazeli*: Nellie Parker. *Kondjé-Gal*: Mabel Irvine. *Pandemonia*: Gertie Clarke. *Lena*: Aggie Vars. *Haideez*, the Sultan's sister: RICHARD F. CARROLL, JR. *Chorus of odalisques, harem girls, slaves, Algerians disguised as Arcan Amazons, Moors disguised as Malay pirates, attendants and Janizaries.*

The action takes place in Turkey. *Time*: You pays your money and you take your choice.

Act 1: The Courtyard of the Sultan's Seraglio. (Thompson.)

Act 2: Interior of the Harem. (Gates and Morange.)

MUSICAL NUMBERS[14]

"Why Am I Not Like the Rest of Us Girls?"

"Singing in Vain for the Moon"
L. MacNichol

"Physical Culture"
J. St. Henry

"Just One Kiss"
L. MacNichol

"Do You Like Tutti-Frutti?"

"Terror, Terror"

"Tuzzie Marie"

"Friendship" (Duet)
L. MacNichol, A. Boucicault

1895.22 FLEUR-DE-LIS

A Comic Opera in Three Acts. Libretto by J. Cheever Goodwin. Adapted from the French "Pervenche" by Henri Cheviot and Alfred Duru. Music by William Furst. Produced under the direction of (staged by) Richard Barker. Settings by Richard Marston. Costumes by W. Dazian. Musical director, Fred J. Eustis[15]. Produced by the Della Fox Comic Opera Company (Management, Nat Roth). Opened 29 August 1895 at Palmer's Theatre and closed 2 November 1895 after 65 performances[16].

CAST: *The Count Des Escarbilles*, claimant of the Duchy Turbotière: JEFFERSON DeANGELIS. *Frederick*, his son, in love with Fleur-de-Lis: MELVILLE STEWART. *The Marquis De Rosolio*, claimant of the Duchy: ALF. C. WHELAN. *Christophe*, an inkeeper, in love with Charlotte: CHARLES J. CAMPBELL. *The Baron Casoar*, military ally of the Count: Charles Dungan. *Jacob*, Christophe's uncle, an old ex-miller: Edward Knight. *A Notary*: John Dudley. *Baptiste*: Steve Porter. *Isabelle*, daughter of the Baron Casoar: IDA FITZHUGH. *Charlotte*, god-daughter of the Marquis, and betrothed to Christophe: KATE UART. *Madame Jacob*, ex-danseuse, the ex-miller's wife: ALICE CAMERON. *Therese, Nanette, Margot*, in service of the Marquis: Ella Aubrey, Laura Wainsford, Edna Lyle. *Fleur de Lis*, a flower vender: DELLA FOX. *Villagers, soldiers, sabot and clock makers, etc.*

Act 1: Public Square in St. Claude, France. Morning.

Act 2: Esplanade of the Fortress Turbotière. Noon.

Act 3: Interior of Jacob's Mill. Night.

MUSICAL NUMBERS[16a]

"Not That Sort of Girl"
D. Fox

"Good Night" (Act 3)

1895.23 THE BATHING GIRL

A Satirical Comedy-Opera in Three Acts. Libretto by Rupert Hughes. Music by Robert Coverly. Stage production under the direction of A. M. Holbrook. Musical director, Nathan Franko. Opened and closed 2 September 1895 at Henry C. Miner's Fifth Avenue Theatre after 1 performance[17].

CAST: *J. Klingsbury Botts*, of New York: WILLIAM STEPHENS. *Lord Fitzpoodle*, of London: WILLIAM BLAISDELL. *Mr. Van Baalamb, Mr. Peal*: W. D. Kerruish, Arthur Leibbee. *Porter*: J. E. Halton. *Salesgentleman*: John E. Belton. *Policeman*: Oscar Sannaa. *Miss Terriberry*, of Boston: GRACE GOLDEN. *Mrs. Jhones, Mrs. Braune, Mrs. Smythe*, of Society: Drew Donaldson, Blanche Drayton, Katherine MacNeill. *Arabella*: Marjorie Teal. *An Old Lady*: Ella Altman. *Poor Woman*: Julia Wood. *Bathing Girls, Golfers, Tennis Players, Bicyclists, Husbands, Loungers and other Social Stars, Shoppers and Shoppees.*

Act 1: A Seaside Hotel.

Act 2: A Moonlit Beach.

Act 3: A Metropolitan Bazaar.

1895.24 ROB ROY

A Return Engagement of the Romantic Comic Opera in Three Acts[18]. Libretto by Harry B. Smith. Music by Reginald DeKoven. Scenery by Joseph Physioc, D. Frank Dodge, Henry E. Hoyt. Costumes by Catherine Seidle. Musical director, Signor Antonio Tomasi. Stage director, Harry Parker. Produced by the Whitney Opera Company (Fred C. Whitney, Proprietor). Opened 2 September 1895 at the Herald Square and closed 28 September 1895 after 28 performances.

CAST: *Rob Roy MacGregor*, a Highland Chief: WILLIAM PRUETTE. *Janet*, daughter of the Mayor: JULIETTE CORDEN. *Prince Charles Edward Stuart*, called "The Young Pretender": JOSEPH SHEEHAN. *Flora MacDonald*, heiress of a Chief of the Clan MacDonald, a partisan of the pretender: LIZZIE MACNICHOL. *Dugald MacWheeble*, Mayor of Perth: OSCAR GIRARD. *Lochiel*, a Highlander, otherwise Donald Cameron, of the Cameron Clan: WILLIAM H. McLAUGHLIN. *Captain Ralph Sheridan*, of King George's Grenadiers: Anna O'Keefe. *Sandy MacSherey*, town crier: Frederick Chapin. *Tammas McSorlie*, the Mayor's henchman: Harry Parker. *Lieutenant Cornwallis*, of King George's Grenadiers: Mittie Atherton. *Lieutenant Clinton*: Minnie Echard. *Angus McAllister*: Jeanette Pearl. *Duncan Campbell*: Julie

---

[12]Settings uncredited.
[13]Subsequently toured under the auspices of the Carroll-Kerker Opera Company (James S. Lee, Will J. Block, proprietors and managers), under the personal direction of the author and composer.
[14]Musical numbers not listed in programs. List prepared from published piano vocal selection (T. B. Harms, & Co., New York, 1895) and reviews.
[15]Opening night was conducted by the composer.
[16]Also played 28 October 1895 at the Harlem Opera House for 8 performances.
[16a]Musical numbers not listed in programs, no libretto or musical score found.
[17]Producer, scenery, costumes uncredited. Musical numbers not listed in programs.
[18]Originally produced 29 October 1894 at the Herald Square Theatre for 168 performances. For Synopsis of Scenes and Musical Numbers, see original 1894 production.

Senac. *Stuart McPherson*: Ollie Russell. *Donald MacAlpine*: Carrie Rieger. *Nelly*, barmaid of "The Crown and Thistle": Clara Allen. *Jamies*: Ole Norman, Jack Bratton, Henry Rolland, Charles Trowbridge, Norman Parr. *Highlanders, Lowland Townsmen, Watchmen, English Grenadiers, Drummer Boys, etc.*

1895.25 PRINCESS BONNIE

An Operetta in Two Acts. Words (libretto) and music by Willard Spenser. Original stage production directed by Richard Barker. Settings by Ernest M. Gros. Costumes designed by Catherine Seidle. Musical director, William J. Rostetter. Produced by Messrs. D. W. Truss & Company (Frank Williams, Manager). Opened 2 September 1895 at the Broadway Theatre and closed 12 October 1895 after 42 performances.

CAST: *Shrimps*, champion canoeist and village "jack-of-all-trades," in love with Kitty: FRED LENNOX, JR. *Captain Tarpaulin*, of the fishing smack "*Nancy*" and keeper of the light house: GEORGE O'DONNELL. *Roy Stirling*, a follower of Isaak Walton, in love with Bonnie: WILL M. ARMSTRONG. *Admiral Pomposo* of the Spanish Navy, with a hobby of collecting rare antiquities: JOSEPH S. GREENSFELDER. *Count Castinetti Marionetti Flageoletti Falsetti*, an Italian nobleman, betrothed to Bonnie in infancy: ROBERT BRODERICK. *Salvador*, body-guard to Admiral Pomposo: Richard Quilter. *Lieutenant Fuzee*, a Spanish officer: Elmer Ritchie. *Captain Surf*, fisherman: Taylor Williams. *Kitty Clover*, Captain of the Canoe Club and the belle of the village: JENNIE GOLDTHWAITE. *Susan Crabbe Tarpaulin*, Tarpaulin's sister, popularly called "Auntie Crab," assistant keeper of the light house: JENNY DICKERSON. *Donna Pomposa*, wife of Admiral Pomposo: JENNY DICKERSON. *Bonnie*, the Princess Bonnabellavita, adopted daughter of Captain Tarpaulin and niece of Admiral Pomposo: HILDA CLARK. *Canoeists, fishermen, soldiers, villagers, marines, Spanish peasants, Spanish dancers, Spanish students, bridesmaids, etc.*

Act 1: Coast of Maine, near Bar Harbor.

Act 2: Courtyard of Admiral Pomposo's Palace in Spain.

ACT 1[19]

"Fair Weather Sailors" (Opening Chorus)
"Listen Well"
J. Dickerson, Chorus
"Once Upon a Time"
J. Goldthwaite, Chorus
"Slumber So Gently"
H. Clark
"Love Is Like a Dainty Flower"
W. M. Armstrong, H. Clark
"Love Is to All a Dainty Dream"
"My Bark Canoe"
F. Lennox, Jr., All
"For It's Funny How It Goes"
"I Told You So"
G. O'Donnell
"Never, Never, Never Fall in Love"
J. Dickerson, Chorus
"Did You Hear What She Was Saying"
H. Clark
"Dreaming of Love"
"Now, Did You Know?"
G. O'Donnell
"H. Clark, My Queen"
W. M. Armstrong
"You Never Lose a Little Fish"
F. Lennox, Jr., W. M. Armstrong
"Ah My Heart With Fear Is Rending"
T. Williams, G. O'Donnell, H. Clark, J. Dickerson, J. Goldthwaite, F. Lennox, Jr.
"Merry Maids of Spain"
"Those Happy Days" ("Days of Old")
H. Clark
March
"Fortune Overwhelms Me" (Finale)

[19]Musical numbers not listed in programs. List prepared from production typescript and published piano vocal score (W. H. Keyser & Co., Philadelphia, 1893).

ACT 2

"Merry, Merry Maids of Spain" (Opening Chorus)
"I am the Great Pomposo"
J. S. Greensfelder
"Lovely Bonnabellavita"
J. Dickerson
"Whisper Words of Love"
Banjo Dance
J. Goldthwaite
"I'm Just a Little Indian, Nothing More"
W. M. Armstrong, F. Lennox, Jr.
"Come, Hurry Up!"
"Ha! Ha! You Are Too Late"
"Love, First Love"
H. Clark
"A Summer Girls Love"
F. Lennox, J. Goldthwaite
"Bridesmaids' Chorus"
"He Came Right Up"
R. Broderick
"Thrice Happy the Wooing" (Finale)

1895.26 THE CHIEFTAIN

A Comic Opera in Two Acts. Libretto by Francis C. Burnand. Music by Arthur Sullivan. Produced under the direction of Richard Barker. Settings by Richard Marston. Costumes by Percy Anderson. Musical director, Antonio deNovellis. Produced by Francis Wilson Company (Management, Al H. Canby). Opened 9 September 1895 at Abbey's Theatre and closed 26 October 1895 after 54 performances.

CAST: *Peter Adolphus Grigg*, a British tourist in search of the picturesque: FRANCIS WILSON. *Count Vasquez de Gonzago*: RHYS THOMAS. *Ferdinand de Roxas*, Chieftain of the Ladrones, disguised as Pietro Slivinski, a Polish courier: JOHN E. BRAND. *Sancho*, First Lieutenant of the Ladrones: JOSEPH C. MIRON. *José*, Second Lieutenant of the Ladrones: EDWARD P. TEMPLE. *Pedro Gomez*, consulting lawyer, astrologer and keeper of the archives of the Ladrones: PETER M. LANG. *Blazzo*: A. Amadeo. *Escatero*: Osborne Clemson. *Pedrillo*, a goatherd: Bessie Lee. *Rita*, an English lady engaged to Count Vasquez; and in Act 2, the Countess of Gonzago: LULU GLASER. *Inez de Roxas*, Chieftainess of the Ladrones: LILLIAN CARLLSMITH. *Dolly*, Mrs. Grigg, Peter A. Grigg's wife: CHRISTIE MacDONALD. *Juanita*, the dancing girl of the Ladrones: ALICE HOLBROOK. *Maraquita*: Agnes Martyne. *Zitella*: Jeanette Emery. *Anna*: Martha Stein.

Act 1: Mountain pass between Compostella and Seville.

Act 2: Exterior of a Posada on the River Sil.

ACT 1[20]

"Hush! not a step" (Duet with Chorus)
J. C. Miron, E. P. Temple, Chorus
"My parents were of great gentility" (Song and Chorus)
L. Carllsmith, Chorus
"The Law and Tradition of the Ladrones" (Recitative)
P. M. Lang, Chorus
"'Tis very hard to choose" (Trio)
L. Carllsmith, J. C. Miron, E. P. Temple
"Only the night wind sighs" (Song)
L. Glaser
"Hand of Fate" (Quintet and Chorus)
L. Glaser, L. Carllsmith, R. Thomas, E. P. Temple, J. C. Miron
"A guard by night" (Duet)
L. Glaser, R. Thomas
"From rock to rock" (Song)
F. Wilson
"Hullo! what's that?" (Trio)
F. Wilson, E. P. Temple, J. C. Miron
Finale
L. Glaser, L. Carllsmith, R. Thomas, F. Wilson, P. M. Lang, A. Amadeo, E. P. Temple, Sanchez, Chorus

[20]Musical numbers not listed in programs. List prepared from published piano vocal score (Boosey, London, 1895).

"(Hymn of) The Sacred Hat"
Chorus of Girls
Dance
The Gay Hussar" (Song)
R. Thomas, Chorus

ACT 2

"Wake, then, awake!" (Introduction and Song)
R. Thomas
"The River! The River!"
Chorus
"The Legend of the River" (Two Happy Gods)(Song with Chorus)
L. Glaser, Chorus
"Ah, oui, j'étais" (Duet)
L. Glaser, R. Thomas
"Bustle! bustle!" (Song with Chorus)
J. E. Brand, Chorus
"To Spain, said my husband" (There Seemed to Be Something in That)(Song)
C. MacDonald, with L. Glaser, R. Thomas, F. Wilson, J. E. Brand
"There are cases" (Truth in the Well) (Trio)
L. Glaser, R. Thomas, F. Wilson, with C. MacDonald, J. E. Brand
"La Criada" (Song)
J. E. Brand
"There's no one, I'm certain" (Quintet)
A. Holbrook, L. Carllsmith, P. M. Lang, E. P. Temple, J. C. Miron
"What is the matter, Peter?" (Trio)
C. MacDonald, L. Carllsmith, F. Wilson
"We quite undertand" (Be Mum) (Sestette)
A. Holbrook, L. Carllsmith, P. M. Lang, F. Wilson, E. P. Temple, J. C. Miron
"The Chieftain is found" (Finale)L. Glaser, C. MacDonald, A. Holbrook, L. Carllsmith,
R. Thomas, P. M. Lang, F. Wilson, J. E. Brand, E. P. Temple, J. C. Miron, Chorus

1895.27 THE WIDOW JONES

A Farcical Conceit (Farce Comedy) in Three Acts. Play by John J. McNally. Staged by R. A. Roberts. Settings by John Thompson. Music arranged by John C. Sorg. Produced by (Isaac B.) Rich and (William) Harris. Opened 16 September 1895 at the Bijou Theatre and closed 9 November 1895 after 64 performances; re-opened 16 February 1896 at the Bijou Theatre and closed 16 May 1896 after 104 additional performances. Total: 168 performances[21].

CAST: *Billy Bilke*, a promoter, whatever that is: JOHN C. RICE. *John James Jones*, a social derelict: JACQUES KRUGER. *Beatrice Byke*, the Widow Jones: MAY IRWIN. *Senor Romero Canovas*, erratic and artistic: GEORGE W. BARNUM. *Felicity Jones*, the derelict's daughter: ADA LEWIS. *Mike McCarthy*, a Maine farmer: JOSEPH M. SPARKS. *Seeking Theatrical Preferment (4)*: *Cassie Cartee*, his daughter: Sally Cohen. *Flossie Cartee*, his other daughter: Kathleen Warren. *Janet Johnson*: Grace Vaughn. *Daisey Davis*: Agnes Milton. *Clifford Prout*, in love with Felicity: Richard J. Jones. *Marcia Mendelshonn*, with marital complications: Maud M. Chandler. *Marie Pose*, a French model: Mabel Power. *A. J. Premium*, insurance detective: Roland Carter. *Mandy Noir*, maid of Beatrice: Gertrude Mansfield. *Farm Hand*: John H. Connolly. *Baby Flo*, a realistic actor: Herself. *Some others and Summer Boarders.*

Act 1: McCarthy's Farm at Maranacook, Maine.

Act 2: Apartment in Paris.

Act 3: Home of Beatrice Bike, Thousand Islands.

ACT 1[22]

Dance
J. C. Rice, S. Cohen
Grand Medley Introduction
Duet from PRINCE PRO TEM
M. Irwin, J. C. Rice, Entire Company
(*Music by* Lewis S. Thompson. *Lyrics by* R. A. Barnet.)
"Rosey Is a Gaiety Girl"
J. C. Rice
"The Streets of Cairo (or, The Poor Little Country Maid)"
S. Cohen
(*Music and Lyrics by* James Thornton.)
"Love's Dream after the Ball"
G. Mansfield
"Be Good, Be Good"
J. M. Sparks
"My Girl (Is a Plain Girl)"
R. Carter
"I Want Yer, Ma Honey"
M. Irwin
(*Music and Lyrics by* Fay Templeton.)
Pickaninny Dance
S. Cohen, K. Warren, G. Mansfield, G. Vaughan

ACT 2

Negro Song and Chorus
M. Irwin
May Irwin's "Bully Song"[23]
M. Irwin
(*Music and Lyrics by* Charles E. Trevathan.)

ACT 3

"Celeste" (from THE ALGERIAN)
M. Irwin, Company
(*Music by* Reginald DeKoven. *Lyrics by* Glen MacDonough.)
"When Bloom the Roses"/"Every Rose Must Have Its Thorn"
G. Mansfield
Songs
M. Irwin

[21]Costumes uncredited. Also played New York area return engagements 11 November 1895 at the Harlem Opera House for 8 performances, 19 October 1896 at the Harlem Opera House for 8 performances, 2 November 1896 at the Grand Opera House for 8 performances, and 28 March 1898 at the Columbus Theatre for 8 performances.

[22]Interpolated during the run or tour, as per published sheet music:
"Hot Tamale Alley"
M. Irwin
(*Music by* George M. Cohan. *Lyrics by* May Irwin.)
"I Love My Honey, Yes I Do"
M. Irwin
(*Music and Lyrics by* Will C. Carleton.)
"I've Been Hoodooed" (Comic Song and Refrain)
M. Irwin
(*Music and Lyrics by* Gussie L. Davis.)
"His Legs Are Assorted Sizes"
M. Irwin
(*Music by* George H. Wilder. *Lyrics by* Lawrence J. Sheehan.)
"There'll Be Murder Tonight"
J. M. Sparks
(*Music and Lyrics by* Francis J. Bryant.)
May Irwin's "Frog Song"
M. Irwin
(*Music and Lyrics by* Charles E. Trevathan.)

[23]Replaced by:
"The New Bully"
M. Irwin
(*Music and Lyrics by* Joseph E. Howard.)
Also published was:
"De New Bully"
M. Irwin
(*Music by* J. W. Cavanagh. *Lyrics by* Will C. Carleton.)

1895.28 HÄNSEL AND GRETEL

Sir Augustus Harris' London Opera Company in a Dainty Fairy Opera in Three Acts. Libretto by Adelheid Wette, adapted from the fairy tale "Hänsel und Gretel" by Jakob and Wilhelm Grimm. English adaptation by Constance Bache. Music by Engelbert Humperdinck. Staged by Augustus Harris. Scenery by L. W. Seavey. Costumes designed by Comelli, London. Conductor, Anton Seidl. Produced by Augustin Daly. Opened 7 October 1895 at Daly's Theatre and closed 16 November 1895 after 48 performances; reopened 23 December 1895 at Daly's Theatre and closed 4

January 1896 after 16 additional performances. Total: 64 performances.

CAST: *Peter*, a broom-maker: Jacques Bars, Wilberforce Franklin. *Gertrude*, his wife: Grace Damian, Alice Gordon. *Hänsel, Gretel*, their children: MARIE ELBA or CECILE BRANI; JEANNE DOUSTE or JESSIE HUDDLESTON. *The Witch*, who eats children: LOUISE MEISSLINGER, ALICE GORDON. *Sandman*, the sleep fairy: Miss (Eone) Delrita, Cecile Brani. *Dewman*, the Dawn Fairy: Edith Johnston, Maud Franklin. *Choir, Angels, Children, etc.*

Act 1: At home.

Act 2: In the Forest.

Act 3: The Witch's House.

1895.29 HIS EXCELLENCY

A Comic Opera in Two Acts. Libretto by W. S. Gilbert. Music by Dr. Osmond Carr. Produced (staged) by John Gunn. Dances arranged by John D'Auban. Settings by Ernest Gros and Edward G. Unitt. Costumes by Percy Anderson. Musical director, Gustave Howig. Produced by Al Hayman and Charles Frohman by arrangement with George Edwardes. Opened 14 October 1895 at the Broadway Theatre and closed 21 December 1895 after 63 performances.

CAST: *The Prince Regent*, disguised as Nils Egilsson, a strolling player: JULIUS STEGER. *Governor Griffenfeld*, Governor of Elsinore: CAIRNS JAMES. *Erling Sykke*, a young sculptor: WILLIAM PHILP. *Tortenssen*, a young physician: AUGUSTUS CRAMER. *Mats Munck*, Syndic of Elsinore: JOHN LeHAY. *Corporal Harold* of the King's Hussars: Ernest Snow. *A Sentry*: Tim Ryley. *First Officer*: C. Clements. *Second Officer*: J. Jamison. *Christina*, a ballad singer: NANCY McINTOSH. *Thora, Nanna*, Griffenfeld's daughters: ELLALINE TERRISS, GERTRUDE AYLWARD. *Dame Hecla Courtlandt*, a lady of property: ALICE BARNETT. *Blanca*, a Vivandière: Mabel Love.

Act 1: Market-place of Elsinore. 1801. (Gros.)

Act 2: Courtyard of the Castle. (Unitt.)

ACT 1[24]

"See the merry bunting flying" (Opening Chorus)
J. LeHay, Chorus
"Good sir, although I sit apart all day" (Recitative and Ballad)
N. McIntosh
"When I bestow my bosom's store" (Song)
W. Philp
"Oh my goodness, here's the nobility!" (Duet)
G. Aylward, E. Terriss
"If all is as you say" (Quartette)
G. Aylward, E. Terriss, W. Philp, A. Cramer
"Here are the warriors all ablaze"
Elsa, Chorus of Girls
Soldiers' Dance
"Now what would I do if you proved untrue" (Duet)
C. James, A. Barnett
"Oh what a fund of joy" (Trio)
C. James, G. Aylward, E. Terriss
"A King though he's pestered with cares" (Song)
J. Steger
"I've grasped your scheme" (Duet)
J. Steger, C. James, Chorus
"Now all that we've agreed upon, O—" (Duet)
Dame, J. LeHay, Chorus
"My wedded life" (Song)
G. Aylward
"Come hither, every one" (Finale)
W. Philp, A. Cramer, All
"After a travelling troublesome" (Trio)
C. James, G. Aylward, E. Terriss
"This is our opportunity—" (Sextette)
W. Philp, A. Cramer, J. LeHay, E. Snow, N. McIntosh, A. Barnett
"When two days old at most" (Ballad)
E. Terriss

ACT 2

"With anger stern" (Opening Chorus)
"Be comforted—his downfall I foresee" (Recitative)
N. McIntosh
"A Hive of bees, as I've heard say" (Song with guitar)
N. McIntosh
"Hail, oh Regent"
Principals, Chorus
Ballet of Hussars
"My people, who've submitted to the Governor's absurdities" (Song)
J. Steger
"Your orders I am trying to obey" (Ensemble)
J. Steger, C. James, W. Philp, G. Aylward, E. Terriss, Harold, A. Cramer, J. LeHay, Principals, Chorus
"Quixotic is his enterprise" (Song)
C. James
"One day, the Syndic of this town" (Quartette)
J. LeHay, A. Barnett, Sentry, C. James
"When a gentleman supposes" (Patter Trio)
C. James, G. Aylward, E. Terriss
"So this is how you'd have us sue you" (Dancing Quartet)
W. Philp, A. Cramer, G. Aylward, E. Terriss
"When you approach the Royal Presence" (Trio)
N. McIntosh, G. Aylward, E. Terriss
"Ring the bells and bang the brasses!" (Chorus)
Chorus
"Now all that we've agreed upon, O—" (Finale)
All
"The Magnet and the Churn"
N. McIntosh

1895.30 MAVOURNEEN

A Revival of the Comedy Drama in Four Acts, 7 Scenes[25]. Play by George H. Jessup and Horace Townsend. Songs by W. J. Scanlan. Staged by Augustus Pitou. Scenery by Homer F. Emens, H. L. Reid, John Young. Musical director, Albert Krausse. Produced by Augustus Pitou. Opened 14 October 1895 at the 14th Street Theatre and closed 26 October 1895 after 16 performances[26].

CAST: *Terence Dwyer*: CHAUNCEY OLCOTT. *John Dwyer*: Daniel Gilfether. *Captain Marchmont*: C. F. Gotthold. *Abbe Maloney*: J. W. Hague. *Colonel*: Edwin Richards. *Shamus Corrigan*: Luke Martin. *Mark*: Frank Peters. *Cossack*: Dan J. Fingleton. *Club Porter*: William Jones. *Lady Caroline Dwyer*: Etta Baker Martin. *Lady May Tyrell*: Rolenda Bainbridge. *Mrs. Dwyer*: Lizzie Washburn. *Kate Morris*: LOUISE CLOSSER. *Helen Dwyer*: Imogene Washburn. *Georgie Dwyer*: Kenneth Barnes. *Susie Morris*: Dot Clarendon. *Kitty Morris*: Imogene Washburn. *Peasants, Guests, Officers, Chair-Bearers and Link-Boys.*

1895.31 LEONARDO

A Romantic Comic Opera in Three Acts. Libretto by Gilbert Burgess. Music by T. Pearsall Thorne. Staged by James C. Duff. Settings by Walter Burridge, Homer F. Emens and Ernest Albert. Costumes designed by Percy Anderson. Musical director, Gustave Kerker. Produced by James C. Duff. Opened 21 October 1895 at the Garrick Theatre and closed 9 November 1895 after 21 performances.

---

[24]Musical numbers not listed in programs; list prepared from published libretto (T. B. Harms, New York, 1894).

[25]Originally produced in New York 28 September 1891 at the 14th Street Theatre for 104 performances. For Synopsis of Scenes and Musical Numbers, see original 1891 production. Olcott sang all the musical numbers. For this revival, "Mrs. Reilly's Party" and "Bye-bye, Baby, Bye-bye" were omitted, and "Mavourneen" (composed by W. J. Scanlan) was added. At the Grand Opera House engagement, the following were added: "Ring the Bells," "The Snowy Breasted Pearl," (*Music*, traditional Irish; *Lyrics by* Stephen deVere.) and "She and I Together." (The latter may not be composed by W. J. Scanlan.)

[26]Costumes uncredited. Later played return engagements with Chauncey Olcott in New York 2 January 1896 at the 14th Street Theatre for 32 performances, 25 May 1896 at the Grand Opera House for 8 performances, and 10 May 1897 at the 14th Street Theatre for 1 week.

CAST: *Leonardo*, a young sculptor: GEORGE E. DEVOLL. *Angelo*, his friend and fellow student: AUBREY BOUCICAULT. *Fra Patchouli*, a mathematician: J. H. RYLEY. *Duke Ludivici of Milan*: HOBART SMOCK. *Marco*, a chamberlain: ALBERT McGUCKIN. *Giovanni*, a student: Grant Odell. *Bruno*, a student: A. Adams. *Andrea*, a curiosity dealer: J. Weisner. *The Lady Beatrice*: MARGUERITE LEMON. *Cecelia*, a poetess: VIRGINIA EARLE. *Lucretia*, a lady of the Court: LUCILLE SAUNDERS. *Artists' Models (4)*: *Tessa*: Winifred Williams. *Lauretta*: Dawn Griffith. *Maria*: Francis Campbell. *Francesca*: Virginia Laurie. *Students, models, soldiers, pages, court ladies, citizens, etc.*

Act 1: A street in Florence. Fifteenth century. (Burridge.)

Act 2: Before the Cathedral in Milan. (Emens.)

Act 3: A Garden in Livorno. (Albert.)

ACT 1[27]

Opening Chorus and Recitative;
Song (There is no need for you to sing so loud)
J. H. Ryley, Chorus
Song (Art is for me no other love)
G. E. Devoll
Ballad (I sing of Doffa-down-dillies)
V. Earle, Chorus
Trio (We've just arrived from the court of Milan)
M. Lemon, A. McGuckin, L. Saunders
Duet (Fair lady, since you deign to shed)
G. E. Devoll, M. Lemon
Song (A mighty King, the story's told)
M. Lemon
Finale (When hearts and young and light)
Principals, Chorus

ACT 2

Opening Chorus (We have donned our silks and satins)
Chorus of Soldiers (Oh a military life)
Song (I feel quite humorous)
A. Bouciault, V. Earle
Song (Two little turtle doves sat on a tree)
L. Saunders
Trio (Prithee, Miss, what are you doing?)
M. Lemon, L. Saunders, G. E. Devoll
Duet (I sing no songs, but songs of thee)
M. Lemon, G. E. Devoll
Song (Northwind a-blowing through the trees)
J. H. Ryley, Chorus
March, Recitative and Song (When first the world began)
H. Smock
Finale (Is Leonardo here?)
Principals, Chorus

ACT 3

Introduction, Gavotte and Chorus (We are people of the very finest quality)
Song (When Man goes forth to make his way)
G. E. Devoll
Trio (Who'd have thought of seeing you here?)
V. Earle, A. Boucicault, J. H. Ryley
Duet (When a gifted lady chooses)
V. Earle, A. Boucicault
Song (Under the blue summer sky)
L. Saunders
Chorus of Men (Boldly behaving, epaulettes craving)
Song (Night is past and the morn is breaking calm and clear)
H. Smock, Chorus
Finale (Hail, Leonardo and his royal bride)
Principals, Chorus

1895.32 THE SHOP GIRL

A Musical Farce in Two Acts. Libretto by Harry J. W. Dam. Music by Ivan Caryll. Additional numbers by Adrian Ross and Lionel Monckton. Staged by A. E. Dodson. Dances arranged by Willie Warde. Settings by Ernest Gros. Costumes by Wilhelm. Musical director, Barter Johns. Produced by Al Hayman and Charles Frohman by arrangement with George Edwardes. Opened 28 October 1895 at Palmer's Theatre and closed 28 December 1895 after 72 performances[28].

CAST: *Mr. Hooley*, proprietor of the Royal Stores: W. H. RAWLINS. *Charles Appleby*, a medical student: SEYMOUR HICKS. *Bertie Boyd*, one of the boys: GEORGE GROSSMITH, JR. *John Brown*, a millionaire: MICHAEL DWYER. *Sir George Appleby*, a solicitor: Walter McEwen. *Colonel Singleton*, retired: George Honey. *Count St. Vaurien*, secretary to Mr. Brown: A. Nillson-Fisher. *Mr. Tweets*, financial secretary to Mr. Brown: Alfred Asher. *Mr. Miggles*, shopwalker at the Royal Stores: BERTIE WRIGHT. *Bessie Brent*, The Shop Girl": ETHEL SYDNEY. *Lady Dodo Singleton*, Charlie's cousin: Annie Albu. *Miss Robinson*, fitter at the Royal Stores: Marie Faucett. *Lady Appleby*, Charlie's mother, wife of Sir George: Leslie Greenwood. *Ada Smith*, an apprentice at the Royal Stores: CONNIE EDISS. *Lady Appleby's daughters (3)*: *Faith*: May Beaugarde. *Hope*: Minnie Sadler. *Charity*: Winnie Rose.
Of the Gaiety Theatre: *Maud Plantagenet*: Adelaide Astor. *Eva Tudor*: Violet Dene. *Lillie Stuart*: Ida Wallace. *Ada Harrison*: Hylda Galton. *Mabel Beresford*: Nellie Huxley. *Florence White*: Zara deLome. *Birdie Waudesfaude*: Nellie Langton. *Maggie Jocelyn*: Violet Durkin. *Violet Deveney*: Annie Vivian. *Principal Dancer*: Dorothy Douglass.

Act 1: The Royal Stores.

Act 2: Fancy Bazaar at Kensington.

ACT 1[29]

"The Royal Stores" (Opening Chorus)
"By Special Appointment" (Song)
W. H. Rawlins, E. Sydney, Chorus
"We'll proceed to search for Ada" (Quartet)
W. McEwen, A. Nilsson-Fisher, W. H. Rawlins, G. Honey
Chorus of Stage Beauties (In us of course you'll see)
(*Music by* Lionel Monckton.)
"Superfluous Relations" (Song)
S. Hicks, Foundlings
(*Music by* Lionel Monckton. *Lyrics by* Adrian Ross.)
"The Song of the Shop" (I stand at my counter)
E. Sydney
(*Music by* Lionel Monckton. *Lyrics by* Adrian Ross.)
"Hush-a-bye" (Perambulator Duet)
E. Sydney, S. Hicks
"Over the Hills" (Valse Song)
"Foundlings are we" (Concerted Piece)
G. Grossmith, Foundlings
"The Vegetarian" (Song)
B. Wright
(*Music by* Ivan Caryll. *Lyrics by* H. J. W. Dam.)
"The Foundling" (Song)
C. Ediss, Chorus
"Farewell, farewell" (Finale)
Principals, Chorus

ACT 2

"Charity, charity!" (Opening Chorus)
"The Smartest Girl in Town" (Song)
(*Lyrics by* Adrian Ross.)
"Louisiana Lou" (Song)
(*Music and Lyrics by* Leslie Stuart.)
"Love on the Japanese Plan" (Duet and Dance)
B. Wright, M. Faucett
(*Music by* Ivan Caryll.)
"Brown of Colorado" (The Millionaire)
M. Dwyer
(*Music by* Lionel Monckton. *Lyrics by* Adrian Ross.)
"Too clever by half" (Trio)
W. McEwen, A. Nilsson-Fisher, G. Honey
(*Lyrics by* Adrian Ross.)

---

[27]Musical numbers not listed in programs. List prepared from published piano vocal score (T. B. Harms & Co., New York, 1894).

[28]Later played a New York return engagement 24 February 1896 at the Harlem Opera House for 8 performances.

[29]Musical numbers not listed in programs; list prepared from published English piano vocal score (Hopwood & Crew, London, 1894, 1895) which may necessarily not reflect interpolations, cut songs, etc. for the American production.

"We're now to have some mystery" (Chorus)
"The man in the moon" (Song)
A. Albu
"Beautiful, bountiful Bertie" (Song)
G. Grossmith, Jr., Chorus
(*Music by* Lionel Monckton. *Lyrics by* George Grossmith, Jr.)
"The show, the show" (Chorus)
"Walk up, walk up! (The Show Song)
V. Durkin
(*Lyrics by* Adrian Ross.)
"Now joy is in the air" (Finale)
Principals, Chorus

SUPPLEMENTARY NUMBERS
"Oh! my dummy!" (Song)
"The Little Mad'moiselle" (Song)
(*Music and Lyrics by* Leslie Stuart.)
"I want yer, ma Honey" (Song)
(*Music and Lyrics by* Fay Templeton.)
"The Little Chinchilla" (Song)
(*Music and Lyrics by* Paul Rubens.)
"What could the poor girl do?" (Song)
(*Music by* Emilie Alexandra. *Lyrics by* Adrian Ross.)
"(And) Her Golden Hair Was Hanging Down Her Back"
S. Hicks
(*Music by* Felix McGlennon. *Lyrics by* Monroe Rosenfeld, revised by Adrian Ross.)

1895.33 THE WIZARD OF THE NILE

A Comic Opera in Three Acts. Libretto by Harry B. Smith. Music by Victor Herbert. Presented under the stage direction of Napier Lothian, Jr. Scenery by Ernest Albert. Costumes designed by Catherine Seidle. Musical director, Frank Palma. Orchestrations by Victor Herbert. Produced by the Frank Daniels Opera Company (Kirk LaShelle, Arthur F. Clarke, Proprietors and Managers). Opened 4 November 1895 at the Casino Theatre and closed 1 February 1896 after 105 performances[30].

CAST: *Kibosh*, a Persian magician, making a professional tour of Egypt: FRANK DANIELS. *Abydos*, his apprentice: LOUISE ROYCE. *Ptolemy*, King of Egypt: WALTER ALLEN. *Simoona*, Ptolemy's second wife: MARY PALMER. *Cleopatra*, a princess who knows naught of love: DOROTHY MORTON. *Ptarmigan*, Cleopatra's music teacher: EDWIN ISHAM. *Cheops*, the royal weather bureau: Louis Casavant. *Obeliska*, captain of the Amazons: Helen Redmond. *Netocris*, lieutenant of the Amazons: Claudia Carlstedt. *Merza*, first maid-of-honor to Cleopatra: Grace Rutter. *Royal Guards, Nobles, Citziens, Pages, Maids-of-Honor, Dancing Girls, Galley Slaves, etc.*
The action takes place in ancient Egypt.

Act 1: Public Square in Alexandria.

Act 2: Terraced roof of the King's palace.

Act 3: Interior of the King's private pyramid.

ACT 1[31]
"Father Nile, Keep Us in Thy Care" (Opening Chorus)
Boatmen, Water-carriers
"Song of the Optimist" (Duet and Chorus)
H. Redmond, L. Casavant, Chorus
"Strew the Way with Flow'rets Blooming" (Oriental March)
Almehs (Dancing Girls), Amazons
"I am the Ruler" (Duet with Chorus)
W. Allen, M. Palmer, Chorus
"That's One Thing a Wizard Can Do" (Solo with Chorus)
F. Daniels, Chorus
"Pure and White Is the Lotus"
Chorus
"I Have Been A-Maying" (Solo with Chorus)
D. Morton, Chorus
"What Is Love?" (Duet)
F. Daniels, D. Morton
"When the Bugles Are Calling" (Solo)
E. Isham
"Bang, Bang, the Most Harmonious Song"/
Chorus
"Incantation"/
M. Palmer, Chorus
"A Cheer for Kibosh" (Finale Act 1)
Principals, Chorus

ACT 2
"List to Our Matin Serenade" (Opening Serenade)
L. Royce, L. Casavant, Pages
"If I Were a King" (Duet)
E. Isham, D. Morton
"On Cleopatra's Wedding Day" (Quintette)
D. Morton, L. Royce, M. Palmer, W. Allen, L. Casavant
"My Angeline" (Song of the Human Snake)
F. Daniels, Chorus
Finale Act 2
Principals, Chorus

ACT 3
"Stonecutters' Song" (Work Away with a Song, My Boys)
E. Isham, Chorus
"In Dreamland" (Solo)
D. Morton
"Star Light, Star Bright" (Waltz Quintette)
L. Royce, M. Palmer, F. Daniels, L. Casavant, F. Daniels
"To the Pyramid" (Pages' Chorus)
L. Royce, Chorus
"The Echo Song" (Duet and Chorus)
F. Daniels, W. Allen, Chorus of Pages
Finale Act 3
Principals, Chorus

[30]Later played return engagements in New York 17 February 1896 at the Harlem Opera House for 8 performances, and 28 September 1896 at the Harlem Opera House for 8 performances.
[31]No song list in the program. List prepared from published piano vocal score (E. Schuberth & Co., New York, 1895).

1895.34 THE NIGHT CLERK

A Farce Comedy in Three Acts. Play by John J. McNally. Produced under the personal direction of Frank Tannehill, Jr. Settings by John A. Thompson. Musical director, Rene Stretti. Produced by (Isaac B.) Rich and (William) Harris. Opened 11 November 1895 at the Bijou Theatre and closed 28 December 1895 after 56 performances[32].

CAST: *Owen More*: PETER F. DAILEY. *Adelaide Starr*, an Actress: JENNIE YEAMANS. *Lord Willie Wilt*, Owen's Chum: RAYMOND HITCHCOCK. *Barney Brogan*: JOHN G. SPARKS. *Conn A. More*, Owen's father: Michael Sullivan. *Lotta More*, his daughter: Freda Depew. *Hannah More*, his sister: Gertrude Fort. *Lizzie Lester*, his ward: Rita Emerson. *Dolly Dent*: Ida Rock. *Violet Ballou*: Nellie Parker. *Kitty Clive*: Eva Butler. *William Lumber*, Theatrical Manager: Hugh Mack. *Gutsy Ladd*, Errand Boy: Bertie Dyer. *Hardy Upp*, One of Many: Charles Sturgis. *Sergeant Grabb*: William Keough. *Jones*, from the West: Peter Randall. *Roundsman Rush*: Lawrence Sheehan. (*Specialty*: The Olympia Quartette.)
The action takes place in greater New York in the nineteenth century.

Act 1: Owen More's apartments.

Act 2: Police Station, Tenderloin Precinct.

Act 3: The Hotel Blase.

ACT 1
"The Debutante" (Song)
J. Yeamans
A little (more or Less) Grand Opera
(*Music by* Rene Stretti.)

ACT 2
"The New York Police" (Song)
Olympia Quartette
Grand Medley
Entire Company

[32]Costumes uncredited.

ACT 3
"Independent Cadets"
Olympia Quartette
Eccentric Dance
G. Fort
Mr. Dailey will make the best of the worst of it ["Red Hot Member"]
"American Girls" (Characteristic Song)
Six of Them
"The Girl from Gay Paree"
J. Yeamans
"Down By the River Side"

1895.35 THE MERRY COUNTESS

A Musical Comedy in Three Acts. Book by Charles Klein. Based on the French play "Niniche" by Maurice Hennequin and Albert Millaud. Music by Johann Brandl. Lyrics by Thomas Frost. Produced under the direction of Eugene W. Presbrey. Settings by John H. Young. Miss Jansen's costumes by Mme. Lessing; other costumes designed by Catherine Seidle. Musical director, Edward Poelz. Produced by Messrs. Steiner and Hahn. Opened 12 November 1895 at the Garrick Theatre and closed 20 November 1895 after (10) performances.

CAST: *Count Vernondorff*, a diplomat: EDWIN STEVENS. *Vicompte De Beaupersil*, a Parisian: DAN DALY. *Medor*, the bathing master: CHARLES DICKSON. *Dupiton*, the angler: Benson Pierce. *Desablettes*, the secretary: Fred W. Peters. *Monsieur Darcey*, a guest: Fred Lotto. *Bath Attendant*: Charles Dade. *Narcisse*, *Jean*, waiters: Ernest Walcott, Edwin Stone. *Hotel manager*: Dwight Smith. *Baptiste*: Theodore Brown. *Commissary*: Charles Moore. *A Swell*: H. R. Forbes. *Madame Pommery*: MAUDE GRANGER. *Hortense*, Lurette's maid: Lillian Burkhart. *Victorine*: Marie Carlyle. *Annette*, maid to the Countess: Elizabeth Leslie. *Amanda*: Belle Hamilton. *Cora*: May Terriss. *Pauline*: Carolyn Lawrence. *Castagnette*: Minnie Bowen. *The Countess (Lurette)*: MARIE JANSEN. *Tourists, Soldiers, Bathers, Attendants, etc.*

Act 1: On the beach at Trouville. Present day.

Act 2: Lurette's Apartments, Paris.

Act 3: Grand Hotel, Paris.

1895.36 THE BICYCLE GIRL

A Musical Farce Comedy in Three Acts. Play by Louis Harrison. Produced by Nellie McHenry (John Webster, Proprietor and Manager) Opened 18 November 1895 at the Grand Opera House and closed 23 November 1895 after 8 performances.

CAST: *Baron Byke*: JOHN WEBSTER. *Stephen Stillwell*: CHARLES P. MORRISON. *John Potipher*, the fully developed man of the future: HENRY LAURENT. *Tom Tipton*: F. W. Richmond. *Twister*, a tramp rider: W. E. Ritchie. *Nathaniel*, waiter at the Briarwood Club-house: James Bowen. *Joseph Hardtack*: James McGrath. *Henry Stubbins*: Henry Moore. *Messenger*: Walter Cole. *Mrs. John Potipher*, the coming woman: LAURA BENNETT. *Blanche Harcourt*: Delle Jackson. *Rose Thorne*: Julia Glover. *Berlina Cortland*: Ethel Tyler. *Clarice Hollywood*: Lillian DeGross. *Grace Fordyce*, "The Bicycle Girl": NELLIE McHENRY.

Act 1: Interior of the Briarwood Bicycle Club.

Act 2: The bicycle clam-bake.

Act 3: The bicycle meet.

ACT 1
"The Girl Who Rides the Wheel" (Opening Chorus)
N. McHenry, Company
"Cannibal King"
C. P. Morrison
"Long Ago"
N. McHenry, C. P. Morrison, H. Laurent
"Joie and Vasaline"
N. McHenry, C. P. Morrison
"The Princess of Trébizonde" (Finale)
Company
(*Music by* Jacques Offenbach.)

ACT 2
"Oh, Honey" (Invisible Chorus)
"Clam-Bake"
N. McHenry, Company
"Ridin' on de Golden Bike"
N. McHenry, Company
Operatic Selections
D. Jackson
"At Eve" (Quartette)
D. Jackson, L. Bennett, C. P. Morrison, H. Laurent
Grand Medley of Popular Songs
Company

ACT 3
Parodies on Popular Songs
C. P. Morrison
Yodelling and Negro Melodies
L. Bennett
"The Bicycle Girl" (Song and Dance)
D. Jackson, J. Glover, L. DeGross, E. Tyler
["Ben Bo It" in German] "Trilby O'Farrell"
N. McHenry, Company
Grand Finale
Company

1895.37 A HAPPY LITTLE HOME

A Musical Comedy Satire in Three Acts. Play by Charles Klein. Produced under the personal direction of Nick Long. Musical conductor, Frank Saddler. Produced by Robert B. Monroe. Opened 25 November 1895 at the 14th Street Theatre and closed 7 December 1895 after 17 performances[33].

CAST: *Owen Moore*, a young lawyer: GEORGE W. MONROE. *Cornelius Gayfeather*, a gay old bird: HARRY HOTTO. *Hector Savanac*, his friend: NICK LONG. *Theophilus Doolittle*, man about town: George W. Howard. *Burke*, a detective detected: Frank Bell. *Boker*, a servant: Harry C. Stanley. *Waiter*: M. T. Tray. *Pantata*, a guardian of the peace: G. L. Tallman. *Mrs. Gayfeather*, an up-to-date wife: MAGARET FITZPATRICK. *Victoria Gayfeather*, her daughter: IDALENE COTTON. *Rose Meredith*, her ward, in love with Moore: CORA MACY. *Carrie*, a maid: JOSIE INTROPODI. *Lulu Montmorency*, a premiere danseuse: Dorothy Drew. *Mrs. Magruder* from Maine: BLANCHE CHAPMAN.

Act 1: Drawing room of "A Happy Little Home."

Act 2: Same as Act 1.

Act 3: Reception room of the Bicycle Club.

ACT 3
Baritone Soloist
G. W. Howard
Chic and Up-to-Date Songs
B. Chapman
Tenor Soloist
G. L. Tallman
Imitations of Vesta Tilley and Mlle. Paquerette
I. Cotton
Clarionette Solos
H. C. Stanley
Songs and High Kicking
D. Drew

1895.38 EXCELSIOR, JR.

A New and Beautiful Entertainment (Musical Comedy) in Three Acts, 4 Scenes. Libretto by R. A. Barnet. Music by George Lowell Tracy, A. Baldwin Sloane. With a few numbers by Edward E. Rice. Entire production presented under the immediate and personal supervision of Edward E. Rice. Settings by Henry E. Hoyt and Frank Rafter. Costumes by Mrs. Mary L.

[33]Costumes, settings, director, and musical direction uncredited. Specialties changed throughout the tour to accomodate cast changes. Later played return engagements in New York 16 March 1896 at the Columbus Theatre for 8 performances, 6 April 1896 at the Third Avenue Theatre for 8 performances, 28 September 1896 at the People's Theater for 8 performances, 5 October 1896 at the 14th Street Theatre for 8 performances, 30 November 1896 at the Star Theatre with THE YELLOW KID for 16 performances, and 13 December 1897 at the Grand Opera House for 8 performances.

Dowling. Orchestra under the direction of John J. Braham. Produced by Rice's Olympia Burlesque Company (E. E. Rice, C. E. Rice, Proprietors). Opened 25 November 1895 at Hammerstein's Olympia Theatre and closed 28 March 1896 after 144 performances; moved 30 March 1896 to the Broadway Theatre and closed after 24 additional performances. Total: 168 performances[34].

CAST: *H. W. Excelsior, Jr.*, a youth who bore mid snow and ice a banner, and whose sole business is to simply flag a mountain: FAY TEMPLETON. *Courier Gyde*, a director of personally conducted tours: CHARLES E. BIGELOW. *William Tell*, whose overture is much admired, and whose shooting apple business is a well-known matter of record: WALTER JONES. *Sammy Smug*, an Old Salt: WALTER JONES. *'Arry*, a costermonger: WALTER JONES. *Ben Bolt*, a little off his nut, driven from home by the hand organs, son of a rich mother: Mathew Ott. *Sig. Vendetta, Sig. Mafia*, Venetians to the backbone: Charles A. Pusey, Arthur Dunn. *Tomagnio Dereske Tenorini*, a tenor of the old school with a rattling voice and the usual high C, Santootsie's prospective husband: RICHARD CARLE. *Four of Crutzner's Laughing Monks*: *Friar Tope*: D. L. Don. *Friar Mope*: Wallace Black. *Friar Phillip*: George F. Campbell. *Friar Tock*: Harry Earle. *Walter Furst, Hildegarde*, two Swiss villagers: Irene Vera, Lillian Cooley. *Hans Auf De Mauer*, the champion wrestler of Switzerland: Hugo Gerber. *William Tell's Hired Son*: W. W. Black. *Valets of Excelsior, Jr. (5)*: *James O*: David Abrahams. *James I*: Kittie Connor. *James II*: Helen Smith. *James III*: May Hamilton. *James IV*: Lillian Cooley. *Paul Jones, Willis Page*, two up to date boys of the period: Violet Potter, Florence Hengler. *St. Bernard Dog*: David Abrahams. *Bertha Gessler*, proprietress of the Gessler Inn, with a penchant for William Tell, large hats and a donkey ride: THERESA VAUGHN. *Mary Vanderbuilt Lamb*, a New York heiress on tour impersonally conducted: IRENE PERRY. *Blanche Calve Santootsie*, with a foreclosed tradition and a yearnin' for connubial bliss: MARIE CAHILL. *'Arriette*, a Coster girl: MARIE CAHILL.

American Book Tourists, personally conducted: *Lucretia Astor Bolt*: Dottie Neville. *Gertie Gigglestone*: Valira Douglas. *Lucy Stuyvesant*: Clara Palmer. *Eunice Oglethrope*: Alice Arnold. *Clara MacPherson*: Mamie Hengler. *Harriet Todd*: Annette Clarette. *Dolly Parrot*: Carrie May. *Evaline*: D. L. Don. *Swiss Men, Swiss Maidens, Swiss Mandolinists, Monks, Watteans, Wattenesses. Olympia Duet Dancers*: Hengler Sisters. *Excelsior Snow Ballet*: Misses Ida Fairbanks, Emma Marsh, Minnie Ashley, Josie Fairbanks, Minnie Gaylor, Nettie Walz, Nina Walsh, Clarette Nanon. *Solo Dancer*: (Mlle. Blanche) DEYO.

Prologue: The Warning to Excelsior.

Act 1: Switzerland in the Snow, Corner of Tell Avenue and Gessler Road. (Rafter.)

Act 2: On the Alps, Visitors' and Recreation Apartment in the Monastery. (Rafter.)

Act 3, Scene 1: Chamounix, the Roccoco Salon in the Grand Hotel. (Hoyt.) *Scene 2*: Atrium of the Grand Hotel. Abode of the Snow King. Final triumph of Excelsior, Jr. (Hoyt.)

ACT 1[35]

"Paraphrase on Upidee"
(*Music by* George Lowell Tracy.)

"Morning Breakfast" (Opening Chorus)
(*Music by* George Lowell Tracy.)

"Grandpa's Hat" (Song)
W. Jones, Chorus
(*Music by* A. Baldwin Sloane.)

"My Love Is Fair" (Yodel Song)
T. Vaughn
(*Music by* Edward E. Rice.)

"Hush, Silence" (Quartette)
(*Music by* A. Baldwin Sloane.)

"I Love You, Evaline" (Waltz Serenade)
M. Cahill, Characters
(*Music by* George Lowell Tracy.)

"I'm a Very Fly Conductor" (Song with Chorus)
C. A. Bigelow
(*Music by* A. Baldwin Sloane.)

"Men, Men, You Foolish Men" (Song and Dance)
I. Perry
(*Music by* George Lowell Tracy.)

Snow Ballet
(*Music by* A. Baldwin Sloane.)

Solo Dance
Mlle. Deyo
(*Music by* A. Baldwin Sloane.)

"I'm Excelsior" (Entrance March and Song)
F. Templeton
(*Music by* George Lowell Tracy.)

"When a Youth and a Maid Pine and Love" (Waltz Song)
(*Music by* A. Baldwin Sloane.)

"The Alpine Horn" (Finale)
(*Music by* George Lowell Tracy and A. Baldwin Sloane.)

"Olympia Gavotte"
(*Music by* Edward E. Rice.)

ACT 2

"A Friar's Life" (Opening Music and Madrigal)
(*Music by* George Lowell Tracy.)

"The 20th Century Girl"
F. Templeton, I. Perry
(*Music by* George Lowell Tracy.)

"Take Him to Evaline" (Finale)
(*Music by* George Lowell Tracy and A. Baldwin Sloane.)

Excelsior March
(*Music by* Edward E. Rice.)

ACT 3

Gavotte and Solo Dance
Mlle. Deyo
(*Music by* A. Baldwin Sloane.)

"My Little Sunday Girl" (Song)
T. Vaughn
(*Music by* A. Baldwin Sloane.)

Duet, Continuous Show
F. Templeton, W. Jones

"Wedding Bells" (Quartette and Dance)
(*Music by* Edward E. Rice.)

"Excelsior" (Finale)
(*Music by* George Lowell Tracy.)

1895.39 A RUNAWAY COLT

A Farcical Play in Four Acts. Play by Charles H. Hoyt. Entire production directed by Julian Mitchell. Scenery by Arthur Voegtlin. Musical director, Harry Braham. Produced by (Charles H.) Hoyt and (Frank) McKee's Comedy Company. Opened 2 December 1895 at the American Theatre and closed 21 December 1895 after 24 performances.[36]

CAST: *The Bishop*: Logan Paul. *The Reverend Chesterfield Manners*: MADISON COREY. *Manley Manners*, his elder son: EDWIN HOLLAND. *Dolton Manners*, his younger son: GAGE CLARKE. *Rankin Haight*, a bank cashier: Clarence Heritage. *Will Haight*, his brother: Walter Turner. *Tennyson Greenfield*, a gentleman of up-to-date ideas: W. F. BLANDE. *Sleigh Bells*, the Mascot: Frank Price. *I. O. A. Savage*, tourist: MADISON COREY. *E. Z. Dunn*, tourist: Logan Paul. *The Judge," "The General,"* devoted to the game: Harry Moulton, C. Madison. *Lange, Everett*, Chicago Ball Club: E. S Metcalfe, Joseph F. Sparks. *Poney Sager*, ground keeper: Edward Leahy. *Catlett Brown*, Manners' servant: James A. Leahy. *Sypher*, waiter Ponce-de-Leon: Ed. Magee. *The Score Card Man*: Dan Sullivan. *Mrs. Manners*, the Doctor's wife: Mrs. Cecile Rush. *Dolly Manners*, her daughter: Alice Evans. *Mercy Given*: GERTRUDE PERRY. *Rosie Hope*, rich but eccentric: JENNIE WEATHERSBY. *Virginia Blood*: Nellie Butler. *Kate Lakeside*, of Chicago: Aggie Vars. *Marie Early*, of Brooklyn: Gene Garland. *Lulu Kidd*, of New York: Sallie Randall. *Daisy Dresser*: Nancy Atherton. *Helena Rush*: Ella Mortimer. *The Captain of the Chicagos*: ADRIAN C. ['Cap'] ANSON.

Act 1: Reception room of Rev. Dr. Manners' house in a town near Chicago. Captain Anson captures the Runaway Colt.

Act 2: Balcony around the swimming pool at the Casino, St. Augustine, Florida. Captain Anson takes the Colts South.

Act 3: Gymnasium adjacent to base ball grounds, Chicago. Captain Anson breaking the colts to harness.

Act 4: Upper tier of the Grand Stand, Chicago Base Ball Park. Captain Anson plays ball.

MUSICAL NUMBERS

1895.40 THE NEW 8 BELLS

A Second Edition of the Nautical Pantomimic Comedy (Acrobatic Pantomime) in Three Acts, 7 Scenes[37]. Written and invented by John F.

[34]Later played a return engagement in New York 12 October 1896 at the Harlem Opera House for 8 performances.

[35]Interpolated as per published sheet music: "My Black Baby Mine"M. Cahill (*Music and Lyrics by* Thomas LeMack.) "I Want Dem Presents Back" (*Music and Lyrics by* Paul West.)

[36]No musical numbers listed in programs.

[37]The First Edition of 8 BELLS was produced in New York 7 September 1891 at the Union Square Theatre for 16 performances, returning 21 November 1892 to the Grand Opera House for an additional 9 performances.

Byrne. Music adapted and arranged by Frank Lorenz. Mechanical effects invented by John F. Byrne. Produced by the Brothers Byrne (Walter Loftus, Manager). Opened 9 December 1895 at Henry C. Miner's People's Theatre and closed 14 December 1895 after 8 performances.

CAST: *Charles Fitzgerald*, in love with Rose O'Connor: J. ED. DONNELLY. *Gussie Blotter*, a tender youth: Harry E. Baker. *Detective Grabb*, from Scotland Yard, with a gun: Wally Melrose. *Henry*, servant to Fitzgerald: John Melrose. *Dan*, a bad boy: Frank Melrose. *Harry Maynard*, a policeman: Joe LaMartine. *Peter*, a good boy: Frank LaMartine. *Sammy Smuggs*, a waiter at Hastings Dock: Ed. Prevost. *Jules*, a French waiter: Henry Kammerer. *Station Agent*, London and Northwestern Railway of England: William H. Miller. *Hard-a-Lee*, a sailor on the S. S. *Norwich*, Charles Cheney. *Monsieur LaTour*, a French detective: William Dale. *Captain of the S.S. Norwich*: Harry Vane. *Rose O'Connor*, McGozzle's niece: BESSIE PHILLIPS. *Mamie White*, her schoolmate: Gladys St. John. *Kate Florence*, another schoolmate: Miss Charlotte. *Madam Blotter*, a schoolmarm: HELENE BYRNE. *Harry*, Servant to Fitzgerald: JAMES BYRNE. *Beeswax*, the schoolmaster: ANDREW BYRNE. *Antoine Macarone*, the deserted Frenchman: ANDREW BYRNE. *Daniel McGozzle*, in love with the ladies but not with his name: JOHN F. BYRNE. *Scholars, statues, animals, etc.*: THE BYRNE TROUPE OF ACROBATS.

Act 1: School days.

Act 2, Scene 1: The railroad station and steamship dock. *Scene 2*: Where is McGozzle? *Scene 3*: Adjoining staterooms aboard the steamship *Norwich*. The chase. The wreck.

Act 2, Scene 1: Safe in France. *Scene 2*: On the warpath. *Scene 3*: The duel. Acrobatic Quadrille.

SPECIALTIES

Specialties (Act 2)
J. F. Byrne, H. Byrne, Misses St. John, Charlotte

Acrobatic Specialties (Act 3)
B. Phillips, John Byrne Troupe of Acrobats

Acrobatic Quadrille (Finale, Act 3)

1895.41 BONNIE SCOTLAND

A Romantic Picturesque Drama in Four Acts. Play and lyrics by Sidney R. Ellis. Music by Albert Anderson. Orchestra under the direction of Albert A. Anderson. Produced by Sydney R. Ellis. Opened 16 December 1895 at the 14th Street Theatre and closed 28 December 1895 after 17 performances[38].

CAST: *Walter MacFarlane*, a young Highland chief of a broken clan: Frank Lander. *Humphrey Colquhoun* of Clan Colquhoun, Douglas on the Clyde: George Klint. *Murdoch Buchanan*, brother of the claimant of Clan Buchanan Auchmere: George A. D. Johnson. *Tam Duncan Faa*, a Highland Laddie: JOHN R. CUMPSON. *Lochburn McCale*, a traveling showman: HORACE LEWIS. *Wallace Dugald*, devoted to MacFarlane: J. L. ASHTON. *Henbane McWharry*, an old retainer of Clan Colquhoun: ROBERT V. FERGUSON. *Captain Hagedorn*, a vassal from the lowlands: Harry Thompson. *Landlord of Holly Inn*: R. Edgar Vance. *Soldier* under Hagedorn: Robert Ireland. *Messenger*: L William Cameron. *Mary Colquhoun*, Humphrey's sister: SELMA HERMAN. *Catherine Epsworth*, devoted to Buchanan: LOUISE RIAL. *Nannie Dugald*, a Highland Lassie: Christie MacLean. *Jean MacFarlane*, Walter's sister: Violet Black. *Bag-pipers, Dancers, Hunters, Soldiers, Yeoman, Drummers, Hghlanders, Buglers, Clansmen, etc.*

Highland Quartette: Sydney G. Tovey, Ashton Nicholls, J. A. Wollerstedt, J. W. Squires. *Royal Pipers*: Robert Ireland, William Cameron, Farquhar Beaton, Alexander Grey, James A. Centre.

The action takes place in Scotland.

Act 1: The Braes of Arroquhar. Post for the stage coach traveling in North Dumbartonshire.

Act 2: "The Roost," a deserted castle. Home of Dugald.

Act 3: Interior of Arroquhar Castle.

Act 4: Heart of the Highlands. The Encampment of Clan MacFarlane.

MUSICAL NUMBERS[39]

"Highland Weather"

"King of Glen and Crag"

"Come Under My Plaidee"

"Wave the Tartan Plaid"

Selections by the Highland Quartette and the Royal Pipers

1895.42 A STAG PARTY, or, A Hero In Spite of Himself

A Musical Travesty in Three Acts. Libretto by Bill Nye and Paul M. Potter. Music composed and arranged by Herman Perlet. Produced under the direction of Richard Barker. Scenery painted by Richard Marston. Costumes by Dazian, from designs by F. Richard Anderson. (Musical director, Herman Perlet.) Produced by A. M. Palmer. Opened 17 December 1895 at the Garden Theatre and closed 28 December 1895 after 16 performances.

CAST: *General Cuyler Van Tassel*, Attorney General of the State of New York, President of the Adirondack Gun Club, and author of "Jungle Life in Cheyenne, or How to quell a Grizzly Bear": LOUIS HARRISON. *Count Otto Witzky*, Son-in-Law of Van Tassel, the butcher of fierce carnivora; a jealous and bilious officer of the Russian Army, sitting constantly on the safety-valve of his imaginary fury: LEO DITRICHSTEIN. *The Countess Magdalen Witzky*, his wife; the silent partner in the possession of his title: SADIE McDONALD. *Ruth Van Tassell, her twin sister*: GERALDINE McCANN. *Freddy Van Tassell*, her small brother; enjoying life first-rate; better in fact than those with whom he is thrown in contact: BESSIE ABBOTT. *Georgia Vest*, a San Francisco heiress; scanning the wide horizon of life for a hero: MARIE DRESSLER. *John Lyttleton, Esq.*, Of the New York Bar; yearning for distinction and Ruth: DAVID TORRENCE. *Joseph Coke*, an English butler, also an authority on the peculiarities of Crowned Heads: Charles Coote. *Paul Brown*, a guide; also, an untutored liar of the Piney Woods: Charles A. Burke. *Captain Richard Brackenburg*, Sheriff of Franklin County; once a corrupt politician, now pure as the beautiful snow: GILBERT CLAYTON. *Lieutenant Goliah Wagstaff*, U.S.A., the Bogie Man of the Adirondacks: GILBERT GREGORY. *Mose*, an old Coon: Mr. Ducrow. *Pete, Sam*, selfmade bears: Daniel Baker, John Slevin. *Phoebe Farintosh*, Ruth's maid: Jessie Abbott.

The Scene is laid at Saranac Lake in the Adirondacks. The time is toward the close of the present century.

Act 1: Exterior of the Gun Club. Evening.

Act 2: A tangle of woods in the mountains. Early morning.

Act 3: Interior of the Club. Night.

MUSICAL NUMBERS

"Obedient Mary"

Barnyard song

Burlesque Spanish Trio (Act 3)

Acrobatic Dance
Messrs. Ducrow, D. Baker, J. Slavin

1895.43 AN ARTIST'S MODEL

A Comedy with Music (Musical Comedy) in Two Acts. Book by Owen Hall. Music by Sidney Jones. Lyrics by Harry Greenbank. Staged by Sydney Ellison. Dances by John D'Auban and Mr. Lefranc. Settings by Edward G. Unitt. Orchestra under the direction of W. W. Furst. Produced by Al Hayman and Charles Frohman, by arrangement with George Edwardes. Opened 23 December 1895 at the Broadway Theatre and closed 15 February 1896 after 56 performances.

CAST: *Adèle*, a rich widow, formerly an Artist's Model: NELLIE STEWART. *Daisy Vane*, Sir George St. Alban's ward: MARIE STUDHOLME. *Mme. Amélie*, a schoolmistress in Paris: CHRISTINE MAYNE. *Lady Barbara Cripps*: Gladys Homfrey. *Amy Cripps*: LOUIE POUNDS. *Lucien*, a school-boy: Nina Cadiz. *Geraldine*, a model: Alison Skipworth. *Art students (6)*: *Jessie*: Cissie Neil. *Rose*: Minnie Cathcart. *Maud*: Lucy Golding. *Violet*: Lillie Pounds. *Ruby*: Amy Reimer. *Mathilde*: Alice Nixon. *Schoolgirls (3)*: *Lucille*: Madge Greet. *Claire*: Elsie Dare. *Lena*: Lucy Nixon. *Rudolph Blair*, an art student: JOHN COATES. *Carbonnet*, an art student: MAURICE FARKOA. *Earl of Thamesmead*, Lady Barbara's brother: LAWRENCE D'ORSAY. *Sir George St. Alban*, a diplomatist: PERCY MARSHALL. *Algernon St. Alban*, his son: Harry Eversfield. *Art Students (3)*: *Apthorpe*: Gilbert Porteous. *Maddox*: Frank Lambert. *Hatfield*: E. Lovat Fraser. *James Cripps*, Lady Barbara's husband: FRED WRIGHT, JR. *Smoggins*: E. W. GARDEN.

Act 1: An Artist's Studio in Paris.

Act 2: Ballroom in Daisy Vane's country house.

[38]Settings and costumes uncredited; director uncredited, presumably the author-producer.

[39]Incidental to the play the Band of Royal Scottish Bag Pipers will render choice selections. Scotch Singers and Scotch Dancers in a varied and interesting repertoire of Scotch Songs and Dances.

ACT 1[40]

"With brush in hand" (Opening Chorus)
F. Lambert, M. Farkoa, G. Porteous,
L. Pounds, M. Cathcart, L. Golding, Chorus

"Gay Bohemi-ah" (Song)
M. Farkoa

"The popular art of the day" (Song)
P. Marshall

"My school is most select" (Song)
C. Mayne

"Is love a dream" (Song)
J. Coates

"Little Daisy with the dimple" (I wonder why)(Song)
M. Studholme

"Queen of the Studio" (Chorus and Recitative)
N. Stewart, Chorus

"On y revient toujours" (Students' Song)

"Oh maid of witching grace"/

"Though all the world of women fair" (Scena and Duet)
J. Coates, N. Stewart

"Six little Misses" (Entrance of school girls)
C. Mayne, Schoolgirls

Finale (Ah here is the truant at last!)

ACT 2

Opening Chorus (The Lancers, Fifth Figure)

"The Gay Tom-tit" (Song)
M. Studholme

"We've reached our destination" (Concerted piece)
C. Neil, M. Farkoa, A. Reimer,L. Pounds, F. Lambert, M. Studholme, P. Marshall, C. Mayne, G. Homfrey

"Antici-tici-pation" (Trio)
H. Eversfield, P. Marshall, C. Mayne

"Give Me Love" (Song)
N. Stewart

"Queen of the Sea and Earth" (Song)
J. Coates

"The Laughing Song"
M. Farkoa

Fancy Dress Lancers

"Music and Laughter" (Valse Chantée)
N. Stewart, J. Coates

"The Lady Wasn't Going That Way" (Song)
C. Mayne

"Sir Roger de Coverly" (Dance)

"Mine (Oh my love) at last" (Song)
J. Coates

Finale (On y revient toujours)

"Umpty Umpty Aye"
M. Studholme

"Ah Yes"
L. D'Orsay

Parisian Quadrille
A. Nixon, L. Nixon, G. Porteous, M. Studholme

Dance
A. Nixon

"I Love Him Only"
N. Stewart

1895.44 THE SCHOOL GIRL

A Musical Comedy in Three Acts. Libretto by George Manchester. Music by Albert Maurice. Arranged and produced for America under the direction of William Gill. Dances arranged by Carl Marwig. Settings by D. Frank Dodge and Arthur Voegtlin. Musical director, Fred Perkins. Produced by Messrs. Taylor, (Frank W.) Conant and Garrison. Opened 30 December 1895 at the Bijou Theatre and closed 4 January 1896 after 8 performances.

CAST: *Professor Gainsbury*: WILLIAM GILL. *Jack Gadsden*: WILLIAM E. WILSON. *Timothy O'Flannigan*: Richard O'Gorman. *Policeman*: Emmet Devoy. *Cheeks*: Lucia Hartford. *Mrs. Allason*: Jenny Dickerson. *Madge Gainsbury*: Frances Rousseau. *Bella Gladsden*: Maud Noel. *Susianah St. Aubyn*: Minerva Adams. *Georgianna Godalphin*: Melytha Adams. *Aminta Armitage*: Annie Pomeroy. *Guests (3)*: *Frederick Fitzjuggles*: George E. Muzzey. *Algy Clayton*: M. J. Thomas. *Montmorency*: H. L. Conley.

The School Girls: *Philips Plantagone*: Cecile Murray. *Frances Fitzwilliam*: Agnes Murray. *Hyacinth Hamilton*: Lucia Hartford. *Olga Oliphant*: Flora Echard. *Florence Fitzherbert*: Addie Starr. *Beatrice Bannerman*: Frankie Peterson. *Alice Argyll*: Minnie Thomas. *Mabel Marmaduke*: Jeannette Hills. *Maggie Macgregor*: Lillian Tulane. *Aggie Forest*: Marion Carlton. *Louisa Allison*, Little Miss Loo: MINNIE PALMER.

Act 1: Courtship. Dodge.)

Act 2: Hardship. (Dodge.)

Act 3: Partnership. (Voegtlin.)

ACT 1

"Working and Scrubbing"

"Ornamental Slaves"

"So Mama Says"

Letter Song

"Song of the Professor

"Oh Cruel Love"

"How Would You Like It Yourselves"

Cigarette Duet and Dance

ACT 2

Serenade and Trio

Boa Dance

Postman Chorus

"Life's a Bubble"

"Keep the Golden Gates Wide Open"

"Madge's Ballad"

"The French Translation"

"Work Is Over" (Chorus)

ACT 3

Waltz and Chorus

"Paradise Alley"

"Marquis de Boulogne-sur-Mer"

"Tim's Songs and Jokes"

"The Sweetest Story Ever Told"

Explanation Quartette and Dance

Finale

1896.01 GENTLEMAN JOE, or, The Hansom Cabby

A Musical Play in Two Acts[41]. (Book and lyrics by Basil Hood. Music by Walter Slaughter.) Scenery by Joseph Physioc. Musical director, Frederick Intropodi. Produced under the stage direction of Willard Lee. Produced by M. B. Curtis. Opened 6 January 1896 at the Henry C. Miner's Fifth Avenue Theatre and closed 14 January 1896 after 9 performances.[42]

CAST: *The Earl of Donnybrook*: HENRY HALLAM. *Mr. Ralli-Carr*: JOSEPH C. FAY. *Mr. Hughie Jaqueson*: ARTHUR PACIE. *Mr. Pilkington Jones*: GEORGE K.

[40]Musical numbers not listed in programs. List prepared from published English piano vocal score (Hopwood & Crew, London, 1895) which may necessarily not reflect interpolations, cut songs, etc. for the American production.

[41]This first unauthorized production was halted by injunction. See authorized production 30 January 1896 for Synopsis of Scenes and Musical Numbers. Musical numbers not listed in programs. One reviewer remarked upon the following which did not appear in the "authorized" production's song list:

"The Ballad of Miss Prim"
A. Meyers

[42]Authors uncredited in programs. Costumes uncredited, musical numbers not listed in programs.

FORTESCUE. *William*, a page boy: Eugene B. Sanger. *Dawson*, the butler: Gus Bruno. *Photographer at Margate*: A. W. Maflin. *Iky*, his assistant: Louis Miller. *James*, a footman: John W. Lawes. *Postman*: Paul Dana. *Policeman*: Wesley Johnstone. *Mons. Plonpoln*, a fakir: Charles F. Lang. *Ciogias*, a longshoreman: Harry Brooks. *Duke Marriotte*, a flip youth: L. H. Croxson. *Tommy Atkins*: Bergh Morrison. *Chef* to Ralli-Carr: Hillyer Burr. *Baker*: William Dunbar. *Hon. Miss Mabel Kavanaugh*: LAURA MOORE. *Mrs. Ralli-Carr*, a lady of position: CARRIE [Caro] ROMA. *Miss Lalage Potts*: ADELAIDE WORTH. *Heiresses (4)*: *Miss Pilkington Jones*: Leonora Cousens. *Miss Amy Pilkington Jones*: Ida M. Godbold. *Miss Lucy Pilkington Jones*: Marina Godoy. *Miss Ada Pilkington Jones*: Viola Fortescue. *Joe's Cabby Pals (4)*: *Dickie Stock*: Phila May. *Dan Bludges*: Camille Dagmar. *Hal Franks*: Minnie Carleton. *Adolphus Linn*: Ione Newhall. *Marid Hilt*, the cook: Lillian Knowles. *Nanette*: Ena Welsh. *Irene*: Bertha King. *The Slavey*: Grace Benedict. *The Head Nurse*: Alberte True. *The Chambermaid*: Myretta Waite. *The Governess*: Leila Williams. *Emma*, an upper servant: ANNIE MEYERS. *Gentleman Joe*: WILLARD LEE[43]. *Ladies, Gentlemen, Servants, etc.*

A BLACK SHEEP,
1896.02 And How It Came Out in the Wash

A Musical Farce in Three Acts. Play by Charles H. Hoyt. Songs by Richard Stahl, Charles H. Hoyt, William Devere, Otis Harlan, Mr. (Harry) Conor, and Mr. Kelly. (Staged by Julian Mitchell.) Settings by Arthur Voegtlin. Costumes by Dazian. Musical director, Richard Stahl. Produced by (Charles H.) Hoyt and (Frank) McKee's Musical Comedy Company. Opened 6 January 1896 at Hoyt's Theatre and closed 9 May 1896 after 144 performances[44].

CAST: *Hot Stuff*, alias Mr. Goodrich Mudd, the black sheep of a distinguished family: OTIS HARLAN. *Percy Vere*, his cousin, a perfect lamb: Joseph Frankau. *Goodfellow Gunning*, editor of the Tombstone (Arizona) "Inscription": WILLIAM DEVERE. *Jarvis Field*, a New York lawyer: Harry Luckstone. *Jack Aspen*, theatrical manager: Joseph Natus. *Slater*, bartender of Tombstone: WILLIAM F. MACK. *Under Dog*, Hot Stuff's partner: Steve Maley. *M. T. Sells*, sheriff at Tombstone: William Hatter. *Count Smorltork*, visiting America: SNITZ EDWARDS. *Phil Glass*, an old servant: John W. Mitchell. *Wetherbee Fowle*, one of Aspen's troupe: CHARLES BRADFORD. *Buffers Ryder*, another of Aspen's troupe: JOHN GILROY. *Old Subscriber*: Charles Diehl. *Hyde Sinn*: Herman Sheldon. *Jimmy Work*, a burglar: Henry Sanger. *John L. Fitz James*, Chesterfield of the P.R.: WILLIAM F. MACK. *Willcut Luce*, a miner on a drunk: John W. Mitchell. *Miss Lida Skiddons*, the "Queen of Burlesque," and star of Aspen's troupe: ADA DARE. *Ada Steele*, cousin of Hot Stuff, and bequeathed to him by will: AGNES ROSE LANE. *Mr. Aspen's troupe (7)*: *Daisy Singer*: Agnes Paul. *Etta Mellon*: Hattie Wells. *May Wing*: Etta Gilroy. *Cora Fay*: Nellie Butler. *Nattie Stile*: Rose Sutherland. *Nora Marks*: Frankie Bailey. *Premiere Danseuse*: BESSIE CLAYTON.

Act 1: Bar-room of Morgue Hotel, Tombstone, Arizona. The lost heir is found.

Act 2: Library at Mudd Mansion, Fifth Avenue, New York City. The wandering boy returns. (Several months are supposed to elapse, but no attempt at realism will be made by having the entr'acte unusually long.)

Act 3: Parlor of the Mudd Mansion. Back from Europe. The will complied with.

ACT 1

College Songs

Medley, including "Onward Soldiers"[45]
(*Music and Lyrics by* Richard Stahl.)

A few minutes of physical exertion by a lady
(*Music by* Richard Stahl.)

"(Sweet) Daisy Stokes"[46]
(*Music and Lyrics by* Charles H. Hoyt.)

"Whistling Colored Boy"[47]
(*Music and Lyrics by* William Devere.)

ACT 2

"Convivial Man"[48]
(*Music and Lyrics by* William Devere.)

Medley, including "Some Things Are Better Left Unsaid"
(O. Harlan)
(*Music by* Richard Stahl. *Lyrics by* Charles H. Hoyt.)

"Armorer's Song"[49] (from ROBIN HOOD)
(*Music by* Reginald DeKoven. *Lyrics by* Harry B. Smith.)

"(She Is) My Picnic Girl"
O. Harlan
(*Music and Lyrics by* Harry Conor.)

ACT 3

"(It's) English as You See It on Broadway" (from A MILK WHITE FLAG)
(*Music and Lyrics by* Charles H. Hoyt and Otis Harlan.)

"Kiss 'Liza"[50]
(*Music and Lyrics by* Herbert Dillea.)

Miss Clayton in new dances

"My First and Only Love"[51]
(*Music and Lyrics by* Richard Stahl.)

Terpsichorean Trio

The Band

1896.03 GIRL WANTED

A Farce Comedy in Three Acts. Produced under the direction of Thomas H. Davis and William T. Keough. Musical director, Charles Hoffman. Opened 6 January 1896 at the 14th Street Theatre and closed 11 January 1896 after 8 performances[52].

---

[43]Role intended for M. B. Curtis who withdrew because of legal difficulties. Curtis' name appears in programs, whereas Lee was seen by reviewers.

[44]Later played return engagements 14 September 1896 at the Harlem Opera House for 8 performances, 5 April 1897 at Hoyt's Theatre for 8 performances, and 30 August 1897 at the Grand Opera House for 8 performances.

[45]Replaced during the run by:
"The Home Guard(s)"
(*Music and Lyrics by* Richard Stahl.)

[46]Replaced in the last month of the run and for subsequent tour by:
"Nancy"
(*Music by* Andrew Mack. *Lyrics by* Otis Harlan.)

[47]Replaced duirng the run by:
"His Parents Haven't Seen Him Since"
O. Harlan
(*Music and Lyrics by* William Devere.)
Which was replaced by
"La Pas Ma La"
(*Music by* Ernest Hogan.)

[48]Replaced in the last month of the run and for subsequent tour by:
"Always Look Cheerful"
(*Music and Lyrics by* Charles H. Hoyt and Richard Stahl.)

[49]Replaced during the run by:
"Laugh, and the World Laughs with You" (Bass Solo)
(*Music and Lyrics by* Louis F. Gottschalk.)
Which was replaced for the end of the run and tour by:
"The Turnkey" (Bass solo) (from ROB ROY)
(*Music by* Reginald DeKoven. *Lyrics by* Harry B. Smith.)

[50]Replaced during the run by :
"Love Me, Honey, Do"
(*Music and Lyrics by* Richard Stahl.)
Which was replaced for subsequent tour by:
"Deed I Do" (a shady fancy)
(*Music and Lyrics by* Richard Stahl.)

[51]Replaced during the run by:
"The Clock Will Never Strike Again the Hours That Have Passed"
Joseph Natus
(*Music and Lyrics by* John T. Kelly.)
Which was later replaced by:
"It Don't Seem Like the Same Old Smile"
(*Music and Lyrics by* Mr. Thornton.)
Which was later replaced by:
"Words Cannot Tell"
(*Music and Lyrics by* Richard Stahl.)
Which was later replaced for the end of the run and tour by:
"The Girl You Dream About"
Joseph Natus
(*Music and Lyrics by* Richard Stahl.)

[52]Direction, settings, costumes not credited.

CAST: *Edwin Forest Smith*, the Stranded Song and Dance Man, who assumes the following guises: FRANK BUSH. *Jabez Runyon*, a "Reuben" from the rustic shades of Vermont: FRANK BUSH. *Billie Brittles*, a tough Waiter from the Bowery: FRANK BUSH. *Pauline Hauser*, a German Damsel from braided blonde locks: FRANK BUSH. *Isaac Wasselowski*, a Hebrew who undertakes to manage the Hurry-Up Restaurant: FRANK BUSH. *Andy McGovern*, a cantankerous Irishman: FRANK BUSH. *Lillian Highnote*, a Prima Donna whose salary is $973.67 per week: FRANK BUSH.

Jethru Larkin, the Yankee inventor, flat owner and restaurant proprietor: Ed Chrissie. *Patricius McNabb*, the industrious janitor of Larkin's flats: James Lee. *Ragged Edges*, the gentleman of leisure: JOHN DILLON. *Gottlob Schloss*, the grocer's boy with a tender heart: Ed. Stanford. *Cholly Plum*, a precious young thing: HARRY DILLON. *Jabez Runyon*, the real Runyon, a visitor from Vermont: Charles Sanders. *Officer Doherty*: Harry Sheldon. *Dorothy Daisy*, the girl wanted by Smith: MABEL FLORENCE. *Delia Mulcahey*, the girl wanted by Schloss: *Hepsibah Spruceby*, the girl wanted by nobody: Jessie Charron. *Clara and Molly*, girls willing to be wanted by the right man: Maud Winston, Sadie Spencer. *Reform Policemen, Unwilling Customers and Others.*

ACT 1

Monologue
F. Bush

Song and Dance
S. Spencer, M. Winston, assisted by the Dillon Brothers

"Old Reuben Rube"
C. Sanders

ACT 2

"Budget of up-to-date songs"
M. Florence

Specialty
E. Sanford, J. Lee

Hebrew Eccentricities
F. Bush

Medley Melange
Full Company

ACT 3

Selected Ballad
H. Sheldon

Parodies, Original[53]
J. Dillon, H. Dillon

DOWN ON THE SUWANEE RIVER

1896.04

An Afro-American Spectacular, Fantastical, Farcical and Musical Comedy in Three Acts[54]. Play by R. N. Stephens. Produced under the direction of George F. Marion. Scenery by John H. Young. Costumes by Paul Vernon. Opened 27 January 1896 at Henry C. Miner's People's Theatre and closed 1 February 1896 after 8 performances[55].

CAST (Act 1): *Thomas Gorham*, a slave-hunter: ALEXANDER C. BUTLER. *Reverend Atkins*, a missionary: JOHN H. KEARNEY. *Peter Pillsbury*, a negro adventurer: WILLIAM McCLAIN. *Boom-De-Aye*, King of Bakuba: CHARLES A. WALKER. *Yambanga*, a prophet and fetch-man: HARRY SINGLETON. *Kli-Ye*, a warrior: FRANK SUTTON. *Gorilla*: Jessie Mitchell. *Bully Garo, Tarantum*, the King's attendants: George Bundy, Walter Aurcher. *Loo-Loo*, Belle of Bakuba: Mme. CORDELIA. *Wa-Wa*, one of the King's wives: Maude Singleton. *Blab-Lub*, one of the King's mothers-in-law: May Walker. *Natives of Bakuba, Slave-Hunters, etc.*

(Act 2) *Thomas Gorham*, a planter: ALEXANDER C. BUTLER. *Mose Willoughby*, an overseer: JOHN H. KEARNEY. *Fairfax Lacombe*, a planter: JAMES E. LEYLAND. *Peter Pillsbury*, a free negro: WILLIAM McCLAIN. *Nicodemus*, a slave: CHARLES A. WALKER. *Uncle Joe*, a slave: HARRY SINGLETON. *Napoleon*, a slave: FRANK SUTTON. *Little Jeff*, a slave: Sherman Coates. *Lafayette*, a slave: George Weston. *Daniel*, a slave: William Asher. *Lulu*, a slave: Mme. CORDELIA. *Snowball*, wife of Nicodemus: Maude Singleton. *Chloe*, a slave: May Walker. *Slaves, Union Soldiers, etc.*

(Act 3) *Lawyer Pillsbury*, a sable Salon: WILLIAM McCLAIN. *Nick Washington*, a policy king: CHARLES A. WALKER. *Rev. Zion Johnson*: HARRY SINGLETON. *Napoleon Gorman*: FRANK SUTTON. *Lafayette*: William Stewart. *Sam Smith*: William Asher. *Lulu Pillsbury*: Mme. CORDELIA. *Mrs. Nick Washington*: Maude Singleton. *Mamie*, a fortune-teller: May Walker. *Dalilia*: Henrietta Weston. *Drum Major and Cake Master*: W. H. Stewart. *Dancers, Cake Walkers, Brass Band, etc.*

Act 1: Royal Village of Bakuba, Africa.

Act 2: Down on the Suwanee River.

Act 3: Rafferty Hall, Thompson Street, New York.

GENTLEMAN JOE, THE HANSOM CABBY

1896.05

A Comedy Operettta in Two Acts[56]. Words (book) and lyrics by Basil Hood. Music by Walter Slaughter. Produced under the direction of Richard Barker. Dances arranged by Rose Beckett. Scenery by Elmer E. Swart, Arthur Voegtlin. Costumes by Catherine Seidle. Musical director, Herman Perlet. Produced by Rudolph Aronson. Opened 30 January 1896 at the Bijou Theatre and closed 29 February 1896 after 48 performances.

Gentleman Joe: JAMES T. POWERS. *Mr. Ralli-Carr*: LOUIS DE LANGE. *Mr. Pilkington Jones*: GEORGE K. FORTESCUE. *Lord Donnybrook*: DAVID TORRANCE. *Hughie Jaqueson*: V. M. DeSilke. *William*, a page boy: Dorothy Usher. *Dawson*, a butler: William Cullington. *James*, a footman: Arthur T. Foster. *Photographer*: G. H. Brooks. *Mrs. Ralli-Carr*: GRACE HUNTINGTON. *Miss Lalage Potts*: FLORENCE (Flo) IRWIN. *Hon. Mabel Kavanaugh*: Ida Brooks. *Daughters of Pilkington Jones (4 Heiresses)*: *Miss Pilkington Jones*: Grace Belasco. *Miss Lucy Pilkington Jones*: Fannie Briscoe. *Miss Ada Pilkington Jones*: Josie Allen. *Miss Amy Pilkington Jones*: Mabel Montgomery. *Cook*: Brownie Wells. *Pals of Gentleman Joe (4)*: *Tom*: May Levigne. *George*: Edna Lyle. *Leonard*: Stella Alexander. *Henry*: Millie Rollins. *Emma*, a Lady's Maid: CLARA WIELAND.

Act 1: Garden of Mr. Ralli-Carr's house, London. (Swart.)

Act 2: The Beach at Margate. (Voegtlin.)

ACT 1[57]

Opening Chorus (Master and missus have been away. .)
Maids and Men Servants

"The Wink of His Eye"
C. Wieland

"I've Always Been Brought Up Polite"
J. T. Powers

"Only Fancy" (Trained Horse Duet)
J. T. Powers, C. Wieland

"Won't You Come to Margate" (Duet)
C. Wieland, J. T. Powers, Full Chorus

Maids and Men Exit Chorus

"It's Money That Makes the World Go Round"[58]
I. Brooks

Song of the Four Heiresses (We are heiresses who)
4 Heiresses

"Lalage Potts, That's Me"
F. Irwin, 4 Heiresses

"In Gay Paree" (Duet)
J. T. Powers, F. Irwin

Chorus Finale

ACT 2

Opening Chorus of bathers, visitors, etc. at Margate (Oh, Margate's many visitors)

---

[53]Authors of "Put Me off at Buffalo," "What right has he on Broadway," "Do, Do My Huckleberry Do" and all the songs they sing.

[54]Billed as presenting 45 of the greatest colored performers on the stage, in a satire on the missionary in Africa, humorous features of the slavery days in Black America, and a skit on the fin-de-siecle negro of Thompson Street. New York.

[55]Musical director and producer uncredited. No songs listed. New York was but a one-week stop of this national tour.

[56]This was the authorized production; the unauthorized production whose run was halted by injunction opened 6 January 1896 at the Henry C. Miner's Fifth Avenue Theatre and closed 14 January 1896 after 10 performances.

[57]Musical numbers from New York program. English piano vocal score (E. Ascherberg & Co, London, 1896) consulted; Act 1 remained largely unchanged. Act 2 indicates that most English numbers had been jettisoned for American specialties.

[58]Replaced for subsequent tour by:

"My Dream of You"
I. Brooks

Dance of the Bathing Girls
"The Moulin Rouge"
C. Wieland
"(Honey,) Does You Love Your Man"
F. Irwin
(*Music by* John W. Bratton. *Lyrics by* Walter Ford.)
"Day Nigger Wid a White Spot on His Face" (The Coon with the Big White Spot)
F. Irwin
(*Music and Lyrics by* Frank J. Gurney.)
"Put It Down"
G. Huntington
Dance of the Heiresses
"In Me 'Ansom"
J. T. Powers, Chorus of 4 Cabbies
Photographing Scene
"She Wanted Something to Play With"
J. T. Powers
(*Music by* Ella Chapman. *Lyrics by* W. S. Laidlaw.)
Bathing Scene
J. T. Powers, G. K. Fortesque
Joe's Diamonds
Clara Wieland's Impersonations (Vanoni, Yvette Guilbert, Chevalier, Paulus, herself)
"Trovatore" (Duet)
J. T. Powers, G. Huntington
"Sweethearts" (Duet)
J. T. Powers, C. Wieland
Finale

1896.06 THE LADY SLAVEY

An Operatic (Musical) Comedy in Two Acts. Book by George Dance. Americanized and staged under the personal direction of George Lederer. Music by Gustave Kerker[59]. Lyrics by Hugh Morton. Scenery by D. Frank Dodge. Costume designs by Mme. Catherine Seidle. Musical director, Gustave Kerker. Produced by Thomas Canary and George W. Lederer. Opened 3 February 1896 at the Casino Theatre; Second Edition[60] opened 30 March 1896 and closed 23 May 1896 after 128 performances[61].

CAST: *Roberts*, sheriff's officer: CHARLES DANBY. *William Endymion Sykes*, assistant to Roberts: DAN DALY. *Vincent Evelyn*, an America millionaire: CHARLES DICKSON. *Major Tolliver*, an impecunious English gentleman: HENRY NORMAN. *Lord Lavender*, an awful swell: RICHARD CARLE. *Ikey Dinkelbinkel*, another swell, of a different type: Charles Kirke. *Artemus Snipe*, a grocer: NICHOLAS BURNHAM. *Krackowitsky*, a tailor: Talmadge Baldwin. *Phyllis*, the Lady Slavey: VIRGINIA EARLE. *Flo Honeydew* of the Music Halls: MARIE DRESSLER. *Major Tolliver's Daughters (4)*: *Beatrice*: Linda DaCosta. *Maud*: Delia Stacy. *Grace*: Jessie Carlisle. *Marjorie*: Mabelle Wallace Howe. *Harriet Snipe*, the grocer's daughter: Babette Rodney. *Mme. Pontet*: Sylvia Holt. *Bessette, Sissette, Dollette*, Modistes: Mabel Potter, Helen Marlborough, Isabel Haslam. *Rossette, Evette, Pepette*, Milliners: Florence Farrington, Josie Zella, Emma Levey. *Fanette, Nanette, Hannette*, Hairdressers: Genie Uniss, Dawn Griffith, Mamie Moore. *Marette, Isette, Lollette*, Manicurists: Ida Moreland, Beatrice Orne, Laurel Atkins. *Tailors, Grocers, Cooks, Haberdashers, Footmen, Undertakers, Clairvoyants, Shoemakers, etc.*: Ladies and Gentlemen of the Chorus. *Graceful Pas Seul* (Act 2 Specialty): LA PETITE ADELAIDE.

Act 1: The Rookholme Manor, England. Now.

Act 2: The house of Artemus Snipe.

MUSICAL NUMBERS[62]
"Baby, Baby"
"The Beautiful Human Fly"
"Cachuca Song"
"Come Down, Ma Honey Do"
(*Lyrics by* J. H. Wagner.)
"Golf Song"
"Nellie Kept on Smiling"
"Twinkle Twinkle"
"Whoop-De-Dooden-Do" (Hoop De Dooden Do)
"The Harmless Little Girlie (with the Downcast Eye)"
"The Blow Almost Killed Father"
D. Daly
(*Music and Lyrics by* James MacAvoy.)
"And Then He Woke Up Father"
D. Daly
(*Music and Lyrics by* Philander Johnson.)
"I Love to See My Poor Old Mother Work"
(*Music and Lyrics by* J. H. Keating.)

1896.07 MARGUERITE

A Spectacular Opera and Ballet in One Act, 2 Scenes (preceded by a vaudeville program). Libretto and music by Oscar Hammerstein. Produced under the personal direction of the composer. Director of ballet, Signor A. Francioli. Musical director, Herr Fritz Scheel. Produced by Oscar Hammerstein. Opened 10 Febuary 1896 at Hammerstein's Olympia Music Hall and closed 11 April 1896 after 54 performances[63].

CAST: *Marguerite*: ALICE ROSE. *Martha*: MARIE BRANDIS. *Faust*: THOMAS EVANS GREENE. *Mephisto*: ADOLPH DAHM-PETERSEN. *Ballet Specialties*: Countess Nina Conti (Premier Danseuse of the Vienna Opera House), Fatima (the Greatest of oriental dancers), the Seven Grigolates. *Vaudeville Specialties*: P. Castor Watt (change artist), Carl Herz (illusionist) with Mlle. D'Alton, O'Gust (French clown), Virginia Aragon (wire act), Leamy Troupe (Nellie, Emmie, Kate/trapeze act).

Scene 1: Faust's Studio. *Scene 2*: The Palace of Flowers.

1896.08 ROBIN HOOD

A Revival of the Comic Opera in Three Acts[64]. Libretto by Harry B. Smith. Music by Reginald DeKoven. Orchestra under the direction of Samuel L. Studley. Produced by the Bostonians (Tom Karl, W. H. MacDonald, Henry Clay Barnabee, Proprietors). Opened 10 February 1896 at the Broadway Theatre for 18 April 1896 after 70 performances[65].

CAST: *Sheriff of Nottingham*: HENRY CLAY BARNABEE. *Robin Hood*: HAROLD BLAKE. *Outlaws (4)*: *Little John*: W. H. MacDONALD. *Will Scarlet*: EUGENE COWLES. *Alan-a-Dale*: JESSIE BARTLETT DAVIS. *Friar Tuck*: GEORGE FROTHINGHAM. *Guy of Gisborne*: C. E. LANDIE. *Maid Marian*: HELEN BERTRAM HENELY. *Dame Durden*, a widow: JOSEPHINE BARTLETT. *Annabel*, her daughter: ALICE NIELSEN. *Villagers, Milkmaids, Outlaws, King's Foresters, Archers, Pedlars, etc.*

1896.09 THE IRISH ARTIST

A Revival of the Comedy Drama in Four Acts, 7 Scenes[66]. Play by Augustus Pitou and George H. Jessop. Songs by Chauncey Olcott. (Staged by Augustus Pitou.) Settings by John H. Young. Costumes by H. A. Ogden. Musical director, Albert Krausse. Produced by Augustus Pitou. Opened 24

---

[59]The original English score by John Crook with abundant interpolations was discarded but for the lyrics to two songs, "Whoop-De-Dooden-Do" and "The Harmless Little Girlie with the Downcast Eye."
[60]For the Second Edition, Walter Jones succeeded Charles Danby as Roberts; new specialties were introduced.
[61]Later played return engagements 1 March 1897 at the Grand Opera House for 8 performances, 8 March 1897 at the Harlem Opera House for 8 performances.
[62]Musical numbers not listed in programs. List prepared from published sheet music, reviews, etc.

[63]Settings and costumes uncredited. Played a return engagement at the Olympia Music Hall 14 September 1896 with Ethan Allen replacing Adolph Dahm-Petersen. Theodore John was musical director; Signor Marchetti, Director of Ballet.
[64]First produced in New York 28 September 1891 at the Standard Theatre for 35 performances, followed by a return engagement 16 May 1892 at the Garden Theatre for 42 performances. Total: 77 performances. For Synopsis of Scenes and Musical Numbers, see original 1891 production.
[65]Stage direction, scenery and costumes uncredited.
[66]First produced in New York 1 October 1894 at the 14th Street Theatre for 48 performances. For Synopsis of Scenes and Musical Numbers, see original 1894 production.

February 1896 at the 14th Street Theatre and closed 29 February 1896 after 8 performances.

CAST: *Maurice Cronin*: CHAUNCEY OLCOTT. *Sir Robert Dean*: DANIEL GILFETHER. *Edmund Dean*: Charles F. Gotthold. *Cormac Cronin*: Frank Peters. *Father Denis Mahone*: J. W. HAGUE. *Jerry Sweeney*: Luke Martin. *Paddy Blake*: Dot Clarendon. *Mike*: Dan J. Fingleton. *Gardner*: George Wallace. *Kate Mahone*: ROLINDA BAINBRIDGE. *Lady Katherine Dean*: Etta Baker Martin. *The Widow Blake*: Effie Germon. *Maggie Cronin*: Louise Closser. *Bridget Cronin*: Lizzie Washburn. *Mary Dean*: Imogene Washburn. *Villagers, Fishermen, Smugglers.*

1896.10 HE GODDESS OF TRUTH

An Opera Comique in Two Acts. Libretto by Stanislaus Stange. Music by Julian Edwards. Produced under the direction of Max Freeman. Settings by Henry E. Hoyt. Costumes by Mme. Catherine Seidle and Castel-Bert. Musical director, Paul Steindorff. Produced by the Lillian Russell Opera Company (Henry E. Abbey, John B. Schoeffel and Maurice Grau, Directors). Opened 26 February 1896 at Abbey's Theatre and closed 4 April 1896 after 45 performances.

CAST: *Timiski*, King of Bulgaria: JOSEPH W. HERBERT. *Olgai*, King of Roumania: FREDERIC SOLOMON. *Prince Artel*, his son: LEO DITRICHSTEIN. *Michael*, a Bulgarian sculptor: RICHIE LING. *Siski*, King Olgai's physician: Owen Westford. *Lysik*, Captain Royal Bulgarian constabulary: A. Holbrook. *Queen Marie*, King Timiski's wife: ROSE BEAUDET. *Princess Nitso*, sister of King Olgai: JENNIE WEATHERSBY. *Wilmai, Caril*, Pages of the Bulgarian court: Julie Senac, Florence Willis. *The Goddess of Truth, Princess Alma*: LILLIAN RUSSELL. *Members of the Bulgarian Constabulary, Nobles, Ladies of the Roumanian and Bulgarian Court, Starostes of the Lower Danube and Members of the Skouptschina.*

The action takes place in a historically inaccurate period.

Act 1: Gardens of the Royal Palace of Bulgaria—with the view of the Danube.

Act 2: Morning Room in the Royal Palace.

MUSICAL NUMBERS

"The Sweet Old Story"
"A Princess I"
"On Probation"
"The Little Weather Vane"
"I Am Bulgaria's King"
"'Tis the Spirit Not the Letter"
"Ah Love, Sweet Fragrant Flower"
"Hush! Say Nothing"
"Auf Weidersehn"
"Love the Magician"
"I Wish That You Wouldn't Do That"
"If You Should"
"When a Good King Reigns"
"One Smile From Thee"
"St Peter and the Fool"

1896.11 THE MINSTREL OF CLARE

A Play (with Music) in Three Acts[67]. Play by Fred Marsden. Musical director, Albert Krausse. Produced by Augustus Pitou. Opened 2 March 1896 at the 14th Street Theatre and closed 4 April 1896 after 35 performances[68].

CAST: *Larry O'Lynn*: CHAUNCEY OLCOTT. *Robert Wynbert*: DANIEL GILFETHER. *Mat. Dougan*: Luke Martin. *Morris Cregan*: Frank Peters. *Dan Cregan*: Charles Gotthold. *Jerry Malone*: Daniel Fingleton. *Nellie Cregan*: Rolinda Bainbridge. *Maggie McKay*: Kitty Coleman. *Bridget McKay*: Effie Germon. *Mrs. Malone*: Mrs. Washburn. *Tommy McKay*: Dot Clarendon. *Tessie McKay*: Imogene Washburn. *The Malone Children*: Masters, Winkleman, Dollman, Bert Buckley, Beatrice Morrison. *Male and female peasants.*

Act 1: Exterior of Morris Cregan's Cottage.

Act 2: Interior of Morris Cregan's Cottage.

Act 3: Pak of Craig-na-Doyle.

MUSICAL NUMBERS

"The Minstrel Boy"
C. Olcott
(*Music*, Old Irish Air, "The Moreen." *Lyrics adapted from* Thomas Moore.)
"The Young Rose"
C. Olcott
(*Music* traditional. *Lyrics adapted from* Thomas Moore.)
"Rory Darlin'"
C. Olcott
(*Music and Lyrics by* Hope Temple.)
Olcott's "Home Song" (Look to That Old Spot)
C. Olcott
(*Music and Lyrics by* Chauncey Olcott.)
"Love Remains the Same"
C. Olcott
(*Music and Lyrics by* Chauncey Olcott.)

1896.12 THE LITTLE DUKE

A Revival of the Opera Comique in Three Acts, in English[69]. (Original French libretto to "Le Petit Duc" by Henri Meilhac and Ludovic Halévy.) Adaptation for this company by Max Freeman. Music by Charles Lecocq. Produced under the direction of Max Freeman. Scenery by Henry E. Hoyt. Costume designs by Catherine Seidle. Musical director, Paul Steindorff. Produced by the Lillian Russell Opera Company (Henry E. Abbey, John B. Schoeffel and Maurice Grau, Proprietors.) Opened 6 April 1896 at Abbey's Theatre and closed 18 April 1896 after 14 performances[70].

CAST: *The Duke of Parthenay*: LILLIAN RUSSELL. *De Montelandry*, Captain in the Duke's Dragoon Regiment: RICHIE LING. *Frimousse*, a Tutor: JOSEPH HERBERT. *Bernard*, a Corporal: Owen Westford. *Blanche*, Duchess de Parthenay: ALEEN BURKE. *Officers (4)*: *De Montchevrier*: Leon Parmette. *De Tanneville*: Camillo Stubel. *De Campvallon*: M. Stone. *De Merignac*: A. Jury. *Pages (3)*: *Roger*: Vira Rial. *Gerard*: Martha Habelman. *Gontran*: Anita Austin. *Helene*, Lady of Honor: Suzanne Leonard. *Diana*, Chanoinesse de Lansac: FREDERIC SOLOMON. *Mlle. de la Roche*: Alice Read. *Mlle. Cleopatra*: Florence Wragland. *Mlle. de la Brune*: Margie Yates. *Mlle. Anemone*: Grace Florence. *Mlle. Ninette*: Katharine Gay.

Act 1: In the Chateau L'Oeil de Boeuf, Versailles. Eighteenth century.

Act 2: In the Pension at Luneville.

Act 3: In the Camp.

1896.13 EL CAPITAN

A Comic Opera in Three Acts. Book by Charles Klein. Music by John Philip Sousa. Lyrics by Charles Klein and Tom Frost. Produced under the stage direction of H. A. Cripps. Settings by Ernest Gros. Costumes by Mme. C. F. Siedle. Musical director, J. S. Hiller. Produced by DeWolf Hopper Comic Opera Company. Opened 20 April 1896 at the Broadway Theatre and closed 25 July 1896 after 112 performances[71].

CAST: *Don Errico Medigua*, recently appointed Viceroy of Peru: DeWOLF HOPPER. *Senor Amabile Pozzo*, Chamberlain: ALFRED KLEIN. *Don Luis Cazarro*, ex-Viceroy: THOMAS S. GUISE. *Count Hernando Verrada*, a Peruvian gentleman: EDMUND STANLEY. *Scaramba*, an insurgent: John Parr. *Montalba, Nevado*, his companions: Harry P. Stone, Robert Pollard. *General Herbana*, Commander of King Philip's forces: Louis Schrader. *Estrelda*, Cazarro's daughter: EDNA WALLACE-HOPPER. *Isabel*, Medigua's daughter: BERTHA WALZINGER. *Princess Marghanza*, Medigua's wife: ALICE HOSMER. *Taciturnez*: Louise Carlisle. (*Spanish and Peruvian Ladies and Gentlemen, Soldiers, etc.*)

The action is set in sixteenth century Peru.

---

[67]A revised version of THE IRISH MINSTREL which was previously produced in New York 9 April 1888 at the Harry Miner's People's Theatre for 8 performances, and 18 March 1889 at the Grand Opera House for 8 performances, and 9 March 1891 at the 14th Street Theatre for 8 performances. A new musical score was used for this production.

[68]Direction, settings and costumes uncredited.

[69]First produced in New York in French 17 March 1879 at Booth's Theatre, and in English 4 August 1884 at the Casino Theatre for 63 performances. This was an all-new adaptation for the Lillian Russell Opera Company. Musical numbers not listed in programs; no libretto or musical score found for this adaptation.

[70]Later played a return engagement 18 May 1896 at the Harlem Opera House for 8 performances.

[71]Later played a return engagement 21 September 1896 at the Harlem Opera House for 8 performances.

Act 1: Viceroy's Palace. (Sunset.)

Act 2: The Gates of Tampoza. (Day.)

Act 3: Plaza Limatamba. (Night.)

ACT 1[72]

"Nobles of Castilian Birth" (Opening Chorus)/
"Oh, beautiful land of Spain" (Recitative and solos)/
"From Peru's majestic mountains" (Recitative Solo and Chorus)
B. Walzinger, A. Hosmer, E. Stanley, Mixed Chorus
"Don Medigua, all for thy coming wait" (Chorus)/
"If you examine human kind" (Solo and Chorus)
B. Walzinger, A. Hosmer, D. Hopper, Chorus
Melodrama/
"When we hear the call for battle" (Solo and Chorus)
E. Wallace-Hopper, T. S. Guise, Mixed Chorus
"Oh, spare a daughter" (Solo and Chorus)
B. Walzinger, Mixed Chorus
"Lo, the awful man approaches" (Chorus)/
"You see in me" (Solo and Chorus)
D. Hopper, E. Wallace-Hopper, T. S. Guise, J. Parr, Chorus
"Bah! Bah!" (Finale)
E. Wallace-Hopper, D. Hopper, T. S. Guise, A. Klein, Chorus

ACT 2

Introduction/
"Ditty of the Drill" (Solo and Opening Chorus)
J. Parr, Chorus
"Behold El Capitan" (Solo and Chorus)
D. Hopper, Men
"I've a most decided notion" (Duet)
E. Wallace-Hopper, D. Hopper
"Bowed with tribulation" (Double Chorus and Solo)
B. Walzinger, A. Hosmer, E. Wallace-Hopper, D. Hopper, Spanish and Peruvian Ladies
"Oh, Warrior Grim!" (Recitative, Solo and Chorus)
B. Walzinger, Chorus
"Don Medigua, here's your wife" (Sextette)
B. Walzinger, A. Hosmer, E. Wallace-Hopper, D. Hopper, A. Klein, T. S. Guise
"He can not, must not, shall not" (Finale)
Principals, Chorus

ACT 3

"Sweetheart, I'm Waiting" (Introduction, Duet and Refrain)
B. Walzinger, E. Stanley, Chorus
"When some serious affliction" (Song)
D. Hopper
"A typical tune of Zanzibar" (Ditty)
D. Hopper, E. Wallace-Hopper, J. Parr
Chorus and Entrance of Spanish Troops
Chorus
"We beg your kind consideration" (Finale)
Principals, Chorus

1896.14

MYLES AROON

A Revival of the Irish Comedy Drama in Four Acts, 8 Scenes[73]. Play by George H. Jessop and Horace Townsend. Music and lyrics by Andrew Mack. Stage manager, James Vincent. Musical director, John Stromberg. Produced by Andrew Mack (D. W. Truss, Manager). Opened 20 April 1896 at the American Theatre and closed 9 May 1896 after 24 performances[74].

CAST: *Myles Aroon*: ANDREW MACK. *Harry Meehan*: ANDREW MACK. *Myles Aroon*: ANDREW MACK. *Squire Raymond Thurston*: Ogden Stevens. *Mike Carney*: JAMES VINCENT. *Gerald Fosdyke*: Frank Ambrose. *Pat Phelan*: William D. Mason. *Joe Upton*: J. Palmer Collins. *Lady Glover*: LIDA McMILLAN. *Mrs. Farrell*: MILLIE SACKETT. *Maggie Farrell*: DOROTHY KENT. *Nellie Glover*: FLORENCE OLP. *Mother Bett*: Charles R. Webster. *Lucy O'Shea*: Adele Olp. *Nora*: Adele Olp. *Minnie*: Adele Olp. *Annie O'Connor*: Alice Smith. *Katie*: Alice Smith.

The Hibernian Madrigal Boys: *Johnny Doyle*: James Plunkett. *Barney Brannagan*: Joseph Walker. *Danny Dwyer*: Frank Meehan. *Patsy McCarthy*: Joseph Ludwig. *Hughey O'Brien*: Joseph Plunkett. *Connie Leary*: Harry Meehan.

MUSICAL NUMBERS[75]

"I'm Proud I'm Irish"
"Dooley's Wedding"
(*Lyrics by* Thomas LeMack.)
"Maggie My Own" (Maggie Me Own)
"Mack's Swing Song"
"The Art of Making Love"
"An Irish Lad's Wooing"

1896.15

THE SUNSHINE OF PARADISE ALLEY

Pictures of New York Life (a Musical and Pictorial Entertainment) in Four Acts. Written by Messrs. George W. Ryer and Denman Thompson. Incidental music by Thomas W. Hindley[76]. Staged by Ben Teal. Scenery by Homer F. Emens. Produced by Messrs. Ryer and Thompson. Opened 11 May 1896 at the 14th Street Theatre and closed 13 June 1896 after 40 performances.

CAST: Act 1: *Jimmie Powers*: John Walsh. *Huntington New*: Frank Currier. *Officer Oliver*: Thomas E. Clifford. *Eddie Duke*: Ben D. Ryer. *Stuttering Joe*: RICHARD J. JOSE. *Shorty Bob*: Frank Mara. *Bridgeport Bill*: Leonard Spencer. *A Would-Be Suicide*: Walter Lennox, Sr. *Nellie McNally* (Sunshine): JULIE RING. *Widow McNally*: Mrs. CHARLES PETERS. *Helen Rich*: Marie Carlyle. (*Dance Specialty*: JOHN P. HOGAN, LOTTA FAUST.)

Act 2: *Uncle Dan*: Walter Lennox, Sr. *Jimmie Powers*: John Walsh. *Dr. Henry Curtis*: H. W. Frillman. *John James O'Grady*: John D. Griffin. *Eddie Duke*: Ben D. Ryer. *Little Danny Mara*: Master Mara. *Nellie McNally* (Sunshine): JULIE RING. *Widow McNally*: Mrs. CHARLES PETERS. *Mrs. John James O'Grady*: Emily Stowe. *Jennie Watson*: Miss Mara.

Act 3: *Uncle Dan*: Walter Lennox, Sr. *Jimmie Powers*: John Walsh. *Huntingdon New*: Frank Currier. *John James O'Grady*: John D. Griffin. *Officer Oliver*: Thomas E. Clifford. *Pat Mara*: Frank Russell. *Stuttering Joe*: RICHARD J. JOSE. *Shorty Bob*: Frank Mara. *Eddie Duke*: Ben D. Ryer. *Little Danny Watson*: Master Mara. *Nellie McNally* (Sunshine): JULIE RING. *Widow McNally*: Mrs. CHARLES PETERS. *Mrs. John James O'Grady*: Emily Stowe. *Helen Rich*: Marie Carlyle. *Mrs. Pat Mara*: Emma Chase. *Jennie Mara*: Miss Mara.

Act 4: *Uncle Dan*: Walter Lennox, Sr. *Jimmie Powers*: John Walsh. *Dr. Henry Curtis*: H. W. Frillman. *John James O'Grady*: John D. Griffin. *Stuttering Joe*: RICHARD J. JOSE. *Eddie Duke*: Ben D. Ryer. *Mr. Tom Oliver*: Thomas E. Clifford. *Sandy McPherson*: Frank Currier. *Ferguson McCuddie*: Frank Mara. *The Chef*: J. W. Myers. *Little Danny Mara*: Master Mara. *Nellie McNally* (Sunshine): JULIE RING. *Widow McNally*: Mrs. CHARLES PETERS. *Mrs. John James O'Grady*: LIZZIE MAY ULMER. *Helen Rich*: Emma Chase. *Mrs. Tom Watson*: Mrs. Frank Mara. *Kittie Forsythe*: Ethel Paine. *Jennie Clark*: Lotta Faust. *Jennie Watson*: Miss Mara.

(*Specialties*: Lotta Faust, May Abby McKay, John Day, John J. Flynn. *Male Quartette*: Roger Harding, Louis H. Croxson, Thomas E. Clifford, H. W. Frillman. *Female Quartette*: Blanche Edwards, Phila May, Lizzie Farrell, Marie Blanchard.)

Act 1: An East River Dock, with a view of Brooklyn Bridge.

Act 2: Widow McNally's Apartments in Paradise Alley.

Act 3: Paradise Alley.

Act 4: Autumn Scene in Bronx Park.

ACT 1

Choruses
Company

[72]Musical numbers not listed in programs. List prepared from published piano vocal score (John Church Co., Cincinnati, 1896).

[73]First produced in New York 21 January 1889 at the 14th Street Theatre for 16 performances. For Synopsis of Scenes and Musical Numbers, see original 1889 production. Also published: "Live My Love, Oh Live."

[74]Played return engagements 20 April 1891 at the Grand Opera House for 8 performances, 27 April 1891 at Miner's People's Theatre for 8 performances. Costumes uncredited. For this revival, "Moonlight at Killarney" was dropped.

[75]Andrew Mack composed a new score for this revival and sang all the songs. Not in performance order.

[76]A hugely popular song with the title "Sunshine of Paradise Alley" (*Music by* John W. Bratton, *Lyrics by* Walter H. Ford.) was originally interpolated into A TRIP TO CHINATOWN, and was most certainly performed in this production as well.

Irish Song
J. Walsh
"Alone" (Song)
R. J. Jose
Dance
J. P. Hogan, L. Faust

ACT 3
"It don't seem like the same old smile" (Song)
L. H. Croxson
(*Music and Lyrics by* James Thornton.)
"The Clock of the Universe"
J. W. Myers
(*Music and Lyrics by* Walter A. Phillips.)

ACT 4
"Autumn Song" (Verdi Ladies' Quartette)
Misses Edwards, May, Farrell, Blanchard
"The Red Scarf"[77]
T. E. Clifford
"Serenade"
Messrs. Jose, Croxson, Clifford, Frillman
"Time and Tide"
R. J. Jose, Double Quartette
"Rastus on Parade" (Grand Finale)
Company
(*Music and Lyrics by* Kerry Mills.)

1896.16 THE BOHEMIAN GIRL

A Revival of the Romantic Opera in Three Acts[78]. (Libretto by Alfred Bunn, after Jules-Henri Vernoy de Saint-Georges' ballet-pantomime "The Gypsy.") Music by Michael William Balfe. Conductor, Paul Steindorff. Produced by Paul Steindorff and Thomas Ebert. Opened 11 May 1896 at the American Theatre and closed 16 May 1896 after 8 performances.

CAST: *Count Arnheim*, Governor of Presburg: JOSPEH LYNDE. *Thaddeus*, a proscribed Pole: JOSEPH F. SHEEHAN. *Florestein*, nephew of the Count: W. H. Fitzgerald. *Devilshoof*, chief of the Gypsies: W. H. CLARKE. *Captain of the Guard*: E. C. Edmonds. *Arline*, daughter of the Count: LAURA MILLARD. *Buda*, her attendant: Emma Millard. *Queen of the Gypsies*: FLORA FINLAYSON. *Chorus of Nobles, Soldiers, Gypsies, Retainers and Peasants.*

1897.17 THE MIKADO, or, The Town of Titipu

A Revival of the Comic Opera in Two Acts[79]. Libretto by William S. Gilbert. Music by Arthur Sullivan. Conductor, Paul Steindorff. Produced by the Paul Steindorff and Thomas Ebert. Opened 18 May 1896 at the American Theatre and closed 6 June 1896 after 24 performances.

CAST: *The Mikado of Japan*: J. W. KINGSLEY. *Nanki-Poo*, his son, disguised as a wandering minstrel in love with Yum-Yum: RICHARD [Richie] LING. *Ko-Ko*, Lord High Executioner of Titipu: CHARLES DREW. *Pooh-Bah*, Lord High Everything Else: JOSEPH LYNDE. *Yum-Yum, Pitti-Sing, Peep-Bo*, three sisters, wards of Ko-Ko: DOROTHY MORTON, DICKIE MARTINEZ, CLARA RANDALL. *Katisha*, an elderly lady in love with Nanki-Poo: FLORA FINLAYSON. *Chorus of School Girls, Nobles, Guards and Coolies.*

[77]Replaced for subsequent tour by:
"The Holy City"
T. E. Clifford
(*Music by* Frederic E. Weatherly. *Lyrics by* Stephen Adams.)

[78]First produced in New York 25 November 1844 at the Park Theatre for 17 performances. For Synopsis of Scenes and Musical Numbers, see original 1844 production.

[79]First presented in New York 20 July, 10-29 August 1885 at the Union Square and People's Theatres for 22 performances. First authorized production presented 19 August 1885 at the Fifth Avenue Theatre by Richard D'Oyly Carte for 250 performances. For Synopsis of Scenes and Musical Numbers, see 19 August 1885 D'Oyly Carte production.

1896.18 IN GAY NEW YORK

An Annual Review, a Kaleidoscopic Retrospect of the Hour, in Three Acts, 6 Scenes[80]. Libretto by Hugh Morton. Music by Gustave Kerker. Staged by George W. Lederer. Ballets arranged by Signor Francioli. Settings by D. Frank Dodge. Costumes by Mme. C. F. Siedle. Conductor, Gustave Kerker. Produced by Thomas Canary and George W. Lederer. Opened 28 May 1896 at the Casino Theatre and closed 5 September 1896 after 110 performances[81].

CAST, ACT 1: *Mrs. DeShyster Van Shoddie*, a millionairess: VIRGINIA EARLE. *Miss Flora Van Shoddie*, her daughter: Jeanette Bageard. *Sally Tompkins*, Johnny Brown's bride: LILLIAN SWAIN. *Mrs. Tompkins*, Sally's mother: Rosa Cook. *Susie Tarbox*, a bridesmaid: Sylvia Holte. *Essie, Tessie, Jessie, Bessie*, the Marmalade Sisters, variety artists: CATHARINE LINYARD, SYLVIA THORNE, MADGE LESSING, GERTRUDE ZELLA. *Miss Peroxide McTushtush*, a leading lady: Ida Moreland. *Miss Fairy Fullmeasure*, an actress: Nanette Nixon. *Prince Rouge-et-Noir*: JULIUS STEGER. *Edgardo Macready Boothand Barrett Todd*, a stranded actor: WALTER JONES. *Johnny Brown*, a country bridegroom: John Keefe. *Lemuel Tompkins*, Sally's father: E. S. Tarr. *Duke of Mulligatawny*, a British fortune-hunter: DAVID WARFIELD. *Si Perkins*, a bumpkin: Charles L. Dox. *Pastor Podgett* of the Meeting House: H. L. Traub. *Deacon Stackpole*, of Huckleberry Center: J. A. Furey. *Grand Central Pete*, a bunco steerer: RICHARD CARLE. *Burglar Bill*: Frank Blair. *Perkins*, a butler at Hotel Waldorf: Frank Blair. *Sandbag*, the strong man: Henry Norman. *Muddy Mike*, a gold-brick bandit: Henry Norman. *Colonel Waring*: Henry Norman. *Policeman Spitzpupheimer*: LEE HARRISON. *Frank Daniels*, the Wizard of the Nile: LEE HARRISON. *White Wings*, one of Colonel Waring's angels: Gilbert Gregory. *Lord Dunraven*: Gilbert Gregory. *Paderewski*: Gilbert Gregory. *Jimmy the Slim*, a light-fingered gentleman: JOHN SLAVIN. *The Central Park Chimpanzee*: JOHN SLAVIN. *Thirsty Bob, Webfoot Willie*, friends of Grand Central Pete: Charles L. Dox, J. A. Furey. *Artificial Arthur*: Ross Snow. *Woozy Whiskers*, a scorching hobo: W. E. Ritchie. *Svengali Trilby*, an actor: George Haynes. *Swipes*, a newsboy: William Torpey. *Pitchpenny*, an urchin: *John, James*, servants to Rouge-et-Noir: Pelham Wilkes, Frank Farrington.

ACT 2: *Treasurer Standoff*, ticket seller at the Casino: LEE HARRISON. *Solomon Solomon*: DAVID WARFIELD. *Mrs. Maryland Leslie Ta Ta*: DAVID WARFIELD. *Henry Macbeth Irving*: DAVID WARFIELD. *Dottie Doodimpe*: MADGE LESSING. *Hattie Allhat*: Ursula Gurnett. *Reginald Tomtit*: William Dunlay. *Little Boy Blue*: William Dunlay. *Harris*, footman: Frank Farrington. *The Spirit of Burlesque*: CATHARINE LINYARD. *Mrs. O'Brien, Mrs. Mulcahey*, Casino scrub women: Gilbert Gregory, John Slavin. *Johnny Brown*: John Keefe. *Sally Brown*: Lillian Swain. *Essie, Tessie, Jessie, Bessie*, the Marmalade Sisters: Catharine Linyard, Sylvia Thorne, Madge Lessing, Gertrude Zella. *Edgardo Macready Boothandbarrett Todd*: WALTER JONES. *Colonel Kellard*: WALTER JONES. *Rudolph*, Prisoner of Zenda: WALTER JONES. *Captain Barrymore*: Frank Blair. *Hogan*, the sexton: E. S. Tarr. *Lemuel Tompkins*: E. S. Tarr. *Mrs. Tompkins*: Rosa Cooke. *His Excellency Don José*: JULIUS STEGER. *Carmen Calve*: Mabel Potter. *Carmen Nethersole*: Getrude Zella. *Yvette Guilbert's Sisters (5)*: *Youbette*: Virginia Earle. *Getwette*: Jeanette Bageard. *Dontfrette*: Catharine Linyard. *Tolette*: Madge Lessing. *Mypette*: Gertrude Zella. *Romeo*: Sylvia Thorne. *Elaine Umty-Tiddly*, Lettie Lind's cousin: Virginia Earle. *Hot Stuff*, a Hoyt hero: Charles Kirke. *Oscar Hammerstein*: Charles Kirke. *Allen*, night watchman: J. A. Furey. *Mr. Rusty Kicker*, the man in the Balcony: J. A. Furey. *Harry*, clerk of the coat-room: Himself.

ACT 3: *Benzeene*, the Circassian girl: JOHN SLAVIN. *Mr. Openface*, a dime museum "barker": Henry Norman. *Lurline*, the Water Queen: Virginia Earle. *Mrs. Deshyster Van Shoddie*: VIRGINIA EARLE. *Edgardo Macready Boothandbarrett Todd*: WALTER JONES. *Snapshot*, a photographer: Gilbert Gregory. *Miss Flora Van Shoddie*: Jeanette Bageard. *Prine Rouge-et-Noir*: JULIUS STEGER. *Duke of Mulligatawny*: DAVID WARFIELD. *Lemuel Tompkins*: E. S. Tarr. *Mrs. Tompkins*: Rosa Cooke. *Johnny Brown*: John Keefe. *Sally Brown*: LILLIAN SWAIN. *Grand Central Pete*: RICHARD CARLE.

Ballet: Misses Ray Allen, Sophie Witt, Rosie Witt, Lottie Dickens, Bertha Wasserman, Marie George, Mabelle Howe, Grace Franton, Clara Franton, Mamie Holden, La Petite Adelaide (Première Danseuse).

Act 1, Scene 1: Village Green of Huckleberry Centre, Maine. *Scene 2*: Exterior of Grand Central Depot. *Scene 3*: Exterior of Hotel Waldorf.

Act 2, Scene 1: Lobby of the Casino, Broadway and 39th Street, New York. *Scene 2*: Stage of the Casino.

Act 3: The Breezy End of Happy Coney Island.

[80]Billed as Canary & Lederer's third annual Casino review.

[81]Later played return engagements under the auspices of Klaw & Erlanger 28 December 1896 at Wallack's Theatre for 8 performances, 15 February 1897 at the Harlem Opera House for 8 performances, 30 August 1897 at the Metropolis Theatre for 8 performances, and 7 February 1898 at the Columbus Theatre for 8 performances.

MUSICAL NUMBERS[82]

"The Cripple Creek Bandits"
H. Norman, Chorus
"Girlie Girl"
L. Swain, Others
"In Gay New York"
"Jim Jam"
"Jusqu'la"
"Lurline" (Waltz Song)
"Mollie" (Molly)
"Take Me Down to Coney Island"
"A Trip Around the Town"
"It's Forty Miles from Schenectady to Troy"
"Turn Your Great Eyes on Me" (Turn Thy Great Eyes Upon Me)
"Just a Little Lump of Sugar for the Bird"[83]
V. Earle
Illustrative Dance of English Peers and American Heiresses (Act 1, Scene 3)
Ballet
The Icicle Ballet
Newspaper Ballet (Act 2, Scene 2)
Ballet, La Petit Adelaide
Specialties:
Newhouse and Waffle, the Wandering Minstrels of Palmer Cox's "Brownies"
The Sisters Witt (Dance Duet)
Ross Snow (the Tuneful Tramp)

[82]Musical numbers, apart from ballets, not listed in programs. List prepared from published sheet music, reviews, not in performance order. For the December 1896 return engagement at Wallack's, Lucy Daly and Gilbert Gregory introduced a new specialty in Act 3 entitled "Yer Baby's A-Comin' to Town," (*Music and lyrics by* John T. Kelly).

[83]Added to the production 18 July 1896.

1896–1897 SEASON

Edward Harrigan in MARTY MALONE (Photo: J. U. Stead)
Billy Rose Theatre Collection, New York Public Library for the Performing Arts

1896–1897 SEASON

H.M.S. PINAFORE,
1896.19 or, The Lass That Loved a Sailor

A Revival of the Comic Opera in Two Acts[1]. Libretto by William S. Gilbert. Music by Arthur Sullivan. Produced under the direction of W. H. Fitzgerald. Costumes by Mrs. Kelly. Orchestra under the directon of Paul Steindorff. Produced by Paul Steindorff and Thomas Ebert. Opened 8 June 1896 at the American Theatre, moved 22 June 1896 to the Herald Square Theatre and closed 27 June 1896 after 21 performances.

CAST: *The Rt. Hon. Sir Joseph Porter, K.C.B.*, First Lord of the Admiralty: R. E. GRAHAM. *Captain Corcoran*, Commander of the *H.M.S. Pinafore*: JOSEPH LYNDE. *Ralph Rackstraw*, Able Seaman: JOSEPH F. SHEEHAN. *Dick Deadeye*, Able Seaman: WILLIAM DANFORTH. *Bill Bobstay*, Boatswain: William McLaughlin. *Bob Becket*, carpenter's mate: A. Greer *Josephine*, the Captain's Daughter: DOROTHY MORTON. *Hebe*, Sir Joseph's First Cousin: Henrietta Lee. *Tom Tucker*, midshipmite: Georgie Bryton. *Little Buttercup*, Mrs. Cripps, a Portsmouth bum-boat woman: FLORA FINLAYSON. *First Lord's Sisters, his Cousins, his Aunts, Sailors, Marines, etc.*

1896.20 THE CHIMES OF NORMANDY

A Revival of the Comic Opera in Three Acts, 6 Scenes[2]. (Original French libretto to the opéra comique 'Les Cloches de Corneville' by Clairville and Charles Gabet.) Music by Robert Planquette. Stage director, William T. Carleton. Produced by Carleton's Opera Company (William T. Carleton, Proprietor). Opened 1 June 1896 at the Grand Opera House and closed 6 June 1896 after 8 performances.

CAST: *Serpolette*, the good-for-nothing: MARIE BELL. *Germaine*, the lost Marchioness: RENA ATKINSON. *Susanne*: Nancy Michal. *Gertrude*: IDA ROCK. *Henri*, Marquis of Corneville: WILLIAM T. CARLETON. *Jean Grenicheux*, a fisherman: JAY C. TAYLOR. *Gaspard*, an old miser: TOM RICKETTS. *The Bailli*: W. H. West. *Chorus of Peasants, Sailors, Servants, Coachmen, Waiting-Maids, etc.*

1896.21 OLIVETTE

A Revival of the Comic Opera in Three Acts[3]. (Original French libretto to the opéra comique 'Les Noces d'Olivette' by Henri Chivot and Alfred Duru.) Music by Edmund Audran. Produced under the personal direction of W. H. Fitzgerald. Costumes by Eaves. Orchestra under the direction of Paul Steindorff. Produced by Paul Steindorff and Thomas Ebert. Opened 29 June 1896 at the Herald Square Theatre and closed 4 July 1896 after 8 performances.

CAST: *Captain De Merimac*: HALLEN MOSTYN. *Valentine*: JOSEPH F. SHEEHAN. *Duc Des Ifs*: THOMAS RICKETT. *Coqulicot*: Ben Lodge. *Marvejol*: Joseph Lynde. *Countess of Rousillon*: FLORA FINLAYSON. *Veloutin*: PAULA EDWARDS. *Moustique*: Georgie Bryton. *Olivette*: DOROTHY MORTON.

PATIENCE,
1896.22 or, Bunthorne's Bride

A Revival of the Comic Opera in Two Acts[4]. Libretto by William S. Gilbert. Music by Arthur Sullivan. Produced under the stage direction of W. H. Fitzgerald. Musical director, Paul Steindorff. Produced by Paul Steindorff and Thomas Ebert. Opened and closed 10 July 1896 at the Herald Square Theatre and closed after 1 performances[5].

CAST: *Patience*: LILLIAN RUSSELL. *Rapturous Maidens (4)*: *The Lady Jane*: FLORA FINLAYSON. *The Lady Saphir*: Dorothy Morton. *The Lady Angela*: SADIE MARTINOT. *The Lady Ella*: LILLIAN SWAIN. *Reginald Bunthorne*: HENRY E. DIXEY. *Archibald Grosvenor*: WILLIAM T. CARLETON. *Officers of the Dragoon Guards (3)*: *Colonel Calverley*: WILLIAM McLAUGHLIN. *Major Murgatroyd*: AUBREY BOUCICAULT. *Lieutenant, The Duke of Dunstable*: JOSEPH F. SHEEHAN.

1896.23 POOR JONATHAN

A Revival of the operette 'Der arme Jonathan' in Three Acts, in German[5a]. Opened 23 July 1896 at the Terrace Garden Theatre in repertory with DIE FLEDERMAUS.

CAST: *Poor Jonathan*: EDMUND LOEWE. *Molly*, his wife: ROSITA GOLDECK. PHILLA WOLFF, FERDINAND SHUETZ.

1896.24 MARTY MALONE

A Local Play (with Songs) in Three Acts. Play (and lyrics) by Edward Harrigan. Music by David Braham. Staged by Edward Harrigan. Musical director, George F. Braham. Produced by Edward Harrigan. Opened 31 August 1896 at the Bijou Theatre and closed 26 September 1896 after 32 performances.[6]

CAST: *Marty Malone*: EDWARD HARRIGAN. *Hippolite Ducrow*: DAN COLLYER. *Moses Guggenheimer*: Harry Rogers. *Heinrich Vanderdam*: HARRY A. FISHER. *Bernard Kelly*: Thomas LeMack. *Gilbert Gillis*: George Merritt. *Bobbitt Babbitt*: Charles Sturges. *Captain Ernest Duncan*: Maurice Drew. *Asa Munday*: William West. *Lord John Foxwood*: JOHN HOLLIS. *Easter Munday*: Dave Braham, Jr. *Antonio Pinto*: EDWARD MACK. *Butt Baxter*: James Cassidy. *Terwilliger Truffles*: Charles Coffey. *Doolittle Dunn*: Thomas Granger. *Delia Dugan*: JOHN BRENNAN. *Policeman*: James McCullough. *Sally Jordan*: CATHERINE LEWIS. *Marie Pinto*: MAGGIE FIELDING. *Henrietta Van Snyder*: Jane Burby. *Pauline Jordan*: Pauline Train. *Mandy Lucas*: Gussie Hart. *Ballad Monger*: Dan McCarty[7].

Act 1: Sally Jordan's Sailors' Lodging-House. "The Shanghai."

Act 2: Handsome Apartment at the house of Marie Pinto's, Riverside Drive. "All for Cuba."

Act 3: Country House and Grounds of Marie Pinto, Whitestone, Long Island. "Quits."

MUSICAL NUMBERS[8]

"The Hole in the Wall"
Sailors

"Savannah Sue"
D. Collyer, D. Braham, Jr., G Hart

"(Sweet) Mary Mullane"

"Pride of the London Stage"

1896.25 THE CALIPH

A Comic Opera in Three Acts. Libretto by Harry B. Smith. Music by Ludwig Engländer. Produced under the direction of Richard Barker. Settings by Ernest M. Gros and Homer F. Emens. Costumes by Mme. C. F. Siedle. Musical director, Fred J. Eustis. Produced by the Jefferson DeAngelis Comic Opera Company (Nat Roth, Manager). Opened 3 September 1896 at the Broadway Theatre and closed 17 October 1896 after 48 performances.

CAST: *Hardluck XIII*, Caliph of Bagdad: JEFFERSON DeANGELIS. *Brikbrak*, his Vizier (and trouble-maker extraordinary): ALFRED C. WHELAN. *Abu Ben Adhem*, a Pirate Chief (brother of the Caliph and rightful heir to the throne): MELVILLE STEWART. *Ahmed*, a Slave in the Caliph's household (and enamored of Gulnare, the

---

[1]Originally presented in New York 15 January 1879 at the Standard Theatre for 175 performances. For Synopsis of Scenes and Musical Numbers, see original 1879 production.

[2]Adaptation uncredited; most likely the published version by Henry B. Farnie and R. Reece. First produced in New York 22 October 1877 at the Fifth Avenue Theatre for 16 performances. Conductor uncredited. No program found for this engagement.

[3]First produced in New York 25 December 1880 for 63 performances; reopened 18 April 1881 at the Fifth Avenue Theatre for 35 additional performances. Total: 98 performances. For Synopsis of Scenes and Musical Numbers, see original 1880 production. English language adaptation uncredited.

[4]First presented in New York 22 September 1881 at the Standard Theatre for 177 performances. For Synopsis of Scenes and Musical Numbers, see original 1881 production.

[5]Scenery and costumes uncredited.

5aPreviously produced in New York in English 14 October 1890 at the Casino Theatre for 208 performances.

[6]Played an additional week's return engagement 5 October 1896 at the Harlem Opera House in what the New York Times called "a somewhat condensed and improved version."

[7]The New York Times reviewed Kitty Rampone in this role opening night.

[8]Not necessarily in performance order. Added during the New York run: "The Castaways" from MULLIGAN'S SILVER WEDDING. In subsequent touring programs, "The Castaways" was dropped, and added was "Tally-Ho" (from NOTORIETY).

Caliph's daughter): PHILIP BRANSON. *Kasrac*, Chief of Police (with a grudge against the Caliph): EDWARD KNIGHT. *Hafiz*, a Slave Merchant: Clifford Wiley. *Backsheesh*, an Irish Pirate: Frank Walsh. *Baalbec*, a German Pirate: Steve Porter. *Hashisch*, an Italian Pirate: Richard Gaunt. *Gulnare*, daughter of the Caliph (in love with Ahmed): IRENE PERRY. *Djemma*, beloved by Abu, but betrothed to the Caliph: MINNIE LANDERS. *Bulbul*, wife of Brikbrak (but represented as the wife of the Caliph): MATHILDE COTTRELLY. *Seleim*, Captain of Merchantman: DREW DONALDSON. *Ali*, Captain of Caliph's Guards: Drew Donaldson. *Cassia*, a waitress: Pauline Graves. *Zolaida*: ADA BERNARD. *Chorus of Pirates, Citizens, Soldiers, Prisoners, Slave Girls, Sailors, etc, etc.*

Act 1: Garden of the Caliph's Palace at Bagdad. (Emens.)

Act 2: The Public Square in Bagdad. (Gros.)

Act 3: The Deck of a Merchant Vessel. (Gros.)

ACT 1[9]

Opening Ensemble and Scene (Aurora o'er the mountains brightly glows)
Milkman, Watchmen, E. Knight
Entrance of Slave Girls (We are bargains most amazing)
C. Wiley, Slave Girls
Chorus of Pirates (With a cautious cheer and a hushed hurrah)
M. Stewart, Pirates

Duet (Another day of vain pretension)
A. Bernard, M. Cottrelly

Chorus (Yonder comes our Caliph gay)
Chorus

Grotesque March of Convicts

Song of the Criminals (All these criminals capricious)
A. C. Whelan, Convicts

"The Monkey and the Parrot" (Song)
J. DeAngelis, Chorus

Lullaby (Sleep, thou pretty, winsome creature)
A. Bernard, M. Cottrelly, Chorus

Finale:
Duet (Although we're rough and savage men)
M. Stewart, A. Bernard
Chorus (Dancing dervishes are we)
Pirates' Chorus

ACT 2

Sailor's Song and Hornpipe (A sailor's life is a jolly, jolly life)
J. DeAngelis, M. Stewart, A. C. Whelan, S. Porter, R. Gaunt, F. Walsh

Song (I oft have dreamed of such a face)
I. Perry

Duet (There once was a china shepherdess)
A. Bernard, M. Stewart

Song (There was a king in the olden days)
J. DeAngelis, Chorus

Finale (March)(While the Caliph is away)
Chorus

Waltz (Afar o'er the sea)
J. DeAngelis, Pirates

ACT 3

Opening Chorus (When the sea is calm there is just one thing to do)
Chorus

Barcarolle
A. Bernard, I. Perry, M. Cottrelly, P. Branson, E. Knight, D. Donaldson

Chorus of Pirates reprise (With a cautious cheer and a hushed hurrah)
Pirates

"The Wishing Cap" (Sextette)
J. DeAngelis, A. Bernard, M. Cottrelly, A. C. Whelan, P. Branson, E. Knight

Finale
All

1896.26 THE ART OF MARYLAND

A Burlesque in One Act, 2 Scenes, preceded by an Olio. A Burlesque of David Belasco's play "The Heart of Maryland." Libretto by Joseph Herbert. Music by John Stromberg. Produced under the stage direction of Joseph Herbert. Dances and ballets by Leon Franchi. Designs by Jean DeLange. Costumes by Mme. Dowling. Scenery by William P. Murphy. Musical director, John Stromberg. Produced by Joseph Weber and Lew M. Fields. Opened 5 September 1896 at Weber and Fields' Broadway Music Hall and closed 3 October 1896 after 33 performances.

Olio: Alburtus & Bartram (The College Boys); Thomas J. Ryan (Comedian and Dancer); (Charles J.) Ross and (Mabel) Fenton in Travesty; Lottie Gilson (The Little Magnet): "Don't Give Up the Old Love for the New," "You're Not the Only Pebble on the Beach" (*Music by* Stanley Carter [Frederick J. Redcliffe]. *Lyrics by* Harry Braisted [Harry B. Berdan]; Joseph Weber and Lew M. Fields (German Senators; Poolroom sketch)

CAST: *Hawlin Hayrick*, a Popocratic commander: JOHN T. KELLY. *Colonel Warp*, who straddles the political fence, and goes it blind: CHARLES K. ROSS. *Major Tom Coon*, of Coonsboro: YOLANDE WALLACE. *Un-Alloyed Calvert*, pure and simple, Maryland's brother by marriage: LILLIAN SWAIN. *Sergeant Grunt*, an ex-jailer at Hogwog: SAM BERNARD. *Orderly*: Frankie Bailey. *Maryland*, an emotional of the made-to-order school: MABEL FENTON. *Mrs. McFadden*: THOMAS RYAN. *Lieutenant Sultzer*: Florence Bell. *Lieutenant Depew*: Maude Gilbert.

Popocrats: *Weary Watkins*: Walter West. *Sockless Simpson*: Seth Miller. *Twister Tillman*: Joseph Brown. *Asbestos Altgeld*: Fred Murray. *Pfrowsky Pfeffer*: William Hodges. *Tinker Teller*: George Avery.

Of Hogan's Alley: *Mickey Doogan*: John Zahn. *Baldie Sours*: Britton Stephens. *Marty Malone*: Rose Beaumont. *Sally Walters*: Gladys Lamoyne. *Maggie Murphy*: Nellie Beaumont. *Katie Connor*: Carrie Boyer. *Soldiers, Popocrats, Citizens, Goats, Chickens, all à la Maryland.*

Scene 1: The Lilocks. The 7th encamped on grounds of the Hotel Maryland. *Scene 2*: Colonel Warp's headquarters.

MUSICAL NUMBERS[10]

Scene 1

Opening Chorus and Song
Y. Wallace

"Maryland" (Song and Chorus)

"Thespian Art"

"I Love You, Dear (Tommy)" (Song)

"My Young Man" (Song)

"A Bunch of Bewhiskered Populists" (Song)

"I'm the Heavy-Bearded Villain" (Song)
C. J. Ross

"Kids in Hogan's Alley" (Song and Chorus)

"Ignatius McFadden's Debut" (Song)

"Let him be shot!"

Finale

Scene 2

"Bring in the prisoner"

"He is saved!"

Finale

1896.27 THE GEISHA

George Edwardes' Japanese Musical Comedy in Two Acts. Book by Owen Hall. Music by Sidney Jones, (additional numbers by) Lionel Monckton. Lyrics by Harry Greenbank. Staged by Augustin Daly. Settings by Henry T. Hoyt after designs and models of the original by W. Telbin. Costumes by Percy Anderson. Produced by Augustin Daly. Opened 9 September 1896 at Daly's Theatre in repertory with "As You Like It" and closed 6 February 1897; returned in repertory with "The Wonder" the week of 29 March 1897, and in repertory with "The Tempest" the week of 12 April 1897, and closed 21 April 1897 after a total of 161 performances.

CAST: *The Marquis Imari*, Governor of the Province: EDWIN STEVENS. *Lieutenant Katasna* of the Imperial Japanese Artillery: Neil McCay. *Police Sergeant Takemini*: Robert Shepherd. *A Buyer*: William Hazeltine. *Wun-Hi*, of the Teahouse of Ten Thousand Joys: WILLIAM SAMPSON. *O Mimosa San*, a Geisha: DOROTHY MORTON. *Juliette (Diamant)*, a French Girl attendant on the Tea-house: HELMA NELSON. *Nami*: Sarina Alexe. *Mousme attendants on the Tea-house (5)*: *O Hana San*, Blossom: Lila Convere. *O Kiku San*, Chrysanthemum: Mabel Thompson. *O Kinkoto San*, Golden Harp: Mabelle Gilman. *Komurasaki San*, Little Violet: Maud Carter. *Other Attendants on the Tea-house*: Lena Loraine, Anne Caverly, Clara St. Clair, Alethe Craig, Isadora Duncan, Belle D'Arcy, Elsie Bennett, Clara Hollywood, Lillian Lipyeat, Mabel Strickland, Alice Winston, Margarete Whiticar, Ellen Mortimer, Maud

[9]Musical numbers not listed in programs. List prepared from production typescript.

[10]Additional song added, as per published sheet music:
"Appearances Were Against Her"
L. Swain

Vincent, Marion Marshall, Lottie Moore, Marjie Carl, Eugene Taylor, Alice Burke, Marguerite Barre.

English Visitors: *Officers of H.M.S. Thistle (6)*: *Lieutenant Reginald Fairfax*: VAN RENSSELAER WHEELER. *Hon. Reginald St. Pancras*: Eric Scott. *Dick Cunningham*: HERBERT GRESHAM. *Arthur Cuddy*: GEORGE LESOIR. *George Grinston*: Henry Gunson. *Tommy Stanley*, Middy: Clara Emory. *A Touring Party just landed from this yacht (5)*: *Lady Constance Wynne*: Marie St. John. *Miss Marie Worthington*: Pauline French. *Miss Ethel Hurst*: Gerda Wisner. *Dorothy Sweet*: Maym Kelso. *Mabel Evant*: Annette Spencer. *Molly Seamore*, also of the Touring Party: VIOLET LLOYD.

The action takes place in Japan outside the Treaty Limits, at the present time.

Act 1: The Tea House of Ten Thousand Joys.

Act 2: A Chrysanthemum Fete in the Palace Gardens.

ACT 1[11]

"Happy Japan" (Opening Chorus)

"Here they come" (Entrance of Officers)
Chorus, Officers

"Jack's the boy" (Song)
V. R. Wheeler, Officers
(*Music by* Lionel Monckton.)

"The dear little Jappy-Jap-Jappy" (Song)
H. Gresham

"The Amorous Goldfish" (Song)
D. Morton

"The Kissing" (Duet)
D. Morton, V. R. Wheeler

"If you will come to tea" (Concerted Piece)
D. Morton, Chorus

"Lamentation" (Oh, will they sell our master up)(Chorus)
Chorus, Geishas

"We're going to call on the Marquis" (Concerted Piece)
V. R. Wheeler, H. Gresham, Officers, Geishas, Chorus

"The Toy" (Duet)
V. Lloyd, V. R. Wheeler

"A Geisha's Life" (Song)
D. Morton

"Attention, pray!" (Recitative)
R. Shepherd, E. Stevens, N. McCay, V. R. Wheeler, Chorus

"Chivalry" (Song)
V. R. Wheeler, Chorus

"Chon Kina" (Song)
V. Lloyd, Chorus

"Thought of staying too long" (Finale)
Principals, Chorus

ACT 2

"Day born of love" (Chorus)

"The Toy Monkey" (Song)
V. Lloyd, Chorus
(*Music by* Lionel Monckton.)

"Ching-a-ring-a-ree!" (Duet)
H. Nelson, W. Sampson

"Geisha are we" (Concerted Piece)
Four Geishas, Officers, H. Gresham, English Girls

"Star of my soul" (Song)
V. R. Wheeler

"If that's not love—what is?" (Song)
H. Nelson

Entrance of Chorus (Japanese March)
Chorus

"With splendor auspicious" (Entrance of Geishas)
Geishas

"Chin, Chin, Chinaman" (Song)
W. Sampson, Chorus

"Love! Love!" (Song)
V. R. Wheeler, Chorus

"Hey-diddle-diddle! when man is in love" (Song)
H. Gresham, Chorus

[11]Musical numbers not listed in programs. List prepared from published English piano vocal score (Hopwood & Crew, Ltd., London, 1896).

"The Interfering Parrot" (Song)
V. Lloyd, Chorus

"Before our eyes" (Finale)
Ensemble

SUPPLEMENTARY NUMBERS[12]

"What will the Marquis do?" (Quartette)
D. Morton, V. R. Wheeler, H. Gresham, W. Sampson

"Jolly young Jacks are we" (Trio)
V. R. Wheeler, H. Gresham, G. Lesoir

"The Jewel of Asia" (Song)
D. Morton
(*Music by* James Philp.)

"I can't refrain from laughing"
(*Music by* Napoléon Lambelet.)

"The Wedding" (Song and Chorus)
(*Lyrics by* Adrian Ross.)

"Violet Lloyd's Mine Song"
V. Lloyd
(*Lyrics by* Adrian Ross.)

"It's coming off to-day" (Song)
E. Stevens, Chorus

"C'est moi" (Song)
H. Nelson, Chorus
(*Music by* Frank E. Tours. *Lyrics by* Percy Greenbank.)

"If to be True"[13]
V. R. Wheeler, D. Morton
(*Music and Lyrics by* Lawrence Kellie.)

1896.28

HALF A KING

A Comic Opera in Three Acts. Libretto by Harry B. Smith. Adapted from the French (opérette "Le Roi de carreau," libretto by Eugène Leterrier and Albert Vanloo[14]). Music by Ludwig Engländer. Produced under the direction of Richard Barker. Settings by Henry E. Hoyt and Richard Marston. Costumes designed by Percy Anderson. Musical direction, W. H. Batchelder. Produced by Francis Wilson (Management, A. H. Canby). Opened 14 September 1896 at the Knickerbocker Theatre and closed 7 November 1896 after 64 performances.

CAST: *Tireschappe*, a mountebank: FRANCIS WILSON. *Mistigris*, his factotum: PETER LANG. *Duke de la Roche-Trumeaux*: JOHN BRAND. *Duke de Chateau Margaux*: JOSEPH C. MIRON. *Honore*, his son: CLINTON ELDER. *Benoit*, his major-domo: EDWARD P. TEMPLE. *Vagabonds (3)*: *Jean de Loup*: H. J. West. *Gigolet*: William Laverty. *Casin Challie*: Samuel Chadwick. *Officer*: Joseph T. Chaillee. *Pierette*, Tireschappe's adopted daughter: LULU GLASER. *Lucinde*, daughter of Duke de la Roche-Trumeaux: CHRISTIE MacDONALD. *Simplice*, secretary to Duke de la Roche-Trumeaux: Agnes Paul. *Stella*: Agnes Martyne. *Duchess*: Blanche Plunkett. *Chorus of grisettes, students, vagabonds, servants, soldiers, wedding guests, etc.*

The action takes place in Paris, in the eighteenth century.

Act 1: Public Garden in Paris, on the Banks of the Seine. (Hoyt.)

Act 2: Interior of the Palace of the Duke de Chateau Margaux. (Marston.)

Act 3: The Court of Miracles. (Hoyt.)

MUSICAL NUMBERS[15]

"Bold Pierre"

"Bon Jour"

"Convent Song"

"If I Were Really a King"
F. Wilson

"Love Makes the World Go Round, Boys"

[12]Interpolations which accompanied the published score; these may or may not have been performed in New York.

[13]Interpolated for Marie Tempest and C. Hayden Coffin in the original London production; this song may or may not have been performed in New York.

[14]The original French score by Théodore de Lajarte was not used in the American adaptation.

[15]Musical numbers not listed in programs. List prepared from published sheet music, reviews.

"Lovely Lady"
"My Boy, You're in Society"
"Serenade"
"Would You Ask?"

1896.29 LOST, STRAYED OR STOLEN

A Comedy with Music in Four Acts. Libretto by J. Cheever Goodwin. Freely adapted from the French play "Le Baptême du Petit Oscar" by Eugène Grangé and Victor Bernard. Music by Woolson Morse. Staged by Ben Teal[16]. Dances arranged by Rose Becket. Settings by Walter Burridge. Costumes designed by F. Richard Anderson. Musical director, John McGhie. Produced by (Henry C.) Miner & Brooks. Opened 16 September 1896 at the Fifth Avenue Theatre and closed 28 November 1896 after 77 performances[17].

CAST: Act 1: *Bidart*, the florist: LOUIS HARRISON. *Chachignon*, from the south of France: M. A. Kennedy. *Courte Botte de Roquencourt*, of the Ancient Regime: JOSEPH HERBERT. *Galampois*, the family notary: Claude Brooke. *Jolivet*, a poor relative: John Gilroy. *Honorine Girardin*, the godmother: FANNIE BULKLEY. Catherine, a wet nurse: ROSE BEAUDET. *Pauline*: Caroline Leigh. *Clerks of both sexes in Bidart's employ, ladies and gentlemen with and without visible means of support, Christening guests, etc.*

Act 2: *Gaston de Champignol*, an aristocratic conscript: CYRIL SCOTT. *Captain La Tour*, a military martinet: Edward Wilks. *Corporal Bridoux*, a victim of circumstances: Daniel Packard. *Achille*: David Torrence. *Commissioned and non-commissioned officers, privates, etc. of the 22nd regiment.*

Act 3: *Rose d'Été*, an opéra bouffe prima donna: GEORGIA CAINE. *Julie*, lady's maid to Rose: Florence Thornton. *Cerise*, a soubrette: May Cuthbert. *Mlle. Doucy*, a contralto: Maude Chandler. *Esteban Pacheco*, a jealous Cuban: Henry Bergman. *Members of the Rose d'Été Opera Bouffe Company, incoluding as danseuses* Misses Emma Janvier, May Cuthbert, Julie Baird, Alice Cook.

Act 4: *Papa Pantin*, a Napoleonic veteran: Edward Wilks. *Papa Bigot*, a companion-at arms: Max Rosen. *Renaud*, a gendarme: Horace Sparks. *Françoise*, a downtrodden nursemaid: IRENE VERONA. *Ninette*, fond of the military: Sue Meade. *Louise*, another nursemaid: Emma Janvier. *Nursemaids, soldiers, gendarmes and typical Parisians of both sexes and all classes.*

The action takes place in Paris at the present time.

Act 1: Bidart's parlor salesrooms. The steeplechase begins. An even start.

Act 2: The 22nd's barracks at Pepinière. Galampois comes to grief at the first hurdle.

Act 3: The Boudoir of Rose d'été. A killing pace forces Chachignon to pull up.

Act 4: In a corner of the Garden of the Luxembourg. Roquencourt falls at the water leap, Bidart is distanced, and the dark horse Jolivet, wins.

MUSICAL NUMBERS[18]

"Our Hearts They Are Light" (When Two Hearts Love)
"Buy a Balloon"
"Ootchy-Cootchy" (Baby Song)
"A Kiss in the Dark"
"When I Joined the Army"
"(When) It's a Boy"
L. Harrison
"Two Heads Are Better Than One"
G. Caine, C. Scott
"Jean and Jacques Were Twins"

1896.30 THE GOLD BUG

A Musical Blend (Musical Farce) in Three Acts. Libretto by Glen MacDonough, adapted from a story by G. A. Pierce. Music by Victor Herbert. Produced under the stage direction of Max Freeman. Scenery by Richard Martson, Frederick Dangerfield. Costumes designed by Catherine Siedle. Orchestra under the direction of Gustave Kerker. Orchestrations by Victor Herbert. Produced by Thomas Canary and George W. Lederer. Opened 21 September 1896 and closed 10 October 1896 after 21 performances.

CAST: *Lotta Bonds*, the banker's daughter: VIRGINIA EARLE. *Honorable Willet Float*, a man with a past: MAX FIGMAN. *Wawayanda*, the girl he left behind him: MOLLY FULLER. *Penn Holder*, the private secretary: FREDERICK HALLEN. *Lady Patty Larceny*, a celebrated case: MARIE CAHILL. *Doolittle Work*, a social highwayman: HENRY NORMAN. *Constant Steele*, the politician: ROBERT FISHER. *Lingard Long*, one of the shadows of a great city: Charles Wayne. *The Mysterious Stranger*, a dark secret: HARRY KELLY. *Pauncefort*, a limited Male: Matthew Ott. *Lord Tudor Clare*, a gilded fool: PHILIP H. RYLEY. *The French Minister*, a gay Parisian: JOHN SLAVIN. *The Spanish Minister*, the Squire of Dames: Daniel Baker. *Bandmaster*: Arthur Etherington. *Boatswain*: Talmadge Baldwin. *Daughters of Lingard Long (4)*: *Essie*: Ada Dare. *Bessie*: Babette Rodney. *Jessie*: Rose Figman. *Tessie*: Sallie Randall. (*Specialties*, Act 2: BERT WILLIAMS, GEORGE WALKER, TITENIA.) *Lobbyists, Athletic Girls, Office-Seekers, Naval Reserves, Marines, etc.*

The Indians: Elsie Davis, Hattie Clifford, F. MacGlynn, T. Baldwin, W. Hethart, G. C. Ogle, O. Clemson, Arthur Etherington, W. Manning. *The Athletic Girls*: Ada Dare, Babette Rodney, Chrissie Carlyle, Sadie Evans, Emma Levy, Flossie Ellis, Pauline Bradley, Nelly Chamberlain, Connie Constantine, Meta Caldwell, Teddie DuCoe, Aimee David, Henrietta Williams, May Sherwood, Nellie Parks, Louise Hemming, Emma Batlo, Sally Randall. *The Lobbyists*: Nanette Nixon, Beatrice Manning, Ethel Valerie, Ivy Health, Justine Batlo, Bertha Whitney, Florence Townshend, Ida Moreland, Rose Figman, Kittie Shields, Estelle Hoyt, Bessie Sutherland, Mamie Moore, Ida Willhelmie, Mabelle Howe, Bobbie Burns, Sylvia Holte, Estelle Smith, Martha Habelman.

The action takes place in early summer.

Act 1: Lawn at the Secretary of the Navy's residence, Washington, D.C. (Marston.)

Act 2: Deck of the Naval Reserve Cruiser "Gold Bug." (Dangerfield.)

ACT 1

"One for Another"
"The Owl and the Thrush"
"The Gold Bug March"
"When I First Began to Marry, Years Ago"
M. Cahill

ACT 2

Specialties
C. Wayne, T. Baldwin (whistler), Williams and Walker,Slavin and Baker, F. Hallen and V. Earle
Specialty (Sand, buck, jig and wing terpsichore)
Titenia

1896.31 A PARLOR MATCH

A Revival of the Farce Comedy in Three Acts[19]. Play by Charles H. Hoyt. Stage director, James T. Galloway. Director of orchestra, William Potter Brown. Produced by Florenz Ziegfeld. Opened 21 September 1896 at the Herald Square Theatre and closed 31 October 1896 after 42 performances[20].

CAST: *I. McCorker*, a literary man: CHARLES E. EVANS. *Old Hoss*, collector for an auction room: WILLIAM HOEY. *Captain William Kidd*, a lineal descendant of the famous pirate: JAMES T. GALLOWAY. *Ephraim Bellomont*, his next-door neighbor, and descendant of Governor Bellomont, who captured the Pirate Kidd: M. J. SULLIVAN. *Ralph Bellomont*, his son, in love with Lucillle: WILLIAM M. ARMSTRONG. *McKee*, of Allon, M.P.: Hugh Mack. *Asa High*, a sport: William Keough. *Abel Leever*, a spiritualist: Stuart Conover. *St. Clair Todd*, a Harvard student: Peter Randall. *Euphonia Allen*, the Captain's maiden sister-in-law: Harriett Sheldon. *Lucille Kidd*, in love with Ralph: ALLENE CRATER. *Aline Kidd*, with a preference for Harvard: Aimee Van Dyne. *Friends of the Family (5)*: *Vesta Bule*: Beatrice Tait. *Gladys Riche*: Millie Tait. *Marie Quick*: Grayce Scott. *Lida Little*: Estelle Henriques. *Nora Marks*: Lillian Claiborne. *Innocent Kidd*, her papa's angel child: Minnie French. *Specialties*: ANNA HELD (Étoile de Paris), Annie St. Tel, Olympia Quartette.

Act 1: Morning. Captain Kidd's home. Digging for the treasure.

Act 2: Noon. McCorker's Headquarters. Still digging.

Act 3: Evening. Parlor in Captain Kidd's House. Finding the treasure.

[16]Direction of subsequent tour credited to Edward E. Rice; Max Bleiman credited as producer of the tour.

[17]Later played return engagements 11 January 1897 at the Harlem Opera House for 8 performances, and 22 March 1897 at the Casino Theatre for 16 performances.

[18]Musical numbers not listed in programs. List prepared from published sheet music, reviews, etc.

[19]Originally produced in New York 22 September 1884 at Tony Pastor's 14th Street Theatre for 16 performances. This revival billed as the Eleventh Evergreen year of Evans & Hoey's success.

[20]Later played return engagements 28 December 1896 at the Columbus Theatre for 8 performances, and 17 April 1899 at the Star Theatre for 8 performances. Costumes and scenery uncredited.

ACT 1[21]

"Somebody" (Duet)
W. M. Armstrong, A. Crater
Sailor Chorus
Company

ACT 2

"A Parlor Match" (Medley)
Company
"Ah There"
M. French
"Sweetheart, I Love But Thee"
W. M. Armstrong
"Spanish Fantasie"
C. E. Evans, Followers
"Dear Golden Days"
A. Crater
"The Diamond King"
W. Hoey
"(Tell Them) Yer Baby's Comin' to Town"
Company
(*Music and Lyrics by* John T. Kelly.)
Materializations from the Mysterious Cabinet:
Characteristic Dance
Sisters Helene
Introduced by Minnie French as Pierrot
March and Drill—N.G.S.N.Y.
Olympia Quartette
Specialty
A. Held
["Come Play with Me" (I Have Such a Nice Little Way with Me)
(*Music by* Alfred Plumpton. *Lyrics by* G. P. Hawtrey.)]
Finale—Review Internationale
England—"Algy"[22] (from ALGY)
Sisters Tait
(*Music and Lyrics by* Harry B. Morris.)
Germany—"Schaffmeister"
A. Crater, W. M. Armstrong
Russia—"Danse Russe"
Misses Scott, Claiborne
Italy—"The Gondoliers" (Selection)
Messrs. Sullivan, Randall, Connover
(*Music by* Arthur Sullivan. *Lyrics by* William S. Gilbert.)
Paris—"The Gay Parisienne" (from THE GAY PARISIENNE[22a])
Miss Van Dyne
(*Music by* Ivan Caryll.)
China, Japan—"Chon Kina" (from THE GEISHA)
Mr. Keough (Li Hung), Miss French (Geisha)
(*Music by* Sidney Jones. *Lyrics by* Harry Greenbank.)
Scotland—"Pipe His Blues"
Mr. Hoey
Ireland—"The Harp That Once"
Mr. Mack
(*Words by* Thomas Moore.)
Spain—"Estudiantina"
Sisters Helene
(*Music by* Paul Lacome.)
America—"Uncle Sam"
Mr. Galloway
Miss Colombia
Miss Sheldon

ACT 3

"Seance Seekers" (Song)
Messrs. Sullivan, Keough, Armstrong, Randall
"It Never Troubles Me" (Song)
W. Hoey
Finale
Company

[21]Specialty interpolated as per published sheet music:
"As They Did in Days of Yore"
W. Hoey
(*Music by* George B. Severs. *Lyrics by* Charles House.)

[22]First introduced and popularized by Vesta Tilley.

[22a]This London success THE GAY PARISIENNE would repeat its success in New York later this season under the title THE GIRL FROM PARIS.

1896.32 THE BLACK CROOK!

A Revival of the Musical Extravaganza in Four Acts, 16 Scenes[23]. Play by Charles M. Barras. (Music by Thomas Baker, others.) Direction, U. D. Newell. Opened 21 September 1896 at the 14th Street Theatre and closed 26 September 1896 after 8 performances.

CAST: MORTALS: *Hertzog*, surnamed the Black Crook, alchemist and sorcerer: FREDERICK MELVILLE. *Greppo*, his drudge: John W. World. *Rudolphe*, a poor artist: VERNON RAMSDELL. *Count Wolfenstein*: S. S. WHELBECK. *Puffengruntz*, his Steward: CHARLES E. GRAHAM. *Casper*, a villager: William Norton. *Wolfgar*, a Gypsy ruffian: Frank Rand. *Bruno*, his companion: Sid Chappel. *Amina*, betrothed to Rudolphe: VERA WILSON. *Dame Barbara*, her foster-mother: Connie Thompson. *Rosetta*: Carroll Clover. *Carline*: LILLIAN HARPER. *Peasants, Villagers, Guards, Attendants, etc.*

IMMORTALS: *Stalacta*, Queen of the Golden Realm: DOROTHY LATHROP. *Dragonfin*, an attendant sprite: A. Borani.

INFERNALS: *Zamiel*, the Arch-Fiend: E. K. STANTON. *Redglare*, Recording Demon: H. Borani. *Skudawelp*, familiar to Hertzog: George Nixon. (*Fairies, Naiads, etc. Ballet.*)

1896.33 SANTA MARIA

A Romantic Comic Opera in Three Acts. Book (libretto) and music by Oscar Hammerstein. Stage director, Max Freeman. Musical director, J. Luckstone. Produced by Oscar Hammerstein. Opened 24 September 1896 at Hammerstein's Olympia Theatre and closed 12 December 1896 after 92 performances.[24]

CAST: *Santa Maria*, (the Prince of Holland): CAMILLE D'ARVILLE. *Sarracco*, (a Gypsy): LUCILLE SAUNDERS. *Princess Terese de Savoy*: MARIE HALTON. *Queen of Holland*: Juliette Preston. *Elise von Hagen*: Eleanor Elton. *Clairette Styrberg*: EDNA MAY PETTIE [Edna May]. *Amida*: Alice Rice. *Lieutenant Bertrand*: JULIUS STEGER. *Moccareli*, (the Judge): JAMES T. POWERS. *King Henry William*: H. W. Tredennick. *Marquis de Villadon*: Joseph Frankau. *Bombazine*: Frederick Bach. *Sheriff*: Albert McGucken. *Captain François*: Albert Lellman. *Fisher Girls, Soldiers, Townspeople, Women Jury, Gypsy Dancing Girls, Courtiers, etc.*

Act 1: Holland in the eighteenth century.

Act 2: The town of Zambazoo in Italy, three years later.

Act 3: Holland again.

MUSICAL NUMBERS[25]

"Santa Maria March"
"Down by the Hillside I Met Her"
"Divorce Song"
"Eskimo's Song"
"Let Us Jolly Be"
"Santa Maria, my joy, my pride"
"Bring Me Back to My Childhood Days"
"When I Found My First (One) Gray Hair"

1896.34 THE MERRY TRAMPS

The Lilliputians in a Grand Spectacular Play (with Music) in Four Acts, 11 Scenes. Play by Robert Breitenbach. Music by Carl Pleininger. Director, Carl Rosenfeld. Acting Manager, Ludwig Rosenfeld. Settings and costumes designed by Carl Rosenfeld. Musical director, Carl Pleininger. Produced by Carl and Theodore Rosenfeld. Opened 28 September 1896 at the Star Theatre and closed 31 October 1896 after 40 performances; reopened 21 December 1896 at the Star Theatre and closed 2 January 1897 after 16 additional performances. Total: 56 performances.

CAST: (*Professor*) *Willard*, an inventor: A. Durand. *Mary*, his daughter: BERTHA JAEGER. *Pisang*, a man ape: LUDWIG MERKEL. *Joe Muller*, baker: SELMA GOERNER. *Bob*, butcher: FRANZ EBERT. *Jim*: ADOLF ZINK. *Kruschke*, owner of a mill: HERMANN RING. *Cordula*, his sister: Mrs. Griebe. *Annie*, his niece and ward: ELISE LAU. *Edward*, miller's help: MAX WALTER. *Patrick*: Mr. Wollner. *Fred, John,*

[23]First produced in New York 12 September 1866 at Niblo's Garden for 475 performances.

[24]Scenery and costumes uncredited.

[25]No musical numbers listed in programs. List includes published songs only. Announced for the 50th performance on 4 November 1896 was a new finale and quartet.

Willard's servants: Messrs. Moritz, Klein. *First Policeman*: Mr. Griebe. *Second Policeman*: Mr. Heimann. *A Farmer*: Mr. Rabe. *Millers, Farmers, Soldiers, Servants, Police Officers, etc.*

Act 1, Scene 1: At the Laboratory. Scene 2: The Ride through Clouds. Scene 3: The Tramps on the Farm. Scene 4: At the Granary. Scene 5: The Harvest Festival.

Act 2: The Mill at the Brook.

Act 3, Scene 1: The Contrary Partners. Scene 2: In the Realm of Light.

Act 4, Scene 1: The Grateful Friends. Scene 2: Silver Laces. Scene 3: Final Apotheosis.

ACT 1

The Harvest Festival:

Reapers, Grape-pickers, Wheat, Corn, Hops, Wine, Cornflowers, Poppies.

Introduction by the Lilliputians, "The Dudes of New York."

ACT 3

The Ballets of Lights and Lamps.

Bronze Figures, Torches, Oil Lamps, Candles, Lanterns, Gaslights, Incandescent Lights.

ACT 4

The Ballet of Silver Laces:

Introduction by the Lilliputians, "The Up-to-Date Chansonettes."

1896.35 EVANGELINE

A Revised Version of the American Opera Bouffe (Spectacular Extravaganza) in Two Acts, 7 Scenes[26]. Libretto by J. Cheever Goodwin. Music by Edward E. Rice. Staged by Edward E. Rice. Scenery by Frank Rafter, John Thompson, Henry Hoyt. Orchestra under the direction of Edward E. Rice. Produced by Edward E. Rice. Opened 1 October 1896 at the Garden Theatre, moved 2 November 1896 to the Lyric Theatre and closed 7 November 1896 after 44 performances.

CAST: *Evangeline*, the heroine of an enduring affection which very nearly proves her ruin: THERESA VAUGHN. *Catherine*, Gabriel's aunt, an antidote for melancholy—"Love's young dream becomes a nightmare": GEORGE K. FORTESCUE. *Eulalie*, her confidante—confidently hoping for women's rights: Violet Potter. *Mary Anne*, Eva's maid: Josephine Fairbanks. *Marie, Rose*, in Eva suite—two sweet to need description: Ida Fairbanks, Emma Marsh. *Elaine*, Evangeline's sister: Yvonne LaGuerre. *LeBlanc*, the notary,—although notary coroner, in quest of somebody, and led to believe that there's a good deal in a name: FREDERIC SOLOMON. *Gabriel*, Eva's worshipper: CHERIDAH SIMPSON. *Felician*, Eulalie's sweetheart: May Baker. *Captain Dietrich* of the Queen's own, familiar with hard-tack and "Hardies Tactics": CHARLES A. BIGELOW. *King Boorioboola Gha*, a sufferin' sovereign: Charles Seagrave. *Basil*, the blacksmith, who believes black myths until convinced to the contrary by his daughter Eva: EDWARD CHAPMAN. *Hans Wagner*, corporal, but fond of the spiritual: Thomas F. Kierns. *Chief of Police*, a "peeler": Sherman Wade. *The Headsman*, a mimic, very clever at taking off blockheads: Louis DeSmith. *Fritz, Rudolph*, Captain Dietrich's aides: Grace Belasco, Florence Wilson. *Maurice*: Beatrice Hamilton. *Hubert*: May Hamilton. *Billy Bowline, Tom Braceway*, two deserters from Her Majesty's ship: J. W. Harris, George Gans. *Unambebe*, Captain of the Amazons: Grace Rutledge. *The Heifer*, two of a kind: Messrs. Sherman Wade, James Lee. *The African Monkey*, the greatest yet discovered: James Reynolds. *Four Drummer Boys*: Misses Mamie Forbes, Josie Winner, May Lavigne, Millie Norton. *Water Nymphs*: Misses May Lavigne, Helen Whiting, Anita Wilson, Millie Norton, Mamie Forbes, Belle Waters, Millie Wilson, Lillian Menzies. *Premier Danseuse*: Mlle. Mirella (from Grand Opera House, Paris.). *Villagers, Fishermen, Amazons, Diamond Diggers, etc. The Lone Fisherman*, a mystery (first time): HENRY E. DIXEY.

Chorus: *Ladies*: Miss May Lavigne, Nellie Wilson, Anita Wilson, Helen Whiting, Lizzie Shaw, Georgie Black, Millie Norton, Florence Carlisle, Lottie Prince, Jessie Banks, Jessie Thompson, Millie Tate, Josie Winner, Annie Winner, Etta Stetson, Helen Smith, May Hamilton, Mable Waite, Georgie Delorme, Arabella DeThein, Arlien Potter, Adele Archer, Beatrice DeThein, Maud Banks, Clara Astor, Elaine Proctor. *Gentlemen*: Messrs. William Howard, Pierre Loring, C. B. Powell, Frank Abbott, Otto Schuster, John P. Savage, Edward Thomas, Henry Amberg, Otto Neilig, Warren A. Cook, Basil Telson, Louis DeSmith, Augustus Kramer, Francis Lavelle, Otto Kreiling, George Astor.

Act 1, Scene 1: Evangeline's Cottage by the Sea, in Autumn. Scene 2; A Lane near by. Evangeline's Home. (All by Rafter.)

Between the acts will be shown for the first time the shipwreck of the English man-of-war off the coast of Africa. (Rafter.)

Act 2, Scene 1: The Diamond Fields of Africa. (Thompson.) Scene 2: Exterior of the King's Palace on a Cold Day. (Hoyt.) Scene 3: Dungeon of the King. (Rafter.) Scene 4: Courtyard of the Palace. (Hoyt.)

[26]Originally produced in New York 27 July 1884 at Niblo's Garden Theatre for 14 performances in a 3-Act version.

ACT 1

"We Must Be Off" (Opening Chorus)

"One Moment, Pray" (Recitative)

"There's a Man" (Song)
C. Simpson

"Thinking, Love, of Thee" (Ballad)
T. Vaughn

"I'm a Fascinating Notary" (Song)
F. Solomon

"Into the Water We Go" (Bathing Quintette)
T. Vaughn, V. Potter, G. K. Fortescue, I. Fairbanks, E. Marsh

Ballet Music

"She's Saved! She's Saved!" (Choral)

"Laughing Eyes of Blue" (Song and Dance)
C. Simpson

"Sammy Smug" (Descriptive Song)
F. Solomon, Chorus

"My Heart" (Ballad)
T. Vaughn, Y. LaGuerre (harp)

"Golden Chains" (Duet)
T. Vaughn, C. Simpson

"Sweet Evangeline"[27] (Gavotte)(Entrance Music of the Shepherds and Shepherdesses)

Dance of the Heifer
(S. Wade, J. Lee)

"In Us You See" (Soldiers' Chorus and Septette)

"He Says She Must Go"[28] (Grand Finale/Quartette)

ACT 2

"Clink, Clank"[29] (Miners' Chorus)

"I'm in Lofe" (Song)
C. A. Bigelow

"The (Six) Miserable Ruffians" (Grand Chorus)

"We Are Off to Seek for Eva" (Duet)
F. Solomon, G. K. Fortescue

"Let's Quietly Steal Away"[30] (A Musical Trifle)

"Kissing Goes by Favor" (Duet)
C. Simpson, T. Vaughn

"Twelve O'Clock, and All Is Well" (Chant)

"Prowling 'Round the Diamond Fields" (Policeman's Narrative)

"Come to the Heart That is Thine" (Romanza)
T. Vaughn

"Where Are Thou Now, My Beloved?" (Romanza)
C. Simpson

"March of the Royal Amazons"[31]

"(King) Polimenicho" (Song)
C. Simpson, Chorus

"She's Acquitted, (He's Outwitted)" (Finale)

1896.36 THE GEEZER

A Burlesque in One Act, 2 Scenes, preceded by an Olio. A Respectful Parody of "The Geisha."[32]. Libretto by Joseph Herbert. Music by John Stromberg. Produced under the stage direction of Joseph Herbert. Costumes by Mrs. M. Dowling. Musical director, John Stromberg. Produced by Joseph M. Weber and Lew M. Fields. Opened 8 October 1896 at Weber and Fields' Broadway Music Hall and closed 17 February 1897 after 148 performances.

[27]Newly composed for this production.
[28]Newly composed for this production.
[29]Newly composed for this production.
[30]Newly composed for this production.
[31]Newly composed for this production.
[32]The Comic Opera with book by Owen Hall, music by Sidney Jones, lyrics by Harry Greenbank. Opened 9 September 1896 at Daly's Theatre for 161 performances.

Olio[33]: Farrell and Taylor (Comedy, Music); Johnson, Davenport and Lorella (The Football Players and the Farmer); John Kernell (Irish Comedy); Imogene Comer (Vocalist); Fields and Lewis (Comedians and Song Authors); The Rays (Johnnie, Emma)(Comedy)

CAST: *Lord Dunraving*: CHARLES J. ROSS. *Two-Hi*, a Chinaman, proprietor of a Doyers Street tea house: SAM BERNARD. *Li Hung Chang*, the Geezer: JOHN T. KELLY. *Nellie Fly*, a newspaper correspondent and tuft-hunter: MABEL FENTON. *Kantaker*, a wandering minstrel: YOLANDE WALLACE. *Lieutenant Conville, Lieutenant Runingham, Lieutenant Brimstone, Mr. Midshipman Fanley*, of the "*Valkyrie*": Maude Gilbert, Genevieve Clifton, Florence Bell, Frankie Bailey. *Ballet girls who have married titles (3)*: *Lady Faith*: Josephine Allen. *Lady Hope, Lady Charity*: Rose Beaumont, Nellie Beaumont [Beaumont Sisters]. *O Le Mosa Sam*, Chinese prima donna: LILLIAN SWAIN.

Chinese buds (4): *Golden Rod*: Ada Walker. *Apple Blossom*: Minnie Walker. *Geranium*: Bobbie Byrnes. *Wood Violet*: Edith Merrill. *Preservers of peace and prosperity (4)*: *A. Roosevelt*: Walter West. *B. Roosevelt*: Seth Miller. *C. Roosevelt*: Fred Murray. *D. Roosevelt*: Joseph Brown. *Weary Watkins* of Waukesha, a citizen of the world: THOMAS J. RYAN. *Hogan's Kid*, attendant to Li Hung Chang: John Zahn.

SYNOPSIS and MUSICAL NUMBERS[34]

Scene 1: Opening Chorus. Doyers Street festivities. Dunraving goes a-slumming. "Sea Song." Two-Hi's woes. Li Hung Chang, the ambassador and diplomat. Song. A true bohemian. Return of the footlight favorites. Trio Ensemble. Misplaced confidence. Nellie Fly's plan. Dunraving's perfidy. Kantaker objects. The ambassador's rage. "(The) Passionate Codfish" (Song). Two-Hi's ruin. The auction. "Off to China" (Finale).

Scene 2: Opening Chorus. Arrival of the Ladies Faith, Hope and Charity. "Get Out Your Hammers, Girls" (Gossiping chorus). Arrival of Dunraven on the "*Valkyrie*." No passenger boats in the way. On time. "What Would His Ludship Say?" (Octette). Weary takes the Emperor's place. Kantaker unfolds his scheme. Darkey Song (sung by Y. Wallace). Li Hung Chang's plea. Between two stools. The Emperor gives commands. Remove his yellow jacket. Li Hung Chang's discomfiture. Weary as a capitalist. Home again. Finale.

1896.37

A GOOD THING

A Farce Comedy with Songs in Three Acts. Play by John J. McNally. Staged by R. A. Roberts. Musical director, James C. McCabe. Produced by H. B. Harris and E. Rosenbaum. Opened 12 October 1896 at the Casino Theatre and closed 31 October 1896 after 21 performances[35].

CAST: *Billy Biddall*, auctioneer's clerk: PETER F. DAILEY. *Timothy Coogan*, an Irish auctioneer, in love with Mrs. Millett: JAMES T. KELLY. *Lemuel Bradbury*, farmer and horse-breeder, in love with Mrs. Millett: CHARLES J. STINE. *Sam Settle*, mischievous country boy: William Barry, Jr. *Professor Preach* of the Metropolitan School of Languages: Joseph Swickard. *Billy Porter*, porter at Coogan's auction rooms: Arthur Earle. *Sam Gally*: O. M. Scott. *Dan McCarthy*: George Lynn. *Sadie Bradbury*, niece of Bradbury—has been on the stage: FLORA [Flo] IRWIN. *Mrs. Minerva Millett*, President of the Minerva Seminary for Girls—giddy but classic: OLLIE EVANS. *Ouida Merritt*, schoolgirl, Coogan's ward: MATTIE NICHOLS. *Minnie Millett*, Mrs. Millett's daughter, in love with Billy: AGNES MILTON.

Pupils of the Millett Seminary: *Sally Rastus*: Delcie V. Walker. *Bella Ringer*: Edna Elsmere. *Flossie Wool*: Jessie Clark. *May Day*: Helen Marlborough. *Haida Heath*: Emma Levey. *Sunny Dell*: Crissie Carlyle. *Carrie Waite*: Mamie Moore. *Josie Goode*: Hattie Harvey.

Servant: Bert A. Williams. *Waiter*: George W. Walker. (*The Americus Comedy Quartette*: O. M. Scott, Arthur Earle, Joseph Swickard, George Lynn).

Time: Today will be yesterday tomorrow.

Act 1: The Millett Seminary, near New York.

Act 2: Coogan's Auction-Room, Bowery, New York.

Act 3: Coogan's Residence, New York.

ACT 1[36]

"While Wheeling with the Girl You Love" (Bicycle Song and Dance)
(*Arranged by* James T. Kelly)
M. Nichols, A. Milton, D. V. Walker, E. Elsmere, J. Clark

Grand Medley Finale

"Rosy Elixir" (from THE KNICKERBOCKERS)(Opening Chorus)
Entire Company
(*Music by* Reginald DeKoven.)

"That's What, by Gosh!"
C. J. Stine

"Sweet Little Rosey Posey"
E. Elsmere

"Hugh McCue"
J. T. Kelly

"Jones Said I'll Be One"
F. Irwin

"Baby's Dream"
Americus Comedy Quartette

"(Tell Them) Yer Baby's Comin' to Town"[37]
P. F. Dailey, Company
(*Music and Lyrics by* John T. Kelly.)

ACT 2[38]

"The Lovers' Quarrel" (Duet)
J. T. Kelly, O. Evans

The Americus Comedy Quartette

"I'm Willie Off the Yacht"
P. F. Dailey, Company
(*Music and Lyrics by* John L. Golden.)

ACT 3

Specialties
J. T. Kelly; F. Irwin; Williams and Walker; P. F. Dailey

1896.39

ON BROADWAY

A Local Comedy Melodrama in Four Acts. Play by Clay M. Greene and Ben Teal. Produced under the stage direction of Ben Teal. Scenery by H. L. Reid. Musical director, William J. Rostetter. Produced by Harry Williams Amusement Corporation. Opened 12 October 1896 at the Grand Opera House and closed 17 October 1896 after 8 performances; returned 23 November 1896 to the Murray Hill Theatre for an additional 8 performances; returned 15 March 1897 to the Grand Opera House for an additional 8 performances, moved 22 March 1897 to the People's Theatre for 8 performances, and 29 March 1897 to the Columbus Theatre for an additional 8 performances. Total this season in New York: 40 performances.

CAST: *Mary Brady*, a womanly woman with a man's nerve: MAGGIE CLINE. *Nellie Crane*, her adopted sister. The innocent victim of a gentleman's perfidy: BEATRICE MORGAN. *Mrs. Scarborough*, a charitable woman and an uncharitable step-mother: Isabel Waldron. *Grace*, her daughter, with a yielding nature, and an obstinate heart: Alice Thill. *"Rags,"* a waif of the slums: Helene Thill. *Ms. Googan*, an unfortunate: Mrs. Wilson. *Thomas Brady, Esq.*, a bankrupt contractor and a doting father with an infirmity: JOHN G. SPARKS. *Thomas Jefferson Brady*, his son, who won "The Suburban" to lose his liberty: FRED W. PETERS. *Harry Scarborough*, educated for the law, but inclined toward missionary work in the Police Department: George W. Howard. *John Moorhead*, an upright man of business with downtown proclivities in the direction of "Sport": BEN T. RINGGOLD. *Philip Pentfield*, a gentleman by connection, and a knave by choice: John T. Burke. *Cornelius Kerr*, a contractor, whose houses are built of sand: E. S. Metcalf. *Bill Masters*, an man with a friendless past and a hopeless future: Jerome Stansill. *Officer Michael Marks*, a Hebro-Hibernian policeman: James A. Leahy. *Dan McCloskey*, the hero of the famous song "Throw Him Down,

---

[33]Other vaudeville acts which appeared in the Olio over the course of the run included: The Russell Brothers, Lizzie B. Raymond, Caron & Herbert, Stanley and Moore (musical comedians); Thomas J. Ryan (Irish comedian and dancer); Charles J. Ross and Mabel Fenton (presenting a melodramatic sketch from Charles Dickens' "Oliver Twist"; Bessie Bonehill (character and descriptive vocalist); McIntyre and Heath (Ethiopian comedians).

[34] Added after the opening: The Hen and the Door-Knob; Kissing Song; Aloft, Below!; Li Hung Chang; Ultra Propriety. Incidental to the Burlesque will be introduced the 5 Embarrassing Sisters and Gertie Reynolds and the Yellow Kid.

[35]Costumes and settings uncredited. Played return engagements 16 November 1896 at the Murray Hill Theatre for 8 performances, 14 December 1896 at the Grand Opera House for 8 performances, and 21 December 1896 at the Harlem Opera House for 8 performances.

[36]Interpolated as per sheet music:
"Honey Does Yer Love Yer Man"
F. Irwin
(*Music by* John W. Bratton. *Lyrics by* Walter Ford.)
"It's Honey All De Time!"
F. Irwin
(*Music and Lyrics by* J. W Wheeler.)

[37]Also interpolated into this season's revival of A PARLOR MATCH.

[38]Added to Act 2 for subsequent tour, after "The Lovers' Quarrel":
"I'll Have Money to Burn" (Acrobatic Song and Dance)
M. Nichols, W. Barry, Jr.

McCloskey": HARRY B. BRADLEY. *Frank Raig*, his dusky opponent, known as the "Harlem Hyena": Jerry Hart. *The Broadway Quartette, Bookmakers, Men About Town, Prisoners, Laborers, Policemen, Firemen, etc.*

Act 1: The Home of the Bradys. A woman of tender heart and iron nerve. The mysterious shot.

Act 2, Scene 1: The Banker's Friend. A brother's bail and a Prize Fighter's stake. *Scene 2*: Exterior of "The Tombs." McCloskey and the Harlem Hyena. A waif of the slums. *Scene 3*: Foot of Twenty-Sixth Street and the East River. Pleasure by the side of woe. "Off for Blackwell's Island." A fatherless child finds a new mother, and McCloskey a backer.

Act 3, Scene 1: Another room in the Brady home. Waiting for the verdict. *Scene 2*: Madison Square. The cable cars blocked, which threatens to check a woman contractor's plan. McCloskey's training versus the cable's speed. *Scene 3*: Skyscrapers near City Hall. A false contractor and a false building. A house built on the sands. The sensational collapse of a building.

Act 4: From Lower Broadway to Madison Square. An evening reception. Four pairs of lovers and one betrothal. Two crimes that bear their own punishment.

MUSICAL NUMBERS[39]

"Throw Him Down, McCloskey"
M. Cline
(*Music and Lyrics by* J. W. Kelly.)

"A Transplanted Shamrock"
M. Cline
(*Music by* Gilbert Tompkins. *Lyrics by* Juliet Wilbor Tomkins.)

1896.40 A NIGHT AT THE CIRCUS

A Revival of the Circo-Comedy in Three Acts[40]. Play by H. Grattan Donnelly. Opened 19 October 1896 at the Grand Opera House and closed 24 October 1896 after 8 performances; re-opened 9 November 1896 at the Standard Theatre and closed 14 November 1896 after additional 12 performances.

CAST: Acts 1 and 2: *Archibald Banger* of Friske and Banger: M. J. Kearney. *Nicholas Friske*, one of the (old) boys: Joe Dailey. *Signor Bonanza*, Manager of the Imperial Circus: J. H. Bradbury. *Pinkerton Kopp*, a private detective: James R. Adams. *Kicker*, an ambitious office boy: Charles G. Patterson. *Dixey Weed*: Ben F. Grinnell. *Bill Sticker*: F. C. Jones. *Calliope Friske*, with an eye on everybody: ANN WARRINGTON. *Belvidere Banger*, a jealous wife: PAULA EDWARDS. *Remi Riter*, a Hammond operator: Kitty Wolfe. *Bud Manhattan*, a New York debutante: Jennie Leary. *Oriole Ogontz*, a Philadelphia Venus: Lottie Leary. *Ida Vassar*, a Boston beauty: Kittie Miley. *Twin Sisters (2)*: *Mlle. Electra*, queen of the arena: FANNY BLOODGOOD. *Mlle. Madeline Milan*, a visiting governess: FANNY BLOODGOOD.

Act 3: *Circus Specialties*: Josie Ashton, Mamie Forepaugh (Equestrienne), Hines & Colby (Perch Act), Ernest Melville, Robert and Rose Stickney (Wire Act), James R. Adams (Stilts), Robert Stickney's Trained Dogs and Charles Lowery's "Ding" (Baby Elephant).

1896.38 HOGAN'S ALLEY

An Irish Farce Comedy in Three Acts. Play by Barney Gilmore and John F. Leonard. Based on the comic strip of the same name. Stage manager, Jack Gardner. Orchestra under the direction of Dave Braham. Manager, Eugene Wellington. Opened 12 October 1896 at the People's Theatre and closed 17 October 1896 after 8 performances; returned 8 February 1897 to the Grand Opera House for 9 additional performances (with The Yellow Kid), 5 April 1897 at the Columbus Theatre for 8 additional performances, moved 12 April 1897 to the People's Theatre for 8 additional performances. Total in New York this season: 33 performances.[41]

CAST: *Mr. Michael Hogan*, owner of the Alley: JOHN F. LEONARD. *Mr. Martin Brogan*, his bosom friend: BARNEY F. GILMORE. *Charley Duno*, too rich for the Alley: WILLIAM J. HAGAN. *John Collier*, won't stay out of the Alley: Thomas Clark. *Ike Arnheim*, won't leave the Alley: Nick Adams. *Luke Murphy*, terror of the Alley: Jack Gardner. *Joe Diablo*, sticks to the Alley: Dan Gardner. *Darby Brogan*, returns to the Alley: Dan Gardner. *Mickey Dugan*, Yellow Kid: DICK GARDNER. *Officer Porter*, One of the Finest: Fred Ward. *Col. Waring White Wings*, keeps the Alley clean: James Curdy. *Mrs. Michael Hogan*, controls the Alley: Joseph E. Conlan. *Nellie Hogan*, Belle of the Alley: Mina Shirley. *Josie Hogan*, pride of the Alley: Lillian Shirley. *Millie Diablo*, dancer of the Alley: Gladys Hayden. *Mamie Callahan*, sunlight of the Alley: Lulu Leslie. *Liz*, Luke's steady: Hulda Halvers. *Annie Ryan*, too good for the Alley: Eva Urline. *Kittie Foley*, Flirt of the Alley: Capitola Urline. *Paddy McGee*, Mickey's chum of the Alley: Joseph Kane. *Organ Grinders, Kids and Rabble from the Alley.*

Act 1: Hogan's Alley.

Act 2: Interior of Hogan's Home.

Act 3: Hogan's Alley.

MUSICAL NUMBERS[42]

Mandolin Quintette (Act 2)

"Down to Coney Isle"
J. F. Leonard, B. F. Gilmore
(*Music by* John F. Leonard. *Lyrics by* Barney Gilmore.)

"The Dugan Kid Who Lives in Hogan's Alley"
J. F. Leonard, B. F. Gilmore
(*Music by* John F. Leonard. *Lyrics by* Barney Gilmore.)

1896.41 BRIAN BORU

A Romantic Opera in Three Acts, 4 Scenes. Book and lyrics by Stanislaus Stange. Music by Julian Edwards. Production under the stage direction of John F. Nash. Fairy Ballet arranged by Signor F. Marchetti. Settings by D. Frank Dodge. Costumes designed by Catherine F. Seidle. Musical direction, Julian Edwards. Produced by the Whitney Opera Company (Fred C. Whitney, Director) Opened 19 October 1896 at the Broadway Theatre and closed 2 January 1897 after 88 performances.[43]

CAST: Irish Characters: *Brian Boru*, Ireland's Champion: MAX EUGENE. *O'Donovan*, his foster brother: SAMUEL I. SLADE. *O'Connor*, his standard bearer: BRUCE PAGET. *Erina*, O'Connor's sister: GRACE GOLDEN. *O'Reilly*, an Irish chieftain: Fred M. Marston. *Johnny Dugan*, O'Hara's rival: JOHN C. SLAVIN. *Baby Malone*, the child of a giant: AMELIA SUMMERVILLE. *Mona*, O'Connor's betrothed: Helen Brackett. *Fairy Queen*, the Spirit of Ireland: Louise Margot. *Banshee*: Annie Cameron. *Bishop*: J. L. Andrews. *Pat O'Hara*, Brian's henchman: RICHARD F. CARROLL.

English Characters: *Elfrida*, an English Princess: AMANDA FABRIS. *Lord Edward*, Commander of the English forces: George O'Donnell. *Fitz-Stephen*, a knight: THOMAS RICKETTS. *Egbert*, Edward's envoy: Andrew J. Lynam. *Oswald*, an English monk: Fred Summerfield. *Herald* (Standard Bearer): John Hendrick. *Athelstone*, a messenger: Ole L. Norman.

Fairies, Elves, Witches, Goblins, Irish Warriors, English Knights, Monks, Maids of Honor, Bards, English Pages, Knights of Red Branch, Irish Colleens, Irish Standard Bearers, Amazons, etc.

The action takes place at the end of the tenth century.

Act 1: Wicklow Hills; St. Kevins Keep R.; Malone's Cottage. Midnight.

Act 2: Great Hall of Dublin Castle. English Headquarters. Noon of the following day.

Act 3, Scene 1: Irish camp outside of Dublin. Afternoon of the same day. *Scene 2*: Old Dublin Street. St. Patrick's Cathedral and view of Dublin Bay.

ACT 1[44]

Chorus of Fairies (The world is dreaming, the stars are gleaming)
L. Margot, R. F. Carroll, M. Eugene, A. Cameron, G. Golden, Chorus

"I'm a Giant's Little Baby" (Solo)
A. Summerville, R. F Carroll

"The Irish Patriot" (Solo)
B. Paget

"(We are the) Guardians of Beauty" (March and Chorus)

"The Heart's Richest Dower" (Solo)
A. Fabris

"Fare-Thee-Well" (Trio and Chorus)
M. Eugene, B. Paget

---

[40]First produced in New York 21 December 1891 at the Park Theatre for 8 performances, and a return engagement 21 March 1892 at the Bijou Theatre for 32 performances. This production boasted new cast, new music and new scenery. For Synopsis of Scenes and Musical Numbers, see original 1891 production.

[41]Played a return engagement 17 January 1898 at the Star Theatre for 8 additional performances.

[42]Not in performance order. List prepared from program advertisement, published sheet music, etc.

[43]Returned 5 April 1897 to the Academy of Music for an additional 8 performances.

[44]Vocals not identified in programs, but verified from published vocal score.

"There's a Lad That I Know" (Solo)
G. Golden
"(There's) A Picture in My Heart" (Duet)
S. I. Slade, G. Golden
"(We Are) Simple Irish Colleens" (Chorus)
"My Name Is Pat O'Hara" (Solo)(Paddy's Legs)
R. F. Carroll
Jig
"Sing the Song of Great Brian" (Finale)

ACT 2
"Sing a Merry Rondelay" (Chorus)
"An Englishman's Toast" (Solo)
T. Ricketts, Chorus
"The Open Gates" (Ensemble)
G. Golden, A. J. Lynam, G. O'Donnell, T. Ricketts
"No Spy Am I" (Solo and Chorus)
G. Golden, Chorus
"A Fool Am I" (Solo) (A fool is he)
S. I. Slade
"Paddy and His Pig" (Solo)
R. F. Carroll
"When Ere You Leave" (Duet)
A. Fabris, M. Eugene
"Sheathe the Sword" (Song and Chorus)
M. Eugene, Principals, Chorus
"Fill Up the Loving Cup" (Ensemble)
A. Fabris, M. Eugene, Principals, Chorus
"The Boys and the Girls" (Duet)
A. Summervile, R. F. Carroll
"Pride Goes Before a Fall" (Finale)

ACT 3
"Clink, Clank" (Chorus)
"Where Is Thy Heart, Oh Brian the Brave?" (Solo and Chorus)
B. Paget, Chorus
"For Ireland" (Solo and Chorus)
M. Eugene, Chorus
"All Hope Has Flown" (Solo)
G. Golden
"The Irish Cuckoo" (Quintette)
A. Summerville, R. F. Carroll, J. C. Slavin, J. Hendrick, T. Ricketts
Finale

1896.42 IN MEXICO—1848 (A War-Time Wedding)

A Comic Opera in Three Acts[45]. Book (and lyrics) by Charles T. Dazey. Music by Oscar Weil. Direction, Frank L. Perley. Musical director, Samuel L. Studley. Produced by the Bostonians (Henry Clay Barnabee, William H. MacDonald, Proprietors). Opened 19 October 1896 at the Murray Hill Theatre and closed 24 October 1896 after 7 performances in repertory.[46]

CAST: *Ramon Falcon*, a guerilla: WILLIAM H. MacDONALD. *Felipe*, a peon, formerly Ramon's servant: EUGENE COWLES. *Don Diego D'Alvarez*, a Mexican gentleman: C. E. Landie. *Guerillas (3)*: *Manuel*: Charles R. Hawley. *Tete*: L. B. Merrill. *Jose*: J. F. Boyle. *Captain Harry Selden*, Second U. S. Dragoons: WILLIAM E. PHILP. *Ezra Stebbins*, late sutler's clerk, now soldier in Second Dragoons: HENRY CLAY BARNABEE. *Soldiers in Second Dragoons serving as Mounted Infantry (5)*: *Tom Atkins*: Charles Robinson. *Larry Murray*: John Walsh. *Pat Burns*: J. E. Miller. *Shorty*: Harry Dale. *Sergeant Blake*: David T. Moore. *Mariquita Mason*, Don Diego's niece: HILDA CLARK. *Mariquita's companions at the convent (3)*: *Anita*: Gracia Quive. *Paquita*: Louise Cleary. *Carita*: Marie Morelle. *Peasant Girls (3)*: *Lilla*: Bertha Lovejoy. *Agnese*: Marcia Von Dresser. *Theresa*: JESSIE BARTLETT DAVIS. *Young Ladies from Convent, Peasant Girls, Dragoons, Muleteers, Orderly, Priests, etc.*

Act 1: Hacienda de la Portales, near the city of Mexico. Morning, 14 September 1847.

Act 2: Same as Act 1.

Act 3: Grove near Hacienda de la Portales.

[45]Toured under the title A WAR-TIME WEDDING, or In Mexico in 1847.
[46]Scenery and costumes uncredited. No musical numbers listed in programs; no libretto or musical score found.

1896.43 PRINCE ANANIAS

A Revival of the Comic Opera in Two Acts[47]. Libretto by Francis Neilson. Music by Victor Herbert. Produced under the stage direction of Frank L. Perley. Settings by Ernest Albert. Costumes designed by Catherine F. Seidle. Musical director, Samuel L. Studley. Produced by the Bostonians (Henry Clay Barnabee, W. H. MacDonald, Proprietors). Opened 26 October 1896 at the Murray Hill Theatre and closed 31 October 1896 after 7 performances in repertory with THE BOHEMIAN GIRL.

CAST: *Boniface*, King of Navarre: GEORGE B. FROTHINGHAM. *Killjoy*, Chamberlain to the King: Harry Dale. *Louis Biron*, (Prince Ananias) a vagabond poet and adventurer: W. H. MacDONALD. *George Le Grabbe*, an Outlaw: EUGENE COWLES. *La Fontaine*, manager of a band of strolling players: HENRY CLAY BARNABEE. *Eugene*, his assistant: T. KELLY COLE. *Jacques*, an innkeeper: James E. Miller. *Felicie*, Countess of Pyrenées, sister to Killjoy: JOSEPHINE BARTLETT. *Mirabel*, daughter to Killjoy: LEONORA QUITO. *Ninette*, a village belle: ALICE NIELSEN. *Idalia*, La Fontaine's leading lady: JESSIE BARTLETT DAVIS. *Lords, Ladies, Heralds, Pages, Halberdiers, Players, Villagers, Attendants, etc.*

1896.44 (THE STRANGE ADVENTURES OF) JACK AND THE BEANSTALK

A Musical Extravaganza in Three Acts, 6 Scenes. Libretto by R. A. Barnet. Music by A. Baldwin Sloane. Staged under the direction of Ben Teal. Ballets arranged by Carl Marwig. Settings by Ernest Albert. Mechanical effects by Claude Hagen. Properties and tricks by Robert Cutler. Dresses (costumes) designed by F. Richard Anderson. Musical conductor, Gustave Kerker. Produced by (Marc) Klaw and A. [Abraham] L. Erlanger (Edwin H. Price, Manager). Opened 2 November 1896 at the Casino Theatre and closed 26 December 1896 after 60 performances[48].

CAST: *Old King Cole*: HENRY V. DONNELLY. *Sinbad the Sailor*: EDDIE GIRARD. *Jack Hubbard*: MADGE LESSING. *Mr. Rusé*, a giant: H. M. MORSE. *Sir Harry Haitewurk*, Captain of the Forte Thieves: HUBERT WILKE. *Neverwash*, a thief, andante largo: H. L. Traub. *Evertyred*, a thief, allegro adagio: J. Craig. *The Marquis de Carabas*, Consort of Puss-in-Boots: HILDA HOLLINS. *Rowland*, King Cole's first royal page: __. *Oliver*, King Cole's second royal page: Kitty Perry. *Sir Guy Coffin*, R.S.S., King Cole's Court Physician: A. C. Butler. *Princess Mary*—"Mary, quite contrary": MAUDE HOLLINS. *Little Miss Muffett* "who sat on a tuffet," Princess Mary's companion: MERRI OSBORNE. *Puss 'n' Boots*: MARIE GODOY. *Sonanum Tuberoseum*, Queen-Dowager of the Fairies: ROSS SNOW. *Mrs. Rusé*, nee "Old Woman who lived in a shoe": John Wilson. *Willie Wilkins*: John Wilson. *Asparagus Blossom*: Donna Dean. *Caterpillar*: Meta Caldwell. *Old Mother Hubbard*, "who went to the cupboard," Jack's mother: CARRIE PERKINS. *Silvia*, a dairymaid: Bertha Waring. *Cyclometrix*, on Sinbad's trail: NELLIE LYNCH. *The Eight Pretty Maids*: Misses Mills, Leslie, Warner, Howe, Ashton, Sanford, Davis, Browne. *The Ten Good Fairies*: Misses Major, Caldwell, Knight, Warren, Schwartz, Borani, Curtis, Dean, Mayer, Cassenelli.

Some of the Forte Thieves: *Jack Sheppard*: Archie Gillis. *Joe Blueskin*: Fred Lewis. *Jonathan Wild*: Carl Kahn. *Dick Turpin*: Dion Wallace. *Sixteen-String Jack*: William Dorfman. *Robert Macaire*: Robert McGlynn. *Jacques Strop*: William Bassett. *Claude Duval*: William Morgan. *Lafitte*: William Pullman. *Captain Kidd*: George Pyke. *Robin Hood*: Charles Wilson. *Jim Alias*, all-around thief: Henry Verney.

Act 1, Scene 1: A Forest on an Autumn Morning. *Scene 2*: The Garden of Old Mother Hubbard.

Act 2, Scene 1: A Room in the Giant's Palace. *Scene 2*: The Giant's Courtyard. *Scene 3*: The Giant's Cliff and Jack's Beanstalk.

Act 3: The Family Estate of Mrs. Hubbard-Bean-Storke, at Cowhurst-by-the-Canal. (Introducing H. Harndin's patented electrical effect, The Birth of the Firefly.)

ACT 1[49]
"'Tis the dawn" (Opening Chorus)
"A Captain Bold"
H. Wilke, Thieves
The Coming of the Fairies (Fairies fay, do not stay)

[47]First produced in New York 20 November 1894 at the Broadway Theatre for 55 performances. For Synopsis of Scenes and Musical Numbers, see original 1894 production.
[48]Played a return engagement 5 April 1897 at the Harlem Opera House for 8 performances.
[49]Musical Numbers not listed in programs. List prepared from published piano vocal score (White-Smith Music Publishing Co., Boston, 1896). Interpolations from individually published song sheets, reviews, etc.

"I'm a cute little king" (Entrance of King Cole)
H. V. Donnelly, Chorus
"Come Along with Me" (Plantation Song)
M. Lessing, E. Girard, Chorus
"I've Sold My Cow"
M. Lessing, Chorus
"Looking for Another Occupation" (Topical Trio)
R. Snow, M. Lessing, E. Girard
"Now Behold a King"
Chorus
"'Tis with Love" (Duet)
M. Lessing, M. Hollins
Finale (Pray, remember Sir)
Principals, Chorus

ACT 2
"The Butcher, the Baker, the Candlestick Maker"
H. M. Morse, Octette
"Tell Me Truly, Daisy"
M. Lessing
"I am the old woman that lived in a shoe" (Song of the Shoe)
M. Lessing, H. V. Donnelly, E. Girard, A. C. Butler, M. Collins, M. Osborne, J. Wilson
"Hail, hail noble Rusé" (Entrance of Rusé) (Song and Chorus)
Chorus
Drinking Song (Once on a time we got so gay)
M. Lessing, M. Hollins, M. Osborne, E. Girard, H. V. Donnelly
Slumber Song (Peacefully slum'bring the hours away)
M. Lessing, M. Hollins, M. Osborne, C. Perkins, E. Girard, H. V. Donnelly
Finale (Now see the traitor)
Principals, Chorus

ACT 3
"Once There Lived a Little maid"
M. Hollins
Duet (O little Miss Muffet, one day on a tuffet)
E. Girard, M. Hollins
"Perhaps He Would"
H. V. Donnelly
"Guard of honor we" (Entrance of Carabas and Puss)
H. Hollins, M. Godoy, Chorus
Finale (Merry, merry chimes are ringing)(Wedding Ceremony)
Principals, Chorus

INTERPOLATIONS
"A Lock of Hair" (Act 1)
(*Music by* Gustave Kerker.)
"Comprenez-vous?" (Com-pren-a-voo?)
M. Osborne
(*Music by* John L. Golden. *Lyrics by* W. A. Jennings.)
"De Frogtown Terror"
M. Lessing
(*Music by* A. Baldwin Sloane. *Lyrics by* Herbert Farrar.)
"Pretty Polly Palmer"
(*Music and Lyrics by* Arthur Seldon.)
"Dangerous Girls, or Our Git Up and Git" (March and Song)(Act 3)
8 Pretty Maids
(*Music by* Paul Schindler. *Lyrics by* Sidney Rosenfeld.)
"Lucy Lou"[50]
G. Thatcher, E. Marble
(*Music by* A. Baldwin Sloane. *Lyrics by* R. A. Barnet.)
"Hush yo' business, Oh Go On"
M. Osborne
(*Music by* Maurice Levi. *Lyrics by* A. Midgeley.)

1896.45 THE MANDARIN

A Comic Opera in Three Acts. Libretto by Harry B. Smith. Music by Reginald DeKoven. Produced under the direction of Richard Barker. Dances arranged by Samuel Marion. Settings by Frederick Dangerfield. Costumes by Catherine F. Siedle. Musical director, Antonio DeNovellis. Produced by the DeKoven-Smith Opera Company (Charles E. Evans, W. D. Mann, Proprietors and managers). Opened 2 November 1896 at the Herald Square Theatre and closed 5 December 1896 after 37 performances[51].

CAST: *The Emperor of China*: HENRY NORMAN. *The Mandarin of Foo-Chow*: GEORGE HONEY. *Fan-Tan*, a vagabond: GEORGE C. BONIFACE, JR. *Hop-Sing*, leading tragedian of the Imperial Theatre: JOSEPH SHEEHAN. *The Court Physician*: Samuel Marion. *Jesso*, the wife of Fan-Tan: BERTHA WALTZINGER. *Ting-Ling*, the Mandarin's favorite wife: ADELE RITCHIE. *Sing-Lo*, chaperone to the Mandarin: ALICE BARNETT. *Ping-Tee*, one of the wives of the Mandarin: Helen Redmond. *Kwei-Tso*, valet to the Mandarin: Claudia Carlstedt. *Pekoe*: Vila Sayne. *Bohea*: Amy Hartley. *Souchong*: Belle Harper. *Oolong*: Helen Redmond. *Wives of the Mandarin (4)*: *Jasmine*: Mildred Meade. *Lotos Lily*: Louise Harlowe. *Chrysanthemum*: Louise St. Cyr. *Cherry Blossom*: Della Niven. *Officers of the Guard*: Edna Lyle, Etta Montrose. *Turnkey*: Florence Pemberton. *Policemen*: Benjamin Follett, David Marion. *Fee-Fum, Wun-Wing*, companions of Fan-Tan: William H. Corliss, Sam Marion. *Imperial Heralds*: J. A. Wallenstedt, J. H. McQuaid, Walter H. Langley. *Hi-Ti, Wing-Lee*, twin sons of Fan-Tan and Jesso: Isabel Barriscale, Louise Ravel. *Nobles, Tradesmen, Imperial Guards, Attendants of the Mandarin, Nursery-maids, Wives of the Mandarin, etc.*

Act 1: A street in the city of Foo-Chow.

Act 2: The garden of the Mandarin's palace.

Act 3: Public square during a feast of lanterns.

ACT 1[52]
Opening Chorus of Citizens (Yen hua ya liu hsiang[53])
V. Sayne, Chorus
Ensemble (Here's a bacchanalian toast we bring you)
Heralds, All
Entrance Chorus (Hail, O Mandarin portentous!)
All
Song (I am a Mandarin romantic)
G. Honey, A. Barnett, All
Song (My sweetheart has her faults in plenty)
J. Sheehan
Duet (There once was a china shepherdess) ("A Dresden China Love Affair")
A. Ritchie, J. Sheehan
Serenade (O lady of the almond eyes and neck of alabaster)
G. C. Boniface, Chorus
Song (The lotos lily dreams upon the river)
B. Walzinger
Finale (What ho! Without there, myrmidons and minions!)

ACT 2
Chorus of Mandarin's Wives (A dozen little widows we)
Wives
Chant of Praise (With Chinese fiddle and Chinese fife)
Wives
Lullaby Dance of Nursery Maids (By lo! By lo!)
Nursery maids
Song (Ting-Ling was a mandarin's daughter) (A Japanese Elopement)
A. Ritchie, Chorus
Nuptial Chant (Hail, happy pair!)
H. Redmond, All
Duet (Two mandarins in blue and white)
G. C. Boniface, A. Ritchie
Duet (Some damsels sigh that they but once can love)
B. Walzinger, J. Sheehan
Processional Chorus (Our most stupendous potentate is here)
C. Carlstedt, All
Song (A truculent, turbulent emperor am I)
H. Norman
Finale (This fundamental law is sound)

[50]Added for a New York cast replacement or on subsequent tour.

[51]Played an additional week 7 December 1896 at the Columbia Theatre for 8 performances.

[52]Musical numbers not listed in program. List prepared from published libretto (Harry B. Smith, New York, 1896).

[53]From the words of a Chinese popular song entited "The Haunts of Pleasure."

ACT 3

Chorus of Lantern-Bearers

Umbrella Dance

Misses Winship, Briscoe, Lyle, Harlowe, Willey, V. Montrose, S. Marion, D. Marion

Song (His Majesty looked at me, he did)

B. Walzinger

Duet (To adequately prove the greatness of my love)

H. Norman, B. Walzinger

Sextette (From his business cares so thrifty)

B. Walzinger, A. Ritchie, G. C. Boniface, G. Honey, H. Norman, J. Sheehan

Finale (Our Emperor! Our Emperor!)

1896.46 ORIENTAL AMERICA, or, In the Isle of San Domingo

A Triple Bill of a Spectacular Operatic Absurdity (MADAME TOUSSANTE L'OVATURE'S RECEPTION), a Vaudeville program and a Selection from Grand and Comic Operas. (Conceived and staged by John W. Isham.) Incidental music by John Villers Stamford. Scenery by John H. Young and Ernest Albert. Costumes by Henry Dazian, the Eaves Company and Mme. Lynd. Musical director, John Villers Stamford. Produced by John W. Isham and ? Graff. Opened 16 November 1896 at the Third Avenue Theatre and closed 21 November 1896 after 12 performances.

ACT 1

MADAME TOUSSANTE L'OVATURE'S RECEPTION), an up-to-date travesty, introducing all the latest and most popular vocal selections, the company being handsomely gowned and the scenic display adequate.

CAST: *Mme. Toussante L'Ovature*: MATTIE WILKES. *Mr. Waldorf*: R. BYRON SHELTON. *Mrs. Henrietta Johns*, guest of Mrs. Waldorf: Mayme Calloway. *Mrs. Van Austin*, a retired songbird: BELLE DAVIS. *Senator Van Puff*: Harry Fidler. *Tired Jimmie*, a tramp: BILLY ELDRIDGE. *Augustus Fetchmequick*, a waiter: BILLY ELDRIDGE. *Weary White Wings*, a tramp: JESSE A. SHIPP. *Jerome Fairbanks*, an author: JESSE A. SHIPP. *Washington Phillips*, chief cook: JUBE JOHNSON. *Freddie*: Lottie Meredith. *Clarence*: Daisy Brown.

These charming maidens sometimes affect Japanese dress (4): *Lottie Aultman*: Fannie Rutledge. *Daisy Fiskel*: Alice Mackey. *Maud Carson*: PEARL MEREDITH. *Jennie Langhorne*: CARRIE MEREDITH.

Members of the Magnolia Golf Club (8): *Clarence Wheeler*: Ollie Burgoyne. *Madeline Garland*: Eleanor Harbor. *Ethel Murdock*: Marcelina Sledge. *Blanche Stone*: Oniada DeLeon. *Jennette Silvers*: Mamie Smith. *Fannie Edwards*: Josie Lamont. *Josie Spencer*: Ada Guy. *Pauline Franklin*: Stella Dorsey.

Six interesting ladies from the Grove Lawn Tennis Club: *Mamie Craighill*: Ida Ennis. *Inetta Falkland*: Jennie Eldridge. *Carrie Tennis*: Esther White. *Grace Meecham*: Nettie Holton. *Ollie Sumpter*: Mamie Roberts. *May Belle Duryea*: Clara Stair.

Not a bit strong indeed, but all wear bloomers when out cycling (4): *Gwendoline Parker*: Pauline Swan. *Mazie Irwin*: Blanche Wentworth. *Stella Tracey*: Jennette Wintree. *Della Reed*: Julia Gaylor. *Guests at the Waldorf (12)*: *James Whitney*: William Elkins. *Edward Platt*: J. R. Johnson. *Thomas Hill*: Henry N. Jackson. *Robert Cleveland*: Alfred R. Roberts. *George Hanna*: Arthur H. Payne. *Theodore Fowler*: W. L. Brown. *Charles Barnum*: Sidney Coward. *Wilson James*: Melvin J. Chisum. *Conried Nelson*: John A. Phillips. *Myer Cohen*: Charles E. Robbins. *Nelson Mills*: Theodore Smith. *Fred Roberts*: Ed. J. Sherman.

MUSICAL NUMBERS

Opening Chorus

Entire Company

"Oh, Mr. Johnson"

J. Johnson

"Our Navy Boys Return"

E. Winn, Chorus

"I'se Coming to Town, Honey"

J. Shipp, Chorus

"Love Is the Tenderest of Themes"

M. Wilkes, Chorus

"High-Born Colored Lady"

Misses Meredith; Messrs. Eldridge, J. Shipp, J. Johnson

"I Want Yer, Ma Honey" (request number) (from THE SHOP GIRL)

B. Davis

(*Music and Lyrics by* Fay Templeton.)

"Four Little Japs"

Misses Meredith, Mackey, Meredith, Rutledge

"Hot Tamale Alley" (request number)

B. Eldridge, Entire Company

(*Music by* George M. Cohan. *Lyrics by* May Irwin.)

ACT 2

Select Repertoire of vocal gems

Margaret Scott

(Specialty) Descriptive Vocalists

J. Shipp, E. Winn

The Manhattan Sports, a Pleasing Travesty

The 20th Century Bicycle Maids

A few moments with the Frisky Funsters, Billie and Jennie Eldridge

The Flower Ballet, a Dancing Divertissement

Premier: Baby Ray. *Coryphées*: Alice Mackey, Lottie Meredith, Ida Ennis, Ethel White, Fannie Rutledge, Daisy Brown, Ollie Burgoyne, Lillie Bacon, Carrie Meredith, Josie Lamont, Mamie Smith, Pearl Meredith.

"Nature's Repose" (the Charming Choral Arrangement)

Inez Clough (soloist)

ACT 3

Forty Minutes of Grand and Comic Opera, with the correct costumes and scenic effects, introducing the American Tenor SIDNEY WOODWARD, assisted by Mme. Dessario Plato, Belle Davis, Margaret Scott, Mattie Wilkes, Mayme Calloway, Inez Clough, J. Rosamund Johnson, William Elkins, L. C. Urling, Louis Archer, S. J. Liggins, and a grand chorus:

Opening Chorus from THE BELLS OF CORNEVILLE

(*Music by* Robert Planquette.)

Waltz from FAUST

(*Music by* Charles Gounod.)

"Armorer's Song" (from ROBIN HOOD)

J. R. Johnson

(*Music by* Reginald DeKoven.)

"Martha" (from MARTHA)

S. Woodward

(*Music by* Friedrich von Flotow.)

"Hunting Scene"

I. Clough

"Dreaming" (Duet)

M. Wilkes, L. C. Urling

"The Last Rose of Summer" (from MARTHA)

M. Wilkes

(*Music adapted by* Friedrich von Flotow. *Lyrics by* Thomas More.)

Quartette from RIGOLETTO

M. Scott, D. Plato, S. Woodward, J. R. Johnson

(*Music by* Giuseppi Verdi.)

"Coming thro' the Rye"

M. Calloway

March—"Oriental Huzzars"

B. Davis (Captain)

"Bridal Chorus" Sextette from LUCIA DE LAMMERMOOR

M. Calloway, D. Plato, S. Woodward, L. C. Urling, W. Elkins, J. R. Johnson

(*Music by* Gaetano Donizetti.)

Grand Finale

Entire Company

1896.47 A NIGHT IN NEW YORK

A Musical Comedy in Two Acts. Play by H. Grattan Donnelly. Produced by Nellie McHenry. Opened 30 November 1896 at the Harlem Opera House and closed 5 December 1896 after 8 performances; returned 1 February 1897 to the People's Theatre and closed 6 February 1987 after 8 additional performances. Total: 16 performances.[54]

CAST: NELLIE McHENRY, John Webster, Charles P. Morrison, John T. Ball, Charles Eastwood, Albert Maher. Henrietta Lee, Francis Brooke, Viola Raymore, La Petite Rosa, Kitty Holden, Mamie Holden, Edith St. Clair, Marie Gomez.

[54]No program available.

1896.48

THE GIRL FROM PARIS

A Musical Comedy in Two Acts[55]. Book (and lyrics) by George Dance. (Adapted from the English musical "The Gay Parisienne.") Music by Ivan Caryll. Staged by Frank Smithson. Dances arranged by H. Fletcher Rivers. Settings by Frank Rafter and D. Frank Dodge. Costumes by Mme. M. L. Dowling. Musical director, Herman Perlet. Orchestrations by George Hayes. Produced by Edward E. Rice. Opened 8 December 1896 at the Herald Square Theatre and closed 10 July 1897 after 248 performances; re-opened 28 August 1897 at the Herald Square Theatre and closed 25 September 1897 after 33 additional performances. Total: 281 performances.[56]

CAST: *Mr. Ebenezer Honeycomb*, "a shining light": CHARLES A. BIGELOW. *Mrs. Honeycomb*, his wife: PHOEBE COHEN. *Norah*, their daughter: CHERIDAH SIMPSON. *Mabel*, Nora's friend: WILLIS NORTON. *Major Fossdyke*, of the Battersea Butterfly Shooters: FRANK SMITHSON. *The Major's Daughters, Bicycle Girls (8)*: *Angela*: Adele Archer. *May*: Josie Fairbanks. *Ethel*: Nina Ainscoe. *Gladys*: Ida Rock. *Maud*: Anita Willson. *Edith*: May Hamilton. *Violet*: Olivia Astor. *Rose*: Millie Willson. *Amos Dingle*, Honeycomb's friend: Edward Chapman. *Tom Everleigh*, a barrister: CHARLES DICKSON. *Algernon P. Ducie*, an American: HAROLD VIZARD. *Percy Tooting, Cecil Smythe*, Ducie's friends: Sydney Tovey, John Savage. *Blatterwatter*, a gendarme: Thomas Kierns. *Hans*, proprietor of the Spa Hotel, Schoffenburgen: Louis Mann. *Servants (3)*: *Gretchen*, (with dance): May Lavigne. *Anna*: Grace Belasco. *Fritz*: Matthew Ott. *Ruth*, Honeycomb's servant: JOSEPHINE HALL. *Mr. Auguste Pompier*, a French spy: JOSEPH W. HERBERT. *Julie Bon-Bon*, the Gay Parisienne: CLARA LIPMAN. (*Dance Specialty*: Mlle. (Blanche) DEYO. *Dancers in the French Quadrille*: Misses Anita Wilson, Millie Wilson, May Levige, Helen Whiting; Messrs. Charles Dickson, Henry Bizard, George Courtney, Sidney Tovey.)

Act 1: Honeycomb's lawn, Kingston-on-Thames.

Act 2: The Spa Hotel, Schoffenburgen.

ACT 1[57]

"Hi! for the Thames on a Summer's Day" (Opening Chorus)

"So Take You a Warning" (Song)
C. A. Bigelow, Chorus

"Somebody" (Duet)
C. Dickson, C. Simpson

"The Battersea Butterfly Shooters" (Song)
F. Smithson, Chorus

"I'm All the Way from Gay Paree" (Duet)
C. Lipman, J. W. Herbert

"Then Off We Go" (Concerted Piece)

"Tweedledum and Tweedledee" (Duet)
C. A. Bigelow, C. Lipman

"Cock-a-doodle" (Quartette)
C. Lipman, J. W. Herbert, P. Cohen, C. A. Bigelow

"Hail, the Hero of the Day" (Finale)

ACT 2

"Isn't It Wonderful?" (Opening Chorus)

Saltarelle[58]

"The Festive Continong" (Quartette)
C. Dickson, S. Tovey, J. Savage, H. Vizard

"It's a Good Thing to Have"[59] (Duet)
C. A. Bigelow, C. Lipman

"Sister Mary Jane's Top Note" (Song)
J. Hall, Chorus
(*Lyrics by* F. Bowyer.)

"Oh, Tender Remembrance"[60] (Waltz Song)
C. Simpson, Chorus

"Tootle, Tootle" (Quartette)
P. Cohen, F. Smithson, J. Hall, J. W. Herbert

"Ding-Dong"[61] (Concerted Piece)

Pas de Quatre[62]

"Upon the Stage Let's Have a Fling"[63] (Duet)
J. Hall, F. Smithson

Finale[64]

INTRODUCED DURING THE PERFORMANCE[65]

"Just For a Kiss" (Song)

"The Girl from Paris" (You Would Like to Hug and Kiss, or "N'est pas"/"Restez-là")
C. Lipman
(*Music by* Nat D. Mann. *Lyrics by* Edgar Smith.)

"He Took It in a Good-Natured Way" (Topical Song)
(*Music by* Frank David. *Lyrics by* Edgar Smith.)

[55]Also billed as the latest London novelty.
[56]Played a return engagement 22 November 1897 at the Harlem Opera House for 8 performances.
[57]Program note: The selection between the acts is descriptive of the escape of Honeycomb from England to Germany.
[58]Dropped during the run.
[59]Replaced during the run by: "The Proper Air" (Duet) Alexander Clark [Honeycomb], C. Lipman
[60]Replaced during the run by:
"Now, Darling We Must Part" (Duet)C. Simpson, Chorus (*Music and Lyrics by* Will P. Brown.)

1896.49

DARKEST AMERICA

An Exalted and Modern Amusement Idea, embracing the better elements of drama, farce, comedy, comic opera, vaudeville and minstrelsy (Musical Revue) in Two Acts. John W. Vogel, Sole Proprietor and Manager. Costumes designed by Gil Geary. Amusement director, Billy McClain. Director of band, Henderson Smith. Musical conductor, Oscar Lindsay. Produced under the direction of Al. G. Field and Oliver Scott. Opened 21 December 1896 at the People's Theatre and closed 26 December 1896 after 9 performances; returned 13–18 December 1897 to the Third Avenue Theatre for an additional 8 performances.[66]

ACT 1

CAST: *Uncle Amos Jackson*: JOHN RUCKER. *Aunt Becky Beasly*: Gil Geary. *Saul Beverly*, a shiftless negro: George Bailey. *Juba Lynch*: WALTER JACKSON. *Nicodemus*: Pete Hampton. *Jasper*: Charles Johnson. *Hannibal*: G. P. Brown. *Pompey*: Frank Kirk. *Zeke*: Ernest Wagner. *Apus*, "The Devil": William Porter. *Clementina*: Ella Dawson. *Lucinda*: Helen Scott. *Daffney*: Sallie Lee. *Colonel Charlotte*, a Planter: Robert Irving. *Mate of the Steamer, Robert E. Lee*: Robert Irving. *Jim Goodhealth*, so bad he's scared of his life: George Bailey. *Levee Bill*: William Porter. *Tobacco Jack*: William Lewis. *Mobile Jim*: Frank Kirk. *Goose Foot Ike*: Ernest Wagner. *Blue Gob*, first cousin to thee Devil: Cliff Brooks. *Auntie Fowlthief*, who runs lunch stand: Gil Geary. *Golden Hair Nell*, terror of the Levee: Lawrence E. Chenault. *Hot Foot Sue*: Ella Dawson. *Amelia Kidder*: Helen Scott. *I. D. Clare*, too young to learn: Sallie Lee. *Hoodoo Hanah*, nothing on her mind but her hat: Charles Johnson.

Act 2: *Juba Lynch*: BILLY MILLER. *Saul Beverly, Dusty Roads, Dusty Roads*, Twins de Bum: George Bailey, Frank Kirk, William Porter. *Uncle Amos*: JOHN RUCKER. *Lucky Steve*: Cliff Brooks. *Chuck A. Look*: G. P. Brown. *Keno*: William Lewis. *Willie*, Giant Policeman, 18 years old, and 7 foot 3: Madison Johnson.

Act 1, Scene 1: Colonel Charlotte's tobacco barn. *Scene 2*: Emancipation. *Scene 3*: First years of Freedom. Life on the Levee.

Act 2, Scene 1: Interior of Rabbit Foot Saloon. The vicious side and sunny side of darkey life.

ACT 1

America's Greatest Negro Monologue Artist in his latest songs and sayings
B. Miller

The Charleston Shouters, introducing the champion negro flat-footed buck and wing dances of America
J. Rucker, F. Kirk, C. Brooks, E. Wagner, W. Johnson

The act terminates with the realistic race between the steamers *Robert E. Lee* and the *Natchez*.

ACT 2

The Black Annies (Misses Scott, Dawson, Lee; Messrs. Chenault, Bailey, Brooks, Geary, Wagner):

"Naughty Girl from Paris"
S. Lee

"The Cake Walk Swell"
H. Scott

[61]Dropped during the run.
[62]Dropped during the run.
[63]Replaced during the run by (as above):
"Reste là" (Song)
C. Lipman
[64]Later in the run the Finale was identified as "Carnival."
[65]As it appears in the program. Late in the run this listing disappears.
[66]Program detail from return engagement at Third Avenue Theatre.

"First Wench Done Turned White"
E. Dawson
"Mama's Little Pumpkin Colored Coons"
H. Waters
"The Alabama Blossom"
J. Rucker

Steam will be seen issuing from the shoes of each member at the finish, for the Policeman and Twins de Bum will cause a hot time in the old town before the "close in."

Olio of Celebrities:
"The Sport and the Crank," Hampton & Johnson, Mirth provoking musical artists
An Old Thing (the acme of ebony comiques in their droll absurdity)
Billy and Mlle. Cordelia McClain
America's Premier Descriptive Vocalist in his own creation, "Policeman 42"
E. Winn
See the finish, an up-to-date satire, "The Operatic Ball"
Prima Donna: Mlle. C. McClain. *Tenor*: L. E. Chenault. *Baritone*: E. Winn. *Elyucutan*: B. McLain. And the Company.

1896.50 DORCAS

An Operatic Comedy in Three Acts. Libretto by Harry Paulton and Edward Paulton, adapted from an old German romance. Original music composed and arranged by Clement Lockname and Watty Hydes. Produced under the personal direction of Edward Paulton. Tour under the direction of [produced by] John F. Harley. Opened 28 December 1896 at Hammerstein's Olympia Theatre and closed 9 January 1897 after 16 performances.[67]

CAST: *Arnold, Lord Lambourne*: WILLIAM BRODERICK. *Lord Beauregard*, his friend, passing as Master Roland: CHARLES O. BASSETT. *Lubin Mugby*, Mine Host at Lambourne Arms: FRED FREAR. *Meredith*, Steward of the Lambourne Estate: Arthur R. Seaton. *James*, Footman at Lambourne Hall: Charles Earle. *Jawkins*, ye 'ostler of Lambourne Arms: Charles Meyer. *Dora, Lady Lambourne*: Marie Millard. *Lady Honoria*, Sister of Lord Lambourne: DREW DONALDSON. *Joan*, Maid to Lady Honoria: Marie Davenport. *Dorcas*, newly married to Lubin Mugby: MINNIE JARBOE. *Griselda*, Nurse and Companion to Lady Lambourne: EVA DAVENPORT.

Act 1: Ye Lambourne Arms. Noon. 1790.

Act 2: Drawing room at the Hall. Evening.

Act 3: Morning-room at the Hall. Morning.

MUSICAL NUMBERS[68]
"This Green Young Man from Town"
F. Frear
"Drinking Song" (Act 1)
(*Music by* Watty Hydes.)
"In Waltzing There Is Pleasure"
"A Peddler Am I"
"Because I Love Thee"
"Chess Duet"
"I Love My Love Always"
"To My Love Ever True" (Duet)(Act 3)
"How To be a Lass" (The Way to Be a Lass)
"Were He a Man"
"The Spinning Wheel Song"
"In Time"
"Trusting Above"
"Must I Remind You"
Minuet (Act 2)
(*Music by* Watty Hydes.)
"A Cup of Tea"
E. Davenport
(*Music by* Frederic Solomon.)

1896.51 AN AMERICAN BEAUTY

A Musical Comedy in Three Acts. (Libretto) Written by Hugh Morton. Music by Gustave Kerker. Staged by George W. Lederer. Settings by Ernest Gros, D. Frank Dodge and Ernest Albert. Costumes by Mme. (Catherine) Siedle. Conductor of music, Paul Steindorff. Produced by Lillian Russell Opera Company (Thomas Canary, George W. Lederer, Direction). Opened 28 December 1896 at the Casino Theatre and closed 6 March 1897 after 72 performances[69].

CAST: *Gabrielle Dalmont*, an American beauty: LILLIAN RUSSELL. *Miriam Firenza*, an Oriental woman: SUSANNE LEONARD. *Dottie Muffet, Tottie Bopeep*, two Casino girls: Sadie Kirby, Mabel Bouton. *Baroness Perkily*: Georgie Hawley. *Richard Grenville*, Earl of Beverly: HAROLD BLAKE. *Proprietors of the Greatest Show On or Off the Earth (3)*: *Bayley Bangle*: JEROME SYKES. *Rose Budd*: CATHERINE LINYARD. *Barney Bingle*: WILLIAM CAMERON. *Prince Schwepps*, an aged suitor for the hand of Gabrielle: OWEN WESTFORD. *Ikey Eisenstein*, a money-lender: Alexander Clark. *Lord Algy Prettybird, Tommy Tucker*, a pair of "Johnnies": Willard Simms, Randolph Curry. *Count Bobo*, aide-de-camp to Prince Schwepps: Albert Juhre. *James, William*, footmen: R. J. Struck, Charles L. Dox.

The action takes place at the present time.

Act 1: The Gardens on Mrs. Dalmont's estate at Newport. (Gros.)

Act 2: The Circus Ball given by Mrs. Dalmont at her Newport home. (Dodge.)

Act 3: Terrace of the Casino at Monte Carlo. One year later. (Albert.)

MUSICAL NUMBERS[70]
"Phizzy-Wiz-Wiz"
L. Russell
"Bonjour Monsieur"
"Fat Boy"
"Heigh Ho for the Feminine Sex"
"Ikey Eisenstein"
"Inherited from My Aunt"
"Little Dickey Doubleday"
"Truly, Truly"
"When I Met You"
"Little Dottie, Little Tottie"
"Love Me, Love Me"

1896.52 COURTED INTO COURT

A Combination of Farce, Comedy and Music in Three Acts. Play by John J. McNally. Produced under the direction of (staged by) R. A. Roberts. Settings by Joseph Physioc. Music program arranged by John C. Sorg. Produced by (Isaac B.) Rich and (William) Harris. Opened 26 December 1896 at the Bijou Theatre and closed 22 April 1897 after 137 performances.

CAST: *Dottie Dimple*, an actress: MAY IRWIN. *Worthington Best, Jr.*, in love with Dottie: JOHN C. RICE. *Worthington Best, Sr.*: RAYMOND HITCHCOCK. *Mrs. Worthington Best, Sr.*: CLARA PALMER. *Helen Best*, her daughter: HATTIE WILLIAMS. *Mlle. Nocodi*, eccentric German dancer: ADA LEWIS. *General Baron Vladimir Vladistoff*, in love with Nocodi: George W. Barnum. *Judge Jeremiah Geoghan*: JOSEPH M. SPARKS. *Pop Dooley*, stage doorkeeper, in love with Nocodi: JACQUES KRUGER. *Sylvia Rosebud*, Dottie's maid: Sally Cohen. *Mortimer Morton*, actor: Roland Carter. *Sharp Lawyer*: Roland Carter. *Gertie*, Mrs. Worthington's maid: Etta Gilroy. *Hal Ford*, a janitor: Charles Church. *Clerk of Court*: Charles Church. *Ladies of the Dottie Dimple Company (4)*: *Mollie Mavourn*: Margery Teal. *Della Carte*: Mabel Power. *Stella Argent*: Belle Steele. *Eunice Colbee*: Maud Gray.

Act 1: Courtship. Morning room of Dottie Dimple, a popular actress. Time is the present.

Act 2: Marriage. Apartments of Worthington Best, Sr.

Act 3: Divorce. Modern courtroom of a trial justice.

---

[67]Prior to its New York premiere, a production of DORCAS by the Pauline Hall Opera Company toured nationally in 1895 under the auspices of Nelson Roberts and Frank B. Arnold. The production was billed as a comic opera, and its musical selections (J. Strauss, Czibulka, Millöcker, Zeller, and Max Hirschfield) and interpolations differed substantially from those used in the New York production. Pauline Hall sang "Take It Home and Give It to the Baby" (*Music by* William Furst, *Lyrics by* C. M. S. McLellan), according to published sheet music.

[68]Musical numbers, with the exception of Drinking Song, Minuet and "A Cup of Tea" not listed in programs. Other titles appear only in reviews from outside New York.

[69]Played a return engagement 15 March 1897 at the Harlem Opera House for 8 performances.

[70]Musical numbers not listed in programs. List prepared from published sheet music *T. B. Harms & Co., New York, 1896).

ACT 1[71]

"Cake Walk Jubilee" (Grand Medley Introduction)
Entire Company
"Young America"[72]
J. C. Rice
"The Oompah"
A. Lewis
"Maloney's Leg"
J. M. Sparks
"Crappy Dan" (De Spo'tin' Man)
M. Irwin
(*Music and Lyrics by* Charles A. Trevathan.)

ACT 2

"Ma Lulu"
M. Irwin
Dance Eccentric
J. C. Rice, S. Cohen
"(There'll Be a) Hot Time in the Old Town To-night"[73]
M. Irwin, Zobo Band
(*Music by* Theodore H. Metz. *Lyrics by* Joe Hayden.)

ACT 3

"Mistah Johnson, Turn Me Loose"[74]
M. Irwin
(*Music and Lyrics by* Ben Harney.)

1897.01 A CONTENTED WOMAN

A Farce Comedy with Music in Four Acts[75]. Play by Charles H. Hoyt. Music by Richard Stahl. Staged by Charles H. Hoyt. Settings by Arthur Voegtlin. Musical director, Richard Stahl. Produced by Charles H. Hoyt and Frank McKee. Opened 4 January 1897 at Hoyt's Theatre and closed 20 February 1897 after 56 performances[76].

CAST: *Benton Holme*, rich and politically ambitious: WILLIAM H. CURRIE. *Cutting Hintz*, his bachelor brother-in-law: Frank Lane. *Aunt Jim*, an earnest advocate of Woman's suffrage: Amy Ames. *Uncle Todie*, Jim's other half—better or worse as you choose: George Ober. *Miss Helen Wrangell, Mrs. Watson Chin*, strongminded friends of Jim: Rose Snyder, Adelaide Ober. *Mrs. Ebbsmith*, considered notorious: Grace Thorne. *Bella*, Benton's sister: Sarah Miskel. *Calliope Ayres*, a girl friend of Grace: Edna Pettie. *Rose Bud* a girl friend of Grace: Marie Millard. *Brighton Betts*, gambling saloon: Frank J. Keenan. *Phil Boyles*, bar keeper: EDWARD GARVIE. *Boyle Dowle*, prize fighter: Gus Hennessy. *Vandyke Beard*, Holme's butler: Will H. Bray. *E. Quinn Holder*, Mrs. Ebbsmith's coachman: F. Baldwin. *Mary Peet*, lady's maid: Eleanor Falk. *Etta Bird*, parlor maid: Emma Lewis. *Dandy Trotter*, messenger: Jean McIlmoyne. *Dodge Carr*, messenger: May Stuart. *Independent Voter*: Frank Baldwin. *Grace Holme*: CAROLINE MISKEL-HOYT.

The action takes place in and about the house of Benton Holme, in a fashionable quarter of Denver, Colorado.

Act 1: Morning-room.

Act 2: Hallway.

Act 3: Hallway.

Act 4: Lawn.

MUSICAL NUMBERS[77]

"The Next President's Goin' to be a Coon"
W. H. Bray
"We're Goin' to Have a Barbecure"
W. H. Bray
"Caroline" (March)
(*Music by* Richard Stahl.)
"Do You Want to Hear the Rest?"
F. Lane
(*Music by* Richard Stahl. *Lyrics by* Charles H. Hoyt.)
War Song
Ladies' Campaign Club
"Dainty Saintly Erica"
C. Miskel-Hoyt
(*Music and Lyrics by* Eugene Ellsworth.)

1897.02 KISMET, or, Two Tangled Turks

A Revival of the Turkish Comic Opera in Two Acts[78]. Libretto by Richard F. Carroll. Music by Gustave A. Kerker. Produced under the personal direction of Richard F. Carroll and Gustave A. Kerker. Dances arranged by A. Francioli. Settings by Fred Dangerfield and Street. Costumes designed by Catherine Seidle. Musical director, Gustave A. Kerker. Produced by The Carroll-Kerker Opera Company (James S. Lee, Will J. Block, Proprietors and Managers). Opened 4 January 1897 at Wallack's Theatre and closed 23 January 1897 after 21 performances[79]

CAST: *Kismet*, the Sultan of Turkey: CAMILLE D'ARVILLE. *Chinchilla*, the Grand Vizier: WILLIAM STEIGER. *Dan De Lyon*, an Irish free lance: WILLIAM HATCH. *Ovah*, the Moor: Henry Leoni. *Sum*, Dey of Algiers: Edward S. Wentworth. *So-Jah*, the Aga of Janizaries: Lillian Cooley. *The Muezzim*, the crier of prayers: Fred A. Tracey. *A-Jeeb, B-Jeebers*, attendants in charge of the harem: Julian Horton, Charles Randolph. *Absinthea*, the Sultan's favorite wife: Belle Bucklin. *Ramadamus*, the Sultana Valdé (the Sultan's Mother): ROSE LEIGHTON. *Odalisques (5)*: *Fat-Mah*: Crissie Carlyle. *Lazeli*: Nellie V. Parker. *Kondjé-Gal*: Emma Levy. *Pandemonia*: Edith Atkinson. *Lena*: Grace Freeman. *Haideez*, the Sultan's sister: RICHARD F. CARROLL, JR. *Chorus of odalisques, harem girls, slaves, Algerians disguised as Arcan Amazons, Moors disguised as Malay pirates, attendants and Janizaries.*

1897.03 SHAMUS O'BRIEN

A Romantic Irish Opera (Musical Comedy) in Three Acts[80]. Libretto by George H. Jessop. (Based on the poem of the same name by Joseph Sheridan Le Fanu.) Music by Charles Villiers Stanford. (Scenery designed by Robert Caney and Joseph Harker. Costumes designed by Comelli.) Dances arranged by Edward Murphy. Musical director, S. P. Waddington. Produced by Messrs. Cowdery and James C. Duff. Opened 5 January 1897 at the Broadway Theatre and closed 20 February 1897 after 56 performances[81].

CAST: *Shamus O'Brien*, on his keeping—outlawed: DENIS O'SULLIVAN. *Captain Trevor* of the British Army: REGINALD ROBERTS. *Mike Murphy*, a peasant farmer: JOSEPH O'MARA. *Father O'Flynn*, the P.P. of Ballyhamis: A. G. CUNNINGHAM. *Sergeant Cox* of Captain Trevor's Company: Walter Leland. *Lynch*, a piper: P. Tuohey. *Little Paudeen*, the heir of the O'Briens: Master Henry. *Nora O'Brien*, wife of Shamus: ANNIE ROBERTS. *Peggy*, a peasant girl: Helen Marvin. *Kitty O'Toole*, sister to Norah: LUCY CARR-SHAW. *Music of the Banshee*: Augusta Schiller. *Soldiers, Peasants, Villagers, etc.*

The action takes place immediately after the suppression of the Rebellion of 1798.

Act 1: Village of Ballyhamis, in the mountains of Cork. (Caney.)

Act 2: The Barrack Square. (Harker.)

---

[71]Added during the run to Act 1 (end):
"My Girl"
R. Carter
[72]Dropped after opening.
[73]Late in the run replaced by:
"Mamie, Come Kiss Your Honey Boy"
M. Irwin, Zobo Band
[74]During the run, replaced by "Song, selected (by) May Irwin." Among those ascribed was:
"All Coons Look Alike to Me"
M. Irwin
(*Music and Lyrics by* Ernest Hogan.)
[75]Billed as Hoyt's Sketch of the Fair Sex in Politics.
[76]Costumes uncredited. Played return engagements 22 February 1897 at the Harlem Opera House for 8 performances, 6 September 1897 at the Grand Opera House for 8 performances.
[77]Musical numbers not listed in program. First 5 numbers appear in a Taunton, Massachusetts tryout program, and are therefore representative of the musical selections, if not necessarily correct. Latter titles from published sheet music.
[78]Originally produced in New York 12 August 1895 at the Herald Square Theatre for 24 performances. For Synopsis of Scenes and Musical Numbers, see original 1895 production.
[79]Played a return engagement 1 February 1897 at the Harlem Opera House for 8 performances.
[80]Subtitled A Story of Ireland 100 Years Ago.
[81]Advertised "with the original cast, scenery and costumes." Direction uncredited; most likely, the direction of the original English production by Augustus Harris was recreated by the stage manager J. G. Shuter. Returned 6 December 1897 to the Star Theatre for 1 week.

Act 3: A Country Road (in County Cork). (Harker.)

ACT 1[82]

"It's Bitter News" (Chorus)
Chorus

"Peace Be With You" (Recitative)

"I'll Give ye to Next Michaelmas" (Song)
A. G. Cunningham

"Let the Army Come On" (Chorus)

"Where Is the Man That Is Coming to Marry Me?" (Song)
L. Carr-Shaw

"He's as Straight as a Dart" (Trio)
J. O'Mara, R. Roberts, L. Carr-Shaw

"Well, He'd Take Me by the Hand" (Duet)
L. Carr-Shaw, R. Roberts

"I've Sharpen'd the Sword the Sake of Ould Erin"
D. O'Sullivan

"Come, Boys, Come" (Quartet)
A. Roberts, L. Carr-Shaw, D. O'Sullivan, A. G. Cunningham

"From the Moor, from the Hill" (Chorus)
Chorus

"Is It Shamus You Seek?" (Trio and Ensemble)
R. Roberts, D. O'Sullivan, A. G. Cunningham, Chorus

"Push the Jug Around" (Finale)
L. Carr-Shaw, A. G. Cunningham, A. Roberts,

"A Grave Yawns Cold" (Song)
A. Roberts

"The Soldiers Are Safe" (Song)
D. O'Sullivan Reel

"Come All Ye True Bred Irishmen" (Chorus)

ACTS 2 and 3

"My Heart Is in Thrall to Kitty's Beauty" (Song)
R. Roberts

"What the Devil Are You Doing" (Duet)
R. Roberts, J. O'Mara

"Ochone, When I Used to be Young!" (Song)
J. O'Mara

"Walk, Girls, Walk" (Ensemble)

"So It's Kisses You're Craving" (Duet)
L. Carr-Shaw, R. Roberts

"Darling, Darling" (Duet)
A. Roberts, D. O'Sullivan

Ensemble and Melodrama

"They're Taking Him from the Jail" (Chorus and Ensemble)
A. Roberts, L. Carr-Shaw, A. G. Cunningham

Finale
"Listen to Me Men" (Solo)
D. O'Sullivan

1897.04

A BOY WANTED

A Musical Extravaganza in Three Acts. Libretto by Charles E. Blaney. Music by Harry James. Staged by Charles E. Blaney. Dances arranged by Lillie Sutherland. Musical director, Harry James. Produced by Charles E. Blaney. Opened 18 January 1897 at the Star Theatre and closed 30 January 1897 after 16 performances; returned 15 February 1897 to the Murray Hill Theatre for 8 performances, 8 March 1897 to the People's Theatre for 8 performances, 12 April 1897 at the Columbus Theatre for 8 performances. Total: 40 performances[83].

CAST: *Phoney Dice*, a sample of the rising generation. Does he look like Corbett?: HARRY CLAY BLANEY. *Willie Settle*? I Think not. Always looking for a good thing, and gets it: Raymond Finlay. *Herman Highball*, a rich brewer. A good thing for everybody: KNOX G. WILSON. *Howland Rant*, a Shakespearean student: CLAUDE GILLINGWATER. *Pat Hawkeye*, a policeman: Frank Young. *Weekly Feeble*, an invalid at Starview Hotel: Frank Young. *Zeake Sylas*: Frank Young. *Tommy Run*, foreman Evening Keg: Sam Miller. *Cough Drop Ed*, a fighter by trade: George Dawson. *Highball's German Band*, Sousa's only opposition (3): *Nicholas Trombone*: Charles R. LaValy. *Hendrick Fleatzer*: Charles Bryant. *Louie Bowhard*: Edward Miller. *Helen Blazes*, Highball's adopted daughter: NELLIE O'NEIL. *Mrs. Herman Highball*, the brewer's wife: LAURA BENNETT. *Madame LeGrand*, a prima donna: LAURA BENNETT. *Lillie Barnstorm, Rose Barnstorm*, twin sisters: LILLIE SUTHERLAND, ROSE SUTHERLAND. *Clam Bake Anna*, a Bowery girl: LILLIE SUTHERLAND. *Clarence Scoop*, a reporter on the Evening Keg: Lillie Allyn. *Widow Twice*, a happy woman: Georgie Lingard. *Charles Wales*, knows the Prince: Flora Evans. *Mary Soon*, a society belle: Belle Tufts. *Carrie Age*, a rival: Bell Garrick. *Winna Beau*: Bonita Loring. *Dora*: Eva Mayhew. *Cora*: Amandita Rivera. *Mora*: Cecil Lorrain. *Miss Rialto Lunch, Miss Ever Fedd*: The Malletta Sisters. *Miss Iva Jagg*: Miss Thurston. *Miss P. Roxide*: Miss Morton. *Miss Sally Forth*: Miss Gilson. *Miss Allie Hogan*: Miss Vreeland. (*Buck dancing Specialty*: Frank Young, champion soft-shoe dancer of the world). *Typesetters, Hotel Guests, etc.*

Act 1: Evening Keg office.

Act 2: Starview Hotel and bathing beach.

Act 3: Cafe and sitting-room, Starview Hotel.

ACT 1

Opening Chorus of Typesetting Girls
Misses Sutherland, Tufts, Lingard, Morton, Rivera, Lorrain, Thurston

"I'm the Boy" (Song and Chorus)
H. C. Blaney, Chorus

Entrance Song and Dance of the Soubrette
Misses Sutherland, Evans, Tufts, Lingard, Morton, Rivera, Lorrain, Mayhew, Gilson

"The Girl with the Naughty Wink" (Song and Chorus)

German Specialty
K. Wilson

Buck dancing
F. Young

"Oriental March" (Grand Finale)
Entire Company

ACT 2

"My Polly is a Peach" (Opening Chorus)
Company

"The Modern Century Girls"
Misses Sutherland, Thurston, Rivera,
Tufts, Evans, Lingard, Allyn, Morton, Lorrain, Loring, Mayhew, Gilson

"The Same Thing Over Again"
R. Findlay, assisted by F. Evans

"Julienne" (Chorus by ladies)
Misses Allyn, Lingard

"The Ideal Girls" (Grand Finale)

Entrance and Recitative of "Cupid"

Entrance of Monster Dragon

College Girls' Song and Dance

Solo
Misses Sutherland, Evans
["Sally, the Pride of Dorothy's Alley"
(*Music and Lyrics by* Walter Hawley.)]

"The Up-to-Date Policeman" (Song and Chorus)
Messrs. Finlay, Young, Bryant, Gillingwater

"Hot Tamale Alley" (Song, Chorus and Acrobatic Dance)
H. C. Blaney, Misses O'Neil, Sutherland
(*Music by* George M. Cohan. *Lyrics by* May Irwin.)]

"The Handicap" (Grand vocal descriptive march)
Entire Company, German Band

ACT 3

"Sweet Little Rosey Posey" (Song and Chorus)
B. Tufts, Company

Original Negro Melodies
L. Bennett

Bryant and Savile (Those creative musical comedians)

Songs and Dances
H. C. Blaney

Acrobatic Dancers
Misses O'Neil, Sutherland

[82]Musical numbers not listed in programs. List prepared from published English piano vocal score, set in Two Acts (Boosey & Co., London, 1896).
[83]Settings and costumes uncredited. Played a return engagement 21 February 1898 at the Third Avenue Theatre for 8 performances.

"I'm the Boy" (Closing Chorus)
H. C. Blaney, Entire Company

1897.05 A RUN ON THE BANK

A Revival of the Farce Comedy in Three Acts[84]. Play by Charles E. Blaney. Tour directed (produced) by E. D. Stair. Opened 18 January 1897 at the Murray Hill Theatre and closed 23 January 1897 after 8 performances; returned 1 March 1897 to the Star Theatre and closed 6 March 1897 after 8 performances.

CAST: *Lord Percy Soakup, Baron Harold DeCanter*, Gentlemen of unlimited nerve and experience: "HAPPY" WARD, HARRY VOKES. *Bow Legs*, crooked by nature: CHARLES GUYER. *General Note Shaver*, a banker to bank on: Tony Williams. *August Riewer*: Charles A. Mason. *Coonie Acker*, a counterfeiter: Charles A. Mason. *Con Mann*, a gentleman of leisure: Joe Kelly. *Barley Corn*, a rustic: Cyrus Riddell. *Bill Booze*, a bar fly: Cyrus Riddell. *Eagle Eye*, a blind man: T. Wilmot Eckert. *Adam Shame*, a depositor: T. Wilmot Eckert. *Clubs R. Trumps*, a policeman: T. Wilmot Eckert. *Lager Hops*, a brewer: T. Wilmot Eckert. *Makin Noise*: W. B. Rock. *Nera Man*, a female book agent: Gilberti Learock. *Estelle Shaver, Belle Shaver*, the Banker's daughters: Emma Berg, Martha Franklin. *Hasty Writer*, a private secretary: Emma Francis. *Sassy Moll*, a tough girl: MARGUERITE DALY VOKES. *Minnie Apolis, Carrie Romance, Grace Church*, friends of the family: Nellie Daly, Sadie Whitcomb, Adelaide Prucilla. *Miss Fit*: Alma Desmond. *Belle Ringer*: Hattie Bernard. *Miss Fire*: Lotta Miranda. *Barbara Shaver*: Grace Archer. *Mona Moe*: Belle Varney.

1897.06 SWEET INNISCARRA

A (Romantic) Drama (with Songs) in Four Acts, 6 Scenes[85]. Play by Augustus Pitou. Music and lyrics by Chauncey Olcott. Dramatic music by David Braham. Staged by Augustus Pitou. Settings by Lewis C. Young, John H. Young, Homer F. Emens. Costumes designed by H. A. Ogden. Musical director, Albert Krausse. Produced by Augustus Pitou. Opened 25 January 1897 at the 14th Street Theatre, closing 10 April 1897; re-opened 19 April 1897 with a new third act and closed 8 May 1897 after 104 performances[86].

CAST: *Gerald O'Carroll*, alias Gerald Otway, the Unknown: CHAUNCEY OLCOTT. *Lawrence Eyre*, a Dublin attorney: Paul Gilmore. *Squire O'Donoghue*: DANIEL GILFETHER. *Captain Robert O'Donoghue*, of the H. M. S. *"Dolphin"*: Charles Riegel. *Squire John Creswick*: W. J. Dean. *Pat Quinn*, a fiddler: Luke Martin. *Michael*, landlord of the Shamrock Inn: W. H. Burton. *Dennis Roach*, hostler at the Inn: J. C. Hickey. *Gerald Otway*, the schoolmaster: Edward Powell. *Boatswain of the H. M. S. "Dolphin"*: Edward Richards. *Pat, Mike*, Quinn's twins: Imogene Washburn, Ada Vanden Gilbert. *Hogan*: George Wallace. *First Sailor*: Frank Bonn. *Second Sailor*: William Jones. *Mr. Donnelly*, secretary: I. Washburn. *Notary*: William Howe. *Kate O'Donoghue*, daughter of Squire O'Donoghue: GEORGIA BUSBY. *Bridget Quinn*, wife of Pat Quinn: Mrs. LIZZIE WASHBURN. *Nora Roach*, chambermaid at the Inn: Kitty Coleman. *A Fishwife*: Lea Templeton. *An Old Mother*: Etta Baker Martin. *Male and Female Peasants, the Pressgang, Sailors, Marines.*

The scene is laid at Inniscarra, on the River Lee, near Cork. 1812.

Act 1: The Shamrock Inn at Inniscarra. The New Schoolmaster. (L. Young.)

Act 2: Three months and one day later. Glen Fail. (The Glen of Destiny.) The Trysting-Stone. (Emens.)

Act 3, Scene 1: The River Lee. One day later. (J. Young.) *Scene 2*: The road to the river. (L. Young.) *Scene 3*: *H.M.S. Dolphin*. The Pressgang. (L. Young.)

Act 4: Apartment in the Castle of Inniscarra. One day later. The Marriage Contract. (L. Young.)

MUSICAL NUMBERS[87]

"Sweet Inniscarra"
C. Olcott

"Kate O'Donoghue"
C. Olcott

"The Old Fashioned Mother"
C. Olcott

"The Fly Song" (Olcott's Fly Song)
C. Olcott

"Songs of Araby"[88]
C. Olcott
(*Music and Lyrics by* James Frederic Clay.)

1897.07 AT GAY CONEY ISLAND

A Farce Comedy in Three Acts. Book by Levin C. Tees. Music and lyrics by J. Sherrie Mathews and Harry Bulger. Additional music by Maurice Levi. Staged by Julian Mitchell. Dances arranged by H. Fletcher Rivers. Settings by John H. Young. Mechanical effects by P. J. McDonald. Produced by Julian Mathews[89]. Opened 1 February 1897 at the Columbus Theatre and closed 6 February 1897 after 8 performances; returned 13 September 1897 to the Grand Opera House and closed 18 September 1897 after an additional 8 performances[90].

CAST: *D. Aiken Payne, Hi Price*, a Plumber (the cause and the effect): J. SHERRIE MATHEWS, HARRY BULGER. *Uncle Goodrich Payne*, with a fortune in stage money: Frank Russell. *M. Pinaud Shampoo*, who shaves those who stand it: Thomas Evans. *Mique La Maque*, an arm of the law with one arm: Mark Hart. *Noyse E. Barker*, King of Coney Island: James Harrigan. *Tom Ginn*, the honest bar boy. Watch him closely: James Harrigan. *Abel Skinner*, a medicine man, with voice attached: Basil Booth. *Billie Dew*, not old enough to know: Marie Touhey. *Lay M. Low*, an undertaker: Clarence King. *Phil Sells, M. T. Sells*, policemen, "hope to die if we ain't": Theodore Romaine, William Kellan. *Will I. Ketcham*, a collector—"It's your move": Harold Montrose. *George Goodhealth*, so bad, he's afraid of himself: Alex Brown. *Daisy Kidder*, who knows her place but won't keep it: LOUISE MONTROSE. *Della Ware*, with money to burn and no matches: JOSIE DeWITT. *Miss Ann Teck*, alias Mrs. Aiken Payne: JESSIE RALPH. *Allie Hogan*, of Hogan's Alley last house: May Devere.

Of the Dramatic School (5): *Ida Clare*: Gladys Clare. *Mattie Nay*: Agnes Martyne. *May Wynne*: Kittie Raymond. *Rose Early*: Virginia Neilson. *Pearl Beach*: Maude Mayo. *A Cornucopia of Terpsichorean Confections (6)*: *Minnie Fish*: Ada Wallace. *Belle Tower*: Flo Piggott. *Etta Coyne*: Louise Sheppard. *Carrie Money*: Lillie Devere. *Annie Howe*: Nellie Devere. *May Wood*: May Devere. (Incidental to Act 2, America's foremost Lady Cornetist, Bessie Gilbert, will appear.)

Time: When the mercury is soaring high.

Act 1: Dr. Payne's Office, New York.

Act 2: Astorbilt Hotel, Sheepshead Bay, Long Island.

Act 3: Gay Coney Island.

MUSICAL NUMBERS[90a]

"Shooting Craps"
L. Montrose

"On Sunday Morning" (Willie's Misfit Pants)

"My Love's a Gamblin' Man"
(*Music by* Maurice Levi. *Lyrics by* J. Sherrie Mathews and Harry Bulger.)

1897.08 TATA-TOTO

A Vaudeville in Three Acts, in German. Libretto by Victor Leon. Music by Antoine Anatole Banès. Director, Heinrich Conried. Costumes by H. Eumicke. Musical arrangements and musical direction by Wilhelm Wolf. Opened 11 February 1897 at the Irving Place Theatre in repertory.

CAST: *Bernard Kaufmann*: Herr LE BRÊT. *Toto (Bernard)*, sein Sohn. Militärzogling: Frl. ELLY BENDER. *Tata (Bernard)*, seine Tochter: Frl. ELLY BENDER. *Gaston Ferrier*: Herr. JOH. PAULSON. *Dupalet*, Director enier Mititävorbereitungs-Anstalt: Herr SCHAFF. *Aurelie*, seine Schwester: Frl. Pitsch. *Blanchart*, Militar-Schulinspector: Herr Link. *Theodore Cabestan*, Schulaufseher: HERR SENIUS. *Cesarine Bassinet*: Frl. REICHARDT. *Der Exerciermeister*: Herr

[84]No program available for this engagement. First produced in New York 14 January 1895 at the Bijou Theatre for 8 performances; return engagements 25 March 1895 at the Columbus Theatre for 8 performances, and 23 March 1896 at the Grand Opera House for 8 performances. For Synopsis of Scenes and a List of Musical Numbers and Specialties, see original 1895 production.

[85]Subititled "On the Banks of the Lee."

[86]Played return engagements 29 November 1897 at the Columbus Theatre for 8 performances; 31 January 1898 at the Fourteenth Street Theatre for 40 performances; 14 March 1898 at the Grand Opera House for 8 performances; 19 September 1898 at the Columbus Theatre for 8 performances; 31 October 1898 at the 14th Street Theatre for 16 performances.

[87]Not necessarily in performance order.

[88]Replaced during the run by: "Only To Love Her" C. Olcott (*Music and Lyrics by* Charles Santley.)

[89]Subsequent tour presented under the auspices of A. M. Miller, Jr. and Fred Peel.

[90]Costume designs not credited.

[90a]Musical numbers not listed in programs. List prepared from published sheet music.

Frischer. *Zöglinge (4)*: *Anatole*: Frl. Loibl. *Ernest*: Frl. Hartner. *Raoul*: Frl. Dücos. *Benjamin*: Frl. Collmer. *Der Coporal*: Frau Hänseler. *Der Portier*: Herr Roland. *Ein Gensdarm*: Herr Brügmann. *Ein Kellner*: Herr Lindner. *Ein Diener*: Herr Rode. *Feuerwehrleute, Gäste, Zöglinge.*

Act 1: A preparatory school for pupils to the military academy in a small provincial town in France.

Act 2: Bernard's residence.

Act 3: The Railway Hotel.

1897.09

UNDER THE RED GLOBE

An Operatic Burlesque in Two Acts, preceded by an Olio. Produced by Joseph Weber and Lew M. Fields. Opened 18 February 1897 at Weber and Fields Music Hall and closed 21 April 1897 after 75 performances.

ACT 1

Olio[91]: Alburtus and Bartram (The College Boys) 3-Avolos-3 (Musical Wonders); Lew Hawkins (Black-face Comedian); Lottie Gilson (The Little Magnet); Caron and Herbert (Gymnastic Comedians)

ACT 2

UNDER THE RED GLOBE, a Burlesque in Two Acts. Suggested by Edward Rose's play "Under the Red Robe," adapted from Stanley Weyman's novel. Libretto by Joseph Herbert. Music by John Stromberg. Produced under the stage direction of Joseph Herbert. Costumes by Mrs. M. Dowling. Musical director, John Stromberg.[92]

CAST: *Gil d'Asphalt*: CHARLES ROSS. *Cardinal Fishglue*: JOHN T. KELLY. *M. Coachanfour*: Sylvia Thorne. *Captain Payroll*: SAM BERNARD. *Sir Thomas Grunt*: FRANKIE BAILEY. *Plon-Plon*: Joseph Donohue. *Mlle. Renee Coachandfour*: MABEL FENTON. *Madame Coachandfour*: Yolande Wallace. *Johnnie Juggins*. Lillian Swain. *The Non-Peroxide Sisters (3)*: *Meda*: Rose Beaumont. *Leda*: Nellie Beaumont. *Reda*: Josephine Allen. *Sally Salt*: Inez Rae. *Winnie Wave*: Maud Gilbert. *Flossie Foam*: Cora Carlyle. *Jean Neuchatel*: Florence Bell. *Pierre Parmesan*: Miss Dunbar. *Soupçon Stilton*: Miss Clifton. *Clevalier Camembert*: Edith Merrill.

Act 1: At Long Branch.

Act 2: Not at Long Branch.

MUSICAL NUMBERS[93]

"Love Lorn Lobster"
S. Bernard

1897.10

EL CAPITAN

A Revival of the Comic Opera in Three Acts[94]. Book and lyrics by Charles Klein. Music by John Philip Sousa. Produced under the stage direction of H. A. Cripps. Settings by Ernest M. Gros. Costumes by Mme. Catherine F. Siedle. Musical director, J. S. Hiller. Produced by DeWolf Hopper Comic Opera Company (B. D. Stevens, Manager). Opened 22 February 1897 at the Broadway Theatre and closed 20 March 1897 after 32 performances[95].

CAST: *Don Errico Medigua*, recently appointed Viceroy of Peru: DeWOLF HOPPER. *Senor Amabile Pozzo*, Chamberlain: ALFRED KLEIN. *Don Luis Cazarro*, ex-Viceroy: Thomas S. Guise. *Count Hernando Verrada*, a Peruvian gentleman: EDMUND STANLEY. *Scaramba*, an insurgent: John Parr. *Montalba, Nevado*, his companions: Harry P. Stone, Robert Pollard. *General Herbana*, Commander of King Phillip's forces: Louis Schrader. *Estrelda*, Cazarro's daughter: EDNA WALLACE HOPPER. *Isabel*, Medigua's daughter: NELLA BERGEN. *Princess Marghanza*, Medigua's wife: ALICE HOSMER. *Taciturnez*: May Weber.

[91]Other performers appearing in the Olio during the run: Beaumont Sisters (Rose, Nellie), A Burlesque of the Corbett-Fitzsimmons prize fight, The Artist's Dream (sketch), The Lobsterscope (burlesque of motion pictures) with Sam Bernard.
[92]Scenery uncredited.
[93]Musical numbers not listed in programs.
[94]Originally produced 20 April 1896 at the Broadway Theatre for 112 performances. For Synopsis of Scenes and Musical Numbers, see original 1896 production.
[95]Played return engagement 4 October 1897 at the Harlem Opera House for 8 performances.

1897.11

LA FALOTE

An Operetta in Three Acts. American libretto by J. Cheever Goodwin. Based on the French opérette of the same name with libretto by Armand Liorat and Maurice Ordonneau. Music by Louis Varney. Produced under the personal direction of James C. Duff. Dances arranged by Rose Beckett. Scenery by John H. Young, Ernest Albert, Ernest Gros. Costumes designed by Catherine Siedle. Musical conductor, Paul Steindorff. Produced by J. T. Cowdery. Opened 1 March 1897 at the Casino Theatre and closed 13 March 1897 after 14 performances.[96]

CAST: *Baron de la Hoguette*: W. J. LeMOYNE. *Pierre*: JULIUS STEGER. *Captain Mirasol*: GUY STANDING. *Canteleu*, innkeeper: Seth Crane. *Baroness de la Hoguette*: GEORGIA POWERS. *Therése*: YVONNE DE TRÉVILLE. *Mariolle*: PAULA EDWARDES. *Mme. Pigeonet*, innkeeper: EVA DAVENPORT. *Mathurine*: Minnie DeReu. *Julia*: Helen Marvin. *Berthe*: Ida Blossom. *Germaine*: MAY NORTON. *Chorus of Villagers, Sailors, Waitresses, Tourists, etc.*

Act 1: A square in Mt. St. Michel. (Young.)

Act 2: Hall of the Chevaliers. (Albert.)

Act 3: Interior of the Hotel Pigeon. (Gros.)

1897.12

THE BOYS OF KILKENNY

An Irish Drama in Five Acts, 6 Scenes. Play by Townsend Walsh. Songs by Joseph F. Healy, Charles Sullivan, Edward Harrigan and George F. Braham. Opened 15 March 1897 at the Star Theatre and closed 20 March 1897 after 8 performances.[97]

CAST: *Darby O'Hara*, the richest man in Kilkenny, and the meanest: TOWNSHEND WALSH. *Mona O'Hara*, his daughter: TESSIE DEAGLE. *Dick O'Hara*, his son: JOSEPH MANOR. *Matt Annesley*: JOSEPH F. HEALEY. *Tim, Ellen*, O'Hara's servants: CHARLES SULLIVAN, Bessie Lea Lestina. *Father Roche*: Charles Drake. *Beresford Dugan*: Walton Townshend. *Dick's Companions, Boys of Kilkenny (4)*: *Barry Sweeney*: FREDERICK KELLY. *Jack Cassidy*: PAUL SHEA. *Charlie McElroy*: N. F. BRADY. *Bob Callahan*: J. J. McARDLE. *Big Pat*, the Piper: John Marron. *Murtaugh*, the jailer: James Francis. *Sergeant Reilly*: Ogden Marks. *Irish Terpsichore Specialty*: WILLIAM McGONIGAL.

The action takes place in Kilkenny, Ireland, in 1840.

Act 1: The farm of Darby O'Hara. A matchmaking, and its consequences.

Act 2: The Hayfield. The quarrel.

Act 3: The home of the miser. The night attack and robbery.

Act 4, Scene 1: Kilkenny Jail. *Scene 2*: The cabin in the bog. Tim's strategy. The chapel across the lake. The signal light from the old round tower.

Act 5: The priest's garden. The return from America. Five years later.

MUSICAL NUMBERS[98]

"The Rose"
J. F. Healey
(*Music and Lyrics by* Joseph F. Healey.)

"Only a Tear"
J. F. Healey
(*Music by* George F. Braham. *Lyrics by* Edward Harrigan.)

"The Real Old Mountain Dew"
C. Sullivan

"The Vagrants of Erin"
C. Sullivan

Selections
Kilkenny Quartette

Bagpipe Specialty
J. Marron

Jig and Reel Dance Specialty
W. McGonigal

1897.13

THE SERENADE

A Comic Opera in Three Acts. Book and lyrics by Harry B. Smith[99]. Music by Victor Herbert. Staged by W. H. Fitzgerald. Scenery by Walter Burridge, Ernest Albert and Alfred Williams. Musical direction by Samuel L. Studley.

[96]Musical numbers not listed in programs; no libretto or musical score found.
[97]Stage direction, scenery, costumes and musical direction uncredited.
[98]Not in performance order.
[99]Program note: The theme of the libretto was suggested by and adapted from an interlude by Carlo Goldoni.

Produced by the Bostonians Opera Company (Frank L. Perley, director; Henry Clay Barnabee, William H. MacDonald, Proprietors). Opened 16 March 1897 at the Knickerbocker Theatre and closed 22 May 1897 after 79 performances in repertory[100].

CAST: *The Duke of Santa Cruz*, a self made nobleman, in love with Dolores, and pursuing the singer of the Serenade: HENRY CLAY BARNABEE. *Carlos Alvarado*, Baritone of the Madrid Opera, who loves Dolores, as he has quite rarely loved before; a fugitive from his creditors—also from Yvonne, whom he has jilted: W. H. MacDONALD. *Romero*, President of the Royal Madrid Brigandage Association, Limited, the head of an influential syndicate of robbers. He commits crimes one day and repents them the next as a monk in a monastery: EUGENE COWLES. *Lopez*, Secretary of the same corporation: WILLIAM E. PHILP. *Gomez*, a tailor in love with Dolores, and trying to learn the serenade in order to win her affections: GEORGE FROTHINGHAM. *Colombo*, formerly a grand opera tenor, now reduced to playing the devil in pantomime: HARRY BROWN. *Yvonne*, his daughter, a ballet dancer at the Madrid Opera, in love with Alvarado, for whom she is looking with a wealth of devotion—and a stiletto: ALICE NIELSEN. *The Mother Superior* of the Convent of St. Ursula: JOSEPHINE BARTLETT. *Schoolgirls (3)*: *Juana*: Marcia Van Dresser. *Isabella*: Leonora Guito. *Mercedes*: Louise Cleary. *El Gato*, a brigand: Charles R. Hawley. *The Abbot of the Monastery of St. Benedict*: James E. Miller. *Fra Anselmo*: Harry Dale. *Fra Timoteo*: A. Warmouth. *Manuelo*, the duke's cook: Bertha Lovejoy. *Dolores*, the Duke's ward, in love with Alvarado: JESSIE BARTLETT DAVIS.

Act 1: The Main Office of the Royal Madrid Brigandage Association, near a haunted castle in the mountains. (Burridge.)

Act 2: The Garden of the Monastery of St. Benedict, adjoining the convent school of St. Ursula. (Albert.)

Act 3: Same as Act 1.

ACT 1[101]

- "Song of the Carbine" (Opening Chorus)
  E. Cowles, Chorus
- "Peering Left and Peering Right"
  Chorus of Duke's Attendants
- "With Cracking of Whip and Rattle of Spur"
  W. H. MacDonald
- "The Funny Side of That"
  H. C. Barnabee
- "I Love Thee, I Adore Thee" (Serenade)
  W. H. MacDonald, J. B. Davis
- "The Singing Lesson"
  A. Nielsen, H. Brown

ACT 2

- "In Our Quiet Cloister"
  Chorus of Monks
- "In Fair Andalusia"
  A. Nielsen, Chorus of Monks
- "The Monk and the Maid"
  E. Cowles
- "Woman, Lovely Woman"
  H. C. Barnabee
- "The Angelus"
  J. B. Davis
- "Cupid and I"
  A. Nielsen

ACT 3

- Opening Chorus
- "Don José of Sevilla"
  J. B. Davis, W. H. MacDonald
- "I Envy the Bird" (Romance)
  W. E. Philp
- "Dreaming, Dreaming" (Trio)
  H. C. Barnabee, A. Nielsen, G. Frothingham
- Finale

[100]Costumes uncredited.

[101]Musical Numbers not listed in programs. List prepared from published libretto (The Bostonians, 1896).

1897.14 GAYEST MANHATTAN, or, Around New York in Ninety Minutes

A Vaudeville in One Act, 3 Scenes, preceded by an Olio. Book and lyrics by Harry B. Smith. Music by Ludwig Engländer. Two songs by Matt Woodward. Produced by (John) Koster and (Albert) Bial. Opened 22 March 1897 at Koster and Bial's Music Hall and closed 22 May 1897 after 65 performances[102].

Olio: Sisters Hawthorne, Mary Arniostis, Professor Leonidas, Fannie Leslie.

CAST: *Delsarte Flam*, a retired tragedian: HENRY E. DIXEY. *Auditorium Shortribs* from Chicago: R. A. ROBERTS. *Anheuser Froth* of St. Louis: Robert E. Graham. *Adamantine Nerve*: Frank B. Blair. *Cholly Regaul*: Frederick Hill. *Willy Flounders*: Harry Sommers. *Wally Holdhands*: June Stone. *Totty Shortribs*: FLO IRWIN. *Daisy Patty Cake*: MERRI OSBORNE. *Ophelia*: Nettie Lyford. *Marguerite*: Katharine Lucille Foot. *Nursemaid*: Beatrice Goldie. *Dance Specialty*: Misses Saharet, Middleton, LaGarete, Dean.

Scene 1: The Mall in Central Park. *Scene 2*: The Stock Exchange. *Scene 3*: Koster & Bial's.

OLIO

- The Hawthorne Sisters (3):
  ["The Daughter of Officer Porter"
  "Daughters of the Guard"
  (*Music and Lyrics by* Leslie Stuart.)
  "The Willow Pattern Plate"
  (*Music and Lyrics by* Leslie Stuart.)]
- Mary Arniostis (a strong woman)
- Professor Leonidas (trained dogs and cats)

MUSICAL NUMBERS

- "She Always Does Exactly as She's Told"
  F. Irwin
- "Gayest Manhattan"
- "That's All"
  M. Osborn
- "Blackbirds"
  F. Irwin
- Dances, Imitations
  H. E. Dixey

1897.15 MISS MANHATTAN

A Dream (Musical Comedy Extravaganza) in Three Acts, 7 Scenes. Book (and lyrics) by George V. Hobart. Music by F. Puehringer and Herman Perlet. Settings by Richard Marston. Produced by Thomas D. Van Osten. Opened 23 March 1897 at Wallack's Theatre and closed 24 April 1897 after 40 performances.[103]

CAST: *"Father" Nicholas Knickerbocker*: REUBEN FAX. *"Chollie" Knickerbocker*: WILLIAM CAMERON. *Dodge Kay-Belkars*: John Young. *Ephraim Washington Hytes*: AL HOLBROOK. *Nipit*, a valet de chambre: Taylor Williams. *Buttsy*, a bootblack: Budd Ross. *Everett Rest*, a weary one: Budd Ross. *Cigsy*, another bootblack: Harry B. Watson. *Patrolman Pynche*, an official: Harry B. Watson. *Conway Leighlow*: Paul B. Brackett. *Bun Kojames*: H. G. Vernon. *Typsim*, a waiter: F. Anderson. *Kuttynge Kornes*: Elmer T. Ritchie. *Irving Playce*: F. D. Carr. *Senator Plattsee*: William Powers. *DeWolf Stopper*: Andrew Powers. *Chauncey DePeach*: James Powers. *A. B. Ummel*: Master McTernan. *M. E. Phisto*: James Clarenze. *Captain Snapman*: W. Ward Beam. *Greene S. Grass*, a old friend: John Keefe. *Marjorie Manhattan*: MAMIE GILROY. *Mrs. Vanastorgool*, Marjorie's aunt: GENEVIEVE REYNOLDS. *Hattie Harlem*, Marjorie's friend: HELEN BYRON. *Grace Goulet-Reims*, a Prince of the Arions: Inez Mecusker. *Maggie Fitzsimmons*, the champion housemaid: May Stevens Boyesen. *Clara Clinton*: Regina Collins. *Lillian Rustling*: Grace Pierrepont. *Miss Span-Wrestler*: Adele Francis. *Anna Geld*: Frankie Peterson. *Miss Krewgle Krewgle*: Estelle Vincent. *Bessie Broadway*: Lillie Collins. *Captain Ep. Paulet, Lieutenant Shol Der Strap, Second Lieutenant and Una Forme*, in charge of Squadron A: Helen Welch, Maud Francis, Adele Francis.

[102]An altogether different entertainment of the same title, but by different authors, but still billed as "Koster & Bial's Spectacular Production" subsequently played engagements 25 October 1897 at the Grand Opera House for 8 performances (see separate entry in 1897-98 season), 3 January 1898 at the Star Theatre for 8 performances, and 19 September 1898 at the Harlem Opera House for 8 performances.

[103]Stage director, musical director uncredited in programs. No musical numbers listed; no libretto or musical score found.

Act 1, Scene 1: "Chollie" Knickerbocker's apartments. *Scene 2*: The Lotos Club, Fifth Avenue. (Marston.)

Act 2, Scene 1: On the Rialto. (Marston.) *Scene 2*: Union Square. (Marston.) *Scene 3*: The Arion Ball. (Marston.)

Act 3, Scene 1: The Casino, Central Park. (Marston.) *Scene 2*: The ballroom of the Knickerbocker mansion.

1897.16 MRS. RADLEY BARTON'S BALL IN GREATER NEW YORK

A Local Burlesque in Three Acts, preceded by a vaudeville bill.[104] Words and lyrics by Oscar Hammerstein. Production staged by Frederic Solomon. Musical director, A. C. Prioner. Produced by Oscar Hammerstein. Opened 26 March 1897 at the Hammerstein's Olympia Music Hall, moved 3 May 1897 to the Olympia Roof Garden and closed 8 May 1897 after 46 performances.[105]

CAST [in order of appearance]: *Mrs. Radley Barton*: GEORGE W. MONROE. *Mr. Radley Barton*: FREDERICK BACH. *Princess Shemay*: ALICE ROSE. *Rigo*: Blanca Benedetto. *Francois*: Mme. Alexia. *Michael Angelo*: Sam J. Ryan. *Friedrich Wilhelm Kimmelfritze*: Thomas O'Brien. *Mr. Oldpot*: W. H. Tredennick. *Mr. Hertz*: A. Froom. *Miss Charity*: Blanca Benedetto. *Bridgetine McCarthy*: GEORGE W. MONROE. *Mrs. Turnout*: Dorothy Usner. *Mrs. Wadsworth*: Madeline Vera. *Mrs. Fettingill*: Frances Lee. *Mlle. Flora*: Flora Leonard. *The Four Unsophisticated Cousins*: Rose Whiting, Leonara Ruiz, Madeleine Vera, E. Louise Elam. *The Four Sleeping Beauties*: Lucille Sturges, Cissy Wilson, Amy Johnston, June Deschamp. *The Four Wideawake Beauties*: Ellen Rinquest, Annie Dagwell, Frances Lee, Lea Martin. (*Specialties*: O'Brien & Havel, The Eldridges.)

Act 1: Mrs. Radley Barton's Parlors. New York City.

Act 2: Longacre Square.

Act 3: Apartments of the Princess Shemay.

1897.17 THE WEDDING DAY

A Comic Opera in Three Acts. Libretto by Stanislaus Stange. Based on the French operette "La Petite Fronde," (libretto by Henri Chivot and Alfred Duru, music by Edmond Audran). Music by Julian Edwards. Produced under the stage direction of Richard Barker. Settings by Ernest Albert and Walter Burridge. Costumes by Caroline Seidle. Orchestra under the direction of Julian Edwards. Produced by the Lillian Russell-Della Fox-Jeff DeAngelis Comic Opera Combination (Frank Murray, Director). Opened 8 April 1897 at the Casino Theatre and closed 8 May 1897 after 36 performances[106].

CAST: *Duc de Bouillon*, General of the Frondist Army: WILLIAM PRUETTE. *Raoul, Vicomte de Bragelonne*, his nephew: TOM GREENE. *Sergeant Sabre* of the Frondist Army: Winfield Blake. *Corporal Souffle* of the Frondist Army: Leonard Savoy. *Laubert*, Madame Montbazon's major-domo: Eugene Desmond. *Polycop*, baker and caterer: JEFFERSON DeANGELIS. *Planchette*, his head cook and first baker: ALF C. WHELAN. *Pomade*, a barber: ALBERT McGUCKIN. *Madame Montbazon*, a leader of the "Fronde": LUCILLE SAUNDERS. *Lucille D'Herblay*, the Queen's messenger: LILLIAN RUSSELL. *Aunt Hortense*, Polycop's aunt: Louise Rial. *Rose-Marie*, Polycop's Normandy bride: DELLA FOX. *Dancers from "La Folie" (4)*: *Mlle Renée*: Sally Randall. *Mlle. Courcey*: May Cuthbert. *Mlle. Villiers*: Grace Freeman. *Mlle. Varney*: Marguerite Leon. *Frondist Soldiers, Parisian Tradesmen, Grisettes, Laundresses, Vivandières, Lords, Ladies, Pages, Drummers, etc.*

Act 1: Polycop's Shop, Rue Arbre Sec, near the Porte St. Germain, (Paris). 1649. Noon. (Albert.)

Act 2: Madame Montbazon's Palace. 3 P.M. (Albert.)

Act 3: Frondist outpost on the road to Reuil. 5 P.M. (Burridge.)

ACT 1[107]
Introduction
"Planchette, Planchette" (Chorus)
A. C. Whelan, L. Savoy, Chorus
"Soldiers of the Parliament" (Song)
A. McGuckin, Chorus
"He Never Said a Word" (Song)
A. C. Whelan
"Life Is But Short at Best" (Song)
T. Greene
"Rose Marie" (Ensemble and Song)
A. McGuckin, A. C. Whelan, Chorus
"I am a Simple Norman Maid" (Chorus and Song)
T. Greene, J. DeAngelis, D. Fox, Chorus
"The Maid and the Officer" (Duet)
T. Greene, L. Russell
"Mon Général" (Ensemble and Song)
D. Fox, L. Russell, T. Greene, W. Pruette, Chorus
"Though the years (have made him mellow)" (Ensemble)
A. McGuckin, J. DeAngelis, D. Fox, Chorus
"The Mermaid and the Whale" (Song)
J. DeAngelis
"At last I find you in" (Finale)
J. DeAngelis, A. C. Whelan, A. McGuckin, D. Fox, W. Pruette, L. Russell, Chorus

ACT 2
"A Woman's Tact" (Chorus and Song)
T. Greene, L. Saunders, Chorus
"How I danced away" (Song)
J. DeAngelis, Chorus
"Ladies , I am sorry" (Ensemble)
L. Saunders, S. Randall, M. Cuthbert, G. Freeman, M. Leon
"The Days of Long Ago" (Song)
L. Saunders
"Love's Prescription" (Duet)
L. Russell, W. Pruette
"This is the Hour" (Ensemble)
L. Russell, T. Greene, L. Saunders, W. Pruette, W. Blake, Chorus
"Come my dearest" (Quartet)
T. Greene, W. Pruette, L. Russell, D. Fox
"Confiding Woman" (Duet)
J. DeAngelis, D. Fox
"A Rogue lies hid in the Wine" (Trio)
L. Russell, D. Fox, W. Pruette
"A Nation's Fate" (Finale)
D. Fox, J. DeAngelis, A. C. Whelan, L. Russell, T. Greene, Chorus

ACT 3
"Gaily marches the Soldier" (Chorus)
A. C. Whelan, Chorus
"The Tomtit and the Nightingale" (Song)
L. Russell
"Vivandiers" (Chorus)
Chorus
"The Wise Little Maid (of France)" (Song)
D. Fox
"It is really too good to be true" (Song)
J. DeAngelis
"The General has relented" (Finale)
Principals, Chorus

1897.18 THE WIZARD OF THE NILE

A Revival of the Comic Opera in Three Acts[108]. Libretto by Harry B. Smith. Music by Victor Herbert. Produced under the stage direction of Napier

[104]After the first night, the show was known simply as IN GREATER NEW YORK. Beginning 12 April, Dan Leno appeared as a star vaudeville attraction between Acts 1 and 2 of IN GREATER NEW YORK.
[105]Scenery and costumes uncredited. No musical numbers listed in programs. Specialties performed by Dorothy Usner, O'Brien & Havel, and the Eldridges were interpolated. Following the show's closing, ballet and vaudeville elements of the show were retained in an ongoing vaudeville entertainment for the balance of the season.
[106]Played a return engagement 28 February 1898 at the Harlem Opera House for 8 performances; revived 18 April 1898 at the Broadway Theatre for 32 performances (see separate entry in next season).

[107]Musical numbers not listed in programs. List prepared from published piano vocal score (John Church Co, Cincinnati, 1897).
[108] Originally opened 4 November 1895 at the Casino Theatre for 105 performances. For Synopsis of Scenes and Musical Numbers, see original 1895 production.

Lothian, Jr. Scenery designed by Ernest Albert. Costumes designed by Catherine Seidle. Musical director, Frank Palma. Orchestrations by Victor Herbert. Produced by the Frank Daniels Opera Company (Kirk LaShelle, Arthur F. Clarke, Proprietors). Opened 19 April 1897 at the Broadway Theatre and closed 8 May 1897 after 21 performances.

CAST: *Kibosh*, a Persian magician, making a professional tour of Egypt: FRANK DANIELS. *Abydos*, his apprentice: LOUISE ROYCE. *Ptolemy*, King of Egypt: WALTER ALLEN. *Simoona*, Ptolemy's second wife: Greta Risley. *Cleopatra*, a princess who knows naught of love: ADELE RITCHIE. *Ptarmigan*, Cleopatra's music teacher: LEONARD WALKER. *Cheops*, the royal weather bureau: LOUIS CASAVANT. *Obelisk*, Captain of the Amazons: Sadie Emmons. *Netocris*, lieutenant of the Amazons: Florence Ritchie. *Merza*, first maid-of-honor to Cleopatra: Edna Thornton. *Captain of the Royal Guards*: Frederic M. Knight. *McIbis, O'Pasha*, policemen: Sinclair Nash, Harry Collins. *Chop-Chop, Chopum*, Headsmen: Carl Hartberg, John Odell. *Royal Guards, Nobles, Citizens, Pages, Maids-of-Honor, Dancing Girls, Galley Slaves, etc.*

"Echo" (Song)
(*Music by* William T. Francis.)
Ensemble
(*Music by* William T. Francis and John Stromberg.)
"Dickery Dock" (Duet)
(*Music by* William T. Francis.)
"King of Ruritania" (Trio)
(*Music by* William T. Francis.)
"Eccentrique" (Ballet)
(*Music by* John Stromberg.)
"The Kiss" (Song)
(*Music by* John Stromberg.)
Finale
(*Music by* William T. Francis.)

1897.19 MR NEW YORK, ESQ.

A Travesty in Two Acts, preceded by an Olio. Produced by Joseph Weber and Lew M. Fields. Opened 22 April 1897 at Weber & Fields Music Hall and closed 6 June 1897 after 52 performances.

Olio: John C. Fox and Katie Allen in 'The Flat Next Door'; Alburtus and Bartram (The College Boys); Josie DeWitt (The Fiddle and I); Mr. and Mrs. Sidney Drew in their latest satirical success, When Two Hearts Are Won, by Kenneth Lee. *Mr. & Mrs. Shellington Shumley*: Mr. and Mrs. Drew. *Cara*: That — Dog.

MR. NEW YORK, ESQ., a Travesty in Two Acts. Book (and lyrics) by Joseph Herbert. Music by John Stromberg, William T. Francis. (Staged by Joseph Herbert.) Musical director, John Stromberg.[109]

CAST: *Mr. New York, Esq.*, a Bohemian: HENRY E. DIXEY. *Brunette Mike*, a victim of heredity: CHARLES J. ROSS. *Captain Spats*: JOHN T. KELLY. *Villainous minions in the employ of Mike (3)*: *Rupert*: JOSEPH WEBER. *Krafstein*: LEW FIELDS. *Benzine*: SAM BERNARD. *Fritz*, in love with Eleda: Yolande Wallace. *Eleda*, in love with Fritz: Sylvia Thorne. *Princess Caviar*, sweet sixteen—for reasons: Ada Deaves. *Three Graces*: *Lady Faith*: Josephine Allen. *Lady Hope*: Rose Beaumont. *Lady Charity*: Nellie Beaumont. *Hans*: Frankie Bailey. *Ole Mosa Sam*: Lillian Swain. *Tess of the W'Eberfields*: MABEL FENTON. *Peasants, Soldiers, Courtiers and other people—common or otherwise—to Ruritania.*

The action takes place in Ruritania, on the borders of Bohemia. *Time*: Allegro.

Act 1: Outdoors. *Act 2*: Indoors.

ACT 1
Opening Chorus
(*Music by* William T. Francis.)
Quartette
C. J. Ross, J. Weber, L. Fields, S. Bernard
(*Music by* William T. Francis.)
Trio
J. Allen, R. Beaumont, N. Beaumont
(*Music by* John Stromberg.)
"Mr. New York, Esq."
(*Music by* John Stromberg.)
"Misplaced Confidence"
(*Music by* John Stromberg.)
Lullabye
(*Music by* William T. Francis.)
"When I'm the King" (Trio)
(*Music by* William T. Francis.)
"Love's Dream Is O'er" (Duet)
(*Music by* William T. Francis.)
Finale
(*Music by* William T. Francis.)

ACT 2
Opening Chorus
(*Music by* William T. Francis.)
"Knock, Knock, Knock" (Song and Chorus)
(*Music by* John Stromberg.)
"Hi-diddle-diddle" (Septette)
(*Music by* John Stromberg.)

[109]Stage director, scenery and costumes uncredited in programs.

1897.20 THE CIRCUS GIRL

A Musical Play in Two Acts, 4 Scenes. Book by James T. Tanner and Walter Pallings [Pallant][110]. Music by Ivan Caryll; additional numbers by Lionel Monckton. Lyrics by Harry Greenbank and Adrian Ross. Produced under the direction of J. E. A. Malone. Dances arranged by Carl Marwig. Settings by Ernest M. Gros and Henry E. Hoyt. Costumes by Comelli. Musical director, Paul Steindorff. Produced by Augustin Daly. Opened 23 April 1897 at Daly's Theatre and closed 26 June 1897 after 75 performances; re-opened 16 August 1897 at Daly's Theatre[111] and closed 6 November 1897 after 97 additional performances. Total: 172 performances[112].

CAST: *Biggs*, an American bartender: JAMES T. POWERS. *Sir Titus Wemyss*: HERBERT GRESHAM. *Dick Capel*: CYRIL SCOTT. *Drivelli*, Proprietor of Circus: SAMUEL EDWARDS. *Hon. Reginald Gower*: Eric Scott. *Auguste*, Clown: Edward Hanford. *Albertini*, Ring Master: Douglas Flint. *Commissaire of Police*: Augustus Cook. *Vicomte Gaston*: Neil McCay. *Toothick Pasha*, the Terrible Turk: Hobart Bosworth. *Rudolph*, the Cannon King: Pierre Young. *Proprietor of the Café de la Régence*: Deane Pratt. *Flobert*: Abner Symmons. *Cocher*: Richard Quilter. *Sergeant de Ville*: Fingleton David. *Valliand*: Hans Roberts. *"La Favorita"*, the Circus Girl: NANCY McINTOSH. *Lucille*, a Slack Wire Walker: BLANCHE ASTLEY. *Mrs. Drivelli*: MARIE SANGER. *Lady Diana Wemyss*: EFFIE GERMON. *Marie*: Helma Nelson. *The Serpentina Quartette (4)*: *Louise*: Mabel Gilman. *Liane*: Grace Rutter. *Emilie*: Edith Miller. *Juliette*: Rita Davis. *Comtesse d'Epérnay*: Matilde Preville. *Marquise de Millefleurs*: Rose Davies. *Mme de Grouchy*: Ruth Holt. *Mlle. Rose Gompson*: Bessie Ashbaugh. *Dora Wemyss*: VIRGINIA EARLE.

Act 1: On the Boulevards. Outside the Café de la Regence. (Gros.)

Act 2, Scene 1: In the Ring at Drivelli's Circus. *Scene 2*: Bureau of the Commissaire of Police. *Scene 3*: The Artists' Ball. (Hoyt.)

MUSICAL NUMBERS
"A Simple Little String"
(*Music by* Lionel Monckton.)
"The Way to Treat a Lady"
(*Music by* Lionel Monckton.)
"Clowns"
(*Music by* Lionel Monckton.)
"Professions"
"La Favorita" (Houp-La)
(*Music by* Lionel Monckton. *Lyrics by* Harry Greenbank.)
"In the Ring"
"A Wet Day"
(*Music by* Lionel Monckton.)
"She Never Did the Same Thing Twice"
"Wine, Women and Song"
"Now That You Know Your Way"
"The Barman's Song"
"Dull Duet and Dance"
(*Music by* Lionel Monckton. *Lyrics by* E. Payne.)

[110]The authors acknowledge Act 2, Scenes 1 and 2 to have been suggested by "Eien Tolle Nacht."
[111]The cast was substantially the same for the return engagement except that May Young succeeded Blanche Astley as Lucette.
[112]Later played a return engagement 3 January 1898 at the Harlem Opera House for 8 performances; also revived 2 May 1898 at Daly's Theatre for 40 performances (see separate entry).

1897.21

THE ISLE OF GOLD

A Musical Burlesque in Three Acts. Book and lyrics by C. A. Byrne. Music by Herman Perlet. Produced under the direction of (staged by) W. H. Lytell. Dances arranged by H. Fletcher Rivers. Costumes by Ehrich Brothers, Mme. Dowling. Musical direction, Maurice Levi. Produced by Oscar Hammerstein. Opened 26 April 1897 at Hammerstein's Olympia Theatre and closed 1 May 1897 after 7 performances.

CAST: *Croesus*, the millionaire monarch of the Isle of Gold: J. ALDRICH LIBBEY. *Pipe McSodar Jones*, a plumber: W. H. Sloan. *Austinel*, an ardent lover, with a soul above the sordid: HENRY HALLAM. *Shake-for-the_Drinks*, an Indian, the last of his race: Mart E. Heisey. *William Pennland*, the Reservation Agent: Ben F. Dillon. *Hypo*, Lord Chief Justice: Ben Lodge. *Geneva*, standing with unwilling feet, where the brook and the river meet: Eleanor Elton. *Superba*, wedded to Croesus, but with an eye on the women of the future: MAYME TAYLOR. *Sophia Maria*, a domestic: MADELINE MARSHALL. *Croesus' daughters (4)*: *Lady Angelina*: Tedde DuCoe. *Lady Betty*: Blanche Howard. *Lady Sapphira*: Maude Williams. *Lady Maud*: Gladys Claire. *Four delightful solutions of the much-vexed quardi-metallic question*: *Goldena*: Jennie Collins. *Silvera*: Cora D'Anguera. *Coppera*: Genevieve Hill. *Plattina*: Florence Hess. *Bridget, Euphemia*, Ladies of the Dustpan: Julia Raymond, Frances Wilson.

Marie March: Helen Baker. *Annie April*: Madge Dunbar. *Minnie May*: Louise Pardee. *Jennie June*: Agnes Keill. *Josie July*: Lillie Dunbar. *Aimee August*: Edith Lovelace. *Susie September*: Julia Lake. *Ollie October*: Marie Tuohey. *Nonnie November*: Persie Evans. *Daisy December*: Alice Lovelace. *Jessie January*: Belle Latone. *Fannie February*: Mae Hezera. *Laundry Maids, Conspirators, Merry Makers, and all the familiar ensemble of a Modern Musical Farce.*

Act 1: Exterior of Palace of Isle of Gold.

Act 2: Garden of Palace.

Act 3: Interior of Palace.

MUSICAL NUMBERS

"Dollars as a Wedge" (Solo and Chorus)
"If I Were Called Upon to Rule" (Trio)
"Susie Smith from Troy" (Solo and Chorus)
"I Am King Croesus" (Solo)
"The Tiger in His Lair" (Quartette)
"Love Is a Fancied Dream" (Solo)
"Sophia Maria" (Solo and Chorus)
"She Has No Past" (Duet)
"Paris, Vienna, London, New York" (Quartette)
"Last of His Race" (Solo)
"Billy of the Olden Days" (Trio)
"Love In an Attic" (Octette)
"(The) Echo Song" (Solo)
"(The) New Woman" (Solo)
"Old Maids' Dance" (Sextette)
"Money to Burn" (Solo and Ensemble)
"Washboard Dance" (Double Sextette)
"Has Anyone Seen" (Solo and Chorus)
Patriotic Hymn (Ensemble)
"Hush, Hush" (Septette and Chorus)
"Ma Little One, or Ma Baby" (Quintette)
M. Marshall
(*Music by* William B. Gottlieb. *Lyrics by* Charles A. Byrne.)

1897.22

AT THE FRENCH BALL

A Musical Farcical Trifle in Three Acts and a Prologue. Adapted by Frederick F. Schrader from the German schwank "Drei Paar Schuhe" [Three Pairs of Shoes]. Musical director, Julius Simonoff. Produced by Fanny Rice (G. W. Purdy, Manager). Opened 3 May 1897 at the Bijou Theatre and closed 15 May 1897 after 16 performances.

CAST: Act 1: *Lawrence Patch*, a shoemaker: John S. Terry. *Tommy Smart*, a newsboy: Reba Haight. *Joe Lightfoot*, a dancer: Ralph Bicknell. *Erasimous*, a colored servant: John Conley. *Thomas Barton*, a banker: GEORGE EDESON. *Mary Barton*, a young wife: Agnes Murray. *Dolly Green*, a dangerous friend: Alice Gaillard. *Nancy Patch*, just a woman: FANNY RICE. Act 2: *Geraldine*, a prima donna: KATE MICHELENA. *Lisette*, a maid: Reba Haight. *Hammermyerstern*, an impressario: CHARLES H. DREW. *Duke of Gargoil*, a title for sale: GEORGE BRODERICK. *Nancy*: FANNY RICE. *Country relatives, etc.* Act 3: *Major Slyboots*, a gay old deceiver: GEORGE BRODERICK. *Viola Slyboots*, a suspicious wife: Mabella Baker. *Nightbird*, a dissipated roué: Mr. Gaillard. *Ajax*, a Brownie king: CHARLES H. DREW. *Erasimous*, the waiter: John Conley. *Patch*, the shoemaker: John S. Terry. *The Little He, the Little She*, two dancers: Ralph Bicknell, Reba Haight. *Dolly Green*: Alice Gaillard. *Daisy Darling*: Agnes Murray. *Nancy*: FANNY RICE.

Prologue and Act 1: The Home of the Shoemaker and the Home of the Banker.

Act 2: Home of the Prima Donna.

Act 3: A Refreshment Balcony at the French Ball.

MUSICAL NUMBERS, SPECIALTIES

Sextette from LUCIA DiLIAMMERMOR
(*Music by* Gaetano Donizetti.)

1897.23

THE WIDOW GOLDSTEIN

A Farcical Character Sketch in Three Acts. Play by Lillian Lewis and Lawrence Marston. Produced by Joel Marks. Opened 17 May 1897 at the 14th Street Theatre and closed 22 May 1897 after 8 performances[113].

CAST: *Sam Brittle*, the man with acres, lots and blocks of gold: W. J. FERGUSON. *Cyrus Russell*, the skinner who gets skinned: R. F. COTTON. *Jay Simpkins*, he means well but can't help himself: GEORGE W. WESSELLS. *Carl Donnerwetter*, looking for trouble and gets it: Sol Aiken. *Willing Boy*, don't care what he does, and does it: Phil Ott. *Brother Ben*, willing to spend anybody's money: Harrison Armstrong. *Baby Bobbie Goode*, has lots of friends, but little money: Matthew Ott. *Slick Waiter*, needs watching: Charles J. Carter. *Butler*, doesn't say much, but thinks a lot: John DeGez. *Clerk*, very tired, but keeps on working: T. H. Withett. *Collection Clerk*, wants nothing but money: Walter Ryder. *Mrs. Hettie Goldstein*, contact with men in business made her what she is: JENNIE REIFFARTH. *Iza Simpkins*, knows that figures don't lie—so has it figured out: LAURA BURT. *Cora Arabella*, wants eddication and her corners rounded off: GERTIE REYNOLDS. *Judith Simpkins*, in town to see the sights: SARAH McVICKER. *Waiters*, The Eagle Quartette: Messrs. Bohanon, Hicks, Ryder, Parmet. *Football Boys and Their Girl Friends, "The Widow Goldstein's" Serenading Band.*

Act 1: The Simpkins' home. 5:30 P.M. Constancy and Faith.

Act 2: The office. 10 A.M. the next day. They don't do a thing to Russell.

Act 3: The restaurant. Ten minutes after Act 2. Christen Baby Sam—The Widow Goldstein.

1897.24

ERMINIE

A Revival of the Comic Opera in Three Acts[114]. Libretto by Harry Paulton (and Claxson Bellamy). Based on the melodrama (L'Auberge des Adrets by Benjamin Antier, Saint-Amand and Paulyanthe, adapted into English as) Robert Macaire. Music by Edward Jakobowski. Produced under the stage direction of Max Freeman. Orchestra under the direction of Ernest Neyer. Produced by the Bijou Comic Opera Company (H. B. Sire, Proprietor; Rudolph Aronson, Manager) by special arrangement with Francis Wilson & Co. Opened 23 May 1897 at the Bijou Theatre and closed 5 June 1897 after 14 performances[115].

CAST: *Erminie*: HELEN BERTRAM. *Princess*: JENNIE WEATHERSBY. *Cerise*: STELLA LIPSON. *Javotte*: Delia Stacy. *Marie*: Mamie Sutton. *Delauney*: JULIE SENAC. *Lieutenant*: Katherine Gay. *Benedict*: Minnie Campbell. *First Swell Girl*: Lottie Prince. *Second Swell Girl*: Annie Cameron. *Third Swell Boy*: Estella Hoyt. *Fourth Swell Boy*: June Dale. *Ravannes*: WILLIAM BRODERICK. *Cadeaux*: FREDERIC SOLOMON. *Eugene*: Charles Campbell. *Marquis*: Richard Guise. *Chevalier de Brabazon*: GEORGE HONEY. *Dufois*: Al Holbrook. *Simon*: Sol Solomon. *V. de B.* (Viscomte de Brissac): Frank Lynden.

1897.25

A ROUND OF PLEASURE

A Modern Extravaganza (Musical Comedy) in Three Acts, 6 Scenes. Book (and lyrics) by Sydney Rosenfeld. Music by Ludwig Engländer. Produced under the stage direction of Ben Teal. Ballets arranged by Carl Marwig. Settings by Ernest Albert. Costumes designed by F. Richard Anderson. Musical director, Paul Schindler. Produced by (Marc) Klaw and (Abraham L.) Erlanger. Opened 24 May 1897 at the Knickerbocker Theatre and closed 3 July 1897 after 42 performances; re-opened as ONE ROUND OF

[113]Musical numbers and specialties not listed in programs.
[114]First produced in New York 10 May 1886 at the Casino Theatre for 648 performances in a series of three engagements. For Synopsis of Scenes and Musical Numbers, see original 1886 production.
[115]Scenery and costumes uncredited.

PLEASURE (see detail immediately below) 23 August 1897 at the Knickerbocker Theatre and closed 4 September 1897 after 14 additional performances. Total: 56 performances[116].

CAST: *Welkin Ring*, who gives the "Round of Pleasure": JEROME SYKES. *Dr. Edson Beaten*, an inventor: WALTER JONES. *Duke of Marlinspike*, in whose honor the "Round" is given: RICHARD CARLE. *Moses Geezenbaum*, who tickets the Duke on the "Round": CHARLES KIRKE. *Domino Boomps, Dromio Schrumm*, a groom and a steward, who assist at the "Round of Pleasure": GUS ROGERS, MAX ROGERS. *Harry Spaulding*, in love with Aurora: Richard C. Bennett. *Ring's Daughters (2): Aurora*, Pride of My Heart: MARGUERITE SYLVA. *Niobe*, Pride of My Soul: MARIE CELESTE. *Miss Winsome*, Chief Executive of the Spinsters' Club: EVA DAVENPORT. *Mimi*, a French maid: JEANNETTE BAGEARD. *Mrs. Van Ogden*, one of society's leaders: Babette Rodney. *Willie Win*: Jessie Carlisle. *Jolly Game*: Clara Franton. *Soh Tyred*: Jessie Haynes.

Welkin Ring's Caddies: Misses Carlisle, Franton, Haynes, Curtis, Earle, Harris, Knell, Egan, Mayfield, Spencer, Hamilton, Harvey. *Welkin Ring's Golfing Guests*: Misses Dupont, Millward, Cramer, May, Haviland, DeLoen, Arthur, Sinclair, Clay, Benedict, Baird, Stone. Messrs. Weeks, Stanley, McKinley, Haines, Cheney, Sparks, Laidlaw, Farrington, Hammond, Kilrain, McGovern, Smiley, Soulea, Simonds, Stevens, Griniert. *Edson Beaten's Apprentices*: Misses Haynes, Franton, Marsh, Curtis, Skillman, Sennett, Hamilton, Chapman. *Members of the Spinster's Club*: Misses Egan, Baird, May, Spencer, DeLeon, Cramer, Wood, Harvey.

Act 1: Welkin Lodge.

Act 2, Scene 1: The Knickerbocker Theatre stage, and the Shakespearian Festival. *Scene 2*: In front of the Knickerbocker Theatre. *Scene 3*: Lobby of Madison Square Garden. *Scene 4*: Madison Square Garden.

Act 3: The Ballroom and Costume Ball.

ACT 1[117]

"Time Is Money"
W. Jones
(*Music and Lyrics by* James Thornton.[118])

Three Merry Cons
R. Carle, W. Jones, C. Kirke

Medley Trio
J. Bageard, G. Rogers, M. Rogers

The Dagger Dance
Misses Rochte, Piggott, Massoney, Hoope, Coogan, Ross, Hoope, Middleton.

ACT 2

Scene 1

Shakespearean Revue (Festival)
Othello, the dark horse: J. Sykes. *Iago*, the easy boss: W. Jones. *Hamlet*, the stubborn candidate: R. Carle. *Brutus, Cassius*, two ward heelers: G. Rogers, M. Rogers. *Richard III*: G York. *Shylock*, Chairman of the Committee: C. Kirke. *King Lear, Henry VIII*, Shakespearean kings out of a job: Mr. Farrington, Mr. Sparks. *Lady Macbeth*, leader of the opposition: E. Davenport. *Juliet*: M. Sylva. *Ophelia*: M. Celeste. *Romeo*: B. Rodney. *Desdemona*: J. Carlisle. *Others, more or less well-known*: Messrs. Weeks, Stevens, Stanley, Hain, McGovern, McKinley, Cheney, Laidlaw, Hammond, Grenoat, Simonds, Soulea. *Shakespeare's Heroines*: Misses Sennett, Millward, May, Arthur, Cramer, Baird, Uart, Benedict, Haviland, Martin, Skillman, Delaro, Harris, Wood, Harvey, Dupont, Sinclair, Stone, Mayfield, Davis. *Standard-Bearers, Courtiers, Pages*: Misses Rochte, Piggott, Massoney, Hoope, Coogan, Ross, Hoope, Middleton. *Jesters*: Misses Haynes, Franton, Knell, Curtis, Spencer, Egan, Marsh, DeLeon, Hamilton, Chapman, Earle, Clay.

The Vanishing Ballet

"Everybody Knows My Name"
J. Sykes
(*Music and Lyrics by* Charles Trevathan.)

Scene 2

A Bunch of Pleasure
G. Rogers, M. Rogers

Scene 4

Horse Show
Horse Show Guests: Misses Carlisle, Millward, Clay, Stone, Skillman, Hamilton, Martin, Dupont, Marsh, Mayfield, Benedict, Delaro, Hoope, Haviland, Sennett, Hoope, Coogan, Ross. Messrs. Weeks, Stevens, Stanley, McKinley, Hain, Cheney, Sparks, Laidlaw, Farrington, Hammond, Kilrain, Griniert, McGovern, Smiley, Soulea, Simonds. *Grooms*: Misses Franton, Haynes, Chapman, Knell, Harris, Earle, Curtis, Hamilton.

ACT 3

"The Villain Still Pursued Her"
W. Jones
(*Music and Lyrics by* James Thornton.)

"I Really Don't Know What You Mean"
E. Davenport, W. Jones
(*Music and Lyrics by* Richard Carle.)

Quadrille d'Honneur
Ladies and Gentlemen of the Company

PUBLISHED SCORE

"(In) The (Gay) Tenderloin" (Act 2)

"A Hard Boiled Egg"

"Teedelum, Tadelum" (Duet)

"I'm a Popular Man"

"The Easy Boss"

"Brain Wafers"
W. Jones

"I'm Going to Soliloquize"

"Nancy and I"

[116]Played a return engagement 1 November 1897 at the Harlem Opera House for 8 performances.

[117]Musical Numbers not listed in program for first month of the run, and interpolations only thereafter.

[118]Published sheet music credits authorship of this song to Walter Tilbury and Fred J. Barnes.

1897.25 ONE ROUND OF PLEASURE

A Revised Version of the Modern Extravaganza (A Round of Pleasure), in Two Acts, 4 Scenes. Book by Clay M. Greene and Syndey Rosenfeld. Music by Ludwig Engländer. Produced under the personal stage direction of Ben Teal. Ballet master, Carl Marwig. Produced by Messrs. (Marc) Klaw and (Abraham L.) Erlanger. Opened 23 August 1897 and closed 4 September 1897 after 14 performances.[119]

CAST: *Bluffingsby Flash*, as his name would imply, a humbug, exceedingly flippant and fly: WALTER JONES. *Moneyton Burn*, he had daughters twain, and of them and his money he was uppishly vain: H. W. TREDENICK. *Azalea Burn* was his queenly firtstborn, and she had a beau who was sadly love-lorn: IDA BROOKS. *Peone Burn* was her sister—a sprite, who upset papa's marital views with delight: MARIE CELESTE. *Ike Plum* was a barber; the plot of the play made him Duke of Westchester, a dude in his way: RICHARD CARLE. *Moses Rosenbaum* set all the traps of the plot, and sprung them as simply as dimes in a slot: CHARLES KIRKE. *Harry Undercover*, as you may have heard, was the beau who the heart of Azalea stirred: ROBERT A. MANSFIELD. *Pinochle*, a flunkey; supremely grotesque, such as are inevitable in burlesque: MAX ROGERS. *Schlopp* was his dread rival in love and in fun, and—well briefly, let's count these two mummers as one: GUS ROGERS. *Miss Winnie Weigh*, of the strong-minded type, exceedingly plump, fair and not over-ripe: Clara Wisdom. *Mimi*, a maid—French—bubbling over with grace, with all the chic and aplomb of her race: Edith St. Clair. *Then Golfers and Gypsies and Guests in array, completing the mis-en-scène with a Ballet.*

Characters in Shakespearean Festival in Act 2: *William Shakespeare*: W. Jones. *First Grave Digger*, Pat O'Toole: W. Jones. *Othello*: H. W. Tredenick. *Hamlet*: R. Carle. *Richard III*: R. A. Mansfield. *Brutus*: M. Rogers. *Cassius*: G. Rogers. *Shylock*: C. Kirke. *Lady Macbeth*: C. Wisdom. *Romeo*: I. Brooks. *Ophelia*: M. Celeste. *Juliet*: E. St. Clair. *Others more or less well known*: Messrs. Weeks, McKinley, Cheney, Laidlaw, Symonds, Wigley, Kilrain, Niles, McPherson, Harvey, Sparks, Kilduff, Rosen, Worthington.

Moneyton Burn's Caddies: Misses Franton, Knell, Curtis, Marsh, Skillman, M. Marsh, Hart, L. Hamilton, Harvey, Earle, Clay, Harris. *Moneyton Burn's Golfers*: Misses May, Cramer, Benedict, Millward, Williams, K. Hamilton, Dunne, Irving, Costello, Gordon, Gilson, Uart. Messrs. Cheney, McKinley, Harvey, Niles, Laidlaw, Sparks, Weeks, Kilduff, Rosen, Worthington, McPherson, Symonds. *Bluffington Flash's Apprentices*: Misses Franton, N. Marsh, Curtis, Skillman, Harris, L. Hamilton, Gilson, Earle. *Members of the Spinster's Club*: Misses May, Spencer, Cramer, Livingstone, Dunne, Harvey, Costello, Gordon, King. *Dagger Dance*: Misses Piggott, Ross, Massoney, Coogan, Gerard, Mabel Hart, Clayton, Roggiero. *Shakespeare's Heroines*: Misses May, K. Hamilton, Cramer, Livingstone, Benedict, Dunne, Harvey, Dore, Costello, Lee, Millward, Uart, M. Marsh, Jerome, Donelson, King, Selkirk, Jaxone, Gordon, Irving. *Standard Bearers, Courtiers, Pages*: Misses Piggott, Ross, Massoney, Coogan, Gerard, Roggiero, Clayton, Harte. *Jesters*: Misses Franton, Knell, N. Marsh, Curtis, Skillman, Harris, Earle, Gilson, L. Hamilton, Clay, Harte, Williams.

Act 1: Moneyton Lodge.

Act 2, Scene 1: The Knickerbocker Theatre Stage. *Scene 2*: Front of the Knickerbocker Theatre. *Scene 3*: The Ballroom.

[119]Scenery, costumes and musical director not credited in programs.

1897.26 THE WHIRL OF THE TOWN

A Musical Review (Comedy) in Three Acts, 7 Scenes[120]. Libretto by Hugh Morton. Music by Gustave Kerker. Staged by George W. Lederer. Ballets arranged by Signor A. Francioli. Settings by D. Frank Dodge and Frederick Dangerfield. Costumes designed by Mme. Caroline Siedle. Musical director, Gustave Kerker. Produced by George W. Lederer. Opened 25 May 1897 at the Casino Theatre and closed 25 September 1897 after 127 performances.

CAST: Act 1: *Jerry Flipflap*, formerly in the saloon business, now the Napoleon of the Theatrical World. His polish is that of the stove: LOUIS HARRISON. *Willie Badboy*, a rich kleptomaniac, the most fashionable thief to be found in the "smart set." The management cannot be responsible for jewelry, opera glasses, hats, umbrellas or false hair while Willie is in the theatre: DAN DALY. *Jakey*, of the firm of Jakey and Fritzy, music hall proprietors. If Welsh rarebits could talk, their language would probably sound like Jakey's: JOHN SLAVIN. *Fritzy*, Jakey's partner, who speaks Jakey's language, added to his own. Fritzy has to employ an interpreter to find out what he himself is talking about: HARRY MACDONOUGH. *Twiggum Knitt*, a lynx-eyed ferret from Scotland Yard, who will change his clothing several times during the evening without the use of a net: DAVID WARFIELD. *Captain Chapman*, a hero, whos historical whiskers cast a shade like the foliage of the oak over the iniquity of the Tenderloin: Henry Norman. *Homicidal Harry*, a patient assassin, who contributes to the gaiety of nations by working the grip of a cable car: Henry Norman. *Peter Salt*, a Skaneateles sailor, with main-top-gallant whiskers and a shifting quid: Henry Norman. *Bejaze Finnerty*, keeper of the Battery Park Aquarium, who possesses a brogue which requires investigation by the Board of Health: D. L. Don. *Jed Higgins*, from Pipville, Cattauraugus County, full of deviltry and doughnuts: GEORGE A. SCHILLER. *Marky Stayer*, a cheerful bird of night, who goes to bed only once in three days: Lee Harrison. *Mr. Tatters*, who runs into a Broadway cable car and is sued for damages by the managers of the road: Randolph Curry. *Terrence Dooley*, the driver of the night hawk, whose horse is occasionally run over by his cab: J. A. Furey. *Mr. Spangle*, the keeper of a wet restaurant in the neighborhood of Forty-Second Street: W. A. McCormick. *Officer McPhelim*, a copper-toed cop: William Black. *Biff, Bing*, a pair of host waiters in Spangles: George F. Campbell, Harry Earle. *Dimples*, a duck of a mermaid. She is a duck that the whole world chases: MADGE LESSING. *Evangeline Earlybird*, the Queen of the Night in upper Broadway, who eats her breakfast at nine in the evening: Catherine Linyard. *Dolly Twinklefoot*, a young lady with volatile limbs, who passes her life trying to kick the stars out of the sky: Marie George. *Molly*, a match girl, who has fire insurance on her life: HELEN BRACKETT. *A Quartette of vaudeville artists imported from London and Paris via Hackensack and Bergen Point*: *Velvet Kookoo*: Paula Edwards. *Cream Kookoo*: Claudia Carlstedt. *Peach Kookoo*: Ursula Gurnett. *Plush Kookoo*: Dorothy Drew. *Lona Barrison*, who is good to her horse: Marie George. *Teddie Trott*, a dear boy: Nelsy Chamberlain. *Gon Rong*, a Chinese giant: William Baker. *Major General Crumb*, a midget: Master Gustav Alexander. *Little Dot*, a fat lady: Marie Peters. (*Grand Pas de Seul*, Act 1: LA PETITE ADELAIDE.)

Chappies: Misses Nanette Nixon, Hattie Moore, Irene Bentley, Crissie Carlyle, Lucy Escott, Jane English, Nelsy Chamberlain, Lulu Harris, Mabel Power, Grace Pierrepont. *Soldiers, Sailors, German, Italian, Turkish Immigrants, Bowery Boys and Girls, Newsboys, Cab Drivers, Dime Museum Curiosities, Cable Car Gripmen, etc.*

Act 2: *Jerry Flipflap*, now manager of the Metropolitan Music Hall: LOUIS HARRISON. *Bill Martin*, a blooming buccaneer: LOUIS HARRISON. *La Hammersteena*, a premiere danseuse: LOUIS HARRISON. *Willie Badboy*, still stealing skillfully: DAN DALY. *Twiggum Knitt*, disguised as Solomon Solomon: DAVID WARFIELD. *Jakey, Fritzy*, whose dialect thickens with the plot: JOHN SLAVIN, HARRY MacDONOUGH. *Goosefoot Googan*, a dealer in Mick's drinks: D. L. DON. *Rusharound Whizz*, a base drummer for a wholesale cloak house: W. A. McCormick. *John Rosemary Drew*: GEORGE A. SCHILLER. *Beppo*, the same old innkeeper: LEE HARRISON. *Magnificent monuments of the past, now in ruins (4)*: *Charles Frohman*: Frank Casey. *Daniel Frohman*: Charles L. Dox. *A. M. Palmer*: Harry Earle. *Augustin Daly*: Randolph Curry. *O Mimosa San*, Queen of the Geishas: MADGE LESSING. *Mlle. Otero*, who dances with her voice and sings with her feet: GERTRUDE ZELLA. *Ruth*, the Josie Hall girl: Catherine Linyard. *The Kookoo Sisters (4)*: *Tottie*: Paula Edwards. *Maude*: Claudia Carlstedt. *Annabelle*: Ursula Gurnett. *Cora*: Dorothy Drew. *Mrs. Jerry Flipflap*, Jerry's wife, who is as loud as Sousa's Band: Helen Brackett. *Jean De Reszke*: W. Hethart. *El Capitan*: William Black. *Mme. Bernhardt*: Ray Allen. *Mme. Calve*: Catherine Linyard. *McJones*, a detective: Randolph Curry. *Dreamful Charley*, a District Telegraph Messenger: William Dunlay. *Flower Girls*: Misses Rose Witt, Bobby Burns, Irene Bentley, Alice Loraine, Nellie Loomis, Beatrice Lennox, Sophie Witt, Ida Doerge. *Geisha Girls and Boys*: *Girls*: Misses Jane English, Ray Allen, Grace Franton, Sophie Witt, Rosie Witt, Irene Bentley, Nelsy Chamberlain, Margie Lytton, Lulu Harris, Ida Doerge. *Boys*: Bobby Burns, Kitty Lawrence, Nellie Loomis, Adele McKaye, Alice Lorraine, May Sherwood. *Pirates, Villagers, Sailors, Waiters, Men-about-town, etc.*

Act 3: *Jerry Flipflap*: LOUIS HARRISON. *Willie Badboy*: DAN DALY. *Neptune*, Monarch of the Ocean, including Manhattan Beach: D. L. DON. *Mr. Fitzsimmons*, a lobster: W. A. McCORMICK. *Twiggum Knitt*: DAVID WARFIELD. *Dimples*: MADGE LESSING. *A Mermaid*: Hattie Moore. *Bicycle Girls*: Misses Paula Edwards, Dorothy Drew, Ursula Gurnett, Claudia Carlstedt, Crissie Carlyle, Rosie Witt, Sophie Witt, Nelsy Chamberlain. *Mermaids, Naiads, and Sailors.*

Act 1, Scene 1: The Interior of the Aquarium on Battery Park, New York. *Scene 2*: The Front of Jakey and Fritzy's Music Hall on Broadway. *Scene 3*: Broadway and Forty-Second Street at 1 A.M. (All painted by D. Frank Dodge.)

Act 2, Scene 1: The Parterre Promenade in the Metropolitan Music Hall, formerly the Metropolitan Opera House. *Scene 2*: A Lobby in the Metropolitan Music Hall. *Scene 3*: The Stage of the Metropolitan Music Hall, during the performance of a review entitled "In Gay Hoboken." (All painted by D. Frank Dodge.)

Act 3: The Cave of Jewels, Neptune's Summer Home off Coney Island. (Painted by Frederick Dangerfield.)

MUSICAL NUMBERS[121]

"What Would They Say"
M. Lessing
"The Original Todd"
"Lead On, Ebeneezer"
"Cable Car Gripman"
"Darling Little Yum Yum"
"From the Battery to Harlem"
"I'm a Captain Bold and Haughty"
"A Girl Is Nothing But a Rose" (Girls Are Nothing But Roses)
"One, Two, Three"
"My Estelle"
"Louisa"
"Little Yaller Boy"
"Mary Ellen Brown"
"Little Birds Learning to Fly"
"The Old Days"
"Nancy Hogan's Ball"
"Tricky Little Sarah"
"Oh, Willie Boy!" (Oh Willie, Don't You Lose Me)
The Ballet of Night Owls and Innocent Birdies (Scene 3)
Birdies: Misses Rosie Witt, Ida Doerge, Ada LaRose, Alice Loraine, Agnes Enright, Nannie Devere. *Owls*: Misses Sophie Witt, Ray Allen, Lulu Parker, Grace Franton, Agnes Baker, Benne Hoffman. Mlle. Catherina Bartho. *Spirit of Champagne* (Grand Pas de Seul): La Petit Adelaide.
"Meet Me Down at Huyler's"
"Pull Away, Boys, Said the Captain"
"Roxiana Dooley"
"When the Clock Strikes Two in the Tenderloin"
"Wine, Wine, Wine"
"Nobody Was in Love"

[120]Billed as the Fourth Annual Review at the Casino, presented by George W. Lederer.

[121]Interpolated during the run as per published sheet music:
"Sadie, My Lady"
Theresa Vaughn
(*Music by* John W. Bratton. *Lyrics by* Walter H. Ford.)

1897–1898 SEASON

James T. Powers in THE CIRCUS GIRL (Photo: Sarony, April 23, 1897)
Museum of the City of New York, Gift of Mrs. James T. Powers, 46.246.238

1897–1898 SEASON

1897.27 CAPTAIN COOK

A Comic Opera in Three Acts. Libretto by Sands W. Forman. Music by Noah Brandt. Production by E. Arden Nobelett and D. E. Barnet. Musical director, Noah Brandt. Opened 12 July 1897 at Madison Square Garden and closed 24 July 1897 after 14 performances.[1]

CAST: *King Kalanopan*: ETHAN ALLEN. *Captain (James) Cook*: FRED MARSTON. *Mairley*: FRED FREAR. *Cupples*: Camm Mauvel. *Gaffsail*: Fred Runnells. *Buntline*: Sol Solomon. *Reefer*: Pauline Rellum. *Captain Franklin*: William Gillon. *Oponuii*: TOM GREEN. *Koko Bola*: FRED SOLOMON. *(Princess) Ia Ia*: MARIE CELESTE. *Like Like*: Laura Pardy. *Hula Hula*: Ruth White. *Attendant*: JENNIE ST. CLAIR. *Pele*, the Goddess: Amelia Mayeroffer. *Kahawale*: Alberto Biancifori.

Scene: Hawaii.

1897.28 VERY LITTLE FAUST AND MUCH MARGUERITE

An Opera Bouffe in Three Acts, 4 Scenes. Book and lyrics by Richard F. Carroll, "with due apologies to Gounod and Goethe." (Adapted from the French opéra-bouffe "Le Petit Faust," libretto by Hector Crémieux and Adolphe Jaime.) Music by Florimond Hervé and Fred J. Eustis[2]. Added lyrics by Clement King. Stage director, Alf. C. Whelan. Scenery by R. Brunton. Costumes by Mmes. Kelly and Eaves. Musical director, Fred J. Eustis. Produced by the Parry Opera Company (William Parry). Opened 23 August 1897 at Hammerstein's Olympia Theatre and closed 4 September 1897 after 16 performances.[3]

CAST: *Marguerite*, the Maiden: DOROTHY MORTON. *Mephisto*, the Devil: TRULY SHATTUCK. *Jess Tryon*, the Prize Scholar: ALLENE CRATER. *The School Girls (3)*: *Lisette*: Alice Campbell. *Aglae*: Floye Redlidge. *Frosch*: Bettie Kennedy. *Siebel*, the Boy: Delia Stacey. *Faust*, the Doctor: HARRY LUCKSTONE. *H. Moses*, the Tutor: ALF C. WHELAN. *Phul*, the Cabby: Edward H. Carroll. *J. Norman Bull*, the Anglo-Saxon: ALF C. WHELAN. *The School Boys (4)*: *Wagner*: Henrietta Austin. *Altmeyer*: Anne Verdell. *Fritz*: Lee Easton. *Franz*: June Dale. *Tips, Taps*, the Waiters: Ernest Arthur, Jack Hayes. *B. Brummell*, the Old Chappy: John Belton. *Corporal Junks, Captain Jinks*, the Officers: Beatrice Hamilton, Florence Bell. *Valentine*, the Comic: RICHARD F. CARROLL. *Chorus of Scholars, Soldiers, Saxons, Students, Sinners, Sprites, and Spirits*. Performance concludes with Luigi Albertieri's realistic pantomimic sketch, "A Night in Naples."

Act 1: Dr. Faust's Kindergarten.

Act 2: Jardin de Rouffe, Paris.

Act 3, Scene 1: Marguerite's Boudoir. Scene 2: Mephisto's Palace.

1897.29 NATURE

A Grand Elaborate Spectacle in Four Acts, 9 Scenes. Play by William E. DeVerna and James Schönberg. Original vocal and instrumental music composed by Frederick Clifton. Directed by William Lytell. Ballets invented and arranged by Mlle. Bonfanti and Signor Baratti. Marches and processions arranged by William Lytell. Settings by Frank Platzer, M. E. Bloom and Hugh Logan Reid. Costumes by Hugo Baruch & Co. (Berlin), Mme. Chrisdie and Mlle. Millie Gray (New York). Properties, accessories and appointments by William E. DeVerna, his sons Frederick and William, William Perkins. Mechanical effects by William Crane, Robert Murray and William Vail. Produced by William E. DeVerna and Benjamin Cohen. Opened 26 August 1897 at the Academy of Music and closed 9 October 1897 after 52 performances.[4]

CAST: Mortals: *Sir John Hampton*, Commander of the *"Erebus"* Polar Expedition: EDWIN C. HOFF. *Hans Schultz*, a faithful Teuton: JOSEPH CAWTHORN. *Lieutenant Hugh Bassett*, First Officer of the *"Erebus"*: Lloyd Melville.

Crew of the "Erebus": *Brace*: Frank Melrose. *Gordon*: F. Lyden. *Galley*: J. Witt. *Scudder*: D. Moore. *Ratline*: W. A. Lawrence. *Tug*: H. Verney. *Scupper*: F. A. Smiley. *Rowlock*: W. V. Gaffney. *Bowline*: Neil Gray. *Lawyard*: H. Steinmann. *Sharp*: A. H. Ransome. *Hamper*: J. C. Cheviot. *Belayer*: R. Rudolfy. *Spike*: O. Saunse. *Keelson*: H. Rowe. *Rudder*: T. G. Goodwin.

Katrina, a schöne Fräuleine: Marie Osborn. *Alice Woodfern*, Sir John's affianced: Annie Dagwell.

Esquimaux Women, Immortals: *Nature*: AMELIA BINGHAM. *Psyche*, Queen of Iscalia: ELAINE GRYCE. *Vacuna*, her attendant: Lillian Comyns. *Una*, Queen of the White Spirits: HELEN BORIS. *Cupid*, Son of Venice: ROSO MARSTON.

Ladies of King Rap's Court: *Sulphurine*: J. Lavis. *Demonia*: R. Miley. *Rimmoni*: J. Howard. *Nicerina*: E. Hoffman. *Ahrimanne*: L. Jeffreys. *Styxadi*: F. Sherwood. *Noxetta*: K. Spero. *Vertutta*: A. Cameron. *Emonide*: B. Hardy. *Azraeli*: Alice Potter. *Satanee*: E. Vincent. *Ezzelini*: A. May. *Luciferi*: B. Sannee. *Zamiello*: N. McGuire. *Plutorini*: M. Glover. *Lethero*: A. Newton. *Venomee*: A. Gray. *Sturgato*: A. E. Cameron. *Fairies Niads, Nymphs of Iscalia, Kelpies, Amazonian Warriors, White Spirits*.

Rap, King of Fire: FREDERICK CLIFTON. *Demons, Gnomes, Imps, Guards, Banner and Trophy Bearers, Sprites, Grotesques, and Attendants on Rap*. *Sprites*: The Lessard Family. (*Ballet*: Mlle. AMELIA SBERNA, Mlle. ADDIE RENNÉE, Fifty Coryphees.)

1897.30 THE GOOD MR. BEST

Rich & Harris' All-Star Comedy Company in a Musical Farce in Three Acts. Libretto by John J. McNally. Music by Henry J. Sayers, Tom LeMack, and Frederick Dana. Produced under the stage direction of R. A. Roberts. (Dances arranged by Sam Marion.) Settings by Joseph Physioc and John A. Thompson. Costumes by Simpson, Crawford & Simpson; and Mme. Hughes, New York. Music arranged by Jesse Williams. Produced by (Isaac B.) Rich and (William) Harris. Opened 30 August 1897 at the Garrick Theatre and closed 11 September 1897 after 16 performances.

CAST: *Tom Best*, exploiter of difficulties: R. A. ROBERTS. *Maximilian Juraez O'Keefe*, an Irish Cuban, his uncle: JOHN G. SPARKS. *Mrs. Isabella Best*, Tom's wife: CAMILLE CLEVELAND. *Marion Agnes McAleer*, minus a past, seeking a future: Mrs. ANNIE YEAMANS. *Gretchen Slowe*, a maid of muddles: JOSIE SADLER. *Bessie*, O'Keefe's daughter: Mae Crossley. *Marmaduke Mush*: JOSEPH COYNE. *Dick Ranger*, man of mystery: JULIUS P. WITMARK. *Marcelle Renaud*, who improves an opportunity: Kate Dale. *Hardis Lotte*, terpsichorean artist: SAM MARION. *Will Fetch*: James H. Cavanaugh. *Ed Kauffman*: J. J. Fisher. *Captain Watchhalle*: J. J. Fisher. *Charlie Onatime*: C. H. Weston. *Jim Holden*: Lawrence J. Sheehan. *Nanette*: Georgie Lawrence. *Lizette*: Emma Levey. (*Specialties*: CLAYTON SISTERS.)

Ladies of the Marcelle Melodramatic Company: *Lottie*: Ruby Capen. *Tottie*: Edith Shaw. *Dottie*: Marie Roselle. *Hattie*: Carrie Francis. *Mattie*: Eva Lowell. *Mamie*: Jennie St. Clair. *Sadie*: Laura Loesch. *Kittie*: Ada LeRoy. *Bertie*: Lillian Jerome. *Haidie*: Florence Raymond. *Carrie*: Julie Raymond.

Act 1: Tim Best's taxidermist shop. New York City.

Act 2: Tom Best's Turkish smoking parlors, New York City.

Act 3: Tim Best's home, New York City.

ACT 2

"Flowers of the Harem" (Opening Chorus)
Clayton Sisters, Company

"Mammy's Little Pumpkin-Colored Coons" (Plantation Slumber Song)
J. P. Witmark, Company
(*Music by* Sideny Perrin. *Lyrics by* George Hillman.)

"Puff, Puff"
C. Cleveland, Clayton Sisters, G. Lawrence,
C. Francis, E. Levey, R. Capen, L. Pardy, M DeLeon

"The Dancing Turk"
A. Yeamans

"Zim Boom Ta-ra" (Medley)
J. J. Fisher, Misses St. Clair, Loesch, Roselle, Shaw, Lowell, LeRoy

"Waltz of the Mazy"
C. Cleveland, Company

"The Swellest Thing in Town"
J. Coyne, assisted by Misses Lawrence, Dueth, LeRoy, Company

"Sadie, My Lady"
J. P. Witmark, Company
(*Music by* John W. Bratton. *Lyrics by* Walter H. Ford.)

Topical Trio
R. A. Roberts, J. G. Sparks, C. Cleveland

"Beautiful, Gay Paree" (Song and Dance)
S. Marion, J. Coyne, L. Young, I. Winship
Attendants: Misses F. Raymond, J. Raymond, L. Jerome. *Visitors*: Misses Pardy, Levey, Dueth, Messrs. Cavanaugh, Lang, Haynes.

[1] No program available.
[2] Hervé provided the music for the original French production; Eustis provided the American interpolations.
[3] No musical numbers listed in programs.
[4] No musical numbers listed in programs.

ACT 3

"O'Dooley's First Five O'Clock Tea"
J. G. Sparks, Company
(*Music by* Frederic Dana. *Lyrics by* Paul West [Philip Waldron].)

"If I Could Only Get a Decent Sleep"
J. Sadler

"Beautiful, Gay Paree" (Finale)
Company

1897.31

THE GLAD HAND/ SECRET SERVANTS

A Burlesque in Two Acts, preceded by an Olio. Book (and lyrics) by Kenneth Lee. Music by John Stromberg. Produced under the direction of Julian Mitchell. Costumes from Simpson, Crawford & Simpson. Musical direction, John Stromberg. Produced by Joseph M. Weber and Lew M. Fields. Opened 2 September 1897 at Weber & Fields' Broadway Music Hall and closed 1 December 1897 after 103 performances.

OLIO[5]

Carbos Brothers (Marvelous Acrobats)

McIntyre and Heath (Bad Man from Montana)

Marie Loftus (England's great character vocalist)

CAST: *Micah Book*: PETER F. DAILEY. *The Lord of Bashbury Beach*: CHARLES J. ROSS. *Mike Koffupski*: JOSEPH M. WEBER. *Augustus Miller*: LEW M. FIELDS. *Harold Meyer*: SAM BERNARD. *Bowles*, the landlord: JOHN T. KELLY. *The Katrina*, his daughter: Lillian Swain. *Lieutenant Astorbilt*: Sylvia Thorne. *Pietro*, the Pirate: Gertrude Mansfield. *Dora, Flora*: The Beaumont Sisters. *Nora*: Josephine Allen. *Little Klondike*: FRANKIE BAILEY. *First Officer*: FRANKIE BAILEY.

Cadets: Misses Florence Bell, Genevieve Clifton, Helen Dunbar McLellan, Edith Merrill. *Sailors, Summer Girls, Waitresses, etc.*: Misses Dunbar, Cora Carlisle, Margot Hobart, Dora Webb, Ida Moreland, Lucy Escott, Genevieve Dolaro, Natta Stromberg, Frankie Loeb, Della Clayton, May Guthbert, Helen Robinson, Marion Langdon, Minnie Poore, Alma Monte. *Waiters, Soldiers, etc.*: Messrs. M. Renner, G. Thomas, W. Russel, W. West.

During Act 2, the thrilling drama SECRET SERVANTS (a Burlesque of the play by William Gillette "Secret Service")[6] for the Sailors' Mothers-in-Law Fund.

SECRET SERVANTS CAST: *Edith Blarney Mitford*: MABEL FENTON. *William Gellatine*: CHARLES J. ROSS. *Peter Dumont Arrelsford*: PETER F. DAILEY. *Whatsisname*: JOHN T. KELLY. *Sergeant Wilson*: JOSEPH M. WEBER. *Sergeant Ellington*: LEW M. FIELDS. *Corporal Matson*: SAM BERNARD. *Telegraph Operator*: G. Thomas.

Act 1: Bowles Hotel, at Bashbury Beach. Departure of the "*Glad Hand*."

Act 2: On the deck of the "*Glad Hand*." Performance of "Secret Servants" for the Sailors' Mothers-in-Law Fund.

MUSICAL NUMBERS[7]

"How I Love My Lou"
P. Dailey
(*Lyrics by* Edgar Smith and Louis deLange.)

"If You Love Me Truly"
S. Thorne

"The Glad Hand"

1897.32

IN TOWN

Mr. George Edwardes' London Gaiety Theatre Burlesque Company in a Musical Farce in Two Acts. Libretto by Adrian Ross and James T. Tanner[8]. Music by Dr. F. Osmond Carr. Staged by J. E. A. Malone. Dances arranged by Willie Warde. Costumes by Wilhelm. Musical direction by Harold Vicars. Produced by Al Hayman and Charles Frohman. Opened 6 September 1897 at the Knickerbocker Theatre and closed 9 October 1897 after 40 performances[9].

CAST: *Captain Arthur Coddington*, a man about town: W. LOUIS BRADFIELD. *The Duke of Duffshire*: LAWRENCE CAIRD. *Lord Clanside*, his son: FLORENCE LLOYD. *Rev. Samuel Hopkins*, his chaplain: LEEDHAM BANTOCK. *Hoffman*: Fritz Rimma. *Benoli*: Arthur Hope. *Shrimp*, a call boy: Claire Romaine. *Bloggings*, a solicitor's clerk: E. G. Woodhouse. *Duchess of Duffshire*: MRS. EDMUND PHELPS. *Lady Gwendoline Kincaddie*, her daughter: MARIE STUDHOLME. *Kitty Hetherton*, a Prima Donna: MINNIE HUNT. *Maud Montresor*, a Gaiety girl: Maud Hobson. *Flo Fanshawe*, a Dancer: Rosie Boote.

Gaiety Girls: *Edith*: Violet Trelawny. *May*: Daisy Jackson. *Lottie*: Kitty Adams. *Lillie*: Marjorie Pryor. *Ethel*: Lottie Williams. *Rose*: Dora Nelson. *Clara*: Norma Whalley.

Juliet Belleville: JULIETTE NESVILLE. *Pas de Trois*: Mlles. Lottie Williams, Daisy Jackson, Rosie Boote.

Act 1: Vestibule of the Hotel Caravanserai.

Act 2: Green Room of the Gaiety Theatre.

ACT 1[10]

"The Hotel Caravanserai" (Opening Chorus)

"Welcome, welcome" (Chorus and Entry of Duke)
Chorus

"The House of Lords"
L. Caird, M. Studholme, F. Lloyd, L. Bantock, Mrs. E. Phelps, Chorus

"Dear Mamma" (Duet)(The Golden Mean)
Mrs. E. Phelps, M. Studholme

"The Man About Town" (Song)
W. L. Bradfield

"Tarradiddle" (Trio)
W. L. Bradfield, L. Bantock, F. Lloyd

"Ambiguity Girls" (Chorus)

"A Heart That is Still the Same" (Song)
M. Hunt, Chorus

"A Balcony Scene" (Duet)(The Waltz Refrain)
W. L. Bradfield, M. Hunt

"Drinks of the Day" (Song)
W. L. Bradfield

Pas Seul
R. Boote

"Hurrah for the Girls" (Finale)

ACT 2

"Romeo and Juliet" (Opening Chorus)

"The Call-Boy" (Call-Boy's Song)
C. Romaine

"Dreamless Rest" (Song)
M. Hunt

"The Strict Game" (Duet)
F. Lloyd, W. L. Bradfield

Pas de Deux
R. Boote, F. Lloyd

"The Maid with a Wink in Her Eye" (Ballad)
M. Hunt

"Milord Sir Smith"[11] (Song)
W. L. Bradfield

"My Propensities Are All the Other Way" (Song)
L. Caird

"I Do Not Mind" (Duet)
L. Caird, L. Bantock

"Friar Larry" (Song and Chorus)
W. L. Bradfield, Chorus

Finale

1897.33

A HOT OLD TIME

A Musical Farce in Three Acts. Play, music and lyrics by Edgar Selden. Scenery by C. W. Valentine. Musical director, Emil Biermann. Produced by the Rays (Johnny, Emma). Management, Edgar Selden. Opened 6

[5]No musical numbers listed in programs.
[6]Scenery uncredited. SECRET SERVANTS was replaced after opening by THE WORST BORN, a Burlesque of Francis Powers' play "The First Born" produced by Belasco. For detail, see entry at 2 December 1897.
[7]Musical numbers not listed in programs.
[8]In London the libretto was credited to Adrian Ross and James Leader.
[9]Played a return engagement 29 November 1897 at the Harlem Opera House for 8 performances.

[10]Musical numbers not listed in programs. List prepared from published English vocal score (J. Williams, London, 1892). Published music indicates that Ross did the lyrics.
[11]Published sheet music calls this The Famous Cafe Chantant Song.

September 1897 at the Third Avenue Theatre and closed 11 September 1897 after 8 performances; returned 27 December 1897 to the Grand Opera House and closed 1 January 1898 after 8 additional performances.[12]

CAST: *Larry Mooney*, of Mooney's Express: JOHNNY RAY. *General Stonewall Blazer*, great man—in his mind: JOHN C. LEACH. *Jack Treadwell*, quarter back at Yale: FRANK LALOR. *Alkali Ike*, from the wooly West: BERNARD DYLLYN. *Cholly Knickerbocker*, too sweet to live: Eva A. Gambles[13]. *O'Donovan Dunn*, M. P., first to visit America: Hugh Converse. *Officer Chase*, a suburban policeman: George Sparkes. *Prairie Pete*, a Yellowstone guide: James Talbert[14]. *Blossom Blazer, Cherry Blazer*, the General's daughters, ripe for picking: BLANCHE WASHBURN, RENE WASHBURN[15]. *Marjorie Daw*, their city chum: Josie Claflin. *Sallie Waters*, their country chum: Pearle Alexander. *Juno Hawthorne*, a Summer girl: Mabel Bonner. *Winifred Mayfair*, a merry maiden: Lillian Marlborough. *Mrs. General Stonewall Blazer*, boss of the whole outfit: EMMA RAY.

Act 1: Blazer Villa on the Hudson.

Act 2: The Library.

Act 3: Yellowstone Park.

MUSICAL NUMBERS[16]

"A Hot Old Time"

"Can't Understand It at All"

"Alkali Ike"

"On the Yellowstone"

Specialties
Washburn Sisters; B. Dyllyn; the Rays

1897.34 A STRANGER IN NEW YORK

Hoyt and McKee's Musical Comedy Company in a Farce Comedy with Music in Three Acts. Play and lyrics by Charles H. Hoyt. Music by Richard Stahl. Staged by Charles H. Hoyt. Settings by Arthur Voegtlin. Costumes by Will H. Barnes. Produced by Charles H. Hoyt and Franklin McKee. Opened 13 September 1897 at the Garrick Theatre, moved 6 November 1897 to Hoyt's Theatre and closed 8 January 1898 after 136 performances[17].

CAST: *A Stranger in New York*—name, residence and business not stated: HARRY CONOR. *Wright Innit*, a gentleman of leisure. Address Manhattan, Lotos or Lambs clubs: LLOYD WILSON. *Carroll Sweet*, his particular friend. Same address: ARTHUR PACIE. *Cumming Swift*, a Chicago clubman, well known in New York: CHARLES WARREN. *J. Collier Downe*, his friend, celebrated as a brilliant wit: GEORGE A. BEANE. *Baron Sands*, one of the old guard of Delmonico's: HARRY GILFOIL. *Will Chase*, a lady's brother: John Hyams. *Wiley Fox*, a private detective: William F. Ryan. *Handel Grubb*, a colored waiter: Jules Jordan. *Haight Work*, a colored valet: Joseph Williamson. *Cal O. Mellish*, officer of Board of Health: William F. Ryan. *Doolittle*, doorman, Hoffman House: Jules Jordan. *Clymen*, hall-boy, Hoffman House: Joseph Williamson. *Ida Dowhe*, wife of I. Collier Downe, a soft thing: Margaret Fitzpatrick. *Virginia Pryde*, a Richmond belle: Nellie Butler. *May Ketchum*, a society spy: AMELIA STONE. *Rosie Hope*, of the chorus: Aimee Angeles. *Kittie Wins*, of the chorus: Leah Angeles. *Wanda Knights*, who has "spoken lines": Amy Muller. *Fairy Storey*, one of the crowd: Grace Freeman. *Hattie*, "the best fellow of them all": SADIE MARTINOT.

Act 1: In the reception-room of the Hoffman House.

Acts 2 and 3: A room in the Madison Square Garden, in the city of New York, on the day and evening of the famous "French Ball."

MUSICAL NUMBERS[18]

"The Broadway Beauty Show"

"Love's Serenade"

Quintette

"Hattie"

"Lou and Sue"

"The Swellest Cullud Lady of Them All" (A Dead Swell Cullud Lady)

"The Gayest Old Sport"

"Mary Jane Marie"
S. Martinot

"The Sign of Love"

"Miss Helen Hunt"
H. Conor
(*Music and Lyrics by* Harry Conor.)

"When Someone Pulls the String"

"Walter's Dancing School"
(*Music by* A. Baldwin Sloane.)

"Father, Won't You Speak to Sister Mary"
(*Music by* A. Baldwin Sloane.)

1897.35 THE FAIR IN MIDGETTOWN

The Lilliputians in a Spectacular Play with Music in Four Acts, 11 Scenes, in German and English. Play by Robert Breitenbach. Music by Victor Hollaender. (Produced under the stage direction of Carl Rosenfeld.) Produced by Carl and Theodore Rosenfeld. Opened 20 September 1897 at the Star Theatre and closed 6 November 1897 after 56 performances.

CAST: *The Lilliputians*: *Brickfellow*: Mr. Wilke. *Maggie*: Mrs. Griebe. *Mary*: ELISE LAU. *Dr. Brown*: Mr. Hartwig. *Fatman*: HERMANN RING. *Allen*: TONI MEISTER. *Joe, Freelunch*: MAX WALTER, FRANZ EBERT. *Soap*: ADOLPHE ZINK. *Azale*: SELMA GOERNER. *First Lackey*: Mr. Ludwig. *Second Lackey*: Mr. Zeidler. *Valet*: Mr. Juhnke. *First Policeman*: Mr. Korn. *Second Policeman*: Mr. Werner. *General Grant*: HELENE LINDNER. (*Dance Solos*: Pepitta, Rositta.)

Act 1, Scene 1: In Stockfellow's House. *Scene 2*: The Voyage to Midgettown. *Scene 3*: The Fair in Midgettown. *Scene 4*: The Five Senses.

Act 2, Scene 1: Transmigration. *Scene 2*: Newspaperdom.

Act 3, Scene 1: Disturbed Slumbers. *Scene 2*: Bathing: The Fatal Cinematograph. *Scene 3*: Rulers of the World.

Act 4, Scene 1: Japanese Dreams. *Scene 2*: At Home.

ACT 1
Scene 4

The Five Senses (Ballet): Dream Sylphides-Touch, Taste, Smell, Sight, Hearing
Corps de Ballet

Chorus of the Spaniards
Lilliputians

ACT 2
Scene 2

Newspaperdom (Ballet): Telegraph Boys, Reporters, Editors, Letters, Figures, Advertisements
Corps de Ballet

Black and White (Ballet Solo)
Pepitta, Rositta
The Lilliputians and Newsboys of New York

---

[12]Revised by George M. Cohan for subsequent tour the following season and advertised as Second Edition, Management of Edward A. Braden. Added to the score were:

"Rag-Time Night on Broadway," "A Funny Little Man," "A Dangerous Man from Denver," "Hero of the Football Game," "A Hot Old Time," "Why Did They Sell Killarney?," "Dewey's Reception," "I Guess I'll Have to Telegraph My Baby," "I Guess I'll See His Finish Pretty Soon," "The Wild and Wooley West," "True Daughters of Old Uncle Sam," "Are You Done, Mr. Dunn" etc.

[13]Succeeded for return engagement by Gilbert Girard.

[14]Succeeded for return engagement by B. D. Smith.

[15]Succeeded for return engagement by Kitty Nelson and Madeline Marshall.

[16]Interpolated for subsequent tour, as per published sheet music:

"Playing Da Golden Strings"
(*Music and Lyrics by* Samuel H. Speck.)

"The Blue and the Gray, or a Mother's Gift to the Country"
The Rays
(*Music and Lyrics by* Paul Dresser.)

[17]Also played return engagements 10 April 1898 at the Star Theatre for 8 performances, 29 August 1898 at the Harlem Opera House for 8 performances, 14 November 1898 at the Grand Opera House for 8 performances, and 28 November 1898 at the Columbus Theatre for 8 performances.

[18]Not listed in programs. List prepared from published sheet music, reviews, etc. Added for subsequent tour, as per published sheet music:

"You Once Were Excess Baggage, Now You'se Only Common Freight"
A. Boyd
(*Music by* A. Baldwin Sloane. *Lyrics by* Sanmenig and Robb.)

ACT 3
Scene 3
World's Armies (Ballet): Procession; Americans at Revolutionary Times; Frenchmen, American Cadets and Cavalary; Russians; English Guard; Prussian Infantry and Guards; the Lilliputians as George Washington, Napoleon I, Nicholas II, Queen Victoria, General Grant, Emperor I, Bismarck. Apotheosis.

1897.36 HALF A KING

A Revival of the Comic Opera in Three Acts[19]. Libretto by Harry B. Smith. Adapted from the French (opérette "Le Roi de carreau," libretto by Eugène Leterrier and Albert Vanloo[20]). Music by Ludwig Engländer. Produced under the direction of Richard Barker. Settings by Henry E. Hoyt and Richard Marston. Costumes designed by Percy Anderson. Musical direction, W. H. Batchelor. Produced by Francis Wilson and Company (Management, Ariel Barney). Opened 20 September 1897 at the Broadway Theatre and closed 23 October 1897 after 35 performances[21].

CAST: *Tireschappe*, a mountebank: FRANCIS WILSON. *Mistigris*, his factotum: PETER LANG. *Duke de la Roche-Trumeau*: JOHN BRAND. *Duke de Chateau Margaux*: JOSEPH CHARLES MIRON. *Honore*, his son: Clinton Elder. *Benoit*, his major-domo: Edward P. Temple. *Vagabonds (3)*: *Jean de Loup*: Charles H. Bowers. *Gigolet*: William Laverty. *Casin Challie*: Samuel Chadwick. *Officer*: Joseph T. Chaillee. *Pierette*, Tireschappe's adopted daughter: LULU GLASER. *Lucinde*, daughter of Duke de la Roche-Trumeau: CELESTE WYNN. *Simplice*, secretary to Duke de la Roche-Trumeau: Albert Parr. *Stella*: Della Niven. *Duchess*: Bessie Howard. *Chorus of grisettes, students, vagabonds, servants, soldiers, wedding guests, etc.*

1897.37 THE FRENCH MAID

A Musical Comedy in Two Acts[22]. Libretto by Basil Hood. Music by Walter Slaughter. Staged by Frederick A. Leon. Ballets arranged by Augustus Sohlke. Settings by Frank Rafter and D. Frank Dodge. Costumes by Mme. M. L. Dowling. Musical director, Herman Perlet. Produced by Edward E. Rice. Opened 27 September 1897 at the Herald Square Theater and closed 19 February 1898 after 170 performances.

CAST: *Admiral Sir Hercules Hawser*, K.C.B.: JOHN GOURLAY. *The Maharajah of Punkapore*: HENRY LEONI. *General Sir Drummond Fife*, V.C.: EDWARD S. WENTWORTH. *Charles Brown*, a waiter: CHARLES A. BIGELOW. *Jack Brown*, a sailor: HALLEN MOSTYN. *Paul Leguire*, a gendarme: HENRY NORMAN. *Monsieur Camambert*, maître d'hotel: GEORGE HONEY. *Lieutenant Harry Fife*, R.N.: WILLIAM ARMSTRONG. *Alphonse*, French waiter: Charles E. Sturgis. (*Willie Splint*: Charles E. Sturgis.) *Dorothy Travers*: ANNA ROBINSON. *Lady Hercules Hawser*: EVA DAVENPORT. *Madame Camambert*: Yolande Wallace. *Marie*, a chambermaid: Leonora Ginto. *Jeanette*: Florence Wells. *Suzette*, the French maid: MARGUERITA SYLVA. (*Dance Specialty*: Saharet, the Great Australian Dancer.) *Tourists, Peasants, Garçons, Femmes de Chambres, etc.*

Bon Bon Ballet: Maud Sohlke, Frances Wilson, Mazie Follette, May Bradley, Carol Glover, Mollie Gaylor, Minnie Gaylor, Carrie May. *Froliques Française*: Gypsey Grant, Fannie Burkhardt, Millie Tait, Beatrice Tait. *Carnival Promenade Ballet*: Alma Desmond, Dorothy Kendall, Maud Chandler, Gabrielle DeThien, Florence Dressler, Netta Scarsez, Edna Lyle, Fannie Bradley, Margie Wade, Josie Winner, Violet Carlstadt, Bertha Dowling.

Act 1: Courtyard of the Hotel Anglais, Boulogne.

Act 2: Gardens of the Casino, Boulogne.

ACT 1
"Chambermaids" (Opening Chorus)
"Pretty Suzette" (Song)
H. Norman
"The Maharajah" (Chorus and Entrance of the Prince and Sir Drummond Fife)
"Do Not Jump at Your Conclusions"[23] (Song)
C. A. Bigelow
Solo Dance
"The Femme de Chambre" (Song)
M. Sylva
"Charity's Useful Disguise" (Duet)
A. Robinson, W. Armstrong
"Love That Is True" (Song)
W. Armstrong
Chorus (Entrance of Sailors)
Sailors, Chambermaids
"Twas Twenty-Seven Bells by the Waterbury Watch" (Song)
H. Mostyn
(*Music by* Donald MacGregor. *Lyrics by* Arthur Augustus Powers.)
"The Twin Duet"
C. A. Bigelow, H. Mostyn
"The Admiral" (Song and Chorus)
(*Music by* Donald MacGregor. *Lyrics by* Arthur Augustus Powers.)
Finale
(*Music by* Herman Perlet.)

ACT 2[24]
Opening Chorus/Dance
"Jolly British Tar" (Song and Chorus)
"I'll Lead You Such a Dance" (Duet)
H. Mostyn, M. Sylva
"Je ne le comprends pas" (Song)
G. Honey
"Rhapsodie Table d'Hôte" (Song)
C. A. Bigelow
(*Music by* Edward E. Rice. *Lyrics by* William Barton.)
"The Gay Gendarme" (Song and Chorus)
H. Norman
(*Music by* Herman Perlet. *Lyrics by* Henry Norman.)
"You Can Read It in My Eyes"[25] (Duet)
A. Robinson, W. Armstrong
"It's Ever My Endeavor"[26] (Song)
J. Gourlay
"It Is Their Nature To" (Trio)
H. Mostyn, C. A. Bigelow, H. Norman
"I've Her Portrait Nex' to My 'Eart" (Song)
H. Mostyn
Finale

1897.38 McFADDEN'S ROW OF FLATS

A Farcical Review (Farce Comedy) in Three Acts. Play by Edward W. Townsend. Based on characters drawn from R. W. Outcault and G. B. Luke's cartoons from the New York Journal. Music by Ivan L. Davis. Staged by Glen MacDonough. Scenery by Joseph Hart, P. J. McDonald, Louis C. Young. Costumes by Mme. Hill, E. Romer, and Dazian. Musical direction by Ivan L. Davis. Produced by Gus Hill. Opened 27 September 1897 at the People's Theatre and closed 2 October 1897 after 8 performances; returned 8 November 1897 to the Grand Opera House, moved 15 November 1897 to the Columbus Theatre and closed 20 November 1897 after 16 additional performances[27].

---

19 First produced in New York 14 September 1896 at the Knickerbocker Theatre for 64 performances. For Synopsis of Scenes and Musical Numbers, see original 1896 production.

20 The original French score by Théodore de Lajarte was not used in the American adaptation.

21 Also played a return engagement 6 December 1897 at the Grand Opera House for 8 performances.

22 Also billed as "Rice's production of the Frisky English Novelty."

23 Dropped after the New York opening.

24 After opening, the running order to Act 2 was revised, and "I've Her Portrait Next to My Heart" was moved to the end of Act 2, preceeding the Finale.

25 Dropped during the run and replaced by :
The Bon Bon Ballet

26 Dropped during the run.

27 Apart from the cast list, program detail from Grand Opera House and Columbus Theatre engagements. This production toured extensively after its New York run. A March 1903 engagement at the New Star Theatre (Lexington Avenue at 107th St) caused a riot in protest over ethnic caricatures, resulting in many arrests.

CAST: *Tim McFadden*, a power in his ward, candidate for alderman: RICHARD K. MULLEN. *Jacob Baumgartner*, another power, also a candidate: CHARLES A. LODER. *Mrs. Murphy*, queen of the Flats: Mrs. LIZZIE CONWAY. *Mary Ellen (Murphy)*, her mother's daughter: ESTELLE WELLINGTON. *Terence McSwatt*, poet of McFadden's Flats: GEORGE LESLIE. *Della Dunnigan*, a sharp flatette: Annie Dunn. *Abraham Levi*, overloaded with heart: Lester Powell. *Jack A. Shore*[28]: Curtis Speck. *Bill Cannon*[29]: Harry Speck. *Kelly*, a McFaddenite bouncer: Al Edwards. *Krau*, a Baumgartner bouncer: Edward Howard. *Tempy*, a black wing: Mark Bennett. *Kerrigan*, a fly cop: Charles L. Newton. *Marty*, handy waiter: J. J. Shaw. *Swipes*, the drum-major of the Flats: John Cullen. *The Twins*: Speck Brothers. *Mickey Duggan*, the fast mail: Joseph Armstrong. *Clerk of Drug Store*: Frank Russell. *McFadden's daughters (3)*: *Evelyn McFadden*: Ruby Lytton. *Angeline McFadden*: Lillian Walton. *Em McFadden*: Hilda Hawthorne. *Baumgartner's Daughters (3)*: *Lillie Baumgartner*: Etta Chatham. *Minnie Baumgartner*: Kittie Lampp. *Liz Baumgartner*: Daisy Rieger. *Female Athletes, Little German Band, Immigrant Girls, Swiss Warblers, Ball Guests, Street Urchins, etc.*

Act 1: Five Points, in New York. A busy street. (Hart.)

Act 2: Rival masquerade ball at Tammany Hall. (McDonald.)

Act 3: Drug store in Hoffman House, New York. (Young.)

MUSICAL NUMBERS, SPECIALTIES

The Famous Four Emperors of Music
Messrs. Howard, Russell, Edwards, Whiting
Miss Estelle Wellington, the picturesque character danseuse
The Funny Sparring Dwarfs
Speck Brothers
Eccentric Dancing Specialty
G. Leslie
The Six Mountain Maids, Tyrolean Warblers
Original Up-to-Date Specialty
C. A. Loder
Up-to-Date Specialty
E. Wellington, G. Leslie
The Pretty Athletic Girls
Misses Lytton, Dunn, Rieger, Chatham, Florence, Hawthorne, Lampp
Novel Specialty
Bicycle Girls
Irish Specialty
R. K. Mullen
Brass Band Choruses
Imperial Brass Band
Boxing Specialty (Act 3)
Speck Brothers
Novelty Finale
Imperial Brass Band, Entire Company

1897.39 THE BELLE OF NEW YORK

A Musical Comedy in Two Acts, 6 Scenes. Libretto by Hugh Morton [C.M.S. McLellan]. Music by Gustave Kerker. Staged by George W. Lederer. Ballets arranged by Signor Francioli. Settings by Ernest Albert, Ernest M. Gros and D. Frank Dodge. Costumes by Caroline Siedle. Musical director, Gustave Kerker. Produced by George W. Lederer. Opened 28 September 1897 at the Casino Theatre and closed 13 November 1897 after 56 performances; re-opened 20 December 1897 at the Casino Theatre and closed 26 December 1897 after 8 additional performances. Total: 64 performances.

CAST: *Ichabod Bronson*, President of the Young Men's Rescue League and Anti-Cigarette Society of Cohoes: DAN DALY. *Harry Bronson*, his son, a young spendthrift: HARRY DAVENPORT. *Karl von Pumpernick*, a polite lunatic: DAVID WARFIELD. *"Doc" Snifkins*, the Father of the Queen of Comic Opera: GEORGE K. FORTESCUE. *"Blinky Bill" McGuirk*, a mixed-ale pugilist: WILLIAM CAMERON. *Kenneth Mugg*, low comedian of the Angelique Comic Opera: GEORGE A. SCHILLER. *Count Ratsi Rattatoo, Count Patsi Rattatoo*, twin Portuguese noblemen: JOHN SLAVIN, WILLIAM SLOAN. *Mr. Twiddles*, Harry Bronson's private secretary: Harry Dodd. *Billy Breeze*, a man-o-war's-man: Winfred Goff. *Fricot*, a French chef: Lionel Lawrence. *Mr. Snooper*, a newspaper reporter: Lionel Lawrence. *Ah Bung*, a Chinaman: Lionel Lawrence. *Mr. Peeper*, a Photographer: L. T. MacDonald. *William*, a Butler: Austin Walsh. *Mr. Snuffy*: Austin Walsh. *Violet Gray*, a Salvation lassie: EDNA MAY. *Fifi Fricot*, a little Parisienne: PHYLLIS RANKIN. *Cora Angelique*, The Queen of Comic Opera: ADA DARE. *Kissie Fitzgarter*, a Music Hall Dancer: MARIE GEORGE. *Pansy Pinns*, a soubrette: Babette Rodney. *Mamie Clancy*, a Pell Street Girl: PAULA EDWARDES.

Cora's Bridesmaids: *Marjorie May*: Mabel Howe. *Myrtle Mince*: Helen Lord. *Gladys Glee*: Harriet Bond. *Dorothy June*: Sylvia Holte. *Queenie Cake*: Rose Witt. *Birdie Seed*: Crissie Carlyle.

Mrs. Snuffy: Minnie Varrell. *Little Miss Flirt*: Mabel Howe. *Dandy Pay*, "Blinky Bill's" pal: Himself.

Corps de Ballet: Sophie Witt, Agnes Enright, Laura Witt, Ida Doerge, Venie Hoffman, May Knight, Bettie Dauble, Molly Hoffman, Anna Baldarsara, Marie Steinberg, Maud Robinson, Clarice Middleton. *Dance Specialty*: La Petite Adelaide.

Act 1, Scene 1: The Dining Room of Harry Bronson's house on Riverside Drive, New York. (Albert.) *Scene 2*: The Conservatory of Harry Bronson's house. (Albert.) *Scene 3*: Pell Street, New York, on the Chinese New Year's Eve. (Dodge.)

Act 2, Scene 1: Smyler's Candy Store, Broadway, New York. (Gros.) *Scene 2*: The Interior of Grand Central Station, New York. (Gros.) *Scene 3*: On the Lawn of the Casino at Narragansett Pier. (Albert.)

ACT 1[30]
Scene 1
"When a Man is Twenty-one" (Opening Chorus)
H. Davenport, Chorus
"Oh Naughty Mr. Bronson" (Chorus of Housemaids)
Chorus
"When I Was Born the Stars Stood Still" (Queen of Comic Opera)
A. Dare, Chorus
"Little Sister Kissie" (Song and Dance)
G. A. Schiller, M. George, W. Cameron
"Teach Me How to Kiss, Dear" (Song)
P. Rankin
"We Come This Way" (March and Chorus)
"The Anti-Cigarette Society" (Song)
D. Daly
"Wine, Woman and Song" (Song and Chorus)
H. Davenport, Chorus
Scene 2
"La Belle Parisienne" (Song)
P. Rankin, Bridesmaids
"My Little Baby" (Song)
D. Daly
Scene 3
"Pretty Little China Girl" (Chinese Divertissement)
Chorus, Corps de Ballet
"They All Follow Me" (Song)
E. May, Chorus
"She Is the Belle of New York" (Song and Dance)
W. Cameron
Finale (Your life, my little girl)(The Belle of New York)(reprise)
D. Daly, H. Davenport, E. May, Chorus

ACT 2
Scene 1
"Oh! Sonny!" (Opening Chorus)
H. Davenport, Chorus
"When We Are Married" (Duet)
P. Rankin, H. Davenport
Entrance of Brass Band
"The Purity Brigade" (Song and Chorus)
E. May, Chorus
"I do, so there!" (Song and Chorus)
E. May, D. Daly, Chorus
Scene 2
"Take Me Down to Coney Island" (Duet)
W. Cameron, P. Edwardes
"On the Beach at Narragansett" (Song)
D. Daly, Others

[28]Later programs rename this character Alex, on pleasure bent.
[29]Later programs rename this character George, likewise bent.

[30]Musical numbers not listed in programs. List prepared from production typescript. The supplementary numbers were drawn from much-revised English piano vocal score (Ascherberg, Hopwood & Crew, Ltd.) and published sheet music.

Scene 3
"For the twentieth time we'll drink" (Opening Chorus)
Chorus
Ballet of Bo Peeps (Oh little Bo Peep)
Chorus
"At ze naughty Folies Bergere" (Song)
E. May
"For in the field" (Finale)
Principals

SUPPLEMENTARY NUMBERS
"You and I" (Song)
D. Daly
"Grogan's Fancy Ball" (Song)
W. Cameron
"Maiden of Gentle Grace" (Duet)
H. Davenport, E. May
"Father of the Queen of Comic Opera" (Song and Chorus)
G. K. Fortescue, Female Chorus
"We'll Stand and Die Together" (Song and Chorus)
Chorus
"Don't You Know" (or, The Languid Man)(Song)
(*Music by* Richard Stahl. *Lyrics by* Edmund Vance Cooke.)

1897.40 COURTED INTO COURT

A Revival of the Farce Comedy with Music in Three Acts[31]. Play by John J. McNally. Musical direction and arrangements by John C. Sorg. Produced by (Isaac B.) Rich and (William) Harris (Henry B. Harris, Manager). Opened 18 October 1897 at the Harlem Opera House and closed 23 October 1897 after 8 performances; re-opened 1 November 1897 at the Grand Opera House and closed 6 November 1897 after an additional 8 performances.

CAST: *Dottie Dimple*: MARIE DRESSLER. *Worthington Wirth, Jr.*: JOHN C. RICE. *Worthington Wirth, Sr.*: OSCAR L. FIGMAN. *Mrs. Worthington Wirth, Sr.*: CLARA PALMA. *Helen Wirth*, her daughter: AGNES MILTON. *Molly Miltum*, Dotty's understudy: Maud Huth. *Dickey Daggett*, in love with Milly: Billy Clifford. *Judge Jeremiah Geoghan*: JAMES F. CALLAHAN. *Pop Dooley*, stage doorkeeper, uncle of Dottie: JACQUES KRUGER. *Sylvia Rosebud*, Dottie's maid: Sally Cohen. *Mortimer Morton*, actor: Damon Lyon. *Sharp*, Lawyer: Damon Lyon. *Gertie*, Mrs. Worthington's maid: Blanche R. Verona. *Hal Ford*, a janitor: John Frees. *Court Officer*: John Frees. *Clerk of Court*: Harry Ertheiler. *Ladies of the Dottie Dimple Company (4)*: *Mollie Mavourn*: Fannie Briscoe. *Della Carte*: Blanche Ward.

ACT 1[32]
"When You're in Love" (Medley Finale)
S. Cohen, Company
"Miss Modesty"
M. Dressler
(*Music and Lyrics by* Dave Reed, Jr.)
"Why I Became a Sailor" (Song and Dance)
J. G. Rice
Grand Finale Cake Walk
Clifford & Huth, Others

ACT 2
"Susie This Coon Has Got the Blues"
M. Dressler, Company
"(There'll Be a) Hot Time in the Old Town To-night"
M. Dressler, Company
(*Music by* Theodore H. Metz. *Lyrics by* Joe Hayden.)

ACT 3
"Taking a Chance" (Song and Dance)
M. Dressler, J. C. Rice

1897.41 LA POUPÉE

A Comic Opera in Two Acts, 4 Scenes. Adapted from the French opéra-comique with libretto by Maurice Ordonneau. English adaptation by Arthur Sturgess. Music by Edmond Audran. Produced by Oscar Hammerstein. Opened 21 October 1897 at the Lyric Theatre and closed 3 November 1897 after 14 performances[33].

CAST: *Hilarius* (an inventor): G. W. ANSON. *Lancelot* (a novice): FRANK RUSHWORTH. *Father Maxime*: ARTHUR CUNNINGHAM. *Chanterelle* (a Baron): FERRIS HARTMAN. *Lorremois* (a friend of the Baron's): W. STEIGER. *Balthazar*: Mr. Vroom. *Agnelet*: Mr. Rolland. *Benoit*: C. S. Fredericks. *Basilique*: Mr. Ridgeley. *Madame Hilarius*: ROSE LEIGHTON. *Guduline* (Alesia's companion): Miss Rousseau. *Henri* (an apprentice): TRIXIE FRIGANZA. *Pierre*: Miss Cook. *Jacques*: Miss Shields. *Marie* (a servant): Miss Bradley. *Fifine*: Miss Stone. *Alésia* (Hilarius' daughter): ANNA HELD.

Act 1, Scene 1: The Monastery. *Scene 2*: Hilarius' Workshop.

Act 2, Scene 1: Chanterelle's Country House. *Scene 2*: The Monastery (another part).

ACT 1[34]
Scene 1
Opening Chorus (Alas! with lean and empty scrip)
A. Cunningham, F. Rushworth, All
Song (Youth is ever vain)
A. Cunningham
Finale (Hark! how the bell is ringing)
A. Cunningham, F. Rushworth, All
Scene 2
Opening Chorus (We are workmen waiting for our payment)
Song (With careless eye I saw him there)
A. Held
Song (I went to town a simple youth)
F. Rushworth
Song (I can sing and dance and chatter)
A. Held
Duet (I love you very dearly)
F. Rushworth, A. Held
Finale
F. Rushworth, Miss Rousseau, All

---

[31]First produced in New York 26 December 1896 at the Bijou Theatre for 140 performances. A different musical score was used for that production. This was a touring company, making weeklong tour dates; costumes, settings and direction uncredited. For Synopsis of Scenes, see original 1896 production.

[32]The musical score, authorship uncredited, continued to change throughout the tour: Added were:
"Mamie Reilly" (Medley Finale)
S. Cohen, Company
"Bon Jour Monsieur"
May Duryea [Molly Miltum], Company
"The Swellest Thing in Town" (from THE GOOD MR. BEST)
O. Figman, Company
"Ram-a-Jam, or I Want That Man"
M. Dressler
(*Music and Lyrics by* Francis J. Bryant.)
"If That Ain't Winning a Home, I Don't Know"
M. Dressler, J. C. Rice
"Ma Lulu"
M. Dressler, Company
"O'Dooley's First Five O'Clock Tea" (from THE GOOD MR. BEST)
John G. Sparks [Judge Jeremiah Goeghan], Company
(*Music by* Frederic Dana. *Lyrics by* Paul West.)
"(I'm the) Daughter of the Leader of the Band"
M. Dressler, Company
(*Music by* Summit L. Hecht. *Lyrics by* Sigmund B. Alexander.)
"Whoop De Dooden Doo" (from THE LADY SLAVEY)
(*Music by* Gustave Kerker.)
"The Oompah"
Ada Lewis
(*Music by* John S. Baker. *Lyrics by* Fred Bowyer.)

[33]Bankruptcy procedings forced the production's sudden closure. Austin Daly presented a new production of LA POUPÉE later this season 15 April 1898 at Daly's Theatre for 18 performances. See full detail at that date below.

[34]Musical numbers not listed in programs. List prepared from Sturgess' published libretto (Hopwood & Crew, Ltd., London, 1897).

ACT 2

Scene 1

Opening Chorus (How we appear)

"Pistoli Carabi" (Duet)(This wicked world I've wandered round)
F. Hartman, W. Steiger

Trio (Ah, Lancelot is not yet here)
A. Held, F. Hartman, W. Steiger

Quartette (Though manners change)
F. Hartman, F. Rushworth, W. Steiger, G. W. Anson

Song (Happy world, such maidens possessing)
F. Rushworth

Marriage Contract Chorus (Here are the wedding guests come)
F. Hartman, F. Rushworth, A. Held, (Notary), G. W. Anson, Chorus

Final Chorus (Now after them we go)
All

Scene 2

Opening Chorus ('Tis night)

"A Jovial Monk" (Song)
A. Cunningham

Chorus of Monks (Oh, strange device)
Messrs. Vroom, Fredericks, Rolland, Ridgeley, All

Song (A poor little dummy am I)
A. Held

Duet (Was it a kiss)
A. Held, F. Rushworth

Finale (And now I mean to leave this place)
F. Rushworth, A. Cunningham, F. Hartman, A. Held, All

1897.42

THE IDOL'S EYE

A Comic Opera in Three Acts. Libretto by Harry B. Smith. Music by Victor Herbert. Produced under the stage direction of Julian Mitchell. Settings by Ernest Albert. Costumes by Mme. Caroline Siedle. Director of music, Frank Pallma. Produced by Kirke LaShelle. Opened 25 October 1897 at the Broadway Theatre and closed 11 December 1897 after 56 performances[35].

CAST: *Abel Conn*, an aeronaut who seeks and find adventure: FRANK DANIELS. *Ned Winer*, an American novelist in search of material and Maraquita: MAURICE DARCY. *Jamie McSnuffy*, the last of the McSnuffys, of Castle McSnuffy, a kleptomaniac, drummed out of a Highland regiment: ALF C. WHELAN. *Don Pablo Tobasco*, a Cuban planter traveling in India in search of big game: WILL DANFORTH. *Corporal O'Flannagan*, devoted to the Colonel: Arthur Nash. *Chief Priest* of the Temple of the Ruby: Newton Westbrook. *Emissiaries from the Rajah of Jabalpur*, in search of the stolen ruby (3): *First Brahmin*: Arthur Carleton. *Second Brahmin*: Lee Latta. *Third Brahmin*: Wensley Thompson. *Damayanti*, favorite Nautch girl of the Rajah of Jabalpur: NORMA KOPP. *Maraquita*, daughter of Don Paolo, in love with Ned: HELEN REDMOND. *Bidalia*, oldest daughter of Corporal Wattles, nurse to her brothers and sisters; looking for the right man to release her from domestic bondage: BELLE BUCKLIN. *Chief Priestess* of the Temple of the Ruby: CLAUDIA CARLSTEDT. *Second Priestess*: Jane English. *Lieutenant Desmond*: Claudia Carlstedt. *Officers' Daughetrs (3)*: *Viola*: Jane English. *Blanche*: Mae Emmons. *Berenice*: Florence Ritchie. *Housemaids in Officers' Families (4)*: *Mollie*: Edith Joyce. *Dollie*: Nellie Hughes. *Pollie*: Eva Palmer. *Ollie*: Dora Zephlin. *Soldiers, Brahmins, Priests, Hindoo Servants, Officer's Wives and Daughters, Nautch Girls, Priestess, etc.*

The action takes place at the present time in India.

Act 1: Officers' quarters of an English regiment.

Act 2: Interior of the Temple of the Ruby.

Act 3: Same as Act 1.

ACT 1[36]

Opening Chorus

"Pretty Isabella and Her Umbrella" (Duet)
H. Redmond, M. Darcy

"Cuban Song"
W. Danforth, Chorus

Grand Chorus and Entrance of Brahmins

"I Just Dropped In"
F. Daniels, Chorus

"Minding the Baby"
B. Bucklin, Chorus

"Captain Cholly Chumley of the Guards"
F. Daniels, Chorus

"Lady and the Kick"
N. Kopp, Chorus

Finale

ACT 2

Opening Chorus and Dance of the Nautch Girls

Song of the Priestess
C. Carlstedt, Priests, Chorus

"The Tattooed Man"
F. Daniels, Chorus

Finale

ACT 3

Opening Chorus

"Talk about Yo' Luck" (The Rabbit's Foot)
F. Daniels, Chorus

"Fairy tales" (Waltz-Sextette)
F. Daniels, H. Redmond, B. Bucklin, N. Kopp, M. Darcy, W. Danforth

Finale

1897.43

THE GRIP

A Revival of the Farce (with Songs) in Three Acts[37]. Play and lyrics by Edward Harrigan. Music by David Braham. Musical director, Charles Leve. Produced by Edward Harrigan. Opened 1 November 1897 at the Grand Opera House, moved 8 November 1897 to the Third Avenue Theatre and closed 13 November 1897 after 17 performances.

CAST: *Sergeant Hickey*: EDWARD HARRIGAN. *Colonel August Grobie*: HARRY A. FISHER. *Ellen Quinlen*, an Irish beauty: M. J. KEARNEY. *Ike Bowser*: M. J. KEARNEY. *Lipsey Warren*, the Ice Man: M. J. KEARNEY. *Albert Wrinkles*: James Cassady. *Tobias Wrinkles*, Albert's father: GEORGE MERRITT. *Lionel Caldwell*: GEORGE MERRITT. *Clementina Jarr*, a saucy wench: DAVE BRAHAM, JR. *Solomon Donovan*, the Sailor: Tom Granger. *Horace Hartley*, an English Butler: James Kearney. *Gillegen*, the detective: James Kearney. *Rossilin Grobie, Jr.*: Rose Braham. *Mary Caldwell*: Bessie Wyatt. *Rossilin Grobie*: ANNIE YEAMANS.

MUSICAL NUMBERS

"The Ould Dudeen"
E. Harrigan

"Rare Old Mountain Dew"
E. Harrigan

"She's My Girl"
J. Cassady, G. Merritt

"Sergeant Hickey of the G.A.R." (from THE WOOLEN STOCKING)
Company

1897.44

THE GEISHA

A Revival of the Musical Comedy in Two Acts[38]. Book by Owen Hall. Music by Sidney Jones and Lionel Monckton. Lyrics by Harry Greenbank. Staged by Herbert Gresham. Dances by Willie Warde. Settings by Henry T. Hoyt after designs and and models of the original by William Telbin. Costumes by Percy Anderson. Orchestra under the direction of Sebastian Hiller.

[35]Also played a return engagement 24 January 1898 at the Harlem Opera House for 8 performances.

[36]Musical numbers not listed in programs; list prepared from published vocal score (E. Schuberth & Co., New York, 1897).

[37]First produced in New York 30 November 1885 at Harrigan's Park Theatre for 88 performances. For Synopsis of Scenes, see original 1885 production. Musical Numbers are altogether different from the original production. Settings and costumes were uncredited.

[38]Originally produced 9 September 1896 at Daly's Theatre for 161 performances in repertory. For Synopsis of Scenes and Musical Numbers, see original 1896 production.

Produced by Augustin Daly. Opened 8 November 1897 at Daly's Theatre and closed 27 November 1897 after 24 performances in repertory[39].

CAST: *Marquis Imari*: HERBERT GRESHAM. *Lieutenant Katana*: NEAL McCAY. *Police Sergeant Takemini*: Deane Pratt. *A Buyer*: Abner Symmons. *Wun-Hi*: JAMES T. POWERS. *O Mimosa San*: NANCY McINTOSH. *Juliette Diamant*: Helma Nelson. *Nami*: Lila Convere. *O Hana San*: Carolyn Gordon. *O Kiku San*: Mathilde Preville. *O Kinkoto San*: Corinne Parker. *Kommyasaki San*: Maud Carter. *Lieutenant Reginald Fairfax*: JULIUS STEGER. *Dick Cunningham*: CYRIL SCOTT. *Arthur Cuddy*: George Heath. *George Grimston*: Eric Scott. *Tommy Stanley*: Eugene Taylor. *Lady Constance Wynne*: Marie St. John. *Marie Worthington*: Beatrice Morgan. *Ethel Hurst*: Edith Cameron. *Dorothy Sweet*: Isabel Moore. *Mabel Grant*: Alice Toland. *Miss Molly Seamore*: VIRGINIA EARL.

1897.45 THE SWELL MISS FITZWELL

A Comedy (with Songs) in Three Acts. Play by Henry A. duSouchet. Stage production under the direction of W. H. Post. Settings by Henry E. Hoyt. Musical director, R. Stretti. Produced by the May Irwin Company (direction of E. Rosenbaum). Opened 15 November 1897 at the Bijou Theatre and closed 26 February 1898 after 122 performances[40].

CAST: *Marquis de Cagiac*: WILLIAM BURRESS. *Count de Cagiac*, his son: IGNACIO MARINETTI. *Countess de Cagiac*, known as Miss Fitzwell: MAY IRWIN. *O'Donovan Dugan*, the Count's partner: JOSEPH M. SPARKS. *Rudolph Kleinagle*, a professional witness: Charles Jackson. *Louise Laredo*, M.D., a friend of the Countess: Alice Johnson. *Colonel Julio Laredo*, a Cuban patriot: Ed Mack. *Mlle. Guinivieve Otello*, of the Vaudeville Francaise: Marion Giroux. *J. Robinson Butts*, an Oklahoman lawyer: Ronald Carter. *Caroline Maguire*, forewoman at Miss Fitzwell's: Jane Burby. *Sibyl*: Gussie Hart. *Marie*: Julia Baird. *Laura Butler*: Marcia Treadwell. *Nellie Morton*: Harriet Bond. *Clara Thompson*: Roland Davis. *Parker*, a butler: Ned Wayburn. *Janitor*: George Gelder.

Act 1: Interior of Miss Fitzwell's dressmaking establishment, in New York City. Trouble.

Act 2: Dr. Laredo's office. TROUBLE.

Act 3: Summer residence of O'Donovan Dugan. TROUBLE.

MUSICAL NUMBERS[41]

"Honey on My Lips"
M. Irwin
(*Music and Lyrics by* Charles E. Trevathan.)

'Rag Time' piano accompaniment to the negro melodies has been specially arranged by Ned Wayburn.

"The Frog Song"
(*Music and Lyrics by* Charles E. Trevathan.)

"On the Dummy Line"

"Oh, What a Beautiful Ocean"

"Can't Bring Him Back" (A Coon Delusion)
M. Irwin
(*Music and Lyrics by* King Kollins.)

"He Cert'nly Was Good to Me"
M. Irwin
(*Music by* A. Baldwin Sloane. *Lyrics by* Jean C. Havez.)

"When a Nigger Keeps You Guessing"
(*Music and Lyrics by* Andrew Mack.)

"Syncopated Sandy"

"The Pickaninny's Lullaby" (Act 3)

1897.46 1999

A Comic Opera in Three Acts. Book (and lyrics) by Herman Lee Ensign. Music by Eduard Holst. Scenery by Joseph Physioc. Produced under the stage direction of Gerald Coventry. Settings by Joseph Physioc. Costumes by Catherine Siedle. Musical director, Gustave Kerker. Opened 15 November 1897 at the Casino Theatre and closed 18 December 1897 after 40 performances[42].

CAST: *Alieophon*, King of Mars: WARWICK GANOR. *Alieosa*, the Prince, his son: HUGH CHILVERS. *Van Duzer Packer*, a supposed millionaire: FERRIS HARTMAN. *Kip*, his accomplice: Ben Lodge. *Alonzo*, a college boy: Miro Delamotta. *Officious Official*, emissary of the law: Tom Ricketts. *His Trusty Men*: Will Spencer, Charles Cantor, John Cantor, Joe W. Harris. *Professor Mme. Brent*, astronomer and inventor: CLARA ALENE JEWELL. *Her daughters (2)*: *Corona*: BERTHA WALTZINGER. *Electra*: CLARESSE AGNEW. *Countess de Cordova*, a Spanish lady of royal blood: MATHILDE COTTRELLY. *Ziegali*, her maid: Annie Wheatley. *Titled Fortune Hunters*: Florence Knight, Alice May, Rosalie Wells, Lillian Blieman, Anita Austin, Margaret McDonald, Lucille Sturgess, Emma Janvier.

Time: During the year 1999 A.D.

Act 1: Quadrangle of a New York College.

Act 2: Interior of the Observatory.

Act 3: Botanical Gardens, near the College.

1897.47 AN IRISH GENTLEMAN

A Play of Life in Ireland in Three Acts. Play by Ramsay Morris. Produced under the directon of R. A. Roberts. Settings by Joseph Physioc. Incidental music by Louie Maurice. Musical director, Louie Maurice. Produced by (Isaac B.) Rich and (William) Harris. Opened 29 November 1897 at the 14th Street Theatre and closed 22 January 1898 after 64 performances[43].

CAST: *Jack Shannon*, a rolling stone: ANDREW MACK. *Stephen Tyrrell*, a treacherous companion: Adolph Jackson. *Clifford Sherlock*, a country gentleman: RICHARD J. DILLON. *Lacy Sherlock*, Clifford Sherlock's son: Edwin Brandt. *Father Lawler*, everybody's friend: GEORGE W. DEYO. *Hugh Dillon*, Sherlock's neighbor: Thomas Jackson. *O'Donoghue*, servant at Old Court: W. J. Mason. *Officer*, a disappointed man: B. Williams. *Maura Sherlock*, Clifford Sherlock's daughter: OLIVE WHITE. *Mrs. Fairleigh*, a wily widow: Florence Ashbrooke. *Easter*, housekeeper at Old Court: Marie Bates. *Peggy*, Clifford Sherlock's niece: Little Florence Olp.

Act 1: A summer morning in the grounds at Old Court. Present time.

Act 2: The morning room at Old Court. Two weeks later.

Act 3: The drawing room at Old Court. One day later.

ACT 1[44]

"An Irish Street Singer (or Honest John McCool)"
A. Mack
(*Music by* Andrew Mack. *Lyrics by* Thomas LeMack.)

"Mack's Love Song"
A. Mack

ACT 2

"My Sweetest Girl"
A. Mack
(*Music by* Andrew Mack. *Lyrics by* Leander Richardson.)

ACT 3

"My Heart's Delight"
A. Mack
(*Music by* Andrew Mack. *Lyrics by* "Alice.")

1897.48 POUSSE CAFÉ/ THE WORST BORN

A Double Bill of Burlesques, prececed by an Olio. Book (and lyrics) by Edgar Smith and Louis de Lange. Music by John Stromberg. Produced under the stage direction of Julian Mitchell. Scenery painted by John Young. Costumes designed by Will R. Barnes. Musical director, John Stromberg. Produced by Joseph M. Weber and Lew M. Fields. Opened 2 December 1897 at Weber & Fields' Broadway Music Hall and closed 1 June

[39]See separate entry for return engagement 21 March 1898 at Daly's Theatre below. Played return engagements 31 January 1898 at the Harlem Opera House for 8 performances, and 26 December 1898 at the Harlem Opera House for 8 performances.

[40]Also played return engagements 14 March 1898 at the Harlem Opera House for 8 performances, and 21 March 1898 at the Grand Opera House for 8 performances. Costumes uncredited.

[41]No songs listed in programs. List prepared from press clippings, published sheet music, etc. Most if not all songs were sung by May Irwin.

[42]Neither producer nor director was credited in programs, nor identified in reviews. Musical numbers not listed in programs.

[43]Played return engagements 7 March 1898 at the Columbus Theare for 8 performances, and 2 January 1899 at the Columbus Theatre for 8 performances. Costumes uncredited.

[44]Also published from the score: "The Dove Song."

1898 after 208 performances.

ACT 1

POUSSE CAFÉ, A (Burlesque of "La Poupée") Dramatic Impossibility in Two Acts.

CAST: *Lord Chumpley* of England's aristocracy, seeking an alliance with America's democracy: CHARLES J. ROSS. *Herr Weishaben*, inventor of "La Pooh Pooh," a mechanical doll: SAM BERNARD. *A Syndicate of Angels Backing the Inventor (2): Herr Weinschoppen*: JOSEPH M. WEBER. *Herr Bierheister*: LEW M. FIELDS. *Abel Stringer*, European buyer for several New York vaudeville houses: PETER F. DAILEY. *Michael McCann*, a wealthy Irish-American: JOHN T. KELLY. *Fiacre*, a Parisian cabby: William West. *Electro*, a musical clown: W. Russell. *Freaka*, a glass eater: G. Thomas. *Deadun*, a minstrel: M. Renner. *Clorinda McCann*, an American girl, ambitious to be a lady of quality: MABEL FENTON. *La Pooh Pooh*, the doll: ROSE BEAUMONT. *Magnesia*, Weilhaben's daughter, with leaning towards Henny: LILLIAN SWAIN. *Henny*, Weishaben's apprentice, also leanings: Sylvia Thorne. *A Brace of Parisian Tenderloiners (2): Julie Bumbum*: Josephine Allen. *Boozette*: Nellie Beaumont. *Sergeant Deville*, a French Captain Chapman: Frankie Bailey. *Jouvin*, a French kid: Gertrude Mansfield. *Fortune Hunters (6): Duke of Thameswater*: Genevieve Clifton. *Lord Weakchester*: Florence Bell. *Sir Hardup Fewacres*: Helen Dunbar. *Earl of Piccadilly*: Edith Merrill. *Viscount of Whitechapel*: Dora Webb. *Sir Hanover Square*: Louise Gould. *Gelatine*, a gay Parisian: Belle Robinson. *Three who find Paris slow after Broadway: Shanley Burnsmartin*: Lucy Escott. *Cable Rhodes*: Inez Rae. *Dodge Carr*: May Edward. *Broadway Walker*: May Cuthbert.

Act 1: On the Boulevard, Paris.

Act 2: McCann's villa, near Paris. The Fête Champêtre.

ACT 1 MUSICAL NUMBERS

"In Gay Paree" (Opening Chorus)

"The Self-Made Man" (Song and Ensemble)

"All That Sort of Rot" (Song)

"The Foreign Vaudevillians" (Song and Ensemble)

(a) The London Comic Singer, (b) Tyrolean Warblers, (c) The Spanish Dancers, (d) The British Minstrel "How I Love My Lu"
(P. Dailey)
(*Lyrics by* Edgar Smith and Louis deLange.)

"I Love Thee, Oleander"[45] (Song)

"I Am a Doll" (Song and Ensemble)

Finale

ACT 2

THE WORST BORN, A Dramatic Impossibility (Burlesque of Francis Powers' play "The First Born" as produced by David Belasco) in Two Acts. Libretto by Edgar Smith and Louis deLange. Music by John Stromberg.

CAST: *Sham Boy*, the Worst Born: PETER F. DAILEY. *Sham Man*, his pa: CHARLES J. ROSS. *Highbinders (3): Chane Gang*, alias Doctor Pow Wow: SAM BERNARD. *Hop Tea*: LEW FIELDS. *Cue Hay*: JOSEPH WEBER. *Cold Deckhand*, on a secret mission: JOHN T. KELLY. *General Viler*, out of place in Chinatown—or anywhere else: Allen Whitman. *Machete*, an insurgent: Willie Pratt. *Stick Kee*, a bill-poster: G. Thomas. *Dam Low Neck*, a Chinese villain: G. Thomas. *Chinks (3): Ace Hi*: M. Renner. *Li Low*: W. Russell. *Chin Low*: W. West. *Ki Yi*, a Chinese dog: Rover. *Looney Thing*, a Chinatown belle: MABEL FENTON. *Sham She*, the Worst-Born's ma: Sylvia Thorne. *Sissy Nearus*, a Cuban girl: Lillian Swain.

Additional characters in Act 2: THE WEE MINISTER:

Cast: *Spavin Dishwater*, the Wee Minister: CHARLES J. ROSS. *Tammas Wahoo, Handy Mealticket, Neal Dow*, 3 hot Scotches: LEW M. FIELDS, JOSEPH M. WEBER, SAM BERNARD. *Lady Gabby*: MABEL FENTON. *Lord Pinpool*, Lady Gabby's father: Gertrude Mansfield. *Captain Ballywell*, Lady Gabby's fiancé: FRANKIE BAILEY. *Annie Laurie, Nannie Webster, Maggie Bruce*, Scotch lassies: Rose Beaumont, Nellie Beaumont, Josephine Allen. And the Five Whirlwinds.

ACT 2 MUSICAL NUMBERS

Scotch Medley Song (with bagpipe obligato)

"Song Tow" (Chorus)

"The Learned Dr. Pow Wow" (Chinese Ditty)

Chinese Intermezzo

Finale

On 20 January 1898, THE WORST BORN was replaced by THE WAYHIGHMAN, a Burlesque of the comic opera "The Highwayman" (libretto by Harry B. Smith, music by Reginald deKoven). Libretto by Edgar Smith, music by John Stromberg.

THE WAYHIGHMAN Cast: *Jesse James*, a spirit: LEW M. FIELDS. *Mick Fitzgargle*, the highlowman: CHARLES J. ROSS. *Quitter*, a defective detective: PETER F. DAILEY. *Tony Wrinkle*, boots at the "Fat and Griddle": JOSEPH M. WEBER. *Captain Kidney* of the Naval Reserve: SAM BERNARD. *Humpy*, driver of the coach: Allen Whitman. *Doll Rumnose*, servant lady at the "Fat and Griddle": MABEL FENTON. *Lady Constantly Singqueer*, a society bud, in love with Mick: ROSE BEAUMONT. *Lieutenant Leftface* of the Militia: Grace Freeman. *Hunters, Soldiers, Farmers, Detectives, etc.*

ACT 2: MUSICAL NUMBERS:

Japanese Divertissement[46]
Misses Dunbar, Clifton Bell, Merrill, Escott, Rae, Webb, Gould, Robinson, Maginn, Edwards, Cuthbert, Loeb, Dolaro, Monti, Poore

Scotch Medley Song (bagpipe obligato)

"Song Tow" (Japanese March)

"Horny-Handed Farmers" (Chorus)

"Sing Hey for the Aniseeed Bag" (Hunting Chorus)

"Sure, Blarney's the Art of Stealing a Heart" (Song)
(C. J. Ross)

"The Farmer and the Con Gent" (Song and Ensemble)
(P. F. Dailey)

"How I Love My Lu" (Finale)
(P. F. Dailey, Ensemble)
(*Lyrics by* Edgar Smith and Louis deLange.)

On 17 March 1898 THE WAYHIGHMAN was replaced by THE CON-CURERS, a burlesque of the play by Paul Potter "The Conquerors" in 3 Scenes. Libretto by Edgar Smith, music by John Stromberg.

THE CON-CURERS Cast: *Eric von Roeshad*, Lieutenant of Uhlans: CHARLES J. ROSS. *Captain Korker, Lieutenant Highball, Lieutenant Payrent*, of the Grocerymen's Own: JOSEPH M. WEBER, LEW M. FIELDS, SAM BERNARD. *Mayor Von Wolffacen*, in command at the castle: JOHN T. KELLY. *Jean Badun*, called Bumface, an innkeeper: PETER F. DAILEY. *Pullet*, a back number: Gilbert Sarony. *Doggybark*, a cook: George Thomas. *Flaskar, Rubynose*, fishermen: W. West, M. Renner. *Sergeant Schmierkase*: W. Russell. *Yvonne Grandpiano*: MABEL FENTON. *Baby Grandpiano*, her sister: ROSE BEAUMONT. *Jane Mary Badun*: NELLIE BEAUMONT. *Acheata*: Nellie Beaumont. *Nogo*, Baron Grandpiano: Frankie Bailey. *Lieutenant Bierheister*: Helen Dunbar. *Melodeone*: Nellie Butler. *Verinete*: Belle Robinson. *Rotita*: Mae Edwards. *Mariette*: Bonnie Maginn. *Creaky*: Lucy Escott. *Corporal Limburger*: Genevieve Clifton. *Captain Heiffeldemel*: Florence Bell. *Pierrot*: May Cuthbert.

The action takes place at Guttenberg, France, just before the battle of Union Hill.

Scenes 1 and 2: Castle of Grandpiano. *Scene 3*: Cabaret of "The Silver Spout."

MUSICAL NUMBERS

"When These Uniforms We Got" (Trio)

"'Tis Eventide" (Vocal Waltz)

"Roll Dem Bones, Sah" (Minstrel Overture)

"Dear Old Father's Knee" (Burlesque Ballad)

"Her Name Is Mandy, or Dar'll Be Trouble in the Tenderloin Tonight" (Negro Song and Ensemble)
Beaumont Sisters

1897.49 MY BOYS

A Farce Comedy with Musical Annex in Three Acts. Play by William Gill. Staged by Walter Turner. Musical director, William C. Ott. Produced by George Richards and Eugene Canfield. Opened 6 December 1897 at the Manhattan Theatre and closed 18 December 1897 after 16 performances[47].

CAST: *Silas Plummer*, a well-to-do stock raiser: GEORGE RICHARDS. *Sam Plummer*, his youngest son: EUGENE CANFIELD. *Charley Plummer*, his next youngest son: Madison Corey. *Jack Plummer*, his second son: George H. Rickets. *Dan Plummer*, his eldest son: GEORGE E. MARTIN. *David Dauber*, a painter with hopes of a title: Philip Robson. *Jessie Sterling*, Plummer's ward: Florence Earl. *Alice Jones*, a typewriter: Harriet Willard. *Beatrice Throgmorton*, a poetess: May Montford. *Clara Celestene*, an opera singer: CARRIE [Caro] ROMA. *Barbara Allen*, maid-of-all-work: SALLIE STEMBLER. *Mrs. Ione McCune*, a neighbor of Plummer's: MATTIE KEENE. *Four Little Plummers, One Little Dauber*: Themselves. (*Dance Specialty*: Annie St. Tel.)

Act 1: On the Lawn of the Farmhouse.

Act 2: Living Room in Farmhouse.

Act 3: Reception Room in same.

---

[45]Replaced for subsequent tour by:
"Oh, What a Row and Rumpus" (Finale)

[46]The Japanese Divertissment preceded THE WEE MINISTER.

[47]Settings, costumes uncredited.

ACT 1

Irish Songs (comic)
M. Keene

ACT 2

"Blue Eyes" (Waltz Song)
G. E. Martin

Comic Duet
E. Canfield, S. Stembler

ACT 3

Operatic Solo
C. Roma

"Asthore"
M. Keene

Burlesque Operatic Trio
G. Richards, E. Canfield, S. Stembler

Sensational Fantasie Dances
A. St. Tel

"Silas, My Darling" (Final Chorus)
Entire Company

1897.50 THE HIGHWAYMAN

A Comic Opera in Three Acts. Libretto by Harry B. Smith. Music by Reginald DeKoven. Staged by Max Freeman. Dances arranged by Carl Marwig. Settings by John H. Young. Costumes by Caroline Siedle. Musical director, Signor A. DeNovellis. Produced by the Broadway Theatre Opera Company (Andrew A. McCormick, Manager). Opened 13 December 1897 at the Broadway Theatre and closed 16 April 1898 after 144 performances[48].

CAST: *Dick Fitzgerald*, an Irish soldier of fortune; ruined by marked cards and loaded dice, he takes to the "road," and gains notoriety as Captain Scarlet: JOSEPH O'MARA. *Lady Constance Sinclair*, a belle of the Court, in love with Dick: HILDA CLARK. *Sir Godfrey Beverley*, a baronet of sporting proclivities: George O'Donnell. *Lady Pamela*, his daughter: Maud Williams. *Captain Rodney*, an officer serving with Nelson, in love with Lady Pamela: VAN RENSSELAER WHEELER. *Constable (Foxy) Quiller* of Bow Street Office, in pursuit of Captain Scarlett and a thousand pounds reward: JEROME SYKES. *Doll Primrose*, barmaid of the Cat and Fiddle Tavern, with a romantic admiration for highwaymen: NELLIE BRAGGINS. *Toby Winkle*, 'ostler of the cat and the Fiddle, in love with Doll: HARRY MACDONOUGH. *Lord Kilkenny*, an Irish nobleman: William S. Corliss. *Sir John Hawkhurst*, a Government attaché, whose finesse with cards and dice was the cause of Dick Fitzgerald's adopting the trade of knight of the road: Edwin White. *Lieutenant Lovelace* of the miltia searching for Captain Scarlet and the reward of a thousand pounds: REGINALD ROBERTS. *Landlord Jarvey* of the Cat and Fiddle: William S. Corliss. *Mrs. Jarvey*: Marion Chase. *Jack Middleton*: William Mackay. *Lady Olivia Fairfax*: Jean St. Clair. *Humphreys*, coachman of the York Mall: H. Steinman. *Bow Street Constables*: T. F. Moore, E. A. Tester, William Steiger, John E. Belton, Edward Everett, Harry Henderson. *Chorus of Fox Hunters, Militia, Farm Laborers, Gypsies, Guests and Servants of the Cat and Fiddle Tavern, Country Squires and Dames, Tenantry as Wedding Guests, etc.*

Act 1: The Cat and Fiddle Tavern on the York Road.

Act 2: Forest near the York Road.

Act 3: The Park of Beverley Manor.

ACT 1[49]

Opening Ensemble (Although I am a 'Dook')
H. Macdonough, N. Braggins, W. Corliss, Chorus

"Bread, Cheese and Kisses" (Duet)
N. Braggins, H. Macdonough

"Marching Away" (Song and Chorus)
R. Roberts, H. Macdonough, J. Sykes, Mixed Chorus

"The Highwayman" (Song)
J. O'Mara, Chorus

"In London Town" (Gavotte Quintette)
M. Williams, R. Roberts, N. Braggins, H. Macdonough, G. O'Donnell, Mixed Chorus

"Vive La Bagatelle" (Ensemble and Song)
H. Clark

"Gretna Green" (Song)
V. R. Wheeler

Finale Act 1
Principals, Chorus

ACT 2

"Kitty O'Brien" (Song)
J. O'Mara

Chorus of Villagers (It's hey for home, enough for a day)

"The Farmer and the Scarecreow" (Duet and Chorus)
H. Macdonough, J. Sykes, Chorus

"A Moonlight Song"[50] (Song)
H. Clark

"Do You Remember, Love?" (Duet)
H. Clark, J. O'Mara

"Gipsy Song"[51] (Gypsy Song)
J. Sykes, Chorus

Finale Act 2

ACT 3

Opening Chorus and Dance (It's hey for a wedding on May Day)

"While the Four Winds Blow" (Sea Song)
V. R. Wheeler

"On the Track" (Song)
J. Sykes, Constables

"Farewell to the King's Highway" (Song)
J. O'Mara

Finale Act 3

1897.51 PROTECTO

A Fairy Trick Pantomime in Three Acts, 11 Scenes. Written and arranged by George H. Adams and James R. Adams. Management, E. G. Lane. Opened 20 December 1897 at the People's Theatre and closed 25 December 1897 after 8 performances.[52]

CAST: *Pico*, the Village Trouble: GEORGE H. ADAMS. *Old One, Two, Buckle My Shoe*: Edward O'Connel. *Dr. Faust*, afterwards Little Boy Blue: JOHN F. RAYMOND. *Little Bo Peep*: Lily Adams. *"Protecto,"* the Fairy Queen: TONINA ADAMS. *Little Miss Bright Eyes*: Becky Taylor. *Little Red Riding Hood*: ROSINA COOKE. *Satanic*, King of Hades: ERNEST G. ADAMS. *Pluto*, his right bower: JEAN HOWARD. *Spero*, a sprite: JAMES R. ADAMS. *Nimo*, a sprite: W. Walla. *Pongo*, a monkey: Charles O'Brien. *Miss Prim*, a flower girl: Rebecca Morgan. *Miss Knowit*: Mamie Morgan. *Policeman Hitemhard*: Richard Mack. *Witches, Demons, Villagers, Firemen, etc.*

Act 1, Scene 1: Council of war. Pluto sent to Earth to move and evil lend. *Scene 2*: Dr. Faust's studio. "Oh, to be young again!" The tempter foiled. *Scene 3*: The village of fun. Pico's arrival. Fun begins.

Act 2, Scene 1: A street in town. Pico tries a smoke, and the sad results. *Scene 2*: Among the Rockies. Out in the cold world. A welcome hut. Pico gets left, but meets witha warm welcome. One in a box.The outcast. "Me poor child." The Indians on the trail. "Who will save me child?" Pico to the rescue. Leap for life. All happy. *Scene 3*: Pico gets a shock, and tries to shock the whole world. *Scene 4*: Hall of Statues.

Act 3, Scene 1: Pico in lots of trouble, ending in a flare-up. Pico's brave fire department. *Scene 2*: Pico joins the force. *Scene 3*: In Hades. Pico lost, but finds lots of friends, who make it warm for Pluto. Sudden appearance of Protecto, and grand transformation scene. *Scene 4*: Home of the fairies. Pico bids all good night.

SPECIALTIES, MUSICAL NUMBERS

Act 2, Scene 3

---

[48]Played a return engagement 12 December 1898 at the Broadway Theatre for 8 performances. The cast was the same except for: *Captain Rodney*: REGINALD RODNEY. *Toby Winkle*: JOHN MAYON.

[49]Musical numbers not in programs. List prepared from published vocal score (T. B. Harms & Co., New York, 1898). Songs not included in vocal score: "The Beau of Georgian Days," "In the Morning," "A Sailor's Song," "Town and Country."

[50]Replaced during the run by:
"For This" (Song)
H. Clark
(*Lyrics by* Leontine Stanfield.)

[51]May have been dropped during the run.

[52]No additional credits in programs for scenery, costumes, musical director; no list of musical numbers.

Mons. Tessier, the marvel of the slack wire

The Meeting of the King and Emperor of Stilts, George H. and James R. Adams.

(The only act of its kind on the American stage.)

Bright, Up-to-date Songs and Dances

Adams Sisters (Tonina and Lily)

Spanish Dance

Adams Sisters

Repertoire of Songs

J. Howard

1897.52 THE BALLET GIRL

A Musical Comedy in Two Acts[53]. Book by James T. Tanner. Music by Carl Kiefert. Lyrics by Adrian Ross. Produced under the personal supervision of James T. Tanner and Frederic A. Leon. Ballets by Augustus Sohlke. Settings by Frank Rafter, Hugh L. Reid and Alfred Williams. Costumes by W. A. Barnes. Musical director, Joseph Van Den Berg. Produced by Edward E. Rice. Opened 21 December 1897 at the Manhattan Theatre and closed 5 February 1898 after 56 performances[54].

CAST: *Reuben van Eyt*, an artist: DAVID H. LYTHGOE. *The Earl of Kilbeggan*, impecunious fortune-hunting peer: THOMAS RICKETTS. *Lord Comarthy*, his son: CHARLES ARTHUR. *Eugene Taradelle*, director of the Folies Theatre: EDOUARD JOSE. *Perch*, Earl's valet: Christopher Bruno. *Kopsdoppen*, landlord of the Three Bells: SNITZ EDWARDS. *Baton Blanc*, a composer: FREDERIC SOLOMON. *Floots*, regisseur at the Folies Theatre: Charles Seagrave. *Vizier*: DAVE ABRAMS. *Vrouw Schomberg*, Nita's aunt: Christine Blessing. *Gretchen, Minna*, just plain, ordinary singing peasant girls: Lillian Cooley, Violet Potter. *Fritz*, peasant boy at Heerenbergen: Irene Vera. *Bedalia*, Nita's Irish nurse: Marie Hilton. *Violette*, premiere danseuse at the Folies Theatre: ARLINE [Allene] CRATER. *Nita Vanderkoop*, an American heiress: LOUISE WILLIS-HEPNER. (*Ballet Specialty*, Act 2: AMORETTE.)

Leading Actress: Lillian Cooley. *First Actress*: Marjory Relyea. *Second Actress*: Lila Haynes. *Third Actress*: Gabriella deThien. *Fouth Actress*: Vashti Earl. *Leading Milliner*: Violet Potter. *First Milliner*: Maud Emmerson. *Second Milliner*: May Hamilton. *Third Milliner*: Gladys Kensington. *Fourth Milliner*: Lillian Kensington. *Leading Heiress*: Irene Vera. *First Heiress*: Caroline Rhodes. *Second Heiress*: Mabel Belton. *Third Heiress*: Emma Guthrie. *Fourth Heiress*: Nettie Scarsez. *Leading Widow*: Rose Flores. *First Widow*: Clarice Middleton. *Second Widow*: Phyllis Baranco. *Third Widow*: Suzie Hale. *Fourth Widow*: Mazie Follette. *Dutch Flower Girls, Villagers, Members of the Ballet at the Folies Theatre, Sellers, Figurantes, etc.*

Act 1: Heerenbergen, on the shores of the Zayder Zee. (Rafter.)

Act 2: Stage of the Folies Theatre, Paris, set for a Moorish Ballet. (Reid.)

ACT 1[55]

"Beside the Zuyder See" (Opening Chorus)(Here you see beside the zuyder)

Chorus

"In America" (Song)(I have made the most remarkable discoveries)

L. Willis-Hepner, Chorus

"A Stitch in Time" (Duet)(There is a clever artist)

L. Willis-Hepner, D. H. Lythgoe

"The Elopement" (Duet)(We've broken our tether)

A. Crater, C. Arthur

"Wedding Bells" (Quintette)(Oh, happy bells of marriage)

L. Willis-Hepner, A. Crater, [B'lindy], D. H. Lythgoe, C. Arthur

"Is It So?" (Chorus and Song)(Is it so? Have you heard?)

T. Ricketts

"Song and Dance" (Song)(At any solemn evening perpendicular)

A. Crater

"Infant Marriage" (Trio)(Did'ums was a pertty 'ickle darling)

L. Willis-Hepner, A. Crater, C. Arthur

"My Home" (Song)(Long have I wandered like the swallow)

D. H. Lythgoe

"A Boom" (Duet)(If you want to run your shows)

D. H. Lythgoe, E. Jose

"Janken and Mieken" (Duet)(Now where are you going so early?)

S. Edwards, C. Blessing, Chorus

"What Occurrence" (Finale)(What occurrence has affected)

ACT 2

"Clear! Clear! (Clear!)" (Chorus)

"Dancing" (Song)(Of all the gifts that grace)

E. Jose

"Vanity of Human Wishes" (Song)(When you and I were dear little boys)

D. H. Lythgoe

"At the Old Stage Door" (Song)

(*Music and Lyrics by* Edward E. Rice.)

Waltz (This is a serious matter)

"In the Ballet" (Song)

M. Hilton

"The Pizzicato Quartette"

S. Edwards, F. Solomon, C. Bruno, C. Seagrave

(*Music and Lyrics by* Edward E. Rice.)

Ballet

(Amorette)

"A Little Bird" (Song)(A little bird chirped in the ear of a maid)

L. Willis-Hepner

"She's the Girl I Love" (Song)

D. H. Lythgoe

Bal Bullier Ballet Quadrille

(*Music by* Edward E. Rice.)

"Romance" (Duet)(If I were poor and mean)

L. Willis-Hepner, D. H. Lythgoe

"The Ballet Girl" (Finale)(Though I am wealthy still)

1897.53 THE QUEEN'S LACE HANDKERCHIEF

A Revival of the Comic Opera in Three Acts.[56] (Original Viennese operette libretto 'Das Spitzentuch Der Königin' by Bohrmann-Riegen[57] and Richard Genée. American adaptation by James Frenor.) Music by Johann Strauss, Jr. Scenery by Frank King (Acts 1, 3), Joseph Clare (Acts 2, 3). Conductor, Adolph Liesegang. Produced by the Castle Square Opera Company (Henry W. Savage, Proprietor). Opened 25 December 1897 at the American Theatre and closed 1 January 1898 after 10 performances.

CAST: *The King*: LIZZIE MacNICHOL. *The Queen*: NITA CARRITTE. *Donna Irene*, the Queen's confidante: GRACE GOLDEN. *Marquise of Villareal*: CLARA WISDOM. *Cervantes*, a poet: JOSEPH F. SHEEHAN. *Count Villaiobois y Rodriguez*, Prime Minister and Head of the Regency: WILLIAM G. STEWART. *Don Sancho de Avellaneda y Villipinguedones*, tutor to the King: RAYMOND HITCHCOCK. *Marquis de la Marceha Villareal*, Minister of War: Frank Wooley. *Duke of Feria*, Minister of Finance: Charles Whyte. *Count San Gregorio*, Minister of Interior: R. Ridgeley. *Count Ermos*, Minister of Navy: W. C. Brockmeyer. *Don Diego de Barados*, Minister of Police: R. Johns. *Dancing Master*: E. Danton. *Master of Ceremonies*: Ruth White. *Antonio*, inkeeper of the Sierra Nuaro: John Read. *Students, Doctors, Ladies and Gentlemen of the Court, Toreadors, Brigands, etc.*

1897.54 THE TELEPHONE GIRL

A Musical Comedy in Two Acts. Libretto by Hugh Morton. Adapted from the French operetta "La Demoiselle du Telephone" by Maurice Désvallières, Anthony Mars, Gaston Serpette. Music by Gustav Kerker.

---

[53]Also billed as Edward E Rice's production of the latest English novelty.

[54]Also played a return engagement 28 March 1898 at the Harlem Opera House for 8 performances.

[55]Interpolated as per published sheet music:

"Her Memory Brings Me No Regret"

L. Willis-Hepner

(*Music* by Charles Graham. *Lyrics by* Howard Graham.)

[56]First produced in New York 21 October 1882 at the Casino Theatre for 8 performances; re-opened 30 December 1882 at the Casino Theatre for 72 additional performances; re-opened 11 June 1883 at the Casino Theatre for 28 additional performances. Total: 113 performances. For Synopsis of Scenes and Musical Numbers, see original 1882 production.

[57]Heinrich Bohrmann and Julius von St. Albino Nigri (whose pen name was Riegen) wrote the first version of the libretto.

Produced under the personal stage direction of George W. Lederer. Ballets arranged by Signor Francioli. Settings by D. Frank Dodge, Ernest Albert. Costumes by Mme. Catherine Seidle. Musical director, Gustav Kerker. Produced by George W. Lederer and George B. McLellan. Opened 27 December 1897 at the Casino Theatre and closed 26 March 1898 after 104 performances; re-opened 27 June 1898 at the Casino Theatre and closed 16 July 1898 after 24 additional performances. Total: 128 performances[58].

CAST: *Hans Nix*, inspector of telephones: LOUIS MANN. *Colonel William Goldtop*, an old beau: CHARLES DICKSON. *Dick Marvel*, a young broker: EDWARD S. ABELES. *Senor Velasquez*, a Brazilian: Henry Bergman. *Ebeneezer Fairfax*, father of Beauty Fairfax: Nicholas Burnham. *Snuffles*, errand boy in the telephone office: JAMES F. McDONALD. *Saunders*, a butler: Benjamin J. Dillon. *A Ballet Master*: Signor FRANCIOLI. *Estelle Coocoo*, the telephone girl: CLARA LIPMAN. *Beauty Fairfax*, music hall favorite: ELEANOR ELTON. *Samanthy Fairfax*, Beauty's mother: Sarah McVicker. *Mrs. Puffaway*, in charge of telephone office: Rosa Cooke. *Toots*, errand girl in telephone office: Millicent Willson. *Clementine*, captain of telephone girls: Anita Willson. *Rosie*, a lady's maid: BESSIE WYNN. *The Telephone Girls*: *Susie*: Helen Dupont. *Sallie*: Edith St. Clair. *Totsie*: Jane English. *Seraphine*: Grace Spencer. *Viola*: Lily Ward. *Adele*: Evelyn Byrd. *Pauline*: Heleyn Whiting. *Lillian*: Emma Levey.

Act 1: Interior of a Central Telephone Office. (Dodge.)

Act 2: A Salon in the House of Beauty Fairfax. (Albert.)

MUSICAL NUMBERS[59]

- "Oh, Willie Boy!"
- "I Wouldn't Do Anything Wrong"
- "And the Bell Goes Ting-a-Ling-Ling"
- "Lead On, Ebeneezer"
- "Mary Ellen Brown"
- "Little Yaller Boy" (Negro Song)
- "I Want to Be a Dancer"
- "My Estelle"
  J. F. McDonald
- "The Old Days"
  E. S. Abeles, C. Lipman
- "Tricky Little Sarah" (Keep Your Eye on Pretty Sarah)
- "Nancy Hogan's Ball!"
  (*Lyrics by* J. H. Wagner.)
- "Little Birdies Learning How to Fly" (Act 2)
  C. Dickson, Ladies
- "Rough Riders"
- "Would You If You Could"
- "Uptown Downtown"
- "The Telephone Girl"
- Hans Nix Telephones Sing Sing (monologue)

1897.55 MISS PHILADELPHIA

A Musical Satire in Three Acts, 6 Scenes. Libretto by Edgar Smith. Music by Herman Perlet and Frederick Gagel. Staged by Junius Howe. Costumes by Madame Nordick. Musical director, Frederick Arundel. Produced by W. R. Howe. Opened 27 December 1897 at the Star Theatre and closed 1 January 1898 after 8 performances.

CAST: *Ruth Springgarden*, a Quaker bud: ELVIA CROX-SEABROOKE. *Daisy Walker*, that rara avis, a sensible girl: QUEENIE VASSAR. *Miss Jane Brownsmith*, Ruth's aunt: JESSIE VILLARS. *Vera Gray*: Georgia Stewart. *Captain Bullitt* of the City Troop: Georgia Stewart. *Etta Candee*, a real sweet thing: Olga Lambert. *Lulu Temple*, a favorite with the boys: Nellie McNulty. *William Penn*, a visitor from spirit land: WILLIAM H. WEST. *Dodge Trolleys*, a rapid young man about town: O. S. Fitz-Gerald. *Butsey*, a bootblack: Harry Robinson. *Shiners*, Butsey's pal: Arthur Connelly. *Nipit*, Penn Jr.'s pal: Frank Lynden. *Bilke*, a waiter at Drinkwater Inn: Robert Boyd. *Willie Treat*, a practitioner of the bar: Arthur Newell. *Owing Taylor*, a social highwayman: Owen McCormack. *Girard Coolidge*, a barnacle on papa's pocket: Edmund Mulkay. *Three Racers*: *Rhoda Wheel*: Nelly McNulty. *Getta Wheel*: Lily Collins. *Iona Wheel*: Regina Collins. *William Penn, Jr.*, an up-to-date Philadelphian: JOSEPH CAWTHORN.

Act 1, Scene 1: William Penn Jr.'s bachelor apartments. *Scene 2*: Exterior of Union League Club with a glimpse of Bellevue Hotel.

Act 2, Scene 1: The Mint and Wanamaker's Store. *Scene 2*: Ninth and Chestnut Streets.

Act 3, Scene 1: Drinkwater Inn, on the Wissahickon. *Scene 2*: Ballroom in William Penn Jr's mansion.

ACT 1

- "Strolling Chorus"
  (*Music by* Frederick Gagel.)
- "A Maid Demure" (Song)
  E. Crox-Seabrooke
  (*Music by* Herman Perlet.)
- "Another Pair of Shoes" (Trio)
  E. Crox-Seabrooke, J. Cawthorn, W. H. West
  (*Music by* Herman Perlet.)
- "Maidens Tender Glances" (Duo)
  Q. Vassar, O. S. Fitz-Gerald
  (*Music by* Frederick Gagel.)
- "March of the City Troops" (Finale)
  (*Music by* Frederick Gagel.)

ACT 2

- "These Words May Have Meaning for Thee" (Song)
  W. H. West
  (*Music by* Herman Perlet.)
- "Pale Moonlight" (Quartette)
  E. Crox-Seabrooke, Q. Vassar, J. Cawthorn, O.S. Fitz-Gerald
  (*Music by* Herman Perlet.)
- "Bootblack Quartette"
  A. Connelly, H. Robinson
- "Love's Sweet Lay" (Song)
  E. Crox-Seabrooke
  (*Music by* Frederick Gagel.)
- Quartette
  E. Crox-Seabrooke, Q. Vassar, J. Cawthorn, O. S. Fitz-Gerald
  (*Music by* Herman Perlet.)
- "El Capitan" Dance (from EL CAPITAN)
  L. Collins
  (*Music by* John Philip Sousa.)
- "Baby Lou" (Song)
  E. Crox-Seabrooke
  (*Music by* Frederick Gagel.)
- Specialty
  J. Cawthorn

ACT 3

- "Mid Shady Groves"
  Chorus
  (*Music by* Herman Perlet.)
- "Tally Ho" (Song and Chorus)
  E. Crox-Seabrooke
  (*Music by* Herman Perlet.)
- "My Love, My Own" (Song with Chorus)
  O. S. Fitz-Gerald
  (*Music by* Frederick Gagel. *Lyrics by* Matt Woodward.)
- Specialty
  J. Villars
- "Jack and Jill" (Quartette and Dance)
  Misses Stewart, Kampt, L. Collins, R. Collins

1897.56 THE NANCY HANKS

A Comedy (Musical Farce) in Three Acts. Play by Frank Tannehill, Jr. Produced under the stage direction of Frank Tannehill, Jr. Songs and music specially arranged by Isadore Witmark. Musical director, Albert Elias. Produced by Marie Jansen, Frank Tannehill (Arthur F. Warde, Charles H.

[58]Also played return engagements 12 September 1898 at the Harlem Opera House for 8 performances, and 1 October 1900 at the Grand Opera House for 8 performances.

[59]No song list in program. List prepared from published vocal selections, not in performance order. Song titles beginning with "Rough Riders" not in vocal selection, but credited to the show in reviews, etc.

Beede, Management). Opened 27 December 1897 at the Garden Theatre and closed 8 January 1898 after 14 performances[60].

CAST: *Jim*, the Dresser: F. W. Caldwell. *Seizer*, deputy sheriff: F. Harvey. *Madison Broadway*, of the world wordly: Clayton E. White. *Marquis de la Rochelle*: HARRY BERESFORD. *Richard Chandos* of the principal theatres: FRANK TANNEHILL, JR. *Zona*, a flower from nature's fields: Emma Dunn. *Frances Lakewood*, the newest woman: Pauline Fletcher. *Henrietta Dash*, she only needs an example: JESSIE BRADBURY. *Aunt Hetty Evergreen*, whose mind is always made up: F. [FRANK] A. TANNEHILL. *Pearl Dodo*, a popular price favorite: MARIE JANSEN.

Act 1: Mrs. Grundy's Boarding House, New York City, 9 A.M.—Fate.

Act 2: Pearl Dodo's Flat. 12 oc'clock the same day.—Severed lives.

Act 3: Aunt Hetty's House. Larchmont on the Sound, 5P.M. the same day, misunderstandings misunderstood.

MUSICAL NUMBERS[61]

"Mary"
M. Jansen

"Willie Off the Yacht"
M. Jansen

1898.01 GAYEST MANHATTAN

A Burlesque Extravaganza in Three Acts[62]. Libretto (book) by W. H. Lytell. Music by W. H. Batchelor. Lyrics by John F. Harley. Direction of John F. Harley. Scenery by Voegtlin, Operti and Dangerfield. Costumes by Van Axe and Mme. Cameron. Musical director, W. H. Batchelor. Produced by Koster & Bial. Opened 3 January 1898 at the Star Theatre and closed 8 January 1898 after 8 performances; returned 19 September 1898 to the Harlem Opera House and closed 24 September 1898 after an additional 7 performances.

CAST: *Hiram Prindle*: RICHARD GORMAN. *Melinda*, his daughter, a graduate at the Collar and Cuff Institute of Troy, New York: GERTIE REYNOLDS. *Nathaniel Mansfield Belgraff*, teacher of elocution: GUS PIXLEY. *Tess* of the Aristooks, Prindle's eldest daughter: JENNIE L. LEWIS. *Society Girls (2)*: *Miss Waldorf*: Kate Michelena. *Miss Van Astor*: Mabel Montgomery. *Countess de Blaine*, French, but willing to be Americanized: Grace Sherwood. *Louis Spitzberger*, a German waiter: JAMES A. KIERNAN. *Willie Way* of Broadway and Fifth Avenue: Jean McIlmoyle. *Jack Fairum*, an enthusiastic lover: Thomas Kiernan. *Count DiGarcia*, from Havana or Sumatra: Matt Alexander. *Knott Chapman*, a light-fotted and quick-witted policeman: Robert Watson. *Shine M. Quick*: Carrie Cameron.

Act 1: The Mall. Central Park.

Act 2: Ball room. The Waldorf.

Act 3: Promenade Floor. Koster & Bial's.

ACT 1[63]

"The Ruler of Central Park" (Chorus)
"I'm a Practical Politican" (Solo and Chorus)
"For Sweet Charity's Sake" (Solo and Chorus)
"Susie Smith from Troy" (Solo)
"The Dandy Sparrow Cops" (March Song)
"The Good Old Palmy Days" (Solo and Chorus)
"From Skowhegan, Maine, B'gosh" (Solo)
"Gayest Manhattan" (Ensemble and Finale)

ACT 2

"Ring the Praises Merrily" (Opening Chorus)
"When Love Was Born" (Solo)
"For Thee, My Love" (Solo)
"My Husband Taught Me to be One of the Boys" (Solo and Chorus)
"But Wasn't It an Odd Place to Do It" (Solo)
"Flirtation Duet"
"My Thoughts Would Still Be with Thee" (Solo and Quartette)
"And Mrs. Grundy Winked" (Solo)
"Will Somebody Tell Me Why?" (Topical Quintette)
"Life Is What We Make It" (Ensemble and Chorus)

ACT 3

"Roses and Thorns" (Octette)
"March of the New York Dailies"
Specialty
J. A. Kiernan, G. Reynolds, Pickaninnies
Extracts from the Vaudevilles
G. Pixley
The Monarch Four (Quartette)
Midland Beach Potpourri (Finale)

[60]Scenery and costumes uncredited. Musical numbers not listed in programs.

[61]Musical numbers not listed in programs. Interpolated as per published sheet music for tour:

"I Want Dem Presents Back"
A. Boyd
(*Music and Lyrics by* Paul West.)

[62]Not to be confused with an earlier vaudeville entertainment, also produced by Koster & Bial, with the title GAYEST MANHATTAN, or Around New York in Ninety Minutes, but with different authors and cast, presented 22 March 1897 at Koster & Bial's.

[63]Song list prepared from Harlem Opera House return engagement.

1898.02 THE GOVERNORS

A Variety Farce in Three Acts. Play by Fred Gibbs. Produced by E. D. Stair. Opened 3 January 1898 at Hoyt's Theatre and closed 15 January 1898 after 14 performances[64].

CAST: *The Governor of Idaho*, by Percy: HAPPY WARD. *The Governor of Oregon*, by Harold: HARRY VOKES. *The Bell-Boy*, by Rubber Neck: JOHNNY PAGE. *Tyhe Bunco Man*, by Keen S. Harper: GUS C. WEINBERG. *Our Country Cousin*, by J. Ott: John Keefe. *Our Landlord*, by Col. Peach: Hal S. Stephens. *Scorcher*, by Rider Bike: JAMES CHERRY. *Guests, Drummers and Bummers*, by Willie Stringer, Bill Board, Mill Wauke, Willie Wright: Nat Nixon, Louis N. Powers, James Johnson, G. H. Shields. *A Club Man*, by a Policeman: Theodore Moross. *Lumber Mercant*, by Willie Stick: Budd Beverly. *Post Man*, by Kerry Mail: William B. Rock. *An Old Settler*, by Brig. Ham. Young: A. H. Scott. *Ice Man*, by Diamond Joe: H. W. Kelly. *Coy Boy*, by William H. Bull: Richard Williams. *The Plot of Our Play*: Our Dog "Boe." *The Foolish Girl*, by Edie Ott: MARGARET DALY VOKES. *The New Woman*, by Winna Man: Vila Sayne. *The Female Suffragist*, by Mrs. Cap'Vour: Hattie Bernard. *The Society Girl*, by Fay Tague: Effie Kamman. *The Summer Girl*, by May Knott: Sadie Whitcomb. *The Choir Singer*, by Annie Price: Mary Hughes. *The Bicycle Girl*, by Minn U. Vour: Patti Lataine. *The Gum-Chewer*, by Or A. Vour: Violet Wein. *Miss Tandem*, by A. Wheeler: Bessie Campbell. *Job Lots*, by Miss Fitts: Nina Walsh. *Miss Star*, by Tillie Twinkle: Anna Chance. *The Female Barber*, by Miss Muggs: Belle Lorraine. *Whirlwind*, by Kittie Hurricane: Arline Athens. *The Giddy Girl*, by Em Peach: LUCY DALY.

Act 1: Exterior summer hotel. Time, twilight. Temperature, normal.

Act 2: Hotel office. Any old time. Temperature, blood heat.

Act 3: Parlor in Winna Man's mansion. Just in time. Temperature, Klondike fever.

During the action of "The Discord" the following specialties will be introduced.

ACT 1

"Six Beautiful Maids"
N. Walsh, M. Hughes, H. Bernard, S. Whitcomb, A. Chance, A. Athens

"Sadie"
L. Daly, Company

"Conversation Dance"
H. Ward, H. Vokes, L. Daly, M. Daly Vokes

John Keefe's "Hey Rube," assisted by James Cherry

"Like Kelly Did"
H. Ward, G. C. Weinberg, H. S. Stephens, J. Cherry, W. B. Rock

"Queen of the Vaudeville, à la Anna Held"
L. Daly, J. Page, assisted by
Misses H. Bernard, S. Whitcomb, A. Chance, M. Hughes, N. Walsh, A. Athens

Troubadour Four
N. Wilson, L. N. Powers, J. Johnson, G. H. Shields

"The Way Duffy Used to Call"
Company

[64]Also played return engagements 24 January 1898 at the 14th Street Theatre for 8 performances, 21 February 1898 at the Columbus Theatre for 8 performances, and 6 March 1899 at the Metropolis Theatre for 8 performances.

ACT 2
"Flo" and "Willie Off the Yacht" by Johnny Page and Lucy Daly

ACT 3
"The Baby on the Shore" (Comic Hymn)
M. D. Vokes, J. Keefe
"Percy and Harold" (Famous Specialty)
H. Ward, H. Vokes
Gus Weinberg and His Original "Register"
Lucy Daly in her famous Pickaninny Specialty, assisted J. Page
"You Ain't As Warm as You Look"

1898.03 A HIRED GIRL

A Farce Comedy in Three Acts. Play by Charles E. Blaney. Music by Harry James. Stage production under the direction of James T. Kelly. Scenery by D. Frank Dodge. Costumes by Evans & Company. Musical director, Harry James. Produced by Charles E. Blaney. Opened 10 January 1898 at the Star Theatre, moved 17 January 1898 to the Third Avenue Theatre and closed 22 January 1898 after 16 performances; re-opened 14 March 1898 at the 14th Street Theatre and closed 19 March 1898 after 8 performances; re-opened 22 August 1898 at the Star Theatre and closed 27 August 1898 after 8 additional performances. Total: 32 performances.

CAST: *Johanna Quinn*, the Hired Girl: JAMES T. KELLY. *Lord Green Goods*, an adventurer: JAMES F. DOLAN. *Chef*: WILLIS P. SWEATNAM. *Crappy Dan*, a waiter: WILLIS P. SWEATNAM. *Link Missing*: WILLIS P. SWEATNAM. *Professor Ver Blotz*, of Vassar: John R. Cumpson. *Officer Swift*: Waldo Whipple. *Dusty Rhodes*: Waldo Whipple. *Ref. E. Ree*, of Yale: John Munger. *Mrs. Ver Blotz*: Ida Lenharr. *U. Bet Gilbert*, a female detective: TRIXIE WADE. *Sylvia Gold*, an heiress: Dorothy Carter. *Miss Weiner*, a German vender: Rose Sutherland. *Sue Brette*, a maid: Stella Bonheur. *Katie Tacks*: BELLE GOLD. *Vassar Girls (6)*: *Fannie Frotchschild*: Alice Nichols. *Marie Knockafellow*: Adelaide Leeds. *Susette Whipney*: Eva Kelly. *Belle Guntington*: Georgie Black. *Babettes Hope*: Blanche Althea. *Rosie Greene*: Lillian Althea. *Waiters, Attendants, Pages, etc.* (*Dance Specialty*: DuHELD SISTERS, Alice, Georgia, Blanche, Lillian.)

Act 1: In the Conservatory at Vassar College.

Act 2: Commencement Day, on the Campus at Vassar.

Act 3: Banquet Room at Vassar. Celebration of the winning of the Hired Girl's lawsuit. Arrest of the Lord, etc.

ACT 1[65]
"Mamie O'Relly" (Opening Chorus)
Waiter Girls
Buck Dances
T. Wade
"You'll Find a Girl to Please You Here in Town" (Chorus and Dance)
"Jolly Josephine" (Song, Chorus and Dance)
Vassar Students
Songs
B. Gold
The Tough Girl (Song and Chorus)
R. Sutherland
"The Rag Time Dance"
Ladies of the Company
"What'll I Do to McAdoo"
J. T. Kelly, Ladies of the Company
"But Time Will Tell" (Grand Concerted Trio)
J. F. Dolan, J. R. Cumpson, S. Bonheur
"The Hired Girl's Pink Tea"
J. T. Kelly, Hired Girls
"The Parisienne Grisettes" (Song, Chorus and Dance)
T. Wade, Company
"A Man Burglar, (Don't Let Him Out)" (Finale)
Entire Company

ACT 2
Opening Chorus and Dance (Medley)
"The Queens of the Rose and Gray"
T. Wade, F. Fields, S. Bonheur, D. Carter
La Folée (The Four DuHeld Sisters in their latest Parisian dances)
Miss Alice, Miss Georgia, Miss Blanche, Miss Lillian
"Genevieve" (Song and Chorus)
Ladies of the Company
Trick and Nerve Dancing
W. Whipple
The Yale and Vassar Football Chorus

ACT 3
Opening Chorus
Ladies of the Company
Miss Rose Sutherland, the terpsichorean wonder
Monologue
W. P. Sweatnam
Burlesque Travesty on "The Sporting Duchess"
Dolan and Lenharr
The arrest of Lord Green Goods
Closing Chorus/Good Night

[65]During the tour, Fannie Fields joined the cast with her specialty songs and dances (Act 2).

1898.04 THE FENCING MASTER

A Revival of the Romantic Opera (Opéra Comique) in Three Acts.[66] Libretto by Harry B. Smith. Music by Reginald DeKoven. Scenery by Joseph Clare, Frank King. Musical director, Adolph Liesegang. Produced by the Castle Square Opera Company (Henry W. Savage, Proprietor). Opened 10 January 1898 at the American Theatre and closed 15 January 1898 after 8 performances.

CAST: *Duke of Milan*: ARTHUR WOOLEY. *Fortunio*, his nephew, rightful heir to the ducal throne: WILLIAM G. STEWART. *Torquato*, Court Fencing Master: WILLIAM SCHUSTER. *Francesca*, his daughter, known as Francesco, and brought up as a boy: GRACE GOLDEN. *Pasquino*, the Duke's private magician and astrologer: OSCAR GIRARD. *Count Guido Malespino*: JOSEPH F. SHEEHAN. *The Doge of Venice*: Oscar Voigt. *Filippa*, the Duke's ward: NITA CARRITTE. *Marchesa di Goldoni*, a young widow: HELEN G. JUDSON. *Theresa*, daughter of a Milanese money lender, betrothed to the Duke: FLORENCE RELDA. *Pietro*, an innkeeper: Ruth White. *Rinaldo*, Captain of the Guard: W. C. Brockmeyer. *Isatella*, a Venetian girl: Emma King.

1898.05 THE GIRL FROM PARIS

A Return Engagement of the Musical Comedy in Two Acts[67]. Libretto by George Dance. (Adapted from the English musical "The Gay Parisienne.") Music by Ivan Caryll. Staged by Frank Smithson. Incidental dances arranged and directed by H. Fletcher Rivers. Settings by Frank Rafter and D. Frank Dodge. Costumes by Mme. M. L. Dowling. Musical director, John J. Braham. Orchestrations by George Hayes. Produced by Edward E. Rice. Opened 17 January 1898 at Wallack's Theatre and closed 12 February 1898 after 32 performances[68].

[66]First produced in New York 14 November 1892 at the Casino Theatre for 120 performances. For Synopsis of Scenes and Musical Numbers, see original 1892 producton.

[67]Also billed as Edward E. Rice's production of the latest London novelty. First produced in New York 8 December 1896 at the Herald Square Theatre for 266 performances; re-opened 28 August 28 1897 at the Herald Square Theatre for 33 additional performances. Total: 299 performances. For Synopsis of Scenes and Musical Numbers, see original 1896 production. For this engagement, "Now Darling We Must Part" (Act 2) was replaced by:
"Remembrance of Love" (Waltz Song)
A. Lorraine, Chorus
"Reste Là" (Act 2) was replaced by:
"N'est Pas" (Song) .
G.Caine

[68]Returned 19 December 1898 to the Columbia Theatre.

CAST: *Mr. Honeycomb*, "a shining light": FRED LENNOX. *Mrs. Honeycomb*, his wife: ROSE BEAUDET. *Norah*, their daughter: ANDREE LORRAINE. *Mabel*, Nora's friend: HATTIE WILLIAMS. *Major Fossdyke*, of the Battersea Butterfly Shooters: WILLIAM BRODERICK. *The Major's Daughters, Bicycle Girls (6)*: *Angela*: Mamie Forbes. *May*: Bessie Bonneville. *Ethel*: Mayme Kealty. *Gladys*: Bessie Wilton. *Maud*: Mabel Dixey. *Edith*: Willie Norton. *Amos Dingle*, Honeycomb's friend: Harry Earle. *Tom Everleigh*, a barrister: AUGUSTUS KRAMER. *Algernon P. Ducie*, an American: SYDNEY deGRAY. *Percy Tooting, Cecil Smythe*, Ducie's friends: Victor Moore, James Lee. *Blatterwatter*, a gendarme: W. Wallace Black. *Hans*, proprietor of the Spa Hotel, Schoffenburgen: D. L. DON. *Servants (3)*: *Gretchen*: Agnes Wadleigh. *Anna*: Margaret Trew. *Fritz*: George F. Campbell. *Ruth*, Honeycomb's servant: ANNA BUCKLEY. *Mr. Auguste Pompier*, a French spy: THOMAS F. KIERNS. *Julie Bon-Bon*, the Gay Parisienne: GEORGIA CAINE. *Dance Specialty*: MABEL CLARK.

Chorus Ladies: Misses Mabel Dixey, Mamie Forbes, Ione Chamberlin, Mayme Kealty, Jessie Calef, Carrie Seiden, Mary Webb, Vinnie Danvers, Bessie Wilton, Annie Franko, Lena Dykstra, Susie Hale, Etta Stetson, Nina Gianetti, Lulu Hesse, Sophia Brosehart, Gertie Clark. *The Bicycle Girls*: Misses Mamie Forbes, Willie Norton, Bessie Wilton, Mayme Kealty, Bessie Bonneville, Mabel Dixey. *Chorus Gentlemen*: Messrs. A. F. Hermann, E. H. Aiken, A. Stewart, Edwin Thomas, J. Leigh, Frank Stetson, Irving Chauncey, John P. Savage, Victor Moore, F. L. Hill, J. F. Gray, James F. Woods. *The Ballet*: Mamie Forbes, Gertie Clark, Helene Lucas, Vinnie Danvers, Frank Stetson, Sydney deGray, James Lee, Irving Chauncey.

1898.06

LILY OF KILLARNEY, The Colleen Bawn

A Revival of the Romantic Opera in Three Acts, 8 Scenes[69]. (Libretto by John Oxenford and Dion Boucicault. Based on the play "The Colleen Bawn" by Dion Boucicault, adapted from the novel "The Collegians" by Gerald Griffin.) Music by Julius Benedict. Scenery by Joseph Clare, Frank King. Musical director, Adolph Liesegang. Produced by the Castle Square Opera Company (Henry W. Savage, Proprietor). Opened 17 January 1898 at the American Theatre and closed 22 January 1898 after 8 performances.

CAST: *Father Tom*: ARTHUR WOOLEY. *Eily O'Connor*, the Colleen Bawn: GRACE GOLDEN. *Hardress Cregan*: JOSEPH F. SHEEHAN. *Anne Chute*, the heiress: GERTRUDE QUINLAN. *Sheelah*: Ruth White. *Danny Mann*: William Wolff. *Myles na Coppaleen*: THOMAS H. PERSSE. *Corrigan*: RAYMOND HITCHCOCK. *Mrs. Cregan*, Hardress' mother: Gertrude Rutledge. *O'Moore*: John Reidy. *Sergeant*: Charles Scribner. *Mike, Mary*, Irish dancers: Edward H. Bradley, Thomas F. Watson. *The Piper*: James C. McCauliffe.

The action is set in Ireland.

Act 1, Scene 1: Dining-hall at Tore Cregan. (Clair.) *Scene 2*: The path leading to the Rock of Dunloe. *Scene 3*: Room in Eily's cottage. (Clair.)

Act 2, Scene 1: Exterior of Tore Cregan. (King.) *Scene 2*: Exterior of Eily's cottage. (King.) *Scene 3*: Devils' Rock at the Cave Entrance (King.)

Act 3, Scene 1: Exterior of Myles' cottage. (King.) *Scene 2*: Ballroom at Castle Chute. (Clair.)

1898.07

PAUL JONES

A Revival of the Opéra (Comique) in Three Acts[70]. [Original French libretto ("Surcouf") by Heni Chivot and Alfred Duru. English adaptation by H. B. Farnie.] Music by Robert Planquette. Scenery by Frank King. Musical director, Adolph Liesegang. Produced by the Castle Square Opera Company (Henry W. Savage, Proprietor). Opened 31 January 1898 at the American Theatre and closed 5 February 1898 after 8 performances.

CAST: *Paul Jones*, the celebrated nautical hero: LIZZIE MACNICHOL. *Rufino de Martinez*, a Spanish naval officer: JOSEPH F. SHEEHAN. *Bicoquet*, a St. Malo Ship Chandler: RAYMOND HITCHCOCK. *Don Trocadero*, Spanish Governor of the Island Estrella: OSCAR GIRARD. *Captain Kestral*, Skipper of a Yankee Privateer: John Read. *Bouillabaisse*, old smuggler: WILLIAM WOOLF. *Petit Pierre*, Fisher Lad of St. Malo: ARTHUR WOOLEY. *Rainez*: Herman Haynes. *Goujon*: F. S. Heck. *Yvonne*, Niece of Bicoquet: AMY HARTLEY. *Chopinette*, wife of Bouillabaisse: BESSIE FAIRBAIRN. *Malaguena*, Niece of Don Trocadero: RUTH WHITE. *Alva*: Amy Travis. *Fernando*: C. Franklyn. *Riboso*: C. Jupyeat. *Delphine*: F. Relda. *Fishermen, Sailors, Smugglers, Lassies of St. Malo, Ladies of the Chateau, Spanish Officers, Pages, Creoles, etc.*

1898.08

WHO IS WHO?

A Comedy of Complication with Vaudeville Trimings (Musical Farce Comedy) in Three Acts. Play by Herbert Hall Winslow. Director, Herbert Dillea. Stage director, Griffith P. Evans. Produced by F. W. Stair and George H. Nicolai. Opened 7 February 1898 at the Third Avenue Theatre and closed 12 February 1898 after 8 performances.

CAST: *Jack Hartland*, junior member of the firm of Nemo & Hartland, attorneys at law, New York City: JOE KELLY. *Peter Von Baumbach*, of the Consoldated Soap Trust: CHARLES A. MASON. *Jeff Barclay*, a man of fashion with a skeleton in his closet: Griffith P. Evans. *Tony Tracy*, a persistent bill collector: EDDIE GIGUERE. *Dennis O'Dowd*, janitor of the Equitable Building: Johnnie LaFevre. *Willie*, on the spot, Nemo & Hartland's office boy: J. Ed. Goggin. *John*, servant to Von Baumbach: Charles Davis. *Mabel Von Baumbach*, reared in luxury: ANNIE DACRE. *Tillie Coombs*, who runs the office: BLANCHE BOYER. *Mrs. Martha Sackett*, proprietress of "Sackett's Balm": Fannie Denham Rouse. *Angelica*, her daughter: Georgie Tompkins. *Coral*, an unwelcome visitor from Chicago: Eva Randolph. *Mabel*, the Long Branch girl: Evelyn Forbes. *Members of the Condemned Murderers' Floral Association (6)*: *Pansy Sells*: Nelle Blanchard. *Myrtle Boltz*: Maud Bank. *Rosie Doom*: Evelyn Woodward. *Lillie Stripes*: May Whiting. *Violet Shakles*: Lillian Whiting. *Daisy Bars*: Belle Tufts.

Time: The Present.

Act 1: Law Office of Nemo & Hartland, Broadway, New York. "In partnership."

Act 2: Exterior of "Sackett's Balm" cottage, adjoining Hon. Peter Von Baumbach's Lawn, on the Hudson. "The partnership dissolved."

Act 3: Lapse of one week. Library in the Hon. Peter Von Baumbach's summer home. "The consequence of the partnership."

ACT 1

"The Typewriter Girls"
Misses Boyer, Wood Sisters, Whiting Sisters, Blanchard, Tufts

"The German Singing Society" (Dutch Saengerfest)
Messrs. Goggin, Davis, Giguere, LaFevre, Mason; P. Von Baumbach, conductor

"Jolly Convicts and Their Admirers"
Misses Wood, Blanchard, Tufts, Whiting; Messrs. Goggin, Davis

"Villains We See at the Play"
A. Dacre, Messrs. Kelly, Mason

ACT 2

"Flirting with the Man in the Moon"
Misses Boyer, Tompkins, Blanchard, Forbes, Dacre, Whiting Sisters, Tufts

Goggin and Davis in the peer of all acrobatic specialties

ACT 3

"The Race Track Girls"
A. Dacre, Ladies of the Condemned Murderers Association

(Specialty) Operatic Duettists
Misses Tompkins, Tufts

Original Specialty
Kelly and Mason

Cornet Duets
Whiting Sisters

(Specialty) A little comedian and singer, and a little soubrette and dancer
Giguere and Boyer

"Who Is Who"
Company

1898.09

H.M.S. PINAFORE, or The Lass That Loved a Sailor

A Revival of the Comic Opera in Two Acts[71] (presented on a double bill with the opera 'Cavalleria Rusticana' by Pietro Mascagni). Libretto by

[69]First produced in New York 1 January 1868 at the Academy of Music, returning 11 May 1868 to the Theatre Français for several performances in repertory. For Synopsis of Scenes and Musical Numbers, see original 1868 production.

[70]First produced in New York 6 October 1890 at the Broadway Theatre for 35 performances. For Synopsis of Scenes and Musical Numbers, see original 1890 production.

[71]Originally presented in New York 15 January 1879 at the Standard Theatre for 175 performances. For Synopsis of Scenes and Musical Numbers, see original 1879 production.

William S. Gilbert. Music by Arthur Sullivan. Stage manager, A. W. F. MacCollin. Scenery by Frank King. Conductor, Adolph Liesegang. Presented by the Castle Square Opera Company (Henry W. Savage, Proprietor). Opened 14 February 1898 at the American Theatre and closed 26 February 1898 after 17 performances.

CAST: *The Rt. Hon. Sir Joseph Porter, K.C.B.*, First Lord of the Admiralty: ARTHUR WOOLEY. *Captain Corcoran*, Commanding the *H.M.S. Pinafore*: WILLIAM G. STEWART. *Ralph Rackstraw*, Able Seaman: JOSEPH F. SHEEHAN, CHARLES O. BASSETT. *Dick Deadeye*, Able Seaman: JAMES STURGESS. *Bill Bobstay*, Boatswain: E. N. Knight. *A Silent Marine*: Charles Scribner. *Josephine*, the Captain's Daughter: ELSA MAY, JESSIE CONANT. *Little Buttercup*, a Bumboat Woman: LIZZIE MACNICHOL. *Hebe*, Sir Joseph's First Cousin: MAY HAMPTON, RUTH WHITE. *Chorus of Sailors, Sisters, Cousins, Aunts, etc.*

1898.10 A BAGGAGE CHECK

A Farce Comedy in Three Acts. Play by Charles E. Blaney. Produced by Charles E. Blaney. Opened 14 February 1898 at the Star Theatre and closed 19 February 1898 after 8 performances.

CAST: *Isa Conboy*, who recognizes no law: RAYMOND FINDLEY. *Robin Steele*, whose highest ambition is to be low: WILLIAM MITCHELL. *Willy Waite*, wealthy, but witless: Edward Sharpley. *Daffy Dan*, a pleasant gentleman to know: Frank Vanetta. *Oiler Can*, an advocate of temperance: Harry McFadden. *Has A. Scent*, health officer: William Mitchell. *Handy Clubber*, night officer: W. E. Horton. *Mrs. Ultra O'Brien*, awoman of experience: ANNIE SANFORD. *Mora Conway*, a mere child: Eva Kelly. *Connie Summay*, a product of France: TRIXIE WADE. *Violet Wilde*, a daughter of the Bowery: LOTTIE BURKE. *Lillie Pond*: Estelle Warde. *Daisy White*: CARRIE BRAUNNECK. *Rose Bush*: ALFA BRAUNNECK. *Peach Bloom*: Margaret Aston. *Ivy Vine*: Charlotte Gale. *May Flower*: Pauline Von Hell. *Messenger Boy*: Alice Kelly. *Billy Butts*, a youth of no importance: JAMES T. KELLY. (*Specialty*: MAGGIE CLINE.)

Act 1: House of Isa Conboy in the Malaria suburbs a few miles from a certain city.

Act 2: The Rip and Tear Laundry, situated in a certain large city.

Act 3: Mrs. Ultra O'Brien's residence in a certain large city.

ACT 1

"You'll Find a Girl to Please You Here in Town"
Lady Members of the Company

"Margaret"
Misses Wade, Burke, Kelly, Warde, Ashton, Gale, Braunneck Sisters

"You'll Miss Me When I'm Gone"
R. Findley, A. Sanford

"Lovers' Quarrel"
J. T. Kelly, T. Wade

"Mr. Van Dyke from Klondyke"
R. Findley

"The Gay Soubrettes"
Braunneck Sisters

"The Girl from Paris"
T. Wade, Company

"I Want My Lulu" (Lew Dockstader's Great Coon Song)
J. T. Kelly, Entire Company

ACT 2

"The New York Laundry Girls"
Ladies of the Company

"Grisette"
T. Wade, Company

"The Laundry Strike"
Company

ACT 3

Potpourri of Coon Melodies
Company

Specialties by Trixie Wade, Mitchell and Sharpley, Raymond Findley, Lottie Burke, James T. Kelly, Maggie Cline.

1898.11 LILLI TSE

An Operetta in One Act[72] (preceded by a revival of the play "The Country Girl," adapted by Augustin Daly from David Garrick's adaptation of William Wycherly's play[73]). English libretto adapted from the German original by Wolfgang Kirchback. Music by Franz Curti. Staged by Augustin Daly. Settings by Henry E. Hoyt. Conductor, Frederic Hiller. Produced by Augustin Daly. Opened 17 February 1898 at Daly's Theatre and closed 12 March 1898 after 28 performances[74].

CAST: *Kiki Tsum*, a Jarinska man: FRANK RUSHWORTH. *Lilli Tse*, his betrothed: MARGUERITE LEMON. *Ming-Ming*, a Priest of Buddha: ARTHUR CUNNINGHAM. *Taima*, a young friend of Lilli Tse: BELLE HARPER. *Miss Whirlbottle*, an English globe-trotter: MARIE ST. JOHN. *A State Offical*: Clement Hopkins.

Scene: A remote Japanese village.

1898.12 A NORMANDY WEDDING

A Comic Opera in Three Acts. Libretto by J. Cheever Goodwin and Charles Alfred Byrne. Based on the French play "La Gardeuse d'Oies" [The Goose Girl] by Leterrier and Vanloo. Music by William Furst. Staged by A. M. Holbrook. Settings by D. Frank Dodge, Walter Burridge. Costumes by Mme. (Catherine) Siedle. Musical director, Antonio Moreale. Staged under the personal direction of Fred C. Whitney. Produced by Whitney Opera Company. Opened 21 February 1898 at the Herald Square Theatre and closed 19 March 1898 after 32 performances[75].

CAST: *Papa Campistrat*, a Normandy cider merchant: RICHARD F. CARROLL. *Denise*, his daughter: DOROTHY MORTON. *Griolette*, a goose-girl: MERRI OSBORNE. *Muscadel*, in love with Griolette: WILLIAM NORRIS. *Farandol*, Campistrat's sea-faring nephew: LEONARD WALKER. *Simone*, Denise's foster-mother: Adela Barker. *Hochepot*, a notary: H. H. Harris. *Jean*: Ole Norman. *Margotte*, a maid-of-all-work: MABEL BOUTON. *Jervais*: Fannie Briscoe. *Bridesmaids (4)*: *Claudine*: Minnie Gaylor. *Eloise*: Carrie May. *Laurie*: Ruth Richards. *Angele*: Mollie Gaylor. *Peasants, Bridesmaids, Villagers, Shepherds, etc.*

The action takes place in a small Normandy village in 1830.

Act 1: Courtyard of Papa Campistrat's house.

Act 2: Street in a Normandy village.

Act 3: Reception-room in Papa Campistrat's house.

MUSICAL NUMBERS[76]

"Papa" (The Charming Papa Song)
G. Cameron

"Come Seven, Come Eleven" (Come Seben, Come Eleben)(The Hi Hi Hi Song)
R. P. Carroll, Chorus

1898.13 EL CAPITAN

A Revival of the Comic Opera in Three Acts[77]. Book by Charles Klein. Music by John Philip Sousa. Lyrics by Charles Klein and Tom Frost. Produced under the stage direction of H. A. Cripps. Settings by Ernest Gros. Costumes by Mme. Catherine F. Siedle. Musical director, H. A. Cripps. Produced by DeWolf Hopper and His Company (B. D. Stevens, Manager). Opened 21 February 1898 at the Fifth Avenue Theatre and closed 5 March 1898 after 14 performances.

CAST: *Don Errico Medigua*, recently appointed Viceroy of Peru: DeWOLF HOPPER. *Senor Amabile Pozzo*, Chamberlain: ALFRED KLEIN. *Don Luiz Cazarro*, ex-Viceroy: THOMAS S. GUISE. *Count Hernando Verrada*: EDMUND STANLEY. *Scaramba*, an insurgent: John Parr. *Montalba, Nevado*, his companions: Harry P. Stone, Robert Pollard. *General Herbana*, Commander of King Philip's forces: Louis Schrader. *Estrelda*, Cazarro's daughter: EDNA WALLACE HOPPER. *Isabel*, Medigua's daughter: EDNA WALLACE HOPPER. *Princess Marghanza*, Medigua's wife: ALICE HOSMER. *Taciturnez*: Katherine Carlisle.

[72]Replaced a one-act comedietta "Subleties of Jealousy" as the curtain raiser, opening 11 February 1898 and withdrawn after 20 performances.

[73]Which opened 1 February 1898 at Daly's Theatre.

[74]No musical numbers listed in program. "New" costumes (designer unnamed) announced in the program.

[75]Played 21 March 1898 at the Harlem Opera House for 8 performances.

[76]Musical numbers not listed in programs. List prepared from reviews, clippings.

[77]Originally opened 20 April 1896 at the Broadway Theatre for 112 performances. For Synopsis of Scenes and Musical Numbers, see original 1896 production.

1898.14

THE GYPSY BARON

A Revival of the Comic Opera in Three Acts. Original Viennese libretto ('Der Zigeunerbaron') by Ignaz Schnitzer, based on the story 'Saffi' by Mór Jókai.[78] Music by Johann Strauss, Jr. Scenery by Frank King. Stage manager, A. W. F. MacCollin. Conductor, Adolph Liesegang. Produced by the Castle Square Opera Company (Henry W. Savage, Manager). Opened 28 February 1898 at the American Theatre and closed 5 March 1898 after 8 performances.

CAST: *Sándor Barinkay*, the Gypsy Baron: JOSEPH F. SHEEHAN. *Count Homonay*, recruiting officer: W. G. STEWART. *Count Carnero*: E. N. KNIGHT. *Kalman Zsupán*, a rich hog raiser: WILLIAM WOLFF. *Ottokar*, son of Mirabella: ARTHUR WOOLEY. *Pali, Zoszi*, gypsies: Charles Scribner, W. E. Brockmeyer. *Sáffi*, a young gypsy girl: NITA CARRITTE. *Czipra*, an old gypsy woman: LIZZIE MACNICHOL. *Arsena*, daughter of Zsupán: Grace Golden. *Mirabella*: Bessie Fairbairn. *Musicians, Students, Soldiers, Gypsies, etc.*

1898.15

NANON

A Revival of the Comic Opera (Opéra Comique) in Three Acts[79]. (Original Viennese libretto, 'Nanon, die Wirthin vom goldenene Lamm,' by F. Zell, based on the play "Ninon, Nanon et Madame de Maintenon" by Emmanuel Théaulon, Armand d'Artois and Lesguillon.) Music by Richard Genée. (American translation by Sydney Rosenfeld.) Stage manager, A. W. F. MacCollin. Scenery by Frank King. Conductor, Adolph Liesegang. Produced by the Castle Square Opera Comapny (Henry W. Savage, Proprietor). Opened 7 March 1898 at the American Theatre and closed 12 March 1898 after 8 performances.

CAST: *Marquis de Marsellac*: OSCAR GIRARD. *Hector*, his nephew: CHARLES CAMPBELL. *Marquis Henri d'Aubigne*, the King's Henchman: W. T. CARLETON. *Bombardine*, his henchman: Charles Scribner. *Louis XIV*: GEORGE BRODERICK. *Monsieur l'Abbé*: Richard Ridgley. *The Notary*: William Voigt. *Nanon*, Mistress of the Golden Lamb: GRACE GOLDEN. *Ninon d'l'Enclos*, a famous beauty: MILDRED MEADE. *Ninon's friends (2)*: *Mme. de Frontenac*: Amy Travis. *Countess Honliers*: Ruth White. *Gaston*, Page to Ninon: GERTRUDE QUINLAN. *Mme. de Maintenon*, the King's consort: BESSIE FAIRBAIRN. *Nanon's Country Relations (7)*: *Cousin Pierre*: John Read. *Uncle Matthew*: Richard Beale. *Papa Bertrand*: W. C. Brockmeyer. *Cousin Joe*: E. Danton. *Mother Lizette*: Hattie Havens. *Aunt Theresa*: Nellie Berwick. *Cousin Marion*: Georgie French. *Jacqueline*: Nancy France. *Sergeant*: Richard Ridgley. *Chorus of Peasants, Soldiers, Country Relations, Courtiers, Ladies, etc.*

1898.16

SINBAD, or The Maid of Balsora

A Revival of the Spectacular Extravaganza in Four Acts, 9 Scenes[80]. Libretto by Harry B. Smith. (Music written and arranged by W. H. Batchelor.) Stage manager, A. W. F. MacCollin. Scenery by Frank King, Walter Burridge. Conductor, Adolph Liesegang. Produced by the Castle Square Opera Company (Henry W. Savage, Proprietor). Opened 14 March 1898 at the American Theatre and closed 19 March 1898 after 8 performances.

CAST: *Sinbad*, a Dashing Young 'Prentice: LOUISE ROYCE. *Count Maledetto Spaghetti*, a Nobleman from foreign shores: JOSEPH F. SHEEHAN. *Ninetta*, Sinbad's' sweetheart: MARIE CELESTE. *Snarleyow*, a Villain who woos and tries to wed Ninetta: ED G. KNIGHT. *Fresco*, the Idle Apprentice who blossoms into a Cannibal King: OSCAR GIRARD. *Salamagundi*, Snarleyow's Lieutenant: GERTRUDE QUINLAN. *Nicolo*, father of Ninetta: RAYMOND HITCHCOCK. *Old Man of the Sea*: A. W. Maflin. *Maraschino*, who wins the Count: BESSIE FAIRBAIRN. *Angelo*, Faimetta's sweetheart: Ruth White. *Rafael*, Zerlina's sweetheart: Maud Vincent. *Fiametta*, in love with Angelo: Lillian Lipyeat. *Zerlina*, in love with Rafael: Emma King. *Cupid*, the Guardian Fairy: Marion Berg. *Tuesday, Wednesday*, Ethiopian slaves: Messrs. Ali, Beni. *Apprentices, Milkmaids, Smugglers, Cannibals, Persians, etc.*

[78]English adaptation uncredited; very likely by Sydney Rosenfeld.
[79]First produced in New York as NANON, The Hostess of the Golden Lamb, 29 June 1885 at the Casino Theatre for 152 performances. For Synopsis of Scenes and Musical Numbers, see original 1885 production.
[80]First produced in New York 27 June 1892 at the Garden Theatre for 105 performances. Harry B. Smith's name did not appear in New York programs in 1892; conversely, Batchelor's name does not appear in programs for this revival. For Synopsis of Scenes and Musical Numbers, see original 1892 production. Interpolated for this revival, per published sheet music:

"I'm the Man"
O. Girard
(*Music by* Gustav Luders. *Lyrics by* M. E. Rourke.)

1898.17

MONTE CARLO

A Musical Comedy in Two Acts[81]. Libretto by Sydney Carlton [Harry Greenbank]. Music by Howard Talbot. Lyrics by Harry Greenbank. Additional lyrics by Edgar Smith and Joseph W. Herbert; additional music by Edward E. Rice and Herman Perlet[82]. Staged by Frank Smithson. Ballets staged by F. Marchetti. Settings by Frank Rafter. Costumes designed by Will R. Barnes. Musical director, Herman Perlet. Produced by Edward E. Rice. Opened 21 March 1898 at the Herald Square Theatre and closed 30 April 1898 after 48 performances.

CAST: *Sir Benjamin Currie*, Q.C., M.P., the Attorney General: THOMAS K. KEARNS. *General Frederick Boomerang*, V.C.: FRANK SMITHSON. *Lieutenant Fred Dorian*, a lieutenant in the Southshire Regiment: Augustus Cramer. *James*, a waiter: Alexander Clark. *Harry Verinder*, a briefless barrister: Sidney deGray. *Professor Lorrimer*, a retired gymnast: Edward Chapman. *Belmont, Standring*, visitors at Monte Carlo: Edward Thomas, Frank H. Crane. *Captain Rossiter* of the steam yacht *"Silver Swan"*: Neil McNeill. *Francois*, Sir Benjamin's valet: James Grant. *Midshipman*: Susie Brown. *First Sailor*: Edward Thomas. *Second Sailor*: Frank H. Crane. *Mrs. Carthew*: JEANNIE WINSTON. *Dorothy*, Mrs. Carthew's daughter: MARGUERITA SYLVA. *Ethel Boomerang*, General Boomerang's daughter: Helen Tuesart. *Bertie Gelatine, Gertie Gelatine*, the Sisters Gelatine: MARIE CAHILL, SADIE KIRBY. *Suzanne*, a chambermaid at the Hotel de Paris: Gerome Edwardy. *Little Jemima* of the East End Music Halls: JOSIE SADLER.

Ladies of the Chorus: Mazie Trew, Estelle Cameron, Gypsy Grant, Frances Wilson, Susan Brown, Kittie Burton, Bessie Bonneville, Mollie Gaylor, Jessie Banks, Nonie Dore, June Jackson, Millie Tait, Lena Dykstra, Agnes Wadleigh, Nina Ainscoe, Minnie Gaylor, Maude Terriss, Marie Lachere, Florence Dressler, Agnes Elliott, Bessie Wilton, Grace Pierrepont, Sophie Brochard, Carrie May.

Gentlemen of the Chorus: Messrs. Dunn, Savage, Amodeo, McBride, Tetson, Cameron, Thomas, Hill, Shuster, Crane, Vernon, Aiken, Mears, Terry.

Act 1: Gardens and Terrace at Monte Carlo.

Act 2: Off Malta, on board *"The Silver Swan."*

ACT 1[83]

"Here at Monte Carlo" (Opening Chorus)
"Here's a Chance for Visitors" (Song)
"How Can Harry Marry" (Duet)
"Ditto Ditto" (Trio)
"Land of Heart's Desire" (Romanza)
"Along the Way Where Lovers Go" (Duet)
"The Use of French" (Duet)
"Red Is the Wine" (Song and Chorus)
"General Boomerang" (Song and Chorus)
"Sisters Gelatine" (Quartette and Dance)
"Waiting for Me" (Song)
"Hi Boys, Ho Boys" (Song)
Billiard and Baccarat Ballet (Pool and Baccarat Ballet)
C. May, F. Wilson, F. Dressler, J. Jackson, Mollie Gaylor, N. Ainscoe, Minnie Gaylor, M. Tait
(*Music by* Edward E. Rice. *Arranged by* Professor H. Marchetti.)
"The Dancing Dean" (Duet)
Hornpipe Trio
Finale
(*Music by* Herman Perlet. *Lyrics by* Edgar Smith.)

ACT 2

"We're an Able Bodied Crew" (Opening Chorus)

[81]Also billed as Rice's recherche production of the new English two-act combination of mirth, melody and nonsense.
[82]Messrs. Smith, Herbert, Rice and Perlet's contributions were interpolations for the American production.
[83]Added interpolation as per published sheet music, not in programs:

"A Little Boy For Sale"
(*Music by* Harry Robson.)
"My Ann Elizer" (tour)
A. Atherton
(*Music and Lyrics by* Malcolm Williams.)

"The Melodramatic Captain" (Song)
"The Ladies' Maid" (Trio and Chorus)
"The Sparrow and the Bullfinch" (Song)
"In the Medieval Ages" (Color Duet and Dance)
"I Only Know I Love Thee" (Song)
"If I Only Knew the Way" (Song)
"At the 'Alls" (Duet)
(*Music by* Herman Perlet. *Lyrics by* Joseph W. Herbert.)
"Very Careful, If You Please" (Song)
The Sailor (Boy) Ballet
(*Music by* Edward E. Rice. *Arranged by* Professor H. Marchetti.)
"Barcelona Girls" (Duet)
"The Summer Girl" (Song)
"Captain Rossiter" (Scene)
Grand Finale[84], with Original Patriotic Effects
(*Arranged by* Edward E. Rice.)

1898.18

THE GEISHA

A Return Engagement of the Musical Comedy in Two Acts[85]. Book by Owen Hall. Music by Sidney Jones and Lionel Monckton. Lyrics by Harry Greenbank. Staged by Herbert Gresham. Dances by Willie Warde. Settings by Henry T. Hoyt after designs and and models of the original by William Telbin. Costumes by Percy Anderson. Orchestra under the direction of Sebastian Hiller. Produced by Augustin Daly. Opened 21 March 1898 at Daly's Theatre and closed 9 April 1898 after 22 performances.

CAST: *O Mimosa San*: MARGUERITE LEMON. *Juliette Diamant*: Helma Nelson. *Nami*: Belle Harper. *O Kiku San*: Sandol Milliken. *O Hana San*: Bessy Ryan. *O Kinkoto San*: Marion Stuart. *Komurasaki San*: Marie Murphy. *Lady Constance Wynne*: Ethel Hornick. *Marie Worthington*: Beatrice Morgan. *Ethel Hurst*: Virginia Navarro. *Mabel Grant*: Louise Draper. *Dorothy Sweet*: Corinne Parker. *Molly Seamore*: MABELLE GILMAN. *Reginald Fairfax*: FRANK RUSHWORTH. *Dick Cunningham*: CYRIL SCOTT. *Arthur Cuddy*: Charles Bates. *George Grimston*: Frederic Truesdell. *Tommy Stanley*: Lillian Coleman. *Captain Katana*: Neil McCay. *Takemine*: George Wharnock. *Wun-Hi*: JAMES T. POWERS. *Marquis Imari*: JOSEPH HERBERT. *Gerald St. Pancras*: Eric Scott.

Ensemble: Ida Hawley, Belle d'Arcy, Lena Lorraine, Margaret Hoyt, Francis Gordon, Carolyn Gordon, Margurite Barre, Misses Ashton, Mills, Carrington, Carlisle, Clements.

1898.19

MARITANA

A Revival of the Romantic Opera in Four Acts. Libretto by Edward Fitzball, adapted from Adolphe Phillippe d'Ennery and Philippe François Dumanoir's play "Don César de Bazan." Music by William Wallace. Stage manager, A. W. F. MacCollin. Scenery by Frank King. Conductor, Adolph Liesegang. Produced by the Castle Square Opera Company (Henry W. Savage, Proprietor). Opened 21 March 1898 at the American Theater and closed 26 March 1898 after 8 performances.

CAST: *Maritana*, a gypsy: GRACE GOLDEN. *Charles II*, King of Spain: DASHEILL MADEIRA. *Don José de Santarem*, his minister: MAX EUGENE. *Don Caesar de Bazan*: JOSEPH F. SHEEHAN. *Marquis de Monntefiori*: OSCAR GIRARD. *Lazarillo*: Ruth White. *Marchioness de Montefiori*: BESSIE FAIRBAIRN. *Captain of Guard*: John Read. *Alcade*: Richad Beale. *Chorus of Nobles, Soldiers, Men at Arms, Citizens, Ladies of Court, etc.*

1898.20

IN GAY NEW YORK

A Revival of the Annual Review, a Kaleidoscopic Retrospect of the Hour, in Three Acts, 6 Scenes[86]. Libretto by Hugh Morton. Music by Gustave Kerker. Produced under the stage direction of George W. Lederer. Ballets arranged by Signor Francioli. Settings by D. Frank Dodge. Costumes by Mme. C. F. Siedle. Conductor, George P. Towle. Produced by George W. Lederer and George B. McClellan. Opened 28 March 1898 at the Casino Theatre and closed 23 April 1898 after 32 performances[87].

CAST, ACT 1: *Prince Rouge-et-Noir*: JULIUS STEGER. *Mrs. DeShyster Van Shoddie*, a millionairess: CHRISTINE BLESSING. *Miss Flora Van Shoddie*, her daughter: JEANETTE BAGEARD. *Sally Tompkins*, Johnny Brown's bride: GERTRUDE ZELLA. *Mrs. Tompkins*, Sally's mother: Christine Blessing. *Susie Tarbox*, a bridesmaid: Erminie Earle. *Essie, Tessie, Jessie, Bessie*, the Marmalade Sisters: Violet Jewell, Rene Egan, Jessie Haines, Josephine Stanton. *Miss Peroxide McTushtush*, a leading lady: Heloise Dupont. *Miss Fairy Fullmeasure*, an actress: Chrissie Carlyle. *Edgardo Macready Boothand Barrett Todd*, a stranded actor: WALTER JONES. *Johnny Brown*, a country bridegroom: ARTHUR V. GIBSON. *Lemuel Tompkins*, Sally's father: E. S. Tarr. *Duke of Mulligatawny*, a British fortune-hunter: James G. Peakes. *Si Perkins*, a bumpkin: Frank H. Hammond. *Deacon Stackpole*, of Huckleberry Center: James A. Furey. *Pastor Podgett* of the Meeting House: Herman Greinert. *Grand Central Pete*, a bunco steerer: LEE HARRISON. *Frank Daniels*, the Wizard of the Nile: PETER CURLEY. *Burglar Bill*: JAMES G. PEAKES. *Perkins*, a butler at Hotel Waldorf: James A. Furey. *Sandbag*, the strong man: William Sellery. *Muddy Mike*, a gold-brick bandit: William Sellery. *Colonel Waring*: William Sellery. *White Wings*, one of Colonel Waring's angels: William Torpey. *Policeman Spitzpupheimer*: LOUIS WESLEY. *Jimmy the Slim*, a light-fingered gentleman: PETER CURLEY. *Thirsty Bob, Webfoot Willie*, friends of Grand Central Pete: Horace Hain, Frank Stevens. *Woozy Whiskers*, a scorching hobo: Harry Watson. *Svengali Trilby*, an actor: J. C. Newell. *Swipes*, a newsboy: William Torpey. *Pitchpenny*, an urchin: Roy Cutter. *John, James*, servants to Rouge-et-Noir: George Hall, William Alexander. (*Premiere Danseuse*: MINNIE SENNETT.)

ACT 2: *Treasurer Standoff*, ticket seller at the Casino: LEE HARRISON. *Mrs. Maryland Leslie Ta Ta*: CHRISTINE BLESSING. *J. Wellington Cohen*: Gus Yorke. *Henry Macbeth Irving*: Gus Yorke. *Isador Rosinskil*: Nick Adams. *Dottie Doodimple*: Jeanette Bageard. *Hattie Alihat*: Violet Jewell. *Reginald Tomtit*: William Torpey. *Harris*, footman: Sherman Rowles. *The Spirit of Burlesque*: Josephine Stanton. *Mrs. O'Brien, Mrs. Mulcahey*, Casino scrub women: LOUIS WESLEY, JOHN C. SLAVIN. *Johnny Brown*: Arthur V. Gibson. *Sally Brown*: GERTRUDE ZELLA. *Essie, Tessie, Jessie, Bessie*, the Marmalade Sisters: Violet Jewell, Rene Egan, Jessie Haines, Josephine Stanton. *Edgardo Macbeth Boothand Barrett Todd*: WALTER JONES. *Colonel Kellard*: WALTER JONES. *Captain Barrymore*: Sherman Rowles. *Orderly Bludso*: Louis Wesley. *Hogan*, the sexton: E. S. Tarr. *Lemuel Tompkins*: E. S. Tarr. *Mrs. Tompkins*: Christine Blessing. *Yvette Guilbert's Sisters (5)*: *Youbette*: Jeannette Bageard. *Getwette*: Jessie Haines. *Dontfrette*: Josephine Stanton. *Tolette*: Nellie Uart. *Mypette*: Violet Jewell. *Romeo*: Rene Egan. *Don José*: JULIUS STEGER. *Carmen Calve*: Crissie Carlyle. *Carmen Nethersole*: GERTRUDE ZELLA. *Elaine Umty-Tiddly*, Lettie Lind's cousin: Winnie Sennett. *Fraulein Wiegehts*, a Zeitung soubrette: Heloise Dupont. *Allen*, night watchman: J. C. Newell. *Mr. Rusty Kicker*, the man in the Balcony: James A. Furey. *Harry*, clerk of the coat room: Martin Bennett. *The Coachman*: William Alexander. *Drum-Major*: William Torpey.

ACT 3: *Benzeene*, the Circassian girl: Peter Curley. *Mr. Openface*, a dime museum "barker": William Sellery. *Lurline*, the Water Queen: Josephine Stanton. *Mrs. Deshyster Van Shoddie*: CHRISTINE BLESSING. *Edgardo Macready Boothand Barrett Todd*: WALTER JONES. *Goose-foot Googin*: LOUIS WESLEY. *Miss Flora Van Shoddie*: Jeanette Bageard. *Duke of Mulligatawny*: James G. Peakes. *Lemuel Tompkins*: E. S. Tarr. *Mrs. Tompkins*: CHRISTINE BLESSING. *Johnny Brown*: ARTHUR V. GIBSON. *Sally Brown*: GERTRUDE ZELLA. *Grand Central Pete*: LEE HARRISON. *Senor Exterio Explosio Torpedo Bomshello*: Martin Bennett. (*Danse Specialty*: Titenia.)

Act 1, Scene 1: Village Green of Huckleberry Centre, Maine. *Scene 2*: Exterior of Grand Central Depot. *Scene 3*: Exterior of Hotel Waldorf.

Act 2, Scene 1: Lobby of the Casino, Broadway and 39th Street, New York. *Scene 2*: Stage of the Casino.

Act 3: The breezy end of Coney Island.

ACT 1[88]
Scene 3
"The Wedding of the Chinee and the Coon"
W. Jones, J. Bageard
Illustrative Dance of English Peers and American Heiresses
Icicle Ballet
Misses Benedict, Shearer, Gardner, L. Sennett, Cohen, Franton, Marsh, Gorden
"Molly"
J. Steger

[84]Including the New York Herald Topical song, "The Ready, Steady Sailor Man," music by Herman Perlet, lyrics by Albert Bigelow Paine.
[85]First produced in New York 9 September 1896 at Daly's Theatre for 161 performances. For Synopsis of Scenes and Musical Numbers, see original 1896 production.
[86]Originally opened 25 May 1896 at the Casino Theatre for 120 performances under the auspices of Klaw and Erlanger. At the conclusion of its national tour, Klaw & Erlanger sub-licensed the touring production to Messrs. Lederer and McClellan, who chose to bring this revised version back to New York.
[87]Also played 7 March 1898 at the 14th Street Theatre for 8 performances.
[88]Program does not list musical numbers, only Ballets and Specialties.

Ballet Solo
M. Sennett
"Song of the Tenderloin"
L. Harrison

ACT 2
Scene 2
Burlesque on "Carmen"
J. Steger, C. Carlisle, G. Zella
"The Casino Scrub Women"
L. Wesley, J. C. Slavin
Hebraic Specialty
G. Yorke, N. Adams
"The Lover's Frolic" (Pas de Quatre devised by Ray Allen.)
W. Sennett, L. Sennett, G. Franton, J. Shearer
"The Devil's Adventures"
W. Jones

ACT 3
Specialty: La Danse Cosmopolitan; Danse L'Amerique; The Staircase
Titenia
Specialty: Louis Wesley as 'Roxiana Dooley' from THE WHIRL OF THE TOWN
Impersonation of The Tramp Cyclist
H. Watson

1898.21 THE MIKADO, or The Town of Titipu

A Revival of the Comic Opera in Two Acts[89]. Libretto by William S. Gilbert. Music by Arthur Sullivan. Scenery by Frank King. Conductor, Adolph Liesegang. Produced by the Castle Square Opera Company (Henry W. Savage, Proprietor). Opened 28 March 1898 at the American Theatre and closed 9 April 1898 after 16 performances.

CAST: *The Mikado of Japan*: OSCAR GIRARD. *Nanki-Poo*, his son, disguised as a wandering minstrel in love with Yum-Yum: JOSEPH F. SHEEHAN. *Ko-Ko*, Lord High Executioner of Titipu: RAYMOND HITCHCOCK. *Pooh-Bah*, Lord High Everything Else: WILLIAM G. STEWART. *Pish-Tush*, a Noble Lord: Dashiell Madeira. *Nee-Ban*, umbrella carrier to the Mikado: Charles Scribner. *Yum-Yum, Pitti-Sing, Peep-Bo*, three sisters, wards of Ko-Ko: GRACE GOLDEN, LILLIAN SWAIN, EMMA KING. *Katisha*, an elderly lady in love with Nanki-Poo: BESSIE FAIRBAIRN. *Chorus of School Girls, Nobles, Guards and Coolies.*

1898.22 A TRIP TO COONTOWN

A Roaring, Racy, Rollicking Musical Comedy in Two Acts, 4 Scenes. Book, music and lyrics by Robert Cole and Billy Johnson. Produced under the personal supervision of Robert Cole and Billy Johnson. Stage manager, Jesse A. Shipp. Musical director, William Carle. Produced by Robert Cole and Billy Johnson. Opened 4 April 1898 at the Third Avenue Theatre and closed 9 April 1898 after 8 performances[90].

CAST: *Willie Wayside*, (a tramp) who has seen better days: BOB [Robert] COLE. *Jim Flimflammer*, a bunco Steerer (confidence man): BILLY JOHNSON. *Silas Green, Jr.*, with a $5,000 pension: ROBERT A. KELLEY. *Silas Green, Jr.*, his wayward son: JESSE A. SHIPP. *A Sly Cop of the Coontown police force*: JESSE A. SHIPP. *Bily Binkerton*, a detective: Tom Brown. *Rube*: Tom Brown. *Italian*: Tom Brown. *Hebrew*: Tom Brown. *Chinaman*: Tom Brown. *Captain Fleetfoot*, of the Gallant 54th of Massachusetts: Walter Dixon. *The Black DeReske of the Coontown Opera Company*: Lloyd G. Gibbs. *Sam*, a waiter: George Brown. *Reverendly*: Hen Wise. *Bill Pulaski*, a razor inspector: Hen Wise. *Mrs. Fannie Brown*, a widow with a boarding house: Vincent Bradley. *Fannie Brown*, her daughter: Pauline Freeman. *Florinda*: Lena Wiser. *Rotinda*: Marguerite Rhodes. *Lucinda*: May Wynder. *Flotinda*: May Wynder. *Marinda*: Sadie Robinson. *Aminda*: Belle King. *Balinda*: Clara Freeman. *Boarders, Pleasure Seekers, etc.*
The action takes place at the present time in the suburbs of New York.

Act 1, Scene 1: Lawn of Widow Brown's Boarding House. *Scene 2*: En route to Coontown. *Scene 3*: The Heart of Coontown.

Act 2: Parlor in Silas Green's Home.

ACT 1[91]
"The Famous Black Moguls"
W. Dixon
"I Hope These Few Lines Will Find Thee Well"
J. A. Shipp [Silas Jr.]
"Old Kentucky Home"
L. Wiser
"Two Bold Bad Men"
B. Cole, B. Johnson
"A Trip to Coontown"
B. Johnson
"A Trip to Coontown" (reprise)
Chorus
"The Czar of the Tenderloin"
J. A. Shipp [Sly Cop]
"The Italian Man"
T. Brown
"The Christening of a Little Black Coon"
Freeman Sisters
"The Equilibrist"
Jim Wilson
"(Play) 4-11-44"
M. Wynder, M. Rhodes, B. Cole, B. Johnson
"The Wedding of the Chinee and the Coon"
B. Cole, B. Johnson, T. Brown, J. A. Shipp, M. Rhodes
Finale
Company

ACT 2
A Coontown Frolic—"Midnight Kisses"
Company
A Collection of Characters
T. Brown
The Greatest Living Black Tenor
L. G. Gibbs
A Few Moments with the Prince
Himself
The Trio from Attilla, introducing the great singer (Novelty)
Mme. Plato

1898.23 ROBIN HOOD

A Revival of the Comic Opera in Three Acts[92]. Libretto by Harry B. Smith. Music by Reginald DeKoven. Stage director, W. H. Fitzgerald. Musical director, Samuel L. Studley. Produced by the Bostonians. Opened 4 April 1898 at Wallack's Theatre and closed 30 April 1898 after 28 performances[93]

[89]First presented in New York 20 July, 10-29 August 1885 at the Union Square and People's Theatres for 22 performances. First authorized production presented 19 August 1885 at the Fifth Avenue Theatre by Richard D'Oyly Carte for 250 performances. For Synopsis of Scenes and Musical Numbers, see 19 August 1885 D'Oyly Carte production.

[90]Played return engagements 12 September 1898 at the Grand Opera House for 8 performances, and 10 June 1899 at the Casino Roof Garden as part of a vaudeville program.

[91]Pursuant to an advertisement in the NY Clipper 24 September 1898, the following songs were written and introduced by Cole and Johnson in A TRIP TO COONTOWN (on tour if not in New York): "There's a Warm Spot in My Heart, Baby," "In Dahomey," "You'll Have to Choose Another Baby Now," "I Wonder What Is That Coon's Game," "La Hoola Boola," "Miss Amorinta Jackson's Promenade," "The Black 400's Ball," "My Old Country Home."
Interpolated as per published sheet music:
"All I Want Is Ma Chickens"
R. Cole
(*Music and Lyrics by* Deas and Wilson.)

[92]First produced in New York 28 September 1891 at the Standard Theatre for 35 performances, followed by a return engagement 16 May 1892 at the Garden for an additional 42 performances. For Synopsis of Scenes and Musical Numbers, see original 1891 production.

[93]Settings, costumes uncredited.

CAST: *Sheriff of Nottingham*: HENRY CLAY BARNABEE. *Robin Hood*: W. E. PHILP. *Little John*: W. H. MacDONALD. *Will Scarlet*: EUGENE COWLES. *Alan-a-Dale*: JESSIE BARTLETT DAVIS. *Friar Tuck*: GEOGE FROTHINGHAM. *Guy of Gisborne*: W. H. FITZGERALD. *Maid Marian*: ALICE NIELSEN. *Dame Durden*: JOSEPHINE BARTLETT. *Annabel*: Elenoire Giusti.

1898.24

BILLEE TAYLOR

A Double Bill of Revivals of the Comic Opera in Two Acts[94] (followed by "I Pagliacci" by Leoncavallo). Libretto by H. P. Stephens. Music by Edward Solomon. Scenery by Frank King. Musical director, Adolph Liesegang. Produced by the Castle Square Opera Company (Henry W. Savage, Proprietor). Opened 11 April 1898 at the American Theatre and closed 23 April 1898 after 16 performances.

CAST: *Captain the Hon. Felix Flapper*, R.N., of H.M.S. *"Thunderbomb"*: RAYMOND HITCHCOCK. *Sir Mincing Lane*, Knight, self-made man: RICHARD RIDGELEY. *Billee Taylor*, a gardener: JAY TAYLOR. *Ben Barnacle*, bosun of the *"Thunderbomb"*: E. N. KNIGHT. *Christopher Crab*, an ancient schoolmaster: OSCAR GIRARD. *Phoebe Farleigh*, a village maiden, betrothed to Billee: MARIE CELESTE. *Arabella Lane*, Sir Mincing Lane's daughter, Phoebe's rival: RUTH WHITE. *Eliza Dabsey*, an old flame of Barnacle's: BESSIE FAIRBAIRN. *Susan*: Emma King. *Chorus of Sailors, Volunteers, Peasants, Charity Girls, etc.*

1898.25

THE BRIDE-ELECT

A Comic Opera in Three Acts. Book and music (and lyrics) by John Philip Sousa. Produced under the stage direction of Ben Teal. (Ballet master, Carl Marwig.) Settings by Ernest M. Gros. Costumes by F. Richard Anderson. Musical director, Paul Steindorff. Produced by Messrs. (Marc) Klaw, (Abraham L.) Erlanger and B. D. Stevens. Opened 11 April 1898 at the Knickerbocker Theatre and closed 4 June 1898 after 64 performances[95].

CAST: *Papagallo XIII*, King of Timberio: ALBERT HART. *Guido*, Duke of Ventroso, his nephew: FRANK POLLOCK. *Frescobaldi*, Prime Minister of Timberio: CHARLES H. DREW. *Gambo*: MELVILLE STEWART. *Buscato*: HARRY LUCKSTONE. *Pietro*, an innkeeper: E. G. Schaeffer. *Sardinia*, a jailer: Wesley Johnstone. *La Pastorella*, a female brigand: NELLA BERGEN. *Bianca*, Queen of Capri: [Emma] MABELLA BAKER. *Minutezza*, Princess of Capri, her daughter: CHRISTIE MacDONALD. *Margherita*: Ursula Gurnett. *Rea*: Alice Campbell. *Zedena*: Bertha Davis. *Rosamunda*: Nana Fairhurst. *The Curate*: Charles A. Goettler.

The action takes place on the island of Capri.

Act 1: A street in Capri.

Act 2: The fold of the shepherdess.

Act 3: Fortress of Anacapri.

ACT 1[96]

"If ninety-nine percent the papers print" (Chorus)
M. Baker, Chorus

"One day King Papagallo sent a note" (Recitative, Solo and Chorus)
M. Baker, M. Stewart, H. Luckstone, Chorus

"When this old coat was in the Style" (Scene and Romance)
H. Luckstone, M. Stewart, Chorus

"Come, Cavalier" (Scene, Duet and Chorus)
H. Luckstone, M. Stewart, Chorus

"Oh, Princess Minutezza" (Recitative, Solo and Chorus)
C. MacDonald, Chorus

"Our Customary Attitude" (Chorus)
Chorus

"Kind Friends, This Deference" (Song and Chorus)
A. Hart, Chorus

"Should You Marry Ma" (Duet)
C. MacDonald, A. Hart

"Before the Moor was master of the hills of old Iberia" (Song)
N. Bergen

"To marry or not to marry" (Recitative, Solo and Chorus)
N. Bergen

"You remember 'twas six months ago" (Trio)
N. Bergen, M. Stewart, H. Luckstone

"In a matter of such grave import" (Octette)
N. Bergen, C. MacDonald, H. Luckstone, M. Stewart, U. Gurnettt, A. Campbell, B. Davis, N. Fairhurst

Finale: "Oh, Stars that form the Milky Way" (Song)
A. Hart

"Let Poets sing" (Ensemble)
N. Bergen, C. MacDonald, A. Hart, H. Luckstone, M. Stewart, Chorus

ACT 2

Introduction/"The rose tint leaves the sky" (Romance)
F. Pollock

"Here's a pack" (Song)
N. Bergen

"He's here" (Trio)
N. Bergen, A. Hart, H. Luckstone

"Love, light of my heart" (Duet)
C. MacDonald, F. Pollock

"We cannot see the reason why" (Chorus and Solo)
Chorus, A. Hart

Tarantella

"Bright star of love" (Invocation)
N. Bergen, H. Luckstone, M. Stewart, Chorus

"An act to purify our band" (Solos and Chorus)
Principals, Chorus

"The Snow Baby" (The Ice Baby)
C. MacDonald, F. Pollock, A. Hart

Finale: "An awkward complication this"/
"Unchain the dogs of war"
Principals, Chorus

ACT 3

Introduction

"These are our sentiments" (Male Quartette)
F. Pollock, A. Hart, H. Luckstone, M. Stewart

"The iceman works" (Song and Chorus)
A. Hart, H. Luckstone, M. Stewart

"Cuckoo" (Cong and Chorus)
N. Bergen, Girls

"Love, light of my heart" (Chorus)
N. Bergen, M. Stewart, H. Luckstone, Chorus

"The Goat" (Song)
A. Hart, N. Bergen, M. Stewart, H. Luckstone, Chorus

Finale: "The God of Love presides"
Principals, Chorus

1898.26

LA POUPÉE

A Revival of the Comic Opera in Two Acts[97]. Original French libretto by Maurice Ordonneau. American adaptation by Arthur Sturgess. Music by Edmond Audran. Conductor, Sebastian Hiller. Produced by Augustin Daly. Opened 15 April 1898 at Daly's Theatre and closed 30 April 1898 after 18 performances.

CAST: *Master Hillarius*, the Doll Maker: JAMES T. POWERS. *Madame Hillarius*, his wife: CATHERINE LEWIS. *Henry*, his favorite apprentice: ETHEL HORNICK. *Allesia*, his daughter: VIRGINIA EARLE. *Gudaline*, her companion: Belle Harper. *The Brother Chanterelle*: HERBERT GRESHAM. *Lorremois*, an antique friend of his: JOSEPH HERBERT. *Brother Maxime*: FRANK CELLI. *Launcelot*, the novice: FRANK RUSHWORTH. *Brother Sebastian*: Frederic Truesdell. *Brother Basil*: William Gilbert. *Notary*: Robert Kelly. *Pierre, Jean*, in the Baron's Service: Messrs. Aitken, Taylor. *Marie*: Grace Rutter. *Dolls*: Blanche Carlisle, Jennie Cobin, Carolyn Gordon, Beatrice Clements.

[94]First opened in New York 19 February 1881 at the Standard Theatre for 101 performances; re-opened 6 June 1881 for an additional 16 performances. Total: 117 performances. For Synopsis of Scenes and Musical Numbers, see original 1881 production.

[95]Played a return enagagement 17 October 1898 at the Harlem Opera House for 8 performances.

[96]Musical numbers not listed in programs; list prepared from published vocal score (J. Church Co., Cincinatti, 1898).

[97]Originally opened 21 October 1897 at the Lyric Theatre for 46 performances under the auspices of Oscar Hammerstein.

1898.27

THE WEDDING DAY

A Revival of the Comic Opera in Three Acts[98]. Libretto by Stanislaus Stange. Based on the French operette "La Petite Fronde" (libretto by Alfred Duru and Henri Chivot, music by Edmond Audran). Music by Julian Edwards. Produced under the stage direction of R. H. Burnside. Settings by Ernest Albert and Walter Burridge. Costumes by Mme. Caroline Siedle. Orchestra under the direction of Julian Edwards. Produced by the Lillian Russell-Della Fox-Jeff DeAngelis Comic Opera Combination (Frank Murray, manager). Opened 18 April 1898 at the Broadway Theatre and closed 14 May 1898 after 32 performances.

CAST: *Duc de Bouillon*, General of the Frondist Army: William Pruette. *Raoul, Vicomte de Bragelonne*, his nephew: Tom Greene. *Sergeant Sabre* of the Frondist Army: Wilfred Arling. *Corporal Souffle* of the Frondist Army: Louis D. Hadley. *Laubert*, Madame Montbazon's major-domo: Eugene Desmond. *Polycop*, baker and caterer: JEFFERSON DeANGELIS. *Planchette*, his head cook and first baker: Charles W. Allison. *Pomade*, a barber: Albert McGuckin. *Madame Montbazon*, a leader of the "Fronde": Lucille Saunders. *Lucille D'Herblay*, the Queen's messenger: LILLIAN RUSSELL. *Aunt Hortense*, Polycop's aunt: Neta Rosa. *Rose-Marie*, Polycop's Normandy bride: DELLA FOX. *Dancers from "La Folie" (4)*: *Mlle Renée*: Ada Bernard. *Mlle. Courcey*: Juno Hilton. *Mlle. Villiers*: Minnie Salvn. *Mlle. Varney*: Ruby Capon. *Frondist Soldiers, Parisian Tradesmen, Grisettes, Laundresses, Vivandières, Lords, Ladies, Pages, Drummers, etc.*

1898.28

THE LADY SLAVEY

A Revival of the Operatic Comedy in Two Acts[99]. Libretto by George Dance. Revised for America by Hugh Morton. Music by Gustave Kerker. Stage production by George W. Lederer. Scenery by D. Frank Dodge. Costumes by Catherine Seidle. Produced by Thomas Canary and George W. Lederer. Opened 25 April 1898 at the Casino Theatre and closed 25 June 1898 after 72 performances.

CAST: *Roberts*, sheriff's officer: WALTER JONES. *William Endymion Sykes*, assistant to Roberts: RICHARD CARLE. *Vincent Evelyn*, an American millionaire: JULIUS STEGER. *Major Tolliver*, an impecunious English gentleman: James Lackaye. *Lord Lavender*, an awful swell: Willard Simms. *Ikey Dinkelbinkel*, another swell of a different type: Charles Kirke. *Artemus Snipe*, a grocer: LEE HARRISON. *Krackowitzky*, a tailor: Lester W. Brown. *Phyllis*, the Lady Slavey: GLADYS WALLIS. *Flo Honeydew* of the Music Halls: MARIE DRESSLER. *Major Tolliver's Daughters (4)*: *Beatrice*: Daisy Dixon. *Maud*: Zella Frank. *Grace*: Delia Stacey. *Marjorie*: Teddie DuCoe. *Harriet Snipe*, the grocer's daughter: MAY MONTFORD. *Mme. Pontet*: CRISSIE CARLISLE. *Modistes (3)*: *Bessette*: May Shearer. *Sissette*: Erminei Earle. *Dollette*: Nellie Berwick. *Milliners (3)*: *Rosette*: Nettie Uart. *Evette*: Nellei Marsh. *Pepette*: Grace Franton. *Fanette*: Louise Skillman. *Nanette*: Lotta Ettinger. *Hannette*: Rhoda Blackburn. *Manicurists (4)*: *Marette*: Helen Moore. *Isette*: Modesta Miner. *Lollette*: Beulah Coolidge. *Trisette*: Miller Fernando. (*Premiere Danseuse*: MABEL CLARK.) *Tailors, Grocers, Cooks, Haberdashers, Footmen, Undertakers, Clairvoyants, Shoemakers, etc.*: Ladies and Gentlemen of the Chorus.

[98]First produced in New York 8 April 1897 at the Casino Theatre for 36 performances. For Synopsis of Scenes and Musical Numbers, see original 1897 production.

[99]Originally opened 3 February 1896 at the Casino Theatre for 128 performances. For Synopsis of Scenes and Musical Numbers, see original 1896 production. For this revival, only specialties and interpolations were listed in the program as follows:

"Why Do I Love Thee" (Act 1)
J. Steger
(*Music by* Robert A. Keiser. *Lyrics by* M. J. Clarence Harvey.)

"O, Lovely Maiden" (Act 2)(from HIS EXCELLENCY)
J. Steger

"She's a Spectable Married Collud Lady" (Act 2)
M. Dressler, W. Jones
(*Music and Lyrics by* E. C. Center and Jackson Gouraud.)

"The Aching Heart" (Act 2)
R. Carle
(*Music and Lyrics by* Richard Carle.)

"Yankee Doodle Boys" (Act 2)
W. Jones
(*Music and Lyrics by* Charles Burke and Morris Levi.)

Grand Pas Seul (Act 2)
:M. Clark

1898.029

THE CIRCUS GIRL

A Return Engagement of the Musical Comedy in Two Acts[100]. Book by James T. Tanner and W. Pallings [Walter Pallant]. Music by Ivan Caryll and Lionel Monckton. Lyrics by Harry Greenbank and Adrian Ross. Staged by J. A. E. Malone. Dances arranged by Carl Marwig. Settings by Ernest M. Gros and Henry E. Hoyt. Costumes by Comelli. Musical director, Sebastian Hiller. Produced by Augustin Daly. Opened 2 May 1898 at Daly's Theatre and closed 4 June 1898 after 40 performances.

CAST: *Sir Titus Wemyss*: HERBERT GRESHAM. *Dick Capel*: CYRIL SCOTT. *Drivelli*: JAMES HERBERT. *Hon. Reginald Gower*: Eric Scott. *Albertoni*: Douglas Flint. *Vicomte Gaston*: Neil McCay. *Commissaire of Police*: George Lesoir. *Auguste*: William Gilbert. *Toothick Pasha*: Randolph Roberts. *Rudolph*: Frederic Truesdale. *Cafe Proprietor*: Mr. Stanley. *Flobert*: Mr. Taylor. *Cocher*: Mr. Regis. *Sergeant de Ville*: Mr. Kelly. *Valliand*: Mr. SMith. *Biggs*: JAMES T. POWERS. *Lucille*: Mabelle Gillman. *La Favorita*: IRENE PERRY. *Mrs. Drivelli*: CATHERINE LEWIS. *Lady Diana Wemyss*: ETHEL HORNICK. *Marie*: Carolyn Gordon. *Louise*: Matilde Preville. *Liane*: Marion Carlton. *Emilie*: Rosa Vera. *Juliette*: Margaret Ashton. *Marquise de Millefleurs*: Edith Hutchings. *Comtesse d'Epernay*: Grace Rutter. *Mlle. Rose Gompson*: Violet Goodall. *Dora Wemyss*: VIRGINIA EARLE. *Mme. de Grouchy*: Francesca Gordon.

1898.30

THE BEGGAR STUDENT

A Revival of the Comic Opera in Three Acts, 4 Scenes[101]. (Original Viennese libretto "Der Bettelstudent" by F. Zell and Richard Genée, based on "Fernande" by Victorien Sardou and "The Lady of Lyons" by Edward Bulwer-Lytton. American adaptation by Emil Schwab.) Music by Carl Millöcker. Scenery by Frank King. Conductor, Adolph Liesegang. Stage manager, A. W. F. MacCollin. Produced by the Castle Square Opera Company (Henry W. Savage, Proprietor). Opened 2 May 1898 at the American Theatre and closed 7 May 1898 after 8 performances.

CAST: *Symon Symonovitz*, the Baggar Student: THOMAS H. PERSSE. *Janitsky*, his friend: JAY C. TAYLOR. *General Ollendorf*, Military Governor of Krakow: WILLIAM WOLFF. *Enterich*, a jailer: RAYMOND HITCHCOCK. *Puffki*, jailer: O. Risley. *Major Holtzheim*: E. C. Edmunds. *Sitzky*, an innkeeper: Charles Scribner. *Countess Palmetica*: JENNIE REIFFARTH. *Laura, Bronislava*, her daughters: Edith Mason, Gertrude Quinlan. *Eva*: Bernice Holmes. *Onophrie*: C. Scribner. *Lieutenant Poppenburg*: Lillian Swain. *Lieutenant Schweinitz*: W. C. Guard. *Lieutenant Wangerheim*: F. S. Heck. *Burgomaster*: W. E. Brockmeyer. *Bogumil*: P. O. Depew. *Chorus of Prisoners, Peasants, Soldiers, Musicians, Courtiers, Pages, Maids, Children, etc.*

1898.31

THE KOREANS

A 'Chinese-Japanese' (Comic) Opera in Three Acts, 4 Scenes. Libretto by Emerson Cooke. Music by Lucius Hosmer. Production supervised and stage directed by W. H. Lytell. Scenery by Joseph A. Physioc. Costumes designed by Miss A. Z. Straight. Director of Orchestra, Herman Perlet. Opened 3 May 1898 at the Herald Square Theatre and closed 7 May 1898 after 7 performances.[102]

CAST: *George Washington Tree*: RICHARD F. CARROLL. *Heinrich Brooke*: SAMUEL EDWARDS. *Singeton Bell*: CHARLES HILDESLEY. *The Four Ancestors (the Mimic Four)*: *Ding Dong*: James Horan. *Young Hyson*: Arthur Brock. *Old Hyson*: William van Deuser. *Mum Tung*: Paul F. Nicholson, Jr. *Wah Tell*: John Hoey. *Fidelia*: ALICE HOLBROOK. *Woo Me*: GERTIE REYNOLDS. *Columbia Hale*: MARCIA MURIAZ. *Sed So*: Eugenie Barker. *Oo Long*: Helene Mortimer.

Officers: Beatrice Hamilton, Mollie Swift, Louise Lear, Virginie Kendall. *Geisha Girls*: Eleanor Kendall, Clara Whitney, Carrie May, Ilene May. *Japanese Boys*: Netta Adams, May Sidonie, Josie Kirk, Mabel Hart. *Korean Girls*: Bertha Whitney, Sallie DePeyster, Julie Caldwell, Willametta Brown. *Sailor Boys*: Eva Lovelace, Annie Young, Florence Warden, May Massony.

Ladies of the Chorus: Misses Josie Moore, Emily Nash, Hattie Crabtree, Lillian Berry, Hattiy Durcell, Madeline Estelle, Marguerite Keil, Marie LeGreig, Lillian Dean, Emile Pouchez, Mabel Hedrickson, Etta Cuerbo, Mina Hunt, Daisy Hunt.

[100]First produced in New York 23 April 1897 at Daly's Theatre for 75 performances; re-opened 16 August 1897 at Daly's Theatre for 97 additional performances. Total: 172 performances. For Synopsis of Scenes and Musical Numbers, see original 1897 production.

[101]First produced in New York 29 October 1883 at the Casino Theatre for 110 performances. For Synopsis of Scenes and Musical Numbers, see original 1883 production.

[102]Producer not identified in programs.

Gentlemen of the Chorus: Messrs. Bechtel, Piner, Trew, Cook, Conway, Pleus, Cochrane, Nichols, Hellig, Lawrence, Nagel, Gibbons, Martin, Douglass, Leonard. *The Japonica Ballet*: Created for this production by H. Fletcher Rivers, to music by Rudolph Aronson. *Ladies in the Ballet*: May Sidonie, Mable Hunt, Eva Lovelace, Annie Young, Florence Warden, May Massony, Hattie Durcell, Marguerite Keil, Marie LeGrieg, Etta Cuerbo, Daisy Hunt, Lillian Dean. *Character Dance*: GERTIE REYNOLDS.

Act 1: A street in the village of Hiti.

Act 2: Garden adjoining Heinrich Brooke's house.

Act 3, Scene 1: The ancestral tombs. *Scene 2*: The Throne-room of Confucius.

MUSICAL NUMBERS[103]

"I'm Georgie Tree" (Entrance Song)
R. F. Carroll

"The Daughter of Today"
M. Muriaz

"We Are Dusty Travellers Three" (Bicycle Trio)
M. Muriaz, C. Hildesley

"In Anthem Old"
S. Edwards

"Dream Boat"

"Dolly Doane"
G. Reynolds

Kissing Duet
R. F. Carroll, G. Reynolds

1898.32 WAR BUBBLES

A Musical Extravaganza Conceit in One Act, following a vaudeville program. Libretto and music by Oscar Hammerstein. Staged by Oscar Hammerstein. Produced by Oscar Hammerstein. Opened 16 May 1898 at Hammerstein's Olympia Music Hall and closed 4 June 1898 after 26 performances.

CAST: ALLENE CRATER, CHERIDAH SIMPSON, CHRIS BRUNO, OSCAR FIGMAN, GUS YORKE and NICK ADAMS, LUCY NELSON, FRANCES LEE.

Scene: The stage of the Metropolitan Opera House.

MUSICAL NUMBERS and SPECIALTIES[104]

"Dewey March"

Levy and Cohen on Baxter Street
G. Yorke, N. Adams, etc.

Songs
C. Simpson

Philippine Song and Dance
C. Bruno, 4 Men

La Cubana in her Bird Specialty
L. Nelson

Wrestling Bout between Roeber and Yousouf

"Misere" from IL TROVATORE
A. Crater

Patriotic Airs/"The Star Spangled Banner" (Finale)
F. Lee

1898.33 FRA DIAVOLO

A Revival of the Comic Opera in Three Acts[105]. Music by Daniel François Esprit Auber. Original French libretto by Eugène Scribe. Stage manager, Charles H. Jones. Conductor, John McGhee. Scenery by Frank King. Produced by the Castle Square Opera Company (Henry W. Savage, Proprietor). Opened 16 May 1898 at the American Theatre and closed 21 May 1898 after 8 performances[106].

CAST: *Zerlina*, Matteo's daughter, in love with Lorenzo: EDITH MASON. *Fra Diavolo*, a bandit chieftain, disguised as the Marquis of San Carlo: THOMAS H. PERSSE. *Beppo, Giacomo*, bandits, followers of Fra Diavolo: William Wolff, Frank Ranney. *Lord Allcash*, an English tourist: Arthur Wooley. *Lady Allcash*, newly wedded to Lord Allcash: Bessie Fairbairn. *Roberto*: Gertrude Blancke. *Matteo*, landlord of the Inn: Dashiell Madeira. *Lorenzo*, Captain of the Caribineers: Jay C. Taylor. *Francesco Verona*, the bridegroom: J. C. GIBSON. *Chorus of Peasants, Carbineers, etc.*

1898.34 THE ISLE OF CHAMPAGNE

A Revival of the Comic Opera in Three Acts, 5 Scenes[107]. Libretto by Charles Alfred Byrne and Louis Harrison. Music by William W. Furst. Production staged by Karl Formes, Jr. Scenery by Walter Burridge (Acts 1, 3), Richard Marston (Act 2). Costumes designed by Madame Calame. Musical director, Edward Buechner. Produced by David Biers. Opened 18 May 1898 at the Broadway Theatre and closed 28 May 1898 after 12 performances.

CAST: *King Pommery Second*, Ruler of the Isle: THOMAS Q. SEABROOKE. *Apollinaris Frappe*, his prime minister: Walter Allen. *Prince Kissingen*, his son: Frederick Knights. *Moet, Chandon*, his army: Tot Ducrow, W. Connors. *Marquis Mumm, Baron Heidsic*, conspirators: Arthur Carleton, Winifred Arling. *Sam Binnacle*, ship-wrecked sailor of New Bedford, Massachusetts: JOHN MAYON. *Count Roederer*: W. Kinder. *Bridgitte*, Diana's companion: Aggie Vars. *Artea, Sophie*, Archers: Beatrice Hamilton, Martha Hybelmann. *Charmantine*: Julia Coldwell. *Pages in the Champagne Palace (5)*: *Chick*: Kittie Nice. *Petite*: Nellie King. *Jolie*: Kitty Gardner. *Billie*: Helene DeVoe. *Chummy*: Marie Minturn. *Lillee*: Bertha Dickens. *Abigail Peck*, Priscilla's aunt of New Bedford, Massachusetts: BLANCHE CHAPMAN. *Diana*, the belle of the Isle: LILLIAN BURNHAM. *Priscilla*, a New England maiden: Katherine Germaine. *Ballet*: Bertha Wasserman, Llly Brink, Grace Stickley, Aggie Vars, Maude Robinson, Lillian Kirk. *Archers, Citizens, Citizenesses, Cherry Girls, Cobweb Girls, Flower Girls, Ladies and Gentlemen of the Court of Champagne, Sailors, Doctors, etc.*

1898.35 LE RËVE

A Novelty (Operetta) in One Act, preceded by a Vaudeville program. Libretto by Joseph Herbert. (Based on the legend of Pygmalion and Galatea.) Music by Max Gabriel. Staged by Joseph Herbert. Scenery designed by Albert Operti. Musical director, Max Gabriel. Produced by Koster & Bial (Albert E. Aarons, General Manager). Opened 23 May 1898 at Koster & Bial's Music Hall and closed 30 May 1898 after 8 performances.

Vaudeville: Rogers Brothers, Dutch comedians; May Belfort, comedienne in "What's Wrong?"; Josie DeWitt, violiniste; Ouda, the aerial marvel; The Pantzer Brothers, head balancers; Bud Snyder, trick bicyclist; Hector and Lauraine, grotesques; Servais LeRoy, illusionist.

CAST: *Michel*, an artist: THOMAS GREEN. *Leander*: THOMAS GREEN. *Mlle Daubigne*: ADELE RITCHIE.

Scene: An Artist's Studio in Paris.

MUSICAL NUMBERS

1898.36 ERMINIE

A Revival of the Comic Opera in Three Acts[108]. Libretto by Harry Paulton (and Claxson Bellamy). Based on the melodrama "L'Auberge des Adrets" by Benjamin Antier, Saint-Amand and Paulyanthe, adapted into English as "Robert Macaire." Music by Edward Jakobowski. Staged by Edward P. Temple. Scenery by Homer Emens, Henry Marston. Costumes by Percy Anderson. Director of music, A. DeNovellis. Produced by George W. Lederer and George B. McLellan. Opened 23 May 1898 at the Casino Theatre and closed 25 June 1898 after 40 performances.

CAST: *Erminie*: PAULINE HALL. *Javotte*: LULU GLASER. *Cerise*: CELESTE WYNN. *Princess de Gramponeur*: JENNIE WEATHERSBY. *Marie*: Miriam Lawrence. *Captain Delaunay*: KATE UART. *Cadeaux, Ravennes*, two thieves: FRANCIS X. WILSON, HENRY E. DIXEY. *Eugene Marcel*: Clinton Elder. *Chevalier de Brabazon*: EDWARD P. TEMPLE. *Marquis de Ponvert*: Arthur Cunningham. *Dufois*: Murry Woods. *Simon*: Edmund Lawrence. *Vicomte de Brissac*: Charles H. Bowers. *Sergeant*: Joseph Chaillee.

[103]No songs listed in program.
[104]No program available; songs and specialties not in performance order.
[105]First produced in New York 20 June 1833 at the Park Theatre in French.
[106]English adaptation uncredited.

[107]Originally produced 5 December 1892 at the Manhattan Theatre for 50 performances. For Synopsis of Scenes and Musical Numbers, see original 1892 production.
[108]First produced in New York 10 May 1886 at the Casino Theatre for 648 performances in a series of three engagements. For Synopsis of Scenes and Musical Numbers, see original 1886 production.

Act 1: Inn at Ponvert. (Emens.)

Act 2: The Pink Ball Room of Chateau Ponvert. (Marston.)

Act 3: Corridor and staircase of same. (Marston.)

1898.37 THE BLACK HUSSAR

A Revival of the Operetta in Three Acts[109]. [Original Viennese libretto ('Der Feldprediger') by Hugo Wittmann and Alois Wohlmuth. English adaptation by Sydney Rosenfeld.] Music by Carl Millöcker. Stage manager, Charles H. Jones. Scenery by Frank King. Conductor, Adolph Liesegang. Produced by the Castle Square Opera Company (Henry W. Savage, Proprietor). Opened 30 May 1898 at the American Theatre and closed 4 June 1898 after 9 performances.

CAST: *(Friedrich von) Helbert*, Captain in Black Hussars, disguised as an Army Chaplain: THOMAS H. PERSSE. *(Hans von) Waldmann*, his companion: RICHARD RIDGELY. *(Theophil) Hackenback*, Magistrate of Trautenfeld: DOUGLAS FLINT, WILLIAM WOLFF. *Piffkow*, his man-of-all-work: ARTHUR WOOLEY. *(François) Thorilliere*, Major in Napoleon's Army: Frank Moulan. *Hetman*, Captain of the Cossacks: A. Barbara. *Mifflin*, an actor: RICHARD BEALE. *Hackenback's Daughters (2)*: *Minna*: EDITH MASON. *Rosetta*: GERTRUDE QUINLAN, RUTH WHITE. *Barbara*, (an Orphan, Hackenback's Housekeeper): BESSIE FAIRBAIRN. *Ricca*: Emma King. *Goddess of Liberty*: Josephine Neale. *Germania*: Ida Clark. *First Citzien*: Frank Ranney. *Second Citizen*: Charles Scribner.

[109]First produced in New York 4 May 1885 at Wallack's Theatre for 104 performances. For Synopsis of Scenes and Musical Numbers, see original May 1885 production.

1898–1899 SEASON

Anna Held in THE FRENCH MAID (Photo: Chickering)
Billy Rose Theatre Collection, New York Public Library for the Performing Arts

1898–1899 SEASON

1898.38 COOK'S TOUR

A Musical, Terpsichorean, Pantomimic, Dramatic Salad, seasoned with a generous sprinkling of Patriotic Allspice in Two Acts, 9 Scenes[1]. Book by Joseph W. Herbert. Music by Max Gabriel. Staged under the personal direction of Joseph W. Herbert. Scenery by Operti. Musical director, Max Gabriel. Produced by Koster & Bial (Alfred E. Aarons, General Manager). Opened 6 June 1898 at Koster & Bial's Music Hall and closed 6 August 1898 after 72 performances.

CAST: *Timothy Cook*, night-porter at the Waldorf-Castoria: EDDIE GIRARD. *Diogenes Doolittle*, a citizen of the world: JOE OTT. *Mr. Krawlanger*, manager of the "Swell of New York" company: HARRY KELLY. *Dopey de Lome*, a letter-writer; incidentally a diplomat: JOHN SLAVIN. *Phineas Flakey*, a reformer: JACQUES KRUGER. *Dod Slowun*, ditto in a different line: HARRY O'KEEFE. *Captain Watkins*: Frank Cheesman. *Waiter*: Franz Schuster. *Johnnies (3)*: *Algie Albermarle*: Archie Craven. *Bertie Brass*: Edward Fielding. *Percy Peweter*: James Forrest. *Lords (3)*: *Marquis of Gooseberry*: James Carroll. *Duke Allover*: John Gilroy. *Count Cranberry*: Arthur O'Keefe. *Measles*, of the lower five: JOSIE HALL. *Lady Soap*: MARIE DRESSLER[2]. *Fanny Frivol*, a voiceless prima donna: GEORGIA CAINE. *Mamie Muggins*, a Montana soubrette: ADA LEWIS. *Arabella*, a Quakeress: DAISY DIXON. *Patti de Fois-Gras*: Florence Laverne. *Newsboy*: Edith Francisco. *Messenger*: Ethel Jackson. *Promising Soubrettes of the "Swell of New York" Company (8)*: *Minnie Middling*: May Lavigne. *Gertie Grabenheim*: Helen Marlborough. *Dela O'Fait*: Martha Habelman. *Clara Cacklesbaum*: Beatrice Hamilton. *Miranda Maguire*: Crissie Carlyle. *Daisy Duffy*: Irene Bentley. *Flossie Flanagan*: Mabel Montgomery. *Annie Asparagus*: Polly Marriott. *One of the Finest*: Ed Aiken. *Gendarme*: Anton Heilig. *La Perche*: Frl. Hechter. *La Framboise*: Frl. Svorg. *La Bar-le-Duc*: Mlle. Christian. *La Gervaise*: Signora Mella.

Characters incidental to the Ballet: *General Lee*: Anton Heilg. *General Miles*: Walter Roland. *English Consul*: Frank Savage. *General Weyler*: Frank Cheesman. *Conspirator*: Harry Nichols. *John Bull*: Frank Squires. *Uncle Sam*: William Church. *Columbia*: Frl. Habelman. *Cuba*: Signora Pinta. *Goddess of Liberty*: Maud Terriss. *Spaniards, Cubans, American and Spanish Soldiers, American Jack Tars, Red Cross Nurses, Reconcentrados, etc.*

Act 1, Scene 1: American Steamship Pier, New York. Depature of the *"Paris"* for Southampton. *Scene 2*: Deck of the *"Paris"* mid-ocean, six days out. *Scene 3*: Cecil Hotel courtyard, facing Strand, London. *Scene 4*: Boulevard de Capucins, front of Grand Hotel, Paris. *Scene 5*: Moulin Rouge.

Act 2, Scene 1: Home again. American Pier, New York. *Scene 2*: Waldorf-Castoria anteroom. *Scene 3*: Lobby of ballroom *Scene 4*: Stage of ballroom, Hotel Castoria.

ACT 1[3]

"We're Going Abroad" (Opening Chorus)
"In Dear Old London"
"Over-trained Soubrette"
"Dopey de Lome"
"Sailing Over the Bright Blue Sea"
"They Didn't Want the Likes of Me"
"Deacon and the Parrot"
"Just Two Days Since We Arrived"
"Little Flossie Flip"
"Sallie Nipp and Jimmie Jones"
"Take Me Back to Brooklyn"
"She Just Walks On"
"Hurrah, for We're in Clover"
"Strolling Along the Boulevard"
"Moulin Rouge, Gaiety's Treadmill"
"The Continong"
Dance Eccentrique
Pas de Quatre
"We Don't Do That in Philadelphia"
"Champagne" (Trio)
"Can Can"

ACT 2

"Home Again"
"We're Back from Abroad"
"What We Saw on the Boulevard"
"Zizzie za zim" (Zizzy-Ze-Zum-Zum Zum)(A Ragtime Nightmare)
J. Hall
(*Music by* Lyn Udall. *Lyrics by* Karl Kennett.)
Liberty's Triumph (Ballet)

1898.39 THE BOHEMIAN GIRL

A Revival of the Romantic Opera in Three Acts[4]. Libretto by Alfred Bunn, after Jules-Henri Vernoy de Saint-Georges' ballet-pantomime "The Gypsy." Music by Michael Balfe. Stage manager, A. W. F. MacCollin. Scenery by Frank King. Conductor, Adolph Liesegang. Produced by the Castle Square Opera Company (Henry W. Savage, Proprietor). Opened 6 June 1898 at the American Theatre and closed 11 June 1898 after 8 performances.

CAST: *Count Arnheim*, Governor of Presburg: WILLIAM BRODERICK. *Thaddeus*, a proscribed Pole: JOSEPH F. SHEEHAN. *Florestein*, nephew of the Count: Arthur Wooley. *Devilshoof*, chief of the Gypsies: DOUGLAS FLINT. *Captain of the Guard*: E. C. Edmonds. *Arline*, daughter of the Count: GRACE GOLDEN. *Buda*, her attendant: Lillian Lipyeat. *Queen of the Gypsies*: LIZZIE MACNICHOL, MARION IVELL. *Chorus of Nobles, Soldiers, Gypsies, Retainers and Peasants.*

1898.40 MADELEINE, or, The Magic Kiss

A Revival of the Comic Opera in Three Acts[5]. Libretto by Stanislaus Stange. Music by Julian Edwards. Stage manager, A. W. F. MacCollin. Scenery by Frank King. Conductor, Adolph Liesegang. Produced by the Castle Square Opera Company (Henry W. Savage, Proprietor). Opened 13 June 1898 at the American Theatre and closed 18 June 1898 after 8 performances.

CAST: *Baron de Grimm*, a centenarian: WILLIAM G. STEWART. *Dr. Gourmet*, his physician: OSCAR GIRARD. *Jules Le Meagre*, his scribe: FRANK MOULAN. *Francois*, his steward: Charles Campbell. *Emile*, his major-domo: Charles Scribner. *Auguste Deutsch*, alias Frederic Ribeau: WILLIAM BRODERICK. *Madeleine*, the Baron's Ward: LOUISE EISSING. *Matrimonial Mary*, a Sextette Widow: BESSIE FAIRBAIRN. *Margot, Vivette*, Dr. Gourmet's daughters: Maude Burke, Cecil Lorraine. *Chorus of Villagers, Courtiers, etc.*

1898.41 RICE'S SUMMER NIGHTS

Variety Entertainment (Vaudeville) in One Act. Staged by Edward E. Rice. Ballet master, Augustus Sohlke. Orchestra under the direction of John J. Braham. Produced by Edward E. Rice. Opened 18 June 1898 at the Casino Roof Garden and closed 20 August 1898 after 55 performances.

CAST (in order of appearance): ETTA STETSON, ELSA MARTENS, WALTER ROGERS, JUNE JACKSON, EDWIN FRENCH, MARGUERITE SYLVA, NELLIE HAWTHORNE, LAFAYETTE, ALICE ATHERTON, AMORITA THE FAWN, the original WATERMELON QUARTETTE, HARRY S. MARION.

Later attractions included: Ernest Hogan, Pearl Meredith, Mamie Emerson, Maud Courtney, The 8 Phaseys, The Midgelys, Shedman's Dog Circus, Harvey Sisters, Hale Sisters, Rice's Cornstalk Ballet, Williams & Hood, Cooper & Reynolds, William English, Charles B. Ward, Sisters Meredith, American Musical Three, Knox Wilson, Rice's March of Amazons, Grand Orchestra of Selected Artists.

SPECIALTIES

Promenade Concert
Ella Stetson: "The Patti Waltz"
Elsa Martens: (an odd "phantasy")

---

[1]Also billed as Koster & Bial's summer olla-podrida. Reviewers referred to the show as an extravaganza.
[2]Joined the cast in the second or third week of the run.
[3]Added during the run:
"Ram-a-Jam, (I Want That Man)" (from COURTED INTO COURT)
M. Dressler

[4]First produced in New York 25 November 1844 at the Park Theatre for 17 performances. For Synopsis of Scenes and Musical Numbers, see original 1844 production.
[5]First produced in New York 25 February 1895 at the Bijou Theatre for 80 performances. For Synopsis of Scenes and Musical Numbers, see original 1895 production.

Walter Rogers (Cornet solo)

June Jackson (patriotic dance)

Edwin French (banjo)

Marguerite Sylva (3 songs)

Nellie Hawthorne in her entirely new costume songs[6]:
"The Girl in the White Silk Dress," Our Lodger," and "The Boys of the Empire"

Lafayette

Alice Atherton:
"The Barmaid"
"The Laughing Song"
(*Music by* John Crook. *Lyrics by* George Dance.)
"Ma Ann Elizer" (My Ann Elizer, The Rag Time Girl)
(*Music and Lyrics by* Malcolm Williams.)

Amorita, the Fawn, in a Ballet Divertissement (with 8 Girls)

The original Watermelon Quartette

Harry S. Marion (illustrated songs)

SPECIALTIES (added during the run)

THE ORIGIN OF THE CAKE WALK, or CLORINDY[7]:
A Sensational African Singing and Dancing Novelty by Paul Laurence Dunbar. Music by Will Marion (Cook). Produced by Ernest Hogan. Musical director, Will Marion (Cook). With Ernest Hogan, Pearl Meredith, Mamie Emerson, and Chorus. Musical Numbers: "Who Dat Say Chicken in Dis Crowd?" (The Great Chicken Song), "Every Coon Had a Lady Friend But Me," "Hottest Coon in Dixie," "Darktown Is Out To-night" [*Music and Lyrics by* Will Marion (Cook)], "Jump Back, Honey."

Rice's Divertissement Croupier

Sisters Meredith

Williams and Hood

Charles B. Ward

Miss Maude Courtney (in the old songs of Bygone Days)

The 8 Phaseys

Knox Wilson

Rice's Cornstalk Novelty

William English

Hale Sisters

Cooper & Reynolds

Harvey Sisters

American Musical Three

Rice's March of Amazons

Shedman's Dog Circus

Way Up East, Richard Carle's screaming burlesque of the rustic drama 'Way Down East'

1898.42 THE GONDOLIERS, or, The King of Barataria

A Revival of the Comic Opera in Two Acts[8]. Libretto by William S. Gilbert. Music by Arthur Sullivan. Scenery by Frank King. Stage manager, A. W. F. MacCollin. Conductor, Adolph Liesegang. Produced by the Castle Square Opera Company (Henry W. Savage, Proprietor). Opened 20 June 1898 at the American Theatre and closed 25 June 1898 after 8 performances.

CAST: *Duke of Plaza-Toro*, a Grandee of Spain: DOUGLAS FLINT, WILLIAM BRODERICK. *Luiz*, his attendant: CHARLES CAMPBELL. *Don Alhambra Del Bolero*, The Grand Inquisitor: RAYMOND HITCHCOCK. *Marco Palmieri, Giuseppe Palmieri, Antonio*, Venetian Gondoliers: JOSEPH F. SHEEHAN, WILLIAM G. STEWART, J. F. BOYLE. *Duchess of Plaza Del Toro*: BESSIE FAIRBAIRN. *Gianetta*: LOUISE EISSING. *Casilda*: RUTH WHITE. *Tessa, Fiametta, Vittoria, Giulia*, Contadine: GERTRUDE QUINLAN, Julie Cotte, L. Martinez, Lillian Lipyeat. *Inez*, The King's Foster-Mother: Dolly Delroy. *Francesco, Giorgio*, Venetian Gondoliers: Charles Scribner, P. O. Depew. (*Chorus of Gondoliers, Contadine, Men-at-Arms, Heralds and Pages.*)

1898.43 YANKEE DOODLE DANDY

An Extravagant (Musical) Extravaganza in Two Acts, 6 Scenes. Book (and lyrics) by Hugh Morton. Music by Gustave Kerker. Staged by George W. Lederer. Settings by Ernest Albert and D. Frank Dodge. Costumes designed by Mme. Catherine Siedle. Orchestra under the direction of Thomas H. Joyce. Produced by George W. Lederer and George B. McLellan, by arrangement with Augustus Pitou. Opened 25 July 1898 at the Casino Theatre and closed 8 October 1898 after 74 performances[9].

CAST: *Theophilus Borax*, a theatrical property man, afterwards the partner of Terwilliger: WALTER JONES. *Paul Croquette*, an art student, afterwards a naval lieutenant: JULIUS STEGER. *Don Alfonzo Alcantara*, Admiral of the Spanish Fleet: J. C. MIRON. *Pasquale de Mackeral*, Lieutenant in the Spanish Navy: RICHARD CARLE. *Terrible Tommy*, Captain of Tommy's Tough Riders: EUGENE O'ROURKE. *Corporal Redneck*, officer of the squad: EUGENE O'ROURKE. *Don Corkey Riley*, Captain of the Fusileers of Cherry Hill: LOUIS WESLEY. *Mistah Razzers*, the Beau of Mistah Johnsing's Chowder Party: LOUIS WESLEY. *Professor Smeere*, an art professor: J. A. Furey. *Hon. William Willaloo*, 14th Assistant Secretary of War: J. A. Furey. *Husky Hardmugg*, a Jailor: LEE HARRISON. *Phelim Pheeney*, an Irishman: D. L. DON. *Domf Dreisengacker*, a German citizen: D. L. DON. *Sisseretta Fraser*, the belle of Mistah Johnsing's chowder party: D. L. DON. *Larry*, a ticket-chopper: Will A. McCormack. *Captain Hawkshaw*, U.S.A., a detective: Will A. McCormack. *Pinch*, a police captain: Will A. McCormack. *Private Muzzle, Private Breach*, sentries: J. Cogley, Lester Brown. *Officer Clubbem, Officer Biffem*, Metropolitan police officers: G. Courtney, J. B. Jordan. *Jabber*, bulletinist of *The Daily Microbe*: Horace Hair. *Gabber*, bulletinist of *The Morning Screamer*: M. Maerschert. *Waxtree Snaggsby*, a newsboy: Paul Kain. *Pietro Bananapeelie*, a vendor: J. L. Baldwin. *Private Plum*: Randolph Curry. *Hon. Gideon Terwilliger*, President of the International Infant Incubator Company, Limited: THOMAS Q. SEABROOKE. *Fair Honoria*, the sincere girl, afterward disguised as Juanita: MADGE LESSING. *Angela Swansdowne*, a soubrette: MARIE GEORGE. *Filomena*, an Italian Street Singer: GERTRUDE ZELLA. *Minnie Harkaway*, an art student: Margaret McDonald. *Dutch Lena*, Vivandiere of the Fusileers of Cherry Hill: Christine Blessing.

Incubator Girls (8): *Violet Ink*: ??.*Ruby Ink*: Susie Drake. *Azure Ink*: Nellie Thomas. *Cherry Ink*: Bertha Wood. *Emerald Ink*: Modesta Miner. *Pinkie Ink*: Jeanette Bageard. *Sapphire Ink*: Mignon Haun. *Rosie Ink*: Violet Holls. *Wartime Soubrettes (4)*: *Clarisse Martini*: Jeanette Bageard. *Roseletta Manhattan*: Jeannette Bageard. *Gladiola Fizz*: Margaret McDonald. *Sappho Giggle*: ??. *Teddy Twoshoes*, an art student, and lieutenant in the New York Naval Reserves: EDNA WALLACE HOPPER. *Pas de Deux*: Mlle. Franchonette, Lillian Brink.

United States Soldiers, Men-o'-War Men, Spanish Soldiers and Sailors, Naval Reserves, Camp Followers, Tough Riders, West Point and Annapolis Cadets, Harvard, Yale and Princeton and Pennsylvania Students, Art Students, Mistah Johnsing's Chowder Party, Citizens, Emigrants, Elevated Railroad Guards, Bulletin Cranks, Flower Girls, Vendors, Newsboys, etc: Grand Chorus and Corps de Ballet.

Act 1, Scene 1: A class room in the New York Academy of Design. (Albert.) *Scene 2*: On the platform of the 23rd Street Station of the Sixth Avenue Elevated Railway. (Dodge.) *Scene 3*: The Battery, New York, in war time, showing the Spanish Fleet in the harbor. (Dodge.)

Act 2, Scene 1: Printing House Square, New York, at night. (Dodge.) *Scene 2*: Interior of a New York Police Station, down among the cells. (Albert.) *Scene 3*: Pennsylvania Avneue, Washington, D.C., at dawn, looking up at the Capitol. (Albert.)

MUSICAL NUMBERS[10]

Colonial Anglo-American Ballet

"The Boys of Yankee Land"

"The Cherry Hill Fusileers"

"Fair Honoria"

"Flora"

Frivolity Ballet
(*Music by* Edward E. Rice.)

---

[6]Replaced during the run by:
"My Little Lady"
"My Susianah from Louisiana"
(*Music by* Sidney L. Perrin. *Lyrics by* Tom McGuire.)
"The Toreador Am I."

[7]Added 5 July 1898. After RICE'S SUMMER NIGHTS closed, CLORINDY continued as part of a vaudeville program with Richard Carle's 'Way Up East,' until 17 September 1898 for an estimated 65 performances.

[8]First produced in New York 7 January 1890 at the Park Theatre for a total of 103 performances. For Synopsis of Scenes and Musical Numbers, see original 1890 production.

[9]Also played return engagements 17 October 1898 at the Grand Opera House for 8 performances, and 31 October 1898 at the Harlem Opera House for 8 performances.

[10]Musical numbers not listed in programs. List prepared from published sheet music, reviews, etc.

"From the Distant Town of Cadiz"
"The Girl with the Strawberry Mark"
"Golly, Charlie!"
"If You Do It in the Proper Sort of Way"
"I Love a Girl Who is Made of Stucco"
"The Infant Incubator"
"Have You Seen Maudie? She's All Right"
"Here's to Our Alma Mater"
"Juanita"
"May I?"
"Mr. Johnsing's Chowder"
"Oh, How Would You Like to Pet?"
"The Old, Old Story"
"Poor O'Hoolahan (Held the Fuse)"
T. Q. Seabrooke
"Louisa"
"Meet Me Down at Huyler's"
"Oh, Willie! Don't You Love Me?"
"Rosie"
"Rough Riders"
"Roxiana Dooley"
W. Jones
"Wine, Wine, Wine"
"When the Clock Strikes Two in the Tenderloin"
"Would You If You Could"
College Ballet
"The Jelly Fish Song"
(*Music by* Jackson Gouraud. *Lyrics by* W. Emmons White.)
"Thou Art Mine Own One"
J. Steger
(*Music and Lyrics by* Henry Bauer.)

1898.44 IN ATLANTIC CITY

A Musical Comedy with a Touch of Pathos (Farce Comedy) in Three Acts. Settings by Walter Burridge. Musical director, Louis Jacobson. Produced by Stewart Lithgow. Opened 13 August 1898 at the Star Theatre and closed 20 August 1898 after 9 performances[11].

CAST: *Otto Buch*, a wealthy retired brewer: FRANK M. WILLS. *Charles Buch*, proud of his sire: WALTER McCOLLOUGH. *Chaucey Van Cott*, a distinguished gentleman: WILTON TAYLOR. *Reginald Van Cott*, a disappointment: JOHN S. TERRY. *Butts*, contented with his lot: PAT ROONEY. *Violet*, with fragrance of the conservatory: MABEL MONTGOMERY. *Rose*, by any other name would smell as sweet: ESTELLA WELLS. *Clementine*, with amorous intentions: ALICE GILMOUR. *Lize*, a sweetheart of Butts: MATTIE ROONEY. *Adeline*: Kitty Helston. *Alethea*: Gussie Helston. *Alicia*: Dollie Helston. *Angelica*: Irene Stewart. *Aurelia*: Emilie DeVera. *Antoinette*: Leslie Marion. *Herald Square Quartette*: G. D. Cuningham, Jay Binkley, George Ovey, Harry Turner.

Act 1: Hotel Lawn at Atlantic City.

Act 2: Hotel Parlor in Atlantic City.

Act 3: Board Walk in Atlantic City.

ACT 1
Opening Chorus
"Ann Eliza"
Entire Company
Duet
W. McCollough, M. Montgomery
Grand Finale
Entire Company

ACT 2
"Dainty Little French Maids"
Helston Sisters, M. Rooney
Specialty (Coon song)
A. Gilmour
"A Quarrel" (Top-boot Dance Specialty)
J. S. Terry, Helston Sisters
Grand Finale
Entire Company

ACT 3
Novelty Act, introducing "Yiddisher Trick"
J. B. Wills, E. Wills
Specialty
P. Rooney, M. Rooney
Travesty of "Hamlet"
W. McCollough, M. Montgomery
Ballads
J. S. Terry
Specialty
F. M. Wills, Herald Square Quartette
Grand Finale
Entire Company

1898.45 THE OLD HOMESTEAD

A Revival of the Rural Melodrama in Four Acts[12]. Play by Denman Thompson and George W. Ryer. Staged by Frank Knapp. Scenic artist, Homer F. Emens. Musical director, H. Braham. Organist, Fred Rycroft. Manager, Frank Thompson. Opened 15 August 1898 at the Academy of Music and closed 24 September 1898 after 48 performances; returned 27 March 1899 to the Academy of Music and closed 4 May 1899 after an additional 48 performances. Total this season: 96 performances[13].

CAST: Act 1: *Joshua Whitcomb*: DENMAN THOMPSON. *Cy Prime*: WILL M. CRESSY. *Happy Jack*: FRED CLARE. *Frank Hopkins*: LOUIS CROXSON. *Eb. Ganzey*: JOHN BARKER. *John Freeman*: FRANK KNAPP. *Aunt Matilda Whitcomb*, Joshua's sister: Mrs. LOUISA MORSE. *Rickety Ann*: ANNIE THOMPSON. *Miss Annie Hopkins*: Mary F. Sherwood. *Nellie Freeman*: Ella Ittner. *Minnie Freeman*: Bertha E. Mason. *Maggie O'Flaherty*: Celia Baker. Act 2: *Henry Hopkins*: GUS KAMMERLEE. *Judge Patterson*: R. E. Rogers. *François Fogarty*: Stephen Baker. *Mrs. Henry Hopkins*: Annie Thompson. *Nellie Patterson*: Helen Ludington. Act 3: *Jack Hazzard*: FRED CLARE. *Reuben Whitcomb*, Joshua's son: HAL E. PAYNE. *Hoboken Terror*: Dan Regan. *One of the Finest*: R. E. Rogers. *U. S. Letter Carrier*: George L. Patch. *Mrs. McGuire*: Marie Kimball. Act 4: *Seth Perkins*: Charles H. Clark. *Len Holbrook, Warren Ellis*, Country Fiddlers: George L. Patch, P. Redmond. *Dave Willard*: Himself. *Pat Clancy*: James F. Callahan. *Mrs. Anna Maria Murdock*: Kathryn Miller. *The Three Stratton Gals* (Eleanor, Jane, Bessie): Katheryn Miller, Sadie F. Cullen, Bertha A. Brierly. *Double Quartette*: A. C. Orcutt, Hal E. Payne, Jr., L. H. Croxson, S. Baker, R. E. Rogers, A. B. Meyers, G. Kammerlee. F. Clare.

SPECIALTIES
"The Palms"
W. C. Weeden, Fred Rycroft (organist)

1898.46 A RUNAWAY GIRL

A Musical Comedy in Two Acts, 3 Scenes. Book by Seymour Hicks and Harry Nichols. Music by Ivan Caryll and Lionel Monckton. Lyrics by Avery Hopwood and Harry Greenbank. All dances and movements by Herbert Gresham. Settings by Henry E. Hoyt. Costumes designed by Wilhelm;

[11]Subsequently moved to the Columbia Theatre. No authors or composers billed in programs, or credited in reviews; costumes uncredited.

[12]First produced in New York 10 January 1887 at the 14th Street Theatre for 155 performances. For Synopsis of Scenes, see original 1887 production. For this revival the following were added:
"When the War Is O'er" (Act 1)
Double Quartet
"I'll Take Care of You, Grandma"
(*Music and Lyrics by* John Quinn.)

[13]THE OLD HOMESTEAD was joined by Denman Thompson's "Songs Illustrated and Illuminated" for Wednesday matinees and Sunday matinees. THE OLD HOMESTEAD later played return engagements in New York 6 January 1897 at the Harlem Opera House for 1 week, 18 October 1897 at the Academy of Music for 40 performances, 15 August 1898 at the Academy of Music for 48 performances, 21 November 1898 at the Harlem Opera House for 1 week, and 27 March 1899 at the Academy of Music for 48 performances.

carnival costumes by Dazian. Orchestra under the direction of Sebastian Hiller. Produced by Augustin Daly. Opened 25 August 1898 at Daly's Theatre, moved 21 November 1898 to the Fifth Avenue Theatre and closed 25 February 1899 after 216 performances.[14]

CAST: *Guy Stanley*, Lord Coodle's nephew: CYRIL SCOTT. *Lord Coodle*, a Cook's tourist: WILFRED CLARKE. *Professor Tamarind*, , Teacher at the School of St. Pierre: HERBERT GRESHAM. *Signor Polloni*, Consul at Corsica: Henry Stanley. *Hon. Bobby Barclay*, a Tourist: ERIC SCOTT. *Sir William Hake*, another: Paul McAllister. *Mr. Creel*, an Entomologist and Disciple of Walton: THOMAS HADAWAY. *Leonello*, chief of a band of Wandering Musicians: Arthur Donaldson. *Pietro Pescara*, his aider and abettor: George Lesoir. *Members of the Band (3)*: *Santa Cruz*: Frank Regis. *Boccaccio*: Charles Bates. *Doloroso*: Percy Smith. *Gendarmes*: Randolph Roberts, Frank Evans. *Waiter*, at the Hotel in Ajaccio: John Taylor. *Flipper*, a Jockey: JAMES T. POWERS. *Dorothy Stanley*, a Cook's tourist: YVETTE VIOLETTE. *Lady Coodle*: CATHERINE LEWIS. *Mrs. Creel*, on her wedding tour: GERDA WISNER. *Fraulein Ehrenbreitstein*, a tourist: Belle Harper. *Agatha*, a school girl: Blanche Carlisle. *Martha*, another: Marion Stuart. *Dolly Dudley*: Beatrice Morgan. *Maude Brook*: Mabel Thompson. *Grace Arlington*: Violet Goodall. *Bertie Wales*: Edith Hutchins. *Jessie Portman*: Rosa Vera. *Georgie St. George*: Edna Hunter. *Eva Grosvenor*: Hazel Pughsley. *Dancers in the Carnival Scene*: Misses Francesca Gordon, Elsa Ryan, Elsie Sarracco. *Folly*, in the Carnival Dance: Carolyn Gordon. *Flower Girls*: Misses Edna Archer, Ida Hawley, Florence Smyth, Louise Kitteridge. *Postillions*: Misses Cecilia Garrick, Edith Terry, Adelaide Phillips, Katherine Clinton, Hilda Henning, Ida Hobson. *Sabot Girls*: Misses Alice Mills, Blanche Carlisle, Beatrice Clements, Marie Murphy, Winnifred Wolcott, Victoria Stone. *Alice*, Lady Coodle's maid: MABEL GILMAN. *Carminita*, one of the band: PAULA EDWARDES. *Winnifred Gray*, an orphan: VIRGINIA EARL.

Act 1, Scene 1: Corsica, near the school grounds of St. Pierre. *Scene 2*: Corsica, a street in Ajaccio.

Act 2: Venice; a square near the Grand Canal.

ACT 1[15]

"Breathe Soft, Wind of the South" (Opening Chorus)

"The Sly Cigarette" (Cigarette Song)
V. Earl, Chorus
(*Music by* Lionel Monckton. *Lyrics by* Aubrey Hopwood.)

"My Kingdom" (Solo and Trio)
G. Lesoir, C. Bates, P. Smith, F. Regis

"Not The Sort of Girl I'd Care About" (Song)
C. Scott, Chorus
(*Music by* Lionel Monckton.)

"I'm Only a Poor Singing Girl" (Song)
V. Earl, Chorus

"No One in the World Like You" (Duet)
V. Earl, C. Scott
(*Music by* Alfred D. Cammeyer.)

"Follow the Man from Cook's" (Concerted Piece)
J. T. Powers, Principals

ACT 2

"The Soldiers in the Park" (Song)
Y. Violette, Chorus
(*Music by* Lionel Monckton.)

"Beautiful Venice" (Song)
V. Earl, Chorus

"Tarantella" (Song, Chorus and Dance)
H. Gresham, P. Edwardes, Chorus

"The Boy Guessed Right (the Very First Time)" (Song)
V. Earl, Chorus
(*Music and Lyrics by* Lionel Monckton.)

"The Pickaninnies" (Duet)
M. Gilman, J. T. Powers
(*Music by* Ivan Caryll.)

"High Society" (Oh, I Love Society) (Song)
P. Edwardes, Chorus
(*Music by* Lionel Monckton. *Lyrics by* Lionel Monckton and Harry Greenbank.)

[14]Stage direction uncredited.

[15]Musical numbers not listed in New York programs. List prepared from subsequent Boston tour (1899), and published English vocal score (Chappell & Co. Ltd., London, 1898). Additional musical numbers which may have been interpolated: "Oh! Listen to the Band" (sung by Y. Violette), "I Love You, My Love, I Do" (sung by May Baker, also Adele Ritchie, per published sheet music, *Music and Lyrics by* Dave Reed, Jr., "English version" by Aubrey Hopwood); Grand March for the Carnival Entrée (*Music by* Sebastian Hiller), "The Convent Bell," "We Have Left Pursuit Behind Us," "Sea-Girt Land of My Home" (*Music by* Ivan Caryll).

1898.47

A DAY AND A NIGHT IN NEW YORK

A Farce Comedy in Three Acts[16]. Libretto by Charles H. Hoyt. Music by Richard Stahl, Charles H. Hoyt, Edmund Vance Cooke, William Devere, Safford Waters, Henri Christiné and Charles Zimmerman. Staged by Charles H. Hoyt. Dances arranged by Thomas Evans. Settings by Arthur Voegtlin. Costumes designed by Barnes and Jackson. Musical director, Charles Zimmerman. Produced by Charles H. Hoyt and Franklin McKee. Opened 30 August 1898 at the Garrick Theatre and closed 22 October 1898 after 54 performances[17].

CAST: *Lyonn Hart*, Commander U. S. Navy, retired: WILLIAM DEVERE. *Fuchsia*, his wife: JANE COOPER. *Marble Hart*, their son: OTIS HARLAN. *Savage Noyes*, his uncle: Ed Wonn. *Routt Booker*, Manager, National Theatre, New York: W. H. CURRIE. *Members of His Company and Staff (11)*: *Handel Schwein*, musical director: CHARLES ZIMMERMAN. *N. Gage Chipps*, stage manager: Thomas Evans. *Will Hammer*, carpenter: Robert Cowan. *Dewing Munkittrick*: Jules Jordan. *Iona Brougham*: Clairisse Agnew. *Fay Kerr*: Nellie O'Neil. *Rhoda Race*: Grace Rutter. *Lura Mann*: HATTIE WILLIAMS. *Sue Brett*: Alma Kramer. *The Clean Man*, stage doorkeeper: Lew Bloom. *Annette Winner*, who gets an engagement: LOUISE GUNNING. *Otto B. Packingham*, who doesn't: Ed Wonn. *Servus Wright*, Booker's servant: Sidney Mansfield. *Ada Marr*, known professionally as Mlle. Bawn Touraine: Mae Lowery.

Act 1: Stage of the National Theatre during a morning rehearsal.

Acts 2 and 3: Music-room of Mr. Booker's house, adjoining the theatre.

ACT 1[18]

"Dutch Comedians"
(*Music by* Richard Stahl. *Lyrics by* Charles H. Hoyt.)

"Ladies from France"
(*Music and Lyrics by* Safford Waters.)

"Can You Forget?"
(*Music and Lyrics by* Safford Waters.)

ACT 2

"Jolly Old Tar"
(*Music and Lyrics by* William Devere.)

"Love Is a Spell"
(*Music and Lyrics by* Safford Waters.)

Dance
(*Music and Lyrics by* Charles Zimmerman.)

"Robin Adair" (Traditional Irish Air)
L. Gunning

"(My Bonnie, Sweet Bessie, the) Maid of Dundee"
L. Gunning
(*Music and Lyrics by* J. L. Gilbert.)

"She Used to Take Me on Her Knee"
(*Music and Lyrics by* Safford Waters.)

ACT 3

"I Want to Be a Soldier" (The Reg'lar Army Man)
H. Williams
(*Music by* Mason Gill. *Lyrics by* H. A. Barr.)

[16]Also billed as Hoyt's 'Report of the doings of a gentleman from New Jersey during a day and a night in New York.'

[17]Also played a return engagement 14 November 1898 at the Harlem Opera House for 8 performances.

[18]Added during the run:

"A Perfect Gentleman" (Act 1)
(*Music by* Henri Christiné. *Lyrics by* Charles H. Hoyt.)

"A Bird, a Bottle and a Cigarette"
(*Music and Lyrics by* Safford Waters.)

"Susie" (Act 2)
(*Music and Lyrics by* ? Brown.)

"The New Belle of New York, '98"
(*Music and Lyrics by* Charles H. Hoyt.)

"They All Know Better Now" (Act 3)
(*Music by* Safford Waters. *Lyrics by* Charles H. Hoyt.)

"The Languid Man"
O. Harlan
(*Music by* Richard Stahl. *Lyrics by* Edmund Vance Cooke.)
"Lucy, Tell Me I'm Your Beau" (Lucie)
O. Harlan
(*Music and Lyrics by* Safford Waters.)
"He Had His Rabbit's Foot with Him" (Rabbit's Foot)(A Coon Superstition)
O. Harlan
(*Music and Lyrics by* William Devere.)
"(As Long as It) Pleases the Ladies"
O. Harlan
(*Music by* Richard Stahl. *Lyrics by* Charles H. Hoyt.)

1898.48

THE CHARLATAN

A Comic Opera in Three Acts. Book (and lyrics) by Charles Klein. Music by John Philip Sousa. Produced under the stage direction of H. A. Cripps. Scenery by Ernest M. Gros. Costumes designed by Catherine F. Siedle. Music under the direction of Paul Steindorff. Conductor, William T. Francis. Produced by DeWolf Hopper Opera Company (E. R. Reynolds, Manager). Opened 5 September 1898 at the Knickerbocker Theatre and closed 8 October 1898 after 35 performances[19]; reopened 11 May 1899 at the Fifth Avenue Theatre and closed 17 June 1899 after 39 additional performances. Total: 74 performances.

CAST: *Demidoff*: DeWOLF HOPPER. *Prince Boris*: EDMUND STANLEY. *Gogol*: MARK PRICE. *Jelikoff*: ALFRED KLEIN. *Captain Peshofski*: George W. Barnum. *Grand Duke*: ARTHUR CUNNINGHAM. *Koreff*: Harry P. Stone. *Showman*: Charles Arthur. *Anna*, alias Princess Ruchkowski: NELLA BERGEN. *Katrinka*: ALICE JUDSON. *Sophia*: Katherine Carlisle. *Grand Duchess*: Adine Bouvier.

The action takes place in Russia in the early nineteenth century.

Act 1: Village of Bohkara.

Act 2: Gogol's House.

Act 3: Courtyard Grand Duke's Palace.

ACT 1[20]
"Mountebanks, Come Waken from Your Dreaming" (Chorus)
Chorus
"Good Morning" (Recitative)
C. Arthur
"She Was a Maid of Sweet Simplicit-ee" (Ballad)
E. Stanley
"The Philosophic Tale is Told" (Solo, Quadrille and Chorus)
E. Stanley, C. Arthur
"As the Agent" (Introduction and Solo)
A. Judson
"Pluto's Partner I" (Song and Chorus)
D. Hopper, A. Judson
"Social Laws" (The Etiquette Quartette)
N. Bergen, A. Judson, D. Hopper, A. Klein
"Venus, Goddess of Love" (Scene)
N. Bergen, A. Judson, E. Stanley, D. Hopper, Chorus
"When the Wintry Moon Is Bright" (Song and Chorus)
N. Bergen, A. Judson, K. Carlisle, A. Klein, D. Hopper, M. Price, Chorus
"Love's the Pleasure" (Finale)
N. Bergen, A. Judson, E. Stanley, A. Klein, D. Hopper, M. Price, Chorus

ACT 2
"I'm the Seventh Son of a Seventh Son" (Melodrama and Refrain)
D. Hopper, E. Stanley, M. Price, G. W. Barnum, Male Quartette
"Before the Twilight Shadows Change" (Duet and Chorus)
N. Bergen, E. Stanley, Chorus
"The Matrimonial Guards" (Duet)
A. Judson, D. Hopper
"Day of Joy" (Chorus)
Chorus
"The Lilies of Your Love May Die" (Recitative and Solo)
N. Bergen, E. Stanley
"Friends, Dear Friends" (Recitative)
E. Stanley, D. Hopper, A. Cunningham, A. Judson
"It's a Well-Established Fact" (Song and Chorus)
D. Hopper
"Ammonia"
A. Judson, E. Stanley, A. Cunningham, D. Hopper, A. Klein, Chorus
"After Due Consideration" (Finale)
Principals, Chorus

ACT 3
Mazurka
"Oh, Sunlit Sea!" (Meditation)
N. Bergen
"I am the Seventh Son of a Seventh Son" (Melodrama and Refrain)
D. Hopper, Chorus
"The Legend of the Frogs" (Song and Chorus)
D. Hopper, Chorus
"The College Man" (Finale)
Principals, Chorus

1898.49

BOCCACCIO

A Revival of the Comic Opera in Three Acts[21]. English libretto adapted from the Viennese operette by F. Zell and Richard Genée. Music by Franz Von Suppé. Stage director, Edward P. Temple. Scenery by Frank King. Musical director, Adolph Liesegang. Produced by the Castle Square Opera Company (Henry W. Savage, Proprietor). Opened 5 September 1898 at the American Theatre and closed 10 September 1898 after 8 performances.

CAST: *Boccaccio*, novelist and poet: LIZZIE MACNICHOL. *Leonetto*, his friend and student: HARRY L. CHASE. *Pietro*, Prince of Palermo: JOSEPH F. SHEEHAN. *Lotteringhi*, a cooper: WILLIAM G. STEWART. *Lambertuccio*, a grocer: RAYMOND HITCHCOCK. *Scalza*, a barber: FRANK MOULAN. *Frateli*, a bookseller: S. P. Veron. *Majordomo*: Frank Ranney. *The Unknown*: Sol Philip. *Checco*, a beggar: O. W. Risley. *Fresco*, the cooper's apprentice: Maud Marean. *Fiametta*, Lambertuccio's adopted daughter: VILLA KNOX *Beatrice*, Scalza's daughter: ATTALIE CLAIRE. *Peronella*, Lambertuccio's sister: ROSE LEIGHTON. *Filippa*: Emma King. *Oretta*: Marie Stuart. *Chorus of Beggars, Students, Citizens, Coopers, Courtiers, etc.*

1898.50

HURLY-BURLY

Another of those things, being to some extent a continuation of "Pousse Café" (a Burlesque) in Two Acts, 3 Scenes[22], preceded by an Olio. Libretto by Harry B. Smith and Edgar Smith. Music by John Stromberg. Scenery painted by John Young. Costumes designed by Will R. Barnes. Musical director, John Stromberg. Produced by Joseph M. Weber and Lew M. Fields. Opened 8 September 1898 at the Weber & Fields Music Hall and closed 5 April 1899 after 264 performances.

Olio: Billy Hart (Comedian); Henry Lee in his unique artistic novelty, Great Men—Past and Present. Words by Henry Tyrell, Music by John Crook. Overture, Introduction, Bismarck, Pope Leo XIII, General Lord Roberts, Rudyard Kipling, Gladstone, David B. Hill, General Ulysses S. Grant, General Robert E. Lee, Major-General Fitzhugh Lee, Colonel Theodore Roosevelt, Commodore Sampson, Commodore Schley, Commodore Dewey.

CAST: *Lord Chumpley*, now known as "King of the Klondike": CHARLES J. ROSS. *Herr Weinschoppen, Herr Bierheister*, with a mummy on their hands: JOSEPH M. WEBER, LEW M. FIELDS. *Solomon Yankle*, a theatrical shoemaker: DAVID WARFIELD. *Abel Stringer*, proprietor of all the theatres in London: PETER F. DAILEY. *Michael McCann*, with a desire to be back on Broadway: JOHN T. KELLY. *Guests at the Stringer Villa, Bilgewater-on-Thames (5)*: *H.R.H., the Prince of Wales*: Allen Wightman. *Sir Peter Routt*: George W. Thomas. *Baron von Hoffbrau*: W. Renner. *Count Fromage de Cammembert*: W. Russell. *Lord Targekilt*: W. West. *Cleopatra*, who has been in a trance for a small matter of 2,000 years: FAY TEMPLETON. *Clorinda McCann Stringer*, with the chafing dish habit: Mabel Fenton. *Suzzanah*, a slavey with

[19]Also played a return engagement 5 December 1898 at the Harlem Opera House for 8 performances.

[20]Vocalists not identified in programs, but prepared from the published vocal score (J. Church, Cincinnati, 1899).

[21]First produced in New York in English 17 May 1880 at the Union Square Theatre for 28 performances. For Synopsis of Scenes and Musical Numbers, see original 1880 production for details.

[22]A sequel to the authors' "Pousse Café" of the preceding season. A few weeks after the opening, Weber & Fields introduced a burlesque of the play "The Turtle" adapted by Joseph Herbert from Leon Gandillot's French original "La Tortue."

the stage fever: Rose Beaumont. *Tottie Cambridge, Sissy Oxford*, with athletic tendencies: Nelly Beaumont, Josephine Allen. *Sweetie Glucose, Stickie Glucose*, "the Glucose Sisters" from the States: Aimee Angelis, Lear Angelis. *Charles Fizz*, representing Booze et Fils "Blue Label": Frankie Bailey. *Ponsonby*, footman at Stringer's: Stubby Ainscoe. *Footlight Divinities (5)*, who came to London with Stringer and married into the nobility: *Pudgy Plumpers*: Belle Robinson. *Ruby Sunburst*: Lucy Escott. *Dizzy Fainter*: May Cuthbert. *Birdie Nestor*: Julia Baird. *Merrie Lafta*: Ada Wyatt. *Husbands of the above (5)*: *Sir Harold Stoneybrooke*: May Edwards. *Duke of Porkingham*: Bonnie Maginn. *Lord Surreyside*: Minnie Gaylor. *Hon. St. John Wood*: Florence Bell. *Sir Westminster Abbey*: May Sherwood. *Guests (4) at Stringer's Vegetable Ball*: *Don Manilla Ponce de Santiago*: Helen Dunbar. *Count Penutti Banan*: Miss Gibson. *Baron Koffupdecoinski*: Miss Moore. *Col. Vanderduiffel*: Nettie Armstrong.

ACT 2: *Lord Chumpley, Mark Antony*, a Roman man-about-town: CHARLES J. ROSS. *Herr Weinschoppen, Herr Bierheister, Solomon Yankle*, who under the influence of Cleopatra's hypnotic power and the authors' vivid imagination, visit Egypt several thousand years before they were born: JOSEPH M. WEBER, LEW M. FIELDS, DAVID WARFIELD. *Abel Stringer, Dinkedidides*, janitor of the Cleopatra Flats: PETER F. DAILEY. *Michael McCann, Octopus Sneezer*, Emperor of Rome: JOHN T. KELLY. *Roman Soldiers (4)*: *Perfidius*: George W. Thomas. *Saleratus*: W. Russell. *Taurus*: M. Renner. *Pegasus*: W. West. *Cleopatra*, Queen of Egypt: FAY TEMPLETON. *Octavia*, wife of Antony: Mabel Fenton. *Charmian, Iras*, maids of honor to Cleopatra: Rose Beaumont, Josephine Allen. *Belladona, Peroxides*, Egyptian officers: Nellie Beaumont, Helen Dunbar. *Komplainia*, a flat-dweller: Aimee Angelis. *Messenger of Egypt D. T. Co.*: Lea Angelis. *Charley Fizz*, on duty at the Royalty Music Hall: Frankie Bailey. *Eros*, Antony's man: Stubby Ainscoe. *Romans (6)*: *Spurius Cassius*: Frankie Bailey. *Gratuitous Omnibus*: Bonnie Maginn. *Penurius Incubus*: Minnie Gaylor. *Infamus Scandalus*: May Sherwood. *Mutinus Caucus*: Florence Bell. *Frivolus Titus*: Lucy Escott. *Egyptian Girls (3)*: *Kleptomania*: Belle Robinson. *Bacteria*: May Cuthbert. *Hirolla*: Olma Desmond. (*Dance Specialty*, La Danse Arab, Act 2, Scene 2: BESSIE CLAYTON.)

Act 1: Stringer's villa at Bilgewater-on-Thames.

Act 2, Scene 1: Bar of the Royalty Music Hall. *Scene 2*: Roof of the Clepatra Flats,.

ACT 1[23] Egypt

"The Progressive Poker Game" (Opening Chorus)

"Little Old New York Is Good Enough for Me" (Song)
J. T. Kelly

"Who'll Help Me Spend My Money?" (Ensemble)
C. J. Ross, Chorus

"A Loidy What Is Studyin' for the Stoige" (Trio)
J. Weber, L. Fields, R. Beaumont

"There Was a Time When on Broadway" (Song)

"The American Serio-Comic"

"The Irish Sidewalk Conversationalists"
P. F. Dailey

"Kiss Me, Honey, Do" (Dinah Song)
P. F. Dailey

"I Think I Shall Learn, Don't You?" (Duet)
C. J. Ross, F. Templeton

"The Vegetable Party" (Finale)

ACT 2

"In the Music Hall Bar When the Curtain Is Down"
Chorus

"Clink, Clink" (Barmaids' Chorus)

"Great Cleopatra Comes" (Ensemble)

"A Large Cold Bottle and a Small Hot Bird" (Song)
F. Templeton

"Keep Away from Emmaline" (Song and Ensemble)
F. Templeton

Finale

During the run, HURLY BURLY was shortened, and CYRANOSE, (a Burlesque of Edmond Rostand's "Cyrano de Bergerac") a New and Prominent Feature, amputated from the French and disfigured without permission by Harry B. Smith and Edgar Smith, was added 3 November 1898; it closed 18 January 1899 after 92 performances.

CYRANOSE DE BRIC-A-BRAC. A burlesque of Edmund Rostand's play "Cyrano de Bergerac" in One Act, 3 Scenes. Libretto by Edgar Smith and Harry B. Smith. Music by John Stromberg. Produced under the stage direction of Julian Mitchell. Including THE HEATHEN, a short travesty on Hall Caine's play "The Christian".[24]

CAST: *Cyranose de Bric-a-Brac*, champon middle-weight duellist, poet, meddler, rubber-neck and nose specialist: LEW M. FIELDS. *Ragamuffin*, the baker poet, author of half-baked verses; the only poet who ever has any "dough": JOSEPH WEBER. *Christmas De Newcadet*, long on books, short on brains: CHARLES J. ROSS. *Le Fret*, Cyranose's press agent and legal adviser: DAVID WARFIELD. *Count de Peach*, the only real gent in the cast: PETER F. DAILEY. *Captain Carbonic de Gassycon* of the Cadets: JOHN T. KELLY. *Sellrows*, a manager and ticket speculator: LEE HARRISON. *Roxy*, who is looking for an impossible combination of good looks, brains and "sand": FAY TEMPLETON. *Liz*, Ragamuffins' wife; driven from home by his poetry, she goes to work as Roxy's maid: ROSE BEAUMONT. *Eclaire*, a lunch-counter siren: NELLIE BEAUMONT. *Clairette, Juliette, Soubrette*, attractions of Ragamuffin's café: Josephine Allen, Aimee Anglelis, Leah Angelis. *Count Absinthe-Frappé* of the Gascony Cadets: Frankie Bailey. *The Bold Cadets of Gascony (6)*: *Count Patsy de Clam*: Bonnie Maginn. *Count A Bas Toutlemonde*: Lucy Escott. *Count Vive l'Armée*: Florence Bell. *Count Chateau Lafitte*: Helen Dunbar. *Count Crackerjack de Hackensack*: May Edwards. *Count Bordeaux de Marseillaise*: Julia Baird. *An Old Gent*: Allen Wightman. *His Son*: Aimee Angelis. *M. Rostaire*, a dramatic critic: Sol Fields. *Gall Cocaine*, a dramatic autor: Walter West. *Duchesse de Maraschino*: Belle Robinson. *Duchesse de Crême de Menthe*: Minnie Poore. *Gascon Musketeers (4)*: *Baron Nicnac de Kodac*: Minnie Gaylor. *Baron de Jumpingjac de Maniac*: Stubby Ainscoe. *Baron Almamanc de Sealsac*: May Sherwood. *Baron Canvasbac de Hypochondriac*: Stella Gray. *Chef*: Sadie Harrison. Incidental to Scene 3: Cissie Loftus (mimic).

Incidental to Scene 1, THE HEATHEN (Not the Christian), a Problem Play, designed merely to elevate the stage.

CAST: *Glory Hallelujah*, a serio-comic hospital nurse: MABEL FENTON. *John Sloppyweather*, theatrical shoemaker and sole-saver: CHARLES J. ROSS. *Horatio Steak*, a good thing: JOHN T. KELLY. *Lord Robber Poor*, a villain with an eye-glass: LEE HARRISON. *Trixie Plantagenet, Trottie Montmorenci*, emotional serio-comiques, jealous of Glory's flat: Josephine Allen, Aimee Angelis. *Scene 1*: A show at the Hotel de Begorra. *Scene 2*: The tart bakery. *Scene 3*: The fire-escape of Roxy's flat. The kick.

MUSICAL NUMBERS[25]

Dance (Scene 1)
B. Clayton

"Kiss Me, Honey, Do" (Dinah Song)
P. F. Dailey

"Keep Away from Emmaline"[26]
F. Templeton

"Oh, Dinah, the Moon am Shining"
P. F. Dailey

"Perhaps You May Not Like It"
Angelis Sisters, J. Allen, N. Beaumont

Champagne Polka

"Moonlight Serenade" (Chorus)
J. T. Kelly

CATHERINE, A Little Bunch of Nonsense, masquerading as a travesty (of the play) "Catherine" by Henri Lavedan. (A Burlesque in One Act, 3 Scenes). Dialogue by Edgar Smith. Music by John Stromberg. Lyrics by Harry B. Smith. Produced by Joe Weber and Lew Fields. Opened 19 January 1899 at the Weber & Fields Music Hall and closed 27 May 1899 after 146 performances.

CAST: *Duke de Coocoo*, looking for a matrimonial sinecure: CHARLES J. ROSS. *George Mantelpiece*, a sacrificer: JOHN T. KELLY. *Paul, Frederick*, the only rivals of the Katzenjammer Kids: JOSEPH M. WEBER, LEW M. FIELDS. *Monsieur Villun*, Catherine's father, with the scissors habit: DAVE WARFIELD. *Monsieur Lowcuss*, a cigarette manufacturer: LEE HARRISON. *Duchess de Coocoo*, a society leader: PETER F. DAILEY. *Catherine Villun*, with a mania for supporting her family: FAY TEMPLETON. *Helene de Gristle*, with a mortgage on the Duke: MABEL FENTON. *Blanche Villun*, too strong to work: ROSE BEAUMONT. *Madeleine*, the Duke's sister: NELLIE BEAUMONT. *Baron Frozenhard*, Helene's guardian: NELLIE BEAUMONT. *__??*: FRANKIE BAILEY. *Baroness Frozenhard*: Josephine Allen. *Jeanne*, maid at the Villuns': Aimee Angelis. *Cigarette makers (5)*: *Clairette*: Helen Dunbar.

[23]Also interpolated during the run:

"Mrs. Patrick Casey's Swell Pink Tea"
P. F. Dailey
(*Lyrics by* Edgar Smith.)

"Maud"
J. T. Kelly

"(I'm Making a Bid for) Popularity"
J. T. Kelly

[24]No program available. Musical numbers assembled from reviews, published music, etc.

[25]Not in performance order.

[26]Transferred from the shortened HURLY BURLY.

Marie: May Edwards. *Jeanette*: Bonnie Maginn. *Julia*: Lucy Escott. *Fanchon*: Belle Robinson. *Of the push (4)*: *Countess de Brie*: Minnie Poore. *Baroness de Roquefort*: Mollie Gaylor. *Count de Monnae*: Minnie Gaylor. *Count de Spoons*: May Sherwood. (*Specialty*, Scene 2: The Angelis Sisters.)

Scene 1: The home of the Villuns. *Scene 2*: Gardens at the Castle. *Scene 3*: Castle of the Duke de Coocoo.

MUSICAL NUMBERS

"Puff! Puff!"
Chorus

"Because We Are So Innocent, You Know" (Song and Dance)

"Show My Coronet"[27]
Chorus

"What, Marry That Gal!" (Song)
F. Templeton

1898.51

THE FRENCH MAID

A Return Engagement of the Musical Comedy in Two Acts[28]. Libretto by Basil Hood. Music by Walter Slaughter. Production staged and ballets arranged by Augustus Sohlke. Settings by Frank Rafter and D. Frank Dodge. Costumes designed by Will R. Barnes. Musical director, Will P. Brown. Produced by Edward E. Rice. Opened 12 September 1898 at the Herald Square Theater and closed 1 October 1898 after 24 performances[29].

CAST: *Admiral Sir Hercules Hawser*, K.C.B.: EDWARD J. HERON. *The Maharajah of Punkapore*: RICHARD RIDGELEY. *General Sir Drummond Fife*, V.C.: MATT WOODWARD. *Jack Brown*, a sailor: HALLEN MOSTYN. *Paul Lecuire*, a gendarme: EDOUARD JOSÉ. *Monsieur Camembert*, maître d'hôtel: George Honey. *Lieutenant Harry Fife*, R.N.: William Armstrong. *Willie Splint*, French waiter: Charles E. Sturgis. *Alphonse*: Charles E. Sturgis. *Lady Hercules Hawser*: EVA DAVENPORT. *Dorothy Travers*: GERRY AMES. *Madame Camembert*: Yolande Wallace. *Marie*, a chambermaid: Mamie Forbes. *Suzette*, the French Maid: OLIVE REDPATH. *Charles Brown*, a waiter: CHARLES A. BIGELOW. *Tourists, Peasants, Garcons, Femmes de Chambre, etc.*.

Sailor Boys: Misses Valeria Douglas, May Toriani, Alice Cameron, Florence Pemberton, May Dickson, Rose Ricci, Lillian DeGrosse, Monte Elmo. *Femmes de Chambre*: Misses Emma Ballard, Florence Raymond, Mabel McKenna, Marie Peterman, Jessie Nelson, Bessie Montgomery, Lee Riggs, Louise Hoope, Belle Lovejoy, Mabel Harte, Carol Clover, Carrie Manning, Maud West. *Carnival Quadrille*: Misses Jessie Nelson, Monte Elmo, Louise Hope, Belle Lovejoy, Mabel McKenna, Bessie Montgomery, Mabel Harte, Carol Clover. *Ballet de Surprise*: Mamie Forbes, Mabel Harte, Carol Clover, Jessie Nelson, Louise Hoope, Belle Lovejoy, Monte Elmo, Herr AUGUSTUS SOHLKE (Grotesque Dancer). *Carnival Promenade Ballet*: Valeria Douglas, May Toriani, Eleanor Kendall, Florence Raymond, Alice Cameron, Emma Bellard, May Dickson, Marie Peterman, Rose Ricci, Lillian DeGrosse, Lee Riggs, Florence Pemberton, Maud West.

1898.52

IOLANTHE, or, The Peer and the Peri

A Revival of the Comic Opera in Two Acts[30]. Libretto by William S. Gilbert. Music by Arthur Sullivan. Stage director, Edward P. Temple. Scenery by Frank King. Musical director, Adolph Liesegang. Produced by The Castle Square Opera Company (Henry W. Savage, Proprietor). Opened 12 September 1898 at the American Theatre and closed 17 September 1898 after 8 performances.

CAST: *The Lord Chancellor*: RAYMOND HITCHCOCK. *Earl of Mountararat*: HARRY L. CHASE. *Earl of Tolloller*: JOSEPH F. SHEEHAN. *Strephon*, an Arcadian shepherd: W. G. STEWART. *Private Willis* of the Grenadier Guards: JOHN CARRINGTON. *Train-bearer*: Frank Ranney. *Male Chorus of Dukes, Marquises, Earls, Viscounts and Barons*. *Queen of the Fairies*: LIZZIE MACNICHOL. *Iolanthe*, Strephon's mother: LAURA DENIO. *Phyllis*, an Arcadian shepherdess and ward in chancery: GERTRUDE QUINLAN. *Fairies (3)*: *Leila*: Mae Burt. *Celia*: Alice Campbell. *Fleta*: Stella Madison. *Female Chorus of Fairies*.

[27]Replaced during the run by:
"Fair American Maid"
Chorus

[28]Originally opened 27 September 1897 at the Herald Square Theater for 175 performances. For Synopsis of Scenes and Musical Numbers, see original 1897 production.

[29]Later played a return engagement 17 April 1899 at the Grand Opera House for 8 performances. Toured with Anna Held as the French Maid, with interpolations as per published sheet music:
"Honey You've Done Me Wrong"
A. Held

[30]First presented in New York 25 November 1882 at the Standard Theatre for 105 performances. For Synopsis of Scenes and Musical Numbers, see original 1882 production.

1898.53

THE GOLDEN HORSESHOE

The Lilliputians in a Grand Spectacular Play in Four Acts, 12 Scenes. Play by Robert Breitenbach, adapted from the German "Das Goldene Hufeisen". Music composed and arranged by Carl Pleininger. Staged by Carl Rosenfeld. Produced by Carl and Theodore Rosenfeld. Opened 15 September 1898 at the Irving Place Theatre and closed 29 October 1898 after 46 performances[31].

CAST: *The Lilliputians*: *Mr. James McKee*, a mechanic: Mr. Oesfeld. *Dick*, *Bob*, his nephews: ADOLPH ZINK, FRANZ EBERT. *Eulalie*, called Princess: BERTHA JAEGER. *Tootsie*, her sister: HELENE LINDNER. *Harry Tall*: MAX WALTER. *Will B. Gay*, actor: SELMA GOERNER. *Rose*, his sister: MRS. TONI MEISTER. *Luke Sharp*, Sheriff of Kalamazoo: HERMANN RING. *Eva*, his daughter: MRS. ELISE EBERT-LAU. *Mrs. Servia Quick*, innkeeper: Mrs. Klaussen-Koch. *Mariam, Adaline*, her daughters: Miss Schlueter, Mrs. Steinmann. *Knight Walker*, impressario: Mr. Wilke. *Ike Catchem*: Mr. Schrader. *Sam*, porter: Mr. Meyer. *Jacob*, McKee's servant: Mr. Lindner. *First Servant*: Mr. Bilder. *Second Servant*: Mr. Krause. *Mr. Mueller*: Kraft Walton.

Act 1, Scene 1: Mechanic's shop. *Scene 2*: Fancy Athletic Club. *Scene 3*: Pink masquerade.

Act 2, Scene 1: Square in Kalamazoo. *Scene 2*: Before the curtain. *Scene 3*: Music festival.

Act 3, Scene 1: In the Swamps. *Scene 2*: Sea weeds. *Scene 3*: At the bottom of the sea.

Act 4, Scene 1: Stage. *Scene 2*: Living pictures from the war. *Scene 3*: Apotheosis.

1898.54

THE LITTLE CORPORAL

A Comic Opera in Three Acts. Book (and lyrics) by Harry B. Smith. Music by Ludwig Engländer. Produced under the stage direction of Richard Barker. Settings from the studio of Richard Marston. Costumes by Percy Anderson. Lighting by James Pennefather. Musical director, John McGhie. Produced by Francis Wilson Opera Company (Francis Wilson, Samuel F. Nixon & J. Fred Zimmerman, Proprietors; Ariel Barney, Manager). Opened 19 September 1898 at the Broadway Theatre and closed 12 November 1898 after 62 performances; re-opened 16 January 1899 at the Broadway Theatre and closed 28 January 1899 after 14 additional performances. Total: 76 performances.

CAST: *Pierre Petipas*, Servant of the Marquis de St. Andre: FRANCIS WILSON. *The Marquis de St. Andre*, a proscribed nobleman: DENIS O'SULLIVAN. *Jacques Grognard*, Sergeant of Grenadiers: LOUIS CASAVANT. *Amulet Bey*, a Mameluke Chieftain: John Brand. *Gilet*, a Regimental Tailor: A. M. Holbrook. *Jean Planche*, a Village Cobbler: Ambrose Dailey. *Urban*, the Village Blacksmith: Samuel Chadwick. *Roger Nicole*, a Tavern Keeper: George Stevens. *Corporal Vignon*: J. T. Chaillee. *Corporal Renard*: George Pelzer. *Leon*, a fisherman: Charles H. Bowers. *Jean Falcon*, a Chouan leader: W. Laverty. *Officers of Bonaparte's Staff*: George Pelzer, H. T. Morey, F. Stanton Heck. *Jacqueline*, Belle of Breton Village, Adele's foster sister: LULU GLASER. *Adele de Tourville*, an Aristocrat: MAUD LILLIAN BERRI.

Village Girls, Drummer Boys and Wives of Amulet Bey: *Babette, Agenor, Sultanetta*: Allene Crater. *Marton, Musaron, Nephtali*: Maude Bagley. *Clairette, Kassime*: Mathilde Preville. *Yvonne, Bertrand, Gouchale*: Florence Relda.

Act 1: Fishing Village on the Coast of Brittany.

Act 2: Public Square in Alexandria, Egypt.

Act 3: Bedouin Camp on the Desert.

ACT 1[32]

Prelude and Opening Ensemble (Saint Simon was a fisherman)

"Gros Jean and P'tit Pierre" (Jeanette, the farmer's daughter)
L. Glaser, Chorus

Duet (An exile is my heart)
M. L. Berri, D. O'Sullivan

Entrance of Petipas

"The Cobbler's Ghost" (As Jean Nigaud, the Cobbler sat)
F. Wilson, Chorus

Rustic Duet (Within a cote our door above)
L. Glaser, F. Wilson

[31]Settings and costumes uncredited. No songs listed in program.

[32]Musical numbers not listed in programs. List prepared from published vocal score (Breitkopf & Haertel, New York, 1898).

"The Song of the Grenadier" (Ho Master Taylor perch on your marrow bones)
L. Casavant
Drill Scene and Song (Left a wife and seven children)
L. Casavant, F. WIlson, Male Chorus
Finale (Act 1)(Yo ho, St. Simon was a fisherman)

ACT 2
Opening Chorus (Hera us Allah mighty pow'r)
"The Old War Horse" (A bold dragoon had an old graynag)
L. Glaser, L. Casavant, Chorus
Hornpipe (Entrance of Petipas)
"We Haven't Discovered It Yet" (Although I'm a scientist fully as wise)
F. Wilson, Chorus
"The Song of the Lampoon" (Upon a little island there was born a great little man)
D. O'Sullivan, F. Wilson, Chorus
Duet (Let me hold once more your hand in mine)
M. L. Berri, D. O'Sullivan
"The Song of the Drum" (Oh here's a song for the drum)
L. Glaser, Chorus
Finale Act 2 (Peering left and peering right)

ACT 3
Opening Chorus and Song (Here let us pitch our tents for the night)
Quintette (Oh, the love of a Bedouin maiden)
F. Wilson, 4 Arab Girls
Finale Act 3 (Upon a little island there was born a great little man)

1898.55 WINE, WOMEN AND SONG

A Prismatic Comique (Musical Comedy) in Three Acts. Book and lyrics by Edward Corbett. Music by Carl Schilling. Entire production under the personal direction of George Paxton. Settings by Frank E. Gates and Edward A. Morange. Costumes by Madame Thompson. Musical director, Carl Schilling. Orchestra under the direction of Thomas H. Joyce. Produced by the John W. Isham Company. Opened 19 September 1898 at the Grand Opera House and closed 24 September 1898 after 8 performances.

CAST: *Max Kruppnit*, storekeeper, P.M., Town Clerk, etc. of Sleepy Hollow, New York: EMIL HEWSEL. *Brothers and Heirs (3): Felix Van Dinkle*, station agent: EDWARD A. SANDFORD. *Rip Van Dinkle, Jr.*, an aeronaut: LOUIS CARROLL. *Ludwig Van Dinkle*, a globe-trotter: EDWARD RYAN. *Sir Royal Goldbrick*, an ex-rope walker of the Andes, alias Rip, Jr.: JAMES HORAN. *Pedro*, an ex-Spaniard: Edward Dermody. *Train Flagman*: Robert Quigley. *Eb*, a village wit: George Quigley. *Cy*, a Sleepy Hollow sage: WILLIAM BALDWIN. *Notary*: Charles Sanford. *Queenie Alhambra*, a London music hall singer: GERTRUDE SAYE. *Princess Sappho*, a French chanteuse, formerly of Sleepy Hollow: RUTH ROBINSON. *Lulu Dimples*, a village belle: MARIE SITA. *Dolly Cinch*, of the Hollow: Mabel Habelman. *Little Sally*, a canal slavey: Jennie Jackson. *Postmistress*: Maude Ellston. *Rip Van Dinkle*: —.

Grape Harvesters, End-of-Century Feminine Athletiques, etc.: Misses Williams, Dwight, Lambert, Jones, Clemens, Princeton, Jackson, Roy, Dillon, Murphy, McGoldrie, Doyle, Peters, Cobb, Pixley, Franklin, Watson, Johnson, Elton, Marcel, McVicker, Prior, Smith, Samson, Nelson; Mr. Boyle.

Act 1: Sleepy Hollow, New York. Time is now.

Act 2: Café Waldorf-Castoria.

Act 3: Greeley Square.

MUSICAL NUMBERS
"Imprisoned" (Opening Chorus)
"Whip-poor-Wills" (Cy's solo)
W. Baldwin
"I Sail the Airy Blue" (Highflyer's Solo)
L. Carroll
"Madiens Aquatic"
Chorus
"Rah-Rah-Rah"
Chorus
"Pop, Pop, Pop"
G. Saye, R. Robinson, Chorus
"Along the Old Canal" (Solo)
"Maybe You Think I Did"
J. Horan, Chorus
"Old Rip Was Flip"
Chorus
"Tale of a Decent Married Hen" (Solo)
"The Wedding Bells Won't Ring Tonight" (Finale)
"It Fills Me with Distress"
Lunch Girl
"Fastest Man in New York" (Trio)
"The Highball Syndicate"
Misses Elton, Sampson, Williams, Dwight
"Royal Waitresses" (Quartette)
Misses Clemens, Roy, Princeton, Jackson
Dances of Long Ago (1830):
Minuet; Hungarian; Egyptian; France; Wooing Sextette
Rough Riders (Solo and Chorus)
J. Horan, Chorus
"Girls of the Midnight Matinee" (Ensemble)
Misses Roy, Cobb,
Jackson, Clemens, Princeton, Dwight, Murphy, Williams
"We Didn't Come Back That Way"
Champagne Ballet (Act 1)
Misses Williams, Dwight, Lamber, Jones, Clemens,
Princeton, Jackson, Jones, Elton, Peters, Cobb, Dillon, Gnomes;
Messrs. Dermody, Thompson, Boyle
Gold and Silver Ballet (Act 3)
Specialty
R. Robinson
"Melindy"
G. Saye

1898.56 IN GOTHAM

A Burlesque in Two Acts, 4 Scenes, preceded by an Olio. Manager, Alfred E. Aarons. Opened 19 September 1898 at Koster & Bial's Music Hall and closed 5 November 1898 after 56 performances.

Olio: The Six Senetts (Grotesque Comedians from the Winter Garden, Berlin); Mlle. Blanche Deliere; Three Sisters Merkel (Marvelous Equilibrists from the Empire Music Hall, London); The Brothers Avolo [Rodolfo, ?] (Musical Artists from the Tivoli Music Hall, London).

IN GOTHAM. A Burlesque in Two Acts, 4 Scenes. Libretto by Joseph W. Herbert. Music by Max Gabriel. Stage production by John E. Nash. Dances arranged by Alberteri. Scenery by L. Seavey & Company; Operti. Costumes designed by Martin J. Jackson. Musical director, Max Gabriel.

CAST: *Mr. Winkle* of Sleepy Hollow: DICK BERNARD. *Charley Swivel*, Skiegel & Skooper's Bueau of Information: RICHARD CARLE. *Ike Slopsky*, President of the Cloakmaker's Union and Captain of the Chrystie Street Brigade: William H. Sloan. *Judge Keenan*, one of New York's best: Richard Guise. *The Bowery Chicken*, a tough bird: Peter M. Lang. *Hendrick Hudson* of the Catskills: F. M. Marston. *Officer Mulcahy*, a club friend: Tony Sullivan. *Yap*, the countryman: Tony Sullivan. *Chips*, elevator boy who has his ups and downs: Billy Barry, Jr. *Mr. John Ribbons*: Harry Rolland. *Boss of the Gnomes*: F. Abraham. *Schneider*, the dog: F. Abraham. *Rag-Time Liz*, the Bowery Queen: JOSEPHINE HALL. *Captain Johnnie*, of the 71st: CHERIDAH SIMPSON. *Miss Winkle*, head saleslady at Skiegel & Skooper's: Laura Millard. *Bella Donna*, pet of the 71st: IRENE BENTLEY. *Mrs. Slopsky*, who makes sweaters in the sweatshop: Helen Marlborough. *Corporal of Cadets*: Daisy Dixon. *Mrs. Milligan*: May Duryea. *Shoppers (3): Mrs. Flint*: May Bedford. *Mrs. Gresham*: Crissie Carlyle. *Mrs. Norman*: Buelah Coolidge. *Miss Nevertired*, saleslady at Skiegel & Skooper's: Bertha Dowling. *Queen of the Nymphs*: Jennie Praegre. *Chystie Street Brigade, Shoppers, Salesladies, Clerks, Floorwalkers, Corset Models, Milliners, Cloak Models, Chappies, Cadets of the 71st, etc.*

Act 1: Skiegel & Skooper's Store. (Seavey.)

Act 2, Scene 1: Woodland Glade in the Catskills. *Scene 2*: Stage door, Windsor Theatre, Bowery. *Scene 3*: Jefferson Market Police Court. (Operti.)

ACT 1
"The Big Department Store" (Opening Chorus)
"Bargain Day"
Chorus
"Oh My"
L. Millard
"Her Front Name Was Sally"
P. M. Lang
"The Boys of the 71st"
C. Simpson

"Hark Hark"
Chorus
"It Was Different When I Awoke"
D. Bernard
"She Only Had a Dollar in Her Purse"[33]
J. Hall
Finale
Entire Company

ACT 2
Scene 1[34]
"Sleep Sleep"
L. Millard
Chorus and Dance of Gnomes (Dance of the Pygmies)
"What Shall We Do With Him"
W. Sloan, Chorus
"We're Indulging in a Frolic" (Song)
F. M. Marston, Chorus
"Katzenjammer Is a Village" (Song)
Chorus
Scene 2
"The Dudelet in the Front"
C. Simpson
"Rag Time Liz"
J. Hall
(*Music by* Alfred E. Aarons. *Lyrics by* Richard Carle.)
"Turn Over Leaf"[35]
R. Carle
"Sing-Bad the Sailor" (A Comic Opera in Five Minutes)
J. Hall, R. Carle
(*Music and Lyrics by* Richard Carle.)
"The Chrystie Street Brigade" and Hebrew Cake-Walk
W. Sloan, Chorus
Scene 3
"In Court"[36]
Chorus
Finale
Entire Company

Added during the run to IN GOTHAM, Second Edition, 17 October 1898:

SIR ANDY DE BOOTJACK, a Twenty Minute Review of Richard Carle's impressions of Cyrano de Bergerac, exploited in 3 Scenes. Music by Alfred E. Aarons. Scenery by Operti. After IN GOTHAM closed, SIR ANDY DE BOOTJACK continued, accompanied by an olio, and closed 26 November 1898 after 48 performances.

Olio: (Bert) Williams and (George) Walker and a cast of 40 in a program of songs and dances; The Sisters Hawthorne in "The Lily of Laguna," Music and Lyrics by Leslie Stuart.

CAST: *Sir Andy De Bootjack*: DICK BERNARD. *Christian Endeavor*: RICHARD CARLE. *Jagonyou*: WILLIAM SLOANE. *Mount Flewey*: Tony Sullivan. *Augustin Dooley*: Peter M. Lang. *Richyard Manzfield*: Richard Guise. *The Oldhenna*: May Duryea. *Mollie Owe*: Nellie Butler. *Roxiana Reehan*: JOSEPHINE HALL.

Act 1, Scene 1: The Theatre. *Scene 2*: The Bakery. *Scene 3*: The Balcony.

Act 2: Stage door Windsor Theatre, Bowery.

1898.57 DOROTHY

A Revival of the Comic Opera in Three Acts[37]. (Libretto by B. C. Stephenson.) Music by Alfred Cellier. Stage director, Edward P. Temple. Scenery by Frank King. Musical director, Adolph Liesegang. Produced by the Castle Square Opera Company (Henry W. Savage, Proprietor). Opened 19 September 1898 at the American Theatre and closed 24 September 1898 after 8 performances.

CAST: *Dorothy Bantam*, Squire Bantam's daughter: ATTALIE CLAIRE. *Lydia Hawthorne*, her cousin: LIZZIE MACNICHOL. *Priscilla Privett*, a widow: ROSE LEIGHTON. *Phyllis*, Tuppet's daughter: GERTRUDE QUINLAN. *Geoffrey Wilder*, Bantam's nephew: JOSEPH F. SHEEHAN. *Harry Sherwood*, Wilder's chum: WILLIAM G. STEWART. *Squire Bantam*, of Chanticleer Hall: HARRY L. CHASE. *Lurcher*, a sheriff's officer: RAYMOND HITCHCOCK. *Tuppet*, the village landlord: FRANK MOULAN. *Tom Grass*, in love with Phyllis: Algernon Aspland. (*Chorus of Hop-Pickers, Peasants, Guests, Bridesmaids, etc.*)

1898.58 THE MARQUIS OF MICHIGAN

A Farcical Comedy in Three Acts. Libretto by Glen MacDonough and Edward W. Townshend. Music by A. Baldwin Sloane. Incidental music by Louie Maurice. Stage production under the direction of J. K. Adams. Produced by Sam Bernard (Management, E. Rosenbaum). Opened 21 September 1898 at the Bijou Theatre and closed 29 October 1898 after 46 performances.

CAST: *Hermann Engel*, a young artist, and the particular friend of the late Rev. Athanasius Dunn: SAM BERNARD. *Bob Tyke*, a hard luck story: CHARLES JACKSON. *Leaky Loomis*, a sentimental burglar: DAN COLLIER [Collyer]. *Chevalier Maginnice*, a sleight-of-hand artist: WILLIAM BURRESS. *Abner Gooch*, the Sheriff of Hopkins County, New York: WILLIAM BURRESS. *Ambulance Surgeon*: George Rollins. *Helen Hastings*, councillor-at-law, the foster daughter of the late Rev. Athanasius Dean: HARRIET STERLING. *Tony Tostevin*, councillor-at-law, Helen's friend and legal partner: Maud White. *Georgianna Dunn*, *Evelina Dunn*, daughters of the late Rev. Athanasius Dunn: Grace Freeman, Helen Potter. *Aurelia Staggers*, a "Family Fireplace" novelist: Helene Lacey. *Birdie Egg*, *Gertie LaPlatz*, *Frixie Fritters*, members of the Eldorado vaudeville Company: Vivian Townsend, Annie Black, Lillian Collins. *Mme. Etna Vesuvius*, famous for her muscle and her music: ALICE ATHERTON.

Act 1: Law office of Hastings & Tostevin. Last summer.

Act 2: Hermann Engel's summer home on the Hudson.

Act 3: Hermann Engel's town residence, New York City.

MUSICAL NUMBERS[38]
"English as She Should Be Spoke"
S. Bernard
Laughing Song
A. Atherton
(*Music by* John Crook. *Lyrics by* George Dance.)
"Lazy Bill" (A Volunteer of Rest)
A. Atherton
(*Music by* A. Baldwin Sloane. *Lyrics by* Glen MacDonough.)
"Various Types of Mashers"
A. Atherton
(*Music by* Edward E. Rice. *Lyrics by* Richard Carle.)

1898.59 KILLARNEY AND THE RHINE

A Play with Songs in Four Acts. Play by Edwin Jerome. Acting manager, John Lane. Musical director, Lawrence Johnson. Produced by J. E. Toole (Edwin Jerome, Manager). Opened 26 September 1898 at the People's Theatre and closed 1 October 1898 after 8 performances.[39]

CAST: *Conrad*, a German wanderer in Ireland: J. E. TOOLE. *Squire Delaney*: James McDonald. *Harvey Lemoyne*: John E. Lane. *Bazel Fitzsimmons*: Clarence Bellaire. *Larry Kernan*: Charles Brandon. *Reginald Carey*: HENRY HALLAM. *Sergeant Douglas*: F. M. Woods. *Rose Delaney*: Doddie Siddon. *Mary O'Connell*: ANNIE CROUCH. *Elly O'Neil*: Lillian DeWolf. *Mrs. O'Connell*: Hilda Vernon.

Scene: Ireland.

1898.60 THE FORTUNE TELLER

A Comic Opera in Three Acts. Libretto by Harry B. Smith. Music by Victor Herbert. Staged by Julian Mitchell. Settings by Joseph Physioc. Costume

[33]Dropped for second edition.
[34]All of Act 2, Scene 1 was dropped for second edition, and replaced by SIR ANDY DE BOOTJACK.
[35]Replaced for second edition by:
"The Vaudevilles"
R. Carle, J. Hall
(*Music and Lyrics by* Richard Carle.)
[36]Dropped for second edition.
[37]First produced in New York 5 November 1887 at the Standard Theatre for 48 performances. For Synopsis of Scenes and Musical Numbers, see original 1887 production.

[38]No songs listed in programs.
[39]No program available.

designs by Catherine Siedle. Musical direction by Paul Steindorff. Produced by Frank L. Perley for the Alice Nielsen Opera Company. Opened 26 September 1898 at Wallack's Theatre and closed 29 October 1898 after 40 performances.

CAST: *Musette*, a gypsy fortune-teller: ALICE NIELSEN. *Irma*, a pupil in the ballet school of the opera at Buda-Pesth: ALICE NIELSEN. *Fresco*, ballet master and stage master at the opera house: RICHARD GOLDEN. *Count Berezowski*, a Polish composer and pianist: JOSEPH W. HERBERT. *Sandor*, a gypsy musician: EUGENE COWLES. *Captain Ladislas*, a Hungarian hussar: FRANK RUSHWORTH. *Boris*, a gypsy, father of Musette: JOSEPH CAWTHORN. *Mlle. Pompon*, a prima donna: MARGUERITE SYLVA. *Vaninka*: Marcia Van Dresser. *Rafael*: Jennie Hawley. *General Korbay*: Paul Nicholson. *Pupils of the ballet school (3)*: *Wanda*: Fanny Briscoe. *Etelka*: May Boley. *Vera*: Frances Sears. *Matosin*, a gardener: William Brown. *Waldemar*, prompter at the opera house: E. Percy Parsons. *Lieutenant Almir*: Jennie Hawley. *Lieutenant Timar*: Annie Clay. *Jan*, a tailor's boy: Fanny Briscoe. *Paul*, a baker's boy: Nelly Marsh. *A Violinist*: P. J. Worthington. *A Pianist*: John T. Gray. *A Trombone player*: William C. Deusing. *First Detective*: J. B. Henrichs. *Second Detective*: W. H. Grimke. *A wounded hussar*: J. Smith. *Chorus of Ballet Pupils, Hungarian Hussars, Drummers, Cadets, Tradesmen, etc.*

Act 1: Courtyard of the Opera House, adjacent to the Ballet School.

Act 2: Garden of the Chateau of Count Berezowski.

Act 3: Camp of the Hungarian Army, near Buda-Pesth.

ACT 1[40]

Introduction and Opening Ensemble
E. P. Parsons, R. Golden, Ladies Chorus
"Always Do as People Say You Should" (Entrance Song)
A. Nielsen, Ladies Chorus
"Hungaria's Hussars" (Chorus of Hussars)
F. Rushworth, Hussars
"Ho! Ye Townsmen" (Entrance Song)
E. Cowles
"Romany Life"
A. Nielsen, E. Cowles, M. Van Dresser, J. Cawthorn, J. Hawley, Chorus
"Czardas" (Dance)
Finale
Principals, Chorus

ACT 2

Opening Chorus
"Signor Monsieur Moldoni"
R. Golden, Chorus
"The Serenade of All Nations"
A. Nielsen, J. Herbert, R. Golden, J. Cawthorn, Mixed Chorus
"Gypsy Love Song" (Slumber On, My Little Gypsy Sweetheart)
E. Cowles, A. Nielsen, Chorus
"Only in the Play" (Duet)
M. Sylva, F. Rushworth
Finale

ACT 3

"Gypsy Jan"
E. Cowles, Chorus
"The Power of the Human Eye" (Duet)
J. Cawthorn, J. Herbert
"The Lily and the Nightingale" (Waltz Song)
A. Nielsen
Finale
Entire Company

1898.61

A SURE CURE

A Musical Farce-Comedy in Three Acts. Play by Harry Doel Parker. Staged by Harry Doel Parker. Scenery by Reisig & Company. Costumes by V. DeGray. Musical director, Carlton Burton. Produced by Harry Doel Parker. Opened 26 September 1898 at the Star Theatre and closed 1 October 1898 after 8 performances.

CAST: *Rusher Tips; Lord Knowswho*, full of schemes for getting there, has a good thing, and works it: CHARLES WAYNE. *Daffodille Ringoose*, a gentleman of leisure, who believes a true aristocrat never works: JAMES P. SMITH. *Adolphus Newrich*, works himself to death in the city while his family go to the country—"nit": C. Jay Williams. *Mr. Sub Rosa*, a good thing for Rusher, and he wishes he wasn't: Charles B. Hawkins. *Cholly Lighttop, Weginald Featherbrain*, fashionably dressed followers of Daffodille's sentiments: Mart M. Fuller, Orral Humphrey. *Officer Gilhooley*, half a dozen of "the Finest": Lee Dougherty. *Hank Hayseed*, knows as much as "city folks": Charles L. Newton. *Daisy Rosa*, going to be a star if $20,000 will make her one: ANNA [Anne] CALDWELL. *Pertie Cashe*, smiles at the men, and they never count their change: EVA TANGUAY[41]. *Sally Tuff*, a lady, if she don't have good clothes, see!: CARRIE SCOTT. *Dolly Doo, Lillie DeStyle*, the latest assortment in tailor-made girls: Elinor Hale, Claudia Petite. *Mrs. Adolphus Newrich*; lords are scarce and come high, but she means to have one in the family: Beatrice Bonner. *Goldie Newrich*, a daughter after her own mother's heart—and a lord's hand: Gracie Gray. *Sadie Silence*, not so quiet as her name: Josie Hart. *Fluffy Feathers*, light and airy: Maybelle Davis. *Mary Jane Hayseed*, able to take care of herself, and Hank too: Anna Caldwell. *Waiters, Porters and others.*

Act 1: Interior of Sub Rosa's "Table d'Hote" Restaurant, New York City.

Act 2: Exterior of "Rusher's Rural Retreat and Sanitarium" at Swampville, New Jersey.

Act 3: Parlor in the sanitarium.

ACT 1

"The Stuttering Man"
"Susette"
E. Tanguay
"On the Stage" (Trio)
E. Tanguay, C. Scott, J. P. Smith
"The Charming Little Actress" (Duet)
A. Caldwell, C. Wayne
Drinking Song
C. J. Williams, Company
"Break the News to Mother" (Solo)
E. Hale
(*Music and Lyrics by* Charles K. Harris.)
An Old-Time Song and Dance
C. Wayne, J. P. Smith, A. Caldwell, C. Scott
Sailor's Hornpipe
E. Tanguay
"The Patriotic Coon" (Finale)
Entire Company
(*Music and Lyrics by* George M. Cohan.)

ACT 2

"The Lord Knowswho"
C. Wayne, Company
(*Music and Lyrics by* George M. Cohan.)
"East and West Side"
"Mr. Johnston, You Are Knocking Your Own Game"
C. Scott
"Bathing in the Sea"
E. Tanguay, G. Gray, E. Hale, C. Petite
"I'm Getting More Devilish"
C. Wayne

ACT 3

"Pickaninny's Dream"
Entire Company
Operatic Duet
E. Hale, C. Petite
"A Few Foolish Ideas"
C. Wayne, J. P. Smith
Grand Finale
Entire Company

[40]Interpolation published after opening (2 October 1898):
"The Bold Dragoon"
M. Van Dresser, F. Rushworth, Chorus

[41]Eva Tanguay's name appears in reviews, Annie Martell's name in the programs.

1898.62 A TRIP TO AFRICA

A Revival of the Comic Opera (Opéra Comique) in Three Acts[42]. (Original Viennese libretto to the operette, 'Die Afrikareise,' by Richard Genée and Moritz West.) Music by Franz von Suppé. Stage director, Edward P. Temple. Scenery by Frank King. Musical director, Adolph Liesegang. Produced by the Castle Square Opera Company (Henry W. Savage, Proprietor). Opened 26 September 1898 at the American Theatre and closed 1 October 1898 after 8 performances.

CAST: *Titania Fanfani*, (a young heiress): VILLA KNOX. *Fanfani Pasha*, her uncle: RAYMOND HITCHCOCK. *Miradello*, a European: WILLIAM G. STEWART. *Antarsid*, Prince of the Maronites: JOSEPH F. SHEEHAN. *Tessa*, a young milliner: LIZZIE MACNICHOL. *Buccametta*, her mother: ROSE LEIGHTON. *Pericles*, a hotel keeper: Harry L. Chase. *Nakid*, a Koptic in poison and perfumes: FRANK MOULAN. *Siebel*, an Abyssinian slave: GERTRUDE QUINLAN. *Hosh*, servant to Pericles: Frank Ranney. *A Muezzin*: F. P. Vernon. *Majordomo*: R. Edmonds. *A Fais*: A. Underwood. *Maronites, Hotel Servants, Guests of Fanfani Pasha, Slave Traders, Muleteers, Dancers, Greek and Arabian People.*

1898.63 HOTEL TOPSY TURVY

A Parisian Vaudeville Operetta (Musical Comedy) in Three Acts. French libretto (to the vaudeville opérette "L'Auberge du Tohu-Bohu") by Maurice Ordonneau. American adapation by Arthur Sturgess and Edgar Smith[43]. Music by Victor Roger; additional music by Lionel Monckton. Stage direction by Frank Smithson. Ballets arranged by John Wagner. Settings by Frank Rafter, D. Frank Dodge. Orchestra under the direction of Herman Perlet. Produced by Charles Frohman. Opened 3 October 1898 at the Herald Square Theatre and closed 24 December 1898 after 102 performances[44].

CAST: *Paul*, art student, friend of Louis: AUBREY BOUCICAULT. *Lebeau*, a clown: EDWIN [Eddie] FOY. *Laforce*, a strong man: Henry Norman. *Dremer*, father of Cecile: Douglas Flint. *Louis*, nephew to Moulinet: FRANK DOANE. *Comte Zarifouli*: Alex Law-Gisiko. *Moulinet*, who likes peace and tranquility: Edward J. Connelly. *Joseph*, servant to Dremer: Randolph Curry. *Latour, Gracieux*, acrobats especially engaged: George Ali, George Beni. *Mme. Moulinet*, wife to Moulnet: Emma Brennan. *Cecile*, daughter of Dremer: Ethel Jackson. *Mariette*, servant to Moulinet: Virginia Ross. *Marcelle*, companion of Cecile: BEATRICE McKENZIE. *Mme. Malicorne*, landlady of the White House Inn: CARRIE PERKINS. *Members of the Circus (3)*: *Estelle*: Marjorie Relyea. *Rose*: Marie Miller. *Jennie*: Bobbie Burns. *Flora*, proprietress of Cluny's Colossal Combination: MARIE DRESSLER. *Acrobats, French Peasants, Fruit Sellers, Villagers, etc.*

Act 1: The White Horse Inn, Bourg-Fleury. (Rafter.)

Act 2: Interior of Moulinet's House. (Dodge.)

Act 3: The same, later on.

ACT 1[45]

Opening Chorus (Alas! alas! Alas! When will our misfortunes pass?)

Song (Sigh not if fate should frown)
M. Dressler

Song (Oh, what is the use of this life)
A. Boucicault
(*Music by* Lionel Monckton.)

Chorus of Villagers (Hark! the drum again is restive)

"Walk up, walk up" (Song)(This is the finest show on earth)
M. Dressler
(*Music by* Lionel Monckton.)

"The Shifting of the Sign" (Quintet) (Silently, creeping, While they are sleeping)
M. Dressler, A. Boucicault, F. Doane, E. Foy, H. Norman

Finale (Welcome! This hostelry is noted)

Valse-Song (Tip-toe! Now go)
M. Dressler, E. Jackson, A. Boucicault, etc.

ACT 2

Opening Chorus (Welcome! this hostelry is noted)

"A little overdoing it" (Song)(All the world's a stage)
F. Doane
(*Music by* Lionel Monckton.)

Duet (How peaceful is this domesticity)
E. J. Connelly, E. Brennan

"Toujours" (Song)(If a man would married be)(Air "Les Blondes")
E. Jackson
(*Music by* H. Fragson and A. Stanislaus.)

"How to kiss" (Duet)(Should you chance to meet a charming little miss)
E. Jackson, A. Boucicault
(*Music by* N. Lambelet. *Lyrics by* Roland Carse.)

Quartet (When a dinner you cook)
F. Doane, A. Boucicault, E. Jackson, B. McKenzie
(*Music by* Lionel Monckton.)

Chorus (We bow our heads)/

Song (Note my most distiguished bearing)
E. Foy

Serenade and Chorus (Ongree was a London jongdarm)
A. Boucicault

Finale (Now 'tis still)

ACT 3

Opening Chorus (Whatever is about to happen now)

"The Boolyvar de Paree" (Song)(When I and brother Harry)
E. Foy
(*Music by* Lionel Monckton.)

Ensemble (How can it be?)

"I Should Like to Know" (Song)(In youthful days)
M. Dressler
(*Music by* Lionel Monckton.)

Chorus and Dance (Here at the break of day)
(*Music by* Lionel Monckton.)

Song (Heed not the tear)
M. Dressler

Finale (Now out little play is done)

Quartet (Addenda)(We started quite badly)
E. Jackson, B. McKenzie, D. Flint, R. Curry
(*Music by* Lionel Monckton.)

AMERICAN INTERPOLATIONS

"I Happened to Be There"
E. Foy
(*Music by* Eddie Foy. *Lyrics by* William M. Dunlevy.)

"My Own Cecile"
A. Boucicault
(*Music and Lyrics by* H. Fragson and Ad. Stanislas.)

"It's Not the Weather Cock That Changes, It's the Wind" (Act 2)
A. Boucicault, E. Jackson
(*Music and Lyrics by* Aubrey Boucicault.)

"The Gingerbread Doll" (Act 3)
M. Dressler
(*Music and Lyrics by* Aubrey Boucicault.)

"Dreaming of Mother and Home" (tour)
V. Ross
(*Music by* John S. Ross. *Lyrics by* Arthur J. Lamb.)

"Hello, Ma Baby" (tour)
(*Music and Lyrics by* Joseph E. Howard and Ida Emerson.)

1898.64 GOING TO THE RACES

A Spectacular Pantomimic Absurdity in Three Acts, 7 Scenes. Music arranged by Frank Lorenz. Play written and mechanical effects invented by John F. Byrne. Stage director, Henry Kammerer. Musical director, Frank

---

[42]First produced in New York 23 December 1884 at the Standard Theatre for 62 performances. For Synopsis of Scenes and Musical Numbers, see original 1884 production. English adaptation uncredited. Most likely by Emil Schwab and Adolph Neuendroff, whose names appear in a November 1884 Boston program, which producer James C. Duff credits as his inspiration for the first New York production.

[43]Sturgess prepared the first London production under the title THE TOPSY TURVY HOTEL, which was then 'Americanized' by Edgar Smith.

[44]Also played return engagements 13 February 1899 at the Harlem Opera House for 8 performances, and 20 February 1898 at the Grand Opera House for 8 performances.

[45]Musical numbers not listed in programs. List of musical numbers prepared from published English vocal score (Chappell & Co., Ltd., London, 1898). Known American interpolations follow.

Lorenz. Produced by John F. Byrne (Management, W. E. Flack). Opened 3 October 1898 at the Grand Opera House and closed 8 October 1898 after 8 performances[46].

CAST: *Silas Fairfield*, a sporting gentleman: FRED B. SAWYER. *Gamble Green*, valet pro tem to Willie Winn: H. M. HERBERT. *Augustus Rubber*, race track dude: Ed Moreland. *Walker Beat*, station policeman: E. M. Resserd. *High Hurdle*, trainer at Goodspeed's stable: Forrest Walton. *Given Odds*, a bookmaker: Dave Walton. *Annie Place*, Winnie's aunt on a visit: Orlie Walton. *Fuller Prunes*, a stout boy; Frank Lafose. *Bailey Hayes*, bartender at station: Larry Vondale. *Reuben Marks*, a laundryman: William Hall. *Sandy Track*, engineer of fire engine: Henry Kammerer. *Jonah Tip*, attendant at lunch counter: John Harden. *A-dam Rabbi*, officer of air-ship: William Dale. *Bill Sticker*, a bill poster: HARRY VANE. *Reader Novel*, a news agent: John Kenann. *Luke Warm, August Filly*: race touts: Frank Long, Ed Bates. *Jockeys (6)*: *Brewster Buggy*: Walter Whyburn. *Howell Ewin*: Bob Alberts. *Justin Longshot*: George McLaughlin. *Able Trotter*: Ralph Osmond. *Canter Handsdown*: Martin Green. *Jay Ridder*: William Wapshire. *Favorites of the Suburban Race (2)*: *Daredevil*: Mingo II. *Firefly*: Templestowe. *Entries for Suburban (4)*: *Chanteuse*: Chanteuse. *Elmont*: Elmont. *Top Tackle*: Top Tackle. *High and Lofty*: High and Lofty. *Winnie Fairfield*, in love with Willie Winn: ALICE NEAL. *Ina Bunch*, a salvation lassie: Kate Benneteau. *Bettie Straight*, a nursemaid: Maude Collins. *Carrie Overwieght*, maid to Winnie Fairfield: HELENE BYRNE. *Call Turner*, Willie Winn's companion: JAMES BYRNE. *Gallop Longgreen*, a man about town, owner of horse Firefly: ANDREW BYRNE. *Willie Winn*, circus clown and manager, owner of horse Daredevil: JOHN F. BYRNE. *Stablemen, sports, touts, book makers, firemen, passengers, policemen*: Company.

Act 1, Scene 1: Apartment house in Washington. *Scene 2*: The burning hotel.

Act 2, Scene 1: Depot of the Aerial Navigation Company. Off to the races. *Scene 2*: Restaurant and station lunch room. *Scene 3*: On the airship. The start.

Act 3, Scene 1: The arrival at the races. The paddock. *Scene 2*: At the track. The race.

1898.65 PATIENCE, or Bunthorne's Bride

A Revival of the Comic Opera in Two Acts[47]. Libretto by William S. Gilbert. Music by Arthur Sullivan. Stage director, Edward P. Temple. Scenery by Frank King. Musical director, Adolph Liesegang. Produced by the Castle Square Opera Company (Henry W. Savage, Proprietor). Opened 3 October 1898 at the American Theatre and closed 8 October 1898 after 8 performances.

CAST: *Reginald Bunthorne*, a Fleshly Poet: RAYMOND HITCHCOCK. *Archibald Grosvenor*, an Idyllic Poet: WILLIAM G. STEWART. *Officers of Dragoon Guards (3)*: *Colonel Calverley*: Harry L. Chase. *Major Murgatroyd*: Frank Moulan. *Lieutenant The Duke of Dunstable*: JOSEPH F. SHEEHAN. *Bunthorne's Solicitor*: Frank L. Ranney. *Chorus of Dragoon Guards*. *Rapturous Maidens (4)*: *Lady Angela*: MARY PALMER. *Lady Saphir*: GERTRUDE QUINLAN. *Lady Ella*: Zetti Kennedy. *Lady Jane*: ROSE LEIGHTON. *Patience*, a milkmaid: BELLE THORNE. *Chorus of Maidens*.

1898.66 HAVE YOU SEEN SMITH?

A Farce Comedy in Three Acts. Play by Scott Marble. Produced by Davis and Keogh. Opened 3 October 1898 at the Star Theatre and closed 8 October 1898 after 8 performances[48].

CAST: A *Bleecker Knight*: JAMES F. DOLAN. *I. Work Days*: JACK TUCKER. *Baron Moquette*: MURRAY WOODS. *Will B. Dunn*: BOBBY MACK. *John J. Smith*: JOE NATUS. *J. Jay Smith*: A. H. FITZ. *Dupay Denero*: James E. Elliott. *Marshall Knott*: W. W. Scott. *I. Will Leavitt*: W. H. Raymond. *Easy Rugg*: Charles Snyder. *Mr. Bass*: C. B. Ronalds. *Mr. Dough*: H. F. Singer. *Mr. Touch*: Frank N. Dale. *Lewey*: W. C. Smiley. *Charlie*: H. J. Smith. *Fritz*: Charles P. Fuller. *Admiral Dot*: J. W. Hyde. *Mrs. Fern Ann Days*: IDA LENHARR. *Mrs. B. Laight Knight*: EVA M. WILLIAMS. *May B. Dunn*: SYLVIA HOLT. *Kitty Hyde*: GERTIE GILSON. *Helen Beer*: MAUD HARVEY. *Constant Swett*: EDYTHE HARVEY. *Ida Kline*: Grace Leonard. *Vera Kruse*: Minnie Daly.

The action takes place in the home of the Days and the Knights in Harlem.

SPECIALTIES[49]

"She Was Bred in Old Kentucky"
G. Gilson
(*Music by* Stanley Carter. *Lyrics by* Harry Braisted.)

"Military Mollie"
G. Gilson

Songs
Harvey Sisters

"Sweet Savannah"
J. Natus
(*Music and Lyrics by* Paul Dresser.)

1898.67 A HIGH-BORN LADY

A Musical Farce-Comedy in Three Acts. Book, music and lyrics by Herbert Hall Winslow. Musical director, Sidney Springer. Produced by William [Billy] Clifford and Maud Huth. Opened 10 October 1898 at the Star Theatre and closed 15 October 1898 after 8 performances[50].

CAST: *Cornelius O'Donovan*, landlord of a professional boarding house, possessed of aristocratic aspirations, but keeps his eye on the main chance: HARRY E. FISHER. *Dr. Sickewell, M.D.L.A.S.S.*, who cures all the ills flesh is heir to "except broken hearts": SAMUEL J. ADAMS. *Buck Ragtime*, the actor who is his own author and originator of everything he does—all others are merely copies: Joseph J. Carroll. *Casey*, O'Donovan's long-lost friend: Joseph J. Carroll. *Harold Brown*, who says the proper thing in the proper place: William C. Lowther. *Yvette Yellow Label*, with a devotional love for Willie that causes her to waste her sweetness on the desert air: Lydia Trenaman. *Beatrice Bunchlight*, who knows more of other people's affairs than necessary, but who kindly keeps her mouth shut: Gladys Leslie. *Sophie Sudden* (O'Donovan's Hebe), who believes brevity to be the soul of wit: Bijou Russell. *Fannie Farle Foote*, who loves bonbons, pepsin gum and the "Duckesess novels": Francis Bayless. *Tottie Spangleback*, a lover of small birds and large bottles: Estelle Hamilton. *Lucille Lovingbyrd*, who intends someday to outrival Bernshardt: Valerie Montague. *Hypatia Highstepper*, whose sole ambition is to be a comic opera queen: Marguerite Adams. *Dolly Ducketts*, a dear little duck, who would not say boo to a goose: Pearl Ridings. *Smut, Dot Short*, members of the colored four-hundred: Tommy Edwards, Maggie Harris. *Sue Brette, Dorothy Dimple*, the Petite Dresden dancing dolls: The Esher Sisters. *Policeman*: Walter Brown. *Flossie O'Shaughnessy* (nee Featherstone), who never borrows trouble, as she has enough without it: MAUD HUTH. *Willie Du-Much*, the arch-plotter, who caused all the trouble: BILLY S. CLIFFORD.

Act 1: New York City. Any time.

Act 2: O'Donovan's new home. One week later.

Act 3: A quiet nook in Central Park. Next day.

MUSICAL NUMBERS[51]

"Reggie the Reigning Rage"
B. S. Clifford

"The Doodle Doodle Wagon's Done Got You at Last"
M. Huth

"Ram-a-Jam, (I Want That Man)" (from COURTED INTO COURT)
(*Music and Lyrics by* Francis J. Bryant.)

"Winning a Home"

"Dusky Lil from Louisville"

Irish Specialty
H. E. Fisher, J. J. Carroll

1898.68 THE BELLE OF NEW YORK

A Return Engagement of the Musical Comedy in Two Acts, 6 Scenes[52]. Libretto by Hugh Morton [C.M.S. McLellan]. Music by Gustav Kerker. Staged by George W. Lederer. Ballets arranged by Signor Francioli. Settings by Ernest Albert and D. Frank Dodge. Costumes by Madame Caroline Siedle. Orchestra conductor, Theodore Bendix. Produced by George W. Lederer and George B. McLellan. Opened 24 October 1898 at the Casino Theatre and closed 5 November 1898 after 14 performances.

CAST: *Ichabod Bronson*, President of the Young Men's Rescue League and Anti-Cigarette Society of Cohoes: DAN DALY. *Harry Bronson*, his son, a young spendthrift: ED TYLER. *"Blinky Bill" McGuirk*, a mixed-ale-pugilist: WILLIAM CAMERON. *Carl Von Pumpernick*, a polite lunatic: D. L. DON. *"Doc" Snifkins*, the father of the Queen of Comic Opera: E. S. TARR. *Kenneth Mugg*, low comedian of the Angelique

---

[46]Musical numbers not listed in programs. Act 2 included specialties by John F and Helene Byrne; Act 3 specialties by the John Byrne Troupe of Acrobats. Settings and costumes uncredited.

[47]First produced in New York 22 September 1881 at the Standard Theatre for 177 performances. For Synopsis of Scenes and Musical Numbers, see original 1881 production.

[48]Returned 9 January 1899 to the Grand Opera House for an additional 8 performances. No program available.

[49]No program available.

[50]Stage direction, scenery and costumes uncredited.

[51]Musical numbers not listed in programs. Specialties performed by Clifford and Huth, Fisher and Carroll, Samuel J. Adams, and Esher Sisters.

[52]First produced in New York 28 September 1897 at the Casino Theatre for 56 performances; re-opened 20 December 1897 at the Casino Theatre for an 8 additional performances. Total: 64. For Synopsis of Scenes and Musical Numbers, see original 1897 production.

Comic Opera Company: OWEN WESTFORD. *Count Ratal Kattstoo, Count Ratal Rattstrio*, twin Portuguese noblemen: H. Daniel Kelly, Joseph Kane. *Mr. Twiddles*, Harry Bronson's private secretary: Robert Dunbar. *Billy Brown*, a man-o'-war's-mate: Robert Dunbar. *Mr. Snooper*, a newspaper reporter: Robert Dunbar. *Violet Gray*: EDNA MAY. *(Fifi) Fricot*, a little Parisienne: LOUISE BEAUDET. *Cora Angelique*, the Queen of Comic Opera: HELEN LORD. *Kissie Fitzgarter*, a music hall dancer: NELLA WEBB. *Mamie Clancy*, a Pell Street girl: QUEENIE VASSAR. *Patsy Pines*, a soubrette: Tessie Thompson.

1898.69 KATE KIP, BUYER

A Farce Comedy in Three Acts. Play by Glen MacDonough. Incidental music by Watty Hydes. Production under the personal direction of (staged by) May Irwin. Musical director, Watty Hydes. Produced by May Irwin (William D. Andreas, Manager). Opened 31 October 1898 at the Bijou Theatre and closed 18 February 1899 after 128 performances[53].

CAST: *The Hon. Wilhelm Coogan*, of the State Senate, under two flags: JOSEPH SPARKS. *The Hon. Montenzuma Gashwiler*, of the State Senate, a child of the prairie: STEPHEN MALEY. *The Hon. Flashby Keene*, of the State Senate, a volunteer in the late Chino-Japanese War and present colonel of New Rome's crack regiment: V. M. DeSILKE. *Gustave L'Aloulette*, an anarchist: IGNACIO MARTINETTI. *Kate Kip*, foreign buyer for Ketchum & Dewham's, New York: MAY IRWIN. *Tom Kip*, her brother, a lawyer for New Rome: Robert Lowe. *Mme. Yomi Tano*, a transplanted Japanese chrysanthemum: Marcia Treadwell. *Mrs. Wilhelm Coogan*: Helen Brackett. *Mrs. Montezuma Gashwiler*: Helena Lacy. *Polly Parsons*, doing general work on the *New Rome Evening Star*: JANE BURBY. *Willie Trailer*, a detective: Roland Carter. *Gladys Brown*, secretly engaged to Tom Kip: Vivian Blackburn. *Lucy Brown*, her sister: Faie Beresford. *Miss Breeze*, Tom Kip's typewriter: Ailleen May. *Lillie Laubenheimer*, a German prima donna: Mlle. ALEXA. *Mr. Johnston*, a carpenter: Harry Wachter. *Mr. Smith*, a head waiter: Harry Wachter. *The Twins*: Beth Ehrlich, Bobbie Victor.

The action takes place now Out West.

Act 1: Tom Kip's office, New Rome. 6:30 P.M.

Act 2: Room in the Hotel Coogan, New Rome. 7:30 P.M.

Act 3: Ante-room adjoining Senate chamber in the temporary capitol, at New Rome. 8:30 P.M.

MUSICAL NUMBERS[54]

"When Yo' Ain't Got No Money Yo Needn't Come Round"
M. Irwin
(*Music by* A. Baldwin Sloane. *Lyrics by* Clarence Brewster.)

"My Rainbow Bride, or Beautiful Rose Marie"
I. Martinetti, M. Irwin
(*Music by* Ignacio Martinetti. *Lyrics by* Glen MacDonough.)

"If I Were You"
M. Irwin
(*Music and Lyrics by* Cissie Loftus.)

"When the Leaves Came Drifting Down"
M. Irwin
(*Music and Lyrics by* Hattie Nevada.)

"She's a Thoroughbred"
M. Irwin
(*Music and Lyrics by* Ned Wayburn.)

"I Got Him 'Dead'" (A Darktown Sinecure)
M. Irwin
(*Music and Lyrics by* Arthur Dunn.)

"Dar's Somethin' About Yer I Like"
M. Irwin
(*Music and Lyrics by* John T. Kelly.)

1898.70 THE FINISH OF MR. FRESH

A Farce Comedy in Three Acts. Play by Thomas H. Davis and William T. Keough. Music by Dave Braham. Produced under the stage direction of Max Freeman. Scenery by John H. Young. Musical director, John Braham. Produced by Thomas H. Davis and William T. Keough. Opened 7 November 1898 at the Star Theatre, moved 14 November 1898 to the Metropolis Theatre and closed 19 November 1898 after 17 performances.

CAST: *Judge E. Z. Mark*: AL H. WILSON. *U.R. Fresh*: JOHN T. TIERNEY. *Major Minor*: GEORGE W. DAY. *Morse Wire*: GEORGE W. DAY. *I. Tooker Sniffen*: Frank Glenn. *Pike Gish*: Harry Earle. *Young Dock Weed*: Harry Earle. *Lawyer Hummelhowe*: Thomas Ripley. *Con McCann*: Tom Flynn. *Chuck*: Charles B. Ward. *Musty Miller*: John McCarthy. *Mrs. Hawke*: Anna Barclay. *Cherry Pye*: BELLE STEWART. *Ruby Hawke*: Fanny Bloodgood. *Mrs. E. Z. Mark*: Nellie McCarthy. *Phyllis Bloom*: MAY STEWART. *May June*: Mabel Williams. *Meta Mann*: Kathryn Klare. *Pearl Knott*: May Montford.

Act 1: The Manicure Parlors. "The Start."

Act 2: The Fresh House at Slight Plains. "In the Stretch."

Act 3: The Courtroom. "The Finish."

ACT 1

"The Manicure Maidens" (Opening Chorus)

"Mr. Fresh" (Song)
J. T. Tierney

Parlor Imitations of both sides of life

"I Guess I'll Have to Telegraph My Baby" (Song and Chorus)
G. W. Day, Company
(*Music and Lyrics by* George M. Cohan.)

ACT 2

"The Original Bowery Boy" (Song)
C. B. Ward

"With a Heart" (Song)
F. Bloodgood

"She Was Bred in Old Kentucky"
K. Klare
(*Music by* Stanley Carter. *Lyrics by* Harry Braisted.)

"Timely Topics"
G. W. Day

Finale
Entire Company

ACT 3

German Monologue and Songs
A. H. Wilson

Grand Finale
Entire Company

1898.71 THE PIRATES OF PENZANCE, or, The Slave of Duty

A Revival of the Comic Opera in Two Acts[55]. Libretto by William Gilbert. Music by Arthur Sullivan. Stage director, Edward P. Temple. Scenery by Frank King. Musical director, Adolph Liesegang. Produced by the Castle Square Opera Company (Henry W. Savage, Proprietor). Opened 7 November 1898 at the American Theatre and closed 12 November 1898 after 9 performances.

CAST: *Major General Stanley* of the British Army: FRANK MOULAN. *Richard*, a Pirate Chief: WILLIAM G. STEWART. *Samuel*, his Lieutenant: John Carrington. *Frederic*, a Pirate Apprentice: JOSEPH F. SHEEHAN. *Edward*, Sergeant of Police: HARRY L. CHASE. *Mabel, Kate, Edith, Isabel*, General Stanley's Daughters: ADELAIDE NORWOOD, GERTRUDE QUINLAN, Zetti Kennedy, Lorle Eddinger. *Ruth*, a Piratical Maid-of-all-work: MARION IVEL. *Chorus of Pirates, Police and General Stanley's Daughters.*

1898.72 A DANGEROUS MAID

A Musical Play in Three Acts, 7 Scenes. American libretto by Sydney Rosenfeld. Adapted from the German original ("Heisses Blut"[56] by Carl Lindau and Leopold Krenn, music by Heinrich Schenk). Music by Leopold Schenck and Frederick J. Eustis. Additional lyrics by Louis Harrison. Entire

[53]Settings and costumes uncredited. Also played a return engagement 3 August 1899 at the Grand Opera House for 8 performances.

[54]Musical numbers not listed in program. List prepared from published sheet music, reviews, etc.

[55]First presented in New York 31 December 1879 at the Fifth Avenue Theatre for 91 performances in two engagements. For Synopsis of Scenes and Musical Numbers, see original 1879 production.

[56]Known also by its British adaptation "Victorine, or I'll Sleep on It." One reviewer remarked that the Act 2 duel scene between Laura Burt and Madge Lessing was inspired by a European painting "Un Affair d'Honneur" in which two beautiful women are stripped to the waist and fight with rapiers.

production under the personal stage direction of George W. Lederer. Settings by D. Frank Dodge and Ernest Albert. Costumes by Mme. Catherine Seidle. Musical director, Frederick J. Eustis. Produced by George W. Lederer and George B. McLellan. Opened 12 November 1898 at the Casino Theatre and closed 7 January 1899 after 65 performances; re-opened 27 February 1899 at the Casino Theatre and closed 4 March 1899 after an additional 8 performances. Total: 73 performances[57].

CAST: *Kokos*, a wealthy Hungarian landowner: CHARLES PLUNKETT. *Ilona*, his daughter: MADGE LESSING. *Miklos*, bethrothed to Ilona: JULIUS STEGER. *Biros*, Burgomaster: James G. Peakes. *Aranka*, his daughter: Helen Marvin. *Count Istvan*: SYDNEY BOOTH. *Schmaltz*, a Viennese wig-maker: SAM BERNARD. *Lena*, his wife: MARIE GEORGE. *Panagl*, a Viennese art patron: WILLIAM NORRIS.

Members of the Vienna Theatre: *Mr. Marks*, Stage Manager: RICHARD F. CARROLL. *Fanchette*, Leading Lady: LAURA BURT. *Diana*: Nellie Delves. *Dingler*, Comedian: Eugene Clarke. *Acker*, Prompter: Alfred Kappelar. *Garrotte*, the Author: Sol Aiken. *Chorus of Prima Donnas*: Edna Aug, Agnes Yates, Mabel Russell, Elaine Selover, Sallie Randall, Anna Knell, Saditha Evans, Frances Palmer.

Henry Jingle, Theatrical Agent: Sol Aiken. *Firenzi*, Hungarian soldier: Willard Harvey. *Juleska*, Hungarian servant: Christine Blessing. *Anna*, Maid to Ilona: Margaret McDonald. *Villagers, Gypsies, Citizens, Theatre Attachés, etc. Specialty (Chansonettes, Act 2, Scene 2)*: CLARA LARDINOIS [Blanche Arral].

Act 1, Scene 1: Ilona's Home in Hungary. The Horn on the Hill. *Scene 2*: At the Viennese Wig-Maker's. A New Arrival. *Scene 3*: Stage of the Burg Theatre. The Rehearsal. (All scenes by D. Frank Dodge.)

Act 2, Scene 1: Ilona's Boudoir. A Desperate Plan. *Scene 2*: The Vienna Gardens at Night. The Challenge. (All scenes by Ernest Albert.)

Act 3, Scene 1: In the Woods. The Duel. *Scene 2*: Ilona's Home. The Awakening. (All scenes by D. Frank Dodge.)

ACT 1[58]

Duet
S. Bernard, M. George
(*Lyrics by* Louis Harrison.)

Pousse Cafe Ballet
Mlle. Fanchonette, L. Brink, Corps de Ballet

"Kiss Me, Honey, Do" (from HURLY BURLY)
(*Music by* John Stromberg. *Lyrics by* Edgar Smith.)

"Oh Days of Yore"
J. Steger
(*Music by* L. Sprowacker. *Lyrics by* Sidney Rosenfeld.)

"He Cert'nly Was Good to Me" (from THE SWELL MISS FITZWELL)
R. F. Carroll
(*Music by* A. Baldwin Sloane. *Lyrics by* Jean C. Havez.)

ACT 2[59]

Two Chansonettes
C. Lardinois

"Song of the Mormon"
W. Norris
(*Lyrics by* Louis Harrison.)

Specialty Song
M. Lessing, 8 Prima Donnas
(*Lyrics by* Louis Harrison.)

1898.73 THE JOLLY MUSKETEER

A Comic Opera in Two Acts. Libretto by Stanislaus Stange. Music by Julian Edwards. Produced under the stage direction of Richard Barker. Settings by Ernest M. Gros and Walter W. Burridge. Costumes designed by Catherine F. Seidle. Musical director, A. Krausse[60]. Produced by Jefferson DeAngelis Opera Company (B. D. Stevens, Manager). Opened 14 November 1898 at the Broadway Theatre and closed 10 December 1898 after 32 performances; re-opened 5 June 1899 at the Casino Theatre and closed 17 June 1899 after 16 additional performances. Total: 48 performances[61].

CAST: *Henri*, Count de Beauprêt, Lieutenant of "King's Own Musketeers": JEFFERSON DeANGELIS. *Francois*, Marquis de Chantilly, Captain of the "King's Own Musketeers": VAN RENSSELAER WHEELER. *Capote*, Corporal of the "King's Own Musketeers": WINFIELD BLAKE. *Antoine, Gaston*, Musketeers: Joseph Smiley, Ole Norman. *Didot Blanc*, Proprietor of the Café Richelieu: HARRY MacDONOUGH. *Yvette*, his daughter: MAUD HOLLINS. *Verve*, his niece: BERTHA WALTZINGER. *Jacqueline, Marie*, flower girls: Helena Frederick, Edith Hendee. *Chorus of Musketeers, Flower Girls, Ladies of the Court, etc.*

The action takes place in Amiens, France, during the siege of that city by the Spaniards in 1634.

Act 1: The Flower Market. A Morning in June. (Burridge.)

Act 2: Ball-room in Chateau, Chantilly. Evening of the same day. (Gros.)

ACT 1

Introduction
H. Frederick, E. Hendee, B. Walzinger, H. MacDonough

"The King's Own Musketeers" (Song and Chorus)
V. R. Wheeler, W. Blake, H. Frederick, E. Hendee, Chorus

"The Wishing Well" (Ensemble)
V. R. Wheeler, M. Hollins, B. Walzinger, H. Frederick, E. Hendee, J. Smiley, O. Norman, W. Blake, Chorus

Entrance of Henri de Beauprêt

"Just To Pass the Time Away" (Song and Chorus)
J. DeAngelis, Chorus

"The Dancing Lesson" (Duet)
M. Hollins, J. DeAngelis

"The Letter from Papa" (Ensemble)
H. Frederick, E. Hendee, O. Norman, J. Smiley, M. Hollins, J. DeAngelis, B. Walzinger, H. MacDonough, Chorus

"Sweet the Birds Were Singing" (Quintette)
B. Walzinger, M. Hollins, H. MacDonough, V. R. Wheeler, W. Blake

"That Sweet Oblivion Drink" (Duet)
H. MacDonough, F. Wilson

Finale

ACT 2

Introduction
Principals

"Willful Woman" (Song and Chorus)
J. DeAngelis, Chorus

"Friends" (Song and Chorus)
V. R. Wheeler, Chorus

"An Explanation I Demand" (Trio)
V. R. Wheeler, F. Wilson, M. Hollins

"This Is Most Exciting" (Ensemble)
Principals

"Love for an Hour" (Song)
B. Walzinger

"Courtship" (Duet)
H. MacDonough, J. DeAngelis

"Wicked Man" (Quartette)
B. Walzinger, M. Hollins, H. Frederick, E. Hendee

Finale

1898.74 THE CHIMES OF NORMANDY

A Revival of the Comic Opera in Three Acts, 6 Scenes[62]. (Original French libretto to the opéra comique 'Les Cloches de Corneville' by Clairville and Charles Gabet. Music by Robert Planquette. Stage director, Edward P. Temple. Scenery by Frank King. Conductor, Adolph Liesegang. Produced by the Castle Square Opera Company (Henry W. Savage, Proprietor). Opened 21 November 1898 at the American Theatre and closed 26 November 1898 after 9 performances.

CAST: *Serpolette*, the good-for-nothing: VILLA KNOX. *Germaine*, the lost Marchioness: ADELAIDE NORWOOD, ZETTIE KENNEDY. *Susanne*: MAUDE POOLE. *Jeanne*: GEORGIE DELAND. *Henri*, Marquis of Corneville: WILLIAM G. STEWART. *Jean Grenicheux*, a fisherman: JOSEPH F. SHEEHAN. *Gaspard*, an old

[57]Played a touring engagement 6 March 1899 at the Harlem Opera House for 8 performances.

[58]Musical numbers not listed in programs. Not necessarily in performance order.

[59]For the subsequent tour, Cissie Loftus joined the cast, and in Act 2, Scene 2, gave her musical imitations of Ada Rehan, Marie Tempest, Fay Templeton, May Irwin, among others.

[60]Initial performance conducted by the composer, Julian Edwards.

[61]Also played a touring engagement 2 January 1899 at the Harlem Opera House for 8 performances.

[62]First produced in New York 22 October 1877 at the Fifth Avenue Theatre in repertory. For Synopsis of Scenes and Musical Numbers, see original 1877 production.

miser: EDWARD P. TEMPLE. *The Bailli*: Frank Moulan. *The Notary*: Frank Ranney. *Chorus of Peasants, Sailors, Servants, Coachmen, Waiting-Maids, etc.*

1898.75 A SPRING CHICKEN

A Farce Comedy in Three Acts. Play by Edgar Selden. Opened 5 December 1898 at the Star Theatre and closed 10 December 1898 after 8 performances.

CAST: *Henry Chickweed*, the Spring Chicken: SAM COLLINS. *Fuller Coyne*: THOMAS C. CLEARY. *Woodbury Mann*: WALTER J. TALBOT. *Wayback Lovejoy*: Fred Lucier. *Con Daily*: Glen Emery. *Happy Hicky*: Leo Hardy. *Lotta Noyse*: Vivian Cerise. *Mrs. Lobelia Coyne*: KITTY WELLS. *Mrs. Spooner*: Ethel Clerise. *Liza Wright*: Bessie Marlowe. *Ann Tique*: Myra C. Brooks. *Emerald Green*: Pearl Radcliffe. *Violets Sweet*: Maude Ellison. *Ida Hoe*, the Dresden Doll: MADELINE MARSHALL.

1898.76 THE BOHEMIAN GIRL

A Return Engagement of the Revival of the Romantic Opera in Three Acts, 6 Scenes[63]. Libretto by Alfred Bunn, after Jules-Henri Vernoy de Saint-Georges' ballet-pantomime "The Gypsy." Music by Michael Balfe. Stage manager, Edward P. Temple. Scenery by Frank King. Conductor, Adolph Liesegang. Produced by the Castle Square Opera Company (Henry W. Savage, Proprietor). Opened 19 December 1898 at the American Theatre and closed 24 December 1898 after 8 performances.

CAST: *Count Arnheim*, Governor of Presburg: HARRY L. CHASE. *Thaddeus*, a proscribed Pole: JOSEPH F. SHEEHAN. *Florestein*, nephew of the Count: Frank Moulan. *Devilshoof*, chief of the Gypsies: E. N. KNIGHT. *Captain of the Guard*: H. L. Owens. *Arline*, daughter of the Count: ADELAIDE NORWOOD. *Buda*, her attendant: Georgie Deland. *Queen of the Gypsies*: LIZZIE MACNICHOL. *Chorus of Nobles, Soldiers, Gypsies, Retainers and Peasants.*

1898.77 THE LITTLE HOST

A Musical Comedy in Two Acts. Libretto by Edgar Smith and Louis deLange. Music by William T. Francis and Thomas Chilvers. Production staged by Max Freeman. Dances arranged by John C. Slavin. Settings by Frank Gates and Walter Burridge. Musical director, W. T. Francis. Produced by Della Fox (Nat Roth, Management). Opened 26 December 1898 (matinee) at the Herald Square Theatre and closed 14 January 1899 after 21 performances[64].

CAST: *Josiah Dashington, Sr.*, whose reputation for probity receives a rude shock: R. E. GRAHAM. *Jack Dashington*, his son, leading a double life: HUGH CHILVERS. *William Reilly*, known as "Honest Bill": EUGENE O'ROURKE. *Herr Einesang*, composer of opera: JOHN C. SLAVIN. *Friends of Jack (4)*: *Charles Horsley*: Charles Wallace. *Bob Upperton*: Bert Carter. *Dodge Taylor*: Wilford Arling. *Fuller Boozeby*: Frank Kelly. *Dick Hammersley*: Harry Rigby. *Mink*, Jack's valet: H. D. Blakemore. *Diggs*, a gardener at Josiah's villa: H. D. Blakemore. *Olympia Longacre*, a prima donna, known as the "Queen of Song": ALICE JOHNSON. *Aunt Jane Hawkins*, a theatrical "has been": Adella Barker. *Susie Jones*, an inocent: MABEL BOUTON. *Mrs. Dashington*, Jack's stepmother: Emily Francis. *Daisy Dandler*: Emma Levey. *Mazie Spanker*: Annie Black. *Dottie Lightfoot*: Florine Murray. *Flossie Flitterby*: Beatrice Darlington. *Rosie Redpath*: Daisy Dwyer. *Mamie Mangen*: Edith Burbank. *Beatrice Bennington*: Lou M. Harlow. *Minnie Mingle*: Jessie Jordon. *Gertie Gertby*: Kitty Nugent. *Lottie Longhouse*: Mabel Seymour. *Bessie Brownhill*: Hattie Clark. *Harriet Henderson*: Caroline Cook. *Ollie Armstrong*: Lettie Bryan. *Edith Eddington*: Norma Bell. *Margery Dazzle*, Jack's sweetheart, masquerading as Willie Everdrop: DELLA FOX.

Act 1: Jack Dashington's bachelor apartments, on Fifth Avenue, New York City. (Gates.)

Act 2: Lawn of Josiah Dashington's country residence, at Dedbury-on-the Hudson. (Burridge.)

MUSICAL NUMBERS[65]

[63]First produced in New York 25 November 1844 at the Park Theatre for 17 performances. For Synopsis of Scenes and Musical Numbers, see original 1844 production. This revival previously produced by the Castle Square Opera Company 6 June 1898 at the American Theatre for 8 performances.

[64]Also played touring engagements 16 January 1899 at the Harlem Opera House for 8 performances, and 13 March 1899 at the Grand Opera House for 8 performances. Costumes uncredited.

[65]Musical numbers not listed in programs. List prepared from published sheet music. Interpolated for subsequent tour as per published sheet music:

"Ma Lady Lu" (A Darky Love Lament)
Ruth White
(*Music by* Edwin S. Brill. *Lyrics by* Charles W. Doty.)

"I Wouldn't Be a Lady If I Could"
D. Fox
(*Music by* Herman Perlet. *Lyrics by* Aubrey Boucicault.)

"Honey You'se My Turtle Dove"
D. Fox
(*Music by* William T. Francis. *Lyrics by* Edgar Smith.)

1898.78 A FEMALE DRUMMER

A Farce Comedy in Three Acts. Libretto by Charles E. Blaney. Music and Lyrics by Frank David. Produced by Charles E. Blaney. Opened 26 December 1898 at the Star Theater and closed 31 December 1898 after 8 performances; re-opened return engagements 20 February 1899 at the Star Theatre for 16 additional performances, and 8 May 1899 at the Manhattan Theatre for an additional 16 performances.[66].

CAST: *Haza Bargain*, a female drummer: JOHNSTONE BENNETT. *The Baby*: JOHNSTONE BENNETT. *Saleslady*: JOHNSTONE BENNETT. *Gwendolin Dugan*, an America type: JOHNSTONE BENNETT. *Tong Morton* an America type: JOHNSTONE BENNETT. *Maudie Pearl* an America type: JOHNSTONE BENNETT. *Wood B. Smooth*, senior member of Smooth, Silk & Co.: GEORGE RICHARDS. *Uptown Downs*, called Buttons: EUGENE CANFIELD. *Super Stitious*, porter of Smooth, Silk & Co.: WILLIS P. SWEATNAM. *Finas Silk*, junior member of Smooth, Silk & Co.: Antonio Williams. *Corset Staye*, the floor-walker: OSCAR FIGMAN. *Mr. Buyer* of Buyer, Seller & Co., opposition dry goods house: Charles B. Burke. *Mr. Stiff*, the undertaker: Charles LaVallay. *Barkeeper*: Gus Stetson. *Carrie Nash*, *cash-girl*: NELLIE O'NEILL. *Mrs. Wood B. Smooth*: Helena Salinger. *Florence Silk*: Beatrice Reinhart. *Miss Cashmore*, cashier: Georgia Rush. *Meery Notes*: Sadie Miner.

Haza's Bargain Couriers, The Drummer Girls: *Captain Sampson*: Minnie Lee. *Lieutenant Hobson*: Stella Borland. *Captain Philips*: Maud Terriss. *Lieutenant Wainwright*: Della Nivens. *Captain Clark*: Eva Holbrook. *Captain Sigsbee*: Caroline Boyer. *Captain Schley*: Mary Hughes.

Tuxedo Girls and Shop Girls: *Miss Pettie Coat*: Hattie Greene. *Lacie Challies*: Georgia Rush. *Pinkie Ribbons*: Grace Harley. *Kid Gloves*: Marie Allen. *Hattie Flowers*: Beatrice Reinhart. *Baby Blue*: Sadie Spencer. *Rose Color*: Bertha Whitney. *Reddie Maid*: Annabel Nivens. *Silkie Stockings*: Mabel Nivens. *Shoppers, Policemen, Bargain Day Buyers, etc. Colored Porters and the Dandy Waiters of the Golden Light.*

Imperial Quartette: Philip Portlock (first tenor), W. H. Tucker (second tenor), W. B. Collins (baritone), G. W. Pickett (bass).

Act 1: Private Office, Smooth, Silk & Co.'s dry goods house, adjoining main salesroom.

Act 2: Main salesroom, Smooth, Silk & Co., on a busy day.

Act 3: Palisade Heights, on the Hudson, at night. The salesladies' ball.

ACT 1[67]

"Opening Chorus"
Salesladies

"Monday and Tuesday"
Salesladies

"A Female Drummer"
J. Bennett, Chorus

"Hannah Jackson Greene"
N. O'Neil, G. Richards, E. Canfield

ACT 2

"In the Department Store"
Ensemble

"The Salesladies' Annual Ball"
N. O'Neil, Company

"The Singing Models"
D. Nivens, C. Boyer

"Burlesque Trio"
B. Reinhart, G. Richards, E. Canfield

ACT 3

"Dandy Waiters of the Golden Light"
W. P. Sweatnam, Imperial Quartette

[66]Also played touring engagements 23 January 1899 at the Grand Opera House for 8 performances; 13 February 1899 at the Columbus Theatre for 8 performances; 3 April 1899 at the Columbus Theatre for 8 performances; 1 May 1899 at the Grand Opera House for 8 performances.

[67]Interpolated during subsequent tour, as per published sheet music:

"I've Got Another Baby"
N. O'Neil
(*Music and Lyrics by* Frank David.)

"You Ain't One, Two, Three"
Imperial Quartette
"The Swellest Thing"
O. Figman, Chorus
"Pinkey, My Darling"
J. Bennett
"My Own Best Love"
J. Bennett
"A Terpsichorean Trifle"
J. Bennett
"Kitty More"
N. O'Neil, E. Canfield
Original Specialty
W. P. Sweatnam
Ground and Lofty Dancing
N. O'Neil
Finale
Ensemble

1899.01 A ROMANCE OF ATHLONE

An Irish Play (Romantic Drama with Songs) in Four Acts. Play by Augustus Pitou. Music and lyrics by Chauncey Olcott. Dramatic music by Gustav Salzer. Staged by Augustus Pitou. Settings by Lewis C. Young. Costumes designed by Caroline Seidle. Produced by Augustus Pitou. Opened 9 January 1899 at the 14th Street Theatre and closed 25 March 1899 after 88 performances[68].

CAST: *Sir Philip Ronyane*: DANIEL GILFETHER. *Margaret Ronyane*, his wife: Etta Baker Martin. *Francis Ronyane*, his elder son: DUSTIN FARNUM. *Dick Ronyane*, his younger son: CHAUNCEY OLCOTT. *Daisy Ronyane*, his daughter: Tottie Carr. *Jack O'Brien* of Munster, brother of Mrs. Ronyane: Luke Martin. *Major Martin Manning* of Dublin: Paul Everton. *Rose Manning*, his daughter: OLIVE WHITE. *Eleanor McBride*, his ward: Grace Freeman. *Hon. Standish Fitzsimmons*, a friend of Francis: Richard Malchien. *Stephen O'Grady*, servant of Sir Philip's household: J. C. Hickey. *Ann Shea*, servant of Sir Philip's household: Lizzie Washburne. *Robin McMahon*, a gypsy: Charles R. Gilbert. *Molly McMahan*, his wife: Argyle Gilbert. *Mary MacMahon*, a gypsy girl: Louise Marcelli. *Ruth*, a gypsy child: Marguerite Diamond. *Bill*, a gypsy: Frank Bonn. *Servant*: W. L. Jones. *Prince*: Himself.

The action takes place near Athlone, Ireland in 1800.

Act 1: Exterior of Philip Ronyane's house.

Act 2: A room in Sir Philips' house. Two months later.

Act 3: Ruins of the old abbey and gypsy camp by moonlight. The night following.

Act 4: At the "Giant Beech Tree" in the park adjoining Sir Philip Ronyane's house. The second morning after.

MUSICAL NUMBERS
"Many Years Ago"
C. Olcott
"We'll Drown It in the Bowl"
C. Olcott
"Olcott's Lullaby"
C. Olcott
"The Irish Swell"
C. Olcott
"My Wild Irish Rose"
C. Olcott

1899.02 LA BELLE HELENE

A Revival of the Opera Bouffe in Three Acts[69], in English. English adaptation by Louis Harrison. Music by Jacques Offenbach. Staged by Frederic Solomon under the supervision of George W. Lederer. Scenery painted by D. Frank Dodge. Costumes designed by Catherine Siedle. Musical director, Ludwig Engländer. Produced by the George W. Lederer Stock Opera Company. Opened 12 January 1899 at the Casino Theatre and closed 25 February 1899 after 52 performances.

[68]Played touring engagements 3 April 1899 at the Harlem Opera House for 8 performances; 29 May 1899 at the Grand Opera House for 8 performances.
[69]First produced in New York 26 March 1868 at the French Theatre.

CAST: *Helene*, Queen of Sparta: LILLIAN RUSSELL. *Bacchis*, her maid: Carolyn Minerva Heustis. *Aspasia*, one of Sparta's society ladies: MAY TEN BROECK. *Leona*: Vashti Earle. *Parthenis*: Ilma Pratt. *Nemea*: Marie Tuohey. *Paris*, son of King Priam: WILLIAM E. PHILP. *Menelaus*, King of Sparta: JOHN E. HENSHAW. *Calchas*, Grand Augur of Jupiter: THOMAS Q. SEABROOKE. *Agamemnon*, King of Kings: JOSEPH C. MIRON. *Orestes*, his son: EDNA WALLACE-HOPPER. *Ajax I*, King of Salamis: William W. Black. *Ajax II*, King of Locriens: Sol Solomon. *Philicome*, Attendant on Calchas: William Carter. *Enthycles*, a Blacksmith: Henry Rollands. *A Slave*: Wensley Thompson. *Guards, Slaves, Citizens, Warriors, Flower Girls, Priests, etc.*

Act 1: Exterior of Jupiter's Temple. Afternoon.

Act 2: Queen Helene's Apartment in the Royal Palace. Evening.

Act 3: A Seaside Resort near Sparta. Noon of Next day.

INTERPOLATIONS[70]
"That Is Fate"
T. Q. Seabrooke
(*Music by* Ludwig Engländer. *Lyrics by* Louis Harrison.)
"I Arrived in Time to Get It"
J. E. Henshaw
(*Music by* Ludwig Engländer. *Lyrics by* Louis Harrison.)
"It's in the Air"
E. Wallace-Hopper
(*Music by* Ludwig Engländer. *Lyrics by* Louis Harrison.)
"Keep One Eye on Your Country"
T. Q. Seabrooke, E. Wallace-Hopper, J. E. Henshaw
(*Music by* Julius Einodshofer. *Lyrics by* Louis Harrison.)
"For Ever and For Aye"
L. Russell
(*Music by* Ludwig Engländer. *Lyrics by* Louis Harrison.)

1899.03 THE RAGGED EARL

A Comedy Drama in Three Acts[71]. Play by Ernest Lacy and Joseph Humphreys. (Music by Andrew Mack. *Lyrics by* "Alice.") Stage direction of Joseph Humphreys. Scenery by Joseph Physioc. Costumes by Miller. Musical director, John C. Sorg. Produced by (Isaac B.) Rich and (William) Harris. Opened 16 January 1899 at the Academy of Music and closed 11 February 1899 after 32 performances.

CAST: *Gerald Fitzgerald*, Earl of Kildare: ANDREW MACK. *Patrick O'Kellar*, an old scholmaster: W. J. Mason. *Larry Donovan*, one of the Earl's retainers: JAMES VINCENT. *Maurice O'Brian*, a tenant: Thomas Jackson. *Father Barry*, a priest: John C. Fenton. *Sir Henry Hardcastle*, Kathleen's step-brother: HENRY HERMAN. *Ralph Forester*, one of his retainers: Edwin Brandt. *James*, Sir Henry's footman: Thomas Mackay. *Lord Wildbrook*, an old English roué: B. T. [Ben Turner] RINGGOLD. *A Process Server*: J. T. Thomas. *Reegan*: Barney Williams. *Mrs. Fitzmaurice*, Sir Henry's mother: MINNIE MONK. *Kathleen Fitzmaurice, Una Fitzmaurice*, her step-daughters, Kathleen disguised as Edward at the Castle: JOSEPHINE LOVETT, GEOGIA FLORENCE OLP. *Sarah McHugh*: ANNIE WARD TIFFANY. *Retainers of the Earl and Sir Henry.*

Act 1: Exterior of Kilkea Castle.

Act 2: Drawing Room, Sir Henry's House, Dublin.

Act 3: The Ruined Abbey, County Kildare.

MUSICAL NUMBERS[72]
"My Sweet Maid"
A. Mack
"Mack's Lullaby"
A. Mack
"The Cruiskeen Lawn"
A. Mack

[70]Interpolations only were listed in the program.
[71]Elsewhere billed as a Romantic Irish Drama.
[72]Also performed by Andrew Mack in THE RAGGED EARL during its extensive tour, as per published sheet music:
"Oh, Lonely Heart" (*Lyrics by* George Cooper.)
"If You Love as I Love"
"Litle Band of Gold" (*Lyrics by* E. E. Price.)
"The Princess of Mulberry Bend" (*Lyrics by* Leander Richardson.)

1899.04 THE EVIL EYE, or the Many Merry Mishaps of Nid and the Weird Wonderful Wanderings of Nod

A Mechanical Trick Entertainment in Three Acts[73]. Play by Sydney R. Ellis. Music composed and arranged by Alfred J. Kuttner. Management (staging) by the author. Scenery by H. L. Reed. Costumes designed by McIlvaine. Produced by Charles H. Yale. Opened 16 January 1899 at the Grand Opera House, moved January 23 1899 to the Columbus Theatre and closed 28 January 1899 after 16 performances.

CAST: *Peleg Philemon* of New York: WILLIAM BLAISDEL. *Evil Eye Wartburg*, a Jettatore: GEORGE A. D. JOHNSON. *Jeppe Jans*, a mountebank: JAMES F. GREEN. *Nid, Nod*, his two comic geniuses: ROBERT ROSAIRE, THOMAS ELLIOTT. *Bertrand*, a Hollander: ZEPH GOUDREAULT. *Puggie*, an innkeeper: Edward Caron. *Dumb Gretchen*, his maid-of-all-work: George D. Melville. *Pokroyskia*, secret police: James F. Green. *Boisdeffre*, landlord Cafe Eccentrique: George D. Melville. *Moskos, Strephing, Peter, Hanajka*, Russian students (The Monarch Four): T. William Sturgeon, Harry Webster, Louis Franklin, Oren Hooper. *Tagansky*, a typical nihilist: Edward Caron. *General Michael Alexander*, with a lost cognomen: H. R. Richards. *Slovinsky, Ladowsky, Barowsky*, Polish musicians: M. G. Deville, W. B. Harrison, S. W. Thomas. *Tucson Tom, Phoenix Pete, Alkali Abe*, Arizonian products: James Carolton, J. D. Anderson, G. Z. Ransem. *Roue*, a memory of Paree: H. S. Williams. *Captain O'Flynn*, of the Rhine boat *"Lurline"*: John Sharpley. *Shade of the Von Spitz-en-Hoffers*: Edward Caron. *Adora Van de Voort*, of New York: CLARA LAVINE. *Gerda Jans*, a bit of nature: LILLIAN COLEMAN. *Thurings, Adelina, Zaria, Elisa*, American girls: Rose Kessner, Julia Ruppell, Florie Mousley, Anna Courtney. *Mme. Bosaic, Mme. Antoinette*, relics of the past: Rose Kessner, Julie Ruppell. *La Marie, La Rouise*: The Althea Twins. *Grape-pickers, Holland Peasans, Gendarmes, Young Swells, Officers, Opera Ladies, Nihilists, Tourists, etc.*

Act 1: A Holland Village.

Act 2: Café Eccentrique. St. Petersburg Winter Season.

Act 3: The Ruined Castle Drachenfels, overlooking the River Rhine.

ACT 1

Sabot Dance of the Grape-Pickers
Misses R. Kessner, J. Ruppell, F. Mousely, A. Kessner, A. Courtney, Althea Twins

Acrobatic Revels
R. Rosaire, T. Elliott

Aerial Surprises
R. Rosaire, T. Elliott

"By Your Side" (Ballad)
Z. Goudreault

"A-m-e-r-i-c-a"
C. Lavine, Misses Kessner, Ruppell, Mousley
(*Dance words by* Lee Haney.)

"That Is Love" (Duet and Dance)
W. Blaisdell, C. Lavine

Animated Tableaux (featuring a sensational comic revolving effect)

ACT 2

"The Jolly Students"
Monarch Four

A Dainty Ballad Offering
L. Coleman

"La Militaire Claribelle and Her Army"
C. Lavine, assisted by R. Rosaire, T. Elliott

"Chantant Palpitations" and Acrobatic Gaieties
Althea Twins, Ensemble

And many other features of a most varied character, which culminate in a most extraordinary and laughable sensation

ACT 3

Electric Ballet (the latest scientific achievement, invented and manipulated by Mr. C. P. Armstrong)

The mysterious "Shades of the Von Spitzenhoffers"

"The Legend of the Rhine" (with minuet accompaniment)
Z. Goudreault, Ensemble

[73]First produced in New York 4 April 1831 at the Bowery Theatre.

1899.05 THE QUEEN'S LACE HANDKERCHIEF

A Return Engagement of the Revival of the Comic Opera in Three Acts[74]. (Original Viennese operette libretto 'Das Spitzentuch Der Königin' by Bohrmann-Riegen[75] and Richard Genée. American adaptation by James Frenor.) Music by Johann Strauss, Jr. Stage director, Edward P. Temple. Scenery by Frank King. Conductor, Adolph Liesegang. Produced by the Castle Square Opera Company (Henry W. Savage, Proprietor). Opened 23 January 1899 at the American Theatre and closed 28 January 1899 after 8 performances.

CAST: *The King*: LIZZIE MacNICHOL. *The Queen*: ELOISE MORGAN. *Donna Irene*, the Queen's confidante: LAURA MILLARD. *Marquise of Villareal*: JOSIE INTROPODI. *Cervantes*, a poet: JOSEPH F. SHEEHAN. *Count Villaiobois y Rodriguez*, Prime Minister and Head of the Regency: HENRY NORMAN. *Don Sancho de Avellaneda y Villipinguedones*, tutor to the King: FRANK MOULAN. *Marquis de la Marceha Villareal*, Minister of War: Frank Ranney. *Duke of Feria*, Minister of Finance: J. G. Gibson. *Count San Gregorio*, Minister of Interior: O. W. Risley. *Count Ermos*, Minister of Navy: Albert Juhre. *Don Diego de Barados*, Minister of Police: W. H. PRINGLE. *Dancing Master*: Charles Scribner. *Master of Ceremonies*: MAUDE LAMBERT. *Antonio*, inkeeper of the Sierra Nuaro: W. H. Brown. *Students, Doctors, Ladies and Gentlemen of the Court, Toreadors, Brigands, etc.*

1899.06 THE THREE DRAGOONS

A Comic Opera in Three Acts. Libretto by Harry B. Smith. Music by Reginald DeKoven. Produced under the stage direction of Julian Mitchell. Settings by Frank E. Gates, Edward A. Morange, Walter Burridge and Richard Marston. Costumes designed by Archie Gunn. Musical director, Antonio DeNovellis. Produced by Broadway Theatre Opera Company (Andrew McCormick, Manager). Opened 30 January 1899 at the Broadway Theatre and closed 11 March 1899 after 48 performances.

CAST: *Jack Sheridan* of the Irish Dragoons: JOSEPH O'MARA. *Bob Leslie*, aide-de-camp of General Wellesley: WILLIAM H. CLARKE. *Archie Cameron*, of the Scots Greys: Robert S. Pigott. *Don Bamboula Bambolio*, Chief Cook of the King of Portugal: JEROME SYKES. *The King of Portugal*: JEROME SYKES. *Larry O'Brien*, Jack's servant: RICHARD F. CARROLL. *Japes*, Bob's servant: Charles Hildesley. *Fergus*, Archie's servant: Edwin Carroll. *Pavane*, the usual family lawyer with the customary will: George Gaston. *A Sergeant*: William G. Gaunt. *A Postillion*: J. A. Wallerstedt. *Don Inez de Lara*: MARGUERITE LEMON. *Rosita*, waitress at the Posada: LINDA DaCOSTA. *Marcella*, a Gypsy girl: Leonora Gnito. *Pedrillo*, Don Bamboula's valet: FANNIE BRISCOE. *Maraquita*: Millie Stoller. *Estrella*: Adele Archer. *Juana*: Della Nevin. *Michaela*: Marguerite Leon. *Isabella*: Phyllis Baranco. *Pepita*: Mazie Follette. *Francesca*: Jessie Wood. *Dolores*: Carrie May. *British and Portugese Soldiers, Smugglers, Gypsies, Harlequins, Columbines, Pierrots, Harlequinettes.*

The action takes place during the peninsular war in 1809.

Act 1: A Posada on the road to Lisbon. (Burridge.)

Act 2: The royal palace at Lisbon. (Marston.)

Act 3: An old fortress near Lisbon, used as a military prison. (Gates & Morange.)

ACT 1[76]

"Then With a Cachuca, Fandango and Bolero" (Chorus)

"Fill Up Again, Warriors" (Arioso)

"Who Would Not Be a Soldier's Bride?" (Solo and Chorus)
W. Gaunt, L. DaCosta, Chorus

"Officers of the Calvary" (Trio)
J. O'Mara, R. S. Pigott, W. H. Clarke

"When Cupid Comes A Tapping at the Door" (Duet)
R. F. Carroll, L. DeCosta

"Bow with air ceremonious" (Chorus)
Chorus

[74]First produced in New York 21 October 1882 at the Casino Theatre for 8 performances; re-opened 30 December 1882 at the Casino Theatre for 72 performances; re-opened 11 June 1883 at the Casino Theatre for 28 additional performances. Total: 113 performances. For Synopsis of Scenes and Musical Numbers, see original 1882 production. This production previously produced by the Castle Square Opera Company 25 December 1897 at the American Theatre for 10 performances.

[75]Heinrich Bohrmann and Julius von St. Albino Nigri (whose pen name was Riegen) wrote the first version of the libretto.

[76]Musical numbers not listed in program; list prepared from published piano vocal score (J. Church, Cincinnati, 1899).

"I'm a Self-Made Nobleman" (Song and Chorus)
J. Sykes, Chorus
"A Runaway" (Ensemble and Chorus)
M. Lemon, L. DeCosta, R. S. Pigott, G. Gaston, W. H. Clarke, Chorus
"'Twas Over Winding Mountain Roads" (Song)
M. Lemon, L. DeCosta, R. S. Pigott, W. H. Clarke, Chorus
"Say That You Cannot Forget" (Duet)
J. O'Mara, L. Lemon
Finale Act 1(To Lisbon town we must away)

ACT 2
"Carnival is King Tonight" (Prelude and Masquerade Scene)
Chorus
"The Naughty Little Clock" (Chansonette)
L. DeCosta, Chorus
"We're a Party of Gay Serenaders" (Serenade and Trio)
J. O'Mara, R. S. Pigott, W. H. Clarke
"The Bold Dragoon" (Song)
J. O'Mara
"In Lisbon Gay" (Romanza)
M. Lemon
"Hail, Our King" (March)
Chorus
"The Smart Set" (Song and Chorus)
J. Sykes, Chorus
"Soldiers of All Nations" (Song and Chorus)
R. F. Carroll, Chorus
Finale Act 2 (All hail the King)

ACT 3
"Camerados, all is clear" (Introduction and Chorus)
"With Ev'ry Heart" (Chorus)
"He Is a Bluff" (Song and Chorus)
R. F. Carroll, Soldiers' Chorus
"One Heart to Thee" (Duet)
M. Lemon, J. O'Mara
"The Legend of the Donkey" (Song and Chorus)
J. Sykes, Chorus
"Philosophy" (Quartet)
W. H. Clarke, R. S. Pigott, A. Archer, M. Stoller
Finale Act 3 ("In Battle or Upon Parade")

1899.07 H.M.S. PINAFORE, or The Lass That Loved a Sailor

A Return Engagement of the Revival of the Comic Opera in Two Acts[77]. Libretto by William S. Gilbert. Music by Arthur Sullivan. Stage director, Edward P. Temple. Scenery by Walter Burridge. Conductor, Adolph Liesegang. Presented by the Castle Square Opera Company (Henry W. Savage, Proprietor). Opened 6 February 1899 at the American Theatre and closed 18 February 1899 after 16 performances.

CAST: *The Rt. Hon. Sir Joseph Porter, K.C.B.*, First Lord of the Admiralty: FRANK MOULAN. *Captain Corcoran*, Commanding the *H.M.S. Pinafore* : WILLIAM G. STEWART; RICHARD RIDGLEY; HARRY L. CHASE. *Ralph Rackstraw*, Able Seaman: CLINTON ELDER. *Dick Deadeye*, Able Seaman: HENRY NORMAN. *Bill Bobstay*, Boatswain: H. L. Butler. *Sergeant of Marines*: William Anthony. *Josephine*, the Captain's Daughter: ELOISE MORGAN. *Little Buttercup*, a Bumboat Woman: LIZZIE MACNICHOL. *Hebe*, Sir Joseph's First Cousin: MAUDE LAMBERT. *Chorus of Sailors, Sisters, Cousins, Aunts, etc.*

[77]Originally presented in New York 15 January 1879 at the Standard Theatre for 175 performances. For Synopsis of Scenes and Musical Numbers, see original 1879 production. For the first week of this revival, PINAFORE was followed by the opera "I Pagliacci" by Leoncavallo; for the second week, PINAFORE was followed by the opera 'Cavalleria Rusticana' by Pietro Mascagni. This double bill previously presented by the Castle Square Opera Company 14 February 1898 at the American Theatre for 17 performances.

1899.08 BROWN'S IN TOWN

A Farce Comedy in Three Acts. Play by Mark E. Swan. Staged by James O. Barrows. Settings by St. John Lewis. Produced by J. J. Rosenthal. Opened 20 February 1899 at the Bijou Theatre and closed 4 March 1899 after 16 performances.

CAST: *Dick Preston*: EDWARD S. ABELES. *Abel Preston*, his father: JAMES O. BARROWS. *Arthur Howard*, a dentist: John Lancaster. *Worth Carew*, a gentleman of leisure: Edward Poland. *Pollock*, the gardener: Andrew Lee. *Suzanne Dacre*, who knows a thing or two: Anna Belmont. *Letty*, Dick's wife: Kathryn Osterman. *Freda von Hollenbeck*, a German heiress: JOSIE SADLER. *Primrose*, the "lady" cook, with a reputation: BELLE DAVIS.
The action takes place in one day at Honeysuckle Lodge.

Act 1: Morning. Complications-Much.

Act 2: Noon. Complication-More.

Act 3: Night. Complications—Plenty.

MUSICAL NUMBERS[78]
Specialty (Coon Songs)
B. Davis
"One Little Angry Word"
(*Music and Lyrics by* Isabel Leaman.)
"Which Is Brown?"
(*Music and Lyrics by* Delcher and Hennessy.)

1899.09 JOHNNY ON THE SPOT

A Farce Comedy in Three Acts[79]. Produced by (Ned) Munroe and (William Kellar) Mack. Opened 27 February 1899 at the Columbus Theatre and closed 4 March 1899 after 8 performances.

CAST: *Wood B. Con*: NED MUNROE. *William Was Easy*: WILLIAM KELLAR MACK. *Watch Mee*: Charles H. Boyle. *Arthur Falsehood*: William Collins. *Hugh B. Haha*: James Dixon. *Smoke Herrin*: Harry Elvin. *Billy Bluff*: Joseph Dokes. *Spots*: William Lippincott. *E. N. Glish*: James Collins. *Mrs. Easy*: Lenni Marley. *Mrs. Conn*: Elinor Hale. *Prudence Cutte*: May Donohue. *Marion Ohio*: Annie Revere. *Esta Boula Harbor*: Mildred Revere. *Beatrice Nebraska*: Katherine G. Warren. *Helena Montana*: Minnie Teal. *Sou Brette*: Carrie Graham.

1899.10 THE GRAND DUCHESS

A Revival of the Comic Opera in Three Acts, 4 Scenes[80] (Original French libretto to the opéra-bouffe 'La Grande-Duchesse de Gérolstein,' by Henri Meilhac and Ludovic Halévy. English translation and adaptation by Charles L. Kenney and Edgar Smith.) Music by Jacques Offenbach. Stage director, Edward P. Temple. Scenery by H. Logan Reid. Musical director, Adolph Liesegang. Produced by the Castle Square Opera Company (Henry W. Savage, Proprietor). Opened 27 February 1899 at the American Theatre and closed 4 March 1899 after 8 performances.

CAST: *The Grand Duchess*: LIZZIE MACNICHOL. *Wanda*: GERTRUDE QUINLAN. *Iza*: MAUDE LAMBERT. *Olga*: Rita Harrington. *Prince Paul*: FRANK MOULAN. *General Boum*: HENRY NORMAN. *Baron Puck*: RAYMOND HITCHCOCK. *Baron Grog*: Charles Scribner. *Fritz*: CLINTON ELDER. *Nepomuc*: Albert Juhre.
Lords and Ladies of the Court, Maids-of-Honor, Pages, Ushers, Soldiers, Vivandieres, Country Girls, etc: Misses Ella Altman, Belle Archer, Mildred Ashland, Grace Bauer, Mae Burt, Mildred Bruce, Helen Darling, Marquita Dwight, Charlotte Franklyn, Belle Franklyn, Rita Harrington, Effie Hamilton, Celia King, Emma King, Maude Lambert, Stella Madison, Lillie Martinez, Ruby Paine, Cora Scribner, May Selbach, Frankie Sherwood, Dolly Weston, Tassa White, Katherine White, Eva Andrews, Ollie Bennett, Dot Young, Alice Clark, Julie Cotte, Georgie Deland, Lolie Eddinger, Georgie French, Pearl Hamlin. Messrs. George Arnand, William H. Brown, Chris Bryde, J. J. Cluxton, William Douglas, E. C. Edmonds, J. G. Gibson, H. Haynes, Frank Howard, Albert Juhre, E. Koch, H. L. Owen, W. A. Pringle, O. W. Risly, J. Rose, H. O. Seigel, Charles Scribner, A. L. Underwood, E. L. Weston, William White.

[78]Musical Numbers not listed in programs. List prepared from published sheet music, reviews.
[79]Authorship uncredited. No program available.
[80]This adaptation first produced in New York 25 February 1890 at the Casino Theatre for 100 performances. For Synopsis of Scenes and Musical Numbers, see original 1890 production.

1899.11 BY THE SAD SEA WAVES

A Musical Vaudeville Comedy in Three Acts. Libretto by J. Sherrie Mathews and Harry Bulger. Music by Gustav Luders. Staged by Barney Fagan[81]. Settings by Lamphier and Buhler, Chicago. Costumes by Ned Wayburn. Musical director, Gustav Luders. Produced by Dunne and (Thomas W.) Ryley. Opened 28 February 1899 at the Herald Square Theatre and closed 8 April 1899 after 47 performances[82].

CAST: *Palmer Coin*, sleight of hand and strong of nerve: J. SHERRIE MATHEWS. *Boston Budge*, the answer to an advertisement: HARRY BULGER. *Colonel Campwell*, fond of America and other things: Gus Mortimer. *Algernon Campwell*, the Colonel's son—"It makes me so angry.": WILL WEST. *Judge Grace*, who has patience with his patients: Robert Vernon. *General Smiles*, good for a laugh; a soldier who thinks he thinks: NED WAYBURN. *Professor Wagner Flat*, a musician playing for a place: GILBERT GREGORY. *John Phillips*, who imagines he is Sousa: GILBERT GREGORY. *Professor Vaulter Barr*, instructor of athletics and talk designer: W. H. Macart. *Silas Perry*, attendant in sanitarium: W. H. Macart. *Jimmie Gun*, a continuous burglar by permission: J. Doctor. *Van Winkle*, sleep-walker, who left a call and did not call for it: Van Huntington. *Dodge Bell*, a waiter—it serves him right: Gordon Eldrid. *J. Pullem*, a policeman with badge: Sandy McDermott. *Yank M. Inn*, another policeman, also a club man: Benjamin Hopkins. *Earl E. Frost*, ice man. Do you want any? Get up!: William Butters. *Sharpley Hunt*, detective, finds them out when they are in: Charles Jacklin. *Charity Grace, Faith Grace, Hope Grace*, the Three Graces, daughters of the Judge: NELLIE HAWTHORNE, JOSIE DeWITT, LIZZIE SANGER. *Sis Hopkins*, an heiress to ills imaginary; too honest to take medicine, unless it is given to her: ROSE MELVILLE. *Babette*, who has a bad habit of forming habits: Eva Leslie. *Miss Lavinia Primmer*, school mistress of Finishville Academy: JULIA RALPH. *Effie Eastman*, she of the wedding breakfast eye: Agnes Saye Wayburn.

Pupils of Finishville Academy: *Vera White*: Bessie Challenger. *Sousie Southern*: Carrie Vincent. *Naomi North*: Helen Budd. *Winnie Western*: Lizzie Creese. *Rennie Redpath*: May Norton. *Georgie Greenwall*: Lottie Ettenger. *Viola Ramedell*: Mabel Rother. *Effie Greenway*: Bessie Bruno. *Susie Short*: Sarah Carr. *Tillie Tallman*: Mattie Lill. *Daisy Dresser*: Lulu Cosgrove. *J. Wood Winham*: Estelle Hamilton. *Billie Deux*: Belle Miller. *Glory Christian*: Agnes Gildea. *Phila Glass*: Margaret York.

Act 1: At the quarters. Finishville Habit-Cure Sanitarium.

Act 2: At the half. Reception room in hallucination ward of sanitarium.

Act 3, Scene 1: In the stretch. Military ward in sanitarium. Under the wire. *Scene 2*: Lawn of sanitarium. A Japanese finish.

ACT 1[83]

"In Dear Old London"[84] (Song and Chorus)
W. West, Chorus
(*Music by* Gustav Luders.)

"Operatic Most Emphatic" (Finale)
Company
(*Music by* Gustav Luders.)

ACT 2[85]

Opening Chorus[86]
Ladies of the Seminary

"Calisthenic Song and Dance"
J. S. Matthews, E. Leslie, Ladies of the Seminary
(*Music by* Barney Fagan.)

"Bell Chorus"
Ladies of the Seminary
(*Music by* DeWitt.)

"Buttercups and Daisies"
J. S. Matthews, H. Bulger,
N. Wayburn, W. H. Macart, G. Mortimer, G. Gregory, Company
(*Music by* Harry Bulger, J. Sherrie Mathews.)

"Honolulu Lady"
N. Hawthorne, J. DeWitt, Ladies
(*Music by* Harry Bulger, J. Sherrie Mathews.)

Sis, with voice attached
R. Melville

["I've Waited, Honey Waited Long for You"
(R. Melville [Sis Hopkins], W. West)
(*Music and Lyrics by* George A. Nichols.)]

Original Rag-Time Specialty
N. Wayburn

"Yankee Banners"
J. S. Matthews, H. Bulger, Company
(*Music by* Harry Bulger, J. Sherrie Mathews.)

ACT 3[87]

"The Military Model"
W. West, N. Hawthorne, J. DeWitt, Ladies
(*Music by* Harry Bulger, J. Sherrie Mathews.)

"The Willow Pattern Plate"
N. Hawthorne
(*Music and Lyrics by* Leslie Stuart.)

"Fiddle and I"
J. DeWitt
(*Music by* Harry Bulger, J. Sherrie Mathews.)

Specialty
J. S. Matthews, H. Bulger

"La-Par Micado" (Ragtime Opera)
W. West, Ladies
(*Music by* Harry Bulger, J. Sherrie Mathews.)

Finale
Company
(*Music by* Charles Gebest.)

1899.12 A REIGN OF ERROR

A Vaudeville in Three Acts. Libretto by John J. McNally. Music by Maurice Levi. Produced under the stage direction of Ben Teal. Dances arranged by Carl Marwig and Rogers Brothers. Scenery by Ernest Albert. Costumes by F. Richard Anderson. Musical arrangements by Maurice Levi. Orchestra under the direction of Maurice Levi. Produced by (Marc) Klaw and (Abraham L.) Erlanger. Opened 2 March 1899 at Hammerstein's Victoria Theatre and closed 10 June 1899 after 102 performances.

CAST: *Hans Wurzt*, with a face for a place: GUS ROGERS. *Carl Leetlewurzer*, with a place for a face: MAX ROGERS. *Mlle. Georgie Gelee*, cool name with warm disposition:

---

[81]On tour and for the Grand Opera House engagement Ned Wayburn was credited with direction.

[82]Played a return engagement 5 March 1900 at the Grand Opera House for 8 performances.

[83]Interpolated per sheet music:

"La Pas Ma La"
(*Music and Lyrics by* Ernest Hogan.)

"Wing Lee's Rag-Time Clock"
J. S. Mathews, H. Bulger
(*Music and Lyrics by* Al Trahern.)

[84]Replaced for subsequent tour by:

"Ragtime Mixes My Brain"
W. J. Deming {Algernon Campwell}, Chorus
(*Music by* Gustav Luders.)

[85]For tour and Grand Opera House engagement, all the songs in Act 2 following Calisthenic Song were dropped and replaced by:

"This Dear Little Fellow Was Cupid"
Jane Lennox {Lily Flower}
(*Music by* Gustav Luders.)

"The Man Who Invented Ragtime"
N. Wayburn

"The Undertakers' Frolic"
J. S. Matthews, H. Bulger, N. Wayburn, W. Macart, Thomas A. Kiernan, Tony Hart, Chorus
(*Music by* Gustav Luders.)

Cornet Solo
Vinie DeWitt {Rose Flower}

"You Told Me Yo' Had Money in the Bank"
J. S. Matthews, H. Bulger, Louise Rosa {Daisy Flower}, Company
(*Music by* Gustav Luders. *Lyrics by* J. Sherrie Mathews and Harry Bulger.)

[86]Dropped for tour.

[87]For tour and Grand Opera House engagement, all the songs in Act 3 were dropped and replaced by:

"Soldiers in Love's War"
Misses Rosa, DeWitt, Lennox, Sanger, Chorus
(*Music by* Gustav Luders.)

Plastique Poses

"Japanese Baby" (Song)
J. Lennox, Company
(*Music by* Gustav Luders.)

"I'se Found Yo', Honey, Found Yo', Now Be Mine" (Song)
J. S. Matthews, Bessie Challeger {Sis Hopkins}

GEORGIA CAINE. *Dr. Dago Daggeri*, would be a consistant stage villain if specialties permitted: GEORGE F. MARION. *Weina Cavaya*, who wants to marry Weina Wurzt: MAUDE RAYMOND. *Clementine Clapper*, an undeveloped clairvoyant: ADA LEWIS. *Jack Ballister*, doesn't care for money, and proves it by backing a show: JOHN PARR. *Irene Orsini*, dreamy and romantic because her voice is soprano: Carrie Elberts. *Marie Manila*, who wants to be a Leetlewurzer: Georgia Laurence. *Justin Soke*, fortune put him in the show business, misfortune keeps him there: Budd Ross. *Neuna Glove*, a fresh kid, Soke's daughter: LA PETITE ADELAIDE. *Mlle. Bon Seconde*: EDITH ST. CLAIR.

Sirens of Superior Sterling's Startlers: *Aurora*: Hattie Walters. *Flora*: Winnie Sennett. *Mora*: Marguerite Haviland. *Nora*: May Warner. *Cora*: Madge Pierce. *Dora*: Miss E. Davis. *Lora*: Gertrude Saye. *Vora*: Camilla Smith.

Captain Flim; Lengi Corsini: Will T. Hodge. *First Officer Flam; Custom House Inspector*: Robert A. Mansfield. *Bill Keelon; Policeman O'Sullivan*: Pete Curley. *Jim Jibe, Detective Sleuth*: H. C. Brown. *Hy Jinks; Augutus Van Dyke Smith*: Frank V. LeMone. *Newsboy; Drum-Major*: Willie Torpey.

Act 1: On board Jack Ballister's yacht, mid-ocean.

Act 2: The dock, New York City.

Act 3: Ancestral hall of Balderini, Brazil.

ACT 1[88]

"Sailing" (Opening Chorus)
Company

"Mlle. Gelee"
G. Caine

Medley Trio
M. Raymond, Rogers Brothers

ACT 2[89]

"Bonnie Little Johnnie"
G. Caine, Chorus

"Long Ago in Alcala"[90] (Solo)
J. Parr
(*Music by* André Messager. *Lyrics by* Adrian Ross.)

"I'm the Manager of the Show"[91]
B. Ross, Misses Haviland, Watters, Sennett, Davis, Warner, Saye, Smith, Pierce

Original Parodies and Sayings[92]
Rogers Brothers

[Parodies: "Get Your Money's Worth"; "I Love You in the Same Old Way"; "He Certainly Was Good to Me"; Parody on "The Banks of the Wabash"; Parody on "Take Back Your Gold"; "Break the News to Mother"; "Do, Do, My Huckleberry, Do"; Original Parody "Coming Through the Rye." Sayings: Meal Ticket; Roaches; Old Age; What a Woman Can Do; The Auction Room; Poetry]

"I Am a Dago"
G. F. Marion, Chorus

"Sweethearts to Burn" (Character Specialty)
Rogers Brothers, A. Lewis, M. Raymond

"The Origin of the Coon Song"
Chorus

"U.S. March"
Entire Company

ACT 3[93]

Opening Chorus
Company

La Petite Adelaide's (Famous Rag-time) Toe Dances

"When I Need You Most, You Throws Me Down"[94]

"You've Got to Play Rag-Time" (Hoot Mon!)[95]
M. Raymond, Chorus
(*Music by* A. Baldwin Sloane. *Lyrics by* Jean C. Havez.)

Finale
Company

[88]Interpolated as per published sheet music:
"First You Do the Rag, Then You Bombashay" (Dat's How De Rag-time Dance Is Done)
Rogers Brothers, M. Raymond
(*Music by* Harry Von Tilzer. *Lyrics by* Andrew B. Sterling.)

[89]Added during the run, after Rogers Brothers Parodies and Sayings:
"Mesmerize Magee" (Dope Song)
A. Lewis
(Music and Lyrics by M. M. Ellis.)
Added in late May to follow "Long Ago in Alcala:"
"Waldorf "Hyphen" Astoria"
J. Parr
(*Music by* Jackson Gouraud. *Lyrics by* E. C. Center.)
During the run, a burlesque of "The Three Musketeers" in One Act entitled "The Eight Must-Get-Theres" was added between Acts 2 and 3; this was later dropped when "Mlle. Ka-za-za" was added 1 May 1899.
THE EIGHT MUST-GET-THERES. Cast: *D'Artagnan de Broadwai*: GUS ROGERS. *D'Artagnan de Knickerbockaire*: MAX ROGERS. *Lady de Winter*, a branded peach: GEORGIA CAINE. *Louis XIII*, King of France: BUDD ROSS. *Anne of Austria*, Queen of France: MAUDE RAYMOND. *Cardinal Richelieu*: GEORGE F. MARION. *Duke of Buckingham*: JOHN PARR. *Felton*: Robert A. Mansfield. *Marron*, Innkeeper: Pete Curley. *Rochefort*: Frank V. LeMone. *Athos, Porthos, Aramis*, friend of D'Artagnan de Broadwai: N. Judels, F. Todd, H. Brown. *Athos, Porthos, Aramis*, friend of D'Artgnan de Knickerbockaire: W. T. Hodge, William Torpey, John Eichburger. *Gabrielle de Callous*: Carrie Elberts. *Toinette*: Winnie Sennett. (No songs from this Act appear in the program.)

[90]Introduced in MIRETTE (London, 1894) and THE LITTLE MICHUS (London, 1897).

[91]Also performed in this spot, per published sheet music:
"End of the Century Girls"
Misses Haviland, Waters, Sennett, Curtis, Warner, Kealty, Belton, Pierce

[92]Details from published sheet music.

1899.13 THE AIR SHIP

A Farce Comedy in Three Acts. Play by Joseph M. Gaites. Opened 13 March 1899 at the Metropolis Theatre and closed 18 March 1899 after 8 performances[96].

CAST: *Johnny Wise*: RAYMOND FINDLAY. *Major Tammany*: JAMES T. KELLY. *Noah Lott*: Ben Welch. *Long Green*: E. D. Coe. *Short Card Cy*: George Erroll. *Pig Iron Pete*: James Newman. *Lop Eared Lou*: Michael Smith. *Harry Harold*: M. J. Garrick. *Fred Morton*: C. W. Arthur. *Hoboken Spider*: BEN SHIELDS. *Jack Carr*: MAX MILLIAN. *Mut*: LOTTIE BURKE. *Hariet Harkaway*: Nana Bascom. *Biddia Binkham*: MARIE STUART. And Maryland Tyson, Marie Wilson, Dorothy Carter, Helen Steele, Marie Tillotson, Stella Blair, Lillian Dougherty.

1899.14 OLIVETTE

A Revival of the Comic Opera in Three Acts[97]. (Original French libretto to the opéra comique 'Les Noces d'Olivette' by Henri Chivot and Alfred Duru.) Music by Edmond Audran. Stage director, Edward P. Temple. Scenery by H. Logan Reid. Musical director, Adolph Liesegang. Produced by the Castle Square Opera Company (Henry W. Savage, Proprietor). Opened 13 March 1899 at the American Theatre and closed 18 March 1899 after 8 performances.

[93]On 1 May 1899 MLLE. KA-ZA-ZA (a burlesque of "Zaza") by John J. McNally, music by Maurice Levi, was added as Act 4, following A REIGN OF ERROR. Cast: *Farmer Refrain*: GEORGE MARION. *Ash-Cart*, partner of Mlle. Ka-Za-Za: GUS ROGERS. *Soke*, stage manager: BUDD ROSS. *Moony Van Sully*, one time matinee idol: W. T. Hodge. *Rosa Bumm*, Mlle. Ka-Za-Za's aunt: Ada Lewis. *Madame Refrain*: Pete Curley. *Alice*: Carrie Elberts. *Fido*: Max Rogers. *Scatterlee*: MAUDE RAYMOND. *Mlle. Ka-Za-Za*: GEORGIA CAINE. *Call-boy*: Willie Torpey.

[94]Dropped late in the New York run. Also performed in this spot, per published sheet music:
"The Yankee Doodle Girls"
Misses Lewis, Elberts, Lawrence,Sinclair, Waters, Haviland, Sennett, Curtis, Warner, Pierce, Kealty, Belton

[95]Also performed in this spot, per published sheet music:
"I Wonder What Is That Coon's Game?"
M. Raymond, Chorus
(*Music by* Billy Johnson. *Lyrics by* Robert Cole.)

[96]Also played a subsequent week 27 March 1899 at the Grand Opera House for 8 performances.

[97]American adaptation uncredited. First produced in New York 25 December 1880 for 63 performances. Re-opened 18 April 1881 at the Fifth Avenue Theatre for 35 additional performances. Total: 98 performances. For Synopsis of Scenes and Musical Numbers, see original 1880 production.

CAST: *Captain de Merrimac* of the man-o'-war *Cormorant*: HENRY NORMAN. *Valentin*, officer of the Rousillon Guards: JOSEPH F. SHEEHAN, CLINTON ELDER. *Duc des Ifs*, cousin and heir-presumptive to the Countess: RAYMOND HITCHCOCK. *Marvejol*, local puralist, Seneschal to the Countess, and Marie Perpignan: WILL H. HATTER. *Olivette*, daughter of the Seneschal Marvejol: MAY BAKER. *Bathilde*, Countess of Rousillon, in love with Valentine: ADELAIDE NORWOOD. *Veloutine*, the Seneschal's housekeeper: GERTRUDE QUINLAN. *Moustique*, Captain's boy, on board the "*Cormorant*": Lorle Eddinger. *Chorus*: (same as in The GRAND DUCHESS, above).

1899.15 IN GAY PAREE

A Spectacular Musical Farce in Three Acts, 5 Scenes. Book by Clay M. Greene adapted from a French farce. Music by Ludwig Engländer. Lyrics by Grant Stewart. Entire production under the personal stage direction of Ben Teal. Ballets and dances arranged by Carl Marwig. Settings by Ernest Albert, Walter Burridge and Ernest Gros. Dresses designed by F. Richard Anderson. Musical director, Herman Perlet. Produced by George W. Lederer. Opened 20 March 1899 at the Casino Theatre and closed 29 April 1899 after 42 performances.

CAST: *Henri Distrait*, a Gay Deceiver: HARRY DAVENPORT. *Jean Ravicot*, His Uncle and Accomplice: ROBERT F. COTTON. *Theodore Lacour*: EDWARD B. TYLER. *Eucevious Bartavel*, a Mercenary Father: GEORGE A. BEANE. *Hector von Donnerblitz*, a Page out of the Past: CHARLES DICKSON. *Canuchet*, a Wine Cellarer: Samuel Edwards. *Joseph*, Servant to Bartavel: Perkins Fisher. *Simon*, a Village Bridegroom: C. Harry Kittredge. *Louisette Gireaud*, a Jilted Dressmaker: MABEL GILMAN. *Denise*, a Village Bride: Marie George. *Emilie Bartavel*, a Promised Bride: MARGARET WARREN. *Ludovica Bartavel*, a Maiden Aunt with a Past: ALICE HOSMER. *Melanie*: Susie Drake. *Fanchette*: Emma Levey. *ClementineFirst MaidSecond MaidFirst Peasant Girl*: Lilly Brink. *Second Peasant Girl*: Madge Dean. *First Vine Dresser*: Jane English. *Second Vine Dresser*: Lillian Lester. *Commissary of Police*: Joseph Marston. *Logerot*, an Inn Keeper: Anthony Sullivan. *Vitevite*, a Waiter: Thomas Collins. *Station Master*: Thomas Whitbread. *Conductor*: _. (*English Dance Specialty, Act 2*: VIOLET HOLMES.) *Guests, Passengers, Gendarmes, Villagers, Bridesmaids, Housemaids, Village Girls, etc.*

The action takes place in and about Paris at the present time.

Act 1, Scene 1: A room in the home of the Bartavels. (Albert.) *Scene 2*: Exterior of the Cafe Robinson. (Burridge.)

Act 2: Vineyards of Argenteuil. (Gros.)

Act 3[98], *Scene 1*: Another part of the Vineyards. (Gros.) *Scene 2*: Another room in the home of the Bartavels. (Albert.)

MUSICAL NUMBERS

"Love Letters"
M. Gilman
(*Music by* Ludwig Engländer. *Lyrics by* Grant Stewart.)

"The Little Dickey Birds"
M. Warren

1899.16 THE MIKADO, or, The Town of Titipu

A Return Engagement of the Revival of the Comic Opera in Two Acts[99]. Libretto by William S. Gilbert. Music by Arthur Sullivan. Stage diector, Edward P. Temple. Scenery by H. Logan Reid. Conductor, Adolph Liesegang. Produced by the Castle Square Opera Company (Henry W. Savage, Proprietor). Opened 27 March 1899 at the American Theatre and closed 1 April 1899 after 8 performances.

CAST: *The Mikado of Japan*: FRANK MOULAN. *Nanki-Poo*, his son, disguised as a wandering minstrel in love with Yum-Yum: JOSEPH F. SHEEHAN, CLINTON ELDER. *Ko-Ko*, Lord High Executioner of Titipu: RAYMOND HITCHCOCK. *Pooh-Bah*, Lord High Everything Else: HENRY NORMAN. *Pish-Tush*, a Noble Lord: Will H. Hatter. *Nee-Ban*, umbrella carrier to the Mikado: Frank Ranney. *Yum-Yum, Pitti-Sing, Peep-Bo*, three sisters, wards of Ko-Ko: LAURA MILLARD, GERTRUDE QUINLAN, EMMA KING. *Katisha*, an elderly lady in love with Nanki-Poo: LIZZIE MacNICHOL. *Chorus of School Girls, Nobles, Guards and Coolies*: (same as THE GRAND DUCHESS above).

1899.17 HELTER SKELTER

A Double-Bill of Burlesques in Two Acts, 4 Scenes. Dialogue by Edgar Smith. Music by John Stromberg. Lyrics by Harry B. Smith. Staged by Julian Mitchell. Musical director, John Stromberg. Produced by Joseph Weber and Lew M. Fields. Opened 6 April 1899 at the Weber & Fields Music Hall and closed 27 May 1899 after 56 performances.

ACT 1

HELTER SKELTER, a Mad Scramble of Tomfoolery in One Act.

CAST: *Lord Shaggy Shetland*, with a talent for picking the losing horse: CHARLES J. ROSS. *Branigan Sudsby*, proprietor of Sudby's Soap, and ambitious to get into society: JOHN T. KELLY. *Conby Frontrow*, purveyor of amusement to the swell set: PETER F. DAILEY. *Isidore Nosenstein*, a detective from Scotchitch Yard: DAVID WARFIELD. *Moritz Longman, Ikay Shortman*, the diamond gang: LEW M. FIELDS, JOSEPH WEBER. *Smalley Gimlett*, a jockey, masquerading as "Bonnie Prince Charlie": LEE HARRISON. *Montague*, Sudsby's footman: Mr. West. *Mrs. Brannigan Sudsby*, who walks in her sleep: FAY TEMPLETON. *Lady Shaggy Shetland*, who coppers her husband's bets: Josephine Allen. *Little Bo-Peep*: JOSIE SADLER. *Lord Qualmy*, Shaggy's good brother: FRANKIE BAILEY. *Guests at Sudbsy's Masquerade Ball (4)*: *Lord Panorama*: Helen Dunbar. *Lady Mildew*: Allie Gilbert. *Hammersley*: May Edwards. *Bilkington*: Bonnie Maginn.

Incidental to the Act, a Skit on "Zaza" (play by Pierre Berton and Charles Simon).

CAST: *Zaza*: MABEL FENTON. *Bernard Fewbrains*, Zaza's steady company: PETER F. DAILEY. *Toto*: Richard Garnella. *Alice Moral*, Zaza's friend: Belle Robinson. *Madame Rummy*, Zaza's aunt: Minnie Poore. *Marquis de Gripsacke*: M. Renner. *Maid*: May Edwards. (*Dance Specialty*, Finale, Something Oriental: BESSIE CLAYTON.)

ACT 1

"The Dinner Party" (Opening Chorus)

"(I'm Making a Bid for) Popularity" (Song)(from HURLY BURLY)
J. T. Kelly

"The Musketeers"/"Trelawny"/"My Josephine" (Song and Ensemble)
P. Dailey

"I'm All Right" (Song)

"The Alarm Clock" (Song)

Oriental Serenade (Guards March)
B. CLayton

Finale (March)

ACT 2

CATHERINE, a Little Bit of Nonsense in One Act, 3 Scenes. (Travesty upon "Catherine" by Henri Lavedan.) For production details, see entry above at HURLY BURLY, 8 September 1898.

1899.18 FINNIGAN'S 400

A Farce Comedy in Three Acts[100]. Musical director, William H. Freer. Produced by James D. Flynn. Opened 10 April 1899 at the People's Theatre and closed 15 April 1899 after 9 performances.[101]

CAST: *Connor Casey*, Finnigan's friend: CHARLES MURRAY. *Danny Casey*, always in the push: John Fields, Jr. *Dusty Rhodes*, alias Willie Getit No. 2: Charles Barry. *H. Arvard Yale*, from Cornell: Ed. A. Kerr. *Terry Tuff*, justa second: Harry Snow. *District Messenger*: Robert Murray. *A Swell Dog*: Himself. *Willie Getit*, from California: Harry Buckley. *Kittie Finnigan*, a beauty bright: Bonnie Bonita Loring. *Leonora Casey*, quite a good housekeeper: Hulda Halvers. *Effie Sharp*, the music teacher: Lonnie Deane. *Cleopatra Finnigan*, a sad affair: Alice Adams. *A Bunch of bewitching beauties (4)*: *Essie*: Annetta Reed. *Bessie*: Editha Wiltshire. *Tessie*: Nettie Knowles. *Jessie*: Musette Gibbs. *Timothy Finnigan*, leader of the "400": JAMES MACK.

Act 1: Finnigan's Flats, New York. One day.

Act 2: Casey's home. Next day.

Act 3: Hotel de Finnigan, Timothyville. Day after.

---

[98]During the run, Act 3 was revised and redesigned as one scene, the Railroad Depot of Argenteuil, designed by John H. Young.

[99]First presented in New York 20 July, 10-29 August 1885 at the Union Square and People's Theatres for 22 performances. First authorized production presented 19 August 1885 at the Fifth Avenue Theatre by Richard D'Oyly Carte for 250 performances. For Synopsis of Scenes and Musical Numbers, see 19 August 1885 D'Oyly Carte production. This revival previously presented by the Castle Square Opera Company 28 March 1898 at the American Theatre for 16 performances.

[100]Billed as "Those Funny Men, Murray and Mack and their Gigantic Company of Artists in the Third Chapter of Timothy."

[101]No credits in program for author, director, scenery or costumes.

ACT 1
"Mary Jane"
Ladies
"Two Dead Game Sports"
C. Murray, J. W. Mack
The Baseball Girls
Misses Loring, Reed, Knowles, Wiltshire, Gibbs
Burlesque Boxing Match
C. Murray, J. W. Mack
"Dandy Dan"
J. Fields, Jr., Misses Loring, Reed, Knowles, Wiltshire, Gibbs
"Lou-Lou"
C. Barry, Ladies
"Susan Simpson, Mary Lou"
C. Murray, J. W. Mack, Company

ACT 2
The 400 Ball and Double Dip
C. Murray, J. W. Mack, Misses Loring, Reed, Knowles, Wiltshire, Gibbs
Ragtime Dance
B. Loring, Misses Loring, Reed, Knowles, Wiltshire, Gibbs
"The Other Foot"
C. Murray, J. W. mack
A Dramatic Pousse-Café
C. Murray, L. Deane
Singing and Acrobatic Dancing
Reed and Halvers
Artistic Melange
B. Loring, J. Fields
The Electric Quartette
Kerr, Barry, Buckley, Fields
(*Devised by* Mr. Kerr.)
Medley of National Airs
C. Murray, J. W. Mack, Company

ACT 3
"Miss Harvard of Yale"
Misses Halvers, Reed, Gibbs Wiltshire
"Weary Willie's Wanderings"
C. Barry
Exercises Athletiques
J. Fields, Loring
"The Serenade"
C. Murray, J. W. Mack, Company

1899.19 THE MAN IN THE MOON

A Spectacular Fantasy in Three Acts, 7 Scenes. (Libretto) Written by Louis Harrison and Stanislaus Stange. Music by Ludwig Engländer, Gustave Kerker and Reginald DeKoven. Entire presentation staged by George W. Lederer. Ballets arranged by Professor Carl Marwig. Scenery painted by D. Frank Dodge, Henry E. Hoyt, St. John Lewis, Ernest Albert. Costumes designed by Mme. Caroline Siedle. Electrical effects by Messrs. Joseph Lee and J. Whalen. Musical director, Gustave Kerker. Produced by George W. Lederer. Opened 24 April 1899 at the New York Theatre; revised version THE MAN IN THE MOON, JR.[102] opened 3 October 1899 and closed 4 November 1899 after 192 performances.

CAST: *Willie Bullion*: JOHN E. HENSHAW. *Continuous Proctor*: WALTER JONES. *Sherlock Holmes*: FERRIS HARTMAN. *Jimmy Donohue*: LOUIS WESLEY. *Prairie Dog Pete*: JOSEPH C. MIRON. *Whaley*, a Champion Heavyweight: JOSEPH C. MIRON. *Pianissimo*, Viola's Musical Director: Frank Whitman. *Alphonse*, a French Butler: Daniel Baker. *Slipsey*, a Street Arab: Daniel Williams. *Dangerous Dugan*, Elevator Boy: Daniel Williams. *McCue*: Daniel Williams. *Police Captain*: Will A. McCormick. *'Arry*: Charles Walton. *Senator Tim Sullivan*: William Sellery. *Mr. McGovern*: Lynn Welcher. *The Creditors (8)*: *Smokeheimer*: J. A. Furey. *Flameberg*: Paul Musaeus. *Goldbricksky*: William Arling. *Swindlefresser*: Charles L. Dox. *Putzelschitzer*: Abner Symons. *Shamrockmeyer*: Charles Courtney. *Boodlestein*: Charles Fitz. *Twelvepercentsky*: Mylo Joyce. *Conan Doyle*, Father of Sherlock Holmes: SAM BERNARD. *Viola Alum*: MARIE DRESSLER. *Diana*: CHRISTIE MacDONALD. *Spirit of Mischief*: Norma Whalley. *Endymion*: Catherine Linyard. *Kitty Lorraine*, a Maid: JEANETTE BAGEARD. *Mlle. Fifi*: JEANETTE BAGEARD. *Miss Tryphenia Bullion*: MAY TEN BROECK. *Punch Sloan*, a Jockey: ZELLA FRANK. (*Specialty*: Honest John Kelly.)

The Leading Ladies: *Psyche*: Violet Holls. *Fuschia*: Vashti Earle. *Ceres*: Nora Gratley. *Ivy*: Miss Margotine. *Clio*: Marie Clements, *Dahlia*: Ruby Reid. *Charity*: Rita Riley. *Fern*: Helen Lacey. *Sapphira*: May Lavigne. *Verbena*: Lou Harlow. *Ruby*: Lottie Medley. *Sweetpea*: Marie Reynolds. *Azalea*: Ivy Claire. *Dewdimple*: Vivian Blackburn. *Carnation*: Marie Allen. *Pansy*: Ethel Elberton. *Mrs. McCue*: Rosa Cooke. *Pansy*: Rosa Cooke.

Liza Ellen: LOUIE FREEAR.

The Ballets: *Danseuse*: LA LISKA. *Le Quatre Danseurs Excentrique*: Misses Sally Lomas, Lily Lawnton, Madelaine Anderton, Marie Millward. *Pony Ballet* (secured thrugh John Tiller, London England): Misses Flo Farmer, Ada Robertson, Eva Marlow, Carrie Poltz, Marie Sanford, Lizzie Lyons, Jennie Makepeace, Mabel Sabin, Maud Corbett, Lizzie Hawman, Alice Donaldson, Cissie McNeill, Maggie Taylor, Aida Harley, Flo Glenville, Beatie Liddle.

Act 1, Scene 1: The Home of Willie Bullion on Riverside Drive. (Dodge.) *Scene 2*: Exterior of the Coney Island Jockey Club, at Sheepshead Bay. (Hoyt.) *Scene 3*: Madison Square Roof Garden. (Hoyt.)

Act 2, Scene 1: The River Front. (Dodge.) *Scene 2*: Matrimonial Agency. (Lewis.) *Scene 3*: The Barn at Bullionhurst. (Dodge.)

Act 3: The Halls of Columbia. The Bullion Scene. (Albert.)

ACT 1[103]

Scene 1
"The Creditors' Chorus"
(*Music by* Ludwig Engländer.)
"Liberty Hall"
J. E. Henshaw, Ensemble
(*Music by* Ludwig Engländer.)
"She Just Walks On"
L. Freear
The Spirit of Mischief and Sprites
(*Music by* Ludwig Engländer.)

Scene 2
"The Jockey Chorus"
Z. Frank, Pony Ballet
(*Music by* Ludwig Engländer.)

Scene 3
"The Orchid Ballet"
(*Music by* Reginald DeKoven.)

---

[102]Reconstructed version had much the same cast with the following changes: *Willie Bullion*: JULIUS STEGER. *Sherlock Holmes*: JOSEPH C. MIRON. *Senator Tim Sullivan*: Frank Ahearn. *Flameberg*: Ferdinand Payton. *Putzelschitzer*: Abner Symons. *Shamrockmeyer*: George Courtney. *John Storm*: Archie Gillis. *Viola Alum*: LOTTIE MEDLEY. *Spirit of Mischief*: Violet Hollis. *The Girl from Maxim's*: TRIXIE FRIGANZA. *Endymion*: LOUISE HARLOW. *Kitty Lorraine*: LOUISE HARLOW. *Punch Sloan*: BEATRICE LIDDELL. (*Continuous Proctor, Jimmy Donohue, Prairie Dog Pete, Whaley, McCue, Mr. McGovern, Mlle. Fifi* dropped.) Additional songs changes:
Coon Song
F. Templeton
Travesty of "The Tyranny of Tears"
F. Templeton
"Be Aisy"
M. Cline
Irish-Spanish Song
M. Cline
"La Masseuse"
E. Fougère
Sea Song with hornpipe
Ponies
English Music Hall song
Eight Mascottes
Sleigh Bell Dance
Eight Mascottes

[103]Interpolated per published sheet music:
"The Boy I Love!"
C. MacDonlad
(*Music by* Gustave Kerker. *Lyrics by* Stanislaus Stange and Louis Harrison.)

"Perhaps I Will, Perhaps I Won't"
L. Freear, L. Wesley
"The Man in the Moon"
J. E. Henshaw
(*Music by* Ludwig Engländer.)
Animation of Diana
(*Music by* Ludwig Engländer.)
Finale
Principals, Ensemble
(*Music by* Gustave Kerker.)

ACT 2[104]

Scene 1

"My Sunday Girl"
C. MacDonald
(*Music by* Gustave Kerker.)
"How It Occurred"
J. E. Henshaw
(*Music by* Ludwig Engländer.)
"'E Didn't Know Exactly What to Say"
L. Freear
"Slumming on the River"
L. Wesley
(*Music by* Gustave Kerker.)
"In Spite of Puck and Judge"
S. Bernard, F. Hartman
(*Music by* Ludwig Engländer.)
"The Telephone Fighters"
J. C. Miron, J. Kelly, L. Wesley
(*Music by* Gustave Kerker.)
"Billy, You're Off Again"
W. Jones
(*Music by* Gustave Kerker.)
"The Timothy D. Sullivan Chowder Party"
M. Dressler, Ensemble
(*Music by* Gustave Kerker.)

Scene 2

"The Husband-Hunters"
C. MacDonald, Leading Ladies
(*Music by* Gustave Kerker.)
"The Rebellious Leg"
S. Bernard
(*Music by* Gustave Kerker.)

Scene 3

"The Bellamy Dance"
Ensemble
(*Music by* Ludwig Engländer.)
"Ring dem Wedding Chimes"
M. Dressler, Ensemble
(*Music by* Gustave Kerker.)
"The Flat on the Opposite Side"
L. Freear
(*Music by* Gustave Kerker.)
"Ballet of the Four Seasons"/Finale
(*Music by* Ludwig Engländer.)

ACT 3

Grand Pageant and Review (The Genius of Freedom)
"Columbia" (New national anthem)
(*Music by* Reginald DeKoven.)

[104]On 15 May 1899 a travesty of the Empire Theatre's production of Shakespeare's "Romeo and Juliet" was added to Scene 3, featuring Sam Bernard (Juliet), Marie Dressler (Romeo) and Walter Jones (Hackett Mercutio). Also added:
"Rastus Surely Loves Me Because He Say He Do" (Cakewalk)
M. Gehrue, C. Bruno
(*Music by* Fred Solomon. *Lyrics by* George Waugh Arnold.)

1899.20 TRIAL BY JURY, or, Love and Duty

A Revival of the Dramatic Cantata (Comic Opera) in One Act[105], (following Rossini's "The Barber of Seville"). Libretto by William S. Gilbert. Music by Arthur Sullivan. Stage director, Edward P. Temple. Musical director, Adolph Liesegang. Produced by the Castle Square Opera Company (Henry W. Savage, Proprietor). Opened 24 April 1899 at the American Theatre and closed 29 April 1899 after 8 performances.

CAST: *Judge*: EDWARD P. TEMPLE. *Usher*: H. L. Butler. *Defendant*: CLINTON ELDER. *Counsel*: HARRY LUCKSTONE. *Foreman*: S. H. Ford. *Plaintiff*: LIZZIE MACNICHOL.

1899.21 AN ARABIAN GIRL AND 40 THIEVES

An Entertainment (Musical Comedy) in Four Acts, 8 Scenes. Libretto by J. Cheever Goodwin. Based upon the story of 1001 Nights. Music by W. H. Batchelor, John J. Braham, Jessie Williams, Myer Lutz. Produced (staged) by Julian Mitchell. Settings and mechanical effects invented and designed by Fred Dangerfield, painted by Fred Dangerfield, Henry E. Hoyt, Frank Rafter, D. Frank Dodge. Costumes by Will R. Barnes, Howard Russell. Electrical effects by John Welch. Ballets arranged by Filiberto Marchetti. Orchestral direction, John J. Braham. Produced by David Henderson. Opened 29 April 1899 at the Herald Square Theatre and closed 27 May 1899 after 33 performances.

CAST: *Ali Baba*, a poor woodcutter, formerly a member of Bagdad's 400, but now in very hard luck: DOROTHY MORTON. *Morgiana*, a slave girl, the only property now owned by Ali Baba, which property is in love with the owner: CLARA LANE. *Nicotina Zaza*, the leading female vaudevillian of the Caliph's troupe of mountebanks in love with her art: BLANCHE CHAPMAN. *Ganem*, the post-boy of Bagdad, Ali Baba's intimate friend: FRANKIE RAYMOND. *Abdallah*, captain of the Forty Thieves, a distingué young criminal, and leader in kleptomaniac society: MAUD GILBERT. *Hassan*, his aide-de-camp, a dashing young Communist, who enjoys life with his ill-gotten gains: Amalia Karle. *Zamora*, daughter of Araby Gorrah, in love with Ganem, whose suit does not fit papa: Agnes Paul. *Cassim D'Artagnan*, Ali Baba's brother, a vagabond; the world owes him a living, which he collects: EDDIE FOY. *Arraby Gorrah*, chief of the Bagdad police, and conservator of the city's morality; professor of purloining; tutor of the Forty Thieves in crime: J. K. MURRAY. *Hackaback*, brief but bold, a vaudevillian: Johnny Page. *Alibazan*, the best Caliph Bagdad ever had, elected on the platform: "The Forty Thieves must go!" As the platform does not go, he afterwards assumes the role of policeman and cobbler of Bagdad: JOSEPH DONER. *Akour*, a cobbler: Joseph Ratcliff. *Amineh*, *Seraphina*, dancing girls belonging to the Caliph's seraglio: Marie Lachere, Ruth Ralston. *Ali Bab'as Donkey*: George Ali. *A Lion*: Beni. *Menah*: Gladys Lester. *Mestour*: Pearl Livingston. *Veramah*, *Backsheesh*, *Sequin*, officers of the band: Grace D'Arvigne, June Dale, Jeannette Ivel. *Salaam*: Marie Bregnazzi. *Minaret*: Estelle Hoyt. *Raschid*: Ollie Cook. *Mustapha*: William Farbeau. *Oriental Watchmen and Members of Arraby Gorrah's Staff* (8): *Bismillah*: J. H. Plunkett. *Aleikum*: Sully Guard. *Abuben*: Zack Gilbert. *Adhem*: H. O. Crane. *Haroun*: R. Marsh. *Alieka*: William Scott. *Muza*: Julian Walsh. *Abreka*: George Roland. *Al Raschid*: W. M. Neil.

Dancers: Misses F. Ellis, Henrietta Rosche, Julie Praeger, Louise See, Ella Ringquest, Nellie Weston, C. Persione, Hettie Rigo, Minnie Murray, H. Konrath, G. Dauble, Kitty Lynch, Lillian Sterling, Clara Street, Josie Kirke, J. Dingham, May Deyo, Kathie Dameling, Nellie Simmons, Anni Mulvihill, Gladys Blake, Josie Devere, Fannie Quick, Conchita Ruiz, Emma Praeger, Daisy Beni, Matti Martini, T. Dingham, Phyllis Lehman, Lizzie Hacrow, Norah Ross, Josie Graham, E. Doner, Emily Russell, M. Edgerly, Catherine Bartho (Premiere Danseuse) Fannie Baldwin, Marcil and Omet.

Act 1: Public square of Bagdad, on the heights, overlooking the city.

Act 2, Scene 1: Ali Baba's humble home. *Scene 2*: Panorama through the wood. *Scene 3*: Exterior of the Cave. Enchanted forest of falling water.

Act 3, Scene 1: Exterior of the Caliph's Palace. *Scene 2*: Interior of the Cave of Forty Thieves. Illuminated Cavern of Coins.

Act 4, Scene 1: Street in Bagdad. *Scene 2*: The Garden of the Dolphins.

ACT 1[106]

[105]First presented in New York 15 November 1875 at the Eagle Theatre for 8 performances. For Synopsis of Scenes and Musical Numbers, see original 1875 production.

[106]Interpolated, as per published sheet music:
"Honey, You'se My Turtle Dove"
D. Morton
(*Music by* W. T. Francis. *Lyrics by* E. Smith.)

Opening Chorus
Entrance of Ganem
"Detectives Bold" (Song)
J. K. Murray, Chorus
"Dashing Militaire" (Duet)
D. Morton, C. Lane
Procession of citizens, slaves, nobles, peasants, dancers
Entrance of Abdallah and Hassan
"Hail to the Caliph" (Grand Chorus)
Danse Egyptienne
Misses F. Ellis, H. Rosche, J. Praeger, L. See, E. Ringquest, N. Weston, Persione, H. Rigo, M. Murray, Konrath, Dauble, Omet.
Entrance of the Caliph
"An Honest Man" (Song)
Alizaban's select troupe of vaudevillians
"Operatic Mountebanks" (Duet)
B. Chapman, J. Page
Entrance of Cassim D'Artagnan (Song)
"Song of the Forty Thieves" (Forty Gallant Thieves Are We)
"Let's Away" (Finale)

ACT 2
Scene 1
"I'm a Little Lady" (Song)
C. Lane
Trio
J. Doner, C. Lane, G. Ali
"To the Cave Away" (Quartette)
D. Morton, C. Lane, F. Raymond, A. Paul
"Virginia Skedaddle"
Scene 3
"Forty Gallant Thieves Are We" (reprise)
Chorus
"Open Sesame"
"Combat Chorus"
Danse Diabolique
Misses C. Street, N. Ross, M. Martien, L. Sterling, G. Balke, F. Quick, A. Mulvehill, E. Praeger, D. Beni, C. Ruiz, Kittie Lynch, J. Dignam.

ACT 3
Scene 1
"We Are the Band"
"Sunshine of Love" (Song)
D. Morton
Scene 2
Drinking Chorus
Grand Ballet Orientale
The Frunga
Misses K. Lynch, L. Stering, C. Street, J. Kirke, J. Dignam, Marcell
The Murgian
Misses M. Deyo, K. Dameling, N. Simons, A. Mulvihill, G. Blake, J. Devere
The Almazor
Misses F. Quick, C. Ruiz, E. Praeger, D. Beni, M. Martini, T. Dignam
The Zid-El-Mar
Misses P. Lehman, L. Hacrow, N. Ross, J. Graham, E. Donner, G. Dauble
The Sormutt
Misses J. Praeger, H. Rigo, E. Russell, M. Murray, M. Edgerly, H. Konrath
The Kadiya
Misses N. Weston, H. Rosche, E. Ringquest, L. See, F. Baldwin, C. Persione
Danse Classique
C. Bartho
Danse Fantasique
J. Praeger

"Memories"
D. Morton
(*Music and Lyrics by* Louise Tunison.)

Grand Ensemble
Finale

ACT 4
Scene 1
"Cobblers We" (Opening Chorus)
"The Wedding Bells" (Song and Chorus)
F. Raymond
"Pictures" (Duet)
E. Foy, B. Chapman
"Sweet William" (Song)
J. K. Murray, Chorus
Scene 2
"Orb Divine" (Duet)
D. Morton, J. K. Murray, Chorus
The Pickaninny Dance
"The Hoo-doo-doo-doo-Man"
D. Morton, E. Foy, Chorus

1899.22 MOTHER GOOSE

A Musical Extravaganza in Three Acts. Libretto by Edgar Smith and Louis deLange. Music by Frederick Gagel and Frederick Eustis. Production staged by Max Freeman. Costumes by Simpson, Crawford and Simpson; Mme. Dowling; Frank Hayden. Augmented orchestra under the direction of J. E. Nicol. Produced by Junius Howe. Opened 1 May 1899 at the 14th Street Theatre and closed ?13 May 1899 after 10? performances.

CAST: *The Knave of Hearts*, known to the world as Jack Horner. A youngster of winning ways. He began life by stealing his mother's tarts, then as Jack Horner stole plums from the Christmas Pie, then stole Little Bo-Peep's heart, and then stole away. He would have been arrested, but he proved at the right moment that he was of royal blood, and was therefore nothing more nor less than the original kleptomaniac: OLIVE REDPATH. *Little Boy Blue*, always blowing his own horn. Jack's hated and unsuccessful rival. He is not the last unsuccessful candidate that is continually blowing his own horn: KITTY MITCHELL. *Simple Simon*, who doesn't know enough to come in when it rains (rainy weather is the best time for fishing). He uses his skull to grow a face and hair on, and for no other purpose: Willard Simms. *Jack*, a partner of Jill: ARNOLD KIRALFY. *The King's Herald*, a disseminator of the latest news: Olga Lambert. *Tom Tom*, the Piper's son. The original pork packer—continually running into debt: Eugene Clowes. *Jack Sprat*, anti-fattist. A mean, miserable, miserly misogynist: James Horan. *Tommy Tucker*, the Jean de Reszke of nursery rhymes: Jennie Graham. *Rags*, a beggar: Eugene Sheldon. *Bunco Pete*: Eugene Sheldon. *A. Pieman*, the Delmonico of Banbury Cross: Frank Lynden. *Greedy*: Edward Mullaney. *Slow*: Arthur Connelly. *Baby Bunting*: Little Hazel Kirke Clarke. *First Fakir*: Charles Thaw. *Second Fakir*: William B. Atwood. *Peter Piper*, the pepper-picker, the symphony orchestra of the army. He is not the Pied Piper of Hamelin, and is not the paid piper of the army, as salary has been in arrears for a long time: ALEXANDER CLARK. *King Cophetua*, otherwise known as the "King of Hearts," who , when the Queen of Hearts died and the Knave of Hearts ran away, tired of the game with the Court Suit, and fain would play "Beggar Thy Neighbor" if he could only find the right beggar maid: HUBERT WILKE. *Mother Goose*, principal of the best (and only) school in Banbury Cross, with journalistic inclinations. The oldest known lady journalist: FRANK BLAIR. *Little Sally Waters*, a mystery. Why did she remain young so long? The only recognized beggar in the Kingdom of Nowhere: Jessie Villars. *Mrs. Jack Sprat*, a plump little dumpling of a woman, with highly tidy habits. When she wasn't licking the platter she was licking Bo-Peep: IDA MULLE. *Goody Two Shoes*, not too goody, just two shoes: Countess OLGA VON HATZFELDT. *Jill*, a partner of Jack: Dora Lambert. *Margery Daw*: Grace Cannon. *Little Red Riding Hood*, a wolf-feeder: Avis Folger. *Mother Goose's Musical Pupils*: Violetta Beasley, Jennie Beasley, Butterfly Beasley, Mayflower Beasley. *Little Bo-Peep*, a sweet little, dear little, careless little shepherdess, who lost her sheep on a bet. Though apparently a loser, she really was a winner, as every boy in the neighborhood could tell you: MARIE CELESTE. *Vivandiers, Coryphees, Peasants, Schoolgirls, Nursery Maids, Mothers, Grandmothers, and Maiden Aunts.*

Act 1: The village of Banbury Cross, in the Kingdom of Nowhere.

Act 2: Mother Goose's schoolroom, showing girls' dormitory.

Act 3: Banbury Fair grounds.

ACT 1[107]
"Mother Goose" (March)
(*Music by* Frederick Gagel.)

---

[107]Interpolated, as per published sheet music:
"I Won't Do Your Washin' Any More"
O. Redpath
(*Music by* Frederick Gagel. *Lyrics by* Jean C. Havez.)

"School is Out" (Opening Chorus)
(*Music by* Frederick Eustis.)
"Jack and Jill" (Ensemble)
(*Music by* Frederick Gagel.)
"Bo-Peep" (Tales of Mother Goose)(Song)
(*Music by* Frederick Eustis. *Lyrics by* George Bowles.)
"Bag Pipe" (Song)
(*Music by* Frederick Gagel.)
"Shine On, Bright Sunlight" (Quintette)
(*Music by* Frederick Eustis.)
"One Little Girl I Know" (Song)
(*Music by* Frederick Gagel.)
Ensemble
(*Music by* Frederick Eustis.)
Finale
(*Music by* Frederick Gagel.)

ACT 2
"Nursery Melodies" (Opening Chorus)
(*Music by* Frederick Gagel.)
"Little Bo-Peep" (Song)
(*Music by* Frederick Eustis.)
"Scare Crow" (Song)
(*Music by* Frederick Eustis.)
Ensemble
(*Music by* Frederick Eustis.)
"Darling, My Darling" (Duet)
(*Music by* Frederick Eustis.)
"At the Vaudeville Show" (Duet)
(*Music by* Frederick Gagel.)
Burlesque Overture
(*Music by* Frederick Gagel.)
Finale
(*Music by* Frederick Gagel.)

ACT 3
Opening Chorus
(*Music by* Frederick Eustis.)
"From the Philippines We Come" (Ensemble)
(*Music by* Frederick Gagel.)
"(Ma) Belle of the Philippines"
(*Music by* Frederick Gagel.)
Finale
(*Music by* Frederick Gagel.)

1899.23

ADONIS

A Revival of the Fascinating Burlesque in Two Acts, 6 Scenes[108]. Libretto by Edward E. Rice and William Gill[109] Original music by Edward E. Rice. (Selected music 'cheerfully contributed by Beethoven, Audran, Suppé, Planquette, Offenbach, Strauss, Mozart, Haydn, Dave Braham, John Eller, Henry Sator and many others too numerous to individualize.') Stage director, Charles Seagraves. Musical director, Henry Sator. Produced by Henry E. Dixey. Opened 9 May 1899 at the Bijou Theatre and closed 20 May 1899 after 15 performances[110].

CAST: *Adonis*, an accomplished young gentleman of undeniably good family, whose name, by the way, is Marble, and who, to avoid serious complications, is obliged during the action of the piece to assume the following disguises: HENRY E. DIXEY, as *Henry Irving* (with song, "It's English, You Know"), *Pepita Petticoat* (with recitations), *Wilson Barrett* (as Clito), *Gussie Gervaise* (a dry goods clerk who sells), *Quinine Quilt* (a druggist who drugs), *Moses Moss* (a clothing merchant who clothes), *Dempsey Brown* (a model barber who barbs).

Marquis de Baccarat, a highly polished villain. It is well to describe his character, as no one would think it to look at him: Sydney DeGrey. Bunion Turke, afther of Rosetta, an unblushing appropriator of the stock in trade of a well-known and worthy histrionic old miller: EDWARD CHAPMAN. Talamea, a sculptress, who like most of her sex, is in love with her own creation: Ruth White. Artea, a goddess, patroness of the fine arts: Hilda Hollins. Duchess of Area, aesthetic to the verge of eccentricity, rich to the verge of millionarism, sentimental to the verge of gush: Bessie Fairbairn. Four Daughters of the Duchess: Lady Nattie: Therese Renold. Lady Hattie: Maud Francis. Lady Mattie: Gracie Cannon. Lady Pattie: Adele Francis. Timmins: Thomas Kiernan. Miss Doolittle: May Engleman. Gladys Needlework: Julie Durya. Susie Mangle: Julie Glover. Poor Blind Man: Bob Watson. Mr. Nervine, who believes in shaving himself: Harry Earl. Mr. Skinner: J. Wallace Black. Miss Perkins: Helen Davidge. Rosetta: AMELIA SUMMERVILLE.

Excelsior Quartette: J. Wallace Black, Harry Earle, Harry Amberg, George Wallace. *The Little Four*: John Coughlin, James Kiernan, Robert Watson, W. B. Fordham. *The Original Tigers*: Walter Long, Oliver Howe, James Carroll, Gillie Gregory, Thomas McGuire, Thomas Kiernan.

1899.24

ERMINIE

A Revival of the Comic Opera in Three Acts[111]. Libretto by Harry Paulton (and Claxson Bellamy). Based on the melodrama ("L'Auberge des Adrets" by Benjamin Antier, Saint-Amand and Paulyanthe, adapted into English as) "Robert Macaire." Music by Edward Jakobowski. Staged by Max Freeman. Settings designed by Homer Emens, Richard Marston. Costumes designed by Percy Anderson. Director of Music, John McGhie. Produced by Francis Wilson Company (Francis Wilson, Samuel F. Nixon & J. Fred Zimmerman, Proprietors; Ariel Barney, Manager). Opened 9 May 1899 at the Casino Theatre and closed 3 June 1898 after 25 performances.

CAST: *Erminie*: LILLIAN RUSSELL. *Javotte*: LULU GLASER. *Cerise*: JOSEPHINE KNAPP. *Princess de Gramponeur*: JENNIE WEATHERSBY. *Marie*: Miriam Lawrence. *Captain Delaunay*: MATHILDE PREVILLE. *Cadeaux, Ravennes*, two thieves: FRANCIS X. WILSON, THOMAS Q. SEABROOKE. *Eugene Marcel*: Clinton Elder. *Chevalier de Brabazon*: MAX FREEMAN. *Marquis de Ponvert*: W. T. Carleton. *Dufois*: Murry Woods. *Simon*: Edmund Lawrence. *Vicomte de Brissac*: Charles H. Bowers. *Sergeant*: Joseph Chaillee. *Benedict*: E. B. Knight.

Act 1: Inn at Ponvert. (Emens.)

Act 2: The Pink Ball Room of Chateau Ponvert. (Marston.)

Act 3: Corridor and staircase of same. (Marston.)

108First produced in New York 4 September 1884 at the Bijou Theatre for 603 performances. Interpolated in this revival as per published sheet music:
"She Was Bred in Old Virginia"
R. White
(*Music by* Robert E. Whittemore. *Lyrics by* J. Vickery Langhorne.)

109Original production credited William Gill as Rice's collaborator, but most subsequent productions credited Dixey as co-author.

110Settings, costumes uncredited. Dixey recreated his original role.

111First produced in New York 10 May 1886 at the Casino Theatre for 648 performances in a series of three engagements. For Synopsis of Scenes and Musical Numbers, see original 1886 production.

1899–1900 SEASON

Lillian Russell in WHIRL-I-GIG (Photo: Falk)
Billy Rose Theatre Collection, New York Public Library for the Performing Arts

1899–1900 SEASON

1899.25 THE ROUNDERS

A Vaudeville (Musical Comedy) in Three Acts, 4 Scenes. Book and lyrics by Harry B. Smith. Based on the libretto to "Les Fêtards" by Antony Mars and Maurice Hennequin[1]. Music by Ludwig Engländer. Staged by Max Freeman. Scenes by D. Frank Dodge. Costumes by Mmes. Ripley and Caughley. Musical director, Antonio DeNovellis. Produced by George W. Lederer. Opened 12 July 1899 at the Casino Theatre and closed 14 October 1899 after 97 performances.

CAST: *Duke du Paty de Clam*, who has tried everything and found nothing in it: DAN DALY. *Marquis de Bacarat*, the moth for whom Thea is the flame: HARRY DAVENPORT. *Siegfried Gotterdammerung*, leader of a German Street Band: JOSEPH CAWTHORN. *A First Nighter*: Frederick Urban. *Joseph*, Head Waiter in the Hotel Royal Biarritz: MAX FREEMAN. *Maginnis Pasha*, an Irish Turk: THOMAS Q. SEABROOKE. *Priscilla*, wife of the Marquis, an American Girl belonging to a worthy family of Quakers: MABELLE GILMAN. *Stella Giltedge*, an up-to-date American Girl: MARIE GEORGE. *Madame Seraphine*, Thea's "mother": CARRIE PERKINS. *La Paloma*, a Spanish Belle: CRISSIE CARLISLE. *Angelique*, an innocent: IRENE BENTLEY. *Adele Vere de Vere*, a type of English beauty: SUSIE DRAKE. *Fanchonette*, a little Parisienne: MARGARET WARREN. *Jolivet*, a young reporter: Eva Kelly. *Ladies of the Ballet (5)*: *Florentine*: Nella Webb. *Olympe*: Avis Folger. *Celestine*: Mabel Russell. *Octavine*: Cora Leslie. *Rosine*: Pauline Chase. *Raoul*: Grace Spencer. *Swells, Patrons of the Ballet (3)*: *Gaston*: Ida Rock. *Honore*: Seline Say. *Gustave*: Harry Clifford. *Call Boy*: Zella Frank. *Schlitz*, leading cornetist: Sol Solomon. *Members of Siegfried's Band (5)*: *Fritz*: Arthur Etherington. *Blitz*: Joseph Kane. *Snitz*: Tom Collins. *Litz*: Horace Hayne. *Ritz*: Gustave Key. *The Bathing Master*: Henri Chaille. *Thea*, a dancer, and mistress to the Marquis: PHYLLIS RANKIN.

Act 1: The Beach at Biarritz by the Hotel Royal.

Act 2, Scene 1: The Star Dressing Room of a Theatre in Paris. *Scene 2*: Salon at Maginnis Pasha's House in Paris.

Act 3: Corridor of the Hotel de Lusignan, Paris.

ACT 1[2]

Opening Chorus (Here we gather ev'ry summer)
"They Play Those Marches, They Play Those Waltzes"
J. Cawthorn, Chorus, Street Band
Chorus for Entrance of Duke de Baccarat
"In Philadelphia"
M. Gilman, Chorus
"We're Adding Local Color" (Trio)
M. George, D. Daly, H. Davenport
"Life Is a Toyshop" (Duet)
M. Gilman, H. Davenport
Entrance of Maginnis Pasha
"Only a Hundred Girls (in the World for Me)"
T. Q. Seabrooke
Finale
Chorus, Principals

ACT 2

Opening Chorus (Fair Gitana tell us what the cards say)
"Same Old Story, Nothing New"
D. Daly
"De Stories Uncle Remus Tells"
M. George, Chorus
"Oh, Where Is Dancer" (Ensemble and Song)
P. Rankin, Chorus
"When You Know These Men" (Song and Duet)
M. Gilman, P. Rankin
Finale
Chorus, Principals

[1]The original French musical score by Victor Roger was discarded in lieu of an entirely new American score by Ludwig Engländer.

[2]Musical numbers not listed in programs. Song list prepared from published vocal score (Edward Schuberth & Co., New York, 1899). Interpolated, as per published sheet music:
"Love Letters" (from IN GAY PAREE)
(*Music by* Ludwig Engländer. *Lyrics by* Grant Stewart.)

"Object Matrimony" (Trio)
M. Gilman, P. Rankin, D. Daly

ACT 3

"She Didn't Understand"
M. George
"The Rounders' Song" (Trio)
D. Daly, H. Davenport, T. Q. Seabrooke
Finale
Chorus, Principals

1899.26 THE MAID IN THE MOON

A Burlesque in One Act, 3 Scenes, preceded by a vaudeville program. Libretto by Richard Carle. Music by Frederic Solomon. Ballet by H. Fletcher Rivers. Produced under the stage direction of Edward E. Rice. Produced by Edward E. Rice. Opened 31 July 1899 at the Casino Roof Garden and closed 2 September 1899 after 30 performances.

CAST: *Luna*: Ruth White. *Sherlock Bernard Doyle*: Gilbert Gregory. *Louie Freak*: JOHN C. SLAVIN. *Richard Choker*: CHARLES KIRKE. *Victor Hendlestein*: CHARLES KIRKE. *Manager Ice*: RICHARD CARLE. *Englander Kerker DeKoven*: RICHARD CARLE. *Harrison Stange*: LEE HARRISON. *Spirit of Mischief*: HARRY KELLY. *Waiter*: William Gould. *Lawyer Hoss*: Lionel Lawrence. *Piano Forte*: Will Dunlay. *The Three Fire Brothers*: Lee Harrison, William Gould, Lionel Lawrence. *Fraud Sloan*: Gladys Van. *Married Wrestler*: Edward Begley. *Carrie Off*: Olive Wallace. *Maudie Mince*: Annabelle Moore. *Roof Garden Habituées, waiters, policemen, toughs, etc.*: Emma Leslie, Kathryn Powell, Amy Ashmore, Marie Lachere, Sadie Nelson, Marie Seville, Joe Lanswell, Anna Archer, Teresa Downing, Julia Levine, Vic Brinkley, Mary Gibson.

Scene 1: Madison Square Garden. *Scene 2*: Exterior New York City. *Scene 3*: Rooms of the Mazet Committee.

VAUDEVILLE

Rice's "March of the Amazons;" Gladys Van (soubrette); Annabelle Moore; Richard English (walking act); Christine Blessing (German dialect songs); Rice's Cornstalk Novelty; Ruth White; Amorita (dancer); Maude Courtney (old time songs); Richard Carle's travesty of "Way Down East" entitled WAY UP EAST with the following cast: *Squire Bartlett Pears*: William P. Sprague. *Louise Bartlett Pears*: LEE HARRISON. *David Bartlett Pears*: William Gould. *Rube Whiffletree*: HARRY KELLY. *Lenox Lyceum*: RICHARD CARLE. *Ann Moore Besides*: Edward Begley.

BURLESQUE[3]

Burlesque on Cissie Loftus
E. Begley
Imitation of Sam Bernard
G. Gregory
"Reckless Reddy"
O. Wallace
Song
J. C. Slavin, Quartette
Song
R. White
Ballet of the Four Seasons (Ballet)

1899.27 THE LAST OF THE ROHANS

A Romantic Irish Drama in Three Acts, 5 Scenes. Play by Ramsay Morris. Songs by Andrew Mack. Produced under the stage direction of Joseph Humphries. Settings by Joseph Physioc. Costumes by Maurice Hermann. Incidental music arranged by John C. Sorg; musical director, John C. Sorg. Produced by Andrew Mack (Isaac B. Rich & William Harris, Management). Opened 31 August 1899 at the Academy of Music and closed 7 October 1899 after 45 performances.[4]

CAST: *Clifford Rohan*, known as Clifford Carew, the heir: ANDREW MACK. *Squire Kerrigan*, the tenant of Castle Rohan: B. T. RINGGOLD. *Neil McNeil*, a bird of prey: Edwin Brandt. *Father Bernard*, of the St. Anthony's Monastery: GEORGE W. DEYO. *Neddy Larey*, a blind basket maker: Ernest E. Warde. *McCarthy*, servant at Castle: James Vincent. *Bristle*, a wandering vagabond: W. J. Mason. *Kelly*, Bristle's companion: Thomas E. Jackson. *Brother Hugh, Brother John*, of St. Anthony's Monastery: John Vance, Harry Sutter. *Tim*: Himself. *Mary Lee*, the mistess of Castle Rohan:

[3]No program available. Not in performance order.

[4]Played a return engagement 30 April 1900 at the Metropolis for 8 performances.

JOSEPHINE LOVETT. *Cauth*, a wandering prophetess: Mrs. SAMUEL CHARLES. *Sheila*, a child, Cauth's companion: Georgia Olp. *Rosie Bantry*, servant at Castle: Jennie Satterlee. *Monks, Peasants, Beggars, etc.*

The action takes places in Ireland in 1812.

Act 1: A summer morning in the courtyard of Castle Rohan.

Act 2: Same as Act 1. Two months later. Halloween.

Act 3, Scene 1: The ruined chapel of St. Finbar's just before midnight. Halloween. *Scene 2*: Road to the Castle. *Scene 3*: Grand Hall at Castle Rohan. One hour later.

MUSICAL NUMBERS

"Pat and His Pipes" (Act 1)
A. Mack

"Grandmother's Songs" (Act 2)
A. Mack

"The Story of the Rose" (Heart of My Heart I Love You)(Act 2)
A. Mack
(*Lyrics by* "Alice.")

"Jack O'Lantern Song" (Act 3)
A. Mack

1899.28 CYRANO DE BERGERAC

A Comic Opera in Three Acts. Book by Stuart Reed. Based on the play of the same name by Edmond Rostand. Music by Victor Herbert. Lyrics by Harry B. Smith. Staged by A. M. Holbrook. Scenery by Richard Marston. Costumes designed by Percy Anderson. Orchestra under the direction of John McGhie. Produced by Francis Wilson Opera Company (Francis Wilson, [Sam] Nixon & [J. F.] Zimmerman, Proprietors), under management of Ariel Barney. Opened 18 September 1899 at the Knickerbocker Theatre and closed 14 October 1899 after 28 performances.

CAST: *Cyrano de Bergerac*, a soldier of fortune: FRANCIS WILSON. *Christian de Neuvillette*, of the Cadets of Gascony: CHARLES H. BOWERS. *Ragueneau*, pastrycook, devoted to the muses: PETER LANG. *Captain Castel-Jaloux*, Commander, Cadets of Gascony: JOHN E. BRAND. *Count de Guiche*, Christian's rival: ROBERT BRODERICK. *Montfleury*, an actor of the company of the Hotel de Bourgogne: A. M. HOLBROOK. *A Friar*: A. M. HOLBROOK. *A Captain of the Musketeers*: Joseph M. Ratliff. *Roxane*, Cyrano's cousin: LULU GLASER. *Lise*, wife of Ragueneau: JOSEPHINE KNAPP. *Duenna*: JOSEPHINE [Josie] INTROPODI. *An Actress* of the company of the Hotel de Bourgogne: Bessie Howard. *An Actor* of the same company: F. S. Heck. *A Young Lord*: William Laverty. *A Doorkeeper*: Charles F. Dodge. *A Pickpocket*: Frank Scott. *First Cadet*: Bessie Howard. *Second Cadet*: Stella Koetter. *Third Cadet*: Martha Stein. *First Poet*: Karl Stall. *Second Poet*: Thomas deVassey. *Third Poet*: H. L. Owen. *Page*: Clara Hollywood. *First Cook's Boy*: Lotta Watson. *Second Cook's Boy*: Laura Wise. *Musketeers*: F. S. Heck, Carl King, H. L. Owen, Karl Stall.

Act 1: Hall of the Hotel Bourgogne.

Act 2: Interior of Ragueneau's Cook and Pastry Shop.

Act 3: Exterior of castle and fortress on outskirts of Aras. (The French camp.)

ACT 1[5]

Opening Chorus (The clock is on the stroke of eight)
Chorus (First, Second, Third, Fourth Cavaliers, Citizen, Flower Girl, First Actor)

"Come the Gallants of the Court" (Chorus of Cavaliers)
Male Chorus

"I Am a Court Coquette" (Song)
L. Glaser, Male Chorus

"I Come from Gascony" (Song)
F. Wilson, Chorus

"I Must Marry a Handsome Man" (Duet)
F. Wilson, L. Glaser

"The King's Musketeers" (Combat Chorus and Solo)
C. H. Bowers, R. Broderick, F. Wilson, Chorus

"Since I Am Not for Thee" (Trio)
L. Glaser, F. Wilson, C. H. Bowers

Finale
L. Glaser, C. H. Bowers, F. Wilson, J. M. Ratliff, Chorus

ACT 2

"In Ragueneau's Cafe" (Opening Chorus)
J. Knapp, Chorus

"Chorus of Poets"
P. Lang, K. Stall, J. Knapp, Chorus

"Song of the Nose"
F. Wilson, Chorus

"Cadets of Gascony" (Song)
J. E. Brand, Chorus

"I Wonder" (Cupid Song)(Waltz Song)
L. Glaser

Finale
L. Glaser, J. Knapp, F. Wilson, C. H. Bowers, J. E. Brand, Cadets, Chorus

ACT 3

"In Bivouac Reposing" (Opening Chorus)
Male Chorus

"Diplomacy" (Song)
F. Wilson, Chorus

"Over the Mountains" (Song)
L. Glaser, Chorus

"'Neath Thy Window" (Serenade)
J. E. Brand, Chorus

"Let the Sun of Thine Eyes" (Trio)
F. Wilson, C. H. Bowers, L. Glaser

Finale
F. Wilson, Full Ensemble

1899.29 (THE ROGERS BROTHERS) IN WALL STREET

A Vaudeville Farce with Music in Three Acts[6]. Book by John J. McNally. Music by Maurice Levi. Lyrics by Richard Carle. Scenery designed by Gates and Morange, Joseph Physioc. Costumes by F. Richard Anderson. Musical director, Maurice Levi. Produced by (Marc) Klaw & (Abraham L.) Erlanger. Opened 18 September 1899 at Hammerstein's Victoria Theatre and closed 30 December 1899 after 108 performances[7].

CAST: *Leo Schwartz, Fritz Weiss*, owners of "The Little Donkey": GUS ROGERS, MAX ROGERS. *Terrence Rafferty*, rich and eccentric: JOHN G. SPARKS. *Otto Winne*, a promoter: ROSS SNOW. *Regi Maitwell*, in love with Patrice: *Stillman Hunt*, a detective: LEE HARRISON. *Mike Scrapwell*: Peter Curley. *Jim Bunns*: Willie Torpey. *Policeman B. Hinde*: Albert Froome. *Purchase Short*: Harry Brown. *Georgette Jollier*: GEORGIA CAINE. *Letta Winne*, Otto Winne's daughter: MAUDE RAYMOND. *Lotta Hintz*, a detective: ADA LEWIS. *Rafferty's Daughters (3)*: *Patrice Rafferty*: LOUISE GUNNING. *Carrie Rafferty*: JEANETTE BAGEARD. *Florence Rafferty*: Carolyn Elberts. *Blanche Winters*: Edith St. Clair. *Messenger Boys (4)*: *Willie Want*: Elsie Davis. *Arthur Snow*: Hattie Waters. *Andrew Flush*: Winnie Senett. *Adam Kidd*: Gertrude Saye. *Members of the Bronx Borough Ladies' Athletic Association (5)*: *Millie*: Rosita Rivera. *Tillie*: Marguerite Haviland. *Dillie*: Armandita Rivera. *Lillie*: May Taylor. *Collie*: Madge Pierce. *Guests, Waiters, Brokers, Customers, etc.*

Act 1: Manhattan Beach.

Act 2: Office of Winne & Company, Wall Street.

Act 3: Grounds surrounding Hollywood Hotel, Elberon.

ACT 1[8]

"On the Beach at Gay Manhattan" (Opening Chorus)

"The Promoter"
R. Snow, Full Chorus

"The Belle of Murray Hill"
L. Gunning, Full Chorus
(*Lyrics by* Willis Clark.)

Burlesque Opera

"Licorice Lize"
(*Music and Lyrics by* Richard Carle.)

"The Three Cops"
Rogers Brothers, M. Raymond

ACT 2

"In Wall Street" (Opening Chorus)

---

[5]Musical numbers not listed in programs. Song list prepared from published vocal score (M. Witmark & Sons, New York, 1899). Other number not in vocal score which may have been performed in New York: "Those Were the Good Old Times."

[6]The first in the annual series of musical comedies starring the Rogers Brothers continuing until Gus Rogers' death in 1908.

[7]Played a return engagement 26 February 1900 at the Grand Opera House for 8 performances.

[8]Interpolated during the run or subsequent tour, as per published sheet music:
"I Don't Care to Be Your Lady Friend No More"
(*Music by* Gus Edwards. *Lyrics by* Will D. Cobb.)

Ballad Selections
J. Parr
["You Are the Only Girl I'll Ever Care About"
(*Music by* Gus Edwards. *Lyrics by* Will D. Cobb.)]
"Gay Georgette"
G. Caine, Full Chorus
Sayings and Parodies
Rogers Brothers
"Athletic Girls"
M. Raymond, Full Chorus
"(Beware of) An Innocent Maid" (Always Happy)(Quartette)
J. Bageard, E. St. Clair, Rogers Brothers
"An Ethiopian Mardi Gras"
Full Company
(*Music by* Maurice Levi.)

ACT 3[9]
"At the Hollywood" (Opening Chorus)
"Busy Liz"
A. Lewis, Rogers Brothers
"The Summer Man"[10]
G. Caine, Messenger Boys, Ladies Athletic Association
Scotch Songs[11]
["To Day"
L. Gunning
(*Music and Lyrics by* Arthur Trevelyan.)]
Coon Songs
M. Raymond
["I Certainly Got My Man"
(*Music and Lyrics by* Arthur Dunn.
"You Told Me You Had Money in the Bank" (from BY THE SAD SEA WAVES)
(*Music by* Gustav Luders. *Lyrics by* J. Sherrie Mathews and Harry Bulger.)]
Finale
Full Company

1899.30 WHIRL-I-GIG

A Dramatic Conundrum in Two Guesses (Double Bill of Vaudeville and a Burlesque in Two Acts). Dialogue (book) by Edgar Smith. Music by John Stromberg. Lyrics by Harry B. Smith. Produced under the direction of Julian Mitchell. Scenery by John Young. Costumes designed by Will R. Barnes. Musical director, John Stromberg. Produced by (Joseph M.) Weber and (Lew M.) Fields. Opened 21 September 1899 at Weber and Fields' Music Hall and closed 5 May 1900 after 270 performances.

VAUDEVILLE
Ali and Beni (Egyptian Whirlwinds)
Fielding (Comic Juggler)

FIRST GUESS (ACT 1)

CAST: *Josh Boniface*, proprietor of the "Stars and Stripes," an hotel in the suburbs of Paris, during the Exposition: PETER F. DAILEY. *Sigmund Cohenski*, a wealthy Hebrew, and President of the Matzo Trust: DAVID WARFIELD. *Captain Kingsbridge*, of the United States Navy: CHARLES J. ROSS. *Herman Dillpickel*, inventor of the Flotsascope, a machine for throwing living pictures on the naked air: JOSEPH M. WEBER. *Wilhelm Hochderkaiser*, an architect, with the plans for a jail with all the comforts of home: LEW M. FIELDS. *Harold Gilhooly*, a gypsy king, with a trained bear: JOHN T. KELLY. *Bolivar*, the bear: George Ali. *Jacques, Francois, Adelbert, Andre*, porters: G. W. Thomas, Michael Renner, Walter West, Augustus Smith. *Mademoiselle Fifi Coocoo*, a Parisian, Queen of Bohemia: LILLIAN RUSSELL. *Uneeda Cohenski*, heiress to Cohenski's millions: Irene Perry. *Count Castellane, Countess Castellane*, with revolutionary ideas: Pearl Andrews, Ilma Pratt. *Captain Vivelarmee*: FRANKIE BAILEY. *Of the U.S. Navy (5)*: *Lieutenant Speedway*: Helen Dunbar. *Lieutenant Decke*: Florence Bell. *Ensign Turrett*: Frankie Bailey. *Ensign Binnacle*: Stella Grey. *Columbia, Shamrock*, friendly rivals: Allie Gilbert, Ilma Pratt. *Dauber*, an artist: Helen Dunbar. *Florette*: Minnie Poore. *Babette, Margot*, Bohemians: Bonnie Maginn, Allie Gilbert. *Banani, Peanutta*, gypsies: Grace Pierrepoint, May Cuthbert. *Chambermaids (4)*: *Marie*: Allie Gilbert. *Pierette*: Bonnie Maginn. *Annette*: Lena Hilbon. *Sylvia*: Belle Robinson. *Pierre, Jean*, bell-boys: Goldie Mohr, "Stubby" Ainscoe. *Henri, Francis*, waiters: May Edwards, Carrie May. *Dance Specialty ("De Sun Do Move")*: BESSIE CLAYTON.

Scene: Exterior of "Stars and Stripes" Hotel.

MUSICAL NUMBERS[12]
"Strike, Strike" (Chorus)
"Marie Antoinette" (March)
"(The) Kissing Bug" (Song)
P. F. Dailey
"Queen of Bohemia" (Ensemble and Song)
L. Russell
"Say You Love Me, Sue" (Song)
P. F. Dailey
"Old Glory" (Sailor Song)
C. Ross
"De Sun Do Move"[13] (Danse Eccentrique)
B. Clayton
"The Dancing Bear" (Finale)

SECOND GUESS (ACT 2)

THE GIRL FROM MARTIN'S, a bit of a fling at the Parisian Comedy Craze, (A Burlesque in One Act, 2 Scenes, suggested by the French farce "The Girl from Maxim's" by Georges Feydeau.) Closed 25 October 1899 after 40 performances.

CAST: *Praline*, an eminently proper young person, who gets into the wrong bed: LILLIAN RUSSELL. *Doctor Petitpois*, a rising young dentist with a taste for comical furniture: CHARLES J. ROSS. *General Petitpois*, the doctor's uncle, who has just run up from Africa for a few moments: PETER F. DAILEY. *Tarroller, Sarsaparilla*, looking for trouble: LEW M. FIELDS, JOSEPH M. WEBER. *The Duke de Swellfront*, a blasé youth of twenty: JOHN T. KELLY. *Fromage*, friend of Doctor Petitpois: DAVID WARFIELD. *Etienne*, valet to the doctor: G. W. Thomas. *Cementine*, the general's niece: Irene Perry. *Madame Petitpois*, addicted to spirits: Mabel Nichols. *Duchess de Swellfront*, mamma to the Duke: Lulu Nichols. *Madame Verabum*, the village dressmaker: Helen Dunbar. *Madame Vinordinaire*: Allie Gilbert. *Madame Sassibrat*: Bonnie Maginn. *Madame Gourmette*: May Edwards. *Madame Vincenti*: Minnie Poore. *Lieutenant Chambertin*: Frankie Bailey. *Lieutenant Cogniac*: Grace Pierrepont. *Lieutenant Medoc*. Florence Bell. *Guests, Officers, Children, etc.*

Scene 1: Office of Pettipois. *Scene 2*: The General's Villa at Tureen.

MUSICAL NUMBERS
Newsboys Quintette
"The (Little) Brunette Soubrette" (Chansonette)
L. Russell
Finale

THE OTHER WAY, a Burlesque of the Freeman Wills' play "The Only Way," replaced THE GIRL FROM MARTIN'S on 26 October 1899; it closed 6 December 1899 after 49 performances; this was then replaced 7 December 1899 by BARBARA FIDGETY, a Burlesque of the Clyde Fitch drama "Barbara Freitchie," closing 7 March 1900 after 107 performances, which was followed 8 March 1900 by SAPOLIO, a Burlesque of the Clyde Fitch drama "Sapho," for the last 9 weeks of the WHIRL-I-GIG run, 68 performances.

THE OTHER WAY, a bit of riotous nonsense, in which the following cast will take liberties with the immortal characters of Dickens (Burlesque in One Act, 3 Scenes).

CAST: *Kidney Tartun*, with a fatal resemblance: PETER F. DAILEY. *Charles Darnation*, otherwise the Marquis St. everybody: DAVID WARFIELD. *Mr. Sorry*, agent for Tellson's bank: DAVID WARFIELD. *Ernest de Fog*, with a brother's past: CHARLES J. ROSS. *Marquis de Balloon*, an aristocrat: JOSEPH M. WEBER.

---

[9]The Gavotte and "Dewey Two-Step" in Act 3 arranged (staged) by Mme. Malvina.

[10]Replaced for subsequent tour by:
"Walks and Talks"
G. Caine, Messenger Boys, Ladies Athletic Association

[11]Dropped for subsequent tour.

[12]The running order of songs was repeatedly revised during the run. Added were:
"King Gilhooly"
J. T. Kelly
(*Lyrics by* Edgar Smith.)
"In Paris Gay"
"If All the Stars Were Mine"
L. Russell
"Serenade of the Blue and the Grey" (Grand Ensemble)
"Tally Ho!" (Finale)

[13]Later in the run billed as "De Cake Walk Dream" which may be the same song.

President of Tribunal: JOSEPH M. WEBER. *Marquis de Fidget*, an aristocrat: LEW M. FIELDS. *Public Posecutor*: LEW M. FIELDS. *Doctor Manicure*: JOHN T. KELLY. *Sergeant*: Walter West. *A Soldier*: M. Renner. *Another*: George W. Thomas. *Another*: Augustus Smith. *The Vengeance*, a picturesque lady, addicted to knitting and giving it to aristocrats in the neck: LILLIAN RUSSELL. *Lucie Manicure*, Darnation's wife: Irene Perry. *A Citizeness*: Lulu Nichols. *A Citizen*: Ilma Pratt. *Another*: Belle Robinson. *Another*: May Edwards. *Another*: May Cuthbert. *Another*: Minnie Poore. *Another*: Grace Pierrepont. *Another*: Carrie May. *Jailer*: Leona Hilbon. *Duke de Marron Glacé*: Helen Dunbar. *Baron de Caramel*: Frankie Bailey. *Count de Trop*: Bonnie Maginn. *Marquis de Rigeur*: Allie Gilbert. *Count de Porozza*: "Stubby" Ainscoe. *Aristocrats, Citizens, Soldiers, Mob, etc.*

Scene 1: The Tribunal. *Scene 2*: Cell in La Conciergerie Prison. *Scene 3*: Hall in La Conciergerie Prison.

MUSICAL NUMBERS

"We're the Mob Erratic" (Chorus)

"Come Along" (Trio)

"I'm a Humorist" (Laughing Song)

"When Chloe Sings (a Song)" (Coon Song)[14]
L. Russell

Finale

BARBARA FIDGETY, which is modestly tendered to the good-natured public as a care-chaser in One Act, 3 Scenes. Staged by Julian Mitchell.

CAST: *Captain Grumbler*, a Northener, and candidate for Mayor of Frederic on the Republican ticket: CHARLES J. ROSS. *Colonel Jagley*, veteran of many political intrigues: PETER F. DAILEY. *Jack Jagley*, his son, dippy over Barbara: DAVID WARFIELD. *Tim Greentz, Fred Giblets*, heelers for Captain Grumbler, but like true politicians, with a penchant for shifting as the wind blows: JOSEPH M. WEBER, LEW M. FIELDS. *Mr. Fidgety*, a Southern "gemman," with decided Democratic views: JOHN T. KELLY. *Arthur Fidgety*, Barbara's brother, active in the cause of Brickwall Johnson: Paerl Andrews. *Doctor Gurld*, Frederic's crack physician: George W. Thomas. *Brickwall Johnson*, Democratic candidate for Mayor of Frederic: John Miller. *A Boy*: George Ali. *A Girl*: Minnie Poore. *Barbara Fidgety*, the belle of Frederic: MABEL FENTON. *Sue Voyce, Laura Voyce, Sally Jagley*, chums of Barbara: Irene Perry, Allie Gilber, Nettie Lyford. *Mrs. Shouter*, the Methodist minister's wife: Mabel Nichols. *Mammy Glue*, the Fidgety's hired girl: Lulu Nichols. *Dr. Hal Bird, Edgar Weeks*, gay young Southerners, with a passion for walking in the cemetary: Helen Dunbar, Frankie Bailey. *Sergeant Smith, Corporal Jones*, of Captain Grumbler's torchlight company: Bonnie Maginn, Leona Hilbon. *Republican Paraders*: Stubby Ainscoe, May Edwards, Helen Walton, Belle Robinson, Grace Pierrepont. *Democratic Paraders*: Carrie May, Goldie Mohr, May Sherwood, Florence Bell, Frankie Loeb.

Time: Frederic, Maryland, just after the War. *Scene 1*: Street in Frederic. Evening. *Scene 2*: Room in Rev. Mr. Shouter's house. Morning. *Scene 3*: Hall in Fidgety Residence. Night.

MUSICAL NUMBERS

"The Colonel" (For That They Made Me Colonel)
P. Dailey

"(Serenade of) The Blue and the Grey" (Serenade)
Entire Company

Medley of War Songs

SAPOLIO, a Farrago of Foolishness which may pass for a Clean Travesty upon "Sapho" (A Burlesque in One Act, 4 Scenes).

CAST: *Jean Gaussin*, a provincial in paris for a good time: PETER F. DAILEY. *Flamant*, victim of a moral crusade: CHARLES J. ROSS. *Caesaire*, an old beau, and uncle to Jean: DAVID WARFIELD. *Fra Gournee*, an artists; LEW M. FIELDS. *Francine*, a servant lady: LEW M. FIELDS. *Caoudal*, an artist: JOSEPH M. WEBER. *Joseph*, Flamant's angel child: JOSEPH M. WEBER. *Hettema*, a suburbanite: JOHN T. KELLY. *De Potter*, in the guise of Cupid: JOHN T. KELLY. *Concierge*: Harold T. Morey. *Porter*: Walter West. *Cabby*: William Gaunt. *Inspectaire de Thompson*: William Gaunt. *Clown*: Augustus Smith. *Fanny Legrand*, nicknamed "Sapolio;" a moral crusader: MAY ROBSON. *Margot*, French Folies Bergere: IRENE PERRY. *Madame Hettema*, Fanny's neighbor at Lonesomehurst: Pearl Andrews. *Dechelette*, a blasé Parisian: Helen Dunbar. *Mimi*, an artist's model: Bonnie Maginn. *Toto*, a dancer: Jane Fortuna. *Clarice*, a singer: Leona Hilbon. *Rosa*, a circus rider: Belle Robinson. *Tini*, a Prima Donna: May Edwards.

A few masqueraders who were never arrested: *Frou Frou*: Inez Rae. *Adrienne*: "Stubby" Ainscoe. *Nana*: Grace Pierrepont. *Camille*: Ilma Pratt. *Zaza*: Violet Jewell. *Cyprienne*: Helen Walton. *Alixe*: Carrie May. *Fernande*: Dorothy Kendall. *Cora*: Dappy Grey. *Messalina*: Stella Grey. *Mrs. Ebbsmith*: Florence Bell. *Mrs. Tanqueray*: Eugenie Bashford. *Mrs. Trevelyan*: Florence Dressler. *Cleopatra*: Mazie Follette. *Becky Sharp*: Minnie gaylor. *Theodora*: Martha Franklin. *Nero*: Eva Allen. *Sir Francis Levison*: Lillian Heckler. *Baron Chevrial*: Maud Kempton. *Naughty Anthony*: May Sherwood. *Henry VIII*: Florence Deshone. *Richard III*: Anna Franko. *Jachiamo*: Vera Wadsworth. *Marc Anthony*: May Sherwood. *Armand*: Myra Smith. *Dufresna*: Harold T. Morey. *Don Juan*: William Gaunt. *Gay Lord Quex*: Walter West. *Lord Steyne*: Augustus Smith.

Scene 1: The Ball at Dechelette's. *Scene 2*: Hallway at Jean's. *Scene 3*: Jean's Lodgings. *Scene 4*: The Little House in the Woods.

MUSICAL NUMBERS[15]

Prelude and Tableau

"Chorus of Masqueraders

Pierrot

"The Bohemian Artist" (Laughing Song)

"He Is My Steady" (Coon Song)
I. Perry

Finale

1899.31 (ISHAM'S) OCTOROONS

A Musical Review (7-11-77) in One Act[16], followed by an Olio and a Selection from the Operas. Managing director, John W. Isham. Ballets, dances and marches by Prof. H. Fletcher Rivers. Scenery by Gates and Morange. Costumes designed by W. Rolff & Son. Electrical effects by N.Y. Calcium Light Co. Musical director, Carl Schilling. Produced by John W. Isham. Opened 2 October 1899 at the Third Avenue Theatre and closed 7 October 1899 after 9 performances.

ACT 1

7-11-77, an Original Ragtime Ethiopian Satire in One Act. (Book and lyrics) Written by Robert Cole. Music by William J. Accooe. Staged under the personal direction of Robert Cole.

CAST: *Bill Blivins*, "The Bull": GEORGE WALKER. *Sam Jones*, "The Bear": WALTER SMART. *Dimon Joe*, a policy writer: BILLY MILLER. *Dandy Jack*, a dream interpreter: William M. English. *Elder Johnson*, a hardshell: Charles Johnson. *Desperate Pete*, a dangerous coon: P. G. Hampton. *Officer McSweeney*, a dangerous foe: Joe Britton. *Midnight*, a lazy coon: ——. *Lucinda Green*, a washwoman: BELLE DAVIS. *Clotilda Brown*, a dark secret: Sadie Britton. *Filipino Few, Sopina Sly*, of cullud society: Alberta Ormes, Marion Henry. *Nurse Girls, Chamber-maids, Cooks, Barbers, Waiters, Crap-shooters, Rounders, et al.*

Scene: A policy shop in operation. Monday morning, 9 A.M. to 12 noon.

MUSICAL NUMBERS

"Any Kinder Coon" (Opening Chorus)
Entire Company

"Gwine to Ketch a Gig"
B. Davis, Company

"Kings of de Policy Shop"
W. Smart, G. Walker

"Play 7-11-77"
W. Smart, G. Walker, Company

"When de Wheel Goes Roun' and Roun'"
Entire Company

"The Policy Players Ball"
B. Davis, Entire Company

ACT 2

Olio: Billy Miller, Monologue Artist; The Brittons (Joe and Sadie). the World's Greatest Grotesque Comedy Dancers; Hampton and Johnson, Musical Mokes; Miss Belle Davis, the Star of Her Race, the Greatest Rag-Time Cantatrice of the day, assisted by her Pickaninny Actors; Smart and Williams, Comedians and Authors, assisted by Marion Henry; William Mozambique English, the Beau Brummel of Blackville

ACT 3

THIRTY MINUTES AROUND THE OPERAS, John W. Isham's initial success. Original Music by Carl Schilling. Cast to the full strength of this matchless company, an aggregation of superior talent, absolutely the most accomplished of their race, introducing Mlles. DeLYON and WALKER, Dramatic Prima Donnas, and P. L. PANKEY, the Distinguished Tenor, and P. H. Hampton, (Misses Ross, Ormes, Booker, Henry, Briston, Lee, Wells, Swanson), in conjunction with a phenomenal chorus of 35 voices:

---

[14]Later moved back to Act 1, WHIRL-I-GIG.

[15]Also interpolated, as per published sheet music:
"De Cake-walk Queen" (Dance)
B. Clayton

[16]Billed as the Sixth Annual Review of John W. Isham's Octoroons, 35 Artists of Popularity.

Opening Chorus
Entire Company
"General Siss-Boom-ah" (Solo)
P. H. Hampton
Cavalleria Dance
Entire Company
Duet (Selection)
Mlle. DeLyon, P. L. Pankey, Company
Soprano Solo
Mlle. DeLyon
"Cuba Girls" (Ballet)
Misses Ross, Ormes, Booker, Henry
"Porto Rico Girls" (Ballet)
Misses Briston, Lee, Wells, Swanson
"Oh, Listen to the Band" (Soldiers in the Park)(from A RUNAWAY GIRL) (Finale)
B. Davis, Company
(*Music by* Lionel Monckton.)

1899.32 THE OLD HOMESTEAD

A Revival of the Rural Melodrama in Four Acts[17]. Play by Denman Thompson and George W. Ryer. (Staged by Denman Thompson.) Scenic artist, Homer F. Emens. Musical director, H. Braham. Organist, Fred Rycroft. Manager, Frank Thompson. Opened 9 October 1899 at the Academy of Music and closed 11 November 1899 after 40 performances.

CAST: Act 1: *Joshua Whitcomb*: DENMAN THOMPSON. *Cy Prime*: CHARLES CARTER *Happy Jack*: FRED CLARE. *Frank Hopkins*: LOUIS H. CROXSON. *Eb. Ganzey*: FRANK KNAPP. *Rickety Ann*: ANNIE THOMPSON. *Aunt Matilda Whitcomb*, Joshua's sister: LOUISA MORSE. *Miss Annie Hopkins*: Ethel Ormonde. *Maggie O'Flaherty*: Celia Baker. *Nellie Freeman*: Satie McNeel. *Bertha Freeman*: Bertha Estelle Mason. Act 2: *Henry Hopkins*: GUS KAMMERLEE. *Judge Patterson*: R. E. Rogers. *François Fogarty*: Steve Baker. *Mrs. Henry Hopkins*: Annie Thompson. *Nellie Patterson*: Bertha Estelle Mason. *Mrs. Patterson*: Helen Ludington. Act 3: *Jack Hazzard*: Fred Clare. *Reuben Whitcomb*, Joshua's son: HAL E. PAYNE. *Hoboken Terror*: Dan Regan. *One of the Finest*: R. E. Rogers. *U. S. Letter Carrier*: E. J. Hanna. *Mrs. McGuire*: Marie Kimball.

1899.33 THE POLICY PLAYERS

A Musical Farce Comedy in Two Acts, 3 Scenes. Book (and lyrics) by George W. Walker. Music (and lyrics) by Bert Williams. (Additional songs by William J. Accooe, Cecil Mack and Tom Lemonier.) Williams and Walker's original idea adapted for the stage by Jesse A. Shipp. (Stage director, Jesse A. Shipp.) Musical director, Will Marion Cook. Produced by Hurtig (Brothers) and (Harry) Seamon. Opened 16 October 1899 at the Star Theatre and closed 21 October 1899 after 8 performances; returned 2 April 1900 to Koster & Bials' Music Hall for an additional 8 performances, and 7 May 1900 to the Star Theatre for an additional 8 performances.[18]

CAST: *Mrs. Readymoney*, a seamstress in the Asterbilt family: Mazy Brook. *Mrs. Tubly*, a wash lad: Lola Launchmere. *Mrs. Diamond Joe*: Lola Launchmere. *Kioka, Kama*, a pair of Honolulu Bells: AIDA OVERTON (WALKER), GRACE HALLIDAY. *Miss Gushington*, of other times: LOTTIE THOMPSON. *Canon Nador Lize*, a hard propositon: Mamie Emerson. *Capricious Young*, but more than seven at that: Ollie Burgoyne. *Nurses*: Maggie Davis, Estelle Pugsley, Mattie Evans, Effie Wilson. *Pastry Cooks*: Eugeneia Wadsworth, Daisy Harris. *Up-to-Date Girls (5)*: *Ruby*: Florence Ellsworth. *Pearle*: Anna Cooke. *Rosa*: Madge Warren. *Lilly*: Odessa Warren. *Violet*: Maude Thompson Jones. *Cadenza Animato*, a prima donna out of a job: MATTIE WILKES. *Diamond Joe*, President, Manager and Chief Clerk of the Liberal Investment Company: Joe Hodges. *Dandy Jack Rugby*, a footman, also dream interpreter: FRANK MALLORY. *Clarence Whipley*, a coachman: ED MALLORY. *Canon Nader*, an awful tough man: Fred Douglass. *Mr. Readymoney*, a butler in the Asterbilt family, wants to become a member of the black 400: Ed Harris. *Elder Berry*, not a bush, but a preacher: W. C. Elkins. *One Lung*, not sick, but a Chinaman: GEORGE CATLIN. *Officer Rush*, but not everyday: Richard Connors. *Shiner*, a bootblack: Arthur Reese. *Extra*, newsboy: Ollie Reese. *Barbers*: Frank Johnson, William W. Orme, Frank B. Williams, W. H. Chappell. *Cooks*: Ed Thomas, Joseph Smith. *Members of the Windjammers Association*: Frank Johnson, Albert Washington, Wilfred Day, Rufus Wilson, Lewis Hunster. *Dusty Cheapman*, living just for fun: BERT A. WILLIAMS. *Happy Hotstuff*, combines business with pleasure: GEORGE W. WALKER.

Act 1, Scene 1: Thompson Street, New York City. *Scene 2*: Interior of policy shop. *Act 2*: Asterbilt Residence on the Hudson by moonlight.

ACT 1[19]
"Who's Going to Make the Lucky Play?" (Opening Chorus)
The Famous Chinese Impersonator
G. Catlin
Vocalists and Dancers
Hodges and Launchmere
"Dream Interpreter"
E. Mallory, F. Mallory, Chorus
"Honolulu Belles" (Duet)
A. O. Walker, G. Halliday
"Gwine to Catch a Gig To-day" (Gambling Song)
E. Harris, Chorus
"Toughest in de Place"
F. Douglass, M. Emerson, Chorus
"Kings of the Policy Shop"
G. Walker, B. Williams
"The Medicine Man"
G. Walker, B. Williams, Chorus
"The Band"
Entire Company

ACT 2
Refined Musical Artists (Specialty)
Mallory Brothers, Brooks
"Moonlight"
Entire Company
"Uncle Sam"
J. Hodges, L. Lauchmere, Chorus
Williams and Walker Quartette
E. Thomas, W. C. Elkins, W. W. Orme, B. Williams
Acrobatic Comique and Gun Spinners
Douglass and Reese Brothers
"The Man in the Moon Might Tell"
G. Walker, B. Williams, A. Overton, G. Halliday, Thompson
"Five Little Haytian Maidens"
Evans, M. Davis, M. Warren, E. Wilson, E. Pugsley
"The Broadway Coon"
G. Walker, A. Overton
Soprano Solo (Specialty)
M. Wilkes
"Asterbilts Welcome Home"
Entire Company

1899.34 THE SINGING GIRL

A Comic Opera in Three Acts. Book by Stanislaus Stange. Music by Victor Herbert. Lyrics by Harry B. Smith. Staged by Julian Mitchell. Settings by Joseph Physioc. Orchestra under the direction of Paul Steindorff. Produced by Alice Nielsen Opera Company (Frank L. Perley, Manager). Opened 23 October 1899 at the Casino Theatre and closed 6 January 1900 after 80 performances.

CAST: *Duke Rodolph*, Governor of Linz: EUGENE COWLES. *Count Otto*, looking for his "well-beloved": RICHIE LING. *Prince Pumpernickel*, one whom age cannot wither, nor custom stale: JOSEPH W. HERBERT. *Aufpassen*, Minister of Police: JOSEPH CAWTHORN. *Stephan*, brother of the Singing Girl: JOHN C. SLAVIN. *Officers of the Austrian Army (5)*: *Frederick*: Edward F. Metcalfe. *Francis*: Louis Kelso. *Felix*: Albert McGuckin. *Karl*: George Tennery. *Ludwig*: H. W. Humphreys. *Peasants (5)*: *Ferdinand*: Frank Edwards. *Oelrich*: William Bechtel. *Herman*: R. Wallace. *Fritz*: Albert Busby [J. A. Wallerstedt]. *Hans*: M. H. Lorenz. *Marie*, Sister of Duke Rudolph: LUCILLE SAUNDERS. *Elsa*: Jennie Hawley. *Minnie*: Ursula Gurnett.

Girls of Linz: *Alma*: Clara Isham. *Elizabeth*: Eunice Drake. *Margaret*: Louise Hilliard. *Katrina*: Lillian Samuels. *Lena*: Nellie Marsh. *Freda*: May Boley. *Netta*: Winifred Williams. *Tolfta*: Louise Lawton. *Xesia*: Nellie Devere. *Vida*: May Devere. *Paula*: Ruby Capen. *Villagers, Peasants, etc.*

Greta, the Singing Girl: ALICE NIELSEN.

---

[17] First produced in New York 10 January 1887 at the 14th Street Theatre for 155 performances. For Synopsis of Scenes, see original 1887 production.

[18] Scenery and costumes uncredited.

[19] Interpolated during the tour into Act 1, Williams & Walker Specialty spot:
"The Ghost of a Coon"
G. Walker, B. Williams
Added during the tour:
"I Don't Like No Cheap Man"
A. O. Walker

Act 1: The Haupt Platz, or Public Square, rising from the river Danube. Noonday in Linz, Austria, 1 July 1820.

Act 2: Bridal apartments in the Palace of Duke Rodolph at Linz. Evening of the same day.

Act 3: Scloss and convent overlooking Linz. Daybreak of the following morning.

ACT 1[20]

Opening Chorus (Fill up)

"Allow Me to Inform You" (Entrance Song)
J. Cawthorne, Chorus

"The Well Beloved" (Song)
R. Ling, Chorus

Entrance of Duke Rodolph
Chorus

"By My Mien" (Song)
E. Cowles, Chorus

Entrance
A. Nielsen, Chorus

"The Song of the Danube"
A. Nielsen, Chorus

"If You Were Only Mine" (Song)
L. Saunders

Finale
A. Nielsen, L. Saunders, U. Gurnett, J. Hawley, E. Cowles, J. Cawthorne, J. Herbert, J. C. Slavin, L. Kelso, E. Metcalfe, Chorus

ACT 2

Opening Chorus (To these noble halls)
U. Gurnett, J. Hawley, Chorus

"Don't Talk to Me of Marriage" (Chink! Chink!)(Song)
J. Herbert, Chorus

"Love Is Tyrant (So I Bid You Beware)" (Waltz Song)
A. Nielsen

"The Siren of the Ballet" (Trio)
J. Herbert, J. Cawthorne, J. C. Slavin

"Wedding Music"
E. Cowles, Principals, Chorus

"The Wonderful Magician" (Love, the Marvelous Magician)
E. Cowles

Ensemble (Good night)
A. Nielsen, L. Saunders, U. Gurnett, J. Hawley, R. Ling, E. Cowles, J. Herbert, L. Kelso, E. Metcalfe, Chorus

"Here's an End to Vacillation" (Duet)
A. Nielsen, R. Ling

Finale
A. Nielsen, L. Saunders, U. Gurnett, J. Hawley, R. Ling, E. Cowles, J. Cawthorne, J. Herbert, L. Kelso, E. Metcalfe, Chorus

ACT 3

Opening Chorus (The grey dawn is breaking)
Chorus

"The Alpine Horn" (Tyrolean Song)
A. Nielsen

"Lovely Nature, Fare Thee Well" (Septet)
A. Nielsen, U. Gurnett, L. Saunders, J. Hawley, R. Ling, L. Kelso, E. Metcalfe

Topical Trio (Just suppose that I am going to arrest you)
J. Herbert, J. Cawthorne, J. C. Slavin

Finale
A. Nielsen, Principals, Chorus

1899.35 SISTER MARY

A Farce Comedy in Three Acts. Play by Glen MacDonough. Staged by Herbert Gresham. Scenery by Henry E. Hoyt. Musical director, Watty Hydes. Produced by May Irwin. Opened 27 October 1899 at the Bijou Theatre and closed 17 February 1900 after 120 performances[21].

---

[20]Musical numbers not listed in programs. List prepared from published piano vocal score (M. Witmark & Sons, New York, 1899). Other musical numbers not in vocal score: "Do You Follow Me?," "Love Is Merest Folly," "Mazurka," "Our Native Land," "The Singing Girl," "So I Bid You Beware," "To Be a Little Singing Girl."

[21]Costumes uncredited. Played a return engagement 19 March 1900 at the Grand Opera House for an additional 8 performances.

CAST: *Percival Penn*, a young gentleman of leisure and a dilletante dentist: HERBERT GRESHAM. *Alicia Penn*, the undiscovered author of the book of the hour, "For Better or Worse": MAY IRWIN. *Cornelia Spiggott*, Alicia's aunt, a specialist in temperance and other people's business: LOUISE RIAL. *Charlemagne Spiggott*, her husband, who has no voice in the matter: Roland Carter. *William Guy*, a sentimental dentist: JOSEPH M. SPARKS. *Mrs. William Guy*, who can't forget the men she *might* have married: Ola Humphry. *John Wemple*, who can't understand why a woman needs money: CHARLES PRINCE. *Mrs. John Wemple*, the wife with a catechism: Amy Muller. *Man from the Storage Company*: Theodore Brown. *Willie Dew*, in love with Lucy Lingard: MELVILLE ELLIS. *Scribner McHarper*, the publisher of "For Better or Worse": GEORGE A. BEANE. *Lucy Lingard*, a semi-fiancée: Madelon Temple. *Harold Cholmondeley*: Charles Church. *Amy Gray*, Alicia Penn's cousin: Aileen May. *Amanda Cracher*, maid at Penn's: Gussie Jones. *Pansy Hollyhock*: Dorothy Livingstone. *Daisy Rose*: Lillie Lawton. *Violet Buttercup*: Marie Millward. *Mignonette Marshmallow*: Madeleine Anderton. *Mrs. Kitty Wood*, a widow, in pursuit of happiness—and mankind: QUEENIE VASSAR.

Act 1: The Penn's Apartment.

Act 2: The Penn's Apartment, one week later.

Act 3: The Adirondacks, early autumn. Three days later.

ACT 1[22]

"Not The Proper Way to Treat a Lady"[23]
("The Way to Treat a Lady" from THE CIRCUS GIRL)
M. Irwin
(*Music by* Lionel Monckton. *Lyrics by* Harry Greenbank, Adrian Ross.)

"I Don't Want to Be Yo' Lady Fren' No' Mo'"
M. Irwin
(*Music by* Gus Edwards. *Lyrics by* Will D. Cobb.)

"Mary Was a Housemaid" (What Did Mary Do?)(from POT POURRI, London)
M. Irwin
(*Music by* Napoleon Lambelet. *Lyrics by* W. H. Risque.)

ACT 2[24]

Descriptive Music and a Study on the Black Keys
M. Ellis
(*Music by* Melville Ellis.)

"My Bed Is Like a Little Boat" (Rocking Song)
M. Irwin
(*Music by* Cissie Loftus. *Lyrics by* Robert Louis Stevenson.)

"In Japan"[25]
M. Irwin
(*Music by* Cissie Loftus. *Lyrics by* Cissie Loftus and Louis Harrison)

"(The) Midnight Serenade" (Cake Walk)
M. Irwin
(*Music by* Cissie Loftus. *Lyrics by* Glen MacDonough)

ACT 3[26]

A Creole Love Song and Dance (Opening Chorus)
M. Irwin

---

[22]Additional musical numbers interpolated as per published sheet music:
"I Likes His Way"
M. Irwin
(*Music and Lyrics by* Albert H. Fitz.)
"Gabie"
M. Irwin
(*Music by* Albert H. Fitz. *Lyrics by* Frank Tannehill.)

[23]Otherwise known as "The Way to Treat a Lady" in THE CIRCUS GIRL.

[24]Added during the run to Act 2, after "My Bed Is Like a Little Boat:"
"Louisiana Lize"
M. Irwin
(*Music by* Billy Johnson. *Lyrics by* Robert Cole.)

[25]Replaced during the run by:
"The Cake-Walk"
M. Irwin
(*Music and Lyrics by* Cissie Loftus.)

[26]Added during the run to Act 3:
"I Couldn't Stand to See My Baby Lose" (to follow A Creole Love Song)
M. Irwin
(*Music by* Gus Edwards. *Lyrics by* Will D. Cobb.)
"Why Don't My Baby Write?" (to follow "He Certainly Has a Soft Spot.")
M. Irwin
(*Music by* J. Rosamond Johnson. *Lyrics by* Robert A. Cole.)

"De 'Possum Chase"[27] (Song)

M. Irwin

(*Music by* Watty Hydes.)

"He Certainly Has a Soft Spot for Me" (Dat Coon's Got a Soft Spot for Me)

M. Irwin

(*Music and Lyrics by* Herbert Cawthorn.)

1899.36

'ROUND NEW YORK IN 80 MINUTES

The Merry, Gingery, Snappy, Clean Well-Costumed Skit on City Life (Musical Comedy) in Two Acts, 11 Scenes, preceded by an Olio. Book by James T. Waldron and Edward Fales Coward. Music original and selected by Edward E. Rice and John J. Braham. Lyrics by J. Cheever Goodwin. Settings by Frank Rafter, Albert Operti, Frank Dodge. Costumes by Carrie E. Perkins. Produced under the personal stage direction of William A. Brady. Produced by William A. Brady. Opened 6 November 1899 at Koster & Bial's Music Hall and closed 16 December 1899 after 50 performances; returned 5 February 1900 to Koster & Bial's Music Hall, moved 19 February 1900 to the Star Theatre and closed 24 February 1900 after an additional 24 performances. Total: 74 performances.

OLIO: Ed Lauri (English Dancer and Comedian); Phoites-Pinaud Troupe (Great Acrobats from Empire Theatre, London); Latest Moving Pictures projected by the American Vitograph.

CAST: *Otto Snitzel*, a champagne agent: DICK BERNARD. *Isaac Mordecai*, representing a famous brewery: JESS DANDY. *Jim Corbett*, a sportsman: JAMES J. CORBETT. *Prince Logy Boolah*, a South Sea Island potentate: ALEXANDER CLARK. *Lieutenant St. Regent*, the Prince's left hand man: DAVID TORRENCE. *Oscar Hobo*, a tramp above the average: HARRY KELLY. *Henry Noseit*, a Scotland Yard detective: Harry Brown. *Commissioner O'Hooley*, who controls all the subways: BOBBY GAYLOR. *Ikey Johnson*, a upper Broadway colored light: Chris Bruno. *Willy Dudah*, a Tenderloin butterfly: (Mr.) June Stone. *William Morrison*, a famous boxer: James J. Jeffries. *John Patterson*, an aspirant for the championship: Thomas Sharkey. *Sergeant of Police*, regular force: WILLIAM SELLERY. *Jasper*, the terror of Thompson Street: Dan Baker. *Policy Pete*, a tough citizen: Carl Williams. *Mr. Rector*, proprietor of the Café Rector: Ulric B. Collins. *Mr. Carl Essner*, his partner: August Kremer. *Policeman Dandy*, regular force: Horace Thrumm. *Inspector McLaughlin*: Tony Baker. *Mr. Edwin Marble*, on a pedestal: Edwin Murphy. *Bob*, a newsboy: Agnes Riley Morse. *Chappie Deluke*, very rich: Margaret McDonald. *Algernon Smart*: Madge Dean. *Princess Monti*, a music hall singer with a foreign reputation: MARGUERITE SYLVA. *Kitty O'Brien*, a Bowery girl: KITTY MITCHELL. *Dottie, Lottie*, The Arlington Sisters, music hall dancers: Leah Angeles, Aimee Angeles. *Mrs. Boore*, habitué of midnight restaurants: Frances R. King. *Mrs. Furnished Flats*: Vera Rosa. *Annie O'Hare*, a beauty rare: Kathlyn Warren. *Liza Jane Bohee*, a cullud lady, disappointed in love: Ed. J. Begley. *Minnie*, the 23rd Street newsgirl: Madge Deane. *Mandy Smith*, who speaks for herself: Hattie Delaro. *Annie Gadfly, Annie Agnew, Clara Vanderpool*, three of a kind beats two pair: Rose Parker, Eunice Hill, Maud Gilbert. *Amelia Lestaux*, who leads the march: May Hamilton. *You meet them wherever you go (6)*: *Evangeline Benedict*: Julia Glover. *May Gabriolet*: Mignon Arlinstaht. *Daisy Deane*: Aimie Ashmore. *Angela Beatrix*: Annie Hurman. *Hortense Goodspeed*: Gussie Joyce. *Jennie Startquick*: Mabel Russell. *Clara Speedway*: Ethel Lowell. *Julia Marthur*: Helen Marvin. *Dudes ahead of the times (6)*: *Tommy Atkins*: Sadie Nelson. *Percy Wilkes*: Dora Webb. *Willy Ware*: Maud Emerson. *Charlie Dilkie*: Florence Adams. *Freddie Hairpin*: Phyllis Berton. *Teddy Allcash*: Maud Gilbert. *Colonel of the Revelers*: Miss Harlow. *Prominent Men, Poets, Painters, Artists, Rounders, Masqueraders, and all sorts of characters you meet in everyday life*: Chorus and others.

Act 2, Scene 1: THE ZANGWILL PLAY, Richard Carle's burlesque of 'Children of the Ghetto,' "Children of the Get-Dough." CAST: *Pop Schmenl*, a clothing dealer: ALEXANDER CLARK. *Hannah*, his daughter: CARRIE E. PERKINS. *David Cohen*, in love with Hannah: Chris Bruno. *The Fire Woman*: Harry Kelly. *Five Musketeers of the pen*: *I. Zangwill*: JESS DANDY. *Hall Caine*: BOBBY GAYLOR. *William Shakespeare*: Harry Brown. *Alexandre Dumas*: Ed J. Begley. *Henry Irving*: DAVID TORRENCE. *Firemen, Peddlers, etc.*

Act 2, Scene 2: SHARP BECKY, a Burlesque on "Becky Sharp" by Clay M. Greene.

CAST: *Becky Sharp*: ETTA BUTLER. *Amelia Sedley*: HARRY KELLY. *Lady Bareacres*: Vera Rosa. *Lady Blanche*: Frances R. King. *Lady Jane Crawley*: Rose Parker. *The Marquis of Steyne*: ALEXANDER CLARK. *Rawdon Crawley*: DICK BERNARD. *Pitt Crawley*: Tony Baker *William Dobbin*: Horace Thrumm. *The Duke of Richmond*: Bobby Gaylor. *George Osborne*: June Stone. *Joseph Sedley*: Carl Williams. *Soldier*: Chris Bruno. *Ta-Ma-Nee*, a stranger in a strange land: Ulric B. Collins. *(Specialty*: The Wonderful Cragg Family.) *Soldiers, Guests, etc.*

Act 2, Scene 3: La Sylphe (Classical and Eccentric Dancer), in the Grand March of the Revelers, and Can Can Finale.

For the fourth week of the run and subsequent tour, the Zangwill burlesque was replaced by another burlesque, THE REMARKABLE PIPE DREAM OF MR. SHYLOCK HOLMES, by Clay M. Greene:

Act 2, Scene 1: *The Remarkable Mr. Holmes*: ALEXANDER CLARK. *Mr. Ditto, Professor Moriarty*: BOBBY GAYLOR. *The Heavy Mr. Mr. Larrabee*: HARRY KELLY. *The Villainous Mr. Bassick*: Harry Brown. *The Assistant Villainous Mr. Leary*: Horace Thrumm. *The Assistant Villainous Mr. McTague*: ULRIC B. COLLINS. *The Pugnacious Billy*: Edward Begley. *The Peculiar Miss Faulkner*: Carrie E. Perkins. *The Wicked Mrs. Larrabee*: Helen Marvin. *The Pipe*: Itself. *Time and Place*: Unknown.

Act 1, Scene 1: Exterior of Rector's. (Rafter). *Scene 2*: Interior of Rector's at night. (Rafter). *Scene 3*: Herald Square. (Operti). *Scene 4*: The Dewey Arch and Madison Square. (Dodge). *Scene 5*: Thompson Street. (Dodge). *Scene 6*: Cake-walk Hall on a busy night. (Dodge).

Act 2, Scene 1: The East Side. (Operti). *Scene 2*: The place where they meet. (Operti). *Scene 3*: The French Ball at Madison Square Garden. (Operti).

Act 3, Scene 1: Exterior Coney Island Clubhouse. (Operti). *Scene 2*: Coney Island Athletic Club. (Operti).

MUSICAL NUMBERS[28]

"Cora (Won't You Tell Me That You Love Me Too?)" (Song and Dance Finale)

(*Music by* Robert A. Keiser. *Lyrics by* George Totten Smith.)

M. Russell, C. Bruno, K. Warren, Angeles Sisters, Archer Colored-Cake Walkers

The Grand March of the Revelers

"When I'm a Man Like You"

K. Mitchell

(*Music and Lyrics by* Louis Weslyn Jones.)

"The Latchstring Is Always Hanging Out for You"

Eugenie Fougere

(*Music and Lyrics by* Paul Cohn and Fred J. Hamill.)

"Dear Old Broadway"

M. Sylva

(*Music by* Edward E. Rice. *Lyrics by* J. Cheever Goodwin.)

Novelty

C. Bruno, Angeles Sisters

Can Can Finale

1899.36

IN GAY PAREE

A Revised Version of the Extravaganza (Musical Farce) in Two Acts, 3 Scenes[29]. Reconstructed libretto by Edgar Smith (from the original of Clay M. Greene). Music by Ludwig Engländer. Staged by Fred Solomon. Produced by George W. Lederer. Opened 6 November 1899 at the New York Theatre and closed 16 December 1899 after 48 performances.

CAST: *Theodore Lacour*, an acrobat, in love with Emilie: WILLIAM CAMERON. *Count Henri Distrait*, Louisette's sweetheart: FERRIS HARTMAN. *Ravigot*, his valet: JOSEPH OTT. *Bartavel*, a rich farmer: NICK BURNHAM. *Colonel Hector von Donnerblitz*, retired officer: HERBERT CAWTHORNE. *Simon*, a country bridegroom: GILBERT GREGORY. *Canuchet Catawba*, a wine cellarer: WILLIAM GOULD. *Joseph*, servant to Bartavel: F. Bernard. *Logerot*, proprietor of Café Robinson: W. Arling. *Guijot*, a traveling showman: J. Simmonds. *Gendarme*: Ed. Knight. *M. Carrion*, proprietor of a stranded theatrical company: F. Bernard. *Station-Master*: M. Rawlins. *Louisette Catawba*, a jilted dressmaker: CHRISTIE MacDONALD. *Denise*, a village bride: KITTY LOFTUS. *Emilie Bartavel*, a promised bride: MARY YOUNG. *Lodovica*, her aunt, an old maid with a past: SUSIE FORRESTER. *Up-to-date Girls (4)*: *Melanie*: Miss Selovar. *Fanchette*: Bobbie Burns. *Clementine*: Edith Moyer. *Annette*: Miss Gerard. *Specialities*: NICK LONG, IDALENE COTTON, EUGENIE FOUGERE. *Guests, Passengers, Gendarmes, Villagers, Bridesmaids, Housemaids, Merrymakers, Tourists.*

Act 1, Scene 1: Parlor in Bartavel's House. *Scene 2*: Exterior of the Café Robinson.

Act 2: Catawba's vineyards at Argenteuill.

MUSICAL NUMBERS, SPECIALTIES[30]

3 new songs (Act 2)

E. Fougere

[27]Dropped early in the run.

[28]Musical numbers, apart from "Cora," were not listed in programs; above list prepared from published sheet music, reviews. Fougère's specialty, including an impersonation of Fay Templeton, was added during the run.

[29]First produced in New York 20 March 1899 at the Casino Theatre for 40 performances. For Synopsis of Scenes and Musical Numbers, see original 1899 production.

[30]Incomplete program included neither scenes nor musical numbers.

Les Italiennes (Act 2)
N. Long, I. Cotton
Burlesque of Mrs. Leslie Carter in "Zaza" (Act 3)
N. Long, I. Cotton
The Grand Wine Ballet

1899.37 PAPA'S WIFE

A Musical Comedy in Three Acts. Book and lyrics by Harry B. Smith. Based on the libretti to two French vaudevilles "La Femme à Papa" by Alfred Hennequin and Albert Millaud, and "Mam'zelle Nitouche" by Henri Meilhac and Albert Millaud[31]. Music by Reginald DeKoven. Settings painted by D. Frank Dodge, Richard Marston. Costumes designed by W. R. Barnes. Musical director, Herman Perlet. Produced by Florenz Ziegfeld. Opened 13 November 1899 at the Manhattan Theatre and closed 31 March 1900 after 147 performances.

CAST: *Anna*, a convent pupil, on her bridal tour, Papa's wife: ANNA HELD. *Baron Florestan de la Boucanière*, "Papa," a model Austrian widower, but hardly a model bridegroom: HENRY BERGMAN. *Major Bombardos*, Papa's rival, a military Lothario, who is always deceived: GEORGE MARION. *Aristide*, Papa's son, a musical enthusiast, who has great difficulty in bringing up his father: HENRY WOODRUFF. *Coralie*, formerly Babette, a nursery maid, now the Queen of Burlesque, and Papa's latest: EVA DAVENPORT. *Tobias*, Papa's valet, a woman-hater: DAN COLLYER. *The Governess of the Convent*: Agnes Findlay. *Pierette*, a country girl: Olive Wallace. *Gabrielle*: Sallie Randall.

Prima Donnas of the future, friends of "Papa": *Fifine*: Vivian Blackburn. *Paula*: Emma Levey. *Fanchon*: Frances Wilson. *Zizi*: May Levigne. *Ninette*: Anna Archer. *Tita*: Marie Allen. *Eugenie*: Caecilia Rhode. *Tili*: Jessie Thompson.

Lieutenant Mercier: Anita Austin. *Lieutenant Gallifet*: Gladys Claire. *Lieutenant Gonse*: May Levigne. *Lieutenant Boisdeffre*: Valerie Douglas. *Lucienne*: Adelaide Orton. *A Porter*: Charles Sinclair. *Antoine*: Charles Sturges. *Waiters*: William Sisson, Royal Cutter, Max Rosen, William Gillow. *Professor Celestine*, teacher of music at the convent, with only two blots on an otherwise blameless past, one a burlesque, the other a love affair: CHARLES A. BIGELOW.

Act 1: Convent of St. Dorothy, near Fontainebleau. (Dodge.)

Act 2: Reception room in Golden Lion Hotel, formerly a chateau, showing a portion of Coralie's apartment. (Marston.)

Act 3: Military Barracks near Fontainebleau. (Dodge.)

ACT 1
Opening Chorus (My Summer Girl)
Song (They Wouldn't Do in the Orient the things that we do here)
Aristede, Girls
"Mistakes Are Apt to happen" (Duet)
Aristede, Celestin
"Socrates Jackson" (Song)
Jackson, Girls
"In the Convent They Didn't Teach Me That"
A. Held
(*Music by* Hervé.)
"Dreamy Eyes" (Duet)
Anna, Celestin
Song
Celestin
"O Summer Bathing Girl" (Ziegfeld Specialty)
Men, Girls
Chansonette "Cut High, Cut Low"
A. Held
"Automobile Song" (Finale)(You may talk about your horses)
A. Held, Girls

ACT 2

ACT 3[32]
"Wedding Anthem"
"A Private Affair"
"I'd Like to Have a Photograph of That"
H. Woodruff
"The Dissolute Mosquito"
"This Wine's All Right"
"Professor, Won't You Teach Me All You Know?"
"Oh, That's the Worst of Girls"
"From la Femme à Papa"
(*Music by* Hervé.)
"Inconsistency"
"My Honolulu Queen"
A. Held
(*Music by* William Penn. *Lyrics by* James O'Dea.)
"I'm Fraid dis Snap is Most too Good to Last"
(*Music by* A. Baldwin Sloane. *Lyrics by* Frank Sloane.)
"I've Been Dreaming of You, Baby"
A. Held
(*Music by* A. Baldwin Sloane. *Lyrics by* Harry B. Smith and Frank Sloane.)
"The Other Page Is Missing (You'll Have to Guess the Rest)"
C. Bigelow
(*Music by* A. Baldwin Sloane. *Lyrics by* Glen MacDonough.)
"The Song of the Colonel"
(*Music by* Hervé.)

[31]The original French score by Hervé was largely discarded.
[32]Musical numbers not listed in programs. List prepared from published sheet music, reviews, etc.

1899.39 A GREEK SLAVE

A Musical Comedy in Two Acts[33]. Book by Owen Hall. Music by Sidney Jones. New numbers, Lionel Monckton. Lyrics by Harry Greenbank and Adrian Ross. Staged by Julian Mitchell. Scenery by Joseph Harker and T. E. Ryan. Produced by Fred C. Whitney, by arrangement with the estate of Augustin Daly. Opened 28 November 1899 at the Herald Square Theatre and closed 23 December 1899 after 29 performances.

CAST: *Antonia*, a relative of Caesar: KATE MICHELENA. *Melanopis*, housekeeper of Heliodorus: MARION SINGER. *Circe*, a slave: Ethel Brougham. *Patricians (5)*: *Licinea*: Inez Rae. *Flavia*: Adine Bouvier. *Tullia*: Mittie Atherton. *Cornelia*: Minnie Halsey. *Iris*, a Greek slave, confidential maid to Antonia: MINNIE ASHLEY. *Diomed*, a Greek slave: HUGH CHILVERS. *Heliodorus*, a Persian soothsayer: RICHARD CARLE. *Archias*, another Greek slave: ALBERT A. PARR. *Patricians (4)*: *Manlius*: W. H. Thompson. *Silius*: William Maitland. *Lollius*: Ole Norman. *Curius*: Arthur Stanford. *Marcus Pomponius*, Prefect of Rome: HERBERT SPARLING. *Maia*, daughter of Heliodorus: DOROTHY MORTON.

Act 1: Villa of Heliodorus on the Heights of Rome, about 90 A.D. (Harker.)

Act 2: Antonia's Villa at Baiae. (Ryan.)

ACT 1[34]
"On the Dial" (Opening Chorus)
Female Slaves
"The Wizard" (Song)
R. Carle
"By Bacchus" (Quartette and Chorus)
W. Maitland, O. Norman, W. H. Thompson, A. Stanford, Chorus
"Confidential" (Song)
M. Ashley
"Freedom" (Song)
H. Chilvers
(*Lyrics by* Henry Hamilton.)
Oracle Scene and Quartette
I. Rae, A. Bouvier, M. Atherton, M. Halsey, E. Brougham
"The Lost Pleiad" (Song)
D. Morton, R. Carle, H. Sparling
"All Is Fair" (Duet)
H. Chilvers, D. Morton
"I Cannot Love" (Song)
K. Michelena
"I Should Rather Like to Try"
M. Ashley
(*Music by* Lionel Monckton.)
"Whirligig" (Trio)
H. Sparling, M. Ashley, R. Carle
"Processional March"/"Chorus of Welcome"
Chorus
"What Homage of Human Lovers" (Invocation)
D. Morton, K. Michelena, Chorus

[33]Billed as the London Comic Opera Success. In London the production was sub-titled A Story of Ancient Rome.
[34]Musical numbers do not appear in programs. List prepared from published English piano vocal score (Hopwood & Crew, Ltd., London 1898). Added after London opening: "Love in Mine Eyes."

"Far Above You is My Throne" (Scene)
H. Chilvers, D. Morton, K. Michelena, Chorus
"Bear the God of Love Along" (Finale)
Chorus, D. Morton, R. Carle

ACT 2
"Here at Baiae on the Bay" (Opening Chorus)
Chorus
"A Song of Love" (Song)
K. Michelena
"Oh, What Will Be the End of It?" (Duet)
M. Ashley, R. Carle
(*Music by* Lionel Monckton.)
"The Golden Isle" (Song)
D. Morton
"Topsy-Turvy" (Concerted Number)
I. Rae, A. Bouvier, W. H. Thompson, A. A. Parr, Chorus
"Chorus of Saturnalia"/Tarantella
Chorus
"The Revels" (Song)
A. A. Parr, Chorus
"The Girl of My Heart" (Song)
H. Chilvers, Chorus
"I Want to Be Popular" (Song)
H. Sparling, Chorus
(*Music by* Lionel Monckton.)
"I'm a Naughty Girl" (Song)
M. Ashley, Chorus
(*Music by* Lionel Monckton.)
"A Frog He Lived in a Pond" (Song and Chorus)
M. Ashley, Chorus
"Nothing But Nerves" (Song)
R. Carle, Chorus
"Forgive!" (Duet)
D. Morton, H. Chilvers
"Hail! Antonia, Hail!" (Finale)
Chorus

1899.40 THE AMEER

A Comic Opera in Three Acts. Libretto by Frederick M. Ranken and Kirke LaShelle. Music by Victor Herbert. Produced under the stage direction of John Stapleton. Director of stage and music, Fred Eustis. Dances arranged by H. Fletcher Rivers. Scenery painted by Richard Marston, Frank Gates and E. A. Morange, Ernest Gros. Costumes designed by Archie Gunn. Music director, L. F. Gottschalk. Produced by Kirke LaShelle. Opened 4 December 1899 at Wallack's Theatre and closed 20 January 1900 after 51 performances[35].

CAST: *Iffe Khan*, Ameer of Afghanistan: FRANK DANIELS. *Heezaburd*, Lord Chamberlain: W. F. ROCHESTER. *Crackasmile*, the Court Jester: WILLIAM CORLISS. *Blackjack*, Chief of Brigands for Cut and Slash: WILL DANFORTH. *Ralph Winston*, Captain of British Guards: GEORGE DEVOLL. *Knifem*, a bad brigand: J. J. Martin. *Slicem*, another: Frank Rainger. *Lieutenant of British Guards*: Sadie Emmons. *Benjaboo*, a peasant: Harry L. Arthur. *A Weaver*: Robert Delius. *A Dyer*: Howard Lawrence. *Constance*, an American girl: HELEN REDMOND. *Fanny*, her friend: NORMA KOPP. *Mirzah*, an Oriental dame: KATE UART. *Sereza, Nana, Ayali*, peasant girls: Mae Emmons, Jane Mandeville, Virginia Karroll. *A Dressmaker*: Tunnie Leslie. *Peasants, Nobles, Brigands, Soldiers, Palace Guards, Pages, Nautch Girls, etc.*

Act 1: Public Square, Cabul, (Afghanistan). Morning. (Marston.)

Act 2: Brigands' stronghold in the mountains. Afternoon. (Gates & Morange.)

Act 3: Throne room in Ameer's palace. Evening. (Gros.)

ACT 1[36]
"Another Shout" (Opening Chorus)
Chorus
"Oh! What Is the Matter?"
Ensemble
"Cupid Will Guide" (Song)
H. Redmond
"I'd Like It" (Entrance and Song)
F. Daniels
"Let Those Who'd Wed" (Scene)
F. Daniels
"Ah Woe Is Me" (Recitative and Song)
K. Uart
"I Am a Practical Brigand, Highwayman"
F. Daniels
"Away With Him" (Finale)

ACT 2
"With Stealthy Footsteps Falling" (Male Chorus)
Brigands
"If There's Any Kind of Crime" (Song)
W. Danforth
"Let Others Boast" (Brigand's Song)
F. Daniels, Brigands
"Surprise, Surprise Astounding" (Quartette)
H. Redmond, N. Kopp, G. Devoll, W. Danforth
"Old Maids Are Willing to Please" (Duet)
W. F. Rochester, K. Uart
"Soldiers All"
Female Chorus
"A Soldier Needs No Truer Friend" (Song)
G. Devoll
"The Armored Knight" (Duet)
N. Kopp, W. Danforth
"The Rubber Man" (Song)
F. Daniels
"Surrender, Surrender" (Finale)

ACT 3
"Soft to Sensuous Music Swaying" (Chorus)
Nautch Girls, Pages
"The Little Poster Maid" (Song)
N. Kopp
"Continuous Performances" (Trio)
F. Daniels, W. Corliss, W. F. Rochester
"On Thy Lattice" (Serenade)
H. Redmond, Chorus
"In Old Ben Franklin's Days" (Song)
F. Daniels
Finale

1899.41 THREE LITTLE LAMBS

A Musical Comedy in Two Acts, 3 Scenes. Book and lyrics by R. A. Barnet. Music by Edward W. Corliss. (Additional musical numbers by H. L. Heartz, G. L. Tracy, W. Chadwick. Lyrical assistance by F. W. Arnold, Jr., W. M. Browne.) Settings by Henry E. Hoyt and Ernest Gros. Costumes designed by M. J. Quimby. Musical director, J. E. Nicol. Produced by Fifth Avenue Theatre Musical Company (Edwin Knowles, Manager). Opened 25 December 1899 at the Fifth Avenue Theatre and closed 3 February 1900 after 49 performances.

CAST: *Jack Harwicke*, of the firm of Harwicke & Tooke: WILLIAM E. PHILP. *David Tooke*, President, Harwicke & Tooke Trust Company, alias Beau Brummel Bob, a thief: RAYMOND HITCHCOCK. *Hungry Jim*, well known to the police: EDMUND LAWRENCE. *Colonel Bogey Bulger*, President St. Ananias Golf Club, a Harwicke Trustee: HAROLD VIZARD. *Willie Putter*, Secretary, St. Ananias Club, a Harwicke Trustee: Thomas Hadaway. *Dakota Dick*, a Cow Boy, up to date: WILLIAM T. CARLETON. *O'Hara*, the bank watchman: THOMAS WHIFFEN. *Algy Vandemeer*, an enthusiastic golf-player: Richard Ridgely. *Janet Vane*, Paying Teller: Ida Hawley. *Bank Messenger*: Beatrice Clements. *Mr. James Meek*, a bank depositer: John Taylor. *Head porter*: James Castle. *Lieutenant Barker*, a Naval Officer: Thomas E. Whitbread. *Organ-grinder*: Percy Smith. *John Wilson*, bank manager: George Williams. *Detective*: Lawrence Flynn. *Mr. William Chatham*, Bank Manager: Robert Warring. *Policeman No.1*: Randolph Jones. *Policeman No. 2*: Frank Wise. *First Waiter*: Lionel Varnum. *Second Waiter*: H. G. Hoffman.

Beatrice Jerome, Bank Secretary: ADELE RITCHIE. *Gretchen Dare* of the Jollity Ballet: NELLIE BRAGGINS. *Phyllis Argyle*, Bride of Hungry Jim: MARIE CAHILL. *Patience More*, cashier: CLARA PALMER. *Mrs. Stuyvesant Van Brunt*: Gerry Ames. *Mrs. Miles Standish Cabot*: Suzanne Santje. *Mrs. J. Winston Von Becker*: Marion Carlton. *Miss Mayflower Kiddle*: Gertrude Townshend. *Miss Daisy Smith Chattering*:

[35] Played a return engagement 8 April 1901 at the Grand Opera House for 8 performances.

[36] Musical numbers do not appear in programs. List prepared from published piano vocal score (M. Witmark & Sons, New York, 1899). Other songs not in vocal score: "Sweet Clarissa" (Darky Love Song), "Fond Love, True Love."

Laura Loesch. *Miss Marie Livingston*: Lita Castello. *Mrs. J. Martha Raymond*: Blanche Ward. *Mrs. P. Nichols Van Houlten*: Louise Lloyd.

The Jollity Theatre Ballet: *Dotty Spensir*: Francesca Gordon. *Rhoda Huggins*: Berta Hobson. *Cora Fay*: Florence Raymond. *Esther Day*: Marion Longfellow. *Vallie Van de Beer*: Nellie Plummer. *Cissie Larks*: Louise Averill. *Alice Bolt*: Lillian Collins. *Bank Depositors, Bank Maids, Investors, Naval Officers, Sailors, Policemen, Cubans, Spanish girls and men. Bank Maids*: Misses Baetz, Bonnington, Clark, Lamar, Walsh, Street, Darley, Echard, Renold, Saracco, Underwood, Selten. *Bank Depositors*: Messrs. Whitbread, Chambers, Hoffman, Williams, Wilson, Beall, Flynn, Lawrason, Warring, Morey.

Act 1: Offices of Harwicke & Tooke Safe Deposit and Trust Company, 400 Wall Street, New York City, U.S.A.

Act 2, Scene 1: Grounds of the Hotel. Porto Rico. *Scene 2*: The Casino of the Hotel, Porto Rico.

ACT 1

- Opening Chorus
- "Hurdy Gurdy Man"
  A. Ritchie, W. E. Philp
- Duet and Chorus
  Children, Chorus
- "The Dresden China Girl"
  A. Ritchie, Double Male Quartette
- "Three Little Lambs" (trio)
  M. Cahill, R. Hitchcock, E. Lawrence
- "Mistress Muse"
  M. Cahill, E. Lawrence, Chorus
- "The Jollity Ballet"
  Eighty Jollity Girls
- Bugaboo Song ("The Bugaboo Man")
  N. Braggins, Pickaninnies, Chorus
  (*Music by* J. E. Nicol.)
- "Dakota Dick"
  W. T. Carleton, Chorus
- "Long Ago" (Duet)
  W. T. Carleton, N. Braggins
- "What You Don't Know" (Quartette)
  H. Vizard, T. Hadaway, C. Palmer, I. Hawley
- "Only a Heart" (Duet)
  W. E. Philp, A. Ritchie
- "Peggy Blake"
  T. Whiffen, Chorus
- Grand Finale
  Full Company

ACT 2

- "Dreamily Dream"
  W. E. Philp, Chorus
- "The Pussy Cat"
  N. Braggins, Chorus
- "(That Naughty Little, Sporty Little) Gay Golf Ball"
  H. Vizard, Chorus
- "Willye Wyllie"
  C. Palmer, Jollity Girls
- "Down on the Farm" (Trio)
  R. Hitchcock, E. Lawrence, M. Cahill
- "Dramatic Patrol" (Trio and Chorus)
  W. E. Philp, W. T. Carleton, A. Ritchie, Chorus
- "Little Lola Little" (Trio and Chorus)
  R. Hitchcock, E. Lawrence, M. Cahill, Directors
- "Charity Bazaar"
  Full Chorus
- "The Man Behind the Gun"
  A. Ritchie, Full Chorus
- Grand Finale
  Entire Company

1899.42 THE BEGGAR STUDENT

A Return Engagement of the Revival of the Comic Opera in Three Acts, 4 Scenes[37]. (Original Viennese libretto by F. Zell and Richard Genée, based on "Fernande" by Victorien Sardou and "The Lady of Lyons" by Edward Bulwer-Lytton. American adaptation by Emil Schwab.) Music by Carl Millöcker. Stage manager, A. W. F. MacCollin. Costumes by Fritz Schoultz & Co. Musical director, Clarence West. Produced by the Castle Square Opera Company (Henry W. Savage, Proprietor). Opened 25 December 1899 (matinee) at the American Theatre and closed 30 December 1899 after 9 performances.

CAST: *Countess Palmatica*: BESSIE TANNEHILL. *Laura, Bronislava*, her daughters: ELOISE MORGAN, GERTRUDE QUINLAN. *Symon Symonovitz*, the Beggar Student: WILLIAM G. STEWART. *Janitsky*, a Polish noble: REGINALD ROBERTS. *General Ollendorf*, Military Governor of Krakow: LOUIS CASAVANT. *Lieutenant Poppenburg*: May Huntington. *Major Holzhoff*: Pierre Young. *Lieutenant Wangenheim*: Bee Jackson. *Captain Henrici*: John Barry. *Cousins of Palmatica (2)*: *Bogumil*: Herman Brand. *Eva*: Elizabeth Riker. *Burgomaster*: A. Barbara. *Enterich*, a jailer: FRANK MOULAN. *Piffke*, his assistant: Alfred Walle. *Sitzka*, an innkeeper: Arthur Evans *Onouphrie*: Charles Meyer. *(Chorus of Prisoners, Peasants, Soldiers, Musicians, Courtiers, Pages, Maids, Children, etc.)*

1900.01 CHRIS AND THE WONDERFUL LAMP

An Extravaganza in Three Acts. Book (and lyrics) by Glen MacDonough. Music by John Philip Sousa. Produced under the stage direction of Ben Teal. Dances arranged by Madame Malvina. Settings by Homer Emens, Frank Gates, E. A. Morange, Ernest Gros. Costumes by F. Richard Anderson. Musical director, Albert Krause. Produced by (Marc) Klaw and (Abraham L.) Erlanger, B. D. Stevens. Opened 1 January 1900 at Hammerstein's Victoria Theatre and closed 24 February 1900 after 58 performances.

CAST: *The Genie*, the origial Slave of the Lamp: JEROME SYKES. *Chris Wagstaff*, a "boy about town": EDNA WALLACE HOPPER. *Scotty Jones*, a boy of all work at Miss Prisms' Academy: Johnny Page. *Lovemoney*, a New England money-lender: Randolph Curry. *The Grand Vizier in Etheria*: Randolph Curry. *Pettingill*: Herbert Carter. *Al Khizar*, chief of Etheria's Secret Police: Herbert Carter. *Selwell*, an auctioneer: Charles H. Drew. *Captain of the Guards*: Frank Todd. *Fanny Wiggins*, star pupil at Prisms' Academy: ETHEL IRENE STEWART. *Aladdin*, Prince of Etheria: EMILIE BEAUPRE. *Miss Prisms*, principal of the Academy: MABELLA BAKER. *Amine*, a talking doll in Etheria: Nellie Lynch. *Pupils of Prisms' Academy, and talking dolls in Etheria (5)*: *Stella*: Edna Hunter. *Della*: Edith Barr. *Bella*: Violet Jewell. *Ella*: Adele Nott. *Nella*: Stella Madison. *Queen of Dreams*: May Norton. *Guards, Attendants, Slaves, Dancers, etc.*

Act 1, Scene 1: A room in the New England home of Professor Cypher. (Emens.) *Scene 2*: Grounds surrounding Miss Prisms' Academy. (Emens.) *Scene 3*: (a) Grand Central Depot, 42nd Street, New York City. (b) Aboard ship. (c) The Land of Etheria, Aladdin's Home. (Gates & Morange.)

Act 2: Aladdin's Palace. (Gros.)

Act 3: Gardens surrounding Aladdin's Palace. (Gros.)

MUSICAL NUMBERS

- "The Fourth of July"
- "The Patter of the Shingle"
- "I'm a High-Toned Genii"
- "We Seniors Are"
- "The Bob-o-link"
- "The College of Hoop-Dee-Doo"
- "In Posterland"
- "Above the Slim Minaret"
- "Mamma, Papa"
- "Sweetheart of All the Words of Love"
- "The Lamp"
- "The Patient Egg"
- "Young Torah Tep Was the Boy for Me"
- "Where Is Love?"
- "He Couldn't Do a Single Thing Without Me"
- "The Man Behind the Gun"
- "Fanny"
- "The Hump-Backed Whale"
- The Doll Ballet
- The Electric Ballet

[37]First produced in New York in German 19 October 1883 at the Germania Theatre, and in English 29 October 1883 at the Casino Theatre for 110 performances. This revival previously presented by the Castle Square Opera Company 2 May 1898 at the American Theatre for 8 performances.

1900.02 DIE FLEDERMAUS

A Revival of the Comic Opera in Three Acts[38]. (Original Viennese libretto to the comic operette by Carl Haffner and Richard Genée, based on "Le Reveillon" by Henri Meilhac and Ludovic Halévy. Viennese lyrics by Richard Genée.) Music by Johann Strauss. Stage director, A. W. F. MacCollin. Costumes by Fritz Schoultz & Co. Musical director, Clarence West. Produced by the Castle Square Opera Company (Henry W. Savage, Proprietor). Opened 1 January 1900 (matinee) at the American Theatre and closed 6 January 1900 after 9 performances[39].

CAST: *Eisenstein*: REGINALD ROBERTS. *Alfred*: Rhys Thomas. *Frosch*: FRANK MOULAN. *Frank*: WILLIAM G. STEWART. *Dr. Blind*: Charles Meyers. *Dr. Falke*: A. W. FLEMING. *Ivan*: Alfred Walle. *Ali Bey*: John Barry. *Murray*: Pierre Young. *Cancorny*: A. Collins. *Rosalind*: D. ELOISE MORGAN, DAISE THORNE. *Prince Orofski*: BELLE D'ARCY. *Adele*: GERTRUDE QUINLAN. *Ida*: Mattie Reeves. *Melenie*: M. Zabelle. *Faustina*: Maude Townshend. *Side*: Adelaide Phillips. *Felicita*: Elizabeth Riker.

1900.03 LITTLE RED RIDING HOOD

The Famous English Extravaganza in Two Acts, 12 Scenes. Book by George T. Richardson. Original and selected music by Edward E. Rice, Charles Dennee, Fred J. Eustis, others. Lyrics and alterations by Harrison Ward. Produced under the stage direction of William Seymour. Dances arranged and directed by Marquette. Settings by Albert Operti, Frank Rafter, John Thompson. Costumes by Angel (London), Carrie E. Perkins (New York). Music director, Fred J. Eustis. (Produced by Edward E. Rice.) Opened 8 January 1900 at the Casino Theatre and closed 20 January 1900 after 24 performances[40].

CAST: *Little Red Riding Hood*, a pretty little girl who loved her granny: ETHEL JACKSON. *The Fairy Queen*: BELLE THORNE. *Little Miss Muffet*, well known for her weakness for curds and whey: GERTY CARLISLE. *Mary, Mary*, quite contrary: Clara Havel. *Jack*, of the well-known fim of Jack and Jill, professional tumblers: Lila Bow. *Jill*, a careless little maid who came tumbling after: Amorita. *Margery Daw*, whose principal occupation is seesawing on what is going on: MAYME GEHRUE. *The Spider*, who attracts all to her web: MAYME GEHRUE. *Granny*, the village schoolmistress: HALLEN MOSTYN. *Simple Simon*, a successful idiot: SAGER MIDGELY. *Johnny Green*, a very bad boy sometimes: THOMAS O'BRIEN. *Johnny Stout*, a good boy, almost always: SNITZ EDWARDS. *Baron Moxnixious*, a mass of German villainy: William Burress. *Jack Horner*, a little boy with a weakness for getting "corners" on mince pies: Kitty Mitchell. *Kitty O'Brien*, a ding, dong belle, from the east Side: Kitty Mitchell. *Tom, Tom*, the son of the man who filled the air with a "concord of sweet sounds": Blanche Sherwood. *The Wolf*, very fond of Lambs without mince sauce: J. M. McQuaid. *Peter Piper*, who ate a peck of peppers: J. M. McQuaid. *The Cat, the Donkey*, two very interesting specimens of the educated brute: DAVE ABRAHAMS. *Little Boy Blue*, the pink of perfection: MADGE LESSING. *Villagers, schoolboys, and girls, fairies, birds, etc.*

Act 1, Scene 1: The Wolf's Lair. (Operti.) *Scene 2*: The Village of Ding-Dong-Dell. (Rafter.) *Scene 3*: The Fringe of the Forest. (Rafter.) *Scene 4*: The Fairy Glade. (Rafter.)

Act 2, Scene 1: Granny's School. (Thompson.) *Scene 2*: The Fairies' Bower. (Rafter.) *Scene 3*: The Forest by Moonlight. (Rafter.) *Scene 4*: In Mid-Winter. (Rafter.) *Scene 5*: Exterior of Granny's Cottage. *Scene 6*: Interior of Granny's Cottage. (Operti.) *Scene 7*: Borders of Toyland. (Operti.) *Scene 8*: Toyland. (Operti.)

ACT 1

"Pretty Little Girl That I Know" (Trio and Dance)

"Away, Away" (Chorus)
(*Music by* Charles Dennee.)

Maypole Dance
(*Music by* Charles Dennee.)

"Simple Simon" (Song)
(*Music by* Fred J. Eustis.)

Maypole Chorus
(*Music by* Fred J. Eustis.)

"Jack and Jill" (Song and Chorus)
(*Music by* Charles Dennee. *Lyrics by* Charles Emerson Cook.)

"A Soldier Bold" (Entrance Song and Chorus)
M. Lessing
(*Music by* Edward E. Rice.)

"Naughty Boys" (Song)
E. Jackson
(*Music by* Edward E. Rice.)

The Circus
S. Edwards, T. O'Brien, D. Abrahams
(*Music by* Fred J. Eustis, Edward E. Rice.)

"At My Time of Life" (Song)
H. Mostyn
(*Music by* T.W. Conner.)

"When Granny is Elected" (Ensemble)

"The Art of Love-Making" (Duet)
S. Midgely, G. Carlisle

Song ("The Legend of the Stork")
B. Thorne
(*Music by* Frank Perlet.)

Duet ("Love Is an Infant")
M. Lessing, E. Jackson
(*Music by* Charles Dennee. *Lyrics by* Charles Emerson Cook.)

Quintette ("Little Boy Blue, Come Blow Your Horn")
M. Lessing, E. Jackson, H. Mostyn, S. Midgely, K. Mitchell
(*Music by* Charles Dennee.)

"Off to the Hunt" (Finale)
(*Music by* Charles Dennee, Fred J. Eustis, Edward E. Rice.)

"Shot and Shell" (March)
(*Music by* Edward E. Rice.)

ACT 2

School Dance
M. Gehrue

"Alphabet Song and Essence"
All Principals
(*Music by* Edward E. Rice.)

"Larry Barry"
K. Mitchell
(*Music by* Edward E. Rice.)

"Susie-Ue"
M. Lessing
(*Music and Lyrics by* B. Gilbert.)

"Shadows Are Falling" (Song)
E. Jackson

"The Midgely's Bogie Man" (Rose Ballet)
S. Midgely, G. Carlisle

"Nothing To Do with You" (Duet)
S. Midgely, G. Carlisle

Grand Toy Dances
(*Music by* Fred J. Eustis.)

Cake Walk Par Excellence
M. Gehrue, Escort

Barnyard Ballet
(*Music by* Fred J. Eustis.)

"Off to Fairyland" (Grand Finale)

1900.04 IOLANTHE, or, The Peer and the Peri

A Return Engagement of the Revival of the Comic Opera in Two Acts[41]. Libretto by William S. Gilbert. Music by Arthur Sullivan. Stage manager, A. W. F. MacCollin. Musical director, Clarence West. Produced by The Castle Square Opera Company (Henry W. Savage, Proprietor). Opened 8 January 1900 at the American Theatre and closed 13 January 1900 after 8 performances.[42]

---

[38]First produced in New York in German 21 November 1874 at the Stadt Theater, and in English 15 March 1885 at the Casino Theatre for 42 performances. English adaptation uncredited. For Synopsis of Scenes and Musical Numbers, see March 1885 production.

[39]English adaptation uncredited.

[40]Played a schedule of two performances daily.

[41]First presented in New York 25 November 1882 at the Standard Theatre for 105 performances. For Synopsis of Scenes and Musical Numbers, see original 1882 production. This revival previously presented by the Castle Square Opera Company 12 September 1898 at the American Theatre for 8 performances.

[42]No program available.

CAST: *The Lord Chancellor*: FRANK MOULAN. *Earl of Mountararat*: RHYS THOMAS. *Earl of Tolloller*: REGINALD ROBERTS. *Strephon*, an Arcadian shepherd: W. G. STEWART. *Private Willis* of the Grenadier Guards: LOUIS CASAVANT. *Male Chorus of Dukes, Marquises, Earls, Viscounts and Barons. Queen of the Fairies*: BESSIE TANNEHILL. *Iolanthe*, Strephon's mother: GERTRUDE QUINLAN. *Phyllis*, an Arcadian shepherdess and ward in chancery: ELOISE MORGAN. *Fairies (3)*: *Leila*: Belle D'Arcy. *Celia*: Adelaide Phillips. *Fleta*: ?. *Female Chorus of Fairies.*

1900.05 THE BELLE OF NEW YORK

A Revival of the Musical Comedy in Two Acts, 6 Scenes[43]. Libretto by Hugh Morton [C.M.S. McLellan]. Music by Gustave Kerker. Staged by George W. Lederer. Ballets arranged by Signor Francioli. Settings by Ernest Albert, Ernest M. Gros and D. Frank Dodge. Costumes by Caroline Siedle. Musical director, W. H. Batchelor. Produced by George W. Lederer. Opened 22 January 1900 at the Casino Theatre and closed 10 February 1900 after 24 performances.

CAST: *Karl von Pumpernick*, a polite lunatic: JAMES E. SULLIVAN. *Ichabod Bronson*, President of the Young Men's Rescue League and Anti-Cigarette Society of Cohoes: E. J. CONNOLLY. *Harry Bronson*, his son, a young spendthrift: W. P. CARLETON. *"Blinky Bill" McGuirk*, a mixed-ale pugilist: WILLIAM CAMERON. *"Doc" Snifkins*, the Father of the Queen of Comic Opera: GEORGE K. FORTESCUE. *Kenneth Mugg*, low comedian of the Angelique Comic Opera: GEORGE A. SCHILLER. *Count Ratsi Rattatoo, Count Patsi Rattatoo*, twin Portuguese noblemen: WILLIAM BARRY, JOHN GILROY. *Mr. Twiddles*, Harry Bronson's private secretary: Lafayette McDonald. *Mr. Snooper*, a newspaper reporter: Lionel Lawrence. *Fricot*, a French chef: Lionel Lawrence. *Mr. Peeper*, a Phottographer: R. J. Struck. *William*, a Butler: R. J. Struck. *Mr. Snuffy*: Austin Walsh. *Violet Gray*, a Salvation lassie: EDNA MAY. *Fifi Fricot*, a little Parisienne: Toby Claude. *Mamie Clancy*, a Pell Street Girl: ELLA SNYDER. *Cora Angelique*, The Queen of Comic Opera: HATTIE MOORE. *Kissie Fitzgarter*, a Music Hall Dancer: Ida Doerge. *Pansy Pinns*, a soubrette: Babette Rodney. *Betty*, the Bat: Martha Franklin.

Cora's Bridesmaids: *Myrtle Mince*: Florence Carlisle. *Queenie Cake*: Jessie Carlisle. *Birdie Seed*: Natalie Olcott. *Gladys Glee*: Erminie Earle. *Marjorie May*: Elaien Selover. *Dorothy June*: Vinie Snyder. *Rosy Love*: Marie Wilson. *Kitty Peach*: Mabel Power.

Little Miss Flirt: Alice Sullivan. *Drummer Boys*: Laura Witt, Teddy Ducoe. *Dance Specialty*: La Belle Americaine/La Belle Dazie.

1900.06 THE MAGIC MELODY, or, Fortunio's Song/ AT THE LOWER HARBOR

A Double Bill of an Operetta in Two Acts, followed by a Lyric Drama in Three Acts. Stage director, Edward P. Temple. Costumes by Fritz Schoultz & Co. Produced by the Castle Square Opera Company (Henry W. Savage, Proprietor). Opened 22 January 1900 at the American Theatre and closed 27 January 1900 after 8 performances.

ACT 1

THE MAGIC MELODY, or Fortunio's Song. An Operetta in Two Acts[44]. (Original French libretto to the opéra-comique 'La Chanson de Fortunio' by Hector Crémieux and Ludovic Halévy in one act.) Music by Jacques Offenbach. Scenery by Thomas G. Moses. Musical director, Clarence West.

CAST: *Arnold*: REGINALD ROBERTS. *Dorick*: LOUIS CASAVANT. *Toby*: FRANK MOULAN. *Grace*: D. ELOISE MORGAN. *Betty*: GERTRUDE QUINLAN. *Will*: Belle D'Arcy. *Ralph*: MAUDE LAMBERT. *Med*: Belle Bartlett. *Basil*: May Gooch. *Charles*: Mae Huntington.

The scene is laid in Germany.

Act 1: Dorick's law office.

Act 2: Garden of Dorrick's house.

ACT 2

AT THE LOWER HARBOR. A Lyric Drama in Three Acts (from the Italian 'A basso porto') by Eugene Checchi, based on "Scenes from Neapolitan Life" by Goffredo[45]. Music by Nicolla Spinelli. Scenery by C. H. Ritter. Conductor, Romualdo Sapio.

CAST: *Maria*: SELMA KRONOLD, MARY LINCK. *Sesella, Luigino*, children of Maria: MARY CARRINGTON, Harry Davies. *Cicillo*, a spy: WILLIAM PRUETTE, WILLIAM G. STEWART. *Pascale*, innkeeper: Frank H. Belcher. *Pichillo*, one of the Cammorristi: Herman Brand. *Sailors, Smugglers, Fishermen, Laborers, Marketwomen, Vagrants, etc.*

Act 1: The Lower Harbor, Naples in the 1860s. Afternoon.

Act 2: The Interior of Pascale's Tavern. The Cammorristi's Rendezvous. Evening.

Act 3: The Lower Harbor. Night.

1900.07 BROADWAY TO TOKIO

A Spectacular Fantasy in Three Acts, 6 Scenes. (Book and lyrics) Written by Louis Harrison and George V. Hobart. Music by A. Baldwin Sloane and Reginald DeKoven. Produced and staged by Max Freeman. Ballets arranged by Carl Marwig. Settings by Ernest Albert, D. Frank Dodge and Henry E. Hoyt. Costumes designed by Mme. Catherine Seidle. Electrical effects by John Whalen. Music arranged by Karl L. Hoschna and Frank Sadler. Orchestra under the direction of Signor Antonio DeNovellis. Opened 23 January 1900 at the New York Theatre and closed 7 April 1900 after 88 performances.

CAST: *Calcium Lightwayte*, an operatic manager: OTIS HARLAN. *Dynamite D'Cognac*, ex-fencing master to the Khedive of Egypt: IGNACIO MARTINETTI. *Salter Lake*, a Mormon elder: JOSEPH OTT. *Payday Donovan*, foreman of a gang of laborers: JOSEPH SPARKS. *Albert Wazleigh*, modeler at the Eden Musée: Bert C. Thayer. *Bonaparte Bilkington*, inventor of Bilkington's Bungaloo Bitters: Edgar Halstead. *Coogan*, an attendant at the Eden Musée: William Gould. *Airbrake Peterson*, conductor of Pullman Car: William Gould. *Tenderloin Charlie*, knight of the hypnotic hand: William Gould. *Pilsner*: Gilbert Gregory. *Train Boy*: Gilbert Gregory. *Count Tabledotti*, an Italian ruin: NICK LONG. *Lee High Hung*, pursued by Highbinders: Charles Kirke. *Stiletto*, a bric-a-brac dealer: James F. Lee. *Touchby Typps*, porter of Pullman Car: Frank White. *Henderson carter*, a tropical baby from Minetta Lane: Lew Simmons. *President Board of Alderman*: George W. Ryan. *Higgins*, a tough: Lew Foley. *Stars*, an astronomer: James Horan. *Captain Breezebreaker*: James Horan. *Ezra Pipkin*: James Horan. *Jean Singlooski*: Julian Myers. *Policeman*: E. B. Knight. *Messenger Boy*: Joseph Smith. *News Boy*: Joseph Smith. *Patti Cadenza*, a prima donna: ALICE JUDSON. *Mrs. Barbara Bilkington*, an advanced woman: ANNA BARCLAY. *Gretchen*: JOSIE SADLER. *Mrs. Payday Donovan*: JOSIE SADLER. *Keziah Pipkin*: Christine Blessing. *Ladies Maid*: Christine Blessing. *Mamie*: Buela Montrose. *Daisy*: Maude Frederick. *Countess Tabledotti*: Idalene Cotton. *Mormon Wives (7)*: *Dorcas*: Maude Francis. *Hepzibah*: Rose Frife. *Cynthia*: Dottie Goodyear. *Huldah*: Catherine Jefferson. *Rosalind*: Alice Ackman. *Jurusha*: Helen Rutledge. *Mabel*: Nancy Sadler. *Cordial Sisters (4)*: *Anisette*: Mayme Kelso. *Benedictine*: Mildred Stoller. *Calisaya*: Gertrude Mayo. *Chartreuse*: Maud Calvert. *Cleopatra*, the Serpent of the Nile: FAY TEMPLETON. *Premiere Danseuses*: Fanchonette, Sisters Mahr.

Act 1, Scene 1: The Eden Musée. (Hoyt.) *Scene 2*: Interior of Pullman car. (Hoyt.) *Scene 3*: Cliff House and Golden Gates. (Dodge.)

Act 2, Scene 1: Long Acre Square. (Dodge.) *Scene 2*: Deck on Pacific Mall steamship. (Hoyt.) *Scene 3*:

Act 3: Tokio. (Albert.)

ACT 1[46]

Opening Chorus

Incantation

"The Serpent of the Nile"
F. Templeton

"Alive Again"
Chorus

"Salvation Hymn
Chorus

"We're a Comic Opera Company"
Chorus

[43]First produced in New York 28 September 1897 at the Casino Theatre for 56 performances; re-opened 20 December 1897 at the Casino Theatre for 8 additional performances. Total: 64 performances. In the program management claims falsely that the original production ran for more than 250 nights at this theatre; this return engagement of the London company after its 697 performance run suggests that changes incorporated in the London production were presented here for this engagement.

[44]English language premiere in New York; no credit for English adaptation. Previously produced in New York in French 21 December 1868 at Pike's Opera House for 14 performances in repertory.

[45]English adaptation uncredited. A vocal score translated into English by Percy Pinkerton was published in London in 1896, and may possibly have been used.

[46]All music by A. B. Sloane, except where indicated. Also performed as per published sheet music:

"Susie, Mah Sue" (Specialty)
F. Templeton
(*Lyrics by* F. J. Sloane.)

"When I'm Traveling on the Road"
O. Harlan, Chorus
"Firefly Ballet" (Firefly's Revel)
(*Music by* Reginald DeKoven.)
"The Love Lorn Lilly"
A. Judson, Chorus
"Story of the Dance"
F. Templeton, O. Harlan, I. Martinetti, C. Kirke
Finale
Principals, Ensemble

ACT 2
"Dig, Ye Dagos, Dig"
"The Dago" (Specialty)
N. Long, I. Cotton
"When O'Donohue Presided at the Grip"
J. Sparks, Chorus
"The Johnnies of Long Acre Square"
Pony Ballet
"Hunting for a (Happy Little) Home in Harlem"
J. Ott, Wives
(*Music by* A. Baldwin Sloane. *Lyrics by* Louis Harrison and George Hobart.)
"Now I'se Got Some Money, Well, I'm Comin' 'Round"[47]
F. Templeton
(*Music by* A. Baldwin Sloane. *Lyrics by* Frank Sloane.)
Finale
Principals, Ensemble
Barcarole
A. Judson, Chorus
Character Medley
J. Ott
Danse Eccentrique
Mahr Sisters
The Warrior's Story
O. Harlan
Imitation of Fougere
F. Templeton
Ballet Eccentrique
Finale
Principals, Ensemble

ACT 3
Opening Chorus
The Cherry Blossom Ballet
Fanchonette, Sisters Mahr
(*Music by* Reginald DeKoven.)
Finale
Principals, Chorus

1900.08 THE FLOOR WALKERS

A Farce Comedy in Two Acts. Music by Herbert Dillea. Musical director, Herbert Dillea. Produced by E. D. Stair. Opened 29 January 1900 at the Grand Opera House and closed 3 February 1900 after 8 performances[48].

CAST: *Lord Percy Hardup*: HAP WARD. *Lord Harold Poorpay*: HARRY VOKES. *J. Doyle Smart*: WILL WEST. *Isy Mark*: GEORGE SIDNEY. *Will E. Doo*: LOUIS POWERS. *Dr. Kelly*: JOHN W. EARLY. *Adam Shame*: Harry Thornton. *A Club Mann*: Nat Wixon. *I. N. Hand*: J. E. Cain. *Cold Feet*: William Morris. *Ask Me*: MARGARET DALY VOKES. *Mrs. Waldorf-Castoria*: HATTIE BERNARD. *Pearl*: Leslie Lyle. *Cora Fay*: Belle Lorraine. *Eva Ready*: Langtry Ashton. *May Towle*: May Gardiner. *Top Not*: Gertrude Tyson. *Sue Brett*: Hazel Burroughs. *May Due*: Lettie West. *Stella Star*: Maude Taylor. *Minnie Apolis*: Valerie Montague. *May Shine*: Grace Gorden. *Vera Vane*: Hazel Selkirk. *Belle O'Dell*: Kittie Stevens. *Rosie O'Grady*: Annie Hill. *Ima Winner*: Adeline Weeks. *Ina Minnitt*: Evelyn Waren. *Fifi Castoria*: LUCY DALY. *Chicago Ladies Quartette*: Bertha Hollenbeck (soprano), Sadie L. Farley (mezzo-soprano), Josephine Comstock (contralto), Alice M. Raymond (alto).

Act 1: A Charity Bazaar under the auspices of Mrs. Waldorf Castoria.

Act 2: The House of the Millionaires' Club on "Ladies Night."

ACT 1[49]
"The Charity Bazaar" (Opening Chorus)
"Conversation Dance"
H. Ward, H. Vokes, L. Daly, M. D. Vokes
"Tommy Was a Bad, Bad Boy"
H. Ward, Company
"I Shall Have to Tell It to Albert, Prince of Wales"
L. Daly, Company
"The Mick Who Sent the Pick"
B. Haverly, Men
"Mah Butterfly"
L. Daly, Company

ACT 2
"Bohemia" (Opening Chorus)
"Hush Thee, Now, My Babe" (Quartette)
H. Bernard, L. Ashton, B. Lorraine, J. W. Early, H. Thornton, L. Powers
"Absence Makes the Heart Grow Fonder" (Longing to Be Near Your Side)
J. W. Early, Company
(*Music by* Herbert Dillea. *Lyrics by* Arthur Gillespie.)
"Percy and Harold" Specialty
H. Ward, H. Vokes
"We Heard What You Said"
H. Ward, H. Vokes, M. D. Vokes
"The Sousa Girl"
L. Daly, Chorus
Specialty
M. D. Vokes, G. Sidney
Travesty on Real Acting
H. Ward, H. Vokes, W. West, G. Sidney, L. Daly, M. D. Vokes
Finale

1900.09 THE CHIMES OF NORMANDY

A Return Engagement of the Comic Opera in Three Acts, 6 Scenes[50]. Original French libretto to the opéra-comique 'Les Cloches de Corneville' by Clairville and Charles Gabet. Music by Robert Planquette. Stage manager, A. W. F. MacCollin. Conductor, Clarence West. Produced by the Castle Square Opera Company (Henry W. Savage, Proprietor). Opened 29 January 1900 at the American Theatre and closed 3 February 1900 after 8 performances.[51]

CAST: *Serpolette*, the good-for-nothing: GERTRUDE QUINLAN. *Germaine*, the lost Marchioness: D. ELOISE MORGAN. *Susanne*: M. Zabelle. *Jeanne*: Mattie Martz. *Henri*, Marquis of Corneville: WILLIAM PRUETTE. *Jean Grenicheux*, a fisherman: REGINALD ROBERTS. *Gaspard*, an old miser: FRANK MOULAN. *The Bailiff*: Louis Casavant. *The Notary*: Charles Meyers. *Chorus of Peasants, Sailors, Servants, Coachmen, Waiting-Maids, etc.*

1900.10 A ROMANCE OF ATHLONE

A Return Engagement of the Irish Play (Romantic Drama with Songs) in Four Acts[52]. Play by Augustus Pitou. Music and lyrics by Chauncey Olcott. Staged by Augustus Pitou. Settings by Lewis C. Young. Costumes designed by Caroline Seidle. Produced by Augustus Pitou. Opened 29

[47]An answer to May Irwin's popular "When You Ain't Got No Money, You Needn't Come Around" sung in KATE KIP, BUYER. Dropped after first month.

[48]Played a return engagement 14 January 1901 at the Grand Opera House for 8 performances.

[49]No program available from this engagement. Musical numbers prepared from a touring program dated 9 September 1900.

[50]First produced in New York 22 October 1877 at the Fifth Avenue Theatre for 16 performances. This production previously appeared in New York 21 November 1898 at the American Theatre for 9 performances. For Synopsis of Scenes and Musical Numbers, see original 1877 production. English adaptation uncredited; most likely the English version by H. B. Farnie and Robert Reece or the American by M. A. Conley was used.

[51]No program available.

[52]First produced in New York 9 January 1899 at the 14th Street Theatre foer 88 performances. Played touring engagements 3 April 1899 at the Harlem Opera House for 8 performances; 29 May 1899 at the Grand Opera House for 8 performances. For Synopsis of Scenes and Musical Numbers, see original 1899 production.

January 1900 at the 14th Street Theatre and closed 3 March 1900 after 41 performances[53].

CAST: *Sir Philip Ronyane*: DANIEL GILFETHER. *(Lady) Margaret Ronyane*, his wife: ETTA BAKER MARTIN. *Francis Ronyane*, his elder son: DUSTIN FARNUM. *Dick Ronyane*, his younger son: CHAUNCEY OLCOTT. *Daisy Ronyane*, his daughter: Tottie Carr. *Jack O'Brien* of Munster, brother of Mrs. Ronyane: Luke Martin. *Major Martin Manning* of Dublin: Paul Everton. *Rose Manning*, his daughter: OLIVE WHITE. *Eleanor McBride*, his ward: Mabel Wright. *Hon. Standish Fitzsimmons*, a friend of Francis: Richard Malchien. *Stephen O'Grady*, servant of Sir Philip's household: George Brennan. *Ann Shea*, servant of Sir Philip's household: (Mrs.) Lizzie Washburne. *Robin McMahon*, a gypsy: Charles R. Gilbert. *Molly McMahan*, his wife: Argyle Gilbert. *Mary MacMahon*, a gypsy girl: Louise Marcelli. *Ruth*, a gypsy child: Marguerite Diamond. *Bill*, a gypsy: Frank Bonn. *Servant*: William L. Jones. *Prince*: Himself.

1900.11 THE PIRATES OF PENZANCE, or, The Slave of Duty

A Return Engagement of the Revival of the Comic Opera in Two Acts[54]. Libretto by William Gilbert. Music by Arthur Sullivan. Stage manager, A. W. F. MacCollin. Musical director, Clarence West. Produced by the Castle Square Opera Company (Henry W. Savage, Proprietor). Opened 5 February 1900 at the American Theatre and closed 12 February 1900 after 8 performances.[55]

CAST: *Major General Stanley* of the British Army: FRANK MOULAN. *Richard*, a Pirate Chief: WILLIAM PRUETTE. *Samuel*, his Lieutenant: Frank Belcher. *Frederic*, a Pirate Apprentice: REGINALD ROBERTS. *Edward*, Sergeant of Police: LOUIS CASAVANT. *Mabel, Kate, Edith, Isabel*, General Stanley's Daughters: D. ELOISE MORGAN, GERTRUDE QUINLAN, Belle D'Arcy, Mattie Martz. *Ruth*, a Piratical Maid-of-all-work: MAUDE LAMBERT. *Chorus of Pirates, Police and General Stanley's Daughters.*

1900.12 THE PRINCESS CHIC

An Opera Comique in Three Acts. Libretto by Kirke LaShelle. Music by Julian Edwards. Staged by Julian Mitchell. Dances arranged by Julian Mitchell. Settings designed by E. Castel-Bert. Costumes by Caroline Siedle. Lighting by Joseph Menchen. Orchestra under the direction of William E. MacQuinn. Produced by Kirk LaShelle. Opened 12 February 1900 at the Casino Theatre and closed 3 March 1900 after 22 performances.

CAST: *Charles the Bold*, Duke of Burgundy: WINFIELD BLAKE. *Louis XI*, King of France: MELVILLE COLLINS. *Francois*, Marquis of Claremont, his friend: EDGAR TEMPLE. *Chambertin*, Steward to the Duke: RICHARD GOLDEN. *Brevet, Brabeau*, swaggering soldiers of fortune: JOSEPH C. MIRON, WALTER A. LAWRENCE. *Pommard*, Steward to the Princess: Harry Brown. *Herald* to the King: E. S. Beverly. *Captain* of the Duke's Guard: F. S. Dearduff. *Herald* to the Princess: Lawrence Frye. *Followers of the Duke (4)*: *Valmond*: F. Hammond. *Marius*: Harold Lynn. *Jerome*: James Daly. *Raoul, Piquet* of the envoy's escort: Flora Enright, Emilie Knapp. *Marie, Felise, Denise*, Ladies' maids: Margaret Sayre, Kate Franklin, Toni Savelli. *Lorraine*, Page to the Princess: MATHILDE PREVILLE. *Estelle*, Daughter of Chambertin: LOUISE WILLIS HEPNER. *Princess Chic of Normandy*: CHRISTIE MacDONALD. *Huntsmen, Retainers, Men-at-Arms, Peasants, Cavaliers, and Courtiers.*

The action takes place in Peronne, Burgundy, in 1468.

Act 1: Courtyard of the Duke's Chateau.

Act 2: Grand Hall of the Chateau.

Act 3: Same as Act 1.

ACT 1[56]

Opening Chorus
Male Chorus

Ensemble
L. W. Hepner, E. Temple, Male Chorus

"A Lover True" (Song)
L. W. Hepner, Male Chorus

Entrance of W. Blake
W. Blake, Male Chorus
W. Blake, Chorus

"A Soldier of Fortune" (Trio)
J. C. Miron, W. A. Lawrence, R. Golden

"Cavaliers" (Chorus)
Female Chorus

"An Envoy's Duty" (Song)
C. MacDonald, M. Preville, H. Brown, Full Chorus

"The Foolish Swallow" (Song)
R. Golden, Female Chorus

Septette
C. MacDonald, L. W. Hepner, M. Preville, W. Blake, E. Temple, R. Golden, H. Brown

"Weak As a Woman" (Song)
C. MacDonald, Chorus

"The Love Light in Your Eyes" (Song)
M. Preville

Finale
C. MacDonald, L. W. Hepner, M. Preville, E. Temple, W. Blake, R. Golden, H. Brown, J. C. Miron, W. A. Lawrence, E. S. Beverly, Chorus

ACT 2

Opening (A gallant goes a-courting)
E. Temple, Chorus

"The Days of Magic" (Duet)
J. C. Miron, W. A. Lawrence

Entrance
Chorus

"Come Love, Go Love" (Song)
C. MacDonald, Chorus

"The Story Book" (Duet)
L. W. Hepner, E. Temple

"How Are We to Know" (Quartette)
J. C. Miron, W. A. Lawrence, R. Golden, H. Brown

Ensemble
C. MacDonald, L. W. Hepner, M. Preville, E. Temple, W. Blake, W. A. Lawrence, R. Golden, H. Brown, J. C. Miron, W. A. Lawrence, E. S. Beverly, Chorus

"The Wood Nymph and the River God" (Song)
C. MacDonald

Finale
C. MacDonald, L. W. Hepner, M. Preville, E. Temple, W. Blake, R. Golden, H. Brown, J. C. Miron, W. A. Lawrence, Chorus

ACT 3

Opening Chorus (There's a feeling of war in the air)
Male Chorus

"War Is a Bountiful Jade" (Song)
J. C. Miron, Male Chorus

"A Fighting Man" (Trio)
L. W. Hepner, J. C. Miron, W. A. Lawrence

"Love Came to Me One Day" (Quartette)
C. MacDonald, W. Blake, E. Temple, M. Preville

Entrance of Princess Chic
Male Chorus

"Love and War" (Song)
C. MacDonald, Chorus

Finale
C. MacDonald, W. Blake, Principals, Chorus

1900.12 MARITANA

A Return Engagement of the Revival of the Romantic Opera in Four Acts[57]. Libretto by Edward Fitzball, after Adolphe Philippe d'Ennery and Philippe François Dumanoir's play "Don César de Bazan." Music by William

[53]Returned 30 April 1900 to the Harlem Opera House for an additional 8 performances.

[54]First presented in New York 31 December 1879 at the Fifth Avenue Theatre for a total of 91 performances in two engagements. This production previously appeared in New York 7 November 1898 at the American Theatre for 9 peformances. For Synopsis of Scenes and Musical Numbers, see original 1879 production.

[55]No program available.

[56]Musical numbers appear in no programs; list prepared from published piano vocal score (M. Witmark & Sons, New York, 1899).

[57]First produced in New York 4 May 1848 at the Bowery Theatre. This production previously appeared in New York 21 March 1898 at the American Theatre for 8 performances. For Synopsis of Scenes and Musical Numbers, see original 1848 production.

Vincent Wallace. Additional lyrics by Alfred Bunn. Stage manager, A. W. F. MacCollin. Musical director, Clarence West. Produced by the Castle Square Opera Company (Henry W. Savage, Proprietor). Opened 12 February 1900 at the American Theater and closed 17 February 1900 after 8 performances.[58]

CAST: *Maritana*, a gypsy: D. ELOISE MORGAN, MAUDE LILLIAN BERRI, MARY CARRINGTON. *Charles II*, King of Spain: FRANK H. BELCHER. *Don José de Santarem*, his minister: WILLIAM PRUETTE. *Don Caesar de Bazan*: JOSEPH F. SHEEHAN, MIRO DELAMONTE. *Marquis de Monntefiori*: FRANK MOULAN. *Lazarillo*: Catherine Condon. *Marchioness de Montefiori*: MAUDE LAMBERT. *Captain of Guard*: LOUIS CASAVANT. *Alcade*: John Barry. *Chorus of Nobles, Soldiers, Men at Arms, Citizens, Ladies of Court, etc.*

1900.14 THE MASCOT

A Revival of the Comic Opera in Three Acts[59]. (Original French libretto to the Opéra-Comique "La Mascotte" by Henri Chivot and Alfred Duru.) Music by Edmond Audran. Stage manager, A. W. F. MacCollin. Scenery by Thomas G. Moses. Musical director, Clarence West. Produced by the Castle Square Opera Company (Henry W. Savage, Proprietor). Opened 19 February 1900 at the American Theatre and closed 24 February 1900 after 9 performances.[60]

CAST: *Lorenzo XVII*, Prince of Piombino: FRANK MOULAN. *Frederick*, Prince of Pisa: CLINTON ELDER. *Pippo*, a shepherd: MIRO DELAMOTTE. *Rocco*, a farmer: CHARLES MEYERS. *Matheo*, an innkeeper: JOHN BARRY. *Parafaute*, a sergeant: Arthur Evans. *Doctor*: Harold DeBray. *Antonio*: Pierre Young. *Bettina*, the Mascot: CISSIE LOFTUS. *Fiametta*, daughter of Lorenzo: MAUDE LILLIAN BERRI. *Francesca*, a peasant girl: Frances Wilson. *Angelo, Luigi*, Heralds: Lucille Egan, Sylvia Egan. *Paola*: Belle Bartlett. *Marco*: Mattie Martz. *Carlo*: May Emory.

Peasants, Pages, Lords and Ladies, Soldiers, etc.: Misses Mayme Allen, Teresa Benedict, Katherine Braidwood, Belle Bartlett, Bessie Campbell, Marie Desmond, May Emory, Sylvia Egan, Lucille Egan, Bessie Goodrich, Nellie King, Katherine Logan, Winfred Lamar, Gladys Leslie, Mabelle McKenna, Mabel Marsh, Nora MacGahan, Kitty McNulty, Elsie Patterson, Mattie Martz, Ada Strang, Maude Townshend, Mildred Tremaine, Mae Tobin, Frances Wilson, Lotta Wilbur. Messrs. Charles A. Bowes, Jack Barry, A. Barbara, Herman Brand, Addison Braidwood, A. W. Collins, Hilliard Campbell, J. C. Deane, Harold DeBray, A. E. W. Engberg, Arthur Evans, L. C. Fitzroy, John Hess, G. B. Jackson, H. D. Johns, Arthur Marvin, James Pilling, Pierre Young, Britton Stephens, J. Wiebley, Lawrence Wilbur, R. W. Wier.

1900.15 AUNT HANNAH

A Musical Farce in Three Acts. Book by Matthew J. Royal. Music by A. Baldwin Sloane. Lyrics by Clay M. Greene. Produced under the direction of Joseph R. Grismer, assisted by Kirtland Calhoun. Produced by William A. Brady and Joseph R. Grismer. Opened 22 February 1900 (matinee) at the Bijou Theatre and closed 10 March 1900 after 21 performances.

CAST: *Aunt Hannah*: AGNES FINDLAY. *Jack Hammersley*, her nephew: FREDERICK HALLEN. *Mike McCarty*, his valet: BOBBY GAYLOR. *Grimes*, her butler: Charles W. Butler. *Jim Madden*, her footman: Bud Ross. *Martha*, her maid: Bella Bucklin. *Nora*, her cook: Louise Lehman. *Mary*, her housemaid: Louise Hilton. *Polly Madden*, an actress: Molly Fuller: *Grosvenor Montmorenci*, an ex-opera singer: JOHN H. BUNNY. *Evelyn*, his daughter: CARO GORDON LEIGH.

His (Montmorenci's) Pupils: *Ottie*: Harriet Kendall. *Lottie*: Maud Morrison. *Dottie*: Catherine Robinson. *Tottie*: Lethe Collins. *Lillie*: Anna Williamson. *Tillie*: Catherine Douglas. *Phillie*: Nellie Burbank. *Millie*: M. Zabelle.

Scene: Reception-room in Aunt Hannah's house at Mattewan.

Time: The present. There is no lapse of time during the action of the play. Events begin at 4 o'clock in the afternoon and end at 7 o'clock the same day.

MUSICAL NUMBERS[61]

"She's My Tiger Lily"
Company

"When the Cat's Away the Mice Will Play"

"(It Was) The Same Old Story"
C. G. Leigh

"What's the Matter with Hannah"
B. Bucklin

"Ma Tiger Lily" (March Cake Walk)

"Little Bo-Peep" (Act 3)
B. Bucklin

1900.16 MAM'SELLE 'AWKINS

A Musical Comedy in Three Acts. Book (and lyrics) by Richard Carle. Music by Herman Perlet, (Alfred E. Aarons). Produced under the stage direction of Frank Smithson. Scenery by Gates & Morange, D. Frank Dodge. Costumes designed by Archie Gunn. Musical director, Frank Gabriel. Produced by Alfred E. Aarons Musical Comedy Company. Opened 26 February 1900 at Hammerstein's Victoria Theatre and closed 31 March 1900 after 35 performances.

CAST: *Lord Bobby Belford*, a bankrupt benedict: WILL ARMSTRONG. *Fitzroy Cavendish*, a crank on physical culture: ETIENNE GIRARDOT. *Dennis MacGregor O'Brien*, a Scottish Celt: GEORGE C. BONIFACE, JR. *Noah Snuffles*, who runs the hotel: CHARLES DANBY. *Rev. Jonathan Job Meacham*, alias "Slippery Jack": RICHARD CARLE. *Julius Ippic*, a money-lender: SNITZ EDWARDS. *Lady Janet Belford*, on her honeymoon: MARGUERITE SYLVA. *Mrs. Snuffles*, who runs Noah: Mrs. McKEE RANKIN. *Hester Wright*, an authoress: Maude Creighton. *Dolly Hawkins*, cousin and companion of Honorah: MAMIE GILROY. *Sally Seltzer, Sadie Seltzer*, an America sketch team: ROSE BEAUMONT, NELLIE BEAUMONT. *Dinah Mite*: Elfie Fay. *Reggie Ralston*: LAURENCE WHEAT. *Pierre*: Hattie Delaro. *Guests (8)*: *Miss Behave*: Georgia Carhart. *Miss Chance*: Marjorie Relyea. *Miss Hap*: Madge Dean. *Miss Fortune*: Elaine Selover. *Miss Judge*: Jean Caskie. *Miss Trust*: Ethel Moore. *Miss Lay*: Lucille Verna. *Miss Construe*: Rose Clarke. *Mam'selle (Honorah) 'Awkins*, an heiress in search of a title: JOSEPHINE HALL. *Guests, Poster Girls, Physical Culture Girls, Gold Boys, Hunting Girls, Grooms, etc.*

Act 1: Lawn in front of a private hotel in Eastbourne, England. Afternoon. (Gates & Morange.)

Act 2: Reception room in same hotel. Evening. (Dodge.)

Act 3: Rear of same hotel. Morning. (Dodge.)

MUSICAL NUMBERS[62]

"It's a 'Andy Thing to 'Ave About the 'Ouse" (Act 1)
J. Hall
(*Music by* Alfred E. Aarons.)

"Ippleberger, Hirsch and Mayer" (Act 1)
S. Edwards

"There Must Be Something Wrong About My Face"
J. Hall
(*Music by* Alfred E. Aarons.)

"Cruel Love"
(*Music by* Alfred E. Aarons.)

"Roy, Roy, Tam O'Shanter O'Brien"
(*Music by* Alfred E. Aarons.)

"That'll Be About All of That"
(*Music by* Alfred E. Aarons.)

"Drink and Let's Be Gay"
(*Music by* Alfred E. Aarons.)

Waltz Song (Opening)
(*Music by* Alfred E. Aarons.)

"Don't Believe a Tale Like That" (Trio)
J. Hall, E. Girardot, W. Armstrong
(*Music by* Alfred E. Aarons.)

"Don't Start No Argerments with Him" (Coon Song with Cakewalk)
Beaumont Sisters
(*Music by* Alfred E. Aarons.)

"You're Talking Rag-Time"
Beaumont Sisters
(*Music and Lyrics by* the Beaumont Sisters.)

"Dolly"

March Song (Finale, Act 2)
(*Music by* Alfred E. Aarons.)

"The Sousa Girl" (Act 3)
(*Music by* Ben M. Jerome. *Lyrics by* Matt C. Woodward.)

---

[58]No program available.

[59]First produced in New York in English 5 May 1881 at the Bijou Opera House for 108 performances. For Synopsis of Scenes and Musical Numbers, see original 1881 production.

[60]English libretto uncredited. No credit for costumes in program.

[61]No musical numbers listed in programs; list prepared from published sheet music, reviews, etc. Not in performance order.

[62]Program lists only the interpolations by Alfred E. Aarons. List prepared from published sheet music, reviews, etc. Not in performance order.

1900.17

FALKA

A Revival of the Comic Opera in Three Acts[63]. (Original French libretto to the opérette 'Le Droit d'aînesse' by Eugene Leterrier and Albert Vanloo. English adaptation by H. B. Farnie.) Music by Francis Chassaigne. Stage manager, A. W. F. MacCollin. Scenery by Thomas G. Moses. Musical director, Clarence West. Produced by the Castle Square Opera Company (Henry W. Savage, Proprietor). Opened 5 March 1900 at the American Theatre and closed 10 March 1900 after 8 performances.

CAST: *Folbach*, Military Governor of Montgratz: WILLIAM PRUETTE. *Tancred*, his nephew, usher in a village school: FRANK MOULAN. *Arthur*, student, son of a rich Hungarian farmer: REGINALD ROBERTS. *Lay Brother Pelican*, Doorkeeper of the Convent: Charles Meyers. *Konrad*, Captain of the Governor's Pages: Hattie Martz. *Tekeli*, Sergeant of the Patrol: A. Barbara. *Boleslas*, Chief of the Tzigani: LOUIS CASAVANT. *The Seneschal*, Folbach's steward: Britton Stephens. *Falka*, niece of Folbach at the convent school: D. ELOISE MORGAN. *Edwidge*, Sister of Boleslas: MAUDE LAMBERT. *Alexina de Kelkirsch*, a young heiress: GERTRUDE QUINLAN. *Minna*, her maid: Belle Bartlett. *Janotha*, Landlady of the Inn: Nora McGahan. *Military Pages, Soldiers of the Watch, Maids of Honor, Peasants, Bohemians, etc.*

1900.18

FRA DIAVOLO

A Return Engagement of the Revival of the Comic Opera in Three Acts[64]. Music by Daniel François Esprit Auber. Original French libretto by Eugène Scribe. Stage manager, A. W. F. MacCollin. Scenery by Thomas G. Moses. Musical director, Clarence West. Produced by the Castle Square Opera Company (Henry W. Savage, Proprietor). Opened 12 March 1900 at the American Theatre and closed 17 March 1900 after 8 performances.[65]

CAST: *Fra Diavolo*, a bandit chieftain, disguised as the Marquis of San Carlo: REGINALD ROBERTS. *Beppo, Giacomo*, bandits, followers of Fra Diavolo: William Pruette, Frank Moulan. *Lord Allcash*, an English tourist: Charles Meyers. *Lorenzo*, Captain of the Caribineers: Rhys Thomas. *Matteo*, landlord of the Inn: LOUIS CASAVANT. *Roberto*: Mae Emory. *Zerlina*, Matteo's daughter, in love with Lorenzo: MAUDE LILLIAN BERRI, GERTRUDE QUINLAN, SYBIL FRANCIS. *Lady Allcash*, newly wedded to Lord Allcash: MAUDE LAMBERT. *Chorus of Peasants, Carbineers, etc.*

1900.19

THE REGATTA GIRL

A Musical Burletta in Two Acts, followed by a Ballet "Progress". Burletta adapted by Clay M. Greene from a comedy by J. Cheever Goodwin and Charles Bradley. Music by Harry McLellan. Settings painted by Gates and E. A. Morange. Ballet by Luigi Manzotti; produced under the direction of Vincenzo Romeo; music by Romauldo Marenco and John J. Braham. Produced by (John) Koster and (Albert) Bial (Salisbury, Manager). Opened 14 March 1900 at Koster & Bial's Music Hall and closed 31 March 1900 after 22 performances.[66]

CAST: *Count Bricque D'Or*: WILLIAM T. TERRISS. *McManus O'Kimberly*: EDDIE GIRARD. *Charles Beresford*: ALBERT PARR. *Frascati Fauxpas*, the Ballet Master: GIOVANNI PERUGINI. *Inspector Short*: ALEXANDER CLARKE. *Lord Harwood*: JENNIE YEAMANS. *Modus*: HENRI LEONI. *Dick Beamish*: STEPHEN MALEY. *Reggie Squires*: Margaret Macdonald. *Bertie Dunlop*: Blanche Sherwood. *La Duchesse des Effets-Verts*: ATTALIE CLAIRE. *Marjorie*, the Regatta Girl: ETHEL JACKSON. *Matilda*: AMELIA SUMMERVILLE. *Lady Paynton*: LAURA JOYCE BELL. *Tillie*: Olive Ulrich. *Lola*: Leonore Harris.

Ballet (Act 3): *Principal Danseuses*: MLLE. LEONTINE, SIGNORA CHITTEN. *Eccentric Dance Specialty*: ARNOLD KIRALFY. *Progress*: ANGELE PESSIONI. *Ignorance*: VINCENZO ROMEO. *A Turk*: Ella Rice. *A Chinaman*: Jennie Cassie. *A Mexican*: Marguerite Mullen. *A Slave*: Signorina Cara.

Act 1: Kensington Gardens.

Act 2: A Villa on the Thames at Henley during regatta week.

Act 3: Covent Garden Theatre. *Scene 1*: Ruins of an old city. *Scene 2*: The interior of the Palace of Progress. *Scene 3*: The Laboratory of Volta. *Scene 4*: Greytown, Nicaragua, on festal day.

1900.20

THE CASINO GIRL

A Musical Comedy in Three Acts[67]. (Book and lyrics) Written by Harry B. Smith. Music by Ludwig Engländer, (Harry T. MacConnell, Arthur Nevin). Staged by George W. Lederer. Settings by D. Frank Dodge, Ernest Albert. Costumes by Mme. Caroline Siedle. Music director, Antonio DeNovellis. Produced by George W. Lederer. Opened 19 March 1900 at the Casino Theatre, closing 9 June 1900 after 105 performances for summer vacation; re-opened in a revised version 8 April 1901 at the Knickerbocker Theatre[68].

CAST: *The Khedive of Egypt*, an Oriental Lothario. Just why the Kedive speaks Egyptian with strong English accent is not stated; but this is not a monograph on Oriental languages: SAM BERNARD. *Fromage*, alias Ben Muley, chief of a gang of thieves: ALBERT HART. *Potage*, his minion: LOUIS WESLEY. *Reuben Bey*, an Orientalized Yankee in the slave trade: GEORGE A. SCHILLER. *Roquefort*, a Gendarme: J. A. FUREY. *Caviare*, another: James McQuaid. *Laura Lee*, The Casino Girl, persecuted by offers of marriage from the nobility; she goes to Cairo and becomes a milliner: MABELLE [Mabel] GILMAN. *Mrs. H. Malaprop Rocks*, a society leader from a Western metropolis: CARRIE E. PERKINS. *Roxy Rocks*, her breezy daughter: ELLA SNYDER. *Lotta Rocks*, her cultured daughter: IRENE BENTLEY. *Carrie Rocks*, her tomboy daughter: MAYME GEHRUE. *Miss Broadway* of New York: Susie Drake. *Miss Bunker* of Boston: Belle Armstrong. *Miss Chestnut* of Philadelphia: Elizabeth Ryker. *Miss Bridge* of San Francisco: Louise Lloyd. *Miss Capitol* of Washington: Jessie Wood. *Miss Wabash* of Chicago: Clara Selton. *Miss Foote* of St. Louis: Emma Lenox. *Miss Pilsner* of Milwaukee: Eleanor Burns. *Hassan*, the Khedive's page: Goldie Mohr. *Cigarette Girls (5)*: *Zuleika*: Katherine Bartlett. *Fatima*: LOTTA FAUST. *Lalla Rokh*: Jessie Jordan. *Zobediya*: Adelaide Phillips. *Amina*: Blanche Cramer. *Odaliska*, the Khedive's favorite Dame: Vina Snyder. *Percy Harold Ethelbert Frederick Cholmondeley*, an English Earl: VIRGINIA EARLE.

Chorus of Odalisques, Cigarette Girls, American and European Tourists, Egyptian Merchants, Khedive's Guards, Masqueraders, Donkey-Boys, etc.

Act 1: A Square in Cairo. (Dodge.)

Act 2: The Khedive's Palace, during his birthday masquerade, "The Fête of Parrots" (Albert.)

ACT 1[69]

Opening Chorus
(*Music by* Ludwig Engländer.)

"Slave Dealer's Song"
G. A. Schiller
(*Music by* Harry T. MacConnell.)

"Song of the Drum Major"
E. Snyder
(*Music by* Harry T. MacConnell.)

"My New York"
M. Gilman
(*Music by* Ludwig Engländer.)

Entrance Chorus of the Khedive
(*Music by* Harry T. MacConnell.)

"I'll Put a Tax"
S. Bernard
(*Music by* Harry T. MacConnell.)

Descriptive Song
V. Earle
(*Music by* Harry T. MacConnell.)

"How Actresses Are Made" (Duet)
V. Earle, M. Gilman
(*Music by* Harry T. MacConnell.)

Finale
(*Music by* Ludwig Engländer.)

ACT 2

Opening Chorus
(*Music by* Ludwig Engländer.)

"Mam'selle"
M. Gilman
(*Music by* Arthur Nevin.)

---

[63]First produced in New York 14 April 1884 at the Casino Theatre for for 110 performances; returned 12 July 1886 at Wallack's Theatre in two engagements for 35 performances. For Synopsis of Scenes and Musical Numbers, see original 1884 production.

[64]First produced in New York 17 October 1831 at the Chatham Theatre in French. This revival previously presented by the Castle Square Opera Company 16 May 1898 at the American Theatre for 8 performances.

[65]English adaptation uncredited.

[66]No list of musical numbers found.

[67]After two weeks, the show was revised into two acts.

[68]For detail, see entry in following season.

[69]See 1901 revival for additional interpolations. Added during the run to Act 1, after "My New York:"

Duet and Dance
S. Collins, A. Hart
(*Music by* Harry T. MacConnell.)

"Down de Lovers' Lane"
V. Earle
(*Music by* Wll Marion Cook.)
"From Africa"
Chorus
(*Music by* Harry T. MacConnell.)
"Chink! Chink!"
A. Hart
(*Music by* Harry T. MacConnell.)
"Variety" (Sextette)
A. Hart, S. Collins, L. Wesley, C. E. Perkins, E. Snyder
(*Music by* Harry T. MacConnell.)
"The Casino Girl"
I. Bentley, A. Paul
(*Music by* Harry T. MacConnell.)
Finale
(*Music by* Ludwig Engländer.)

1900.21

PATIENCE, or, Bunthorne's Bride

A Return Engagement of the Revival of the Comic Opera in Two Acts[70]. Libretto by William S. Gilbert. Music by Arthur Sullivan. Stage manager, A. W. F. MacCollin. Musical director, Clarence West. Produced by the Castle Square Opera Company (Henry W. Savage, Proprietor). Opened 19 March 1900 at the American Theatre and closed 24 March 1900 after 8 performances.[71]

CAST: *Reginald Bunthorne*, a Fleshly Poet: FRANK MOULAN. *Archibald Grosvenor*, an Idyllic Poet: RHYS THOMAS. *Officers of Dragoon Guards (3): Colonel Calverley*: LOUIS CASAVANT. *Major Murgatroyd*: Charles Meyers. *Lieutenant The Duke of Dunstable*: REGINALD ROBERTS. *Bunthorne's Solicitor*: Harold DeBray. *Chorus of Dragoon Guards. Rapturous Maidens (4): Lady Angela*: GERTRUDE QUINLAN. *Lady Saphir*: BELLE D'ARCY. *Lady Ella*: Florence DeLuce. *Lady Jane*: CARRIE GODFREY. *Patience*, a milkmaid: D. ELOISE MORGAN. *Chorus of Maidens.*

1900.22

THE BOHEMIAN GIRL

A Return Engagement of the Revival of the Romantic Opera in Three Acts[72]. Libretto by Alfred Bunn, after Jules-Henri Vernoy de Saint-Georges' ballet-pantomime The Gypsy, based on Miguel de Cervantes' La Gitanilla. Music by Michael Balfe. Stage manager, A. W. F. MacCollin. Musical director, Clarence West. Produced by the Castle Square Opera Company (Henry W. Savage, Proprietor). Opened 26 March 1900 at the American Theatre and closed 31 March 1900 after 8 performances.[73]

CAST: *Count Arnheim*, Governor of Presburg: WILLIAM PRUETTE. *Thaddeus*, a proscribed Pole: REGINALD ROBERTS. *Florestein*, nephew of the Count: FRANK MOULAN. *Devilshoof*, chief of the Gypsies: LOUIS CASAVANT. *Captain of the Guard*: John D. Barry. *Arline*, daughter of the Count: ADELAIDE NORWOOD. *Buda*, her attendant: Mattie Martz. *Queen of the Gypsies*: MAUDE LAMBERT. *Chorus of Nobles, Soldiers, Gypsies, Retainers and Peasants.*

1900.23

NANON

A Return Engagement of the Revival of the Comic Opera (Opéra Comique) in Three Acts[74]. (Original Viennese libretto, 'Nanon, die Wirthin vom goldenene Lamm,' by F. Zell, based on the play "Ninon, Nanon et Madame de Maintenon" by Emmanuel Théaulon, Armand d'Artois and Lesguillon.) Music by Richard Genée. (American translation by Sydney Rosenfeld.) Stage manager, A. W. F. MacCollin. Scenery by Thomas G. Moses. Musical director, Clarence West. Produced by the Castle Square Opera Company (Henry W. Savage, Proprietor). Opened 2 April 1900 at the American Theatre and closed 7 April 1900 after 8 performances.

CAST: *Marquis de Marsellac*: FRANK MOULAN. *Hector*, his nephew: REGINALD ROBERTS. *Marquis Henri d'Aubigne*, the King's Chamberlain: MIRO DELAMOTTE. *Bombardine*, his henchman: Harold DeBray. *Louis XIV*: LOUIS CASAVANT. *Monsieur l'Abbé*: WILLIAM PRUETTE. *The Notary*: A. W. Collins *Nanon*, Mistress of the Golden Lamb: D. ELOISE MORGAN. *Ninon d'l'Enclos*, a famous beauty: DREW DONALDSON. *Ninon's friends (2): Mme. de Frontenac*: Belle D'Arcy. *Countess Honliers*: Mattie Martz. *Gaston*, Page to Ninon: GERTRUDE QUINLAN. *Mme. de Maintenon*, the King's consort: MAUDE LAMBERT. *Nanon's Country Relations (7): Cousin Pierre*: Arthur Evans. *Uncle Matthew*: A. Barbara. *Papa Bertrand*: Pierre Young. *Cousin Joe*: J. Wiebley. *Mother Lizette*: Gladys Leslie. *Aunt Theresa*: Naomi Arnold. *Cousin Marion*: Maude Townshend. *Jacqueline*: Mae Huntington. *Sergeant*: J. Barry. *Chorus of Peasants, Soldiers, Country Relations, Courtiers, Ladies, etc.*

1900.24

A HOT OLD TIME

A Revival of the Musical Farce in Three Acts[75]. Play, music and lyrics by Edgar Selden. Scenery by C. W. Valentine. Produced by the Rays (Johnny, Emma). Opened 2 April 1900 at the Victoria Theatre and closed 28 April 1900 after 28 performances.[76]

CAST: *Larry Mooney*, of Mooney's Express: JOHNNY RAY. *General Stonewall Blazer*, great man—in his mind: WILLIAM KELLER MACK. *Jack Treadwell*, quarter back at Yale: FRANK LALOR. *Alkali Ike*, from the wooly West: J. BERNARD DYLLYN. *Cholly Knickerbocker*, too sweet to live: Harry Hayes. *O'Donovan Dunn*, M. P., first to visit America: Harry Dull. *Rogers*: Louis Hunting. *Sergeant O'Casey*: John Hunting. *Officer Mulligan*, a suburban policeman: Harry Elvin. *Willie Swift*: Martin Healy. *High Tenor*: Franklyn Wallace. *Blossom Blazer, Cherry Blazer*, the General's daughters, ripe for picking: QUERITA VINCENT, EMMA FRANICS. *Marjorie Daw*, their city chum: Mollie Hunting. *Sallie Waters*, their country chum: Fanny Mora. *Ethel Thorne*, a Summer girl: Vernie Rose. *Stella Drew*: Minerva Adams. *Mrs. General Stonewall Blazer*, boss of the whole outfit: EMMA RAY.

1900.25

THE VICEROY

The Bostonians in a Comic Opera in Two Acts. Libretto by Harry B. Smith. Music by Victor Herbert. Staged by William H. Fitzgerald. Orchestra under the direction of Samuel L. Studley. Orchestrations by Victor Herbert. Produced by the Bostonians (Henry Clay Barnabee and William H. MacDonald, Proprietors), (Marc) Klaw and (Abraham L.) Erlanger. Opened 9 April 1900 at the Knickerbocker Theatre and closed 5 May 1900 after 28 performances[77].

CAST: *The Viceroy of Sicily*: HENRY CLAY BARNABEE. *Corleone*, Captain of Militia: WILLIAM H. MacDONALD. *Bastroco*, Sergeant of Militia: GEORGE B. FROTHINGHAM. *Barabino*, Minister of Police: WILLIAM H. FITZGERALD. *Luigi*, a fisherman: FRANK RUSHWORTH. *Ruffino*, a jailor: John Dunsmure. *Tivolini*, a pirate chieftain: HELEN BERTRAM. *Fioretta*, the viceroy's daughter: MARCIA VAN DRESSER. *Beatrice*, for whose hand the Viceroy and Tivolini are rivals: GRACE CAMERON. *Ortensia*, wife of Bastroco: JOSEPHINE BARTLETT. *Tivolini's Men (4): Stiletto*: Harry Dale. *Vermicelli*: Adam Warmouth. *Spaghetti*: David White. *Macaroni*: James E. Miller. *Waitress*: Edith Hendee. *First citizen*: Arthur T. Earnest. *Second citizen*: Henry Miller.

The action takes place in Palermo, Sicily, in the sixteenth century.

[70]First produced in New York 22 September 1881 at the Standard Theatre for 177 performances. This production previously appeared in New York 3 October 1898 at the American Theatre for 8 performances. For Synopsis of Scenes and Musical Numbers, see original 1881 production.
[71]No program available.
[72]First produced in New York 25 November 1844 at the Park Theatre. This production previously appeared in New York 6 June 1898 at the American Theatre for 8 performances. For Synopsis of Scenes and Musical Numbers, see original 1844 production.
[73]No program available.
[74]First produced in New York as NANON, The Hostess of the Golden Lamb, 29 June 1885 at the Casino Theatre for 152 performances. This revival previously presented by the Castle Square Opera Company 7 March 1898 at the American Theatre for 8 performances. For Synopsis of Scenes and Musical Numbers, see original 1885 production.
[75]First produced in New York 6 September 1897 at the Third Avenue Theatre for 8 performances; returned 27 December 1897 to the Grand Opera House for 8 additional performances. For Synopsis of Scenes, see original 1897 production. All specialties were changed for this revival.
[76]Revised by George M. Cohan for subsequent tour the following season and advertised as Second Edition, under the management of Edward A. Braden. Added to the score were:
"Rag-Time Night on Broadway" (*Music and Lyrics by* George M. Cohan.), "A Funny Little Man," "A Dangerous Man from Denver," "Hero of the Football Game," " A Hot Old Time" (*Music and Lyrics by* George M. Cohan.), "Why Did They Sell Killarney?," "Dewey's Reception," "I Guess I'll Have to Telegraph My Baby" (*Music and Lyrics by* George M. Cohan.), "I Guess I'll See His Finish Pretty Soon," "The Wild and Woolly West," "True Daughters of Old Uncle Sam," "Are You Done, Mr. Dunn" etc.
[77]No credits for settings or costumes.

Act 1: The Lido, the public promenade on the sea wall, Palermo.

Act 2: A public square in Palermo.

Act 3: The Pirates' cave.

ACT 1[78]

"We Come to the Lively Market Square" (Opening Chorus)

"With Military Pomp" (Song)
G. B. Frothingham, Chorus

"We'll Catch You at Last, Tivolini" (Song/Legend)
W. H. MacDonald, Chorus

"Hear Me!" (Tivolini's Serenade)
H. Bertram, Chorus

"I'm a Leader of Society" (Song)
H. C. Barnabee, Chorus

"Just For To-day" (Song)
F. Rushworth

"By This Sweet Token" (Quartette)
H. C. Barnabee, G. Cameron, J. Bartlett, M. Van Dresser

Finale
H. Bertram, M. Van Dresser, G. B. Frothingham, W. H. MacDonald, W. H. Fitzgerald, Soldiers, Chorus

ACT 2

"Thy Subjects Are We" (Opening Chorus)

"The Robin and the Rose" (Song)
G. Cameron

"Eyes of Black and Eyes of Blue" (Song)
W. H. MacDonald, Chorus

"A Sailor's Life" (Quartette)
H. C. Barnabee, W. H. MacDonald, G. B. Frothingham, W. H. Fitzgerald

"'Neath the Blue Neapolitan Skies" (Song)
H. Bertram, Chorus

"So They Say" (Duet)
H. C. Barnabee, M. Van Dresser

"I See by Your Smile" (Duet)
M. Van Dresser, J. Dunsmure

"Since I am Queen of the Carnival" (Song)
M. Van Dresser, Chorus

Finale
Principals, Chorus

ACT 3

"In a Smuggler's Cave" (Opening)
Solo, Chorus

"All Men Have Their Troubles" (Song)
W. H. MacDonald, Chorus

"One Fellow's Joy Is Another Fellow's Woe" (Quintette)
M. Van Dresser, J. Bartlett, F. Rushworth, W. H. Fitzgerald, W. H. MacDonald

"That's My Idea of Love" (Duet)
H. Bertram, M. Van Dresser

"On My Nuptial Day" (Sextette)
G. Cameron, M. Van Dresser, J. Bartlett, F. Rushworth, W. H. MacDonald, W. H. Fitzgerald

Finale
Principals, Chorus

1900.26 H.M.S. PINAFORE, or, The Lass That Loved a Sailor

A Return Engagement of the Revival of the Nautical Comic Opera in Two Acts[79]. Libretto by William S. Gilbert. Music by Arthur Sullivan. Stage director, Edward P. Temple. Musical director, Clarence West. Produced by the Castle Square Opera Company (Henry W. Savage, Proprietor). Opened 9 April 1900 at the American Theatre and closed 14 April 1900 after 8 performances.

CAST: *The Rt. Hon. Sir Joseph Porter, K.C.B.*, First Lord of the Admiralty: FRANK MOULAN. *Captain Corcoran*, Commander of H.M.S. Pinafore: HARRY LUCKSTONE. *Ralph Rackstraw*, Able Seaman: MIRO DELAMOTTE, REGINALD ROBERTS. *Dick Deadeye*, Able Seaman: WILLIAM PRUETTE. *Bill Bobstay*, Boatswain's Mate: LOUIS CASAVANT. *Becket*: A. Barbara. *Josephine*, the Captain's Daughter: D. ELOISE MORGAN. *Little Buttercup*, Mrs. Cripps, a Portsmouth Bum-Boat Woman: CARRIE GODFREY. *Hebe*, Sir Joseph's First Cousin: Gertrude Quinlan. *First Lord's Sisters, His Cousins, His Aunts, Sailors, Marines.*

preceded by

TRIAL BY JURY, or, Love and Duty
A Return Engagement of the Revival of the Dramatic Cantata (Comic Opera) in One Act[80]. Libretto by William S. Gilbert. Music by Arthur Sullivan. Stage director, Edward P. Temple. Musical director, Clarence West.

CAST: *Judge*: EDWARD P. TEMPLE. *Plaintiff*: GERTRUDE QUINLAN. *Defendant*: REGINALD ROBERTS, MIRO DELAMOTTE. *Counsel*: HARRY LUCKSTONE. *Usher*: Harold DeBray. *Foreman*: Pierre Young. *First Bridesmaid*: Florence DeLuce.

1900.27 THE MIKADO, or, The Town of Titipu

A Return Engagement of the Revival of the Comic Opera in Two Acts[81]. Libretto by William S. Gilbert. Music by Arthur Sullivan. Stage manager, A. W. F. MacCollin. Conductor, Clarence West. Produced by the Castle Square Opera Company (Henry W. Savage, Proprietor). Opened 16 April 1900 at the American Theatre and closed 21 April 1900 after 8 performances.[82]

CAST: *The Mikado of Japan*: HALLEN MOSTYN. *Nanki-Poo*, his son, disguised as a wandering minstrel in love with Yum-Yum: REGINALD ROBERTS. *Ko-Ko*, Lord High Executioner of Titipu: FRANK MOULAN. *Pooh-Bah*, Lord High Everything Else: WILLIAM PRUETTE. *Pish-Tush*, a Noble Lord: Louis Casavant. *Nee-Ban*, umbrella carrier to the Mikado: Harold DeBray. *Yum-Yum, Pitti-Sing, Peep-Bo*, three sisters, wards of Ko-Ko: D. ELOISE MORGAN, GERTRUDE QUINLAN, MATTIE MARTZ. *Katisha*, an elderly lady in love with Nanki-Poo: MAUDE LAMBERT. *Chorus of School Girls, Nobles, Guards and Coolies.*

1900.28 A RUNAWAY GIRL

A Revival of the Musical Play in Two Acts[83]. Book by Seymour Hicks and Harry Nicholls. Music by Ivan Caryll and Lionel Monckton. Lyrics by Aubrey Hopwood and Harry Greenbank. Directed by B. D. Stevens and Edwin H. Price. Produced by Daniel Frohman. Opened 23 April 1900 at Daly's Theatre and closed 2 June 1900 after 40 performances.

CAST: *Flipper*, a Jockey: JAMES T. POWERS. *Guy Stanley*, Lord Coodle's nephew: VAN RENSSLAER WHEELER. *Lord Coodle*, a Cook's tourist: MAURICE ABBY. *Professor Tamarind*, teacher at the school of St. Pierre: JOSEPH C. FAY. *Hon. Signor Poloni*, Consul at Corsica: Henry Stanley. *Hon. Bobby Barclay*, a Tourist: CHARLES RUTHVEN SMITH. *Mr. Creel*, an entomologist and disciple of Walton: SPOTTISWOOD AITKEN. *Leonello*, chief of a band of wandering musicians: Arthur Cunningham. *Pietro Pescare*, his aider and abetter: George Lesoir. *Members of Band (3)*: *Santa Cruz*: Frank Regis. *Boccaccio*: Robert M. O'Neil. *Doloroso*: Joseph Cauto.

[78]Musical numbers not listed in the program; list prepared from published piano vocal score (M. Witmark & Sons, 1900).

[79]Originally presented in New York 15 January 1879 at the Standard Theatre for 175 performances. This production previously appeared in New York twice: 14 February 1898 at the American Theatre on a bill with "Cavaleria Rusticana" for 8 performances, and 6 February 1899 at the American Theatre for 16 performances. For Synopsis of Scenes and Musical Numbers, see original 1879 production. There exists extant contradictory programs for this 1900 revival in which PINAFORE and TRIAL BY JURY each appear to have been performed first.

[80]First presented in New York 15 November 1875 at the Eagle Theatre for 8 performances. For Synopsis of Scenes and Musical Numbers, see original 1875 production. Castle Square Opera Company previously presented TRIAL BY JURY as the second half of a double bill with THE BARBER OF SEVILLE 24 April 1899.

[81]First presented in New York in an unauthorized version 20 July 1885, 17-29 August 1885 at the Union Square and Henry Miner's People's Theatres for 22 performances. Presented 19 August 1885 at the Fifth Avenue Theatre by Richard D'Oyly Carte for 250 performances. For Synopsis of Scenes and Musical Numbers, see original 1885 D'Oyly Carte production. This revival previously presented by the Castle Square Opera Company 28 March 1898 at the American Theatre for 16 performances.

[82]No program available.

[83]First produced in New York 31 August 1898 at Daly's Theatre for 216 performances. For Synopsis of Scenes and Musical Numbers, see original 1898 production.

Gendarmes: Messrs. Roerke, Symonds. *Waiter* at the hotel in Ajaccio: William J. Welch. *Winnifred Grey*, an orphan: MARIE CELESTE. *Alice*, Lady Coodle's maid: RACHEL BOOTH. *Carmenita*, one of the band: PAULA EDWARDES. *Dorothy Stanley*, a Cook's tourist: MAY BAKER. *Lady Coodle*: CARRIE LOCKE. *Mrs. Creel*, on her wedding tour: CAROLYN GORDON. *Fraulein Ehrenbreitstein*, tourist: Jane Schenck. *Agatha*, a schoolgirl: Mamie Walsh. *Martha*, another: Ollie Craig. *Members Lady Coodle's Tourist Party*: *Pearl Nelson*: Frances Tyson. *Dolly Dudley*: Carrie Locke. *Maud Brook*: Beth Marr. *Grace Arlington*: Isobel Hall. *Bertie Wales*: Jeanette Ivel. *Jessie Portman*: Eleanor Burton. *George St. George*: Almira Forrest.

Eva Grosvenor: Babe Stanley. *Dancers at the Carnival*: Misses Locke, Armstrong, Ivel, Gunderman. *Folly in the Carnival Dance*: CAROLYN GORDON. *Flower Girls*: Misse Rudd, Weigant, Holt, Howe. *Postillons*: Misses Welch, Harris, Armstrong, Ashlyn, Knight, Noel. *Sabot Girls*: Misses Tyson, Stanley, Craig, Conly, Guderman, Forrest. *Peasants, Gondoliers, Brigands, etc.*

1900.29

THE BLACK HUSSAR

A Return Engagement of the Revival of the Operetta in Three Acts[84]. (Original Viennese libretto 'Der Feldprediger' by Hugo Wittmann and Alois Wohlmuth. English adaptation by Sydney Rosenfeld.) Music by Carl Millöcker. Stage director, A. W. F. MacCollin. Scenery by Thomas G. Moses. Costumes by Fritz Schoultz & Co. Musical director, Clarence West. Produced by the Castle Square Opera Company (Henry W. Savage, Proprietor). Opened 23 April 1900 at the American Theatre and closed 28 April 1900 after 8 performances.

CAST: *(Friedrich von) Helbert*, Captain in Black Hussars, disguised as an Army Chaplain: REGINALD ROBERTS. *(Hans von) Waldmann*, his companion: RICHARD RIDGELY. *(Theophil) Hackenback*, Magistrate of Trautenfeld: WILLIAM PRUETTE. *Piffkow*, his man-of-all-work: FRANK MOULAN. *(François) Thorilliere*, Major in Napoleon's Army: Eugene Danton. *Hansiber*, a Prussian officer: J. Barry. *Hetman*, Captain of the Cossacks: A. Barbara. *Mifflin*, an actor: Charles Meyers. *Hackenback's Daughters (2)*: *Minna*: D. ELOISE MORGAN. *Rosetta*: GUELMA L. BAKER. *Barbara*, (an Orphan, Hackenback's Housekeeper): CARRIE GODFREY. *Ricca*: Mattie Martz. *Germania*: Naomi Arnold. *First Citizen*: Arthur Evans.

1900.30

A NIGHT IN VENICE

A Revival of the Comic Opera in Three Acts[85]. Original German libretto (to the operette 'Eine Nacht in Venedig') by F. Zell and Richard Genée, based on "Le Château Trompette" by Jules Cormon and Michel Carré. Music by Johann Strauss. Stage manager, A. W. F. MacCollin. Musical director, Clarence West. Produced by the Castle Square Opera Company (Henry W. Savage, Proprietor). Opened 30 April 1900 at the American Theatre and closed 5 May 1900 after 8 performances.[86]

CAST: *Duke of Urbino*: WILLIAM G. STEWART. *Seators of Venice (3)*: *Bartholomeo Delacqua*: WILLIAM PRUETTE. *Stefano Barbaruccio*: RAYMOND HITCHCOCK. *Georgia Testaccio*: Charles Meyer. *Caramello*, the Court Barber: HARRY DAVIES. *Pappacoda*, a Macaroni Cook: FRANK MOULAN. *Enrico Piselli*, Nephew of Delacqua: LOUIS CASAVANT. *Centurio*, Page: Mattie Martz. *Balbi*, Guard: Harold DeBray. *Annina*, a Fisher Girl, and foster sister to Barbara: CLARA LANE. *Ciboletta*, Delacqua's Cook: GERTRUDE QUINLAN. *Barbara*: Guelma Baker. *Agricola, Constantia*, Senators' Wives: Maude Lambert, Nora MacGahan. *Peppino*: John Barry. *Macedonia*: Frances Wilson. *Thedolinda*: Naomi Arnold.

1900.31

ROBIN HOOD

The Bostonians in a Revival of the Comic Opera in Three Acts[87]. Libretto by Harry B. Smith. Music by Reginald DeKoven. Musical direction by Samuel L. Studley. Produced by The Bostonians (Henry Clay Barnabee and William H. MacDonald, Proprietors), (Marc) Klaw and (Abraham L.) Erlanger. Opened 7 May 1900 at the Knickerbocker Theatre and closed 12 May 1900 after 8 performances[88].

CAST: *Robert of Huntington*, afterwards Robin Hood: FRANK RUSHWORTH. *Sheriff of Nottingham*: HENRY CLAY BARNABEE. *Sir Guy of Gisborne*: W. H. FITZGERALD. *Little John*: WILLIAM H. MacDONALD. *Will Scarlet*: JOHN DUNSMURE. *Friar Tuck*: GEORGE B. FROTHINGHAM. *Alan-a-Dale*: MARCIA VAN DRESSER. *Lady Marian Fitzwater*: HELEN BERTRAM. *Dame Durden*: JOSEPHINE BARTLETT. *Annabel*: GRACE CAMERON. With Harry Dale, Adam Warmouth, David White, James E. Miller, Edith Hendee, Arthur T. Earnest, Henry Miller.

1900.32

THE SERENADE

The Bostonians in a Revival of the Operetta in Three Acts[89]. Book and lyrics by Harry B. Smith. Music by Victor Herbert. Staged by William H. Fitzgerald. Scenery by Walter Burridge, Ernest Albert and Alfred Williams. Musical direction by Samuel L. Studley. Produced by the Bostonians (Henry Clay Barnabee and William H. MacDonald, Proprietors), (Marc) Klaw and (Abraham L.) Erlanger. Opened 14 May 1900 at the Knickerbocker Theatre and closed 19 May 1900 after 8 performances.

CAST: *The Duke of Santa Cruz*, a self made nobleman, in love with Dolores, and pursuing the singer of the Serenade: HENRY CLAY BARNABEE. *Carlos Alvarado*, Baritone of the Madrid Opera, who loves Dolores, as he has quite rarely loved before; a fugitive from his creditors—also from Yvonne, whom he has jilted: W. H. MacDONALD. *Romero*, President of the Royal Madrid Brigandage Association, Limited, the head of an influential syndicate of robbers. He commits crimes one day and repents them the next as a monk in a monastery: JOHN DUNSMURE. *Lopez*, Secretray of the same corporation: FRANK RUSHWORTH. *Gomez*, a tailor in love with Dolores, and trying to learn the serenade in order to win her affections: GEORGE FROTHINGHAM. *Colombo*, formerly a grand opera tenor, now reduced to playing the devil in pantomime: W. H. FITZGERALD. *Yvonne*, his daughter, a ballet dancer at the Madrid Opera, in love with Alvarado, for whom she is looking with a wealth of devotion—and a stiletto: GRACE CAMERON. *The Mother Superior* of the Convent of St. Ursula: JOSEPHINE BARTLETT. *Schoolgirls (4)*: *Juana*: Edna Floyd. *Isabella*: Essie Lyons. *Mercedes*: Alice Radcliffe. *Corona*: Leslie Drake. *El Gato*, a brigand: William McDonald. *The Abbot of the Monastery of St. Benedict*: James E. Miller. *Fra Anselmo*: Harry Dale. *Fra Timoteo*: A. Warmouth. *Manuelo*, the duke's cook: Bertha Lovejoy. *Dolores*, the Duke's ward, in love with Alvarado: MARCIA VAN DRESSER.

---

[84]First produced in New York 4 May 1885 at Wallack's Theatre for 104 performances. For Synopsis of Scenes and Musical Numbers, see original May 1885 production. This revival previously produced by the Castle Square Opera Company 30 May 1898 at the American Theatre for 9 performances.

[85]First produced in New York in English 26 April 1884 at Daly's Theatre for 33 performances. For Synopsis of Scenes and Musical Numbers, see original 1884 production.

[86]No program available. American adaptation uncredited.

[87]Originally presented in New York 28 September 1891 at the Standard Theatre for 35 performances, returning that season to the Garden Theatres for 42 additional performances. For Synopsis of Scenes and Musical Numbers, see original 1891 production.

[88]Stage direction, scenery and costumes uncredited.

[89]First produced by the Bostonians in New York 16 March 1897 at the Knickerbocker Theatre for 79 performances in repertory. For Synopsis of Scenes and Musical Numbers, see original 1897 production.

1900–1901 SEASON

James T. Powers in SAN TOY (Photo: Falk, 1900)
Museum of the City of New York, Gift of Mrs. James T. Powers

1900–1901 SEASON

1900.33 THE "NEW" ROUNDERS

A Return Engagement of the Musical Comedy in Three Acts, 4 Scenes[1]. Book (and lyrics) by Harry B. Smith. Based on the libretto to "Les Fêtards" by Antony Mars and Maurice Hennequin[2]. Music by Ludwig Engländer. Staged by Max Freeman. Scenery by D. Frank Dodge, Ernest Albert. Costumes designed by Mme. Catherine Seidle. Orchestra under the direction of Ludwig Engländer. Produced by George Lederer. Opened 25 June 1900 at the Casino Theatre and closed 28 July 1900 after 36 performances[3].

CAST: *Maginnis Pasha*, an Irish Turk: THOMAS Q. SEABROOKE. *The Duke De Paty Du Clam*, who has tried everything and found nothing in it: JOSEPH HERBERT. *The Marquis de Baccarat*, the Moth for whom Thea is the flame: HARRY DAVENPORT. *Siegfried Gotterdammerung*, leader of a German street band: DAVE LEWIS. *Joseph*, head waiter at the Hotel Biarritz: H. W. Nowell. *Priscilla*, wife of the Marquis, an American girl, belonging to a worthy family of Quakers: MADGE LESSING. *Stella Giltedge*, an up-to-date American girl: IRENE BENTLEY. *Madame Seraphine*, Thea's "mother": SARAH McVICKER. *La Paloma*, a Spanish belle: TRIXIE FRIGANZA. *Angelique*, an innocent: Ruby Reid. *Adele Vere de Vere*, a type of English beauty: Susan [Suzie] Drake. *Fanchonette*, a little Parisienne: Lillie Madison. *Jolivet*, a young reporter: Paula Allen. *Ladies of the Ballet (5)*: *Celestine*: LOTTA FAUST. *Olympe*: Vincie Twohey. *Justine*: Eleanor Burns. *Octavine*: Marie Deene. *Rosine*: Martha Marlowe. *Joan*: Pollie Gibson. *Jacque*: Josie Nagle. *Raoul*: Daisy Lucas. *A First Nighter*: James A. Furey. *Swells, Patrons of the Ballet (3)*: *Gustave*: Burrell Barbaretto. *Gaston*: Florence May. *Honore*: Sadie Gerard. *Call Boy*: Zella Frank. *Ludwig Dollar*, leading cornetist: Sol Solomon. *Members of Siegfried's Band (5)*: *Fritz*: George Nagle. *Blitz*: James Callahan. *Snitz*: Tom Collins. *Littz*: Horace Hayne. *Ritz*: Edd West. *The Bathing Master*: Geoge Schramm. *Thea*, a ballet dancer: PHYLLIS RANKIN.

And Eileen Florence, Helen Lucas, Edith Moyer, Gertie Moyer, Margaret Wynn, Mabel Florence, Edith Potter, Frankie Barrington, Mildred Lorella, Valerie Fernando, Julia Caldwell, Marion Grant, Clem Herschel, Otto Heilig, Will Sissons, Thomas Hayden, George Rollands, Ed. Dossert, Will Walsh, Henry Dixey, Percy Hart, Albert Amadeo, others.

Act 1: The beach at Biarritz, by the Hotel Royal.

Act 2, Scene 1: The star dressing-room of a theatre in Paris. *Scene 2*: Salon at Maginnis Pasha's house in Paris.

Act 3: Corridor of the Hotel Metropole, Paris.

1900.34 THE CADET GIRL

A Musical Comedy in Three Acts, 6 Scenes. Book and lyrics by Harry B. Smith. Adapted from the French libretto for "Les Demoiselles de Saint-Cyriens" by Paul Gavault, Victor de Cottens. Music by Louis Varney and Ludwig Engländer[4]. Staged by George Marion. Scenery painted by D. Frank Dodge, La Moss. Costumes designed by Archie Gunn. Music director, Frederic Solomon. Produced by A. H. Chamberlyn. Opened 25 July 1900 at the Herald Square Theatre and closed 8 September 1900 after 48 performances.

CAST: *Baron Chartreuse*, his own best friend, a gentleman of scientific tastes looking for curiosities for a museum: DAN DALY. *Pelopidas*, a veteran of many wars—fond of romantic literature: JOSEPH C. MIRON. *Popo*, private secretary to the Baron: WILLIAM CAMERON. *Lucien*, a cadet of St. Cyr, in love with Marguerite: WILLIAM PROPERT CARLETON. *Georges*, his friend, in love with Daisy: CHARLES H. BOWERS. *Berg-ap-Zoom*, a Swiss scientist: GEORGE A. SCHILLER. *Griffard*, host of the Café de la Gare at St. Cyr: Charles Danby. *Calicot*, a notary: Charles Dox. *Edouarde*, a cadet: Adele Farrington. *Comemblers*, the oldest inhabitant: Fred Urban. *Station Master* of the village of Pic-en-Pointe: James Kane. *Marguerite*, pupil of Mme. Majeste's institution: ADELE RITCHIE. *Antoinette* Griffard's wife: CHRISTIE MacDONALD. *Daisy*, an American girl: TOBY CLAUDE. *Mme. Majeste*, proprietress of the institute: CATHERINE LEWIS. *Baroness*: Hattie Moore. *Margot*: Nella Webb. *Javotte*: Ollie Wallace. *Clairette*: Tessie Mooney. *Genevieve*: Lulu Mooney. *Jeanette*: Pauline Chase. *Francene*: Laura Witt. *Artine*: Florence Carlisle. *Leontine*: Mildred Meade. *Susette*: Erminie Earl. *Fanchette*: Dolly Anderson. *Nanette*: Grace Spencer. *Yvette*: Bessie Wynn. *Marie*: Kathryn Pearl. *Nanine*: Dorothy Lester.

Monitors, School Girls, Vivandieres: Misses Rita Riley, May Page, Ada Vreeland, Addie Orton, Helen Chester, Rose Boyer, Pauline Patz, Mabel Jordan, May Davis, Lulu Farrance, Mary Morris, Bertha Wilson, Estelle Franklin, Annie Schiller, Lida Lewis, Laura Stanley, E. Enright, Belle Wheeler. *Cadets of St. Cyr*: Messrs. Fairchild, Kissee, Hamilton, McGuire, Vail, Cox, Wichlow, Smith, Earle, Law, Ware, Meehan, Millholland, Chaille, Martin. *Trumpeters*: Arthur Etherington, Roy Richards,

Act 1: Garden in front of Madame Majeste's Seminary at Villepreux, near St. Cyr.

Act 2, Scene 1: Café de la Gare and Sumemr Garden at St. Cyr. *Scene 2*: Entrance to the Café de la Gare. *Scene 3*: Official Hall in Chateau of Camembert. (La Moss.)

Act 3, Scene 1: Pavilion of Love, Camembert. *Scene 2*: Exterior of Castle Camembert.

ACT 1

Opening Chorus
(*Music by* Ludwig Engländer.)

"The Demon of the Deep" (Song)
(*Music by* Ludwig Engländer.)

"When a Girl Doesn't Know What She Is" (Song)
T. Claude
(*Music by* Ludwig Engländer.)

Military Ensemble
(*Music by* Louis Varney.)

"The Cadets of St. Cyr" (Quartette)
(*Music by* Louis Varney.)

"I Annex It" (Duo)
D. Daly?
(*Music by* Ludwig Engländer. *Lyrics by* J. Cheever Goodwin.)

"In My Museum Now" (Song)
(*Music by* Ludwig Engländer.)

Finale
(*Music by* Louis Varney.)

ACT 2

"Cantineer of the Regiment" (Opening Chorus)
(*Music by* Louis Varney.)

"Ve Vas Germans" (Trio)
D. Daly, T. Claude, ?
(*Music by* Ludwig Engländer.)

Champagne Waltz and Chorus
A. Ritchie
(*Music by* Louis Varney.)

"The Special Train" (Song and Chorus)
(*Music by* Louis Varney.)

"We Cannot Let You Go" (Ensemble)
(*Music by* Louis Varney.)

Chorus of Notables
(*Music by* Louis Varney.)

"They Are Nothing But Girls"
D. Daly
(*Music by* Ludwig Engländer.)

"We Are the Heiresses" (Ensemble)
(*Music by* Louis Varney.)

"Come, Gentle Stranger" (Waltz Ensemble)
(*Music by* Louis Varney.)

Finale
(*Music by* Ludwig Engländer.)

ACT 3

"The Pavilion of Love" (Ensemble and Waltz)
(*Music by* Louis Varney.)

"Gottet Got" (Eccentric Song)
(*Music by* Louis Varney. *Lyrics by* J. Cheever Goodwin.)

Duo
(*Music by* Ludwig Engländer.)

"Battalion of France"
(*Music by* Louis Varney.)

Finale
(*Music by* Ludwig Engländer and Louis Varney.)

1900.35 THE CASINO BOY

A Burlesque in One Act, preceded by the Casino Beauty Minstrels and followed by a vaudeville program. Book and lyrics by Robert Smith. Music by Harry T. MacConnell. Music director, Arthur Weld. Produced by George W. Lederer. Opened 31 July 1900 at the Casino Roof Garden and closed 9 September 1900 after 35 performances.[5]

[1] First produced in New York 12 July 1899 at the Casino Theatre for 97 performances. For Synopsis of Scenes and Musical Numbers, see original 1899 production.

[2] The original French musical score by Victor Roger was discarded in lieu of an entirely new American score by Ludwig Engländer.

[3] Musical numbers not listed in program.

[4] Varney wrote the score for the original French production; Engländer provided the American interpolations.

[5] No program available.

Vaudeville: *The Casino Beauty Minstrels*: Ada Gardner (interlocutor), Andy Gardner, Frank White, Lew Simmons, Robert Ward, Jack Gardner, John Queen, Arthur F. Miller.

CAST: *Ginger Early*: ANNA LAUGHLIN. *Willie K. Seeno*: Countess von HATZFELDT. *Padlock Homes*: JACK GARDNER. *Nether Saphosole*: GEORGE K. FORTESCUE. *Mr. Nero*: GILBERT GREGORY. *Dennie*: SOL SOLOMON. *Matilda*: BELLE WILLIAMS. *Dakota Ethelbert*: JOHN QUEEN. *Cabman*: Robert Ward. *1900 A.D.*: Zella Frank. *The Whistling Newsboy*: Louis M. Granat. *Pajama*: William J. Conlan. *Bloomer*: Franklin J. Smith. *Trouser*: Mark S. Smith. *Pantaloon*: R. Edgar Vance. *Truly Would*: Minerva Courtney. *Surely Could*: Libbie Hart. *Really Should*: Louise Middleton. *Wholly Good*: Bessie Keyes. *Sincerely Thine*: Alice Lane. *Absolutely Mine*: Laura Lane. *Superbly Fine*: Pony Menzies. *Brightly Shine*: Josephine Nagle. *Cornell*: Amie Hadden. *Columbia*: Lettie Bryan. *Yale*: Isabel Carroll. *Harvard*: Maud Vincent. *Princeton*: Hattie Hilton. *Amherst*: Geraldine Cook. *Pennsylvania*: Helen Gordon. *Wisconsin*: Agnes Keller.

Vaudeville: The Three Gardners (Ada, Andy, Jack, in a musical act), Three Lane Sisters (acrobatic song and dance), Frank Manning (German comedy), Bailey and Madison (comedy), Lew Simmons and Frank White (blackface), Mlle. Alma (plastique poses), the World's Comedy Four, Cakewalk (Jack Gardner and 16 Girls).

1900.36 THE REBEL

A Drama of the Irish Rebellion in Four Acts, 6 Scenes. Play by James B. Fagan. (Music and Lyrics by Andrew Mack.) Produced under the stage direction of Joseph Humphries. Scenery by Joseph Physioc. Costumes by M. Hermann and Charles Chrisdie. Incidental music arranged by John C. Sorg, Musical director. Produced by (Isaac B.) Rich and (William) Harris. Opened 20 August 1900 at the Academy of Music and closed 20 October 1900 after 57 performances.

CAST: *Jack Blake*, one of the leaders of the rebelllion: ANDREW MACK. *Squire Bagenall*, an old country gentleman: George W. Deyo. *"Ned" Bagenall, Jr.*, his son, a boy of 19: John C. Ince, Jr. *Captain Armstrong*, of the Yeomanry: EDWIN BRANDT. *Father Teeling*, the village priest: John C. Fenton. *Concerned in the rebellion (4): Quire Fallon*: Henry Sutur. *"Hellcat" Ryan*: Edward Aiken. *Jimmy Keogh*: Thomas Jackson. *Counsellor O'Mahan*: William J. Morgan. *Colonel Desmarets*, an emissary from France: George Pullman. *"Dark" Michael Ogie*, a blind pedlar: Giles Shine. *Mick Raffery*, the village tailor: Charles MacDonald. *Andy*, Squire Bagenall's butler: Ben T. Ringgold. *Dr. Considine*, physician at Kilmarnham prison: Daniel O'Connell. *Gaoler*, at Kilmarnham prison: Edward Daley. *Lame Shaun, Larry "The Snatcher"*: Charles Walton, John Sylvester. *Corporal*: John Frees. *Sergeant*: John Frees. Jr. *Nora Bagenall*, the squire's daughter: JOSEPHINE LOVETT. *Bridget*, her maid: CLARA KNOTT. *Rebels, Soldiers, Peasants, etc.*

The action is set in Ireland in 1798.

Act 1, Scene 1: The Hall at Dunlecky. *Scene 2*: The meeting of the Rebels.

Act 2: A Chamber at Dunlecky.

Act 3, Scene 1: A Corridor in Kilmarnham Prison. *Scene 2*: The Vaults under the Church of St. Olaf.

Act 4: The Hall at Dunlecky.

MUSICAL NUMBERS

- "Mack's Serenade" (Oh, my love!)
  A. Mack
- "Freedom and Ireland" (Tara, you shall hear the harp once more)
  A. Mack
- "Little Tommy Murphy"
  A. Mack
- "Eyes of Blue"
  A. Mack

1900.37 THE ROSE OF PERSIA, or, The Story Teller and the Slave

A Comic Opera in Two Acts. Libretto by Basil Hood[6]. Music by Arthur Sullivan. Produced under the stage direction of Richard Barker. Scenery by Edward G. Unitt. Dresses designed by Percy Anderson. Musical director, William Furst. Produced by Charles Frohman, by arrangement with Richard D'Oyly Carte. Opened 6 September 1900 at Daly's Theatre and closed 29 September 1900 after 25 performances.

CAST: *The Sultan Mahmoud*: CHARLES ANGELO. *Hassan*, a philanthropist: JOHN LeHAY. *Yussuf*, a professional story-teller: SIDNEY BRACY. *Abdallah*, a priest: HERBERT CLAYTON. *The Grand Vizier*: Stuart Hyatt. *The Physician-in-Chief*: John Doran. *The Royal Executioner*: Arthur Barry. *The Sultana Zubedyeh*, named Rose-in-Bloom: RUTH VINCENT. *Her favorite slaves (3)*: *Scent-of-Lilies*: Hettis Lund. *Heart's Desire*: Isabelle Dillon. *Honey-of-Life*: Hilda Stephens. *Dancing Sunbeam*, Hassan's first wife: AMY MARTIN. *Blush-of-the-Morning*, his twenty-fifth wife: MARY CONYNGHAM. *Wives of Hassan (4)*: *Oasis-in-the Desert*: Doris Latour. *Moon-upon-the-Waters*: Hetty Hertzfeld. *Song-of-Nightingales*: Marguerite Trew. *Whisper-of-the-West-Wind*: Nell Meissener. *Chorus, Act 1*: Hassan's Wives, Mendicants, and Sultan's Guards. *Chorus, Act 2*: Royal Slave-Girls, Palace Officials, Guards.

Act 1: Court of Hassan's house.

Act 2: Audience Hall of Sultan's Palace.

ACT 1[7]

- "As We Lie in Languor Lazy" (Opening Chorus)
  Chorus of Girls
- "I'm Abu-el-Hassan" (Song)
  J. LeHay
- "When Islam First Arose" (Song)
  H. Clayton, Chorus of Girls
- "Dancing Sunbeam"[8] (Song)
  A. Martin
- "If a Sudden Stroke of Fate" (Trio)
  M. Conyngham, A. Martin, H. Clayton
- "If You Ask Me to Advise You" (Trio)
  R. Vincent, H. Lund, I. Dillon
- "'Neath My Lattice" (Song)
  R. Vincent
- "Tramps and Scamps"
  Chorus
- "When My Father Sent Me to Ispahan" (Song)
  J. LeHay, Chorus
- "I Care Not If the Cup I Hold" (Song)
  S. Bracy, Chorus
- "Mystical Maidens Are We" (Ensemble with Dance and Chorus)
  R. Vincent, H. Lund, I. Dillon, H. Stephens, J. LeHay, Chorus
- "We Have Come to Invade"
  H. Clayton, J. LeHay
- "What Will Become of Me?" (Octette)
  J. LeHay,
  A. Martin, D. Latour, H. Hertzfeld, M. Trew, N. Meissener, M. Conyngham, Wives
- "I'm the Sultan's Vigilant Vizier" (Dervish Quartet)
  S. Hyatt, J. Doran, A. Barry, C. Angelo
- Finale (Oh, luckless hour!)

ACT 2

- "Oh, What Is Love?" (Song)
  I. Dillon, S. Bracy
- "If You or I Should Tell the Truth" (Quartet)
  H. Lund, H. Stephens, I. Dillon, S. Bracy
- "From Morning Prayer to Sultan"
  S. Hyatt, J. Doran, A. Barry, Chorus
- "Let a Satirist Enumerate a Catalogue of Crimes" (Song and Chorus)
  C. Angelo
- "In My Heart of Hearts I've Always Known" (Septette)
  A. Martin, M. Conyngham, H. Stephens, M. Trew, C. Angelo, S. Hyatt, J. Doran
- "Suppose—I Say, Suppose" (Duet)
  R. Vincent, C. Angelo
- "Laughing Low, on Tip-toe"
  Chorus
- "Where Am I?"
  J. LeHay, S. Hyatt, J. Doran, Chorus
- "It's a Busy Day" (Quintet and Chorus)
  H. Lund, A. Barry, S. Bracy, I. Dillon, J. LeHay
- "Our Tale Is Told" (Song)
  S. Bracy
- "What Does It Mean?" (Recitative and Quartet)
  A. Martin, M. Conyngham, S. Bracy, A Soldier of the Guard

[6] Inspired by the tale of "Abu Hassan, or The Sleeper Awakened" from the "Arabian Nights."

[7] Musical Numbers not listed in program; list prepared from New York production typescript and published English vocal score (Chappell & Co., Ltd., London, 1900).

[8] Not in English vocal score.

"It Has Reached Me a Lady Named Hubbard" (Septette)
A. Martin, H. Lund, S. Bracy, J. LeHay, Others
"Hassan, the Sultan with His Court Approaches"
S. Hyatt, J. Doran, A. Barry, Chorus
"There Once Was a Small Street Arab" (Song)
J. LeHay
Finale

1900.38 FIDDLE-DEE-DEE

A Knockout Blow to the Demons of Care and Melancholy (Musical Burlesque) in Two Acts. Dialogue and lyrics by Edgar Smith. Music by John Stromberg. Produced under the direction of (staged by) Julian Mitchell. Scenery painted by John R. Young. Costumes by Will R. Barnes. Music director, John Stromberg. Produced by (Joseph M.) Weber and (Lew M.) Fields. Opened 6 September 1900 at Weber and Fields' Music Hall and closed 20 April 1901 after 262 performances[9].

ACT 1

FIDDLE-DEE-DEE, A Potpourri of Dramatic Fol-di-rol, in 2 Scenes.

CAST: *Hoffman Barr*, an athletic young American, with nothing but money and nothing to do but spend it: DeWOLF HOPPER. *Shadrach Leschinski*, a Hebrew prestidigitateur: DAVID WARFIELD. *Michael Krautknuckle, Rudolf Bungstarter*, on a pleasure trip to the Paris exposition: JOSEPH M. WEBER, LEW M. FIELDS. *Ignatius McSorley*, doing the continent for the first time: JOHN T. KELLY. *Birdie McSorley*, his niece, from Ireland: Charles Fostelle. *Leo*, a St. Bernard dog: GEORGE ALI. *Ingambe*, an acrobat: Benjamin Hapgood (Burt). *Pourboire*, a waiter: Harold T. Morey. *Mrs. Waldorf Meadowbrook*, a young widow, with a longing to do something to startle society: LILLIAN RUSSELL. *La Belle Zara*, a chanteuse Parisienne: FAY TEMPLETON. *Fantine, Frizette*, birds of prey: Josephine Allen, Irene Vera. *Mariette, Googoo*, automatic dolls: Bonnie Maginn, Belle Robinson. *Bilkarine*, a collector: Margaret Sayre. *Nervie Tartington*, an embryo Bernhardt: Goldie Mohr. *American youths doing Paris (7)*: *Nestor Puffer*: Bonnie Maginn. *Sterling Kane*: May Sherwood. *Dodge Carr*: Leona Hilbon. *Charley Horseleigh*: Goldie Mohr. *Madison Parks*: Jessie Richmond. *Claremont Riverside*: Vernie Wadsworth. *Asbury Sands*: Genevieve Dolaro. *Cinqcentime*, a valet: May McKenzie. *Allez*, a gendarme: Myra Smith.

Hoffman Barr's String of Beauties: Gladys Canby, Marie Early, Rhoda Wheeler, Dottie Ryder, Mazie Walzinger, Merrie Andrews, Carrie Waite, Blondie Dyer, Lotta Fellows, Poney Upton, Cora Appleby, Olive Green, May Kissam, Violet Jewell, Inez Rae, Ilma Pratt, Grace Pierrepont, Mae Sherwood, Georgia Stewart, Florence Bell, Phyllis LaFond, Mazie Follette, Eva Allen, Florence Deshone, Clara Selden, May Page. *Forrest Holmes*, aerobat: Nata Stromberg. *Fourchette*, a chanteuse: Florence Dressler. *Spanish dancers (4)*: *Bolero*: Phyllis LaFond. *Cachuca*: Belle Robinson. *Seguedilla*: Violet Jewell. *Fandango*: Mazie Follette. *Lingerie Sisters (4)*: *Garta*: Grace Pierrepont. *Valencienne*: Carrie Willis. *Torchon*: Ilma Pratt. *Basbleu*: Virginia Foltz. *Shirt-waist men (4)*: *Duryea Starchleigh*: Leona Hilbon. *Wilton Warmington*: Lillian Heckler. *J. Withers Belton*: Dappy Grey. *Budd Carmichael*: Virginia Foltz. *Specialty Dance* (La Danse d'Afrique): BESSIE CLAYTON.

Scene 1: Rue de Paris, at the Exposition. *Scene 2*: The Swiss Village, at the Exposition.

ACT 1

"Come One, Come All, and See the Sights" (Opening Chorus)
"The Tips of Gay Paree"[10] (Song)
J. T. Kelly
"Nothing Doing"[11] (Song)
D. Hopper
"I Sigh for a Change" (Song)
L. Russell
"Comic Opera" (Duet)
L. Russell, D. Hopper
"Je ne le comprends pas"[12]
"Ma Blushin' Rosie, Ma Posie Sweet" (Rosie, You Are My Posey)
F. Templeton, Ensemble
"Fiddle-dee-dee March"[13] (Dance)
B. Clayton
Swiss Yodel (Swiss Warble and Dance)
G. P. Watson, Ensemble
"Come Back, My Honey Boy, to Me"
L. Russell
Finale

ACT 2

QUO VASS ISS?, a Burlesque by Edgar Smith on the drama "Quo Vadis" by Stanislaus Stange, from the novel by Henry Sienkiewicz. Closed 17 October 1900 after 48 performances.

CAST: *Petrolius*, an oily Roman gent, in high favor with Zero: DeWOLF HOPPER. *Marcus Finishus*, a Tribune: CHARLES J. ROSS. *Zero*, Emperor of Rome: JOHN T. KELLY. *Fursus*, a strong man: JOSEPH M. WEBER. *Smallus*, a Roman kid: LEW M. FIELDS. *Hilo*, a hobo philosopher: DAVID WARFIELD. *Tickeliritus*, a general: Harold T. Morey. *Starvus*, a poet: Margaret Sayre. *Punctus Tireas*, a freedman: Harold T. Morey. *Deodorus*, a merchant: Violet Jewell. *Porus Plasta*, a centurion: Grace Pierrepont. *Chirpnos*, a musician: Leona Hillbon. *Infamous Touchus*, a pickpocket: Ben Hapgood. *Plain, everyday Romans (4)*: *Quininius Malarius*: Carrie Willus. *Duflikus Tumatus*: May Sherwood. *Bogus Extrus*: Virginia Foltz. *Peddlus Potatus*: Eva Allen. *Sparrus Copus*, a Roman park policeman: George Ali. *Lythia*, of the Rome W.C.T.U.: FAY TEMPLETON. *Popcornea*, Empress of Rome: Josephine Allen. *Spoonice*, slave to Petrolius: Bonnie Maginn. *Numonia*, maid of honor to the Empress: Belle Robinson. *Acta, Pumpia*, friends of Lythia: Goldie Mohr, Mazie Follette. *Rubba, Catapilla*, ladies of Zero's court: Phyllis LaFond, Ilma Pratt. *Gladiators (6)*: *Stabba*: Myra Smith. *Killa*: Georgia Stewart. *Slashus*: Inez Rae. *Jabba*: Florence Bell. *Solus*: Marie Worthington. *Plexus*: Clara Selden.

Scene: Public gardens in Rome adjoining the palace of Zero, the residence of Petrolius, and the Arena.

MUSICAL NUMBERS

"We Are Citizens of Rome"
Chorus
"Signor Gazamma" (Song)
D. Hopper, Ensemble
"(Come) Fetch Your Baby Home" (Song)
F. Templeton, Ensemble
Finale

QUO VASS ISS? was replaced 18 October 1900 by ARIZONA, a burlesque on Augustus Thomas' play of the same name, for 73 performances. Dialogue and lyrics by Edgar Smith. Music by John Stromberg. Staged by Julian Mitchell.

CAST: *Henry Cannedbeef*, owner of the Aridvapor Ranch: DeWOLF HOPPER. *Of the 11th U.S. Cavalry (7)*: *Colonel Bunjam*: JOHN T. KELLY. *Captain Hogman*: DAVID WARFIELD. *Lieutenant Tention*: CHARLES J. ROSS. *Sergeant Killer*: LEW M. FIELDS. *Doctor Felon*: Harold T. Morey. *Lieutenant Stung*: Bonnie Maginn. *Lieutenant Frolic*: Virginia Foltz. *Pony Mustango*, a cow gent: George P. Watson. *Ham Song*, a boxer: George Ali. *Sarsaparilla*, the colonel's wife and Bonita's sister: LILLIAN RUSSELL. *Bonita*, daughter of the owner of the Aridvapor Ranch: FAY TEMPLETON. *Lena Killer*, the sergeant's daughter: JOSEPH M. WEBER. *Mrs. Cannedbeef*: Charles Fostelle. *Miss MacCrullers*, a school teacher: Ilma Pratt. *Montezuma Matt*, a puncher: Leona Hilbon. *El Paseo Pete*, another: Belle Robinson. *Alkali Bill*, another: Goldie Mohr. *Lariat Luke*, another: Phyllis LaFond. *Buck Saddler*, another: Margaret Sayre. *Hi Roper*, another: Violet Jewell. *"Pop" Gunner*, another: Mae Sherwood. *Apache Charley*, another: Grace Pierrepont. *Cherokee Kid*, another: Mazie Follette. *Antonio Alamo*, a vaquero: Carrie May. *Durango Colorado*, a vaquero: Myra Smith. *Chiaca Tamale*, a vaquero: Georgia Stewart. *Pupa Chihuahua*, a vaquero: Florence Bell. *Juan Sombrero*, a vaquero: May McKenzie. *Soldiers of the 11th U.S. Cavalry*: Misses Dappy Grey, Jessie Richmond, Eva Allen, Lillian Heckler, Grace Heckler, Vernie Wadsworth, Mamie Gould, Edna Birch, Ethel Jewett, Madge Adae, Nettie Barton.

MUSICAL NUMBERS

"Beautiful Arizona" (Song)
D. Hopper
"Uncle Sam's Boys in Blue" (Chorus)
"Puff Puff" (Song)
Finale

ARIZONA was replaced 20 December 1900 by EXHIBIT II, comprised of burlesques of "The Gay Lord Quex" and "The Royal Family", a composite affair which may pass for a brief review of several more serious dramatic morceaux[14]. Dialogue and lyrics by Edgar Smith. Music by John Stromberg. Produced under the direction of Julian Mitchell. This closed 20 April 1901 after 141 performances.

---

[9]A much revised touring version (without Weber & Fields) played a return engagement 23 February 1902 at the Grand Opera House for 8 performances.

[10]Replaced for subsequent tour by:
"McSorley's Trip to Paris 'Cafe Chantants' with Spanish, Scotch and Irish Dances"

[11]Dropped early in the run.

[12]Dropped for subsequent tour.

[13] Replaced for subsequent tour by:
"In the Good Old Summer Time"
(*Music by* George Evans. *Lyrics by* Ren Shields.)

[14]A 20-minute burlesque of "Captain Jinks of the Horse Marines" was added 28 March 1901 to Exhibit II. Cast: *Madame Trentoni*, as played by Ethel Barrymore: FAY TEMPLETON. *Professor Bellarti*, as played by Edwin Stevens: DeWOLF HOPPER. *Captain Jinks*, as played by H. Reeves-Smith: DAVID WARFIELD. *Ballet Girls*: Messrs. Weber, Fields, Kelly, Fostelle, and Ali. *Bell-boy*: Virginia Foltz.

CAST: *The Gay Lord Quex*, or rather Hoffman Barr, masquerading as such: DeWOLF HOPPER. *Prince Victor Constantine*, masquerading as Count Bernadine: FRITZ WILLIAMS. *Rudolf Bungstarter*, masquerading as King Louis, in the Royal Family: LEW M. FIELDS. *Michael Krautknuckle*, masquerading as Prince Ferdinand, in the Royal Family: JOSEPH M. WEBER. *Shadrach Leschinski*, masquerading as Queen Ferdinand , in the Royal Family: DAVID WARFIELD. *Ignatius McSorley*, masquerading as Baron Grogstein, in the Royal Family: JOHN T. KELLY. *Tipit*, a butler: GEORGE ALI. *Ingambe*, an acrobat: Ben Hapgood. *Pourboire*, a waiter: Harold T. Morey. *Mrs. Meadowbrook*, masquerading as the Princess Angela, in the Royal Family: LILLIAN RUSSELL. *Sophy Fullgally*, a manicure hartiste, with designs on Gay Lord Quex: FAY TEMPLETON. *Baron Holdfaste*, friend of Prince Constantine: Bonnie Maginn. *Flossie, Dossie, Bossie*, three flirts: BONNIE MAGINN, ALLIE GILBERT, BELLE ROBINSON. *Patrons of the Manicuring Art (6): Dodge Carr*: Leona Hilbon. *Sterling Kane*: May Sherwood. *Madison Parks*: Virginia Foltz. *Claremont Riverside*: Dappy Grey. *Asbury Sands*: May McKenzie. *Charlie Horseleigh*: Genevieve Dolaro. *Manicure Girls (6): Miss Fyles*: Belle Robinson. *Miss Emery*: Allie Gilbert. *Miss Rosaline*: Violet Jewell. *Miss Brummell*: Ilma Pratt. *Miss Towle*: Ruth Rollins. *Miss Cutter*: Lillian Heckler. *Duchess of Prude*: Margaret Sayre. *Flames of Lord Quex (5): Countess of Elmhurst*: Irene Vera. *Lady Lowbridge*: Inez Rae. *Lady Syosset*: Grace Pierrepont. *Lady Hempstead*: Jessie Richmond. *Lady Westbury*: Madge Adae. *Lacqueys (6): Chilton*: Mamie Gould. *Chomondley*: Vernie Wadsworth. *Hammersley*: Grace Heckler. *Cortland*: Alice Curtis. *Bleeker*: Minnie Garretty. *Essex*: Sissie Garretty.

Scene: Grounds of a Villa near Paris, occupied by Hoffman Barr.

MUSICAL NUMBERS[15]

"The Latest Cure for Ennui"
Chorus
"That's About the Size of It" (Song)
D. Hopper
"I'm a Respectable Working Girl" Song)
F. Templeton
"Tell Us, Pretty Ladies" (Song and Dance Sextette)
"Fads" (Song)
L. Russell
Finale

1900.39 THE MONKS OF MALABAR

A Comic Opera in Three Acts. Libretto by J. Cheever Goodwin. Music by Ludwig Engländer. Staged by Al. M. Holbrook. Settings by Henry E. Hoyt. Costumes by Dazian. Music director, Emerico Morealle. Produced by Messrs. (Sam) Nixon & (J. F.) Zimmerman. Opened 14 September 1900 at the Knickerbocker Theatre and closed 20 October 1900 after 39 performances.

CAST: *Boolboom*, merchant of Malabar[16]: FRANCIS WILSON. *Daru*, Nabob of Khari-Khali: VAN RENSSELAER WHEELER. *The Maharajah of Malabar*: HALLEN MOSTYN. *The Nabob's Chums (3): Bitoby*: H. Arling. *Bakari*: SIDNEY JARVIS. *Macassar*: J. Ratliff. *Anita Tivoli*, A Parisienne: MADGE LESSING. *Cocodilla*, a lady's maid: MAUD HOLLINS. *Zizibar*, her lover: EDITH BRADFORD. *Boolboom's Servants (3): Djelma*: CLARA PALMER. *Ninika*: Louise Lawton. *Zoloe*: Edith Hutchins. *The Monks, Nobles, Bayaderes, Guards, Citizens of Malabar, Slaves, etc.*

Act 1: Under the Taj Mahal in Malabar.

Act 2: Outside the Maharajah's Palace of Pearls.

Act 3: Inside the Maharajah's Palace of Domes.

ACT 1[17]

"Hail the Groom and Hail the Bride" (Prelude and Opening Chorus)
"I Love My Love" (Solo)
E. Bradford
"Where He Goes We Go Too" (Solo)
M. Hollins
"The Monks of Malabar" (Solo)
F. Wilson, Chorus
"The Dear Little French Grisette" (Duet)
F. Wilson, V. R. Wheeler
"Singing and Dancing"
Ensemble
"In Gay Paree" (Solo)
M. Lessing, Chorus
"Article 213" (Sextette)
F. Wilson, E. Bradford, M. Hollins, C. Palmer, L. Lawton, E. Hutchins
"Joseph, James and John" (Duet)
F. Wilson, M. Lessing
"Go On and Marry!" (Finale)

ACT 2

"With Keen Anticipation" (Opening Ensemble)
"Hear! Hear!" (Solo)
H. Mostyn
"You Know That I Adore You" (Duet)
E. Bradford, M. Hollins
"Ebb and Flow" (Solo)
V. R. Wheeler, Chorus
"With Glad Acclaim"
Chorus
"Then, If I Understand Right" (Duet)
F. Wilson, M. Lessing, Chorus
"No More Weighted Down by Sorrow"(Finale)

ACT 3

"Ha! Ha! Ha! Ha! Ha! Ha!" (Quartette)
E. Bradford, M. Hollins, E. Hutchins, C. Palmer
"Here We Are Sir" (Servants' Chorus)
Chorus
"Ere I Wed You" (Trio)
F. Wilson, M. Lessing, V. R. Wheeler
Finale

1900.40 THE ROGERS BROTHERS IN CENTRAL PARK

A Vaudeville Farce in Three Acts. Book by John J. McNally. Music by Maurice Levi. Lyrics by J. Cheever Goodwin. Staged by Ben Teal. Scenery painted by Ernest Gros. Dresses designed by F. Richard Anderson. Electrical effects by Edw. Ocker. Music director, Maurice Levi. Produced by (Marc) Klaw & (Abraham L.) Erlanger Comedy Company. Opened 17 September 1900 at the Hammerstein's Victoria Theatre and closed 24 November 1900 after 72 performances[18].

CAST: *Marcus Blatter*: GUS ROGERS. *Lucas Stucke*: MAX ROGERS. *Al Money*, an explorer: EUGENE O'ROURKE. *George Merri*, driven to gaiety: WILLIAM WEST. *Ben Dunne*, but still doing: LEE HARRISON. *Sam Clippe*, office-boy: JOHN PAGE. *Lavord*, proprietor Casino, Central Park: Carl King. *Con Maguffin*: James Cherry. *Park Policeman*: James Cherry. *Chief Inspector*: James Cherry. *Inspector Wotts*: Joseph Merrick. *Inspector Dotts*: George H. Nagel. *Inspector Botts*: Carl King. *Tom Swift*: Willie Torpey. *Belle Money*, Money's divorced wife: DELLA FOX. *Rose Merri*, George's wife: GRACE FREEMAN. *Floretta Diggs*, George's aunt: MARION LANGDON. *Marie LeHaute*: JEANNETTE BAGEARD. *Bettina Betts*: EDITH ST. CLAIR. *Constance Strain*, stenographer: Emma Francis. *Daisy Money*: Leonie Dueth. *Ezi Money, Helen Money*, Money's nieces: Gertrude Saye, Dollie Wiggins. *Alona Money*: Hattie Waters. *Sisie Camera*: Madge Pierce. *Lucy Ricky*: May Taylor. *Cora De Fitzmaurice*: Margaret Stewart. *Carrie Page*: Elsie Davis. *Charlie Plenty*: Ruth Renard. Willie Want: Mildred Claire. *French Girls, Spanish Girls, Irisg Girls, Grass Widows, American Girls, Guests, Attendants, etc.*

The action takes place in New York today.

Act 1: Money's Matrimonial Agency.

Act 2: The Casino, Central Park.

Act 3: Roof of the Waldorf-Astoria (night).

ACT 1

Opening Chorus
"The Matrimonial Agent"
E. O'Rourke, Full Chorus
"The Duchess of Central Park"
J. Bageard, Full Chorus
"Lina, My Lady"/"Barnacle Jim and Binnacle Tim" (Specialty)
Rogers Brothers, D. Fox

---

[15] Added to The Royal Family burlesque 28 March 1901 in burlesque of the song 'Tact' from FLORODORA:
"Nerve"
F. Templeton

[16] Vocal score identifies Boolboom as a French merchant living in India.

[17] Musical numbers not listed in program. List prepared from published piano vocal score.

[18] Played a return engagement 1 April 1901 at the Grand Opera House for 8 performances.

ACT 2
"In Central Park" (Opening Chorus)
"A Bottle and a Bird"
D. Fox, Full Chorus
Songs
W. West
Sayings and Parodies[19]
Rogers Brothers
"The Brave Hussar" (Military March)
M. Langdon, Full Chorus
"Is It Yes, or Is It No?" (Specialty)
J. Page, E. Francis
"When Reuben Comes to Town" (Quartette)
J. Bageard, D. Fox, Rogers Brothers
"Darktown Barbecue" (Finale)
Full Company
ACT 3
"Up on the Roof" (Opening Chorus)
"Sally" (Song)
G. Freeman, Full Chorus
"If Cabby Told Half What He Knows" (Cabby Specialty)
D. Fox, assisted by
H. Waters, E. Davis, D. Wiggins, M. Pierce, G. Saye, M. Taylor, M. Claire, L Dueth
"Run, Brudder Possum, Run" (Specialty)
Rogers Brothers, Full Chorus
(*Music by* C. Rosamond Johnson. *Lyrics by* Bob Cole and James Weldon Johnson.)
Finale
Full Company

1900.41 THE BELLE OF BOHEMIA

A Musical Farce in Two Acts, 4 Scenes. Book and lyrics by Harry B. Smith. Music by Ludwig Engländer. Staged by George W. Lederer. Ballets arranged by Sig. Aurelia Coccia. Settings by D. Frank Dodge, Ernest Albert and Joseph Physioc. Costumes by Mme. Caroline Siedle. Orchestra under the direction of Paul Steindorff. Produced by George W. Lederer. Opened 24 September 1900 at the Casino Theatre and closed 10 November 1900 after 55 performances.

CAST: *Adolph Klotz*, a wandering photographer: SAM BERNARD. *Rudolph Dinkelhauser*, a brewer: DICK BERNARD. *Phelim McDuffy*, an influential politician and amateur musician: D. L. DON. *Algy Cuffs*, a matinee ideal, leading at a popular New York theatre: PAUL F. NICHOLSON. *Yellowplush*, Dinkelhauser's English Tiger: FREDERICK SOLOMON. *Chick Riley*, the pride of the Bowery: JOHN HYAMS. *Doctor Pillsbury*, a veterinary surgeon: JAMES A. FUREY. *'Arris, 'Awkins*, song and dance men: Sol Solomon, Stanford Wylie. *Hooligan, Mulligan*, two of the finest: Fred Titus, Clement Herschel. *Friends of Klotz (6)*: *Cammembert*: Otto Heilig. *Vermicelli*: Thomas F. Hayden. *Doeumpsky*: Benjamin Schwartz. *Ole Olson*: Percy Hart. *Machaggis*: Julian Myers. *Murphy*: Gilbert Schramm. *Paquita*, formerly Spanish dancer, wife of Dinkelhauser: MARIE DAINTON. *Geraldine McDuffy*, a Matinee girl: IRENE BENTLEY. *Mame*, otherwise La Sahara, a snake-chamer and fortune-teller: ANNA LAUGHLIN. *Brassie*, a golf caddy: Zella Frank. *Swift*, a messenger boy: Zella Frank. *Chloe*, colored nurse to Dinkelhauser: Trixie Friganza. *Little Katie, Little Leopold*, Klotz's children: Virgie Martin, A. Gentle. *Rosie Mulberry* of "de Bowery": BONNIE CLARK.

Matinee Girls: *Sadie Stuyvesant*: Susie Drake. *Mamie Livingstone*: Ruby Reid. *Carrie Van Cortlandt*: Lotta Faust. *Daisy Manhattan*: Eugenie White. *Laura Astergilt*: Teddie DuCoe. *Hattie Van Twiller*: Eleanor Burns. *Netty Rubygold*: Katherine Broughton. *Polly Lafayette*: Geraldine Fair. *Jessie Jefferson*: Minnie Edwards. *Myrtle Claremont*: Cecilia Garrick.

Rural Visitors to Coney Island: *Si. Muggins*: JAMES A. FUREY. *Mrs. Muggins*: Trixie Friganza. *Ebenezer*: J. Myers. *Samanthy*: Lillian Madison.

Katie, wife of Klotz, and a serio-comic singer, known as Mlle. Clarisse: VIRGINIA EARLE.

Act 1: Klotz's Tin-type Gallery at Coney Island. (Dodge.)

Act 2, Scene 1: Dinkelhauser's Villa at Newport. (Albert.) *Scene 2*: Garden of same. (Dodge.) *Scene 3*: Chateau in Switzerland. (Physioc.)

ACT 1
Opening Chorus
"Strolling thro' the River" (Duet; Song and Dance)
A. Laughlin, J. Hyams
"The Serio-Comic"/"Plain Kitty McGuire"/"Mlle. Zizi"[20]
V. Earle, Chorus
March and Chorus Entrance of Dinkelhauser
"Beer, Beautiful Beer" (Song)
D. Bernard, Chorus
"Never Again" (Song)
S. Bernard
"Matinee Girls" (Song)
P. F. Nicholson, Chorus
"The Girl Who Is Up to Date" (Song)
I. Bentley
"Always Make Allowances for Love" (Quartette)
S. Bernard, P. F. Nicholson, I. Bentley, L. Faust
"(It's) What Eve Said to Adam"[21] (Song)
V. Earle
Spanish Chorus and Entrance of Paquita
"Be Clever" (Song)
M. Dainton
Finale
ACT 2
Scene 1
Opening Chorus
"The Blue Ribbon Girls"/"The Champagne Waltz" (Song)
M. Dainton, Corps de Ballet
"Fairies' Lullaby" (Song)
I. Bentley
"The Wishing Cap"[22] (Song)
V. Earle
"The Amateur Entertainer"[23] (Song)
M. Dainton
Hungarian Chorus Entrance of Katie
"Tell Me Where I Shall Find Him" (Song with Mandolin Accompaniment)
V. Earle
"The Belle of Bohemia" (Song and Finale)
Scene 2
"He Was a Married Man" (Song)
S. Bernard
Scene 3
Opening Chorus
Yodel Quartette
"The Lady in the Moon" (Quartette and Chorus)
V. Earle, I. Bentley, P. F. Nicholson, D. L. Don
Specialty Trio
J. Hyams, A. Laughlin, B. Clark
Finale

1900.42 A MILLION DOLLARS

A Melodious Medley of Mirth and Madness (An Extravaganza) in Three Acts, 6 Scenes. Book by Louis Harrison and George V. Hobart. Music by A. Baldwin

[19]Added to Sayings and Parodies for subsequent tour:
"Vandyke and Klondyke"
Rogers Brothers
(*Music and Lyrics by* Matthew Ott.)

[20]Replaced for subsequent tour by:
"My Mobile Gal"
Sadie Kirby [Katie], Chorus
(*Music by* Harry T. MacConnell. *Lyrics by* Robert B. Smith.)

[21]Replaced for subsequent tour by:
"She Never Loved a Man as Much as That"
S. Kirby
(*Music by* Harry T. MacConnell. *Lyrics by* Robert B. Smith.)

[22]Replaced for subsequent tour by:
"When I Am By Her Side"
S. Kirby, Chorus

[23]Dropped for subsequent tour.

Sloane. Lyrics by George V. Hobart. Staged by Frank Smithson. Ballets arranged by Carl Marwig. Settings by Lewis & Macoughtry, D. Frank Dodge, James Fox. Orchestra under the direction of Jose Van den Berg. Produced by Messrs. (Meyer L. and Henry B.) Sire. Opened 27 September 1900 at the New York Theatre and closed 20 October 1900 after 28 performances.

CAST: *Prince Punxatawney* from the Philippines: JOE OTT. *Consomme de Noodle*, (a barber): IGNACIO MARTINETTI. *Wishbone McManus*: JOSEPH SPARKS. *Cecil Roads*: NAT M. WILLS. *Harold Spotwood*: Grafton Baker *Chasem, Clutchem, Clipem*, a firm of lawyers: GILBERT CLAYTON, CHARLES H. PRINCE, JOHN MAYON. *Slats*: Pat Rooney, Jr. *Ragtime Duster*: Lew Simmons. *Peddler*: Archie Gillies. *Policeman*: Louis Foley. *Bazazza*, the elephant: Pat Rooney, Jr., Harry Fitch. *Aurora Borealis*, a professional adventuress: CORA TANNER. *Tryphena Shoolz*, DeNoodle's housekeeper: JOSIE SADLER. *Phyllis Vandergold*: IDA HAWLEY. *Iona Bond*: Blanche Sherwood. *Gracie Bullion*: Ethel Everton.

Coney Island Soubrettes: Maude Francis, Virginia Barnes, Georgie Kelly, Ethel Kelly, Ernestine Kingston, Maud Rose, Ethel Goodyear, Lottie Medley. *Scotch Girls*: Zaza Belasco, Fanny Dudley, Rita Dean, Anna Snyder, Lillie Leslie, Jane Morrison, Maude Harlow, Corniel Williams.

Ballet Specialties: Lillie Brink, Aggie Vars, Mlle. Leontine, Ernestine Kingston. Mlle. Editha. *Ballet*: Misses Courtney, Kessner, LaChere, Hazlewood, Murray, Palmer, J. Hoope, Nelson, Belmont, Carter, G. Florence, L. Florence, M. Florence, Menzies, Diamond, Travers, Harcourt, Garrett, B. Lovelace, N. Lovelace, Robinson, Young, Payne, Townshend, Gordon, C. Ruiz, L. Ruiz, Horton, Fennell, Collins, Troy, DeFord, Chapin, Wile, Marcelle, Leslie, Armstrong, Bonner, Parker, Reid, Stern, Sawyer, West, Maitland, Harvey, Earle.

Act 1, Scene 1: Law office of Chasem, Clutchem & Clipem. (Lewis & Macoughtry.) *Scene 2*: The barber shop of DeNoodle. (Dodge.) *Scene 3*: Battery Park. (Dodge.) Incidental to this scene, the March of the Allies.

Act 2, Scene 1: Mansion on the Hudson. (Lewis & Macoughtry.) *Scene 2*: Coney Island. (Fox.) Incidental to this scene, the Riotous Revel of the Merry-go-round.

Act 3: The Jeweled Arch (Fox.) Incidental to this scene, the Gold, Silver and Rose Ballet.

ACT 1
Scene 1
"Divorce Hunters' Chorus"
"We Are the Men of the Law"
G. Clayton, C. H. Prince, J. Mayon
Scene 2
"Barbers Are We"
"I Am a Millionaire"
I. Martinetti, Chorus
Scene 3
"The March of the Allies"
(*Arranged by* Carl Marwig.)
France: Misses Courtney, Kessner, LaChere, Hazelwood. *Germany*: Misses Murray, Vars, Harvey, Earle. *Russia*: Missses Palmer, J. Hoope, Nelson, L. Hoope. *Italy*: Misses Blemont, G. Florence, Carter, L. Florence. *Austria*: Misses Menzies, Diamond, Travers, Harcourt. *Japan*: Misses Garrett, B. Lovelace, Robinson, Young. *England*: Misses Payne, Townsend, M. Florence, Gordon. *Scotland*: Misses C. Ruiz, Horton, N. Lovelace, Fennell. *Ireland*: Misses Brink, Collins, Troy, M. Chapin. *America*: Misses L. Ruiz, Wile, Chapin, Marcelle. *Columbia*: Mlle. Leontine. *The Flag-Bearers*: Misses Parker, Millard, Schooth, Reid, Stern, Sherod, Sawyer, West, Maitland. *America*: E. Kingston.
"Believe Me"
I. Hawley
"McManus"
J. Sparks, Chorus
"I'm a Prince"
J. Ott, Chorus
Finale
Ensemble
ACT 2
Scene 1
"Phoebe, Dear, I Love You"
G. Baker, [Thomas[24]]
"He's a Man of Mystery"
Ensemble
Scene 2
"If I Could Only Get a Chance to Cook"
J. Sadler
"Merely a Matter of Habit"
J. Ott, I. Martinetti

[24] No character named Thomas appears in the cast list.

"Front!"
Bell Girls
Scene 3
The Ballet on the Beach at Coney Island
The Boys and Girls on the Merry-go-round: Misses Garrett, Lovelace, Belmont, Harcourt, Vars, Murray, Hazelwood, Lovelace. *Quadrille*: Misses Chapin, Courtney, Earle, Young, Horton, Howard, Robinson, Ruiz. *Pas a Trois*: Misses Leontine, Chitten, Brink. *The Rough Riders*: Misses L. Ruiz, Payne, Hoope, Hoope. *Golf Boys and Girls*: Misses Chapin, Gordon, Troy, LaChere.
"On the Beach"
B. Sherwood, Coney Island Soubrettes
"Good Night, O Sea" (Sea Song)
C. Tanner
Ragtime Dancing
P. Rooney, Jr.
"Hoot, Mon"
J. Ott, Chorus
A Tramp's Trip to the Paris Exposition
N. M. Wills
"The Christening"
J. Sparks, Chorus
Finale
Ensemble
ACT 3
The Gold, Silver and Rose Ballet (Sixteen to One)
Premieres: Mlles. Leontine, Chitten (First), Brink, Editha (Second), A. Vars (Cupid). *Coryphees*: Ballet Ensemble.
Finale
Ensemble

1900.43 SAN TOY

A Chinese Musical Comedy in Two Acts[25]. Book by Edward Morton. Music by Sidney Jones. Lyrics by Harry Greenbank and Adrian Ross. Production under the personal supervision of J. C. Duff. Dances arranged by Willie Warde. Scenery by Ernest Gros and Henry E. Hoyt. Ladies' costumes by Miss Fisher, London, and Colin Eaves, New York; gentlemen's costumes imported from China. Musical director, George P. Towle. Under the direction of B. D. Stevens and Edwin H. Price. Produced by Daniel Frohman by arrangement with the Augustin Daly Estate. Opened 1 October 1900 at Daly's Theatre and closed 24 November 1900 after 65 performances. Reopened a return engagement 4 March 1901 at Daly's Theatre and closed 1 June 1901 after 103 additional performances. Total: 168 performances.

CAST: *Li*: JAMES T. POWERS. *Captain Bobby Preston*, son of Sir Bingo: MELVILLE STEWART. *Sir Bingo Preston*, British Consul at Pynka Pong: WILFRED CLARKE. *Sing Hi*, President of the Board of Ceremonies: J. L. Weber. *Lieutenant Harvey Tucker*: Henry Girard. *Fo Hop*, a Chinese student: JOSEPH GOODEROWE. *Hu Pi, Wai Ho*, Jewelers of Pynka Pong: Joseph Cauto, Robert M. O'Neil. *Li Hi, Li Lo*, Tartar Guards: W. W. Scott, George A. Roarke. *The Emperor*: Sarony Lambert. *Yen How*, a Mandarin: GEORGE K. FORTESQUE. *Wun Lung*, Corporal of the Emperor's own: Florence Newcombe. *Ko-Fan* of the Emperor's own: Isobel Hall. *Trixie, Rose Tucker* with Pas-Seul in Act 2: Carolyn Gordon. Frances Gordon. *The Six Little Wives of Yen-How*: *Yung-Shi*: Elgie Bowen. *Me-Koui*: Marie Welch. *Siou*: Nora Lambert. *Shuey-Pin-Sing*: Jeannete Palmer. *Li-Kiang*: Mary Kier. *Hu-Yu*: Elsie Thorne. *Mrs. Harley Streeter*: Eva Randolph. *Hon. Mrs. Hay Stackpole*: Stella Krumm. *Dudley*, Poppy's maid: MINNIE ASHLEY. *Poppy*, daughter of Sir Bingo: FLORA ZABELLE. *San Toy*, daughter of Yen-How: MARIE CELESTE.

Act 1: A street in Pyunka Pong. (Gros.)

Act 2: Hall in the Emperor's Palace, Pekin. (Hoyt.)

ACT 1[26]
"We'll Keep the Feast in Pynka Pong" (Opening Chorus)
"The Mandarin" (Quintette and Chorus)
"Six Little Wives" (Kow Tow)(Song)
G. K. Fortesque, Wives

[25]The original English production contained a subtitle: SAN TOY, or The Emperor's Own.
[26]Musical numbers not listed in program. List prepared from program for 1905 Broadway revival, the published piano vocal score (Keith Prowse & Co, London, 1899), and newspaper clippings. Added songs were:
"Shine On, Bright Star"
M. Stewart

"The Petals of the Plum Tree"[27] (Song)
E. Bowen
"A B C" (Duet)
M. Celeste, M. Stewart
"The Lady's Maid" (Song)
M. Ashley
(*Music by* Lionel Monckton.)
"The Moon" (Concerted Number)
"Pynka Pong" (Quartette)(Song and Dance)
"Love Has Come from Lotus Land" (Lotus Land)(Song)
M. Stewart
"When You Are Wed to Me" (Duet)(Scene)
M. Celeste, J. Gooderowe
"Samee Gamee" (Duet)
M. Ashley, J. T. Powers
"We Have Come Here Now" (Finale Act 1)

ACT 2
Chorus of Mandarins (We're the Cream of Courtly Creatures)
"I'm So Fond of a Little Bit of Fun" (Song)
M. Celeste
"We Have Come to See" (Concerted Number and Dance)
Six Wives
"Rhoda and Her Pagoda" (Song)
M. Ashley
(*Music by* Lionel Monckton.)
"The Emperor's Own" (Chorus and Entrance of Body Guards)
"Entrance of English Visitors" (Chorus and Scene)
"Somebody" (Song)
M. Celeste
"(Private) Tommy Atkins" (Song)
M. Stewart, Chorus
(*Music and Lyrics by* L. S. Potter.)
"I Mean to Introduce It into China" (Song)
G. K. Fortesque
"Pletty Little Chinee" (Chinese Duet)
M. Ashley, J. T. Powers
"The Little China Maid" (Duet)
M. Celeste, M. Stewart
"Chinee Soje-Man" (Song)
J. T. Powers
(*Music by* Lionel Monckton.)
Finale

1900.44 THE MILITARY MAID

A Musical Farce in Two Acts. Book and lyrics by George V. Hobart, adapted from the French. Music by Alfred E. Aarons. Produced by Alfred E. Aarons and David Henderson. Opened 8 October 1900 at the Savoy Theatre and closed 13 October 1900 after 8 performances.

CAST: *The Baron (Blynkinwinkin)*: HENRY BERGMAN. *Captain Gerald Fitzgerald*: DAVID TORRENCE. *The Marquis (Mouchoir)*: SIDNEY DeGRAY. *Adolphe*: FRANK DOANE. *Colonel Castlemaine*: Charles H. Riegel. *Major Lefevre*: TAYLOR GRANVILLE. *Lieutenant Pierre d'Norville*: Bertram Yost. *The Baroness*: PHOEBE COYNE. *Bebe Castlemaine*: Sallie Berg. *Marquise Mouchoir*: Mrs. Matt B. Snyder. *Clarissa*: Lucille Verna. *Calanthe*: Gertrude Lewis. *Caroline*: Emma Levy. *Catherine*: Elaine Selover. *Clorinda*: Leonore P. Harris. *Orderly Eclair*: Maude Calvet. *Soldier Soupcon*: Maude Lyle-Cortenay. *Annette*: Daisy Deane. *Georgia*: Le Clair Bernard. *Madeleine*: Libbian Diamond. *Suzanne*: Ethel Moore. *Fleurette d'Norville*: JOSEPHINE HALL.

Act 1: The Chateau d'Norville.

Act 2: The Barracks of the Madagascar Musketeers.

MUSICAL NUMBERS[28]
"Sister Mary Has the Measles"
"The Tin Gee Gee"

[27]By mid-October, "The Petals on the Plum Tree" was replaced by:
"It's Nice to be a Boy (Sometimes)" (Song)
M. Celeste
(*Music by* Lionel Monckton.)

[28]Program found contains no list of musical numbers.

1900.45 SHOOTING THE CHUTES

A Musical Farce in Three Acts. Play by George E. Emerick. Opened 8 October 1900 at the Metropolis Theatre and closed 13 October 1900 after 8 performances.[29]

CAST: *Con Connelly*: CHARLES A. MURRAY. *Roger Sweeney*: OLLIE MACK. *Erastus Bugg*: LEO HARDMAN. *Doolittle Wright*: JOHN McVEIGH. *Lord Blesshugh*: GEORGE S. BETTS. *Tired Tompkins*: Pete Curley. *Rudolph Schattermann*: Pete Curley. *Acton Barnes*: Harry E. Lester. *Percy Vere*: Ed. S. Jolly. *Reverend Spoutwell*: Boyd J. Gilmour. *Junie Bugg*: KITTIE BECK. *Lillie White Swansdown*: Lonnie Deane. *Katarina Katzenjammer*: MARYLAND TYSON. *Ina Mann*, Mlle. Prymm Adonna: GILBERTIE LEAROCK. *Cora Singe*: Nonie Reynolds. *Carrie DeLong*: Jessie Sharp. *Justa Phillip*: Rose Collins. *May Remaine*: Edith Dunlap. *Annie Glitz*: May McKee. *Aggie Glotz*: Rose Mee. *Daisy Bell*: Ethel Gibbs. *Annie Rooney*: Bertha Else. *Maggie Mooney*: Nellie Verna. *Uneeda Biscuit*: Winnie Jolly. *Susie Snodgrass*: Nellie Bernard. *Dora Bishop*: Katharine LaTour. *Maud Bixby*: Estelle Holland. *Tille*: Kathrine Roberts.

Act 1: First Round. Bugg's Hotel, Bunco Beach.

Act 2: Second Round. Parlor in Bugg's Hotel.

Act 3: Third Round. Bunco Race Track.

1900.46 SONS OF HAM

A Musical Comedy in Two Acts, 6 Scenes. Book by Stephen Cassin and Jesse A. Shipp. Music and lyrics by Bert Williams and George Walker. Production staged by Jesse A. Shipp. Produced by (Jules) Hurtig and (Harry) Seamon. Opened 15 October 1900 at the Star Theatre and closed 20 October 1900 after 8 performances; returned 29 April 1901 to the Grand Opera House and closed 4 May 1901 after 8 additional performances. Total: 16 performances.[30]

CAST: *Hampton J. J. Flam*, the old man: PETER HAMPTON. *Jeneriska Hassambad, Aniesta Babdola*, his sons: GREEN H. TAPLEY, RICHARD CONNORS. *Professor Switchen*, the faculty of Risk College: JESSE A. SHIPP. *Willie Wataboy*, Caroline Jenkins' cute brother-in-law: ?. *Ben Jenkins*, always looking for trouble: ?. *Joe Jenkins*, a student ?. *Tobias Wormwood*, always with a kick: BERT WILLIAMS. *Harty Lafter*, always with a scheme on tap: GEORGE WALKER. *Patsy Patterson, Dinah Patterson*: CLARA FREEMAN, ANNA E. COOK. *Caroline Jenkins*, a college girl: AIDA OVERTON WALKER. *Specialties*: The Golden Gate Quartette.

New York Company also included George Harris, James McDonald, Fred Douglas, W. H. Chappelle, Fred W. Simpson, John C. Pittman, Arthur Coats, Frank Sutton, Henry Winfred, James Burris, Sheppard H. Edmonds, Will Murray, George Pickett, Will Marion Cook, Charles Moore, The Reese Brothers (Arthur, Ollie), ABBIE MITCHELL COOK, Marie Williams, Nellie Wells, Fannie Windred, Odessa Warren, Estelle Ware, Lavine Jones, Maggie Davis, Jennie Scheper, Pauline Freeman, Maggie Rector, Florence Ellsworth.

Act 1, Scene 1: The Home of Ham, Swampville, Tennessee. *Scene 2*: Foot path between Riske College and Crytal Spring. *Scene 3*: Riske College.

Act 2, Scene 1: Interior of Ham's Home. *Scene 2*: Exterior of Town Hall, Swampville, Tennessee. *Scene 3*: Interior of Town Hall, Swampville, Tennessee.

ACT 1 (Second Edition)[31]
"Down Where the Cotton Blossoms Grow"
A. Cook
"Old Man's Song and Dance"
P. Hampton
(*Music and Lyrics by* George Walker and Bert Williams.)
"Miss Hannah from Savannah"
A. O. Walker
(*Music by* Richard C. McPherson [Cecil Mack]. *Lyrics by* Tom Lemonier.)

[29]No program available.

[30]No program available from original New York engagement. Cast list prepared from the New York Clipper and Dramatic Mirror. The cast and song list changed frequently during a two year tour. Played a return engagement at Hurtig & Seamon's Music Hall. Scenery by Gradt; Gates & Morange; Physioc; Moses & Hamilton. Song list from subsequent tour. Additional songs published by Williams and Walker which may have been interpolated for the tour before or after New York:
"My South Car'lina Gal" (Does You Love Your Baby)
"When Cupid Hunting Goes"
"I'se Promoter of the Coon Society"

[31]Also interpolated, as per reviews:
"She's Gettin' More Like White Folks Every Day"
B. Williams
(*Music and Lyrics by* George Walker and Bert Williams.)

"Calisthenics"
Students of Riske College
(*Music and Lyrics by* George Walker and Bert Williams.)
"Maria"
A. Mackey
In Africa: "My Little Zulu Babe"
B. Williams, G. Walker
(*Music and Lyrics by* ? Esterman and Brymm.)

ACT 2[32]
"Leading Lady"
A. O. Walker
"The Phrenologist Coon" (Fortune Telling Man)
B. Williams
(*Music by* William J. Accooe. *Lyrics by* Ernest Hogan.)
"(When It's) All Goin' Out and Nothin' Comin' In"
B. Williams
(*Music and Lyrics by* George Walker and Bert A. Williams.)
"(The) Leader of the Ball"
G. Walker
(*Music by* Richard C. McPherson [Cecil Mack]. *Lyrics by* Tom Lemonier.)
"Good Afternoon, Mr. Jenkins"
G. Walker
(*Music by* Richard C. McPherson [Cecil Mack]. *Lyrics by* Tom Lemonier.)
"Elegant Darky Dan"
G. Walker
(*Music by* Richard C. McPherson [Cecil Mack]. *Lyrics by* Tom Lemonier.)
"Beyond the Gates of Paradise"
L. Gibbs
"The Promoters"/"Ragtime Schottische"
Company
(*Music by* William J. Accooe.)

CAST: *Hampton J. J. Flam*, the old man: PETER HAMPTON. *Aniesta Babdola, Jenarusha Hassambad*, his sons: ARTHUR REESE, OLLIE REESE. *Professor Switchen*, the faculty of Risk College: JESSE A. SHIPP. *Willie Wataboy*, Caroline Jenkins' cute brother-in-law: FRED DOUGLAS. *Ben Jenkins*, always looking for trouble: G. W. Washington. *Joe Jenkins*, a student: W. G. Pickett. *Joshua Pipes*: Richard Connors. *Joseph Simkins*: Ed. Chappell. *Samantha Johnson*, the wife of Ham: FLORENCE ELLSWORTH. *Caroline Jenkins*, a college girl: AIDA OVERTON (WALKER). *Gabb Slangtry*, a modern linguist: LOTTIE WILLIAMS. *Patsy Patterson, Dinah Patterson*: CLARA FREEMAN, ANNA E. COOK.

Schoolgirls: *Mariah*: Alice Mackey. *Millie*: Maggie Davis. *Tillie*: Jennie Scheper. *Fluffy*: Pauline Freeman. *Tuffy*: Mamie Rector. *Lou*: Nellie Glenn. *Daphne*: Marie Williams. *Sou*: Nellei Wells. *Mollie*: Fannie Winfred. *Polly*: Odessa Warren. *Jane*: Mamie Emerson. *Lize*: Lavine Jones.

The Golden Gate Quartette: *Frank*: (Frank) Sutton. *Arthur*: (Arthur) Coates. *James*: (James) Burris. *Henry*: (Henry) Winfred. *Tobias Wormwood*, always with a kick: BERT WILLIAMS. *Harty Lafter*, always with a scheme on tap: GEORGE WALKER. *Farm Hands, Students, etc.*

New York Company also included George Harris, James McDonald, , W. H. Chappelle, Fred W. Simpson, John C. Pittman, Arthur Coats, Frank Sutton, Henry Winfred, James Burris, Sheppard H. Edmonds, Will Murray, George Pickett, Will Marion Cook, Charles Moore, The Reese Brothers (Arthur, Ollie), ABBIE MITCHELL COOK, Marie Williams, Nellie Wells, Fannie Windred, Odessa Warren, Estelle Ware, Lavine Jones, Maggie Davis, Jennie Scheper, Pauline Freeman, Maggie Rector, Florence Ellsworth.

Act 1, Scene 1: The Home of Ham, Swampville, Tennessee. *Scene 2*: Foot path between Risk College and Crytal Spring. *Scene 3*: Risk College.

Act 2, Scene 1: Interior of Ham's Home. *Scene 2*: Exterior of Town Hall, Swampville, Tennessee.

[32]Added for Second Edition the following season:
"Good Morning, Carrie"
G. Walker, B. Williams
(*Music by* Richard C. McPherson [Cecil Mack]. *Lyrics by* Elmer Bowman and Chris Smith.)
"Society"
A. Overton-Walker
(*Music by* William J. Accooe.)
"Josephine My Jo"
Alice MacKay
(*Music by* Richard C. McPherson [Cecil Mack]. *Lyrics by* James T. Brymm.)
"My Castle on the (River) Nile"
B. Williams
(*Music by* J. Rosamond Johnson. *Lyrics by* Robert Cole and James Weldon Johnson.)
P. F. Dailey, C. MacDonald, Entire Company

ACT 1 3/29/01 GOH
"(Royal) Sons of Ham"
P. Hampton, Chorus
(*Music by* Richard C. McPherson [Cecil Mack]. *Lyrics by* Tom Lemonier.)
"When the Corn Is Waving"
Clara Freeman, Quartette
New Anthem (invisible)
(by Will Accooe)
"Sparkling Ruby"
A. Overton
"Health Exercise" (original specialty)
Freeman Sisters
"Dinah"
A. Mackey, Chorus
Douglass and Reese Brothers novel specialty
"(My Little) Zulu Babe"
Williams, Walker, Company
(*Music and Lyrics by* Esterman and Brymm.)

ACT 2
"Cairo" (by Will Marion Cook)
Ensemble
"When the Heart is Young" (by F. Green Tapley)
Catlin (Chinese Impersonator)
"Fortune-Telling Coon"
B. Williams
"She's Getting More Like White Folks Every Day"
B. Williams
"Blackville Strutters"
G. Walker
The Acme of Scientific Coonology (Novel Finale)

1900.47

HODGE, PODGE & CO.

A Musical Comedy in Three Acts. Book by George V. Hobart. Based on the German posse "Im Himmelshof."[33] Music by John W. Bratton. Lyrics by Walter Ford. (Interpolated songs by Gus Edwards, Herman Perlet, Dave Reed, Jr., Harry T. MacConnell and Robert B. Smith.) Produced under the stage direction of R. A. Roberts. Settings by Arthur Voegtlin. Costumes by Will R. Barnes. Orchestra under the direction of Herman Perlet. Produced by Frank McKee. Opened 23 October 1900 at the Madison Square Theatre and closed 22 December 1900 after 73 performances[34].

CAST: *Rudolf Roastemsum*, the pride of two doting papas: PETER F. DAILEY. *Hiram Hodge, Philip Podge*, of the firm of Hodge, Podge & Co., perpetrating posters: GEORGE W. BARNUM, STEPHEN MALEY. *Don Antonio d'Careera Cararra*, a Spanish noble: WILLIAM BRODERICK. *Christopher Chinchilla*, a young lawyer: Robert S. Pigott. *L. Hyde*, a patrolman: EDWARD GARVIE. *Ledger d'Main*, bookkeeper of the firm of Hodge, Podge & Co.: Edward Wonn. *A. Poze*, photographer: Lawrence Sheehan. *Captain Kaufcatchem* of the local militia: William Strong. *William Plantes*, a gardener: Charles Winters. *Priscilla Hodge, Evangeline Hodge*, daughters of Mr. Hodge and his first wife: CHRISTIE MacDONALD, AMY LESSER. *Carmenita Hodge*, Mr. Hodge's second wife: JENNIE HAWLEY. *Marquita Tarantara*, daughter of Carmenita and her first husband: Mamie Forbes. *Minnie Rausmittem*, maid to Mrs. Hodge: Georgie Lawrence. *Members of the Howlinghurst Golf Club (8)*: *Mabellina*: Frankie Bailey. *Laurelina*: Lea Amrose. *Gracellina*: Mae Edwards. *Estellina*: Frances Wilson. *Rosalina*: May Blanchard. *Claralina*: Martha Steyne. *Sarahlina*: Mary E. Post. *Lucylina*: Winnie Kramer. *Poetic Poster Girls (4)*: *Sheeza Dream*: Frankie Bailey. *Guessah Genn*: Mamie Forbes. *Ainshee Grayt*: Helen Cheston. *Eulalia Lee*: Frances Wilson. *A Bugler*: Marguerite Binford.

Members of Golf Club, Poster Girls, Local Militia, Villagers, etc.: Misses Lea Amrose, Bessie Seymour, Maude LeMonde, Helena Cheston, Lillian Harris, Lottie Ettinger, Alice May, Sarah LeMonde, Gussie Bertrand, Gertrude Arden, Muriel Ulmer, Maud Sloane, Mabel Cameron, Marion Harland, Corinne Mayo, Josie Nagle, Kitty Harvey. Messrs. Bradley, Weaver, Austin, Stevens, others.

The action takes place at Howlinghurst-on-the-Hudson at the present time.

Act 1: Lawn in front of Mr. Hodge's villa, overlooking the Hudson.

Act 2: Hodge, Podge & Co.'s poster studio.

Act 3: Garden in the rear of Mr. Hodge's villa.

[33]Original libretto by Jean Kren, music by Max Schmidt, lyrics by Alfred Schönfeld.
[34]Played a return engagement 22 April 1901 at the Grand Opera House for 8 performances.

ACT 1

"Springtime Bells" (Opening Chorus and Song)
C. MacDonald, Full Chorus

"My Sunflower Sue"
P. F. Dailey

"A Billet Doux" (Trio)
P. F. Dailey, C. MacDonald, A. Lesser
(*Music by* John W. Bratton. *Lyrics by* George V. Hobart and Walter Ford.)

"Mine, All Mine"[35]
C. MacDonald

"A Soldier of Love Am I"
W. Broderick

Finale:

"Away to the Links"
Full Chorus

"My Gay Golf Girl"
C. MacDonald

"I'm a Scion of the House of Highball"
P. F. Dailey, Company, Chorus

ACT 2

"Modest Model Maidens We" (Opening Chorus)

"You're Altogether Model Girls"
P. F. Dailey, Chorus

"You Never Can Tell What a Kiss Will Do"
P. F. Dailey, C. MacDonald

"Good Night"[36]
J. Hawley

"What a Funny Story" (Sextette)
C. MacDonald, J. Hawley, A. Lesser, W. Broderick, Bradley[37], R. S. Pigott
(*Music by* Herman Perlet.)

"'E Didn't Seem to Know Just Wot to Soy"
C. MacDonald, P. F. Dailey
(*Music and Lyrics by* Harry Pleon.)

"Cindy (I Dreams of You)" (A Coon Love Tale)(Finale)
P. F. Dailey, C. MacDonald, Full Company, Chorus
(*Music and Lyrics by* Dave Reed, Jr.)

ACT 3

Opening Chorus and March

Mr. Dailey's version of "The Blue and the Gray, or A Mother's Gift to Her Country"
(*Music and Lyrics by* Paul Dresser.)

"I Love You Babe, and You Love Me"
P. F. Dailey, C. MacDonald
(*Music by* Harry T. McConnell. *Lyrics by* Robert B. Smith.)

"The Town Folks Will Be Pleased"[38] (Duo)
E. Garvie, G. Lawrence

"My Charcoal Charmer"[39]
P. F. Dailey, Full Chorus
(*Music by* Gus Edwards. *Lyrics by* Walter Ford.)

"Dream Days of Seville"[40]
W. Broderick, J. Hawley

Finale

1900.48 THE BELLE OF BRIDGEPORT

A Farce in Three Acts. Play by Glen MacDonough. (Music by J. Rosamond Johnson. Lyrics by Bob Cole and James Weldon Johnson. Additional songs by William Jefferson, Cissie Loftus and William J. Accooe.) Stage director, George A. Beane. Scenery by Louis & Macaughtry, Fox & Vincent. Musical director, Watty Hydes. Produced by May Irwin. Opened 29 October 1900 at the Bijou Theatre and closed 8 December 1900 after 45 performances.[41]

CAST: *John Smith*, founder and proprietor of the largest department store in America: GEORGE A. BEANE. *Ariel Smith*, John Smith's eldest daughter: MAY IRWIN. *Mrs. John Smith*, Ariel's stepmother: JANE BURBY. *Jessica*, Ariel's half-sister: Mabel Florence. *Alonzo Topping*, John Smith's general manager: Charles Prince. *Dr. Luke Craven*, John Smith's family physician: Roland Carter. *Miss Roberts*, one of John Smith's store detectives: Edith Blair. *Malcolm Crane*, John Smith's confidential secretary: BERT THAYER. *Agnes Crane*, Malcolm's sister: Sadie Peters. *Phil Bonhomie*, Malcolm's chum: Charles Church. *A. J. Factor*: Frank M. Johnson. *Bokhara Skitbollitski*, the musical lion of the moment: RAYMOND HITCHCOCK. *Ferdinand*, his man: Jacques Kruger. *Ethelbert Box*, looking for $98.50: Frank H. White. *Parepa Box*, his sister, dresser of the Momus Club: Gussie Jones. *Roundsman Sharp*, a policeman: James McDonough. *Mamie Cassidy, Mary Doyle*, cash girls at John Smith's store: Lillie Collins, Alice Howard. *Miss Green, Miss Black, Miss White*, Officers of the New York Woman's Athletic Club: Grace Almy, Ruth Grey, Anne Woodward. *Mrs. Marion Colby*, a social struggler: Helen Rainsley. *Miss Popkins*, an amateur playwright: Queenie Vassar.

Act 1: John Smith's Office at his store. Morning.

Act 2: Malcolm Crane's apartment. Evening.

Act 3: Room in the New York Woman's Athletic Club. Afternoon.

ACT 1

"Mabel Moore"
M. Irwin
(*Music and Lyrics by* William J. Accooe.)

"Dandy Soldier Coon" (My Dandy Soldier Boy)
M. Irwin
(*Music and Lyrics by* William J. Accooe.)

"I Ain't Gwine to Work No Mo'"
M. Irwin

ACT 2

"Why Don't the Band Play?"

"(I've Got) Troubles of My Own"

"Dance on Friday Night"
(*Music and Lyrics by* William Jefferson.)

ACT 3

"(Magdalene, My) Southern Queen"

"Bullfrog Ben"
(*Music and Lyrics by* Cissie Loftus.)

"(I'm Gwine to Marry) Angeline"
(*Music and Lyrics by* Cissie Loftus.)

1900.49 NELL-GO-IN

A Bill of a Burlesque, Ballet and Vaudeville. Produced by the Messrs. (Meyer L. and Henry B.) Sire. Opened 31 October 1900 at the New York Theatre and closed 17 November 1900 after 25 performances.[42]

ACT 1

NELL GO IN, a Burlesque of "Nell Gwynne." Play and lyrics by George V. Hobart, suggested by Henrietta Crosman's play "Nell Gwynn." Music by A. Baldwin Sloane.

CAST: *King Charlie, Two Times*: JOSEPH OTT. *P. Green O'Jowl*: JOSEPH SPARKS. *Duck of Buckwheats*: FRANK DOANE. *Jim*: Grafton Baker. *Strings D'Brass*: John Mayon. *Jack Knife*: W. H. Macart. *Shorty Hoyle*: Joseph Harrington. *Feathers*: PAT ROONEY. *Philip*: Lou Foley. *First Second*: Charles Fitz. *Wezzie*, Duchess of Gingerbread: AMELIA SUMMERVILLE. *Moll*: Venie Henshaw. *Lady Hammoneggs*: Attalie Claire. *Lady Auburf Hugh*: Jeanne Caskie. *Nell-Go-In*: MABEL FENTON.

MUSICAL NUMBERS

"My Honey Nell"

ACT 2

"Le Bal champêtre aux Champs Elysées," a Ballet arranged by Carl Marwig.

"The Forget-Me-Nots," a Ballet arranged by Carl Marwig.

---

[35]Dropped for subsequent tour.
[36]Dropped for subsequent tour.
[37]No actor or character by the name of Bradley in program.
[38]Added in Medley with "Town Folks Will be Pleased" for tour:
"A Picture No Artist Can Paint"/
"Since My Linda's in Da Syn-de-cate"
E. Garvie, G. Lawrence
[39] Dropped for subsequent tour.
[40] Dropped for subsequent tour.

[41] Many songs and similar characters were retained for May Irwin's next vehicle MADGE SMITH, ATTORNEY which opened 10 December 1900 at the Bijou Theatre.
[42] No program available.

CAST: LILLIE BRINK, FANCHONETTE, Editha, N. Lovelace, Aggie Vars, J. Hoope, the Cloinis, and Corps de Ballet.

ACT 3

Vaudeville program: George Fuller Golden; Emma Carus singing "Beyond the Golden Gates of Paradise;" Signor Jules Perotti and Mme. Ilka Kossuth; Snitz Edwards; Pat Rooney and Mayme Gehrue; Lew Hawkins; American Comedy Four; the Eight Mascots.

1900.50

FOXY QUILLER

A Comic Opera in Three Acts. Libretto by Harry B. Smith[43]. Music by Reginald DeKoven. Staged by Ben Teal. Dances arranged by Mme. Malvina. Scenery painted by Ernest Gros. Costumes by F. Richard Anderson. Musical director, A. DeNovellis. Produced by the (Marc) Klaw & (Abraham L.) Erlanger Opera Company. Opened 5 November 1900 at the Broadway Theatre and closed 22 December 1900 after 50 performances.

CAST: *Foxy Quiller*, the quintessence of all human intelligence: JEROME SYKES. *Paganino*, a Corsican with a vendetta on his hands: JULIUS STEGER. *Ned Royster*, Captain of a ship trading in the Spanish main; in love with Daphne: W. G. STEWART. *Walsingham Binks*, a neglected genius: HARRY MacDONOUGH. *Kimono*, the World-Famous Japanese Drawf: ADOLPH ZINK. *Abel Gudgeon*, a rich ship-builder: LOUIS CASAVANT. *Splicer*, Abel Gudgeon's foreman: Arthur T. Earnest. *Six inferior intellects*, minions of the unparalleled Quiller (6): *Ferrett*: Albert Farrington. *Padlock*: Albert S. Sykes. *Dodge*: Louis Kelso. *Weasel*: Owen J. McCormick. *Sherlock*: Edward Everett. *Lovecraft*: Frank Todd. *Governor of Corsica*: H. C. Nichols. *Antonio Purloino*: George P. Smith. *Garabaldi Filcho*: L. C. Fitzroy. *La Colomba*, Paganino's sister, who helps in the vendetta business: HELEN BERTRAM. *Daphne*, Abel Gudgeon's daughter: GRACE CAMERON. *Polly Prime*, barmaid at the sailor's tavern, "The Jolly Dolphin," Portsmouth: GEORGIA CAINE. *Belladonna*, the original cause of the vendetta, now the leading sorceress of Corsica, doing a fine trade in spells, horoscopes, love filters, etc.: JOSIE INTROPODI. *Marjorie*, Daphne's maid: Edna Hunter. *Mrs. Plumduff*, bum-boat woman: Clara Bancroft. *Serpentina*, a snake charmer: Almira Forrest. *Leona*, a tight-rope dancer: Edith Barr. *Longina*, a giantess: H. A. Poot.

Act 1: Dock Yards, Portsmouth, England. 1825.

Act 2: Sea Coast, Corsica.

Act 3: Castle and Fortress, Residence of the Governor of Corsica.

ACT 1

"The Shipbuilders' Song" (Opening Chorus)

"Winding, Winding, My Love and I"
W. G. Stewart, G. Cameron

"The Mountebank's Song"
W. Banks, Chorus

Entrance of Foxy Quiller
J. Sykes, Chorus

"The Song of the Vendetta"
H. Bertram, J. Steger

Finale (Over the Rolling Sea)

ACT 2

"The Legend of the Tarantella"
H. Bertram

"The Cheating Peddler"
J. Sykes

"The Golden Age"
W. G. Stewart, G. Cameron

"Here at Thy Window, Love"(Mandolin Serenade)
J. Steger

ACT 3

"Bivouac Song"
Soldiers' Chorus

"The Song of the Sword"
J. Steger, Chorus

"The Song of the Watchman's Rattle"
J. Sykes, Chorus

"Poor Shepherds We"
H. Bertram, G. Caine

"For Foxy Has the Brain"
Company

[43] Conceived as a sequel to THE HIGHWAYMAN (13 December 1897, Broadway Theatre, 144 performances) in which Jerome Sykes first introduced the character of Foxy Quiller. Toured under the title FOXY QUILLER (IN CORSICA).

1900.51

FLORODORA

The English Musical Comedy in Two Acts, 3 Scenes. Book by Owen Hall, revised for America by Frank Pixley. Music by Leslie Stuart. Lyrics by Ernest Boyd-Jones, Paul Rubens and Leslie Stuart. Produced [staged] by Lewis Hooper, under the personal supervision of Willie Edouin. Settings by Moses & Hamilton. Orchestra under the direction of Arthur Weld. Produced by John W. Dunne, Thomas Ryley, John C. Fisher. Opened 10 November 1900 at the Casino Theatre, moved 14 October 1901 to the New York Theatre and closed 25 January 1902 after 505 performances[44].

CAST: *Cyrus W. Gilfain*, proprietor of the Island and the perfume of Florodora: R. E. GRAHAM. *Captain Arthur Donegal*, Fourth Royal Life Guards, Lady Holyrood's brother: CYRIL SCOTT. *Frank Abercoed*, Manager for Mr. Gilfain of the Island of Florodora: SYDNEY DEANE. *Leandro*: Nace Bonville. *Gilfain's clerks (6)*: *Tennyson Sims*: Ernest Pym, *Max Aepfelbaum*: Reginald Langdale. *Paul Crogan*: John Scott, *George DeLong*: Lewis Hooper. *Edward Gore*: Joseph Welsh. *Thomas A. Kiernan*: Joseph S. Colt. *Anthony Tweedlepunch*, showman, phrenologist, hypnotist, palmist: WILLIE EDOUIN. *Dolores*, (Frank's fiancée): FANNIE JOHNSTON. *Valleda*, maid to Lady Holyrood: Guelma L. Baker. *Florodorean girls, Heads of the Various Farms (5)*: *Inez*: Elaine Van Selover. *Jose*: Sadie Lauer. *Juanita*: Adelaide Phillips. *Violante*: Aline Potter. *Calista*: Mabel Barrison. *Angela Gilfain*: MAY EDOUIN. *(Sextette)*: *Daisy Chain*: Margaret Walker. *Mamie Rowe*: Vaughn Texsmith. *Lucy Ling*: Marie L. Wilson. *Cynthia Belmont*: Marjorie Relyea. *Lottie Chalmers*: Agnes Wayburn. *Clare Fitzclarence*: Daisy Greene. *Lady Holyrood*: EDNA WALLACE HOPPER. *Florodorean Farmers, Laborers, Flower Girls, Welsh Peasants, etc.*

Act 1: The Island of Florodora in the Philippines.

Act 2, Scene 1: Abercoed Castle, Wales. *Scene 2*: Grand Ball-room in the Castle.

ACT 1

"Flowers a-blooming so gay" (Opening Chorus)

Musical Number[45]
Clerks

"The Silver Star of Love"[46] (Song)
F. Johnston
(*Lyrics by* Leslie Stuart.)

Chorus of Welcome
(*Lyrics by* Ernest Boyd-Jones.)

"Come and See Our Island" (Musical Number)
Clerks, English Girls

"When I Leave Town" (Song)
E. Wallace-Hopper
(*Lyrics by* Paul Rubens.)

"The Fellow Who Might Be"/"Galloping" (Duet Song and Dance)
M. Edouin, C. Scott
(*Lyrics by* Ernest Boyd-Jones.)

"I Want to Marry a Man, I Do" (Trio)
E. Wallace-Hopper, R. E. Graham, W. Edouin
(*Lyrics by* Paul Rubens.)

"Phrenology" (Song)
R. E. Graham, Chorus
(*Lyrics by* Ernest Boyd-Jones.)

"(When) An Interfering Person"[47] (Quartette)
E. Wallace-Hopper, M. Edouin, C. Scott, W. Edouin

[44] Immediately after closing 25 January 1902, the Winter Garden Company presented another production of FLORODORA 27 January 1902 at the Winter Garden Theatre for 48 additional performances; see entry in following season.

[45] Later billed as a Sextette Overture, performed by the Clerks and Chorus; at end of run billed as:

"The Credit's Due to Me" (Sextet)
Clerks, Chorus

[46] Replaced in the run by:

"Somebody" (Duet)
Kate Condon {Dolores}, S. Deane
Which was replaced late in the run by:

"He Loves Me—He Loves Me Not" (Duet)
Helen Redmond {Dolores}

[47] Dropped early in the run.

"(Under) the Shade of the Palm"
S. Deane
(*Lyrics by* Leslie Stuart.)
Finale
(*Lyrics by* Ernest Boyd-Jones.)

ACT 2
Scene 1
Opening Chorus
"Tact" (Song)
E. Wallace-Hopper, Chorus
(*Lyrics by* Paul Rubens.)
"When You're a Millionaire" (Song)
R. E. Graham, Chorus
(*Lyrics by* Ernest Boyd-Jones.)
"Tell Me, Pretty Maiden" (Musical Number[48])
Clerks, English Girls (Sextette)
(*Lyrics by* Leslie Stuart.)
"We Get Up at 8 A.M." (Duet Song and Dance)
N. Bonville, G. L. Baker
"Willie Was a Gay Boy"[49] (Song)
M. Edouin
(*Lyrics by* Alfred Murray.)
"When We're on the Stage"(We're Both on the Stage) (Song)
F. Johnston, W. Edouin
"I've an Inkling" (Song)
E. Wallace-Hopper
(*Music and Lyrics by* Paul Rubens.)
"(The) Queen of the Philippine Islands" (His Only Love)(Song)
F. Johnston
(*Music and Lyrics by* Paul Rubens.)

Scene 2
Barn Dance[50]
"I Want to Be a Military Man" (Song)
C. Scott, Chorus
(*Lyrics by* Frank A. Clement.)
Finale

1900.52 STAR AND GARTER

A Vaudeville Farce in Three Acts. Book by John J. McNally. Music by John W. Bratton. Lyrics by Walter Ford. Staged by Bean Teal. Dances arranged by Ned Wayburn. Settings by Joseph Physioc. Costumes by F. Richard Anderson. Lighting by Peter King. Produced by Frank McKee. Opened 26 November 1900 at the Victoria Theatre and closed 15 December 1900 after 22 performances.

CAST: *Willette Work*: JOSEPH COYNE. *Otto Work*: William Blaisdell. *Bennett Work*: Thornton Cole. *Madame Piquet*: MARIE CAHILL. *Carrie Waite*: May Lowery. *Mollie Fyer*: Margaret Knight. *Lotta Goode*: Nellie Lynch. *Willie Tyre*: OTIS HARLAN. *Terence McCann*: JOHN G. SPARKS. *Taylor Hede*: Lionel Hogarth. *Annie Howe*: Carolina Locke. *Maida Coup*: Florence Norwood. *Tall Tout*: Robert Kelly. *Tim Fleece*: C. H. Bates. *Jack Tippem*: J. F. Leary. *Jennie*: Nellie Murray. *Binnie*: Aimee Gerarde. *Minnie*: Margaret Leon. *Mattie*: Babette Robinson. *Specialty* (Act 2): Monsieur AGOUST and THE MARVELOUS AGOUST FAMILY (Juggling Act).

Act 1: A Dressmaking shop.

Act 2: Star and Garter Restaurant.

Act 3: Morris Park Racetrack.

MUSICAL NUMBERS[51]
Opening Chorus
"After the Show"
"Auto-Mo-Biling"
(*Music and Lyrics by* Matthew Woodward.)
"Dickie the King of the Dudes"
(*Music by* Arthur Trevelyan.)
"Every Inch a Lady"
(*Music by* Herman Perlet. *Lyrics by* Matthew Woodward.)
"(Give Me Back My) Liza"
(*Music and Lyrics by* Dave Reed, Jr.)
"I Wouldn't Mind a Job Like That"
"My Hannah Lady"
(O. Harlan)
(*Lyrics by* William Jerome.)
"My Lady Bug"
(O. Harlan)
"3:33 in the Morning"
(M. Lowery)
(*Music and Lyrics by* Dave Reed, Jr.)
"When Sousa Leads the Band"
(M. Cahill)
(*Music by* Frederick V. Bowers and Charles Horwitz. *Lyrics by* William Jerome.)

1900.53 THE KATZENJAMMER KIDS

A Farce Comedy in Three Acts. Play by Edward Blondell. Based on the popular comic strip by Rudolph Dirks. Stage director, Edward Blondell. Musical director, Ludwig Heck. Produced by (Edward) Blondell and (William) Fennessy. Opened 26 November 1900 at the Third Avenue Theatre and closed 1 December 1900 after 8 performances.

CAST: *Jeb Arnold*: EDWARD BLONDELL. *Bessie Palmer*: LIBBIE ARNOLD BLONDELL. *Adolph Katzenjammer*, to whom all troubles flow: JOHN HENNINGS, SR. *Mr. Quarkerly*: Frank Mudge. *Archie Mason*: Louis Pritzkow. *Happy Hulligan*: Henry Dunn. *Hans Von Gugenheimer*: John Hennings. *James Monroe*: M. Franks. *Willie Get Sweet*: Don Hanley. *Dick Dempsey*: Harry Jenks. *Officer McGinnis*: Howard Howe. *Uneeda Bisquet*: Mallie Little. *Lillian Moore*: Maybelle Eckert. *Gertrude Moore*: Augustine Morton. *Florette*: Mlle. Bertina. *Marie*: Mamie Hennings. *Jeb Dimple*: Leo Edwards. (*Specialties*: Sisters Brannick, Eckert & Heck.)

Act 1: The Living Room in the Katzenjammer Home.

Act 2: The Lawn of the Katzenjammer Home.

Act 3: The Music Room of the Katzenjammer Home.

SPECIALTIES[52]
Dance Specialty
J. Hennings, Jr., M. Hennings
Song
F. Mudge
Song
A Morton
Duet
L. Pritzkow, M. Little
Songs
Sisters Brannick
Contortion Dances
Eckert & Heck, Mlle. Bertine

1900.54 SWEET ANNE PAGE

A Comic Opera in Three Acts. Book by Louis DeLange and Edgar Smith[53]. Music by William Harold Neidlinger. Staged by Max Freeman and J. K. Adams. Settings by D. Frank Dodge. Costumes by F. Richard Anderson. Music director, Albert Krausse. Produced by Lulu Glaser & Company (Management, Frank W. Martineau). Opened 3 December 1900 at the Manhattan Theatre and closed 29 December 1900 after 29 performances.

CAST: The Ridworth Folk: *Anne Page*: LULU GLASER. *Squire Pius Page*, her uncle, a close-fisted country gentleman; an adherent of the Stuarts: FRED FREAR. *Dame Martha Page*, the thorn in Squire Page's side as well as his best rib: JOSIE INTROPODI. *Tom Styles*, a yeoman; master of his own farm, and Anne's heart; the biggest, bravest and best lad in all Devon: ARTHUR DONALDSON. *Jan, Rab, Abram*, yeomen: Frank Smiley, Randolph Curry, Thomas E. Whitbread. *Liz, Judy, Ellen*, rustic belles: Daisy King, Marquita Dwight, Grace Blake. *Elspeth, Bet*, Dame Page's maids: May Gooch, Addie Randolph. *Yeomen, Villagers, Maypole Dancers, Domestics, etc.*

48Often referred to as the "Florodora Sextette;" in later programs billed as a Double Sextette.

49Replaced late in the run by:
"The Fellow Who Might" (Song)
Jeannette Lowrie {Angela}

50Replaced late in the run by:
"The Island of Love"
H. Redmond, Chorus
(*Music by* Ivan Caryll. *Lyrics by* Aubrey [Percy] Hopwood.)

51Not in performance order.

52Musical numbers and specialties not listed in programs.

53DeLange wrote the book, Smith the lyrics.

Exeter Folk: *Justice Fuddlestone Portleigh*: Gilbert Clayton. *Lady Arabella Portleigh*: May Gooch. *Sir Huntley Fox*: Frank Smiley. *Clerk of Court*: Randolph Curry. *Constable*: W. C. White. *Landlord of "The King's Arm"*: Thomas E. Whitbread. *Clutch Crimsonbeak*, a prisoner: Harry Wiegand. *Crier*: Ole Norman. *Tipstaff*: L. D. Schlenk. *Courier*: Osborne Clemson. *"Kirke's Lamb," "Ladies of Quality," Pages, Gentry of the Hunting Club, Cooks, Housemaids, Postboys, Townsfolk, Court Officers, Constables, etc.*

Torbay Folk: *Uncle Davy*, who sighs for the good old days of "Noll Cromwell": Gilbert Clayton. *Young Davy*, Uncle Davy's crew, likewise his grandson: W. S. Smith. *Micah*, a fisherman: Thomas E. Whitbread. *Meg*, a fishwife: Daisy King. *Fishermen, Fishwives, Lads and Lasses.*

London Townfolk: *The Chevalier St. Henry*, the sweetest, drollest gossip of the truly inner circle, from the court of St. James: Harold Blake. *Sally Peachum*, leading lady, orchestra and treasurer of "The Royal Mummers": Greta Risley. *Adrastus Kafoozalum*, conjurer, pantomimist, tragedian, clown, fakir and owner of "The Royal Mummers": ALEXANDER CLARK. *Players of "The Royal Mummers" Troupe.*

Holland Folk: *William*, Prince of Orange: RANDOLPH CURRY. *Mynheer Van Schaak*, from the Zuyder Zee, dealing in schemes, secrets and schnapps: William Herman West. *Nobles, Courtiers, Ladies, Pages, Soldiers, Sailors, etc.*

Act 1: The town common, Ridworth, Devon. 1688.

Act 2: The big hall in the "St. George and the Dragon Inn," Exeter.

Act 3: The wharf at Lyme-Regis.

MUSICAL NUMBERS[54]

"It Is Difficult to Shimmer in Society" (Duet)
"Mr. Noddy Knows a Thing or Two"
"The Mad Sequedilla of Gay Seville"
"A Simple Little Maid"
"I Met a Jolly Sailor Man" (Laughing Song)
"When (I Was) in Flanders"
"By the Gallants I Am Feted" (Chevalier Song)
"When Another Cherub Sings" (Duet)
"There Is Something Hidden in This Chaffing"
"Spanish Song"
"Tom and Yeomen"
"Mummer's Art"
"The Court Is With You, Little Lady"
"Be Off! Be Off!"
"Fairies Gayly Dancing"
"Drinking Song"
"O Golden Leaves"
"The Daffodils and Daisies Bow to Sweet Anne Page"

1900.55 MADGE SMITH, ATTORNEY

A Comedy-Farce (with Music) in Three Acts. Play by Ramsay Morris. (Songs by A. Baldwin Sloane, Theodore H. Northrup, Dave Reed, Jr., Francis Bryant, Ernest Hogan.) Staged by Louis Harrison. Settings by Lewis and MacCoughtry. Music director, Watty Hydes. Produced by May Irwin. Opened 10 December 1900 at the Bijou Theatre and closed 12 January 1901 after 38 performances[55].

CAST: *John Smith*, Mrs. Smith's husband: GEORGE A. BEANE. *Mrs. Madge Smith*, a member of the Hackensack, New Jersey bar: MAY IRWIN. *Ajax O'Shaughnessey*, brother of an important man: JOSEPH M. SPARKS. *Count Cotton*, who came back: IGNACIO MARTINETTI. *Gunnington Swift*, a commercial traveller: Bert Thayer. *Wilson*, Mrs. Smith's private secretary: JACQUES KRUGER. *Montressor Bing* of the Folly Theatre: Roland Carter. *Judge of Police Court*, and other things: Roland Carter. *Upson Downes*: Frank W. Johnson. *Clerk of Police Court*: Charles Church. *Detective*: James M. MacDonough. *Another Detective*: Edward Bowen. *Clarice Gay*, a flame of other days: Mabel Florence. *Of the Folly Theatre (5)*: *Bijou Leech*: Sadie Peters. *Cissy Peachblow*: Anne Woodward. *Flossy Greensleeves*: Grace Amy. *Kate Maxwell*: Alice Sands. *Diana Blush*: Edythe Blair.

Act 1: Morning-room in John Smith's house, Hackensack, New Jersey.

Act 2: Clarice Gay's apartments, New York City. Twenty-four hours later.

Act 3: Haymarket Police Court, New York City. One hour later.

"I Ain't Gwine to Work No Mo'"
M. Irwin

ACT 1[56]

"Why Don't the Band Play?" (from THE BELLE OF BRIDGEPORT)
I. Martinetti, Company
(*Music by* J. Rosamond Johnson. *Lyrics by* Cole Cole and James Weldon Johnson.)

"I've Got Troubles of My Own" (from THE BELLE OF BRIDGEPORT)
M. Irwin
(*Music by* J. Rosamond Johnson. *Lyrics by* Cole Cole and James Weldon Johnson.)

"I Ain't Going to Work No More" (from THE BELLE OF BRIDGEPORT)
M. Irwin
(*Music by* J. Rosamond Johnson. *Lyrics by* Cole Cole and James Weldon Johnson.)

ACT 2

"Oui! Oui! Mademoiselle"
I. Martinetti

"When I'm By Her Side"
W. Burress

"I've Laid Him on de Shelf"
M. Irwin

"Bull-frog Ben"
M. Irwin
(*Music and Lyrics by* Cissie Loftus.)

"(Give Me Back My) 'Liza"
M. Irwin
(*Music and Lyrics by* Dave Reed, Jr.)

"I'm Gwine to Marry Angeline" (Cake Walk)(from THE BELLE OF BRIDGEPORT)
Company
(*Music and Lyrics by* Cissie Loftus.)

"The Turkey and the Turk"
J. Sparks
(*Music and Lyrics by* Francis Bryant.)

"My Little Jungle Queen" (My Congo Queen)
M. Irwin

1900.56 THE GIDDY THRONG

A Burlesque-Review in One Act, 5 Scenes, preceded by a Vaudeville Program. Book and lyrics by Sydney Rosenfeld. Music by A. Baldwin Sloane. Staged by Frank Smithson. Scenery painted by St. John Lewis and McCoughtry. Produced by Messrs. (Meyer L. and Henry B.) Sire. Opened 24 December 1900 at the New York Theatre and closed 11 May 1901 after 164 performances[57].

ACT 1[58]

---

[54] No song list in program. List prepared from published vocal selections (M. Witmark & Sons, New York, 1900) and Century Library Inc. catalogue; not in performance order.

[55] Many songs and similar characters were retained from May Irwin's previous vehicle THE BELLE OF BRIDGEPORT which opened 29 October 1900 at the Bijou Theatre. First produced at a special matinee 6 December 1900. No musical numbers listed for Act 3. Costumes uncredited. Played a return engagement 25 March 1901 at the Grand Opera House for 8 performances.

[56] Added for tour as opening to Act 2:
"Dance on Friday Night" (from THE BELLE OF BRIDGEPORT)
Company
(*Music and Lyrics by* William Jefferson.)

[57] Costume design, musical direction uncredited.

[58] The vaudeville portion of the bill changed frequently. During the run, the following were added: THE DEVIL'S DREAM, a Spectacular Ballet arranged by Carl Marwig. CAST: *Fair Rosamund*: LILLY COLLINS. *Andree*: LILLY BRINK. *Satan*: LAURA LYNDE. And a Corps de Ballet of 200.

MELVILLE and STETSON, the Queens of Comedy.

EDNA AUG (The winsome comedienne)

AFTER OFFICE HOURS, Being a Bundle of Music Tied with a String of Nonsense. The String and the Songs by George V. Hobart. Music by A. Baldwin Sloane. Staged by Frank Smithson. Settings by St. John Lewis. Cast: *Peter Pensywayte*, an amateur from Pennyville: DANIEL McAVOY. *Percy Flawgs*, manager of the costume shop: CHARLES H. PRINCE. *The Shine Brothers, Pollish and Glisten*, two bad minstrel men with worse jokes: CHARLES H. PRINCE, WILLIAM BURRESS. *Sizzleina*, a somewhat saucy soubrette: Jessie May. *Deale Ebetreen*, subdued but soubrettish: Mamie Gilroy. *The Princess*: Ixoria Pinaud. *Chorus of Fifth Avenue Girls, School Girls, Baby Girls and Other Girls.*

Vaudeville program: Grafton Baker in the first scenic spectacular presentation of the Southern Idyl "Ma Mississippi Belle" by Cole and Johnson, and "Roaming in the Gloaming" by Northrup and Arnold. Assisted by the Misses Kelly, Fair, Goodyear, Chapin, Ruiz, Stilson, Tuoey, Marcelle, Palmer, Pepper, Payne, Blye, Wile; Messrs. Fitz, Foley, Peters, Levere. Staged by Lionel E. Lawrence. Scenery by Lewis & McCoughtry.

A Few Minutes with Jessie May and Company

Fred Niblo (The Premier Monologuist)

Emma Carus (The Female Baritone) in the new Spectacular Scenic Production "Ma Samoan Beauty." Staged by Lionel E. Lawrence. Scenery by Lewis & McCoughtry.

Torcat, the Musical Eccentric. (First appearance in America)

The Meeting Of The Allies at the Gates of Pekin. Carl Marwig's Gorgeous Pageant introducing Military Movements and Wall Scaling by detachment of Company B, Second Regiment under command of Captain M. H. Kelly (scaling 20 feet wall in 20 seconds).

ACT 2

THE GIDDY THRONG, a Burlesque-Review in One Act, 6 Scenes[59]. Book and lyrics by Sydney Rosenfeld. Music by A. Baldwin Sloane. Staged by Frank Smithson. Settings by Lewis and McCoughtry.

CAST: *Lady Muriel Despair*, the "real thing" in English girls, betrothed to lord Quex: MAY YOHE [Lady Francis Hope], EMMA CARUS (alternate). *Lord Quex*, who afterwards becomes transformed into—but why betray the plot?: LOUIS HARRISON. *Sophy Fulgarney*, a manciure, with apologies to the shop next door: MABEL FENTON. *The Duchess of Sirood*, who owns a boudoir, without which there could not have been this play: AMELIA SUMMERVILLE. *Richard Carvel*, who was dramatized from a novel—and shows it: FRANK DOANE. *Dorothy Manners*, who suffers similarity with a leaning toward Richard: Mamie Gilroy. *David Harum*, who tries to sell a horse under difficulties: William Gould. *Foxy Quiller*, a detective in the employ of Lord Quex and others: CHARLES H. PRINCE. *Flambeau*, a French grenadier (save the mark!): DANIEL MacAVOY. *Lady Allover*, a typical walking lady: Vera Morris. *Mr. Noble Rohman*, a great theatrical manager: Joseph Harrington. *A Tenor Hero*: Grafton Baker. *The Doctor*: Grafton Baker. *An Office Boy*: PAT ROONEY. *A Drummer Boy*: Pat Rooney. *His Sweetheart*: MAYME GEHRUE.

Florodora Girls: Marie Baldwin, Muriel Milton, Mattie Chapin, Georgia Kelly, Ethel Goodyear, Ethel York. *San Toy Boys*: Attalic Claire, Leonora Ruiz, Lilly Brink, Inez Marcelle, Pearl Stilson, Beulah Montrose. *Characters in the Visions (3)*: *A Noted President*: Louis Foley. *A Noted Chief* (The Rough Rider): Charles E. Fitz. *A Typical Tenderloiner*: Miss Binford. *A New Reformer*: Theodore Peters. *Groups from "L'Aiglon," "Arizona," "Richard Carvel," etc., Amazons, Drummer Boys.*

Scene 1: Office of Manager Noble Rohman. *Scene 2*: The Carvel-Quex Manor. *Scene 3*: The Manicure's Office. *Scene 4*: The Duchess' Boudoir. *Scene 5*: At the Manicure's. *Scene 6*: The Battlefield of Wagram.

MUSICAL NUMBERS[60]

"Powder Your Nose"
A. Summerville
"Kiss Me to Sleep" (Scene 2)
M. Yohe
(*Music by* Ivan Caryll.)
"Down By the River" (Scene 2)
M. Yohe
(*Music by* Ivan Caryll.)
"Since Sally's in the Ballet"
E. Carus
(*Music by* Mike Bernard. *Lyrics by* Vincent P. Bryan.)

1900.57

A ROYAL ROGUE

An Operatic Comedy (Comic Opera) in Two Acts. (Book) Written by Charles Klein. Music by William T. Francis. Lyrics by Grant Stewart. Staged by R. H. Burnside. Settings by D. Frank Dodge. Costumes by Caroline Seidle. Music director, William T. Francis. Produced by Jefferson DeAngelis (Sam S. Shubert, Manager). Opened 24 December 1900 at the Broadway Theatre and closed 19 January 1901 after 30 performances.

CAST: *Baptiste Ballou*, (an anti-royalist cut-throat): JEFFERSON DeANGELIS. *Members of the Chapeau Rouge Society (4)*: *Couval*: Henry Norman. *Pillot*: Charles Dungan. *Ristac*: John Dudley. *Cadaux*: Leonard Savoy. *Cadet Georges Girodet*: F. NEWTON LINDO. *La Blanc*: HAROLD VIZARD. *Captain Dubois* of the War Office: George Rolland. *Lieutenant Chambois*: J. Canduit. *Prefect of Police*: Frederic K. Logan. *First Gendarme*: George Schofield. *Servant*: C. V. Clarke. *Stephanie*, Ballou's daughter: JOSEPHINE HALL. *Madame Girodet*: EVA DAVENPORT. *Madame Duclos*: Hilda Hollins. *Bejazine, Coralie*, of the Theatre Varietes: Adine Bouvier, Maude Poole. *Madame Hilaire*: Emily Francis. *Waitresses at Ballou's Cafe, Grisettes, Students, Officers, Gendarmes, etc.*

Act 1: Ballou's Cafe on the Boulevard des Jardin, Paris. 1797.

Act 2: Garden and Conservatory of Madame Girodet's House near Paris.

ACT 1[61]

"When You Are Found Out"
A. Bouvier, A. M. Poole
"Pop, Pop, Pop!"
"In Bohemia"
"When Socialism Has Full Sway" (Quintette)
"No One Thinks of Me"
"Something Burning"
"I Once Had a Chef"
J. DeAngelis
"(We Won't Do a Thing to) Mamma's Millions" (Duet)
J. DeAngelis, ?
"Make Way for the Wealthy Widow" (I'm the Widow Girodet)
"They Will Put Him in a Cell" (Concerted Number)
"Two is Company" (Waltz Song)
"A Double-Eyed Assassin"
J. DeAngelis
"Wanted: A Cook in a Restaurant"
"All the World to Me"
"(The) Daughters of a Minister"

ACT 2

"Ding-Dong-Ding" (Bell Song)
"When I'm Are Married" (Duet)
F. N. Lindo, ?
"A (Gallant) Would-Be General"
J. DeAngelis
"Dinner, Dinner" (Quartette)
"Not Yet"

1900.58

MISS PRINNT

An Evening's Entertainment (Farce Comedy) in Three Acts. (Book) Written by George V. Hobart. Music (and lyrics) by John L. Golden. Scenery painted by A. Operti. Music director, Clarence Rogersoll. Produced by Joseph Immerman. Opened 25 December 1900 at Hammerstein's Victoria Theatre and closed 19 January 1901 after 28 performances[62].

CAST: *Helen Prinnt*, a woman and a good fellow always: MARIE DRESSLER. *Mrs. Van Asteroid*, related to the "400" by money: JOBYNA HOWLAND. *Breezie Fairweather*, a soubrette from the country where the cyclone grows: Zella Frank. *Mabel Morningside*, Helen's niece: CHARLOTTE WALKER. *Dolly Darling*, a reporter who finds the men always willing to be interviewed: ADELE FARRINGTON. *Mrs. Bonsonrocks*, who husband has money to burn, but no matches: Julia McCoy. *Remington Typewriter Girls (4)*: *Rosalind*: Lottie Medley. *Clarisa*: Mabelle Howe. *Dorothy*: KITTY NUGENT. *Yeobel*: Mayme Harnish. *Helene*: Lona DuBois. *Mollie*: June Dechamp. *Richmond Blackstone*, a lawyer and therefore to be trusted with a watchful eye: THEODORE BABCOCK. *Sneezovitch Snoozlelotski*, an anarchist who believes in highballs, horror and hair: DAVE LEWIS. *Count Boney Cashkacheck*, an importation from France whose linguistic wires are crossed: Leon Kohlmar. *Dick Tait*, city editor of the Somerset Turnover: ARTHUR STANFORD. *Eaton Spayce*, the sport-

For subsequent tour, AFTER OFFICE HOURS was replaced by THE MARCH OF OLD GLORY, Captain M. A. Kelly's masterwork, introducing his famous company of Second Regiment of Volunteers, entire chorus and corps de ballet of the New York Theatre. "March of Old Glory" Music by A. Baldwin Sloane.

[59]Featuring characters from current Broadway hits "The Gay Lord Quex," "Richard Carvel," "L'Aiglon," "David Harum," Lost River," "Florodora," "San Toy." Revised during the run.

[60]Musical numbers not listed in programs. The Ivan Caryll songs presumably originated with earlier English shows.

[61]Additional musical numbers published: "Found Out," "Down, Down with Everything," "Shall I?"

[62]Staging, presumably by the author, was uncredited; acting manager, W. A. McConnell; costumes uncredited.

ing editor and wise guy even as a guy is wise: THOMAS EVANS. *Latherup Leatherbe*, still in the shadow of his Zulu ancestry: Lew Simmons. *Kid McGinnis*, a sporting remnant: James F. Grant. *Ponsonby Pewtertop*, a writer of up-to-date songs but otherwise perfectly harmless: John McCauley. *Galley B. Jinks*, a devil among the printers: Frederick Richter.

Ensemble: Lala Hoffman, Eugene Whiston, Clara Wood, Margaret Leon, Maude Lee, Edith Daniels, Maude Francis, Clara Carrigan, Wilma Gilmore, Burleigh Murray, Leslie Mayo, Florence Norwood, Queenie Winslip, Bena Hoffman, BESSIE CLAYTON, Aimee Geraide, Irene Wentworth, Stella Adams, Blanche Alwens.

Incidental to Act 3, Miss Dressler will introduce a burlesque[63] on Rostand's masterpiece "L'Aiglon" written by James Clarence Harvey, with apologies to Mme. Bernhardt and Miss Adams.

The action takes place to-day, near by.

Act 1: Good morning. Editorial rooms of the Daily Somerset Turnover.

Act 2: Good afternoon. The law offices of Richmond Blackstone.

Act 3: "To-morrow." The exterior of Miss Prinnt's suburban villa.

MUSICAL NUMBERS[64]

"I'm Looking for an Angel (without Wings)"
M. Dressler

"The Mosquito Song"

"Sweet Saturday"
M. Dressler
(*Music and Lyrics by* J. B. Mullen.)

"I'm Gettin' So Thirsty"
M. Dressler
(*Music and Lyrics by* Jean C. Havez.)

1900.59 THE BURGOMASTER

A Musical Comedy in Two Acts and a Prologue, 5 Scenes. Book and lyrics by Frank Pixley. Music by Gustav Luders. Staged under the direction of Thomas Ricketts. Musical diretor, Gustav Luders. Produced by Dearborn Theatre Management (W. W. Tillotson, director). Opened 31 December 1900 at the Manhattan Theatre and closed 26 January 1901 after 33 performances.

CAST (Prologue): *Peter Stuyvesant*, Burgomaster of New Amsterdam: HENRY E. DIXEY. *Doodle Van Kull*, his secretary: KNOX WILSON. *Captain Krall*, Commander of the Burgher forces: WILLIAM RILEY HATCH. *Captain Spuyten* of the Dutch ship *"Blitzen"*: JOSEPH S. WELSH. *Blue Feather*, Chief of the Tammany Tribe: BEAUMONT RALSTON. *Terrence Rafferty*, a saloon keeper: James T. Kelly. *William Haagen*, Town Councillor: George Town. *Jan de Peyster*, Town Counsillor: Harry Andrews. *Dame Stuyvesant*, wife of the Burgomaster: ADA DEAVES. *Katrina Vanderbeck*, Doodle's sweetheart: SALLIE RANDALL. *Lieutenant Sweetzer* of the Dutch cadets: RUTH WHITE. *Indians, Dutch Cadets, Burgher Soldiers, Village Girls, Sailors, etc.*

CAST (Act 1): *Peter Stuyvesant*, after his nap: HENRY E. DIXEY. *Doodle Van Kull*, who has also overslept: KNOX WILSON. *E. Booth Talkington*, an actor in hard luck: RAYMOND HITCHCOCK. *"The Harlem Spider,"* a professional pugilist: WILLIAM RILEY HATCH. *Officer Clancey* of the Broadway squad: George E. Romaine. *Foreman of the Street Gang*: E. W. Lewis. *Grogan*, a street laborer: James T. Kelly. *Newsboy*: Annette Duval. *Willie Van Astorbilt*, "a midnight son": ZELMA RAWLSTON. *Phoebe Kummagin*, a Theosophist: ADA DEAVES. *Ruth*, the girl from Chicago: Ruth White. *Daisy*, a roof garden favorite: JOSEPHINE NEWMAN. *Broadway Soubrettes (8)*: *Pansy*: Alice Sweet. *Pink*: Luella Drew. *Rose*: Nellie Follis. *Violet*: Lillian Austin. *Mignonette*: Grace Gray. *Lilly*: Van Huntington. *Dahlia*: Gladys Mitchell. *Fern*: Della Rosa. *Rainy Daisies (8)*: *Sunny Shine*: Evelyn Clemons. *Mannie Fair*: Nellie Boyd. *Fannie Clear*: Flora Arkell. *Gertie Bright*: Lena Kamp. *Minnie Zephyr*: Ethel Hoag. *Nellie Breeze*: Maude LeRoy. *Cissy Twilight*: Florence Hayes. *May Change*: Annie Ott. *Miss Madison*: Sallie Randall. *Primroses from Miss Prim's Seminary (8)*: *Miss Beacon*: May Morris. *Miss Walnut*: Dora Carrier. *Miss Chestnut*: Annette Duval. *Miss Lexington*: Eva Gunning. *Miss Kearney*: Gertrude Arden. *Miss Olive*: Franes Palmer. *Miss Speedway*: Emerony James. *Miss Boulevard*: Constance Vale. *College Boys, Football Teams, Workingmen, Street Vendors, etc.*

CAST (Act 2): *Peter Stuyvesant*, who is "Seeing the Elephant": HENRY E. DIXEY. *Doodle Van Kull*: KNOX WILSON. *"The Harlem Spider"*: William Riley Hatch. *E. Booth Talkington* of the International Dime Museum: RAYMOND HITCHCOCK. *Marmaduke*: Harry Murdock. *Phoebe Kummagin*: Ada Deaves. *Willie Van Astorbilt*: ZELMA RAWLSTON. *Ruth*, the summer girl: RUTH WHITE. *Mrs. Splurger*, of the New York "400": Jeanne Caskie. *Seaside Fairies, Fakirs, Yachtsmen, etc.*

Burlesque—"Leg Long"

CAST: *The Duke*: ADA DEAVES. *Matternix*: RAYMOND HITCHCOCK. *Scrambo*: WILLIAM RILEY HATCH. *English Visitors in Search of an Heiress*: Messrs. James Henner, Hery Bird, Cecil Lane, W. R. Lintol, Albert Hutches, A. L. Collis, V. L. Bray, George N. Dodge. *Members of the Larchmont Yacht Club*: Messrs. Ralph Briggs, O. P., Rupont, Brady Grear, Willard Mears, DeWitt Mott, Henry DePack, Samuel Fox, George Nagle, H. R. Webester, George A. Pringle, Walter Cook, Alex Kaut, George Lewis. *Burlesquers, French Dancers, etc.*

Prologue: The Town Hall of New Amsterdam, now New York, in 1660 showing the ancient Whitehall.

Act 1: Printing House Square. Today.

Act 2, Scene 1: The Seashore. *Scene 2*: Wall Street, New York. *Scene 3*: The Ball-room at Mrs. Splurger's City Residence.

PROLOGUE[65]

"Love Can't Say No" (Opening Chorus and Song)
S. Randall, Dutch Girls

"Good-Bye, New Amsterdam" (Ensemble)
W. R. Hatch, Burgher Soldiers

"(Just) Keep Cool" (Song)
H. E. Dixey

"We're Civilized Now" (Indian Chorus)
B. Ralston, Indians

"The Dutch Cadets" (Military Song)
R. White, Soldiers

"I Drink from My Heart to You" (Drinking Song)
J. S. Welsh, Dutch Girls, Sailors

Finale

ACT 1

"We Always Work the Public-Not the Job" (Opening Chorus)
E. W. Lewis, Workingmen

"The Land of Midnight Son"[66] (Solo and Chorus)
Z. Rawlston

"The (Little) Soubrette" (Song)
J. Newman, Soubrettes

"Merely a Matter of Form"

"(In) Dear Old College Days" (Ensemble)
College Boys

"The Modern Gladiator" (Solo and Chorus)
W. R. Hatch, Tough Girls

"The Tale of the Kangaroo" (Song and Chorus)
H. E. Dixey, Z. Rawlston, R. White

"The Liberty Girl"

Finale

ACT 2[67]

"The Bathing Girls" (Opening Chorus)
J. Newman, Chorus

"We Haven't Discovered Him Yet" (We've Never Discovered Him Yet)

(Comic Song)
R. Hitchcock, Chorus

---

[63]After the opening, this was replaced by THE VILLAGE BEAUTY, an entirely unoriginal comic opera bluffe, freely adapted from everything you ever saw· Worded by J. Clarence Harvey. Musiced by John L. Golden. Cast to the full strength of the daily Somerset Turnover staff: *The Usual King*: THOMAS EVANS. *The Real Lover*: ARTHUR STANFORD. *The Villanous Villain*: DAVE LEWIS. *First Prima Donna of the Chorus*: ADELE FARRINGTON. *Another First Prima Donna of the Chorus*: CHARLOTTE WALKER. *The Village Beauty*: MARIE DRESSLER.

[64]No New York program available. Musical numbers from published sheet music, reviews, etc.

[65]Vocals were not indicated in opening night program; vocals have been assigned on the basis of the vocal score. Vocal score (M. Witmark & Sons, New York, 1900) published prior to New York production. Included in vocal score, but presumably dropped prior to New York

"The Rainy Daisies" (Scene)
Female Chorus

"Cupid Does Not Marry" (Duet)
R. White, Z. Rawlston

Performed in show as per published sheet music:

"If I Were a Hypnotist" (The Hypnotist)

[66]Replaced for subsequent tour by:

"Mademoiselle New York"
(*Music by* John W. Bratton. *Lyrics by* Paul West.)

[67]Act 2 varies substantially from the published vocal score.

"I Love You (Dear, and Only You)" (Ballad)
R. White
"The Summer Girl"
"The Aristocracy"
"Yo Ho for a Jolly Good Sail"
"In Gay Paris"
Knox Wilson's Specialty
"Reaching for the Cake" (Darkey Song)
J. Newman, Chorus
Finale—"Painting Chicago Red"

1901.01 THE GIRL FROM UP THERE

Charles Frohman's Musical Comedy Company in a Musical Comedy in Three Acts. Book and lyrics by Hugh Morton. Music by Gustave Kerker. Produced under the stage direction of Julian Mitchell. Settings by Ernest Gros, Ernest Albert. Costumes by Caroline Seidle. Orchestra under the direction of Gustave Kerker; music director, George L. Humphrey. Produced by Charles Frohman. Opened 7 January 1901 at the Herald Square Theatre and closed 30 March 1901 after 96 performances.

CAST: *King Flash* of West Polaria: HARRY KELLY. *King Flush* of East Polaria: OTIS HARLAN. *Bertie Tappertit*, Captain of the Royal Guards: HARRY DAVENPORT. *J. Angostura Pickles*, a disagreeable man: HARRY CONOR. *Colonel Marcellus Whizzle*, U.S.A., an inventor: Charles W. Young. *Captain Hiram Hardtack*: Alf C. Whelan. *Jack Hemingway*, a young explorer: J. FARREN SOUTAR. *Skeets*, a burglar: Charles T. Aldrich. *Solomon Scarlet*, a pirate chief: DAVID MONTGOMERY. *Christopher Grunt*, one of the pirate crew: FRED STONE. *Binks*, an innkeeper: LAWRENCE WHEAT. *Olga*, the ice maiden: EDNA MAY. *Phyrnette*, prima donna of the Aurora Borealis Opera Company: VIRGINIA EARL [Earle]. *Thyrza, Margot*: Grace Belmont. *Lais, Bebe*: EDNA AUG. *Theresa, Mimi*: Nella Webb. *Mabel*: Leonore Harris. *Sister Heartease*: Jane May. *Ortrud*: Bobby Burns. *Christina*: Mabel Powers. *Althea*: Louise Monti. *Zenobia*: Marie Allen. *Sibylla*: Maude Harlow.

Opera Girls: Misses Estelle Moyer, Gertrude Moyer, Mabel Powell, Connie Powell, Nellie Paine, Miss T. Roggerio, Miss N. Hoffman, Georgie Irving, Vivian Austin, Leila Romer, Gladys Earlcott.

Act 1: Polaria, six miles from the North Pole. (Albert.)

Act 2: Crackrib Crescent, on the Island of Kokoriko. (Albert.)

Act 3: On the Boulevards, Paris (Gros.)

MUSICAL NUMBERS[68]
"When Seraphina Plays the Concertina"
E. Aug
"Don't You Believe Those Eyes"
"Fair Phrynette"
"I Was Walking Round the Ocean"
"Susie"
"We'll Never Eat"

1901.02 GARRETT O'MAGH

A Comedy (with Music) in Four Acts. Play by Augustus Pitou. Music and lyrics by Chauncey Olcott. Staged by Augustus Pitou. Scenery painted by Louis C. Young. Costumes designed by H. A. Ogden. Dramatic music composed by Gustave Salzer. Musical director, Gustave Salzer. Produced by Augustus Pitou. Opened 7 January 1901 at the 14th Street Theatre and closed 16 March 1901 after 81 performances[69].

CAST: *Garrett O'Magh*: CHAUNCEY OLCOTT. *Mrs. Mary Devlin*, his aunt: MARGARET FITZPATRICK. *Roger Nagle, Esq.*, a Dublin attorney: CHARLES ABBOTT. *Eileen Nagle*, his daughter: EDITH BARKER. *May Nagle*, his daughter: TOTTIE CARR. *Sir Horace Wilton*, an English diplomat: DANIEL GILFETHER. *Louise Wilton*, his daughter: Louise Marcelli. *Alfred Spencer*, his nephew: Richard Malchien. *Rufus Hardy*, an American trader: Paul Everton. *Josephine*, a French maid: Katherine Willard. *Jerry Quigley*, an old gardener: George Brennan. *Military attache*: Henry Watson. *Darby Lynch*, the innkeeper: Luke Martin. *Maggie Lynch*, his wife: Elizabeth Washburne. *Old Mrs. Lynch*, his mother: Etta Barker Martin. *Lynch's children (4)Darby Lynch, Jr.*: Clara Cubitt. *Pat Lynch*: Bert Buckley. *Nora Lynch*: Gretta Carr. *Mollie Lynch*: Pese Glaser. *Dennis*: Ernest Havens. *Annie*: Mabel Andrews. *Peasant man*: Edward Smith. *Peasant woman*: Jennie Buckley. *Constable and Aids, Male and Female Peasants*.

Act 1: Mrs. Devlin's House in the suburbs of Dublin. 1812.

Act 2: Room in Mr. Nagle's house in Dublin. Two months later.

Act 3: Darby Lynch's Inn, near Dublin.

Act 4: Mrs. Devlin's house, in the suburbs of Dublin.

MUSICAL NUMBERS
"Paddy's Cat"
C. Olcott
"Ireland A! Gra Ma Chree"
C. Olcott
"The Lass I Love"
C. Olcott
"My Sweet Queen"
C. Olcott

1901.03 MR. CONEY'S ISLE

A Farce Comedy in Three Acts. Opened 14 January 1901 at the Third Avenue Theatre and closed 19 January 1901 after 8 performances.[70]

CAST: *General Rufus Stanton*: Warren F. Hill. *Tom Stanton*: M. Farnum. *Ralph Curtis*: W. B. Johns. *Ned Walters*: B. Hilliard. *Harry Walters*: H. Glayton. *Dr. Lawrence*: John H. W. Byrne. *Wigson*: John H. Lewis. *Matthews*: Frederick Collier. *Oliver*: Ted Tobell. *Three Pugilists: Arthur Thorndyke*: JOHN P. DUNN. *Jimmy Hardman*: MATTY MATTHEWS. *Walter Beecher*: JIMMY HANDLER. *Daisy Howard*: Zuida LeClair. *Isabel Armstrong*: Anna Lavigne. *Mrs. Walters*: Louise Pugh. *Rose Stewart*: Amelia Stoddard. (*Specialty*, Champion Lightweight of the World: HARVEY PARKER.)

Act 1: The Albemarle Hotel.

Act 2: The Bloomingdale Sanitarium.

Act 3: The Coney Isle Sporting Club.

1901.04 THE NIGHT OF THE FOURTH

A Vaudeville (Musical Comedy) in Three Acts, 4 Scenes. (Book by George Ade[71].) Music by Max Hoffman. Lyrics by J. Sherrie Mathews. Production staged by Ned Wayburn. Scenery painted by Gates & Morange. Costumes by Belle Coughley. Musical director, Max Hoffman. Vocal arrangements by George Wiseman. Produced by ? Dunne and Thomas W. Ryley. Opened 21 January 1901 at Hammerstein's Victoria Theatre and closed 2 February 1901 after 14 performances.

CAST: *Keenan Swift*, a lawyer: JOSEPH COYNE. *Eli Frost*, a retired iceman: HARRY BULGER. *Joseph Kidder*, boy detective: TONY HART[72]. *Pierpont Von Graft*, son of his parents: PHILIP H. RYLEY. *Judge Erasmus Boliver* of the Circuit Court: A. J. BODE. *Arthur Strong*, looking for work: WALTER JONES. *Hiram Lowe*, vaudeville agent: WALTER JONES. *Augustus Handle*, warden of the Nutville Asylum: George Weisman. *Mr. Sokum*, proprietor Summer Rest Hotel: George Weisman. *Dr. X. Rays Cuticle*, specialist and expert witness: Dave Andrada. *W. Ruff*, keeper Nutville Asylum: Alexander Thompson. *Charley Hunter* Deputy Sheriff: L. J. Hall. *Cuthbertson Carruthers*: Ralph Bicknell. *Cloyster, Oyster*, lackeys: Charles McNevins, Gus Mebus. *Elise Boliver*, just from school: BESSIE TANNEHILL. *Laura Jane Frost*, the iceman's sister: BESSIE TANNEHILL. *Kitty*, a ready maid: Bertha Dowling[73]. *Summer Girls (5): Jacque Rose*: MAUD COURTNEY. *Lily Bud* Helen Dunlap. *Sophie Thorn*: Adlyn Estee. *Nanette Blossom*: Anne Dale. *Jennie Clover*: Daisy Gehrue.

Miss Judge: Gertrude Hayes. *Miss Behave*: Grace Field. *Miss Cellaneous*: Eva Burnham. *Miss Chief*: Grace Vaughn. *Miss Construe*: Edna Barclay. *Miss Fortune*: Reba Bicknell. *Miss Take*: Agnes Marsh. *Miss Informed*: Amy Forsslund. *Miss Trust*: Florence McNeil. *Miss Nomer*: Blanche Alwens. *Miss Lead*: LeClair Bernard. *Miss Happ*: Florence Borden. *Miss Gyde*: Ida Lester. *Miss Rule*: Cornell Williams. *Miss Deed*: Laura Rowe. *Miss Give*: Blanche Sherwood.

Act 1: Exterior of the Summer Rest Hotel. Evening of 4 July. Absolute calm.

Act 2: Reception room and law office of Swift, McClure & Skinner. 5 July. Several conspiracies.

Act 3, Scene 1: Warden's office, Nutville Private Asylum. *Scene 2*: Evening of 5 July. "All serene."

---

[68]Musical numbers not listed in programs; list prepared from published vocal score, reviews, etc. Press clippings note revised version premiered 24 February 1901.

[69]Played a return engagement 27 January 1902 at the 14th Street Theatre for 24 additional performances.

[70] Author uncredited. No program available.

[71] George Ade had withdrawn his name from the production prior to its New York opening.

[72] Nephew to the famous Tony Hart of Harrigan & Hart.

[73] Contrary to program credit, some reviewers saw Josie DeWitt in this role.

ACT 1
"Stepsons of the Revolution"
A. Estee, Chorus
"Walk, (You Sucker, Walk)"
J. Coyne, H. Bulger, W. Jones
"Love Me Lize"
J. Coyne, Chorus
ACT 2
"Wiseman's Serenaders"
D. Andrada, L. J. Hall, G. Wiseman, A. J. Bode
Parodies
H. Bulger
"You've Hardly Known Me Long Enough for That"
J. DeWitt, P. H. Ryley
Whirlwind Dances
Ralph and Reba Bicknell
"Stars of the Vaudeville"
M. Courtney, G. Hayes, D. Gehrue, W. Jones, Chorus
"M-O-N-E-Y Spells Money"
B. Tannehill, Company
ACT 3
Parodies
H. Bulger
"Fiddle and I"
J. DeWitt
Finale
Company

1901.05 VIENNA LIFE

An Operetta in Three Acts. Original Viennese libretto ("Wiener Blut") by Victor Léon and Leo Stein. English adaptation and lyrics by Glen MacDonough. Music by Johann Strauss[74]. Staged by A. F. MacCollin. Scenery painted by D. Frank Dodge, Ernest Albert. Costumes by Mme. M. L. Dowling. Electrical effects by Joseph George. Music director, Selli Simonson. Produced by Rudolph Aronson. Opened 23 January 1901 at the Broadway Theatre and closed 23 February 1901 after 35 performances[75].

CAST: *Count Zedlau*, Ambassador from Reuss-Griez-Schliez: THOMAS H. PERSSE. *Prince Gindelbach* of Reuss-Griez-Schliez: CHARLES H. DREW. *Rudolph Kaegler*, father of Franziska: RAYMOND HITCHCOCK. *Josef*, valet of Count Zedlau: William Blaisdell. *Captain of Gendarmes*: E. B. Knight. *Franziska Cagliari*, a ballet dancer: AMELIA STONE. *Countess Zedlau*: ETHEL JACKSON. *Pepi*, a milliner's model: OCTAVIE BARBE. *Betty*, maid to Franziska Cagliari: Rosemary Glosz. *Theresa*, Tyrolean Danseuse: Arlie Arlington. *Prince Bitowski*: MAUD THOMAS. *Marguerite*: Theresa Renold. *Ursula*: Marie Wheeler. *Marie*: Kitty Lynch. *Luise*: Julia Raymond. *Hortense*: Ethel Lyman. *Agnes*: Daisy Dwyer. *Amelia*: Kathleen Franklin. *Rose*: Marie Franklin. *Katrina*: Ella Devine. *Rodolfo*: Margaret Trew. *Milliners*: Misses Marie Franklin, Kathleen Franklin, Kitty Lynch, Ella Devine, Theresa Renold, Mabel Miller, Daisy Dwyer, Julia Raymond. *Bird-sellers, Peddlers, Peasants, Lancers, Pages, Maids of Honor, Court Ladies, Tyrolean Singers, etc.*

Act 1: The villa of Count Zedlau, in the environs of Vienna. (Dodge.)

Act 2: Ball-room in Prince Bitowski's palace. (Albert.)

Act 3: Casino at Hietzing, near Vienna. (Dodge.)

1901.06 MY LADY

A Romantic Extravaganza in Three Acts. Book and lyrics by R. A. Barnet, (a burlesque of) "The Three Musketeers" by Alexandre Dumas. Music by Harry Lawson Heartz. Additional musical numbers by Edward W. Corliss, Robert G. Morse, D. K. Stevens, Clifton Crawford. Entire production under the stage directon of Will A. McCormick. Ballets in Act 3 arranged by M. B. Gilbert. Scenes, William Gill. Costumes by M. Sullivan, Boston; Dazian, New York. Music director, Paul Schindler. Produced by A. H. Chamberlyn. Opened 11 February 1901 at Hammerstein's Victoria Theatre; second edition introduced 18 March 1901[76]; and closed 4 May 1901 after 93 performances.

CAST: *Raoul d'Artagnan*, "The Musketeer": LILLIAN GREEN. *Cardinal Richelieu*[77]: CHARLES J. ROSS. *Henri de Rochefort*: ARTHUR NELSTONE. *"The Three (Musketeers)*, a drop of Irish, a drop of Dutch, a drop of Scotch: *Ah-Those*: GILBERT CLAYTON. *Pork-House*: GILBERT GREGORY. *Arrah-Miss*: CLIFTON CRAWFORD. *George Villiers*, Milord Duke of Buckingham: LOTTA FAUST. *Louis XIII*: Carle Stowe. *De Jussac*, Captai of the Cardinal's Guard: Ethel Moore. *The Cardinal's Guard (4)*: *Aubonn*: G. H. Williams. *Bicarat*: J. H. Boyle. *Cahuzac*: Gilbert DeVoy. *Dernajoux*: C. Day. *Messenger Boy*: Tom Browne. *Henri*: G. H. Stevens. *Cantaniers (4)*: *Juliquet*: Frances Belmont. *Mimette*: Olive Ulrich. *Manette*: Dean Wilkie. *Bellette*: Minner Rudolph. *A Feeble Old Citizen of Calais*: A. J. Morris. *Clearice, Countess de Winter, "Miladi"*: MERRI OSBORNE. *Gabrielle du Chalus*, the Queen's Confidante: EVA TANGUAY. *Anne of Austria*, Queen of France: VIOLET HOLLIS. *Mignonette*, a spy of the Cardinal: Mlle. Proto. *Fanchonette*, the Queen's Confidential Maid: Alexia Bassian. *Captain Roche, Captain François*, Officers: Natalie Olcott, Florence Carlisle. *The Queen's Maids-in-Waiting (6)*: *Marie*: Pauline Chase. *Annette*: Tessie Mooney. *Mabelle*: Isabelle D'Armand. *Mamette*: Jessie Jordan. *Hortense*: Laura Stone. *Cecile*: Leonora Carlisle. *Jeanne*: Ethel Grey.

Interpolated specialties: Tom Browne (Whistling solos), Czarina (Premiere danseuse in her terpsichorean act), Arthur Nelstone and Misses Pauline Chase and Tessie Mooney in a Danse Eccentrique, Mlle. Proto (Novel dances).

Act 1: Old Paris. The handkerchief.

Act 2: Calais. The purple pawn ticket.

Act 3: The Louvre. The Ballet of La Merlaiason.

ACT 1
"A Soldier's Life is a Game of Strife" (Opening Chorus)
Soldiers, Maidens
"He's a Military 'Beaut'!"
A. Nelstone, E. Tanguay
"Maids in Waiting"
Maids' Chorus
"O'er the Sea of Dreamland Sky"
V. Hollis
"Ma Chère Paris"
L. Green, M. Osborne
"The Three Musketeers" (Rat-a-tat-tat! Zing-boom!)
G. Clayton, G. Gregory, C. Crawford, Chorus
"(My) Bobby and I"
L. Green
"Richelieu"
C. J. Ross, Chorus
Finale (Before another act's recess)
Principals, Chorus
ACT 2
"The Good Old Days" (Opening)
E. Tanguay, Maids-in-Waiting, Chorus
"The Idol of the Day"
L. Green, G. Clayton, G. Gregory, C. Crawford
"On the Wrong Quay"
C. J. Ross, A. Nelstone, M. Osborne
"One for All, All for One!"
L. Green, V. Hollis, Chorus
(*Music and Lyrics by* Edward W. Corliss.)
"Such Good Little Girls"
Maids-in-Waiting
"Miladi!"
L. Green, Chorus
(*Music and Lyrics by* Edward W. Corliss.)
Finale (When the wind is no' no' ee')
Principals, Chorus
ACT 3
"When Maggie Dooley Scrubs the Floor"
M. Osborne, Chorus
"I Told You So"
C. J. Ross, A. Nelstone, G. Clayton, G. Gregory, C. Crawford, M. Osborne, V. Hollis, Mlle. Proto
"My Heart Is Ever True" (March Song and Chorus)
L. Green
(*Music and Lyrics by* D. K. Stevens.)

---

[74]Music taken from the works of Johann Strauss and arranged by Adolf Müller, Jr.

[75]Musical numbers not listed in program.

[76]Second edition included a longer list of interpolated vaudeville specialties.

[77] During the run, this character was renamed Looloo, the personal representative of Cardinal Richelieu.

Pas de Fleur (Ballet)
(*Introduction by* H. L. Heartz)
I. "Come Let Us Dance"
(Chorus)
(*Music and Lyrics by* D. K. Stevens.)
II.
(*Music by* H. L. Heartz.)
III.
(*Music by* R. G. Morse.)
IV. Finale
(*Music by* R. G. Morse.)
"And That's What He Taught Me to Do"
E. Tanguay

INTERPOLATIONS[78]
"After the Fancy Ball"
"The Sword Song"
"Simple Little Sister Mary Green"
C. Crawford
(*Music and Lyrics by* Clifton Crawford.)
"Our Land of Dreams"
C. Crawford
(*Music and Lyrics by* Clifton Crawford.)
"Automobile Song" (Act 2)

1901.07 THE GOVERNOR'S SON

A Musical Farce in Three Acts. Book, music (and lyrics) by George M. Cohan[79]. Staged by R. A. Roberts[80]. Settings by C. Walsh Valentine. Costumes by Thomas McIlvane. Lighting by Julian C. Lavin. Musical director, Charles J. Gebest. Produced by L. C. Behman. Opened 25 February 1901 at the Savoy Theatre and closed 23 March 1901 after 32 performances[81].

CAST: *Benjamin Curtis*, just married and jealous: JERRY J. COHAN. *Algy Wheelock*, the governor's son: GEORGE M. COHAN. *Honorable Theodore Wheelock*, Governor of the State: William Keough. *Dicky Dickson*, a runaway husband: WILL H. SLOAN. *Martin McGovern*, proprietor of the Vacation Inn: JAMES H. MANNING. *Bill Swift*, Mrs. Dickson's brother: M. J. SULLIVAN. *Mr. Johnson*, the Governor's secretary: Hugh Mack. *Webster*, in and out: Peter F. Randall. *Percy*, bell boy: Walter W. Stockwell. *Harold*, porter: Ed. B. Platt. *Emerald Green*, a little bit of a girl: ETHEL LEVEY. *Mrs. Franklin-Jones-Berrymore*, a widow for the third time: JOSEPHINE KIRKWOOD.

This is a beautiful bunch of busy birds though not of a feather they flock together: *Ruby Robin*: Helene Bronner. *Susan Sparrow*: Alice Kellar. *Clara Canary*: Ruby Raymond. *Cissie Crow*: Cecile Early. *Polly Parrot*: Hilda Hawthorne. *Edith Eagle*: Daisy Thompson. *Ollie Ostrich*: Katherine Gordon. *Daisy Dove*: Edythe Tyler. *Queenie Quail*: Claire Murray. *Sarah Swan*: Sophie Stewart. *Peachie Peacock*: Amy Williams. *Nina Nightingale*: Helen Grey. *Onnie Thrush*: Elfay White. *Minnie Lark*: Georgie White. *Maud Snype*: Jeannette King. *Lottie Owl*: Minnie Sinn.

Mrs. Benjamin Curtis, anxious to meet the Governor: HELEN F. [Nellie] COHAN. *Mrs. Dickie Dickson*, in pursuit of her husband: JOSEPHINE COHAN.

Act 1: Vacation Inn. Morning.

Act 2: Parlor in Vacation Inn. Afternoon.

Act 3: Same as Act 2. Night.

ACT 1[82]
"The Real Girls"
Ladies of the Chorus
"A Widow's Wile"
J. Kirkwood, Female Chorus
"A Regular William Gillette"
W. H. Sloan, Company
"Behold the Governor"
W. Keough, Company
"The Story of the Wedding March" with Characteristic Dance
Josephine Cohan, G. M. Cohan
"Ma Honey Babe"[83]
E. Levey, Entire Company

ACT 2
"Jolly Good Fellow"[84]
Company
"Too Many Miles from Broadway"[85]
G. M. Cohan, Company
"We Live to Love"[86]
E. Levey
"The Governor's Son"
Josephine Cohan, G. M. Cohan, Company

ACT 3
"Oh! Mr. Moon" (Serenade)
E. Levey, Female Chorus
"And the Manager Said—"[87] (Medley)
G. H. Cohan and Josephine Cohan; E. Levey and W. H. Sloan
"Never Breathe a Word of This " (Conversational Duet)
W. Keough, G. M. Cohan
"The Quakertown Cadets"[88]
E. Levey, Olympia Quartette, Entire Company
Finale
Enire Company

1901.08 THE CASINO GIRL

A Revised Version of the Musical Comedy in Two Acts[89]. (Book and lyrics) Written by Harry B. Smith. Music by Ludwig Engländer, (Harry T. MacConnell, Will Marion Cook, Arthur Weld). Staged by George W. Lederer. Settings by D. Frank Dodge, Ernest Albert. Costumes by Mme. Caroline Siedle. Music director, Antonio DeNovellis. Produced by George W. Lederer. Opened 8 April 1901 at the Knickerbocker Theatre and closed 4 May 1901 after 32 performances.

CAST: *Pilsener Pasha*, a brewer, whose introduction of beer into Egypt won for him his title: JAMES E. SULLIVAN. *Ben Muley*, chief of a gang of thieves; a deserter from the French army: ALBERT HART. *Potage*, his lieutenant: SAM COLLINS. *Percy Harold Ethelbert Van Stuyvesant*, a young doctor in love with the casino girl: HARRY FAIRLEIGH. *J. Offenbach Gaggs*, know as Signor Hasbeeni, a Grand Opera tenor, who takes a company to Cairo and meets with reverses: CHARLES DOX. *First Officer*: Joseph Sullivan. *Second Officer*: Roy Richards. *Errand Boy*: "Rastus." *Dolly Twinkle*, leading dancer of the opera company managed by J. Offenbach Gaggs: KATIE SEYMOUR. *Laura Lee*, formerly The Casino Girl, known in Cairo as Mlle. Estelle, a French milliner: ELLA SNYDER. *Miss Roxana Rocks*, an heiress from Chicago: Emlily Herve. *Lotta Rocks*, *Carrie Rocks*, sisters of Roxana: Grace Milburn, Claudine Sharp. *Mrs. H. Malaprop Rocks*, a leader of Chicago society, better half of "Rocks & Co.," pork-packers of the Western Metropolis: CARRIE E. PERKINS. *Miss Broadway*

78No song list in programs. List prepared from an earlier published vocal score as MILADI AND THE MUSKETEER (White-Smith Music Publishing Co., Boston, 1900). List of interpolations prepared from published sheet music, reviews, etc.

79Adapted from his own vaudeville sketch for The Four Cohans.

80The subsequent tour and return engagement were staged by Ned Wayburn, produced by Fred Niblo.

81Played a return engagement 14 April 1902 at the Grand Opera House for 8 performances.

82Added for subsequent tour, as per published sheet music:
"Maudie"
Josephine Cohan

83Replaced for subsequent tour by:
"Lucy"
E. Levey, Entire Company

84Replaced for subsequent tour by:
Rosie"
G. M. Cohan, Finale Chorus
Which was then later replaced by:
"Wine Divine"
J. Kirkwood, Entire Company

85Late in subsequent tour, replaced by:
"Then I'd Be Satisfied with Life"
G. M. Cohan, Company

86Dropped for subsequent tour.

87Late in subsequent national tour, this was replaced by:
"Yankee Doodle Doings"
G. M. Cohan, Josephine Cohan, E. Levey, Irving Brooks {Dicky Dickson}

88Late in subsequent national tour, this was replaced by:
"The Soldiers of the Stage"
E. Levey, Female Chorus

89Originally opened in New York 19 March 1900 at the Casino Theatre for 105 performances. This revised 1901 version incorporates substantial personnel, character and song changes made for the London production.

of New York: Ruby Reid. *Miss Chestnut* of Philadelphia: Vina Snyder. *Miss Wabash* of Chicago: Marie Twohey. *Miss Charles* of Baltimore: Maud Thomas. *Miss Lindell* of St. Louis: Irene L. Cameron. *Miss Kearney* of San Francisco: Mona Sydney. *Miss Capitol* of Washington: Ocia Thompson. *Miss Tremont* of Boston: Kathleen Franklin. *Fatima*: Minnie Cline. *Cigarette Girls (8)*: *Zuleika*: Marie Tyler. *Lalla Rookh*: Ella Doyle. *Zobedia*: Minerva Courtney. *Amina*: Kathrin Bartlett. *Roseka*: Margot Hobart. *Ernina*: Edna Lawrence. *Alexia*: Ivy Jay. *Rofixa*: Josie Lawrence. *Selim*, a page: Rose Krohe. *Odaliska*, the Pasha's favorite Dame: Louise Lloyd.

International Quartette: Misses Emma Franks, Gertie Tullett, Nellie Pike, May Lucas. *Pony Ballet Octette*: Misses Beatrice Liddell, Maggie Taylor, Sippie McNeil, Lizzie Nawman, Eva Marlow, Eugenie Makepeace, Ada Robertson, Carrie Poltz. *Chorus of Odalisques, Cigarette Girls, American and European Tourists, Egyptian Merchants, Pasha's Guards, Slaves, Masqueraders, Donkey Boys, etc.*

Act 1: A Street in Cairo. (Dodge.)

Act 2: The Pasha's Palace. (Albert.)

MUSICAL NUMBERS[90]

"Society"
C. E. Perkins, Chorus
(*Music and Lyrics by* William J. Accooe.)

"Mam'selle"
(*Music by* Arthur Nevin.)

"Millie"

"The Casino Girl"

"Chink, Chink"
(*Music by* Harry T. MacConnell.)

"Variety"
(*Music by* Harry T. MacConnell.)

"A Lesson in Acting"
(*Music by* Harry T. MacConnell.)

"Money"

"In Disguise" (Masquerade Song)
K. Seymour
(*Music by* Arthur Weld.)

"Annie More"

Moon Dance (Eccentric Dance)
English Pony Ballet Octette

"Bygone Days Are Best"
(*Music by* Will Marion Cook. *Lyrics by* L. Lamprey.)

"Whatever the Hue of Your Eyes"
(*Music by* Will Marion Cook. *Lyrics by* Harry B. Smith.)

"Romance"
(*Music by* Will Marion Cook. *Lyrics by* Harry B. Smith.)

"Love Has Claimed Its Own"
H. Fairleigh
(*Music by* William J. Accooe. *Lyrics by* Stephen B Cassin.)

"(Down de) Lovers' Lane" (A Plantation Croon)
E. Snyder
(*Music by* Will Marion Cook. *Lyrics by* Paul Laurence Dunbar.)

1901.09 THE PRIMA DONNA

A Musical Farce in Three Acts. Book and lyrics by Harry B. Smith. (Based on an adaptation by George Hoey of the French farce "La Siège de Grenade" by Henri Chivot and Alfred Duru.) Music by Aimé Lachaume. Staged by W. F. Rochester. Settings painted by D. Frank Dodge. Costumes designed by Archie Gunn. Musical director, Aimé Lachaume. Produced by A. H. Chamberlyn. Opened 17 April 1901 at the Herald Square Theatre and closed 18 May 1901 after 36 performances.

CAST: *Angela Chumpley*, the Prima Donna: LULU GLASER. *Peggy*, maid to the Prima Donna: TOBY CLAUDE. *Amina*, an Egyptian, rival of the Prima Donna: ETTA BUTLER. *Mrs. Chumpley*, mother of the Prima Donna, and manager of the Frivolity Theatre: CATHERINE LEWIS. *Aboo Ben Adhem*, an Egyptian, patron of the arts, who patronizes the Prima Donna: GILBERT CLAYTON. *Abdallah*, a young Egyptian, who thinks he falls in love with the Prima Donna: W. P. CARLETON. *Meyerbeer Supnoodle*, who composes an opera for the Prima Donna: HERBERT CAWTHORNE. *McNab*, a Deputy Sheriff, who seizes the Prima Donna: WILLIAM CAMERON. *M. Justin*, chief clerk of a hotel in Paris: CHARLES B. BOWERS. *M. Baptiste*, proprietor of the hotel: Eugene Redding. *Miss Daisy Devonshire*, a leading lady: Hattie Moore. *Miss Violet Plantagenet*, another leading lady: Madeline Bouton. *Miss Clytemnestra Vere*, still another: Mazie Follette. *Miss Margie Violette*, yet one: Mabel Arnold. *Miss Zippie Montmorenci*, an ingenue: Mabel Courtney. *Miss Dottie Delancey*, another: Blanche West. *Miss Pansy Devereaux*, yet one: Dorothy Lester. *Miss Queenie Kenilworth*, a soubrette: Minnie Britton. *Miss Cillie Canterbury*, another: Estelle Franklyn.

Waiting Maids (6): *Clairette*: Mabel Barrison. *Babette*: Miss Bertel. *Suzette*: Miss Belmont. *Pierette*: Miss Dameling. *Jacquette*: Miss Tyler. *Ninette*: Miss Williams. *Among those present (4)*: *Mlle. Cleopatra*: Claire Lorraine. *Mlle. Vivienne*: Miss Rinquest. *Mlle. Circe*: Loie Stern. *Mlle.; Phrynette*: Lucille Bowles. *Odalisques of Aboo's Seraglio (6)*: *Blush-of-Morning*: Lucy White. *Rose-of-Springtime*: Lucille Dole. *Lotos-Blossom*: Graham May. *Star-of-Evening*: Hazel Vanderhoff. *Song-of-Nightingale*: Miss Stanton. *Violet-Eyes*: Miss Cook. *Orchestra players of the Frivolity Theatre (4)*: *Dumkoff*: Mr. Bennett. *Spitzbub*: J. F. Kent. *Schwarzbrod*: Mr. Alexander. *Hofbrau*: Mr. Griffin. *Nokes, Stokes*, Deputy Sheriffs: Mr. White, Winfield Young. *Achmet, Muley*, Aboo's Servants: Fred Jackson, George Cantor. *Woffington Binks*, an actor of the old school: M. Laurason. *F. Forest Juggins*, of the same school: F. L. Wilson. *Macready Muggs*, the only "Hamlet" since Yorrick: Mr. Vail. *Superfluous Laggs*, the veteran of the stage: Mr. Constant. *Snail*, a call-boy: Miss Fitzgerald. *Narcisse, Alphonse*, servants at the hotel: Ida Doerge, Marion Morse.

Act 1: Green-room of the Frivolity Theatre, London.

Act 2: An apartment in the Hotel Lion d'Or, Paris.

Act 3: Aboo's Palace, Cairo.

ACT 1

Chorus of Discontented Actors

"They're Going into Vaudeville" (Duet)

"If Only I Were a Boy" (Solo)
T. Claude

Entrance Chorus

"The Absent-Minded Girl" (Song)
L. Glaser

Duet
L. Glaser, H. Cawthorne

Entrance Chorus and Song
G. Clayton

"On the Stage" (Solo)
L. Glaser

Finale

ACT 2

Chorus of Hotel Servants

"The Hotel Clerk"
C. B. Bowers

"Life Is a Revel" (Solo)
W. P. Carleton

Serenade
W. P. Carleton

"Cherchez la Femme"
L. Glaser, Chorus

Irish Song (introduced)
T. Claude, Chorus

March—Trio

"The Course of True Love" (Duet)
E. Butler, W. P. Carleton

Finale

ACT 3

Oriental Chorus

"In the Harem of the East"

Oriental Ballet

Spanish Song
E. Butler

Solo
L. Glaser

Finale

"The Honeysuckle and the Bee"
(*Music and Lyrics by* Fitz and Arthur Penn.)

1901.10 FRA DIAVOLO

A Revival of the Romantic Opera in Three Acts[91]. Original French libretto (to the Opéra-comique 'Fra Diavolo, or L'Hotellerie de Terracina') by

[90] Musical numbers not listed in programs. Listed are known interpolations, as per published sheet music, reviews, not in performance order.

[91] First produced in New York in English as THE DEVIL'S BROTHER 20 June 1833 at the Park Theatre. Previously revived in an uncredited adaptation 11 August 1884 at the Bijou Theatre for 7 performances. English adaptation uncredited for this revival.

Eugène Scribe. Music by Daniel Auber. Produced by the Maud Daniel Opera Company Opened 29 April 1901 at Koster & Bial's and closed 4 May 1901 after 12 performances.[92]

CAST: *Zerlina*: HATTIE RICHARDSON. *Fra Diavolo*: GUSTAVE VAUGHN. *Lorenzo*: J. C. CONLY. *Lord Allcash*: ?. *Lady Allcash*: ?. *Beppo, Giacomo*, Two Italian bandits: FRED FERRAR, HARRY LANE. *Matteo*, Zerlina's father: ?. *Soldiers, Peasants, Bandits, etc.* Company also included Helena Salinger, May Williams, Robert Lett, Charles Vaughan.

1901.11 NELL GWYNNE

A Revival of the Comic Opera in Three Acts[93]. Libretto by Henry B. Farnie (based on the play 'Rochester' by W. T. Moncrieff). Music by Robert Planquette. Produced by the Maud Daniel Opera Company. Opened 6 May 1901 at Koster & Bial's and closed 11 May 1901 after 12 performances.[94]

CAST: *King Charles II*: BERTIE DALE. *Buckingham*, Exile from Court: GUSTAVE VAUGHN. *Rochester*, Landlord and waiter at the Dragon: J. E. CONLY. *Falcon*, a Strolling Player: Post Mason. *Weasel*, Village Usurer and Pawnbroker: Harry Lane. *The Beadle*, the local authority: ALLAN RAMSAY. *Hodge, Podge*, villagers: Charles Vaughn. Charles Hoskins. *Peregrine*, Buckingham's page: Annie Moore. *Nell Gwynne*: MAY BAKER. *Zaphet*, a gypsy: MAY BAKER. *Lady Clare*, ward of Charles II: HELENA SALINGER. *Jessamine*, Old Weasel's niece: KATHRYN HOWLAND. *Marjorie*, Weasel's servant: Florie Graff. *Villagers, Huntsmen, Nobles, Pages, Ladies of Court, etc.*

1901.12 THE KING'S CARNIVAL

A Burlesque in Two Acts, 9 Scenes, preceded by a Spectacular Ballet and Vaudeville. Book and lyrics by Sydney Rosenfeld. Music by A. Baldwin Sloane. Additional lyrics by George V. Hobart. Staged by Frank Smithson. Settings by St. John Lewis. Costumes by Caroline Seidle. Director of music and conductor, J. Sebastian Hiller. Produced by Sydney Rosenfeld. Opened 13 May 1901 at the New York Theatre, closing 6 July 1901 after 64 performances; re-opened 9 September 1901 at the New York Theatre and closed 12 October 1901 after 38 additional performances. Total: 102 performances[95].

ACT 1[96]

THE AGLOS TRIO (The most wonderful novelty ever imported)

A Few Minutes with BILLY LINK

AFTER OFFICE HOURS, Being a Bundle of Music Tied with a String of Nonsense[97]. The String and the Songs by George V. Hobart. Music by A. Baldwin Sloane.

CAST: *Peter Pennywayte*, an amateur from Pennyville: DANIEL McAVOY. *Percy Flawge*, manager of the costume shop: CHARLES H. PRINCE. *The Shine Brothers, Polish and Glisten*: CHARLES H. PRINCE, WILLIAM BURRESS. *Sizzleina*, a somewhat saucy soubrette: JESSIE MAY. *Besie Blossom*, subdued but soubrettish: MAMIE GILROY. *The Princess*, a breeze frm the South: Ixoria Pinaud. *Chorus of Fifth Avenue Girls, School Girls, Baby Girls and Other Girls.*

ACT 2

THE KING'S CARNIVAL, a Burlesque in Two Acts, 9 Scenes[98]. Book and lyrics by Sydney Rosenfeld. Music by A. Baldwin Sloane. Additional lyrics by George V. Hobart. Staged by Frank Smithson. Settings by St. John Lewis. Costumes by Caroline Seidle.

CAST (in order of appearance): *Adonis*, the King's jester: FRANK DOANE. *Officers (4) of the Royal Guard with various other duties*: *Don Tarara*: John Ford. *Don Mendoza*: EDGAR HALSTEAD. *Don Robusto*: CHARLES H. PRINCE. *Don Eduaido*: William Link. *Ladies of Honor (4)*: *Princess of Eboli*: Nina Farrington. *Duchess of Aloa*: Florence Crosby. *Countess of Medina*: Ethel Elberton. *Baroness of Baume*: Vera Morris. *King Philip of Spain*: LOUIS HARRISON. *Sidonia*, the King's dancer: MAYME GEHRUE. *The Prophetess*: Jessie May. *Dolores de Mendoza*: Laura Burt. *Don John of Austria*: FRANK DOANE. *King Henry VIII of England*: HARRY BULGER. *Lady Jane Bolingbroke*, friend of Mary Tudor: EMMA CARUS. *Bombastes Furioso*, a first murderer: DANIEL McAVOY. *Anne*, Queen of Spain: MARIE DRESSLER. *Inez*, her daughter: AMELIA SUMMERVILLE. *Pedro*, a page: Tobie Craig. *Mary Tudor*: ADELE RITCHIE. *Anne Boleyn*: Georgia Kelly. *Mencia*, another royal dancer: Lilly Brink. *Grandees, Guardsmen, Pages, Lords and Ladies, Climbers*: Chorus.

Act 1, Scene 1: The Corridor of the Palace. *Scene 2*: The Throne Room of the Palace. *Scene 3*: The Queen's Bridechamber. *Scene 4*: The Queen's Reception Room. *Scene 5*: The Royal Conservatory. *Scene 6*: Chellala Gorge.

Act 2, Scene 1: The Villa Alyussa. *Scene 2*: The Conservatory. *Scene 3*: "Bohemia."

MUSICAL NUMBERS[99]

"Ragtime Will Be Mah Finish"
M. Dressler
(*Lyrics by* George V. Hobart.)

"And the Band Began to Play"
A. Ritchie
(*Lyrics by* George V. Hobart.)

"If I Had a Little Boy to Love Me"
A. Ritchie
(*Lyrics by* George V. Hobart.)

"My Sailor Boy"
E. Carus
(*Lyrics by* George V. Hobart.)

"My Evaline" (Darkey Love Song)
(*Music and Lyrics by* Mae Anwerda Sloane.)

"When Mr. Shakespeare Comes to Town" (or I Don't Like Them Minstrel Folks)
H. Bulger
(*Music by* Jean Schwartz. *Lyrics by* William Jerome.)

Dance
M. Dressler, L. Harrison, D. McAvoy

[92]Performed twice daily. During the interval, a vaudeville program was presented: Joe Welch (Yiddish parodies), Bettina Girard (songs), Madge Fox (vocal solos), The Fall of Babylon (living picture), an Amazon March.

[93]First produced in New York 8 November 1884 at the Casino Theatre for 38 performances. For Synopsis of Scenes and Musical Numbers, see original 1884 production.

[94]Performed twice daily. During the interval, a vaudeville program was presented: Florence Bindley and Ida Morrelle in specialties, The Fall of Babylon (living picture), and an Amazon March.

[95]For return engagement, Marion Winchester, Junie McCree and Mabelle Gilman succeeded Mayme Gehrue, Harry Bulger and Adele Ritchie, respectively. A Carl Marwig ballet titled "L'Amour" was added, and a burlesque SUPPER AT SHERRY'S, Libretto by George V. Hobart, Music by A. Baldwin Sloane, featuring Dan McAvoy, Laura Burt and others.

[96]The vaudeville portion of the program preceding AFTER OFFICE HOURS and THE KING'S CARNIVAL changed weekly. Among other offerings were: Mayme Gehrue and John Ford (America's Greatest Dancers). Da McAvoy & Company, as seen on Fifth Avenue. THE DEVIL'S DREAM, a Spectacular Ballet Arranged by Carl Marwig. Headed by the following famous Premiers: *Fair Rosamond*: Lilly Collins. *Andree*: Lilly Brink. *Satan*: Mlle. Ronco. And a Corps de Ballet of 200. For the return engagement: SUPPER AT SHERRY'S, being a dramatization of a Bill of fare. Play, (lyrics) by George V. Hobart. Music by A. Baldwin Sloane. Produced under the direction of Frank Smithson. Scenery painted by St. John Lewis. The Menu Card (Cast): *Sherry McTadd*, Inventor of the fishless codfish-cake: DAN McAVOY. *General Goosedipper*, lookng for a good thing from New Jersey: CHARLES H. PRINCE. *Will O'Fare*, a waiter who waits a long time: Jay Roberts. *Chappie Chappingham*, a chap from Chapmanville: Edwin Walker. *Duebill Doolittle*, a hungry man from Harlem: EDGAR HALSTEAD. *Dolly Dime*, the cashier at Sherry's: Zella Frank. *Terpsie Koar*: Lydia Arnold. *Chorus of Broadway Girls, Waitress Girls, Other Girls.*

MUSICAL NUMBERS (interpolations only listed)

"On Broadway"
(*Music by* Mae Anwerda Sloane.)

"Sallie, Ma Hot Tamale"
D. McAvoy
(*Music by* Mae Anwerda Sloane.)

[97]Previously presented as part of this theatre's previous attraction 24 December 1900 on a bill with THE GIDDY THRONG and THE DEVIL'S DREAM for 164 performances.

[98]Reviews remarked that the playwright had chosen to burlesque characters and incidents from current Broadway successes 'When Knighthood Was in Flower,' 'The Climbers,' 'In the Palace of the King' and Under Two Flags.'

[99]Program listed interpolations only; list prepared from published sheet music. Added for subsequent tour:

"Fifth Avenue"
D. McAvoy
(*Lyrics by* George V. Hobart.)

1901–1902 SEASON

Lulu Glaser in DOLLY VARDEN (Photo: Falk)
Billy Rose Theatre Collection, New York Public Library for the Performing Arts

1901–1902 SEASON

1901.13 THE STROLLERS

Francis Wilson and His Company in a Musical Comedy in a Prologue and Two Acts. Book and lyrics by Harry B. Smith, adapted from a German libretto "Die Landstreicher" by Leopold Krenn and Carl Lindau[1]. Music by Ludwig Engländer. Staged by A. M. Holbrook under the direction of George W. Lederer. Settings by D. Frank Dodge, Ernest Albert. Costumes by Caroline Seidle. Orchestra under the direction of Signor A. DeNovellis. Produced by (Sam) Nixon and (J. F.) Zimmerman. Opened 24 June 1901 at the Knickerbocker Theatre and closed 31 August 1901 after 70 performances.

CAST: *August Lump*, a wandering philosopher: FRANCIS WILSON. *Prince Adolar de Bomsky*: HARRY GILFOIL. *Kamfer*, a jailor: EDWIN [Eddie] FOY. *Don Juan del Tabasco*, an amateur lothario: D L. DON. *Roland*, a magistrate: Benjamin Howard. *Rudi von Rodenstein*, *Muki von Muggeheim*, Lieutenants: Wilmer Bentley, Harry Stuart. *Bratwurst*, an innkeeper: James Darling. *Sprat*, proprietor of a restaurant and leader of a singing society: Fred Urban. *Rollo*, a shopkeeper: James Furey. *Mimi*, a ballet dancer: MARIE GEORGE. *Bertha*, wife of August Lump: IRENE BENTLEY. *Anna*, Roland's betrothed: Louise Lawton. *Frau Bratwurst*: Lizzie McCall.

Ballet Girls from the Opera House, Vienna, on an automobile trip: *Elsa*: Mona Sydney. *Ortruda*: Maud Thomas. *Senta*: Lou Middleton. *Zieglinde*: Bernice Norcross. *Isolde*: Edna Hunter. *Wilhelmina*: Maud Furniss. *Ermina*: Mazie Follette. *Laura*: Bessie Wynne. And Kathryn Pearl. (*Act 2 Pas de Seul Specialty*: Katie Seymour.) *Heidelberg Cadets, Soldiers, Villagers, Travelers, etc.*

Prologue: The Village Jail. Austria. (Dodge.)

Act 1: The Mountain Hotel. (Dodge.)

Act 2: The Fête of the Fans. (Albert.)

PROLOGUE[2]

"Capital Punishment"
L. Lawton, H. Fairleigh

"Gossip Chorus and March"
Chorus

"Song of the Strollers" (Strollers We, Our Life Is Free)
F. Wilson, I. Bentley, Chorus

"Heaven's Best Gift" (Duet)
M. George, D. L. Don

Melodrama

Finale
Principals

ACT 1

Opening Ensemble/"Song of Loretta"
H. Fairleigh, Chorus

"Little Daffy Pipe Dreams" (An English Coon Song)
F. Wilson, Chorus

"Automobile Ensemble"
M. George, F. Wilson, Girls

"A Lesson in Flirtation" (Song)
I. Bentley, Officers

"The Bold Hussars"
M. George, W. Bentley, H Stuart, Chorus

Song
E. Foy

Finale (Hail to the Bridegroom)
Chorus

ACT 2

Opening Ensemble and Ballet

"When the Orchestra Plays" (Song)
F. Wilson, Chorus

Finale

INTERPOLATIONS

"Baby Mine"
(*Music by* Leo Friedman. *Lyrics by* Raymond A. Browne.)

"The Cuckoo Bird"
F. Wilson
(*Music and Lyrics by* Fred Meyer.)

"I'm Tired" (The Tired Man)
E. Foy
(*Music by* Jean Schwartz. *Lyrics by* William Jerome.)

"Good-bye, Little Girl, Good-bye"[3]
George Lydecker, May Bouton
(*Music by* Gus Edwards. *Lyrics by* Will D. Cobb.)

"Look It Up in the Dream Book"
F. Wilson
(*Music by* Harry T. MacConnell. *Lyrics by* Robert B. Smith.)

"Loretta"
(*Music by* Ludwig Engländer. *Lyrics by* Harry B. Smith.)

"(My) Lady Bird"
May Bouton
(*Music by* Evans Lloyd. *Lyrics by* Jeff T. Branen.)

"Alone on My Honeymoon"
(*Music by* ? Sawyer. *Lyrics by* Jeff T. Branen.)

1901.14 THE ROBBER BARON

A Romantic Musical Comedy (Comic Opera) in Three Acts. Book by John Arthur Fraser. Music composed and arranged by Wilhelm Schaffer [William Schaefer]. Produced by the Parry Opera Company. Opened 15 July 1901 at the Terrace Garden and closed 20 July 1901 after 8 performances.[4]

CAST: *Maurice*: HUBERT WILKE. *Mousqueton*: Frank Deshon. *Le Loup*: George R. Callahan. *Marc*: T. William Sturgeon. *Doloreux*: Harry Carter. *Count De Cliquot*: Harry Davies. *Marquis de Grassi*: J. E. Wheeler. *Redarm*: Harry Poot. *Eloise*, a flower girl: Villa Knox. *Babette*: Helen Byron. *Julie*: Bonnie May. *Mignonette*: MATHILDE COTTRELLY. And Chorus.

The action takes place in Sixteenth century France.

1901.15 TOM MOORE

A Romantic Drama (with Songs) in Four Acts. Play by Theodore Burt Sayre. (Songs by Andrew Mack; poems as lyrics by Thomas Moore.) Staged by William Seymour. Scenery by Joseph Physioc. Costumes by M. Herrmann, C. Kunisch. Musical director, William P. Brown. Produced by (Isaac B.) Rich & (William) Harris. Opened 31 August 1901 at the Herald Square Theatre and closed 5 October 1901 after 40 performances[5].

CAST: *Tom Moore*, Ireland's favorite poet: ANDREW MACK. *Prince of Wales*, Regent of England: MYRON CALICE. *Sir Percival Lovelace*, boon companion to the Prince: GEORGE F. NASH. *Lord Moira*, Moore's friend and patron: THEODORE BABCOCK. *Robin Dyke*, an Irish minor poet: George W. Deyo. *Sheridan*, the famous wit: Giles Shine. *Beau Brummell*, a leader of society: Harry P. Stone. *Terence Farrell*, a young Irishman: Frank Mayne. *Buster*, Moore's servant: Edward J. Heron. *McDermott*, a publisher: Richard J. Dillon. *Servant*: John Napier.

School children: *Mickey*: Johnny Cooke. *Willie*: Willie Cooke. *Patsey*: Augustus Wilkes. *Dicky*: Georgie Cadieux. *Johnny*: Johnny Wilkes. *Tommy*: Harold Grau. *Lizzie*: Vivian Martin. *Nellie*: Ethel Clifton. *Maggie*: Mary McManus. *Katie*: Sylvia Cashin. *Bridget*: Isabel Barrcacole. *Mary*: Loretta Ruge.

Bessie Dyke, an Irish girl: JOSEPHINE LOVETT. *Winnie Farrell*, an heiress: Susie Wilkerson. *Lady Fitz-Herbert*, the Prince's favorite: JANE PEYTON. *Mrs. Malone*, Moore's landlady: Maggie Fielding. *Courtiers, Ladies, Footmen, Servants, etc.*

Act 1: The District School, Dalkey, Ireland.

Act 2: Moore Garret, London. One year later.

Act 3: Sir Percival Lovelace's Mansion, London. Four months later.

Act 4: Moore's Garret, London. One week later.

MUSICAL NUMBERS[6]

"Eveleen's Bower"
(Music traditional. *Lyrics by* Thomas Moore.)

---

[1]The American production retained none of the original musical score by E. M. Ziehrer.

[2]Musical numbers not listed in program; list prepared from published vocal score (Edward Schuberth & Co., New York, 1901), reviews, etc. is in performance order, with the exception of interpolations which follow at the end.

[3]Presumably interpolated for a late tour, as the song is copyrighted 1904.

[4]No program available.

[5]Played a return engagement 27 October 1902 at the Grand Opera House for 8 performances.

[6]As listed in the program, but not necessarily in performance order.

"Love's Young Dream"
(Music traditional[7]. *Lyrics by* Thomas Moore.)
"The Last Rose of Summer"
(Music traditional. *Lyrics by* Thomas Moore.)
"Believe Me, if All Those Endearing Young Charms"
(Music traditional. *Lyrics by* Thomas Moore.)
Mack's "Song Games"
(*Music and Lyrics by* Andrew Mack.)
"The Story of the Rose"
(*Music and Lyrics by* Andrew Mack.)

1901.16

THE ROGERS BROTHERS IN WASHINGTON

A Vaudeville Farce (with songs) in Three Acts. Book by John J. McNally. Music by Maurice Levi. Lyrics by Harry B. Smith. Produced under stage direction of (staged by) Ben Teal. Settings by Ernest Gros. Costumes designed by F. Richard Anderson. Musical director, Maurice Levi. Produced by (Marc) Klaw & (Abraham L.) Erlanger. Opened 2 September 1901 at the Knickerbocker Theatre and closed 12 October 1901 after 49 performances.

CAST: *Carlos Chauffs*: GUS ROGERS. *Louis Lauffs*: MAX ROGERS. *Alf. Harriman*: WILLIAM WEST. *Judge Braley*: Eugene Jepson. *Fuller Guffe*: GUS C. WEINBURG. *Johnny Lift*: PAT ROONEY. *Tough Boy*: JAMES CHERRY. *Burglar Jim*: John B. Hendricks. *B. Tardy*: WILLIAM TORPEY. *Maizi Mahoni*: HATTIE WILLIAMS. *Maude Braley*, the Judge's niece: Grace Freeman. *Margy*: Emma Francis. *Clara Braley, Bessie Braley*, the Judge's daughters: JEANNETTE BAGEARD, EDITH ST. CLAIR. *Bertha Snap*: May Taylor. *Esther Pace*: NORA BAYES. *Nona Eclat*: Elsie Davis. *Tottie Chic*: Gertrude Saye. *Edith Idem*: Jessie Richmond. *Alice Agyle*: Nettie Uart. *Lillie Longery*: Clara Franton. *Susie Swish*: Stella Maury. *Queener Diamonds*: Lottie Uart. *Acie Hartz*: Lillian Collins. *Ann Other Acie*: Julia Eastman. *The Other Acie*: Lucille Fallon. *Messenger Boy*: Kathleen Murray.
(*Ensemble*): May Kimball, Helen Brookes, Leslie Lyle, Lillian Stanford, Lily Hart, Minnie Woodbury.

Act 1: Reception-room of the Democratic Club, New York City.

Act 2: Section of the Botanical Gardens, Washington, D.C., showing the Capitol in the background.

Act 3: The Court of Fountains at the Pan-American Exposition, Buffalo, New York.

ACT 1
"The Girl of Greater New York" (Opening Chorus)
"Get Next to the Man with a Pull" (Song)
G. C. Weinberg, Full Chorus
"In the Swim" (Song)
J. Bageard, Full Chorus
"Ma Ebony Belle" (Specialty)
Rogers Brothers, H. Williams
(*Lyrics by* Ed. Gardenier.)

ACT 2
"1776-1901" (Opening Chorus)
"Diplomacy" (Song)
H. Williams, Full Chorus
Sayings and Parodies
Rogers Brothers
"Watermelon Party" (Specialty)
N. Bayes, Full Chorus
"An Englishman's Idea of Rag-time" (Specialty)
W. West
"The Game of Love" (Specialty)
E. Francis, P. Rooney
"The Wedding of the Reuben and the Maid, or, They Were On Their Honeymoon"
(Quartette)
Rogers Brothers, J. Bageard, E. St. Clair
"The Electric Light Cadets" (Finale)
Entire Company

ACT 3
"At the Pan-American" (Opening Chorus)
"My (Little) Bunco Queen" (Burlesque Song and Dance)
Rogers Brothers, assisted by M. Taylor, E. Davis, G. Saye, L Collins, J. Richmond,
M. Kimball, J. Eastman, H. Brookes, C. Franton, L. Lyle, S. Maury,
L. Stanford, N. Uart, M. Woodbury, L. Hartland, K. Murray

1901.17

HOITY-TOITY

A Giddy Little Skit on Things Dramatic and Otherwise (A Burlesque) in Two Acts. Dialogue and lyrics by Edgar Smith. Music by John Stromberg. Produced under the direction of (staged by) Julian Mitchell. Settings by John Young. Costumes by Will R. Barnes. Orchestra under the direction of John Stromberg. Produced by (Joe) Weber and (Lew) Fields. Opened 5 September 1901 at Weber and Fields' Music Hall and closed 19 April 1902 after 259 performances[8].

CAST (Act 1): *General Steele*, an American billionaire, on a purchasing tour in Europe: DeWOLF HOPPER. *Harvard Yale*, a young collegian touring with the college minstrels: FRITZ WILLIAMS. *Philip Sauerbraten*, a wealthy delicatessen purveyor: JOE WEBER. *Herman Kaffekuchen, Frederich Schnitzel*, friends of Sauerbraten, and engaged in the friendly occupation of helping him to spend his money: LEW M. FIELDS, SAM BERNARD. *King Kazoo*, a monarch by force of circumstances: JOHN T. KELLY. *Reuben Hunter*, a Graduate of the "Alley" and Lady Grafter's right hand man: LEE HARRISON. *Baron Barbon*, an aged roué: GEORGE ALI. *4 of the College Minstrels*: *Canby Hurd*: May. M. McKenzie. *Rufe Rayser*: Edna Birch. *Tony Singer*: Genevieve Dolaro. *Cord Barber*: Carrie Bowman. *Lady Grafter*, a society leader, addicted to the fashionable habit of short-card playing: LILLIAN RUSSELL. *Cho-Cho San*, known as "Madame Butterscotch," and in search of a lost husband: FAY TEMPLETON.
Daughters of General Steele (7): *Sprite*: BONNIE MAGINN. *Petrolia*: MAYME GEHRUE. *Glucosa*: Goldie Mohr. *Nicotina*: Belle Robinson. *Coffeea*: Estelle Moyer. *Cornea*: Gertie [Gertrude] Moyer. *Fifi Rougepaynt*: Margaret Sayres. *Zuzuki*, a Japanese maid: Bonnie Maginn. *British officers (5)*: *Kensington Earlscourt*: Myra Smith. *Grosvenor Rhodes*: Mae Sherwood. *Battersea Parks*: Margaret Sayres. *Paddington Harrow*: Eva Allen. *Cecil Langham*: Kathryn Howland. *Society Moths (5)*: *Scorchleigh*: Virginia Foltz. *Flitterly*: Vernie Wadsworth. *Singeton*: Florence Dressler. *Burnsby*: Mona Desmond. *Mothmiller*: Elisabeth Young. *Japanese Lads and Lassies (5)*: *Nagasaki*: Estelle Moyer. *Ki Owta*: Gertie Moyer. *Kloy Sonay*: Grace Heckler. *Shaki Fan*: Lillian Heckler. *Chu Chu Gum*: Annie Miller. *Buds of various nations (7)*: *Albia*: Madge Adea. *Tokia*: Inez Ray. *Viennanetta*: May Bradley. *Parisetta*: Dora Senac. *Sevilla*: Pauline Bradley. *Bosphora*: Ilma Pratt. *Miss Freeport*: Natta Stromberg.
Act 2: *Cambridge Backbeigh, Boylston Tremont*, Harvard Students: L. Diamond, Ella Gilroy. *Scheffield Schooley, Dodge Chapelle, Kane Rush*, Yale students: Virginia Foltz, Mae Sherwood, Doris Mitchell.

ACT 2

1901.17

Incidental to Act 2, DEPLEURISY, A Travesty (Burlesque) upon Victorien Sardou's masterpiece ("Diplomacy"), by permission of Charles Frohman and T. Henry French.

CAST: *Julian Beauclerc*, a young diplomatist: SAM BERNARD. *Henry Beauclerc*, Julian's brother: LEW M. FIELDS. *Count Orloff*, a Russian diplomatist: JOSEPH M. WEBER. *Baron Stein*, a German diplomatist: JOHN T. KELLY. *Antoine*, a valet: GEORGE ALI. *Policeman*: A. Smith. *Countess Zicka*, an adventuress: DeWOLF HOPPER. *Dora*, Julian's wife: FAY TEMPLETON.

Act 1: Lady Grafter's Villa near Monte Carlo.

Act 2: The Yale Campus at New Haven.

ACT 1[9]
"Beautiful Monte Carlo"
Ensemble

[7] Some sources credit Michael William Balfe or Sir John Stevenson with the music.

[8] The Burlesques were revised repeatedly through the run, as detailed below. The road version was presented for the first time 17 April 1902 prior to the closing.
[9]Added to Act 1 in November 1901:
"Easy Money" (Ma Poppy Belle)
F. Templeton
Added to HOITY-TOITY on 2 January 1902:

"King Kazoo of Kakaroo" (Song)
J. T. Kelly
"Poor Little Fluttering Moths" (Song)
L. Russell
"I'm an American Billionaire" (The American Billionaire)(Song)
D. Hopper
"My Japanese Cherry Blossom" (Song)
F. Templeton
"When Two (Little) Hearts Are One" (Duet)
D. Hopper, L. Russell
"De Pullman Porters' Ball" (Song)
F. Williams
"Gold! Gold! Gold!" (Finale)
L. Russell, D. Hopper, Ensemble

ACT 2
"Under the Elms at Old New Haven"
Ensemble
"As On Moonlit Waves We Ride"
L. Russell, Ensemble
"Mary Black"
F. Templeton
Finale
Ensemble

1901.17

DEPLEURISY was replaced 8 November 1901 by A MAN FROM MARS (Burlesque on 'A Message From Mars' by Richard Ganthony[10]).

CAST: *An A.D.T. Man from Mars*: DeWOLF HOPPER. *Horrid Sparker*: FRITZ WILLIAMS. *Mr. Dizzy*: JOSEPH M. WEBER. *A Tramp*: LEW M. FIELDS. *A Policeman*: SAM BERNARD. *An Ambulance Surgeon*: Lee Harrison. *A Waiter*: Lee Harrison. *A Trolley Victim*: George Ali. *Minnie*: FAY TEMPLETON. *Aunt Martha*: JOHN T. KELLY. *Cella*: AIMEE ANGELES. *A Beggar Woman*: BONNIE MAGINN. *A Chorus Girl*: Belle Robinson. *A Newsboy*: Goldie Mohr. *A Bootblack*: Edna Birch. *Dodge Ruinart*: May McKenzie. *Harry Pommery*: Mae Sherwood. *Phil Cliquot*: Carrie Bowman. *Moet Chandon*: Grace Heckler. *Georgie H. Mumm*: Elizabeth Young. *Dryden Monopole*: Bena Hoffman. *Willie Heidseick*: Mollie Hoffman. *Perry Jouet*: Kathryn Howland. *Lythia Waters*: Inez Rae. *Vera Fuller*: Ilma Pratt. *Etta Lott*: Ella Gilroy. *Carrie Loader*: Fanny Dupre. *Daisy Drinker*: Doris Mitchell. *Goldie Buck*: Madge Adea. *Meta Fellows*: Dora Senac.

1901.17

A MAN FROM MARS was replaced 2 January 1902 by THE CURL AND THE JUDGE (Burlesque of 'The Girl And The Judge' by Clyde Fitch) which closed 12 March 1902 after 117 performances.

CAST: *Judge Charges*: DeWOLF HOPPER. *Tankton*: John T. Kelly. *Chin*: Lee Harrison. *Broom*: BONNIE MAGINN. *Mikey Hockenstein*: Abie Rose. *Winifred Tankton*: FAY TEMPLETON. *Mrs. Tankton*: LEW FIELDS. *Mrs. Broom*: SAM BERNARD. *Mrs. Charges*: Fritz Williams. *Mrs. Hockenstein*: JOSEPH M. WEBER. *Vera Shapeleigh*: Frankie Bailey. *Leda March*: Violet Jewell. *Ona Brougham*: Beulah Martin. *Daisy Stringer*: Mae Sherwood. *Neva Ketchum*: Fanny Dupre. *Jewell Winner*: Eva Allen. (*Dance Specialty*: Bessie Clayton.)

MUSICAL NUMBERS
"Down the Line"
F. Templeton
"We Are Three Perfect Ladies"
J. Weber, L. Fields, S. Bernard

1901.17

THE CURL AND THE JUDGE was replaced 13 March 1902 by DuHURRY (Burlesque of 'DuBarry' by David Belasco) for 40 performances. A brief parody on "DuBarry" by Edgar Smith. Music by John Stromberg.

CAST: *Louis Quince*, King of France: SAM BERNARD. *Gussie de Brickbat*, who picked violets and lost: JOSEPH M. WEBER. *Dennis*, a faithful servitor: LEW M. FIELDS. *Comte Bluejeans DuHurry*, the family trouble: FRITZ WILLIAMS. *Duc de Brickbat*, Gussie's Papa and Captain of the Royal Supers: JOHN T. KELLY. *Duc de Richleon*, who has a pull with the crown: Lee Harrison. *A clarinet player*: Augustus Smith. *Jeanette d'Aubarabair, later La DuHurry*: FAY TEMPLETON. *Sophie*, maid to La DuHurry: Bonnie Maginn. *Metoo*, Lord Manicurist, and other things: Frankie Bailey. *Marie Antoinit*: Goldie Mohr. *Duchesse d'Eggbouillon*: Leona Hilbon. *Duchesse de Cheesey*: Belle Robinson. *A page*: May MacKenzie. *Another*: Fanny Dupre. *A gypsy hag*: Genevieve Dolaro.

Scene: The boudoir of La DuHurry.

MUSICAL NUMBERS
"When Mr. Shakespeare Comes to Town"
(*Music by* Jean Schwartz. *Lyrics by* William Jerome.)

1901.18

THE LADIES' PARADISE

A Musical Extravaganza in Two Acts, 4 Scenes. Book and lyrics by George Dance. Music by Ivan Caryll. Stage direction of William Parry. Produced under the personal direction of Richard Carle. Ballets by M. Albertieri. Produced by Alfred E. Aarons. Opened 16 September 1901 at the Metropolitan Opera House and closed 28 September 1901 after 14 performances[11].

CAST: *Mademosielle Antoinette*, known as Sans Souci: QUEENIE VASSAR. *M. Pomade*, her father: JOHN HYAMS. *Mullins*, a stage door tender: JOHN HYAMS. *The Duke of Beaumont*: ALEXANDER CLARK. *The Duchess of Beaumont*: Phoebe Coyne. *Lord Allington*, their son, posing as Harold Ripley: TEMPLAR SAXE. *Camembert*, an author: DAVE LEWIS. *Samuel Peashooter*, the Sausage King: LOUIS WESLEY. *Maud, Anastasia*, his daughters: LUCILLE VERA BURNHAM, JOSEPHINE HALL. *Sarah*, Souci's sister: ETHELE GORDON. *Marie, Pincher*, Souci's servants: LYDIA WEST, RICHARD CARLE.

Friends of Sans Souci: *Lisa*: Caroline Heustis. *Adele*: Kathryn Pearl. *Nella*: Florence Relda. *Della*: Jessie Jordan. *Stella*: Frances Wilson. *Bella*: Reine Davies. *Ella*: Maud Barnard. *Dolly*: Nonie Dore. *Polly*: June Dale. *Molly*: Sylvia Star. *Folly*: Minnie Fisher. *Minnie*: Anna Leslie. *Winnie*: Pearl Henri. *Hunting Boys, Vacationists, Guests and Members of San Souci's Theatrical Company*.: Chorus of 100.

Dance Specialty (Act 2): LA TORTAJADA[12]. And Ballet Company of 250.

Act 1: Sans Souci's Hotel, Versailles.

Act 2, Scene 1: San Souci's home, Paris. *Scene 2*: Outside the theatre. *Scene 3*: Greenroom of the Follies Theatre.

ACT 1[13]
"Think It Over" (Quartette)
L. Wesley, D. Lewis, J. Hyams, A. Clark
(*Music by* Alfred E. Aarons. *Lyrics by* Richard Carle.)
Finale
Entire Company
(*Music by* Alfred E. Aarons. *Lyrics by* Richard Carle.)

ACT 2
"Antoinette" (Waltz Song)
D. Lewis, Chorus
(*Music by* Alfred E. Aarons. *Lyrics by* Richard Carle.)
"Miss Clementina and Her Beau"
J. Hyams
(*Music by* Alfred E. Aarons. *Lyrics by* Richard Carle. *Produced by* John Hyams.)
"Love's Advent"
T. Saxe
(*Music by* Alfred E. Aarons. *Lyrics by* T. Saxe.)

MUSICAL NUMBERS[14]
"Bobbing"
"Fiddle Dee Dee"
"The Dreamland Dimple"
"When a Man's in Love"
"The Social Polkarette"

La Danse Afrique
Bessie Clayton
Added to the show as per published sheet music:
"The Queen of Society"
L. Russell

[10]Reviewers remarked on the slight musical content of A MAN FROM MARS.

[11] Toured subsequently in a revised form as MY ANTOINETTE.

[12] Critics remarked that La Tortajada did not appear on opening night, but was expected to appear soon.

[13] Program lists only the interpolations, not the musical numbers by Messrs. Caryll and Dance.

[14] Additional musical numbers by Messrs. Caryll and Dance not in program, but published in the United States. Not in performance order.

"Le Petit Caporal"
"Gustave Gigot's Band"

1901.19 THE MESSENGER BOY

A Musical Comedy in Two Acts, 4 Scenes[15]. Book by James T. Tanner and Alfred Murray. Music by Ivan Caryll and Lionel Monckton. Lyrics by Adrian Ross and Percy Greenbank. Staged by Herbert Gresham. Settings by Joseph Harker and T. E. Ryan. Costumes by F. Richard Anderson. Orchestra under the direction of Louis F. Gottschalk. Produced by Messrs. (Sam) Nixon and (J. F.) Zimmerman. Opened 16 September 1901 at Daly's Theatre and closed 4 January 1902 after 128 performances.

CAST: *Hooker Pasha*, Commissioner of the Nile: GEORGE HONEY. *Cosmos Bey*, agent to Hooker Pasha: PAUL NICHOLSON. *Clive Radnor*, a King's messenger: JOHN B. PARK. *Captain Pott* of the S.S. *"Shark"*: HARRY KELLY. *Professor Phunckwitz*, a German Egyptologist: Tom Hadaway. *Comte de Fleury*: George DeLong. *Mr. Tudor Pyke*, a financier: George Heath. *Lord Punchestown*, Governor of El Bara: Harold C. Crane. *Captain Naylor* of the *P. & O.S.S. "Sirdar"*: JOHN P. KENNEDY. *Mr. Trotter*, an amateur journalist: Herbert Darley. *Purser, S. S. "Sirdar"*: Herbert Darley. *Dedong*, a waiter: Armand Cortes. *Tommy Bang*, a district messenger: JAMES T. POWERS. *Nora*, Lady Punchestown's step-daughter: GEORGIA CAINE. *Mrs. Bang*, Tommy's mother: MAY ROBSON. *Lady Punchestown*, a leader of London society: JOBYNA HOWLAND. *Isabel Blyth*: FLORA ZABELLE. *Lady Winifred*: Hattie Waters. *Cecilia Gower*: Agnes Wayburn. *Dorothy Majoribanks*: Helen Chichester. *Pepita*: Miss Fanchonette. *Rosa*, Lady Punchestown's Maid: RACHEL BOOTH.

Carpet Sellers: Messrs. Abner Seymour, George Pullman, J. W. Styles. *Society Ladies*: Misses Florence Redmond, Bertha Hunter, Agnes Blake Wadleigh, Caroline Lock, Sally McNeil, Louis Murry, Dene Woodruff, Leonora Crum.

Act 1, Scene 1: Hotel de Luxe, Thames Embankment, (London). (Harker.) *Scene 2*: Brindisi.

Act 2, Scene 1: Cairo. (Ryan.) *Scene 2*: Paris Exhibition Garden. (Harker.)

ACT 1

"Charity Bazaar" (Opening Chorus)
(*Music by* Ivan Caryll. *Lyrics by* Adrian Ross.)

"Ask Papa" (Song)
G. Caine, J. Park
(*Music by* Ivan Caryll. *Lyrics by* Percy Greenbank.)

"Bradshaw" (Bradshaw's Guide)(Song)
F. Zabelle, P. Nicholson, G. DeLong, T. Hadaway, H. Darley, H. Waters
(*Music by* Ivan Caryll. *Lyrics by* Adrian Ross.)

"The Messenger Boy" (Song)
J. T. Powers, Full Chorus
(*Music by* Lionel Monckton. *Lyrics by* Percy Greenbank.)

"Aspirations" (Song)
R. Booth, J. T. Powers
(*Music by* Lionel Monckton. *Lyrics by* Adrian Ross.)

"Tarantella" (Dance)
Miss Fanchonette, Full Chorus
(*Music by* Ivan Caryll.)

"Off to Cairo" (Song)
J. Kennedy, P. Nicholson, H. Kelly
(*Music by* Ivan Caryll. *Lyrics by* Adrian Ross.)

Dance
H. Kelly, J. Kennedy

"Wash! Wash! Wash!" (In the Wash)(Song)
M. Robson, Chorus
(*Music by* Lionel Monckton. *Lyrics by* Adrian Ross.)

"Has Anybody Seen My Cat?" (Has Anybody Seen Our Cat?)(Song)
J. T. Powers, assisted by Misses M. Robson, R. Booth, F. Zabelle, H. Waters, Messrs. H. Kelly, P. Nicholson, T. Hadaway, G. DeLong
(*Music and Lyrics by* T. W. Conner. *Additional Verses by* J. T. Powers.)

Finale
J. T. Powers, H. Kelly, J. Kennedy;
Misses R. Booth, G. Caine, M. Robson, Full Chorus

ACT 2

"Sheltered from the Noonday Glare" (Opening Chorus)
(*Music by* Lionel Monckton. *Lyrics by* Percy Greenbank.)

"A Perfectly Peaceful Person"[16] (Song)
J. Park
(*Music and Lyrics by* Paul Rubens.)

"Can't You Take My Word" (Song)
J. T. Powers, Chorus
(*Music by* Bert Brantford. *Lyrics by* Harry Boden and James T. Powers.)

"Maisie" (Song)
F. Zabelle, Chorus
(*Music by* Lionel Monckton. *Lyrics by* Leslie Mayne.)

"Dervish" (Song and Dance)
J. T. Powers, Chorus
(*Music by* Lionel Monckton. *Lyrics by* Adrian Ross.)

"They Are All After Pott" (Captain Pott)(Song)
H. Kelly, Chorus
(*Music by* Lionel Monckton. *Lyrics by* Adrian Ross.)

"To the Paris Exposition" (Chorus)
Full Chorus
(*Music by* Lionel Monckton. *Lyrics by* Adrian Ross.)

"The Mummies" (Duet)
J. T. Powers, R. Booth
(*Music by* Ivan Caryll. *Lyrics by* Adrian Ross.)

"The Volunteers"[17] (Song)
M. Robson, Full Chorus
(*Music by* Lionel Monckton. *Lyrics by* Adrian Ross.)

"The Messenger Boy March" (Finale)
(*Music by* Lionel Monckton. *Lyrics by* Percy Greenbank.

1901.20 THE HOTTEST COON IN DIXIE

A Musical Comedy in Two Acts. Book and lyrics by Phil R. Miller. Music by William J. Accooe. Stage director, Bob A. Kelly. Produced by Phil R. Miller. Opened 16 September 1901 at the Third Avenue Theatre and closed 21 September 1901 after 8 performances.[18]

CAST: *Lem Loose*: BOB A. KELLY. *J. Thompson Talbart*: JOE HODGES. *Ebeneezer Day*: WALTER DIXON. *Dewman Day*: BOB RUSSELL. *Jimmie Lightfoot*: Sam Davis. *Johnnie Push*: Ed. Furber. *Sammie Jackson*: Norris Smith. *Willie Hotair*: Fletcher Cole. *Joshua Jenkins*: Walter Gaston. *Pap*: George Brown. *Mrs. Knight*: LOLA LAUNCHMERE. *Madame Alburtis*: KATE GRASSES. *Susie*: Pauline Freeman. *Dinah*: Clara Freeman. *Miss Virginia*: MOLLIE SULLIVAN. *Lucy*: Lavinia Ellis. *Georgie*: CASSIE BROWN. *Kitty*: Ida Harris. *Sally*: Nellie Wells. *Toby*: Marie Washington. *Chloe*: Maud Turner. *Georgie*: Cassie Brown. *Carrie*: Pauline Humphreys. *Hattie*: Annetta Fagin.

1901.21 THE LIBERTY BELLES

Klaw & Erlanger's Troubadours in a Musical Comedy in Three Acts. Book and lyrics by Harry B. Smith. (Music by John W. Bratton, Clifton Crawford, Aimé Lachaume, Harry Von Tilzer, A. Baldwin Sloane.) Produced under the stage direction of Herbert Gresham. Settings by Ernest Albert. Costumes by F. Richard Anderson. Orchestra under the direction of Aimé Lachaume. Produced by (Marc) Klaw and (Abraham L.) Erlanger. Opened 30 September 1901 at the Madison Square Theatre and closed 28 December 1901 after 104 performances[19].

---

[15] Billed as George Edwardes' London Gaiety Theatre success.

[16]Replaced for subsequent tour by:
"Your Own" (Ballad)
J. Park
"Pansy" (Song and Dance)
H. Waters, G. Caine, Full Chorus
(*Music and Lyrics by* Pat Rooney.)

[17]Replaced for subsequent tour by:
"The Dialect Soubrette" (Song)
M. Robson, Chorus
(*Music by* Lionel Monckton. *Lyrics by* Adrian Ross.)

[18]No program available. It's likely that this touring show was built around the hit song of the same title by Will Marion Cook and Paul Laurence Dunbar introduced in CLORINDY. THE HOTTEST COON IN DIXIE toured the country in many editions by different authors up to 1912.

[19]Played a return engagement 19 January 1902 at the Grand Opera House for 8 performances.

CAST: *Margery Lee*, who is a trifle stagestruck: Etta Butler. *Dorothy Grey*, who is more than a trifle in love: Sandol Milliken. *Virginia Dean*, devoted to music: Augusta Glosé. *Daisy Field*, a novel-reading girl: Edna Hunter. *Geraldine Fair*, who has a fondness for practical jokes: LOTTA FAUST. *Kathleen Gay*, with an appetite for bonbons: Pauline Chase. *Mildred Ross*, a romantic schoolgirl: Margaret Walker. *Edith May*, who has absorbed the conversational style of her five brothers: Grace Kimball. *Ethel Love*, who stutters a little: Edith Barr. *Gladys Somers*, who lisps a good deal: Marie Tuohey. *Ruth Leslie*, whose parents are Quakers: Dorothy Lester. *Elaine Tennyson*, devoted to poetry: Louise Middleton. *Juana Gomez*, a Cuban girl sent to America to be educated: Helene Lucas. *Omyama San*, a Japanese girl sent to America to be educated: Marie Murphy. *Schoolgirls (6)*: *Laura Carroll* from Richmond: Violet Jewell. *Dora Van Ness* from New York: Bobby Burns. *Ada Randolph* from Baltimore: Laura Stone. *Maria Morris* from Boston: Elsie Ferguson. *Priscilla Penn* from Philadelphia: Katharine Roberts. *Celia Brown* from Cleveland: Esther Lyons. *Teresa Corsini*, an Italian singer: LOTTA FAUST. *Mrs. Dr. Sprowl*, L.L.D., B.R., President of the Hudson Academy for Young Ladies: Crissie Carlysle. *Jack Everleigh*, a cadet at Annapolis: HARRY DAVENPORT. *Phil Fullerton*, Columbia 1902: JOHN SLAVIN. *Uncle Jasper Pennyfeather*, an inventor: HARRY GILFOIL. *Captain Hiram Ketcham* of the whaling vessel "*Polly Ann*": J. C. MARLOWE. *Peterson*, a janitor: D. Mack Lumsden. *Kiley*, *McFadden*, police officers: L. D. Wharton, Nat K. Cafferty. *Thomas*: Edward Pooley.

Act 1: Dormitory of a young ladies' seminary.

Act 2: The cooking school of the Liberty Belles.

Act 3: A Florida hotel.

ACT 1[20]

"Supper Chorus"
Ensemble
(*Music by* Aimé Lachaume.)

"A Lesson with a Fan"

"A Billet-Doux"[21] (from HODGE, PODGE & CO.)
(*Music by* John W. Bratton, Harry Von Tilzer. *Lyrics by* George V. Hobart and Walter H. Ford.)

"To Marry a Millionaire"
A. Glosé

"A Little Child Like Me"
(*Music by* A. Baldwin Sloane.)

"Jack O'Lantern" (The Great Will-o'-the-Wisp Song)[22]
E. Butler
(*Music by* Mae Anwerda Sloane.)

ACT 2[23]

"Shopping" (Song of Spring Fashions)
Chorus
(*Music by* Mae Anwerda Sloane.)

"Spring Hat" (Song)
E. Hunter, M. Walker, L. Stone, Chorus
(*Music by* A. Baldwin Sloane.)

"(The Song of a) Yankee Tar" (Song)
J. C. Marlowe, Chorus
(*Music by* Louis F. Gottschalk. *Lyrics by* Irving Claxton.)

"De Trop" (Song)
H. Davenport, Ensemble
(*Music and Lyrics by* Clifton Crawford.)

"Starlight"[24] (Song and Characteristic Dance)
J. Slavin, assisted by E. Hunter, E. Barr, M. Murphy, B. Burns, P. Chase, E. Ferguson, L. Middleton, L. Stone, M. Tuohey, V. Jewell
(*Music and Lyrics by* Clifton Crawford.)

Finale
Ensemble
(*Music by* Alfred E. Aarons, Aimé Lachaume.)

ACT 3[25]

"In Florida"[26] (Chorus)
Ensemble
(*Music by* Louis F. Gottschalk.)

"(I'd Like to Be) A Gunner in the Navy"[27] (Song)
H. Davenport, Ensemble
(*Music by* William J. Accooe.)

Spanish Dance/"An Ethiopian Essence"[28]
J. Slavin, Chorus
(*Music by* Aimé Lachaume.)

Finale
Ensemble
(*Music by* Aimé Lachaume.)

1901.22

CIRCUS DAY

A Musical Farce. Book by Owen Davis. Music by George E. Nichols. Staged by Ned Wayburn. Management of Davis and Cooke. Opened 30 September 1901 at the Metropolis Theatre and closed 5 October 1901 after 8 performances.[29]

CAST: *Elephant Toots*, proprietor of the circus: SIM WILLIAMS. *Rubber Ike*: JOE ADAMS. *Little Lancy-Lot*: FRANK E. McNISH. *Herr Scholoagare*: LOUIS MARTINETTI. *Herculese Sap*: Harry Shunk. *Kenneth Strings*: Burt Smith. *Ephreum North*: Ed Coe. *Joseph Hart*: Charles Doty. *Nellie North*: Maude Meredith. *Primrose Scubbins*: LILLIE SUTHERLAND. *Blanche*: Edna Mitchell. *Fifi*: Mamie Mitchell.

1901.23

THE NEW YORKERS

A Musical Play in Two Acts. Book by Glen MacDonough. Music by Ludwig Engländer. Lyrics by George V. Hobart. Staged by George W. Lederer. Settings by D. Frank Dodge and Ernest Albert. Costumes by Caroline Seidle. Orchestra under the direction of Selle Simonson. Produced by George W. Lederer. Opened 7 October 1901 at the Herald Square Theatre and closed 30 November 1901 after 64 performances.[30]

CAST: *Upson Downes*, an American promoter in London temporarily reduced to driving a cab: DAN DALY. *De Long Green*, an American billionaire with a frantic fear of dying rich: GEORGE A. SCHILLER. *Lorenzo Lenz*, proprietor of an American photograph gallery near Earl's Court, London: WILLIAM GOULD. *Paul Patoff*, a Russian detective: NICK LONG. *Ricardo*, an Italian detective employed as a butler at Blithering Towers, Worcestershire: Frank Tannehill, Jr. *Alkali Ike*, late of the Wild West: WILLIAM CAMERON. *Bryton Beach*, an American horseman: Thomas Evans.

---

[20]Interpolated, as per published sheet music:
"The Way That Walker Walked Away"
(*Music by* Harry T. MacConnell. *Lyrics by* Robert B. Smith.)

[21]Dropped for subsequent tour.

[22]Replaced for subsequent tour by:
"My Gal Sal"
Katie Rooney {Margery Lee}
(*Music by* Albert Rezlitt.)[Note: Rezlitt may be an anagram for Albert Von Tilzer. Not the famous song by Paul Dresser, copyright 1905.]

[23]Added to Act 2 for subsequent tour:
"Just to Know What's Going on in New York Town"
Violet Dale {Dorothy Grey},
K. Rooney, Harry Linton {Jack Everleigh}, John Gilroy {Phil Fullerton}
(*Music by* Harry Linton. *Lyrics by* John Gilroy.)

[24]Replaced for subsequent tour by:
"The Instrumental Man"
H. Gilroy, Chorus
(*Music by* Harry Linton. *Lyrics by* John Gilroy.)

[25]Added during the run after Ethiopian Essence":
"Oh, What a Lovely Dream"
H. Gilfoil
(*Music by* Harry Von Tilzer.)
Which was later replaced during the subsequent tour by:
"Beautiful Fairy tales"
H. Gilfoil
(*Music by* Harry Von Tilzer.)

[26]Dropped during the run and replaced by:
"Lesson Book Song" (Opening Chorus)
E. Hunter, M. Walker, L. Faust, M. Murphy, E. Barr, Ensemble
(*Music by* Aimé Lachaume.)
"The Quaker Maids" (Characteristic Dance)
McCoy Sisters
(*Music by* Aimé Lachaume.)

[27]Dropped during the run and replaced by:
"Follow the Man That Leads the Band"
H. Davenport, Ensemble
(*Music by* Aimé Lachaume.)

[28]Dropped during the run and replaced by:
"My Filipina Pet"
J. Slavin, Ensemble
(*Music by* Aimé Lachaume.)

[29]No program available.

[30]Played a return engagement 5 May 1902 at the Grand Opera House for 8 performances.

Dr. Kerr, an American dog doctor: William Black. *Herr Fitzenstatts*, a fortune-seeking German-American: Frank Farrington. *Bobby Bobbett*, a policeman: James A. Fuery. *G. Reginald Dobbs*, a chappie: POWERS GOURAUD. *R. Witherington Bobbs*, another chappie: Fred Titus. *Olive Green*, daughter of De Long Green: VIRGINIA EARLE. *Olga Patoff*, Paul's sister, also a detective: IDALENE COTTON. *Sallie Waters*, an American soubrette: ROSE BEAUMONT. *Jennie O'Jones*, a title-hunting aunt: CARRIE E. PERKINS. *Her Nieces (3)*: *Lotttie Lee*: ANNA LAUGHLIN. *Mary Lamb*: MARGUERITE CLARKE. *Matinee Girls (4)*: *Clytie*: Florence Parker. *Clorinda*: Isabelle D'Armond. *Cleo*: Tessie Mooney. *Calypso*: Kathryn Bartlett.

Titled Guests at Blithering Towers: Ruby Reid, Vernie Snyder, Nell Gwenn, Geraldine Fair, Ethel Jewett, Mildred DeVerre, Jessie Banks, Belva Don Kerlsey, Gertrude Blanke, Pauline Karmen.

Act 1: An American photograph gallery, near Earl's Court, London. Morning. (Dodge.)

Act 2: Conservatory at Blithering Towers, Worcestershire. Night; three days later. (Albert.)

ACT 1[31]

Opening Chorus
(*Music by* Arthur Weld.)

Octette
Misses Beaumont, Perkins, Laughlin, Clarke;
Messrs. Cameron, Evans, Black, Farrington

"Keb, Sir? Want a Keb?"
D. Daly
(*Music by* Arthur Weld.)

"Russia, the Fatherland"
I. Cotton, N. Long

"When You Sail for Paris in the Spring"
V. Earle
(*Music by* Jackson Gouraud.)

"Strolling in Society" (Quartette)
V. Earle, D. Daly, G. A. Schiller, W. Gould

"The Kodak Girl"
R. Beaumont, W. Gould, Chorus

Finale

ACT 2

Opening Chorus

"Honolulu Lu"
A. Laughlin, W. Cameron, Chorus
(*Music by* Emil Bierman. *Lyrics by* George Totten Smith.)

"Take Me Back to Herald Square"
D. Daly

"And the Band Began to Play"
V. Earle, Chorus

"There's a Lobster Left for Me"[32]
R. Beaumont

"Oh! Fudge!"
D. Daly
(*Music by* Paul Schindler. *Lyrics by* George Sidney.)

"The Gossip Song"[33]
V. Earle, Male Chorus

"'Is Old Man's 'At Won't Fit 'Im"/"Three Women to Every Man"
W. Gould

Imitation of "Fougere"
I. Cotton

"(Ragtime Girl), Dat's All"
R. Beaumont, M. Clarke, A. Laughlin, Chorus
(*Music by* Will Marion Cook.)

"If I Should Say Good-bye"
V. Earle, D. Daly

Finale

[31]Additional songs interpolated as per published sheet music:
"My Dixie Queen"
A. Laughlin
(*Music and Lyrics by* Sidney L. Perrin.)
"Down Among the Pines"
"Della, Della, Della"

[32]Dropped during subsequent tour.

[33]Dropped during subsequent tour.

1901.24

SWEET MARIE

A Musical Comedy in Three Acts, 5 Scenes. Book and lyrics by W. Brown[34]. Music by R. Jackson. Musical conductor, N. B. Emanuel. Produced by Oscar Hammerstein's Musical Comedy Company. Opened 10 October 1901 at Hammerstein's Victoria Theatre and closed 2 November 1901 after 28 performances[35].

CAST: *Marie Malonie, Adele Malonie*, (two sisters): JAMES RUSSELL, JOHN RUSSELL. *Castafore*: Rhyce Thomas. *Eduardo Gumpshion*, (engaged to Marie): LOUIS MONTGOMERY. *François Sceemere*, (engaged to Adele): ALBERT LaMAR. *Ysaba*: E. C. Rogers. *Provoss*: William H. Grimke. *Cabbillard*: O. W. Risley. *Paul Grevin*: Robert Gemp. *Mons. Kick*: MASTER GABRIEL. *Bayal-Passandro*: F. Archambauldt. *Del-cannate*: Francis Lee. *Nubiani*: ELEANOR FALK. *Adrette*: Countess OLGA VON HATZFELDT.

The Scholars of the Magician Castafore (Act 2, Scene 3): *In the Tyrol*: Gertrude Adams, Florence Brown, Clara Bernard, Lillian Vogel. *In Spain*: Clara Ballantine, Lulu Whalen, Evelyn Carett, Lillian Bernard. *In France*: Madge Hobart, Ella Ray, Marie deGarmour, Marie Troy. *In Germany*: Sylvia Lysle, Amy Haddon, Blanche Alwin, Minnie Britton. *In America*: Georgie Miller, Marie Parks, Dorothy Palmer, Ada Russell. *The Pierrots*: Rose Earl, Alice Delamour, Sylvia Diamond, Elizabeth Elliott.

Act 1: The bird store of Marie and Adele Malonie in Saterne, France.

Act 2, Scene 1: Himalaya Square, Bombay, India. *Scene 2*: Apartments of Marie and Adele, Bombay, India. *Scene 3*: The Palace of Magic, Bombay, India.

Act 3: Riding Academy of Duval & Company, Paris.

MUSICAL NUMBERS[36]

"Once I Loved the Girl Cecelia"
(*Music and Lyrics by* Oscar Hammerstein.)

"Cecelia and Amelia"
E. Falk, Chorus

1901.25

THE LITTLE DUCHESS

A Musical Comedy in Three Acts. Book and lyrics by Harry B. Smith.[37] Music by Reginald DeKoven. Stage director, George Marion. Settings by Ernest Albert. Costumes designed by Mrs. Catherine Seidle, Will R. Barnes, Archie Gunn. Orchestra under the direction of Herman Perlet. Produced under the personal direction of Florenz Ziegfeld, Jr. Presented by the Florenz Ziegfeld Musical Comedy Company. Opened 14 October 1901 at the Casino Theatre and closed 8 February 1902 after 136 performances.[38]

CAST: *Gustave*, a bathing master and a hero: CHARLES A. BIGELOW. *Maurice de Champignon*, fencing master and duellist: JOSEPH W. HERBERT. *Captain Ralph Edgerton*, an English officer in love with "The Little Duchess": SYDNEY BARRACLOUGH. *Count Casabinca*, a gambler with an infallible system, Claire's uncle: GEORGE MARION. *Baron Koffupsky*, of the Russian secret service, a jealous husband fond of shooting: Chales Swain. *Baptist*, valet to Maurice: JOSEPH WELCH. *Director of the Casino*: Harold T. Morey. *Alfonso*, waiter: B. McGahen. *Drum Major*: Robert Fairchild. *Baroness Juliette Koffupsky*: EVA DAVENPORT. *Annette*: Billy Norton. *Georgette*: BESSIE WYNN. *Philomene*: Anna St. Tel.

Friends of Clare de Brion: *Cora*: Vivian Blackburn. *Nanette*: Frankie Bailey. *Francine*: Adele Orton. *Pierette*: Helen Planchet. *Susette*: Phyllis LaFond. *Lucienne*: Lillian Harris. *Nanon*: Blanche West. *Gabrielle*: Elaine Van Selover. *Tina*: Ruth Rennard. *Fifine*: Daisy Dean. *Liane*: Minnie Gaylor. *Janette*: Katherine Bell. *The Little Duchess*: ANNA HELD. *Clare de Brion*: ANNA HELD.

Ladies Ensemble, Sadie Girls, etc.: Misses Gaylor, Monti, Harris, Rennard, West, Belle, Blackburn, James, LaFond, Selover, Planchet, Selton, Orton, Wyn, Ettinger, Vestor. *Men's Ensemble*: Messrs. Fairchild, Hooper, Flanagan, Morey, Tester.

Act 1: Ostend.

Act 2: The Boudoir of Claire de Brion, Paris.

Act 3: Fencing Academy of Maurice, Paris.

[34]The Dramatic Mirror reported that W. Brown and R. Jackson were pseudonyms for producer Oscar Hammerstein. Program for the week of 28 October 1901 credits Oscar Hammerstein with book and music.

[35]Settings and costumes not credited.

[36]Extant programs contain no song list; list compiled from press reviews, published songs.

[37]Incidents in Act 1 based on the vaudeville operetta "Niniche."

[38]Played a return engagement 21 April 1902 at the Grand Opera House for 8 performances.

ACT 1[39]

"Ostend" (Opening Chorus)
Chorus

"Won't You Come and Float Me"
Chorus

"Flirtation on the Beach"[40]
J. W. Herbert

Duet[41]
C. A. Bigelow, E. Davenport

"A Dip in the Ocean" (Song)
A. Held

"Make Allowance for Love"[42] (Duet)
A. Held, C. Bigelow

"Wading We Go" (A Seaside Episode)
Misses Wynn, Selover, Norton, Orton; Messrs. Tester, Welsh, Becca, Fairchild

"The Swimming Master" (Song)
C. A. Bigelow

Pantomime Dance[43]
Misses Gaylor, Monti, Harris, Bennard, West, Belle; Messrs. Fairchild, Hooper, Flanagan, Morey, Tester

Finale
Company, Chorus, Band

ACT 2

"The House Maids"[44] (Song, Flo)
Chorus

"Those Great Big Eyes"[45] (Song)
A. Held
(*Music by* Leo LeBrunn.)

"Violets" (Ballad)
S. Barraclough
(*Music by* Ellen Wright. *Lyrics by* Julian Fane, after the German poem by Heinrich Heine.)

"Menagerie Song"[46]
C. A. Bigelow

"Chloe, "I'm Walkin'" (Banjo Serenade)
A. Held, Chorus

Hand Organ Song and Dance[47]
G. Marion, A. St. Tel

"The Man with the Tamborine" (Song and Dance)
J. W. Herbert, Misses B. Norton, B. Wynn
(*Lyrics by* William Jerome.)

"Sadie"
A. Held, 13 Sadie Girls
(*Music by* Leo LeBrunn. *Lyrics by* J. P. Harrington.)

Finale
Company, Chorus, Band
(*Music by* Herman Perlet.)

ACT 3

"(Sweet) Salome"
J. Welsh
(*Music by* J. Rosamond Johnson. *Lyrics by* Robert Cole.)

"The Fencing Girls"
Chorus

"My Dandelion"[48]
A. Held, Chorus
(*Music by* A. Baldwin Sloane.)

Satire on French Duel

"The Military Girl"[49]
S. Barraclough, Chorus

Finale
Company, Chorus, Band

1901.26 A TIPPERARY CHRISTENING

A Musical Farce Comedy in Three Acts. Play by Ramsdill and Asher. Direction by Joseph McKever. Opened 14 October 1901 at the Third Avenue Theatre and closed 19 October 1901 after 9 performances.[50]

CAST: *Mr. Jeremiah McSweeney, Mr. Owen McCarthy*, contractors: TONY KENNEDY, JOHN J. SHEEHAN. *Joe McSweeney*: EDWARD HAYES. *Colonel Bunker Hill*, ex-senator: JOSEPH RUSSELL. *Guggenheimer*, policeman: Harry Willis. *Hasty Hastings*, tramp: James Mooney. *Mr. Joseph Dawley*: Frank Rushmore. *Mr. Harry Fairweather*: George J. Werner. *Kitty McCarthy*: MONA WYNNE. *Mrs. McCarthy*: JOSEPH CONLAN. *Mrs. McSweeney*: IDA HOLBEIN. *Miss Seeley*: Mable Walsh. *Carry Grant*: May Burton. *May Savage, Nellie Yohe*: Annetta Reid, Cecilia Reid (acrobatic dancers). *Jessie Fairfield*: Louise Kennedy. *Alice Evans*: Florence Leslie. *Emma Miner*: Clara O'Neil. *Minnie Slavin*: Eugenie Thayer. *Lottie Moore*: Beatrice Morelin. *Hattie Hazard*: Mable Morelin.

---

[39] Added during subsequent tour:
"Soldiers" (Act 1, after Opening Chorus)
Hubert Wilke {Mahdi Khanpore}
"Since Sister Nell Heard Paderewski Play" (Act 1, before "Won't You Come and Float Me")
G. Marion
(*Music by* Jean Schwartz.)
Other interpolations, as per published sheet music:
"Maiden with the Dreamy Eyes"
(*Music by* J. Rosamond Johnson. *Lyrics by* Robert Cole.)
"Strollin' Along the Beach"
(*Music by* J. Rosamond Johnson. *Lyrics by* Robert Cole.)

[40] Dropped during the run. The subsequent tour in Boston includes a different song:
"Little Girl"
J. Welsh
A Chicago tour includes a new song in this spot:
"If I But Knew!"
Frank Rushworth {an American in love with the Little Duchess}
(*Music by* W. A. Pratt. *Lyrics by* W. A. Pratt and J. W. Baume.)

[41] Dropped after opening.

[42] Replaced during subsequent tour by:
"The Maiden with the Dreamy Eyes"
A. Held, J. W. Herbert
(*Music by* J. Rosamond Johnson. *Lyrics by* Robert Cole.)
This was replaced thereafter by:
"Strolling Along the Beach"
A. Held
(*Music by* J. Rosamond Johnson. *Lyrics by* Robert Cole.)

[43] Replaced for subsequent tour by:
"What'd Yo' Do Wid' De Letter Mr. Johnson?" (Song)
A. Held, G. Marion, Chorus
(*Music and Lyrics by* Monroe H. Rosenfeld.)
Which was later replaced by:
"Susan Anna Anna"
A. Held, G. Marion, Chorus

[44] Replaced during the run by:
"Pretty Betsy Brown" (Song)
G. Marion, Chorus
Which was later replaced by:
"Mandy" (Song)
G. Marion, Chorus

[45] Replaced during subsequen tour by:
"L'Amoureuse" (Song)
A. Held

[46] Replaced during subsequent tour by:
"Silas" (Song)
J. W. Herbert
This was subsequently replaced by:
"But You Couldn't Hardly Notice It at All"
C. A. Bigelow

[47] Replaced after opening by:
"De Dago, De Org' and De Monk" (Song and Dance)
G. Marion, A. St. Tel
(*Music and Lyrics by* Harry Von Tilzer.)

[48] Replaced after opening by:
"(Pretty) Mollie Shannon" (She's the Real, Real Thing)
A. Held {as a Paris Street Gamin}
(*Music by* Walter Woolf. *Lyrics by* George H. Ryan.)

[49] Dropped after opening.

[50] Program tearsheet incomplete.

1901.27

THE SLEEPING BEAUTY AND THE BEAST

A Musical Extravaganza in Three Acts, 12 Scenes. (Original English book) Written and invented by J. Hickory Wood and Arthur Collins. Adapted for the American stage by John J. McNally and J. Cheever Goodwin. Music by J. M. Glover and Frederick Solomon. Lyrics by J. Cheever Goodwin. Staged by Ben Teal, Marshall Moore[51]. Ballets by Ernest D'Auban. Settings by Julian Hicks, R. C. McCleery, R. Caney, H. Emsden, Bruce Smith. Costumes designed by Attilio Comelli[52]. Musical director, Frederick Solomon. Business direction, Joseph Brooks. Produced by (Marc) Klaw and (Abraham L.) Erlanger. Opened 4 November 1901 at the Broadway Theatre and closed 31 May 1902 after 241 performances.

CAST: *King Bardout*: HARRY BULGER. *Queen Spadia*: CHARLES J. ROSS. *Lena*: JOSEPH CAWTHORNE [Cawthorn]. *President Petit*: John Page. *Doctor Squills*: John Hyams. *Princess Beauty*: ELLA SNYDER. *Prince Charming*: VIOLA GILLETTE. *Malevolentia*, a witch: PHOEBE COYNE. *Benevolentia*, the Fairy Queen: NELLIE THORNE. *Lord Jocelyn*: May Hengler. *Flossie*: Florence Hengler. *Algie, Reggie, Johnnie, Freddie*, Prince's chums: Nora Cecil, Jane Whitbeck, Annabelle Whitford, Nina Fitzwilliams. *Fairy Godmothers (6)*: *Columbine*: Susie Rusholme. *Eglantine*: Kathryn Colvin. *Violet*: Pearl Landers. *Daffodil*: Lillian Hudson. *Mignonette*: Kittie Norman. *Jessamine*: Viola Kellogg. *Gwendoline, Mariana, Evelina*: Myrtle Steele, Susie Rusholme, Pearl Landers. *Guests at Aix-and-Pains (5)*: *Maudie*: Lelia Lewis. *Claudie*: Virginia Voorhees. *Dora*: Anna Carr. *Cora*: Bessie Stanton. *Nora*: Maude Cummings. *Spirit of the Air*: Nellie Reed. *Witch's Attendant*: Mlle. Martina. *Dash, Flash*: Jeannette Mozar, Lillian Rice.

The Royal Guard: Messrs. Sullivan, Mathias, Smith, Beall. *Sportsmen, Prince's Friends, etc.*: Misses Follette, Martin, Geach, Wild, Tyler, Walter, Carr, Murray, Weldon, Ralston. *Fairies, Demons, Imps, Courtiers, Guards, Sportsmen, Patients, Attendants, Barmaids, etc.*

Act 1, Scene 1: The Fairy Parliament. (Hicks.) *Scene 2*: The Hydro at Aix-and-Pains. (Hicks.) *Scene 3*: The Haunted Vaults of the Castle. (Carey.) *Scene 4*: The Royal Aviary. (McCleery.)

Act 2, Scene 1: The Tangled Forest. (McCleery.) *Scene 2*: Entrance to the Castle Grounds. (McCleery.) *Scene 3*: The Deserted Castle. (Caney.) *Scene 4*: Beauty's Awakening (Emden.)

Act 3, Scene 1: The Palace of the New Republic. (Hicks and Brooks.) *Scene 2*: Exterior of the National Museum. (Smith.) *Scene 3*: The Prince's Orange Grove. (Smith.) *Scene 4*: The Enchanted Crystal Garden and Illuminated Fountains. (Smith.)

ACT 1[53]

Scene 1

"Fairies We" (Fairy Opening Chorus)

"Was Ever a Daintier Infant Seen?"
Fairy Chorus

"Take Thy Way to Earth" (Finale)

The Birth of Beauty. The Fairies' Gifts. The Witch's Evil Prophecy. Beauty Is Sent to Earth.

Scene 2

"Cure or Kill" (Opening Chorus)

"Hygiene" (Duet)
H. Bulger, C. J. Ross

"Multi-Millionaires"
Chorus

"Tell Me, Dusky Maiden" (Specialty)
H. Bulger, C. J. Ross, assisted by
Misses Stead, Daly, Taylor, Poston, Claire, Pepper, M. Luby, L. Luby, Steele, Remley, Willard, Keene, Solomon, Sharpe, Craig, W. Siegrist
(*Music by* J. Rosamond Johnson. *Lyrics by* Bob Cole, James Weldon Johnson.)

"The Royal Pair Are Off To-Day" (Finale)

The King and Queen Take the Mud Cure. Beauty's Sixteenth Birthday. Hasty Departure of the Royal Couple.

Scene 3

"Years Ago" (Song)
P. Coyne

The Witch's Magic Spell. Beauty in Danger.

Scene 4

"The Princess We Adore" (Opening Chorus)

"Day Dreams" (Ballad)
E. Snyder

"Nursery Rhymes" (Specialty)
J. Cawthorne
(*Music by* Jean Schwartz. *Lyrics by* William Jerome.)

"Let Them Go" (Quartette)
E. Snyder, M. Hengler, F. Hengler, J. Cawthorne

Parodies
H. Bulger

"Drowsily, Dreamily" (Finale)

Beauty Celebrates Her Birthday. Her Nurse Gives Her Advice. Arrival of the King and Queen. The Witch's Gift. Beauty Tries the Spinning Wheel. One Hundred Years of Sleep.

ACT 2

Scene 1

"Bang, Bang, Bang" (Hunting Chorus)

"It's a Dream That Never Comes True" (Ballad)
V. Gillette

"Onward" (March Finale)

Prince Charming and His Hunting Suite. The Fairy Queen Appears. She Tells of the Sleeping Beauty. Days of Romance and Chivalry Not Over. The Prince to the Rescue.

Scene 2

"Spirits of the Midnight Spell" (Incantation Chant)

Incidental Ballet
Grigolatis Troupe of Aerialists, assisted by Corps de Ballet

"Rip Van Winkle (Was a Lucky Man)" (Song)
H. Bulger
(*Music by* Jean Schwartz. *Lyrics by* William Jerome.)

The Witches at Work. They Try to Induce Prince Charming to Abandon His Search. The King and Queen Awake from Their Hundred Years' Sleep.

Scene 3

Concertina Specialty
J. Cawthorne

"B'gosh!" (Comic Trio)
H. Bulger, C. J. Ross, J. Cawthorne

Beauty's Nurse Turns Somnambulist. The King, Queen and Nurse Finally Awake. Prince Charming Still in Quest of Sleeping Beauty.

Scene 4

"Beauty's Awakening" (Grand Ballet)(A Dream of the Year)
Grigolatis Troupe of Aerialists, Grand Corps de Ballet, introducing St. Valentine's Guards, Shamrocks, Palm-Bearers, Nest-Bearers, April Fools, Primroses, Daisies, Wisterias, Laburnums, May-Queen, Pink Roses, Yellow Harvest Boys and Girls, Ceres, Autumn Leaves, Holly, Snow, Swallows, etc.

The Fairies Inspire Pleasant Dreams. Prince Charming Finds Beauty at Last. Love's First Kiss.

ACT 3

Scene 1

"Vive la Liberté" (Opening Chorus)

"President Am I" (Specialty)
J. Page, assisted by Misses Medley, Whitford

"Dinah" (Come Out, Dinah, on the Green)(Darkey Serenade)
V. Gillette, Chorus
(*Music by* J. Rosamond Johnson. *Lyrics by* Bob Cole, James Weldon Johnson.)

---

[51]As directors, Teal represented producers Klaw & Erlanger, and Moore represented author Arthur Collins.

[52]Except costumes in "Dusky Maiden" specialty and "Flora, I Am Your Adorer" designed by F. Richard Anderson.

[53]Added late in the run, as per published sheet music:
"Kitty"
Hengler Sisters (Flo, ?)
(*Music by* Frederic Solomon. *Lyrics by* J. Cheever Goodwin.)

"Flora, I Am Your Adorer"[54] (Song)
H. Bulger, assisted by Misses
W. Siegrist, Landers, S. Rusholme, Stead, L. Luby, M. Luby, Willard, Claire
(*Lyrics by* Vincent Bryan.)

"Take her away!" (Finale)

The President Has Unexpected Visitors. They demand Royal Honors. Confusion and Arrests. The Doctor's Unpaid Bill. The Wedding of Beauty and Prince Charming Is Interrupted. The Witch Transforms Prince Charming into a Beast.

Scene 2

The King and Queen, assisted by Beauty's Nurse, burglarize the Museum in search of their Crown Jewels. An Unfortunate Mishap.

Scene 3

"A Cure for Love"[55] (Specialty)
J. Hyams, assisted by
(Boys) Misses Remley, Kayser, Bonner, Thurgate, Williams, Follette,
(Girls) Taylor, Schilt, Poston, Craig, Sharpe, Hatfield

"The Moon and the Owl"[56] (Song)(Nobody's Lookin' But the Owl and the Moon)
E. Snyder
(*Music by* J. Rosamond Johnson. *Lyrics by* Bob Cole, James Weldon Johnson.)

"Kitty" (Specialty)

Dance (*Music by* Maurice Levi.)
Hengler Sisters

"Death Be His Doom"[57] (Chorus)

Beauty Laments Her Lost Happiness. The King and Queen Pluck the Enchanted Rose. The Prince's Edict. The King and Queen Condemned to Die. One Means of Escape. Beauty's Kiss Removes the Witch's Spell. The Beast Is Changed into the Prince. Beauty and Prince Charming are Reunited Amid General Rejoicing.

Scene 4

Xylophone Ballet Movement

"By Love Undying, Crowned" (Finale)

The Palace of Crystal and Prismatic Fountains!

1901.28 FOL-DE-ROL

A Musical Burlesque. Produced by Ida Emerson and Joseph E. Howard. Music and Lyrics by Ida Emerson and Joseph E. Howard. Opened 11 November 1901 at the Third Avenue Theatre and closed 16 November 1901 after 8 performances.[58]

CAST: *Mrs. Meadowbrook*: IDA EMERSON. And LAURA COMSTOCK, JOSEPH E. HOWARD, BOBBY HARRIS, JAKE BERNARD, AL. JOHNSTON, John Fox, Joe Abacco. *Specialties*: The Musical Johnstons (xylophone), the Young American Quintette, biograph views of President McKinley's funeral.

Scene: The Pan-American Exposition.

MUSICAL NUMBERS[59]

"The Rosie Posie Girls"

"Hello Ma Baby"

"I've Lost Ma Baby"

"The Queen of Charcoal Alley"
(*Lyrics by* Andrew B. Sterling.)

"My Georgia Lady Love"
(*Lyrics by* Andrew B. Sterling.)

1901.29 THE SUPPER CLUB

A Musical Comedy in Three Acts. Book by Sydney Rosenfeld. Music and lyrics by A. Baldwin Sloane, Mae Anwerda Sloane, J. Rosamond Johnson and Robert Cole, Ben Jerome and ? Black, William Penn, Will D. Cobb and Gus Edwards, others. Staged under the direction of Lionel E. Laurence. Scenery by St. John Lewis. Costumes designed by Will E. Barnes. Musical director, Genaro Saldierna. Produced by the (Meyer L. and Henry B.) Sire Brothers. Opened 23 December 1901 at the Winter Garden (atop the New York Theatre) and closed 25 January 1902 after 40 performances.[60]

CAST (in order of appearance): *Bess*, daughter of Dingtuttle: MAUDE WILLIAMS. *Castor Beane*, her lover: DONALD BRIAN. *John*, butler: STUART HYATT. *Louise*, chambermaid: JOSIE SADLER. *Ichabod Bender*, a grafter: AL HART. *Pop Dingtuttle*, who has risen from the ranks: THOMAS Q. SEABROOKE. *Kate*, his oldest daughter, married to Hopkins: ADA LEWIS. *Bert Hopkins*, a fashionable dentist: LIONEL LAWRENCE. *The Marquis de Castalenne*: ALEXANDER CLARKE. *Nettie, Hettie, Lettie*, three of his nine daughters: Adele Archer, Oriska Worden, Effie Hamilton. *Nan*, youngest daughter of Dingtuttle: TOBY CLAUDE. *Old Beane*, father of Castor: Richard Brown. *Mrs. Flighty*: Nina Farrington. *Mrs. Golightly*: Vera Morris. *Mrs. Springhtly*: Gertrude Lewis. *Mrs. Knightly*: Eugenie Bashford. *Mrs. Winifred Darling Smith*, President of the Progressive Dames: VIRGINIA EARLE. *The Dummy*: JUNIE McCREE. *Singing Trio*: The DeRigney Sisters. *Master of Ceremonies*: GEORGE FULLER GOLDEN. *Tom*, butler at the Supper Club: John Ford. *Three Noted Politicians*: *Boss Richard*: JOHN W. RANSONE. *Chief William*: EUGENE O'ROURKE. *Boss Thomas*: GEORGE FULLER GOLDEN.

The Progressive Dames (6): Mazie Follette, Florence Carlisle, Natalie Olcott, Maude Frances, Ethel Perry, Jessie Thompson. *Living Fashion Plates (9)*: Adelle Archer, Orisha Warden, Lillian Bond, Jessie Thompson, Grace Maitland, Grace Rogers, Effie Hamilton, Stella Kenny, Bessie Wynne. *Guests, Daughters, Dames, Dancers.*

Act 1: Dingtuttle's home, New York.

Act 2: The Supper Club, New York.

MUSICAL NUMBERS[61]

"When the Band Plays Ragtime"
(*Music by* J. Rosamond Johnson. *Lyrics by* Robert Cole.)

"Don't Butt In"
(*Music by* J. Rosamond Johnson. *Lyrics by* Robert Cole.)

"The Maiden with the Dreamy Eyes"
T. Q. Seabrooke
(*Music by* J. Rosamond Johnson. *Lyrics by* Robert Cole.)

1901.30 THE WIDOW JONES

A Revival of the Farce Comedy in Three Acts[62]. Play by John J. McNally. Produced under the stage direction of R. A. Roberts. Scenery painted by St. John Lewis. Musical director, Charles Zimmerman. Produced by May Irwin. Opened 23 December 1901 at the Bijou Theatre and closed 25 January 1902 after 40 performances.

CAST: *Beatrice*, the Widow Jones: MAY IRWIN. *Billy Bilke*, a promoter: HANS F. ROBERT. *John James Jones*, a social derelict: W. H. POST. *Felicity Jones*, his daughter: FLORENCE REED. *Senor Romero Canovas*, an erratic artist: Christoper Bruno. *Marcia Mendelsonn*, a divorcée: GENEVIEVE REYNOLDS. *Mike McCarthy*, a farmer: Roland Carter. *Cassie Cartee*, his daughter: Mabel Florence. *A. T. Premium*, insurance detective: John James. *Clifford Prout*, just rich, that's all: Charles Church. *Perchance Pedro*, a plumber: Louis Foley. *Hetherington O'Donell*: Russell Lennon. *Osbaldistan Daye*: Frank M. Johnson. *Pansy Weed*: Mabel Russell. *Marie*, an artist's model: Grace Vaughan. *Daisy Davis*: Louise Hollister. *Mandy Noir*, housemaid: Helene Dunlap. *Flossie Zazin*, a tourist: Edith Blair. *Stella Gould*: Charlotte Nolting. *Clara Newman*: Genevieve Day.

Act 1: McCarthy's summer boarding house at Maranacook, Maine.

Act 2: (Apartment in) Paris.

Act 3: Home of Beatrice, Thousand Islands.

MUSICAL NUMBERS[63]

"I'se Gwine to Save To' Soul"
(*Music by* Nat D. Mann. *Lyrics by* Ed. S. Abeles.)

---

[54]Replaced during the run by:
"My Princess Zulu Lou" (Song)
H. Bulger, assisted by Chorus of Misses
(*Music and Lyrics by* Dave Reed, Jr.)

[55]Dropped after opening.

[56] Dropped after opening.

[57] Dropped after opening.

[58] No program available.

[59] Not in performance order.

[60]Two weeks after opening the show was revised from three acts to two acts.

[61]No songs listed in program.

[62]First produced in New York 16 September 1895 at the Bijou Theatre for 168 performances in two engagements.

[63]Musical numbers not listed in programs; list prepared from published sheet music; others such as May Irwin's "Bully Song" may have been retained from the original production.

"De Darkey Cavaliers"
(*Music and Lyrics by* Dave Reed, Jr.)

1902.01

THE TOREADOR

A Musical Play in Two Acts[64]. Book by James T. Tanner and Harry Nichols. Music by Ivan Caryll and Lionel Monckton. Lyrics by Adrian Ross and Percy Greenbank. Staged by Herbert Gresham. Scenery by Ernest Gros. Costumes by Dazian and Mme. Freisinger; dresses designed by F. Richard Anderson, Wilhelm. Orchestra under the direction of Louis F. Gottschalk. Produced by Messrs. (Sam) Nixon & (J. F.) Zimmerman. Opened 6 January 1902 at the Knickerbocker Theatre and closed 3 May 1902 after 121 performances[65].

CAST: *Augustus Traill* of the British Consulate at Villaya: MELVILLE ELLIS. *Pettifer*, a dealer in wild animals: William Blaisdell. *Sir Archibald Slackett, Bart*: JOSEPH COYNE. *Rinaldo*, Carlist: Robert A. Evans. *Governor of Villaya*: EDWARD GORE. *Bandmaster*: W. H. Thompson. *Carajola*, a toreador: WILLIAM BRODERICK. *Mr. Probitt*, a solicitor: Joseph Fay. *Moreno*, Carajola's friend: Harry L. Wallace. *Sammy Gigg*, a tiger: FRANCIS WILSON. *Nancy Staunton*: CHRISTIE MacDONALD. *Dora Selby*, a ward in chancery: ADELE RITCHIE. *Susan*, proprietress of the Magazin des Fleurs, Grand Hotel, Biarritz: QUEENIE VASSAR. *Mrs. Malton Hoppings*, a widow: MAUD RAYMOND. *Donna Teresa*: JENNIE HAWLEY.

Lady Visitors: Sadie Peters, Mabel Redfern, Stella Krum, Helen Chichester, Belle Chamberlain, Sylvia Lisle, Emma Millard, Eleanor Brudell. *Bridesmaids*: Marjorie Relyea, Hermione Hazelton, Margot Hobart, Lucille Verna, Maude Furniss, Margaret McDonald, Nonie Dore, Essie Lyons. *Shop Girls*: Lillian Wallace, Elizabeth Innes.

Act 1: Interiro of Susan's flower shop, Biarritz.

Act 2: Maarket Square, Villaya.

ACT 1

"Where the Gigantic Ocean Atlantic" (Opening Chorus)
(Chorus)
(*Music by* Ivan Caryll. *Lyrics by* Adrian Ross.)

"We're All of Us Lovely and Young" (Chorus of Bridesmaids)
(Bridesmaids)
(*Music by* Lionel Monckton. *Lyrics by* Adrian Ross.)

"I'm Romantic" (I Have Always Had a Passion")(Song)
M. Raymond, Chorus
(*Music by* Lionel Monckton. *Lyrics by* Adrian Ross.)

"Toreador's Song" (I'm the Glory and the Pride of the Land of Spain)(Song)
W. Broderick, Chorus
(*Music by* Ivan Caryll. *Lyrics by* Adrian Ross.)

"Won't It Be a Lark" (We're Dear Little Girls)(Trio)
A. Ritchie, C. MacDonald, Q. Vassar
(*Music by* Ivan Caryll. *Lyrics by* Percy Greenbank.)

"Everybody's Awfully Good to Me" (I'm an Awfully Simple Fellow)(Song)
J. Coyne
(*Music and Lyrics by* Paul Rubens.)

"If Ever I Marry" (Duet)
Q. Vassar, F. Wilson
(*Music by* Lionel Monckton. *Lyrics by* Percy Greenbank.)

"My Zoo" (Whenever You're My Way)(Song)
W. Blaisdell, Chorus
(*Music by* Ivan Caryll. *Lyrics by* Percy Greenbank.)

"(Away to) Espana" (Quartette)
A. Ritchie, C. MacDonald, M. Ellis, J. Coyne
(*Music by* Ivan Caryll. *Lyrics by* Adrian Ross.)

"The Language of Flowers" (If You Want to Show Your Passion) (Song)
C. MacDonald, Chorus
(*Music by* Lionel Monckton. *Lyrics by* Percy Greenbank.)

"Oh, Senor, Pray" (Scena)
J. Hawley, F. Wilson
(*Music by* Ivan Caryll. *Lyrics by* Percy Greenbank.)

"Hear Me, Amelia" (Finale)
(*Music by* Ivan Caryll. *Lyrics by* Adrian Ross.)

ACT 2

"With All the Town in Bright Array" (Opening Chorus)
(Chorus)
(*Music by* Lionel Monckton. *Lyrics by* Percy Greenbank.)

"The Governor of Villaya" (We Are That Person Glorious)(Song)
E. Gore, Chorus
(*Music by* Ivan Caryll. *Lyrics by* Adrian Ross.)

"Yaller Boy and the Moon"[66]
C. MacDonald, J. Coyne

"My Toreador" (La Belle Bolero)(Hark to the Sound of Multitudes)(Song)
J. Hawley
(*Music and Lyrics by* Paul Rubens.)

"The Hall of Fame" (Song)
F. Wilson
(*Music by* John W. Bratton. *Lyrics by* Robb.)

"Keep Off the Grass" (When the Children Go to Play)(Song)
A. Ritchie, Bridesmaids
(*Music by* Lionel Monckton. *Lyrics by* Leslie Mayne.)

"Here They Come in Glittering Glory" (Grand Chorus and March)
Chorus
(*Music by* Lionel Monckton. *Lyrics by* Adrian Ross.)

"Archie" (Sir Archie was a Subaltern)(Song)
J. Coyne, Chorus
(*Music by* Lionel Monckton. *Lyrics by* George Grossmith, Jr.)

Finale

1902.02

THE HEAD WAITERS

A Farce Comedy in Two Acts. Play by Edmund Day. Music by Thomas H. Chilvers and Herbert Dillea. Musical director, Hugo Marks. Produced by E. D. Stair. Opened 20 January 1902 at the Grand Opera House and closed 25 January 1902 after 8 performances; Second edition opened 2 March 1902 at the Grand Opera House and closed 7 March 1902 after 8 performances.

CAST: *First edition*: *Percy Negligee, Harold Negligee*: HAPPY WARD, HARRY VOKES. *Izzy Mark*: George Sidney. *Imaginary Thomas*, an opium devotee: Joe Kelly. *Little Willie*, a pugilistic sport: Lew Miller. *Harry Solace*, a real pebble: Harry Thornton. *Wagner Mozart*, a dancer: Cecil Lean. *Ringer*, the bell boy: Louis Powers. *Gotrox Bywine*, an ancient sport: Lew Miller. *Hi Binder* from Maine: Frank Willing. *Hiram Over*, a cook: Jess Cain. *Sam Sun*, a strong man: Fred Whitfield. *Joe Kerr*, the town clown: Bert Wainwright. *High Perch*, a fish dealer: John Motz. *Leilac Held*, a flower girl: MARGARET DALY VOKES. *Allie Mooney*, a flirt: Hallie White. *Chloe Ridley*, a real actress: Maude Alice Kelly. *Josie Daly*: Josie Daly. *Polly Footlights*, a Casino girl: LUCY DALY.

CAST: *Second edition*: *Percy Negligee, Harold Negligee*: HAPPY WARD, HARRY VOKES. *Izzy Cohen*, Izzy Mark's cousin: Allan Curtis. *Imaginary Thomas*, an opium devotee: Joe Kelly. *Gotrox Bywine*, an ancient sport: Tony Williams. *Little Willie*, a pugilistic sport: Tony Williams. *Ringer*, the bell boy: Eddy Judge. *Harry Solace*, a real pebble: Louis Powers. *Hiram Over*, a cook: Jess Cain. *Sam Sun*, a strong man: Fred Whitfield. *Joe Kerr*, the town clown: Bert Wainwright. *Wagner Mozart*, a dancer: Carlos Hopkins. *Hi Binder* from Maine: George Ives. *High Perch*, a fish dealer: Dan Coleman. *Leilac Held*, a flower girl: MARGARET DALY VOKES. *Allie Mooney*, a flirt: Helen Norton. *Rosey Real*: Marie Gellert. *Lettie*, her real name: Lettie West. *Josie*, a seashore girl: Lettie West. *Addie*, her real name: Adele Kessner. *Chloe Ridley*, a real actress: Olive Street. *Liza*, her real name: Lizzie Purcel. *Mata Nee*, a girl baritone: May Murray. *Maud*, her real name: Maud Bredel. *Rose*, her real name: Rose Williams. *Elita*, her real name: Catharine Konnen. *Nellie*, her real name: Nellie Sterling. *Alma*, her real name: Alma Bauer. *Polly Footlights*, a Casino girl: LUCY DALY.

The Tuxedo Ladies' Band: *Cornet and Saxophone*: Gussie G. Dial. *Cornet*: Bertha M. Silsby. *Saxaphone*: Martha Sandager. *Baritone*: Anna Hall. *French Horn*: Janet Hall. *French Horn and Saxaphone*: Martha Hall. *Tuba and Saxaphone*: Blanche Hall. *Cornet*: Elizabeth Banks. *Cornet*: Alice Banks. *Clarinet*: Bertha Davis. *Drum*: Lydia WIlhelm. *Trombone*: Lottie Gary. *Directress*: Gussie G. Dial.

Act 1: Exterior of the Hotel Maybe, Cape Maybe, Perhaps County, State of Guess Where.

---

[64]Billed as George Edwardes' reigning London Gaiety Theater success.

[65]Played a return engagement 22 February 1904 at the Academy of Music for 16 performances.

[66]Replaced during the run by:
"Moon Moon"
C. MacDonald
(*Music and Lyrics by* Nat D. Mann.)
"In the Moonlight"
C. MacDonald
(*Music by* Theodore F. Morse. *Lyrics by* Raymond A. Browne.)

Act 2: Interior of the Shamrock Rathskeller.

ACT 1 (Second edition)[67]

"The Song of Summer Time" (Opening Chorus)

"'Tis You I Love"
L. Powers, Missses. Norton, Daly, Street, Bauer, Kessner, Sterling, Williams

"Nez Pas"
L. Daly, Messrs. Cain, Hopkins, Wainwright, Ives, Coleman, Whitfield

"Conversation Dance"
H. Ward, H. Vokes, L. Daly, M. D. Vokes

"The Martial Music of the Fife and Drum"
L. Daly, Company

"I Was Just Going to Ask You About That" (a seesaw talk)
H. Ward, H. Vokes

"The Art of Exercising"
T. Williams, Messrs. Hopkins, Powers, Cain, Ives, Whitfield, Wainwright

"My Morning Glory"
L. Daly, Full Company

ACT 2

The Hard Shell Baptist Choir
D. Coleman, assisted by Messrs. Wainwright, Powers, Ives, Cain, Whitfled and Hopkins

"Gayety"
B. Wainwright, Company

"Lenore"
F. Whitfield, assisted by J. Daly, M. Murray

Something different in the "Percy and Harold" line
H. Ward, H. Vokes

"My Ping Pong Girl"
L. Daly

"Mary Jane"
M. D. Vokes, introducing E. Judge

Selections
Tuxedo Ladies' Band

A War Drama, in which the following artists will fight to a finish:
H. Ward, H. Vokes, A. Curtis, J. Kelly, J. Cain, M. D. Vokes, L. Daly

1902.03 DOLLY VARDEN

The Lulu Glaser Opera Company in a Comic Opera in Two Acts. Libretto by Stanislaus Stange. (Based on the novel "Barnaby Rudge" by Charles Dickens.) Music by Julian Edwards. Produced (staged by) Al E. Holbrook, under the personal direction of Stanislaus Stange and Julian Edwards. Court dances and minuets arranged by Cervallo. Settings by Homer Emens and John H. Young. Costumes by Caroline Seidle. Director of Music and conductor, W. E. Macquinn. Produced by F. C. Whitney. Opened 27 January 1902 at the Herald Square Theatre and closed 28 June 1902 after 154 performances[68].

CAST: *Captain Richard Belleville*, an English officer: VAN RENSELLAER WHEELER. *Captain Horace Harcourt* of the English Navy: ALBERT PARR. *Lord Gayspark*, a London exquisite: MARK SMITH. *John Fairfax*, Dolly's guardian: TOM DANIEL. *Lieutenant Marlow, Lieutenant Cragsby* of the English Navy: Harry Lott, Percy Stephens. *Letitia Fairfax*, a London belle: ESTELLE WENTWORTH. *Lady Lucette, Lady Alice*, ladies of fashion: Ada Palmer Walker, Ila Niles. *Dolly Varden*: LULU GLASER. *Court Ladies, Belles and Beaux of London, Naval Officers, etc.*

The action takes place in 1730 during the reigns of King George I of England and Louis XV of France.

Act 1: Garden of Beauchamp Towers, London-on-Thames. The home of Lady Letitia Fairfax.

Act 2: Reception hall in Beauchamp Towers.

ACT 1

"Swing, My Petty One, Swing" (Introduction)
M. Smith, A. P. Walker, I. Niles, Female Chorus

"My Ship's the Girl for Me" (Song)
A. Parr, Chorus

"(For) The Knot There's No Untying" (Song)
E. Wentworth

"Dolly Varden" (Song)
V. R. Wheeler

"An Aural Misunderstanding" (I'm Whirling, Twirling)(Trio)
L. Glaser, V. R. Wheeler, Chorus

"What Love Means" (Duet)
L. Glaser, V. R. Wheeler

"We Met in Lovers' Lane" (Song)
T. Daniel

"When Lovers Are Alone" (Duet)
E. Wentworth, A. Parr

"The Cannibal Maid"[69] (Song)
L. Glaser, Chorus

"He Must Be Punished" (Finale)
Principals, Chorus

ACT 2

"Lovable Love" (Quartette)
E. Wentworth, I. Niles, H. Lott, P. Stephens, Company

"The Girl You Love" (Song)
A. Parr, Chorus

"The Navy" (Song)
E. Wentworth, Chorus

"For the Benefit of Man" (Quartette)
E. Wentworth, L. Glaser, A. P. Walker, I. Niles

"The Lay of the Jay" (Song)
L. Glaser

Ensemble
Principals, Chorus

"To Be with Thee"
V. R. Wheeler

"The Song of the Sword" (Song)
T. Daniel, Male Chorus

"Brides and Grooms" (Octette)
E. Wentworth, L. Glaser, A. P. Walker, I. Niles,
A. Parr, V. R. Wheeler, H. Lott, P. Stephens

Finale II
Principals, Chorus

1902.04 MAID MARIAN

The Bostonians in a Romantic Comic Opera in Three Acts[70]. Libretto by Harry B. Smith. Music by Reginald DeKoven. Staged by Herbert Gresham. Scenery designed by Ernest Gros. Costumes designed by F. Richard Anderson. Musical director, Samuel L. Studley. Management, (Marc) Klaw and (Abraham L.) Erlanger. Produced by the Bostonians (Henry Clay

---

[67]No program available for first edition. Also performed in THE HEAD WAITERS as per published sheet music:

"Absence Makes the Heart Grow Fonder"
(*Music by* Herbert Dillea. Lyrics by Arthur Gillespie.)

"Perhaps Love's Dream Will Last Forever"
F. Whitfield
(*Music by* Herbert Dillon. *Lyrics by* Arthur Gillespie. *Additional verse by* Frederic Whitfield.)

"The Girl Who Leads the Band"
L. Daly
(*Music by* Herbert Dillon. *Lyrics by* Arthur Gillespie.)

"Mah Midnight Lou" (A Scared Coon's Serenade)
L. Daly
(*Music by* Herbert Dillea. *Lyrics by* C. J. Campbell and Ralph M. Skinner.)

"'Tis Better to Have Loved and Lost than Never to Have Loved at All"
(*Music by* Herbert Dillea. *Lyrics by* Arthur Gillespie.)

"Tell Me Honey"
L. Daly
(*Music by* Herbert Dillea. *Lyrics by* George Sidney.)

[68]Played a return engagement 29 December 1902 at the Grand Opera House for 9 perofrmances.

[69] Dropped late in subsequent national tour.

[70] Billed as a sequel to ROBIN HOOD, which opened 28 September 1891 at the Standard Theatre.

Barnabee, W. H. MacDonald, proprietors). Opened 27 January 1902 at the Garden Theatre and closed 22 March 1902 after 64 performances.

CAST: *Sheriff of Nottingham*: HENRY CLAY BARNABEE. *Little John*: W. H. MacDONALD. *Robin Hood*: FRANK RUSHWORTH. *Will Scarlett*: ALLEN C. HINCKLEY. *Friar Tuck*: GEORGE B. FROTHINGHAM. *Alan-a-Dale*: ADELE RAFTER. *Guy of Gisbourne*: WILL H. FITZGERALD. *Dame Durden*: JOSEPHINE BARTLETT. *Giles, Geoffrey*, gamekeepers: J. J. Fennessey, W. J. Sullivan. *Yussuf*, a Slave Merchant: J. J. Martin. *Sir H. Ven deVere, Sir Hugh Montford*, Knights of St. George: Albert Wilder, Henry Brown. *Messenger*: Harry Dale. *Herald*: Albert Watson. *Amida*, a snake charmer: Helene Gordon. *Lady Vivian*: Belle Harper. *Maid Marian*: GRACE VAN STUDDIFORD. *Huntsmen, Men-at-Arms, Saracen Warriors, Mummers, Crusaders, etc.*

Act 1: The park surrounding the castle of the Earl of Huntington.

Act 2: The camp of the crusaders in the desert, with the city of Acre in the distance.

Act 3: The great banqueting hall of Huntington Castle on Christmas day.

ACT 1[71]

Introduction and Opening Chorus

"Annabel Was Fairest" (Song)
B. Harper

"The Cellarer's Toast" (Song)
A. C. Hinckley, G. B. Frothingham, Chorus

"Song of the Falcon"
G. Van Studdiford, Chorus

Entrance of Sheriff
Chorus

"Sheriff's Song" (I Am the Sheriff)
H. C. Barnabee, Chorus

"The Forester's Song"
W. H. MacDonald, Chorus

"Love May Come and Love May Go" (Madrigal Quintette)
G. Van Studdiford, A. Rafter, W. H. MacDonald, A. C. Hinckley, J. J. Fennesey

"Never in the Wide, Wide World" (Trio)
B. Harper, W. H. MacDonald, J. Bartlett

Finale Act 1 (The Dew Is on the Heather)
Chorus

ACT 2

The Crusaders' March

Opening Chorus
Crusaders

"The Monk and the Magpie" (Song)
A. C. Hinckley, Chorus

"Song of the Outlaw"
F. Rushworth, Chorus

"A Popular Tune" (Serenade)
H. C. Barnabee, Chorus

"The Man at Arms" (Trio)
F. Rushworth, A. C. Hinckley, W. H. MacDonald, Chorus

"Tell Me Again, Sweetheart" (Song)
A. Rafter

"Snake Charmer's Song"
G. Van Studdiford, Chorus

"If You Were I and I Were You" (Quartet)
H. C. Barnabee, J. Bartlett, W. H. Fitzgerald, G. B. Frothingham

"True Love Is Not for a Day" (Duet)
G. Van Studdiford, F. Rushworth

"Song of the Crusader" (Guard Ye the Banner)
F. Rushworth, Male Chorus

Finale Act 2

ACT 3

Introduction and Ensemble (God save ye merry gentlemen)
Chorus

"Under The Mistletoe Bough" (Song)
B. Harper, Chorus

"The Cobbler and the Flies" (Sextette)
F. Rushworth, W. H. Fitzgerald,
H. C. Barnabee, W. H. MacDonald, G. B. Frothingham, A. C. Hinckley

Finale Act 3

[71]Musical numbers not listed in the program. List prepared from published piano vocal score (E. Schuberth & Co., New York, 1901).

1902.05 FLORODORA

A Revival of the English Musical Comedy in Two Acts[72]. Book by Owen Hall, revised by Frank Pixley. Music by Leslie Stuart. Lyrics by Ernest Boyd-Jones, Paul Rubens, Leslie Stuart. Produced (staged) by Lewis Hooper. Scenery by St. John Lewis. Costumes designed by Will E. Barnes. Director of Music and Conductor, Philip Klatzkin. Produced by John C. Fisher and Thomas W. Ryley. Opened 27 January 1902 at the Winter Garden (atop the New York Theatre) and closed 8 March 1902 after 48 performances.

CAST: *Cyrus W. Gilfain*, proprietor of the Island and the perfume of Florodora: ALBERT HART. *Captain Arthur Donegal*, Fourth Royal Life Guards, Lady Holyrood's brother: DONALD BRIAN. *Frank Abercoed*, Manager for Mr. Gilfain of the Island of Florodora: SYDNEY BARRACLOUGH. *Leandro*, overseer of farms: Stuart Hyatt. *Gilfain's clerks (6)*: *Tennyson Sims*: Arthur Miller. *Ernest Pym*: W. H. Pringle. *Max Aepfelbaum*: J. F. Cronin. *Paul Crogan*: C. M. Sharpsten. *Reginald Langdale*: Francis Stuart. *John Scott*: Richard Spencer. *William*, a footman: Lou Abrams. *Anthony Tweedlepunch*, showman, phrenologist, hypnotist, palmist: THOMAS Q. SEABROOKE. *Dolores*, (Frank's fiancée): DOROTHY MORTON. *Valleda*, maid to Lady Holyrood: Lillie Collins. *Estelle Lamont*, typewriter to Gilfain: Rhoda Ferner. *Florodorean Girls, Heads of the Various Farms (5)*: *Mona*: Lillian DeRigney. *Inez*: Maud Mullen. *Jose*: Elba Kenney. *Juanita*: Sadie Knapp. *Violante*: Mazie Follette. *Calista*: Isabelle Carroll. *Angela Gilfain*: TOBY CLAUDE. *(Sextette)*: *Daisy Chain*: Effie Hamilton. *Mamie Rowe*: Agnes Wayburn. *Lucy Ling*: Pearl Stilson. *Cynthia Belmont*: Eugenie Bashford. *Lottie Chalmers*: Ethel Perry. *Clare Fitzclarence*: Isabel Whitlock. *Lady Holyrood*: VIRGINIA EARLE. *Florodorean Farmers, Laborers, Flower Girls, Welsh Peasants, etc.*

ACT 1

Opening Chorus

"The Credit's Due to Me" (Sextet)
Clerks, Chorus

"He Loves Me—He Loves Me Not" (Duet)
D. Morton

Chorus of Welcome
(*Lyrics by* Ernest Boyd-Jones.)

"Come and See Our Island" (Musical Number)
Clerks, English Girls

"When I Leave Town" (Song)
V. Earle
(*Lyrics by* Paul Rubens.)

"The Fellow Who Might Be"/"Galloping" (Duet Song and Dance)
T. Claude, A. Hart
(*Lyrics by* Ernest Boyd-Jones.)

"I Want to Marry a Man, I Do" (Trio)
V. Earle, A. Hart, T. Q. Seabrooke
(*Lyrics by* Paul Rubens.)

"Phrenology" (Song)
A. Hart, Chorus
(*Lyrics by* Ernest Boyd-Jones.)

"(Under) the Shade of the Palm"
S. Barraclough
(*Lyrics by* Leslie Stuart.)

Finale
Ensemble
(*Lyrics by* Ernest Boyd-Jones.)

ACT 2

Scene 1

Opening Chorus
Chorus

"Tact" (Song)
V. Earle, Chorus
(*Lyrics by* Paul Rubens.)

"When You're a Millionaire" (Song)
A. Hart, Chorus
(*Lyrics by* Ernest Boyd-Jones.)

[72] First produced in New York 10 November 1900 at the Casino Theatre and closed 25 January 1902 after 505 performances. For Synopsis of Scenes, see original 1900 production.

"Tell Me, Pretty Maiden" (Double Sextette)
Clerks, English Girls (Sextette)
(*Lyrics by* Leslie Stuart.)
"We Get Up at 8 A.M." (Duet Song and Dance)
S. Hyatt, L. Collins
"The Fellow Who Might" (Song)
T. Claude
"When We're on the Stage" (We're Both on the Stage)(Song)
D. Morton, T. Q. Seabrooke, Chorus
"I've an Inkling" (Song)
V. Earle
(*Music and Lyrics by* Paul Rubens.)
Scene 2
"The Filipino Maid"
D. Morton, Chorus
"I Want to Be a Military Man" (Song)
D. Brian, Chorus
(*Lyrics by* Frank Clement.)
Finale
Ensemble

1902.06 THE HALL OF FAME

An Elaborate Pictorial Review in Three Acts, 10 Scenes. (Book) Constructed and written by Sydney Rosenfeld. Music by A. Baldwin Sloane. Lyrics by George V. Hobart. Staged by Ned Wayburn. Ballet directed by Carl Marwig. Scenes painted by St. John Lewis. Costumes designed by Will R. Barnes. Electrical effects by John Whalen. Musical director, Genaro Saldierna. Produced by the Messrs. (Meyer L. and Henry B.) Sire Brothers. Opened 5 February 1902 at the New York Theatre and closed 4 June 1902 after 137 performances.

CAST (in order of appearance): *Fame*: AMELIA SUMMERVILLE. *The Nine Muses*: *Clio*: Edythe Moyer. *Euterpe*: Marguerite Binford. *Melpomene*: Dorothy Zimmerman. *Thalia*: Julia Woodruff. *Erato*: Esther Brunette. *Terpsichore*: Lilly Brink. *Polyhymnia*: Eithel Kelly. *Urania*: Mildred Mead. *Calliope*: Florence Hayes. *Don Caesar II*: CHARLES H. PRINCE. *Will Haverstraw*, an actor who plays many parts, ever in search of fame: DAN McAVOY. *"Kinky,"* the familiar name of a soldier of fortune disguised as a Chinaman: JUNIE McCREE. *A Little Confederate*: Will Archie. *Prosper le Gai*, a Crusader: LOUIS HARRISON. *Matt o' the Moor*, a peasant: Edgar Halstead. *Roy*, a page: EMMA CARUS. *Don Galors*: CHARLES H. PRINCE. *Lady Oblivion*: MARIE DRESSLER. *Lady Ambrosia*: Nina Farrington. *Isoult*, the Desirous, a forest child: MABELLE GILMAN. *The Jailer*: Edgar Halstead. *Griselda*, the jailer's daughter: Georgia Kelly. *Ethelbert, Ethelinda*, dancers in the Feather Ballet: Lilly Brink, Marion Winchester. *Chamberlain*: Leon Kohlmer. *Major John Drew Bingham*, Second in Command: FRANK DOANE. *The Unwelcome Mrs. Hatch*: ADA LEWIS. *Tabitha*, hostess of "The Black Cat Inn": NELLA WEBB. *Lachlan Campbell*, Host of "The Black Cat": Edgar Halstead. *Heinz*, waiter at "The Black Cat": Leon Kohlmer. *Roy*, the girl: EMMA CARUS. *Lady Patrick Tanqueray Campbell*: ADA LEWIS. *Rachel*, her maid: JOSIE SADLER. *Prosper*, disguised as a comic singer: LOUIS HARRISON. *Haverstraw*, disguised as "The Auctioneer": DAN McAVOY. *"Kinky,"* disguised as "The Messenger from Mars": JUNIE McCREE. *Fame*, modernized for the moment (and her 9 muses): AMELIA SUMMERVILLE. *Maude Adams Throssell*: MABELLE GILMAN. *Louise*, her maid: GEORGIA KELLY. *Major Domo*: Leon Kohlmer. *Monsieur Richard Beaucaire Mansfield*: FRANK DOANE. *Premieres danseuses in "The Maid of the Mist" Ballet*: Marion Winchester, Lilly Brink. *"The Only DuBarry"*: ALEXANDER CLARK. *The Royal Announcer*: Edgar Halstead. *Countess de Rouge et Noir*: Mildred Mead. *Marquise de Pinky Panky Poo*: Eithel Kelly. *Marie Antoinette*, the Dauphine: Nina Farrington. *The Marquise Tarara Boom De Ay*: Julia Woodruff. *King Louis*: JUNIE McCREE. *Cosse*, the lover: DAN McAVOY. *Jean DuBarry*: John Ford. *Fame*, as a guide: AMELIA SUMMERVILLE. *Andrew Cairngorm*, a public benefactor: LOUIS HARRISON. *A Dancer*: John Ford. *Kinky* as himself: JUNIE McCREE. *Captain Valentine Brown*: FRANK DOANE. *Columbia*: MABELLE GILMAN.

Act 1, Scene 1: The Grove of Fame. *Scene 2*: Lady Oblivion's Park. *Scene 3*: Lady Oblivion's Jail. *Scene 4*: Lady Oblivion's Palace.

Act 2, Scene 1: The Switchback Valley. *Scene 2*: The Blue Room in Quality Street. *Scene 3*: The Falls of Niagara.

Act 3, Scene 1: The DuBarry Bedchamber. *Scene 2*: The Exterior of the Hall of Fame. *Scene 3*: The Hall of Fame.

ACT 1
"Hail, Fame"
Opening Chorus
"If I've Got What You Want"
D. McAvoy, J. McCree
"The Wandering Hero"
L. Harrison
"Hunting Song"
M. Dressler, Chorus
"Forest Loafers" (Forest Song)
M. Gilman, L. Harrison
"I Am the Keeper"[73] (Solo)
E. Halstead
"Love Is a Jailer" (Trio)
G. Kelly, D. McAvoy, J. McCree
(*Music by* Mae Anwerda Sloane.)
"Nick Carter"[74]
J. McCree
"Feather Ballet"
(*Music by* Henry Waller.)
"Ah Is It I?"[75]
M. Gilman
"Stay, Won't You Stay" (Medley Ensemble)

ACT 2
"The Black Cat Inn"
N. Webb, Chorus
"Nancy"
E. Carus, Chorus
(*Music by* Mae Anwerda Sloane.)
"Romance and Reality"
L. Harrison
"When Charlie Plays the Slide Trombone"[76]
M. Dressler
(*Music by* Mae Anwerda Sloane.)
"Quality Street"[77]
A. Summerville, Muses
"Darling Lou"
M. Gilman
"The Sunflower and the Sun" (Duet)
M. Gilman, F. Doane
"The Rainbow Ballet"
M. Winchester, L. Brink, Corps de Ballet
"Let's Find Him"[78]
Ensemble Chorus

ACT 3[79]
"My Pajama Beauty"
N. Webb, Chorus
(*Music by* Mae Anwerda Sloane.)
"Alive to Tell the Tale"
L. Harrison
"Living Pickles" (Trio)
M. Dressler, J. McCree, F. Doane
"March of the Heroes"
M. A. Kelly, Company

---

[73]Dropped during the run.
[74]Replaced during the run by:
"My Angemima Greene" (previously in Act 3)
D. McAvoy, L. Harrison
(*Music by* Billy Johnson. *Lyrics by* Bob Cole.)
[75]Replaced during the run by:
"(Maiden with the) Dreamy Eyes" (from THE SUPPER CLUB)
M. Gilman, Chorus
(*Music by* J. Rosamond Johnson. *Lyrics by* Robert Cole.)
[76]Dropped during the run.
[77]Dropped during the run.
[78]Dropped during the run.
[79]Immediately after the opening, Act 3 was rewritten, all the songs, except "My Pajama Beauty" and the Finale, were dropped, and were replaced by: ("My Angemima Greene" re-assigned to Act 1)
"Meet Me When the Sun Goes Down"
E. Carus, Quintette
"There Is No North, There Is No South"
M. Gilman, Chorus
(*Music and Lyrics by* Paul Dresser.)

Introducing Kelly Zouaves, who scales a 15 foot wall in 15 seconds.
(*Arranged by* Captain M. A. Kelly.)
"The Army of Peace"
M. Gilman, Chorus
(*Music by* Raymond A. Brown. *Lyrics by* Theodore F. Morse.)
"My Angemima Greene"
D. McAvoy, L. Harrison
(*Music by* Billy Johnson. *Lyrics by* Robert Cole.)
Finale
Entire Company

1902.07 MISS SIMPLICITY

An Operatic Comedy in Two Acts. Book and lyrics by R. A. Barnet. Music by H. L. Heartz. Additional musical numbers by E. W. Corliss and Clifton Crawford. Produced under the personal stage direction of R. A. Barnet. Dances arranged by M. B. Gilbert and Albertieri. Scenery painted by Joseph Physioc. Costumes designed by C. F. Seidle. Musical director, Fred Eustis. Produced by Kirke LaShelle. Opened 10 February 1902 at the Casino Theatre and closed 29 March 1902 after 56 performances.

CAST: *"My Man Blossoms"*: FRANK DANIELS. *Philip Montford*: DAVID LYTHGOE. *Lord Bob, Arthur Tammons, Esq.*, Montford's Pals: OWEN WESTFORD, LAWRENCE WHEAT. *Dr. Willie Pellet*, an Enthusiast: WILLIAM DANFORTH. *Sergeant Jean Thomas Michel* of the King's Own: TOM RICKETTS. *Faon, Benet, Pygmee*, Michel's Companions: Harry Holliday, Frank Conway, Sinclair Nash. *The Men of the English Party (4)*: *Tom Blessington*: J. S. Northern. *Matthew Rugby Northcote*: HARRY COLLINS. *Stafford Coombe*: Ambrose Daly. *Jack Drummond*: Alphonse Fuguet. *Mademoiselle Clair de Loinville*: HELEN LORD. *Patty Yarrell*, her Duenna: GRACE BELMONT. *Rosalie*, a Beggar maid: ALLENE CRATER. *Lady Dorothea Walsingham Bagges*, the Chaperon of the Montfort Party: KATE UART. *Margery Bagges*: GRACE MYERS. *Madame Michel*: Florence Gammage. *The Girls of the English Party (4)*: *Constance Strafford*: Mildred Forrest. *Emily Map Dalyrymple*: Lottie Vernon. *Theodora Mowatt*: Marie deGrue. *Roggy Edwards*: Rosalie Boyer.

Belles of Sauterelle: *Gabrielle*: Frances Palmer. *Babet*: Eva James. *Dorothee*: Helen Bartlett. *Octavia*: Amy Forsslund. *Clio*: Gladys Earlcott. *Vistonette*: Bertha Northern. *Antoinette*: Grace Gordon. *Junie*: Margaret Hastings. *King's Own Body Guards, Villagers of Sauterelle, etc.*

Act 1: Square in Sauterelle.

Act 2: Grand Hall in the Chateau Loinville.

ACT 1[80]
"The King's Own" (Opening Chorus)
T. Ricketts, Chorus
"Stand Back" (Song)
A. Crater
"Sweet Ecstasy" (Entrance and Song)
H. Lord
"You'd Better Take It Back" (Song)
G. Belmont, Belles of Sauterelle
"With All Proprieties" (Song)
K. Uart, O. Westford, G. Myers, L. Wheat, English Party
"Charity" (Song)
H. Lord
"Some Do, Some Don't" (Duet)
H. Lord, D. Lythgoe
"Don't Mind Me"
F. Daniels
(*Music by* Clifton Crawford.)
"The Chestnutty Language of Lovers"[81]
F. Daniels
"Roses Begin with R, Love" (Song)
G. Myers, L. Wheat, English Party
"An Innocent City Maid" (Song)
A. Crater, T. Ricketts
"The (Good Little) Sunday School Boy"
F. Daniels
"Rosalie" (Song)
D. Lythgoe
(*Music by* E. W. Corliss.)
Finale
Omnes
ACT 2
"Oh What Delight to Be Dancing" (Song)
Chorus
"He Did It So Politely" (But He Said It So Politely) (Song)
W. Danforth
"The Interrogative Child"[82] (Mrs. Wimple's Party)(Song)
F. Daniels
(*Music by* Clifton Crawford.)
"When You Were Shy Eighteen" (And You Were Shy Eighteen)(Duet)
K. Uart, O. Westford, English Party
"Love Me Little, Love Me Long" (Duet)
G. Myers, L. Wheat, English Party
"Foreign Ditties"[83] (Ensemble)
F. Daniels, A. Crater, Chorus
"When Will My Dream Come True"[84] (Duet)
D. Lythgoe, H. Lord
Finale
Omnes

[80]Added the last week of March 1902, after "Foreign Ditties":
"Living Your Own Life"
F. Daniels, W. Danforth, A. Crater, G. Belmont
(*Music and Lyrics by* Benjamin Hapgood Burt.)

[81]Dropped for subsequent tour.

[82]Replaced for subsequent tour by:
"Babette" (Song)
F. Daniels
(*Music by* Benjamin Hapgood Burt. *Lyrics by* Paul West.)

[83]For subsequent tour, performed in tandem with:
"Don't Forget You're Talking to a Lady"
F. Daniels, Mai Lowery {Rosalie}, Chorus
(*Music by* George A. Spink. *Lyrics by* Henry W. Blossom.)

[84]Replaced for subsequent tour by:
"Phoebe"
Grace Orr Myers {Mlle. Claire de Loinville}

1902.08 FOXY GRANDPA

A Musical Snapshot (Comedy) in Three Acts. Book by R. Melville Baker. Based on the comic strip/stories of the same name by Carl E. Schultze. Music, (lyrics) by Joseph Hart. (Staged by R. Melville Baker.) Orchestra under the direction of William H. Batchelor. Orchestrations by William H. Batchelor. Produced by William A. Brady. Opened 17 February 1902 at the 14th Street Theatre and closed 31 May 1902 after 125 performances[85].

CAST: *Goodelby Goodman*, who believes that boys will be boys, and proves himself a Foxy Grandpa: JOSEPH HART. *Horace Goodman*, his youngest brother, who thinks Goodelby should have a guardian: J. R. ARMSTRONG. *Chub*, Goodelby's grandson, who thinks Grandpa is a wonder: GEORGIE MACK. *Bunt*, Goodelby's grandson, who thinks Grandpa is a wonder: BOBBIE BARRY. *Signor Bolero*, a facial artist, who makes a living by looking like other people: EUGENE REDDING. *Jack Richman*, who is English, with a strong fondness for the Yankee girl: CLIFTON CRAWFORD. *His Chums (3)*: *Dan Harper*: Bert Young. *Tom Walker*: Charles Wilson. *Bob Summers*: Maurice Stone. *Hiram Hopper*, proprietor of the Green Mineral Springs: John Keefe. *Hank*, his bell boy, night clerk, head waiter, porter, anything else the occasion demands: Charles A. Bates. *Weary Waggles*, who has no fixed habitation: Arthur Borani. *Henry Wilson, Nelson Stone*, attendants at Dr. Holden's private sanitarium: Fred Haines, E. F. Van Rennselaer. *Three from the House of Colonna, who constitute a Neapolitan Trio*: *Pietro*: Charles A. Bates. *Giorgio*: Bert Young. *Michello*: Maurice Stone. *Polly Bright*, who is Grandpa's protege and, if her sex would permit it, her right hand man: CARRIE DeMAR. *Signorina Colonna*, who takes Grandpa into her confidence: BEATRICE LIEB. *Dorothy Goodman, Millicent*, Horace's daughters: Fleurette DeMar, Louise Moore. *Jallma*, who tells fortunes: Margaret Knight. *Guests, Fakirs, Tourists.*

Guests at the Green Mineral Springs: *Elsa Vane*: Gertrude Arden. *Mildred Winters*: Florence Worden. *Violet Young*: Grace Pomeroy. *Agnes Ward*: Margaret Knight. *Charltte Fuller*: Mabel Dwight. *Millie Love*: Dorothy Armington. *Mary Sweet*: Eula Jordan. *Ethel Hunt*: Judith Shaw. *Betty Moore*: Loretta Long. *Dolly Munn*: Marie Franklin. *Lucy Snap*: Helene Chadwick. *Daisy Deane*: Minnie Packard.

Act 1: The Green Mineral Hotel. Afternoon.

Act 2: Picnic Grounds at Lake Hopper. Afternoon of the next day.

[85]Played a return engagement 9 February 1903 at the Grand Opera House for 8 performances.

Act 3: Interior of the barn at Green Mineral Hotel that evening. Barn dance.

ACT 1[86]

"Before and After Taking" (Opening Chorus)
Guests
"Military Charlie"
C. DeMar, Chorus
Comic Medley
G. Mack, B. Barry
"Story of the Two Bad Boys"
J. Hart, G. Mack, B. Barry
"Polly"
C. Crawford, Chorus
"The Tight Rope Walker"
J. Hart, Company

ACT 2

"Neapoli" (Neapolitan Trio)
C. Wilson, B. Young, M. Stone
"The Country Club"
C. DeMar, F. DeMar, C. Crawford, Chorus
"The First Submarine Boat"
J. Hart, G. Mack, B. Barry
"The Funny Family"[87]
J. Hart, C. DeMar
"(The) Bathing Lesson"
G. Mack, B. Barry, Girls
"Friska Linda" (Barcarole)
C. Wilson, B. Young, M. Stone

ACT 3

"Country Quadrille"
Guests
"La Parisienne"[88] (Solo Dance)
F. DeMar
"My Clementine"
L. Moore, Chorus
"Dancing Dollies"[89]
C. Crawford, C. DeMar
"Banjo Dance"
J. Hart, G. Mack, B. Barry
"The Barn Dance"
Company

1902.09 HAPPY HOOLIGAN

A Farce Comedy in Three Acts. Play by Frank Dumont. Based on the popular comic strip by Frederick Opper. Music by Nicholas Brown. Produced by Gus Hill. Opened 10 March 1902 at the Metropolis Theatre and closed 15 March 1902 after 8 performances; returned in revised form[90] 4 May 1903 to the New Star Theatre for an additional 8 performances.

CAST: *Happy Hooligan*, a victim of hard luck: ROSS SNOW. *Smooth Con*, cause of trouble: WILLIAM HALLIDAY. *Michael O'Shaughnessy*: PAUL QUINN. *Peter Gugenheimer*: FRANK OTTO. *Maken Welcome*, Hooligan's partner: WILFRED GERDES. *Mickey Whale*, a tough citizen: CHRIS WHELAN. *Bill Simkins*, a jay: William Zinell. *Isaac Kahn*, a button merchant: James Cardiff. *Broncho Bill*, a cow-puncher: WILLIAM HALLIDAY. *No Hair*: Edwin Stockwell. *Had Hair*: J. F. Leonard. *Lost Hair*: J. Jay Shaw. *Want Hair*: P. A. Kennedy. *The Dutchess*, a female lawyer: ADELAIDE MARSDEN. *Liz Snow*, a tough proposition: CARRIE EZIER. *Bridget Moriarty*, suddently wealthy: MAGGIE WESTON. *Miss Sales*: Jennie Donna. *Miss Bargain*: Rossita Rivera. *Nurse Girl*: Bessie Montgomery. *Vera Spring*, a military girl: Rita Merrill. *Mabel Summers*, a summer girl: Dora Price. *Stella Autumn*, a soubrette: Marie Young. *Maudie Winters*, a concert girl: Alice Hornig. *Mystic Figures*: Minnie Searles. *Garnet Ring*: Eleanore Telford. *Mamie Mumm*, a bicycle girl: Nellie Sawyer. *Susie Supers*, an auto girl: Winnie Erlanger. *Specialty*: The Pan-American Quartette.

Act 1: The barber shop. A busy day.

Act 2: The trolley car. Hustling for money.

Act 3: The court room. A hot finish.

ACT 1

Opening Chorus
"Balmoral Chorus"
"What You Don't Expect"
"Happy Hooligan"
Specialty Operatic
"I Will Love You, Always Love You"
"As the Boys Go Marching By"
"Dat's My Girl"
Specialty
W. Halliday, P. Quinn
"Whoa Bill"
Medley Overture, Happy Hooligan

ACT 2

"Hold Fast" (Chorus)
A Bit of Everything
Up-to-date Specialty
C. Whelan, F. Otto
Specialty
C. Ezier
"The Dutchess of Central Park"
Novelty Singing
"An American Thoroughbred" (Chorus)

ACT 3

"Old Court-house Chorus"
"My Lucky Star"
"Bachelors and Maids"
"Our United Emblem"

1902.10 THE BELLE OF BROADWAY

A Musical Comedietta in One Act, followed by a vaudeville program. Book by William H. Post. Music by A. Baldwin Sloane and others. Lyrics by George V. Hobart. Staged by Ned Wayburn. Produced by the (Meyer L. and Henry B.) Sire Brothers. Opened 15 March 1902 at the New York Winter Garden (atop the New York Theatre) and closed 29 March 1902 after 17 performances.[91]

CAST: *Hannibal Jerome*: THOMAS Q. SEABROOKE. *Ebeneezer Halleck*: ALEXANDER CLARK. *Count Boney Parte*: Charles Caverly. *Baron Von Blitzern*: Edward Raymond. *Tom Finch*: DONALD BRIAN. *Michael Fitzallen*: Malachi Kelly. *Reverend Krupp Gunn*: CHARLES PRINCE. *Freeman Woods*: Stuart Hyatt. *Speaking Waiter*: George Evers. *Silent Waiter*: George Woolsey. *Cook*: Bob Cole. *Policeman*: Lou Abrams. *Mr. Chalmers*: Arthur Miller. *Mrs. George Washington Honeywell*: GENEVIEVE WHITLOCK. *Mrs. Letiticia Halleck*: Maude Williams. *Geraldine Morningstar*: Marion Winchester. *Susan Gunn*: Lillie Collins. *Typewriter*: Essie Knapp. *Grace Shanley*: Agnes Wayburn. *Nellie Rector*: Effie Hamilton. *Gertie Sherry*: Lillian Bond. *Jenny Delmonico*: Isabelle Whitlock. *Phoebe Martin*: Ivy Moore. *Cissy Burns*: Nellie Payne. *Mary Jack*: Ocia Thompson.

Vaudeville program: Carl Marwig Ballet; Madge Fox, Sydney Barraclough; The Dope Fiend (sketch) with Junie McCree, Nina Farrington, Lilly Collins, Charles H. Prince; Ernest Hogan (coon songs); James Richmond Glenroy; George Fuller Golden; Juan Caicedo (wire act); "Cleopatra"[92] (Ballet by Carl Marwig) with Lilly Brink, Elphye Snowden.

---

[86] Added for a late tour, 1904, as per published sheet music:
"I'll Be Your Dewdrop Rosey"
C. DeMar, J. hart
(*Music by* Tom Lemonier. *Lyrics by* Richard H. Gerard.)

[87] Replaced for subsequent tour by:
"Different Ways of Proposing"
J. Hart, C. DeMar

[88] Dropped for subsequent tour.

[89] Replaced for subsequent tour by:
"I'm Not at Liberty to Tell"
John McVeigh {Jack Richman}, C. Demar

[90] The principals remained the same, with the addition of BELLE DARLING in a new role as Liz Snow, with two new songs "Honey, Send Home for the Money" and "Bake, O Babe."

[91] No program available.

[92] Though scheduled, "Cleopatra" was not performed on opening night, but was added later.

Scene: Manhattan Beach.

MUSICAL NUMBERS

"There's a Little Street in Heaven Called Broadway"
T. Q. Seabrooke

1902.11 A TRIP TO BUFFALO

A Musical Extravaganza (Musical Comedy) in Three Acts. Book (and lyrics) by Harry B. Marshall. Music by William Lorraine. Stage director, Eugene Rogers. Scenery by Gates & Morange, William V. McNamara, Lee Lash. Musical director, William Lorraine. Produced by Charles P. Salisbury. Opened 24 March 1902 at the New Star Theatre and closed 29 March 1902 after 9 performances.

CAST: *Orientals*: *Abdul Damit XXX*, an erratic Sultan who longs for a new harem: EUGENE ROGERS. *Michael O'Rafferty* (known as Muley Rafferty), chief of the Sultan's secret service: MARTIN O'NEILL. *Hans Schloss* (known as Muley Bey), his confidential advisor: JACK MARSHALL. *Ameta*, the flower of the harem, with a mind all her own: FLORENCE WOLCOTT. *Kalesha*, another flower, but a faded one: FANNY DABOLL. *Sallie*, the Sultan's American protégé—a harem attendant: Venus Arnold.

Americans: *Jack Dual*, showman and tourist—Envoy from the Pan-American Exposition: GEORGE E. BEBAN. *Willie Sport*, also an Envoy and backer of the Exposition: GRACE DARE. *Bessie Bussell*, an American newspaper correspondent: ANNA McNABB. *Vanity Vassar* (Willie's finacée), a London society belle: Cora Folsom. *Mrs. Vassar*, her mother: Dawn Leroy.

In the Sultan's Service: *Captain Seafar*, in the Turkish Navy: Morey Long. *Binnacle*, first mate: Howard Stevens. *Ned*, *Ted*, cabin boys: Bessie Clifford, Elsie Harvey. *Zamona*, the Sultan's chief dancer: VESTA BERGEA. *Mulah Nitt*, master of the harem: Howard Stevens. *Aboo Haman*, a slave: James Ryan. *Abdullah*, captain of the palace guards: CHARLES JUDELS. *Ali Ben*, lieutenant of the palace guards: Thomas F. Reilly. *Omar*, *Hassim*, Royal Guards: Mina Jurgens, Indiola Arnold.

The Royal Turkish Dancers: *Narcissus*: Bessie Clifford. *Saphira*: Elsie Harvey. *Zarina*: Marie Nelson. *Amina*: Tillie Monroe. *Saloma*: Charlotte Scott. *Alesha*: Vesta Bergea.

The Harem: *Neula*: Bertha Dean. *Zuellka*: Lottie Maydock. *Farina*: May Raymond. *Suelima*: Marie Nelson. *Zaliah*: Indiola Arnold. *Fatima*: Florence Hawkins. *Talmina*: Venus Arnold. *Zebona*: Jessie Clark. *Blush-of-Rose*: Alice Forman. *Star-of-Night*: Emma Carl. *Turkish Subjects, Guests, Sailors, Exposition Visitors, Guards, etc.*

Act 1: Turkey. The Sultan's Private Gardens, adjoining his Palace in Constantinople.

Act 2: The Atlantic Ocean. The Sultan's flagship.

Act 3: Buffalo, New York, U.S.A. The Pan-American Exposition.

ACT 1

"'Neath Oriental Skies" (Opening Chorus)
Chorus

Chorus of Welcome
Chorus

"A Bit of Diplomacy" (Song and Chorus)
J. Marshall, Chorus

"The Sultan's Policy" (Entrance Solo and Ensemble)
E. Rogers, Chorus

"In Buffalo" (Trio)
A. McNabb, G. Dare, G. E. Beban

Octette
E. Rogers, F. Wolcott, A. McNabb,
C. Folsom, D. Leroy, G. E. Beban, G. Dare, J. Marshall

"An Oriental Maid" (Solo)
F. Wolcott, Chorus

Oriental Ballet

Ensemble and Finale

ACT 2

"On the Bounding Main" (Opening Chorus)

"A Seaman Bold" (Solo)
M. Long

"The Rounder" (Solo)
G. E. Beban, illustrated by Misses Dean, Bergea, Arnold

"A Pirate Trinity" (Trio)
F. Daboll, M. O'Neill, J. Marshall

"Be Careful of The Hoo-Doo Man" (Solo and Chorus)
A. McNabb, Chorus

"Land, Ho!" (Finale)

ACT 3

"Midway Reminders" (Opening Chorus)

Scene 1

"In Buffalo"
Chorus

"A Midway Flirtation" (Octette)
Misses Arnold, Raymond, Bergea, Dare,
Messrs. C. Judels, Stevens, Ryan, Long

"Maidee Come Be My Lady" (Solo)
F. Wolcott, assisted by Mr. Long

Scene 2

"Rafferty Bey" (Song and Chorus)
M. O'Neill, Chorus

Scene 3

"Nobility on the Midway" (Character Sketch)
G. E. Beban, assisted by Miss Folsom

Scene 4

"I Left My Heart in Dixie" (Solo and Chorus)
H. Stevens, assisted by G. Dare, V. Arnold

Ensemble and Finale

1902.12 SAN TOY

A Return Engagement of the Musical Comedy in Two Acts[93]. Book by Edward Morton. Music by Sidney Jones. Lyrics by Harry Greenbank and Adrian Ross. Staged by B. D. Stevens and Edwin Price. Dances arranged by Willie Warde. Orchestra under the direction of John J. Braham. Produced by the Daniel Frohman for the Austin Daly Musical Company. Opened 7 April 1902 at Daly's Theatre and closed 3 May 1902 after 32 performances.

CAST: *Li*: SAMUEL COLLINS. *Captain Bobby Preston*, son of Sir Bingo: MELVILLE STEWART. *Sir Bingo Preston*, British Consul at Pynka Pong: HAROLD VIZARD. *Sing Hi*, President of the Board of Ceremonies: Damon Lyon. *Lieutenant Harvey Tucker*: R. S. Pigott. *Fo Hop*, a Chinese student: JOSEPH CAUTO. *Hu Pi*, *Wai Ho*, Jewelers of Pynka Pong: William Wallace, Robert M. O'Neil. *Li Hi*, *Li Lo*, Tartar Guards: Archie Gilles, George A. Roark. *The Emperor*: Sarony Lambert. *Yen How*, a Mandarin: GEORGE K. FORTESQUE. *Wun Lung*, Corporal of the Emperor's own: Annie Cameron. *Ko-Fan* of the Emperor's own: Isobel Hall. *Trixie* with Pas-Seul in Act 2: Nora Lambert. *The Six Little Wives of Yen-How*: *Yung-Shi*: Elgie Bowen. *Me-Koui*: Marie Welch. *Siou*: Helen Maynard. *Shuey-Pin-Sing*: Jeannette Palmer. *Li-Kiang*: Mary Kier. *Hu-Yu*: Dorothy Maynard. *Mrs. Harley Streeter*: Margaret Yorke. *Hon. Mrs. Hay Stackpole*: Ella Rocke. *Dudley*, Poppy's maid: MINNIE ASHLEY. *Poppy*, daughter of Sir Bingo: Ella Rocke. *San Toy*, daughter of Yen-How: MARIE CELESTE.

1902.13 LES CLOCHES DE CORNEVILLE

A Revival of the Opéra-comique in Three Acts, in French[94]. Libretto by Clairville and Charles Gabet. Music by Robert Planquette. Stage director, Messr. Moreau. Produced by Oscar Hammerstein. Opened 21 April 1902 at Hammerstein's Victoria Theatre and closed 26 April 1902 after 8 performances.[95]

CAST: *Le Marquis*: Messr. VILETTE. *Grenicheux*: Messr. QUEYLA. *Gaspard*: Messr. Douchet. *Le Bailli*: Messr. GABEL. *Le Tabellion*: M. Gervais. *Fouinard*: Messr. Ritter. *Grippardin*: Messr. Godin. *Cachalot*: Messr. Arthur. *Serpolette*: Mlle. DELIANE. *Germaine*: Mlle. DE TER. *Gertrude*: Mlle. Lespinasse. *Jeanne*: Mlle. Gillet. *Manette*: Mlle. Lambert. *Peasants, Sailors, Coachmen, Maid-servants, Domestics, etc.*

---

[93]Originally produced 1 October 1900 at Daly's Theatre for 65 performances. Re-opened a return engagement 4 March 1901 at Daly's Theatre for 103 additional performances. Total: 168 performances. For Synopsis of Scenes and Musical Numbers, see original 1900 production.
[94]First produced in New York in English as THE CHIMES OF NORMANDY 22 October 1877 at the Fifth Avenue Theatre for 16 performances. First produced in New York in French 13 May 1878 at the Park Theatre in repertory. For Synopsis of Scenes and Musical Numbers, see original 1878 production.
[95]No program available.

1902.14

WEARY WILLIE WALKER

The Original Lilliputians in a Spectacular Comedy in Three Acts. Play by John Fowler. Opened 28 April 1902 at the New Star Theatre and closed 3 May 1902 after 8 performances.[96]

CAST: *Mr. Sparks*: Major JAMES J. DOYLE. *Mrs. Sparks*: ANNIE NELSON. *Mr. Larks*: CASPER WEIS. *Mrs. Larks*: HELEN LINDNER. *Miss Larks*: BERTHA SHULTZ. *Tired Mike*: JAMES E. ROSEN. *Weary Willie*: LOUIS MERKLE. *Backem Downs*: George Liable. *Manager Angel*: T. J. Sharpler. *Toddy Grimes*: Howard Knowles. *Dooley*: Joseph Algere. *Paddy Dolan*: John Church. *Sol Soakem*: C. O. Mack. *Only Sick*: August Barth. *Bud Ticem*: Howard Knowles. *Dollie Dimple*: Della Ranney. *Solomon Diverksy*: JOSEPH E. MACK. *Jocko*: Howard Knowles. *Hi Hubbard*: Joseph Algere. *Sickem Finlay*: Fred Spanter. *Mrs. Dimity*: May Valentine. *May Jarndyce*: Della Ranney. *Eunice Divinity*: Adele Spencer.

Act 1: A street in New York.

Act 2: Interior of a famous restaurant.

Act 3: A haunted castle, with transformation scene.

1902.15

THE SHOW GIRL, or The Cap of Fortune

A Jolly Bit of Tomfoolery (Musical Comedy) in Two Acts, 4 Scenes. Book and lyrics by R. A. Barnet. Music by H. L. Heartz and Edward W. Corliss. Lyrical assistance, D. K. Stevens. Entire production under the stage management of Edward P. Temple. Dances aranged by Joseph C. Smith. Scenery painted by Frank Rafter. Costumes by Will R. Barnes. Lighting by Joseph Menchen. Orchestra directed by Edward E. Rice. Produced by Edward E. Rice. Opened 5 May 1902 at Wallack's Theatre and closed 28 June 1902 after 64 performances[97].

CAST: *Dionysus Lye*[98], manager, leading man, dramatic author, lightning calculator, second sighter, Sophocles Dramatic Company: FRANK LALOR. *Lord Cadwallader Dyce*, high commissioner of Cyprus: CLARENCE HARVEY. *Captain E. Ross Armor* of the Northumberland Guards, on leave: STANLEY HAWKINS. *Jhonnie Jhonnes*, property man, Sophocles Dramatc Company: CHARLES GUYER. *Garrick Forrest McCready*, juvenile, Sophocles Dramatic Company: ROBERT L. DAILEY. *Max Rothkopfsky*, a peripatetic hatter: DAVID ABRAHAMS. *Wessex Fusiliers (4)*, stationed at Cyprus: *Captain Cornwallis*: Louis McGowan. *Lieutenant Dale*: J. L. Fitzroy. *Sergeant Higgins*: R. Noble. *Corporal Egge*: R. Hudson. *4 from the English steam yacht "Gnat,"* Royal yacht squadron: *Captain*: Paul J. Chute. *Mate*: F. Garfield. *Purser*: Henry Dale. *Surgeon*: E. T. Giles. *Lady Betty Pringle*, the fiancée of Lord Dyce: PAULA EDWARDES. *Miss Cecilia Gay*, the Show Girl, Sophocles Dramatic Company (her patrents are highly connected): MARION PARKER. *Lady Clarissa*, sister of Lord Dyce: Yolande Wallace. *Vivien Epps*, ingenue, Sophocles Dramatic: Marie Hilton. *Swagger debutantes, professionally known as "The Rainbow Sisters" (4)*: *Maerie Jhones*: Agnes Dailey. *Suesann Jhones*: Rose Barnett. *Jaynne Jhones*: Ada St. Clair. *Elighza Jhones*: Frances Wilson. *Maids of Cyprus (4)*: *Diana*: Catherine Hutchinson. *Chloris*: Bertha Blake. *Helen*: Nina Blake. *Lotis*: Agnes Wadleigh. *Katrina*, a German waif: ALONZO PRICE. *Specialties: Dancing Girl of the Cyprus Theatre*: Amorita. *The Remarkable Kitty*: David Abrams. *Learning to Dance by Book*: Frank C. Young, Bessie DeVoie. *Other Maids of Cyprus, Men of the Wessex Fusiliers, Band and Drummers of the Wessex Fusiliers*: Auxiliary Company of 70.

Act 1, Scene 1: Esplanade of the Shrine, Cyprus. *Scene 2*: Exterior of the wished for villa.

Act 2, Scene 1: Grove near Cyprus. *Scene 2*: Lord Dyce's Gardens at Cyprus.

ACT 1[99]

"Oh, Shrine of Psyche" (Opening Ensemble)
Officers of the Fusiliers, Maids of Cyprus, Chorus
(*Music by* H. L. Heartz.)

"That's the Way of a Sailor" (Song)
P. Edwardes, C. Harvey
(*Music by* H. L. Heartz.)

"Sometimes—Perhaps" (Quartette)
S. Hawkins, C. Harvey, P. Edwardes, Y. Wallace
(*Music by* L. S. Thompson.)

"We Are Trying to Support Our Only Mother" (Quintette)
C. Guyer, Rainbow Sisters
(*Music by* M. W. Daniels.)

"Invocation to Pie"[100] (Concerted Number)
F. Lalor, M. Parker, C. Guyer, R. L. Dailey, M. Hilton, Rainbow Sisters
(*Music by* M. W. Daniels.)

"By-and-by"[101] (Song)
P. Edwardes
(*Music by* William T. Francis.)

"I'm a Simple Author-Manager"[102] (Song)
F. Lalor, Others, Chorus
(*Music by* H. L. Heartz.)

"As the Prince Waked the Princess" (Duet)
M. Parker, S. Hawkins
(*Music by* H. L. Heartz.)

"The Family Ghost" (Trio)
Y. Wallace, C. Harvey, F. Lalor
(*Music by* H. L. Heartz.)

"Psyche" (Song)
S. Hawkins
(*Music by* Edward W. Corliss.)

"Champagne and Terrapin, Vision Darling!" (Finale)
Tutti
(*Music by* H. L. Heartz.)

ACT 2

"Where Jasmine Flowers Are Twining" (Opening)
M. Parker, Chorus
(*Music by* Edward W. Corliss.)

"Reggie's Family Tree" (Quartette)
F. Lalor, C. Harvey, P. Edwardes, Y. Wallace
(*Music by* H. L. Heartz.)

"Love Is Just the Same"[103] (Octette Song and Dance)
Officers of the S.S. "Gnat", Rainbow Sisters
(*Music by* H. L. Heartz.)

"Lovers' Lane"[104] (Song)
S. Hawkins
(*Music by* H. L. Heartz.)

---

[96]No New York program available; the Dramatic Mirror indicates the show is "bountifully supplied with musical numbers, including popular songs and many choruses."

[97]Played a return engagement 23 August 1902 at the Grand Opera House for 9 performances. Later toured under the auspices of B.C. Whitney as THE SHOW GIRL, or, The Magic Cap, with the following published interpolations:

"Nellie Kelly"
(*Music by* Harry I. MacConnell. *Lyrics by* Sid H. Forrester.)

"Come Down Mister Man in the Moon"
(*Music by* Harry I. MacConnell. *Lyrics by* Sid H. Forrester.)

"I'm Crazy to Go on the Stage"
(*Music by* Gus Edwards. *Lyrics by* Will H. Cobb.)

"Tippecanoe"
(*Music by* Egbert Van Alstyne. *Lyrics by* Harry Williams.)

"In Zanzibar"
(*Music by* Gus Edwards. *Lyrics by* Will H. Cobb.)

"Dolly Dimple" Song
(*Music and Lyrics by* Dustin and Haines.)

"Seminole"
(*Music by* Egbert Van Alstyne. *Lyrics by* Harry Williams.)

[98]Renamed Dionysius Fly for subsequent tour.

[99]Interpolation also performed, as per opening night program:

"(Be) My Little Apple Dumplin', Do"
(*Music by* John W. Bratton. *Lyrics by* Paul West.)

Added for subsequent tour to Act 2, after "Where Jasmine Flowers Are Twining":

"Susie Anna" (Song)
Y. Wallace, R. L. Dailey, Chorus

[100]Replaced for subsequent tour by:

"(In) Spotless Town" (interpolation)
F. Lalor
(*Music by* Jean Schwartz. *Lyrics by* William Jerome.)

[101]Dropped for subsequent tour.

[102]Replaced for subsequent tour by:

"Waltz Me Down the Alley, Sally" (Song)
Anna McNabb, Neil McNeil {Jhonnie Jhones}

[103]Dropped for subsequent tour.

[104]Replaced for subsequent tour by:

"The Lily and the Dew" (Song)
David Lythgoe {Armor}, Quartette
(*Music and Lyrics by* C. E. Billings and Karl L. Horchus.)

"Advice"[105] (Song)
C. Harvey
(*Music by* H. L. Heartz.)
"In Gay Japan"[106] (Duet)
F. Lalor, P. Edwardes
(*Music by* M. W. Daniels.)
"The Fates"[107] (Processional March)
Omnes
(*Music by* H. L. Heartz.)
"Adeline"[108] (Song and Dance)
C. Guyer, R. L. Dailey, M. Hilton
(*Music by* Edward W. Corliss.)
"One That He Loves Best" (March Song and Chorus)
S. Hawkins, Men
(*Music by* Edward W. Corliss.)
"Katrina" (Waltz Song and Chorus)
C. Hutchinson, Chorus
(*Music by* Edward W. Corliss.)
"A Rose and a Lily"[109] (Finale)
S. Hawkins, M. Parker
(*Music by* Edward W. Corliss.)

1902.16 THE WILD ROSE

A Musical Comedy in Two Acts. Book (and lyrics) by Harry B. Smith and George V. Hobart[110]. Music by Ludwig Engländer. Staged by George W. Lederer. Dances arranged by Adolph Neuberger. Settings by D. Frank Dodge. Costumes by Caroline Seidle. Musical director, Frederic Solomon. Produced by George W. Lederer. Opened 5 May 1902 at the Knickerbocker Theatre and closed 30 August 1902 after 136 performances

CAST: *Paracelsus Noodles*, formerly a subject for a traveling hypnotist, now in business for himself: EDDIE FOY. *Mahomet*, a gypsy lothario: ALBERT HART. *Victor Hugo de Brie*, a novelist who lives his novels: JUNIE McCREE. *Rudolph von Walden*, lieutenant of hussars: David Lythgoe. *Count von Lahn*, colonel of Uhlans: William Wallace Black. *Major Hauptmann*: Richard Lambert. *Aristotle*, a old gypsy who dabbles in science: E. H. O'Connor. *Scipio*, leader of a trained bear: William Wallace Black. *Lieutenant Henri St. Bris*, who stutters a little: Louis Kelso. *Lieutenant Pierre de Rastignac*, devoted to the fair sex: Charles Hooker. *Lieutenant Marcel de Talleyrand-Perigord*, a duellist: David Bennett. *Lieutenant Franz von Richter*: Henry Miller. *Lieutenant Leopold*: Charles Morton. *Lieutenant Conrad*: V. H. Lee. *Lieutenant Walther*: Averell Harris. *Rose Romany*, daughter of Count von Lahn, brought up by gypsies as Mirabel's daughter: IRENE BENTLEY. *Vera von Lahn*, Mirabel's daughter, brought up as the daughter of Count von Lahn, colonel of Uhlans, in love with Victor: MARIE CAHILL. *Lieutenant Gaston Gardennes*: MARGUERITE CLARK. *Mirabel*: CARRIE E. PERKINS. *Vashti*: Evelyn Florence [Nesbit]. *Rafael*: Ida Gabrielle. *Beppo*: Helga Howard. *Rosalie*: Mollie Sherwood. *"Baby"*: George Ali. *Fritz*: Archie Guerin. *Lieutenant Goetz*: Viola Carlstedt. *Lieutenant Drachenfels*: Mai Walker. *Lieutenant Bourbon*: Louise DeRigney. *Lieutenant Charlevoix*: Elba Kenny.

Parisian Actresses: *Eve Bonheur*: Madge Marston. *Michelline*: Neva Aymer. *Diane D'Ivry*: Madge Adae. *Petite Singe*: Mazie Follette. *Germinie*: Belva Don Kersley. *Philomele*: Elsie Ferguson. *La Radieuse*: Madge Brooks. *La Boulotte*: Marion Alexander. *Rigolette*: Maida Van Buren. *La Rouleuse*: Nina Randall. *Fanchonette*: Irene Bishop. *La Joyeuse*: Ethel Jewett. *Cigale*, Danseuse: Ma Belle Davis. *Waitresses (4)*: *Gretchen*: Teddie DuCoe. *Lisa*: Minna Blackman. *Barbara*: Hazel Manchester. *Lena*: Theresa Barron.

Act 1: Gypsy Camp on the banks of the Rhine, near Strassburg, Germany.

Act 2: Cafe Michele, Strassburg.

MUSICAL NUMBERS[111]
"Cupid Is the Captain"
I. Bentley
(*Lyrics by* Harry B. Smith.)
"The Soldier's Story"
"Love's Young Dream" (Waltz Song)
"The Gipsy's Wedding Song"
"I Sing a Little Tenor"
"The Land That's Far Away"
E. Foy
(*Music by* Harry Linton. *Lyrics by* John Gilroy.)
"They Were All Doing the Same" (Act 2)
E. Foy
(*Music and Lyrics by* Ren Shields.)
"Nancy Brown" (A Bucolic Wail) (Act 2)
M. Cahill
(*Music and Lyrics by* Clifton Crawford.)
"My Little Gypsy Maid" (The Little Gypsy Maid) (Act 1)
I. Bentley
(*Music by* Will Marion Cook. *Lyrics by* Harry B. Smith and Cecil Mack.)
"What Would You Be A-Doing"
I. Bentley
(*Music by* Will Marion Cook. *Lyrics by* Harry B. Smith and Cecil Mack.)
"She Did It All Herself"
I. Bentley
(*Music by* Will Marion Cook. *Lyrics by* Harry B. Smith and Cecil Mack.)
"It Must Have Been Svengali in Disguise"
E. Foy
(*Music by* Harry Von Tilzer. *Lyrics by* Vincent Bryan.)
"Smiles, Smiles, Smiles"
A. Hart
(*Music and Lyrics by* William H. Penn.)
"Those Things Cannot Be Explained"
(*Music by* Ben Jerome. *Lyrics by* Junie McCree.)
"The World of a Star"
(*Music by* Melville Ellis. *Lyrics by* George V. Hobart.)
"I'm Unlucky"[112] (A Most Unlucky Man)
(*Music by* Jean Schwartz. *Lyrics by* William Jerome.)

1902.17 RUDOLPH AND ADOLPH

A Farcical Melange (Farce Comedy) in Three Acts. Play by Charles Newman [George H. Broadhurst]. Produced by Broadhurst and Currie. Opened 5 May 1902 at the Metropolis Theatre and closed 10 May 1902 after 8 performances.

CAST: *Rudolph Dinkelspiel*: DAN MASON. *Adolph Dinkelspiel*: CHARLES A. MASON. *Jack Marden*: LEW H. NEWCOMB. *Isidore Hinkleheimer*: Robert Mack. *The Gasman*: Thomas Williamson. *The Janitor*: Thomas Teetzel. *The Expressman*: Frank Welderhoff. *Anna Gilbert*: Jessie Mae Hall. *Mrs. Rudolph Dinkelspiel*: CLARA REYNOLDS SMITH. *Mrs. Adolph Dinkelspiel*: GLORIA ALONZO. *Stella Comstock*: BEATRICE McKENZIE. *Rosalind McGovern*: Nellie Maskell. *Flo*: Anita Lawrence. *Tessie Brown, Jessie Brown*: SISTERS LAWRENCE.

Acts 1 and 2: Home of Dinkelspiel.

Act 3: Adolph's dress-designing establishment.

MUSICAL NUMBERS[113]
"The Melody of Parodies"
D. Mason, C. A. Mason
Shaving Duet
D. Mason, C. A. Mason
Popular Song Medley
L. H. Newcomb, B. McKenzie
Acrobatic Dance Specialty
Lawrence Sisters
Electric Parasol Dance (Specialty)
Lawrence Sister

1902.18 KING DODO

A Comedy-Opera in Three Acts. Book and lyrics by Frank Pixley. Music by Gustav Luders. Produced under the direction of (staged by) Charles H. Jones. Settings by Walter Burridge. Costumes by Fritz Schultz, Voeglin,

105 Dropped for subsequent tour.
106 Dropped for subsequent tour.
107 Dropped for subsequent tour.
108 Dropped for subsequent tour.
109 Dropped for subsequent tour.
110 According to Eddie Foy's biographer, the libretto was adapted from a German story "The Bohemian Girl." (Eddie Foy, a biography of the early stage comedian, by Armond Fields, McFarland & Company, Inc., Jefferson, North Carolina, 1999).
111 No songs listed in programs. List prepared from published sheet music, not in performance order.

112 Added after New York opening.
113 No New York program available.

Mme. Freisinger. Musical director, Frank N. Darling. Produced by Daniel Frohman in arrangement with Henry W. Savage. Opened 12 May 1902 at Daly's Theatre and closed 5 July 1902 after 64 performances.[114]

CAST: *King Dodo*, a ruler by divine right only: RAYMOND HITCHCOCK. *Pedro*, court chamberlain: ARTHUR DEAGON. *Dr. Fizz*, court physician: EUGENE O'ROURKE. *Mudge*, court historian: Charles W. Meyer. *Sancho*, an innkeeper: Albert Juhre. *Bonilla*, Prime Minister to Queen Lili: William Corliss. *Lo Basswood*, a sign of the times: Frederick Meek. *Lopez*, a soldier: William J. Wilson. *Citizens (4)*: *Diego*: John Barry. *Jose*: Lawrence Wilbur. *Unio*: Ray Aldrich. *Marco*: Madge Burpee. *Queen Lili*, ruler of the Spoopjus: GRETA RISLEY. *Angela*, the king's ward, bethrothed to Piola: MARGARET McKINNEY. *Piola*, soldier of fortune: CHERIDAH SIMPSON. *Annette*, daughter of Sancho: GERTRUDE QUINLAN. *Poursuivant*: Florence Willey. *Heralds (2)*: Linda DaCosta, Hermione Besserer. *Citizens, Soldiers, Guards, etc.*

Act 1: Exterior of King Dodo's Palace in Dodo Land.

Act 2: Gardens fronting Queen Lili's Palace in Spoopju Land.

Act 3: The same. Moonlight.

ACT 1[115]

"Merrily, Cheerily" (Opening Chorus)

"Joy Rules the Day" (Solo and Chorus)
G. Quinlan

"Look in the Book and See" (Solo and Chorus)
C. W. Meyer

"I'll Do or Die" (Solo and Chorus)
C. Simpson

"The Eminent Dr. Fizz" (Solo and Chorus)
E. O'Rourke

"On This Festal Day"
Chorus

"A Jolly Old Potentate" (Solo and Chorus)
R. Hitchcock

"When You Are Mine" (Solo)
A. Deagon

"Two Hearts Made One" (Duet)
C. Simpson, M. McKinney

"The Miller's Cats" (Cats' Quartette)
C. Simpson, M. McKinney, G. Quinlan, A. Deagon

"Old Father Time" (Solo and Chorus)
C. Simpson

"In Lands Unknown" (Quintette)
C. Simpson, G. Quinlan, M. McKinney, A. Deagon, E. O'Rourke

"Let's Away" (Solo and Chorus)
C. Simpson

"Behold the Call to Arms" (Finale)

ACT 2

"Gently the Breeze of Summer" (Opening Chorus)

"For Love I Live Alone" (Solo and Chorus)
G. Risley

"Diana" (Solo and Chorus)
M. McKinney

"I'll Shut My Eyes (and Think It's You)" (Duet)
G. Quinlan, A. Deagon

"Claim Thou Thine Own" (Solo)
G. Risley

"The Lad Who Leads" (Solo and Chorus)
C. Simpson

"The Tale of a Bumble-Bee" (Duet and Chorus)
R. Hitchcock, G. Quinlan

"Let Music Sound"
Chorus

Ensemble and Finale

ACT 3

"We Are Conspirators" (Opening Chorus)

"Serenade"
C. Simpson, Chorus

"They Gave Me a Medal For That" (Solo and Chorus)
R. Hitchcock

Ensemble and Finale

---

114 Played a return engagement 4 May 1903 at the Grand Opera House for 8 performances.

115 A 1904 national tour under the auspices of Henry Savage, starring Richard Golden as King Dodo, featured a revised score, including the following songs: ""Star of My Life," "Troubadours," "In the Spring," and Romping Chorus.

1902–1903 SEASON

Blanche Ring in JEWEL OF ASIA (Photo: Schloss, 1903)
Museum of the City of New York

1902–1903 SEASON

1902.19 A CHINESE HONEYMOON

The English Musical Comedy in Two Acts. Book and lyrics by George Dance. Music by Howard Talbot. American production under the direction of (staged by) Gerald Coventry. Settings by D. Frank Dodge. Costumes by Caroline Seidle[1]. Electrical effects by Joseph C. Menchen. Orchestra under the direction of Gustav Kerker. Orchestrations by Gustave Kerker. Produced by Sam S. Shubert and (Sam) Nixon and (J. F.) Zimmerman. Opened 2 June 1902 at the Casino Theatre and closed 25 April 1903 after 364 performances.

CAST: *Mr. Samuel Pineapple*: THOMAS Q. SEABROOKE. *Hang Chow*, Emperor of Ylang-Ylang: EDWIN STEVENS. *Chippie Chop*, Lord Chancellor: WILLIAM BURRESS. *Hi Lung*, Lord High Admiral: WILLIAM PRUETTE. *Tom Hatherton*: VAN RENSELAER WHEELER. *Mrs. Pineapple*: ADELE RITCHIE. *Mrs. Pineapple's Bridesmaids (9)*: *Florrie*: Aline Redmond. *Millie*: Pauline Elliott. *Gertie*: Genevieve Whitlock. *Violet*: Aline Potter. *Beatrice*: Helen Dixey. *Margaret*: Mae Fellon. *Frances*: Sylvia Lisle. *Gwendolin*: Nonie Dore. *Nettie*: Adelaide Phillips. *Genevieve*: Mabel Gribbon. *Soo Soo*, the Emperor's niece: AMELIA F. STONE. *Yen Yen, Sing Sing*, Soo Soo's maids of honor: Nella Webb, Edith Barr. *Mi Mi*, a waitress: Aimee Angeles. *Mrs Brown*, the official mother-in-law: MRS. ANNIE YEAMANS. *Fi Fi*, waitess at the hotel: KATIE BARRY. *Chinese Maidens, Tea Girls, Chinamen, Sailors, Courtiers, etc.*

The action takes place in China at the present time.

Act 1: The Gardens of the Hotel at Ylang-Ylang.

Act 2: Room in the Emperor's palace.

ACT 1[2]

"In Ylang-Ylang" (Opening Chorus)
Ensemble

"Roly-Poly"
W. Pruette

"A Paper Fan"
A. F. Stone

"The Emperor Hang Chow"
H .W. Tredenick

"A Chinese Honeymoon"
T. Q. Seabrooke, A. Ritchie

"The à la Girl"
A. Ritchie

"Nursery Rhymes" (Sextette)
N. Webb, A. Yeamans, K. Barry, H . W. Tredenick, T. Q. Seabrooke, V. R. Wheeler
(*Music by* Jean Schwartz. *Lyrics by* William Jerome.)

"The Twiddley Bits"
K. Barry
(*Music by* Ernie Woodville. *Lyrics by* George Dance and H. Adams.)

"A Royal Honeymoon" (Finale)
Ensemble

ACT 2

"With Weary Hearts" (Opening Chorus)

"I Want to Be a Lidy"[3]
K. Barry
(*Music by* George Dee.)

"Dolly with a Dimple on Her Chin"[4]
A. Ritchie
(*Music by* Ivan Caryll. *Lyrics by* Alfred Murray.)

"Welcome, Official Mother-in-Law"
Chorus

"Tidbits from the Plays"
A. Angeles, W. Pruette

"Martha Spanks the Grand Pianner"[5]
K. Barry

"He Is the Bridegroom" (Finale)

1902.20 THE CHAPERONS

Frank L. Perley's Comedians in a Musical Comedy in Two Acts. Book and lyrics by Frederic Ranken. Music and lyrics by Isidore Witmark. Orchestra under the direction of Max Hirschfeld. Produced under the stage direction of George W. Lederer. Produced by Frank L. Perley. Opened 5 June 1902 at the New York Theatre, moved 30 June 1902 to the Cherry Blossom Grove (atop the New York Theatre) and closed 26 July 1902 after 60 performances.

CAST: *Adam Hogg*, a pork packer of Cincinnati and President of the International Society for the Investigation and Suppression of Vice: HARRY CONOR. *Augustus*, his valet: George K. Henery. *Algernon O'Shaunessy*, studying rapid transit in Paris: WALTER JONES. *Signor Ricardo Bassini*, proprietor of a stranded Opera Company: JOSEPH C. MIRON. *Schnitzel*, a bill poster: Edd Redway. *Tom Schuyler*, an American student of vocal music at the Paris Conservatory: ALBERT FARRINGTON. *Student friends of Tom (4)*: *Pierre*: D. G. Ruthven. *Paul*: E. H. Randall. *Philip*: Jake Weilby. *Jacques*: T. H. Burton. *Francois*, a head waiter: Carl Hartberg. *Amaranthe Dedincourt*, managing director of the English and Continental Order of Trained Chaperons: TRIXIE FRIGANZA. *Phrosia*, an admirer of Old Sleuth: EVA TANGUAY. *Violet Smilax*, a ward of Adam Hogg, and masquerading as Caraola in the Paris Conservatory of Chaperons: NELLIE FOLLIS. *Hortense*, prima donna contralto in Bassini's Company: MAY BOLEY. *Jacqueline*, prima donna soprano in Bassini's Company: WINIFRED FLORENCE.

Show Girls in Bassini's Opera Company (8): *Serpolette*: Katherin Coll. *Antoinette*: Sybil Clifton. *Jeanette*: Lucille Egan. *Genevieve*: Maude Wycherly. *Mignonette*: Lillian

---

[1]Miss Ritchie's costumes designed and made by Lord & Taylor.

[2]The English vocal score (Hopwood & Crew Ltd., London, 1901) contains many songs not used in the American production. "Nursery Rhymes" acquired altogther new music and lyrics for America. Added after opening to Act 1, after "A Paper Fan":

"Could I But Tell You"
V. R. Wheeler

Which was replaced late in the subsequent tour by:

"I Knew At First Sight That I Loved You"
Benjamin Howard {Tom Hatterton}

Added during the run to Act 2, before "Welcome, Official Mother-in-Law":

"Mister Dooley" (introduced in THE DEFENDER)
T. Q. Seabrooke
(*Music by* Jean Schwartz. *Lyrics by* William Jerome.)

Added for subsequent tour to Act 1, after "Mister Dooley":

"The Old Oak Tree and the Twining Vine"
Miss Claude, W. H. Clarke

Added during the New York to Act 2, after "I Want to Be a Lidy":

"Perhaps"
A. F. Stone, V. R. Wheeler
(*Music and Lyrics by* Melville Ellis.)

Added to the production as per publised sheet music:

"Could You Be True to Eyes of Blue If You Looked into Eyes of Brown?"
V. R. Wheeler
(*Music by* Leo Edwards. *Lyrics by* Will D. Cobb.)

"Oolong Li" (added for tour, 1904)
(*Music by* Edward James Howe, Jr. *Lyrics by* Joseph E. Miller.)

"Sunlight and Shadow"
Catherine Cooper
(*Music by* Louis Tocaban. *Lyrics by* Marc Sylvan.)

[3]On subsequent tour, listed in programs as "I Want to Be a Loidy."

[4]Replaced after opening by:

"The Leader of Frocks and Frills"
A. Ritchie
(*Music by* Melville Ellis. *Lyrics by* Robert B. Smith.)
Which was later replaced by:

"My Little Hong Kong Baby"
A. Ritchie
(*Music by* John W. Bratton. *Lyrics by* Paul West.)
Which was replaced late in the tour by:

"Roses Red and White"
M. DeSousa, B. Howard
(*Lyrics by* Harry Greenbank.)

[5]Dropped for subsequent tour.

Germaine. *Cigarette*: Grace Cornish. *Madelin*: Emily Fulton. *Yvette*: Hattie Forsythe. *Charlotte*, a flower girl: Sadie Harris. *Edward, Jack*, Eton boys: Geralda Malone, Mazoa Bradcome.

Chorus Girls in Bassini's Opera Company: *Pinzonette*: Mae Stebbins. *Caromella*: Sophia Williams. *Suzanola*: Nina Gillet. *Jacquimot*: Geraldine Cook. *Fanchon*: Elsie Baird. *Mimi*: Lillie DeVere. *Mignon*: Emma King. *Fantine*: Anna Bell Gordon. *Marie*: Ruby Paine. *Valerie*: Isabell Franklin. *Annette*: Sallie Fisher. *Fifi*: Margaret Striker. *Toto*: Florence Striker. *Claire*: Marie Striker.

Act 1: Scene in Latin Quarter, Paris.

Act 2: Court yard of Alexandria Hotel, Alexandra, Egypt.

ACT 1[6]

"Vive la Bohemia" (Opening Chorus)

"(When I Sang) My Low C"
J. C. Miron, Chorus

"In My Official Capacity"
H. Conor, M. Boley, W. Florence

"Flowers"
T. Friganza

"The Little Girl That Couldn't Say No" (The Little Maid That Couldn't Say No)
N. Follis

"Talk, Talk, Talk"
W. Jones, E. Tanguay, E. Eddway

"We're All Good Fellows"
A. Farrington, Male Chorus
(*Lyrics by* Frederic Ranken.)

"The Bois de Boulogne"
H. Conor, W. Florence, M. Boley, Chorus

"To Stop a Marriage" (To Stop This Marriage)(Finale)

ACT 2

"Oh, Love, Airy Like, Fairy Like"
Mandolin Club

"Egypt Land" (Oriental Dance)
M. Stebbins, Chorus

"The Comic Opera Bandits"[7]
J. C. Miron, Chorus

"The Man Behind the Scenes"
H. Conor, J. C. Miron, T. Friganza

"Somehow It Made Him Think of Home"[8]
W. Jones

"He Winked at Me"
N. Follis, Chorus

"My Sambo" (Darky Love Song and Dance)
E. Tanguay, Chorus
(*Lyrics by* Isidore Witmark.)

"(Just) A Gentle Touch"
H. Conor, T. Friganza

"Just a Gentle Buck" (Dance)
W. Jones, E. Redway

Finale

[6]Published piano vocal score, pre-New York, is in Three Acts (M. Witmark & Sons, New York, 1901), which does not credit Witmark with lyrics. Published separately from the vocal score, most likely added:

"It Seems Like Yesterday," "Love In a Palace is Better" (Duet), "You Musn't Blame the Copper, Blame the Cook," "The Chaperon," "A Dream of a By-Gone Day" (Duet), "Happy When We Eat," "Millinery Mary."

Interpolated as per published sheet music:

"Blooming Lize"
(*Music by* Ben M. Jerome. *Lyrics by* Matt C. Woodward.)

[7]Novelty introducing strains from favorite comic operas.

[8]Also known as "Somehow It Made Me Think of Home."

1902.21

THE DEFENDER

A Yachtical Musical Extravaganza in Three Acts. Words (book, lyrics) by Allen Lowe. Music by Charles Dennée. Scenery by D. Frank Dodge. Staged by Frank Smithson. Settings by D. Frank Dodge. Costumes designed by Archie Gunn. Orchestra under the direction of George P. Towle. Produced by A. H. Chamberlyn. Opened 3 July 1902 at the Herald Square Theatre and closed 23 August 1902 after 60 performances.

CAST: *Sir Thomas Ceylon Teaton*, who longs to lift the cup: HARRY DAVENPORT. *Mr. Tom Pinkson*, the Copper King: GEORGE ALISON. *Charles Dare*, Lord Hautboys, who wants an American girl, but not her money: RICHIE LING. *Mr. Ivory D. Queers* (Good gracious , have you used Queer's Soap?): GILBERT CLAYTON. *Han Kuff*, bo'sun on Sir Thomas yacht, the *Hibernia*: Gordon Tomkins. *Snip*, cabin boy: Peggy Edwardes. *Pinkie Winkerton*, a detective in a measure: CHARLES WAYNE. *Sam Keno*, a fallen star: ALEXANDER CLARK. *Mrs. Jack Orchard*, with a strong interest in anything new—and old—that can resemble a fad: EMMA CARUS. *Miss Hilda Shipton*: SANDOL MILLIKEN. *Mrs. Everly Chase*, "the dear girls must be provided for": Maym Kelso. *"The dear girls" (3)*: *Winsome*: Edith Eldridge. *Caprice*: Grace Spencer. *Modeste*: Aimee Ashmore. *Millie Canvass*, but she 'as 'opes: BLANCHE RING. *Jellie Canvass*, queen of the ring: PAULA EDWARDES.

Yachting Editors: Misses Wayne, Davis, Francis, Warren, Howe, Staley, Thornton, Powers, Lorraine. *Citizens*: Misses Carlyle, Weir, Hunt, Faulkner, Denning, Miller, Van Ness, Scott. *Boating Boys*: Misses Bremont, Bird, Brown, Anderson, Parks, L. Pope, Murray, Averell. *Yachting Girls*: Misses Salvatore, Hasty, Conquest, Lansing, West, Mathews, J. Cook. *Dancers*: Misses Telford, K. Pope, Daggert, E. Cook. *Conspirators*: Harry Murray, Joe Worthington, Norman Lillie, Messrs. Edwardes, Robinson, McFadden, Eaton, Brooks. *Seamen*: Messrs. Black, Parr, Brooks, Lee, Willing, Hutton, Cuttle, Kent, Meehan, Williams, Walsh.

Time: Past, present or future.

Act 1: Landing at Yacht Club.

Act 2: Deck of the *"Hibernia,"* by moonlight,

Act 3: Garden at Newport.

ACT 1[9]

Opening Chorus (The Yachting King)

"Hail to the Baronet"

"Lift the Cup"
H. Davenport

"Lighthouse and the Boat"
R. Ling

"Whiskerettes"[10]
A. Clark

"Queens of Society"
E. Carus

"Welcome, Jellie Canvass"
Chorus

"Sammie"[11]
P. Edwardes

"Heart-to-Heart Talks" (Duet)
P. Edwardes, A. Clark

Finale

[9]Running order of songs revised after opening and for tour. Added for subsequent tour:

"Satisfied with Life" (prior to Act 1 Finale)
Dan McAvoy {Sam Keno}

[10]Replaced after opening by:

"Houp-la"
P. Edwardes
Replaced for subsequent tour by:

"Queen of the Circus Ring"
Edna Floyd {Jellie Canvas}

[11]Dropped after opening. Most likely the same song as "Sammy," music by Edward Hutchison, lyrics by James O'Dea, a popular song later interpolated with success by Grace Kimball, then Lotta Faust into THE WIZARD OF OZ.

ACT 2[12]

Barcarole (The Moon Shines Bright)
Male Chorus

"Vesper Bells"
M. Thornton

"Cup of Tea"[13]
H. Davenport

"Conspirators' Chorus"
(Consirators)

"Love Is the Queen of the Sea" (Waltz Song)
E. Eldridge

"I'll Be Your Rainbow"[14]
E. Carus

"Love Is Queen of the Sea"[15] (Waltz Song)
E. Eldridge

"(Naughty) Little Fly" (Duet)
S. Milliken, H. Davenport

"Good Night"
P. Edwardes

"Ocean's Fond Caress"[16] (Duet)
E. Eldridge, R. Ling

Superstition Trio[17]
M. Kelso, A. Clark, F. Smithson

"Pinky, Panky Poo" (Duet)
B. Ring, C. Wayne
(*Music and Lyrics by* Andy Louis.)

"The Boys Before the Mast" (March Finale)

ACT 3

"In the Good Old Summertime" (Song and Chorus)
B. Ring
(*Music by* George Evans. *Lyrics by* Ren Shields.)

"Pretty New England Pink"[18]
E. Eldridge

Vaudeville Duet[19]
P. Edwardes, A. Clark

"Anglo-Saxons of To-day"
R. Ling

Gavotte (Sound the Bell) and Finale

JAPAN BY NIGHT/THE MIKADO, or The Town of Titipu

1902.22

A Double Bill of a Japanese Vaudeville Novelty in Three Acts and a Revival of the Comic Opera in Two Acts[20], Libretto by William S. Gilbert. Music by Arthur Sullivan. Opera staged by Milton Aborn. Ladies' orchestra (for vaudeville) conducted by Theodore Deventhal. Produced by Messrs. Kushibiki and Arai. Opened 7 July 1902 at the Madison Square Roof Garden and closed 13 September 1902 after 70 performances.

Vaudeville: Lillian Hollis, Frances Lamar, Aeolian Four, Kudara's Trained Dogs, T. Akagi, Y. Kogema, Otokichi, Kataro, Tokimtasse.

CAST for THE MIKADO: *The Mikado of Japan*: NICK BURNHAM. *Nanki-Poo*, his son: GRAFTON BAKER. *Ko-Ko*, Lord High Executioner of Titipu: FRED FREAR. *Pooh-Bah*, Lord High Everything Else: WILLIAM SCHUSTER. *Pish-Tush*, a Noble Lord: JOHN HENDRICKS. *Three Sisters, Wards of Ko-Ko*: *Yum-Yum*: GRACE MEYERS. *Pitti-Sing*: URSULA MARCH. *Peep-Bo*: FLORENCE LITTLE. *Katisha*: HATTIE ARNOLD.

ACT 1

Colonel Goettings (March)
(*Music by* White.)

Overture to "Fra Diavolo"
(*Music by* Daniel François Esprit Auber.)

Kudara's Japanese Trained Dogs, the only dogs of their kind in America

"Birds of Paradise" (Waltz)
(*Music by* Henri Kling.)

Aeolian Four

"American (Patrol)"
(*Music by* F. W. Meacham.)

ACT 2

"American Volunteers" (March)
(*Music by* Tobain.)

T. Akagi and Y. Kogema, graduates from the fencing school at Tokio, in a bout with the Shinai, the Japanese fencing sword.

KING DODO Selections
(*Music by* Frank Pixley.)

"When Eyes Meet Eyes" (Vocal Solo)
L. Hollis

"Darkies' Jubilee" (Descriptive Selection)
(*Music by* Turner.)

"Theodora" (Gavotte)
(*Music by* Hurdley.)

ACT 3

"Admiral" (March)
(*Music by* Friedman.)

"Tell Me" (Vocal Solo)
F. Lamar

Von Tilzer Medley Overture

Otokichi and Kataro (double barrel kicking)

Tokimtasse (Wire walker)

Finale (Galop)

SALLY IN OUR ALLEY

1902.23

A Musical Comedy in Two Acts. Book and lyrics by George V. Hobart. Music by Ludwig Engländer. Personally staged by George W. Lederer. Settings by D. Frank Dodge and Edward G. Unitt. Costumes designed by Mme. Caroline F. Siedle. Musical director, Max Hirschfield. Produced by George W. Lederer. Opened 29 August 1902 at the Broadway Theatre and closed 25 October 1902 after 68 performances; re-opened 24 November 1902 at the New York Theatre and closed 13 December 1902 after an additional 24 performances. Total: 92 performances[21].

---

[12]Added after opening before Finale, Act 2:
"The Man Who Hypnotized McCarthy"
A. Clark

[13]Dropped after opening.

[14]Replaced for subsequent tour by:
"Shine On, Silvery Moon"
Lizzie B. Raymond {Mrs. Jack Orchard}

[15]Dropped after opening.

[16]Dropped after opening.

[17]Dropped after opening.

[18]Replaced after opening by:
"Jack o' Lantern Man"
E. Carus
Replaced for subsequent tour by:
"Down Where the Congo Flows"
L. B. Raymond, Chorus

[19]Replaced for subseequent tour by:
"Sally, Hot Tamale Alley"
D. McAvoy

[20]THE MIKADO was added to JAPAN BY NIGHT in the second week of the run with a shortened vaudeville program. THE MIKADO was first presented in New York 20 July, 10-29 August 1885 at the Union Square and People's Theatres for 22 performances. First authorized production presented 19 August 1885 at the Fifth Avenue Theatre by Richard D'Oyly Carte for 250 performances. For Synopsis of Scenes and Musical Numbers, see 19 August 1885 D'Oyly Carte production.

[21]Also played 10 November 1902 at the Harlem Opera House for 8 performances.

CAST: *Sally*, named after the alley by her father: MARIE CAHILL. *Izzy*, her father and proprietor of the Heterogeneous Emporium: DAN McAVOY. *Captain Dan O'Reilly*, Izzy's steadfast friend and counsellor: RICHARD F. CARROLL. *Louis Henri Fleuret*, an artist, in love with Sally: JULIUS STEGER. *Damon Marigold*, rich and retired, but not retiring: JOSEPH W. HERBERT. *Calanthe Marigold*, wife of the rich and retired, but tireless: CATHERINE LEWIS. *Virginia Marigold*. daughter of the rich and retired, but industrious: MARGARET MARSTON. *Cassandra*, maid of the rich and retired, but industrious: GEORGIA CAINE. *Leopold*, Izzy's infant industry, nicknamed "Swifty": LOUIS WESLEY. *Little Norah Ryan*, the apple that fits the eye of "Swifty": Georgie Lawrence. *Paul Smith*, poor but not particularly proud of it: HARRY FAIRLEIGH. *Marian Von Beekman, Marcia Von Beekman*, two society girls: Georgia Kelly, Viola Carlstedt. *The Prince of Fezalone*, an Algerian title in search of a Bradstreet bride: Frank Bernard. *Jonathan*, one of Izzy's buyers: Frank Bernard. *Favorel*, a butler: Edward Ellkors.

Friends of Izzy (6): *Wilhelm Shauerbat*: J. T. Chaillee. *Nels Nelsen*: Dan Smith. *Michael Ryan*: James A. Furey. *Aunt Seelah Ryan*: Agnes Wayburn. *John McGuff*: Fred J. Titus. *Terry McCue*: James A. Furey. *Friends of the Marigold family (4)*: *Hon. Doolittle Dunn*: Harry Brown. *Mrs. Doolittle Dunn*: Rita Dean. *Cornelia Pewtertop*: Anna Delaney. *Ponsonby Pewtertop*: May Miller. *Minister Wing Ling Lang*: Fred J. Titus. *The Governor of North Carolina*: Roger DeCoverly. *The Governor of South Carolina*: Ruddy Struck. *General Stonefence*: Wheeler Earl.

Socety Buds: *Miss Rose*: Gertrude Blancke. *Miss Pansy*: Mildred Devere. *Miss Heliotrope*: Ray Gilmore. *Miss Violet*: Reine Davies. *Miss Daffodil*: Dora Cheever. *Miss Daisy*: Ethel Kelly. *Miss Hyacinth*: Minnie Edwards. *Miss Lilly*: Madeline Martin. *Chorus of Shop Girls, Society Girls, Bridesmaids, etc.*

Act 1, Scene 1: A Street in New York near the corner of "Sally's Alley." *Scene 2*: Interior of the Heterogeneous Emporium. (Dodge.)

Act 2: A reception hall in the Fifth Avenue mansion of Damon Marigold. (Unitt.)

MUSICAL NUMBERS[22]

"I Want To Be a Soldier Lady"

"When I Am Yours, Dear" (Duet)
P. Fairleigh, M. Marston

"My Queen of Ping Pong"

"Nora Ryan"

"Whistling Bill"

INTERPOLATIONS

"When the Troupe Comes Back to Town"
M. Cahill
(*Music by* Harry Von Tilzer. *Lyrics by* George Totten Smith.)

"The Girlie with the Baby Stare" (Septette)
(*Music by* William H. Penn. *Lyrics by* Ernest Hanegan.)

"Sally in Our Alley"
(*Music and Lyrics by* Henry Carey.)

"When It's All Goin' Out and Nothin' Comin' In"
(*Music and Lyrics by* Bert A. Williams, George Walker.)

"Under the Bamboo Tree"
M. Cahill
(*Music by* J. Rosamund Johnson. *Lyrics by* Robert Cole.)

"My Matilda"
L. Wesley
(*Music by* William F. Peters. *Lyrics by* Henry Blossom.)

1902.24

THE ROGERS BROTHERS IN HARVARD

A Vaudeville Farce in Two Acts[23]. Book by John J. McNally. Music by Maurice Levi. Lyrics by J. Cheever Goodwin and Ed Gardenier. Staged by Ben Teal. Settings by Ernest Gros. Costumes by F. Richard Anderson. Electrical effects by Harry Bissing. Music director, Maurice Levi. Produced by (Marc) Klaw and (Abraham L.) Erlanger. Opened 1 September 1902 at the Knickerbocker Theatre and closed 25 October 1902 after 63 performances.

CAST: *Milo Kross*: GUS ROGERS. *Christopher Karlstadt Kavenhuller*: MAX ROGERS. *Harry Hart*: William Gould. *Clarence Cholmondeley*: George Honey. *Colonel Hotchkiss*: Eugene Jepson. *Major Gaulle*: LEE HARRISON. *T. Stanislaus McGurk*: PAT ROONEY. *Jem Tip*: Emil Heusel. *Joe O'Rourke*: JAMES CHERRY. *Head Waiter*: M. Cortez. *Boy*: Willie Torpey. *Madame Pélisse*: HATTIE WILLIAMS. *Blanche Reveres*: CLARA PALMER. *Peggy Clip*: EMMA FRANCIS. *Ida Claire*: EDITH ST. CLAIR. *Daisy Sten*: NEVA AYMAR. *Gertie Tell*: Stella Maury. *Clara Stone*: Olive Ulrich. *Ena*: Nettie Uart. *Mena*: Lillian Collins. *Mona*: Julia Eastman. *Mae*: Minnie Woodbury. *Jessie*: Mary Conwell. *Bessie*: Helen Brooks. *Tessie*: Nellie Victoria. *Ray*: PAULINE FREDERICKS. *Fay*: Lily Hart. *Violet*: Nellie Florede. *Gipsy*: Lottie Uart. *Millie*: Lillian Stanford. *Willie*: Kitty Murray. *Myria*: Minerva Courtney.

Boys: Nettie Uart, Lillie Hart, Minnie Woodbury, May Wood, Nellie Victoria, Sue Stuart, Helen Bare, Helen Morrison, Elsie Davis, Edith Rockwell, Lottie Uart, Dorothy Watson. *Girls*: Lillie Collins, Jolly Matthews, Helen Brooks, Della Freese, Julia Eastman, Harriet Burt, Irene Brown, Minerva Courtney, Irna Molyneux, Pauline Fredericks, Esther Marks.

Act 1: The Gardens of Claremont, New York City.

Act 2: Campus at Harvard College, Class Day.

Act 3: Entertainment Hall, Eden Musee, New York City.

ACT 1

"Sporting Girls" (Opening Chorus)
(*Lyrics by* J. Cheever Goodwin.)

"I'm Getting Quite American, Don't You Know" (Song)
G. Honey, Full Chorus
(*Lyrics by* J. Cheever Goodwin.)

"Mary, Be Wary" (Song)
C. Palmer, Full Chorus
(*Lyrics by* Ed. Gardenier.)

"Dream of Love" (Trio)
Rogers Brothers, H. Williams
(*Lyrics by* Vincent Bryan.)

"Ma Starlight Queen"
Rogers Brothers, H. Williams
(*Lyrics by* Ed. Gardenier.)

ACT 2

"College Girls" (Opening Chorus-Class Day)
(*Lyrics by* J. Cheever Goodwin.)

"I'm a Lady"
H. Williams, Full Chorus
(*Lyrics by* Ed. Gardenier.)

Songs
W. Gould

Sayings and Parodies
Rogers Brothers

Rainbow Specialty
C. Palmer, Full Chorus
(*Lyrics by* J. Cheever Goodwin.)

"Pretty Peggy" (Specialty[24])
P. Rooney, E. Francis

"The Troubles of the Reuben and the Maid" (Quartette)
(Trouble Began to Brew)
Rogers Brothers, E. St. Clair, N. Aymar
(*Lyrics by* J. Cheever Goodwin.)

"Dear Old College Days" (Finale)
(*Lyrics by* J. Cheever Goodwin.)

ACT 3

"Round the Town" (Opening Chorus)
(*Lyrics by* J. Cheever Goodwin.)

"Upper Broadway After Dark" (Song)
L. Harrison, Full Chorus
(*Lyrics by* Ed. Gardenier.)

"Linda, Look Out de Windah"
Rogers Brothers, assisted by Chorus
(*Lyrics by* Ed. Gardenier.)

[22]Programs list no Engländer-Hobart songs, only the interpolations. List is prepared from published piano vocal selection.

[23]Billed as their fifth annual tour.

[24]Traditional Irish song and dance "performed with immense success by Pat Rooney" as per published sheet music, for which Rooney takes credit.

1902.25 THE EMERALD ISLE, or The Caves of Carrig-Cleena

A Comic Opera in Two Acts. Libretto by Basil Hood. Music by Arthur Sullivan and Edward German. Staged by R. H. Burnside. Produced by the Jefferson de Angelis Opera Company (Sam S. Shubert, Managing Director). Opened 1 September 1902 at the Herald Square Theatre and closed 18 October 1902 after 50 performances.

CAST: *Professor Bunn*, Shakespearean reciter, character impersonator, etc.: JEFFERSON DeANGELIS. *The Earl of Newtown, K.P.*, Lord Lieutenant of Ireland: CHARLES DUNGAN. *Dr. Fiddle, D.D.*, his private chaplain: F. Stuart Hyatt. *Terence O'Brien*, a young rebel: EDMUND STANLEY. *Pat Murphy*, a fiddler: GERALD GEROME. *Black Dan, Mickie O'Hara*, Irish peasants: Charles Dungan, John Dudley. *Sergeant Pincher, Private Perry*, H M. 11th Regiment of Foot: Frank Belcher, Frederick K. Logan. *The Countess of Newtown*: AMELIA FIELDS. *Lady Rosie Pippin*, her daughter: HELENA FREDERICK. *Molly O'Grady*, a peasant girl: KATE CONDON. *Susan*, Lady Rosie's maid: Edna Burd. *Nora*: Audrey Kingsbury. *Kathleen*: Lois Garneau. *Irish Peasants and Soldiers of 11th Regiment of Foot.*

The action takes place about a hundred years ago.

Act 1: Outside the Lord Lieutenant's country home.

Act 2: The Caves of Carrig Cleena.

ACT 1[25]

"Have ye heard the brave news" (Opening Chorus and Dance)

"My friends!—A Saxon stranger" (Recitative)
E. Stanley

"I'm descended from Brian Boru" (Song)
E. Stanley, Chorus

"Of Viceroys though we've had" (Song)
G. Gerome, Chorus

"If you wish to appear as an Irish type" (Song)
J. DeAngelis, Chorus

"On the heights of Glentann there's no voice" (Trio)
K. Condon, E. Stanley, G. Gerome

"Two is company—Three is none" (Quartette)
H. Frederick, E. Burd, E. Stanley, J. DeAngelis

"I am the Lord Lieutenant" (Entrance of Lord Lieutenant, Countess, Chaplain)

"At an early stage of life" (Song)
C. Dungan, H. Frederick, A. Fields, F. S. Hyatt

"When Alfred's friends their King forsook" (Song)
A. Fields

"Oh setting sun, you bid the world good-bye" (Song)
H. Frederick

"Their courage high, you may defy" (Quintette)
H. Frederick, E. Burd, K. Condon, E. Stanley, J. DeAngelis

"That we're soldiers no doubt you will guess" (Entrance of Soldiers)

"Now this is the song of the Devonshire men" (Song)
F. Belcher, Chorus

"It is past my comprehension" (Entrance of Bunn)

"Many years ago I strode" (Song)
J. DeAngelis, Chorus

"Their fathers fought at Ramillies" (Finale)

ACT 2

"Is there anyone approachin'?" (Opening Chorus)

"Bedad, it's for him that we'll always employ" (Chorus and Dance of the Peasants)

Jig

"Och, the Spalpeen! Let him drown!" (Chorus of Peasants)

"Oh, have you met a man in debt" (Song)
E. Stanley, Chorus

"'Twas in Hyde Park beside the Row" (Duet)
H. Frederick, E. Stanley, Chorus

"I cannot play at love" (Ensemble)

"Oh, the age in which we're living" (Song)
J. DeAngelis

"Sing a rhyme of 'Once upon a time'" (Concerted Piece and Dance)

"Listen! Harken, my lover" (Scena)

"Good-bye, my native town" (Song)
G. Gerome

"I love you ! I love you!" (Duet)
K. Condon, G. Gerome

"There was once a little soldier" (Song)
E. Stanley, Chorus

"With a big shillelagh" (Finale)

[25]Musical numbers not listed in programs. List prepared from English piano vocal score (Chappell & Co. Ltd., London, 1901).

1902.26 CODFISH ARISTOCRACY

A Musical Comedy in Three Acts. Book, music and lyrics by A. H. Woodhull. Opened 1 September 1902 at the Metropolis Theatre and closed 6 September 1902 after 8 performances.[26]

CAST: *Paul Buster*: WILLIAM MITCHELL. *Fred Dove*: JOHN CAIN. *Chuck Bonners*: GEORGE TOPACK. *Alphonse*: George Herbert. *Gaston*: Frank Willing. *Mr. Astorcraven*: Charles Wilson. *Mons. LaFarge*: William Cetti. *Policeman*: Andrew Wilson. *Porter*, Hotel Carlton: Edward H. Clark. *Mrs. Ton Flipps*: James Lee. *Miss Van Tassel*: DELIA STACEY. *Mrs. Paul Buster*: Lillian Tyce. *Mrs. Fred Dove*: ETHEL TILLSON. *Nell Bonners*: LILLIE WASHBURN. *Mlle. Helene*: Jennie Crovini. *Mlle. Fifi*: Edyth Murray. *Madame Trimeaux*, Modiste: EMMA SEIBERT. ——: Beth Nudo. *Suzette*: Hazel Dunham. *Marie*: Sadie Long. *Annette*: Kathryn Leslie. *Aimee*: Laura Waldo. *Blanch*: Amy Haddon. *Julie*: Delia Lee Campbell. *Paula*: Tessie Burns. *Judith*: Viola MacDonald. *Stephanie*: Lillian Langweed. *Honore*: Marie Brenner. *Serpolette*: Angie Dickens. *Frances*: Carrie Montell. *Clarice*: Anna Howard. *Valentine*: Flora Gilmore. *Eloise*: Annie Peters.

1902.27 KING HIGHBALL

A Comic Opera in Two Acts and a Prologue. Libretto by Charles Horwitz. Based on "The Understudy" by Rupert Hughes. Music by Frederick V. Bowers. Staged by Edward E. Rice. Ballets by Carl Marwig. Produced by Edward E. Rice. Opened 6 September 1902 at the New York Theatre and closed 4 October 1902 after 33 performances.

CAST: *King Highball*: CHARLES STURGES. *Blancus Theophilus Edison Dunn*: GEORGE H. CARR. *Diedrich Von Stumph*: WILL H. SLOAN. *Prince Reginald*: Miro Delamotta. *Gaggy*: SYDNEY de GREY. *Booster*: CHARLES GUYER. *Adelina*: LOUISE MOORE. *Dotty*: JEANETTE LOWRIE. *Pansy*: STELLA TRACEY. *Violet*: Blanche Homans. *Imogene*: (Miss) Frances Wilson. *Elicia*: Adele Archer. *Beatrice*: Nina Randall. *Jeanette*: Margaret Knight. *Hortense*: Lou Harlow. *Phyllis*: Maybelle Courtney. *Elaine*: Bertha Blake. *Louella*: Beatrice Hastings. *Cynisca*: Florence Maybe. *Pomponi*: Jennie Thompson. *Thisbe*: Ocia Thompson. *Eliat*: Paula Desmond. *Dors*: Grace Walton. *Stacia*: Esther Brubette. *Ex-Queen Tarantula*: MARIE DRESSLER.

MUSICAL NUMBERS

"Nother High Ball"
S. deGrey

"I'm Lookin' for an Angel"
M. Dressler

"The Girl from Mars"

1902.28 ROBIN HOOD

A Revival of the Comic Opera in Three Acts[27]. Libretto by Harry B. Smith. Music by Reginald DeKoven. Acting manager, Charles R. Bacon. Scenery by Ernest Gros. Costumes by Mme. Freisinger. Director of music, Samuel

[26]No New York program available.

[27]Originally presented in New York 28 September 1891 at the Standard Theatre for 35 performances, returning that season to the Garden Theatre for 42 additional performances. For Synopsis of Scenes and Musical Numbers, see original 1891 production.

L. Studley. Produced by the Bostonians (Henry Clay Barnabee, William H. MacDonald, Proprietors). Opened 8 September 1902 at the Academy of Music and closed 4 October 1902 after 32 performances.

CAST: *Sheriff of Nottingham*: HENRY CLAY BARNABEE. *Little John*: WILLIAM H. MacDONALD. *Robert of Huntington*, afterwards Robin Hood: HAROLD GORDON. *Will Scarlet*: ALLEN C. HINCKLEY. *Alan-a-Dale*: OLIVE CELESTE MOORE. *Friar Tuck*: GEORGE B. FROTHINGHAM. *Guy of Gisborne*: CAMPBELL DONALD. *Dame Durden*: JOSEPHINE BARTLETT. *Annabel*: SABERY D'ORSELLE. *Maid Marian*: GRACE VAN STUDDIFORD.

1902.29

TWIRLY-WHIRLY

The Weber & Fields All-Star Company in a Merry-Go-Round of Fancy and Foolishness (a Musical Comedy and a Burlesque) in Two Whirls, 3 Scenes. Dialogue by Edgar Smith. Music by W. T. Francis and John Stromberg. Lyrics by Edgar Smith and Robert B. Smith. Produced under the stage direction of Julian Mitchell. Settings by John Young. Costumes designed by Will R. Barnes. Musical director, W. T. Francis. Produced by (Joseph L.) Weber and (Lew M.) Fields. Opened 11 September 1902 at the Weber & Fields Music Hall and closed 11 April 1903 after 247 performances.

ACT 1

1902.29

TWIRLY-WHIRLY, a Musical Comedy in Two Acts, 3 Scenes, including I, MARY McPAIN, a Burlesque in One Act[28].

CAST: *Bob Upton*, of Wall Street, endeavoring to boom Texas Oil Stock in Europe: WILLIAM COLLIER. *Buck Winger*, otherwise known as "The King of Vaudeville": PETER F. DAILEY. *Michael Schlaatz, Meyer Ausgaaben*, formerly of New York, but late of the German Army and the unwilling possessors of an airship: JOE WEBER, LEW FIELDS. *Ebeneezer Doolittle* of Chicago, stepfather of Mrs. Stockson Bond and something of a "romeo": CHARLES A. BIGELOW. *Roger McCracken*, bos'un of Mrs. Bond's yacht, *"Runashor"*: JOHN T. KELLY. *Hanki Panki Poo*, a pet monkey: WILL ARCHER. *Walker Tighe*, an actor: WILL ARCHER. *Mrs. Stockson Bond*, a wealthy young American widow, engaged in the world-wide introduction of the game of ping-pong: LILLIAN RUSSELL. *Maud Moraine*, a typical chorus lady: FAY TEMPLETON. *May MacPain* of Butte, Montana, author of "The Pipe Story of Mary MacPain": LOUISE ALLEN. *Lieutenant Connyngtower*, U.S.S. *"Hoboken"*: Bonnie Maginn. *Henri*, a valet: Mabel Barrison. *Pirouetta, Paseula*, dancing girls: Estelle and Gertie Moyer. (*Specialty*: BESSIE CLAYTON.)

Of the Spanish Four Hundred (9): *Don Carrara*: Frankie Bailey. *Don Muskeeta*: Virginia Foltz. *Don Guavajelli*: May McKenzie. *Don Cheroota*: Mabel Lynn. *Donna Vetta*: Ilma Pratt. *Donna Gazabo*: Lillian Harris. *Senora Andante*: May Leslie. *Senora Fricadillo*: Anna Leslie. *Senorita Adagio*: Carrie Bowman. *Toreadors (4)*: *Senor Stabbatatauro*: Annie Revere. *Senor Climafensa*: Carolyn Fostelle. *Senor Dogeaquicca*: Edna Birch. *Senor Runafasti*: Emily Francis. *Senor Spunkiflagga*: Vernie Wadsworth. *Senor Jumpigooda*: Katherine Howland. *Senor Wavaraggi*: Frankie Loeb.

Spanish Students: *Plunkageeta*: Agnes Lynn. *Pikastringa*: Eugeie Bashford. *Tremuloso*: Laura Senac. *Lazilofer*: Grace Heckler. *Wall Street Wizards (5)*: *Reuben Skinner*: Mamie Chapin. *Cortright Lamb*: Elizabeth Young. *Cunningham Goode*: Mattie Chapin. *Waldorf Bragg*: Molly Hoffman. *Cummings Low*: Bena Hoffman. *Lotta Munn*: Anna Miller. *Sue Ayres*: Ethel Jewett. *Villa Atwater*: Gracie Bishop. *Mrs. Parke Ryder*: Peggy Donaldson. *Mrs. Colton Stryker*: Gertrude Taylor. *Nevers Ober*: Eva Allen. *Malden Mayer*: Lillian Diamond. *Fuller Dewar*: Eleanor Kendall. *Jay Mariner*: Eva Merrill. *Will Knott*: May Harris. *Wagner Recker*: Edith Caine. *Stryker Carr*: Jean Hassall. *Tode Holmas*: Ollie Hatfield. *Chase Kidd*: Winnie Siegrist.

Whirl 1, Scene 1: Grounds of Mrs. Stockson Bond's Castle, near Seville. *Scene 2*: Ruin near same.

Whirl 2: Ping Pong Court of Mrs. Stockson Bond's Castle.

ACT 1[29]

"Ping Pong" (Opening Ensemble)
(*Music by* W. T. Francis, John Stromberg. *Lyrics by* Robert B. Smith.)

"Romeo" (Song)
C. A. Bigelow
(*Music by* W. T. Francis. *Lyrics by* Edgar Smith.)

"Strike Out, McCracken"(Song)
J. T. Kelly
(*Music by* W. T. Francis. *Lyrics by* Edgar Smith.)

"In Stage Land" (Duet)
W. Collier, L. Allen
(*Music by* W. T. Francis. *Lyrics by* Edgar Smith.)

"The Long Green"[30] (Song and Ensemble)
L. Russell
(*Music by* W. T. Francis. *Lyrics by* Robert B. Smith.)

"Kit"[31] (Song)
W. Collier
(*Music by* W. T. Francis. *Lyrics by* Edgar Smith.)

Potpourri Ensemble[32]:
P. F. Dailey
"The Vaudeville King"
(*Music by* W. T. Francis. *Lyrics by* Edgar Smith.)
"Susie Woosie"
(*Music by* John Stromberg. *Lyrics by* Edgar Smith.)

"Priscilla" (Dance)
B. Clayton
(*Music by* W. T. Francis.)

ACT 2

Potpourri Ensemble:
F. Templeton

"A Buenna Senorita Am I"
(*Music by* W. T. Francis. *Lyrics by* Edgar Smith.)

"Dream One Dream of Me"
(*Music by* W. T. Francis, John Stromberg. *Lyrics by* Edgar Smith.)

"Tell Us, Jolly Sailors"[33]
J. Weber, L. Fields, P. Dailey, W. Collier, B. Maginn, M. Barrison, Moyer Sisters
(*Music by* W. T. Francis. *Lyrics by* Edgar Smith.)

"After Dinner"[34] (Ensemble)
(*Music by* W. T. Francis. *Lyrics by* Edgar Smith.)

"Come Down, My Evenin' Star" (Song)
L. . Russell
(*Music by* John Stromberg. *Lyrics by* Robert B. Smith.)

"My Intimate Friend" (Song)
F. Templeton
(*Music by* W. T. Francis. *Lyrics by* Wilton Lackaye.)

"Big Pound Cake"[35] (Quartette Song and Dance)
J. Weber, L. Fields, P. Dailey, W. Collier
(*Music and Lyrics by* John T. Kelly.)

Finale

1902.29

HUMMING BIRDS AND ONIONS, a Burlesque in 2 Scenes. Libretto by Edgar Smith. Music by W. T. Francis. Opened 6 November 1902.

HUMMING BIRDS CAST: *Lord Bummy*, an amateur scientist: WILLIAM COLLIER. *Gufstaple*, on a mission of revenge: LEW M. FIELDS. *Signor D'Oreilly*, a home

[28]After six weeks, I, MARY McPAIN was replaced by another burlesque on 6 November 1902, HUMMINGBIRDS and ONIONS, parodying "The Mummy and the Humming Bird" and "Carrots."After seven weeks, this was replaced by another burlesque on 18 December 1902, THE STICKINESS OF GELATINE, parodying "The Stubbornness of Geraldine" by Clyde Fitch, for eleven weeks. On 26 February 1903 this was succeeded by THE BIG LITTLE PRINCESS, a parody of "The Little Princess" by Frances Hodgson Burnett, for the remaining 7 weeks of the run.

[29]Running order revised after opening.

[30]Replaced during the run by:
"Sailing"
J. Kelly
(*Music by* W. T. Francis. *Lyrics by* Edgar Smith.)
"Little Widow Brown"
L. Russell
(*Music by* W. T. Francis. *Lyrics by* Edgar Smith.)

[31]Dropped during the run.

[32]Added after opening between "Vaudeville King" and "Susie Woosie:"
"Clog Dance"
(*Music by* W. T. Francis.)

[33]Dropped after opening.

[34]Dropped during the run.

[35]Dropped during the run.

wrecker: JOHN T. KELLY. *Lord Rounder*, trying to butt into the family: MABEL BARRISON. *Jagson*, an upper servant: Will Archie. *Lady Bummy*, a neglected wife: Louise Allen. : *Ruth*, Bummy's niece: May Mackenzie. ONIONS CAST: *Mr. Lippy*, looking for peace with a gun: PETER F. DAILEY. *Mrs. Lippy*, a household terror: CHARLES A. BIGELOW. *Onions*, their son: FAY TEMPLETON. *Annette*, a servant lady: JOSEPH M. WEBER. *Felix*, a dog: Pongo. *Onion's Schoolmates (5)*: *Margot*: Estella Moyer. *Jean*: Gertie Moyer. *Francois*: May Mackenzie. *Pierre*: Eva Allen. *Fiffine*: Ilma Pratt. *Others*: Misses Hatfield, Chapins, Hoffmanns, Pratt, Revere, Howland, Leslies, Harris, Lynn, Senac, Bowman, Fostelle, Birch, Mitchell, Jewett, Heckler, Siegrist. Costumes designed by Will R. Barnes. Settings by John Young.

Scene 1: Lady Bummy's Study. *Scene 2*: The Lippy Home at Camambert Park, near Paris.

MUSICAL NUMBERS

"Come With Us"
Ensemble
(*Music by* W. T. Travers. *Lyrics by* R. B. Smith.)

A Bunch of Imitations[36]
F. Templeton

Finale

1902.29

THE STICKINESS OF GELATINE, a Travesty in One Act, by Edgar Smith. Music by W. T. Francis. Lyrics by Robert B. Smith. Scenery by John Young. Opened 18 December 1902.

CAST: *Count Careless Kidney*, a hungry Hungarian: LEW M. FIELDS. *Lord Spillberries*, an expatriated "Johnnie": PETER F. DAILEY. *Mr. Brightun*, a model husband: CHARLES A. BIGELOW. *Ship's Doctor*: Tom Collins. *Steward*: Joseph Torpey. *Hungarian Band [Ossman Banjo Quartette] (4)*: *Paprika*: V. L. Ossman. *Goulash*: Henry Six. *Buda*: F. E. Dunn. *Pesth*: F. A. Hopp. *Gelatine Pang*, a tearful young person with a gum-arabic disposition: FAY TEMPLETON. *Vi Bumpson* of Tombstone, Arizona: WILLIAM COLLIER. *Fraulein Krank*, companion to Gelatine: JOSEPH M. WEBER. *Mrs. Brightun*, who means well, but— —: Louise Allen. *Stewardess*: Mabel Barrison. *Miss Lansing* of Michigan: Ilma Pratt. *Passengers on the Cunarder "Pneumonia" (9)*: *Dodges Meales*: Frankie Bailey. *Innis Roome*: Mabel Lynn. *Poole Winner*: Carrie Bowman. *Knott Eaton*: Edna Birch. *Merrie Tripp*: Doris Mitchell. *Mona Little*: Annie Leslie. *May Raines*: May Leslie. *Daisy Saylor*: Laura Senac. *Dottie*: Eva Allen.

Scene: Promenade Deck of the S. S. "Pneumonia."

MUSICAL NUMBERS

"Ho! for the Sea" (Ensemble)
(*Music by* W. T. Francis. *Lyrics by* R. B. Smith.)

"Etiquette"
P. F. Dailey
(*Music by* W. T. Francis. *Lyrics by* R. B. Smith.)

"I Never Loved a Man as Much as That"
F. Templeton
(*Music by* W. T. Francis. *Lyrics by* R. B. Smith.)

Medley (includes "Ramble")
Company, accompanied by the Ossman Banjo Quartette

1902.29

THE BIG LITTLE PRINCESS. A Burlesque in One Act, 2 Scenes. Dialogue and Lyrics by Edgar Smith. Music by W. T. Francis. Directed by Lew M. Fields. Scenery by John Young. Costumes designed by Will R. Barnes. Opened 26 February 1903.

CAST of S.P.C.C. Immunes: *Sarah Crude*, star pupil at Miss Pinchin's academy for young criminals: FAY TEMPLETON. *Rottie*, the baby of the school: PETER F. DAILEY. *Erminegarter*, who learns all her lessons by proxy: WILLIAM COLLIER. *Specky*, a servant lady: LEW M. FIELDS. *Miss Pinchin*, main squeeze of Pinchin's Academy: CHARLES A. BIGELOW. *Mr. Borrow*, a wardman: JOHN T. KELLY. *Mr. Carisford*, a wealthy and retired housebreaker: JOHN T. KELLY. *Mrs. Patmichael*, a patron of the Academy: Louise Allen. *Miss Familiar*, a teacher at the Academy: Emily Francis. *Dam Dass*, an East Indian: Mabel Barrison. *Spee Kup*, a Lascar: Frankie Bailey. *Mrs. Patmichael's interesting family (4)*: *Ronaldo*: Will Archie. *Pantaletta*: Elizabeth Young. *Craisie*: Frankie Loeb. *Snora*: Libbie Diamond. *Freshie*, a spiteful pupil: MAY McKENZIE.

[36]Imitations of Marie Cahill singing "Under the Bamboo Tree" from SALLY IN OUR ALLEY and Thomas Q. Seabrooke singing "Mr. Dooley" from A CHINESE HONEYMOON.

Little students at the fountain head of wisdom: *Vanilla*: Topsy Siegrist. *Sarsparilla*: Estelle Beardsley. *Peachie*: Carrie Bowman. *Oragine*: Mona Desmond. *Cherrie*: Ollie Hatfield. *Lemona*: Agnes Lynn. *Nectarina*: Mabel Lynn. *Orgea*: Edna Birch.

Ralston, head jailer at the academy: Joseph Torpey. *Lascars (5)*: *Chut Knee*: Eva Allen. *Khur Ree*: Doris Mitchell. *How Dhu*: Irene Bishop. *Chu Gum*: Mazie Follette. *Rowdi Dhow*: Laura Senac. *Scholars, Servants, Lascars.*

Scene 1: School room at Miss Pinchin's Academy. *Scene 2*: Garret at same.

MUSICAL NUMBERS

"We Dearly Love Our Teachers" (Opening Ensemble)

"Miss Pinchin's Boarding School" (Song)
C. A. Bigelow, Ensemble

"The Bugaboo Man" (Song)
F. Templeton, Ensemble

"Softly Stealing, Lanterns Gleaming"
Ensemble

Finale

1902.30

A COUNTRY GIRL, or Town and Country Life

A Musical Play in Three Acts[37]. Book by James T. Tanner. Music by Lionel Monckton. Lyrics by Adrian Ross, additional lyrics by Percy Greenbank. Additional lyrics and numbers by Paul Rubens. Settings by Walter Burridge and Henry E. Hoyt. Costumes by Percy Anderson. Electrical effects by George McCurdy. Director of music, J. Sebastian Hiller. Produced by Augustin Daly Musical Company under the direction of J. C. Duff. Opened 22 September 1902 at Daly's Theatre and closed 27 December 1902 after 112 performances.

CAST: *Geoffrey Challoner*: MELVILLE STEWART. *Quinton Raikes, the Rajah of Bhong*: HALLEN MOSTYN. *Sir Joseph Verity*: HAROLD VIZARD. *Douglas Verity*: PAUL NICHOLSON. *Granfer Mummery*: CLARENCE HARVEY. *Lord Anchester*: W. E. Philp. *Lord Grassmere*: Lawrence Earle. *Major Vicat*: W. H. Smith. *Sir Charles Cortelyou*: Jefferson Egan. *Tzanticheff*: Robert Chawner. *Rube Fairway*: N. C. Shaw. *Barry*: WILLIAM NORRIS. *Marjorie Joy*: GRACE FREEMAN. *Princess Mehelaneh*: GENEVIEVE FINLAY. *Nan*: HELEN MARVIN. *Mrs. Quinton Raikes*: ADINE BOUVIER. *Nurse*: Marion Singer. *Lady Anchester*: Isobel Delmont. *Miss Powyscourt*: Helen Sherwood. *Lady Arnott*: Isobel Yates. *Miss Courtlands*: Grace Gresham. *Miss Ecroyd*: Julia Millard. *Miss Sydney*: Mary Welch. *Miss Ormonde*: Alice Campbell. *Miss Selwyn*: Susie Kelleher. *Attedants of Sophie*: Lena Wright, Leila Benton. *Madame Sophie*: MINNIE ASHLEY. (*Dance Specialty*: BLANCHE DEYO[38].)

Act 1: A Devonshire Landscape. (Burridge.)

Act 2: Interior of the Ministry of Fine Arts. (Hoyt.)

ACT 1[39]

Opening Chorus (When the birds begin to sing)

Song (Young Jan he were a harvester)
C. Harvey

"Try Again, Johnnie" (Song)
H. Marvin

"Coo!" (Song)
G. Freeman
(*Music by* Paul Rubens. *Lyrics by* Percy Greenbank.)

"The Sailor's Life" (Traditional Song)
M. Stewart

"Yo Ho, Little Girls (Yo Ho)" (Song and Chorus)
W. Norris, Chorus

"Boy and Girl" (Duet)
G. Freeman, M. Stewart

[37]Billed as Mr. George Edwardes' latest musical play at Daly's Theatre, London.

[38]Shortly after opening assigned the character name of Miss Carruthers.

[39]Programs for the original 1902 production contain no song lists. List was prepared from the published English vocal score (Chappell & Co. Ltd, London, 1902) and 1911 Boston revival program. Interpolated as per published sheet music (1904) for subsequent tour:

"My Darling Girlie"
M. Stewart
(*Music by* Alfred D. Moulton. *Lyrics by* John P. Wilson.)

"The Rajah of Bhong" (Chorus and Scene)
H. Mostyn, G. Finlay, Chorus
"Molly the Marchioness" (Song and Chorus)
H. Marvin, Chorus
"The Arcadians" (Chorus and Scene)
Chorus
"Two Little Chicks" (Duet)
W. Norris, M. Ashley
(*Music by* Paul Rubens. *Lyrics by* Percy Greenbank.)
"Under the Deodar" (Song)
G. Finlay
Finale (Hurrah for the Squire)
Principals, Chorus

ACT 2
Opening Chorus (The Reception)
Chorus
"Take Your Pretty Partner (to the Ball)" (Sextette)
G. Freeman, H. Marvin, M. Ashley, H. Mostyn, P. Nicholson, L. Earle
"Me and Mrs. Brown" (Song)
W. Norris
(*Music by* Paul Rubens. *Lyrics by* Percy Greenbank.)
"My Own Little Girl" (Song)
M. Stewart
"Peace! Peace!" (Song and Chorus)
H. Mostyn, Chorus
"Quarrelling Duet"
M. Ashley, W. Norris
(*Music by* Paul Rubens. *Lyrics by* Percy Greenbank.)
Finale

1902.31 DOLLY VARDEN

A Return Engagement of the Comic Opera in Two Acts[40]. Libretto by Stanislaus Stange. (Based on the novel "Barnaby Rudge" by Charles Dickens.) Music by Julian Edwards. Staged by Al Holbrook. Court dances and minuets arranged by Cervallo. Settings by Homer Emens and John H. Young. Costumes by Caroline Seidle. Orchestra under the direction of Enrico Morreale. Produced by F. C. Whitney. Opened 22 September 1902 at Hammerstein's Victoria Theatre and closed 4 October 1902 after 14 performances.

CAST: *Lord Gayspark*, a London exquisite: MARK SMITH. *Captain Richard Belleville*, an English officer: HARRY GIRARD. *Captain Horace Harcourt* of the English Navy: ALBERT PARR. *John Fairfax*, Dolly's guardian: GEORGE O'DONNELL. *Lieutenant Marlow, Lieutenant Cragsby* of the English Navy: Edward Mulkay, Edward Martindell. *Letitia Fairfax*, a London belle: ESTELLE WENTWORTH. *Lady Lucette, Lady Alice*, ladies of fashion: Ada Palmer Walker, Cecilia Quinn. *Dolly Varden*: LULU GLASER. *Court Ladies, Belles and Beaux of London, Naval Officers, etc.*

1902.32 THE DOINGS OF MRS. DOOLEY

A Farce in Three Acts. Book by Sidney Wilmer and Walter Vincent. Musical numbers composed by Charles Miller. Production staged by George W. Monroe and Raymond Finley. Musical numbers staged by George Marion. Musical director, Charles Miller. Produced by (Sidney) Wilmer and (Walter) Vincent. Opened 22 September 1902 at the Grand Opera House and closed 27 September 1902 after 8 performances; returned 17 November 1902 to the West End Theatre and closed 22 November 1902 after 8 additional performances; returned 5 January 1903 to the Metropolis Theatre and closed 10 January 1903 after an additional 8 performances. Total: 24 performances.

CAST: *Mrs. Michael Dooley*, formerly Rosie McGee: GEORGE W. MONROE. *Dennett Mink*, a player of parts. He's wise: RAYMOND FINLEY. *Gloomy Gus*, he leads a dog's life: JOHN DONAHUE. *Timothy O'Brien*, a Democrat: James Lee. *Wannie Maker*, a brilliant thing: MART FULLER. *Isadore Isaacs*, a generous man: Harry Walters. *Gaston*, a waiter at Sunset: Edward Loper. *Flip*, Mrs. Dooley's adopted daughter: MATTIE NICHOLS. *Sherry Martin*, cashier at Sunset Villa: LOTTIE BURKE. *Mrs. DeKalb Fulton*, a society woman: BESSIE BURR. *Carrie Money*, a widow and a lawyer: FANNIE FRANKEL. *Zaza DuBarry*, actress at the Casino: May Melbane. *Dolores Huntsworth*: Dorothy Brandon.

Casino Girls and Summer Boarders: *Ruble Pearl*: Fannie Franke. *Barbara Sapho*: Virgie Ware. *Effie Ebbsmith*: Ada Gifford. *Daffodil Pink*: Marie Lee. *Lucy Lee*: Nellie Young. *Ruby Pearl*: Nellie Millette. *Katie DeVoe*: Belle Millette. *Emma Marsh*: Lenoir Maine. *Mary Manning*: Mabel Hawthorne. *Leslie Chester*: Evelyn Gray. *Mazie Color*: Mable Lawrence. *Vera Jack*: Pauline Marshall. *Tessie Taft*: Gussie Gray. *Vivian Splash*: Lydia Franklin. *Omega Rubb*: Emily Palmer.

Act 1: Susnet Villa and the Dizzy House. Bath Beach. New York.

Act 2: Dining room of the Dizzy House. Bath Beach. New York.

Act 3: Reception Room at Mrs. Dooley's. Riverside Drive.

ACT 1[41]
"Down Where the Ocean Breezes Blow" (Opening)
Chorus
"I'm Momma's Pet"
M. Fuller, Chorus
"The horse I used to dry my old clothes on"
G. Monroe, Chorus
Singing and Dancing Specialty
F. Frankel
"Mrs. Dooley on Parade" (Grand Finale)
G. Monroe, Entire Company

ACT 2
"There is no such thing as a Bogie man"
B. Burr, Company
Monologue
G. W. Monroe
Statute Clog
Misses Burke, Nichols, Burr, Kenwick
Burlesque
G. W. Monroe, R. Finley, J. Donahue, J. Lee
"John Would Never Do That" (Finale)
R. Finley, Company

ACT 3
"When the heart is young"
A. Kenwick, Chorus
High Class Singing
F. Frankel, M. Melbane
"Just the same old story" (A Vaudeville Travesty)
R. Finley, L. Burke
Singing, Dancing and Acrobatic Comedy Duo
J. Donahue, M. Niichols
Wait for the Finale—Different from all others

1902.33 IN POSTERLAND

The Royal Liliputians in a Spectacular Musical Comedy in Three Acts. Music arranged and directed by W. H. Rostetter. Musical numbers arranged, adapted and directed by Gus Sohlke. Produced by Gus Hill. Opened 20 October 1902 at the Metropolis Theatre and closed 25 October 1902 after 8 performances; returned 23 March 1903 at the 14th Street Theatre and closed 28 March 1903 after an additional 8 performances.[42]

CAST: The Famous ROYAL LILIPUTIANS: *Larry Dooley*, a sporty old boy and something of a sparker: Major JAMES J. DOYLE. *Mrs. Dooley*, who stands on her dignity: Annie Nelson. *Mr. Larks*, a larkish neighbor of Sparks: Major A. J. CRIQUI. *Mrs. Larks*, who stands in her rights: Martha Weis. *Miss Larks*, who doesn't care where she stands: INEZ LEWIS. *Tired Mike*, brothers in rest, but—: JAMES E. ROSEN. *Weary Willie*, always gets there: LOUIS MERKEL. *Toddy Grimes*, the grocer's boy: HOWARD KNOWLES. *Foxy Grandma*, you know her: CHARLES SAUNDERS.

[40]Originally produced in New York 27 January 1902 at the Herald Square Theatre for 156 performances. For Synopsis of Scenes and Musical Numbers, see original 1902 production.

[41]No program available for Grand Opera Hosue engagement; song list prepared from West End Theatre program.
[42]No credits in programs for stage director.

Little Mickey Dooley, the fat boy: Al Rice. *Back'em Down*, a car superintendant: George Laible. *Happy Hooligan*, old Happy: George Laible. *Bud Ticem*, a tough proposition: Joe Mack. *Sol Soakem*, the bartender: B. F. Kelly. *Hi Hubbard*, a rube: Robert Angle. *Dottie Dimple*, from the Gayety: BEATRICE COOPER. *Only Sick*, a consumptive: Frank King. *Sickem Finley*, a tough from the Bowery: Howard Knowles. *Mrs. Dimity*, who chases her baby: May Valentine. *Phebe Jarndyce*, of the Gayety company: Helen Bates. *Eunice Divinty*, of the same company: Emma West. *The Giant Policeman*: B. F. Kelly.

Gems of Lustre Highly Necessary to the Setting: *La Belle Martine*: May Valentine. *La Grande Sabartine*: Beatrice Cooper. *La Petite Boulevard*: Helen Bates. *La Poses Plastique*: Emma West. *La Vera Chartreuse*: Carrie Larson. *La Verde Modiste*: Mabel Morelyn. *La Belle Medici*: Beatrice Morelyn. *La Neyve Duriand*: Lottie McCree. *La Petite Thisbe*: Nelie Hazelwood. *La Fargaro Reynault*: Carrie Edney. *La Etoile Sapho*: Bessie Leyland. *La Natalie Silphide*: Rita Love. *Baby, Charmer*: The Pony.

Act 1: A Street in Chinatown. Tired Mike and Weary Willie engage as conductors. Lively competition for pasengers—a mix-up with no transfers—any destination you want. The jealous neighbors. A lively time for Dooley and Larks. A triple invitation for supper. Look out for the Indian. Arrival of the Tom Thumb Coach—who got the baby—a hot chase after the kidnapper. Arrval of the police patrol with the police horses, Baby and Charmer. A combination riot with the Liliputians on top.

Act 2: In Posterland. The Hilarity Troupe Supper given by Foxy Grandma. Trouble with the turkey and trouble all around—a mixed company—and a mix-up in general. Mike and Willie monarchs of all they survey. Dooley and Larks make a mash, get mashed and then samshed. Dooley gets mixed up with a looking-glass. Good times alla round.

Act 3: The Golden Gardens. The windy boys. Listen to the echo. What is an echo? A meeting of the Busy Bees. Foxy Grandma as a "Coochie Cooche Dancer." "Who gets the honey?" "You Get it." A catchel of money. All is fish that comes to the net.

ACT 1[43]

"On the Avenue"

"Welcome To-night at the Ball"

"I'm Lucky"
Major J. A. Doyle

"Roses and Lillies"
I. Lewis, Chorus

"Conversation Song and Dance"
J. E. Rosen, L. Merkel, B. Cooper C. Larsen

"I'm a Millionaire" (Song and Dance)
H. Knowles

Chinese Medley with light effects
Full Company

"Laughing Song"
A. Rice

ACT 2

"We Are Out for a Jolly Good Time, Suzie Anna"

Tyrolean Song and Dance

"The Gay Castinets"
Chorus

"When a Lady Leads the Band"

The Colibris Midgets (Acrobatic wonders)

ACT 3

"The Windy Boys"
J. D. Doyle, J. E. Rosen, L. Merkel, H. Knowles, A. Rice

The Minuet

"The Good Old Summer Time"

"The Amazon March" (Finale)
(Chorus)

1902.34

TOMMY ROT

A Musical Comedy in Two Acts[44]. including a Joseph Herbert parody of "Iris" called "Cyris." Dialogue (book) by Rupert Hughes. Music and lyrics by Safford Waters. Staged by Mrs. Osborn, Joseph Herbert and Lewis Hooper. Gowns by Mrs. Osborn Co. Scenery designed by Physioc & Co., Frank Dodge. Musical director, William F. Peters. Produced Mrs. Osborn. Opened 21 October 1902 at Mrs. Osborn's Playhouse and closed 22 November 1902 after 39 performances.

CAST: *Thomas Rottingdean*: CHARLES BUTLER. *Eric Leicester*: FLETCHER NORTON. *Hawtrey Treebohm*: ALFRED HICKMAN. *Lord Dope*: RICHARD LAMBARD. *Marchese Reminesca*: George Herbert. *Reporter*: Richard Lee. *Stage Doorkeeper*: Richard Lee. *Call Boy*: Henry Hyde. *Innocence Demure*: BLANCHE RING. *Phoebe Dare*: GRAYCE SCOTT. *Mrs. Green Carnation*: MARGARET HUBBARD AYER. *Uneeda, Zuzu*, her twin daughters: HENGLER SISTERS (Flora, May). *Miss Never Getleft*: DRINA DeWOLFE. *Miss Always There*: Evelyn Florence Nesbitt. *Lady Dope*: Pauline von Arnold. *Grace Lloyd*: Alice Hills. *Sadie Vere*: Helen Chichester. *Messenger Boy*: John Pemberton.

Nearly Ballet Girls: Rosa Earle, Madlyn Summers, Claudine Sharp, Laura Stone, Vida Whitmore, Kathleen Clifford. *Men-About-Town*: Jack Lyles, Yale Benner, A. J. Marshall, Jack Henderson, Franklin Jones, Samuel Sandgrain, Echlin P. Gayer, William B. Daly.

CAST of "Cryris" introduced in Act 2: *Cryris*: BLANCHE RING. *Fannie Sloven*: GRAYCE SCOTT. *Hot Tomale Oscar*: GEORGE HERBERT. *Lawrence Trenwithout*: ALFRED HICKMAN. *Croker Sturgis*: CHARLES BUTLER. *Footman*: Henry Hyde.

Act 1: Open air performance of "As You Like It" at Country Club at Newgansett. (Physioc.)

Act 2: Green Room of the "Bandbox Theatre." (Dodge.)

ACT 1

"History Class"
M. H. Ayer, Chorus

"Every Dog Must Have Its Day, and Every Puss Her Afternoon"
D. DeWolfe, Chorus

"I Want to Be One of the Smart Set"
Hengler Sisters, Chorus

"The Only Thing That Makes Life Worth Living"
G. Scott, F. Norton

"In the Press"
A. Hickman, Chorus

"There's a Strange Fascination About the Stage"
B. Ring, Chorus

"She Used to Take Me on Her Knee"
G. Scott, Chorus

"The Hit of the Season"
A. Hickman, Septette

"Mike McCarthy's Wake"
B. Ring

Finale Act 1

ACT 2

Opening Chorus

"Oh, for a Great Idea"
A. Hickman, R. Lambard, J. Herbert

"Belle of Avenue A"
B. Ring, Chorus

"An Actress and a Lady"
B. Ring, G. Scott

"Island of Love"
F. Norton

"Sally"
R. Lambard, 6 Ballet Girls

"When the Girls Come Back to Town"
M. H. Ayer, Chorus

"I Come from Sunny Dixie"
Misses Earle, Summers, Sharp, Stone, Whitmore, Clifford

"Boo-Ra-Boo"
B. Ring, Chorus

Finale Act 2

---

[43]No New York program found. Songs taken from 16 March 1903 Brooklyn tour.

[44]Revised as FAD AND FOLLY which opened 27 November 1902 at Mrs. Osborn's Playhouse for 34 performances.

1902.35

THE SILVER SLIPPER

A Musical Comedy in Two Acts, 5 Scenes[45]. Book by Owen Hall, re-arranged for America by Clay M. Greene. Music by Leslie Stuart. Lyrics by W. H. Risque. (Additional music by Arthur Weld; additional lyrics by Leslie Stuart, Charles H. Taylor, George Rollitt.) Staged by James Francis, assisted by Harry B. Burcher. Costumes by Charles Alias. Scenery by Ernest Albert. Orchestra under the direction of Arthur Weld. Produced by John C. Fisher. Opened 27 October 1902 at the Broadway Theatre and closed 14 March 1903 after 165 performances[46].

CAST: *Henry Bismarck Henschs*, showman, card sharp and all round fakir: SAM BERNARD. *Sir Victor Shallamar*, an astronomer: SNITZ EDWARDS. *Berkeley Shallamar*, of the Household Brigade, Nephew of Sir Victor: CYRIL SCOTT. *Donald Gregor* of the Royal Navy: MACKENZIE GORDON. *Roland Western*: Harry B. Burcher. *Duval*: John Ardisonne. *The Queen of Venus*: MAI deVILLIERS. *Belle Jimper*, servant of Sir Victor: JOSIE SADLER. *Stella*, the girl from Venus: HELEN ROYTON. *Brenda*, niece of Sir Victor: Susan Drake. *Judicia*: Daisy Greene. *Susette*: Clarita Vidal. *Dolly*, the maid: Rebecca Kaufman. *Wrenne*: EDNA WALLACE HOPPER.

Venus Girls (5): *Cleo*: Gertrude Douglas. *Dione*: Margaret Walker. *Ira*: Marie Allen. *Astria*: Alice Toland. *Lydia*: Marjorie Relyea.

Students of Shallamar College: *Cynthia Grey*: Edith Blair. *Minnie Lomas*: Frances Hill. *Mary Estelle*: Clarita Vidal. *Jennie Vercker*: Sadie Hollister. *Maisie Brooks*: Louise Lonsdale. *Ella Hatfield*: Maud Thomas. *Roland Western*: Harry Burcher. *Harry Powler*: Jack Taylor. *Algernon Hepworth*: Benjamin H. Burt. *Claude Coucher*: Fred Walsh. *Fred Rollins*: W. H. Pringle. *Douglas Wharton*: Atherton B. Furlong.

English Dancing Girls: Sallie Lomax, Dollie Corke, Beatrice Grenville, Rose Martin, Maggie Taylor, Lillie Lawton; *Dancing Getlemen*: Messrs. Hoey, Marsden-Robinson, Hodson, Hirschberger. *Student Boys and Girls, Flower Girls, Nurse Girls, Soldiers, Gendarmes, Troubadours, Waiters, Attendants.*

Act 1, Scene 1: The Gardens of College of Sir Victor Shallamar. *Scene 2*: Hall of Justice on the Planet Venus.

Act 2, Scene 1: Neuilly Fair, France. *Scene 2*: Students' Ball at the Art Club, Paris

PROLOGUE

"Invocation of Venus"
M. deVilliers, Female Chorus
(*Lyrics by* Leslie Stuart.)

"A Glimpse" (A Glimpse-impse-impse)
H. Royton, Venus Chorus

ACT 1[47]

Opening Chorus[48]

"To-night's the Night"
S. Edwards, Chorus

"Fun on a Motor"[49]
C. Scott, Chorus
(*Music by* Landon Ronald. *Lyrics by* George Rollit.)

"Two Eyes of Blue"
M. Gordon
(*Lyrics by* Charles Taylor.)

"If I Were a Girl Instead"[50]
E. W. Hopper
(*Lyrics by* Leslie Stuart.)

Finale

ACT 2[51]

Scene 1

Opening Chorus

"The Baby with the Dimple and the Smile"
E. W. Hopper, Female Chorus

"The Detrimental Man"[52]
C. Scott, Chorus
(*Lyrics by* Charles Taylor.)

"Ping-Pong" Duet
E. W. Hopper, C. Scott
(*Music by* Ivan Caryll. *Lyrics by* Percy Greenbank.)

Duet ("If Hearts But Knew")
M. deVilliers, M. Gordon
(*Music by* Arthur Weld.)

"Come Little Girl, (and Tell Me Truly)" (Sextette)
Misses Walker, Douglas, Allen, Toland, Relyea, Greene;
Messrs. Burcher, Taylor, Burt, Walsh, Pringle, Furlong
(*Lyrics by* Leslie Stuart.)

Champagne Dance
English Dancing Girls, Gentlemen

Scene 2

Dance (Slow Waltz)
(*Music by* Arthur Weld.)

"Because I Love You Dear"[53]
M. Gordon

"Four and Twenty Little Men"
E. W. Hopper, 24 Men

"Class"
J. Sadler, Chorus
(*Lyrics by* Charles Taylor.)

Finale

[45]After opening, revised to a Prologue and Two Acts, Four Scenes; revised to Three Scenes for tour.

[46]Played a return engagement 31 August 1903 at the Grand Opera House for 8 performances.

[47]The show was revised for its subsequent tour. English score published by Francis Day & Hunter (London, 1901). Interpolated for subsequent tour, as per published sheet music:

"Never Had to Work"
Sam Collins
(*Music and Lyrics by* Benjamin Hapgood Burt.)

"My Celia"
George Tennery
(*Music and Lyrics by* Jerome Kern and John L. Golden.)

[48]Also known as "Our College Gowns" in the original English production.

[49]Replaced during the run by:

"Although I Am a Soldier, I Prefer a Private Life"
C. Scott, Chorus
(*Music and Lyrics by* Melville Ellis.)
Which was replaced for the tour by:

"Soldiers of the Army"
C. Scott, Chorus
(*Music by* John Sebastian Hiller.)

[50]Replaced for subsequent tour by:

"You and Me"
Ann Tyrell {Wrenne}, C. Scott

[51]Added during the run and for tour to Act 2, after "The Detrimental Man:"

"(Then) I'd Be Satisfied with Life"
S. Bernard, Student Boys
(*Music and Lyrics by* George M. Cohan.)
Added for subsequent tour after the Champagne Dance:

"The Girl You Love" (from THREE LITTLE MAIDS)
A. Tyrell, Student Boys
(*Music and Lyrics by* Paul A. Rubens.)

[52]Replaced (from English production) for subsequent tour by:

"She Didn't Know Enough About the Game"
C. Scott, Chorus
(*Lyrics by* George Rollitt.)

[53]Replaced during run and for subsequent tour by:

"Tessie, You Are the Only, Only, Only"
Stanley Hawkins {Donald Gregor}
(*Music and Lyrics by* Will R. Anderson.)

1902.36

OLD LIMERICK TOWN

An Irish Drama (with Music) in Four Acts. Play by Augustus Pitou. Music and lyrics by Chauncey Olcott. Staged by Augustus Pitou. Produced by Augustus Pitou. Opened 27 October 1902 at the 14th Street Theatre and closed 13 December 1902 after 56 performances[54].

CAST: *Neil O'Brien*: CHAUNCEY OLCOTT. *Kate Darcy*, a widow, Neil's sister: ALICE TAYLOR. *William Darcy*, her son: Tottie Carr. *Lajahan*, a Hindoo, servant to Neil: EDWIN B. TILTON. *Peter Burke*, a country gentleman: MATT B. SYDER. *Margaret Burke*, his wife: Rose Snyder. *Noreen Burke*, his daughter: MIRIAM NESBITT. *Oonah Burke*, his daughter: Blanche Alexander. *Thomas Burke*, Noreen's twin

[54]Costume and scenic credits, musical director unknown.

brother: HARRY MESTAYER. *Captain Boswell* of the English garrison: Bertram Godfrey. *Captain Leffingham* of the English garrison: Percy Jennings. *Count de Chalveres*, an adventurer: Emile LaCroix. *Matthew O'Rierdon*, an attorney: Edmund Hogan. *Dan O'Shea*, superintendent of a lace factory: William H. Gough. *Molly Dooley*, a widow, Neil's housekeeper: Elizabeth Washburn. *Ann Corrigan*, her maiden sister: Blanche Sweet. *Phil Doyle*, master of Neil's stable: George Brennan.

The action takes place on the banks of the River Shanon, near Limerick, Ireland, from 1835-1836.

Act 1: Neill O'Brien's Estate on the River Shannon, near Limerick. September 1835. The Hunt Breakfast.

Act 2: The Estate of Peter Burke on the River Shannon near Castle Connell, showing the Falls of Doonas. November 1836. The Conspiracy to ruin Neil.

Act 3: A room in Neil's house. A few days later. The attempted robbery of the funds of the Monte de Piete.

Act 4: Same scene. The following mornng. The scent of violets. Neil's reward.

MUSICAL NUMBERS[55]

"Every Little Dog Must Have His Day"
C. Olcott

"Limerick Girls"
C. Olcott

"Noreen Mavourneen"
C. Olcott

"The Voice of the Violet"
C. Olcott

1902.37 THE MOCKING BIRD

A Romantic Comic Opera in Three Acts. Libretto by Sydney Rosenfeld. Music by A. Baldwin Sloane. Staged by Robert (R. H.) Burnside. Scenery built by John Cunningham. Costumes designed by Will R. Barnes. Orchestra under the direction of Max Knauer. Produced by the Messrs. (Meyer L. and Henry B.) Sire. Opened 10 November 1902 at the Bijou Theatre and closed 5 January 1903 after 64 performances; re-opened a return engagement 25 May 1903 at the Bijou Theatre and closed 6 June 1903 after 14 additional performances. Total: 78 performances[56].

CAST: *General Aubrey*, Governor of Louisiana: ROLAND CARTER. *Eugene DeLorme*, the Governor's Secretary: SYDNEY DEANE. *Maxime Grandpre*, a wealthy citizen of New Orleans: ROBERT ROGERS. *Yvette Millet*, his ward: MABELLE GILMAN. *Manon de Lange*, an Immigrant: Violet Holls. *Jean Le Farge*, a gentlemanly pirate, traveling as Jacques Villiers: FRANK DOANE. *Bob Finchley*, a Virginian: EDGAR ATCHISON-ELY. *Captain Beloit*, a French soldier: Claude Boyer. *Don Aurelio de Mendez*, a Spanish envoy: Walter C. Shannon. *The Marquise de Villebois*: Louise Mackintosh. *The Countess Bellaien*, her niece: Maude Alice Kelly. *Duc de la Volta*: Ivy Moore. *Estelle Favor*: Edythe Truran. *Pierre*, a Negro butler: John F. Parry. *Javotte*, the Governor's Housekeeper: Stella Adams. *Chloe*, a Slave: Sarah Osgood.

Immigrants: Monte Elmo, Florence Hayes, Eullah Lee, Frankie Trumbo, Mildred Thornwall, Edith Thayer, Grace Walton, Daisy Binford, Elise Sargent, Hattie Forsythe.

The action takes place in New Orleans at the close of the eighteenth century.

Act 1: The Place d'Armes, New Orleans.

Act 2: The Salon of the Marquise de Villebois. A few days later.

Act 3: The Garden of the Marquise. The same evening.

ACT 1[57]

Opening Chorus (Ship Ahoy!)

"The Governor's Song" (The King of France)
R. Carter, Chorus

Entrance of Immigrants
Girls' Chorus

"The Flash of the Skipper's Eye" (Song and Chorus)
V. Holls

"France, Glorious France" (Song and Chorus)
S. Deane

"One I Love, the Other I Abhor" (Trio)
M. Gilman, R. Rogers, S. Deane

"From a Different Point of View" (Duet)
F. Doane, E. Atchison-Ely

Finale Act 1

ACT 2

Opening Chorus:

"The Gossipers" (Oh have you heard the news)
Chorus

"A Stale World and a Pale World"
L. Mackintosh, M. A. Kelly, Chorus

"The Lion and the Mouse" (Duet)
M. Gilman, F. Doane

"Just a Kiss" (Duet)
M. Gilman, S. Deane

"Carried Off" (Octette)
R. Carter, M. A. Kelly, V. Holls, I. Moore, E. Truran, F. Doane, E. Atchison-Ely, S. Deane

"The Rigadoon" (Song)
E. Atchison-Ely

Finale Act 2
W. C. Shannon, M. Gilman, Quartette

"The Sly Musette"
M. Gilman, Chorus of Women

ACT 3

"In Silence" (Song)
S. Deane

"(If You Couldn't) Change Your Mind" (Song)
M. Gilman

"What's the Matter with the Moon To-night?" (The Moon Song)
M. Gilman, E. Atchison-Ely, Chorus

"The Lion and the Mouse" (reprise/Exit of LaFarge)
M. Gilman, F. Doane

Finale Act 3

1902.38 SOUTHERN ENCHANTMENT

The Smart Set in a Spectacular Extravaganza (Musical Comedy) in Three Acts, 7 Scenes[58]. Book and lyrics by F. B. Cassin[59]. Music by Ernest Hogan. Produced under the personal direction of Edgar Temple[60]. Scenery by Lee Lash Studio, Ernest Albert and Mosher and Hamilton. Costumes designed by Will H. Barnes. Electrical effects by Joseph Menching. Orchestrations and musical direction by James F. Dougherty. Produced by Gus Hill. Opened 10 November 1902 at the New Star Theatre and closed 15 November 1902 after 8 performances; returned 23 February 1903 to the 14th Street Theatre and closed 7 March 1903 after an additional 16 performances. Total: 24 performances.

CAST: *George Washington Bullion*, an American millionaire (The Lone Star): ERNEST HOGAN. *Grafton Smooth*, a slick article: BILLY McCLAIN. *Planter Caine*, a wealthy sugar planter: BEN HUNN. *Lieutenant Leon Mildew*, a British officer: HENRY JACKSON NORRIS. *Willie Slope*, not such a fool as he appears: Russell Brandow. *Titus Barnes Ketchum*, one of Pinkerton's finest: J. M. Thomas. *Mrs. Waldorf*, a widow, Honolulu society leader: Mme. CORDELIA McCLAIN. *Dollie Dupree*, news correspondent: MATTIE WILKES-HOGAN[61]. *Lucy*, Willie's sweetheart: Pauline Freeman[62]. *Moana*, a lost gem: IDA FORCEN[63]. *Mrs. Ferguson*, housekeeper

[55]Not in performance order. Song list prepared from touring programs and reviews.
[56]Also played a New York area return engagement 30 March 1903 at the Grand Opera House for 8 performances.
[57]Musical Numbers not listed in the program. List prepared from published piano vocal score (Joseph W. Stern & Co., New York, 1902).

[58]This production continued to tour as late as 1906 (Metropolis, 7 May 1906) with changing cast and all new musical numbers.
[59]For return engagement, book credited to Billy McClain.
[60]For return engagement, Temple's credit as direction was dropped; added was the credit "Additional musical numbers and ensembles by Gus Sohlke."
[61]For the return engagement, Dollie Dupree was played by MARION HENRY.
[62]For the return engagement, Lucy was played by Miss Settle.
[63]For the return engagement, Moana was played by MINNIE RINGGOLD.

Hilo Hotel: Mrs. BEN HUNN. *Manthy*, a flower girl: Marguerite Jordan. *Fluffy, Cinthy*, Honolulu Girls: Marguerite Jordan, Stella Wiley. *Parson*: Ladson Alston[64]. *Dinwiddie Quartette*: S. C. Rex (first tenor); J. C. Meredith (second tenor); H. B. Cover (first bass); J. M. Thomas (second bass). *Soldiers, Sailors, Flower Girls, Honolulu Belles, Honolulu Dancers, Native Singers.*

Act 1, Scene 1: Mrs. Duer's gardens at Waikili, Honolulu. *Scene 2*: Street in front of Royal Rooster's Lodge. *Scene 3*: Royal Rooster's Lodge. Initiation of Bullion.

Act 2: Plantation. City of Waikili in the distance.

Act 3, Scene 1: Parlor in the Rio Hotel, Honolulu. *Scene 2*: In the Park. *Scene 3*: The Duel in the Forest.

ACT 1

Opening Chorus
Company

"Sing a Little Tenor"[65]
Linton, Gilroy

"Dolly Dupree"[66]
McPherson, Brymur

"The Missionary Man"
S. B. Casson, E. Hogan

Selections ["Come Out Dinah on the Green"]
Dinwiddie Quartette

"Chicken Song" (Royal Rooster's Ensemble)
J. R. Rayner, E. Hogan

ACT 2[67]

"Levee Jamboree"
S. B. Casson, E. Hogan

"Leonora Lee"
B. Johnson

"Roll On, Mr. Moon"
B. McLain, E. Hogan

"Gabie"
Himself

"Florence"
B. McLain, E. Hogan

Hot Foot Finale
Entire Company

ACT 3[68]

"The Gypsy Maid" (from THE WILD ROSE)
WM. Cook, P. L. Dunbar

"Wood Nymphs' Call"
Langston Williams

"(Tell Me) Dusky Maiden"
(L: J R Johnson) E. Hogan, M. Henry

"Honor Points the Way"
J A. Raynes, E. Hogan

Ensemble Finale
(Logan-E Hogan) Entire Company

[64]For the return engagement, the Parson was played by Jerry Mills.
[65]Replaced for return engagement by:

"If I Was a Millionaire"
B. McClain

[66]Dropped for return engagement.
[67]For the return engagement, only "Roll On, Mr. Moon," "Gabie" and Hot Foot Finale were retained. Added were:

"(The) Army of Peace" (Grand March)
H. J. Norris, Company

Specialty: "Turkey in the Straw"/"Jinnie My Own Love"
B. Hunn

"My Sweet Moana"
Mme. C. McClain, Company

[68]For the return engagement, "Honor Points the Way" was dropped. Added were:

"Honey, Will You Miss Me When I'm Gone"
H. J. Norris, Company

1902.39 A PRINCE OF TATTERS

A Play (with songs) in Four Acts. Play (and lyrics) by Sidney R. Ellis. Music by Al. H. Wilson. Scenery by Thomas Neville and Arthur Overpeck. Costumes designed by McIlvaine. Musical director, Louie Maurice. Produced by Charles H. Yale and Sidney R. Ellis. Opened 17 November 1902 at the Metropolis Theatre and closed 22 November 1902 after 8 performances.

CAST: *Prince Hugo Von Reppert*, an exiled Austrian: AL H. WILSON[69]. *Earl Richard Bellomont*, English Governor of New York: GEORGE RIDDLE. *Henry Belloment*, his son and secretary: A. J. Coleman. *Lord Edward Gray*, uncle and guardian of Lady Helen: MARK PRICE. *Captain John Schoonhaven*, of the ship *"Goede Vrow"*: HARRY FISHER. *Wandle Podincroft*, a Dutch burgher: Lawrence Gay. *Admiral Marcisse*, of the French fleet: R. J. Lans. *Old Bleecker*, a fisherman: John Baldwin. *Cooper Spiegle*, jailer of St. George: Al. H. Holstein. *Captain of Dragoons*, in the Governor's pay: Lew Stoddard. *Bill Bobstay*, mate of the *"Goede Vrow*: J. H. Heck. *Little Spiegel*, a privileged character: Little Fraunces Clinton. *Lady Helen*, from England's court: KATE BENETEAU. *Ann Clattercrop*, a Burgher's daughter: FANNY BLOODGOOD. *Lady Bellomont*, the Governor's wife: Eva Byron. *Jessemine*, Lady Helen's maid: Isabelle Stevens. *Mother Bleecker*, Fisherwoman: Lillie Clinton. *Buccaneers, Dragoons, etc.*

Act 1: On the coast of Long Island. Old New York, 1700.

Act 2: The Governor's House in Fort George one week later.

Act 3: Lady Helen's apartments in Fort George, the same night.

Act 4: The Yard and Guardhouse of Fort George, three days later.

MUSICAL NUMBERS[70]

"The Winding of the Yarn" (Waltz)
A. H. Wilson

"The Mermaid and the Buccaneer" (Comic Descriptive)
A. H. Wilson

"Whispering Breeze" (Yodel)
A. H. Wilson

"Memory" (Ballad)
A. H. Wilson

"When Your Ship Comes Home" (Descriptive)
A. H. Wilson

"The Echo"
A. H. Wilson

1902.40 FAD AND FOLLY

A Musical Melange (Comedy) in Two Acts[71] (including a Joseph Herbert parody of "Iris" called "Cyris"). Book, music and lyrics by Safford Waters and Rupert Hughes[72], revised by Paul West. Stage director, Lewis Hooper. Scenery by (Joseph) Physioc & Co., D. Frank Dodge. Musical director, William F. Peters. Produced by Mrs. Osborn. Opened 27 November 1902 at Mrs. Osborn's Playhouse and closed 27 December 1902 after 34 performances.

CAST: *Hezekia Goop*, D.O.M.: HARRY CONOR. *Sammy*, a messenger boy: FELIX HANEY. *Tommy Rottingham*: E. LOVATT FRASER. *Lord Dope*: R. PEYTON CARTER. *Reuben Haytop*, a Countryman: Richard Lee. *Hawtrey Treebohm*, an Actor: RICHARD LAMBART. *Eric Leicester*: Jack Henderson. *Innocence Demure*: BLANCHE RING. *Mrs. Immortelle*: DRINA DeWOLFE. *Lady Dope*: MARGARET HUBBARD AYER. *Phoebe Dare*: Claudine Sharp. *Flirta Little*: Alice Toland. *Flytie Bird*: Marie Allen. *Grace Lloyd*: Alice Hills. *Sadie Vere*: Helen Chichester.

Sally: Rose Earl, Marion Mathey, Laura Stone, Vida Whitmore, Madlyn Summers, Kathleen Clifford. *Men-About-Town* A. J. Marshall, Louis Dupre, Samuel C. Sangrain, Echlin P. Gayer, William B. Daly, Philip F. Leigh, Arthur Taylor.

CAST of "Cyris" introduced in Act 2: *Cyris*: BLANCHE RING. *Fannie Sloven*: Claudine Sharp. *Hot Tomale Oscar*: HARRY CONOR. *Lawrence Trenwithout*: RICHARD LAMBART. *Croker Sturgis*: E. LOVATT FRASER. *Footman*: Henry Hyde.

[69]Billed as the "Great German Dialect Comedian and Golden Voiced Singer."
[70]Not necessarily in performance order; "The Echo" does not appear in programs, but its music was publsihed.
[71]FAD AND FOLLY was a revised version of TOMMY ROT which was produced 20 October 1902 at Mrs. Osborn's Playhouse for 39 performances.
[72]The TOMMY ROT program credits Hughes with the book and Waters with music and lyrics.

Act 1: Grounds of the Country Club at Newgansett.

Act 2: Green Room of the Bandbox Theatre, New York.

MUSICAL NUMBERS[73]

"There's a Strange Fascination About the Stage"
B. Ring, Chorus

"Belle of Avenue A"
B. Ring, Chorus

"Sally"
R. P. Carter, 6 Ballet Girls

"I Come from Sunny Dixie"
Misses Earle, Summers, Sharp, Stone, Whitmore, Clifford

NEW MUSICAL NUMBERS

"What's It All About?" (Opening Chorus)
(*Music by* Henry Waller. *Lyrics by* Paul West.)

"Doing Well"
E. L. Frazer
(*Music by* Safford Waters. *Lyrics by* Paul West.)

"Try, Try Again"
D. DeWolfe
(*Music by* Safford Waters. *Lyrics by* Paul West.)

"Run, Boy, Run"
F. Haney, Chorus
(*Music by* Henry Waller. *Lyrics by* Paul West.)

"Microbes"
H. Conor
(*Music by* Safford Waters. *Lyrics by* Paul West.)

"Lover's Roost"
B. Ring
(*Music and Lyrics by* George Evans.)

"She'll Do"
E. L. Frazer
(*Music and Lyrics by* Jackson Gowraud.)

"The Smoke Goes Up the Chimney Just the Same"
H. Conor
(*Music and Lyrics by* F. Chandler.)

"She Reads the New York Papers Every Day"
D. DeWolfe
(*Music by* John W. Bratton. *Lyrics by* Paul West.)

"Chansonettes"
M. Ayer

"I'se Been A-lookin' for You"[74]
B. Ring
(*Music by* W. F. Peters.)

Dance (following "Sunny Dixie")
(B. Ring)
(*Music by* W. F. Peters.)

"My Kimona Queen"
J. Henderson
(*Music by* W. F. Peters. *Lyrics by* Henry Blossom, Jr.)

1902.41

WHEN JOHNNY COMES MARCHING HOME

A Spectacular Military Opera in Three Acts, 4 Scenes. Book (and lyrics) by Stanislaus Stange. Music by Julian Edwards. Staged by Al M. Holbrook. Scenery by D. Frank Dodge, Homer Emens, Ernest Albert. Costumes by Mme. Caroline Siedle. Orchestra under the direction of William Maquinn. Entire production under the personal direction of F. C. Whitney. Produced by the Whitney Opera Company (F. C. Whitney). Opened 16 December 1902 at the New York Theatre and closed 14 February 1903 after 71 performances.

CAST: *Colonel John Graham*: WILLIAM G. STEWART. *Felix Graham*: ALBERT McGUCKIN. *General William Allen*: HOMER LIND. *Jonathan Phoenix*: GEORGE BACKUS. *Major Geoffry Martin*: MAURICE DARCEY. *Major George Buckle*: ALGERNON ASPLAND. *Major William Walker*: W. H. THOMPSON. *Uncle Tom*: Will H. Bray. *Cordelia Allen*: MAUDE LAMBERT. *Amelia Graham*: THELMA FAIR. *Susan Garham*: BERTHA DAREL. *Mrs. Constance Pemberton*: LUCILLE SAUNDERS. *Kate Pemberton*: ZETTI KENNEDY. *Robert Pemberton*: JULIA GIFFORD.

Southern Belles: *Mabel Tracey*: Beatrice Dilworth. *Minnie Courtney*: Lotti Maydoe. *Mary Rivers*: Minnie Salvin. *Jessie Fairfax*: Helen Carr. *Nellie Jefferson*: Maude George. *Bella Montrose*: Formosa Henderson. *Lottie Allyn*: Virginia Tyler-Hudson. *Bessie Beauregard*: Ella Doyle. *Honie Chisholm*: Olive Jennings-Cox. *Carrie Sadler*: Maude Smythe. *Fannie Ludlow*: Etta Bigelow. *Jennie Holly*: Leila May Parker. *Susie Manning*: Georgia Sage. *Mamie Brixom*: Margaret Naethie. *Kittie Colfax*: Elizabeth Brinswade. *Sadie Culver*: Agnes Charbonneau.

Federal Officers: *Of the Artillery (4)*: *Captain Tate*: Joseph Royce. *Captain Kellard*: Joseph DeVens [Divans]. *Captain Hume*: Eugene Kahn. *Captain Vaughn*: George Hall. *Of the Infantry (4)*: *Captain Mawin*: C. C. Robinson. *Captain Anderson*: Forest Doolittle. *Captain Totten*: Lafayette Neber. *Captain Hopkinson*: Chanders Lightner. *Of the Cavalry (8)*: *Captain Hunter*: Edward Berg. *Captain Summers*: Fred Hornly. *Captain Hudson*: Hillion Campbell. *Captain Maltby*: Wilbur Cox. *Captain Butler*: Fred N. Stevens. *Captain Holcomb*: Howard Stephens. *Captain Byrne*: Frank Emerson. *Captain Briggs*: Benjamin Wilbur.

Act 1: Interior, General Allen's Headquarters. Cordelia's Brithday Party. (Dodge.)

Act 2: Exterior. On the Banks of the Mississippi. Felix Graham's Plantation. (Emens.)

Act 3, Scene 1: Encampment of the Federal Army. *Scene 2*: Prior to Declaration of Peace. (Albert.)

ACT 1[75]

Opening Chorus
M. Lambert, A. Aspland, W. H. Thompson, Male Chorus

"I Could Waltz On Forever (with You)"
T. Fair, M. Lambert, A. Aspland, M. Darcey, W. H. Thompson, Chorus

"Twas Down in the Garden of Eden"[76]
M. Lambert, M. Darcey

"My Own United States"
W. G. Stewart

"Just Marry the Man and Be Merry"
L. Saunders, T. Fair, B. Darel, A. Aspland, W. H. Thompson, Chorus

"When Our Lips in Kisses Met"
L. Saunders, H. Lind

"Fairyland"
Z. Kennedy, Chorus

"Who Knows"
Z. Kennedy, W. G. Stewart

"While You're Thinking"
M. Lambert, Female Chorus

"The Suwanee River"
Z. Kennedy, L. Saunders, J. Gifford, W. G. Stewart, H. Lind
(*Music and Lyrics by* Stephen Foster.)

Finale
Principals, Chorus

ACT 2

Introduction and Chorus[77]

"My Honeysuckle Girl" (Ma Honeysuckle Gal)
W. H. Bray, Chorus

"Love's Night"
Z. Kennedy, W. G. Stewart

---

[73]Not in performance order. The first 4 were in TOMMY ROT, and the "new" musical numbers were conceived for this production of FAD AND FOLLY, whose songs are listed in performance order.

[74]Replaced during the run by:
"Boo Ra Boo"
B. Ring

[75]Added to the show for subsequent tour:
"I'm So Upset" (added to Act 2, after "Love's Light")
Fin Reynolds {Phoenix}
"Why Girls Marry" (added to Act 2, after "Katie, My Southern Rose")
Albert Dorris{Geoffry}, Bertha Davis {Cordelia}
"Ootsey Totsey" (added to Act 2, before Finale)
A. McGuckin {General Allen}, Lucille Saunders {Constance}, A. Dorris, B. Davis, Chorus

[76]Dropped for subsequent tour.

[77]Touring programs identify this opening chorus as "Sing, Darkies, Sing," sung by Plantation Darkies. Whether this was the Act 2 opening is not known.

"Spring, Sweet Spring"
Z. Kennedy
"Katie, My Southern Rose"
W. G. Stewart
"Good Day, Yankees!" (Ensemble)
T. Fair, B. Darel, M. Darcey, W. H. Thompson, Chorus
"Years Touch Not the Heart"
L. Saunders
Finale II
Principals, Chorus

ACT 3
"Flag of My Country"[78] (Introduction and Chorus)
W. G. Stewart, Chorus
"But They Didn"t" (Did He, No, He Didn't)
M. Lambert, Female Chorus
"The Drums"[79] (Ensemble)
Z. Kennedy, L. Saunders, M. Lambert, W. G. Stewart, H. Lind, Chorus
Finale III
Principals, Chorus

1902.42 ALPHONSE AND GASTON

A Cartoon Comedy Extravganza in Three Whirls (Acts). Play by Gus Hill. Based on the popular comic strip by Frederick Opper. Produced under the direction of Gus Hill. Opened 29 December 1902 at the Metropolis Theatre and closed 3 January 1903 after 8 performances.

CAST: *Alphonse, Gaston*, two French Inventors in search of Capital and Fame: GEORGE E. BEBAN, BEN F. GRINNELL. *Larry Finnegan*, a retired contractor with money to invest: JOHN PRICE. *Hans Pumpernickle*, Finnegan's friend, with eyes on Mrs. Garrity: DENMAN MALEY. *Weary Walker*, a tramp and a stowaway: Harry Watson. *Captain Breeze*, of the good yacht *"Roly Poly"*: JEHAN BEDINI. *Jack Scupper*, first mate of the *"Roly Poly"*: Arthur Shaw. *Officer Sleepwell*, a minion of the law: Arthur Shaw. *Unlucky Jim*, a gambler: Frank Edwards. *Horace Rushby*, valet to Alphonse and Gaston: Mr. Arthur. *Captain Chapman*, a fly cop: Henry Wilson. *Uncle Heinie*, a sailor: Henry Hoff. *The Monkeys*, by themselves: Mr. Arthur, D. B. Carber. *Mrs. Delia Garrity*, a widow with an eye of Finnegan: JENNIE LAMONT. *Miss Evelyn Finnegan, Miss Agnes Finnegan*, Finnegan's daughters who are after a title: ANNIE LLOYD, ELLA GARDNER. *Birds of a Feather, Rainy Daisy Girls*.

Act 1: On board the good ship *"Roly Poly."* In the swim.

Act 2: Temple of Fortune. You cannot win.

Act 3: Boardwalk, Atlantic City. You cannot lose.

ACT 1[80]
"Jackies of Parade" (Opening Chorus)
"After You Alphonse"
G. E. Beban, B. F. Grinnell, Chorus
"Blooming Lize"
A. Lloyd
"In the Sweet Bye and Bye"
H. Watson, Ladies
"The Automobile Girls"
E. Gardner, Chorus
"Pretty Lulu Lu"
D. Maley, H. Watson, E. Gardner, A. Lloyd, Chorus

ACT 2
"Temple of Fortune"
Chorus
"A Bunch of Nonsense"
B. F. Grinnell, G. E. Beban
Specialty
J. Bedini, Mr. Arthur
"My Old High Hat"
J. Price, Chorus
"A Mild Flirtation"
G. E. Beban, A. Lloyd

ACT 3
"Pretty Little Bathers"
Ladies
"Yankee Doodle Dandy"
B. F. Grinnell, Ladies
Comedy Bicycle Act
H. Watson
"The Fifer of the Old Drum Corps"
L. English, Ladies

1902.43 THE BILLIONAIRE

A Musical Farce in Three Acts. Book and lyrics by Harry B. Smith. Music by Gustave Kerker. Staged by Herbert Gresham. Dances arranged by Ned Wayburn. Scenery painted by Ernest Albert. Costumes by F. Richard Anderson. Orchestra under the direction of Antonio deNovellis. Management, B. D. Stevens and Frank L. Perley. Produced by (Marc) Klaw and (Abraham L.) Erlanger. Opened 29 December 1902 at Daly's Theatre and closed 28 March 1903 after 104 performances[81].

CAST: *John Doe*, Owner of a Controlling Interest in the Earth: JEROME SYKES. *Lieutenant Ladislas*, a Hungarian Officer addicted to duelling: JULIUS STEGER. *Baptiste*, a Waiter in a hotel in Nice: HARRY MACDONOUGH. *Tim Lafferty*, a Light-Weight Pugilist who goes to France to show the Superiority of Fists over Feet: HARRY KELLY. *Monsieur Achille Petipas*, a Savateur: JOHN P. KENNEDY. *M. Cardenes*, a Hotel Proprietor: Fred Scott. *Mrs. Peppercorn*, an ambitious American mother: MAY ROBSON. *Mr. Peppercorn*, Mrs. Peppercorn's Husband, that's all: THOMAS C. LEARY. *Flora, Rosalba*, their daughters, somewhat different: SALLY FISHER, MARIE DORO. *Wally Peppercorn*, their son: HANS F. ROBERT. *Pansy Good*, who has traveled all the way from Bird Centre, Iowa, to study music in Paris: NELLIE FOLLIS. *Ping Pong*, Doe's Valet: Abraham Friedland. *Miss Flossie Frivol*: Hattie Waters. *Miss Gotham* of New York: Lillian Hudson. *Miss Lakeside* of Chicago: Gertrude Saye. *Miss Tremont* of Boston: Sally McNeel. *Miss Capitol* of Washington: Vera Cameron. *Miss Tulane* of New Orleans: Sadie Peters. *Miss Memphis* of Tennessee: Elfie [Elphye] Snowden. *Mr. Herman Rheinheister*, a stout Theatre-goer: John Steppling. *Messenger Boy*: Charles Sinclair. *First Ticket Speculator*: L. C. Fitz Roy. *Second Ticket Speculator*: Walter James. *A Stage Carpenter*: Frank Todd. *Mirandy Hopkins, Hiram Hopkins*, a Bridal Couple: Gertrude Saye, Albert Sykes. *A Page*: Marion Bent. *Mr. Gummel*, a First Nighter: James Grant. *Mr. Fidget*, a Nervous Theatre-goer: William Havens. *Hot Stuff Jake*, a Cowboy: L. B. Foley. *Southern Gent*: Edward Everett. *Little Leopold*: A. Rosenthal. *First Theatre-goer*: R. A. Beale. *Second Theatre-goer*: George Dolan. *Third Theatre-goer*: George Lyman.

Act 1: Nice, (France), during Carnival Time.

Act 2: Doe's Theatre in New York.

Act 3: The Race Track, Longchamps.

ACT 1[82]
Opening Chorus of Spaniards, Chinese, Russians (To this most entrancing fête)
Chorus

---

[78]Replaced for subsequent tour by:
"Of the Stars and Stripes I Am Dreaming"
W. H. Thompson {John Graham}, Chorus

[79]Dropped for subsequent tour.

[80]No New York program available. List of musical numbers prepared from Elizabeth, New Jersey tryout 21 November 1902. Interpolated per reviews:
"Under the Bamboo Tree" (from SALLY IN OUR ALLEY)
(*Music by* J. Rosamond Johnson. *Lyrics by* Bob Cole.)

[81]Played a return engagement 6 April 1903 at the Grand Opera House for 8 performances.

[82]No song list appears in the program. List prepared from published vocal selection (incomplete), early production typescript and reviews.Also performed, as per published sheet music:
"Miss Dinah"
J. Sykes
(*Music by* Harry Armstrong. *Lyrics by* Bartley C. Costello.)
"Glory" (A Military Ballad)
J. Steger
(*Music by* William E. Bock. *Lyrics by* Edward F. Cogley.)

"Americans We" (Quartette)
T. C. Leary, H. F. Robert, S. Fisher, M. Doro
"To Be Truly Refined" (Song)
M. Robson, Chorus
Duet Blasé (People sometimes travel round the world to spend their wealth)
H. F. Robert, T. C. Leary
Entrance Chorus (Oh, toss the ready cap)
Chorus
"The Money Burner" (Song)
J. Sykes, Chorus
Exit Chorus (We're demanding satisfaction)
Chorus
"Morality's a Matter of Geography" (Duet)
J. Sykes, N. Follis
"Defeat We Never Know" (Song)
J. Steger, Chorus
"Such a Dear Little Man as You" (Quartette)
J. Steger, S. Fisher, M. Doro, H. Macdonough
"The Kangaroo" (Song)
H. Kelly, J. P. Kennedy
"Grace Personified" (Song)
M. Robson
"For a Sight of Old Broadway" (Song)
J. Sykes
Finale (We represent the power)

ACT 2

Opening Chorus (To the opening of a playhouse we have all been invited)
"The Money Burner" (reprise)
J. Sykes, Chorus
"There Are Tricks in Every Trade" (Duet)
J. Sykes, M. Robson
"Such a Dear Little Wife as You" (Quartette/reprise)
J. Steger, S. Fisher, M. Doro, H. Macdonough
"Rap, Rap, Rap" (Ensemble)
Chorus
"The Lives of Famous Men" (Song)
J. Sykes
"Flora" (Waltz Song)
Song
M. Doro
Specialty
H. Kelly, J. P. Kennedy
Specialty
H. Macdonough
"Pansy" (Song)
N. Follis, Chorus
Burlesque Drama
"The Drink of All Nations" (Toast Song/Finale)
J. Sykes, Company

ACT 3

Opening Chorus (Then horses all expectantly)
Chorus
"Don't You Care" (Song)
H. F. Robert, Girls
"Here Comes Pansy" (Trio)
N. Follis, H. Kelly, J. P. Kennedy
"Truly Refined" (Song)
M. Robson
"In the Land of Romance" (Duet)
"Just 'Cause the Moon Was Shinin'"
J. Sykes, Chorus
"The Money Burner" (Finale)
J. Sykes, Chorus

1902.44 THE SULTAN OF SULU

A Musical Satire in Two Acts. Book and lyrics by George Ade. Music by Alfred G. Wathall. Dances arranged by Joseph C. Smith. Scenery by Walter Burridge. Costumes by Will R. Barnes, John T. McCutcheon. Orchestra under the direction of Alexander Spencer. Produced by Henry W. Savage. Opened 29 December 1902 at Wallack's Theatre and closed 13 June 1903 after 192 performances[83].

CAST: *Ki-Ram*, the Sultan of Sulu: FRANK MOULAN. *Colonel Jefferson Budd* of the Volunteers: WILLIAM C. MANDEVILLE. *Lieutenant William Hardy* of the Regulars: TEMPLAR SAXE. *Hadji Tantong*, the Sultan's Private Secretary: FRED FREAR. *Datto Mandi* of Parang: Frank Rainger. *Wakeful M. Jones*, agent and salesman: PAUL NICHOLSON. *Dingbat*, Captain of the Guards: Frank Hunter. *Sergeant Standpipe*, U. S. Army: Basil Millspaugh. *Rastus, Didymos*, Nubian slaves: John J. Fogarty, Edward J. Flanagan. *Henrietta Budd*, the Colonel's daughter: MAUDE LILLIAN BERRI. *Pamela Francis Jackson*, Judge-Advocate: BLANCHE CHAPMAN. *Chiquita*, Wife No. 1: GERTRUDE QUINLAN. *Galula*, the faithful one: Victory Gale. *Wives of Ki-Ram (6)*: *Mauricia*: Loris Scarsdale. *Ramona*: Nellie Adams. *Pepita*: Beryl Gomez. *Natividad*: Mabel Wilbur. *Natalia*: Effie Hasty. *Selina*: Marian McLean. *The Schoolm'ams from Boston (4)*: *Miss Roxbury*: Aurora Piatt. *Miss Dorchester*: Charlotte Groves. *Miss Cambridge*: Jane Mandeville. *Miss Newton*: Memay Kennedy. *U.S. Soldiers, Marines, American Girls, Salves, Natives and Attendants.*

Act 1: Exterior of Sultan's Palace, Island of Sulu, in the Phillippines.

Act 2: Hanging gardens of the Sultan's Palace.

ACT 1

"Salute" (Opening Chorus)
"(Man, Man,) Fickle Man"[84]
G. Quinlan, Chorus
"Hike" (Soldier's Song)
T. Saxe, Ensemble
"Palm Branches Waving"[85]
M. L. Berri, Chorus
"The Peachy Teacher"
Schoolma'ams, Chorus
"(The) Smiling Isle"
F. Moulan, Chorus
"Oh, What a Bump!" (Topical Trio)
P. Nicholson, W. C. Mandeville, F. Moulan
"(We Are) Engaged in a Sort of Way" (Duet)
T. Saxe, M. L. Berri
"If I But Knew"[86]
T. Saxe
"My Sulu Lulu Loo"
G. Quinlan, Ki-Ram's Wives
(*Music by* Nat. D. Mann.)
"Till the Volunteers Return" (Finale)
T. Saxe, Chorus

ACT 2

"Slumber On" (Lullaby)(Opening Chorus)
"R-E-M-O-R-S-E"
F. Moulan

---

[83]Direction uncredited, presumably by the author. Played a return engagement 23 November 1903 at the Grand Opera House for 8 performances.
[84]Replaced early in the run by:
"The Queer Little Ostrich"
G. Quinlan, Chorus
(*Music and Lyrics by* Maurice Pratt Dunlap.)
Which was later replaced by:
"Ki-Ram Wedding March"
G. Quinlan, Chorus
(*Music by* George L. Brun.)
[85]Replaced for subsequent tour by:
"(In the) U.S.A."
Cheridah Simpson {Henrietta}, Chorus
[86]Replaced for subsequent tour by:
"A Song of Yesterday"
Walter Laurence {Lieutenant Hardy}
(*Music by* Anton Heindl. *Lyrics by* Rida Johnson Young.)

"Imperial Guards' March"
Imperial Guards, Chorus

"(The) Old Jay Bird"
W. C. Mandeville, Chorus

"Since I First Met You" (Drippling Sunshine)
F. Moulan, M. L. Berri, T. Saxe,G. Quinlan, F. Frear, V. Gale, P. Nicholson, W. C. Mandeville, others

"Always Late"
G. Quinlan, F. Moulan

Medley of Popular Songs:

"Rosabella Clancy"
P. Nicholson, F. Moulan, W. C. Mandeville, T. Saxe, Chorus

"(Come Back to) Manistee"
F. Moulan, Male Chorus

"Delia"
G. Quinlan, Chorus

"Ten Little Gentlemen of Spooney Town"[87]
P. Nicholson, Schoolma'ams

"Carmena"
M. L. Berri

"Foolish Wedding Bells"
T. Saxe, M. L. Berri, G. Quinlan, W. C. Mandeville, Chorus

"Candidates' March"
Ensemble

Finale

1903.01

ZIG-ZAG ALLEY

A Spectacular Trick Farce in Three Acts. Written by James Gorman. Staged by James Gorman. Incidental music by Karl Weixelbaum. Produced by W. E. Flack and Walter Floyd. Opened 19 January 1903 at the Star Theatre and closed 24 January 1903 after 8 performances[88].

CAST: *Colonel Slick, Major Slack,* a Pair hard to beat: JOLLY ZEB, HAPPY ZARROW. *Michael Moriarty,* the Politician of the Alley: BEN T. DILLON. *Terrence Moriarty,* his son, the Beau Brummel of the Alley: ANDREW O'NEIL. *Johnny Wise,* the author's idea of messenger service: James Farley. *Isaac Goldstein,* the restive pawn-broker of the Alley: Goff Phillips. *Melancholy Ike,* a wandering misfit, always in the way: Frank Kennebel. *Adam On,* his shadow: Frank Rice. *Patrick Duffy,* guardian of the Alley: John Church. *Clarence Heavysides,* a weight of trouble: Allen Schrock. *Willie Yell,* train announcer: Charles Kennebel. *Hardly Abel,* a tough proposition: George Dempsey. *Cregan, Dregan,* Depot Agents: Harry Kammerer, Frank Markey. *Sally,* who lives in the Alley: Irene Young. *Mrs. Donahue,* the Queen of the Alley: Louise Dempsey. *Annie Goldstein,* the Pride of the Alley: ELLA SHIELDS. *Margery Lovestock, Ida Simmonds,* from Atlantic City: LILLIE SIEGER, Anna Casselle. (*Specialties*: Sol Bloom, Doty and Brill.)

Belles of the Alley: *Kittie Reed*: Elsinore Richmond. *Daisy Deen*: Lizzie Purcelle. *Hazel Wood*: Orient Anson. *Effie Brown*: Lillian DeSchoen. *May Snow*: Josephine Leslie. *Sadie Ryan*: Nettie Frederick. *Maude Dunn*: Ella Stuart. *Mabel Vane*: Emma Lipman. *Helen Morris*: Mabel Ware. *Nellie Jackson*: Grace Ellison. Other characters too numerous to mention will appear and disappear at will.

Act 1: Zig-Zag Alley in all its glory.

Act 2: New Underground Station, Pennsylvania Railroad, New York.

Act 3: The Board Walk—Atlantic City.

MUSICAL NUMBERS[89]

"Belles of Zig-Zag Alley"
K. Weixelbaum, Company

"Queen of the Alley"
K. Weixelbaum, L. Dempsey, Misses Sieger, Eckert, Mortimer, Anson

"When I'm an Alderman"
K. Weixelbaum, B. T. Dillon, Company

"Sally in Our Alley" (from SALLY IN OUR ALLEY)
A. O'Neil
(*Music and Lyrics by* Henry Carey.)

Cyclone Finish

"Under the Bamboo Tree" (from SALLY IN OUR ALLEY)
L. Purcelle
(*Music and Lyrics by* Bob Cole and J. Rosamund Johnson.)

"The Italian Organ Grinder"
A. O'Neil

"Off for Atlantic City"
K. Weixelbaum, Company

Cornet Solo
L. Sieger

"The Girl with the Banjo Eyes"
J. Farley, I. Gray, E. Shields

"Sunny Afternoon"
A. O'Neil

"Pinky Panky Poo" (from THE DEFENDER)
S. Bloom, Company
(*Music and Lyrics by* Andy Louis.)

"The Southern Nightingale"
E. Shields

"We Are Four Actors"
J. Zeb, H. Zarrow, B. Dillon, G. Phillips

"Is It Love"
Doty and Brill, A. O'Neil

"Dreaming on the Ohio"
Doty and Brill, A. O'Neil, Company

"Kitty Kitty"
K. Weixelbaum, B. Dillon, A. Mortimer

The Zeb and Zarrow Trio, the Daredevils of the Wheel,

introducing William C. Hoefler, America's Champion Trick Bicycle Rider; European Gymnasts, The Brothers Damm.

Finale

1903.02

MR. PICKWICK

A Musical Production in Two Acts. Book by Charles Klein. Based on Charles Dickens' masterpiece "The Pickwick Papers." Music by Manuel Klein. Lyrics by Grant Stewart. Staged by George Marion. Scenery by D. Frank Dodge[90]. Costumes by Van Horn. Musical director, Manuel Klein. Produced by the DeWolf Hopper Opera Company. Opened 19 January 1903 at the Herald Square Theatre and closed 21 March 1903 after 65 performances[91].

CAST: *Pickwick*: DeWOLF HOPPER. *Sam Weller*: DIGBY BELL. *Tony Weller*: HENRY NORMAN. *Alfred Jingle*: GRANT STEWART. *Winkle*: Louis Payne. *Mr. Wardle*: J. K. Adams. *Snodgrass*: George Chapman. *Tupman*: Augustus Coletti. *Fat Boy*: Guy H. Bartlett. *Colonel Bulder*: George Rolland. *Dr. Slammer*: Phillip Connor. *Landlord*: George Williams. *Arabella*: LOUISE GUNNING. *Mrs. Bardell*: LAURA JOYCE BELL. *Polly*: MARGUERITE CLARK. *Miss Wardle*: GRACE FISHER. *Miss Tompkins*: Mary Davis. *Liza, Lally, Sue,* Mrs. Bardell's Nieces: Alice Maude Poole, Marion Lee, Ruth Halbert. *Seminary Girls, Huntsmen, Gamekeepers, etc.*

Act 1: Dingley Dell Arms.

Act 2: Manor Farm.

ACT 1

Opening Chorus (We gather at the Dingley Arms)
(M. Davis, Chorus)

"Golden Rules" (Solo)
G. Stewart

"Love" (Duet)
L. Gunning, M. Clark

---

[87]Dropped early in the run.

[88]No New York program found. Credits taken from Chicago program prior to New York; costumes, settings uncredited.

[89]No New York program available. List of musical numbers assembled from reviews and touring programs, not necessarily in performance order.

[90]Settings uncredited in New York programs; credited to D. Frank Dodge for tryout and subsequent tour.

[91]Played a return engagement 27 April 1903 at the Grand Opera House for 8 performances.

"Gratitude" (Trio)
H. Norman, D. Bell, M. Clark
"What's the Latest News from Town?"
Chorus
"The Pickwick Club" (Solo)
D. Hopper, Chorus
"The Lady of the Merry Ha, Ha" (Quartette)
D. Hopper, G. Chapman, L. Gunning, M. Clark
"I'll Have the Law, I'll Have My Right" (Octette)
L. J. Bell, A. M. Poole, M. Lee,
R. Halbert, D. Hopper, A. Coletti, G. Chapman, H. Norman
"Boys Will Be Boys" (Trio)
D. Hopper, J. K. Adams, H. Norman
"Speak Low" (Solo)
L. Gunning, School Girls
(*Lyrics by* Hermann Klein.)
Finale

ACT 2
Opening Chorus (Hay, Hay, a wagon of hay)
(L. Gunning, M. Clark, M. Davis, D. Bell, H. Norman, Chorus)
"The Story of the Rainbow" (Solo)
L. Gunning, School Girls
"On the Side"[92] (Solo)
D. Bell
"Pickwick's Horse Brigade" (Solo)
D. Hopper, Chorus
(*March composed by* George A. Spink.)
"The Forest Air"[93] (Madrigal)
D. Hopper, D. Bell, L. Gunning, M. Clark
"Acting" (Solo)
M. Clark, School Girls
Finale

1903.03 THE WIZARD OF OZ

A Musical Play in Three Acts, 6 Scenes. Book and lyrics by L. Frank Baum. Based on his own novel "The Wonderful Wizard of Oz." Music by Paul Tietjens and A. Baldwin Sloane. Staged by Julian Mitchell. Settings by Walter Burridge, Fred Gibson, John Young. Costumes by Mrs. Edward (Caroline) Siedle. (Electrical effects by James Finn.) Orchestra under the direction of Charles Zimmerman. Produced by Fred R. Hamlin. Opened 20 January 1903 at the Majestic Theatre and closed 3 October 1903 after 306 performances[94].

CAST (in order of appearance): *Dorothy Gale*, a Kansas girl, the victim of a cyclone: ANNA LAUGHLIN. *The Cow named Imogene*, Dorothy's playmate: EDWIN J. STONE. *Farmhands*: Misses Grace Bond, Marie Fitzhugh, Etta Diamond, Virginia Kendall, Marie Burnell, Kathleen Flynn, Grace Pomeroy, May DuFrene, Mary Jackson, Grace Igoe, Messrs. Albert Cleveland, Irving Christerson, George Young, William Van Brunt. *Tom Piper*: IDA DOERGE. *Munchkins (7)*: *Peter Boq*: Mabel DeVere. *Simon Powder*: Ella Gilroy. *Antonia*: Georgia Baron. *Sophronia*: Edna Adams. *Premonia*: Lillian DeVere. *Malvonia*: Stubby Ainscoe. *Semponia*: Albertina Benson. *Munchkin Youths*: Misses Erna Evans, Elsie Mertens, Clara Pitt, Josephine Clayton, Helen Blye, Anna Leon, Laura Young, Clara Selton, Anna Fitzhugh, Rae Dixon, Emma Clarke, Genevra Gibson, Messrs. Field, Dewey, Rogers, Wyckoff, Hoskins, Sargent, Mansfield, Wiegand. *Munchin Maidens*: Misses Leta Shaw, Nancy Poole, Lola Gordon, Marie Clayton, Nellie Payne, Emily Fulton, Lucile Bryant, Margie Griffith. *Cynthia Cynch*, the lady lunatic, a Munchkin maiden: HELEN BYRON. *The Witch of the North*, a friend in need: EDITH HUTCHINS. *Sir Dashemoff Daily*, Poet laureate: BESSIE WYNN. *The Army of Pastoria*: JOSEPH SCHRODE. *Pastoria II*, ex-King of the Emerald City, with a conspiracy to regain his throne: GILBERT CLAYTON. *Tryxie Tryffle*, prospective Queen of the Emerald City: GRACE KIMBALL. *Brigadier General Riskitt*, commanding Pastoria's army: HAROLD P. MOREY. *The Scarecrow*, looking for brains: FRED A. STONE. *The Cowardy Lion*: Arthur Hill. *Mick Chopper*, the Tin Woodman in search of a heart: DAVID C. MONTGOMERY. *The Poppy Queen*: IDA DOERGE. *Poppy Flowers*: Misses Diamond, Burnell, Gordon, Selton, Poole, Young, Blye, M. Clayton, Gilroy, Payne, Kendall, Leon, Griffith, Bond, J. Clayton, Adams, Diamond, Evans, Flynn, Dixon, Ainscoe, DuFrene, Bryant, Pomeroy, Jackson, Fulton, Clark, Igoe, Pitt. *Snow Queen*: Georgia Baron. *Snow Boys*: Genevia Gibson, Ella Gilroy, Mabel DeVere, Anna Fitzhugh, Lillian DeVere. *Snow Girls*: Elsie Mertens, Albertine Benson, Lita Shaw, Ailene Potter. *Leo*, Captain of the Relief Guards: Robert D. Fairchild. *Captain of the Phantom Guards*: Georgia Baron. *Phantom Guards*: Misses Adams, Leon, Selten, Diamond, Bond, Flynn, DuFrene, Griffith, Dixon, M. Fitzhugh, Gordon, Gibson, Pomeroy, Kendall, Clark, Igoe. *Alonzo*, a confederate: Joseph Schrode. *Sir Wiley Gyle*, a conspirator, who scorns all magical arts: STEPHEN MALEY. *The Wizard's Wise Men (4)*: *Silicus*: Earl Dewey. *Sophocles*: Charles Hoskins. *Pericles*: Irving Christenson. *Diogenes*: William Van Brunt. *Bardo*, the Wizard's factotum: Geneva Gibson. *Oz*, the Wonderful Wizard, Past Master of Magic, ruler of the Emerald City and Potentate of the Land of Oz: BOBBY GAYLOR. *Witches*: Misses Doerge, Gilroy, M. DeVere, L. DeVere, Benson, Pitt. *Pierrot Boys*: Misses Young, A. Fitzhugh, J. Clayton, M. Clayton, Payne, Mertens. *Alberto*, Captain of the Guard: IDA DOERGE. *Waitresses (6)*: *Gloriana Jane*: Mabel DeVere. *Gladys Ann*: Ella Gilroy. *Leontine Em*: Albertine Benson. *Vera Ellen*: Lillian DeVere. *Aileen Nance*: Elsie Mertens. *Pansy Lil*: Josephine Clayton. *Cooks (4)*: *Francois Giblets*: Genevra Gibson. *Jean deChar*: Anna Fitzhugh. *Remnante Sauté*: Marie Clayton. *Pungue DeSert*: Lola Gordon. *Laundresses*: Misses Flynn, Fulton, Shaw, Igoe. *Captain of the Royal Guards*: Ida Doerge. *Royal Guards*: Misses Baron, Adams, Blye, Selten, Bond, Diamond, Young, Griffith, Clark, Pomeroy.

Act 1, Scene 1: A Kansas Farm. (Painted by Fred Gibson from designs by Walter W. Burridge). *Scene 2*: Transformation. The Country of the Munchkins. (Young). *Scene 3*: The Road through the Forest. (Gibson). *Scene 4*: The Poppy Field. (Young). The Poppy Field in Winter.

Act 2: The Courtyard of the Wizard's Palace. (Burridge).

Act 3: The Borderland, dividing the Kingdom of Oz from the Dominions of the Good Witch. (Young).

ACT 1[95]
"Life in Kansas" (Opening)
(*Music by* Paul Tietjens.)
"Niccolo's Piccolo"
H. Byron
(*Music by* A. Baldwin Sloane. *Lyrics by* Glen MacDonough.)
"In Michigan"
G. Clayton
(*Music by* A. Baldwin Sloane. *Lyrics by* Glen MacDonough.)
"When the Circus Comes to Town" (Duet)
G. Kimball, G. Clayton
(*Music by* Bob Adams. *Lyrics by* James O'Dea.)
"Carrie Barry" (Carry Barry)
A. Laughlin
(*Music by* A. Baldwin Sloane. *Lyrics by* Glen MacDonough.)
"Alas for the Man Without Brains" (The Scarecrow)
F. A. Stone
(*Music by* Paul Tietjens.)
"That Is Love" (That Must Be Love)
B. Wynn
(*Music and Lyrics by* Maurice Steinberg.)
"When You Love, Love, Love"
F. A. Stone, D. C. Montgomery, A. Laughlin
(*Music by* Paul Tietjens.)
"Poppy Chorus"
(*Music by* Paul Tietjens.)

ACT 2
"Phantom Patrol"
Chorus
(*Music by* Paul Tietjens.)

---

[92]For subsequent tour, replaced by:
"The Potato Song"
D. Bell

[93]For subsequent tour, replaced by:
"Five Little Piggies" (Three Little Piggies)
D. Hopper

[94]A Second Edition with a revised score played New York 21 March 1904 at the Majestic and New York Theatres for 72 performances. See separate entry in 1903-1904 season.

[95]Interpolated in 1904 as per published sheet music:
"Mary Canary" (Novelty Song with Refrain)
B. Wynne
(*Music by* Seymour Furth. *Lyrics by* Edward P. Moran.)

"Pay Night" (On a Pay Night Evening)
B. Gaylor
(*Music by* Bruno Schilinski. *Lyrics by* John W. West.)

"The Witch Behind the Moon"[96]
H. Byron, Chorus
(*Music by* Charles Albert. *Lyrics by* Louis Weslyn.)

Medley: Ball of All Nations (Dance of All Nations)
(*Music by* A. Baldwin Sloane. *Lyrics by* Edgar Smith.)

"Connemara Christening"
B. Gaylor
(*Music by* A. Baldwin Sloane. *Lyrics by* Edgar Smith.)

"Spanish Bolero"
F. A. Stone

"Wee-High and Mon" (Wee Highland Mon)
D. C. Montgomery
(*Music by* A. Baldwin Sloane. *Lyrics by* Edgar Smith.)

"Rosalie" (Coon Song and Cakewalk)
A. Laughlin
(*Music by* Gus Edwards. *Lyrics by* Will D. Cobb.)

"I Love Only One Girl in the Wide, Wide, Wide World"
B. Wynn
(*Music by* Gus Edwards. *Lyrics by* Will D. Cobb.)

"Sammy"
G. Kimball, Chorus
(*Music by* Edward Hutchison. *Lyrics by* James O'Dea.)

"Hurrah for Baffin's Bay" (Nautical Nonsense)
F. A. Stone, D. C. Montgomery
(*Music by* Theodore Morse[97]. *Lyrics by* Vincent Bryan.)

"Star of My Native Land" (Finale)
Ensemble
(*Music by* A. Baldwin Sloane. *Lyrics by* Glen MacDonough.)

ACT 3[98]

Opening Chorus[99]
Waitresses, Cooks, Laundresses
(*Music by* A. Baldwin Sloane. *Lyrics by* Glen MacDonough.)

"Pimlico Malinda"[100] (A Cockney Negro Song)
D. C. Montgomery, F. A. Stone
(*Music by* Bob Adams. *Lyrics by* James O'Dea.)

"Honey, My Sweet" (Honey is Sweet)
A. Laughlin
(*Music by* George Spink. *Lyrics by* Henry Blossom.)

1903.04 MR. BLUEBEARD

The Great Spectacular Entertainment from the Theatre Royal, Drury Lane, London, in Three Acts, 12 Scenes. Book by J. Hickory Wood and Arthur Collins, adapted for America by John J. McNally. Music by Frederic Solomon. Lyrics by J. Cheever Goodwin. Additional songs by William Jerome and Jean Schwartz, Alfred Bryan and Theodore Morse, Gus Edwards and Alfred Bryan, Bob Cole and J. Rosamond Johnson, William Jerome and Matt Woodward, Dan McAvoy. Presented under the stage direction of Herbert Gresham and Ned Wayburn. Ballets by Ernest D'Auban. Settings by Bruce Smith, H. Emden, Ernest Albert, R. C. McCleary, Hicks & Brooks. Costumes by Comelli. Musical director, Frederic Solomon. Produced by (Marc) Klaw & (Abraham L.) Erlanger. Opened 21 January 1903 at the Knickerbocker Theatre and closed 16 May 1903 after 135 performances.

CAST: *Mr. Blue Beard*: DAN McAVOY. *Sister Anne*: EDDIE FOY. *Fatima*: FLORA PARKER. *Selim*: ADELE RAFTER. *Imer Dasher*: BONNIE MAGINN. *Abdallah*: Norma Kopp. *Mustapha*: WILLIAM DANFORTH. *Irish Patsha*: HERBERT CAWTHORNE. *Hatrac*: Thomas O'Brien. *Korafai*: BESSIE DeVOIE. *Abaddin*: Sam Reed. *Abumun*: Frank Young. *Mirza*: Clara Havel. *Blue Beard's Six Pretty Wives*: *Zaidee*: May Taylor. *Amina*: Edith Palmer. *Zara*: Helga Howard. *Nadie*: Rose Earle. *Beca*: Myrtle Arlington. *Zoli*: Nellie Simmons. *Blue Beard's Six Ugly Wives*: *Laidoff*: Harry Murdoc. *Dunfor*: George A. Cameron. *Knouse*: Fred Walsh. *Badun*: Abner Symmons. *Hacnum*: W. H. White. *Passai*: Chauncey Holland. *Stella*, Queen of the Fairies: Georgia Kelley. *Pony Ballet*: Seppie McNeil, Lonie Hauman, Ada Robertson, Beatrice Liddell, Elizabeth Hauman, Eva Marlowe, Dorothy Marlowe, Carolyn Poltz. Elephant and Head Tricks by Dane and Seymour. (*Specialty*: The Grigolatis Troupe of Aerialists. Elsa Huerting, Premiere.)

Act 1, Scene 1: The Market Place on the Quay near Bagdad. (Smith.) *Scene 2*: On board Blue Beard's Yacht. (Smith.) *Scene 3*: The Isle of Ferns. (Emden.) *Scene 4*: The Land of Ferns. (Emden.)

Act 2, Scene 1: The Castle Terrace and Gardens. (McCleery.) *Scene 2*: Chamber of Curiosities. (McCleery.) *Scene 3*: Home of the Old Woman who lived in a Shoe. (Albert.) *Scene 4*: Hall in Blue Beard's Palace. (Albert.) *Scene 5*: Triumph of the Magic Fan. (Emden.)

Act 3, Scene 1: Hall of Pleasures in Blue Beard's Palace. (Albert.) *Scene 2*: Below the Ramparts. (Hicks & Brooks.) *Scene 3*: The Fairy Palace. (Smith.)

ACT 1[101]

Scene 1

Opening Chorus:

"Come Buy Our Luscious Fruit"

"Oriental Slaves Are We"

"We Come from Dalmatia"

"Algerian Slave Song and Chorus"

Grand Entrance, Blue Beard's Retinue. Medley Ensemble

"A Most Unpopular Potentate" (Song)
D. McAvoy, Chorus

"Poor Unfortunate Sister Anne"[102] (Sister Ann)(Song)
E. Foy
(*Music by* Matt Woodward. *Lyrics by* William Jerome.)

"Welcome Fatima"

"I'm as Good as I Ought to Be" (Song)
F. Parker

"Then Away We Go" (Finale)

Scene 2

"There's Nothing Like the Life We Sailors Need" (Opening Chorus)

Medley
D. McAvoy

"(You'll Have to) Read the Answer in the Stars"
(*Music by* Harry Von Tilzer. *Lyrics by* Vincent Bryan.)

"I'm a Poor Unhappy Maid"
(E. Foy)
(*Music by* Jean Schwartz. *Lyrics by* William Jerome.)

Duet
A. Rafter, F. Parker

---

[96]Replaced by mid-March 1903:
"Things That We Don't Learn at School" (There's a Lot of Things You Never Learn at School)
Jeanette Lowrie {Cynthia}
(*Music by* Edwin S. Brill. *Lyrics by* Edward Gardenier.)

[97]In programs music credited by Charles Zimmerman, the show's conductor.

[98]Added to the close of Act 3, by the second week; then dropped in June 1903:
"That's Where She Sits All Day"
D. C. Montgomery, F. A. Stone
(*Music and Lyrics by* Frank Leo.)

[99]Replaced during the run by:
"The Traveler and the Pie"
F. A. Stone, Chorus
(*Music by* Paul Tietjens.)

[100]Replaced by the second week by:
"Must You?"
D. C. Montgomery, F. A. Stone
(*Music by* Bert Branford. *Lyrics by* Harry Boden. *Additional lyrics by* David C. Montgomery.)

[101]Interpolated by Eddie Foy as per published sheet music:
"Stories Adam Told to Eve"
E. Foy
(*Music by* Jean Schwartz. *Lyrics by* William Jerome.)

[102]Dropped during the run.

"Marriage Is Sublime"
(*Music by* Theodore Morse. *Lyrics by* Alfred Bryan.)
"He's Gone" (Finale)
Scene 4
Ballet of Ferns—Procession and Weaving of the Magic Fan
Fairies, Grand Corps de Ballet
ACT 2
Scene 1
"Daylight Is Dawning" (Opening Chorus)
"Songbird of Melody Lane"
(*Music by* Gus Edwards. *Lyrics by* Alfred Bryan.)
"(The) Beer That Made Milwaukee Famous"
(*Music and Lyrics by* Dan McAvoy.)
Sister Anne and Pet Elephant
"In the Pale Moonlight" (Let Us Swear It by the Pale Moonlight)
(*Music by* Ben M. Jerome. *Lyrics by* Matt C. Woodward.)
"When the Colored Band Comes Marching Down the Street"
(*Music by* J. Rosamond Johnson. *Lyrics by* Bob Cole.)
Scene 3
Pierrot Dance
"The Old Woman Who Lived in a Shoe"
(*Music by* Theodore Morse. *Lyrics by* Alfred Bryan.)
Scene 4
Dancing Specialty
F. Young, B. DeVoie
(*Music by* C. Herbert Kerr.)
Scene 5
The Land of Palmas; Egypt; India; Japan; Rarisian Rose Garden; Spanish Rose Garden; Electric Apotheosis.
Grigolatis Troupe of Aerialists, Grand Corps de Ballet
ACT 3
Scene 1
"Let Us Be Jolly as Long as We Can" (Opening Chorus)
"Billy Gray, U.S.A., (O.K.)"
(*Music by* Gus Edwards. *Lyrics by* Will D. Cobb.)
U.S.A. March
B. Maginn, Chorus
Pony Ballet Specialty
(*Music by* Jean Schwartz.)
"Julie"
H. Cawthorne, Chorus
(*Music by* Jean Schwartz. *Lyrics by* William Jerome.)
"Raving"
D. McAvoy
(*Music by* Theodore F. Morse. *Lyrics by* Vincent Bryan.)
"Hamlet Was a Melancholy Dane"
E. Foy
(*Music by* Jean Schwartz. *Lyrics by* William Jerome.)
Scene 2
"The Yankee Tourist Girl"
(*Music by* Matt Woodward. *Lyrics by* William Jerome.)
Scene 3
Entrance and Triumph of the Fairy Army
Grand Transformation Scene

1903.05 SPOTLESS TOWN

Gus Hill's Comedians in a Musical Comedy in Three Acts[103]. Play by Whitcomb Reilly. Musical numbers, ballets and ensembles by Gus Sohlke. Produced by Gus Hill.Opened 9 February 1903 at the Metropolis Theatre and closed 14 February 1903 after 8 performances; returned 2-7 April 1903 to the 14th Street Theatre for an additional 8 performances.

CAST: *Dietrich Schnitzel, Ludwig Sauerbraten*, engaged in the friendly occupation of helping each other spend his money: BOB CARLIN, NAT BROWN. *Butcher Delicatessen*, the festive caterer: DAVE CONROY. *Policeman O'Rafferty*, guardian to the quiet little town: PHIL McFARLAND. *Dr. Grafter*, hard to beat: CHARLES E. FLYNN. *Mayor Wise*, "who owns the town": GEORGE W. KERR. *Tips*, the waiter, hard to lose: CURTIS SPECK. *Chips Stake*, out to win: HARRY SPECK. *Alkali Ike*, a tough proposition: GEORGE W. KERR. *Avor Du Pois*, a copper: Frank Raymond. *Harvard Yale*, just home from college: CHARLES E. FLYNN. *Kitty Topnote*, the maid of Spotless Town: ADELAIDE MARSDEN. *Lady Bountiful*, society leader, but prefers to be an actress: MARIE RICHMOND. *Mary Ann*, the cook, who runs the house: LILLIAN TYCE. *Vera Swell*, from the suburbs: Frances Kelcy. *Villa Parks*, very exclusive: Nelly Kelcy. *Princella Rustic*, a village maiden: Kate Kelcy. *Zaza DuBarry*, a little gay: Allie Palmer.

Prima Donnas of the Halls (4): *Miss Canby Hurd*: Lillian Lewis. *Miss Rufe Raiser*: Marie Young. *Miss Cora Singer*: Antoine Allen. *Miss Carrie Holdit*: Madelien Reynard. *Coy Maidens of the Spotless Town Choir* (6): *Miss Flora Day*: Vera Belmont. *Miss Birdie Sunshine*: Stella Warner. *Miss Flossie Footlight*: Winnie Erlinger. *Miss Bessie Bunchlight*: Helen Bellew. *Miss Lillie Limelight*: Lillian Clements. *Miss Sophie Spotlight*: Marie Adams.

Act 1: Streets of Spotless Town. Scenes of everyday life.

Act 2: Public Square in Spotless Town. The "Get Rich Quick" stores.

Act 3: Spotless Town Hotel in active operation.

ACT 1
Opening Number
A. Marsden, Chorus, Police Corps
"Things Are Not What They Used to Be" (Sextet)
A. Marsden, L. Tyce, C. E. Flynn, G. W. Kerr, D. Conroy, P. McFarland
"I Wants to Be an Actor Lady"
M. Richmond, Full Chorus
(*Music by* Harry Von Tilzer. *Lyrics by* Vincent Bryan.)
Songs and Sayings
B. Carlin, N. Brown
"In Spotless Town" (Song)
D. Conroy, P. McFarland, Principals and Chorus
Specialty
Sisters Kelcy (Australia Triplets in their Biograph Dances)
Specialty
L. Tyce
Spotless Town Firemen March
M. Richmond, Messrs. G. W. Kerr, C. E. Flynn, Chorus
ACT 2
"In the Sweet Bye and Bye" (Opening Number)
A. Marsden, C. E. Flynn, Chorus
(*Music by* Harry Von Tilzer. *Lyrics by* Vincent Bryan.)
Specialty (Funny Sayings)
D. Conroy, P. McFarland
Specialty (Boxing Act)
C. Speck, H. Speck
Operatic Specialty ("Violets")
A. Marsden
Jockey Song and Dance
M. Richmond, Chorus
"Spotless Town Cadet Trio"
"Herald Square Song"
G. W. Kerr, Entire Company in Character
ACT 3
"Oh, the Girls" (Opening Number)
M. Richmond, Chorus
"The Gypsy Maid"
A. Marsden, Company
Medley of all the Latest popular and classical songs
Entire Company
Grand Divertissement and Transformation Finale

[103]Billed as "a facetious feast of frolic and frivolity." On tour the authorship was credited to Whitcomb *and* Reilly.

1903.06 THE JEWEL OF ASIA

A Musical Comedy (Comic Opera) in Two Acts. Book and lyrics by Frederic Ranken and Harry B. Smith. (Music) Composed by Ludwig Engländer. Produced (staged) under the personal stage direction of George W. Lederer. Settings by D. Frank Dodge, Ernest Albert. Orchestra under the direction of Max Hirschfeld. Produced by George W. Lederer. Opened 16 February 1903 at the Criterion Theatre and closed 11 April 1903 after 64 performances.

CAST: *Pierre Lerouge*, an artist who is forced by necessity to act as a waiter in the cafe of Madame Hersillie: JAMES T. POWERS. *Simoon Pasha*, Minister of Police, with up-to-date ideas: GEORGE O'DONNELL. *Mufti*, janitor of the Pasha's domestic establishment: WILLIAM CAMERON. *Yussuf Potiphar*, a young Turkish noble, heir of his uncle, the late Badeg Pasha: CLIFTON CRAWFORD. *Sergeant Lafitte*, the only surviving member of Napoleon's old guard: HARRY SHORT. *Hashish, Backsheesh*, Bodyguards of Simoon Pasha: E. B. Knight, Frank Symonds. *Anatole*, a student: Paul Decker. *Francois*, a student: Thomas Miller. *A Gendarme*: Frank G. Hill. *Ali*, the Pasha's favorite swordsman: Frank G. Hill. *Zaidee*, called the Jewel of Asia, favorite better half of Simoon Pasha: BLANCHE RING. *Mimi*, daughter of Sergeant Lafitte, employed in Mme. Hersillie's cafe: RACHEL BOOTH. *Hersillie*, proprietress of a café: CARRIE PERKINS. *Corinne, Consuelo*, sisters in the millinery trade: Reine Davies, Ida Gabrielle. *Bebe*, an Oriental innocent, with no knowledge of the world: Bessie Graham. *Pierette, Babette*, Grisettes: Ermine Earle, Maude Wycherly. *Avali, Salali*, Favorite wives of Simoon Pasha: Harriet Burt, Blanche Brooks.

The Wives of Simoon Pasha (10): *Medora*: Cecile Rhoda. *Delilah*: Mildred Kearney. *Zobeide*: Teresa Bryant. *Zaza*: Mabel Slocum. *Peruna*: Ada Verne. *Sapolia*: Mabel Verne. *Peroxida*: Gladys Hancock. *Cassia*: Yvonne Rivers. *Wanda*: Louise DeRigney. *Nyanza*: Agnes Errington. *A Parisian Thief*: Tom Collins. *First Beggar*: Milo Joyce. *Second Beggar*: Ross Dale. *The Pasha's favorite dancers (4)*: *Zumra*: Ida Gabrielle. *Tutu*: Lillie Brink. *Dudu*: Ella Ray. *Hatdee*: Ethel Gilmore. *Chorus of Act 1*: Parisians, Wives of Pasha, Grisettes, Flower Girls, Gens d'Armes, Students, Soldiers, etc. *Chorus of Act 2*: Wives inherited by Pierre, Turkish Guards, etc.

Act 1: Paris. Café and Boulevard. (Dodge).

Act 2: Turkish Asia. Interior of the late Badeg's Harem. (Albert).

ACT 1[104]

Opening Chorus (The nations of dear Paree)
(*Lyrics by* Harry B. Smith.)

"Pierre" (Solo and Chorus)
R. Booth, (Ensemble)
(*Lyrics by* Frederic Ranken.)

"Beggars' Chorus"
Double Sextette
(*Lyrics by* Frederic Ranken.)

"Please Don't Move" (Solo and Chorus)
J. T. Powers, Ensemble
(*Lyrics by* Frederic Ranken.)

"We Say We'll Do a Thing (and Don't Do It)"
J. T. Powers
(*Lyrics by* James T. Powers.)

"Twelve Pretty Wives from Turkey" (Solo and Chorus)
W. Cameron, Show Girls
(*Lyrics by* Frederic Ranken.)

"The Same Old Crowd"
B. Ring
(*Music by* Theodore F. Morse. *Lyrics by* Fred F. Farrell; extra verses by Joseph C. Farrell.)

"I Am the Pasha"
G. O'Donnell
(*Lyrics by* Harry B. Smith.)

"Off to Turkey" (Finale)
J. T. Powers, G. O'Donnell, Ensemble
(*Lyrics by* Harry B. Smith.)

ACT 2

Opening Chorus (Mufti! Wake thee from thy slumber)
(*Lyrics by* Frederic Ranken.)

"My Honey Bunch" (interp)
R. Booth, Ensemble

"I Love You, Dolly" (Blanche Ring's Doll Song)
B. Ring

"Oh, What's the Use?"
J. T. Powers, G. O'Donnell, W. Cameron

"Everybody Wants to Hold the Baby" (Everybody Wants to See the Baby)(interp)
J. T. Powers, Chorus

"In Dreamland"
J. T. Powers, H. Short, C. E. Perkins

Grand Finale

[104] Programs early in the New York run contain no song list. List prepared from programs late in the New York run. Published vocal score from Boston tryout contains a wholly different score for Act 2. Other songs: "Love Is a Game," "Better late than Never," "Wanted, a Fly" (Spider and Fly), "The Chicago Girl," "Oh! Thou Art fair, My Love," "For Love," "We Never Do That in the Orient."

1903.07 NANCY BROWN

A Musical Comedy in Two Acts. Book and lyrics by George H. Broadhurst and Frederic Ranken. Music by Henry K. Hadley. Staged by Frank Smithson. Settings by Frank E. Gates and E. A. Morange. Costumes designed by Mme. Caroline Seidle. Musical director, George P. Towle. Produced by Daniel V. Arthur. Opened 16 February 1903 at the Bijou Theatre and closed 16 May 1903 after 104 performances[105].

CAST: *Muley Mustapha*, Bey of Ballyhoo: EDWIN STEVENS. *Mara Mustapha*, his son, the Crown Prince: ALBERT PARR. *Socrates Finis*, Chairman of his Board of Strategy: Harry Brown. *Noah Little*, an agent for a susbstitute firm: AL GRANT. *Venderhyphen Jenks*, an only son: ALFRED HICKMAN. *Four members of the Amalgamated Order of Impecunious Noblemen*: *Count Fromage de Brie*: GEORGE BEBAN. *Baron Sauerbraten*: Henry Vogel. *Lord Worcestershire*: John Havens. *The Grand Duke of Drinkamutchsky*: Frank Dearduff. *Hullybaloo*, landlord of the Outside Inn: MADISON SMITH. *Nancy Brown*, a marriage broker: MARIE CAHILL. *Muriel*, her stenographer: GRACE CAMERON. *The Princess Barboo*, only daughter of the Bey: Judith Berolde. *Mrs. John Jenks*, of Porkopolis: Jean Newcombe. *The Dancer*: Mlle. Proto. *Tutu, Zuzu, Tulu*, Maidens of Ballyhoo: Alice Knowlton, Lita Castello, Helen Lathrop.

American Heiresses (8): *Gwendolen*: Maud Francis. *Maud*: Adele Archer. *Sally*: Leslie Mayo. *Gracie*: Ruby Paine. *Alice*: Edythe Moyer. *Sadie*: Maud Sloan. *Rena*: Helen Curzon. *Nara*: Aline Boyd. *Strolling Minstrels*: Evelyn Botsford, Harry Burgess.

Maidens of Ballyhoo: Misses Elizabeth Cummings, Gertrude Doremus, Florence French, Ada Bartlett, Gertrude Cochrane, Anna Bennett, Minna Blackman, Ethel Carroll, Gertrude Cochrane, Adelaide Howland, Agnes Hinton, Estelle Rogers, Margaret Johnson, Elizabeth King, Eva Lewis, Rose Stevens, Isabelle Stuart, Gladys Earlcott, Lou Egener, Farron Gray, Beth Titus, Mabel Gardner, Alice Brown, Ella Mann, Julie Fenton, Sadie Harris, Maude Stillman, Jennie Hardy, May Bordley. *Nobles and Guards of Ballyhoo*: Messrs. W. W. Meehan, T. R. O'Brian, V. A. Rose, Daniel Corse, Henry Borden, Mason Smith, G. M. Vale, Philip Dale.

Act 1: A Public Square in Ballyhoo.

Act 2: A Room in the Palace.

ACT 1[106]

Opening Chorus
Company
(*Music by* C. Rosamond Johnson. *Lyrics by* Bob Cole, James Weldon Johnson.)

"Strange, Odd, Queer"
G. Beban, H. Vogel, J. Havens, F. Dearduff

[105] Played a return engagement 26 October 1903 at the Grand Opera House for 8 performances.

[106] Song list did not appear in program until midway through the run. Among the songs published but not in later songs lists were:

"Just for Me" (An Awful Bore)

"Fill Up Your Tankards" (Male Chorus and Quartette)

"I Jot It Down" (Stenographers' Song)

"What the Band Played"
J. T. Powers
(*Music and Lyrics by* John Madison Reid.)

The show was wholly revised for its subsequent tour and Grand Opera House engagement. Cole and Johnson Brothers were added to principal program credits following Henery K. Hadley. Among the new songs added and dropped during the tour were:

"Navajo" (Navaho)(Act 2)
M. Cahill
(*Music by* Egbert Van Alstyne. *Lyrics by* Harry Williams.)

"It Is a Most Disagreeable Thing to Do"
E. Stevens, Ensemble

"You Can't Fool All the People (All the Time)"
M. Cahill

"American, Oh, Girls?"
The Heiresses

"The Little Bird Told Me So" (A Little Birdie Told Me So)
A. Hickman, G. Cameron

"(The) Katydid, the Cricket and the Frog"
M. Cahill, E. Stevens, A. Grant
(*Music by* C. Rosamond Johnson. *Lyrics by* Bob Cole, James Weldon Johnson.)

"The Glow-worm and the Moth"
M. Cahill, Ensemble
(*Music by* Max S. Witt. *Lyrics by* Frederick Ranken.)

"Red, White and Blue Girl" (Finale)
Company

ACT 2

Opening Chorus
Company

"Two Eyes"
Student
(*Music by* C. Rosamond Johnson. *Lyrics by* James Weldon Johnson.)

"The Melancholy Marshmallow"[107]
M. Cahill
(*Music by* Louis G. Munz. *Lyrics by* Aaron S. Hoffman.)

"I'm Glad I'm Not Methusalem"
H. Brown, E. Stevens, A. Grant
(*Music and Lyrics by* Eugene Ellsworth.)

"Cupid's Ramble"
M. Cahill, A. Hickman, Heiresses
(*Music by* C. Rosamond Johnson. *Lyrics by* Bob Cole, James Weldon Johnson.)

"The Military Band"
A. Parr, Company
(*Lyrics by* Frederick Ranken.)

"The Royal Crocodile" (Act 1)
George C. Boniface (Muley Mustapha), Chorus (*Music by* Theodore F. Morse. *Lyrics by* Edward Madden.)

"I Could Be Happy with Either One" (Act 1)
Julius Steger (Mara Mustapha), Heiresses
(*Music by* Silvio Hein.)

"June" (Act 1)
M. Cahill
(*Music and Lyrics by* Clare Kummer.)

"Octette to Bacchus" (Come Fill Your Glass and Drink with Me)
Nobles and Guards of Ballyhoo
(*Music by* C. Rosamond Johnson. *Lyrics by* Bob Cole, James Weldon Johnson.)

"In Gay Ballyhoo"
Entire Chorus
(*Music by* C. Rosamond Johnson. *Lyrics by* Bob Cole, James Weldon Johnson.)

"A Wise Old Owl" (Act 2)
G. C. Boniface, H. Brown, A. Grant
(*Music by* Theodore F. Morse. *Lyrics by* Edward Madden.)

"The Soldier Is the Idol of the Nation" (Act 2)
J. Steger, Chorus
(*Music by* C. Rosamond Johnson. *Lyrics by* Bob Cole, James Weldon Johnson.)

"I'm Going to Change My Man" (Act 2)
M. Cahill
(*Music and Lyrics by* Clare Kummer.)

"Save It for Me" (Act 2)
M. Cahill
(*Music by* C. Rosamond Johnson. *Lyrics by* Bob Cole, James Weldon Johnson.)
"Que Voulez Vous" (Act 2)
M. Cahill, Geoge Beban (Count Fromage de Brie)
(*Music by* Theodore F. Morse. *Lyrics by* Edward Madden.)

[107]Replaced during the run by:

"Sweet Nellie Wood" (authors uncredited in sheet music)
M. Cahill

"(Marie Cahill's) Congo Love Song"
M. Cahill
(*Music by* C. Rosamond Johnson. *Lyrics by* Bob Cole, James Weldon Johnson.)

Finale
Company

1903.08 DAHOMEY

A Musical Farce in Three Acts, 5 Scenes. Book by Jesse A. Shipp. Music by Will Marion Cook. Lyrics by Paul Laurence Dunbar. Additional music and lyrics by James Vaughan and Alex Rogers. Scenery painted by Moses & Hamilton. Costumes designed by Mme. Pauline Reed. Musical director, James Vaughan. Produced by (Jules) Hurtig & (Harry) Seamon. Opened 18 February 1903 at the New York Theatre and closed 4 April 1903 after 53 performances[108].

CAST: *Shylock Homestead*, called "Shy" by his friends: BERT A. WILLIAMS. *Rareback Pinkerton*, "Shy's" personal friend and advisor: GEORGE W. WALKER. *Cicero Lightfoot*, president of a colonization society: PETE HAMPTON. *Dr. Straight* in name only, street fakir: Fred Douglas. *Mose Lightfoot*, brother of Cicero, thinks Dahomey a land of great promise: William Barker. *George Reeder*, keeps an intelligence office: ALEXANDER ROGERS. *Henry Stampfield*, letter carrier, with an argument against immigration: Walter Richardson. *Me Sing*, keeps a chop suey factory: George Catlin. *Hustling Charley*, proprietor of Got-the-Coin Syndicate: J. A. SHIPP. *Leather*, a bootblack: RICHARD CONNORS[109]. *Officer Still*: George W. Pickett. *Messenger Rush*, but not often: Theodore Pankey. *Bill Primrose*: James Leubrie Hill. *Cecilia Lightfoot*, Cicero's wife: HATTIE McINTOSH. *Mrs. Stringer*, dealer in foresaken patterns, also editor of fashionnotes in "Beanville Agitator:' LOTTIE WILLIAMS. *Rosetta Lightfoot*, a troublesome young thing: AIDA OVERTON WALKER. *Colonists, natives, etc.*: (Misses Hattie Hopkins, Ellis, Wallace, Davis, Bowman; Messrs. Lloyd Gibbs, Elkins, L. H. Saulsbury, Green Henry Tapley.)

Act 1: Public Square, Boston

Act 2, Scene 1: Exterior of Lightfoot's Home, Gatorville, Florida. *Scene 2*: Road, one and a half miles from Gatorville. *Scene 3*: Interior of the Lightfoot home.

Act 3, Scene 1: Swamp in Dahomey. *Scene 2*: Garden of Caboceer, governor of a province. Execution tower in the distance.

ACT 1

"Dat Gal of Mine" (Medicine Fakir Quartette)
Messrs. Vaughn, J. L. Hill, G. Pickett, Henderson
(Music and Lyrics by *Benjamin L. Shook.*)

"Organ Quartette"
Messrs. Elkins, Saulsbury, R. Connor, Tapley

"Molly Green" (Mollie Green)(Song)
H. Troy, Company
(*Lyrics by* Will Marion Cook and Cecil Mack.)

"When Sousa Comes to Coontown"
G. W. Walker, Company
(*Music by* James Vaughn *and Tom Lemonier. Lyrics by* Alex Rogers.)

"(On) Broadway in Dahomey (Bye and Bye)"
B. Williams, G. Walker, Chorus
(*Music by* Al Johns. *Lyrics by* Alex Rogers.)

ACT 2

"Leader of (the) Colored Aristocracy"
H. McIntosh, Company
(*Lyrics by* James Weldon Johnson.)

"Society"
H. Hopkins, A. O. Walker, Mrs. McIntosh,
L. Gibbs, R. Connors, A. Rogers, F. Douglas, B Williams
(*Music by* Will Marion Cook and Will Accooe.)

"The Jonah Man" (I'm a Jonah Man)(Song)
B. Williams
(*Music and Lyrics by* Alex Rogers.)

"I Want to Be a Real Lady"
A. O. Walker
(*Music by* Tom Lemonier. *Lyrics by* Alex Rogers.)

---

[108]Following their European triumph, a "New" IN DAHOMEY played 27 August 1904 at the Grand Opera House for 17 performances, many changes were made in the cast, text and musical score. See separate entry at that date.

[109]Later programs identify him as Richard Conner.

"The Czar" (Chorus and Solo)
G. Walker, assisted by Misses Ellis, Wallace, Davis, Bowman, Company
(*Music by* John H. Cook and Will Marion Cook. *Lyrics by* Alex Rogers.)

"(On) Emancipation Day"
B. Williams, G. Walker, Company

ACT 3

"Caboceers' Choral"
Company

Finale
Company

1903.09 BUSY IZZY

A Sparkling Musical Entertainment (a Musical Comedy) in Two Acts. Written by Jingo. Some songs by James O'Dea and Bob Adams, some by me and some by him. Produced under the stage direction of Matt C. Woodward. Musical direction, Warner Crosby. Produced by E. D. Stair. Opened 16 March 1903 at the 58th Street Theatre and closed 21 March 1903 after 8 performances; returned 21 March 1904 to the 58th Street Theatre and closed 26 March 1904 after 10 additional performances.[110]

CAST: *Izzy Mark*, yet easier: GEORGE SIDNEY. *Gee Whiz*, blew in from Yorkville: FRED WYCKOFF. *Yube Quick*, fast and slow: Edward Clark. *Jim Crow*, hard to take: Daniel Sullivan. *Hooley Hapigan*, always happy: CHARLES LoMIER. *Willie Cheat*: FRANK GIBBONS. *Harry Smart*, a wise guy: WILL J. HAGAN. *Will Walk*, all the time: Walter Scott. *Seld M. Seels*, a drummer: ED. GILMORE. *Sil E. Kid*, a foolish man: ED. GILMORE. *Jim Pansy*: ED. GILMORE. *Knight Stick*, a club man: ALFRED C. TRUSCHEL. *Charles River*, a salesman: Earl Stanley. *Little Jack Horner*: Freddie West. *Billie Bench*, take a seat: Andrew West. *Sammy Simmer*, growing dimmer: John West. *Eddie Fication*: Fred West. *Rob Burr*, takes well: Ed. C. Earle. *Dan Yube*, very deep: Barney Smith. *Y. Knott*, he doesn't know: Clyde Luther.

Rilly Fine, a fact: ANNIE MARTELL. *Miss Yoosed* and misplaced: Lisle Bloodgood. *Daisy Dell*, a real daisy: Maude Campbell. *May Bell*, just like May: Edythe Gibbons. *Dolly Varden*, a Lulu: Meta Peinze. *Allie Way*, her own way: Lillian Beard. *Laide Ray*, full of hope: Helen Shafer. *Lottie Lee*, doesn't know Fitzhugh: Evelyn Westcott. *Mae Noe*, and may not: Ettie Drew. *Ophelia Pulse*, go ahead: Helen LoMier. *Madge Enary*, can't help it: Gertrude Walcott. *Cloe Zinn*, it's getting late: Frances Berg. *Minnie Fish*, what kind: Madeline Broughton. *Helen Dutch*, what is it in English?: Annie Newell. *Annie How*, and finally: Dorothy Fair. *Celia Lipp*, talk is cheap: Rose Fowler. *Delia Hand*, a good card: Marie Philips. *Ray Ning*, Mackintosh's sister: Kathryn Denning. *Sara Cuse*, from New York: Rennie Thorne. *Carrie All*, no trouble: Bessie Hirst.

CAST (Return engagement): *Izzy Mark*, yet easier: GEORGE SIDNEY. *Gee Whiz*, blew in from Yorkville: FRED WYCKOFF. *Yube Quick*, fast and slow: Edward Clark. *Archie Tect*, a planner: FRANK GIBBONS. *Alphonse*: FRANK GIBBONS. *Jim Crow*, hard to take: Dan H. Mellen. *Hooley Hapigan*, Always happy: CHARLES LoMIER. *Harry Smart*, a wise guy: WILL J. HAGAN. *Will Walk*, all the time: Walter Scott. *Seld M. Seels*, a drummer: Charles Burton. *Sil E. Kid*, a foolish man: ED. GILMORE. *Knight Stick*, a club man: ED. GILMORE. *Charles River*, a salesman: William Walsh. *Billie Bench*, take a seat: Harvey Winkler. *Sammy Simmer*, growing dimmer: Wilson Franks. *Rob Burr*, takes well: Ed. C. Earle. *Dan Yube*, very deep: Barney Smith. *Y. Knott*, he doesn't know: Clyde Luther. *Mamselle Paree*, a Paree damsel: CARRIE WEBBER.

Rilly Fine, a fact: MAUD CAMPBELL. *Miss Yoosed* and misplaced: Langtry Ashton. *Daisy Bell*, a real daisy: Madeline Broughton. *May Bell*, just like May: Rose Maurer. *Dolly Varden*, a Lulu: Katherina Denning. *All E. Way*, her own way: Meri Dumont. *Sadie Ray*, full of hope: Frances Berg. *Lottie Lee*, doesn't know Fitzhugh: Evelyn Westcott. *Mae Noe*, and may not: Helene LoMier. *Ophelia Pulse*, go ahead: Marie Phillips. *Madge Enary*, can't help it: Helen Shafter. *Cloe Zinn*, it's getting late: Etta Drew. *Minnie Fish*, what kind: Mera Pelnze. *Helen Dutch*, what is it in English?: Gertrude Walcott. *Annie How*, and finally: Blanche Stella. *Celia Lipp*, talk is cheap: Beri Marsden. *Delia Hand*, a good card: Alice Packard. *Ray Ning*, Mackintosh's sister: Ivy Williams. *Sara Cuse*, from New York: Florrie Franks. *Carrie All*, no trouble: Eleanor May. *Lu Weeze*, very woozy: Cora Fields. *Miller Terry*, can soldier: Hattie Wynn. *Anna Leen*, to do or dye: Phyllis Shields. *Amy Able*, and affable: Daisy Kyle.

Act 1: Busy Izzy's Fun Emporium.

Act 2: Busy Izzy's Dizzy Hotel.

MUSICAL NUMBERS[111]

[110]No program available for first engagement. Cast and production detail taken from 1904 return engagement.

[111]No program available.

"Mr. Dooley" (from THE DEFENDER)
G. Sidney
(*Music by* Jean Schwartz. *Lyrics by* William Jerome.)

"Lovely Day for a Walk"
G. Sidney, E. Gibbons, F. Wyckoff, A. Newell, M. Broughton, R. Fowler

"Sallie Mine"
E. Clark, M. Campbell, assisted by "tough" chorus

"On Daddy's Back"

"Daffy Down Dilly"
M. Campbell

"The Bell Boy"
E. Clark, Company

"At Night"[112]
(*Music and Lyrics by* Luce Pagani.)

ACT 1 (Return engagement)

"Back to Work" (Opening Chorus)
Shop Girls, Company

"I Want to Go Back to London"
W. Hagan. Company

"Pettie Mignon"
C. Webber, Company

"Busy Izzy Oo"
G. Sidney, Company

"I Never Had Such a Time"
F. Wyckoff, Company

"Tommy and Me"
M. Campbell, E. Clark, assisted by the Company

Character Specialty
F. Wyckoff

"Something Nice and Foolish"
S. Sidney, C. Webber

"My Dixie Anna"
M. Campbell, Entire Company

ACT 2

"On a Summer's Night"
M. Campbell, Hotel Guests

"Beautiful Dream, Come True"
C. LoMier

"Hiawatha in Fun"
G. Sidney, Company

"The Absurd Four"
G. Sidney, C. LoMier, W. Hagan, E. Gilmore

"Can We Stroll with You" (Sextette)
Misses Broughton, Maurer, Denning; Messrs. Sidney, Wyckoff, Gibbons

"The Bell Boy"
E. Clark, Company

"A Minstrel Take Off"
G. Sidney, C. Webber, F. Wyckoff

Finale
Entire Company

1903.10 THE PRINCE OF PILSEN

A Musical Comedy in Two Acts. Book and lyrics by Frank Pixley. Music by Gustav Luders. Staged by George Marion. Scenery by Walter Burridge. Costumes by Will R. Barnes. Orchestra under the direction of Gustav Luders. Produced by Henry W. Savage. Opened 17 March 1903 at the Broadway Theatre and closed 18 July 1903 after 143 performances.

CAST: *Carl Otto*, the Prince of Pilsen, a student at Heidelberg: ARTHUR DONALDSON. *Hans Wagner*, a Cincinnati brewer, traveling abroad: JOHN W. RANSONE. *Lieutenant Tom Wagner*, of the U.S. Cruiser "Annapolis": ALBERT PARR. *Arthur St. John Wilberforce*, Lord Somerset: EDGAR NORTON. *Francois*, Concierge, Hotel

[112]Interpolation copyrighted 1904 for tour.

Internationale: Sherman Wade. *Cook's Courier*, Vassar Girl's pilot: J. L. Sutherland. *Sergeant Brie*, of the Gendarmes: J. L. Sutherland. *Jimmy*, a bell boy: Eva Westcott. *Mrs. Madison Crocker*, from New York: HELEN BERTRAM. *Edith Adams*, a Vassar girl: ANNA LICHTER. *Sidonie*, Mrs. Crockers' French maid: Jeanette Bageard. *Nellie Wagner*, Hans Wagner's daughter: LILLIAN COLEMAN.

The Heidelberg Boys (8): *Rudolph*: Clyde L. McKinley. *Adolph*: Henry Taylor. *Heirich*: Linford R. Jefferson. *Fritz*: John H. Pratt. *Ludwig*: Francis Stuart. *Carl*: Edward J. Burns. *Oscar*: Charles W. Hawkins. *Wilhelm*: Walter C. White.

The American Girls (9): *Frankie Friskie*, San Francisco: Pearl Guzman. *Dolly Dixie*, New Orleans: Diamond Donner. *Pansy Penn*, Philadelphia: Blanche Cramer. *Priscilla Plymouth*, Boston: Jeannett French. *Mazie Manhattan*, New York: Carroll McComas. *Missy Rivers*, St. Louis: May Arno. *Illie Noyes*, Chicago: Mabel Spencer. *Olive Oriole*, Baltimore: Luoida Hilliard. *Goldie Dome*, Washington: Queenie LeRoi.

The Sea Shell Grls: *White Capps*: Camile Clifford. *Pearlie Beach*: Jane Patison. *Fomie Crest*: Ella Warren. *Brinie Deep*: Grace Holmes. *Bessie Barnacle*: Loretta LaPitre. *Weedie Sea*: Marie Price. *Daisie Dolphin*: Marion Hartwell. *Birdie Petrel*: Myrtle Marsh. *Coralie Shell*: Helen Hutchins. *Sylvia Waves*: F. Caldwell Holmes. *Lottie Fogge*: Margaret MacDonald. *Pleasant Sayle*: May Pratt.

The Bathing Girls: *Amthyst*: Florence Radcliff. *Opal*: Florence Bergea. *Emerald*: Vesta Bergea. *Diamond*: Rose Botley. *Turquoise*: Hazel Clayton. *Sapphire*: Florence Huntley. *Coral*: Mamie Botley. *Ruby*: Gertie Nickerson. *Pearl*: Eleanora Bergea. *Cameo*: Louise LaSalle. *Agate*: Rhea Lusby. *Onyx*: Ada Brown. *Carnelian*: Mabel Kent.

American Tourists (3): *Claudia Belmont*: Mignon D'Allencon. *Ester Morgan*: Lillian Whitton. *Bessie DePew*: Margaret Messinger. *The Gendarmes (6)*: *Vidocq*: Charles Strombold. *Sherlock*: Peter Swift. *Hawkshaw*: Charles F. Sullivan. *Sleuth*: Allan Ramsey. *Carter*: O. W. D'Lanais. *Doyle*: C. W. Wilson. *Flower Girls, Naval Cadets, Fox Hunters, French Maids, Waiters, etc.*

The action takes place in Nice, France, now.

Act 1: Garden of the Hotel Internationale. Afternoon.

Act 2: Court of the Hotel Internationale. The next morning.

ACT 1

"The Modern Pirate"
S. Wade, Chorus of Waiters

"We Know It's Wrong to Flirt"
A. Lichter, Ensemble

"Artie" (Solo)
E. Norton, Chorus of Vassar Girls

"A Season at the Shore" (Solo)
H. Bertram, Chorus of Golf Girls

"Hail to Our Noble Guest" (Entrance of Hans and Nellie)
Ensemble

"The Message of the Violet" (Duet)
A. Parr, A. Lichter

"Biff! Bang!" (Solo)
A. Donaldson, Chorus of Heidelberg Students

"The Stein Song;" "Heidelberg."

"The Widow" (Trio)
H. Bertram, A. W. Ransone, E. Norton

"Keep It Dark"
E. Westcott, J. Bageard, Chorus of Butlers and Maids

"Pictures in the Smoke" (Duet)
A. Donaldson, L. Coleman

Finale ("Auf Widersehen")
General Ensemble

ACT 2

"The Field and Forest" (Fox Hunters)(Chorus with Solo)
A. Lichter, Ensemble

"He Didn't Know Exactly What to Do" (Solo)
J. H. Ransone

"The American Girl" (Song of the Cities)
H. Bertram, Picture Girls

"The Tale of the Sea-Shell"
A. Donaldson, L. Coleman, Ensemble

"Back to the Boulevards"
S. Wade, J. Bageard

"Our Floral Queen"
H. Bertram, Ensemble

"Fall In" (March Solo)
A. Parr, Naval Cadets, Ensemble

Finale
Principals, Chorus

1903.11 RUNNING FOR OFFICE

The Four Cohans and Their Company of Comedians in the Newest Musical Frivolity (Musical Comedy) in Three Acts. Book, music, (lyrics) by George M. Cohan. Staged by George M. Cohan and James Gorman. Scenery painted by C. W. Valentine. Costumes by Lord & Taylor. Orchestra under the direction of Charles J. Gebest. Orchestrations by Charles J. Gebest. Produced by Fred Niblo. Opened 27 April 1903 at the 14th Street Theatre and closed 6 June 1903 after 48 performances.

CAST: *Andrew Riley*, Mayor of Tigersvile: James H. Manning. *Sam Gayhand*, the popular man: William Keough. *Peter Pinchem*, the constable: Peter F. Randall. *Herman Helberger* Gussie's cllege chum: Jo Smith Marba. *Franklyn Flusher*, a theatrical manager: M. J. Sullivan. *Dan Timmons*, Riley's right-hand man: Hugh Mack. *Boliver Bixby*, Gayland's servant: Joseph Leslie. *Captain Hicks*, of New Hampshire football: William Forrest. *Quick Hall*, sergeant of police: Charles Bachman. *Jim Fizz*, a temperance crank: Maurice Robinson. *Alf Bach*, a football player: Fred Williams. *William Raid*, a policeman: Walter Stockwell. *John Tiger*, a Prohibition candidate: JERRY J. COHAN. *Augustus Wright*, "Rah, Rah, Rah": GEORGE M. COHAN. *Mrs. John Tiger*, formerly Mrs. Wright: HELEN F. COHAN. *Madeleine Tiger*, New Hampshire '04: JOSIE COHAN. *Gertie Gayland*, a noisy kid: ETHEL LEVEY. *Susie Springtling*, "Jeanetta Zanfretta": Gertrude Rutledge. *Mary*, Mr. Tiger's servant: Florence Little.

The New Hampshire Girls: *Minerva Chase*: Mollie Newell. *Gracie Earl*: Rosella Rhodes. *Octavia Davies*: Agnes Gildea. *Eden DeFoe*: Mamie Gildea. *Olive Ellsworth*: Jessie Joyce. *Vivian Stanton*: Bert Montclair. *Leyla Delmont*: Carrie Ward. *Clarence Wellington*: Jane Barry. *Pearl Belmont*: Clara Barnes. *Senora Dutton*: Wilma Gilmore. *Electa Sylvester*: Marie DeRonne. *Mildred Vantine*: Sophie Palmer. *Cecille Rockwell*: Mattie Rivenberg. *Vesta Mansfield*: LaReine Cumley. *May Blossom*: Nadine Sidney. *Rosie Budd*: Cora Carter.

The Tigersville Girls: *Violet Sweet*: Marion Watts. *Lily Blossom*: Mary Tobin. *Daisy Flower*: Josephine Boston. *Pansy Bloom*: Mabel Leigh. *Hella Thropp*: Zu Zonne. *Cynthia High*: Marie Ireland. *Daisy Dill*: Frances Bradford. *Pinky May*: Frankie Scott. *Minnie Dew*: Minerva Brooks. *Tillie Wells*: Katherine Lacy. *Dora Beach*: Maud Wilson. *Kittie Cute*: Della Gale. *Visitors, Strangers, Town Folks, Politicians, Ward Heelers, etc.*

The action takes place in Tigersville, Vermont, last November.

Act 1: Exterior of Gayland Hotel.

Act 2: Interior of John Tiger's home. Three weeks later.

Act 3: The public square. That night.

MUSICAL NUMBERS

"The Football Boys and Girls"
Ladies and Gentlemen of the Company

"Sweet Popularity"
W. Keough, College Girls

"Root for Riley"
J. H. Manning, Ensemble

"They Are Hypnotized"
G. Rutledge, Ladies

"Kid Days"
E. Levey, Her Playmates

"Flirtation on the Beach"
Josephine Cohan, G. M. Cohan

"In a One Night Stand"
M. J. Sullivan, His Friends

"If I Were Only Mr. Morgan"
G. M. Cohan

"I Want to Go to Paree, Papa"
Josephine Cohan, Ensemble

"Johnny Get Off the Corner"
C. Bachman, 'the Force'

"I'll Be There—in the Public Square"
E. Levey, the Smat Set

"The Elopement" (dance)
Josephine Cohan, G. M. Cohan

"The Reubens on Parade"
E. Levey, Company

Finale—Medley
The Four Cohans and Company

1903.12

MY LADY PEGGY GOES TO TOWN

A Comedy (with Songs) in Four Acts. Book and play by Frances Aymar Mathews, revised by Eugene W. Presbrey. Songs by Roy Newton Hair, (William Jerome, Jean Schwartz). Staged by Eugene W. Presbrey. Scenery by Harley Merry. Costumes by Mme. Marie Cummings, Dazian, Charles Chrisdie. Musical director, Roy Newton Hair. Produced by Mrs. (Cecil) Spooner. Opened 4 May 1903 at Daly's Theatre and closed 23 May 1903 after 24 performances.

CAST: *The Earl of Exham*, Peg's father: EDWARD LOCKE. *Sir Percy de Bohun*, Peg's suitor: WALTER HALE. *Sir Robin McTart*, of Robinswold, Kent: ETIENNE GIRARDOT. *Mr. George Brummell*, fashion's arbiter: Lynn Pratt. *Lord Kennaston* of Kennaston Castle, Peg's twin: Mortimer Weldon. *Dr. Nicholas*, the Vicar of Rhoinsgold: Edwin H. Curtis. *The "Ton" (4): Lord Chalmers*: Ashley Miller. *Lord Lovell*: J. H. Montgomery. *Sir Charles Wyatt*: Lee Daniel. *The Duke of Escombe*: Gray B. Towler. *Biggs*, Constable of Brook-Armsleigh: Ogden Wight. *Binks, Stubs*, his posse: Edward C. Rooney, Frank Stanton. *Bickers*, gardener at Kennaston: Charles C. Palmer. *Grigson*, Sir Percy's own man: Ogden Wight. *Tompers*, Mr. Brummell's own man: Frederick Guest. *First Assassin*: C. Russell Sage. *Second Assassin*: Edgar Allen. *Landlord of the "Queen and Artichoke"*: Charles C. Palmer. *Michael*, his stableboy: Charles Gibson. *Dan, Dick, Jake*, hostlers: Earl Ford, Comer W. Breedlove, Charles F. Blair. *Chalk*, the tailor's boy: Jeffrey Blaine. *Harlequin*, in Vauxhall Gardens: Robert Kosciusko. *The Duchess of Escombe*: Catherine Belle. *Laddy Peggy Burgoyne* of Kennaston Castle: CECIL SPOONER. *The"Fair" (5): Lady Diana Weston*: Lillian Avann. *Lady Biddy O'Toole*: Mildred Lawrence. *Lady Vernon*: Frances Lloyd. *Lady Wooton*: Marion Miller. *Hon. Dolly Tarleton*: Cora Morlan. *Jane Chockey*, Lady Peggy's own woman: Clara Coleman. *Frowse*, charwoman at Lark Lane: Reta Villiers. *Bess*, barmaid at the "Queen and Artichoke": Helen Barker. *Hester, Nancy, Jean*, milkmaids at Kennaston: Florence Sweeney, Frances Lloyd: Katherine Morgan. *Folly* in Vauxhall Gardens: Ethel Dwyer. *Pleasurers at Vauxhall, Servants, Stablemen, Waiters, etc.*

Act 1: Transpires during the late afternoon of a June day, in the yard and buttery of Kennaston Castle, Surrey, England.

Act 2: Transpires late the following night at Lord Kennaston's lodgings in Lark Lane, a mean quarter of London.

Act 3: Transpires at the Vauxhall Gardens the next evening, where all London goes a-pleasuring at the bidding of Mr. Brummell.

Act 4: Transpres at daybreak the following morn, before the "Queen and Artichoke," on the road to Kennaston Castle.

MUSICAL NUMBERS[113]

"When George the Third Was King"

1903.13

MICKEY FINN

A Farce Comedy in Three Acts. Play by Bernard Kling and J. H. Perry. Based on the popular comic strip. Opened 4 May 1903 at the Third Avenue Theatre and closed 9 May 1903 after 8 performances.[114]

CAST: *Roger Sweeney*: J. H. Perry. *Michael Finn*: J. B. LEONARD. *Paul Fairweather*: LEW WATSON. *Gloomy Gus*: VIC STONE. *John Unit*: JOE KELLY. *Mike Mose*: TOM DOWNEY. *Deputy Sheriff*: C. F. Edwards. *Daisy Donot*: LILLIAN PERRY. *Dora Sweeney*: Edna Tillyne. *Mrs. Finn*: Rose Kelly. *Bedella Finn*: Helen Gilbert. *Gladys Izz*: Madaline Dorsch. *Carrie Fuller*: Georgia DeGraff. *Clare Williams*: Dolores DeGraff. *Carrie Wood*: Clara Mann. *Carrie Seen*: Nell DeVore. *Cora Lee*: Judith LeMoyne. *Carrie Lee*: Grace Leslie. *Minnie Spry*: Christine LeLang. *Nellie Haveakiss*: BAB SHELDON. *Mickey Finn*: EDDIE RUSSELL.

1903.14

THE RUNAWAYS

An Elaborate Musical Extravaganza (Musical Comedy) in Two Acts. Book (and lyrics) by Addison Burkhardt. Score (music) by Raymond Hubbell. Produced under the supervision of (staged by) Gerald Coventry. Dances staged by Sam Marion. Scenes painted by D. Frank Dodge. Costumes by Caroline Seidle. Musical director, Arthur Weld. Produced by Sam S. Shubert, (Sam) Nixon and (J. F.) Zimmerman. Opened 11 May 1903 at the Casino Theatre and closed 17 October 1903 after 167 performances[115].

[113]No others listed in program.

[114]No program available.

[115]Frederick Ranken was hired by the producers to rewrite and restage the show, which opened its Second Edition 15 June 1903 to the critics, with song changes as noted below. Programs however do not credit individual songs to him.

CAST[116]: *General Armour Hardtack*, U.S. Army, a dyspeptic in search of a cure: ALEXANDER CLARK. *Dave Budd*, his son, a tout: WILLIAM GOULD. *Robert Gray*, a wine agent and friend of the general: VAN RENSSELAER WHEELER. *(Diagnosius) Fleecem*, a patent medicine fakir with smoldering ambitions: AL FIELDS. *Blutch*, his confederate: ARTHUR DUNN. *The Giant Rooster*[117]: WALTER STANTON, JR. *Lieutenant Hobson Funston*, who displays good military form: SUZANNE HALPREN. *Beef*, Lord High Chancellor of the Isle of Table d'Hote: WILLIAM WOLF. *Josey May*, the regulation much-married prima donna, only more so: DOROTHY DORR. *Dorothy Maynard*, an army nurse, also ward of the general: HELEN LORD. *The Princess Angelcake*, of the Isle of Table d'Hote: AMELIA STONE. *Jeanette Darling*: Mabel Carrier. *Beatrice Wheeler, Mary Ann Garland*, two lady reporters, afterwards Love Editors on the Table d'Hote Bulletin: FLORA HENGLER, MAY HENGLER. *Widows of His Late Majesty Goulash III, whose sauce of life they were (6)*: *Tobasco*: Mabel Carrier. *Paprika*: Edna Goodrich. *Chili*: Florence Worden. *Mint*: Daisy Leighton. *Pepper*: Katherine Bell. *Chutney*: Alice Campbell. *Skip, Flip*, messenger boys: Blanche Wood, Elise Barney. *Slim*: Mlle. May's press agent: Sadie Lauer.

Josie May's Comic Opera "Queens": *Mabel Montmorenci*: Rose Wilson. *Lyllyan Lancaster*: Loretta Ward. *Helene Huntington*: Esther Brunette. *Reina Rivington*: Eleanor Tierney. *Erntrude Fairfax*: Frances Ingraham. *Violet Verrington*: Addie Marze. *Sybil Sinclair*: Josephine LaMotte. *Elayne Ellyngton*: May Maloney. *Vivian Van Bibber*: Mildred Forrest. *Ethylene Newcastle*: Nellie Plummer. *Signor Fausturo Di Bosco, M. Pierre Plantagenet*, Josie May's basso and tenor: Alphosne Fuguet, R. M. Dolliver. *Dancers in the Rose Ballet*: Maybelle Davies, Estelle D'Arville, Babette D'Arville (Premieres); Doris Townsend, Eloise DeFord, Vida Whitmore, May Carlisle, Jean Collins, Miriam Falconer. *Society Ladies and Gentlemen, U.S. Soldiers and Sailors, Policemen, Jockeys, Stable Boys, Touts, Pickpockets, Courtiers, Dancing Girls, Pages, Heralds, etc.*

Act 1: The club house and race track at Saratoga.

Act 2: (Salad Glen in) the Isle of Table d'Hote.

ACT 1[118]

"The Suburban" (Opening Chorus)
(Jockeys, Swells, Chorus)

"If I Were a Bright Little Star"[119]
V. R. Wheeler, F. Hengler, M. Hengler

"In Swell Society"[120]
D. Dorr, Her Comic Opera Queens

"How I'd Write a Comic Opera" (How to Write a Comic Opera)
D. Dorr, V. R. Wheeler

"Pretty Maid Adelaide"
F. Hengler, M. Hengler, A. Dunn, A. Fields

"My Queen of the Track"[121] (Queen of the Track)
V. R. Wheeler, W. Gould

[116]During the run character names were revised, changed and reassigned among the cast.

[117]Later programs assign the name *Henry Pullet*, pet rooster of the Princess Angelcake

[118]The running order of songs was repeatedly revised during the run. Added during the run:

Imitations
Fay Templeton {Josey May}
Added to Act 1 for tour:

"Forever and a Day"
A. Stone, W. Gould

"If I Should" (If I Told You That I Loved You)
W. Gould, Mabel Carrier {Dorothy Maynard}
(*Music by* Leo Friedman. *Lyrics by* Bartley C. Costello.)
Added for tour as per published sheet music:

Fay Templeton's "Woodchuck Song"
F. Templeton
(*Music by* Theodore F. Morse. *Lyrics by* Robert Hobart Davis.)

[119]Dropped during the run run and replaced by:

"In a General Sort of Way" (after "The Suburban")
A. Clark

[120]Dropped late in the run and replaced by:

"Summer Girl"/"Yes I'm the Same Little Girl"
F. Templeton
(*Music by* Raymond Hubbell. *Lyrics by* Frederic Ranken.)

[121]Replaced during the run by:

"The Maiden and the Jay"
V. R. Wheeler, W. Gould
(*Music by* William Gould.)

"Our Cause Is the Cause"[122]
A. Clark, Brigade
"Tra la la la"[123]
A. Dunn, A. Fields, Comic Opera Queens
"Strolling"
H. Lord, Swells
"To the Island" (Finale)
Company

ACT 2[124]
"Sadly I Wait" (For thee I'm sighing)(Opening Chorus)
Ensemble
"My (Radiant) Firefly"
A. Stone, Natives
"I Am the Royal Chancellor"
W. Wolf, Natives
"Love Is an Ailment"[125]
H. Lord
"(Miss) Susanna from Urbana"
W. Gould, Comic Opera Queens
"I Would Be Your Romeo"[126] (Duet)
A. Stone, V. R. Wheeler
"A Kiss for Each Day in the Week"
A. Dunn, Widows
"I'm Going Back to Dixieland"[127]
F. Hengler, M. Hengler, Company
"One Hundred Years From Now"[128]
A. Clark, Widows
"The Land I Love"
A. Stone, Sailors, Company
Finale

---

[122]Dropped during the run and subsequent tour.
[123]Dropped during the run and subsequent tour.
[124]Added during the run to Act 2:
"The Rose Ballet" (after "Susanna from Urbana")
Mlles. D'Arville
(Published as The Rose Dance, a March by Raymond Hubbell.)
"Dance of All Nations" (after "Way Down South")
F. Hengler, M. Hengler
Smart English Dance; Dance Français; Dance Bolero; Berliner Tanz; The American Dance
Added to Act 2 for subsequent tour:
"My Little Girlie" (Guess Little Girlie, Who Loves You)
V. R. Wheeler, A. Stone
(*Music and Lyrics by* Ernest R. Ball.)

[125]Dropped during the run.
[126]Replaced during the run by:
"My Little Hindoo Belle"
F. Templeton
(*Music by* Raymond Hubbell. *Lyrics by* Addison Burkhardt.)
"Hiawatha"
A. Stone, V. R. Wheeler
(*Music by* Neil Moret. *Lyrics by* James O'Dea.)
[127]Replaced during the run by:
"Way Down South"
F. Hengler, M. Hengler
[128]Replaced during the run by, then later dropped:
"Teach Us the Subtle Art of Kissing"
A. Clark, Company
(*Music by* Raymond Hubbell. *Lyrics by* Addison Burkhardt.)

1903–1904 SEASON

Raymond Hitchcock in THE YANKEE CONSUL (Photo: Marceau)
Billy Rose Theatre Collection, New York Public Library for the Performing Arts

1903–1904 SEASON

1903.15 PUNCH, JUDY AND COMPANY

A Spectacular (Musical) Extravaganza in One Act, preceded by a program of vaudeville. Book, music and lyrics by Oscar Hammerstein. Musical numbers staged by Frank Tannehill and Gertrude May Hoffman. Produced by Oscar Hammerstein. Opened 1 June 1903 at (Hammerstein's) Paradise Roof Garden[1] and closed 5 September 1903 after 83 performances.

Vaudeville: Riccabona's Horses. Robert Cole and J. Rosamund Johnson (songs). Hoosier Zouaves (dance act). The Four Nightons. The Chamberlin's (lassoo act). the Marco Twins. Galletti's Monkeys. Joseof Dumond (violin), assisted by Mlle. Dumond, etc.

CAST: *Mefistole*: JOSEPHINE SABEL. *Satania*: LOUISE DeRIGNEY. *Ulka*: ELSA HARTUNG. *Bettina*: Charlotte Stemmer. *Francisca*: GERTRUDE MAY HOFFMAN. *Punch*: KITTY DONOGHUE. *Judy*: GLADYS SHAW. *The Policeman*: Lulu Whalen. *Joey*: Angy Wemis. *The Beadle*: Emilie Wellington. *The Nigger*: MADELINE SOMERS. *The Chinaman*: Julie Curtis. *The Doctor*: Rose Earle.

Members of the Punch and Judy Club: May Gunderman, Lillian Vogelle, Lillie Bernard, Georgia White, Martha Edmond, Myrtle King, Amy Laurens, Katharine Powell, Sadie Raymond, Mabel Gordon, Catherine Pope, Harriet de Norma, Helen Courtney, Fern Ballentine, Nina Gillette, Miriam Norris. *The Royal Guard*: Charlotte Danbridge, Tina Alberts, Dorothy Downing, Lola Hoffman, Ede Tyler, Louise Ferguson. *Nurses*: Gertrude May Hoffman, Katharine Powell, Georgia White, Ede Tyler.

MUSICAL NUMBERS[2]

"The Stork Ballet"
E. Hartung, Nursemaids, Storks, Babies
"The Girl in Blue"
L. DeRigney
"If I Again Would Be a Baby"
J. Sabel
"There's But One New York"
J. Sabel
Finale
Entire Company

1903.16 THE BLONDE IN BLACK

A Musical Farce-Comedy in Three Acts[3]. Book and lyrics by Harry B. Smith. Music by Gustave Kerker. Staged by Max Freeman. Entire production under the personal direction of George W. Lederer. Dances by Carl Marwig. Settings by D. Frank Dodge. Costumes by Archie Gunn. Electrical effects by Joseph George. Orchestra under the direction of Gustave Kerker. Produced by George W. Lederer. Opened 8 June 1903 at the Knickerbocker Theatre and closed 11 July 1903 after 35 performances.

CAST: *Flossie Featherly*, who goes to Paris to teach the cake-walk, but whose ambition is to play Camille: BLANCHE RING. *Gaston Roulette*, Ladies' Tailor, Matrimonial Agent, and President of the "Domestic Fidelity Trust Co., Limited": HARRY CONOR. *Walker Foote*, formerly a humble Shakespearean actor, now anything: ALBERT HART. *Bettine*, Roulette's wife, who fad is art cookery, tempered by sentiment: ROSE BEAUMONT. *Van Dyck Beard*, an American painter, completing his education in Paris: CHARLES H. BOWERS. *M. Carrousel Ladjos*, a Hungarian ballet master and producer of spectacular ballets: MAX FREEMAN. *Elsa Beckmesser-Carrousel*, his wife, a Wagnerian prima donna: VIOLET HALLS. *Claude Rapin*, a studio apprentice, very unhandy about the house: Wilmer Bentley. *Claudine*, his fiancée: Reine Davies.

Members of Carrousel's Theatrical Company (8): *Eugenie*: Mabel Verne. *Albertine*: Ada Verne. *Victorine*: Mignon Hardt. *Antoinette*: Adelaide Lorraine. *Francine*: Madeleine Martin. *Wanda*: Georgia Russell. *Julie*: Mildred DeVere. *Celine*: Stella Hammerstein. *Paulette, Pierrette*, art students: Helga Howard, Bess Evylyn Gibson. *Mlle. Lemaire*, forewoman of Roulette's shop: Lillian Hudson. *Toine*: Addie Sharpe. *Margot*: Sadie Probst. *Babette*: Elba Kenney. *Jeanne*: R. Rothwell. *Natalie*: Madeleine Martin. *Claire*: Georgia Russell. *Denise*: Mignon Hardt. *Celeste*: Kate Gothold. *Roulette's customers (6)*: *Madame De Bargeton*: Hazel Manchester. *Lady Brewer-Muggs*: Frieda Salber. *Mrs. Mushroom Smart*: Lillie Hart. *Madame D'Espard*: Lillian Seville. *Mrs. Startup*: Katherine Kellogg. *Frau Muller*: Leila Benton. *Art Students (5)*: *Jules*: David Bennett. *Jean*: Paul Decker. *Raoul*: Vernon Lee. *Robert*: Wheeler Earl. *Adolphe*: Cecil Summers.

The action takes place in Paris at the present time.

Act 1: Gaston Roulette's establishment.

Act 2: Van Dyke Beard's studio.

Act 3: Gaston Roulette's establishment.

ACT 1[4]

"Men Are Ambitious" (Opening Chorus)
"Don't Overdo It" (Trio)
"The Yankee Girl" (Song and Chorus)
(B. Ring)
"Any Old Thing" (Song)
Quartette
Finale (Cake-Walk Song)
(B. Ring, Chorus)

ACT 2

"(Twas) Love All the Day" (Artist and Model)(Opening Chorus)
"My Ideal" (Song)
"(When) She Walks Like This" (Song)
Spanish Song and Chorus
"Awake Ma Chile" (Coon Song and Chorus)
"Although I'm So Demure" (Champagne Song)
(R. Beaumont)
Finale

ACT 3

"Country Belles"/"Cynthia Jane" (The Sewing Machine Chorus)
(B. Ring)
"(They Are) Angels Without Wings" (Trio)
(B. Ring, H. Conor, A. Hart)
Finale

1903.17 THE KNICKERBOCKER GIRL

The Alfred E. Aarons Musical Comedy Company in a Musical Comedy in Two Acts. Book and lyrics by George Totten Smith. Music by Alfred E. Aarons. Musical numbers staged by Ad. Newberger. Scenery by D. Frank Dodge. Costumes designed by Archie Gunn. Director of music, Anton Heindl. Produced by Frank Howe, Jr. Opened 15 June 1903 at the Herald Square Theatre and closed 27 June 1903 after 14 performances.[5]

CAST: *Sanford Merton*, a society politician: SYDNEY DEANE. *Terry*, his political adviser: John Keefe. *Professor Herman Wartz* from Heidelberg University, Germany: WILL H. SLOANE. *Abner Merton*, proprietor of "Merton's Rejuvenating Springs," Oxbow Centre, Vermont: HARRY KELLY. *Don Carlos Estrobana*, leader of the Independent Party of Danero, South America: GEORGE HONEY. *Messenger Boy*: Alice Clifford. *Baldwin*, superintendent of the Club House: Edgar Halstead. *Captain Barnacle* of the launch *Josephine*: CHARLES JUDELS. *Meigal Rosaros*, Estrobana's rival: Edgar Halstead. *Captain Nunez*: CHARLES JUDELS. *Eleanor de Reuyter*, descendant of a good old Knickerbocker family: GRACE BELMONT. *La Rosa Estrobana*, Don Carlos' sister: NELLIE BEAUMONT. *Roxie*, Miss de Reuyter's maid: AIDA HEMMI.

Society Buds: *Trixie Tiller*: Nina Randall. *Miss Madison*: Helen Irwin. *Members of the Westchester Country Club*: *Daisy Deuce*: Ada Bernard. *Miss Lexington*: Caroline Locke. *Miss Grammercy*: Edythe Moyer. *Murray Hill*: Maud LeRoy. *Miss Riverside*: Ollie Woolford. *Miss Larchmont*: Beatrice Flint. *Miss Englewood*: Clara MacCord. *Miss Pelham*: Florence Campbell. *Miss Irvington*: Minnie Johnston. *Miss Piermont*: Georgia Campbell. *Miss Woodford*: Edna Kerr. *Miss Hoffman*: Effie Leslie. *Miss Waldorf*: Louie Sprague. *Miss Million*: Ione Kerr.

Inez: Sadie Long. *Dolores*: Gwendoline Coate. *The Tough Girl*: Kittie Hamilton. *Mehitabel Merton*, living advertisement for "Merton's Rejuvenating Spring Water": JOSEPHINE HALL. *Golfers, Bathers, Yachters, Tennis Players, Denizens of Danero, Soldiers, Stewards.*

Act 1: The Westchester Golf Club, New York.

Act 2: The public square in the town of Danero, South America.

ACT 1

Opening Chorus
"Just a Smile"

---

[1]Atop the Victoria and Belasco Theatres.
[2]No program available; musical numbers not in performance order.
[3]Billed as George W. Lederer's annual summer presentation. Revised from three acts to two acts during the run.

[4]Vocals not credited in program; listing from late in the run. Opening night reviewers remarked upon additional songs not in the later program: "Friendship is a Lovely Thing," "(I Love) Ze American Ragtime," "What's the Use of Love?" and "A Banjo Serenade."
[5]Stage direction uncredited in New York; in Philadelphia prior to New York direction credited to L. Lawrence.

S. Deane, H. Irwin, N. Randall
"To-day"
G. Belmont, Chorus
"Contrary Mary"
C. Judels, Chorus
(*Lyrics by* M. E. Rourke)
"Country Life"
H. Kelly, J. Hall
"Lalla"
H. Kelly, Chorus
"A Little Bird Is Watching All the Time"
P. Hall, W. H. Sloan, H. Kelly
"(I Only Know) I Love You"
S. Deane
"I Wouldn't, Would You?"
A. Hemmi
"Brother Bill"
J. Hall
"Hear the Band"
S. Deane, Chorus

ACT 2
Opening Chorus
"Dolly Daily"
P. Hall, Chorus
"Devotion"
A. Hemmi
"Pretty Polly Primrose"
A. Hemmi, Show Girls
"Espanola Viva"
P. Hall
"My Linda Love"
N. Beaumont, Chorus
"She's All Right"
P. Hall, Clarenze Quintette, Chorus
Finale

1903.18 (GEORGE W. LEDERER'S) MID-SUMMER NIGHT FANCIES

A Double Bill of Burlesques ("The Darling of the Gallery Gods" and "The Dress Parade") and Vaudeville Specialties. Book by George V. Hobart. Music by Ben M. Jerome. Lyrics by Matthew C. Woodward, John Gilroy and Nicholas H. Biddle. Entire entertainment under the personal stage direction of George V. Lederer. Settings painted by D. Frank Dodge. Costumes by Mme. Ripley. Orchestra under the direction of Max Hoffmann. Produced by George W. Lederer. Opened 22 June 1903 at the Crystal Gardens and closed 18 July 1903 after 24 performances.

Frobel and Ruge (Aerial Comedians on the Revolving Pole)
Rooney and Francis

ACT 1

THE DARLING OF THE GALLERY GODS. A Musical Comedy in Seven Spasms (Scenes). Book by George V. Hobart. Music by Ben M. Jerome. Lyrics by Matthew C. Woodward and John Gilroy.

CAST: The Men: *Karl*, Outlaw Prince and Leader of the "Short Card" Band: JUNIE McCREE. *Sakkookoo*, the Minister of War: D. L. DON. *Doggon*, the Prince of Toosoon: WILLIAM CAMERON. *Dandy Doo*: JOHN GILROY. *Dippy Dott*: HENRY DYER. *Beau Beau*: PAT ROONEY. *Mr. Black Bear*: George Ali. *Tom Tumbo*, nephew of Minister of War: FRANK BERNARD. *Jig Jug*, secretary to the Minister of War: Cecil Summers. *Pitty Pat*, servant of the Prince of Toosoon: James Furey. *Victims of Prince Karl and His "Short Card" Men (3)*: *Sir Buyup Junk*: Milo Joyce. *Lord Fudge*: John Talbot. *Admiral Fatt Head*: Wilfred Gerdes. *Shad Roe*, a fisherman: JOSEPH KANE. *Spies of the Minister of War (6)*: *Gum Shoo*: Frank Hill. *Peep Long*: Fred Titus. *Butt Inn*: Joseph Chaillee. *Ketch Up*: Harry Brown. *Sneek Hi*: Theodore Peters. *Tot So*: Charles Wentz. *Tan Sun*, the Governor's slave, who is Whoa San's slave: William W. Black. *Prince Karl's Band of "Short Card" Men (6)*: *Too Much*: Ollie Norman. *Whooa Deal*: Charles Edwards. *No Belt*: Henry Elkins. *Antie Up*: Ben Schwartz. *Tutt Tutt*: Edward Bingham. *Ham Manny*: Charles Wentz.

The Women: *Whoa San*, daughter of the Prince of Toosoon: EMMA CARUS. *Rosy Dawn*, champion long-distance Geisha: MAMIE GILROY. *Goo Goo San*, friend of Whoa San: May Taylor. *Bri Ton*, Who San's maid: Kathryn Bartlett. *Too Too San, Foo Foo San, Woo Woo San*, three little maids: Lillie Brink, Helen Lucas, Elphie Snowden. *Whoa San*, daughter of the Prince of Toosoon: TRIXIE FRIGANZA.

Geisha Girls: Misses Slocum, Errington, Seymour, J. Eagan, DeVere, Bryant, Lucas, Maguire. *Mikado Girls and Japanese Girl in general*: Misses Maurice, Girvin, Smith, Skeer, Parker, Rogers, Vorhees, Rice, McClure, Walsh, Wilson, Bradcome, Upton, R. Lewis, J. Lewis, Milliken, Denham, others.
DaKolta, Frobel and Ruge.

Scene 1: The Strike of the Thousand Dagoes. The lost subway in the Boulevard Mountains, near 60th Street, Tokio. Can anybody change a five spot? *Scene 2*: Picking Pork Chops in the garden of the Prince of Toosoon. A pair of deuces beats a four flush. *Scene 3*: The Great State Hall during the night of "The Feast of a Thousand Come-ons." Who opened that jackpot? *Scene 4*: Whoa San's Shoji in the Palmleaf Flats. 114th Street and Amsterdam Avenue, Tokio, at the hour of the Tenderloin (? A.M.) The Faces in the Window. *Scene 5*: The old sleuth room in the house of Sakkookoo, the Minister of War. He held up a kicker. *Scene 6*: Under the Bamboo Trees. Give me five cards, please. *Scene 7*: One thousand years later. The swimming lesson at Soles River near the Battery, Tokio. Arrived.

MUSICAL NUMBERS[6]
"Kiyomori" (Japanese Intermezzo)
(*Music by* Ben M. Jerome.)
"My Japanese Baby"
T. Friganza
(*Music by* A. Baldwin Sloane. *Lyrics by* Arthur Ambrose.)
"If Ever You Want a Favor, Mention Me"
J. McCree, Chorus
(*Music by* A. Baldwin Sloane. *Lyrics by* Arthur Ambrose.)
"Oshi Dori"[7]
M. Gilroy, Chorus
(*Music by* Ben M. Jerome. *Lyrics by* Matthew Woodward.)
"Whoa San"[8]
T. Friganza, J. McCree
(*Music by* Ben M. Jerome. *Lyrics by* Matthew Woodward.)
"Omi Omai"
D. L. Don
"Ida Bell"
T. Friganza, E. Carus, M. Gilroy, M. Taylor,
J. McCree, W. Cameron, J. Gilroy, D. L. Don
(*Music by* Ben M. Jerome. *Lyrics by* Matthew Woodward.)
"Mozart Lincoln"
E. Carus, Chorus
(*Music by* Ben M. Jerome. *Lyrics by* John Gilroy.)
"Solo Koko"
M. Taylor, J. Gilroy, P. Rooney, W. Cameron, F. Bernard
(*Music by* Ben M. Jerome. *Lyrics by* John Gilroy.)
"Watch Me To-night in the Torchlight Parade"
E. Carus, Entire Company
(*Music by* Ben M. Jerome. *Lyrics by* Arthur Lamb.)

ACT 2

NED WAYBURN'S MINSTREL MISSES. Devised and personally staged by Ned Wayburn. Words and music by Max Hoffmann.

CAST: *Bones*: Madge Pierce, Estella Sine, Jane Lovell, Maud Gillett. *Tambos*: Bertie Herron, Hattie Burdell, Teresa Roggerio, Dolly Shilton. *Interlocutor*: Elona Leonard. *In the Uniforms*: Emmilie Victoria, Sadie Burdell, Eleanor Telford, Myra Dalton, Heloise Horton, Belle Heath, Daisy Johnston, Edith Warren.

ROTATION OF SPECIALTIES
Parade
The Minstrel Misses
First part
The Good Old Songs Our Mammys Sang
Olio
My Dixie Land Daisy
English Pony Ballet (just returned from extended European tour)
Selections by Harris' Orphan Boys' Band (W. H. Rohrer, director)

---

[6]Composer and lyricist credits from published sheet music. Added during the run:
"Hinkey Dee"
J. McCree, Chorus
(*Music and Lyrics by* Harry Morris.)

[7]Dropped during the run.

[8]Dropped during the run. Sheet music also credits Emma Carus as the vocalist.

ACT 3

THE DRESS PARADE, a Bundle of Nonsense Tied Up with a String of Music. Nonsense by George V. Hobart. Music by Ben M. Jerome. Lyrics by Matt Woodward and John Gilroy. Dances arranged by Pat Rooney.

CAST: *The Earl of Pawtucket*: JUNIE McCREE. *The Girl with the Green Eyes*: EMMA CARUS. *The Sultan of Sulu*: D. L. DON. *The Messenger from Mars*, master of ceremonies: WILLIAM CAMERON. *Dorothy* from "The Wizard of Oz": MARGUERITE CLARK. *Sis Hopkins*: CARRIE GRAHAM. *Kon Kushan*, an imported violinist: Joe Kane. *Juliet*: Elphie Snowden. *The Prince of Pilsen*: Wilfred Gerdes. *The Sleeping Beauty*: May Taylor. *Romeo*: Lilly Brink. *The Billionaire*: Fred Titus. *Mr. Pickwick*: Wallace W. Black. *Prince Charming*: Daisy Lucas. *The Blonde in Black*: Lucille Eagan. *Silver Slipper*: Charlote Leslay. *The Mocking Bird*: Kathryn Bartlett. *Jewel of Asia*: JOHN GILROY. *The Old Homestead*: Harry Brown. *A Gentleman of France*: Charles Wentz. *The Starbucks*: Milo Joyce. *The Toreador*: Tom Collins. *'Way Down East*: Joseph Chaillee. *Benoit*, head waiter: JOHN BEDINI. *Snowface*, a waiter: ARTHUR ARTHUR. (Also Wheeler Earl.)

Show Girls: Misses Bryant, Slocum, Errington, Seymour, Devere, Maguire, Leslay, Maurice, Girvin, Smith, Skeer, Parker, Rogers, Voorhees. *Outing Girls*: Misses McClure, Walsh, Wilson, Rice, Bradcome, Upton, R. Lewis, J. Lewis, Milliken, Denham, others.

Scene: Exterior of the Hotel de Pipe, on the Foolish River, near Laughing Gas City, Lotus County, in the State of Ridiculous.

MUSICAL NUMBERS[9]

Opening
Chorus

"Down Where Two Lovers Sat"[10]
M. Gilroy, Chorus

"Ella"
T. Friganza, Chorus
(*Lyrics by* Nicholas Biddle.)

"Keep on a Shining, Silvery Moon"
E. Carus, Chorus
(*Lyrics by* Nicholas Biddle.)

"The Marriage of the Daffodil and Daisy" (Old Time Song and Dance)
P. Rooney,
J. Gilroy, W. Cameron, T. Collins, W. Earl, L. Brink, M. Taylor, E. Snowden, L. Rice
(*Lyrics by* Nicholas Biddle.)

"Willie"[11]
E. Carus, D. L. Don

Finale
Entire Company

On 27 July 1903, a new burlesque LIFTING THE CUP replaced THE DRESS PARADE; the order of the program was also reversed, so that LIFTING THE CUP preceded THE DARLING OF THE GALLERY GODS.

LIFTING THE CUP, a Nautical Nonsensicality in One Knot. Log Book by George V. Hobart. Music by Ben M. Jerome. Lyrics by Matt C. Woodward and Nicholas H. Biddle. Dances devised by Ned Wayburn.

Complete Passenger List (Cast): Landlubbers: *Sir Thomas Liftit*, a genuine sportsman: JAMES FUREY. *The Earl of Pawtucket*, a visitor: JUNIE McCREE. *August Sauerberger*, the leader of a band: D. L. DON. *Conrad Puffenlotz*, the player of a piccolo: Joseph Kane. *Members of Band (4)*: *Giovanni*: George Ali. *Ludwig*: Tom Collins. *Carlo*: Willie Collins. *Otto*: Ben Schwartz. *Sandy Hook, Jr.*, official mascot: Wilfred Gerdes. *A.D.T. McSlow*, the messenger boy: Edna McClure. *Thomas J. Invention*: JOHN GILROY.

Lady Landlubbers: *Helen Type*, a newspaper girl: EMMA CARUS. *Prunella Prue*: REINE DAVIES. *Breezie Day*, a soubrette girl: May Taylor. *Miss Sarah Snap*, Kodak girl: Bessie Evelyn Gibson.

The Crew: *Mike McGuire*, the Irish captain: JUNIE McCREE. *Henry Hawkins*, the English mate: WILLIAM CAMERON. *Sandy Gillis*, the Scotch bo'sun: Wallace W. Black. *Jolly Jack*, the deep sea juggler: JEHAN [John] BEDINI. *Sambo Heavyfeet*, the African cabin boy: Arthur Arthur. *Ole Olsen*, the Swedish sailor: Ollie Norman. *Paulovitch*, the Russian sailor: Fred Titus. *Pierre Baptiste*, the French sailor: Joseph Chaillee. *Felipe*, the Spanish sailor: Theodore Peters. *Patrick Shamrock, Jr.*, the leader of the Shamrock boys: Elizabeth Hawman. *Tom Redwitenblue, Jr.*, the leader of the Columbia boys: Adah Robertson.

Scene: The Deck of the "Erin."

MUSICAL NUMBERS

"Yea Ho, My Lads, Heave Oh"
W. W. Black, Sailors

"Ella"
M. Taylor, W. Cameron

"Flirtation Song"
E. Carus, Sailor Boys

"Bee, Be My Honey Bee"
R. Davies, Chorus

"The Marriage of the Daffodil and the Daisy"
M. Taylor, E. Snowden, L. Rice, J. Gilroy, W. Cameron, T. Collins, W. Earl

"Will Lifton Lift the Cup?"
J. McCree, Pony Ballet

"New York Forever"
E. Carus, Entire Company

1903.19 OTOYO/JAPAN BY NIGHT

A Japanese Comic Opera in Two Acts[12]. Book by Henry Pincus and Melvin G. Winstock. Music by William Frederick Peters. Lyrics by Robert L. Beecher. Produced under the personal direction of Gus Sohlke. Scenery painted by I. Hasegawa and K. Takahashi. American costumes by DeGrey. Musical direction, William Frederick Peters. Produced by (Messrs.) Kushibiki and Arai (Henry Pincus, Business Manager). Opened 1 July 1903 at the Madison Square Roof Garden and closed 5 September 1903 after 57 performances.

CAST: *Ten Yen*, Lord Mayor of Tokio, the worst Lord Mayor Tokio ever had: JAMES F. MacDONALD. *Arthur Roberts*, an American gentleman: HOBART SMOCK. *Con Slick*, a San Francisco confidence man: ABBOTT DAVISON. *Sallie Scraggs*, an old-time ballet girl: HATTIE ARNOLD. *Pollie Roberts*, sister of Arthur: IRENE JERMON. *San Ke*, private secretary of Ten Yen: Jefferson Hall. *Matsuba*, an old Japanese military hero: MARK LANE. *Toki*, the Mikado's official message bearer: Harry Truax. *Willie Scraggs, Mignonette Scraggs*, children of Sallie Scraggs: Harry McKee, Rose Parker. *Yama, Toma*, companions of Otoyo: Viola Prince, Naomi Arnold. *Undertaker*: Samuel Sandgran. *Otoyo*, daughter of Ten Yen, betrothed to Matsuba: BETTINA GERARD. *Guards, Attendants, Workmen, Geisha Girls, etc.*

Octette of Tourists: Viola Prince, Grace Naesmith, Naomi Arnold, Cora Carter, Samuel Sandgran, Adrien Bellevue, Ambrose Daly, Frank McCullough. *White Pickaninnies*, led by Irene Jermon: Jeanette Thomas, Ledyard Pope, Rena Aubray, Stella Madisan, Marie Tunison, Emma West, Mildred Cooke, Helen Clifton, Margaret Hastings, Mabel Lloyd, Allie Marshall, Vivian Marston. *Dance Specialty*: Hermenese.

Act 1: Gardens of Ten Yen at Tokio, (Japan). Present time.

Act 2: Council Chamber of the Lord Mayor of Tokio.

ACT 1

Opening Chorus
Chorus

"Kemo Kimo" (Duet)
N. Arnold, V. Prince
(*Lyrics by* Arthur Burrows.)

"Pity My Pitiful Plight"
B. Gerard
(*Lyrics by* Arthur Burrows.)

"A Toast to the Moon"
B. Gerard
(*Lyrics by* Arthur Burrows.)

"The Garden of Youth"
H. Smock

"O! Mystic Moon in Sapphire Sea" (Ensemble)
Chorus

[9]Added during the run:
"Sis Hopkins"
C. Graham
"Won't Go Home Till Morning"
J. McCree, G. Ali, Quartette

[10]Dropped during the run.

[11]Dropped during the run.

[12]Preceded by a light orchestral concert by the Boston Ladies Orchestra; the performance was followed by the Japanese Magicians, Sono Sonetaro and Company.

"The Mayor of Tokio"
J. F. MacDonald
"Welcome to Foreign Princes" (Ensemble)
Chorus
"I Wouldn't Do That, Would You?" (Trio)
J. F. MacDonald, A. Davison, H. McKee
(*Lyrics by* Arthur Burrows and Robert L. Beecher.)
"The Silver Sea of Love" (Duet)
B. Gerard, H. Smock
Finale
Chorus, Principals

ACT 2
Opening Chorus
Chorus
(*Lyrics by* Arthur Burrows and Robert L. Beecher.)
"The Tale of a Monkey"
B. Gerard
(*Lyrics by* Arthur Burrows.)
"Are You On?"
A. Davison
"The Idol and the Maid"
B. Gerard
(*Lyrics by* Arthur Burrows.)
"My Lallapaloosa Girl"
I. Jermon
"We're a Scientific Band" (Octette)
V. Prince, G. Naesmith, N. Arnold, C. Carter,
S. Sandgran, A. Bellevue, A. Daly, F. McCullough
"ZuZu and ZaZa" (Duet)
H. Arnold, J. F. MacDonald
"Yankee Noblemen"
H. Smock
Finale
Principals, Chorus

1903.20 A SON OF REST

A Musical Farce in Two Acts. Book, music and lyrics by George Weston. Musical numbers and dances staged by Sam Marion. Scenery by P. Dodd Ackerman. Costumes by Eaves. Musical director, Max S. Witt. Produced by Broadhurst and Currie. Opened 17 August 1903 at the 14th Street Theatre and closed 22 August 1903 after 8 performances; returned 22 February 1904 to the 14th Street Theatre and closed 27 February 1904 after an additional 8 performances.[13]

CAST: *Hunting Grubb*: NAT M. WILLS. *Willie*, Grubb's friend: GABRIEL. *Professor Fulton*, who knows a few things about microbes: John Allison. *Frank Fields*, in love with Bessie: Al. Lamar. *Timothy Snodgrass*, who runs the village: Thomas J. Grady. *Budd*, Tim's assistant: Edward Hayes. *Captain Warren*, an unexpected arrival: Frank Dearduff. *John West*, a friend of Frank's: William Hodson. *Mrs. Warren*, the Captain's wife: Susanne Rocamora. *Mrs. Spruceby*, who keeps the seminary: MAUD ALLISON. *Bessie Atherton*, a seminary girl: MONA WYNNE. *Mariola*, the high priestess: Katheryn Manning. *Gwendolin, Guinevere*, the soda water girls: Ruth Baine, Georgie Irving. *Constance, Marjorie*, their friends: Nora Johnson, Dorothy Marlow. *Annie*, who loves the shop: Edith O'Reilly. *Mildred*, the canine's friend: Linnet Fiske. *Idadene*, just a shopper: Madge Melbourne. *Viola*, another shopper: Maude Elliott.

Some of Mrs. Spruceby's Seminary Girls (8): *Georgia*: Rosie Earle. *Marcia*: Lou Gillette. *Flora*: Gertrude Merrill. *Helena*: Pauline Pearl. *Editha*: Marie Young. *Gloria*: Gertrude Cogan. *Bertha*: Sylvia Diamond. *Florida*: Loie Mack. *And these young ladies are the village belles (8)*: *Anabel*: Georgia White. *Amy*: Stella Warner. *Ada*: Vivian Van Sickle. *Alice*: Inez Bayard. *Agnes*: Carrie Lawson. *Adele*: Frances Lawson. *Aline*: Bertha Field. *Attalie*: Elfay Durst. *The Summer Men*: Archie Scott, Nick Grist, Perry Belmont, Charles T. Parr, Arthur Caville, James Lee, Benjamin Benard, F. Beese.

Act 1: A village in Connecticut. Morning.

Act 2: The drug store. Evening.

ACT 1
"Glorious Summer"
Chorus
"The Song of the Flowing Stein"
A. Lamar, Chorus
"Demure and Shy"
M. Allison, Seminary Girls
"Had She Only Let Me Dream an Hour More"
N. M. Wills
"The Flag and the Girl I Love"
S. Rocamora, Sea Shore Girls
"Hail! the Sacred Cat"
Entire Company, Chorus
"Plain Jane Payne"
T. J. Grady, A. Lamar, E. Hayes, M. Allison, M. Wynne
"General Four Flush" (Finale)
N. M. Wills, Entire Company

ACT 2
"In the Evening Time"
E. O'Reilly, K. Manning, Chorus
"My Little 'Rang Outang"
M. Wynne, assisted by Seminary Girls, Village Belles
Dancing Couple: E. Hayes, M. Wynne.
(*Music by* Theodore F. Morse. *Lyrics by* Edward Madden.)
"My Dixie Anna"
A. Lamar, Gabriel
Songs and Parodies
N. M. Wills
"Sukey-Sue"
S. Rocamora, Full Chorus
(*Music by* Max S. Witt. *Lyrics by* Frederic Ranken.)
Finale
N. M. Wills, Company

1903.21 A PRINCESS OF KENSINGTON

An Original Romantic Comic Opera in Two Acts. Libretto by Basil Hood. Music by Edward German. Produced under the stage direction of Cyril Scott. Costumes by Alias, London; Mme. Freisinger. Musical director, J. Sebastian Hiller. Produced by John C. Fisher. Opened 31 August 1903 at the Broadway Theatre and closed 3 October 1903 after 41 performances.

CAST: *Of the H.M.S. "Albion" (4)*: *William Jelf*: JAMES T. POWERS. *Bill Blake*: FRED HUNTLEY. *Will Weatherley*: Bernard Tieman. *Jem Johnson*: P. J. Worthington. *Sir James Jellicoe*, a banker: George B. Jackson. *Puck*, the Imp of Mischief: WILLIAM STEPHENS. *Lieutenant Brook Green* of the Kensington Rifles: RICHIE LING. *Yapp*, a policeman: Walter S. Craven. *Mr. Reddish*, proprietor "Jolly Tar," Winkelmouth: STANLEY H. FORDE. *Old Ben*: George Mudie, Jr. *James Doubleday*: C. H. Hillman. *Oberon*, King of Fairies: JACK TAYLOR. *Azuriel*, a mountain spirit: EDWARD MARTINDELL. *Recruiting Sergeant*, Royal Marines: Thomas Shannon. *Zephyrus*: Loyd Hoey. *Joy*, daughter of Sir James Jellicoe: CECIL ENGELHARD. *Nell Reddish*, niece of Mr. Reddish: AMELIA FIELDS. *Titania*, Queen of Fairies: PAULINE FREDERICK. *Fairies (6)*: *Butterfly*: Lily Bircham. *Dragonfly*: Nellie Emerald. *Peaseblossom*: Estelle Ward. *Moth*: Leila Williams. *Cobweb*: Elsie Gibbons. *Mustardseed*: Pauline de la Paz. *Lady Jellicoe*: Angela May. *Kenna*, daughter of Oberon: DORA DeFILIPPE.

The action takes place at the present time.

Act 1: Kensington Gardens, near "The Basin." Morning.

Act 2: Winkelmouth-on-Sea. Afternoon.

ACT 1
"Fairies, Fairies Come Forth" (Opening Chorus)
Girls
"From Where the Scotch Mountains" (Chorus and Duet)
J. Taylor, P. Frederick
"If We Pass Beyond the Portals" (Song with Chorus)
W. Stephens
"Seven O'Clock in the Morning" (Duet)
C. Engelhard, R. Ling
"Who That Knows How I Love You, Love" (Sextette)
D. DeFilippe, A. Jellicoe, C. Engelhard, R. Ling, W. Stephens, E. Martindell

[13]Touring programs 16 months later credit music to Max S. Witt; only four songs were retained from the original score.

"(We're) Four Jolly Sailormen" (Hornpipe)(Quartette)
J. T. Powers, Three Sailors
"Oh! What Is Woman's Duty" (Song)
A. Fields
"We're Butchers and Bakers and Candlestick-Makers" (Chorus)
Dance
L. Bircham
"Twin Butterflies That Fitfully Fall"
E. Ward
"Now, Here's to the 'Prentices'" (Song and Chorus)
R. Ling
"At the Seaside" (Song)
J. T. Powers
(*Music by* Ernest Shand. *Lyrics by* C. H. Bovill. *Additional Lyrics by* J. T. Powers.)
"If Love in a Cottage Be All That They Tell" (Trio)
C. Engelhard, R. Ling, W. Stephens
"Till the Day of My Majority" (Finale)
Ensemble

ACT 2[14]
"High and Dry Let Her Lie" (Opening Chorus)
"A Mountain Stood Like a Grim Outpost"[15] (Song)
D. DeFilippe
"By a Piccadilly Cab Stand"[16] (Song)
J. T. Powers
"If You Will Spare the Time" (Trio with Chorus and Dance)
J. T. Powers, D. DeFilippe, W. Stephens, Chorus
Gipsy Dance
D. DeFilippe, Chorus
"See a Rainbow Arch" (Bridal March, Chorus, Duet, Ensemble)
"A Sprig of Rosemarie"[17] (Song)
R. Ling
"A German Prince May Wed Me Since" (Trio)
A. Fields, W. Stephens, W. T. Powers
"It's a Pressing Invitation That I Bring" (Song, Ensemble and Chorus)
"Seven O'Clock in the Evening" (Finale)
Ensemble

1903.22 THREE LITTLE MAIDS

A Musical Comedy (Musical Play) in Three Acts. Book, music and lyrics by Paul Rubens. (Additional numbers by Percy Greenbank and Howard Talbot.) Acting manager, Charles N. Richards. Scenic artist, Edward G. Unitt. Orchestra under the direction of Frank E. Tours. Produced by Charles Frohman and George Edwardes. Opened 1 September 1903 at Daly's Theatre, moved 16 November 1903 to the Garden Theatre and closed 26 December 1903 after 130 performances[18].

CAST: *Daughters of the Reve. Theodore Branscombe (3)*: *Ada Branscombe*: MADGE CRICHTON. *Edna Branscombe*: DELIA MASON. *Hilda Branscombe*: ELSA RYAN. *Lady St. Mallory*: MAUD HOBSON. *Proteges of Lady St. Mallory (3)*: *Lady Rosemary Beaulieu*: Vera Edwardine. *Venetia Grafton*: Eva Kelly. *Lady Marjorie Crichton*: Kathleen Warren. *Miss Deare*, Postmistress at Market Mallory: Barbara Huntley. *Miss Crane*, a village girl: Vera Vallis. *Miss Price*, Manageress of the Tea Shop: Marie West. *Louisa* of the Tea Shop: Pollie Emery. *Lord Cheyne*, nicknamed "Daisy": G. P. HUNTLEY. *Brian Molyneux*: J. Edward Fraser. *Reverend Branscombe*, Vicar of Market Mallory: R. St. George. *Cupid*, a caddie: GEORGE CARROLL. *M. de l'Orme* of the French Embassy: MAURICE FARKOA.
Visitors: Misses Kuzelle, Brooks, Watts. Tunison, Maurice, Robinson. Messrs. Armstrong, Lipson, Finley, Alston, Ozab, Weaver, Cutter, Featherstone. *Tea Girls*: Misses Daincourt, Thorne, Vallis, Callan, Gordon, Wright, Sanford, Lucie.

Act 1: Golf Links at Market Mallory, near London.

Act 2: A Bond Street Tea Shop, London.

Act 3: Lady St. Mallory's Drawing-room at Market Mallory.

ACT 1[19]
Opening Chorus (Since daybreak the sun . . .)
(*Music by* Howard Talbot. *Lyrics by* Percy Greenbank.)
"Me and the Post" (Song)
B. Huntley
"Three Little Maids" (Trio)
D. Mason, E. Ryan, M. Crichton
"The Town and Country Mouse" (Sextet)
Country Girls, London Girls
"I'm Only the Caddie" (Song)
G. Carroll
(*Music by* Walter Rubens. *Lyrics by* Percy Greenbank.)
"Love, You're a Wonderful Game" (Song)
M. Farkoa
"Do You Think That You Have Known Me Long Enough" (Duet)
D. Mason, J. E. Fraser
(*Music by* Walter Rubens. *Lyrics by* Percy Greenbank.)
"(My Gal) Sal" (Song)
M. Crichton
"Golf" (Duet)
M. Crichton, G. P. Huntley
Finale (All the luggage has been put upon the cart. .)
(*Music by* Howard Talbot. *Lyrics by* Percy Greenbank.)

ACT 2
Opening Chorus (When society goes shopping. .)
(*Music by* Howard Talbot. *Lyrics by* Percy Greenbank.)
"(She Was) the Miller's Daughter" (Song)
E. Ryan
"I'll Dream of You" (Song)
M. Farkoa
"That's a Very Different Thing" (Song)
D. Mason
"Men" (Song)
M. Crichton
"Girls, girls, girls" (Song)
G. Carroll
"Algy's Simply Awfully Good at Algebra" (Song)
M. Farkoa
"Tea and Cake Walk" (Trio)
D. Mason, E. Ryan, M. Crichton
"Suppose we have a Breakdown" (Sextet)
M. Crichton, D. Mason, E. Ryan, G. P. Huntley, J. E. Fraser, M. Farkoa
(*Music by* Howard Talbot. *Lyrics by* Percy Greenbank.)
Finale (instrumental)
(*Music by* Howard Talbot.)

ACT 3

---

[14]Added after opening or for tour (following "High and Dry Let Her Lie"):
"(Here's to the) Nut Brown Ale"
S. H. Forde
(*Music and Lyrics by* Theodore [Harry] Northup.)

[15]Replaced during the tour by:
"If All the Stars Were Mine" (Song)
D. DeFilippe

[16]Replaced after opening or for tour by:
"Yarns" (Song)
J. T. Powers

[17]Replaced during the tour by:
"For What Thou Art" (Song)
R. Ling

[18]No director (J. E. A. Malone, director of original London production), costume designer (Hawes Craven, Joseph Harker from London production) or song list in programs. Transfer to the Garden Theatre billed "new songs, new features."

[19]Musical numbers not listed in programs. Above list prepared from published English piano vocal score (Chappell & Co., London, 1902). Published in vocal score addenda:
"A Real Town Lady" (Song)
E. Ryan
Additional numbers published for American production:
"Do I Like Love"
(*Music by* Paul Rubens. *Lyrics by* F. E. Weatherley.)
"My Little Girlie"
(*Music by* Frank E. Tours. *Lyrics by* Leedham Bantock.)

Opening Chorus (Lady St. Mallory's friends. .)
(*Music by* Howard Talbot. *Lyrics by* Percy Greenbank.)
"What Is a Maid to Do" (Song)
D. Mason
"The Fishes in the Sea" (Song)
E. Ryan
"There Really Must be Something Nice About Me" (Something Sweet About Me)(Song)
M. Crichton
"Je vous adore" (Duet)
E. Ryan, M. Farkoa
"Wedding March" (Sextet)(Oh what a splendid thing . . .)
M. Crichton, D. Mason, E. Ryan, G. P. Huntley, J. E. Fraser, M. Farkoa
Finale

1903.23 THE ROGERS BROTHERS IN LONDON

A Farce Comedy with Music (Musical Comedy) in Three Acts[20]. Book by John J. McNally. Music by Max Hoffmann and Melville Ellis. Lyrics by George V. Hobart and Ed. Gardenier. Staged by Herbert Gresham and Ned Wayburn. Scenes painted by Ernest Gros, Ernest Albert. Costumes designed by F. Richard Anderson. Musical director, Max Hoffmann. Produced by (Marc) Klaw and (Abraham L.) Erlanger. Opened 7 September 1903 at the Knickerbocker Theatre and closed 31 October 1903 after 64 performances[21].

CAST: *Ferdinand Falls*: GUS ROGERS. *August Furst*: MAX ROGERS. *Harold Harvey*: JOSEPH COYNE. *Will Conn*: LEE HARRISON. *Marie Patricia*: LILLIAN COLEMAN. *Rosie Lotte*: CARRIE REYNOLDS. *Lord Harry Hartford*: MELVILLE ELLIS. *Charley Cortright*: GEORGE AUSTIN MOORE. *Barney Barnegat*: William J. Cale. *Evelyn Birmingham*: Neva Aymar. *Peggy Prued*: Sue Stuart. *Dorothy Dorchester*: Frances Tyson. *Claire Harte*: Minerva Courtney. *Mabel Strong*: Julia Eastman. *Mrs. Finch*: May B. Wood. *Tom Helper*: James Cherry. *Mike Dugan*: Harry Brown. *Dick Decker*: WILLIAM TORPEY. *Welter Waite*: J. S. Thompson. *Captain of the "Kronprinz Wilhelm"*: Ole Norman.

Ensemble: Nellie Uart, Florence Carrette, Jean Baxter, Vinnette Bradcome, Frances Bradford, Helen Barrett, Isabelle Scott, Davida Hawthorne, Lillie Hart, Franes Folsom, Abby Hyatt, Pauline Montreau, Bessie Leyland, Estelle Wilmott, Josephine Clairmont.

Act 1: Deck of the North German Lloyd Steamship, *"Kronprinz Wilhelm."*. (Gros.)

Act 2: Trafalgar Square, London. (Albert.)

Act 3: "Meet Me at the Fountain"—Siegel-Cooper's. (Gros.)

ACT 1
"Going Home" (Opening Chorus)
(*Music by* Max Hoffmann.)
"On a Starlight Night" (Duet)
C. Reynolds, G. A. Moore, Full Chorus
(*Music by* Melville Ellis. *Lyrics by* Ed Gardenier.)
"Queen of the Bungalow" (Trio)
Rogers Brothers, N. Aymar
(*Music by* Max and Gus Rogers. *Lyrics by* Ed Gardenier.)
"You'll Dream of Me"[22] (You Dream of Me Love)(Song)
L. Coleman
(*Music by* Melville Ellis. *Lyrics by* George V. Hobart.)

ACT 2
"King Edward's Subjects" (Opening Chorus)
(*Music by* Max Hoffmann. *Lyrics by* George V. Hobart.)
Original Sayings and Parodies
Rogers Brothers
"The American Beauty" (Song)
G. A. Moore, Chorus
(*Music by* Max Hoffmann.)
"Mr. Breezy (Was an Easy Mark)" (Octette)
Rogers Brothers, Misses Reynolds, Aymar, Stuart, Tyson, Courtney, Eastman
(*Music by* Melville Ellis. *Lyrics by* Ed Gardenier.)
"By the Sycamo Tree"
L. Coleman, G. A. Moore
(*Music by* Max Hoffmann. *Lyrics by* George V. Hobart.)
"The Coster's 'Oliday" (The Coster's Holiday)(Finale)
(*Music by* Max Hoffmann. *Lyrics by* George V. Hobart.)

ACT 3
"Shopping" (Opening Chorus)
(*Music by* Max Hoffmann. *Lyrics by* Ed Gardenier.)
"It's Awfully Hard to Shop" (Song)
J. Coyne, Chorus
(*Music by* Melville Ellis. *Lyrics by* George V. Hobart.)
"In Gay New York" (Song)
L. Harrison, Chorus
(*Music by* Max Hoffmann. *Lyrics by* Ed Gardenier.)
"Say You'll Be a Friend of Mine" (Song)
Rogers Brothers
(*Music by* Theodore F. Morse. *Lyrics by* Vincent Bryan.)

[20]Billed as the sixth annual tour (of the Rogers Brothers).
[21]Played return engagements 23 November 1903 at the Harlem Opera House for 8 performances, and 28 December 1903 at the Grand Opera House for 8 performances.
[22]Dropped during the run.

1903.25 ARRAH-NA-POGUE

A Revival of the Scenic (Irish) Drama in Three Acts, 10 Scenes[23]. Play by Dion Boucicault (and E. H. House). (New music and lyrics by Andrew Mack.) Incidental music is the original used by Dion Boucicault. Stage direction, William Seymour. Scenery by Joseph Physioc from sketches made in Ireland. Costumes by M. Herman (New York), Van Horn & Son (Philadelphia), Schultz (Chicago), and the Boston Museum Musical director, William P. Brown. Produced by (Isaac B.) Rich & (William) Harris, by special arrangement with Louise Thorndyke Boucicault. Opened 7 September 1903 at the 14th Street Theatre and closed 31 October 1903 after 65 performances.

CAST: *Shaun, the Post*, a Wicklow Carman: ANDREW MACK. *Colonel Bagenal O'Grady*: THOMAS J. McGARNE. *Beamish McCoul*: JOHN S. ROBERTSON. *Major Coffin*, an English officer: Daniel Gilfether. *Michael Feeny*, a process server: LUKE MARTIN. *The Sergeant*: Thomas E. Jackson. *Of the Sept of "The McCoul" (7)*: *Oiny Farrell*: John Birch. *Andy Regan*: John Napier. *Moran*: Edward Aiken. *Patsey*: Frank M. Kendrick. *Tim Cogan*: O. Mann. *Lanagan*: G. L. Baker. *Pat Ryan*: Thomas Paulton. *Followers of "The O'Grady" (5)*: *Tim Conolly*: S. Anderson. *Paddy Finch*: N. Mackey. *Con Reilly*: Joseph French. *Murtagh Delaney*: V. Hathaway. *Barney Nolan*: M. Reddy.

Arrah Meelish, nicknamed by the peasantry "Arrah na Pogue," or Arrah of the Kiss: EDITH BARKER. *Fanny Power*, of Cabinteely: ANNE LEONARD. *Katty Walsh*: Maggie Fielding. *Norah Cavanaugh*: Lizzie Sanger. *Elsie O'Brien*: Emma Scully. *Molly Ryan*: Anna Wilson. *Eileen O'Donnell*: Beatrice Harris. *Kathleen Boyle*: Marie Dibrook. *Ducie Tiernan*: Anna Turner. *Bridget Maguire*: Marie Napier. *Anne Shaughnessy*: Florence Russel. *Molly McCarthy*: May Wilson. *Irish Peasants, English Soldiers, etc.*

Act 1, Scene 1: Glendalough, the Ruins of St. Kevin's Abbey. (1798.) *Scene 2*: Arrah's cottage at Larragh. *Scene 3*: Armory at O'Grady's house. *Scene 4*: Arrah's cottage, as before.

Act 2, Scene 1: Glen near Ballybetagh Castle. *Scene 2*: A prison in the castle. *Scene 3*: The court-room in the castle.

Act 3, Scene 1: The armory. *Scene 2*: The prison. *Scene 3*: The battlements.

MUSICAL NUMBERS[24]
"We'll Hurry to Church and Get Married"

[23]First produced in New York as ARRAH-NA-POGUE, or, The Wicklow Wedding, 12 July 1865 at Niblo's Garden for 66 performances; returned 15 November 1865 to Niblo's Garden for an additional 24 performances; moved 25 December 1866 to the New Bowery Theatre for an additional 12 performances. Total: 102 performances.
[24]With the exception of "The Wearing of the Green" from the original production, all of Andrew Mack's songs were written by him for this production. Later interpolations for the subsequent tour:
"The Heart of the Rose"
(*Music and Lyrics by* Andrew Mack.)
"Good Night, My Love, Good Night"
(*Music and Lyrics by* Andrew Mack.)
"The Joys of an Irish Dance"
(*Music and Lyrics by* Barney Fagan.)

A. Mack
"You Are My Star, for I Love You"
A. Mack
"An Irishman's Lilt"
A. Mack
"For Home and Ireland"
A. Mack
"The Wearing of the Green"
(*Music by* traditional. *Lyrics by* Dion Boucicault and E. H. House.)
A. Mack

1903.24

PEGGY FROM PARIS

A Musical Comedy in a Prologue and Two Acts. Book and lyrics by George Ade. Music by William Lorraine. Staged by George Marion. Settings by Walter Burridge and Edward LaMoss. Produced by Henry W. Savage. Opened 10 September 1903 at Wallack's Theatre and closed 21 November 1903 after 85 performances[25].

CAST: Prologue: *Captain Alonzo Plummer*, the village dignitary: GEORGE RICHARDS. *Hon Jabez Flanders*, the village orator: Goodwal Dickerman. *Walt Quackenbush*, the village joker: Dan Baker. *Jim Peasley*, the village station agent: E. H. O'Connor. *Lutie Plummer*, the village soprano: Guelma L. Baker. *Mrs. Homer Ketcham*, the village news bureau: Esta Reed. *Lem Harvey*, the village tenor: Harry Benham. *Tessie Higgins*, helping in the kitchen: Olivette Haynes.

Acts 1 and 2: *Cicero J. Grampis*, king of the prairie actors: Paul Nicholson. *Captain Alonzo Plummer* of Hickory Crick: GEORGE RICHARDS. *Montague Fish*, a banker with a private ambition: GEORGE A. BEANE. *Alexander Nerveen*, collegian: JOHN P. PARK. *Reginald Hickey*, a useful boy: ARTHUR DEAGON. *M. Hommard, M. Folies-Bergere*, of the Franco-American League: Dan Baker, E. H. O'Connor. *Dickey Drexel*: George F. Bennett. *Peggy Plummer*, known as Mlle. Fleurette Caramelle: GEORGIA CAINE. *Lutie Plummer*, her half sister: Guelma L. Baker. *Sophie Blatz*, Mlle. Caramelle's maid: JOSIE SADLER. *Mrs. Montague Fish*, a wife: ALICE HAGEMAN. *Lilly Ann Lynch*, the grown-up article: Helen Hale. *Mrs. Tuft-Hunter*, a society top-notcher: Blanche Gilson.

Society Leaders: Misses Reed, Frizelle, Williamson, Jansen, Olga Fredericks, Packer, Carlton, Evans. *Chappies*: Misses Rice, Aldrich, Harlow, Gardner, Mack, Lilja, Earl, Gorman. *Debutantes*: Misses Arnold, Anderson, Willard, Lee, Henderson, Alton, Hill. *Cupids*: Misses Olivette, Rae, Marik, Dalghren, Norman, Francis, Collette. *Clubmen*: Messrs. Davis, Benham, Chadwick, Moore, Wells, Hull, Carlson, E. Wells. *Flunkies*: Messrs. Randall, Carshone, Hollenbeck, Minor.

This effort is supposed to deal, more of less indirectly, with the strictly American habit of paying homage to the foreign artist. We have had musical plays dealing with London, New York, Paris, Japan, China, Turkey, the Philippines, Egypt and various cannibal islands. Why not Illinois?

Prologue: In Hickory Crick, Illinois.

Act 1: Chicago.

Act 2: Chicago.

PROLOGUE[26]
"Happy, Happy Illinois"
"Highfalutin Music"
"Old Fashioned Songs"
"The (Regular) Limited Train"

ACT 1
"We Are the Principals" (Opening Chorus)
"(We're True to the) College Days"
"Art"
"(My) Emmaleen"
"The Girl Who Comes in From the West"
"Welcome"
"Gay Fleurette"
Finale

ACT 2
"When He's Not Near"
"The Little Tip"
"Chappies' Song"
"Autograph Girls' Song"
"Henny" (Come and hear the orchestra play)
J. Sadler
Between scenes, "Henny" and "(My) Emmaleen"
"Here's Happy Days to You" (Ensemble)
"Come Little Chic"[27]
"Imported, Yes We Are"[28]
"Lil, I Like You" (I Like You, Lil, For Fair)
"I Left My Heart in Dixie"
(*Lyrics by* Harry Marshall.)
Finale

1903.26

UNDER COVER

An Original Play (with Music) in Three Acts, 5 Scenes. Play and words (lyrics) by Edward Harrigan. Music composed and arranged by George Braham. Staged by Edward Harrigan. (Scenery) Painted by Frank Gates and Edward A. Morange. Musical director, George Braham. Produced by Liebler and Company (Theodore Liebler, George C. Tyler). Opened 14 September 1903 at the Murray Hill Theatre and closed 28 November 1903 after 90 performances[29].

CAST: *Lizzie Lutz*: JANE ELTON. *Minnie*: Ida Braham. *Paula*: Ada Wild. *Toddy Tingle*: Joseph Davis. *Choo Foo*: Joseph Davis. *"Hiny" Muller*: Arthur O'Keefe. *Peter Hochady*: James McCullough. *Royal Moffit*: George L. Stout. *Philo Pinkham*: George Merritt. *Dorcas Moffit*: Lillie Eldridge. *Myrtle Pinkham*: Addie Gibbons. *Alonzo Bileover*: DAN COLLYER. *Emma Holdup*: JOSEPH SPARKS. *First Waiter*: Dave McCall. *Bob Blinker*: George L. Stout. *Owney Gilmartin*: EDWARD HARRIGAN. *Nancy Delaney*: MRS. ANNIE YEAMANS. *August Rhinehart*: HARRY FISHER. *Dixie Merryall*: Maude Knowlton. *Second Waiter*: F. Ryan. *Third Waiter*: Will Berkes. *Fourth Waiter*: Fred Johnson. *Al Singleton*: Jay Wilson. *Helene*: ADELAIDE MANOLA. *Eliza Bluepoint*: George E. Pierce. *Beau Marshall*: William S. Gill. *Mamie Delaney*: Elizabeth King. *Winnie Merryall*: Gilbert Fitzgerald. *Syd Slaughter*: WILL H. BRAY. *Michael Quigley*: James H. Corbley. *(Boozie) Susie*: JENNIE YEAMANS. *Beppo*: George Lambert. *Major Allison*: F. Bond Burke. *Sogee Mike*: James F. Corbley. *Maggie Nugent*: W. Watson. *Betty Prig*: Louie Wild. *Cigarettes*: Georgie Snyder. *Country Girl*: Jennie Stewart. *Mrs. Choo Foo*: Margaret Manning. *Touts, Waiters, Lodgers, Colored People, etc.*

Act 1: Merryall Roadhouse. Flyaway's Victory.

Act 2, Scene 1: Interior of Nancy Delaney's Farmhouse. "When Mame, Sweet Mamie's a Bride." *Scene 2*: Exterior of "Gilmartin & Co." Poolroom. Who will be the leader? *Scene 3*: The New Waldorf Lodging House. Fire the Coons!

Act 3: Merryall Roadhouse, night. They're off!

MUSICAL NUMBERS[30]
"Oh, What's the Use?"
J. Elton
"Limerick's Running Yet"
E. Harrigan
"When Mamie, Sweet Mamie's a Bride"
E. Harrigan
"The Fringe of Society"
J. Yeamans
"A Coon Will Follow a Band"
D. Collyer, J. Sparks
"Lulu's Honeymoon"
A. Manola

---

[25]Costumes, musical director uncredited in New York programs. Played a return engagement 18 April 1904 at the Grand Opera House for 8 performances.

[26]Program does not credit vocalists. The Prologue's musical numbers are listed as Act 1, Scene 1; Act 1's numbers are listed as Act 1, Scene 2. Interpolated per published sheet music:
"Tell-Tale Eyes"
G. Caine
(*Music by* W. C. Powell. *Lyrics by* S. E. Kiser and C. P. McDonald.)

[27]Interpolated.

[28]Interpolated.

[29]Costumes uncredited. By late October, the program was augmented by the appearance of Miss Vesta Tilley, the English music hall star, in her own program of impersonations and songs, between Acts 2 and 3 of UNDER COVER.

[30]Also performed: "Under Cover" (Waltz).

1903.27 THE JERSEY LILY

A Musical Comique (Comedy) in Two Acts, 4 Scenes. Book and verses (lyrics) by George V. Hobart. Music by Reginald DeKoven. (Additional music and lyrics by Max Hoffman, William Jerome and Jean Schwartz.) Production staged by George W. Lederer. Dances arranged by Joseph C. Smith. Settings painted by D. Frank Dodge. Costumes by Archie Gunn. Orchestra under the direction of Daniel Dore. Produced by George W. Lederer. Opened 14 September 1903 at the Victoria Theatre and closed 3 October 1903 after 24 performances.

CAST: "*Liliandra*, sometimes called "The Jersey Lily": BLANCHE RING. *Rosie Bauer*, housekeeper of the hotel: MAUDE RAYMOND. *Senorita Marquita*, searching for the Terpsichorean honors: ROSE BEAUMONT. *Sara de Vries*, the bride elect: Aida Hemmi. *Estelle de Vries*, engaged to John: Reine Davies. *Fifi de Vries*, engaged to James: Mignon Hardt. *Florine de Vries*, engaged to Joseph: HARRIET BURT. *Gwendolyn*, maid to Liliandra: Bessie Evelyn Gibson.

Frivolity Girls in the Frivolity Theatre at Trouville: *Babette*: Miss St. Clair. *Maizette*: Miss Broske. *Nicolette*: Miss Clayton. *Mariette*: Miss Adams. *Dadette*: Miss Cobb. *Suzette*: Miss Devere. *Florette*: Miss Hunter. *Lizette*: Miss Ellwood.

Doctor Bolivar, a veterinary surgeon and hereditary mayor: BILLY B. VAN. *Edam d'Brie*, a lawyer: D. L. DON. *Don Pedro de la Platza*, a South American diplomat: LOUIS HARRISON. *Lieutenant Edgar Jefferson*, of the American Navy: BILLEE TAYLOR. *Baron Bourgeois*, proprietor of the Frivolity Theatre: Joe Kane. *Max Bennett*, stage manager and maitre d'ballet of the Frivolity Theatre: WILLIAM CAMERON. *Offenbach Veriverdi*, composer and juggler: Jehan Bedini. *Paul*, the boy from the doctor's office: Wilfred Gerdes. *Bill Dawson*, a sailor: Arthur Arthur. *Pretty Polly*, a parrot: George Ali. *Philippe*, a waiter: Joseph Chailee. *Dan Petrel*, a coast guard: James Furey. *John*, engaged to Estelle: Charles Wentz. *James*, engaged to Fifi: Wheeler Earl. *Joseph*, engaged to Florine: Cecil Summers. *Anthony*, another coast guard: Milo Joyce.

The action takes place last Wednesday and Thursday.

Act 1: The "Square" in St. Helier, on the Isle of Jersey, in the English Channel.

Act 2, Scene 1: The stage of the Frivolity Theatre, Trouville, an hour before the rehearsal begins. *Scene 2*: A view of the boxes in the Frivolity Theatre. *Scene 3*: The stage of the Frivolity Theatre set for a performance.

ACT 1

"Welcome the Bride" (Opening Chorus)

"The Gingerbread Boy" (Sextette)

"Patsy Bolivar"
B. B. Van

"The New Cook"
M. Raymond

"Some Beautiful Day"
B. Ring
(*Music by* George W. Lederer.)

"The Ump-pum Man"
B. Ring, B. B. Van

"Old Glory"
B. Taylor

"The Lily's Promenade" (Octette)
(*Music by* George W. Lederer. *Lyrics by* Ernest Hanegan.)

"Sweetheart Mine"
A. Hemmi, B. Taylor

"My Dear Old Jersey Home" (Finale)

ACT 2

Opening Chorus
W. Cameron, Ensemble

"(The) Lobster and the Lady"
L. Harrison
(*Music and Lyrics by* Ernest Hanegan.)

"Bedelia" (Bedelia)
B. Ring
(*Music by* Jean Schwartz. *Lyrics by* William Jerome.)

"Looey"
M. Raymond
(*Music and Lyrics by* George Hobart and Max S. Witt.)

"Dreaming, (Dreaming)" (The Moon Song)
A. Hemmi

"Aurora"
B. Ring, L. Harrison

"On a Chinese Honeymoon"/"Neath Thy Window, Senorita"
G. Hoffman, B. Taylor, G. Hoffman Dancing Girls
(*Devised and staged by* Gertrude Hoffman. *Music and Lyrics by* Max Hoffman.)
Chinese Lantern Girls and Senoritas: Misses Sadie Probst, Elphye Snowden, Ethyl Daves, Sadie Burdell, Hattie Burdell, Hazel Manchester, Julia Mooney, Sadie Raymond, Lulu Whalen, Edith Girvin, Amie Lawrence, Lillian Rice, Edna McClure, Beatrice Walsh, Bessie Ariel, Daisie Lucas.

"Rosie Lee"
R. Beaumont, W. Cameron

"(My) Dear Old Jersey Home" (Finale)

"Reve d'Amour" (Waltz)

Finale

1903.28 WHOOP-DEE-DOO

The Weber & Fields All-Star Company in a Jumble of Jollities (Musical Extravaganza) in Two Whoops (Acts), 3 Scenes. Written (book, lyrics) by Edgar Smith. (Music) Composed by William T. Francis. Realized (staged) by Ben Teal. Settings by John H. Young. Costumes designed by Caroline F. Seidle. Conductor, W. T. Francis. Produced by (Joseph M.) Weber and (Lew) Fields. Opened 24 September 1903 at Weber and Fields' Music Hall and closed 30 January 1904 after 151 performances; re-opened a return engagement 16-28 May 1904 at the New Amsterdam Theatre for an additional 14 performances. Total: 165 performances.

WHOOP 1 (ACT 1)

WHOOP-DEE-DOO

CAST: *Josh Kidder*, a citizen of the world at present engaged in the promotion of ragtime in Europe: PETER F. DAILEY. *Pilsener Hofbrau*, proprietor of a German beergarden in the environs of Paris: LOUIS MANN. *Michael Suppegreentz*, a retired New York corner grocer looking for a safe investment: JOSEPH M. WEBER. *Meyer Schmartgeeser*, ambitious to be a financier but lacking the price: LEW FIELDS. *P. Dennis O'Shea*, a wealthy New York subway contractor, doing Paris for the first time: JOHN T. KELLY. *Pierrepont Grimes*, whose father desires him to win the blue ribbon for general worthlessness: CARTER DeHAVEN. *Monsieur Saisir*, a French deputy-sheriff: Willie Archie. *Henri*, man of all work at the Kaiser Wilhelm Bier-haus: Charles Halton. *The Countess de Quartierlatin*, engaged in unloading the art treasures of Europe on the American market: LILLIAN RUSSELL. *Bridgeeta O'Shea*, with a 'hunch' for the drama: EVIE STETSON. *Gladys Snowflake, Maid Snowflake*: Lizzie McCoy, Nellie McCoy. *Mlle. Dumonde*: Helen duHeron. *Nathalie*: Eva Allen. *Fifine*: Jane Mandeville. *Jeanette*: Maud Morris. *Lieutenant Montmartre*: Marie Christie. *Monsieur Bonmarche*: Bena Hoffman.

Models (5): *Marie*: Vera Morris. *Jeanne*: Maude LeRoy. *Annette*: Ethel Kelly. *Margot*: Dorothy Watson. *Clementine*: Mildred Meade. *Art Students (5)*: *Dauber*: Mae Sherwood. *Vergette*: Ilma Pratt. *Palette*: Ruth Pierce. *Maulstick*: Loretta McDonald. *Crayonne*: May Chapin. *Dancers at the Kaiser Wilhelm Bier-haus (6)*: *Hans*: Gertie Moyer. *Chris*: Winnie Seigrist. *Lena*: Carrie Bowman. *Gretel*: Agnes Lynn. *Lotten*: Ollie Hatfield. *Katrina*: Rose Malvene. *Waiters and Waitresses at the Kaiser Wilhelm Bierhaus (6)*; *Kartuffle*: Freda Linyard. *Schnitzel*: Mattie Chapin. *Kaffeline*: Helen Brooks. *Steinetta*: Mabel Lynn. *Salatina*: Madeline Somers. *Bratwuest*: Daisy Thompson. *Cashiers (4)*: *Nudelina*: Minnie Britton. *Kanerer*: Helga Howard. *Geldia*: Libbie Diamond. *Gecchie*: Angie Weimars. *Heidelberg Art Students (6)*: *Fertig*: Edna Chase. *Parieren*: V. Dolaro. *Fechten*: Jessie Richmond. *Aufgepasst*: Hattie Forsythe. *Steiner*: Mollie Hoffman. ——: Minnie Whitmore. *German Officers (4)*: *Cornet Trompette*: Irla LaBaara. *Cornet Fueret*: Sophie Jordan. *Cornet Pompomstein*: Marion Alexander. *Cornet Sabrelitz*: Florence Averill. *Captain Campsdemars, Lieutenant Bombarde*, French offciers: Myrtle Arlington, Myrtle King.

Scene 1: The Kaiser Wilhelm Bier-haus in the environs of Paris. Afternoon. *Scene 2*: Statuary Gardens of same. Evening.

MUSICAL NUMBERS

Scene 1

"Hoch! Hoch! Hoch!" (Opening Ensemble)

"The Good Old U.S.A." (U.S.A.)(Song)
J. T. Kelly

"Papa Wouldn't Care for That" (Trio)

"On the Boulevard" (Song)
L. Russell
(*Music by* Alfred Müller-Norden.)

Pot-pourri: "Rag-time in Europe"

"My Goo-goo Queen"

Scene 2

"Paris on a Moonlight Night" (Ensemble)

"The Flowers of Dixie Land"[31]

(*Music by* J. Rosamond Johnson. *Lyrics by* Bob Cole and Edgar Smith.)
The Rose; The Sunflower; The Magnolia.

"If I Were an Actress" (Song)

Finale

(*Music and Lyrics by* W. T. Francis, Alfred Müller-Norden and Edgar Smith.)

WHOOP 2 (ACT 2)

LOONEY PARK, a Comic Supplement in One Scene, with due acknowledgement to the artists who designed the various characters and the newspapers that made them famous. (Burlesque of "Luna Park"). Closed 9 December 1903.

CAST: *Little Buster*: PETER F. DAILEY. *Happy Hooligan*: LEW M. FIELDS. *Gloomy Gus*: JOSEPH M. WEBER. *Uncle Heinie*: LOUIS MANN. *The Admiral*: JOHN T. KELLY. *Mr. E. Z. Mark*: CARTER DeHAVEN. *Lige*: Willie Archie. *Johnnybostonbeans*: Willie Archie. *The Policeman*: Charles Halton. *Noah*: Roger D. Coverly. *The Lynx*: John H. Davis. *The Bear*: Herman Owens. *The Elephant*: John Devins. *The Monkey*: Al Lewis. *Lady Bountiful*: LILLIAN RUSSELL. *Toodles*: EVIE STETSON. *Mrs. E. Z. Mark*: Emily Francis. *Mrs. Kidd*: Eva Allen. *Beach strollers, attendants, officials, side showman, etc.*

MUSICAL NUMBERS

"Down by the Ocean Strand" (Ensemble)

"Looney Park" (Song)

"(The) Maid of Timbuctoo"

(*Music by* J. Rosamond Johnson. *Lyrics by* Bob Cole.)

Finale

LOONEY PARK was replaced on 10 December 1903 by WAFFLES for the balance of the run. CATHERINE formed Act 2 for the return engagement.

WAFFLES, a Travesty upon the play "Raffles" in 2 Scenes. Play by Edgar Smith. Music by W. T. Francis. Staged by Ben Teal.

CAST: *Waffles*: PETER F. DAILEY. *Captain Dedwood*, an amateur detective: LOUIS MANN. *Croshay*, an honest, hardworking burglar: LEW M. FIELDS. *Bunny*, a good audience for Wafflfes: CHARLES HALTON. *Lord Ansometeeth*, an aristocrat: JOHN T. KELLY. *Lord Prowley*, his son, a social pickpocket: CARTER DeHAVEN. *Certon*, a Scotland Yarder: CARTER DeHAVEN. *Coldguy*, a footman: Roger DeCoverly. *Baroclothes*, a janitor: Mae Sherwood. *Mrs. Flygal*, a trouble maker: Vera Morris. *Lady Smelrose*, proprietor of the Smelrose Diamonds: EVIE STETSON. *Gwendolyn Congame*, fond of Waffles: Mildred Meade. *Marie*, a French maid: JOSEPH M. WEBER. *Ethel*: Ilma Pratt. *Guests and Occupants of the "Alimony" Apartment House, London.*

MUSICAL NUMBERS

"After Dinner" (Opening Chorus)

Finale

CATHERINE, a Little Bunch of Nonsense masquerading as a travesty upon the drama "Catherine" by Henri Lavedan, in 2 Scenes. Play by Edgar Smith. Music by W. T. Francis. Staged by Ben Teal.

CAST: *Duke de Coocoo*, in search of a wife to support him: CHARLES J. ROSS. *George Mantelpiece*, a chronic sacrificer: JOHN T. KELLY. *Monsieur Villun*, Catherine's father who bemoans his inability to do less towards the support of his family: LOUIS MANN. *Freddy*, aged forteen, and *Paul*, aged twelve, two young villains, only rivals of the Katzenjammer Kids: JOSEPH M. WEBER, LEW M. FIELDS. *Monsieur Lowcuss*, a wealthy dealer in pinwheels: CHARLES HALTON. *Duchess de Coocoo*, a society leader, looking for an easy job for her son: PETER F. DAILEY. *Helene de Gristle*, who has a mortgage on the Duke for an hour: LILLIAN RUSSELL. *Catherine Villun*, with a mania for supporting a family: MABEL FENTON. *Blanche Villun*, an invalid who is dying from too much health: Mildred Meade. *Jeanne*, maid at Villun's: Mabel Lynn. *Baron Frozenhard*: Frankie Bailey. *Baroness Frozenhard*: Vera Morris.

Scene 1: Catherine's Garret House. *Scene 2*: The Duke's Conservatory.

MUSICAL NUMBERS

Opening Chorus

"Maid of Timbuctoo" (from LOONEY PARK)

(*Music by* J. Rosamond Johnson. *Lyrics by* Bob Cole.)

Finale

[31]Replaced during the run by:

"In Dreamland, (In Dreamland)"

L. Russell

(*Music by* William T. Francis. *Lyrics by* Edward S. Abeles.)

1903.29 THE FISHER MAIDEN

A Comic Opera in Two Acts. Libretto by Arthur J. Lamb. Music by Harry Von Tilzer. Production staged by and under the personal supervision of Harry Von Tilzer. Dances by Joseph C. Smith. Scenery by Ernest Albert. Costumes by Dazian and Wanamaker. Orchestra under the direction of Fred Perkins. Produced by the Von Tilzer Opera Company (Harry Von Tilzer). Opened 5 October 1903 at the Victoria Theatre and closed 31 October 1903 after 32 performances.

CAST: *Sir George Gilding*, an English nobleman traveling for his health: ROBERT LETT. *Dullovitch*, *Grimsky*, Secret Society Members: AL SHEAN, CHARLES WARREN. *Benedict Sevan*, a naturalist: HARRY SHORT. *Jack Tuggs*, a sailor: J. Francis Sullivan. *Bob Bobstay*, a sailor: Tom Collins. *Harry Goodwill*, a poor soldier in love with Marjory: GEORGE TENNERY. *Robert Luckstone*, a rich youth in love with Marjory: GEORGE J. MacFARLANE. *Simon Sax*, Marjorie's father, an inn-keeper: AL. H. WESTON. *Dr. Grip*, Sir George's physician: Frank Smiley. *Minister*: Sydney A. Harris. *Photographer*: James Wallace. *Marjorie*, the belle of the village: EDNA BRONSON. *Maydee*, a South Sea Island lady: BESSIE TANNEHILL. *Georgianna*, *Ethel*, *Mabel*, Sir George's daughters: Rose LaHarte, Elaine Selover, Dorothy Jardon. *Tippie*: Frances Cameron. *Village Lads and Lassies, Musicians, Secret Society Members, Apple Blossom Girls, Shore Girls, Fisher Boys and Girls, Rose Girls, etc.*

Act 1: A New England village near Newport during the Apple Blossom Celebration.

Act 2: Gardens of Robert Luckstone's mansion, Newport, during the fete given in honor of Marjorie.

ACT 1

Opening Chorus

"Oh Marjorie"
G. Tennery, G. J. MacFarlane, A. H. Weston

"Laughing Song"
A. H. Weston, Chorus

"I'm in Love with the Beautiful Bugs"
H. Short

"I'm a Fisher Maiden"
E. Bronson, Chorus

"Let the Band Play (a Pleasing Tune)"
R. Lett, Chorus

"On a Beautiful Distant Land"
E. Bronson, Chorus

"We're Secret Society Members"
C. Warren, A. Shean

"He Dangled Me on His Knee"
E. Bronson, R. Lett, F. Smiley

Ensemble

"Maydee" (Pretty Little South Sea Island Lady)
B. Tannehill, Chorus

"Under the Mulberry Tree" (Finale)
Entire Company

ACT 2

Opening Chorus

"A Daughter of the Moon Am I"
E. Bronson

"The Highly Important Fly"
H. Short, B. Tannehill, C. Warren, A. Shean

Ensemble

"Roses for the Girl I Love"
R. LaHarte, Chorus

"Down on a South Sea Isle"
G. Tennery, B. Tannehill

"A Sail on the Tail of a Whale"
J. F. Sullivan, C. Warren, A. Shean

"When You Go to London Town, (Gay Paree or Dixie Land)"
E. Bronson, Chorus

"Cooe-Cooe-Coo" (Coo-ee Coo-ee)
R. Lett, B. Tannehill

"Secret Society" (Ensemble)
C. Warren, A. Shean, Chorus

Finale
Entire Company

1903.30 WIDOW DOOLEY'S DREAM

A Musical Farce in Three Acts. Play by William F. Carroll. Produced by George B. Reno. Opened 5 October 1903 at the Grand Opera House and closed 10 October 1903 after 8 performances.[32]

CAST: *Bridget Gallagher*, the boss of the house: GEORGE W. MONROE. *Herman Coodlefleck*, an inventor: WILLIAM F. CARROLL. *Tom Montrose*, father of Felix: HARRY LINTON. *Demosthenes Bluff*, an attorney at law: ABBOTT DAVIDSON. *Jack Ward*, a young Army officer: Charles E. Flynn. *Rap McGonigle*, an expressman: George M. Darling. *Rufus Leaking*, a constable: Joe Mack. *Nora Whiting*, Jack's best girl: VIOLET STALEY. *Elirra Coppsem*, pretty and from Paris: ANITA LAWRENCE. *Katie Gallagher*, Bridget's niece, known as "Scrapp": VIRGINIA ACKERMAN. *Lucy Montrose*. Tom's wife and mother of Felix: Bessie Burr. *Aunt Hattie*, Tom's aunt from Chicago: AIDA RIVERS. *Maxie Mumm*, the real brand: Ada Gifford. *Carrie Taylor*, a French maid: Pauline Harice. *Mrs. Tayles*, a human cyclone: Emily Jordan. *Oscaleeta*, the Indian princess: JANETTE WEBB. *Belle Holdsem*: IRENE ZIPEY. *Carrie Behr*: Mabel Dillingham.

MUSICAL NUMBERS[33]

"My Hong Kong Lady"
H. Linton

"The Old Jokes' Home"
H. Linton, W. F. Carroll

"Bedelia" (from THE JERSEY LILY)
(*Music by* Jean Schwartz. *Lyrics by* William Jerome.)

1903.31 BABES IN TOYLAND

A Musical Extravaganza in a Prologue and Three Acts, 11 Scenes. Libretto (book, lyrics) by Glen MacDonough. Music by Victor Herbert. Staged by Julian Mitchell. Settings by John Young, Homer Emens. Costumes by Caroline Seidle. Orchestra under the direction of Max Hirschfeld. Produced by Fred R. Hamlin and Julian Mitchell. Opened 13 October 1903 at the Majestic Theatre and closed 19 March 1904 after 192 performances[34].

CAST (in order of appearance): *Alan*, nephew of Barnaby: WILLIAM NORRIS. *Jane*, Barnaby's niece: MABEL BARRISON. *Uncle Barnaby*, a rich miser in love with Contrary Mary: GEORGE W. DENHAM. *The Widow Piper*, a lonely widow with 14 children: HATTIE DELARO. *Contrary Mary*, the Widow Piper's eldest daughter: AMY RICARD. *Tom Tom*, her eldest son: BESSIE WYNN. *Jill*, who helps Jack: Nellie Daly. *Bo-Peep*, who is a careless shepherdess: NELLA WEBB. *Red Riding Hood*, who is devoted to her grandmother: Susie Kelleher. *Sallie Waters*, who wants to get married: Mary Welsh. *Curly Locks*, who wants to wed a title: Elizabeth Roth. *Miss Muffett*, who is afraid of spiders: Irene Cromwell. *Simple Simon*, who is fond of fairs: Virginia Foltz. *Peter*, who has a passion for pumpkin pie: Bertha Krieghoff. *Tommy Tucker*, who sings for his supper and everything else: Doris Mitchell. *Jack*, who does chores: Mae Naudain. *Boy Blue*, who wants to be a farmer: Stella Beardsley. *Bobby Shaftoe*, who wants to be a sailor: MyrtleMcGrain. *Roderigo*, a sentimental ruffian: Frank Hayes. *Gonzorgo*, his hard-hearted partner: Charles Barry. *Hilda*, maid of all work in the Piper household: Hulda Halvers. *The Master Toymaker*, who designs the toys of the world: DORE DAVIDSON. *Grumio*, apprentice at the Master Toymaker's workshop: CHARLES GUYER. *Inspector Marmaduke*, of the Toyland Police: GUS PIXLEY. *Max*, the toymaker's apprentice: Margaret Sutherland. *The Brown Bear*: Walter Schrode. *The Sun Queen*: Georgia Baron. *The Spirit of Maple*: Margaret Sutherland. *The Spirit of Oak*: Mae Naudain. *The Spirit of Pine*: Katherine Howland. *The Spirit of Willow*: Mabel Frenyear. *The Moth Queen*: Albertina Benson. *Mima*: Grace Field. *The Volcano Queen*: Minnie Murray. *The Giant Spider*: Robert Burns.

Act 1: *Dandies*: Misses Georgia Baron, Albertina Benson, Elsie Mertens, Minnie Murray. *Butterflies*: Misses Katherine Fairfax, Jean Carnegie, Vincie Twohey, Ethel Ricketts, Gertrude Standley, K. Murray, Jessie Thompson, Edith Sheppard, May Leslie. *Flower Girls*: Misses Elsie Mertens, Dix Carruthers, Gladys Earlcott. Act 2: *French Dolls*: Misses Irene Cromwell, Myrtle McGrain, Albertina Benson, Grace Field. *Punches*: Misses Mabel Frenyear, Lesbia Grealls, Mabel Powell, Toldie Boley. *Dutch Dolls*: Misses Ethel Ricketts, Helen Hilton, Edith Curtis, Elsie Mertens, Marguerite Spencer, Vincie Twohey, Thisba Knight, Marie Troy. *Toy Soldier Captains*: Misses Georgia Baron, Katherine Howland. *Trumpeters*: Misses Maude deRigney, Evelyn Ware, Gertrude Carson, K. Fairfax, L. Osborn, May Bishop. *Drummers*: Misses Flo Edney, May Haywood, Daisy Carson, Dix Carruthers, May Wilson, Jessie Thompson. Act 3: *Widows*: Misses Katherine Howland, Mabel Frenyear, Albertina Benson, Edith Curtis, Grace Field, Marie Troy, Helen Hilton, Minnie Murray, Mabel Powell, Vincie Twohey, Eslie Mertens, May Leslie, Carolyn Fostelle. *Justices*: Misses Margaret Sutherland, Katherine Fairfax, L. Osborn.

Prologue, Scene 1: Exterior of Uncle Barnaby's house. *Scene 2*: Electrical storm at sea and wreck of the "Galleon."

Act 1, Scene 1: Country fête in Contrary Mary's garden. *Scene 2*: Garden wall back of the garden. *Scene 3*: The Spider's Forest. *Scene 4*: The Floral Palace of the Moth Queen.

Act 2, Scene 1: The Christmas Tree Grove in Toyland. *Scene 2*: A street in Toyland. *Scene 3*: The Master Toymaker's workshop. (Emens.) *Scene 4*: Exterior of Master Toymaker's castle.

Act 3: The courtyard of the Toyland Palace of Justice. (Emens.)

ACT 1

"Don't Cry, Bo-Peep" (Never Mind, Bo-Peep, We Will Find Your Sheep)
N. Webb, B. Wynn, Widow Piper's Children

"Floretta"
W. Norris, Chorus

"Mary Mary" (Entrance of Contrary Mary)
Chorus

"Barney O'Flynn"
A. Ricard, Chorus

"I Can't Do the Sum"
M. Barrison, Widow Piper's Children

"Slumber Deep"
M. Naudain, Wood Spirits

ACT 2

"Christmas Fair Waltz"
Chorus

(Our Castle in Spain) "The Legend of the Castle"[35]
F. Marie, Chorus

"Rock-a-bye Baby"
W. Norris, Chorus

"Toy Soldiers' March and Military Ball"
W. Norris, M. Barrison, Full Chorus

"The Toymakers (Shop)"
Male Chorus

"Toyland"
B. Wynn, Male Chorus

"My Rag Doll Girl" (The Rag Doll)
C. Guyer, N. Daly

ACT 3

"An Old-Fashioned Rose"
B. Wynn

"Before and After"
W. Norris, A. Ricard

"Jane"[36]
M. Barrison, C. Guyer, C. Barry, Chorus

"Maybe the Moon Will Help You Out"
N. Webb

Finale
Ensemble

1903.32 ERMINIE

A Revival of the Comic Opera in Three Acts[37]. Libretto by Harry Paulton (and Claxson Bellamy). Based on the melodrama ("L'Auberge des Adrets" by Benjamin Antier, Saint-Amand and Paulyanthe, adapted into English as)

[32]Later toured under the title OUR BRIDGET'S DREAMS.

[33]No program available.

[34]Played a return engagement 2 January 1905 at the Majestic Theatre for an additional 25 performances. See entry in that season for detail.

[35]Dropped during the run.

[36]Replaced during the run by:

"He Won't Be Happy 'Till He Gets It"
M. Barrison, W. Norris, C. Barry, Chorus

[37]First produced in New York 10 May 1886 at the Casino Theatre for 648 performances in a series of three engagements. For Synopsis of Scenes and Musical Numbers, see original 1886 production. Interpolated for this revival:

"Two Eyes of Brown"
J. B. Davis
(*Music by* Stephen Howard. *Lyrics by* Edward Madden.)

"A Gainsborough Girl"
(*Music and Lyrics by* Bernard Rolt.)

'Robert Macaire.' Music by Edward Jakobowski. Scenery by Henry E. Hoyt. Musical director, John McGhie. Produced by Francis Wilson, Messrs. (Sam) Nixon and (J. F.) Zimmerman (Arthur Miller, Manager). Opened 19 October 1903 at the Casino Theatre and closed 28 November 1903 after 42 performances.

CAST: *Cadeaux* (Caddy): FRANCIS WILSON[38]. *Ravennes* (Ravvy): WILLIAM BRODERICK. *Chevalier de Brabazon*, the Marquis' guest: Signor (John) PERUGINI. *Eugene Marcel*, the Marquis' secretary: Albert Parr. *Marquis de Pomvert*: ROBERT BRODERICK. *Captain Delauney*: JESSIE BARTLETT DAVIS. *Simon*, Waiter at the Lion d'Or: William Laverty. *Dufois*, Landlord of the Lion d'Or: Patrick Wallace. *Vicomte de Brissac*: J. C. Jackson. *Sergeant*: Charles Arling. *Benedict*: George Dunham. *Erminie*: MARGUERITE SYLVA. *Princess de Gramponeur*: JENNIE WEATHERSBY[39]. *Cerise Marcel*, Erminie's companion: Laura Butler. *Marie*: Lucille Egan. *Javotte*: MADGE LESSING. *Gainsborough Girls*: Misses Egan, Van Ness, Ellis, Norris, Chester. *Flower Girls, Soldiers, Peasants, Clowns, Lords and Ladies, etc.*

1903.33 THE GIRL FROM KAY'S

A Musical Play in Three Acts. Book and lyrics by Owen Hall[40]. Music by Ivan Caryll. (Additional songs by Paul Rubens, Adrian Ross, Claude Aveling, Cecil Cook, Howard Talbot, Percy Greenbank, Clare Kummer, Maurice J. Stonehill). Scenery by Edward G. Unitt and Homer Emens, Ernest Gros. Costumes by Mrs. Robert Osborn Company. Orchestra under the direction of Gus Salzer. Produced by Charles Frohman and George Edwardes. Opened 2 November 1903 at the Herald Square Theatre and closed 28 May 1904 after 205 performances; re-opened a return engagement 18 August 1904 at the Herald Square Theatre and closed 3 September 1904 after an additional 18 performances. Total: 223 performances[41].

CAST: *Max Hoggenheimer*: SAM BERNARD. *Harry Gordon*: HARRY DAVENPORT. *The Hon. Percy Fitzthistle*: ERNEST LAMBERT. *Mr. Chalmers*: George R. Sprague. *Theodore Quench, K.C.*: Homer Granville. *Joseph*, Hall Porter at Flacton Hotel: Winchel Smith. *Archie Pembridge*: Maurice Lavigne. *Pepper*, Page Boy at Flacton Hotel: Emil Heusel. *Frank*, Waiter at Savoy Restaurant: Paul Decker. *Winnie Harborough*, The Girl from Kay's: HATTIE WILLIAMS. *Nora Chalmers*: GRACE FREEMAN. *Ellen*, her maid: Grace Dudley. *Mrs. Chalmers*: Maude Granger.

Assistants at Kay's (6): *Nancy Lowley*: MARIE DORO. *Mary Methuen*: Leonore Harris. *Clara Butler*: ELSIE FERGUSON. *Cora Paget*: Sadie Peters. *Mabel Donald*: Vera Cameron. *Hilda French*: Elise Barney. *Norah's Bridesmaids (6)*: *Ella Winton*: Margaret Malcolm. *Rhoda Cantaur*: Teddie DuCoe. *Maud Ebor*: Olive Ullrich. *Gertrude Sarum*: Lillian Seville. *Olive Manton*: Belva Don Kersley. *Joan Ely*: Mabel Clarke. *Jane*: Blanche Wood. *Blanche*: May Harding.

Act 1: Chalmers' Flat (Unitt & Emens).

Act 2: Grand Hotel, Flacton-on-Sea. (Gros).

Act 3: The Savoy Restaurant. (Unitt & Emens).

ACT 1[42]

Opening Chorus
(*Music by* Cecil Cook. *Lyrics by* Adrian Ross.)

"Bride's Song" (As I came up the aisle)
G. Freeman, Chorus
(*Music and Lyrics by* Bernard Rolt.)

"Tips"
G. Dudley, Bridesmaids
(*Music by* Cecil Cook. *Lyrics by* Adrian Ross.)

"Bonnet Shop"
H. Williams
(*Lyrics by* Adrian Ross.)

"Matilda and the Builder"
H. Davenport
(*Music by* Ernest Bucalossi. *Lyrics by* J. Hickory Wood.)

Finale
Chorus
(*Music by* W. Meyer Lutz. *Lyrics by* Adrian Ross.)

ACT 2

Opening Chorus
(*Music by* Cecil Cook. *Lyrics by* Adrian Ross.)

"Semi-Detached"
H. Davenport, G. Freeman
(*Lyrics by* Adrian Ross.)

"Customers at Kay's"
H. Williams, Chorus
(*Lyrics by* Adrian Ross.)

"Bob and Me"
G. Dudley, Chorus
(*Music by* Howard Talbot. *Lyrics by* Claude Aveling.)

"Egypt"
Pierrot Quartette
(*Music and Lyrics by* Clare Kummer.)

"Smiling Sambo"
M. Doro, Chorus
(*Music by* Howard Talbot. *Lyrics by* Percy Greenbank.)

"My Little Love Bird"
H. Williams
(*Music and Lyrics by* Maurice J. Stonehill.)

"I Don't Care"
H. Davenport
(*Music and Lyrics by* Paul Rubens.)

Finale
G. R. Sprague, H. Granville, S. Bernard
(*Music by* Cecil Cook. *Lyrics by* Adrian Ross.)

ACT 3

Opening Chorus

"Make It Up"
H. Williams, H. Davenport
(*Lyrics by* Claude Aveling.)

"Sufficiency"
S. Bernard
(*Music and Lyrics by* Clare Kummer.)

"A High Old Time"[43]
H. Davenport, Chorus
(*Music by* A. D. Cammeyer. *Lyrics by* Claude Aveling.)

"Birthday Party Song" (My Birthday Party)
E. Lambart, M. Doro, P. Decker, G. Dudley
(*Music by* Paul Rubens. *Lyrics by* Percy Greenbank.)

"Mrs. Hoggenheimer of Park Lane"
H. Williams, S. Bernard
(*Lyrics by* Adrian Ross.)

Finale

1903.34 THE OFFICE BOY

A Musical Comedy in Two Acts. Book and lyrics by Harry B. Smith. Based on the French farce ("Le Jockey malgré lui") by Maurice Ordonneau and Paul Gavault. Music by Ludwig Engländer. Staged by Al Holbrook. Scenery painted by Homer Emens and Edward G. Unitt, Joseph Physioc. Costumes designed by F. Richard Anderson. Musical director, Watty Hydes. Produced by Charles B. Dillingham. Opened 2 November 1903 at Hammerstein's Victoria Theatre and closed 2 January 1904 after 66 performances[44].

CAST: *Noah Little*, an office boy: FRANK DANIELS. *Rider Little*, a famous jockey: ALFRED HICKMAN. *Tobias Van Twiller*: SYDNEY TOLER. *Damon Ketcham*:

[38]Recreating his original role.
[39]Recreating her original role.
[40]Alleged to have been based, without credit, on the French farce "La Mariée recalcitrante" by Léon Gandillot.
[41]Played a return engagement 20 March 1905 at the Grand Opera House for 8 performances.
[42]Programs early in the run contain no song list. Added for subsequent tour, then later dropped:

"Lucy Linda Lady" (Act 2, after "Bob and Me")
Pierrot Quartette
(*Music and Lyrics by* Dave Reed, Jr.)
Added for tour or return engagement, as per published sheet music:

"Miranda"
H. Williams
(*Music and Lyrics by* Clare Kummer.)

"I Love You All the Time"
H. Williams
(*Music and Lyrics by* Will R. Anderson.)

[43]Dropped for subsequent tour.
[44]Played a return engagement 18 January 1904 at the Grand Opera House for 7 performances.

GILBERT CLAYTON. *Pythias Cheatham*: JAMES C. REANY. *Reggy Higgins*: DAVID BENNETT. *Percy Wiggins*: LAURENCE WHEAT. *McNab*: W.[Walter] C. KELLY. *Scales*: Leavitt James. *Euphemia*: LOUISE GUNNING. *Claire de Lune*: EVA TANGUAY. *Paquita*: Violet Halls. *Jeanette*: Marion Harte. *Florine*: Ida Gabrielle. *First Messenger* in Law Office: May Sheridan. *Second Messenger* in Law Office: Maude Welsh. *Miss Harvard, Miss Yale*, Guests of Van Twiller: Gwendolyn Valentine, Gertrude Doremus. *Spike Muggins*: Frank Conway. *Thug Magafa*: J. Lafayette. *Typewriter girls, telephone girls, clerks, guests, bookmakers and jockeys.*

Act 1: Law offices of Ketcham and Cheatham.

Act 2: Van Twiller's villa and private race course.

ACT 1[45]

Opening Chorus (First, put the date!)
J. C. Reany, Chorus
"After Business Hours" (Song)
G. Clayton, M. Harte, I. Gabrielle, Chorus
"Bohemia" (Song)
E. Tanguay, L. Wheat, D. Bennett, Chorus
"I Thought Wrong"[46]
F. Daniels, Company
(*Music by* R. G. Knowles. *Lyrics by* Richard Morton.)
"Will You Be My Hero, Noble Sir?"[47] (Duet)
F. Daniels, L. Gunning
"Because He Told Me So"[48] (Waltz Song)
L. Gunning
"Plain Mamie O'Hooley" (Quartette)
F. Daniels, E. Tanguay, L. Wheat, D. Bennett
Finale
F. Daniels, Company

ACT 2

Opening Chorus (Patrons of the turf are we)
"If I Were the Bride of a Soldier" (Song of the Drum and Fife)
L. Gunning, Chorus
"I'm on the Water Wagon Now"
F. Daniels
(*Music by* John W. Bratton. *Lyrics by* Paul West.)
"Signs" (Song)
F. Daniels, L. Gunning, S. Toler
"Summer Proposals"[49] (Song)
E. Tanguay
"An Embassy Burglarious" (The Burglars)(Quartette)
E. Tanguay, G. Clayton, L. Wheat, D. Bennett
"A Maiden's Heart" (Ballad)
L. Gunning, Chorus
Finale
F. Daniels, Company

[45]Interpolated for subsequent tour, per published sheet music:
"Trials of a Simple Maid"
Clara Belle Jerome
(*Music by* Robert Hood Bowers. *Lyrics by* Raymond Peck.)

[46]Replaced for subsequent tour by:
"I Never Had to Work"
F. Daniels, Chorus
(*Music and Lyrics by* Benjamin Hapgood Burt.)

[47]Replaced during the run by:
"The Proper Way to Kiss"
F. Daniels, L. Gunning
(*Music by* Theodore Morse. *Lyrics by* Raymond Browne.)

[48]Published in vocal score as "Because I Love You So."

[49]Replaced during the run by:
"When the Band Plays Ragtime"
E. Tanguay
(*Music and Lyrics by* Bob Cole and James Weldon Johnson.)
Replaced for subseqeuent tour by:
"The Trials of a Simple Maid"
Clara Belle Jerome {Claire de Lune}
(*Music by* Robert Hood Bowers. *Lyrics by* Raymond Peck.)

1903.35 MRS. DELANEY OF NEWPORT

A Musical Farcical Comedy in Three Acts. Book and lyrics by William Jerome. Music by Jean Schwartz. Produced by James Hyde. Opened 2 November 1903 at the Grand Opera House and closed 7 November 1903 after 8 performances.

CAST: *Michael McGuire*, from the Klondike: FRANK MURPHY. *William Hardup*, out for the goods: C. EDDIE MORTON. *Slithers Merry*, his accomplice: THOMAS HARRIS. *Squire Dorchester*, who wrote a play: Elmer Jerome. *Count Moustache Strappedo*, who lost a wife: George Gorman. *Jeems Jubbins*, the butler: Peter H. Maguire. *Charley Wood*, in love with Rose: Charles C. Barrett. *Lord Isnt Hecute*, who detects: Charles A. Cartmell. *Lord Helpus*, who reports: Claudius A. Lightner. *Tom Type*, who assists: Harry Earl. *Mrs. Gotrocks*, member of Society: Pearl Hamlin. *Carry Coal*, the maid: Laura Harris. *Bedelia Delaney*, a widow: KATE ELINORE. *Rose Delaney*, her daughter: MAY ELINORE.

MUSICAL NUMBERS[50]

"I Want to Break into Society"
K. Elinore
"Hula-Lula Girl"
M. Elinore
"Irish Eyes of Blue" (Her Eyes of Irish Blue)
M. Elinore
"Bedelia" (from THE JERSEY LILY)
K. Elinore, F. Murphy, Chorus
(*Music by* Jean Schwartz. *Lyrics by* William Jerome.)
"The Hobo Solo Band"
P. Hamlin
"Spain, Beautiful Spain"
"The Latest Thing in Swell Society"
"Whistling Sue"
"Baby, My Little Baby"
"Barney"
(*Music and Lyrics by* Ed Rogers.)

1903.36 RED FEATHER

A Romantic Opera in Two Acts. Book by Charles Klein. Music by Reginald deKoven. Lyrics by Charles Emerson Cook. Staged by Joseph W. Herbert and Max Figman. Dances arranged by Joseph C. Smith. Scenery painted by Ernest Albert. Costumes designed by Caroline Seidle. Electrical effects by T. J. Clarke, Al Hawkes, Joseph Menchen. Orchestra under the direction of Louis F. Gottschalk. Produced by Florenz Ziegfeld, Jr. Opened 9 November 1903 at the Lyric Theatre and closed 2 January 1904 after 60 performances[51].

CAST: *Countess Hilda von Draga*, "Red Feather": GRACE VAN STUDDIFORD. *Mlle. Fifine*, a fashionable milliner: Mlle. ELISE DeVERE. *International Girls (4)*: *Anita*, a Spanish Girl: OLIVE CELESTE MOORE. *Prada*, an Australian Girl: Lillian Sefton. *Daphne*, an English Girl: Margaret Hubbard Ayer. *Victorine*, a French Girl: Floye Redledge. *Fiancées of Diplomats (4)*: *A Baroness*: Louise Hollister. *A Duchess*: Dean B. Dulany. *A Marquise*: Cora Tracey. *A Countess*: Daisy R. Fuguet. *Milliners (4)*: *Cara*: Mona Desmond. *Rita*: Mina Rudolph. *Nana*: Grace Kimball. *Maria*: Dorothy Maynard. *Captain Trevors*: GEORGE L. TALLMAN. *H.R.H. Crown Prince of Romancia*: STANLEY HAWKINS. *Friends of "Red Feather" (3)*: *Baron Bulverstrauss*: THOMAS Q. SEABROOKE. *Colonel McPatrick*: LOUIS CASAVANT. *Bagstock Bowler*: F. Stuart Hyatt. *Royal Guards of Romancia (2)*: *Colonel Furbis*: Benjamin McGahen. *Colonel Neva*: Thomas E. Whitbread. *Diplomatic Corps (4)*: *Count Zeegan*: Myron P. Davis. *Lieutenant Reger*: William J. Sullivan. *Captain Baget*: Philip Connor. *Senor Romboza*: J. Frank Gibbons. *Chief of Police*: Fred J. Titus. *Lieutenant Detrich*: Charles Fitz. *Trumpeters*: Messrs. Brown, Speck.

White Lace Officers: Misses Allen, Bartlett, Bertrand, Carlisle, Daigneau, Gordon, Kaye, Lavis, Ormsby, Vester, Wheaton, Wilkins. *Conspirators*: Misses Allen, Bartlett, Bertrand, Carlisle, Dagwell, Daigneau, Francis, Gordon, Kaye, Landers, Lavis, Merrill,

[50]No program available. Musical numbers from published sheet music and reviews, not in performance order.

[51]Played a return engagement 25 April 1904 at the Grand Opera House for 8 performances. A touring production (1908) starring Cheridah Simpson under the auspices of producer Joseph M. Gaites contained the following interpolation:
"Carissima"
C. Simpson {Countess Hilda von Draga}
(*Music and Lyrics by* Arthur A. Penn)

Orsmby, Vester, Wheaton, Wilkins. Messrs. Coley, Delmore, Engle, Harn, Jenkins, Kenny, Miller, Platt, Power, Rover, Wall. *Waitresses*: Misses Bertrand, Gordon, Kaye, Kinsgubry, Ormsby, Tracy, Vester, Wheaton. *Servants*: Messrs. Engel, Jenkins, kenny, Power. *Court Gentlemen*: Messrs. Fuguet, Hadley, Leaf, Wall, Way, Whitney, Wilson. *Court Ladies*: Misses Black, Brunette, Dulany, Francis, Fuguet, Hollister, Kidder. *Townspeople*: Misses Allen, Bartlett, Beaudrey, Boyt, Carlisle, Cummings, Daigneau, Dagwell, Freeman, Kidder, Landers, Lavis, Merrill, Purcell, Rice, Rose, Wilkins, Wilson. *Dancers*: Misses Maynard, Desmond. *Royal Guards, Gendarms, Waiters, Attendants, Milliners, Nobility, Townspeople*.

Act 1: Town of Romancia.

Act 2: Castle of Countess von Draga.

ACT 1

Choral Prelude ("A Boatman")
B. McGahen

"Conspirators" (Trio)
T. Q. Seabrooke, L. Casavant, S. Hyatt

"The Little Milliner"
E. DeVere, Milliners

"Song of the Guards"
G. L. Tallman, Chorus of Guards

"(A) Prince of Good Fellows"[52]
S. Hawkins, Chorus

"Entrance of Hilda"
G. Van Studdiford

"Lessons in Verse"
E. DeVere, O. C. Moore, T. Q. Seabrooke, S. Hawkins

"To Call Thee Mine" (Duet)
G. Van Studdiford, G. Tallman

"If I Only Had a Mustache Like the Kaiser"[53]
T. Q. Seabrooke

Finale

ACT 2

"The Conspirators" (Opening Chorus)

"The Merry Cavalier"
G. Van Studdiford

"The Humorous Ghost"
L. Casavant, Chorus

"There's a Little Street in Heaven (That They Call Broadway)" (From THE BELLE OF BROADWAY)[54]
T. Q. Seabrooke
(*Music by* A. Baldwin Sloane. *Lyrics by* James T. Waldon and A. Baldwin Sloane.)

"Garden of Dreams"
G. Van Studdiford

"A Madrigal" (Quartette)
G. Van Studdiford, O. C. Moore, G. Tallman, L. Casavant

"The Rose and the Breeze"
O. C. Moore

"Bird Song"[55]
Misses Brunette, Rose, Dulany, Black, Tracey, Fuguet, Kidder, Landers, Boyt, Metrill, Francis, Dagwell, Hollister

"Mo Tichi-titi"[56]
E. DeVere

"Arrest Him" (Ensemble)

"Triumph March (Finale)

[52]Moved to Act 2, following "Bird Song" for subsequent tour.
[53]Interpolation, composer and lyricist unknown. Dropped for subsequent tour.
[54]Replaced for subsequent tour by:
"They All Looked at Me"
William J. McCarthy {Baron Bulverstrauss}
[55]Most likely the same as the published song "Tale of a High Born Rooster."
[56]Dropped for subsequent tour.

1903.37

BABETTE

A Comic Opera in Three Acts. Libretto by Harry B. Smith. Music by Victor Herbert. Produced (staged) by Fred G. Latham and A. M. Holbrook. Settings by Homer Emens and Edward G. Unitt. Costumes by F. Richard Anderson. Orchestra under the direction of John Lund. Presented by Charles B. Dillingham. Opened 16 November 1903 at the Broadway Theatre and closed 9 January 1904 after 59 performances.

CAST: *Babette*, a village letter writer, afterward a court prima donna: FRITZI SCHEFF. *Mondragon*, a soldier of fortune: EUGENE COWLES. *Marcel*: RICHIE LING. *Baltazar*: EDWARD J. CONNELLY. *Vinette*: Ida Hawley. *Van Tympel*: LOUIS HARRISON. *Eva*: JOSEPHINE BARTLETT. *The King of France*: ERROL DUNBAR. *Guzman*: Madison Smith. *Schnapps*: William Sissons. *Captain Walther*: Alfred S. Ely. *Jan, Quentin*: Frank Boyle, James Beals. *Margot, Greta, Joan*: Rosa Earle, Edna Luby, Adele Nott. *Coachman*: J. T. Chaillee. *Footman*: Charles Emerson. *Maids of Honor (3)*: *Mlle. de la Motte*: Bertha Willoughby. *Mlle. de Rohan*: May Seeley. *Mlle. de Fontanges*: Mildred Forest. *A Court Lady*, with solo: Mary Smith. *Courtiers (3)*: *Marquis de Villette*: George Williamson. *Count de Courville*: Arthur Blanchard. *Duc de St. Michel*: Henry Wilkinson. *Pages (5)*: *Francois*: Georgia Campbell. *Henri*: Rita Dean. *Gaston*: Helen Planche. *Jacque*: Aline Redmond. *Laurent*: Gertrude Adams. *Teresa*: Emily Montague. *Katrina*: Florence Belleville.

Peasants, Courtiers, Maids of Honor, etc.: Mesdames Florence Campbell, Lotta Waymire, Nellie Parks, Emma King, Ada Meade, Margaret Berrien, Mary Smith, Bessie Penn, Dorothy Palmer, Grace Spencer, Olive Cox, Barbara Farres, Ada Pratt, Edith Warner, Julie Cotte, Florence Wilson, Bartha Holly, Clara Freedel, Maude Harlow, Teckla Morton, Inez Kalms, Rose Ginsburg, Margaret Harding, Mildred Herbert, Grace Emmons, May Lannig, Belle Chamberlain, Agnes Williamson, Charlotte Uart, Gertrude Adams. Messrs. Bernard Milton, Robert Hunt, Robert Hayes, Arthur Widdowson, Ralph P. Lancaster, James A. Beale, Gus Smith, Nicholas Parker, H. Rosemire, A. Schander, Arthur M. Pergain, Radford D'Orsay, C. W. Emerson, E. J. Wunder, David Lieberman, Maurice Hoffman, Fred Vokes, George W. Smythe, James J. McClusky, Frank L. Thomas, A. Parker.

The action takes place in the seventeenth century.

Act 1: Garden of Van Tympel's House, near Antwerp.

Act 2: A Roadside Inn, near Brussels.

Act 3: Versailles.

ACT 1

Opening Chorus

"My Honor and My Sword" (Borrow Trouble)
E. Cowles, Chorus

"On the Other Side of the Wall" (Duet)
E. Cowles, I. Hawley

Entrance of Babette
Chorus

"Letter Writing Song" (Letters I Write All the Day)
F. Scheff

"Clockmaker's Song" (He Who'd Thrive Must Rise at Five)
L. Harrison, Chorus

"I'll Bribe the Stars" (Duet)
F. Scheff, R. Ling

Finale

ACT 2

Opening Chorus

"Tony the Peddler"
E. Cowles, Chorus

"To the Sound of the Pipe and the Roll of the Drum"
F. Scheff, J. Bartlett, L. Harrison, Chorus

"Pierrot Song" (Be Kind to Poor Pierrot)
F. Scheff

"There Once Was an Owl" (Sextette)
J. Bartlett, E. Luby, R. Karle, E. Cowles, R. Ling, L. Harrison

"The Life of a Bold Free Lance"[57]
M. Smith, Chorus

[57]Replaced for subsequent tour by:
Re-entrance of Players
"Vivienne the Vivandiere"
F. Scheff, Chorus
"On the Stage"
L. Harrison

Finale

ACT 3

"Pavanne"
J. Bartlett, R. Ling, E. Cowles

"It's a Way We Have in Spain"
L. Harrison, Chorus

"My Lady of the Manor" (Madrigal)
I. Hawley, R. Ling, E. Cowles

"Where the Fairest Flowers Are Blooming" (Butterfly Waltz Song)
F. Scheff

Finale

1903.38 WINSOME WINNIE

A Musical Comedy in Two Acts. Book and lyrics by Edward Jakobowski. Music by Harry Paulton. Adaptation and lyrics by Frederic Ranken; (additional) music by Gustave Kerker. Staged by R. H. Burnside. Stage director, Frank Smithson. Scenery by D. Frank Dodge. Costumes designed by Caroline Seidle. Musical conductor, Gustave Kerker. Produced by Sam S. Shubert and Messrs. (Sam) Nixon and (J. F.) Zimmerman. Opened 1 December 1903 at the Casino Theatre and closed 16 January 1904 after 56 performances.

CAST: *Lord Poverish*, an impecunious nobleman: DICK TEMPLE. *Lady Arabella*, his wife: JOBYNA HOWLAND. *Desmond Poverish*, his son: W. P. CARLETON. *Aileen Poverish*, his daughter: HELEN REDMOND. *Captain Cotterill*, his sailing master: WILLIAM E. PHILP. *Marjorie Bell*, Lord Poverish's American Ward: Isobel Hall. *Dr. Krause*, proprietor "Krause's Tiny Tablets:" JAMES E. SULLIVAN. *Henrietta*, his daughter: Daisy Green. *Honoria*, another daughter: Mildred Kearney. *Pericles*, proprietor Plucked Pigeon Inn and Chief Brazen Bandits: JOSEPH C. MIRON. *Demetrius*, his assistant in both enterprises: William S. Corliss. *James*, Winnie's assistant: William Leonard. *Zora*, a disciple of Claude Duval: Annie Cameron.

Paying Guests on Board Lord Poverish's yacht "Anita": *Lady Clare*: Stella Hammerstein. *Lady Maude*: Edna Sidney. *Lady Dorcas*: Clara Pitt. *Lady Eudora*: Mazie Follette. *Lady Mabel*: Julia Sanderson. *Lady Frances*: Louise DeRigney. *Lady Vivian*: Mildred Thornwall. *Lady Gracia*: May Hopkins. *Lady Loona*: Cecila Rhode. *Lady Angela*: Grace Spencer.

Flower Girls: *Daisy*: Marjorie Walton. *Pansy*: Edna Gatecher. *Rose*: Carla Byron. *Lily*: Laura Hyland.

Waitresses: *Ayali*: Jeanne Calducci. *Sereza*: Edith Sanders. *Zumra*: Alice Coleman. *Tutu*: Ita Kamph.

Montenegrin Peasant Girls: *Mirza*: Ruth Russell. *Zametta*: Cordelia L. Carron. *Dudu*: Bessie Merrill. *Lira*: Carlotta Coleman. *Maru*: Helen Hahn. *Salili*: Martha Seborn Jones. *Murali*: Carlton Dudley. *Alisett*: Alice Mark.

Montenegrin Peasant Boys: *Marco* Marcella Tasche. *Alex*: Olive Haskell. *Mourico*: May Bonner. *Pepe*: Dollie Bonner.

Winnie Walker, known as Winsome Winnie, an American Soubrette: PAULA EDWARDES.

Male Octette: W. B. Daly, C. Comersford (first tenors); H. Haynes, A. A. Densmore (second tenors); M. Hood, F. Bishop (baritones); L. Parmet, W. C. Brockmeyer (bassos). *Chorus of Paying Guests, Sailors, Waiters, Brigands.*

Act 1: The Landing at Cataro, Montenegro.

Act 2: The Lair of the Brazen Bandits.

ACT 1

"There's a Yacht Come In" (Opening Chorus)
(*Music by* Gustave Kerker. *Lyrics by* Frederic Ranken.)

"The Englishman" (Song)
W. E. Philp
(*Music by* Edward Jakobowski. *Lyrics by* Harry Paulton.)

"Oh, the Paying Guests" (Entrance)
Chorus of Ladies
(*Music by* Edward Jakobowski. *Lyrics by* Harry Paulton.)

"Cities I Love" (Song)
J. E. Sullivan
(*Music by* Edward Jakobowski. *Lyrics by* Frederic Ranken.)

"I Love You Only" (Duet)
H. Redmond, W. E. Philp
(*Music by* Gustave Kerker. *Lyrics by* Frederic Ranken.)

"They're Looking for Me"
P. Edwardes
(*Music by* Gustave Kerker. *Lyrics by* Frederic Ranken.)

"In the Good Old Days" (Trio)
J. C. Miron, H. Redmond, W. E. Philp
(*Music by* Gustave Kerker. *Lyrics by* Frederic Ranken.)

"Rose, Rose, Rose"
D. Temple
(*Music and Lyrics by* Dick Temple.)

"Miss Walker of Kalamazoo" (Ensemble)
P. Edwardes, Principals
(*Music by* Edward Jakobowski. *Lyrics by* Harry Paulton.)

"Everything Is Big in Chicago" (Song)
P. Edwardes
(*Music by* Gustave Kerker. *Lyrics by* Frederic Ranken.)

"I Don't Remember That" (Duet)
P. Edwardes, W. P. Carleton
(*Music by* Gustave Kerker. *Lyrics by* Frederic Ranken.)

"Way Down South" (Quartette)
P. Edwardes, J. C. Miron, J. E. Sullivan, W. S. Corliss

"Loud Let the Bugle Sound" (March)
(*Music by* Gustave Kerker. *Lyrics by* Frederic Ranken.)

ACT 2

"Hola" (Opening Chorus)
Brigands
(*Music by* Gustave Kerker. *Lyrics by* Frederic Ranken.)

"Oh, Maiden" (Male Octette)
(*Music by* Gustave Kerker. *Lyrics by* Frederic Ranken.)

"The Maid and the Miller" (Song)
J. C. Miron
(*Music by* Gustave Kerker. *Lyrics by* Frederic Ranken.)

"Two Little Doves" (Duet)
H. Redmond, W. E. Philp
(*Music by* Gustave Kerker. *Lyrics by* Frederic Ranken.)

"Jenny"
I. Hall
(*Music by* Edward Jakobowski. *Lyrics by* Harry Paulton.)

"Montenegrin Patrol"
J. C. Miron
(*Music by* Edward Jakobowski. *Lyrics by* Harry Paulton.)

"Heroes"
P. Edwardes, D. Temple, J. E. Sullivan
(*Music by* Gustave Kerker. *Lyrics by* Frederic Ranken.)

"Winsome Winnie"
W. P. Carleton
(*Music by* Gustave Kerker. *Lyrics by* Frederic Ranken.)

"Sing Song Lee"
P. Edwardes
(*Music by* Gustave Kerker. *Lyrics by* Frederic Ranken.)

"Ach Louise"
J. E. Sullivan
(*Music and Lyrics by* Gus Edwards.)

Finale
(*Music by* Gustave Kerker. *Lyrics by* Frederic Ranken.)

1903.39 MOTHER GOOSE

A Musical Extravaganza (Pantomime) in Three Acts, 13 Scenes[58]. Original libretto by J. Hickory Wood and Arthur Collins. Adapted for the American stage by John J. McNally. Music by Frederick Solomon. Lyrics by George V. Hobart. (Interpolated numbers by William Jerome and Jean Schwartz, George M. Cohan, Clifton Crawford, Billy Johnson, William H. Penn, Will Heelan and J. Fred Helf, J. M. Glover and Matthew Woodward.) Presented under the stage direction (of) Herbert Gresham and Ned Wayburn. Ballets by Ernest D'Auban. Settings by R. Caney, R. C. McCleery, C. Formilli, Henry Emden and Bruce Smith. Costumes by Comelli, London. Electrical effects by H. Bissing & Co. Music director, Frederick Solomon. Business direction, Joseph Brooks. Produced by (Marc) Klaw & (Abraham) Erlanger. Opened 2 December 1903 at the New Amsterdam Theatre and closed 27 February 1904 after 105 performances.

CAST: *Mother Goose*: JOSEPH CAWTHORN. *Jack*, her son: HARRY BULGER. *The Laird of Borderland*: W. McCART. *Mayor of Chatham*: CLIFTON CRAWFORD. *Alexander*, the Laird's brother: PAT ROONEY. *Jill*, daughter of Mother Goose: LEILA McINTYRE. *Colin*, Jill's sweetheart: VIOLA GILLETTE. *Caroline Evelyn Gwendolyn Scraggs*: AIMEE ANGELES. *Ida*, the Laird's sister: EDITH ST. CLAIR. *Eric*, Ida's

[58]Billed as "the latest Drury Lane Spectacle."

sweetheart: Adele Archer. *Maud*: Marion Garson. *Duchess*: Hattie Waters. *Vicomte Boreham*: George Clennett. *Inez*: Emma Francis. *Fairy Queen*, heartsease: Edith Hutchins. *Demon*: Charles A. Fuller. *Priscilla*, the Golden Goose: Walter Stanton. *Donkeys and Horse*: Dawe & Seymour. *King Goose*: Allan Ramsay. *Queen Goose*: Harry Wigley.

Act 1, Scene 1: The Ruined Belfry. (Smith). *Scene 2*: The Cottage of Mother Goose. (Smith). *Scene 3*: The Hall of Gold. (Smith). *Scene 4*: The Palace of Fantasy. (Formilli).

Act 2, Scene 1: The Meet at the Laird's. (McCleery). *Scene 2*: The Path to the Magic Pool. (Emden). *Scene 3*: The Magic Pool. (Emden). *Scenes 4 and 5*: The Mountain of Fire and the Land of Frost and Ice. (Emden). *Scene 6*: The Land of Heartsease. (Emden).

Act 3, Scene 1: The Wishing Gate. (McCleery). *Scene 2*: Home of the Demon. (Caney). *Scene 3*: Gooseland; Transformation. (Caney).

ACT 1[59]

Scene 2

Opening Chorus
Villagers, Policemen

"Rafferty" (Song)
C. Crawford, Chorus
(*Music and Lyrics by* Clifton Crawford.)

"Under the Mistletoe Bough (Duet)
H. Bulger, A. Angeles
(*Music by* J. Fred Helf. *Lyrics by* Will Heelan.)

"Our Goose Has a Mint in Her Little Inside" (Song)
J. Cawthorn, Chorus

Scene 3

Chorus of Snobs

Parodies
H. Bulger

"When I Do the Highland Fling" (Song and Chorus)
W. McCart, Chorus
(*Music by* J. Fred Helf. *Lyrics by* Will Heelan.)

Scene 4

Grand Chorus, March and Ballet

ACT 2[60] \

Scene 1

Hunting Chorus

"Laughing Water" (Song)
H. Bulger, Chorus
(*Music by* Frederick W. Hager. *Lyrics by* George Totten Smith.)

"Social Eclat" (In the Ladies Home Journal)
J. Cawthorn
(*Music and Lyrics by* Clifton Crawford.)

"On the Go" (Song)
J. Cawthorn, Chorus

Scene 2

"Sweeter dan a Sugar Cane"
L. McIntyre
(*Music and Lyrics by* Billy Johnson.)

"Always Leave Them Laughing When You Say Goodbye" (from RUNNING FOR OFFICE)
H. Bulger
(*Music and Lyrics by* George M. Cohan.)

Scene 3

"Girls Will Be Girls and Boys Will Be Boys"
C. Crawford, E. St. Clair, Chorus

"The Time to Love" (Ballad)
V. Gillette

"We Marched Away" (Trio)
J. Cawthorn, H. Bulger, W. H. McCart

Scenes 4 and 5

Grand Ballet

Scene 6

"Pansy Faces" (Song)
M. Garson
(*Music and Lyrics by* William H. Penn.)

Grand Ballet and Chorus

ACT 3

Scene 1

"Everybody's Loved By Someone" (Chorus)

"I Don't Want to be a Lady"[61] (Song)
A. Angeles
(*Music and Lyrics by* J. M. Glover.)

"Rube Song"
H. Bulger, Chorus
(*Music and Lyrics by* George M. Cohan.)

"Stories Adam Told to Eve" (Song)
J. Cawthorn, Chorus
(*Music by* Jean Schwartz. *Lyrics by* William Jerome.)

"The Rose of the Riviera" (Song)
L. McIntyre, Chorus
(*Music by* Bernard Rolt.)

"Still in the Front Line" (Song)
J. Cawthorn, H. Bulger, W. H. McCart, Chorus
(*Music and Lyrics by* Matthew Woodward.)

Scene 3

Contentment (Finale)

[59]Interpolated during the run, per published sheet music:

"The Evolution of Ragtime"
(*Music by* J. Rosamond Johnson. *Lyrics by* Robert Cole, James Weldon Johnson.)

"There's Nobody Just Like You"
V. Gillette
(*Music by* William H. Penn. *Lyrics by* Ed. Gardenier.)

"Hiss for Shame"
L. McIntyre
(*Music and Lyrics by* Albert H. Fitz.)

"Honey Boy"
L. McIntyre
(*Music by* William H. Penn. *Lyrics by* Clayton Kennedy.)

"Jingles, Jokes and Rhymes"
J. Cawthorn
(*Music and Lyrics by* Benjamin Hapgood Burt.)

Interpolated for subsequent tour, as per published sheet music:

"Blue-Eyed Sue"
Neva Aymar
(*Music and Lyrics by* James Reece Europe.)

[60]Added to Act 2, Scene 6, after Grand Ballet and Chorus, for subsequent tour:

"Pansy March"

1903.40 MAM'SELLE NAPOLEON

A French Vaudeville (Musical Play) in Three Acts, 5 Scenes. (Libretto) Adapted by Joseph W. Herbert. Based on the French original ("Mlle. Mars") by Jean Richepin. Music by Gustav Luders. Staged by Joseph W. Herbert. Settings by Ernest Albert. Orchestra under the direction of Herman Perlet. Produced by Florenz Ziegfeld. Opened 8 December 1903 at the Knickerbocker Theatre and closed 16 January 1904 after 43 performances.

CAST: *Napoleon*: ARTHUR LAURENCE. *Miche, Flute*, agents of the Secret Police: JOSEPH W. HERBERT, FRANK MOULAN[62]. *Fouché Duc D'Otrante*, Minister of Police: HENRY BERGMAN. *Choupille*, a friend of Mars, pensionnaire of the Comédie Française: REGINALD CARRINGTON. *Noel Gilot*, officer of the Imperial Guard and Mars' fiance: FRANK RUSHWORTH. *Le Marechal Le Febvre*: Robert Hickman. *Talma*, the great tragedian, Societaire of the Comédie Française: Harry M. Blake. *Constant*, valet de chambre of the Emperor: Harry M. Blake. *The Marquis d'Estizac, The Viscount Maubreiul*, Body Guards of King Louis XIV: Robert Hickman, Richard Wallace. *Écrévisse*, call boy of the Comédie Française: Franz Ebert. *The Abbe Delille*, member of the French academy: Fletcher Norton. *Ducis*, the poet: Francklyn Wallace. *David*, the great painter, member of the institute: Edward Gore. *Commissaire of Police*: E. A. Tester. *A Young Elegant*: Alfred Pyke. *An Old Financier*: Karl Becca. *Joachim Murat*, King of Naples: J. S. Northern. *The Marechal Ney*: S. P. Pulen. *Roustan*, the Emperor's Mamelouck: J. S. Dunlevy. *The Emperor of Austria*: Howard Stevens. *The Emperor of Russia*: M. Sharpe. *Mme. Phillipard*: MATHILDA [Mathilde] COTTRELLY. *Flora*, maid of Mlle. Mars: BILLY NORTON. *Mlle. Raucourt*,

[61] Dropped for subsequent tour.

[62] Frank Moulan withdrew from the cast after the opening, pursuant to an injunction against him by Henry W. Savage, and was replaced by Dan McAvoy.

Societaire of the Comédie Française: Adelaide Orton. *Madame Sans-Gene*, La Marechal Le Febvre: Edythe Moyer. *Dancers*: BESSIE McCOY, NELLIE McCOY. *Duchess d'Abrante*: Nina Randall. *Mme. Recamier*: EDNA GOODRICH. *Mlle. Contat*: Elsie Baird. *Mademoiselle Mars* (of the Comédie Française): ANNA HELD.

Act 1: The Artist's Foyer of the Comédie Française, 1803.

Act 2: Kiosk on the Lake at the Chateau de Compiegne.

Act 3, Scene 1: Interior of the Grand Opera House, Paris, 1809. Opera Ball in progress. *Scene 2*: A glade in the Wood at Dauphine. The Ambush at the Mill. *Scene 3*: On to Paris.

ACT 1

"The Stage and Fashion Hand in Hand" (Opening Chorus)
Chorus

"Life Is Not an Airy Bubble" (Life's No Blooming Airy Bubble)
J. W. Herbert

"Hit Enormous"
Chorus

"The Language of Love"
A. Held

"Flowers, Feathers, Ribbons, Laces" (Quintette)(Art Cannot Improve the Rose)
A. Held, B. Norton, M. Cottrelly, F. Rushworth, R. Carrington

"The Cockatoo and the Chimpanzee" (The Story of the Monkey and the Parrot)
A. Held

"I Love You Then as Now" (Then as Now)
A. Held, F. Rushworth

Finale: "The Art of Stimulation"/"Queen of the Comédie Française"
A. Held, Ensemble

ACT 2

"Nymphs and Satyr" (Opening)
Fantasia Mythologique

"Too-Whoo" (My Heart Will Be True to You)(Trio)
M. Cottrelly, J. W. Herbert, F. Moulan

"Le Lion et la Souris" (The Lion and the Mouse)
A. Held

ACT 3

Scene 1

"Long Live Folly" (Opening Chorus)
Chorus

"The Brave Soldier Boy" (March)
Miltary Girls, J. S. Northern, H. M. Blake

"Out with the Boys"
J. W. Herbert, Ensemble

"The Rigodon"
Ensemble

Saint and Prude; Polka Militaire; Pas de Deux; Solo Espagnole; Finale.

"The à la Mode Girl"
A. Held, Ensemble

"The Two Dolls and the Glory of France" (Finale)
A. Held, Ensemble

Scene 2

"The Song of the Grenadier" (Brave Comrades Rise)
F. Rushworth, Grenadiers

"On to Paris" (Finale)
Ensemble

1903.41 A GIRL FROM DIXIE

A Musical Comedy in Two Acts, 3 Scenes. Book by Harry B. Smith. (Music by J. Rosamond Johnson, Will Marion Cook, Max Witt, A. Baldwin Sloane, George Norton, M. G. Watson, Kerry Mills, Ben Jerome, Ludwig Engländer, Theo Tobani, etc. Lyrics by Harry B. Smith, Robert Cole, M. G. Watson.) Staged by R. H. Burnside. Musical director, Selli Simmonson. Produced by the Sam S. Shubert and the Messrs. (Sam) Nixon and (J. F.) Zimmerman. Opened 14 December 1903 at the Madison Square Theatre and closed 2 January 1904 after 25 performances.

CAST: *Lord Dunsmore*, object matrimony: FERDINAND GOTTSCHALK. *Angelo Catalani*, village music teacher: ARNOLD DALY. *Jack Randolph*, professor of everything at the Grammar School, Tamarack, Maryland: ALBERT HART. *Squire Mink* of the Tamarack Bar, legal and otherwise: GEORGE A. SCHILLER. *Edward Brandon*, a lawyer's clerk: CHARLES H. BOWERS. *Nick Calvert*, a schoolboy: Wilmer H. Bentley. *Napoleon Lee*, who worked for deCalverts when dey all was rich: Charles K. French. *Maria Louisa*, his wife: Charles H. Sheffer. *Jefferson Payne, Bob Marshall*, school boys: Albert J. Marshall, Vernon H. Lee. *Bill Douglas*: D. M. Lumsden. *Jim Small*: W. L. Hobart. *Kitty Calvert*, best old family in Maryland, and the worst clothes: IRENE BENTLEY. *Bess Jackson*: EVELYN NESBIT. *Maud Mabel Earle*, whose father owns the cigar factory: Dorothy Donner. *Imogenia*: Rose Hart. *Sally Sumpter, Malvina Carrol*, school girls: Esther Lyons, Belle Desmond. *Dora*, a college girl: Mabel Verne. *Alice*, another: Ade Verne. *Edith*, another: Olga May. *Helen*, another: Lorraine Osborne.

Members of the Horse Shoe Hunt Club: Misses May, Smyth, Grant, Muller, Holmes, Verne, Osborne. Messrs. Marshall, Lee, Booley, O'Brien, Hobart, Bentley. *Ushers at Kitty's Wedding Rehearsal*: Messrs. Roberts, Bohannon, Pooley, Brengle, Lumsden, McArthur, Hall, O'Brien, Hobart, Lee, Marshall. *Bridesmaids*: Misses Grant, May, Osborne, A. Verne, M. Verne, Holmes, Smyth, Muller.

Act 1: Interior of School House, Tamarack, Maryland.

Act 2, Scene 1: Garden of Oxbridge College. *Scene 2*: Ballroom of Kitty Calvert's New York home.

ACT 1[63]

"Love in an Orchard"
(*Music by* Ben Jerome.)

"The Lovers' A.B.C."
(*Music by* Max Witt. *Lyrics by* M. E. Rourke.)

"Mary from Maryland"
(*Music and Lyrics by* George A. Norton.)

"Angels Without Wings"
(*Music by* Gustave Kerker.)

"The Dissipated Kitten"
(*Music by* A. Baldwin Sloane. *Lyrics by* Harry B.Smith.)

Finale

ACT 2

Scene 1

"The Sunflower and the Sun"
(*Music by* Will Marion Cook.)

"When the Moon Comes (Peeping) O'er the Hill"
(*Music by* J. Rosamond Johnson. *Lyrics by* Robert Cole.)

Waltz—Finale
(*Music by* Ludwig Engländer.)

Scene 2

Minuet and March
(*Music by* George Rosey.)

"Bubbles"
(*Music by* Max Witt. *Lyrics by* Harry B. Smith.)

"An American Heiress"
(*Music by* Theo M. Tobani.)

"Johnny Strong"
(*Music by* E. D. Prussian. *Lyrics by* Harry Raymond.)

"Happy Days in Dixie"
(*Music by* Kerry Mills.)

"There's Nothing Like a Friend"
(*Music by* Max Witt.)

"Huzza" (part song for male voices)
(*Music by* Dudley Buck.)

"Honey"
(*Music by* H. J. Green.)

1904.01 MY LADY MOLLY

A Musical Comedy in Two Acts. Book and lyrics by George H. Jessop. Music by Sidney Jones. (Additional lyrics by Percy Greenbank and Charles H. Taylor.) Produced under the stage direction of (staged by) Gilbert Laye.

[63]Additional musical numbers per published sheet music:

"When I Look into Those Lovey Dovey Eyes"
(*Music by* Manuel Klein. *Lyrics by* Rida Johnson Young.)

"You, You, You"
(*Music and Lyrics by* E. H. Pendleton.)

"Pansy Faces"
I. Bentley
(*Music and Lyrics by* William H. Penn.)

Orchestra under the direction of W. P. Brown. Produced by Charles Frohman. Opened 5 January 1904 at Daly's Theatre and closed 16 January 1904 after 15 performances[64].

CAST: *Captain Harry Romney*: SIDNEY DEANE. *Lionel Bland*: RAY YOUNGMAN. *Sir Miles Coverdale*: DAVID TORRENCE. *Mickey O'Dowd*, servant to Captain Harry: RICHARD F. CARROLL. *Landlord*, of Coverdale Arms: LUKE MARTIN. *Head Waiter*: Francis Motley. *Head Groom*: Edward Chappell. *Judge Romney*, father to Harry: John Henderson. *Lady Molly Martingale*: VESTA TILLEY. *Hester*, her confidential maid: Alice Judson. *Alice Coverdale*, daughter to Sir Miles: ADELE RITCHIE. *Mademoiselle Mirabeau*, governess to Alice: ANNA BOYD. *Housekeeper*, at Coverdale Arms: Oriska Worden. *Owen*, servant at Coverdale Arms: W. J. Morgan. *Chambermaids (2)*: *Lucy*: Amy Lesser. *Allison*: Belle Robinson. *Servants at Coverdale Castle (2)*: *Roger*: Arthur Rice. *Martin*: E. Matthews.

The Bridesmaids: Misses Amy Lesser, Belle Robinson, Claire Moore, Mary McLane, May Densmore, Ruby Petrie, Mae Clark, Anna Baker. *Huntresses*: Misses Elizabeth Sanger, Clara Eckstrom, Jeanne Bernard, Sadie Melles, Isabel Cheshire, Maud Nelson, Margaret Masi, Viola Clayton. *Ladies of the Court*: Misses Lillian Jones, Blanche Morrell, Aline Potter, Sadie Melles, Amy Forsland, Kate Haddon, Dorothy Allen, Vera Pindor. *Hunters*: Messrs. Bent, Rice, Matthews, Bentley, Daley, Parry, Baker, Hudson. *Gentlemen of the Court*: Messrs. Morgan, Voltaire, Brady, Bastick, Aiken, Emerson, C. S. Calhoun. *Grooms, Country Girls, Maid Servants, etc.*

The action takes place in the middle of the eighteenth century.

Act 1: Courtyard, Coverdale Arms. Morning.

Act 2: Coverdale Castle. Night.

ACT 1[65]

Opening Chorus (Brushes and brooms)
Chorus
"There Is the Key" (Solo)
L. Martin
"A Man May Know No Voice of Friend" (Song)
L. Martin
"There's a Little Maid (I Know)" (Song)
R. Youngman
(*Lyrics by* Percy Greenbank.)
"The Land of Make Believe" (Duet)
A. Ritchie, R. Youngman
"But, Oh Beware" (Quartette)
A. Boyd, A. Ritchie, R. Youngman, L. Martin
"Ballinasloe" (Song)
R. F. Carroll
"Oh! I'll Greet Him Soft and Slow" (Duet)
V. Tilley, A. Judson
"(Ye) Wear 'em Wid an Air" (Trio)
R. F. Carroll, V. Tilley, A. Judson
"Hurrah for the Field" (Chorus and Song)
D. Torrence, L. Martin, Chorus
"The Merry Medieval Maid"
A. Ritchie
(*Lyrics by* Percy Greenbank.)
"Topers fling your glasses aside"
Chorus
"Though You May Choose" (Duet)
S. Deane, R. Youngman
"Here's a nice to do"
Chorus
"We saw the swords"
Chorus
"To You, Sir Miles" (Song)
S. Deane
Finale (Rougue detected)
Principals

ACT 2

Opening Chorus (How do you do)
"I Mean to Be a Good Girl Now" (Song)
A. Ritchie, Chorus
"A Regular Parley-voo" (Duet)
R. F. Carroll, A. Boyd
"Once Too Often" (When a Maiden Is Wooed by a Man)(Song)
V. Tilley
"Kiss lad and never tell" (Trio)
D. Torrence, V. Tilley, A. Ritchie
"At My Lady's Feet" (Song)
S. Deane
"Suppose a highwayman you were" (Quartette)
A. Ritchie, R. Youman, S. Deane, V. Tilley
Entrance of Bridesmaids and Song (Trousseau)
A. Judson
Flower Chorus (A chance dear girls)
Chorus
"Don't Whistle So Loud" (Song)
R. F. Carroll
Bridal March and Chorus (Now the chancel waits)
Chorus
"Opeless ze state of me" (Sad Is Ze Fate of Me)(Song)
A. Boyd
"What's the Matter" (Chorus)
Chorus
"To-day" (Duet)
V. Tilley, S. Deane
Finale
Principals

[64]Settings, costumes uncredited.
[65]Musical numbers not listed in program. Above list is prepared from the English vocal score; revisions and interpolations are certain, and many of the songs above were not performed in New York. During the tryout Andrew Mack was replaced by Richard F. Carroll, and Ethel Levey by Vesta Tilley, resulting in many changes and interpolations. Reviews acknowledged the following in New York reviews: "When a Maiden Is Wooed (Once Too Often)," "Ye Wear 'Em Wid an Air," "Don't Whistle So Loud," "Ballinasloe," "There's a Little Maid," "At My Lady's Feet," "Oh! I'll Greet Him Soft and Slow," "I Mean to be a Good Girl Now," "The Merry Medieval Maid." Reviewers remarked upon four songs not in English vocal score:
"Not at Home"
V. Tilley
"The Seaside Sultan"
V. Tilley
"Go Back to Work"
V. Tilley
"Algy" (The Piccadilly Johnny with the Little Glass Eye)
V. Tilley
(*Music and Lyrics by* Harry B. Morris.)

1904.02

TERENCE

A Picturesque Irish Comedy (with Songs) in Four Acts. Play by Mrs. Edward Nash Morgan, adapted from the novel by Mrs. B. M. Croker. Music and lyrics by Chauncey Olcott. Production (staged) by Augustus Pitou. Produced by Augustus Pitou. Opene 5 January 1904 at the New York Theatre and closed 20 February 1904 after 56 performances.

CAST: *Terence*, the mail coach driver: CHAUNCEY OLCOTT. *Sir Greville Fanshawe*, an English sportsman: HARRY HANSCOMBE. *Captain Lovell*, an English officer: H. S. Northrup. *Simon Foulcher*, a lawyer: Augustus Cook. *Pat Ryan*, a pensioner: Matt B. Snyder. *Tim O'Brien*: George Brennan. *Hogan*: C. N. Schaeffer. *Danny*, *Connie*, little sweethearts: Dolly Forde, Blanche Alexander. *Maureen D'Arcy*: ADELAIDE KEIM. *Lady Fanshawe*, Maureen's half-sister: AMANDA WELLINGTON. *Mrs. Malpas*, Maureen's aunt: ROSE SNYDER. *Lady Flashe*: Edith Miller Cook. *Mrs. O'Hara*, landlady of the Inn at Shule: ELIZABETH WASHBURNE. *Mad Sheela*: Mary Moran. *Judy*, a housemaid: Eugenie Forde.

The action of the play takes place at Ballybay, Shule and Dublin, Ireland. Present day.

Act 1: The "Fly and Fish" Inn at Ballybay. Terence, the Coachman.

Act 2: Mrs. O'Hara's Inn at Shule. Saddling the Wrong Horse.

Act 3: Road near Ballybay, "The Devil's Elbow." The Temptation of Terence.

Act 4: Reception Room in the House of Sir Greville Fanshawe, Dublin. The Last of the Desmonds.

MUSICAL NUMBERS

"My Own Dear Irish Queen"
C. Olcott

"The Girl I Used to Know"
C. Olcott
"My Sonny Boy" (Rocking, Rocking)
C. Olcott
"Tick Tack Toe" (Tic Tac Toe)
C. Olcott

1904.03 THE MEDAL AND THE MAID

A Musical Comedy in Two Acts. Book and lyrics by Owen Hall. Music by Sidney Jones. Staged by Cyril Scott. Dances and ensembles by Tom Terriss. Settings by (Thomas G.) Moses & Hamilton. Costumes by Alias, London; Greek costumes by Zuccaro, Greece. Orchestra under the direction of Arthur Weld. Produced by John C. Fisher and Thomas W. Ryley. Opened 11 January 1904 at the Broadway Theatre and closed 20 February 1904 after 49 performances[66].

CAST: *Merva Sunningdale*: RUTH VINCENT. *Josephine*: CECIL ENGELHEART. *Miss Ventnor*: JEANNETTE LOWRIE. *Mrs. Habbicombe*: EMMA CARUS. *Elsie Habbicombe*: Edna McClure. *Simon Pentweazle*: JAMES T. POWERS. *Admiral Lord Belton*: W. T. CARLETON. *Allen Blythe*, R.N.: CYRIL SCOTT. *Levanter*: IGNACIO MARTINETTI. *Darien*: STANLEY H. FORDE. *Lionel Habbicombe*: Tom Terriss. *Sergeant (Blakeley)*: Frank D. Nelson. *Jungo*: George Jackson. *Kalim*: W. May. *Gerdes*: C. Brabin. *Maud Hersham*: Manola Mada Hurst. *Sarah Sevenoaks*: Carla Byron. *Ilma Malden*: Laura Stone. *Galdys Combe*: Bessie Denham. *Mona Vale*: Lillian Harris. *Ada Bray*: Virginia Sargent. *Lillian*: Beatrice Walsh. *Violette*: Lillian Rice. *Daisy*: Grace Wilson. *The No Frill Girl*: Lou Wheelan. *Antoinette*: Lily Collins. *Vi*: Sadie Raymond. *Rosa*: Lelia Benton. *Tita*: Edith Girvin. *Conchita*: Avita Sanchez. *Marie*: May Willard. *Jeanette*: Ita Kamph. *Cora*: Mary Lachere. *Lady Visitors at Cannes (6)*: *Edith Melville*: Mary Clayton. *Blanche Densmore*: Mildred Devere. *Vera Smythe*: Martha Garver. *Gertrude Crawford*: Gladys Lockwood. *Frances Rentworth*: Susan Parker. *Florence Meredith*: Grace Vaughn. *Polo Boys (6)*: *Blakely*: Harris Pyke. *Grant*: Leon de Lisle. *Melville*: M. M. Johnson. *Kingsley*: Lawrence Howell. *Wheeler*: Nat K. Cafferty. *Gatacre*: Frank Garfield.

Act 1: Outside Miss Ventnor's School at Cannes.

Act 2: The Island of Karagovina, Greece.

ACT 1[67]
Opening Chorus (We have come from the ends of the earth)
"Polo" (The Polo championship we claim)
Ensemble
"In My Curriculum"
J. Lowrie
"Who'll Buy My Flowers"
C. Engelheart
"Come, Kind Gentlemen"[68]
R. Vincent, C. Engelheart
"Any Sort of Girl"
I. Martinetti
"(A) Prize for That"
J. T. Powers
"(The) Frills Upon The Petticoats"
J. Lowrie
"I'm Going to Be a Marquis"
E. Carus, J. T. Powers, I. Martinetti
Finale

ACT 2
Opening Chorus
"Brigand Chief"[69] (The Philosophic Brigand)
S. H. Forde
"Publicity"
J. Lowrie
"Consequences"
R. Vincent, C. Scott
(*Music and Lyrics by* Paul Rubens.)
"(In) Zanzibar" (My Little Chimpanzee)[69a]
E. Carus
(*Music by* Gus Edwards. *Lyrics by* Will D. Cobb.)
"Hide and Seek"
C. Engelheart, T. Terriss
"If Girls Had Wings"
R. Vincent
"Vanderdecken"[70]
I. Martinetti
Finale
Ensemble

1904.04 AN ENGLISH DAISY

A Musical Comedy in Two Acts, 4 Scenes. Original English libretto by Seymour Hicks. Rearranged for the American stage by Edgar Smith. Music by Walter Slaughter, with added music by Alfred Müller-Norden. Lyrics by Edgar Smith. (Added lyrics by Percy Greenbank.) Staged by Ben Teal. Settings by John H. Young. Produced by (Joseph) Weber and (Lew) Fields. Opened 18 January 1904 at the Casino Theatre and closed 20 February 1904 after 41 performances[71].

CAST: *Daniel Crab*, an American in hard luck: CHARLES A. BIGELOW. *Hiram Smart*, his companion in misfortune: FRED LENOX. *Of the Royal Artillery Quartered at Dover (4)*: *Major Bickersdyke*: George A. Beane. *Lieutenant Charles Lambton*: TEMPLAR SAXE. *Lieutenant Dick Pepler*: George P. Smith. *Lieutenant Tom Brown*: Alfred Truschel. *Bliffkins*, Landlord of the Kursaal Hotel at Ostend: FRANK LALOR. *Bert*, Hall Boy and Call Boy and Boy of all work: Louis Wesley. *The Compte Dubois*, a French Don Juan: HENRY LEONE [Leoni]. *Henri, Gustave, Adolphe*, Young French Swells: Franc V. LeMone, Osborne Clemson, Arthur Stanford. *Joe Tents*, a Menagerie Owner: Frank Hammond. *A Waiter*: Walter Van Allen. *Daisy Maitland*, the "English " Daisy: CHRISTIE MacDONALD. *Celestine*, a Footlight Divinity: TRULY SHATTUCK. *Henriette*, a Maid: Clara Belle Jerome. *Lavinia Squib*, Bliffkins' neice: KITTY BALDWIN. *Lady Lauderdale*, an aristocrat: Jean Newcombe. *Cherie*, a Dancer: Nora Sarony. *Belles of Ostend (5)*: *Josephine*: Lillian Maure. *Clotilde*: Emily Sanford. *Lucille*: Helen Wilmer. *Marie*: Lola Hoffman. *Jacqueline*: Katherine Cooper. *Smart English Girls (3)*: *Lady Marjorie*: Lillian Marshall. *Lady Winifred*: Carrie B. Munroe. *Lady Mabel*: Jane Tyrell. *Flower Girls, Bathing Girls, Dancers, Guests, etc.*: Misses Elmo, Gray, Winnship, Egan, Marshall, Monroe, Appell, Howell, Franklin, Grant, Roome, Bell, Forrester, Millard, Cooper, Carrette, Hickey, Hobart, Maure, Tyrell, Hoffman, Dore, Marshall, Monroe, Wilmar, Sanford. Messrs. Stanford, LeMone, Gaunt, Truschel, Clemson, Smith, McClasky, Hammond, Pogue, Baker.

The action takes place during Carnival Time in Ostend, (England)[72].

Act 1: Outside the Kursaal Hotel, Ostend.

Act 2, Scene 1: The Artistes' Dressing Room in the Kursaal Hotel. Night. *Scene 2*: The Gardens of the Kursaal.

ACT 1
Opening Chorus
(*Music by* Walter Slaughter, Alfred Müller-Norden. *Lyrics by* Percy Greenbank.)

---

[66]Played a return engagement 14 March 1904 at the Grand Opera House for 8 performances.
[67]Added during the run (from London production), after "In My Curriculum:"
"Katie and Her Kodak" (Click went the Kodak)
McCoy Sisters, Chorus
Added during the run, after "Frills Upon Their Petticoats:"
"My Love I Dare Not Tell (Thee)"
R. Vincent
(*Music by* S. Stenhammer. *Lyrics by* Bartley C. Costello.)
Added during the run, after "I'm Going to Be a Marquis:"
"Rain or Shine"
C. Scott
[68]Replaced during the run by:
"A Well Bred Girl"
R. Vincent, C. Engelheart

[69]Replaced by the following interpolation, as per published sheet music:
"Beware of the Brigand Bold"
S. H. Forde
(*Music by* Theodore H. Northrup. *Lyrics by* Stanley H. Forde.)
[69a]Also interpolated into the 1904 tour of THE SHOWGIRL, 1902.
[70]Replaced during the run by:
"The Man Behind"
W. T. Powers
Dance
McCoy Sisters
[71]Later toured under the auspices of Joseph M. Gaites and J. F. Arnold.
[72]No description of the scene locations appears in American programs. Scene breaks taken from an English program, which divided into Two Acts, 3 Scenes.

"I Adore a Certain Party" (Duet)
L. Wesley, C. B. Jerome
(*Music by* Alfred Müller-Norden. *Lyrics by* Edgar Smith.)
"The Military Man" (Song)
T. Saxe, Ensemble
(*Music by* Gus Edwards. *Lyrics by* Edgar Smith.)
"I'm a Little English Daisy" (I am the English Daisy)(Song)
C. MacDonald, Ensemble
(*Music by* Alfred Müller-Norden. *Lyrics by* Percy Greenbank.)
"To the End of the World Together" (Duet)
C. MacDonald, T. Saxe
(*Music by* Jerome Kern. *Lyrics by* Edgar Smith.)
"At the Music Hall" (Comic Duet)
C. A. Bigelow, C MacDonald
(*Music by* Jean Schwartz. *Lyrics by* Edgar Smith.)
Finale
(*Music by* Walter Slaughter, Alfred Müller-Norden. *Lyrics by* Percy Greenbank.)

ACT 2
"You Couldn't Get on Without Me, Girls" (Song)
L. Wesley, Ensemble
(*Music by* Alfred Müller-Norden. *Lyrics by* Percy Greenbank.)
"Wine, Wine" (Song)
T. Shattuck, Ensemble
(*Music by* Jerome Kern. *Lyrics by* Edgar Smith.)
"The Coon, the Moon and the Little Octoroon" (Song)
C. MacDonald
(*Music by* Maud Nugent. *Lyrics by* Will A. Heelan.)
Opening Chorus, International Number:
Spanish Dance
Ladies' Ensemble
(*Music by* Alfred Müller-Norden.)/
"Big Indian Chief"
C. B. Jerome, F. Lenox
(*Music by* J. Rosamond Johnson. *Lyrics by* Robert Cole.)
"Spin Again" (Song)
H. Leone, Ensemble
(*Music by* Alfred Müller-Norden. *Lyrics by* Percy Greenbank.)
"Prepossessing Maid" (Song)
C. MacDonald, Semi-Chorus
(*Music by* J. Rosamond Johnson. *Lyrics by* Robert Cole.)
Finale

1904.05 SERGEANT KITTY

The Virginia Earl Opera Company in a Military Comic Opera in Two Acts. Book and lyrics by R. H. Burnside. Music by A. Baldwin Sloane. Staged by R. H. Burnside. Scenery by D. Frank Dodge. Costumes designed by Archie Gunn, Mme. Caroline Seidle, Mme. Freisinger. Musical direction, Carl Burton. Orchestrations by Frank Saddler. Produced by George R. White. Opened 18 January 1904 at Daly's Theatre and closed 12 March 1904 after 55 performances.

CAST: *General Dubois*, a choleric old martinet: SYLVAIN LANGLOIS. *Henri de Marrillac*, Lieutenant 22nd Hussars, his nephew: HARRY STONE. *Lucien Vallière*, Lieutenant 24th Hussars, in love with Kitty: ALBERT PARR. *Jacques Jonquiniere*: JUNIE McCREE. *Jean Cornichon*, proprietor of the hotel : Charles Renwick. *Pierre Picorin*, Kitty's uncle, a pastry cook: Harry Braham. *Celestin Brideaux*, Lucien's orderly: GEORGE E. MACK. *Sergeant Lefevbre*: Charles J. Goode. *Notary Le Van*: J. A. Furey. *First Gendarme*: Lawrence Hilliard. *Second Gendarme*: W. C. Roberts. *Private Danton*: Harmon Anderson. *Louise de Marrilac*, Henri's wife: ESTELLE WENTWORTH. *Mme. Angelique*, Kitty's aunt: CARRIE E. PERKINS. *Ninon*, a florist: GRACE BELMONT. *Suzette*, Picorin's daughter: Nellie Emerald. *Babette*, Mme. de Marrilac's maid: Ethel Lloyd. *Kitty LaTour*, in love with Lucien: VIRGINIA EARL. *Soldiers, Peasants, Flower Girls, Pastry Cooks, Milkmaids, Vivandieres, Bugler Boys, etc.*: Ladies and Gentlemen of the Chorus.

The action takes place in the morning and afternoon of the same day in France, 1830.

Act 1: Exterior of Cornichon's Hotel at Montigny.

Act 2: The Camp of the 22nd Hussars.

ACT 1
"Buy, Buy, Come and Buy" (Opening Chorus)
"Cupid's Cure" (Duet)
G. Belmont, N. Emerald, Chorus
"I'm the King of Bakers" (Song)
H. Braham, Chorus
"An Accident" (Ensemble)
G. Belmont, Chorus
"True Love Lives But in Our Dreams" (Song)
E. Wentworth
"The One That I Love the Best Gave That to Me" (Song)
J. McCree
"Love" (Waltz Song)
V. Earl
"Strange Things Happen Every Day" (Song)
V. Earl, J. McCree
"I Have Thought of a Scheme" (Trio)
V. Earl, H. Braham, G. E. Mack
Finale

ACT 2
"A Soldier's Life" (Opening Chorus)
"War!" (Song)
S. Langlois
"The Girl He Left Behind Him" (Duet)
H. Stone, E. Wentworth
"Oh, Kitty" (Song)
V. Earl
"Ninon's Father Doesn't Seem to Mind" (Song)
J. McCree
"Love Laughs at Locksmiths" (Duet)
V. Earl, A. Parr
"Just Take Things as They Come" (Duet)
J. McCree, C. E. Perkins
"What Is a Poor Girl to Do" (Song)
V. Earl
"Oh, Star of Hope" (Song)
A. Parr
"We Are a Gallant Regiment" (March Song)
V. Earl, Chorus
"To the Guard House" (Ensemble)
Company
Grand Finale

1904.06 THE FUNNY MR. DOOLEY

A Musical Farce Comedy in Three Acts. Book, music and lyrics by Frank D. Bryan, Paul E. Quinn and Charles H. Smith. (Based on the newspaper columns of Finley Peter Dunne.) Musical director, Harry Trappert. Produced by Frank D. Bryan. Opened 8 February 1904 at the Metropolis Theatre and closed 13 February 1903 after 8 performances.

CAST: *Mr. Dooley*: PAUL E. QUINN. *Dr. Jollian Skinem*: Charles H. Smith. *Hans Dinkelspiel*: Frank Manning. *Nothin Doin*: Thomas Glenroy. *E. Z. Mark*: Edgar Flavelle. *Leander Fairweather*: EMMET O'CONNOR. *Noan Lott*: WILLIAM P. HAYES. *Lean Hamlet*: James F. Casey. *Handy Andy*: Walter C. White. *Kani Ketchum*: Edward Hall. *Arizona Pete*: S. Henry Wilson. *Clarence*: Sam Walters. *Pokerhauntus*: Elmer Vincent. *Mercie Onus*: Will E. Franks. *Four-Legged Towser*: Himself. *Sadie Lightweight*: Frank Jones. *Mrs. Phillius McFadden*: Maggie LeClair. *Minerva McFadden*: May Walsh. *Miss Gotthe Goods*: MAY WALSH. *"Sassy Sal"*: Edyth Murray. *Miss Carolina Cotton*: Edyth Murray. *Bashful Beatrice*: Annette Morrow. *Society Shoppers, Sales Ladies.*

Act 1: "Bunco Square," 34th Street and Broadway, New York City. Noon, Monday.

Act 2: "Skinem's Drug Store." Noon, Tuesday.

Act 3: Dooley's Department Store. Noon, Wednesday.

MUSICAL NUMBERS
"Virginia Reel"
Shoppers, Clerks, Pedestrians
"Chicago"
P. E. Quinn, Company
"Who's Your Friend"
M. Walsh
"Chauffeurs"
Men of the Company
"Pastimes"
E. Murray, W. P. Hayes

"Miss Margie"
E. O'Connor, Show Girls
"(I'm a) Yankee Doodle Dandy"
Company
(*Music and Lyrics by* George M. Cohan.)
"Kiss Song"
W. C. White, E. O'Connor, Sales Ladies
"Physical Culture Girls"
M. Walsh, Show Girls
"I Love Them All"
E. O'Connor, Show Girls
"Go Where the Crowd Goes"
C. H. Smith, M. Walsh, Company
"Shoppers and Clerks"
E. O'Connor, Show Girls
"Follow Me"
P. E. Quinn, Company
"Let Go, Mr. Coon"
M. Walsh, Show Girls
"Good Night"
Company

1904.07 THE GOOD OLD SUMMERTIME

A Musical Farce in Three Acts. Book (and lyrics) by Ren Shields. Music by George Evans. Costumes by Archie Gunn. Chorus directed by Frank Smithson. Produced by the Shea Amusement Company. Opened 8 February 1904 at the 14th Street Theatre and closed 20 February 1904 after 17 performances.[73]

CAST: *Tommy Todd*, a jockey: GEORGE "Honey Boy" EVANS. *Con Mahoney*, a sporting politician: JOHN CONROY. *Macon Goode*, a bookmaker: CHARLES M. McDONALD. *Spike McGuire*, ex-welterweight champion: JOE NATUS. *Bob Mahoney*, Con's son: Karl Stahl. *Hans Upp*, a brewer: GOFF PHILLIPS. *Oarlock Bones*, Scotland Yard detective: Charles Seagrave. *I. Doolittle*, a waiter: Harlan Knight. *Murphy's sister* (poetic): Dorothy LaMar. *Ima Mahoney*, Con's daughter: ANNIE MARTELL. *Rosie Riley*, from the Bowery: PEARL REVERE. *Kitty Did*, one of the girls: Marie Hylands. *Petty Cash*, she runs for Bob: Della Freese. *Annie Work*, a maid: Lucy Gover. *Lillie Vesta*: Esther Marks. *Hi Yell* race track announcer: Al Price. *E. Z. Bet*: Ted Sharkoff. *Vanderbilt Smith*: Lee Miers. *Pickaninnies*: Blanche Wilmot, Elizabeth Elliott. *It is?*: A horse. *Show girls, summer girls, college girls, girls and girls, college boys, race men, tourists, yacht owners, etc.*

Scene: A seaside hotel and near a race track.

MUSICAL NUMBERS
"In the Good Old Summertime"
"(You're) The Sweetest Flower That Grows in Tennessee"
"Sunday Morning When the Church Bells Ring"
"Tom Mahoney"
"America"
"Keep Away from Rosie"
"My Little Japanee"
P. Revare
"When the American Eagle Screams"
"In the Sweet Spring Time"
"Don't Never Look for It Among the Irish"
"Just a Mile and a Half from Town"
"Walks"
"Bimbo"

1904.08 GLITTERING GLORIA

A Comedy with Music in Three Acts. Book by Hugh Morton. (Adapted from his English farce of the same name.) Music by Bernard Rolt. Lyrics by Hugh Morton and Bernard Holt. Produced by John C. Fisher and Thomas W. Ryley. Opened 15 February 1904 at Daly's Theatre and closed 5 March 1904 after 22 performances[74].

CAST: *Jack James*: CYRIL SCOTT. *Archie Toddleby*, his friend: PERCY F. AMES. *Zebedee Poskett*, a rural solicitor: FERDINAND GOTTSCHALK. *Colonel Pasquale Gallegher*, from El Paso, Texas: Forrest Robinson. *Algernon Entwistle*, the Colonel's Secretary: GEORGE A. SCHILLER. *Samuel Slapton*, a Bond Street jeweler: Edward Gore. *Robert Shreve*, Slapton's partner: E. Lovat Fraser. *Mr. Griddletop*, Third Assistant superintendent of luggage, Euston Station: EUGENE O'ROURKE. *First Porter*: John Hendy. *Gloria Grant*, known as "Glittering Gloria": ADELE RITCHIE. *Mrs. Jack James*, Jack's wife: ADELAIDE PRINCE. *Dorothy Kenworthy*, Archie's fiancée: PHYLLIS RANKIN. *Sarah*, maid to Gloria: May Hengler. *Herbert*, "Buttons," at Coddlesmere mansions: Flora Hengler. *Ariadne*: Marie L. Wilson. *Irene*: Gertrude Douglas. *Ethel*: Edna Farrell. *Kathleen*: Belva Don Kersley. *Rosamund*: Sybil Anderson. *Brenda*: Marie Allen.

Friends of Gloria, Passengers, Shoppers, etc: Misses F. Salber, Carol Oty, Sibyl Anderson, May Hopkins, Lottie Vernon, Katherine Black, Olive Haskell, Lotta Ettinger, Ethel Intropodi, Viola E. Clayton, Amy Forsland, Jessie Radcliffe.

The action takes place in London at the present time.

Act 1: Interior of Slapton & Shreve's Fashionable Jewelry Shop in Bond Street. Forenoon.

Act 2: Apartments of "Glittering Gloria" in Kensington. Afternoon of the following day.

Act 3: Luggage Room of the Euston Railway Station. The next morning.

MUSICAL NUMBERS[75]
"Glittering Glor-i-a"
A. Ritchie
"Laura Bell"
A. Ritchie
"The Hothouse on Broadway"
A. Ritchie
"Saphira"
C. Scott
"Little Mary"
C. Scott
"Cordelia (Malone)"[76]
E. O'Rourke
(*Music by* Jean Schwartz. *Lyrics by* William Jerome.)
"Tell Me Why, Why, Why"
P. Ames
"Margate Sands"
"Susan"
Isadore Rush
(*Music by* A. Baldwin Sloane. *Lyrics by* Edward S. Abeles.)
"When I Come Out of Here"
"No Wedding Bells for Her"
P. Rankin

1904.09 THE TENDERFOOT

An Operatic (Musical) Comedy in Three Acts. Book and lyrics by Richard Carle. Music by H. L. Heartz. Production staged by Richard Carle. Scenery by Sheppard and Slipper. Costumes by F. Shoultz & Company, Marshall Field & Company. Musical director, Fred J. Eustis. Produced by The Dearborn Theatre Management. Opened 22 February 1904 at the New York Theatre and closed 30 April 1904 after 81 performances.

CAST: *Professor Zachary Pettibone, L.L.D., B.A*: RICHARD CARLE. *Texas Rangers (5)*: *Colonel Paul Winthrop*: EDMUND STANLEY. *Sergeant Bill Barker*: CHARLES WAYNE. *Captain O'Reilly*: Dan J. Moyles. *Captain Vincent*: Edwin Baker. *Captain Todd*: Gwilym Edwards. *Honest John Martin*, gambler: Henry Norman. *Hop Lee*, servant: WILLIAM ROCK. *Reckless Reddy*, cowboy: H. S. Austin. *Bigg Bluff*: William Russell. *White Pill*, medicine man: Edward Beck. *Abe Splicer*, parson: Milton Baldwin. *Marion Worthington*, heiress: HELENA FREDERICK. *Sally*, maid: MARGARET SAYRE. *Flora Jane Fibby*, authoress: Agnes Paul. *Patsy*, waif: Ethel Johnson. *Seminary Girls (10)*: *Miss Gotham*: Louise Gardner. *Miss Narragansett*: Louise Grignon. *Miss Manhattan*: Virginia Neal. *Miss Asbury*: Ethel Kirkpatrick. *Miss Niagra*: Ella Fitch. *Miss Knickerbocker*: Adelaide Ackland. *Miss Newport*: Vilette Stanley. *Miss Amsterdam*: Dollie Williams. *Miss Cohasset*: Mabelle Smith. *Miss Nantucket*: Vena Brunk. *Rupert*: Himself.

Cow Boys: Messrs. Burns, Starr, Jenkins, Peters, Lyons, Farr, Beck. *Cow Girls*: Misses Conley, Cramer, Palmer, Allen, Cochran, Farrelly, Hamilton, Eastman, Lorena, Baldwin. *Mexicans*: Messrs. Beck, Austin, Baldwin, St. John, Rooney, Starr, Burns,

[73]No program available; songs not in performance order.

[74]Played a return engagement 4 April 1904 at the Grand Opera House for 8 performances. No credits on programs for stage directory, scenery, costumes, or musical director.

[75]Musical numbers not listed in programs.

[76]Perhaps an adaptation of these authors' successful hit song "Bedelia" introduced in THE JERSEY LILY.

Locke, Jenkins, Peters, Lyons, Farr, Harry Tolin, Tom Gippel, George M. Bogues, Edwin Mack. *Mexican Girls*: Misses Adams, Elliott, White, Castle, Mazurette, Pearl, Stanley, Dalroy, Huntington, Cordelia. *Texas Rangers*: Messrs. Beck, Austin, Baldwin, St. John, Rooney, Starr, Burns, Locke, Jenkins, Peters, Lyons, Farr, 4 other men. *Bridesmaids*: Misses Adams, Elliott, White, Castle, Mazurette, Pearl, Stanley, Dalroy, Huntington, Cordelia, Conley, Cramer, Palmer, Allen, Cochran, Farrelly, Hamilton, Eastman, Lorena, Baldwin. *Soldiers*: Misses Grigarou, Gardner, Neat, Kirkpatrick, Fitch, Ackland, Stanley, Williams, Brunk, Smith, Adams, Elliott, White, White, Mazurette, Pearl, Stanley, Dalroy, Huntington, Cordelia, Conley, Cramer, Palmer, Allen, Cochran, Farrelly, Hamilton, Eastman, Lorena, Baldwin. Adams, Elliott, White, Castle, Mazurette, Pearl, Dalroy, Huntington, Cordelia, Kirkpatrick, Grigarou.

Act 1: Courtyard of the house on Marion Worthington's ranch. Afternoon.

Act 2: Interior of the ranch barn. Evening.

Act 3: An Indian camping ground. Morning a week later.

ACT 1

"Washing Song"
W. Rock

"Texas Rangers"
Male Chorus

"Marriage Is a Lottery"
A. Paul, H. Norman

"A Gay Lothario"
C. Wayne, Male Chorus

"I'm a Peaceable Party"
R. Carle, Seminary Girls

"Only a Kiss" (Entrance of Mexicans, Cow Girls, and a Song)
H. Frederick, Chorus

"The Soldiery"
M. Sayre, Chorus

"A Soldier of Fortune"
E. Stanley

Finale

ACT 2

Opening Chorus

Dance
E. Johnson, W. Rock

"Love Is Elusive"[77]
H. Frederick

"My Alamo Love"
R. Carle, Chorus

"Adios"
E. Stanley

"The Tortured Thomas Cat"
R. Carle, C. Wayne, H. Norman, Misses Cramer, Palmer, Lorena

Finale

ACT 3

Opening Chorus

"Dancing"
E. Johnson, M. Sayre, C. Wayne, R. Carle

Finale

1904.10 THE YANKEE CONSUL

A Comic Opera in Two Acts. Book and lyrics by Henry M. Blossom. Music by Alfred G. Robyn. Staged by George Marion. Settings by Walter Burridge, Edward LaMoss. Costumes by Will R. Barnes. Orchestra under the direction of Frank N. Darling. Produced by Henry W. Savage. Opened 22 February 1904 at the Broadway Theatre and closed 2 July 1904 after 115 performances[78].

CAST: *Don Rafael Deschado*, Governor of Puerto Plata: WILLIAM DANFORTH. *Herr Gebubler*, his secretary: JOHN E. HAZZARD. *Captain Leopoldo* of the Dominican Army: HUBERT WILKE. *Lieutenant Jack Morrell*, commanding U.S. Gunboat *"Vixen"*: HARRY FAIRLEIGH. *Carlos*, water carrier: Parker Coombs. *Sancho*, proprietor of Los Dos Toros restaurant: Frank Ranney. *Nunez*, chef of Los Dos Toros restaurant: Albert Juhre. *Felipo*, telegraph operator: J. H. McLean. *Rodrigo, Miguel*, local officers under Leopoldo, Local Army: Basil Millspaugh. John Pratt. *Donna Teresa Rebera-y Uruburu*, a wealthy widow: EVA DAVENPORT. *Bonita*, her daughter: FLORA ZABELLE. *Papinta*, her neice: ROSE BOTTI. *Blanca*, a bar maid: Sally McNeel. *Inez*, Sancho's wife: Estrella Carmichael. *Juanita*, a flower girl: Adelaide Orton. *Estrella*, a fruit girl: May Wheeler. *Friends of the Girls (7)*: *Anita*: Mae Darling. *Jacinta*: Lila Conquest. *Francesca*: Madge Burpee. *Panilla*: Lillian Eldredge. *Maria*: Sophie Witte. *Leonora*: M. C. Flavin. *Bella*: Gertrude O'Neill. *Abijah Booze*, American Consul in Puerto Plata: RAYMOND HITCHCOCK.

Spanish Students: Misses Conquest, Fairbanks, O'Neill, Merritt, Marsh, Proctor, Wallace, Desmond. *Mosquito Girls*: Misses Turten, Fallon, Dunne, Welch, Botti, Marshall, Fredericksen, Burt. *Senoritas*: Misses Freda Rica, M. Burpee, Darling, L. Burpee, Eldredge, Flavin, Witte, Carmichael, McNeel, Vance, Chandler, Carroll, Wheeler, Shaw, Eckstrom, Simpson, Croker. *Spanish Dancers*: Misses Flavin, S. Witte, L. Whitte, Eldredge. *Soldiers*: Messrs. Addison, Templeton, Remy, Jenkins, Green, Armour, Books, Hanlon, Wallace, DeCourcey, Purvionce, Owen. *Senors*: Messrs. Pugh, Seley, Peck, Colishaw.

The action takes place in Puerto Plata, Santo Domingo, at the present time.

Act 1: A public square in Puerto Plata. The Fiesta Forenoon. (Burridge.)

Act 2: Exterior of Governor's Mansion. The Governor's Ball. Night of the same day. (LaMoss.)

ACT 1

"Viva, the Gay Fiesta" (Opening Chorus)

"The Hammers Will Go Rap, Rap, Rap"
W. Danforth, Chorus

"(Ye Ho!) Oh Glad Is the Life of a Sailor at Sea"
H. Fairleigh, Chorus

"In Old New York"
R. Hitchcock, Chorus

"Hola!" (Entrance Song)(Bolero)
F. Zabelle, Chorus

"I'd Like to Be a Soldier" (Military Duet)
H. Wilke, R. Botti, Chorus

"We Were Taught To Walk Demurely" (Trio)
F. Zabelle, R. Botti, E. Davenport

"Cupid Has Found My Heart" (Ballad)
H. Fairleigh

"Tell Me"[79] (Duet)
H. Fairleigh, F. Zabelle

Finale

ACT 2

"Gossip's Chorus"
Eight Girls

"The Mosquito and the Midge"
R. Botti, Chorus of Girls

"Ain't It Funny What a Difference Just a Few Hours Make"
R. Hitchcock

"My San Domingo Maid"
F. Zabelle, Chorus

"We Come of Castilian Blood" (Male Chorus)
H. Wilke, Twelve Soldiers

Ensemble Number (includes San Domingo Dance by Miss Anne St. Tel.)

"In the Days of Old"
R. Hitchcock, Chorus

Finale

1904.11 A PAIR OF PINKS

An Offering of Music and Fun (a Musical Comedy) in Two Acts. Music and lyrics by Bob Adams and James O'Dea. Staged by Joseph C. Smith. Musical director, Emil Bierman. Produced by E. D. Stair. Opened 7 March 1904 at the 58th Street Theatre and closed 12 March 1904 after 9 performances.[80]

---

[77]Replaced after opening by:
"Fascinating Venus"
H. Frederick

[78]Played a return engagement 24 January 1905 at Wallack's Theatre for 47 performances; see separate entry below in following season.

[79]Dropped during the run.

[80]Book uncredited; no credits for scenery or costumes. The following year a revised version of A PAIR OF PINKS, with music by Fred Schwartz, lyrics by Will West and Harry Vokes, toured Wilkes-Barre, etc.

CAST: *Percy Barr Gaites, Harold Bolton Sells*, a pair of Pinkerton Detectives: HAP WARD, HARRY VOKES. *Ikey Lock*, Ayer's gatekeeper: CHARLES HOWARD. *Billion Ayer*, the richest man on earth: TONY WILLIAMS. *Fuller Ayer*, Ayer's son: David DeWolf. *Mons. Fibber*, Ayer's liar: Gus Bruno. *Tuft Nut*, Ayer's burglar: Lou Miller. *Thomas*, Ayer's butler: DAN COLEMAN. *Kidder Little*, Ayer's Too: DAN COLEMAN. *Bell Boy*, Fuller Ayer's valet: EDDIE JUDGE. *Bell Boy*, Ayer's "hurry up": EDDIE JUDGE. *Dunn Brown*, Ayer's friend: Harry Hemenway. *Messenger Boy*, Ayer's limit: E. J. Gunther.

Among those present: *Mister Train*: Lewis Powers. *Mister Carr*: Willie Daly. *Mister Cabb*: Walter Pearson. *Mister Lotz*: Edward Mumford. *Mister Chance*: William Phillips. *Mister Fortune*: Richard Barry. *Mister Friend*: George Johnson. *Mag Knette*, Ayer's 'scrub-lady': MARGARET DALY VOKES. *Bon Ayer*, Ayer's daughter: VINIE DALY. *Carry Ayer*, Ayer's latest wife: Helen Norton. *Mrs. Dunn Brown*, Ayer's Waterloo: Florence Hawkins. *Ophelia Way*, Ayer's society actress: Celeste Carter.

Some Social Problems: *Miss Underwood*: Corinne Charles. *Miss Judge*: Florence Phillips. *Miss Doubt*: Rose Williams. *Miss Trust*: Alma Bauer. *Miss Fortune*: Bessie Stewart. *Miss Fitz*: Emily Frost. *Miss Fashion*: Bertha Silsby. *Miss Form*: Alice Mayo. *Miss Print*: Katherine Gould. *Miss Quote*: Neva Ellis. *Miss De Votion*: Dottie Wilson. *Miss Chief*: Donna Foster. *Miss Stepp*: Lettie West. *Miss Govern*: Maud Bredell. *Miss Place*: Rose Bird. *Miss Happ*: Madge Mason. *Miss Shape*: Helen Duval. *Miss Deed*: Tillie Gorman. *Miss Take*: Eva Fox.

Charlotte Russe, just the right flavor: LUCY DALY. (*Dance Specialty*: Joseph C. Smith.)

ACT 1

"Just For a Day" (Opening Chorus)
Company

"When Linda Smiles"
D. Coleman, Male Chorus

"The Maiden I Left in Hong Kong"
L. Daly, Chorus

"It's Best Not to Say Too Much About It"
M. D. Vokes, Company

"Root"
H. Ward, H. Vokes, L. Daly, V. Daly

"Flirting with the Bees"
M. D. Vokes, C. Howard

"Pimlico Malinda"
H. Ward, V. Daly, Chorus

"On Our Honeymoon"
C. Howard

"The Sweetest Girl in Dixie" (Finale)
L. Daly, V. Daly, M. D. Vokes, Dixie Girls

ACT 2

"Cupid's Fancies" (Opening Chorus)

"If I Had You"
E. Mumford, Chorus

"Reuben and Betsy"
M. D. Vokes, E. Judge, Chorus

"Aerial Waltz"
V. Daly, J. C. Smith

Medley Finale
Entire Company

1904.12 A CHINESE HONEYMOON

A Revival of the Musical Play in Two Acts[81]. Book and lyrics by George Dance. Music by Howard Talbot. Staged by Gerald Coventry. Settings by D. Frank Dodge. Costumes by Caroline Seidle. Orchestra under the direction of Alexander Spencer. Orchestrations by Gustave Kerker. Produced by Sam S. Shubert and (Sam) Nixon and (J. F.) Zimmerman. Opened 7 March 1904 at the Academy of Music and closed 2 April 1904 after 31 performances.

CAST: *Mr. Samuel Pineapple*: FRED W. MACE. *Hang Chow*, Emperor of Ylang-Ylang: GEORGE BRODERICK. *Chippie Chop*, Lord Chancellor: JOSEPH E. MILLER. *Hi Lung*, Lord High Admiral: WILLIAM PRUETTE. *Tom Hatherton*: BENJAMIN HOWARD. *Mrs. Pineapple*: JULIA SANDERSON. *Mrs. Pineapple's Bridesmaids (8)*: *Florrie*: Gertrude Wallace. *Millie*: Frances Darrington. *Gertie*: Helen Morrison. *Violet*: Rose Wilson. *Beatrice*: Florence Worden. *Margaret*: Regina McAvoy. *Frances*: Charlotte Palmer. *Gwendolin*: Edna Hixon. *Princess Soo Soo*, the Emperor's niece: MAY DeSOUSA. *Yen Yen, Sing Sing*, Soo Soo's maids of honor: Gene Luneska, Eveleen Dunmore. *Mi Mi*, a waitress: Marie Louise Gribbon. *Mrs Brown*, the official mother-in-law: (Emma) MABELLA BAKER. *Fi Fi*, waitress at the hotel: KATIE BARRY. *Chinese Maidens, Tea Girls, Chinamen, Sailors, Courtiers, etc.*

1904.13 THE WIZARD OF OZ

A Return Engagement (Second Edition, or Edition DeLuxe) of the Musical Play in Three Acts, 7 Scenes[82]. Book and lyrics by L. Frank Baum. Based on his own novel "The Wonderful Wizard of Oz." Music by Paul Tietjens and A. Baldwin Sloane. Staged by Julian Mitchell. Settings by Walter Burridge, Fred Gibson, John Young. Orchestra under the direction of Charles Zimmerman. Produced by Fred R. Hamlin[83]. Opened 21 March 1904 at the Majestic Theatre, moved 2 May 1904 to the New York Theatre and closed 21 May 1904 after 72 performances[84].

CAST (in order of appearance): *Dorothy Gale*, a Kansas girl, the victim of a cyclone: ANNA LAUGHLIN. *The Cow named Imogene*, Dorothy's playmate: JOSEPH SCHRODE. *Golfman*: George Fields. *Farmhands*: Misses Fisher, Donalson, Burnell, Von Brune, Costello, Townsend, Moffatt, Gerard, Diamond, Wilton, Arnold. Messrs. Christian, Cleveland, Devlin, Young. *Munchkins (8)*: *Tommie Top*: Anna Fitzhugh. *Peter Pop*: Elizabeth Young. *Simon Slick*: Emily Fulton. *Antonia*: Sadie Emmons. *Sophronia*: Ella Gilroy. *Premonia*: Lillian DeVere. *Malvonia*: Stubby Ainscoe. *Semponia*: Josephine Clayton. *Munchkin Youths*: Misses Clara Selton, May DuFrene, May Gunderman, M. DeVere, Emma Clark, Nellie Lane, Helen Turner, Virginia Kendall, Osia Thompson. Messrs. Steele, Bingham, Diskins, Hoskins, Nichols, West. *Munchin Maidens*: Misses Merle Mathey, Anna Leslie, Laura Young, Minna Doerge, Edna Leach, Nancy Crawford, Lola Gordon, Nellie Payne, Beatrice Gilbert. *Cynthia Cynch*, the lady lunatic, a Munchkin maiden: ALLENE CRATER. *The Witch of the North*: Albertina Bensen. *Sir Dashemoff Daily*, Poet laureate: MAY DeSOUSA. *The Army of Pastoria*: Earl Dewey. *Pastoria II*, ex-King of the Emerald City, with a conspiracy to regain his throne: OWEN WESTFORD. *Tryxie Tryffle*, prospective Queen of the Emerald City: LOTTA FAUST. *Brigadier General Riskitt*, commanding Pastoria's army: HAROLD P. MOREY. *The Scarecrow*, looking for brains: FRED A. STONE. *The Cowardly Lion*: Arthur Hill. *Mick Chopper*, the Tin Woodman in search of a heart: DAVID C. MONTGOMERY. *Sir Wiley Gyle*, a conspirator who scorns all magical arts: Stephen Maley. *The Poppy Queen*: Josephine Clayton. *Poppy Flowers*: Misses Moffat, Fisher, Townsend, Leslie, Leach, Gunderman, Gerard, Dean, Clark, Von Brune, Lane, Gilbert, Diamond, Burnell, Gordon, Selton, Young, Blye, Kendall, DuFrene, Costello, Arnold, Thompson, Doerge, Donalson. *Snow Queen*: Nellie Payne. *Snow Boys*: Ella Gilroy, Lillian DeVere, Marie Mathey, Anna Fitzhugh, Emily Fulton. *Snow Girls*: Elizabeth Young, Sadie Emmons, M. DeVere, Helen Wilton. *Leo*, Captain of the Relief Guards: George B. Field. *Captain of the Patrol*: Sadie Emmons. *The Patrol*: Misses Gerard, Lane, Donalson, Dean, Thompson, Costello, Gunderman, Arnold, Diamond, Von Brune, Clark, Kendall, Fisher, Turner. *Alonzo*, the Wizard's Confederate: EARL DEWEY. *The Wizard's Wise Men (4)*: *Silicus*: H. Devlin. *Sophocles*: F. Kelsee. *Pericles*: Irving H. Christian. *Diogenes*: Charles Hoskins. *Bardo*, the Wizard's factotum: Ella Gilroy. *Oz*, the Wonderful Wizard, Past Master of Magic, ruler of the Emerald City and Potentate of the Land of Oz: CHARLES SWAIN. *Alberto*, Officer of the Day: Sadie Emmons. *Waitresses (8)*: *Gloriana Jane*: Nancy Crawford. *Violet Victoria*: M. DeVere. *Gladys Ann*: Ella Gilroy. *Leontine Em*: Emily Fulton. *Vera Ellen*: Lillian DeVere. *Aileen Nance*: Elizabeth Young. *Pansy Lil*: Josephine Clayton. *Lavinia Loo*: Lolo Gordon. *Cooks (8)*: *Claude Cliquot*: Nellie Payne. *Alphonse Fripon*: Osie Thompson. *Marcel Moreau*: Stubby Ainscoe. *Louis LeBeau*: Vernon Arnold. *Francois Giblets*: May DuFrene. *Jean DeChar*: Anna Fitzhugh. *Remnante Saute*: Marie Clayton. *Pungue DeSert*: Edna Leach. *Laundresses*: Misses Gilbert, Gunderman, Burnell, Wilton, Thompson, Von Brune, Costello, Doerge, Leslie, Mathey, Moffat, Fisher. *Royal Guards*: Misses Townsend, Turner, Donalson, Kendall, Selton, Diamond, Young, Gerard, Dean, Clark, Lane.

Act 1, Scene 1: A Kansas Farm. (Painted by Fred Gibson from designs by Walter W. Burridge). *Scene 2*: Transformation. The Country of the Munchkins. (Young). *Scene 3*: The Road through the Forest. (Young). *Scene 4*: The Poppy Field. (Young). *Scene 5*: The Poppy Field in Winter. (Young).

Act 2: The Courtyard of the Wizard's Palace. (Burridge).

Act 3: The Borderland, dividing the Kingdom of Oz from the Dominions of the Good Witch. (Young).

[81]First produced in New York 2 June 1902 at the Casino Theatre for 376 performances. For Synopsis of Scenes and Musical Numbers, see original 1902 production.

[82]First edition produced in New York 20 January 1903 at the Majestic Theatre for 293 performances. For Synopsis of Scenes and Musical Numbers, see original 1903 production.

[83]After Hamlin's death 27 November 1904, Julian Mitchell and William Gray assumed production credit and responsibility for the ongoing tour. Production rights were sub-contracted to Hurtig & Seamon in November 1906.

[84]Played New York return engagements 7 November-31 December 1904 at the Academy of Music for 66 performances, and 30 October-25 November 1905 at the Academy of Music for 33 performances.

ACT 1[85]
"Life in Kansas" (Opening)
(*Music by* Paul Tietjens.)
"Nicolo's Piccolo"
A. Crater
(*Music by* A. Baldwin Sloane. *Lyrics by* Glen MacDonough.)
"The Tale of the Cassowary"[86] (The Tale of a Monkey)
A. Crater
(*Music by* Gus Edwards. *Lyrics by* Will D. Cobb.)
"Down on the Brandywine"[87] (Duet)
L. Faust, O. Westford
(*Music by* J. B. Mullen. *Lyrics by* Vincent Bryan.)
"Carry Barry" (Carrie Barry)
A. Laughlin
(*Music by* A. Baldwin Sloane. *Lyrics by* Glen MacDonough.)
"Alas for the Man Without Brains" (Scarecrow)
F. A. Stone
(*Music by* Paul Tietjens.)
"I Love You All the Time"[88]
M. DeSousa
(*Music and Lyrics by* W. Anderson.)
"Mary Canary"[89]
M. DeSousa
(*Music by* Seymour Furth. *Lyrics by* Edward P. Moran.)
"When You Love, Love, Love"
F. A. Stone, D. C. Montgomery, A. Laughlin
(*Music by* Paul Tietjens.)
"Poppy Chorus"
(*Music by* Paul Tietjens.)

ACT 2[90]
"The Tale of the Red Shirt"[91]
C. Swain
(*Music and Lyrics by* Brackett and Medor.)
"It's Enough to Make a Perfect Lady Mad"[92] ('Twas Enough to Make a Perfect Lady Mad)
A. Crater
(*Music by* J. B. Mullen. *Lyrics by* Vincent Bryan.)
Medley: Dance of All Nations (Ball of All Nations)[93]
(*Music by* A. Baldwin Sloane. *Lyrics by* Edgar Smith.)
"Connemara Christening" (Irish Song)
C. Swain
(*Music by* A. Baldwin Sloane. *Lyrics by* Edgar Smith.)
"Gooda-bye, Fedora"[94]
F. A. Stone
(*Music by* Robert J. Adams. *Lyrics by* Harry H. Williams.)
"Wee-High and Mon" (Wee Highland Mon)(Scotch Song)
D. C. Montgomery
"Under a Panama"
A. Laughlin
(*Music by* J. B. Mullen. *Lyrics by* Vincent Bryan.)
"An Afternoon Tea" (Dance)
F. A. Stone, D. C. Montgomery, A. Laughlin
"Johnnie, I'll Take You"[95]
L. Faust
(*Music by* Gus Edwards. *Lyrics by* Will D. Cobb.)
"I Never Loved a Love as I Love You"[96]
M. DeSousa
(*Music by* Gus Edwards. *Lyrics by* Will D. Cobb.)
"The Nightmare"[97] (Duet)
F. A. Stone, D. C. Montgomery
(*Music by* J. B. Mullen. *Lyrics by* Vincent Bryan.)
"I'd Like to Go Halves in That"[98]
F. A. Stone, D. C. Montgomery
(*Music by* David C. Montgomery.)
Finale

ACT 3
"The Traveler and the Pie"
F. A. Stone
(*Music by* Paul Tietjens.)
"Must You"
D. C. Montgomery
"The Sweetest Girl in Dixie"[99]
A. Laughlin
(*Music by* Bob Adams. *Lyrics by* James O'Dea.)

1904.14 THE AWAKENING OF MR. PIPP

A Musical Farce in Three Acts, 5 Scenes. Book, music and lyrics by George Totten Smith and Charley Grapewin[100]. Staged under the direction of Fred Wayne. Musical director, John Kurkamp. Management, Samuel L. Tuck. Opened 21 March 1904 at the 14th Street Theatre and closed 26 March 1904 after 8 performances; returned 1 May 1905 to the Murray Hill Theatre for an additional 9 performances.[101]

CAST (in order of appearance): *Fat*, a butcher boy: Luke Sylvester. *Dropsy*, a poor relative of Mr. Pipp: LOUISE GALLOWAY. *Mugsy*, a messenger boy: AL. W. MADDOX. *Adam Payne*, the man-about-town: C. Al. Clarke. *Mrs. Hebe Payne*, Pipp's mother-in-law: Amie L. Travis. *Mrs. Pipp*, Pipp's better half: ANNA CHANCE. *Florrie Payne*, Pipp's sister-in-law: BEATRICE RAY. *Reggie Payne*, Pipp's brother-in-law: FRED WAYNE. *Tom Murray*, Reggie's chum: JULES C. REIFF. *Jack Edwards*, Reggie's chum: GEORGE W. REIFF. *Mr. Pipp*, a lawyer: CHARLEY GRAPEWIN. *Tony*, a bootblack: Frank Owen. *Jimmy*, a newsboy: George Donaldson. *Big Bill*, a

---

[85]Added to Act 1 for subsequent tour in Chicago:
"Only You"
Virginia Foltz {Sir Daily Dashemoff}
(*Music by* Charles Zimmerman. *Lyrics by* Frank Keesee.)
"When the Heart Is Sad"
V. Foltz
(*Music by* Charles Zimmerman. *Lyrics by* ? Hollister.)

[86]Not in first version.

[87]Not in first version.

[88]Not in first version.

[89]Not in first version.

[90]Added to the production's Act 2 for subsequent tour, 1905: (all songs after Dance of All Nations dropped)
"Julie Dooley" (after Opening, "Phantom Patrol")
James K. Wesley {Wizard}
(*Music by* Joe Howard.)
"The Tale of a Stroll" (after Dance of All Nations Medley)
Marion Stanley {Tryxie}
(*Music by* Byrd Dougherty. *Lyrics by* George Totten Smith.)
"My Own Girl" (following above)
V. Foltz
(*Music by* Gus Edwards.)
"Football" (follows above)
F. A. Stone, D. C. Montgomery
(*Music by* Charles Zimmerman.)
"Marching Through Port Arthur" (follows above)
F. A. Stone, D. C. Montgomery
(*Music by* Charles Zimmerman.)
Added to touring production in 1905, as per published sheet music:
"Can't You See I'm Lonely"
M. Stanley
(*Music by* Harry Armstrong. *Lyrics by* Felix Feist.)

[91]Not in first version.

[92]Not in first version.

[93]Dropped for 1905 tour were "Goodbye, Fedora," "Under a Panama" and "An Afternoon Tea." Added to Dance of All Nations for 1905 tour:
"Sitting Bull" (Indian Song); "Green Corn Dance"
F. A. Stone
(*Music by* Charles Zimmerman.)

[94]Not in first version.

[95]Not in first version.

[96]Not in first version.

[97]Not in first version.

[98]Not in first version.

[99]Not in first version.

[100]According to critics, the book was adapted from a successful vaudeville sketch of the same name performed by Charley Grapewin and Anna Chance.

[101]No program available from the first New York engagement. Song list prepared from return engagement. No credits for scenery, costumes or producer. By late 1906 Wells, Dunne and Harlan were billed as producers on tour.

policeman: Tom Craven. *"Kid" Curtis*: Clarence Prouty. *Miss Ables*: Irena Golden. *Miss Caine*, her friend: Burleigh Murray. *Tessie Tiptoe*, from the Jollity Theatre: NELLIE BEAUMONT. *Professor Carter*, one of Dore's patrons: Frederick Clarenze. *Ida Nough*, his friend: Joyce Thorne. *Hadda Nuff*, his friend: Mabel Melvin. *Paul*, his friend: John Burns. *William*, waiter at Dore's: Arthur Curtis. *Max*, waiter at Dore's: Chris Allworth. *Henry*, waiter at Dore's: George Donaldson. *Miss Greene*: Isabel Arlington. *Miss White*: Angie Quaid. *The Intruder*: Charles Morton. *Brown*: John Burns. *Smith*: Charles Prouty. *Lizzie Johnson*, from Boston: Lizzie McCall. *Nora*: Lizzie McCall.

Act 1, Scene 1: Pipp's garden. 6 P.M. *Scene 2*: Exterior of Dore's Restaurant. 9 P.M. *Scene 3*: Interior of Dore's restaurant, 11:30 P.M.

Act 2: Pipp's sleeping apartments, 6 A.M. the following morning.

Act 3: Reception room. Pipp's house, ten days later.

ACT 1[102]

"The Races" (Song and Chorus)
Company
(*Music by* Theodore Winthrop.)

"(It's) Pie" (Song and Chorus)
C. Grapewin, Company
(*Music by* Theodore Winthrop.)

Song
C. Grapewin

ACT 2[103]

"When the Brass Band Played" (Song and Chorus)
N. Beaumont, Company

Pantomime Juggling
C. Grapewin

"You'll Be Sorry in the Morning"
C. Grapewin, Company

ACT 3

"Blue Bell" (Song)
L. Galloway, A. W. Maddox

"The Old Oaken Bucket for Mine" (Song)
C. Grapewin
(*Music by* George Nichols. *Lyrics by* George Toffen Smith.)

"Callie" (Song)
N. Beaumont, Company

"I Can Think Of Nothing Else But You, Lou" (Song)
A. Chance

1904.15 PIFF! PAFF!! POUF!!!

A Musical Cocktail (Comedy) in Two Acts. Book by Stanislaus Stange. Music by Jean Schwartz. Lyrics by William Jerome. Staged by Gerard Coventry. Dances by Gus Sohlke. Settings by (Homer) Emens and (Edward G.) Unitt. Costumes by Mme. Caroline Seidle. Electrical effects by Joseph Menchen. Orchestra under the direction of John Sebastian Hiller. Orchestrations by Frank Saddler. Produced by F. C. Whitney. Opened 2 April 1904 at the Casino Theatre and closed 19 November 1904 after 264 performances[104].

CAST (in order of appearance): *Dick Daily*: Maurice Darcy. *Lord George Piffle*: TEMPLAR SAXE. *Macaroni Paffle*: JOHN HYAMS. *Bedelia*: Abby Stange. *August Melon*: JOSEPH C. MIRON. *Mrs. Lillian Montague*: ALICE FISCHER. *(His Daughters, 4)*: *Nora Melon*: MABEL HOLLINS. *Cora Melon*: GRACE CAMERON. *Encora Melon*: HILDA HOLLINS. *Rose Melon*: AMELIA STONE. *Peter Pouffle*: EDDIE FOY. *Joe Silver*: George Wiseman. *The Original English Pony Ballet (8)*: *Miss Cotton*: Evelyn Marlowe. *Miss Slow*: Beatrice Liddell. *Miss Turtle*: Seppie McNeil. *Miss Delaware*: Lizette Hawman. *Miss Bacon*: Dorothy Marlowe. *Miss Bean*: Louise Hawman. *Miss West*: Carrie Poltz. *Miss Trust*: Ada Robertson.

Easter Girls: Misses Martin, Hahn, Mandeville, Walton, Clayton, Bruce, LeRoy, Griffith. *Bathing Girls*: Misses Goodyear, Darcy, Maloney, Dean, Moore, Crane, Cornish, Wallace, Dudley, Striblen. *Busters*: Misses Falconer, Wharton, Howard, Rohe, Carroll, Scott, Mooney, Walton, Hammond, Hoyt. *Johnnies*: Messrs. Chase, Arnold, Hollingsworth, Slick, Mora, Ireland, Rose, Breslin, Evans, Craig.

Act 1: Board Walk, Atlantic City. In front of the Casino, East time.

Act 2: Grounds of Mrs. Montague's house, "Fairmount-on-Hudson."

ACT 1[105]

"Under Our Lovely Umbrellas" (Opening Chorus)
Chorus

"I Have Interviewed the Wide, Wide World"[106]
M. Darcy, Chorus

"(The) Melancholy Sunbeam and the Rose"
T. Saxe, Chorus

"M.A.C.A.R.O.N.I."
J. Hyams, Chorus

"I Don't Want Any Wurtzberger"
J. Miron, Bathing Girls

"We Really Ought to Be Married" (We Really Ought to Get Married)
A. Fischer, A. Stone, G. Cameron, H. Hollins, M. Hollins, J. Miron

"Under the Goo Goo Tree"
M. Hollins, Easter Girls, Chorus
(*Lyrics by* William Jerome and Stanislaus Stange.)

"Dear Old Manhattan Isle"
J. Miron, Chorus

"Pixie's Entrance"
E. Foy, Pony Ballet

"The Ghost That Never Walked"
E. Foy, Pony Ballet

"My Unkissed Man"
A. Stone
(*Lyrics by* William Jerome and Stanislaus Stange.)

Finale

ACT 2[107]

Opening Chorus

"Good Night, My Own Love"
T. Saxe, Chorus
(*Lyrics by* William Jerome and Stanislaus Stange.)

"Love, Love, Love"
A. Stone, Summer Girls and Boys

"Lutie"
J. Hyams, Chorus

"Barney Donohue"[108]
M. Hollins, Chorus

"I'm So Happy"
E. Foy

"Radium Dance"
Pony Ballet

"Dolly Dimples" (Since Dolly Dimples Made a Hit)
G. Cameron, Chorus

---

[102]Songs added later in the tour (September 1906):

"Ida-ho"
Bessie Kyle [Tessie Tiptoe], the Bucking Broncos

"U.S.A."
Loretta Marshal, Max Reynolds [Dropsy, Muggsy)

"Take Me Back to Paree"
B. Kyle, the Bucking Broncos

[103]According to opening night reviews, also performed (probably as opening of Act 2):

"The Loves of Mary Ann"
N. Beaumont

[104]Played a return engagement 26 December 1904 at the Majestic Theatre for 8 performances. Among the principals, Robert E. Graham replaced Joseph C. Miron as August Melon, Vinie Daly replaced Grace Cameron as Cora Melon, and Blanche Morrison replaced Amelia Stone as Rose Melon. For this engagement, "Love, Love, Love" was dropped from Act 2 and replaced by "My Unkissed Man" from Act 1. In place of "My Unkissed Man" in Act 1 was added the following:

"Waltzing with Jane"
Vinie Daly [Cora Malone}, J. Hyams

[105]During the run, the running order of songs was revised, especially Act 2. Added late in run or for tour, as per published sheet music:

"I Caught You Making Eyes"
Vonnie Hoyt
(*Music by* Richard Tragman. *Lyrics by* Charles H. Lynch.)

[106]Dropped after opening.

[107]Added during the run to Act 2, after "Good Night, My Own True Love:"

"Cordelia Malone" (from GLITTERING GLORIA)
J. C. Miron, Chorus
(*Music by* Jean Schwartz. *Lyrics by* William Jerome. *Staged by* Gus Sohlke.)

[108]Dropped after opening.

"For You"
J. Miron
"March of the Flags"
Principals, Chorus
Grand Finale
Ensemble

1904.16 THE PRINCE OF PILSEN

A Revival of the Musical Comedy in Two Acts[109]. Book and lyrics by Frank Pixley. Music by Gustav Luders. Staged by George Marion. Scenery by Walter Burridge. Costumes by Will R. Barnes. Orchestra under the direction of Gustav Luders. Produced by Henry W. Savage. Opened 4 April 1904 at Daly's Theatre and closed 30 April 1904 after 32 performances.

CAST: *Carl Otto*, the Prince of Pilsen, a student at Heidelberg: ARTHUR DONALDSON. *Hans Wagner*, a Cincinnati brewer, traveling abroad: JOHN W. RANSONE. *Lieutenant Tom Wagner*, of the U.S. Cruiser "Annapolis": ALBERT PARR. *Arthur St. John Wilberforce*, Lord Somerset: VICTOR MORLEY. *Francois*, Concierge, Hotel Internationale: Sherman Wade. *Cook's Courier*, Vassar Girl's pilot: Madison Smith. *Sergeant Brie*, of the Gendarmes: Madison Smith. *Jimmy*, a bell boy: Eva Westcott. *Mrs. Madison Crocker*, from New York: TRIXIE FRIGANZA. *Edith Adams*, a Vassar girl: ISOBEL HALL. *Sidonie*, Mrs. Crockers' French maid: Mattie Nichols. *Nellie Wagner*, Hans Wagner's daughter: MADELINE BEASLEY.

The Heidelberg Boys (8): *Rudolph*: William Stenberg. *Adolph*: Louis Lewis. *Heirich*: Linford R. Jefferson. *Fritz*: Albert Whitney. *Ludwig*: Charles Wilson. *Carl*: T. Henry Coote. *Oscar*: Fred Randall. *Wilhelm*: Nelson Hall.

The American Girls (9): *Frankie Friskie*, San Francisco: Mabel Wilber. *Dolly Dixie*, New Orleans: Idora Porter. *Priscilla Plymouth*, Boston: Margaret Magrath. *Pansy Penn*, Philadelphia: Bessie Clifton. *Missy Rivers*, St. Louis: Ida Stanhope. *Illie Noyes*, Chicago: Mabel Spencer. *Olive Oriole*, Baltimore: Eula Jensen. *Goldie Dome*, Washington: Nell Adams. *Mazie Manhattan*, New York: Camille Clifford.

Making the Grand Tour (4): *See Allott*: Mazie Follette. *Pleasant Daze*: Mildred Kearney. *Charmie Tyme*: Inez Marcel. *Lottie Towers*: Bessie Friganza.

The Sea Shell Grls: *White Capps*: Meta Caldwell. *Pearlie Beach*: Jeannette Patison. *Weedie Sea*: Grace Ballou. *Daisie Dolphin*: Lillian Hollis. *Birdie Petrel*: Helen Scanlan. *Coralie Shell*: Irene Zipsy. *Lottie Fogge*: Florence Holmes. *Pleasant Sayle*: Hattie Hamilton. *Brinie Deep*: Carrie Deming. *Calmie Waters*: Essie Engel. *Foamie Crest*: M. Watkins. *Stormie Waves*: Nellie Emerald.

1904.17 WANG

The DeWolf Hopper Company in a Revival of the Comic Opera (Musical Comedy) in Two Acts[110]. Libretto by J. Cheever Goodwin. Music by Woolson Morse. Staged by Sam S. Shubert. Produced by Sam S. Shubert. Opened 18 April 1904 at the Lyric Theatre and closed 4 June 1904 after 57 performances.

CAST: *Wang*, Regent of Siam: DeWOLF HOPPER. *Colonel Robert Fracasse*, military instructor Siam troops: WILLIAM PRUETTE. *Pepat*, Keeper of the sacred elephant: FRANK CASEY. *Lieutenant Jean Boucher* of the French garrison: DONALD MacLAREN. *Papanti*, Professor of Deportment: Augustus Coletti. *Chow Sury*, innkeeper: George Williams. *Panopim*, Cambodian envoy: Frank Hill. *Mataya*, Crown Prince of Siam: MADGE LESSING. *Le Veuve Frimouse*, widow of French Consul of Pechabury: MARION SINGER. *Marie*, her stepdaughter: NELLA BERGEN. *Gillette*, her eldest daughter: JULIA SANDERSON. *Nanette*, her youngest daughter: Helen Mooney.

More Daughters (8): *Babette*: Edna Hixon. *Claifette*: Frances Darrington. *Fleurette*: Rose Wilson. *Minette*: Lucy Giorgi. *Julie*: Maud Stanley. *Coralie*: Regina McAvoy. *Rosalie*: Helen Morrison. *Suzette*: Charlotte Palmer. *Messenger No. 365*: Lucille Johnson. *Russam*, Royal Elephant: Himself. *Siamese Peasants, Troops, Guards, Pages, Courtiers, Cambodians, Burmese, French Officers, Soldiers, Sailors, etc.*

Act 1: Village and harbor of Pechabury, Siam.

Act 2: Royal Palace at Bangkok.

ACT 1[111]
"Gaily Over the Bounding Billows" (Opening Chorus)
"No Matter What Others May Say" (Trio)
M. Lessing, W. Pruette, D. Maclaren
"A Pretty Girl" (A Summer's Night)
M. Lessing
Entrance March
W. Pruette, Guards
"Where Are You Going, My Pretty Maid?" (Duet)
M. Lessing, N. Bergen
"Mary's Got a Beau" (Solo and Ensemble)
Entrance of Wang
"The Man with an Elephant on His Hands"
D. Hopper
Duet
D. Hopper, M. Singer
"We're Soldiers of the Army"
Soldier Chorus, D. MacLaren
Cambodian's Entrance
Finale

ACT 2
Opening Chorus
"A Rose Without a Thorn" (Every Rose Must Have Its Thorn)
N. Bergen
Cambodian's Entrance
"The Man in the Moon" (Trio)
D. Hopper, M. Lessing, W. Pruette
"When You Were All to Me"
W. Pruette
"Tizan"
M. Lessing
(*Music by* Leo Friedman. *Lyrics by* George Lieb.)
"Baby"
D. Hopper, M. Lessing, Children
"Sharper Than the Serpent's Fang"
Male Chorus
Siamese Wedding March
"Coronation March"
Finale

1904.18 THE MAN FROM CHINA

A Musical Comedy in Two Acts. Book and lyrics by Paul West. Music by John W. Bratton. Entire production staged by Barney Fagan. Scenery painted by Ernest Albert. Costumes designed by A. Wilbur Crane. Orchestra under the direction of Gustave Salzer. Produced by Melville B. Raymond. Opened 2 May 1904 at the Majestic Theatre and closed 4 June 1904 after 41 performances.

CAST: *Reggy Van Pelt*, a handy young man in Palm Beach Society: EDGAR ATCHISON-ELY. *Gustavus Giltedge*, amulti-millionaire, the "Peach King": HARRY RICHARD. *Tommy Dodd*, Peter's assistant: BILLIE TAYLOR. *Count Luigidi Spaghetti*, an Italian nobleman, formerly Peter's partner: EUGENE REDDING. *Sing Hi, Sing Lo*, Two Celestial Detectives: John E. Gorman, George Gorman. *Freddy Folsom*, an athletic youth, engaged to Claudia: John Taylor. *Algy de Peyster*, a pampered young man, Janet's fiancé: JOHN A. ARMSTRONG. *Ben Bolt*: Allston Bent. *Bill Barnacle*: Redford D'Orsay. *Bob Bobstay*: Arthur Engle. *Bick Bickerstaff*: John Drury. *Amorel*, Giltedge's daughter: AMY LESSER. *Anastasia*, his sister: STELLA MAYHEW. *Cerise*, Amorel's maid: AIMEE ANGELES. *Janet Grammercy*, Algy's fiancée: Diamond Donner. *Claudia Courtland*, Freddy's fiancée: Frances Rockefeller King. *Young Matrons (6)*: *Mrs. Maddox*: Caroline McCord. *Mrs. Faddish*: Helen Curzon. *Mrs. Gazzam*: Dorothy Zimmerman. *Mrs. Stoxonbonds*: Nora Seymour. *Mrs. Uppercrust*: Aline Boyt. *Mrs. Innitt*: Anna M. Tyler. *Ornamental Youths (6)*: *Willie*: John Dunton. *Charlie*: Bert D. Harris. *Harold*: George W. Smyth. *Percy*: A. E. Melville.

---

[109]Originally produced in New York 17 March 1903 at the Broadway Theatre for 143 performances. For Synopsis of Scenes and Musical Numbers, see original 1903 production. For this revival, the following changes were made:
"Artie" was replaced by:
"Walk, Mister, Walk" (Solo)
V. Morley, Chorus of Vassar Girls
"He Didn't Know Exactly What to Do" was replaced by:
"It Was the Dutch" (solo)
J. W. Ransone

[110]First produced in New York 4 May 1891 at the Broadway Theatre for 151 performances.

[111]Interpolated as per published sheet music:
"Oolong Li"
(*Music by* Edward James Howe, Jr. *Lyrics by* Joseph E. Miller.)

Georgie: David Hearn. *Horace*: John Drury. *Peter Pudge*, a wandering musician, "The Human Band": CHARLES A. BIGELOW.

People of Fashion, Colored Servants, Clorinda Girls, Humming Birds, Columbine Girls, Esquimaux, etc, etc.

Matrons: Misses McCord, Curzon, Zimmerman, Seymour, Boyt, Tyler. *Clorinda Girls*: Misses Humphrey, Grant, J. Mozar, Shaw, Zaltz, Travis, DeVere, E. Mount, Johnston, N. Williams, Zell, F. Williams, Earle, E. Nagel, G. Field, Skiff. *Columbine Girls*: Misses Greene, Gray, Harris, G. Field, Elmo, Townsend, Daly, Marley. *Fashionables*: Misses Nelson, Conrad, Rellis, Sherwood, Seymour. *Esquimaux*: Misses R. Field, Nagel, Skiff, Earle, F. Williams, Zell, Johnston, N. Williams, E. Mount, DeVere, Trevis, Zaltz, Humphrey, Grant, J. Mozar, Shaw. *Humming Birds*: Misses N. Williams, Zell, F. Williams, Earle, Skiff, Nagel, R. Field, Humphrey, Grant, J. Mozar, Shaw, Zaltz, Trevis, DeVere, E. Mount, Johnston. *Continental Girls*: Misses F. Williams, Earle, Skiff, Nagel, R. Field, Humphrey, Grant, J. Mozar, Shaw, Zaltz, Trevis, DeVere, E. Mount, Johnston, N. Williams, Zell. *Continental Men*: Messrs. Bent, Dailey, D'Orsay, Dunton, Harris, W. Heath, D. Heath, McCormick, Melville, Faber, Smyth, Young, DeMers.

The action takes place in the morning and afternoon of the same day.

Act 1: The Grounds of Peachblow Villa at Palm Beach, Florida.

Act 2: On board Giltedge's Steam Yacht *"The Peach."*

ACT 1

"Just Another Silly Day" (Opening Chorus)
Men, Women

"What Would You Do Without Reggy?" (Song)
E. Atchison-Ely, Chorus

"The Peach King" (Chorus and Trio)
H. Richard, A. Lesser, S. Mayhew, Chorus

"The Human Band" (Chorus and Peter's Entrance)
C. A. Bigelow, Chorus

"Clorinda" (Song)
E. Atchison-Ely, Chorus

"Life Is Too Short to be Wasting Your Time" (Duet)
A. Angeles, B. Taylor

"Ting Tang Kee, or If You Understood Chinese" (Song)
C. A. Bigelow, Chorus

"Columbine" (or The Timid Humming Bird)(Song)
A. Angeles, Chorus

"(There Are) Fifty-Seven Ways to Catch a Man" (Song)
S. Mayhew

"How I Thought I Looked" (Trio)
C. A. Bigelow, E. Atchison-Ely, S. Mayhew

Finale
Principals, Chorus

ACT 2[112]

"The Bashful Moon" (Opening Chorus)
Chorus

"Be a Spy for Love's Sake" (Song)
A. M. Tyler, Chorus

"One Nice Little Million" (Quintette)
H. Richard, F. R. King, J. Taylor, J. A. Armstrong

"Make-Believe" (Septette)
E. Atchison-Ely, Matrons

"For He Was a Married Man" (For I Am a Married Man) (Song)
C. A. Bigelow, Chorus

"Frightened Fawn" (Song)
A. Lesser

"The Amorous Esquimaux" (Duet)
E. Atchison-Ely, A. Angeles

"My Black Cloud" (Duet)
S. Mayhew, B.Taylor

"For Glory and For Love" (Song)
B. Taylor, Chorus

Finale
Principals, Chorus

1904.19 A VENETIAN ROMANCE

A Comedy Opera in Three Acts. Book by Cornelia Osgood Tyler. Music by Frederic Coit Wright. Produced under the stage direction of Al Holbrook. Scenery by (Homer) Emens and (Edward G.) Unitt, Joseph Physioc. Costumes designed by Mme. Caroline Seidle. Orchestra under the direction of A. M. Langstaff. Produced by Frank L. Perley Opera Company. Opened 2 May 1904 at the Knickerbocker Theatre and closed 28 May 1904 after 28 performances.

CAST: *Pietro Palpitini*, Manager of the "Temple of Hymen:" HARRY MacDONOUGH. *Garibaldi Nervusini*, late of the Venetian police: IGNATIO MARTINETTI. *Spaghettini*, Proprietor of the"Belle Venezia" café: Neil McNeil. *Antonio Felipe Foscari*, a poet from Palermo, in love with Nanetta: WALTER PERCIVAL. *Captain Count von Hauptman*, Antonio's rival for the hand of Nanetta: HARRY LANE. *Murderallo*, The Robber of the Hills: JOSEPH MIRON. *Ricardo, Angelo, Stephano*, Three Trusty Thieves: Edd Redway, William Zinell, Harry Short. *Gratiano, Bassanio*, Two Gondoliers: Frank Smiley, Cassius Freeborn. *Conspritto, Holduppo*, Two Robbers: W. C. Smith, P. B. Pratt. *Nanetta*, Marchesa di Santa Molina: GENEVIEVE DAY. *Giulia*, Nanetta's cousin and a capitalist: JOSIE INTROPODI. *Nerissa*, Nanetta's maid: MABEL HITE. *Marianina, Francesca, Selina*, the famous Triplets of Tripoli: May Conwell, Annabelle Whitford, Carroll McComas. *Senorita Anita*, lately returned from Spain: Gertrude Eulalie. *Torturetta*, the daughter of Murderallo: Ethel Intropodi. *Teazeymina*, Murderallo's other daughter: Margot Hobart. *Lucetta*, a robber lady: Daisy Dobrinor. *Robberto*, a robber gentleman: Adele Carson.

Other members and daughters of Merderallo's band, assistants in the office of "the Temple," Merry makers at the feast of Zobia Grassa, Ladies and Gentlemen of Venice, Figurants of the Carnival Parade, Barmaids and Gondolieri, Postillons, Officers and Soldiers.

The action takes place in the fifteenth century.

Act 1: At night in the Plaza San Remo, during the celebration of Zobia Grassa, the Venetian Mardi Gras. (Emens & Unitt.)

Act 2: Interior of the Temple of Hymen, the following morning. (Physioc.)

Act 3: Bandits' retreat in the mountains of the Austrian Tyrol, near Andraz, the same evening. (Physioc.)

MUSICAL NUMBERS[113]

"But Our Charms Do Not Stop Quite There"

"The Goblin Man"
J. Miron
(*Music by* Ted Snyder. *Lyrics by* Ed Rose.)

"Let Us Forget!"
G. Day
(*Music by* T. Mayo Geary. *Lyrics by* Harry J. Breen.)

"My Indian Maiden"
G. Day
(*Music by* Ed J. Coleman. *Lyrics by* Harry Wilson)

"In the Weeping Willow Tree" (A Cuckoo Love Song)
H. MacDonough
(*Music by* Harry Frantzen. *Lyrics by* Joseph C. Farrell.)

"How to Woo and Win"
(*Music by* Harry Frantzen. *Lyrics by* Joseph C. Farrell.)

1904.20 GULLIVER'S TRAVELS

The Lilliputians in a (Musical) Burlesque in Three Acts. Play by John Fowler. Music by William Rostetter. Ballets and musical numbers arranged by Jack Mason. Scenery by Frank Gates and Edward A. Morange; Ernest Albert. Costumes by Hayden and Rowley and Bush and Heiland. Electrical effects by Joseph Menchen. Opened 2 May 1904 at the Metropolis Theatre and closed 7 May 1904 after 8 performances.[114]

CAST: *Lord High Chancellor*: PRINCE GIOVANNI. *Sir Dick Whittington*: LOUIS MERKEL. *Blubberly*, his servant: JAMES E. ROSEN. *The Emperor of Lilliput*: HERBERT RICE. *The Empress of Lilliput*: MARTHA WEIS. *Lemunel Gulliver*: AL. RICE. *Grand Chamberlain*: A. T. Darcey. *Butler of the Royal Court*: William Platt. *Royal Housekeeper*: SELMA GOERNER. *Princess Andrea*: Queen Mab. *Mother Goose*: Louis Waters. *Humpty Dumpty*: PRINCE GIOVANNI. *Little Boy Blue*: MARTHA WEIS. *Jocko*, the Monkey and Sprite: Alfred Latell. *Giant*: B. F. Kelly. *Fairy Golden Rod*: Grace McLeod. *Fairy Ebony Rod*: Della Ranney.

[112] "In a Pagoda" (instrumental) was played between Acts 1 and 2.

[113] Musical Numbers not listed in program.

[114] No New York program available. Musical numbers taken from a Brooklyn tryout program 16 November 1903. No producer credited. The miniature coach used in this production is the original "Tom Thumb Coach" purchased by the Royal Lilliputians Company from the P. T. Barnum estate.

Fairies of Light (6): *Fairy Sunlight*: May Valentine. *Fairy Brightlight*: Gertie Hawkins. *Fairy Sunlight*: Beatrice Morelyn. *Fairy Starlight*: Rita Love. *Fairy Electriclight*: Mona McCarthy. *Fairy Fanlight*: Pearl Franklin. *Fairies of Night (7)*: *Fairy Firefly*: May Valentine. *Fairy Brightlight*: Lilian Jeanette. *Fairy Moonlight*: Vera DeVere. *Fairy Eveninglight*: Fay Steiner. *Fairy Darklight*: Arline Bliss. *Fairy Twilight*: Belle DuBoise. *The Ponies*: Themselves.

ACT 1[115]

Prologue

"Queen of the Night (Opening Chorus)

"My Little Orang-o-Tang"
Chorus

"Laughing Song"
A. Rice

"My Lady Moon"
M. Weis, Company

ACT 2

"Crack of the Whip"
S. Goerner, Chorus

Conversation Song and Dance
J. E. Rosen, P. Giovanni, M. Valentine, B. Morelyn

"Too Many Miles from Broadway"
Company

ACT 3

"The Windy Boys"
J. E. Rosen, L. Merkel, H. Rice, W. Platt

"Roly Poly Sam"
Company

"My Lady"
M. Weis, Chorus

Foster and his musical dog, Mike (Specialty)

"General Hard Tack" (March)
Chorus

1904.21 THE SOUTHERNERS

A Musical (Comedy) Study in Black and White in Two Acts, 4 Scenes. Book and lyrics by Will Mercer and Richard Grant. Score (music) by Will Marion Cook. Personally staged by George W. Lederer. Dances arranged by Joseph C. Smith. Settings by D. Frank Dodge. Costumes by Mme. (Caroline) F. Siedle. Musical director, Antonio DeNovelis. Produced by George W. Lederer. Opened 23 May 1904 at the New York Theatre and closed 25 June 1904 after 36 performances.

CAST: Prologue, 1880: *General Preston*, a relic of the days before the war: WILLIAM GOULD. *Uncle Dan'l*, formerly his coachman, now a pensioner: EDDIE LEONARD. *Parthenia*. Uncle Daniel's grandchild: VINIE DALY.

Play, 1830: *Brannigan Bey*, a Viceroy pro tem of the Isle of Ballyhoo: JUNIE McCREE. *Bob Rutledge*, a combination of black sheep and innocent lamb: ALBERT HART. *LeRoy Preston*, Lieutenant U.S.A.: WILLIAM GOULD. *Dandy Dan*, in love with Parthenia: EDDIE LEONARD. *Colonel Maximilian Easy*, "A Southern Cavalier Sah": W. Wallace Black. *Judge Budge*, of several different bars: Joseph W. Standish. *Cyril Osborn*, Midshipman of the *Louisiana*: WILMER BENTLEY. *Naval Cadets (4)*: *Phil Fuller*: Paul Decker. *Cecil Brown*: Charles Wentz. *Lewis Middleton*: Theodore S. Peters. *Harry Stetson*: Cecil Somers. *Sam Blossom*, also in love with Parthenia: Wheeler Earl. *Uncle Mose*, the oldest landmark on the plantation: Charles Moore. *Aunt Matilda*, his wife: Walter Dixon. *Sing Hi*: Theodore Peters. *Polly Drayton*: ELFIE FAY. *Parthenia*, Miss Preston's maid: VINIE DALY. *Japonica Preston*, LeRoy's sister: REINE DAVIES. *Olivia Pemberton*, Japonica's chum: Louisa Lathrop. *Magnolia Preston*, Japonica's cousin: Bertyne Mortimer. *Mandy Lou*, a slave: ABBIE MITCHELL.

Companions of Olivia and Magnolia (6): *Violet*: Mildred DeVere. *Rose*: Mabel Verne. *Pansy*: Irene Cameron. *Lily*: Florence Arkell. *Daisy*: Belva Don Kerlsey. *Marguerite*: Lorayne Osborne. *The Kiddies (9)*: *Virginia*: Sallie Loomis. *Florida*: Ethel Davies. *Louisiana*: Hattie Burdell. *Alabama*: Edith Girvin. *Carolina*: Ella Ray. *Orleans*: Lillian Rice. *Maryland*: Averta Sanchez. *Georgia*: Bessie Moulton. *Atlanta*: Violet Pearle. *Planters, Guests, Slaves, etc.*

Act 1, Scene 1: Uncle Dan's cabin in New Orleans. *Scene 2*: The Preston Mansion and grounds. "Monst the Magnolias."

Act 2, Scene 1: Avenue of Oaks. When the Sunflower turns to the Sun. *Scene 2*: On the Levee—at the Barbecue.

[115]No New York program available. Musical numbers from a Brooklyn program dated 16 November 1903.

ACT 1[116]

"I Love the Southland" (Opening Chorus)

"Daisy Deane"
(*Lyrics by* Richard Grant.)

"Swing Along Children"

Duet (A pinafored, pig-tailed girl and a knickerbockered boy)
C. Bentley, R. Davies

"I Love the Southland" (reprise)

"Julep Song" (The good old mint julep for me)
Sextette or Octette
(*Lyrics by* Richard Grant.)

"The Chipmunk and the Squirrel" (The Squirrel and the Chipmunk)
E. Fay

The Ballet of the Squirrels

Chorus for Entrance of the Bey (Agitate the cymbals!)
Chorus

"When I First Went to Turkey" (Song)
J. McCree, Chorus

"Tippecanoe" (A Comic Indian Song)
W. Gould
(*Music by* Egbert Van Alstyne. *Lyrics by* Harry Williams.)

"Dandy Dan"
E. Leonard

"(It's) Allus de Same in Dixie"
(*Lyrics by* Richard Grant.)

"As the Sun Flower Turns to the Sun"
A. Mitchell
(*Lyrics by* Harry B. Smith.)

"Mandy Lou"
A. Mitchell
(*Lyrics by* R. C. McPherson [Cecil Mack].)

"Darktown Barbecue" (Darktown was out at dat Barbecue)
Slaves
(*Lyrics by* Will Marion Cook.)

ACT 2

Opening Chorus (In Oriental nations, in harems of the East)
Chorus

"Clancy Had a Fancy" (Song)
J. McCree

"A Southern Gentleman" (Song)
A. Hart, Chorus

Valse Aeriel
V. Daly, J. C. Smith

"Where the Lotus Blossoms Grow" (Song)
R. Davies

"Sarah Jane" (Song)
W. Gould, Wives

"Good Evenin'" (Duet)
V. Daly, E. Leonard

"The Sunny South" (Song)
E. Fay

Dream Duet
W. Gould, E. Fay

"The Irish Canary" (Song)
J. McCree

"I Love You" (Duet)(In ev'ry land, in ev'ry clime)
E. Fay, J. McCree

Finale

[116]Musical Numbers not listed in program; list prepared from early production typescript, reviews, sheet music. Additional songs:

"The Amorous Star"
(*Music and Lyrics by* Marie Sutherland.)

"Dreamin' Town"

"Val from Vallejo"
W. Gould
(*Music and Lyrics by* William Gould.)

"'Mongst the Magnolias"

"Sweet Dreams, Dear One of Thee" (Slumber Song)

"Teasing"
R. Davies, W. Bentley
(*Music by* Albert Von Tilzer. *Lyrics by* Cecil Mack.)

1904–1905 SEASON

Roland Cunningham and Fritzi Scheff in THE TWO ROSES (Photo: Hall)
Billy Rose Theatre Collection, New York Public Library for the Performing Arts

1904–1905 SEASON

1904.22 **A LITTLE OF EVERYTHING**

A Musical Vaudeville Entertainment in Three Acts, 5 Scenes. Book by John J. McNally. Staged by Herbert Gresham. Dances arranged by Ned Wayburn. Settings by Richard Marsden. Costumes designed by F. Richard Anderson. Musical direction, Frederic Solomon. Produced by (Marc) Klaw and (Abraham L.) Erlanger. Opened 6 June 1904 at the Aerial Gardens (atop the New Amsterdam Theatre), moved 5 September 1904 to the Broadway Theatre and closed 17 September 1904 after 120 performances.

CAST: *John Edward Haggerty*: JOSEPH SPARKS. *Benjamin Franklin Perkins*: GEORGE A. SCHILLER. *John Corteright Muggs*: HARRY KELLY. *Bert Height*: Allan Ramsay. *Barty Lowe*: Charles Hessong. *Billy Hurlingham After*: PETER F. DAILEY. *Miss Lillian Maye*: Leila McIntyre. *Miss Ivy Stringham*: Sabel Johnson. *Miss Daisy Bovine*: Susie Fisher. *Miss Bessie Perkins*: Charlotte Leslay. *Miss Della Haggerty*: Elphye Snowden. *Mrs. Aurora Daye-Knight*: FAY TEMPLETON. *Ladies and Gentlemen, Friends of Mrs. Knight, Servants and Officials of various kinds. (Specialties*: Frank Coomes, Franklin Baily.) And Carl Kahn, Victor Bozardt, Neil McNeil, Frank Coomes, Franklin Baily, Isabelle D'Armonde, Sabel Johnson.

Act 1: The Terrace at Hunting Towers.

Act 2, Scene 1: The Conservatory at Hunting Towers. *Scene 2*: Reception Hall at Hunting Towers. *Scene 3*: The Fens at Huntington.

Act 3: A Chalet in Switzerland.

ACT 1[1]

Opening Chorus

"A Stroll in the Moonlight"
C. Leslay, Chorus
(*Music and Lyrics by* Harding and Kennedy.)

"You Won't Do Any Business If You Haven't Got a Band"
P. F. Dailey, Chorus
(*Music and Lyrics by* George M. Cohan.)

"The Pretty Little Squaw from Utah"
L. McIntyre
(*Music by* J. Rosamond Johnson. *Lyrics by* Robert Cole.)

"A Little Bit of Blarney"
J. Sparks, Chorus
(*Music by* J. Fred Helf. *Lyrics by* Will Heelan.)

"Fishing"[2]
F. Templeton
(*Music by* J. Rosamond Johnson. *Lyrics by* Robert Cole.)

"I Love to Hear a Yankee Doodle Tune"
F. Templeton, P. F. Dailey, Chorus
(*Music and Lyrics by* George M. Cohan.)

ACT 2

Scene 1

Medley of Negro Melodies (arranged by Frederic Solomon)

"There Is Something About You That I Love, Love, Love"[3]
F. Coomes
(*Music by* J. Rosamund Johnson. *Lyrics by* Bob Cole.)

"Hiss, Hiss, Hiss"
J. Sparks, Company
(*Music by* J. Fred Helf. *Lyrics by* Will Heelan.)

"Just a Little Ever-Loving Girl"
L. McIntyre, Chorus
(*Music by* Mullen. *Lyrics by* Bryan.)

"Your Mother Wants You Home, Boy"[4]
F. Baity, Quartette
(*Music and Lyrics by* Paul Dresser.)

"Della and Ella"
H. Kelly
(*Music by* Gus Edwards. *Lyrics by* Robert B. Smith.)

"Oh, Joy"
P. F. Dailey
(*Music by* Mullen. *Lyrics by* Bryan.)

"Como le Gusta Me?"
F. Templeton
(*Music by* J. Rosamund Johnson. *Lyrics by* Bob Cole.)

Scene 2

"Maid of the Mill"[5]
S. Fisher
(*Music and Lyrics by* Stephen Adams.)

Scene 3

"The Evolution of Rag Time" (from MOTHER GOOSE)
G. A. Schiller, P. F. Dailey, F. Templeton, Entire Company
The Voice of the Savage; Echoes of the Day; Essence of the Jug; Darkies' Delights; The Spirit of the Banjo; Sounds of the Times.
(*Music by* J. Rosamond Johnson. *Lyrics by* Robert Cole.)

ACT 3[6]

Opening Chorus
(*Music by* Frederic Solomon.)

---

[1]Added early in the run to Act 1, after "Fishing":

Original Sextette from FLORODORA

A Short Skit burlesquing scenes from CAMILLE

Also performed at the opening, per the New York Dramatic Mirror:

"Turn Those Eyes Away"
S. Johnson
(*Music by* Frederic Solomon.)

"The Maid of the Mill"
S. Fisher

[2]Replaced during the run by:

"Just Leave It to Bill"
F. Templeton
(*Music by* J. Rosamond Johnson. *Lyrics by* Bob Cole.)
Note: Published sheet music for "Leave It to Bill" credits Bob Cole with both music and lyrics.

[3] Dropped after opening.

[4]Replaced after opening by:

"Good-Bye, Little Girl, Good-bye"
Gus Edwards
(*Music by* Gus Edwards. *Lyrics by* Will Cobb.)

[5]Replaced early in the run by:

"Salt of the Sea"
S. Fisher
(*Music by* Arthur Penn. *Lyrics by* Will Cobb.)

"Blue-Eyed Sue" (from MOTHER GOOSE)
S. Fisher
(*Music and Lyrics by* James Reese Europe.)

[6]Shortly after opening, Acts 2 and 3 were combined and shortened, and Act 3 replaced by THE OFFENBACH REVIEW, as successfully presented in the Moulin Rouge, Paris. Costumes by Van Horn.

MUSICAL NUMBERS

Chorus of Brigands and Carabiniers (from LES BRIGANDS)
H. Kelly {Captain of Carabiniers}

"Blue Beard and Eight Wives" (Song and Chorus from BARBE-BLUE)
A. Ramsay {Blue Beard}

Chorus of Kings and Solos of Ajax 1 and 2 (from LA BELLE HÉLÈNE)
G. A. Schiller (Ajax 1), J. Sparks {Ajax 2)

Chorus and Letter Song (from LA PÈRICHOLE)
L. McIntyre (Perichole)

"General Boom" (Chorus and Songs)(from LA GRAND DUCHESSE)
P. F. Dailey (General Boom), H. Kelly (Fritz)

"Chanson de la Bruscambille" (Song and Chorus)(from LA JOLIE PARFUMEUSE)
F. Templeton (Rose)

"The Two Gendarmes" (Duo)(from GENVIEVE DeBRABANT)
H. Kelly, P. F. Dailey

Grand Finale:

"Say to Him" (from LA GRANDE DUCHESSE)
F. Templeton

"Lo Here the Sabre" (from LA GRANDE DUCHESSE)
F. Templeton, Chorus

"Galop" (from ORPHEE AUX ENFERS)
Entire Company

"Pas Seul"
E. Snowden
(*Music and Lyrics by* Frederic Solomon.)

"Turn Those Eyes Away"[7]
S. Johnson
(*Music and Lyrics by* Fred Solomon.)

"Let Him Dream"[8]
P. F. Dailey, Chorus
(*Music by* J. Rosamond Johnson. *Lyrics by* Robert Cole.)

Finale

1904.23 PARIS BY NIGHT

A Musical Julep (Revue) in Two Acts. Book (and lyrics) by Harry B. Marshall. Music by Alfred Solman, (Robert W. Edwards). Staged by Sol Fields. Scenery painted by P. Dodd Ackerman. Costumes furnished by Mrs. (Bertha) Dowling. Orchestra under the direction of Robert W. Edwards. Produced by Weber and Rush. Opened 2 July 1904 at the Madison Square Roof Garden and closed 13 August 1904 after 50 performances[9].

CAST: *Richard Congood*, a theatrical manager who tackled Europe and got the worst of it: EDGAR TEMPLE. *Steve Hickey*, an ex-circus canvasman, astray in Paris: HUGH CAMERON. *Isaac Goldstein*, a retired pawnbroker, who married a society widow on his honeymoon: BEN WELCH. *Orlof Sleuthski*, a Hungarian Detective in the Russian service, searching for Japanese spies: HENRY VOGEL. *Harold Vere de Vere Cushman*, a wealthy young art student: Burnell Pratt. *J. Jeffries Fitzcorbett*, an athletic instructor: Cassius Freeborn. *Eugene*, a musical waiter: George Fields. *Magnolia Goldstein*, Isaac's wife, who married for money: TOMA HANLON. *Cissy Footlytes*, a rag-time prima donna, formerly leading lady of Congood's Vaudevillians: FLEURETTE DeMAR. *Mme. Bon Bon*, a susceptible Parisian landlady: MADGE LAWRENCE. *Marguerita Hottomoleo*, a Spanish girl in love, generally speaking: SYLVIA BEECHER. *Nanette*, head waitress at the Hotel: Bertha Dowling. *Mazie Sharp*, a cunning detective: Mae Sheridan.

Late of Congood's Vaudevillians from New York (6): *Evaline Madison*: Naomi Arnold. *Anna Manhattan*: Edyth Forrest. *Virginia Casino*: Margaret Messinger. *Lillian Knickerbocker*: Linnet Fiske. *Florence Victoria*: Maude Wynne. *Lotta Amsterdam*: Helen Drew.

Parisian Boulevardiers (6): *Mons. Roulette*: Adrian Bellvue. *Mons. La Pierre*: W. R. Paschel. *Mons. Germaine*: Frank McCullough. *Mons. Pallaten*: George Nagel. *Mons. Le Blanc*: Frank Evans.

More of less responsible for making Paris famous (10): *Mlle. Adelaide*: Ceretta Ross. *Mlle. La Miro*: Julia Cook. *Mlle. Pierrot*: Mabelle Bonner. *Mlle. Yvette*: Julia Curtis. *Mlle. Danbere*: Grace Bond. *Mlle. Susette*: Louise Egener. *Mlle. Vigneau*: Alberta Davis. *Mlle. Marie*: Edyth Warren. *Mlle. DuBarry*: Minnie Egener. *Mlle. La Purrell*: Mlle. Guyer. *Waiters, Flower Girls, American Tourists, Models, Students, Spanish Boys and Girls, Cosmopolitans, etc.*

Act 1: The First Night. Garden Café of the Hotel Bon Bon in Paris. A Warm Evening.

Act 2: The Second Night. Office of the Hotel Bon Bon, a week later. A Hot Night.

ACT 1[10]

"In Gay Paree" (Opening Chorus)
(*Music by* Robert W. Edwards.)

"Maudie" (Solo and Ensemble)
M. Lawrence, Chorus

"Waltz, Waltz, Waltz" (Quartette and Dance of All Nations)
F. DeMar, T. Hanlon, H. Vogel, B. Welch, Chorus
(*Music by* L. Bloodgood. *Lyrics by* John E. Hazzard.)

"Dear Old Broadway" (Solo and Chorus)
E. Temple, Chorus
(*Music by* Harry B. Marshall.)

"Seminole" (Solo and Ensemble)
F. DeMar, Chorus
(*Music by* Egbert Van Alstyne. *Lyrics by* Harry Williams.)

"In Sweet Love Land" (Solo and Ensemble)
E. Temple, Chorus
(*Music by* Alfred Solman. *Lyrics [Poem] by* Joan Haden.)

"The Convivial Girl" (Song and Chorus)
F. Demar, T. Hanlon, H. Vogel, B. Welch
(*Music by* Robert Edwards.)

"Sweet Rose of Mexico" (Solo)
M. Lawrence

"I Loves You, Lady, 'Deed I Do" (Sextette Song and Dance)
M. Lawrence, F. DeMar, S. Beecher, H. Vogel?, B. Welch, B. Pratt
(*Music and Lyrics by* Joseph Nathan.)

"Twinkle, Twinkle, Little Star" (Solo and Ensemble)
S. Beecher, Chorus
(*Music by* Robert Edwards, Alfred Solman.)

"Paris By Night" (Finale)
(*Music by* Robert Edwards.)

ACT 2

"The Boulevardiers" (Opening Chorus)
(*Music by* Harry Marshall.)

Solo Dance
F. DeMar

"Turn Those Eyes Away" (Tenor Solo)
E. Temple
(*Music by* Alfred Solman. *Lyrics by* Estella Acres.)

"Louise Schmidt" (Ensemble Song and Dance)
H. Vogel, Chorus
(*Music by* Harry Von Tilzer. *Lyrics by* Andrew B. Sterling.)

"Follow the Crowd (on a Sunday)" (Song and Chorus)
S. Beecher, Chorus
(*Music by* Harry Armstrong. *Lyrics by* James Morrison.)

"The Girl with the Changeable Eyes" (Solo)
T. Hanlon
(*Music by* Alfred Solman. *Lyrics by* Estella Acres.)

"That Horrid Mosquito" (Solo and Chorus)
M. Lawrence, Chorus
(*Music by* Alfred Solman.)

Selected Parodies
B. Welch

"The U.S. Volunteers" (Solo Ensemble and March)
T. Hanlon, Chorus
(*Music by* Julius Adler.)

Finale

1904.24 THE MAID AND THE MUMMY

A Musical Melange in Two Acts. Book and lyrics by Richard Carle. Music by Robert Hood Bowers. Staged by Richard Carle. Ensembles and dances by Adolph Newberger. Settings by D. Frank Dodge. Costume plates by Archie Gunn. Orchestra under the direction of Robert Hood Bowers. Produced by Carle Amusement Company Enterprise (Richard Carle; Charles Marks, Managing director). Opened 25 July 1904 at the New York Theatre and closed 3 September 1904 after 42 performances.

CAST: *Washington Stubbs*, an impecunious curio dealer: RICHARD F. CARROLL. *Bolivar*, his man-of-all-work: EDWARD GARVIE. *Doctor Elisha Dubbins*, a wealthy inventor: GEORGE A. BEANE. *Mac Swat*, a would-be detective: LOUIS WESLEY. *Lord Triverton*, in love with Flo: EDGAR NORTON. *Michael McGovern*, a dime novel fiend: Jess Caine. *Flo Dobbins*, the Doctor's daughter: ADELE ROWLAND. *Trixie Evergreen*, an actress: MAY BOLEY. *Auroria Dubbins*, the Doctor's maiden sister: ANNIE YEAMANS. *Muggsy*, a street urchin: Janet Priest. *Tiger*: Madge Vincent. *Polly Girls (6)*: *Polly*: Myra Dalton. *Betsy*: Inez Bauer. *Dolly*: Jane Grant. *Celia*: Viola Vallori. *Molly*: Janet French. *Ophelia*: Marjorie Eastman. *Poster Girls (6)*: *Creme de l'Amour*: Jessie Stanley. *Fur Sale*: Daisy Yost. *Oper Comique*: Edith Conrad. *Folly To-night*: Jack Boutwell. *Viva Tonique*: Ethel Lloyd. *Juanita Cigarette*: Antonio Stross.

School Girls: Misses French, Grant, Vallari, Eastman, Pelham, Dalton, Stanton, Raymond, Bauer, Morrison, Fredericks, Bernard. *Apprentices*: Misses Vincent,

[7]Dropped early in the run.

[8]Replaced after opening by:

"I Hate to Wake Up"
P. F. Dailey, Chorus
(*Music by* Frederic Solomon.)

[9]Played a return engagement 28 August 1905 at the Murray Hill Theatre for 9 performances.

[10] The following musical numbers were especially written for this production (per program): "In Gay Paree," "Dear Old Broadway," "In Sweet Love Land," "The Convivial Girl," "Twinkle Twinkle, Little Star," "Paris By Night," "The Boulevardiers," "Turn Those Eyes Away," "The Girl with the Changeable Eyes," "That Horrid Mosquito," Finale. Toured subsequently with a most different score: "King Solomon Knew a Thing or Two," "The Naughty Scarecrow," "Katerina," "O, Love Divine," "A Study in Pink," "La Chansonette," "Wine's My Only Pleasure," "My Dew Drop Rosy," "La Saronita," "Roaming with the Romans."

Ardavaini, Roberts, Harris, Yost, Tourisse, Melvin, Selwyn, Fennell, Miner, Brown, Gilber. *Auto Girls*: Misses Rowland, Stross, Stanley, Conrad, Lloyd, Boutwell. *College Boys*: Messrs. Beck, Platt, Dewey, Flynn, Dalton, Collins, Winn, Koldosky.

The action takes place at the present time in New York City.

Act 1: Curio Shop of Washington Stubbs, New York City. Afternoon.

Act 2: Egyptian Ball Room of Dr. Dobbins Seminary in New York City. Next evening.

ACT 1

Opening Chorus

"My Gasoline Automobile"
G. A. Beane, Chorus

"Flo"
A. Rowland, E. Norton, Chorus

"The Sales Lady"
M. Boley, School Girls

"Letters"
M. Boley, R. F. Carroll

"Sad Experiences"
E. Garvie, R. F. Carroll, E. Norton

"Poster Diversity"
The Poster Girls

"It's Great To Be Crazy"
L. Wesley, Chorus

Finale

ACT 2

Opening Chorus

"My Egyptian Queen"
A. Rowland, Chorus

"I'm So Dizzy"
E. Garvie
(*Music by* Richard Carle.)

"I Fell in Love with Polly"
R. F. Carroll, Polly Girls
(*Music by* Richard Carle.)

"The Artful Crocodile"
M. Boley

"Peculiar Julia"
E. Garvie, M. Boley, Chorus
(*Music by* Richard Carle.)

Finale

1904.25 THE ISLE OF SPICE

The Piquant Musical Mixture (Musical Play) in Three Acts[11]. Book and lyrics by Allen Lowe and George E. Stoddard. Music by Paul Schindler and Ben Jerome. Original ensemble pictures, dances and poses arranged and produced (staged) by Gus Sohlke. Settings by W. Franklin Hamilton. Costumes by Arlene Falls, Mme. Freisinger. Electrical effects by Irving Barker. Orchestra under the direction of Paul Schindler. Produced by B. C. Whitney. Opened 23 August 1904 at the Majestic Theatre and closed 29 October 1904 after 80 performances[12].

CAST: *Bompopka*, Sixty-Seventh King of Nicobar: ALEXANDER CLARK. *Lieutenant Harold Katchall*, the Hero of Muddy Mack: GEORGE FISKE. *Mickey O'Grady*, deserter from *U.S.S. "Roosevelt"*: HERBERT CAWTHORNE. *Slubsy Mackinaw*, his tearful companion: GILBERT GREGORY. *Kashon*, an unfortunate Court Treasurer: JOHN HENDRICKS. *Konner*, his jealous brother: James Phelan. *Taric*, a regular Boxer: Harry Truman. *Sam Snap*, a Sergeant of Marines: Otto Booker. *Teresa*, the King's ward: BLANCHE BUCKNER. *Kamorta*, a Queen whose lease has almost expired: MATTIE MARTZ. *Absena*, the ex-Queen of Nicobar: SUSIE FORRESTER. *Trinket*, on a long lease as Queen: MAUDE WILLIAMS. *Young Cupid*: Vivien Prescott. *Mother Witch*: Alice Yorke. *Rickshaw Boys*: Stella Maury, Helen Duval. *Cayenna*: Jessie Maury. *Peppera*: Aida Vaughn. *Court Ladies of Nicobar (4)*: *Anchovia*: May Kennedy. *Saucenna*: Merle Dumont. *Tobasconne*: Ivy Williams. *Radisha*: Minnie Woodberry.

Maids of Nicobar: Stella Maury, Helen Duval, Jessie Maury, Aida Vaughn, May Kennedy, Merle Dumont, Ivy Williams, Minnie Woodberry. *U.S. Marines*: *Drummers*: Camille Lavilla., Helen Gellette, Agnes Merrill, Margie Cogen. *Flag Bearers*: Nellie Waters, Virginia Reynolds, Lola Merrill, Alice Merrill.

The Children of Witchland: *Mother Witch*: Alice Yorke. *Witch Children*: Helne Gellette, Camille Lavilla, Margie Cogen, Trixie Jennery, Alice Merrill, Lola Merrill, Agnes Merrill, Vivian Prescott, Mattie Nelson, Tot Clayton, Lillian Harvey, Eleanor Tilford, Nellie Waters, Mira Lorena. *"Mercenary Mary Ann"*: Stella Maury, Linda Nelson, Merle Dumont, Jessie Maury, Ivy Williams; Messrs. Ferguson, Eggleston, Finlay, Riley, Folly. *"Peggy Brady"*: *Spalpeens*: Camille Lavilla, Helen Gellette, Margie Cogen, Trixie Jennery, Nellie Waters, Agnes Merrill, Alice Merrill, Lola Merrill, Tot Clayton, Vivian Prescott, Gertie Stanley, Eleanor Tilford. *Colleens*: Stella Maury, Merle Dumont, Helen Duval, Jessie Maury, Ivy Williams, May Kennedy, Linda Nelson, Aida Vaughn, Helen Duval, Mattie Nelson, Lillian Harvey, Mamie Britton, Gertrude Dixon, Ivy Teel, Hazel Wright, Mable Loyde, Minnie Woodberry. *Gossoons*: Eleanor Elkins, Edith Depew, Mira Lorena, Virginia Reynolds, Cora Landis, Helen Courtney, Amelia Ames, Evlyn Hagan, Imogene Vickers, Florence Whitmore, Francis Lamar, Daisie Beauta. *Sweethearts*: Messrs. Brandon, Riley, Fraser, Eggleston, Finley, Worthington, Foley, Hopkins, Ferguson, Samuels, Whitmore, Finn, North, Leonard, Hackleton, Lewis, Spaulding. *"Goo-Goo Girls"*: Margie Cogen, Camille Lavilla, Helen Gellette, Trixie Jennery, Mira Lorena, Nellie Waters, Ages Merrill, Alice Merrill, Lola Merrill, Tot Clayton, Vivian Prescott, Mattie Nelson, Lillian Harvey, Eleanor Tilford.

Act 1: Exterior of the King's Palace.

Act 2: Interior of the King's Palace.

Act 3: Outside the Tomb of Silence.

ACT 1

Opening
Full Chorus
(*Music by* Paul Schindler.)

"The Little Maid of Nicobar" (The Maid from Nicobar)
B. Buckner, Court Ladies
(*Music by* Paul Schindler. *Lyrics by* Allen Lowe.)

"Uncle Sam's Marines"
G. Fiske, Male Chorus, Drummer Girls
(*Music by* Paul Schindler.)

"Silly Sailors"
H. Cawthorne, G. Gregory
(*Music by* Paul Schindler.)

"Hail Bompopka"
Full Chorus
(*Music by* Paul Schindler.)

"The Sporting King of Nikobar"[13]
A. Clark, Chorus
(*Music by* Paul Schindler.)

"Star of Fate" (Finale)
B. Buckner, M. Williams, M. Martz, J. Hendricks, O. Booker, G. Fiske, Full Chorus
(*Music by* Paul Schindler.)

ACT 2[14]

Opening
Full Chorus
(*Music by* Ben Jerome.)

"The Witches" (Sohlkes' Creation)
A. Yorke, Her Children
(*Music by* Paul Schindler. *Lyrics by* A. L. Jansson.)

---

[11]Published sheet music carried a sub-title, THE ISLE OF SPICE, or His Majesty of Nicobar.

[12]Revised version, adapted into Two Acts by Frederic Ranken, premiered 23 September 1904.

[13]Dropped for subsequent tour.

[14]Added during the run to Act 2:

"The Ambitious Animals" (Quartette)
M. Martz, M. Williams, H. Cawthorne, G. Gregory
(*Music by* Paul Schindler.)

"A Japanese Umbrella"
B. Buckner

"Sail with Me"
A. Yorke, Chorus

The production was radically revised from 3 to 2 Acts during its run and for subsequent tour. In Act 2, Opening, "The Ambitious Animals," "Mercenary Mary Ann," "A Japanese Umbrella," and "The Witches" were dropped. Added were: "Ching Ling Fong," "The Broomstick Witches," "Take Me Home," "O, April Eyes," "How Can You Tell Till You Try" were added. "You and I" was moved to Act 1.

"Mercenary Mary Ann" (Mercenary Mary)
A. Clark, Girls, Men
(*Music by* Ben Jerome and Paul Schindler. *Lyrics by* Allen Lowe.)

"You and I" (Duet)
B. Buckner, G. Fiske
(*Music by* Ben Jerome.)

"Peggy Brady"
M. Williams, Full Chorus
(*Music by* Paul Schindler.)

"Kow Tow" (Ensemble)
Full Chorus
(*Music by* Paul Schindler.)

Finale
B. Buckner, G. Fiske, Chorus
(*Music by* Paul Schindler.)

ACT 3

Opening
Full Chorus
(*Music by* Ben Jerome.)

"The Goo-Goo Man"
A. Clark, Goo-Goo Girls
(*Music by* Ben Jerome.)

Finale
Company
(*Music by* Paul Schindler.)

1904.26 IN DAHOMEY

A "New" Version of the Musical Farce in Two Acts, a Prologue and 4 Scenes[15]. Book by Jesse A. Shipp. Music by Will Marion Cook. Lyrics by Alex Rogers. Additional music by James Vaughan. Scenery painted by (Thomas G.) Moses & Hamilton. Costumes designed by Mme. Pauline Reed. Musical director, James Vaughan. Produced by (Jules) Hurtig & (Harry) Seamon. Opened 27 August 1904 at the Grand Opera House and closed 10 September 1904 after 17 performances.

CAST: *Je-Je*, a Caboceer (Governor of a Province): George Hammond. *Menki*, Messenger of the King: William Elkins. *Mose Lightfoot*, Agent of Dahomey Colonization Society and Hamilton Lightfoot's brother: JAMES RIVERS. *Shylock Homestead*, called "Shy" by his friends: BERT A. WILLIAMS. *Rareback Pinkerton*, "Shy's" personal friend and advisor: GEORGE W. WALKER. *Hustling Charlie*, promoter of the "Get-the-Coin" Syndicate: J. A. SHIPP. *George Reeder*, proprietor of an intelligence office, one of the "Get-the-Coin": ALEXANDER ROGERS. *Dr. Straight* in name only, street fakir, another "Get-the-Coinist": J. Leubrie Hill. *Hamilton Lightfoot*, President of the Dahomey Colonization Society—henpecked, light and easy: JAMES LIGHTFOOT. *Me Sing*, a Chinese cook: George Catlin. *Archie Brown*, a sailor boy, the son of an old acquaintance of Mrs. Stringers: Green Henry Tapley. *Leather*, a bootblack: RICHARD CONNER[16]. *Henry Stampfield*, a letter carrier: L. H. Saulsbury. *Messenger Rush*, but not often: Theodore Pankey. *James*, a butler: John Edwards. *Officer Still*: George Hammond. *Helper to the Doctor*: W. H. Chappelle. *Cecilia Lightfoot*, Hamilton's second wife, Rosetta's stepmother: HATTIE McINTOSH. *Madame Flash*: Rosa Lee Tyler. *Mrs. Stringer*, dealer in forsaken patterns, and interested in the Dahomey scheme: LOTTIE WILLIAMS. *Rosetta Lightfoot*, a troublesome young thing, Hamilton's pride: ADA OVERTON WALKER. (*Specialty*: Miss Mattie Edwards.) *City folks, country folks, lady folks, men folks, old folks, young folks and others*: (Misses Davis, Day, Martin, Gaston, Hill, Ringold, Ellis, Vaughn, Walker, Carle, Kemp; Messrs. Lloyd G. Gibbs, Elkins, Henderson, Rex, Panckey, Rivers, Saulsbury.)

Prologue: Garden of the Caboceers, Dahomey.

Act 1: Public Square, Boston

Act 2, Scene 1: Exterior of Lightfoot's Home, Gatorville, Florida. *Scene 2*: Road, one and a half miles from Gatorville. *Scene 3*: Interior of the Lightfoot home.

PROLOGUE

"The Attuck's March" (Overture)

"(My) Dahomian Queen" (Song)
M. Edwards, G. H. Tapley, Chorus
(*Music by* J. Leubrie Hill. *Lyrics by* Frank B. Williams.)

"Caboceers' Choral"
Chorus

ACT 1

"Swing Along" (Opening Chorus)
Company
(*Music and Lyrics by* Will Marion Cook.)

"When the Moon Shines (on the Moonshine)"
R. Conner, Chorus
(*Music by* James Vaughan. *Lyrics by* Alex Rogers.)

"Me an de Minstrel Ban'"
G. W. Walker, Chorus
(*Music by* James Vaughan. *Lyrics by Alex Rogers.*)

"(On) Broadway in Dahomey (Bye and Bye)"
B. Williams, G. Walker, Chorus
(*Music by* Al Johns. *Lyrics by* Alex Rogers.)

"Un Oncore" (Entre Act/Waltz)
B. A. Williams

ACT 2

Scene 1

"Why Adam Sinned"
A. O. Walker
(*Music and Lyrics by* Alex Rogers.)

"Chin Chin"
G. Catlin

Selection
R. L. Tyler

"Society"
H. Hopkins, J. Lightfoot,
L. G. Gibbs, G. H. Tapley, R. Conner, E Anderson (soprano solo)
(*Music by* Will Marion Cook and Will Accooe.)

Scene 2

"I May Be Crazy But I Ain't No Fool"
B. A. Williams
(*Music and Lyrics by* Alex Rogers.)

Scene 3

"A Rich Coon's Babe"
A. O. Walker, Male Double Quartette
(*Music and Lyrics by* Alex Rogers[17].)

"A Dream of the Philippines"
G. Walker, B. A. Williams, A. O. Walker, Dancing Filipino Misses

"Dear Luzon"
G. Walker, B. A. Williams, A. O. Walker, Dancing Filipino Misses
(*Music by* Tom Lemonier.)

Finale
B. A. Williams, G. Walker, Company

1904.27 GIRLS WILL BE GIRLS

A Musical Comedy in Three Acts[18]. Book by R. Melville Baker. Music (and lyrics) by Joseph Hart. Production staged by Joseph Hart. Scenery by Bert Tucman and (Thomas G.) Moses & Hamilton. Costumes by van Horn, Hayden and Rowley. Electrical effects, Joseph Menchen. Musical director, H. Harris Ware. Produced by William A. Brady. Opened 27 August 1904 at the 14th Street Theatre and closed 3 September 1904 after 9 performances.[19]

CAST: *Professor Ebeneezer Hezekiah Dodge*, Principal of the Dodge Academy, who is running for Assembly: AL LEECH. *Abner Sankey*, of the Watch and Ward Society: Art Brock. *Sheriff Ketchem*, of the Board of Health, Board of Police, etc.: HUBERT CORTHELL. *Nathan Hanley*, teacher of music: WINIFRED YOUNG. *Tom Sparrow*, who breaks jail: John McVeigh. *Marvin Brown* of the Fire Company: Harry Davies. *Henry Sniffens*, man about Academy: Oscar Watson. *Police Officer Chase*: Harry Wilson. *Police Officer Holdhim*: Ed Schultz. *Ned Raymond*: Ed Mora. *Madeline Scribner*, teacher of society: LILLIAN BAYER. *Martha Young*, governess, who runs the Academy: MARY KARR. *Lonely Sprouts, Esther Sprouts, Brussell Sprouts*: THE THREE ROSEBUDS: ROMA SNYDER, GLADYS CLAIRE and CHRISTINE COOK.

[15]Earlier version of IN DAHOMEY opened 18 February 1903 at the New York Theatre for 53 performances, followed by a national and European tour. Paul Laurence Dunbar was the credited lyricist on the earlier version.
[16]Earlier programs identify him as Richard Connors.

[17]Also credited to Clare Kummer.
[18]Billed as "Just nonsense—that's all—in three acts."
[19]No New York program available. By the time the subsequent tour reached Wilkes-Barre in 1906 the show featured an all-different musical score.

Girls: Margaret Hastings, Mabel Perotty, Mabel Nevins, Edna Snyder, Anna Hoey, Edith Brockley, Helen Daniels, Jean Ward, Louise Striblen, Annabel Nevins, Estelle Franklyn, Gwendoline Coate, Ethel Croley, Pearl Snyder, Dorothy Wood, Myra Crayne, Clara Barnes. *Boys*: William Herman, William Brockley, D. C. Smith, Frank Braid, William Bradley, Harry Linkey, Arthur Rice, Charles Schell, Ed. T. Mora.

Place: Dodgeville. *Time*: Present.

Act 1: The Play Ground.

Act 2: The School Room.

Act 3: Japanese Fete.

ACT 1

"Swinging" (Opening Chorus) (Sloane)
Chorus

"Sally" (Ware)
E. Mora, Chorus

"Arrival of Madeline"
Chorus

"Etiquette" (Sloane)
L. Bayer

"How'dy Do"
A. Leech, Sprout Sisters

"Dora Lane"
Sprout Sisters

"That Little Girl Is You"
W. Young, L. Bayer

"Boys in Blue"
A. Leech, Sprout Sisters

"The Band Played Boom-Ta-Ra"/"Flag Raising" (Sloane)
Company

ACT 2

"This is the Day" (Opening Chorus)
Chorus

"Ah, Bou Ben Ala"
J. McVeigh

"Good Morning, Teacher"
A. Leech

"My Rubber Ball"
A. Leech, Sprout Sisters, Chorus

Eccentric Dance
A. Leech

"Fly, Fly, Fly" (Finale)(Ware)
A. Leech, Company

ACT 3

"Japanese Lullaby" (Opening Number)(Ware)
Chorus

"Signor Lo Bar"
W. Young, Chorus

"My Brown-Eyed Daisy"
L. Bayer, Chorus

"Gee! Wouldn't That Be Great" (Leech)
A. Leech, Sprout Sisters, Chorus

Finale
Company

1904.28 THE ROYAL CHEF

A Musical Extravaganza (Comic Opera) in Three Acts[20]. Book by George E. Stoddard. Music by Ben M. Jerome. Lyrics by Charles S. Taylor. Reproduced (staged) by Frank Smithson. Orchestra under the direction of Ben M. Jerome. Produced by the LaSalle Theatre Company (Will J. Block, Management). Opened 1 September 1904 at the Lyric Theatre and closed 17 September 1904 after 17 performances.

CAST: *Heinrich Lempauser*, from Chicago: DAVE LEWIS. *The Rajah of Oolong*: HENRY LEONE [Henri Leoni]. *Lord Mito*: JOSEPH C. MIRON. *Badso*: Joseph Allen. *Lieutenant Harry Parkes*: JOHN PARK. *Admiral Noble*: J. Allen. *Midshipmen*: George Stevens, Harry Leonard. *Princess Teto*, the Rajah's daughter: AMELIA STONE. *Kitty O'Reilly*: STELLA TRACY. *Mabel Noble*, the Admiral's Daughter: GERTRUDE MILLINGTON. *Court Beauties (8)*: *Triko*: Bertha Blake. *Salamo*: Estelle Libert. *Kamo*: June Lowry. *Tomo*: Ursula Thompson. *Mohat*: Caroline Sylvester. *Kavat*: Marie Glazier. *Mariat*: Daisy Reed. *Bomat*: Dolly Williams. *Court Pages (4)*: Nena Blake, Helen Cheston, Blanche Lemasney, Florence Townshend.

The Spirit of '76: *Drummer Boy*: Florence Townshend. *Fifer*: Harry Scott. *Veteran Drummer*: George Stevens. Incidental to Act 2, IDA RENÉE, the English Song Genius, makes her American debut presenting her original character studies and creations[21]. *Soldiers and Sailors.*

The action takes place on the mythical Isle of Oolong.

Act 1: Exterior of Rajah's Palace.

Act 2: Interior of Rajah's Palace.

Act 3: Rendezvous of the Oolong bands, Kibul Mountans.

ACT 1[22]

Opening Chorus

"As Befits My Rank and Station"
J. C. Miron

"The Tale of the Tailless Frog"
A. Stone

"When Old Glory Floats from Everywhere"
J. Park

"It's a Way They Have in Chicago"
D. Lewis

"Hail the Rajah" (Rajah Bold Am I)
H. Leone, Ensemble

"Would You If You Were I?" (Trio)
A. Stone, S. Tracey, D. Lewis

"Let Me Go Back"
D. Lewis

Finale

ACT 2

"O, Glorious Sun" (Opening Chorus)
Ensemble

"What Color Eyes Do You Love Best?" (Duet)
A. Stone, J. Park

"O'Reilly"
S. Tracey

"An Admirable Admiral"
J. Allen, G. Millington

"Old Mother Goose"
G. Millington

"Away to the Mountains"
Company

Finale

ACT 3

"We Are a Band of Gentlemen"
J. C. Miron, Bandits

"In the Morning"
D. Lewis

"What's the Matter with My Man in the Moon?"
A. Stone

"Napenee"
S. Tracey, J. Park

Finale

---

[20]The published piano vocal score (F. B. Haviland Co, New York, 1904) contains the subtitle, The Mythical Isle of Oolong.

[21]The New York Dramatic Mirror enumerated her 3 specialties: recitation/song on matrimonial deceit, "The Rake's Progress" and "The Maid and the Monk."

[22]Interpolated by the show's authors, as per published sheet music:

"The Maiden and the Kissing Bug"
S. Tracey, J. C. Miron

Interpolated for subsequent tour, as per published sheet music:

"All Through Through the Love of You"
Helen Cheston
(*Music by* Chester Searles. *Lyrics by* P. C. Mason.)

1904.29 THE SCHOOL GIRL

A Musical Play in Two Acts, 3 Scenes. Book by Paul M. Potter and Henry Hamilton. Music by Leslie Stuart. Lyrics by Charles H. Taylor. (Additional songs by Paul West, John W. Bratton, Howard Talbot, W. T. Francis, Benjamin Hapgood Burt, Joseph Rosey and Albert Von Tilzer.) Produced under the stage direction of J. E. A. Malone. Scenery by Ernest Gros. Orchestra under the direction of William T. Francis. Produced by Charles Frohman. Opened 1 September 1904 at Daly's Theatre, moved 24 October 1904 to the Herald Square Theatre and closed 10 December 1904 after 150 performances[23].

CAST: *Lillian Leigh*: EDNA MAY. *Mother Superior*: Mildred Baker. *Marianne*, a French Bonne: Clara Braithwaite. *American Girls (6)*: *Minnie Reckfeller*: Lulu Valli. *Norma Rochester*: Jane May. *Yolande*: Vivian Vowles. *Violette*: Ivy Louise. *Mimi*: Dorothy Dunbar. *Louise*: Barbara Dunbar. *Margot*: Madge Greet. *Saaefrada*, a Model: Lakme Darcier. *Miss Yost*, the Typist: Virginia Staunton. *Mrs. Marchmont*: Mrs. Watt Tanner. *Cicely Marchmont*, her daughter: Constance Hyem. *Kate Medhurst*: Jeannette Paterson. *Mabel*: Joyce Thorn. *Jessie Campbell*: Queena Sanford. *Evelyn Summers*: Eithel Kelly. *Waitress*: Adele Carson. *Edgar Verney*, an Artist: W. TALLEUR ANDREWS. *General Marchmont*: FRED WRIGHT, JR. *Tubby Bedford*: JAMES BLAKELEY. *Peter Overend* of the Stock Exchange: Robert Minster. *Corner*: W. R. Shirley. *George Sylvester, Adolphe Delapoise*, Artists: Harry Hudson, Murri Moncrieff. (*Jacques de Creyert*: Fred Ozab. *Merrion*: Jerome Hayes.) *Sir Ormsby St. Ledger*: GEORGE GROSSMITH, JR.

Act 1, Scene 1: The Convent Lawn. *Scene 2*: The Open Stock Exchange, Paris.

Act 2: Edgar Verney's Studio.

ACT 1[24]

Scene 1

Opening Chorus

"If Ma Says No"[25]
C. Hyem

"When I Was a Girl (Like You)"
M. Baker
(*Lyrics by* Charles Taylor.)

"(The) Daughters of the Guard"
E. May, Chorus
(*Lyrics by* Leslie Stuart.)

Scene 2

Opening Chorus

"American Girls" (Chickoo We're Only Just Sixteen)
Chorus

"Florrie"[26]
G. Grossmith, Jr.
(*Music and Lyrics by* Paul Rubens.)

"(Looking for a) Needle in a Haystack"
J. Blakeley
(*Lyrics by* Adrian Ross, Leslie Stuart.)

"(She's) An English Girl"[27]
W. T. Andrews
(*Lyrics by* Adrian Ross, Leslie Stuart.)

"Call 'Round Again"
E. May
(*Lyrics by* Leslie Stuart.)

Finale

ACT 2[28]

Opening Chorus[29]

"My Little Canoe"
E. May
(*Lyrics by* Leslie Stuart.)

"(We Want to Be) Simpler"
J. Blakeley, F. Wright, Jr., G. Grossmith, Jr.
(*Lyrics by* Leslie Stuart.)

"Jolly Little Japs"[30]
W. T. Andrews, Chorus

"My Cosey Corner Girl"
G. Grossmith, Jr., E. May
(*Music by* John W. Bratton[31]. *Lyrics by* Charles Noel Douglas.)

"One of the Boys"
F. Wright, Jr.
(*Music by* Howard Talbot.)

"In Black and White"[32]
J. Blakeley
(*Music by* John W. Bratton. *Lyrics by* Paul West.)

"Real Town Lady"[33]
E. May, G. Grossmith, Jr.
(*Music and Lyrics by* Paul Rubens.)

"Old English Cake Walk"[34]
G. Grossmith, Jr.
(*Music and Lyrics by* Paul Rubens.)

"A Honeymoon Girl"[35]
C. Hyem
(*Lyrics by* Leslie Stuart.)

Finale

1904.30 A MADCAP PRINCESS

A Comic Opera in Three Acts. Libretto by Harry B. Smith. Based on the novel "When Knighthood Was in Flower" by Charles Major. Music by Ludwig Engländer. Staged by Edward P. Temple. Settings by Homer Emens and Edward G. Unitt. Costumes designed by Klaw & Erlanger Costume Department. Orchestra under the direction of Antonio DeNovellis. Produced by Charles Dillingham. Opened 5 September 1904 at the Knickerbocker Theater and closed 22 October 1904 after 48 performances.

CAST: *Mary Tudor*, Princess of England: LULU GLASER. *Henry VIII*, King of England: WILLIAM PRUETTE. *Charles Brandon*: BERTRAM WALLIS. *Sir Edwin Caskoden*, Master of the Dance: Donald McLaren. *Sir Adam Judson*: Howard Chambers. *Will Somers*, the King's Jester: FRANK REICHER. *Duke of Buckingham*:

---

[23] Costumes uncredited.

[24] Also interpolated into the show, as per published sheet music:
"Little Girl You'll Do"
W. T. Andrews
(*Music by* Alfred Solman. *Lyrics by* Benjamin Hapgood Burt.)

[25] Replaced after opening by:
"A Honeymoon Girl"
C. Hyem
Which was later replaced for the tour by:
"I Love You All the Time"
C. Hyem

[26] Replaced after opening by:
"Belinda on the Telephone" (Belinda on the Line)
G. Grossmith, Jr.
(*Lyrics by* Paul Rubens.)

[27] Replaced for subsequent tour by:
"Little Girl You'll Do"
W. T. Andrews
(*Music by* Alfred Solman. *Lyrics by* Benjamin Hapgood Burt.)

[28] Added during New York run or for tour after "My Cosey Corner Girl:"
"It's a Good World After All"
J. Blakeley
(*Music by* Gus Edwards. *Lyrics by* Vincent Bryan.)

[29] Added after opening to Opening Chorus, Act 2:
"(Oh Woman in) Days of Romance"
W. T. Andrews, Chorus

[30] Replaced during the run or for subsequent tour by:
"Sweet Sano-oo"
W. T. Andrews, Chorus
(*Music by* William T. Francis. *Lyrics by* Vernon Roy.)

[31] Song version of Bratton's instrumental conceit "In a Cosey Corner."

[32] Dropped during the run.

[33] Replaced during the run by:
"Lonesome"
E. May
(*Music by* Albert Von Tilzer. *Lyrics by* Joseph Rosey.)

[34] Replaced during the run by:
"The Lancers"
G. Grossmith, Jr., Chorus

[35] After opening, moved to Act 1 following Opening Chorus. Also known as "The Honeymoon Girl."

Arthur Barry. *Cardinal Wolsey*: Ralph Lewis. *Duke de Longueville*, Envoy of France: Guy Hoffman. *Captain Bradhurst*: Howard Chambers. *Farmer Blake*: Reginald Barlow. *A Friar*: Maurice Sims. *Landlord of "The Bow & String" Tavern*: Herbert Freer. *Goody Blake*: Elsie Thomas. *Queen Katherine*: Maud Ream Stover. *Maids of Honor to Mary Tudor (3)*: *Lady Jane Bolingbroke*: Mary Conwell. *Mistress Jane Seymour*: Gwendolyn Valentine. *Mistress Annie Boleyn*: Rose Earle. *A Page*: Lillian Lipyeat.

Ladies and Gentlemen of the Court, Country Folk, Flower Girls, Attendants, etc.: Misses Estelle deAngelis, Helen Bancroft, Louise Wein, Rita Dean, Kathryn Hale, Mariam Norris, Virginia Courtney, Georgia Sage, Elsie Thomas, Olive Cox, Beatrice Anderson, Sadie Gerschoff, Vera Brewster, Ethel Wynne, Estelle Peterson, Emma Spohr, Elizabeth Murray, Ella Reichter, Lucy Stone, Katherine LaTour,. Messrs. Joseph Frohoff, Louis Helie, Maurice Robinson, Adam Dockray, Charles B. Baker, Joseph Miller, E. J. Kloville, E. F. Drew, Peter Canova, Ambrose Daly.

The action takes place in England in the sixteenth century.

Act 1: Windsor Park on May-day morning.

Act 2: Princess Mary's apartment in Bridewell House, London.

Act 3: "Bow and String" Tavern at Bristol.

ACT 1[36]

"May Day Is Hey Day" (Opening Ensemble)
Chorus

"I'm Bluff King Hal" (Song)
W. Pruette

"May Day Processional" (Chorus)
Chorus

"A Madcap Princess" (Entrance Song)
L. Glaser

"That Beautiful Isle of the Sea" (Song)
L. Glaser, B. Wallis, Chorus

Finale:

"Sir! You Wear a Sword"
Entire Company

"If I Marry the King Of France"
L. Glaser, Chorus

"Let a Good Ship Be Made Ready"
W. Pruette, Chorus

ACT 2

"Maids of Honor to the Princess" (Opening Ensemble)
Chorus

"Woman Rules the King" (Song)
W. Pruette

"If You Were Mine Alone" (Song)
B. Wallis

"Thrice Noble Is He" (Finale)
Entire Company

ACT 3

"Come, Fill Up a Brimming Flagon" (Opening Ensemble)
Entire Company

"The Kings of the Sea" (Quartette and Chorus)

"Cavalier Song" (Song and Chorus)
L. Glaser, Chorus

Finale
Entire Company

1904.31 THE ROGERS BROTHERS IN PARIS

A Vaudeville Farce in Three Acts, 5 Scenes[37]. Book by John J. McNally. Music by Max Hoffmann. Lyrics by George V. Hobart and Ed Gardenier. Staged by Herbert Gresham. Musical numbers staged by Ned Wayburn. Scenery painted by Ernest Gros. Costumes designed by F. Richard Anderson. Electrical effects by Harry Bissing. Music director, Max Hoffmann. Produced by (Marc) Klaw and (Abraham L.) Erlanger. Opened 5 September 1904 at the New Amsterdam Theatre, moved 10 October 1904 to the Liberty Theatre and closed 12 November 1904 after 72 performances.

CAST: *Rudolph Kahn*: GUS ROGERS. *Adolph Finkleleiner*: MAX ROGERS. *George Hamilton Dodge*: GEORGE AUSTIN MOORE. *P. Sarsfield Kelliher*: JOHN CONROY. *Walter Lee Leonard*: FRED NIBLO. *Justin Little*: Joseph Kane. *Leo*, the lion tamer: Louis B. Foley. *Pierre Gorot*: Frank C. Young. *Marjorie Kelliher*: JOSEPHINE COHAN. *Emilie Lamson*: Dorothy Hunting. *Rene Renaud*: Emily Nice. *Clairette Soule*: Bessie DeVoie. *Francois*: Willie Torpey.

Ladies of the Ensemble: Julia Eastman, Florence Folsom, Lillie Luby, Bessie Leyland, Bessie Kyle, Vinnie Bradcome, Lottie Sennett, May Luby, Lily Hart, Pauline Montreau, Helen Brooks, Ida Evon, Florence Carrette, Marjorie Blair, May Lawrence, Helen DeMond, Monta Elmo, Grace Gindell, Polly Allison, Doris Townsend, Vinnie Danvers, Davida Hawthorne, Daisy Ashton, Pearl Perry, Hattie Van Buren, Lillian Collins, Helen Miller, Gladys Crawford, Maud Napier, Stella Adams, Amy Scott, Rosita Lawrence, Gertrude Merrill. *Men's Ensemble*: Messrs. Thompson, Dale, Harclerode, Cochrane, George, Price, Rogers, Sherman, Silliman, Steinman, Strath, Fabian.

Act 1: The Bal Boullier, Latin Quarter, Paris

Act 2, Scene 1: Garden of the Tuilleries, Paris. *Scene 2*: Rue de Rivoli, Paris. *Scene 3*: Place de la Concorde, Paris.

Act 3:The Hagenbach Zoo, St. Louis Exposition.

ACT 1

The Students' Ball"
Ensemble

"Soldier Boy"
D. Hunting, Chorus
(*Lyrics by* George V. Hobart.)

"Belle of the Silvery Nile"
Rogers Brothers, Ladies' Ensemble
(*Lyrics by* Ed Gardenier.)

French Cake Walk (Finale)

Dance Eccentric
F. C. Young, B. DeVoie

"Yankee Land"
Rogers Brothers, Entire Company

ACT 2

"Quarreling Coachmen" (Opening)
Men's Ensemble

"McNabb! (Who Drives the Cab)"
J. Conroy, Coachmen
(*Lyrics by* Ed Gardenier.)

"Society"
J. Cohan, assisted by Ladies of the Ensemble
(*Lyrics by* Ed Gardenier.)

Original Sayings and Parodies
Rogers Brothers

"The American Minstrels in Paris"
B. DeVoie, F. C. Young, assisted by Ladies of the Ensemble

"By the Old Oak Tree" (By the Sycamore Tree)
D. Hunting, G. A. Moore
(*Lyrics by* George V. Hobart.)

Celebration of the Fall of the Bastille (Finale)
Ensemble

ACT 3

"Kindness"
L. B. Foley, Animals

"Pretty Polly"
G. A. Moore, assisted by Ladies of the Ensemble
(*Lyrics by* George V. Hobart.)

"The Village Maid"
Rogers Brothers, J. Cohan, assisted by Ladies Ensemble
(*Lyrics by* Max Hoffmann.)

Finale
Rogers Brothers, Entire Company

---

[36]Musical numbers not listed in program. List prepared from published vocal score. Performed in the show but not listed in the vocal score: "Letter Chansonette," "Lonesome Little Maid," (*Music by* Alfred Solman. *Lyrics by* Benjamin Hapgood Burt.) "Ontario," "Rings of the Sea." Added for subsequent tour:

"A-L-E-X-A-N-D-R-I-A"
Sophie Brandt
(*Music by* Alfred Solman. *Lyrics by* John B. Lowitz.)

[37]Billed as the seventh annual engagement of the Rogers Brothers; the series began in 1899.

1904.32 THE OLD HOMESTEAD

A Revival of the Rural Melodrama in Four Acts[38]. Play by Denman Thompson and George W. Ryer. Produced by Franklin Thompson. Opened 12 September 1904 at the New York Theatre and closed ?5 November 1904 after 61 performances.

CAST [in order of appearance]: *Joshua Whitcomb*: DENMAN THOMPSON. *Cy Prime*: CHARLES CARTER. *Happy Jack*: WALTER GALE. *Frank Hopkins*: Horace Wright. *Eb. Ganzey*: FRANK KNAPP. *John Freeman*: JOSEPH A. HANNA. *Aunt Matilda (Whitcomb)*: LOUISA MORSE. *Rickety Ann*: ANITA L. FOWLER. *Annie Hopkins*: BLANCHE KIRK. *Nellie Freeman*: LAURA BRADFORD. *Maggie O'Flaherty*: LILLIAN CORDON. *Henry Hopkins*: GUS KAMMERLEE. *Judge Patterson*: George R. Clark. *Francois Fogarty*: W. E. Chamberlain. *Mrs. Hopkins*: Annie Thompson. *Reuben Whitcomb*: Hector Dion. *One of the Finest*: Charles Ingoldsby. *Hoboken Terror*: Dan Regan. *Newsboy*: L. M. Roe. *Postman*: Edward J. Hanna. *Seth Perkins*: Charles H. Clark. *Len Holbrook*: George L. Patch. *David Willard*: Himself. *Warren Ellis*: Patrick Redmond. *Anna Maria Murdock*: Venie Thompson. *The Old Homestead Double Quartette*.

1904.33 THE STREET SINGER

A Musical Drama in Four Acts, 6 Scenes. Play by Hal Reid. Music adapted by Victor Colwell. Stage direction by Will J. Dean. Dances arranged by Emil Hansel. Costumes by Van Horn & Sons. Musical director, Victor Colwell. Produced by B. E. Forrester and Harry Mittenthal. Opened 12 September 1904 at the American Theatre and closed 24 September 1904 after 16 performances; returned 17 October 1904 to the West End Theatre and closed 22 October 1904 after an additional 8 performances.[39]

CAST: *Morgan Van Voort*, an octogenarian millionaire: GEORGE PAUNCEFORT. *Lawrence Winfield*, his illegitimate son: BIGELOW COOPER. *William Van Voort*, his legitimate son and heir: GUY LEWIS. *John Vodray*, his confidential book-keeper: ARDA LaCROIX[40]. *Antoine Jean Xavier*, the Count de Villerole: M. W. RALE. *Dr. William West*: Tobie Lyons. *Thomas Jackson*, a detective: John F. Donovan. *John Murray*, a detective: Frederick Morgan. *Patrick Quinn*, a policeman: George Morgan. *Michael Dooley*, a policeman: Joseph W. Herbert, Jr. *James Brown*, butler to Van Voort: Frank Baldwin. *Madge Westervelt*, after Van Voort's millions: CLAIRE GRENVILLE. *Mona Mayme*, the millionaire's toy: AGNES PORTER. *Kathleen Burns*, a cuckoo from Killarney: Katherine Dooling. *Marie Fitch*: Harriet Keyes. *Mazie DuBarry*: Elizabeth Dunphy[41]. *Effie Pearl*: Maud Colwell. *Prudence Villars*: Edna May Donohew. *Winnie Searles*: Eleanore Russell. *Zaza Maloney*: Jeannette D'Arville. *Violet Vodray*, La Belle Violetta, "The Street Singer": FLORENCE BINDLEY.

Act 1: Entertainment on lawn on Van Voort summer home on the Hudson.

Act 2, Scene 1: Violet's apartment. *Scene 2*: Foot of West 23rd Street, Erie Railroad, New York. *Scene 3*: Cathedral, Isle Pine Forest. Lakewood, New Jersey.

Act 3: Street in New York City.

Act 4: Residence of Morgan Van Voort, Fifth Avenue, New York.

ACT 1[42]

"Like Katy Did"
H. Keyes, R. Osborne, M. Colwell, E. Donohew, E. Russell, J. D'Arville

National Airs
F. Bindley, Show Girls

ACT 2
Scene 1

"Billy" (My Billy Boy)
F. Bindley, R. Osborne, M. Colwell, E. Donohew, E. Russell, J. D'Arville
(*Music by* Ted S. Barron. *Lyrics by* Edgar Malone.)

ACT 3

"Carmina"
F. Bindley

"My Dixie Lou"
F. Bindley, Her Girls

1904.34 MR. WIX OF WICKHAM

A Musical Comedy in Two Acts. Book and music by Herbert Darnley. (Adapted from the English musical of the same name.) Additional musical numbers by George Everard, Jerome D. Kern. Re-adaptation and many new lyrics by John H. Wagner. Produced under the stage direction of Tom Ricketts. Scenery by Frank Rafter and Theodore Reisig. Costumes by Madame Ripley. Orchestra under the direction of Whitney Bennington. Produced by Edward E. Rice. Opened 19 September 1904 at the Bijou Theatre and closed 22 October 1904 after 41 performances.

CAST: *Wilfrid Wix*, late of Wickham, England, manager of the Gentleman's Wants Supply Stores: HENRY CORSON CLARKE. *Tom Howard*, Duke's missing nephew, young colonial heir to £3,000,000: DAVID LYTHGOW. *John Smith*, B. A., Tom's school friend, now his tutor: JULIAN (DALTON) ELTINGE. *Duke of Tadminster*: SYDNEY DeGREY. *Shamus O'Scoot*, Duke's private detective: FRANK LALOR. *Mr. Banks*, M.P. for Coddletwon and Colonel in the Coddletown Town Guards: Arthur Wooley. *Mr. Potter*, Mayor of Coddletown and Major in Guards: Douglas Flint. *Mr. Dodd*, Chairman Coddletown and Captain in Guards: Andrew O'Neill. *Mr. Jinks* of the Horse Marines: Fred Waters. *Drinkaweldry*, an Aboriginal Chief: MILT POLLOCK. *Lady Betty*, Duke's daughter: THELMA FAIR. *Maude Benton*, Lady Betty's friend and travelling companion: ALICE MAUDE POOLE. *Madame Marie*, proprietress of the Gentleman's Wants Supply Stores: LAURA GUERITE. *Mrs. O'Scoot*: Catherine J. Hayes. *Susan Flyte*: Frances Wilson. *Tottie Travers*: Cecile Mayer. *The Frolicsome Kangaroo*, his original creation: David Abraham.

Lady Shop Assistants, Business Men, Vivandiers, Soldiers, etc.: Misses Violet Holbrook, Marion Stokes, Frankie Loeb, Lillian MacCeney, Ocia Thompson, Annie Winner, Jessie Thompson, Mabel Douglas, Mildred Tate, Lucille Monroe, Adelaide Ackland, Helen Ryley, Wally Vaughn, Trixie Orient, Ethel Filmore, Sybil Ellwood, Mabel Gilmore, Ethel Gilmore, Kate Young, Maude Stanley, Elsie Yale. Meredith S. Brown; (Messrs.) Joseph Levere, Fred Smythe, William Mowry, Jack E. Sullivan, Fred Lalor, Walter Garfield, Frank White, Jack Howell, Herman Noble.

Act 1: Shop of Madame Curie, Coddletown, Australia.

Act 2: Camp of the Coddletown Guards.

ACT 1

Opening Chorus
(*Music by* George Everard.)

"A Handle to My Name" (Song)
A. M. Poole, Chorus
(*Music by* Herbert Darnley.)

"Her First Can Can" (Song)
L. Guerite, Chorus
(*Music by* Jerome D. Kern. *Lyrics by* J. H. Wagner.)

"The Important Man" (Trio)
A. Wooley, D. Flint, A. O'Neil, Chorus
(*Music by* Jerome D. Kern.)

"One Thing Different" (Song)
H. C. Clarke, Chorus
(*Music by* Herbert Darnley, Jerome D. Kern.)

"(From) Saturday 'Til Monday" (Song)
L. Lawlor, Chorus
(*Music by* Jerome D. Kern. *Lyrics by* John H. Wagner.)

"Cupid's Garden" (Duet)
T. Fair, D. Lythgow
(*Music by* Max C. Eugene [Max Dreyfus].)

"Raindrops" (Aria)
T. Fair
(*Music by* George Everard.)

[38]First produced in New York 10 January 1887 at the 14th Street Theatre for 155 performances. For Synopsis of Scenes, see original 1887 production.

[39] Played New York area return engagements 22 January 1906 at the Metropolis Theatre for 9 performances, 23 April 1906 at the American Theatre for 8 performances, and 30 April 1906 at the West End Theatre for 8 performances.

[40] For return engagement at the West End, John Vodray was played by ROBERT McWADE.

[41] For return engagement at the West End, Mazie DuBarry was played by Rose Osborne.

[42] For subsequent return engagement to the Metropolis Theatre 22 January 1906, all the musical numbers had been changed (except "Billy"):

"Jessamine" (Act 1)
H. Keyes

Xylophone Solo (Act 1)
F. Bindley

"Lolita" (Act 3)
F. Bindley, Chorus

"Waiting for You" (Duet)
J. C. Clarke, L. Guerite, Chorus
(*Music by* Jerome D. Kern. *Lyrics by* John H. Wagner.)

"Susan" (Song)
D. Lythgow, F. Wilson, Chorus
(*Music and Lyrics by* Jerome D. Kern.)

Finale
(*Music by* Herbert Darnley.)

ACT 2

Opening Chorus
(*Music by* Herbert Darnley.)

"Volunteers"
Chorus
(*Music by* George Everard.)

"Rub-a-Dub" (Trio)
A. Wooley, D. Flint, A. O'Neill
(*Music by* Jerome D. Kern.)

"Angling by a Babbling Brook" (Song)
A. M. Poole, Girls
(*Music by* Jerome D. Kern.)

"Googy-oo" (Duet)
F. Lawlor, C. J. Hayes
(*Music by* Edward E. Rice. *Lyrics by* John H. Wagner.)

"Military Maids" (Solo and Chorus)
D. Lythgow
(*Music by* Jerome D. Kern.)

"Because I Am a Duke" (Song)
S. DeGrey, Chorus
(*Music by* Jerome D. Kern. *Lyrics by* John H. Wagner.)

"Bluff" (Song and Recitative)
L. Guerite
(*Music by* Jerome D. Kern. *Lyrics by* John H. Wagner.)

"Love Is King"[43] (Aria)
T. Fair
(*Music by* Waller.)

"Not Like Other Girls" (You'll Find Another Girl)(Song and Specialty)
J. D. Eltinge
(*Music and Lyrics by* Andros Hawley.)

"The Dancing Kangaroo" (Aria)
D. Abraham
(*Music by* Jerome D. Kern.)

"Sergeant Wix" (Song)
J. C. Clarke, Chorus
(*Music by* Herbert Darnley.)

Finale
(*Music by* Jerome D. Kern.)

1904.35 THE WEST POINT CADET

A Musical Comedy in Three Acts. Adapted from the original French by Paul Billaud and Alfred Barré. Music by Alfred Muller Norden. American adaptation by Alfred Muller Norden. Staged by Joseph W. Herbert. Orchestra under the direction of Jose Vandenberg. Produced by Nathaniel Roth. Opened 30 September 1904 at the Princess Theatre and closed 3 October 1904 after 3 performances.

CAST: *Ethan Allen Bernard*: Scott Cooper. *Billie, Lillie*, twins: DELLA FOX. *Ernest Everett*: RICHIE LING. *General Jackson Scott*: ARTHUR CUNNINGHAM. *Aurelia*: Agnes Stone. *Washington Graft*: JOSEPH W. HERBERT. *Alonzo Sheridan Scott*: EDWARD ABELES. *Cesarine Allen*: CLARA PALMER. *Tom*: Madeline Hazlett. *Harry*: Mabel Carrier. *Fred*: Laura Butler. *Ben*: Viola Clayton. *Drill Sergeant*: Robert Ward. *Pat*, the porter: Edward Lehay. *Fritz*, the gardener: James Nichols. *Pierre*, the cook: Joseph Graham. *Waiter*: James Nichols. *Policeman*: Joseph Graham. *Valet*: Roy Cutter.

Flirtation Sextet: Misses Mabel Carrier, Elsa Rheinhardt, Josephine Angela, May Willard, Lucie Georgi, Hazel Roberts. *Gentlemen*: Roy Cutter, Harry DeRango, J. William Stelz, James Cameron, Paul Russell Stone, John Cunningham.

Act 1: The Drill Ground of a Military Academy.

Act 2: The Drawing Room in Bernard's House in New York.

Act 3: A Corridor in a Hotel near Grand Central Station.

MUSICAL NUMBERS

"Dream Song"

"The Good Old G.A.R."

"I'll Be a West Point Cadet"

"Lovely Little Marjorie"

"My Love Forevermore"

"Those Days of Long Ago"

"Two Little Lovebirds"

1904.36 LOVE'S LOTTERY

A Comic Opera in Two Acts. Libretto by Stanislaus Stange. Music by Julian Edwards. Staged by Max Freeman. Produced under the personal supervision of F. C. Whitney. Orchestra under the direction of William E. Macquinn. Produced by F. C. Whitney. Opened 3 October 1904 at the Broadway Theatre and closed 19 November 1904 after 50 performances[44].

CAST: *Sergeant Bob Trivet*: WALLACE BROWNLOW. *Sir Hervey Aston*: GEORGE L. TALLMAN. *Squire Marmaduke Skeffington*: W. H. THOMPSON. *Laura Skeffington*: LOUISE GUNNING. *Sally Lunn*: Delight Barsch. *Barney O'Toole*: JOHN SLAVIN. *Ponsonby Damocles Twiller*: H. W. Tredenick. *Jane Jones*: Margaret Crawford. *Molly Muggins*: Tekla Farm. *Bess Myrtle*: Ivy Clyde. *Gill Poorman*: Lucia Nola. *Tom Ryder*: Heathe Gregory. *Jack Kite*: John H. Duffey. *Bill Butler*: John Norele. *Joe Costar*: Lionel Robsarte. *Lina*, (a German laundress): MME. (ERNESTINE) SCHUMANN-HEINK.

The action takes place in England in 1818 during the reign of George III.

Act 1: Courtyard of Lina's house in the village of Deanswold. Early summer. Morning.

Act 2: A secluded part of Deanswold Park. Afternoon of day of Act 1.

ACT 1

"Song of the Tub" (Quartette)
T. Farm, I. Clyde, M. Crawford, L. Nola

"Behold Our Lady Great" (Quintette)
L. Gunning, T. Farm, I. Clyde, M. Crawford, L. Nola

"What Art Thou?" (Song)
L. Gunning

Entrance of Twiller
H. W. Tredenick, T. Farm, I. Clyde, M. Crawford, L. Nola, Girls' Chorus

"Hoax and Coax" (Duet)
D. Barsch, J. Slavin

"My First True Love" (Song)
G. L. Tallman

"The Village Recruits" (Ensemble)
T. Farm, I. Clyde, M. Crawford, L. Nola,
H. Gregory, J. H. Duffey, J. Norele, L. Robsarte, Chorus

"The Honeymoon" (Duet)
L. Gunning, W. H. Thompson

"Cupid's a Lad" (Quintette)
L. Gunning, E. Schumann-Heink, G. L. Tallman, W. H. Thompson, W. Brownlow

"Kind Fortune Smiles To-day"[45] (Polacca)
E. Schumann-Heink

Finale
Principals, Chorus

ACT 2[46]

"Long Forgotten" (Song)
G. L. Tallman

[43]Dropped after opening.

[44]Settings, costumes uncredited. Played a return engagement 5 June 1905 at the Academy of Music for 7 performances.

[45]Dropped for subsequent tour.

[46]During the run, the following interpolation was added to the program: Mme. Schumann-Heink will introduce in Act 2 the famous Brindisi from the opera "Lucretia Borgia" with the kind permission of Mr. Julian Edwards and Mr. F. C. Whitney.

"A Glimpse of Eden"[47] (Trio)
L. Gunning, G. L. Tallman, W. H. Thompson

"Holday Joys" (Ensemble)
L. Gunning, T. Farm, I. Clyde, M. Crawford, L. Nola, W. H. Thompson, H. Gregory, Chorus

"Follow the Flag" (Song)
W. Brownlow, Chorus

"If We Part" (Trio)
E. Schumann-Heink, G. L. Tallman, W. Brownlow

"The Blarney of Killarney" (Song)
J. Slavin, Girls' Chorus

"Sounds We Love to Hear"[48] (Song)
W. H. Thompson, H. Gregory, J. H. Duffey, J. Norele, L. Robsarte, Chorus

"The Temptation" (Quintette)
L. Gunning, E. Schumann-Heink, G. L. Tallman, W. H. Thompson, W. Brownlow

"Sweet Thoughts of Home" (Song)
E. Schumann-Heink

Finale
Principals, Chorus

1904.37 THE SHO-GUN

A Korean Comic Opera in Two Acts. Libretto by George Ade. Music by Gustav Luders. Produced under the stage direction of George F. Marion. Dances arranged by Sam Marion. Settings by Walter Burridge. Costumes designed by F. S. Neydhart and Will R. Barnes. Orchestra under the direction of John McGhie. Produced by Henry W. Savage. Opened 10 October 1904 at Wallack's Theatre and closed 21 January 1905 after 125 performances.

CAST: *William Henry Spangle*, an energetic pilgrim: CHARLES E. EVANS. *His Excellency Flai-Hai*, the Sho-Gun of Ka-Choo: EDWARD B. MARTINDELL. *General Kee-Otori*, a military grandee: DAVID TORRENCE. *Hanki-Pank*, astrologer and dealer in proverbs: THOMAS C. LEARY. *Tee-To Komura*, a despised bachelor: WILLIAM C. WEEDON. *Beverly Dasher*, Ensign U.S. Navy: Henry Taylor. *O Hung*, a messenger on the dark path: George Ollerenshaw. *Wi-Ju*, a publicity promoter: Arthur O'Bryan. *Sha-Man*, a Head Priest: E. P. Parsons. *Omee-Omi*, widow of the former Sho-Gun: GEORGIA CAINE. *Princess Hunni-Bun*, niece of Sho-Gun: CHRISTIE MacDONALD.

The Dowager Hi-Faloot, first of the exclusives: CARRIE E. PERKINS. *Moo-Zoo May*, first of the Sing-Song girls: GRACE KING. *Kee-Zi*, companion of Hunni-Bun: Loris Scarsdale. *Maids of Honor attending Hunni-Bun (5)*: *U-Ju*: Myra Davis. *Yung-Fun*: Olga Fredericks. *Tiki-Too*: Marie Christie. *Tah-Tah*: Cora Spicer. *Nanni-Fan*: Georgena Leary.

Sing Song Girls: Rose Murray, Osie Williams, Fay Tincher, May Murray, Edna Jackson, Lucille DeMentz, Anita Marik, Elinor Barras, Hertha Engel. *Guards*: Amy LaDew, Olive Hill, Lucille Prince, Muriel Harmon, Pansy Farmer, Eda Chandler, Etta Raynor. *Bachelors*: Arney Henry, Alex B. St. Johns, Whitlock Davis, William Reiske, James Dale, Derby Brown, J. H. Keenan, Frank Blackman, Morris Hiller, Carlyle Sweitler, Albert Cunningham, O. Fowle, P. H. Tazeman, E. O'Connor. *Korean Girls*: Genevieve Freeman, Lucy Tonge, Virgie Ware, Grace Overand, Lulu Hamill, Grace Walsh, Agnes Sheridan, Patsy Rogers. *Priests, Attendants, Soldiers, Watchmen, Coolies, etc.*

The action takes place in the imaginary island of Ka-Choo, in the Sea of Japan, between Japan and Korea.

Act 1: In front of the Ancestral Temple, outside the city wall and near the Gate of Victory of the city of Ka-Choo.

Act 2: The Wistaria Garden of the Forbidden City.

ACT 1[49]

Opening Chorus

"Teach the Young Idea How to Shoot"
T. C. Leary, Chorus

"I Am, Yours Truly"
W. C. Weedon

"Life All Free from Care"
W. C. Weedon, Bachelors' Chorus

"(Keep Your Eye on) The Girl Just Out"
C. MacDonald, D. Torrence, C. E. Perkins, Chorus

"Little Moo-Zoo May"
G. King, Chorus

"Flutter, Little Bird"
C. MacDonald, T. C. Leary, W. C. Weedon, D. Torrence

"Soldiers' Chorus"

""The Irrepressible Yank"
C. E. Evans

"Mourners' Chorus"

"(The) Man She'll Never Meet"
G. Caine, Chorus

"Love Must Be Blind"
G. Caine, C. E. Evans

Finale

ACT 2

Opening Chorus

"Wistaria My Bride"
C. MacDonald, Chorus

"Your Honeymoon Will Last"
C. MacDonald, W. C. Weedon

"Hiko Chorus"

"The Games We Used to Play"
C. E. Evans, G. King, Chorus

"Wedding Chorus"

"The Sho-Gun of Ka-Choo"
E. B. Martindell, Chorus

"The Jackie"
H. Taylor, Chorus

Finale

[47]Dropped for subsequent tour.

[48]Dropped after opening.

[49]After opening, the running order to Act 1 was changed. "The Girl Just Out", "Mourners' Chorus" and "Soldiers' Chorus" were dropped, "Little Moo Zoo May" moved to follow the opening chorus. Added were:

"This Is How I Do"
C. MacDonald, D. Torrence, C. E. Perkins, Chorus

"Schemes"
C. E. Evans, Chorus

"She's Just a Little Bit Different from the Others That I Know"
C. MacDonald, W. C. Weedon

1904.38 A TRIP TO AFRICA

A Musical Comedy in Two Acts. Book and lyrics by John Larkins. Music by Dave Peyton. Musical director, Will Vodery. Produced by W. C. Craine. Opened 17 October 1904 at the Third Avenue Theatre and closed 22 October 1904 after 8 performances.[50]

CAST: *Princess Lulu*: DORA PATTERSON. *King Dowashe*: JOHN LARKINS. *Captain Cinch*: BERT GRANT. *Minstrel Boys*: Bailey & Fletcher. *Uncle St. Johnson*: Earl Harris. *Thomas Jenkins*: William Dewey. *Detna*: J. W. Lamb. *Mrs. Samartha*: Irene Franklin. *Gennette*: CARRIE SMITH. *Chief Boo*: Joseph Smith. With James Watkins, Arthur Rhode, John Hill, James Waite, Ed. Jackson, Bertha Grant, Gertie Watkins, Irene Gaines, Lena Mitchell, Viola Jackson, Mamie White, Ella Cole, Gertrude Miller, Blanch Arlington, Belle King.

Scenes: Georgia; Africa.

MUSICAL NUMBERS

"I Wants a Loving Man"
D. Patterson

"Zongo, My Congo Queen"
D. Patterson

"Without You"
C. Smith

Minstrel Specialty (between acts)
Bailey & Fletcher

[50]No New York program available. A TRIP TO AFRICA continued to tour as late as 1910 with different casts, musical numbers, under the auspices of the Black Patti Musical Comedy Company.

1904.39 HIGGLEDY-PIGGLEDY

Weber and Ziegfeld All-Star Stock Company in a Rigamarole of Fun, Fancy and Foolishness (Musical Farce) in Two Acts. Dialogue and lyrics by Edgar Smith. Music by Maurice Levi. Staged by George Marion. Dances by Sam Marion. Settings by John Young, Ernest Albert. Costumes by Madame (Catherine) Seidle. Produced under the personal direction of Joseph M. Weber and Florenz Ziegfeld. Opened 20 October 1904 at the Weber Music Hall and closed 25 March 1905 after 185 performances. Re-opened a return engagement 26 August 1905 at the Weber Music Hall, closing 9 September 1905 after 17 performances. Total: 202 performances.

CAST: *Adolf Schnitz*, a wealthy mustard manufacturer, touring Europe for rest and recreation: JOSEPH M. WEBER. *Gottlieb Gesler*, a millionaire, President of the American Swiss-Cheese Sandwich Trust, friend of Schnitz, and upona similar mission: HARRY MORRIS. *Sandy Walker*, a "rail-bird" with clipped wings: CHARLES A. BIGELOW. *Charley Stringham*, Gesler's nephew and Paris agent: AUBREY BOUCICAULT. *Waldorf Lamb*, a New Yorker; friend of Stringham: Frank Mayne. *Herr Baedecker*, a courier: Franz Ebert. *Pierre*, a waiter: Sam Marion. *Hans* a tramp bear: Walter Stanton, Jr. *Parisian Friends of Stringham (7)*: *Henri Batignolles*: Harry Hoffmann. *Pierre Montmartre*: W. Douglas Stevenson. *Jean Procope*: Robert Austin. *Honore D'Absinthe*: Richard Dolliver. *Prosper Malheur*: Jarvis Jocelyn. *Maurice De Maxims*: Charles Flynn. *Jacques de Riche*: Bert Hagen. *Chasseur at the Cafe D'Aramonville*: Henry dePackh. *Mimi de Chartreuse*, patron saint of the Parisian "Bohemia": ANNA HELD. *Philopena Schnitz*, heiress to her father's mustard millions: MARIE DRESSLER. *Gertie Keith, Mamie Proctor*, known in American vaudeville circles as "The Little Sparklets": Aimee Angelis, Bonnie Maginn. *Fifine*, a grisette: May McKenzie.

Tourists: *Fuller Bragg* of Boston: Freda Linyard. *J. Rushton Bridges* of Brooklyn: Lillian Harris. *Holmes Meadows* of Elizabeth, New Jersey: Bena Hoffman. *Willie Dodge Carr* of New York: Daisy Leon. *Mrs. Tooker Knapp* of Philadelphia: Vivian Blackburn. *Miss Lotta Crabb* of Baltimore: Addie Orton. *Miss Goldie Gates* of San Francisco: Edyth Moyer. *Miss Ellie Victor* of Chicago: Hattie Loraine.

Swiss Mountain Guides: *Wilhelm*: Edyth Smyth. *Hinrich*: Maude Leroy. *Hans*: Frances Palmer. *Leding*: Belva Don Kersley. *Karl*: Milded Devere. *Heinie*: Ada Verne.

Hurraut, a jockey: Florence French. *Helene*: Grace Kimball. *Marcelle*: Marjorie Relyea. *Elise*: Elaine Selover. *Marie*: Madelaine Martin. *Fantone*: Mabel Verne. *Margot*: Madelaine Martin. *Madelaine*: Esther Brunette.

Milk Maids: *Hilda*: Elsie Davis. *Freda*: Edna Chase. *Helga*: Blanche West. *Olga*: Beatrice Walsh. *Meanie*: Violet Pearl. *Tilly*: Iva Barbier. *Hennie*: Kitty Wheaton. *Lottie*: Beatrice Learwood.

Captain Pompon: Edythe Smythe. *Captain Bombarde*: Irene Bishop. *Lieutenant Fusil*: Belva Donkersley. *Indians (4)*: *Pain in the Face*: Florence Lancaster. *Red Scalp*: Vernie Wadsworth. *Laughing Water*: Maude Seddon. *Standing Dog*: Caroline Green.

Exhibit "A" (Act 1): A Swiss Chalet, near Dampunbad, Lake Lucerne, Switzerland. (Young.)

Exhibit "B" (Act 2): The Cafe Armenonville, in the Bois, Paris. (Albert.)

ACT 1[51]

"Awake! Awake! (Opening Ensemble)

"The Song of the Rifle" (Octette)

"Luck, Luck, Luck"
C. Bigelow, A. Angelis, B. Maginn

"My Beautiful Gay Paree" (In Gay Paree)
A. Held, Held Girls

"A Great Big Girl Like Me"
M. Dressler

"Swiss Porters" (Dance)

"On to Paris à la Automobile"[52]
A. Held, Held Girls

Finale
M. Dressler, H. Morris, J. Weber, A. Boucicault, F. Mayne, A. Angelis, B. Maginn, F. Ebert, Chorus

ACT 2

"The Grand Prix" (Opening Ensemble)

"Nancy Clancy" (Waltz Song)
A. Held, Chorus

I'm So Lonesome"
C. A. Bigelow

"For You, Honey, For You"
A. Boucicault, A. Angelis, B. Maginn, Ensmeble

"A Game of Love"
A. Held, C. A. Bigelow

"The Big Indian and (His) Little Maid"
C. Bigelow, A. Angelis, B. Maginn, Ensemble

"Laughter"[53]
A. Held

"In the Chorus"
M. Dressler

"The Revels of the Jewels" (Finale)

THE COLLEGE WIDOWER, a Burlesque of the George Ade's play "The College Widow" by Edgar Smith. Music by Maurice Levi. Staged by Frank Hatch and Sam Marion. Added 5 January 1905.

CAST: *Professor Witheredloon*: AUBREY BOUCICAULT. *"Stubby"*: JOSEPH M. WEBER. *"Ratty" McGown*: CHARLES A. BIGELOW. *Mrs. Hiram Buttin*: Harry Morris. *Jim Witheredloon*: FRANK MAYNE. *The Town Policeman*: Sam Marion. *A Box Office Victim*: John C. Miller. *A Ticket Seller*: Thomas Sedgewick. *A Doorkeeper*: Henry DePackh. *A Theologue*: W. Douglas Stevenson. *Tilly Buttin*: MARIE DRESSLER. *Hon. Ellen Slick*: AIMEE ANGELES. *"Babe" Slick*: Alexandra Hall. *Polly Mitchell*: Bonnie Maginn. *Dixie MacAllister*: May McKenzie. *Jinny Hopper*: Edythe Moyer. *A Ticket Speculator*: Edythe Moyer. *Sally Cameron*: Addie Orton.

MUSICAL NUMBERS

"The Higher Education"

"Mama's Boarding House"
M. Dressler

"Socrates Jackson" (An Educated Coon)
C. A. Bigelow, Chorus

1904.40 THE CINGALEE

A Musical Play in Two Acts[54]. Book by James Tanner. Music by Lionel Monckton. Lyrics by Adrian Ross and Percy Greenbank. Additional numbers by Paul Rubens. Stage manager, Lewis Hooper. Settings by John Young. Costumes by Mrs. Fields (of Daly's Theatre London, from designs by Percy Anderson). Electrical effects by George McCurdy. Orchestra under the direction of Louis F. Gottschalk. Produced by John C. Duff. Opened 24 October 1904 at Daly's Theatre and closed 19 November 1904 after 33 performances.

CAST: *Lady Patricia Vane*: MARTHA CARINE. *Nanoya*: GENEVIEVE FINLAY. *Peggy Sabine*: BLANCHE DEYO. *Angy Loftus, Molly Loftus*, Sir Peter's daughters: May Hengler, Flora Hengler. *Four Tea Girls on Vereker's Plantation*: *Naitooma*: Julia Millard. *Sattambi*: Kathleen Warren. *Mychellah*: Noel Gordon. *Coorowe*: Dorothy Bertrand. *Angy's Governesses (4)*: *Miss Pinkerton*: Viola Kellogg. *Miss Werner*: Amy Forsslund. *Miss Vernon*: May Hopkins. *Miss Clements*: Myrtle McGrain. *Harry Vereker*, a Tea Planter: MELVILLE STEWART. *Boobhamba*, a Noble of Kandy: HALLYN MOSTYN. *Sir Peter Loftus*, High Commissioner and Judge, Ceylon: HAROLD VIZARD. *Myamgah*, an Indian Servant: Charles Wallace. *Pupils of Vereker on the Tea Plantation (4)*: *Bobby Warren*: George LeSoir. *Dick Bosanquet*: Lionel Hogarth. *Freddie Lowther*: Jordon Osborne. *Jack Clinton*: George Featherstone. *Captain of the Guard*: Edward Gore. *Attendant*: Paul Pancer. *Chambuddy Ram*: WILLIAM NORRIS. *Pas de Deux in Acts 1 and 2*: May Hengler, Flo Hengler. *Grotesque Acrobatic Dance in Act 2*: The Eddies.

Act 1: Vereker Tea Plantation, "Karagama," Ceylon.

Act 2: Boobhamba's Palace, by the Lake of Candy.

ACT 1

Opening Chorus

"Pearl of Sweet Ceylon"
M. Stewart, Tea Girls
(*Lyrics by* Adrian Ross.)

"Reading, Writing, Arithmetic"
G. Finlay, M. Stewart

"Peggy"
Chorus

"With a Boo"
H. Mostyn, Chorus

"Something Devilish Wrong"
W. Norris
(*Music and Lyrics by* Paul Rubens.)

---

[51]An additional song which does not appear in programs: "Next Summer in Dear Old New York."

[52]Dropped within two months of the opening.

[53]Dropped within two months of the opening.

[54]Original London production was titled THE CINGALEE, or Sunny Ceylon.

"My Heart Is at Thy Feet" (My Heart's at Your Feet)
M. Carine
(*Lyrics by* Percy Greenbank.)

"Tea, Tea, Tea"
J. Millard, Tea Girls

"White and Brown Girl"
B. Deyo, W. Norris

"In Gay Ceylon"
Sextette

"My Cinnamon Tree"
G. Finlay
(*Lyrics by* Adrian Ross.)

"Bear Away the Bride" (Finale)

ACT 2

"At the Palace of Boobhamba" (Opening Chorus)

"I'm a Merry Maiden"
G. Finlay, Chorus

"The Crocodile" (On a Crocodile)
W. Norris
(*Music by* James Kendis and Herman Paley. *Lyrics by* James O'Dea.)

"She's All Right"
B. Deyo, Chorus
(*Music and Lyrics by* Paul Rubens.)

"You and I" (I and You)
M. Carine
(*Music and Lyrics by* Paul Rubens.)

"Make a Fuss of Me"
B. Deyo, W. Norris

"The Course of True Love" (True Love)
G. Finlay, M. Stewart, L. Hogarth
(*Lyrics by* Adrian Ross.)

"On the Lake, or The New Year Festival"
Chorus

"The Parahara"
H. Vizard, Chorus

"There's Nothing Much More to Say"
H. Mostyn, Male Chorus
(*Lyrics by* Adrian Ross, Rutland Harrington.)

"The Monkeys"
B. Deyo, W. Norris

"Wedding March" (Finale)

1904.41 THE ERRAND BOY

A Musical Comedy in Two Acts. Book by George Totten Smith. Produced under the personal supervision of Sam Marion. Scenery by Ernest Albert. Costumes by Mme. Freisinger of Paris and New York, designed by McIlvain. Electrical effects by Menchen Electrical Company. Musical director, Edwin L. Walker. Produced by (P. H.) Sullivan, Harris and Woods. Opened 31 October 1904 at the 14th Street Theatre and closed 5 November 1904 after 8 performances.[55]

CAST (in order of appearance): *Pinkerton Pinch*, sheriff: Clem Bevins. *Silas Hemlock*, country merchant: Frank C. Evans. *Jersuha Pickens*, who objects to theatricals: Florence Brooks. *Sally Hemlock*, Silas' daughter: Edith Hart. *MacCullough Muggs*, manager Gloriana Bird Musical Comedy Company: Abbott Davison. *Gloriana Bird*, the leading lady: ROSE BEAUMONT. *Kerry Baggage*, an expressman: Joe Mack. *Patsy Bolivar*, the errand boy: BILLY B. VAN. *Sam Sellars*, a travelling man: Charles Saxon. *May B. Wright*, a female detective: Florinne Sweetman. *R. T. D. Boggs*: William Hart. *Noah Kidhart, Henry Stickney, Orlando Boyce, Dura Chase*, Novelty Comedy Four: W. S. Cetti, Mark Tomsen, William Lawrence, William Arcall. *Tracy Colby*: E. R. Scrimshaw. *Wilber Young*: Dave Coogan. *Austin Russell*: Charles Clovet. *Sweat Perkins*: Richard Stubbs. *Billy Carter*: Dave Davis. *Bo Nagel*: M. J. Anderson. *Luther Chase*: J. A. Mullen. *Bert Martin*: W. E. Whitehall. *Becky Skinner*: Blanch Latell. *Bessie Blush*: Nettie Wheeler. *Jessie Joy*: Helena DaNourie. *Tessie Tease*: May Lloyd. *Mrs. Sawyer*: May Bishop.

Bronchos: *Winnie Wink*: Agnes Marsh. *Kitty Kick*: Lillian Marsh. *Sadie Smile*: Kitty Pope. *Trixy Tirl*: Marguerite Cogan. *Lillie Laugh*: Sylvia Diamond. *Daisy Dance*: Pauline Pearl. *Sally Singer*: Lola Hilton. *Carrie Chirp*: Stella Warner.

Toreadors: *Senor Pesacos*: Rose Gilday. *Rosario Contraro*: Lizzie Southwalk. *Segaro Garcio*: Maud Cecil. *Don Pediero*: Frankie Seymour. *Senor Lopez*: Amy Gillette. *Adamio Patto*: Marcia Loraine. *Manuel Alvorez*: Ida Gerard. *Alonzo Dorez*: Gladys Walker. *Carlos Pedro*: Francis King.

Act 1: Opera House, George's Mills, New Hampshire.

Act 2: Hemlock's Grocery Store and Hotel.

ACT 1

"The Painters and the Rube"
Novelty Comedy Four,
W. E. Whitehall, E. R. Scrimshaw, J. A. Mullen, M. J. Anderson

"The Greatest Show on Earth"
A. Davison, Chorus

"Gloriana"
R. Beaumont, Chorus

"Patsy Bolivar" (from THE JERSEY LILY)
B. B. Van, Chorus

"Girly, Girly" (from HOITY TOITY)
R. Beaumont, C. Saxon
(*Music by* John Stromberg. *Lyrics by* Edgar Smith.)

"Say, Sal"
B. B. Van, E. Hart, Chorus

"Spain, Beautiful Spain'
R. Beaumont, B. B. Van, Chorus

"The Katydid (the Cricket and the Frog)" (from NANCY BROWN)
E. Hart, A. Davison, F. C. Evans, F. Sweetman
(*Music by* James Weldon Johnson. *Lyrics by* Bob Cole.)

"The Battle of the Daisies and the Ferns" (Finale)
R. Beaumont, Entire Company

ACT 2

"Mary Canary" (from THE WIZARD OF OZ)
R. Beaumont, Full Chorus
(*Music by* Seymour Furth. *Lyrics by* Edward P. Moran.)

"(Poor) Robinson Crusoe"
B. B. Van, Chorus
(*Music by* Seymour Furth. *Lyrics by* Edward P. Moran.)

"Isn't It Lovely to Be on the Stage"
R. Beaumont, B. B. Van

Grand Finale
Entire Chorus

1904.42 LITTLE JOHNNY JONES
(The American Jockey)

A Musical Play in Three Acts. Book, music and lyrics by George M. Cohan. Staged by George M. Cohan. Settings by W. F. Hamilton. Costumes by Mme. Freisinger; Lord & Taylor. Orchestra under the direction of Charles J. Gebest. Orchestrations by Charles J. Gebest. Produced by Sam H. Harris. Opened 7 November 1904 at the Liberty Theatre and closed 24 December 1904 after 52 performances. Re-opened a return engagement 8 May 1905 at the New York Theatre and closed 26 August 1905 after 128 additional performances; re-opened 13 November 1905 at the New York Theatre and closed 2 December 1905 after 25 additional performances. Total for 3 engagements: 205 performances[56].

CAST [in order of appearance]: *Anthony Anstey*, an American gambler: JERRY J. COHAN. *Sing Song*, editor of the Pekin Gazette: J. BERNARD DYLLYN. *Timothy D. McGee*, a New York politician and horse owner: SAM J. RYAN. *Henry Hapgood*, who also makes the trip: DONALD BRIAN. *The Unknown*: TOM LEWIS. *Jenkins*, starter at the

---

[55]A Second edition toured the following season under the auspices of P. H. Sullivan Amusement Company. Its New York engagement 28 August 1905 at the 14th Street Theatre for 8 performances, for which no program was found. Additional songs introduced included: "Miss Popularity," "Mollie O," "Strolling," "You Won't Do Any Business If You Haven't Got a Band," "Miss Maloney," "Lucia de Lammermoor" (burlesque), "Rag Bag Man," and "Cannilaler."

[56]Played a return engagement 8 January 1906 at the Grand Opera House for 8 performances.

Cecil: C. J. Harrington. *Captain Squirvy* of the St. Hurrah: C. J. Harrington. *Bell Boy*: William Seymour. *Detective Perkins*: Charles Bachmann. *Stevens*, a waiter: Joseph Leslie. *Chung Fow*: Charles Stevens. *Hong Chung*: Fred Williams. *Johnny Jones*, the American jockey: GEORGE M. COHAN[57]. *Mrs. Andrews Kenworth*, a fanatic on the subject of reform: HELEN F. COHAN. *Florabelle Fly* of the San Francisco Searcher: TRULY SHATTUCK. *Bessie*, an American girl: Edith Tyler. *Goldie Gates*, (Johnny's girl): ETHEL LEVEY. *Rosario Fauchette*: ETHEL LEVEY. *Earl of Bloomsbury*: ETHEL LEVEY. *Female Reformers, American Girls, English Policemen, Life Guards, Sailors, etc.*

Act 1: Hotel Cecil (exterior), London, England.

Act 2: Southampton Pier, "St. Hurrah" docked.

Act 3: Chinatown, San Francisco.

MUSICAL NUMBERS[58]

"The Cecil in London Town"
C. J. Harrington [Jenkins]

"They're All My Friends"
S. J. Ryan

"Mam'selle Fauchette"
E. Levey [Goldie Gates]

"'Op in the 'Ansom"
Cabbies and Reformers

"Nesting in a New York Tree"
T. Shattuck

"(The) Yankee Doodle Boy"
G. M. Cohan

"Off to the Derby"
Company

"Girls from the U.S.A."
T. Shattuck

"Sailors of St. Hurrah"
Sailors

"Captain of the Ten-Day Boat"
C. J. Harrington [Squirvy]

"Good-bye, Flo"
E. Levey [Goldie Gates]

"Good Old California"
D. Brian

"A Girl I Know"
G. M. Cohan, E. Levey [Goldie Gates]

"Give My Regards to Broadway"
G. M. Cohan

"March of the Frisco Chinks"
Company

"Life's a Funny Proposition"
G. M. Cohan

Finale
G. M. Cohan, Company

1904.43 MRS. BLACK IS BACK

May Irwin and Her Company in Her New Offering (a Farce with Songs) in Three Acts. Play by George V. Hobart. Orchestra under the direction of George A. Nichols. (Produced by May Irwin.) Opened 7 November 1904 at the Bijou Theatre and closed 7 January 1905 after 71 performances. Reopened 27 March 1905 to the New York Theatre and closed 1 April 1905 after an additional 8 performances[59]. Total: 79 performances.

CAST: *Mrs. Black*: MAY IRWIN. *Professor Black*, Mrs. Black's second husband: A. S. LIPMAN. *Emily Mason*, Mrs. Black's sister: Jane Burby. *Priscilla Black*, Mrs. Black's sister-in-law: Frances Gordon. *Jack Dangerfield*, Mrs. Black's only son: EDGAR ATCHISON-ELY. *Larry McManus*, Mrs. Black's son's valet: JOHN G. SPARKS. *Don Pedro Degazebe*: Mrs. Black's son's nemesis: NICK LONG. *Tom Larkey*, Mrs. Black's physical culturist: Charles Lane. *Major Thorne*, Mrs. Black's broker: Arthur Sanders. *Bramley Bush*, Mrs. Black's neighbor: John Johnson. *Hank*, Mrs. Black's gardener: Roland Carter. *Lizzie*, Mrs. Black's cook: May Donohue. *Peter Patter*, Mrs. Black's letter carrier: Charles Church.

Young Lady Students in Mrs. Black's Husband's College (6): *Sarah Dale*: Vira Rial. *Ellen Leighton*: Maryland Tyson. *Elizabeth Morgan*: Lillie Lawton. *Caroline Patterson*: Madeline Anderton. *Amelia Brant*: Kate Gotthold. *Agnes Hamilton*: Dorothy Banes.

Act 1: Home of Professor and Mrs. Black on the Hudson River, near New York. Now.

Act 2: Same as previous act. One minute later.

Act 3: Same as previous acts. One hour later.

ACT 1[60]

"Dinner Bells"
Chorus
(*Music and Lyrics by* Harry Brown.)

"Bygone Days Are Best"
Incidental Piano
(*Music and Lyrics by* Will Marion Cook.)

"Nothin' But Talk"[61]
M. Irwin
(*Music and Lyrics by* Harry Brown.)

"Mumm's the Word"[62]
M. Irwin
(*Music by* Gus Edwards. *Lyrics by* Will D. Cobb.)

"Bible Stories"
M. Irwin
(*Music by* Al Johns. *Lyrics by* John Lee Clarke.)

ACT 2

"Can't You Guess?" (Guess, Guess, Guess)
M. Irwin, E. Atchison-Ely
(*Music by* John W. Bratton. *Lyrics by* Paul West.)

"I'm Worried to Death About That"
M. Irwin, E. Atchison-Ely
(*Music and Lyrics by* May Irwin.)

ACT 3

"In the Shadow of the Pyramids"
M. Irwin, Company
Harp Accompanist: Vira Rial.
(*Music by* Ernest R. Ball. *Lyrics by* R. C. McPherson.)

"I Love to Two-Step (with My Man)"
M. Irwin, Company
(*Music and Lyrics by* Hughie Cannon.)

"Sadie"[63]
E. Atchison-Ely, assisted by L. Lawton, M. Anderton
(*Music and Lyrics by* Al. Johns.)

---

[57]Billed as the Yankee Doodle Comedian.

[58]For return engagement, the following song changes were made. Added after "Good-Bye, Flo" was:

"So Long, Sing Song"
Company
"Life's a Funny Proposition After All" was replaced by:

"If Mr. Boston Lawson Had His Way"
G. M. Cohan

[59]Settings, costumes, direction (George V. Hobart) and producer (May Irwin) uncredited in programs. Played return engagements 13 March 1905 at the Grand Opera House for 8 performances, and 30 April 1906 at the Grand Opera House for 8 performances.

[60]Specialty interpolated for tour (1905) as per published sheet music:

"Don't Argify'
M. Irwin
(*Music and Lyrics by* John B. Lowitz.)

[61]Replaced during the run by:

"Expotentisius"
M. Irwin
(*Music and Lyrics by* Shep .)

"The Spanish Coon"
M. Irwin
(*Music and Lyrics by* Mark Beam.)
Replaced for subsequent tour by:

"Tennessee, That's the Place for Me"
M. Irwin
(*Music by* Jean Schwartz. *Lyrics by* Harry Williams.)

[62]Dropped during the run.

[63]Dropped during the run.

1904.44 THE WIZARD OF OZ

A Revival of the Musical Spectacle in Three Acts, 7 Scenes[64]. Book and lyrics by L. Frank Baum. Based on his own novel "The Wonderful Wizard of Oz." Music by Paul Tietjens and A. Baldwin Sloane. Entire production arranged and staged by Julian Mitchell. Settings by Walter Burridge, Fred Gibson, John Young. Orchestra under the direction of Charles Zimmerman. Produced by Fred R. Hamlin. Opened 7 November 1904 at the Academy of Music and closed 31 December 1904 after 66 performances.

CAST (in order of appearance): *Dorothy Gale*, a Kansas girl, the victim of a cyclone: ANNA LAUGHLIN. *The Cow named Imogene*, Dorothy's playmate: JOSEPH SCHRODE. *Farmhands*: Misses Fisher, Donaldson, Von Brune, Benson, Diamond, Gerard, Arnold. Messrs. Cleveland, Devlin, Young. *Munchkins (8)*: *Tommie Top*: Josephine Clayton. *Peter Pop*: Leona Stephens. *Simon Slick*: Catherine Carson. *Antonia*: Sadie Emmons. *Sophronia*: Lola Gordon. *Premonia*: Lillian DeVere. *Malvonia*: Stubby Ainscoe. *Semponia*: Leta Shaw. *Munchkin Youths*: Misses Clara Selton, Mabel Powell, Bert Dean, Helen Blye, Emma Clark, Nellie Lane, Helen Turner, Virginia Kendall, May Fisher. Messrs. Bingham, Diskins, Hoskins, Nichols, Bright. *Munchin Maidens*: Misses Maria Mathey, Peggy Donaldson, Anna Leslie, Ilai Mable, Minna Doerge, Edna Leach, Nancy Poole, Therese Von Brune, Marie Clayton, Grace Heckler. *Cynthia Cynch*, the lady lunatic, a Munchkin maiden: ALLENE CRATER. *The Witch of the North*, a friend in need: Ella Gilroy. *Sir Dashemoff Daily*, Poet laureate: ALBERTINE BENSON. *The Army of Pastoria*: Maxwell Sergeant. *Pastoria II*, ex-King of the Emerald City, with a conspiracy to regain his throne: CHARLES E. MITCHELL. *Tryxie Tryffle*, prospective Queen of the Emerald City: LOTTA FAUST. *Brigadier General Riskitt*, commanding Pastoria's army: HAROLD P. MOREY. *The Scarecrow*, looking for brains: FRED A. STONE. *The Cowardly Lion*: ARTHUR HILL. *Mick Chopper*, the Tin Woodman in search of a heart: DAVID C. MONTGOMERY. *Sir Wiley Gyle*, a conspirator who scorns all magical arts: George B. Field. *The Poppy Queen*: Josephine Clayton. *Poppy Flowers*: Misses Stevens, Fisher, Allien, Mable, Leslie, Leach, M. Clayton, Heckler, Gerard, Dean, Clark, Von Brune, Lane, B. Benson, Gordon, Selton, Wilton, Blye, Kendall, Turner, Arnold, Doerge, Donaldson, Mansfield. *Snow Queen*: Catherine Carson. *Snow Boys*: Lillian DeVere, Sadie Emmons, Mabel Powell, Nancy Poole. *Snow Girls*: Leta Field, Marie Mathey. *Leo*, Captain of the Relief Guards: Charles Hoskins. *Captain of the Patrol*: Sadie Emmons. *The Patrol*: Misses Gerard, Lane, Donaldson, Dean, Diamond, Arnold, Von Brune, Clark, Kendall, Fisher, Turner. *Alonzo*, the Wizard's Confederate: IRVING CHRISTIAN. *The Wizard's Wise Men (4)*: *Silicus*: H. Devlin. *Sophocles*: George Young. *Pericles*: S. Van Bibber. *Diogenes*: W. C. Van Brunt. *Bardo*, the Wizard's factotum: Alice Ainscoe. *Oz*, the Wonderful Wizard, Past Master of Magic, ruler of the Emerald City and Potentate of the Land of Oz: CHARLES SWAIN. *Alberto*, Officer of the Day: Sadie Emmons. *Waitresses (8)*: *Gloriana Jane*: Nancy Poole. *Violet Victoria*: Mabel Powell. *Gladys Ann*: Ilai Mable. *Leontine Em*: Leona Stephens. *Vera Ellen*: Leta Field. *Aileen Nance*: Lillian Devere. *Pansy Lil*: Josephine Clayton. *Lavinia Loo*: Lola Gordon. *Cooks (8)*: *Claude Cliquot*: Helen Turner. *Alphonse Fripon*: Grace Heckler. *Marcel Moreau*: Stubby Ainscoe. *Louis LeBeau*: Vernon Arnold. *Francois Giblets*: Daisy Carson. *Jean DeChar*: Helen Blye. *Remnante Saute*: Marie Clayton. *Pungue DeSert*: Edna Leach. *Laundresses*: Misses Benson, Wilton, Von Brune, Doerge, Leslie, Mathey, Mansfield. *Royal Guards*: Misses Fisher, Donaldson, Kendall, Selton, Diamond, Gerard, Dean, Clark, Lane, Allien.

ACT 1

"Life in Kansas" (Opening)
(*Music by* Paul Tietjens.)

"Niccolo's Piccolo"
A. Crater
(*Music by* A. Baldwin Sloane. *Lyrics by* Glen MacDonough.)

"The Tale of the Cassowary"[65]
A. Crater
(*Music by* Gus Edwards. *Lyrics by* Will. Cobb.)

"Down on the Brandywine"[66] (Duet)
L. Faust, C. E. Mitchell
(*Music by* J. B. Mullen. *Lyrics by* Vincent Bryan.)

"Carry Barry" (Carrie Barry)
A. Laughlin
(*Music by* A. Baldwin Sloane. *Lyrics by* Glen MacDonough.)

"Alas for the Man Without Brains"
F. A. Stone
(*Music by* Paul Tietjens.)

"I Love You All the Time"[67]
A. Benson
(*Music and Lyrics by* Will. R. Anderson.)

"When You Love, Love, Love"
F. A. Stone, D. C. Montgomery, A. Laughlin
(*Music by* Paul Tietjens.)

"Poppy Chorus"
(*Music by* Paul Tietjens.)

ACT 2

"On a Pay Night Evening" (Pay Night)
C. Swain
(*Music by* Bruno Schilinski. *Lyrics by* John W. West.)

"It's Enough to Make a Perfect Lady Mad"[68]
A. Crater
(*Music by* J. B. Mullen. *Lyrics by* Vincent Brian.)

Medley: Ball of All Nations (Dance of All Nations)
(*Music by* A. Baldwin Sloane. *Lyrics by* Edgar Smith.)

"Connemara Christening"
C. Swain
(*Music by* A. Baldwin Sloane. *Lyrics by* Edgar Smith.)

"Gooda-bye, Fedora"[69]
F. A. Stone
(*Music by* Robert Adams. *Lyrics by* Harry H. Williams.)

"Wee Highland Mon"
D. C. Montgomery
(*Music by* J. B. Mullen. *Lyrics by* Vincent Bryan.)

"Rosalie" (Coon Song and Cakewalk)
A. Laughlin
(*Music by* Gus Edwards. *Lyrics by* Will D. Cobb.)

"An Afternoon Tea"[70]
F. A. Stone, D. C. Montgomery, A. Laughlin
(*Music by* A. Baldwin Sloane. *Lyrics by* Edgar Smith.)

"Sammy"
L. Faust, Chorus
(*Music by* Edward Hutchinson. *Lyrics by* James O'Dea.)

"I Never Loved a Love as I Love You"[71]
A. Benson
(*Music by* Gus Edwards. *Lyrics by* Will D. Cobb.)

"The Nightmare"[72]
F. A. Stone, D. C. Montgomery
(*Music by* J. B. Mullen. *Lyrics by* Vincent Bryan.)

Finale

ACT 3

"The Traveler and the Pie"[73]
F. A. Stone
(*Music by* Paul Tietjens.)

"Must You"[74]
D. C. Montgomery
(*Music by* Bert Branford. *Lyrics by* Harry Boden and David C. Montgomery.)

"The Sweetest Girl in Dixie"[75]
A. Laughlin
(*Music by* Bob Adams. *Lyrics by* James O'Dea.)

[64]First edition produced in New York 20 January 1903 at the Majestic Theatre for 293 performances. For Synopsis of Scenes, see original 1903 production. Dropped for this revival were: "In Michigan," "When the Circus Comes to Town," "That Is Love," "Phantom Patrol," "The Witch Behind the Moon," "Spanish Bolero," "I Love Only One Girl in the Wide, Wide, Wide World," "Hurrah for Baffin's Bay," "Star of My Native Land," Opening Chorus (Act 3), "Honey, My Sweet."
[65] Not in original 1903 production.
[66] Not in original 1903 production.
[67]Not in original 1903 production.
[68]Not in original 1903 production.
[69]Not in original 1903 production.
[70]Not in original 1903 production.
[71]Not in original 1903 production.
[72]Not in original 1903 production.
[73]Added during previous New York run.
[74]Added during previous New York run.
[75]Not in original 1903 production.

1904.45 DOWN THE PIKE

A Musical Comedy in Two Acts. Book by W. G. Rose and G. W. Quigley. Music by Egbert van Alstyne. Lyrics by Harry Williams. Scenery by Sosman and Landis. Costumes by Susie Kirwan. Staged by Gertrude Hoffman. Musical director, Adolph Frankenstein. Produced by E. D. Stair. Opened 7 November 1904 at the West End Theatre and closed 12 November 1904 after 9 performances.

CAST: *McCorkle*, the janitor: JOHNNY RAY. *Russell Keene*, a broker: A. A. MUDGE. *Esau Wonder*, a detective: PHIL PETERS. *Uncle Cohen*, a man of interest: Harry First. *Jack Noble*, an ambitious artist: WILBUR HELD. *Blufton West*, a plunger: Harry Collignon. *Harry Wilder*, a sponger: George H. Timmons. *Tips*, the handy boy: Harry Duncan. *Pewee*, an elephant: Tom Leo. *Texas*, a donkey: Tom Leo. *Front*, the bell boy: Will Llewellyn. *Bronco Bill*, from Arizona: Ed. B. Roscoe. *Ima Lune*, a lunatic: J. J. Harvey. *Will U. Touchem*, a burglar: Paul Livingston. *Officer*: Ed B. Roscoe. *Mollie May*, an heiress: SOPHIE BURNHAM. *Flourette*, a milliner: NETTIE PETERS. *Rosie Dawn*: JESSIE CHAPMAN. *Ella Waite*, an old maid: Lucile Deval. *Miss Fortune*, a seeress: Nellie Chilters. (*Specialty*: William Bissett, John Scott.)

Typewriters (10): *Miss Bickensderfer*: Pearl Tyson. *Miss Densmore*: Lena Tyson. *Miss Remington*: Addie Gallant. *Miss Yost*: Elizabeth Sloan. *Miss Underwood*: Patricia Wagner. *Miss Smith-Premier*: Phyllis Proctor. *Miss Caligraph*: Esmerelde McClelland. *Miss Peerless*: Janette Reynolds. *Miss Oliver*: Sura Seamon. *Miss Fox*: Cheleste Fleming.

Maids (8): *Bertie Auto*: Myra Mattison. *Dora Bell*: Julia Sweeney. *Helen Hunt*: Mabel Stanley. *Miss Carr*: Ella Kerr. *Annie Fair*: Margaret Roach. *Carrie Coyne*: Louise Taft. *Arabella Rozenski*: Mazie Harrison. *Miss Take*: Sybil Curtiss.

Bell Boys (6): *Tom*: John Scott. *Jerry*: Will Bissett. *Frank*: John Evans. *William*: John Bird. *Walter*: Charles Warren. *Joseph*: Frank Carlton.

Mrs. Russell Keene: EMMA RAY.

Act 1: Paradise Flats, New York City.

Act 2: The Cascade Building, World's Fair Grounds, St. Louis.

ACT 1[76]

Opening Chorus
Maids, Bell Boys

"If I Were Only You"
W. Held, S. Burnham, Male Chorus

"I Am the Janitor"
J. Ray, Chorus

Burlesque Quartette
J. Ray, P. Peters, H. Collignon and G. H. Timmons

"Back, Back, Back to Baltimore"
E. Ray, Male Chorus

"Farewell, Nellie Mine"
W. Held, Company

ACT 2

"Kentucky Babe" (Song)
S. Burnham

"Snowball Sammy"
J. Chapman, Chorus

"Down the Pike"
N. Peters, Chorus

"Lola"
S. Burnham, Chorus

Champion Clog Dancers
W. Bissett, J. Scott

Grand Finale
Entire Company

1904.46 THE WAY TO KENMARE

An Irish Comedy Drama in Four Acts. Play by Edward E. Rose. Music by Andrew Mack. Opened 7 November 1904 at the 14th Street Theatre and closed 17 December 1904 after 49 performances; returned 14 May 1906 to the Academy of Music and closed 26 May 1906 after an additional 16 performances. Total: 65 performances.

CAST: *Dan Maguire*: ANDREW MACK. *Captain Clement Fairley*: HUGO TOLAND. *Roy Donald*, Rose's brother: William J. Townshend. *The Earl of Kenmare*: George W. Deyo. *Bentley Harden*: Myron Calice. *Baron Gustavus Hergogengarten*: RICHARD GORMAN. *Martin Keen*: EDWARD J. McCORMACK. *Con O'Neil*, half-witted sexton of Kenmare Church: Luke Martin. *Mulkenan Hogan*, landlord of "The Shamrock and the Thistle": EDDIE HERON. *Patrick O'Shale*, who drives the Irish jaunting car: Thomas E. Jackson. *McShane*, poacher and thief: John Napier. *Jerry*: E. Constance. *Rose Donald*: MARGARET ROBINSON. *Miss Honoria Maloney*: ANNIE MACK BERLEIN. *Moira Doolan*: Gertrude Toland. *Julia*: Mae Stevenson.

Act 1: Reception Room, Bentley Harden's. Fifth Avenue, New York.

Act 2: Courtyard of the Shamrock and Thistle, Roadside Inn, Ballyscanlan, Ireland.

Act 3: Inside the Ruined Church, Kenmare.

Act 4: Entrance Hall, Kenmare Castle.

MUSICAL NUMBERS[77]

"Dan, My Darlin' Dan"
A. Mack

"The Legend of the Maguire"
A. Mack

"The Rose of Kenmare"
A. Mack

"She Just Suits Me"
A. Mack

1904.47 HUMPTY DUMPTY

A Musical Spectacle (Pantomime) in Three Acts, 11 Scenes[78]. (Original English) Book by J. Hickory Wood and Arthur Collins. Adapted for the American stage by John J. McNally. Music and lyrics by James W. Johnson, Bob Cole, J. Rosamund Johnson, unless otherwise indicated. (Additional music and lyrics by J. M. Glover, Frederick Solomon.) Produced under the stage direction of Herbert Gresham and Ned Wayburn. Ballets by Ernest D'Auban. Settings by Bruce Smith, R. C. McCleery, R. Caney, C. E. Caney, Henry Emden and Johnstone and Hartford. Electrical effects by H. Bissing & Co. Orchestra under the direction of Frederick Solomon. Produced by (Marc) Klaw and (Abraham L.) Erlanger. Opened 14 November 1904 at the New Amsterdam Theatre and closed 4 March 1905 after 132 performances. Re-opened 12-31 March 1906 at the New York Theatre for an additional 24 performances. Total: 156 performances.

CAST: *Little Mary*, the Cook: FRANK MOULAN. *Peter*, Little Mary's Son: JOHN McVEIGH. *King Sollumm*: GEORGE SCHILLER. *Prince Rudolph*: MAUDE LILLIAN BERRI. *Princess Marie*: NELLIE DALY. *Blossom*, the Lost Princess: LILLIAN COLEMAN. *Humpty Dumpty*: WILLIAM C. SCHRODE. *Pantaloon*: J. H. Powers. *Harlequin*: Joseph C. Smith. *Columbine*: Nora Sarony. *The Fairy Queen of Mirth*: Fredericka Raymond. *The Demon of Misrule*, (also) the Guardian of the Mystic Ring in Act 1, Scene3, and the Parrot in Act 2, Scene 2: Arthur Conquest. *Alice*, a Cat: David Abrams. *Yankee*, a Dog: Hilarion Ceballos. *Undine*: Mlle. Grigolatis. *Neptune*: J. Cleneay Mathews. *The Guardian of the Mystic Ring*, in Act 2, Scene 1: Eugene Everett. *Sprites*: Rosalie Ceballos, Hilarion Ceballos, Frank Connors, William Beattie. *The King's Men, Maids of Honor, Courtiers, Jesters, etc.* And THE GRIGOLATIS TROUPE OF AERIALISTS.

Act 1, Scene 1: The Palace Wall. (Smith). *Scene 2*: The Throne Room. (McCleery). *Scene 3*: An Enchanted Wood. (McCleery). *Scene 4*: The Fairy Forest. (McCleery).

Act 2, Scene 1: The Royal Kitchen. (Caney). *Scene 2*: On the Terrace. (Caney). *Scene 3*: The Sirens' Home; The Anemones' Retreat; The City of Coral. (Emden).

Act 3, Scene 1: Under the Sea. (Caney). *Scene 2*: The Kingdom of Misrule. (Caney). *Scene 3*: The Palace Eyrie. (Johnstone and Hartford). *Scene 4*: The Wedding; The Silver Wedding; The Golden Wedding; The Diamond Wedding. (Smith).

ACT 1
Scene 1

Opening Chorus of King's Guards
(*Music by* J. M. Glover.)

Chorus of Villagers

"Mary from Tipperary" (Song)
F. Moulan

"The Egg Has Fallen Down"
Ensemble

"I Am the King" (Song)
G. Schiller
(*Music by* Frederic Solomon, J. Rosamund Johnson.)

Scene 2

"Will He Ever Smile Again?"
Chorus

[76]Published sheet music features a wholly different score by H. B. Blanke (music) and Arthur Lamb (lyrics).

[77]Not necessarily in performance order.

[78]Billed as "The Latest London Drury Lane Spectacle."

"Pussy and the Bow-Wow" (Duo)
N. Daly, J. McVeigh
(*Lyrics by* James Weldon Johnson.)
"We Go to Find the Ring" (Finale)
Scene 3
Pantomime Bouffe Fantastique
(*Music by* Frederic Solomon.)
"Mexico" (Song)
M. L. Berri
"Fairyland" (Finale)
F. Raymond
Scene 4
The Frolic of the Birds
The Grigolatis Troupe
Grand Finale
(*Music by* J. M. Glover, Frederic Solomon.)
ACT 2
Scene 1
Opening Chorus of Cooks
(*Music by* Frederic Solomon.)
"Sambo and Dinah" (Song)
L. Coleman, J. McVeigh
"Down in Mulberry Bend" (Song)
N. Daly
Scene 2
"Cupid Reigns King"[79](Cupid Is King To-night)
M. L. Berri
(*Music and Lyrics by* Frederick Solomon.)
"Man, Man, Man" (Man! Man! Man!) (Song)
F. Moulan
(*Music by* Bob Cole *Lyrics by* James Weldon Johnson.)
Grand Finale
(*Music by* J. M. Glover, Frederic Solomon.)
Scene 3
The Divertissement Under the Sea
Grigolatis Troupe
ACT 3
Scene 1
Opening[80]
(*Music by* J. M. Glover.)
"I'm a Very Good Soldier on Land"[81] (Song)
F. Moulan
"Down at the Bottom of the Sea"[82] (Quartet)
N. Daly, F. Moulan, J. McVeigh, G. Schiller
Scene 2
Conspirators' Chorus[83]
Scene 3
"On Lalawana's Shore" (Song)
M. L. Berri
(*Lyrics by* James Weldon Johnson.)
Finale
Scene 4
"The Four Seasons of Wedlock"
(*Music by* J. M. Glover, Frederick Solomon.)

[79]Replaced during the run by:
"Kisses"
M. L. Berri
(*Music by* William H. Penn. *Lyrics by* Arthur Penn.)
[80]For return engagement, replaced by:
Opening
(*Music by* Frederick Solomon.)
[81]For return engagement, replaced by:
"War Echoes"
F. Moulan, J. McVeigh, G. A. Schiller, William Pullman
[82]For tour following first engagement, replaced by:
"The Lobster and the Smelt" (Quartet)
N. Daly, F. Moulan, J. McVeigh, G. Schiller
(*Music by* Frederic Solomon.)
For return engagement, replaced by:
"Texas Dan"
N. Daly, J. McVeigh
(*Music by* Jean Schwartz. *Lyrics by* Ben M. Jerome.)
[83]For return engagement, replaced by:
"Kissing" (Kisses)
F. Moulan
(*Music by* William Penn. *Lyrics by* Arthur Penn.)

1904.48 MRS. 'MAC,' THE MAYOR

A Comedy Drama in Four Acts, 7 Scenes. Play by William Gill. Songs by Albert Von Tilzer. Directed by James Carey. Produced by Robert B. Monroe and Fred Irwin. Opened 14 November 1904 at the Metropolis Theatre and closed 19 November 1904 after 8 performances; returned 16 January 1905 to the Murray Hill Theatre for an additional 8 performances.[84]

CAST: *Peggy MacNeill*, known as the "Honest Woman of Silverado." Formerly Pender, formerly Hocksteiner, formerly Carrara (now Mayor of Silverado): GEORGE H. MONROE. *Her children (4)*: *Rose Pender*: MARIE RAWSON. *Lena Hocksteiner*: ESTELLE X. WILLS. *Lucia Carrara*: MARIE FALLS. *Mickey MacNeill*: Dan McCarthy. *Tom Dalton*, part owner of the "Honest Woman" mine: James A. Young. *Lawrence McSwagger MacNeill*, Peggy's fourth: WILLIAM CALE. *Stephen Jenkins*, capitalist and pillar of the social community of Silverado: Maurice Drew. *Charley Patterson*, a young attorney: Ezra Mathews. *Fredrick Carden*, a gambler known as "Gentleman Fred": R. Lee Hill. *Manuel Garcia*, a Mexican miner: J. J. Dougherty. *Anita*, a Mexican girl: Mary Condon. *Minnetonka*, an Indian maiden: Emily Berg. *Sheriff Brandon*, the arm of the law: Fred Burgess. *Madeline Tuterorn*: Sylvia Barnes. *Ladies Brass Band, Political Boosters and Townspeople.*

The action is set in the mining town of Silverado on the border of Mexico at the present time.

Act 1: Exterior of MacNeill's cabin on the outskirts of Silverado.

Act 2: Mayor's office in town hall of Silverado.

Act 3, Scene 1: Ball room of the Little Waldorf-Astoria. *Scene 2*: A Street in Silverado. *Scene 3*: Interior of the Sierra Madre Mine.

Act 4: Interior of Peggy MacNeill's home.

1904.49 A CHINA DOLL

A Musical Play in Two Acts. Book by Harry B. Smith. Music by Alfred E. Aarons. Lyrics by Harry B. Smith and Robert Smith. Staged by Max Freeman. Scenery by Ernest Albert. Musical direction, Alfred E. Aarons. Produced by F. C. Whitney. Opened 19 November 1904 at the Majestic Theatre and closed 3 December 1904 after 18 performances.

CAST: *Wing Lee*, a Mandarin who believes in reform: W. H. MacDONALD. *Pee Chee San*, his daughter: HELEN ROYSTON. *Sing Lo*, Chief of Police: ARTHUR CUNNINGHAM. *Hi See*, his son: CORINNE. *Cerise*, a Paris milliner, imported as governess to Wing Lee's two daughters: Adele Rafter. *Hoochee*, a cannon ball tosser: ALBERT HART. *Hanki*, a juggler: GEORGE C. BONIFACE, JR. *Kwei-Twao*, proprietor of tea-house: Charles J. Wilson. *Wee Nee Wun, Chu-Gum*, tea girls: Ione Kerr, Laura Senac. *Wun Hook*, a fisherman: Charles J. Wilson. *Bridesmaids*: Sadie Long, Louise Elliott, Helouise Lee, Lucie Houston, Ann Ott, Marie Christie. *Citizens, Chinese Schoolboys, Guests, Dancers, Doctors, Attendants, Guards and the Doll.*

Act 1: Market Place in Hong Kong. Present day.

Act 2: The Palace of Sing Lo.

ACT 1[85]

[84]Musical numbers not listed in programs. On tour the show was billed as a musical comedy drama.
[85]No program found. Song list prepared from published piano vocal score (M. Witmark & Sons, New York, 1904), which differs substantially in content and cast list from the New York presentation. The New York production includes no American characters [Walker Foote, Sampson Muckles, Daniel Gaggs, Barker, La Belle Daisy and Bonnie Brierly] which figure prominently in the vocal score. Two additional songs not in published score, but possibly interpolated for New York: "Mistakes Are Apt to Happen," and "The Dew on the Heather."

Opening Chorus (In Hong Kong)
Chorus
(*Lyrics by* Harry B. Smith.)

"I Want to See the Happy Man" (Song)
H. Royston, Chorus
(*Lyrics by* Robert B. Smith.)

"How to be Happy Though Married" (Quartet)
Corinne, H. Royston, A. Cunningham, W. H. MacDonald
(*Lyrics by* Robert B. Smith.)

"Apple Mary Maguire" (Entrance)
[Bonnie]
(*Lyrics by* Harry B. Smith.)

"I Never Took a Lesson in My Life" (Song)
[Bonnie]
(*Lyrics by* Robert B. Smith.)

"One Umbrella Would Be Big Enough for Two" (Duet)
Corinne, H. Royston, Chorus
(*Lyrics by* Harry B. Smith.)

"If I Only Had a Theatre on Broadway" (Song)
[Walker, Gaggs, Muckles, Barker, Daisy, Chorus]
(*Lyrics by* Harry B. Smith.)

"If You Only Know the Way to Pull the Wires" (Song)
[Bonnie]
(*Lyrics by* Robert B. Smith.)

Finale
Principals, Chorus

ACT 2

Opening Chorus
(*Lyrics by* Harry B. Smith.)

"The Tale of the Wedding Bell" (Duet)
Corinne, H. Royston, Chorus
(*Lyrics by* Robert B. Smith.)

"My Little China Doll" (Song)
H. Royston, Chorus
(*Lyrics by* Robert B. Smith.)

"Hist! Hist! Hist!" (Trio and Dance)
[Walker, Daisy, Barker]
(*Lyrics by* Harry B. Smith.)

"That Man" (Song)
[Bonnie]
(*Lyrics by* Robert B. Smith.)

"A Lady with Money" (Song)
[Gaggs, Chorus]
(*Lyrics by* Harry B. Smith.)

"My Lucky Star" (Song)
Corinne, Chorus
(*Lyrics by* Robert B. Smith.)

"What Will China Do"?" (Octett)
H. Royston, H. Royston, A. Cunningham,
W. H. MacDonald, [Walker, Muckles, Gaggs, Barker]
(*Lyrics by* Robert B. Smith.)

"Le Café Chantant" (Song)
[Bonnie}
(*Lyrics by* Harry B. Smith.)

Finale
Principals, Chorus

1904.50 THE BARONESS FIDDLESTICKS

A Musical Satire on society (Comic Opera) in Two Acts, 3 Scenes. Book and lyrics by George de Long. Music by Emil Bruguière. Staged by Al M. Holbrook. Produced by MacDonald and Sullivan. Opened 21 November 1904 at the Casino Theatre and closed 10 December 1904 after 25 performances.

CAST: *Mashaway*, a parvenu: JOHN E. HENSHAW. *Archer*, his stepson, Captain Royal Horse Guards: RICHIE LING. *Jack Elkins*, in love with Isabelle: Alden McClaskie. *Maurel Trenchant*, Archer's friend: Tony Asher. *Cholly*, an exquisite: Walter A. Cluxton. *Algy*, *Monty*, Piccadilly chappies: Mae Sherwood, EDNA McCLURE. *Marionetta*: Anna Johnston. *The Duchess of Reelboro*: Minnie Methot. *Isabelle*, Mashaway's daughter: TOBY CLAUDE. *Geraldine*, her friend: NELLA BERGEN. *Mrs. McGurk*, the cook: Mary Ten Broeck. *Jenkins*, Mashaway's butler: Gustav Koldovski. *Patrina*, the Baroness Fiddlesticks: ANNA FITZHUGH.

Patrina Girls: Violet Conrad, Aline Boyt, Helene Curzon, Freda Salber, Charlotte Waldron, Anna Johnston. *Isabelle's Friends*: Auguste Boulin, Bella deFrates, Mittie Weedon, Velma Berrell, Ruth Langdon. *Debutantes*: Lillian Rice, Angie Weimers, Lillian Spencer, Edith Barr, Lou Whelan, Minthorne Worthley. *Archery Girls*: Geraldine Bruce, Edith Warren, Cora Lee, Florence Skiff. *Tennis Girls*: Charlotte Crane, May Kavanaugh, Lillian Fitzgerald, Marion Ruckert. *Guests*: Imogene Avis, Minerva Walton, Martha Bright, Mary Hall, Madaline Hesser, Madeline Summerville, Jean Hammel. *Johnnies*: Messrs. Gallatin, Peteroff, Williams, Bickford, Abbey, Allaird. *Mashaway's Cronies*: Messrs. DeVarney, Fletcher, Hendee, Koldovski. *Archers*: Messrs. Turner, Beattie, Bradcome, Lyons.

MUSICAL NUMBERS[86]

"Daphne Sue"

"Heigh Ho"

"Spring"
N. Bergen

"Rachel O'Toole"

"When I Drop 'Round"
A. Fitzhugh

"Imogen"

"Could You But Know"

"Listen to the Night a-Singing"

"Mr. Bugaboo"
T. Claude

"Seeing New York"

"When You Love a Little Girl"

"What's the Use of Kisses"

"To Arms! Hear the Cry"

"When You Don't Know"

"Tra-la-La"

"At a Fancy Costume Ball"
T. Claude

"Something or Other Sue"

"I'm Just About as I Ought To Be"
J. E. Henshaw

1904.51 THE TWO ROSES

A Musical Comedy in Two Acts. Book and lyrics by Stanslaus Stange. Based on the play "She Stoops to Conquer" by Oliver Goldsmith. Music by Ludwig Engländer. Staged by Fred G. Latham. Dances and chorus numbers arranged by A. M. Holbrook. Settings by Homer Emens and Edward G Unitt. Costumes by Mme. Caroline Seidle. Orchestra under the direction of John Lund. Produced by Charles B. Dillingham. Opened 21 November 1904 at the Broadway Theatre and closed 17 December 1904 after 29 performances.

CAST (in order of appearance): *Rustics recently appointed to the Grange Servants' Hall (8)*: *Polly Primrose*: Ada Meade. *Alice Tupper*: Grace Spencer. *Annie Parsons*: Ila Niles. *Betty Brown*: Bertha Holly. *Giles Munson*: James Beall. *Peter Dodge*: Roy Penalton. *John Juggins*: Otto Wedemeyer. *Geoffrey Davis*: Frank Boyle. *Susan Knight*, maid to Rose Descourcelles: IDA HAWLEY. *Dr. Thomas Well*, a young physician: M. W. WHITNEY, JR. *Lady Jane*, friend of Rose Decourcelles: LOUISE LeBARON. *Ferdinand Day*, Squire Oldfield's stepson: LOUIS HARRISON. *Mrs. Oldfield*, Ferdinand's mother: JOSEPHINE BARTLETT. *Andrew Oldfield*, Squire of Cobham Manor: CLARENCE HANDYSIDE. *Philip Merivale*, Rose Decourcelles' suitor: ROLAND CUNNINGHAM. *Rose Decourcelles*, Squire Oldfield's ward, at one time known as Rose Marie: FRITZI SCHEFF.

Rustics, Village Committee, Squires and Dames of the Period: Helen Chadwick, Carey Lee, Florence Barbier, Nellie Parkes, Marie Parkes, Mae Baldwin, Emma King, Cecile Buck, Julie Cotte, Helen Clifton, Grace Emmons, Agnes Williamson, Belle Chamberlin, Tekla Morton, Flora Fitzgerald, Lola Allen. Messrs. Widdowson, Smith, Hunt, DeVassey, Emerson, Wunder, Lieberman, Hoffman, Barbara, Pergain.

The action takes place in England in the eighteenth century.

---

[86]Musical numbers not listed in programs. List prepared from published sheet music (M. Witmark & Sons, New York, 1903) and reviews.

Act 1: Farmer Knight's Apple Orchard.

Act 2: Squire Oldfield's House.

ACT 1[87]

"'Tis the Hour" (Opening Ensemble)
Chorus

"A Simple Dimple" (Song)
I. Hawley, Chorus

"A Remarkable Doctor" (Song and Chorus)
M. W. Whitney, Jr.

"Appearances Are Oft Deceitful" (Trio)
L. Harrison, J. Bartlett, C. Handyside

"The Spirit of Mischief" (Song)
R. Cunningham

"Fairest of Roses" (Ensemble)
Entire Company

"Smile and Be Merry" (Quartette)
F. Scheff, L. LeBaron, R. Cunningham, M. W. Whitney, Jr.

"What's a Kiss" (Song)
F. Scheff

"There's Not a Thing I Wouldn't Do" (Song)
L. Harrison

"What May a Lovesick Maiden Do" (Song)
F. Scheff

"Ding Dong, Ding Dong" (Finale)
Entire Company

ACT 2

"Sing Hey, Sing Ho" (Opening Ensemble)
Chorus

"The Making of Woman" (Song and Chorus)
M. W. Whitney, Jr.

"Airy Mary" (Song)
F. Scheff

"The Battle on the Tiles" (Trio)
L. Harrison, C. Handyside, R. Cunningham

"Love's Misgivings" (Duet)
F. Scheff, R. Cunningham

"Jack in the Box" (Song and Chorus)
I. Hawley, Chorus

"Just Three Words"
F. Scheff

"Rose Marie" (Ballad)
R. Cunningham

"Why" (Song)
L. Harrison

Grand Finale
Entire Company

1904.52 WOODLAND

A Musical Fantasy of the Forest in Two Acts. Book and lyrics by Frank Pixley. Music by Gustav Luders. Staged by George Marion. Dances arranged by Sam Marion. Settings by Walter Burridge and Edward LaMoss. Costumes by Archie Gunn. Electrical effects by Joseph Wilson. Orchestra under the direction of Gustav Luders. Produced by Henry W. Savage. Opened 21 November 1904 at the New York Theatre, moved 22 December 1904 to the Herald Square Theatre, and closed 28 January 1905 after 83 performances[88].

[87]Musical numbers not listed in programs. List prepared from published piano vocal score (J. W. Stern, New York, 1904). Interpolation not in vocal score: "The Stolen Jewels" (Ensemble), (*Music by* Gustave Kerker.)

[88]Played return engagements 10 April 1905 at the Grand Opera House for 8 performances, and 19 August 1905 at the Grand Opera House for 9 performances.

CAST: *King Eagle*, ruler of Woodland: CHARLES DOW CLARK. *Prince Eagle*, a college student, heir to the throne: CHERIDAH SIMPSON. *The Blue Jay*, a tramp politician: HARRY BULGER. *Robin Redbreast*, college mate of the Prince: HARRY FAIRLEIGH. *General Rooster*, Chief of Police: FRANK DOANE. *Judge Owl*: STANLEY H. FORDE. *Dr. Raven*, Court Physician: Frank D. Nelson. *Cardinal Grosbeak*, representing the Church: Harry N. Pyke. *Miss Nightingale*, concert singer, betrothed to the Prince: IDA BROOKS-HUNT. *Miss Polly Parrot*, a gossiping widow: Ida Mulle. *Lady Peacock*, a society leader: EMMA CARUS. *Miss Turtle Dove*, a country ingenue: MARGARET SAYRE. *Miss Jenny Wren*: HELEN HALE. *Lady Hawk*, the Prince's cousin: Louida Hilliard. *Miss Mocking Bird*: Lucile Nelson. *The Cold Bottle*: Mattie Nichols. *The Hot Bird*: John Donahue. *Lieutenant Sparrow*, commanding the Cadets: EVA FRANCIS. *Miss Canary*: Grace Walsh.

Canaries: Misses Holt, Farrell, Collins, Luttrelle, Drew, E. Burnett, H. Burnett, (Marion) Ford, Fowler. *Doves*: Misses Reidle, Eagen, Hill, Miller, Randall, Spalding, Pattison, Clifford. *Blackbirds*: Misses (Mabel) Moyles, Francis, Holton, (Louise) LaSalle, (Rose) Deni, (Blanche) Collette, Raynor, H. Burnett. *Peacocks*: Misses (Margaret) Sands, (Lucile) Tozier, Hilliard, (Sally) Carlton, Dennis, Spelman, Miller, Ure. *College Students*: Messrs. Abbott, Berg, Johnson, Creamer, DeLisle, Hudson, Maloon, Murphy, Martin, Black, Holt, Stromblad.

Act 1: King Eagle's royal court in the forest. The action begins just before sunrise.

Act 2: The Birchen Grove—the following morning.

ACT 1

"At Night, (At Night)" (Opening Solo and Chorus)
S. H. Forde, Owls, Full Chorus

"Time Is Flying"
I. B. Hunt

"Dainty Little Ingenue"
H. Fairleigh, C. Lilja

"No Bird Ever Flew So High He Didn't Have to Light"
H. Bulger, Chorus
(*Music by* Harry Bulger. *Lyrics by* Will D. Cobb.)

"Bye-Bye, Baby"
H. Bulger, H. Hale

Entrance of Prince Eagle (Solo with Male Chorus)

When the Heart Is Light"
C. Simpson

"Will You Be My Little Bride?"
E. Carus, Chorus

Finale

ACT 2[89]

"Clear the Way" (Opening Chorus of Sparrows)
E. Francis

"You Can Never Tell Till You Try"
F. Doane, Chorus

"The Valley of Hokus Pocus"
H. Bulger, S. H. Forde, F. Doane, F. D. Nelson

"Society"
E. Carus, Chorus

"The Romance of the Bachelor Bird"
L. Nelson

Singing Contest:

"Keep on Smiling"
G. Walsh, Chorus of Canaries

"The Message of Spring"
I. B. Hunt, Chorus

"If You Love Me Lindy"
H. Hale, Blackbirds

"The Tale of the Turtle Dove"
C. Lilja, Chorus

Ensemble

"They'll Have to Go"
H. Bulger

Finale

[89]Added by second month of run, following "They'll Have to Go:"
"Cheer, Boys, Cheer"
C. Simpson, I. B. Hunt, H. Fairleigh, Chorus

1904.53

FLO-FLO

A Musical Comedy in Two Acts. Book and lyrics by Collin Davis. Music by Howard Whitney. Staged by James Gorman. Produced by E. D. Stair and George H. Nicolai. Opened 21 November 1904 at the West End Theatre and closed 26 November 1904 after 9 performances.

CAST: *Mickey McFen*, Irish at times: MATTHEW KENNEDY. *Lord Smiley Smiles*, an invalid: CHARLES A. PUSEY. *Jackson Paths*, rich and from Chicago: Nat. K. Cafferty. *Lieutenant Barry* of the Battleship *Teddy*: Albert Farrington. *Obadiah Floral*: CHARLES JUDELS. *Scotty*: Gilbert Fitzgerald. *James*, valet to Lord Smiles: Andrew M. Buckley. *Deuteronomy Jones*: John Clahane. *Willie Wring*: IZETTA SPRAGUE. *Minnie Mint*, an actress mistaken for an heiress: ESTHER WALLACE. *Gertie*, a Florida orange blossom: Violet McMillan. *Rachel McFen*, Mickey's wife: LOUISE GOULD. *Rose Bloom*: Julia Rooney. *Violet Blossom*: Josie Rooney. *Flo Floral*: STELLA MAYHEW.

Act 1: Garden of the Ponce de Leon Hotel, St. Augustine, Florida.

Act 2: A Pearl Reef off the coast of Florida.

MUSICAL NUMBERS[90]

"Phelia"
(*Lyrics by* Howard Whitney.)

"Many, Many Ways to Say Good-By" S. Mayhew

"For the Sake of Auld Lang Syne"

"Five Dollars a Seat"

"A Wife Is a Necessary Evil"

"Girl of Pearl"

"Kissing Is One Grand Occupation"

"Rachel"
L. Gould, Men's Chorus

"Miss Wide Awake"

"A Sailor Boy"

"Sleep and Dream Serenade"

"Cupid is a Little Mischief-Maker"

"Your Love for Me, Sweetheart"
(*Lyrics by* Lois Evan Davis.)

Dance Specialty
Rooney Sisters

1904.54

IT HAPPENED IN NORDLAND

A Musical Comedy in a Prologue and Two Acts. Book and lyrics by Glen MacDonough. Music by Victor Herbert. Staged by Julian Mitchell. Settings by John Young. Costumes designed by Mme. Caroline Siedle. Electrical effects by Kleigl Brothers. Orchestra under the direction of Max Hirschfeld. Produced by the Fields Stock Company (Fred R. Hamlin, Julian Mitchell and Lew Fields). Opened 5 December 1904 at Lew Fields' Theatre and closed 29 April 1905 after 154 performances; re-opened a return engagement 31 August 1905 at Lew Fields' Theatre and closed 25 November 1905 after 100 additional performances[91]. Total: 254 performances.

CAST: Prologue: *Queen Elsa of Nordland, Prince George of Nebula, the Duke of Toxen, the Duchess Helene, the Countess Pokota, Prince Karl.*

The Play: *Hubert*, the long lost brother of Katherine Peepfogle: LEW FIELDS. *Prince George of Nebula*, who is ordered by the Czar to marry Queen Elsa of Nordland: HARRY DAVENPORT. *Duke of Toxen*, Prime Minister of Nordland: JOSEPH HERBERT. *Baron Sparta*, Minister of War and Police and enemy to the Duke of Toxen: HARRY FISHER. *Captain Slivowitz*, his chief assistant: Joseph Carroll. *Princess Aline*, Queen Elsa's aunt: MAY ROBSON. *Dr. Otto Blotz*, dermatologist and proprietor of Blotz's pain-killer: JULIUS STEGER. *Parthenia Schmitt*, a country girl, maid to the Princess Aline: BESSIE CLAYTON. *Hugo von Armin*, Lieutenant in the Royal Body Guard: CHARLES GOTTHOLD. *Mayme Perkins*, personal secretary to the American ambassadress: (Miss) Billie Norton. *Dr. Popoff*, proprietor of Popoff's Sanatorium: WILLIAM BURRESS. *Captain Gatling*, of the United States Navy: WILLIAM BURRESS. *Duchess Helene*, Mistress of the Robes and sister of the Duke of Toxon: Rosemary Glosz. *Rudolf*, a peasant, Parthenia's sweetheart: Frank O'Neill. *Prince Karl*, in love with Queen Elsa: Frank O'Neill. *Miss Hicks*, First Secretary of the American Embassy at Nordland: Pauline Frederick. *Countess Pokota*, lady-in-waiting to Queen Elsa: Pauline Frederick. *Katherine Peepfogle*, American Ambassadress to the Court of Nordland: MARIE CAHILL.

Dr. Blotz's Samples (6): *Ethylle*: Indiola Arnold. *Vyvienne*: Maida Athens. *Sylvia*: Harriet Forsythe. *Gladys*: Josephine Karlin. *Imogeyne*: Susan Parker. *Gwendolyn*: Diva Marolda. *General of the Army of Nordland*: Katherien Howland. *Colonels of the Army of Nordland*: Georgia Baron, May Leslie. *Maid at the Baths*: Clara Pitt.

Detective Girls: Grace Field, May Chapin, Mattie Chapin, Carolyn Fostelle, Edna Birch, May Hickey, Loretta MacDonald, Ethel Gilmore, May Leslie, Emily Fulton, Marie Troy, Elizabeth Young, Mabel Gilmore, Jessie Crane, Barbara Farres, Adah Carlyle, Charlotte Palmer, Jessie Richmond, Miss Ray Gilmore, Dorothy Watson, Paula Desmond, Frankie Lee, Maude Mills, Hattie Lowraine, Amalie Karle, Ocie

---

[90]No New York program found. Musical numbers prepared from published sheet music (M. Witmark & Sons, New York, 1904).

[91]During the show's second engagement, IT HAPPENED IN NORDLAND was shortened to allow the interpolation of a burlesque of THE MUSIC MASTER, the comedy drama by Charles Klein produced by David Belasco, added 21 September 1905:

Burlesque by Joseph Herbert. Produced under the personal supervision of Lew Fields and staged by Joseph Herbert. Musical director, Hans Linne. (Scenery uncredited). Cast: *Herr Barewig*, a professional assasin of melody: LEW FIELDS. *Loose Spinach*, who has charge of the Second Violin Department in a Liberty Street cafe, prices reasonable: JULIUS STEGER. *Signor Tag*, who claims to be "it," and has the same trouble: ANTHONY PEARL. *Gus Spoons*, who is endeavoring to play to the label: WILLIAM BURRESS. *Henry Canting*, a modern villain, who in a wild desire to keep before the public has appointed himself a slum worker. This does not interfere with his other business, he being head of a banking house and Chairman of the Auto Oil Trust: JOSEPH HERBERT. *Beverage Kruger*, who is going to college to be cured of the simples: PAULINE FREDERICK. *Mr. Flynn*, delegate of the Snow Shovelers Union: HARRY KELLY. *Tom Dundy*, partner at the "hip": JOSEPH CARROLL. *Jowls*, a footman, always on hand: HARRY KELLY. *Lanny*, a wildflower from Bleecker Street: HARRY MONTGOMERY. *Helen Canting*, a wise child who does not know her own father: BLANCHE RING. *Miss Hoistem* of Little Houston Street: HARRY FISHER. *Jenny*, maid of no work and general dish breaker: GEORGIE LAWRENCE. *Charlotte Stanlaws, Octavie Christy*, not Gibson Girls: Gertrude Whitty, Grace Field. *Mrs. Kruger*: May Naudain. *Pony Ballet*: *Miss Eugenia Burch*: Carrie Bowman. *Miss Queenie Trowbridge*: Helen Gordon. *Miss Helen Nichols*: Loretta MacDonald. *Miss Coy Maid*: Ruthita Field. *Miss Hamburg Belle*: Josie Sylvester. *Miss Beldames*: Ivy Williams. *Miss Tradition*: Gertrude Grant. *Miss Yorkville Belle*: Frankie Lee. *Miss Hope Gonne*: Josephine Karlin. *Miss May B Knott*: Ocie Williams. *Miss Iona Mann*: Indiola Arnold. *Miss Minnie Mumm*: Elba Kenny. *Miss Ida Friend*: Isobel Plunkett. *Miss Anna Sthetic*: Molly McGrath.

Chorus Ladies: *Miss Ida Kline*: Marion Whitney. *Miss Rose Early*: Minnie Martrit. *Miss Lotta Gaul*: Maximilienne Verande. *Miss Maida Noyes*: Elizabeth Young. *Miss Grace Notes*: Molly Hoffman. *Miss Cora Fay*: Edith Palmer. *Miss Nellie B. Haive*: Helen Turner. *Miss Ida Claire*: Ocia Thompson. *Miss Carrie Wood*: Clara Pitt. *Miss Pattie Defoy*: Mattie Chapin. *Miss Pearl Gray*: Eleanor Mansfield. *Miss Emma Grant*: Charlotte Crane. *Miss Della Ware*: Jeanne Crane. *Miss Sara Toga*: May York. *Miss Em. Porium*: Carolyn Lilja. *Miss Sara Cuse*: Jessie Richmond.

College Boys: *Al Toona*: F. A. Reinhardt. *Phil A. Delphia*: Herman Noble. *Willy Mantic*: George V. Dill. *Louis Ville*: Edmund Mortimer. *Bing Hampton*: Raymond Strath. *Willes Barry*: Alex Gibson. *Frank Fort*: Glenwood White. *William Sport*: Alfred Borneman.

MUSICAL NUMBERS

"Castles in the Air" J. Steger
(*Music by* Ralph Lemoyne. *Lyrics by* Joseph Herbert. *Harp accompaniment by* Anthony Pearl.)

Chorus
Chorus
(*Music by* Hans S. Linne. *Lyrics by* Joseph Herbert.)

"Little Houston Street"
H. Fisher
(*Music by* Hans S. Linne. *Lyrics by* Joseph Herbert.)

Exit of Pony Ballet
(*Music by* Hans S. Linne. *Lyrics by* Joseph Herbert.)

"Sneezing Quintette"Messrs. Fiuelds, Steger, Pearl, Burress, Fisher, Miss Lawrence
(*Music by* Hans S. Linne.)

"Same Old Moon"
G. Lawrence
(*Music by* Joseph E. Howard. *Lyrics by* Will M. Hough and Frank Adams.)

"Hiram Green, Good-bye"
B. Ring
(*Music by* C. M. Chapel. *Lyrics by* Henry A. Gillespie.)

Finale
The Company

Williams, Gertrude Grant. *Nordland Boys*: Misses Barbara Farres, Adah Carlyle, Charlotte Palmer, Jessie Richmond, Ray Gilmore, Dorothy Watson, Paula Desmond, May Hickey, Frankie Lee, Mabel Gilmore. *Nordland Girls*: Misses Maude Mills, Hattie Lowarine, Amalie Karle, Edna Birch, Ocie Williams, Gertrude Grant. *Flower Girls*: Fanny Dupre, Jeanne Crane. *Water Girls*: Minnie Whitmore, Ruthita Field. *Masqueraders*: Misses Georgia Baron, May Leslie, Katherien Howland, Harriet Ryamond, Elba Kenney, Ray Gilmore. *Matinee Girls*: Nadine and the Misses Emily Fulton, Paula Desmond, Loretta McDonald, Gertrude Grant, May Chapin, Mattie Chapin, Marie Troy, Carolyn Fostelle, Ethel Gilmore, Mabel Gilmore, Clara Pitt. *King Leopold of Belgium*: Alfred Borneman. *King Edward of England*: Frederick Fair. *Dr. Dowie*, of Zion City: Walter Lindberg. *Fauncey Betrue*, of New York: Jack Hall. *Aide to Prince George*: Edmund Mortimer. *Emil*: W. C. Van Brunt. *Boris*: Jean d'Albert. *Guest*: Herman Noble. *Cook's Tourist Conductor*: Franklin Deland. *General*: R. W. Rosemire. *Waiter*: Parvin White. *Corporal*: George V. Dill.

Prologue: The Railroad Station in Kronenberg, capital of Nordland.

Act 1: Promenade in Elsa Bad, Nordland.

Act 2: Terrace of Queen Elsa's Palace in Kronenberg. The next day.

ACT 1[92]

"Opening Chorus

"Tell It All"[93]
J. Herbert, Chorus

"Absinthe Frappé"
H. Davenport, Chorus

"Dr. Blotz"
J. Steger, Chorus

"Business Is Business"[94]
M. Cahill

"Slippery James"
H. Fisher, Chorus

"Beatrice Barefacts"
M. Cahill, L. Fields

"The Man Meant Well"[95]
B. Clayton, H. Davenport, F. O'Neill {Rudolf}

"The Commanderess-in-Chief"
M. Cahill, Full Chorus

ACT 2

"The Carnival" (Al Fresco)
Full Chorus

"The Knot of Blue"
R. Glosz

"Ding Dong Dell"[96]
M. Cahill

"Matinee Maids"
G. Field, Chorus

Imitations[97]
L. Fields, M. Cahill

"(The) Jack O'Lantern Girl"
B. Clayton

"I Took Them Home to Mother"[98]
L. Fields

"Bandana Land"
M. Cahill, Chorus

Finale

---

[92]At the start of the national tour following the first New York engagement, the following were added to Act 1, replacing "Beatrice Barefacts":

"How Did the Story End?"
L. Fields, Billie Norton {Katherine}

"The Flag He Loved"
H. Fisher

[93]Replaced late in the first engagement by:

"The Woman in the Case"
J. Herbert, Chorus

Dropped during second engagement when "The Music Master" burlesque was added.

For subsequent tour this followed the opening chorus:

"If I Were the Governor of Guam"
J. Herbert, B. Clayton, Chorus

Interpolated for subsequent tour, as per published sheet music:

"I'm Looking for a Sweetheart"
Jeanette Lowry
(*Music and Lyrics by* Raymond A. Browne.)

[94]Dropped after the opening, and replaced from "Ding Dong Dell" from Act 2.

[95]Replaced during the run by:

"My Catamaran"
B. Clayton, H. Davenport

Dropped during second engagement when "The Music Master" burlesque was added.

[96]Interpolated by permission of Victor Herbert. After opening moved to Act 1; Act 2 spot replaced by:

"Any Old Tree" (interpolated by permission of Victor Herbert)
M. Cahill

In January 1905 this was replaced by:

"My Hindoo Man" (interpolated by permission of Victor Herbert)
M. Cahill
(*Music by* Egbert Van Alstyne. *Lyrics by* Harry H. Williams.)

Which was later replaced by:

"A Little Class of One"
M. Cahill, H. Davenport

Dropped during second engagement when "The Music Master" burlesque was added.

[97]Dropped after opening.

[98]Dropped two months into the run. Also known as "I Brought Them Home to Mother."

1904.55 LADY TEAZLE

The Lillian Russell Opera Company in a Musical Play in Two Acts, 3 Scenes. Book (and lyrics) by John Kendrick Bangs[99] and Roderick C. Penfield. Based on the comedy "The School for Scandal" by Richard Brinsley Sheridan. Music by A. Baldwin Sloane. Staged by R. H. Burnside. Produced under the personal supervision of Sam S. Shubert. Settings painted by D. Frank Dodge, Frank Gates and Edward A. Morange. Costumes designed by Mme. Caroline Seidle. Orchestra under the direction of Gustav Kerker. Orchestrations by Saddler-Nelson Bureau. Produced by the Messrs. Shubert. Opened 24 December 1904 at the Casino Theatre and closed 11 February 1905 after 57 performances.

CAST: *Sir Peter Teazle*: W. T. CARLETON. *Sir Oliver Surface*: CLARENCE HANDYSIDES. *Sir Benjamin Backbite*: AUGUSTUS BARRATT. *Sir Harry Taylor*: JACK TAYLOR. *Joseph Surface*: STANLEY HAWKINS. *Charles Surface*: VAN RENSSELAER WHEELER. *Crabtree*: Owen Westford. *Careless*: Albert Wilder. *Moses*: Edmund Lawrence. *Snake*: JOHN DUNSMURE. *Trip*, Joseph's servant: Albert McGuckin. *Mrs. Candour*: Phoebe Coyne. *Maria*: ELSA RYAN. *Mollie*: Nellie McCoy. *Lady Sneerwell*: LUCILLE SAUNDERS. *Lady Teazle*: LILLIAN RUSSELL.

Chorus of Guests, Courtiers, Officers, Macaronis, Actresses, etc.: *Macaroni Boys*: Louise DeRigney, May Maloney, Lou Leighton, Lou Grule, Esther Marks, Rita Dean, Claire Lane. *Concert Hall Girls*: Grace Townshend, Essie Lyons, Marjorie Walton, Madeline Durand, Hattie Waters, Josephine Angela, Margaret Rohe.

The action takes place in London.

Act 1: Garden of Sir Peter Teazle's House. (Dodge.)

Act 2, Scene 1: Library in Joseph Surface's House. *Scene 2*: Ball-room in Sir Oliver Surface's House. (Gates & Morange.)

ACT 1

"The Smart Set" (Opening Chorus)

"The Power of the Press"[100]
J. Dunsmure

---

[99]In published sheet music, John Kendrick Bangs alone is credited with lyrics.

[100]Replaced (during New York run? and) for subsequent tour by:

"The Hypocrite"
S. Hawkins

"You Mustn't Do That in High Society"
L. Saunders

"The Scandal Club"
V. R. Wheeler
"Charity"
L. Russell
"Love By Proxy" (Courting by Proxy)
L. Russell, V. R. Wheeler
"The Widow"[101]
L. Russell
"In (Dear Old) Grandma's Days"
E. Ryan
"Were I Happily Married"
L. Russell, S. Hawkins, W. T. Carleton, J. Dunsmure
"The Power of the Press"
J. Dunsmure
"Roger DeCoverly"
Chorus
"The Gay Divorcée"
L. Russell
Finale
Chorus

ACT 2
Scene 1
"Here's to the Bashful Girl of Fifteen"
J. Taylor
"Dear Old London Town"
S. Hawkins
"The Dance"
N. McCoy
"The Auction"
V. R. Wheeler
"The Consciousness of Innocence"
S. Hawkins, L. Russell
"The Dainty Little Milliner"
L. Russell, W. T. Carleton, S. Hawkins
"The Wherefore and the Why"
L. Russell
Scene 2
Opening Chorus
Chorus
"Macaronis We"
A. Barratt
"You've Lied to Me"
L. Saunders
"Tittle Tattle"
Chorus
"Oh, How Sweet Is the Hour of Victory"[102]
L. Russell
Finale

1904.56

IN NEWPORT

A Musical Burlesque on Fashionable Society in Three Acts. Book by John J. McNally. Music and lyrics by James Weldon Johnson, Bob Cole and Rosamund Johnson. Presented under the stage direction of Herbert Gresham and Ned Wayburn. Settings by Richard Marston, D. Frank Dodge and Ernest Albert. Produced by (Marc) Klaw and (Abraham L.) Erlanger Comedy Company. Opened 26 December 1904 at the Liberty Theatre and closed 14 January 1905 after 24 performances.

CAST: *Alert Pincherton*, a detective: PETER F. DAILEY. *Percy Van Alstyne*, a Traditional English nincompoop: JOSEPH COYNE. *John Bankwell*: LEE HARRISON. *Neil Nelson*: Charles F. MacDonald. *Burton*: Alfred Fisher. *Harvey Hawes*: Louis Kelso. *Jim Props*: Frank Todd. *Viola Cartwright*: VIRGINIA EARLE. *Mrs. Jack Bankwell*: Edith Yerrington. *Belle Martelle*: Sue Stuart. *Maizie Mason*: Lillian Hudson. *Lillian Bankwell*: Elphye Snowden. *Piano Girl*: Florence Brennan. *May*: Alice Palmer. *Fay*: Irene Palmer. *Daisy*: Peggy Lawton. *Millie*: Gussie Bennett. *Carrie*: Mildred Claire. *Lorette*: Edith Milward. *Mlle Fleurette*: FAY TEMPLETON.

The action takes place at the present time in Newport, Rhode Island.

Act 1: Mrs. Jack Bankwell's Villa at Newport.

Act 2: Stage of the Casino.

Act 3: Section of the grounds of the Casino at Newport.

ACT 1[103]
"The House That Jack Built" (Opening Chorus)
"Don't Go Too Dangerously Nigh" (Duet)
V. Earle, J. Coyne
"When I Am the Chief of Police"
P. F. Dailey
"Scandal"
F. Templeton
"The Newport Dip" (Finale)

ACT 2
"The Rehearsal" (Opening)
"Stockings"
V. Earle, Chorus
"Nobody But You"
F. Templeton, J. Coyne
"Hello, Ma Lulu"
P. F. Dailey, Chorus
"Zel-Zel" (Duet)
F. Templeton, V. Earle, Chorus
"Roaming Around the Town" (Finale)
P. F. Dailey, Entire Company

ACT 3
The Football Game: Newport vs. Narragansett
Newport: *Right End*: D. Heath. *Right Guard*: A. Laurens. *Right Tackle*: B. Carrette. *Centre*: E. Carisle. *Left Guard*: M. Farrell. *Left Tackle*: V. DeFord. *Left End*: C. Inge. *Quarter-Back*: M. Wallace. *Right Half-Back*: P. Lawton. *Left Half-Back*: G. Hawkins. *Full-Back*: E. Lyth.
Narragansett: *Right End*: M. Arlington. *Right Guard*: F. Hubbard. *Right Tackle*: J. Trevis. *Centre*: M. Claire. *Left Guard*: A. Morgan. *Left Tackle*: B. Heath. *Left End*: G. Anderson. *Quarter-Back*: G. Wallace. *Right Half-Back*: G. Bennett. *Left Half-Back*: F. Burman. *Full-Back*: E. Mitchell.
"Peggy Is a New Yorker Now"
V. Earle, Chorus
Imitations
F. Templeton
Finale

1904.57

FATINITZA

A Revival of the Comic Opera in Three Acts in English[104]. (Original German libretto by F. Zell and Richard Genée, based on the libretto for "La Circassienne" by Eugène Scribe.) (New American) Libretto adapted by Harry B. Smith. Music by Franz von Suppé. Staged by Max Freeman.

---

[101]Dropped (during the run and) for subsequent tour.
[102]Replaced (during the run and) for subsequent tour by:
"Would You"
E. Ryan, V. R. Wheeler

[103]Reviewers remarked upon 2 musical numbers not in the program:
"Women"
F. Templeton
"How a Monocle Helps the Mind"
P. F. Dailey
[104]First produced in German in New York 14 April 1879 at the Germania Theatre; in English 22 April 1879 at the Fifth Avenue Theatre.

Costumes by Van Horn. Musical director, John Lund. Produced by Charles B. Dillingham. Opened 26 December 1904 at the Broadway Theatre, closing 28 January 1905 after 35 performances; re-opened 13 February 1905 at the Broadway Theatre and closed 25 February 1905 after 14 additional performances. Total: 49 performances[105].

CAST: *Lieutenant Vladimir*: FRITZI SCHEFF. *General Kantchukoff*: ALBERT HART. *Princess Lydia*, his niece: ELAINE DeSELLEM. *Izzet Pasha*, Turkish Governor of Rustschuk: LOUIS HARRISON. *Julian Sinclair*, an American war correspondent: RICHIE LING. *Sergeant Steipann*: ARTHUR CUNNINGHAM. *Hassan Bey*, leader of the Bashi Bazouks: OTTO WEDEMEYER. *Mustapha*, guardian of the harem: Campbell Donald. *Captain Vassili*: F. M. Boyle. *Lieutenant Ossip*: Henry Coote. *Vuila*, a sutler: A. BARBARA. *Hanna*, his wife: Lola Allen. *Cadets (6)*: *Dimitri*: Ida Hawley. *Fedor*: Louise LeBaron. *Ivan*: Ada Meade. *Casimir*: Ila Niles. *Gergor*: Bertha Holly. *Michel*: Grace Spencer. *Marshaldshi*, a Turkish woman: JOSEPHINE BARTLETT. *Izzet Pasha's wives (4)*: *Nurisdam*: Ida Hawley. *Diona*: Louise LeBaron. *Zuleika*: Ila Niles. *Besika*: Ada Meade. *Odalisque*: BESSIE McCOY.

Russian Soldiers, Bashi-Bazouks, Bulgarian Peasants, Turkish Women, etc.: Misses Belle Chamberlin, Agnes Williamson, Flora Barbier, Tekla Morton, Helen Clifton, Helene Chadwicke, Marie Parkes, Margaret Leonard, Nellie Parkes, Mae Baldwin, Emma King, Julia Cotte, Jeannette Paterson, Grace Emmons, Flora Fitzgerald, Meta Carson, Grace Pomeroy, Klillian Raymond. Messrs. Thomas DeVassey, Arthur Widdowson, Bob Hunt, Gus Smith, Edward Wudner, Dave Liberman, Morris Hoffman, Arthur Pergain, Harry Wilson, William Koldovsky, Freda Beal, Louis Blumenthal, Arthur Lea, Andrew Swinton, James Norman, Austin Beatte.

Act 1: The Russian Outposts on the Lower Danube.

Act 2: The Harem of Izzet Pasha.

Act 3: Headquarters of General Kantchukoff at Odessa.

1904.58 ME, HIM AND I

A Fantastic Farcical Frivolity and Musical Spectacle in Three Acts. Book by Willard Holcomb. Score (music) by Max Hoffmann. Lyrics by Vincent Bryan. The play staged and produced under the personal direction of Jules Hurtig. Musical and dancing numbers directed by Gertrude Hoffman. Costumes by Will R. Barnes. Musical director, Will Scheffler. Produced by Jules Hurtig and Harry Seamon. Opened 26 December 1904 at the West End Theatre and closed 31 December 1904 after 8 performances; re-opened 16 January 1905 at the American Theatre and closed 28 January 1905 after 16 performances[106]. Total: 24 performances.

CAST: *U. Kahn*, a German bandmaster: GEORGE BICKEL. *Dusty Dawson*, just a tramp: HARRY WATSON, JR. *Con. Conn*, a Hibernian: ED LEE WROTHE. *Klondyke Charley* of the Chilcoot Patch: John J. McCowan. *Hon. Hiram Rolla*, a Western millionaire: Thomas Carlson. *Willie Rolla* (Swiftwater Willie): Edward B. Adams. *Lord Storm*, an English nobleman: George Germaine. *Vera Hartburn*, an emotional prima donna: Marion Stanley. *Seattle Sal*, a lunch-counter gal: GERTRUDE HOFFMAN. *Costa Rolla*, an heiress: ETTA PEARCE. *Marjory Gold*, Costa's college chum: EMILY SANFORD. *Cissy Butte, Sassy Butte*, from dear old London: Ethel Millard, Esther Morse.

10 of the Eldorado Opera Company: *Winnie Pegg*: Marguerite Clayton. *Helena Montana*: Nelda Noble. *Victoria Columbia*: Morna Campbell. *Adelaide Australia*: Thelma Flanders. *Alta Californa*: Frances Bayliss. *Toronto Ontario*: Eleanor Telford. *Augusta Georgia*: Helen Brandon. *Dallas Texas*: Estelle Baldwin. *Della Ware*: Lillian Hoerlein. *Red Flagg*: Pauline Campbell. *Sons of Toil and Tons of Soil (4)*: *Bill Brakes*: F. H. Mayrose. *Maryland*: James H. Lichter. *Siwash Pete*: James Lee. *Silka Sam*: Hary E. Bickford. *Itinerant Musicians (8)*: *Pian Issimo*: Clay Price. *Fort Issimo*: Sam Bennett. *All Egro*: Lester Charlee. *Mode Rato*: C. W. Wallace. *Show Girls*: *Coryphees*: *Dancers*: *Railroad Men, Sailors, Miners, Tourists, Western Girls, Russian, Japanese and Amercan Soldier Girls.*

Act 1: Railroad Station and Docks at Seattle.

Act 2: On board the yacht *High-Roller* en route to the Klondyke.

Act 3: Main Street, Dawson City, front of the Frozen Dog Salon and Dance House

ACT 1

"All Aboard" (Opening Chorus)
Entire Chorus

"The Self-Made Man"
E. Pearce, E. Sanford, E. B. Adams, T. Carlton

"The Worst Woman on the Stage"
M. Stanley

"Good Night, Evangeline"
G. Hoffman, Messrs. Bickel, Watson, Wrothe

"Henry Dinkelspiel"[107]
E. B. Adams, E. Pearce, E. Sanford, Henny and Lenas

"The Football Girls" (Finale)
Messrs. Bickel, Watson, Wrothe, G. Hoffman, E. Pearce, E. Sanford, Entire Company

ACT 2

"Sailing" (Opening Chorus)

"Over the Moonlit Sea"
M. Stanley, E. B. Adams

"Aber Nit"
Messrs. Bickel, Watson, Wrothe

"My Bonita Conchita"
G. Hoffman, Chorus

"The Professor and His Pupil"[108]
G. Bickel and H. Watson, introducing their original band

"Song of Nations" (Finale)
E. Pearce, G. Hoffman, M. Stanley, Messrs. Bickel, Watson, Wrothe, Entire Company

ACT 3

"In (the) Dear Old Fatherland"
E. B. Adams, Company

"Harry, Harry, (Won't You Marry Me?)"
G. Hoffman, Chorus

"My Yukon Belle"
E. Pearce
Bell Soloists: E. Telford, B. Goldie, E. Baldwin, H. Brandon, M. Reed, E. Millard, N. McDonald, P. Campbell.

Finale
Entire Company

1905.01 BABES IN TOYLAND

A Revival of the Musical Extravaganza in Three Acts, a Prologue and 11 Scenes[109]. Libretto (book, lyrics) by Glen MacDonough. Music by Victor Herbert. Staged by Julian Mitchell. Settings by J. P. McDonald. Costumes by Caroline Seidle. Orchestra under the direction of Silvio Hein. Produced

[105]No individual musical numbers listed. Settings uncredited.

[106]Played return engagements 11 September 1905 at the Grand Opera House for 8 performances, and 4 December 1905 at the 14th Street Theatre for 8 performances.

[107]Replaced during the tour by:
"My Shooting Star"
Al H. Weston {Willie Rolla}, Chorus

[108]Replaced during tour by:
"Travesty on Creatore"
(James Francis Sullivan, leader)
B. Watson, Arthur Whitelaw (Con Conn}, Band

[109]Originally produced in New York 13 October 1903 at the Majestic Theatre for 192 performances. For Synopsis of Scenes and Musical Numbers, see original 1903 production. Added for this revival:

"Don't Be a Villain" (Act 1, after "Barney O'Flynn")
G. A. Stone, J. Rome
(*Lyrics by* Vincent Bryan.)

"Beatrice Barefacts" (from IT HAPPENED IN NORDLAND)(Act 2, after "Rockabye Baby")
M. Barrison, G. Pixley

At the close of Act 2, "My Rag Doll Girl" (now retitled "The Rag Doll") moved to precede "The Toymakers." "An Old-Fashioned Rose" (Act 3) replaced by:

"My Castle in Spain"
B. Wynn

"Maybe the Moon Will Help You Out," "The Legend of the Castle" and "Jane" were dropped.

by Fred R. Hamlin and Julian Mitchell. Opened 2 January 1905 at the Majestic Theatre and closed 21 January 1905 after 25 performances.

CAST (in order of appearance): *Alan*, nephew of Barnaby: IGNACIO MARTINETTI. *Jane*, Barnaby's niece: MABEL BARRISON. *Uncle Barnaby*, a rich miser in love with Contrary Mary: JOHN F. WARD. *The Widow Piper*, a lonely widow with 14 children: ARLINE BOLEY. *Contrary Mary*, the Widow Piper's eldest daughter: MAY DeSOUZA. *Tom Tom*, her eldest son: BESSIE WYNN. *Jill*, who helps Jack: Marguerite Ferguson. *Bo-Peep*, who is a careless shepherdess: KATHERINE MURRAY. *Red Riding Hood*, who is devoted to her grandmother: Katherine Bell. *Sallie Waters*, who wants to get married: Mary Welsh. *Miss Muffett*, who is afraid of spiders: Irene Cromwell. *Simple Simon*, who is fond of fairs: Ethel Donaldson. *Peter*, who has a passion for pumpkin pie: Bertha Krieghoff. *Tommy Tucker*, who sings for his supper and everything else: Ida Doerge. *Jack*, who does chores: Elsie Mertens. *Bobby Shaftoe*, who wants to be a sailor: Jean Carnegie. *Roderigo*, a sentimental ruffian: George A. Stone. *Gonzorgo*, his hard-hearted partner: James Rome. *Hilda*, maid of all work in the Piper household: Helen Hilton. *The Master Toymaker*, who designs the toys of the world: JOSEPH GREENE. *Grumio*, apprentice at the Master Toymaker's workshop: CHARLES GUYER. *Inspector Marmaduke*, of the Toyland Police: GUS PIXLEY. *The Brown Bear*: Walter Schrode. *The Sun Queen*: Maud DeRigney. *The Spirit of Maple*: Helen Burnham. *The Spirit of Pine*: Vincie Twohey. *The Spirit of Willow*: Georgie Betts. *The Moth Queen*: Katherine Murray. *The Volcano Queen*: Minnie Murray. *The Giant Spider*: Robert Burns.

1905.02 HIS HONOR THE MAYOR OF THE BOWERY

A Crazy Conglomeration (Musical Comedy) in Two Acts. Book and lyrics by Everybody. Music by the Orchestra. Produced by the Samuel Blair Company, Inc. Opened 7 January 1905 at the Murray Hill Theatre and closed 14 January 1905 after 9 performances.[110]

CAST (in order of appearance): *Rosa Kohlvetter*, August's niece: GEORGIE KELLY. *Cornelius Van Kroost*, a reformer in politics: JOSEPH P. SWICKARD. *Dolly O'Reilly*, O'Reilly's daughter: VIVIAN PRESCOTT. *August Kohlvetter*, steward of the International Club: JOSEPH W. STANDISH. *Timothy Gilligan*, O'Reilly's friend: THOMAS GRIMES. *Kitty Abott*, a beauty doctor: LOUISE TEMPLE SWICKARD. *Angelica Tibbits*, a husband hunter: ADA RIVERS. *Dennis O'Reilly*, "The Mayor of the Bowery": DAN McAVOY.

Rosa's friends who are supposed to act: *Jessie*: Ethel Pennington. *Bessie*: Pauline Vetter. *Tessie*: Florence Barton Revelle. *Josie*: Blanche LaTour. *Rosie*: Lillian Hall. *Nellie*: Millie Beatrice. *Trixie*: Maud Belle Sewell. *Cora*: Blanch Lund. *Flora*: Edna Gotechair. *Dora*: Bessie Clifford. *Tillie*: Helen Clark. *Lillie*: Lillian Florence.

Friends of O'Reilly, also supposition actors: *Tom*: Earl J. Benham. *Bill*: Cass Burke. *Fred*: King M. Saul. *Harry*: Rupert Chidlow. *Eddie*: T. J. McLaughlin. *Teddie*: Alex. Thompson. *Sam*: William Lennon. *George*: J. Dagnan. *Charlie*: George Dillin. *Billy*: Charles Clugston.

Act 1: Summer Garden near the Bowery.

Act 2: Oh! for a good time at Long Beach on the sea.

ACT 1

Opening
Full Chorus

"To Be Beautiful"
L. T. Swickard, Chorus

"O'Reilly, the Mayor of the Bowery"
G. Kelly, J. P. Swickard,
V. Prescott, J. W. Standish, T. Grimes, L. T. Swickard, A. Rivers, Chorus

Medley of Songs
D. McAvoy

"When I'm With You" (Duet)
L. T. Swickard, J. P. Swickard

"Smile, Please Smile" (Trio)
T. Grimes, V. Prescott, D. McAvoy

"Just Like Jane"
G. Kelly, Chorus

Popular Songs
D. McAvoy

March and Grand Finale
Entire Company

ACT 2

"Big Injun"
J. P. Swickard, Chorus

"Back to Baltimore"
D. McAvoy, assisted by G. Kelly, L. T. Swickard,
V. Prescott, A. Rivers, T. Grimes, J. P. Swickard, J. W. Standish

"(The) Sunbeam and the Morning Glory"
G. Kelly, Chorus

A Few Vocal Efforts
J. P. Swickard, L. T. Swickard

"Smile of the Crocodile"
V. Prescott, Chorus

Grand Finale
Entrie Company

1905.03 FANTANA

The Jefferson DeAngelis Company in a Japanese-American Musical Comedy in Three Acts. Book by Sam S. Shubert and Robert B. Smith. Music by Raymond Hubbell. Lyrics by Robert B. Smith. Staged by R. H. Burnside. Settings by John Young, D. Frank Dodge, Frank E. Gates and Edward A. Morange. Costumes designed by Mme. Caroline Seidle. Music under the direction of Albert Krause. Produced by Sam S. Shubert. Opened 14 January 1905 at the Lyric Theatre and closed 30 September 1905 after 298 performances.

CAST: *Commodore Everett*, a retired naval officer, at present a California wiune merchant, and owner of the vineyard "Fantana": HUBERT WILKE. *Hawkins*, valet to the Commodore: JEFFERSON DeANGELIS. *Lieutenant Sinclair Warren*, of *H.M.S. Pontiac*, anchored off Frisco: FRANK RUSHWORTH. *Fred Everett*, a recent graduate of Annapolis, nephew of Commodore Everett: DOUGLAS FAIRBANKS. *Henri Pasdoit*, a waiter at the Café Odeon, Paris, traveling as a count, and seeking his fortune in the wine business: GEORGE BEBAN. *Hon. Kogora Hirataka*, Japanese Minister to America: Philip Leigh. *The Marquis Kioto*, Governor of Kinshin Province, Japan: Robert Broderick. *Fanny Everett*, his daughter: ADELAIDE RITCHIE. *Jessie*, her maid: KATIE BARRY. *Elsie Sturtevant*, a New York belle, schoolmate of Fanny's: Julia Sanderson. *Mlle. Anita*, a Parisian vaudeville artist and secretly married to Pasdoit: ELEANOR BROWNING. *The Kid*: ADELAIDE SHARP. *Leaders of the Younger Set at the Hotel* (3): *Lillian*: Helen Cheston. *Florence*: Jean Calducci. *Jeanette*: Catherine Cooper. *Leola San, Hela Kora*, Geisha Girls: Lynn D'Arcy, Victoria Stuart.

Vassar Girls visiting their colleague, Fanny Everett: Misses Sybil Anderson, Carlotta Doty, Aurora Piatt, Mabel Courtey, Louise Barthel. *Maids*: Misses Grace Wilson, Lotta Ettinger, Neva West, Carol Oty, Dorothy Knight, Amy Dale. *Valets*: Misses Lynn D'Arcy, Nina Clemens, Olive Quimby, Katherine Hyland, Gertrude Mandell, Marain Bontelle. *Officers of the H.M.S. Pontiac*: Messrs. Harvey A. Kelly, Edward Hallaran, Frank Greene, George Picard, Henry Davis. *Cadets of the Annapolis Naval Academy*: Messrs. R. T. Kirkwood, Charles Wright, Jack Carlyle, Henry Dyer, Francis Cameron.

Act 1: Exterior and grounds of Hotel Del Monterey, California. Present time. (Young.)

Act 2: Exterior palace and residence of Marquis Kioto, Nagasaki, Japan. (Dodge.)

Act 3: On board the Commodore's yacht "*Japonica*," homeward bound. (Gates and Morange.)

ACT 1[111]

"North, South, East or West" (Opening Chorus)
Chorus

"A Lesson in Etiquette"
H. Wilke, A. Sharp, Chorus

"It Is the Girl, Not the Horse That Wins the Prize" (Entrance Song)
A. Ritchie

"La Danse Parisienne vs. La Americaine"
G. Beban, assisted by J. Calducci, C. Cooper

"Drop In on Me at Luncheon" (Entrance Song)
J. DeAngelis, K. Barry

"The Farewell Waltz" (The Waltz Duet)
A. Ritchie, F. Rushworth

[110]No credits in program with regard to authors, composers, director, designers or musical director. The published vocal selections feature a wholly different score by George Nichols (music) and George Totten Smith (lyrics).

[111]Interpolated into the show as per published sheet music:
"G.O.P."
J. DeAngelis
(*Music by* Getrude Hoffmann. *Lyrics by* Vincent Bryan.)

"Darby and Joan" (Duet)
J. DeAngelis, K. Barry
"Hail, Celestial Potentate"
A. Sharp, Chorus
Finale
Company

ACT 2
Lantern Fête (Opening Chorus)
Chorus
"(In) My Rickshaw of Bamboo"
A. Ritchie, Chorus
"Hold the Lanterns High"
Chorus
"Laughing Little Almond Eyes"
F. Rushworth, L. Barthel
"The Secret"[112] (Gossip Song)
J. Sanderson
"My Word"
K. Barry
"Tammany"
J. DeAngelis
(*Music by* Gus Edwards. *Lyrics by* Vincent Bryan.)
Finale
Company

ACT 3
"Song of the Pipe" (Opening)
F. Rushworth, Sailors
"The Girl at the Helm"
H. Wilke
"That's Art"
J. DeAngelis
"Just My Style"
A. Ritchie, F. Rushworth
Finale
Company

1905.04 THE DUCHESS OF DANTZIC

A Romantic Light Opera in Three Acts, 4 Scenes[113]. Book and lyrics by Henry Hamilton. Based on Victorien Sardou and Émile Moreau's "Madame Sans Gêne." Music by Ivan Caryll. Staged by Holbrook Blinn. Dances and chorus business arranged by Willie Warde. Settings by Homer Emens and Edward G. Unitt. Costumes by Percy Anderson. Orchestra under the direction of Barter Johns. Produced by George Edwardes. Opened 16 January 1905 at Daly's Theatre and closed 15 April 1905 after 93 performances.

CAST Act 1: *Catherine Upscher*, known as "Sans Gêne": EVIE GREENE. *Laudresses (6): Lisette*: MAY FRANCIS. *Mathilde*: Helena Byrne. *Jacqueline*: Evelyn Cottee. *Therese*: Ethel Forsythe. *Louise*: Agnes Matz. *Phillipe*, Vicomte de Bethune: LAWRENCE REA. *Captain Reignier*, National Guard: PHILIP H. BRACY. *Napoleon Bonaparte*, Lieutenant of Artillery: HOLBROOK BLINN. *National Guard (3): Sergeant Francois Lefebvre*: LEMPRIERE PRINGLE. *Sergeant Flageot*: A. J. Evelyn. *Corporal Gildon*: Frank Greene. *Papillon*, a Peddler: COURTICE POUNDS. *Laundresses, Soldiers, Mob.*

Acts 2 and 3: *Napoleon I*, Emperor of the French: HOLBROOK BLINN. *Courtiers (3): Comte de Narbonne*: Ridgewell Cullum. *Comte de Chanteloup*: Frank Greene. *Comte de Laborde*: Martin Hayden. *M. D'Alegre*, Chamberlain to the Grand Duchess of Berg: PHILIP H. BRACY. *M. De Montmorenci*, Page to the Empress: Cecil Cameron. *François* Maréchal Lefebvre, afterwards Duke of Dantzic: LEMPRIERE PRINGLE. *Adhémar*, Vicomte de Bethune: LAWRENCE REA. *Papillon*, Court Milliner: COURTICE POUNDS. *Empress Josephine*, Consort of Napoleon: Grace Heyer. *Sisters of Napoleon (2): Caroline Murat*, Grand Duchess of Berg and Cleves: ELIZABETH FIRTH. *Pauline*, Princess Borghese: Mary Grant. *Renée de Saint Mézard*, an Imperial Ward: Adrienne Augarde. *Ladies of the Imperial Court (4): Comtesse de Laborde*: Helena Byrne. *Mme. de Beauffremont*: Ethel Forsythe. *Mme. de Chatel*: Evelyn Cottee. *Mlle. de Legrange*: Agnes Matz. *Lisette*, Maréchal Lefebvre's Maid: MAY FRANCIS. *Catherine*, Maréchale Lefebvre, afterwards Duchess of Dantzic: EVIE GREENE. *Ladies of the Court, Ambassadors, Marshals of France, Chamberlains, Pages, Courtiers, Soldiers, Milliner's Assistants, etc.*

Act 1: Sans Gêne's Laundry, in the Rue Royale, Paris.

Act 2: Gardens of the Palace of Fontainebleau.

Act 3, Scene 1: The Tuilleries. Apartments of the Maréchale Lefebvre. *Scene 2*: The Throne Room.

ACT 1[114]
Chorus of Laundresses (Here you may gaze upon a bevy of beauty)
M. Francis, E. Cottee, H. Byrne, Laundresses
"When the trumpets sound to arms" (Chorus of Soldiers)
Soldiers
"Wine of France" (Drinking Song and Chorus)
L. Pringle, All
"My Sabots" (Song)
E. Greene
"Do You Remember?" (Duet)
L. Pringle, Catherine
Recitative (Dear François)
E. Greene, L. Pringle, C. Pounds, L. Rea
Song (Forgive me, pray)
L. Rea
Finale (The tyrant is shaken)
Soldiers, Mob, Laundresses (Chorus)
Air (Aha, my boy, I give you joy)
P. H. Bracy
"Brothers in Arms" (Song) (Let sober maiden sit at home)
E. Greene
Chorus (Then haste to the wedding)

ACT 2
Opening Chorus (Old days have come again in full felicity)
P. H. Bracy, M. Grant, E. Firth, Ladies, Courtiers
"La Petit Caporal" (Song)
A. Augarde, Chorus
(*Lyrics by* Adrian Ross.)
"Here in big boxes we bear" (Chorus of Assistants)
Chorus
"I'm the Milliner Monarch of Paris" (Song and Chorus)
C. Pounds, Chorus
"La Midinette" (Song)
M. Francis, Chorus
Entrance of Napoleon (Chorus)
Ladies, Courtiers
Finale (Assent to no divorce I can)
E. Greene, L. Pringle, H. Blinn, L. Rea, Courtiers

ACT 3
Scene 1
"Mirror Song" (Mirror, in thy glass we scan)
E. Greene
Scene 2
Chorus (Once the lips the Bourbon owned)
Ladies, Courtiers
"The Legend Olden" (Duet)(Tho' throned in majesty)
E. Greene, H. Blinn

---

[112]Dropped during the run.
[113]Billed as "Mr. George Edwardes' original company from the Lyric Theatre, London."
[114]Musical numbers not listed in program. List prepared from English published libretto and vocal score.

1905.05 BUSTER BROWN

Melville Raymond's Cartoon Comedy (with Songs) in Two Acts. Written by Charles Newman and George Totten Smith[115], by special arrangement with New York Herald and R. F. Outcault. Rewritten by Melville B. Raymond. Staged by James Gorman and Melville B. Raymond. Scenery by Ernest Albert. Costumes designed by A. Wilbur Crane. Musical director, Karl Weixelbaum. Produced by Melville B. Raymond. Opened 24 January 1905 at the Majestic Theatre and closed 8 April 1905 after 95 performances[116].

CAST: *Buster Brown*, a regular boy: MASTER GABRIEL. *Tige*, Buster's dog: GEORGE ALI. *Jack Wynn*, in love with Susie: AL LAMAR. *Rocky O'Hare*, a much-used man: John Young. *August Yunkle*, a visitor: Bobby North. *Thomas Brown*, Buster's father: George Tennery. *Mary Brown*, Buster's mother: Nellie Butler. *Susie Sweet*, her younger sister: NINA RANDALL. *Mrs. Sweet*, Mrs. Brown's mother: Jennie Reiffarth. *Gladys O'Flynn*, Mr. Brown's cook: Mamie Goodrich. *Mlle. LaGrandre*, Buster's governess: Dorothy Zimmerman. *Sir Donald McIntosh*: William Arnold. (*Specialties*: EMMA FRANCIS, LA BELLE DAZIE, Emilyn Lackaye, Flossie Hope).

Basket-Ball Girls: Esther Mantell (Captain), Trizie Mantell, Trixie Jennery, Mabel Dedlow, Edmund Danton, Jeannette Mozar, Lottie Franklyn, Amy Mortimare, Helen Zaltz. *Gladys Girls*: Mella Drouette, Laura Lyman, Muriel Wilbur, Fanny Edwards, Lottie Merritt, Mabel Merritt, Edmund Danton, Jennie Stuart, Florence Bird, Amy Mortimare, Lottie Franklyn, Trixie Jennery. *French Maids and Boys*: Misses Mabel Dedlow, Lottie Merritt, Jennie Stuart, Edmund Danton, Jeanette Mozar, Fanny Edwards, Lottie Franklyn, Mabel Merritt, Trixie Jennery, Amy Mortimare, Helen Zaltz, Mamie Clauson. Messrs. E. V. Kaynor, Judson Daniels, J. Osterberg, J. Moffett, Charles Vaughn, E. D. Greene, George Wright, Ralph Strong, H. K. Wood, E. C. Eggleston, E. Bronson, William Bolosky. *Buster Girls*: Trixie Jennery, Jeanette Mozar, Trixie Mantell, Edmund Danton, Lottie Franklyn, Amy Mortmare, Jennie Stuart, Caroline Greene.

Bo Peep: *Bo Peeps*: Misses Drouette, Danton, Perrin T. Mantell. *Red Riding Hoods*: Misses Lyman, Edwards, Mozar, Dedlow. *Krisgringles*: Misses Jennery, Franklyn, Mortimare, Zaltz. *Sheep*: Misses Stuart, Fenton, Morrison, Clauson. *Santa Clauses*: Charles Vaughn, Will Bolosky, J. Daniels, George Wright. *Wolves*: Messrs. Greene, Kaynor, Strong, Osterberg. *Shepherds*: Messrs. Wood, Moffett, Eggleston.

Milkmaids: Claire Husted, Esther Mantell, Lucille Allen, Muriel Wilbur, Florence Bird, Mabel Merritt, Josephine Stilba, Rose Hirsch, Josephine Morrison, Fanny Edwards, Caroline Greene. *Scotch Fusiliers*: Misses Allen, E. Mantell, T. Mantell, Laura Lyman, Perrin, M. Merritt, L. Merritt, Danton, Wilbur, Drouette, Stuart, Mortimare, Mozar, Bird, Robinson, Zaltz, Husted, Fenton, Clauson, Dedlow, Stolba, Hirsch, Greene, Morrison.

Act 1: Lawn at Buster's Home.

Act 2: At the Beach.

ACT 1

Opening Chorus
Company

"I'll Be Your Honey"
A. Lamar, Male Double Sextette

"Gladys O'Flynn"
M. Goodrich, Company

"Sue, Sue, I Love You"
N. Randall, A. Lamar, Double Male Sextette

"Buster's Chums"
Master Gabriel, Buster Girls Octette

Miss Emma Francis will introduce her sensational novelty dances, assisted by her two Arabian whirlwinds, Mohammed and Brahmen.

Grand Original Finale
Company

Review of Raymond's Fusilieers, introducing their silent drill, with imposing and complex manoeuvres. (*Invented and staged by* James Gorman.)

ACT 2

Opening Chorus
Company

"Resolved"
Master Gabriel
(*Music by* John W. Bratton. *Lyrics by* Paul West.)

"Sweetheart Lue"
E. Lackaye, Company

"The French Maids"
E. Francis, F. Hope, Double Male and Female Sextette

La Belle Dazie (Eccentric Toe-Dancing)

"Bo Peep"
Master Gabriel, N. Randall, G. Ali, Company

Finale
Master Gabriel, Company

1905.06 THE YANKEE CONSUL

A Return Engagement of the Comic Opera in Two Acts[117]. Book and lyrics by Henry M. Blossom. Music by Alfred G. Robyn. Staged by George Marion. Settings by Walter Burridge (Act 1), Edward LaMoss (Act 2). Costumes by Will R. Barnes. Orchestra under the direction of Frank N. Darling. Produced by Henry W. Savage. Opened 24 January 1905 at Wallack's Theatre and closed 4 March 1905 after 47 performances.

CAST: *Don Rafael Deschado*, Governor of Puerto Plata: WILLIAM DANFORTH. *Herr Gebubler*, his secretary: JOHN E. HAZZARD. *Captain Leopoldo* of the Dominican Army: JOSEPH RATLIFF. *Lieutenant Jack Morrell*, commanding U.S. Gunboat *"Vixen"*: ALBERT PARR. *Carlos*, water carrier: John Pratt. *Sancho*, proprietor of Los Dos Toros restaurant: Frank Ranney. *Nunez*, chef of Los Dos Toros restaurant: James Templeton. *Felipo*, telegraph operator: C. Books. *Rodrigo*, *Miguel*, local officers under Leopoldo, Local Army: Basil Millspaugh, Clyde McKinley. *Donna Teresa Rebera-y Uruburu*, a wealthy widow: EVA DAVENPORT. *Bonita*, her daughter: FLORA ZABELLE. *Papinta*, her niece: ROSE BOTTI. *Blanca*, a bar maid: Sally McNeel. *Inez*, Sancho's wife: Pearl Evans. *Juanita*, a flower girl: Lila Conquest. *Estrella*, a fruit girl: Eva Marsh. *Friends of the Girls (7)*: *Anita*: Mae Darling. *Jacinta*: Grace Proctor. *Francesca*: Madge Burpee. *Panilla*: L. Witt. *Maria*: Sophie Witte. *Leonora*: M. C. Flavin. *Bella*: Gertrude O'Neill. *Abijah Booze*, American Consul in Puerto Plata: RAYMOND HITCHCOCK.

Spanish Students: Misses O'Neill, Merritt, Marsh, Proctor, H. Chaffee, L. Dew, Chandos. *Mosquito Girls*: Misses Dunne, Botti, Pauline Marshall, Fredericksen, Burt, Kitty Marshall, M. Wallace, G. Wallace. *Cerise Girls*: Misses Gomez, Kendall, Mignon, Trevor. *Senoritas*: Misses M. Burpee, Darling, L. Burpee, Evans, Flavin, Witte, Vance, Chandler, L. Witt, Proctor, Marsh, Fairbanks, Nelson, Tina Marshall. *Spanish Dancers*: Misses Flavin, S. Witte, L. Whitte, Vance. *Soldiers*: Messrs. Addison, Templeton, Armour, Hanlon, Pease, German, Conway. *Senors*: Messrs. Pugh, Seley.

1905.07 THE LOST BOY

A Merry Musical Farce in Two Acts. Book, music and lyrics by Edward Blondell. Production staged by and under the direction of Sol Fields. Scenery by John Young. Costumes by Mme. (Bertha) Dowling and F. Hayden. Musical director, Charles P. Burton. Produced by Edward Blondell (Management, Weber and Rush). Opened 30 January 1905 at the Murray Hill Theatre and closed 4 February 1905 after 9 performances.

CAST: *Professor Kookamai*, an M.D.: Joe Fields. *Frank Kookamai*, his son: JACK REIDY. *Doctor Forplatz*, a scientist: Sam Shannon. *Duke Damnno*, on tour: Bert Angeles. *King Ho Ho*, a mummy: Daniel Ferguson. *Lady Chedwick* of London: Charlotte Lambert. *Gladys Passe*, ancient maid: Lulu Dewey. *Lucille Gray*, in love: ELSIE CURRIER. *Lola*, a lost child: JULIA WEST. *Ion*, a lost boy: GLADYS ARNOLD. *King Go Go*, the ruler of all the gypsies: William Mansfield. *Gadzooks*, chief warrior: John Dewey. *Mrs. Smith*, with a baby: Florence Hawkins. *Gertie*, a pert maid: Bertha Dowling. *Bertie*, a pert maid: Eva Lanning. *Officer Oofferty*, the sparrow: Harry Zeda. *Pedro*, a young Spaniard: MABEL DOUGLAS. *The Lost Boy*, *"Ruben Plumb"*: EDWARD BLONDELL.

Guests, Visitors, Sailors, Soldiers, Toreadors, Court Ladies, Indians, Picadors, Gypsies and other characters: Misses Bessie Moulton, Irene Russell, Mabel Douglas, Alice Keen, Irene White, Hay Bartell, Florence Hawkins, Fannie Avery, Dorothy Paget, Ivy Paget, Maud Harrison, Gabrielle Stahl, Freda West, Lillian Raymond, Tilly Munroe, Beulah Hamilton, Edith Lansing, Alice Carle, Belle Banker, Carrie Lukens, Della Larkin, Maud Fulton, Effie Fridley, Frankie Bronson, Grace Mason, Hattie Lawrence, Ida Markley, Josie Raymond, Katie Thompson, Lydia Morgan; Messrs. Wesley D'Arland, George Koenig, William Howard, Edw. Agard, George Fisher, Harry Thomas, Jack Whitecar, Kenneth Young, Larry Nelson, Martin McElroy.

---

[115]During the run Newman and Smith's names were removed as authors, and Richard F. Outcault's name replaced them as "Author, inventor, designer."

[116]Played a return engagement 8 May 1905 at the 14th Street Theatre for 9 performances.

[117]First presented in New York 22 February 1904 at the Broadway Theatre for 115 performances. For Synopsis of Scenes and Musical Numbers, see original 1904 production. "Tell Me" was dropped.

Act 1: Hotel LaBelle, Tampa, Florida.

Act 2: Gypsy King's Castle, island of Flew Flew.

ACT 1

"Progressive Poker Party" (Opening Ensemble)

"Doctor, Doctor, Doctor"
Company

"In the Land of Romance" (Duet)
J. Reidy, E. Currier

"Chappies of the Day" (Solo and Ensemble)
J. West

"Plantation Echoes" (Ensemble)
Company

"Jolly Tars" (Solo and Ensemble)
G. Koenig

"Japanese and Russians" (Ensemble)
Company

Sensational Military Spectacle including quick changes of costume in full view of the audience.

"The Sun That Rose on Thirteen States Now Sets on Forty-Five" (Ensemble)
E. Blondell, J. Reidy, Company

ACT 2

Opening Ensemble
Company

"Caribou" (Solo and Ensemble)
G. Arnold, M. Douglas

"Spanish Serenade" (Solo and Ensemble)
Company

"Belle of Seville" (Solo and Ensemble)
J. West

"Lola" (Solo and Ensemble)
J. Reidy, E. Currier

Finale
Company

1905.08

GIROFLÉ-GIROFLA

A Revival of the Comic Opera (Opéra-bouffe) in Three Acts[118]. Original French libretto by Albert Vanloo and Eugène Leterrier. Music by Charles Lecocq. Produced by Charles B. Dillingham. Opened 31 January 1905 at the Broadway Theatre and closed 11 February 1905 after 16 performances[119].

CAST: *Giroflé, Girofla*, twin daughters of Bolero: FRITZI SCHEFF. *Aurora*, Don Bolero's wife: JOSEPHINE BARTLETT. *Paquita*, attendant on Giroflé, Girofla: ELAINE DeSELLEM. *Pedro*, in love with Paquita: IDA HAWLEY. *Don Boléro d'Alcazar*, Governor of a Spanish province: CAMPBELL DONALD. *Marasquin*, betrothed to Girofla: RICHIE LING. *Mourzouk*, Chief of the Moors: WALLACE BROWNLOW. *Pirate Chief*: ARTHUR CUNNINGHAM. *The Uncle*: Otto Wedemeyer. *A Notary*: Henry Coote. *His Clerk*: Frank Boyle. *Fernando*: Louise LeBreton. *Second Cousin*: Ila Niles. *Third Cousin*: Ada Meade. *Fourth Cousin*: Bertha Holly. *Fifth Cousin*: Grace Spencer. *Sixth Cousin*: Lillian Raymond. *Seventh Cousin*: Jeanette Paterson. *Eighth Cousin*: Thekla Morton.

Other characters: Misses Flora Barbier, Helen Chadwick, Agnes Williamson, Clara Frey, Grace Pomeroy, Margaret Leonard, Mae Baldwin, Marie Parkes, Nellie Parkes, Meta Carson, Grace Emmons, Flora Fitzgerald, Helen Clifton, Emma King, Marion Chase, etc. Messrs. Hunt, DeVassy, Norman, Bergain, Wilson, Lieberman, Hoffman, Beale, Lea, Barbara, Blumenthal, Wunder, Smith, Koldovsky, Beattie, Widdowson, Swinton.

[118]First produced in New York 4 February-20 March 1875 at the Park Theatre.

[119]American adaptation, musical director, settings and costume design uncredited.

1905.09

HOW HE WON HER

A Musical Comedy Drama in Three Acts. Play by Joseph LeBrandt. Produced by C. F. Whitaker. Opened 20 February 1905 at the Murray Hill Theatre and closed 25 February 1905 after 9 performances.[120]

CAST: *Tom Walton*: BILLY (Single) CLIFFORD. *Samuel Walton*: John F. Bolger. *Charles Stone*: FRED GRANT. *Jack Clark*: John Howe. *Sandy White*: Charles Gano. *George Washington White*: Spider Johnson. *Mike*: James Garen. *Professor Wiggins*: John Williams. *Policeman*: George Daniels. *Skip*: Albert Hargraves. *Phoebe Hemingway*: CORNELIA HUNTER. *Madame Durand*: BARBARA DOUGLASS. *Mabel Marvin*: Jennie Austin. *Jessie Marvin*: Clara Austin.

Daisie: Amy Dodge. *Mazie*: Lillian Goldsmith. *Hazie*: Florence Fields. *Lazie*: Helen LaSalle. *Fazie*: Grace Sessler. *Crazie*: Louise Palmer. *Jessie*: Harriet Springer. *Tessie*: Estelle Silveria. *Bessie*: May Leonard. *Flora*: Amy Stone. *Cora*: May Bateman. *Dora*: Helen Kirby. *Mora*: Jessie Golden.

Act 1: A Wall Street brokerage office.

Act 2: The Boardwalk, Atlantic City.

Act 3: The Criterion Hotel Office, Atlantic City.

MUSICAL NUMBERS

"Bunker Hill"

"By the Seaside"

"Won't You Fondle Me?"

"Be Good and You'll Be Happy"
B. Clifford

Just a few minutes with Billy Clifford

"Uncle Jonathan"

(*Music by* Harry Newman. *Lyrics by* Joe Flynn.)

1905.10

SINBAD

The Lilliputians in a Spectacular Musical Extravaganza in Three Acts, 7 Scenes. (Book and lyrics) Written by John Fowler. Music by William Rostetter. Play staged by Michael Heckert. Ballets and ensembles arranged by H. Fletcher Rivers. Scenery by Frank Gates and Edward A. Morange; Lee Lash Studio. Costumes by Frank Hayden. Musical director, William Rostetter. Produced by Thomas R. Henry. Opened 27 February 1905 at the Murray Hill Theatre and closed 4 March 1905 after 9 performances.

CAST (in order of appearance): *Furioso*, a wicked witch: Jennie Lamont. *Sinbad's troublesome servants (2)*: *Firefly*, a demon, afterwards Tad: Willie Baker. *Comet*, a demon, afterwards Shad: George Meeker. *Golden Rod*, a fairy queen: MARY BAKER. *Secretary*: Louis Merkel. *Mary Ann*: ANNIE NELSON. *Margery Daw*: Martha Weis. *Lady Blanca*: QUEEN MAB. *Policeman Ketchemnow*: Jerry Sullivan. *Sinbad*, an extraordinary sailor: CHARLES H. JOHNSON. *Bridget O'Rafferty*, cook of the "*Nancy Jane*": Jennie Lamont. *Mate Mainbrace* of the "*Nancy Jane*": MARY BAKER. *The Giraffe*: (Willie) Meeker and (George) Clark. *Policeman Keepemdowno*: George Laible. *Mrs. Blubberly*: MARTHA WEIS. *Mrs. Wittington*: Annie Nelson. *Wittington*: Louis Merkel. *Blubberly*: JERRY SULLIVAN. *Giant Policeman*: H. A. Beechele. *Boy Blue*: Queen Mab. *Pedestrian*: W. H. Donovan. *A Dude*: George Clark.

Miss Topsail: Marie Daley. *Miss Mainsail*: Dora Price. *Miss Jipsail*: Della Ranney. *Miss Trysail*: Gabrielle Barbier. *Miss Slysail*: Genevieve Gibson. *Miss Mizzensail*: Sadie Hunt. *Miss Foresail*: Helen Von Derlure. *Miss Aftsail*: Louise Bartlett. *Miss Buckstay*: Ethel Rough. *Miss Mainstay*: Ethel Palmer. *Miss Forestay*: Beatrice Wilson.

Act 1, Scene 1: The Witch's Grotto. *Scene 2*: The presidential palace, Lilliputia.

Act 2: A square in Newville.

Act 3, Scene 1: The haunted chamber. *Scene 2*: A street. *Scene 3*: The gardens of Lilliputia. *Scene 4*: Grand Transformation.

ACT 1

Hunting Song
Ladies

"Twenty-Seven Bells by the Waterbury Watch"
Ladies

"Won't You Fondle Me?"
M. Baker, Ladies

"Every Loving Girl"
A. Nelson, Ladies

Medley of Popular Songs, including "Back, Back to Baltimore"
Company

[120]Music uncredited. No program available.

ACT 2

"Ebenezer Brown"
M. Weis, Ladies

"The Village School and Heinie"
C. H. Johnson, Ladies

Comedy Acrobats
Meeker-Baker Trio

"Alexander"
M. Baker, Ladies

Specialty
Queen Mab

"Louise Schmidt"
C. H. Johnson, Ladies

Miniature Acrobat
J. Sullivan

"Follow the Merry Crowd"
Queen Mab, Ladies

Finale
Company

ACT 3

"Dainty Dragon Fly"
Ladies

"Come Down from the Big Fig Tree"
Ladies

"The Windy Boys"
C. H. Johnson, J. Sullivan, G. Laible and L. Merkel

"The Heroes That Wear the Blue"
M. Baker, Ladies

"Listen to the Big Brass Band"
Company

1905.11 BOCCACCIO

A Revival of the Comic Opera (Operette) in Three Acts in English[121]. Original Viennese libretto by F. Zell and Richard Genée. Music by Franz von Suppé. Staged by Max Freeman. Scenery by Frank Gates and Edward A. Morange. Costumes designed by Mme. Catherine Seidle. Musical director, John Lund. Produced by Charles B. Dillingham. Opened 1 March 1905 at the Broadway Theatre and closed 25 March 1905 after 32 performances.

CAST: *Boccaccio*, novelist and poet: FRITZI SCHEFF. *Leonetta*, his friend, a student: RICHIE LING. *Pietro*, Prince of Palermo: Wallace Brownlow. *Lambertuccio*, a grocer: LOUIS HARRISON. *Lotteringhi*, a cooper: ARTHUR CUNNINGHAM. *Scalza*, a barber: Campbell Donald. *Fiametta*, Lambertuccio's adopted daughter: LOUISE LeBARON. *Isabelle, wife of Lotteringhi*: Ida Hawley. *Petronella*, Lambertuccio's sister: JOSEPHINE BARTLETT. *Beatrice*, daughter of Scalza: Ila Niles. *Fratelli*, a bookseller: Otto Wedemeyer. *Checco*, a beggar: Frank Boyle. *Fresco*, the cooper's apprentice: Grace Emmons. *The Unknown*: Henry Coote. *Students 6)*: *Guido*: Bertha Holly. *Tofano*: Jeanette Paterson. *Grotti*: Agnes Williamson. *Coste*: Lillian Raymond. *Lante*: Grace Spencer. *Frederico*: Ada Meade. *Citizens (3)*: *Carla*: Marion Chase. *Lola*: Flora Barbier. *Philipa*: Nellie Parkes.

Students, Citizens, Soldiers, Beggars, etc.: Misses Helene Chadwicke, Clara Frey, Grace Poremoy, Margaret Leonard, Mae Baldwin, Marie Parkes, Meta Carson, Flora Fitzgerald, Julia Weedon, etc. Messrs. Hunt, DeVassy, Norman, Pergain, Wilson, Lieberman, Hoffman, Beal, Lea, Barbara, Blumenthal, Smith, Koldovsky, Beattie, Widdowson, Swinton, etc.

Act 1: A Public Square in Florence on St. John's Day.

Act 2: The Gardens and Houses of Lambertuccio and Lotteringhi.

Act 3: The Gardens of the Ducal Palace.

1905.12 THE WATCH ON THE RHINE

A Romantic Drama in Four Acts. Play (and lyrics) by Sidney Ellis. (Music by Al. H. Wilson.) Stage manager, Harry Fisher. Musical director, Fred R. Hoff. Produced by Sidney R. Ellis. Opened 20 March 1905 at the Murray Hill Theatre and closed 25 March 1905 after 9 performances.[122]

CAST: *Metz Strobel*, a young diplomat: AL. H. WILSON. *Count von Beckman*, in charge of Imperial affairs: ROSS O'NEAL. *Ludwig von Beckman*, his son: GEORGE A. WRIGHT. *Old Fireball*, "thunder and lightning": HARRY H. FISHER. *Ulrich Steinway*, a fugitive: H. H. Greene. *Watson Dobbs*, the Count's son: Al. T. Holstein. *Baron von Strange*, of the Imperial Guard: H. C. Haddock. *Driver of Coach*: Myles Mohn. *First Officer*: Tony Wayland. *Second Officer*: L. H. Mast. *Norma Steinway*, Ulrich's sister: ROLINDA BAINBRIDGE. *Baroness von Menger*, a widow: FLORENCE STOVER. *Telka Gregory*, matrimonially inclined: MANDA HENDRIX. *Mrs. Watson Dobbs*: Aurelie Durand. *Little Dorothy*, a precious one: Margaret Magraw. *Farm Hands, Soldiers, etc.*

Act 1: Interior von Menger Homestead on River Rhine. An October day. The young diplomat arrives on his mission from America.

Act 2: Interior von Menger Homestead. The next afternoon. Metz turns the tables on Old Fireball.

Act 3: The von Beckman Castle. The same evening. Metz made a very startling discovery.

Act 4: The Homestead again. One week later. Metz reveals himself by a song of the past.

MUSICAL NUMBERS[123]

"Johnny in the Army"
A. H. Wilson

"Love Is All in All"A. H. Wilson

"My Little Fraulein"
A. H. Wilson

"Tea Kettel Song"
A. H. Wilson

"In Tyrol"
A. H. Wilson

"The Song of Home"
A. H. Wilson

1905.13 FLORODORA

A Revival of the Musical Comedy in Two Acts, 3 Scenes[124]. Book by Owen Hall, revised by Frank Pixley. Music by Leslie Stuart. Lyrics by Ernest Boyd-Jones, Paul Rubens, Leslie Stuart. Staged by Cyril Scott. New sets and costumes[125]. Produced by John C. Fisher and Tom W. Ryley. Opened 27 March 1905 at the Broadway Theatre and closed 22 April 1905 after 32 performances.

CAST: *Cyrus W. Gilfain*, Proprietor of the Island and the perfume of Florodora: HENRY V. DONNELLY. *Captain Arthur Donegal*, Fourth Royal Life Guards, Lady Holyrood's brother: CYRIL SCOTT. *Frank Abercoed*, manager for Mr. Gilfain, of the Island of Florodora: JOSEPH PHILLIPS. *Leandro*, overseer of farms: Thomas A. Kiernan. *Gilfain's clerks (6)*: *Tennyson Sims*: Edward Gore. *Ernest Pym*: George P. Smith. *Max Aepfelbaum*: D. C. Mott. *Reginald Langdale*: James Hughes. *Paul Grogan*: Ralph Williams. *John Scott*: Jack Standing. *William*, a footman: L. Hazeltine. *Anthony Tweedlepunch*, a showman, phrenologist, hypnotist and palmist: PHILIP H. RYLEY. *Dolores*: MAUD LAMBERT. *Valleda*, maid to Lady Holyrood: Jennie Bolger. *Garland Dancers (6)*: *Monta*: Sallie Lomas. *Inez*: Lillie Lawton. *Jose*: Madeline Anderton. *Juanita*: Jennie Bolger. *Violanta*: Maud Crossland. *Callista*: Maggie Taylor. *Angela Gilfain*: ELSA RYAN. *English Visitors to the Islands (6) [Sextette]*: *Daisy Chain*: Gertrude Douglas. *Maud Rowe*: Elsa Reinhardt. *Cynthia Belmont*: Gladys Lockwood. *Dottie Chambers*: Almeda Porter. *Lucy Ling*: Lottie Vernon. *Clare Fitzclarence*: Kathleen Dealey. *Lady Holyrood*: ADELE RITCHIE. *Florodrean Farmers, Laborers, Flower Girls, Welsh Peasants, etc.*

---

[121]First produced in New York in English 17 May 1880 at the Union Square Theatre for 28 performances. This American adaptation uncredited.

[122]No credits in program for stage direction, scenery or costumes.

[123]Also performed on tour, but not in New York programs:

"My German Rose"
A. H. Wilson

[124]First produced in New York 10 November 1900 at the Casino Theatre for 505 performances. For Synopsis of Scenes and Musical Numbers, see original 1900 production.

[125]Design uncredited.

1905.14 A HOT OLD TIME

A Revival of the Ray's Original Musical Farce in Three Acts[126]. Produced by Harry M. Hill. Opened 27 March 1905 at the Murray Hill Theatre and closed 1 April 1905 after 9 performances.

CAST: *Larry Mooney*, of Mooney's Express: WILLIAM McROBIE. *General Stonewall Blazer*, a great man: JOSEPH WEBER. *Jack Treadwell*, Yale's quarterback: VICTOR STONE. *Alkali Ike*, from the Woolly West: HARRY YOST. *Cholly*, from across the pond: Irving Newhoff. *O'Donovan Dunn*, M. P.: Harry Browning. *Officer Milligan*: William Moulton. *Willie Swift*, another officer: George Scotty. *Canby Strong*, also an officer: George Errol. *Izze Wright*, mountain guide: William Cooley. *Blossom Blazer, Cherry Blazer*, General's daughters, ripe for picking: MINNIE JARBEAU, BABETTE SHELDON. *Sallie Waters*, their country chum: Dodo Phelps. *Marjorie Daw*, their city chum: Beulah Richardson. *Bell Long*: Daisy Dene. *Mrs. General Stonewall Blazer*: FLORENCE HUGHES. *Guests, Serenaders, Cake walkers, etc.*

1905.15 THE SCHOOL FOR HUSBANDS

A Comedy with Music in Four Acts. Play by Stanislaus Stange. (Inspired by Richard Brinsley Sheridan's play "The School for Scandal.") Songs and incidental music by Julian Edwards[127]. Staged by Stanislaus Stange. Settings by Homer Emens and Edward G. Unitt. Costumes by Mme. C. Seidle. Electrical efefcts by Joseph Menchen. Produced by F. C. Whitney. Opened 3 April 1905 at Wallack's Theatre and closed 13 May 1905 after 48 performances.

CAST (in order of appearance): *Betty*, maid to Lady Belinda: Lucy Ashton. *Roger*, servant to Sir John: Charles Bowser. *Captain Lovel* of the Royal Guard: Wilfred North. *Lord Drinkwell, Lord Playmore*, men of "quality": ROBINSON NEWBOLD, Bruce Delamater. *Sir John Manners*, an indifferent husband: JOSEPH KILGOUR. *Lady Belinda Manners*, a devoted wife: ALICE FISCHER. *Clarissa Huntleigh*, her cousin: FRANCES STEVENS. *Prince Assam*, the Nawab of Calicut: ARTHUR FORREST. *Lady Airish*, a butterfly: Grace Filkins. *Lady Speakill, Lady Tattle*, women of fashion: Mrs. Ida Jeffreys-Goodfriend, Mrs. Goldfinch. *Jocko*, an Ethiopian page: William Sampson. *Lord Foppington*, "the glass of fashion and the mould of form": JAMESON LEE FINNEY. *Warrant Officer*: Edward Dresser. *Constable*: Henry Belasco.

The action takes place in London Town in 1720.

Act 1: Hall of Sir John's House. A morning in May.

Act 2: Spring Gardens. Four weeks later.

Act 3: Lady Belinda's Boudoir—Sir John's House. Night of the same day.

Act 4: Same as Act 3, one week later.

1905.16 THE PRINCE OF PILSEN

A Revival of the Musical Comedy in Two Acts[128]. Book and lyrics by Frank Pixley. Music by Gustav Luders. Scenery by Walter Burridge. Costumes by Will R. Barnes. Produced under the personal stage direction of George Marion. Conductor, Adolph Liesegang. Produced by Henry W. Savage. Opened 3 April 1905 at the New York Theatre and closed 6 May 1905 after 40 performances.

CAST: *Carl Otto*, the Prince of Pilsen, a student at Heidelberg: ARTHUR DONALDSON. *Hans Wagner*, a Cincinnati brewer, traveling abroad: JESS DANDY. *Lieutenant Tom Wagner*, of the U.S. Cruiser "Annapolis": IVAR ANDERSON. *Arthur St. John Wilberforce*, Lord Somerset: PERCY F. AMES. *Francois*, Concierge, Hotel Internationale: James Francis Sullivan. *Sergeant Brie*, of the Gendarmes: Peter Swift. *Cook's Courier*, Vassar Girl's pilot: Peter Swift. *Jimmie*, a bell boy: Stella Martine. *Mrs. Madison Crocker*, from New York: LOUISE WILLIS. *Edith Adams*, a Vassar girl: ALMYRA FORREST. *Sidonie*, Mrs. Crockers' French maid: Jeannette Bageard. *Nellie Wagner*, Hans Wagner's daughter: MARIE WELSH.

The Heidelberg Boys (8): *Rudolph*: James Brennan. *Adolph*: Harry Wigley. *Heinrich*: George Alexander. *Fritz*: Eric Maxwell. *Ludwig*: Earl Berry. *Carl*: Harry Weeks. *Oscar*: Plantagenet McCarthey. *Wilhelm*: Leonard Leffeson.

The American Girls (9): *Priscilla Plymouth*, Boston: Isabella Dixon. *Frankie Friskie*, San Francisco: Mabel Wilbur. *Olive Oriole*, Baltimore: Camille Lavis. *Dolly Dixie*, New Orleans: Mabel DeLacy. *Illie Noyes*, Chicago: Blanche Burnham. *Missy Rivers*, St. Louis: Lorie Sprague. *Pansy Penn*, Philadelphia: Elva Baldwin. *Goldie Dome*, Washington: Edith Kendrick. *Mazie Manhattan*, New York: Ida Stanhope.

The Sea Shell Girls: *White Capps*: Christine Stone. *Pearlie Beach*: Maud Daunt. *Weedle Sea*: Peggy Ballou. *Daisy Dolphin*: Helen Cayvan. *Birdie Petrel*: Grace Belmont. *Coralie Shell*: Elsie Gibson. *Lottie Fogge*: Martha Barnard. *Pleasant Sayle*: Adele Johnson. *Brinie Deep*: Carrie Deming. *Bonnie Voyage*: Vera Stanley. *Bounding Billow*: Claudia Clark. *Foamy Crest*: Ella Warren.

The Bathing Girls: *Amthyst*: Pauline Huntley. *Opal*: Ethel Grau. *Sapphire*: Mabel Daunt. *Coral*: Sybil Ellison. *Pearl*: Lelia Smith. *Cameo*: Jennette Drusse. *Agate*: Alice May. *Diamond*: Elizabeth Brook.

The Gendarmes (4): *Vidocq*: James Brennan. *Sherlock*: William Thompson. *Hawkshaw*: Eric Maxwell. *Carter*: Don McLean. *French Girls, Flower Girls, Naval Cadets, Fox Hunters, French Maids, Waiters, etc.*

1905.17 A YANKEE CIRCUS ON MARS/ THE RAIDERS

A Triple Bill of a Musical Extravaganza in 2 Scenes, a Circus Tournament and Ballet, and a War Drama in 2 Tableaux. Produced by Frederic W. Thompson and Elmer S. Dundy. Opened 12 April 1905 at the New York Hippodrome and closed 1 July 1905 after 120 performances; re-opened 30 August 1905 at the Hippodrome and closed 9 December 1905 after an additional 176 performances. Total: 276 performances.

ACT 1

A YANKEE CIRCUS ON MARS. A Musical Extravaganza in 2 Scenes. Arranged by Frederic W. Thompson. Book by George V. Hobart. Music by Manuel Klein and Jean Schwartz. Lyrics by Harry Williams. Stage direction of Edward P. Temple. Settings by Arthur Voegtlin. Costumes by Mme. Dowling, Wanamaker, Dazian, M. Alfredo Edel. Ballet master, Vincenzo Romeo. Dances arranged by Sam Marion. Orchestra under the direction of Manuel Klein.

CAST: *Signor Thunderairo*, Animal King: ALBERT HART. *Andy Wood*, a Sideshow Spieler: FELIX HANEY. *Sheriff Pennybigger*, a Power in the Village: H. F. Siegfried. *Messenger from Mars*, His First Trip to Earth: BENJAMIN F. GRINNELL. *Ike Morgan*, Boss Canvasman: Thomas D. Daly. *Earnest Jay*, an Innocent: Jack Warren. *Woozy*, Wild Man of Borneo: William Fables. *Picturesque Pete*, a Tattooed Man: JAMES CHERRY. *The Bogie Man*: Frederick Bennett. *Jo-Jo*, a Dog-Faced Boy: J. Leando. *Skeleton*: ??. *Rube Policeman*: J. Harry Taylor. *Aurora*, a Saucy Soubrette: BESSIE McCOY. *Mrs. Earnest Jay*, Another Innocent at Home: Laura Morris. *Voltini*, Third Rail, an Electric Lady: Rita Dean. *Henrietta Heavysides*, a Fay Lady: Leila Romer. *Millie Hortense*, a Snake Charmer: Jeanette O'Brien. *Susie Sutherland*, a Long-Haired Lady: Evelyn Graham. *Madam Gazaza*, a Circassian Lady: Georgie Dix. *King Borealis*, Ruler of the Planet Mars: FELIX HANEY. *Princess Peek-a-boo*, daughter of the Ruler: OLIVE NORTH. *The Astrologer*: Vernon Lee. *Rubes, Canvasmen, Boys and Girls, Spielers, Ticket Takers, Ticket Sellers, Townspeople, Butchers, Animal Men, Milkmaids, Chamberlains, Dignitaries, Pages, Royal Guards, Drummers, Amazons, Officers, etc.*: Hippodrome Company.

Scene 1: A Yankee Circus, in dire financial distress, bought to an enjoy from Mars. *Scene 2*: A Yankee Circus performance in the Royal Courtyard of the King of Mars.

ACT 1
Scene 1
Opening Chorus
(*Music by* Manuel Klein.)
"Ruben, Tell Your Mandy"
(*Music by* Jean Schwartz.)
Entrance of Sheriff
Chorus
(*Music by* Manuel Klein.)
Entrance of Soubrette
Chorus
(*Music by* Manuel Klein.)

---

[126]Authorship uncredited; original production credited to Edgar Selden, revised the following season by George M. Cohan. First produced in New York 6 September 1897 at the Third Avenue Theatre for 8 performances; returned 27 December 1897 to the Grand Opera House for an additional 9 additional performances.

[127]No musical numbers listed in the program.

[128]Originally produced in New York 17 March 1903 at the Broadway Theatre for 143 performances. For Synopsis of Scenes and Musical Numbers, see original 1903 production. No credits in programs for scenery or costumes. For this revival, the following changes were made:
"Artie" was replaced by:
"Walk, Mister, Walk" (Solo)
P. F. Ames, Chorus of Vassar Girls
"He Didn't Know Exactly What to Do" was replaced by:
"Imagination" (Solo)
J. Dandy
(*Music by* James B. Mullen. *Lyrics by* Vincent Bryan.)

"Hold Your Horses"
B. McCoy, Chorus
(*Music by* Jean Schwartz.)

"The Bogie Man"
A. Hart, Chorus
(*Music by* Jean Schwartz.)

Entrance of Messenger from Mars
Chorus
(*Music by* Manuel Klein.)

Finale
(*Music by* Manuel Klein.)

Barlow and Powers' elephants will give an entirely new and wholly original variety of performance, and Colonel Gaston Bordeverry, the world's greatest rifle and pistol shot, will exhibit his skill, concluding by disrobing a lady in full evening dress by bullet. Assisted by Mlle. Leonie de Lausanne.

Scene 2

Milkmaids' Chorus
(*Music by* Jean Schwartz.)

Grand Ensemble of Martians
(*Music by* Manuel Klein.)

"Aurora Borealis"
F. Haney, B. McCoy, Chorus
(*Music by* Jean Schwartz. *Lyrics by* Harry Williams.)

Ensemble
Jungle Chauffeurs
(*Music by* Manuel Klein. *Lyrics by* George V. Hobart.)

"Git a Horse"
F. Haney, Chorus
(*Music by* Jean Schwartz.)

Entrance of Yankee Circus
(*Music by* Manuel Klein.)

The Animal King
A. Hart, Freaks, Chorus
(*Music by* Manuel Klein.)

Grand Finale
Entire Company
(*Music by* Manuel Klein. *Lyrics by* George V. Hobart.)

ACT 2

CIRCUS TOURNAMENT (Frank Melville, Equestrian Director)

The Leaping Champions (headed by Dan O'Brien, Joe Artressi); The Sisters Ronay, Clakes (Jockeys), Marceline (the Droll), Teims Troupe (Gymnasts), The Mazettes (Acrobats), The Six Florettes (Acrobats), Albert Carré with Horses and Dogs (from the Circus Carré, the Royal Circus of Holland), Les Perrez (Perpendicular Ladder), Ferry Corwey (Musical Clown), Clarkonians (Flying Trapeze), Coco the Human Monkey.

DANCE OF THE HOURS, a Ballet from La Gioconda. Music by Amilcare Ponchielli. Staged by Vincenzo Romeo.

ACT 3

THE RAIDERS[129] A War Drama in 2 Tableaux. Arranged by Frederic Thompson. Book by Carroll Fleming. Incidental music by Manuel Klein. Staged by Edward P. Temple. Settings by Arthur Voegtlin.

CAST: *Captain Johnes Barnes*, Senior Cadet Officer: VERNON LEE. *Sidney Calhoun*, Brother to Virginia: WILLIAM HAWLEY. *Commandant of Cadets*: HARRY MITCHELL. *Judge Calhoun* of Georgia: HARRY E. CLUETT. *Professor Barnes*, a Northerner: MALCOLM BARRETT. *Virginia Calhoun*, a Daughter of Dixie: OLIVE NORTH. *Northern and Southern Visitors, Soldiers, Guards, Cadets, Orderlies*: Hippodrome Company.

Scene 1: 1861. West Point Military Academy; Ford Sumter Fired Upon. *Scene 2*: 1865. Battle at Rocky Ford Bridge of Men and Horses in which participate the Thompson & Dundy Stud of Plunging Horses; Peace Declared.

---

[129]Replaced in October 1905 by THE ROMANCE OF A HINDO PRINCESS. Book by Carroll Fleming.

1905.18

SAN TOY

A Revival of the Chinese Musical Comedy in Two Acts[130]. Book by Edward Morton. Music by Sidney Jones. Lyrics by Harry Greenbank and Adrian Ross. Additional musical numbers by Lionel Monckton. Produced under the personal direction of John C. Fisher. Dances and general movement invented and produced by Willie Warde of Daly's and the Gaiety Theatre, London. Scenery by Ernest Gros, Henry E. Hoyt. Costumes by Miss Fisher of London; Colin Eaves, New York. Orchestra under the direction of Arthur Weld. Produced by John C. Fisher by arrangement with the Augustin Daly Estate. Opened 17 April 1905 at Daly's Theatre and closed 6 May 1905 after 24 performances.

CAST: *Li*, a chinaman who has traveled: JAMES T. POWERS. *Captain Bobbie Preston*, son of Sir Bingo: FRANK GREENE. *Sir Bingo Preston*, British Consul at Pyunka Pong: HAROLD VIZARD. *Sing Hi*, President of the Board of Ceremonies: Fred W. Huntly. *Lieutenant Harvey Tucker*: Charles Arling. *Fo Hop*, a Chinese student: Fred W. Huntly. *Hu Pi, Wai Ho*, Jewelers of Pyunka Pong: H. H. May, Sydney Harris. *Li Hi, Li Lo*, Tartar Guard: A. A. McDonald, W. C. Justice. *The Emperor*: W. L. Romaine *Yen How*, a mandarin: GEORGE K. FORTESCQUE. *Wun Lung*, a corporal of the Emperor's own: Dorothy Marlowe. *Ko Fan* of the Emperor's own: Bebe Stanley. *The Six Wives of Yen How*: *Yung Shi*: Clara Martini. *Me Kou*: Emelie Wellington. *Si Ou*: Dorothy Bertrand. *Shuey Ping Sing*: Madlyn Summers. *Li Klang*: Esther Mitchell. *Hu Yu*: Vinnie Safford. *Mrs. Harley Streeter*: Corene Uzzell. *Hon. Mrs. Hay Stackpole*: Myrtle Cosgrove. *Dudley*, Poppy's maid: Margaret McKinney. *Poppy*, daughter of Sir Bingo: JULIA MILLARD. *San Toy*: FLORENCE SMITH.

1905.19

SERGEANT BRUE

A Musical Farce in Three Acts, 4 Scenes. Libretto by Owen Hall[131]. Music by Liza Lehmann. (Interpolations by Ben Jerome and Jean Schwartz; John W. Bratton and Paul West; Clare Kummer, D. K. Stevens.) Staged by Herbert Gresham[132]. Settings by Richard Marston. Costumes by F. Richard Anderson. Orchestra under the direction of Watty Hydes. Produced by Charles B. Dillingham, by arrangement with Klaw and Erlanger. Opened 24 April 1905 at the Knickerbocker Theatre, closing 1 July 1905 after 71 performances; re-opened 14 August 1905 and closed 2 September 1905 after 22 additional performances. Total: 93 performances[133].

CAST: *Sergeant Brue* of the C Division: FRANK DANIELS. *Michael Brue*, his son: ALFRED HICKMAN. *Aurora Brue*, his daughter: SALLIE FISHER. *Daisy*, a servant: CLARA BELLE JEROME. *Mabel Widgett*: Anna Fitzhugh. *Members of Lady Bickenhall's Committee (16)*: Vivienne Russell, Elphie Snowden, Louise Clair, Mary Clayton, Florence Latham, Myrtle McGrain, Nellie Mayne, Irene Cameron, Dollie Read, Claire Leslie, Cissie Raynor, Aileen Goodwin, Madge Dawson, Della Connor, Olive Day, Greta Burdick. *Gerald Treherne*: WALTER PERCIVAL. *Matthew Habbishom*, a lawyer: Nace Bonville. *Inspector Gorringe* of the C Division: James Reany. *Rev. John Lamb*, Charity Jim: LAWRENCE WHEAT. *Captain Bay*, Radium Jack: David Bennett. *Percy Proctor*: George Lestocq. *Haddon Wallis*: Louis Fitzroy. *Mr. Crank*, a magistrate: Gilbert Clayton. *Crookie Scrubbs*, a criminal: HARRY MacDONOUGH. *Dot*, a flower girl: Ida Gabrielle. *Pippins*, a newsboy: Sally Daly. *Bill Nokes*, a coster: Leavitt James. *Bridget*, his wife: Leslie Mayo. *Lady Bickenhall*: BLANCHE RING.

Act 1: Michael Brue's hairdressing salon.

Act 2: The Green Park Hotel.

Act 3, Scene 1: Crawlborough Street Police Court. *Scene 2*: A house in Berkeley Square. Lady Bickenhall's Zoological Party.

ACT 1

"Our Emporium" (Opening Chorus)

"Young Man in a Shop"
A. Hickman, Chorus

"Saturday Afternoon"
B. Ring, Chorus
(*Music by* James O'Dea. *Lyrics by* Anna [Anne] Caldwell.)

---

[130]Originally produced in New York 1 October 1900 at Daly's Theatre for 65 performances; revived 4 March 1901 for 103 additional performances. For Synopsis of Scenes and Musical Numbers, see original 1900 production.
[131]In its previous London production, Owen Hall was credited with the book, and J. Hickory Wood with lyrics.
[132]For subsequent tour, dances were credited to Nace Bonville.
[133]Played a return engagement 26 March 1906 at the Grand Opera House for 8 performances.

"A Cup of Tea"
S. Fisher, W. Percival

"I'm a Sergeant of Police"
F. Daniels, Company

"Hail to the Piccadilly Hero" (Finale)
Company

ACT 2

"We Have Dined" (Opening Chorus)

"Old Man Shea"[134]
F. Daniels, Company
(*Music and Lyrics by* Benjamin Hapgood Burt.)

"Put Me in My Little Cell"
H. MacDonough, L. Wheat, D. Bennett
(*Music by* Frederick Rosse. *Lyrics by* P. G. Wodehouse.)

"Welcome Mr. Brue"
Chorus
(*Music and Lyrics by* Benjamin Hapgood Burt.)

"Let Me Sing"
F. Daniels, Company
(*Music and Lyrics by* Frank Leo.)

"Lancers"
F. Daniels, Company

"Oh, Help!" (Finale)
Company

ACT 3

"Hail to the Magistrate" (Opening Chorus)
Chorus

"Zoological Party"
Chorus

"I Was Born on a Friday"
F. Daniels
(*Music by* George Brevard. *Lyrics by* Fred Murray.)

"Dearie"
B. Ring, Chorus
(*Music and Lyrics by* Clare Kummer.)

"Sweet Anastasia Brady"
S. Fisher, Company
(*Music by* Jean Schwartz .*Lyrics by* William Jerome?.)

Finale
Company

SUPPLEMENT

"Saturday After Two"
B. Ring
(*Music and Lyrics by* D. K. Stevens.)

"Sergeant Brue"[135]
(*Music by* John W. Bratton. *Lyrics by* Paul West.)

(All in the) "Line of Duty"[136]
(*Music by* John W. Bratton. *Lyrics by* Paul West.)

"Skating"
C. B. Jerome, F. Daniels
(*Music by* John W. Bratton. *Lyrics by* Paul West.)

"My Irish Molly O"
B. Ring
(*Music by* Jean Schwartz. *Lyrics by* William Jerome.)

"A Message from the Land of Love"
Anna Fitzhugh
(*Music and Lyrics by* Dave Reed, Jr.)

1905.20 THE ROLLICKING GIRL

A Musical Play (Musical Comedy) in Three Acts, 7 Scenes. Book and lyrics by Sydney Rosenfeld. (Adapted from his earlier libretto for "A Dangerous Maid.") Music by W. T. Francis. Staged by Ben Teal. Scenery by Ernest Gros. Costumes by Alfredo Edel, Mme. Caroline Seidle. Lighting by William Remlinger. Orchestra under the direction of Gus Salzer. Produced by Charles Frohman. Opened 1 May 1905 at the Herald Square Theatre and closed 14 October 1905 after 167 performances.

CAST: *Schmaltz*, a Viennese wig-maker: SAM BERNARD. *Panagl*, a Viennese art patron: JOE [Joseph] COYNE. *Miklos*, bethrothed to Ilona: HARRY FARLEIGH. *Count Istvan*: George Howard. *Kokos*, a wealthy Hungarian: A. W. Fleming. *Biros*, burgomaster: Sidney DeGrey. *Karl Vonrad*, director of the Royal Theatre, Vienna: Sidney DeGrey. *Imre von Blenheim*: George Odell. *Robert*, a callboy: Harry Sammis. *Henri*, a head-waiter: Armond Cortez. *Firenzi*, a Hungarian soldier: Eugene O'Brien. *Ilona*, daughter of Kokos: HATTIE WILLIAMS. *Lena*, wife of Schmaltz: AIMEE ANGELES. *Fanchette* of the Royal Theatre, Vienna: Esther Tittell. *Aranka*, daughter of Biros: Thelma Fair. *Members of the Royal Theatre (5)*: *Felicia*: Edna Goodrich. *Lavinia*: Phyllis LaFond. *Clarissa*: Flora Prince. *Sophronia*: Belle Ashlyn. *Dancers of the Royal Theatre (2)*: *Cypyra*: Flossie Hope. *Saffi*: Gertie Moyer. *Julieka*, a friend of Ilona: Marie Kellar. *Anna*, maid to Ilona: Virginia Staunton.

Act 1, Scene 1: Courtyard surrounding Koko's house in Hungary. *Scene 2*: Schmaltz's wig emporium in Vienna. *Scene 3*: Stage of the Royal Theatre, Vienna.

Act 2, Scene 1: Ilona's boudoir. *Scene 2*: The Vienna Gardens.

Act 3, Scene 1: In the woods. *Scene 2*: Courtyard surrounding Koko's house.

ACT 1[137]

Opening Chorus (Drink the wine and sing the song)
T. Fair, Chorus

"The Life of Love" (Duet)
H. Williams, H. Farleigh

Opening, Act 1, Third Scene (Midnight, midnight)
Chorus

"Tricks (or, Put It in Your Repertoire)"
H. Williams
(*Music by* John W. Bratton. *Lyrics by* Paul West.)

"The Contented Caterpillar" (Duet)
S. Bernard, H. Williams

"When Love Begins"
J. Coyne, Female Quartette

"Coonjine"
S. DeGrey, Dancers

"My Little Sunbeam Sue"
S. DeGrey, Dancers
(*Lyrics by* Dave Reed, Jr.)

"Old Time Song and Dance" (All the world is moving)
A. Angeles

Danse de Ballet; Coon Dance
(*Lyrics by* Vernon Roy.)

"Nita"
H. Williams, Chorus
(*Music by* W. Aletter. *Lyrics by* Vernon Roy.)

Finale (Hail to the spirit rare)
Principals, Chorus

ACT 2

"Miranda"[138]
A. Angeles
(*Music and Lyrics by* Clare Kummer.)

"Friends That Are Good and True"
H. Williams
(*Music by* Edmund Eysler. *Lyrics by* Julius Steger.)

"My Native Land" (Opening, Scene 2)
T. Fair, Chorus

"As We Swing, Sweeetheart" (Swing, Swing, Swing)
H. Farleigh, Female Chorus
(*Lyrics by* Vernon Roy.)

Hussar Entrance (A la Patrol)
H. Williams, Female Quartette

---

[134]Listed in return engagement program only.
[135]Not listed in program for return engagement.
[136]Not listed in program for return engagement.

[137]Added for subsequent tour:
"My Cabin Door"
(*Music by* Tom Lemonier. *Lyrics by* Grant Stewart.)
[138]Previously interpolated into the tour of THE GIRL FROM KAY'S for Hattie Williams.

"The Girl I Left in Boston Town" (The Girl From My Own Town)
H. Williams, Chorus
(*Music by* Ernest R. Ball. *Lyrics by* Charles Noel Douglass, John W. Bratton.)

The Dawn (Intermezzo)

"Won't You Be My Lovey Dovey?"
S. Bernard, J. Coyne
(*Music by* Seymour Furth. *Lyrics by* Ed P. Moran.)

ACT 3

Opening Chorus (Oh what lovely wedding presents)
Chorus

Finale (Oh love is not only sorrow)
H. Williams, Chorus

1905.21 MY TOM-BOY GIRL

A Musical Comedy Drama in Four Acts, 10 Scenes. Book by Charles E. Blaney. Original choruses and musical specialties composed and arranged by Wagner Crosby. Incidental music by Thomas Cutty. Production staged by Priestly Morrison. Scenery by Thomas Follis. Costumes by Wanamaker Company; Jones & Son. Electrical effects by Bernie Lewis. Musical director, Warner Crosby. Produced by Charles E. Blaney Amusement Company (Henry H. Winchell, Manager). Opened 1 May 1905 at the Metropolis Theatre and closed 6 May 1905 after 8 performances; re-opened 22 May 1905 at the 14th Street Theatre and closed 27 May 1905 after an additional 8 performances.

CAST: *Colonel T. C. Calvert*, "Old Fury": JOHN A. BOONE. *Herman von Benninghouse*, of the German nobility: AL. LESTER. *Richard Vaughn*, a rascal who poses as a gentleman: WALTER G. HORTON. *James Barton*, a mountain outlaw, known as "Black Joe": ALBERT HALL. *Hon. Blackstone Law*, a judge of the Tombs court: Eugene LaRue. *Rev. Amos Tinker*: Larry Eugene. *Scrappy*, a newsboy: Bart L. Guy [Guy Bartlett]. *Possum*, a lazy nigger: Guy Bartlett. *Policeman Graft*, one of New York's finest: Edward B. Giles. *Giovanni*, a push cart merchant: William Handy. *Members of Black Joe's Band (5)*: *Blustering Bill*: Burton Varr. *Daring Dave*: Howard Bolton. *Stealthy Steve*: GEORGE VAN RENSELLAER. *Hurricane Hall*: ROBERT CAMPBELL. *Foxey Fred*: F. E. WHITEHOUSE. *Lillian Calvert*, sister of Josie: MAUD KELLETT. *Mammy Pullett*, the old negro mammy of Fury Hall: Nellie Maskell. *Diavola*, an octoroon: Harriet Davis. *Bill*, a hostler: STRAP HILL. *Jane*, a maid: Viola McDonald. *Mother Sheppard*, a beggar: Allie Marshall. *Mrs. James*, a charitable old lady: Dorothy Carter.

Octoroons: Claire Husted, Syble Brennan, Dorothy Carter, Theressa Leland, Edyth Forrest, Bertie Houseman, Madge Robinson, Allie Marshall, Viola McDonald, Lizzie Fuller, Madge Henning, Sadie Stanley, Daisy Cline, Jenny Pierson, Annie Hall, Sally Isaacs, May Ferguson, Doris Usher.

Josie, the Tom-Boy Girl: LOTTIE WILLIAMS. *Captain Charlie*: LOTTIE WILLIAMS. *Ragged Joe*: LOTTIE WILLIAMS. *Cabmen, Newsboys, Bootblacks, Outlaws, Waiting Maids, etc.*

Act 1, Scene 1: Pennsylvania Ferry, 33rd Street, New York City. *Scene 2*: Jefferson Market, Police Court. *Scene 3*: Subway Entrance, 42nd Street and Broadway. *Scene 4*: Private Apartment in Waldorf-Astoria Hotel.

Act 2: Grounds of Calvert Mansion, "Fury Hall," Virginia.

Act 3, Scene 1: Josie's bed-chamber, Fury Hall. *Scene 2*: A path in the mountains. *Scene 3*: Cave in the Mountains. Black Jack's stronghold. *Scene 4*: The River.

Act 4: Dining room in Fury Hall.

ACT 1

"The Pride and Pet of the Lane"
G. Bartlett, Company

"The Legitimate Coon"
S. Hill

"The Gossiping Housemaids"
Ladies of the Company

ACT 2

"Down Where the Suwanee River Flows"
Company

Up-to-date Parody
A. Lester

Imitations
S. Hill

"The Merry Masqueraders"
L. Williams, Company

ACT 3

"The Laurel Four"
E. B. Giles, F. E. Whitehouse, G. Van Rensellaer, R. Campbell

"Lazy Moon"
Company

"Let's Drink to the Foaming Stein"
Company

ACT 4

"Thieving Coons"
E. B. Giles, F. E. Whitehouse, G. Van Rensellaer, S. Hill

1905–1906 SEASON

Victor Moore and Fay Templeton in 45 MINUTES FROM BROADWAY (Photo: Hall)
Billy Rose Theatre Collection, New York Public Library for the Performing Arts

1905–1906 SEASON

1905.22 LIFTING THE LID/ A GILBERT AND SULLIVAN REVIEW

A Double Bill of a Local Musical Travesty in Two Acts, 4 Scenes, followed by A Gilbert and Sullivan Review. (Book) Written by John J. McNally. Music by Jean Schwartz. Lyrics by William Jerome. Staged by Herbert Gresham and Ned Wayburn. Scenery by Castle and Harvey; Marston. Costumes by F. Richard Anderson. Orchestra under the direction of Frederic Solomon. Produced by (Marc) Klaw and (Abraham L.) Erlanger. Opened 5 June 1905 at the Aerial Gardens (atop the New Amsterdam Theatre) and closed 26 August 1905 after 72 performances.

Olio: The Automobile Chase, A Parisian Novelty by George Melies. (film)

ACT 1

CAST for LIFTING THE LID: *Mathilde Macartini*, a dressmaker: CORINNE[1]. *Bessie Otis Adams*, a country girl studying for the stage: VIRGINIA EARLE. *Grace Gaston*, a telephone girl: SUE STUART. *Hilda Hilton*, a telephone girl: LILLIAN HUDSON. *Marie Wilton*: DIAMOND DONNER. *I. Just Doothem*, a lobbyist: LOUIS HARRISON. *George Stonefellow*: FRANK GREENE. *Willie Steele*, a Southern gambler, known as "Texas Dan": EDDIE LEONARD. *William T. G. Rome*: JULIUS TANNEN. *Inspector Muchadoo*: Frank Todd. *Inspector McLarfinn*: Edwin Wilson. *Inspector McCluskey*: Henry Coote. *Honest John*: Allan Ramsay. *Weary Willie*: A. Seymour Brown. *Silas, Peleg*, Members of the Assembly: Henry Coote, Henry Schroeder. *Waiter*: James Grant. *Newsboy*: William Torpey. *Detectives*: Messrs. Pulen, Grant, Baci, Brown. *Roundsman*: Allan Ramsay. *Police Officer*: Edwin Wilson. *Mr. McGinty*: James Grant. *Timmy McGinty*: Master Nathan Wallach. *Mickey Flynn*: Master Pincus Lekosky. *Hammerstein*: LOUIS HARRISON. *Employee at Fields' Theatre*: Edwin Wilson. *Common People*: James Grant. *Theatre Trust*: Master Abrahams. *Tom Lawson*: Henry Coote. *Trusts*: Male Chorus. *The Press*: Allan Ramsay. *Abie Damn*: CORINNE. *Coffer Damm*: LOUIS HARRISON. *Mrs. Coffer Damm*: STELLA MAYHEW. *Hans Danzel*: D. L. Don. *Mrs. Hans Danzel*: MAUDE LAMBERT. *U. B. Damm*: Henry Coote. *Mrs. U. B. Damm*: SUE STUART. *I. B. Damm*: Edwin Wilson. *Mrs. I. B. Damm*: LILLIAN HUDSON. *Hebe Damm*: DIAMOND DONER. *Billy B. Damm*: William Torpey. *The Damm Dog*: Himself. *Jerry Tip*: A. Seymour Brown.

Act 2[2]: Lifting the Lid. *Scene 1*: Times Square. (Castle & Harvey.) *Scene 2*: The Circle, showing Columbus Monument. Central Park in background. (Castle & Harvey.) *Scene 3*: Lobby of Fields' Theatre. (Castle & Harvey.) *Scene 4*: Dining Hall at Sherry's. (Marston.)

MUSICAL NUMBERS[3]

Scene 1

"Home With the Milk in the Morning" (Chorus)

"(There's) Nothing Doing in the Old, Old Town"
L. Harrison, Chorus

"Jerome, the Bogey Man"
J. Tannen, Detectives

"Baa, Baa, Black Sheep" (Black Sheep)[4]
V. Earle, Chorus
(*Music by* William C. Polla. *Lyrics by* James O'Dea.)

"Albany"
L. Harrison, Chorus

"(It) Reminds Me of Home, Sweet Home"[5]
Corinne
(*Music and Lyrics by* Frank Bryan.)

Recitative[6]
Chorus

"Texas Dan"
E. Leonard, Full Chorus

Scene 2-4

"How To Get in Central Park"
E. Wilson, Chorus

"Line It Out, (Mr.) Maginnity"[7]
L. Harrison, Chorus

"Over Sunday"[8]
V. Earle, Male Chorus

"Dear Old Dixieland"
H. Coote, Chorus

"Life On the Stage"
L. Harrison
(*Music by* Victor Herbert.)

Imitations
J. Tannen

"Sombrero"[9]
Corinne
(*Music by* William C. Polla. *Lyrics by* James O'Dea.)

"My Syndi-Kate" (Cindy Kate)
F. Greene, Chorus

"Coonland"[10]
E. Leonard, Full Chorus
(*Music and Lyrics by* Kenneth Clark.)

Finale
Entire Company

ACT 2

A GILBERT AND SULLIVAN REVIEW: CAST for PIRATES OF PENZANCE: *Sergeant of Police*: Frank Todd. *Mabel*: Lillian Hudson. PATIENCE: *Buthorne*: LOUIS HARRISON. *Grosvenor*: Frank Greene. *Angela*: Edith Millward. *Patience*: Diamond Donner. THE MIKADO: *Nanki-Poo*: Virginia Earle. *Mikado*: Allan Ramsay. *Katisha*: Lilly Hart. *Koko*: A. Seymour Brown. *Yum-Yum*: Essie Lyons. *Pitti-Sing*: Ethel Green. *Peep-Bo*: Helen Dexter. IOLANTHE: *Phyllis*: Diamond Donner. *Strephon*: Lillian Barbour. *Lord Chancellor*: Edwin Wilson. *Lord Mt. Ararat*: Frank Todd. *Lord Tolleler*: Henry Coote.[11]

---

[1]Reviewers saw CORINNE in this role briefly; Fay Templeton resumed performances during the run.

[2]The program actually billed LIFTING THE LID in Two Acts. Act 1 was Scene 2. Act 2 was comprised of Scenes 2-4.

[3]Also performed as per published sheet music:
"What has the Nighttime to Do with the Girl?"
(*Music by* Jean Schwartz. *Lyrics by* William Jerome.)

[4]Replaced during the run by:
"Making Eyes"
V. Earle, Chorus
(*Music by* Harry Von Tilzer.)

[5]Replaced during the run by:
"What You Want and What You Get"
F. Templeton
(*Music and Lyrics by* R. A. Brown.)

[6]Dropped during the run.

[7]Dropped during the run.

[8]Replaced during the run by:
"Mrs. Maloney"
V. Earle, Chorus

[9]Replaced during the run by:
"Oh, Marie!"
F. Templeton

[10]Replaced during the run by:
"Rosy"
E. Leonard, Full Chorus
(*Music and Lyrics by* J. B. Mullen.)

[11]During the run in July 1905, A Burlesque titled THE WHOLE DAMN FAMILY was performed by the company in lieu of A Gilbert and Sullivan Review. The running order was also reversed, so that LIFTING THE LID preceded THE AUTOMOBILE CHASE; THE WHOLE DAMN FAMILY came last: The Whole Damn Family.

Scene: Banquet Hall at Sherry's.

MUSICAL NUMBERS

"A Cocktail and a Cherry" (Chorus)
(*Music and Lyrics by* Kenneth S. Clark.)

"Nobody But You"
F. Templeton

"Conversational Song"/"Turn Over"/"My First Smoke"
S. Mayhew

"I Love You"
M. Lambert

"Borneo"
M. Lambert, Chorus

"A Moonlight Buggy Ride"
Full Company

Finale

1905.23 WHEN WE ARE FORTY-ONE

An Oslerized Burlesque in Two Doses (Acts), preceded by a program of vaudeville. Book and lyrics by Robert B. Smith. (Burlesque inspired by the farce "When We Were Twenty One" by Henry V. Esmond.) Music by Gus Edwards. Staged under the direction of Edward E. Rice. Musical numbers produced by Joseph Smith, (Gertrude Hoffman). Scenery by Joseph Physioc. Costumes designed by (Thomas) McIlvaine. Orchestra under the direction of Robert Hood Bowers. Produced by Edward E. Rice. Opened 12 June 1905 at the New York Roof Theatre and closed 26 August 1905 after 66 performances.

VAUDEVILLE[12]

Kelly and Reno (Biffo and Buffo)

Nella Webb and the Wistaria Shetlands

DeMarco Twins (Things to Laugh at)

The Astonishing Avalos in a Novelty Bar Act

Johnny McVeigh, assisted by Rosa Daine

Sam Elion (Last time in America)

Coco the Monk

Mosher, Houghton and Mosher (Bicycle Troupe)

Hugh Jeans (The Baseball Equilibrist)

Ferry Corwey (The Musical Clown from the New York Hippodrome)

The Three Zoellers (Direct from the Wintergarden, Berlin)

The Navassar Troupe (Embracing the famous Navajo and Vassar Girls together with the Wistaria Shetlands and concluding with the entire Wistaria Chorus; introducing Armstrong's Electric Dance (Nora, Cecil, Columbia)

ACT 1

Le Domino Rouge (*The Girl with the Red Domino*: Mlle. LA BELLE DAZIE) introducing her much talked of mystic mirror dance.

The Carrolls Three and the Carroll Dog

WHEN WE ARE FORTY-ONE, an Oslerized Burlesque in Two Doses.

CAST (Burlesque, Act 2): *Dr. Hosler*, the Chloroform King: HARRY BULGER. *John de Rocks, Jr.*, the soul proprietor of a young men's class: JOHN McVEIGH. *George Gessler*, a sparkling lothario: CHARLES H. PRINCE. *Charles Vagner*, a simple liver: George Kelly. *Kid Narrow*, a pugilist; hero of the Red Lights: George P. Reno. *Ted Sparks*, a continuous tourist: Percy Janis. *Digby Pipp*, a Gibson man: HARRY MEEHAN. *Frank Penn*, a dramatic critic who rules the roast: James Thompson. *Bennie*, Dr. Hosler's valet: Clara Hathaway. *Tom, Jerry*, Claremont waiters: George P. Reno, George Kelly. *Lady Long-Green*, the Dowie heiress; just escaped from the unkissed son: EMMA CARUS. *Anastasia Pickles*, fresh from the farm: Nellie Daly. *Marian*, the maid: Nella Webb. *Floradora Fisher*, the original pretty maiden: Lucille St. Claire. *Dolly Dimples*, a rollicking girl: Amy Lake. *The Man with the Laughing Whiskers*: William Plunkett. *Rector's Carriage Agent*: George Sanders. *Pete*, a newsboy: Madlyn Sommers.

Pupils in John DeRock, Jr.'s class, the Wistaria Shetlands (8): *Reggie*: Norma Thomas. *Cornelius*: Madlyn Sommers. *Alfred*: Edith Girvin. *Harold*: Bessie Leyland. *William*: Marjorie Bonner. *Theodore*: Rosa Danie. *Harry*: Florence Milton. *Hazen*: Estehr Mitchell.

Me in the Chorus? No Siree! Small parts, but never in the Chorus (6): *Dessa*: Bessie Kyle. *Daisy*: Jeannette Patterson. *Dolly*: Elise Steele. *Daphne*: Anna Berg. *Diana*: Arnette Steele. *Delilah*: Florence Worden.

Columbia Barnard, a "rah, rah" girl: ELSIE JANIS. *Wistaria Shetlands, Cab Drivers, Soubrettes, Summer Girls, College Gils, Zionists, Colleens and Cow Girls.*

Scene: Le Domino Rouge; The Carrolls Three; When We Are Forty-One (Burlesque). *Sponge No 1*: Rector's White Light Palace. Broadway. *Entr'acte*: Kinetoscope views of Osler's pursuit from Longacre Square to Riverside. *Sponge No. 2*: Claremont, Riverside Drive.

A FEW MUSICAL TABLOIDS

"The Goddess of Rector's" (Opening Chorus)

"I Am a Regular Romeo"
C. Prince, Chorus

"Write to Marian the Maid" (Marian the Maid)
N. Webb, Chorus

"(The) Brother Masons"
H. Bulger
(*Music by* Gertrude Hoffman. *Lyrics by* Vincent Bryan.)

"The Advantage of a College Education"
E. Janis, the Summer Girls

"The Man That Leads the Band Leads the Army"
E. Carus, Chorus

Entr'acte—Kinetoscope Pictures—"The Pursuit": Leaving Rector's; Entrance to Central Park; The Casino; One Hundred and Tenth Street; Grant's Tomb; Arrival at Claremont.

"Up and Down the Boardwalk"
E. Carus, Chorus

"Kindly Pass the Chloroform Along" (The Age of Chloroform)
H. Bulger
(*Music by* Gertrude Hoffman. *Lyrics by* Vincent Bryan.)

"Meet Me Under the Wysteria"
R. Daine, Chorus

"Sweet Kitty Kellairs"
E. Carus, Chorus

Shooting Scene
H. Bulger, assisted by J. McVeigh, C. Prince

Imitations[13]
E. Janis

Finale
Entire Company

1905.24 PAPA'S BOY

A Musical Comedy in Three Acts. Book by Frank W. Lloyd. Music and lyrics by Harry B. Lester. Produced by Charles Bowser's Comedians (Frank W. Lloyd, Manager). Opened 19 August 1905 at the Murray Hill Theatre and closed 26 August 1905 after 9 performances.[14]

CAST: *Professor Bluffem*: CHARLES BOWSER. *I. B. Crankie*, Dolly's father: D. J. SULLIVAN. *Dolly (Crankie)*, a mama's boy: HARRY B. LESTER. *Jack Flyboy*: W. R. Samuels. *Captain Doolittle*: G. R. Raymond. *Mrs. Doolittle*: Sue Belle Mead. *Polly*: LOIE ARNOLD. *Madam Tiptoe*: ELIZABETH HESS. *Manicure Girls (4)*: *Pearl Dexter*: Mollie E. Rogers. *Mabel Batton*: Grace Paulding. *Elsie Early*: Etta Mintz. *Dorrie Dimple*: Beck Ryeford.

MUSICAL NUMBERS[15]

"Don't You Wish That You Were Me?" (Act 3)
G. Lester

1905.25 THE PEARL AND THE PUMPKIN

The Unique Imaginative (Musical) Extravaganza in Three Acts, 10 Scenes. Book by Paul West and W. W. Denslow (based on their children's book of the same name). Music by John W. Bratton. Lyrics by Paul West. Staged by Herbert Gresham and Ned Wayburn. Settings and costumes designed by W. W. Denslow[16]. Electrical effects by H. Bissing. Orchestra under the direction of A. M. Langstaff. Business direction, Joseph Brooks. Produced by (Marc) Klaw and (Abraham L.) Erlanger. Opened 21 August 1905 at the Broadway Theatre and closed 4 November 1905 after 72 performances[17].

CAST: MORTALS: *Pearl Pringle*: GERTIE CARLISLE. *Joe Miller*: TAYLOR GRANVILLE. *Johnny Farnum*: SAGER MIDGLEY. *Polly Premier*: IDA HAWLEY. *Sally Simpkins*: ETHEL JOHNSON. *Jimmy Gingerbread*: CARROLL McCOMAS. *Mr. Dudley*: THOMAS WHIFFEN. *Mons. Gigot*, foreman of Canners: Allan Ramsay. *John Doe*: GEORGE RICHARDS. *Ike Cannem*: HARRY MacDONOUGH.

IMMORTALS: *Mother Carey*, the Fairy Queen: KATHRYN HUTCHINSON. *Mother Carey's Chickens (6)*: *Spangle Wings*: Vinnie Bradcome. *Dancing Eyes*: Grace Emmons. *Sunbeam*: Clare Moore. *Thistledown*: Elta Weir. *Bluebell*: Maude Benson. *Zephyr*: Lillian Sterling. *The Corn Dodger*: Joseph Kane. *Davy Jones*: JOHN MAYON. *Captain Blackbeard*: GEORGE COLLINS. *Captain Kidd*: E. A. Anson. *Captain Jinks*: James Caldwell. *John Silver*: Martin Reddy. *Lyonnaise Portugeeser*: Harry Bergman. *Sir*

[12]Vaudeville specialties changed weekly; list is representative and cumulative, incomplete for the run.

[13]Per Elsie Janis' autobiography "So Far, So Good," she performed imitations of George M. Cohan, Fay Templeton, Eddie Foy, Emma Carus, Harry Bulger, and Mlle. Dazie.

[14]No program available.

[15]No program available.

[16]Denslow's scenic designs realized for the stage by R. Marsden (Act 1 and 3), and Ernest Albert (Act 2).

[17]Played a return engagement 20 November 1905 at the Grand Opera House for 8 performances.

Henry Morgan: Edward Wines. *Captain Stede Bonnet*: A. H. Ransome. *Captain Bartholomew Roberts*: Ivan Charteris. *Captain Avery*: Julius Schroeder. *Captain Hick*: Roy Purviance. *Midshipman Easy*: Tao Howard. *Nancy Lee*: FLORENCE QUINN. *Philip Vanderdecken*: Oscar Ragland. *Captain Dolphin*: Allan Ramsay. *Pages to Vanderdecken*: Misses Stella Huehn, Clara Huehn. *McGinty*, the Ancient Mariner: EDWIN STEVENS. *Silver Clarion Quartette*: Misses Darling, Porter; Messrs. Walters, Schroeder. *Chorus of Villagers, Pirates, Children, Fairies, Sprites, Demons, Crew of The Flying Dutchman, Canners, Puckwudgies, Soldiers, etc.*

Act 1, Scene 1: A Fairy Grotto in the Forest. Hallowe'en. *Scene 2*: Interior of Pringle's Barn in Vermont. *Scene 3*: Hallowe'en Hollow, or the Dell of a Thousand Eyes. On the way to the Cornfield. *Scene 4*: Cornfield on the Pringle Farm. Just before midnight.

Act 2, Scene 1: Exterior of Davy Jones' Locker, underneath the sea. *Scene 2*: North Rock off the Coast of Bermuda. *Scene 3*: Mother Carey's Palace Cave.

Act 3, Scene 1: Ike Cannem's Canning Factory, Bermuda. *Scene 2*: A Lily Field, Bermuda. *Scene 3*: On the South Shore.

ACT 1[18]
Scene 1
"The Fairies' Meeting"
Scene 2
Opening Chorus
"Who Makes the Finest Gingerbread?"[19]
G. Richards, Chorus
"My Party"
G. Carlisle, Chorus
"Jack o' Lantern Joe"
S. Midgley, Chorus
"Sitting on the Starboard Tack"[20]
E. Stevens, Chorus
Scene 3
"Stars Are Shining"
Chorus
"Come, My Dear Love" (Come My True Love)
I. Hawley, Chorus
Scene 4
"When the Moon is in the Sky" (Shadow Song)
E. Johnson, Chorus
"We'll Hang Together"
E. Stevens, G. Richards, H. MacDonough
Finale
Full Company

ACT 2[21]
Scene 1
"Pirates (Are) We"[22]
Male Chorus
"Fol-de-iddledy-ido!"
E. Stevens, Pirates, Mermaids
"(I'm) the Daughter of Annie Rooney"
F. Quinn, Male Chorus
"A String of Pearls"
G. Carlisle, Fairies
"Fighters of Flames Are We" (The Submarine Fire Brigade)
K. Hutchinson, Chorus
Scene 2
"Honeymoon Hall"[23]
I. Hawley, C. McComas
Scene 3
"Hail to Our Queen"[24]
Chorus
"My Combination Girl"
H. MacDonough, E. Johnson
"The Phantom Ship" (The Phantom Brigade)
O. Ragland, Chorus

ACT 3
Scene 1
"The Canny Canner"
H. MacDonough, Chorus
Scene 2
"Lily White"
I. Hawley, Chorus
"My Baby Elephant"
G. Carlisle, S. Midgley
Scene 3
"It Is the English"
E. Stevens, Chorus
Finale
Entire Company

[18]Running order revised during the run and for tour.
[19]Dropped for subsequent tour.
[20]Dropped for subsequent tour.
[21]Added to Act 2, Scene 3, after "My Combination Girl" for subsequent tour:
Ercole-Ariaza (Castilian Dancers and Troubadours from the Royal Theatre, Madrid) Specialty
[22]Dropped for subsequent tour.
[23]Dropped during the run, and replaced by "My Little Baby Elephant" from Act 3.
[24]Dropped during New York run.

1905.26 EASY DAWSON

An American Comedy (with songs) in Three Acts. Play by Edward E. Kidder. Staged by George Marion. Scenery by Walter Burridge. Orchestra under the direction of Harry Braham. Produced by Henry W. Savage. Opened 22 August 1905 at Wallack's Theatre and closed 7 October 1905 after 56 performances[25].

CAST: *Ripley Royal Dawson*, inventor, "good fellow" and chief of local fire department: RAYMOND HITCHCOCK. *Henry Titus*, his friend: JOHN BUNNY. *Benjamin Grierson*, a capitalist: Scott Cooper. *Bruce Grierson*, his son: Earle Browne. *Count Giacomo Chinquescudi*: Nick Briglio. *Wellington Bonaparte*, a chauffeur: William Martin. *Hannah Doty*, "Rip's" sister-in-law: GRACE GRISWOLD. *Rose Dawson*, "Rip's" daughter: JULIE HERNE. *Sadie Collins*, the village flirt: FLORA ZABELLE. *Mrs. Churchill-Churchill-Brenton*, an auto enthusiast: JEFFREYS LEWIS. *Ernestine Ormsby*, a New York girl: Lovell Taylor. *Angie Bates*, an irrepressible youngster: Phyllis Sherwood.

Members of Salamander Hose Company, No. 1: Messrs. Lightner, McCaffery, Boyd, Walsh, White, Kramer, Barry, Samlow. *Town Girls*: Misses Fairbanks, Tonge, Desmond, Mills, Smith, Arnold, Kent, Depew.

The action takes place in an American village at the present time.

Act 1: Living room at Ripley Dawson's. An early evening in June.

Act 2: Front yard of Dawson's house. Three months later.

Act 3: Exterior of Dawson's new house, "Easy Villa," one month later.

ACT 1
"And the World Goes On"
(R. Hitchcock)
(*Music by* Harry O. Sutton. *Lyrics by* Jean Lenox.)

ACT 2
"It's a Waste of Time to Worry"
(R. Hitchcock)
(*Music and Lyrics by* Raymond A. Brown.)

ACT 3[26]
"Little Yellow Bird"
(F. Zabelle, Town Girls)
(*Music and Lyrics by* C. W. Murphy and William Hargreaves.)
"Let Her Drown (If the Missus Wants to Go)"
(R. Hitchcock)
(*Music and Lyrics by* Phil Ray.)
"The Fireman's Parade"
(*Music by* Harry O. Sutton. *Lyrics by* Jean Lenox.)

[25]Costumes uncredited. Played a return engagement 6 November 1905 at the Grand Opera House for 8 performances.
[26]Also performed during the entr'acte:
"Easy Dawson March"
(*Music by* Harry Braham.)

1905.27 THE CATCH OF THE SEASON

The London Musical Play in Two Acts, 4 Scenes. Book by Cosmo Hamilton and Seymour Hicks. Music by Herbert E. Haines and Evelyn Baker. Lyrics by Charles H. Taylor. (Musical interpolations by Alfred Solmon and Benjamin Hapgood Burt, Edward Madden and Theodore Morse, Jerome Kern and F. Clifford Harris, Fred Earle, and Dave Reed, Jr.) Staged by Ben Teal. Settings by Ernest Gros. Costumes by Ward. Orchestra under the direction of William T. Francis. Produced by Charles Frohman. Opened 28 August 1905 at Daly's Theatre and closed 25 November 1905 after 93 performances.

CAST *The Duke of St. Jermyns*: FARREN SOUTAR. *Lord Bagdad Monteagle*: FRED KAYE. *Mr. William Gibson*: FRED WRIGHT, JR. *Lord Yatton*: BERT SINDEN. *Sir John Crystal*: W. L. Branscombe. *Talleur Andrews*, of "School-Girl" Company: Talleur Andrews. *Captain Rushpool*: Frank Norman. *Almeric Montpelier*: Jack H. Millar. *Badminton*: Vivian Graham. *W. M. Dorking*: John F. O'Sullivan. *Bucket*: Master Louis Victor. *First Footman*: William Jefferson. *Second Footman*: C. J. Evans. *The Duchess*, St. Jermyns' mother: Mrs. J. P. West. *Lady Caterham*: MAUD MILTON. *Lady Crystal*: ANNIE ESMOND. *Hon. Sophia Bedford, Hon. Honoria Bedford*, her daughters: Jane May, Margaret Fraser. *Angela*: EDNA MAY. *Princess Schowenhöhe-Hohenschowen*: Madge Greet. *Hon. Ermintrude Dorking*: VIVEAN VOWLES. *Lady Louise Dorsay*: Lillian Burns. *Clotilde*: Dora Sevening.

Gibson Girls: Dorothy Zimmerman, Elaine Barry, Ethel Kelly, Dorothy Reynolds, Eda Shirley, Alys Hardy, Mariel St. Quinten, Queenie Pete, Violet Conrad, Evelyn Powys, Helen Morrison, Sylvia Eagan. *French Gibson Girls* from the Folies Bergeres, Parisienne and Ambassadeurs, Paris: Mlle. Elise Delisia, Suzanne Maud, Martha Dufrene, Suzanne Mallot, Angele Lerida, Germaine deValeral, Marguerite DeManges, Suzanne LaPage.

Act 1: Lady Crystal's House, Mayfair.

Act 2, Scene 1: Ballroom at the Duchess of St. Jermyns. *Scene 2*: Angela's Wedding. *Scene 3*: Same as Scene 2.

ACT 1[27]

Opening Chorus (Tea and tittle tattle)
A. Esmond, B. Sinden, J. H. Millar, Footmen, Chorus
(*Music by* Herbert E. Haines.)

Entrance of Gibson Girls (We've become the great attraction)
Gibson Girls
(*Music by* Evelyn Baker.)

"(It's) All Done by Kindness"
F. Wright, Jr.
(*Music by* W. T. Francis.)

"I'll Be a Good Little Girl"
E. May
(*Music by* Herbert E. Haines.)

"If I Were King of Babylon" (Song)
M. L. Victor
(*Music by* Evelyn Baker.)

"(My Little) Buttercup" (Song and Chorus)
E. May
(*Music by* Luke Forwood.)

Finale (Fairy attendants!)
D. Sevening, E. May, M. Milton, Assistants
(*Music by* Herbert E. Haines.)

ACT 2

Opening Chorus (Every years there's somebody)
Chorus
(*Music by* Herbert E. Haines, Evelyn Baker.)

"Sylvia the Gibson Girl" (Entrance of Gibson Girls)
S. Eagan, Gibson Girls
(*Music by* Hugh Rumbold. *Lyrics by* Frank Compton.)

"Seaweed"
F. Wright, Jr.
(*Music and Lyrics by* Fred Earle.)

"Hail! Miss O'Halloran"
Chorus
(*Music by* Evelyn Baker.)

"Molly O'Hallorhan" (Edna May's Irish Song)
E. May
(*Music and Lyrics by* Jerome Kern.[28])

"A Little Bit of Dinner (with a Friend)"[29]
B. Sinden
(*Music by* W. T. Francis.)

"Suppose" (Duet)
E. May, F. Soutar
(*Music by* Herbert E. Haines.)

"Auf Wiedersehn" (Song and Chorus)
T. Andrews
(*Music by* W. T. Francis. *Lyrics by* Vernon Roy.)

"The Church Parade" (Song and Chorus)
F. Soutar
(*Music by* Herbert E. Haines.)

Dance
V. Vowles

"Back to Harrow" (Duet)
F. Wright, Jr., B. Sinden
(*Music by* W. T. Francis. *Lyrics by* J. Montague.)

"Rainbow" (Song and Chorus)
E. May
(*Music by* Henry E. Pether. *Lyrics by* Fred. W. Leigh.)

Finale (Scene 1)

"Rosy Petals We Will Shower" (Dance)
(*Music by* W. T. Francis.)

"Cinderella! You Have Won!"
E. May
(*Music by* W. T. Francis.)

Finale
(Ensemble)
(*Music by* Herbert E. Haines.)

1905.28 THE HAM TREE

A Musical Vaudeville in Three Acts. Book by George V. Hobart. Music by Jean Schwartz. Lyrics by William Jerome. Staged by Herbert Gresham. Musical numbers staged by Ned Wayburn. Scenery painted by Ernest Gros. Costumes designed by F. Richard Anderson. Musical director, John C. Sorg. Produced by (Marc) Klaw and (Abraham L.) Erlanger. Opened 28 August 1905 at the New York Theatre and closed 11 November 1905 after 90 performances[30].

CAST: *Alexander Hambletonian*: JAMES McINTYRE. *Henry Jones*: T. K. HEATH. *Sherlock Baffles*, a mystery: W. C. FIELDS. *Ernest Everhart*, Manager of the Georgia Minstrels: FORREST HUFF. *Lord Spotcash*, of the English nobility: David Torrence. *Lawrence Nickelbacker*, a rich old New Yorker: Alfred Fisher. *Mrs. Nickelbacker*, his wife: Jobyna Howland. *Tessie Nickelbacker*, his daughter: Caroline Gordon. *Desdemona*, Mrs. Nickelbacker's colored maid: Belle Gold. *Jimpsey*, landlord of the hotel: John Dobson. *Ponsonby*, valet to Lord Spotcash: Otto F. Johnson. *Bill Peters*, a drummer: Harry Dudley. *Ike Mainstem*, another drummer: Ed. Pooley. *Dan Dawson*,

---

[27]Musical numbers not listed in New York program, only interpolation credits. List prepared from published American vocal score. Interpolated in the show, but not in vocal score:

"Little Girl, You'll Do" (dropped for tour)
T. Andrews
(*Music by* Alfred Solmon. *Lyrics by* Benjamin Hapgood Burt.)

"(A) Quaint Old Bird" (dropped for tour)
F. Wright, Jr.
(*Music by* Theodore Morse. *Lyrics by* Edward Madden and Charles H. Taylor.)

"Raining" (most likely replaced "Rainbow")
E. May
(*Music by* Jerome D. Kern. *Lyrics by* F. Clifford Harris.)

"Cupid Is the Captain of the Army"
(*Music and Lyrics by* Dave Reed, Jr.)

"Won't You Kiss Me Once Before I Go?" (dropped for tour)
(*Music by* Jerome Kern. *Lyrics by* Fred W. Leigh.)
Added for subsequent tour:

"Around the World"
(*Music by* Cassius Freeborn and Grant Stewart.)

[28] According to vocal score, composed by Evelyn Baker; authorship commonly ascribed to her.

[29] Dropped for subsequent tour.

[30] Played return engagements 9 April 1906 at the Grand Opera House for 8 performances; 30 July 1906 at the New York Theatre for 40 performances. For detail on the latter, see entry in 1906-1907 season. Toured as late as 1913 under the auspices of John Cort.

also a drummer: Pierre Young. *Bob Hughes*, a drummer: D. M. Lumsden. *Mollie of Chicago*: Pauline Montreau. *Dolly Jones*, of Fargo: Margery Ganes. *Bashful Nan*, of Olean: Helen Whitney. *Nancy Brown*, of San Francisco: May Whitney. *Jane*, of Kansas City: Myrtle Recker. *Wisome Kitty*, of Brooklyn: Lily Hart. *Daisy*, of Savannah: Jane Lovell. *Lola*, of Havana: Jennie Cannar. *Flo* of Buffalo: Edna Arend. *Nellie McGowan*, of Harlem: Eleanor Dobson. *Millie* of New Jersey: Dorothy Paget. *Sleepy Kate* of Philadelphia: Ivy Paget. (*Specialty*: E. Murry, M. Fisher, V. Furst.)

Misses Whitford, Laurens, Nevins, Howard, R. Luby, Larkin, Mayo, Lowe, Wilmot, Hazel, Losee, Hertraise, Brown, Carey, Golden, Dupree, Polo, Hamilton. Messrs. Barry, Coleman, Corcoran, Gros, Harrison, Kennedy, Mann, Paul, Ryan, Jaffie, Garfield.

Act 1: Exterior of "The Travellers' Rest," a country hotel in Marion, North Carolina.

Act 2, Scene 1: At a water tank of P.Q.R.R.R., near Dover, Delaware. *Scene 2*: Woods near the railroad, Dover, Delaware.

Act 3: Drawing room in Mrs. Nicklebacker's Fifth Avenue Mansion, (New York City).

ACT 1
- "Walking" (Opening Chorus)
  Athletic Girls, Trainers
- "Desdemona"
  B. Gold, Athletic Girls, Trainers
- "Sweethearts in Every Town" (Drummer Song)
  H. Dudley, Quartette, Sweethearts
- "The Merry Minstrel Band" (Finale)
  Chorus

ACT 2
- "Good-Bye, Sweet Old Manhattan Isle" (Opening)
  E. Pooley, Passengers, Tourists
- "A New Way to Play Tennis"
  W. C. Fields
- "Honey, Love Me All the Time"
  Honey Girls, Honey Boys
- "The Ham Tree Barbecue" (Finale)
  Chorus

ACT 3
- "When the Cat's Away" (Opening)
  Parlor Maids, Flunkeys, Butlers
- Specialty Dance
  E. Murry, M. Fisher, V. Furst
- "On an Automobile Honeymoon"
  F. Huff, J. Lovell, Auto Girls
- Finale
  Everybody

1905.29 MISS DOLLY DOLLARS

A Musical Comedy in Two Acts. Book and lyrics by Harry B. Smith. Music by Victor Herbert. Staged by Al Holbrook. Scenery painted by Homer Emens and Edward G. Unitt. Costumes by Mme. (Caroline) Seidle. Orchestra under the direction of Antonio DeNovellis. Orchestrations by Victor Herbert. Produced by Charles B. Dillingham. Opened 4 September 1905 at the Knickerbocker Theatre, moved 16 October 1905 to the New Amsterdam Theatre and closed 21 October 1905 after 56 performances[31].

CAST: *Dorothy Gay*, an American known as "Dolly Dollars": LULU GLASER. *Lord Burlingham*, in favor of an Anglo-American alliance: MELVILLE STEWART. *Finney Doolittle*, an educated fool: RALPH C. HERZ. *Samuel Gay*, a condensed soup magnate: CHARLES BRADSHAW. *Mrs. Gay*, his better fifty per cent: CARRIE PERKINS. *Guy Gay*, who pays a fellow to study for him at Oxford: CARTER DeHAVEN. *Bertha Billings*, Dorothy's maid, with a fondness for romance: OLIVE MURRAY. *Celeste*: ELSIE FERGUSON. *Lieutenant von Richter*, of the German Army: HENRY VOGEL. *Miggs*, Lord Burlingham's valet: Byron Ongley. *Members of the Club of Friendly Rivals (8)*: *The Hon. Percy Fitzboodle*: William Naughton. *The Marquis de Baccarat*: James Leahy. *Baron von Rheinheister*: Carl Hartberg. *Count Runoffsky*: James Reany. *Count Chianti*: Enrico Oremonte. *Duke de Bolero*: John Ardizone. *Prince Umskyvitch*: Sidney Harris. *Captain Sheridan Barry*: Edward Leahy. *Costers (6)*: *'Arry*: J. Leahy. *Bobby*: E. Oremonte. *H'Alfred*: S. A. Harris. *'Arriet*: Lillie Van Arsdale. *Jane*: Minerva Hall. *Matilda*: Beatrice Anderson. *Eton Boys (4)*: *Hon. Montague Bank*: Bessie Holbrook. *Hon. Mayland Bank*: Sadie Probst. *Hon. Algy Sydney*: Elizabeth Doddridge. *Hon. Reggy Chumpley*: Mildred Cecil. *Margery*: Lilian Spencer. *Millicent*: Queenie Hewlitt. *Vera Vane*: Marion Chase. *Vashti Pearl*: Gladys Zell. *First Bailiff*: Joseph Frohoff. *Second Bailiff*: L. F. Sampson. *The Summer Girls (6)*: *Freda Dressler*: Elsa Rheinhardt. *Estelle DeLange*: Vida Whitmore. *Greta Giltedge*: Aline Redmond. *Ruth Delamere*: Helen Marlborough. *Vena Rodriguez*: Leila Benton. *Miriam Odell*: Susanne Parker.

Act 1: A Villa on the Thames at Henley.

Act 2: The Garden of a Hotel in Paris.

ACT 1[32]
- Opening Choruses
  Company
- "The Self-Made Family" (She's a Lady with Money)(Trio)
  C. Perkins, C. Bradshaw, C. DeHaven
- "An Educated Fool" (It Keeps Me Guessing All the Time)
  R. C. Herz
- Entrance of Dolly
  Chorus
- "Just Get Out and Walk" (Song)
  L. Glaser, Chorus
- Entrance of the Friendly Rivals' Club
- "An American Heiress" (Song)
  L. Glaser, Noblemen
- "Dolly Dollars" (Song)
  C. DeHaven
- "My Fair Unknown" (Song)
  M. Stewart
- Finale
  L. Glaser, Company

ACT 2
- Opening Chorus
  Company
- "It's All in the Book You Know" (Ollendorff Duet)
  L. Glaser, H. Vogel
- "Life's a Masquerade" (Quartette)
  C. Perkins, C. Bradshaw, E. Ferguson, C. DeHaven
- "The Moth and the Moon" (Song)
  L. Glaser, Chorus
- "Walks"[33] (Song)
  C. DeHaven, Girls
- "A Woman Is Only a Woman, But a Good Cigar Is a Smoke"[34]
  (A Good Cigar Is a Smoke)(Puff, Puff, Puff)(Song)
  M. Stewart
- "(American Music) 'Tis Better Than Old Parsifal to Me"
  Principals, Chorus
- "Queen of the Ring"[35] (Circus Song)
  L. Glaser, Chorus
- Finale
  L. Glaser, Company

1905.30 THE ROGERS BROTHERS IN IRELAND

A Musical Play in Three Acts. Book by John J. McNally. Music by Max Hoffmann. Lyrics by George V. Hobart. Staged by Herbert Gresham and Ned Wayburn. Scenery painted by Ernest Gros. Costumes designed by F. Richard Anderson. Electrical effects by Harry Bissing. Music director, Max Hoffmann. Produced by (Marc) Klaw and (Abraham L.) Erlanger. Opened 4 September 1905 at the Liberty Theatre, closing 28 October 1905

[31] Played return engagements 4 December 1905 at the Grand Opera House for 8 performances; 8 October 1906 at the New York Theatre for 16 performances; see separate entry for cast and credit detail in 1906-1907 season for latter production.

[32] Musical numbers not listed in program for original New York engagement; list prepared from published vocal score, subsequent Boston and Grand Opera House tour programs. Running order revised during the tour.

[33] Dropped during subsequent tour.

[34] Title drawn from Rudyard Kipling's "The Betrothed."

[35] Dropped during subsequent tour.

after 56 performances, re-opened 29 January 1906 at the New York Theatre and closed 10 March 1906 after 50 additional performances. Total: 106 performances[36].

CAST: *Heinrich Punk*: GUS ROGERS. *Nicholas Knox*: MAX ROGERS. *Alice O'Grady*: CORINNE. *Gerald Fitzgerald*: MAURICE DARCY. *Anastasia O'Hoolihan*: JOSIE INTROPODI. *Mary O'Gaffeny*: ETHEL INTROPODI. *Hannah Dooley*: Bessie deVoie. *Dan O'Hoolihan*: Charles F. McCarthy. *Pat Lynch*: Edward O'Connor. *Dr. Philpot-Gavan O'Gaffeny*: John Conroy. *Sheila Rhue*: Julia Eastman. *Pat Shields*: William Torpey. *Nora*: Lillian Collins. *Peggy*: Pauline Thorne. *Maggie*: Lynn D'Arcy. *Lizzie*: Grace Grindell. *Murty*, an officer: Arthur V. Gibson. *The Piper*: George Earle. (*Chorus*: Misses Polly Addison, Elona Leonard, Beth Harrison, Frances Folsom, Marguerite Farrell, Pauline Thorne, Bessie Kyle, Grace Grindell, Florence Carrette, Marie McDonald, Lottie Sennett, Julia Curtiss, Gail Crandall, Clara Inge, Abita Morgan, Daisy Ashton, Lynn D'Arcy.)

Act 1: Glendalough.

Act 2: The Lakes of Killarney.

Act 3: Blarney Castle—the Blarney Stone.

ACT 1
"Maids of Killarney" (Opening Chorus)
Ensemble
"The Irish Girl I Love"
M. Darcy, Corinne, Chorus
"My Irish Maid"
G. Rogers, M. Rogers, Corinne, B. deVoie
(*Lyrics by* George V. Hobart, Max Hoffmann.)
Finale
Roger Brothers, Entire Company

ACT 2
"The First Time We Rode on the Cars" (When I Rode on the Choo-Choo Cars)
Misses E. Intropodi, J. Eastman
"Mike Doolin's Jaunting Car"
Corinne, Chorus
"St. Patrick's Day"
B. deVoie, Chorus
Original Sayings and Parodies[37]
G. Rogers, M. Rogers
"The Shamrock of Erin" (Finale)
Corinne, Chorus

ACT 3
"The Tourists"
Ensemble
"The Blarney Stone"
M. Darcy, Chorus
"So Different"
Corinne
"Hannah Dooley"
G. Rogers, M. Rogers, B. deVoie, assisted by Boys and Girls
Finale
G. Rogers, M. Rogers, Entire Company

1905.31 BANKERS AND BROKERS

A Fantastic Musical Comedy in Two Acts. Book and lyrics by George Totten Smith and Aaron Hoffman. Music by Gus Salzer. Ensemble numbers staged by John P. Kennedy. Scenery by John Young. Costumes designed by Archie Gunn. Musical director, Eugene Salzer. Produced by B. E. Forrester. Opened 4 September 1905 at the West End Theatre and closed 9 September 1905 after 8 performances; returned 9 October 1905 to the American Theatre and closed 21 October 1905 after 16 additional performances; returned 6 November 1905 to the Metropolis Theatre and closed 11 November 1905 after 8 additional performances. Total: 32 performances.

CAST: *Pincus, Plonsky*, bankers and brokers: GUS YORKE, NICK ADAMS. *B. Dunne Goode* their partner: JAMES J. COLLINS. *Wood B. Holmes*, a little below par: Bert Thayer. *Senor Santos Colozo*, foreign stock: F. T. S. Buckley. *Billy Boobs*, the office boy: Eddie Barto. *Orpheus Dippe*, the shorn lamb: Earl Barry. *Bill S. Higher*, the gas man: Ralph Beals. *Ord. R. Round*, Manager Palm Beach Casino: Linton DeWolf. *Allie Gator* from Florida: Dick Burch. *Lulu Larchmont*, the Florida Nightingale: RITA REDMOND. *Molly Sweet*, preferred stock: ANNA WILKES. *Jessie Jenks*, a telephone girl: Mamie Lafferty. *Rosebuds (6)*: *Jacquinette*: Eathel Golden. *La France*: Laurier DeWolf. *Beauty*: Viola Macey. *Bride*: Sylphette. *June*: Lolette Names. *Moss*: K. Wing. *Amalga Mated*: Margie Catlin. *Miss Ouri*: Daisy Dickerman. *Con Solidated*: Helen Phillips. *Tennie See*: Isabel Monroe. *Western Union*: Kathleen Adair. *Atchy Son*: Nettie Lyons. *Texas Pacific*: Sadie Morris. *Balty Moore*: Mabel Croft. *Inter Borough*: Eleanor Ingham. *Goldie Bonds*: Mildred Newman. *Lake Superior*: Carrie Cooper. *Sugar Trust*: Bertha Reed. *Erie First*: Gussie Bettels. *Lehigh Common*: Helen Grant. *Pensy Vania*: Mazie Freeman. *Alton Rhodes*: Laura Perry. *I. N. Vestor*: Joseph Evers. *S. P. Eculator*: Walter Gunther. *I. Dabble*: Herman Walthers. *Justa Flier*: Kenneth Junor. *Putson Calls*: Burt LaShure. *A. J. Ticker*: Charles Manners. *Specualtors, Bulls, Bears and Lambs, Hotel Guests, Summer Girls, etc.*

Act 1: Interior of B. Dunne Goode's office on Wall Street.

Act 2: The Casino Grounds at Palm Beach, Florida.

ACT 1
"On a Strike"
Chorus
"She Just Suits Me"
M. Lafferty, E. Barto, Chorus
"I'll Be Your Lady Love If You'll Be My Beau"
A. Wilkes, J. J. Collins
"My Pretty Rosebud" (Rosebud)
R. Redmond, Rosebuds
"That Never Happened in Wall Street"
G. Yorke, N. Adams
"Miss Maloney"
A. Wilkes, Chorus
"Searchlight Eyes"
E. Barto, M. Lafferty, Chorus
"Bulls and Bears"
R. Redmond
Finale
Entire Company

ACT 2
"Way Down in Florida"
Chorus
"Under the Palm Tree Shade"
J. J. Collins, Chorus
"The 'Gator and the Coon"
A. Wilkes, Chorus
"What Would You Do"
R. Redmond, A. Wilkes, G. Yorke, N. Adams
"Lovelight"
R. Redmond
"I Love to Wear That Uniform of Blue"
B. Thayer, Chorus
"Hindoo Belle"
R. Redmond, Chorus
Parodies
G. Yorke, N. Adams
"Honey Dew"
M. Lafferty, E. Barto, the Ponies
Finale

1905.32 A JOLLY BARON

A Musical Fantasy in Two Acts. Book by Joseph LeBrandt. Music by Harry Von Tilzer. Produced under the stage direction of Jeff D. Bernstein. Produced by Charles F. Whitaker. Opened 4 September 1905 at the 14th Street Theatre, moved 11 September 1905 to the Metropolis Theatre and closed 16 September 1905 after 16 performances.

CAST: *Louis Baron*, nicknamed "A Jolly Baron": BILLY S. CLIFFORD. *Chris Baron*, his father, President National Glue Company: JOE FIELDS. *Jacob Schmidt*, Julia's father, President International Glue Company: MARK WOOLEY. *Willy-of-the-Yacht*, who has never been to sea, see?: LEO HAYES. *Zack Housem*, who owns the mill and inn, and is in on Paradise Springs: W. H. White. *Baron Von Holstein*, an Ambassador of Germany: George Nagel. *Police Officer*: Charles T. Parr. *Julia Bauer*, in love with Louis: JEANNETTE MARCELLE. *Maydee*, a lady from Porto Rico: MATHILDE PREVILLE. *Maria*, a lady slavey: Madge Pierce.

[36] Played a return engagement 16 April 1906 at the Grand Opera House for 8 performances.

[37] Among those songs parodied were "If You Ask Me If I Love You" and "In the Shade of the Old Apple Tree."

The College Club: *Charley*: Earl Lloyd. *Clarence*: Eugene D'Andelet. *Wally*: John J. Coyne. *Reggie*: Louis Reyals. *Sammy*: Glee C. T. Page. *Billy*: Jack Cahill. *Jimmy*: Charles T. Parr. *Gussy*: George Nagel. *Horace*: Charles Matthews. *Wilbur*: H. E. Rosebrough.

Society Girls: *Edna*: Bayde Kellermann. *Alice*: Helene Drew. *Olga*: Myrtle Lorimer. *Helen*: Frances Gerard. *Vera*: Louise Palmer. *Clare*: Anna Beaty. *Bertie*: Edith Field. *Mildred*: Genevieve Marison. *Maude*: Edna Goodrich. *Violet*: Carrie Cornel.

Village Cut-Ups: *Flossie*: Sayde Kellermann. *Kittie*: Cecelia Hall. *Dollie*: Ethel Hall. *Tillie*: Violet Pardue. *Myrtle*: Anna Stone. *Dora*: Daisy Barrett. *Flora*: Mazie Temple. *Gay*: Ethel White. *Mary*: Flora Sutro. *Fay*: Blanche Leslie. *Lulu*: May Callam. *Daisy*: Elizabeth Lowe.

ACT 1[38]

"Oh! Marjory"

"I'm the Miller's Daughter"

(*Lyrics by* Arthur J. Lamb.)

"Let the Band Play a Pleasing Tune"

"Maydee"

"Mum's the Word"

(*Lyrics by* Addison Burkhardt and Aaron S. Hoffman.)

"The Highly Important Fly"

ACT 2

"(A Sail on) The Tail of a Whale"

"Kalamazoo Is No Place for You"
(*Lyrics by* Addison Burkhardt and Aaron S. Hoffman.)

"Down On the South Sea Isle"

"In Vacation Time"
(*Lyrics by* Addison Burkhardt and Aaron S. Hoffman.)

"The Magic Man"
(*Lyrics by* Addison Burkhardt and Aaron S. Hoffman.)

"Laughing Song"

1905.33 THE DUKE OF DULUTH

An Operatic Farce in Two Acts[39]. Book and lyrics by George H. Broadhurst. Music by Max S. Witt. Staged by George H. Broadhurst. Musical numbers and dances staged by Sam Marion[40]. Scenery by D. Frank Dodge, Frank Gates and Edward A. Morange. Costumes by Will R. Barnes. Orchestra under the direction of Max S. Witt. Produced by Broadhurst and Currie. Opened 11 September 1905 at the Majestic Theatre and closed 30 September 1905 after 24 performances; returned 9-14 October 1905 to the 14th Street Theatre for an additional 8 performances; returned 1-6 January 1906 to the West End Theatre for an additional 8 performances. Total: 40 performances[41].

CAST: *Darling Doolittle*, a tramp: NAT M. WILLS. *Kiakka IV*, King of the Land of Wot: Henry Norman. *Dennis O'Hara*, Captain in the King's Army: Stanley Hawkins. *Guiseppi Barratta*, the bogus Italian ambassador: Robert Paton Gibbs. *Jasper Washington Green*, Barratta's servant: Frank White. *The High Priest*: Frank Dearduff. *Messenger*: A. G. Franklin. *Ameera*, daughter of the King: EDITH DECKER. *Princess Flirtino*, the King's sister: Hattie Arnold. *Jhansi*, another daughter of the King: Catherine Call. *Bianca*, Barratta's niece: Diva Marolda. *Assistant to the High Priest*: May Harrison. *Lieutenant*: Gertrude Merrill. *Terpsio, Ballera*, the King's dancers: Eleanor Brooks, Georgia Brooks.

The Dresden Girls: Misses Elenor Brooks, Georgia Brooks, Etta Carlton, Edmond Danton, Goldie Daymon, Elizabeth Elliott, Carolyn Greene, Gertrude Merrill, Blanche Morrell, Lillian Singleton, Lottie Wesner, Violette Curtis, Vinnie Danvers, Verna Dalton, Margaret Love, Lillian Nicholson, Beatrice Lindsey, Ida Manierre, Carrie Baird, Inez Jones, Glora Mason, Jeannette Allen, May Blake. *The Peaches*: Misses Sadie Wyman, Grace Cooke, Edith Duryea, Margaret Fealey, Georgie Irving, Madge Melbourne, M. Nevin, Anna Raymond, Charlotte Tillman, Maude Elliott, Annabel Niven, Lillian Nicholson, Margaret Love, Muriel Wilbur, Josephine Arden, Bessie Stillman, Elphie Phillips, Ada Mack, Blanche Grosjean, Sadie Wyman, Florence Bain. *The Rosita Girls*: Misses Elenor Brooks, Georgia Brooks, Etta Carlton, Edmond Danton, Goldie Daymon, Elizabeth Elliott, Carolyn Greene, Gertrude Merrill, Blanche Morrell, Lillian Singleton, Lottie Wesner, Violette Curtis, Vinnie Danvers, Verna Dalton, Ida Manierre, Carrie Baird, May Blake, Jeannette Allen. *The King's Guard*: Messrs. Adolph Ethel, Edward Lawrence, M. M. Moore, J. E. Campbell, Danill Day, Edgar F. Hill, George McIntosh, J. Richard, Carl Taxwood, Edward Beck, C. Danielson, Nic Grist, W. S. Horton, Carl Schell, John O'Donnell.

The action is supposed to take place in the land of Wot, the usual suppositious country in the usual suppositious location.

Act 1: A public square. (Dodge.)

Act 2: The gardens of the King. (Gates & Morange.)

ACT 1[42]

Opening Chorus and "The Land of Wot"
H. Norman, Chorus

"There's One Sweetheart I'll Never Forget" (Sweetheart of My Childhood)
S. Hawkins

"While in My Submarine"[43]
N. M. Wills, Chorus

"My Dainty Dresden Shepherdess"[44]
C. Call, Dresden Girls

"Zenedee" (Zenadee)
E. Decker, Male Chorus

Ensemble

"The Sweetest Part of Loving is to Dream"
H. Arnold, N. M. Wills

"Nicodemus"
C. Call, Chorus

"If My Man Could Do It for Me"
N. M. Wills, Chorus

"Strenuous" (Finale)
N. M. Wills, Entire Company

ACT 2[45]

"My Sweet Wild Rose"[46]
E. Decker, Chorus

"No Peach Hangs Too High for Him Then" (No Peach Hangs Too High for Me)
H. Norman

"Through All Eternity" (Duet)
E. Decker, S. Hawkins

"Rosita"
N. M. Wills, Dancing Girls

"(Give Me) Death or Victory"
S. Hawkins, Chorus

Parodies
N. M. Wills

"G.O.P." (from FANTANA)
N. M. Wills
(*Music by* Gertrude Hoffman. *Lyrics by* Vincent Bryan.)

Finale

---

[38]Program missing song list. List prepared from published sheet music from prior Chicago production, presented as THE JOLLY BARON, or The Miller's Daughter, a Modern Comic Opera as presented by the LaSalle Theatre Company. Book by Addison Burkhardt and Aaron S. Hoffman. Lyrics by Arthur J. Lamb. Also mentioned in the New York reviews: "Tip Your Hat to Uncle Sammy."

[39]Billed as a musical farce on subsequent tour.

[40]For subsequent tour, Jack Mason shared credit for staging of dances and musical numbers.

[41]Played a return engagement 4 December 1905 at the American Theatre for 8 performances.

[42]The running order was revised for subsequent tour.

[43]For subsequent tour, "While in My Submarine" was paired with:
"The Dream"
N. M. Wills

[44]Replaced for subsequent tour by:
"The Trolley Line"
Etta Pearce {Jhansi}, Male Chorus

[45]Added for subsequent tour, after "Rosita":
"Take a Trip in My Auto"
E. Pearce, May Harrison {Bianca}, Chorus

[46]Replaced for subsequent tour by:
"I Like Your Way"
Margaret Witt {Ameera}, Chorus
(*Lyrics by* J. J. Walker.)
"Percy"
E. Pearce, the Ponies
(*Music by* Gertrude Hoffman. *Lyrics by* Vincent Bryan.)

1905.34 TOM, DICK AND HARRY

A Musical Concoction (Musical Comedy Extravaganza) in Two Acts. Book and lyrics by Aaron Hoffman and Harry Williams. Music by Egbert Van Alstyne. Produced under the direction of Al. H. Woods and Will N. Drew. Musical numbers staged by Gertrude Hoffman. Musical director, Melville Brown. Produced by Al H. Woods. Opened 25 September 1905 at the American Theatre and closed 30 September 1905 after 8 performances; returned 20-25 November 1905 to the 14th Street Theatre for 8 performances, 27 November-2 December 1905 to the West End Theatre for 9 performances; 1-6 January 1906 to the Metropolis Theatre for 8 performances; 15-20 January 1906 to the American Theatre for 8 performances. Total: 41 performances.[47]

CAST: *Late Flipper Brothers Circus (3)*: *Tom*: GEORGE L. BICKEL. *Dick*: HARRY WATSON, JR. *Harry*: ED LEE WROTHE. *Colonel Bluff*, commander U.S.A.: HARRY BOND. *Lieutenant Manley*, second in command, U.S.A.: FRANK THORNDYKE. *Don Garcia*, President of the Port O'Domingo: Robert Athon. *Spanish Spies disguised as musicians (3)*: *Gallic*: Tom O'Brien. *Reverse*: Clay Price. *Malto*: John Henry. *Congo*, the President's servant: Frank Stapleton. *Carson*, a waiter: James Lichter. *The Great Mogul*: Frank Bernard. *I'm a Trailer*: Frank McCue. *Senorito Riccardo*, Spanish spy: JEANNETTE LaBEAU. *Lillian Bluff*, Colonel's daughter: Bessie Clifford. *Mrs. Ella Noyes*, a widow: DOROTHY LaMAR.

Yearlings: Misses Spaeth, J. Raymond, B. Raymond, K. Hawkins, V. Hawkins, Falk, Melville, Baldwin, Ranney, Fitzgerald, B. Hawkins, McAvoy, Dawn, Brown, Leigh, Frank. *Show Girls*: Misses Hunter, Armstrong, LeRoy, Stanley, Clayton, Hay, Hoppe, Richardson. *Cadets and Turks*: Messrs. Bernard, Price, Purdy, Young, Blair, McCarty, Grasser, Lichter.

Act 1: Parade Grounds, West Point.

Act 2: President's Court, Port O'Domingo.

ACT 1[48]

"At West Point" (Chorus)
Company
"Be My Girl"
B. Clifford, F. Thorndyke
"Nicodemus" (from THE DUKE OF DULUTH)
B. Clifford, G. L. Bickel, H. Watson, E. L. Wrothe
(*Music by* Max S. Witt. *Lyrics by* George H. Broadhurst.)
"My Nightingale"
J. LaBeau, Chorus
"Rufus Rastus Johnson Brown"
B. Clifford
"(Down in) Lovers' Lane"
D. LaMar, Chorus
"Fight Them Like Your Dear Old Dad" (Finale)
F. Thorndyke, G. L. Bickel, H. Watson, E. L. Wrothe, Company

ACT 2

"Because He Wears That Hat" (Opening Chorus)
R. Athon, Chorus
"I Forgot the Rhyme"
G. L. Bickel, H. Watson, E. L. Wrothe
"Bonita Cachelti"[49]
J. LaBeau, Chorus
"Cholly"
B. Clifford, Chorus
"Professor and His Pupil"
G. L. Bickel, H. Watson, introducing their original comedy band
"Back to U.S.A." (Finale)
G. L. Bickel, H. Watson, E. L. Wrothe, Entire Company

1905.35 THE BEAUTY DOCTOR

A Musical Comedy in Two Acts. Book by Howard M. Shelley. Music by Fred Hylands, C. H. Kerr. Lyrics by Thomas W. Prior, Phil M. Hacker. Directed by Will Philbrick. Scenery by Arthur Voegtlin. Costumes by Wolff Fordin. Musical director, Fred Hylands. Produced by Fred E. Wright. Opened 25 September 1905 at the 14th Street Theatre, moved 2 October 1905 to the Metropolis Theatre and closed 7 October 1905 after 16 performances.

CAST: *Julia De la Creme*: CLAIRE GRENVILLE. *Geraldine Bohemia*: Lottie Uart. *Flora*: MARIE HYLANDS. *Valeria Veronica*: Susie Winner. *Walsingham Gayboy*: Dan Moyles. *Ebenezer Lester*: WILL PHILBRICK. *Ketchum Quick*: Earl Redding. *Solomon Cohen*: JAMES R. WATERS. *Jack Lester*: H. D. Johns. *Expressman*: L. A. Rogers. *Waiter*: Al. Ohlendorf. *Pansy*: Jessie Cardownie.

MUSICAL NUMBERS[50]

"My Scarecrow Coon"
"The Pretty Little Maid of Zanzibar"
"Where Was Moses When the Lights Went Out?"
(*Music and Lyrics by* C. H. Kerr.)
"I Never Would Believe It" (Duet)
"Will You Have a Gin Rickey?" (Drinking Song)
"Hiram Green, Goodbye"
(*Music and Lyrics by* Henry A. Gillespie and Clarence M. Chapel.)

1905.36 HAPPYLAND, or, The King of Elysia

A Comic Opera in Two Acts. Libretto by Frederic Ranken. Music by Reginald DeKoven. Staged by R. H. Burnside. Scenery by Ernest Albert. Costumes by Eaves Costume Company. Orchestra under the direction of Herman Perlet. Produced by Sam S. and Lee Shubert. Opened 2 October 1905 at the Lyric Theatre and closed 9 December 1905 after 82 performances; reopened 12 March 1906 at the Casino Theatre, closing 7 April 1906 after 32 performances; re-opened 7 May 1906 at the Majestic Theatre and closed 2 June 1906 after 32 additional performances. Total: 146 performances.

CAST[51]: *Ecstaticus*, King of Elysia: DeWOLF HOPPER. *Sphinxus*, his confidential adviser and keeper of secrets: WILLIAM WOLFF. *Altimus*, King of Altruria: WILLIAM DANFORTH. *Fortunatus*, Crown Prince of Fortunia: Joseph Phillips. *Pedro*, his servant: Frank Casey. *Appollus*, Captain of the Elysian Hussars: John Dunsmuire. *Pedro*, his servant: Frank Casey. *Adonis*, Lieutenant of the Elysian Hussars: Carl Haydn. *Paprika*, a lady of Altruria: Ada Deaves. *The Lady Patricia, the Lady Alicia*, Elysian Ladies of Honor: Estelle Wentworth, Bertha Shalek. *Sylvia*, daughter of King Ecstaticus: MARGUERITE CLARK. *Horse Guards, Troubadours, Elysian Maidens, Altrurian Soldiers, Flower Maidens, Courtiers, Reaper Girls, etc.*

Act 1: The Courtyard of the Imperial Palace in Elysia.

Act 2: In the Elysian Fields.

ACT 1[52]

Opening:
"Hail, Gentle Eros"
E. Wentworth
"Oh, Goddess" (Entrance)
Elysian Maidens
Entrance and Sickle Dance
Reaper Maids
"Royal Hussars Are We" (Entrance of Hussars)
(Hussars)
"A Soldier of Love Am I" (Song)
J. Dunsmuire

---

[47]Scenery and costumes uncredited

[48]Song list from West End program. During subsequent national tour, a Third Act was added, set in the interior of the St. Regis Hotel, New York City.

[49]Replaced for second engagement by:
"Senorita Papeta"
LaBeau, Chorus

[50]No New York program available; list of musical numbers taken from published vocal selections (Wright Music Publishing Co, New York). Additional musical numbers from Toledo and Wilkes-Barre programs from 1907: Opening Chorus, "Angel Voices", "A Chorus Girl's Longing", "College Days", "Come Down, Mr. Man in the Moon", "Culture Drill", "Flirtation Sextette", "Hail to the Queen of Beauty", "Loved One, So Pure and Tender", "My Flower of the South", "My Little Simi San", "Myron Brown, Farewell", "Nobody", "On a Paper and Comb", "The Queen of Beauty Am I", "Stop, Thief."

[51]Characters added for the Casino and Majestic Theatre engagements: *Strephon, Phyllis*, Pages to the King: Anita Brady, Dolly Ashton.

[52]Running order changed for tour. Added to Act 1 (after "Behold the King of Altruria") for tour:
"Music" (Song)
W. Woolf

"A Sickening Sadness Sits on Me" (Entrance)
D. Hopper
"Robin (Redbreast)" (Recitation and Song)
M. Clark
"What's a Maiden?" (Trio)
M. Clark, D. Hopper, W. Woolf
"Under Wicket" (Entrance)
Troubadours
"(Pretty) Pretty Maiden" (Serenade)
J. Phillips
"Cupid's Grammar" (Duet)
J. Phillips, M. Clark
"Behold the King of Altruria" (Entrance)
Altrurians
"Take Her, My Boy; She's Yours" (Finale)
Ensemble

ACT 2
"Shy Strephon" (Opening Chorus)
Arcadian Shepherds
"The Black Sheep"
J. Dunsmuire
"'Twas the Rose" (Song)
M. Clark
"Mimette, My Human Mermaid"[53] (Song)
D. Hopper
"What Is the Difference?" (Song)
M. Clark
"Happy is the Summer's Day"[54] (Madrigal)
J. Dunsmuire, C. Haydn, E. Wentworth, B. Shalek
"How I Love Flowers!" (Duet)
D. Hopper, W. Danforth
"Surrender" (Music Scene)
Soldiers of Fortunatus
"Charge, Boys, Charge!"
J. Phillips
Finale
Ensemble

1905.38 EDMUND BURKE

A Romantic Irish Drama in Four Acts, 5 Scenes. Play by Theodore Burt Sayre. (Music and Lyrics by Chauncey Olcott.) Stage direction by Edgar Selwyn. Scenery by Lewis C. Young. Costumes by H. A. Ogden. Musical director, Frank A. Mandeville. Produced by Augustus Pitou. Opened 2 October 1905 at the Majestic Theatre and closed 28 October 1905 after 28 performances[55].

CAST: *Edmund Burke*: CHAUNCEY OLCOTT. *Oliver Goldsmith*: DANIEL JARRETT. *Prince of Wales*, (Frederic): MACE GREENLEAF. *Lord Nugent*: VERNER CLARGES. *Sir Hugh Vivian*: THOMAS DAVID. *Captain Guliver*: Richard Malchien. *Maurice Desneyer*: Macy Harlam. *Terry*: George Brennan. *Haversham*: Charles Ogle. *Slogger Murphy*: Charles Ogle. *Lord Archie*: Lottie Milbourne Smith [Lotte Pickford]. *Micky Murphy*: Lottie Milbourne Smith [Lotte Pickford]. *Lord Bertie*: Gladys Milbourne Smith [Mary Pickford]. *Lady Phyllis*: Edith Milbourne Smith [Jack Pickford]. *Mary Nugent*: EDNA PHILLIPS. *Mrs. O'Grady*: Elizabeth Washburne. *Gabrielle LeJeune*: Eleanor Browning. *Mona*: Charlotte Milbourne Smith.

Act 1: The Rose Garden near Lord Nugent's London House. Middle of the eighteenth century, London.

Act 2: Burke's Lodgings in the house of Mrs. O'Grady. Two months later.

Act 3, Scene 1: The Wall surrounding the Garden of the Prince. Thirty minutes later. *Scene 2*: An Upper Room in the Prince's Love-Nest.

Act 4: Burke's Lodgings. A year later.

MUSICAL NUMBERS[56]
"(A) Little Bird's Story"
C. Olcott
"Miss Mary"
C. Olcott
(*Music and Lyrics by* Chauncey Olcott and Theodore Northrup.)
"You Can Sail in My Boat"
C. Olcott
"Your Heart Alone Must Tell"
C. Olcott
"In the Garden of the Gods" (Waltz)
(*Music by* Frank A. Mandeville.)

1905.37 BREAKING INTO SOCIETY

A Musical Farce in Three Acts. Book by Lee Arthur and Robert B. Smith. Music and lyrics by Gus (and Leo) Edwards. Lyrics by Robert B. Smith. Directed by Percy G. Williams. Opened 2 October 1905 at the West End Theatre and closed 7 October 1905 after 8 performances; returned 4-9 November 1905 to the 14th Street Theatre for 8 performances, 2-7 April 1906 to the Metropolis Theatre for 8 performances, 30 April-5 May 1906 to the American Theatre for 8 performances, 7-12 May 1906 to the Yorkville Theatre for 8 performances. Total: 40 performances.

CAST: *Major Mike O'Donovan*: SAM MORTON. *Jack Montague*: PAUL MORTON. *Aileen O'Donovan*, his daughter: CLARA MORTON. *Margaret O'Donovan*, his wife: KATE MORTON. *August Montague*: James Cooper. *Conreid Hammerschmidt*: FORD STERLING. *Reginald Carlyle*: Echlin P. Gayer. *Sergeant Clark*: Harry Hearn. *Mafia Dynamito*: John H. Smiley. *Jenkins*: Arthur Lee. *Simpson*: Paul Train. *Casey*: E. D. W. Tannehill. *Murphy*: Edward Cutler. *Mulligan*: Cornelius Lembach. *Hoolihan*: Howard Ordway. *Trixie Gibson*: GRACE BELMONT. *Miss DePeyster*: Mildred Claire. *Miss Van Mott*: Adelaide Kornay. *Maggie Casey*: Emma Lamoine. *Tessie Burns*: Rita Gray. *Miss Harrie*: Violet Hart.

Act 1: A Public Square on the East Side.

Act 2: The fancy Dress Ball at the Montague House, Riverside Drive. A year later.

Act 3: The Lawn of Montague House.

MUSICAL NUMBERS[57]
"The Bashful Chappie"
"Columbia's Colleen"
"The Daughter of the Regiment"
(*Music by* Gus Edwards and Leo Edwards.)
"If Women Had Their Way"
"I'm the Boy"
"Jolly Yourself Along"
"Marriage Game"
"My Senorita"
"Ping Pong"
(*Music by* Gus Edwards and Leo Edwards.)
"Standing Pat"
(*Music by* Gus Edwards and Leo Edwards.)
"That's What the Papers Say"
"Ting-a-Ling-a-Ling Ping Pong"
"Up and Down the Boardwalk"

1905.39 THE BELLE OF AVENUE A

A Musical Comedy in Three Acts. Book and lyrics by Harry Williams and Aaron Hoffman. Music by Egbert Van Alstyne. Staged by Edward E. Rose. Musical numbers by John Hymes. Scenery by Charles H. Yale Studios. Costumes by Bloodgood. Musical director, Edward Walker. Produced by A. H. Woods. Opened 9 October 1905 at the Grand Opera House and closed 14 October 1905 after 8 performances; returned 6-11 November 1905 to the American Theatre for 8 performances; returned 27 November-2 December

[53]Replaced late in subsequent tour by:
"Birdie" (Song)
D. Hopper
[54]Dropped by the time of the Majestic Theatre engagement.
[55]Played a return engagement 7 May 1906 at the Grand Opera House for 8 performances.

[56]Not necessarily in performance order.
[57]No New York program available; musical numbers from American Song: The Complete Musical Theatre Companion, by Ken Bloom, Schirmer Books, 1996.

1905 to the Metropolis Theatre for 9 performances; 1-6 January 1906 to the 14th Street for 8 performances; 8-13 January 1906 to the West End Theatre for 8 performances. Total: 41 performances.

CAST: *George Fairfax*: HAL CLEMENTS. *Judge Stuyvesant Green-de-Mint*, George's uncle: JOSEPH SLAYTOR. *Lord Cecil Cavendish*, George's chum: FRANK HOLLINS. *Spike McNeil*, a "Pug": BILLY KENT. *Carl Klatz*, the Corner Saloon: NAT FIELDS. *Solomon Bloom*, Unredeemed Pledges: HARRY FIELDS. *Snatchem*, Constable: Francis McGuire. *Straight, Jacket*, Officers: Robert Wade, Eugene Ryan. *Marie Fairfax*, George's Sister: MARIE DUMONT. *Sophronia Cambridge*, from Vassar: MAUDE EARL. *Mrs. McCluskey*, of Avenue A: Ada Boschell. *Bernice Deriga*, a Parisian importation: Mildred Adams. *Maggie Burns*, the Belle of Avenue A: ELFIE FAY.

Of Avenue A: *Katie Cowan*: Estha Mitchell. *Ethel O'Brien*: Alyce Gilrain. *Georgie MacGuire*: Ida Mahler. *Mabel Martan*: Estelle St. Clair. *Gertrude Vivian*: Ages Colton. *Martha Hallan*: Hattie Palmer. *Ethel Kingsland*: Bly Brown. *Helen Campbell*: Ida Scott. *Minnie McLaine*: Florence Fair. *May Quinn*: Adelaide Walsh. *Jerry Sullivan*: Ward Barton. *A Newsboy*: J. C. Wheat. *An Organ Grinder*: Walter Wellman. *An Officer*: Edwin Ash. *A Bootblack*: Alfred Lewis. *A Street Vendor*: Orison Swett.

Of Fifth Avenue: *Charlotte Gilman*: Violet Wilson. *Adalaide Somers*: Blanche Huntlew. *Madillade Fisher*: Dasyl Taylor. *Julia Hungerlord*: Gladys Shaw. *Elizabeth Crabtree*: Florence Major. *Trixie Botelle*: Carline Lanson. *Elfleta Larkin*: Fay Barton. *Josephine Forbes*: Della Dumond. *Vancie Cook*: Ada Marvin. *Wallace Irving*: Robert Wade. *Harrison Burgess*: George Fay. *Strickland Gillian*: Royal Byron. *Stephen Kirby*: George Clark. *Dudes, Butlers, Maids, Society Women, etc.*

Act 1: Avenue A. (New York)

Act 2: The Reception Room of George Fairfax's Mansion.

Act 3: Garden of Fairfax Home.

ACT 1

"The Hurdy Gurdy Man" (Opening Chorus)
Company

"There's a Little Fighting Blood in Me"
B. Kent, Ponies

"I Would Like to Have a Photograph of You"
M. Earl, Show Girls

"You're the Candy" (You're All the Candy with Me)
E. Fay, B. Kent

"The Belle of Avenue A"
E. Fay, Company

ACT 2

"Society"
Company

"In College" (I May Go to College and Still May Be a Fool)
E. Fay, H. Clements

"The Cobweb Man"
M. Dumont, Ponies

"When the Band of Rubensville Turns Out" (The Band of Rubenville)
E. Fay, Company

ACT 3

"Happy Days"
M. Dumont, Company

Parodies
H. Fields

"Why Don't You Try" (The Rolling Chair Song)[58]
M. Earl, Show Girls

Finale
Company

Entire Company

1905.40 THE SAMBO GIRL

A Musical Comedy in Two Acts.[58a] Book (and lyrics) by Harry B. Smith. Music by Gustave Kerker. Musical director, Charles E. Candee, Jr. Produced by Eva Tanguay (Joseph Gaites, Management). Opened 16 October 1905 at the West End Theatre, moved 23 October 1905 to the American Theatre and closed 28 October 1905 after 16 performances.

CAST: *Raphael Rubens*, an artist with American ideas of art and commercialism: MELVILLE S. COLLINS. *Henri DuPont*, a Parisian modist of "A Worth" trademark: GEORGE K. HENERY. *Willie Runabout*, who was half-back at college, but is away back now: HARRY LANE. *Angelo Martini*, ballet master, but no master of Mme. Martini: ARTHUR O'KEEFE. *Celeste*, wife of Henri DuPont, a professor of home cooking: MARIE GRIBBEN. *Mme. Martini*, Signor Samson, one of the Olympian circus, but with aspirations for grand opera: FLORENCE MORRISON. *Julie*: Helen Rockwell. *Antoinette*: Mildred Ashland. *Francine*: Helen Coyne. *Natalie*: Lucia Hartford. *Madaline*: Bessie Hively. *Adelaide*: Lottie Dethloff. *Lisette*: Grace Sessler. *Helene*: Jean Macnamee. *Susette*: Isabelle Burnside. *Mascotte*: Dora Goodwin. *Flora*: May Franklin. *Bella*: Genevieve Richmond. *Lilla*: Annie Lane. *Etta*: Margaret Hamilton. *Marie*: Hilda Hollins. *Carlotta Dashington*, the Sambo Girl: EVA TANGUAY.

ACT 1

"At DuPont's" (Opening Chorus)

"I Don't Care"
E. Tanguay
(*Music by* Harry Sutton. *Lyrics by* Jean Lenox.)

"I'm a Bohemian"
M. S. Collins
(*Music and Lyrics by* Melville S. Collins.)

"The Artist and His Model"
M. Gribben

"I'm for You—Eva Tanguay"
E. Tanguay
(*Music and Lyrics by* Melville S. Collins.)

"Flirting"
M. S. Collins, M. Gribben
(*Music by* Harry Sutton. *Lyrics by* Jean Lenox.)

"Mlle. Kek-Kek" (Finale)
E. Tanguay, Entire Company

ACT 2

Chorus of Students

"My Ideal" (from THE BLONDE IN BLACK)
M. Gribben, Chorus

"The Firefly" (My Little Firefly)
E. Tanguay, M. S. Collins
(*Music by* Harry Sutton. *Lyrics by* Jean Lenox.)

"Toreador"
H. Lane

"(The) Banjo Serenade"
E. Tanguay, Chorus

"From the Circus to the Grand Opera Is Only a Step"
F. Morrison

"(The) Drinking Song" (Trio)
E. Tanguay, M. S. Collins, G. K. Henery

Three Minutes with a Piano
M. S. Collins

"Eva Tanguay's Love Song" (I love but only one, and that is you)
E. Tanguay
(*Music and Lyrics by* Melville S. Collins.)

Finale

1905.41 FRITZ IN TAMMANY HALL

A Musical Play in Three Acts. Book by John J. McNally. Music by Jean Schwartz. Lyrics by William Jerome. Staged by Herbert Gresham and Ned Wayburn. Scenery by Frank Platzer and Meixner. Costumes by F. Richard Anderson. Lighting by H. Bissing. Music director, Anton Heindl. Produced by Messrs. (Marc) Klaw and (Abraham L.) Erlanger. Opened 16 October 1905 at the Herald Square Theatre and closed 18 November 1905 after 43 performances.

CAST: *Fritz von Swobenfritz*: JOSEPH CAWTHORN. *Pat McCann*, district captain: MARK HART. *Bella McCann*, his daughter: Sue Stuart. *Elena McCann*, McCann's second wife: Alison Skipworth. *J. Edward Corley*, a politician: JULIUS TANNEN. *Charles Hart*, Mrs. Judson's brother: Frank W. Shea. *Lil McGrain*, A Manicure Girl: ADA LEWIS. *Susette Sorbonne*, soubrette: NEVA AYMAR. *Alfred Hines*, bank cashier: GEORGE AUSTIN MOORE. *Millie Meyers*, school teacher: Suzanne Halpren. *Grant Bellyne*, millionaire: MELVILLE ELLIS. *Teddy Mullane*: Charles MacDonald. *Fergus O'Flaherty*, policeman: Robert O'Connor. *Tim Sullivan*, newsboy: Henry E. Valois. *Slim Jim*: EARL J. BENHAM. *"Fatty" Dupois*: Eli J. Brouillette. *Mat McGregor*: Charles Close. *Bessie*: Corinne Uzell. *Tessie*: Violet Barnes. *Letty*: Alva Holland. *Betty*:

[58]Produced [staged] by Jack Mason.

[58a]A revised version of THE BLONDE IN BLACK which opened 8 June 1903 at the Knickerbocker Theatre for 35 performances.

Beryle Dare. *Pincus*: P. Lekosky. *Waiter*: Eugene Roder. *Mrs. Hart-Judson*: STELLA MAYHEW. *Twin City Quartette, Children, Chorus.*

Act 1: Cooper Union, New York.

Act 2: Donnelly's Grove, College Point, Long Island.

Act 3: Ball-room, Tammany Hall.

ACT 1

"In Old New York" (Opening Chorus)
Tammany Chorus

"East Side Lil"
A. Lewis, Chorus

"My Sweet"
E. J. Benham, Twin City Quartette, Chorus

"When You're in Love"
S. Mayhew

"In Bad Man's Land"
J. Cawthorn, Children

"The Dear Little Wise Old Bowery" (Finale)
J. Cawthorn, Company

ACT 2

"East Side Walk" (Opening Chorus)
N. Aymar, Chorus

"I'm a Woman of Importance"
S. Mayhew

"I Don't Want a Little Canoe"
G. A. Moore, Chorus

"Yankee Doodle Boodle" (Yankee Boodle)(Trio)
S. Mayhew, M. Hart, J. Cawthorn

"The Man Behind the Club" (Finale)
Tammany Chorus

ACT 3

"The Tammany Ball" (Opening Chorus)
Company

Grand March

"In Tammany Hall"
M. Hart, Chorus

"The Dear Old Farm"
VJ. Cawthorn

"My Irish Daisy"
G. A. Moore, C. McDonald, M. Ellis, Quartette, Children, Chorus
(*Music by* Maude Nugent and Jean Schwartz.)

"Tammany Hall" (Finale)
Entire Company

1905.42 IN NEW YORK TOWN

A Musical Comedy in Three Acts. Book (and lyrics) by Willard Holcomb and Loney Haskell. Music by Albert Von Tilzer. Staged by Jules Hurtig. Musical numbers and ensembles arranged by Charles Nevins. Scenery by Charles Brothers. Costumes designed by Will R. Barnes. Electrical effects by Kleigl. Musical director, Clifford W. Meech. Produced by (Jules) Hurtig and (Harry) Seamon Comic Players. Opened 23 October 1905 at the West End Theatre and closed 28 October 1905 after 8 performances; moved 30 October-4 November 1905 to the 14th Street Theatre for 8 performances; returned 11-18 November 1905 to the Metropolis Theatre for 9 performances; 26-31 March 1906 to the American Theatre for 8 performances; 14-21 May 1906 to the Yorkville Theatre for 9 performances. Total: 42 performances.

CAST: *Baron Heinrich von Essigs*, working as a waiter: CLIFF GORDON. *Ikey Skinalski*, with political aspirations: CHARLES HOWARD. *Rag Time Jimmy*, a Bowery bartender: CHARLES NEVINS. *Knox Knox*, a knocker from Knoxville: TEDDY BURNS. *Cumming Swift*, a theatrical manager: Tell Taylor. *Baron Ludwig von Essigs*, Heinrich's brother: Frank Nagle. *Mock Duck*, a Mongolian diplomat: Loney Haskell. *Will Vanderslip*, too wealthy to work: D. F. Crossman. *Headwaiter*, imported for Hotel Astor: L. B. Sachs. *Patrolman Casey*, an East Side Policeman: Harry Ward. *Muzzy Liz*, the belle of the Bowery: VINNIE HENSHAW. *The Rummager*, queen of the pipe slaves: Georgia Fransioli. *Rosa Rosetta*, an Italian flower girl: Lillian Shaw. *Miss Vanderclip*, an heiress: IDA EMERSON. *Gwendolyn Westside*, her chum: GRACLYN WHITEHOUSE. *Birdie Flip*, the red soubrette: MAY WARD. *Libbie Wurst, Wienie Wurst*, a sister act: CLARA AUSTIN, JENNIE AUSTIN.

Miss St. Regis: Margaret Sloan. *Miss Waldorf*: Carrie Landers. *Miss Astoria*: Blanche Landers. *Miss Imperial*: Maude Landers. *Miss Holland*: Lucille Tallier. *Miss Savoy*: Josephine Carr. *Miss Breslin*: Caribel Davis. *Miss Astor*: Belle Carlton. *Miss Gilsey*: Gertrude Carter. *Miss Bartholdi*: Flo Kimball. *Miss Hoffman*: Henrietta Herbert. *Miss Marlborough*: Marion Hunnewell. *Miss First*: Lydie Franklin. *Miss Madison*: Florence Jeffries. *Miss Lexington*: Etta Mintz. *Miss Park*: Lillian Barton. *Miss Lenox*: Ethel Adams. *Miss Manhattan*: Libbie Barry. *Miss Amasterdam*: Carrie Wilson. *Miss St. Nicholas*: Josie Melville. *Miss Columbus*: Libbie Bell. *Miss Riverside*: Elsie Gilliland. *Miss Sturtevant*: Lizzie Ward. *Miss West End*: Alice Chadwick. *Miss Waverly*: Josephine Moore. *Miss Washington*: Marion Campbell. *Miss Lafayette*: Kitty Morgan. *Mr. Macy*: George Nevins. *Mr. Sachs*: George Lloyd. *Mr. Hearn*: Herbert Henry. *Mr. McCreery*: Fred Clifton. *Mr. Altman*: Howard Griffith. *Mr. Ehrlich*: Richard Schuyler.

Members of the Dizzy Dozen Extravaganza Company, Bowery Types, City Girls, Lasso Lassie Girls, Blacksmiths, Salvation Army Girls, Italian Girls, Chinese Girls, Hungarian Girls, Society Ladies. Show Girls: Margaret Sloan, Carrie Landers, Blanche Landers, Maude Landers, Julia Kidder, Josephine Carr, Clarabel Davis, Belle Carlton, Gertrude Carter, Flo Kimball, Henrietta Herbert, Marion Hunnewell. *Dancers*: Kitty Morgan, Lydia Franklin, Myra Franklin, Florence Jeffries, Etta Mintz, Lillian Barton, Ethel Adams, Libbie Barry, Carrie Wilson, Josie Melville, Stella Kline, Elsie Gillen, Lizzie Ward, Lavender Byers, Alice Chadwick, Florence Chadwick, Marion Campbell.

Act 1: A Bowery Concert Hall.

Act 2: A Street in Chinatown.

Act 3: The Hotel Astor Roof Garden.

ACT 1[59]

Opening Chorus

Unique Concert Hall First Part

"Rosa Rosetta"
L. Shaw, Chorus
(*Lyrics by* Earle C. Jones)

"I'd Like to See It"
C. Gordon

"Down to Delaware"[60]
M. Ward

"Come Down, Ma' Evening Star" (Imitation, Lillian Russell)
G. Whitehouse, Show Girls

"Lulu" (Imitation, Pete Dailey)
T. Burns, Austin Sisters

"Have You Seen My Henry Brown" (Imitation, Katie Barry)
L. Shaw

"(It's) New York Town for Mine"
I. Emerson, G. Whitehouse, C. Nevins, Company

ACT 2[61]

"Lasso Lassie"
C. Nevins, C. Austin, Chorus

"Be Polite" (Polite)
G. Fransioli
(*Lyrics by* Junie McCree.)

"Chinese Finale"
Entire Company

ACT 3

Hungarian Dance
K. Morgan, L. Franklin, Solo Dancers

"The Moon Has His Eyes on You"
I. Emerson, T. Taylor
(*Lyrics by* Billy Johnson.)

"Beauty Lane"
C. Nevins, M. Ward
(*Lyrics by* Junie McCree.)

---

[59]Musical numbers prepared from Metropolis Theatre engagement. Other musical numbers: "The Belle of New York Town", "Espanita", "I Can't Find Another Girl Like You", "My Georgiana", "Stein Song."

[60]Dropped after first engagement and replaced by:

"Lady Lindy Love"
J. Austin

"Listen to the Popping of the Corks"
I. Emerson

[61]Added after opening to Act 2, following "Lasso Lassie":

"A Word to the Wise"
T. Burns

Parodies
C. Howard
Finale
Entire Company

1905.43 IT'S UP TO YOU, JOHN HENRY

An American Farce Comedy with Music in Three Acts. Book by George V. Hobart, based on his farce "John Henry." Produced under the stage direction of Richard F. Carroll. Musical director, A. Ellis. Produced by Frank Howe, Jr. Opened 23 October 1905 at the Grand Opera House and closed 28 October 1905 after 8 performances; returned 18-23 December 1905 to the West End Theatre for 8 performances. Total: 16 performances.[62]

CAST: *John Henry*: CHARLES E. GRAPEWIN. *Bunch Jefferson*, his pal: EDWARD C. GILLESPIE. *Kid Dawson*, of Vaudeville fame: NAT KOLB. *Senator Peter Grant*, John's Guardian: FRED MOWER. *William Gray*, John's admirer: James Allen. *Harmony Diggs*, the "Sherlock" of Ruraldene: Harry Crandall. *Bono Bonoscari*, John's pet aversion: Victor Malley. *O'Hara*, the little furniture mover: John Dillon. *McGarr*, the big furniture mover: John Dillon. *Thompson*, clerk at the Hotel Manhattan: C. D. Burnham. *Biff*, the bell boy: William Tammany. *Mike*, the hotel porter: Arthur Saunders. *'Rastus*, Station Master of the C. R. R. of N. J.: Hugh H. Decker. *The Man Who Gets Up and Goes Out*: Charles Morton. *Clara J*, "Peaches," who occupies the only furnished room in John's heart: ANNA CHANCE. *Mrs. Peter Grant*, everybody's Aunt Martha: ANNE E. WINTER. *Alice Gray*, the fiancée of John's friend Bunch: KATHRYN PEARL. *Countess Natalie Delmonte Veccio*, the real owner of Dove Nest Villa: BLANCHE HOWARD. *Jubilee Diggs*, with social aspirations: Emma Morey. *Flora Madura*, who supplies John's "smokes": Ruth Black. *His fiancée's Five Friends*, Members of the Keep-Awake Club: *Marietta*: Virginia Sanford. *Lucy*: Myrtle Dale. *Molly*: Stella Hill. *Gladys*: May Williams. *Caroline*: Daisy Fair.

Act 1: The Hotel Manhattan, New York.

Act 2: Dove's Nest Villa, Ruraldene, New Jersey.

Act 3: Get-Off Junction on the Pennsylvania Railroad.

ACT 1
An Old Time Song and Dance
C. E. Grapewin, N. Kolb
"Aristocratic Annie"
A. Chance, Girls of the Keep-Awake Club
"Right in This Old Town"
C. Grapewin

ACT 2
"Strolling"
A. Chance, C. Grapewin
"My Lonesome Louisiana Lady"
A. Chance, Chorus

ACT 3
The St. Cecelia Quartette
E. Morey, V. Sanford, B. Howard, A. E. Winter
A Christian Science Game of Pool
C. Grapewin
Finale
Entire Company

1905.44 WONDERLAND

A Fantastic Musical Play in Three Acts, 8 Scenes. Book (and lyrics) by Glen MacDonough. Based on the story "The Dancing Princess"[63] by the Brothers Grimm. Music by Victor Herbert. Staged by Julian Mitchell. Settings by John Young, Edward G. Unitt. Costumes designed by Caroline Siedle. Electrical effects by Kleigl Brothers. Orchestra under the direction of Carl Styx. Orchestrations by Victor Herbert. Produced by Julian Mitchell. Opened 24 October 1905 at the Majestic Theatre and closed 23 December 1905 after 73 performances.

CAST: *Dr. Fax*, a specialist in love and its cure; head of the Hospital for Broken Hearts: SAM CHIP. *Phyllis*, a Dresden shepherdess: EVA DAVENPORT. *Gladys*, Dr. Fax's daughter: Aimee Angeles. *Hildegarde Figgers Fax*, daughter of Dr. Fax, a teacher at the Asylum for the Children of the Homeless Rich: LOTTA FAUST. *Prince Fortunio*: BESSIE WYNN. *Captain Montague Blue, James the Stoker*, two professional heroes recently in employed as crew of the airship "Peekaboo": CHARLES BARRY, GEORGE McKAY. *King of Hearts*, disguised as Perrico, a gypsy musician: J. C. MARLOWE. *Leander*: Doris Mitchell. *Margot*, the favorite daughter of the King of Hearts: SUE KELLEHER. *Gertrude*: Hulda Halvers. *Rollo*: James Harris, Eugene Kelly. *Chief of Gendarmes*: William McDaniels. *Daughters of the King of Hearts (7)*: *Margaret*: Emily Fulton. *Marguerite*: Helen Hilton. *Meg*: Alice Eis. *Marjorie*: Lucille Eagen. *Margherita*: Phoebe Loubet. *Madge*: Adele Gordon. *Maggie*: Minnie Woodbury. *The Princes of the Enchanted Castle (6)*: *Romeo*: Marie Franklyn. *Antony*: Kathryne Howland. *Orlando*: Georgia Barron. *Lothario*: Louise Burpee. *Paolo*: Sadie Emmons. *Giovanni*: Madge Burpee. *Bassanio*: Rose Fredricks. *Monitors*: May Leslie, Lillian Devere.

Students in the Nature Classes: *Freshmen*: Misses Mordaunt, Hickey, Madison, Smith, Barthold, Allen, Cameron. *Sophomores*: Misses Raymond, Mansfield, Ward, Winters, Madison, Ackland, Allien, Chadwick. *Shop Girls*: Misses Leslie, DeVere, Mordaunt, Raymond, Ward, Gordon, Hickey, Smith. *Companions of Prince Fortunio*: Misses May Leslie, Lillian DeVere, Ethel Donaldson, Bessie Skeer, Ada Gordon, Lillian Raymond, Eleanor Mansfield, Jean Cameron, Maurie Madison, May Hickey, Pauline Winters, Lelia Smith, Gertrude Barthold, Jean Ward, Helen Chadwick, Lillian Allen, Adolida Ackland, Flora Madison, Mabel Mordaunt.

Act 1, Scene 1: Dr. Fax's cottage in the King's Park. *Scene 2*: The painted desert. *Scene 3*: The Square of the Houses that make Faces.

Act 2, Scene 1: The King's Park. (Unitt.) *Scene 2*: The exterior of a department store. *Scene 3*: A department store. *Scene 4*: The Lake of the Enchanted Castle.

Act 3: Ball-room of the Enchanted Castle.

ACT 1
"Until We Meet Again" (Opening Chorus)
Chorus
"Nature Class"
Chorus
"Peek-a-Boo"
L. Hayes, C. Barry, A. Angeles, Chorus
"When Perrico Plays"
W. Cameron, Chorus
"No Show To-night"
S. Chip
"Jografree" [Geography]
A. Angeles, Chorus
"Love's Golden Day"[64]
B. Wynn
"The Ossified Man"
S. Chip, C. Barry, L. Hayes
"Broadway Favorites"[65]
A. Angeles
"Companions of the Bride"
B. Wynn, Chorus

ACT 2
Opening Chorus
"The Only One"
B. Wynn, Chorus
"Popular Pauline"
L. Faust, Chorus
"The Voice For It"
S. Chip, A. Angeles, Chorus
Eccentric Dance
L. Hayes, C. Barry

ACT 3
Opening Waltz
Chorus
Minuet and Barbarian Dance
Chorus
"Me, Myself and I"
S. Chip, Chorus
(*Lyrics by* Vincent Bryan.)

1905.45 MOONSHINE

A Musical Play in Two Acts. Book and lyrics by Edwin Milton Royle and George V. Hobart. Music by Silvio Hein. Staged by Frederick Perry.

[62]No credits for music and lyrics, scenery and costumes.
[63]Also known as "The Twelve Dancing Princesses."
[64] Dropped late in subsequent tour.
[65] Dropped for subsequent tour.

Musical numbers arranged by Gertrude Hoffman. Scenery by Frank Gates and Edward A. Morange. Costumes by Eaves Costume Company. Orchestra under the direction of Silvio Hein. Produced by Daniel V. Arthur. Opened 30 October 1905 at the Liberty Theatre and closed 2 December 1905 after 37 performances; re-opened 25 December 1905 at the Majestic and closed 6 January 1906 after 16 additional performances[66]. Total: 53 performances.

CAST: *Lord Dumgarven*, of the home office: ROY ATWELL. *Hon. Lionel Longacre*, in the Diplomatic Service: DICK TEMPLE. *Lady Gweneth*, his sister: FRANCES GORDON. *Earl of Broadlawns*, his father: J. WARD KETT. *Countess of Broadlawns*, late of "The Belle of New York": LEONA ANDERSON. *Molly Moonshine*, formerly of the U.S. Secret Service: MARIE CAHILL. *Sadie Short*, her secretary: SADIE HARRIS. *"Plunger Dawson,"* late of Sheepshead Bay, posing as a mystic: William Ingersoll. *Marcel Barbier*: GEORGE BEBAN. *Lola Charmion*: CLARA PLAMER. *Terence O'Fogg*: H. R. Roberts. *General Moroff*, Russian Ambassador: H. Guy Woodward. *Baron Hosaki*, Japanese Minister: Frederic Paulding.

Guests: Misses Blanche West, Anella Martin, Virginia Steihart, Louise McDonald, Lucile Monroe, Marion Mosby, Olga May, Therese Baron, Harriet Van Buren, Mabell Douglas. Margaret Berrien, Marion Watts, Anna Mooney, Leslie Deane, Margaret Brooks, Edith MacBride, Ernestine Brady. Messrs. George Lyman, Whitlock Davis, William Wood, James Ludwig, Dore Rogers, James Lyons, Franklyn Ardelle, Alfred DuChemin.

The action takes place immediately preceding the breaking out of the Russo-Japanese War.

Act 1: During Lord Dumgarven's houseboat party, Heather Banks, near Henley on Thames.

Act 2: An evening in the Rose Pergola at Lord Dumgarven's country place, The Terraces.

ACT 1

Opening Chorus
Ensemble

"A Hundred Years from Now" (Sextette)
L. Anderson, F. Gordon, S. Harris, R. Atwell, H. R. Roberts, J. W. Kett

"In My New Submarine"
R. Temple, Chorus
(*Lyrics by* George V. Hobart.)

"I Want to Go Back to the Boulevard"
C. Palmer, G. Beban
(*Lyrics by* George V. Hobart.)

"Robinson Crusoe" (Robinson Crusoe's Isle)
M. Cahill
(*Music and Lyrics by* Benjamin Hapgood Burt.)

"How Happy Could This Chappie Be"[67]
R. Atwell, S. Harris, F. Gordon, Chorus
(*Lyrics by* George V. Hobart.)

"(They Never Do That) In Our Set"
M. Cahill, R. Temple
(*Lyrics by* George V. Hobart.)

Finale (including Waltz Song "Friendship")
M. Cahill, Entire Company

ACT 2

"The Musical Gypsy" (Opening)
R. Temple, Ensemble

"Don't Be What You Ain't"
M. Cahill

"All She Could Say Was 'Oui'"[68]
C. Palmer, Chorus

"Foolish"
M. Cahill, R. Temple, R. Atwell
(*Lyrics by* George V. Hobart.)

"Napoleon Bonaparte" (Mister Bonaparte)
G. Beban, Chorus
(*Lyrics by* Benjamin Hapgood Burt.)

"I Am Looking for My Ten" (I'm a-Looking for My Ten)
M. Cahill
(*Lyrics by* George V. Hobart.)

Finale
M. Cahill, Entire Company

[66] Toured under the title MOLLY MOONSHINE.
[67] Also known as "How Happy Would This Chappie Be" in published sheet music.
[68] Replaced during the run by:
"I Like You Very Much"
C. Palmer, Chorus
(*Lyrics by* George V. Hobart.)

1905.46 VÉRONIQUE

Mr. George Edwardes' Company in a Comic Opera in Three Acts. Original French libretto ("Véronique") by Albert Vanloo and Georges Duval. English adaptation by Henry Hamilton. Music by André Messager. English lyrics by Lillian Eldée and Percy Greenbank[69]. Produced (staged) by Sydney Ellison. Settings by Joseph Harker, Julian Hicks. Musical director, Arthur Wood. Produced by (Marc) Klaw and (Abraham L.) Erlanger, and George Edwardes. Opened 30 October 1905 at the Broadway Theatre and closed 13 January 1906 after 81 performances[70].

CAST: *Florestan de Valiancourt*: LAWRENCE REA. *Monsieur Loustot*, a Bailiff: Aubrey Fitzgerald. *Seraphin*, a groom: Ralph Nairn. *Octave, Felicien*, Florestan's friends: John Malcolm, Leslie Rainey. *Max, Achilles*, Waiters: James Grant, Max Shapiro. *Orderly*, of the National Reserve: Richard Dolliver. *Monsieur Coquenard*: John LeHay. *Ermerance*, Countess de Champ Azur: Lena Maitland. *Agatha*, Madame Coquenard: KITTY GORDON. *Aunt Benoit*: Emmie Santer. *Denise*, her niece: VALLI VALLI. *Sophie, Elisa, Zoe, Lucille*, Florists: Madge Vinten, Ruby Delmar, Florence Plunkett, Beulah Martin. *Hélène de Solanges*: RUTH VINCENT. *Chorus*.

Act 1: Coquenard's Flower Shop, Paris. 1840. (Harker.)

Act 2: The Tourne Bride, Romanville. (Harker.)

Act 3: Reception Room, The Tuileries. (Hicks.)

ACT 1[71]

Opening Chorus (Flowers of springtime, sweetly scented)

Song (Oh, what a dainty profession)
K. Gordon, Chorus

"Out on the Breezy Morning Air" (Trio)
R. Vincent, L. Maitland, R. Nairn

"Please, Sir, We Want If We May" (Song)
R. Nairn, Chorus

"Life Is Short, My Dear Friends" (Song)
L. Rea, Chorus

"Between Us All Is O'er" (Quartette)
R. Vincent, K. Gordon, L. Maitland, L. Rea

"Now the Carriages All Are Waiting" (Finale)
R. Vincent, K. Gordon, L. Maitland,
J. LeHay, L. Rea, A. Fitzgerald, Flower Girls, Young Men, Soldiers

"As Along the Street We Wander" (Take Estelle, and Véronique)(Song)
R. Vincent, Chorus

ACT 2

"Come Drink a Toast to Man and Wife" (Opening Chorus)
Chorus

"At Weddings as a General Rule" (Song)
R. Nairn, Chorus

"When Not Engaged in Fighting" (Chorus)
(K. Gordon,) Male Chorus

"The Bloom of the Apple Tree" (One day, 'neath an apple tree laden) (Song and Chorus)
K. Gordon, Chorus

"Trot Here and There" (Donkey Duet)
R. Vincent, L. Rea

"You Are Laughing" (Swing Song)
R. Vincent, L. Rea

"I've Got a Little Hubby Now" (Song)
Valli-Valli

"Sweet Lizette, So People Say" (Country Dance)
K. Gordon, Chorus

"You're a Charming Little Maiden"
L. Rea

[69] The published vocal score credits Lilian Eldée with lyrics, and Percy Greenbank with alterations and additions.
[70] Costumes uncredited. Toured under the title THE FLOWER GIRL.
[71] Musical Numbers not listed in New York playbills. Program song list prepared from published vocal score and subsequent Boston tour program.

Finale (Now then, where is the blushing bride?)
Company
"Farewell, I Go" (The Letter Song)
L. Rea

ACT 3
"Hush, Hush, She's Meditating" (Opening Chorus)
Chorus
"The Garden of Love" (Like the bee to the garden of roses)(Song)
L. Maitland
"While I' Am Waiting" (Auntie, please tell me)(Valse Song)
R. Vincent
"Come One and All" (Chorus and Duet)
K. Gordon, J. Le Hay, Chorus
"O Strange Situation" (Quartette)
R. Vincent, K. Gordon, L. Maitland, J. LeHay
"Ah Well, We'll Try to Be Precise" (Duet)
R. Vincent, L. Rea
Finale (Now my little story's ended)
Company

1905.47 SIMPLE SIMON SIMPLE

A Cartoon Musical Extravaganza in Three Acts. Book by Otis F. Wood, Charles H. Brown. Based on the popular comic strip. Music and lyrics by Charles Puerner, Carlos Curti, Theodore Bendix, Rollin Bond, Henry J. Koenig, Bert Howard and Arndt Morris. Staged by Lewis Morton. Dances arranged by Joseph Dawson. Produced by Sam Nixon & J. F. Zimmerman's Opera Company (Fred C. Nirdlinger, Manager). Opened 30 October 1905 at the West End Theatre and closed 4 November 1905 after 8 performances.

CAST: *Simple Simon*: NEIL McNEIL. *Mose*, his pal: JERRY D. SULLIVAN. *Judge Simple*: TOM SPRINGER. *Mrs. Simple*: JENNETTE MILLS. *Mandamus Backstone*: JACK J. CLARK. *Hulda Spiegelberger*: ANNA McNABB. *Hans Spiegelberger*: WALLY CLARK. *Mammy Johnsing*: BERTIE DALE. *Dinah Mite*: Trizie Cadiz. *Hiram Swatem*: George E. Murphy. *Sig Saute*: J. K. Adams. *Tony DeBumski*: HORACE WRIGHT. *Li Hung Chang*: Tom Gipple. *Tillie Collie-Wabbs*: Louise Goodwin. *Alma Vassar*: MAY KILCOYNE.

MUSICAL NUMBERS[72]
"Bachelor Girls"
(*Music by* MacArthur.)
"Bargain Day"
(*Music by* Theodore Bendix.)
"The Bull Frog and the Coon" (Froggie Frog)
(*Music by* MacArthur.)
"(Dear Old) College Days"
(*Music by* Theodore Bendix. *Lyrics by* Charles Brown, Otis Wood.)
"A Coy Young Maid"
(*Music by* MacArthur.)
"Dear Old Pals"
(*Music by* MacArthur.)
"Holding Hands" (You Don't Say Nothing at All)
(*Music by* Albert Von Tilzer. *Lyrics by* Jack Norworth.)
"La Tiddle De Um"
"Love Me and the World Is Mine"
(*Music by* Ernest R. Ball. *Lyrics by* David Reed, Jr.)
"Ma Southern Oriole"
(*Music by* Henry J. Koenig. *Lyrics by* Charles Brown.)
"Nursery Rhyme Dances"
(*Music by* Theodore Bendix.)
"Oskaloosa Lou"
"Pickaninny Mose"
(*Music by* Bond.)
"The Sand Man"
(*Music by* MacArthur and Varley.)
"Shine, Shine, Shine"
(*Music by* MacArthur.)
"Venetia"
(*Music by* Albert Von Tilzer.)
"Yankee Doodle-Up-to-Date"
Finale
(*Music by* Carlos Curti, Theodore Bendix.)

[72]No New York program available; musical numbers from 4 January 1907 Wilkes-Barre tour and American Song: The Complete Musical Theatre Companion, by Ken Bloom, Schirmer Books, 1996.

1905.48 THE WHITE CAT

A Musical Spectacle in Three Acts, 13 Scenes[73]. Original English book by J. Hickory Wood and Arthur Collins. Adapted to the American stage by Harry B. Smith. Music by Ludwig Engländer. Lyrics by Harry B. Smith. Additional lyrics and music by William Jerome and Jean Schwartz. Presented under the stage direction of Herbert Gresham and Ned Wayburn. Ballets by Ernest D'Auban. Settings designed by Matt Armbruster, R. C. McCleery, R. Caney, Henry Emden, Bruce Smith. Costumes designed by Comelli; F. Richard Anderson (specialties). Orchestra under the direction of Frederic Solomon. Produced by (Marc) Klaw and (Abraham L.) Erlanger. Opened 2 November 1905 at the New Amsterdam Theatre and closed 9 December 1905 after 46 performances.

CAST: *Methuselina*, a Veteran Fairy: WILLIAM MACART. *Jonah the Thirteenth*, King of Malaria: WILLIAM T. HODGE. *Simeon*, the Missing Link, his protege: HUGH J. WARD. *Prince Paragon*: EDGAR ATCHINSON-ELY. *Prince Plump*: HERBERT CORTHELL. *Prince Peerless*: MAUDE LAMBERT. *Hecate*, a Bad Fairy: Harriet Worthington. *Migonet*, her son: SEYMOUR BROWN. *Princess Chiffon*, the King's Ward: EDITH ST. CLAIR. *The Fairy Queen*: Harriette Cropper. *Cupid*: Maida Snyder. *Popula*: Monte Elmo. *Aristo*: HELEN LATHROP. *The Mother*: Inez Shannon. *Court Herald*: Robert Harold. *First Nurse*: Sarah Hollister. *Knocko, Jocko*, Simeon's Parents: Patrick Dawe, Harry Seymour. *Chorus*. (*Dance Specialties*: Tiller Sextette; Ercole-Ariaza Dancers and Troubadours, from the Royal Theatre, Madrid. Senorita Salvita (Premiere Ballerina); Josef and Amalia Zapata, Eliza and Paulina Lopez, Carmen Garcia, Elvra Guiterrez, Pilar Gacia, Pilar Ferrer, Cardoso, Eduardo Martinez, San Martin (tenor).)

Act 1, Scene 1: Palace and Cottage. (Armbruster.) *Scene 2*: The Palace of Hardluck XIII, King of Malaria. (McCleery.) *Scene 3*: The Fairy Pavilion. (Caney.) *Scene 4*: Walls of the Magic Garden. (Emden.) *Scene 5*: The Fairy Orchard. (Emden.)

Act 2, Scene 1: The City of Phantasia. (Caney.) *Scene 2*: The Home of Methuselina. (Smith.) *Scene 3*: The Road to the Island. (Caney.) *Scene 4*: A Desert Island. (McCleery.) *Scene 5*: The Triumph of Hymen. (McCleery.)

Act 3, Scene 1: The Palace of the White Cat. (Emden.) *Scene 2*: Homeward Bound. (Emden.) *Scene 3*: The King's Banqueting Hall. (Smith.)

ACT 1
Scene 1
"Sailing Away" (Opening Chorus)
H. Cropper, Chorus
"Girls and Boys" (Finale)
Scene 2
"A Court Is Like a Chessboard" (Opening Chorus)
"Graft"
W. T. Hodge, Chorus
"Let the Trumpets Sound"
Chorus
"Where Broadway Meets Fifth Avenue" (Song)
E. St. Clair, E. Atchison-Ely
(*Music and Lyrics by* Lester Keith and John Kemble.)
Scene 3
"Good-Bye, Maggie Doyle" (Song)
M. Lambert, Chorus
(*Music by* Jean Schwartz. *Lyrics by* William Jerome.)
"Antonio"
W. T. Hodge, H. J. Ward, H. Seymour, P. Dawe
(*Music by* Jean Schwartz. *Lyrics by* William Jerome.)
Scene 5
"The Ballet of Fruits" (Grand Divertissement)

[73]Billed as Klaw and Erlanger's annual Drury Lane spectacle.

"Cherries Ripe"
H. Cropper, Chorus
Cherry Gavotte; Grape Ballet; Fruit March; Orange Ballet; Cupid's Ballet; Ribbon Ballet; Finale.

ACT 2
Scene 1
"A Year and a Day" (Opening Chorus)
Chorus
"The Golden Net"
"Highland Mary" (Song)
M. Lambert, Chorus
(*Music by* Jean Schwartz. *Lyrics by* William Jerome.)
Scene 2
"Henny Klein"
M. Snyder, S. Brown, Chorus
(*Music by* Jean Schwartz. *Lyrics by* William Jerome.)
"Get the Money" (Quartet)
W. T. Hodge, W. Macart, H. J. Ward, H. Corthell
(*Music by* Jean Schwartz. *Lyrics by* William Jerome.)
Scene 4
"The Penang-Ourang-Outang"
H. J. Ward, assisted by Messrs. Dawe, Seymour
(*Music by* Philip Braham.)
Scene 5
"The Glory of Nations" (Grand Divertissement)
Triumphant March of Hymen
Russia; Norway; Hungary; Greece; Holland; France; Italy; Spain.
Grand Finale

ACT 3
Scene 1
"Catland" (Opening Chorus)
Dance Nouveau
Tiller Sextette
(*Music by* Frederic Solomon.)
"Meet Me on the Fence (Tonight)"
E. St. Clair, S. Brown, Chorus
(*Music by* Jean Schwartz. *Lyrics by* William Jerome.)
"My Lady of Japan"
M. Snyder, Chorus
(*Music by* Jean Schwartz. *Lyrics by* William Jerome.)
Scene 2
The Famous Ercole-Ariaza Castilian Dancers and Troubadours (Specialty)
Scene 3
"Down the Lane with Arabella"
E. Atchison-Ely, Chorus
(*Music by* Jean Schwartz. *Lyrics by* William Jerome.)
Grand Finale: "The Christmas of All Nations"

1905.49 THE EARL AND THE GIRL

The Merry English Musical Whirl (Musical Comedy) in Two Acts. Book by Seymour Hicks. Music by Ivan Caryll. Lyrics by Percy Greenbank. Produced (staged) by R. H. Burnside. Scenery painted by Ernest Albert and D. Frank Dodge. Costumes designed by Caroline Siedel. Electrical effects by Thomas J. Cleland. Musical director, Clarence West. Organization under the personal direction of Frank L. Perley. Produced by Sam S. and Lee Shubert, Inc. Opened 4 November 1905 at the Casino Theatre and closed 10 March 1906 after 148 performances.

CAST: *Jim Cheese*, a dog trainer: EDDIE FOY. *Dick Wargrave*: VICTOR MORLEY. *Hon. Crewe Boodle*: TEMPLAR SAXE. *A. Bunker Bliss*, an American: J. BERNARD DYLLYN. *Mr. Downham*, a New York solicitor: W. H. Armstrong. *Hazell*, landlord of the Fallowfield Arms: W. H. Denny. *Dudley Cranbourne*: John Peachey. *Bellam*: Dudley E. Oatman. *George*: Allan Campbell. *Elphin Haye*. a little school girl: GEORGIA CAINE. *Eliza Shodham*: ZELMA RAWLSTON. *Mrs. Shimmering Black*: AMELIA SUMMERVILLE. *Daisy Fallowfield*: NELLIE McCOY. *Miss Virginia Bliss*: Violet Holls. *Lady Gussie*: Louise DeRigney. *Lady Muriel*: Edna Jeans. *Lady Gwendoline*: Jane Hall. *Lady Violet*: Ruth Langdon. *Lady Maud*: Katherine Hyland. *Lady Geraldine*: Beatrice Adams. *Lady Millicent*: Enid Forde. *Lady Gladys*: May Lewis. *Lady Ethel*: Violet Adams. *Lady Marguerite*: Grace Walton. (*The Famous English Champagne Dancers*: Lillian Lawton, Maude Crossland, Jennie Boylan, Madeline Anderson.)

Inn Party Ladies: Misses Hall, Langdon, Highland, B. Adams, Forde, Lewis, V. Adams, Walton. *Inn Party Men*: Messrs. Oatman, Harder, Marshall, Handee, Strauss, Pyke, Lanning, Dennison. *Hunting Girls*: Misses Chandler, Clayton, L. Alexander, Stanley, Ayer, M. Alexander, Watson. *Hunting Boys*: Misses Chandler, L. Alexander, Taylor, Raymond, Gibbons, Howard. *Hunting Men*: Messrs. Campbell, Goodman, Weick, Zerger, LaDoux, Boyce. *Waitresses*: Misses Heath, Traves, Rice, Weimers, Zimmerman, De LaPaze. *Fishing Girls*: Misses Heckler, Fitzgerald, Wellington, Myers, Courtney, Aroval. *Ladies' Maids*: Misses Raymond, Howard, L. Alexander, Taylor, Gibbons, Chandler. *Spooning Girls*: Misses Hall, Langdon, Highland, V. Adams, Forde, Lewis, Walton, B. Adams. *Spooning Boys*: Misses Fitzgerald, Heath, Traves, Rice, Weimers, Heckler, Alexander, De LaPaze. *Grenadiers*: Misses Weimers, Adams, Manchester, Chandler, Zimmerman, Taylor, Raymond, Heath, Alexander, Traves, Rice, De LaPaze, Heckler, Fitzgerald, Myers, Courtney, Aroval. *Nurse Maids*: Misses Wellington, Clayton, Stanley, Ayres, Alexander, Taylor, Howard.

Act 1: Exterior of Fallowfield Arms.

Act 2: Ball room in the manor of the Earl of Stole.

ACT 1[74]
Opening Chorus
Ensemble
"Sporting Song"
N. McCoy, Chorus
"Little Lady in Distress"
Inn Party
"Shopping"
N. McCoy, Inn Party Ladies
"When the Right Little Girl Comes Along" (Song)
T. Saxe
(*Music by* E. Ray Goetz. *Lyrics by* Paul Barnes.)
Trio[75]
J. B. Dyllyn, W. H. Armstrong, A. Summerville
Duet
G. Caine, V. Morley
"I Would Like to Marry You" (Song)
G. Caine
(*Music and Lyrics by* Edward Laska.)
Specialty[76]
E. Foy
"Mediterranean Blue"
V. Morley, Chorus
"One Night Only"
V. Morley, G. Caine, E. Foy, Z. Rawlston
Finale
Ensemble

[74]The original English production was rife with American interpolations. Likewise, the American production witnessed many interpolations. The following were published as vocal numbers (M. Witmark) from Sam S. Shubert's production of the London success, but do not appear in extant programs:
"Dangerous Little Maid"
(*Music and Lyrics by* R. Melville Ellis.)
"School Boy and Girl Dance"
(*Music and Lyrics by* R. Melville Ellis.)
"Come Along with Me"
(*Music by* R. Melville Ellis. *Lyrics by* R. H. Burnside.)
"Ma Daphne Sue"
(*Music by* Emile Bruguiere. *Lyrics by* George DeLong.)

[75]Replaced for subsequent tour by:
"Cheyenne"
J. B. Dyllyn, Chorus
(*Music by* Egbert Van Alstyne. *Lyrics by* Harry Williams.)

[76]According to Eddie Foy's biographer, once Foy was transformed into the Earl, "in lavender tights, medal-studded chest, monocle, red wig and crown—Eddie impersonated Admiral Togo (Japanese officer in the Russo-Japanese War), the Czar, President Theodore Roosevelt, and J. D. Rockefeller." (Eddie Foy, A biography of the early stage comedian, by Armond Fields, McFarland & Company, Inc., Jefferson, North Carolina, 1999).

ACT 2[77]

"My Southern Belle"[78] (Opening Chorus)
J. Peachey, Chorus
(*Music by* Max C. Eugene [Max Dreyfus]. *Lyrics by* Jerome Kern.)

"The Poor Little Marionette"
N. McCoy
(*Music and Lyrics by* R. A. Browne and William H. Penn.)

"Cupid's Mistake"[79] (Song)
V. Morley

Domino Dance
English Champagne Dancers

Entrance of the Earl of Stole
Chorus

Gavotte
E. Foy, V. Morley, J. Peachey, V. Holls, L. DeRigney, J. Hall, T. Saxe, Chorus

"I Want a Man Made to Order for Me" (Song)
Z. Rawlston
(*Music by* Nat D. Mann. *Lyrics by* Nat D. Mann and Arthur Gillespie.)

"Won't You Change Your Name (from Miss to Mrs.)?" (Song)
E. Foy
(*Music by* Albert von Tilzen. *Lyrics by* Addison Burkhardt.)

"How Would You Like to Spoon With Me?" (How'd You Like to Spoon with Me?)
V. Morley, G. Caine, Chorus
(*Music by* Jerome Kern. *Lyrics by* Edward Laska.)

"Grenadiers" (March)
T. Saxe, Chorus

Finale
Ensemble

1905.50 THE BELLE OF THE WEST

A Musical Comedy in Three Acts. Book and lyrics by Harry B. Smith. Music by Karl Hoschna. Directed by Edward W. Rose. Opened 13 November 1905 at the Grand Opera House and closed 18 November 1905 after 8 performances.

CAST: *Bob Randolph*: JACK RANDOLPH. *Tarantula Jake*: JOSEPH GREENE. *Sir Montmorenci Montague*: GEORGE B. JACKSON. *August Winer*: ERNEST OTTO. *Henry Schnitzel*: ARTHUR OTTO. *Methusalem Jones*: Jimmy Lee. *Glad Hand Bill*: J. E. Miller. *Dakota Dan*: Ernest D. Wood. *Short-Card Charley*: Wallace F. Beery. *Ah Chew*: Joseph W. Herbert, Jr. *Mirandy Jane*: Harriette Keyes. *Nora*: Leona Ambrose. *Cora*: Ioma D'Autry. *Dora*: Tina Hunt. *Flora*: Hazel Wise. *Aurora*: Elsie Artz. *Laura*: BESSIE CLIFFORD. *Virginia Lee*: FLORENCE BINDLEY.

MUSICAL NUMBERS[80]

"The Frog and the Owl"
F. Bindley

"Holding Hands"
F. Bindley

"My Little Lasso"
F. Bindley

"Where the Flag Is Waving"
F. Bindley

Dutch Specialty
A. Otto, E. Otto

Horse-Play Dance
J. Lee

"Down by the Blue Rio Grande"

"It's So Different in London"

"The Land of Romance"

"My Little Sioux Sue"

"There Are Lots of Things Teacher Does Not Know"

"Those Were Happy Days"

"The Waltz" (Song)

[77]Running order of Act 2 revised after opening.

[78]Replaced for subsequent tour by:
"Mexicana Anna" (Opening Chorus)
T. Saxe, Chorus

[79]Dropped early in the run.

[80]No New York program available; musical numbers prepared from reviews and published sheet music (M. Witmark & Sons, New York, 1905).

1905.51 HOW BAXTER BUTTED IN

A Musical Comedy in Four Acts. Book by Owen Davis. Music and lyrics by Sidney Toler. Produced by Vance & Sullivan. Opened 13 November 1905 at the Murray Hill Theatre and closed 18 November 1905 after 8 performances; returned 11-16 December 1905 to the 14th Street Theatre for 8 performances. Total: 16 performances.

CAST: *Billy Baxter*: SIDNEY TOLER. *Erastus Winch*: LOUIS FEIRCE. *Zenus Meek*: George McCabe. *Abner Meek*: Robert W. Smiley. *Ezra Quick*: J. E. NICHOLS. *Ed. Dale*: Kingsley Benedict. *Lute Halstead*: WILLARD S. LOUIS. *Eben Titmouse*: H. A. Pearson. *Biddy*: Arthur Lipson. *Ben Jitson*: Arthur Cobb. *Miranda Winch*: May Maurice. *Nell Dale*: DELLA CLARKE. *Tabitha Tully*: LOUISE VALLENTINE. *Fanny Smalley*: Ruth Baine. *Rose Quigley*: Maud Louis. *Hope Sawtell*: Jessie Elliott. *Sue Jarvis*: Vivian Marston. *Laura Spruce*: May Guyer. *Rose Smith*: Virginia Harms. *Hattie Wilson*: Frances Clark. *Jack Mason*: J. Joe Seley. *Frank Judson*: Kenneth Ross.

Act 1: The Office of the Elm Hotel, Beaver Creek, New Hampshire.

Act 2: The Beaver Creek Church.

Act 3: The Judge's Office. *Scene 2*: The Apple Orchard and Cider Press.

Act 4: The Office of the Elm Hotel.

MUSICAL NUMBERS[81]

"Billy Baxter's Swing Song" (Act 1)
S. Toler

"The Same Thing"

"All Eternity" (Act 2)
W. S. Louis

"Billy Baxter's Jack-o-Lantern Boogieman" (Act 3)
S. Toler

"The Same Thing" (burlesque)(Act 4)
S. Toler, L. Vallentine, W. S. Louis, J. E. Nichols

1905.52 THE PRESS AGENT

A Musical Comedy in Two Acts. Book by Mark E. Swan and John P. Wilson. (Music by William Lorraine. Lyrics by John P. Wilson.) Produced under the direction of (staged by) Frank Smithson. Production revised by R. H. Burnside. Produced by Sam S. and Lee Shubert. Opened 29 November 1905 at Lew Fields' Theatre and closed 30 December 1905 after 40 performances.

CAST: *Benton Scoops*, a press agent who afterwards becomes a war correspondent: PETER F. DAILEY. *Bunny Hare*, an amateur hero: FRANK LALOR. *General Bustamento Y. Cabrillo Y. Gonzales*, a rebellion promoter: THEODORE FRIEBUS. *Francis Seabrooke*, Commander of the Revolutionary Expedition: Bertram Wallace. *Captain Gattling*, skipper of the ship *La Libertad*: ALBERT FROOM. *Silas Fosdick*, an American capitalist: W. F. Rochester. *Bitter Creek Benson*, known as "Fighting Bill," a bad man from Texas: Charles Chappelle. *Salvador Garcia*, secretary to President Castelar: Walter Neale. *Joseph Rutherford*, a speculator; Fosdick's rival: Charles Sitgreaves. *Bolivar*, a private soldier in the Army of Concarne: Adam Dockery. *Bill Bobstay*, bosun of *La Libertad*: John P. Pursell. *Adams*, a customs inspector: Fred Sherman. *Landlord*, owner of the Inn Concarne: C. R. Larkin. *Enchilada*, a lieutenant in the Army of Concarne: A. M. Pollock. *Sangrez, Pedrillo*, followers of the General: F. S. Lalor, T. F. Reynolds. *Dolores Yznaga*, the heroine of the latest revolution: KATE CONDON. *Bouncing Betty*, the ship's mascot: Carrie Graham. *Dolly Dashington*, Mr. Fosdick's niece: Isobel Hall. *Celia Courtney*, in love with a sailor: Jeanne LaCrosse. *Rosalie*, a chorus girl: Norma Seymour. *Pepita*, a Concarne beauty: Vera Stanley. *Yvonne*, another: Almeda Potter. *Excursionists, Boys, Girls, Revolutionists, Soldiers, etc.*

Act 1: The dock of the Spanish American Transport Company, New York.

Act 2: A public square in the City of Concarne.

MUSICAL NUMBERS

"Alexis from Texas"
P. F. Dailey, Chorus
(*Music by* Raymond Hubbell.)

"In Gay Manhattan"
P. F. Dailey

"The Simple Life"
P. F. Dailey

[81] No New York program available.

"Moonlight"
K. Condon
"Away to Spain"
K. Condon, P. F. Dailey
"Nightmare Land"
F. Lalor, C. Graham, Chorus
"Love, Love, Love"
F. Lalor, C. Graham, P. F. Dailey, Chorus
"Good-bye, Sweetheart"
F. Lalor, I. Hall
(*Music by* Gustave Kerker.)
"Here's to Your Eyes, Sweetheart"
F. Lalor
"In a Hammock"
I. Hall
"The Concarne Vivandières"
I. Hall
"Yo Ho"
"(I Think) It Must be Love"
(*Music by* Leo Friedman. *Lyrics by* Raymond Browne.)
"Moon Dear"
"Not a One Compares with Me"
"We All Love Our Dear Jack"
"Concarne for Me"
"Away, Away, We Sail Today"
"Float Me Charlie"
(*Music by* Jean Schwartz. *Lyrics by* William Jerome.)
"Sombrero" (Opening Chorus, Act 2)
A. Potter, Chorus

1905.53 THE MAYOR OF TOKIO

A Farcical Opera in Two Acts. Book and lyrics by Richard Carle. Music by William Frederick Peters. Entire production under the personal supervision of the author[82]. Dances arranged by Ad Neuberger. Scenery by J. Frank Dodge and Thomas Bradley. Costumes by E. S. Freisinger, Marshall Field & Co., Fisher & Co., Madame Ena Welch. Electrical effects by Harry Bising and Eugene Dupuis. Musical director, Alfred Moulton. Produced by Richard Carle[83]. Opened 4 December 1905 at the New York Theatre and closed 13 January 1906 after 50 performances.

CAST: *Kow Tow*, the Mayor of Tokio: FRED FREAR. *General Satake*, a conspirator: Sylvain Langlois. *Ivan Orfulitch*, a Russian spy: Jo Smith Marba. *Tanake*, Court Physician: Jess Caine. *Nikko*, the Royal Messenger: Edwin Baker. *Awaki*, a body guard: William H. Platt. *Betsy Lincoln*, an American heiress: ADELE ROWLAND. *Oloto San*, daughter of Kow Tow: HORTENSE MAZURETTE. *Kimono, Ylang Ylang, Toma, Yamo*, friends of Oloto: Lillian Doherty, Florence Willarde, Ethel Lloyd, Ada Mitchell. *Chub*, a cabin boy: Madge Vincent. *The Ostrich*: Rollo Carnegie.

Members of Kidder's Konsolidated Komiques: *Julian Lincoln*, the Tenor: Albert Wellerstedt. *Rusty*, the Song Book Boy: WILLIAM ROCK. *Madame Stitch*, the Wardrobe Mistress: EMMA JANVIER. *Birdie Talcum*, the Soubrette: MINERVA COURTNEY. *The Peanut Ballet*: Madge Vincent, Olive Roberts, Inez Bauer, Irene O'Donnell, Marie Salisbury, Helen Brandon, Daisy Johnstone, Beatrice Mack, Lucille Adams. *Marcus Orlando Kidder*, impressario: RICHARD CARLE. *Geisha Girls, Japanese Soldiers, Yachting Girls, Sailors, Japanese Dancing Girls, Maids of Honor, Tokio Bebo Men*.

Yachting Girls: Effie Hamilton, Florence Meigs, Adelaide Thompson, Jane Griffith, Laura Castle, Marjorie Elliott, Violet Mack. *Yachtmen*: Georges Bogues, Harry Smith, John Flynn, Robert Laidlaw, J. W. Cunningham, Harry Irwin, Ross Harvey, Clarence Caldren. *Sailor Ladies*: Ida Lind, Daisy Johnstone, Jane Grant, Bert Dodsworth, Jeannette Despres, Lillian McCeney, Alice Grey, Florence Jones, Inez Bauer, Olive Roberts, Irene O'Donnell, Marie Salisbury, Helen Brandon, Beatrice Mack, Lucille Adams, Adele Hertrais. *Maids of Honor*: Ethel Lloyd, Ada Mitchell, Lillian Doherty, Florence Willarde. *Dancing Girls*: Ida Lind, Laura Castle, Florence Jones, Alice Grey, Bert Dodsworth, Daisy Johnstone, Jane Griffith, Lillian McCeney. *Geisha Girls*: Effie Hamilton, Florence Meigs, Jeannette Despres, Adelaide Thompson, Jane Grant, Violet Mack, Marjorie Elliott, Cecile Gray, Laura Casle, Jae Griffith, Ida Lind, Bert Dodsworth, Florence Jones, Daisy Johnstone, Lillian McCeney, Alice Grey.

Act 1: A Public Garden in Tokio.

Act 2: Outside Sing Song, the Japanese Jail, near Tokio Harbor.

ACT 1
"Bridal Song"
Company
"Tokio"
A. Rowland, Chorus
"Conspirators Are We"
S. Langlois, J. S. Marba
"Welcome, Oloto"
F. Warde, L. Doherty, E. Lloyd, A. Mitchell
"Pity My Pitiful Plight"
H. Mazurette, Chorus
(*Lyrics by* Arthur Burrows.)
"Cheer Up Everybody"
R. Carle, E. Janvier, W. Rock, M. Courtney, the Peanuts
"Entrance of Kow Tow"
Chorus
(*Lyrics by* Robert I. Beecher.)
"The Mayor of Tokio"
F. Frear, Chorus
"A Comic Opera Capsule"
A. Rowland, R. Carle
"Kidder's Reception"
Chorus
Finale
Company

ACT 2
"Festival of Mourning"
Company
(*Lyrics by* Robert I. Beecher, James R. Montague.)
"Cruising Home"
R. Carle, F. Frear, W. Rock
"(The) Silver Sea of Love"[84]
H. Mazurette, A. Wellerstedt
"When Ocean Breezes Blow"
A. Rowland, Chorus
(*Lyrics by* Arthur Gillespie.)
"Foolishness"
R. Carle
(*Lyrics by* Arthur Gillespie.)
"Is Marriage a Failure?"[85]
F. Frear, E. Janvier
"I Like You"
R. Carle, Chorus
(*Lyrics by* Richard Carle, Charles J. Campbell and Ralph M. Skinner.)
"La Dance Blanche et Noire"
W. Rock, M. Courtney, Peanut Ballet
Finale
Company

1905.54 A SOCIETY CIRCUS

A Musical Extravaganza in Two Acts, 5 Scenes. Book by Sidney Rosenfeld. Music by Manuel Klein and Gustav Luders. Lyrics by Sidney Rosenfeld and Manuel Klein. Arrangement and production by Frederic Thompson. Staged by Edward P. Temple. Dances arranged by Vincenzo Romeo. Settings by Arthur Voegtlin. Costumes by Alfredo Edel and Archie Gunn. Electrical effects by Charles deSoria, Hugh S. Thomas. Produced by Frederic Thompson and Elmer S. Dundy. Opened 13 December 1905 at the Hippodrome and closed 2 June 1906; re-opened 1 September 1906 and closed 24 November 1906 after 596 performances.

CAST: *Bolesla*, King of the Gypsies: FRANCIS J. BOYLE. *Draga*, Queen of the Gypsies: LEILA ROMER. *Esmeralda*, Gypsy Fortune-teller: OLIVE NORTH. *Paul Pasky*: EDWIN A. CLARKE. *Radsky, Ladsky, Badsky*, Gypsy Lieutenants: James Cherry, Harry F. Siegfreid, Thomas J. Daly. *The Lady Volumnia*: ROSE LaHARTE. *Fizz Fluka*, her factotum: MARCELINE. *Page*: Rita Dean. (*Gypsy Bride*: Stella Martine. *Gypsy Bridegroom*: H. E. Cluett.[86]) *The Major Domo*: FELIX HANEY. *His Shadow*: FRANK SILVERS OAKLEY. *Waiters*: Messrs. Bennett, Scott, Soley. *Florette*: Miss Riano.

[82]Staged by Richard Carle.
[83]Tour presented under the auspices of Joseph Gaites.

[84]Dropped for subsequent tour.
[85]Dropped for subsequent tour.
[86]The Gypsy Bride and Bridegroom do not appear in the earliest cast lists.

Circus Specialties: CLAIRE HELIOT and Her 12 Lions, Barlow's Elephants, Miss Marquis and Ponies, Ralph Johnstone, Mlle. Leris, Marguerite and Hanley, Sisters O'Meers, The Four Marnos, The Flying Dunbars, The Four Rianos.

Act 1, Scene 1: A Gypsy Camp, strangely invaded. *Scene 2*: A Society Circus. Spaciously beautiful terrace of Lady Volumnia's Palace.

Act 2, Scene 1: In the Jungle. *Scene 2*: Garden of the Golden Peristyles. *Scene 3*: Court of the Golden Fountains.

ACT 1
Scene 1
Morning in the Gypsy Camp
Arrival of Gypsies
Formation of Camp
Gypsy Wedding Ceremony and Festivities
Appearance of Lady Volumnia and Court
"Tainted Gold" (Song)
R. LaHarte
(*Music by* Manuel Klein. *Lyrics by* Sydney Rosenfeld.)
Exit of Lady Volumnia
Breaking of Gypsy Camp
Claire Heliot and Her 12 Lions
Scene 2
Opening Chorus and Gavotte of Courtiers
Entrance of Major Domo and His Shadow
"But It Ain't" (Song)
F. Haney
Entrance of Lady Volumnia and Court
"The Laughing School" (Song)
R. LaHarte
(*Music by* Manuel Klein. *Lyrics by* Sydney Rosenfeld.)
Entrance of Gypsies
"The Conspiracy" (Song)
F. Haney, Marceline, Gypsies
"Let the Circus Now Appear" (Exit March)
All
Circus Events[87]:
Barlow's Elephants, Miss Marquis and Ponies; Marguerite and Hanley (Equilibristic Novelty Act); Caicedo (King of the Bounding Wire); Sisters O'Meers (Tight Wire artists); Sisters Powell (Etoil Equestriennes); Albert Crandall (Burlesque Equestrian); Heras Family (Acrobats); August Family (Jugglers); The Four Marnos (Acrobats). Frank Melville, Equestrian Director.
Grand Wedding March and Chorus
"Moon, Dear" (Song)
E. A. Clark
(*Music and Lyrics by* Manuel Klein.)
"They Have Carried the Bridegroom Off" (Finale)
Omnes

ACT 2
Scene 1
The Four Rianos
"The Good, Kind, Jolly Man" (Song)
F. J. Boyle
(*Music and Lyrics by* Manuel Klein.)
Scene 2
The Kaufman Troupe (12 Bicycle performers)
"Song of the Flowers" (Ballet)
(*Music by* Gustav Luders.)
Entrance of Wedding Guests
"In Bright Array"[88] (March Chorus)
"Everybody Must Be Happy" (Ensemble)
Omnes
Scene 3
Aquatic Tableau

[87]Other Circus Specialities during the run included The Flying Dunbars, The Four Rianos (Simian Impersonators); Cottrell-Powells (Riding Extraordinary); Ralph Johnstone, Mlle. Leris; Wulff's Leaping Hounds; Five Lecussons (Novelty Equestrians); Mlle. Natalina Rossi (Equestrienne); The Bporsinis (Rolling-Globe Artists); Manello-Manitz Troupe (Musical Equilibrists); The Flying Meteos (Aerial Marvels); The Bonhair-Gregory troupe (Acrobats Unparalleled); Ralph Johnstone (Bicyclist Extraordinary).

[88]Dropped after opening. Re-instated for return engagement.

1905.55 THE BABES AND THE BARON

An English Musical Extravaganza in Two Acts, 10 Scenes. Story by A. M. Thompson and Robert Courtneidge. Music by H. E. Haines and other composers. Lyrics by Charles M. Taylor. American version and additional lyrics by Robert B. Smith. Staged by R. H. Burnside, assisted by J. Paul Callam. Settings by T. Holmes, E. H. Ryan, Philip Howden, R. C. McCleery and Stafford Hall. Costumes designed by Wilhelm, Paris; Hugo Bauch, Berlin. Orchestra under the direction of Arthur Weld. Produced by John C. Fisher (and the Messrs. Sam S. and Lee Shubert). Opened 25 December 1905 at the Lyric Theatre and closed 27 January 1906 after 45 performances.

CAST: *The Baron*, alias Bill Burke: JUNIE McCREE. *Robin Hood*, Earl of Huntington, an outlaw: MAUDE LAMBERT. *Jack Tuff, Bill Ruff*, the two robbers: JAMES C. MARLOWE, LOUIS WESLEY. *Will Scarlet, Little John, Allan A'Dale*, members of Robin Hood's Band: Mabel Wilbur, Vera Cameron, Margaret King. *Charlie, Cissie*, the two babes: WILL ARCHIE, ADELE COX. *Touser*, a collie dog: Alfred Latell. *The Cowardly Policeman*: EDDIE GARVIE. *The Dude*: Edward Craven. *Chinaman*: David Rogers. *Cinderella*: LILLIAN COLEMAN. *Lena Pickles*, the nurse: CARRIE BEHR. *Clorinda, Thysbie*, Cinderella's sisters: Florence Guise, Florence Trevillion. *The Fairy God Mother*: Lillian English. *Dorothy, Dorcas, Phyllis*, beloved of Will Scarlet, Little John, and Allan A'Dale: Gertrude Douglass, Margaret von Keeze, Marie Leuyllemn. *Royal Messenger*: Mildred Warde. *The Laughing Steed*: The Brothers Ward. *Pas de Seul*: LA PETITE ADELAIDE. *The Toy Soldier*: FRED WALTON. *Archers, Living Toys, Villagers, Shoppers, Guards, Knights, etc.*

Act 1, Scene 1: The Market Square, Nottingham. (Holmes.) *Scene 2*: A Country Lane. (Ryan.) *Scene 3*: The Fair Grounds at Nottingham. (Holmes.) *Scene 4*: The Nursery. (Howden.) *Scene 5*: The Toy Country: Outside the Gates, and The Toy Capital. (Howden.)

Act 2, Scene 1: The Baron's Bazaar. (Holmes.) *Scene 2*: The Edge of the Forest. (McCleery.) *Scene 3*: The Heart of the Forest. (McCleery.) *Scene 4*: Interior of a Restaurant. (Ryan.) *Scene 5*: Ball-room of Robin Hood's Castle. (Hall.)

ACT 1
Opening Chorus
(*Music by* H. E. Haines.)
"(It's a) Jolly Good Thing To Be Alive"
C. Behr, A. Cox, W. Archie
(*Music by* H. E. Haines.)
"An Outlaw Bold"
M. Lambert, Chorus
(*Music and Lyrics by* Arthur Weld.)
"Robin Hood's Arrest"
Ensemble
(*Music by* H. E. Haines.)
"I Didn't Mean No Harm"
W. Archie
(*Music by* J. Fred Helf.)
"The English Bow"
Ensemble
(*Music by* H. E. Haines.)
"The Firefly and the Rose"
L. Coleman, Chorus
(*Music by* Nat D. Mann)
"I Would Like to Be Your Pal"
J. McCree, C. Behr, Chorus
(*Lyrics by* Junie McCree.)
"How D'Ye Do?"
M. Lambert, L. Coleman
(*Music and Lyrics by* F. R. Babcock.)
"March of the Toys" (Farewell, Dear Toys)
Chorus
(*Music by* Jerome D. Kern.)
"The Music of the Band"
Chorus
(*Music by* Dan Lipton. *Lyrics by* Raymond Browne.)

ACT 2
Opening Chorus
(*Music by* Raymond Hubbell.)

"Tailor's Dummy"
L. Coleman, Chorus
(*Music by* H. E. Haines.)
"Milo (You're Just My Style-O)" (A Romance of Turkey)
J. McCree, Chorus
(*Music by* Alfred Solman. *Lyrics by* Benjamin Hapgood Burt.)
"Knock Wood"
J. McCree, J. C. Marlowe, L. Wesley
(*Music by* Raymond Hubbell.)
"(By) The Light of the Honeymoon (or Kiss Me and Say You'll Be Mine)"
M. Lambert, Chorus
(*Music by* Anna [Anne] Caldwell. *Lyrics by* James O'Dea.)
"If I But Dared"
M. Lambert
(*Music and Lyrics by* Nat D. Mann.)
"Gee, But This Is a Lonesome Town"
E. Garvie
(*Music and Lyrics by* Billy Gaston.)
"Think It Over"
J. McCree, E. Garvie, J. C. Marlowe, L. Wesley
(*Music by* Alfred E. Aarons.)
Finale
Chorus

1905.56 THE GINGERBREAD MAN

A Fanciful Fairyesque (Musical Play) in Two Acts. Book and lyrics by Frederic Ranken. Music by A. Baldwin Sloane. Stage director, Charles Sinclair. Settings designed by Ernest Albert. Costumes designed by Archie Gunn, Will R. Barnes and J. Hegeman. Musical director, Louis F. Gottschalk. Produced by Harry E. Converse and Mason Peters. Opened 25 December 1905 at the Liberty Theatre and closed 6 January 1906 after 16 performances; re-opened 14 May 1906 at the New York Theatre and closed 26 May 1906 after 16 additional performances. Total : 32 performances[89].

CAST: *Kris Kringle*, known as Santa Claus: J. P. MacSWEENEY. *Machevelius Fudge*, a dealer in Black Art, Second Hand Curses and Evil Omens: HOMER LIND. *Mme. Santa Claus*, a very fair Fairy Queen: Ross Snow. *Doughnut*: Gus Weinberg. *Marshmallow*: Gilbert Gregory. *Wonderous Wise*, a Solomon in Judgement: W. H. Mack. *Jack Horner*, a baker's apprentice: HELEN BERTRAM. *Simon Simple*, author of nursery rhymes and Christmas jingles: Joseph Welsh. *Taffy*, a friend of Jack's: Lillian Leon. *Coffee*: Uria Rottger. *The Gingerbread Man*, a mere outline, but in danger of being obliterated: EDDIE REDWAY. *The Fiery Dragon*: H. L. Zeda. *Cookie*: Frankie Bailey. *Duke of Pie*: Frankie Bailey. *Mazie Bon-Bon*, a Confectioner's Sales Girl; afterward Princess Sugar Plum: ALMYRA FORREST. *King Bunn*, with 1000 things to think of: Gus Weinberg. *Sallie Lunn*: Harriet Burt. *Margery Daw*, the village tom-boy: Nellie Lynch.

Baker Boys: Misses Edwards, Kramer, Lane, Leighton, Mooney, Rivenberg. *Baker Girls*: : Misses Ainslie, Barber, Bradbury, Clifford, Maxwell, Sawyer. *Village Boys*: Misses Belasco, Buhl, Fairfax, Meridan, Millard, Proctor, Wilson. *Village Girls*: Misses Appleton, Browne, Ivy, Merritt, Winifred Jordan, Miller, Morrison, Tyler. *Sales Girls*: Misses Abbott, Barnes, Brown, Dunne, Gaffney, Marie Jordan, Kennedy, Murray. *Pastry Cooks*: Messrs. Becca, Bowman, Damerel, Devlin, Lindermann. *Toy Makers*: Messrs. Ertz, Fitz, Hobart, Jenkins, Tiemann. *Fairies*: Misses Abbott, Appleton, Barnes, Brown, Browne, Dunne, Gaffney, Ivy, Marie Jordan, Kennedy, Millard, Miller, Meridan, Morrison, Murray, Proctor. *Reindeer*: Misses Abbott, Barnes, Brown, Dunne, Gaffney, Kennedy, Proctor.

Subjects of King Sugar Plum: *Peasant Girls*: Misses Barnes, Brown, Dunne, Kennedy. *Maids*: Misses Miller, Meridan, Wilson. *Waitresses*: Misses Appleton, Winifred Jordan, Buhl and Tyler. *Pastry Cooks*: Messrs. Becca, Bowman, Damerel, Devlin, Lindermann.

Subjects of King Bunn: *Peasant Girls*: Misses Browne, Gaffney, Marie Jordan, Murray. *Waitresses*: Misses Ivy, Millard, Morrison, Proctor. *Maids*: Misses Belasco, Merritt, Fairfax. *Toy Makers*: Messrs. Ertz, Fitz, Hobart, Jenkins, Tiemann. *Courtiers*: Misses Edwards, Kramer, Lane, Leighton, Mooney, Rivenberg; Messrs. Becca, Bowman, Damerel, Devlin, Lindermann, Ertz, Fitz, Hobart, Jenkins, Tiemann. *Court Ladies*: Misses Ainslie, Barber, Bradbury, Clifford, Maxwell, Sawyer. *Chocolate Eclairs*: Misses Ainslie, Barber, Bradbury, Edwards, Kramer, Lane, Mooney, Rivenburg. *Gingerbread Cadets*: Ladies of the Chorus.

Act 1: A street scene in Santa Claus Land.

Act 2: The dividing line between the Realms of King Bunn and King Sugar Plum.

[89]The production subsequently toured under the auspices of Nixon & Zimmerman Company.

ACT 1[90]
Opening Chorus
"That Awful Bogie Man"
H. Lind, Chorus
"(The) Evil Eye"
N. Lynch, H. Lind, J. Welsh, W. H. Mack
"Mazie"
H. Bertram, Chorus
"Beautiful Land of Bon-Bon"
H. Bertram, A. Forrest
"Incantation"
H. Lind, Chorus
"John Dough" (John Doe)
E. Redway, Fairies
Finale
Ensemble

ACT 2[91]
Opening Chorus
"Queen of My Dreams" (King of My Dreams)
H. Lind, Male Chorus
"Old Ramses"
G. Weinberg, G. Gregory, Chorus
"Nursery Rhymes"
N. Lynch, E. Redway
"Moon, Moon, Moon" (The Moon Song)
H. Bertram, Chorus
"Every Little Something"
N. Lynch, H. Burt, L. Leon, G. Weinberg, G. Gregory, W. H. Mack
(*Lyrics by* Brandon Burst.)
"Gin-Gin-Ginger Boy"[92]
E. Redway, Chocolate Eclairs
Finale
Ensemble

1905.57 MLLE. MODISTE

A Comic Opera in Two Acts. Libretto by Henry Blossom. Music by Victor Herbert. Staged by Fred G. Latham. Settings by Ernest Gros, (Homer) Emens and (Edward G.) Unitt. Dresses executed by John Wanamaker, Mlle. Dazian, Lord & Taylor; Miss Scheff's mdoern gowns by Mme. Jacqueline. Music director, John Lund. Produced by Charles Dillingham. Opened 25 December 1905 at the Knickerbocker Theatre and closed 16 June 1906 after 202 performances; re-opened 1 September 1906 at the Knickerbocker 1 September 1906 and closed 22 September 1906 after 22 additional performances. Total: 224 performances.

CAST: *Henri de Bouvray*, Comte de St. Mar: WILLIAM PRUETTE. *Captain Etienne de Bouvray*, his nephew: WALTER PERCIVAL. *Hiram Bent*, an American millionaire: CLAUDE GILLINGWATER. *Gaston*, an artist, Mme. Cécile's son: LEO MARS. *General Le Marquis de Villefranche*: George Schraeder. *Lieutenant René La Motte*, engaged to Marie Louise: Howard Chambers. *François*, porter at Mme. Cécile's: R. W. Hunt. *Mme. Cécile*, proprietress of a Parisian hat shop: JOSEPHINE BARTLETT. *Fanchette*, *Nanette*, her daughters: Edna Fassett, Blanche Morrison. *Marie Louise de Bouvray*, Etienne's sister: Louise LeBaron. *Bébé*, dancer at the Folies Bergère: Miss LaMora. *Fleurette*: Ada Meade. *Mrs. Hiram Bent*: Bertha Holly. *Fifi*: FRITZI SCHEFF.

Milliners, Guests, Dancers, Soldiers, Servants: Flora Barbier, Lillian Lipyeat, Grace Spencer, Mae Baldwin, Marie Parkes, Bellie Parkes, Jeanette Paterson, Grace Cornish, Janet Pawsey, Olive Cox, Adelaide Ott, Cecile Rowe, Gertrude Reeves, Pauline Georgi, Thekla Morton, Edna Cecil, Dix Carruthers, Grace Bond, Alice May, Ailsa Craig,

[90] Added for subsequent tour:
"I Must Have Been Mistaken" (Act 1, after "Evil Eye")
J. M. Holden {Good Fairy}, Chorus
"Kisses" (Act 2, after Every Little Something")
R. Snow {Wondrous Wise}, Chocolate Eclairs

[91] Added to Act 2 for return engagement, after "Moon, Moon, Moon:"
"Do You Believe in Santa Claus?"
H. L. Zeda, E. Redway, N. Lynch

[92] Replaced for return engagement by:
"March On (O Soldier)"
H. Bertram, Gingerbread Cadets

Kathryn Mertens, Nancy Poole, Carli Benson, Thomas DeVasey, A. Widdoson, G. V. Hurlock, F. Lademan, A. F. Burchly, Herman Walters, Frank W. Boyle, Charles H. Page, Peter Canova, A. Swinton, A. M. Pergain, H. Margan, James Quarrinton.

Act 1: Mme. Cecile's hat shop. Rue de la Paix, Paris. (Gros.)

Act 2, Scene 1: Comte. de St. Mar's private dining room. One year later. *Scene 2*: The Charity Bazaar in the Gardens of the Chateau de St. Mar. (Emens, Unitt.)

ACT 1

Opening Chorus (Furs and Feathers, Buckles and Bows)
E. Fassett, B. Morriosn, Girls

"When the Cat's Away the Mice Will Play"
E. Fassett, B. Morrison, J. Bartlett

"The Time, the Place and the Girl"
W. Percival, Chorus

"If I Were on the Stage" (Kiss Me Again)
F. Scheff

"Love Me, Love My Dog"
L. Mars

"Hats Make the Woman"
F. Scheff, Female Chorus

Finale
Entire Company

ACT 2

Scene 1

Chorus of Footmen (Servants' Chorus)

"I Want What I Want When I Want It"
W. Pruette

Scene 2

Opening Chorus

Ballet
LaMora

"Ze English Language"
L. Mars

"The Mascot of the Troop" (Mascot of the Moon)
F. Scheff, Male Ensemble

"The Dear Little Girl Who is Good"
H. Chambers, Female Ensemble

"The Keokuk Culture Club"
B. Holly, Ensemble

"The Nightingale and the Star" (Waltz Song)
F. Scheff

Finale
Entire Company

1906.01 TWIDDLE-TWADDLE

Joe Weber's All-Star Company in a Merry-Go-Round of Mirth, Melody and Madness (a Musical Burlesque) in Two Goes (Acts). Dialogue (book) and lyrics by Edgar Smith. Music by Maurice Levi. Produced under the stage direction of (staged by) Al M. Holbrook. Settings by Ernest Albert. Costumes designed by Mrs. Caroline F. Siedle. Lighting effects by Thomas Smith. Orchestra under the direction of Maurice Levi. Produced by Joe Weber. Opened 1 January 1906 at Joe Weber's Music Hall and closed 2 June 1906 after 159 performances[93].

CAST: Act 1: *Philip Grabfelder*, a Cincinnati multi-millionaire sojourning at Marienbad for the reduction of the embonpont of his person and his purse: JOE WEBER. *Ebenezer Dodge*, an American insurance nabob on a mission involving business and the faith cure: CHARLES A. BIGELOW. *Richard Jones*, a former showman and present gambler, better known in the Golden West as "Denver Dick": Edward J. Connelly. *Hon. Algernon Fitz-Haggis*, twenty-second Earl of Fininhaddie; reduced to the necessity of introducing the titled pauper to the untitled rich for a monetary consideration: ERNEST LAMBART. *The Grand Duke Josef*, indulging in a welcome incognito, at Marienbad: BONNIE MAGINN. *Captain Schmitt*, a superannuated army relic: Sam Marion. *Emperor Franz Josef* of Austria: Sam Marion. *American College Youths (4)*, with the self-imposed mission of waking up Europe: *Jack Potter*: Jarvis Jocelyn. *"Toots" Horne*: Jack Joyce. *Charley Hawes*: James Nugent. *Howell Goode*: W. Douglas Stevenson. *Patients at Marienbad (4)*: *Herr Bierheister*: Joseph Kaufman. *Herr Drinkenstein*: H. W. Robinson. *Herr Krautundwurst*: J. McLaughlin. *Herr Katzenjammer*: John D'Arcy. *Egyhaza*, a gypsy peddler: Ambrose Ball. *Rangypoot*, an East Indian: T. C. Diers, Jr. *Colonel Fez*, a Turkish officer: David R. Locke. *Monsieur Montmarte*, a Turkish officer: Al. T. Darling. *Matilda Grabfelder*, whose social aspirations cause much trouble for her worthy father, and cure her of a desire to mingle with the nobility: MARIE DRESSLER. *Mrs. "Jack" Van Shaik*, a New York society divorcée, and milliner in particular to the smart set: TRIXIE FRIGANZA. *Maggie McGurk*, a saleslady: May Montfort. *Gladys Dodge*, a society "broiler": Erminie Earle. *Count Ladislas*, of the Austrian Army: Edith Moyer. *Cheata*, a "billeteur': Edith Moyer. *Count Rudolf*, of the Austrian Army: May Grant. *Vera Shapeleigh*, a "society bud": May Grant. *Flower Girls (4)*: *Mignetta*: Minerva Coverdale. *Rosa*: Mae Carlisle. *Violetta*: Madlyn Jane Summers. *Verbena*: Vonnie Hoyt. *Bonne*: Mattie Boorum. *Society Buds (8)*: *Polly Parrott*: Alice Atwater. *Daisy Ryder*: Arline LaCrosse. *Elsie Avenue*: Evelyn Mitchell. *Rhoda Heights*: Frieda Ricca. *Cassie Boulevard*: Grace Spencer. *Angie Rhodes*: Lolita Gordon. *Sadie Strasse*: Vida Whitmore. *Vienna Cocottes (4)*: *Grisette*: Freda Linyard. *Collette*: Kitty Wheaton. *Anette*: Fay Tincher. *Nanette*: Dorothy Bertrand. *Mazooka, Mazaaka*, gypsies: Helen Heins Lucy Tonge. *Bavarian Girl*: Eva Francis. *Hungarian Girl*: Lillian Fitzgerald.

Butterflies of Fashion: *Lillie*: Kitty Wheaton. *Millie*: *Tillie*: Bessie M. Skeer. *Dollie*: Ethel Donaldson. *Mollie*: Freda Linyard. *Collie*: Gertrude Barthold. *Hattie*: Dorothy Bertrand. *Mattie*: Helen Heins. *Captain Cannonski, Major Lipthauer*, officers: Alice Atwater, Arline LaCrosse.

Of the Vienna Smart Set: *Herr Ladidaski*: Frieda Ricca. *Herr Damenkilla*: Arline LaCrosse. *Herr Eingang*: Irene Carlisle. *Herr Ausgang*: Vida Whitmore. *Fraulein Stefansplatz*: Evelyn Mitchell. *Fraulein Waldquelle*: Grace Spencer. *Fraulein Rausmitter*: Selma Mantell. *Fraulein Aufderheida*: Lillian Barrington. *Fraulein Wunderlich*: Lolita Gordon. *Fraulein Tannenbaum*: Vernie Wadsworth. *Fraulein Holzapfel*: Phoebe Loubet.

Go 1: The Esplanade at Marienbad at the promenade hour.

Go 2: "Venedig," The Coney Island of Vienna, by night.

ACT 1[94]

"When You've Pampered Your Adipose Tissue" (Opening Ensemble)
Young America Quintette, Chorus

"A Little Bunch of Daisies" (Octette)
College Boys, Flower Girls

"Days of My Boyhood"[95] (Song)
C. A. Bigelow

"Society Buds" (Song)
T. Friganza, Ensemble

"It's Hard To Be a Lady in a Case Like That"[96] (Song)
M. Dressler

"(For) You and the Girl You Love" (Song)
B. Maginn, Ensemble

"Hats" (Trio)
M. Dressler, T. Friganza, E. Lambart, Ensemble

"My Syncopated Gypsy Maid" (Song)
C. A. Bigelow, Ensemble

"'Tis Dreadful!" "'Tis Astounding!" (Finale)
M. Dressler, J. Weber, C. A. Bigelow,
E. J. Connelly, E. Lambart, T. Friganza, Ensemble

ACT 2[97]

---

[93]Played a return engagement the following season 12 November 1906 at Weber's Music Hall for 32 performances; see separate entry in following season.

[94]Late in the run, 'The Jays', a skit burlesquing The Fays, was introduced near the close of Act 1. Joe Weber appears as Mr. Jay, and Marie Dressler appears as Mrs. Jay.

[95]Replaced during the run by:
"(Everybody's) Looking for a Sure Thing" (Song)
E. J. Connelly

[96]Replaced during the run by:
"(Hard Luck) Stories of the Stage"
M. Dressler

[97]During the run (26 February 1906), the two acts were combined into one, and a burlesque (THE SQUAW MAN'S GIRL OF THE GOLDEN WEST) was added to form a new Act 2. The burlesque was inspired by David Belasco's play "The Girl of the Golden West" and Edwin Milton Royle's comedy-drama "The Squaw Man", and was retained for the subsequent tour. Program note: "The Indian language used by Mr. Kaufman as Topictowna and Miss Montford as Scratchoritch is genuine Bute, and if you don't understand it, we can't help it."

"Venedig, Fair Venedig"[98] (Ensemble)
Young America Quintette, Chorus
"Buttterflies of Fashion"[99] (Song and Dance)
B. Maginn, Ensemble
"Oh, Heigh-Ho!"[100] (Song)
J. Weber, Ensemble
"Hard Luck Stories of the Stage"[101] (Song)
M. Dressler
Finale
Company

Added during the run:

THE SQUAWMAN'S GIRL OF THE GOLDEN WEST

A Good-natured Swat at the Popular Craze for Atmospheric Melodrama[102] (A Burlesque in One Act). Dialogue (book) and lyrics by Edgar Smith. Music by Maurice Levi. Staged by Al Holbrook. Opened 26 February 1906 and closed 2 June 1906 after 102 performances.

CAST: *Captain Winstake*, the Squaw Man: ERNEST LAMBART. *Jack Chance*, the Sheriff: EDWARD J. CONNOLLY. *Rash Tawkins*, the Bad Man: JOE WEBER. *Topictowna*, the Chief: CHARLES A. BIGELOW. *Tick*, the Bartender: LEE HARRISON. *Snoring Jim*, the Miner: SAM MARION. *Scrappy Holiday*: David R. Locke. *Trinidad Moe*: Joseph Kaufman. *Silent Jake*: Jack Joyce. *Jim Leakins*, the Guzzler: Jarvis Jocelyn. *The Parson*: W. Douglas Stevenson. *Shako Fight*: T. C. Diers. *Cut-Throat Billy*: Ambrose Ball. *Royal Rustlers Minstrels and Chair Warmers (5)*: *Jose Castoff*: James Nugent. *Willy Welshrabbit*: Al. T. Darling. *Joe Miller*: John D'Arcy. *Phil Graves*: H. W. Robinson. *Ike Kiljoy*: Joseph Kaufman. *Lottie Lee*: Mattie Boorum. *The Girl*: MARIE DRESSLER. *Scratchoritch*: May Montfort. *Little Hal*, the Papoose: BONNIE MAGINN. *Banana*, the Lady: FLORA ZABELLE. *Papooses, Cow Gents, Tourists*.

Scene: Long Horn Tavern, California, in 1849.

MUSICAL NUMBERS
"Hurrah for the Beautiful Golden West" (Opening Chorus)
Ensemble
"Poor Little Red Pappoose"
B. Maginn, Ensemble
"The Girls of Forty-Nine"
F. Zabelle, Ensemble
Finale
Company

1906.02 FORTY-FIVE MINUTES FROM BROADWAY

A Music Play in Three Acts. Book, music and lyrics by George M. Cohan. Staged by George M. Cohan. Setings by John Young, Ernest Albert, Frank Marsden. Costumes by F. Richard Anderson. Electrical effects by Harry Bissing. Orchestra under the direction of Frederic Solomon. Business direction, Sam H. Harris. Produced by (Marc) Klaw and (Abraham L.) Erlanger. Opened 1 January 1906 at the New Amsterdam Theatre and closed 17 March 1906 after 90 performances[103].

CAST: *Mary Jane Jenkins*, the housemaid: FAY TEMPLETON. *Flora Dora Dean*, a footlight favorite: LOIS EWELL. *Mrs. David Dean*, her mother: JULIA RALPH. *Mrs. Purdy*, a resident of New Rochelle: Marion Singer. *Tom Bennet*, the heir-at-law: DONALD BRIAN. *Kid Burns*, his secretary: VICTOR MOORE. *James Blake*, Public Administrator, man about town: Charles Prince. *Daniel Cronin* in the mining business: JAMES H. MANNING. *Andy Gray*, the butler: LOUIS R. GRISEL. *Station Master*: Maurice Elliot. *Police Sergeant*: Floyd E. Francis. *Messenger Boy*: Nat Royster. *New Rochelle Girls (8)*: *Polly Poughkeepsie*: Mabel Ellis. *Pauline Peekskill*: Fern Minard. *Tessy Tarrytown*: Desiree Lazard. *Fannie Fordham*: Hazel Cox. *Rose Rye*: Madeline LeBoeuf. *Minnie Melrose*: Marguerite Lane. *Teresa Tuckahoe*: Nevada Maynard. *Winnie Wakefield*: Margaretta Masi. *Reporters*: Messrs. Eugene McGregor, Joe Simons, A. Claire Heath, Alf DeBall. *Policemen*: Messrs. J. S. Donnelly, Ned Achard, Frank Benor.

Act 1: Exterior of Castleton Mansion in New Rochelle. Morning. (Young.)

Act 2: Interior. Evening. (Albert.)

Act 3: Railroad Station. Next morning. (Marsden.)

MUSICAL NUMBERS
"Gentlemen of the Press"
Policemen, Reporters
"(I Want to Be a) Popular Millionaire"
D. Brian, Chorus
"Mary is a Grand Old Name"
F. Templeton
"Forty-Five Minutes from Broadway"
V. Moore, Chorus
"So Long, Mary"
F. Templeton, Chorus

1906.03 MR. BLARNEY FROM IRELAND

An Irish-American Musical Comedy-Drama in Four Acts. Play by Charles E. Blaney. (Music and lyrics by Fiske O'Hara.) Staged by Charles E. Blaney. Produced by Charles E. Blaney Amusement Company. Opened 1 January 1906 at the American Theatre and closed 6 January 1906 after 8 performances; returned 12 March 1906 to the West End Theatre and closed 17 March 1906 after 8 performances. Total: 16 performances.[104]

CAST: *Daniel Blarney*, a son of old Ireland: FISKE O'HARA. *Michael Murphy*, a wealthy real estate owner: J. P. SULLIVAN. *Charles Murphy*, his son: EDWIN A. SPARKS. *Samuel Barker*, Murphy's superintendent: W. F. WALCOTT. *Patrick Croker*, a foreman: John Martin. *Jimmie Drake*, a Bowery kid: GEORGE COOPER. *Buck Trainer*, a ward heeler: HOWARD CRAMPTON. *Foxy Tabor*, a process server: Herbert Jones. *Thomas Wilson*, a broker: A. R. Voight. *Henry Thomas*, Murphy's chauffeur: C. A. Ward. *Felix Watts*, a gardener: W. J. Walsh. *Isadore Cohen*, a merchant: J. S. Floyd. *Henry Foster*, a clerk: Charles T. Parr. *P. H. Dermott*, a policeman: William Trent. *James Conly*, a messenger: Albert Retnor. *Song Foy*, a laundryman: Henry Farwell. *Kate Murphy*, Michael's daughter: EUGENIE HAYDEN. *Sadie Croker*, Patrick's daughter: FLORENCE ROSSLAND. *Nora Scallen*, Michael's housekeeper: MAGGIE WESTON. *Little Mary McCann*, an East Side waif: QUEENIE MARBLE. *Mollie Callahan*, Kate's friend: Blanche Marble. *Mabel Jolly*, a fly girl: Nellie Barnard. *Mother Quinn*, an unfortunate: Grace Marble. *Jennie Cluett*, a stenographer: Lou Oberlie. *Winnie Thomas*, a book-keeper: Olive Carr. *Arline Mercer*, a maid: Myrtle Lorimer. *Myrtle Walton*, a clerk: Marie D. Stuart. *Tillie Dawson*, a book-keeper: Marie Bennett. *Mrs. Isadore Cohen*: Olga Wagner. *Fannie Clark*, a cloak model: Josephine Carr. *Sally Parker*, an East Side Spieler: Lavender Byers.

The action is set in New York City.

MUSICAL NUMBERS[105]
"Rollicking Blarney O"
"Like My Own Mother Dear"
"One Little Baby"
"Sunbeam of My Heart"
"(Little Girl) If You'll Be Good"

1906.04 COMING THRO' THE RYE

A Satiretta (Song Play/Musical Comedy) in Two Acts. Play (book, lyrics) by George V. Hobart. Music by A. Baldwin Sloane, J. Sebastian Hiller. Stage under the direction of Lewis Hooper. Dances arranged by Joseph C. Smith. Scenery designed by Ernest Albert. Costumes designed by F. Richard Anderson. Orchestra under the direction of Paul Schindler. Produced under the personal supervision of George V. Hobart and Will J. Block. Produced by

[98]Dropped at the time the burlesque was added to Act 2.
[99]Dropped at the time the burlesque was added to Act 2.
[100]During the run, moved to Act 1, following "Society Buds."
[101]Dropped at the time the burlesque was added to Act 2.
[102]The cast was enlarged during the run, and the running order of songs revised.
[103]Played a return engagement 13 May 1907 at the Grand Opera House for 8 performances.
[104]Played a return engagement 11 March 1907 at the American Theatre for an additional 8 performances.
[105]Not in performance order. List prepared from management press materials.

Will J. Block Amusement Company. Opened 9 January 1906 at the Herald Square Theatre and closed 10 February 1906 after 34 performances[106].

CAST: *Ippy Ipstein*, the tailor: DAN McAVOY. *Lord Battersbee*, the Englishman: FRANK DOANE. *Vandyke Brown*, the artist: JOHN PARK. *William Cactus Claude*, the cowboy: WILLIAM RILEY HATCH. *Macon Spayce*, the press agent: Burt C. Weston. *Augustus Petro*, the magazine writer: Percival Jennings. *Eaglefeather*, the Indian: Charles Swayne. *Flip*, the valet: Allen K. Foster. *Van Tweedle, Van Toodle, Van Toddle*, the Three Rounders: Harry K. Francis, Paul T. Case, Louis E. Wagner. *Broncho Boy*: Himself. *Mrs. Kobb*, the capitalist: ALICE FISHER. *Loleta*, the model: AMELIA STONE. *Bossie Claude*, the cowgirl: NENA BLAKE. *Diana Conway Black*, the magazine writer: GEORGIA KELLY. *Countess Christiana*, the imposter: Joseph Standish.

A Sweet Bouquet of Newports' Flora of Fashion: *Daisy Field*: Bessie Evelyn Gibson. *Rosy Day*: Florence Martin. *Pansy Potts*: Natalie Olcott. *Lily White*: Agnes Dasmar. *Pinky Lawson*: Ethel Kirkpatrick. *Violet Hughes*: Florence Randick. *Primrose Bank*: Bertha Blake. *Poppy Tulips*: Maud Mills.

Gee Gee Girls: May Murray, Esther Petrine, Janet McDonald, Maud Mills, Irene Farber, Constance Farber, Alice Sullivan, Daisy Dean, Bertha Behan.

Act 1: The temporary studio of Vandyke Brown, in Mrs. Kobb's mansion at Newport.

Act 2: At the Newport Casino.

ACT 1[107]

Opening Chorus
Ensemble
(*Music by* J. Sebastian Hiller.)

"Whoa, Bill"
R. Hatch, Chorus
(*Music by* A. Baldwin Sloane.)

"When in Love"
F. Doane

"(I Love You) Because You Are You, (Dear)"
J. Park
(*Music by* A. Baldwin Sloane.)

"Mother, Pin a Rose on Me"
D. McAvoy
(*Music by* Bob Adams, Paul Schindler. *Lyrics by* Bob Adams, Sam M. Lewis.)

"My Little Canoe" (In My Canoe)
A. Stone, Chorus
(*Music by* Ted Snyder. *Lyrics by* Ed Rose.)

[106]Played a return engagement 21 January 1907 at the Grand Opera House for 8 performances. Design and dance credits appear in out of town programs only.

[107]The show was radically rewritten and revised for its subsequent tour. All of the score (excepting "Because You Are You," "My Broncho Boy" and "The Sand Man") was dropped. Added were:

"I Know a Girl Like You"
Stella Mayhew {Mrs. Kobb}, J. Park, Billee Taylor {Macon Spayce}
(*Music and Lyrics by* Billee Taylor.)

"Mary, My Prairie Fairy"
W. R. Hatch, Chorus
(*Music by* George Lederer.)

"Spoofing"
F. Doane

"It Must Be Love"
Frank Lalor {Nott}, Florence Townshend {Lizzette, Mrs. Kobb's maid}
(*Music and Lyrics by* Raymond Brown and Leo Friedman.)

"A Woman of Importance"
S. Mayhew

"I Guess I'll Take the Train Back Home"
B. Taylor, Male Chorus
(*Music by* Billee Taylor. *Lyrics by* Jeff T. Branen.)

"Won't You Let Me Put My Arms Around You?" (or That Certainly am 'Zulu Love')
J. Park, Chorus
(*Music and Lyrics by* Bob Adams.)

"Clancy"
F. Lalor, Male Chorus

"Don't Forget"
Alma Youlin {Loleta}, Chorus

"Camp Meetin' Time"
S. Mayhew

"You're an Indian"
S. Mayhew
(*Music by* Evans Lloyd. *Lyrics by* Jeff T. Branen.)

Finale
Ensemble

ACT 2[108]

"I Don't Want to Be a Sailor"
B. Weston, Mr. Leonard[109], Chorus

"Spoontime"
J. Park, A. Stone
(*Music by* Albert Von Tilzer. *Lyrics by* Addison Burkhardt.)

"My Broncho Boy"
N. Blake, Chorus
(*Music by* A. Baldwin Sloane.)

"They Are Waiting (There) for Me"
D. McAvoy
(*Music and Lyrics by* Dave Lewis.)

"Fiji"
A. Stone, Chorus
(*Music by* A. Baldwin Sloane.)

"The Sandman"
N. Blake, Chorus

Finale
Ensemble
(*Music by* J. Sebastian Hiller.)

1906.05 THE VANDERBILT CUP

An 8-Cylinder Comic Machine Carrying Three Shoes and Eight Tubes (A Musical Comedy in Three Acts, 8 Scenes). Book by Sydney Rosenfeld. Music by Robert Hood Bowers. Lyrics by Raymond Peck. Staged by Hugh Ford. Scenery by Frank Gates and Edward A. Morange. Lighting effects by Benjamin Beerwald. Moving picture effects by The Kinetograph Company and Kliegl Brothers. Orchestra under the direction of Robert Hood Bowers. Produced by Liebler and Company (Theodore Liebler, George C. Tyler). Opened 16 January 1906 at the Broadway Theatre and closed 1 June 1906 after 143 performances[110].

CAST (People in the car, in the order in which they are likely to be hit): *Newt Offut*, a hill climber: Charles Dow Clark. *Mrs. Willets*, mother of Dorothy: Grace Gaylor Clark. *Theodore Banting*, an Equitable attorney at law, and other things: OTIS HARLAN. *Miss Carstairs*, Dorothy's music teacher and chaperone: Blanche Chapman. *Dorothy Willetts*: ELSIE JANIS. *Dexter Joyce*, a wine agent: AUBREY BOUCICAULT. *Clerk of the Marjorie Wellington Hotel*: Charles Dickson. *Detective in the Marjorie Wellington Hotel*: Lillian Nicholson. *Stockholders (6) in the Marjorie Wellington Hotel*, known as the Six Crusty Dames: *Mrs. Hillrace*: Helen Weathersby. *Mrs. Sylvester*: Kate Mayhew. *Mrs. Filestrom*: Grace Griswold. *Mrs. Herkimer*: Blanche Rice. *Mrs. Dillenberg*: Sallie Berge. *Mrs. Ostrand*: Marie Messner. *Bell-girls of the Marjorie Wellington Hotel (8)*: *Winnifred*: Bessie Mills. *Eloise*: Lillian Nicholson. *Gwynne*: Kate Buckley. *Elaine*: Bessie Graham. *Pearl*: Muriel Wilbur. *Marion*: Daisy Leon. *Freda*: Blanche Morrell. *Maude*: Margaret Love. *Leon*, waiter at the Garden City Hotel: Percy Janis. *Celeste*, elevator girl at the Marjorie Wellington Hotel: Kate Graham. *Kate Croops*, the porter: Ella Hatton. *Inkie North*, Western Union Messenger Girl: Violet Duval. *Gaspard*, an honest French chauffeur: HENRY BERGMAN. *Curt Willetts*, who "got rich quickly," uncle of Dorothy: HENRY V. DONNELLY. *Clarinda Larkspur*, who objects to a speed limit: EDITH DECKER. *Mr. Boxwood*. President of the Gasoline Trust: JACQUES KRUGER. *Arthur*, his chainless hopeless: F. Newton Lindo. *Flowers of the Comic Opera (4)*: *Rose*: Dorothy Kent. *Lily*: Gertrude Grant. *Violet*: Eloise Steele. *Pansy*: Elsa Rheinhardt. *Male Quartette*: Messrs. Tomasso, Odell, Mertimer, Bosher. (*Whirlwind Dance Specialty*: The Constantine Sisters). *Garage Owners, Other Robbers, Bell-Girls, Guests, Naval Officers, Cadets, Sailors, Sight-seers, and others.*

Act 1, Scene 1: The Willett's Home. (No gasoline.) *Scene 2*: En route to New York. (Get a horse.) *Scene 3*: The Marjorie Wellington Hotel, New York City. (An Up-to-Date Garage.)

Act 2, Scene 1: The Veranda of the Garden City Hotel, Long Island. 5 A.M. (The perfect clutch.) *Scene 2*: Parking place at Mineola, Long Island. (The start. Space $50 a foot.) *Scene 3*: A glimpse of a race. Introducing Barney Oldfield's great mechanical effect, showing two automobiles going at the rate of a mile a minute. *Scene 4*: The finish.

[108]Incidental to Act 2 was a Burlesque of "The Squaw Man." Program note: "The music used during the "Squaw Man" travesty was composed by Theodore Bendix, and loaned by him for this production."

[109]No Mr. Leonard appears in the cast list.

[110]Costumes uncredited. Played a return engagement the following season 7 January 1907 at the New York Theatre for 40 additional performances; 1 April 1907 at the Grand Opera House for 8 performances. See separate entry in that season.

Act 3: The Willett's Club House on Long Island.

ACT 1

Overture and Pastoral

"So I've Been Told" (Duet)
A. Boucicault, E. Janis

"Vanderbilt Cup" Gallop

"The Lament of the Crusty Dames"

"The Little Chauffeur"
E. Decker

"If You Were I, and I Were You" (If I Were You, and You Were I)
A. Boucicault, Male Quartet

Finale

ACT 2[111]

Descriptive Opening

"Somewhere in the World (There's a Little Girl for Me)"
A. Boucicault, Male Quartet

"Wine, Women and Song"
O. Harlan, Girls of the Comic Opera
Introducing the Constantine Sisters (Whirlwind Dancers).

"The Ride to the Course" (Descriptive)

"My Houseboat Beau" (Let Me Be Your Houseboat Beau)[112]
E. Janis, Chorus

Finale

ACT [113]

"If You Were Lost to Me"[114]
E. Decker

Elsie Janis

"The Fatal Curse of Beauty"
Crusty Dames

Elsie Janis

Finale

1906.06 HAPPY HOOLIGAN'S TRIP AROUND THE WORLD

A Spectacular Musical Comedy in Three Acts. Constructed for Laughing Purposes Only. Book and lyrics by Maurice Hagerman. Music by James T. Brymn. Directed by M. L. Heckert. Chorus and ensembles by J. Fletcher Rivers. Scenery by Ernest Albert. Costumes by Will R. Barnes. Music director, Leo Merriman. Produced by Joe Pettingill. Opened 22 January 1906 at the Murray Hill Theatre and closed 27 January 1906 after 8 performances; returned 9 April 1906 to the Thalia Theatre for an additional 8 performances. Total: 16 performances.

CAST: *Happy Hooligan*, a national character, in and out of luck: JACK LYLE. *Donald McGregor*, a schemer, in love with the widow: JOSEPH J. SULLIVAN. *Max Guggenheimer*, another schemer, looking for wealth: AL LEWIS. *Charley Flipp*, secretary to the widow, in love with Rose: CHARLES HANLEY. *Widow Johnson*, suddenly wealthy, on a tour of the world: VIOLET STALEY. *Rose*, her niece, in love with Mr. Flipp: Mlle. VALESCA. *Station Master*: William Jackson. *First Cadet*: S. Bohannan. *Second Cadet*: Bill Pooley. *Third Cadet*: S. Boas. *A Spikey*: Chris. Alsworth. *Dudesky*: Cyril Alden. *Minister*: Dudley McAdee. *Hiram Green*: John Welsh. *Russian Guard*: William Norman. *Jap General*: Rel Worthall. *Policeman*: Bert Cannon. *Mr. Con-Sumptive*: Tom Sharkey.

Automobile Girls (6): *Mabel*: Maria Marshall. *Coral*: May Collier. *Pearl*: Millie Dermott. *Sapphire*: Lucille Elliott. *Camelia*: Bess Hirst. *Rosetta*: Blanche Buegler. *Russian Maidens (6)*: *Katiesky*: Margie Howard. *Lenasky*: Hattie Fox. *Fritsisky*: Salina Marshall. *Whilamenasky*: Marie Bailey. *Philopemasky*: Anna Courtney. *Katarsnasky*: Louise Richards. (*Trans-Atlantic Four*: S. Bohannan, B. Pooley, W. Norman, S. Boas.)

Act 1: Waiting Room at Kidalova Railroad Station, near Manchuria, close to the firing line, between the Russians and Japanese.

Act 2: Menlo Park, Tokio. The Feast of the Cherry Blossoms. A Japanese Street Car in action.

Act 3: Pawnbrokers Shop on Market Street, San Francisco, California. Six months later.

ACT 1[115]

Opening Number
C. Alsworth, W. Jackson, S. Boas, S. Bohannan

"The Russian Maidens"
Company

"Why Don't You Try?"
C. Hanley, Mlle. Valesca

"Molly O"
J. Sullivan, Company

Specialty
J. Lyle, Company

Military Drill
Chorus

"Railroad" (Finale)
Company

ACT 2

"Moonlight"
Mlle. Valesca, Company

Specialty
Trans-Atlantic Four

Specialty
C. Hanley, Mlle. Valesca

"Cherry Blossoms"
Company

"Yokahama"
Mlle. Valesca, Company

ACT 3

"Auction Day"
Company

"Easy Street"
A. Lewis, Company

"Bull Frog and Coon"
V. Staley, Company

"The Old Black Crow"
J. Lyle, Company

"Away to the Dungeon Cell"
Company

"To Our Homes We'll Go" (Finale)
Company

1906.07 MEXICANA

A Comic Opera in Three Acts. Book and lyrics by Clara Driscoll and Robert B. Smith[116]. Music by Raymond Hubbell. Staged by R. H. Burnside. Orchestra under the direction of Herman Perlet. Produced by Sam S. and Lee Shubert (Inc.) Opened 29 January 1906 at the Lyric Theatre and closed 7 April 1906 after 82 performances[117].

CAST: *Johnny Rocks*, a Wall Street broker: THOMAS Q. SEABROOKE. *Tita*, an Indian girl, vender of pottery: CHRISTIE MacDONALD. *Captain Carmona*, an officer in the Mexican army: JOSEPH HERBERT. *Juan Adrian*, an Indian pulque seller: EDWARD MARTINDEL. *Senorita Margarita Juarez*, daughter of the governor of a Mexican state: CARO ROMA. *Rodrigo Cortinez*, a Mexican of wealth and leader of the revolutionists: Edmund Stanley. *Senora Mendoza*, aunt to Tita: Maggie More. *Ines*: Blanche Deyo. *Manuel*: Harry Wallace. *Pedro*: Almon Knowles. *Duena to Margarita*: Helene St. John. *Chorus of Market People, Vacqueros, Senoritas, Rurales, Peons, Haciendados, Caballeros, Cargadores and Revolutionists.*

[111]Miss Janis will introduce her imitations during Act 2. During the intermission, Miss Janis' imitation of Yvette Guilbert will precede Act 3.
[112]Also known as "My Household Beau."
[113]During Act 3, will be introduced a little burlesque of "The Lion and the Mouse" by William Oakland.
[114]Replaced after opening by:
"The Light That Lies in Girlish Eyes" (The Light of Girlish Eyes)
E. Decker

[115]No New York program available. Cast credits and musical numbers prepared from a program dated 29 January 1906 at the Grand Opera House, Boston, Massachusetts.
[116]Published sheet music credits Robert B. Smith alone with lyrics, not Driscoll.
[117]Settings, costumes uncredited.

Act 1: The Market Square of a Mexican town. Early morning.

Act 2: The patio of the hacienda of Rodrigo Cortinez. Noon of the next day.

Act 3: The Borda Gardens on the night of a fiesta.

ACT 1
- Opening Chorus
- "How (Now) Do You Account for That?"
  - J. Herbert, Chorus
- "United We Stand"
  - E. Stanley, Chorus
- "Take Care, Senor"
  - C. Roma, E. Stanley
- "Hark to the Voice of Your Lover"
  - E. Martindell
- "The Fickle Weather Vane"
  - C. MacDonald
- Entrance of Johnny Rocks
  - Chorus
- "(I Am) The Wizard of Wall Street"
  - T. Q. Seabrooke
- "Graft"
  - T. Q. Seabrooke, C. MacDonald, Chorus
- Finale

ACT 2
- Opening Chorus
- "(The) Lorelei"
  - E. Martindell
- "We've Got a Lot to Learn"
  - T. Q. Seabroke, C. MacDonald
- "Mrs. O'Ho"[118]
  - T. Q. Seabrooke
- "Major Margery"
  - C. MacDonald, Chorus
- "I've Heard So Much About You"
  - E. Stanley, C. MacDonald
- Finale

ACT 3
- Opening Chorus
- "The Bolero"
  - C. Roma, T. Q. Seabrooke, J. Herbert, M. Moore
- "I Was Just Supposing"
  - C. MacDonald, E. Stanley, M. Moore
- Finale

1906.08 RUFUS RASTUS

A Musical Extravaganza in Two Acts. Book by William D. Hall. Music and lyrics by Ernest Hogan and Tom Lemonier; ensemble numbers by Joe Jordan and H. Lawrence Freeman. Lyrics by Frank Williams. Production staged by J. Ed Green[119]. Scenery painted by Castle & Harvey. Costumes designed by Will Barnes. Musical director, H. Lawrence Freeman. Produced by (Jules) Hurtig & (Harry) Seamon. Opened 29 January 1906 at the American Theatre, moved 5 February 1906 to the Metropolis Theatre and closed 10 February after 16 performances; returned 26 February 1906 to the West End Theatre for an additional 8 performances. Total: 24 performances.

CAST: *John Drake*, second waiter at the Ponce de Leon Hotel: J. F. Morres. *Dr. Fo-Jo*, dealer in lucky charms: J. LEUBRIE HILL. *Sophronia*, housekeeper at Ponce de Leon Hotel: ANNA COOKE PANKEY. *Hugo*, the porter, successful and satisfied: Harry Fiddler. *Noah Beasley*, head waiter at the Ponce de Leon Hotel: J. ED. GREEN. *Angelica Newcomb*, looking for a job for her friend: A. D. Byrd. *Bill B. Dam*: Will Wilkins. *Reverend Nightingale*, Slipback Newcomb, a man of many callings: Robert A. Kelly. *Federica*, their educated daughter: ALICE MACKEY. *Snowflack*, their youngest offspring: Muriel Ringold. *Enoch*, the bell boy: Theodore Pankey. *Cousin Monk*: Theodore Pankey. *Catasterphe*: Theodore Pankey. *Lazarus Tuttle*, stage manager and theatrical promoter: HENRY TROY. *Selina Giltedge*, prima donna of Coontown 400: CARITA DAY. *Mandy Jones*, leading soprano of Ragtime Opera Company: MAMIE EMERSON. *Rufus Rastus*, unfortunate: ERNEST HOGAN. *Samson Strong*, with hallucinations: Harry Gilliam. *Officer*: William Spicer. *Belmoral*, Hugo's sweetheart: Pauline Hackney. *Floor Manager*: Bill Moore. *Floor Help, Jubilee Singers, Minstrels, Terpsichorean Artists, Masqueraders.*

Scrub Women: Pearl Lavan, Sarah Green, Amy Leslie. *Nurse Girls*: Pearl Brown, Jeannette Foster, Madge Warren, Bertha Gillespie. *Chambermaids*: Nellie Dansy, Georgia Mickey, Maude Jones, Mollie Sullivan. *Laundresses*: Pauline Hackney, Pinky Cooper, Marie Thomas, Anita Wilkins. *Bell Boys*: Jennie Thompson, Maude Turner, Mabel Turner. *Yardmen*: Billy Moore, Matt Houseley, George Lynnier, William Spicer. *Waiters*: Will Wilkins, Angelo Housely, R. C. Baker, J. F. Morres. *Footmen*: William Pierce, J. L. Grant, Beverly Housley. *Chefs*: James Worles, Edward Gray, Walter Robertson, John Hill. *Newsboys*: Pearl Brown, Maude Turner, Amy Leslie, Jennie Thompson, Sarah Green, Jeanette Foster, Mabel Turner, Madge Warren.

Act 1, Scene 1: Rotunda of Ponce de Leon Hotel, St. Augustine, Florida. Two days before opening of season. *Scene 2*: Tenement Row. Treasury Street, the quarters of the help. *Scene 3*: Palmetto Bower. (Original conception by Ernest Hogan.)

Act 2, Scene 1: The Wharf at St. Augustine. *Scene 2*: Exterior of Madison Square Garden. *Scene 3*: Interior of Madison Square Garden.

ACT 1[120]
- "What We're Supposed to Do"
  - Ensemble
- "Mammy"
  - (R. A. Kelly, A. D. Byrd, A. Mackey, M. Ringold, T. Pankey [Enoch])
- "My Mobile Mandy"
  - (M. Emerson)
- "Oh (Say) Wouldn't It Be a Dream?"
  - (E. Hogan)
  - (*Music by* Joe Jordan. *Lyrics by* Earl C. Jones.)
- "Cockadoodle Doo"
- "Watermelon"
- "Consolation"
  - (H. Troy)
- "Is Everybody Happy?"
  - (E. Hogan)

ACT 2
- "The (Beautiful) Isle of Repose"
  - (A. C. Pankey)
  - (*Music by* H. Lawrence Freeman.)
- Songs and Dance of the South
- ["Old Kentucky Home"
  - S. Green]

---

[118]Dropped during the run.

[119]During subsequent tour, Ernest Hogan assumed directorial credit.

[120]The production, especially Act 2, was substantially revised during its subsequent tour. A Brooklyn program dated 10 December 1906 indicates that "My Mobile Mandy," "Cockadoodle Doo," "Watermelon" and all the songs in Act 2 had been replaced by:
- "Dixie Anna Lou" Act 1)
  - A. Mackey
- Musical number for scene of Palmetto Bower
- Bones and Tambourines
  - Chorus
- Medley
  - Company
- "Grandma's Kitchen Floor" (Act 1)
  - H. Troy
- Character Impersonations
  - H. Fidler
- "Enjoy Yourself with Me" (Act 1 Finale)
  - E. Hogan, Company
- "Old Kentucky Home" (Act 2)
  - G. Harvey
- "I'll Love You All the Time" (Act 2)
  - C. Day, E. Hogan
- "Moon Boy" (Act 2)
  - Chorus
- "The Song of the Monkey and the Bear" (Act 2)
  - L. Turner [Snowflake], A. Gillam [Cousin Monk]
  - (*Music by* Ernest Hogans. *Lyrics by* Lester Walton.)
- "Toreador" (Act 2)
  - F. F. Brown [Signo Brury], L. Knox [Mandy Jones], Chorus

"If Peter Was a Colored Man"
"Good-bye, Old Dixie Land"
"Newsboys' Life"
"The Hornet and the Bee"
(C. Day)
"Lilly's Wedding Day"
Finale

1906.09

THE GRAFTER

A Musical Storyette (Musical Play) in Three Acts. Book by Guy F. Steeley. Music by W. C. Polla. Lyrics by James O'Dea. Staged by James Gorman. Produced by E. D. Stair. Opened 29 January 1906 at the Grand Opera House and closed 3 February 1906 after 8 performances; re-opened 12 February 1906 at the West End Theatre for an additional 8 performances. Total: 16 performances.[121]

CAST: *Bill Grafter*, watch his method: HAP WARD. *Bud Wilson*, in great demand: WILLIAM FRIEND. *Baron Von Hirsh*, somebody in the Old Country: William Maxwell. *Jack Desmond*, an artist: CHARLES BATES. *Mr. Burton*, has a wife and daughter: Donald Harold. G. *Horace Homer*, a real author: Tony Williams. *Borne G. Jones*, Jack's friend: Richard Barry. *Ella Burton*, an only daughter: WINNIFRED SPAULDING. *Mrs. Burton*, President of the Homer Club: May Thompson. *Mrs. Wilson*, mislaid her husband: Daisy Dudley. *Mercy Hanks*, the deserted bride: LUCY DALY. *Phoebe*, servant: LUCY DALY.

Jack's artist friends, models, bellboys and waitresses, Ladies and Gentleme of the Hunt Club: Kitty Parks, Helen Clark, Kitty Melville, Virginia Royden, Emma Marshall, Elizabeth Vizzard, Francisca Parker, Carrie Donnell, Helen Byrnes, Meta Pienza, Kitty Wood, Mildred Baron, Minnie Mason, Nellie DeGrasse, Lillie DeGrasse, Eva Fortesque, Opal Pursell, Rosalie Williams, Mabel Porter, George Johson, William Toland, Charles Ray, Tom Fisher, Jack Manley, William Igar, Harry Sickford, Harry Humphreys, D. E. Latham, Tommy Waddell, Morris Tangua.

Act 1: Jack Studio, New York City. Morning.

Act 2: St. Regis Court, New York City. Next afternoon.

Act 3: Mr. Burton's Country home. Next evening.

ACT 1
"Artists and Models" (Opening Chorus)
Company
"My Picture of You"
C. Bates, W. Spaulding, Company
"They Sent for Me"
H. Ward, Company
"My Bungalow Babe" (My Babe of the Bungalow)
L. Daly, Company

ACT 2
"Coachmen and Maids"
Company
"In Dear Old Grandma's Day"
W. Maxwell, Company
"I Could Use Five"
H. Ward, W. Friend
"(On) Independence Day"
L. Daly, Company

ACT 3
"Hear the Hunter's Horn"
Company
"Guess Again"
C. Bates, W. Spaulding, Company
"My Indian Summer Moon"
W. Spaulding, Company
"(Little) Mary Wise"
L. Daly, Company
(*Music by* William C. Pola and W. Dailey.)
Finale
Company

[121]Scenery, costumes and musical director uncredited.

1906.10

GAY NEW YORK

A Comedy with Music in Two Acts. Book (and lyrics) by Maurice Hageman[122]. Music by Harry Trappert. Staged by M. L. Heckert. Ensemble arranged by Edward B. Adams. Scenery by Ernest Albert, C. W. Valentine. Costumes by Will R. Barnes, Frank Hayden, J. Henry Rowley. Electrical effects by Joseph Menchen. Produced by Charles E. Barton. Opened 5 February 1906 at the Murray Hill Theatre and closed 10 February 1906 after 8 performances.

CAST: *Herman Schultz*, a fashionable ladies' tailor: DAN MASON. *Bertha Schultz*, his wife: LOUISE SANFORD. *Julia Schultz*, their daughter: LEAH KEINZ. *Frank Swift*, a photographer, Schultz's nephew: CHARLES E. FOREMAN. *Mlle. Florizell*, a famous dancer: LILLIAN HOERLEIN. *Marie Darcey*, M.D., Vassar College: KATHRYN BARTLETT. *Hon. W. B. Jennings*, Judge of the Supreme Court: Theodore Peters. *Wilbur Jennings*, his only son: EDWARD B. ADAMS. *Walter Brook Jennings* of the Swedish Massage Establishment: Ed. Brennan. *Sam*, servant of the Schultz family: Joseph F. Willard. *Officer Ketchim*: William Butler. *Swifty*, a lively up-to-date messenger: Dan W. Mack. *Fannie*, a maid of the Schultz family: Carroll Hamilton. *Polly Primrose*, a cloak model: Bessie Bartell. *Dolly Van Tassel*, the pet of the Schultz establishment: Lulu Lee. *Donna Dean*, queen of the golf links: Viole Rio. *Marjorie Darje*, a military girl: Nellie Cameron. *Chorus of Marie's friends, cloak models, college students, military girls, golf girls, paraders, etc.*

Models and Students: Lulu Lee, Nellie Cameron, Helen Lawton, Myrtle Paul, Dottie Williams, May Martin, Hazel Claire, Kittie Chester, Lillie Belmont, Bessie Bartell, Louise Mason, Violet Rio. *Newport Girls*: (same as Models and Students). *Kinkee Dee Girls*: Lulu Lee, Nellie Cameron, Helen Lawton, Myrtle Paul, Violet Rio, Lillie Belmont, Kittie Chester, Hazel Claire, May Martin, Pansy LeRoy, Marie Roy, Marie Daley, Louise Mason, Bessie Bartell. *Congress of Nations*: America: Nellie Cameron, Carroll Hailton; England: Lillie Belmont, Hazel Claire; Scotland: Bonnie Grace, Marie Daley; Ireland: Bessie Bartell, Helen Lawton; France: Lulu Lee, Louise Mason; Russia: Myrtle Paul, Kittie Chester; Italy: Violet Rio, Pansy LeRoy; Germany: May Martin, Dottie Williams.

Act 1: Schultz's Fifth Avenue Residence, New York. Present time.

Act 2: Schultz's summer villa, Long Island.

ACT 1[123]
"Why So Late" (Concerted Medley)
C. E. Foreman, Company
"The Model's Complaint"
D. Mason, Company
"Explanation"[124] (Duet)
L. Hoerlein, C. E. Foreman
"Gay New York" (Trio)
D. Mason, L. Hoerlein, C. E. Foreman
"Newport by the Sea" (Solo)
E. B. Adams
"Message from Mars" (Song)
"Students on a Lark" (Finale)
Entire Company

ACT 2[125]
"On the Links" (Concerted Number)
L. Hoerlein, Company
"Julia" (Song)
E. B. Adams, Company
"Julia" (Quartette)
L. Hoerlein, L. Keinz, E. B. Adams, C. E. Foreman, Company
"Dainty Mignon"
K. Bartlett

[122]Adapted from an unidentified old German farce.
[123]Musical numbers prepared from a New Rochelle program dated 19 February 1906.
[124]Replaced during subsequent tour by:
"Carissima" (Valse de Concert)
L. Hoerlein
(*Music and Lyrics by* Arthur Penn.)
[125]Added during subsequent tour to Act 2:
"Nightingale" (Song)
L. Hoerlein, Company
"Sallie" (Character Song and Dance)
E. B. Adams, C. Hamilton, Company
"Chu-Chu-Cars" (Quartette)
L. Hoerlein, L. Keinz, E. B. Adams, C. E. Foreman, Company

"Hinkee Dee" (Song)
D. Mason, Company
March
C. E. Foreman, Company
Finale

1906.11 GEORGE WASHINGTON, JR.

A Musical Play in Three Acts, 4 Scenes[126]. Book, music and lyrics by George M. Cohan. Staged by George M. Cohan. Settings by John Young, Ernest Albert. Costumes designed by F. Richard Anderson. Music arranged and conducted by Charles J. Gebest. Produced by Sam H. Harris. Opened 12 February 1906 at the Herald Square Theatre and closed 21 April 1906 after 81 performances[127].

CAST: *James Belgrave*, a United States Senator: JERRY J. COHAN. *William Hopkins*, a United States Senator: EUGENE O'ROURKE. *Lord Rothburt*: Cleveland Nicholson. *George Belgrave*, the Senator's son: GEORGE M. COHAN. *Eaton Ham*, of Alexandria: HARRY MONTGOMERY. *Superintendent Dodge* of Mt. Vernon: Frank McNish, Jr. *Bell boy*, of Willard Hotel: Frank McNish, Jr. *McFadden*, a tourist: Joseph Leslie. *Hotel clerk*: John Kauffman. *Page*, at Mt. Vernon: Walter Olcott. *Colonel Greene*: Earl C. Stanley. *Colonel Browne*: William Leyle. *Colonel Pincus*: John Willard. *Colonel Williams*: Joseph Levere. *Porter*, of Willard Hotel: Lee Myers. *Drums*: Samuel Avedon. *Mandolin and Guitar Quartette*: Messrs. Butin, Tipaldi, Rostain, Whitlaw. *Mrs. Stebbins*, Senator Belgrave's widowed sister: HELEN F. COHAN. *Evelyn Rothburt*, the Lord's accomplice: TRULY SHATTUCK. *Telephone operator*: Margie Rhodes. *Dolly Johnson*, Senator Hopkins' niece: ETHEL LEVEY.

Act 1: Exterior Washington's home, Mt. Vernon, Virginia, facing the Potomac. (Young.)

Act 2: Corridor Willard Hotel, Washington, D.C. (Albert.)

Act 3, Scene 1: Hallway leading to ball-room, Willard Hotel. One year later, during Senator Belgrave's campaign for Governor of Rhode Island. (Young.) *Scene 2*: Exterior Senator Belgrave's residence, Pawtucket, Rhode Island. (Young.)

MUSICAL NUMBERS
"He Was a Wonderful Man"
Guides, Old Ladies
"Virginia" (Ethel Levey's Virginia Song)
E. Levey
"The Grand Old Rag"[128]
G. M. Cohan
"I'll Be There With Bells On"
Chorus
"I've Never Been Over There"
T. Shattuck, Chorus
"All Aboard for Broadway"
Chorus
"Wedding of the Blue and Gray"
E. Levey, G. M. Cohan
"Colonial Chorus"
Chorus
"If Washington Came to Life"
G. M. Cohan
Finale
Company

1906.12 JUST A JOKE

A Miniature Musical Comedy in One Act, devised as a curtain raiser to the play "Lucky Miss Dean" by Sidney Bowkett[129]. Book, music and lyrics by Porter Emerson Brown. Produced by Katie Barry. Opened 12 February 1906 at the Madison Square Theatre and closed 17 February 1906 after 8 performances.[130]

[126]Billed as "The Yankee Doodle Comedian in His Latest American Musical Play," or on tour as "His National Song Show."
[127]Played a return engagement 11 February 1907 at the New York Theatre for 32 performances. For detail see separate entry in that season.
[128]In later programs titled "The Grand Old Flag."
[129]JUST A JOKE replaced a curtain-raiser drama called "The Daughter Of The Tumbrills" by Walter E. Grogan which opened, along with "Lucky Miss Dean," 5 February 1906 at the Madison Square.
[130]No program available. Katie Barry performed her musical specialties.

CAST: KATIE BARRY, GEORGE WILSON, JOHN ALDEN.

Scene: A Hotel.

1906.13 LOVERS AND LUNATICS

A Musical Farce in Two Acts. Play and music by Walter Coleman Parker. Directed by Charles Sinclair. Scenery by P. Dodd Ackerman. Costumes by J. Henry Kowley. Musical director, Herman A. Meybohm. Produced by the Mittenthal Brothers Amusement Co., Inc. Opened 19 February 1906 at the Metropolis Theatre and closed 24 February 1906 after 8 performances; returned 5-10 March 1906 to the West End Theatre for 8 performances. Total : 16 performances.

CAST: *Richard Hamilton*: JOHNNY FORD. *Ikey Rosenstein*: JOE MORRIS. *Heinrich Dinkelspiel*: SAM SHANNON. *Lieutenant George Richmond*: GEORGE P. WATSON. *Cornelia Dinkelspiel*: J. Maurice Holden. *Nellie Richmond*: Florence Little. *Nell*: Henrietta Tedro. *Nellie Huntington*: MAYME GEHRUE.

Escaped Lunatics (4): *Admiral Togo*: Philip Zuker. *Napoleon*: J. A. Byrne, Jr. *Caesar the Great*: J. Davenport Hamilton. *Czar of Russia*: William W. Benedict.

Gentlemen Tourists (4): *Mr. Henderson*: Albert Michaelson. *Mr. Bradley*: Charles A. Cummins. *Mr. Condon*: John T. Barrett. *Mr. Denton*: Charles W. Green.

The Carolina Girls (11): *Raleigh*: Marie Landis. *Henderson*: Bessie Moulton. *Monroe*: Mae Tobin. *Hatteras*: Edythe James. *Beaufort*: Dorothy Clarke. *Madison*: Kathryn Wolfe. *Clayton*: Amy Berry. *Darlington*: Rose Ford. *Alston*: Madeline Keene. *Columbia*: Olive Claremont.

Debutantes (6): *Anita Ainsmere*: Maude Kyles. *Gladys Merryweather*: Frances Fairfield. *Irma Irving*: Flo Mardell. *Beatrice Braithwaite*: Marguerite Vinton. *Gwendoline Carew*: Sarah Kyles. *Angelet Lamour*: Cannie Culpepper. *Hunters, Auto Girls, Maids, Hussars, Lunatics, Flower Girls, Beaus and Belles.*

Act 1: House and grounds of Heinrich Dinkelspiel adjoining the State Lunatic Asylum.

Act 2: Drawing room, Dinkelspiel Manor.

ACT 1[131]
"Off to the Hunt"
S. Shannon, Chorus
"The Four Lunatics"
W. W. Benedict, J. A. Byrne, Jr., J. D. Hamilton, P. Zuker
"Sly Old Fox"
S. Shannon, Chorus
"The Lovers' Quarrel"
G. P. Watson, F. Little
"My Own Boy"
M. Gehrue, Hussars
"The Parody Man"
J. Morris
"Roll On, Silver Moon"
G. P. Watson
"Automobiling"
J. Ford, Auto Girls
Finale
General Ensemble

ACT 2
"Dainty Housemaids We"
Housemaids' Chorus
"True Blue"
F. Little, Housemaids
"Prince of Borneo"
J. Morris, Yiddish Chorus
"Georgianna Dunn"
J. Morris
"You're the Kind of a Girl I Like"
J. Ford, Summer Girls
"Carolina"
M. Gehrue, P. Zuker, Carolina Girls
"Would You Do It?"
M. Gehrue, J. Ford

[131]No New York program available. Song list prepared from a Wilkes-Barre, Pennsylvania program dated 20 September 1906. Also performed as per reviews: "He's Ma Romeo", "I'se Juliet", "I Read About It in a Book" (sung by S. Shannon).

"Would You Do It?" (reprise)
J. Morris, J. M. Holden
Finale
General Ensemble

1906.14 ABYSSINIA

A Musical Oddity (Comedy) in One Act, a Prologue and 4 Scenes. Book and lyrics by Jesse A. Shipp and Alex Rogers. Music by Will Marion Cook and Bert A. Williams. Additional lyrics by Earl C. Jones. Staged by Alex Rogers and Jesse A. Shipp. Dances arranged by Aida Overton Walker. Scenery by Ernest Albert, Louis Young. Costumes by Eaves. Orchestra under the direction of James J. Vaughn. Director of vocal music, W. C. Elkins. Produced by Melville Raymond. Opened 20 February 1906 at the Majestic Theatre and closed 17 March 1906 after 31 performances.[132]

CAST: *From the U.S.A.*: *Jasmine Jenkins*, always with the money: BERT A. WILLIAMS. *Rastus Johnson*, U.S.A.,——"The Money": GEORGE W. WALKER. *Elder Fowler*, pastor of the largest colored Baptist church in Wilson County, Kansas: Charles H. Moore. *Miss Primly*, a dear friend of Ras' family: LOTTIE WILLIAMS. *Aunt Callie Parker*, Ras' aunt and leading sister in Fowler's flock: Hattie McIntosh. *Wong Foo*, a Chinese cook: George Catlin. *Serena*, Miss Primly's niece: Maggie Davis. *Lucinda, Nettie, Daphne, James*, friends of Ras' and members of Fowler's choir: Lavinia Rogers, Ada Guigesse, Aline Cassel, Craig Williams.

From Abyssinia: *King Menelik II*, king of kings of Abyssinia: R. HENRI STRANGE. *The Affa Negus Tegulet*, King Menelik's chief justice: J. A. SHIPP. *Shambal Bollasso*, Tegulet's nephew, a captain in King Menelik's army: ALEX ROGERS. *Zamish*, Tegulet's trusted servant: J. E. Lightfoot. *Omreeka, Semra*, Shambal Bollasso's escort: Charles L. Moore, William Foster. *Hadji*, a messenger: William C. Elkins. *Tai Tu*, queen of Abyssinia: ANNIE ROSS. *Varinoe, Allamo*, market girls: Hattie Hopkins, Katie Jones. *Miriam*, also a market girl: AIDA OVERTON WALKER.

Flower Girls, Sweet Sellers, Tej Girls, Ribbon Girls, Wood Carriers, Water Carriers, Citizen Types, etc.: Misses Clarke, Christian, DePas, DeMoss, E. Brady, B. Brady, Busch, Tapley, Payne, Martin, Hawkins, Meredith, Day, Ellis, Vaughn, Puggsley, Allen, Barnes, Bolden, Mitchell, Adams, M. Brown, L. Brown, Ringgold. *Soldiers, Servants, Priests, Donkey Boys, Citizens, etc.*: Messrs. Tapley, Payne, F. Williams, Henderson, Gibbs, Rex, Chenault, R. Young, Thomas, Hall, Guillaume, Saulsbury, Lillard, Randall, Roberts, Johnson.

Prologue: Mountain Pass near the capital, Addis Ababa. An Abyssinian Guard House. Monday evening. *Scene 1*: Borema Spring, the last camping place before reaching Addis Ababa, the capital of Abyssinia. Tuesday at sunset. (Albert.) *Scene 2*: Market place outside the walls of Addis Ababa. Wednesday. (Albert.) *Scene 3*: King Menelik's audience chamber. Thursday, 5 A.M. All affairs of state and official business in Abyssinia transacted at this hour. (Young.) *Scene 4*: King Menelik's throne room. Thursday evening, the queen's birthday. (Young.)

MUSICAL NUMBERS[133]
Prologue[134]
"Ode to Menelik"
Male Chorus
"Jolly Jungle Boys"
C. Young, Male Chorus
(*Music by* Bert A. Williams. *Lyrics by* Earle C. Jones.)
Scene 1
"Ode to the Sun"
Entire Chorus
(*Lyrics by* Earle C. Jones.)
"Where My Forefathers Died"[135]
H. McIntosh, Chorus
(*Music by* Bert A. Williams. *Lyrics by* Alex Rogers.)
"Twilight at Home, Sweet Home"
C. Williams
Scene 2
"Holiday in the Market" (Opening)
Entire Chorus
"Rastus Johnson, U.S.A."
G. W. Walker, Chorus
(*Music by* Bert A. Williams. *Lyrics by* Alex Rogers.)
"Answers That You Don't Expect to Get"
L. Williams, assisted by A. Rogers, B. A. Williams
(*Lyrics by* Earle C. Jones.)
"The Lion and the Monk (Die Trying)"[136]
A. O. Walker, 9 Abyssinian Maids
(*Music by* Bert A. Williams. *Dance arranged by* A. O. Walker.)
"It's Hard to Find a King Like Me"[137]
G. W. Walker, Chorus
(*Music by* James J. Vaughn.)
"The Capture of Yaraboo" (Finale)
B. A. Williams, G. W. Walker, Chorus
Scene 3
"Here It Comes Again"[138]
B. A. Williams
(*Music by* Bert A. Williams. *Lyrics by* Alex Rogers and Earle C. Jones.)
Scene 4
"Menelik's Tribute to Queen Tai Tu"/
The Court Procession with Tai Tu and Menelik, followed by the Priests of Gondar.
The Dance of the Falasha Maids/
The Dance of the Amhara Maids
A. O. Walker, B. A. Williams, G. W. Walker,
assisted by the Drum Majors, Randall, Roberts, Johnson and the Dixie Ballet
(*Arranged by* Aida Overton Walker.)
"Good-Bye, Ethiopia"
B. A. Williams, G. A. Walker,
assisted by the Drum Majors, Randall, Roberts, Johnson, The Dixie Ballet
(*Music by* James J. Vaughn.)

1906.15 HIS MAJESTY

A Musical Diversion (Play) in Two Acts. Book, music and lyrics by Shafter Howard. Staged by Richard F. Carroll. Dances by Hugh Flaherty. Orchestra under the direction of Clarence Rogerson. Produced by Nelson Roberts. Opened 19 March 1906 at the Majestic Theatre and closed 7 April 1906 after 24 performances.

CAST: *His Majesty*: VAN RENSSELAER WHEELER. *Abel Stringham*, an operatic manager: HARRY KELLY. *Daffy Dan*: Knute Erickson. *The Hon. J. Norman Bull*: Walter F. Dyett. *R. Redington Rogers*: Herbert Carter. *Napoleon I*: William H. White. *Swifty*: Hughey [Hugh] Flaherty. *Scat*: Gus Alexander. *Dolly Dainty*: ANNA LAUGHLIN. *Miss Stella Bright*: MAY A. NAUDAIN. *Miss Back Bay*: Alice Hageman. *Sans Gene*: Emmalyn Lackaye. *Gladys Glitter*: Margaret Malcolm. *Clara Clatter*: Indiola Arnold. *Mrs. Brown* of Chicago: BLANCHE RING. *Imps, Devils, Pages, Dancers, Isabel Girls, Members of Opera Company, Summer Boys, etc.*

---

[132]Played return engagements 23 April 1906 at the West End Theatre for 8 performances, and 18 August 1906 at the Grand Opera House for 9 performances.

[133]For Grand Opera House return engagement the running order changed, and the following songs were added to the score:
"Varinoe" (Scene 1)
James Marshall

[134]For subsequent tour the prologue and Scene 1 were combined.

[135]Early in tour and for return engagement, "Twilight at Home" was replaced by:
"The Island of By-and-By"
A. O. Walker, 8 Abyssinian Maids, Double Male Quartette
(*Music by* Bert A. Williams. *Lyrics by* Alex Rogers.)
Later in the tour, "Where My Forefathers Died" was dropped.

[136]Replaced for subsequent tour by:
"I'll Keep a Warm Spot in My Heart for You"
A. O. Walker
(*Music by* J. Rosamond Johnson. *Lyrics by* James Weldon Johnson.)
Which was later replaced (also for return engagement) by:
"Build a Nest for Birdie"
A. O. Walker, Chorus
(*Music by* J. Tim Brymn. *Lyrics by* R. C. McPherson.)
And then later (1907) replaced by:
"Sweetie Dear"
A. O. Walker

[137]Replaced later in tour by:
"I'm a Rular" (I'm a R-U-L-A-R)
G. W. Walker, Chorus

[138]Replaced for return engagement and tour by:
"Let It Alone"
B. A. Williams
(*Music by* Bert A. Williams. *Lyrics by* Alex Rogers.)

Act 1: Lobby of the Styxview Hotel.

Act 2: An Island near Palm Beach.

ACT 1[139]

Opening Chorus
Imps, Devils

"His Majesty" (Entrance Song and Chorus)

"The Maid from Boston Town" (Trio)
A. Hageman, W. F. Dyett, H. Carter

Duet
V. R. Wheeler, M. A. Naudain

Songs
B. Ring

Pages' Chorus and Dance

"Conspirators"
Quintette, Male Chorus

"My Own" (Waltz Song)
M. A. Naudain

"Are You a Single or Married Man?"
B. Ring
(*Music and Lyrics by* James Reilly and Henry Gillespie.)

Finale

ACT 2

"Fairies' Chorus"

"Isabel"
W. F. Dyett

"The Maid of Arcadie"
M. A. Naudain

Song ("My Bahama Baby")
B. Ring, Male Chorus

"The Brat"
A. Laughlin

Serenade
V. R. Wheeler

"Jemima Green"
A. Hageman

"Crazyisms"
K. Erickson

(Specialty)
H. Carter, Girls

Finale

1906.16 THE PRINCE OF PILSEN

A Revival of the Musical Comedy in Two Acts[140]. Book and lyrics by Frank Pixley. Music by Gustav Luders. Staged by George Marion. Scenery by Walter Burridge. Costumes by Will R. Barnes. Produced by Henry W. Savage. Opened 19 March 1906 at the Grand Opera House and closed 24 March 1906 after 8 performances; returned 2 April 1906 to the New York Theatre and closed 14 April 1906 after 16 performances. Total this season: 24 performances.

CAST (in order of appearance): *Carl Otto, the Prince of Pilsen*, a Heidelberg student: ARTHUR DONALDSON. *Hans Wagner*, a Cincinnati brewer, travelling abroad: JESS DANDY. *Lieutenant Tom Wagner*, of the U.S. Cruiser *Annapolis*: IVAR ANDERSON. *Arthur St. John Wilberforce, Lord Shrimpton*: J. HAYDEN CLARENDON. *François*, concierge, Hotel Internationale: James E. Rome. *Sergeant Brie* of the Gendarmes: Peter Swift. *Cook's Courier*, Vassar Girl's pilot: Peter Swift. *Jimmie*, a bellboy: Pauline Huntley. *Mrs. Madison Crocker* from New York: IDA STANHOPE. *Edith Adams*, a Vassar girl: RUTH PEEBLES. *Sidonie*, Mrs. Crocker's French maid: Marguerite Ferguson. *Nellie Wagner*, Hans Wagner's daughter: MARIE WELSH.

The Heidelberg Boys (8): *Rudolph*: Ernest Armour. *Adolph*: Roy Berry. *Heinrich*: William Stenberg. *Fritz*: Frank Randall. *Ludwig*: George McAlister. *Carl*: Joseph Colville. *Oscar*: Henry Holt. *Wilhelm*: Samuel Chadwick. *American Girls (8)*: *Priscilla Plymouth*, Boston: Marie Stoner. *Frankie Friskie*, San Francisco: Hilda Eldridge. *Olive Oriole*, Baltimore: Beulah Parker. *Dollie Dixie*, New Orleans: Peggy Ballou. *Goldie Dome*, Washington: Christine Stone. *Nellie Noyes*, Chicago: Ethel Gordon. *Miss Rivers*, St. Louis: Adelaide Lee. *Pansy Penn*, Philadelphia: May Darling. *Miss Manhattan*: Ida Stanhope.

Arctic and Sea Shell Girls (8): *White Caps*: Christine Stone. *Pearlie Beach*: Flossie Brooks. *Weedie Sea*: Marie Goodwin. *Birdie Petrel*: Maude Mordaunt. *Lottie Fogge*: Helen O'Neill. *Pleasant Sayle*: Adele Johnson. *Brinie Deep*: Estelle Labart. *Bounding Billow*: Lulu Carroll. *The Bathing Girls (10)*: *Amethyst*: Pauline Huntley. *Opal*: Polly Dorsey. *Sapphire*: Grace Waldo. *Coral*: Martha Bernard. *Topaz*: Elise Krebs. *Cameo*: Marion Lyons. *Agate*: Edna Bontaine. *Diamond*: Edna Wallace. *Pearl*: Madeline May. *Emerald*: May Wilson. *The Gendarmes (4)*: *Vidocq*: Henry Holt. *Sherlock*: William Thompson. *Hawkshaw*: Eric Maxwell. *Carter*: Robert Mallory. *French Girls, Flower Girls, Naval Cadets, Fox Hunters, French Maids, Waiters.*

1906.17 THE SOCIAL WHIRL

A Musical Comedy in Two Acts. Book by Charles Doty and Joseph Herbert. Music by Gustav Kerker. Lyrics by Joseph Herbert. (Interpolated songs by George A. Spink, E. Ray Goetz, James O'Dea, Anne Caldwell, and Charles J. Ross.) Staged by R. H. Burnside. Costumes by Mme. (Caroline) Siedle. Orchestra under the direction of Gustav Kerker. Produced by Sam S. and Lee Shubert (Inc.). Opened 9 April 1906 at the Casino Theatre and closed 15 September 1906 after 195 performances[141].

CAST: *Violet Dare*, a Broadway favorite: ADELE RITCHIE. *Mrs. James Ellingham*, a society leader: MABEL FENTON. *Beezy*, colored attendant in manicure parlors: MAUDE RAYMOND. *Germaine Du Monde*, owner of the manicure parlors: BLANCHE DEYO. *Mrs. Hoover Thorpe*, a society widow: Caroline Locke. *Kittie La Verne*, soubrette from the West: ADA LEWIS. *Julian Endicott*, a self-made man: CHARLES J. ROSS. *James Ellingham*, on the right side of the market: FREDERIC BOND. *Jack Ellingham*, his son: WILLARD CURTISS. *Artie Endicott*, representative of "The Social Whirl": JOSEPH COYNE. *Sandy Graham*, son of James Ellingham: Mark E. Heisey. *Lem Hicks*, his friend: Charles Halton. *Jacob Enderman*, the professor: Charles Halton. *Babette*, a manicure: Elizabeth Brice. *Wagstaffe*: J. Rider Glynn. *Court Clerk*: Edward Craven. *Policeman*: Edward Craven. *Stable Boy*: Henry Williams.

Society Girls: (Misses) Eugenie Cole, Irene Hobson, Madge Allen, Sybilla Thorne, Evelyn Wood, Almeda Potter, Claudia Hubbard, Della Spray, Frances Alexander, Della Spray, Katherine Deahy, Estelle Christy, Sadie Melles, Marie Hammett, Mattie Rivenburg, Margaret Cobb, Bessie Friganza, Pauline Neff, Beatrice Walsh, Violet Jewell. *Cashier*: Grace Studdiford. *Manicures*: (Misses) Alice Clifford, Carolyn Green, Edna Mayo, Paula Marr, Marie Arnold, Belle Lorimer, Irma Dickson, Lillian Warde, Katherine Hunton, Ethel Wheeler, Grace Wallis, Madge Wallis, Louise Elton, Eleanor Lund, Violet Jewell. *Hunting Girls*: (Misses) Katherine Deahy, Frances Alexander, Mattie Riverberg, Margaret Cobb, Pauline Neff, Claudia Hubbard. *Shoe Blacks*: (Misses) Alice Clifford, Carolyn Green, Edna Mayo, Louise Elton, Grace Wallis, Madge Wallis, Ethel Wheeler, Irma Dickson. *Blue Girls*: (Misses) Katherine Deahy, Margaret Cobb, Pauline Neff, Sybilla Thorne, Mattie Rivenburg, Beatrice Walsh, Frances Alexander, Almeda Potter. *Casino Girls*: (Misses) Beatrice Walsh, Pauline Neff, Sadie Melles, Mattie Rivenburg, Paula Marr, Margaret Cobb, Almeda Potter, Katherine Hunton. *Golf Boys*: (Misses) Edna Mayo, Louise Elton, Ethel Wheeler, Carolyn Green. *Golf Girls*: (Misses) Alice Clifford, Grace Wallis, Madge Wallis, Marie Arnold. *Johnnies*: Messrs. Vanesse, Wheeler, Arnold, Rider, Lutz, Krauner, Scott, Barlab, Wales. *Hair Dressers*: Messrs. Berges, Benoit. *Porter*: Mr. Kramer. *Policemen*: Messrs. Benoit, Deahy. *Hunters*: Messrs. Arnold, Scott, Wheeler, Vanesse, Rider, Glyn, Deahy, Wales, Barlab. *Butler*: Mr. Benoit. *Waiters*: Messrs. Berges, Deahy. *Grooms*: Messrs. Lutz, Wales. *Driver*: Mr. Gould. *Footman*: Mr. Kramer.

Act 1: Interior of Germaine Du Monde's manicure parlors.

Act 2: Exterior of Bronxville club house.

ACT 1[142]

Opening Number
Chorus

"The Profession of a Manicure"
B. Deyo

"Vi, Vi!"
A. Ritchie, Johnnies

---

[139]New York programs contain no song list. Song list prepared from Boston tryout, with different director and cast. Also published:
"At the Telephone"
B. Ring
(*Music by* Anna Caldwell. *Lyrics by* James O'Dea.)

[140]First produced in New York 17 March 1903 at the Broadway Theatre for 143 performances. For Synopsis of Scenes and Musical Numbers, see original 1903 production.

[141]Settings uncredited.

[142]Added to Act 1 late in subsequent tour, following "Bill Simmons":
"Can You Keep a Secret"
C. J. Ross, E. Brice, Chorus

"Old Man Manhattan"
C. J. Ross
(*Music by* Anna Caldwell. *Lyrics by* James O'Dea.)
"A Rainy Day"
Shopping and Shoe Blacks
"Bill Simmons" (I've Got to Dance Till the Band Gits Through)
M. Raymond
(*Music and Lyrics by* George A. Spink.)
Finale
Ensemble

ACT 2
Opening Number
E. Brice, Chorus
"Love Among the Freaks"
J. Coyne
"Just Kids"
A. Ritchie, C. J. Ross, F. Bond
(*Music and Lyrics by* Charles J. Ross.)
"Run Away, Naughty Man"[143] (Song)
B. Deyo
(*Lyrics by* Hugh Morton.)
"(You're) Just the One I'm Looking For"[144]
A. Ritchie, W. Curtiss, Huntsmen
(*Music and Lyrics by* E. Ray Goetz.)
"We'll Blow the Jolly Horn" (Tally Ho!!!)(Duet)
C. J. Ross, J. Coyne
Racing Scene
Ensemble
Finale
Ensemble

1906.18 THE FREE LANCE

The Sousa Opera Company in a Military Comic Opera in Two Acts. Book (and lyrics) by Harry B. Smith. Music by John Philip Sousa. Staged by Herbert Gresham. Scenery by Ernest Albert of the Lee Lash Studio. Costumes by F. Richard Anderson. Orchestra under the direction of Anton Heindl. Produced by (Marc) Klaw and (Abraham L.) Erlanger. Opened 16 April 1906 at the New Amsterdam Theatre and closed 19 May 1906 after 35 performances[145].

CAST: *Siegmund Lump*, a Brigand Chief: JOSEPH CAWTHORN. *Duke of Graftiana*: ALBERT HART. *Emperor of Braggadocia*: FELIX HANEY. *Pertinax*, Court Censor of Braggadocia: Sim Pulen. *Prince Florian*, his son: GEORGE TALMAN. *Dagonet*, Minister of the Interior of Graftiana: Louis Haines. *Herald*: Henry J. Santra. *Princess Yolande*, daughter of the Emperor of Braggadocia: NELLA BERGEN. *Griselda*, a goose girl: JEANETTE LOWRIE. *Mopsa*, a Sorceress: Fanny Migley. *Leandre, Silvandre*, Pages: Geraldine Malone, Monte Elmo. *Jacqueline, Diane*, Maids of Honor: Estelle Thebaud, Dorothy Southwick. *Lords and Ladies of the Court, Pages, Maids of Honor, Warriors of Graftiana, Amazons and Members of Siegmund's Band of Brigands*.

Act 1: Garden of Emperor's Palace, Braggadocia.

Act 2: Border line dividing Braggadocia and Graftiana. At left, tent of Duke of Graftiana. At right is tent of Emperor of Braggadocia.

ACT 1
"All Lovely Art, We Worship at Thy Shrine" (Chorus)
Mixed Voices
"Three Love Stories" (Song)
N. Bergen
"I Do It All By Proxy" (Chorus and Song)
F. Haney, Chorus
"The Goose Girl" (Song)
J. Lowrie
"Friendship's Sacred Touch" (Scene and Duet)
A. Hart, F. Haney, Male Chorus
"(It Depends Upon the) Hair" (Song)
J. Cawthorn
"Assembling of the Two Courts" (Scene)
Principals, Chorus
"Come, My Dear" (Quartette)
N. Bergen, G. Talman, J. Lowrie, J. Cawthorn
"On to Victory" (Finale)
Princpals, Chorus

ACT 2[146]
"Come, Ye Heroes All"[147] (Scene)(The Emperor's War Song)
F. Haney, Amazons
"The Legend of the Sons of Samson" (Song)
G. Talman, Chorus
"The Mystery of History" (Duet)
J. Lowrie, J. Cawthorn
"The Carrier Pigeon" (Song)
N. Bergen
"Release That Man!" (Ensemble)
Principals, Chorus
"Conundrums"[148] (Trio)
J. Cawthorn, F. Haney, A. Hart
"The Song of the Free Lance" (Song)
J. Cawthorn
Finale
Principals, Chorus

1906.19 THE DISTRICT LEADER

A Musical Comedy Drama in Two Acts. Book, music and lyrics by Joseph E. Howard. Staged by Joseph E. Howard. Settings by Frank Platzner and Maxner. Costumes by Mme. Osborne and M. Simowitch. Produced by Frank J. Sardam and Walter C. Lindsay. Opened 30 April 1906 at Wallack's Theatre and closed 5 May 1906 after 8 performances.

CAST: *Mr. Partridge*, Clerk of the Hotel: Fred J. Barnes. *Ezra Whittle*, from Teaneck, New Jersey: Charles M. McDonald. *The Man Who Wants to Bet*: Mark Sullivan. *Sam Grady*, Halloran's campaign manager: MARK HART. *Grace Lowton*, the woman he loves: FLORENCE SINNOTT. *Tom Cole*, reporter on the Comet: DAVE LEWIS. *Clinton Goddard*: Allen Bennett. *Dan Lowton*, Republican nominee for senator: Joseph Allen. *Valeska Granger* from Denver: Ida Emerson. *Florrie Fenshaw*: DIAMOND DONNER. *Hop Lee*, proprietor of an opium joint: Leonard B. Hoyt. *Tim Halloran*, a candidate for the state senate: HARRY STONE. *Willie Carter*, a rich young man: William S. Davis. *The Belle of Chinatown*: Leona Pam. *Jim Halloran*, Tim's twin brother: HARRY STONE. *Dutch*, Dan Lawton's lieutenant: E. G. Stockwell. *Jack Dunning*, a young New Yorker: JOSEPH E. HOWARD.

Chinese Maidens: Misses M'Neill, Porter, Fanchonetti, DuPree, Barnes, West, Stockwell, Urmazy, Jenkins, Gordon.

Act 1: Lobby of the Kauffman House. Night before election.

Act 2, Scene 1: Pell Street, Chinatown. After midnight. *Scene 2*: Union Square. Election Day.

ACT 1[149]

---

[143]Dropped late in subsequent tour.
[144]Also known in its published sheet music as "You're Just the Girl I'm Looking For."
[145]Played a return engagement 7 January 1907 at the Grand Opera House for 8 performances.

[146]Added for subsequent tour, after "Release That Man!":
"I Never Was Right in My Life" (Topical Song)
J. Cawthorn
[147]For subsequent tour, replaced by:
Opening Chorus
Ensemble
Chant Militaire
J. Lowrie, Chorus
[148]Dropped after opening.
[149]Added during subsequent tour:
"Way Down in Jersey," "Home Is Home," "Won't You Be My Girlie?," "When You Go Out to Dine," "There's Something Doing Around My Heart."
"The Same Old Story"
(*Lyrics by* Arthur Gillespie.)
"You're the Sweetest Girl I Know"
(*Lyrics by* Arthur Gillespie.)
"Make Your Own Sunshine"
(*Lyrics by* Collin Davis.)
"So?"
(*Lyrics by* Collin Davis.)

Opening Chorus
Full Chorus
"One and One Make One"
F. Sinnott, Chorus
"A Heart to Let"
D. Donner, D. Lewis
Finale
Chorus

ACT 2
Scene 1
"Sing Sung Sammy" (Sing Sing Sammy Sen)
L. Pam, Chorus
"What's the Use of Dreaming?"
H. Stone, Chorus
Scene 2
"Old Broadway"
F. J. Barnes, Chorus
"The Big Banshee"
J. E. Howard, Chorus
"Union Square"
Misses Porter, Fanchonetti, Stockwell, Barnes,
Gordon, Urmanzy, Throne, DuPree, McNeill, Jenkins, Sextette
Finale
Entire Company

1906.19 OLD LAVENDER

A Revival of the Local Play in Four Acts, 6 Scenes[150]. Play (and lyrics) by Edward Harrigan. (Music by David Braham.) Staged by Edward Harrigan. Produced by B. K. Bimberg. Opened 21 May 1906 at the 14th Street Theatre and closed 26 May 1906 after 8 performances.

CAST: *Philip Coggswell*: THOMAS F. FALLON. *Paul Cassin*: Harry Cowan. *John Filbert*: WILLIAM SHELDON. *Smoke*: JACK WELCH. *Dick*: WILLIAM HARRIGAN. *Pop Jones*: J. A. Nunn. *Dick Jingle*: George Donaldson. *Martin Reilly*: Jonathan A. Larkin. *Zolla Brown*: Henry Paris. *Silas Longmetre*: Otto Paris. *Henry Mercer*: William Paris. *John Stone*: Harry Frederick. *Lascar Joe*: Roy Fairfield. *Morris Hopkins*: Rob Hooley. *Louis Donnetti*: Jonathan A. Larkin. *Marcus Cyclone*: Henry Waters. *Tom Romnious*: Jean Seplow. *Mother Crawford*: ANNIE YEAMANS. *Laura Coggswell*: Adelaide Matthews. *Sally Stacy*: Jose Lovering. *Nellie Slocum*: Janet Shaw. *Mrs. Stone*: Winifred Lowerie. *Mrs. Goslow*: Margaret Smythe. *Mrs. Mercer*: Pauline Sothern. *Miss Keepcool*: Clara Bertram. *Martha Hollis*: Flara Wells. *Old Lavender*: EDWARD HARRIGAN. *Serenaders, Street Characters, Sailors, etc.*

Act 1, Scene 1: Interior of the Owl Club House. *Scene 2*: Ante-room of the Club-house. *Scene 3*: The Banking House of Philip Coggswell.

Act 2: The River Front.

Act 3: The Interior of Mother Crawford's Sailor's Boarding House.

Act 4: Private Office of Philip Coggswell, Banker.

MUSICAL NUMBERS
"Poverty's Tears Ebb and Flow"
"Extra, Extra"
"(The) Jolly Old Owls"
"Get Up, Jack; John, Sit Down"
"Sweetest Love"
"Please to Put That Down"

1906.20 HIS HONOR THE MAYOR

A Summer Entertainment (Musical Comedy) in Two Acts. Book and lyrics by Charles J. Campbell and Ralph M. Skinner. Music by Julian Edwards, Alfred E. Aarons, (Gus Edwards, Will Cobb and Ren Shields). Staged by J. S. Murray. Business director, William Raymond Sill. Musical director, Daniel Dore. Produced by Alfred E. Aarons. Opened 28 May 1906 at the New York Theatre, moved 30 July 1906 to Wallack's Theatre and closed 25 August 1906 after 104 performances; re-opened 17 September 1906 at Wallack's Theatre and closed 29 September 1906 after 16 additional performances. Total: 120 performances[151].

CAST: *Hon. Teddy Todd*, Mayor of Kankakee: CLARENCE HARVEY. *Daisy*, a milliner girl: MABEL HOLLINS. *May Flood*: Madelyn Marshall. *T. Chesterfield Prebble*, an Anglicized native of Kankakee: FLETCHER NORTON. *"Jack" Thayer*, his chum: Arthur Earnest. *Deacon Flood*, May's father: HARRY KELLY. *"Reddy" Samson*, a cowboy: William W. Black. *Mrs. Vayne*, a young widow: LOIS E. TABOR. *Marjorie Vayne*, her stepdaughter: Lora Lieb. *Solomon Syphonstein*, a Parisian marriage-broker: E. E. Van Rensellaer. *Captain Rudolph Zitzky* of the Royal Hungarian Hussars: JOHN H. PRATT. *Dauber Brush*, an art student: Hal Pearson. *Lieutenant Schnipp* of the Royal Hungarian Hussars: Catherine Tanner. *R. LaCarte*, manager of LaCarte's Hotel: James S. Murray. *Jozef*, waiter at LaCarte's Hotel: L. F. Botsford. *Katrinka*: BLANCHE RING. *Chorus of Arts Students, Tourists, Parisians, French Officers, Gendarmes, Hungarian Nobles and Peasants, Slavs, Chikos, etc.*

The Original English Pony Ballet: Beatrice Liddell, Elizabeth Hawman, Carrie Poltz, Dorothy Marlow, Seppi McNeil, Louise Hawman, Eva Marlow, Ada Robertson.

Shoppers: Misses Ocia Thompson, Marion Whitney, Isobel Plunkett, Jessie Carr, Helen Turner, Ella Bernard, Jessie Thompson, Bessie Fennell, Elinor Mansfield, Helen Howard. *American Art Students* (Girls) Misses Marion Alexander, Grace Andrews, Birdice MacLaughlin, Rose Berg, Lillian DeGrasse; (Boys) Florence May, Kitty Marsh, Alice Keese, Camille Darnton, Anna Nelson, Jessie Cameron, Kitty Parks, Nellie DeGrasse, Julia Burns. *Clients of Syphonstein*: Misses Catherine Tanner, Marion Alexander, Rose Bird, Anna Nelson, Grace Andrews, Lillie DeGrasse. *Gendarmes* Messrs. Edward Melandy, Hal Pearson, E. R. Edwards, Charles Robinson. *Hungarian Officers*: Messrs. Fred Walton, John Belton, Archie Falk, Leon Botsford. *Gypsys*: Messrs. E. R. Edwards, Charles Robinson, Edward Melandy, Hal Pearson. *Gypsy Girls*: Misses Jessie Carr, Grace Andrews, Lillie DeGrasse, Eva Marsh, Florence May, Elinor Mansfield, Alice Keese, Julia Burns. *Gypsy Boys*: Misses Marion Alexander, Helen Turner, Isobel Plunkett, Ocia Thompson, Nellie DeGrasse, Kitty Parks, Ella Bernard, Birdice MacLaughlin, Rose Bird. *Visitors to the Isle*: Misses Jessie Thompson, Marion Whitney, Camille Darnton, Bessie Fennell. (*Skating Specialty*: Morris and Kramer.)

Act 1: Courtyard of Hotel LaCarte, Paris. Present time.

Act 2: The Isle of Margitsziget, on the Danube River, between Buda and Pesth, Hungary.

ACT 1[152]
Opening Chorus
Full Chorus
(*Music by* Julian Edwards.)
"Flower Song"
L. Lieb
"The Dainty Milliners"
Pony Ballet, M. Hollins
(*Music by* Alfred E. Aarons.)
"The Little Girl from Illinois"
M. Hollins, Ponies
(*Music by* Julian Edwards.)
"Come Take a Skate with Me"[153]
B. Ring, J. S. Murray, Morris and Kramer
(*Music by* Gus Edwards. *Lyrics by* R. A. Browne.)
"The Mayor of Kankakee" (Entrance of Todd)
C. Harvey, Chorus
(*Music by* Julian Edwards.)
"I'll Travel the Links with You"
C. Harvey, Chorus
(*Music by* Alfred E. Aarons.)

---

[150]This full length version of OLD LAVENDER was first produced in New York 31 August 1885 at Harrigan's Park Theatre for 100 performances. Previous shorter versions of OLD LAVENDER were presented for one week engagements 3 September 1877, 22 April 1878, and 26 August 1878 all at the Theatre Comique for a total of 24 performances. This revival's one week engagement was one small part of a larger regional tour.

[151]Played return engagements 17 December 1906 at the Grand Opera House for 8 performances, and 3 June 1907 at Wallack's Theatre for 16 performances (see separate entry in 1907-1908 season), 27 November 1907 at the Circle Theatre for 17 performances.

[152]Harry Kelly continued to tour in this show until the 1911-1912, and the show was revised to suit his talents. Interpolated into the show as per published sheet music:
"Roxana's Song"
(*Music by* William Furst.)

[153]Replaced for subsequent tour by:
"There's Nothing Better Than Beer"
Claire Maentz (Katrinka)
(*Music by* Julian Edwards.)

"The Land You Left Behind"
Sextette
(*Music by* Julian Edwards.)

"(She's All My Own) Mary Ann"
A. Earnest, Chorus
(*Music by* Julian Edwards.)

Imitations[154]
B. Ring

"Call Around on Sunday"
Ponies
(*Music by* Alfred E. Aarons.)

Finale and Burlesque
Full Company
(*Music by* Julian Edwards.)

ACT 2

Opening Chorus and "Sweet Tokay"
J. H. Pratt, Chorus
(*Music by* Julian Edwards.)

Hungarian Dance
Pony Ballet

"Military Willie"
F. Norton, Chorus
(*Music by* Julian Edwards.)

"Magyar Maid"
B. Ring, J. H. Pratt
(*Music by* Julian Edwards.)

Skipping Rope Dance
Pony Ballet

Rube Dance
H. Kelly, M. Marshall

"A Little Girl Like Me"
M. Hollins, Full Chorus
(*Music by* Alfred E. Aarons.)

"Waltz Me Around Again, Willie" ('Round-'Round-'Round)
B. Ring
(*Music by* Ren Shields. *Lyrics by* Will D. Cobb.)

Fougere Dance
Pony Ballet
(*Music by* Alfred E. Aarons.)

Finale and Medley
Full Company

[154]Replaced for subsequent tour by:
"(Sweet) Anastasia Brady"
Nella Webb {Daisy}
(*Music by* Jean Schwartz. *Lyrics by* William Jerome.)

1906–1907 SEASON

Mrs. Fred Stone, David Montgomery, Fred Stone, and Ethel Johnson in THE RED MILL
Billy Rose Theatre Collection, New York Public Library for the Performing Arts

1906–1907 SEASON

1906.21 THE GOVERNOR'S SON

A Revival of the Summer Song Show (Musical Farce) in Three Acts[1]. Play (book, lyrics) and music by George M. Cohan. (Adapted from his own vaudeville sketch for the Four Cohans.) Scenic production by John Young. Costumes by Klaw and Erlanger Costume Company. Electrical effects by Kleigel Brothers and Globe Electric Company. Music arranged and orchestra under the direction of Charles J. Gebest. Staged by George M. Cohan and Herbert Gresham. Produced by Sam H. Harris. Opened 4 June 1906 at the Aerial Gardens (atop the New Amsterdam Theatre) and closed 25 August 1906 after 75 performances.

CAST: *Benjamin Curtis*, just married and jealous: JERRY J. COHAN. *Hon. Theodore Wheelock*, Governor of the State: WILLIAM KEOGH. *Dickey Dickson*, the Runaway: JULUS TANNEN. *Martin McGovern*, owner of the vacation hotel: John Conroy. *Bill Swift*, Mrs. Dickinson's brother: Jack Webster. *Webster*, of the Vacation Hotel: Frank McNish, Jr. *Johnson*, Secretary to the Governor: Cleveland I. Nicholson. *Messenger Boy*: Nat Royster. *Algy Wheelock*, the governor's son: GEORGE M. COHAN. *Mrs. Franklin Jones Berrymore*, a three times widow: TRULY SHATTUCK. *Mrs. Benjamin Curtis*, who married for love and money: HELEN F. [Nellie] COHAN. *Emerald Green*, a little bit of a girl: ROSE GREEN. *Mrs. Dickey Dickson*, the Runaway's wife: ETHEL LEVEY. *Chorus*.

MUSICAL NUMBERS

Opening Chorus

"Push Me Along in My Pushcart"
Lee Meyers, Chorus

"(The) Mysterious Maid"
T. Shattuck, Chorus

"If Bill Gillette Could Only See Me Now"
J. Tannen

"Governor of the State"
W. Keogh, Chorus

"The Story of the Wedding March"
E. Levey, G. M. Cohan

"I Want My Rag Time"
G. M. Cohan, Chorus

"I Love Everyone in This Wide, Wide World"
T. Shattuck, Chorus

"Never Breathe a Word of This to Mother"
W. Keogh, G. M. Cohan

"The Governor's Son"
G. M. Cohan, Chorus

"Night Time"
E. Levey

"Nothing New Beneath the Sun"
G. M. Cohan

"(The) Soldiers of the Stage"
Company

Finale

1906.22 SEEING NEW YORK

A Musical Snapshot (Farce) in One Act, Six Snaps (scenes), preceded by a vaudeville program. Worded, songed and tuned by Joseph Hart, Clifton Crawford and A. Baldwin Sloane[2]. Staged by Joseph Hart. Scenery painted by H. Robert Law. Costumes by Will R. Barnes. Electrical effects by Kleigl Brothers. Matters of tone, developer (conductor), N. Harris Ware. Produced by William A. Brady and Joseph Hart. Opened 5 June 1906 at the Wistaria Grove (atop the New York Theatre) and closed 18 August 1906 after 75 performances.

CAST: *Professor Danby Parsons* of Holyoke, Massachusetts, seeing New York: AL LEECH. *Sir Montiford Knight*, a wealthy Englishman, in love with Dolly: CLIFTON CRAWFORD. *Grace Van Alstyne*, prima-donna of the Society Theatre: CHERIDAH SIMPSON. *George Pabst*, whose father made a place famous: Thomas Fortnum. *Sniggers*, page at the Hotel Astor, with yearnings to be a sleuth: John E. Brennan. *J. Riley Shannon*, who controls a few political wards: Charles F. McCarthy. *Daisy Bell, Mary Green*, Show Girls of the Society Theatre: Fleurette DeMar, Maud Grey. *Sylvia Stone, Frances Payne*, Dancers of the Society Theatre: Aileen Flavin, Beatrice McKey. *Gertie Dixon*, friend of Shannon's: Marion Mills. *Varney*, head-waiter of Hotel Astor: A. Bates. *Sergeant of Bingham Police*: Harry Linkey. *A cabman*: Wilfred Thompson. *The Second-Story Man*: Louis Morton. *Dolly Dan*, comedienne of the Society Theatre: CARRIE DeMAR.

Social Debutantes: Misses Eula Jordan, Shirley Clifford, Virginia Marshall, Claire Lane, Sadie Long, Madge Melbourne, Louise King, Maybelle Adams, Marion Mills, Regina Johnson, Leonora Johnson, Lily Dean Hart, Marie Proctor, Blanche Turner, Claire Calhoun, Isabelle Carroll, Bessie Edwards, Louise Hinkson, Hattie Williams, May Willard, Ada Nelligan. *Waiters*: Messrs. Harry Linkey, William Herman, A. Bates, James Fuller, Wilfred Thompson, J. A. Reid, Herbert Frank, Lloyd Peddrick, Morris Avery. *Chappies*: Misses Beatrice McKey, Willard, Edwards, Calhoun, Williams, Turner Proctor, Carroll. *General Bingham's Squad*: Mr. Linkey (Sergeant); Messrs. Herman, Bates, Fuller, Reid, Avery, Thompson, Frank, Peddrick. *The Flatiron Building Sightseers*: Messrs. Linkey, Herman, Bates, Fuller, Reid, Chapman, Tevis, Frank, Peddrick.

Act 1: Vaudeville program.

Act 2, Scene 1: La Orangerie, Hotel Astor. *Scene 2*: Mike's Place, the Bowery. *Scene 3*: Madison Square and the Flatiron Building. *Scene 4*: Forty-second and Broadway. *Scene 5*: A bill-posting location. *Scene 6*: The Casino, Central Park.

ACT 1: SOME VERY HIGH VAUDEVILLE[3]

The Dandy Dixie Minstrels

Yamamoto Brothers (Japan's Greatest Perch Artists)

The Spissel Brothers and Mack in their acrobatic sketch, Scenes in a Cafe.

The Six Proveanies (Best of Women Bicyclists)

Salerno (Europe's Novelty, the World's Greatest Juggler)

ACT 2[4]

"The Hotel Astor"
Chorus

"Tell the Band to Play an Irish Tune"
M. Mills

"My Blushing Rose"
C. Simpson, Chorus

"The Different Girls on Broadway"
C. DeMar, Chorus

"General Bingham's Squad"
H. Linkey, Chorus

"At the Party" (Specialty)
C. Crawford

"The Misfit Family"
C. DeMar

"Howdy Do?"
A. Leech, Three Rosebuds

Eccentric Dance
A. Leech

"I'm Not Particular"
C. Crawford, F. Demar, Chorus

(A Flatiron Flare on an Un-nice Day.)

"Miss Daisy Gown"
C. Simpson, Sextette

"Puff! Puff! Puff!"[5]
T. Fortune, Men's Chorus

Finale
Ensemble

---

[1]Originally produced 25 February 1901 at the Savoy Theatre for 32 performances. For Synopsis of Scenes and Musical Numbers, see original 1901 production.

[2]More precisely: Book and lyrics by Clifton Crawford and Joseph Hart; Music by A. Baldwin Sloane.

[3]During the run, the Musical Farce was moved up to Act 1, with the Vaudeville to follow. Vaudeville bill changed weekly.

[4]Added during the run, after "General Bingham's Squad:"
"(On) The Shady Side of Broadway"
C. Crawford, Sextette
(*Music and Lyrics by* Clifton Crawford.)

[5]Replaced during the run by:
"The Mimetic Doll"
C. DeMar

1906.23 MAMZELLE CHAMPAGNE

A Musical Bubble[6] (Revue) in Two Acts. Book and lyrics by Edgar Allan Woolf. Music by Cassius Freeborn. Staged by Lionel Lawrence. Produced by Henry Pincus. Opened 25 June 1906 at the Madison Square Garden Roof and closed 1 September 1906 after 60 performances; returned 24 October 1906 to the Berkeley Lyceum for an additional 4 performances.

CAST: *Mr. Fuller Spice*, an American Theatrical Manager in search of a novelty: HARRY SHORT. *Mr. Gustavus Hicks*, formerly a Plumber, now husband of an authoress: Edwin Fowler. *Mr. Jack McAllister*, an American all through: ARTHUR STANFORD. *Henri LaTour*, a French Sherlock Holmes: Alfred Hudson. Jr. *Mamzelle Champagne*, only a Bubble: VIOLA DeCOSTA. *Violet Stuyvesant*, an American Heiress: MAUDE EARL. *Diana Hicks*, authoress, seeking atmosphere: SYLVIA STARR. *Bessie Lonely*, her maid: Ida Crispi. *Mabel Chatterton*, with little to say: Maud Fulton. *Siebelle*, Waitress at Maxim's: Alberta Davis. *American Art Students in Paris (6)*: *Percy Yale*: Harry Hudson. *Walter Harvard*: Frank McCullough. *Phillip Cornell*: Fred J. Ozab. *Martin Browne*: Fred Woodward. *Prince Towne*: Walter Liebmann. *George Carlisle*: Walter Pascal. *Head Waiter at Maxim's*: Edward Giles. *A Burglar*: Fred J. Ozab. *A Gendarme*: James E. Ludwig. *Spices Big "6" American Show Girls*: *Pansy Lovejoy*: Alice Chase. *Bianca Armour*: Janette Andrietta. *Myrtle Granger*: Edna Hixon. *Winnie Darling*: Alice Robinson. *Mazie Huyler*: May Rollins. *Dolly Lakefront*: Elfia White. *Iona Lott, Tiny Timmyon*, Dancers Maxim's: Sadie Etherton, Inez Marcelle. *Masqueraders, Flower Girls, Waitresses, Reporters, Gendarmes, etc.*

The action takes place at Maxim's, Paris, France, at the present time.

First Bottle: Night. *Second Bottle*: Next morning.

MUSICAL NUMBERS[7]

"I Could Love a Million Girls"
"Somewhere"
"I'm in Search of a Novelty"
"(The) Moonlight, You and I"
"Could I Fascinate You?" (Fascination)
"(The) Land of Golden Dreams"
"(A Cottage to Let Down) Lovers' Lane"
"Gloriana"
"(The) Tale of the Tadpole and the Frog"
"Peter Pan"
"Goddess of Liberty"
"Never Again"

1906.24 THE HAM TREE

A Return Engagement of the Musical Vaudeville in Three Acts[8]. Book by George V. Hobart. Music by Jean Schwartz. Lyrics by William Jerome. Staged by Herbert Gresham. Musical numbers staged by Ned Wayburn. Scenery painted by Ernest Gros. Costumes designed by F. Richard Anderson. Musical director, Alfred Langstaff. Produced by Marc Klaw and Abe L. Erlanger. Opened 30 July 1906 at the New York Theatre and closed 1 September 1906 after 40 performances.

CAST: *Alexander Hambletonian*: JAMES McINTYRE. *Henry Jones*: T. K. HEATH. *Sherlock Baffles*, a mystery: W. C. FIELDS. *Ernest Everhart*, Manager of the Georgia Minstrels: FREDERICK V. BOWERS. *Lord Spotcash*, of the English nobility: David Torrence. *Lawrence Nickelbacker*, a rich old New Yorker: Alfred Fisher. *Mrs. Nickelbacker*, his wife: Jeanne Towler. *Tessie Nickelbacker*, his daughter: Carolyn Gordon. *Desdemona*, Mrs. Nickelbacker's colored maid: Belle Gold. *Jimpsey*, landlord of the hotel: Stephen Paul. *Ponsonby*, valet to Lord Spotcash: Otto F. Johnson. *Molly*, of Chicago: Adele Kesner. *Dolly Jones*, of Fargo: Helen Whitney. *Bashful Nan*, of Olean: Jennie Meyers. *Nancy Brown*, of San Francisco: Inez Marcel. *Jane*, of Kansas City: Belle Court. *Wisome Kitty*, of Brooklyn: Daisy Lyle. *Daisy*, of Savannah: Jane Lovell. *Lola*, of Havana: Lizzie Smith. *Flo* of Buffalo: Felcitas Haubell. *Nellie McGowan*, of Harlem: Harriet Rehfeld. *Lillie* of New Jersey: Corinne Lincoln. *Sleepy Kate* of Philadelphia: Alice Wayland.

Chorus: Misses Nevins, Marshall, Golden, Freda Haubeil, Wilmott, Bellew, Hawkins, Claywood, Olive, Hazel, Brown, Rose, Hayden, Seton, Salisbury, Thornton, Briggs, Morris, Lovell, Lyle, Kesner, Marcel, Court, Felicitas Haubeil, Smith, Whitney, Lincoln, Meyers, Wayland, Rehfeld. Messrs. Foy, Scheck, Harrison, Jaffie, Baron, Fitzsimmons, Huebner, Barry, Coleman, Smith, Kennedy.

Act 1: Exterior of "The Travellers' Rest," a country hotel in Marion, North Carolina.

Act 2, Scene 1: At a water tank of P.Q.R.R.R., near Dover, Delaware. *Scene 2*: Woods near the railroad, Dover, Delaware.

Act 3: Drawing room in Mrs. Nickelbacker's Fifth Avenue Mansion, (New York City).

ACT 1

"Walking" (Opening Chorus)
Athletic Girls, Trainers
"(Desdie, My)Desdemona"
B. Gold, Atyhletic Girls, Traners
"Sweethearts in Every Town"
F. V. Bowers, Sweethearts
"The Merry Minstrel Band" (Finale)
Chorus

ACT 2

"Good-Bye, Sweet Old Manhattan Isle" (Opening)
F. V. Bowers, Passengers, Tourists
"A New Way to Play Tennis"
W. C. Fields
"Honey, Love Me All the Time"
Honey Girls, Honey Boys
"The Ham Tree Barbecue" (Finale)
Chorus

ACT 3

"When the Cat's Away" (Opening)
Parlor Maids, Flunkeys, Butlers
"On an Automobile Honeymoon"
F. V. Bowers, Auto Girls
Finale
Everybody

1906.25 THE LITTLE CHERUB

A Musical Comedy in Three Acts. Book and lyrics by Owen Hall. Music by Ivan Caryll. (Additional music by Paul Rubens, Frank E. Tours; additional lyrics by George Grossmith, Jr., W. H. Risque.) Staged by Ben Teal. Settings by Ernest Gros. Costumes by Mrs. Robert Osborn, Pascaud of Paris. Orchestra under the direction of William T. Francis. Produced by Charles Frohman. Opened 6 August 1906 at the Criterion Theatre and closed 28 December 1906 after 160 performances[9].

CAST: *Earl of Sanctobury*: TOM WISE. *Lord Congress*: ANDREW HIGGINSON. *Algernon Southdown*: JAMES BLAKELEY. *Shingle*: WILL WEST. *Captain Hereward*: Martin Haydon. *Alderman Briggs*: Richard Chawner. *Mr. Grimble*, Landlord: Charles Gibson. *Ethelbert*: John Mayon. *Police Sergeant*: David Bennett. *Crumm*: John F. Rogers. *Sir John Monteith*: Harold F. Hendee. *Miss Molly Montrose*: HATTIE WILLIAMS. *Daughters of the Earl of Sanctobury (4)*: *Lady Isobel Congress*: MAY NAUDAIN. *Lady Dorothy Congress*: Mabel Hollins. *Lady Agnes Congress*: WINONA WINTER. *Lady Rosa Congress*: Grace Field. *Letty*, Chambermaid at Hotel: Beth Stone. *Mrs. Briggs*: Emily Francis.

Actresses: *Miss Cuckoo Vanblane*: Dorothy Zimmerman. *Miss Kitty Cranbourne*: Elsa Reinhardt. *Miss Maud Rochester*: Eithel Kelly. *Miss Mabel Ducross*: Clara Pitt. *Miss Mary Macclesfield*: Grace Kimball. *Miss Olive Manderville*: Edna Sidney.

Act 1: Room in Lord Sanctobury's Town House.

Act 2: Hotel at Dunbridge Baths.

Act 3: Reception Room at Lord Sanctobury's Town House.

ACT 1[10]

Opening Chorus
"Olympian Octette"
M. Naudain, M. Hollins, W. Winter, G. Claire, Ensemble
"As a Friend"[11]
W. West

[6]Also billed as an "Effervescent Frivolity."

[7]Incomplete program contained no song list; songs not in performance order.

[8]First produced in New York 28 August 1905 at the New York Theatre for 90 performances. For Synopsis of Scenes and Musical Numbers, see original 1905 production.

[9]Played return engagements 30 December 1906 at the Grand Opera House for 8 performances, 4 February 1907 at the Grand Opera House for 8 performances.

[10]Interpolated as per published sheet music:
"When We Get Married"
W. West
(*Music and Lyrics by* Theodore Murray and Fred Leigh.)

[11]Replaced during the run by:
"The Valet"
W. West

"It's the Girls"[12]
H. Williams
(*Lyrics by* Adrian Ross.)
"Dear Little Girls"[13]
W. Winter, M. Naudain, G. Claire, M. Hollins
Finale

ACT 2[14]
Opening Chorus
"My Wife Will Be My Lady"[15]
R. Chawner
"Won't You Waltz?"
B. Stone
"Little Willie Browne"
J. Blakeley
(*Music and Lyrics by* Charles Collins.)
"I Should So Love to Be a Boy"
G. Claire, M. Naudain, M. Hollins, W. Winter
(*Music by* Frank Tours. *Lyrics by* C. H. Bovill.)
"The Supper Girls" (The Girl You Take Out to Supper)
[Tommy]
(*Lyrics by* George Grossmith.)
"Experience"
H. Williams
(*Lyrics by* Adrian Ross.)
Finale

ACT 3
"Pierrot and Cupid" (Pierrot and Pierrette)
G. Claire
(*Music by* Frank Tours. *Lyrics by* Adrian Ross.)
"My Irish Rosie"
H. Williams
(*Music by* Jean Schwartz. *Lyrics by* William Jerome.)
"The Doggie in Our Yard"
H. Williams, J. Blakeley
(*Music and Lyrics by* Marie Doro.)
"Cupid's Rifle Range"[16]
M. Hollins
(*Music by* Frank Tours. *Lyrics by* Adrian Ross.)

"Meet Me at Twilight"
W. Winter
(*Music by* Jerome Kern. *Lyrics by* Clifford Harris.)
Finale

1906.26 THE TOURISTS

A Musical Comedy in Two Acts. Book and lyrics by R. H. Burnside. Music by Gustave Kerker. Staged by R. H. Burnside. Settings by George H. Williams. Costumes designed by Caroline Seidle. Lighting by George Morgan. Orchestra under the direction of Gustave Kerker. Produced by Sam S. and Lee Shubert (Inc.). Opened 25 August 1906 at the Majestic Theatre and closed 8 December 1906 after 124 performances.

CAST: *John Duke*, registered at the Hotel Oriental as the "Duke of Plymouth": ALFRED HICKMAN. *Timothy Todd*, his tutor and guardian: RICHARD GOLDEN. *Benjamin Blossom*, an American millionaire: PHIL H. RYLEY. *Gopal Singh*, the Rajah of Rangapang: WILLIAM PRUETTE. *Askeema*, his former court physician: Fred Frear. *Noorian*, captaij of the Rajah's body guard: Howard Chambers. *Loofah*, proprietor of the Hotel Oriental: ALBERT FROOM. *Kalih*, John Duke's servant: F. Kek Schilling. *Ram-Dow* (Jambo-Ree): ALFRED CAHILL. *Mr. Blossom's daughters* (6): *Dora*: JULIA SANDERSON. *Caroline*: Anna C. Wilson. *Katherine*: Mabel Wilbur. *Dorothy*: Edna Chase. *Eleanor*: Edna McClure. *Letitia Hemingway*, their governess: Anna Boyd. *Julia Jellicoe*, a newspaper correspondent: GRACE LaRUE. *Princess Cholulu*, the Rajah's Daughter: VERA MICHELENA. *In love with Mr. Blossom's daughters (4)*: *Archie Lawrence*: Jack Henderson. *Reginald Wilberforce*: Robert Algier. *Gregory Marston*: Fred W. Cousins. *Theodore Walsingham*: Philip Leigh.

The action takes place at the present time on the afternoon and evening of the same day in Hindustan.

Act 1: Courtyard at exterior of Hotel Oriental, Rangapang.

Act 2: Interior of the Rajah's palace, near Rangapang.

ACT 1
Opening Chorus
"Keep on Doing Something" (Song)
A. Froom, Chorus
"Here They Come" (Ensemble Entrance)
"Dear Old Broadway" (Song)
P. H. Ryley, J. Sanderson, Chorus
"When You Take a Trip" (Ensemble Entrance and Song)
R. Golden, Chorus
"Mary's Lamb" (Song)
G. LaRue
Ensemble Entrance of Rajah and Chorus
"A Game of Hearts" (Duet)
H. Chambers, V. Michelena
"Which One Shall We Marry?" (Quartette)
Tourists
"We're the Gnomes" (Dancing Specialty)
Chorus
"Natives" (Entrance)
Male Chorus
"He's Gone" (Finale)
Ensemble

ACT 2
"In Rangapang" (Opening Chorus)
Ensemble
"They Lived to Be Loved in Vain" (Song)
V. Michelena
"Love Is a Wonderful Thing" (Trio)
W. Pruette, V. Michelena, H. Chambers
Ensemble
Chorus
"She Always Told the Truth" (Song)
A. Boyd
"That's the Time" (Song)
R. Golden
"Different Girls" (Song)
G. LaRue
"It's Nice to Have a Sweetheart" (Song)
J. Sanderson, Chorus
Finale

1906.27 MARRYING MARY

A Musical Play in Three Acts. Book by Edwin Milton Royle. Based on his farce "My Wife's Husbands." Music by Silvio Hein. Lyrics by Benjamin Hapgood Burt. Staged by Edward Milton Royle. Musical numbers staged by Al Holbrook. Scenery by Frank Gates and Edward A. Morange. Costumes designed by Lord & Taylor. Orchestra under the direction of Silvio Hein. Produced by Daniel V. Arthur. Opened 27 August 1906 at Daly's Theatre and closed 6 October 1906 after 43 performances.

CAST: *Mary Montgmery*: MARIE CAHILL. *Fleurette*, her maid: Annie Buckley. *Senator David Bunchgrass*, No. 1: H. GUY WOODWARD. *Bishop Brigham Smudge*, No. 2: MARK SMITH. *Willie Drinkwater*, No. 3: ROY ATWELL. *Ormsby Kulpepper*, No. 4: WILLIAM COURTLEIGH. *Colonel Henry Clay Kulpepper*, his father: EUGENE COWLES. *Kitty Kulpepper*, Ormsby's sister: Virginia Staunton. *Reverend Thorley Throcmorton*: George Backus. *M. Archambeau*, proprietor Hotel Alamo: Ben F. Grennell. *Porter*: James A. Reid. *Head Waiter*: William Herman. *Eph*: Franklyn Ardelle. *Bell-Boy*: George Lyman.

---

[12]Replaced during the run by:
"Popular Songs"
H. Williams
(*Music and Lyrics by* Clare Kummer.)
[13]Dropped for subsequent tour.
[14]Added to Act 2 late in the run, before Finale:
Burlesque Imitations
H. Williams, Henry V. Donnelly {Earl of Santcobury}
[15]Dropped for subsequent tour.
[16]Replaced for subsequent tour by:
"Love's Last Word"
M. Naudain

Guests of the Hotel: *Miss Curley*: Blanche West. *Miss Greene*: Anna Mooney. *Miss Smith*: Anna Belle Gordon. *Miss Keene*: Frances Carruthers. *Miss Savage*: Olga May. *Miss Wiley*: Elizabeth King. *Miss Longsince*: Virginia Steinhardt. *Miss Longfront*: Elsie Shaw. *Miss Arbuckle*: Ethel Shaw. *Miss Verdon*: Sadie Long. *Miss Brown*: Bessie Graham. *Miss Morton*: Jane Hewitt.

The action take place at the present time in Florida.

Act 1: Courtyard of the Hotel Alamo. Evening.

Act 2: Same as Act 1. The morning following.

Act 3: Parlor of the Wedding Suite in same hotel.

ACT 1

Opening Waltz

"Looking for a Man By the Name of Smith"[17]

(Is There Anyone Here by the Name of Smith?)

B. S. Grennell, Guests

"Old Reliable Jokes"[18]

H. G. Woodward, R. Atwell, M. Smith, B. West, A. Mooney, B. A.Gordon

"He's a Cousin of Mine"

M. Cahill

(*Music by* Silvio Hein, Chris Smith. *Lyrics by* Cecil Mack [R. C. McPherson].)

"Noah Knew a Thing or Two"[19]

R. Atwell, Guests

ACT 2

Opening

Ensemble

"Three Men in a Boat"

H. G. Woodward, R. Atwell, M. Smith

"The Last One Is Best of All" (I Love the Last One Best of All)

E. Cowles

"Mr. Cupid"

M. Cahill, W. Courtleigh

Finale

M. Cahill, Company

ACT 3

"Gwendolyn (and Her Mandolin)"[20]

A. Buckley, Guests

"My Hottentot"[21] (A Hottentot Love Song)

M. Cahill, Guests

(*Music by* Bob Cole. *Lyrics by* J. Rosamond Johnson.)

Finale

M. Cahill, Company

[17]Replaced for subsequent tour by:

"I Want to Go Back to the Boulevard"

CharlesJudels {M. Archambeau}, Nellie Lynch {Fleurette}, Chorus

[18]Replaced for subsequent tour by:

"Nobody Knows the Answer"

W. T. Clark {Buchgress}, M. Smith, William Clifton {Drinkwater}, C. Judels, Anne Mooney {Kitty}, A. B. Gordon {Daisy Calhoun}, Daisy Devere

(*Music by* Silvio Hein. *Lyrics by* Benjamin Hapgood Burt.)

[19]Replaced for subsequent tour by:

"Rock, Rock, Rock"

W. Clifton, A. B. Gordon, A. Mooney, Chorus

Finale

M. Cahill, Company

[20]Replaced for subsequent tour by:

"I Want to Wed a Soldier Boy"

N. Lynch, Chorus

[21]Replaced for subsequent tour by:

"Do, Re, Mi, Fa, Sol, La, Si, Do"

M. Cahill, E. Cowles

(*Music by* Benjamin Hapgood Burt. *Lyrics by* William Cahill.)

"I Love You in My Dum, Dum, Dummy Way" (The Dummy Love Song)

M. Cahill

(*Music and Lyrics by* Marie Cahill.)

Added to Act 2 after "Won't You Waltz?"

"Oh, How I Love My Teacher"

W. West

Then later replaced by:

"Come Along, Pretty Eliza"

W. West

Which was replaced for subsequent tour by:

"I Haven't Told Him"

W. West

1906.28 A ONE HORSE TOWN

A Musical Fun Show in Two Acts. Book by George Totten Smith. Directed by New Wayburn. Produced by the Times Square Amusement Company. Opened 27 August 1906 at the Yorkville Theatre and closed 1 September 1906 after 8 performances.

CAST: *Herman Dingle*: JOE KANE. *Porcupine Peters*: Louis B. Foley. *Dunlap Young*: James Norval. *Taddy*: Willie Solar. *Sammy Sunset*: Earl J. Benham. *Doc Dolittle*: Lores Herman. *Jimmie Twodrinks*: W. J. Hammernic. *Knight Stands*: John C. Brownell. *Evangeline Glitter*: GERTRUDE RUTLEDGE. *Catastrophe Kate*: SADIE CONNOLY. *Nancy Peters*: JANET PRIEST.

Act 1: The Town of Lemonville.

Act 2:

MUSICAL NUMBERS[22]

"Hurdy Gurdy Man"

G. Rutledge

"Alamo"

1906.29 ABOUT TOWN

Lew Fields' All-Star Company in a Musical Revue in Two Acts. Book and lyrics by Joseph Herbert. Music by Melville Ellis and Raymond Hubbell. Interpolated numbers by Jack Norworth, Albert Von Tilzer, Cobb and Edwards. Produced under the direction of (staged by) Julian Mitchell. Settings by Arthur Voegtlin, Edward G. Unitt and Homer Emens. Costumes by Mrs. Carolyne Siedel and Mrs. Robert Osborn. Orchestra under the direction of William E. MacQuinn. Produced by Lew Fields. Opened 30 August 1906 at Lew Fields' Herald Square Theatre, closing 10 November 1906 after 85 performances; re-opened 15 November 1906 in shortened form (see following entry), accompanied by a burlesque "The Great Decide"[23] and closed 29 December 1906 after 53 additional performances. Total: 138 performances[24].

[22]No program found.

[23]Suggested by the drama "The Great Divide" by William Vaughn Moody.

[24]ABOUT TOWN subsequently toured with an Act 2 Travesty of "The Music Master" (previously added to IT HAPPENED IN NORDLAND) in 2 Scenes. Cast: *Herr Barewig*, a professional assassin of melody: LEW FIELDS. *Loose Spinach*, who has charge of the Second Violin Department in a Liberty Street cafe, prices reasonable: LAWRENCE GROSSMITH. *Signor Tag*, who claims to be "It," and has the same trouble: GEORGE BEBAN. *Gus Spoons*, who is endeavoring to play to the label: Joseph Herbert, Jr. *Henry Canting*, a modern villain, who, in a wild desire to keep before the public, has appointed himself a slum worker. This does not interfere with his other business, he being head of a banking house and Chairman of the Auto Oil Trust: LAWRENCE GROSSMITH. *Beverage Kruger*, who is going to college to be cured of the simples: Joseph Herbert, Jr. *Mr. Flynn*, delegate of the Snow Shovelers' Union: PETER F. DAILEY. *Tom Dundy*, partner at the "Hip": Cecil B. Summers. *Jowls*, a footman; always at hand: PETER F. DAILEY. *Lanny*, a wild flower from Bleecker Street: Vernon Castle. *Helen Canting*, a wise child who does not know her own father: BLANCHE RING. *Mrs. Hoistem*, of Little Houston Street: HARRY FISHER. *Jenny*, maid of no work and general dish breaker: LOUISE DRESSER. *Charlotte Stanlaws, Octavie Christie*, not Gibson Girls: Edith Ethel MacBride, Frances Harris. *Mrs. Kruger*: EDNA WALLACE HOPPER. *Pony Ballet, Society Pests, Chorus Ladies, College Boys*.

Scene 1: Mrs. Hoistem's Boarding House, in Houston Street, New York. *Scene 2*: The Home of Henry Cantling.

MUSICAL NUMBERS

Chorus

Chorus

"Little Houston Street"

H. Fisher

(*Music by* Hans S. Linne. *Lyrics by* Joseph W. Herbert.)

"Sneezing Sextette"

L. Fields, L. Grossmith, G. Beban, J. Herber, H. Fisher, L. Dresser

CAST: *Baron Blitz*, a brash cab driver: LEW FIELDS. *The Duke of Slushington*, seeking the Golden Girl: LAWRENCE GROSSMITH. *Laird o' Findon Haddock*, his uncle in more ways than one: JOSEPH HERBERT. *Bertie*, a boulevardier from Pittsburgh: HARRY FISHER. *Jack Doty*, a social arclight: JACK NORWORTH. *Marquis de Rectori*, a famous swordsman: GEORGE BEBAN. *Count Sherri, Viscomte Martino*, at the Human Bench Show: JOSEPH HERBERT, JR., VERNON CASTLE. *Julius*, an infant prodigal: Little Major. *Lackey*: Mr. Summers. *Waiter*: Mr. Summers. *Watchman*: Mr. Dill. *Policeman*: Mr. Dolliver. *Mr. B. O'Graf*, interested in moving pictures: Mr. Reinhard. *Jenny*, a horse, North End: Joseph Schrode. *Jenny*, a horse, South End: Mr. Dill. *Gertie Gibson*, a girl with a black and white past: LOUISE DRESSER. *Millie Bounder*, a society pest: Coralie Blythe. *Lottie Limejuice*, just plain chorus: LOUISE ALLEN COLLIER. *Mrs. Frivol*, a stage mommer: ELITA PROCTOR OTIS. *Fannie Frivol*, a prima donna with no voice in the matter: EDNA WALLACE HOPPER.

Carrie, Sadie, occasional show girls: Topsy Siegrist, Gertrude Moyer. *Marianne*, Gertrude's maid: Edith Ethel McBride. *Maude, Rose, Madeline*, in the merry: Marion Whitney, Ray Gilmore, Jane Murray. *Tea Maid*: Lillian Raymond. *Debutantes (8)*: *Kate Demedicis*: May Leslie. *Josie Beauharnais*: Jessie Richmond. *Lucy Borgia*: Jessie Richmond. *Mamie Tudor*: Ray Gilmore. *Lola Montez*: Lillian Harris. *Annie Boleyn*: Jane Murray. *Camille Gautier*: Viola Hopkins. *Mamie Antoinette*: Bessie Skeer.

Grizettes: Misses Gertrude Moyer, Lillian Devere, May Leslie, Mattie Chapin, Ruth Fields. *French Wives*: Misses Topsy Siegrist, Ida Doerge, Loretta MacDonald, Della Connor, Gladys Zell. *Frenchmen*: Misses Mae Murray, May Hickey, Lynn D'Arcy, Fredo Linyard, Elsie Davis. *Piccadilly Crawl*: Misses Gertrude Moyer, Topsy Siegrist, May Leslie, Lillian Devere, Ida Doerge, Loretta MacDonald, Mae Murray, Ruth Fields. Messrs. Summers, Dill, Dolliver, Reinhard, Laughlin, Miller, King, Schraeder, Potts. *In Amsterdam*: Misses Gertrude Moyer, Topsy Siegrist, May Leslie, Lillian Devere, Ida Doerge, Loretta MacDonald, Mae Murray, Ruth Field, May Hickey, Freda Linyard, Elsie Davis, Gladys Zell, Lynn D'Arcy, Della Connor.

Act 1: Grounds of the Heiress' Club, New York. (Unitt and Emens.)

Act 2, Scene 1: Out All Night Bank. *Scene 2*: Le Jardin Fin de Siecle, Paris. (Voegtlin.)

ACT 1

Opening Chorus
Entire Chorus
(*Music by* Raymond Hubbell.)

"Seeing the Town in a Yap Wagon"
L. A. Collier
(*Music by* Melville Ellis.)

Duet
G. Beban, C. Blythe
(*Music by* Melville Ellis.)

"The Gibson Girl"
L. Dresser
(*Music by* Raymond Hubbell.)

"The Piccadilly Crawl"
L. Grossmith, Chorus
(*Music by* Melville Ellis.)

"I'm a Fickle Maid"
E. W. Hopper
(*Music by* Melville Ellis.)

"Baby in the House"
C. Blythe
(*Music by* Melville Ellis.)

"The Girl in the Baby-Blue Tights"
E. P. Otis
(*Music by* Melville Ellis. *Lyrics by* Addison Burkhardt.)

"In Amsterdam"
E. W. Hopper
(*Music by* Melville Ellis.)

"When Tommy Atkins Marries Dolly Gray"
J. Norworth, E. W. Hopper, Chorus
(*Music by* Gus Edwards. *Lyrics by* Will D. Cobb.)

ACT 2

Scene 1

"Gossip" (Solo and Ensemble)
H. Fisher, Chorus
(*Music by* Raymond Hubbell.)

"The Great White Way"
J. Norworth
(*Music by* Raymond Hubbell.)

Scene 2

"A French Tonic"
Chorus
(*Music by* Raymond Hubbell.)

"I'm Sorry"
L. Dresser
(*Music by* Albert Von Tilzer. Lyrics by Jack Norworth.)

Finale
Entire Company
(*Music by* Melville Ellis and Raymond Hubbell.)

1906.29

ABOUT TOWN and THE GREAT DECIDE

Revised version of the Musical Revue in One Act, accompanied by a burlesque of William Vaughn Moody's drama of the Southwest, "The Great Divide" in One Act, 3 Scenes. (All credits same as above.) Opened 15 November 1906 at Lew Fields' Herald Square Theatre and closed 29 December 1906 after 53 performances.

ABOUT TOWN, a Musical Revue in One Act. Scenery by Homer Emens and Edward G. Unitt.

CAST: *Acton Alday*, known as "King of the Continuous," owner and manager of the leading American vaudeville theatres: PETER F. DAILEY. *Baron Blitz*, a New York cabman: LEW FIELDS. *Countess de Rectori*, who marries in Paris to repent in New York: BLANCHE RING. *Count de Rectori*, a source of supply for the leading French cemetaries: GEORGE BEBAN. *Carrol Sweet*, a popular song writer with a thirst for society: HARRY FISHER. *Duke of Ehwattiington*, an imported nobleman with a financial conscience: LAWRENCE GROSSMITH. *Duchess of Ehwattington*, a Pittsburgh peeress: EDNA WALLACE HOPPER. *Mrs. Acton Alday*, who trusts her husband implicitly (when she is with him): ALICE HAGEMAN. *Mrs. Astormont Vanderbell*, a rich and weary widow: LOUISE DRESSER. *Count Sherri, Viscomte Martino*, at the Human Bench Show: Joseph Herbert, Jr., Vernon Castle. *Lottie*, Mrs. Vanderbell's maid: Edith Ethel McBride. *Tottie Limejuice*, just plain chorus: Topsy Siegrist. *Sadie*, occasional show girl: Gertrude Moyer. *Watchman*: Mr. Dill. *Policeman*: Mr. Moore. *Jenny*, a horse, North End: Joseph Schrode. *Jenny*, a horse, South End: Mr. Dill. *Mr. B. O'Graf*, interested in moving pictures: Mr. Reinhard. *Hortense*, maid to Countess de Rectori: Lynn D'Arcy.

Vaudeville Volunteers: *Kate Demedicis*: May Leslie. *Josie Beauharnais*: Jessie Richmond. *Lucy Borgia*: Jessie Richmond. *Mamie Tudor*: Ray Gilmore. *Lola Montez*: Ida Doerge. *Annie Boleyn*: Jane Murray. *Camille Gautier*: Viola Hopkins. *Mamie Antoinette*: Bessie Skeer. *Dora Wagner*: Frances Harris.

Piccadilly Crawl: Misses Gertrude Moyer, May Leslie, Lillian Devere, Ida Doerge, Loretta MacDonald, Mae Murray, Ruth Fields. Messrs. Laughlin, Dill, Summers, Reinhard, Miller, Potts. *In Amsterdam*: Misses Gertrdue Moyer, Topsy Siegrist, May Leslie, Lillian Devere, Ida Doerge, Loretta MacDonald, Mae Murray, Ruth Fields, Freda Linyard, Elsie Davis, Gladys Zell, Lynn D'Arcy, Della Connor, Elsie Davis. *Southern Boys*: Misses Mae Murray, Freda Linyard, Mae Sherwood, Elinor Kershaw. *Southern Girls*: Misses Gertrude Moyer, Topsy Siegrist, Loretta MacDonald, Ruth Fields. *Summer Boys*: Misses Gladys Zell, Dorothy Webb, Della Connor. *Broadway Girls*: Misses Jessie Richmond, Viola Hopkins, Marion Whitney, Eleanor Mansfield. *New York Girls*: Misses Bettie Dodsworth, Helen Turner.

Scene: Exterior of Hotel Carlton, Westchester, New York.

ACT 1

Opening Chorus
Entire Chorus
(*Music by* A. Baldwin Sloane.)

"Gossip"[25] (Solo and Ensemble)
H. Fisher, Chorus
(*Music by* Raymond Hubbell.)

"Dinner Time"
L. Grossmith, Chorus
(*Music by* Addison Burkhardt.)

"The Piccadilly Crawl"
P. F. Dailey, Chorus
(*Music by* Melville Ellis.)

"Little Class of One"[26] (from IT HAPPENED IN NORDLAND)
B. Ring, P. F. Dailey
(*Music by* Victor Herbert. *Lyrics by* Glen MacDonough.)

Imitations
B. Ring

Finale
Company

[25]Dropped for subsequent tour.

[26]Replaced for subsequent tour by:
"Tipperary Nora"
B. Ring, P. F. Dailey
(*Music by* Ted Snyder. *Lyrics by* Ren Shields.)

"The Same Old Girl"
L. Dresser

"I'm a Fickle Maid"
E. W. Hopper
(*Music by* Melville Ellis. *Lyrics by* Addison Burkhardt.)

Imitations
B. Ring

"In Amsterdam"[27]
E. W. Hopper, Chorus
(*Music by* Melville Ellis.)

"When Tommy Atkins Marries Dolly Gray"
B. Ring, E. W. Hopper, Chorus
(*Music by* Gus Edwards. *Lyrics by* Will D. Cobb.)

ACT 2

THE GREAT DECIDE, a Burlesque in 3 Scenes. Scenery by Frank Gates and Edward A. Morange.

CAST: *Steve*: PETER F. DAILEY. *Philip Jordanmarsh*: GEORGE BEBAN. *Winthrop Duxbury*: EDNA WALLACE HOPPER. *Dutch*: LEW FIELDS. *Pedro*: LAWRENCE GROSSMITH. *Polly*: HARRY FISHER. *Ruth Jordanmarsh*: BLANCHE RING. *Lon Anderson*: Joseph Herbert, Jr. *A Contractor*: Vernon Castle. *Messenger Boy*: Topsy Siegrist. *Katonah*: Gertrude Moyer. *Lakoleta*: Topsy Siegrist. *Mattahnac*: May Leslie. *Indians*: Misses Lillian Devere, Ida Dorge, Mae Murray, Freda Linyard, Stacia Leslie, Lynn D'Arcy, Elsie Davis, Ruth Field, Bessie Skeer, Gladys Zell, Mae Sherwood, Loretta MacDonald. *Cowboys*: Misses Vera Pindar, Bessie Skeer, Lynn D'Arcy, Elsie Davis. *Ranch Girls*: Misses Lillian Devere, Mae Leslie, Ida Doerge, Stacia Leslie.

Scene 1: Philip Jordanmarsh's road house at Gory Gulch, on the Alkali Desert of Arizona. *Scene 2*: The marriage at the office of the Justice of the Peace. *Scene 3*: Steve's cabin by Haunted Canon.

MUSICAL NUMBERS

Scene 3

"Legend of the Mojaves"
G. Moyer, T. Siegrist, M. Leslie, Chorus
(*Music by* Gustav Kerker.)

Imitations[28]
B. Ring

"A Girl from Everywhere"
P. F. Dailey, Chorus
(*Music by* A. Baldwin Sloane.)

1906.30 THE MAN FROM NOW

A Musical Fantasy in Two Acts and a Prologue. Book by John Kendrick Bangs and Vincent Bryan. Music by Manuel Klein. Lyrics by John Kendrick Bangs, Vincent Bryan, (Manuel Klein). Staged by George Marion. Settings by Walter Burridge. Costumes by Archie Gunn. Musical conductor, John McGhie. Produced by Henry W. Savage. Opened 3 September 1906 at the New Amsterdam Theatre and closed 29 September 1906 after 28 performances.

CAST (in order of appearance): *Forecasta*, Professor of Physics, Usona College: EDWARD B. MARTINDELL. *Jack Raleigh*, a student at Usona: Walter Lawrence. *John P. Pennypacker*, a billionaire: PHIL BRANSON. *Eli Beasley*, a rural sleuth: GILBERT GREGORY. *Steve Waffles*, "The Man from Now": HARRY BULGER. *Samsonia*, Captain Gassar College Tug of War Team: HELEN HALE. *Matricula*, President of Gassar College 2906: Hattie Arnold. *Dora*, a student at Gassar: SALLIE FISHER. *Electra*: Marie Keller. *Zeroine*, captain of Liquid Air Police: Lucy Tonge. *Comahn*, a lecturer at Screamland: William Murphy. *Gasolina*, the gasoline maid: HELEN HALE.

(*Ensemble*): *Classical*: Misses MacPhie, Schriebley, Montclair, Tichenor, Erickson, Mason, Dalrymple, Spencer. *Samsonian*: Misses Daggett, Dupont, Helen Burnett, Myles, Holton, Stover, Edwardes, Merritt. *Fox-Glove*: Misses Randall, Eva Burnett, Johnston, Drew. *Pansy*: Misses Flower, Marshall, Dunne, Cramer. *Daisy*: Misses LaDew, Spaulding, Mack, Richmond. *Tiger Lily*: Misses Despres, Berg, Hackett, Riedel. *Astronomical*: Misses MacPhie, Schriebley, Montclair, Tichenor, Erickson, Mason, Dalrymple, Spencer. *Culinary*: Misses Daggett, Dupont, Helen Burnett, Moyles, Holton, Stover, Edwards, Merritt. *Electric*: Misses Randall, Cramer, Mack, Richmond, Despres, Berg, Hackett, Riedel. *Coaxing*: Misses MacPhie, Schriebley, Montclair, Erickson, Mason, Mack, Richmond, Depres. *Belles*: Misses Mason, Dalrymple, Spencer, Berg, Hackett, Riedel. *Music Maids and Automatic Girls*: Misses Daggett, Dupont, Helen Burett, Moles, Holton, Stover, Edwards, Merritt, Randall, Eva Burnett, Johnston, Drew, Flower, Marshall, Dunne. *Students*: Messrs. Murphy, Hudson, Brand, Hessong, Books, Cramer, Winstrom.

Prologue: Laboratory of Professor Forecasta, Usona College, 1906.

Act 1: Campus, Gassar College, 2906.

Act 2:"Screamland," National Amusement Park, 2906.

PROLOGUE

"Oh,) It's Rah! Rah! Rah!"
Students

"Science" (Recitative and Song)
E. B. Martindell, Students

ACT 1

"Daisy Chain"
Gassar Girls

"Girls, Just Girls"
H. Hale, Girls
(*Lyrics by* Isabel deWitt Kaplan.)

"Love's Lesson" (The Only Way to Love)
S. Fisher, Gassar Girls
(*Lyrics by* Manuel Klein.)

Concerted number:
"We Are the Laddies" (Entrance of College Students)
Students
"Come Along, My Boys"
H. Arnold
"Lunch Is Ready"
Students

"I Will Love You Forever, (My Dear)"
W. Lawrence
(*Lyrics by* Manuel Klein.)

"What's the Matter with Our Team?" (Song and Dance)
H. Hale, Athletic Girls
(*Music by* Harry Von Tilzer.)

"There Isn't Anything That Can't Be Cured"
H. Bulger
(*Music by* Harry Bulger. *Lyrics by* Vincent Bryan.)

Scientific Classes:
"Astronomy"
S. Fisher, Astronomic Girls
"The Wireless Telephone"
M. Keller, Electric Girls
"Liquid Air"
H. Hale, Liquid Air Girls
"Mary Ann"
H. Arnold, Culinary Girls
"Liquid Air Police"
L. Tonge, Police

"In Pity, Spare Them" (Finale)
Company
(*Lyrics by* Manuel Klein.)

ACT 2

Opening Chorus
Automatic Girls

"My Gasoline Maid"
H. Hale, Automatic Girls

"The Irresistible Tune" (Song and Dance)
H. Bulger, Chorus
(*Lyrics by* Manuel Klein.)

"I Want to Go Home Now" (Quartette)
H. Hale, E. B. Martindell, P. Branson, G. Gregory
(*Lyrics by* John Kendrick Bangs.)

"Coaxing"
W. Lawrence, S. Fisher, Girls
(*Music by* Bernard Rolt.)

[27]Replaced for subsequent tour by:
"Deutschland"
E. W. Hopper, Chorus
(*Music and Lyrice by* Herman Paley and James Kendis.)

[28]Dropped during the run.

"The Dainty Music Maid"
S. Fischer, Music Girls
(*Lyrics by* Manuel Klein.)

"College Chums"
H. Bulger
(*Music and Lyrics by* Gertrude Hoffman and Vincent Bryan.)

"What Says Your Heart" (Duet)
H. Bulger, H. Arnold

Finale
Company

1906.31

PANHANDLE PETE

Panoramic Musical Comedy in Three Acts. Book by Willard Holcomb. Based on the popular cartoon strip by George McManus. Music by Samuel Lehman. Lyrics by David Kemp and Edward Laska. Musical director, Oscar Goodfriend. Produced by Abe Levy. Opened 10 September 1906 at the Metropolis Theatre and closed 15 September 1906 after 8 performances.

CAST: *Panhandle Pete*: JAMES HARRIGAN. *Willie Newlywed*: Emmet Lennen. *Lyman Lyter*: William H. Conley. *Francois*: William H. Conley. *Biddy Tucker*: William H. Conley. *Kelly McCan*: WILLIAM MAUSSEY. *Danny Tucker*: Vic Milo. *Abijah O'Grady*: Abe Leavitt. *Algy Astor*: Matt Taylor. *Reggy Rector*: Frank Gerard. *Officer Onspot*: Ed. Roscoe. *Filmore Fokus*: T. A. Brown. *Mrs. William Newlywed*: EDDIE EDWARDS. *The Jolly Girls (2)*: *Molly Jolly*: ROSE BERGERE. *Dolly Jolly*: FLORENCE BERGERE. *Mayme Madigan*: BERTIE DOUGLAS. *"Aunt Jane"*: Jane Adelaide Hood. *Dancing Girls*: *Tough Girls*: *Police Girls*: *Duster Girls*: *Policemen*: *Summer Girls*.

The action takes place in New York at the present time.

Act 1: Times Square. Night.

Act 2: Ballroom at the Hotel Astor. Same night.

Act 3: Claremont, Central Park. Same day.

ACT 1[29]

Opening Chorus

"California Belle"
B. Douglas

"You'll Have to Get Off and Walk"
J. Harrigan

"Luna"

"We're the Handy Dandy Cops"
Company

Finale
Entire Company

ACT 2

Opening Chorus Act 2
Duster Girls

"(When) Two Hearts Beat as One"
The Spooners

"Going on the War Path"
M. Madigan

Finale
Entire Company

ACT 3

"Pleasant Day" (Opening Chorus)
Summer Boys and Girls

German Specialty
E. Husel, B. Douglas

"Jennie Jones"
J. Harrigan

Won't You Be My Honey?"
B. Douglas

"Columbia (You're My Girl)"

Finale
Entie Company

[29]No New York program available; musical numbers taken from a Cedar Rapids tour, September 1907. Additional songs mentioned in New York reviews: "I Got Another One," "I'd Like to Call You Mine," "I'm a Natural Born Hoodoo," "Everybody Hands Me a Lemon."

1906.32

MY LADY'S MAID, or, Lady Madcap

A Musical Play in Two Acts[30]. Book by Paul Rubens and (Colonel) N. Newnham-Davis. Revised (for America) by Edward Paulton, R. H. Burnside, (Percy Greenbank). Music by Paul Rubens. Lyrics by Paul Rubens and Percy Greenbank. Staged by R. H. Burnside. Costume design by Caroline Seidle. Orchestra under the direction of Clarence West. Produced by Sam S. Shubert and Lee Shubert (Inc.). Opened 20 September 1906 at the Casino Theatre and closed 27 October 1906 after 44 performances[31].

CAST: *East Anglian Hussars (4)*: *Colonel Layton*: Joseph Maylon. *Major Blatherswaite*: Claude Flemming. *Lieutenant Somerset*: John Dudley. *Captain Harrington*: FRANK RUSHWORTH. *Bill Stratford*, known as "Stony" Stratford: ROBERT E. GRAHAM. *Posh Jenkins*, his confederate: WALTER E. PERKINS. *Count Manuelo de Colonna*: HENRY BERGMAN. *Giuseppe*, his servant: George R. Stevens. *Lord Framlingham*: Charles W. Dungan. *Corporal Ham*: GEORGE CARROLL. *Palmer*, Butler to Lord Framlingham: Nicholas Burnham. *Old Huntsman*: Prince Miller. *Oroya Brown*, known as Trooper Smith of the East Anglian Hussars: JOSEPH COYNE. *Gwennie Holden*, friend of Lady Betty: DELIA MASON. *Susan*, maid to Lady Betty: ELSA RYAN. *Mrs. Layton*, Colonel Layton's wife: Edith Blair. *Lady Betty Framlingham*, Lord Framlingham's daughter—the Madcap: MADGE CRICHTON.

Footmen: Messrs. Dearduff, Fletcher, Lingo, Rogers. *Officers of Yeomanry*: Messrs. Hobart, Dealy, McCaffrey, D'Orsay, Wright, Chapin, Rauch, O'Keefe. *Archery Girls*: Misses Gibson, Roetger, Marr, Mohr, Maguire, Whitlock, Martrit, Coffin, Thompson, Grealis. *Society Ladies*: Misses Berge, Richmond, Dealy, Taylor. *Pages*: Misses Lancaster, Ford, M. DeVere, Scotten, Campbell, LeRoy. *Maids*: Misses Snyder, D. DeVere, Taylor, Els, Ashby, Jewett.

Act 1: Garden at Framlingham Castle.

Act 2: Hall at Framlingham Castle.

ACT 1[32]

Opening Chorus (We're simple rustic folk)
Society Ladies, Country Girls, Game Keepers
(*Music by* Howard Talbot.)

"(Pretty) Primrose"
D. Mason

Entrance of Yeomanry (Here they are, don't you see)
F. Rushworth, Officers

"Mum's the Word"
D. Mason, M. Crichton, E. Ryan

"My Lady's Maid"
M. Crichton, Maids
(*Music and Lyrics by* Paul Rubens.)

"I've No Patience with a Soldier"
E. Ryan, G. Carroll

"A Way We Have in the Army"
F. Rushworth, Chorus

Finale
Company

ACT 2[33]

Opening Song[34]
F. Rushworth

Entrance of the Pages and Maids (We're pert little, plump little page-boys!)
Ensemble

[30]Previously produced in London as LADY MADCAP.
[31]Settings uncredited.
[32]Also performed per opening night reviews:
"They Handed Me a Lemon"
J. Coyne
(*Music by* J. Fred Helf. *Lyrics by* Ed Gardenier.)
[33]Added during the run to Act 2 after Entrance of the Pages and Maids:
"Hard to Understand the Ladies"
J. Coyne
[34]Dropped during the run.

"(I'd Love to Have a) A Soldier of My Own"
M. Crichton, Chorus
(*Music and Lyrics by* Paul Rubens.)
"I Love You in Velvet" (I Like You in Velvet)
F. Rushworth, D. Mason
(*Music and Lyrics by* Paul Rubens.)
"Don't You Care"
W. E. Perkins, Chorus
(*Music by* Harold Orlob. *Lyrics by* Joseph E. Miller.)
"All I Want Is You" (I Want You)
M. Crichton
(*Music by* Jerome Kern. *Lyrics by* Paul West.)
"It's Lovely When Your Love Loves You"
E. Ryan, Chorus
(*Music and Lyrics by* E. Ray Goetz.)
"I'd Like to Call You Mine"
J. Coyne, M. Crichton, F. Rushworth, D. Mason, R. E. Graham, E. Ryan, Chorus
(*Music and Lyrics by* Samuel Lehman.)
Finale

1906.33 THE RED MILL

A Musical Play in Two Acts. Book and lyrics by Henry Blossom. Music by Victor Herbert. Staged by Fred G. Latham. Settings by Frank E. Gates, E. A. Morange ; Homer Emens, Edward G. Unitt and Joseph Wickes. Costumes by Wilhelm. Orchestra under the direction of Max Hirschfield. Orchestrations by Victor Herbert. Produced by Charles Dillingham. Opened 24 September 1906 at the Knickerbocker Theatre and closed 29 June 1907 after 318 performances.

CAST: *Con Kidder, Kid Conner*, two Americans 'doing' Europe: FRED A. STONE, DAVID MONTGOMERY. *Jan Van Borkem*, Burgomaster of Katwyk-ann-Zee: EDWARD BEGLEY. *Franz*, Sheriff of Katwyk-ann-Zee: Charles Dox. *Willem*, keeper of the Red Mill Inn: David L. Don. *Captain Doris Van Damm*, in love with Gretchen: JOSEPH M. RATLIFF. *The Governor of Zeeland*, engaged to Gretchen: NEAL McCAY. *Joshua Pennefeather*, Solicitor, Lincoln's Inn Fields, London, automobiling with his daughters through Holland: Claude Cooper. *Gretchen*, the Burgomaster's daughter: AUGUSTA GREENLEAF. *Bertha*, the Burgomaster's sister: ALINE CRATER. *Tina*, barmaid, Willem's daughter: ETHEL JOHNSON. *Countess de La Tere*, automobiling with her sons through Holland: Juliette Dika. *Flora*: Constance Eastman. *Dora*: Kitty Howland. *Lena*: Paula Desmond. *Anna*: Cleo Sweninger. *Phyllis*: Estelle Baldwin. *Madge*: Sadie Probst.

Peasants, Artists, Aides de Camp, Burghers, etc.: Misses Carew, Kendal, Dean, Gabrielle, Leslie, Scott, Hengler, Emmons, Stokes, Howard, White, Belmont, Braun, Robinson, Green. Messrs. Fuller, Avery, Arnold, Emerson, Fletcher, Stelz, Callihan, Kelly, Mills, Dodge, Walsh, McGee, Gibson, Drumheller, Whiting, Howland.

The action takes place in Katwyk-ann-Zee, Holland, at the present time.

Act 1: At the sign of The Red Mill. (Gates and Morange.)

Act 2: A Hall in the Burgomaster's House. (Emes, Unitt and Wickes.)

ACT 1[35]
"By the Side of the Mill" (Opening Chorus)
Chorus
"Mignonette"
E. Johnson, Girls
"You Can Never Tell About a Woman"
E. Begley, D. L. Don
"Whistle It" (Trio)
D. Montgomery, F. Stone, E. Johnson
"A Widow Has Ways"
A. Crater
"(In) The Isle of Our Dreams"
J. M. Ratliff, A. Greenleaf
"(Always) Go While the Goin' Is Good"
F. A. Stone, D. Montgomery, E. Johnson, A. Crater
"An Accident" (Ensemble)
J. Dika, E. Johnson, Chorus
"Moonbeams" (Finale)
A. Greenleaf, J. M. Ratliff, Male Chorus

ACT 2
"Gossip Song" (Opening Chorus)
A. Crater, Chorus
"(The) Legend of the Mill"
A. Crater, Chorus
"Good-a-bye, John"
F. Stone, D. Montgomery
(*Music by* Egbert Van Alstyne. *Lyrics by* Harry Williams.)
"I Want You to Marry Me!"
E. Johnson, Chorus
"Every Day Is Ladies' Day With Me"
N. McCay, Male Chorus
"Because You're You!"
A. Crater, N. McCay
"The Streets of New York" (In Old New York)
F. Stone, D. Montgomery, Chorus
Entrance of Wedding Guests (The Wedding Song)(Wedding Bells)
N. McCay, Chorus
"The Streets of New York" (Finale)
Entire Company

1906.34 THE GIRL AND THE GAMBLER

A Comedy with Music in Four Acts. Play by Hal Reid. Produced under the direction of Byron Ongley. Scenery by John Young. Musical director, J. P. Corin. Produced by B. E. Forrester. Opened 1 October 1906 at the American Theatre and closed 6 October 1906 after 8 performances.

CAST: *David Maxwell*, the lover: DARWIN KARR. *Douglass Blanchard*, the broker: Bigelow Cooper. *François Maurice DuBois*, the Frenchman: Arthur A. Klein. *S.S. Smith*, the porkpacker: J. P. MacSweeeney. *Walter Lawrence*, the father: John McKee. *John Anderson*, the detective: Albert DeRocher. *Parkins*, the butler: Frank Baldwin. *Reverend Ambrose*, the minister: William Lyons. *Nellie Lawrence*, the sister: Lillian Goldsmith. *Helene Marshall*, the wedge: Anne Leonard. *Mrs. Annie Lawrence*, the mother: Inda Palmer. *Lucinda Brown*, the black: "Carlotta." *Geraldine's friends (12)*: Clara Walton, Georgie Holman, Mabel Hance, Sue Barker, Mamie Wilson, Jennie Maynard, Estelle Colbert, Percie Judah, Lillian Kimball, Edith Gill, May G. Lyon, Maud Young. *Geraldine Lawrence*, the little burglar: FLORENCE BINDLEY.

Act 1: The Lawrence homestead. Driven from the fold.

Act 2: The library of Walter Lawrence's New York home. The Little Burglar.

Act 3: The millionaire's mansion on Riverside Drive. The Girl and the Gambler.

Act 4: The interior of the old home. Back to the fold.

ACT 1
"Mooney Time"
F. Bindley, Girls
(*Music by* Joseph Nathan. *Lyrics by* Felix Feist.)
"Let's Get Acquainted" (Duet)
F. Bindley, D. Karr
(*Music and Lyrics by* Albert Von Tilzer.)

ACT 3
"Sunflower"
F. Bindley, Girls
(*Music by* Joel Corin. *Lyrics by* Felix Feist.)

ACT 4
Imitation
F. Bindley
"How'd You Like to Like a Girl Like Me?"
F. Bindley, D. Karr, Girls
(*Music by* Joseph Nathan. *Lyrics by* Felix Feist.)

1906.35 A LUCKY DOG

A Musical Play in Three Acts. Book (and lyrics) by Mark E. Swan. Music by George Nichols. Musical director, George Nichols. Produced by Broadhurst and Currie. Opened 1 October 1906 at the Yorkville Theatre and closed 6 October 1906 after 8 performances.[36]

[35]Musical Numbers do not appear in original programs. List prepared from published vocal score. Score credits Herbert and Blossom as authors of "Good-a-Bye, John."

[36]Director, scenery and costumes uncredited.

CAST: *Happy Holmes*, a peripatetic philosopher: NAT M. WILLS (The Happy Tramp). *Reuben Haskins*, a Yankee inventor: CHARLES W. UDELL. *Lal Chunder*, a Hindoo priest: Joseph Eggenton. *Herbert Dalton*, a man of the world: James Vincent. *Sam Lurk*, a friend of Dalton: Peter Griffin. *Victor Strong*, a young inventor: Millar Bacon. *Gregory Kent*,a collector of curios: Fred Runnells. *Ram Dass*, an East Indian: Morley Peake. *Joe Simmons*, an officer: Jay Shaw. *Tom Porter*, his mate: David Rosenthal. *Madeline Grey*, an heiress: CARRIE THOMAS. *Angeline Pettijohn*, a maid servant: Delia Stacy. *Cora Norman*, Dalton's wife: ANITA ZORN. *Sarah Darnley*, the schoolmistress: Lee Hobbs Martin. *Alice Vaughn*, a pupil at Fenwood: MAE HARRISON: *Phyllis Cavanaugh*, another: Edna Michell. *Babette St. Vrain*, a young French musician: NINON de VARENNE.

Susy Norwood: Sybil Brennon. *Georgia Dallas*: Mae Lawrence. *May Anderson*: Eleanor Fay. *Maud Bessemer*: Alice Brophy. *Dora Armour*: Elimore Russell. *Vivian Sinclair*: Vivian Pickard. *Estelle Weatherford*: Ethel Seymour. *Cora Temple*: Anna Morgan. *Isabel Van Schuyler*: Clara Pickard.

Act 1: Exterior of Fenwood School. The Wonderful Hypnotic Ring.

Act 2: Interior of Fall Brook Museum. Afternoon of the same day.

Act 3: The Garden at Fenwood School. Evening of the same day.

ACT 1[37]
- Opening Chorus
- "Beautiful Bed"
  N. M. Wills

ACT 2
- "Just Like Jane"
  M. Harrison, N. de Varenne, Girls
- "When I'm with You" (Duet)
  C. Thomas, M. Bacon
  (*Music by* Ovett.)
- Trio
  D. Stacy, C. W. Udell, N. M. Wills
- "By the Pyramids"
  D. Stacy, Girls

ACT 3
- "Mexico"
  P. Griffin, C. W. Udell, Girls
- Dancing Specialty
  P. Griffin
- A Few Parodies
  N. M. Wills
- Finale
  Entire Company

1906.36 THE SPRING CHICKEN

A Musical Play in Three Acts[38]. Book by George Grossmith, Jr. Based on Adolphe Jaime and Georges Duval's farce "Coquin de Printemps." Music by Ivan Caryll and Lionel Monckton. Lyrics by Adrian Ross and Percy Greenbank. American adaptation by Richard Carle. (Interpolated songs by M. E. Rourke, Robert Hood Bowers, Milton W. Lusk and Richard Carle.) Entire production under the personal supervision of Richard Carle. Dances arranged by Adolph Neuberger. Orchestra under the direction of Frank Palma. Produced by Richard Carle, by arrangement with (Marc) Klaw and (Abraham L.) Erlanger and the Gaiety Theatre Company, Ltd., Management of Charles Marks. Opened 8 October 1906 at Daly's Theatre and closed 1 December 1906 after 66 performances; re-opened 10 December 1906 at the New Amsterdam Theatre and closed 29 December 1906 after 25 additional performances. Played a return engagement 1 April 1907 at Daly's Theatre and closed 20 April 1907 after 24 additional performances. Total: 115 performances.[39]

[37]Subsequent national tour presented by E. D. Stair included the following interpolations: "All for You," "Cinderella," "I Would Do Anything in the World for You," "Morning Sky," "Rueben's Holiday," "A Sad Affair," "Willing to Learn."
[38]Billed as "Richard Carle presents himself in George Edwardes' success of two London seasons."
[39]Settings, costumes uncredited.

CAST: *Gustave Babori*, advocate: VICTOR MORLEY. *Boniface*, his head clerk: Richard Ridgely. *Baron Papouche*, his client: SYLVAIN LANGLOIS. *Felix*, head waiter at "The Crimson Butterfly": SYLVAIN LANGLOIS. *Stephen-Henry*, Girdle's son: Arthur Conrad. *Dr. Brabazon*, a specialist: Tony Sullivan. *Lafitte*, proprietor of "The Crimson Butterfly": Horace Whitaker. *Alexis, Ferdinand*, Babori's clerks: J. N. Roseland, J. A. Nugent. *Henri, Pierre*, waiters: James Yates, C. H. Beardsley. *Joseph Boniface*, an artist: H. A. Smith. *Inspector of Police*: J. H. Purcell. *Rosalie*, a maid: BESSIE McCOY. *La Belle Sissi*: BLANCHE DEYO. *Dulcie*, Babori's wife: May Bouton. *Baroness Papouche*: ADELE ROWLAND. *Emmy-Lou*, Girdle's niece: Amy Dale. *Silvie, Therese*, Clients of Babori: Frankie Douglas, Burleigh Murray. *Friends of Felix (4)*: *Clarice*: Gertrude Gibbens. *Sybele*: Violet Handy. *Celeste*: Florence Averell. *Tessa*: Helen St. John. *Page Boy*: Leila Smith. *Artist's Model*: Vivian Rushmore. *Otto*, a Dutch boy: Lois Fennell. *Mrs. Girdle*: EMMA JANVIER. *Ambrose Girdle*: RICHARD CARLE.

Maids: Misses Pouts Barell, Alain, O'Donnell. *Clients*: Misses Handy, Warner, Averell, St. John, Morton, Capron, Fisher, Aroval, Gibbens, Lorena, Murray, Nelligan, Bennett, Windsor, Ashland, Rushmore, Courtney, West, Mansfield, Douglas, Williams. *Grisettes*: Misses Crandall, Leonard, D'Arville, Smith, Raymond, (Avita) Sanchez. *Dutch Boys*: Misses Barrell, Alain, Crandall, Leonard, D'Arville, Smith, Sanchez, Raymond. O'Donnell, Capron, Lorena, Bennett, Windsor, Ashland, West, Cullom, Boley, Mansfield, Warner, Fisher.

Act 1: Office of M. Babori, at his residence in Paris.

Act 2: The Crimson Butterfly Restaurant, Malmaison.

Act 3: A Studio at Malmaison.

ACT 1
- Opening
- "Baron Papouche"
  S. Langlois, Chorus
- "I've Come Along to Paris"
  B. McCoy
  (*Music by* Lionel Monckton. *Lyrics by* Leslie Mayne.)
- "All the Girls Love Me"
  R. Carle, Chorus
  (*Music and Lyrics by* Richard Carle.)
- "Beautiful Spring"
  Chorus
  (*Lyrics by* George Grossmith, Jr.)
- "I Don't Know, But I Guess"
  E. Janvier, Chorus
  (*Music by* Lionel Monckton. *Lyrics by* Adrian Ross.)
- "Baby and Nursie"
  B. McCoy, R. Carle
  (*Music by* Robert Hood Bowers. *Lyrics by* Richard Carle.)
- "Coquin du Printemps"
  V. Morley, Chorus
  (*Lyrics by* George Grossmith, Jr.)
- Finale
  Ensemble

ACT 2
- Opening
- "In Seville"
  B. Deyo, R. Carle, Chorus
  (*Music by* Milton W. Lusk. *Lyrics by* M. E. Rourke.)
- "A Modest Little Maiden"[40]
  A. Dale, A. Conrad
- "Waiting for a Certain Girl"
  V. Morley
  (*Music by* Milton W. Lusk. *Lyrics by* Richard Carle.)

ACT 3
- "In Rotterdam"
  B. McCoy, Dutch Boys
  (*Music by* Lionel Monckton. *Lyrics by* Percy Greenbank, Leslie Mayne.)
- "A Lemon in the Garden of Love"
  R. Carle, Chorus
  (*Music by* Richard Carle. *Lyrics by* M. E. Rourke.)
- Finale
  Ensemble

[40]Dropped after opening.

1906.37 THE RICH MR. HOGGENHEIMER

A Musical Comedy (Farce) in Three Acts. Book and lyrics by Harry B. Smith Music by Ludwig Engländer. Interpolated songs by Jerome D. Kern, Paul West, William Jerome, Jean Schwartz. Staged by Ben Teal. Scenery by Ernest Gros. Costumes designed by Mme. Caroline Siedle. Musical director, Louis F. Gottschalk. Produced by Charles Frohman. Opened 22 October 1906 at Wallack's Theatre and closed 30 March 1907 after 187 performances[41].

CAST: *Mr. Hoggenheimer* ("Piggy"): SAM BERNARD[42]. *Guy*, his son: EDWIN NICANDER. *Hon. Percy Vere*, a society pet: PERCY AMES. *Ned Brandon*, an American college athlete: Ivar Anderson. *Lord Tyrone*: A. G. Krantz. *Hon. Reggie Gordon*: Charles Kenyon. *Lord Bantam*: Dwight Williams. *Chianti*, an Italian tenor: John Ardizone. *Alacarte*, a French basso: Armand Cortes. *Perkins*, butler: Milo Joyce. *Williams*, a valet: William Sleck. *Footman*: Donald dePont. *First Customs Inspector*: Charles Burrows. *Second Customs Inspector*: Arthur Wood. *Carl Wagner*, a steward: Victor LeRoy. *Cabman*: Chris O'Hara. *Policeman*: William Jarratt. *Head Waiter*: Eugene Maurice. *Flora Fair*, an actress: GEORGIA CAINE. *Mrs. Hoggenheimer*: Josephine Kirkwood. *Lady Mildred Vane*: Kathryn Hutchinson. *Amy Leigh*, a shop girl: MARION GARSON. *Miss Wadsworth*: Edith Whitney. *The Duchess of Bedlam*: Helen Morrison. *The Countess of Farnham*: Mattie Rivenberg. *Lady Deadbroke*: Jane Hall. *Lady Doughmore*: Molly McGrath. *Hon. Maud Guest*: Edna Hixon. *Lady Benedict*: Josephine Angela. *Hon. Dolly Berresford*: Rae Irvin. *Sara Land*, a novelist: Lillian Seville. *Marie*, maid: Grace Walsh. *Tom Brown*, a messenger boy: Flossie Hope. *Violet Moss*, flower girl: Carrie Bowman.

Act 1: Mr. Hoggenheimer's drawing-room. Park Lane, London , W.11

Act 2: Dock, North German Lloyd S. S. Company, Hoboken.

Act 3: Mrs. Van Bunk's Garden, great Neck, Long Island.

ACT 1
- "Five O'Clock Tea" (Opening Chorus)
- "Be Demure" (Song)
  G. Caine
- Finale

ACT 2
- "Homeward Bound" (Opening Chorus)
- "Little Old America for Me"[43] (Song)
  I. Anderson
- "Don't You Want a Paper, (Dearie)?"
  G. Caine,
  assisted by Misses Hope, Bowman, Rudd, Sanford, Walsh, Kernell, Walton, Moore
  (*Music by* Jerome Kern. *Lyrics by* Paul West.)
- "Any Old Time at All"
  M. Garson, E. Nicander
  (*Music by* Jean Schwartz. *Lyrics by* William Jerome.)
- "The Bagpipe Serenade"
  G. Caine
  (*Music and Lyrics by* Jerome Kern.)
- Finale

ACT 3[44]
- "For Charity's Sake"/"Cupid's Auction Sale" (Opening Chorus)
  K. Hutchinson
- "Poker Love" (Card Duet)
  F. Hope, C. Bowman
  (*Music by* Jerome Kern. *Lyrics by* Jerome Kern and Paul West.)
- "This World Is a Toy Shop" (Song)
  G. Caine
- Finale

[41]Played a return engagement 25 November 1907 at the Grand Opera House for 9 performances.
[42]Sam Bernard created the character of Mr. Hoggenheimer in the musical THE GIRL FROM KAY'S.
[43]Late in the run replaced by:
"The Homesick Yankee, (or You're Thinking of Home Sweet Home)"
I. Anderson
(*Music and Lyrics by* Kenneth S. Clark.)
[44]Added late in the run to Act 3, following "Poker Love":
"(Au Revoir, My Little) Hyacinth" (Song)
K. Hutchinson, M. Garson, I. Anderson, E. Nicander,
Assisted by Misses Rudd, Sanford, Walsh, Kernell, Walton, Moore, Holtz, Belle, Merrill, Poole
(*Music* by Herman Darewski. *Lyrics by* A.E. Sidney Davis.)

1906.38 EILEEN ASTHORE

A Romantic Irish Drama in Four Acts. Play by Theodore Burt Sayre, founded on the old song "Eileen Alannah, Eileen Asthore." Music and lyrics by Chauncey Olcott. Staged by Augustus Pitou. Scenery painted by Homer Emens, Edward G. Unitt and Joseph Wickes. Orchestra under the direction of Gus Salzer. Produced by Augustus Pitou. Opened 22 October 1906 at the New York Theatre and closed 3 November 1906 after 16 performances.[45]

CAST: *Richard Temple*: CHAUNCEY OLCOTT. *Sir Geoffrey Loftus*: GEORGE E. LESSEY. *Terence O'Donnell*: RICHARD J. DILLON. *Rodney O'Donnell*: ARTHUR JARRETT. *Corney Delaney*: Daniel Jarrett. *McBride*: Charles Ogle. *Dineen*: John Dunne. *Captain McGuire*: William Walters. *O'Toole*: George Brennan. *Dougherty*: Ned Reardon. *Reilly*: Quincey C. Bass, Jr. *Eileen O'Donnell*: FLORENCE LESTER. *Kate Fitzgerald*: Mildred Beverly. *Kitty Duane*: Willa Keys. *Mrs. O'Flanigan*: GERTRUDE D. STANLEY. *Norah O'Toole*: Olive McVine.

Act 1: Lodgings of Richard Temple in Dublin, (1804). Richard falls in love at first sight and pauses on the "Road to Ruin."

Act 2: One year later. A shady spot on the grounds of Terence O'Donnell, near Dublin. Richard Temple goes awooing, angers a rival and saves a friend from arrest.

Act 3: Two months later. Lodgings of Richard Temple in Dublin. Richard Temple breaks his pledge and plays trick for trick with a scoundrel for love and happiness.

Act 4: The following morning. The Harp and Shamrock Inn, near Dublin. Richard Temple meets an old acquaintance, outwits a villain and wins a wife.

MUSICAL NUMBERS[46]
- "Day Dreams"
  (C. Olcott)
- "Eileen Asthore"
  (C. Olcott)
- "For Love of Thee" (Olcott's Love Song)
  (C. Olcott)
- "Wearers of the Green"
  (C. Olcott)
- "The Eyes That Come from Ireland"
  (C. Olcott)
  (*Lyrics by* Richard LeGalliene.)

1906.39 PAINTING THE TOWN

A Musical Hurrah (Farce) in Three Acts. Book by W. F. Carroll. Based on the popular comic strip "Hogan Alley." Music and lyrics by Herman Perlet. Dances arranged by Aurelio Coccia. Produced by Charles H. Yale. Opened 22 October 1906 at the Metropolis Theatre and closed 27 October 1906 after 8 performances.

CAST: *Michael Hogan*: JOHN F. LEONARD. *Martin Brogan*: WILL HALLIDAY. *Captain Thomas Fowler*: ALMON KNOWLES. *Clarice Truffles*: MAZIE KING. *Nellie Duchateau*: EDITH LOWE. *Mrs. Michael Hogan*: LOUISE SANFOD. *Mr. Martin Brogan*: JAMIE LYNCH. *Bob*: Lizzie Oakland. *J. Carl Bedford*: James Johnson. *Max Hoffbrau*: Fred. Borneman. *Felix Lightwait*: Edward Pooley. *Ferrie Deepe*: Edgar S. Allyn. *Justin Voice*: T. H. Bohannon. *U. B. Seeted*: Edward Connelly. *Corkscrew*, the Head Waiter: Aurelio Coccia.

Act 1: Hogan's Alley.

Act 2: The stage of the Folly Music Hall.

Act 3: The Jolie Cafe.

MUSICAL NUMBERS[47]
- "Le Danse des Harlequines"
  M. King
- "All Aboard"
- "By the Seaside"

[45]Costumes uncredited.
[46]Musical Numbers not listed in programs. List prepared from reviews and published sheet music.
[47]No New York program available; musical numbers from a Cedar Rapids tour November 1907.

"Bohemia Is the Life for Me"
"The Dainty Little Maid"
"Dressing Room Echoes"
"Drink Up"
"Emigrants"
"Fatima the Fair"
"Fifteen Minutes"
Grand Operatic Finale Act 2
"The Great Ram-Jam"
"He's a Jolly Good Fellow"
"Hoolah Goolah Stone"
"List to the Pleading"
"The Night Bird Is Calling"
"The One Night Stands"
"Painting the Town"
"Salaam Salaam"
"The Tail of a Kite"
"The Waiters"
"The Walking Family"
"When There Isn't a Girl About"

1906.40 AROUND THE CLOCK

A Musical Farce Comedy in Three Acts. Book by Steve B. Cassin. Music by Lee Orean Smith. Lyrics by J. S. Hiller. Directed by M. L. Heckert. Dances arranged by Dan Dody. Scenery by Ernest Albert, Frank Gates and Edward A. Morange. Costumes by Will R. Barnes. Musical director, J. Albert Brown. Produced by the Sparkling Comedy and Travesty Company (Walter F. Westcott, Manager). Opened 29 October 1906 at the American Theatre and closed 3 November 1906 after 8 performances.[48]

CAST: *Billie Smith*, a drunk, the man from nowhere: BILLIE RITCHIE. *Johnny Mack*, the bell-boy, full of mischief: RICH McALLISTER. *Tom Wilson*, sometimes a liar in the U.S. Army: Ben S. Mears. *Hank Wilson*, Tom's uncle from the Far and Wooly West: JOE F. WILLARD. *Emile Muller*: Sid Franklin. *Edwin Uptown*, a waiter who mixes things: JACK LLOYD. *Deacon Mayfield*, Nellie's father, who adds to the confusion: C. F. Cardon. *Mrs. Muller*: Eda Maley. *Susie*, a maid who maid mischief: Winifred Frances. *Nellie Wilson*, Tom's wife, the cause of it all: SALLIE STEMBLER.

Supplementary Characters in Act 3, by Richie's Pantomime Company: *Gene Holbrook*, an elocutionist: Arthur Spears. *Professor Boni re Burro*, a magician: Leon Kahn. *Pardello*, "the terrible": Harry Taylor. *George Siller*, the referee: Ken Rodgers. *Ben Speal*, stage manager: James E. Garvin. *Tillie*, the program girl: NINA VERNON. *Marie*, her assistant: Dora Dean. *Helen Desmond, Viola Desmond*, the Dancing Soubrettes: Rhea Marble, Jessie LeRoy. *Diana Morley*, coon shouter: Nellie Mason.

Among those present: Maudie Cochrane, Nellie Mason, Phyllis Proctor, Irene Esop, Gabriel Barbier, Genevive Gibson, Elenore Rose, Phoebe Hienes, Julia Kelly, Mabel Bradford, Santo Bernard, Celia St. Clair, Josephine Hamilton, Carrie Dewey, May Taylor, Susie Milton.

Act 1: Mrs. Abbott's home in the outskirts of Philadelphia. New Year'.

Act 2: Same place the next day. The trouble increases.

Act 3, Scene 1: Lobby of Music Hall. *Scene 2*: A stage upon a stage at the vaudeville. More trouble, and lots of it.

ACT 1[48a]
"Hark to the Chimes" (Opening Ensemble)
Chorus
"Idaho" (Cowboy Song)
J. F. Willard, Chorus
"Playland"
S. Stembler, Chorus
"Father Penn"[49] (Grand Ensemble)
Entire Company

ACT 2
"The Waiter Girl"[50]
N. Vernon, Chorus
"The Mighty Dollar" (Topical Song)
S. Franklin, B. S. Mears, J. Lloyd
"Sarah of Sahara"
W. Frances, J. Lloyd
"Rag Bag Man"
J. F. Willard
"Spooning" (Duet)
W. Frances, J. Lloyd
"The Gay and Merry Play"[51] (Grand Ensemble)
Full Company

ACT 3
"The Military Maid"
Chorus
"The Football Girls at Vassar"
J. Lloyd, Chorus
"Around the Clock" (Grand Finale)
Full Company

1906.41 THE BLUE MOON

An English Musical Comedy in Two Acts. Book by Harold Ellis. Music by Howard Talbot and Paul A. Rubens. Lyrics by Percy Greenbank and Paul A. Rubens. (Interpolated numbers by Addison Burkhardt and Gus Edwards.) Produced [staged] by Frank Smithson. Settings by Ernest Albert , Homer Emens, Edward G. Unitt and Joseph Wickes. Costumes by Susie Kerwin. Musical director, Albert Krause. Presented by the Shubert Theatrical Company (Messrs. Shubert). Opened 3 November 1906 at the Casino Theatre and closed 5 January 1907 after 76 performances.

CAST: *Major Vivian Callabone*, head of the garrison at Naga: EDWARD M. FAVOR. *Captain Jack Ormsby*, Lady Brabasham's nephew: TEMPLAR SAXE. *Bobbie Scott*, a journalist: DICK TEMPLE. *Moolraj*, idol maker, juggler and marriage broker: PHIL RYLEY. *Private Charlie Taylor*, acting bandmaster of the Royal Muzzerver-nugger native band: JAMES T. POWERS. *The Prince Badahur Sanatsinjhi*, of Kharikar: Arthur Donaldson. *Hon. Archie May*: Louis Franklin. *Clive Mansfield*: Arthur Bell. *Leslie Arbuthnot*: Joseph West. *Lady Brabasham*: EDITH SINCLAIR. *Evelyn Ormsby*: GRACE LaRUE. *Chandra Nil*, the Blue Moon, a singing girl: ETHEL JACKSON. *Millicent Leroy*, Evelyn's maid: CLARA PALMER. *Miss Lovehill*: Kathryn Robinson. *Miss Lillian Moore*: Lillian Leon. *Oma*, a native: Marjorie Nevin. *Chua*, a native: Lucy Jane Johnstone. *Bingo*: Ada Gordon. *Abdul*: Donald Archer. *Hafiz*: Richard Knollenberg. *Beggarmen*: Max Sharpe, O. W. Risley. *Mail Carrier*: John Kuester. *Private Atkins*: Clarence Satchell. *Dancing Girls*: Lillian Rice, Angie Weimers.

(Dancers) in the Crocodile and Bunny Dances: Maude Carey, Ruth Julien, Effie LaVarre, Loreen Bordman, Ethel Mostyn, Dolly Honey, Elizabeth Hawman, Lillian Rice, Angie Weimers, Virginia Cameron, Blanche Wilmot, Gertrude Barnes, Lillian Boardman. *Tootsa* (imported from England by Moolrai): LA PETITE ADELAIDE. *Original English Pony Ballet, Double Quartette, Officers of the English Army and Navy, English and Native Ladies, Ayahs, Retainers,of the Nizam, Coolies, Jugglers, Natives, Flower Girls, Fruits Sellers, etc.*

Act 1: The Bungalow at Naga. (Albert.)

Act 2: The Ruby Palace at Kharikar. (Emens, Unitt and Wickes.)

ACT 1[52]

---

[48]Returned the following season in revised form 6 January 1908 at the American Theatre for 9 performances; see separate entry in that season.
[48a]Song list prepared from a Wilkes-Barre, Pennsylvania, tour program dated 6 October 1906.
[49]Replaced for subsequent tour by:
"The Gay and Merry Play" (Grand Ensemble)
Full Company

[50]Replaced for subsequent tour by:
"Hello, Miss Liza Green"
B. S. Mears, Company
[51]Replaced for subsequent tour by:
"In Yankee Land"
Full Company
[52]Added for subsequent tour to Act 1:
"Juggler" Dancing March (after "All My Girls")
Pony Ballet
"My Maid of Mandalay" (before Finale, Act 1)Frank Rushworth {Captain Ormsby}
(*Music by* Hans Scherber. *Lyrics by* Roderic Penfield.)
Which was then replaced by (and later dropped):
"If You Only Knew (How Much I Loved You)"
F. Rushworth
(*Music by* Gilbert von Bein. *Lyrics by* Edward Oxenford.)

Opening Chorus
Company
"Major's Song"
E. M. Favor, Company
"Pit-a-Pat"
J. T. Powers, C. Palmer
"All My Girls"
J. T. Powers, E. M. Favor, D. Temple, T. Saxe, Chorus
"(Little) Blue Moon"
E. Jackson
(*Music by* Howard Talbot. *Lyrics by* Percy Greenbank.)
"The Loveland Volunteers"[53]
G. LaRue, Pony Ballet
"The Lady's Maid"[54]
C. Palmer, Pony Ballet
Specialty
La Petite Adelaide
Finale
Company

ACT 2
Opening Chorus
Company
"Burmah Girl"
E. M. Favor, Chorus
(*Music and Lyrics by* Paul Rubens.)
"She Didn't Know"[55]
C. Palmer
(*Music and Lyrics by* Paul Rubens.)
"(Oh, Be Careful of the) Crocodile"
J. T. Powers, Chorus
(*Music and Lyrics by* Paul A. Rubens.)
"Fairest of the Fair"
Company
"La Koguette"
Pony Ballet
"(Don't You Think It's) Time to Marry?"
G. LaRue, D. Temple, Chorus
(*Music by* Gus Edwards. *Lyrics by* Addison Burkhardt.)
Entertainments
C. Palmer, J. T. Powers
Bridal Chorus
Company

1906.42 FORTY-FIVE MINUTES FROM BROADWAY

A Return Engagement of the Play with Music in Three Acts[56]. Book, music and lyrics by George M. Cohan. Staged by George M. Cohan. Settings by John Young (Act 1), Ernest Albert (Act 2), Frank Marsden (Act 3). Costumes by F. Richard Anderson. Electrical effects by Harry Bissing. Orchestra under the direction of Frederic Solomon. Business direction, Sam H. Harris. Produced by Marc Klaw and Abraham L. Erlanger. Opened 5 November 1906 at the New York Theatre and closed 1 December 1906 after 32 performances.

CAST: *Mary Jane Jenkins*, the housemaid: FAY TEMPLETON. *Flora Dora Dean*, a footlight favorite: EMMA LITTLEFIELD. *Mrs. David Dean*, her mother: JULIA RALPH. *Mrs. Purdy*, a resident of New Rochelle: Marion Singer. *Tom Bennet*, the heir-at-law: DONALD BRIAN. *Kid Burns*, his secretary: VICTOR MOORE. *James Blake*, Public Administrator, man about town: Charles Prince. *Daniel Cronin* in the mining business: JAMES H. MANNING. *Andy Gray*, the butler: LOUIS R. GRISEL. *Station Master*: Maurice Elliot. *Police Sergeant*: Floyd E. Francis. *Messenger Boy*: Charles Friedland. *New Rochelle Girls (8)*: *Polly Poughkeepsie*: Tessie Solomon. *Pauline Peekskill*: Lillian Leroy. *Tessy Tarrytown*: Katherine Melton. *Fannie Fordham*: Dorothy Lee. *Rose Rye*: Madeline LeBoeuf. *Minnie Melrose*: Marguerite Lane. *Teresa Tuckahoe*: Clara Dollard. *Winnie Wakefield*: Evelyn Francis. *Reporters*: Eugene McGregor, Joe Simons, A. Claire Heath, Alf DeBall. *Policemen*: Messrs. J. S. Donnelly, Ned Achard, Frank Benor.

1906.43 MRS. WILSON, THAT'S ALL

A Comedy with Songs in Three Acts[57]. Play by George V. Hobart. Orchestra under the direction of John C. Sorg. Produced by May Irwin. Opened 5 November 1906 at the Bijou Theatre and closed 22 December 1906 after 52 performances[58].

CAST: *Mrs. Wilson*: MAY IRWIN. *Colonel Andrews*, her second venture: ADOLPH JACKSON. *Gerald McSweeney*[59], a messenger from the past: JOHN E. HAZZARD *Mrs. Gilsey*: LILLIAN DIX. *Manuel Gettenheimer*, a Jew (her broker): VICTOR CASSMORE. *Rhoda Kingston*, her confidante: Mary K. Taylor. *Mrs. Kate Clancy*,, her janitress: May Donohue. *Walter Roberts*, her brother: C. Russell Sage. *Mabel Keswick*, her brother's ideal: Madelon Temple. *James*, her cook: J. Early Hughes. *Centipede Sam*, her cowboy: BEN ROTH. *Pierre*, her dressmaker's apprentice: Herbert Burton. *Godolphin Haggerty*, her surprise: Willie Gray. *Hausenbauer*, her calamity's barber: Henry Hoster. *Her society friends (4)*: *Mrs. Garrett*: Kate Gotthold. *Mrs. Beckwith*: Tilley Monroe. *Mrs. Bostwick*: Dorothy Baines. *Miss Morrison*: Maude Forrest.

The action takes place in a New York Apartment House.

Act 1: Morning.

Act 2: Afternoon, two weeks later.

Act 3: Evening.

MUSICAL NUMBERS[60]
"Dan"
(*Music by* May Irwin. *Lyrics by* Earl Jones.)
"Matrimony"
(*Music and Lyrics by* William J. McKenna.)
"Moonshine"
(*Music by* Silvio Hein. *Lyrics by* George V. Hobart and Edward Montagu.)
"Honora Doolin"
(*Music by* Ted Snyder. *Lyrics by* Bowman Brothers.)
"Moses Andrew Jackson, Goodbye"
(*Music by* Ted Snyder. *Lyrics by* Ren Shields.)

1906.44 MAMSELLE SALLIE

A Musical Comedy in Two Acts. Book and lyrics by Robert B. Smith. Book revised by George Totten Smith. Music by Raymond Hubbell. Staged by Charles H. Jones. Music under direction of Frank P. Paret. Produced by the John C. Fisher Company. Opened 26 November 1906 at the Grand Opera House, moved 3 December 1906 to the New York Theatre and closed 15 December 1906 after 24 performances[61].

CAST: *Mamselle Sallie*, a ladies' hairdresser: KATIE BARRY. *Jonathan Joy*, masquerading as an English lawyer, in reality a waiter: JOHN SLAVIN. *Professor Marrow*, professor of archaeology in the seminary: GEORGE E MACK. *Muriel Oliver*, one of Mme. Woodbury's pupils: FLORENCE QUINN. *Elaine*, Mme. Woodbury's daughter: AGNES FINLEY. *Marco Bazzaris*, a Greek nobleman: WILLIAM P. CARLETON, JR. *Anthony Oliver*, Muriel's father: Sydney deGrey. *Emile Martell*, a cadet in French

[53]Dropped during the run.
[54]Replaced for subsequent tour by:
"Why Don't You Take Out One Little Boy"
C. Palmer
(*Music and Lyrics by* Will R. Anderson.)
[55]Replaced for subsequent tour by:
"I Told a Friend of Mine"
C. Palmer
[56]First produced in New York 1 January 1906 at the New Amsterdam Theatre for 90 performances. For Synopsis of Scenes and Musical Numbers, see original 1906 production.

[57]After two weeks the play's title was changed to MRS. WILSON ANDREWS.
[58]Settings, costumes uncredited.
[59]After two weeks, character was renamed Herman Schultz, her calamity.
[60]Not necessarily in performance order, all sung by May Irwin. Added for subsequent tour in 1907:
"Save a Little Money for a Rainy Day"
M. Irwin
(*Music by* Maxwell Silver. *Lyrics by* Ren Shields.)
[61]Revised by its authors and presented the following season as KNIGHT FOR A DAY, 16 December 1907 at Wallack's Theatre for 176 performances.

military school: JACK HENDERSON. *Mme. Woodbury* of the Woodbury Seminary for Young Ladies: DELLA NIVEN. *The Mysterious Greek*: Joseph Monahan. *Gendarmes*: Harry St. Clair, George W. Wilson.

School Girls (12): *Miss Genevieve Devere Devoe*: Olive Roberts. *Miss Angeline Boucicault*: Pauline Winters. *Miss Alice Collins*: Monte Blair. *Miss Gertrude Summers*: Gertrude Scott. *Miss Mildred Rollins*: Virginia Calvert. *Miss Marie Monroe*: Eleanor Rose. *Miss Henrietta Wetherby*: Adelaide Arnold. *Miss Laura Williard Witcherly*: Mabel Morris. *Miss Helen Hudson*: Beatrice deRuelle. *Miss Mary Winters*: Rose Doyle. *Miss Judith Judson*: Lucille Losee. *Miss Virginia Lee*: Octavie Hague. *Cupid*: Rita Walker.

Lady Visitors: Misses Maude Morrison, Kathleen Moore, Carolyn Barber, Mabel Fairfax, Louise Tozier, Theresa Van Brune, Beryl Gomez, Lucille Georgi. *Art Students*: Messrs. Reginald Newman, Charles West, Tracie Clark, Charles Kain, Theodore Whitehill, H. A. Robe, H. B. Hillier, Irvin Klinger. *Military Cadets*: Messrs. Joseph Craven, Charles Vandivere, George W. Wilson, J. C. Sheridan, Frank Reilly, Harry St. Clair, A. D. Morton, G. R. Stevens. *Hairdressers*: Misses Santa Bernard, Anna Goodwin, Ethel Merriles, May Roche, Leah Lang, Helen Keers. *Butterfly Dancers*: Misses Margaret Taylor, Vera Birke, Ada Burgess, Amy Burgess, Emme Walker, Cissie Petherbridge. *Greek Peasants*: Misses Anna Goodwin, Ethel Merriles, Leah Lang, Santa Bernard, May Roche, Kathleen Moore, Beryl Gomez, Helen Keers. *Greek Men*: Messrs. George W. Wilson, Harry St. Clair, Tracie Clark, Charles West, Charles Kain, H. A. Robe, Erwin Klinger, H. B. Hillier, J. C. Newell, Theodore Whitehill.

Act 1: Auburn Manor. The Grounds of Mme. Woodbury's Saminary. The Riviera, France.

Act 2: An Old Estate in the Mountains of Thessaly, Greece.

ACT 1

"The Sweet Girl Graduate" (Opening Chorus)
Ensemble

"Every Little Object Has a History" (Song)
G. E. Mack, School Girls

"A Million" (Ensemble)
Chorus

"I'm a Lawyer" (Entrance Song)
J. Slavin, Chorus

"Another Situation"
K. Barry

"Life Is a See-Saw" (Duet)
F. Quinn, W. P. Carleton, Chorus

"Farewell, Prosperity"
J. Slavin
(*Music by* Lester Keith. *Lyrics by* John Kemble.)

Finale
Ensemble

ACT 2

"Thessaly" (Opening Chorus)
Chorus

"Her Portrait" (Song)
W. P. Carleton, Chorus

"La Parisienne" (Dance)
Butterfly Dancers

"Love Makes the World Go Round" (Song)
F. Quinn, Chorus

"And I Laughed" (Song)
K. Barry

"You Never Told Me That Before We Were Married" (Song)
A. Finley, J. Henderson

"Hurroo, Hurray, and Hurrah for That" (Song)
J. Slavin

"Whistle When You Walk Out" (Song)
G. E. Mack, Chorus

Finale
Ensemble

1906.45 A PARISIAN MODEL

A Musical Comedy in Three Acts, 4 Scenes. Book and lyrics by Harry B. Smith. Music by Max Hoffmann. (Interpolated numbers by Vincent Bryan, P. H. Christine, Will D. Cobb and Gus Edwards.) Staged by Julian Mitchell. Settings by Ernest Albert. Costumes by Mrs. Caroline Siedle and Landolff, Paris. Lighting by Louis Lamont. Orchestra under the direction of Max Hoffmann. Produced under the personal direction of Florenz Ziegfeld. Presented by Frank McKee. Opened 27 November 1906 at the Broadway Theatre and closed 29 June 1907 after 179 performances[62].

CAST (in order of appearance): *Customers at Callot's (10)*: *Marcelle*: Edith Daniell. *Paulette*: Grace Leigh. *Suzanne*: Grace Russell. *Therese*: Adelaide Orton. *Fleurette*: Phyllis Grey. *Adrienne*: Janet Burton. *Helene*: Aurora Piatt. *Jeanette*: Ada St. Clair. *Heloise*: Dorothy Waldron. *Hortense*: Mabel Spencer. *Callot*, dictator of fashions: EDOUARD DURAND. *Violette* of the Opera Comique: TRULY SHATTUCK. *Hercule* of the Paris Olympia: F. Stanton Heck. *Silas Goldfinch*, who is trying to spend his money: CHARLES A. BIGELOW. *Fifine*, *Titine*, Ballet Girls of the Opera House: Ethel Gilmore, Madlyn Summers. *Anna*, the Parisian model: ANNA HELD. *Carver Stone*, an American sculptor: James H. Bradbury. *Julien de Marsay*, an artist: HENRY LEONI. *Celeste*, a shop girl at Callot's: Adele Carson. *Grand Prix Girls (8)*: *Fanchonette*: Grace Leigh. *Denise*: Phyllis Grey. *Georgette*: Janet Burton. *Francine*: Aurora Piatt. *Diane*: Edith Daniell. *Claudine*: Mabel Spencer. *Josie*: Dorothy Waldron. *Marie*: Adelaide Orton. *Mrs. Silas Goldfinch*: Mabella Baker. *Colombe*, a dancing girl: GERTRUDE HOFFMANN. *Adele*, *Marie*, Anna's maids: Adelaide Orton, Edith Daniell. *Collectors of money and oil paintings (8)*: *Mr. Moregain*: G. B. Scott. *Mr. Rathskeller*: Charles Hessong. *Mr. Cornergie*: W. J. Ford. *Mr. New Depot*: John Abbott. *Mr. Rates*: William James. *Mr. Shark*: C. M. Books. *Mr. Keno*: John Roche. *Mr. Quick*: Carl Morgan. *Director of the "Palais de Patinage"*: Lew Quinn. *El Rio Rey*: Earle Reynolds. *Jeanne*: Bertha Mack.

(*Ensemble*: Misses Marjorie Bonner, Libbie Diamond, Julia Eastman, Ethel Gilmore, Jessie Howe, Madelaine Summers, Gertrude Thayer, Edith Warner, G. Conklin, Dorothy Bertrand, B. Hoffman, I. Howe, L. Marion, E. Marsh, C. Rodgers. Messrs. MacKinley, Books, Ford, Hessong, Roche, Scott.)

Act 1: Callot's dressmaking establishment, Rue de la Paix, Paris.

Act 2: Sculptor's studio.

Act 3, Scene 1: Boudoir of Mlle. Anna de la Fontaine. *Scene 2*: Palais de Patinage—The Skating Rink.

ACT 1[63]

"Trying on Dresses" (Opening Chorus)

"The Only Man I Ever Loved"[64] (Song)
T. Shattuck, Chorus

"I'm the Man (They Talk About So Much)" (Song)
C. A. Bigelow, with M. Bonner, L. Diamond,
J. Eastman, E. Gilmore, J. Howe, M. Summers, G. Thayer, E. Warner

"A Gown for Each Hour of the Day" (Solo)
A. Held, Chorus

(introducing the Paris "La Mattchiche"
A. Held, G. Hoffmann)

"The American Girl in Paris"[65]
H. Leoni, Grand Prix Girls

"A Lesson in Kissing" (Kiss Kiss Kiss)(If You Want to Learn to Kiss)(Duet)
A. Held, C. A. Bigelow

Finale

ACT 2[66]

"Paris Carnival" (Opening Chorus)

"Lots of Good Fish in the Sea"[67] (Song)
H. Leoni, Chorus

---

[62]Played return engagements 30 September 1907 at the Grand Opera House for 8 performances, and 6 January 1908 at the Broadway Theatre for 21 performances (see separate entry).

[63]Added to Act 1, after Opening Chorus, for subsequent tour and return engagements:
"The Story That Never Grows Old"
H. Leoni
(*Music by* Seymour Furth. *Lyrics by* Edward P. Moran.)
Also performed during the run, as per published sheet music:
"When Uncle Sammy Sings the Marseillaise"
H. Leoni
(*Music by* Herman Avery Wade. *Lyrics by* Earle C. Jones.)

[64]Dropped early in the run.

[65]Replaced for subsequent tour and return engagements by:
"The Whistling Yankee Girl"
Edith Decker {Violette}, American Girls
(*Music by* Seymour Furth. *Lyrics by* Edward P. Moran.)

[66]Added during the run to Act 2, after "Artists and Models", and retained for tour and return engagements:
"Won't You Be My Teddy Bear?" (Will You Be My Teddy Bear)
A. Held, Ladies' Ensemble with trained "bears"
(*Music by* Max Hoffmann. *Lyrics by* Vincent Bryan.)

[67]Dropped early in the run.

Dance and Caricatures of Famous Artists[68]

"I (Just) Can't Make My Eyes Behave"

A. Held

(*Music and Lyrics by* Will D. Cobb, Gus Edwards, Harry B. Smith.)

"Artists and Models"[69]

Misses Daniell, Grey, Leigh, Orton, Spencer, Waldron
Messrs. MacKinley, Books, Ford, Hessong, Roche, Scott

"(I Love You) Ma Cherie (My Sweetheart)"[70]

H. Leoni

(*Music and Lyrics by* Paul Rubens.)

"In Washington"

C. A. Bigelow

(*Music and Lyrics by* Vincent Bryan, Max Hoffmann, Harry B. Smith.)

"(On) San Francisco Bay"

T. Shattuck, Company

(*Music by* Gertrude Hoffmann. *Lyrics by* Vincent Bryan.)

Finale

ACT 3

"Bells" (The Bell Song)(Opening Chorus)

Misses D. Bertrand, M. Bonner, A. Carson, G. Conklin,
L. Diamond, J. Eastman, E. Gilmore, B. Hoffman, I. Howe, J. Howe, L. Marion,
E. Marsh, C. Rodgers, M. Summers, G. Thayer, E. Warner

"When We're Married"[71] (Duet)

A. Held, H. Leoni

Finale (Skating Scene) introducing "Skating Song"[72]

L. Quinn, M. Leslie, B. Mack, E. Reynolds, Babette Angleterre {C. A. Bigelow}

1906.46 PIONEER DAYS and NEPTUNE'S DAUGHTER

A Triple Bill of a Spectacular Drama (Pioneer Days) in 3 Scenes, a Program of Circus Events, and an Operatic Extravaganza (Neptune's Daughter) in 3 Scenes. Staged by Edward P. Temple. Scenery by Arthur Voegtlin. Costumes designed by Alfredo Edel. Electrical effects by John F. Corrigan. Musical direction, Manuel Klein. Produced by the Messrs. Shubert and M. C. Anderson. Opened 28 November 1906 at the Hippodrome and closed 25 May 1907; re-opened 31 August 1907 at the Hippodrome and closed 23 November 1907 after 288 performances.

ACT 1

PIONEER DAYS. A Spectacular Drama of Western Life by Carroll Fleming. Music by Manuel Klein. Staged by Edward P. Temple. Scenery by Arthur Voegtlin.

CAST: *Lew Bridger*, Indian Scout, Trapper: W. H. CLARKE. *Sheriff Bart Hickok*: J. P. COOMBS. *Judge Sweezy*: JOHN G. SPARKS. *Big Lige Hawkins*: George Holland. *Deputy Sheriffs (4)*: *Jim Gillan*: Sam Baker. *Mat Riley*: Phil Gilpin. *Jack Hardy*: Jiggs Donohue. *Dan Dawson*: Tom Trimlets. *Jeff Rawlins*, Driver of Coach: Jim Thompson. *Joe Brant*, Guard of Coach: Wyatt Barnes. *Jess Busby*, Pony Messenger: JAMES GABRIEL. *Outlaws (5)*: *Bat Hussey*: J. Artressi. *Nick Horton*: James Balno. *Tom Pew*: Abe Aronson. *Art Hoskins*: John Fleming. *Cy Scribner*: James Ashburn. *Wounded Snake*, a Half Breed: George Melville. *Lone Wolf*, a Half Breed: Jack Warren. *Half Breeds*: James Adams, Clyde Powers, J. Hanson, W. Harris, A. Romeo. *Keeper of Store*: Harry Dale. *The Fiddler*: D. J. McCaffrey. *Ting Wing*, Chinese Laundry Man: Charles Ravel. *Captain Harrington of U.S.A.*: H. J. Siegfried. *Lieutenant Drummond*: H. E. Cluett. *Mounted Orderly*: Frank Melville. *Miss Virginia Harrington*: Eva MacKenzie.

A Band of Sioux Indians from the Pine Ridge Agency in South Dakota, in (the) charge of Scout James Gabriel, formerly dispatch rider for General Nelson A. Miles in the Wounded Knee Campaign of 1890. *Sioux Chiefs*: Black Horn, William Sitting Bull, Iron Bird, White Bone, Bear-in-the-Woods, Lone Wolf. *Medicine Men and Braves*: Blue Shield, Charging Thunder, Spotted Eagle, John Littlke-Elk, James Gray-Blanket, Willie Red-Shirt, Harry White-Blanket, Sweet Mouth, Harry Big-White-Horse, Luke Big-Turnip, Levi Sitting-Hawk, Bluffing Bear, Albert Running-Bear, Frank Good-Buffalo, George Lone-Crow Long Bear, Abraham Good-Crow, George Red-Elk, James Eagle-Spear, Rueben White-Star, Running Bear, Peter Iron-Rope, Alex Iron-Bear, Big Charger, Bawling Bull, Spotted Weasel, Albert Bear-Killer, Nathan Lone-Wolf, Thomas Loafer, John Ledeauk, David Standing-Bear, Daniel Black-Horn. *Squaws*: Mrs. Nellie Big Turnip, Mrs. Mary White Star, Mrs. Lucy Little Elk, Mrs. Amelia Spotted Eagle, Mrs. Jennie LaPointe, Mrs. Ella Long Bear, Mrs. Spotted Weasel, Mrs. Julia Big Charger, Mrs. Lucy Sitting Bull, Miss Rosie Red Bear. *Papooses and Children*: Master Charlie Spotted Eagle, Master Oscar Spotted Eagle, Miss Victoria Spotted Eagle, Master Joseph Long Bear, Master George Washington Spotted Weasel, Miss Susie Big Charger, Miss Nancy Sitting Bull, Miss Rose Gabriel Sitting Bull (aged 3 months). *Interpreter*: Henry Standing Bear.

Scene 1: A Western Town in Pioneer Days. *Scene 2*: In the Mountains. *Scene 3*: The Hold-Up.

MUSICAL NUMBERS

Scene 2

Indian Dance (Indian War Song)

"Hymn To the Sun"

ACT 2

CIRCUS EVENTS. Specialties[73] included Herzog's Performing Stallions (Six Beautiful Animals in an Unequalled Act), The Rowlands (Novel Equestrian Tally-ho Act), Powers' Elephants (The Famous Hippodrome Herd of Trained Pachyderms), "Little Hip" (the Smallest Elephant in the World), The Curzon Sisters (Novel Gymnasts), The Four Holloways (Sensational Wire Act), The Dollar Troupe (Seven Incomparable Acrobats), The Patty-Franks (Extraordinary Acrobats), Eight Flying Jordans (Most Sensational Wire Act Ever Seen) Frank Melville, Equestrian director.

ACT 3

NEPTUNE' S DAUGHTER. A Romantic Operatic Extravaganza in 3 Scenes. Book and lyrics by Manuel Klein and Edward P. Temple. Music by Manuel Klein. Original scenario by H. L. Bowdoin. Scenery by Arthur Voegtlin. Costumes by Alfredo Edel of Paris. Water effects invented by H. L. Bowdoin. Ballet master, Vincenzo Romeo.

CAST: *Jean Dubois*, a well-to-do fisherman: J. PARKER COOMBS. *Margot*, his wife: ROSE LaHARTE. *Hibou*, the Oracle: JOHN G. SPARKS. *Gaston*, a Fisherman: Sam Baker. *François*, a Fisherman: Angelo Barbara. *Richard*, a Fisherman: Harry Dale. *Marianna, Henriette, Fifine*, 3 Fish Wives: Agnes Williamson, Leila Romer, Albertine Glennon. *Pierre*, 6 years old: LeRoy Casling. *King Neptune*: W. H. CLARKE. *Sirene*, a Water-Nymph: MARGARET TOWNSHEND. *Pierre*, (24 years old): EDWIN A. CLARKE. *Annette*, the Foster Child Rescued from the Sea: MARIE LOUISE GRIBBON. *Hibou*, the Oracle: JOHN G. SPARKS. *Tinou*, a Silent Fisherman: Marceline. *Chorus of Sirens, Mermaids, Mermen, Tritons, Crabs, Lobsters and Octopuses*.

Scene 1: A Fishing Port on the Coast of Brittany, France. *Scene 2*: Same as Act 1. Eighteen years later. *Scene 3*: The Court of King Neptune.

---

[68]Replaced for subsequent tour and return engagements by:

"The Gibson Girl"

Otis Harlan {Silas Goldfinch}, F. Stanton Heck {Hercule}, George Wharnock {Carver Stone}

[69]Program footnotes also credit the song (performed by the "Artists and Models"):

"I'd Like to See a Little More of You"

(*Music and Lyrics by* Will D. Cobb, Gus Edwards.)

[70]Added to Act 2, performed along with "Ma Cherie" for subsequent tour and return engagements:

"I Want You Ma' Honey" [in French]

H. Leoni

[71]Replaced during the run by:

"It's Delightful to Be Married" (Duet)

A. Held, H. Leoni

(*Music by* P. H. Christine and Vincent Scotto. *Lyrics by* Anna Held.)
Sheet music notes: Anna Held's version of the Parisian success 'Petite Tonkinese')

[72]Tour and return engagements programs add the credit "Staged by Gertrude Hoffmann."

[73]Other Circus Specialties which performed during the run included Webb's Performing Seals and Sea-Lions, Marceline—the Droll (Most Celebrated Pantomime Artist in the World), The Niards (European Acrobats in Unique Feats), 24 Bedouin Arabs, and The Four Karolys (Royal Hungarian Riders).

MUSICAL NUMBERS
Scene 1
Opening Ensemble
Hornpipe
"The Angelus"
"Red Sky" (Song of the Weather Oracle)
The Storm
Scene 2
Welcome Home of Pierre
"Lucia (My Italian Maid)"
E. A. Clark
Annette's Refusal to Marry Pierre
Appearance of Mermaids
Pierre's Farewell to Earth
Annette's Appeal to Neptune
Arrival of Neptune and Attendants
Annette's Departure
Finale
Scene 3
Chorus of Mermaids and Pierre
E. A. Clark, Chorus
Entrance of Neptune and Annette
Meeting of Annette and Pierre
Preparation for the Wedding
"Under the Sea" (Ballet)
Wedding Procession
Finale

1906.47 THE BELLE OF MAYFAIR

A Musical Comedy in Two Acts. Book and lyrics by Charles H. E. Brookfield and Cosmo Hamilton[74]. Music by Leslie Stuart. Stage under the direction of Harry B. Burcher. Scenery by Young Brothers and Boss. Gowns originated by F. Crew-Jones, John Wanamaker; modern clothes by Ritchie-Harnden & Company. Orchestra under the direction of Antonio DeNovellis. Produced by Thomas W. Ryley. Opened 3 December 1906 at Daly's Theatre and closed 30 March 1907 after 140 performances.

CAST: *The Earl of Mount Highgate*: HARRY B. BURCHER. *Honorable Raymond Finchley*: VAN RENSSELAER WHEELER. *Sir John Chaldicott, Bart, M.P.*: RICHARD F. CARROLL. *Comte de Perrier*: IGNACIO MARTINETTI. *Hugh Meredith*: JACK GARDNER. *Sir George Cheatham, K.C.*: J. Louis Mintz. *Charlie Goodyer*: Cyril Offage. *Bandmaster*: J. Costellanos. *Simpson*, footman to Sir John: Frank W. Shea. *Bramley*, footman to Lord Mt. Highgate: W. Freeman. *H.S.H. Princess Carl of Ehbreneitstein*: IRENE BENTLEY. *The Countess of Mount Highgate*: Honore French. *Lady Chaldicott*: Jennie Opie. *Julia*, her daughter: CHRISTIE MacDONALD. *Duchess of Dunmow*: VALESKA SURATT. *Lady Violet Gussop*: Annabelle Whitford. *Debutantes (8)*: *Lady Jay*: May Hobson. *Lady Paquin*: Elenore Pendleton. *Lady Louise*: Margaret Rutledge. *Lady Lucille*: Hattie Forsythe. *Lady Peter Robinson*: Stella Beardsley. *Lady Hayward*: Clare Cascelles. *Lady Swan*: Elizabeth Whitney. *Lady Edgar*: Rose Beatrice Winter.

Stall-holders: Misses Florence Gardner, Eula Mannering, Beulah Martin, Caroline Lee, Palmyre Monnett, Lillian Earle, Beatrix Tuite-Dalton, Sadie Miner, Bessie Penn, Alice Tallant, Alice Knowlton, Myrtle Lawton, Florence Saville, Viola Bowers, Gene Cole, Maud Faulkland. *Little Buds*: Misses Dorothy Hutchinson, Edith Barr, Effie Wheeler, Ethel Davis, Grace Russell, Rose Eaton, Ethel Vivian. *Guests*: Messrs. Joseph Parsons, Pierre Young, Harry Husk, Walter Grover, William Griffin, Arthur Nestor, Trestell Ayres, J. Sidney, Richard Davis, Harry Hoffman, J. Davis. *Cupid*: Roselle Esposit.

Act 1: A Bazaar in a private park

Act 2: Drawing-room in Sir John Caldicott's house.

ACT 1
Opening Chorus
(*Lyrics by* Basil Hood.)
"Bells in the Morning" (Song)
B. Clayton
(*Lyrics by* William Caine.)
"I'm a Miltary Man" (Song)
H. B. Burcher
(*Lyrics by* William Caine.)
"Eight Little Debutantes Are We" (Song—Concerted Number)
Debutantes
(*Lyrics by* William Caine.)
"I'm a Duchess" (Song)
V. Suratt
(*Lyrics by* Basil Hood.)
"In Gay Mayfair"[75] (Song)
C. MacDonald
(*Lyrics by* William Caine.)
"Welcome to Princess" (Chorus)
(*Lyrics by* Basil Hood.)
"Said I to Myself"[76] (Song)
I. Bentley
(*Lyrics by* Basil Hood.)
"Where You Go Will I Go" (Song)
C. MacDonald
(*Lyrics by* Basil Hood.)
"Come to St. George's"
C. MacDonald, I. Bentley, V. R. Wheeler, J. Gardner
(*Lyrics by* Leslie Stuart.)
Finale
(*Lyrics by* Basil Hood.)

ACT 2
Opening Chorus
(*Lyrics by* Basil Hood.)
"My Lady Fair" (Song)
A. Knowlton, Chorus
"My Little Girl is a Shy Little Girl" (Duet)
B. Clayton, I. Martinetti
(*Lyrics by* Basil Hood.)
"Hello, Come Along Girls" (Song)
J. Gardner, Debutantes, Little Buds
(*Lyrics by* Leslie Stuart.)
"We've Come from Court" (Quintette)
C. MacDonald, I. Bentley, J. Opie, I. Martinetti, J. L. Mintz, Guests
(*Lyrics by* Basil Hood.)
"And the Weeping Willow Wept" (Song)
I. Bentley
(*Lyrics by* George Arthurs.)
"The Little Girl at the Sweet Shop"
C. MacDonald
"What Makes the Woman?"[77] (Song)
V. R. Wheeler
(*Lyrics by* George Arthurs.)
Doll Dance[78]
B. Clayton
"Why Do They Call Me a Gibson Girl?" (Song)
V. Suratt, H. Burcher, Debutantes
(*Lyrics by* Leslie Stiles.)
"I Know a Girl" (Song)
V. R. Wheeler, J. Gardner, I. Martinetti, H. B. Burcher, R. F. Carroll
(*Lyrics by* Leslie Stuart.)
"Come to St. George's" (Finale)

---

[74]Authorship in London previously billed to C. H. E. Brookfield and Basil Hood.

[75]For subsequent tour, replaced by :
"Pierrot" (Song)
Countess Olga Von Hatzfeldt {Julia Caldicott}

[76]For subsequent tour, replaced by:
"Montezuma"
O. Von Hatzfeldt
(*Lyrics by* Leslie Stuart.)

[77]Dropped for subsequent tour.

[78]Dropped for subsequent tour.

1906.48 DREAM CITY and THE MAGIC KNIGHT

A Dramatic Pipe in Two Puffs (A comic opera, DREAM CITY, accompanied by a burlesque, THE MAGIC KNIGHT). Dialogue and lyrics by Edgar Smith. Music by Victor Herbert. Staged by Al Holbrook. Settings by Ernest Albert. Costumes by Will R. Barnes, Mme. Castel-Bert. Musical director, Louis F. Gottschalk. Produced by Joe Weber. Opened 25 December 1906 at Weber's Music Hall and closed 23 March 1907 after 102 performances.

CAST: *Wilhelm Dinglebender*, a Long Island truck farmer, with a dreamy disposition and a chronic distaste for labor: JOE WEBER. *J. Billington Holmes*, a real estate boomer, with the plans of an ideal city: OTIS HARLAN. *Henri D'Absinthe*, an artist seeking rural atmosphere: MAURICE FARKOA. *Seth Hubbs*, village hackman and the oracle of Malaria Center: WILLIAM T. HODGE. *Henry Peck*, a city flat-dweller, spending the week-end with his family in the country: W. L. Romaine. *Willie Peck*, his restless offspring: Lores Grimm. *Old Man Platt*, a relic: Major Johnson. *Joe Snediker, Hank Scudder, Hen Conklin*, village romeos: W. Douglas Stevenson, Ernest Wood, James McCormack. *Tuffie*, an incubator chicken: David Abrams. *Big Bill Hankins*, a farm hand: Will Lodella. *Nancy*, Dinglebender's daughter and the belle of Malaria Center: CECILIA LOFTUS. *Marie Dinglebender*, his wife, with energy enough for two and a bossy disposition: Lillian Lee. *Amanda Boggs*, the "help" at the Dinglebender farm: Madelyn Marshall. *Mrs. Henry Peck*, with alleged society connections in the metropolis: Cora Tracy. *Mabel, Maude, Gladys*, her daughters: Billy Norton, Lois Ewell, Lillian deLee. *Sarah Smith*, a villager: Ella Tate.

Others who assist more or less in this performance are: Isabel Plunkitt, Pauline Barrett, Helen Barrett, Grace Spencer, Elsie Heins, Vonnie Hoyt, Pauline Huntley, Fay Tichner, Kitty Wheaton, Lillian Fitzgerald, Eva Francis, Beatrice Learwood, Martha Bright, Edna Chase, Susie Pitt, Gertrude Grant, Daisy Fair, Minie Martrit, Bertha Compton, Belle Desmond, Dorothy Southwick, Natalie Dagwell, Helene Hall, Alice DeVere, Lillian Wallace, Virginia Richmond, Eunice Mackey, Peggy Ten Brook, Eleanor Wilson, Bertha Wisser, Nellie Wisser, Esther Darrell, Alice Bertrand, Annie Thompson, Lettie Adams, W. H. Vickery, A. Berg, Herbert Aldrich, E. C. Norrington, A. H. Fletcher, J. A. Ried, E. Plummer, W. T. Johnson, M. Fair, Charles McGrath, Addison Stanton, John S. Bowden.

THE MAGIC KNIGHT, A Dash at Grand Opera (Burlesque of Richard Wagner's opera "Lohengrin.") incidental to Puff 2. Music by Victor Herbert. Libretto by Edgar Smith.

CAST: *Elsa*, a typical grand-operatic maiden in the usual distressing predicament: LILLIAN BLAUVELT. *Ortrud*, her contralto aunt, given to dabbling in the art of magic: CORA TRACY. *Frederick*, her hen-pecked uncle: OTIS HARLAN. *The King*, a base monarch: FRANK BELCHER. *Lohengrin*, a professional rescuer of distressed maidens: MAURICE FARKOA. *The Herald*, a medieval news announcer: W. L. Romaine. *The Swan, Godfrey*, an item in a foul conspiracy: Lores Grimm. *Lastnite, Tunite, Tumaronite*, three knights: Billy Norton, Lois Ewell, Lillian deLee. *Knights, maidens, men-at-arms, pages, vassals and other minor details of grand opera.*

Time: The immediate future, according to current real estate advertisements.

Puff 1: The Dinglebender Farm at Malaria Center, Long Island.

Puff 2: (a) The principal square in Dream City. (b) Interior of Dream City Opera House.

PUFF 1 (Act 1)[79]

"Oh, the heat and the skeet!" (Opening Chorus)
Ensemble

"Down a Shady Lane" (Sextette)
B. Norton, L. Ewell, L. Lee, W. D. Stevenson, E. Wood, J. McCormack

"A Farmer's Life" (Song)
J. Weber, Ensemble

"Improvements" (Song)
O. Harlan, Ensemble

"A Shy Suburban Maid" (Song, with imitations)
C. Loftus

"(Nancy,) I Fancy You" (Song)
M. Farkoa

Finale:

Rustic Patrol
Ensemble

"The Volunteer Fireman" (Song)
W. T. Hodge

March
W. T. Hodge, O. Harlan, M. Marshall, L. Grimm, J. Weber, Ensemble

PUFF 2 (Act 2)[80]

Opening Ensemble:

"Beautiful Dreamtown"; Pas de Nuit
Ensemble

"I Don't Believe I'll Ever Be a Lady" (Song)
M. Marshall

"Hannah"[81] (Song)
C. Loftus, Ensemble

"On the 'Phone"[82] (Song)
M. Farkoa, Ensemble

"Going to the Opera" (Ensemble)
J. Weber, M. Marshall, W. T. Hodge, L. Lee, etc.

"In Vaudeville" (Duet)
C. Loftus, O. Harlan

Intermezzo
Orchestra

THE MAGIC KNIGHT: MUSICAL NUMBERS[83]

"Our King Is Here" (Opening Chorus)
Ensemble

"The Court Is Called to Order"
F. Belcher

"Elsa Is Accused"
O. Harlan, L. Ewell

"I'm Such a Modest Maiden"
L. Blauvelt

"The Human Canary"
L. Blauvelt

"The Magic Knight Is Summoned"
W. L. Romaine

"Oh, Look Who's Here"
L. Blauvelt, Chorus

"Ta Ta, My Dainty Little Darling"
M. Farkoa

"The Cake-Walk Duel"
M. Farkoa, O. Harlan

"The Confession"
C. Tracy

Finale
Company

Finale
Company

1906.49 THE STUDENT KING

A Romantic Light Opera in Three Acts. Book and lyrics by Frederic Ranken and Stanislaus Stange. Music by Reginald DeKoven. Staged by George Marion. Settings by Walter Burridge. Costumes by A. Comelli. Electric display by Joseph P. Wilson. Orchestra under the direction of Arthur Weld.

---

[79] For subsequent tour, another intermission was added after Finale (Rustic Patrol; The Volunteer Fireman; March); the show was advertised as a Dramatic Pipe in Three Puffs. Added to Act 1 after "Down a Shady Lane:"
Duet
M. Marshall, W. T. Hodge

[80] Dance Incidental to Puff 2 by Miss Helen Heins. For subsequent tour, added to Act 2 before "I Don't Believe I'll Ever Be a Lady:"
"I Love You" (Song)
M. Farkoa
(*Lyrics by* Al. Holbrook.)
After early touring engagements, THE MAGIC KIGHT was dropped and replaced by a Selection from Grand Operas performed by Lillian Blauvelt.

[81] Dropped after opening.

[82] Dropped after opening.

[83] Musical Numbers for THE MAGIC KNIGHT were not listed in New York programs. Above list is prepared from the Boston tour which immediately followed the New York run.

Produced by Henry W. Savage. Opened 25 December 1906 at the Garden Theatre and closed 26 January 1907 after 40 performances.

CAST: *Francis*, the Student King: HENRY COOTE. *Rudolph*, King of Bohemia: ALEXANDER CLARK. *Grumblekoff*: Frank Hayes. *Merrilaff*: Thomas C. Leary. *Cupid*: Dorothy Buscher. *Klingel*: Detmar Poppen. *Heinrich*: James E. Feeney. *Wilhelm*: J. R. Phillips. *Frederich*: Percy Parsons. *Ferdinand*: Albert Pellaton. *Ilsa*, Princess of Tyrol: LINA ABARBANELL. *Pantine*: EVA FALLON. *Lady Anne*: FLAVIA ARCARO. *Milka*: Lenora Watson. *Gretchen*: Ellanore Brooks. *Frieda*: Georgie Brooks. *Chorus of Students, Men at Arms, Tyrolean Maids and Swains, Ladies in Waiting, Courtiers, Gypsies, Clowns, Pantaloons, Columbines and Town People.*

The action takes place in Prague, Bohemia, in 1600 A.D.

Act 1: University Place, Summer.

Act 2: Garden of Royal Palace. Night.

Act 3: Fest Hall of the University. About 11:30 P.M.

ACT 1

Opening Chorus
Students' Corp
"Opposites Are We"
T. C. O'Leary, F. Hayes, Male Chorus
"Election of the Student King"
H. Coote
"Pray, Pretty Maid"
E. Fallon, A. Pellaton
"Tyrolean Maid"
L. Abarbanell, Girl Chorus
"Give Me Thy Heart, Love"
H. Coote
"His Majesty Advances"
Chorus
"I Took Them All"
A. Clark, Chorus
Finale
Ensemble
Crowning the Student King
"(I Play on) My Old Bassoon"
(A. Clark)
Entrance of Lady Anne

ACT 2

"Tarantella"
L. Watson, Chorus
"Czardas"
F. Arcaro, Chorus
"Off to Paris"
L. Abarbanell, Chorus
"In Bohemia"
A. Clark, F. Hayes, T. C. O'Leary
"Would You Like a Little Girl Like Me?"[84]
E. Fallon, Chorus
"The Jolly Pair"
L. Abarbanell, H. Coote
"To Arms"
L. Abarbanell
"The Same Old Game"
A. Clark, E. Brooks, G. Brooks
Finale
Ensemble

ACT 3

"The Students' Kneipe"
J. E. Feeny, P. Parsons, H. Coote, Male Chorus
Entrance of Innsbruck Students
Girl Chorus
"Nudel, Nudel, Nupp, Nupp"
L. Abarbanell, Chorus
Finale
Ensemble

[84]Arranged by John Mason.

1906.50 MATILDA

A Farce in Three Acts, with a Song Now and Then[85]. Book by I. N. Morris. Music by George T. Gartlan. Lyrics by Everett Ruskay. Produced under the stage direction of George Foster Platt. Musical director, John J. Braham. Produced by Walter N. Lawrence. Opened 31 December 1906 at the Lincoln Square Theatre and closed 12 January 1907 after 17 performances[86].

CAST: *Sir Duncan Claymore*, grand uncle to Matilda: CHARLES LANE. *Lord Jermyngham*, bequeathed to Matilda: LIONEL WALSH. *Lester Markham*, betrothed to Matilda: JOSEPH TUOHY. *"Tod" Archer*, friend to Matilda: ALFRED HICKMAN. *Incidental to Matilda (4)*: *Dr. Lamb*: Edwin Middleton. *Dr. Short*: Robert Newcombe. *Bo'sun*: J. Homer Hunt. *Steward*: Frederick C. Patterson. *Lady Arabella Jermyngham*, presumptive mother-in-law to Matilda: Clara Thompson. *Constance Lamb*, friendly to Matilda: Katherine Emmet. *Edna Raymond*, attached to Matilda: MAUDE FULTON. *Matilda*: AMY RICARD.

Act 1: Matilda's apartment, New York City. Morning.

Act 2: Deck of the steam yacht, "*Water Witch*." Afternoon.

Act 3: Main Cabin of the "*Water Witch*." Evening.

ACT 1

"Love Me in the Winter"
A. Hickman
"Affinity"
A. Ricard, J. Tuohy
"The Innocent Debutante"
M. Fulton

ACT 2

"What Is Life—What Is Love?"
K. Emmet
"Wow-Yip-Po"
A. Hickman
"Roll On"
A. Hickman, K. Emmet, L. Walsh
"I Wonder If the Thing's Worth While"
A. Ricard, M. Fulton, J. Tuohy, A. Hickman

ACT 3

"Who's Your Gen'man Frien'?"
A. Hickman
"Mermaids"
A. Ricard
Finale
Company

1907.01 PRINCESS BEGGAR

A Fantastic Comedy Opera in Two Acts. Libretto by Edward Paulton. Music by Alfred G. Robyn. Staged by Frank Smithson. Scenery designed by Ernest Albert, Edward G. Unitt. Miss Edwardes' costumes by Castel-Bert, London; Altman, New York. Musical director, Arthur Pell. Produced by Sam S. and Lee Shubert, Inc. Opened 7 January 1907 at the Casino Theatre and closed 9 February 1907 after 40 performances.

CAST: *King Otto XXX* of Vagaria: EDDIE GARVIE. *Prince Karl*, his only son: BERTRAM WALLIS. *Count Rollo*, Karl's friend: JAMES G. REANEY. *Casper*, Elaine's foster father: Ernest Graham. *Hans von Sprudel*, an insurance doctor: HARRY MacDONOUGH. *Baron Lombardo*, a financier: STANLEY L. FORDE. *Father Boniface*, the hermit: D. J. Flanagan. *Rowena*, Baron Lombardo's daughter: CECILIA RHODA. *Antickia*, the royal housekeeper: Adele Barker. *Elaine*, a girl from the woods: PAULA EDWARDES. *The Princesses (8)*: *Edith of England*: Suzanne Boyd. *Margaret of Scotland*: Mildred Cooke. *Kathleen of Ireland*: Mabelle Courtney. *Josephine of France*: Ella Rock. *Helen of Greece*: Genevieve Fenwick. *Zuleika of the Orient*: Theresa Powers. *Dolores of Castille*: Evelyn Mitchell. *Gretchen of Prussia*: Ursula Thompson. *Adela, Frieda*, Elaine's Schoolmates: Edith Fraser, Daisy Fuguet. *Max, Ferdinand*, Court Attendants: J. W. Murphy, Edward Stone. *Hussars, Court Ladies, Retainers, Flunkies, Forest Girls and Boys, Huntsmen, etc, etc.*

Act 1: Throne Room in King Otto's Palace. (Albert.)

Act 2: Hermitage on the Island of Ferns. (Unitt.)

ACT 1

Opening Chorus

[85]Also advertised as a Screaming Farce in Three Explosions.
[86]Settings, costumes uncredited.

"Love, Love, Love"
B. Wallis, Chorus
"Waiting for Me"
E. Garvie, Chorus
"Beautiful Maidens (Are We)" (Entrance of Princesses)
Ensemble
Song
P. Edwardes
"I Want It All"
S. L. Forde, Male Chorus
"I Don't Love You" (Quintette)
E. Garvie, B. Wallis, S. L. Forde, J. G. Reaney, C. Rhoda
"Wouldn't You Like to Learn to Love Me?"
P. Edwardes, Entire Company
(*Music and Lyrics by* Edward Montagu.)
"Madrigal"
P. Edwardes, S. L. Forde, B. Wallis
"All Hail the Queen" (Entrance of the Queen)
P. Edwardes, E. Garvie, Chorus
"You're the Only One for Me"
J. G. Reaney, C. Rhoda
Finale

ACT 2
Opening Chorus
"Huntsman's Song"
J. G. Reaney, Chorus
"Echo"
B. Wallis, Princesses
(*Music by* Leo Friedman. *Lyrics by* Edward Montagu.)
"(When It's) Raining"
P. Edwardes, Chorus
"All the Same to Me"
E. Garvie, H. MacDonough
"Elaine (Girl of My Heart)"
B. Wallis
"The Chimes of Long Ago"
P. Edwardes, Chorus
"Sad, Sad World" (Hermit Trio)
P. Edwardes, E. Garvie, H. MacDonough
"O Tell Me, Daisy" (Dear Little Daisy)
C. Rhoda, Chorus
Finale

1907.02 THE VANDERBILT CUP

A Return Engagement of the 8-Cylinder Comic Machine Carrying Three Shoes and Eight Tubes (Musical Comedy in Three Acts, 8 Scenes)[87]. Book by Sydney Rosenfeld. Music by Robert Hood Bowers. Lyrics by Raymond Peck. Staged by Hugh Ford. Scenery by Frank E. Gates and Edward A. Morange. Lighting effects by Benjamin Beerwald. Moving picture effects by The Kinetograph Company and Kliegl Brothers. Orchestra under the direction of Albert Dalby. Produced by Liebler and Company (Theodore Liebler, George C. Tyler). Opened 7 January 1907 at the New York Theatre and closed 9 February 1907 after 40 performances[88]

CAST (People in the car, in the order in which they are likely to be hit): *Newt Offut*, a hill climber: Charles Dow Clark. *Mrs. Willets*, mother of Dorothy: Grace Griswold. *Theodore Banting*, an Equitable attorney at law, and other things: ROBERT F. DAILEY. *Miss Carstairs*, Dorothy's music teacher and chaperone: Blanche Chapman. *Dorothy Willetts*: ELSIE JANIS. *Dexter Joyce*, a wine agent: ARTHUR STANFORD. *Clerk of the Marjorie Wellington Hotel*: Albert Cowles. *Detective in the Marjorie Wellington Hotel*: Midde White. *Stockholders (6) in the Marjorie Wellington Hotel,* known as the Six Crusty Dames: *Mrs. Hillrace*: Helen Weathersby. *Mrs. Sylvester*: Kate Mayhew. *Mrs. Filestrom*: Grace Griswold. *Mrs. Herkimer*: Mary Greville. *Mrs. Dillenberg*: Louise Sylvester. *Mrs. Ostrand*: May Quinette. *Bell-girls of the Marjorie Wellington Hotel (8)*: *Winnifred*: Erma Green. *Eloise*: Lelia Maillon. *Gwynne*: Birdnye Zuber. *Elaine*: Jane Oakes. *Pearl*: Jacque Bradley. *Marion*: Daisy Leon. *Freda*: Orma Nagle *Maude*: Leona Drew. *Leon*, waiter at the Garden City Hotel: Percy Janis. *Celeste*, elevator girl at the Marjorie Wellington Hotel: Genevieve Victoria. *Kate Croops*, the porter: Ella Hatton. *Inkie North*, Western Union Messenger Girl: Emma Naylor. *Gaspard*, an honest French chauffeur: HAL DeFORREST. *Curt Willetts*, who "got rich quickly," uncle of Dorothy: CLARENCE HANDYSIDES. *Clarinda Larkspur*, who objects to a speed limit: EDITH DECKER. *Mr. Boxwood*. President of the Gasoline Trust: JACQUES KRUGER. *Arthur*, his chainless hopeless: F. Newton Lindo. *Flowers of the Comic Opera (4)*: *Rose*: Amy Lake. *Lily*: Joan Sawyer. *Violet*: Eloise Steele. *Pansy*: Helen Case. *Olga, Nadine*, Russian whirlwind Dancers: The Constantine Sisters. *Male Quartette*: Messrs. Tomasso, Williams, Mertimer, Bosher. *Garage Owners, Other Robbers, Bell-Girls, Guests, Naval Officers, Cadets, Sailors, Sight-seers, and others.*

1907.03 THE MIMIC AND THE MAID

A Merry Musical Comedy in Three Acts. Book and lyrics by Allen Lowe. Music by A. Baldwin Sloane. Staged by Tom Collins. Produced by The Herman Oppenheimer Company, Inc. Opened 11 January 1907 at the Bijou Theatre and closed 12 January 1907 after 2 performances.

CAST: *Treadwell Track*: GUS WEINBURG. *Harry B. White*: Maurice Darcy. *Terence Tracy*: HARRY B. WATSON. *Obadiah Stough*: GEORGE OBER. *Lem Jones*: GEORGE RICHARDS. *Amos Trout*: Fred J. Waedler. *The Landlord Bold*: Thomas W. Lane. *Mrs. Randolph Dexter*: Janet Melville. *Figaro*: EVIE STETSON. *Nellie Butler*: Alice Kraft Bentson. *Lillian Saddart*: DOROTHY RUSSELL. *Marie Tempest*: Doris Godwin. *Tidy Annie*: HATTIE PALMER. *Snip Williams*: Elfie Rue. *Lou Dillon*: Rose Leslie. *Nancy Hanks*: Vaughn Sargeant. *Belle Hamlin*: Virginia Tyler Hudson. *Flora Temple*: Kathryn Montague. *Lucille Golddust*: Ray Gilmore. *Neva Simmons*: Emily Ward. *Hazel Wilkes*: Lillian Berrian. *Virginia Evans*: Jane Murray. *Lily Star*: Margaret Derrian.

Act 1: A Palm Garden.

Act 2:

Act 3: The Stage of a Rural Theatre.

MUSICAL NUMBERS[89]
"Teddy Bears"
D. Russell, D. Goodwin, Chorus
"Dear Love"
A. K. Bentson
"The Auto Song"
D. Goodwin
"Everybody Seemed to be Invited"
G. Weinburg
(*Music and Lyrics by* Gus Weinburg.)

1907.04 THE GIRL FROM BROADWAY

A Musical Comedy in Three Acts. Book by Herbert Hall Winslow. Music by Karl Hoschna. Lyrics by Charles Noel Douglass. Directed by Charles Sinclair. Produced by Aubrey Mittenthal. Opened 14 January 1907 at the 14th Street Theatre and closed 19 January 1907 after 8 performances.

CAST: *Walter Pallette*: James A. Smith. *Jeremiah Skeeters*: ARTHUR JENNINGS. *Jack Dawson*: ROBERT H. WILSON. *Abraham Blonstein*: Ernest Otto. *Mike Hercules*: Arthur Otto. *Nanette*: GRACE EDMOND. *Luna Rosebud*: MAY FLORINE EDMOND. *Rattles*, a tramp: HARRY FENTELLE. *Mrs. Cutadash Moneypile*: LEONA LEIGH. *Lillian*: Josephine Reade. *James*: Weston F. McLain.

MUSICAL NUMBERS[90]
"Cupid"
G. Edmond
"Dat's the Way I Lubs You, Honey Mine"
"Eccentricities"

[87]First produced in New York 16 January 1906 at the Broadway Theatre for 143 performances. For Synopsis of Scenes and Musical Numbers, see original 1906 production. All changes made during the run retained for this engagement and the national tour.
[88]Costumes uncredited. Played a return engagement 1 April 1907 at the Grand Opera House for 8 performances.

[89]No program available.
[90]No New York program available. Musical numbers taken from an October 1906 tryout.

"The Girl from Broadway"
G. Edmond
"He Loves Me, He Loves Me Not"
G. Edmond
"The Hobo Man"
"Hoop La"
"I Cannot Marry You All"
"It's Up to You to Do the Rest"
G. Edmond, R. H. Wilson
"Love Me as You Used to Do"
"Love's Language"
M. F. Linden
"Millionaire's Daughters"
"Oh, Joe, with Your Fiddle and Bow"
"Rocky Road to Dublin"
"Something Happened"
"Tally-Ho"
"That's Easy for a Little Girl to Do"
"We'll Never Make a Lady Out of You"
G. Edmond
"When I Dream of Annie Laurie"

1907.05

THE BELLE OF LONDON TOWN

A Comedy with Music in Four Acts. Book and lyrics by Stanislaus Stange. Music by Julian Edwards. Staged by R. H. Burnside. Orchestra under the direction of Herman Perlet. Produced by the Messrs. Sam S. and Lee Shubert (Inc.). Opened 28 January 1907 at the Lincoln Square Theatre and closed 9 February 1907 after 16 performances.

CAST (in order of appearance): *Betty*, maid to Lady Belinda: Kathleen Clifford. *Roger*, servant to Sir John: Joseph Frohoff. *Captain Anthony Lovell* of the Royal Guard: Giorgio Majeroni. *Sir John Manners*, an indifferent husband: KARL STALL. *Men of Quality (4)*: *Lord Drinkwell*: ORVILLE HARROLD. *Lord Playmore*: Hal Pearson. *Lord Plausible*: Arthur D. Wood. *Lord Muddle*: Herman Steinman. *Lady Belinda Manners*, a devoted wife: CAMILLE D'ARVILLE. *Clarissa Huntleigh*, her cousin: RUTH PEEBLES. *Prince Assam*, the Nawab of Calicut: EDMUND STANLEY. *Lady Airish*, a fashionable widow: Belle Thorne. *Lady Speakill*, *Lady Tattle*, Women of Fashion: Hortese Mazurette, Hilda Hollins. *Lord Poppington*, the glass of fashion and the mould of form: FRANK FARRINGTON. *Warrant Officers, Constables, Servants, etc.*

Act 1: Hall in St. John's House, London.

Act 2: Spring Gardens, London.

Act 3: Lady Belinda's Apartments, Sir John's Huse.

Act 4: Same as Act 3. One week supposed to have elapsed.

ACT 1
"To Drink We Have No Fear" (Opening Ensemble)
"The Light That Lies in Woman's Eyes"
"Magician Love"
(C. D'Arville)
"I Was Born to Rule" (Men Are Born to Rule)
"I Cannot Wait 'til Monday"
(R. Peebles, E. Stanley)
"They Pictured Me Like This"
(B. Thorne)
Finale

ACT 2
"Let Us Gossip of the Latest Court Flirtation" (Opening Chorus)
"Fairy Beauty's Queen" (Ensemble)
"The Lady of Society"
(C. D'Arville)
"(The) Hindoo Paradise"
"I Should Have Been Offended If My Waist You Had Not Squeezed"
(R. Peebles, E. Stanley)
"When Fortune Smiles"
Finale

ACT 3
"Guardians of the House"
(K. Clifford, J. Frohoff)
"The Little Weather Vane"
"Drink With Me the Night Away"
(C. D'Arville)
Quintette Finale

ACT 4
Opening Ensemble
"Love's Secret"
"Still the World Rolls On, On, On"
(F. Farrington)
Finale

1907.06

THE LITTLE MICHUS

An Original Musical Play in Three Acts[91]. (Original French opéra-comique libretto) Book by Albert Vanloo and Georges Duval. English version by Henry Hamilton. Music by André Messager. (English lyrics by Percy Greenbank.) Staged by J. E. A. Malone. Dances arranged by Willie Warde. Settings by Walter Hann, Joseph Harker. Orchestra under the direction of Augustus Barratt. Produced by James C. Duff. Opened 31 January 1907 at the Garden Theatre and closed 23 February 1907 after 29 performances.

CAST: *The Little Michus* (2): *Marie-Blanche*: ALICE JUDSON. *Blanche-Marie*: RUTH JULIAN. *Madame Michu*, Michu's wife: ELITA PROCTOR OTIS. *Mlle. Herpin*, school mistress: May Tunison. *Mlle. Julie*, assistant school mistress: Ruth Baine. *Gaston Rigaud*, captain of Hussars: WILLIAM C. WEEDON. *Pierre Michu*, provision merchant GEORGE FORTESQUE. *Bagnolet*, soldier servant to General Des Ifs: ERNEST LAMBART. *Aristide Vert*, his assistant: Harold Crane. *Sebastion*, old gardener: Sarony Lambert. *Guests (4)*: *Madame du Tertre*: FLAVIA ARCARO. *Madame Rousselin*: May Griffiths. *Madame de Saint-Phar*: Lillian Grey. *Madame d'Albret*: Mabel Cox. *Schoolgirls (8)*: *Ernestine*: Ethel Mostyn. *Loie*: Violet Zell. *Irma*: Frances DuBarry. *Pamela*: Emily Wellington. *Palmyra*: Zelda Saunders. *Ida*: Lotta Parker. *Francine*: Harriet DuBarry. *Estelle*: Ethel Dudley. *General Des Ifs*: GEORGE GRAVES. *Solo Dance, Act 2*: Nora Sarony. *Guests, Ladies, School Girls, Customers, Soldiers, etc.*

The action takes place in Paris in 1810.

Act 1: Playground of Mlle. Herpin's School. Morning.

Act 2: Salon at General Des Ifs. Evening.

Act 3: Michu's Shop (The Halles). Morning.

ACT 1
Opening Chorus
"Blind Man's Buff" (Song)
F. DuBarry
"Michu! Michu!" (Trio)
A. Judson, R. Julian, W. C. Weedon
Entrance of Soldiers
"The Song of the Regiment" (Song)
W. C. Weedon, Chorus
"He Wouldn't Have to Ask Me Twice" (Trio)
G. Fortesque, E. P. Otis, H. Cane
Song
E. P. Otis
"Our Fairy Godmamma" (Concerted Number)
"The Donkey and the Hay" (Song)
H. Crane
"This Little Girl and That" (Song)
E. Lambart
Finale

ACT 2
Opening Chorus

[91]Billed as the first performance here of Mr. George Edwardes' latest success from Daly's Theatre, London.

"Miss Nobody from No-Where" (Song)
F. Arcaro
Dance
(N. Sarony)
"It's No Use Crying for the Moon" (Song)
W. C. Weedon
Trio
A. Judson, R. Julian, W. C. Weedon
Prayer ("A Prayer to St. Valentine")
A. Judson, R. Julian
Finale
Song
A. Judson, Chorus

ACT 3
Opening Chorus
"The Regiment of Frocks and Frills" (song)
E. Lambart
Chorus
"The Mice Will Play"
E. P. Otis, Chorus
(*Music and Lyrics by* Augustus Barratt.)
Sextet
Finale

1907.07 THE GIRL AND THE GOVERNOR

The Jefferson DeAngelis Opera Company in a Comic Opera in Two Acts. Book (and lyrics) by S. M. Brenner. Music by Julian Edwards. Produced under the personal supervision of (staged by) Jefferson DeAngelis. Scenery by John Young, Ernest Albert. Costumes designed by Caroline Siedle. Musical director, Albert McGuckin. Produced by The Jefferson DeAngelis Opera Company (Frank McKee, manager). Opened 4 February 1907 at the Manhattan Theatre and closed 23 February 1907 after 26 performances.

CAST: *Don Pascal de Mesquita*, Governor of La Guayra: JEFFERSON DeANGELIS. *Tacoma*, South American Indian Medicine Man: JOSEPH C. MIRON. *Dick Kingsley*, an English officer: RITCHIE LING. *Pedrillo*, Lieutenant to the Governor: ANDREW BOGART. *The Governor's Secretaries (3)*: *Vascalia*: Arthur Barry. *Tremolo*: Russell Lennon. *Staccato*: Roland Carter. *Messenger*: Frank Holmes. *Ruth Granville*, an English girl: ESTELLE WENTWORTH. *Donna Isadora*, a Spanish lady: ANNA BOYD. *Carita*, her maid: LILLIAN RHOADES. *Happigowonda*, Tacoma's daughter: Myrtle Gilbert. *Paula*: Loraine Bernard. *Bianci*: Victoria Stuart. *Lorello*: Marion Chase. *Waseto*: Veve Morton.

Peasants, Court Ladies, Wedding Attendants: Miss Grace Sage, Marve Chase, Helena Gilbert, Georgianna Mould, Nannette Fallon, Mabel Claire, Imogene Morton, Estelle Clark, Myrtle Clark, Effie Delle, Virginia Stuart, Jane Ettinger, Lillian Hanlon, Stella Foy, Patricia Wade, Phyllis Shearer, Gloriana Whitley, Guvinne Jones, Catherine Carter, Ethel Grey, Mary Priddy, Margaret Alferris, Inez Gomez, Carmen Castro, Mabello Serrano, Juanita Mutricio, Pepita Fernandez, Silvio La Bara, Marie Dresser, Minerva Wilson, Laura Emment, Julia LaFarge, Helen Estell, Martha Hallan, Lethia Howell, Beatrice Galloway, Mary Stanton. *Soldiers, Indians, Lords, Knights, Sailors*: Rober Fabian, Thomas Holmes, Julian Baliss, Grant Smith, Herbert Vaughan, Willison Huber, Simms Brady, Richard Frank, William Sands, Russell Frank, Robinson Merriman, Constant Brothers, John Graham, Termont Reader, Thomas Logan, Richard Spangler, Charles Halsted, Matt Myers, James Earle, William Ogle, Walter Mansfield.

The action takes place in a Spanish settlement in South America in 1590.

Act 1: The fort overlooking the harbor of La Guayra.

Act 2: The Banquet room in the Governor's Palace.

ACT 1
Opening Chorus
Governor's Guards
"I Am So Fair" (Quintet)
A. Boyd, A. Bogart, A. Barry, R. Lennon, R. Carter
"(Said) The Governor" (Song)
A. Bogart, Company
"Don Pascal de Mesquita" (Song and Chorus)
J. DeAngelis, Company
"I've a Very Nasty Temper" (Song)
E. Wentworth, Company
"Farewell Fond Dreams (of Love)" (Duet)
E. Wentworth, R. Ling
"Wouldn't It Puzzle You?" (Trio)
E. Wentworth, J. DeAngelis, R. Ling
Finale
J. DeAngelis, Company

ACT 2
"The Musical Bullfrog" (Song)
J. C. Miron, Male Chorus
"The Serenade" (Septette)
J. DeAngelis, J. C. Miron, R. Ling, A. Bogart, A. Barry, R. Lennon, R. Carter
"My Love and I" (Song)
E. Wentworth
"The First Kiss" (Duet)
L. Rhoades, J. DeAngelis
"The Bolero" (Ensemble and Dance)
"Who Would a Bachelor Be?" (Song)
R. Ling
"Fire Water" (Song)
J. C. Miron
"When a Maiden Won't" (Quintet)
A. Boyd, J. C. Miron, A. Barry, R. Lennon, R. Carter
"Have You Ever Heard It Told That Way Before?" (Topical Song)
J. DeAngelis
Finale
J. DeAngelis, Company

1907.08 THE ROSE OF THE ALHAMBRA, or The Magic Lute

A Comic Opera in Three Acts, 4 Scenes. Book and lyrics by Charles Emerson Cook. Based on a story by Washington Irving. Music by Lucius Hosmer. Staged by Charles Emerson Cook. Settings by Frank E. Gates, Edward A. Morange, Homer Emens, Edward G. Unitt. Musical director, Joseph E. Nicol. Produced by the Opera Comique Company (F. C. Whitney). Opened 4 February 1907 at the Majestic Theatre and closed 23 February 1907 after 26 performances.

CAST: *Philip V*, King of Spain: EDDIE HERON. *Elizabetta*: GRETA RISLEY. *Ruyz*, favorite page: LEY VERNON. *Brother Nicolo*, a musician, attached to the Court of Philip: LOUIS CASAVANT. *Peregil*, the royal physician, attached to the Court of Philip: OWEN WESTFORD. *Fredegonda*, Jacinta's aunt and guardian: Isabelle Winloche. *Spirit of Zorahavda*, the Moorish Princess: GRETA RISLEY. *Boraldo*, chief of the band of brigands: HENRY NORMAN. *Estrella*, the "Mascot" of his band: LILLIAN HUDSON. *Mario, Roberto*, members of his band: Augustino Baci, W. L. Thorne. *Captain Vivar*, of the King's Guard: Frank M. Kelly. *Sancho*, a water carrier: Augustino Baci. *Don Alvaro, Don Rodrigo*, Gentlemen of the Court: George Eaton Collins, Joseph Little. *Dona Camilla, Dona Felisha*, and other Ladies of the Court: Alma Osbrne, Tessie Bunchu, Margaret Warren, Elizabeth Anglin, Lydia Dumpere, Burdella Patterson. *Pedro, Pepita, Frasquita*, Citizens of Granada: William James, Betty Ohls, Hazel Neason. *Jacinta*, The Rose of Alhambra: AGNES CAINE BROWN. *Ladies and Gentlemen of the Court, Residents of the Alhambra, Citizens of Granada, Bandits, Guardsmen, Spirits of Moorish Warriors, Peasants, etc.*

Act 1: The Rose Garden of the Tower of the Princesses. Granada. 1730.

Act 2, Scene 1: Interior of the Tower of the Princesses. Midnight. *Scene 2*: The Old Moorish Mill in the Mountains on the road to Seville. Sunrise.

Act 3: The Hall of the Ambassadors in the Alcazar, or Royal Palace, Seville.

ACT 1
Opening Chorus: "All the Kings' Horses and Men"
"The Falcon" (Song)
L. Vernon
"Weaving" (Solo)
A. C. Brown
"Give Him a Welcome Quite Spanish" (Chorus)
Entrance Song
E. Heron
"(The Burlesque) Serenade"
E. Heron, L. Casavant, O. Westford
Chorus of Friars

"Long Live the King" (Requiem)
"Slash! Dash! Bang!" (Song)
H. Norman
Quartette
A. C. Brown, L. Vernon, L. Casavant, I. Winloche
Finale

ACT 2
Scene 1
Scene of the Apparition
A. C. Brown, G. Risley
"Love's Eternal Song" (Recitative and Aria)
A. C. Brown
Scene 2
Song of the Millers
L. Hudson, H. Norman, Bandits
"The Pilgrim of Love" (Solo)
L. Vernon
"The Nightingale and the Rose" (Duet)
L. Hudson, L. Vernon
"Castles in Spain"
E. Heron, L. Hudson, O. Westford, H. Norman
Finale

ACT 3
"We're the Royal M.D.'s"
H. Norman, Male Chorus
"Sevillana"—"Manana" (Ensemble)
L. Casavant, Chorus
"O, Won't You Shed One Little Tear for Me?"
E. Heron
"The Lay of the Lute" (Scene and Aria)
A. C. Brown
Finale

1907.09 GEORGE WASHINGTON, JR.

A Return Engagement of the National Song Show (Musical Comedy) in Three Acts, 4 Scenes[92]. Book, music and lyrics by George M. Cohan. Staged by George M. Cohan. Settings by John Young (Acts 1, 3), Ernest Albert (Act 2). Costumes designed by F. Richard Anderson. Music arranged and conducted by Charles J. Gebest. Produced by Sam H. Harris. Opened 11 February 1907 at the New York Theatre and closed 9 March 1907 after 32 performances[93].

CAST: *James Belgrave*, a United States Senator: JERRY J. COHAN. *William Hopkins*, a United States Senator: J. Willard. *Lord Rothburt*: H. B.Kay. *George Belgrave*, the Senator's son: GEORGE M. COHAN. *Eaton Ham*, of Alexandria: WILLIS P. SWEATNAM. *Superintendent Dodge* of Mt. Vernon: Frank McNish, Jr. *Bell boy*, of Willard Hotel: Frank McNish, Jr. *McFadden*, a tourist: Joseph Leslie. *Hotel clerk*: Frank N. Boyle. *Page*, at Mt. Vernon: Harold Forbes. *Colonel Greene*: Earl C. Stanley. *Colonel Browne*: William Leyle. *Colonel Pincus*: William E. Doyle. *Colonel Williams*: Joseph Levere. *Porter*, of Willard Hotel: Lee Myers. *Drums*: Samuel Avedon. *Mandolin and Guitar Quartette*: Messrs. Butin, Tipaldi, Rostain, Whitlaw. *Mrs. Stebbins*, Senator Belgrave's widowed sister: HELEN F. COHAN. *Evelyn Rothburt*, the Lord's accomplice: Leona Anderson. *Telephone operator*: Mary Gildea. *Dolly Johnson*: Vinie Daly.

1907.10 THE WHITE HEN

A Musical Comedy in Two Acts. Book by Roderic C. Penfield. Music by Gustave Kerker. Lyrics by Roderic C. Penfield and Paul West. Staged by Julian Mitchell, J. C. Huffman. Settings painted by Ernest Albert, Arthur Voegtlin. Produced by the Messrs. Sam S. and Lee Shubert, Inc. Opened 16 February 1907 at the Casino Theatre and closed 18 May 1907 after 94 performances.[94]

CAST: *Hensie Blinker*, proprietor of "The White Hen," a hotel in the Austrian tyrol: LOUIS MANN. *Eric Weiss*, attorney at law: RALPH C. HERZ. *Paul Blancke*: Robert Michaelis. *Lieutenant Wilhelm Klopstock* of the Austrian Infantry: Otis Sheridan. *Heinrich*, head waiter at "The White Hen": William F. Carroll. *Pepi Gloeckner*, of the Burgstrasse Theatre, Vienna: LOUISE GUNNING. *Sonia Matemoff*, a Viennese marriage broker: CARRIE E. PERKINS. *Lisa Sommer*, secretary to Attorney Weiss: LOTTA FAUST. *Lottchen Spring*, secretary to Mme. Matemoff: Leona Stephens. *Hedwig*, a "relatif" of Blindner: Beatrice Bertrand. *Emmy, Toni, Sofie*, three young women in search of husbands: Dessa Gibson, Hattie Lorraine, Elsa Reinhart. *Eduard*: himself. *Clients, Waiters, Villagers, Guests at "The White Hen"*.

Act 1: The Offices of Mme. Matemoff and Erich Weiss. A morning late in May. (Albert.)

Act 2: "The White Hen," an Inn in the Austrian Tyrol. Two weeks after. (Voegtlin.)

ACT 1
Opening Chorus and Song
L. Faust
"A Man Is Only a Man"[95]
C. E. Perkins, Chorus
Exhibit
C. E. Perkins
"Follow, Follow"
L. Gunning, Chorus
"Follow the Good Advice"
R. C. Herz, Chorus
"Edelweiss"[96]
R. Michaelis
"The Prima Donna"
The Buds
Finale
Company

ACT 2[97]
"Waiting for the Bride" (Opening Chorus)
Chorus
"Mountain Maids"
Tyrolean Yodelers
"Everything Is High Nowadays"
L. Faust
"That's Why the Danube Is Blue"
L. Gunning, Chorus
"At Last We Are Alone"
L. Gunning, R. Michaelis
"Very Well Then"
R. C. Herz
"The Thrush and the Star"
L. Stephens, Chorus
"Printemps"
L. Gunning
"Smile (Smile Smile)"
L. Faust, L. Mann
(*Music by* Martin G. Brown. *Lyrics by* Louis Mann.)
Finale
Company

1907.11 THE TATTOOED MAN

A Comic Opera in Two Acts. Book by Harry B. Smith and A.N.C. Fowler. Music by Victor Herbert. Lyrics by Harry B. Smith. Produced under the

[92]Originally produced in New York 12 February 1906 at the Herald Square Theatre for 81 performances. For Synopsis of Scenes and Musical Numbers, see original 1906 production. "The Grand Old Rag" now listed in the program as "The Grand Old Flag."

[93]Played a later engagement 18 March 1907 at the Grand Opera House for 8 performances.

[94]Costumes, conductor uncredited. Dr. Ralph Horner was credited as musical director during subsequent tour.

[95]For subsequent tour, replaced by:
"Keep Cool"
William Armstrong {Erich Weiss}

[96]Replaced during the run by:
"Fishing"
R. Michaelis, Chorus

[97]Act 2 was substantially revised for the subsequent tour, and the following were dropped: "Mountain Maids," "Everything Is High Nowadays," "The Thrush and the Star," "Printemps," and "Smile." Added after "Waiting for the Bride": "(Because) I'm Married Now" Adelaide Sharpe {Hedwig} (*Music and Lyrics by* Herbert Ingraham.)

stage direction of Julian Mitchell. Scenery painted by Homer Emens, Edward G. Unitt and Joseph Wickes. Costumes by Caroline Siedle. Orchestra under the direction of Arthur Weld. Orchestrations by Victor Herbert. Produced by Charles Dillingham. Opened 18 February 1907 at the Criterion Theatre and closed 15 April 1907 after 59 performances.

CAST: *Omar Khayam, Jr.*, astrologer, poet and sworn foe to temperance: FRANK DANIELS. *Abdallah*, an Arab chief: WILLIAM P. CARLETON. *Algy Cuffs*, a matinee idol: HARRY CLARKE. *Hashish*, janitor of the Shah's Harem: NACE BONVILLE. *Muley*, inspector of the mint: George O'Donnell. *Ali*, court nuisance: Gilbert Clayton. *Yussuf*, bad news specialist: Charles Drew. *The Shah (of Persia)*, who travels for his health until very late every evening: HERBERT WATEROUS. A *Muezzin*, who calls the people to prayer, but they don't come: Harold Russell. *Leila*, beloved of Omar, but nothing doing: SALLIE FISHER. *Alma*, daughter of Omar: Gertie Carlisle. *Fatima*, a wall flower: MAY VOKES. *Imported American Bridesmaids (9)*: *Miss Vandergilt*, of New York: Maida Athens. *Miss Penn* of Philadelphia: Jessie Richmond. *Miss Lakeside* of Chicago: Almeda Potter. *Miss Beacon* of Boston: Lottie Vernon. *Miss Bridge* of Brooklyn: Gertrude Doremus. *Miss Frisk* of 'Frisco: Josephine Karlin. *Miss Vine* of St. Louis: Jane Rogers. *Miss Charles* of Baltimore: Leila Benton. *Miss Mint* of Washington: Gene Cole. *Omar's Four Wards* (being translations of their Oriental names): *Star of Evening*: Reina Swift. *Blush of Dawn*: Mabel Croft. *Rose of Summer*: Daisy DeVere. *Bird of Paradise*: May Field. *Mutti*: Maida Athens. *Omar's Nephews, educated in American colleges (4)*: *Ahmed*: Edna Birch. *Selim*: Bessie Holbrook. *Hassan*: Claudia Clark. *Canem*: Jessie Carr.

Dancing Slaves: Misses Birch, Carr, Lloyd, Swift, Wilson, Everett, Holbrook, Richardson. *Snake Charmers*: Misses Croft, DeVere, Field, Baker, Quinby, Bernard, Williams, Vesta Field, Roche, Major.

The action takes place at the present time in Persia.

Act 1: The Courtyard of the Regent's Palace.

Act 2: The Rose Garden of the Shah.

ACT 1[98]

Opening Chorus
N. Bonville, C. Drew, Slave Girls, Muezzins
(Hear me, O master mine)
Slave Girls
"Things We Are Not Supposed to Know"
N. Bonville, G. O'Donnell, C. Drew, G. Clayton
Entrance of Arabs (Galloping over the desert I ride)
W. P. Carleton, Chorus
Entrance of Omar (Oriental March)
Chorus
"Omar Khayyam"
F. Daniels, Chorus
"Boys Will Be Boys and Girls Will Be Girls"
Girls, Boys
"Hear My Song of Love"
W. P. Carleton, Girls
"The (Beautiful) Land of Dreams"
S. Fisher
Finale

ACT 2

Opening Chorus (Noble stranger, gentle guest)
"Legend of the Djin"
W. P. Carleton, Chorus
"The Floral Wedding" (Wedding of the Lily and the Rose)
S. Fisher, Chorus
"Watch the Professor"
F. Daniels, W. P. Carleton, S. Fisher
"Take Things Easy"
N. Bonville, G. Clayton, C. Drew, G. O'Donnell
"Nobody Loves Me"
M. Vokes
"There's Just One Girl I'd Like to Marry"
H. Clarke, G. Carlisle, Girls
Entrance of Shah (Shout and sing and laurels bring)
Chorus
"The Never Never Land"
F. Daniels, All
Finale

1907.12 NOT YET, BUT SOON

A Comedy Cackle in Two Lays (Musical Comedy in Two Acts). Music by Egbert Van Alstyne. Lyrics by Harry Williams. Musical numbers staged by Joseph C. Smith. Produced by E. D. Stair. Opened 4 March 1907 at the American Theatre and closed 9 1907 after 8 performances.[99]

CAST: *Bill Nerve*: HAP WARD. *Keeper Sane*: FRED WYCOFF. *Professor Nutt*: *Dr. Von Cure'm*: Abe Friedland. *Whis Keey*: Richard Barry. *Will Smoke*: John C. Hart. *Upan Down*: Harry Parent. *Canne Catchem*: CHARLES 'Sandy" CHAPMAN. *Clarence Nerve*: Lee Allen. *Charley Overweight*: Jack Manley. *Captain Nelson A. Feet*: Richard Barry. *O'Leary the Walker*: Sam Martin. *Hez E. Wheels*: George Johnson. *Ratty*: Charles T. Ray. *Miss Gooden Smart*: Helen Clark. *Lady Bug*: Dorothy Wells. *Miss Cute*: Marian Merrill. *May Nerve*: Madeline Buckley. *Mary Wise*: LUCY DALY.

Time: Not yet but soon.

Act 1: Interior of Sanatarium "Bughouse on the Hudson."

Act 2: Exterior of "Bughouse on the Hudson."

ACT 1[100]

"Nurse Girls and Doctors" (Opening Chorus)
H. Parent, Company
"I'm Wise"
L. Daly
"I'm the Leading Lady"
D. Wells, Company
"Way Down on the Farm"
F. Wycoff
"My Irish Girl" (My Irish Gal)
M. Merrill, D. Wells, Company
"Wonderland"
H. Ward, L. Daly
(*Music and Lyrics by* Thomas Allen.)
"Things That Happen Every Day"
H. Ward, F. Wycoff, M. Merrill, M. Buckley
"San Antonio"
C. Chapman, Company
Grand Finale
Entire Company

ACT 2

Opening Chorus
"Some Day When Dreams Come True"
C. Chapman, Company
(*Music and Lyrics by* Phil Staats.)
"O, Come My Lou"
M. Buckley, J. Manley, G. Johnson, Boys, Girls
"Mary Wise"
L. Daly, Boys and Girls
"The Wedding of the Blue and Grey"
M. Merrill, D. Wells, Company
Grand Finale

1907.13 THE GRAND MOGUL

A Musical Comedy in Three Acts. Book and lyrics by Frank Pixley. Music by Gustav Luders. Staged by Herbert Gresham. Manager, Edwin H. Price. Scenery painted by Ernest Albert. Costume design by F. Richard Anderson. Produced by (Marc) Klaw and (Abraham L.) Erlanger. Opened 25 March

[98] Musical Numbers do not appear in programs. List prepared from the published piano vocal score (M. Witmark & Sons, New York, 1907).

[99] Book writer uncredited.

[100] No New York program available; song list prepared from January 1907 tour. Also performed as per reviews: "Camp Meetin' Time," "I Like You Too," "Larry," "Mam'selle," "Playmates."

1907 at the New Amsterdam Theatre and closed 27 April 1907 after 40 performances[101].

CAST: *Hon. Josephus Walker*, Provisional Governor of Hawaii: JOHN DUNSMURE. *Lieutenant-Commander Newton*, in command of U.S. Gunboat *Cleveland*: GEORGE MOORE. *Lofty Baldwin*, an aeronaut with soaring ambitions: W. H. Macart. *Professor Muggs*, F.R.G.S., travelling in the interest of science: Sager Midgley. *Jack Marlin*, skipper of the schooner *Kate Flyaway*: J. R. Williams. *Hannibal*, colored body servant to Governor Walker: A. Seymour Brown. *Yu Li*, celestial assistant to Baldwin: Eugene Moulan. *The Grand Mogul*, ruler of the Island of Inde: JOHN DUNSMURE. *Lumbago*, the Moguls' prime minister: A. Seymour Brown. *Officer of the Guards*: J. V. Tullar. *Ruth Walker*, daughter of Governor Walker: MAUDE LILLIAN BERRI. *Lola*, a half-caste Kanaka girl: EDITH ST. CLAIR. *Dolly Muggs*, daughter of Professor Muggs: Elsa Ryan. *Fuzzywudge*, the Mogul's wife: Laura Clement. *Middy*, messenger to Newton: Pauline Thorne. G. *Washington Barker*, a former circus side-show man: FRANK MOULAN.

Lotus Buds: Norine Williams, Babe Stanley, Daisy Green, Margaret Emerson, Evelyn Carleton, Lillian Sterling, Mae Gunderman, Aimee Williams, Helen Bertrand, Isabelle Strange, Edith Williams, Lucy Harrison. *Double Male Quartette*: B. Milton, Frank LaSalle, James Frostick, Louis Mason, Abe Strizik, Sol Rosen, Lewis Allen, George Wilson.

Act 1: Grounds of the Royal Palace, Honolulu. Summer of 1898.

Act 2: Throne Room of the Grand Mogul's Palace, Island of Inde.

Act 3: Fortified Square outside of the Grand Mogul's Palace. The next morning.

ACT 1

Opening Chorus of Kanakas

"Honolulu" (Solo)
E. St. Clair

"Annexation" (Solo)
J. Dunsmure

"Help Yourself" (Solo)
A. S. Brown

"The Circus Band" (Solo and Ensemble)
F. Moulan, Chorus

"Aloha (I Love You)"
Mixed Chorus

"The Land Which My Heart Calls Home"
Double Male Quartette

"By-and-By" (Bye and Bye) (Solo)
G. Moore

"My Hula-Hula Girl" (Duet)
F. Moulan, E. St. Clair, Chorus of Hula Dancers, Kanakas

Ensemble with SolosG. Moore, J. Dunsmure, F. Moulan, M. L. Berri, Full Chorus

ACT 2

Chorus of Invocation
Chorus, A. S. Brown, L. Clement

"The Lotus" (Solo)
E. St. Clair, Lotus Buds

"The Military Man" (Solo)
M. L. Berri, Male Chorus

"Cupid's Private Code" (Solo)
E. Ryan, Male Chorus

"Nestle By My Side" (Duet)
F. Moulan, M. L. Berri, Full Chorus

Grand Ensemble with Solos
J. Dunsmure, F. Moulan, S. Midgley, W. H. Macart, M. L. Berri, E. St. Clair

ACT 3

"The Good Old-Fashioned Way" (Solo)
F. Moulan

"Cheer Up" (Chorus)
Lotus Buds

"(Love Is) Not for a Day" (Solo)
M. L. Berri

Fete Scene and Drill
Ensemble

Finale

[101]Conductor uncredited. Played a return engagement 9 September 1907 at the Grand Opera House for 8 performances. At that time Frank Pallma was credited as Musical director.

1907.14 THE LAND OF NOD and THE SONG BIRDS

A (Musical) Extravaganza in Two Acts, 4 Scenes, followed by an Operatic Outburst. Book (and lyrics) by Frank R. Adams and Will M. Hough. Rearranged by George V. Hobart. Music by Joseph E. Howard. Interpolated numbers by Joseph Hart. Music for "The Song Birds"[102] by Victor Herbert. Produced by The Will J. Block Amusement Company. Opened 1 April 1907 at the New York Theatre and closed 15 April 1907 after 17 performances.

CAST (in order of appearance) Act 1: *Bonnie*: MABEL BARRISON. *Bonnie's Mother*: Emily Hoff. *The Jack of Hearts*: HELEN BERTRAM. *The Weather Man*: William Sellery. *The Chorus Girl*: CARRIE DeMAR. *The Joker*: GUS C. WEINBERG. *The April Fool*: Knox Wilson. *The Welsh Rarebit*: Neil McNeil. *The Telephone*: Henry Gibson. *The Hair Tonic*: Walter Blair. *The Man in the Moon*: JOSEPH E. HOWARD. *The Sandman*: WILLIAM BURRESS.

THE SONG BIRDS (Act 2): *Pat McGuire*, Hammy's doortender: John Barrett. *The Principal Birds (2)*: *Oscar Hammerstein*: WILLIAM BURRESS. *Con, the Conried*: GUS C. WEINBERG. *Connie's Birds (3)*: *Robinson Caruso*: Notty Lyberopoulo. *Peter Pantson*: Percy Smith. *Emma Screams*: CARRIE DeMAR. *Hammy's Birds (4)*: *Alessandro Bouncey*: Charles Edward Wright. *A. La Monday*: WILLIAM SELLERY. *Madame Yellba*: HELEN BERTRAM. *Wright Rong*, a Magazine Bird: Neil McNeil.

The Chorus Birds: *Diewacht Amrhine*: Fred McGurk. *Achdu Liebe*: Mary Rhodes. *Dubist Ferícht*: George Blair. *Aus Gespiel*: Hazel Templeton. *Raus Mittim*: Arthur Wright. *Wasist Los*: Molly Prince. *Auf Wiedersehn*: Henry Clair. *Gesund Heit*: Louis Berri. *Giva Dakiss*: Lona Zytell. *Louda Dascream*: John Harper. *Mucha Dayell*: Laura Castle. *Makea Damash*: Frank Adams. *Bigga Dashine*: Powdy Moran. *Sweeta Dapeach*: Grace Millard. *Fatta Daslob*: Frank Demers. *Sella Banan*: Peggy O'Neil. *And Possibly Other Birds.*

Act 1, Scene 1: The Garden at Bonnie's Home, where, tired after playing all through the Summer's day, she falls asleep and dreams of the many things she has talked about or has heard discussed. *Scene 2*: The Land of Nod, a quaint Kingdom with its Castle of Cards and Peppermint River, where Bonnie meets with many strange adventures, and which is inhabited by the fanciful and Grotesque creatures of Slumberland. The Land of Nod is bounded on the North by the Sea of Sentiment, on the South by the Mountains of Mirth, on the East by the Lake of Laughter, and on the West by the Hills of Harmony.

Act 2, Scene 1: The Sandman's Palace of Dreams. Here the good old Sandman, in a friendly effort to entertain his royal guests, brings about a meeting of the Impressarii, and thereby precipitates a grand opera quarrel which results in the Battle of B-flat. *Scene 2*: Sunset in the Garden at Bonnie's home.

ACT 1[103]

[102]Previously played ??as a Lamb's Gambol?.

[103]The running order was revised for subsequent tour. Added for subsequent tour to Act 1:

"Blame the Weather Man" (after "Love Contagious")
W. Sellery, Four Assistants

"If You Grow Tired, Little Girl"
H. Bertram

"Come On, Let's Two Step"
M. Barrison, J. E. Howard, Chorus

Interpolated for tour under the management of Sam E. Rork, as per published sheet music (1908):

"I've Taken Quite a Fancy to You"
Grace Drew [Jack of Hearts]
(*Music by* Theodore Morse. *Lyrics by* Edward Madden.)

"I Could Learn to Love You If You'd Only Let Me Try"
Sue Smith
(*Music by* Harry Armstrong. *Lyrics by* Felix E. Feist.)

Opening Chorus
Full Company
"Love Contagious"
H. Bertram, M. Barrison
"The Belle of Bald Head Row"
C. DeMar, Chorus
"Just One More"
G. C. Weinburg
"The Wedding of the Chafing Dish"[104]
N. McNeil
"Cross Your Heart"
M. Barrison, J. E. Howard
"Ain't It Foolish?"[105]
K. Wilson
"You Look Good to Father"[106]
M. Barrison, Chorus
"Sneeze Time" (Duet)
C. DeMar, G. C. Weinberg
(*Music and Lyrics by* Joseph Hart.)
"The Same Old Moon"
J. E. Howard, Chorus

ACT 2[107]
"My Cinderella"
H. Bertram, Chorus
"(The) Same Old Story"
J. E. Howard, M. Barrison
"Amateur Night"
C. DeMar
(*Music and Lyrics by* Joseph Hart.)
"The Devils' Cake Walk"
W. Sellery

Incidental to "The Song Birds"
"Hammerstein"
Chorus
"Mazuma" (Trio)
H. Bertram, C. E. Wright, W. Sellery
"Yankeeland" (Trio)
C. DeMar, N. Lyberopoulo, P. Smith
The Song Contest
Hammerstein's and Conreid's Forces

THE EPILOGUE[108]
"The Awakening of Bonnie"
Children
"The Lullaby"
H. Bertram, Chorus

---

[104]Replaced for subsequent tour by:
"You Can't Keep a Good Man Down"
N. McNeil, Ensemble
[105]Dropped for subsequent tour.
[106]Replaced for subsequent tour by:
"How Was I to Know"
M. Barrison, Ensemble
[107]Added to the Opening of Act 2 for subsequent tour:
"The Nightmare March"
Company
"Bonnie (Briar Bush)"
M. Barrison, J. E. Howard, Double Sextette
[108]Added to the end of Act 2 for subsequent tour, replacing the Epilogue:
"Jingles and Jokes"
M. Barrison, J. E. Howard
"It's Great to Be an Actor"
J. E. Howard, C. DeMar
"Once More to Dream"
H. Bertram, Company

1907.15 THE ORCHID

An English Musical Entertainment (Comedy) in Two Acts, 3 Scenes. Book by James T. Tanner and Joseph W. Herbert. Music by Ivan Caryll and Lionel Monckton. Lyrics by Adrian Ross and Percy Greenbank. Produced under the direction of (staged by) Frank Smithson. Dances arranged by William Rock. Orchestra under the direction of Alexander Spencer. Produced by the Messrs. Sam S. and Lee Shubert (Inc.). Opened 8 April 1907 at the Herald Square Theatre, moved 2 September 1907 to the Casino Theatre and closed 14 September 1907 after 178 performances.[109]

CAST: *Caroline Vokins*, of a matrimonial turn: TRIXIE FRIGANZA. *Lady Violet Anstruther*, principal pupil at the horticultural college: AMELIA STONE. *Zelie Homberg*, an adventuress: LAURA GUERITE. *Thisbe*, private secretary to Chesterton: MAUDE FULTON. *Countess Anstruther*, Violet's mother: Jean Newcombe. *Josephine Zaccary*, pupil at the horticultural college: IRENE FRANKLIN. *Dr. Ronald Fausset*, a country practitioner: MELVILLE ELLIS. *Hon. Guy Scrymageour*, Chesterton's nephew: ALFRED HICKMAN. *Aubrey Chesterton*, a rich American residing in England: George C. Boniface, Jr. *Toby Blockett*, champion pugilist and wrestler: JOSEPH W. HERBERT. *Professor Zaccary*, a professional orchid hunter: WILLIAM ROCK. *Registrar*: Barrington Foote. *Lady Warden*: GRACE (VAN) STUDDIFORD. *Masker*: Marietta diDio. *Fluerette*: Urla Rottger. *Annette*: Estelle Coffin. *Clarice*: Margaretta Masi. *Jeannette*: Charlotte Corbett. *Marie*: Mabel Weeks. *Lizzette*: Veronique Banner. *Master of Ceremonies*: Arthur Warren. *M. Beauclasse*, French Minister of State: Marc Ducharme. *Commissaire of Police*: William Moore. *Cocher*: Marc Ducharme. *Gendarme*: R. L. McAndrews. *Ice Cream Vendor*: George Pullman. *Marchand d'Nez*: J. C. Newell. *Artie Choke*, gardener at the horticultural college: EDDIE FOY.

Pupils and Dancers: Misses A. Ford, F. Royce Elton, Calvert, Pouts, Holmes, Merrilles, M. Ford, Foster, Franklin, Fairfax, Barthold. *Debutantes*: Misses Weeks, Banner, Corbett, Masi. *Guests, Gardeners and Flunkies*: Misses Brennan, Doherty, DeNourie, Weldon, E. Royce, Leslie, Cameron, Clayton, Snyder, Archer, Beckwith, Melles, Jarrett, Creagh and Kingdon. Messrs. McAndrew, Neilson, Brady, Lyman, King, Kirtland, Smith, Newell, Pullman, McCann, Warren, Rose, Carpenter, Beem, Toland. *Maskers, Harlequins, Pierrots, Clowns, Flower Girls, etc.*

Act 1: Countess of Barwick's Horticultural College.

Act 2, Scene 1: Square at Nice—Carnival. *Scene 2*: Bal-Blanc, Opera House at Nice.

ACT 1[109a]
"This High Horticultural College"
Chorus
(*Music by* Ivan Caryll. *Lyrics by* Adrian Ross.)
"(The) Lady Secretary"
M. Fulton, Chorus
(*Music by* Lionel Monckton. *Lyrics by* Adrian Ross.)
"Ladies in Society"
Debutantes, Chorus
(*Music by* Lionel Monckton. *Lyrics by* Adrian Ross.)
"Oh, Mr. Registrar"
A. Stone, I. Franklin, A. Hickman, M. Ellis
(*Music by* Lionel Monckton. *Lyrics by* Percy Greenbank.)
"A Perfect Lady"
T. Friganza
(*Music by* Hugo Frey. *Lyrics by* Harold Atteridge.)
"(And They Say He Went to) College"
E. Foy, Chorus
(*Music by* Seymour Furth. *Lyrics by* Edward P. Moran.)
"I Don't Want the Dark"
A. Stone, Chorus
(*Music by* Lionel Monckton. *Lyrics by* Percy Greenbank, Leslie Mayne.)
"(From) Far Peru"
W. Rock, Chorus
(*Music by* Ivan Caryll. *Lyrics by* Adrian Ross.)
Finale
Company

---

[109]Settings, costumes uncredited.
[109a]Jerome Kern wrote two songs for interpolation into the American production of THE ORCHID which did not appear in extant programs for the New York run (*Lyrics by* Paul West): "Come Around on Our Veranda," and "A Recipe."

ACT 2[110]
Scene 1
"Up and Down, Over the Town" (Opening Chorus)
Chorus
(*Music by* Lionel Monckton. *Lyrics by* Percy Greenbank.)
"Come Along to the Zoo"[111]
L. Guerite, Debutantes and Chorus
"He Goes to Church on Sunday"
E. Foy
(*Music by* E. Ray Goetz. *Lyrics by* Vincent Bryan.)
"Little Blanche Marie"
A. Stone, Dancers
(*Music by* Lionel Monckton. *Lyrics by* Adrian Ross.)
"No Wedding Bells for Me"
T. Friganza
(*Music by* Seymour Furth. *Lyrics by* Edward P. Moran, Will Heelan.)
"Liza Ann" (A Yorkshire Idyll)
M. Fulton, W. Rock
(*Music by* Lionel Monckton. *Lyrics by* Leslie Mayne.)
"I Must Propose to You"
I. Franklin, A. Hickman
(*Music and Lyrics by* Paul Rubens.)
Scene 2
Pianologue
(*Music by* Jerome Kern.)
M. Ellis
"Fancy Dress"[112]
T. Friganza, Chorus
(*Music by* Lionel Monckton. *Lyrics by* Adrian Ross.)
"Little Chimney Sweep"[113]
A. Stone, Picaninnies
(*Music by* Lionel Monckton. *Lyrics by* Adrian Ross.)
"La Promenade Anglais"
M. Fulton, W. Rock, Dancers
(*Music by* Lionel Monckton. *Lyrics by* Adrian Ross.)
Burlesque
E. Foy
Finale
Company

[110]Added two months into the run:
"Why Do They Call Me a Gibson Girl?" (from THE BELLE OF MAYFAIR)
E. Foy
(*Music by* Leslie Stuart. *Lyrics by* Leslie Stiles.)
Added during the run to Act 2, Scene 2, after "La Promenade Anglaise":
Dance of the Orchid
La Petite Adelaide [Premiere danseuse]
(*Music by* Hugo Frey.)
[111]Replaced late in the run by:
Zoo Song
M. DiDio {Zelie Homberg}
Which was later replaced by:
"Paree"
M. diDio
(*Music and Lyrics by* Gus Edwards.)
[112]Replaced during the run by:
Character Song
T. Friganza, Chorus
[113]Replaced two months into the run by:
"I Do, I Do, I Do!"
A. Stone
(*Music by* Dave Reed, Jr.)
"Mulberry Street" (Moolbarri)
E. Foy
(*Music and Lyrics by* Junie McCree.)

1907.16 LITTLE JOHNNY JONES

A Revival of the Musical Comedy in Three Acts[114]. Book, music and lyrics by George M. Cohan. Produced (staged) under the personal supervsion of George M. Cohan. Scenery painted by John Young. Costumes by Mme. Freisinger. Music arranged by Charles Gebest. Conductor, E. T. Howe. Produced by Sam H. Harris. Opened 22 April 1907 at the Academy of Music and closed 1 May 1907 after 16 performances.

CAST: *Anthony Ansley*, an American gambler: Jack Raffael. *Sing Song*, editor of the "Pekin Gazette": Frank Montgomery. *Timothy D. McGee*, a New York politician and horse owner: Sam J. Ryan. *Henry Hapgood*, who also makes the trip: William E. Meehan. *Leslie*, valet to Earl of Bloomsbury: William E. Meehan. *The Unknown*: TOM LEWIS. *Jenkins*, starter at the Cecil: C. J. Harrington. *Captain Squirvy* of the "St. Hurrah": C. J. Harrington. *Bellboy*: William Seymour. *Inspector Perkins*: ——. *Stevens*, a waiter: Edw. Sheehan. *Hung Chung*: ——. *Johnny Jones*, the American jockey: GEORGE M. COHAN. *Mrs. Andrew Kenworth*, a fanatic on the subject of reform: Lottie Medley. *Florabelle Fly*, of the "*San Francisco Searcher*": ADELE RAFTER. *Bessie*, an American girl: ETHEL DEANE. *Earl of Bloomsbury*: STELLA TRACEY.*Rosario Fauchette*: STELLA TRACEY.*Goldie Gates*: STELLA TRACEY.

MUSICAL NUMBERS
"The Cecil in London Town"
C. J. Harrington
"They're All My Friends"
S. J. Ryan
"Mam'selle Fauchette"
S. Tracey
"'Op in the 'Ansom"
Cabbies, Reformers
"Nesting in a New York Tree"
A. Rafter
"Yankee Doodle Boy"
G. M. Cohan
"Off to the Derby"
Company
"Girls from the U.S.A."
A. Rafter
"Sailors of the St. Hurrah"
Sailors
"Captain of the Ten-Day Boat"
Company
"So Long, Sing Song"
Company
"Always Leave Them Laughing When You Say Goodbye"
G. M. Cohan
"A Girl I Know"
G. M. Cohan, S. Tracey
"Give My Regards to Broadway"
G. M. Cohan
"March of the 'Frisco Chinks"
Company
"Nothing New Beneath the Sun"
G. M. Cohan
Finale
Entire Company

1907.17 THE PRINCE OF PILSEN

A Revival of the Musical Comedy in Two Acts[115]. Book and lyrics by Frank Pixley. Music by Gustav Luders. Staged by George Marion. Costumes designed by Will R. Barnes. Musical conductor, Frank Darling. Produced by Henry W. Savage. Opened 6 May 1907 at the Academy of Music and closed 1 June 1907 after 32 performances[116].

[114]Originally produced in New York 7 November 1904 at the Liberty Theatre for 52 performances. For Synopsis of Scenes and Musical Numbers, see original 1904 production.
[115]First produced in New York 17 March 1903 at the Broadway Theatre for 143 performances. For Synopsis of Scenes and Musical Numbers, see original 1903 production.
[116]Settings uncredited.

CAST (in order of appearance): *Carl Otto, the Prince of Pilsen*, a Heidelberg student: GEORGE LYDECKER. *Hans Wagner*, a Cincinnati brewer, travelling abroad: JESS DANDY. *Lieutenant Tom Wagner*, of the U.S. Cruiser *Annapolis*: HENRY COOTE. *Arthur St. John Wilberforce, Lord Shrimpton*: J. HAYDEN CLARENDON. *François*, concierge, Hotel Internationale: Robert O'Connor. *Sergeant Brie* of the Gendarmes: Peter Swift. *Cook's Courier*, Vassar Girl's pilot: Peter Swift. *Jimmie*, a bell-boy: Elinore Delmore. *Mrs. Madison Crocker* from New York: PAULINE GUZMAN. *Edith Adams*, a Vassar girl: ALBERTINE BENSON. *Sidonie*, Mrs. Crocker's French maid: Jeannette Bageard. *Nellie Wagner*, Hans Wagner's daughter: MARIE WELSH.

The Heidelberg Boys (8): *Rudolph*: Ernest Armour. *Adolph*: Roy Berry. *Heinrich*: William Stenberg. *Fritz*: Frank Randall. *Ludwig*: George McAlister. *Carl*: Joseph Colville. *Oscar*: Henry Holt. *Wilhelm*: Samuel Chadwick. *American Girls (8)*: *Priscilla Plymouth*, Boston: Marie Stoner. *Frankie Friskie*, San Francisco: Hilda Eldridge. *Olive Oriole*, Baltimore: Beulah Parker. *Dollie Dixie*, New Orleans: Peggy Ballou. *Goldie Dome*, Washington: Christine Stone. *Nellie Noyes*, Chicago: Ethel Gordon. *Miss Rivers*, St. Louis: Adelaide Lee. *Pansy Penn*, Philadelphia: May Darling. *Miss Manhattan*: Ida Stanhope.

Arctic and Sea Shell Girls (8): *White Caps*: Christine Stone. *Pearlie Beach*: Flossie Brooks. *Weedie Sea*: Marie Goodwin. *Birdie Petrel*: Maude Mordaunt. *Lottie Fogge*: Helen O'Neill. *Pleasant Sayle*: Adele Johnson. *Brinie Deep*: Estelle Labart. *Bounding Billow*: Lulu Carroll. *The Bathing Girls (10)*: *Amethyst*: Pauline Huntley. *Opal*: Polly Dorsey. *Sapphire*: Grace Waldo. *Coral*: Martha Bernard. *Topaz*: Elise Krebs. *Cameo*: Marion Lyons. *Agate*: Edna Bontaine. *Diamond*: Edna Wallace. *Pearl*: Madeline May. *Emerald*: May Wilson. *The Gendarmes (4)*: *Vidocq*: Henry Holt. *Sherlock*: William Thompson. *Hawkshaw*: Ernest Armour. *Carter*: Robert Mallory. *French Girls, Flower Girls, Naval Cadets, Fox Hunters, French Maids, Waiters.*

1907.18 FASCINATING FLORA

A Musical Comedy in Two Acts, 3 Scenes. Book by R. H. Burnside and Joseph W. Herbert. Music by Gustave Kerker. (Lyrics by R. H. Burnside. Interpolated numbers by Jerome Kern, James O'Dea, Harry O. Sutton, Jean Lenox, John Kemble and Lester Keith, Paul West, Louis Harrison.) Staged by R. H. Burnside. Dances arranged by Jack Mason. Settings by Frank E. Gates and Edward A. Morange. Costumes by Caroline Seidle. Orchestra under the direction of Gustave Kerker. Produced by (R. H.) Burnside and (F. Ray) Comstock, Inc. Opened 20 May 1907 at the Casino Theatre and closed 7 September 1907 after 113 performances[117].

CAST: *Alphonse Allegretti*, in love with his voice: LOUIS HARRISON. *Gulliver Gayboy*, in love with his money: FRED BOND. *Professor Ludwig Wagner*, in love with his money: JAMES E. SULLIVAN. *Jack Graham*, in love with Dolly: ARTHUR STANFORD. *Baron Reynard*, in love with the girls: Charles Jackson. *Edouard Valliere*, in love with his art: EDWARD M. FAVOR. *Mr. Ferret*, in love with nobody: Frank Miller. *Reuben Brown*, in love with Oshkosh: Edward Craven. *Butler*, in love with his job: E. S. Kinslow. *Winnie Wiggles*, in love with her prospects: ADA LEWIS. *Dolly Wagner*, in love with Jack: ELLA SNYDER. *Rose Gayboy*, in love with the tenor: Kathleen Clifford. *Fifi*, in love with everybody: Fremont Benten. *Flora Duval*, in love with America: ADELE RITCHIE.

Pupils, in love with their teachers: Misses Danton, Whiteford, Murray, Davis, Linyard, Wheeler, Carlisle, Chase. *Bathing Girls*, in love with the water: Misses Leslie, Montague, Rivenburg, Cobb, Griffith, Mercer, LeRoy, Dagwell, Pindar. *Johnnies*, in love with the chorus: Messrs. Dealy, Sullivan, Lutz, Connor, Karlyle, Cousins, Kirkwood, Dutson. *Messenger Boys*, in love with their sleep: Misses Danton, Whiteford, Murray, Davis, Linyard, Wheeler, Carlisle, Chase. *Pink Girls*: Misses Florence Ravel, Julia Mills, Dorothy Bertrand, Alice Clifford, Alice Eis, May Millard.

Act 1: Reception room of Signor Allegretti's conservatoire of music in Paris.

Act 2, Scene 1: Office of Graham & Co., Stockbrokers, Wall Street, New York. *Scene 2*: Manhattan Beach Hotel.

ACT 1[118]

"It's Going to Be a Pretty Wedding" (Opening Chorus)

"In Paris" (Song)
E. Snyder, Chorus

"Money"[119] (Song)
J. E. Sullivan, Chorus

"Katie Was a Business Girl"[120] (Song)
A. Ritchie
(*Music by* Jerome Kern. *Lyrics by* Paul West.)

Entrance of American Girls

"I Am a Marvelous Musician" (Song)
L. Harrison

"What Will Happen Then" (Trio)
A. Ritchie, L. Harrison, F. Bond

"Right Now"[121] (Duet)
A. Stanford, E. Snyder
(*Music by* Fred Fisher. *Lyrics by* Jerome Kern.)

"The Subway Express"
A. Ritchie, L. Harrison
(*Music by* Jerome Kern. *Lyrics by* James O'Dea.)

"Off to New York" (Finale)

ACT 2[122]

"Bulls and Bears" (Opening Chorus)

"Romance and Reality" (Song)
L. Harrison
(*Music by* A. Baldwin Sloane. *Lyrics by* Louis Harrison.)

Dancing Specialty
Messenger Boys

"Nice Little Girls and Boys" (Song)
L. Harrison

"Old Yankee Land for Me" (Yankee Land)(Song)
A. Ritchie
(*Music by* Harry O. Sutton. *Lyrics by* Jean Lenox.)

Ensemble

"Come Along In, the Water's Fine" (Octette)
American Girls

"Oshkosh" (Song)
E. Craven
(*Music and Lyrics by* John Kemble, Lester W. Keith.)

"Ballooning" (Song)
A. Ritchie, Chorus
(*Music by* Jerome Kern. *Lyrics by* Paul West.)

Finale
Ensemble

1907.19 LITTLE DOLLY DIMPLES

A Musical Playlet in Two Acts with vaudeville. Play by C. Herbert Kerr. Produced by the Grace Cameron Opera Company (C. Herbert Kerr, Management). Opened 27 May 1907 at the 14th Street Theatre and closed 1 June 1907 after 9 performances.

CAST: *Little Dolly Dimples*: GRACE CAMERON. *Mayme Green*: MAUD MORRIS. *Aunt Matilda Dunn*: DAISY KING CAMERON. *Betsy*: PHOEBE CARDOWNIE. *Fannie*: Jessie Cardownie. *Hiram Skinner*: AL LAWRENCE. *Alexander Comstock*: WILLIAM PHILBRICK. *Robert Lorraine*: JOHN B. WILSON. *Cy Prime*: John Bohlman. *Zeke Heatherspoon*: Al Thorson. *Bill Spivins*: Frank Campbell. *Harry Hale*: Otto Wichart. *Tom Dashington*: V. L. Newman. *Ned Hathaway*: H. Thurmon Morse. *Fred Gibson*: Harry H. Wiel. *George Astergould*: John

---

[117]Played a return engagement 23 September 1907 at the Grand Opera House for 8 performances.

[118]Running order of songs revised during the run.

[119]Replaced during the run by:
"Zuyder Zee"
Harry Davenport {Jack Graham}, Chorus
(*Music and Lyrics by* Kerry Mills and Scott.)

[120]Published as "Katy Was a Business Girl." Replaced during the run by: (moved to follow "I Am a Marvelous Musician")
"Fascinating Flora" (Entrance Song)
A. Ritchie
Interpolations published during the run, as per published sheet music:
"The Little Church Around the Corner"
(*Music by* Jerome Kern. *Lyrics by* M. E. Rourke.)

[121]Dropped during the run.

[122]Act 2 running order revised during the run. Added were:
"I'd Rather Two-Step Than Waltz, Bill" (added after "Nice Little Girls and Boys")
A. Ritchie
(*Music and Lyrics by* Benjamin Hapgood Burt.)
"Won't You Come and Splash Me" (You Splash Me and I'll Splash You)(after "Oshkosh")
A. Ritchie, Chorus
(*Music by* Alfred Solman. *Lyrics by* Arthur J. Lamb.)

L. Huddleston. *Ben Swagger*: Al Thorson. *John Boldman*: Frank Campbell. *Gildie Lightfeather*: John Bohlman. *Specialties*: Phoebe Cardownie and the Pony Ballet; Klein, Ott Brothers, and Nicholson; Al Lawrence (mimic); Emma King (Russian and Hungarian Dancer); Rita Curtis (lady violinist); Church City Quartette.

MUSICAL NUMBERS[123]

"Good-Bye, Old Home"
G. Cameron

"Because I Am So Shy"
G. Cameron

"Lullaby"
G. Cameron

"(Since)Little Dolly Dimples—Made a Hit" (from PIFF! PAFF!! POOFF!!!)
G. Cameron
(*Music by* Jean Schwartz. *Lyrics by* William Jerome.)

"Jennie Jones"
W. Philbrick

"Bobby"
M. Morris

"Naughty Kid Song"

"The Girl That I'd Call Mine"

Double Sextette

"At Night in My Brilliant Salon"
M. Morris

"Friends of Long Ago"

"What D'you Mean You Lost Your Dog?"

"I'm Going Back to Carolina"

[123]No New York program available.

1907–1908 SEASON

Elsie Janis (Photo: Walery)
Billy Rose Theatre Collection, New York Public Library for the Performing Arts

1907–1908 SEASON

1907.20 THE HONEYMOONERS

A New Edition of the Musical Farce in Three Acts. Book, music and lyrics by George M. Cohan. (Adapted from George M. Cohan's musical comedy "Running for Office."[1]) Staged by George M. Cohan. Produced by Sam H. Harris[2]. Opened 3 June 1907 at the Aerial Gardens (atop the New Amsterdam Theatre) and closed 24 August 1907 after 72 performances.

CAST: *John Tiger*, a prohibition candidate: JERRY J. COHAN. *Sam Gayland*, the popular man: WILLIAM KEOUGH. *Andrew Riley*, Mayor of Hazelnut: James H. Manning. *Franklyn Flusher*, a theatrical manager: Jack Webster. *Peter Pinchum*, the constable: Jonathan Keefe. *Herman Highberger*, Gussie's college chum: Jo Smith Marba. *Bolivar Bixby*, Gayland's servant: Joseph Leslie. *Dan Timmons*, Riley's right hand man: Frank McNish, Jr. *Captain Hicks*, of New Hampshire football team: Howard Stevens. *Augustus Wright*, Rah, Rah, Rah: GEORGE M. COHAN. *Mrs. John Tiger*, formerly Mrs. Wright: HELEN F. COHAN. *Madeline Tiger*: GETRUDE HOFFMAN. *Susie Sprightling*, "Jeanetta Zanfretta": Leona Anderson. *Gertie Gayland*, a noisy kid: Liola Rhodes. *Mary*, Mrs. Tiger's servant: Alice Merrill. *Drums*: S. M. Avedon. *Dance Specialty*: GERTRUDE HOFFMAN. *Visitors, Strangers, Town Folks, Politicians, Ward Heelers, etc.*

Act 1: Hazelnut, Vermont. A quarter of too.

Act 2: Tiger's Home. Two weeks later.

Act 3: Public Square. Same night.

MUSICAL NUMBERS[3]

"Let's Take an Old-Fashioned Walk" (Opening Chorus)

"I'm a Popular Man"
W. Keough, Chorus

"Make a Lot of Noise"
J. H. Manning, Chorus

"The Musical Comedy Maid"
G. Hoffman, Chorus

"Kid Days"
G. M. Cohan, Baby Ballet

"Honey Babe" (Ensemble)
G. M. Cohan, Chorus

"In a One Night Stand"
L. Anderson, J. Webster, Chorus

"Nothing New Beneath the Sun"
G. M. Cohan

"Mysterious Maid"
L. Anderson

"I'll Be There in the Public Square"
L. Anderson, Chorus

"(If) Goin' to Die, (I'm) Goin' to Have Some Fun"
G. M. Cohan

"The Story of the Wedding March"
G. Hoffman, G. M. Cohan

"Pupolar March"
Chorus

Finale
Entire Chorus

1907.21 HIS HONOR THE MAYOR

A Revival of the Musical Entertainment (Musical Comedy) in Two Acts[4]. Book and lyrics by Charles J. Campbell and Ralph M. Skinner. Music by Julian Edwards, Alfred E. Aarons, (Gus Edwards, Will Cobb and Ren Shields). Staged by J. K. Adams. Costumes by Joseph C. Fischer. Musical director, Daniel Dore. Produced by Alfred E. Aarons. Opened 3 June 1907 at Wallack's Theatre and closed 15 June 1907 after 16 performances. Re-opened 25 November 1907 at the Circle Theatre and closed 7 December 1907 after 17 performances. Total: 33 performances.[5]

CAST: *Hon. Teddy Todd*, Mayor of Kankakee: CLARENCE HARVEY. *Daisy*, a milliner girl: MABEL HOLLINS. *May Flood*: Janet Priest. *T. Chesterfield Prebble*, an Anglicized native of Kankakee: FLETCHER NORTON. *"Jack" Thayer*, his chum: Harry Stuart. *Deacon Flood*, May's father: HARRY KELLY. *"Reddy" Samson*, a cowboy: William W. Black. *Mrs. Vayne*, a young widow: LOIS E. TABOR. *Marjorie Vayne*, her stepdaughter: Lora Lieb. *Solomon Syphonstein*, a Parisian marriage-broker: FREDERICK VAN RENSSELAER. *Captain Rudolph Zitzky* of the Royal Hungarian Hussars: JOHN H. PRATT. *Lieutenant Schnipp* of the Royal Hungarian Hussars: Nellie DeGrasse. *R. LaCarte*, manager of LaCarte's Hotel: James Murray. *Josef*, waiter at LaCarte's Hotel: E. G. Melendy. *Alphonse*, a waiter: Dan Evans. *Treadau*, a waiter: Harry Evans. *Katrinka*: CATHERINE TANNER. *Chorus of Arts Students, Tourists, Parisians, French Officers, Gendarmes, Hungarian Nobles and Peasants, Slavs, Chikos, etc.*

Alfred E. Aarons Dancing Dolls: Misses Eva Marlow, Carie Poltz, Maude Crossland, Martha Edmonds, Ethel Rosebud, Florrie Poltz, Lilly DeGrasse.

Act 1: Courtyard of Hotel LaCarte, Paris. Present time.

Act 2, Scene 1: The Isle of Margitsziget, on the danube River, between Buda and Pesth, Hungary. *Scene 2*: Ice Palace, Buda Pesth.

1907.22 THE SHOO-FLY REGIMENT

A Musical Comedy in Three Acts. Book by Bob Cole. Music by J. Rosamund Johnson. Lyrics by James Weldon Johnson. Staged by Bob Cole. Luneta dances arranged by Siren Nevarro. Costumes by Siren Nevarro. Settings by Ernest Albert. Musical director, James Reese Europe. Produced by Melville Raymond. Opened 3 June 1907 at the Grand Opera House and closed 8 June 1907 after 8 performances; re-opened 6 August 1907 at the Bijou Theatre and closed 17 August 1907 after an additional 15 performances. Total: 23 performances.

CAST: *Professor Maxwell*, principal of Lincolnville Institute: Arthur Talbot. *Randolf*, a farmer: Arthur Ray. *Wlliamson*, a blacksmith: Frank DeLyons. *Virginia*, Ned's sister: Nettie Glenn. *Uncle July Jackson*, Ned's father: Henry Gant. *Aunt Phoebe Jackson*, Ned's mother: Elizabeth Williams. *Rose Maxwell*, the professor's daughter: FANNIE WISE. *Ophelia*, the village pride: ANDREW TRIBBLE. *Mailman*, Lincolnville Post Office: J. T. Porter. *Brother Doolittle*, "Bode Edjicashun": WESLEY JENKINS. *Brother Doless*, "Bode Edjicashun": SAM LUCAS. *Hunter Wilson*, janitor, Lincolnville Institute: BOB COLE. *Edward Jackson*, a graduate of Tuskegee: J. ROSAMUND JOHNSON. *Dilsey Lumpkins*, a widow with a family: Mollie Dill. *Napoleon Bonaparte Lumpkins*, the snowball: ARTHUR RAY. *Martha Jones*, lady principal, Lincolnville Institute: Anna Cook Pankey. *Lieutenant Dixon*, Co. G., 54th U.S.V.: Theodore Pankey. *Orderly*, Co. H., 54th U.S.V.: William Phelps. *Grizelle*, a Filipino dancer: SIREN NEVARRO. *A Filipino Spy*: Herbert Amos. *The Graduates, The Sewing Class, The Pickaninnies The Farmers, The Cooks, The Blacksmiths*: Chorus.

Act 1: Lincolnville Institute in Alabama.

Act 2: Philippines.

Act 3: Same as Act 1.

ACT 1[6]

---

[1]RUNNING FOR OFFICE was first produced in New York 27 April 1903 at the 14th Street Theatre for 48 performances.

[2]The show subsequently toured with a different cast under the auspices of Hope & Welsh.

[3]Program note: During Act 3, Miss Gertrude Hoffman will give imitations of The Gibson Girl from "The Belle of Mayfair," Eddie Foy and Anna Held.

[4]Originally produced in New York 28 May 1906 at the New York Theatre for 120 performances. For Synopsis of Scenes and Musical Numbers, see original 1906 production. Act 2 was divided into 2 scenes. For this revival, the following songs were dropped: Flower Song," "Come Take a Skate with Me," Hungarian Dance, "My Irish Rose." In Act 1, Imitations and "Call Around on Sunday" were replaced by:

"Anastasia Brady" (Song)
L. E. Tabor
(*Music by* Jean Schwartz. *Lyrics by* William Jerome.)

Pageantry March
Dancing Dolls
(*Music by* Alfred E. Aarons.)

In Act 2, "Waltz Me Around Again, Willie" was replaced by:

"My Roller Skating Girl"
M. Hollins
(*Music by* Alfred E. Aarons.)

[5]Settings uncredited.

[6]No New York program found. Song list prepared from 9 December 1906 tryout. Additional numbers credited to the show:

Opening Chorus
Company
"De Bo'd of Education" (De Bode o' Edicashun; Bode O' Edjicashun)
W. Jenkins, S. Lucas
(*Music by* J. Rosamond Johnson. *Lyrics by* James Weldon Johnson.)
"The Little Choo-Choo, Gee-Gee"
J. R. Johnson, B. Cole
"Just How Much I Love You"
J. R. Johnson
"If Adam Hadn't Seen the Apple Tree"
B. Cole, Picks
(*Music and Lyrics by* Robert Cole.)
"I'll Always Love Old Dixie"
A. C. Pankey, Girls
"Run, Brudder Rabbit, Run" (Run, Brudder Possum, Run)
A. Ray, A. Tribble
(*Music by* J. Rosamond Johnson. *Lyrics by* James Weldon Johnson.)
Finale
Entire Company

ACT 2
"Southland"
J. R. Johnson, A. C. Pankey, Male Chorus
"Li'l Gal"
J. R. Johnson, Chorus
(*Music by* J. Rosamond Johnson. *Lyrics by* Paul Laurence Dunbar.)
"The Ghost of Deacon Brown"
B. Cole, Chorus
"On the Gay Luneta"[7]
T. Pankey, Chorus
(*Music by* James Reese Europe. *Lyrics by* Robert Cole.)
Ballet
S. Nevarro, Dancers
"Lemmons"
B. Cole

ACT 3
Opening Chorus
"We've Been to Boston Town"
Company
"Who Do You Love?"
A. Ray, A. Tribble
(*Lyrics by* Robert Cole.)
"Floating Down the Nile"
J. R. Johnson
(*Music by* J. Rosamond Johnson. *Lyrics by* James Weldon Johnson.)
"Down in the Philippines"
B. Cole, S. Nevarro
"The Old Flag Never Touched the Ground" (Finale)
Entire Company

1907.23 THE MAID AND THE MILLIONAIRE

A Musical Comedy in Two Acts. Book, music and lyrics by Frederick Chapin, (others). Produced by Mortimer Theise and Henry Pincus. Opened 22 June 1907 at the Madison Square Garden Roof and closed 31 August 1907 after 72 performances.

CAST: *John Van Hostetter*: FRED WYCKOFF. *Walter Van Hostetter*: HARRY LINKEY. *Barney Cosgrove*: Charles Burke. *Tell M. Strong*: JOHN C. HART. *Goodand Slow*: Ed Morton. *Blenkins*: Albert Davis. *Nannette*: TOMA HANLON. *Glorianna Warrener*: Maude Alice Kelley. *Mademoiselle Marie*: Mildred Morton. *Blossom*: Lilla Brennan.

Act 1: Isle of Guam.

Act 2:

MUSICAL NUMBERS[8]
"Kitty O'Neill"
T. Hanlon
"I Like You, I Love You, I Want You"
"My Coney Island Queen"

1907.24 FOLLIES OF 1907

The Ziegfeld Musical Revue in Two Acts, 13 Scenes[9]. Words (sketches) by Harry B. Smith. Music by Everybody (Seymour Furth, Gertrude Hoffman, Gus Edwards, E. Ray Goetz, Silvio Hein, Jean Schwartz, Billy Gaston. Lyrics by Edgar Selden, Vincent Bryan, Will D. Cobb, Billy Gaston, William Jerome, Matt Woodward). Principals directed by Herbert Gresham. Chorus directed by Julian Mitchell; Doll numbers and others arranged by Joseph C. Smith; drummer girls instructed by John O'Neil. Costumes by W. H. Matthews, Mme. E. S. Freisinger. Settings by Peter V. Griffin, T. Bernard McDonald and John H. Young. Electric effects by Harry Bissing. Musical director, Max Hoffman. Conceived and produced by Florenz Ziegfeld. Opened 8 July 1907 at the Jardin de Paris (atop the New York and Criterion Theatres), moved 26 August 1907 to the Liberty Theatre and closed 7 September 1907 after 70 performances[10].

CAST (in order of appearance): *The Idol of the People*: HARRY WATSON, JR. *His Vocal Proxy*: Frank Mayne. *Mr. Harryman*, a railway guide: James Manley. *A Wife and Mother*: LILLIAN LEE. *The Hero of a "Nature Story"*: John Kennedy. *Captain J. Smith*, a reincarnated adventurer: DAVID LEWIS. *An Inquisitive Girl*: Adele Carson. *Another One*: Madlyn Summers. *Another*: Edna Snyder. *Pocahontas*, in the cigar business: GRACE LaRUE. *Chauncey Depot*, a railway porter: Frank Mayne. *Tony Cornstock*, in search of the immoral: GEORGE BICKELL. *An Easy Mark*: CHARLES J. ROSS. *An Antique Bridegroom*: HARRY WATSON, JR. *His Bride*: LILLIAN LEE. *Topsy*, a soubrette lady: EMMA CARUS. *A Cigarette Fiend*: FLORENCE TEMPEST. *Officer Schmaltz*: GEORGE BICKELL. *Officer O'Finnegan*: Dan Baker. *A Smart Setter*: Grace Leigh. *The District Attorey for the Defense*: HARRY WATSON, JR. *A Wild West Napoleon*: CHARLES J. ROSS. *Her Honor the Judge*: GRACE LaRUE. *Mrs. Central Park*: EMMA CARUS. *Brago*, the monk: Dave Abrams. *Signor Crusoe*: Frank Mayne. *A Lady Expert*: LILLIAN LEE. *Still More*: Sherwood Alston. *Mrs. Newlywed*: Grace Leigh. *Her Husband*: Dave Abrams. *A Lady in Search of Bargains*: Edith Moyer. *Another One*: Mabel Spencer. *A Poor Weak Woman*: LILLIAN LEE. *Mr. Biersteiner*: GEORGE BICKELL. *Dolly*: Mlle. DAZIE. *John Philip*: DAVID LEWIS. *Victor O'Herbert*: C. M. Brooks. *Miss Mimique*: Edna Luby. *Daughter of the Regiment*: EMMA CARUS. *Drum Major*: Willie Torpey. *Mr. Cornfeed*: DAVE LEWIS. *Salome*, the one who sings: EMMA CARUS. *Salome*, the one who dances: Mlle. DAZIE. *A Show Girl*: Natalie DeLonton. *A Showy Girl*: Stacia Leslie. *The Showiest Girl*: May Emery. *A Mere Star*: Roma Snyder. *A Property Mother*: Edith Moyer. *Miss Edna Might*: Edna Luby. *Miss Maytell Steelman*: Pauline Thorne. *A Girl Who Married a Millionaire*: May Leslie. *Adam Rounder*: CHARLES J. ROSS. *Cremo*, a milkman: W. H. Powers. *Scrub Lady*: Adele Carson. *John D*: James Manley. *Andy C*: CHARLES J. ROSS. *An Undesirable Citizen*: HARRY WATSON, JR. *Miss Ginger*, of Jamaica: GRACE LaRUE. *An Honest Pugilist*: HARRY WATSON, JR. *A Belle of the Beach*: Marion Sunshine. *A Belle of the Sands*: Angie Weimer. (*Specialty*: PRINCE TOKIO.)

Act 1, Scene 1: Jamestown Exposition Grounds. *Scene 2*: Weary Railroad Station. *Scene 3*: The Home of the Murad. *Scene 4*: Court Room. *Scene 5*: The Shopping District. *Scene 6*: Broadway, a month after a snowstorm.

Act 2, Scene 1: Atlantic City. *Scene 2*: The Beach. *Scene 3*: The Surf. *Scene 4*: The Future Library. *Scene 5*: Gymnasium. *Scene 6*: Broadway Theatre Stage Door. *Scene 7*: Metropolitan Opera House.

ACT 1[11]

"I Think an Awful Lot of You"
(*Music by* Joe Jordan. *Lyrics by* Alfred Anderson.)
"I Can't Think of Nothing in the Wide, Wide World But You"
J. R. Johnson, B. Cole
(*Music by* J. Rosamond Johnson. *Lyrics by* Bob Cole.)
"My Sweetheart's a Soldier (in the Army)"
"That Still Small Voice"
"There's Always Something Wrong"
(*Music by* J. Rosamond Johnson. *Lyrics by* Bob Cole.)
"Won't You Be My Little Brown Bear?"

[7]Also appears as "On the Gay Lunette."

[8]No program available.

[9]The first in the annual series of revues produced by Florenz Ziegfeld. Billed as "Another One of Those Things in Thirteen Acts."

[10]Played a return engagement 4 November 1907 at the Grand Opera House for 9 performances.

[11]Running order revised frequently during the run; musical numbers and specialties added and dropped. Added during New York run to Act 1:
Doll Dance (*Arranged by* Joseph C. Smith.)
Mlle. Dazie, J. C. Smith

"(My) Pocahontas"
G. LaRue, Chorus
(*Music by* Seymour Furth. *Lyrics by* Edgar Selden.)
"Budweiser" (Budweiser's a Friend of Mine)
C. J. Ross
(*Music by* Seymour Furth. *Lyrics by* Vincent Bryan.)
"Little Murad"[12]
"Mother's the Boss of Our House"[13]
E. Carus
(*Music and Lyrics by* Herbert Ingraham.)
"Re-Incarnation"[14]
D. Lewis
(*Music by* E. Ray Goetz. *Lyrics by* Vincent Bryan.)
"I Want to be a Drummer Boy" (Finale)
E. Carus, 16 Drummer Boys
(*Music by* Silvio Hein. *Lyrics by* Matt Woodward.)

ACT 2[15]

"The Man Who Built the Subway"
C. J. Ross
(*Music by* Max Hoffman. *Lyrics by* Vincent Bryan.)
Incidental Music in Court Room Scene, Operatic Selections
F. Mayne, Entire Company
"Cigarette"
F. Tempest, Girls
(*Music by* Max Hoffman. *Lyrics by* Vincent Bryan.)
Which was replaced for subsequent tour by:
"(They) All Look Alike to Mary"
F. Tempest
(*Music and Lyrics by* Billy Kent.)
"That's What the Rose Said to Me" (dropped for tour)
M. Mooney
(*Music by* Gus Edwards. *Lyrics by* Will Cobb.)
Added for subsequent tour (Grand Opera House engagement) in Act 1, then later dropped:
"A Foolish Song"
N. Bayes
Interpolated as per published sheet music:
"Meet Me with Spangles and Bells On"
N. Bayes
(*Music and Lyrics by* Martin G. Brown.)
"On the Grand Old Sands"
F. Tempest, Bathing Beauties
(*Music by* Gus Edwards. *Lyrics by* Will Cobb.)
"That's How He Met the Girl"
(*Music by* E. Ray Goetz. *Lyrics by* Vincent Bryan.)
"I Think I Oughtn't Auto Anymore"
D. Lewis
(*Music by* E. Ray Goetz. *Lyrics by* William Jerome.)
"Miss Ginger of Jamaica"
G. LaRue, C. J. Ross
(*Music and Lyrics by* Billy Gaston.)
"Handle Me with Care"
E. Carus, H. Watson, Jr.
(*Music by* Jean Schwartz. *Lyrics by* William Jerome.)
"Jiu Jitsu" Waltz
Mlle. Dazie
"If We Knew What the Milkman Knows"[16]
C. J. Ross
(*Music by* E. Ray Goetz. *Lyrics by* Vincent Bryan.)
"(Come Down) Salomy Jane"[17]
E. Carus
(*Music by* E. Ray Goetz. *Lyrics by* Vincent Bryan.)
The (Vision of) Salome Dance; "La Kraquette"
Mlle. Dazie
(*Music by* Frederic Solomon.)

1907.25

THE TIME, THE PLACE AND THE GIRL

A Musical Comedy in Three Acts. Chatter (book, lyrics) by Will M. Hough and Frank Adams. Jingles and tunes (music) by Joseph E. Howard. Produced under the stage direction of (staged by) Ned Wayburn. Dramatic portion of the play directed by Arthur Evans. (Scenery) Designed by Will R. Barnes. Costumes by Spitzer and Harris; Eaves. Conductor, Edward Howe. Produced by Harry Askin and (Mort H.) Singer Company, Inc. Opened 5 August 1907 at Wallack's Theatre and closed 31 August 1907 after 32 performances.[18]

CAST (in order of appearance): *Pietro*, an organ grinder: William Ricciardi. *Mrs. Talcott*, a widow: HARRIET BURT. *Molly Kelly*, a nurse: ELENE FOSTER. *Bud Simpson*: John C. Rowe. *Jasper Simpson*, a thrifty farmer: George Ebner. *Laurie Farnham*, a black sheep: JAMES NORVAL. *An Attendant*: Barney McConnell. *Margaret Simpson*, "The Girl": VIOLET McMILLEN. *Tom Cunningham*, a rich man's son: GEORGE ANDERSON. *"Happy" Johnny Hicks*, a gambler: ARTHUR DEAGON. *Willie Talcott*, a spoiled child: Hubert Hornsby. *A Chauffeur*: Clyde Hunnewell. *A Coal Heaver*: George Johnson. *A Police Sergeant*: William O'Day.

Nurses, Guests, Boarding School Girls, Sanitarium Attendants, etc.: *Summer Girls*: Misses Albertine Marr, Violet Inglish, Eleanor Rose, Berkeley Perrin, Gertrude O'Conner, Victoria Stuart, Sylvia Evlyn. *Nurses*: Misses Mattie Vance, Effie Hamilton, Alice Chase, Josephine Howard, Lillian Brown, Theresa Powers, Virginia Richmond. *Boarding School Girls*: Misses Camille LaVilla, Nellie DeForest, Ethel Cantor, Nan Pomery, Bertha Peck, Fannie Bradshaw, Ruth Pollo, Blanche Cosley, Minnie Carruthers, Grace Lane, Lillian Gilman. *Honeymoon Girls and Boys*: Misses Mattie

---

[12]Dropped after opening.
[13]Replaced late in the run by: (then later dropped)
"(The) Band Box Girl"
N. Bayes
(*Music by* Seymour Furth. *Lyrics by* Edgar Selden.)
[14]Dropped during subsequent tour.
[15]Added during the New York run:
"The Gibson Bathing Girls"
A. Whitford, others
(illustrating Charles Dana Gibson's Sketches of the Seaside, by permission of the Management of "The Belle of Mayfair.")
(*Music by* Alfred Solman. *Lyrics by* Paul West.)
"Come and Float Me, Freddie Dear" (How'd You Like to Float Me?)
G. Leigh
(*Music by* E. Ray Goetz. *Lyrics by* Vincent Bryan.)
"In the Surf"/"The Heart Breaker"
"The Fencing Girls"
(*Music by* E. Ray Goetz. *Lyrics by* Vincent Bryan.)
"I Don't Want an Auto"
G. LaRue, Chorus
(*Music by* Seymour Furth. *Lyrics by* William Jerome.)
Imitations
E. Luby
Musical Specialty
G. Bickel, H. Watson, Their Famous Band
The Peacock Girls
Grand Ballet (an Innovation in Operatic Ballets)
"Bye-Bye, Dear Old Broadway"
Entire Company
(*Music by* Gus Edwards. *Lyrics by* Will D. Cobb.)
Added during subsequent tour to Act 2 (Grand Opera House engagement), but subsequently dropped:
"Oh, Marie"
N. Bayes, M. Libby
"Bridget Salome"
N. Bayes
Added late in subsequent tour to Act 2, after "In the Surf/"The Heart Breaker":
"Way Down on the Strand"/"That's All"/"Be Good"
Lucy Weston
Added to Act 2 after "Jiu Jitsu Waltz" late in subsequent tour:
"Dixie Dan" (from THE GAY WHITE WAY)
G. LaRue, Chorus
(*Music by* Seymour Furth. *Lyrics by* Will D. Cobb.)
[16]Dropped during the New York run.
[17]Dropped during the New York run.
[18]Played a return engagement 31 August 1908 at the Grand Opera House for 8 performances.

Vance, Virginia Richmond, Albertine Marr, Alice Chase, Lillian Brown, Effie Hamilton, Berkeley Perrin, Sylvia Evlyn; Messrs. Barney McGee, Larry Deagon, Henry Alderson, Joseph Simpson, Harry Willard, Clyde Hunnewell, Guy Primeau, Richard McCullum. *Harlem Girls*: Misses Lillian Brow, Theresa Powers, Victoria Stuart, Virginia Richmond. *New York Girls*: Misses Josephine Howard, Alice Chase, Effie Hamilton, Mattie Vance. *Mexican Girls*: Sylvia Evlyn, Berkeley Perrin, Violet Inglish, Gertrude O'Conner. *Spanish Girls*: Misses Fannie Bradshaw, Nan Pomery, Eleanor Rose, Albertine Marr. *Dixie Girls*: Misses Camille LaVilla, Nellie DeForest, Ethel Cantor, Minnie Carruthers, Bertha Peck, Ruth Polo, Blanche Cosley, Grace Lane, Lillian Gilman.

The action takes place in a sanitarium and hotel in the mountains of Virginia.

Act 1: Grounds of sanitarium, Thursday 27 September. Shortly after noon.

Act 2: Veranda of hotel. Late afternoon and evening of the same day.

Act 3: Grounds of sanitarium, Thursday 11 October. Afternoon. Two weeks later.

ACT 1

Opening Chorus
Ensemble

"Blow the Smoke Away"
J. Norval, Chorus

"I Don't Like Your Family"
V. McMillen, Chorus

"Thursday's My Jonah Day"
A. Deagon, Chorus

ACT 2

"First and Only"
G. Anderson, Company

"The Waning Honeymoon"
H. Burt, Chorus

"Lonesome" (It's Lonesome Tonight)
V. McMillen

"Uncle Sam's Best Girl"/

"Dixie, I Love You"
H. Burt, Company

ACT 3

"Don't You Tell"
V. McMillen, A. Deagon

Finale—Medley
Entire Company

1907.26

THE ALASKAN

A Comic Opera in Two Acts and a Prologue. Book by Max Figman and Joseph Blethen. Music by Harry Girard. Lyrics by Joseph Blethen. Staged by Max Figman. Dances arranged by Joseph C. Smith. Gowns by A. Morton Oppenheim; eskimo suits by Warnock Uniform Company. Conductor, Oscar Radin. Produced by John Cort. Opened 12 August 1907 at the Knickerbocker Theatre and closed 7 September 1907 after 29 performances.[19]

CAST: *Richard Atwater*, a prospector: HARRY GIRARD. *Totem Pole Pete*, foreman of Discovery Claim: EDWARD MARTINDEL. *Smallberry Strander*, a Broadway favorite: Teddy Webb. *Meadowbrooke Blazes*, Ph. D. of the Metropolitan Museum: HAROLD VIZARD. *Teddy Bear*, the real thing: William Fables. *U. S. Mail Driver*: M. V. L. Smith. *Eskimo Chief*: John Wheeler. *Arlee Easton*, an heiress: AGNES CAIN BROWN. *Mrs (Lydia) Good-Better-Best*, the chaperon: ANNE ADAIR. *Claudie Cluster*, a wardrobe mistress: Amy Leicester. *Trixie*: Jessie Brown.

Sextette Girls: Florence Paulin, Pearl Girard, Alice Loasby, Eloise Reed, Lillian Norton, Genevieve Reed. *Eskimo Girls*: May [Mae] Murray, Daisy Lucas, Ellen Tate, Daisy Johnstone, Marie Goodner, Ethel Little, Reta Kent, Geraldine Cook, Ida Gabrielle, Pearl Gabrielle, Bertha Perl, Ellen Dompierre. *Show Girls*: Vivienne Fraser, Mazie Hartford, Anna Hudson, Lela Williams, Marjory Ganes, Pauline Turner.

Alaskan Miners: Messrs. Derbyshire, Bretland, Thatcher, Wheeler, Reed, Forest, Dolliver, Loomis, Abbott, Jones, Huddlestone, Silverman, Kalich, Ludwig, Little, Rough, Sharp, Bagge.

The action takes place at the present time in Alaska.

Prologue: On the trail. Midwinter.

Act 1: Long Chance Creek, near Nome. Late fall.

Act 2: Arlee Easton's Bungalow at Dawson. New Year's Eve.

PROLOGUE

Prelude—Introduction—Finale

ACT 1

Opening Chorus

"Yup and Away"
E. Martindel, Chorus

"The Trouble Tree"
T. Webb, Chorus

"The Fossil Man"
H. Vizard, Eskimo Girls

"Song of the Riffles"
H. Girard, Ensemble

"Party of the Second Part"
A. C. Brown

"Glittering Gold"
A. C. Brown, A. Adair, T. Webb

"Rainbow and Thistle"
A. C. Brown, H. Girard

"(My) Totem Pole"
E. Martindel, Chorus

Finale
Ensemble

ACT 2

"There Is Gold Along the Rivers"
Male Chorus

"Mother Did"
A. C. Brown, Male Chorus

"Bah, Bah, Black Sheep"
T. Webb, Chorus

"Alimony"
A. Adair

"Naughty Little Lady, O"
E. Martindel, Chorus

"Arlee"
H. Girard, Ensemble

"My Eskimo"
Ensemble

1907.27

THE YANKEE TOURIST

A Musical Farce in Three Acts. Book by Richard Harding Davis based on his play "The Galloper." Music by Alfred G. Robyn. Lyrics by Wallace Irwin. Staged by George Marion. Scenery designed by Walter W. Burridge. Costumes by Mme. Herman. Electrical effects by Joseph Wilson. Orchestra under the direction of John McGhie. Produced by Henry W. Savage. Opened 12 August 1907 at the Astor Theatre and closed 9 November 1907 after 103 performances[20].

CAST: *Copeland Schuyler*, of New York: RAYMOND HITCHCOCK. *Kirke Warren*, War correspondent of the "Republic": Harry West. *Mr. Hewitt*, war correspondent of "Collier's": Wallace Beery. *Captain Anstruther*, war correspondent of the "London Times": Phillip Smalley. *Mr. Griggs*, war correspondent of the London "Imperialist": HERBERT CAWTHORN. *Billy Ashe*, manager for the "Republic" at Athens: E. R. Phillips. *Captain O'Malley* of the Foreign Legion: Harry Lane. *Colonel Osten* Turkish Army: E. PERCY PARSONS. *Innkeeper*: M. W. Rale. *Grace Whitney*: FLORA ZABELLE. *Blanche Bailey*: HELEN HALE. *Mrs. Sybil Schwartz*: Susie Forrester Cawthorn. *Chief Steward*: EVA FALLON. *A Greek Girl*: Mabel Breen. *Captain Mouzaffer*, Turkish Army: Frederick Corbin. *Crown Prince of Greece*: W. M. Cheesman. *First Officer*, Transport to Volo: Fred Johnston. *First Officer*, Transport to Constantinople: Murray D'Arcy. *Sergeant*: O. J. Van Asse. *Boatswain*: Victor Clarke. *Captain Zonya*, Foreign Legion: Herman Ruepke. *Herr Muller*, proprietor Hotel Angleterre: M. W. Rale.

Vaudevillians: Misses Marshall, Moyles, Dunn, (Clara) Noelke, Doddridge, Honehan, Darville, Paon. *Correspondents*: Misses Winters, Despres, Allen, Newell. *Flower Girls*: Misses Breen, Land, Chase, Desmond. *Foreign Legion*: Messrs. Oden, Supraner, Murphy, Feeney, Davis, Lawrence, Drew.

[19]Scenery uncredited in programs.

[20]Played a return engagement 18 November 1907 at the Grand Opera House for 8 performances.

Act 1: Hotel Angleterre, Athens.

Act 2: The wharf at Piraeus.

Act 3: Mountain pass between Grecian and Turkish lines.

ACT 1

Opening Chorus

"The Teddy Girl"[21]
H. Hale, Vaudevillians
(*Music by* Jean Schwartz. *Lyrics by* William Jerome.)

"Golden Sails"
F. Zabelle, Men

"The Yankee Millionaire"
R. Hitchcock, Girls

Finale

ACT 2

Opening Chorus[22]:

"Longshoremen's Chanty"
Enseble

"Stewards' Song"
E. Fallon, Girls

"Stokers' Song"
Men

"Would You Like a Sweetheart?" (Wouldn't You Like to Have Me for a Sweetheart?)
H. Hale, F. Zabelle, E. Fallon

"When a Girl is Born to Be a Lady"
S. F. Cawthorn

"Irish Memories"
H. Lane, Legion

"So Long, Bill"[23] (Take Care of Yourself)
R. Hitchcock
(*Music by* Alfred G. Robyn. *Lyrics by* Wallace Irwin.)

Finale

ACT 3

Opening Chorus:

Greek Dance
E. P. Parsons, Chorus

"Saracen Song March"
E. P. Parsons, Chorus

"Come and Have a Smile with Me"[24]
R. Hitchcock, H. Hale, F. Zabelle, H. West, H. Lane, E. R. Phillips

"Rainbows"
F. Zabelle, Girls

Finale

1907.28 THE HIRED GIRL'S MILLIONS

A Musical Melodrama in Four Acts. Book by Charles E. Blaney. Staged by James R. Garey, General Stage Director. Musical director, Jules Friquet. Produced by Charles E. Blaney. Opened 12 August 1907 at the Lincoln Square Theatre and closed 17 August 1907 after 9 performances; returned 9 December 1907 to the 14th Street Theatre and closed 14 December 1907 after an additional 8 performances. Total : 17 performances.[25]

CAST: *Frau Sweinburger*: JAMES RUSSELL. *Betsy Brief*: JAMES RUSSELL. *Jeannette*: JAMES RUSSELL. *Jim McCann*: JAMES RUSSELL. *John McCann*: JOHN RUSSELL. *Mary MacGregor*: JOHN RUSSELL. *Houlihan*: JOHN RUSSELL. *Antonio Carreno*: JOHN RUSSELL. *Sally Brief*: JOHN RUSSELL. *Raymond Strong*: Charles J. Diem. *Norman Canby*: Lewis J. Cody. *Lemon Squeeze*: JOHN RUSSELL, JR. *Cough Drop Ed*: James A. Marcus. *Sampson Sly*: James A. Marcus. *Smoke*: Harry S. Fisher. *Judge Sly*: A. J. Sucram [James A. Marcus]. *Jeremiah Lockem*: Victor Scott. *Jennie McCarthy*: FLORA BONFANTO RUSSELL. *Mrs. Vander Gould Potter*: ANNIE C. RUSSELL. *Mrs. Stidgers*: Lillian Hathaway. *Torpedo Till*: Lillian Hathaway.
Salesladies: May Mayfield, Christine McLain, Josephine McLain, Tessie Flirt, Agnes King, Dolly Dimples, Mayble Gilmore, Grace Manning, Ethel Gilmore, Georgie Frills, Florence Wilmont, Daisy Darling, Jessie May, Ada Throps, Anna Day, Teresa Cutler, Daisy Dash, Ethel Southgate, Mazie Huyler, Tessie Graham.

Act 1: Cooper-Macy's Store.

Act 2: East Side Tenement Attic.

Act 3: Long Island Summer Hotel.

Act 4: Same as Act 3; 24 hours later.

ACT 1[26]

"When the Band Plays Yankee Doodle" (Opening Medley)

"School Days"
(*Music and Lyrics by* Gus Edwards.)/

"Torpedo Till"/

"Bye-bye, My Caroline"/

"I Couldn't Make a Hit with Molly"[27]
J. Russell, Jr., Chorus

ACT 2

Scotch Song
John Russell

Imitations
James Russell

ACT 3

"I'd Rather Two-step Than Waltz"[28] (From FASCINATING FLORA)
McLain Sisters, Chorus

Wooden Shoe Dancing (Specialty)
McLain Sisters

Russell Brothers' Specialty

"Where the River Shannon Flows"
John Russell
(*Music and Lyrics by* James Russell.)

"Killarney"
Russell Brothers, Chorus

"Handle Me with Care" (From FOLLIES OF 1907)
J. Russell, Jr., Chorus

"Any Old Time at All" (from THE RICH MR. HOGGENHEIMER)
F. B. Russell, Chorus
(*Music by* Jean Schwartz. *Lyrics by* William Jerome.)

ACT 4[29]

"Let Me Put My Arm Around You"
H. Fisher, Chorus

---

[21]Replaced for subsequent tour by:
"Hello Bill"
H. Hale, Vaudevillians

[22]Added for subsequent tour to Act 2 Opening Chorus after "Stokers' Song":
"Perhaps"
Ensemble

[23]Replaced after opening by:
"So What's the Use?" (What's the Use?)
R. Hitchcock
(*Music and Lyrics by* Edward Montagu.)
Which was replaced for subsequent tour by:
"She Was Not Like Other Maidens"
R. Hitchcock

[24]Replaced for subsequent tour by:
"Ebenezer Frye" (Wal, I Swan!)
R. Hitchcock, H. Hale, F. Zabelle, H. West, H. Lane, E. R. Phillips
(*Music and Lyrics by* Benjamin Hapgood Burt.)

[25] Songs, scenery and costumes uncredited.

[26] A composite score assembled from popular songs of the day.

[27] Medley replaced during tour by:
"They All Look Alike to Mary"
J. Russell, Jr.

[28] Song and Specialty by the McLain Sisters replaced during subsequent tour by:
"Laughing Eyes"
Florence Wilmont
Parisian Toe Dancing (Specialty)
F. Wilmont

[29] Added during subsequent tour:
"Tropical Moon" (Song and Dance)
H. Fisher, Chorus

Dancing Specialty
H. Fisher
Dancing Specialty
F. B. Russell

1907.29 CAPTAIN RUFUS

A Military Musical Comedy in Three Acts. Book and lyrics by J. Ed. Green and Alfred Anderson. Music by H. Lawrence Freeman. Staged by J. Ed. Green. Dances by Bill Johnson. Produced by the Pekin Stock Company (Robert T. Motts, Manager). Opened 12 August 1907 at the Harlem Music Hall and closed 17 August 1907 after 8 performances.[30]

CAST: *Corporal Higgins*: Leon P. Rooks. *Sergeant Huyke*: Don Wormley. *Colonel Warsaw*: Clifton Ross. *Major Drummond*: JERRY MILLS. *Lieutenant Stokes*: CHARLES GILPIN. *Lucy Warsaw*, the Colonel's daughter: JENNIE RINGGOLD. *Cheteka*: Lottie Grady. *U. R. Swift*, Jones' companion in misfortune: MAT MARSHALL. *Leon Carlos*: L. E. Chenault. *Julia Gray*: Pearl Brown. *Russell Wallstreet*: GEORGE WHITE. *May Wallstreet*: Nettie Lewis. *Rufus Jones*, a shipwrecked vagabond: HARRISON STEWART. *Captain Rufus*: J. FRANCIS MORES.

Scene: Philippine Islands.

MUSICAL NUMBERS[31]

"The Great I Am with a Capital I"
H. Stewart, M. Marshall
"Morning Is Dawning"
"I've Got Good Common Sense"
"The Tale of the Monkey and the Snake"
"Song of the Witches"
"The Lilly"
"The Voodoo King"
"Girls of the U.S.A."
"Chief of the Aggregation"
"You Ain't Said Nothing Yet"
"Lilly's Wedding Day"
"The Sword and the Flat"
"The Wanderer"

1907.30 THE LADY FROM LANE'S

A Musical Comedy in Three Acts. Book and lyrics by George Broadhurst. Music by Gustave Kerker. Produced under the stage direction of Thomas Wise. Musical numbers under the direction of Lewis Hooper. Settings by D. Frank Dodge, Frank Gates and E. A. Morange. Costumes by Mlle. Frederica DeWolfe and Mood. Orchestra under the direction of Herman Perlet. Produced by Broadhurst and Currie. Opened 19 August 1907 at the Lyric Theatre, moved 19 September 1907 to the Casino Theatre and closed 28 September 1907 after 47 performances.

CAST: *Singleton Seabright*, who assumes the name of Bassett: THOMAS WISE. *Wayland Clingstone*, one of the boys of long ago: ROBERT PEYTON CARTER. *Arthur Gilbert*, Seabright's nephew: PERCY BRONSON. *Lieutenant King*, stationed at Fortress Monroe: WALTER PERCIVAL. *Lord Choppentott*: Lionel Walsh. *Front*, who runs the hotel: William Barrows. *Johnson*, a fearless detective: Frank Kelley. *Florence Gilbert*, Seabright's niece: IDA HAWLEY. *Mamie Morris*, Miss Gilbert's maid: Georgie Lawrence. *Arabella Clingstone*, an appropriated angel: Mrs. E. A. Eberle. *Adelaide Forster*, (The Lady) from Lane's detective agency: TRULY SHATTUCK. *Henry Andrews*, a policeman: John Brander. *William Darrow*, a policeman: Frank Unger.

Cashiers: Miss Marie Barry, Margaret Fealey, Myrtle Lawton, Mabel Shepherd, Georgia Snyder, Polly Stanley, Gertrude Taylor, Mary Harris. *Telephone Girls*: Misses Edith Williams, Virginia Laurance, Irene Chandler, Georgie Sage, Florence Westervelt, Edna Clark, Helen Courtney, Beula Montroise, Irene Love. *Typewriters*: Misses Anna Hall, Julie Newell, Alice Packard, Lucille Parrish, Edith Sladden, Dorothy Watson, Eleanor Russell. *Bell-Boys*: Messrs. Charles Melville, Arthur Lichty, Charles Wedlake, Frank Williams. *Porters*: Messrs. Harold Russell, John Meagher, Joseph Wells, J. W. Murphy.

Act 1: Parlor of Hotel at Old Point Comfort, Virginia. Today.

Act 2: Sun Parlor in same hotel. Next morning.

Act 3: The parade grounds at Fortress Monroe. Afternoon of same day.

ACT 1

Opening Chorus
"Take a Maid" (Duet)
I. Hawley, P. Bronson
"That Really Was a Lovely Place for Me"
G. Lawrence
"It Takes a Woman to Catch a Man"
T. Shattuck
"(Rock-Rock-Rock Let Me Rock in) My Old Rocking Chair"
T. Wise, Chorus
(*Music and Lyrics by* George Spink.)

ACT 2

Opening Chorus, including "I Met My Love in a Restaurant"
W. Percival, Chorus
"I Never Do It Now"
R. P. Carter, P. Bronson, W. Barrows
"You, Just You"
I. Hawley, Chorus
"Story Book Days"
W. Percival
"(The) Correspondence School"
G. Lawrence
Finale
Company

ACT 3

"Ladies' Day Parade"
W. Percival, Chorus
"Woman, Lovely Woman"
T. Wise
"The Sweetest Words That E'er Were Said" (Duet)
I. Hawley, W. Percival
Finale

1907.31 THE HUSBAND (?)

A Musical Comedy in Two Acts. Book and lyrics by Aubrey Lyles and Flournoy Miller. Music by Joe Jordan and James T. Brymn. Staged by J. Ed Green. Produced by the Pekin Stock Company (Robert T. Motts, Manager). Opened 19 August 1907 at the Harlem Music Hall and closed 24 August 1907 after 8 performances.

CAST: *Punk Willis*: HARRISON STEWART. *John Durant*: Jerry Mills. *Tom Jenkins*: Mat Marshall. *Arthur Voss*: J. F. Mores. *George Overstreet*: George White. *Dishrag George*: CHARLES GILPIN. *Ice Cream Jimmy*: Ras Jones. *Pigankle Charlie*: Charles Foster. *Ruth Overstreet*: Lottie Grad. *Alice*: Jennie Ringgold. *Clara*: Beulah White. *Rose Joyce*: Nettie Lewis. *Mrs. Overstreet*: Oma Crosby. *Hannah Willis*: PEARL BROWN. *The Cook*: Madeline Cooper.

MUSICAL NUMBERS[32]

"Take Your Time"
H. Stewart
"Lulu"
"Oh You Kid"
"Good Evening Caroline"
"You Dear"
"Dissipation"
H. Stewart
"Happiness"
"I've Got Good Common Sense"
H. Stewart
"Friend of the Family"
M. Marshall
"Mine, All Mine"
J. Ringgold
"Susanna"
(*Music and Lyrics by* Bob Cole and J. Rosamond Johnson.)
"I'm Running Wild"

---

[30]No complete New York program found, incomplete song list.
[31]Not in performance order.

[32]No New York program available. Song list prepared from Chicago 1909 production.

1907.32 THE DAIRYMAIDS

A Farcical Musical Play in Two Acts. Book by Alexander M. Thompson and Robert Courtneidge. Music by Paul A. Rubens and Frank E. Tours. (Lyrics by Arthur Wimperis.) Staged by A. E. Dodson. Dances arranged by Adolph Neuberger. Settings by Ernest Gros. Costumes by Mrs. Osborn Company; Dazian. Musical director, William T. Francis. Produced by Charles Frohman. Opened 26 August 1907 at the Criterion Theatre and closed 16 November 1907 after 86 performances.

CAST: *Lady Brudenell*: Ruby Ray. *Sam Brudenell, Frank Brudenell*, her nephews: GEORGE GREGORY, Langford Kirby. *Captain Fred Leverton*: DONALD HALL. *Dr. O'Byrne, R. N.*: EUGENE O'ROURKE. *Peggy*, a dairymaid: JULIA SANDERSON. *Winifred*, her sister: BESSIE DeVOIE. *Helène*, their half-sister: THELMA RAY. *Miss Penelope Pyechase* of Pyechase Academy: Emily Francis. *Eliza*, a maid of all work at Pyechase's: Flossie Hope. *Joe Mivens*, A. B., servant to Dr. O'Byrne: HUNTLEY WRIGHT. *Farm Hands (3)*: *Daisy*: Beatrice McKay. *Betty*: Hazel Neason. *Joan*: Florence Wilson. *Dairymaids (3)*: *Jenny*: Frieda Weigold. *Mag*: Edna Dodsworth. *Nancy*: Wilma Wood. *Schoolgirls (4)*: *Rosie*: Dorothy Gibson. *Gertie*: May Gerson. *Cecilia*: Minna Martrit. *Bessie*: Isabelle Meyers. *The Sandow Girls*: Misses Rose Leslie, Hatty Lorraine, Maude LeRoy, Enid Gibson, Grace Lindsay, Lillian LeRoy, May Yerby.

Act 1: Lady Brudenell's Model Dairy, at Hindstead.

Act 2: Gymnasium at Miss Pyechase's Academy.

ACT 1[33]

Opening Chorus
(*Music by* Frank E. Tours.)

"Home Again"
(*Music by* Frank E. Tours.)

"It's Naughty to Be Kissed" (Duet)
(J. Sanderson)
(*Music by* William T. Francis. *Lyrics by* J. B. Loughrey.)

"(I Must Have) A Lot of Little Girls All 'Round Me"
(H. Wright)
(*Music by* Frank E. Tours. *Lyrics by* Paul Rubens.)

Quarrel Duet
(*Music and Lyrics by* J. J. Montague and Paul Rubens.)

"I've a Million Reasons Why I Love You"
(*Music by* Jerome Kern. *Lyrics by* M. E. Rourke.)

"How the Winds Blow"
(*Music by* Frank E. Tours.)

"Lazyland"[34]
(*Music by* Paul Rubens.)

"Tinker, Tailor"
(J. Sanderson, Male Chorus)
(*Music by* Paul Rubens.)

"Poaching" (Duet)
(H. Wright)
(*Music by* Paul Rubens.)

Finale

ACT 2

"Gymnasium Chorus"
(*Music by* Paul Rubens.)

"Hello, Little Stranger" (Hullo! Little Stranger!)
(B. DeVoie)
(*Music by* Paul Rubens. *Lyrics by* Arthur Wimperis.)

"(Never Marry a Girl with) Cold Feet"
(*Music by* Jerome Kern. *Lyrics by* M. E. Rourke.)

"(The) Sandow Girl"
(J. Sanderson)
(*Music and Lyrics by* Paul Rubens.)

"(Let's All Go) Down the Strand"
(*Music and Lyrics by* E. G. McLellan and Bernard Rolt.)

"Mary McGee"[35]
(E. O'Rourke)
(*Music by* Jerome Kern. *Lyrics by* M. E. Rourke.)

"(In) Barcelona"
(*Music by* James W. Tate. *Lyrics by* Eustace Baynes and Vernon Roy.)

"Oh, Mr. Brown"
(*Music by* Harry Von Tilzer. *Lyrics by* Andrew B. Sterling.)

"Dat Friend of Mine"
(*Music by* Egbert Van Alstyne and Harry Williams.)

"I'd Like to Meet Your Father"
(J. Sanderson, G. Gregory)
(*Music by* Jerome Kern. *Lyrics by* M. E. Rourke.)

"Good Night"
(*Music by* Paul Rubens.)

"In the Twi-Twi-Twilight"[36]
(*Music and Lyrics by* Charles Wilmot and Herman E. Darewski, Jr.)

[33]Musical numbers not listed in the program for New York run. List in performance order prepared from subsequent tour, by which time a number of interpolations had been added for American audiences. Among the songs mentioned by opening night reviewers but not found in the touring song list were:

"Wild Rose"
T. Raye

Swimming song
T. Raye

Also published as an "extra number" (interpolation) for the American production:

"The Hay Ride"
(*Music by* Jerome Kern. *Lyrics by* M. E. Rourke.)

[34]Identified in the New York Times as a new interpolation as of 18 September 1907.

[35]Identified in the New York Times as a new interpolation as of 18 September 1907.

[36]Dropped during the tour.

1907.33 THE ROGERS BROTHERS IN PANAMA

A Musical Play in Three Acts, 5 Scenes. Book by Sylvester Maguire and Aaron Hoffman. Music by Max Hoffmann. Lyrics by Edward Madden. Produced (staged) under the personal direction of Ben Teal. Dances arranged by Pat Rooney. Scenery designed by Walter Burridge, Homer Emens , Ernest Albert. Costumes designed by Will H. Barnes. Electrical effects by Kleigl Brothers. Musical director, John Harding. Produced by Gus Rogers and Max Rogers. Opened 2 September 1907 at the Broadway Theatre, moved 21 October 1907 to the Liberty Theatre, and closed 9 November 1907 after 71 performances[37].

CAST: *Hugo Kisser*: GUS ROGERS. *A. Gustave Windt*: MAX ROGERS. *Hunting Coyne*: ALFRED HICKMAN. *Chub Featherweight*: WALTER WARE. *Camillo Mendoza*: GEORGE LYDECKER. *Jose Amador*: ROBINSON NEWBOLD. *Gruimo DeHabana*: Joseph Kane. *Hon. Gideon Gay*: James A. Bliss. *Diaz*: Bert Ewing. *Gomez*: Frank Conners. *Captain Pedro*: Philip Leigh. *Rose Gay*: MARION STANLEY. *Nita*: MAY HENGLER. *Pequita*: FLO HENGLER. *Bella Amador*: Avita Sanchez. *Lola*: Lottie Greenwood. *Marquita*: Marion Mosby.

Cactus Boys: Misses Fenton, Brown, Kesse, Lloyd, Twohey, McCeney, Handy, Alain. *Flower Girls*: *Rose*: Miss Wilson. *Violet*: Miss Barnard. *Mignonette*: Miss Everett. *Lily*: Miss Green. *Pansy*: Marion Mosby. *Daisy*: Miss Devere.

Restaurant Girls: *Shanley's*: Miss Acklin. *Sherry's*: Miss Clifford. *Martin's*: Miss Vallorie. *Waldorf*: Miss Stanton. *Rector's*: Miss Sinclair. *Churchill's*: Miss Melton.

Act 1: Grounds surrounding President Amador's Residence, Panama. (Burridge.)

Act 2, Scene 1: Exterior of Prison showing Life-saving Station. *Scene 2*: The Isle of Gold. (Emens.)

Act 3, Scene 1: Exterior of the Arena. *Scene 2*: The Arena. (Albert.)

ACT 1

Opening Chorus
Ensemble

"In Panama"
G. Lydecker

"Laugh and the World Laughs Too"
M. Hengler, F. Hengler, A. Hickman, W. Ware

Burlesque Opera
Rogers Brothers, M. Stanley

"Way Down in Colon Town"
Rogers Brothers, M. Stanley

[37]Played a return engagement 6 April 1908 at the Grand Opera House for 8 performances.

Finale and Ensemble
Entire Company

ACT 2

Opening Chorus
Ensemble, Cactus Boys

"My Cigarette"
A. Sanchez

"Sunrise at the Zoo"[38]
M. Hengler, F. Hengler

Original Sayings and Parodies
Rogers Brothers

"Under the Jungle Moon"[39]
M. Stanley, A. Hickman

ACT 3

Opening Chorus—Dance Characteristique
Ensemble

"Each One Has a Way of His Own"
M. Stanley

"(I Could Learn to Love You When You) Smile, Smile, Smile"
Rogers Brothers, M. Hengler, F. Hengler

"Adorable Toreador"
G. Lydecker

Finale
Entire Company

1907.34 PATSY IN POLITICS

A Rural Song Play in Two Acts. Book by Joe Doe. Music by Carl Hand. Lyrics by Seymour Furth. Dances arranged by Al. White. Scenery by Charles E. Boss. Costumes by Frank Hayden; Lord & Taylor, New York. Mechanical effects by George Ormston. Musical director, Carl Hand. Produced by the P. H. Sullivan Amusement Company. Opened 2 September 1907 at the 14th Street Theatre and closed 7 September 1907 after 8 performances.[40]

CAST: *Patsy Bolivar*, the Tabasco Kid: BILLY B. VAN. *Silas Hemlock*, candidate for supervisor: FRANK C. EVANS. *Pinkereton Pinch*, county sheriff: Clem Bevins. *Adam Grouch*, a money lender: J. H. Wright. *FitzMaurice Vincent*, an English nobleman: CHARLES SAXON. *Joel Sprout*, the postmaster: Charles Gray. *Jimmy Swift*, a messenger: Nat Whitestone. *Yank Trunck*, the village drayman: William Stewart. *Jerusha Pickens*, the town tattler and temperance advocate: FLORENCE BROOKS. *Sally Hemlock*, Silas' daughter: MABEL REED. *Becky Skinner*, the village help: Blanche Latell. *Aggie Stammers*, she talks in chunks: Mae Hilliard. *Gloriana Bird*, star of a stranded opera company: ROSE BEAUMONT.

Members of the Merry Merry Party (15): Trixie Twirl: Little Giggler: Terpsi Chore: Carrie Behr: Minnie Soti: Minnie Apolis: Belle Weather: Belle Clapper: Helen Harlem: Mamie Nailem: Sally Doom: Daisy Dancer: Jessie Joy: Winnie Wink: Tessie Tease: Waitresses, Crooks, Porters, Voters, Rubes, Yaps, and Maudie the Mule.

Act 1: Office of Pleasant Home Hotel, Georges Mills, New Hampshire.

Act 2: The Village Square on Election Day.

ACT 1

"Back to Old Broadway" (Opening Chorus)
Chorus

"Miss Ginger from Jamaica"
R. Beaumont, Chorus

"For Old Time's Sake"
C. Saxon

"Much Obliged to You"
B. B. Van, Chorus

"Tipperary"
R. Beaumont

"(Hello) Sweetie"
M. Reed, Chorus

"Budweiser Is a Friend of Mine" (Grand Finale)
Entire Company

ACT 2

"Summer Boarders" (Opening Chorus)
Chorus

"They Say He Went to College"
B. B. Van, Chorus

"(Just) You, Dear, You"
R. Beaumont, C. Saxon

Travesty on Grand Opera
F. Brooks, B. B. Van

"Very Peculiar"
J. H. Wright, F. C. Evans, B. B. Van

"Beautiful Spain"
R. Beaumont, B. B. Van, Chorus

Grand Finale
Entire Company

[38]Replaced during the run by:
"Cupid's Gay Bouquet"
W. Ware, Flower Girls, Restaurant Girls
For subsequent tour, replaced by:
"'Neath the Old Palm Tree"
M. Stanley, Tell Taylor {Hunting Coyne}
(*Lyrics by* Ed Gardenier.)

[39]Replaced for subsequent tour by:
"Are You the Girl that Dined with Me?"
Philip Leigh {Chub Featherweight}, assisted by Ladies Ensemble

[40]Stage director uncredited.

1907.35 FROM ACROSS THE POND

A Musical Comedy in Three Acts. Libretto by Adolf Philipp and Mortimer M. Theise. adapted from the Berlin and Viennese success[41]. Produced by Mortimer M. Theise Opened 7 September 1907 at the Circle Theatre and closed 12 September 1907 after 8 performances.[42]

CAST: *Louis Strumkohl*: ADOLF PHILIPP. *Moishe Rositsky*: BARNEY BERNARD. *Maggie O'Reilly*: ANNA BOYD. *Patrick O'Brien*: WILLIAM CALE. *Robert Melancolique*: Stanley Jessup. *Marie*: Viola deCosta. *Nanon*: Mazie Follette. *Susette*: Ethel Jewett. *Fanchon*: Nettie Lyons. *Florette*: Catherine Black. *Nanon*: FRANKIE BAILEY. *Jean*: Sam Goodman. *Paul*: William Newkirk. *François*: Al. Sanders. *Charles George Edward James Farrington Cherrytree*, Duke of Townsend: R. R. NEILL. *Maladetto*: Lester Bernard. *Tony*: Michael Curran.

Act 1: Ellis Island.

Act 2: Chatham Square.

Act 3: The Bowery.

MUSICAL NUMBERS[43]

"Election Returns"

"Louis Is All Right"

"Marie from Paree"

"The True Irish Girl"

Laughing Song
A. Boyd

1907.36 MLLE. MODISTE

A Revival of the Comic Opera in Two Acts[44]. Book and lyrics by Henry Blossom. Music by Victor Herbert. Staged by Fred G. Latham and Al Holbrook. Settings by Homer Emens, Edward G. Unitt. Costumes by Messrs. Lichenstein, Dazian, Lord & Taylor, Wanamaker. Musical director, John Lund. Produced by Charles Dillingham. Opened 9 September 1907 at the Knickerbocker Theatre and closed 28 September 1907 after 21 performances.

[41]Source is unidentified.

[42]No complete New York program found.

[43]No New York program found.

[44]First produced in New York 25 December 1905 at the Knickerbocker Theatre for 202 performances. For Synopsis of Scenes and Musical Numbers, see original 1905 production.

CAST: *Henri de Bouvray*, Compte de St. Mar: WILLIAM PRUETTE. *Captain Etienne de Bouvray*, his nephew: ROBERT MICHAELIS. *Hiram Bent*, an American millionaire: CLAUDE GILLINGWATER. *Gaston*, an artist, Mme. Cécile's son: LEO MARS. *General Le Marquis de Villefranche*: George Schraeder. *Lieutenant René La Motte*, engaged to Marie Louise: Howard Chambers. *François*, porter at Mme. Cécile's: R. W. Hunt. *Mme. Cécile*, proprietress of a Parisian hat shop: JOSEPHINE BARTLETT. *Fanchette, Nanette*, her daughters: Almaretta Webster, Blanche Morrison. *Marie Louise de Bouvray*, Etienne's sister: Carlyn Strelitz. *Bébé*, dancer at the Folies Bergères: Ethel Bard. *Mrs. Hiram Bent*: Bertha Holly. *Fifi*: FRITZI SCHEFF. *Milliners, Guests, Dancers, Soldiers, Servants.*

1907.37 LOLA FROM BERLIN

A Comedy (with Music) in Three Acts. Book by John J. McNally. Music by Jean Schwartz. Lyrics by William Jerome. Staged by Al Holbrook. Settings by John Young. Costumes by F. Richard Anderson. Electrical effects by Harry Bissing. Music arranged and conducted by Watty Hydes. Produced by Messrs. (Marc) Klaw and (Abraham L.) Erlanger. Opened 16 September 1907 at the Liberty Theatre and closed 19 October 1907 after 35 performances[45].

CAST (in order of appearance): *Edward Lott*, Westervelt's secretary: George LeGuere. *Annie White*, stenographer: Minnette Barrett. *Harry Clarkson*, man-about-town: Walter Pennington. *John Westervelt*, corporation lawyer and man of affairs: DODSON MITCHELL. *Mrs. Jack Westervelt*, his wife: FLORENCE LESTER. *Edith Westervelt*, daughter of John Westervelt: LILLIAN SPENCER. *Barstowe*, butler: Wallace Owen. *Arthur Paget*, novelist, in love with Lola: JACK STANDING. *Lotchen von Breckenhaussett*, known as Lola: LULU GLASER. *Beatrice Courtlandt*, in love with Harry: Lavinia Shannon. *Billy Needham*, in love with Edith: William Glaser. *Richard Winchester Chorttle*, an actor of the old school: R. [Ralph] C. HERZ. *Dollie Chorttle*, his niece: Vinnie Bradcome.

German Girls: Misses Edith Warner, Bessie Carrette, Lulu Martell, Gladys Zell, Katherine Daly, Billee Florence, Geraldine Malone, May Willard. *College Boys*: Messrs. Jackson Karlyle, Homer Potts, Howard W. James, Thomas Phillips, Arthur Bell, W. J. Readon, J. D. Miller, Al. S. Dowling.

Act 1: Library in the house of John Westervelt.

Act 2: Drawing-room in the house of John Westervelt.

Act 3: Summer house of Westervelt, overlooking the Hudson.

ACT 1

"Madchenlied"/

"Altdeutscher Liebersreim"

L. Glaser

ACT 2

"I Think of You the Whole Year Round" (Duet and Dance)

L. Spencer, W. Glaser

"I'd Sooner Be a Has-Been (Than a Never-Was)" (Song)

R. C. Herz

"Unter der Linden (in Germany)" (Song)

L. Glaser

ACT 3

"Beneath the Moon" (Duet and Male Octette)

L. Spencer, L. Glaser

"Just Home from College" (Chorus)

"Poor Little Foolish Man" (Song and Chorus)

L. Glaser

"Signs" (Song)

R. C. Herz

"There's Not Another Girlie in the World Like You" (Song and Chorus)

L. Glaser

[45]Played a return engagement 28 October 1907 at the Grand Opera House for 8 performances. Produced the following season for national tour by J. M. Welch Amusement Company with Corinne top-billed as Lola. The following songs were added: (Act 1) "Yodel Song," "None of Them's Got Anything on Me," Meet Me in Rose Time, Rosey;" (Act 2) "Good-Bye, Mr. Ragtime;" (Act 3) "Always You," I Won't Go Home Until Morning" "I'm Awfully Strong for You" from COHAN AND HARRIS MINSTRELS, "So Different" from THE ROGERS BROTHERS IN IRELAND

1907.38 THE BOY WITH THE BOODLE

A Musical Comedy Drama in Four Acts. Book by Howard Hall. Produced by Howard Hall Amusement Company. Opened 16 September 1907 at the Metropolis Theatre and closed 21 September 1907 after 8 performances.[46]

CAST: *Skidoo*, a shoeshine boy: GEORGE OVEY. *Tammany Ann*, his girl friend, also known as Nevada: LOUISE HORNER. *Pokey*: Harry Sheppell. *George Milton*: FRED E. WRIGHT. *Judge Fairfield*: FRED E. WRIGHT. *Hiram Rogers*: V. C. Armstrong. *Joe Franks*: Charles H. McCloskey. *Antoine*: Morris Cole. *Mary Nesbit*: NEVA BOUTWELL. *Zamora*: NEVA BOUTWELL. *Annie Laurie*: Poppy Robbins. *Rachel*: Ruth Galbraith. *Fedora*: Ray Morris. *Fluffie Ruffles*: Gladys Turner. *Katie, the Kicker*: Marie Nelson. *Mag Foley*: Violet Long. *Plug Ugly*, a kidnapper: JOSEPH WEBER. *Tom Lawton*: William Stafford. *John DeRock*: Fred George. *Abe Cohen*: Billy Tyler. *Charlie Hays*: William Stafford. *Mike Casey*: Charles Good. *Yen Louie*: E. B. Will. *Buster Bill*: Jack Youngs. *Shakespeare*: Pete Depew.

Act 1: The Williamsburg Bridge, with Skidoo's Castle.

Act 2: Judge Fairfield's Villa near Goldfield, Nevada.

Act 3: A Street in Goldfield and a view near Tonopah.

Act 4: The Judge's House, New York City; the Swan Lake in Central Park.

MUSICAL NUMBERS[47]

"Antoine"

N. Boutwell

1907.39 THE HURDY GURDY GIRL

A Musical Comedy in Three Acts, 4 Scenes. Book and lyrics by Richard Carle. Music by H. L. Heartz. Entire production staged under the personal supervision of Richard Carle. Dances arranged by Richard Carle, Adolph Neuberger. Settings by Oliver P. Bernard. Costumes by Miss Ena Welch and the Warnock Company (Act 1), Felix, Worth, Paquin and Lafirriere of Paris (Acts 2, 3). Orchestra under the direction of Alfred Dalby. Orchestrations by Robert Hood Bowers and Alfred Dalby. Produced by Charles Marks. Opened 23 September 1907 at Wallack's Theatre and closed 12 October 1907 after 24 performances.

CAST: *Lola*, the Hurdy Gurdy Girl: BERTHA MILLS. *Judge Terence Fitzgerald*: JOHN E. HAZZARD. *Gwendolyn Fitzgerald*, his wife: MAYME KELSO. *Mary Fitzgerald*, their daughter: ADELE ROWLAND. *Otto Ludwig Otis*, the Sausage King: JOHN W. RANSOME. *Sara Otis*, his wife: ANNIE YEAMANS. *Tom Otis*, their son: WALTER LAWRENCE. *Felix Bunn*, a hotel clerk: Harry Stone. *Old Bunn*, his father: JACQUES KRUGER. *Miss Cuticle*, a manicure: MAY BOLEY. *Milo*, a street musician: SYLVAIN LANGLOIS. *Roma*, his wife: James Hunter. *Mrs. McShane*: Tony Sullivan. *Ethelbert*, the Otis family's butler: Tony Sullivan. *Mr. Wheels*: Nat Kolb. *A Walking Delegate*: Nat Kolb. *Chuck Bixby*, a bell boy: Hughie Flaherty. *Porter No. 1*: Victor Bozart. *Porter No. 2*: Oscar Jones. *The Kicker*: James Russell. *Policeman Ajax*: F. S. Scholl.

Milkmen: Rita Stanwood, Marie Sydney, Ethel Daggett, Peggy Merritt. *Postmen*: Marjorie Gerald, Hattie Williams, Evelyn Meredith, Jewell Meredith. *Newsboys*: Bertha May, May Barrell, Minnie Mason, Edith Kimball. *White Wings*: Marion Vose, Nellie Fallon, Dot Cloudman, Josie Magee.

Act 1, Scene 1: Office of the Hotel Castor, New York City. *Scene 2*: Times Square, New York City.

Act 2: Otto Otis' summer home in Larchmont. A week later.

Act 3: Ballroom of the Otis residence in Fifth Avenue, New York city. A month later. Le Bal Noir et Blanc.

ACT 1

"Bluff"

V. Bozart, Bunco Men

"The Sausage King"

J. W. Ransome, Chorus

"Scrub, Scrub, Scrub"

Scrub Women

Ensemble

Cabbies, Wine Agents, Tradesmen, Laborers

"Hope On"

M. Calder, S. Langlois

[46]No New York program available.

[47]No New York program found.

"The Hurdy Gurdy Girl"
W. Lawrence, Chorus
Finale

ACT 2
"The Croquet Game"
Opening Chorus
"I'm a Mischievous Girl"[48]
A. Rowland, Chorus
"The Modest Manicure"
M. Boley
"Come, Little Dearie"
M. Calder, A. Rowland, W. Lawrence, H. Stone
"In Bohemia"
W. Lawrence, Chorus
(*Music by* Richard Carle.)
"Stories"
J. E. Hazzard, J. W. Ransome, J. Kruger
Finale

ACT 3
"Style"
M. Boley, Chorus
"She's the Apple of My Eye"
H. Stone, Chorus

1907.40

THE MAZUMA MAN

A Musical Burlesque in Two Acts. Book (and lyrics) by Frank Kennedy. Music by William J. McKenna. E. D. Stair, Manager. Opened 30 September 1907 at the Yorkville Theatre and closed 5 October 1907 after 8 performances.[49]

CAST: *Izzy Mark*, the Mazuma Man: GEORGE SIDNEY. *Will Steele*: Ezra Mathews. *Lem Soakum*: Fred Law. *Sylvester Parbola*: Victor Casmore. *Flip*: Johnny Philliber. *Clipper Bond*: Frank Gibbons. *Wash Bailey*: Frank Gibbons. *Tee Totaler*: Ray Montgomery. *Rosetta Kremona*: CARRIE WEBBER.

MUSICAL NUMBERS[50]
"To Be an Actor"
G. Sidney, F. Law, C. Webber
"Dot's Right"
G. Sidney, Company
"Around the Town"
Company
"Zoo Loo"
E. Mathews, Company

1907.43

THE OLD HOMESTEAD

A Revival of the Rural Melodrama in Four Acts[51]. Play by Denman Thompson and George W. Ryer. Stage director, Frank Knapp. Settings by Homer Emens and Edward G. Unitt. Produced by Franklin Thompson. Opened 30 September 1907 at the Academy of Music and closed 26 October 1907 after 40 performances.

CAST (in order of appearance): *Joshua Whitcomb*: DENMAN THOMPSON. *Cy Prime*: HORACE RUSHBY. *Jack Hazard*: FRED CLARE. *Frank Hopkins*: Harry R. Webster. *Eb. Ganzey*: FRANK KNAPP. *John Patterson*: J. T. Calkins. *Aunt Matilda (Whitcomb)*: LOUISA MORSE. *Rickety Ann*: ANITA L. FOWLER. *Annie Hopkins*: LAURA BRADFORD. *Nellie Patterson*: MARGARET BOUSTEAD. *The Old Homestead Double Quartette*: Harry R. Webster, J. T. Calkins, Roy Purviance, Charles Ingoldsby, F. Kek Schillings, E. F. Cochran, Gus Kammerlee, Fred Clare. *Henry Hopkins*: GUS KAMMERLEE. *Judge Patterson*: E. F. Cochran. *Francois Fogarty*: F. Kek Schillings. *Mrs. Hopkins*: Annie Thompson. *One of the Finest*: Charles Ingoldsby. *Reuben Whitcomb*: Roy Purviance. *Harlem Spider*: Frank Knapp. *Postman*: George L. Patch. *Seth Perkins*: Charles H. Clark. *Len Holbrook*: George L. Patch. *David Willard*: David Willard (himself). *Warren Ellis*: P. Redmond. *Anna Maria Murdock*: Venie Thompson. *Eleanor Stratton*: Maude Pleasants. *The Stratton Girls, Holbrook Boys, and the Eames's.*

MUSICAL NUMBERS, SPECIALTIES
"The Palms"
C. Ingoldsby, Old Homestead Choir, Anita Fowler (organist)

1907.41

THE GIRL BEHIND THE COUNTER

A Musical Comedy in Three Acts. Book by Leedham Bantock and Arthur Anderson, freely adapted and reconstructed by Edgar Smith. Music by Howard Talbot. Lyrics by Arthur Anderson. Produced under the direction of J. C. Huffman and Julian Mitchell. Scenery by Arthur Voegtlin. Costumes designed by William H. Matthews. Conductor, William E. MacQuinn. Produced by Sam S. and Lee Shubert, Inc. and Lew Fields. Opened 1 October 1907 at the Herald Square Theatre and closed 6 June 1908 after 282 performances[52].

CAST: *Henry Schniff*, a soldier of misfortune, dazzled by the sudden transition from a half bedroom existence in Gower street to a butterfly life in Easy street: LEW FIELDS. *Mrs. Henry Schniff*, formerly Mrs. Willoughby, his former landlady and present spouse, in whom the unexpected accession wealth has awakened a desire for social conquest: CONNIE EDISS. *Winnie Willoughby*, her daughter, with rather sound ideas concerning life in general, and matrimony in particular: MAY NAUDAIN. *Millie Mostyn*, overlady at "The Universal," an American department store in London: LOUISE DRESSER. *Ninette Valois*, of the millinery department of the same: LOTTA FAUST. *Susie Scraggs*, assistant cashier: TOPSY SIEGRIST. *Mrs. M. Whittington*: Edith Ethel McBride. *Mrs. Crossley-Shoppington*: Lottie Fremont. *Dudley Cheatham*, cashier at "The Universal," imbued with American ideas of high finance: IGNACIO MARTINETTI. *Lord Augustus Gushington*. familiarly known as "Gussie"—the proprietor of an empty purse, an empty title, and an equally empty head: DENMAN MALEY. *Charley Chetwynd*, a self-made young millionaire: JOSEPH RATLIFF. *Henri Duval*, expert in millinery and lingerie, and manager of "The Universal": GEORGE BEBAN. *John Blobbs*, a waiter at the Jardin de Paris: VERNON CASTLE. *Maggie*, of the wrapping department of "The Universal": 'Patsy' Mitchell. *Hon. Aubrey Battersea, Lord Rumbold*, friends of Lord Gushington: VERNON CASTLE, Hubert Neville.

Original English Pony Ballet: *French Milliners, Zylophone Girls, Salvation Army Lassies*: Beatrice Liddell, Ada Robertson, Dorothy Marlowe, Louise Hawman, Seppie McNeil, Elizabeth Hawman. *Ponsonby*, a chauffeur: Vincent Cooper.

Shoppers: *Lottie Munn*: Elsa Reinhardt. *Dottie Styles*: Claire Casscles. *Daisy Lyons*: Helen Turner. *Hattie Tryon*: Mae Allen. *Trixie Coates*: Marion Whitney. *Kitty Ermine*: Nan Brennan.

Patrons of "The Universal": *Mrs. Canby Dunn*: Viola Hopkins. *Lady Stonybroke*: May Burnett. *Mrs. C.O.D. Billings*: Dorothy Williams. *Mrs. Mark Down*: Jane Grant. *Mrs. Uneeda Wafer*: Frances Harris. *The Hon. Eunice Byington*: Ruth Humphries. *Lady Cheapington-Jones*: Olive Menton. *Lady Bargyn-Hunter*: Winifred Vaughan.

Salesladies: *Vera Leight*: Ida Doerge. *Winnie Fellows*: Anna C. Wilson. *Willa Ketchum*: Reina Swift. *Grace Church*: Lillian Raymond. *Ida Knowington*: Ethel Millard. *Rita Ruffhouse*: Bettine LeFevre. *Maida Mantell*: Madge Robertson. *Hope Gonne*: Gladys Browne. *Tessie Tardington*: Molly Mack.

Cash Girls: *Sallie Sample*: Lillian Devere. *Tessie Temple*: Daisy Carson. *Winnie Wimple*: Josephine Harriman. *Rhode Rimple*: Erminie Clark. *Montmorency*, footman for Mrs. Schniff: Jack Strause. *DeBelleville*, porter for Millie Mostyn: J. J. Youngs.

Waiters: *Hawkins*: VERNON CASTLE. *Bliffkins*: Joseph Torpey. *Simkins*: Richard Fanning. *Tompkins*: Sebastian Cassie. *John L. Fitz Corbet*: Charles Mitchell. *Booth Attendants*: *Louis*: Radford D'Orsay. *Jean*: John Reinhardt. *Francois*: J. J. McDonald. *Pierre*: A. Van Sant.

Act 1: Interior of "The Universal," an American department store in London

Act 2: The "Jardin de Paris," at Hammersmith, devoted to the first-class entertainment of second-class people.

ACT 1
Opening Chorus
Ensemble
"The Entreprising Frenchman"
G. Beban, Chorus

[48]Dropped during the run.
[49]Toured under the title BUSY IZZY, THE MAZUMA MAN. No New York program available.
[50]No New York program found.
[51]First produced in New York 10 January 1887 at the 14th Street Theatre for 155 performances. For Synopsis of Scenes, see original 1887 production. In Act 3, "Palms" rendered by Charles Ingoldsby and the "Old Homestead" Choir. Anita Fowler, Organist.

[52]Played a return engagement 28 December 1908 at the Grand Opera House for 8 performances.

"Flirting"[53]
I. Martinetti, T. Siegrist
"Eh? Ah? Oh!"[54]
C. Ediss
"Shopping"
Shoppers, Chorus
"(The Best I Get Is) 'Much Obliged to You'"[55]
L. Dresser
(*Music and Lyrics by* Benjamin Hapgood Burt.)
"The Bandbox Girl"
L. Faust, Pony Ballet
"Won't You Buy?"
M. Naudain, J. Ratliff
Finale

ACT 2
"Frivolity" (The Frivolity March)
The Pony Ballet
"I Want to Marry a Man"[56] (I Mean to Marry a Man)
M. Naudain
"(Any Time You're) Passing By"
L. Dresser
"When You Steal a Kiss or Two (Making Love)"
L. Faust
(*Music and Lyrics by* Kenneth S. Clarke.)
"The Cherry in the Glass"
J. Ratliff
(*Music by* Paul Lincke. *Lyrics by* Will D. Cobb.)
"Now I've Married a Millionaire"[57]
C. Ediss
"The Way of Trade"
T. Siegrist, I. Martinetti, Pony Ballet, Chorus
Finale

1907.42 THE GAY WHITE WAY

A Musical Revue[58] in Three Acts. Book and lyrics by Sydney Rosenfeld and J. Clarence Harvey. Music by Ludwig Engländer. Staged by R. H. Burnside. Dances arranged by Ralph Post. Scenery designed by Arthur Voegtlin. Costumes by Castel-Bert; Mme. Lubin; Mme. Ripley. Director of Music, Frank P. Paret. Produced by Sam S. Shubert and Lee Shubert, Inc. Opened 7 October 1907 at the Casino Theatre and closed 4 January 1908 after 105 performances.

CAST: *George Dane*, the detective: JEFFERSON DeANGELIS. *Montgomery Bernstein Brewster*: ALEXANDER CARR. *Favvy Hackettsham*: FRANK DOANE. *Van Cortlandt Knickerbocker*: MELVILLE ELLIS. *Montgomery and Stone*: Post and Russell. *John D. Rock-a-Bye*: Joseph Redmond. *Daniel Frohman*: Joseph Herbert, Jr. *One of the Finest*: Joseph Carey. *Eddie Foy*: Joseph Carey. *Henry Miller*: J. Heron Miller. *David Belasco*: R. P. Galinde. *Mrs. Dane*: BLANCHE RING. *Marion Marshmellow*, a matinee girl: MAUD RAYMOND. *Alla Nazimova*: MAUD RAYMOND. *Rose of the Rancho*: MAUD RAYMOND. *Anna Held*: LAURA GUERITE. *Wee-bit*: Elgie Bowen. *Minnie Dupree*: Elgie Bowen. *Tessie Twinkletoes*: Katherine Bell. *Tottie Twoaday*: Gertrude Moyer. *Lady Daisy Scotland*: Daisy Greene. *Lady Eliot Cornwall*: Estelle Christy. *Lady Tiny Bruterig*: Louise DeRigney. *Lady Belle Portland*: Harriet Forsythe. *Lady Harriet Stewart*: Harriet Merritt. *Lady Alice Beresford*: Maude Stanley. *Trixie Friganza*: Bessie Friganza. *Court Officer*: Edward Cutler.
Picture Girls: Misses Grace Walton, May Clifford, Helen Doyle, Bessie Friganza, Flo Ridge, Maybelle Dean. *The Eight English Primroses*: Misses Flossie Bell, Kitty Bell, Nancy Simpson, Rita Mason, Cissie Shotten, Dora West, Dottie Duval, Marie Hughes. *Golf Girls*: Misses Lillian Loraine, Florence Lancaster, Angela Conlin, Jean Crane. *Golf Boys*: Misses Luzerne Van Orden, Mollie Hoffman, Lillian Rogers, Eleanor Chrystie. *Flower Girls*: Misses Edna Broderick, Florence Blake, Julia Douglas, Mayme Dupont, Grace Lester, Mona Trieste, Grace E. Wilson. *The Six Johnnies*: Messrs. Jack Hall, John Laughlin, A. V. MacDonald, Herman Robie, John Wickes, Charles Blackwell. *Policemen*: Messrs. James Ryley, Joseph Galton, Thomas Shannon, Eugene Roder, Edward Cutler, Harold Smith. *Waiters*: Messrs. Eugene Roder, Earl Dean, James Ryley, Joseph Galton, Thomas Shannon, Alfred Dubois, Hugh Brady.

Act 1: Garden of Rooseveltia.

Act 2: Actors' Fund Fair at the Metropolitan Opera House.

Act 3: At Murray's, New York.

ACT 1[59]
Opening Chorus
"Great White Way" (Duet)
J. DeAngelis, M. Raymond
"The Broadway Show"
L. Guerite, Primroses, Chorus
"Brewster the Millionaire"
A. Carr, Chorus
"(Love's) Merry-Go-Round"
B. Ring, Chorus
(*Music by* Louis Hirsch. *Lyrics by* E. Ray Goetz.)
"Somebody's Been 'Round Here (Since I've Been Gone)"
M. Raymond
(*Music by* John Bratton. *Lyrics by* Paul West.)
"Climbing the Ladder of Love" (Duet)
B. Ring, A. Carr
"Theodore"[60]
J. DeAngelis, Chorus
Finale
All Principals

ACT 2[61]
Opening Chorus
Imitation of Trixie Friganza
B. Friganza
Imitation of Eddie Foy
J. Carey

---

[53]Replaced early in the run by:
"If You'll Walk with Me"
I. Martinetti or William Rock, T. Siegrist
(*Music by* Paul Rubens. *Lyrics by* Edgar Selden.)

[54]Replaced during the run by:
"Now I've Married a Millionaire"
C. Ediss

[55]Replaced after opening by:
"The Minstrel Show" (I've Got to See de Minstrel Show)
L. Dresser
(*Music by* Harry Von Tilzer. *Lyrics by* Vincent Bryan.)
Which was later replaced by:
"I Want to Be Loved Like a Leadin' Lady"
L. Dresser
(*Music by* Herman Avery Wade. *Lyrics by* Paul West.)
Also performed during the New York run, as per published sheet music:
"Just Because He Couldn't Sing 'Love Me and the World Is Mine'"
L. Dresser
(*Music and Lyrics by* Bert Fitzgibbons.)

[56]Replaced after opening by:
"The Glow-Worm"
M. Naudain
(*Music by* Paul Lincke. *Lyrics by* Lilla Cayley Robinson.)

[57]Replaced after opening by:
"When I Was in the Chorus at the Gaiety"
C. Ediss
(*Music by* Harry Von Tilzer.)

[58]Billed as a musical review devised for the purpose of affording an evening's entertainment during which the authors make no attempt at providing a plot.

[59]Running order revised repeatedly during the run. Added late in the run after "Somebody's Been 'Round Here" and retained for subsequent tour:
"Aren't You the Girl I Met at Sherry's?" (from TWO ISLANDS)
F. Doane, Chorus
(*Music by* Louis A. Hirsch. *Lyrics by* E. Ray Goetz.)

[60]Replaced during the run by: (not used in tour)
"Rain in the Face"
J. DeAngelis, Chorus

[61]Added briefly during the run before Act 2 Finale:
"Little Johnny Jones" (George M. Cohan impression)
Paul Russell Stone

Imitation of Montgomery and Stone
Post and Russell
"School of Acting" (Duet)
B. Ring, J. DeAngelis
"A Different Girl Again"[62]
F. Doane, Chorus
"If You Must Make Eyes at Someone (Won't You Please Make Eyes at Me)"[63]
L. Guerite
(*Music by* Leo Edwards. *Lyrics by* Leo Edwards and Matt Woodward.)
"Dixie Dan"
B. Ring, Chorus
(*Music by* Seymour Furth. *Lyrics by* Will D. Cobb.)
Finale

ACT 3
Opening Chorus
"Le Kic-King" (Dance)
The Primroses
Specialty
M. Ellis
"My Irish Gibson Girl"[64]
B. Ring, Gibson Girls
(*Music by* Jean Schwartz. *Lyrics by* William Jerome.)
Finale

1907.44 HIP! HIP! HOORAY!

Joe Weber and His Company in Another Foolish Affair, A College Yell (a Musical Comedy) in Two Shouts (Acts), 3 Scenes. Dialogue and lyrics by Edgar Smith. Music by Gus Edwards. Produced under the direction of Julian Mitchell. Settings painted by Ernest Albert. Costumes by Mme. Castel-Bert, Mme. DeWolfe, Cora MacGeachy, William H. Matthews, J. Henry Rowley. Lighting by Tom Smith. Orchestra under the direction of Anton Heindl. Produced by Joe Weber. Opened 10 October 1907 at Weber's Theatre and closed 7 December 1907 after 64 performances.

CAST: *Julius Grienbacher*, a retired capitalist, financially interested with his friend Schultz in exploiting a new breakfast food: JOE WEBER. *Michael Schultz*, a smart little business man: DICK BERNARD. *Charley Horsley*, Grienbacher's nephew, and familiarly known at Doolittle University as "Babe": HARRY TIGHE. *Washington Deecy*, a colored brother with ambitions in the line of pugilism: TOM LEWIS. *Punch Hardy*, boxing instructor of the college boat club under the title of "Professor Wallop": WILLIAM GOULD. *Grey Matterson*, a serious student: Howard Estabrook. *Rush Lyons*, an athletic student: W. Douglas Stevenson.

More Students: *Dope Stickney*: Walter Paschel. *Bat Strycker*: Ernest Wood. *Owen Taylor*: Joe Burry. *Tode Marks*: Max Scheck. *Bob Upton*: William J. Tuite. *Kid Glover*: Beatrice Learwood. *Chip Chase*: Fay Tincher. *Butt Innis*: Martha Bright. *Wright Holmes*: Georgia Howard. *Toots Horne*: Dorothy Bertrand. *Dad Payson*: Edna Chase. *Tote Flagg*: Susie Pitt. *Hen Hussey*: Eleanor Rose. *Dawdlers (4)*: *A. Thorley Budd*: Ernest Wood. *O. Willie Drinkwater*: Walter Paschel. *H. Astor Cortwright*: Joe Burry. *J. Withers Carr*: Raymond St. Elmo. *Tootsie Tripper*, bright particular star of "The Parisian Pets" Burlesque Company: BESSIE CLAYTON. *Ivy Green*, the belle of the college town: AMELIA STONE. *Mrs. Vera Shapeleigh*, a wealthy young widow with a taste for athletics: VALESKA SURATT.

Town Girls: *Eve Walker*: May Hopkins. *Carrie Waite*: Mabelle Courtney. *Daisy Stringer*: Mabel Snyder. *Lota Boyes*: Peggy Ten Brooke.

The Parisian Pets: *Cheta Singer*: Helen Heins. *Vera Laight*: Bonny Hoyt. *Erminie Rellick*: Helen Barrett. *Georgette Marion*: Pauline Barrett. *Alvie Holbrook*: Ruby Lewis. *Maxine Freeman*: Lillian Fitzgerald. *Pettie Fynes*: Selma Mantell. *Jewel Winner*: Sylvia Beecher. *Iona Banker*: Eunice Mackay. *Hattie Josephs*: Lillian Harris. *Diamond Davis*: Kitty Wheaton. *Julie Tooker*: Minerva Walton.

Of The Swell Set: *Mrs. Lowe Bridges*: Grace Middleton. *Hazie Knight*: Agnes Dasmar. *Dottie Fisher*: Florence Schenck. *Ruby Tanner*: Sylvia Beecher[65].

Oarsmen: *Tom Steers*: Susie Pitt. *Will Rowe*: Beatrice Bertrand. *Harry Brokaw*: Georgie Howard. *Dodge Work*: Beatrice Harris. *Jack Tarr*: Elenor Rose. *Pipe Trainor*: Ethel Pony Cantor. *Orr Locke*: Nathalie Porter. *"Crabb" Ketcham*: Daisy Delmar.

Shout 1: The Campus of Doolittle University.

Shout 2: Interior of the College Boat Club.

SHOUT 1 (Act 1)[66]
"Here on the Fence at Doolittle College" (Opening Ensemble)
"(Let's) Wander Off Nowhere" (Octette)
H. Barrett, P. Barrett, H. Heins, R. Lewis;
Messrs. W. D. Stevenson, M. Sheck, Sadler, E. Wood
"Coon College" (Song)
T. Lewis
"What's the Use?" (Song) (What's the Good?)
H. Tighe
"You'll Never Know What Love Is Until I Love You" (Song)
A. Stone
(*Lyrics by* Will D. Cobb, Matthew C. Woodward.)
"(Little) Tootsie Tripper" (Song)
B. Clayton
"All I Want in the Wide, Wide World Is You, Just You" (Duet)
A. Stone, H. Tighe
"Here in the Moonlight on the Fence" (Finale)

SHOUT 2 (Act 2)
"Leader of Fashion Am I" (Fashion)(Song)
V. Suratt
"Put Me Among the Girls" (Song)
W. Gould
"Zabelle"[67] (Song)
A. Stone
"Old Friends" (Song)
V. Suratt
(*Lyrics by* Sam Ehrlich.)
"The College Boy's Dream" (Song)
H. Tighe, B. Clayton
"Peter Pan"
B. Clayton
The Japanese Tea Girls and Naval Officers
The Premiere Danseuse
B. Clayton
The Spanish Girls and Naval Officers
"The Frolics of Pierrot"
B. Clayton
Finale

1907.45 TWO ISLANDS

A Musical Comedy in Three Acts[68]. Libretto by Adolf Philipp and Mortimer M. Theise. adapted from the Berlin and Viennese success[69]. Produced by

---

62Dropped during the run.
63Replaced during the run by:
"Tiddley om pom"
L. Guerite
(*Music and Lyrics by* ? Leigh and ? Powell.)
64For subsequent tour, replaced by:
"My Irish Fluffy Ruffles"
B. Ring
(*Music by* Albert Gumble. *Lyrics by* Will Heelan.)
65Unidentified in opening night program; Beecher's name appears in subsequent programs.

66Beginning 23 November 1907, a burlesque of "The Thief" with C J Ross and Mabel Fenton was added. Added during the run after Shout Two:
Opening Chorus
A. Stone, H. Tighe, Chorus
"In Philadelphia"
W. Gould
(*Lyrics by* Whitford Watson.)
"Mandy"
A. Stone, Chorus
Finale
67Replaced after opening with:
"How Would You Like to Take Me Home with You?"
A. Stone
(*Lyrics by* Will D. Cobb.)
68A revised version of the musical FROM ACROSS THE POND, which opened 7 September 1907 at the Circle Theatre for 8 performances.
69Source is unidentified.

Mortimer M. Theise Opened 14 October 1907 at the Circle Theatre and closed 9 November 1907 after 34 performances.

CAST: *Moishe Rositsky*: BARNEY BERNARD. *Stella Somers*: LOTTIE KENDALL. *Helen Hunt*, an American soubrette: GULEMA BAKER. *Tobe Terris*, an English singer: LILLIAN DOREEN. *Sarah Rositzky*: Leila Remer. *Two Italian Immigrants*: Lester Bernard, Michael Curran. With JACK VINCENT, RICE and CADY.

Act 1: Landing at Ellis Island.

Act 2: Exterior of a Bowery Museum.

Act 3: Chatham Square on Election Night.

MUSICAL NUMBERS[70]

"Mexico"
L. Kendall

"Mooney Time"
L. Kendall

"My Sunny Sunbeam"
L. Kendall

"Aren't You the Girl I Met at Sherry's?"
Octette
(*Music by* Louis A. Hirsch. *Lyrics by* E. Ray Goetz.)

"Aren't You the Girl I Met at Sherry's?" (reprise)
B. Bernard, Rice and Cady

"Stephen (Was a Minister)"
L. Doreen
(*Music by* Harold Orlob. *Lyrics by* Addison Burkhardt.)

1907.46 THE HOYDEN

A Musical Comedy in Three Acts. Book by Cosmo Hamilton. Based on "La Soeur" by Tristan Bernard. Music (and lyrics) by Paul Rubens, John L. Golden and Robert Hood Bowers. Staged by Ben Teal. Scenery by Homer Emens. Costumes by Mlle. Dazian. Musical director, Robert Hood Bowers. Produced by Charles Dillingham. Opened 19 October 1907 at the Knickerbocker Theatre, moved 2 December 1907 to Wallack's Theatre and closed 14 December 1907 after 58 performances[71].

CAST: *Thomas Talbot* of New York: Samuel Reed. *Harry Talbot* of London, a long distance connection: ARTHUR STANFORD. *Major Algernon Fitzhugh Finch*, retired: ROBERT LETT. *Dr. Julian Gousse*: ARMAND KALISZ. *Hon. Bertie Cecil Grahame*, a friend of Harry: Lionel Walsh. *Louis*, a chauffeur: Robert Ward. *Theobold*, another: Larry Ward. *Lucy Talbot*: Kathryn Hutchinson. *Joan Talbot*, known as "The Hoyden": ELSIE JANIS. *Elsie Janis*: ELSIE JANIS. *Miss Herminia Smith*, their maiden aunt: ANNIE ESMOND. *Henriette*, Joan's maid: Isabel D'Armond. *Ritz Santacierci*: NELLIE BEAUMONT. *M'lle La Clairette*: La Noveta. *Rita's friends (3): Maud de Maulan, Chris Angier, Thais Coutier*: Ella Rock, Elsie Steele, Eleanor Pendleton. *Danton*: Harry Depp. *Gaston*: Mabel Croft.

Guests of the Bon-Ton Hotel, Dieppe: *Fleurette*: Clara Pitt. *Elise*: May Emory. *Bebe*: Marjorie Norton. *Marianne*: Lottie Vernon. *Violette*: Jane Rogers. *Beatriz*: Leila Benton. *Nanine*: Evelyn Mitchell. *Nanette*: Nita Pierson. *Other characters by*: Misses Mae Murray, Bena Hoffman, May Chapin, Daisy Johnstone, Dorothy Webb, Edith Livingstone, Minnie Whitmore, Pauline Walden, Libbian Diamond, Lillian McMillan, Florence Major, Della Dolvan, Bertha Morrell, Jane Archer, Ellen Beckwith, Lura Wentworth, Marjorie Norton. Messrs. J. M. Colosanti, W. C. Wood, J. Robb, S. M. Burbank, E. W. Bosher, J. Brady, W. Toland, F. R. Fenn, L. Beck, J. Rose, L. Harkins.

Act 1: Morning. Garden of Talbot's chateau, Normandy.

Act 2: Afternoon. Terrace of the Hotel Bon-Ton, Dieppe, France.

Act 3: Evening. Aunt Herminia's Home. The pension, Normandy.

ACT 1[72]

Opening Chorus
(*Music by* Robert Hood Bowers.)

"Every Fellow Wants to Love Me"
I. D'Armond
(*Music by* Robert Hood Bowers. *Lyrics by* Raymond W. Peck.)

"Love's Prescription" (Duet)
K. Hutchinson, A. Kalisz
(*Music and Lyrics by* John L. Golden.)

"A Solitary Finish"
E. Janis
(*Music by* Egbert Van Alstyne. *Lyrics by* Harry Williams.)

"That's Why I Never Married"
R. Lett
(*Music by* John L. Golden. *Lyrics by* John L. Golden and Joseph Cawthorn.)

ACT 2

Opening Chorus and Dance
(*Music by* Robert Hood Bowers.)

"(Let's Go and Sit) On the Piazza"
N. Beaumont
(*Music and Lyrics by* George A. Spink.)

"Gretchen" (Graetchen Madchen Mine)
E. Janis, R. Lett
(*Music and Lyrics by* John L. Golden.)

"I'm Growing Fond of You"
E. Janis, A. Stanford
(*Music and Lyrics by* John L. Golden.)

Finale
(*Music by* Robert Hood Bowers and John L. Golden.)

ACT 3

Opening
(*Music by* Robert Hood Bowers. *Lyrics by* Raymond W. Peck.)

"(I'd Like to) Lock You in My Heart" (Lock Your Heart)
K. Hutchinson
(*Music by* Robert Hood Bowers. *Lyrics by* Raymond W. Peck.)

Ballet
(*Music by* Robert Hood Bowers.)

Imitations
E. Janis

"My Father's Wooden Leg" (Quartette)
J. Cawthorn, S. Jarvis, L. Walsh, A. Stanford
(*Music by* Harry Dillon. *Lyrics by* Joseph Cawthorn.)

"Put Me Amongst the Girls"
R. Lett
(*Music by* Dan Lipton. *Lyrics by* George Arthurs.)

"You're the Girl I Love"
K. Hutchinson

"Finishing School" (Finish)
E. Janis

"Advertising"
N. Beaumont

1907.47 THE TOP O' TH' WORLD

A Musical Extravaganza in Two Acts, 4 Scenes. Book by Mark E. Swan. Music by Manuel Klein and Anna [Anne] Caldwell. Lyrics by James O'Dea. Staged by Frank Smithson. Dances by William Rock and Signor Luigi Albertieri. Settings by Platzer and Dodge. Costumes by Archie Gunn. Musical director, Albert Krausse. Produced by J. M. Allison. Opened 19 October 1907 at the Majestic Theatre, moved 3 February 1908 to the Casino Theatre and closed 22 February 1908 after 156 performances.

CAST (in order of appearance): *Kris Kringle*, the Toymaker: Russell Bassett. *Kankakee*, an Eskimo Chief: Roger Dolan. *Maida*, a little girl who wants to grow up: KATHLEEN CLIFFORD. *Billy*, apprentice of Kris Kringle: Bessie Franklin. *Shellman*, a balloonist, pledged not to discover the North Pole: HARRY FAIRLEIGH. *Westinghouse Morse*, a hustling inventor: JOHN McVEIGH. *Kokomo*, an Eskimo belle: ANNA LAUGHLIN. *Jack in the Box* a Wonderful Toy: Fred Bailey. *The Candy Kid*, an Arctic Practical Joker:

---

[70]No New York program found. Incomplete song list not in performance order.

[71]Played a return engagement 27 January 1908 at the Grand Opera House for 8 performances.

[72]Musical Numbers not listed in the program. Song list prepared, excepting the last 4 songs, from Chicago tour. The show was revised after its opening; Joseph Cawthorn joined the cast in the newly written role of Baron Hugo Weybach, replacing the part of Major Algernon Fitzhugh Finch, played by Robert Lett. Sydney Jarvis succeeded Armand Kalisz. Published, but not in Chicago program:

"Finish" (Finishing School)
(*Music by* John L. Golden. *Lyrics by* Henry Blossom.)

"You Want Someone to Love You"
(*Music by* Egbert Van Alstyne. *Lyrics by* Harry Williams.)

Ralph Austin. *The Friendly Bear*, a Stretch of Imagination: Arthur Hill. *Stalacta*, an Ice Vestal: BLANCHE WAYNE. *Prince Tinymite*: Helene Montrose. *Jack Frost*, King of the North Wind: GEORGE MAJERONI. *Ice Guards*: Mary Mooney, Carolyn Barber. *Aurora Borealis*, Queen of the North: GEORGE W. MONROE. *Chief of Police*: Bobbie Nolan.

Collies: *Tip*: Jane Quirk. *Collo*: Florrie Royce. *Bee-Bee*: Virginia Calvert. *Sunny Jim*: Elsie Gilbert. *Snow Boy*: Anna Ford. *Frost King*: Daisy Virginia.

Gnomes: Harry Ali, Rudolph Allen, John Gibbons, Sam Diamond, Julian Alfred, Fred Steinman, Artie Pratt, George Campbell, Wellington Cross, Benjamin Tieman, Robert Merriman, Dixie Kirtland, Carl Taxwood, Simeon Tomars, Jud Brady. *Marionette Dolls*: Virginia Calvert, Jean Barnette, Madora Williams, Aida Klein, Anna Ford, Dorothy Honey, Vivian Danvers. *Pierrots*: Harry Ali, Dixie Kirtland, Julian Alfred, Wellington Cross. *Tyroleans*: Elsie Gilbert, Daisy Virginia, Florrie Royce, Mabel Mordaunt. *Grenadiers*: Jane Quirk, Grace Whiteley, Margaret DeBohmar, Virginia Guest, Ruth Hartman, Alice Mark, Edith Newman. *Ice Guards*: Jane Ward, Nettie Uart, Nell Adams, Susanne Boyd, Henriette Herbert, Ida Mordaunt, Tempe Evans, Helen Desmond, Lucille Monroe, Marjorie Jordan. *Ice Maidens*: Ruth Hartman, Edith Newman, Nita Dermond, Alice Mark, Virginia Guest, Margaret DeBohmar, Dorothy Cooper, Grace Whiteley, Jane Loras. *The One Girl*: Bobbie Nolan, Dixie Kirtland, Virginia Calvert, Elsie Gilbert, Madora Williams, Harry Ali, Florrie Royce, Vivian Danvers, Aida Klein, Anna Ford, Mabel Mordaunt, Jane Ward, Daisy Virginia, Dorothy Honey, Mary Mooney, Marjorie Jordan, Carolyne Barber, Margaret DeBohmar.

Act 1, Scene 1: Kris Kringle's work shop in Xmas Land. *Scene 2*: A Pass in the Mountains. *Scene 3*: Palace of Aurora Borealis.

Act 2: Plaza in the City of Illusia.

ACT 1[73]

Opening Chorus
Gnomes
(*Lyrics by* Joseph W. Herbert.)

"O'er the Snows" (Ensemble)
Eskimo Kiddies, Gnomes

"Busy Mr. Bee" (Duet Dance)
A. Laughlin, J. McVeigh
(*Music by* Anna Caldwell.)

"How'd You Like to Be My Bow-Wow-Wow?" (Song and Dance)
Kiddies, Collies
(*Music by* Anna Caldwell.)

"Where Fate Shall Guide" (Solo)
H. Fairleigh
(*Music by* Anna Caldwell.)

"Riddle-Ma-Ree" (Trio and Dance)
K. Clifford, F. Bailey, R. Austin

"Hail to Aurora" (Ensemble)
Chorus

"Aurora from Aurora, Illinois" (Solo and Chorus)
G. W. Monroe

"Hand Me Out a Laugh" (Trio and Dance)
G. W. Monroe, F. Bailey, R. Austin

"Why Don't You?" (Song and Chorus)
A. Laughlin
(*Music by* Anna Caldwell.)

"My Dolls" (Ensemble and Dance)
Entire Company
(*Ballet music by* Manuel Klein.)

Finale

ACT 2[74]

Opening Chorus and Policeman Song
(*Music by* Manuel Klein.)

"Yankee Doodle Yarns"
F. Bailey, R. Austin

"Cupid and You and I" (Duet)
K. Clifford, H. Fairleigh
(*Music and Lyrics by* Manuel Klein.)

"Little Brown Hen" (Song and Dance)
A. Laughlin, J. McVeigh

"(Sailing in a) Sea-going Hack" (Ensemble and Song)
G. W. Monroe, Chorus
(*Lyrics by* Joseph W. Herbert.)

"My Shaggy Old Polar Bear" (Song and Dance)
K. Clifford, A. Hill

"The One Girl" (Ensemble, Song and Dance)
Affinities and Divinities

"Side By Side"[75] (Song and Chorus)
A. Laughlin, Company
(*Music by* Manuel Klein.)

Finale

[73]The running order of both Acts 1 and 2 was revised during the run.
[74]Added during the run, after "Sea-going Hack": "Good-Bye, Dinah" (Song and Dance) A. Laughlin, Company (*Music by* Gus Edwards. *Lyrics by* Ed Gardenier.) Added for subsequent tour, as per published sheet music: "Perfectly Terrible" Emma Janvier (*Music by* Anna Caldwell. *Lyrics by* James O'Dea.)

[75]Dropped during the run.

1907.48 THE MERRY WIDOW

An Operetta in Three Acts. (Original Viennese) Book ("Die Lustige Witwe") by Victor Léon and Leo Stein after "L'Attaché d'ambassade" by Henri Meilhac. Music by Franz Lehár. English lyrics by Adrian Ross. Production staged by George Marion. Settings by Walter Burridge. Costumes by Percy Anderson, Mme. Hermann, Mme. Zimmerman. Orchestra under the direction of Louis F. Gottschalk. Produced by Henry W. Savage. Opened 21 October 1907 at the New Amsterdam Theatre, moved 29 June 1908 to the Aerial Gardens (atop the New Amsterdam), returned 31 August 1908 to the New Amsterdam Theatre and closed 17 October 1908 after 416 performances.[76]

CAST: *(Baron) Popoff*, Marsovian Ambassador: R. E. GRAHAM. *Natalie*, his wife: LOIS EWELL. *Prince Danilo*, Embassy attaché: DONALD BRIAN. *Sonia*, a young widow: ETHEL JACKSON. *Camille de Jolidon*: WILLIAM C. WEEDON. *Marquis Cascada*: Walter C. Wilson. *Raoul de St. Brioche*: Charles Meakins. *Khadja*, (Counselor of Legation): Harry Hyde. *Malitza*, his wife: Margaret Dalrymple. *Nova Kovich*, of the Embassy: F. J. McCarthy. *Olga*, his wife: Frances Cameron. *Nisch*, messenger of Embassy: Fred Frear. *Praskovia*: Blanche Rice. *Little Willie*: Harry H. Meyer. *An Englishman*: Ralph Whiting. *Head Waiter*: Gerald Lane. *Orchestra Leader at Maxim's*: Nicholas Szabo.

(Girls at Maxim's): *Zo-Zo*: Frances Cameron. *Fi-Fi*: Eva Bennett. *Lo-Lo*: Aurora Piatt. *Do-Do*: Pauline Winters. *Jou-Jou*: Marion Armstrong. *Frou-Frou*: Jean Ward. *Clo-Clo*: Clara Tichenor. *Margot*: Portia Belma. *Zu-Zu*: Bernice Harte. *Sapho*: Sophie Witt.

Guests: Misses Murray, Davees, Duryea, Witt, Wadham, Corwin, Schiebly, Creagh. Messrs. Alberti, Livington, Cassidy, Whiting, Holt, Hastings, Meyer, Lane, Smith. *Servants*: Messrs. Miller, Doyle, Hamilton. *Marsovian Dancing Men*: Messrs. Bauer, Boone, Ransome, Taylor, Von Calish, Ellinger, Fisher, Manchester. *Marsovian Troubadours*: Messrs. Walda Marjanovich, Alekx Hursau, Koszta Kolarszky, Cira Lozarne, Emil Demetorad, Nicholas Szabo.

Act 1: The Marsovian Embassy in Paris.

Act 2: Gardens of Sonia's Residence in Paris.

Act 3: Cafe Maxim, Paris.

ACT 1

Opening Chorus

Ball-Music

"A Dutiful Wife"
L. Ewell, W. C. Weedon

"In Marsovia"
E. Jackson, Chorus

Ball-Music

"Maxim's" (Girls, Girls, Girls)
D. Brian

Finale

ACT 2

Opening Chorus

[76]English libretto uncredited. Kurt Gänzl in his "Encyclopedia of the Musical Theatre" states that the American libretto was based on the uncredited English libretto, variously ascribed to Edward Morton or Basil Hood.

"Vilia"
E. Jackson
"The Cavalier"
E. Jackson, D. Brian
"Women"
Septet
Duet
E. Jackson, D. Brian
"Oh, Say No More"
L. Ewell, W. C. Weedon
"Love in My Heart"
W. C. Weedon
Finale

ACT 3
Opening Scene
"The Girls at Maxim's"
F. Cameron, Girls, Chorus
"Butterflies" (Dance)
E. Bennett, Chorus
"I Love You So" (The Merry Widow Waltz)
E. Jackson, D. Brian
Finale

1907.49 MISS POCAHONTAS

A Musical Comedy in Two Acts. Book by R. A. Barnet and R. M. Baker. Music by Dan J. Sullivan, Augustus Barratt and Carl Willimore. Lyrics by R. M. Baker. Staged by R. A Barnet. Orchestrations by Albert M. Kanrich. Produced by R. L. Giffen Opened 28 October 1907 at the Lyric Theatre and closed 9 November 1907 after 16 performances.[77]

CAST: *Captain John Smith*: WALTER JONES. *Pow-Ha-Tan*: GEORGE LeSOIR. *Mighty Medicine Man*: NEIL McNEIL. *Soan-Ge-Ta-Ha*: HAROLD CRANE. *John Rolfe*: GEORGE FOX. *Freckled-Thunder-Cloud*: John Peachey. *Man-Who-Soaked-Father*: L. N. Lawson. *Splinter-in-his-Foot*: Jean Millar. *Deep-Voice-in-His Chest*: J. E. Scott. *Contractor McLaughlin*: Daniel Hall. *Not Afraid of-a-Lunch*: John O'Hanlon. *Panting-Pants-of-the-Panther*: C. Vandiver. *Jane Rolfe*: BLANCHE DEYO. *Kee-Kee-Kee-Wan-Da-See*: ANNA McNABB. *Wah-Wah-Tay-See*: Violet Zell. *Shaw-Shaw*: Emilie Wellington. *Ne-Ne-Moo-Sha*: Gladys Eagan. *O-Pee-Chee*: Loraine Bernard. *Questionia Plim*: Marie Terry. *Messenger Boy*: Loraine Bernard. *Bride*: Violet Zell. *Bridegroom*: Lester Allen. *Pocahontas*: MARIE DUPUIS. *Black Face Specialty*: The Nichols Sisters.

Act 1: Jamestown, Virginia, as it might have been in the days of Pocahontas and Captain John Smith.

Act 2, Scene 1: Big Chief Pow-ha-tan's more or less primeval Forest. *Scene 2*: Big Chief O'Toole's [ne Pow-ha-tan] Made-to-Order City in Modern Somewhere.

ACT 1
"If Things Were Only Different"
W. Jones
"Up, Up, Help a Fellow Up"
B. Deyo
"Every Little Bit"
W. Jones, N. McNeil, G. LeSoir, A. McNabb
"What Remarkable Things"
W. Jones, N. McNeil, G. LeSoir, A. McNabb

ACT 2
"Twang of My Rusty Bow"
H. Crane
(*Music by* Carl Wilmore. *Lyrics by* Harry H. Luther.)
"A Papoose Lullaby" (Mama, Do Not Leave Your Papoose)
"Won't You Say Yes (to Me)?"
M. Dupuis, Male Octette
"In a Dory"
(*Music by* Carl Wilmore. *Lyrics by* Harry H. Luther.)

[77] No New York program found. Song list prepared from Boston tryout.

1907.50 THE CANDY KID

A Musical Melodrama in Two Acts. Book and lyrics by Lem B. Parker. Music by W. R. William. Produced by Kilroy and Britton (Managers). Opened 28 October 1907 at the Yorkville Theatre and closed 1 November 1907 after 8 performances.[78]

CAST: *Eddy Edson*, the Candy Kid: RAY RAYMOND. *Emanuel Lopez*, a patriot from South America: TAYLOR BENNETT. *Captain Robert Bosworth*: WILLIAM J. MADDERN. *August Aurbach*: Richard C. Maddox. *Consul Bosworth*: Ed. F. Settle. *Clerk*: Henry S. Sylvester. *Drayman*: Ed. O'Haus. *Bonnie Bosworth*: WANDAH LUDLOW. *Coral Reeves*, an adventuress: ALICE BOLTON. *Kitty Cary*, daughter of Erin: Mattie Edwards.

Act 1: Yale College.

Act 2: Drawing room of Coral Reeves.

MUSICAL NUMBERS
"The Past, the Present and Future"
R. Raymond
"Bye, Bye, Dreamy Eyes" (Bye Bye Drowsy Eyes)
R. Raymond
"Hark to the Scream of the Eagle"
R. Raymond, Chorus
Parodies
R. C. Maddox

1907.51 TOM JONES

An English Comic Opera in Three Acts. Book by Robert Courtneidge and A. M. Thompson. Based on the novel by Henry Fielding. Music by Edward German. Lyrics by Charles H. Taylor. Produced [staged] under the personal direction of by Edward German and Robert Courtneidge. Dances arranged by Dave Marion. Settings by Walter Burridge. Costumes by Mme. Herman. Lighting by Joseph Wilson. Orchestra under the direction of Herman Perlet. Produced by Henry W. Savage. Opened 11 November 1907 at the Astor Theatre and closed 4 January 1908 after 65 performances.

CAST: *Tom Jones*, a foundling: VAN RENSSELAER WHEELER. *Mr. Allworthy*, a Somersetshire magistrate: Albert Pellaton. *Blifil*, his nephew: Vaughan Trevor. *Benjamin Partridge*: WILLIAM NORRIS. *Squire Western*: Henry Norman. *Gregory, Grizzle, Dobbin*, his servants: John Bunny, Bernard Gorcey, Henry Turpin. *Friends of Squire Western's (3)*: *Squire Cloddy*: E. P. Foster. *Pimlott*: E. W. Bowman. *Tony*: E. A. Clark. *An Officer*: Percy Parsons. *Highwaymen*: E. J. Oden, T. D. Crittenden. *Post Boy*: William Herman. *Waiter*: John Frolisch. *Colonel Hamstead*: Banning Willis. *Tom Edwardes*: Charles Kingsland. *Colonel Wilcox*: John Hassan. *Sophia*, Squire Western's daughter: LOUISE GUNNING. *Honour*, maid to Sophia: GERTRUDE QUINLAN. *Lady Bellaston*, a lady of quality: LAURA BUTLER. *Etoff*, her maid: Madge Marston. *Hostess of the Inn at Upton*: Florence Burdett. *Bessie Wiseacre, Letty Wheatcroft*, friends of Sophia: Marjorie Fairbanks, Odette Bordeaux. *Rosie Lucas*: Louise Meyers. *Susan*, serving maid at Upton: Lucy Tonge. *Betty, Peggy*, waiting maids: Evelyn Smith, Anna Hall.

Farmers' Daughters: Misses Bordeaux, Meyers, Norton, Hall, Lang, Aubrey. *Squires' Daughters*: Misses Bownes, Carroll, Crantzell, Von deMuehlen, Peters, J. Standish, Stoner, Vernon, Weeks, Blanchard. *Squires' Wives*: Misses Curtis, Leslie, Rankin, Smith, M. Standish. *Ladies of Quality*: Misses Curtis, Fairbanks, Smith, Weeks. *Farmers*: Messrs. Clark, Fay, Fougerard, Pearson, Kearns, Supraner. *Squires*: Messrs. Edwardes, Hammond, Foster, Frolisch, Hassan, Hammond, Kingsland, Fenton, Terry. *Soldiers*: Messrs. Bowman, Foster, Hammond, Kingsland, Willis.

Act 1: The lawn at Squire Western's.

Act 2: The Inn at Upton.

Act 3: Ranelagh Gardens.

ACT 1
"Don't You Find the Weather Charming?" (Opening Chorus)
"On a January Morning (in Zummersetscheer)"
H. Norman, Chorus
"West Country Lad"
V. R. Wheeler, Chorus
"I Wonder"
L. Gunning

[78] No New York program available.

"Wisdom Says 'Festina Lente'"
L. Gunning, G. Quinlan, V. R. Wheeler
"The Barley Mow"
G. Quinlan, J. Bunny, E. Smith, A. Hall, H. Turpin, B. Gorcy
"Here's a Paradox for Lovers" (Madrigal)
L. Gunning, G. Quinlan, V. R. Wheeler, A. Pellaton
"For Aye, My Love" (Finale)

ACT 2
"Hurry, Bustle" (Opening Chorus)
F. Burdett, P. Parsons, Chorus
"Benjamin Partridge, a Person of Parts"
W. Norris, Chorus
"Dream o' Day Jill"[79]
L. Gunning
"Uncle John Tappit"[80]
J. Bunny, Chorus
"My Lady's Coach Has Been Attacked"
F. Burdett, Chorus
"Let's Be Merry"
G. Quinlan, W. Norris, J. Bunny
"Love Maketh the Heart a Garden Fair" (Finale)

ACT 3
"Glass of Fashion" (Opening Dance and Gavotte)
"All for a Green Ribbon"
G. Quinlan, Male Chorus
"Beguile, Beguile, with Music Sweet"
L. Gunning
"King Neptune" (from MERRIE ENGLAND)
W. Norris, Chorus
(*Lyrics by* Basil Hood.)
"Hark, The Merry Marriage Bells" (Finale)

1907.52 THE GIRLS OF HOLLAND

A Comedy Opera in Three Acts. Book and lyrics by Stanislaus Stange. Music by Reginald DeKoven. Staged by Al Holbrook. Conductor, Antonio DeNovellis. Produced by Sam S. and Lee Shubert (Inc.). Opened 18 November 1907 at the Lyric Theatre and closed 30 November 1907 after 15 performances[81].

CAST: *Max of Holland*, a troubadour, sculptor, musician and a 'boon companion': HARRY MACDONOUGH. *Dr. Franz*, a penniless student: HARRY FAIRLEIGH. *Little Snowdrop*, a new student: EDWARD F. FAVOR. *Alvarez y Toledo*, a Spanish captain: PACIE RIPPLE. *Otto Van Biere*, son of Frau Van Biere: George Callahan. *Jan*, a notary: KARL STALL. *Ariella*, a female cousin of Mephisto: VERA MICHELENA. *Frau Trinkette Van Biere*, widow of Van Biere, the brewer: CARRIE E. PERKINS. *Freda, Minna, Gretel*, Frau Van Biere's nieces: Mary Nash, Ellen Tate, Leona Stephens. *A Nun*: Erla Rottger. *A Waitress*: Louise Montague.

Dutch Girls: Misses Marie Lawrence, Olga May, Willa Sterrett, Henrietta Pouts. *Dutch Boys*: Misses Reba Kent, Grace Conklin, Alice Simmons, Marie Ford. *Citizenesses*: Misses Charlotte Tillman, Floretta Crosby, Bess Foye, Erla Rottger, Mildred Thall, Minerva Mills, Catherine McGraw, Mabel Stewart. *Drummer Boys*: Misses Kitty Waldon, Madge Styles, Bessie Allen, Leonora Edie. *Trumpeters*: Misses Clara DeBeers, Mae Willard, Florence Hayden, Corinne Crosby. *Burghers*: Messrs. Jesse Willingham, John Van Aspe, Philip Watson, Charles Williams, John Mundinger, James Tiernan, Al McFeeters, John McDonough. *Soldiers*: Messrs. Charles Senna, George Devine, James Hall, Walter Macadam, Howard Hall, Charles Campbell, Aoli Cellini, Herman Noble.

Act 1: A street in Liege, Flanders, during the Spanish occupation of the Netherlands in 1687. A day in May.

Act 2: Hall of Frau Van Biere's home in Bruges. The next day.

Act 3: Garden of Frau Van Biere's home. Afternoon of the same day.

ACT 1
"We Sing a Jubilee"
K. Stall, Chorus
Sabot Dance
K. Stall, Chorus
"The Men of Spain" (Ensemble)
K. Stall, Chorus
"Captain Cupid"
P. Ripple, Chorus
"Our Doctor Comes" (Ensemble)
"I'm the Doctor"
H. Fairleigh, Chorus
"Could You Love Me?" (Quartette)
P. Ripple, K. Stall, E. Tate, L. Stephens
Entrance of Ariella
"Ariella"
V. Michelena
"The Unveiling of the Statue"
Company
Finale

ACT 2
"The Wedding Day" (Ensemble)
"Oh, Boy!" (Duet)
H. Fairleigh, M. Nash
"The Spanish Grandee"
H. Macdonough, Chorus
"The Gay Fusilier"
L. Stephens, Chorus
"Why Is It?" (Duet)
H. Macdonough, E. M. Favor
Ensemble
"(I Want You for) My All Time Girl"
H. Fairleigh, Chorus
"The Joy of a Kiss"
V. Michelena
Finale

ACT 3
Ensemble
"My Ladye Faire"
P. Ripple, Male Chorus
"The Rooster and the Lark"
H. Macdonough, M. Nash
"(Serenade) D'Amour"
V. Michelena
Finale

1907.53 KING CASEY

A Hodgepodge of Mirth and Melody (Musical Farce) in Two Acts. Book by Aaron Hoffman. Produced by E. D. Stair. Opened 18 November 1907 at the West End Theatre and closed 23 November 1907 after 8 performances.[82]

CAST: *Dan Casey*: JAMES RAY. *Pat Casey*, the King of Lalla Pa Zaza: DAN COLEMAN. *Orphiz Noodle*: FORD STERLING. *Rocky Mountain Jack*: John B. Morris. *Mons. LaFroge*: Jack Clahane. *Lieutenant Tom Hardy*: FRANK E. ROSE. *Chief Casey*: Grover Land. *Police Officer*: H. Duncan. *Captain of the Bell Boys*: William Llewllyn. *First Guard*: Joseph C. Ames. *Second Guard*: Leslie Feathers. *Princess Eulah*: JUNE MAY. *Materia*: Julia Sweeney. *Goldie Mine*: EMMA RAY.

Act 1: Waldorf-Astoria Hotel.

Act 2: The Island of Lalla Pa Zaza.

MUSICAL NUMBERS
"'Neath the Old Cherry Tree"
F. E. Rose

---

[79] Replaced late during subsequent tour by:
"The Road to Yesterday"
L. Gunning
(*Music and Lyrics by* Clare Kummer.)
[80] Dropped late in subsequent tour.
[81] Settings, costumes uncredited.

[82] No New York program found.

"Deutschland"
J. May
"My Dixie Girl"
J. May
"Prairie Mary"
E. Ray, Chorus
"Uncle Sam Land"
F. E. Rose
"I'll Teach You How"
J. Ray

1907.54 THE AUTO RACE

A Triple Bill of a Historical Spectacle in 2 Scenes, a Musical Melange and Spectacle in Two Acts, including a Novelty Circus and a Ballet. Story and lyrics by Manuel Klein and Edward P. Temple. Music composed and directed by Manuel Klein. Arranged and staged by Edward P. Temple. Dances arranged by Vincenzo Romeo. Scenery designed by Arthur Voegtlin. Produced by the Messrs. Shubert and G. M. Anderson. Opened 25 November 1907 at the Hippodrome and closed 23 May 1908 after 312 performances.

ACT 1

THE BATTLE OF PORT ARTHUR, a Historical Spectacle in 2 Scenes, by Owen Davis. Music composed and directed by Manuel Klein[83]. Arranged and staged by Edward P. Temple. Scenery designed by Arthur Voegtlin.

CAST: *Japanese*: *Captain Tonkoka* of the Japanese Army, arrested as a spy: WILLIAM R. HAWLEY. *Major Yamoko*: H. Dale. *Okopa*: Charles Ravel. *Chigi*, Japanese Secret Agent at Port Arthur: James R. Adams. *Riuka*, Daughter of Colonel Ochigi and in love with Captain Tonkoka: Miss E. McKenzie. *Russians*: *Colonel Ostag*, of the Russian Army at Port Arthur: J. PARKER COOMBS. *Captain Garabedioff*, Aide to Colonel Ostag: Sam Barker. *Barnsky* of the Prison Guard: C. Caldron. *Olaf*, an old peasant: A. Barbara. *Lyoff*, a Drunken soldier: W. C. Moore. *Mounted Aide*, Russian Army: John Fleming. *Mounted Messenger*, Russian Army: W. Williams. *Picket*, Russian Army: H. Mansfield. *Wounded Soldier*, Russian Army: Nat Harris. *Tatiana*, A Soldier's Wife: Miss M. England. *Garasun*, an Old Peasant: Charlotte Weir. *Russian Soldiers, Japanese Soldiers, Russian Populace, Cossacks, Japanese Prisoners, etc.*

Scene 1: At Port Arthur. A Public Square, near the outer gate. *Scene 2*: The Capture of 203 Metre Hill. The Battle in the Rain.

ACT 2

THE AUTO RACE[84], a Musical Melange and Spectacle in 2 Scenes. Story and lyrics by Manuel Klein and Edward P. Temple. Music composed and directed by Manuel Klein. Arranged and staged by Edward P. Temple. Scenery designed by Arthur Voegtlin. Costumes by Mme. Frances Ziebarth.

CAST: *Mrs. Gay Spanker*, known as "Lady Gay": ROSE LaHARTE. *Mr. Dick Spanker*, her husband: EDWIN A. CLARKE. *Miss Virginia Carter*, her cousin: Marie Louise Gribbin. *Mr. William Worthington*, her father: WILLIAM H. CLARK. *Mr. Arthur Fitz Wilkins*, fiancé of Virginia: John Norman. *Sergeant Ruggles*, Mounted Squad: J. PARKER COOMBS. *Sergeant O'Rafferty*, Foot Patrol: JOHN G. SPARKS. *Tony*, The Head Waiter: MARCELINE. *Singing Waiters*: Messrs. H. Dale, H. S. Cluett, Sam Barker, L. Blumenthal, J. Carrol, D. Sheehan, J. Warren, E. Vary. *Acrobatic Waiters*: Messrs. George Hollnad, Charles Ravel, James R. Adams, James Balno, Nat W. Harris, Frank Hanson, Otto Fenn, H. Shaw, A. Romeo, Clyde Powers, Abe Aronson, Leo Brunswick. *Chorus of Chauffeurs, Rube Men, Rube Women, Peddlers, Flower Girls, Sandwich Women, Patrolmen, Mounted Policemen, Male and Female Automobilists, etc. The Ice Maiden* (Four Seasons): MARGARET TOWNSHEND.

Novelty Circus: *Clowns*: Charles Ravel; James R. Adams; James Balno; Nat Harris; Frank Hanson; George Holland; Clyde Holland; Clyde Powers; Angelo Romeo. (*Specialties:*) Marcel and Rene Philippart; Daisy Hodgini, Equestrienne; The Five Cliftons; The Seven Grunathos; The Six Bonsettis; The Mirza Golem Troupe of Persian Gymnasts and Acrobats; Hagenbeck's Troupe of 12 Performing Elephants.

Scene 1: Gardens and Exterior of Lady Gay Spanker's Mansion. *Scene 2*: A secluded part of the Spanker Estate on the edge of a lake.

[83]At the end of THEATTLE OF PORT ARTHUR, Tschaikowsky's "March-Slav" was interpolated.
[84]By February 1908, THE AUTO RACE had been renamed LADY GAY'S GARDEN PARTY.

MUSICAL NUMBERS[85]
Scene 1
"Riding in a Motor Car"
R. LaHarte
"Sweet is the Perfume of Summer Flowers"
M. L. Gribbin
"Those Days Gone By"
W. H. Clark
"Starlight Maid"
E. A. Clark
Scene 2
"The Four Seasons" (Ballet)
Vocal and Ensemble
(*Dances arranged by* Vincenzo Romeo. *Costumes by* Alfredo Edel.)
First Tableau: Spring. *Second Tableau*: Summer. *Third Tableau*: Autumn. *Fourth Tableau*: Winter. All Concluding with The Winter Carnival.

1907.56 O'NEILL OF DERRY

A Romantic Irish Drama in Four Acts. Play by Theodore Burt Sayre. Songs by Chauncey Olcott. Settings by Homer Emens, Edward G. Unitt and Joseph Wickes. Costumes by Van Horn. Musical director, Gus Salzer. Produced by Augustus Pitou. Opened 25 November 1907 at the Liberty Theatre and closed 21 December 1907 after 33 performances.[86]

CAST: *Bryan O'Neill*, an Irish cavalier: CHAUNCEY OLCOTT. *Sir Graham Croft*, English Governor of Londonderry: LEONARD SHEPHERD. *Major Duncan*, Chief of the Secret Police: George A. Lessey. *Laurence Desmond*, an Irishman serving in the Foreign Legion of France: EDWIN CAREWE. *Hugh Farrell*, a Fencing Master: Arthur Jarrett. *Barney McGee*: Daniel Jarrett. *McVane*: John Dunne. *O'Toole*, Keeper of "The Floating Bowl" Inn: Ned Reardon. *Captain*: Nelson Riley. *Lieutenant of City Guard*: Quincy C. Bass, Jr. *Sergeant*: Charles Howard. *Servant*: Jerome Hayes. *Waddy Fitzsimmons*, an adventurous youth: Anna Wilks. *Juggler*: Henry Newton. *Lieutenant Beraud* of the French Navy: George Brennan. *Citizen*: Martin Haydon. *Peasant*: William Jones. *Kate Fitzroy*, Half Sister of Hugh Farrell: ROSE CURRY. *Lady Croft*: Mildred Beverly. *Mrs. McGuire*: Maggie Fielding. *Elly O'Toole*: Alice Farrell. *First Violinist*: B. T. Glasser.

Act 1: Interior of the Flowing Bowl Inn. (Ireland at the time of Cromwell.) (Emens.)

Act 2: Rear Yard of Hugh Farrell's House. The same evening. (Unitt & Wicks.)

Act 3: Library in the house of Sir Graham Croft. Later, the same evening. (Unitt & Wicks.)

Act 4: The ramparts of the ruined Castle of Glenarvon. The dawn of the next day. (Emens.)

MUSICAL NUMBERS[87]
"A Bowl of Roses"
C. Olcott
"Every Star Falls in Love with Its Mate"
C. Olcott
(*Music and Lyrics by* Chauncey Olcott and Charles E. Casey.)
"Michael McGinnity"
C. Olcott
(*Music and Lyrics by* Chauncey Olcott and Manuel Klein.)
"One Little, Sweet Little Girl"
C. Olcott
(*Music and Lyrics by* Chauncey Olcott and Daniel J. Sullivan .)
"A Rose of Old Derry"
C. Olcott
(*Music and Lyrics by* Chauncey Olcott, J.J. Dillon and William G. Kopp.)

[85]Also performed, per production souvenir book, though not listed in program:
"We Have to Tramp and Tramp and Tramp"
J. G. Sparks
[86]Stage direction, presumably by Augustus Pitou, uncredited in programs.
[87]Not necessarily in performance order.

1907.55 THE OYSTER MAN

A Spectacular Song Comedy in Two Acts, 4 Scenes. Book by Flournoy E. Miller and Aubrey L. Lyles, based on a story by Hal Reid. Music by Will Vodery and Ernest Hogan. Lyrics by Henry S. Creamer, (Lester Walton). Musical numbers, dances, ensembles and play staged by Ernest Hogan. Costumes by Will R. Barnes. Scenery by Angevine. Music director, Will Vodery. Produced by (Jules) Hurtig and (Harry) Seamon. Opened 25 November 1907 at the Yorkville Theatre and closed 30 November 1907 after 10 performances; returned 16 December 1907 to the Grand Opera House, moved 23 December 1907 to the Metropolis Theatre, moved 30 December 1907 to the 14th Street Theatre and closed 4 January 1908 after a total of 36 performances.

CAST (in order of appearance): *Thief*: James Worles. *Policeman 4-11-44*: William Wilkens. *Panama Jack*, sailor: Charles Foster. *Matilda Jeusharp*, Rufus' best girl: MURIEL RINGGOLD. *George Oramos*, detective: Greg. Williams. *Samuel Austen*, promoter of Blazassus scheme: LAWRENCE DEAS. *Brother Peter Smith*: ROBERT A. KELLY. *Sisters of his flock (5)*: *Mrs. Pocketbook*: Emma Robinson. *Mrs. Change*: Ora Henry. *Mrs. Chance*: Dolly Thorpe. *Mrs. Chinn*: Maggie Thomas. *Mrs. Short*: Ella Anderson. *Aunt Jemima*, Brother Smith's better half: AL F. WATTS. *Angeline Gaillard*, who graduated at Tuskegee: CARITA DAY. *Belle Cowan*, her girl chum: Ella Deas. *Sunny Sam*, Rufus' side partner: JOHN RUCKER. *Useless*, Rufus' dog: HARRY REED. *Rufus Rastus*, The Oyster Man: ERNEST HOGAN. (*Specialty*: CRAIG WILLIAMS.) *Pony Ballet*: Esmeralda Statham, Gertie Peterson, Louise Salisbury, Rose Brown, Beatrice Bowen, Ruth Belmont, Minnie Robinson. *Yankee Belles*: Pinkey Cooper, Blanche Arlington, Louise Salisbury, Beatrice Bowen, Rose Brown, Annie Smith, Gertie Peterson, Esmeralda Statham, Minnie Robinson, Ruth Belmont. *Jubilee Chorus*: Misses Blanche Arlington, Rose Brown, Pinkey Cooper, Louise Salisbury, Beatrice Bowen, Esmeralda Statham, Gertie Peterson, Ora Henry, Dolly Thorpe, Maggie Thomas, Annie Smith, Bertha Lee, Violet Somers, Sophie Reed, Florence Osgood, Ruth Belmont, Minnie Robinson, Emma Robinson. Messrs. George Lynnier, Gus Hall, Charles Foster, Billie Moore, William Wilkens, John L. Grant, James Worles, Joseph Lyllard, James R. Marshall, Newell Morse, William Cowen, Fred Miller, Frank Tracey, Arthur Thomas, George Taylor. *Whitewash Brigade*: Charles Foster, Gus Hall, Billie Moore, William Wilkens, John L. Grant, James Worles, Joseph Lyllard, James R. Marshall, Newell Moore.

Act 2: *Gazook Seventh Eleventh*, ruler of Blazassus: BILLIE MOORE. *Ho Bo*, prime minister: GEORGE LYNNIER. *Gazabo*, chancellor of the exchequer: GUS HALL. *Koldo, Keno*, Royal Guards: Newell Morse, J. R. Marshall. *Debility, Delivery*, Generals of the Revolutionary Army: James Worles, J. L. Grant. *Princess Itto*, the king's favorite daughter, heiress to the throne: ELLA ANDERSON. *La La, Ba La*, Serving Maids: Blanche Arlington, Louise Salisbury. *Zamazi*, the Royal Seeress: ORA HENRY. *Dagalo*, sacred dog: HARRY REED. *Signeto*: Esmeralda Statham. *Ponno*: Ruth Belmont. *Watcho*: William Wilkens. *Palace Guards*: *Natives*: *Cowbys, Cossacks, Indians' Soldiers, Arabs, etc.*

Act 1: Oyster Fisheries, Baltimore. Present time.

Act 2, Scene 1: The Isle of Blazassus. Cast adrift. *Scene 2*: Road to Blazassus. *Scene 3*: Palace of Blazassus.

ACT 1[88]

"Fish Chorus"
Ensemble

"Mina"
M. Ringgold, Pony Ballet, Chorus

"Yankee Doodle Coon"
L. Deas, Yankee Belles

"White Wash"
J. Rucker, Male Chorus

"To-morrow"
C. Williams, Chorus of Beaus and Belles

"Contribution Box"
E. Hogan, Jubilee Chorus

"I Just Can't Keep My Eyes Off You"
C. Day, E. Hogan
(*Lyrics by* Lester Walton.)

"To Blazassus" (Finale)
Entire Company

ACT 2

"Roll On, Mighty Wave"
Mermaid Chorus

"Enough, (That's Enough)"
E. Hogan

"All Hail the King"
G. Hall, Native Chorus

"Dogalo" (Doggielow)
Native Chorus

"Meeet Me at the Barber Shop"
R. Brown, N. Morse, Double Octette

"When Buffalo Bill and His Wild West Show First Came to Baltimore"
O. Henry, Entire Company

Finale (Medley)
(Company)

[88]Program detail from Grand Opera House engagement includes minor cast changes. Also performed at the West End, but not at the Grand Opera House:

"Suwanee River," and "You Didn't, Yes I Did."
S. H. Forde, Chorus

"Gee, Ain't I Glad I'm Home"
V. Moore, Chorus

1907.57 THE TALK OF NEW YORK

A Musical Play in Four Acts. Book, music and lyrics by George M. Cohan. Produced under the personal direction of George M. Cohan. Settings by John Young, Edward G. Unitt and Joseph Wickes. Costumes by Richard Anderson. Orchestra under the direction of Gus Kleinecke. Orchestrations by Charles J. Gebest. Produced by Sam H. Harris and George M. Cohan. Opened 3 December 1907 at the Knickerbocker Theatre and closed 18 April 1908 after 157 performances[89].

CAST: *Kid Burns*: VICTOR MOORE. *Joe Wilcox*: JACK GARDNER. *Dudley Wilcox*: STANLEY H. FORDE. *Freddie Stevens*: JOE SMITH MARBA. *Martin McFadden*: John Conroy. *Mrs. Wilcox*: Lorena Atwood. *Isabelle McFadden*: Emma Littlefield. *Grace Palmer*: NELLA BERGEN. *Geraldine Wilcox*: Saidie Harris. *Jockeys*: Gertie [Gertrude] Vanderbilt, Rosie Green. *Andy Grey*: Harry Gwynette. *Commissioner Thompson*: William Thompson. *Captain of Bell Boys*: Maurice Elliott. *Mounted Policeman*: William Thompson. *Bicycle Policeman*: A. J. Thornton. *Special Policeman*: William Leyle *Head Waiter*: Maurice Elliott.

The action takes place during the summer of 1907.

Act 1: Exterior of Club House, Sheepshead Bay Race Track.

Act 2: Lobby of Astor Hotel, New York. The following day.

Act 3: Booth Lawn at Claremont. Riverside Drive, New York. Two weeks later.

Act 4: Exterior Home of Kid Burns, New Rochelle, New York. Four days later.

MUSICAL NUMBERS[90]

"Follow Your Uncle Dudley"
S. H. Forde, Chorus

"Put a (Little) Bet Down for Me"
Chorus

"Mr. Burns of New Rochelle"
V. Moore, Chorus

"When We Are M-A-double-R-I-E-D"
J. Gardner, N. Bergen

"Burning Up the Boulevard"
N. Bergen, Chorus

"Busy Little Broadway"
Chorus

"When a Fellow's on the Level with a Girl That's on the Square"
V. Moore, Chorus

"I Want You"[91]
N. Bergen, Chorus

"Claremont"
J. S. Marba, Chorus

"I Want the (Whole) World to Know I Love You"[92]
J. Gardner

[89]Played a subsequent week's engagement 20 April 1908 at the Grand Opera House for 8 performances, and another return engagement 21 September 1908 at the same venue for 8 performances.
[90]Running order of songs revised for tour.
[91]Replaced for subsequent tour by:

"That's Some Love"
N. Bergen, Chorus

[92]Dropped for subsequent tour.

"Under Any Old Flag at All"
V. Moore, Chorus
"Drink With Me"

1907.58 **THE LANCERS**

An Entertainment with Music in Three Acts. Play by Rida Johnson Young and J. Hartley Manners. Adapted from the German (original "Krieg im Frieden" {War and Peace} by Von Moser and Schoenheim)[93]. (Music and lyrics by Cecilia Loftus, George Spink, others.) Staged by Frank Smithson. Scenery by Edward G. Unitt and Joseph Wickes. Dancing dresses by Madame Ripley. Musical director, George Martens. Produced by Sam S. and Lee Shubert (Inc.) by arrangement with the executors of the estate of Augustin Daly. Opened 5 December 1907 at Daly's Theatre and closed 14 December 1907 after 12 performances.

CAST: *Marcia Tremaine*: CECILIA LOFTUS. *Mrs. D'Esterre*: PHOEBE COYNE. *Evangeline D'Esterre*: GRACE FISHER. *Ruth Fellowes*: ELLEEN ANGLIN. *Marcia's Friends (6)*: *Miss Woodgate*: Suzanne Rusholme. *Miss Marsh*: Roma Thorne. *Miss Vernon*: Margaret Cobb. *Miss Lafrenaye*: Jane Brown. *Miss Eversley*: Theresa Bryant. *Miss Rutherford*: Ethel Peyton. *Miss Loring*: Lillias Wilde. *Cook*: Dora Cameron. *Maid*: Maud Rowland. *Mr. D'Esterre*: Arthur R. Lawrence. *Dr. Chrystal*: BEN FIELD. *Pierre*: J. Stapleton Kent. *Of the 17th Lancers (7)*: *Colonel O'Connor*: Fred Tyler. *Surgeon Patrick O'Connor*: Hubert Harben. *Lieutenant Gordon Willoughby*: A. H. VAN BUREN. *Lieutenant Jack Graham*: HENRY COOTE. *Lieutenant Ainslie*: Bertram Allen. *Lieutenant Burroughs*: George Hollis. *Lieutenant Neville*: Cyril Chadwick. *Captain Cecil Fitzherbert*: LAWRANCE D'ORSAY.

Heatherbells: Misses Violet Curtis, Mollie Hall, Evelyn Honohan, Stella Warner, Anna Millward, Edna Merrill. *Guests*: Messrs. J. F. Fitzgerald, H. B. Eirick, William J. Ellis, Cyril Sully, Leon Bailey, Percival Norton, Master Harold Kehoe.

The action takes place in Quebec.

Act 1: At Mr. D'Esterre's house.

Act 2: The same.

Act 3: The grounds at Mr. D'Esterre's.

MUSICAL NUMBERS[94]

"Our Brave Lancers" (Minuet, Act 3)
(*Music and Lyrics by* Cecilia Loftus.)
"Come Out in the Moonlight"
(*Music and Lyrics by* Cecilia Loftus.)
"Any Little Girl"
(*Music by* Milton Lusk. *Lyrics by* H. A. Evans.)
"Captain D'Arcy" (of the Guards)
(*Music and Lyrics by* George Spink.)
"(Pretty Little) Heatherbell"
C. Loftus
(*Music and Lyrics by* George Spink.)
"(The) Voodoo Man"
C. Loftus
(*Music and Lyrics by* George Spink.)
"Twinkling Star"
(*Music by* Arthur Gumble. *Lyrics by* C. P. McDonald.)

1907.59 **A KNIGHT FOR A DAY**

A Musical Farce in Two Acts. Book and lyrics by Robert B. Smith[95]. Music by Raymond Hubbell. Staged by Gus Sohlke. Settings by D. Frank Dodge. Costumes by Arlene Falls. Orchestra under the direction of Paul Schindler. Produced by B. C. Whitney. Opened 16 December 1907 at Wallack's Theatre and closed 16 May 1908 after 176 performances[96].

CAST (in order of appearance): *Mme. Woodbury*, pincipal of the Evanston Seminary for Young Ladies: Mayme Taylor. *Elaine*, Mme. Woodbury's daughter: Lottie Kendall. *Emile Sheldon*, a university student: PERCY BRONSON. *Marceline*, the seminary chef, originator of His Own Meat Sauce: SHERMAN WADE. *Sir Anthony Oliver*, Muriel's father: Gavin Harris. *Muriel Oliver*, one of Mme. Woodbury's pupils: SALLIE FISHER. *Marco*, a Corsican, in search of affinity: WILL P. CARLETON. *Tillie Day*, a servant lady: MAY VOKES. *Jonathan Joy*, a self-alleged lawyer, by profession a waiter: JOHN SLAVIN. *Adam*, an expressman: Gavin Harris.

Visiting Alumnae: Misses Bonnie Bunyea, May Bennett, Bobbie Roberts, Josie Sylvester, Marcel Lamb, Evelyn Smith, Phyllis Gordon, Frances LeClair, Georgia Snyder, Virginia Adams. *Graduates*: Misses Hazel Templeton, Blanche LaMasney, Claire Bourne, Lillian Piper, Pearl Dawson, Jane Cook, Lilia Loraine, May Roche. *Under-Graduates*: THE ORIGINAL EIGHT BERLIN DANCING MADCAPS. *College Students*: Harry DeBanks, George Headley, Carl Norti, Arthur Cardinal, Harry Quinlan, Lee DeBold, Harry Loomis, Harold Reynolds, Otto Goffney. *Corsican Youths*: Bonnie Bunyea, Bobbie Roberts, Josie Sylvester, Marcel Lamb, Evelyn Smith, Phyllis Gordon, Frances LeClair, Georgie Snyder, Virginia Adams. *Corsican Flower Girls*: Hazel Templeton, Blanche LaMasney, Claire Bourne, Lillian Piper, Pearl Dawson, Jane Cook, Lilia Lorraine, May Roche. *Corsican Dancers*: THE ORIGINAL EIGHT BERLIN DANCING MADCAPS. *Corsican Banditti*: Harry DeBanks, George Headley, Carl Norti, Arthur Cardinal, Harry Quinlan, Lee DeBold, Harry Loomis, Arthur Callignan, Otto Goffney.

Act 1: Fairview Villa, Mme. Woodbury's Seminary for Young Ladies at Evanston.

Act 2: An estate upon the Island of Corsica.

ACT 1[97]

"The Sweet Girl Graduate" (Opening Chorus)
"Marceline's Meat Sauce" (Song)
S. Wade, Chorus
"I'd Like Another Situation Just Like That" (Situation)(Song)
M. Vokes
(*Lyrics by* M. Stephen.)
"What Fools We Mortals Be" (Duet)
J. Slavin, M. Vokes
"Life Is a See-Saw" (Duet)
S. Fisher, W. P. Carleton, Chorus
"My Very Own"[98] (Song)
S. Fisher
(*Music and Lyrics by* Clare Kummer.)
Finale

ACT 2

"Corsica" (Opening Chorus)
"(The) Little Girl in Blue" (Duet)
S. Fisher, J. Slavin
"The Bold Banditti"[99] (Song)
Madcaps, S. Wade
"Hurrah, Hurrah and Hurroo for That" (Song)
J. Slavin
"I'm Afraid to Go Home in the Dark"[100] (Song)
S. Fisher
"Whistle As You Walk Out" (Whistle When You Walk Out)(Song)
J. Slavin, Chorus
Finale

1907.60 **THE CAT AND THE FIDDLE**

A Great Musical Trick and Comic Spectacle in Three Acts, 20 Scenes. Book and lyrics by Lincoln J. Carter. Music by Clarence N. Sinn. Produced by

---

[93]Adapted into English as "The Passing Regiment"/"Our Regiment" and produced by Augustin Daly.
[94]Not in performance order.
[95]A revised version of the authors' MAMSELLE SALLIE which opened 26 November 1906 at the Grand Opera House for 24 performances.
[96]Played a return engagement 9 November 1908 at the Grand Opera House for 8 performances.
[97]Added to Act 1 (after Opening Chorus) for subsequent tour:
"You Never Told Me That Before We Married" (Duet)
Earle Dewey {Emile}, Grace DeMar {Elaine}
(*Music by* Raymond Hubbell. *Lyrics by* Robert D. Smith.)
[98]Replaced during the run by:
"(The) Garden of Dreams"
S. Fisher
(*Music and Lyrics by* Clare Kummer.)
[99]Replaced during the run by:
"Grosartiga Tanzerinnen" (Dance)
The Madcaps
[100]This may well be an interpolation of the popular song by Egbert Van Alstyne and Harry Williams. Replaced for subsequent tour by:
"Hang Out the Front Door Key" (Song)
M. Vokes

Lawrence J. Carter. Opened 16 December 1907 at the West End Theatre and closed 21 December 1907 after 8 performances.[101]

CAST: *Happy*: Charles A. Sellon. *Hans*: Fred J. Guillard. *Captain Bluff*: Ogden White. *Mike*: Will H. Bruno. *Wilfred*: Ben N. Mulvey. *Polly*: Jennie Elmore. *Aunt Matilda*: Edesse Fowler. *Circe*: Lotta Emmons. *The Genii*: Florence Willis. *Great Gobs*: Harry Farnum. *The Cat*: LAWRENCE GOTHARD.

Scenes: Farm of Captain Bluff in New York State; Enchanted Isle of Eye; Egyptian Cave under the Catskills.

MUSICAL NUMBERS[102]

"The Mosquito and the Whale"

"Under the Sea"

"Lota from South Dakota"

"Irish Lullaby"

"Long Ago"

"Lady Mine"

"Rabbit Foot"

"Rags and Patches"

"My Sailor Boy"
J. Elmore

1907.61 THE BAD BOY AND HIS TEDDY BEARS

An Extravaganza of Fun, Music and Pantomime in Three Acts. Book by Charles E. Blaney. Music by Ted Coleman. Lyrics by Frank Dupree. Staged by James R. Graey. Dances arranged by Harry Pilcer. Scenery by Elmer E. Swart. Costumes by Hayden; bear costumes by Edward Seidle. Produced by Charles E. Blaney. Opened 23 December 1907 at Blaney's Lincoln Square Theatre and closed 18 January 1908 after 44 performances.[103]

CAST: *The Bad Boy's Friends (4)*: *Papa Bear*: WILLIAM RHODES. *Mama Bear*: LEW ENGEL. *Teddy Bear*: E. T. SCOTT. *Flossie Bear*: WILLIAM PLATT. *Chips*, the Bad Boy: WILLIAM BARROWS. *Henry Harrington*, railroad magnate: RICHARD BURTON. *Percy Harrington* his son: HARRY PILCER. *Badly Cook*, innkeeper: George C. Clennett. *Harry Clayton*, station agent: William Naughton. *Archibald Overton Sherlock*, the XXXth Century Policeman: JOHNNY INGLIS. *Martin West*, First Vice-President of the Railroad: Robert Laidlaw. *Marcus Perkins*, road master: Tim Faust. *Jacques Floto*, summer boarder: William A. Watkins. *Ignates Farrira*, foreign representative: Richard H. Smith. *Alice Cook*, the innkeeper's daughter: EILEEN SHERIDAN. *Rosie*, maid at the hotel: JOSEPHINE BARROWS. *Angelica*, old maid, hotel guest: Flora Finch. *Health Seekers (6)*: *Margaret*: Helene Martin. *Florence*: Hilda Hoffman. *Elizabeth*: Regina Lynch. *Katherine*: Gertrude Lynch. *Caroline*: Florence Lynch. *Winifred*: Rosalie Lynch. *Reuben Simkins*, Sheriff of Raccoon County: R. H. Smith.

Tourists: *Minnie*: Madge Cullom. *Mamie*: Laura Witt. *Mercy*: Gertie Hawkins. *Marie*: Kitty Hawkins. *Frieda*: Grace Falk. *Fannie*: Beth Harrison. *Fernie*: Frances Folsom. *Flora*: Polly Allison. (*Vaudeville Specialties*: Rhodes and Engel (comedy acrobats); Harry Pilcer; *The X.L.C.R. Four*—Messrs. Smith, Watkins, Faust, Laidlaw; Josephine Barrows; *The Six Dancing Bells*: Gertie Hawkins, Kitty Hawkins, Grace Falk, Beth Harrison, Frances Folsom, Polly Allison.)

Act 1: Mountain View Hotel and Health Resort.

Act 2: Home of the Teddy Bears.

Act 3: The barn dance and society circus.

ACT 1

Opening Chorus
Company

"Tell Me Again"
E. Sheridan, W. Naughton

"When the Teddy Bears Come to Life"
W. Barrows, J. Barrows, W. Rhodes, L. Engel, E. T. Scott, W. Platt

"Only a Story from Fairy Tales"
J. Barrows, E. T. Scott, Primer Girls

"The Man Who's Got a Mortgage on the Mint"
R. Burton, Company

"When the Minstrels Come to Town"
H. Pilcer, Company

Finale
Company

ACT 2

Opening Chorus
Little Red Hiding Hoods and Their Teddy Bear Friends

"You've Made a Hit with Me"
W. Barrows, J. Barrows

"The Teddy-Bear and the Bee"
E. Sheridan, Company

ACT 3

Opening Chorus
Company

"You Are Not the One for Me"
E. Sheridan, H. Pilcer

"I'm a Real Carnegie Hero"
J. Inglis, Company

Vaudeville Stunts:

Rhodes and Engel; Harry Pilcer; The X.L.C.R. Four; Josephine Barrows; The Six Dancing Bells.

Finale
Company

1907.62 PLAYING THE PONIES

A Musical Comedy in Two Acts[104]. Book by Aaron Hoffman. Music by Theodore Morse. Lyrics by Edward Madden. Staged by Frank Smithson. Scenery by Frank Gates, Edward A. Morange. Costumes by Mme. Freisinger. Musical director, Al Smythe. Produced by B. E. Forrester. Opened 23 December 1907 at the New Circle Theatre and closed 18 January 1908 after 32 performances.[105]

CAST: *Pincus*: GUS YORKE. *Plonsky*: NICK ADAMS. *Hal Merritt*: HARRY B. LESTER. *Bill Welch*: CHARLES H. PRINCE. *Colonel Honey*: Joseph Clark. *I. M. Onne*: Linton DeWolfe. *Bud McGuiness*: GEORGIE MACK. *Tippen Offen*: Jack Clinton. *Skeets Carter*: Russell Hill. *Grace Honey*: Maude Campbell. *Vera Montfort*: ADELE RAFTER. *Mame*: Josephine Davis.

Act 1: A Race Track.

Act 2: Luna Park.

MUSICAL NUMBERS[106]

"Cupid's Wedding Bells"

"The Family Tree"
M. Campbell

"I Could Give My Heart to You"

"I Would Like to Flirt with You"

"I Would Rather Be a Lobster than a Wise Guy"
H. B. Lester

"(In) a Cosy Little Cottage by the Sea"
A. Rafter

"Love, Love, Love"

"Moon Beams"
A. Rafter

"Wind Yourself Around Me, Dearie" (Twine Yourself Around Me Dearie)

"When I Count Three"
G. Mack, J. Davis, Chorus

Opening Chorus (Act 2)

[101]No New York program available.
[102]List of musical numbers prepared from published piano vocal selections (Clarence E. Sinn & Bros, Chicago, 1907), excepting the last title, drawn from reviews.
[103]Musical director, uncredited.

[104]A sequel to BANKERS AND BROKERS which opened 4 September 1905 at the West End Theatre.
[105]No New York program available. Revised as a touring vehicle for (C. William) Kolb and (Max) Dill the following season with a different cast and musical score.
[106]No program available; songs not in performance order.

1907.63 MISS HOOK OF HOLLAND

The Dutch Musical Incident (Musical Comedy) in Two Acts. Chatter (book) by Austen Hurgon and Paul Rubens. Jingles and tunes (music, lyrics) by Paul Rubens. Staged by T. Reynolds. Scenery by Edward G. Unitt and Wickes. Costumes by Dazian. Musical director, W. T. Francis. Produced by Charles Frohman. Opened 31 December 1907 at the Criterion Theatre and closed 11 April 1908 after 119 performances[107].

CAST: *Mr. Hook*, a widower, a wealthy liquor distiller: TOM WISE. *Sally Hook*, his daughter: CHRISTIE MacDONALD. *Mina*, his maid: GEORGIA CAINE. *Captain Adrian Papp, Lieutenant de Coop, Bandmaster Van Vuyt*, of the Mounted Artillery quartered at Arndyk: BERTRAM WALLIS, GLEN WHITE, JOHN McCLOSKEY. *Simon Slinks*, a loafer by the canal at Arndyk: WILL WEST. *Ludwig Schnapps*, foreman of distillery: Richard L. Lee. *An Old Policeman*: Tom Collins. *Van Eck*, a very ordinary Dutchman: William B. Wood. *Freda Voos*: Catherine Cooper. *Clara Voos*: Marion Little. *Gretchen*, manageress of the distillery: FLORENCE NASH. *An Old Market Woman*: Eleanor Mansfield. *Chorus of Market Folk, Soldiers, Cheese Merchants, Villagers, Assistants in the Liquor Distillery, etc.*

Act 1: The Cheese Market at Arndyk, on the borders of the Zuyder Zee.

Act 2: The Interior of the Liquor Distillery. Amsterdam.

ACT 1
- Opening Chorus
- "Miss Hook" (Song)
  - Policemen, Chorus
- "Knitting Sextette"
  - Orphans
- "Fly Away, Kite"
  - C. MacDonald
- "Cheese Chorus"
- "Soldiers of the Netherlands"
  - B. Wallis, Chorus
- "(The) Sleepy Canal"
  - C. MacDonald, J. McCloskey
- "Flying Dutchman"
  - G. Caine, Chorus
- "A Little Bit of Cheese"
  - R. L. Lee, W. West, T. Wise, Chorus
- "Tra-La-La"
  - J. McCloskey, Chorus
- Finale

ACT 2[108]
- Opening Chorus
- "Bottles" (Madrigal)
- "Little Miss Wooden Shoes"
  - C. MacDonald, Chorus
- "A Pink Petty from Peter"
  - G. Caine
- "I Want To Be Your Wife"[109]
  - C. MacDonald
- "The House That Hook Built"
  - F. Nash, Chorus
- "The Violincello"
  - J. McCloskey
- "Amsterdam"
  - C. Cooper, Chorus
- "Cream of the Sky"
  - C. MacDonald, Chorus
- Finale

---

[107]Toured under the name HOOK OF HOLLAND. Interpolated for tour:
"Gee, I Certainly Hate These Trousers"
Frank Daniels
(*Music by* Edwin Burch. *Lyrics by* Billy Kent.)

[108]For subsequent tour, added to Act 2 (after "The House That Hook Built"):
"Salome Jackson"
T. Wise

[109]Dropped for subsequent tour.

1908.01 BURLESQUE OF THE MERRY WIDOW

A Burlesque of "The Merry Widow"[110] in Three Acts. Book (and lyrics) by George V. Hobart. Music by Franz Lehár, by permission of Henry W. Savage. Staged by Julian Mitchell. Settings by John Young. Gowns and fancy costumes designed by William J. Matthews; male and character costumes by Eaves. Music production under the direction of Anton Heindl. Orchestrations and entr'acte music arranged by Hugo Frey. Produced by Joe Weber. Opened 2 January 1908 at Weber's Music Hall and closed 16 May 1908 after 156 performances[111].

CAST: *Baron Copoff*, Farsovian Ambassador at Paris: ALBERT HART. *Prince Dandilo*, a waiter at Maxim's: CHARLES J. ROSS. *Caramel de Jollidog*, a journeyman lover: PETER F. DAILEY. *Disch*, a janitor at the Embassy: JOE WEBER. *Raoul St. Grouche*, an attaché: W. Douglas Stevenson. *Marquis Cascara*, a diplomat: Max Scheck. *Katcha*, another: Robert Dunlap. *Byron Lizst*, author and composer: Major Criqui. *Napoleon Bernstein Archer*, soldier, playwright and critic: Carl Gordon. *Fonia*, a Farsovian widow with means: LULU GLASER. *Fatalie*, the Baroness Copoff: MABEL FENTON. *Kickette De Lingerie*, a visitor at Maxim's: BESSIE CLAYTON. *Perfect Ladies* (6): *Ko-ko*: Kitty Wheaton. *Jo-jo*: Ruby Lewis. *Coo-coo*: Edna Chase. *Goo-goo*: Gladys Zell. *Do-do*: Ethel Donaldson. *Jo-ko*: Loretta McDonald. *Perfect Gentlemen* (4): *Mons. Duval*: Selma Mantel. *Mons. Charpentier*: Beatrice Learwood. *Mons. Verdun*: Edna Mayo. *Mons. Robideau*: Martha Bright.

Guests at the Embassy (9): *Mlle. Celeste*: Nathalie Dagwell. *Mlle. Angelique*: Nina Collins. *Mlle. Babette*: Stacie Leslie. *Mlle Yvonne*: Violet Jewell. *Mlle. Antoinette*: Ida Doerge. *Mlle. Clochette*: Helen Willis. *Mlle. Piquette*: Agnes Dasmar. *Mlle. Nannette*: Edna Dodsworth. *Mlle. Bettine*: Edith Villa. *Senorita Concarne*, from Spain: Letita Gordon. *Mlle. Cateline*, late of the Moulin Rouge: Lillian Fitzgerald. *Flowers of the Embassy Wall*, facetiously known to the younger set as 'battle-axes' (6): *Miss Marathon*: Ruby Lewis. *Miss Bosworthfield*: Gladys Zell. *Miss Waterloo*: Violet Zell. *Miss Brandywine*: Beatrice Learwood. *Miss Plevna*: Edna Mayo. *Miss Balaclava*: Lillian Fitzgerald. *Farsovian Guests* (6): *Miss Goulasche*: Vonnie Hoyt. *Miss Wienerschnitzel*: Irene Howley. *Miss Pumpernickle*: Minerva Walton. *Miss Zwiebach*: Lynn D'Arcy. *Miss Kaffeeklatsch*: Florence Wilson. *Miss Kolsbratten*: Maud Kent. *An Englishman*: Edna Chase. *Mlle. Champagne*: Gladys Zell. *Mlle. Creme Yvette*: Ethel Donaldson. *Mlle. Burgundy*: Ruby Lewis. *Mlle. Creme de Menthe*: Lynn D'Arcy. *Male Guests*: The Messrs. Heath, Miller, Robinson, Ball, Atwell, Huber, Steinmann, Senna, Sidney.

Act 1: The Farsovian Embassy.

Act 2: Garden at Fonia's residence.

Act 3: Maxim's.

ACT 1
- "We've a Feeling" (Ensemble)
- "(I Am) a Beautiful Wife" (Duet)
  - M. Fenton, P. F. Dailey
- "In Farsovia" (Entrance Number)
  - L. Glaser, Ensemble
- "I Am a Waiter at Maxim's"
  - C. J. Ross
- Finale
  - Company

ACT 2
- Opening Ensemble and Dance
- "Vilia" (Song)
  - L. Glaser, Ensemble
- "Silly Bingham Cavalier" (Duet)
  - C. J. Ross, L. Glaser
- "Women" (Sextette)
  - C. J. Ross, A. Hart, J. Weber, P. F. Dailey, R. Dunlap, W. D. Stevenson
- Dance
  - B. Clayton

---

[110]THE MERRY WIDOW opened 21 October 1907 at the New Amsterdam Theatre for 416 performances. Its book ("Die Lustige Witwe") was by Victor Léon and Leo Stein after "L'Attaché d'Ambassade" by Henri Meilhac. (English libretto uncredited.) Music by Franz Lehár. English lyrics by Adrian Ross.

[111]A revised version of the BURLESQUE OF THE MERRY WIDOW, known as THE MERRY WIDOW AND THE DEVIL, was produced by Joe Weber 3 November 1908 at the West End Theatre, returning 18 January 1909 to Weber's Theater for 24 performances. See separate listing in the 1908-1909 season.

Waltz
L. Glaser, C. J. Ross
Finale
Company

ACT 3
Opening Ensemble
Dance
B. Clayton
"Wine, Girls and Gay Paree"
A. Hart, Ensemble
Duet (Merry Widow Waltz)
L. Glaser, C. J. Ross
Finale
Company

1908.02 AROUND THE CLOCK

A Revival of the Musical Farce Comedy in Three Acts[112]. Book by Steve B. Cassin. Music by Lee Orean Smith. Lyrics by J. S. Hiller. Directed by Charles E. Foreman. Musical numbers staged by M. Fenton. Scenery by Ernest Albert, Frank Gates and Edward A. Morange. Costumes by Will R. Barnes. Produced by Gus Hill. Opened 6 January 1908 (matinee) at the American Theatre and closed 11 January 1908 after 9 performances.

CAST: *Billie Smith*, the drunk, the man from nowhere: BILLIE RITCHIE. *Perkins*, the bell-boy, full of mischief: RICH McALLISTER. *Tom Wilson*, a lawyer sometimes; a liar at all times: CHARLES E. FOREMAN. *Hank Wilson*, Tom's uncle from the Far and Wooly West: JOHN MOORE. *Algie Abbott*, an English lord, who married for money: Dan Dawson. *Edwin Uptown*, a waiter who mixes things: George Hall. *Deacon Mayfield*, Nellie's father, who adds to the confusion: JACK LLOYD. *Mrs. Abbott*, a jealous wife and Algy's shadow: Gertrude Fort. *Susie*, a maid who maid mischief: WINIFRED FRANCIS. *Nellie Wilson*, Tom's wife, the cause of it all: FLORENCE CLEMENTS.

Supplementary Characters in Act 3, by Richie's Pantomime Company: *Gene Holbrook*, an elocutionist: Jack Lloyd. *Professor Boni de Burro*, a magician: D. Dawson. *Pardello*, "the terrible": Mike Heffernan. *George Siller*, the referee: John Griffith. *Ben Speal*, stage manager: Harry Bristow. *Tillie*, the program girl: Sophie Mordecal. *Viola Desmond, Helen Desmond*, the Dancing Soubrettes: Winifred Francis, Nina Vernon. *Diana Morley*, coon shouter: Nina Vernon.

Among those present: Maud Cochrane, Nellie Mason, Julie Kelly, Genevieve Gibson, Gabriel Barbier, Phyllis Proctor, Corinne Brown, Nina Vernon, Bella Anderson, Ina Thomas, Genevieve Crawley, Edna Britton, Meta Caldwell, Jeanette Crawford.

ACT 1
"Lizzie Green"
C. E. Foreman, Chorus
"In the Land of the Buffalo"
J. Moore, Chorus
"Playland"
F. Clements, Chorus
Finale Act 1 (Grand Ensemble)
Full Company

ACT 2
"Sound of the Rolling Drums"
F. Clements, Company
Trio
B. Ritchie, R. McAllister, D. Dawson
"Don't Be Angry"
W. Francis, Chorus
"I Love Them All"
D. Dawson, Chorus
Finale Act 2
Entire Company

ACT 3
"Sugar Mine"
J. Lloyd, Chorus
"Dear Heart"
F. Clements
"Around the Clock" (Grand Finale)
Entire Company

[112] Substantially revised from previous production. First produced in New York 29 October 1906 at the American Theatre for 8 performances. For Synopsis of Scenes, see original 1906 production.

1908.03 FUNABASHI

A Musical Comedy in Three Acts. Book by Irwin S. Cobb. Music and lyrics by Safford Waters. (Additional lyrics by Paul West, Carolyn Wells, Wallace Irwin, Vincent Rose and Ted Snyder). Staged by Al M. Holbrook. Settings by Edward G. Unitt, Homer Emens , Young Brothers and Boss. Gowns by Whitmore & Lyden; Japanese costumes by A. W. Tams; uniforms by Warnock Company. Orchestra under the direction of Frank Palma. Produced by Thomas W. Ryley. Opened 6 January 1908 at the Casino Theatre and closed 1 February 1908 after 32 performances.

CAST: *Tecumseh J. Carter*, U.S. Secretary of War: JOSEPH MIRON. *Jack Carter*, his son: WALTER PERCIVAL. *Nan Livingston*, a New York widow: ALICE FISCHER. *Polly Rivers*, an American girl: VERA MICHELENA. *Monty Beauchamp*, an American clubman: PERCY AMES. *Owney McGehee*, a refugee from Forty-Second Street: WILLIAM ROCK. *Macy Bloomingdale Saks* of Sixth Avenue: Maude Fulton. *Hon. Miss Gwyndolin Hillary-Hoops*, a British heiress: MARGARET RUTLEDGE. *Wilkinson*, a chauffeur: Charles Butler. *Hi Low*, a poor conversationalist: D. W. Merket. *WIlliam Harrison*, H.M.S. Troublesome: W. S. Freeman. *Meouma*, a light-weight Japanese wrestler: Harry Husk. *Kitty*, a maid: Margaret Calvert. *Big Bumps, Little Bumps*, case-hardened sailors: George S. McCone, Sam Burns. *Debutantes (8)*: *Miss Claire Mont*: Rose Winter. *Miss Knicker Bocker*: Madge Melbourne. *Miss Astor Court*: Jeannette Horton. *Miss Holland Howes*: Lillian Carleton. *Miss Mercedes Carr*: May Faulkner. *Miss Owna Panhard*: Belle Ashlyn. *Miss Newport Hitt*: Eleanor Pendleton. *Miss Effie Vessant*: Margaret Cobb. *Able Seamen of the H.M.S. Troublesome (10)*: *O. Stilton*: C. W. Emerson. *Y. Hyson*: W. W. Benedict. *T. Marmalade*: F. W. Holmes. *B. Crumpets*: Holmstead. *J. Muffins*: J. F. McDonough. *H. Toast*: R. F. Cushing. *F. Periwinkle*: William Cohan. *G. Whelks*: O. H. McCartney. *A. Bivalve*: DeG. Robinson. *S. Whitbait*: Robert Buchannan. *Midshipmen of the U.S. Pacific Fleet (8)*: *Master Paducah*: Aimee Berry. *Master Keokuk*: Grace Emmons. *Master Wheeling*: Ethel Lawrence. *Master Duluth*: Jean Ward. *Master Savannah*: Ione Montgmoery. *Master Topeka*: Grace Conklin. *Master Tacoma*: Florence Jennings. *Master Mobile*: Grace Russell.

Tea Girls: Alice Gray, Trudie Hatch, Billie Sterrett, Reba Kent, Beatrix Doane, Helen Howell, Edna Merrill, Kitty Walden, May Reid, Helen Heilman, Lillian McMillan, Madeline Rellis, Bertha Carlisle, Violet Von Nichols, Katherine Peters, Adelaide Rankin.

Act 1: A bungalow on the seashore. Morning. (Unitt, Emens.)

Act 2: Garden, outside of bungalow. Noon. (Young Bros., Boss.)

Act 3: Tea room in the bungalow. Evening. (Unitt, Emens.)

ACT 1
"In Old Japan"
Chorus
"The Dear Old Story"
V. Michelena, Chorus
"A Little Japan Lady" (Duo)
V. Michelena, M. Calvert
"Her Baggage Was Checked for Troy" (Duo)
W. Percival, P. Ames
"One, Two, Three All Over (Down and Out)"
W. Rock
(*Lyrics by* Paul West.)
"(Love Is) My Matrimonial Bon-Bon"
W. Percival, V. Michelena
"The Girl behind the Man behind the Gun"
W. S. Freeman, Chorus
"The Girls of Every Land"/
"Miss Yankee Doodle"/
(*Lyrics by* Carolyn Wells.)
"Hi Yah" (Chinese Song)
W. Rock, Chorus
"Ambassador of Peace"
J. Miron, Chorus
Finale

ACT 2
"For a Girl Can Love a Sailor"
Chorus
(*Lyrics by* Wallace Irwin.)

"The Island of Love"
W. Percival
"When I've Made Up My Mind to a Thing"[113]
J. Miron
"I've Been Discharged by Them All"[114]
M. Fulton
(*Lyrics by* Paul West.)
"The Butterfly and the Rose"
W. Percival, V. Michelena, D. W. Merket
"Entrance of Meouma"[115]
Chorus
Finale
V. Michelena, Chorus

ACT 3
"Boo Ra Boo"
M. Calvert, Chorus
"Diplomats"
"Flirtation"
Debutantes, Diplomats
"Love Is Victor"[116] (Trio)
W. Percival, V. Michelena, J. Miron
"I Walked Around"
J. Miron, W. Rock, A. Fischer, M. Fulton, C. Butler
(*Lyrics by* Rose and Snyder.)
"I'd Guess You"
W. Rock, M. Fulton
(*Lyrics by* Carolyn Wells.)
Finale

1908.04 A PARISIAN MODEL

A Return Engagement of the Musical Comedy in Three Acts, 4 Scenes[117]. Book and lyrics by Harry B. Smith. Music by Max Hoffman. (Interpolated numbers by Vincent Bryan, P. H. Christine, Will D. Cobb and Gus Edwards.) Staged by Julian Mitchell. Settings by Ernest Albert. Costumes by Mrs. Caroline Siedle and Landolff, Paris. Lighting by Louis Lamont. Musical director, Watty Hydes. Produced by Florenz Ziegfeld[118]. Opened 6 January 1908 at the Broadway Theatre and closed 25 January 1908 after 21 performances.

CAST (in order of appearance): *Customers at Callot's (6)*: *Marcelle*: Edith Daniell. *Paulette*: May Leslie. *Suzanne*: May Emery. *Therese*: Lillian Wiggins. *Fleurette*: Sadie Emmons. *Adrienne*: Evelyn Dale. *Models (4)*: *Helene*: Bertha Blake. *Jeanette*: Louise Burpee. *Heloise*: Evelyn Westbrook. *Hortense*: Jeanne DeFoye. *Callot*, dictator of fashions: EDOUARD DURAND. *Violette* of the Opera Comique: EDITH DECKER. *Hercule* of the Paris Olympia: F. STANTON HECK. *Julien de Marsay*, an artist: HENRI LEONI. *Silas Goldfinch*, who is trying to spend his money: OTIS HARLAN. *Fifine, Titine*, Ballet Girls of the Opera House: Madlyn Summers, Marjorie Bonner. *Anna*, the Parisian model: ANNA HELD. *Carver Stone*, an American sculptor: GEORGE WHARNOCK. *Celeste*, a shop girl at Callot's: Roma Snyder. *American Girls (8)*: *Fanchonette*: Edith Daniell. *Denise*: Bertha Blake. *Georgette*: May Leslie. *Francine*: May Emery. *Diane*: Louise Burpee. *Claudine*: Lillian Wiggins. *Josie*: Sadie Emmons. *Henriette*: Evelyn Westbrook. *Mrs. Silas Goldfinch*: Mabella Baker. *Marie*, Anna's maid: Edith Daniell. *Jean*: Charles Hessong. *Collectors of money and oil paintings (8)*: *Mr. Moregain*: Charles Books. *Mr. Rathskeller*: Charles Hessong. *Mr. Cornergie*: C. T. Cunningham. *Mr. New Depot*: F. Noel. *Mr. Rates*: John Roach. *Mr. Shark*: H. Bouvier. *Mr. Keno*: C. S. Morton. *Mr. Quick*: H. Smith. *El Rio Rey*, director of the 'Palais de Patinage': Earle Reynolds. *Jeanne, Henriette* of the 'Palais de Patinage': Bertha Mack, Nellie Donegan.

1908.05 LONESOME TOWN

A Comedy with Music in Two Acts. Book and lyrics by Judson D. Brusie. Based on a story of "Watts," a boom town in California. Music by J. A. Raynes. Additional numbers by Witmark & Sons. Staged by Frank Smithson for New York. Dances arranged by Kolb and Dill. Scenery by Homer Emens. Costumes by Eaves. Orchestra under the direction of J. A. Raynes. Produced by Max M. Dill and C. William Kolb. Opened 20 January 1908 at the New Circle Theatre and closed 4 April 1908 after 88 performances.

CAST: *Chico Charlie*, tramping for his health: C. WILLIAM KOLB. *Bakersfield Bill, Fresno Phil*, tramps by choice: MAX M. DILL, BEN T. DILLON. *Wise, Hip*, promoters: ROBERT G. PITKIN, WILMER BENTLEY. *Hiram Diggs*, a constable of Watts: George Wright, Sr. *Eazy*, a native son of Watts: Arthur Van. *Lounnie Dippe*, proprietor of Hotel Watts: WILMER BENTLEY. *Mrs. A. Marvellous Wonder*, a New York widow: MAUDE LAMBERT. *Hazy Fogg*, a native daughter of Watts: GEORGIA O'RAMEY. *Ima Peach*, a product of San Francisco: Edna Dorman. *Anne Nother*: Irma Croft. *Cow*: Charles McGaffney.

Summer Girls: Misses Elenore Russell, Evangeline Dixie, Alice Willard, Faye Stewart, Julie Newell, Marie Lamar, Frances Paon, Lillian Nortn, Rhoda DeVourney, Myrtle DeSota, Jennie E. Orr, Austina Mason, Marion Miller, Loretta Wilson, Marion Vose, Carlita Ricard, Marion Lewis, Lottie McCree, Marie Propp, Mabel Orr, Anna Wilson. *Golf Boys*: Messrs. Herbert Lancaster, Louis Fletcher, Clyde Allen, B. Case, Graham Velsey, R. J. Bellaire, L. Lawson, Charles McCaffrey. *Townspeople, Golf Players, Summer Boarders of Watts, Hotel Attachés, Bus Drivers, Baggagemen, Porters, Waiters, etc.*

The action takes place in Watts in the summer of 1902.

Act 1: Morning. Country road leading to Watts.

Act 2: Afternoon. Court Garden of Hotel Watts.

ACT 1
"California Sunrise"
Orchestra
"The Game of Golf"
Chorus
"I'm Running After Nancy"
E. Dorman, I. Croft, R. G. Pitkin, W. Bentley
Specialty[119]
A. Van
"Gee! But This Is a Lonesome Town"[120]
C. W. Kolb, M. M. Dill, B. T. Dillon
(*Music and Lyrics by* Billy Gaston.)
"The Old Barn Dance"[121]
G. O'Ramey, A. Van, Chorus
"The Lanky, Yankee Boys in Blue"[122]
C. W. Kolb, M. M. Dill, B. T. Dillon
(*Music by* Theodore Morse. *Lyrics by* Edward Madden.)
Finale

ACT 2
"Mission Bells" (Opening)
Chorus
"Just Some One"[123]
M. Lambert, Summer Boys, Girls
(*Music and Lyrics by* Will R. Anderson.)
"Big Chief Smoke"
C. W. Kolb, M. M. Dill, B. T. Dillon, Indians

---

[113]Dropped during the run.
[114]Replaced during the run by (following "The Butterfly and the Rose):
"When There Isn't a Girl About"
W. Rock, Middies
[115]Replaced during the run by:
"It's Only a Piece of Advice"
A. Fischer, Debutantes
[116]Dropped during the run.
[117]First produced in New York 27 November 1906 at the Broadway Theatre for 179 performances. For Synopsis of Scenes and Musical Numbers, see original 1906 production. Note revisions to musical numbers contained in footnotes. For this engagement "La Vie" [sung in French by Henri Leoni] joined "I Love You, Ma Cherie" in Act 2.

[118] Previous 1906 engagement presented by Frank McKee, under the personal direction of Florenz Ziegfeld. Program for this engagement drops McKee's billing to below the title, below Ziegfeld's billing, and names him as President of Interstate Amusement Company.
[119] Dropped late in the run.
[120] Dropped late in the run.
[121] Replaced for subsequent tour by (then later dropped):
"So Long Bill"
Harris McQuire {Easy}, M. M. Dill
[122] Alternate title or replacement song for tour: "The Yankee Soldier Boy."
[123] During subsequent lengthy tour (1911), replaced by:
"There's a Big Cry Baby in the Moon"
Laura Oakley {Mrs. A. Marvelous Wonder}, Chorus

"My Cigarette Maid"[124]
R. G. Pitkin
"When the Moon Plays Peek-a-Boo"[125]
M. Lambert, Chorus
Medley—Finale
Company

1908.06 A WALTZ DREAM

An Operetta in Three Acts. (Original Viennese) Book ("Ein Walzertraum") by Felix Dörmann and Leopold Jacobson. Based on a story "Nux der Prinzgemahl" from Hans Müller's "Buch der Abenteuer" [Book of Adventures]. English book and lyrics by Joseph W. Herbert. Music by Oscar Straus. Production staged by Herbert Gresham. Settings by Homer Emens. Costumes by F. Richard Anderson. Orchestra under the direction of Arthur Weld. Produced by The Inter-State Amusement Company, Inc. (Frank McKee, President). Opened 27 January 1908 at the Broadway Theatre and closed 2 May 1908 after 111 performances.

CAST: *Joachim XIII*: CHARLES A. BIGELOW. *Princess Helene*: MAGDA DAHL. *Prince Lothar*: JOSEPH W. HERBERT. *Lieutenant Niki*: EDWARD JOHNSON. *Lieutenant Montschi*: Harry Fairleigh. *Friedericke*: MAYME KELSO. *Wendolin*: Bruce Smith. *Sigismund*: Joseph Carey. *Franzi Steingruber*: SOPHIE BRANDT. *Fifi*: JOSIE SADLER. *Anneri*: Geraldine Malone.

Viennese Orchestra: *Directress*: SOPHIE BRANDT. *Bass Drum*: Josie Sadler. *Piano*: Louisa Valentine. *Harmonium*: Camille Toulmin. *First Violin*: Geraldine Bruce. *First Violin*: Irma Schueler. *Second Violin*: Donna Garcia. *Flute*: Mrs. Paul Philipp. *D. Bass*: Anna Kessler. *Drums*: May Sheinert. *Trumpeter*: Rosie Geiger. *Trumpeter*: Julia Geiger. *'Cello*: Geraldine Malone. *Alternate Soprani*: Misses Romani, Chase. *Alternate Alti*: Misses Matin, Harrington. *Alternate Tenor*: Harry Fairleigh. *Alternate Baritone*: Edward Wilson.

Act 1: Festival Hall in Prince Joachim's Castle at Flausenthurn.

Act 2: Garden Restaurant.

Act 3: Drawing-Room in the Castle at Flausenthurn.

ACT 1
Opening Chorus
M. Kelso, J. Carey, B. Smith
"A Soldier Stole Her Heart" (Song)
M. Kelso, J. Carey, Chorus
Wedding March and Hymn
Ensemble
"Love Cannot Be Bought" (Song)
E. Johnson
"A Husband's Love" (Duet)
M. Dahl, M. Kelso
"The Family's Ancient Tree" (Terzette)
M. Kelso, E. Johnson, C. A. Bigelow
"Love's Roundelay" (Waltz Duet)
E. Johnson, H. Fairleigh
Duet and Finale
M. Dahl, E. Johnson, M. Kelso, J. W. Herbert, C. A. Bigelow

ACT 2[126]
"Kissing Time" (March)
Ladies' Orchestra, Chorus
"Life Is Love and Laughter" (Song)
S. Brandt, Chorus
"(The) Sweetest Maid of All" (Kiss Duet)
S. Brandt, E. Johnson
"Lesson in Love" (Terzette)
M. Dahl, S. Brandt, M. Kelso
"Piccolo" (Duet)
S. Brandt, J. W. Herbert
"When the Song of Love Is Heard" (Buffo Duet)
J. Sadler, C. A. Bigelow
(*Music by* Arthur Weld.)
Finale
Ensemble

ACT 3[127]
Gavotte
"I Love and the World Is Mine" (Song)
E. Johnson
(*Music by* Charles Gilbert Spross. *Lyrics by* Florence Earl Coates.)
"Two is Plenty" (Madrigal Trio)
E. Johnson, J. W. Herbert, C. A. Bigelow
"A Country Lass and a Courtly Dame"[128] (Duettino)
J. Sadler, S. Brandt
Finale
M. Dahl, S. Brandt, E. Johnson

1908.07 THE SOUL KISS

A Musical Entertainment in Two Acts, 10 Scenes. Book and lyrics by Harry B. Smith. Music by Maurice Levi. Staged by Herbert Gresham and Julian Mitchell. Settings by John Young, Ernest Albert, Frank E. Gates and Edward A. Morange. Costumes by F. Richard Anderson, Pancaud of Paris. Aerial evolutions arranged by Herr H. Schultz. Mlle. Genée's divertissements arranged by Mons. Alexander Genée; music by Cuthbert Clark; costumes designed by Wilhelm. Orchestra under the direction of Max Schmidt. Produced by Florenz Ziegfeld. Opened 28 January 1908 at the New York Theatre and closed 23 May 1908 after 122 performances.

CAST (in order of appearance): *Maurice*, a sculptor: Mortimer H. Weldon. *Therese*, a model: Amelia Rose. *Suzette*, a model, in love with Maurice: FLORENCE HOLBROOK. *Reggie*, a school boy: Almeda Potter. *Mr. Fogg* of London: Albert Froom. *Mrs. Fogg*: Marguerite Lane. *Angela*, their daughter: Jane Hall. *J. Lucifer Mephisto*: RALPH C. HERZ. *Mephisto's Daughters (6)*: *Lucia*: Eva Francis. *Satanella*: Freda Linyard. *Diabola*: Elphye Snowden. *Sulphuria*: Daisy Rudd. *Demona*: May Willard. *Impia*: Florence Walton. *Sol. Skevinsky*, traveling for pleasure: BARNEY BERNARD. *Cleo*, the belle of the Tabarin: STELLA TRACEY. *Ketcham Short* of Wall Street: CECIL LEAN. *Francine*: Edith Whitney. *Parisiennes (6)*: *Manon*: Grace Rankin. *Camille*: Hattie Forsyth. *Celeste*: Marian Hartman. *Yvonne*: Florence Ardell. *Liane*: Dos Howard. *Denise*: Jane Hall. *Fifine*, dancer at the Bal Tabarin: Madeleine Anderton. *Carmen*: Billy Norton. *Marguerite*: Grace Rankin. *Cleopatra*: Clara DeBeers. *Phrynette*: Elphye Snowden. *A Gibson Bathing Girl*: Jane Hall. *Captain Bulwinkle*, a promoter: Lee Harrison. *Custom House Inspector*: Albert Froom. *A Manager*: Harry Stone. *Anna Held*, "Parisian Model": Eva Francis. *Ethel Jackson*: Mildred Fay. *Edna May*: Almeda Potter. *Mrs. Carter*: Marian Hartman. *Rose Stahl*: Jane Hall. *Ethel Barrymore*: Dos Howard. *Margaret Illington*: Grace Rankin. *Mme. Nazimova*: Mildred DeBeers. *Fritzi Scheff*: Hattie Forsyth. *Henrietta Crosman*: Florence Arkell. *Fay Templeton*: Marguerite Lane. *Bessie Clayton*: Madeliene Anderton. *Bonnie Maginn*: Ethelyn Wilmot. *Leonora Brandt* ("Waltz Dream"): May Harris. *Mary Garden*: Irene Blair. *Maud Adams*: Elaine Gordon. *Maxine Eliot*: Francesca Gordon. *Florence Rockwell* ("The Round Up"): Mae Bevan. *Billee Burke*: Mae Doherty. *Ethel Levey*: Margaret Vingut. *Vesta Victoria*: Gretta Gleason. *Hattie Williams*: Dorothy Furniss. *Grace Larue* ("Follies of 1907"): Amelia Rose. *Harry Woodruff*: Cecil Sully. *Maclyn Arbuckle*: Henry Bergman. *George Cohan*: Stella Tracey. *Arnold Daly*: Homer Potter. *Donald Brian*: R. A. Allen. *The Dancer*: ADELINE GENÉE.

Dancing Girls from the Empire Theatre, London, accompanying Mlle. Genée: Emily Peters (Premiere), Belle Logan, Kitty Underdale, Millie Peers, Emily Nash, Florrie Bacon, Laurie Hart, Ada Rickwell, Florence Burke, Miss Benton.

Act 1, Scene 1: Studio of Maurice. *Scene 2*: Exterior of Bal Tabarin, New Year's Eve. *Scene 3*: Bal Tabarin, Paris, New Year's Night. *Scene 4*: Promenade, Monte Carlo.

---

[124]During subsequent tour, replaced by:
"I've Been Told"
Billy Clifford {Fresno Phil}
Which was later (1911) replaced by:
"Woman's Eyes"
Percy V. Bronson {Fresno Phil}

[125]During subsequent lengthy tour (1911), replaced by:
"Whistle When You're Lonely"
Charlotte Woods {Anne Nother}, Boys

[126]Added for subsequent tour:
"Vienna" (Act 2, after "Sweetest Maid of All")
{Fifi, Joachim, Lothar, Orchestra Girls, Chorus}
(*Music by* Jerome D. Kern. *Lyrics by* Adrian Ross.)
"The Prater" (Act 2, after "Vienna")
{Monschi, Chorus}
(*Music by* Ivan Caryll.)

[127]For subsequent tour, all of Act 3 was revised, to include only an Opening {Monstschi, Chorus}, and a Finale.

[128]Dropped during the run.

Scene 5: Treasury, Monte Carlo.

Act 2, Scene 1: View of New York at Night from the Singer Building. *Scene 2*: Pier of Cunard Line, New York. *Scene 3*: Mlle. Genée's Dressing Room, New York Theatre. *Scene 4*: Exterior of New York Theatre. *Scene 5*: The Hunt Meadowbrooke.

ACT 1[129]

"When the Swallows Return in the Spring"
S. Tracey, Male Chorus

"Meet Me at the Tabarin"[130]
Chorus

"That Wasn't All" (Song)
R. C. Herz
(*Music by* Louis A. Hirsch. *Lyrics by* Addison Burkhardt, Matt Woodward.)

"The Dances of the Tabarin"
Ensemble

"The Dollar Sign"[131] (Song)
B. Bernard, Mephisto's Daughters
(*Music by* Fleta Ian Brown. *Lyrics by* Jessie Villars.)

"My Affinity" (Duet)
S. Tracey, B. Bernard

"(I'm) The Human Night-Key of New York" (Song)C. Lean, Parisiennes, Ensemble

"Let's Pretend" (Duet)
F. Holbrook, C. Lean

"The Soul Kiss (Just for You from Above)"
R. C. Herz, M. H. Weldon,
B. Norton, G. Rankin, C. DeBeers, E. Snowden, J. Hall
(*Lyrics by* Lewis Gates.)

The Dance of the Soul Kiss
A. Genée, (Dance Ensemble)

"My Diabolo Beau"
S. Tracey
(*Music and Lyrics by* Kenneth S. Clark.)
Poodles: Misses Crane, Daly, Martell, Hamilton, Lytell, Thayer. *Poodle Girls*: Misses Cameron, Rudd, Walton, Francis, Lingard, Willard.

"Happy Day March" (Finale)
Money Ballet

Grand Balabille
A. Genée, (Dance Ensemble)

ACT 2

"I Wonder Where They'll Go" (Song)
R. C. Herz

"A Quiet Sunday in 1920"[132]
Collins & Hart

Medley of Harry Lauder Songs:
Lauder Girls: *Blue Bell*: E. Snowden. *Saftie*: D. Rudd. *Parted on the Shore*: F. Linyard. *Daisy*: M. Willard. *Fou Enoo*: E. Francis. *Tickling John*: F. Walton.

"I'm Glad to Get Back to New York"
S. Tracey, Ensemble

"There Were Actors Then" (They Were Actors Then)
R. C. Herz

"Any Old Place (in the World) with You" (Duet)
F. Holbrook, C. Lean

Pas de Fascination[133]
A. Genée, (Dance Ensemble)

"Those College Yells" (Rah! Rah! Rah!)(Song)
C. Lean, Male Chorus
(*Music by* C. M. Chapel. *Lyrics by* Cecil Lean.)

Danse de Chasse (Hunting Ensemble)
A. Genée, (Dance Ensemble)

Finale

1908.08 BANDANNA LAND

A New Creation (Musical Comedy) in Three Acts. Book and lyrics by J. A. Shipp and Alex Rogers. Music by Will Marion Cook. Staged by the authors. Musical numbers staged by Aida Overton Walker. Scenery by Carns, New York. Costumes by Mme. Pauline Reed (women's), Richie Harnden Company (men's); Max Marx (Mr. Walker's). Orchestra under the direction of Will Marion Cook and James J. Vaughan. Produced by F. Ray Comstock. Opened 3 February 1908 at the Majestic Theatre and closed 18 April 1908 after 89 performances[134].

CAST (in order of appearance): *Amos Simmons*, who owns the property that all the fuss is about: ALEX ROGERS. *Mandy Lou*, niece of Amos: ABBIE MITCHELL COOK. *Sophie Simmons*, Amos' wife: Hattie McIntosh. *Cynthia*, niece of Amos: Bertha Clark. *Dinah Simmons*, Amos' daughter: AIDA OVERTON WALKER. *Pete Simmons*, Amos' brother: Charles H. Moore. *Dinah's Schoolmates (4)*: *Julia Smothers*: Maggie Davis. *Sue Higgins*: Bessie Vaughan. *Babe Brown*: Ida Day. *Amelia Green*: Bessie Brady. *Sis Black, Becky White*, the two kids: Marguerite Ward, Katie Jones. *Angelina Diggs*, teacher in the County School and President of the R.L.B.H. Society: ADA REX. *Fountain Lewis*, owner of the Carrollton Hotel barber shop: R. Henri Strange. *Si Springer*, janitor of the G.U.O.O.F. Hall: Mord Allen. *Mr. Wilson*, large shareholder in the corporation: James E. Lightfoot. *Mr. Jones*, large shareholder in the corporation: Sterling Rex. *Sandy Turner*, chairman of the corporation meeting: J. LEUBRIE HILL. *Deacon Sparks*: Lloyd G. Gibbs. *Jack Dimery*, Uncle Apple Jack: George Catlin. *Board of Trustees of the T.S.C.R. Co. (10)*: *Sid Morgan*: James M. Thomas. *Neil Carter*: Matt Hously. *Dick Beel*: H. B. Guillaume. *Bill Hayden*: Angelo Hously. *Jim Strode*: Charles Hall. *Mr. White*: Arthur Payne. *Abe Milum*: L. H. Saulsbury. *Mr. Black*: J. P. Reed. *Mr. Brown*: G. Henry Tapley. *Mr. Green*: Frank H. Williams. *Sleepy Jim Harper*: W. H. Chappelle. *Jim Harper Jr.*: Ada Vaughan. *Mr. Collins*, Secretary of the Corporation: HENRY TROY. *Mose Blackstone*, a lawyer and founder of the T.S.C.R. Co.: J. A. SHIPP. *Skunkton Bowser*, the missing heir: BERT WILLIAMS. *Bud Jenkins*, Bon Bon Buddie: GEORGE W. WALKER. (*Doc Foster*, the Conjure Man: J. Francis Mores[135].) *Sadie Tompkins*: LAVINIA ROGERS. *Fred Lewis*, Fountain Lewis' nephew: Henry Troy.

Act 1: Back yard of Amos Simmons' home.

Act 2: Basement of the Odd Fellows' Hall. Three weeks later.

Act 3: "Bandanna Land." Five weeks later.

ACT 1[136]

"Corn Song"
A. M. Cook, Male Quartette, Chorus

"Kinky"[137]
A. O. Walker and the "Kinky Girls," Misses Jones, Brad, Davis, Day, B. Vaughan, Ward
(*Lyrics by* Mord Allen.)

"'Tain't Gwine to Be No Rain"
A. Rogers, Male Chorus

"Exhortation"
L. G. Gibbs, Male Chorus

"Until Then"[138]
B. A. Williams, G. W. Walker, Male Chorus

---

[129]Added late in the run to Act 1, after "My Diabolo Beau":
"Very Well, Then" (from THE WHITE HEN)
R. C. Herz
(*Music by* Gustave Kerker. *Lyrics by* Paul West.)

[130]Replaced during the run by:
"Meet Me at the Masquerade" (The Tabarin)
Chorus
(*Music by* Paul Lincke. *Lyrics by* Harry B. Smith.)

[131]Replaced during the run by:
"Under the Bargain Tree"
B. Bernard, Mephisto's Daughters

[132]Dropped during the run.

[133]For subsequent tour, Mlle. Genée's dance specialty became a Divertissement "Sir Roger de Coverly."

[134]Played a return engagement 28 August 1908 at the Grand Opera House for 8 performances.

[135]Character added during the New York run.

[136]Additional numbers not listed in New York programs examined:
"(My) Bandana Land"
J. L. Hill
(*Lyrics by* Mord Allen.)
"Saucy Little Sadie"

[137]Replaced during run, but reinstated for subsequent tour, by:
"Dinah"
J. A. Shipp, Ensemble

[138]Replaced during the run by:
"The Man from Conjure Land"
J. F. Mores

ACT 2

"Minuet"
J. A. Shipp
Assisted by M. Davis, Misses Jordan M. Brown, L. Brown, Rex, Rogers, Fowler; Messrs. Chappelle, Rex, A. Housley, M. Housley, Hill, Saulsbury.

"Red, Red Rose"[139]
A. M. Cook
(*Lyrics by* Alex Rogers.)

Specialty
R. H. Strange

"When I Was Sweet Sixteen"
A. Rex
(*Music by* J. Leubrie Hill. *Lyrics by* Mord Allen.)

"It's Hard to Love Somebody (When Your Somebody Don't Love You)"[140]
A. O. Walker, assisted by G. H. Tapley, Messrs. A Housley, M. Housely, Rex, Saulsbury, Thomas
(*Music by* Chris Smith. *Lyrics by* Cecil Mack.)

"Just the Same"

"Somewhere"[141]
H. Troy, Chorus
(*Music and Lyrics by* F. H. Williams, Joe Jordan.)

"Late Hours"[142]
B. A. Williams, assisted by W. C. Elkins
(*Music by* Bert A. Williams. *Lyrics by* David Kempner.)

"Bon Bon Buddie" (Bon-Bon-Buddy)
G. W. Walker
(*Lyrics by* Alex Rogers.)

ACT 3[143]

Drill
G. W. Walker, Men

"Ethiopia" (Ballet)
A. O. Walker, Girls
(*Music by* Al Johns. *Created by* Aida Overton Walker.)
Introducing "The Merry Widow Waltz" in Black.

"Me to Me Is Me"[144]
B. A. Williams

Finale
B. A. Williams, George W. Walker

Replaced for subsequent tour by:

"Any Old Place in Yankee Land Is Good Enough for Me"
B. A. Williams, G. W. Walker, Company

[139]Replaced during the run by:

"When I Was Sweet Sixteen"
L. Williams

[140]Published as "It's Hard to Love Somebody (Who's Loving Somebody Else)." During the subsequent tour, "Hard to Love Somebody" was joined in medley by "I'm Just Crazy 'Bout You." Later replaced by:

"The Sheath Gown in Darktown"
A. O. Walker, assisted by Sheath Girls
(*Music by* J. Leubrie Hill. *Lyrics by* Mord Allen.)

[141]During the New York run, joined in medley by "Somewhere":
(*Music by* Bert Williams, Joe Jordan, F. H. Williams. *Lyrics* by Dave Kemper, Joe Jordan, F. H. Williams.)

Both were replaced during subsequent tour by:

"In My Own Home"
H. Troy, Chorus
(*Music by* Tom Lemonier. *Lyrics* by Mord Allen.)

[142]Replaced at different times for subsequent tour by:

"At Peace Wid de World"
B. A. Williams
(*Music by* Bert Williams. *Lyrics* by Mord Allen.)
"Drinkin'"
B. A. Williams

[143]Between Acts 2 and 3 an Intermezzo was added during the New York run and tour:

"Maori" (A Samoan Dance)
William H. Tyers

For subsequent tour, Act 3 was thoroughly revised as follows:

The Dancing of Salome (later dropped)
A. O. Walker
(*Music and Orchestrations by* Joseph Jordan.)

"Southland"
Miss Clough, Chorus
(Very likely interpolated from THE SHOO-FLY REGIMENT, *Music by* J. Rosamond Johnson, *Lyrics by* James Weldon Johnson.)

"Down Among the Sugar Cane"
Muriel and Jennie Ringgold

"I'm Tired of Eatin' in Restaurants"
B. A. Williams

"(You're in the) Right Church But the Wrong Pew"
B. A. Williams
(*Music by* Chris Smith. *Lyrics* by R. C. McPherson.)

Finale
Entire Company

[144]Replaced after opening by:

"I'd Rather Have Nothin' All de Time Than Somethin fo' a Little While"
B. A. Williams
(*Music by* Bert Williams. *Lyrics* by John Lowitz.)
Which was then replaced by:

"Somebody Lied to Me" (Nothing Personal)
B. A. Williams
(*Music and Lyrics* by Jeff T. Branen, Evans Lloyd, adapted by Bert Williams.)

[145]Played a subsequent week 2 March 1908 at the Grand Opera House for 8 performances.

1908.09 FIFTY MILES FROM BOSTON

A Rural Play with Music in Three Acts. Book, music and lyrics by George M. Cohan. Directed by George M. Cohan. Settings by Ernest Albert, Young Brothers and Boss Company. Costumes by F. Richard Anderson. Orchestra under the direction of Al E. Gaylord. Orchestrations by Charles J. Gebest. Produced by Sam H. Harris and George M. Cohan. Opened 3 February 1908 at the Garrick Theatre and closed 29 February 1908 after 32 performances[145].

CAST: *Joe Westcott*: LAURENCE WHEAT. *Nathan Westcott*, Joe's father: JAMES H. BRADBURY. *Dave Harrigan*, the Brookfield dude: GEORGE PARSONS. *Tim Harrigan*, Dave's father: JAMES C. MARLOWE. *Moseley*, Westcott's man: Richard Nesmith. *Eddie Moseley*, boy around the barn: Master LORES GRIMM. *Jed Woodis*, Sadie's brother: JOHN WESTLEY. *Foreman Brookfield Hose*: Sim Pulen. *Fat Boy*: Russell Pincus. *Brainerd*: Frank Bouman. *John*: Charles Cartwell. *Mary*: Laura Harris. *Mrs. Westcott*, Joe's mother: Mrs. Louise Rial. *Mrs. Tilford*, everybody's favorite: EMMA JANVIER. *Nellie Harrigan*, Tim Harrigan's daughter: Hazel Lowry. *Aunt Kate*: Alice Parks Warren. *Sadie Woodis*, the Postmistress: EDNA WALLACE HOPPER. *Town Girls, High School Boys, Firemen, Salesladies, Base Ball Players, Brookfield Band, etc.*

Town Girls: Misses Elizabeth Young, Nellie Young, Beatrice Harris, Evelyn Meredith, Jewel Meredith, Madalin Frank, Flossie Martin, Sylvia Clarke, Ethel Vivian, Bertha Arnold, Dot Courtney. *High School Boys*: Messrs. Lester Templeton, John Edwards, Lawrence Dowd, John Meehan, William Sissons, Kent Ebersal, John Harrington, Stanley Fields, E. Paul Souther, Ernest Sharrock.

Act 1: Exterior of Westcott House. (Young Brothers, Boss.)

Act 2: Interior of Woodies Home. (Albert.)

Act 3: Public Square, Brookfield. Two hours later. (Young Brothers, Boss.)

MUSICAL NUMBERS

"Jack and Jill"
E. W. Hopper, Chorus

"A Small Town Gal" (The Small Town Girl)
L. Wheat, Chorus

"(The) Boys Who Fight the Flames"
L. Grimm, Chorus

"Waltz with Me"
L. Wheat, E. W. Hopper, Chorus, C. Cartmell, L. Harris

"Ain't It Awful"
E. Janvier

"Harrigan"
J. C. Marlowe, Chorus

1908.10 NEARLY A HERO

A Farce with Music in Three Acts. Book by Harry B. Smith. Music by Seymour Furth. Lyrics by Edward B. Claypoole and Will Heelan. Staged by George Marion and J. C. Huffman. Dances arranged by William Rock. Settings by Arthur Voegtlin, Edward G. Unitt. Costumes by Castel-Bert, Miss Finch; men's costumes by Ritchie Harnden, Charles Swarns. Orchestra under the direction of Oscar Radin. Produced by Sam S. Shubert and Lee Shubert (Inc.). Opened 24 February 1908 at the Casino Theatre and closed 6 June 1908 after 116 performances[146].

CAST: *Ludwig Knoedler*, nearly the hero of the day: SAM BERNARD. *Jabez Doolittle*, with padlocks on his hip pockets: SAM EDWARDS. *Moreau*, a theatrical costumer: Robert Paton Gibbs. *Fred Doolittle*: BURRELL BARBARETTO. *Harold Percy Montague*: EDGAR NORTON. *Wade Waters*, a bathing master: Franklyn Roberts. *Plympton*, an English footman: R. Franklyn. *Count Orloff*: Louis Helie. *Angeline DeVere*, a queen of musical comedy: ETHEL LEVEY. *Gwenolyn Doolittle*, a matinee girl of romantic dispositions: ADA LEWIS. *Edith*, the girl next door: NEVA AYMAR. *Mrs. Doolittle*, who does not care what she does with her husband's money: ZELDA SEARS. *Francine*, a French maid: ELIZABETH BRICE. *Marie*, cashier at Moreau's shop: Daisy Greene. *Estelle Puffenkranz*: Virginia Marshall. *Geraldine Murphy*: Lillian Harris. *Pussy Foote*: Vaughn Sargent. *Marian Love*: Maxine Revillion. *Hildegarde Jones*: Susan Pitt. *Laura Lee*: Dorothy Watson. *Connie Moore*: Albertine Sargent. *Nora Mooney*: Doris Cameron. *Hazel Dayton*: Marian Alexander.

Others who sing and dance are: (Misses) Ethel Laurence, Miss Carr, Rita Lancaster, Dorothy Lancaster, Alice Knowlton, Jane Brown, Adelaide Lehr, Edith Gervan, Alice Eis, Ethel Wheeler, Edith Warner, Josephine Kernell, Nancy Poole, Katherine Robertson, Violet Moore. Messrs. W. F. Fair, W. A. Hungerford, Louis Austin, Fred Gray, Cyril Chadwick, William Davis, Victor LeRoy, Samuel Lindsay, W. Slick, Richard J. Kirkwood.

Act 1: A bridge whist party and fancy dress German at the residence of Mr. Doolittle, Riverside Drive. (Unitt).

Act 2: The fitting room at Moreau's costuming establishment. (Voegtlin).

Act 3: Mr. Doolittle's villa at Seabright. (Voegtlin).

ACT 1[146a]

Opening Chorus

"Bridge"
Z. Sears

"After Office Hours"
B. Barbaretto, Chorus

"I Don't Want to Marry You"
B. Barbaretto, N. Aymar
(*Music and Lyrics by* Edward B. Claypoole.)

"(My) Sahara Girl" (My Sahara Belle)
E. Levey
(*Music by* Edward B. Claypoole. *Lyrics by* Harry B. Smith.)

"Waltz and Two-Step" (Minuet)
E. Levey, N. Aymar, A. Lewis

Finale

ACT 2

"Stitch, Stitch"[147] (Opening Chorus)

"Don't You Ever Tell I Told You"
D. Greene, Chorus

"I'm So Particular"[148]
E. Levey
(*Music by* Louis A. Hirsch. *Lyrics by* Matt Woodward.)

"I Was a Hero (Too)"
S. Bernard
(*Music by* Egbert Van Alstyne. *Lyrics by* Harry Williams.)

"My Washy Washy Beau"[149]
Chorus of Girls

"Not Really"
E. Norton, Girls

"Mary! My Heather Belle" (Mary! My Heather Queen)
B. Barbaretto, Girls
(*Music by* Louis A. Hirsch. *Lyrics by* John B. Lowitz.)

"The Queen of Belle Parce"
E. Levey, Men

Finale

ACT 3[150]

Opening Chorus

"I Want a (Fine Little) Steam Yacht"
E. Brice, Chorus
(*Music by* Herman Avery Wade. *Lyrics by* Paul West.)

"The Drawing Lesson"[151]
Octette

"The Walking Tour"
N. Aymar, D. Greene, E. Brice, Chorus

Specialty
E. Levey

"A Singer Sang a Song"
S. Bernard
(*Music by* Seymour Furth. *Lyrics by* Will Heelan.)

Finale

[146]Played a return engagement 19 October 1908 at the Grand Opera House for 8 performances.

[146a]Interpolated after opening as per published sheet music:
"What Makes the World Go Round"
N. Aymar
(*Music by* Egbert Van Alstyne. *Lyrics by* Harry Williams.)

[147]Dropped after opening.

[148]Replaced for subsequent tour by: "I Was Married Once" (Song) Grace LaRue {Angeline DeVere} Which was later replaced by:"La Belle Lizette" Daisy Leon {Francine}, Chorus "Highland Mary" (from THE WHITE CAT) G. LaRue (*Music by* Jean Schwartz. *Lyrics by* William Jerome.)

[149]Dropped after opening.

[150]The running order of Act 3 was revised during the run. Added to Act 3 after "The Drawing Lesson":
"When Miss Patricia Salome Dances the Do-La-Palome" (From FOLLIES OF 1907)
N. Bayes
(*Music by* Harry Von Tilzer. *Lyrics by* Vincent Bryan.)

[151]Replaced for subsequent tour by:
"It's a Matter of Opinion After All"
G. LaRue

1908.11 THE BIG STICK

The Four Mortons in a Play with Music in Three Acts. Play by George V. Hobart. Stage direction by Charley Grapewin. Musical director, Leon Polachek. Manager, John P. Daly. Opened 24 February 1908 at the West End Theatre and closed 29 February 1908 after 8? performances; returned 16 March 1908 at the Metropolis Theatre and closed 21 March 1908 after 9 performances.

CAST (in order of appearance): *Guinevere*, the cook: May Thompson. *Egbert Penrose*, not himself!: Frank Sheen. *Mrs. Donahue*: KATE MORTON. *Danny Donahue*: PAUL MORTON. *Vecchio Giovani*, a padrone: Ernest Mack. *Dolly Donahue*: CLARA MORTON. *Daniel Donahue*, a contractor: SAM MORTON. *John Flint*, a money shark: Butler Mandeville. *Professor Bauerschmidt*, a music teacher: Tony Hart. *Gladiolus Montgomery*, in employ of Flint: Marion Sherwood. *Mrs. Fitzhugh*, who minds everybody's business: Margaret Flavin. *Muggins*, a servant: Butler Mandeville. *American Ladies' Quartette*: *Marie Lusardi*: Agnes Williamson. *Gertrude Fitzgerald*: Edyth Warner. *Gladys Howard*: Jeanne Edwards. *Edan Hyde*: Lexie Clarke.

Act 1: Sitting-room of Donahue's residence. Long Island City, New York. Present.

Act 2: Exterior of Donahue's home. Two weeks later.

Act 3: Future home of (the) Donahue's, Riverside Drive, New York. Two days later.

MUSICAL NUMBERS

"I (Would) Still Love You"
C. Morton
(*Music by* C. W. Murphy. *Lyrics by* Harry Castling.)

"Christine Swanson"
P. Morton

The American Ladies' Quartette
J. Edwards, L. Clarke, A. Williamson, E. Warner

"Since Arrah Wanna Married Barney Carney"
C. Morton
(*Music by* Theodore Morse. *Lyrics by* Jack Drislane.)

Instrumental Ensemble
The Four Mortons
"I'm Afraid to Come Home in the Dark" (from A KNIGHT FOR A DAY)
C. Morton
(*Music by* Egbert Van Alstyne. *Lyrics by* Harry Williams.)
"Too a roi-oor a Loi-a"
C. Morton
Piano Dance
The Four Mortons

1908.12 BUSY IZZY'S BOODLE

A Musical Comedy in Two Acts[152]. Book by Frank Kennedy. Music and lyrics by William J. McKenna. Staged by Frank Mason. Scenery by Resig's. Electrical effects by Kliegl Brothers. Musical director, G. W. Herdicks. Produced by E. D. Stair. Opened 6 April 1908 at the West End Theatre and closed 13 April 1908 after 9 performances.[153]

CAST: *Busy Izzy Mark*, with the Mazuma: GEORGE SIDNEY. *Will Steele*, a Promoter: EZRA MATTHEWS. *Lem Soakum*, the Sheriff: FRED LAW. *Silvester Parbola*, in love with Rosetta: VICTOR CASMORE. *Hooley Happigan*, always butting in: Charles LoMier. *Flip*, the office boy: Nick Basil. *Clipper Bond*, a Banker: Frank Gibbons. *Ben Barnacle*, an old sea dog: Frank Gibbons. *Tee Totaler*, on the wagon: Ray Montgomery. *Eleanor Bond*, Clipper's daughter: Mabel Melvine. *Fluffy*, Flip's sweetheart: Trixie Mantell. *Maria Nightmare*, looking for her affinity: Helen LoMier. *Fortune Teller*: Freda Florence. *Rosetta Kremona*, the Italian organ-grinder: CARRIE WEBBER. *Bankers, Brokers, Sailors.*

Act 1: The Bank.

Act 2: The Boat.

ACT 1
Opening Chorus
Company
"My Sweet"
N. Basil, T. Mantell
"That's What My Organ Plays"
C. Webber, Company
"Dot's Right"
G. Sidney, Company
"Zoo Loo"
E. Matthews, Company
"To Be an Actor"
G. Sidney, F. Law, C. Webber
"Under the Mazuma Tree"
G. Sidney, C. Webber, Company
"When You're Sailing"
Company
"Good-Bye Sweetheart"
M. Melvine, Company
"Four Onions"
G. Sidney, L. Law, C. LoMier, F. Gibbons

ACT 2
"Nonsense"
G. Sidney, C. Webber
"Cherry"
G. Sidney, Company
"I Want a Gibson Man" (Double Octette)
"The Circus Queen"
C. Webber, Company
"The Breakway"
Company

[152]A sequel to BUSY IZZIE (16 March 1903, 58th Street), and revised version of THE MAZUMA MAN (30 September 1907, Yorkville), with which it shares much plot, characters, songs and actors in common.
[153]Costumes uncredited.

1908.13 THE FLOWER OF THE RANCH

A Comedy with Music (Musical Comedy Melodrama[154]) in Three Acts. Book, music and lyrics by Joseph E. Howard. Dramatic staging by Joseph E. Howard. Ensemble numbers staged by Ned Wayburn. Musical director, Dayton C. Paine. Produced by Joseph E. Howard Amusement Company, Inc. Opened 20 April 1908 at the Majestic Theatre and closed 2 May 1908 after 16 performances[155].

CAST: *Pete*, the barkeep at Little Flower's shack: Ike Oliver. *Shorty*, a cowpuncher from Farnum's Big Horn Ranch: Frederick Rogers. *Sergeant McGinty*, U.S.A., of the garrison at Fort Custer: J. P. McSweeney. *O'Kinahoke*, the Navajo Chief: MART LORENZ. *Dick Spaulding*, a graduate of West Point: John Todd. *Cheyenne Charlie* of the days of '49: FREDERICK KNIGHT. *Toni Miguel*, a greaser: A. A. Klein. *Judge Hopper*, foster daddy to Little Flower: William Betts. *Skivers*, a tenderfoot from Maine: EDWARD HUME. *Timberline Ike*, a bad man from Farnum's Big Horn Ranch: Earl Stanley. *Bob Brandon*, the sheriff: Severin DeDeyn. *Waunetta*, the dancing girl: LA PETITE ADELAIDE. *Margaret Merron*, the new schoolmarm: Alma Youlin. *Little Flower*, a California bud: MABEL BARRISON. *Jack Farnum*, the owner of Big Horn Ranch: JOSEPH E. HOWARD. *Friends of Margaret from the East (6): Miss Behave*: Forest Doolittle. *Miss Fortune*: Katherine Tormey. *Miss Taken*: Verna Miller. *Miss Judge*: Leona Remington. *Miss Trust*: Ruth Addington. *Miss Understand*: Ella Brandle.
Broncho Busters: Misses Jessie Buckley, Janet MacDonald, Margaret Davis, Lol Marlow, Emma Amsler, Camille Aster, Camille LaVille, Claudine Tienette. *Cow Punchers*: Messrs. Pickering, Williams, Delaney, Rogers, Short, Fagin, Marion. *Indians, Soldiers, U. S. Officers, etc.*

The action takes place at the present time in Tomahawk, California.

Act 1: Interior Little Flower's general store and Post Office. Late in the afternoon.

Act 2: Jack Farnum's camp on his Big Horn Ranch. Early the next morning.

Act 3: Exterior officers' quarters and barracks at Fort Custer, Tomahawk. The shank of that evening.

ACT 1
"In the Shack That Little Flower Built" (Opening Chorus)
"The Light That Lies in Women's Eyes"
A. Youlin, Male Chorus
"California, (Claremont)"
M. Barrison, Male Chorus, Broncho Busters
(*Lyrics by* Collin Davis.)
"Just Say You Care"
M. Barrison, J. E. Howard
"The Round-Up"
Ensemble
"Worried"
M. Barrison, E. Hume
(*Lyrics by* Collin Davis.)

ACT 2
"Lo-Lo" (My Lolo Maid)
M. Lorenz, Chorus
(*Lyrics by* Collin Davis.)
"That's What a Fellow Does When He's in Love"
M. Barrison
"Love Up a Tree"
E. Hume, Chorus
(*Lyrics by* Collin Davis.)
"What's the Use of Dreaming"
J. E. Howard
"In the Days of '49"
F. Knights, Chorus

ACT 3
"The Garrison Ball" (Opening):
Ensemble
Grand March; "Come On, the Music Is Fine"; Solo Dance
La Petite Adelaide
"(The Big) Banshee"
J. E. Howard, Chorus
(*Lyrics by* Frank R. Adams, Will M. Hough.)

[154]Billed as a Western Play with Music on its sheet music in its Chicago production prior to New York.
[155]Prior to its Broadway run, THE FLOWER OF THE RANCH played 9 March 1908 at the West End Theatre in Harlem for 1 week.

"The Pajama and the Nightie"
M. Barrison, E. Hume, Chorus
"The Same Old Story"
M. Barrison, J. E. Howard
(*Lyrics by* Arthur Gillespie.)
Imitation of "The Merry Widow" Waltz Scene[156]
M. Barrison, J. E. Howard
Finale
Entire Company

1908.14 THE YANKEE PRINCE

A Timely Satire on Titled Fortune Hunters (Musical Play) in Three Acts[157]. Book, music and lyrics by George M. Cohan. Staged by George M. Cohan. Scenery by John Young. Costumes by Klaw and Erlanger's Costume Company. Orchestra under the direction of Charles J. Gebest[158]. Orchestrations by Charles J. Gebest. Produced by Sam H. Harris and George M. Cohan. Opened 20 April 1908 at the Knickerbocker Theatre, closing 11 July 1908 after 84 performances; re-opened 3 August 1908 at the Knickerbocker Theatre and closed 29 August 1908 after an additional 28 performances. Total: 112 performances[159].

CAST: *Franklin Fielding*: JERRY J. COHAN. *Percy Springer*: GEORGE M. COHAN. *Whiteside Webster*: JACK GARDNER. *Karl of Weymouth*: FRANK HOLLINS. *Steve Daly*: TOM LEWIS. *John Fagan*: SAM J. RYAN. *DeVrie*: J. Liquel Lanoe. *Duke of Dollsford*: Robert Emmett Lennon. *Mrs. Fielding*: HELEN F. COHAN. *Evelyn Fielding*: JOSEPHINE COHAN. *Lillian Lloyd*: ESTELLE WENTWORTH. *Gertrude Spivans*: STELLA HAMMERSTEIN. *Detective*: William Leyle. *Guard*: William Leyle. *Waiter*: Donald Crisp. *Policeman*: Donald Crisp. *Bellboy*: John Jarrott.

Pages to the Court Ladies: Misses Grace Kimball, May Maloney, Elizabeth Young, Helen Morrison, Edna Hixon, Gussie Girard, Etta Woodward, Larene Cumley. *Ladies of the Court*: Misses Lila Rhodes, Aline Bartlett, Clara Whiteford, Beatrice Whiteford, Mamie Gilbert, Ethel Fairbanks, Vinie Danvers. *Tourists*: Misses Mamie Gildea, Vivian Densmore, Helen Gardner, Edna Marsh, Amelia Linden, Rose Walden, Daisy Thompson, Eleanor Richmond. *The King's Guards*: Messrs. O'Keefe, Blackford, Leonard, Hovey, Cody, Klendon, Deagon, Cushing, Fried, Gilmore, McCartney, Loomis, Turpie, Murphy. *Coster Boys and Girls*: Lila Rhodes, Mr. O'Keefe, Aline Bartlett, Mr. Cody, Clara Whiteford, Mr. Klendon, Beatrice Whiteford, Mr. Cushing, Mamie Gilbert, Mr. Gilmore, Grace Russell, Mr. Halstead, Ethel Fairbanks, Mr. McCartney, Vinie Danvers, Mr. Hovey.

Act 1: Tea Room, Savoy Hotel, London, England.

Act 2: Exterior, Windsor Castle.

Act 3: Exterior, Fielding Home, Chicago.

ACT 1
"Showing the Yankees London Town"
J. Gardner, Chorus
"Come On Down Town"
S. J. Ryan, Chorus
"Villains in the Play"
J. Gardner, E. Wentworth
"I'm Going to Marry a Nobleman"
Josephine Cohan, Chorus
"Characteristic Waltz" (Yankee Prince Waltz)
G. M. Cohan, Josephine Cohan
(*Music by* George M. Cohan and Charles J. Gebest.)
"Yankee Doodle Come to Town"
G. M. Cohan, Company
ACT 2
"Soldiers of the King"
Chorus
"I'm Awfully Strong for You"
J. Gardner
"I Say, Flo"
Coster Boys and Girls
"The A-B-Cs of the U. S. A."
G. M. Cohan, Josephine Cohan
"M-O-N-E-Y" (Comedy Quartette)
G. M. Cohan, S. J. Ryan, J. Gardner, T. Lewis
"Tommy Atkins, You're All Right"
E. Wentworth, Chorus
"A Song of the King"
R. E. Lennon, Chorus
(March and Drill arranged by James Gorman.)
ACT 3
Opening Chorus
"From the Land of (My) Dreams"
E. Wentworth, Chorus
"Think It Over Carefully"[160]
G. M. Cohan
"(Cohan's) Rag Babe" (New Kind of Two Step)[161]
G. M. Cohan, Josephine Cohan, Chorus
Finale
Company

1908.15 THE MERRY-GO-ROUND

A Musical Comedy in Two Balmy Breaths from Bohemia (Two Acts), 5 Scenes. Book by Edgar Smith. Music by Gus Edwards. Lyrics by Paul West. Production staged by George Marion. Chorus numbers and dances staged by Joseph C. Smith. Scenery by Frank Dodge and Matt. Morgan. Costumes designed by William H. Matthews. Produced by the Circle Production Company. Opened 25 April 1908 at the Circle Theatre (Gus Edwards' Music Hall) and closed 18 July 1908 after 97 performances.

CAST: *"Hen" Stubbs*, a Reuben with Metropolitan tastes and a hankering for vaudeville: JAMES J. MORTON. *Morris Nosenstein*, a promoter of vaudeville sensations: BOBBY NORTH. *Casimir de Cliquot*, aristocrat by birth and Bohemian by fate: IGNACIO MARTINETTI. *Jack Saudners*, a young American artist: MELVILLE STEWART. *Hiram Spavin*, a veteran of the G.A.R.: Jonathan Keefe. *Richard Niebelung*, former operatic artist and present proprietor of the Cafe Boheme: JAMES B. CARSON. *Alec Smart*, a side-show barker: GEORGE McKAY. *Bill Graftly*, a policeman: GEORGE McKAY. *Ratsy*, newsboy: JOHN CANTWELL. *Swiper*, a pick-pocket: JOHN CANTWELL. *Violet Nearstar*: May Hopkins. *A Side-Show Man*: Arthur Morrison. *A Bearded Lady*: William Sissons. *A Glass Eater*: William Sadler. *A Merry-Go-Round Man*: Jim Kane. *A Farmer*: Vernon Milton. *Another*: Mr. Gibbs. *Martha Scraggs*, a rural maid-of-all-work: MABEL HITE. *Mrs. Wheatly Bungalow*, a young society widow with the usual hunch for a title: DOROTHY JARDON. *Samantha Spavin*, who keeps boarders: Louise Carter. *Jeanne Danvray*, of the Bohemian set: Rita Perkins. *Maggie*, of the candy booth: Mabel Russell. *A Fortune Teller*: Edna Belmont. *A Snake Charmer*: Ethel Southgate. *Dancing Girls*: Lillian Rice, Angie Weimers.

Show Girls: Misses May Hopkins, Ellen Beckwith, Alice Lazar, Joan Sawyer, May Thatcher, Rita Dean, Hilda V. Lawrence, Virginia Adams. *Jockeys, Belles, Country Girls, Flower Girls, Shop Girls, Show Girls, Models, Sightseers, Burglars*: Misses May Hopkins, Ellen Beckwith, May Thatcher, Mae Murray, Bobby Manning, Rita Dean, Alice Lazar, Virginia Adams, Julia Mooney, Lillian Hazel, Regina Connelly, Jeanette Alpine, Gypsy Mooney, Ethel Kelly, Ocie Willaims, Maude Adams, Marjorie Stewart, Flora Crosbie, Jean Davidson, Edna Belmont, Ethel Southgate, Edythe Graham, May Barrell, Millie Woods, May Kingdon, Marjorie Race, Fay Tincher, Stella Mauray, Florence Jackson, Erna Evans, Suzanne Johnston, Viola Adams, Pearl Gabrielle, Jeanne Macpherson.

Act 1: The County Fair Grounds, Mineola.

Act 2, Scene 1: The Shopping District, New York City. *Scene 2*: Jack Saunders' Studio, four months later. *Scene 3*: Exterior of Café La Boheme. *Scene 4*: New Year's Eve at La Boheme.

---

[156]Courtesy of Henry W. Savage.
[157]Billed as "George M. Cohan and His Royal Family in a Timely Satire on Titled Fortune Hunters."
[158]Special drum effects by Samuel Avedon.
[159]Played a return engagement 1 February 1909 at the Grand Opera House for 7 performances.

[160] Replaced during subsequent tour by:
"Nothing New Beneath the Sun"
G. M. Cohan
[161] Replaced during subsequent tour by:
"The Dancing Ceremony"
G. M. Cohan, Josephine Cohan, S. J. Ryan, Chorus

ACT 1[162]

"It's a Fair Day for a Fair-day" (Opening Chorus)

"Rubens on Broadway"[163]
G. McKay, J. Cantwell, M. Russell

"I Like Them Just Like You, Little Girl"
I. Martinetti, Swells, Belles

"I'm a Two-Horse Fellow in a One-Horse Town"
J. J. Morton, Company

"Stupid Mr. Cupid"
M. Hite
(*Music by* Theodore Morse. *Lyrics by* Edward Madden.)

"Betty You're the One Best Bet"
J. Cantwell, L. Rice, A. Weimers, Jockey Shrimps

"I Won't Be Home for Dinner" (I Won't Be Home Tonight)
D. Jardon

"I'm the Captain of the Mineola Guards" (Finale)
M. Stewart, Company

ACT 2[164]

Scene 1

"Shopping" (Opening Chorus)

"Have You Seen My Baby?"
M. Russell

Burlesque Medley of Grand Operas
B. North

"I Really Hate to Talk About Myself"[165]
M. Hite

"The Shop Window Girls"[166]
I. Martinetti
(*Lyrics by* Will D. Cobb.)

James J. Morton in a Merry Monologue

Scene 2

"In a Studio" (Opening Chorus)
D. Jardon, Artists and Models

"When the Music Starts to Play"
M. Stewart
(*Cello accompaniment by* Miss Rita Perkins.)

"He's A-my Brud" (My Brud Sylvest)
M. Hite
(*Music by* Fred Fisher. *Lyrics by* Jesse Lasky.)

Scene 3

"(We're the) Orchids of the Opera"
Opera Goers

Scene 4

"Goodbye Old Year, Welcome New" (Opening Chorus)

"Gold Cure Dance"
L. Rice, A. Weimers

"The Tipsy Swell and the Messenger Boy"
G. McKay, J. Cantwell

"I Met Her at the Metropole (But I Lost Her at Jack's)" (My Cafe Girl)
I. Martinetti

[162]Interpolated as per published sheet music:
"My Boy Bill"
M. Russell
(*Music by* John W. Bratton. *Lyrics by* Paul West.)

[163]Replaced early in the run by:
"Down on the Foolish Farm"
M. Russell, G. McKay, J. Cantwell

[164]The running order of songs was revised during the run and for tour.
Added late in the run:
"Recollections" (Scene 2, before "He's a my Brud")
Raymond Hitchcock {Hen Stubbs)
"There Comes a Night" (Scene 4, before "I Met Her at the Metropole")
R. Hitchcock
"Obadiah McIntire"
R. Hitchcock
(*Music and Lyrics by* Dan J. Sullivan.)

[165]Replaced for subsequent tour by:
"I Want to Be Loved Like a Leading Lady"
Cathryn Rowe Palmer {Martha Scraggs}

[166]Replaced early in the run by:
"My Little Tailor Maid"
I. Martinetti
(*Lyrics by* Will D. Cobb and Paul West.)

1908.16 THE GAY MUSICIAN

A Comic Opera in Two Acts. Book and lyrics by Edward Siedle and Charles Campbell[167]. Music by Julian Edwards. Staged by Julian Edwards. Dances arranged by Roger Gray. Settings by James Fox, Ernest Albert. Costumes by Mme. Castel-Bert. Orchestra under the direction of Antonio DeNovellis. Produced by John P. Slocum for The Amusement Producing Company, Inc. Opened 18 May 1908 at Wallack's Theatre and closed 6 June 1908 after 21 performances.

CAST: *Eugene Dubois*, an ambitious young composer: WALTER PERCIVAL. *Mr. Samuel Lyons*, manager of the Novelty Theatre, New York: EDWARD MARTINDELL. *The Hon. Clarence Beresford*: CHARLES WELLESLEY. *Captain George Fish*, retired sea captain: JOSEPH C. MIRON. *A. Corker*, retired wine merchant: Charles Campbell. *Hank Hickory*: L. R. Lefferson. *Members of the Glee Club (4)*: *Harry Woods*: F. W. Faber. *Walker Baker*: Eugene Herbert. *John Smith*: Thomas B. McCormick. *Tom Murray*: A. L. Whitman. *Maude Granville*, prima donna of the Novelty Theatre, New York: AMELIA STONE. *Marie Dubois*, wife of Eugene: SOPHIE BRANDT. *Matila Yager*, his mother-in-law: Martha George. *Hilda Branson*, soubrette of the Novelty Theatre, New York: OLGA VON HATZFELD. *Kitty Connor*, servant of Marie: Katherine Moran. *Suzanne*, French maid in service of Maude: Katherine Moran. *Delia*, servant of Maude: Dollie Eads. *Members of the Glee Club (4)*: *Dorothy*: Florence Lindley. *Helen Knowles*: Francesca LeClair. *Olie Weber*: Gabrielle Bacot. *Lilly Sherwood*: Jean Erickson. *Modistes*: Gertrude Williams, Jacquette Murphy, Gertrude Thurston. *Milliners*: Grace Wilson, Margaret Von Keese, Lorie Sprague, Katherine Howland. *Shop Girls*: Camille Lavis, Jean Pearson, Gertrude Gibbons. *Messengers*: Messrs. A. L. Whitman, T. B. McCormick. *Servants in Maude's House*: Messrs. Eugene Herbert, F. W. Turner. *Delivery Drivers*: Messrs. Thomas W. Faber, Roy Torrey, George Coburn, A. Strizck. *Members of the Glee Club, Modistes, Milliners, Shop Girls, Footmen, Servants, Florists, Messengers, etc.*

Act 1: The Home of Eugene Dubois, Bensonhurst. (Fox.)

Act 2: Hall in the Home of Maude Granville, New York City. (Albert.)

ACT 1

"We Won't Do a Thing to His Opera" (Opening Chorus)
Members of the Glee Club

"Hail to the Queen of Beauty" (Ensemble)
W. Percival, Chorus

"Lovelight" (The Lovelight Beaming from Your Eyes)(Ballad)
W. Percival

"That's How I Got Treated" (Song)
J. C. Miron

"The Saucy Sparrow" (Song)
S. Brandt

"My Dashing Soldier Boy" (My Soldier Boy)(Ensemble and Song)
A. Stone, Chorus

"The Box Office Tells the Story"[168]
E. Martindell, Chorus

"That Melody" (Quartette)
A. Stone, M. George, S. Brandt, W. Percival

"At Last, at Last (I Hold You)" (Octette)
A. Stone, O. Von Hatzfeld, S. Brandt, M. George, W. Percival, E. Martindell, C. Wellesley, J. C. Miron

"Daintily Lightly" (Ensemble and Song)
E. Matindell, Ladies of the Glee Club

"D'une Coquete" (Dance)
O. Von Hatzfeld

"Allez! Houp La!" (Finale)

[167] Subsequent touring programs credit the book to Siedle and lyrics to Campbell.

[168] Dropped for subsequent tour.

ACT 2

"What a Dry World This Would Be" (Opening Chorus)
O. Von Hatzfeld, Chorus

"A Cup of Tea"
A. Stone, O. Von Hatzfeld, Chorus

"(It's) The Unexpected Happens"
A. Stone, O. Von Hatzfeld, E. Martindell, C. Wellesley

"I Have My Doubts" (Duet)
A. Stone, W. Percival

"(It's) A Long, Long Time" (Quintette)
W. Percival, E. Martindell, C. Wellesley, J. C. Miron, C. Campbell

"Not as Simple as I Look" (Song)
S. Brandt

"I Want to be Your (Blue-Eyed) Baby Boy" (Duet)
M. George, J. C. Miron

"Come Along, It's a Trifling Affair"
Ensemble

"Take That" (Duet)
A. Stone, S. Brandt

Finale

1908.17

MARY'S LAMB

A Musical Gambol (Comedy) in Three Acts. Book, music and lyrics by Richard Carle. Based on the French farce "Mme. Mongodin"[169]. Staged by Richard Carle. Scenery by ?. Costumes by Klaw and Erlanger Costuming Company, Ena Welch[170]. Orchestra under the direction of Frank Darling. Produced by Richard Carle (Manager, Charles Marks). Opened 25 May 1908 at the New York Theatre and closed 18 July 1908 after 64 performances; re-opened 24 August 1908 at the New York Theatre and closed 5 September 1908 after 16 additional performances. Total: 80 performances.

CAST: *Alan Townshend*, an artist: JOHN B. PARK. *"Bill" Blackwell*, from Idaho: FRANK H. BELCHER. *Clyde Wetherbee*, a secretary: Ray Youngman. *Sylvester Q. Nightingale*, a servant: Harry Montgomery. *Judge Henry Gibson*: Abbott Adams. *Mary Miranda Lamb*, a monarch: ELITA PROCTOR OTIS. *Sylvia Montrose*, a retired actress: HENRIETTA LEE. *Mercedes*, her maid: EDITH ST. CLAIR. *Phyllis Atwood*, Lamb's niece: BERTA MILLS. *Weenie*, a Dutch girl: Winifred Gilraine. *Guests (4)*: *Celia Dale*: Marion Mills. *Edna Sydney*: Carmen Espinoza. *Viola Fair*: Rita Stanwood. *Lucille St. John*: Evelyn Richman. *Cadets (4)*: *Horace Drummond*: Walter Paschal. *Willis Brooks*: Howard Hall. *Guy Whitaker*: Paul Souther. *Stacy Miller*: Herman Noble. *Aphrodite*: Herself. *Leander Lamb*, a martyr: RICHARD CARLE. *Guests, Cadets, Maids, Grisettes, Parisian Dandies, Models, Dutch Girls, Cow-Girls.*

The action takes place during the afternoon and evening of the same day at Haverstraw, New York.

Act 1: Drawing-room in Lamb's house, 2 P.M.

Act 2: Alan's Studio, 8 P.M.

Act 3: Same as Act 1, 10 P.M.

ACT 1

"Marching" (from THE SPRING CHICKEN)
M. Mills, Cadets, Guests

"Never Borrow Trouble"
B. Mills, F. H. Belcher

"Betsy's the Belle of the Bathers"[171]
R. Carle, J. B. Park

"Letters"[172] (from THE MAID AND THE MUMMY)
E. St. Clair, J. B. Park
(*Music by* Robert Hood Bowers.)

"Jamais d'La Vie" (French Song)
H. Lee, Chorus

"If No. 1 Met No. 2" (If Number One Met Number Two)
R. Carle, Guests

Finale

ACT 2

"My Madagascar Maid"
J. B. Park, Boys

"The Modest Little Model"
H. Lee, Models

ACT 3

"We're Hollandaise"
W. Gilraine, Dutch Girls

"Love Is Elusive"[173] (from THE TENDERFOOT)
B. Mills
(*Music by* H. L. Heartz.)

"I Idolize Ida"
F. H. Belcher, Boys, Girls

Finale

[169]Adapted into English and produced as "Mrs. Ponderbury's Past."
[170]Costume credits appear only in tryout programs. Settings uncredited.

[171]Published as "Belle of the Bathers."
[172]Replaced for subsequent tour by:
"(Baby and) Nursie" (from THE SPRING CHICKEN)
Mina Davis {Florence N. Gale}
(Music by Robert Hood Bowers.)
[173]Replaced for subsequent tour by:
"Fascinating Venus" (from THE TENDERFOOT)
Nellie Brewster {Phyllis Atwood}

1908–1909 SEASON

Anna Held in MISS INNOCENCE (Photo: Otto Sarony Co., 1908)
Museum of the City of New York

1908–1909 SEASON

1908.18 **THREE TWINS**

A Musical Play in Two Acts. Book by Charles Dickson. Based on Mrs. R. Pacheco's farce "Incog." Music by Karl Hoschna. Lyrics by Otto A. Hauerbach [Harbach]. Staged by Gus Sohlke. Settings by P. Dodd Ackerman. Costumes by Orange Manufacturing Company. Orchestra under the direction of C. DeWitt Coolman. Produced by Joseph M. Gaites. Opened 15 June 1908 at the Herald Square Theatre, closing due to fire 22 December 1908 after 214 performances; re-opened 18 January 1909 at the Majestic Theatre and closed 20 March 1909 after 75 additional performances. Total: 289 performances.

CAST: (in order of appearance): *Ned Maryland*, in love with Isabel: MARTIN BROWN. *General Stanhope*, a martyr to dyspepsia: Joseph Allen. *Tom Stanhope*, his father's son: CLIFTON CRAWFORD. *Kate Armitage*. Tom's sweetheart: ALICE YORKE. *Isabel Howard*, the General's ward: Florence Willard. *Mrs. Dick Winters*, a cheerful weeper: Frances Kennedy. *Molly Sommers*, always happy: BESSIE McCOY. *Dick Winters*, somewhat nervous: Joseph Kaufman. *Harry Winters*, Molly's expected bridegroom: WILLARD CURTISS. *Matthew*, an attendant: Tom McMahon. *Dr. Siegfried Hartman*, B.U.G. N.U.T.: W. J. McCarthy. *Bessie Winters, Richard Winters*, Dick's children: Jo. McIntyre, Connie Farber.

Summer Girls: Misses Jessica Berg, Irene McLaughlin, Virginia Steinhardt, Jessie Stoner, Theresa Powers, Florence Blake, Mona Trieste, Hattie DeVon, Ida Adams, Clara Stanton. *Bathing Girls*: Misses Blanche LaMasney, Ethel Fawcett, Alice Packard, Florrie Madison, Daisy Appelt, Viola Grant, Rae Dixon. *Boating Boys*: Misses Connie Farber, Irene Farber, Bessie Leonard, Hazel Williams, Laura Gaynelle, Eva Mull, Mabel Elmore, Dixie Leigh, Helen Falconer, Jo McIntyre. *Tennis Boys*: Messrs. T. C. MacMahon, Harry Collins, George Ross, Walter Jenkins, C. McKinley, George Mansfield, W. J. Ford, S. Sommerville, Ernest Geyer, Charles Fitz. *Boo Hoo Tee Hee Girls*: Misses Jessica Berg, Irene McLaughlin, Virginia Steinhardt, Jessie Stoner, Theresa Powers, Florence Blake, Mona Trieste, Hattie DeVon, Blanche Wilson, Flora Madison, Clara Stanton, Rae Dickson, Ida Adams. *Trained Nurses*: —. *Sanitarium Visitors*: Misses Jessica Berg, Irene McLaughlin, Virginia Steinhardt, Jessie Stoner, Theresa Powers, Florence Blake, Mona Trieste, Hattie DeVon. *Attendants*: Messrs. T. C. MacMahon, Harry Collins, George Ross, Walter Jenkins, C. McKinley, George Mansfield, W. J. Ford, S. Sommerville, Ernest Geyer, Charles Fitz. *Yama Yama Girls*: Misses Connie Farber, Irene Farber, Bessie Leonard, Hazel Williams, Laura Gaynelle, Eva Mull, Mabel Elmore, Dixie Leigh, Helen Falconer, Jo McIntyre.

The action takes place at the present time in the summer.

Act 1: On the beach at Sea View. (Morning of the boat race.)

Act 2: Reception room of Dr. Hartman's sanitarium. (Visiting day.)

ACT 1

"Summer Pastimes" (Opening Chorus)

"Over There"[1]
C. Crawford

"Good Night, Sweetheart"
C. Crawford, A. Yorke

"Boo-Hoo-Tee-Hee (Ta-Ha)"
F. Kennedy, B. McCoy, Girls

"Cuddle Up a Little Closer, Lovey Mine"
A. Yorke, Chorus
Introducing the Original Tableaux arranged by Gus Sohlke:
Tableau 1: The Seven Ages of Cuddling. *Tableau 2*: Home Again. *Tableau 3*: The Reunion.

Finale

ACT 2

Opening Chorus

"At a Reception"
C. Crawford

"Little Miss Up-to-Date"
M. Brown, F. Willarde

"The Hypnotic Kiss"
C. Crawford, B. McCoy

"The (Little) Girl Up There"[2]
A. Yorke

"(The) Yama Yama Man"
B. McCoy, Yama Yama Girls
(*Lyrics by* Collin Davis.)

Finale

[1]Replaced during the run and for subsequent tour by:
"The Fifth Avenue Brigade"
C. Crawford

[2]Programs refer to a unique device, "a faceograph", invented and patented by Charles DeSoria

1908.19 **(ZIEGFELD) FOLLIES OF 1908**

A Musical Revue in Two Acts, 10 Scenes[3]. Words (Sketches and lyrics) by Harry B. Smith. Music by Maurice Levi. Principals directed by Herbert Gresham. Ensemble numbers produced by Julian Mitchell. Settings by John H. Young. Costumes by Alfredo Edel, F. Richard Anderson, Mme. E. S. Freisinger, Hafleigh, William H. Matthews. Lighting by Tony Greshoff. Orchestra under the direction of Frederic Solomon. Conceived and produced by Florenz Ziegfeld. Opened 15 June 1908 at the Jardin de Paris, moved 7 September 1908 to the New York Theatre and closed 26 September 1908 after 120 performances.

CAST: (in order of appearance): Act 1: *Eve*: LUCY WESTON. *Adam*: BARNEY BERNARD. *Satanette*: NORA BAYES. *Cain and Abel*: Daisy Green, Gertrude Vanderbilt. *A Mosquito from New Jersey*: Grace Leigh. *Miss Manhattan*: GRACE LaRUE. *Nervy Nat*: HARRY WATSON. *Leery Louie*: GEORGE BICKEL. *Diamond Dan*: ARTHUR DEAGON. *An American Heiress*: Elphye Snowden. *Another*: Eva Francis. *Flower Girl*: May Mackenzie. *Italian Boy*: NORA BAYES. *Prince de Jagon*: William Powers. *Count Boneless*: Seymour Brown. *Duke d'Aboozy*: William C. Schrode. *Earl of Yabra*: Billie Reeves. *Goldie Rocks*: Lillian Lee. *Phil Fuller*: Billie Reeves. *The Latest Parisian Creation*: MLLE. DAZIE. *Miss Columbia*: Lucy Weston. *Carmen*: William C. Schrode. *Marguerite*: William Powers. *Cleopatra*: Billie Reeves. *Coquette*: GEORGE BICKEL. *"My Policy"*: ARTHUR DEAGON. *Ruler of the Universe*: HARRY WATSON. *Big Hats Girls*: Misses Emory, Paul, Vernon, Washburn, Bowers, Summers.

Act 2: *A Perfect Lady*: Lillian Lee. *A Perfect Gent*: Billie Reeves. *Mrs. Smarte*: Grace Leigh. *Toy Dresser*: Lee Harrison. *Captain of the Precinct*: Alfred Froome. *Red Leary*: ARTHUR DEAGON. *Nibsy Hooligan*: HARRY WATSON. *The Nell Brinkley Girl*: Annabelle Whitford. *Brinkley Girls*: Misses Washburn, Paul, V. Powers, M. Leslie, Vernon, Clark, West, Daniels, Murray. *Mr. Wiseheimer*: BARNEY BERNARD. *Walker*: HARRY WATSON. *Rider*: GEORGE BICKEL. *Madame Sneezeankoffsky*: Grace Leigh. *Girl Orchestra Leader*: Elphye Snowden. *Girls of Orchestra*: Misses Daniels, Washburn, Paul, V. Bowers, Westbrook. *Two Musicians*: HARRY WATSON, GEORGE BICKEL.

Groups in the International Merry Widow: *Spanish*: Florence Walton, Daisy Clark. *Bowery*: Florence Mackenzie, May [Mae] Murray. *Dutch*: Ruby Lewis, Marjorie Bonner. *Irish*: Evelyn Carlton, Beatrice Learwood. *Coon*: Rosie Greene, Gertrude Vanderbilt. *Lieutenant Moxie*: May Leslie. *White Rooster*: Elsie Hamilton.

Act 1, Scene 1: The Garden of Eden. *Scene 2*: New Jersey Tube. *Scene 3*: On Board the Lusitania. *Scene 4*: New Amsterdam Theatre, New York. *Scene 5*: Interior of the Capitol at Washington. *Scene 6*: Naval Review—Presentation of Sword to Admiral Evans—Around the World with Uncle Sam.

Act 2, Scene 1: Smart Set Athletic Club, New York. *Scene 2*: Nell Brinkley's Studio. *Scene 3*: Beaux Arts, Huntington, Long Island. *Scene 4*: Old Vienna.

ACT 1[4]

Scene 1

"Mosquito Song"[5]
G. Leigh, Chorus

Scene 2

"The Duchess of Table d'Hote"
G. LaRue

Scene 3

"You Will Have to Sing an Irish Song"[6]
N. Bayes
(*Music by* Albert Von Tilzer. *Lyrics by* Jack Norworth.)

[3]The second in the annual series of revues presented by Florenz Ziegfeld beginning in 1907.

[4]For subsequent tour, the following songs were added:
"Over on the Jersey Side" (Scene 2, before "Duchess of Table d'Hote")
J. Norworth
(*Music and Lyrics by* Jack Norworth.)

[5]Replaced for subsequent tour by:
"The Girls I Left Behind"
William Powers {Adam}

[6]For subsequent tour, replaced by:
"Sing Me a Come-All-Ye (Like My Daddy Sang to Me)"
N. Bayes
(*Music and Lyrics by* Nora Bayes and Jack Norworth.)

"The Rajah of Broadway"
A. Deagon, Chorus
"Titles"
Principals, Chorus
Scene 4
"Nothing Ever Troubles Me"[7] (Nothing Ever Ever Ever Hardly Ever Troubles Me)
N. Bayes
(*Music by* Albert Von Tilzer. *Lyrics by* Jack Norworth.)
"The Big Hats"[8] (Hat Song)
A. Deagon, Chorus
"The Taxicab" (Take Me Round in a Taxi)
G. Leigh, Chorus
(*Music by* Melville Gideon. *Lyrics by* Edgar Selden.)
Scene 5
Dance Harlequinette
Mlle. Dazie
"The Candidate," Burlesque of 'The Soul Kiss' (Staged by Julian Mitchell.)
Scene 6
The Naval Review: Song of the Navy ("Follow the Flag")(Finale)
Admiral Evans: A. Froome. *King of England*: Mr. Bergman. *King of Germany*: Mr. Hessong. *Emperor of Japan*: Mr. DeBall. *President of France*: Mr. Books. *King of Spain*: Mr. Abbott. *Czar of Russia*: Mr. Royer. And Dancing American Girls.

ACT 2
Scene 1
"Society"[9] (Opening Chorus)
Dance du Directoire
Mlle. Dazie
Scene 2
"The Nell Brinkley Girl"[10]
A. Whitford
Scene 3
Pony Ballet
English Dancing Dolls
"When the Girl You Love Is Loving You"[11]
L. Weston
(*Music by* Jean Schwartz. *Lyrics by* William Jerome.)
Scene 4
"The International Merry Widow"[12]
A. Deagon, Chorus
"Since Mother Was a Girl"
N. Bayes
(*Music by* Albert Von Tilzer. *Lyrics by* Jack Norworth.)
Bickel and Watson's Burlesque Orchestra
Finale
E. Hamilton, the Rooster Girls, the Famous Drummer Girls, Entire Company

[7]For subsequent tour, replaced by:
"Shine On, Harvest Moon"
N. Bayes, J. Norworth
(*Music and Lyrics by* Nora Bayes and Jack Norworth.)
[8]Dropped for subsequent tour.
[9]Dropped for subsequent tour.
[10]Later programs list a series of tableaux as follows:
(a) A Row of Geese. (b) A Row of Betsies. (c) In a Canoe. (d) 'Between Love and Duty.' (e) 'Faces in the Waves.' (f) The Riding Girl. (g) All the Brinkley Girls.
[11]Replaced for subsequent tour by:
Cartoons in Song
J. Norworth
Which was later replaced by:
"Let's Get the Umpire's Goat"
J. Norworth
(*Music and Lyrics by* Nora Bayes and Jack Norworth.)
[12]Replaced for subsequent tour by:
"I Wonder If They're All True to Me" (later dropped)
A. Deagon

1908.20

SKI-HI

A Musical Comedy in Two Acts. Book, music and lyrics by Charles Alphin. Chorus numbers and dances staged by Robert A. Marks. Produced by N.I.M. and A. Company. Opened 20 June 1908 at the Madison Square Garden Roof Theatre and closed 4 July 1908 after 15 performances.[13]

CAST: *Ski-Hi*: WILLIAM CONLEY. *Otto Car*: Harry Short. *Prince de Rageon*: Joseph Carey. *Harrycane*: Joseph Carey. *Kuhla*: Frank Kelley. *Goto*: THOMAS FORTUNE. *Ricksha*: George Powers. *Paul Light*: Charles McGhee. *Willie Pipe*: George Elliott. *Claudius Cloud*: Harry Adams. *Will I. Killum*: William Smith. *Terry Ferma*: William Grant. *Astoria Vandergould*: LOTTIE KENDALL. *Mrs. Courtington*: Adella Barker. *Tee Foo*: Gertrude Black.

Act 1: Tokio, Japan.

Act 2: Jupiter.

MUSICAL NUMBERS[14]
"The Girl Worth the While"
L. Kendall
"Dance of Sing Ling Foo"
"My Tokio Queen"
T. Fortune
"Pretty Little Japanese Lady"
"Tamamura"
"Honey, Do You Love Me Dearly"

1908.21

THE MIMIC WORLD

A Musical Review in Two Acts, 7 Scenes. Book by Edgar Smith[15]. Music by Ben M. Jerome and Seymour Furth. Lyrics by Edward Madden and Addison Burkhardt. Staged by J. C. Huffman. Musical numbers conceived and executed by Ned Wayburn. Settings by H. Robert Law, Arthur Voegtlin. Costumes by Matthews; Madame Freisinger; Mme. Ripley. Orchestra under the direction of Oscar Radin. Produced by Sam S. and Lee Shubert (Inc.) and Lew Fields. Opened 9 July 1908 at the Casino Theatre and closed 26 September 1908 after 92 performances[16].

CAST: *Prince Danillo*, husband of the Merry Widow, and engaged with her in a fruitless search for their native land of Marsovia: WALTER LAWRENCE. *Lemuel Sawwood*, an American business man, who, late in life, develops sporting tendencies, with the usual luck of the beginner: HARRY CORSON CLARK. *Jack Witchinghour*, a gentleman gambler, with a gift of thought-transference: WILLIAM BONNELLI. *Colonial Bridau*, a custodian of his family's honor: Will West. *Kid Burns*, an authority on the races, and an adapt in the art of slinging slang: Arthur MacWatters. *George Cohan*, a pop-up clip-up: SEYMOUR FELIX. *Three Woman Haters*: *Ludwig Knoedler*, a near hero: Sam Collins. *Henry Schniff* a solider of misfortune: Sam Sidman. *Mr. Disch* of the Marsovian embassy: Charles Sharp. *Lord Dundreary*, a ghost from the humorous past: ROY ATWELL. *Richard Thief*, a worthy gentleman, whose fame rests upon his possession of a kleptomaniacal wife: Frank Mayne. *Tom Sawwood, William Sawwood*, father's boys: Bert Von Klein, DAVE LEWIS. *Artie*, an American college chap: CHARLES KING. *Captain Champmars*, a Parisian: Jack Laughlin. *Henri Montmarty*: Bert French. *Pierre Ambigu*, a French actor: William Moore. *Victor*, head-waiter at La Cascade: Louis Franklin. *Arretta*, a gendarme: Frank Thomas. *Baron Savogaire*, a diplomat: George Pierce. *Prince Distingu*, another: Jack Gordon. *Evans*, a butler: Joe Hadley. *Sonia*, formerly the Merry Widow, whose second matrimonial adventure is marred by her husband's habit of generalizing his affections: IRENE BENTLEY. *Mrs. Richard Thief*, whose kleptomaniacal tendencies contribute materially to the family bank roll: GRACE TYSON. *Mademoiselle Ou La La*: LOTTA FAUST. *Phoebe Snow*: LOTTA FAUST. *Miss Tiny Daley*, of Chicago: GEORGE W. MONROE. *Pamela, Kate Violet*, members of the Man Hater's Association: Doris Cameron, Ada Gordon, Marjorie Cortland. *Mrs. Guilford*, a society leader: VERNON CASTLE. *Polly* of the circus: Gladys Claire. *Molly Carey*: Nellie King. *Ninette*, a gay Parisienne: Grace Shannon. *Maxim's girls (8)*: *Flo Flo*: Dorothy Davidson. *Ho Ho*: Grace (Von) Studdiford. *Ko Ko*: Lillian Graham. *Coo Coo*: Ellen Worth. *Lu Lu*: Elizabeth Gardner. *Frou Frou*: Hattie Lorraine. *Goo Goo*: Bessie Stevens. *Jo Jo*: Marian Hartman. *Bessie Clayton*: Mazie King. *Jacqueline*, a female coacher: Theresa Bercien. *Salome*: Gladys Moore. *Six American Daisies*: Misses L. Franklin, E. Franklin, P. Franklin, V. Earl, H.

[13]No program available.
[14]No program available; song list from published sheet music.
[15]Program note: The management desire to state that they make no pretence at plot, but simply strive to amuse with a review of the successes of the current season.
[16]Played an additional week 28 September 1908 at the Grand Opera House for 8 performances.

Pillard, Gladys Moore. *Tourists, Cocottes, Race-goers, Diplomats, Gamblers, etc.* (*Miss Hook of Holland Burlesque Specialty*: Gladys Caire.)

Act 1, Scene 1: "La Cascade" Restaurant in the Bois de Boulogne. *Scene 2*: Paddock at Longchamps Race Tracks, Paris. *Scene 3*: Grand Stand, Long Champs, on the day of the "Grand Prix." (Law.)

Act 2, Scene 1: A furnished room in Paris. (Law.) *Scene 2*: Outside of Marsovia. (Law.) *Scene 3*: Garden of Witchinghour's Palace of Chance, Marsovia. (Voegtlin.)

ACT 1

Opening Chorus

"Any Old Nag at All"
A. MacWatters, Company
(*Music by* Seymour Furth. *Lyrics by* Addison Burkhardt.)

"All the Stars and Stripes Belong to Me"
S. Felix

"Mademoiselle"
L. Faust, Father

"(Yours Lips Say No, But) Your Eyes Say Yes"
I. Bentley, Ensemble
(*Music by* Ben M. Jerome. *Lyrics by* Edward Madden.)

"Richard Carle"
S. Felix

"Rogers Brothers"[17]
S. Felix, G. Caire

"When Tetrazzini Sighs High F"
G. Tyson

"Mary Carey" (My Little Blarney Stone, or Tipperary Mary Cary)
W. Lawrence, Ensemble
(*Music by* Benjamin Hapgood Burt. *Lyrics by* John B. Lovitz and Benjamin Hapgood Burt.)

"When Johnny Comes Marching Home (from College) Again"
L. Faust, Ensemble
(*Music by* Louis A. Hirsch.)

"Woman, Lovely Woman"
I. Bentley, G. Tyson, H. C. Clark

"Two Hearts Beat As One"
C. King, N. King

"I'm No Stingy Romeo"
W. Lawrence, Directoire Ladies

"Rag Man, Music Man" (Ragtime Minstrel Man)
C. King, Ensemble
(*Music by* Louis A. Hirsch.)

ACT 2[18]

Burlesque on Girls

"Phoebe Snow"
L. Faust, D. Lewis, Ensemble

"Chip Along"
Ensemble

"My Lady Wine"
W. Lawrence, Ensemble
(*Music by* Carl Rehman. *Lyrics by* Addison Burkhardt.)

"Miss Hook of Holland"[19]
G. Caire

"Fred Stone" (burlesque)
S. Felix

"Bessie Clayton" (burlesque)
M. King

Specialty
G. Moore

"Yankee Prince Waltz"[20]
S. Felix, G. Caire

"(In) Monte Carlo Town"
W. West, Ensemble
(*Music by* Ben M. Jerome. *Lyrics by* Edward Madden.)

"Making Eyes"
G. Tyson

"Ambassador's March"
W. Lawrence, Ensemble

Finale

[17]Dropped during the run.
[18]Running order was revised during the run. Added during the run to Act 2:
Vision of Salome (*Music by* Melville Ellis.)
Gertrude Hoffmann
"On a Pullman Honeymoon"
C. King, N. King, Ensemble
(*Music by* Carl Rehman. *Lyrics by* Edgar Smith.)
[19]Dropped during the run. No Gladys Caire appears in the cast list.
[20]Dropped during the run.

1908.22 COHAN AND HARRIS MINSTRELS

An Entertainment Embracing Minstrelsy, Vaudeville, Burlesque and Musical Comedy, in Two Acts, 4 Scenes. Book, music and lyrics for "The Bellė of the Barbers' Ball" by George M. Cohan. Staged director, Harry M. Morse. Dances arranged by James Gorman. Scenery painted by Ernest Albert. Costumes by Klaw and Erlanger Costume Company; First part and Parade costumes by Max Marx. Orchestra under the direction of Carl Schilling. Produced by George M. Cohan and Sam Harris. Opened 3 August 1908 at the New York Theatre and closed 22 August 1908 after 24 performances[21].

CAST: GEORGE EVANS (and 100 HONEY BOYS): EDDIE LEONARD, JULIAN ELTINGE, ARTHUR ALEXANDER, GEORGE THATCHER, Waterbury Brothers, Rice and Prevost, John King, George W. Lewis, F. McGinniss, W. Freeze, L. Freeze, Joe LeStrange, W. Brazil, Harry M. Morse, Ernest Tenney.

ACT 1

Scene1

In the Glade of the Orchids (A Transformation First Part Scene of Poetic Beauty)
Interlocutor: H. M. Morse. *Comedians*: G. Thatcher, E. Leonard, J. King, E. Tenney, G. W. Lewis, J. LeStrange, F. McGinniss, W. Brazil, W. Freeze, L. Freeze.

"I'll Be True to My Honey Boy"
Entire Ensemble

Introducing the Popular Minstrel Jesters, John King and Ernest Tenney

"Good Bye, Mr. Ragtime"
J. King

"Meet Me in Rose Time, Rosie"
E. Benham

"Answer"/

"Love Days"
F. Morrell

Introduction of those famous fellows, George Thatcher and Eddie Leonard

"Big Brown Boo Loo Eyes"
E. Leonard

Yodel Song
M. Keefe

Arrival of the "Honey Boy", George Evans

"Kiss Your Minstrel Boy Good Bye"
(G. Evans)

Scene 2

A Vaudeville Program of Star Features:
(a) George Evans presenting an entirely new repertoire of unconventional wit, a heart to heart talk by Minstrelsy's Most Famous Comedian
(b) The Dancing Marvel, Eddie Leonard, assisted by Two Gordon Boys and the Cohan & Harris Dancing Corps, in an entirely new Terpsichorean Divertissement. Introducing Joe (Rags) LeStrange, the eccentric dancer.
(c) An Artist from the land of Finesse, Julian Eltinge, in his marvelous imitations of feminine characters, introducing his latest and most remarkable creation, The Salome Dances, as studied by him in the principal European cities and now presented by this wonderful artist for the first time in America.
(d) A New and Sensational Marching Feature, After the Battle, conceived, arranged and produced by James Gorman.

[21]Billed as the Inaugural Tour. Later played a return engagements 11 January 1909 at the Grand Opera House for 8 performances, 16 August 1909 at the New York Theatre for 16 performances (see separate entry in that season). COHAN & HARRIS' MINSTRELS continued to tour with varied casts and musical content.

ACT 2

Scene 1

The Emperors of Wit and Melody, Waterbury Brothers and Tenney.

The Acrobatic Comedy Stars, (James) Rice & (Johnny Bell) Prevost, presenting their funny absurdity, 'Bumpty Bumps.'

Scene 2

THE BELLE OF THE BARBER'S BALL, A New Minstrel One-Act Musical Comedy by George M. Cohan.

Kid Jones: G. Evans. *Bill Simmons*: E. Leonard. *Algernon Duclos*: G. Thatcher. *Johnson*: F. Morrell. *Henry Beeson*: E. Tenney. *Carolina Brown*: J. King. *Annabelle Bascom*: J. Eltinge. *Guests at the Ball and Other Characters*: Entire Company.

MUSICAL NUMBERS

"At the Barbers' Ball"
Chorus

"Rag Time Quadrille"
Dancing Corps

"The Gibson Coon"
J. Eltinge, Chorus

"Oh! You Coon"
G. Evans, J. Eltinge, Chorus

1908.23 THE GIRL QUESTION

A Musical Comedy in Three Acts. Book and lyrics by Will M. Hough and Frank Adams. Music by Joseph E. Howard. Staged by George F. Marion. Scenery by John H. Young. Costumes by Eaves; Leavitt & Grossman. Produced by Askin-(Mort H.) Singer Company. Opened 3 August 1908 at Wallack's Theatre and closed 29 August 1908 after 32 performances.[22]

CAST: (in order of appearance): *Elsie Davis*, the cashier: ISABEL D'ARMOND. *A Reporter*: Dan Bruce. *T. P. G. Sears*, a magnate: Edwin Maynard. *"Jo" Forster*, a waitress: GEORGIE DREW MENDUM. *Con Ryan*, the head waiter: JUNIE McCREE. *Billy*: George Morgan. *Harold Sears*: JACK HENDERSON. *Mrs. Jessie Sears*: HELEN ROYTON. *Baron Max von Tesmar*: Carl H. George. *"Bud" McGinty*, a plumber: Harry Hanlon. *"Kid" Hennessey*, a prize fighter: Lester Brown. *"Skinny" Jones*, President of the Steel Workers' Union: Lew Fuller. *Jake Schwartzberger*, a delicatessen dealer: William Davis. *A Bailiff*: J. D. Miller. *Solo Dancing*: Morgan and McGarry. *College Men, Waitresses, Stenographers, Sheriffs, Show Girls, Broilers.*

Act 1: A Restaurant in the Times Square District, New York. Noon hour.

Act 2: Same as Act 1. New Year's Eve.

Act 3: Same as Acts 1 and 2. Temporary office of T. P. G. Sears.

ACT 1

Opening Chorus
Ensemble

"Be Sweet to Me, Kid"
J. McCree, I. D'Armond, Chorus

"Waltz with Me 'Till I'm Dreamy"
H. Royton, Chorus

"There Is No Place Like Home"
I. D'Armond, Chorus

"College Days"
J. Henderson, Male Chorus

"The Girl You Dream About"
Entire Company

ACT 2

"The Old Buck and Wing"
J. McCree, Chorus
(*Music by* Hilding Anderson, Joseph E. Howard.)

"I Like to Have You Call Me Honey"
I. D'Armond, Broilers

"When Eyes Like Yours Look into Eyes Like Mine"
J. Henderson, I. D'Armond

"It's Bye-Bye, Pal" (It's Goodbye, Pal)
H. Royton, Chorus

[22]Musical director uncredited.

ACT 3

"I Hate to Work on Mondays"
Clerks, Stenographers, Post Card Kiddies, etc.

"Do Something"
J. McCree

1908.24 ALGERIA

A Musical Play in Two Acts[23]. Book and lyrics by Glen MacDonough. Music by Victor Herbert. Staged by George Marion. Settings by Ernest Albert. Costumes designed by Alfredo Edel. Lighting by Kleigl Brothers. Orchestra under the direction of John McGhie. Produced by Frank McKee. Opened 31 August 1908 at the Broadway Theatre and closed 10 October 1908 after 48 performances.

CAST: *Zoradie*, Sultana of the Barakeesh, the ruler of a powerful desert tribe, seen in Act 1 as Miriam, Mistress of the Bayadères: IDA BROOKS HUNT. *General Petipons*, Governor General and uncle of Captain DeLome: WILLIAM PRUETTE. *Captain DeLome*, in command at the oasis of Sidi Ahmoud: GEORGE LEON MOORE. *Millicent Madison*, M.D., an American girl who is practicing medicine in the East: HARRIET BURT. *Soldiers of Fortune (3)*, who have enlisted in and deserted from the Foreign Legion of the French Army: *C. Walsingham Wadhunter*, a straggler from Bohemia: GEORGE MARION. *Van Cortland Park*, an ex-cotillion leader out of work: ERNEST LAMBART. *Trainor Crewe*, a college athletic instructor in hard luck: WILLIAM CAMERON. *Mr and Mrs. Billings F. Cooings*, a recently married couple from Paterson, on their honeymoon bound for nowhere in particular: EUGENE P. ARNOLD, FLORENCE NASH. *Ali Kohja*, chief of police to the Sultana of the Barakeesh, seen in Act 1 as the Arab story-teller: Joseph Carey. *Mimi* of the Latin Quarter: May Willard. *Nella*, the Sultana's confidante: Grace Rankin. *Ladies in Waiting to the Sultana (4)*: *Zaphirie*: Katherine Howland. *Aouda*: Madge Richardson. *Mirzah*: Carolyn Barber. *Lakme*: Jane Grover. *Lieutenant Bertrand*: Richard M. Dolliver. *Lieutenant Dubonnet*: Franklin Foster.

Bayadères and Nurses: Misses (Helen) Broderick, Richardson, Benyusuf, Willard, Desmond, Breen, Lang, Meyers, Valliere, Lawrence, Dupont, Baldwin, Warren. *Artists' Models*: Misses Race, Clarke, Leidy, Angela. *Grisettes*: Misses Bennett, Perry, Mack, Ware. *Candy Sellers*: Misses Bennett, Clarke, Perry, Parker, Kendal, Race. *Flower Sellers*: Misses Howland, Mack, Gordon, Vingut, Ware, Donelson. *Hasheesh Vendors*: Misses Burpee, Madden, Angela. *Kabyle*: Misses Leidy, Grover, Rankin. *Fruit Sellers*: Misses Barber, Richardson, Hansen, Arnold, Cuppia, Peters. *Chorus Gentlemen*: *Water Carrier*: Mr. Foster. *Rich Arab*: Mr. Carey. *Rug Merchants*: Messrs. Goeble, Corse, Kern. *Jewel Merchants*: Messrs. Walsh, Reinhardt, Kline. *Pottery Merchants*: Messrs. Groves, D'Angelo, Rome. *Hasheesh Vendor*: Mr. Maxwell.

Act 1: The walled oasis of Sidi Ahmoud in the Sahara.

Act 2: Exterior of an old palace at Mustapha Superieur, Algiers, two days later.

ACT 1[24]

Opening Chorus

"The Boule' Miche"
G. L. Moore

"I've Been Decorated"

"Rose of the World"
I. B. Hunt

"The Great White Easiest Way"

"You'll Feel Better Then"
H. Burt

"The Same Old Two"

Finale
Ensemble

ACT 2

Opening Chorus

"Love Is Like a Cigarette"
G. L. Moore

"Ask Her While the Band Is Playing"

"Only One of Anything"

"Twilight in Barakeesh"
I. B. Hunt

[23]Revised by its authors the following season as THE ROSE OF ALGERIA, which opened 20 September 1909 at the Herald Square Theatre for 40 performances.

[24]Musical numbers not listed in program. List prepared from published vocal score, reviews. Other musical number not in vocal score: "In Jail" (Trio). Additional songs published but not in vocal score: "I'll Dream of Thee," "Thanksgiving Day," and "He Was a Soldier Too," all with lyrics by Vincent Bryan.

"Bohemia, Good-bye"
"Little Bird of Paradise"
Finale

1908.25 THE GIRLS OF GOTTENBERG

A Musical Comedy in Two Acts, 3 Scenes. Book by L. E. Berman and George Grossmith, Jr. Music by Ivan Caryll and Lionel Monckton. (Lyrics by Adrian Ross and Basil Hood.) Staged by J. E. A. Malone. Orchestra under the direction of W. T. Francis. Produced by Charles Frohman. Opened 2 September 1908 at the Knickerbocker Theatre and closed 28 November 1908 after 103 performances.[25]

CAST: *Max Moddelkopf*: JAMES BLAKELEY. *Otto*, Prince of Saxe-Hildesheim: LIONEL MACKINDER. *Brittbottl*, Sergeant of Hussars: JOHN E. HAZZARD. *General the Margrave of Saxe-Nierstein*: Ross Clifford. *Officers of the Blue Hussars (5)*: *Colonel Finkhausen*: ERNEST COSSART. *Fritz*: WARWICK WELLINGTON. *Herman*: Overton Moyle. *Franz*: Ridgwell Cullum. *Carl*: Henry Vincent. *Albrecht*, Captain of Dragoons: WALLACE McCUTCHEON. *Burgomaster*: EDWARD GARVIE. *Kannenbier*, an innkeeper: Sarony Lambert. *Adolf*, town clerk: R. R. Neill. *Policeman*: Theodore Walters. *Waiters*: Messrs. Grant and Leech. *Corporal Riethen*, *Private Schmidt*, Blue Hussars: Guy Maingy, Herman Brand. *Elsa*, the General's daughter: MAY NAUDAIN. *Clementine*, the Burgomaster's daughter: LOUISE DRESSER. *Lucille*, maid to Elsa: Edith Kelly. *Kathie*: Hazel Neason. *Hana*: Grace Riopel. *Hilda*: Ethel Vivian. *Minna*, Captain of College: Mabel Hollins. *Freda*, head of Alemannia Corps: Clara Pitt. *Anna*, head of the Pomerania Corps: Molly McGrath. *Eva*, head of the Saxonia Corps: Mary Lee. *Lina*, head of the Borussia: Adelaide Kornau. *Katrina*, the only girl in Rottenberg: Louise Brunelle. *Barbara Briefmark*, the Postmaster's daughter: Grace Walsh. *Betti Berncastler*, the Doctor's daughter: Esther Robinson. *Mitzi*, the Innkeeper's daughter: GERTIE MILLAR.

Act 1, Scene 1: The Barracks, Rottenberg. *Scene 2*: The Market Place, Gottenberg.

Act 2: The Gardens of "The Red Hen," across the river near Gottenberg.

ACT 1[26]
Scene 1
Opening Chorus
(*Music by* Ivan Caryll. *Lyrics by* Adrian Ross.)
"The Only Girl"
W. Wellington
(*Music by* Ivan Caryll. *Lyrics by* Basil Hood.)
"Off to Gottenberg" (Trio)
L. Mackinder, O. Moyle, H. Vincent
(*Music by* Ivan Caryll. *Lyrics by* Adrian Ross.)
Scene 2
Opening (Chorus) of Scene 2
(*Music by* Ivan Caryll. *Lyrics by* Adrian Ross.)
"Girls of Gottenberg"[27] (Song)
M. Hollins
(*Music by* Ivan Caryll. *Lyrics by* Adrian Ross.)
"Clementine"[28] (Song)
L. Dresser
(*Music by* W. T. Francis. *Lyrics by* J. B. Loughrey.)
"What Is It?" (Entrance Song)
Chorus
(*Music by* Lionel Monckton. *Lyrics by* Basil Hood.)
"A Glass of Beer" (Song)(The Beer Girl)
G. Millar
(*Music and Lyrics by* Lionel Monckton.)
"Otto of Roses" (Song)
L. Mackinder
(*Music by* Ivan Caryll. *Lyrics by* George Grossmith, Jr.)
"The Titsy Bitsy Girl" (Duet)
G. Millar, J. Blakeley
(*Music by* Lionel Monckton. *Lyrics by* Basil Hood.)
"Freda" (Song)
M. Naudain
(*Music by* Jerome Kern. *Lyrics by* M. E. Rourke.)
Finale

ACT 2
Opening Chorus
(*Music by* Lionel Monckton. *Lyrics by* Adrian Ross.)
"Here's to the Girl"(Song)
W. Wellington
(*Music and Lyrics by* Will R. Anderson.)
"Always Come Back to You"[29] (Duet)
L. Mackinder, E. Kelly
"(Do You Know) Mr. Schneider" (Song)
G. Millar
(*Music by* Lionel Monckton. *Lyrics by* George Grossmith, Jr. and Lionel Monckton.)
"Birds in the Trees" (Duet)
L. Dresser, J. Blakeley
(*Music by* Ivan Caryll. *Lyrics by* Adrian Ross.)
"Sprechen sie Deutsch (Mein Herr?)"[30] (Trio)
G. Millar, J. Blakeley, L. Mackinder
(*Music by* Lionel Monckton. *Lyrics by* Adrian Ross.)
Song and Dance[31]
E. Kelly, W. McCutcheon
"I Can't Say That You're the Only One" (Duet)
L. Mackinder, M. Naudain
(*Music by* Jerome Kern. *Lyrics by* C. H. Bovill.)
"(Two Little) Sausages" (Duet)
G. Millar, J. Blakeley
(*Music and Lyrics by* Lionel Monckton.)
"Queenie (Was There) with Her Hair in a Braid" (Song)
L. Dresser
(*Music by* W. T. Francis. *Lyrics by* John L. Hazzard.)
"Berlin (on the Spree)"
G. Millar
(*Music by* Lionel Monckton. *Lyrics by* Basil Hood.)
Finale
(*Music by* Ivan Caryll. *Lyrics by* Adrian Ross.)

[25]Settings, costumes uncredited.
[26]Interpolation, as per published sheet music:
"Kate O'Brien"
L. Dresser
(*Music by* W. T. Francis. *Lyrics by* J. B. Loughrey.)
"I Will Be Waiting for You"
M. Naudain, Girls
(*Music by* W. T. Francis. *Lyrics by* David J. Clark.)
[27]Dropped for subsequent tour.
[28]Replaced for subsequent tour by:
"I Remember You" (Song)
L. Dresser
(*Music by* Harry Von Tilzer. *Lyrics by* Vincent Bryan.)
Another specialty interpolated during the run, as per published sheet music:
"She Had a Lot of Things When She Came Back"
L. Dresser
(*Music by* W. T. Francis. *Lyrics by* John L. Hazzard.)

1908.26 SPORTING DAYS

A Triple Bill of a Spectacular Melodrama, a Ballet, and a Spectacle. Staged by R. H. Burnside. Settings by Arthur Voegtlin. Costumes designed by Mme. Frances Ziebarth. Orchestra under the direction of Manuel Klein. Produced by Messrs. Shubert and Anderson. Opened 5 September 1908 at the Hippodrome and closed 29 May 1909 after 448 performances.

ACT 1

SPORTING DAYS, A Spectacular Melodrama (with Music) in One Act, 5 Scenes. Book by R. H. Burnside. Music and lyrics by Manuel Klein. Staged by R. H. Burnside. Settings by Arthur Voegtlin. Costumes designed by Mme. Frances Ziebarth. Orchestra under the direction of Manuel Klein.

CAST: *John P. Vanderveer*, a Millionaire: J. PARKER COOMBS. *Jack Vanderveer*, his eldest son: Edwin A. Clark. *Paul Vanderveer*, his youngest son: George Mordecai. *Kitty*

[29]Dropped for subsequent tour.
[30]Dropped for subsequent tour.
[31]Dropped for subsequent tour.

Vanderveer, his daughter: MARIE TYLER. *Doctor Dawson*, head of Newtown College: William H. Clarke. *Matt Morgan*, Mr. Vanderveer's trainer: George Melville. *Tommy Swift*, formerly a jockey in Mr. Vanderveer's employ: HARRY DALE. *Peter Barker*, Proprietor of Barker's Circus: Frank Melville. *Toby*, the clown: MARCELINE. *Willie Bibbs, Jimmy Bobbs*, 2 tramps: GEORGE HOLLAND, NAT W. HARRIS. *Baron Henri de Belleville*: HERBERT MANSFIELD. *Countess of Scarborough*, his sister: NANETTE FLACK. *Dick Seymour*, in love with Kitty: Adrian Bellvue. *Mrs. Stuyvesant Mills*: ELLA SMYTH. *Jim Brice*, Cambria coach: Sam Baker. *Joe Van Dyck*, Newtown coach: Harry E. Cluett. *Newtown Leader*: Sam Baker. *Cambria Leader*: Urolin Edwards. *Umpire*: Jack C. Warren. *Mickey Bryan*, Vanderveer's jockey: J. Donohue. *First Crook*: Peter Lyon. *Second Crook*: John Fleming. *Village Policeman*: J. Harry Taylor. *Chauffeur*: Herbert Ross. *The Spring Girl*: Gabrielle Bacot. *The Summer Girl*: Violet Williams. *The Autumn Girl*: Gertrude Williams. *The Winter Girl*: Gene Hassell.

Circus Program: George Melville (Equestrian, Director); Frolic of the Hippodrome Clowns, including Marceline; the Eight Brazilian Equestrians; Paul Sandor's Dog Circus; Oscar Lowande (Bareback Rider); Four Kirston-Mariettis (Equilibrists); The Four Riegos (Acrobats); The Four Poncherrys (Wire Act); Albert's 10 Performing Polar Bears

Scene1: Baseball Field of Newtown College. The Ball Game. Arrival of the Circus. The Circus Performance. *Scene 2*: Outside the Newtown Boathouse. *Scene 3*: The Boat Race. *Scene 4*: The Paddock at Saratoga. *Scene 5*: The Race for the Saratoga Cup.

MUSICAL NUMBERS

"Good Old Cambria" (Opening Chorus)
Ensemble
"When the Circus Comes to Town" (Song)
M. Tyler
"Rowing" (Song)
Coaches, Chorus
"The Racing Game" (Song)
J. P. Coombs
"The Whole Year Round"[32] (Song)
E. A. Clark

ACT 2

THE THREE WISHES, or The Land Of The Birds[33]. A Ballet in Two Tableaux. Written and produced by R. H. Burnside. Music composed and directed by Manuel Klein. Dances arranged by Vincenzo Romeo. Scenery designed by Arthur Voegtlin. Costumes designed by Alfredo Edel.

CAST: *The Bird Trapper*: VINCENZO ROMEO. *His Wife*: MARGARET TOWNSEND. *His Daughter*: Blanche Boone. *The Wood Chopper*: Charles Ravel. *His Wife*: Eva Mackenzie. *His Son*: Lillian Daven. *The Eagle*: Adrian Bellvue. *The Canary*: NANETTE FLACK. *The Stork*: William Moore. *The Sentinel Bird*: MARCELINE. *The Dove*: Mlle. ESTHER ZANINI. *The Devil Bird*: SIGNOR G. BONFIGLIA. And the Famous Flying Ballet.

Scene 1: On the Edge of a Forest near the Hartz Mountains. *Scene 2*: The Land of the Birds.

MUSICAL NUMBER

"The Canary Song"[34]
"Giving Three Wishes"

ACT 3

THE BATTLE OF THE SKIES, a Spectacle in 4 Scenes. Invented by Arthur Voegtlin. Written and produced by R. H. Burnside. Music composed and directed by Manuel Klein. Costumes designed by Hy. Mayer.

CAST: *Count Lucca Malini*, an Italian officer: J. PARKER COOMBS. *Madam Servaroff*, a Russian adventuress: ELLA SMYTH. *Baron Rudolph von Amberg*, a German attaché: GEORGE HOLLAND. *Geoffrey Gedison*, a young inventor: EDWIN A. CLARK. *Alice Gedison*, his sister: NANETTE FLACK. *General Fairfax*, Commander of the United States Aero-Plane Army: WILLIAM H. CLARK. *Diana Fairfax*, his daughter: MARIE TYLER. *Captain*: Herbert Mansfield. *Lieutenant*: Jack C. Warren. *First Citizen*: John Fleming. *Captain Norendorff*: George Melville.

Scene 1: Street in a City in the United States. *Scene 2*: Fortifications of a City in Europe. Arrival of the Airship. Destruction of the City. *Scene 3*: The Open Sea. *Scene 4*: The Golden Garden. Concluding with an Apotheosis of Victory.

Opening Chorus
Ensemble
"What a Scene of Beauty Glorious"
W. H. Clark
"A Toast to the King of War"
W. H. Clark
"Love Is King"
N. Flack
"Dear Motherland" (Victory)
E. A. Clark

---

[32]Replaced during the run by:
"I'm Looking for a Sweetheart (and I Think You'll Do)" (Song)
E. A. Clark, N. Flack, Chorus

[33]Titled changed in ads and billing to THE LAND OF BIRDS on 13 September 1908.

[34]Not listed in programs; as per published sheet music.

1908.27 FLUFFY RUFFLES

A Musical Melange in Three Acts. Book by John J. McNally. Based on the "Fluffy Ruffles" comic strip (by Wallace Morgan from the New York Herald). Music by William T. Francis, (Jerome Kern). Lyrics by Wallace Irwin. Staged by Ben Teal. Settings by Edward G. Unitt and Jospeh Wickes; Hugo Baruch. Costumes by Mme. Adrienne King, Alfredo Edel. Orchestra under the direction of Gus Salzer. Produced by Charles Frohman. Opened 7 September 1908 at the Criterion Theatre and closed 17 October 1908 after 48 performances.

CAST: *Fluffy Ruffles*: HATTIE WILLIAMS. *Noggie Noggles*: BERT LESLIE. *Dave Dill*, Fluffy's Uncle: JOHN BUNNY. *Herbert Henshaw*: JACK GARDNER. *Francois Franconi*: Edouard Durand. *Boggs*, Proprietor of Ducks and Drakes Inn: Charles R. Burrows. *Toby*, boy of all work: VICTOR HYDE. *Tom Jones*, a waiter: Frank Lewis. *Anatole*, waiter at Armenonville: Victor LeRoy. *An Old Policeman*: F. G. Dillabough. *Henry Peck*: EDWARD O'CONNOR. *Andre*: Roy Dennison. *Madame Shonts*: LIDA McMILLAN. *Mrs. Herbert Henshaw*: Nellie Butler. *Isobelle Barlow*: Josephine Drake. *Louise, Sadie*, Uncle Dave's nieces: ADELE ROWLAND, FLORENCE MARTIN. *Mattie Swizzle*: Bessie Clifford. *Celeste*: Marie Annis. *Mme. Molly Maloni*: MATTIE O'BRIEN. *Carrie Crewe*, a youthful suffragette: Violet Hemming. *Belle Binks*, a bride: Elsie Drews. *Jane Jorkins*, a bridesmaid: Hazel Jocelyn. *Lucille*: Jane Hall. *Clairette*: Eithel Kelly. *Estelle*: Helen Morrison. *Clarabelle*: Madge Melbourne. *Marguerite*: Ethel Filmore. *Pauline*: Mabel Mercer. *Sarah Scruth*: Florence Averill. *Hon. Augustus Traddles*: GEORGE GROSSMITH, JR.

Act 1: Madame Shonts' Employment Emporium, New York City. (Unitt and Wickes.)

Act 2: The Ducks and Drakes Inn on the Thames, near London. (Unitt and Wickes.)

Act 3: Armenonville, Paris. (Baruch.)

ACT 1

Opening Chorus
(*Music by* Jerome Kern.)
"(There's Something Rather Odd About) Augustus"[35]
G. Grossmith, Jr.
(*Music by* Jerome Kern. *Lyrics by* C. H. Bovill.)
"(I Love to Sit and) Look at You"
J. Gardner
(*Music by* Pat Rooney. *Lyrics by* Edward Madden.)
"Fluffy Ruffles"
H. Williams
"Evolution"
H. Williams, G. Grossmith, Jr.
Finale
(*Music by* Jerome Kern.)

ACT 2

Opening Chorus
(*Music by* Jerome Kern.)
"I Wonder Why"
B. Leslie
"(Go and) Get Your Partner for the Barn Dance"
J. Gardner
(*Music by* Joel P. Corin. *Lyrics by* Felix F. Feist.)
"Willie's Got Another Girl Now"
H. Williams
(*Music by* Leigh. *Lyrics by* Paul Potter.)
"(Won't You) Let Me Carry Your Parcel"
A. Rowland, F. Martin, V. Twohey, V. LeRoy, E. O'Connor
(*Music by* Jerome Kern. *Lyrics by* C. H. Bovill.)

---

[35]Replaced for subsequent tour by:
"He Wanted a Girl"
William Norris {Augustus}

"(Sweetest Girl, Silly Boy,) I Love You" (Reckless Boy, I Love You")[36]
H. Williams, G. Grossmith, Jr.
(*Music by* Jerome Kern. *Lyrics by* Wallace Irwin.)

"Jane Is a Suffragette"
E. O'Connor

Finale

ACT 3

"Echo of My Heart"[36a] (Opening Chorus)
M. Annis
(*Music by* Jerome Kern.)

"Dining Out"
G. Grossmith, Jr.
(*Music by* Jerome Kern. *Lyrics by* George Grossmith, Jr.)

"(In) Love's Bouquet"
J. Gardner
(*Music and Lyrics by* E. S. Brill.)

"Burlesque Imitations"
H. Williams, G. Grossmith, Jr.

Finale

"My Moonbeam Dream"
J. Gardner

1908.28

SCHOOL DAYS

Gus Edwards' Kids in a Young Musical Play in Three Acts. Book by Will D. Cobb[37]. Music by Gus Edwards. Lyrics by Edward Gardenier and Gus Edwards. Staged by Ned Wayburn. Scenery by J. Frank Dodge. Costumes by Castel-Bert, and Browning, King & Company. Direction of Jeff D. Bernstein. Produced by Gus Edwards. Opened 14 September 1908 at the Circle Theatre and closed 10 October 1908 after 32 performances.

CAST: (in order of appearance): *Biff Dugan*, from the East Side: MILFRED BERRICK. *Carl Dachshund*, brought up under the bureau: Daniel Murphy. *Sassy Little*, very sassy: GYPSY MOONEY. *Ima Lemon*, she stutters: Ethel Wayne. *Lizzie Brown*, she lisps: Jeannette Alpine. *Johnny Boston Beans* Webster-on-a-Bridge: GREGORY KELLY. *Timmy, Jimmy*, the Hold-up Twins: JOHN HINES, Isabor Rabino. *Lotta Gold*, very rich: Berenice Faye. *Tommy Tatters*, tattered and torn: JOE KENO. *Freshy Buttinsky*, a nosey little thing: AGNES LYNN. *Hazel Nutty*, very nutty: Ethlyn Wilmont. *Van Cortland Perry*, dead swell: Jesse Keppler. *Nonnie*, anonymous: JANET PRIEST. *Tony*, the florist: Nat Baker. *Pat Kelly*, the grocer: Harry Siedel. *Izzy Levi*, greenhorn, just over: HERMAN TIMBERG. *Captain Bugham*, one of the finest: Harry Evans. *Miss Take*, our teacher: Hazel Cox. *Sunbonnet Sue*, very popular: Carolyn Waide. *Little Dot*, of the Paper Hat Brigade: Loraine Lester.

Dancing Devils: Misses Mooney, Alpine, Noack, Elaine, Irving, Carlyle, Etta Wainman, Jeannette. *Graduates*: Misses Crawford, Kuba, Wilmont, Greene, Gilbert, Clark, Russell, Gurkin, Edwards, Miller. *Singing Boys*: Messrs. Webster Aurimenia, Marion, Moss, Klein, F. Timberg, Price, Levine, White. *Dancing Boys*: Messrs. Starr, Zinnaman, O'Donnell, Bargalla, Golden, Kessler, Mackler, Evans, Weston.

Act 1: The School Yard. First day of school.

Act 2: The School Room. Two weeks later.

Act 3: Lotta's Home on the Hudson. Two weeks later.

ACT 1

"Childhood's Happiest Moments" (Opening Ensemble)
Chorus

"The Fighting Kid"
M. Berrick, Chorus
(*Lyrics by* Edward Gardenier.)

"Going to Fight the Indians"[38]
I. Rabino, J. Hines, Chorus

"Katie Gray"[39]
J. Priest, Chorus

"Whe I'm an American Citizen"[40]
H. Timberg

"You're Just the Boy for Me"
H. Timberg, J. Priest, Boys, assisted by E. Wainman, W. Aurimenia
(*Lyrics by* Edward Gardenier.)

"It Takes the Cop to Cop the Girls"
H. Evans, Chorus
(*Lyrics by* Vincent Bryan.)

ACT 2

"My Country 'tis of Thee" (National anthem)
Ensemble

"The Calendar of Love"
A. Lynn, M. Berrick, Chorus
(*Lyrics by* Edward Gardenier.)

"Sunbonnet Sue" (When I Was a Kid So High)
C. Waide, Chorus
(*Lyrics by* Will D. Cobb.)

"Little Tittle Tattle (Tale)"
A. Lynn, J. Keno, Chorus
(*Lyrics by* Edward Gardenier.)

"Get on the Merry Go Round"
M. Berrick, H. Timberg, J. Priest, E. Wayne, J. Keno, A. Lynn, Chorus
(*Lyrics by* Edward Gardenier.)

ACT 3

"Maybe It's a Bear"
H. Cox, Babies, Chorus
(*Lyrics by* Vincent Bryan.)

"Everybody's Going to the Devil in New York"
H. Timberg, Dancing Devils

"You Have Me"
J. Keno, A. Lynn

"My Old Lady"[41]
H. Timberg, J. Priest, Boys' Quartette

"The Paper Hat Brigade"
L. Lester, Band, Fife, Drums, Chorus
(*Lyrics by* Vincent Bryan.)

"School Days (When We Were a Couple of Kids)" (Finale)
Entire Company

1908.29

MLLE. MISCHIEF

An Operetta in Three Acts. (Original Viennese) libretto ("Ein tolles Mädel") by Curt Kraatz, Wilhelm Sterk, Heinrich Stobitzer. English libretto by Sydney Rosenfeld. Music by Carl M. Ziehrer. Play staged by J. C. Huffman. Musical numbers staged by Ned Wayburn. Scenery by H. Robert Law. Costumes by Melville Ellis. Electrical effects by John Whalen. Produced by Sam S. and Lee Shubert (Inc.). Opened 28 September 1908 at the Lyric Theatre, moved 30 November 1908 to the Casino Theatre, and closed 19 December 1908 after 96 performances.[42]

CAST: (in order of appearance): *Andre Clair*, an artist: ROBERT DEMPSTER. *Susanne*, his aunt: JOSIE INTROPODI. *Meline*: ALEXANDER CLARK. *Mrs. Meline*: ADA HENRY. *Freddy Meline*: ROY ATWELL. *Colonel Romber*: Robert Broderick. *Lucie*, his wife: Jean Newcombe. *Lieutenant Berner*: W. T. CARLETON. *Gaston*, a cadet: Oliver Follansbee. *Sergeant Dubaer*: Frank Farrington. *Paul*, an art student: William Arnold. *Victor*: J. Ryder Glyn. *Policeman*: Mark Harrison. *Charlotte*: ETHEL INTROPODI. *Lola*: ELIZABETH BRICE. *Mimi*: GERTRUDE DARRELL.

---

[36]Replaced during the run and for subsequent tour by:
"Won't You Harmonize with Me?"
H. Williams
(*Music by* C. W. Murphy. *Lyrics by* George Arthurs.)

[36a]An "Echo Song" by W. T. Francis and Wallace Irwin was also published.

[37]Based on Gus Edwards' vaudeville sketch of the same name. Contrary to the playbill, reviewers credit Aaron Hoffman with the book. For subsequent tour, the book was credited to Edward Gardenier and Gus Edwards. For many years during the next decade, different productions titled SCHOOL DAYS toured the United States successfully under varying auspices, with many different authors, casts and musical numbers, all drawing their inspiration from Gus Edwards' original novelty.

[38]Replaced for subsequent tour by:
"Omaha"
John Hines {Jimmy}, Irving Robbins {Timmy}, Chorus

[39]Replaced for subsequent tour by:
"Mary Mack"
J. Priest

[40]Dropped for subsequent tour.

[41]Dropped for subsequent tour.

[42]Musical director uncredited.

Rosette: LULU GLASER.

Act 1: Studio of Andre Claire.

Act 2: The Barracks at Fremstadt.

Act 3: Outside of the Barracks.

ACT 1

Opening Chorus
Models, Painters

"Verily, Merrily" (Trio)
L. Glaser, R. Dempster, A. Clark

"Le Coeur de Ninon" (Solo)
G. Darrell

"Ev'ry Hour Brings Its Flower" (Quartette and Chorus)
E. Brice, G. Darrell, R. Dempster, R. Atwell

"To the Regiment We'll Go" (Finale)

ACT 2

"The Army Corps" (Opening Chorus and Solo)
W. T. Carleton, Male Chorus

"The Joy Duet"
L. Glaser, W. T. Carleton

"A Single Day"[43]
L. Glaser, A. Clark

"She Knew a Thing or Two" (She Knows a Thing or Two)
L. Glaser

"Sweetheart" (Finale)

ACT 3

Opening
L. Glaser

"My Own Vienna" (Trio)
E. Brice, G. Darrell, R. Atwell

"Ladies Beware"
A. Clark, Show Ladies

Finale

"I'll Forget to Remember the Rest"
W. T. Carleton

1908.30 MARCELLE

An Operetta in Two Acts, 3 Scenes. Book and lyrics by Frank Pixley. Music by Gustav Luders. Staged by Frank Smithson. Dances directed by David Bennett. Scenery built by George Williams. Costumes designed by Melville Ellis. Orchestra under the direction of Clarence Rogerson. Produced by Sam S. and Lee Shubert (Inc.). Opened 1 October 1908 at the Casino Theatre and closed 28 November 1908 after 68 performances.

CAST: *Baron von Berghof*, hereditary proprietor of the Berghof estates: JESS DANDY. *Lieutenant Karl von Berghof*, his nephew in the German Army: FRANK RUSHWORTH. *Dumm*, cellar master of Castle Berghof: HENRY NORMAN. *Herr Schwindle*, burgomaster of Berghof: HERBERT CAWTHORNE. *Klug*, a lawyer, friend of Karl: GEORGE BONIFACE, JR. *"Bud" Wilson* from Kalamazoo, an "innocent abroad": LAWRENCE WHEAT. *Pierre*, a Parisian painter: Robert O'Connor. *Corporal Frisch* of the Schwindle Corps: David Bennett. *Fritz*: George Reed. *Marcelle*, a Parisian actress: LOUISE GUNNING. *Lucille*, her maid: Edith Girvan. *Fraulein Elsa von Berghof*, the Baron's adopted daughter: Elsa Ryan. *Mitzi*, her maid: Marion Ford. *Mrs. Darlington*, preceptess of a young ladies' seminary: Leona Anderson. *Baroness von Berghof*: Nettie Black.

The American Girls: Florence Arkell, Margarite MacDonald, Mae Rollins, Nan Parkhurst, Eileen Kearney, Mae Allen, Louise Tozier. *Dancers*: Della Connor, Marion Ford, Irene Spencer, Bessie Carrette, Bessie Skeer, Bertha Perl, Lucille Jardon, Ollie Stewart. *Peasants, Servants, Officers, Militia Men, Seminary Girls, etc.*

The action takes place in the small German town of Berghof, near the French border, at the present time.

Act 1: The Garden and Exterior of Castle Berghof. Afternoon.

Act 2, Scene 1: An open place near the old ruined Castle of Berghof. The Duelling Ground. Evening. *Scene 2*: The reception Hall of Castle Berghof. Same evening.

ACT 1

Opening Chorus

"Drink and Be Jolly To-Day"
H. Norman

"It's Not the Proper Thing"
L. Anderson, American Girls

"Love, the Magician"
E. Ryan

Entrance of the Baron

"Kalamazoo"
L. Wheat, Chorus

"The Schwindle Corps"
H. Cawthorne, Chorus

"Mary's Little Lamb" (My Little Lamb)(Duet)
L. Wheat, E. Ryan

Marcelle's Entrance
L. Gunning, Chorus

"My Own Paree"
L. Gunning

"Once in a While"
F. Rushworth

"The Soldier Boy" (Finale)

ACT 2

Watchmen's Chorus

"Forget It" (Ensemble)

"Good Evening"
Chorus

"Something (Is Always Going Wrong)"
J. Dandy

"Cupid—Sly Little Rascal"
L. Wheat, E. Ryan

"Far, Far Away" (Memories Fond and True)
L. Gunning

Battle Song (To Live and Die a Soldier Bold)[44]
F. Rushworth

"The Message of the Red, Red Rose"
L. Gunning, F. Rushworth

Finale

[43]Dropped for subsequent tour.

[44]Replaced for subsequent tour by:
Dance Champagne
E. Girvan, D. Bennett, R. O'Connor

1908.31 THE AMERICAN IDEA

The Cohan & Harris Comedians in a Musical Frivolity (Comedy) in Three Acts. Book, music and lyrics by George M. Cohan. Staged by George M. Cohan. Costumes by F. Richard Anderson. Settings by John Young; Edward G. Unitt and Joseph Wickes. Orchestra under the direction of George A. Nichols[45]. Orchestrations by Charles J. Gebest. Produced by George M. Cohan and Sam Harris. Opened 5 October 1908 at the New York Theatre and closed 28 November 1908 after 64 performances.

CAST: *Pierre Souchet*: GEORGE BEBAN. *Stephen Hustleford*: Robert Dailey. *Daniel Sullivan*: WALTER LeROY. *Herman Budmeyer*: GILBERT GREGORY. *The Mysterious Man*: Hugh Mack. *Henry Budmeyer*: Richard Taber. *Charlie Sullivan*: Harold Forbes. *Bellboy*: Harold Gordon. *Officier*: Richard Tobin. *Mrs. Waxtapper*: TRIXIE FRIGANZA. *Edythe Yellowback*: Stella Hammerstein. *Catherine Budmeyer*: Carrie Bowman. *Nellie Sullivan*: Lola Merrill. *The Mysterious Girl*: Edith MacBride. *Vera*: Rosie Green. *Violette*: Gertie [Gertrude] Vanderbilt.

(*Ensemble*): Misses Hartford, Alexander, Martin, Monroe, Harries, Coyle, Barron, Martrit, Snyder, Brooks, Hartman, Lee, Wilson, F. Martyn, Newell, Troutman, Hay, B. Friganza, Courtney, Watson, McNown, Ford, LeRoy, Earl, E. Ross, F. Ross, Glasson, Hilton, Gilbert, Whiteford. Messrs. Avery, Lorraine, Conway, Shields, Monte, Shattick, Waite, Stevens, Lasher, Doyle, Fink, Day, Levallin, McCormick, Rawley.

Act 1: Court of Elysée Palace Hotel, Paris. (Young.)

Act 2: Drawing-room in the same hotel. (Unitt and Wickes.)

Act 3: Promenade in the Jardin de Paris. (Unitt and Wickes.)

ACT 1

"In Gay Paree"
Chorus

[45]Drum effects by J. E. Lynehan.

"Sullivan"
W. LeRoy, Chorus
"Brothers and Sisters"
R. Taber, H. Forbes, C. Bowman, L. Merrill
"They Always Follow Me"
T. Friganza, Chorus
(*Music by* Jean Schwartz. *Lyrics by* William Jerome.)
"Too Long from Long Acre Square"
R. Dailey, Chorus
Ensemble
Company

ACT 2
"We're Supposed to Be"
Chorus
"Cohan's Pet Names" (That's the Pet Name for Me)
T. Friganza, G. Beban
"That's Some Love"[46]
R. Taber, H. Forbes, C. Bowman, L. Merrill, Chorus
"F-A-M-E"
R. Dailey, W. LeRoy, G. Gregory, G. Beban
"American Ragtime"
R. Dailey, Chorus

ACT 3[47]
"The Garden That Blooms for You" (My Garden That Blooms for You)
R. Tobin, Chorus
(*Music by* Milton W. Lusk. *Lyrics by* William Kendall Evans.)
"The Bold Gendarmes"
Ponies
"Whoop-La-La"
Mlle. Vanity, Misses Doyle, Day, Shields, Lorraine; Misses Gilbert, Whiteford, Hilton, Earl.
"The Gendarmes' Dance"
R. Green, G. Vanderbilt
"French Militaire"
Chorus
March Finale
Company
(*Music by* Charles J. Gebest.)

1908.32 THE OLD HOMESTEAD

A Revival of the Rural Melodrama in Four Acts[48]. Play by Denman Thompson and George W. Ryer. Stage director, Frank Knapp. Settings by Homer Emens and Edward G. Unitt. Produced by Franklin Thompson. Opened 5 October 1908 at the Academy of Music and closed 24 October 1908 after 24 performances.[49]

CAST: (in order of appearance): *Joshua Whitcomb*: DENMAN THOMPSON. *Cy Prime*: FREDERICK MAYNARD. *Jack Hazard*: FRED CLARE. *Frank Hopkins*: Harry R. Webster. *Eb. Ganzey*: FRANK KNAPP. *John Patterson*: Harry A. Jaeger. *Aunt Matilda (Whitcomb)*: LOUISA MORSE. *Rickety Ann*: ANITA L. FOWLER. *Annie Hopkins*: LAURA BRADFORD. *Nellie Patterson*: MINNIE STANSIL. *The Old Homestead Double Quartette*: Jess Calkins, Harry A. Jaeger, Harry R. Webster, E. F. Cochran, Roy Purviance, Gus Kammerlee, Charles Ingoldsby, Fred Clare. *Henry Hopkins*: Gus Kammerlee. *Judge Patterson*: E. F. Cochran. *Francois Fogarty*: Jess Calkins. *Mrs. Hopkins*: Annie Thompson. *One of the Finest*: Charles Ingoldsby. *Reuben Whitcomb*: Roy Purviance. *Harlem Spider*: Frank Knapp. *Postman*: George L. Patch. *Seth Perkins*: Charles H. Clark. *Len Holbrook*: George L. Patch. *David Willard*: David Willard (himself). *Warren Ellis*: P. Redmond. *Anna Maria Murdock*: Margaret Boustead. *Eleanor Stratton*: Jessie Graham. *The Stratton Girls, Holbrook Boys, and the Eames's.*

[46]Replaced for subsequent tour by:
"Order Wedding Bells for Two"
{Henry, Charlie, Nellie, Catherine, Chorus}
(*Music by* Jean Schwartz. *Lyrics by* William Jerome.)

[47]Added for subsequent tour, after "The Garden That Blooms for You":
"Whoop-La-La"
Ensemble

[48]First produced in New York 10 January 1887 at the 14th Street Theatre for 155 performances. For Synopsis of Scenes, see original 1887 production. In Act 3, "Palms" rendered by Charles Ingoldsby and the "Old Homestead" Choir. Anita Fowler, Organist.

[49]Costumes uncredited.

1908.33 MORNING, NOON AND NIGHT

A Musical Comedy in Two Acts. Book by Joseph W. Herbert. Music by Jean Schwartz. Lyrics by William Jerome. Stage manager, Teddy Burns. Musical director, Frederick Perkins. Produced by Mortimer Thiese. Opened 5 October 1908 at the Yorkville Theatre and closed 10 October 1908 after 8 performances.

CAST: *Abraham Goldberg*: JOE WELCH. *Artie Hall*: (Miss) ARTIE HALL. *Herr Otto Seise*: AL SHEAN. *Gusty Bunk*: Charles A. Warren. *Mrs. See Breeze*: Maud Morris. *Bill Sykes*: TEDDY BURNS. *Inspector Martin*: Fred George. *Guffanti Bacigalupo*: Mike Curran. *Inspector Shinners*: Howard Nesbit. *Officer Sullivan*: Henry Ling. *Salome*: ROSECITA MANTILLA. *Eight Little Dancing Friars*. With Richard Smith, Harry Meehan, Violet Winters, Mabel Botto, Anna Proctor, Lioto Fabiono, Irene Gorden, Hazel Allen, Pauline LaVie, Anita Julius, Mamie Brooke, Lyda Franklin, Rose Ferguson, Leslie Greer, Ruth Gilbert, Helen Bertrand, Molly Gilson, Pearl Davis, Flo Maquot, Irene Williams, Irene Gregg, Daisy Moxley, Frankei Smith, Rexford Linn, Frank Clayton, I. A. Martin.

Act 1: Ellis Island.

Act 2: Luna Park.

MUSICAL NUMBERS
"Life's Highway" (Act 1)
(Chorus of 4 men, 4 women)
"Rainbow"
A. Hall
(*Music by* Percy Wenrich. *Lyrics by* Alfred Bryan.)
"None of Them's Got Anything on Me"
T. Burns
(*Music by* Jean Schwartz. *Lyrics by* William Jerome.)
Qua Vadis Upside Down (sketch)
A. Shean, C. Warren
Specialty
(*Music by* Frederick Perkins.)
R. Mantilla
"A Room to Let"
(*Music and Lyrics by* A. Hall.)

1908.34 THE GOLDEN BUTTERFLY

A Comic Opera in Three Acts. Book and lyrics by Harry B. Smith. Music by Reginald DeKoven. Staged by A. M. Holbrook. Scenery designed by Frank Gates and Edward A. Morange, Ernest Albert, Edward G. Unitt and Joseph Wickes. Costumes designed by William H. Matthews. Orchestra under the direction of Anton Heindl. Orchestrations by Reginald DeKoven. Produced by Grace Van Studdiford Amusement Company (Charles Bradley, manager). Opened 12 October 1908 at the Broadway Theatre and closed 21 November 1908 after 48 performances.

CAST: *Bertha*, daughter of Petoffy: Lenora Novasio. *Olga*, her sister: Marion Woods. *Count Androssy*, Colonel of the Hungarian Hussars stationed at Buda-Pesth: CHARLES PURCELL. *Petoffy*, a rich brewer of Buda-Pesth: LOUIS CASSAVANT. *Baron von Affenkoff*, director of the Buda Pesth Opera: LOUIS HARRISON. *Ilma Walden* of the Buda-Pesth Opera: GRACE VAN STUDDIFORD. *Strolling Musicians (6)*: *Schmucke*: Frank Benor. *Schinken*: Charles W. Butler. *Lump*: Robert G. Williams. *Eselbein*: Walter Jenkins. *Puffenkranz*: A. Hanschman. *Schmalz*: Carl Gordon. *Franz*, a music student of the Latin Quarter: WALTER PERCIVAL. *Wanda*, a Gypsy girl: Alice Hills. *Hanska*, stage manager of the Buda-Pesth Opera House: W. J. McCarthy. *Tina Korbay* of the Buda-Pesth Opera Company: Gene Luneska. *Coryphées of the Buda-Pesth Opera Company (6)*: *Hildegarde*: Lenora Novasio. *Freda*: Louise Garrett. *Magda*: Florence Topham. *Duschka*: June Bonnell. *Toni*: Harriet Allen. *Fritzi*: Marion Woods. *Of the Buda-Pesth Opera Company (6)*: *A Costumer*: H. P. Woodley. *A Wigmaker*: R. G. Williams. *A Hairdresser*: Edward Reddy. *A Shoemaker*: Frank Benor. *A Theatrical Tailor*: Robert Graham. *Assistant Hairdresser*: John Carroll. *Call Boy, "To To"* at the opera: Charles W. Butler. *Head Usher* at the opera: A. Hanschman. *Stage Carpenter* at the opera: Walter Jenkins. *Prince Sergius Orloffsky*, a Russian noble: LOUIS CASSAVANT. *Lazlov*, a wine grower: CHARLES PURCELL. *His Wife*: Gladys Coleman.

Act 1: *Show Girls*: Misses Pierce, Allen, Morden, Dare, Vivian, Coburn, Coleman, Livingston, Lange. *Society Girls*: Misses Frances, Garrett, H. Allen, Doane, Bowes, Spencer, Boies, Carmody, Fursman, Southgate, Gardner, Raymond, Elmore, Bonnell, Topham, Wall, Chapelle, Meredith, Fanning, Prentiss, Detrich, Desmond, Elmo, Wallace. *Civilians*: Messrs. Hanschman, Woodley, Hartford, Klisto. *Hussars*: Messrs. Burke, Musser, Reddy, Chapman, Graham, Hovel, Carroll, Camp, Jenkins, Lademan. *Footmen*: Messrs. Williams, Benor.

Act 2: *Ballet Girls*: Misses Frances, Garrett, H. Allen, Doane, Bowes, Spencer, Boies, Carmody, Fursman, Southgate, Gardner, Raymond, Elmore, Bonnell, Topham, Wall. *Columbines*: Misses Chapelle, Meredith, Fanning, Prentiss, Detrich, Desmond, Elmo, Wallace. *Pierrots*: Misses Pierce, Allen, Morden, Dare, Vivian, Coburn, Coleman, Livingston, Lange. *Butterfly Girls*: Misses Frances, Garrett, H. Allen, Doane, Bowes, Spencer, Boies, Carmody, Fursman, Southgate, Gardner, Raymond, Elmore, Bonnell, Topham, Wall. *Gendarmes*: Messrs. Williams, Benor, Woodley, Hartford, Klisto. *A Pantaloon: A Harlequin, A Musical Director*: Richard Hartford, Messrs. Klisto, Hovel. *Ushers*: Messrs. Carroll, Camp, Jenkins, Lademan. *Maid*: Bertha Norfolk.

Act 3: *Peasant Girls*: Misses Frances, Garrett, H. Allen, Doane, Bowes, Spencer, Boies, Carmody, Fursman, Southgate, Gardner, Raymond, Chapelle, Meredith, Fanning, Prentiss, Detrich, Desmond. *Peasant Boys*: Misses Elmo, Bonnell, Topham, Novasio, Woods, Wall, Elmore. *Automobile Girls*: Misses Elmo, Wallace, Pierce, Allen, Morden, Dare, Vivian, Coburn, Coleman, Livingston, Lange. *Peasant Men*: Messrs. Woodley, Hartford, Klisto, Burke, Musser, Reddy, Chapman.

Act 1: The Garden of Petoffy's Villa near Buda-Pesth. Afternoon. (Gates and Morange.)

Act 2: The Green Room of the Opera House, Buda-Pesth. Night. (Albert.)

Act 3: The Vineyard near the Baron's Villa on the outskirts of Buda-Pesth. Next day. Unitt and Wickes.)

ACT 1

Opening Ensemble/"Military Review"
C. Purcell, Ensemble

"Great Musicians"
L. Harrison, Chorus

"Don't Forget Me"
G. Van Studdiford

"Wandering Musicians"
W. Percival, Strolling Musicians

"In Paris" (Duet)
G. Van Studdiford, W. Percival

"Singing Lesson"
G. Van Studdiford, L. Harrison, W. Percival, W. J. McCarthy

Finale

ACT 2

Opening Ensemble
Ensemble, Chorus

"Queen of the Ring"
G. Luneska, Chorus

"The Two-Headed Nightingale"
L. Harrison

"Butterfly and the Clover"
G. Van Studdiford, Chorus

"Off to Russia" (Duet)
G. Luneska, W. Percival

"The Man About Town"
L. Casavant, Chorus

Finale

ACT 3

Opening Ensemble
Ensemble, Chorus

"Legend," "The Elf King"
A. Hills, C. Purcell, G. Coleman, Chorus

"The Bottle Imp"
W. Percival, Chorus

Duet
G. Van Studdiford, W. Percival

Finale
Ensemble, Chorus

1908.35

LITTLE NEMO

A Musical Comedy in Three Acts, 11 Scenes. Book and lyrics by Harry B. Smith. Based on Windsor McKay cartoons (Little Nemo in Slumberland) by permission of New York Herald. Music by Victor Herbert. Staged by Herbert Gresham. Settings by Ernest Albert, John Young, Young Brothers & Boss Co. Costumes by F. Richard Anderson. Orchestra under the direction of Max Hirschfield. Produced by (Marc) Klaw and (Abraham L.) Erlanger.

Opened 20 October 1908 at the New Amsterdam Theatre and closed 23 January 1909 after 111 performances[50].

CAST: *Dr. Pill*, physician to King Morpheus: JOSEPH CAWTHORN. *Flip*, nephew of the Guard of the Dawn: BILLY B. VAN. *The Dancing Missionary*: HARRY KELLY. *Little Nemo*: MASTER GABRIEL. *Morpheus*, King of Poppyland: W. W. BLACK. *An Officer in the Continentals*: A. H. Hendricks. *Gladys*, the cat: DAVE ABRAMS. *Teddy*, the bear: DAVE ABRAMS. *Nutty*, the squirrel: DAVE ABRAMS. *Mons Roma, Mons Graeso*, Olympian wrestlers: (Louis) HART, (Sim) COLLINS *Aide to Officer of the Continentals*: Edward B. Kramer. *Ruler of the Isle of Table d'Hote*: Louis F. Barnes. *The Candy Kid*, Messenger of King Morpheus: FLORENCE TEMPEST. *The Little Princess*: Aimee Ehrlich. *The Valentine Fairy*: Albertine Benson. *The Barometer Girl*: Albertine Benson. *The Weather Vane*: Elphye Snowden. *Mrs. Nemo*: Rose Beaumont. *Sally*, a traveler in Slumberland: Madeline Marshall. *Tilly, Betty*, likewise travelers in Slumberland: Mildred Manning, Sunshine James.

Pages, Attendants to the Princess, Guards of Slumberland, Teddy Bears, Cannibals, Toy Soldiers, Jungle Animals, Continentals, English Soldiers, Naval Officers, Midshipmen, Sailors, etc.

Act 1, Scene 1: The Playroom of the Little Princess in Slumberland. (Young.) *Scene 2*: A Playground in a City Park. (Young.) *Scene 3*: Little Nemo's Bedroom. (Young.) *Scene 4*: The Land of St. Valentine. (Albert.)

Act 2, Scene 1: The Weather Factory Office in Cloudland. (Young Brothers &Boss Co.) *Scene 2*: Wreck of the Ship of Dreams; The Isle of Table d'Hote (Young Brothers & Boss Co.) *Scene 3*: The Amusement Park in the Jungle. (Young Brothers & Boss Co.) *Scene 4*: Little Nemo's Bedroom. (Young Brothers & Boss Co.) *Scene 5*: A Dream of the Fourth of July. (Young Brothers & Boss Co.)

Act 3, Scene 1: Deck of a Battleship. (Young Brothers & Boss Co.) *Scene 2*: Slumberland. (Albert.)

ACT 1

Scene 1

Opening Chorus (Slumberland)

"The Happy Land of Once-Upon-a-Time"
F. Tempest

"There's Nothing the Matter with Me" (Trio)
J. Cawthorn, H. Kelly, W. W. Black
Assisted by S. Collins, L. Hart, M. Marshall.

Scene 2

"Blow Upon Your Bugles"/"Won't You Be My Playmate?" (Chorus)
A. Ehrlich, M. Gabriel, Chorus

"Read the Papers Ev'ry Day" (Newspaper Song)(Trio)
J. Cawthorn, B. B. Van, H. Kelly

Scene 4

"(When) Cupid Is the Postman"/"Won't You Be My Valentine?"
A. Benson, Chorus

Finale (March of the Valentines)

ACT 2[51]

Scene 1

Opening Chorus: Different Kinds of Weather:

Sunbeams
S. James, Chorus

Snowflakes
M. Manning, Chorus

Raindrops
Chorus

"(The Hen and the) Weather Vane" (Trio)
E. Snowden, A. Benson, B. B. Van

Scene 2

"Will o' the Wisp"
F. Tempest, Chorus

"The Barbecue" (Ensemble)

Scene 3

"If I Could Teach My Teddy Bear to Dance"
M. Gabriel
Assisted by D. Abrams, H. Kelly, M. Marshall, Chorus.

---

[50]Played a return engagement 21 March 1910 at the Grand Opera House for 8 performances.

[51]Added during the run and for tour to Act 2, Scene 3, before "The Olympian Games":

"It's the Irish" (They Were Irish)
J. Cawthorn, E. Snowden, Chorus

"The Olympian Games" (Finale)
Scene 4
"I Guess I Talk Too Much"
M. Gabriel
"I Wouldn't Take a Case Like That"
J. Cawthorn
Scene 5
"Remember the Old Continentals"
A. H. Hendricks
"The Chime of the Liberty Bell" (Ensemble)

ACT 3
Scene 1
"Give Us a Fleet" (Opening Chorus)
A. Benson, Chorus
"Happy Slumberland"[52]
M. Gabriel, F. Tempest, A. Ehrlich, E. Snowden, S. James
"Is My Face on Straight?" (Trio)
J. Cawthorn, B. B. Van, H. Kelly
Scene 2
The Subterranean Dream; The Submarine Dream; The Dream of Love; Nightmare; The Celestial Dream
Finale
Entire Company

1908.36 THE BOYS AND BETTY

A Musical Play in Three Acts. Book and lyrics by George V. Hobart. (Based on the play "La Papillion" by Robert Danceny and Rene Peter.[53]) Music by Silvio Hein. Staged by George Marion. Settings by Frank E. Gates and Edward A. Morange. Costumes by Lord & Taylor. Orchestra under the direction of Silvio Hein. Produced by Daniel V. Arthur. Opened 2 November 1908 at Wallack's Theatre and closed 6 February 1909 after 112 performances.

CAST: (in order of appearance): *Tony Arditti*: E. J. DeVarny. *Rudolph Gruber*: JAMES B. CARSON. *Algernon Graham*: EDGAR NORTON. *Baptiste Leveque*: Macy Harlam. *Nanon Duval*: CLARA PALMER. *Izora Deschon*: Annabelle Gordon. *Julie Perret*: Claudia Rodgers. *Minnie Racherre*: Anna Ford. *Cleo Marcette*: Blanche Wilmot. *Betty Barbeau*: MARIE CAHILL. *Marie Antoinette*: Bonnie Maud. *Casimir Barbeau*: JOHN E. KELLERD. *Paul Gerard*: EDGAR ATCHISON-ELY. *Major Gordon, U.S.A.*: EUGENE COWLES. *Grace Gordon*: Anna Mooney. *Elise Rochet*: Camille Buehler. *Valerie Pannier*: Phoebe Loubet. *Laure Moreau*: Florence Holmes. *Virginie Guillaume*: Mary Mooney. *Porter*: Harry Morey. *Mrs. Pranz*: Marguerite Binford. *Servant*: George Deane. *Philippe Fouchet*: A. E. Luzzi.

Shop Girls and Shoppers: Misses Mary Worthington, Jesse Elliott, Evelyn Radcliffe, Claudia Rogers, Dorothy Waldron, Florence Ravel, Louise Shelley, Annabelle Gordon, Carrie Miller, Blanche Wilmot, Fanny Boutelle, Mary Mooney, Anna Ford, Gertrude Barnard, Marie Mayo, Lorie Sprague, Bessie Cottrell, Florence Evans, Tempee Evans, Camille Buehler, Grace Harper, Agnes Ormonde, Josephine Montague, Sadie Henderson.

Act 1: Home of Monsieur and Madame Barbeau. Nice, (France). 5 P.M.

Act 2: Betty's Shop in Paris. Christmas Eve, eighteen months later. 5:30 P.M.

Act 3: The Gardens of Major Gordon's Villa, near Paris, on the Seine. Six months later. 6 P.M.

ACT 1[54]
"I Want to Go to Paris"
C. Palmer, assisted by Misses A. Ford, Rodgers, Wilmot, Gordon, Messrs. Carson, Norton, Harlam, DeVarny
"Take Plenty of Shoes"
M. Cahill
(*Music by* Melville Gideon. *Lyrics by* Will D. Cobb.)
"The Tetrazzini Family"
Themselves
"Auf Wiedersehen"
M. Cahill

ACT 2
Opening
Ensemble
"Girls, Girls, Girls"
E. Cowles, Chorus
"A Little Farther" (A Little Further)
M. Cahill
(*Music and Lyrics by* Frederic Norton.)
"I Love to Go Shopping"
M. Cahill, E. Athison-Ely
"(Down At) The Follies Bergere"
C. Palmer, Chorus

ACT 3
Opening
Storm
"Gee, But You Look Awfully Good to Me"
E. Atchison-Ely, Chorus
(*Lyrics by* Will D. Cobb.)
"The Arab Love Song" (Marie Cahill's Arab Love Song)
M. Cahill

[52]Dropped for subsequent tour.
[53]Source identified in playbills for subsequent tour.
[54]Interpolated as per published sheet music:
"Laura Lee"
M. Cahill
(*Music and Lyrics by* Frederic Norton.)
Interpolated for tour:
"Whoop Her Up with a Whoop-La-La"!
M. Cahill
(*Music and Lyrics by* Will Marion Cook.)
"She Was a Dear Little Girl"
M. Cahill
(*Music by* Ted Snyder. *Lyrics by* Irving Berlin.)

1908.37 TOO MANY WIVES

A Musical Farce in Two Acts, 3 Scenes. Book and lyrics by Charles Horwitz. Music by Frederick V. Bowers. Produced by the Mittenthal Brothers. Opened 2 November 1908 at the Metropolis Theatre and closed 7 November 1908 after 8 performances.

CAST: *Isidor Meyer*, from Kansas City: JOE MORRIS. *Jack Simon*, his nephew: HERBERT E. DENTON. *Bob Lester*: CLAUDE LIGHTNER. *Jimmy Push*: William H. Low. *Miss Dough*: CLIFFORD LYMAN. *Mrs. Josephine Lester*: Jeanette Paterson. *Kate Winchester*: INEZ BUCK. *Mary*: MANOLITA STETSON. *Chorus.*

MUSICAL NUMBERS[55]
"My Honeysuckle Baby"
J. Morris
"In a Lady-like Way"
"Ain't It Grand to Be an Actress"
"I Want Someone to Show Me New York Town"
"L-O-V-E and M-O-N-E-Y"
"Let's Make Love" (Octette)
"Oh, Mister Abrams"
"When the Band Plays the Star-Spangled Banner"
"Big Chief Oi, Oi"
"He's Getting Like His Daddy Every Day"
"How'd You Like to Call Me Dearie"
"When the Moon Shines on Broadway"
"Be Careful That He Doesn't Find It Out"

1908.38 THE MERRY WIDOW AND THE DEVIL

Joe Weber's Travesty Company, Incorporated in a Satire (Burlesque) on 'The Merry Widow' and 'The Devil' (by arrangement with Henry W. Savage) in Three Acts[56]. Libretto by George V. Hobart. Staged by Julian

[55]No New York program available. Detail from published sheet music, the Dramatic Mirror.
[56]An earlier version of the BURLESQUE OF THE MERRY WIDOW was previously produced in New York 2 January 1908 at Weber's Music Hall for 156 performances. THE MERRY WIDOW, operetta in Three

Mitchell. Produced under the personal direction of Joe Weber. Settings by John H. Young. Orchestra under the direction of Hugo Frey. Produced by Joe Weber. Opened 16 November 1908 at the West End Theatre, closing 21 November 1908 after 8 performances; returned 18 January 1909 at Weber's Theatre and closed 30 January 1909 after 16 additional performances. Total : 24 performances[57].

CAST: *Prince Dandilo*, now known as Carl Mahler, an artist: CHARLES J. ROSS. *Heinrich Disch*, his valet: JOE WEBER. *Mimi*, his model: LILLIAN FITZGERALD. *The Devil*, calling himself DeJollidog, a wine agent: WALTER JONES. *Baron Kaughman*, Farsovian ambassador to Paris: ALBERT HART. *Fonia*, his wife, who wants to be a merry widow: BLANCHE RING. *Elsie Eisberg*, an heiress, engaged to Prince Dandilo: GRACE GRISWOLD. *Booze de Grouch, Biff De Grouch, Baz De Grouch*, the Three Twins: R. DUNLAP, E. SPATZ, A. C. HEATH. *English Tourist*: Beatrice McKay.

Nice Girls from the Witching Hour Cafe: *Ko-Ko*: Janet Burton. *Jo-Jo*: Beatrice McKay. *Goo-Goo*: Minerva Walton. *Do-Do*: Sadie Aravol. *Jo-Ko*: Annie Ray. *Coo-Coo*: Violet Laurell. *Dog*: Charlie Ball. *Cat*: Harry Huber. *Mons. Duval*: Major Crique. *Mons. Carpentier*: Neal Harvey. *Mons. Deverdon*: Charlie Ball. *Mons. Robideau*: Harry Huber. *Mlle. Celeste*: Violet Laray. *Mlle. Angelique*: Kittie Sayer. *Mlle. Babette*: Nora Hamilton. *Mlle. Antoiette*: Annie Betterton. *Mlle. Yvonne*: Minnie May Quental. *Mlle. Cochette*: Eunice Mackay. *Mlle. Piquette*: Nellie Howard. *Mlle. Nanette*: Nettie Hamilton. *Mlle. Bettine*: Vivian Howard. *Senorita Concarne*: Maud LeRoy. *Mlle. Marnold*: Marie Hughes. *Mlle. Fatima*: June Marlowe.

Act 1: Reception Hall adjoining Studio of Prince Dandilo.

Act 2: Garden at Fonia's residence.

Act 3: Witching Hour Cafe.

ACT 1[58]

Opening Chorus
Ensemble

"Gee, Ain't I Glad I'm Single"
C. J. Ross
(*Music by* Silvio Hein.)

"In Farsovia"
B. Ring

"I'm the Original Devil" (The Devil)
W. Jones
(*Music by* Silvio Hein.)

Finale
Company

ACT 2

Opening Chorus
Ensemble

"Bonnie, My Highland Lassie"
B. Ring

"She's My Daisy" (Harry Lauder imitation)
C. J. Ross

"Girls" (Sextette)
C. J. Ross, A. Hart, J. Weber, W. Jones, E. Spatz, A. C. Heath

Waltz
B. Ring, C. J. Ross

Finale
Company

ACT 3

Opening Chorus
Ensemble

"The Girls at Maxim's"
A. Hart

"Yip, I Adee, I Aye"
B. Ring
(*Music by* John H. Flynn. *Lyrics by* Will D. Cobb.)

Duet
B. Ring, C. J. Ross

Finale
Company

1908.39 MISS INNOCENCE

A Musical Entertainment in Two Acts, 8 Scenes. Book and lyrics by Harry B. Smith. Music by Ludwig Engländer. Produced under the stage direction of Julian Mitchell. Settings by Ernest Albert, John H. Young. Costumes by Klaw & Erlanger Costume Company. Musical director, Frank Darling. Produced by Florenz Ziegfeld. Opened 30 November 1908 at the New York Theatre and closed 1 May 1909 after 176 performances.[59]

CAST: *Anna*, Miss Innocence, model pupil of a model school: ANNA HELD. *Miss Sniffins*, Proprietor of the School for Innocence; a lady with several "pasts": EMMA JANVIER. *Helen Legarde*, a gay Parisienne: EDITH DECKER. *Claire*, a school girl: EDITH ST. CLAIRE. *Ezra Pettingill*, "the greatest detective in the world": CHARLES A. BIGELOW. *Captain, The Hon. Roland Fitzmaurice Montjoy*, of the First Life Guards: LAWRENCE D'ORSAY. *Pierre de Brissac*, Lieutenant in the French Navy: Leo Mars. *The Duke of Pomerania*: Robert Paton Gibbs. *Bobo*, a poor relation: F. Stanton Heck. *The Marquis de Chabert*: Maurice Hegeman. *Angele*: LILLIAN LORRAINE. *Loulou*: EVA FRANCIS. *Visitors to the L'Abbaye (7)*: *Eugenie*: Vida Whitmore. *Flore*: Virginia Marshall. *Margot*: Grace Rankin. *Diane*: May Hopkins. *Celestine*: Lottie Vernon. *Eve*: Mae Paul. *Felise*: Grace Washburn. *Marie*: Bertha Blake. *Fleurette*: Ethel Donaldson. *Hortense*: Lillian Wiggins. *Clairette*: Edna Chase. *Lolo*: Mabel Snyder. *Ella Lee*, an American serio-comic: SHIRLEY KELLOGG. *Pierrette*: Anna C. Wilson. *Maxine*: Marion Whitney. *Yvonne*: Daisy Rudd. *"Hindoo Honey" Girls (3)*: *Rita*: Edna Birch. *Carita*: Elise Hamilton. *Pepita*: Ruby Lewis. *Sadie*: Dorothy Follies. *Spanish Dancers*: Misses GLADYS ZELL, FLORENCE WALTON, Blanche West, Elise Hamilton. *Count Maxime*: James Clyde. *Albert*, Maitre d'hotel: Pierre Roudil. *Walker*, an American: Dudley Oatman. *Hobbes*, a college boy: Ernest Wood. *O'Brien*, an American athlete: Peter Swift. *Ben Hassan*, an Arab: Alfred Fairbrother. *Prince Yogama*, a Japanese: Lionel Lozier. *Count Sergius Borodin*, a Russian: John S. Brush. *Rastignac*, a student: Charles Barry. *Durand*, an artist: Alfred Rinehart. *Claude*: William Gammage. *Spanish Dancers*: Faico, La Flamencia. *Schmalz*, a ballet master: Maurice Hegeman. *Premiere Danseuse*: Madlyn J. Summers. *Mme. Pompignac*, the Husband Syndicate: EMMA JANVIER. *Alphonse*, attendant at the Hotel de Boheme: Pierre Roudil. *A Postman*: Dudley Oatman. *Dr. Charcot*: Maurice Hegeman. *Pompignac*: CHARLES A. BIGELOW. A *Gendarme*: Ernest Wood. *Sergeant*: John A. Youngs. *Artist Model*: Elise Hamilton.

"Three Weeks with You": Misses Lillian Lorraine, Grace Rankin, Eva Francis, Vida Whitmore, Florence Walton, Edna Chase, Shirley Kellogg. Messrs. Ernest Wood, Dudley Oatman, John A. Young, James Barry, Alfred Rinehart, Albert Fairbrother, John Wentzel. *School Girls*: Misses Burns, Chase, Clark, Davies, Dodsworth, Fennell, Follies, Hamilton, Harriman, Jewell, Kellogg, MacDonald, Mantell, Rudd, Swift. *Maids*: Misses Birch, Bright, Carson, M. Gilmore, Walton, West, Willard, Wilson, Zell. *Railway Number*: Misses Chase, Davies, Follis, Hamilton, Harriman, Jewell, Learwood, Mantell, MacDonald, Willard, Rudd, Summers. *Ballet School*: Misses Lillian Lorraine, Eva Francis, Birch, Bright, Carson, Chase, Clark, Davies, Follis, M. Gilmore, Hamilton, Harriman, Hoyt, Jewell, Learwood, Lewis, MacDonald, Mantell, Rudd, Summers, Swift, Walton, West, Zell. *Specialty*: Faico.

Act 1, Scene 1: Girls' school on Isle of Innocence in the Mediterranean Sea. (Young.) *Scene 2*: Continental Railway Carriage, Marseilles to Paris. (Young.) *Scene 3*: L'Abbaye, Montmartre, Paris. (Albert.)

Act 2, Scene 1: Ballet School, Vienna. (Albert.) *Scene 2*: Flying machine. Paris at night. (Young.) *Scene 3*: Room in Parisian Hotel. (Young.) *Scene 4*: Studio on the Rhine. (Albert.) *Scene 5*: Land of Peach Blossoms. (Albert.)

ACT 1[60]

Opening Chorus

Acts, produced 21 October 1907 at the New Amsterdam Theatre for 416 performances. Original Viennese book by Victor Leon and Leo Stein, music by Franz Lehár, English lyrics by Adrian Ross. THE DEVIL, play in Three Acts by Ferenz Molnar, produced in 2 simultaneous productions 18 August 1908 at the Belasco for 175 performances in a translation by Alexander Konta and William Trowbridge Larned, and at the Garden Theatre in a translation by Oliver Herford for 87 performances.

[57]Costumes uncredited.

[58]Interpolated as per published sheet music:

"Mr. Dinkelspiel"
B. Ring
(*Music by* J. Fred Helf. *Lyrics by* Ed. Moran.)

[59]Re-opened a return engagement 27 September 1909 at the New York Theatre for an additional 16 performances; see separate entry for detail in following season. Total: 192 performances.

[60]Added 15 December 1908, replacing "In My Flying Machine;"

"We Two in an Aeroplane"
A. Held, L. Mars

Added to Act 1 during the run, following "Yankiana Rag":

"Marie, Marie"
C. A. Bigelow

"Am I a Wife, Widow or Maid?"
E. St. Clair
"Please Tell Me What They Mean"[61]
A. Held, C. Bigelow
"My Post Card Girl"[62]
L. Lorraine, School Girls
(*Music by* Louis A. Hirsch. *Lyrics by* Addison Burkhardt.)
"I'm Learning Something Every Day"
A. Held
(*Music and Lyrics by* Nora Bayes and Jack Norworth.)
Railroad Number
Chorus
Spanish Dance
Misses Hamilton, Walton, West, Zell
"(Oh! That) Yankiana Rag"
S. Kellogg, Company
(*Music by* Melville Gideon. *Lyrics by* E. Ray Goetz.)
"I Have Lost My Little Brown Bear"
A. Held
(*Music by* J. Rosamond Johnson, Bob Cole. *Lyrics by* Bob Cole.)
(Specialty)
Faico
Finale

ACT 2
Opening Chorus
"I'm Crazy When the Band Begins to Play"
E. Decker
(*Music by* Jean Schwartz. *Lyrics by* William Jerome.)
"I Wonder What's the Matter with My Eyes"
A. Held
(*Music by* Egbert Van Alstyne. *Lyrics by* Harry Williams.)
"What Kind of a Wife to Choose" (What Kind of a Wife Does a Man Like Best)
L. Mars
(*Music and Lyrics by* Gus Edwards.)
"Perfectly Terrible, Dear"
E. Janvier
(*Music by* Egbert Van Alstyne. *Lyrics by* Harry Williams.)
"In My Flying Machine"
A. Held, L. Mars
"Afraid to Go Home at All"
C. A. Bigelow
(*Music by* Egbert Van Alstyne. *Lyrics by* Harry Williams.)
Students' Chorus
"Three Weeks (with You)"
Misses Lorraine, Rankin, Francis, Whitmore, Walton, Chase, Kellogg; Messrs. Wood, Oatman, Young, Barry, Rinehart, Fairbrother, Wentzel
Pierrot Patrole and Dance
Finale

1908.40 THE PRIMA DONNA

A Comic Opera in Two Acts[63]. Libretto by Henry Blossom. Music by Victor Herbert. Staged by Fred G. Latham. Scenery painted by Homer Emens. Dresses by Mlle. Elsie DeWolfe. Orchestra under the direction of John Lund. Produced by Charles Dillingham. Opened 30 November 1908 at the Knickerbocker Theatre and closed 30 January 1909 after 72 performances.

CAST: *Colonel Dutois*: St. Clair Bayfield. *Captain Bordenave*: WILLIAM K. HARCOURT. *Lieutenant Armand*, Count de Fontenne: WILLIAM RAYMOND. *Lieutenant Fernand Drouillard*: DONALD HALL. *Lieutenant Gaston de Randal*: MARTIN HAYDON. *Lieutenant Prosper Rousseau*: George W. MacNamara. *Lieutenant Eugene de Beaumont*: Robert E. Clark. *Monsieur Beaurivage*, Athenée's father: W. J. FERGUSON. *Herr Max Gundelfinger*, known as "Pop": JAMES E. SULLIVAN. *Signor Giuseppe Ciucicini*: Phil Branson. *Baron de Pompal*: Herbert Ayling. *First waiter*: Armand Cortes. *Second waiter*: Peter Canova. *Mother Justine*, proprietress of the café: Josephine Bartlett. *Mlle. Athenée*, prima donna of the Opéra Comique, Paris: FRITZI SCHEFF. *Margot*: Gwendolyn Valentine. *Mlle. Mathilde, Mlle. Désirée*, Café chanteuses: Grace Delmar, Renee Dyris. *The Dancer*: La Noveta. *The Duchess of Montrose*: RUTH HOLT BOUCICAULT. *Countess Helene*: BLANCHE MORRISON. *Marquise du Perrifonds*: Katherine Stewart. *Cafe-concert girls (4)*: *Celeste*: Margaret Ross. *Mignon*: Gertrude Doremus. *Clairette*: Virginia Reed. *Bebe*: Marguerite May. *Metropolitan Octette*, Act 2: Margaret MacKenzie, Margaret Harrison (soprani); Florence Fisk, Evelyn Jackson (contralti); Albert A. Dennay, Fred. Killeen (tenori); Walter White, Virgil Holmes (bassi).

Other characters by Misses Margaret Harrison, Margaret MacKenzie, Evelyn Jackson, Florence Fisk, Olive Stanley, Eleanor Mansfield, Vina Snyder, Marie Barry, Josephine Gibbons, Katherine Leslie, Evelyn Mitchell, Emma Tritcheler, Alma Picard, Clara Faye, Ada Cooke, Anna Pelham, Gertrude Douglas, Lillian Randolph, Ailsa Craig, Marie Franklin, Grace Crowley, Genevieve Hawes, Vivian Rose, Muriel Harmon, Luivine Frankel, Irene Moyer, Dottie Moyer, La Reve, Evelyn Hall, Beatrice Cummings. Messrs. Albert Denny, Fred Killeen, Walter White, Virgil Holmes, Herman Walters, P. Hahn, H. Russell, H. Semels, F. von Gottfried, Leonard Hartley, I. Goldman, J. S. Duffus, Sidney Glass, W. H. Mytinger.

Act 1: The Pomme d'Or Café, St. Germain.

Act 2: The Club House at Ile de Puteaux in Paris.

ACT 1[64]
Opening Chorus
"There's Only One Rose in the Garden of Love"
"Something Always Happens When It Shouldn't"
J. E. Sullivan
"Here's to My Comrades and Me"
"Dream Love" ('Twas Only Dreaming)
F. Scheff
"A Soldier's Life Is Never Long" and Ensemble
Chorus
"Oh! Oh! Oh!"
Ballet Waltz
"O Mia Speranza"
"A Soldier's Love!"
F. Scheff
Finale
Chorus

ACT 2
Opening Chorus
Ensemble
"The One You're Looking For"
"When Girls Command the Army"
"Everybody Else's Girl Looks Better to Me Than Mine"
M. Haydon
"What Is Love" (Octette)/
"A Man and a Maid" (Octette)
"I'll Be Married to the Music of a Military Band"
J. E. Sullivan
"Espagnola"
F. Scheff
Finale

1908.41 THE PIED PIPER

An Operatic Fantasy (Musical Comedy) in Two Acts, Five Scenes. Book and lyrics by Austin Strong and R. H. Burnside. Music by Manuel Klein. Staged by R. H. Burnside. Orchestra conducted by Manuel Klein. Produced by Sam S. and Lee Shubert (Inc.). Opened 3 December 1908 at the Majestic Theatre and closed 16 January 1909 after 52 performances.[65]

Interpolated after opening, as per published sheet music:
"See What You've Done to Me"
C. A. Bigelow
(*Music and Lyrics by* Benjamin Hapgood Burt.)

[61]Dropped during the run.

[62]Replaced during the run by:
"Shine On, Harvest Moon" (from ZIEGFELD FOLLIES OF 1908)
L. Lorraine, School Girls
(*Music and Lyrics by* Nora Bayes and Jack Norworth.)

[63]Below the show's title in programs appeared the words "Made in America."

[64]Musical Numbers not listed in program. List below prepared from the published vocal score. Other musical numbers not in vocal score: "If You Were I and I Were You" (*sung by* B. Morrison, D. Hall); "You'll Be Surprised"; "Chanson."

[65]Settings, costumes uncredited.

CAST: *The Pied Piper*: DeWOLF HOPPER. *His Offical Adviser*: William Cameron. *His Offical Reminder*: D. L. Baker. *The Board of Aldermen*: W. L. ROMAINE. *The Bad Boy*: Bert Devlin. *Willie Van Cortlandt*: JOHN PHILLIPS. *Sammy Struggles*: EDWARD HERON. *Lizzie Dizzy*: GRACE CAMERON. *The Housekeeper*: Ada Deaves. *The Model Couple*: Frank Laddis, Bonnie Farley. *Romance*: Lillian Thatcher. *Poetry*: Elda Curry. *Song*: Mabel Mordaunt. *Father Time*: WARREN FABIAN. *Elviria*: MARGUERITE CLARK. *Chorus*.

Act 1, Scene 1: The Home of Father Time. *Scene 2*: Saint Valentine's Square in the City of Innocence.

Act 2, Scene 1: The Pied Piper's Boudoir. *Scene 2*: The Nursery. *Scene 3*: Saint Valentine's Square in the City of Innocence.

ACT 1

Introduction

"It's Going to be a Very Busy Day" (Chorus)

"We Tell Him Just What to Do" (Duet)
W. Cameron, D. L. Baker

"(A) Woman's a Wonderful Thing"[66] (Song)
D. Hopper, Chorus

"The Dresden China Plate" (Song)
M. Clark

"Adam and Eve"[67] (Song)
G. Cameron

"I'm Looking for a Sweetheart" (Duet)
M. Clark, J. Phillips

"Love Is a Curious Feeling"[68] (Sextette)
D. Hopper, J. Phillips, E. Heron, M. Clark, A. Deaves, G. Cameron

"It's the Little Things That Count in Life" (Duet)
G. Cameron, D. Hopper

Finale

ACT 2

Opening Chorus

"It All Depends" (Trio)
E. Heron, W. Cameron, D. L. Baker

"It Really Was a Very Pretty Story"[69] (Song)
M. Clark

"I Should Like to Know the Reason" (Duet)
D. Hopper, M. Clark

"Sentimental Sarah"[70] (Song)
G. Cameron

"Nursery Rhymes" (Song)
D. Hopper

"(Tell Me,) Whose Little Girl Are You" (Duet)
M. Clark, J. Phillips

"What Do You Think of That?"[71] (Quartette)
E. Heron, G. Cameron, M. Clark, D. Hopper

1908.42 THE QUEEN OF THE MOULIN ROUGE

A Musical Comedy-Drama in Two Acts, 8 Scenes. Book by Paul M. Potter. Music by John T. Hall. Lyrics by Vincent Bryan. Staged by Frank Smithson. Dances arranged by Joseph C. Smith. Scenery painted by Edward G. Unitt and Joseph Wickes. Costumes by Will R. Barnes. Orchestra under the direction of Charles Zimmerman. Produced by Thomas W. Ryley. Opened 7 December 1908 at the Circle Theatre and closed 24 April 1909 after 160 performances.

CAST: *Princess Marotz Rakovitza*: FLORA PARKER. *Sacha*, King of Orcania: CARTER DeHAVEN. *Sergius*, ex-King of Orcania: RICHARD F. CARROLL. *Daddy Gimble*: RICHARD F. CARROLL. *Italian Waiter*: RICHARD F. CARROLL. *Ma'm Monicart*: RICHARD F. CARROLL. *Monsieur Belschazzar*, loan broker: RICHARD F. CARROLL. *Narcisse*, a tramp: RICHARD F. CARROLL. *Dobrofsky*, an Anarchist: RICHARD F. CARROLL. *Savourette*, art teacher: EDWARD M. FAVOR. *Major General Bonnivard*: Fred Rivenhall. *Olga Zu Linar, Dorothy Wildreck*, Art Students: Berta Mills, Veola Adams. *Anna*, an Orcanian maid; *Telegraph Operator*: Louise Alexander. *Mme. St. Angelo*: Juliette Dika. *Tod McAlpin, Phelim O'Shea*: George Anderson, Edward Wilson. *Van Gosling*: FLETCHER NORTON. *Inspector of Police*: A. Allan Campbell. *Count Kristof*: Frank Sherlock. *Baron St. Etienne*: T. DeVassey. *Philippe*, of the Quat-z-Arts: George Wharnock. *Mariette*: Jeanette Horton. *Alice*: Elizabeth Whitney. *Lea*: Hattie Forsyth. *Chochon*: May Maloney. *Edmee*: Eileen Kearney. *Mathilde*: Doris Cameron. *Margot*: Eleanor Thorne. *Parisette*, a shop girl: Odette Auber. *A Flower Girl*: Patricia Collinge. *Blanchard*, a singer: Reginald DeVeulle. *Durand*, a citizen: Frank X. [Francis] Bushman. *Constant*, a waiter: Harry Humphreys. *Wu Tin*: P. H. Riblet. *Agent of Police*: Russell Price. (*Apache Dancers*: Joseph C. Smith, Louise Alexander.)

Dancing Girls: Misses Grace Russell, Trudie Hatch, Lotta McCree, Ethel Mostyn, Adele Marie, Violet Zell, Gail Crandall, Frances Alain, Anita Pollock, Marguerite St. Clair, Regina Connelly. *Art Students*: Misses Billie Cuppia, Stella Hansen, Irene George, Florence Townshend, Inez Blair, Leila Parker, Ethel Davis, Madeline Seville, Eloise Reed, Genevieve Reed, Grace Lester, Lillian Dowd. *Students*: Messrs. Joel Johnston, Waldo Heineman, Frank Bushman, Joseph Tullar, Stephen Haggery, Horace Blankinship, Harry Dee, Al LaCroix, Edward Crawford, P. H. Riblet, Albert Barlow, Charles Price, Rudolph Allen, Harry Humphreys, Charles Dalton, John Hamilton. *Students, Artists, Art Students, Models, Apaches, Tourists, Street Singers, Gigolos, Gigolettes, Prison Matrons, Grisettes.*

The action takes place in Paris at the present time.

Act 1, Scene 1: Roof of the Academy Savourette, Quartier Montparnasse. *Scene 2*: A telegraph office. *Scene 3*: Cabaret of the Quat-z-arts.

Act 2, Scene 1: "The House with the Green Shutters." *Scene 2*: A Police station. *Scene 3*: Place Pigalle, in front of the "Rat Mort." *Scene 4*: Boulevard Clichy. *Scene 5*: Roof of the Academy Savouertte.

ACT 1

Scene 1

Opening Chorus
Art Students

"Painting Paris" (Come with Me and Paint Paris)
C. DeHaven, Chorus

"The Quarrel" (Duet)
F. Rivenhall, R. F. Carroll {Sergius}

"Shy Little Violet Blue"
F. Parker, Chorus

"Drill of the Coquette Corps"
F. Parker, B. Mills, V. Adams, Students

Scene 2

Drinking Trio
E. M. Favor, F. Rivenhall, L. Alexander

Scene 3

"Quat-z-arts" (Opening Chorus)
Ensemble

French Chanson
R. DeVeulle

"Sweet Rosa Pompetta"
R. F. Carroll {Sergius}, Chorus

"Psychical Society"
E. M. Favor

"Papa's Popular Boy"
F. Norton, Girls

"In Orcania"
C. DeHaven, Chorus

Finale

ACT 2

Scene 1

"The Pleasure Brigade"
Ensemble

"Love's Dream Is Over" (Sextet)(Our Dream of Love Is O'er)
F. Parker, B. Mills, V. Adams, C. DeHaven, E. Wilson, G. Anderson

"I've Waited Long for Thee"
R. F. Carroll, Chorus

Scene 2

"Take That Off, Too" (Chorus)
A. A. Campbell, Girls

---

[66]Replaced for subsequent tour by:
"The Pirate's Doom"
D. Hopper, Children
(*Music by* A. Baldwin Sloane. *Lyrics by* Glen McDonough.)

[67]For subsequent tour, moved to Act 2 following "I Should Like to Know the Reason."

[68]Dropped for subsequent tour.

[69]Dropped for subsequent tour.

[70]Dropped for subsequent tour.

[71]Dropped for subsequent tour.

Scene 3
"The Under-world" (Dance)
J. C. Smith, L. Alexander
"The Kicking Polka"[72]
O. Auber, R. DeVeulle
Scene 4
"Drummed Out"
Ensemble
Scene 5
"Clock Song"
Art Students
"Little Old New York"
F. Norton, Chorus
Finale

1908.43 PEGGY MACHREE

A Romantic Comedy with Music in Three Acts. Play (and lyrics) by Patrick Bidwell[73]. (Original music by Signor Michele Esposito, Clarence Lucas.) Staged by Percy F. Leach. Scenery painted by Frank Platzer. Costumes by Klaw & Erlanger Costume Department. Conductor, Antonio DeNovellis. Orchestrations by Clarence Lucas. Produced by Brooks and Dingwall. Opened 21 December 1908 at the Broadway Theatre and closed 23 January 1909 after 40 performances.

CAST: *Barry Trevor*, (a young English-Irishman traveling in Ireland): JOSEPH O'MARA. *Sir Lawrence Borthwick*, his friend: PERCY F. LEACH. *Captain de la Cour*, Peggy's cousin from France: Marc MacDermott. *Lawyer Keane*, family solicitor to the O'Driscolls: Marcus Moriarty. *Alexander McDougal*, major-domo at Castle O'Driscoll: JOHN D. O'HARA. *Michael Donoghue*, the O'Driscoll's hereditary piper who can't pipe: Dan Fitzgerald. *Bampton*, sergeant in the English army, afterwards Trevor's servant: ARTHUR WYNN. *Priest*: Fred A. Cordes. *Patsy*, a villager: C. P. Waters. *Mike*: Ed Cahill. *The Lady Margaret O'Donnell* (Peggy): ADRIENNE AUGARDE. *Mme. de la Cour*, her aunt: Corah Adams. *The Hon. Emily Pryor*, Trevor's cousin: Belle Daube. *Moira*, the widow Cafferty, Peggy's foster mother: Jennie Lamont. *Molly Cafferty*, Moira's daughter: Katharine Moran. *Nora*, a village girl: Jean Waters. *Cathleen*, a village girl: Stella Baker. *Mrs. Ryan*: Miriam Cordes. *Villagers, Children, Servants, Soldiers*.

The action takes place in Ireland about 1740.

Act 1: Edge of Downkilty Fair. Morning.

Act 2: Courtyard of Castle O'Driscoll. Five years later. Afternoon.

Act 3: Great Hall of Castle O'Driscoll. The evening of the next day.

ACT 1
"Downkilty Fair" {traditional}
Chorus
(*Music arranged by* Michele Esposito.)
"The Colors of the King"
J. Waters, Chorus
(*Music by* Michele Esposito.)
"Maureen"
J. O'Mara, Chorus
(*Music and Lyrics by* Alicia Adelaide Needham.)
"Co-Boss"
K. Moran, Chorus
(*Music by* Clarence Lucas. *Lyrics by* Denis O'Sullivan.)
"The Ould Plaid Shawl"
J. O'Mara
(Traditional, arranged by Clarence Lucas.)
"The Idle Colleen" {traditional}
A. Augarde
(*Music arranged by* Michele Esposito.)
"Peggy Machree"
A. Augarde, J. O'Mara
(*Music arranged by* Michele Esposito.)
"Believe Me (If All Those Endearing Young Charms)" {Moore's melodies}
J. O'Mara

ACT 2
"Follow the Plow" {traditional}
Chorus
(*Music arranged by* Clarence Lucas.)
"The Exile's Return" {traditional}
J. O'Mara
(*Music and Lyrics arranged by* Alicia Adelaide Needham.)
"The Birds Fly South" {traditional}
J. O'Mara
(*Music arranged by* Michele Esposito.)
"(O) Lovely Roses" {traditional}
A. Augarde
(*Music arranged by* Clarence Lucas.)
"Family Pride"
P. F. Leach, A. Augarde
(*Music by* Clarence Lucas.)

ACT 3
"Ladies, We Love You" (Drinking Song)
A. Wynn, Chorus
(*Music by* Clarence Lucas.)
"The Wearin' of the Green"
J. O'Mara
"Scotland Ye Ken" (Bonny Scotland)
J. D. O'Hara, Maids
(*Music by* Clarence Lucas.)
"O, Never Trust to Strangers" {traditional}
A. Augarde
(*Music arranged by* Michele Esposito.)
"Hail to the Deer" {old air}
Chorus
(*Music arranged by* Michele Esposito.)
"Peggy Machree" (reprise)

1908.44 MR. HAMLET OF BROADWAY

A Musical Whimsicality (Comedy) in Two Acts. Book by Edgar Smith. Music by Ben M. Jerome. Lyrics by Edward Madden. Production staged by Ned Wayburn. Scenery by Arthur Voegtlin. Orchestra under the direction of Ben M. Jerome. Produced by Sam S. and Lee Shubert, Inc. Opened 23 December 1908 at the Casino Theatre and closed 6 February 1909 after 54 performances.[74]

CAST: *Joey Wheeze*, late Clown, Bunko Brothers Circus: EDDIE FOY. *Barnaby Bustle*, Business Man: GEORGE A. SCHILLER. *Jonathan Cheatam*, Landlord Starvation Inn: OSCAR ('RAGS') RAGLAND. *Tom Manleigh*, Captain of the "Utica Reds": John H. Pratt. *Monsieur Fourneau*, a waiter at Delmonico's: EUGENE REDDING. *Hank Piper*, Adirondack Guide: Harry Madison. *"Amelie"*, a Trained Bear: JAMES F. COOK. *Arthur Goodrich*, Lieutenant of the "Utica Reds": R. H. Strong. *Sergeant McSweeney*, Sergeant of the "Utica Reds": William Morgan. *Harold Yardstick*, guest: Harry Simpson. *Schippenbach*, guest: Valentine Holman. *Rafferty*, the porter: William Rees. *Blootch*, the waiter: Jud Brady. *Mrs. Daisy Stringer*, New York Cloak Model: LAURA GUERITE. *Molly Brown*, an Adirondack belle: MAUDE RAYMOND. *Mrs. Barnaby Bustle*, President of the Daughters of the Classics: MABELLE BAKER. *Cymbaline Bustle*, her daughter: DAPHNE POLLARD. *Miss Annabelle*, Head Parlor Maid, Starvation Inn: Helene Davis. *"Brakebeam Pete,"* a Tramp Soldier: JAMES F. COOK. *Coal Oil Johnny*, another (tramp soldier): HARRY MADISON. *Miss Take*: Susie Pitt. *Miss Fortune*: Florence Douglas. *Miss Pronounce*: Mollie McGrath. *Miss Behave*: Maude Stanley. *Miss Adventure*: Elizabeth Gardiner. *Miss Understood*: Florence Blake. *Miss Hap*: Cuyler Mitchell. *Miss Deed*: Olga Roller. *Felix*, Head Bell Boy: Marie DuPree. *Patsy*, Second Bell Boy: Octavia Hague. *Blondy*, Third Bell Boy: Vera Maxwell.

Cast for Hamlet: *Hamlet*: EDDIE FOY. *King*: GEORGE A. SCHILLER. *Queen*: MABELLE BAKER. *Horatio*: EUGENE REDDING. *Ophelia*: MAUDE RAYMOND.

Act 1: Starvation Inn—Lake Mosquito, Adirondack Mountains.

Act 2: Summit of Mount Katish—Camp of the Utica Reds.

ACT 1[75]
"We've Been Taken In" (Opening Chorus)

---

[72]Program note: (Performers) especially engaged from the Folies Bergere.

[73]Nom de plume for Mrs. Denis O'Sullivan, who wrote the play as a vehicle for her husband. He died while the show was touring, and Joseph O'Mara premiered it in New York.

[74]Costumes uncredited.

[75]Interpolation as per published sheet music:
"Beautiful Eyes"
L. Guerite
(*Music by* Ted Snyder. *Lyrics by* George Whiting and Carter DeHaven.)

"In a Summer Hotel" (The Man Who Built the Summer Hotel)
O. Ragland, Ned Wayburn's Girls
"Won't You Harmonize with Me"[76]
L. Guerite, Chorus
"Everything Depends on Money"
E. Foy
Ensemble
"Good-Bye, Molly Brown" (Molly Brown)
M. Raymond
"Under the Honeymoon"
J. H. Pratt, D. Pollard
"The Hornpipe Rag"
L. Guerite, Chorus
"Tell Us What's the Row" (Finale)

ACT 2
"In the Golden Dawn"
J. H. Pratt, Male Chorus
"That's as Far as You Can Go"
D. Pollard, J. H. Pratt, Ned Wayburn's Girls
"When I Was a Kid Like You"
E. Foy, Children
"The Dusky Salome"
M. Raymond, Girls
"A Poor Little Girl Like Me"
D. Pollard
"Nobody's Got Anything on Me" (None of Them's Got Anything on Me)
E. Foy, Girls, Chorus
"Dancing Is So Delightful"
J. F. Cook, H. Madison
"Regimental Review"
"I Want to Join the Army"/
"When We Made the Gallant Charge of Bunker Hill"
Ensemble
Finale
Entire Company

1909.01 KITTY GREY

A Musical Comedy in Three Acts, 4 Scenes. (Book and lyrics) Adapted from the French by J. Smyth Pigott[77]. (Based on the play "Les Fêtards" by Antony Mars and Maurice Hennequin.) Music, with Introductions, by Lionel Monckton and Howard Talbot. Produced under the stage direction of Austin Hurgon. Orchestra under the direction of William T. Francis. Presented by Charles Frohman. Opened 25 January 1909 at the New Amsterdam Theatre and closed 6 March 1909 after 50 performances.[78]

CAST: *The Earl of Dulston*: G. P. HUNTLEY. *Sir John Binfield*: F. POPE STAMPER. *Ernest III*, King of Illyria: CHARLES ANGELO. *Count Trenitz*: Frank Perfitt. *Karl*, *Fritz*, the King's attendants: Percy Corray, Robert Corray. *Pontbichet*, manager of the Hotel Royale: Francis Gaillard. *Joseph*, English waiter at the hotel: PERCIVAL KNIGHT. *Lady Binfield*: VALLI VALLI. *Sadie Poulson*, her sister, an American heiress: Eva Kelly. *Madame Pontbichet*: Barbara Huntley. *Susan Bright*, Kitty Grey's dresser: Mabel Sealby. *Queen of Illyria*: Glory Pearce. *Actresses at the Apollo Theatre (6)*: *Gladys*: Gladys Desmond. *Millicent*: Millicent Forsyth. *Ethel*: Ethel Forsyth. *Barbara*: Barbara Dunbar. *Mabel*: Mabel D'Estere. *Dorothea*: Dorothea Temple. *Kitty Grey*: JULIA SANDERSON. *Chorus of Villagers, Flower Sellers, Bathing Attendants, Guests, Actors and Actresses.*

Act 1: Hotel Royale, Biarritz.

Act 2, Scene 1: Kitty Grey's Dressing Room. *Scene 2*: Pinafore Room, Savoy Hotel, London.

Act 3: Duplay's Restaurant, London.

ACT 1
Opening Chorus
Ensemble
"Sweet Kitty (Grey)" (Song)
J. Sanderson
(*Music and Lyrics by* St. John Hammond and Richard Kenneth.)
"Welcome to His Majesty" (Chorus)
"Incognito" (Song)
C. Angelo
"The Tract" (Duet)
F. P. Stamper, V. Valli
"A Gentleman's Gentleman" (Song)
P. Knight, Chorus
Finale

ACT 2
Scene 1
Chorus
"If the Girl Wants You (Never Mind the Color of Her Eyes)" (Song)
J. Sanderson
(*Music by* Jerome Kern. *Lyrics by* M. E. Rourke.)
Finale
Scene 2
"For She's a Jolly Good Fellow" (Chorus)
"King Hal's Gals" (Song)
C. Angelo
(*Music and Lyrics by* St. John Hammond and Richard Kenneth.)
"Mr. Soldier" (Song)
J. Sanderson
(*Music by* Harold Lonsdale. *Lyrics by* Ralph Roberts.)
"M'lle. Pirouette" (Song)
V. Valli
"The Ode" (Trio)
Finale
Ensemble

ACT 3
"Just Good Friends" (Duet)
J. Sanderson, F. P. Stamper
(*Music by* Jerome Kern. *Lyrics by* M. E. Rourke.)
"Kitty's Not Built That Way" (Song)
J. Sanderson
Finale

1909.02 STUBBORN CINDERELLA

A Musical Play in Three Acts. Book and lyrics by Will M. Hough and Frank Adams. Music by Joseph E. Howard. Staged by George Marion. Scenery by Frank Gates and Edward A. Morange. Costumes by Will R. Barnes. Orchestra under the direction of Arthur Pell. Produced by Mort H. Singer. Opened 25 January 1909 at the Broadway Theatre and closed 10 April 1909 after 88 performances.

CAST: (in order of appearance): *Fat*: CHARLES PRINCE. *Skeeter*: ROBERT HARRINGTON. *Sallie*: DOROTHY BRENNER. *Lois*: ALICE DOVEY. *A Tutor*: Alan Brooks. *The President*: Don Merrifield. *Thaddeus Leonardo*, a famous sculptor: Charles Rankin. *A Cab Driver*: John Wheeler. *Police Sergeant*: Ben Turbett. *"Mac"*: JOHN BARRYMORE. *Officer*: Charles Wedlake. *Grid*: Clarence Lutz. *Colonel Hunt*, of the visiting English party: JAMES C. MARLOWE. *Lady Leslie*, daughter of the Earl of Glenkirk: SALLIE FISHER. *Lady Evelyn*, her aunt: Helen Salinger. *An Engineer*: Ben Turbett. *A Porter*: Charles Wedlake. *An Indian*: Don Merrifield. *Hotel Manager*: Frank Magin. *College Boys and Girls, Lady Leslie's Military Escort, English Girls, Italian Laborers, Passengers on the Sunset Flyer, Cowboys, Mexicans, etc.*

"The Little Bowling Alley Sally Ran"
E. Foy
(*Music by* Ben M. Jerome. *Lyrics by* Edward Madden.)
Added for the national tour, second edition which opened 30 August 1909 in Toronto:
"Down Where the Watermelon Grows"
E. Foy
(*Music by* George Evans.)
"Hamlet's Ghost"
E. Foy

[76]Replaced for subsequent tour by:
"She Wanted to be a Show Girl"
Nanon Jacques (Mrs. Stringer), Chorus

[77]Incorrectly billed in the program as J. W. Pigott. First produced in London as a non-musical adapted by J. W. Pigott as KITTY GREY, then subsequently musicalized for London audiences.

[78]Settings, costumes uncredited.

Show Girls: Misses Adams, Baker, Boswell, Carleton, Cecil, Cummings, Deskaw, Downing, Edwards, Everette, Feltes, Francis, Gilbert, Harrington, Harris, Horlock, Houck, Hubbard, Lockwood, Merrill, Miller, Moon, A. Notter, H. Notter, O'Day, Oty, Porterfield, Rodriquez, Shaw, Stephenson, Stone, Stoy, Vose, Webb, White, Young. *Boys*: Messrs. Damarel, Diamond, Gates, Hamilton, Headley, Hutchins, Lansky, Lasher, Lutz, Merrill, McDermott, McKitteridge, Murray, Sampson, Wood, Yorkshire.

Act 1: Campus of Columbus University. Afternoon.

Act 2: A Mountain Wilderness near the Mexican Border. Next day.

Act 3: Natatorium of Hotel del Coronado. Coronado Beach, California, during the progress of the Orange Fête.

ACT 1[79]

Opening Chorus
Ensemble
"Love Me Just Because"
A. Dovey, Chorus
"Don't Be Cross with Me"
S. Fisher, Chorus
"I'm in Love with All the Girls I Know"
R. Harrington, Chorus

ACT 2

"None But the Brave Deserve the Fair"
J. C. Marlowe, Chorus
"The Land of the Sky":
"Adios, Senorita"
D. Brenner, Chorus
"Don't Be Anybody's Moon But Mine"
A. Dovey, Chorus
Cinderella Solo (off stage)
C. R. Wood
Dream Minuet (Finale Act 2)
S. Fisher, Chorus

ACT 3

"Don't Teach Me to Swim Alone"
D. Brenner, Chorus
"If They'd Only Let Poor Adam's Rib Alone"
J. Barrymore, J. C. Marlowe, R. Harrington, C. Prince
"The Orange Fête" introducing
Entrance of the Orange Pickers
Entrance of Orange Blossoms (Ensemble Ballet)
Entrance of Evil Sprite which attempts to destroy the Orange Blossoms. The Orange Pickers defend the Blossoms and destroy the Evil Sprite.
Entrance of the Oranges and the Orange Buyers (Ensemble Ballet)
"When You First Kiss the Last Girl You Love"
S. Fisher

1909.03 THE FAIR CO-ED

A College Comedy with Music (Musical Comedy) in Three Acts. Book and lyrics by George Ade. Music by Gustav Luders. Play staged by Fred G. Latham. Dances arranged by William Rock. Settings designed by Homer Emens. Costumes by Elsie DeWolfe. Orchestra under the direction by Robert Hood Bowers. Produced by Charles Dillingham. Opened 1 February 1909 at the Knickerbcker Theatre, moved 26 April 1909 to the Criterion Theatre and closed 29 May 1909 after 136 performances.

CAST: *Davy Dickerson*, almost a senior: ARTHUR STANFORD. *Wellington Reed*, '78, an old grad: SYDNEY JARVIS. *Josephus Cadwallader*, professor of psychology: Edgar Halstead. *Ernest Grubb*, a scholarship star: H. David Todd. *Freddie Carrington*, a society star: Lionel Walsh. *Bob Chester*, an athletic star: James Reaney. *Captain Peacock*, a military star: Donald McLaren. *Squab Dingle*, freshman: HARRY CLARKE. *Grouch Hubbard*, president of Woman's Haters' League: Leavitt James. *A Sergeant*: Stuart Belknap. *Cynthia Bright*, the only co-ed: ELSIE JANIS. *Angelina Baxter* of Red Wing, Minnesota: Inez Bauer. *Hazel Pinkham* of Worcester, Massachusetts: Constance Eastman. *Byrdie Wheeler* of Boise, Idaho: Marion Mills. *Magnolia Curtis* of Jackson, Mississippi: Elsie Steele.

Town Girls and Visitors: Ella Rock, Bertha Morrelle, Bena Hoffman, Josie Karlin, Effie Wheeler, Leila Benton, Clara Eckstrom, Louise Donovan, May Fields, Lillian Nicholson, Florence Major, Bessie Holbrook, Fanny Robertson, Daisy Johnstone, Jeanette D'Arville, Bella Desmond, Birdice MacLaughlin, E. Mae Davis, Bessie Skeer. *Freshmen, Sophomores, Juniors, Seniors, etc.*: Messrs. Robb, Burbank, Fenn, Beck, Sargent, Revere, Hinds, Stuart, Wood, Bobbe, Strange, Hancock, Baum, Miller, Aveling, Benbow, Kingsland, Roberts, Dietrich, Champlin, Porter, Lloyd, Allen, Fischer, Charwate, Young, Smith, Bernard. *Banjoists*: Messrs. Ward, Carpenter, Wallace. *Waltzers*: Bena Hoffman, L. [Larry] M. Beck.

Act 1: In front of Bright Hall, Bingham College, afternoon of 1 June.

Act 2: Interior of the Armory and Drill Hall, one week alter. The annual Military Ball.

Act 3: On the Campus, the following morning.

ACT 1[80]

Opening Chorus
L. Walsh, Chorus
"Almost"
"The College Military"
"I'll Dream of That Sweet Co-Ed" (College Serenade)
Finale
E. Janis, L. Walsh, H. D. Todd, E. Halstead, J. Reaney, S. Jarvis, D. McLaren, A. Stanford, Chorus

ACT 2

Opening Chorus
Chorus
"(Sing Hey for) The Chaperon" (Entrance Song)
H. Clarke, Girls
"Leave It to the Boys in the Navy"
"Please Don't Keep Me Waiting"
"(The) Day of the Game"
S. Jarvis, Chorus

ACT 3

Opening Chorus
Chorus
"An Isle of the Philippines"
"A Little Girl That's Wise"
I. Bauer, H. Clarke
Finale

1909.04 HAVANA

A Musical Play in Three Acts[81]. Book by George Grossmith, Jr. and Graham Hill. Revised for America by James T. Powers. Music by Leslie Stuart. Lyrics by Adrian Ross and George Arthurs. Entire production staged by Ned Wayburn. Scenery painted by Arthur Voegtlin. Orchestra under the direction of Clarence Rogerson. Produced by Sam S. and Lee Shubert (Inc.). Opened 11 February 1909 at the Casino Theatre and closed 10 July 1909 after 177 performances; re-opened 8 August 1909 at the Casino Theatre and closed 25 September 1909 after 59 additional performances. Total: 236 performances.[82]

CAST: *Senator Bombito Del Campo*, Mayor of Havana, a Cigar Manufacturer, long on birth and short on money: HAROLD VIZARD. *Consuelo*, his niece: EDITH DECKER. *Isabelita*, his sister, a "revolutionista": EVA DAVENPORT. *Don Adolfo*, his son, fresh from an English University: ERNEST LAMBART. *Anita*, a cigar vender, heroine of an obsolete matrimonial adventure: CLARA PALMER. *Pepita, Lolita, Tita*, Cigarette girls employed by Bombito: Daisy Green, Viola Kellogg, Mabel Weeks. *Mamie*, the stenographer at Bombito's establishment: Geraldine Malone. *Gladys*, a newspaper beauty from Pensacola: EDITH KELLY. *Senora Donna Junenez*, a fortune teller: VIOLA KELLOGG. *Teressa*, a flower girl: Violet Hopkins. *Diego de la Concha*, superintendent at Bombito's establishment and a chronic revolutionist: WILLIAM PRUETTE. *J. DePeyster Jackson*, an American yacht owner on a cruise to Cuba: JOSEPH PHILLIPS. *Frank Van Dusen*, his friend: William Phillips. *Reginald Brown*,

[79]Added for subsequent tour after "Love Me Just Because:"
"What's the Use"
{"Mac"}

[80]Musical numbers not listed in program. List prepared from published vocal score. Other musical numbers not in vocal score: "Barn Dance Schottische"; "College Medley" (arranged by Robert Hood Bowers.); "Dans des Hottentots"; "The Girl I Knew"; "Here in the Starlight"; "The Real American Girl"; "Valse (Billet Doux)."

[81]Billed as from "the George Edwardes Gaiety Theatre, London."

[82]Costumes uncredited.

steward on Jackson's yacht *"The Wasp"*: Percy Ames. *Roderigo*, a gallant, in love with Consuelo: Bertram Grassby. *Hilario, Alejandro, Enrigo*, employees of Bombito: ERNEST HARE, Ted Sullivan, Glen Conner. *Senor Patigo*, one of the Cause: Joseph Galton. *Soldaro*: Joseph Galton. *Sentry*: Eugene Roder. *Officer*: Milburry Ryder. *Chiquita*: Little Lillie Feuhrer. *Chiquito, Sammy, Jr.*: Master Robbie Fuehrer. *Julio*, of the Havana Police: Bertram Grassby. *Juan*, servant: Harry Sulkin. *Samuel Nix*, a matrimonial outlaw and Bo'sun of the *"The Wasp"*: JAMES T. POWERS.

Touring Newspaper Beauties: Misses Edith Kelly, Caroline Green, Dolly Filly, Erminie Clark, Elsa Croxton, Cecelia Mayo, Irene Hawley, Julia Mills. *Ladies of Havana*: Misses Emily Monti, B. Ryan, Gladys Alexander, Freda Braun, Helen Broderick, Marion Hartman. *Bombito's Clerks*: Messrs. Glen Conner, Alfred Gerrard, Irwin Harding, Jack Wellekin. *Gentlemen of Havana*: Messrs. Harold Nelson, Jack Brese, Harold Watson, Arthur McSorley, George Allison, Harry Sulkin. *Cuban Soldiers*: Messrs. Jean Roder, Arthur Whitman, Jack Leonard, Harry MacDonough, Jr, Philip Haring, Albert Massour, George Skillman, Milburry Ryder, Alexander Groves. *Cigarette Girls*: Misses Elsie Raymond, Adelaide Rossmi, Suzette Gordon, Isabelle Daintry, Mildred Bright, Lorraine Bright, Mary Murillo, Patsy O'Connor, Libbey Diamond, Mona Sartoris. *Cigar Girls*: Misses Hazel Williams, Dorothy Sayce, Ruth Elton, Irma Dixon, Jeanne McPherson, Miss Holmes, Isabel Cannar, Sylvia Loti, Mildred Dupree, Natalie Harvey.

Act 1: The Cigar Establishment of Bombito, Havana. Noon.

Act 2: The Patio of Bombito's Residence. The same evening.

Act 3: The Harbor, Havana. The next morning.

ACT 1

"'Tis Noon of Tropic Day" (Opening Chorus)

"The Yacht"
D. Green, V. Kellogg, M. Weeks, H. Vizard, E. Hare, T. Sullivan

"My Husband"
C. Palmer

"I'm a Cuban Girl"
E. Decker, Chorus

"Hello People"
E. Lambart, Newspaper Girlies
(*Lyrics by* George Arthurs.)

"The Girl with the Yellow Roses" (Finale)

ACT 2[83]

Opening Chorus:
"The Sun Is Down and Over the Town"
"Zara"
W. Pruette

"My (Little) Deutscher Girl" (My Little Deitscher Girl)
W. T. Powers, Chorus
(*Music and Lyrics by* Frank Leo. *American version by* James T. Powers.)

"On the Shores of Sheepshead Bay"
J. T. Powers, C. Palmer

"Cupid's Telephone"
E. Lambart, Newspaper Girlies
(*Lyrics by* George Arthurs.)

"Welcome to the Lovely Bride to Be" (Finale)

ACT 3

"Way Down in Pensacola"
J. Phillips, E. Kelly, Chorus
(*Lyrics by* Leslie Stuart.)

"How Did the Little Bird Know That?"
J. T. Powers, V. Kellogg

"Would You Like to Motor with Mater?"
E. Lambart, C. Palmer, Newspaper Girlies, Escorts
(*Lyrics by* George Arthurs.)

Final

[83]Added during the run to Act 2 after "My Little Deutscher Girl":
"What Shall I Do with the Rest?" (What Shall We Do with the Rest?)
E. Decker

1909.05

THE NEWLYWEDS AND THEIR BABY

A Musical Comedy in Two Acts, 4 Scenes. Book by Aaron Hoffman and Paul West. Based on the comic strip "The Newlyweds" by George McManus[84]. Music by Nat D. Ayer and John W. Bratton. Lyrics by Paul West and A. Seymour Brown. Staged by Frank Smithson. Dances arranged by Chris Maxwell. Costumes by Cora McGeachy. Electrical effects by Kleigl Brothers and Globe Lighting Company. Settings by P. Dodd Ackerman. Musical director, Eugene Salzer. Produced by The Leffler-Bratton Company (Inc.). Opened 22 March 1909 at the Majestic Theatre and closed 24 April 1909 after 40 performances.

CAST: *Ferdinand Newlywed*, a newlywed father and proud of it: WILLIAM CLIFTON. *Napoleon*, the baby: JAMES E. ROSEN. *Major Knott Much*, an abbreviation: JAMES E. ROSEN. *Tom Travers*, in love with Dolly: FLETCHER NORTON. *Professor August Nicol*, proprietor of infant incubators: IRVING BROOKS. *Adolph Nichol*, his brother: GEORGE P. MURPHY. *Dr. I. Curem*, the family physician: Tom Hadaway. *Mrs. Newlywed*, Baby's Mamma: RUBY RAY. *Gwendolin*, the baby's nurse: FLAVIA ARCARO. *Dolly Jolly*, Mrs. Newlywed's sister and ward of Mr. Newlywed: CARRIE REYNOLDS. *Bolivar*, the bear: Alfred Grady. *Sergeant Daly*, a police officer: Harry Murphy. *Dora, Cora*, incubator nurses: Minnie Higgins, Nancy Neville. *Violet, Rose*, dancing girls: Marguerite Florence, Leona Remington.

Prospective Mrs. Newlyweds: *Mary*: Enid Gibson. *Kate*: Minnie Higgins. *Jane*: Elfay White. *Bess*: Stella LaBelle. *Ray*: Helen Lavelle. *Marta*: Maeola Stockdale. *Ellen*: Irene Hastings. *Polly*: Irene Von Mueller. *Charlotte*: Jennie Lipman. *Louise*: May Wesley.

The Eight Napoleons: Millie Wood, Florence Campbell, Mella Drouet, Leslie Greer, Nancy Neville, Florence Florence, Alma Harding, Leona Remington. *The Pouter Pigeons*: Hazel Earl, May Green, Trixie Warren, Sue Vollmer, Bessie Hale, Minnie Hoffman, Agnes Richter, Irene Gardner.

Act 1, Scene 1: Napoleon's Nursery. The Party. *Scene 2*: The Chase for the Baby. *Scene 3*: The Boogie Boo Babies' Bedtime.

Act 2: A Garden Restaurant near Moonlight Park.

ACT 1[85]

"The King of Babyland"
Ensemble

[84]By arrangement with the New York World.

[85]This production continued to tour for many years after its Broadway run, and many songs were added and dropped. Among the added titles were:
"The Lovelight in My Eyes"
"Our Picture Book" (Act 1)
(Tom, Dolly)
"Begging the Baby to Sleep" (Act 1)
(Mrs. Newlywed)
"Great Big Blue Eyed Baby" (Act 1)
(Mrs. Newlywed)
"I Love You, Oh! Oh! Oh!" (Act 1)
(Tom, Chorus)
"Honeymoon Bells" (Act 1)
(Tom, Dolly)
"I'm Crazy Over You" (Act 1)
(Mrs. Newlywed)
"The Leader of the Band" (Act 1)
(Adolph, Girls)
"Take Me to That Tango Tea" (Act 1)
(Tom, Dolly)
"That Chop Stick Rag" (Act 1)
(Dolly, Chinese Ballet)
"(Be) My Sweitzer Bride" (Act 2)
(Mrs. Newlywed, Dolly, Ensemble)
(*Music by* Frank Stratton. *Lyrics by* Paul West.)
"Santa Rosa Rose" (Act 2)
(Mrs. Newlywed, Girls)
"Nonsensical Nonsense" (Act 2)
(Adolph)
"Minstrels on Parade" (Act 2)
"Down Red Rose Lane" (Act 2)
(Mrs. Newlywed, Rose Maids)
"Mamzelle Fifi" (Act 2)
Mr. Newlywed, Show Girls
"Come on Over Here" (Act 2)
(Gwendolin, Adolph)
"Fuzzy Wuzzy" (Act 2)
(Adolph, Newlywed, August, Dr. I. Curem)

"Teddy, the Jungle Man"
F. Norton, C. Reynolds
(*Music and Lyrics by* Kenneth S. Clark.)
"Napoleon"
W. Clifton, R. Ray, Chorus
"My Black Dove"
F. Arcaro
(*Music by* John W. Bratton. *Lyrics by* Paul West.)
"Love Time" (Loving Time)
F. Norton, M. Florence, L. Remington, Chorus
"The Boogie Boo"
W. Clifton, Boogie Boo Babies
Babies: Misses Hale, Earl, Hoffman, Gardner, Green, Volimar, Warren, Richter.
"I'm So Shy"[86]
C. Reynolds
"Baby's Gone"
Ensemble

ACT 2
"Supper Out of Doors"/
"Every Baby Is a Sweet Bouquet"
M. Higgins, N. Neville, Chorus
"An Operatic Solution"
G. P. Murphy, Chorus
"The Latest Sensation in Girls"
R. Ray, Eight Newlywed Girls
"Girls Who Want to Go Upon the Stage"
F. Arcaro
"Can't You See I Love You"
C. Reynolds, F. Norton, Chorus
(*Music by* Nat Ayer. *Lyrics by* A. Seymour Brown.)
"Valse Fantastique"
R. Ray
"Jig Along, Mr. Jigger"
W. Clifton, L. Remington, M. Florence, Eight Pouter Pigeons
Finale

1909.06 THE PROMOTERS

A Musical Frolic in Two Acts. Book by W. I. Flagg. Music by Joseph M. Daly. Lyrics by R. P. Janette. Produced by (Hap) Ward and (Harry) Vokes. Opened 29 March 1909 at the Metropolitan Theatre and closed 3 April 1909 after 8 performances.

CAST: *Lord Knows*: HAP WARD. *Count Upp*: HARRY VOKES. *Professor Dope*: LEW KELLEY. *Sandy Roads*: CHARLES "Sandy" CHAPMAN. *Willie Come*: JOHN MANLEY. *Mr. Haverway*: John C. Fenton. *Michael Hennessy O'Brien*: Richard Barry. *O. B. Jolly*: David DeWolfe. *Casey*, the dog: EDDIE JUDGE. *Celle Goode*: Ernest Altree. *A. Bunke*: W. W. Scott. *B. A. Round*: Louis LaVine. *Bowery Liz*: Jennie L. Moore. *Sue Brette*: JOSIE DALY. *Letta Haverway*: Marion Merrill. *May Haverway*: Frances Avery. *Sherry Holmes*: LUCY DALY.

MUSICAL NUMBERS[87]
"Sympathetic Sue"
"Tomorrow"
"To the One We Love Best" (In the land of the stein)
"The Only One I Love Is?"
L. Daly
"I'd Like to See Them All Together" (Soldier boys of every land)
"Somewhere There Is Someone I'd Like to Know"
(*Music by* Joseph Daly. *Lyrics by* Joseph Mittenthal.)

1909.07 THE BEAUTY SPOT

A Musical Play in Two Acts. Book and lyrics by Joseph W. Herbert. Music by Reginald DeKoven. Staged by Frank Smithson. Dances arranged by Julian Alfred. Settings by H. Robert Law, Edward G. Unitt and Joseph Wickes. Costumes by Julia Cummings (ladies' dresses), Orange Manufacturing Company (fancy dresses). Musical direction by Frank P. Paret. Produced by F. Ray Comstock and Morris Gest. Opened 10 April 1909 at the Herald Square Theatre and closed 7 August 1909 after 137 performances.

CAST: *General Samovar*, of the Russian legation, at Paris: JEFFERSON DeANGELIS. *Nikolas Kromeski*, his nephew, a Dutch coffee planter from Borneo: Alfred DeBall. *Baron Lecoq*, Chef de Surete, Paris Bureau of Police: W. H. Denny. *Jacques Baccarel*, an American painter from New Orleans, Louisiana: GEORGE MacFARLANE. *Chickoree*, his valet: FRANK DOANE. *Artists, Friends of Baccarel (4)*: *Victor*: Harry Tebbutt. *Gustave*: Francis Tyler. *Jean*: Morgan Williams. *Paul*: Frank Kelley. *Commissionaire*: Mr. Maxwell. *Waiter*: Mr. Smith. *Nichette*, the General's second wife, formerly an actress and model: VIOLA GILLETTE. *Countess Nitsky*, the General's sister: JEAN NEWCOMBE. *Pomare*, wife of Kromeski, a native of Borneo: ISABEL DeARMOND. *Nadine*, the General's daughter: MARGUERITE CLARK. *Artists' Model (4)*: *Zulieka*: Estelle Baldwin. *Naouma*: Grace Benedict. *Mimi*: Arline LaCross. *Ninette*: Muriel Harmon. *Friends of Nichette, The "S" Girls (8)*: *Samis*: Bertha Blake. *Sadhu*: Eileen Kearney. *Sybile*: Lillian Wiggins. *Sorrell*: Alice Lazar. *Sarinne*: Ellen Beckwith. *Suzanne*: Susie Pitt. *Shanley*: Grace Walton. *Shirley*: Elizabeth Brandell. *Bathing Girls*: Misses LaCrosse, Baldwin, Harmon, Benedict, Shattuck, Daisy Fair, Burns, Dunn. *Maids*: Misses Carr, Warren, Bonner, Hazel, Ames, Rogers, Winters, Barrel. *Chairmen*: Messrs. Stone, Werber, Jafolla, Sparks, Baker, Warren, Latsch, Fischer. *Artists, Officers of the Fleet, Sailors, Models, Nautch Dancers, Aborigines, etc, etc.*

Act 1: Grand Hotel at Dinard, in the South of France. (Law.)

Act 2: Tropical gardens adjoining the hotel. (Unitt & Wickes.)

ACT 1[88]
"Wading" (Opening Chorus)
Bathing Girls, Chorus
"She Sells Sea Shells" (Song)
J. DeAngelis, Girls
(*Music by* Harry Gifford. *Lyrics by* Terry Sullivan.)
"The Ballerino"[89] (Duo)
V. Gillette, J. DeAngelis
"A Song of the Sea" (Ensemble)
M. Clark, Chorus
"(The) Boulevard Glide" (Duet)
J. DeAngelis, M. Clark
(*Music by* Melville Gideon. *Lyrics by* E. Ray Goetz.)
"Creole Days" (Romance)
G. MacFarlane, Artists
"Goo-Goo" (Chansonette)
M. Clark
Ensemble
J. DeAngelis, V. Gillette, M. Clark, G. J. MacFarlane
"The Prince of Borneo" (Song)
F. Doane
"Toujours la Politesse" (Trio)
M. Clark, A. DeBall, G. MacFarlane
"Coo-ee" (Song)
I. DeArmond, Artists
Finale
Principals, Chorus

ACT 2
Opening Scene:
Barcarolla
H. Tebbutt
Fete des Fleurs
Chorus
Valse Pas Seul
M. Clark
"Haut École" (Chariot Song; Ballet)
Ladies' Octette, Ensemble

---

[86]Dropped during the New York run.
[87]No New York program available. Song list prepared from published sheet music.

[88]Interpolated during the run as per published sheet music:
"Foolish Questions"
J. DeAngelis
(*Music by* A. Baldwin Sloane. *Lyrics by* William Lee.)
[89]Dropped after opening, then later replaced for tour by:
"Memoirs"
V. Gillette

"(The) Cinematograph"[90] (Song)
J. DeAngelis
"Boys Will Be Boys" (Quintette)
V. Newcomb, Artists
The Fete (Ensemble):
"Salaam" (Entrance)
Chorus
Nautch Dance[91]
Models
"Pretty Punchinello" (Song)
M. Clark
Coconut Dance
Artists
"He Loved Me Tender" (He Loved Her Tender)(Song)
J. DeAngelis, Ensemble
"In a Hammock" (Hammock Love Song, or Swinging the Summer Night Long)
M. Clark, G. J. MacFarlane
"The Jungle Man"[92] (Legend)
I. DeArmond, Maids
"Ode de Aphrodite"[93] (Septette)
V. Newcomb, M. Clark, G. J. MacFarlane, Artists
Finale
Principals, Chorus

1909.08 THE MASCOT

An Elaborate Revival of the Comic Opera in Three Acts[94]. Adapted from the French opéra-comique "La Mascotte," libretto by Henri Chivot and Alfred Duru. Music by Edmond Audran. Staged by Herbert Gresham. Musical director, W. T. Francis. Produced by (Marc) Klaw and (Abraham L.) Erlanger. Opened 12 April 1909 at the New Amsterdam Theatre and closed 8 May 1909 after 32 performances.[95]

CAST: *Bettina*, the Mascot: FLORA ZABELLE. *Fiametta*, daughter of Lorenzo XVII: ESTELLE WENTWORTH. *Pippo*, a shepherd: HENRY COOTE. *Lorenzo XIV*, Prince of Piombino: RAYMOND HITCHCOCK. *Rocco*: EDWARD M FAVOR. *Frederic*, Prince of Pisa: EDGAR ATCHISON ELY. *Matheo*, an innkeeper: Bruce Smith. *Parafante*, a sergeant: Arthur Thalasso. *Physician*: Pony Moore. *Nicola, Gabrini*, pages to Lorenzo XVII: Marie Louise Miller, Marguerite Loveridge. *Adelaide*, a peasant girl: Inez Girard. *Rosa, Rienzi*, peasants: George Pullman, Clarence Coldren. *Pages (6)*: *Carlo*: Nita Manson. *Paolo*: Alice Marrenner. *Angelo*: Flora Crosbie. *Luigi*: Geraldine Bruce. *Marco*: Greta Gleason. *Garri*: Bee Wentworth. *Pages, Peasant Boys and Girls, Servants, Hunting Lads and Ladies, Courtiers, Court Ladies, Pierrots, Drummers, Guards, Waiters, Soldiers.*

Act 1: A Farm in Piombino, Italy. Fifteenth century.

Act 2: Grand Ducal Palace at Piombino.

Act 3: Patio of an Italian Inn. Duchy of Pisa.

ACT 1
Introduction and Opening Chorus/
Drinking Song
"Legend of the Mascot" (Ballad)
H. Coote, Chorus
"Now the Vintage Time"
"Come Now, My Beauty" (Entering Song and Chorus)
F. Zabelle
"Don't Come Too Near" (Song)
F. Zabelle
Chorus and Presage Song
F. Zabelle, E. Wentworth, E. A. Ely, R. Hitchcock, E. M. Favor, Chorus
"Wise Men in All Ages" (Song)
R. Hitchcock
"When the Gay Sport"
Chorus
"When I Behold" (Duet)
F. Zabelle, H. Coote
Finale
F. Zabelle, E. Wentworth, E. A. Ely, H. Coote, R. Hitchcock, E. M. Favor

ACT 2
"O, What Beauty!" (Chorus)
Pages
"Excuse My Boldness" (Couplet)
"Ah, Let Me Be!" (Couplets)
F. Zabelle, R. Hitchcock
"What a Charming Bright Display" (Air of Saltarelle)
"Know'st Thou Those Robes?"
F. Zabelle, H. Coote
"From Courtiers as They Pass"
E. A. Ely
"To Hunt the Stag" (Couplets)
R. Hitchcock
Finale

ACT 3
Chorus of Soldiers
B. Smith
Entrance of the Prince
Song of the Drum
E. A. Ely, Male Chorus
Entrance of the Refugees
E. Wentworth, R. Hitchcock, E. M. Favor, A. Thalasso, Male Chorus
"Orang-Outang Song"
Entrance of Wedding Party/
"I Near the Goal"
E. Wentworth, E. A. Ely, H. Coote, R. Hitchcock
"How Is This, Pippo"
F. Zabelle, H. Coote, R. Hitchcock, E. M. Favor
"Ah, With Wrath"/
"Pray, Tell Me Why?"
E. M. Favor, H. Coote
Finale
Company

1909.09 THE CANDY SHOP

A Summer Entertainment (Musical Comedy) in Two Acts. Book by George V. Hobart. Music and lyrics by John L. Golden. (Additional lyrics by Henry Blossom.) Staged by Fred G. Latham. Scenery painted by Homer Emens, John H. Young. Ladies' dresses and by Elsie DeWolfe, Wachner & Co. Dances arranged by William Rock. Musical director, William E. MacQuinn. Produced by Charles Dillingham. Opened 27 April 1909 at the Knickerbocker Theatre and closed 12 June 1909 after 49 performances.[96]

CAST: *John Sweet*, proprietor of the candy shop: CHARLES ANGELO. *Jack Sweet*, his son: LESLIE GAZE. *Hilda Noble*, a shop girl: MAUDE FULTON. *Saul Wright*, a tailor: FRANK LALOR. *Sally Ann*, his daughter: Bliss Milford. *Gilbert Grand*, a soda fountain attendant: WILLIAM ROCK. *Mrs. Gregory*, a widow: LOUISE DRESSER. *Mrs. Bashfield*, in charge of the candy shop: FLORENCE MORRISON. *Mrs. Montrose Quilligan*, a suffragette: ANNIE YEAMANS. *Ned Johnson*, a proprietor at Coney Island: Malcolm Williams. *Rufus*, a detective: Kinzie Higgins. *Genevieve*, cashier in the candy shop: Eva Francis. *Mr. Squills*, a candy drummer: Edmund Lawrence. *Miss Glick*: Ida Adams. *Miss Meddle*: Esther Brunette. *Sue, Settle*, the Alimony Sisters: ANGIE WEIMERS, LILLIAN RICE. *Pas Seul*: M'lle Rayo.

Friends of Mrs. Gregory: Misses Esther Brunette, Ida Adams, Jane Grant, Elba Warren, Jessie Crane, Irene George. *Shop Girls*: Misses Mona Trieste, Eloise Reed, Genevieve Reed, Mazna Don, Delia Foster, Jeanne Crane, Stella Hansen, Hazel Adele. *Matinee Girls*: Misses Elizabeth Grant, Blanche Babbitt, Helen Tiffany, Josephine Angela, Olive Montague, Estelle Parry, Nellie Allen, Harriet Leidy. *Dancing Girls*: Misses Norma Thomas, Virginia Calvert, Ethel Millard, Olivia Depp, Alice

[90]Replaced during the run by:
"Choose Her in the Morning" (Song)
J. DeAngelis
(*Music and Lyrics by* Paul Barnes and R. Weston.)
[91]Dropped during the run.
[92]Dropped during the run.
[93]Dropped during the run.
[94]Originally produced in New York in English 5 May 1881 at the Bijou Opera House for 200 performances.
[95]English libretto uncredited; settings, costumes uncredited.

[96]Played a return engagement 24 January 1910 at the Grand Opera House for 8 performances.

Keese, Dorothy Gibson. *Chicago Girls*: Misses Kathryn Reynolds, Gertrude Duffy, Hazel Sullivan, Gertrude Carmer, Jeanette Miller, Lillian Hansen, Dorothy Bristol, Mabel Moreheart. *Yachtsmen, etc.*: Messrs. R. C. Bosch, LeMoyne Cox, Victor Royal, Charles Lloyd, H. Harrington, John Strause, Irving S. Carpenter, Louis Strangard, Ralph Pattersan, E. T. H. Bromeley, R. H. Lewis, J. E. Cockeyne, Edward Traver, P. McCarthy.

Act 1: The Candy Shop. (Emens.)

Act 2: Coney Island. (Young.)

ACT 1[97]

Opening Chorus (Working, clerking, selling candies, etc.)

"Now That I've Got It, I Don't Want It" (Solo and Chorus)
J. Hazzard, Girls

"Just We Two" (Duet)
L. Gaze, M. Fulton

"Honey Bunch" (Solo and Ensemble)
L. Gaze, A. Weimers, L. Rice

"I've Been Married Once" (Solo)
F. Lalor

"In Vaudeville" (Duet and Ensemble)
W. Rock, M. Fulton

"You're My Girl" (Duet)
W. Rock, M. Fulton

Finale (Who Among You Stole That Jewel?)
Entire Company

ACT 2

Opening Chorus (There Is an Island)
Entire Company

"By Wireless" (Double Octette)
Boys, Girls

"Help! And the Villain Goes to Jail" (Solo and Chorus)
B. Milford

"Chinese Love Song" (Duet)
W. Rock, M. Fulton

"Mr. Othello" (Solo)
L. Dresser

"Meet Me Down on the Corner"
W. Rock, B. Milford

1909.10 THE RED MOON

An American Musical Comedy in Red and Black, in Three Acts. Book and lyrics by Bob Cole. Music by (J.) Rosamond Johnson. Additional music by James Reese Europe. Additional lyrics by Charles A. Hunter. Additional dances by Benny Jones. Staged by Robert Cole. Tour under the direction of Philip Robson. Musical director, James Reese Europe. Produced by A. L. Wilbur. Opened 3 May 1909 at the Majestic Theatre and closed 29 May 1909 after 32 performances.[98]

CAST: *Slim Brown*, the lawyer they don't expect: BOB COLE. *Plunk Green*, the doctor they don't expect: (J.) ROSAMOND JOHNSON. *Bill Gibson*, the saloonkeeper: HENRY GRANT. *Bill Armour*, the butcher: Wesley Jenkins. *Bill Webster*, the barber: Sam Lucas. *Bill Simmons*, the whitewasher: BENNY JONES. *John Lowdog*, the old chief: ARTHUR TALBOT. *Red Feather*, an educated brave (Minnehaha's Indian father): THEO PANKEY. *Eagle Eye*, the tribe's scout: Frank Brown. *Spread Eagle*, the medicine man: Sam Lucas. *Lucretia Martin*, the old chief's wife: Elizabeth Williams. *Amanda Gibson*, the saloonkeeper's wife: Mollie Dill. *Minnehaha*, the old chief's child: ABBIE MITCHELL. *Lilly White*, the washerwoman: ANDREW TRIBBLE. *Truscalina White*, her actress daughter: Fanny Wise. *Nakomis*, the tribe prophetess: Fanny Wise. *Waneta*, an Indian girl: Marie Young. *Bill Simmons' Kids (3)*: *Sambo Simmons*: Edgar Connor. *Sally Simmons*: Leona Marshall. *Susan Simmons*: Daisy Brown. *The Gibson Gals*: Bessie Tribble, Mayme Butler, Lulu Coleman, Blanche Deas, Tillie Smith, Bessie Simms. *The Dancing Picks*: Daisy Brown, Leona Marshall, Marion Potter, Bessie Oliver, Pearl Taylor, Lottie Gee. *The Ada Girls*: Marie Young, Pauline Hackney, Mattie Harris, Marjorie Sipp, Zennie Hunter, Rebecca Allen. *The College Boys*: Frank DeLyons, William E. Phelps, Lewis Mitchell, Herbert Sutton, Robert Young, Frank Brown. *The Policemen*: Nelson Tunsell, Harry Watson, Samuel Craig, William Hill. *Indian Braves, Squaws, Villagers, Guests, etc.*

Act 1: Swamptown, Virginia. Sunshine Land.

Act 2: The Land of the Setting Sun.

Act 3: Bill Gibson's parlor, Swamptown, Virginia.

ACT 1[99]

Opening Chorus
Company

"(Life Is a Game of) Checkers"
H. Sutton, College Boys

"Keep on Smilin'"
H. Gant, W. Jenkens, S. Lucas, B. Jones

"Don't Tell Tales Out of School"
R. Cole, J. R. Johnson, A. Mitchell, F. Wise

"I Love But You"
J. R. Johnson, A. Mitchell

"Ada (My Sweet Potater)"
B. Cole, Ada Girls
(*Music by* James Reese Europe, Robert Cole. *Lyrics by* Charles A. Hunter.)

Finale
Ensemble

ACT 2

Prelude
Company

"Bleeding Moon"
F. Wise

"The Big Red Shawl"
J. R. Johnson, Chorus

"The Pathway of Love"
A. Mitchell

"On the Road to Monterey"
T. Pankey

War Dance
Braves

ACT 3

"Red Moon To-da-lo" (Two-Step)
E. Connor

"Sambo"
E. Connor, Chorus
(*Music by* James Reese Europe.)

---

[97]Musical numbers not listed in program. List prepared from published piano vocal score (Joseph E. Remick, New York, 1909), reviews. Other musical numbers not in vocal score: "When I Marry My Mary in Maryland"; "The Whitewash Man"; "Oogley, Oogley, Ooo"; "(I Used to Sigh for)The Silvery Moon"; "I'll Follow You." Interpolation, as per published sheet music (may be same as Oogley, Oogley, Ooo" above): "Googy-oo" F. Lalor (*Music and Lyrics by* Edward E. Rice.)

[98]No credits in program for scenery or costume design.

[99]Other musical numbers ascribed to the show, not found in New York programs examined:

"Coola Woola Moola Woola"
J. R. Johnson

"Cupid Was an Indian Pickaninny"
A. Mitchell

"I Want My Chicken"

"My Indian Maid"

"Phoebe Brown"
A. O. Walker

"Red Moon"
(*Music by* James Reese Europe.)

"Wildfire"
A. O. Walker

"Pliney, Come Out in the Moonlight"
(*Music by* James Reese Europe.)

"The Pickaninny Days"
(*Music by* James Reese Europe.)

"I've (Just) Lost My Teddy Bear"
(*Music by* Robert Cole and J. Rosamond Johnson.)

"As Long as the World Goes Round"
A. Mitchell

Pianologue
J. R. Johnson
"Run, Billy Possum, Run" (from THE ROGERS BROTHERS IN CENTRAL PARK)
B. Cole
"I Ain't Had No Lovin' in a Long Time"
A. Tribble, B. Jones
(*Music by* James Reese Europe.)
"Love Me, Baby Mine"
A. Mitchell, Chorus
Finale
Ensemble

1909.11 THE MIDNIGHT SONS

A Musical Moving Picture (Comedy) in Two Acts, 8 Films (Scenes). Words (book, lyrics) by Glen MacDonough. Notes (music) by Raymond Hubbell. Production staged by Ned Wayburn. Settings by Arthur Voegtlin. Costumes by Melville Ellis. Orchestra under the direction of George A. Nichols. Orchestrations by Frank Saddler. Produced by Lew Fields. Opened 22 May 1909 at the Broadway Theatre and closed 1 January 1910 after 257 performances[100].

CAST: *Senator Constant Noyes*, a rich politician with four sons and a burning thirst for head lines and notoriety: GEORGE A. SCHILLER. *The Senator's boys known about town as "The Midnight Sons" (4)*: *Jack Noyes*, who plays at art: JOSEPH M. RATLIFF. *Dick Noyes*, who toys with the ticker: HARRY FISHER. *Harry Noyes*, who trifles with the stage: DENMAN MALEY. *Tom Noyes*, who fusses with sports: FRITZ WILLIAMS. *Merri Murray*, America's leading chorus lady: LOTTA FAUST. *Rose Raglan*, from the country: NORMA BROWN. *Claire Voyant*, a scientific fortune teller: Linden Beckwith. *Pansy Burns*, who won't cook for everybody: GEORGE MONROE. *Lilly Burns*, who won't cook for anybody: LILLIAN LEE. *A Case Daly*, a wine agent: Taylor Holmes. *Sousberry Lushmore*, in search of his home: VERNON CASTLE. *Miss Beatrice Ballast*, a theatre patron: Blanche Sherwood. *Lady Fire-fly*: GLADYS MOORE. *Mlle. DeLeon*: Maybelle Meeker. *The Cynical Owl*: Berchard Dickerson. *The Baby Owl*: Johnnie Hines. *Mercedes Panhard, Harriet Hammer, Katherine Knockwell*, Shoe Store Patrons: Nan J. Brennan, Mollie McGrath, Florence Cable. *Mrs. Carrie Margin*: BLANCHE RING. *Guests, Theatregoers, Tourists, etc, etc.*

Pony Ballet: Misses Elizabeth Hawman, Lousie Hawman, Beatrice Liddell, Dorothy Marlowe, Seppie McNeil, Ada Robertson. *Mary Gardeners, etc.*: Misses Margaret Hawman, Daisy Carson, Grace Heckler, Alice Kelly, Hazel Allen, Clara Lloyd, Sara Luce, Adele LaPierre, Cassie Meade, Josephine Kernell. *Shoppers, etc.*: Misses Elsa Reinhardt, Nan J. Brennan, Mae Tormey, Helen Turner, Mollie Margolies, Lillian Leroy, Nedda Nilsson, Mollie McGrath, Florence Blake, Dessa Gibson, Hazel Troutman. *French Waitresses, etc.*: Misses Edna Merrill, Pearl Ben-Yusef, Nettie Lyon, Ocie Williams, Ida Doerge, Vina Gorden, Edna Merrill, Minnie Monroe, Regina Stone, Grace Pomeroy, Violet Devere, Olga Hempstone. *College Boys, Chauffeurs, etc.*: Messrs. Raymond Strath, Alex Gibson, Henry Dyer, W. C. Van Brunt, Albert Van Sand, R. B. Hamilton, Gus Baci, W. L. Hobart, Harry Wilcox, Frank Ellis, J. J. Keenan, William J. Kline, Edward Grant, H. L. Frost, Harry Prew, Gerald McDonald, R. J. Kirkwood, Billy Cohan, Earl Bruch, Fred Howard.

Act 1, Scene 1: The Farewell Banquet to Senator Noyes in the Sportsman's Room of the Hotel Insomnia, (New York City). *Scene 2*: Exterior of Richard Noyes Shoe Store on Fifth Avenue. A year and a half later. *Scene 3*: Interior of Shoe Store. *Scene 4*: Concourse at the Grand Central Station. *Scene 5*: The Honeymoon Express.

Act 2, Scene 1: Interior of the Merri Murray Theatre. Same afternoon. *Scene 2*: Exterior of the Merri Murray Theatre. *Scene 3*: A Garden Fête at the Pounceuponham Hotel, Billionaire Beach, Florida. Two months later.

ACT 1[101]
Opening Chorus:
"High! High! High!
Guests
"Call Me 'Bill'"
V. Castle, Guests
"My Fire-Fly Lady"
J. M. Ratliff, Guests
"The Soubrette's Secret"
L. Faust, Guests
"The Little Mary Gardeners"
N. Brown, Guests
"Hello, Tu Tu"[102]
B. Ring
"Cinderella at the Shoe Store"
Clerks, Shoppers
"The Billiken Man"
B. Ring, Pony Ballet
(*Music and Lyrics by* Melville Gideon.)
"The Cynical Owl"
J. M. Ratliff, N. Brown, Chorus
"(On a) Yankee Honeymoon"
H. Fisher, B. Ring, Brides, Bridegrooms

ACT 2
"The Harlequin Hoops"
Pony Ballet
(Pianologue Specialty)[103]
M. Ellis, assisted by Pocket Paderewskiettes
"The Human Pin-Wheel"
M. Meeker
"Eily Riley"
B. Ring, Company
"True Blue"
L. Beckwith, Company
"(I've Got) Rings on My Fingers" (Mumbo Jumbo Jijiboo J O'Shay)
B. Ring
(*Music by* Maurice Scott. *Lyrics by* F. J. Barnes, R. P. Weston.)
"Carmen the Second"
L. Faust, Chorus
"Columbines' Courtship"[104]
G. Moore, M. Meeker
Parasol Dance
Pony Ballet
(Whirlwind Dancers, Specialty)
The Marvelous Millers
"Amina, (Queen of the Night or the Arab's Dream)"
B. Ring, Chorus
(*Music by* Paul Lincke, 'Serenade Egyptienne.' *Lyrics by* Ballard Macdonald.)
Finale
Company

1909.12 THE BOY AND THE GIRL

Richard Carle's Whistling Summer Show (A Musical Comedy) in Two Acts. Book and lyrics by Richard Carle. Music by H. L. Heartz. Additional music by Richard Carle; additional lyrics by M. E. Rourke. Staged by Charles Marks. Musical numbers and ensembles arranged by Gus Sohlke. Orchestra under the direction of Arthur Weld. Produced by Richard Carle and Charles Marks. Opened 31 May 1909 at the Aerial Gardens atop the New Amsterdam and closed 19 June 1909 after 18 performances.[105]

---

[100]Played return engagements 3 January 1910 at the West End Theatre for 8 performances, 2 January 1911 at the Circle Theatre for 8 performances.

[101]Interpolated as per published sheet music:
"Goo-Goo Land"
M. Ellis
(*Music by* C. W. Murphy. *Lyrics by* Fred W. Leigh.)
Interpolated for subsequent tour:
"Kelly's Gone to Kingdom Come!"
Maud Lambert
(*Music by* T. W. Thurban. *Lyrics by* Sax Rohmer.)

[102]Replaced immediately after opening by:
"Yip-ie-addyi-ay" (from THE MERRY WIDOW AND THE DEVIL)
B. Ring
(*Music by* John H. Flynn. *Lyrics by* Will D. Cobb.)
Which was replaced late in the New York run and for subsequent tour by:
"My Sist' Tetrazin"
B. Ring
(*Music by* Anatol Friedland. *Lyrics by* Edward J. Madden.)

[103]Dropped early in the run.

[104]Replaced for tour by:
Spring Dance
G. Moore

[105]No credit in programs for costumes or sets.

CAST: *Adolph Allen*, Impressario of Allen's Alcazar: BARNEY BERNARD. *Clarence Percival*, his silent partner: EDWARD M. FAVOR. *Dick Percival*, the boy: BURRELL BARBERETTO. *Professor Zero*, a poetical palmist: TOBY LYONS. *Jasper Plum*, a would-be juggler: Eugene Moulan. *Signor Tomasso*, a juggler, afterwards the Count of Cremo: Felix Fantus. *Headwaiter*: Hugh Fay. *Katie*, the girl: HARRIET STANDON. *Avita*, a Spanish chanteuse: MARION GARSON. *Winona*: Florence Averell. *Evelyn*: Sophia Ralph. *Salome*: Vivian Rushmore. *Marion*: Mabel Howell. *Telegraph Boy*: Claudia Clarke. *A Kodak Fiend*: Nedra Gage. *A Coachman*: Helen St. John. *A Footman*: Audrey Munson. *Gladys De Vine*, an actress: MARIE DRESSLER.

The Sightseers: Edith Thrne, Marie Savage, May Williard, Myrtle Wellington, Ida Crawford, Hazel Campbell, Frankie Hill, Frances Ramsey. *The Carolina Pets*: B. Clarke, Ruth Van, Mattie Crofts, (Misses) Pearl, Kirk, Taylor, Bartlett. *Men of the Ensemble*: Messrs. Lancaster, McShane, Richardson, W. Smith, J. Smith, Graham, Schultz, Schumann-Heink.

Act 1: The Pier Head of Palm Beach, Florida.

Act 2: Rear of Concert Hall, Havana.

ACT 1

Opening Chorus
M. Garson, Chorus

"I'm Only Waiting My Chance"
E. Moulan, Chorus

"Allen's Alcazars"
B. Bernard, Chorus

"My Dearie Dear"
M. Garson, Male Chorus
(*Lyrics by* M. E. Rourke.)

"A Simple Girl"
H. Standon, Chorus

"I'm in a Position to Know"
M. Dressler

"A Poor Working Girl"
M. Dressler

"Kate, Come and Kiss Me"
H. Standon, B. Barbaretto, Chorus
(*Lyrics by* M. E. Rourke and Richard Carle.)

ACT 2

Opening

"Why Are All the Girls So Hungry?"
B. Barbaretto, Chorus

"In Yucatan"
M. Garson, Chorus
(*Music by* Richard Carle.)

"In Ireland"
T. Lyons

"Y'-la"
M. Dressler

"Naughty Cupid"
B. Barbaretto, H. Standon

"Seductive Caroline"
M. Dressler, Chorus
(*Music by* Richard Carle.)

Finale

1909–1910 SEASON

Eva Tanguay in ZIEGFELD FOLLIES OF 1909 (Photo: White Studio)
Billy Rose Theatre Collection, New York Public Library for the Performing Arts

1909–1910 SEASON

1909.13 ZIEGFELD FOLLIES OF 1909

A Musical Revue in Two Acts, 16 Scenes[1]. Sketches and lyrics by Harry B. Smith. Music by Maurice Levi. Staged by Julian Mitchell and Herbert Gresham. Dances arranged by Julian Mitchell. Costumes by Alfredo Edel, William H. Matthews. Settings designed by John H. Young. Orchestra under the direction of Frederic Solomon. Produced by Florenz Ziegfeld. Opened 14 June 1909 at the Jardin de Paris (atop the New York and Criterion Theatres) and closed 7 August 1909 after 64 performances.[2]

CAST (in order of appearance): Act 1: *Venus*: ANNABELLE WHITFORD. *Psyche*: EDNA CHASE. *Cupid*: MAE MURRAY. *Adonis*: ELISE HAMILTON. *Apollo*: Marion Whitney. *Monty Van Swagger*, a man about town: WILLIAM BONELLI. *Miss Manhattan*: LILLIAN LORRAINE. *Managers of Grand Opera (5)*: *Got a Cazzaza*: William Powers. *Herr Dimpel*: William Oatman. *Toscannetti*: David Abrams. *Hurts*: Robert Burns. *Schmaler*: Arthur Hill. *Caruso—The Second*: ARTHUR DEAGON. *A Patroness of Opera*: Arline Boley. *Oscar Hammerstein*: MAURICE HEGEMAN. *Oscar H.*: BILLIE REEVES. *O. Hammerstein*: William Schrode. *Oscar Hammer*: William Powers. *Oscar Stein*: Robert Burns. *O.H.*: David Abrams. *H.O.*: ALBERT FROOME. *Camen La Tosca*, a Prima Donna: NORA BAYES. *Maitre de Ballet*: BESSIE CLAYTON. *The Lucia Sextette*: *Lucia*: Arline Boley. *Maria*: Anna C. Wilson. *Edgardo*: J. Youngs. *Arturo*: A. Oatman. *Tomato*: W. Johnson. *Banano*: Arthur Swift. *Pipe Dream Girl*: LILLIAN LORRAINE. *T.R.*, a Mighty Hunter: HARRY KELLY. *Kermit*: JACK NORWORTH. *The Jungle Queen*: SOPHIE TUCKER. *Animals in Jungle Scene*: *Tiger*: Arthur Hill. *Ostrich*: C. Woodward. *Monkey*: David Abrams. *Lions*: Joseph Schrode, Charles Schrode. *Elephant*: Charles Abbott, W. Hessong. *Giraffe*: Messrs. Silvers, Milliken. *Reuben*: BILLIE REEVES. *Sal*: MAE MURRAY. *The Scarecrow*: Miss McMahon. *A Couple of Kids*: NORA BAYES, JACK NORWORTH. *The Roosevelt of Germany*: WILLIAM BONELLI. *The Kaiser of America*: HARRY KELLY. *The Empress*: ANNABELLE WHITFORD. *President Taft*: ARTHUR DEAGON. *The German Eagle*: GERTRUDE VANDERBILT. *The American Eagle*: Rosie Green.

Act 2: *A Christy Girl*: ANNABELLE WHITFORD. *Christy Girls*: Misses Edna Chase, Virginia Marshall, Marjorie Bonner, Lottie Vernon, Amy Webb, Eunice Mackey, Marion Whitney, Mae Murray. *A Critic*: ARTHUR DEAGON. *Another*: William Oatman. *Yet Another*: William Powers. *Palmy Daze*, a manager: HARRY KELLY. *A Theatregoer*: MAURICE HEGEMAN. *His Escort*: Arline Boley. *A Speculator*: ALBERT FROOME. *William Shakespeare, Esq.*: WILLIAM BONELLI. *A Newsboy*: David Abrams. *A Gaiety Dancer*: BESSIE CLAYTON. *The Aeroplane Girl*: LILLIAN LORRAINE. *Millionaire Prisoners (4)*: *Mr. Skinner*: HARRY KELLY. *Mr. Ketcham*: ARTHUR DEAGON. *Mr. Steele*: MAURICE HEGEMAN. *Mr. Conn*: William Powers. *Mr. Stringham*: ALBERT FROOME. *Jailerettes*: Misses Vanderbilt, Green Murray, Hamilton. *Miss Blarney*: NORA BAYES. *Pearline*, the hypnotist: WILLIAM BONELLI. *Subjects*: HARRY KELLY, ARTHUR DEAGON, Billie Reeves, William Powers, William Schrode, David Abrams, Joseph Schrode, Arthur Hill. *A Doctor*: MAURICE HEGEMAN. *Base Ball Pitcher*: Mr. Montrose. *Base Ball Player*, catcher: Mr. Welsh. *Base Ball Player*, batter: Mr. Mealey. *Base Ball Umpire*: JACK NORWORTH.

Act 1, Scene 1: Court of Venus. (Lee Lash Studios). *Scene 2*: Lobby of Metropolitan Opera House. (Lee Lash Studios). *Scene 3*: Hammerstein's Office, Manhattan Opera House. (Lee Lash Studios). *Scene 4*: Bubbles. (Lee Lash Studios). *Scene 5*: The Jungle. (John Young). *Scene 6*: A Wheat Field. (John Young). *Scene 7*: A Nursery. (John Young). *Scene 8*: The Throne Room. (Hugo Baruch & Company, Berlin). *Scene 9*: The Greatest Navy in the World.

Act 2, Scene 1: Christy Pictures. *Scene 2*: Shakespearian Theatre. (John Young). *Scene 3*: New York Station of the Aero Club. (John Young). *Scene 4*: Millionaires' Ward, the Tombs. (Lee Lash Studios). *Scene 5*: Stage Door of the New York Theatre. (John Young). *Scene 6*: Hypnotic Cabinet. *Scene 7*: Polo Grounds, New York. (John Young).

ACT 1[3]

Opening Chorus

"Madam Venus" (Take a Tip from Venus)
A. Whitford, Chorus

"Linger, Longer, Lingerie"
L. Lorraine, Chorus

"My Cousin Caruso" (from MISS INNOCENCE)
A. Deagon, Chorus
(*Music by* Gus Edwards. *Lyrics by* Edward Madden.)

"Mad Opera House"
N. Bayes
(*Music and Lyrics by* Nora Bayes and Jack Norworth.)

"Dance de Maitre de Ballet"
B. Clayton

"Sextette—Lucia" (burlesque)
A. Boley, A. C. Wilson, J. Youngs, A. Oatman, W. Johnson, A. Swift

"What Every Woman Knows"
6 Maude Adams, 6 John Shands, 6 Blondes

"(It's) Nothing But a Bubble"[4]
L. Lorraine

"Moving Day in Jungle Town"[5]
S. Tucker, Chorus
(*Music by* Nat D. Ayer. *Lyrics by* A. Seymour Brown.)

"(If It Were Not for) Dear Old Father"[6]
J. Norworth
(*Music and Lyrics by* Nora Bayes and Jack Norworth.)

"I Wish I Was a Boy and I Wish I Was a Girl" (I'm Glad I'm a Boy)
N. Bayes, J. Norworth
(*Music and Lyrics by* Nora Bayes and Jack Norworth.)

"Roosevelt of Germany"[7]
Male Chorus

"Rulers of the Earth"[8]
H. Kelly, W. Bonnelli, Misses Vanderbilt, Green

"The Greatest Navy in the World"[9]
Ensemble

ACT 2[10]

"The Christy Girl"[11]
A. Whitford, Girls

"Falling Stars"
N. Bayes, H. Kelly
(*Music and Lyrics by* Nora Bayes and Jack Norworth.)

Song Hits of 1909 (Song Hits of By Gone Days)
Principals, Chorus

---

[1]The third in the annual series of musical revues produced by Florenz Ziegfeld beginning in 1907.

[2]Played a return engagement 6 December 1909 at the Grand Opera House for 8 performances.

[3]The running order was revised during the run; in July, Eva Tanguay joined the cast 12 July 1909 (as Nora Bayes and Jack Norworth departed), appearing in the Mad Opera House sketch, performing "I Wish I Was a Boy" with Lillian Lorraine, and adding the following to Act 2:

"Go As Far as You Like" (after "Up! Up! Up! in My Aeroplane")
E. Tanguay

Songs ["I Don't Care"](prior to Finale)
E. Tanguay

[4]Dropped after opening.

[5]Moved to Act 2 early in the run, and in second month re-assigned to Eva Tanguay as the Jungle Queen.

[6]Moved to Act 2 after opening, then later dropped.

[7]Dropped during the run.

[8]Moved to Act 2 early in the run, then later replaced by:

"Come On, Play Ball with Me, Dearie"
L. Lorraine, Company, Audience
(*Music by* Gus Edwards. *Lyrics by* Edward Madden.)

[9]During the run, "The Greatest Navy in the World" moved to Act 2 Finale. Act 1 closed with its own finale, performed by the principals and chorus.

[10]Act 2 was revised repeatedly during the run. Added were:

"Play That Fandango Rag" (based on Fiaco's original Spanish Dance)
Ensemble
(*Music by* Lewis F. Muir. *Lyrics by* E. Ray Goetz.)

Heinz Is Pickled Again
A. Deagon

"The (Brinkley) Bathing Girls"
A. Whitford, 10 Bathing Girls

"The Parisian Twist"
William Schrode, Evelyn Carlton

[11]Dropped after opening.

"The Gaiety Dance"[12]
B. Clayton
"Up! Up! Up! in My Aeroplane"
L. Lorraine, Chorus
(*Music by* Gus Edwards. *Lyrics by* Edward Madden.)
"Paradise Jail Birds"[13]
Messrs Kelly, Deagon, Powers, Hegeman; Misses Vanderbilt, Green, Murray, Hamilton
"Blarney"[14]
N. Bayes
(*Music and Lyrics by* Nora Bayes and Jack Norworth.)
"Let's Get the Umpire's Goat"[15]
N. Bayes, Chorus
(*Music and Lyrics by* Nora Bayes and Jack Norworth.)
Finale

1909.14 THE MOTOR GIRL

A Musical Comedy in Two Acts. Book and lyrics by Charles J. Campbell and Ralph M. Skinner. Music by Julian Edwards. Staged by Frank Smithson. Dances arranged by Wellington Cross. Scenery painted by Lee Lash. Orchestra under the direction of Ben M. Jerome. Produced by Frank Hennessy. Opened 15 June 1909 at the Lyric Theatre and closed 4 September 1909 after 95 performances.[16]

CAST: *Dorothy Dare*, the Motor Girl: GEORGIA CAINE. *Louise*, Countess of Altenstein: ELIZABETH BRICE. *Wilhelmina Lamm*, a Deutscher maid, in pastures new: ADELAIDE SHARP. *Mrs. Arthur Dare*, lately married: Bessie Franklin. *Lottie Lakeside*: Helen Adair. *Penlope Penn*: Stella Bowe. *Adolphous*, Grand Duke of Noodleberg: GEORGE PAUNCEFORT. *General Bockheister*, Minister of Police: GEORGE MAJORONI. *Dick Willoughby*, chum of Dare's: MARTIN BROWN. *Bill Pusher*: JAMES F. COOK. *Robin Coyne*: JOHN LORENZ. *Mynheer Alehoff*, Burgomaster of Saardam: George Callahan. *Ludwig Liebling*, Secretary to the Duke of Altenstein: James B. Carson. *Captain Ruffhaus* of the German Embassy: Frank Shea. *Felix*, Maitre d'Hotel, Paris: Robert O'Connor. *Arthur Dare* of New York: George Lyman. *President of the Auto Club*: Carroll C. Clucas. *Chauffeur*: Ned Joyce. *(Eight) of the Society of Friends, Philadelphia*: *Ruth Rittenhouse*: Lura Wentworth. *Welthea Walton*: Leota Hingston. *Patience Partridge*: Matie Ten Eyck. *Charity Chambers*: Helen Scotten. *Hope Hapgood*: Flora Crosbie. *Faith Fairleigh*: Nancy Poole. *Priscilla Penrose*: Lillian Foster. *Prudence Pennington*: Anita Pollock. *Lizzette*: Elinor Dayne. *Georgette*: Bessilee Merrill.

American Girls: Misses Elizabeth Young, Elinor Dayne, Sue Duval, Bessilee Merrill, Nancy Newell, Marie Baxter, Anita Claire. *Waitresses*: Misses May Brennan, Dorothy Warrington, Sadie Melles, Alice Clayton, Katherine Robertosn, Mildred DeSilva, Ethel Tanguay. *Milkmaids*: Misses Evelyn Meredith, Julia Meredith, Mayme DuPont, Minnesota Martrit, Corene Uzell, Katherine Warren, Ethel Mostyn, Katherine Walden. *Quakers* of the Society of Friends, Philadelphia: Messrs. Ted Lorraine, Jack Laughlin, Jackson Karlyle, Homer Potts, George O'Rourke, Harry Thornell, Bert Smith, Alvin Morton. *Uhlans*: Messrs. Randolph Brewington, Ross Harvey, Edward McNulty, Fred Bates, John Shaddick, George Lanning, Valentine Homan, Thomas McCormack. *Ladies of the Teazle Period*: Misses Corene Uzell, Ethel Mostyn. *Men (of the Minuet)*: Messrs. Homer Potts, Jack Laughlin.

Act 1: The Plaza of the Holland City of Saardam on Kermess Day.

Act 2: Salon of the Grand Hotel, Paris.

ACT 1
Opening Chorus
"Prosit"
G. Callahan
"Trot-i-ty Trot"
G. Majoroni, Uhlans
"When We Were Twenty-One" (When I Was Twenty-One)
G. Pauncefort, Chorus
"Wilhelmina"
A. Sharp, Dutch Boys and Girls
"(I'm) The Motor Girl"
G. Caine, Chorus
"Out in a Barnyard"
J. F. Cook, J. Lorenz, A. Sharp
"All the World Loves a Lover"
G. Caine, E. Brice, J. B. Carson
"Just Like This"
E. Brice
"Just Suppose You Loved Me"
G. Caine, M. Brown
Finale
G. Caine, Ensemble

ACT 2[17]
"The Honor of Altenstein"
G. Majoroni, Uhlans
"Finesse"
G. Caine, American Girls
"In Philadelphia"
E. Brice, Quakers, Uhlans
"What Can a Fellow Do?"[18]
M. Brown
"When I'm a Duchess"
A. Sharp
"Coffee and Cheese"
G. Caine, A. Sharp, B. Franklin, J. Lorenz, G. Pauncefort, G. Majoroni, M. Brown
"The Belle of the Dairy Lunch"
G. Caine, Chorus
"I'm Old Enough to Think" (I'm Old Enough to Do a Little Thinking)
E. Brice, Chorus
Finale—Medley
Entire Company

1909.15 THE GAY HUSSARS

A Military Operetta in Three Acts. Original Hungarian libretto ("Tatárjárás") by Károly Bakonyi; Viennese adaptation ("Ein Herbstmanöver") by Robert Bodansky. English book by Maurice Brown Kirby. Music by Emmerich Kálmán. English lyrics by Grant Stewart. Staged by George Marion. Scenery painted by Walter Burridge. Costumes of Landorf, Paris. Orchestra under the direction of Gus Salzer. Lighting by Joseph Wilson. Produced by Henry W. Savage. Opened 29 July 1909 at the Knickerbocker Theatre and closed 4 September 1909 after 44 performances.

CAST: *Field Marshall Baron von Lahoney*: William E. Bonney. *Baroness Treszka*, his daughter: FLORENCE REID. *Baroness Risa von Marbach*: ANNA BUSSERT. *Captain von Emmerich* of the 14th Hussars: Alonzo Price. *Captain von Lorenty* of the 14th Hussars: EDWIN WILSON. *Lieutenant von Elekes* of the 14th Hussars: Robert Young. *Volunteer Cadet Marosi* of the 14th Hussars: MURIEL TERRY. *Sub-Lieutenant Wallerstein* of the Reserve Militia: BOBBY NORTH. *Sergeant Turi* of the Reserve Militia: Frank Russell. *Herr Starke*, Steward of Baroness Risa's Estate: W. H. Denny. *Lajos*, a retainer of the Estate: Frank Montgomery. *Virag*, Corporal of the Guard: John O'Hanlon. *Private Fekete* of the Hussars: H. T. Pinkham. *Private Yrmin* of the Reserve Militia: Bernard Lyons. *Corporal Ludwig* of the Reserve Militia: ROBERT CLARKE. *Captain Wulff*: R. M. Frank. *Major von Fritsche*: Arthur Bauer. *Captain Sturmfried*: George Dwyer. *Lieutenant Jiricicz*: George Lamar. *Lieutenant Koppler*: Edward Leech. *First Soldier*: Henry Wilkes. *Second Soldier*: George Bernard. *Third Soldier*: Maxwell Pierce. *Frau von Bergen*: Ilon Bergere. *Countess Olga*: Pauline Winters. *Frau von Schroeder*: Sophie Witt. *Countess Elsa*: Violet Mack. *Baroness Hapsburg*: Mabelle Jones.

---

[12]Replaced during the run by:
"The Dance of the Widow" Mexatexa
B. Clayton
(*Music by* Lewis F. Muir.)
[13]Dropped during the run.
[14]Dropped during the run.
[15]Dropped during the run.
[16]Costumes uncredited. Played return engagements 13 September at the West End Theatre, 20 September 1909 at the Metropolitan Theatre, and 27 September 1909 at the Lincoln Square Theatre, for 8 performances each.

[17]Added for subsequent tour to Act 2, following "What Can a Fellow Do?":
"A Friend of Mine"
J. F. Cook
[18]During the run, a dance specialty was added, performed by M. Brown, J. Lorenz.

(*Ensemble*): *Ladies*: Misses Stewart, Morawski, Clifford, Chase, Willette, Witt, Ballaire, Stuart, Jones, Mack, Ramay, Winters, Olson, Maury, Emmons, Coombs, Marks, Harris, Bizzell, Feegan, Bergere. *Gentlemen, Peasants and Soldiers*: Messrs. Fletcher, Pierce, Willard, Lewis, Gould, Chute, Foster, Leach, Duryea, Humphrey, Taylor, Bauer, Robbins, Lyons, Ellenger, O'Hanlon. *Hungarian Troubadours*: William Corner, Michel Koster, Gorgine Gruja, Sandor Kokos, Rado Milos, James Glu.

The action takes place at the present time.

Act 1: Before the Castle of Baroness Risa von Marbach.

Act 2: The Ballroom of Baroness Risa's Castle.

Act 3: Gardens of Baroness Risa's Castle.

ACT 1[19]

"The Army Directory"
A. Bussert, Ladies

"Love Is a Traitor"
E. Wilson

"The Gay Hussars"
M. Terry, Ensemble

"A Misfit Soldier"
B. North
(*Lyrics by* Maurice Brown Kirby.)

"Vagrant Fancies"[20]
R. Clarke

"A Soldier's Life"
R. Clarke

"Oh, Silver Moon!"
A. Bussert, E. Wilson

Finale

ACT 2

"Hussar's Quadrille"
Ensemble

"(Kitty), Please Give Me a Kiss"
M. Terry, Ensemble

"Sex Delicious"
M. Terry, F. Reed

"Oh, Silver Moon!" (reprise)
A. Bussert, Ensemble

"Heart to Heart"
A. Bussert, Ensemble

"Vagrant Fancies"[21] (reprise)
E. Wilson

Finale
Principals, Ensemble

ACT 3

"Dreaming of Love"[22]
A. Bussert

"My Friend Lebel"
B. North

"Oh, You Bold, Bad Men!"
F. Reid, Ladies
(*Lyrics by* Maurice Brown Kirby.)

Finale—"The Gay Hussars"
Ensemble

1909.16 COHAN AND HARRIS MINSTRELS

A Return Engagement of the Minstrel Entertainment in Two Acts[23]. (Scenery) Conceived and painted by Ernest Albert. Produced by George M. Cohan and Sam Harris. Opened 16 August 1909 at the New York Theatre and closed 28 August 1909 after 16 performances.

CAST: GEORGE EVANS. *Comedians*: Sam Lee, John King, Earl Benham, Harry Van Fossen. *Interlocutors*: Vaughn Comfort, John P. Rogers. And Will Oakland, Thomas Scott, Clarence Marks, Arthur Alexander.

MUSICAL NUMBERS

Scene 1

"When the Minstrels Come to Town"
Entire Company

Scene 2

The Crimson Trellis: Introducing the Popular Jesters, Harry Van Fossen and Sam Lee

Scene 3

"I'm Going Home"
H. Van Fossen

Scene 4

"Any Old Port in a Storm"
J. P. Rogers

Scene 5

Arrival of those funny fellows Harry Van Fossen and Sam Lee

Scene 6

"The Hat My Father Wore" (on St. Patrick's Day)
E. Benham

Scene 7

"The Wedding Bells"
V. Comfort

Scene 8

"Down Where the Watermelons Grow"
J. King

Scene 9

"The Rose of Killarney"
W. Oakland

Scene 10

A Few Happy Moments with the Star of Minstrelsy, the Original Honey Boy:

"These Are the Good Old Days"
G. Evans

[Parodies of "The Rose of Killarney," "School Days," "My Wife's Gone to the Country"]

Scene 11

Scenes from Blackville
E. Benham, J. King, assisted by 50 others

The Most Recent Dancing Creation, conceived and produced by James Gorman

Scene 12

The Fastidious Exponents of the Classy Ethiope
Alexander & Scott from Virginia

["I'm Going Away," "Down Among the Sugar Cane," "Bon Bon Buddy," "Handle Me with Care, Baby."]

Scene 13

Manila, James Gorman's Masterful Production, an Intricate and Perfectly Presented Marching Feature [Sword Drill to "Dixie" and "Yankee Doodle"]

Scene 14

Joe Boganny's Lunatic Bakers

Scene 15

"The Fireman's Picnic"/"The Brinkley Coon"/"Oh, You Chocolate Kid"
(*Music and Lyrics by* George M. Cohan.)
Snowball Livingstone: G. Evans. *Jesimima Brinkley*: A. Alexander. *Monk Anderson*: S. Lee.

1909.17 A BROKEN IDOL

A Musical Farcicality in Two Acts. Book by Hal Stephens. Music by Egbert Van Alstyne. Lyrics by Harry Williams. Staged by Gus Sohlke. Settings

[19]Added to Act 1, after "The Gay Hussars" late in subsequent tour: "Particular Marguerite" F. Reid (*Music and Lyrics by* John L. Golden.) Additional published interpolation: "Shine Out All You Little Stars" (*Music by* Jerome Kern. *Lyrics by* M. E. Rourke.

[20]Dropped late in subsequent tour.

[21]Dropped late in subsequent tour.

[22]Dropped for subsequent tour.

[23]Billed as an entertainment embracing Minstrelsy, Burlesque and Musical Comedy. Previously played 3 August 1908 at the New York Theatre for 24 performances.

designed by D. Frank Dodge. Miss Yorke's gowns by Lord & Taylor; Miss Guerite's gowns by Hayden[24]. Orchestra under the direction of Fred Eustice. Produced by B. C. Whitney. Opened 16 August 1909 at the Herald Square Theatre and closed 18 September 1909 after 40 performances.

CAST (in order of appearance): *Sing Wee*, daughter of Sun Lee Loo: Madge Voe. *Sun Lee Loo*, a Chinese merchant: Lawrence Comer. *Silas Pugsley*, a retired merchant with political ambitions: GEORGE RICHARDS. *Mrs. Lucretia Muddleford*, wife of Ely, with social ambitions: CARRIE E. PERKINS. *J. Ely Muddleford, D.Z.*—in search of bugs: OTTO HOFFMAN. *Jack Mason*: FORREST HUFF. *"Doc Whatt"?*: OTIS HARLAN. *Lord Dunby*, a fortune hunter: DAVID ANDRADA. *Marion Pugsley*, Silas Pugsley's daughter: ALICE YORKE. *Mlle. Marie De Deau* from the Folies Bergere, Paris: LAURA GUERITE. *Officer Jenkins*: Fred Hill. *Henry*, a servant: Maxwell Sargent. *Servant Girl*: Margie Stiles.

Chinese Boys: Misses C. Farber, Lillian Hazel, Gertrude Rutland, Laura Gaynelle, Ethel Aris, Lee Leontine, Gypsy Mooney, Agnes Vars. *Chinese Girls*: Misses Bertie Beaumont, Irene Farber, Marjorie Cogan, Isabel Berclay, Violet Winters. *Reckashaw Boys*: Misses Olivette TreMayne, Millie Woods, Ethel White, Billie Grant. *Sandwich Men*: Messrs. Fuller, Worden, Porter, Bell, Foster, Sullivan, Williams, Van Norden. *Dutch Soldiers*: Misses C. Farber, Hazel, Aris, Gaynelle. *China Dolls*: Misses Vars, Leontine, Barclay, Winters. *Vivandiers*: Misses Beaumont, Lascelles, Harwood, Farber, TreMayne, Baron, Carlisle, Woods, Pauline, LaMar. *Dragon Girls*: Misses Farber, Gaynelle, Cogan, Aris, Hazel, Rutland, Winters. *Chinese Lanterns*: Misses Vars, Mooney, Leontine, Barclay. *Mexican*: Messrs. Porter, Beaumont, Fuller, Miss Baron. *Dutch*: Mr. Bingham, Connie Farber. *Hungarian*: Mr. Van Orden, Miss I. Farber. *Indian*: Gypsy Mooney, Mr. F. Foster. *Gibson*: Mr. Worden, Miss Marie LaMar. *Servant Girl*: Margie Stiles. *Tree Girls*: Misses Vars, Leontine, Mooney, Winters. *Toodle's Kids*: Misses C. Farber, Gaynelle, Aris, Hazel. *Bathing Girls*: Misses LaMar, Baron, TreMayne, Woods. *Yankee Land Boys and Girls*: Misses Lascelles, Harwood, LaRue, Pauline, Styles, Carlisle; Messrs. Sullivan, Bingham, Wilaims, Bell, Foster, Van Norden. *Silver Clog Boys*: Misses Gaynelle, Cogan, Aris, Mooney, Hazel, Rutland. *Daffy Dan Boys*: Misses Beaumont, Vars, White, Maniere, Winters, Barclay. *Gold Dust Twins*: Misses C. Farber, Leontine.

Act 1: Chinatown, Los Angeles, during Chinese New Year's Celebration.

Act 2: Silas Pugsley's Home, Santa Monica, California.

ACT 1

Opening Chorus

"Cured"
O. Harlan, Boys

"(A Little) China Doll"
A. Yorke, Dutch Soldiers, China Dolls

"Marie"
L. Guerite, Vivandiers

"Love Makes the World Go Round" (What Makes the World Go Round)
O. Harlan, A. Yorke, F. Huff, Chorus

Finale

ACT 2[25]

"Happy Days" (Opening Chorus)
(*Music by* Jean Schwartz.)

"(That's the) Sign of the Honeymoon"
A. Yorke, F. Huff

"Bobbing Up and Down"[26]
D. Andrada

"Poor Old Dad in New York for the Summer"
A. Yorke, O. Hoffman, C. E. Perkins, Bathing Girls

"Yankee Land"
L. Guerite, Chorus

"Alabama" (Alabam')
O. Harlan, Girls

Finale

1909.18

IN HAYTI

A Musical Diversion in Three Acts. Book by John J. McNally. Music by Jean Schwartz. Lyrics by William Jerome. Staged by A. H. Holbrook. Musical numbers produced (staged) by Julian Alfred. Scenery by Frank Platzer. Costumes designed by F. Richard Anderson. Orchestrations by Frank Saddler. Produced by (Marc) Klaw and (Abraham L.) Erlanger. Opened 30 August 1909 at the Circle Theatre and closed 16 October 1909 after 56 performances.[27]

CAST: *Geronimo Jobbs*: JAMES McINTYRE. *Jasper Johnson*: THOMAS HEATH. *Bizzy Izzy Rosenstein*: JULIAN ROSE. *Rosey Rosenstein*, his daughter: Mabel Sealby. *Timothy Burke O'Malley*, adventurer: TOBY LYONS. *Colonel Scott*, millionaire: Alfred Fisher. *Clara Scott*, his daughter: MARION STANLEY. *George Scott*, his son: CARL McCULLOUGH. *Harry Holbrook*, newspaper correspondent: John H. Pratt. *Ann Eliza Space*, newspaper woman: Lena Merville. *Ruth Ann Morgan*, a wench: Jane Burby. *Bertie*, an angelette: FLETCHER NORTON. *Florence Forcem*, an actress: ADELE ROWLAND. *Otto Winne*: Otto Johnson.

Act 1: The Casino at French Lick, Indiana.

Act 2: Plaza at Port au Prince, Hayti.

Act 3: Reception room in the Palace at Port au Prince.

ACT 1

"The American Monte Carlo" (Opening Chorus)

"A-L-E"
T. Lyons, Chorus

"I Would Like to Correspond With You"
M. Stanley, J. H. Pratt

"Everybody's Rag Time Crazy" (Finale)
T. Lyons, Ensemble

ACT 2

"Bamboo Lane"
M. Stanley, Chorus

"The Revolutionary Man"
J. Rose

"Come, Toddle Along"
F. Norton, Girls

"Captain Flo"
A. Rowland, Male Chorus

"Chicken" (Finale)
M. Stanley, Chorus

ACT 3

"Good Bye, Miss Liberty"
C. McCullough, Chorus

"Romeo and Juliet" (Love Me Just Like Romeo Loved Miss Juliet)
M. Stanley, J. H. Pratt, Chorus

"Mr. Bizzy Izzy Rosenstein" (Mr. Izzy, Always Busy, Rosenstein)
J. Rose

Finale

1909.19

THE LOVE CURE

A Musical Romance of Stageland in Three Acts[28]. Original Viennese libretto ("Künstlerblut") by Leo Stein and Karl Lindau. Music by Edmund Eysler. American book and lyrics by Oliver Herford. Staged by George Marion. Scenery painted by Walter Burridge. Costumes by Zimmerman, Paris; Madame Moore, New York. Lighting by Joseph Wilson. Orchestra under the direction of Augustus Barratt. Produced by Henry W. Savage. Opened 1 September 1909 at the New Amsterdam Theatre and closed 30 October 1909 after 70 performances[29].

CAST: *Torrelli*, leading man of the Novelty Theatre: CHARLES J. ROSS. *Alfred Blake*: CRAIG CAMPBELL. *Mr. Blake*, his father: Fred Frear. *Major Vaughn*: Joseph Allen. *Mr. Silliman*, a capitalist: Thomas J. Walsh. *James*, a butler: James Horne. *The Leading Old Man*, Novelty Theatre: Arda Lacroix. *Clarence Chauncey*, Assistant District Attorney: Harry Hyde. *Nellie Vaughn*, prima donna of the Novelty Theatre: ELGIE BOWEN. *Mildred Silliman*, an heiress: EVA FALLON. *Mrs. Julia Silliman*,

[24]Out of town costumes credited to Cora McGeachy.

[25]Added to Act 2 after the opening:

"Up in a Balloon" (following "Alabama")
A. Yorke, Chorus

[26]Dropped after opening.

[27]No New York program available; list of musical numbers prepared from Brooklyn program dated 1 November 1909. Musical director for tour, A. M. Langstaff.

[28]During the run, Act 1 was renamed the Prologue, Act 2 became Act 1, etc.

[29]Played a return engagement 3 January 1910 at the Grand Opera House for 8 performances.

her mother: ALICE HOSMER. *The Leading Old Woman*, Novelty Theatre: Blanche Rice. *A Chorus Girls*, Novelty Theatre: Helen Rockefeller. *A Page*: Grace Waldo. *Stage Doorkeeper*: George Pullman. *Policeman*: Pedro Reddiman. *Libretto Boy*: William Kaestner. *Carriage Caller*: Jack Bergman. *Manager of the Novelty Theatre*: George McDermott. *Stage Manager*, Novelty Theatre: Milton Pollock. *Assistant Stage Manager*, Novelty Theatre: Henry Russell.

Ushers, Novelty Theatre: Messrs. McConville, Grahay. *Stage Door Johnnies*: Messrs. McDermott, Kern, Black, McConville, Van Sickle, Whiting, Grahay, Schnager, Miller. *Matinee Girls*: Misses Benson, Everett, Allen, West, Belma, Hart, Rockefeller, Campbell, Burnham, Rellis. *Dancing Girls*: Misses Temple, Sayre, Rogers, Landers, Wellington, Vivian, Renard, St. Clair, Bell, Waldo, Quirk. *Members of the Novelty Theatre Company and Chorus, Stage Hands, Guests, Novelty Theatre Orchestra, Ladies and Gentlemen of the Audience, etc.*

Act 1: Exterior of Novelty Theatre. After the play.

Act 2: Drawing room in Mr. Blake's home. The following night.

Act 3: Behind the scenes of the Novelty Theatre. The 200th performance.

ACT 1[30]

"Oh, Be Jolly"
C. Campbell, Stage Johnnies

"How Fair the World"
C. Campbell

"The Matinee Idol"
C. J. Ross, Matinee Girls

"I Wonder What the Audience Would Say"
E. Bowen

"A Pretty Part for Me to Play" (Finale)
E. Bowen, C. J. Ross, C. Campbell, Johnnies

ACT 2

"Gather Ye Rosebuds"
Opening Chorus

"I Am an Indian"
E. Bowen

"Peek-a-Boo"
A. Hosmer, C. J. Ross

"When Skies Are Bright"
C. Campbell, E. Bowen

"Love and Wine" (Drinking Song)
C. J. Ross

Finale
Ensemble

ACT 3

"Forget Me Not"
E. Bowen

"Cupid's March"
E. Fallon, Chorus of the Novelty Theatre

"A Toast"
E. Bowen, Ensemble

"Just a Play"
C. J. Ross

Finale
Ensemble

1909.20 A TRIP TO JAPAN

A Triple Bill, including a Spectacular Melodrama with Music in 5 Scenes, a Ballet in Two Tableaux, and a Spectacle in 5 Scenes. Music and lyrics by Manuel Klein. Staged by R. H. Burnside. Dances arranged by Vincenzo Romeo. Settings designed by Arthur Voegtlin. Costumes by Mme. Ziebarth. Orchestra under the direction of Manuel Klein. Produced by Messrs. Lee and J. J. Shubert. Opened 4 September 1909 the Hippodrome and closed 21 May 1910 after 447 performances.

ACT 1

A TRIP TO JAPAN, a Spectacular Melodrama with Music in 5 Scenes[31]. Play by R. H. Burnside. Suggested and invented by Arthur Voegtlin. Music and lyrics by Manuel Klein. Staged by R. H. Burnside. Dances arranged by Vincenzo Romeo. Settings designed by Arthur Voegtlin. Costumes by Mme. Ziebarth. Orchestra under the direction of Manuel Klein.

CAST: *Lieutenant Dick Gordon*, U.S. Navy: E. A. CLARK. *Hiram Dixon*, a ship builder: W. H. CLARK. *Tom Dixon*, his son: HARRY GRIFFITH. *Dolly Dixon*, his daughter: MABEL DWIGHT. *Martin Sharpe*, his manager: Herbert Mansfield. *Kirby Dayton*, his secretary: Adrian Bellevue. *Colonel Cook*, Proprietor of the Circus: J. Parker Coombs. *Mary*, his adopted daughter, known as La Belle Marie: Mildred Flora. *Violet Jackson*, Dolly's friend: Lily Lillian. *Kura Yamamora*, a Japanese merchant: Harry Dale. *O Ko San*, a Geisha girl: NANETTE FLACK. *George Washington Jenkins*: HARRY WARDELL. *Marceline*: MARCELINE. *Chinaman*: Frank Hanson. *Bob Binnacle*, a sailor: James R. Adams. *Bill Bobstay*, a sailor: George H. Adams. *Jonathan Gray*, Proprietor of the Hotel: Harry Cluett. *John Wainwright*, American Consul at Tokio: H. L. Barstar. *Mr. Stevens*, Cashier of the Bank: Nat Harris.

ACT 1[32]

Scene 1

Opening Chorus
Ensemble

Finale
Ensemble

CIRCUS PROGRAM: Foureaux and Manetti (Europe's Famous Equestrians); Entrée Marceline; Mme. Louise's Performing Monkeys; Dankmar-Schiller Troupe; Balton Troupe; Four Idianis. George Bonhair Troupe (High Class Risley Act).
Equestrian Director, George Melville.
Scene: Hotel at Old Point Comfort. The Circus Performance by the Sea.

Scene 2

"Our Navy's the Best in the World"
E. A. Clark, Navy Boys

"I'm Going to (the) Sea"
H. Wardell, Chorus
Scene: Exterior of the Ferry House in New York City.

Scene 3

"Goodbye"
Ensemble
Scene: The Steamer lying at her moorings at the dock in Jersey.

Scene 4

"Flower Song" (Fair Flower of Japan)
N. Flack, Chorus

"Meet Me Where the Lanterns Grow"
M. Dwight, H. Wardell
Scene: Street Scene in Tokio, Japan at evening.

Scene 5

Finale
Ensemble
Scene: The Gardens of the Mikado's Palace in Tokio.

ACT 2

THE BALLET OF THE JEWELS, A Ballet in Two Tableaux. Written and produced by R. H. Burnside. Music by Manuel Klein. Dances arranged by Vincenzo Romeo. Scenic effects by Arthur Voegtlin. Costumes designed by Alfredo Edel.

CAST: *Count de San Marco*: GEORGE H. ADAMS. *Carmala*, his daughter: LESLIE LEIGH. *Florian*, a Gondolier, in love with Carmala: NANETTE FLACK. *Hassan*, Prince of Cashmere: CHARLES RAVEL. *Princess Zora*, his wife: MABEL DWIGHT. *Mustapha*, their valet: MARCELINE. *Cupid*, the God of Love: ALBERTINA RASCH. *Scene 1*: Plaza San Marco, Venice. *Scene 2*: The Cave of Jewels.

ACT 3

INSIDE THE EARTH, A Marvelous Scenic and Dramatic Representation of Antipodean Wonders (Spectacle) in 5 Scenes. Written and produced by R. H. Burnside. Music by Manuel Klein. Scenic effects designed by Arthur Voegtlin. Musical director, Manuel Klein.

---

30 Added during the run and for subsequent tour to Act 1 after "I Wonder What the Audience Would Say":
"Flirtation"
E. Bowen, Stage Door Johnnies

31 Though billed as 6 Scenes, only 5 are listed.

32 Also performed, according to souvenir program, but not in the song list:
"Every Girl Loves a Uniform"

CAST: *Oxtacelec*, The Inca: W. H. CLARK. *Dave Allen*, Superintendent and Partner in the Willoughby Mines: E. A. CLARK. *Dan Willoughby*, Owner of the Willoughby Mines: J. PARKER COOMBS. *Miners (5)*: *Jim Harper*: Harry Griffith. *Joe Wallace*: J. H. Taylor. *Billy Jenkins*: Herbert Mansfield. *Harry Carter*: Harry Wardell. *Tom Johnson*: H. L. Barstar. *Ki Wi*, Chief of the Maori: CHIEF KI WI. *Rose Allen*, Dave's wife: NANETTE FLACK. *Mrs. Harper*, Jim's wife: Caroline Weir. *Alice Allen*, in love with Dan: Blanche Boone. And the Maori Tribe (specially engaged for their first appearance outside of New Zealand.)

Scene 1: A Maori Village in New Zealand. *Scene 2*: Summit of the Sacred Mountain. *Scene 3*: Interior of the Volcano. *Scene 4*: The Magic Waterfall. *Scene 5*: The Palace in the Center of the Earth.

1909.21 THE DOLLAR PRINCESS

A Musical Comedy (Operette) in Three Acts. Original Viennese libretto ("Die Dollarprinzessin") by A. M. Willner and Fritz Grünbaum (based on a comedy by Gatti-Trotha). (Book and lyrics) Adapted for the American stage by George Grossmith, Jr. Music by Leo Fall. Staged by J. A. E. [Pat] Malone. Settings designed by Ernest Gros. Musical director, W. T. Francis. Produced by Charles Frohman. Opened 6 August 1909 at the Knickerbocker Theatre and closed 14 May 1910 after 250 performances.[33]

CAST: *John W. Cowder*, president of Coal Trust: EDW. J. CONNOLLY. *Tom Cowder*, his brother, always broke: Albert Hart. *Dick*, his nephew: Frank Tierney. *Freddy Smythe*: DONALD BRIAN. *Marquis de Jolifontaine*: F. POPE STAMPER. *Lord Herbert Fitz-Jones*, one of Cowder's footmen: PERCIVAL KNIGHT. *Ivan Tartaroff*, of the Cirque Tartaroff: WILL WEST. *Paillard*: J. J. Horwitz. *Alice Cowder*, Cowder's daughter: VALLI VALLI. *Daisy*, Cowder's niece: ADRIENNE AUGARDE. *Olga Labinksa*: LOUIE POUNDS. *Blanche*: Jane Hall. *Rose*: Kitty Melrose. *Marie*: Pauline Francis. *Dolly*: Mary Mackid. *Nellie*: Hazel Nelson.

Typewriter Girls: Misses Irene Avon, Frances Curtis, Nan Morgan, Annie Burton, Cynthia Bennett, Elsie Wrede, Adele Kornau, Anna Kuehl, Nonie Torrence, Virginia Richmond, Gretta Gleason, Marie Benedict, Hazel Nelson, Mary Mackid, Elsie Gibson, Clara Heath, Lucy Stone, B. Shirli Rives, Claire Lippincott, Dollie Grey, Oriola Davidson, Maud Worden, Marie Walker. *Tennis Girls*: Misses Mary Mackid, Hazel Nelson, Oriola Davidson, Lucy Stone, Lillian Heim, Claire Leslie, Maude Jackson, May Taylor, Marie Benedict, Mildred Stockvis, Sadie Green, Elsie Gibson, Maud Worden, Mary Lindsay, Dolly Dale, Claudia Esmond, Jessie York, B. Shirli Rives, Annie Burton, Lillian Ogden. *Summer Girls*: Misses Cynthia Bennett, Elsie Wrede, Adele Kornau, Kitty Melrose, Pauline Francis, Irene Avon, Virginia Richmond, Jane Hall, Dolly Grey, Nonie Torrence, Gretta Gleason, Marie Walker, Florence Mac, Charlotte Neumann, Frances Curtis, Claire Lippincott, Nan Morgan, Clara Heath, Anna Kuehl. *Yankee Girls*: Misses Gretta Gleason, Nonie Torrence, Lillian Ogden, Elsie Wrede, Kitty Melrose, Pauline Francis, Jane Hall, Nan Morgan, Oriola Davidson, Cynthia Bennett, Dolly Grey, Marie Walker, Florence Mac, Frances Curtis, Irene Avon, Adele Kornau, Anna Kuehl, Virginia Richmond, Maud Worden, Mary Lindsay. *Clerks, etc.*: Messrs. Ozab, Foley, Carrier, Fink, Vesey, Glanville, Snyder, Sheppard, Vandiver, Linden, Lutz, Jones, D'Orsay, Wilson, Stuart, Simson, Stone, Hall, Sipperly, Walters.

Act 1: An office in Cowder's house. New York City.

Act 2: Winter garden in Cowder's house. New York City.

Act 3: The Franco-British Exhibition. London.

ACT 1

Opening Chorus

"A Self-Made Maiden" (Song)
V. Vali, Typewriter Girls

"Lady Fortune" (Song)
F. P. Stamper

"The Riding Lesson"[34] (Duet)
A. Augarde, F. P. Stamper

"My Dream of Love" (Song)
D. Brian

"Inspection" (Duet)
V. Valli, D. Brian

"Hip, Hip, Hurrah!" (Trio)
L. Pounds, F. Tierney, A. Hart

Finale

ACT 2[35]

Opening Chorus

"Typewriting" (Duet)
V. Valli, D. Brian

"Paragraphs" (Ring O'Roses)(Duet)
A. Augarde, F. P. Stamper

"Love, Love" (Song)
L. Pounds
(*Music by* Frank Tours. *Lyrics by* Adrian Ross.)

"(I Can Say) Truly Rural" (Song)
W. West, P. Knight
(*Music and Lyrics by* George Arthurs, Worton David.)

"The Dollar Princess" (Quartette)
V. Valli, A. Augarde, F. P. Stamper, D. Brian

Finale

ACT 3

Opening Chorus
(*Music by* William T. Francis.)

"Love's a Race" (Song)
D. Brian

"A Boat Sails on Wednesday" (Hornpipe Quintette)
E. J. Connelly, W. West, A. Hart, F. Tierney, P. Knight
(*Music by* Jerome Kern. *Lyrics by* George Grossmith, Jr., Adrian Ross.)

"Reminiscence" (Duet)
A. Augarde, F. P. Stamper

"Then You Go" (Duet)
V. Valli, D. Brian

Finale

1909.25 MISS INNOCENCE

A Return Engagement of the Musical Entertainment in Two Acts, 8 Scenes[36]. Book and lyrics by Harry B. Smith. Music by Ludwig Engländer. Produced under the stage direction of Julian Mitchell. Settings by Ernest Albert, John H. Young (Act 1, Scenes 1, 2; Act 2, Scenes 2, 3). Costumes by Klaw & Erlanger Costume Company. Musical director, Frank Darling. Produced by Florenz Ziegfeld. Opened 27 September 1909 at the New York Theatre and closed 9 October 1909 after 16 performances.

CAST: *Anna*, Miss Innocence, model pupil of a model school: ANNA HELD. *Miss Sniffins*, Proprietor of the School for Innocence; a lady with several "pasts": ALICE HEGEMAN. *Helen Legarde*, a gay Parisienne: GENE LUNESKA. *Claire*, a school girl: FRANCES FARR. *Ezra Pettingill*, "the greatest detective in the world": CHARLES A. BIGELOW. *Captain, The Hon. Roland Fitzmaurice Montjoy*, of the First Life Guards: LAWRENCE D'ORSAY. *Pierre de Brissac*, Lieutenant in the French Navy: JOHN REINHARD. *The Duke of Pomerania*: William Powers. *Bobo*, a poor relation: Peter Swift. *The Marquis de Chabert*: Maurice Hegeman. *Angele*: MILLIE BAKER. *Loulou*: LOTTIE VERNON. *Visitors to the L'Abbaye (14)*: *Eugenie*: Violet Jewell. *Flore*: Virginia Marshall. *Diane*: Elinor Dayne. *Celestine*: Marie LaMar. *Eve*: Mae Paul. *Marie*: May Hickey. *Fleurette*: Janet Burton. *Clairette*: Beatrice Gladstone. *Toto*: Bessie Fennell. *Lolo*: Lorraine Leslie. *Gabrielle*: Myrtle Marsh. *Frances*: Corinne Drexel. *Zolo*: Gertrude Dale. *Zaza*: Dorothy Lancaster. *Zuzu*: Bessie Neil. *Maxine*: Eunice Mackay. *Yvonne*: Marion Thompson. *"Hindoo Honey" Girls (3)*: *Rita*: Alice Leslie. *Carita*: Alice Tyson. *Pepita*: Vonnie Voyt. *Sadie*: Margaret O'Neill. *Spanish Dancers*: Misses Billy Birch, Marjorie Bonner, May Hickey, Frances Leslie. *Count Maxime*: James A. Youngs. *Albert*, Maitre d'hotel: Pierre Roudil. *Walker*, an American: Charles Page. *Hobbes*, a college boy: Edward A. Smith. *O'Brien*, an American athelete: John S. Brusch. *Ben Hassan*, an Arab: Alfred Fairbrother. *Prince Yogama*, a Japanese: Lionel Lozier. *Rastignac*, a student: John Barry. *An American*: Max Scheck. *Claude*: James G. Doyle. *Schmalz*, a ballet master: Clifford B. Saum. *Premiere Danseuse*: Marie Lavelle. *Alphonse*, attendant at the Hotel de Boheme: Pierre Roudil. *A Postman*:

---

[33] Costumes uncredited.

[34] Replaced for subsequent tour by:
"Follow Me Round" (Duet)
A. Augarde, F. P. Stamper

[35] Added during the run to Act 2 (after "Typewriting"):
"Souvenir"
A. Hart

[36] Original production opened 30 November 1908 at the New York Theatre for 176 performances. For Synopsis of Scenes, see original 1908 production. Dropped for this engagement were: "Am I a Wife, Widow or Maid?," "Please Tell Me What They Mean," "My Post Card Girl," Perfectly Terrible, Dear," "Afraid to Go Home at All" and "Shine On, Harvest Moon."

Dudley Oatman. *Dr. Charcot*: Maurice Hegeman. *A Gendarme*: Clifford P. Saum. *Sergeant*: Jerome Van Norden. *Artist Model*: Elise Hamilton.

"Three Weeks with You": Misses Marjorie Bonner, Elinor Dayne, May Hickey, Violet Jewell, Selma Mantell, Eunice Mackey, Millie Baker. Messrs. John A. Youngs, John Barry, Albert Fairbrother, Clifford P. Saum, Harry Hoffman, Edward A. Smith. *School Girls*: Misses Birch, Blake, Bonner, Cheridah, Daly, E. Dana, F. DeVere, M. DeVere, Hamilton, Hoyt, Jewell, Hickey, G. Kingstone, Lavelle, A. Leslie, F. Leslie, Mackey, Mantell, Martin, Mellman, Thompson. *Maids*: Misses Barnette, Chadwick, P. Dana, A. Kingstone, Lavallerie, Maccabe, Voclezka, Wilson. *Railway Number*: Misses Birch, Bonner Daly, E. Dana, D. DeVere, M. DeVere, Hamilton, Hickey, Hoyt, Jewell, F. Leslie, Mantell. *Ballet School*: Misses Barette, Birch, Bonner, Chadwick, Cheridah, Daly, E. Dana, P. Dana, D. DeVere, M. DeVere, Hamilton, Hickey, Hoyt, Jewell, A. Kingstone, G. Kingstone, Lavelle, A. Leslie, Maccabe, Martin, Millman, Wilson.

ACT 1

Opening Chorus

"By the Light of the Silvery Moon" (from ZIEGFELD FOLLIES OF 1909)
F. Farr, School Girls
(*Music by* Gus Edwards. *Lyrics by* Edward Madden.)

"I'm Learning Something Every Day"
A. Held
(*Music and Lyrics by* Nora Bayes and Jack Norworth.)

Railroad Number
Chorus

Spanish Dance
Misses Birch, Bonner, Hamilton, Hickey

"(Oh! That) Yankiana Rag"
G. Luneska, Company
(*Music by* Melville Gideon. *Lyrics by* E. Ray Goetz.)

"I Have Lost My Little Brown Bear"
A. Held
(*Music by* J. Rosamond Johnson, Bob Cole. *Lyrics by* Bob Cole.)

Finale

ACT 2

Opening Chorus

"I'm Crazy When the Band Begins to Play"
G. Luneska, Ballet Girls
(*Music by* Jean Schwartz. *Lyrics by* William Jerome.)

"I Wonder What's the Matter with My Eyes"
A. Held
(*Music by* Egbert Van Alstyne. *Lyrics by* Harry Williams.)

"What Kind of a Wife to Choose" (What Kind of a Wife Does a Man Like Best)
(*Music and Lyrics by* Gus Edwards.)
J. Reinhard

"My Cousin Caruso"
C. A. Bigelow
(*Music by* Gus Edwards. *Lyrics by* Edward Madden.)

"We Two in an Aeroplane"
A. Held, J. Reinhard
(*Music by* Egbert Van Alstyne. *Lyrics by* Harry Williams.)

"I'm Not That Kind of a Girl"
A. Hegeman
(*Music by* Nat. D. Ayer. *Lyrics by* A. Seymour Brown.)

Students' Chorus
F. Farr, Model, E. Hamilton

"Three Weeks (with You)"
Misses Bonner, Dayne, Hickey, Jewell, Mantell, Mackey, Baker; Messrs. Youngs, Barry, Fairbrother, Saum, Hoffman, Smith

Pierrot Patrole and Dance

Finale

1909.22 THE CHOCOLATE SOLDIER

An Opera Bouffe (Comic Opera) in Three Acts. Original Viennese book ('Der tapfere Soldat') and lyrics by Rudolph Bernauer and Leopold Jacks [Jacobson], based on George Bernard Shaw's play "Arms and the Man." American book and lyrics by Stanislaus Stange. Music by Oscar Straus. Staged by Stanislaus Stange. Music ensembles (arranged) by Al. Holbrook. Settings by Hugo Baruch & Cie., Edward G. Unitt and Joseph Wickes. Costumes by Hugo Baruch & Cie. Orchestra under the direction of Antonio DeNovellis. Produced by Whitney Opera Company (F. C. Whitney, Director). Opened 13 September 1909 at the Lyric Theatre, moved 25 October 1909 to the Herald Square Theatre, moved 22 November 1909 to the Lyric Theatre, moved 20 December 1909 to the Casino Theatre and closed 28 May 1910 after 296 performances.

CAST (in order of appearance): *Nadina Popoff*, Daughter of Colonel Popoff: IDA BROOKS HUNT. *Aurelia Popoff*, Her Mother: FLAVIA ARCARO. *Mascha*, Aurelia's Cousin: Edith Bradford. *Lieutenant Bumerli*, the "Chocolate Soldier," (a Swiss Mercenary in the employ of the Servian Army): JACK E. GARDNER. *Captain Massakroff* of the Bulgarian Army: FRANCIS J. BOYLE. *Louka, Stephen*, Popoff's servants: Lillian Poli, George C. Ogle. *Colonel Casimir Popoff* of the Bulgarian Army: WILLIAM PRUETTE. *Major Alexius Spiridoff* of the Bulgarian Army, betrothed to Nadina: George Tallman. *Soldiers of Bulgarian Army, Gentry, Peasants, Wedding Guests, Villagers, Musicians, etc, etc.*

The action takes place near the Dragoman Pass, Bulgaria, in 1885.

Act 1: Nadina's sleeping apartments in Popoff's house. Nightfall. (Hugo Baruch & Cie.)

Act 2: Gardens of Popoff's house. Daytime. (Unitt & Wickes.)

Act 3: Same as Act 2. Sunset. (Unitt & Wickes.)

ACT 1[37]

Soldiers' Chorus (Introduction)

Trio (What Can We Do Without a Man?)
I. B. Hunt, E. Bradford, F. Arcaro

"My Hero" (Song)
I. B. Hunt

"Sympathy" (Duet)
I. B. Hunt, J. E. Gardner

"Seek the Spy" (Scene)
F. J. Boyle, I. B. Hunt, E. Bradford, F. Arcaro, J. E. Gardner, Bulgarian Soldiers

Romanze (Tiralala) and Scene (Finale)
I. B. Hunt, E. Bradford, F. Arcaro

ACT 2

Opening Chorus (Our Heroes Come)
(Ensemble)

Scene (Alexius, the Heroic)
G. Tallman, W. Pruette, Ensemble

"Thank the Lord the War Is Over"
Ensemble

"Never Was There Such a Lover" (Duet)
I. B. Hunt, G. Tallman

"The Chocolate Soldier"
I. B. Hunt, J. E. Gardner

"The Tale of a Coat" (Sextette)
I. B. Hunt, E. Bradford, F. Arcaro, J. E. Gardner, G. Tallman, W. Pruette

"That Would Be Lovely" (Duet)
I. B. Hunt, J. E. Gardner

Finale

ACT 3

"Sweetheart" (Chorus)
Ensemble

"Falling in Love" (Duet)
E. Bradford, G. Tallman

"The Letter Song"
I. B. Hunt

"The Letter" (Duet)
I. B. Hunt, J. E. Gardner

Finale
Ensemble

---

[37]Musical numbers were not listed in earliest programs. The following list was prepared from the published piano vocal score (Joseph Remick, New York, 1909) and programs during the original run.

1909.23

THE ROSE OF ALGERIA

A Musical Play in Two Acts, 4 Scenes[38]. Book and lyrics by Glen MacDonough. Music by Victor Herbert. Entire production staged by Ned Wayburn. Settings designed by Ernest Albert[39]. Costumes by Dazian and Castel-Bert. Orchestra under the direction of Theodore Stearns. Orchestrations by Victor Herbert. Produced by Lew Fields. Opened 20 September 1909 at the Herald Square Theatre and closed 23 October 1909 after 40 performances.[40]

CAST: *Zoradie*, Sultana of the Barakeesh, seen in Act 1 as Miriam the fortune teller: LILLIAN HERLEIN. *Millicent Madison*, M.D., an American doctress who has brought out a trained corps of nurses for the French government: ETHEL GREEN. *Mirzah, Zaphirie*, Ladies in Waiting to the Sultana: Edith Ethel MacBride, Marion Wynne. *General Petipons*, Governor General of Algeria and uncle of Captain deLome: EUGENE COWLES. *Barnum Sells, Bailey Ringling*, two young American circus men, forced by the failure of their circus in Algeria to enlist in the Foreign Legion of the French Army: WILLIAM GASTON, JAMES DIAMOND. *Captain deLome*, a French Captain in command of the military post: FRANK POLLOCK. *Mr. and Mrs. Billings F. Cooings*, a recently married couple on their honeymoon and bound for nowhere in particular: ANNA WHEATON, RALPH NAIRN. *Lieutenant Bertrand*, aide to Captain deLome: Maitland Davies. *Mimi*, of the Latin Quarter: Belle Pallma. *Pierre*, an artist: Edward Tabor. *Philippe*, another: Carl Kahn. *Sergeant Georges*: Ralph Watson. *Fanchon, Camille, Toni*, Café Chantant girls: Carrie Poltz, Florrie Poltz, Nellie Poltz.

Bayaderes and Nurses: Misses Ada Blair, Mabel Gebeau, Dolores Sanasace, Daisy Schwartz, Bessie McCellan, Elsie Clark, Vivian Morton, Alice Evartson, Clara Whitford, Gladys Seymour, Octavia Hague, Henrietta Pillard, Pearl Franklyn. *Flower and Candy Sellers*: Misses Dorothy Sanasace, Maud Martin, Edna Martin, Ethel LeBrower, Grace Russell, Molly Ward, Katherine Dornier, Ray Williams. *Artist's Models and Grisettes*: Misses Dorothy Pope, Virginia Adams, Nancy Rose, Gloria Starr, Virginia Ruppert, Laura Campbell, Fay Stuart, Belle Pallma. *Staff Officers*: Messrs. Tabor, Conn, Birch, LePato. *Soldiers and Merchants*: Messrs. Swalm, Steinman, S. Kolnich, Dillon, Watson, Lingham, Wallace, Chase, Metzger, Mulligan, Taft, Belmont, Hook, Jaffe, Vanderklom, Kahn.

The action takes place at the present time.

Act 1, Scene 1: A French Military Post near the seacoast of Algeria. *Scene 2*: A Gully on the Coast. *Scene 3*: The Open Sea.

Act 2: Terrace of an old palace in the outskirts of the city of Algiers.

ACT 1[41]

"The Lady Sleeps" (Opening Chorus)
L. Herlein, Ensemble

"The Same Old Two"
A. Wheaton, R. Nairn, Chorus

"Boule' Miche"
F. Pollock, Models, Artists, Dolls

"I've Been Decorated"
E. Cowles, Chorus

"You'll Feel Better Then"
E. Green, E. Cowles, Nurses

"The Great White Easiest Way"
E. Green, J. Diamond, W. Gaston

"Rose of the World"
L. Herlein

"Letters from Home"
Ensemble

"Bohemia Good-bye"
E. Green, J. Diamond, W. Gaston

ACT 2[42]

"The Mardi Gras" (Opening Chorus)
Ensemble

"Only One of Anything"
E. Cowles, Chorus

"Ask Her While the Band Is Playing"
E. Green

"Love Is Like a Cigarette"
F. Pollock, Chorus

"Twilight in Barakeesh"
L. Herlein, People of Barakeesh

"The Foolish Gardener"
J. Diamond, W. Gaston

Finale
Ensemble

[38]A revised version of the musical play ALGERIA originally produced 31 August 1908 at the Broadway Theatre for 48 performances.
[39]The surf scene at the finale of Act 1 is patented by Frank D. Thomas.
[40]Played a return engagement 15 November 1909 at the West End Theatre for 8 performances.
[41]Running order revised after opening.
[42]Added after opening to Act 2, after "The Foolish Gardener:"
"Little Birds of Paradise"
M. Davies, Dolls, Chorus

1909.24

THE GIRL AND THE WIZARD

A Romance of the Austrian Tyrol (Musical Play) in Two Acts and a Prologue. Book by J. Hartley Manners. Music by Julian Edwards. Lyrics by Robert B. Smith and Edward Madden. Production staged by Ned Wayburn. Scenery painted by H. Robert Law. Costumes designed by Melville Ellis. Orchestra under the direction of Cassius Freeborn. Produced by the Sam S. and Lee Shubert Inc. Opened 27 September 1909 at the Casino Theatre and closed 18 December 1909 after 96 performances.[43]

CAST: *Herman Scholz*, Lapidary: SAM ASH. *Count Hochstetter*: HARRY CORSON CLARKE. *Felicitas*, his daughter: FLORA PARKER. *Paul*, Schultze's nephew: WILLIAM ROSELLE. *Frantzi*, Felicitas' confidante: HARRIET STANDON. *Mina*: (Little) Bessie Shrednecky. *Gretchen*: Hattie Lorraine. *Jake Juggers*: Charles K. Burrows. *Carl Behrend, Max Andressen*, of the Meiningen Opera Company: Donald Buchanan, Oscar Swartz. *The Baron*, an old friend: Bert Lawrence. *Burgomaster*: Henry Holt. *Sergeant*: Thomas Reynolds. *Captain of the Troop*: Percy Hammond. *Count Hochstetter's Boon Companions (4)*: *Kurt*: Max Robertson. *Raoul*: Charles P. Scales. *Steiffel*: Samuel Keene. *Schwendemann*: Oliver Sterling. *Murietta*, prima donna of the Meiningen Opera Company: KITTY GORDON.

Personnel of the Chorus: *Jewels, etc.*: Misses Hattie Lorraine, Berna DeVore, Nedra Gage, Bertha Montague, Sadie Carr, Helen Edwards, May Hopkins, Arline LaCrosse, Louise Gale, Gladys Alexander. *Tyrolean Boys and Girls*: Misses Ethel Kelly, Anna Stone, Violet Marsden, Sallie Webb, Marguerite Faulkner, Blanche Brayton, Francis Alair, Gracie McMean. *Opera Singers, etc.*: Misses Nellie Neil, Aime Dalmores, Vinnie Danvers, Audrey Munson, Blixie Murrie, Daisy Anderson, Anita Francesca, Estelle Francesca. *Coryphées, etc.*: Misses Cissie Shotten, Dora West, Ray Mordecai, Rita Mason. *Soldiers of Austria, etc.*: Messrs. F. H. Meirose, H. M. Holt, W. Ward, Oliver Sterling, Oscar Swartz, Bert Lawrence, Olin Howland, M. Robertson, L. Garvey, Harry Truelson, F. Trebbie, H. Law, Thomas Reynolds, C. P. Scales, S. Keene. *Tyrolean Kiddies*: Misses Gladys Taylor, Dorothy Scherer, Bessie Shrednecky, Edith Shrednecky, Gertrude Jenkins, Olive Norman.

The action takes place today in a little town in the Austrian Tyrol.

Prologue: A Hill-top. Daybreak.

Act 1: Interior of Herman Schultze's Lapidarium and Museum of Precious Stones.

Act 2: Rotunda, Schultz's Castle.

ACT 1[44]

"Reveille" (Opening Chorus)
Ensemble

"The Land of Love"
F. Parker
(*Lyrics by* Robert Smith.)

"When I Sang Toreador"
K. Gordon, D. Buchanan, O. Swartz, Chorus
(*Music and Lyrics by* Melville Gideon.)

"What Wealth Is Here"
Chorus

"La Belle Parisienne"
H. Standon, Chorus
(*Music by* Louis A. Hirsch. *Lyrics by* Edward Madden.)

[43]Played a return engagement 27 December 1909 at the West End Theatre for 8 performances.
[44]Added for subsequent tour:
"Oh How That German Could Love"
S. Bernard
(*Music and Lyrics by* Irving Berlin.)

"Military Mary Ann"
K. Gordon, Chorus
(*Music by* Louis A. Hirsch. *Lyrics by* Edward Madden.)

"Song of the Heart"
K. Gordon
(*Lyrics by* Edward Madden.)

ACT 2

Opening Chorus
Ensemble

"How Can You Toot (a Toot-Toot)?"
S. Bernard
(*Music by* George Dougherty, Seymour Furth. *Lyrics by* Will Heelan, Ned Wayburn.)

"I Wonder If You're Lonely"
F. Parker, Chorus
(*Music by* George Dougherty. *Lyrics by* Ned Wayburn.)

"Opera Comique"[45]
S. Bernard, K. Gordon
(*Music and Lyrics by* Melville Gideon.)

"(By) The Blue Lagoon"
K. Gordon, Chorus
(*Music by* Jerome D. Kern. *Lyrics by* Percival Knight.)

"Frantzi Frankenstein"
H. Standon, Male Chorus
(*Music by* Jerome D. Kern. *Lyrics by* Percival Knight.)

"The Black Butterfly"
K. Gordon

"The Wedding Fête"
Ensemble

Finale
Ensemble

1909.26 THE MAN WHO OWNS BROADWAY

A Musical Play in Three Acts, 4 Scenes. Book, music and lyrics by George M. Cohan, based on his own play "Popularity." Staged by George M. Cohan. Scenery painted by Ernest Albert, Edward G. Unitt and Joseph Wickes. Ladies' costumes from Klaw & Erlanger Costume Company; men's clothes from Max Marx. Orchestra under the direction of Karl Weixelbaum. Musical numbers arranged by Charles Gebest. Produced by Sam H. Harris and George M. Cohan. Opened 11 October 1909 at the New York Theatre and closed 29 January 1910 after 128 performances.

CAST: *Sydey Lyons*, a Broadway star: RAYMOND HITCHCOCK. *Anthony Bridwell*, a multi-millionaire: STANLEY FORDE. *Tom Bridwell*, his son: SCOTT WELSH. *Sylvia Bridwell*, his daughter: FLORA ZABELLE. *George Burnham*, a villain: GEORGE LYDECKER. *Caroline Curtis*, a villainess: LORA LIEB. *Edith Wilson*, Tom's sweetheart: FRANCES GORDON. *Andrews*, a butler: Mark Sullivan. *Bill Robinson*, Lyons' manager: Mark Sullivan. *Anna*, a maid: Maude Morris. *Butler*: W. J. Ford. *Harry Hathaway*, a young sport: W. J. Ford. *Starter*: Armand King. *Detective*: Ralph Harlow. *Captain at Martin's*: Curt Karpe. *Special Officer*: Thomas Shields.

Show Girls: Misses Elizabeth Young, Edythe Gilbert, Rose Leslie, Paula Leslie, Irma Bertrand, Emily Wilson, Irene Moyer, Lulu Davies, Trixie DeWitt, Marie Caldwell, Marguerite Loveridge, B. Bertrand, Mary Moon, Bonnie Luzon, Catherine Howland, Edythe Thorne, Mollie Hoffman, Polly Stanley, Mary Gordon. *Dancing Girls*: Misses Grace Beaumont, Sadie Livermoore, Ethel Lytle, Dottie Moyer, Frances Ross, Eva Marsh, Mabel Leichman, Maudie Heath. *Boys*: Messrs. Ralph Harlow, Charles L. Tucker, Martin Enwright, Thomas Shields, Armand King, Rokey Johnson, Edward Weinberg, Curt Karpe, Leland Sterns, Leonard Davies, William Hovey, John Gordon, Ernest Band, George Barber, Paul McShane, Harry Glover, William Hobbis. *Dancing Waiters*: Messrs. Johnny Dale, Murry Harris, Eddie Lynn, William Cody. *Servants*: Messrs. Ford, Halowe, Johnson; Misses Gordon, Hoffman.

Act 1: Reception Hall in Anthony Bridwell's New York Home. (Albert.)

Act 2: Martin's Restaurant, 26th and Broadway. (Unitt & Wickes.)

Act 3, Scene 1: Corridor in the Waldorf-Astoria. (Albert.) *Scene 2*: Interior of the National Theatre. Same night. A performance of "King Hobo" is going on.

ACT 1

"My Daughter Is Wed to a Friend of Mine"
Esemble

"I've Always Been a Good Old Sport"
S. Forde, Male Chorus

"I'm in Love with One of the Stars"
F. Zabelle, Chorus

"Secrets of the Household" (When a Servant Learns a Secret)
Servants

"The Man Who Owns Broadway"
R. Hitchcock, Chorus

ACT 2

"You'd Think You Were in Paris"
Ensemble

"Love Will Make or Break a Man"
G. Lydecker, Chorus

"(There's) Something About a Uniform"
L. Lieb, Chorus

"Ona Hundred Different Ships"
R. Hitchcock, Company

"I'm All O.K. with K. & E." (I'm O.K. with K. and O.)
M. Sullivan, Company

"A Nice Little Plot for a Play"
R. Hitchcock, S. Welsh, F. Zabelle, F. Gordon

ACT 3

"In the Waldorf Halls"
R. Harlow, Chorus

"I'll Go the Route for You" (I'll Go the Route with You)
S. Welsh, F. Gordon

"March of the King's Amazons"
Chorus

"Why They Made Him King"
R. Hitchcock

Finale
F. Zabelle, Company

1909.27 MR. LODE OF KOAL

A Musical Show in Three Acts. Book and lyrics by J. A. Shipp and Alexander Rogers. Music by J. Rosamond Johnson; additional music by Bert A. Williams. Orchestra under the direction of James J. Vaughn. Produced by F. Ray Comstock. Opened 1 November 1909 at the Majestic Theatre and closed 4 December 1909 after 40 performances.[46]

CAST: *Chester A. Lode*: BERT WILLIAMS. *Buggsy*: ALEXANDER ROGERS. *Gimlet*: TOM BROWN. *Gluten*, Gimlet's silent partner: Siren Nevarro. *Buttram*: J. LEUBRIE HILL. *Weedhead*: Charles H. Moore. *"Cap"*: Henry Troy. *Singlink*, Court messenger: CHARLES McKENZIE. *"Saig"*: J. E. Lightfoot. *First "Lieut"*: Sterling Rex. *Second "Lieut"*: J. M. Thomas. *Third "Lieut"*: Clarence Redd. *Blootch*: MATT HOUSLEY. *Woozy*: Hattie McIntosh. *Whirlina*: Siren Nevarro. *Mysteria*: Lottie Grady. *A. Saylor*: Ada Banks. *Hoola*: Hattie Hopkins. *Kinklets*: Georgia Gomez. *What*: Bessie Brady. *Ho*: Anita Bush. *Rubeena*: Lavinia Rogers. *Diano*: Maggie Davis. *Osee*: Jessie Ellis. *Discretia*: Ida Day. *Giddina*: Katie Jones. *Citizens, Guards, etc.*: Messrs. Hawks, Payne, Holland, Cooper, Gibbs, Foster, Saulsbury, Tapley, Hilliard, Tulliver, Chappelle. *Flower Girls, Dancers, etc.*: Misses M. Brown, Clough, F. Brown, Lewis, Yorke, Vaughan, King, DeVance, Guiguesse, Payne.

The action takes place between 3 o'clock in the afternoon and 9 o'clock in the evening of the same day.

Act 1: Court outside the Smokery (he goes to sleep.)

Act 2: The same (he dreams).

Act 3: The same (he awakens).

ACT 1

"The Start"
Chorus

"The Can Song"
J. L. Hill, Men

"My Ole Man"
B. A. Williams

[45]Dropped for subsequent tour.

[46]Settings, costumes uncredited.

"The Harbor of Lost Dreams"
G. Gomez, Chorus

"Mum's the Word, Mr. Moon"
L. Grady, Chorus
(*Music by* Leubrie Hill. *Lyrics by* Alex Rogers.)

"In Far Off Mandalay"
A. Banks, Girls
(*Music by* Al Johns. *Lyrics by* Alex Rogers.)

Finale

ACT 2

Opening
Company

"Hodge Podge" (Dance)
S. Nevarro

A Song ["That Is Plenty" (That's a Plenty)]
B. A. Williams

"By-Gone Days in Dixie"
H. Troy, assisted by J. E. Lightfoot, S. Rex, J. M. Thomas, C. Redd

"Lament"
A. Rogers, Men

"Chink-Chink, Chink-Chink, Chinyman"
T. Brown, S. Nevarro

Finale
B. A. Williams, Company

ACT 3

"The Fate of the Veiled Mugs"
Entire Company

"Believe Me"
B. A. Williams, Company

1909.28 THE SILVER STAR

A Musical Play in Three Acts, 4 Scenes. Book and lyrics by Harry B. Smith. Music by Robert Hood Bowers, C. J. M. Glaser, Jean Schwartz, Raymond Hubbell, Al Piantadosi, Karl Hoschna. Staged by Herbert Gresham. Dances arranged by Julian Mitchell. Ballets for Mlle. Genée produced under the personal direction of Alexander Gené. Costumes by F. Richard Anderson; Mlle. Genée's costumes designed by C. Wilhelm. Settings designed by Ernest Albert. Orchestra under the direction of Robert Hood Bowers, C. J. M. Glaser. Produced by (Marc) Klaw and (Abraham L.) Erlanger. Opened 1 November 1909 at the New Amsterdam Theatre and closed 8 January 1910 after 80 performances[47].

CAST: *Professor Alonzo Dingelblatz*: GEORGE BICKEL. *Doctor Algernon Hornblower*: HARRY WATSON. *Mr. Wiseheimer*: BARNEY BERNARD. *Ernest Connor*: Lee Harrison. *Koffitchsky*, a Russian: F. Stanton Heck. *Ned Brandon*: Mortimer Weldon. *Traddles*, a footman: O. C. Mack. *The Colonel*: F. H. Stanton. *The Sergeant*: J. H. Purcell. *Mrs. Vera Willing*: EMMA JANVIER. *Mary Anne*: NELLIE McCOY. *Rosa*, a Gypsy Girl: Gene Ormonde. *Viola*, adopted daughter of the Professor and the Doctor: ADELINE GENÉE. *The Christmas Fairy*: ADELINE GENÉE. *The Spirit of Champagne*: ADELINE GENÉE. *Queen of the Floral Fête*: ADELINE GENÉE. *Ensemble*: (Misses Lewis, Morris, etc.).

Act 1, Scene 1: Exterior Wiseheimer's House on Christmas Eve. *Scene 2*: Interior Wiseheimer's House; a Christmas Party.

Act 2: Grand Opera House, Paris.

Act 3: Mrs. Willing's Country House on the Thames. Springtime. (Painted by Platzer.)

ACT 1
Scene 1

"Sleigh Bells May Be Wedding Bells"
Ensemble
(*Music by* Robert Hood Bowers.)

"To Bring Up a Girl" (Trio)
N. Coy, G. Bickel, H. Watson
(*Music by* Karl Hoschna.)

Scene 2

"Dancing the Cottillion"
Ensemble
(*Music by* Raymond Hubbell.)

"The Cooney Spooney Dance" (That Spooney Dance)(Song)
N. Coy, H. Watson
(*Music by* Jean Schwartz. *Lyrics by* William Jerome.)

"If Only I Were Santa Claus" (Trio)
G. Bickel, H. Watson, B. Bernard
(*Music by* Robert Hood Bowers.)

The Living Christmas Tree:

Fairy Dance; March Militaire; Horn Pipe (dances)
A. Genée
(*Music by* C. J. M. Glaser.)

Finale
A. Genée, Company

ACT 2

"Carnival"
Ensemble
(*Music by* Robert Hood Bowers.)

"They're Not Doing That This Season"
E. Janvier
(*Music by* Albert Gumble.)

"Franco-American Ragtime"
N. McCoy, Ensemble
(*Music by* Jean Schwartz. *Lyrics by* William Jerome.)

"(You Can Have Your 'Oh You Kids' But) It's a Loving Wife for Mine"
H. Watson, G. Bickel, Misses Lewis, Morris
(*Music and Lyrics by* Herbert Ingraham.)

The Silver Grape Arbor
(Painted by Baruch & Company, Berlin)

Ballet (The Spirit of Champagne)
A. Genée
Vermouth Cocktail, Absinthe, Martini, Manhattan Cocktail, Sauterne, Claret, Burgundy, Apricot Cordial, Creme de Menthe, Creme de Violet, Benedictine, Chartreuse, Pousse Café: Ensemble.

ACT 3

"Boat Race Chorus"
Ensemble
(*Music by* Robert Hood Bowers.)

"It May Be So, But I Doubt It" (Song)
E. Janvier, Ensemble
(*Music by* Robert Hood Bowers.)

Springtime (Ballet)
(*Music by* C. J. M. Glaser.)

Reverie
A. Genée

"A Collection of Blue Notes"
G. Bickel, H. Watson

"The Silver Star"[48]
A. Genée, Company
(*Music by* Albert Gumble.)

Finale
Company

1909.29 THE BELLE OF BRITTANY

A Musical Play in Two Acts[49]. (Book) Written by Leedham Bantock and P. J. Barrow. Music by Howard Talbot and Marie Horne. Lyrics by Percy Greenbank. Staged by Frank Smithson. Costumes by Melville Ellis. Orchestra under the direction of Clarence Rogerson. Produced by Sam S. and Lee Shubert (Inc.). Opened 8 November 1909 at Daly's Theatre and closed 8 January 1910 after 72 performances.[50]

[47]Played a return engagement 7 February 1910 at the Grand Opera House for 8 performances.

[48]Late in the run this song was moved to Act 2, following "Carnival," where it was performed by Ann Tasker who had assumed the role of Viola from Mlle. Genée, who retained her other 3 roles.

[49]Billed as the London Musical Success.

[50]Scenery uncredited. Played a return engagement 17 January 1910 at the West End Theatre for 7 performances.

CAST: *Marquis de St. Gautier*: FRANK DANIELS. *Raymond de St. Gautier*, son of the Marquis: FRANK RUSHWORTH. *Comte Victoire de Casserole*, a dandy: GEORGE M. GRAHAM. *Poquelin*, a miller: EDWARD GARVIE. *Old Jacques*, a clarinet player: J. Arthur O'Brien. *Artistes (4)*: *Bertrand*: Hubert Neville. *Eugene*: Story Chipman. *Phillippe*: Joseph A. Bingham. *Vivien*: Jack Loughlin. *Baptiste Boubillon*: MARTIN BROWN. *Toinette*, maid to the Marquis: ELSA RYAN. *Mlle. Denise de la Vire*, ward of the Marquis: DAISY DUMONT. *Madame Poquelin*: FRANCES KENNEDY. *Adele*: Gertrude Douglas. *Christine*: Aline Redmond. *Mitrette*: Eileen Kearney. *Rosaline*: May Hopkins. *Lucille*: Evelyn Mitchell. *Colitte*: Ethel Rose. *Maquette*: Dorothy Perry. *Maline*: Josephine Brandell. *Postillons to the Marquis*: Tracy Elbert, Camille Truesdale. *Babette*, Poquelin's daughter: WINNIE O'CONNOR.

Octet: Misses Louise Elton, Blanche Huntington, Sidney Jacouver, Dixie Compton. Messrs. Story Chipman, Hubert Neville, Joseph A. Bingham, Jack Laughlin. *Postillons*: Misses Blanche Huntington, Tracy Elbert, Louise Elton, Sidney Jacouvier, Dixie Compton, Mudge Harman. *Daffodil Girls*: Misses Eileen Kearney, May Hopkins, Hazel Troutman, Gertrude Douglas, Evelyn Mitchell, Josephine Brandell, Dorothy Perry, Aline Redmond. *Country Mice and Dancing Girls*; Misses Louise Elton, Blanche Huntington, Sidney Jacouvier, Mudge Harmon, Camille Truesdale, Dixie Compton, Tracy Elbert, Helen Mackey.

The action takes place at Daffodil Time in Brittany in the eighteenth century.

Act 1: The Old Mill in the Bois d'Amour, Pont Aven.

Act 2: The Chateau, St. Gautier.

ACT 1[51]

"The Bois d'Amour"
Opening Chorus

"It's Too Late Now"
Octet

"The Trysting Tree"
F. Kennedy, Chorus of Girls

"Daffodil Time" (When Daffodil Time Comes Round)
W. O'Connor, Chorus

"The Girl with the Clocks"[52]
F. Rushworth
(*Music by* Walter Davidson. *Lyrics by* Walter Davidson and T. H. Read.)

Entrance of Marquis de St. Gautier
Chorus

"(Oh!) I Must Go Home To-Night"
F. Daniels
(*Music and Lyrics by* William Hargreaves.)

"The Stepping Stones"
W. O'Connor, F. Rushworth
(*Music by* Marie Horne.)

"I'm Not a Ladies' Maid"
E. Ryan, Artists

Chorus of Welcome (The Hero Proudly Comes)

"Two Giddy Goats"
M. Brown, E. Ryan

"Sing to Your Dear One"
F. Daniels

"The Doggies and the Bone"
E. Ryan, T. Elbert, C. Truesdale

Finale
Company

ACT 2

"Wreathe the Golden Flower" (Opening Chorus)
(*Lyrics by* P. J. Barrow.)

"The Best Brittany"
E. Ryan, Chorus

"The Old Chateau"
F. Daniels, D. Dumont, G. M. Graham, F. Kennedy, E. Garvie

"Little Country Mice"
D. Dumont, (Mice) Girls

"In the Oven"
M. Brown, Cooks, Daffodil Girls, Dancing Girls

"The Dawn of Love"
W. O'Connor
(*Lyrics by* P. J. Barrow and Percy Greenbank.)

"A Little Cafe"
M. Brown, E. Ryan

"In the Chest"[53]
F. Daniels, F. Kennedy

Country Dance (Finale)
Entire Company

1909.30

OLD DUTCH

A Musical Farce in Two Acts, 3 Scenes. Book by Edgar Smith[54]. Music by Victor Herbert. Lyrics by George V. Hobart. Staged by Ned Wayburn. Costumes by Melville Ellis. Scenery by John H. Young. Electrical effects by John Whalen. Orchestra under the direction of Louis F. Gottschalk. Produced by Sam S. and Lee Shubert, Inc. and Lew Fields. Opened 22 November 1909 at the Herald Square Theatre and closed 5 February 1910 after 88 performances.[55]

CAST: *Ludwig Streusand*, absent-minded inventor, familiarly known in his native town as "Old Dutch": LEW FIELDS. *Lisa Streusand*, his daughter: ALICE DOVEY. *Leopold Mueller*, an adventurer: JOHN E. HENSHAW. *Alma Villianyi*, a Viennese music hall singer: ADA LEWIS. *Joseph Cusinier*, proprietor of the Hotel Schoenwald: CHARLES JUDELS. *Franz von Bomberg*, a wealthy Viennese manufacturer, touring the Tyrol: JOHN BUNNY. *Rosa von Bomberg*, his wife: EVA DAVENPORT. *Alfred von Bomberg*, his son, lieutenant in the Royal Light Infantry: WILLIAM RAYMOND. *Honorable Algernon Clymber*, in the Tyrol for his health: VERNON CASTLE. *Jean*, head porter at Hotel Schoenwald: Mack Johnston. *The Girl with the Hair Lip*: Irene Russell. *Sisters of Hon. Algernon Clymber (6)*: *Gwendolyn*: Jane Grover. *Maude*: Marion Whitney. *Mabel*: Billie Cuppia. *Kate*: Josephine Karlin. *Margaret*: Elsie LaBoy. *Julia*: Marise Naughton. *Brother Officers of Alfred von Bomberg (6)*: *Wilhelm*: George Lynch. *Franz*: Harry Harrington. *Adelbert*: Thomas McCormick. *Oskar*: Wood Gobel. *Rudolf*: Fred Roberts. *Gustave*: Joseph Norwich. *Freda, Lois*, Maids at the Schoenwald: May Willard, Ruth Rider. *Gretchen*: Gertrude Grant. *Grenwald*, a mountain guide: John Donnelly. *Messenger*: Victor Hyde. *Gendarmes*: George Dowling, Joseph Torpey. *Allan*: Victor Hyde. *Olga*: Nettie Hyde. *Fleurette*: Rhea Hess. *Babette*: Hannah Hess. *Little Hans*: Master Robert Fuehrer. *Little Mime*: HELEN HAYES. *Lighting Charlie*: Himself. (Dance Specialty: Hortense.)

Tourists, Soldiers, Guides, Peasants, Waitresses, Guests, Children, etc. Mountain Climbers, etc.: Misses Lavinia Mason, Mazie Kimbal, Isabelle Jason, Elsie Raymond, Lillian Foster, Dolly Filly, Charlotte Cushman, Rose Monroe, Opal Scott, Jeanne Crane, Libby Diamond, Lotta Morse. *Cafe Maids, etc.*: Misses Blanche Brooks, Beatrice Priest, Mabel Barnes, Edna Dodsworth. *Waiting Maids, etc.*: Misses Gertrude Grant, Layne Donaldson, Ruth Rider, May Willard. *Peasants, etc.*: Misses Natalie Dare, Evelyn Martin, Sue Duval, Gwenn Sears, Mina Davenport, Miriam Butler. *Guides, etc.*: Messrs. Harry Devine, John Donnelly, Henry Detloff, Louis Boyle, Frank Griffiths, Louis Finnery, Albert Aporta, Arthur Fisher. *Soldiers, etc.*: Messrs. Harry Carmack, George Howe, William Whittaker, Robert O'Neill, Paul Moore, Frank Hallam. *Gypsies, etc.*: Misses Lavinia Mason, Mazaie Kimball, Isabelle Jason, Lotta Morse, Elsie Raymond, Dolly Filly, Lillian Foster, Charlotte Cushman, Rose Monroe, Opal Scott, Jeanne Crane, Libby Diamond. *Dignitaries, etc.*: Messrs. Paul Moore, John Donnelly, Harry Devine, Arthur Fisher, Henry Detloff, Frank Griffiths, Louis Finnerty, Albert Aporta. *Wives of Dignitaries, etc.*: Misses Layne Donaldson, Blanche Brooks, Beatrice Priest, Mabel Barnes, Edna Dodsworth, Gertrude Grant, Ruth Rider, May Willard. *Titled Ladies, etc.*: Misses Sue Duval, Gwenn Sears, Miriam Butler, Mina Davenport, Natalie Dare, Evelyn Smith. *Orientals, etc.*: Messrs. Louis Boyle, William Steyers, Robert O'Neill, Frank Hallam, George Howe, William Whittaker. *French Dancers, etc.*: Misses Lavinia Mason, Mazie Kimball, Isabelle Jason, Lotta Morse, Elsie Raymond, Opal Scott, Jeanne Crane, Libby Diamond, Dolly Filly, Lillian Foster, Charlotte Cushman, Rose Monroe.

---

[51]Running order revised after opening. Added during the run after Chorus of Welcome:

"The Girl with the Clocking on Her Stocking"
M. Brown, Daffodil Girls, Artists

[52]Replaced after opening by (removed from later in Act 1):

"I'm Not a Ladies' Maid"
E. Ryan, Artists

[53]Dropped for subsequent tour.

[54]According to reviewers, the libretto was yet another retelling (uncredited as to its source) of the famous Robert Macaire legend, first introduced on the Paris stage in "L'Auberge des Adrets" and its sequel "Robert Macaire" by Benjamin Antier, Saint-Amand and Paulyanthe; this served as the source for the hugely successful comic opera ERMINIE presented 10 May 1886 at the Casino Theatre for 512 performances.

[55]Played a return engagement 11 April 1910 at the West End Theatre for 8 performances.

Act 1: Exterior of the Hotel Schoenwald in the Tyrol. Afternoon.

Act 2, Scene 1: The Palm Garden of the Hotel Schoenwald. Evening. *Scene 2*: Second floor corridor of the hotel. Night.

ACT 1

Opening Chorus (incidental solo by J. Grover.)
Ensemble

"Algy"
V. Castle, Sisters

"I Want a Man to Love Me"
A. Dovey, Chorus

"I Love ze Parisienne"
C. Judels, Opea Bouffe Girlies

"Rich Man, Poor Man (Beggar Man, Thief)"
Officers, Sisters

"Honor the Brave"
Ensemble

ACT 2
Scene 1

Opening Chorus:

"Drink to the Health of This Great Man"
Ensemble

"That Is Love"
W. Raymond, Chorus

Danse Fantastique
R. Hess, Hortense

Russian Dance
N. Hyde, V. Hyde

"U, Dearie"
W. Raymond, A. Dovey

"My Gypsy Sweetheart"
A. Dovey, Ensemble

Finale

Scene 2

"Pretending"
J. E. Henshaw, A. Lewis

"Mrs. Grundy"
Officers, Sisters

Finale
Ensemble

1909.31 THE GODDESS OF LIBERTY

A Musical Farce in Three Acts. Book (and lyrics) by Frank Adams and Will M. Hough. Music by Joseph E. Howard. Produced (staged) by Ned Wayburn; stage under the direction of Percy Leach. Scenery by John C. Becker, Frank Gates and Edward A. Morange, Ernest Albert, Lee Lash & Co. Costumes designed by Will R. Barnes. Orchestra under the direction of Hugo Fry. Presented by Joseph E. Howard. Opened 22 December 1909 at Weber's Theatre and closed 15 January 1910 after 29 performances.

CAST (in order of appearance): *Lord Algernon Banbury*: Charles Aveling. *Hope Butterworth*: FRANCES DEMAREST. *Mrs. Horace Butterworth*: Marie Richmond. *Lady FitzHugh Murray*: Florence Gerald. *Doris Butterworth*: Stella Tracey. *Horace Butterworth*: LOUIS CASAVANT. *Harry McCormick*, Guardian of Phyllis: Wilton Taylor. *Phyllis Crane*: MAY DeSOUSA. *Bill*, the Barkeep: Myles McCarthy. *Lord Jack's Tailor*: Sol Solomon. *Taxi Driver* from Hotel Knickerbocker, New York: Joseph Clark. *Lord Jack Wyngate*: EDWARD ABELES. *Sigmund*: George W. Dachshund. *Augustus Butterworth*: H. T. Pinkham. *A Detective*: Bert Smith. *Adolph Muscle*, a trainer: Charles Fletcher. *Rudolph Tuscle*, a trainer: Herbert Leonard. *George Spelvin*, an attendant: Edward Noble. *First Coacher, Second Coacher, Third Cocher*: The Frey Trio.

The Hick SistersFifi, a dancer: *Mimi*, a dancer: C. K. Kittridge.

Personnel of Chorus: *Coaching Girls*: Misses Willard, Ancker, Moyer, Earlcott. *Girlies, etc.*: Misses Buckley, Stanley, Grace McMeen, Lauers, Honey, Harrington, Lane, Willard, Ancker, Hartford, Christy, A. Hawley, Sterling, Morton, Moran, Berry, Grindon. *Chorus Men*: Messrs. Morton, Holton, Scanlon, Birch, Pierce, Smith, Gorey.

Act 1: Country Place of Horace Butterworth in the Berkshire Hills. (Becker.)

Act 2, Scene 1: Forest near the Butterworth Estate. *Scene 2*: Reception Room in the Butterworth Mansion. (Gates and Morange.)

Act 3: Dining room in Lord Jack's apartments in New York, overlooking the Hudson River at Claremont. (Ernest Albert, Lee Lash.)

ACT 1[56]

Opening Chorus
Ensemble

"Don't Choose a Gibson Girl"
F. Demarest, Chorus

"I Wonder Who's Kissing Her Now!"
E. Abeles, Chorus

"Lonely"
F. Demarest, Chorus

"Down Goes the Price of Eggs"
M. DeSousa, E. Abeles

"Hail Diana"
Ensemble

"If All the Moons Were Honeymoons"
M. DeSousa, Chorus

ACT 2

"Something" (Duet)
E. Abeles, M. DeSousa

"Honeymoon Trail"
F. Demarest, Chorus

"The Haunted Pool"
L. Casavant, Male Chorus

"Here's to the Last Girl"
M. DeSousa, Chorus

ACT 3

"Hush, I Think I Hear Him"
M. DeSousa, Show Girls

"Here's to the Last Girl" (Finale)
Ensemble

1910.01 THE JOLLY BACHELORS

A Musical Spectacle in Two Acts, 7 Scenes. Book and lyrics by Glen MacDonough. Music by Raymond Hubbell. Entire production staged by Ned Wayburn. Settings by designed by Arthur Voegtlin. Costumes by Melville Ellis. Orchestra conducted by George A. Nichols. Orchestrations by Frank Saddler. Produced by Lew Fields. Opened 6 January 1910 at the Broadway Theatre and closed 28 May 1910 after 165 performances.

CAST: *The Jolly Bachelors (3)*: *Dr. Launcelot Lightfoot*, a nerve specialist: WALTER PERCIVAL. *Howson Lott*, a suburban real estate dealer at present engaged in booming Stringham Terrace: JACK NORWORTH. *Bunbury Tankerville*, social guide and secretary to Mrs. DeFoe Parr: LIONEL WALSH. *Astarita Vandergould*, an orphan heiress with ideas, ideals, and a thirst for romance: NORA BAYES. *Guy (Vandergould)*, her brother: BILLIE TAYLOR. *Carola Gayley*, a society struggler: ELIZABETH BRICE. *Mrs. De Foe Parr*, a society struggler: EMMA CARUS. *Chase Payne*, proprietor of Payne's drug store: AL LEECH. *Harold McCann*, his manager: Robert L. Dailey. *Veronica Verdigris Jackson*, a colored chorus lady, recently on tour with the Nashville Students: STELLA MAYHEW. *Perdita Pears*, in search of a bargain: TOPSY SIEGRIST. *Lily Kraus*, ex-chambermaid at Revere cottage: JOSIE SADLER. *Fannie Faintwell*: Nellie Lynch. *Notta Sound*, employed at Payne's: GERTRUDE VANDERBILT. *Ludwig*, a coat boy with gouty tendencies: NAT FIELDS. *"Pudge" Wilson*, a Revere student: Lew Fullerton. *Hardy Hyde*, the elephant trainer from the Central Park Zoo: Henry Lehmann.

Personnel of the Chorus: *Ned Wayburn's Steppers*: Misses Octavia Hague, Lottie Franklin, Etta Pillard, Virginia Earle, Margaret Brown, Ruby Lewis, Blanche Turner, Flo May, Arria Hathaway, Ethel Kelly. Messrs. Arthur Gros, Harold Atkinson, James Monahan, Addison Meade, Charles McNally, Harry Lowry, Frank Ward, Martin Culhane, Robert Nevins, William Hart, John O'Donnell. *Society Buds, Trans-Atlantic Passengers, etc.*: Misses Florence Cable, Clara Stanton, Sara Carr, Alice Fitch, Alice Chase, Madeline LeBoeuf, Sophia Ralph, Gladys Alexander, Emily Monte, Arline LaCrosse. *Shoppers*: Misses Grace Benedict, Daisy Rudd, Bernice Elsler, Beth McNown, Daisy Anderson, Anna Kellar, Edna Marsh, Belle Robinson, Anitra MacTavish, Mabelle Stewart, Blanche Barnes, Nina Pastorelli, Marie Lachere, Eva Burnett, Adele Marie, Gertrude Thurston, Lucille Oakley, Madge Parsells, Gladys Seymour. *Cadets, Aviators, College Students, etc.*: Messrs. Thomas Everett, Herman Hirschhorn, William Downs, Sidney Atcherson, Lester Baker, Sheldon McCloy, Harry

[56]Song list prepared from touring program. No New York program available.

Wilde, John Dewey, Edward Brown, Arthur Wells, Clay Hill, Roger Davis, Victor Boenea, Austin Clark, Lew Fullerton, Ernest Schnaps, Victor Franco, Joe McShane, Van Sheldon, Frank Hardy, Herman Lehr, Thomas Hughes, Ralph O'Brien, Edward Davies, John Pillard, Leslie Powers, Thomas Connors, Robert Mulligan, Wilmer Bradley, Lester Ostrander.

Act 1, Scene 1: A Red Cross Bazaar in the garden of a Westchester Residence. *Scene 2*: Exterior of Payne's drug store. Two days later. *Scene 3*: Interior of Payne's drug store.

Act 2, Scene 1: Exterior of 1791 dormitory at Revere College on alumni day. Three days later. *Scene 2*: Rear of the airship garage, Mineola. The next day. *Scene 3*: Flight of the airship. That night. *Scene 4*: Fourth of July concert on board the three day ocean greyhound, *"Insania."*

ACT 1

Opening Chorus

"Tax the Bachelors"
B. Taylor, Chorus

"Rosa Rosetta"[57]
W. Percival, N. Bayes
(*Music by* Albert Von Tilzer. *Lyrics by* Earle C. Jones, Jack Norworth.)

"The Red Cross Girl"
B. Taylor, Chorus

"The Luncheon Line"
E. Brice Chorus

"(Has Anybody Here Seen) Kelly?"
N. Bayes
(*Music by* C. W. Murphy, Will Letters. *Lyrics by* William McKenna.)

(Opening of Drug Store:)

"Please, Oh Please"

"Language of Signs"
W. Percival, G. Vanderbilt, Chorus

"What Am I Going to Do to Make You Love Me?"
E. Brice, N Bayes, Bachelors, Chorus

(Specialty)
A. Leech, N. Lynch

"Stop Dat Rag" (Stop That Rag, Keep on Playing Honey)
S. Mayhew
(*Music by* Ted Snyder. *Lyrics by* Irving Berlin.)

"Walk This Way"
A. Leech, E. Brice Girlies

Finale
Ensemble, Steppers

ACT 2[58]

"Freshie, O Freshie" (Opening Chorus)
Students

Medley of College Songs
J. Norworth
(*Music and Lyrics by* Nora Bayes, Jack Norworth.)

"The Single Bird"
L. Walsh, Chorus

"Come Along, (My) Mandy"[59]
N. Bayes, J. Norworth
(*Music and Lyrics by* Nora Bayes, Jack Norworth.)

"We'uns from Dixie"
R. L. Dailey, Ned Wayburn's Steppers

"Savannah"
S. Mayhew

"The Air Ship Joy Ride" (The Aeroplane Joy Ride)
B. Taylor, Chorus

Opening Chorus
Ensemble

"Oh, La, La, La!"[60]
W. Percival

"Young America"[61]
N. Bayes
(*Music and Lyrics by* Nora Bayes, Jack Norworth.)

Finale

[57]An earlier version of the song without Norworth's revised lyrics was previously introduced in the musical IN NEW YORK TOWN in 1905. Replaced for subsequent tour:

"A Little Bit of Blarney"
W. Percival, Lucy Weston (Astarita Vandergould)

[58]For subsequent tour, Act 2 was substantially revised, and the following were added:

"The Mind Reader"
L. Weston

"I've Lost My Gal"
S. Mayhew, B. Taylor
(*Music by* Egbert Van Alstyne. *Lyrics by* Harry Williams.)

"Moon, Moon, Moon"
W. Percival, Chorus

[59]Dropped for subsequent tour.

1910.02 THE OLD TOWN

A Musical Play in Two Acts. Book and lyrics by George Ade. Music by Gustav Luders. Staged by Ben Teal. Settings by Homer Emens. Costumes by Wilhelm of London, Will R. Barnes. Orchestra under the direction of Arthur Pryor. Produced by Charles Dillingham. Opened 10 January 1910 at the Globe Theatre and closed 4 June 1910 after 166 performances.

CAST: *Henry Clay Baxter*, Citified Country Boy: FRED STONE. *Archibald Hawkins*, his Manager: DAVE MONTGOMERY. *The Hon. Dike Bilwether*, a recent Millionaire: CLAUDE GILLINGWATER. *Ernestine Bilwether*, his Ambitious Wife: ALENE CRATER. *Caroline Bristow*, Mrs. Bilwether's Niece: FLO HENGLER. *Diana Bristow*, another Niece: MAY HENGLER. *Gustiana Jimpsen*, a Swedish Maid: ETHEL JOHNSON. *Lieutenant Otto Von Up de Graff*, Mountain Climber: W. J. McCARTHY. *W. Darrell Gimpley*, Self-confessed Genius: Lyndon Law. *Jim Flanders*, a Politician: John Hendricks. *Ethel Trotter*, a Social Secretary: SHIRLEY KELLOGG. *Donald MacGookin*, a Scotch Tourist: Claude Cooper. *Angus Dumfries*, another Scotchman: Fred Perine. *Fawnie Smith*, a Suffragette: Shirley Kellogg. *Serepta Wallace Kitts*, another Suffragette: Nathalie Green. *Gwendolyn Hemenway*, ditto: Alice Belga. *Sylvia Luggs*, Helping to Spend the Money: Eloise Reed. *Florence Etherington*, also Helping: Genevieve Reed. *Marie Swift*, likewise Helping: May Hopkins. *Janet Spangle*, ditto: Clementine Dundas. *Rosalie Band*, Doing What She Can: Margaret Denver. *Jubal Dunkbury*, Sheriff: Charles Mitchell. *Monsieur DeVaux*, a Wire Walker: Harold Russell. *A Vision*: Constance Eastman. *Mortimer*, a Servant: Harry Lillford.

Bagpipe Specialty and Original English Pony Ballet: Misses Beatrice Liddell, Dorothy Marlowe, Ada Robertson, Elizabeth Hawman, Lousie Hawman, Seppie McNeil. *Circus Performers, Guests and Servants of the Bilwethers, Scotch Lassies, Cowboys and Girls, Indian Maidens, U.S. Soldiers, Anglo-Japanese, etc.*: May Ainsworth, Veronique Banner, Dorothy Bertrand, Gene Cole, Grace Crowley, May Ellison, Anice Harris, Virginia Kendall, Evelyn Meredith, Julia Meredith, Vivian Prichard, Jeanette Joen, Verna Dalton, Anita Yonge, Ethel Tanguay, Reba Kent, Regina Stone, Effie Wheeler, Dorothy Gibson. Messrs. Morris Avery, Nat M. Bowes, Albert Dempsey, Charles Dodge, Fred Emerson, Arthur Kuester, Louis Mason, Ed. Reader, Frank Turner, Mack Whiting, C. L. Kelly, R. H. Greenlaw. *Dancing Ensemble*: Blanche West, Florence Walton, Helen Falconer, Gladys Zell, Violet Zell, Mazie LeRoy, Josephine Harriman, Nancy Poole.

Act 1: St. Augustine.

Act 2: The Old Town, California.

MUSICAL NUMBERS[62]

"The Man Who Will Not Love Back" (When You're Yearning, Burning)

"Queen of the One-Ring Show"

"The Noovo Riche"

"Electric Signs"

"When I Would Think of You"
D. Montgomery, F. Stone, F. Hengler, M. Hengler

"What Man Dare Say (My Truant Heart)"

"Weak Little Woman" (Suffragette)

"Keep Your Whip in Your Hand"

"My Japanee" (The Modern Japanee)

"The Militant Suffrage Song"

"Minnesota"
(*Music by* Alfred Robyn. *Lyrics by* Thomas T. Railey.)

[60]Dropped after 2 weeks.

[61]Dropped for subsequent tour.

[62]No song list from programs (M. Witmark, New York, 1909); not in performance order.

"A Popular Song"
(*Music by* Alfred Robyn. *Lyrics by* Thomas T. Railey.)

"Travel, Travel, Little Star"
F. A. Stone, D. Montgomery
(*Music by* Arthur Pryor. *Lyrics by* Vincent Bryan.)

"Goodbye, Christina Swanson"
(*Music by* Terry Sherman. *Lyrics by* Bob Adams.)

1910.03 THE KING OF CADONIA

A Musical Comedy in Two Acts[63]. Book by Frederick Lonsdale. Music by Sidney Jones and Jerome D. Kern. Lyrics by Adrian Ross and M. E. Rourke. Staged by Joseph Herbert. Settings designed by Arthur Voegtlin. Costumes by Melville Ellis. Orchestra under the direction of Hugo Byrk. Produced by the Messrs. Shubert. Opened 10 January 1910 at Daly's Theare and closed 22 January 1910 after 16 performances.[64]

CAST: *Duke of Alasia*, heir presumptive to the throne: WILLIAM NORRIS. *Alexis King of Cadonia*: ROBERT DEMPSTER. *General Bonski*: ALBERT GRAN. *Captain Laski*: MELVILLE STEWART. *Lieutenant Jules*: Donald Buchanan. *Lieutenant Saloff*: William Davis. *Panix*, Secretary to the Duke of Alasia: D. L. DON. *Laborde*, President of the anti-King Society: St. Clair Bayfield. *Bran*, servant to Captain Laski: WILLIAM DANFORTH. *Barber*: Vincent Dusenberry. *Militza*, maid to Princess Marie: CLARA PALMER. *Stephanie*, first lady-in-waiting to Princess Marie: Mabel Weeks. *Duchess of Alasia*: BESSIE TANNEHILL. *Natine*, lady-in-waiting: Addie Marze. *Wanda*, lady-in-waiting: Edna Broderick. *Ottaline*, lady-in-waiting: Carolyn Armstrong. *Princess Marie*, daughter of the Duke of Alasia: MARGUERITE CLARK.

Soldiers, Gardeners, Peasants, Ladies of the Court, etc.: *Cherry Girls*: Misses Richards, Gordon, Ryan, Langhorn, Grant, Sargent. *Dancing Girls*: Misses V. Rose, Hamilton, Weston, Howard, Walters, Williams, A. Rose, Booth, Himes, Dally, Virginia D. d'Irinyi, Wheeler. *Peasants*: Misses Forbes, Summers, Baron, St. John, Winters, McKeon, Flint, Addison, Banta, Ryan, Hempstone, Silver, Stewart. *Ladies of the Court*: Misses Hamilton, Richards, V. Rose, A. Rose, Forbes, Gordon, Summers, Baron, Sheldon, Clifford, Weston, Addison, Grant, Langhorn, St. John, Himes, Dailey, Winters, Stewart, Virginia, Devereux, Flint, Banta, Williams, Booth, McKeon, D. d'Irinyi, Walters. *Anarchists*: Messrs. Wells, Giles, Mayer, Brandell, Bingham, Summerville, Dusen, Kingsley, Ford. *Soldiers*: Messrs. Ford, Warwick, Dodge, Spears, Tedret, Feiner, Carter, Kingsley, Johnston, Searl, Andres, Sleek, Pierce, Alston, Wellikens. *Starters*: Ryan, E. Grant. *Pages*: E. Wheeler, Virginia.

Act 1: The Garden of the Duke of Alasia.

Act 2: Throne Room of the Royal Palace of Cadonia.

ACT 1[65]

Opening Chorus
Ensemble

"It's a Bomb"
S. C. Bayfield, Anarchists

"You're Not the Only Cinder in the Grate"
W. Danforth, C. Palmer

"Hail to the King"
Entire Ensemble

"Barber Song"
M. Stewart, Guards

"Time for the King"
M. Stewart, A. Gran, Guards

"Coo-oo (Coo-oo)"
M. Clark, Ladies in Waiting
(*Music by* Jerome D. Kern. *Lyrics by* Maurice Stonehill.)

"Father and Mother" (Mother and Father)
R. Dempster, M. Clark
(*Music by* Jerome D. Kern. *Lyrics by* M. E. Rourke.)

"Do Not Hesitate to Shoot"
W. Norris, Guards

"Come Along Pretty Girl"
C. Palmer, Soldiers
(*Music by* Jerome D. Kern. *Lyrics by* M. E. Rourke.)

"The Portrait"
M. Clark, Ladies in Waiting

Finale
Entire Company

ACT 2

Opening Chorus
Ensemble

"Catamaran" (Catamarang)
M. Weeks
(*Music by* Jerome D. Kern. *Lyrics by* Percival Knight.)

"Every Girl I Meet"
M. Stewart
(*Music by* Jerome D. Kern. *Lyrics by* Percival Knight.)

"When a Fellow Loves a Girl"
M. Stewart, M. Clark

"(The) Blue Bulgarian Band"
D. L. Don, Girls
(*Music by* Jerome D. Kern. *Lyrics by* M. E. Rourke.)

"Sparrow and Hippopotamus" (The Hippopotamus)
W. Danforth, M. Clark
(*Music by* Jerome D. Kern. *Lyrics by* Adrian Ross.)

"Lena (Lena)"
W. Norris, M. Stewart, W. Danforth, D. L. Don
(*Music by* Jerome D. Kern. *Lyrics by* M. E. Rourke.)

"Disguises"
W. Norris, C. Palmer
(*Music by* Frederick Rosse. *Lyrics by* Arthur Wimperis.)

Grand Finale
Entire Company

[63]Billed as the English Musical Comedy Success.
[64]Moved to the West End Theatre 24 January 1910 for an additional 8 performances.
[65]Songs not otherwise credited have music by Sidney Jones and lyrics by Adrian Ross.

1910.04 THE PRINCE OF BOHEMIA

A Musical Play in Two Acts. Book by J. Hartley Manners. Music by A. Baldwin Sloane. Lyrics by E. Ray Goetz. Staged by Ned Wayburn. Scenery painted by John Young. Costumes designed by Melville Ellis. Orchestra under the direction of John Braham. Produced by Lew Fields. Opened 14 January 1910 at the Hackett Theatre and closed 29 January 1910 after 20 performances.[66]

CAST: *Dick Conyers*: ANDREW MACK. *Ashby Tritton*: W. T. CARLETON. *Allan Tritton*, his son: HAROLD CRANE. *Dominick Kearney*: CHARLES F. McCARTHY. *Montague Head* of Scotland Yard: Henry Norman. *Spencer Twigg*, Manager Hotel Metropole: E. H. KELLY. *Suitors for Angela's Hand (3)*: *Count Cataloni*: John Ardizoni. *Captain Raoul Jacquinard*: Vincent MacCarthy. *Hon. Nigel Woodgate*: Henry Warwick. *Officer*: Sim Pulen. *Mrs. Mary Kelly*: Mary Forrest. *Kate Kearney*: GEORGIE LAWRENCE. *Angela Tritton*: CHRISTIE MacDONALD. *Annette*, Her Maid: Mildred Manning. *Freddie* who whistles: Maudie Brown.

Personnel of the Chorus: *American Girls, etc.*: Misses Rellis, Landers, Hurst, Markert, Livingston, Stowe. *English Girls, etc.*: Misses Taylor, Roming, Wyant, Land, Leidy, Coleman. *Bellboys, etc.*: Misses Whitesill, Fairbanks, Brown, Clarke, Margolies, DeFord. *Maids, etc.*: Misses D'Elma, Campbell, Everett, Olp, Townsend, Manning. *English Tourists, etc.*: Messrs. Higgins, Brady, Hickey. *American Tourists, etc.*: Messrs. Graham, Whitman. *Porters, etc.*: Messrs. Turner, Grieg, Worthing. *Clerks, etc.*: Messrs. Elling, Shannon, Hadley. *Waiters, etc.*: Messrs. Davis, Hynes, Risley. *Debutantes, etc.*: Misses Taylor, Wyant, Leidy, Roming, Land, Coleman, Stowe, Markert, Landers, Livingston, Hurst, Rellis. *Belles, etc.*: Misses Clarke, DeFord, Fairbanks, Olp, Manning, Everett, Campbell Townsend, Margolies, Brown, Whitesill, D'Elma. *Suitors, etc.*: Messrs. Hynes, Turner, Hadley, Graham, Higgins, Hickey, Grieg, Brady, Shannon.

The action takes place in England today.

Act 1: The Palm Garden and Lounge in Hotel Metropole, Westpool.

Act 2: Dominick Kearney's houseboat, *"The Banshee,"* on the Thames. A day later.

ACT 1

Opening Chorus
Ensemble

"Cupid's Wireless Telegraph"
G. Lawrence

[66]Moved 31 January 1910 to the West End Theatre for an additional 8 performances.

"Dollars and Debutantes"
C. MacDonald, Chorus
"(If You'll Only) Say You'll Be a Friend of Mine"
G. Lawrence, H. Crane, M. Brown, Chorus
"The Prince of Bohemia"
A. Mack, Chorus
"Life in the Country"[67]
A. Mack
"Shandon Belles"
H. Crane, Chorus
"Correspondence" (Duet)
A. Mack, C. MacDonald
Finale
Ensemble

ACT 2
Opening Chorus
Ensemble
"Just a Little Bit of Blarney"
C. MacDonald, A. Mack
"Sentimental Tommy"
Chorus
"I Wonder What They're Doing Now in Home, Sweet Home"[68]
A. Mack, Chorus
"Gentle River"
C. MacDonald
"Goodbye, Sweetheart, Goodbye"
A. Mack
"La Donna è mobile" (from RIGOLETTO)
A. Mack
(*Music by* Giuseppe Verdi.)
"Viens Poupoule"
A. Mack
"Go 'Way Mistah Moon"
A. Mack, Chorus
(*Music and Lyrics by* Andrew Mack.)
Finale
Ensemble

1910.05 THE ARCADIANS

A Musical Play in Three Acts. Book by A. M. Thompson and Mark Ambient. Music by Lionel Monckton and Howard Talbot. Lyrics by Arthur Wimperis, (Lionel Monckton). Staged by Thomas Reynolds. Settings designed by Homer Emens. Costumes by Wilhelm; Lord and Taylor. Orchestra under the direction of Watty Hydes. Produced by Charles Frohman. Opened 17 January 1910 at the Liberty Theatre, moved 16 May 1910 to the Knickerbocker Theatre and closed 2 July 1910 after 193 performances[69].

CAST: *James Smith*, of Smith & Co., Caterers, London: FRANK MOULAN. *Simplicitas*, an Arcadian: FRANK MOULAN. *Peter Doody*, a jockey: PERCIVAL KNIGHT. *Jack Meadows*: ALAN MUDIE. *Bobby*: ALFRED KAPPELER. *Sir George Paddock*: Lawrence Grant. *Percy Marsh*: John Paulton. *Reggie*: H. H. Meyer. *Sir Timothy Ryan*: E. H. Lyle. *Harry Desmond*: Tom Collins. *James Withers*: Sam Collins. *Time*: J. Gunnis Davis. *Eileen Cavanaugh*: JULIA SANDERSON. *Mrs. Smith*: CONNIE EDISS. *Lady Barclay*: Vivian Blackburn. *The Hon. Maud Barclay*: Eleanor Pendleton. *Lady Jim*: Eithel Kelly. *Beatrice*: Josephine Howard. *Lucy Selwyn*: Esther Brunette. *Marion*: Grace Eddington.

Arcadians: *Sombra*: ETHEL CADMAN. *Chrysea*: AUDREY MAPLE. *Amaryllis*: Jane Hall. *Daphne*: Marion Mosby. *Astrophel*: STANLEY JESSUP. *Strephon*: HARRY H. MEYER. *Damoetas*: John O'Hanlon.

Ladies of the Ensemble[70]: *"Arcadians" Girls (Act 1)*: Misses Viola Clark, Gertrude Fursman, Beatrice Burrows, Carol Oty, Muriel Parker, Lucile Parsons, Frances Ceratt, Bessie Nelligan, Jeanette Lewis, Ruth Mason, Connie DeTournie, Ethel Vivian, Alice Randolph, Elise Kimber, Antoinette LeComte, Mary Pendleton, Mae D'Arcy, Cherry Gildea. *Ladies of Fashion (Act 2)*: Misses Helen Edwards, Dixie Tabor, Mollie Alexander, Jeanette Singer, Myrtle Lawton, Millie Murray, Irene von Muller, Josephine Angela, Leslie Zannere, Helen Wheeler, Mollie Lorraine. *Arcadian Restaurant Girls (Act 3)*: Misses Beatrice Burrows, Gertrude Fursman, Bessie Nelligan, Ethel Vivian, Frances Seratt, Carrol Oty, Helen Wheeler, Antoinette LeComte, Ruth Mason, Alice Randolph, Connie DeTournie, Lucile Parsons, Mae D'Arcy, Mollie Lorraine, Leslie Zannere, Muriel Parker. *Piccadilly Girls*: Misses Helen Edwards, Dixie Tabor, Mollie Alexander, Jeanette Singer, Elise Kimber, Myrtle Lawton, Millie Murray, Cherry Gildea, Irene von Muller, Josephine Angela, Jeanette Lewis, Mary Pendleton, Viola Clark.

Act 1: Arcadia.

Act 2: Askwood Race Track, near London.

Act 3: The Arcadian Restaurant. London.

ACT 1
Opening Chorus
(*Music by* Howard Talbot.)
"The Joy of Life" (Quartet)
E. Cadman, A. Maple, S. Jessup, H. H. Meyer
Chorus of Fear (Look What Hovers There)
(*Music by* Howard Talbot.)
"The Pipes of Pan (Are Calling)" (Song)
E. Cadman
(*Music by* Lionel Monckton.)
"All a Lie!" (Chorus)
(*Music by* Howard Talbot.)
"Sweet Simplicitas" (Song)
F. Moulan
(*Music by* Howard Talbot.)
Finale
(*Music by* Howard Talbot.)

ACT 2
Opening Chorus
(*Music by* Lionel Monckton.)
"(The) Ladies"[71]
A. Keppeler
(*Music by* Lionel Monckton. *Lyrics by* Adrian Ross.)
"The Girl with a Brogue"
J. Sanderson, Chorus
(*Music by* Lionel Monckton.)
Shower Chorus
(*Music by* Lionel Monckton.)
"Arcady Is Ever Young"
E. Cadman, Chorus
(*Music by* Lionel Monckton. *Lyrics by* Lionel Monckton, Arthur Wimperis.)
"Somewhere" (Duet)
F. Moulan, C. Ediss
(*Music by* Lionel Monckton.)
"Charming Weather" (Duet)
J. Sanderson, A. Mudie
(*Music by* Lionel Monckton. *Lyrics by* Lionel Monckton, Arthur Wimperis.)
Finale
(*Music by* Lionel Monckton.)

ACT 3
Opening Chorus
(*Music by* Howard Talbot.)
"I Like London"
A. Maple, Chorus
(*Music by* Howard Talbot.)
"Light Is My Heart" (Song)
E. Cadman
(*Music by* Howard Talbot.)

---

[67]Dropped for subsequent tour.
[68]Dropped for subsequent tour.
[69]Played a return engagement 21 November 1910 at the Grand Opera House for 8 performances.
[70]Ensemble members not listed individually in programs until the third month of the run.

[71]Replaced for subsequent tour by: ("The Ladies" later restored during tour)
"Back Your Fancy" (Song)
A. Kappeler
(*Music by* Lionel Monckton.)

"Bring Me a Rose"
A. Mudie, Chorus
(*Music by* Lionel Monckton. *Lyrics by* Lionel Monckton, Arthur Wimperis.)

"Cheer for Simplicitas!" (Chorus of Belgravians)
(*Music by* Lionel Monckton.)

"Willy of Piccadilly" (All Down Piccadilly)(Song)
F. Moulan, Ensemble
(*Music by* Lionel Monckton. *Lyrics by* Lionel Monckton, Arthur Wimperis.)

"Truth Is So Beautiful" (Quintet)
F. Moulan, A. Mudie, A. Kappeler, H. H. Meyer, J. Paulton
(*Music by* Lionel Monckton.)

"My Motter" (Song)
P. Knight
(*Music by* Howard Talbot.)

Finale
(*Music by* Lionel Monckton.)

1910.06

RAGGED ROBIN

A Play (with Music) in Three Acts. Play by Rida Johnson Young and Rita Olcott. Music for the fairy scenes composed by Frederick Knight Logan. Staged by Augustus Pitou. Scenery painted by Edward G. Unitt and Joseph Wickes. Costumes designed by Rita Olcott. Musical director, Frederick Knight Logan. Produced by Augustus Pitou. Opened 24 January 1910 at the Academy of Music and closed 5 February 1910 after 16 performances.

CAST: *Ragged Robin*, (later Sir Robert Harcourt): CHAUNCEY OLCOTT. *Andrew Grattan*: MARK PRICE. *Margaret Grattan*: ROSE CURRY. *Sheelah Grattan*: Lottie Smith. *Martin Darcy*: GEROME EDWARDS. *Joan Darcy*: Magda Foy. *Lanty Lanigan*: Andrew O'Neil. *Beth Meehan*: Josie Claflin. *Shaun Casey*: George Brennan. *Barney Riley*: Charles L. Newton. *Casey Sullivan*: William Jones. *Darby*, the harpist: John B. Gasparo. *Meg Manning*: Charlotte Smith. *Bess Riley*: May Morley. *Mary*, the Harpist's daughter: Alice Farrell. *Comrade*, the dog: Himself.

Male and Female Peasants and Fairies: *Fairy of the Well*: Alice Farrell. *The Fairy Host*: Misses Hayden, Waite, Watkins, Lyons. *The Leprahaun*: Margaret Johnson. *The Good Little People*: May Morley, Florence Critchley, Marion Gasparo.

The action takes place at Innishannon, (Ireland) in 1830.

Act 1: Exterior of Andrew Grattan's house.

Act 2: Interior of Andrew Grattan's house, Margaret's wedding day. The flight of the Banshee.

Act 3, Scene 1: Interior of the Inn. The vision. Three years later. *Scene 2*: A wood scene. The Will-o'-the-Wisp. *Scene 3*: The great bog scene. The fireflies. The flight of the fairy host.

MUSICAL NUMBERS[72]

"The Eyes That Came from Ireland"
(*Music by* Chauncey Olcott. *Lyrics by* Richard LeGallienne.)

"Sweet Girl of My Dreams"
(*Music and Lyrics by* Chauncey Olcott and Daniel J. Sullivan.)

"If You'll Remember Me"
(*Music by* Ernest R. Ball. *Lyrics by* George Graff, Jr.)

"The Laugh with a Tear in It" (A Laugh with a Tear in It)
(*Music and Lyrics by* Chauncey Olcott and Manuel Klein.)

"I Used to Believe in Fairies"
(*Music and Lyrics by* George Spink.)

1910.07

THE YOUNG TURK

A Musical Play in Two Acts, 3 Scenes. Book by Aaron Hoffman. Music by Max Hoffmann. Lyrics by Harry Williams. Stage production of Herbert Gresham. Musical numbers produced by Jack Mason. Produced by (Marc) Klaw and (Abraham L.) Erlanger. Opened 31 January 1910 at the New York Theatre and closed 26 February 1910 after 32 performances.[73]

CAST: *Howe Swift, Sr.*, of Keene & Swift, bankers and brokers: CHARLES J. STINE. *Howe Swift, Jr.*, his son: MAX ROGERS. *Otis Knott*, executors of Keene's estate: FREDERICK V. BOWERS. *Oxenham*, a waiter at the Inn: Joseph Carey. *Tipham*, head waiter at the Inn: Walter Paschal. *A Sailor*: Harry Kleinman. *Izzett Ali*, secret envoy of the Sultan: William Edmunds. *Ammi el Emmun*, envoy of the Turkish Revolutionary Society: JOHN DUNSMURE. *The Sultan*: HARRY COWAN. *Tewfik*, favorite servant of the Sultan: J. R. Lemery. *A Turk*: Alex Kleinman. *United States Consul*: W. H. Bentley. *Mrs. Alice Keene*, widow of Keene: MAUDE RAYMOND. *Alice*, her daughter: Violet McMillan. *Mirza*, daughter of Izzett: DORIS GOODWIN. *Fifi*: Mae Murray. (*Specialty*: TOOTS PAKA AND HER HAWAIIANS. *Show Girls, Guests, Waiters, etc.*

Act 1: Arrowhead Inn, New York. Afternoon of 4 July. *Scene 1*: The Sevres tea set. *Scene 2*: On the briny.

Act 2: Audience chamber of the Sultan's palace. Two weeks later.

ACT 1

"At the Arrowhead Inn" (Opening Chorus)

"I'll Be Happy Too"
F. V. Bowers, D. Goodwin

"(The) Parisian Glide"
F. V. Bowers, D. Goodwin, Chorus

"Proposals"
M. Raymond

Parodies
M. Rogers

Finale
Full Company

ACT 2

Opening Chorus; "The Sword Is My Sweetheart True"
J. Dunsmure, Male Chorus

"The Chauffeur"
M. Raymond, C. J. Stine, Chorus

"(Under the) Oriental Moon"
D. Goodwin, F. V. Bowers, Female Chorus

"Did You Ever Hear That in Turkey?"
M. Rogers, Female Chorus

Divertissement
T. Paka and Her Hawaiians

"I Thought I Wanted Opera (but I Changed My Mind)"
M. Raymond, M. Rogers, Company

Finale
Full Company

1910.08

THE YANKEE GIRL

A Musical Comedy in Three Acts. Book and lyrics by George V. Hobart. Music by Silvio Hein. Production staged by Ned Wayburn[74]. Scenery painted by Frank Gates and Edward A. Morange. Costumes by Castel-Bert and Mme. Ripley. Orchestra conducted by William Loraine. Produced by Lew Fields[75]. Opened 10 February 1910 at the Herald Square Theatre and closed 30 April 1910 after 92 performances.

CAST: *The Americans*: *Jessie Gordon*: BLANCHE RING. *Dolly Dean*, her friend: EVA FRANCIS. *Willie Wiggs*, her father's secretary: HARRY GILFOIL. *Captain John Lawrence*, the American consul: WILLIAM P. CARLETON. *J. Phillip Gordon*, her father: JUAN VILLASANA[76].

The Foreigners: *Ambrose Castroba*, President of Brilliantina: WILLIAM BURRESS. *Loleta*, his fiancée: DOROTHY JARDON. *Salvatore*, his secretary of state: William Halliday. *P. C. Gonzabo*, his minister of war: Peter Curley. *Maraquita*, his drummer boy: Naomi Dale. *Oyama*, a Japanese agent: FREDERICK PAULDING. *Rudolph Schnitzel*, a German student: CHARLES J. WINNINGER. *Pedro*, landlord of El Brisa Hotel: E. J. Caldwell. *Angelique*, his wife: Margaret Malcolm. *Nina*, his daughter: Vinnie Bradcome. *Morales, Phillip, Ferdinand, Alfonso*, cigar makers: Henry Bergman, Robert Hamilton, Paul Porter, Louis Franklyn. *Blanco*: Juan Villasana.

American Girls: *Rosie*: Harriet Leidy. *Josie*: Gertrude Grant. *Phrosie*: Edith Offutt. *Posie*: Helen Broderick. *Nell*: Janet Burton. *Dell*: Mildred DeSilva. *Stell*: Lillian Wallace. *Belle*: Florence Douglass. *Dancing Girls*: *Juanita*: Dolly Filley. *Pepita*: Olive

[72]Musical numbers not listed in program. List prepared from press notices and published sheet music; not in performance order.
[73]Scenery and costumes uncredited.

[74]For subsequent tour the direction was credited to Al. Holbrook.
[75]Subsequent national tour was produced jointly by Lew Fields and Frederic McKay.
[76]Contrary to the opening night program, the New York Times reviewed William Graham in the role of J. Phillip Gordon. Graham played the role in the production's tryout.

Carr. *Bonita*: Elsie Raymond. *Eulalita*: Lotta Morse. *Rosita*: Maurie Madison. *Margarita*: Anita Pollock. *Angelita*: Ella Warner. *Zita*: Beck Wood. *Spanish Girls*: Misses Helen Lattan, Isabelle Lattan, Bonnie Clarke, Edith Cramer, Nell Feltas, Evelyn Dare, Theresa Bryant, May Wesley, Irene Palmer, Marie Dupree, Katharyn Pinkerton, Effie Hopkins, May Willard, Nellie Ward, Ada Christy, Sally Webb.

Act 1: The office and courtyard of El Erisa Hotel at Santa Rosa, in the Island Republic of Brilliantina. 7 o'clock Monday evening.

Act 2: Interior of the American Consulate at Santa Rosa. 7 o'clock Tuesday evening.

Act 3: Same as Act 1. 10 o'clock Tuesday night.

ACT 1[77]

Opening Chorus
Ensemble

"The Yankee Girl"
W. P. Carleton, Chorus

"Top of the Morning"
B. Ring, Ensemble

"(That) Hypnotizing Rag"[78]
B. Ring
(*Music and Lyrics by* C. F. Zittel.)

Finale

ACT 2

Opening Chorus

"Where's Mama?" (Quartette)
B. Ring, E. Francis, H. Gilfoil, C. J. Winninger

"Louisiana Elizabeth" (Louisiana Lizabeth)
B. Ring, Chorus

"Maid of Sevilla"
D. Jardon, Chorus

"All Alone"[79]
B. Ring

ACT 3

Opening
D. Jardon, Chorus

"I'll Make a Ring 'Round Rosie"
W. P. Carleton, H. Leidy, Chorus

"Whoop Daddy Ooden Dooden Day"
E. J. Caldwell, H. Bergman, R. Hamilton, P. Porter, L. Franklin

"Nora Malone (Call Me by Phone)"
B. Ring
(*Music by* Albert Von Tilzer. *Lyrics by* Junie McCree.)

Finale

1910.09

BRIGHT EYES

An American Musical (Comedy) Production in Three Acts. Book by Charles Dickson. Based upon the the comedy "Mistakes Will Happen" by Charles Dickson and Grant Stewart. Music by Karl Hoschna. Lyrics by Otto A. Hauerbach [Harbach]. Direction of Morris Uri. Production staged by Frederick A. Bishop. Settings by P. Dodd Ackerman. Costumes by Cora MacGeachy. Lighting by Kliegl Brothers, Charles DeSoria, Frank Callaghan. Orchestra under the direction of Earl Schwartz. Produced by Joseph M. Gaites. Opened 28 February 1910 at the New York Theatre and closed 2 April 1910 after 40 performances.[80]

CAST (in order of appearance): *Quick*, Stage Manager, Morality Theatre: Eugene Sallinger. *Gladys Brady*, Show Girl at the Morality Theatre: Pauline Winters. *Joseph McCann*, Electrician at the Morality Theatre: Manuel A. Alexander. *Linda Kurtz*, German maid of Miss Mayland: Adelaide Sharp. *Dorothy Mayland*, Prima Donna, Morality Theatre: FLORENCE HOLBROOK. *Tom Genowin*, Actor and Author: CECIL LEAN. *John Q. Montague*, Manager of the Morality Theatre: WALTER LAW. *Mr. Hunter-Chase*, President of the Greystone Female Seminary: PERCY LYNDAL. *Mrs. Hunter Chase*, second wife of Mr. Hunter-Chase: VERA FINLAY. *William Hawley*, Coachman of Hunter-Chase: ARTHUR CONRAD. *Reggie Murphy*: Victor.

Show Girls of the Morality Theatre: Misses Grace Wall, Alice Courtland, Olga Britton, Stella Thomas, Florence Averill, Emirza Gordon, Esther Olson, Ida Harris, Pauline Winters, Anna Dexter, Helen Gray. *Broilers and Tom Boy Girls*: Misses Bessie Fontaine, Ethel Grau, Juliet Moore, Agatha Pickard, Ella Valentine, Cecelia Renard, Winkie Worthington, Alice Gordon, Emily Price, Heloise Sheppard, Bunk Middleton, Gypsy Mooney, Juliet Mooney. *Medium Girls*: Misses Billie Ward, Louise Lathrop, Lillian Hager, Mary Billsbury, Marguerite von Keese, Carrie Lillie, Jennie Fielding, Louise Lucas, May Sheldon, Natalie Porter. *Stage Hands, Props, Grips, Chorus Men, etc.*: Messrs. Melendy, St. John, Thompson, Archer, McConville, Skerrett, McMahon, Rodgers, Leech, Simpson, Longley, Wilson.

Act 2: *Footmen in the Employ of Mr. Hunter-Chase*: Messrs. Leech. Melendy, Simpson, Wilson. *Grooms in the Employ of Mr. Hunter-Chase*: Messrs. Rodgers, St. John, McMahon, Longley, Archer, Thompson, Skerrett, McConville. *Housemaids*: Misses Ward, Billsbury, Lathrop, Lillie, von Keese, Lucas, Hager, Sheldon, Fielding, Porter. *Tigers*: Misses Fontaine, Moore, Pickard, Valentine, Grau, Renard, Price, Worthington, Gordon, Sheppard, Middleton, Mooney. *Ladies of the Hunt Club*: Misses Wall, Gray, Olson, Averill, Harris, Winters, Gordon, Britton, Courtland, Dexter, Thomas.

Act 3: *Military Academy Cadets*: Messrs. Leech Melendy, Simpson, St. John, Thompson, Archer, Rodgers, McMahon, Longley, Skerrett, McConville, Wilson. *Automobile Girls*: Misses Courtland, Averill, Thomas, Britton, Gordon, Harris, Winters, Olson, Wall, Gray, Dexter. *Chauffeurs*: Misses Grau, Fontaine, Mooney, Pickard, Moore, Gordon, Worthington, Valentine, Renard, Scott, Sheppard, Middleton, Price. *Maids*: Misses Ward, Billsbury, Lathrop, Lillie, von Keese, Lucas, Hager, Fielding, Sheldon, Porter.

The action takes place last October in New York City and Greystone, Westchester County.

Act 1: Stage of the Morality Theatre, any Monday morning at 10 o'clock, showing gradual setting of scene (Roof Garden of a prominent New York hotel).

Act 2: Carriage-house of Mr. Hunter-Chase in Greystone, Westchester County, the following Thursday afternoon about 2 o'clock.

Act 3: The Hunter-Chase residence, and grounds of Greystone Seminary, three hours later.

ACT 1

"On with the Rehearsal" (Opening Chorus)
Ensemble

"Tom Boy, Tom Boy"
Tom Boy Girls

"For You, Bright Eyes"
F. Holbrook, Chorus

"Cheer Up, My Honey"
C. Lean, F. Holbrook

"The Mood You Are In"
C. Lean, F. Holbrook, P. Lyndal, V. Finlay

"Good Old Days of Yore"
S. Thomas, (Ensemble)

Dance
P. Winters
Indian Braves: Misses Hager, Moore. *Indian Squaws*: Misses Grau, Pickard. *Puritan Men*: Messrs. Rodgers, Skerrett. *Puritan Maidens*: Misses Lillie, Billsbury. *Dutch Men*: Messrs. Melendy, St. John. *Dutch Maidens*: Misses Lathrop, von Keese. *Colonial Dames*: Misses Wall, Gray, Gordon, Fielding. *The Crinolines*: Misses Ward, Sheldon, Lucas, Porter. *Men of 1847*: Messrs. McMahon, Archer, Thompson, McConville. *Bangs and Bustles*: Misses Sheppard, Gordon, Price, Middleton. *Chanticleer Girls*: Misses Olson, Britton, Harris, Dexter. *Evening Gowns*: Misses Averill, Courtland. *Dress Suits*: Messrs. Leech, Simpson, Longley, Wilson. *Fencing Girl*: Miss Mooney. *Football Girl*: Miss Worthington. *Marathon Girl*: Miss Valentine. *Bathing Girl*: Miss Renard. *Skating Girl*: Miss Fontaine.

ACT 2

Opening Chorus:

"That's the Life of a Stable Boy"
Ensemble

"The Man on the Box" (Solo)
A. Conrad

[77]Blanche Ring also reprised her recent hits: "Yip-i-addy-i-ay! (from THE MERRY WIDOW AND THE DEVIL) (*Music by* John Flynn. *Lyrics by* Will Cobb.) "I've Got Rings on My Fingers" (Mumbo Jumbo Jijhiboo J. O'Shea) (from THE MIDNIGHT SONS) (*Music by* Maurice Scott. *Lyrics by* F. J. Barnes and R. P. Weston.) Added for subsequent tour, as per published sheet music (1911): "Yea Boys' Let's Have a Time!" B. Ring (*Music by* Phil Schwartz. *Lyrics by* Harold Atteridge.) "Tell It to Sweeney" (*Music by* Harry Von Tilzer. *Lyrics by* William Dillon.) "My Cavalier" (Spanish Waltz Song) (*Music by* Joseph S. Nathan. *Lyrics by Felix F. Feist.)*

[78]Replaced for subsequent tour by: "The Wise Fisherman" B. Ring, W. P. Carleton

[79]Replaced for subsequent tour by: "That Bandit Man" B. Ring, Chorus

[80]Played a return engagement 2 May 1910 at the Grand Opera House for 8 performances.

"Gallop, Gallop"
Ensemble

"If Only You Would Take a Tip (from Me)"[81]
A. Conrad

ACT 3

Opening Chorus:

"The Angelus"
Ensemble

"Arrival of the Guests"
Ensemble

"The Lines in Molly's Hand"
C. Lean

"Mrs. Casey"
F. Holbrook
(*Music by* Florence Holbrook. *Lyrics by* Collin Davis, Cecil Lean.)

"He's a Fan, Fan, Fan"
C. Lean
(*Music by* Florence Holbrook. *Lyrics by* Cecil Lean.)

Finale
Ensemble

1910.10 A SKYLARK

A Whimsical Musical Comedy in Two Acts. Book and lyrics by William Harris, Jr. Music by Frank G. Dossert. Staged by Ben Teal. Dances arranged by David Bennett. Settings designed by H. Robert Law. Costumes by William H. Matthews. Light effects by Peter W. King. Orchestra under the direction of Theodore Bendix. Produced by Henry B. Harris. Opened 4 April 1910 at the New York Theatre and closed 23 April 1910 after 24 performances.

CAST (Acts 1 and 2): *Tourists*: *Ruben Smith*: JOHN SLAVIN. *Christine Parling*: MAY DeSOUSA. *Elberta Parling*: GRACE KING. *Amelia Parling*, mother of Christine and Elberta: ANNA BOYD. *Billy Kent*: ROBERT PITKIN. *Tom Randolph*: LESLIE GAZE. *Casey*, courier en avant: EDWARD GARVIE. *Of the S. S. Pegasus (3)*: *Captain Cook*: John Dunsmuir. *Dr. Reed*: Jack Terry. *Rosalie*, Flower Girl: GERTRUDE VANDERBILT. *Neptune*: HARRISON BROCKBANK. *Mrs. Elinore Wilmerding*: May Emory. *Helene Whistler*: Jeanette Horton. *May Manton*: May Maloney. *Gladys Currie*: Estelle Perry. *Norma Lawton*: Leila Benton. *Sally Somers*: Stella Beardsley. *Gertrude Kingston*: May Harris. *Ollie Oriton*: Irene George. *Maude Moore*: Myrtle Gillette. (Act 2 only): *The Gods*: *Jupiter*: Frank Belcher. *Mercury*: Jack Terry. *Cupid*: EDWARD GARVIE. *Bacchus*: JOHN DUNSMURE. *Venus*: HAZEL COX. *Juno*: CLARICE VANCE. *Diana*: GERTRUDE VANDERBILT. *Puck*: GERTRUDE VANDERBILT.

Gods, Greek Divinities, Muses, Attendants, etc.: Misses Edna Smith, Florence Wilson, Norma Mali, Ethel Moysten, Marion George, Lura Wentworth, Mella Drouet, Jean King, Goldie Redding, Alice Mariner, Clair Leslie, Beatrice Capulet, Lillian Stiles, Beatrice Allen, Katherine Howland, Eunice Mackay, Nellie Willette, Helen Tomlinson, Frances Alain, Katheryn Robertson, Fayette Perry, Edith Warren, Ethel Wheeler, Helen Brandon, Ida Vantine, Martha Bright, Gertrude Holland, Edith Ross, Laura Gaynelle, Ethel Avis. Messrs. William Davis, Robert Howard, Elmer Leyton, Jackson Carlyle, Emerson Overton, Lloyd Peddrick, Clyde Crawford, Francis Wells, Edward Morrison, W. K. Kemsley, V. P. Dusenberry, George Johnson, Louis Fletcher, Henry Holt, John Kern, James Colville.

Act 1: On Board the S. S. *Pegasus*.

Act 2: Garden of the Gods.

ACT 1

Opening Chorus
Ensemble

"Good-Bye, Yankee Doodle"
Chorus

"I Just Can't Wait"
J. Slavin, R. Pitkin, L. Gaze, E. Garvie, A. Boyd, M. DeSousa, G. King

"I'm Looking For a Little Girl Who's Looking for a Man"
M. DeSousa, G. King, L. Gaze, R. Pitkin

"When the Bloom Is on the Bottle"
J. Slavin, R. Pitkin

"When Love Is There"
M DeSousa

"Any Time at All"
R. Pitkin, Chorus
(*Music by* Joel P. Corin. *Lyrics by* Felix F. Feist.)

"The Chicken and the Frog"
J. Slavin, G. Vanderbilt

Finale
H. Brockbank, Principals, Chorus

ACT 2[82]

"The March of the Gods"

"Oh, Mr. Jupiter"
Chorus

Song Cycle
F. Belcher, J. Dunsmure, H. Cox, Nine Muses, G. Vanderbilt

"And I Believe Him"
C. Vance

"(The) Broadway Lament"
J. Slavin, R. Pitkin, L. Gaze, A. Boyd, M. DeSousa, G. King

"Style, Style, Style"
C. Vance, M. DeSousa, G. King

"The Gallous Old Goddess of Greece"
C. Vance

"Oh, We Know" (Song)
G. Vanderbilt, 12 Little Pucks

"In the Garden"
J. Slavin

Finale

1910.11 MOLLY MAY

An Original Comic Opera in Three Acts. Book and lyrics by Walter Browne. Music by Julian Edwards. Staged by Edward Temple. Scenery by Lee Lash Studios. Costumes designed by William Henry Matthews[83]. Orchestra under the direction of Emil Bierman. Produced by Byron Chandler. Opened 8 April 1910 at the Hackett Theatre and closed 30 April 1910 after 27 performances.

CAST: *Molly May*: GRACE LaRUE. *Senator Sparks*: JAMES E. SULLIVAN. *Sam Scumble*, an artist: JOHN H. GOLDSWORTHY. *Captain Tom Booker*: GEORGE ODELL. *Jenks*, butler at Willoughby's: Frank W. Shea. *Mrs. Sparks*: Kate Rolla. *Ella Willoughby*. Jack's wife: Marie Annis. *Dorothy Dingle*, her sister: HELLEN CULLINAN. *Sophia*, maid at Willoughby's: Audrey Hamilton. *Bebe*, a model: Sadie Melles. *Norah*, Scumble's servant: Velnette Viton. *Jack Willoughby*: SYDNEY GRANT.

Models: Misses Melles, Snyder, Gerard, Roberts, Ivamay, Engle, Ashton, Prescott, LaVere, Blair, McClellan, Vane, Earlcott, Vinton, Messinger, Vaughn, Page, Jackson, Dixon, Dean, Spencer, Slayton, Louis, Tallant, Chambers. *Golf Girls*: Misses Melles, Snyder, Page, Gerard, Jackson, Messinger, Vane, Roberts. *Dancing Maids*: Misses Prescott, LaVere, McClellan, Blair, Vaughn. *Tennis Girls*: Misses Prescott, LaVere, McClellan, Blair, Vaughn. *Polo Girls*: Misses Roberts, Engle, Vinton, Moon. *Riding Girls*: Misses Clayton, Gerard, Ivamay, Jackson. *Football Girls*: Misses Ada Balir, Essie McClellan, Louise Prescott, Maybelle LaVere, Rose Vaughn. *Taxicab Men*: Messrs. Hoyt, Loft, Hamilton, Grom, Mack, Ormsby, Murphy, Wonling, Chossman, Belmont, Conroy, Polen. *Hallowe'en Revellers*: Misses Dixon, Roberts, Clayton, Dean Gerard, Louis, Tallent, Chambers, Page, Jackson, Messinger, Snyder, LaVere, Ada Blair, Louise Precott, Essie McClellan, Rose Vaughn. Messrs. Hoyt, Loft, Hamilton, Wonling, Crossman, Belmont, Fairfax.

Act 1: Jack Willoughby's house (known at the "Dove Côte") near Riverside Drive, New York. Morning.

Act 2: Sam Scumble's studio. Afternoon.

Act 3: Gardens of the "Dove Côte". Evening (Hallowe'en).

ACT 1

"Maids and Mailmen"
Chorus

[81]Replaced during subsequent tour by:

"The Bumble Bee"
Freddie Nice (William Hawley)

"I'll Be Your Chanticleer"
Cecelia Renard (Linda Kurtz), F. Nice, Barnyard Fowl

[82]Order of songs revised during the run.

[83]Miss LaRue's gowns designed by her.

"O.I.C."
A. Hamilton, F. W. Shea
"Though We're Rude in Thus Intruding"
Chorus of Models
"Toot, Toot, the Fog Horn Gay"
Taxicabmen
"When a Girl Leads the Band"
G. LaRue, Chorus
"Molly May"
G. LaRue, Chorus
"Sleep On! Snore On!"
K. Rolla, M. Annis, H. Cullinan
"Love Comes to Stay"
H. Cullinan
"The Way to See Him Home"
G. Odell, Chorus
"I Only Drink for Friendship's Sake" (But I Have a Lot of Friends)
S. Grant, Chorus
"Clap Hands"
G. LaRue
Finale
Entire Company

ACT 2
Opening Chorus
Models and Students
"Art with a Capital A"
J. H. Goldsworthy, Chorus
"Nancy"
G. LaRue, S. Grant
"The Butterfly and the Rose"
H. Cullinan, G. Odell
"My Turkish Maid"
G. LaRue, Chorus
"Posing"
G. LaRue, J. H. Goldsworthy
"Baby Grand"
S. Grant
Finale
Entire Company

ACT 3
"Hallowe'en"
H. Cullinan, G. Odell, Chorus
"Castles in the Air"
G. LaRue
"A Chinese Theatre"
S. Grant
"Photography"
G. LaRue, S. Grant
Finale
Entire Company

1910.12 A MATINÉE IDOL

A Song Comedy (Musical Comedy) in Two Acts, 3 Scenes. Book by Armand and Barnard. Based on Moliere's "Un Médecin malgré lui." Music by Silvio Hein. Lyrics by E. Ray Goetz and Seymour Brown. (Staged by Daniel V. Arthur.) Scenery by Frank Gates and Edward A. Morange. Ladies' gowns designed by Lord and Taylor. Musical director, Albert Krausse. Produced by Daniel V. Arthur. Opened 28 April 1910 at Daly's Theatre, moved 6 June 1910 to the Lyric Theatre, and closed 25 June 1910 after 68 performances[84].

CAST (in order of appearance): *Dick Allen*: JOSEPH SANTLEY. *Lucy Gray*: ETHEL GREEN. *Mr. Layton*: Matt Hanley. *Nellie Wendell*: Trixie Moore. *Polly Brown*: Meta BoMar. *Mrs. Burton*: LOUISE DRESSER. *Dr. Allen*: George Backus. *Medford Griffin*: DeWOLF HOPPER. *Jimmie Grant*: GEORGIE MACK. *Cocher*: Thomas Roberts. *Dr. Gray*: George Wilson. *Marie*: ANNA FORD. *John*: William Jackson. *Mrs. Gray*: Elda Curry. *Seniors*: Misses Houck, Stevens, Williams, Elliott, Lascelles, Klingel.
Juniors: Misses Fortier, Hill, Burnett, Gray, [Katherine] Sainpolis, Weston, Starr, Moore, Adair, [Meta] BoMar, Raymond, Cottrell, Norris, Letsome, Jenkins, Watson, Edwards.

The action takes place on the Coast of Normandy at the present time.

Act 1, Scene 1: The campus of the Valerie Seminary. *Scene 2*: Living room in Dr. Allen's house.

Act 2: Courtyard of the Valerie Seminary.

ACT 1
"Exercise" (Opening Chorus)
Ensemble
(*Lyrics by* E. Ray Goetz.)
"The Yankee Romeo"
E. Green, J. Santley, Ensemble
(*Lyrics by* E. Ray Goetz.)
"Loving Ways"
L. Dresser, Seniors
"Autographs" (Won't You Write Your Autograph in My Album)
D. Hopper, School Girls
(*Lyrics by* E. Ray Goetz.)
"The Dancing Banshee" (That Dancing Big Banshee)
G. Mack, Ensemble
(*Lyrics by* Seymour Brown.)
"I Will Always Love You, Dear"
E. Green, J. Santley
(*Lyrics by* Seymour Brown.)
"Nonsense"
D. Hopper, G. Mack, J. Santley
(*Lyrics by* Seymour Brown.)
"Under the Yum-Yum Tree"[85]
L. Dresser, School Girls
"Hypnotic Waltz" (Hyp-Hyp-Hypnotism) and Finale
D. Hopper, Entire Company

ACT 2
"Little Lady in the Moon" (Opening)
E. Green, Ensemble
(*Lyrics by* Seymour Brown.)
"She's the Only Girl for Me"[86] (She's the Only Girl That I Could Ever See)
G. Mack, A. Ford
(*Lyrics by* Seymour Brown.)
"If You Could Only See Yourself as Other People Do"
D. Hopper, L. Dresser
"Put On Your Slippers, You're In for the Night"[87]
L. Dresser
"(Won't You) Let Me Build a Nest for You" (The Robin and the Wren)
J. Santley, E. Green
(*Lyrics by* Seymour Brown.)
Finale
D. Hopper, Entire Company

---

[84]Played a return engagement 1 May 1911 at the Manhattan Opera House for 8 performances.

[85]Dropped during the run. Added to Act 1, preceding "Nonsense":
"Side By Side by the Seaside"
L. Dresser, School Girls
Which was later replaced by:
"Miss Boodle and Her Poodle"
L. Dresser, Girls

[86]Dropped during the run.

[87]Dropped during the run and replaced by:
"Take a Look at Me Now"
L. Dresser
"I Want to Wed a Soldier Boy"
G. Mack, A. Ford, School Girls
For subsequent tour, this was subsequently revised as: "I Want to Wed a Jockey Boy"

1910.13

TILLIE'S NIGHTMARE

A Mixture of Mirth and Melody (A Musical Comedy) in Two Acts, 8 Scenes. Book and lyrics by Edgar Smith. Music by A. Baldwin Sloane. Entire producton staged by Ned Wayburn. Costumes by Melville Ellis. Settings by John H. Young. Orchestra under the direction of George A. Nichols. Produced by Lew Fields. Opened 5 May 1910 at the Herald Square Theatre and closed 9 July 1910 after 77 performances[88].

CAST: *Tillie Blobbs*, a boarding house drudge: MARIE DRESSLER. *Her Mother*, a voice: Lottie Uart. *Maude Blobbs*, her sister: OCTAVIA BROSKE. *Peroxia Snow*, excess baggage with "Frost and Snow": May Montford. *Slim Pettingill*, a small town genius with metropolitan aspirations: Horace Newman. *Harvey Tinker*, an unappreciated inventor: CLARENCE HARVEY. *Smiley Bragg*, a New York commercial drummer: BURRELL BARBARETTO. *Harry Frost*, of the vaudeville team "Frost and Snow": George Gorman. *A Broadway Policeman*: George Gorman. *Metropole Bill*, a pickpocket: John E. Gorman. *A Taxi Chauffeur*: Sim Pulen. *A Newsboy*: Harry Wilcox, Jr. *Dorset Walkingly*, head floorwalker at Pettingill's: LEW QUINN. *Dr. Rudolf Salve*, of Bargain Ambulance Corps, at Pettingill's: Barry Delaney. *Miss Thompson*, in charge of ribbon counter at Pettingill's: Marie Fanchionette. *Miss Johnson*, in charge of perfume counter at Pettingill's: Nellie DeGrasse. *Mrs. Grouch*, shopping for pink ribbon: Lottie Uart. *Mrs. Jeffries Wolgast Rush*, in search of a bargain: May Brennan. *Mr. Henry Peck*, of East Lemon, New Jersey: Carl Gordon. *Aarons' "Hello" Girls at Pettingill's (4)*: *Bell*: Carrie Poltz. *Dell*: Florrie Poltz. *Nell*: Eva Marlowe. *Stell*: Nellie Wilke. *Captain Fitzpelet*, of the Yacht *"Tillie"*: LEW QUINN. *Nip, Tuck*, Sailors of the Yacht *"Tillie"*: George Gorman, John E. Gorman. *The Ambassadors (6)*, representing: *America*: John E. Gorman. *England*: George Williams. *Italy*: Bernard Lyons. *Germany*: Carl Gordon. *Russia*: Pietro Moutalba. *Mexico*: Fred Hill. *Jean*: Andrew Harper.

Personnel Of Chorus: *Original English Dancing Girls*: Misses Carrie Poltz, Florrie Poltz, Eva Marlowe, Nellie Wilkie. *Chantecleer Models, Yankee Wives, etc.*: Misses Edith Offutt, Harriet Leidy, Virginia Gunther, Susie Pitt, Theresa Allen, Bessie Ryan. *Shoppers, Cocottes, etc.*: Misses Margaret Carlin, Lois Stowe, Gladys Coleman, Mina Schall, Josephine Brandell, May Brennan. *Theatregoers, Chanteuses, etc.*: Misses Kathryn Humphries, Hazel Drouant, Gertrude Barnard, Marie Hurst, Louise Orth, Mildred Livingston. *Society Buds, etc.*: Misses Kathryn Schuyler, Salie Daly, May Hanlon, Meta Caldwell, Hilda Hoffmann, Florence Topham. *Cash Girls, Cafe Maids, etc.*: Misses Mazie Murray, Olive Carr, Ethel Lytle, Ethel Fairbanks, Lillian Hazel, Nora Cotter. *Floorwalkers, Americans, etc.*: Messrs. J. C. Breese, H. T. Pond, Andrew Harper, Harry Laughlin, Ernest Sharrack, Arthur Whitman, Garfield Meixner. *College Boys, Boulevardiers, etc.*: Messrs. Ralph Watson, Barry Delaney, Joseph Hadley, Louis Von Blake, Harry Laughlin, Harry Wilcox, Robert E. Graham, Jr.

Act 1, Scene 1: Mrs. Blobb's Boarding House at Skaneateles, New York. *Scene 2*: 42nd Street, near Broadway, at theatre time. *Scene 3*: Interior of Pettingill's department store. New York.

Act 2, Scene 1: Deck of the Yacht "Tillie." *Scene 2*: Under the deep blue sea. *Scene 3*: Cafe Vaudeville, adjacent to Aeroplane Trial Grounds, Paris. *Scene 4*: In the clouds on Tinker's air ship, "The Eagle." *Scene 5*: Home again.

ACT 1

"Heaven Will Protect the Working Girl"
M. Dressler

"White Light Lane"
Ensemble

"There He Goes" (There Goes Another One)
H. Newman, Chorus

"Shopping"
Ensemble

"Every Pretty Girl"
L. Quinn, Models, Chorus

"Shopping Glide"
L. Quinn, M. Fanchionette

"I Want to Bring You a Ring"
B. Barbaretto, Hello Girls, Chorus
(*Music and Lyrics by* John L. Golden.)

"The Wedding Rehearsal" (Finale)
M. Dressler, Ensemble

ACT 2

"Life Is What We Make It, After All"[89]
O. Broske, Male Chorus

"Shipboard Frolics"
G. Gorman, J. E. Gorman

"Spook Dance"
Aaron's Dancing Dolls

"Be-Bee"
Grisettes, Cocottes, Yankee Wives, Americans, Chanteuse, Boulevardiers, Cafe Maids

"What I Could Do Upon the Stage"
M. Dressler

"Flight of the Air Ship"
Ensemble

[88]Played a return engagement 18 December 1911 at the Manhattan Opera House for 8 performances.

[89]Replaced for subsequent tour by: "Kind Moon Man" O. Broske, Male Chorus (*Music and Lyrics by* John L. Golden.)

1910.14

THE MIKADO, or The Town of Titipu

A Revival of the Comic Opera in Two Acts[90]. Libretto by William S. Gilbert. Music by Arthur Sullivan. Staged by Joseph Herbert and William J. Wilson. Costumes by Melville Ellis. Orchestra directed by John Lund. Produced by the Messrs. Shubert and William A. Brady. Opened 30 May 1910 at the Casino Theatre and closed 9 July 1910 after 48 performances.[91]

CAST: *The Mikado of Japan*: WILLIAM DANFORTH. *Nanki-Poo*, his son disguised as a wandering minstrel, and in love with Yum-Yum: ANDREW MACK. *Ko-Ko*, Lord High Executioner of Titipu: JEFFERSON DeANGELIS. *Pooh-Bah*, Lord High Everything Else: WILLIAM PRUETTE. *Pish-Tush*, a Noble Lord: ARTHUR CUNNINGHAM. *Three Sisters, Wards of Ko-Ko*: *Yum-Yum*: FRITZI SCHEFF. *Pitti-Sing*: CHRISTIE MacDONALD. *Peep-Bo*: CHRISTINE NIELSON. *Katisha*, an Elderly Lady in love with Nanki-Poo: JOSEPHINE JACOBY. *Chorus of School Girls, Nobles, Guards and Coolies.*

1910.15

THE MERRY WHIRL

An Entertainment of Quality (Musical Play) in Two Acts. Book by Don Roth. Music by Leo Edwards. Lyrics by Ed Ray. Staged by Julian Alfred. Dances arranged by Jack Mason. Scenery by John Young, Homer Emens. Costumes by Bush Lubin & Freisinger. Musical director, Aaron Binkow. Produced by Cliff Gordon and Bobby North. Opened 30 May 1910 at the New York Theatre and closed 18 June 1910 after 24 performances[92].

CAST: Act 1: *??Clock*: JAMES C. MORTON. *??Snowman*: FRANK MOORE. *C.U. Damm*, an American millionaire: Phil White. *Lord ? Broke*, an impecunious nobleman: WALTER PEARSON. *?Sikh Anagar*, slave to ring: James Doyle. *?*: Allan Reid. *from the Folies Bergere*: Marie Beaugarde. *?an Rogers*, an American widow: Eleanor L'Estelle. *??*: Grace Hammond. *??*: Noette Aimes. *??*: Alice Emerald. *Guests, Maids, Butlers, Servants, etc.*

Act 2: *Spike McCarthy*, an American pugilist in Paris: JAMES C. MORTON. *Dan McCormick*, his manager: FRANK F. MOORE. *Jacques Frou Frou*, proprietor Jacques Emporium: Phil White. *O. U. Kidd*, an American millionaire doing Paris: ??. *Baron de Cammembert*, a French nobleman: Edwin Jerome. *Mlle. DeBaron*, the prettiest model in Paris: MILDRED ELAINE. *Barronne De Cammembert*, in love with Francoise Dubonet: RITA REDMOND. *Pierre De Saute*, the duelist: ??. *Jacqueline*: Grace Hammond. *Notoslynne*: May Emerald. *Mlle De BrieMme. De SoMme. De NorthMme. DeMondePommeryMoetGuests, Maids, Messenger Boys, etc.Chorus GirlsPoniesMale Chorus*

Lew Harkins. : R. L. McAndrew. : Jack Clendon. : May Florine Linden. : Florence May. : Catherine Holland. : Ray Gilmore. : May Tomlinson. : Dorothy Benton. :

Act 1: Lord Broke's ancestral hall, England. (Young.)

Act 2: Jacques' Ladies' Emporium, Paris. (Emens.)

ACT 1: THE MAGIC RING

Opening Chorus

"Yankee Doodle Girls"
W. Pearson, Show Girls

[90]First presented in New York 20 July, 10-29 August 1885 at the Union Square and People's Theatres for 22 performances. First authorized production presented 19 August 1885 at the Fifth Avenue Theatre by Richard D'Oyly Carte for 250 performances. For Synopsis of Scenes and Musical Numbers, see 19 August 1885 D'Oyly Carte production. Scenery uncredited.

[91]Scenery uncredited.

[92]Previously and subsequently produced in New York under a vaudeville contract performed twice daily.

"The Man with Money"
P. White

"Lima Beans"
J. C. Morton, F. Moore

"La Belle Francaise"
Cherie, Chorus

"Down Havana Way"
W. Pearson, Chorus

"I'll Be There with You"
J. C. Morton, F. Moore, Cherie

"The Rose"
Mrs Morgan

"Play, Play, Play"
J. C. Morton, F. Moore

Finale
Entire Company

ACT 2: THE MERRY WHIRL

Opening Chorus
Ensemble

"A Model of Fashion Am I"
M. Elaine, Johnnies

"Ring the Wedding Bells"
??, M. Elaine

"When I Waltz with You"
R. Redmond, Chorus

"The Paris Push"
??, G. Hammond

"When the Stars Fall in Love with the Moon"
R. Redmond, M. Elaine

"Strike Up a Bagpipe Tune"
M. Elaine, Chorus
(*Music by* Leo Edwards. *Lyrics by* Edward Madden.)

Finale
Entire Company

1910–1911 SEASON

Lina Abarbarnell in MADAM SHERRY (Photo: White Studio)
Billy Rose Theatre Collection, New York Public Library for the Performing Arts

1910–1911 SEASON

1910.16 THE SUMMER WIDOWERS

A Musical Panorama in Seven Views (Two Acts, 8 Scenes). Words (book and lyrics) by Glen MacDonough. Tunes (music) by A. Baldwin Sloane. Entire production staged by Ned Wayburn. Dances arranged by Ned Wayburn. Scenic equipment by Arthur Voegtlin. Costumes designed by Melville Ellis. Orchestra under the direction of George A. Nichols. Orchestrations by Frank Saddler. Produced by Lew Fields. Opened 4 June 1910 at the Broadway Theatre and closed 1 October 1910 after 140 performances.

CAST: *Otto Ott*, a retired German druggist: LEW FIELDS. *Max Ott*, his romantic son: WALTER PERCIVAL. *William Alfred Henry George*, colored janitor of St. Vitus Court: WILLIS P. SWEATNAM. *Salve di Mora*, Otto's most intimate friend, in the grocery and delicatessen line: CHARLES JUDELS. *Guy Stringer*, an automobile agent: FRITZ WILLIAMS. *Hunter Lamb*, a broker: JACK HENDERSON. *Conwell Swift*, press agent for the Folderol Gardens: PAUL NICHOLSON. *Captain Kodak*, an Atlantic City photographer: William Burress. *Pinkie Doolittle*, Mrs. McGuirk's little boy: Will Archie. *Sandy Beach*, a bathing master: Eugene O'Rourke. *Tom Noyes*, a pianist: Burt Green. *Oxford Tighe*, American agent for "Eyzzzst" the new Hungarian cordial: VERNON CASTLE. *Sammy Square*, manager of the Folderol Gardens: Maitland Davies.

Claribel Clews, a perfect lady detective: IRENE FRANKLIN. *Mrs. Guinivere McGuirk*, Celia Carew's older sister, once widowed, twice divorced, but still hopeful: ADA LEWIS. *Celia Carew*, Otto Ott's prospective daughter-in-law: ALICE DOVEY. *Fritzi Fluff*, an absent minded prima donna: Maud Lambert. *Virginia Ham*, her loyal but candid chorus-girl friend: Angie Norton. *Psyche Finnegan*, Pinkie's playmate: HELEN HAYES. *Mrs. Conwell Swift*: Jane Grover. *Mrs. Hunter Lamb*: Jeanne Lansford. *Mrs. Guy Stringer*: Mabel Weeks. *Gertie Gherkin*: Marion Whitney. *Winnie Wildwaves*: Billie Cuppia. (*Specialties*: The Hess Sisters, The Hyde Troupe, The Baxters, Eight Berlin Madcaps.)

Personnel of the Chorus: *Summer Wives, Peaches, Patrons, etc.*: Misses Marise Naughton, Billie Cuppia, Estelle Richmond, Emily Monte, Frances Harris, Marian Whitney, Helen Adair, May Willard, Louise Gale, Jessie Crane. *"Air-esses", Bathers, Shoppers, etc.*: Misses Lillian West, Minnie Monroe, Minna Davenport, Frances Shannon, Ethel Fleming, Ninon DuBal, Beatrice Priest, Inez Borrero, Caroline Wade, Mabel Delmar. *Snapshot Girls, Cashiers, etc.*: Misses Stacia Leslie, Adele LaPierre, Jean Crane, Rose Monroe, Mae Taylor, Libbia Diamond, Morrie Madison, Adelaide Mason, Ella Warner. *Nurses, Maids, Ushers, etc.*: Misses Frances Fulsom, Frances Leslie, Vivian Rogers, Mazie Kimball, Polly Allison, Isabelle Jason, Ethel Sinclair, Dorothy Godfrey, Edna Snyder, Cecelia Pink. *Boardwalk Types, Clerks, Johnnies, , etc.*: Messrs. Henry Detloff, Thomas Reynolds, Robert O'Neill, Douglass Williams, Ralph Whiting, William Nav, Edward McNulty, William Meyer. *Rolling "Chairists", Guests, Brokers, etc.*: Messrs. Fred Bates, Fred Roberts, George Lynch, Robert Waite, Thomas Everett, Russell Summerville, Fred Hazelwood, Lew Finnerty. *Board Walkers, Clerks, Bankers, etc.*: Messrs. Duke Rogers, Frank Sterling, Ralph O'Reilly, Harry Nelson, Martin Hickey, Wood Goebel, Edward Weinberg, Clarence Lutz. *Chair Pushers, Delivery Boys, Waiters*: Messrs. Harry Acheson, Eddie Simms, Fred DuBall, John Cook, Arthur Gros, Joe Mariott, Harry Neimann, Ralph Rose.

Act 1, Scene 1: The Boardwalk, before the Marlborough-Blenheim Hotel, Atlantic City. *Scene 2*: A street in New York. *Scene 3*: Salve di Mora's Delicatessen Shop and Fancy Grocery. *Scene 4*: On the beach, Atlantic City. *Scene 5*: In the surf at the Million Dollar Pier.(*Devised by* Frank D. Thomas.)

Act 2, Scene 1: The Third, Fourth and Fifth Floors of the St. Vitus Apartments, near Amsterdam Avenue, New York. *Scene 2*: Lobby of the Folderol Gardens. *Scene 3*: The Folderol Gardens.

ACT 1[1]

"On the Boardwalk"/"We'll Go to the Minstrel Show" (Opening Chorus)
Ensemble

"I Never Know How to Behave When I'm with Girls, Girls, Girls"
V. Castle, Madcaps, Chorus

"The Calcium Moon"
A. Dovey, Heroes, Heroines, Chorus

"Flying High"
W. Percival, P. Nicholson, F. Williams, J. Henderson, "Air-esses"

"There's No Place Like Home (Boys), When Your Wife Has Gone Away"
J. Henderson, Summer Widowers

Dance[2]
The Jackson Troupe

"I Knew Her When"
I. Franklin
(*Music and Lyrics by* Burton Green and Irene Franklin.)

"(We're Looking for Something in) Peaches"
Ensemble

"Gee, But I'd Like to Furnish a Flat for You (Dear)"
W. Percival, A. Dovey, Ensemble

"Oh You Summertime Romeo"
M. Lambert, Chorus

"Come and Take a Dip in the Sea with Me"
M. Weeks, Bathers, Chorus

ACT 2[3]

"Miss Dennett"
I. Franklin
(*Music and Lyrics by* Burton Green and Irene Franklin.)

"The Lady-Ushers Ball" (The Ladies Usher Ball)
Lady Ushers, Waiters

"Chili-Concarne"[4]
M. Lambert

"Those Were (the) Happy Days"
F. Williams, "Lou," "Rosie," "Dinah," "Star Girls"

"The Sahara Twins"
The Hess Sisters

"Muscovite"
The Hyde Troupe

Dance Eccentrique
The Baxters

Specialty
The Eight Berlin Madcaps

"I'm All That's Left of the First Pony Ballet" (The Pony Ballet Girl)
I. Franklin, "The Phony Ballet"
(*Music and Lyrics by* Burton Green and Irene Franklin.)

"Mandalay"
M. Lambert, Chorus

Finale
Ensemble

[1]Interpolation, as per published sheet music:
"Fireflies" (Idyl)
(*Music by* Paul Lincke. *Lyrics by* Ballard Macdonald.)

[2]Dropped during the run.

[3] Added to Act 2, after "Those Were the Happy Days," for subsequent tour:
"Red Head"
I. Franklin
(*Music by* Burton Green. *Lyrics by* Irene Franklin.)

[4]Dropped during the run.

1910.17 GIRLIES

The Comic Supplement of the Dramatic Season (A Musical Comedy) in Two Acts, 11 Scenes. Book by George V. Hobart. Music by Egbert Van Alstyne. Lyrics by Harry Williams. (Staged by Frederic Thompson.) Dances and ensembles by Jack Mason. Scenery by Sosman & Landis, Chicago; Edward G. Unitt and Joseph Wickes; Lee Lash Studios. Costumes designed by Edel of Paris. Orchestra under the direction of Charles J. Gebest. Produced by Frederic Thompson. Opened 13 June 1910 at the New Amsterdam Theatre and closed 27 August 1910 after 88 performances.

CAST: *Dr. Oscar Speil*, professor of botany: JOSEPH CAWTHORN. *Justin Wright*, professor of Greek: J. B. Hollis. *Gordon Doane*, professor of languages: JED PROUTY. *Billy Murray*, a freshman: ERNEST TRUEX. *Harry Shelby*, a senior: HARRY KERNELL. *The Burglar*: Harry Kernell. *Bud Washington*, a porter: Harry S. Fern. *Seetim*: Harry Breen. *Blitzen*, his dog: David Abraham. *Frank*, a student: Sid M. Ayres. *Walter*: Darl MacBoyle. *Harold*, a student: Walter Clinton. *Carl*, a student: J. W. Cody. *Tom*, a student: Edwin Stone. *Jim*, a student: Den Lownie. *Amos*, a student: Fred Emerson. *Willie*, a student: Jack Henry. *McGregor*, a policeman: Donald Gulland. *Hank*: Harry Breen. *Rubes (3)*: *Getup*: E. Bowers. *Early*: F. Walker. *Plough*: A. Crooker. *Gloriana Gray*, an investigatress: MAUDE RAYMOND. *Marion See*, director of deportment: Carrie E. Perkins. *Bertha Day*, a student: VIOLET MacMILLAN. *Jessie*, a student: Julia Mills. *Gertie Wilson*, a student: Pauline Thorne. *Susie Smith*, a student: Erminie Clark. *Nora Gray*, a student: Edna Hunter. *Bessie*, a student: Teddy Hudson. *Dorothy*, a student: Dorothy Sayce. *Maud*, a student: Emily Sweeney. *Winnie*, a student: May Hennessey.

Girl Students: Misses Josephine Arnold, Pudge Belma, Thelma Belmont, Mildred Bright, Marie Baxter, Zaini Curzon, Dollie Collins, Pony Cantor, Ethel Conlinson, Mabel Clark, Eleanor Carroll, Viola Clark, May Doherty, Jeannette Despres, Marion Finlay, Marion Goodwin, Laura Gaynelle, Gypsy Grau, Marion George, Jerry Girard, Elma Gay, Florence Hayes, Edna Hunter, Teddy Hudson, May Hennessey, Clara Lloyd, Dottie Moyer, Viola Macey, Alice Mariner, Minnie Martrit, Edna Mayo, Audrey Munson, Julia Mills, Irene Moyer, Dolly Pacy, Corienne Penelton, Jess Piper, Paula Pauline, Olive Quimby, Emily Sweeney, Dorothy Sayce, Mildred Sanford, Florence Scott, Clare Schroeder, Rita Trainor, Hazel Troutman, Beatrice Whitney, Florence Wilson, Amy Williams, Lorette Ward. *Boy Students*: Messrs. M. Avery, S. Ayres, W. Clinton, F. Emerson, J. Cody, D. Goolsby, F. Hudler, G. Johnson, J. Henry, D. Lownie, J. McDonald, J. Piper, J. Pierce, E. Stone, R. Van Sickle, F. Wells, A. E. Wilson, D. Gulland, D. MacBoyle.

Act 1, Scene 1: A room in the "Frat" house of the Gamma Gamma Gammu Society at Hightonia Co-ed College, near High Hills, near High Hills, Highland County, U.S. Late afternoon. *Scene 2*: Lover's Lane at Twilight. The same evening. *Scene 3*: A part of the campus decorated for the celebration. The next morning.

Act 2, Scene 1: Gymnasium. *Scene 2*: Front of Crazyquilto Apartment House. *Scene 3*: Crazyquilto Apartment House. *Scene 4*: The Nursery. *Scene 5*: The Dormitory Balcony. *Scene 6*: The Aeroplane. *Scene 7*: The Chapel Walk. *Scene 8*: The River Seine.

ACT 1

Scene 1

Opening Chorus

"(Going) Up in My Aeroplane"
H. Kernell, Chorus

"That's Good"
M. Raymond

"Life Is (Just) a Merry-Go-Round"
J. Cawthorn, Male Students
(*Music by* Benjamin Hapgood Burt. *Lyrics by* John L. Golden.)

Scene 2

"My Irish Girl"[5]
J. Prouty, assisted by E. Hunter

Scene 3

"You Will Read It in the Papers" (You Can Find It in the Papers Every Day)
J. Cawthorn, assisted by Messrs. Truex, Cody, Clinton, Ayres

"Who Were You with To-Night"
M. Raymond, assisted by Misses Clark, Mills, Pendleton, Bright, Dupree, Mayo, Pauline, Sayce

"(The Bull) Frog and the Dove"
V. MacMillan, Dancing Ponies

"Why Be a Hero"—Finale
Principal Characters, Entire Chorus

ACT 2[6]

Scene 1

"Ring Me Up in the Morning"
V. MacMillan, Chorus (Male, Female Students)

Scene 2

"(Play That) Barber Shop Chord"
H. S. Fern

Scene 3

Burlesques:

Mrs. X [A Burlesque on "Madame X," the drama by Alexander Bisson, adopted by John Raphael.]
The Burglar: H. Kernell. *Mrs. X*: D. Mitchell. *Laroquefort*: J. Prouty. *The City Marshall*: J. Cawthorn.
The Spendthrift [A Burlesque on "Seven Days," play by Mary Roberts Rinehart and Avery Hopwood, and "Alias Jimmy Valentine," play by Paul Armstrong from the story "A Retrieved Reformation" by O. Henry.]
Frances: D. Mitchell. *Richard*: J. Cawthorn. *Suffern Katz*: J. Prouty.

Scene 4

"Baby Talk"
Ponies, Male Students

Scene 5

"Concertina"
J. Cawthorn

Scene 6

March
Entire Chorus

Rube Specialty
Messrs. Bowers, Walters, Crooker

"Rowing Song"
Full Chorus

Scene 7

An Attack of the Songfits[7]
H. Breen

Scene 8

"Honolulu Rag"
M. Raymond, Chorus

Finale (Medley)

1910.18 ZIEGFELD FOLLIES OF 1910

A Song (Musical) Revue in Three Acts, 14 Scenes[8]. Words (sketches, lyrics) by Harry B. Smith. Music by Gus Edwards and many others. Staged by Julian Mitchell. Dances arranged by Frank Darling. Costumes by Herr Crage, William H. Matthews. Scenery designed by Ernest Albert, John H. Young. Orchestra under the direction of Frank Darling. Produced by Florenz Ziegfeld. Opened 20 June 1910 at the Jardin de Paris[9] and closed 3 September 1910 after 88 performances.

CAST: FANNY [Fannie] BRICE, ANNA HELD, BERT WILLIAMS, HARRY WATSON, GEORGE BICKEL, LILLIAN LORRAINE, GRACE TYSON, MINDEL KINGSTON, LILLIAN ST. CLAIR, BOBBY NORTH, Jerome Van Nordern, Rosie Green, Maurice Hegeman, Jacques Kruger, Margaret Morris, William [Billie] Reeves, John Quigg, Hazel Robinson, Vonnie Hoye, Elsie Hamilton, Aline Boley, John Reinhardt, Clifford Saum, Arthur McWaters, Alice Hegeman, Charles Scribner, Edward Devlin, May Paul, Henry Johnson, Dudley Oatman, Louise Alexander, Julian Mitchell, Eleanor Pendleton, Arthur Nickerson, Arthur Youngs, W. Wania, Peter Swift, William Schrode, Charles Hessong. Motion picture of Anna Held and Harry Watson.

Misses Maxwell, Holbrook, Mackey, Daly, Renneard, Conway, Whitford, Eleanor St. Claire, Daisy Virginia, Lillian, Vera Olcott, Walker, Beck, Scott, Readmond, Gabrielle, O'Donnell, Mitchell, Wilson, May Hopkins, Averill, Dale, Gardner, Koerner, Stuart, Betty Neil, Webb, Beardsley, L. Vernon, Howe, Christy, Conway. Messrs. Daly, Hoyt, Kent, B. Richardson, Fairbrother, Milton, Gates, Bell.

ACT 1[10]

Scene 1

View of New York from the Metropolitan Tower (*Painted by* John Young.)

"Good Bye, Becky Cohen"
F. Brice
(*Music and Lyrics by* Irving Berlin.)

"Look Me Over Carefully (and Tell Me Will I Do)"[11]
G. Tyson
(*Lyrics by* Will D. Cobb.)
Scene: Dress Rehearsal of the Follies.
Stage Manager Mitchell: H. Watson. *Musical Director Levi*: G. Bickel. *Stage Door-keeper*: J. Van Norden. *Miss Pansy Perkins*: F. Brice. *Mazie Muggs*: R. Green. *Sadie Spooner*: V. Hoye. *Flossie Frost*: V. Maxwell. *Flossie's Mother*: A. Boley. *Ione Carr*: G. Tyson. *Towne Duer*: J. Reinhardt. *A Waiter*: C. Saum.

---

[5]Replaced during the run by:
"Lovelight"
J. Prouty, assisted by the Chorus

[6]After opening, the running order of Act 2 was revised, and the following added to Scene 5:
"Serenade"
Male Students

[7]Dropped during the run.

[8]The fourth in the annual series of revues produced by Florenz Ziegfeld beginning in 1907.

[9]Atop the New York and Criterion Theatres.

[10]Interpolated as per published sheet music:
"(The Dance) of the Grizzly Bear"
(*Music by* George Botsford. *Lyrics by* Irving Berlin.)

[11]Dropped for subsequent tour.

Scene 2

"Nix on the Concertina, Lena"[12]

G. Tyson

(*Music by* Harry Carroll. *Lyrics by* Ballard Macdonald.)

Scene: Office of the Get Poor Quick Syndicate (*Painted by* John Young.)

Andy C: M. Hegeman. *Jim Hill*: A. McWaters. *John D*: J. Kruger. *Hetty G*: A. Hegeman. *J Pierrepont*: C. Scribner. *The Office Boy, The Common People*: E. Devlin. *Iona Carr*: G. Tyson. *Dick the Rat*: G. Bickel. *Gentleman Mike*: H. Watson.

Scene 3

"Sweet Kitty Bellairs"[13]

L. Lorraine

Scene: Lakes of Killarney. (*Painted by* Ernest Albert.)

Scene 4

Taking a Moving Picture (Taking a Fake Picture of the Jeffries-Johnson Fight)

Scene: A Street in Reno. (*Painted by* John Young.)

Jack Johnson's Double: B. Williams. *Jim Jeffries*—in his mind: B. Reeves. *A Promoter*: J. Quigg. *A Moving Picture Man*: A. Nickerson. *An Announcer*: P. Swift. *An Ex-Plug*: J. Kruger. *A Second*: W. Schrode. *An Ex-Heavyweight*: A. McWaters.

Scene 5

Operatic Medley[14] (*by* Aaron Hoffman)

B. North

Scene: Behind the Curtains.

The Ruler of New York: B. North.

Scene 6

"Kidland"[15]

L. Lorraine

(*Lyrics by* Will D. Cobb.)

Scene: The Apple Blossom Grove (The Spring of Youth) (*Painted by* Unitt & Wickes.)

Sweet Girl Graduates: Misses V. Maxwell, Holbrook, Mackey, Morris, Daly, Renney, Conway, Whitford, E. St. Claire, V. Walker, Beck. *Prowler*: B. Reeves.

"Our American Colleges"

(*Musical Arrangements by* Maurice Levi.)

Finale

ACT 2[16]

Scene 1

"The Pensacola Mooch"

M. Kingston, R. Green

(*Music and Lyrics by* Ford Dabney and Will Marion Cook.)

Scene: Café de l'Opera—"Dress suits must be worn." (*Painted by* John Young.)

Boys: Misses Holbrook, Daly, Morris, E. St. Clair, Whitford, Hoyt, Howe, Kent. *Girls*: Misses Maxwell, Mackey, Scott, Walker, Christy, Readmond, Gabrielle, Conway, R. Green, E. Hamilton. *Head Waiter*: M. Hegeman. *Hat Boy*: M. Pendleton. *Coat Boy*: D. Virginia. *Glove Boy*: V. Olcott. *Cane Boy*: L. Walker. *Waiter*: C. Saum. *Weston*: B. Richardson. *A Stranger in New York*: H. Watson. *The Stranger's Friend*: G. Bickel.

Songs

B. Williams

["Constantly"

(*Music by* Bert Williams. *Lyrics by* James Henry Burriss, Chris Smith.)

"Believe Me"

(*Music by* Bert Williams. *Lyrics by* Alex Rogers.)

"In the Evening" (In de Evenin')

"The Black Cat"

"Play That Barbershop Chord"

(*Music by* Lewis F. Muir. *Lyrics by* William Tracey.)]

"You're Gwine to Get Somethin' What You Don't Expect"

(*Music by* Bert Williams. *Lyrics by* Vincent Bryan.)]

Scene 2

"A Woman's Dream" (Song)

L. St. Clair

Scene: A Woman's Boudoir.

A Woman's Necessities: *Bath Robe*: Miss Mitchell. *Slippers*: Miss Trent. *Lingerie*: Miss M. Hopkins. *Garters*: Miss Averill. *Corsets*: Miss V. Bowers. *Perfume*: Miss Gardner. *Jewels*: Miss Koerner. *Flowers*: Miss Stuart. *Gloves*: Miss Neil. *Plumes*: Miss Webb. *Parasol*: Miss Beardsley. *Furs*: Miss L. Vernon.

A Fool There Was

L. Alexander, J. Mitchell

Scene 3

A Band Rehearsal (Roosevelt Band from Cartoons by Rube Goldberg)

G. Bickel, H. Watson

Scene: Metropolitan Tower.

Scene 4

"The Swings" (Swing Me High, Swing Me Low)

L. Lorraine

(*Music by* Victor Holländer. *Lyrics by* Ballard Macdonald.)

(*Accompanied by*) Misses Howe, Christy, Maxwell, Conway, Morris, St. Claire, Mackey, Hoyt. (Bells arranged by John O'Neil.)

ACT 3[17]

Scene 1

"Why Take a Girl Down to Coney" (Don't Take a Girl Down to Coney) (Song)

M. Kingston, Chorus

(*Lyrics by* Will D. Cobb.)

---

[12]Revised subsequently for tour under the title "Nix on the Glow-Worm, Lena."

[13]Replaced for subsequent tour by:

"Come Along My Mandy"

L. Lorraine, H. Pilcer

(*Music and Lyrics by* Irving Berlin.)

[14]Dropped for subsequent tour.

[15]Dropped for subsequent tour.

[16]Added to Act 2, Scene 2 in second month of the run:

Reminiscent Ragtime Revue:

"Yankiana Rag" (from MISS INNOCENCE)

S. Kellogg, (assisted by) R. Green, H. Pilcer, M. Morris, V. Maxwell

(*Music by* Ludwig Englander.)

"Temptation Rag"

L. Lorraine

Cuban Glide

H. Pilcer

"Fandango Rag" (from FOLLIES OF 1909)

M. Kingston, (assisted by) R. Green, H. Pilcer

(*Music by* Lewis F. Muir. *Lyrics by* E. Ray Goetz.)

"Wild Cherry Rag" (Wild Cherries; Coony, Spoony Rag)

F. Brice

(*Music and Lyrics by* Irving Berlin.)

"Italian Rag"

B. North

"Rosey Posey" (Fay Templeton's Greatest Creation)

L. St. Claire

"Rosalie" (Fay Stone's success in THE WIZARD OF OZ)

L. Lorraine

(*Lyrics by* Will D. Cobb.)

"Franco-American Rag"

M. Kingston, M. Morris

Added to Act 2, Scene 1 for subsequent tour:

Medley

B. North

"(Telephone Your) Riskey Issey" (Song)

F. Brice

[17]Added for subsequent tour to Act 3, Scene 1:

"My Yiddisha Colleen"

B. North, S. Kellogg

(*Music by* Leo Edwards. *Lyrics by* Edward Madden.)

"I'm in Love with You"

L. Lorraine

(*Music by* Gus Edwards. *Lyrics by* Harry B. Smith.)

Scene: The Apple Blossom Grove. (*Painted by* Unitt & Wickes.)

Sweet Girl Graduates: Misses Maxwell, Thompson, B. Morris, Morris, Daly, Carlton, Marcelle, DuBarry, Lane, Quinnette, Virginia, Kent. *A Johnnie*: B. Reeves.

Added to Act 3, Scene 2, in second month of the New York run:

"The Chicken Thief Man" (dropped for subsequent tour)

M. Kingston, 16 Broilers

"(I'm the) Cock of the Walk"

B. North

"Lovey Joe" (Lovie Joe)
F. Brice
(*Music by* Joe Jordan. *Lyrics by* Will Marion Cook.)
Scene: Office of a Musical Publisher. (*Painted by* John Young.)
Frank Steel, a song-writer: G. Bickel. *Nibbsie Hooligan*, a piano mover: H. Watson. *Smiley*, a publisher: A. McWaters. *Steele*, a composer: A. Nickerson. *The Dotty Sisters*: F. Brice, A. Hegeman. *Rosie Blow, Puff Bluff*, of Bluff and Blow, the well-known sketch team: G. Tyson, J. Kruger.

Russian Dance (from Imperial Opera House, St. Petersburg)
W. Wania

Scene 2

"I'll Get You Yet"[18] (Duet)
L. Lorraine, H. Watson, 16 Chicks
(*Music by* Harry Von Tilzer. *Lyrics by* Addison Burkhardt.)
Scene: Model Hennery.
A Chanticleer: B. North. *A Dissipated Rooster*: B. Reeves. *Hen Pheasant*: L. Lorraine. *An Ancient Hen*: A. Hegeman. *A Cold Storage Chicken*: A. Boley. *A Rooster*: C. Saum. *A Turkey*: P. Swift. *George*, a Fighting Bantum: W. Schrode.

Songs[19]
B. Williams
["White Folks Call It Chantecler, But It's Just Plain Chicken to Me"
(*Music by* Bert Williams. *Lyrics by* Andrew B. Sterling.)
"I'll Lend You Everything I've Got Except My Wife"
(*Music by* Harry Von Tilzer. *Lyrics by* Jean C. Havez.)]

Scene 3

"Mr. Earth and His Comet Love" (The Comet and the Earth)
L. St. Claire
Scene: Halley's Comet and the Earth.
The Comet: A. Held. *The Earth*: H. Watson.

Scene 4

"The Waltzing Lieutenant"
B. North
Scene: The Return of Roosevelt. (*Painted by* John Young.)
The Rough Riders: *Teddy*: H. Watson. *Bill*: G. Bickel. *Uncle Joe*: J. Kruger. *Goddess of Liberty*: L. Lorraine. And the West Points Cadets. *The Reception Committee*: *Tim Woodruff*: A. Devlin. *His Honor*: B. Reeves. *William Travers*: J. Van Norden. *Chauncey M*: Mr. Fairbrother. *Pulitzer*: Mr. Milton. *Crocker*: C. Saum. *Cornelius Vanderbilt*: Mr. Gates. *Aldrich*: Mr. Reinhardt. *Parkhurst*: D. Oatman. *Dewey*: C. Hessong. *Carnegie*: A. Youngs. *Loeb*: Mr. Bell. *Mr. Morgan*: C. Scribner.

Finale
Entire Company

1910.19 UP AND DOWN BROADWAY

A more or less incoherent resume of current events, theatrical and otherwise (Musical Revue) in Two Acts, 11 Scenes. Book by Edgar Smith. Music by Jean Schwartz, (Irving Berlin, Ted Snyder). Lyrics by William Jerome. Staged by William J. Wilson. Scenery by Lee Lash Studio. Costumes by Melville Ellis. Orchestra under the direction of Oscar Radin. Produced by Sam S. and Lee Shubert (Inc.), (Lew Fields). Opened 18 July 1910 at the Casino Theatre and closed 17 September 1910 after 72 performances.

CAST: *IMMORTALS*: *Momus*, janitor of the High Brow Club on Mt. Parnassus: EDDIE FOY. *Apollo*, president of the club: GEORGE ANDERSON. *Erato*, a high brow poet: MARTIN BROWN. *Nabba*, Parnassus policeman: Harry MacDonough, Jr. *Vicius*, club member: ERNEST HARE. *Terpsichore*, muse of dancing: VIDA WHITMORE. *Thalia*, muse of comedy: Phyllis Gordon. *Euterpe*: Mae Dealy. *Caliope*: Jessica Worth. *Pythagoras*, club-page: Marguerite St. Clair. *Lucius*, club-page: Sylvia Clarke. *Genus*, club-page: Peggy Merritt. *Melpomene*, muse of tragedy, with a mission to highbrowize Broadway: EMMA CARUS.

MORTALS: *George Bumpkin*, a tired business man: Frederick Powell. *Isador Schlameil*, a pants manufacturer: James B. Carson. *Henry Write*, a book-keeper: Harry MacDonough, Jr. *Harry Soakem*, a baseball fan: Hans Robert. *Mrs. Shark*, a landlady: Ricca Allen. *Mrs. Bumpkin*, a stout lady: May Donahue. *Miss Frite*, a young lady: ANNA WHEATON. *Lazia*, a servant lady: Eva Williams. *Vivian Bumpkin*, a young lady: Jessica Worth. *Bunco Bill*, a ticket speculator: Hans Robert. *Dutch McGee*, an Eastsider: Robert Milliken. *Willie Run*, a messenger boy: Robert Milliken. *Officer Casey*, of the traffic squad: ERNEST HARE. *Sing Hi*, a chink: Henry Holt. *Chu Gum*, a chop suey dispenser: Gene Foxcroft. *Jean Garcon*, a head waiter: Harry MacDonough, Jr. *An Umpire*, the usual favorite: Robert Milliken. *Gilligan*, a baseball god: Harold Robe. *George Lushington*, a swell: Ray Dodge. *Mazie Malborough*, a show girl: Gloria Pierce. *Mrs. Shopleigh*, a vaudeville patron: Mae Dealy. *Mrs. Shirkflat*, another: Marie Flood. *Fan Tan*, a Chinese maiden: Melissa Ten Eyck. *Entertainers at the Cafe d'Lobster*: IRVING BERLIN, TED SNYDER. *Special Dancing Feature*: ADELAIDE and J. J. HUGHES.

Opening Chorus: *Pages*: Misses Sylvia Clark, Marguerite St. Clair, Thea Howard, Peggy Merritt, Agnes Richter, Martha Hines, Frankie Rice, Ammie Berry, Armitage, Roderiguez, Kramer, Adele Marie. *Greek Dancing Girls*: Misses Edna Bates, Edna Dodsworth, Frances Halliday, Betty Lavalliere. *Poets*: Misses Marie Flood Patsy Hamilton, Erma LaPierre, Blanche Mell, Lillian Barnett, Lillian Gay, Betty Best, Anna Ber, Lillian Darlington, Bertha Caruthers, Maude Inglesby. *Muses*: Misses Ada Howell, Morien Huben, Blanche Marr, Susie Kerwin, Marguerite Meyers, Beatrice Rose. *Greeks*: Messrs. Potter, Childs, Jones, Schwartz, Rhoder, Ryder, Hagner, Lyman, Holmes, Johns, Merrick, Willingham, Kennedy, Robinson. *Speculators*: Messrs. Hagner, Ryder, Cutler, Jones, Kennedy, Potter, Holmes, Lyman, Mack, Childs, Johns, Robinson, Willingham, Kingsley, Roe, Merrick. *Broadway Girls*: Misses Marr. Huben, Douglass, Meyers, Wier, Howell, Rose, Flood, Berg, Wright, Grailing, Darlington, Hamilton. *Girlies*: Misses St. Clair, Halliday, Warrington, Bates, Dottsworth, Best, Barnett, Rice, Flood, Grayling, LaPierre, Caruthers, Berg, Hamilton, Edwards, Darlington. *Kelly's Ghost*: Misses Berry, St. Clair, Carr, Howard, Rice, Merritt, Armitage, Rodriguez, Richter, Marie, Bates, Lavalliere, Himes. *Military Cadets*: Entire Ensemble. *Chinatown Visitors*: Misses Rubin, Howell, Langhorne, Meyer, Inglesby, Grayling, Rose. *Spanish Ladies*: Misses Darlington, Rose, Edwards, Caruthers, Inglesby, Lavalliere. *Spanish Boys*: Misses Rhoder, Robinson, Jones, Potter, Kennedy, Merrick. *Dollar Princesses*: Misses Langhorne, Grayling, Flood, Wier, Hamilton, Berg, Warrington, LaPierre. *Chocolate Soldiers*: Messrs. Dodge, Hagner, Robe, Cutler, Lyman, Ryder, Mack.

Act 1, Scene 1: High Brow Club upon Mt. Parnassus. *Scene 2*: En route to Earth and Broadway. *Scene 3*: Mrs. Shark's Boarding House in New York. *Scene 4*: Herald Square, in front of Macy's. *Scene 5*: Actors' Field Day at the Polo Grounds.

Act 2, Scene 1: Interior of the Cafe d'Lobster. *Scene 2*: Exterior of the Cafe d'Lobster. *Scene 3*: Chinatown. *Scene 4*: Lobby of the Tabloid Opera Hosue. *Scene 5*: The stage of same, showing four scenes of vaudeville performance. *Scene 6*: Mt. Parnassus.

ACT 1

Opening Ensemble
The High Brow Club

"I Am Melpomene" (Trio)
E. Carus, P. Gordon, V. Whitmore

"Have a Smile with Momus" (Song)
E. Foy

"Go On Your Mission" (Ensemble)
G. Anderson, E. Carus, P. Gordon, E. Foy

"Come Down to Earth, (My Dearie)" (Duet)
G. Anderson, P. Gordon

"I Want a Lot of Girlie Girlies" (Song)
G. Anderson, Ensemble

"(I'm) The Ghost of Kelly" (Song)
E. Foy

"The Pretty Little Girl Inside" (Duet)
M. Brown, V. Whitmore

"(In) 1861" (Song)
E. Carus
(*Music by* Albert Von Tilzer. *Lyrics by* Junie McCree.)

"The Gathering of the Clans"/"(Everybody Is) Bagpipe Crazy"[20]

(Finale)
Ensemble

ACT 2

Opening Chorus
Ensemble

"The Spanish Fandango Rag" (Dreamy Fandango Tune)(Trio)
M. Brown, V. Whitmore, H. Robert

"(Sweet) Italian Love"[21]/"(Oh,) That Beautiful Rag"
I. Berlin,T. Snyder
(*Music by* Ted Snyder. *Lyrics by* Irving Berlin.)

"Chocolate Soldier" (Octette)

"In Chinatown" (Song and Ensemble)
E. Hare, Ensemble

"The Dope Fiend" (Duet and Dance)
M. Brown, M. Ten Eyck
(*Music by* Melville Ellis.)

[18]Dropped for subsequent tour.
[19]See Act 2, Scene 1 above for specialties.
[20]For subsequent tour, replaced by "Chocolate Soldier" Octette from Act 2.
[21]Dropped from production when Berlin and Snyder departed the tour.

"(I'm) The Lily" (Song)
E. Foy
"Mary Ann" (Song)
E. Carus, Ensemble
(*Music by* Albert Von Tilzer. *Lyrics by* Junie McCree.)
"The Ticket Speculators"
H. Robert, Ensemble
"The Military Gilde" (March)
A. Wheaton, Ensemble
Special Dance Features[22]
Adelaide, J. J. Hughes
"(My Operatic) Samson and Delilah"[23]
E. Carus, Ensemble
"When Sist' Tetrazin' Met Cousin Carus" (Duet)
Mr. Diamond, P. Gordon
(*Music by* Louis A. Hirsch and Melville Gideon. *Lyrics by* Edward Madden.)
Finale—Medley
Company

1910.20

THE ECHO

A Summer Singing and Dancing Frolic (Musical Play) in Two Acts. Book and lyrics by William LeBaron, Deems Taylor. Music by Deems Taylor. Staged by Fred G. Latham. Dances arranged by William Rock, Al Holbrook. Costumes designed by Serge de Salomko. Orchestra under the direction of DeWitt C. Coolman. Produced by Charles Dillingham. Opened 17 August 1910 at the Globe Theatre and closed 1 October 1910 after 53 performances.[24]

CAST: *Rudolph W. Sylvester*, a wealthy soap manufacturer: JOHN E. HAZZARD. *Dick Brown*, manager of the "Echo House": DOUGLAS STEVENSON. *Don Ferris*, in love: George White. *Bob Ferris*, in love: Ben Ryan. *Reggie Brewster*, the life of the party: JOSEPH HERBERT, JR. *Cyrus Adams*, a professional hermit: Edgar Halstead. *Horace Randolph*, Echo House bell boy: John J. Scannell. *Mrs. Brewster*, a widow from Boston: EVELYN CARRINGTON. *Molly Brewster*, her daughter: EVA FALLON. *Edith Sylvester, Dorothy Sylvester*, Rudolph W.'s nieces: Rose [Roszika] Dolly, Jennie [Yancsi] Dolly. *Laura Short*, a newspaper correspondent: Georgie Drew Mendum. *Mrs. Sophie Adams*: ANNIE YEAMANS. *Kate*, head waitress at the Echo House: BESSIE McCOY. *Sue, Settle*: waitresses: Angie Weimers, Lillian Rice. *Mr. Bruin*: Arthur Hill.

Summer Boarders, Waitresses, etc.: *Riding Girls*: Louise Donovan, Bertha Morelle, Clara Eckstrom. *Tennis Girls*: Alice Belga, Lillian Nicholson, Lucille Storer. *Golf Girls*: Leila Sprague, Alma Benson, Helen Gilmore. *Canoe Girls*: Blanche Trapp, Verna Dalton, Grace Wendell. *Dancing Girls*: Lillian Rice, Angie Weimers, Olivia Depp, Norma Thomas, Ruth Tompkins, Virginia Calvert, Bonnie Clark, Violet Zell, Gladys Zell, Jean Barnet. *Riding Men*: E. H. Randall, Jr., R. S. Hunason, Howard Dyatt. *Tennis Men*: W. A. DeVens, R. C. Bosch, Louis Strangard. *Golf Men*: Irving Carpenter, E. H. Bromley, Fred Perine. *Canoe Men*: Roy Lloyd, Carl McBride, Earl Cavanaugh. *Picnic Entertainers*: Toots Paka and Her Trio from the Hawaiian Islands.

Act 1: Office and living room of the Echo House, New England. Present time.

Act 2: A Grotto in the Mountains back of the House.

MUSICAL NUMBERS[25]
"The Advertising Man"
D. Stevenson
"To Be Continued"
G. White, B. Ryan, E. Carrington, G. D. Mendum
"Since Jane Heard a Popular Song"
R. Dolly
"The Things You Think Are Not the Things You Say"
J. E. Hazzard
"Clothes Make the Soldier Man"
J. Herbert, Jr., Chorus
"The Course of True Love"
G. White, B. Ryan, R. Dolly, J. Dolly
"Poor Old Solomon"
J. E. Hazzard
"All the World Loves a Lover"
D. Stevenson
"They Never Think About the Man"
D. Stevenson, E. Fallon

MUSICAL SCORE AND INTERPOLATIONS[26]
"Jolly the Boarders Along"
"Mountain Maiden"
"The Little Echo"
"Song of the Songs"
"Never Too Late to Learn"
"My Guiding Star" (When in Joy or Gladness)
(*Music and Lyrics by* James R. Brewers and Edward B. Claypoole.)
"Heigh Ho"
(*Music by* Nat Ayer. *Lyrics by* A.Seymour Brown.)
"Too-Ral-I-Oo-Ral-I-Ay"
"(It's) Never Too Late to Learn"
"I'm Waiting Here for Kate"
(*Music and Lyrics by* Worton David and George Arthurs.)
"I Don't Want to Be a Soldier Boy"
(*Music by* Karl Hoschna. *Lyrics by* George V. Hobart.)
"The Newport Glide"
(*Music by* Jean Schwartz. *Lyrics by* William Jerome.)
"Whistle When You're Lonely"
(*Music by* Jerome Kern. *Lyrics by* M. E. Rourke.)
"The Yankee Doodle Guards"
(*Music by* DeWitt Coolman. *Lyrics by* John L. Golden.)
"You're Just the Girlie That I Adore"
(*Music by* Nathaniel D. Ayer. *Lyrics by* A. Seymour Brown.)
"The French Fandango"
(*Music by* Christiné. *Lyrics by* John L. Golden.)
"Skiddy-mer-rink-a-doo Means I Love You"
(*Music by* Al Piantadosi. *Lyrics by* Felix Feist.)

1910.21

OUR MISS GIBBS

The Gaiety Theatre, London Musical Comedy in Two Acts. Book and lyrics by James T. Tanner. Music by Ivan Caryll and Lionel Monckton. Staged by Thomas Reynolds. Costumes by Lord and Taylor, Dazian. Orchestra under the direction of W. T. Francis. Orchestra under the direction of W. T. Francis. Produced by Charles Frohman. Opned 29 August 1910 at the Knickerbocker Theatre and closed 22 October 1910 after 57 performances.[27]

CAST: *Hon. Hughie Pierrepoint*, an amateur criminal: ERNEST LAMBART. *The Earl of St. Ives*, Lord Eynsford's father: Ernest A. Elton. *Slithers*, an American crook: BERT LESLIE. *Mr. Toplady*, manager at Garrod's: Arthur Laceby. *Lord Eynsford*, in love with Mary: CRAUFURD KENT. *Mr. Beavis*, the Earl's family solicitor: Reginald Sheldrick. *A Taxi Cabby*: Victor LeRoy. *Mr. Amalfy*: Gilbert Coleman. *Timothy Gibbs*, Mary's cousin: FRED WRIGHT. *Lord Arthur*: Edward Leech. *Lord Percy*: Roger Davis. *Lord Harold*: H. Edelman. *Lord Cyril*: Oliver Sterling. *Lord Alfred*: Ralph O'Brien. *Lord Tom Noddy*: Eddie Morris. *Mary Gibbs*, "Our Miss Gibbs": PAULINE CHASE. *Madame Jeanne*, modiste at Garrod's: JEAN ALWYN. *Lady Elizabeth Thanet*, engaged to Lord Eynsford: JULIA JAMES. *The Duchess of Minster*, Lady Thanet's mother: Daisy Belmore. *Mrs. Farquhar*, an impecunious woman of fashion: Mollie Lowell. *Clarita*: KITTY MASON. *Irish girls (3)*: *Kathleen*: Gertrude Vanderbilt. *Sheilah*: Marion Mosby. *Nora*: Ethel Wheeler. *Lady Connie*: Clara Pitt. *Lady Sybil*: Margaret MacKenzie. *Lady Trixie*: Henrietta Pellard. *Lady Angela*: Freda Braun. *Lady Muriel*: Margaret von Keese. *Lady Gwen*: Bert Rice.

Buyers: Misses Ethel Kelly, Helen Morrison, Doris Cameron, Irene [Ina] Claire, Bessie Frewen, Sara Carr, Madelain DeBoeuf, Adel Kornan, Anna Kuehl, Maybelle Dean, Helen Dixon, Natalie Dana, Lillian Smalley. *Attendants*: Misses Nancy Butler, Florence Plunkett, Montacuse Melmen, Lillian Francis, Mary E. Martin, Madge Robinson, Della Dolson, Lillian Shepherd, Dorothy Castle, Lethea Grey, Dorothy Courtney, Mona Sartoris, Nellie Stewart, Louise Louis, Julie Newell, Edith Warren, Edna Dana, Marion Mosby, Glory Gray, Ethel Wheeler, Lillian Stair. (*Gentlemen of the Ensemble*: Edward Leech, Roger Davis, H. Edelman, Oliver Sterling, Ralph O'Brien, Eddie Morris.)

Act 1: Garrod's Department Stores.

Act 2: A Japanese Garden at the Jap-Anglo Exhibition.

---

[22]Dropped for subsequent tour and replaced by:
Special Dance ("While Under the Jungle Moon")
Rhea and Rayo
(*Music by* Nat Vincent.)
[23]Dropped during the tour.
[24]Settings uncredited.
[25]Songs not listed in any programs. List below taken from published vocal score to an earlier production by the New York University's Varsity Dramatic Club, published by William Maxwell Music, New York, 1910.
[26]First five songs published by Joseph W. Stern, NYC, 1910.
[27]Settings uncredited.

ACT 1

Opening Chorus (and Entrance of Irish Girls)
(*Music by* Lionel Monckton. *Lyrics by* Percy Greenbank.)

"(Bridesmaid's) Sextette"
Bridesmaids
(*Music by* Lionel Monckton.)

"Hats" (Song)
J. Alwyn, Chorus
(*Music by* Ivan Caryll. *Lyrics by* Percy Greenbank, Adrian Ross.)

"Betty's Advice" (Song)
J. James, Chorus
(*Music by* Jerome Kern. *Lyrics by* Frederick Day.)

"Correct" (Sextette)
Dudes
(*Music by* Lionel Monckton. *Lyrics by* Adrian Ross.)

"Mary" (Song)
P. Chase, Dudes
(*Music by* Lionel Monckton. *Lyrics by* Adrian Ross.)

"Bertie the Bounder" (Song)
E. Lambart, Bridesmaids
(*Music by* Clarke. *Lyrics by* George Grossmith.)

"Come, Tiny Goldfish to Me" (Duet)
F. Wright, G. Vanderbilt
(*Music by* Harry Marlowe. *Lyrics by* Jerome Kern.)

"Will You Sing This Glee with Me" (Song)
B. Leslie, Chorus
(*Music by* George Arthurs. *Lyrics by* Worton David.)

"Not That Sort of Person" (Duet)
P. Chase, E. Lambart
(*Music by* Lionel Monckton. *Lyrics by* George Grossmith.)

Finale

ACT 2

Opening Chorus

"March of Foreign Commissioners" (Trio)

"Yorkshire" (Song)
P. Chase, Girls
(*Music by* Lionel Monckton. *Lyrics by* Ralph Roberts.)

"Gentlemen" (An English Gentleman) (Sextette)
E. Lambart, A. Laceby, B. Leslie, C. Kent, F. Wright, [Director]
(*Music by* Lionel Monckton. *Lyrics by* Percy Greenbank.)

"Bedtime at the Zoo" (Song and Waltz)
J. James, Chorus
(*Music by* Lionel Monckton. *Lyrics by* Percy Greenbank, Leslie Mayne.)

"I Don't Want You to be a 'Sister' to Me"
P. Chase, E. Lambart
(*Music by* Jerome Kern. *Lyrics by* Frederick Day.)

"I Love MacIntosh" (Song)
(*Music by* Harold Lonsdale. *Lyrics by* George Arthur.)

"Dougal"
J. Aylwin

"Eight Little Girls" (Song)
E. Lambart, Chorus
(*Music by* Jerome Kern. *Lyrics by* M. E. Rourke.)

"Our Farm" (Duet)
P. Chase, F. Wright
(*Music and Lyrics by* Lionel Monckton.)

Dance
K. Mason

March of the Creottes
Chorus

"Moonstruck" (Song)
P. Chase, Chorus
(*Music and Lyrics by* Lionel Monckton.)

"A Little Change" (Duet)
B. Leslie, F. Wright

Finale

1910.22 MADAME SHERRY

A French Vaudeville (Musical Play) in Three Acts. American book and lyrics by Otto Hauerbach [Harbach]. (Adapted from the German of the same name by Benno Jacobson from a libretto by Maurice Ordonneau and Paul Burani, music by Hugo Felix, and the English version adapted by Charles E. Hands and Adrian Ross, produced by George Edwardes.) Music by Karl Hoschna. Staged by George Lederer. Costumes by Mme. Francis, Kate Keeler. Settings designed by Ernest Albert. Orchestra under the direction of Hans S. Linné. Produced by H. H. Frazee, George Lederer and A. H. Woods. Opened 30 August 1910 at the New Amsterdam Theatre and closed 11 March 1911 after 231 performances.

CAST (in order of appearance): *Lulu*, an actress and dancer, Edward's sweetheart: FRANCES DEMAREST. *Catherine*, Edward's housekeeper, Phillippe's wife: ELIZABETH MURRAY. *Phillippe*, janitor, Catherine's husband: IGNACIO MARTINETTI. *Edward Sherry*, a New York man-about-town, nephew of Theophilus Sherry: JACK GARDNER. *Leonard Gomez*, son of the President of Venezuela: JOHN REINHARD. *Pepita*, Leonard's sweetheart: DOROTHY JARDON. *Yvonne Sherry*, a convent girl, niece of Theophilus Sherry: LINA ABARBANELL. *(Uncle) Theophilus Sherry* a millionaire connoisseur of Greek art: RALPH HERZ. *Hectar*, Head steward on the yacht *Yvonne*:. Frank Johnson. (*Bobby*, a guest: Joseph C. Smith.[28])

Pupils at the Sherry School of Aesthetic Dancing: Helen Van Ness: May Hanna. *Florence Brevoort*: Almanore Francis. *Loy De Puyster*: Irene Palmer. *Irene Vandervelt*: Alice Palmer. *Myrtle Stuyvesant*: May Thompson. *Ruth Amsterdam*: Evelyn Westbrook. *Florence Astoria*: Lillian Tucker. *Bertha Von Hutton*: Marcelle Lamb. *Eleanor de Peyster*: Elizabeth Nelson. *Marion Pallerson*: Leslie Stose. *Betty Palmer*: Roselle Lyons. *Dorothy Pelham*: Naomi Dale.

Act 1: Edward Sherry's studio, Manhattan. A morning in July at the present time.

Act 2: The salon of the yacht *Yvonne*, New York Harbor. Same evening.

Act 3: After-deck of the yacht *Yvonne*. Off Coney Island. Same night.

ACT 1[29]

"Aesthetic Dancing"
F. Demarest, Dancing Class

"Theophilus"
J. Gardner, F. Demarest

"Every Little Movement (Has a Meaning All Its Own)"
F. Demarest, J. Reinhard

"The Kiss You Gave"
D. Jardon, F. Demarest, J. Reinhard

"Uncle Says I Mustn't, So I Won't"
L. Abarbanell, J. Reinhard, F. Demarest

"The Birth of the Butterfly"
L. Abarbanell, Fifth Avenue Girls

"You Can't Argue"
R. Herz

"The Smile She Means for You"
L. Abarbanell, J. Gardner, F. Demarest, J. Reinhard, R. Herz, E. Murray

"The Love Dance"
L. Abarbanell, J. Gardner

ACT 2

"Athletic Prancing"
Sherry's Pupils

"Won't Some One Take Me Home"
E. Murray, Girls

"The Other Fellow"
L. Abarbanell, I. Martinetti

"The Dublin Rag"
E. Murray
(*Music by* Phil Schwartz. *Lyrics by* Harold Atteridge.)

"I'm All Right"
L. Abarbanell

"Terzetto Buffo"
R. Herz, F. Demarest, J. Reinhard, I. Martinetti, E. Murray, J. Gardner
(*Music by* Hugo Felix.)

"The Birth of Passion"
J. Gardner, L. Abarbanell

"Off for a Sail" (Finale)

---

[28]Omitted from opening night program, but included thereafter.

[29]Interpolated late in New York run or for subsequent tour:

"When I Woke Up This Morning"
E. Murray
(*Music and Lyrics by* James V. Monaco.)

"Good-bye Old Gal (I'm Going Away on the 2:10 Train)"
Anna Boyd
(*Music by* Albert Von Tilzer. *Lyrics by* Lew Brown.)

ACT 3

An Evening on Deck:[30]

Serenade; "Dunnerwetter"
L. Abarbanell

"Mr. Johnson, Good Night"
E. Murray

"Put Your Arms Around Me, Honey (I Never Knew Any Girl Like You)"
E. Murray
(*Music by* Harry Von Tilzer. *Lyrics by* Junie McCree.)

"The Mad Madrid and the Dance of Danger"
D. Jardon, J. C. Smith
(*Music by* Harry Von Tilzer. *Lyrics by* Edward Madden.)

Intermezzo (*Music by* Hugo Felix.)

"I Want to Play House with You"
L. Abarbanell, J. Gardner

"We Are Only Poor, Weak Mortals (After All)"
R. Herz

"The Seduction"
R. Herz, F. Demarest, D. Jardon, E. Murray
(*Music by* Hugo Felix.)

Finale

1910.23 THE INTERNATIONAL CUP

A Triple Bill of a Spectacular Melodrama with Music (The International Cup) in 7 Scenes, The Ballet of "Niagra" in Two Tableaux, and a Spectacular Melodrama (The Earthquake) in 5 Scenes. Play by R. H. Burnside. Music and lyrics by Manuel Klein. Staged by R. H. Burnside. Settings designed by Arthur Voegtlin. Lighting by Joseph Eisner. Orchestra under the direction of Manuel Klein. Produced by the Messrs. Shubert. Opened 3 September 1910 at the Hippodrome and closed 13 May 1911 after 333 performances.

ACT 1

THE INTERNATIONAL CUP, A Spectacular Melodrama with Music in 7 Scenes. Written and produced by R. H. Burnside. Music and lyrics by Manuel Klein. Scenic effects designed by Arthur Voegtlin. Costumes designed by Mme. Ziebarth. Musical director, Manuel Klein.

CAST: *Colonel David Carewe*, a Confederate veteran: W. H. CLARK. *Roy Carewe*, his son: BEN WAINWRIGHT. *Jasper Grantham*, his lawyer: George Adams. *John Gordon*, who fought with the Northern Army: EDWIN A. CLARK. *Nancy Gordon*, his daughter: SABRY DORSELL. *Mrs. Leslie*, his sister: Mabel Dwight. *Will Leslie*, his nephew: Herbert Mansfield. *Harvey Denton*, an adventurer: ALBERT FROOM. *General Giradot* of the French Army: Gordon Sackville. *Mme. Giradot*, his wife: NANETTE FLACK. *The Duke of Dulchester*: Harry Jackson. *Lady Alice Duffshire*, his sister: Mae Bronte. *George Gulliver, Daisy Dashaway*. an Eloping Couple: NAT HARRIS, MARGARET TOWNSEND. *Matilda Wiggles*, Daisy's Aunt: Caroline Weir. *Sam Wilton, Ira Harris*, Wireless Operators at Seaview, New Jersey: Jack Warren, J. H. Taylor. *Captain Wallace* of the Lifeboat Crew: James R. Adams. *Circus Proprietor*: Gwilyn Edwards. *The Mayor*: HARRY DALE. *Sergeant Lefevre*: HARRY DALE. *Deaf Man*: Charles Ravel. *"Silvers"*: Himself. *Marceline*: Marceline. *Clowns*: Charles Ravel, James R. Adams, George H. Adams, Melise, Stanley Ferguson, Jack Warren, Harry Shaw, Abe Aronson, Mike Hefferman, Angelo Romeo.

Scene 1: A small country town near Paris. Arrival of the Circus: The Circus Performance. *Scene 2*: Railroad Station. *Scene 3*: The Wireless Station at Seaview. *Scene 4*: The Wreck. *Scene 5*: The Boardwalk at Seaview. *Scene 6*: The Yacht Race. *Scene 7*: Garden of Gordon's Summer Home.

MUSICAL NUMBERS

Scene 1

Opening Chorus
Chorus

"The Fighting Regiment"
H. Dale, Chorus

"Hail the Hero of Today" (Finale)
Principals, Chorus

The Circus Performance:
Clown Carnival; Louise Stickney (Equestrienne); The Metzettis (Sensational Aerial Artists); Lidia & Albino (Equilibrists); Lee Serano (Marvelous Hand Balancers); The Three Houcks (French Sensational Equestrians); The Four Lukens (Famous High-Bar Artists); Powers' Elephants; Mueller's Lions; Spellman's Bears.

Scene 2

"Take a Trip to the Seaside" (Song)
M. Townsend, N. Harris

Scene 5

"Loving" (Duet)
S. Dorsell, B. Wainwright, Chorus

"Yachting" (Sailing in a Yacht) (Song)
E. A. Clark, Chorus

(The "Baby Number")
(Chorus)

Scene 7

"The Sons of Every Nation" (Song)
N. Flack

"The North and South of Today" (There Is No North or South Today) (Song)
E. A. Clark, Chorus

ACT 2

The Ballet of "Niagra," in Two Tableaux. Written and produced [staged] by R. H. Burnside. Suggested and invented by Arthur Voegtlin. Music composed and directed by Manuel Klein. Dances arranged by Vincenzo Romeo. Scenic effects designed by Arthur Voegtlin. Costumes designed by Alfredo Edel.

CAST: *Chief Keneu* "The War Eagle": VINCENZO ROMEO. *Ioneta*, his daughter: ALBERTINA RASCH. *Chief Tak-Qua-Menaw* "Rushing River" at war with Keneu: SILVERS OAKLEY. *Os-se-o* "Worker of Magic," Keneu's Medicine Man: Signor Bonfiglio. *The Spirit of the Waters*: NANETTE FLACK. *Chief Mish-E-Mowka* "Great Bear of the Mountain": George H. Adams. *Chief Mon-Da-Min*, "Friend of Man": James R. Adams. *Chief Kwasind* "The Strong One": CHARLES RAVEL. *Chief Way-Wass-I-Mo* "The Lightning': George Melville.

Scene 1: An Indian Encampment. After the Battle. *Scene 2*: The Falls of Niagara.

MUSICAL NUMBERS

"The Legend of Niagara"

ACT 3

THE EARTHQUAKE, A Spectacular Melodrama in 5 Scenes. Written and produced [staged] by R. H. Burnside. Suggested and invented by Arthur Voegtlin. Music composed and conducted by Manuel Klein. Scenic effects designed by Arthur Voegtlin.

CAST: *President Manuel Carrera*: HARRY JACKSON. *General Zeloyo*, The Insurgent Leader: ALBERT FROOM. *Lieutenant Jose Palazzo*: EDWIN A. CLARK. *Captain Estrada*: Bert Wainwright. *Officer of General Zeloyo's Army*: George H. Adams. *Manuel*, a Planter: Nat Harris. *Moraz*, a Planter: Harry Dale. *Benito*: Jack Warren. *Pedro*, Innkeeper: J. H. Taylor. *Kuna Capac*, a Young Aztec: HERBERT MANSFIELD. *Amara*, His Sister: MAE BRONTE. *Juanita*, President's Carrera's Daughter: MABEL DWIGHT. *Colonel Morales*: Gordon Sackville. *Colonel Paradaz*: Charles Ravel. *Captain Lopez*: George Melville. *Queen of the Aztecs*: NANETTE FLACK. *High Priest of the Aztecs*: W. H. CLARK. *Messenger*: James R. Adams.

Scene 1: Camp of the Revolutionists in the Town of Peraquipa. *Scene 2*: On the way to the Capitol. The Race for Life. *Scene 3*: Outside the Capitol, Caragua. *Scene 4*: The Plaza of the Capitol. The Earthquake. *Scene 5*: The Valley of Gold. The Temple of the Moon.

MUSICAL NUMBERS

Procession; Grand March; Finale

1910.24 HANS, THE FLUTE PLAYER

A Comic Opera in Three Acts. Adapted from the French opéra-comique 'Hans, le joueur de flûte' by Maurice Vaucaire and Georges Mitchell. Music by M. Louis Ganne. English lyrics by A. St. John Brennan. Staged by Jacques Coini. Ballet arranged by Pauline Verhoevan. Scenic department,

[30]The musical detail of An Evening on Deck did not appear in the opening night programs (except for "Mr. Johnson, Good Night") but does appear in programs during the first month of the run. "Dunnerwetter" and "Mr. Johnson, Good Night" dropped during the run. For subsequent tour they were replaced by:

"Kissing By Cable"
L. Abarbanell

"He's Coming Back"
E. Murray

Fritz Weisse, Julius F. Dowe. Costumes by Landolff of Paris. Orchestra under the direction of Josiah Zuro. Produced by Oscar Hammerstein I. Opened 20 September 1910 at the Manhattan Opera House and closed 26 November 1910 after 79 performances.

CAST: *The Prologue*: Mr. (FRANK) DOANE. *Hans*: GEORGES CHADEL. *Yoris*: Frank Pollock. *(Burgomaster) Pipperman*: GEORGE W. CALLAHAN. *Van Pott*: FRANK DOANE. *Peetronius*: St. Clair Bayfield. *Willum*: Frank Coombs. *Tantendorff*: Paul L. Warren. *Loskitch*: B. Milton. *Steinbeck*: L. Derman. *Karteifle*: F. C. Chapman. *Night Watchman*: E. Hollander. *A Sergeant*: Mr. Schwenecke. *Lisbeth*: Sophie Brandt. *Ketchen*: Olive Ulrich. *Frau Pipperman*: Alice Gentle. *Else*: Blanche Lipton. *Citizens, Aldermen, Civil Guards, Musicians, Fisherboys, Fisher Girls, Dolls, Milkwomen, Servants, Children.*

The action takes place in Milkatz, the rich capital of an imaginary country, situated between Holland and Flanders.

Act 1: Public Square before the City Hall in Milkatz.

Act 2: Dining Room of Burgomaster Pipperman.

Act 3: The Public Square during Carnival Time.

MUSICAL NUMBERS[31]

"Ah, I Laugh"
"Buy a Kiss"
"Entrance of Hans"
"Father Is a Business Man"
"I Come from Afar"
"I Love Him"
"Listen to My Prayer"
"National Hymn"
"Pray Excuse"
"Prepare the Dolls"
"Read My Sighs"
"Set the Table"
"Song of the Dolls"
"Song of the Flute"
"The Time of Dolls Is Past"
"Triumphant Entry of Hans"
"You Do Not Understand"

1910.25 HE CAME FROM MILWAUKEE

A Musical Comedy in Two Acts. Book by Mark Swan and Edgar Smith. Music by Ben M. Jerome, (Melville Ellis) and Louis A. Hirsch. Lyrics by Edward Madden. Staged by Sidney Ellison. Scenery by H. Robert Law. Costumes by Melville Ellis. Orchestra udner the direction of Ben M. Jerome. Produced by Sam S. and Lee Shubert, Inc. Opened 21 September 1910 at the Casino Theatre and closed 31 December 1910 after 117 performances.

CAST: *Herman von Schellenvein*: SAM BERNARD. *Napoleon Ravachal*, conspirator, of Zurach: LOUIS HARRISON. *Egbert Keskiesko*, Duke of Zurack: GEORGE ANDERSON. *Bruce Chetwynde* companion to the Duke: MARTIN BROWN. *Brokaski*, general of the army in Zurach: Henry Norman. *Lestichy*, conspirator and companion to Napoleon: Charles Burrows. *Lieutenant*, of the army of Zurach: Paul Musaeus. *Sentry*, of the army of Zurach, a conspirator: Henry Holt. *Sergeant*, of the army of Zurach: Dolph Ryan. *Porter*, of the hotel in Ostend: Frank Sargent. *Footman* to the Duke of Zurach: Bert Lawrence. *Constance Harvey*, in love with the Duke: WINONA WINTER. *Terriffa*, circus queen, daughter of the Duke of Zerda: AMELIA SUMMERVILLE. *Betty Winthrop*, cousin to Constance, in love with Bruce: ADELE ROWLAND. *Mrs. Matthew Harvey*, of Ft. Wayne, Indiana, mother of Constance: Alice Gordon. *Leska*, a loyal subject to the Duke: NELLA BERGEN.

Heiresses: Evelyn Hope, Ethel Weir, Mary Mooney, Peggy Goulding, Hortense Kelly, Albertina Sargent, Roselle Lyons, Viola Williams, Vennetta Pressler, Virginia Steinhardt, Bertha Perkins. *Gypsies*: Adele Cheridah, Monte Melman, Anna Stone, Octavia Hague, Annette Woodman, Mae Donnelly, Leota Armitage, Trixie Whiteford, Vera DeFord, Cletoce Caldwell. *Balloon Girls, Postal Girls, Fishermans*: Katherine Grant, Anita Francesca, Estelle Francesca, Billie Grant, Daisy Thompson, May Stone, Lillian Howell, May Borden, Rita White, Margaret Blackburne. *Bohemian Girls*: Adele Cheridah, Monte Melmen, Anna Stone, Octavia Hague, Annette Woodman, Mae Donnelly, Leota Armitage, Trixie Whiteford, Vera DeFord, Cletoce Caldwell, Katherine Grant, Anita Francesca, Estelle Francesca, Billie Grant, Daisy Thompson, May Stone, Lillian Howell, May Borden, Rita White. *Frenchmen, English Lords, Soldiers*: Herbert Connor, Frank Meyrose, Bernard Wallenstein, Bert Lawrence, Joseph Starr, Edwin Tester, Homer Potts, Dolph Ryan, Frank Sergeant, Guy Premo, Louix Berg.

Act 1: Hotel in Ostend.

Act 2: Street in Zurach in front of the Palace.

ACT 1[32]

Opening Chorus
"In Gypsy Land"
N. Berger, Chorus
"When We Are Married to You and Me"[33] (If We Were Married)(Duet)
M. Brown, A. Rowland
(*Music by* Louis A. Hirsch.)
"Love Is Like a Red, Red Rose"
G. Anderson, W. Winter
"Lena" (Bring Back My Lena to Me)[34]
S. Bernard
(*Music by* Ted Snyder. *Lyrics by* Irving Berlin.)
"(Merry) Wedding Bells" (Quartette)
G. Anderson, W. Winter, A. Rowland, M. Brown, Chorus
Circus Ensemble[35]
A. Summerville, Chorus
"The Zinga Zulu Man"[36] (Finale)
S. Bernard, Company

ACT 2

Opening Chorus
"Come Back to Bohemia"
N. Bergen, Chorus
"Consequences"
S. Bernard, Show Girls
"If You Were There with Me"
M. Brown, Dancers
"Tie a Red Ribbon on Me"[37]
L. Harrison
"The Sentimental Moon"
W. Winter, Chorus
"There's an Aeroplane Air About You"
A. Rowland, M. Brown, Chorus
"The Coronation"
Ensemble
Finale

1910.26 ALMA, WHERE DO YOU LIVE?

A French Vaudeville in Three Acts. American book and lyrics by George V. Hobart, adapted from the German original ('Alma, wo wohnst du?[38] by Adolf Philipp, from a French original by Paul Hervé.[39]) Music by Jean Briquet. Produced under the stage direction of Joseph Weber. Orchestra under the direction of Hugo Frey. Produced by Joseph Weber.

[31]Songs not listed in the program. List prepared from published piano vocal selections (Boosey & Co., New York, 1910).

[32]Vocal score does not identify individual composers of the songs.
[33]Published in vocal score as "If We Were Married."
[34]Dropped for subsequent tour.
[35]Dropped during the run and for subsequent tour.
[36]During the run, "The Zinga Zulu Man" and Sam Bernard's vocal credit were dropped, and replaced merely by a Finale. "Zinga Zulu Man" was moved to Act 2, replacing "If You Were There with Me."
[37]Replaced for subsequent tour by:
"The Man I Love"
Anna Wheaton (Betty Winthrop)
[38]First produced in New York in German 25 October 1909 at the Wintergarten 'Zum Schwarzen Adler" (86th Street and Third Avenue) by Adolf Philipp and his Deutsch-Amerikanische Ensemble.
[39]Kurt Gänzl in his Encyclopedia of Musical Theatre (Blackwell, 1994) suggests that Paul Hervé and Jean Briquet were nom de plumes for Adolf Philipp.

Opened 26 September 1910 at the Weber Theatre and closed 15 April 1911 after 232 performances.[40]

CAST: *Theobald*: CHARLES A. BIGELOW. *Gaston*: GEORGE W. LESLIE. *Pierre le Peach*: JOHN McCLOSKEY. *Count Bolivario*: EDOUARD DURAND. *Piquart*, a detective: GEORGE LOANE TUCKER. *Renault*, a notary: Frederick Truesdell. *Dunoir*, a minister: E. F. Nagle. *Alma*: KITTY GORDON. *Antoinette*, Theobald's wife: Georgia Harvey. *Germaine*, his daughter: Ivy Barbour. *Louise*, a housemaid: Charlotte Leslay. *Fleurette*, Alma's maid: Ethel Dovey. *Mimi*, a maid: Daisy James.

Act 1: The house of the Martins. Tuesday morning.

Act 2: Alma's Boudoir. Tuesday evening.

Act 3: The house of the Martins. Wednesday morning.

ACT 1
- "Boo-Hoo-Hoo"
  C. Leslay
- "Never More"
  C. A. Bigelow, G. W. Leslie
- "Alma"
  K. Gordon
- "Girlies" (Don't Let the Girlies Get You)
  J. McCloskey
- "Childhood Days"
  K. Gordon, J. McCloskey
- Finale

ACT 2
- "Boogie Boo"
  K. Gordon, C. A. Bigelow, G. W. Leslie
- "The Land of Beautiful Dreams"
  K. Gordon, J. McCloskey
- "Sail Home"
  K. Gordon
- "Love Me" (The Tom Cat Song)
  J. McCloskey, Ensmeble
- Finale

ACT 3
- Song
  C. A. Bigelow
- "Kiss Me, My Love" (Duet)
  K. Gordon, J. McCloskey
- Finale

1910.27 THE GIRL IN THE TRAIN

An Operetta in Three Acts. American book and lyrics by Harry B. Smith. Adapted from the Viennese original ('Die geschiedene Frau') by Victor Léon. Music by Leo Fall. Staged by Fred G. Latham. Dances arranged by Al Holbrook. Settings designed by Homer Emens. Costumes by Anna Conkwright; Wilhelm. Orchestra under the direction of Anton Heindl. Produced by Charles Dillingham. Opened 3 October 1910 at the Globe Theatre and closed 5 November 1910 after 40 performances.

CAST: *Karel Van Myrtens*, court secretary: MELVILLE STEWART. *Jana*, his wife: VERA MICHELENA. *Pieter Bockenstiegel*, Jana's father: Philip Branson. *Gonda Van Der Loo*, an actress: JUNE GREY. *Judge Van Tromp*: CLAUDE GILLINGWATER. *Van Dender*, Karel's attorney: Henry Vincent. *De Liege*, Jana's attorney: Donald Hall. *William Kroutvliet*, Karel's foster brother: James Reaney. *Martha* his wife, Jana's foster sister: Bessie Franklyn. *Cornelius Scrop*, sleeping car conductor: Martin Hayden. *Professor Wiesum*: Gilbert Clayton. *Adelaine*: Vivian Rushmore. *The Beadle*: Harry Strang.

Court Attendants, Spectators in Court, and other characters: Misses Diana Oste, Estelle Perry, Mabel Ray, Josephine Harriman, Adele Cheridah, Florence Farmer, Dorothy Perry, Constance Crane, Almyra Sessons, Gladys Meyrick, Edna Houck, Ada Holt, Stella Hansen, Alice Belga, Blanche Burnham, Madge Quest, Kitty Porter, Violet Burnham, Edna Hunter, Elsie Raymond, Dorothy Newell, Kathryn Peters. Messrs. Percy Matson, W. S. Allison, Harry Strang, Elliot Fraser, Lee Carrier, John Johnson, Harry Kittredge, F. Von Gottfried, Harry Clinton, Ray Tuller, F. S. Foley, J. S. Duffus, William Lafferty, Charles Kamp, Henry Dyer, Edgar Bryde.

Act 1: A Court Room in Amsterdam.

Act 2: The House of Karel Van Myrtens.

Act 3: Public Square in Makkum, Holland.

ACT 1[41]
- Melodrama and Song
  V. Michelena, C. Gillingwater, D. Hall
- Ensemble and Chorus
  G. Mitchell, C. Gillingwater, The Public
- "Oh, Married Life!" (Quintet)
  V. Michelena, B. Franklyn, G. Mitchell, J. Reaney, C. Gillingwater
- "I'm Fancy Free"
  J. Grey
- Chorus
  The Public
- Finale
  V. Michelena, J. Grey, B. Franklyn, C. Gillingwater, J. Reaney

ACT 2
- Opening Chorus
  B. Franklyn, J. Reaney, Chorus
- "That's Why Lots of People Marry" (Duet)
  J. Grey, G. Mitchell
- Melodrama and Chorus
  The Public
- "Children, You Seem Rather Distant to Me"
  V. Michelena, G. Mitchell, P. Branson
- "Eeny, Meeny, Miny, Mo" (March Sextet)
  J. Grey, G. Mitchell, D. Hall, C. Gillingwater, P. Branson, H. Vincent
- "You Must Be Mine, Dear" (Duet)
  V. Michelena, G. Mitchell
- Finale
  V. Michelena, J. Grey, G. Mitchell, C. Gillingwater, M. Haydon, P. Branson, Chorus

ACT 3
- Opening Chorus (Kermess Dance Song)
  B. Franklyn, J. Reaney, Chorus
- "Follow Me" (Duet)
  J. Grey, M. Haydon
- "Why Not, Why Not?" (Duet)
  V. Michelena, G. Mitchell
- Ensemble (Play the Game)
  V. Michelena, J. Grey, C. Gillingwater, P. Branson, M. Haydon, Chorus
- Finale (arranged by Max Hirschfeld)
  G. Mitchell, V. Michelena, J. Grey, C. Gillingwater, Chorus

Not in score:
- "The Girl in the Train"
- "Gonda Waltzes"
- "In My Dreams of You" [on tour]
  Sallie Fisher
  (*Music and Lyrics by* Clare Kummer.)
- "Let Us Be Married"
- "When Love Is Free"
- "The Women Get the Best of Us"
- "Goodbye"
  (*Music and Lyrics by* Clare Kummer.)

1910.28 THE CHOCOLATE SOLDIER

A Return Engagement of the Comic Opera in Three Acts.[42] Original Viennese operette ('Der tapfere Soldat') by Rudolph Bernauer and Leopold

[40] Settings, costumes uncredited. Played a return engagement 1 May 1911 at the Grand Opera House for 8 performances.

[41] Musical numbers not listed in the program. List below taken from published piano vocal score by M. Witmark & Sons, 1910. Supplement includes interpolations.

[42] First produced in New York 13 September 1909 at the Lyric Theatre for 296 performances. For Synopsis of Scenes and Musical Numbers, see original 1909 production.

Jacks [Jacobson], based on George Bernard Shaw's play "Arms and the Man." American book and lyrics by Stanislaus Stange. Music by Oscar Straus. Staged by Stanislaus Stange. Music ensembles (arranged) by Al. Holbrook. Settings by Hugo Baruch & Cie. (Act 1), Edward G. Unitt and Joseph Wickes (Acts 2 and 3). Costumes by Hugo Baruch & Cie. Orchestra under the direction of Antonio DeNovellis. Produced by Whitney Opera Company (F. C. Whitney, Director). Opened 3 October 1910 at the Circle Theatre and closed 8 October 1910 after 8 performances.

CAST (in order of appearance): *Nadina Popoff*, Daughter of Colonel Popoff: LOIS EWELL, Lilian Poli (alt.). *Aurelia Popoff*, Her Mother: MILDRED ROGERS. *Mascha*, Aurelia's Cousin: Edith Bradford. *Lieutenant Bumerli*, the "Chocolate Soldier," (a Swiss Mercenary in the employ of the Servian Army): HARRY FAIRLEIGH. *Captain Massakroff* of the Bulgarian Army: JOHN DUNSMURE. *Louka, Stephen*, Popoff's servants: Eily Spellman, William Morgan. *Colonel Casimir Popoff* of the Bulgarian Army: GEORGE O'DONNELL. *Major Alexius Spiridoff* of the Bulgarian Army, betrothed to Nadina: George Tallman. *Soldiers of Bulgarian Army, Gentry, Peasants, Weddign Guests, Villagers, Musicians, etc, etc.*

1910.29 THE DEACON AND THE LADY

A Musical Entertainment in Two Acts. Book and lyrics by George Totten Smith. Music by Alfred E. Aarons. Produced by Louis F. Werba. Staged by Alfred E. Aarons. Musical numbers staged by Eddie Clark. Scenery by D. Frank Dodge. Costumes designed by William H. Matthews. Musical director, Ivan Rudisill. Produced by Alfred E. Aarons and Louis F. Werba. Opened 4 October 1910 at the New York and closed 15 October 1910 after 16 performances.

CAST: *Deacon Flood*: HARRY KELLY. *Jack Flood*: FLETCHER NORTON. *Jupiter P. Slick*: ED WYNN. *Hon. Charles Chetwynne*: P. O'MALLEY JENNINGS. *Jim Gruff*: W. W. Black. *Head Waiter*: C. G. Staples. *First Waiter*: George Faust. *Second Waiter*: Milton Silby. *Marie Trouville*: CLARA PALMER. *Mrs. Hunter Grey*: Dorothy Homer. *Millicent Grey*: EVA FALLON. *May Flood*: MADELYN MARSHALL. *Meg*: MAYME GEHRUE. *Flower Girl*: Helen Mooney. *Autograph Girl*: Irene Messenger.

College Boys: Messrs. Robert Hunter, William Izzard, P. G. Riblet, C. G. Thompson, B. Fetherstone, H. W. Gray, P. Wilson, J. Foley, H. Healy, T. Stanton, Charles Hoff. *Seminary Girls*: Misses Katherine MacDonald, Claude Lea, Ida DeCampe, Billy French, Georgie Gardner, Velma Roberts. *Dairymaids*: Misses Jeanette Singer, Estelle St. Clair, Birdie McLaughlin, Arline LaCrosse. *Country Boys*: Misses Aureals Marlow, Nellie Jackson, Beatrice Osgood, Ethel Leyden, Marion Thompson, Beatrice Caplet, Lillian Mansfield, Janis McCann. *Country Girls*: Misses Lillian Baker, Pearl Muis, Anna Bayuk, Lee Leontine, Audrey Mohr, Hazel Mooney, Nellie White, Wanda Dean, Lillian Lippkam, Bessie Hale, Gertie Barreto.

Act 1: Depot Square, Floodville, Vermont.

Act 2: Claremont Gardens, New York City.

ACT 1

Opening Chorus

"It's Queer What a Little Love Will Do"
F. Norton, E. Fallon

"La Belle Parisienne"
C. Palmer, Chorus

"I Want a Wife"
P. O. Jennings, Chorus

"Modest Mazie"
C. Palmer

"Who's Your Hoosier Friend?"
E. Wynn, Chorus

"Naughty Boy"
E. Fallon

"What an Awful Scandal"
H. Kelly, E. Wynn, P. O. Jennings, M. Marshall

"Oh, Mr. Scarecrow Man" (Mr. Scarecrow)
M. Gehrue, Ponies

Finale

ACT 2

Opening Chorus

"Dreams"
E. Fallon, Chorus

"I Must Find Someone"
C. Lee, B. French, K. MacDonald, J. Singer, B. McLaughlin, E. St. Clair, C. Hoff, P. C. Riblet, C. Faust, R. Hunter, M. Silbe, J. Foley

"Tiger Love"
C. Palmer

"The French Flip-Flop"
F. Norton, Chorus

"I Love You Every Hour (of the Day)"
F. Norton, E. Fallon

"Omar"
C. Palmer

"(On a) Hottentot Honeymoon"
M. Gehrue, Chorus

Finale

1910.30 JUDY FORGOT

A Musical Comedy in Two Acts and a Prologue. Book and lyrics by Avery Hopwood. Music by Silvio Hein. (Staged by Daniel V. Arthur.) Dances arranged by Lewis Morton. Costumes by Max & Mahieu. Orchestra under the direction of Anton Heindl. Produced by Daniel V. Arthur. Opened 6 October 1910 at the Broadway Theatre and closed 12 November 1910 after 44 performances.[43]

CAST (in order of appearance): *Freddie Evans*: ARTHUR STANFORD. *Judy Evans*: MARIE CAHILL. *Elsa*, a Maid: Anna Ford. *Francois*, a Waiter: H. P. Woodley. *Dr. Kuno Lauberscheimer*: JAMES B. CARSON. *Trixie Stole*, formerly Trixie Gale: TRULY SHATTUCK. *Dickie Stole*, Trixie's husband: JOSEPH SANTLEY. *John Mugg*, Dickie's uncle: Bert Baker. *Rosa*: ETHEL JOHNSON. *American Debutantes (4)*: *Betty James*: Hazel Kingdon. *Virginia Ellwood*: Emila Barnabo. *Dorothy Lewis*: Evelyn Grahame-Smith. *Fanny DeKalb*: Anna Hoffman.

Peasants: Misses Ford, Wilmot, McNally, Carmen, Spuhler, Van Court, Darling, Evans, Holland, Walton, Sylvester, Crawford, Three Constantine Sisters. *Hussars*: Messrs. Davis, Jenkins, Sheilds, Woodley, Bryan, Yorkshire, Wheeler, Johnson, Stassi, Gillespie, Clarke, Hudson. *Guests*: Misses Cottrell, Tormey, Holmes, Hein, Bennett, Buehler, Berhabo, Kingdon, Hoffman, Wilson, Finney, Smith, Ben-Yusuf, Carlyle, Oberle, Leslie, Merest, Sisters May, DeLima.

Prologue: The reception room of Mr. and Mrs. Freddie Evans' suite in the Swiss Inn at Innsbruck on an evening in June. Judy wants to forget.

Act 1: Colonnade, Kreutzbrunnen, Marienbad. The next afternoon. Judy does forget.

Act 2: Garden of Furstenhof, Marienbad. The same evening. Judy wishes she hadn't.

PROLOGUE

Opening

"Students' Serenade"
M. Cahill, Students

"The Quarrel"
M. Cahill, A. Stanford

ACT 1[43a]

Opening
Ensemble

"The Song of the Honeymoon" (Honeymoon)
T. Shattuck, J. Santley

"Good Morning, Judge"
M. Cahill
(*Music by* John Golden, Silvio Hein. *Lyrics by* John Golden, Avery Hopwood.)

"My Soldier Boy"
E. Johnson, J. B. Carson

"The Star Factory"
Some of the material

"Give Me All the Flowers" (Flower Song)
A. Stanford

Finale
M. Cahill, Company

ACT 2

"The Judy Two-Step"

"(My) Dream, Dream Man"
E. Johnson

[43]Settings uncredited.

[43a]Also performed and interpolated as per published sheet music: "I Want a Little Lovin' Sometimes" M. Cahill (*Music and Lyrics by* Chris Smith.)

"(Whoop 'er Up with a) Whoop-La"
M. Cahill
(*Music by* Will Marion Cook. *Lyrics by* Andrew B. Sterling.)
"(The World Is Full of) Women's Eyes"
J. Santley
"Thinky, Thanky, Thunk"
M. Cahill, A. Stanford
Introducing "The Judy Waltz"
J. B. Carson, J. Santley, G. Stassi, E. Bernabo
"My Toreador"
T. Shattuck
"The Society Circus"
By some who are in it
"Turkish Love Song"
M. Cahill
Finale
Entire Company

1910.31 MADAME TROUBADOUR

An Operetta in Three Acts. (American) Book and lyrics by Joseph Herbert. (Adapted from the Croatian and German operetta of the same name, libretto by Bela Jenbach and Richard Pohl, based on the French comedy "La Petite Marquise.") Music by Felix Albini. Staged by Joseph Herbert. Scenery by H. Robert Law. Gowns worn by Miss LaRue designed by Mme. Frances.[44] Musical director, Oscar Radin. Produced by the Messrs. Shubert. Opened 10 October 1910 at the Lyric Theatre, moved 28 November 1910 to Nazimova's 39th Street Theatre and closed 17 December 1910 after 80 performances.

CAST: *Henriette*, wife of the Marquis: GRACE LaRUE. *Juliette*, a maid: GEORGIA CAINE. *Joseph*, body-servant to the Marquis: EDGAR ATCHISON ELY. *Marquis de Kergazon*, a literary amateur: CHARLES ANGELO. *The Chevalier*, uncle of Henriette: EDGAR NORTON. *Georgette, Martine*, servants: Anna Wheaton, Doris Goodwin. *Vicomte Max de Voigommeux*, a man about town: VAN RENSSELAER WHEELER. *Servants, etc.*

The action takes place at the present time in Paris.

Act 1: Chateau of Marquis de Kergazon.

Act 2: Country home of Vicomte de Voigommeux.

Act 3: Same as Act 1.

ACT 1
Introduction and Duet
G. LaRue, V. R. Wheeler
"Trou-Trou-ba-ba-Troubadour" (Trio)
C. Angelo, G. LaRue, V. R. Wheeler
"Oh, How That Taxi Got on My Nerves" (Duet)
G. LaRue, V. R. Wheeler
Trio
E. Norton, G. LaRue, V. R. Wheeler
Finale
C. Angelo, G. Caine, E. A. Ely, Servants

ACT 2
Duet Pastoral
D. Goodwin, A. Wheaton
Trio and Chimes Song (The Chimes Number)
V. R. Wheeler, A. Wheaton, D. Goodwin
"Yesterday and To-day" (Duet)
G. LaRue, V. R. Wheeler
"Don't Be Rash (Rage Is Blind)" (Trio)
C. Angelo, G. Caine, E. A. Ely
Finale
Ensemble

ACT 3
"Tra-la-la, et-cetera" (Duet)
G. Caine, E. A. Ely
"Please, Please" (Duet)
G. LaRue, V. R. Wheeler
Finale
Ensemble

[44]Other costumes uncredited.

1910.32 THE GIRL IN THE TAXI

A Farce (Musical Play) in Three Acts. Play by Stanislaus Stange. Based on the French original "Fils à Papa." by Anthony Mars. Staged by Carter DeHaven. Produced by A. H. Woods. Opened 24 October 1910 at the Astor Theatre and closed 3 December 1910 after 48 performances.

CAST (in order of appearance): *Mariette*, maid to Mrs. Stewart: Jeanette Bageard. *Clara Stewart*, wife of John Stewart: Jessie Millward. *Walter Watson*, a friend of the family: FRANK FARRINGTON. *John Stewart*, president of the Society for the Prevention of Cruelty to Animals, recently elected a member of "The Society of Arts and Letters": FRED BOND. *Bertie Stewart*, his son: CARTER DeHAVEN. *Mary Peters*, his niece: Fremont Benton. *Percy Peters*, her husband: MORGAN COMAN. *Frederick Smith*, a manufacturer of perfume, also a Major of the 37th New Jersey National Guard: JOHN GLENDINNING. *Mignon*, his wife, "The Girl in the Taxi": LAURA GUERITE. *Mademoiselle Irma*, a vaudeville artiste: Grace Walton. *Rosie*, her friend, an ex-chorus lady: Katherine Smythe. *Alexis*, head waiter at "Cafe Churchill": MAX FREEMAN. *Emile*, one of his assistants: Jerome Nelson. *Policeman*: Joseph Clark. *Dr. Paul*: Clifford Heckinger.

The entire action of the play transpires in 24 hours.

Act 1: Home of John Stewart, Apartment House, Riverside Drive, New York.

Act 2: Private Dining Room in the Cafe Riche, New York.

Act 3: Same as Act 1.

MUSICAL NUMBERS[45]
"Mister Pat O'Hare"
A. Ritchie
(*Music and Lyrics by* Benjamin Hapgood Burt.)

1910.33 GETTING A POLISH

A Farcical Comedy (with Songs) in Three Acts and a Prologue. Play by Booth Tarkington and Harry Leon Wilson. Staged by Hugh Ford. Produced by Liebler & Company (Theodore Liebler, George C. Tyler). Opened 7 November 1910 at Wallack's Theatre and closed 17 December 1910 after 48 performances.[46]

CAST: *Mrs. Jim*: MAY IRWIN. *John Blake*, a miner: George Fawcett. *Remington Blanchard*, a hard-working town-talker: Riley C. Chamberlin. *Georgiana*: Rosalind Coghlan. *Henry*: JOHN DALY MURPHY. *Tommy Kent*: John Junior. *Principe de Campo-Basso*: J. T. Chailee. *Clinton Van Stuyk*: Charles A. Gay. *Mrs Croydon-Jones*: Mary K. Taylor. *Frisch*, a courier: Albert Roccardi. *Pauline*, a milliner: Mary V. Hall. *Marie*, a maid: Florence Glenn. *Louis*, a footman: Frank Bixby. *Auguste*, a page: Edward Liebert.

Prologue: Back yard of Mrs. Jim's Boarding House, in Yellow Dog, Montana.

Act 1: Mrs. J. Sterling Griggs' Apartment in the Hotel Sitz, Paris

Act 2: Garden of the Hotel.

Act 3: Same as Act 1.

MUSICAL NUMBERS
"The Toledo Glide" (That Toledo Tune)
M. Irwin
(*Music by* Lou Piantadosi. *Lyrics by* Joseph McCarthy.)
"The Baltimore Bombashay"
M. Irwin
(*Music and Lyrics by* Stanley Murphy.)
"That Opera Rag"
M. Irwin
(*Music by* Ted Snyder. *Lyrics by* Irving Berlin.)
"Teaching McFadden to Waltz"
M. Irwin
(*Music and Lyrics by* Michael Carey.)

[45]Reviewers remarked that Carter DeHaven performed a dance and 3 songs, unidentified in the program. List prepared from published sheet music. Production with interpolations continued to tour in 1912.
[46]Settings, costumes, musical director uncredited.

1910.34 THE BACHELOR BELLES

A Musical Comedy in Two Acts, 4 Scenes. Book and lyrics by Harry B. Smith. Music by Raymond Hubbell. Staged by Julian Mitchell. Settings by Ernest Albert, Lee Lash Company. Costumes by F. Richard Anderson, Wilhelm. Orchestra under the direction of Albert Krause. Orchestrations by Frank Saddler. Produced by (Marc) Klaw and (Abraham L.) Erlanger. Opened 7 November 1910 at the Globe Theatre and closed 3 December 1910 after 32 performances.

CAST: *Laura Lee*, Mlle Celeste, President of the Bachelor Belles: RUTH PEEBLES. *Tiny Schimmel*, formerly a popular actress, now a costumer: JOSIE SADLER. *Daphne Brooks*, an heiress: EVA FALLON. *Gwendole*, a shop girl: Blanche West. *Susan Jane*, a country girl: Mae Murray. *Eleanor*, an assistant to Mlle. Celeste: Eleanor Pendleton. *Tom Jones*, once a matinee idol, now reduced to playing with amateurs: FRANK LALOR. *Tom Van Cortlandt, Sr.*: Jack Raffael. *Tom Van Cortlandt, Jr.*: LAWRENCE WHEAT. *Charley Van Renssalaer*: JOHN PARK. *Maginnis*, a professor of physical culture: F. Stanton Heck. *The Victim*: Story Chipman. *Mae*, a dentist: Mae Murray. *Eleanor*, a barber: Eleanor Pendleton. *Florence*, a lawyer: Florence Walton. *Grace*, a book agent: Grace Kimball. *Eunice*, a doctor: Eunice Mackay. *Olive*, a policeman: Olive Depp. *Gertrude*, an architect: Gertrude Grant. *Sergeant-at-Arms*: Grace Wendell. *Directoire Model*: Eleanor Pendleton. *Crinoline Model*: Hazel Lewis. *Grecian Bend Model*: Olive Depp. *Hobble Skirt Model*: Ida Gabrielle. *Opera Model*: Eunice Mackay. And ADELINE GENÉE.

(*Dance Specialty*: Messr. Sherer Bekefi; Misses Emily Peters, Winnie Anderson, Cissie Sewell, Minnie Mackenzie, Dolly Mackenzie, Casella Rayshaw, Amy Payne, Dolly Hines. *Chorus*.

Act 1, Scene 1: A Room in a Theatrical Costumer's Shop. *Scene 2*: An Attorney's Office.

Act 2, Scene 1: A Bazaar. *Scene 2*: The Open Air Stage.

ACT 1

"Trying It On" (Opening Chorus)
Chorus

"A Popular Girl"
E. Pendleton, Company

"It's Style That Makes the Girl"[47]
B. West, M. Murray, Chorus

"She Trimmed Them All So Neatly"
E. Fallon, Girls

"The Bachelor Belles"
M. Murray, E. Pendleton, F. Walton, O. Depp, Chorus

"Why Don't You Be Nice to Some Young Fellow?"
L. Wheat, Chorus

"I'm Dying for You"[48]
R. Peebles, L. Wheat

"Everybody Brushes By"[49]
F. Lalor

"The Initiation of Daphne"
Company

"Song of the Fashions"
A. Genée, J. Park, E. Pendleton, H. Lewis, I. Gabrielle, O. Depp, E. Mackay

ACT 2

Opening Chorus:
"In Vanity Fair"
Chorus
"Kisses at Auction"[50]
R. Peebles, Chorus

"If I Just Think of Her" (Song)
L. Wheat, Girls

"You've Been Kissing the Blarney Stone" (Song)
E. Fallon, J. Park

"What Has Become of the Girls I Used to Know?"
F. Lalor, Chorus

"Roses and Butterflies" (Dance)
A. Genée
(a) Music by Charles Gounod (from 'Phelmon and Baucis'), arranged by C. Glaser.
(b) Variation by Claude Debussy.
(c) Waltz by Moritz Moszkowski.
(Assisted by) M. S. Beckefi, Misses E. Peters, W. Anderson, C. Sewell, M. Mackenzie, D. Mackenzie, C. Rayshaw, A. Payne, D. Hines.

"The Summer Girl" (Duet)
R. Peebles, L. Wheat

"Give Us a Ragtime Tune" (Song)
L. Wheat, Chous

"Those Were Happy Days" (Those Good Old Days Can Never Come Again)(Duet)
J. Sadler, F. Lalor

"Carmenita"[51] (Song)
R. Peebles, Chorus

Hungarian Dance
A. Genée, assisted by S. Bekefi

Finale

[47]Dropped for subsequent tour.
[48]Replaced for subsequent tour by "The Summer Girl" from Act 2.
[49]Dropped after opening.
[50]Replaced for subsequent tour by:
"The Bachelor Belles Bazaar"
R. Peebles, Chorus

1910.35 NAUGHTY MARIETTA

A Comic Opera in Two Acts, 3 Scenes. Book and lyrics by Rida Johnson Young. Music by Victor Herbert. Produced under the direction of Jacques Coini. Dances arranged by Pauline Verhoeven. Settings by Julius Dowe, Theodore Reisig. Costumes by Will R. Barnes. Orchestra under the direction of Gaetano Merola. (Orchestrations by Victor Herbert.) Produced by Oscar Hammerstein. Opened 7 November 1910 at the New York Theatre and closed 4 March 1911 after 136 performances.

CAST (in order of appearance): *Simon O'Hara*, Captain Dick's servant: HARRY COOPER. *Etienne Grandet*, son of Lieutenant Governor Grandet, who is also the famous buccaneer, "Bras Pique": EDWARD MARTINDEL. *Lieutenant Governor Grandet*: WILLIAM FREDERICK. *Sir Harry Blake*, an Irish adventurer, friend to Captain Dick: RAYMOND J. BLOOMER. *Rudolfo*, keeper of a Marionette Theatre: James S. Murray. *Florenze*, secretary to the Governor: Howard Morgan. *Manuelo*, a pirate: William Mack. *Night Watchman*: Eugene Roder. *Indian*: Thomas Reynolds. *East Indian*: Bert Leslie. *Knife Grinder*: Philip Hahn. *Marietta D'Altena*: EMMA TRENTINI. *Lizette*, a Casquette girl: Kate Elinore. *Adah*, a quadroon slave of Etienne Grandet: MARIA DUCHENE. *Nanette*, a flower girl: Louise Aichel. *Felice*, a flower girl: Blanche Lipton. *Fanchon*: Vera DeRosa. *Graziella*, an Italian girl: Sylvia Loti. *Franchesca*, an Italian girl: Myrtle Randall. *Captain Warrington*: ORVILLE HARROLD.

Quadroon Belles: Misses von Nichols, Malli, Phelan, Baldwin, Broughton, Netta, Wood, Hathaway, Lee, Johnson, Nelson, Noethinger. *Spanish Girls*: Misses Ricardio, Raymond, Aichel, DeRosa, Griffin, Rice. *San Domingo Girls*: Misses Norton, Irland, Marlotte, Hamilton, Netta, DeVere. *French Girls*: Misses Lipton, Lloyd, Moore, Olcott, Holcomb, Aubin. *Flower Girls, Quadroons, Dancers, Captain Dick's Adventurers, Pirates, Street Sweepers, Mexicans, Spaniards, Indians.*

Act 1: The Place D'Armes. New Orleans, 1780.

Act 2, Scene 1: The Marionette Theatre. *Scene 2*: Ball Room of the Jeunesse Dorée Club.

ACT 1

Opening Chorus
(Vendors, Street Sweepers, Flower Girls)

"Tramp, Tramp, Tramp"
O. Harrold, Chorus

"Taisez-Vous"
Casquette Girls

"Naughty Marietta"
E. Trentini

"It Never, Never Can Be Love"
E. Trentini, O. Harrold

"If I Were Anybody Else But Me"
H. Cooper, K. Elinore

"'Neath the Southern Moon (For Thee)"
M. Duchene

"Italian Street Song"
E. Trentini, Chorus

Finale

[51]Dropped for subsequent tour.

ACT 2
"The Marionette Song"
E. Trentini, J. S. Murray
"(You) Marry an Marionette"
E. Martindel
"New Orleans Jeunesse Dorée"
Male Chorus
"Opening of the Ball" (Loves of New Orleans)
Ensemble
"(The Sweet) By and By"
K. Elinore
"Live for Today"
E. Trentini, M. Duchene, O. Harrold, E. Martindel
"I'm Falling in Love with Someone"
O. Harrold
"It's Pretty Soft For Simon"
H. Cooper, Chorus
"Dream Melody" (Ah, Sweet Mystery of Life)
E. Trentini, O. Harrold
Finale
Ensemble

1910.36 THE GIRL AND THE KAISER

An Operetta in Three Acts.[52] Original Viennese operette ('Die Förster-Christl'), libretto by Bernhard Buchbinder. American adaptation by Leonard Liebling. Music by Georg Jarno. Staged by Sidney Ellison. Scenery by H. Robert Law. Costumes designed by Melville Ellis. Orchestra under the direction of Oscar Radin. Produced by Sam S. and Lee Shubert, Inc. Opened 22 November 1910 at the Herald Square Theatre and closed 14 January 1911 after 64 performances.

CAST: *Kaiser Josef II*: JULIUS McVICKER. *Baron von Loeben*, Imperial master of ceremonial: MELVIN STOKES. *Von Reuter*, gentleman in waiting: Robert Vivian. *Count Sternfeld*, captain in Imperial army: Robinson Newbold. *Tibor Berenyi*, lieutenant in Imperial army: William Bonelli. *Franz Foldessy*, overseer of the Sternfeld Estate: THOMAS RICHARDS. *Hans Lange*, Imperial forester: Albert Wilder. *Peter Wenzel*, tailor at court: HARRY CONOR. *Ludwig*, an old forester: George Leonard. *Sergeant Kolonitzky*, of the Imperial army: Alfred Darling. *Baroness von Graven*, lady in waiting: FLAVIA ARCARO. *Countess von Rendorff*: Mabel Weeks. *Minka*: EDITH DECKER. *Christ'l*, Lange's daughter: LULU GLASER. *(Dance Specialty*: Victor Hyde, Blanche Hyde.)

Ladies of the Court, Peasants, Gypsies, etc.: Natalie Saymure, Clara Heath, Genevieve Tucker, Nell Willette, Lillian Crossman, Camille Barnette, Edna Marsh, Phoebe Phares, Evelyn Ellis, Vinnie Danvers, Florence Summerville, Bessie Morrissey, Marie Andree, Marion Steimer, Margery Earle, Vivian Lawrence, Beatrice Duval, Marion Ford, Bessie Carter, Irene Spence, Arline Lilie, Carrie Lilie, Eleanor Twain, Ruth Walker, Beatrice Gordon, Anna Froehlich, Gladys Feldman, Edna Francis, Blanche Huntington, Edna Fenton, Adele Marie, Mary Richter. *Gentlemen, Guards, Peasants, Gardeners, Lackeys, Civiolians, Cavaliers, Grooms*: George R. Davis, Jr., Jack Reynolds, Robert Krosby, Ralph W. Hastings, Robert Gilbert, Harley Knoles, Harry Law, James Marshall, Jack Leonard, Martin H. Keary, William H. Moore, Harry Pearce, Edward Grant, George Alison, Joseph Pepe, William Bauman, William Cohen, Albert Arling, George Hudson.

The action takes place in and about Vienna in 1764.

Act 1: Exterior Forester's Lodge near Vienna. A Summer morning.

Act 2: Reception Hall at Kaiser's Palace in Vienna. Next evening.

Act 3: Same as Act 1. One week later.

ACT 1
"Only a Gypsy Maid"
E. Decker
"A Tailor Man"
H. Conor
"Laughing and Happy Am I"
L. Glaser
"Butterfly, Butterfly"
T. Richards, M. Weeks
"Hungaria's Rhythmic Air" and Czardas
L. Glaser, E. Decker, T. Richards, Ensemble
Whirlwind Hungarian Dance
V. Hyde, B. Hyde
"O, Kaiser, Dear Kaiser" (Oh Kaiser, My Kaiser)(Finale)

ACT 2
"Free Etiquette"
M. Stokes, Ladies
"At Court" (Duet)
L. Glaser, H. Conor
"With a Glance Demure" (Duet)
L. Glaser, M. Stokes
"Cradled in Thy Arms"
E. Decker, Chorus
"Music of Viol" (When True Hearts Meet in Fond Love's Kiss)
T. Richards, Chorus

ACT 3
Introduction—Incidental Music
"Mine Forever More"
T. Richards
Finale

[52]First produced in German in New York 13 January 1910 at the Irving Place Theatre.

1910.37 THE SPRING MAID

An Operetta in Two Acts, 4 Scenes. Book and lyrics by Harry B. Smith, Robert B. Smith. (Based on the German original "Die Sprudelfee" by Julius Wilhelm and A. M. Willner.) Music by Heinrich Reinhardt. Staged by George Marion. Scenery by D. Frank Dodge. Costumes designed by Will R. Barnes. Orchestra under the direction of Max Bendix. Produced by Louis F. Werba and Mark A. Luescher. Opened 26 December 1910 at the Liberty Theatre and closed 10 June 1911 after 192 performances; returned 20 January 1913 to the New Amsterdam Theatre and closed 1 February 1913 after an additional 16 performances.[53]

CAST: *Princess Bozena*, visiting Carlsbad Spa at the gala season with her father, Prince Nepomuk: CHRISTIE MacDONALD. *Prince Nepomuk*, possessed of more ancestry than income: WILLIAM BURRESS. *Prince Aladar*, a Hungarian nobleman whose aversion to women of his own rank, leads him to a flirtation with Annamirl: LAWRENCE REA. *Annamirl*, the favorite fountain girl at Carlsbad known as "The Spring Maid": ELGIE BOWEN. *Baron Rudi*, a young officer and cousin of Bozena, who, like her, has come to Carlsbad to participate in the annual pageant of the discovery of Carlsbad Spring: RALPH ERROLLE. *Roland*, director of the pageant, the famous English tragedian, whose favorite role is Othello: TOM McNAUGHTON. *Ursula*, one of Roland's admiring matinee patrons: Jessie Bradbury. *Spaetling*, the town sleuth, who imagines his mission in life is to capture Black Wenzel, a notorious robber: Charles W. Meyers. *Evakatl*, at whose popular hostelry are sojourning various American visitors: Blanche Sherwood. *Colonel Boone*, an American who objects to the water cure: Edward Metcalf. *Mr. Lomax*, an American who is trying to get thin: Arthur Thalasso. *Mr. Skinner*, an American who is trying to get stout: Otto F. Hoffman.

Spring Girls: *Gretel*: Irene O'Donnell. *Hanni*: Mae Carlisle. *Josie*: Beatrice McKay. *Fritzi*: Margaret Langdon. *Sophie*: Elizabeth Bell. *Elsie*: Leonie Benzinger. *Barbara*: Anitra Mactavish. *Mazie*: Lexie Mero.

Officers: *Toni*: E. H. Barlab. *Niki*: Joseph Barlowe. *Franz*: William J. Kline. *Fritz*: E. B. MacDonald. *Louis*: Charles A. Minton. *Leo*: Karl Knight. *Vladimir*: Joseph H. Smith. *Eugene*: Albert Van Sand.

Visitors at Carlsbad, Tradesmen, Attendants, Flower Girls, Wood Nymphs, Peasants: Pet Childress, Billie Coviere, Phoebe Hines, Bertha Blake, Florence Bowers, Laura Colfax, Maude Connor, Dorothy Daniel, Ida Doerge, Gretta Gleason, Jane Lovell, Violet Mack, Jean Pierson, Alice Tallent, Ethel West, Mary Whitehurst, George Bobbe, Jack Gibson, Fred C. Jones, Earl Glenn, R. St. John, (Paul Chute).

The action covers three days during the festival season at Carlsbad Springs.

Act 1: A Fountain Square, Carlsbad.

Act 2, Scene 1: The Bee-Farm at Bitterbruennen, Near Carlsbad, the following afternoon. *Scene 2*: Interlude, preparing for the festival celebrating the discovery of Carlsbad Springs. *Scene 3*: The Annual Al Fresco Fête, at Carlsbad.

[53]Cast for the return engagement included Christie MacDonald, Tom Conkey (as Prince Aladar), Tom McNaughton, Ben Hendricks, Jessie Bradbury, Elgie Bowen and Charles J. Hart.

ACT 1[54]
"The Cure" (Opening Chorus)
Chorus
"The Loving Cup" (Song)
E. Bowen, Chorus
(*Music by* Robert Hood Bowers.)
"The Fountain Fay Protective Institution, Limited" (Song)
R. Errolle, Officers
"Day Dreams" (Anticipation) (Song)
C. MacDonald
(*Music by* Heinrich Reinhardt {chorus}, Robert Hood Bowers {verse}.)
"The Next May Be the Right" (Duet)
C. MacDonald, W. Burress
"How I Love a Pretty Face" (Song)
L. Rea
"The Fountain Fay" (Song)
C. MacDonald, Chorus
(*Lyrics by* Robert B. Smith.)
"Two Little Love Bees" (Duet)
C. MacDonald, L. Rea
Finale

ACT 2
Scene 1
"Folk Songs" (Opening Chorus)
Chorus
"Dance with Me"
E. Bowen, Chorus
"Take Me Dear"
C. MacDonald, E. Bowen, R. Errolle, L. Rea
(*Music by* Robert Hood Bowers.)
"Day Dreams" (Realization) (Duet)
C. MacDonald, L. Rea
Finale

Scene 2
Interlude (*Music by* Robert Hood Bowers. *Costumes by* F. Richard Anderson.)
The Water Sprite: B. Stone. *The Huntsman*: P. Chute. *The Rabbit*: E. Bowen.

Scene 3
"The Carlsbad Legend" (Legend)
T. McNaughton
"The Interrupted Allegory"
E. Bowen, T. McNaughton, W. Burress, L. Rea
Finale

1911.01 MARRIAGE À LA CARTE

A Musical Comedy in Three Acts. Book and lyrics by C. M. S. McLellan. Music by Ivan Caryll. Staged by Austen Hurgon. Musical directors, J. Sebastian Hiller, Carl H. Engel. Produced by Liebler & Company (Theodore Liebler, George C. Tyler). Opened 2 January 1911 at the Casino Theatre and closed 25 February 1911 after 64 performances.[55]

CAST: *Napoleon Pettingill*: HARRY CONOR. *The Hon. Richard Miables*: C. MORTON HORNE. *Lord Mirables*: HAROLD VIZARD. *Jimmy Wragge*: NORMAN A. BLUME. *Ponsonby de Coutts Wragge*, the Minstrel: Cyril Chadwick. *Aubrey Hipps*: Quentin Tod. *Eustace Haws*: Jack F. Henry. *Thomas Bolingbroke Mullens*: Joe Doner. *Cuthbert Coddington*: CHARLES BROWN. *Gerald Gifford*: J. R. Torrens. *Young Micklethorpe*: Jack Hagner. *Mr. Pink*: A. W. Fleming. *Footman*: Harry Kelly. *Rosalie*: EMMY WEHLEN. *Sheila Wragge*: ESTHER BISSETT. *Mrs. Ponsonby de Coutts Wragge*: Maria Davis. *Daisy Dimsy*: ELSA RYAN. *Iseult Punchum*: Frances Reeve. *Euryanthe Bowers*: Marie Ashton. *Primrose Farmilow*: Ida Barnard. *Elsie Tattleby*: Diane Oste. *Molly*: Rosina Henley.

Bridesmaids, Wedding Guests, Hussars, Schoolboys, Schoolgirls, Hockey Girls, Cricketeers, etc.

Act 1: The Gardens of Tottminster Hall at Stony Stixford in Surrey.

Act 2: The Dionysian Court. Tottminster Hall.

Act 3: At the Little Green Inn, on the Brighton Road.

ACT 1
"Did You Ever, etc." (Opening Chorus)
"Take Him Away to the Mountains" (Recitative)
E. Bissett
"When Zim Zim Go the Cymbals"
E. Ryan, Q. Tod, J. F. Henry
"What's the Use of Going to Bed"
H. Conor
"Walking on a Wire"[56]
E. Wehlen, C. M. Horne
"Oh, Rosalie"
H. Conor, Chorus
"No Doubt I Ought to Try"
E. Wehlen, Chorus
Finale
Full Ensemble

ACT 2
"Of All Her Sex a Paragon" (Opening Chorus and Solo)
C. M. Horne, Chorus
"Smile, Smile, Smile"
E. Wehlen, Chorus
"Such a Bore"
C. M. Horne, Chorus
"Toddle Go the Girls"[57]
E. Ryan, E. Bissett, M. Ashton, F. Reeve, I. Barnard, N. A. Blume, C. Brown, J. R. Torrens, Q. Tod, J. F. Henry
"Silly Cock-a-Doodle-Doo"
E. Wehlen, C. M. Horne
"Captain Dinklepop"
E. Ryan, Chorus
"Cassie's Not a Bit Like Mother"
C. Brown
Finale
E. Wehlen, Full Ensemble

ACT 3
Opening Chorus
Solos
R. Henley, J. Hagner
"For I'm Just I"
E. Wehlen, Chorus
"You, You"[58]
C. M. Horne, Chorus
"Thrifty Little Mabel"
H. Conor
Finale
Full Ensemble

1911.02 THE SLIM PRINCESS

A Musical Comedy[59] in Three Acts. Book and lyrics by Henry Blossom. Adapted from the story of the same name by George Ade. Music by Leslie Stuart. Staged by Austin Hurgon. Costumes designed by Percy Anderson. Orchestra under the direction of W. E Macquinn??. Produced by Charles Dillingham. Opened 2 January 1911 at the Globe Theatre and closed 1 April 1911 after 104 performances.[60]

CAST: *Hamdi Pasha*, Commander of the Imperial Guards: CARL HAYDEN. *Bokhara, Baluchistan*, Guards: Neil Walton, Arthur J. Engel. *Prince Selim Malagsaki*,

[54]Added after opening, following "The Next May be the Right:"
"(We're) On the Track" (Trio)
T. McNaughton, J. Bradbury, C. W. Meyers.

[55]Settings, costumes uncredited.

[56]Replaced for subsequent tour by:
Waltz Duet (Music by R. Berger).

[57]Dropped for subsequent tour.

[58]Dropped for subsequent tour.

[59]On tour the show was billed as a comic opera.

[60]Settings uncredited.

Governor-General of Borivenia: JOSEPH C. MIRON. *Herr Louis von Schloppenhauer*, tutor of the Princess Kalora: JOSEPH CAWTHORN. *Hon. Crawley Plumston*, British Consul in Borivenia: RALPH NAIRN. *Count Luigi Tincagni Tomasso*: CHARLES JUDELS. *Alex Pike* of Bessemer, Pennsylvania: Wallace McCutcheon. *"Tod" Norcross* of Pittsburgh, Pennsylvania: CHARLES KING. *Harry Romaine*: Eugene Revere. *Tom Golding*: Sam Burbank. *Lucas*, head waiter at Golf Club: Albert Stewart. *Princess Jeneka*, Kalora's younger sister: JULIA FRARY. *Madame Saidis*: Queenie Vassar. *A Visitor*: Harriet Sterling. *Hon. Mrs. Plumston*: Kate Wingfield. *Lutie Longstreet*: ELIZABETH BRICE. *Princess Kalora*: ELSIE JANIS.

Plump Ladies of the Court of Borivenia: Misses Henriette Pouts, Pauline Hathaway, Josephine Lachmar, Jane Bliss. *Caddies*: Masters Albert Lamson, Fred Pirkuritz, Max Brown, Fred Gould. *Other characters by* Misses Mona Trieste, Alys Belga, Elise Steele, Leila Benton, Peggy Preston, Estelle Perry, May Fields, Alice Keyes, Josephine Harriman, Dolly Germaine, Margaret St. Clair, Edna Bates, Babe Beresford, Jackie Beryl, Evelyn Carson, Olive Quimby, Peggy Dana, Anna Pallas, Norah Gourley, Julia Beaubien, Josephine Kernell, Bessie Holbrook, Helen Falconer. Messrs. Armstrong, Burbank, Miller, Johnson, Hinds, Rose, Way, Sullivan, Schulz.

Act 1: Gardens of Prince Selim's Palace Grounds, in Borivenia. Present time.

Act 2: Chevy Chase Golf Club, near Washington, D.C. Six weeks later.

Act 3: Music Room in the Plumston's Home, Washington, D.C. Evening of the same day.

ACT 1[61]

Opening Song and Chorus
J. Frary, Chorus
"When the Guards Go Marching By" (Patrol; Soldiers' Song)
C. Hayden, Male Chorus
"I Like 'Em Plump" (Song)
"Love's Lesson" (Quartette and Chorus)
Female Chorus
"A Little Pot of Tea" (Consul's Song)
R. Nairn, Chorus
"Kalora's Entrance" (Ensemble)
J. C. Miron, E. Janis, Chorus
"My Yankee Doodle Girl"
(*Music by* John L. Golden and Victor Herbert.)
Finale
E. Janis, J. Frary, Guards

ACT 2

Opening Chorus (Caddies' Song)
Girls, Chorus
"We Will Not Live in a Little Bungalow" (Duet)
"Nursery Rhymes" (Quartette)
"I'm Glad My Home Is in the States" (Song)
"The Land of the Free" (Song)
"Do You Belong to Anyone in Particular?" (Octette)

ACT 3

"A Certain Sort of Father" (Song)
"Oh! What a Chance to Take" (Song)
"Queen of My Dreams" (Waltz Song)

1911.03 THE PARADISE OF MAHOMET

An Opéra-bouffe in Two Acts. American libretto by Harry B. Smith and Robert B. Smith. (Adapted from the French "Le Paradis de Mahomet" by Henri Blondeau.) Music by Robert Planquette.[62] (Staged by Daniel V. Arthur.) Groupings and dances by Lew Morton. Scenery by H. Robert Law. Costumes designed by Will R. Barnes. Orchestra under the direction of Silvio Hein. Produced by Daniel V. Arthur. Opened 17 January 1911 at the Herald Square Theatre and closed 4 February 1911 after 23 performances.

CAST (in order of appearance): *Babouch*, brother of Vaninka: FLORENCE KOLB. *Vaninka*, a gypsy girl: BERNICE MERSHON. *Ali*, a cook: Albert Crecelius. *Hassan*, a cook: Joseph Guthrie. *Maboul*, husband of Clarisse: HARRY MacDONOUGH. *Clarisse*, formerly a French music hall artist, now a proprietress of a café: MAUDE ODELL. *Prince Cassim*: GEORGE LEON MOORE. *First Friend of the Prince*: Harry Murphy. *Second Friend of the Prince*: Robert Latsch. *Bengaline*: GRACE VAN STUDDIFORD. *Noah Vale*, an American chauffeur: ROBERT G. PITKIN. *Baskir*, a marriage broker, engaged to marry Bengaline: ARTHUR P. RIPPLE. *Nerestan*, captain of yacht: Charles Knapp. *Nemea*: Marta Spears. *Zeline*: Shirley King. *Alphonse*, fencing master in the Algerian army, first husband of Clarisse: Karl Stall.

Oriental Dancers: Misses Bessie Baker, Helen Berkley, Freda Falz, Harriet Hale, Evelyn Kneen, Jessie Palmer, Evelyn Russell, Etta Ware. *Cook Boys*: Misses Blanc Babbitt, Blanch Betters, Lillian Harding, Evelyn Hope, Grace Miller, Nancy Neville, Peggy O'Neil, Edna Travers. *Bridesmaids*: Misses Laura Chester, Mabel Parker, Frances Ray, Flora Smith. *Wedding Guests*: Misses Dorothy Cloudman, Mabel Don Levy, Anita Fortier, Lillian Francis, Florence Hayes, Martha Jones, Dorothy Landers, Millie Marsden, Gertie Rudd, Lillian Shepherd, Evelyn Sloan, Frankie Wilson. *Guards and Attendants*: Messrs. Wilmer Bradley, Arthur Brooks, Walter Clinton, Edward Erving, Ted Hoffman, William Lisle, Frank Stevens, George Thompson, Harry Titus, Edward Towle, Charles Vale, Will Yates.

Act 1: The Quay of Constantinople and the Turkish Cafe of Clarisse.

Act 2: Oriental Gardens of Prince Cassim.

ACT 1

Opening
Chorus
Song and Hungarian Czardas
B. Mershon, F. Kolb, Chorus
"I've Got To Give Her Her Own Way" (Song)
H. MacDonough, Chorus
"Those Eyes" (Song)
G. L. Moore, Chorus
(*Lyrics by* Harry B. Smith.)
"(The Sun Shines on) My Wedding Day" (Song)
G. Van Studdiford, Chorus
"Look Out! Look Out! Look Out!" (Song)
R. G. Pitkin, Chous
"When His Eyes Look into Mine" (Song)
G. Van Studdiford, G. L. Moore
"You're So Different from the Rest"[63] (Duet)
R. G. Pitkin, M. Odell
"The Gypsy Song" (Song)
B. Mershon, F. Kolb, Chorus
Finale
G. Van Studdiford, Company

ACT 2

"Life Oriental" (Song)
B. Mershon, Chorus
"The Joys of Love" (Song)
G. Von Studdiford, Chorus
"I Have Found Them All" (Song)
G. L. Moore, Chorus
"I Can't Get Enough" (Song)
R. G. Pitkin, Chorus
"Y.M.D." (Song)
H. MacDonough, Chorus
"My Idea of Paradise" (Song)
M. Odell, R. G. Pitkin, H. MacDonough

---

[61]Musical numbers not listed in any program. List below prepared from the published vocal score (Chappell & Co., New York, 1910). Interpolations not found in vocal score:

"That's Why I Never Married" (from THE HOYDEN)
J. Cawthorn
(*Music by* John L. Golden. *Lyrics by* John L. Golden and Joseph Cawthorn.)
"Bless Your Ever Loving Little Heart"
E. Brice, C. King
(*Music by* Henry I. Marshall. *Lyrics by* Stanley Murphy.)
"For I Love Only You"
(*Music by* Herman Darewski. *Lyrics by* Elsie Janis.)
"A Soldier's Life"
(*Music and Lyrics by* John P. Wilson and Alfred G. Robyn.)
"Let Me Live and Stay in Dixieland"
E. Brice, C. King
(*Music and Lyrics by* Elizabeth Brice and Charles King.)

[62]After Planquette's death in 1903, "Le Paradis de Mahomet" was posthumously produced in Paris in 1906, and its score was completed by Louis Ganne, not credited in the American production.

[63]Retitled and perhaps revised during the run and for subsequent tour as: "There's Something About You Dear That Appeals to Me" (Duet) R. G. Pitkin, M. Odell (*Music by* Silvio Hein and John L. Golden. *Lyrics by* Frank Cravens.)

"The Rose of the Orient" (Song)
G. Van Studdiford, Chorus
"When the Cat Comes Back" (Song)
B. Mershon, H. MacDonough, F. Kolb
"Forgive and Forget" (Song)
G. Van Studdiford, G. L. Moore
Finale
G. Van Studdiford, Company

1911.04 BARRY OF BALLYMORE

A Play (Romantic Drama with Music) in Three Acts, 4 Scenes. Play by Rida Johnson Young. (Music by Chauncey Olcott and Ernest Ball.) Staged by Augustus Pitou. Incidental music by Frederic Knight Logan. Scenery painted by Homer Emens, Edward G. Unitt, and Joseph Wickes. Costumes designed by H. Ogden. Musical director, Frederic Knight Logan. Produced by Augustus Pitou. Opened 30 January 1911 at the Academy of Music and closed 11 February 1911 after 16 performances; returned 20 February 1911 to the Grand Opera House and closed 25 February after an additional 8 performances. Total: 24 performances.

CAST: *Thomas Barry*: CHAUNCEY OLCOTT. *Sir Edward Emery*: Howard Chambers. *Lord Bannon*: GEORGE SYDENHAM. *Michael McShane*: Ned Reardon. *Phadrig Bannon*: Nesta de Becker. *Gerald O'Mara*: Arthur Jarrett. *Corney*: Daniel Jarrett. *Lady Mary Bannon*: EDITH BROWNING. *Betty O'Mara*: Alice Martin. *Nanette*: ALICE FARRELL. *Mrs. Barry*: Mary Johnstone. *Biddy*: Marion Gasparo.

The action takes place at Ballymore, Ireland, in 1789.

Act 1: The Armour Room Bannon Castle.

Act 2: The Apothecary's Shop in Ballymore. (Unitt & Wickes.)

Act 3, Scene 1: Small room in Castle Bannon. *Scene 2*: Bannon Woods, at dawn. (Emens.)

MUSICAL NUMBERS[64]
"I Love the Name of Mary"
C. Olcott
(*Lyrics by* George Graff, Jr.)
"Wild Rose"
C. Olcott
(*Music by* Ernest R. Ball. *Lyrics by* Louise Heald.)
"My Land"
C. Olcott
(*Lyrics by* Bartley C. Costello.)
"Mother Machree"
C. Olcott
(*Lyrics by* Rida Johnson Young.)
"In the Sunshine of Your Love"
C. Olcott
(*Lyrics by* Dave Reed, Jr.)
"Macushla"
C. Olcott
(*Music by* Dermot McMurrough. *Lyrics by* Josephine V. Rowe.)

1911.05 THE HEN-PECKS

A Musical Panorama in Two Acts, 6 Pictures (scenes). Words (book) by Glen MacDonough. Notes (music) by A. Baldwin Sloane. Rhymes (lyrics) by E. Ray Goetz. Entire production staged by Ned Wayburn. Color schemes selected by Ned Waynurn. Costume plates by Cora MacGeachy. Orchestra under the direction of George A. Nichols. Orchestrations by Frank Sadler. Produced by Lew Fields. Opened 4 February 1911 at the Broadway Theatre and closed 3 June 1911 after 137 performances; re-opened 7 August 1911 at the Broadway Theatre and closed 23 September 1911 after 50 performances. Total: 187 performances.

CAST (in order of appearance): *Silas*, a farm hand: Sam Watson. *Henoria Peck*, Henry Peck's oldest daughter, brought up in the old-fashioned way by her mother: GERTRUDE QUINLAN. *Henrietta Peck*, Henry's wife: LILLIAN LEE. *Hiram*, a farm hand: Joseph Keno. *Dr. I. Stall*, Cranberry Cove's leading horse doctor: BERT LESLIE. *Henderson Peck*, Henry's son, who after a correspondence course at an engineering institute, is going to New York to help solve the traffic problem: STEPHEN MALEY. *Verbena Peck*, Henderson's newly wedded country bride: Edith Frost. *Zowie*, the Monarch of Mystery, the third and last attraction of the season at the Cove's Temple of Amusement, Melodeon Hall: VERNON CASTLE. *Pansy Marshmallow*: Lillian Rice. *Weenie Wistaria*: Angie Weimars. *Henry Peck*, a farmer, formerly the village barber: LEW FIELDS. *Rufe*, the village fiddler: Frank Whitman. *Henolia Peck*, Henry's second daughter, brought up in the new fashioned way by her father, just home from Swellsley College: ETHEL JOHNSON. *Ayer Castle*, a city real estate promoter who has decided to turn Cranberry Cove into the summer metropolis of Briny Bluff: LAURENCE WHEAT. *Henella Peck*, Henry's youngest daughter, who has run away to new York to bring herself up in the chorus under the name of Carmencita Tabasco: BLOSSOM SEELEY. *Montgomery Muggs*, *Launcelot Gaggs*, of the "Jolly Embalmers": Fred Roberts, Harry Pond. *Ravioli*, a boss barber: Joseph Kane. *Mrs. Murgatroyd*, "Clarence's" owner: Nan Brennan. *Major Manley* of the Salvation Army: Hazel Allen. *Ermengarde* with the Lilliputian voice: Dolly Filley. *Casey Jones*, a policeman: Virgil Bennett. *Mlle. Twinkle Toes*, one of the wedding dinner entertainers: Mazie King.

Town Beauties, Village Belles, Rural Kiddies, Yokele, Barbers, City Chaps, Customers, etc.[65])

Act 1, Scene 1: Henry Peck's Farm, Cranberry Cove, New England. *Scene 2*: Exterior of the Railroad Station, Cranberry Cove. *Scene 3*: Signor Ravioli's barber shop in New York.

Act 2, Scene 1: Times Square, New York. *Scene 2*: A Railway Lunch Counter. *Scene 3*: The court of the "Peckingham," an apartment house built on the site of Henry Peck's farm-house.

ACT 1[66]
Opening
"Don't Forget the Beau You Left Behind" (Don't Forget the Beau You Left at Home)
J. Keno, L. Rice, A. Weimars, Chorus
"Just Tell Me with Your Eyes"[67]
L. Wheat, E. Johnson, Chorus
Finale
Ensemble
"Hail to the Bride"
F. Whitman, Ensemble
"Toddling the Todalo"
B. Seeley
"Next"
Ensemble
"It's the Skirt"
L. Wheat, E. Johnson, Chorus
"Little Italy"
B. Seeley, Chorus

ACT 2[68]
"White Light Alley"[69]
L. Wheat, Chorus
"He's the Wonder of Them All"[70]
B. Leslie

[64]Not necessarily in performance order.

[65]Late in the second month of the run individual chorus names were finally listed.

[66]Late in the New York run, added to Act 1 after "Hail to the Bride":
"The Dancing Fiddler"
F. Whitman

[67]Late in the New York run, replaced by:
"(In the) Shadows"
Charles King (Ayer), Elizabeth Brice (Henolia)
(*Music by* Herman Finck.)

[68]After opening, the running order of Act 2 was revised. Added to Act 2 during the run (27 March 1911), after "He's the Wonder of Them All":
"Wine Maid Divine"
Miss Irene Grange, Chorus

[69]Dropped late in the New York run and for subsequent tour; replaced by an Opening Chorus.

[70] Replaced late in the New York run by:
"Dixie Land"
C. King, E. Brice

"Breezes That Blow"[71]
Ensemble
"It's Not the Trick Itself But It's the Tricky Way It's Done"
V. Castle, Chorus
"The Manicure Girl"[72]
G. Quinlan
(*Music by* Jerome Kern. *Lyrics by* Frederick Day.)
"Lasses Who Live in Glass Houses"[73]
E. Frost
Dancing Specialty
M. King
"Try This On Your Pianna, Anna"[74]
E. Johnson, Chorus
"June"
B. Seeley, Chorus
Finale
Ensemble

1911.06 THE BALKAN PRINCESS

A Musical Play in Two Acts and a Prologue. Book by Frederick Losdale and Frank Curzon. Music by Paul A. Rubens. Lyrics by Paul A. Rubens and Arthur Wimperis. Staged by W. J. Wilson. Scenes painted by H. Robert Law. Costumes designed by Melville Ellis. Orchestra directed by John McGhie. Produced by Sam S. and Lee Shubert Inc. by arrangement with William A. Brady. Opened 9 February 1911 at the Herald Square Theatre, moved 27 February 1911 to the Casino Theatre and closed 13 May 1911 after 108 performances.

CAST: *The Grand Duke Sergius*: ROBERT WARWICK. *Count Boethy*, Prime Minister of Balaria: J. H. Pratt. *Captain Radomir*: Kenneth Hunter. *Lieutenant Varna*: Fritz Macklyn. *Max Hein*, alias "Prince Boris of Matalia": PERCY AMES. *Blatz*, his confederate: Teddy Webb. *Lounger at the Bohemian Restaurant*: Harold de Becker. *Emil*, proprietor of the Bohemian Restaurant: Harry Lewellyn. *Hermann*, commissionaire at the Bohemian Restaurant: Robert Milliken. *Henri*, a waiter: HERBERT CORTHELL. *Magda*, charwoman at the Palace: MAY BOLEY. *Olga*, maid of honor: ALICE BRADY. *Sofia*, an habitué of the Bohemian Restaurant: VIDA WHITMORE.

Other Habitués: *Paula*: Rose Firestone. *Tessa*: Bobby B. Nichols. *Carmen*: Carmen Romero. *Marguerita*: Daisy James. *Teresa*: Peggy Merritt. *Guests at the Bohemian Restaurant*: Robert Milliken, Len Litchfield, Olin Howland. *Cashier at the Bohemian Restaurant*: Sylvia Clark. *Princess Stephanie of Balaria*: LOUISE GUNNING, CHRISTINE NIELSEN (alt.). *Five Nobles of Balaria*: Olin Howland, S. Keen, H. deBecker, Irving Finn, Robert Millikin. *Four Waitresses at the Bohemian Restaurant*: Millie Bright, Grace Kimball, Mabel Ferry, Nanon Welch. *Chorus of Court Ladies, Debutantes, Officers, Footmen, Habitués at the Restaurant, etc.*: (unidentified).

Prologue: A Room in the Palace.

Act 1: The Bohemian Restaurant. The next evening.

Act 2: The Garden of the Palace. A week later.

PROLOGUE[75]
Opening Chorus
"Holidays" (Song)
A. Brady, F. Maclyn, Chorus
"I Char" (Song)
M. Boley, Charwomen
"I Like You All" (Song)
L. Gunning, Chorus of Dukes
Finale
Ensemble

ACT 1[76]
Introduction
Chorus
"Love and Laughter" (Song)
V. Whitmore, Chorus
Entrance of Grand Duke (la, la, la, la)
"Dear Delightful Women" (Song)
R. Warwick, Chorus
"Don't Let's Meet Again" (Duet)
L. Gunning, R. Warwick
"Lady and Gentleman" (Duet)
M. Boley, T. Webb
"(A) Hard Life"[77]
H. Corthell
"Wonderful World" (Song)
L. Gunning
"The Opera Ball" (Sextet)
H. Corthell, P. Ames, T. Webb, V. Whitmore, M. Boley, C. Romero
Finale

ACT 2
"Dreaming" (Opening Number-Song)
A. Brady
"A Man's a Man" (Song)
R. Warwick
"(When) The Sunshine of Springtime"[78] (Song)
L. Gunning
Finale
Toute Ensemble

1911.07 THE HAPPIEST NIGHT OF HIS LIFE

A Musical Comedy in Three Acts. Book and lyrics by Junie McCree and Sydney Rosenfeld. Music by Albert Von Tilzer. Staged by George W. Lederer. Settings designed by Ernest Albert. Costumes by Frazee and Lederer's Costume Department (Kate Keeler, manageress.) Orchestra under the direction of Rudolf Berliner. Produced by (H. H.) Frazee and (George W.) Lederer. Opened 20 February 1911 at the Criterion Theatre and closed 11 March 1911 after 24 performances.

CAST (in order of appearance): *Harry Jelliman*: PHIL RYLEY. *Martha Jelliman*: Julia Ralph. *Popsy*: SALLIE STEMBLER. *Tom Dawson*: JACK HENDERSON. *Minnie Randolph*: ANNABELLE WHITFORD. *Chicago Delegation , Protective Order of Young Widows (8)*: *Mrs. Clark*: Leola Lucey. *Mrs Dearborn*: Lillian Stanton. *Mrs. Washington*: Rose Leslie. *Mrs. Madison*: Maud LeRoy. *Mrs. Monroe*: Dorothy Page. *Mrs. Adams*: Beryl Marsden. *Mrs. Wabash*: Edythe Gilbert. *Mrs. Lake*: Bessie Stewart. *Officer Flannigan*: JUNIE McCREE. *Herman Schultz*: Will A. McCormick. *Dick Brennan*: VICTOR MOORE. *Mrs. Ricketts*: MAE PHELPS. *Jane Ricketts*: GERTRUDE VANDERBILT. *Popsy's Little Sister*: EMMA LITTLEFIELD. *Anastasia McIntyre, Nell Grogan*, Scrub women: Charles E. Walt, Jack Fairbanks. *John*, the grocer: James C. O'Neill. *Dan*, the baker: Victor H. Bozardt. *Tom*, the butcher: George W. Steteler. *Pete*, the milkman: Edward C. Yeager. *Chimmy*, the newsboy: Harry Smithfield. *Post L. Carried*, the letter carrier: Henry Ward.

Act 1: Jelliman's residence, Washington Heights, New York City. Morning.

Act 2: Mrs. Rickett's garage. Same night.

Act 3: Jelliman's residence. Next morning.

ACT 1
Tradesmen Ensemble
"Oh, What a Beautiful Morning"
J. Henderson
"(We Are) Laughing Widows"
A. Whitford, Widows

---

[71]Replaced after opening by "Try This On Your Pianna, Anna," removed from its later position in Act 2.
[72]Dropped late in the New York run and for subsequent tour.
[73]Dropped late in the New York run and for subsequent tour.
[74]Also known as "Try This on Your Piano, Anna" or "Try This On Your Pianny, Annie." Dropped late in the New York run and for subsequent tour.
[75]Added to Prologue for subsequent tour, after "Holdiays":
"Stealing"
Harry P. Gribbon (Hein), T. Webb

[76]Added to Act 1 for subsequent tour after "Don't Let's Meet Again":
"Somebody's Arms" (Double Octette)
Ladies and Gentlemen, Cafe Anglais
[77]Dropped for subsequent tour.
[78]Replaced for subsequent tour by:
"His Return" (Song)
L. Gunning

"Because It Can't Sit Down"
S. Stembler
"New York and Chicago" (Oh You Chicago, Oh You New York)
A. Whitford, V. Moore
(*Lyrics by* Junie McCree.)
"The Happiest Night of His Life"
J. Henderson, V. Moore, P. Ryley
"There's One Born Every Minute"
V. Moore
(*Music by* Phil Schwartz. *Lyrics by* Harold Atteridge.)

ACT 2[79]
"Hurry Boys"
M. Phelps, Chauffeurs
"Etiquette"
J. McCree, M. Phelps
"I'm Just Out of My Teens"
G. Vanderbilt, College Boys
"Nectar for the Gods"
M. Phelps, J. Henderson, V. Moore, P. Ryley
"A Joy Ride"
G. Vanderbilt, J. Henderson
"Blind Man's Bluff"
P. Ryley, J. McCree, Jane's Guests
Dance
E. Littlefield, P. Ryley, J. McCree
"Things Left Unsaid"
V. Moore
"The Fiddler Must Be Paid"
A. Whitford, J. Henderson
Finale

ACT 3
Ensemble
J. Henderson, V. Moore, P. Ryley, Widows
"Jane"
J. Henderson, G. Vanderbilt
"What a Difference When You're Married"
S. Stembler, J. McCree
"Little Church Around the Corner" (Double Octette)
Widows, College Boys
"Twenty-Four Hours of Love" (Musical Poem)
V. Moore
Finale

EVERYWOMAN

1911.09 (Her Pilgrimage in Quest of Love)

A Modern Morality Play in Five Canticles (Acts). Play by Walter Browne. Music by George Whitefield Chadwick. Staged by George Marion. Scenery painted by Walter Burridge. Electrical effects by Joseph G. Wilson. Gowns and costumes designed by Hy. Mayer. Music under the direction of Hugo Frey. Produced by Henry W. Savage. Opened 27 February 1911 at the Herald Square Theatre, moved 29 May 1911 to the Lyric Theatre annd closed 1 July 1911 after 144 performances; returned 19 February-23 March 1912 to the Herald Square Theatre for an additional 45 performances. Total: 189 performances.

CAST (in order of appearance): *Nobody*: H. COOPER CLIFFE. *Everywoman*: LAURA NELSON HALL. *Her Companions (3)*: *Youth*: PATRICIA COLLINGE. *Beauty*: AURORA PIATT. *Modesty*: JULIETTTE DAY. *Conscience*, her handmaiden: WILDA BENNETT. *Flattery*: Frank Lacy. *Truth*, a witch: SARAH COWELL LeMOYNE. *King Love the First*, her son: Edward Mackay. *Bluff, Stuff*, theatre managers: Henry Wenman, John L. Shine. *Puff*, a press agent: Richard Lee. *Passion*, a play actor: SYDNEY JARVIS. *Time*, a call boy: Barry Maxwell. *Wealth*, a millionaire: Frederic de Belleville. *Witless*, a nobleman; Huber Osborne. *Age*: McIntyre Wickstead. *Greed*: Kathleen Kerrigan. *Self*: Jean Barrett. *Vanity*: Vivian Blackburn. *Vice*, a courtesan: Stella Hammerstein. *Charity*, a minister: Detmar Poppen. *Law, Order*, policemen: Richard Fuller, William Calvin. *Grovel, Sneak*, servants: Charles Hayne, David Estoclet.

Chorus Girls: *Pert*: Suzette Gordon. *Flirt*: Eleanor Flowers. *Smiles*: Betty Murdoch. *Dimples*: Rue Brown. *Curls*: Charlotte Carter. *Curves*: Grace Calve. *Shape*: Marjorie Fitch. *Shy*: Alice Kline. *Giggles*: Edna Porter. *Chorus Men. Students, Fools, Rogues, Vagabonds, Revellers, etc.*

Canticle 1: A Room in Everywoman's Home.

Canticle 2: On the stage of a metropolitan theatre.

Canticle 3: Everywoman's apartment in the city.

Canticle 2: New Year's Eve on Broadway.

Canticle 3: A Room in Everywoman's Home.

CANTICLE 1[80]
Trio (Born of a sunbeam's purity)
P. Collinge, A. Piatt, J. Day
Entrance of Everywoman (Melodrama)
There shall come a time when. .
H. C. Cliffe
Melodrama (No stranger I when not active duty)
F. Lacy
Entrance of Truth
Everywoman (Melodrama)

CANTICLE 2
Entrance of Chorus Girls (Two and two at its cue)
Exit of (Modesty and) Chorus (One by one beauty gone)
A little star crept out one night . . .
W. Bennett
Passion Song (Melodrama and Finale) (The sun smiles on virgin snow)

CANTICLE 3
Entrance of Everywoman and Revellers
Conscience's Song (A flow'r was born in a garden fair)
W. Bennett
Melodrama (Be-el-ze-bub!)
L. N. Hall, W. Bennett, All

CANTICLE 4
The Gay White Way
Couplet (Chorus and Dance) (Full of glee, follow me. .)
Melodrama
S. C. LeMoyne
Chorus within the Supper Room (Sing a merry song to Venus. .)
Entrance of Chorus (Solo and Dance) (Happy New Year. .)
Procession to the Chorus (Behold! Time moweth us down. .)

CANTICLE 5
Melodrama
Melodrama
Postlude

JUMPING JUPITER

1911.08

A Farce with Music in Three Acts. Book and lyrics by Richard Carle and Sydney Rosenfeld. Music by Karl Hoschna. Staged by Richard Carle. Settings by Lee Lash Studios, D. Frank Dodge. Gowns by Lucile, Ltd.; Frazee & Lederer Costume Dept. Orchestra under the direction of Hans S. Linne. Produced by H. H. Frazee and George W. Lederer. Opened 6 March 1911 at the New York Theatre and closed 25 March 1911 after 24 performances.

CAST: *Robert Winthrop*, an artist: BURRELL BARBARETTO. *Major Felix Buchanan*, a retired army officer: JOSEPH C. MIRON. *Stephen Buchanan*, his nephew: Lester J. Crawford. *Toby Pebbleford*, his crony: WILL H. PHILBRICK. *Marmaduke Bright*, Genevieve's cousin: JOHN GOLDSWORTHY. *Stilwell*, butler: Murray D'Arcy. *Connie Curtiss*, a former model: EDNA WALLACE HOPPER. *Genevieve Buchanan*, the Major's wife: Isabelle Winloche. *Elsie Buchanan*, her daughter: NATALIE ALT. *Caroline Goodwillie*, the Professor's wife: JESSIE CARDOWNIE. *Molly Pebbleford*, Toby's daughter: Eileen Claire. *Mrs. Anastasia Kidd*, a widow, much: ANNA CHANDLER. *Professor Goodwillie*, an expert on dermatology: RICHARD CARLE.

---

[79]Incidental to Act 2, Miss Emma Littlefield will introduce her Danse Eccentrique.

[80]Musical numbers not listed in programs. List prepared from published vocal score (T. B. Harms, Inc., New York, 1911).

Miss Ranier: Bly Brown. *Miss Chalmers*: Blanche Curtis. *Miss Renault*: Jean Engels. *Miss Packard*: Marie Vernon. *Miss Cadillac*: Ida Harris. *Miss Pierce*: Beatrice Morton. *Miss Locomobile*: Margaret Strasselle. *Miss Lozier*: Estelle St. Clair. *Miss Winston*: HELEN BRODERICK. *Miss Buick*: Betty Scott. *Miss Hupp*: Naomi Dale. *Miss Daimler*: Bessie Skeen.

Act 1: Smoking room in the country home of Major Buchanan. (Lash.)

Act 2: Drawing room, same house. Evening. (Lash.)

Act 3: Garden, same house. Following morning. (Dodge.)

ACT 1[81]

"Give Me a Good Havana"
J. C. Miron, W. H. Philbrick, B. Barbaretto, J. Goldsworthy

"The Mail Man"
Ensemble

"Little Girl I Love You"
N. Alt, B. Barbaretto

"To the Strains of that Wedding March" (It's a Long, Long Walk)
R. Carle, Girls
(*Music by* Grace LeBoy. *Lyrics by* Gus Kahn.)

"I Like to Have a Flock of Men Around Me"
E. W. Hopper, B. Barbaretto, J. C. Miron, W. H. Philbrick, J. Goldsworthy
(*Music by* Harry Auracher [Archer]. *Lyrics by* Francis DeWitt.)

ACT 2

"Oh, Innocent Young Thing"
N. Alt, Girls

"Pet of the Family"
E. Claire, Girls

Imitations (Vesta Victoria, Elizabeth Murry, Harry Lauder)
E. Claire

"Thank You, (Kind Sir!, Said She)"
R. Carle, E. W. Hopper
(*Music by* Irving Berlin. *Lyrics by* Ted Snyder.)

"Snuggle" (Dearie, Won't You Snuggle Close to Me?)
E. Claire, L. J. Crawford, Girls
(*Music by* Harry Auracher [Archer]. *Lyrics by* Francis DeWitt.)

"I Am a Poor Unfortunate" (Finale)
Full Company

ACT 3

"Bill and Coo"
N. Alt, B. Barbaretto, Girls

"Oh You Chicago, Oh You New York" (from THE HAPPIEST NIGHT OF HIS LIFE)
R. Carle, E. W. Hopper
(*Music by* albert Von Tilzer. *Lyrics by* June McCree.)

"Possum Rag"
A. Chandler
"Angle Worm Wriggle"
W. H. Philbrick

"Only a Man"
E. W. Hopper
(*Music by* Grace LeBoy. *Lyrics by* Gus Kahn.)

Finale
Full Company

1911.10 THE BOHEMIAN GIRL

A Revised and Modernized Revival of the Comic Opera in Three Acts, 6 Scenes.[82] Libretto by Alfred Bunn. Music by Michael William Balfe. Staged by Edward P. Temple. Settings by Lee Lash Studios (Act 1), P. Dodd Ackerman (Acts 2 and 3). Costumes by Bagarozy and Odierno. Orchestra under the direction of Max Fichandler. Produced by the Aborn Opera Company (Milton and Sargent Aborn, Managing Directors). Opened 13 March 1911 at the Majestic Theatre and closed 1 April 1911 after 24 performances.

CAST: *Count Arnheim*, an Austrian Noble, afterwards Governor of Presburg: JAMES STEVENS. *Thaddeus*, a Proscribed Polish Noble: HENRY TAYLOR. *Florestein*, the Count's Nephew: MAURICE LAVIGNE. *Devilshoof*, a Gypsy Chief: CHARLES GALLAGHER. *Captain of the Guard*: Ralph Nicholls. *Officer of the Patrol*: Ralph Nicholls. *Servant*: C. Drumheller A *Gypsy Messenger*: H. Ben Ali. *Queen of the Gypsies*: Bertha Shallek. *Arline*, the Bohemian Girl: BLANCHE DUFFIELD. *Buda*, attendant to the Baby Arline: Florrie Sloane.

Austrian Ladies, Peasant Women, Boys and Girls, Gypsies, Ladies of the Court: Female Chorus. *Austrian Noblemen, Hunters, Peasants, Gypsies, Townspeople, Travelling Showmen, Frontier Patrol*: Male Chorus.

1911.11 THE PINK LADY

A Musical Comedy in Three Acts. Book and lyrics by C. M. S. McClellan. Based on the French play "Le Satyr" Georges Berr and Marcel Guillemaud. Music by Ivan Caryll. Staged by Herbert Gresham. Musical numbers staged by Julian Mitchell. Costumes by F. Richard Anderson. Settings designed by Ernest Albert. Lighting by Frank Detering. Orchestra under the direction of Arthur Weld. Produced by (Marc) Klaw and (Abraham L.) Erlanger. Opened 13 March 1911 at the New Amsterdam Theatre and closed 9 December 1911 after 312 performances.[83]

CAST (in order of appearance): *Serpolette Pochet*: Alma Francis. *Desirée*: IDA M. ADAMS. *A Photographer*: Dudley Oatman. *Pochet*: F. Newton Lindo. *The Hungry Man*: Joseph Carey. *Annette*: Ida Gabrielle. *Gilberte*: Olive Depp. *Gabrielle*: Eunice Mackey. *Raymonde*: Trixie Whitford. *Minette*: Florence Walton. *Sophie*: Erminie Clark. *Benevol*: FRED WRIGHT, JR. *Lucien Garidel*: WILLIAM ELLIOTT. *Julie*: Ruby Lewis. *Nini*: Teddy Hudson. *Suzanne*: May Hennessy. *Angele*: ALICE DOVEY. *Maurice D'Uzac*: CRAUFURD KENT. *Bebe Guingolph*: JOHN E. YOUNG. *Claudine*, The Pink Lady: HAZEL DAWN. *Crapote*: Harry Depp. *Madame Dondidier*: ALICE HEGEMAN. *Philippe Dondidier*: FRANK LALOR. *Theodore Lebec*: A. S. Humerson. *Comtesse de Montavert*: LOUISE KELLEY. *Rouget*: Dudley Oatman. *Dr. Mazou*: Maurice Hegeman. *Pan*: W. Jackson Sadler. *Ywaxy*, a violinist: Benjamin Lissit. (*Chorus*: Unidentified.)

Act 1: The Gardens of "Joli Coucou," a restaurant in the forest of Compiezgne, France.

Act 2: Interior of an antique shop in the Rue St. Honoré, Paris.

Act 3: Ball of the Nymphs and Satyrs, at the Vafe Les Satyre, Paris.

ACT 1

Opening Chorus (Here's a Lady)
I. Adams, A. Francis, Victims, Chorus

"Bring Along the Camera"
F. Wright, Jr., Chorus

"When Love Goes Astraying"[84]
A. Dovey, C. Kent

"The Girl by the Saskatchewan"
J. E. Young, I. M. Adams, Victims, Chorus

"(Oh, So) Gently"[85]
H. Dawn, Chorus
(*Lyrics by* George Grossmith, Jr.)

---

[81]Songs not listed in New York programs. Song list below prepared from subsequent Boston tour and published piano vocal score (M. Witmark, New York, 1911) Rosenfeld did not contribute lyrics. Also performed in New York, per opening night reviews:

"Mississippi Dip"
A. Chandler

Also performed as per published sheet music:

"Mee Me To-night at Nine"
(*Music by* Albert Von Tilzer. *Lyrics by* June McCree.)

[82] First produced in New York 25 November 1844 at the Park Theatre. For Synopsis of Scenes and Musical Numbers, see original 1844 production. For this revival, the Dance of the Hours from the opera LA GIOCONDA by Ponchielli was interpolated in Act 3.

[83]Played a return engagement 26 August 1912 at the New Amsterdam Theatre for 24 additional performances. See separate entry in following season for detail.

[84]Replaced shortly after the opening by (but later restored and performed following "I'm Going to Be Married. .):

"I'm Going to be Married in June" (I'm Single for Six Weeks More)
W. Elliott

[85]In the last weeks of the run, replaced by (but restored for the subsequent tour):

"In a French Girl's Heart"
H. Dawn, Chorus

Finale[86]
Ensemble

ACT 2

Opening Chorus[87]
H. Depp, Chorus

"The Intriguers"
W. Elliott, F. Lalor, H. Dawn, H. Depp

"Donny Did, Donny Didn't"
L. Kelley, A. Hegeman, F. Lalor, W. Elliott

"The Kiss Waltz" (The Pink Lady Waltz)
H. Dawn

"Hide and Seek"
A. Francis, F. Lalor

"The Duel"
H. Dawn, A. Francis, W. Elliott, C. Kent

Finale[88]
Ensemble

ACT 3

"Parisian Two-Step"
W. J. Sadler, E. Mackey, A. Francis, Chorus

"I Like It!"
F. Lalor, Chorus

"(My) Beautiful Lady"
H. Dawn, A. Francis

Finale[89]
Ensemble

1911.12 LA BELLE PAREE

A Musical Extravaganza (comprised of) LA BELLE PAREE, a Jumble of Jollity in Two Acts, 11 Scenes, preceded by a Spanish Ballet (Tortajada and Her and Her Sixteen Moorish Dancing Girls), and a Chinese Fantasy Opera (BOW SING) in One Act. Staged by J. C. Huffman and William J. Wilson. Produced by the Winter Garden Company (Messrs. Shubert.) Opened 20 March 1911 at the Winter Garden and closed 10 June 1911 after 96 performances; returned 11-16 September 1911 to the Winter Garden for 8 additional performances. Total: 104 performances.

ACT 1[90]

BOW-SING, a Chinese Fantasy Opera in One Act, 3 Scenes. Libretto by Carroll Fleming and Arthur Voegtlin. Music by Manuel Klein. Staged under the direction of J. C. Huffman and William J. Wilson. Ballet of Harlequins arranged by Ottokar Bartik.

CAST: *Bow Sing*, the Flower of Hong Kong: DOROTHY JARDON. *Eric D'Arcy*, an attaché of the British Legation: Leonard Kirtley. *Mong Gok*, keeper of the tea-house of the Lotus Blossoms: Frederick Gunther. *Katu*, his wife: Josephine Jacoby. *Sing Fang*, a gambler: Robert Dore. *A Mandarin*: ARTHUR CUNNINGHAM. *A Guard*: Arthur Grover. *An Old Musician*: Herbert Frank.

Scene: A Public Square in Hong Kong.

ACT 2

TORTAJADA and 16 Moorish Dancing Girls (in a Spanish Ballet)

ACT 3

LA BELLE PAREE, a Jumble of Jollity (a "Cook's Tour through Vaudeville with a Parisian Landscape") in Two Acts, 11 Scenes.[91] Book by Edgar Smith. Music by Jerome Kern and Frank Tours. Lyrics by Edward Madden. Staged by J. C. Huffman and William J. Wilson. Dances arranged by William J. Wilson. Settings by Arthur Voegtlin. Costumes designed by Melville Ellis.

CAST: *George Ramsbotham*, former undertaker and present man of business to the Widow McShane: Harry Fisher. *Eczema Johnson*, the Widow's mulatto maid: STELLA MAYHEW. *La Duchesse*, Queen of Paris, Bohemia: DOROTHY JARDON. *Fifi Montmartre*, artists' model and sweetheart of Henri: MITZI HAJOS. *La Sylphide*, a danseuse: MLLE. DAZIE. *Henri Dauber*, a young painter: Edgar Atchison-Ely. *Lady Guff Jordan*, a society modiste: KITTY GORDON. *Jack Ralston*, a failure as an art student but a success as a guide about Paris: Paul Nicholson. *Isadore Cohen*, of Bridgeport, U.S.A.: BARNEY BERNARD. *Ike Skinheimer*: Lee Harrison. *Toots Horner*, an American college youth: FLORENZ TEMPEST. *Susie Jenkins*, an American girl: MARION SUNSHINE. *Susan Brown*, a Cook's tour derelict: Ray Cox. *A Violin-ist*: Yvette. *Bridgeeta McShane*, a wealthy Irish-American widow, sojourning in Paris for her health and other people's profit: ARTHUR CUNNINGHAM. *Erastus Sparkler*, a colored aristocrat from San Juan Hill, cutting a wide swath in Paris: AL JOLSON. *Russian Dancers*: HESS SISTERS. *The Marquis de Champignon*: HAROLD A. ROBE. *Madame Clarice*, a modiste: JEAN AYLWIN. *Mimi*, forelady at Mme. Clarice's: GRACE [VON] STUDDIFORD. *Fifine*, a model: Violet Bowers. *Margot*, a model: Bessie Frewen. *Marcelle*, a model: GRACE WASHBURN. *Fifine*: Katherine McDonald. *Juliette*: May Allen. *A Flower Girl*: Sylvia Clark. *A Grisette*: Ida Kramer. *Buck Lyons*, a friend to Toots Horner: Ray Dodge. *A "Cook" Guide*: Lew Quinn. *A Cocher*: Milberry Rider. (*Ballet Specialties*: Signor Bonfiglio, Rhea and Rayo, Vlasta Novotna.)

Models and Attendants: Grace Washburn, Mae Dealy, Doris Cameron, Bessie Frewan, Beatrice Obrey, Anna Berg, May Allen, Katherine McDonald, Gladys Meyrick, Sarah Carr, Blanche Marr, Maud Stanley, Gladys Feldman, Gene Dale, Dolores Devereux, Florence Cable, Natalie Saymore, Hazel Trautman, Eileen Jackson, Jane Lawrence, Bertha Haywood, Sue Parker, Cecele Murn, May Murphy, Violet Bowers, Aileen Barnes, Lucille Page, Viola Ford, Peggy Forbes, Eveline Arnold, Hattie Brooks, Dorothy Parker. *Artists, Tourists, Guides, Grisettes, Peddlers, Apaches, Flower Girls, Gendarmes, Debutantes, etc.*: *Ladies of the Chorus*: Goldie Blair, Margaret Shields, Jennie Callan, Dorothy Wright, Ermina Evans, Ruth Heil, Tao Howard, Gertie Anderson, May Pickard, Ida Kramer, Agnes Richter, Corinne Pickard, Eva Crane, Bessie Carrette, Dorothy Godfrey, Grace Hall, Agnes Hall, Marie Lachere, Jessie Piper, Sylvia Clark, Genevieve Dolaro, Isabella Jason, Edna Hettler, Anna Pauly, Vinnie Mason, Aileen Pickard, Mazie Kimbal, Mathilde Rodriguez, Frankie Rice, Elizabeth Trunkett, Jennie Canner, Claire Burke, Frieda Sanborn, Lucy Leslie, Mona Sartorius, Daphne French, Gladys Dupell, Edith Lenox, Florence Reid, Garnet Arnold, Helen Bancroft, Catherine Call, Beatrice Burnham, Virginia Carvel, Ferrie Berg, Julie Newell, Sadie Mullen, Betty Enwright, Mabel Allen, Mae Allen, Audrey Munson, Agnes Hebron, Nellie Whitman.

The action takes place in Paris at the present time.

Act 1, Scene 1: Exterior of Cook's Office, Avenue de l'Opera. *Scene 2*: In the Place Vendome. *Scene 3*: Modiste Establishment of Mme. Clarice. *Scene 4*: In the Tuilleries Garden. *Scene 5*: Students' Ball.

Act 2, Scene 1: Dauber's Studio in the Latin Quarter. *Scene 2*: In the vicinity of the Louvre. *Scene 3*: Outside a Cafe in the Boulevard des Capucines. *Scene 4*: The Duel in the Bois de Boulogne. *Scene 5*: Street in the Latin Quarter. *Scene 6*: Ballet at the Follies Marigny.

ACT 1

Opening Chorus
Guides, Tourists

"Susan Brown from a Country Town"[92] (Song)
R. Cox

"(I'm) The Human Brush (That Paints the Crimson on Paree)"
F. Tempest, Artists
(*Music by* Jerome Kern.)

"Widows" (Song)
J. Aylwin, Chorus

"Paris Is a Paradise for Coons"[93] (Duet)
S. Mayhew, A. Jolson
(*Music by* Jerome Kern.)

"The Pretty Milliners"
Chorus

"Monte Carlo Moon" (Song)
K. Gordon

"That Deviling Tune" (De Devilin' Rag)(Song)
S. Mayhew
(*Music and Lyrics by* Billee Taylor.)

"Teasing" (Duet)
F. Tempest, M. Sunshine

---

[86]Titled "The Game I Hunt I Never Miss" in English vocal score.
[87]Titled "Oh Fortunate Man Who Has Taste and Gold" in English vocal score.
[88]Titled "Again a Cry" in English vocal score.
[89]Titled "Flow River Flow" in English vocal score.
[90]Early in the run BOW SING and TORTAJADA and Her Dance Specialty were dropped.
[91]Added after the opening:
"That's All Right for McGilligan"
(*Music by* Jerome Kern. *Lyrics by* M. E. Rourke.)
"Look Me Over Dearie"
(*Music by* Jerome Kern. *Lyrics by* Edward Madden.)

[92]Dropped during the run.
[93]Dropped during the run.

"Bosphorous" (Two-Step)
Chorus
"The Edinburgh Wriggle"[95]
J. Aylwin, Chorus
(*Music by* Jerome Kern. *Lyrics by* M. E. Rourke.)
Russian Dance
Hess Sisters, Chorus
Song and March
Yvette, Chorus

ACT 2
Violin Specialty
Yvette
(Red Domino) Dance
Mlle. Dazie
"(Sing) Trovatore" (Song)
D. Jardon
(*Music by* Jerome Kern.)
Specialty[96]
A. Jolson
"Goblins"[97] (De Goblins Glide) (Duet)
F. Tempest, M. Sunshine
(*Music by* Jerome Kern. *Lyrics by* Frederick Day.)
"What Kind of a Place Is This?"[98] (Song)
S. Mayhew
"The Duel"
Mlle. Dazie, G. Washburn, Chorus
The Ballet of Pierrots and Harlequins
Arranged by Ottokar Bonfiglio of the Metropolitan Opera House.
Solos: Mlle. Dazie, Signor Bonfiglio—Plaissanterie Classique.
Finale
Ensemble

1911.13 LITTLE MISS FIX-IT

An Entertainment with Songs (Musical Play) in Three Acts. Book by William J. Hurlbut (and George V. Hobart. Music by Nora Bayes and Jack Norworth. Lyrics by Jack Norworth) and Harry B. Smith. Staged by Gustav von Seyffertitz. Settings by D. Frank Dodge, Frank Gates, and Edward A. Morange. Miss Bayes' dresses by Lucile. Orchestra under the direction of Frederic Solomon. Produced by Louis F. Werba and Mark A. Luescher. Opened 3 April 1911 at the Globe Theatre and closed 20 May 1911 after 56 performances.[99]

CAST: *Delia Wendell*, Little Miss Fix-It: NORA BAYES. *Henry Burbank*: WILLIAM DANFORTH. *Buddie Arnold, Marjorie Arnold*, almost divorced: JACK NORWORTH, GRACE FIELD. *Percy Paget, Bella Ketcham*, almost engaged: Lionel Walsh, Eleanor Stuart. *Harold Watson, Ethel Morgan*, almost married: JAMES C. LANE, Oza Waldrop. *Mary Ann, Edward Doolittle*, almost servants: Annie Buckley, Harry Lillford. *Jimmie, Mazie*, almost grown up: Ernestine Emler, Edith Norman. *Almost Suffragettes (4)*: *Cora Lee*: Bessie Gibson. *Jane Wheatley*: Hazel Cox. *Agnes Marston*: Vivian Rushmore. *May Roberts*: Helen Hilton. *Kate Winthrop*: Estelle Perry. *Rose Lawton*: Alys Belga. *Florence Gordon*: Mona Trieste. *Fred*: Harry Wagner. *Jack*: David Stampler. *Tom*: Egbert T. Roach. *Ned*: Joseph Baumeister. *"Billie"*: W. J. Curtis. *"Cotty"*, almost human: Scottish Lad (a blue ribbon winner).

Act 1: Delia Wendell's Country Home on Long Island in July. (Dodge.)

Act 2: Interior of the Wendell Home. Evening of the same day. (Gates & Morange.)

Act 3: The same. The following morning. (Gates & Morange.)

ACT 1[100]
"Please Go Find My Billie-Boy" (Song)
N. Bayes
(*Music and Lyrics by* Fred Barnes, R. Weston.)
"No More Staying Out Late" (Staying Out Late) (Song)
J. C. Lane, Boys
(*Music and Lyrics by* Nora Bayes, Bert Lee, Jack Norworth.)
"I've a Garden in Sweden"[101] (Garden in Sweden) (Duet)
N. Bayes, J. Norworth
(*Music and Lyrics by* Nora Bayes, Dan Lipton, C. W. Murphy, Jack Norworth, Hugh Owens.)

ACT 2
"Fine Strawberries" (Strawberries)[102]
N. Bayes
(*Music by* James McGhee. *Lyrics by* Herbert Rule.)
"Parlor Games"
W. Danforth, Company
"Turn Off Your Light, Mr. Moon-Man" (Moon Man)
N. Bayes, J. Norworth
(*Music and Lyrics by* Fred Barnes, R. Weston.)

ACT 3
"(For) Months and Months"[103]
J. Norworth
(*Music and Lyrics by* Nora Bayes, Jack Norworth, Joe Tabrar.)
"The Only Bit of Ireland"[104]
N. Bayes
(*Music and Lyrics by* Fred Barnes, R. Weston.)

1911.14 THE LONDON FOLLIES

A Vaudeville and Burlesque (Revue) in Three Acts.[105] (Staged by Norman A. Blumé.) Produced by M. Howard Jones and Norman A. Blumé. Opened 17 April 1911 at Weber's Theatre and closed 21 April 1911 after 11 performances.

CAST: GEORGE E. MACK, GLADYS ARCHBUTT, NORMAN A. BLUMÉ, LAURA JAFFRAY, HELEN LALOR, CHARLES OLCOTT, NATALIE ALT, AGOSTINO BACI, Mr. Baron.

---

[95]Replaced during the run by:
"The Man I Love"
M. Sunshine, Male Chorus

[96]Jolson's Specialty included:
"That Lovin' Traumerei"
(*Music and Lyrics by* Aubrey Stauffer, adapted from Robert Schumann.)
For the tour and return engagement:
"Dat Lovin' Touch"
(*Music and Lyrics by* Leo Bennett and Sam M. Lewis.)

[97]Dropped during the run.

[98]Dropped during the run.

[99]Played a return engagement 27 November 1911 at the Grand Opera House for 8 performances.

[100]For subsequent tour with Alice Lloyd as Delia Wendell, the runing order of songs was substantially revised, and Acts 2 and 3 were combined. Added were:
Opening March (Act 1)
J. C. Lane, Boys
"There Is a Happy Land" (Tale of Woe)(Trio)(Act 1)
J. Norworth, L. Walsh, W. Danforth
(*Music by* Jerome Kern. *Lyrics by* Jack Norworth.)
"Turkey Trot" (Waltz)[instrumental](Act 2)
G. Field, J. C. Lane
(*Music by* Jerome Kern, Dave Stamper.)
"If You'll Be My Eve (I'll Build an Eden for You)"
A. Lloyd
(*Music by* J. Rosamond Johnson. *Lyrics by* James Weldon Johnson.)
"Excuse Me, Mister Moon"
A. Lloyd
(*Music by* J. Rosamond Johnson. *Lyrics by* James Weldon Johnson.)
"Have You Ever Loved Any Other Girl?"
A. Lloyd
(*Music and Lyrics by* J. P. Long and Bennett Scott.)

[101]Credited in program to Messrs. Austin, Barnes and Murphy.

[102]Dropped from subsequent tour when Nora Bayes left the show.

[103]Dropped from subsequent tour when Jack Norworth left the show.

[104]Credited in program to Messrs. Austin, Barnes and Murphy.

[105]Inspired by the success of Pelissier's London success THE FOLLIES, Norman A. Blumé attempted to assemble a similar entertainment for New York audiences.

ACT 1

Opening Chorus
Company
"Our Canadian Canoe" (Duet)
N. Alt, A. Baci
"Belles and Beaux" (Song)
L. Jaffray
"No, No, No!" (Song)
H. Lalor
Satire on Modern Musical Comedy
C. Olcott
"In Moonlight Land" (Song)
N. Alt
"Everything Has Been So Pleasant Up to Now" (Song)
G. E. Mack
"Uz-Guz-Goozle-Um" (Song)
N. A. Blumé
"Won't You Waltz with Me" (Song)
G. Archbutt
"Dear Little Girls of the U.S.A." (Quartette)
N. Alt, L. Jaffray, G. E. Mack, N. A. Blumé
Burlesque of National Music
Company
(a) Spanish, (b) Scotch, (c) Dutch, (d) Swiss.

ACT 2

THE BALKY PRINCESS, a Canned Comedy (Burlesque of "The Balkan Princess"[106]) in Three Tins. Book and lyrics by Charles Brown. Music by Paul A. Rubens.

CAST: *Princess Stiff Annie*: G. E. Mack. *Sofa*: G. Archbutt. *Duke Splurgious*: N. A. Blumé. *Blots*: L. Jaffray. *Porous*: H. Lalor. *Captain*: C. Olcott. *Lieutenant*: N. Alt. *Hennery*, a waiter: A. Baci. *Stage Hand*: C. Olcott.

Tin the First: The Palace. *Tin the Second*: The Cafe des Enfants. *Tin the Third*: Gardens of the Palace.

ACT 3

THE LAMB OF DELFT, a Phantasy in Blue. Libretto and lyrics by Joseph Herbert. Music by Arthur Weld.

CAST: *Bothof*, Burgmaster of Delft: G. E. Mack. *Lena*: G. Archbutt. *Hoek*: H. Lalor. *Van Rooy*: C. Olcott. *Renskop*: L. Jaffray. *Kloof*: Mr. Baron. *Hoch*, the Standing Army: A. Baci. *Jean*: N. A. Blumé. *Valerie*: N. Alt.

1911.15 DR. DE LUXE

A Little Play with a Little Music (Novel Musical Play) in Three Acts. Book and lyrics by Otto Hauerbach [Harbach]. Music by Karl Hoschna. Entire production staged by Frank Smithson. Settings designed by P. Dodd Ackerman, William Castle, and Walter H. Harvey. Costumes by the Orange Manufacturing Co. Musical director, Gustave Salzer. Produced by Joseph M. Gaites. Opened 17 April 1911 at the Knickerbocker Theatre and closed 13 May 1911 after 32 performances.[107]

CAST: *Dr. DePaw*: Taylor Williams. *Miss Barker*: Rena Santos. *Miss Ada Houston*: Marion Ballou. *Sadie*: POLLY PRIM. *Dennis*: ERNEST TRUEX. *Kittie Melville*: JEANETTE CHILDS. *Mrs. Dorothy Melville*: Helen Robertson. *Dr. Robert Melville*: Harry Stone. *Mrs. Clara Houston*: GEORGIE KELLY. *Margie Melville*: ETHEL GREEN. *Donald Houston*: Edward Nicander. *John Truesdale*, otherwise known as Dr. DeLuxe: RALPH HERZ. *Colonel Houston*: WILLIAM PRUETTE. *Hattie Heartsdale*: Lillian Berry. *Francesca Foote*: Ethel Millard. *Annette Armswell*: Verna Dalton. *Lottie LaNerve*: Bessie Muller. *Lillian Legglesby*: Anna Hall. *Louise Lipton*: Julia Mills. *Vera Van Dentine*: Ada Mitchell. *Laura Lashwood*: Florence Campbell. *Toodlums*: Albert Lamson. *Kiddies*: Anna Lichter, Cecilia Renard, Evelyn Lancer, Dixie Costello, Helen Larkins, Jeanette Alpine, Anna Sheldon, Kathryn Sinclair.

Act 1: Dr. DePaw's Pet Emporium, just Off Broadway. A summer afternoon. (Ackerman.)

Act 2: Dr. Melville's Waiting Room and Private Office in the Hotel Lennox, New York City. Toward evening of the same day. (Ackerman.)

Act 3: Summer Garden in the Court of the Hotel Lennox, and just below Mrs. Houston's bedroom window. Evening of the same day. (Castle & Harvey.)

ACT 1

"Mama's Little Pet"
Opening Chorus
"That's the Way to Treat a Little Doggie"
J. Childs, Children
"The Accent Makes No Difference in the Language of Love"
E. Truez, P. Prim
"That Will Keep Him True to You"
G. Kelly, Ladies
"What You Want and What You Get" (What We Want and What We Get)
R. Herz
(*Music and Lyrics by* Edward Laska.)
"War Is Hell, But Oh You Jealousy" (War Is Hell, but Oh You Green-Eyed Monster)
W. Pruette, Ladies
"For Every Boy That's Lonely"
A. Lamson

ACT 2

"The Family Brawl"
Opening Chorus
"No One But You"
R. Herz
Ventriloquist
R. Santos
"For Every Boy That's Lonely There's a Girl Who's Lonely Too"
E. Green

ACT 3

"Hide and Seek"
Opening Chorus
"When the Old Top Hummed" (The Humming Top)
E. Green, Girls
"Skeletons in the Closet"
P. Prim, E. Truex
"The Harum-Scarum"
J. Chidls, Kids
"Love Is a Race"
R. Herz

1911.16 I SALTIMBANCHI

An Opéra-comique in Three Acts, 4 Scenes, performed in Italian. (Original French libretto 'Les Saltimbanques' by Maurice Ordonneau.) Music by Louis Ganne. Impressario, Signor Raimondo. Conductor, Guiseppe Canepa. Management, Max Rabinoff and Ben H. Atwell. Opened 24 April 1911 at the Majestic Theatre and closed 26 April 1911 (matinee) after 3 performances.[108]

CAST: *Marion*: AMELIA BRUNO. *Susanna*: E. CANEPA. *Andreasi Langeat*: G. MERIGHI. *Pagliaccio*: L. GUIDI. *Pingouin*: F. ELEONORI. *Egisto Malicorne*: G. FARRI. *Madama Malicorne*: M. COLAGRANDE. *Il Conte des Etiquettes*: S. Bonanno. *Il Barone Vallengoujon*: L. Giorgi. *La Baronessa Vallengoujon*: A. Verdi. *Il Marchesse Del Libano*: R. Romli. *Bertillard*: L. Campeggi. *Komponnet*: D. Baccarini. *Pisonnet*: N. Grillo. *Simona*: V. Malia. *Geltrude*: A. Brozini. *Toaladette*: R. Margio. *Frigolette*: T. Beccari.

1911.17 A CERTAIN PARTY

A Musical Farce in Three Acts. (Book and lyrics by Edgar Smith.[109]) Based on a comedy ("The Head of the House") by Frank Ward O'Malley and Edward W. Townsend. Music by Robert Hood Bowers. Staged by William

[106] Original libretto for THE BALKAN PRINCESS by Frederick Lonsdale and Frank Curzon, music by Paul A. Rubens, lyrics by Paul A. Rubens and Arthur Wimperis.

[107] Played a return engagement 16 October 1911 at the Grand Opera House for 8 performances.

[108] Italian adaptation uncredited. No credits for costumes, scenery, director or musical director. No musical numbers listed.

[109] Edgar Smith's name does not appear in any New York credits, playbill or reviews. Townsend and O'Malley's names appear as librettist during the tryout, and Edgar Smith's name appear for the subsequent tour.

Collier. Musical numbers arranged by Joseph C. Smith. Costumes by Lucille; Hitchins; Max & Mahieu. Orchestra under the direction of Tom Kelly. Produced by Liebler and Company (Theodore Liebler, George C. Tyler). Opened 24 April 1911 at Wallack's Theatre and closed 13 May 1911 after 24 performances.[110]

CAST: *Homer Caldwell*: JAMES SEELEY. *George Caldwell*, his son: ALFRED KAPPELER. *James Barrett*, a detective sergeant: MIKE DONLIN. *Jerry Fogarty*, a political boss: JOHN T. KELLY. *Sydney Finch*, a gambling house proprietor: HAROLD HARTSELL. *Danny Clark*, Norah's younger brother: Arthur O'Keefe. *Roundsman Timothy Moline*: Richard Garrick. *Atkins*, the Caldwell's butler: John Peachey. *Members of the Jeremiah J. Fogarty Association* (7), they vote early and often: *Larry Dunn*: John Pierce. *Handsome Harry*: Quayle Settliffe. *Buck Powers*: Andrew Brannigan. *Patrick Reilly*: Andrew Brannigan. *Barney Rafferty*: Eddie Cline. *Ikey Finklestein*: George Sullivan. *Jerry Fagan*: Frank Grom. *Mrs. Lorimer*, Caldwell's widowed sister: Beatrice Moreland. *Grace Fairweather*, her step-daughter: Nina Blake. *Mrs. Jeremiah Fogarty*: Louise Dempsey. *Society Girls* (3): *Miss Depuyster*: Marie Ashton. *Miss Brompton*: Esther Bissett. *Miss Ogilvie*: Ruth Lloyd. *Mary*: Susanne Willis. *Maybelle Carrington*, kitchen assistant: Lillian Herbert. *Lena*, housemaid: Carolyn Parsons. *Carrie Keyes*, stenographer: Ruth Lloyd. *Norah*, Grace's maid: MABEL HITE.

The Fogarty Asssociation's Lady Friends: Misses Parsons, Williams, Clements, Welson, Lane, Howard, Holmes, Randall, Harris, Dana, Depp. *Society Boys*: Messrs. Pierce, Jaffola, Setliffe, Grom, Johnson, Brannigan, Cline, Devlin, Rogers.

The action takes place at the present time in Manhattan.

Act 1: The Caldwell Library.

Act 2: The Caldwell Kitchen.

Act 3: The Caldwell Drawing Room.

ACT 1[111]

"I Want Another Situation Just Like That"
M. Hite

"Love's Wireless Telephone"
N. Blake, A. Kappeler, Chorus
(*Lyrics by* Ramond Peck.)

"Walking Delegate"
M. Hite

ACT 2

"Get the Hook"
M. Hite
(*Music by* Tom Kelly.)

"(Why Don't You Get a Sweetheart from the) Emerald Isle"
M. Hite

"Turkey Trot"
M. Hite, M. Donlin, Chorus
(*Music by* Tom Kelly.)

ACT 3

"I Want a Boy"
N. Blake, A. Keppeler, Chorus
(*Music by* Tom Kelly.)

"Fogarty"
J. T. Kelly, Chorus

"You're Going to Lose Your Husband"
M. Hite
(*Music and Lyrics by* Mabel Hite.)

1911.18 HELL/TEMPTATIONS/GABY

A Triple Bill of HELL, a Profane Burlesque in 2 Scenes; TEMPTATIONS, a Ballet in One Act; and GABY, a Satirical Revuette in 3 Scenes. Staged by George Marion. Ballet and ensembles staged by Alfredo Curti. Scenes designed by Ernest Albert. Produced by Henry B. Harris and Jesse L. Lasky. Opened 27 April 1911 at the Folies Bergère Theatre and closed 8 July 1911 after 92 performances.[112]

ACT 1: HELL, a Profane Burlesque in 2 Scenes. Book and lyrics by Rennold Wolf. (Music by Robert Hood Bowers, Maurice Levi, Irving Berlin.) Staged by George Marion.

CAST (in order of appearance): *Maude Adams*: ADA LEWIS. *The Statue of Liberty*: Elizabeth Goodall. *A Herald*: Leslie Leigh. *A Room Clerk*: Arthur Lipson. *The Devil*: OTIS HARLAN. *Mrs. Devil*: ADA LEWIS. *The Janitor*: W. C. Gordon. *A Hell Boy*: Marion Ford. *A Pittsburgh Magnate*: Theodore Marston. *Mrs. Maxon Newrow*: Mayme Kelso. *Phoebe Snow*: LESLIE LEIGH. *A Clergyman*: John Marble. *Mlle. Montparnassus*: MLLE. LENCLUD. *A Prima Donna*: KATHLEEN CLIFFORD. *A Shoe Store Clerk*: KATHLEEN CLIFFORD. *Salome*: LESLIE LEIGH. *A Police Captain*: W. C. Gordon. *A Dancer*: EMILY LEA.

In the Department Store: *A Saleswoman*: ADA LEWIS. *An Actress*: Geraldine Gerard. *An Old Maid*: Mayme Kelso. *Nat Woodwin*: John Marble. *A Loudly Dressed Woman*: LESLIE LEIGH. *An Antique*: Patrick Walsh. *A Matinee Girl*: Kathleen Clifford. *Four Husbands*: Messrs. Hoffman, Hamilton, Wilson, Piper. *A Messenger Boy*: Kittie Devere.

In the Society Prize Fight: *Dreadnaught Drexel*: Arthur Lipson. *Battling Beresford*: Taylor Holmes. *A Second*: Kathleen Clifford. *Another Second*: OTIS HARLAN.

Inhabitants of Hell: Misses Belmont, Johnson, Carson, Mayo, Ford, Devere, Steinhardt, Gray, the Pender Troupe. *Delegates from The Cities of the World*: Misses Richmond, Clark, Romero, Leslie, Thurston, Ralphe, Roller, Gerard, Renon, Landers, Hordlow, Francis, Vincent, Ashe, Robertson, Danvers, Burns, Priest, Davies, Adair, M. Wyatt, B. Wyatt, Barreto, Dodsworth, Mongiardino, Curti, Everett, Tonini, Rose, Patterson, Frey, Walsh. *Shoe Clerks*: Messrs. Heinemann, Wilson, Hoffman, Kittridge, Piper, Townshend, Darling, Hamilton. *Shoe Store Shoppers*: Misses Richmond, Ralphe, Renon, Landers, Hordlow, Ashe, Robertson, Dodsworth. *Messenger Boys*: Misses Belmont, Johnson, Carson, Mayo, Ford, Devere, Steinhardt, Grey. *Lonely Maidens*: Misses Richmond, Clark, Romero, Leslie, Thurston, Ralphe, Roller, Gerard.

Representatives of the New York Clubs: Misses Richmond, Clark, Romero, Leslie, Thurston, Ralphe, Roller, Gerard, Francis, Ashe, Burns, Priest, Mayo, Ford, Devere, Steinhardt, Gray, M. Wyatt, B. Waytt, Barretto, Dodsworth, Mortimer, Curti, Lovelace.

The Infernal Guards: Misses Renon, Landers, Hordlow, Vincent, Robertson, Johnson, Carson, Danvers, Davies, Adair, Sassone, Reine, Florence, Ronayne, Everett, Mongia.

Scene 1: Bedloe's Island. *Scene 2*: The Reception Room in Hell.

MUSICAL NUMBERS

Opening Chorus
Ensemble

March of the Delegations from All Parts of the World
(*Music by* Robert Hood Bowers.)

"How'd You Like to be the Shoe Store Man?"
K. Clifford, Clerks, Shoppers
(*Music by* Maurice Levi.)

Specialty
E. Lea

"Answer Me"[113]
L. Leigh, Lonely Maidens, Messengers
(*Music by* Irving Berlin.)

Valse d'Amour
Mlle. Lenclud, assisted by Mons. Victor

March of the New York Clubs
(*Music by* Maurice Levi.)

March of the Infernal Guards

ACT 2: TEMPTATIONS, a Ballet in One Act. Invented and produced by Alfredo Curti. Music by Edmond Diet. Orchestra conducted by Charles Berton.

CAST: *Rene*, young student: EMILY LEA. *Lily*: FRAULEIN NOVOTNA. *The Spirit of Pleasure, The Spirit of Games*: Signorina Borghini. *Eunuch*: Waldo Heinemann. *Favorita*: Yvonne Renon. *Spirit of Smoke*: Mlle. Cavallori. *Lady Nicotine, Champagne, Voluptuousness*: Mlle. Britta. Assisted by 60 Ladies of Corps de Ballet and the Pender Troupe. Cigarettes, Liquers, Cards, Roulettes, Daughters of Eve, Voluptee, Courtesans and Slaves of Love.

Scene: A Palace in the Kingdom of Pleasure.

---

[110]Settings uncredited.

[111]Also performed as a specialty in the show as per published sheet music, or on tour:

"I'm Going Back to Reno" (I'm On My Way to Reno)
M. Hite
(*Music by* Jean Schwartz. *Lyrics by* William Jerome.)

[112]Costumes, musical director for Act 1 uncredited.

[113]Replaced during the run by:

"Keep a Taxi Waiting, Dear"
L. Leigh, Lonely Maidens, Messengers
(*Music and Lyrics by* Irving Berlin, Ted Snyder, Vincent Bryan.)

Synopsis: In a scene of magical beauty, the tempter in the Court of Pleasure shows Rene, who has deserted his sweetheart Lily, by means of a procession, the Passions of his life. First, Lady Nicotine appears, with all her perfumed train, then Champagne, followed by the most delicious liqueurs; following them, the cards and roulettes show Rene his passion for gaming and love of gold. At last the Voluptees pass before him and offer themselves and when Rene is about to succumb to the temptresses, he hears a strain of music from afar which awakens in him memories of his innocent Lily and her pure love. Rene calls to his fiancée to save him and as he kisses the flower she gave him, Lily appears with outstretched arms. The vanquished passions disappear before her and Rene embraces his bride.

ACT 3: GABY, a Satirical Revuette in 3 Scenes. Book and lyrics by Harry B. Smith and Robert B. Smith. (Music by Robert Hood Bowers, Irving Berlin, Ted Snyder, Vincent Bryan.) Staged by George Marion. Ensembles by Alfredo Curti. Orchestra conducted by Daniel Dore.

CAST (in order of appearance): *Mrs. Lyon Hunter*: Elizabeth Goodall. *Dolly Longreen*: Kathleen Clifford. *The Royal Governess*: ADA LEWIS. *King Manny*: LADDIE CLIFF. *First Messenger Boy*: Erma Bauer. *Second Messenger Boy*: Helen Marlowe. *Gaby*: ETHEL LEVEY. *A Toreador*: W. C. Gordon. *Izzy Smart*: Taylor Holmes. *Martini*: Arthur Lipson. *Wiley Fox*: OTIS HARLAN. *Spanish Dances*: Arenera Duo. And The Pender Troupe.

Toreadors: Misses Richmond, Clark, Romero, Leslie, Thurston, Ralphe, Roller, Gerard, Renee, Landers, Hordlow, Francis, Dorlys, Ashe, Robertson, Belmont, Johnson, Carson, Danvers, Burns, Priest, Davies, Adair, Mayo, Ford, Devere, Steinhardt, Grey, M. Wyatt, Barretto, B. Wyatt, Dodsworth, Sassone, Mortimer, Reine, Florence, Stockton, Curti, Everett, Tonini, Faccioli, Sayer, Morgia, Lovelace; Messrs. Heinemann, Wilson, Hoffman, Kittridge, Piper, Townsend, Darling, Hamilton. *Porters*: Messrs. Heinemann, Wilson, Hoffman, Kittridge, Piper, Townsend, Darling, Hamilton, Borneman, Overton.

The March of the Nations: *Beauties*: *Arabian*: Miss Richmond. *Austrian*: Miss Clark. *Turkish*: Miss Romero. *Russian*: Miss Roller. *Japanese*: Miss Robertson. *English*: Miss Johnson. *German*: Miss Mayo. *American*: Miss Clifford.

Soldiers: *Arabian*: Misses Sassone, Everett, Sayer, Mongiardino. *Austrian*: Misses *Russian*: Misses Carson, Ford, Devere, Gray. Leslie, Thurston, Ralphe, Gerard. *Turkish*: Misses Danvers, Burns, Davies, Steinhardt. *Japanese*: Misses Barretto, Mongia, Lovelace, Curti. *English*: Misses Priest, Adair, M. Wyatt, B. Wyatt. *German*: Misses Hordlow, Francis, Dorlys, Ashe. *American*: Misses Dodsworth, Renon, Landers, Belmont. *Italian*: Misses Walsh, Rose, Patterson, Frey. *French*: Misses Mortimer, Reine, Florence, Stockton. *Nobles*: Misses Knight, Edwards, Faccioli, Graneta, Ronayne, Bertrand, Dean, Dun, Marlowe, Bauer.

MUSICAL NUMBERS

Scene 1

Specialty
La Arenera, assisted by Mons. Victor

Opening Chorus[114]

"Sarasa" (Spanish Dance)
E. Levey

"Don't Stop, Mr. Jenkinson"
L. Cliff

"March of the Toreadors"
(*Music by* Robert Hood Bowers.)

"Spanish Love"
E. Levey
(*Music and Lyrics by* Irving Berlin, Ted Snyder, Vincent Bryan.)

Scene 2

"I Beg Your Pardon, (Dear Old) Broadway"
E. Levey, Porters
(*Music and Lyrics by* Irving Berlin.)

"(Let's All Go) Down the Strand"
E. Levey, L. Cliff
(*Music and Lyrics by* Bernard Rolt, E. G. McLellan.)

Specialty[115]
The Pender Troupe

Scene 3

March of the Beauties of the Nations

Finale
Entire Company

[114]May have been the following published musical number:
"Down to the Folies Bergere"
(*Music and Lyrics by* Irving Berlin, Ted Snyder, Vincent Bryan.)

[115]Dropped during the run.

1911.19 AMOR DI PRINCIPE

An Operetta in Three Acts, in Italian. (Original Viennese libretto "Pufferl"[116] by Ignaz Schnitzer and Sigmund Schlesinger.) Music by Edmund Eysler. Impressario, Signor Raimondo. Conductor, Guiseppe Canepa. Management, Max Rabinoff and Ben H. Atwell. Opened 2 May 1911 at the Majestic Theatre and closed 6 May 1911 after 7? performances.[117]

CAST: *Natalie*: Ines Imbimbo. *Stanislaus*: G. Farri. *Pufferl*: FAUSTO ELEONARI. *Ewald*: Giuseppe Merighi. *Kate*: Virginia Farri. *Chiffon*: Elvira Canepa. *Lili*: Esther Cozzi. *Mimi*: Augusta Verdi. *Fifi*: Gilda Beccardi. *Franz*: Ludovico Guidi. *The Governor*: Silvio Carbone. *Mother Superior*: Adelina Levia. *Countess of Ribord*: MARIA COLOGRANDE. *First Majordomo*: Luigi Campeggi. *Second Majordomo*: Ugo Carranti. *First Lady*: S. Precerutti. *Second Lady*: A. Bronzini. *Maddalena*: E. Galleti. *Eva*: E. Lancetti. *Tecla*: E. Gironetti. *Sofia*: L. Compeggi. *A Groom*: M. Grillo.

1911.20 HIS HONOR, THE BARBER

The Smart Set Company in a Musical Comedy in Three Acts, 7 Scenes. Book by Edwin Hanaford. Music by James T. Brymn. Lyrics by Chris Smith and James Burris. Staged by S. H. Dudley. Produced by the Southern Enchantment Company. Opened 8 May 1911 at the Majestic Theatre and closed 20 May 1911 after 16 performances.[118]

CAST: *Raspberry Snow*: S. H. DUDLEY. *Mose Lewis*: James Burris. *Captain Percival Dandelion*: Will Grundy. *Wellington White*: James Lightfoot. *Lily White*: ELIZABETH HART. *Caroline Brown*: ELLA ANDERSON. *Ella Wheeler Wilson*: Alberta Ormes. *Babe Johnson*: ANDREW TRIBBLE. *Patrick*: The Donkey. *The Lion*: Will Everly. *The Bear*: George McClain. *The Monkey*: John Warren. *Specialty*: AIDA OVERTON WALKER.

MUSICAL NUMBERS[119]

"Caroline Brown"

"Come After Breakfast (Bring 'Long Your Lunch and Leave 'Fore Supper Time)"

"Consolation Time"
(*Music by* Ford Dabney.)

"Corn Shucking Time"

"Cry Baby in Town"

"Gee Ain't America a Grand Old Place"
(*Music and Lyrics by* Chris Smith.)

"Golly, Ain't I Wicked"

"His Dream Is Over"

"I Like That"

"The Isle of Love"

"Let Him Dream"

"Merry Widow Brown"

"Pickaninny Days"

"Porto Rico"
A. O. Walker

"Rainbow Sue"

"Rubber-necking Moon"
E. Hart, Chorus

"Sweetness"
J. Burriss, Chorus

"That's Why They Call Me Shine" (Shine)
(*Music and Lyrics by* Ford Dabney and Cecil Mack.)

"Watermelon Time"

"You Needn't Come at All"
S. H. Dudley

[116]The New York press referred to the Viennese original as "Furstenliebe."

[117]Scenery, costumes, conductor uncredited. No musical numbers listed.

[118]No New York program found.

[119]Not in performance order.

1911.21 H.M.S. PINAFORE, or The Lass That Loved a Sailor

A Star Revival of the Comic Opera in Two Acts.[120] Libretto by William S. Gilbert. Music by Arthur Sullivan. Staged by Lewis Morton. Scenery painted by H. Robert Law. Costumes by Mme. Ripley. Orchestra directed by Silvio Hein. Produced by William A. Brady and the Messrs. Shubert. Opened 29 May 1911 at the Casino Theatre and closed 8 July 1911 after 48 performances.

CAST: *The Rt. Hon. Sir Joseph Porter, K.C.B.*, First Lord of the Admiralty: HENRY E. DIXEY. *Captain Corcoran*, Commanding *H.M.S. Pinafore*: GEORGE J. MacFARLANE. *Ralph Rackstraw*, Able Seaman: ARTHUR ALDRIDGE. *Dick Deadeye*, Able Seaman: DeWOLF HOPPER. *Bill Bobstay*, Boatswain: Eugene Cowles. *Bob Becket*, carpenter's mate: Robert Davies. *Josephine*, the Captain's Daughter: LOUISE GUNNING. *Little Buttercup*, Mrs. Cripps, a Portsmouth bumboat woman: MARIE CAHILL. *Hebe*, Sir Joseph's First Cousin: Alice Brady. *First Lord's Sisters, his Cousins and His Aunts, Sailors, etc*: Full Chorus.

1911.22 A COUNTRY GIRL

A Revival of the Musical Play in Two Acts.[121] Book by John T. Tanner. Music by Paul Rubens and Lionel Monckton. Lyrics by Adrian Ross and Percy Greenbank. Staged by Melville Stewart. Produced by the Gray-Stewart Musical Company. Opened 29 May 1911 at the Herald Square Theatre and closed 24 June 1911 after 32 performances.

CAST: *Geoffrey Challoner*: MELVILLE STEWART. *The Rajah of Bhong*: ROBERT ELLIOTT. *Sir Joseph Verity*: GEORGE E. MACK. *Douglas Verity*: Donald Hall. *Granfer Mummery*: A. W. Flemming. *Lord Anchester*: Cyril Chadwick. *Lord Grassmere*: A. L. Clark. *Major Vicat*: W. L. Doyle. *Sir Charles Cortelyou*: Charles Kamp. *Her Tulzer*: F. von Gottfried. *Rube Fairfax*: J. A. Bingham. *Barry*: JOHN SLAVIN. *Marjorie Joy*: GRACE FREEMAN. *Princess Mehelanch*: GENEVIEVE FINLAY. *Mlle. Sophie*: Laura Jaffray. *Nan*: Florence Burdett. *Mrs. St. Quinton Raikes*: Ada Sterling. *Nurse*: Anna Bell. *Lady Anchester*: Ada Sterling. *Lady Arnott*: Teresa Bryant. *Miss Carruthers*: May Wesley. *Miss Powyscourt*: Edna Houck. *Miss Courtlands*: Madge Gest. *Miss Ecroyd*: Ada Holt. *Miss Fitzroy*: Florence Burnham. *Miss Arundel*: Florence Farmer.

---

[120]Originally presented in New York 15 January 1879 at the Standard Theatre for 175 performances. For Synopsis of Scenes and Musical Numbers, see original 1879 production.

[121]First produced in New York 22 September 1902 at Daly's Theatre for 112 performances. For Synopsis of Scenes and Musical Numbers, see original 1902 production.

1911–1912 SEASON

Julian Eltinge in THE FASCINATING WIDOW
Billy Rose Theatre Collection, New York Public Library for the Performing Arts

1911–1912 SEASON

1911.23 THE RED ROSE

Valeska Suratt and Her Own Company in a Musical Comedy in Three Acts. Book and lyrics by Harry B. Smith and Robert B. Smith. Music by Robert Hood Bowers. Production staged by R. H. Burnside. Dances arranged by Jack Mason. All robes, costumes and scenery designed by Valeska Suratt. Orchestra under the direction of Louis F. Gottschalk. Produced under the management of Lee Harrison. Opened 22 June 1911 at the Globe Theatre and closed 26 August 1911 after 76 performances.[1]

CAST: *Lola, an artists' model*: VALESKA SURATT. *Dick Lorimer, the model's artist*: WALLACE McCUTCHEON. *Alonzo Lorimer*: ALEXANDER CLARK. *Silas Plant*: John Daly Murphy. *Hon. Lionel Talboys*: ERNEST LAMBART. *Daisy Plant*: LILLIAN GRAHAM. *Ludwig Spiegle*: JOHN E. HAZZARD. *Mme. Joyant*: FLAVIA ARCARO. *M. Duprez*: HENRY BERGMAN. *Andre*: CRAIG CAMPBELL. *Gyp*: Carrie Reynolds. *Baron LeBlanc*: LOUIS CASAVANT. *Maxime DuPont*: HENRY BERGMAN.

Wedded to Art: *Tita*: Beatrice Doane. *Celeste*: Edna Bates. *Marie*: May Carlisle. *Rosalie*: Marjorie Dayton. *Denise*: Laura Gaynelle. *Elane*: Dorothy Langdon. *Louise*: Nellie Remmington. *Flane*: Adelaide Warren. *Six English Rosebuds*: Misses Ethel Rosebud, Minna Cook, Nellie Cartner, Sallie Irving, Daisy Atkinson, Grace Lambert. *Members of the Art School*: Misses Jane Warrington, Josie Kernell, Elizabeth Young, Eleanore Dayne, Irene Messenger, Kittie Howland, Myrtle Best, Bessie Holbrook, Helen O'Day. Messrs. Kugler, Kirkwood, Strangard, Ward, Hayes, Willingham, Tuller, Smith.

The action takes place in Paris.

Act 1: The Art School of M. Julian Duprez.

Act 2: The Baron's Chateau. Six months later.

Act 3: The Ball of the Four Arts.

ACT 1

Opening Chorus
C. Campbell, Students
(*Lyrics by* Robert B. Smith.)

"Come Along, Ma Cherie" (Duet)
V. Suratt, W. McCutcheon
(*Lyrics by* Robert B. Smith.)

"Spanish Love"[2] (Song)
V. Suratt, Chorus
(*Lyrics by* Harry B. Smith.)

"(In) the Land of the Free" (Song)
A. Clark, Chorus
(*Lyrics by* Robert B. Smith.)

"If You Can't Sing, Dance" (Duet)
E. Lambert, C. Reynolds
(*Lyrics by* Robert B. Smith.)

"The Old Ballet Days" (Duet)
J. E. Hazzard, F. Arcaro

Finale

ACT 2[3]

Opening Chorus
(*Lyrics by* Harry B. Smith.)

"Wedding Bells" (Duet)
C. Campbell, C. Reynolds

"I'd Like to Go on a Honeymoon with You" (Duet)
J. E. Hazzard, F. Arcaro
(*Lyrics by* Harry B. Smith.)

"The Queen of Vanity Fair" (Song)
V. Suratt, Chorus
(*Lyrics by* Harry B. Smith.)

"Hammock Song" (Then You Swing, Swing, Swing)
E. Lambert, Bridesmaids
(*Lyrics by* Robert B. Smith.)

"Love and Beauty"[4] (Waltz Duet)
V. Suratt, W. McCutcheon

"Buy, Buy, Baby" (Trio)
A. Clark, C. Reynolds, J. D. Murphy
(*Lyrics by* Harry B. Smith.)

Finale

ACT 3[5]

"The Dance of the Seven Saturnalias" (Opening)
V. Suratt, 6 English Rosebuds

"(You Can) Go As Far as You Like with Me"[6]
A. Clark, W. McCutcheon, Chorus
(*Lyrics by* Harry B. Smith.)

"Students' Glide" (Turkey Wing March)
V. Suratt, Chorus

"The Brass Band"[7] (Quartette)
F. Arcaro, J. E. Hazzard, C. Reynolds, C. Campbell

Russian Dance Classique[8]
L. Graham

"Men! Men! Men!"[9] (Song)
V. Suratt, Men
(*Lyrics by* Harry B. Smith.)

[1]Played a return engagement 11 September 1911 at the Grand Opera House for 8 performances.
[2]Dropped for subsequent tour.
[3]Added to Act 2 for subsequent tour, following "Wedding Bells":
"Don't Mention My Name" (Song)
Carlton King (Alonzo Lorimer)
[4]Replaced for subsequent tour by:
"I'm All Thine" (Waltz Duet)
V. Suratt, Al Rauh (Dick Lorimer)
(*Lyrics by* Harry B. Smith.)
[5]Added to Act 3 for subsequent tour:
"Rum-ti-tiddle" (Song)
C. King
"Yo Ho! Yo Ho!" (Song)
C. Campbell
Confetti March and Finale
[6]Dropped for subsequent tour.
[7]Dropped for subsequent tour.
[8]Dropped late in the run and for subsequent tour.
[9]Dropped for subsequent tour.

1911.24 ZIEGFELD FOLLIES OF 1911

A Musical Extravagnaza (Revue) in Two Acts, 13 Scenes.[10] Words (sketches) and lyrics by George V. Hobart. Music by Maurice Levi and Raymond Hubbell. (Additional music and lyrics by Irving Berlin, Jerome Kern, James Blyler, Sid Brown, Vincent Bryan, Henry Marshall, Stanley Murphy.) Staged by Julian Mitchell. Musical numbers arranged by Gus Sohlke, Jack Mason. Settings designed by Ernest Albert, Edward G. Unitt and Joseph Wickes. Costumes by W. H. Matthews. Musical director, Joseph Sainton. Produced by Florenz Ziegfeld. Opened 26 June 1911 at the Jardin de Paris and closed 2 September 1911 after 80 performances.

CAST: LEON ERROL, BERT WILLIAMS, FANNY BRICE, LILLIAN LORRAINE, VERA MAXWELL, BESSIE McCOY, THE DOLLY SISTERS (Rosika, Jenny [Ganesi]), CLARA PALMER, ARLINE BOLEY, STELLA CHATELAINE, THE GORMAN SISTERS (Emma, ?), TOM DINGLE, WALTER PERCIVAL, (Sid) BROWN and (James) BLYLER, Katherine Daly, Eleanor St. Clair, Charles A. Mason, George White, Harry Watson Jr., Charles Hessong, W. J. Kelly, Peter Swift, Leslie Coverra.

Anna Held Girls (75): Elise Belga, Ann Meredith, Ethel Clayton, Dorothy Dalland, Misses Vernon, Abbott, Trieste, Richmond, Mitchell, Aichel, Perry, LeRoy, etc.

ACT 1[11]

Scene 1

The Customs (*Painted by* Ernest Albert.)

"New York (You're the Best Town in Europe)"
W. Percival, Ensemble
(*Music by* Raymond Hubbell. *Lyrics by* Raymond W. Peck.)

Siamese Twins Dance
Dolly Sisters

[10]The fifth in the annual series of revues produced by Florenz Ziegfeld beginning in 1907.
[11]No complete New York program found; New York program from 28 August 1911 found for Act 1, Scenes 1-4. Boston tour program used for all subsequent musical numbers.

"The Widow Wood"
C. Palmer, Ensemble
(*Music by* Maurice Levi. *Lyrics by* Channing Pollock, Rennold Wolf.)
Dance[12]
L. Errol, S. Chatelaine
Folly of 1907: E. Gorman. *Folly of 1908*: E. Belga. *Folly of 1909*: K. Daly. *Folly of 1910*: E. St. Clair. *Folly of 1911*: V. Maxwell. *Inspector Search*: L. Errol. *F. Ziegfeld Jr.*: W. Percival. *Siamese Twins*: Dolly Sisters. *Mrs. Hillside*: A. Boley. *Widow Wood*: C. Palmer. *Miss Prim*, a dancer from abroad: S. Chatelaine.

Scene 2

Jardin de Paris (*Painted by* E. Albert.)
Herr Lauderspiel, from Hamburg: C. A. Mason. With his Saengerbund.

Scene 3

A California Poppy Field (*Painted by* Unitt & Wickes.)
"The Bumble Bee" (Dance)
T. Dingle
(*Music by* James B. Blyler. *Lyrics by* A. Donnelly, Jean Havez.)
Reuben Jay: T. Dingle. *Willie*: R. Dolly. *Jack*: G. Dolly.

Scenes 4-7

Everywife (A Symbolic Play in 4 Scenes) (*Painted by* E. Albert.)
"The Girl in Pink" (Scene 5)
W. Percival, assisted by V. Maxwell, Misses Raynham, Sewell, Virginia, Foster, Gross, McKnight, Dana, Gabrielle
(*Music by* Raymond Hubbell.)
"The Imitation Rag" (Scene 6)
S. Brown, J. Blyler
Time: Yesterday, Today and Always. *Scene 4*: The Home. *Scene 5*: The Stage Door. A month elapses. *Scene 6*: Everyhusband's Club. Another month elapses. *Scene 7*: The Home.
Women: *Everywife*: A. Meredith. *Happiness*: V. Maxwell. *Jealousy*: C. Palmer. *Squabina*: E. Clayton. *Care*: A. Boley. *Dress*: Miss Vernon. *Excitement*: Miss Abbott. *Elegance*: Miss Belga. *Kindness*: Miss Trieste. *Gaiety*: Miss Richmond. *Loveliness*: Miss Dalland. *Grace*: Miss Mitchell. *Amusement*: Miss Aichel. *Vanity*: Miss Perry. *Romantic*: Miss LeRoy.
Men: *Everyhusband*: W. Percival. *Rhyme*: H. Watson, Jr. *Reason*: W. J. Kelly. *Drink*: L. Errol. *Gamble*: P. Swift. *Nobody*: B. Williams.

Scene 8

"Take Care, Little Girl, (Take Care)"
B. McCoy
(*Music by* Raymond Hubbell.)
Scene: The Poppy Field.

Scene 9

New Year's Eve on the Barbary Coast
"Texas Tommy (Swing)"
V. Maxwell, H. Watson, Jr., L. Errol, Ensemble
(*Music by* Sid Brown. *Lyrics by* Val Harris.)
Dance
Dolly Sisters
"Ephraham (Played Upon the Piano)"
F. Brice
(*Music and Lyrics by* Irving Berlin and Vincent Bryan.)
Songs
S. Brown, J. Blyler
["Turkey Gobbler's Ball"
(*Music by* James B. Blyler. *Lyrics by* A. Donnelly; Jean Havez.)
"Whippoorwill (Never Again for Me)"
(*Music by* James B. Blyler. *Lyrics by* Barney Fagan.)
Scene: A San Francisco Cabaret. (*Painted by* Unitt & Wickes.)

ACT 2

Scene 1

H.M.S. Vaudeveel (*Painted by* E. Albert.)
Opening Chorus—Selection from H.M.S. PINAFORE
Sir Glassuf Pilsener, K. E. G.: H. Watson, Jr. *Captain Headliner*: W. Percival. *Ralph Hutlestraw*: C. Hessong. *Dick Deadeye*, imported from Leipsic: C. A. Mason. *Bill Bobstay*: P. Swift. *Gasolene*, the Captain's cheeild: V. Maxwell. *Bebe*, Sir Glassuf's quaint cousin: L. Errol. *Rachel Rossenstein, alias Becky Butternut*: F. Brice. *Sailors, Marines, Midshipmates, Chickens, Broilers, and Squab.*

Scene 2

Tad's Daffydills (*Painted by* Unitt & Wickes.)
"I'm a Crazy Daffy-Dill" (Daffydil)
B. McCoy, T. Dingle
(*Music by* Jerome Kern. *Lyrics by* Bessie McCoy.)
Chief Daffy: B. McCoy. *A Sailor Man*: T. Dingle. *Other Daffys* Misses Gross, McKnight, Heath, Livermore, Foster, Cadiz, Mantell, Thomas.

Scene 3

New York Central Depot. (Now in course of construction) (*Painted by* Unitt & Wickes.)
Rufus Redcap: B. Williams. *Major Waterbrush*: L. Errol.

Scene 4

Exterior of New York Central Depot. (Now in course of construction)
Songs
B. Williams
["Woodman, Woodman, Spare That Tree"
(*Music by* Irving Berlin. *Lyrics by* Vincent Bryan.)
"That's Harmony" (Dat's Harmony)
(*Music by* Bert Williams. *Lyrics by* Grant Clarke.)
"It Was Me"
(*Music by* Seymour Furth. *Lyrics by* George V. Day.)]

Scene 5

A Fifteen Minute Peep at "The Pink Lady" (Burlesque)
Cake Walk
Ensemble
Dance
B. McCoy
"My Beautiful Lady" (from THE PINK LADY)
C. A. Mason, L. Errol, Gorman Sisters
(*Music by* Ivan Caryll. *Lyrics by* C.M.S. McLellan.)
Finale (Ensemble)
The Company
Von Didhepay: L. Errol. *The Pink Lady*: H. Watson, Jr.

1911.25 THE GIRL OF MY DREAMS

A Musical Play in Two Acts. Book by Wilbur D. Nesbit and Otto Hauerbach [Harbach]. Music by Karl Hoschna. Lyrics by Otto Hauerbach. Production staged by Frank Smithson. Scenery by P. Dodd Ackerman Studios. Costumes by Orange Manufacturing Company and Madame Halley Clogg. Orchestra under the direction of C. E. MacArthur. Produced by Joseph M. Gaites. Opened 7 August 1911 at the Criterion Theatre and closed 9 September 1911 after 40 performances.

CAST: (in order of appearance): *Bob Chase*: Harry Humphreys. *Claudie Robinson*: Charles Diamond. *Fred Jackson*: Harry McIntyre. *Doc Hoffman*: Gus Monte. *Members of the "Be Happy Bachelors" Club (5)*: *Harry Luckenbach*: W. C. Mason. *King Bingham*: Frank McEwen. *Dan England*: Joseph Harris. *Vic Sincere*: Ed Swartz. *Will Anderson*: Harry Hynes. *Steve Hexter*: Robert Brown. *Warrie Cahnson*: Frank Timberg. *Moatz Rotewall*: James Clay. *Pigeon Williams*, a doubtful candidate: HAROLD FORBES. *Socrates Primmer*, a disappointed lover: PERCYVAL AYLMER. *Charlotte*, a maid: DOROTHY WILCOCK. *Carolyn (Cuddle) Swifton*, Harry's sister—home from boarding school: CARRIE BOWMAN.

Boarding School Misses: *Edna May*: Helen Pierson. *Anna Dawson*: Dot Miller. *Tillie Cox*: Lynme Thomas. *Ursula Farnum*: Gertrude Rutledge. *Amy Frank*: Adele Boulais. *Josie Griggs*: Ida Dahl. *Margery Towne*: Blanche Barnes. *May Hayden*: Evelyn Downer. *Grace Newton*: Anna Breucher. *Dollie Cushing*: Blanche Benton. *Mildred St. Clair*: Anna Engel. *Perla Little*: Lyle Tayo. *Violet Merriam*: Ethel Marston. *Bessie Quicksee*: Dorothy Honey. *Gladys Wilbur*: Dorothy Wilcox. *Hazel Hartman*: Bessie Millar.

Tucker, Harry Swifton's chauffeur: Joseph Harris. *Harry Swifton*, an all round good fellow: JOHN HYAMS. *Generalissimo Bombastino*, dangerously in love with his wife: EDOUARD DURAND. *Count von Schnigglefits*, a society fad: IRVING BROOKE. *Helen Bombastino*, the General's wife III: HENRIETTA LEE. *Phineas Medders*, Quaker, Lucy's father: RAY L. ROYCE. *Lucy Medders*, Harry's sweetheart: LEILA McINTYRE.

Belles of the Neighborhood: *Ethel Winsor*: Anna Bruecher. *Vivian Darling*: Blanche Benton. *Daisy Farnes*: Anna Engel. *Ruth Stone*: Lyle Tayo. *Frances St. Cloud*: Bessie Millar. *Violet Newman*: Ethel Marston. *Blanche Jerome*: Dorothy Honey. *Hortense Lang*: Dorothy Wilcox. *Daphne Daffington*, Mlle. Daphne, the sentimental milliner: ALICE HILLS. *Messenger Boy*, from "Therese's: Edward Swartz. *Bachelor Boys, Boarding School Misses, Belles of the Neighborhood, Quaker Lads and Lassies, Toy Town Tinkers, etc.*

Act 1: Harry's Suite at Dovecrest—the Swifton Homestead.

Act 2, Scene 1: Grounds and entrance to Dovecrest. *Scene 2*: In the realm of Dr. Tinker.

[12]Replaced for subsequent tour by "Kiss Duet."

ACT 1[13]

"Bachelor Days"
Bachelor Boys

"Belles of the Tally-Ho Boarding School"
C. Bowman, Chorus

"I'm Ready To Quit and Be Good"
J. Hyams, Bachelor Boys

"Quaker Talk"
L. McIntyre, Boys, Girls

"The Girl Who Wouldn't Spoon"
J. Hyams, L. McIntyre

"Story of a Marionette" (Dearest Little Marionette)
H. Forbes, C. Bowman

"My Wife! My Wife"[14] (Finale)
Principals, Chorus

ACT 2

"Something Very Mysterious" (Opening Chorus)
H. Forbes, Ensemble

"(What's) Sauce for the Gander Is Sauce for the Goose" (Trio)
H. Lee, A. Hills, I. Brooks

"(The) Girl of My Dreams"
J. Hyams, L. McIntyre

"Every Girlie Loves Me But the Girl I Love"
H. Forbes, Chorus

"Dear Little Games of Guessing"
J. Hyams, R. L. Royce, P. Aylmer, H. Forbes, L. McIntyre, C. Bowman, Girls

"O-o-h (Maybe It's a Robber)"
L. McIntyre, J. Hyams

"Dr. Tinkle Tinker"
L. McIntyre, Chorus

Finale
Entire Cast, Chorus

1911.26 HELLO, PARIS

A Midnight Revuette in One Act. Dialogue by William LeBaron. Music by J. Rosamond Johnson. Lyrics by J. Leubrie Hill. Staged by Ned Wayburn. Orchestra conducted by Charles Berton. Produced by Henry B. Harris, Jesse Lasky. Opened 19 August 1911 at the Folies Bergère Theatre as a late night attraction for 30 performances through 21 September 1911: re-opened 22 September 1911 in a new Three Act edition, followed by a Satirical Burlesque, A LA BROADWAY, and a vaudeville program, at the Folies Bergère Theatre and closed 30 September 1911 after 8 additional performances. Total: 38 performances.[15]

CAST: *Johnny Sikes*, a young American in Paris for the first time: HARRY PILCER. *Mortimer Sikes*, his father—President of the Folding Bed Trust: JAMES J. MORTON. *Henry Dwight*, Sikes' private bar: ZEKE COLVAN. *Fifi*, of the Café: MINERVA COVERDALE. *Mrs. Mazie Kummer*, a San Francisco grass widow: NITA ALLEN. *Armand*, a waiter: Harry Leonard. *The Newspaper Girlies (6)*: *The Herald*: Frances Folsom. *The World*: Lucille Bloom. *The Times*: Polly Allison. *The Tribune*: Marie Earle. *The American*: Dottie Wang. *The Sun*: Dorothy Godfrey. *The Cafe Charmers (7)*: *Fifi Granier*: Ysobelle Jason. *Liani de Pousy*: Edith Rose. *Mimi Rameaux*: Bessie Gray. *Marie Rejane*: Zaini Curzon. *Helane de Blue*: Ethel Lytle. *Lina Calais*: Lottie Franklyn. *Un Garçon*: Earle Mountain. *"Tommy Atkins" (5)*: *Eric Ponsonby*: Bun Wheeler. *Dwight Scotch-Seltzer*: Harry Leonard. *Harmon Chichester*: Harry Laughlin. *Percy O'Malley Berresford*: Robert O'Neill. *Harold Chatfield-Bodington*: Clyde Hall. *Specialties*: Al White and Melody Maids; Alabama Trio, with Young Alabama and Rena Hoffman; Fougère, assisted by Esther Fougère; Living Statuary Groups, arranged by Jean Marcel.

Scene: The most popular café in Paris. *Time*: the Hour.

MUSICAL NUMBERS

"Hello Paris" (Opening Ensemble)
Chorus

"Look Me Over (and Tell Me)"
M. Coverdale, Chorus

"That Aeroplane Rag"
N. Allen

"Sentimental Tommy"
Ned Wayburn's Steppers
(*Music by* A. Baldwin Sloane. *Lyrics by* E. Ray Goetz.)

Dance Grotesque
C. Hall, E. Mountain

"Lovin' Moon"
M. Coverdale, Chorus

"You're the Nicest Little Girl I Ever Knew"/

"Fascination Waltz"

"The Siberian Whirl" (The Siberian Dip)
H. Pilcer, M. Coverdale

"The 'Frisco Frizz"
H. Pilcer, M. Coverdale, Company
(*Music by* Ned Wayburn. *Lyrics by* Collin Davis.)

ACT 2: A LA BROADWAY

A Satirical Burlesque on all musical comedies in One Act.[16] Book by William LeBaron. Music by Harold Orlob. Lyrics by William LeBaron and M. H. Collins.

CAST: *John Morris*: JAMES BRADBURY. *Archie Mann*: WILL PHILLIPS. *Fitzhugh St. Clair*: Hayden Clifford. *Tom Jackson*: Agostino Vaci. *Jim Jamb*: JAMES COOK. *Nick O'Teene*: JOHN LORENZ. *Smith*: Earl Mountain. *Mrs. Morris*: OCTAVIA BROSKE. *Polly Morris*: RAE MORRIS. *Dorothy Morris*: MAE THOMPSON. *Maggie O'Hara*: MAE WEST. With Harriet Leidy, Emily Monte, Virginia Gunther, Betty Scott, Pat Neaves, Miriam Sanford, Martha Edmonds, Gladys Turner, Florence Warner, Ted Westus, Margaret Taylor, Wallace Nedringhaus, Ernest Collins, Ida Harris, Glenn Eastman, Kitty Kyle.

MUSICAL NUMBERS

"The Philadelphia Drag"

"Antics of the Comics"
J. Cook, J. Lorenz

"In Loving Time"

"Rue Broadway"

"They Were Irish"

"You Have to Hand It to Them"

"You May Kiss Me Good-Night, Dear"

ACT 3: Vaudeville

Jean Marcel's Living Models; Rappo Sisters; Russian Dancers; Weston, Fields and Carroll; Billy Gould and Florence Geneva; Mlle. Bianca; Carter DeHaven; Eight Berlin Madcaps.

1911.27 THE SIREN

A Musical Play in Three Acts. English libretto by Harry B. Smith. Adapted from the Viennese original 'Die Sirene' by Leo Stein and A. M. Willner. Music by Leo Fall. Staged by Thomas Reynolds. Scenery designed by Homer Emens. Gowns by Lord & Taylor; uniforms by Dazian. Orchestra under the direction of Harold Vicars. Produced by Charles Frohman. Opened 28 August 1911 at the Knickerbocker Theatre and closed 16 December 1911 after 116 performances.

CAST: *Baron Siegfried Bazilos*, Minister of Police in Vienna: FRANK MOULAN. *Clarisse*, His Wife: Elizabeth Firth. *Grion*, a Court Official: Gilbert Childs. *Armand, Marquis de Ravaillac*: DONALD BRIAN. *Malipote*, Bazilos' secretary: F. POPE STAMPER. *Lolotte*: JULIA SANDERSON. *Hannibal Beckmesser*, a Veterinary Surgeon: WILL WEST. *Frau Eisenbehr*, Keeper of a Post Tavern: Florence Morrison.

The Sirens (12): *Suzanne*, called the Sweet Mouse: Moya Mannering. *Yvonne*, called the White Rabbit: Pauline Delorme. *Justine*, called the Firefly: Clementina Dundas. *Pepi*, called the Humming Bird: Sara Carr. *Mimi*, called the Mermaid: Jane Hall. *Ninon*, called the Magpie: Beatrice D'Essling. *Franzi*, called the Butterfly: Helen May. *Alberta*, called the Poodle: Gene Cole. *Toni*, called the Kitty cat: Eithel Kelly. *Magda*, called the Dragon Fly: Louise Donovan. *Robertine*, called the Gazelle: Veronique Banner. *Freda*, called the Goldfish: Ethel Davis. *Ladislas*, Bazilos' servant: Victor LeRoy.

Society Women: Jacqueline DuBarry, Florence Mack, Anna Kuehl, Frances Ceratt, Marie Hurst, Audrey Berton, Mollie Alexander, Edith Allen, Sydney Baram, Molly Wyndham, Marie Butler, Florence Farmer, Caroline Puliam, Adelaide Kornau, Clara

---

[13]Added during the run, following "The Girl Who Wouldn't Spoon":
"The Letter You Shouldn't Have Sent"
A. Hills, J. Hyams

[14]Replaced during the run by:
"That Soul Inspiring Sneeze" (Finale)
Principals, Chorus

[15]Settings, costumes uncredited.

[16]No New York program available.

Eckstrom, Minnie Martin, Hazel Flint, Edith Burch, Leah Lennox, Candida Dundas, Alice Ashe, Edith Lennox, Bessie Durant, Constance Hyatt. *Officers*: John O'Hanlon, Walter Gilbert, Robert B. Toms, Gilbert Coleman, Winship Fink, Roger Davis, George Wharton, Charles Vandiveer, Theodore Walters, Edwin Stone, Luther Mott, Edwin Burch, Edward Marshall, Lester Ostrander, Henry Holt, George Johnson, Ralph O'Brien.

The action takes place in Vienna at the present time.

Act 1: Private Office of Bazilos, Minister of Police.

Act 2: Conservatory in the House of Bazilos.

Act 3: Railroad Junction in the Suburbs of Vienna.

ACT 1[17]

Opening

"Wallflower (Sweet)" (Duet)
D. Brian, E. Firth

"Follow Me Round" (Song)
F. P. Stamper, Sirens
(*Lyrics by* Jerome Kern, Adrian Ross.)

"Ancestors Bold" (Duet)
J. Sanderson, F. Moulan

Finale
D. Brian, J. Sanderson, F. Moulan, E. Firth, F. P. Stamper

ACT 2

Opening

"The Donkey (and the Hay)" (Trio)
D. Brian, J. Sanderson, E. Firth

"Waltz Caprice" (Music Caressing of Violins)(Duet)
D. Brian, J. Sanderson

"Cupid the Conqueror"[18] (Song)
F. P. Stamper, Ensemble

"Confidential Source"[19] (Song)
F. Moulan

Finale

ACT 3

Opening
F. Morrison, Ensemble

"Maid from Montbijou" (In the Valley of Montbijou) (Song)
J. Sanderson
(*Music by* Jerome Kern. *Lyrics by* M. E. Rourke [Herbert Reynolds].)

"(Hail,) She Is the One Girl" (Song)
D. Brian

"I Want to Sing in Opera" (Song)
W. West
(*Music by* Jerome Kern, Worton David. *Lyrics by* Jerome Kern, George Arthurs.)

"Little Girls Beware (of the Sirens)" (Song) (
D. Brian, Sirens
Music by Egbert Van Alstyne. *Lyrics by* Herbert Thompson.)

Finale

---

[17]Added during the run, after the Opening:
"Beware of the Sirens (So Fair)" (Song)[Moved from Act 3.]
D. Brian, Sirens
Added for subsequent tour:
"Mon Bijou" (Duet)
D. Brian, J. Sanderson
"The Siren's Honeymoon"
D. Brian
(*Music and Lyrics by* Donald Brian.)

[18]Replaced during the run and for subsequent tour by:
"Follow Me Round" [from Act 1]
F. P. Stamper, Sirens
Which was then replaced by:
"Oh, Do Step the Two-Step" (Duet)
F. P. Stamper, M. Mannering
(*Music by* Howard Talbot. *Lyrics by* Percy Greenbank.)

[19]Replaced during the run by:
"On the Farm"
J. Sanderson, W. West
Which was then replaced for subsequent tour by:
"I Always Come Back to You" (Duet)
J. Sanderson, W. West

1911.28 AROUND THE WORLD

A Series of Superb Spectacles with Music in Three Acts, 15 Scenes. Conceived by Arthur Voegtlin. (Book) Written by Carroll Fleming. Music and lyrics by Manuel Klein. Produced [staged] by Carroll Fleming. Musical ensembles staged by William J. Wilson. Scenic effects designed by Arthur Voegtlin. Costumes by Cora MacGeachy. Musical director, Manuel Klein. Presented by the Messrs. Shubert. Opened 2 September 1911 at the Hippodrome and closed 18 May 1912 after 445 performances.

CAST: MARCELINE, HENRY SANTREY, W. H. CLARKE, ROSA LaHARTE, SABREY DORSELL, HARRY JACKSON, ALBERT PELLATON, MILDRED FLORA, ALBERT FROOME, LILLIAN CARRENO, DAN DAWSON, NELLIE MORDECAI, ELSIE BAIRD, Felix Hanley, Master Ahmedo, George Adams, Gwilyn Edwards, Arthur Beech, Abbas Ben Abdallah, Bobker Ben Ali, Emma Fette, Claudia Scott, Harry Taylor, Harry Dale, Jack Cheviot, Angel Barbara, Kitty Drolet, Marven Morgan, Mlle. Athena, Margaret Townsend, Sylvia Craft, Teresa Hamner, Edgar Allen, May Carlisle, Manuel Valles, Frank Hanson, Jeanette Schacht, Lewis Strong, James Lee, Georgie Russell, Stanley Ferguson, Helen Gilmore, Tommy Mullins, M. J. Anderson, Harry Van Cleve, Daisy Smythe, Frank Graus, Isabel Graus, Aenny Boye, Gus Ochsner, G. Schmitt, Tyrolean Quartette.

ACT 1

Scene 1

"Pretty Little Sunshine"
Chorus

"My Old Town"
H. Santrey, Chorus
Scene: .On the Hudson.
Jason Burlingham, an Eccentric Millionaire: W. H. Clarke. *Mrs. Grantwood Leigh*, His Fiancée: R. LaHarte. *Jean Burlingham*, His Daughter: S. Dorsell. *Paul Burlingham*, His Son, a Polo Champion: H. Jackson. *Rear Admiral Bruce*, U.S.N.: A. Pellaton. *Lillian Bruce*, His Daughter: M. Flora. *Lieutenant Stanley*, U.S. Man of-War *"New York,"* engaged to Jean: H. Santrey. *Swami Vana Kavenda*, an Indian Yogi: A. Froome. *McShane*, Burlingham's Butler: F. Haney. *Babette*, Maid to Mrs. Leigh: B. Boone. *The Earl of Darnay*, Captain of English Polo Team: J. Harvey. *A Marine*, U.S.N.: J. Warren. *Marceline*: Marceline. *Polo Players, Yachtsmen, Society Girls, English Visitors, etc, etc.*
Synopsis: Lawn of Burlingham's Mansion on the Hudson. The Polo Match. Purchase of the Diamond. The Swami's Warning. Farewell to New York and Departure for Europe.

Scene 2

Scene: Burlingham's Yacht *"The Diana"* in Mid-Ocean.

Scene 3

"The Merry Month of May"
Chorus

"'Arry and 'Arriet"
D. Dawson, N. Mordecai, Chorus

"It's a Long Lane That Has No Turning"
S. Dorsell, H. Santrey, Chorus
Scene: Windsor, England. Garden Party at Windsor Castle.
Additional Characters: *'Slippery Bill' Mason,'* an English Crook: A. Froome. *The Spider,'* King of the Costers: D. Dawson. *'Arriet*, His "Doner": N. Mordecai. *The Nipper*: Master Ahmedo. *Head Gameskeeper*: G. Adams. *Coster Boys and Girls, Maypole Dancers, Country Yokels, Beef Eaters, Game-keepers, Constables, etc.*
Synopsis: The Maypole Dance. The Diamond is Stolen. Paul Burlingham and Shane are arrested on a false charge and taken to jail. The thieves depart for Switzerland. The Gretna Green Elopement. "The Long Lane."

Scene 4

"Auf den berg, es ist schon"
Tyrolean Quartette, Male Chorus

"Die vogelein singen in dem wald"
Female Chorus
Scene: Switzerland. The Alps.
Additional Characters: *Alpine Shepherd*; J. Harvey. *A Benedictine Monk*: G. Edwards. *Franz*: A. Beach. *Yodlers*: F. Graus, I. Graus, A. Boye, G. Ochsner. *Tyrolean Peasants, Chamois Hunters, Mountain Guides, Monks, etc, etc.Synopsis*: On the Track of the Thieves. The Spider falls from a rock, but "Slippery Bill" escapes with the diamond. "I'll Get It Back if I Have to Follow Him to the Ends of the Earth."

Scene 5

Egyptian Music, Muezzin Call.
Scene: Egypt—The Sphinx. Daybreak in the Desert.
Additional Characters: *Sheik Diamond*: A. Ben Abdallah. *Sheik Abdallah*: A. Pellaton. *Arab Messenger*: B. Ben Ali. *Bedouins, Berbers, Arab Musicians, Donkey Boys, Camel Drivers, Denizens of the Desert, etc.*

Synopsis: The Muezzin Call. The Passing Caravan. Arab Pastimes. Arrival of "Slippery Bill" and Sheik Abdallah. The battle on Horseback. The Abduction of Jean Burlingham.

Scene 6

Sandstorm Music

Scene: The Desert. The Sandstorm.

Scene 7

Turkish Slaves (Dance)

Oriental Dance

Mlle. Athena

Scene: Constantinople. Garden of the Vizier's Harem.

Additional Characters: *The Grand Vizier*: J. Harvey. *Saidee*, *Zuleika*, His Favorites: C. Scott, E. Fette. *Captain of the Harem Guard*: J. Warren. *American Consul*: H. Tylor. *Chief Eunuch*: H. Dale. *Ebeu*, *Ahmet*, Slave Merchants: J. Cheviot, A. Barbara. *Greek Slave*: K. Drolet. *Circassian Slave*: M. Morgan. *An Oriental Dancers*: Mlle. Athena. *Eunuchs, Circassians, Nubian Slaves, Odalisques, Nautch Dancers, Women of the Harem, Palace Guards, U. S. Marines, Native Soldiers, etc.*

Synopsis: Harem Pastimes. The Nautch Dancers. European Entertainers. The Slave Market Marceline selects his Harem. Arrival of Jean Burlingham as a Slave. Her Purchase by the Grand Vizier. Her Rescue by Lieutenant Stanley and His Men O' War.

Scene 8

Grand Durbar March

"See the Royal Durbar Palace" (The Royal Durbar March)

Principals, Chorus

Scene: India. The Durbar.

Additional Characters: *The Rajah of Rampootra*: A. Froome. *His Maharanee*: M. Townsend. *The Prince of Jeypore*: D. Dawson. *The Prince of Mahratta*: H. Taylor. *The Princess of Jeypore*: S. Craft. *The Princess of Mahratta*: T. Hamner. *The Royal Executioner*: E. Allen. *The Court Astrologer*: A. Barbara. *Hindu Soldiers, Goorkha, Sikhs, Maharajahs, Princes, Nubians, Princesses, Parsees, Dancing Girls, Keepers of the Sacred Idol, English Lancers, Hindu Magicians, Mahouts, Native Fakirs, Europeans, Populace, Beggars, etc, etc.*

Synopsis: McShane finds a new clue to the Diamond. The Americans sail for Italy. During the Ceremonies of the Coronation of the Rajah of Rampootra there will appear the Brothers Merano, Equilibrists, and Sie Hassan Ben Ali's Famous Tribe of Whirlwind Berber Acrobats.

ACT 2

Scene 1

"Venetian Serenade" (In Venice Serenade)

H. Santrey, Male Chorus

Scene: Italy. Venice by Moonlight.

Additional Characters: *An Italian Bravo*: A. Barbara. *The Contessa's Maid*: B. Boone. *Lieutenant Stanley as a Lothario*: H. Santrey. *Gondoliers, Serenaders, Wedding Party, Lazzarone, etc.*

Synopsis: An Interrupted Serenade. The Tryst. Departure for Spain.

Scene 2

"Salute to the Toreador"

S. Dorsell, Chorus

"Sweet Senorita"

R. LaHarte

Scene: Spain. The Bull Ring in Seville.

Additional Characters: *Don Emilio*: A.Pellaton. *The Contessa*: E. Baird. *Senor Lopez*: A. Froome. *Manuel*: Signor Alberto. *Inez*: S. Dorsell. *Dolores*: M. Carlisle. *Pedro*: M. Valles. *A Spanish Captain*: F. Hanson. *A Ticket Seller*: G. Schmitt. *Matadores, Picadores, Muleteers, Cigarette Makers, Hucksters, Donkey Drivers, Citizens, etc, etc.*

Synopsis: The Contessa presents Don Emilio with the Fatal Diamond. The Escape of the Bull. The Panic. The Toreador is Saved. McShane finds the diamond and his bad luck begins.

Scene 3

Hula Hula (Dance)

J. Schacht

Scene: Hawaii. The Harbor of Honolulu. "The Dance of the Flowers."

Additional Characters: *A Kanaka Princess*: J. Schacht. *Officer of Customs*: L. Strong. *Messenger*: J. Lee. *Native Dancers, Kanakas, Mandolin Players, etc.*

Synopsis: The Voyagers visit Honolulu. Letters from Home. *"The Diana"* sails for Ireland.

Scene 4

"Blarney of Killarney"

F. Haney, Chorus

Scene: Ireland. Blarney Castle.

Additional Characters: *Terry Mullane*: F. Hanson. *Nora Mullane*: G. Russell. *Biddy Mullane*: S. Ferguson. *The O'Neill*: G. Adams. *Elly O'Neill*: M. Flora. *Old Meg*, a Witch: H. Gilmore. *Jerry Hogan*: J. Warren. *Mickey Dugan*: H. Taylor. *Dan Doolin*: T. Mullins. *Paddy*, the Piper: M. J. Anderson. *Mickey Flynn*, a Groom: H. Van Cleve. *Pete*, the Mule: Himself. *Colleens, Irish Lads, Squires, Squireens, Peasants, etc.,etc.*

Synopsis: McShane has troubles of his own with Van Cleve and His Mule "Pete." The Witch's Warning. McShane drops the diamond in the Fairies' Well. "All Hands for an Irish Reel." "The Mule's Bewitched."

Scene 5

Ballet of the Butterflies

Music of Forest Fires

(*Conceived by* Arthur Voegtlin. *Written and produced by* Carroll Fleming. *Music composed and directed by* Manuel Klein. *Dances arranged by* Vincenzo Romeo, Ballet Master of the Hippodrome. *Scenic effects designed by* Arthur Voegtlin. *Costumes designed by* Alfredo Edel.)

Tableau 1: Dance of the Butterflies. *Tableau 2*: The Fire in the Forest.

Characters: *The Queen Butterfly*: L. Carreno. *The King Butterfly*: D. Smythe. *The Black Butterfly*: G. Russell.

ACT 3

Scene 1

March of the Elves, Pixies, Fauns, and Satyrs

Scene: The Fairies' Glen. The Magic Waterfall.

Characters: *Woodland King*: W. H. Clarke. *The Forest Queen*: R. LaHarte. *The Fairy Prince*: H. Santrey. *The Princess*: S. Dorsell. *Queen of the Fairies*: B. Boone. *The Gnome King*: D. Dawson. *Wood Nymphs, Elves, Dryads, Fauns, Satyrs, Pixies, Gnomes, Water Nymphs, Woodland Hunters, Archers, Bacchantes, etc,*

Scene 2

Grand Finale and Trumpet Salute to the Magic Waterfall

Scene: Grand Final Tableau. The Golden Barge.

1911.29

MISS JACK

A Musical Comedy in Three Acts. Book and lyrics by Mark E. Swan. Music by William Frederic Peters. Staged by Lewis Morton. Musical numbers and ensembles staged under the personal direction of Bothwell Browne. Settings by H. Robert Law. Costumes by Bothwell Browne. Musical director, William Frederic Peters. Produced by Ben Sangor. Opened 4 September 1911 at the Herald Square Theatre and closed 16 September 1911 after 16 performances.

CAST: *Jack Hayward*, in love with Evelyn: BOTHWELL BROWNE. *Evelyn Stanley*, a pupil at Winterfield College: OLIVE ULRICH. *Nellie Trevor*, her chum: SUZANNE ROCAMORA. *Otto Von Hertz*, professor of psychology: JAMES B. CARSON. *Silas Bean*, gardener and factotum at Winterfield College: Jonathan Keefe. *Eudora Marshall*, principal at Westerfield College: May McCabe. *Bob Marshall*, a college boy: ERNEST F. YOUNG. *Marcie Brook*, a society woman: Rose Baudett. *Olive Brook*, her daughter: HAZEL COX. *Chucky Berton*, a burglar: Carl Stall. *Didon*, a waiter: Harry Browne.

Alice Benton: Kalene Carter. *Dolores Mendoza*: Bessie Sessions. *Inez Calthorpe*: Claire Tiegen. *Nora Fitzgerald*: Viola Williams. *Grace Pendleton*: Gladys Breston. *Kitty Severance*: Kathryn Hurst. *Bessie McGregor*: Billie Francis. *Yvette Lascelles*: Julia Carle. *Genevieve Castleton*: Evelyn Raymond. *Marietta Montgomery*: Charlotte Corbett. *Dollie*: Carrie Watts. *Mollie*: Bernice McCabe. *Pollie*: Graycie Conklin. *Ollie*: Edna Garrick. *Hollie*: Annie Ray. *Maizie*: Helene Weimer. *Daisy*: Mabel VyVan. *Lottie*: Billie Wilburn. *Tottie*: Nora Hamilton. *Dottie*: Nettie Hamilton.

The action takes place at the present time in any college town.

Act 1: Exterior of Winterfield Seminary. Afternoon.

Act 2: Interior of the same. Evening.

Act 3: Oriental lounge of the Bellingham Hotel. One week later.

ACT 1

Opening Chorus

Seminary Girls

"If You Could Fancy Me"

E. F. Young, S. Rocamora, Girls

"Visions of Love"

O. Ulrich, Girls

"(Old) Deacon Pettigue"

J. Keefe, Girls

Finale

Company

ACT 2

"This Is No Place for a Good Little Girl"

S. Rocamora

"The Fencing Girl"

B. Browne, Seminary Girls

"The English Language"
J. B. Carson, Girls
"Slumbertown"
O. Ulrich, Girls
Finale
Company

ACT 3
Opening Chorus
Actresses, Society Girls
"Good-Bye, Little Girl"
H. Cox, Actresses
"That's Peculiar, Isn't It? Very"
E. F. Young, Girls
"There Really Isn't Any More to Tell"
S. Rocamora, J. B. Carson, J. Keefe
"(Song of) The Skylark"
O. Ulrich
Egyptian Ballet
Girls
"The Serpent of the Nile"
B. Browne
Finale
Company

1911.30 THE FASCINATING WIDOW

The Somewhat Different Comedy with Music in Three Acts, 4 Scenes. Book and lyrics by Otto Hauerbach [Harbach]. Music by Frederick W. [Kerry] Mills. Staged by George Marion. Dances arranged by Jack Mason. Scenery by Dodge & Castle. Gowns by Frances (Company), Hayden & Co. (Mr. Eltinge's costumes). Orchestra under the direction of August Kleinecke. Orchestrations by William M. Redfield. Produced by A. H. Woods. Opened 11 September 1911 at the Liberty Theater and closed 28 October 1911 after 56 performances.[20]

CAST: *Lankton Wells*, the college trainer: EDWARD GARVIE. *Tuthill Leffingwell*, a Freshman: JAMES SPOTTSWOOD. *Oswald Wentworth*, a Sophomore: Lionel Walsh. *Reverend Wilbur Watts*, the college chaplain: Charles W. Butler. *Nick Bulgler*, the hotel detective: James E. Sullivan. *John Wilson*, a bus driver: Frank Wentworth. *Mrs. Leffingwell*, matron of the Girls' Dormitory at K (College): Carrie E. Perkins. *Margaret Leffingwell*, her daughter: WINONA WINTER. *Tessie Danforth*, a romp: JUNE MATHIS. *Ivy Tracy*, clinging vine: NATALIE ALT.

Students at K College: *Ethel Ethridge*: Jean Morrell. *Maisie Mannering*: Louise Orth. *Lottie Lovedale*: Gladys Feldman. *Bessie Bothwell*: Marie Baxter. *Harriet Halford*: Blanche Burnham. *Nella Northrup*: Dorothy Sanders. *Rholla Rollins*: Dorothy Wilcox. *Cissie Cyril*: Natalie Seymour.

Mrs. Monte, the Fascinating Widow: JULIAN ELTINGE. *Hal Blake*, a Junior at K (College): JULIAN ELTINGE.

Time: Present. *Place*: The United States.

Act 1: Exterior of a hotel in the mountains. A morning in September.

Act 2, Scene 1: A room in the Boys' Dormitory at K, a co-educational college. A week later—evening. *Scene 2*: A corner in the reception hall in the Girls' Dormitory at K. The same night.

Act 3: The chaplain's study adjoining the K College Chapel. A week later.

ACT 1[21]
"Put Your Arms Around Me"
E. Garvie, N. Alt
(*Lyrics by* Sam M. Lewis.)
"The Fascinating Widow"
J. Eltinge, Girls
(*Lyrics by* E. Ray Goetz.)
"Don't Take Your Beau to the Seashore"
J. Eltinge, Bathing Girls
(*Music by* Irving Berlin. *Lyrics by* E. Ray Goetz.)

ACT 2
"You've Built a Fire Down in My Heart"[22] (from ZIEGFELD FOLLIES OF 1911)
W. Winter
(*Music and Lyrics by* Irving Berlin and Vincent Bryan.)
"Love Is the Theme of My Dream"[23]
N. Alt, Girls
"The Rag Time College Girl"
J. Eltinge, Girls
(*Lyrics by* Sam M. Lewis.)
"Valse Julian" (Oriental Dance)
J. Eltinge
"Don't You Make a Noise"[24]
W. Winter, Girls

ACT 3
"I'm to be a Blushing Bride"
J. Eltinge, Bridesmaids
(*Lyrics by* Sam M. Lewis.)
Finale

1911.31 WHEN SWEET SIXTEEN

A Songplay (Musical Play) in Two Acts. Book and lyrics by George V. Hobart. Music by Victor Herbert. Staged by R. H. Burnside. Settings by Bernard MacDonald. Costumes by Kaufman Costume Company, Everall & Wallach Costume Dept., Dazian. Orchestra under the direction of Frederick Schwartz. Orchestrations by Victor Herbert. Entire production staged under the direction of George V. Hobart. Produced by the Everall & Wallach Company (Harry J. Everall, Samuel H. Wallach). Opened 14 September 1911 at Daly's Theatre and closed 23 September 1911 after 12 performances.

CAST: *John Hammond*: FRANK BELCHER. *Mrs. Hammond*, his wife: JOSIE INTROPODI. *Victoria (Hammond)*, his daughter: HARRIET STANDON. *Jefferson Todd*, his friend: WILLIAM NORRIS. *Stanley Morton*, Todd's secretary: ROY PURVIANCE. *Zeke*, his valet: Harry S. Fern. *Gertie Greene*, a manicure: Eva Williams. *The Laird of Loch Lomond*: GEORGE RIDGWELL. *Monsieur Beaucaire*, a fashionable faker: ARTHUR LIPSON. *Eleanor Bradford*, Victoria's cousin: Mabel Mordaunt. *Mabel Bradford*, her other cousin : Belle Taylor. *Gridley*, a butler: R. M. Dolliver.

Friends of Victoria from the Young Ladies Seminary: *Emma*: Esther Hall. *Annabelle*: Cecelia Pink. *Mary*: Edith Williams. *Rose*: Helene Miller. *May*: Sadie McNish. *Lucy*: Mabel Morton. *Gertrude*: Grace Lind. *Jeannette*: Claire Leslie. *Marion*: Rose Munroe. *Louise*: Mildred Sanford. *Geraldine*: Elinor Carrol. *Florence*: Monte Menden. *Edna*: Ludovica deBeau. *Helen*: Harriet Carter. *Carol*: Ada Blair. *Margaret*: Virginia May.

Act 1: The Living Room in the Country Home of the Hammonds. Wednesday morning, last September.

Act 2: The pine grove on the estate of John Hammond. The following evening at eight o'clock.

ACT 1
"Oh, Those Boys"
M. Mordaunt, B. Taylor
"It's Always Going to be That Way"
J. Intropodi, A. Lipson
"A Man's a Man for a' That"
F. Belcher
"Hearts Are Trumps"
H. Standon, Chorus
"(There's Money in) Graft" (There's a Raft of Money in Graft! Graft! Graft!)
F. Belcher, W. Norris, R. Purviance, A. Lipson
"The Wild Rose"
R. Purviance
"(In) the Golden Long Ago"
R. Purviance, H. Standon

---

[20]Played a return engagement 13 November 1911 at the Grand Opera House for 9 performances.
[21] Interpolated as per published sheet music/perhaps dropped prior to New York:
"Don't Go in the Water, Daughter" (Julian Eltinge's Bathing Song)
J. Eltinge
(*Music by* Jean Schwartz. *Lyrics by* William Jerome.)

[22]Replaced for subsequent tour by:
"All the World Loves a Lover"
W. Winter
[23]Dropped during the run and for tour.
[24]Replaced for subsequent tour by:
"Nightie Parade"
W. Winter, N. Alt, J. Mathis, Girls

"Laughs"
Principals, Chorus

ACT 2

"(Mah) Honey Love"
R. Purviance, Chorus

"My Toast to You"
F. Belcher, R. Purviance, A. Lipson, G. Ridgwell

"(There's None So Sweet as) Rosalind"
B. Taylor, Chorus

Medley of Victor Herbert's operas [for As You Like It]:
Principals
"Absinthe Frappé" (from IT HAPPENED IN NORDLAND)
"Put Down Six and Carry Two" (I Can't Do That Sum) (from BABES IN TOYLAND)
"Kiss Me Again" (from MLLE. MODISTE)
"Love Is Like a Cigarette" (from ALGERIA)
"Star Light, Star Bright" (from THE WIZARD OF THE NILE)
"Dream Love" (from THE PRIMA DONNA)

"(Little) Fifi"
A. Lipson, Chorus

"Has Cupid Laid in Wait for You?"
R. Purviance, H. Standon

Finale
Entire Company

1911.32 THE KISS WALTZ

A Viennese Operetta in Two Acts. American book by Edgar Smith. (Based on the Viennese operette 'Liebeswalzer' by Robert Bodansky and Alfred Grünbaum.) Music by Carl Michael Ziehrer. (American) Lyrics by Matthew Woodward. Staged by J. C. Huffman. Musical numbers staged by William J. Wilson. Dances staged by Gus Sohlke. Scenery by H. Robert Law. Costumes designed by Melville Ellis. Orchestra under the direction of Frank Tours. Produced by Sam S. & Lee Shubert (Inc.). Opened 18 September 1911 at the Casino Theatre and closed 2 December 1911 after 88 performances.

CAST: *Count Arthur Wildenberg*, a jealous husband: WILLIAM PRUETTE. *Jenny*, Countess Wildenberg, a flirtatious wife: ELSA RYAN. *Nella*, Baroness von Bernau, her cousin: FLORA ZABELLE. *Guido Spini*, a composer: Robert Warwick. *Leopold Fuhringer*, a "nouveau riche": CHARLES BIGELOW. *Kathi*, his wife: EVA DAVENPORT. *Antschi*, their daughter: ADELE ROWLAND. *Paul von Gervais*, an impecunious baronet: MARTIN BROWN. *Marquis Roget*, a gossip: George Pauncefort. *Brissard*, maître d'hotel: Robert Milliken. *Jacques*, garcon: Oscar Schwartz [Shaw]. *Guests at the Hotel Elektra (4)*: *Lady Helene*: Lillian Wiggins. *Mlle. Florine*: Olga Hempstone. *Lady Henrietta*: Mae Allen. *Madame Ritzi*: Mildred Manners. *An American Girl*: Ethel Weir. *Bertram, Albert*, Guests at the Villa Wildenberg: Robert Milliken, Oscar Schwarz [Shaw].

Personnel of the Chorus: *Guests*: Anna Berg, Margaret Adair, Blanche Marr, Ethel Dennison, Mae Dealy, Josephine Bramdell, Winifred Browne, Vivian Raymond, Marion George, Mildred Manners, May Von Sommerfeld, Florence Summerville, Agnes Hebron, Florence Mallory, Claudia Esmond, Sue Young, Estelel Grayce, Helen Clagett, Mae Arnold, Violet Marsden. *Waitresses, Guests*: Helen Lloyd, Nemo Ormsden, Camille Truesdale, Elsie Froehlich, Cecile Mayo, Ethel Collinson, Frances Summerville, Annette Woodman. *Officers, Guests, Waiters*: LeRoy Pruette, F. E. Walker, Frank Hempstone, Clarence Lutz, Frederick Hamilton, Isador Snee, Irving Feiner, Louis Finity, George Gray, Robert Gilbert, James Curran, Lew Graham.

Time: The Present.

Act 1: The Hotel Elektra in the Riviera.

Act 2: The Villa Wildenberg.

ACT 1

Opening Chorus

"(The) Belle of Vienne" (The Girl from Vienne)
A. Rowland, Chorus
(*Music by* Leslie Stuart.)

"Do As You Please" (Duet)
E. Ryan, M. Brown
(*Music and Lyrics by* Harry Gifford, Alfred S. Lawrence, Tom Mellor, Martin Brown.)

Entrance
F. Zabelle, Chorus

"Ta-Ta, Little Girl"
M. Brown, Chorus
(*Music by* Jerome Kern.)

"Elevation" (What I Seen I Done)
E. Davenport
(*Music by* Louis Hirsch.)

"(The) Kiss Waltz"
F. Zabelle, R. Warwick

Trio
E. Ryan, A. Rowland, M. Brown

Finale

ACT 2

"O'er the Blue Waters" (Barcarolle)
W. Pruette, Chorus

"Love Is Like a Little Rubber Band" (Hoop Song)
E. Ryan, Chorus
(*Music by* Jerome Kern.)

"Laughing Song"
E. Davenport

"Oh! You Girls!"
R. Warwick, Chorus

"Love's Charming Art" (The Dove Duet)
A. Rowland, M. Brown
(*Music by* Jerome Kern.)

Entrance Lisa
F. Zabelle

Finale

1911.33 THE LITTLE MILLIONAIRE

George M. Cohan and His Own Company in a Musical Farce in Three Acts. Book, music and lyrics by George M. Cohan. Staged by George M. Cohan. Ensembles and drills staged by James Gorman. Scenery painted by Edward G. Unitt and Joseph Wickes. Gowns and Millinery by Schneider-Anderson Company. Musical director, Karl Weixelbaum. Produced by (George M.) Cohan and (Sam) Harris. Opened 25 September 1911 at the Cohan Theatre and closed 9 March 1912 after 192 performances.

CAST: *Henry Spooner*, a millionaire: JERRY J. COHAN. *Robert Spooner*, just as wealthy as his father: GEORGE M. COHAN. *George Russell*, Spooner's secretary: George Parsons. *Bill Costigan*, a wine agent: TOM LEWIS. *Roscoe Handover*, a bad man: SYDNEY JARVIS. *Danny Wheeler*, Robert's chauffeur: EARL BENHAM. *Edward Plumber*, Spooner's butler: Donald Crisp. *Rudolph*, manager "Beaux Art": Donald Crisp. *Starter* at the "Beaux Art": William Ford. *Mrs. Prescott*, Goldie's aunt: Mrs. Helen F. [Nellie] Cohan. *Goldie Gray*, of the "Zig Zag Folly Co.": LILA RHODES. *Berdina Busby*: JULIA RALPH. *Bertha Burnham*, Roscoe's accomplice: JOSEPHINE WHITTELL. *Miss Primper*: Maud Allen. *Mary*, Goldie's maid: Amy Mortimer. *Policeman*: Dore Rogers. *Reverend H. Henry Dodge*: Jack Klendor. *Page Boy*: Charles W. Weil.

Act 1: "Beaux Art," Huntington, Long Island.

Act 2: Spooner's Home. Three weeks later.[25]

Act 3: The Astor Roof. The following night.

ACT 1[26]

Opening Chorus
Company

"(The) New Yorkers"
G. Parsons, Chorus

"(The) Little Millionaire"
G. M. Cohan, Chorus

"Come With Me to My Bungalow"[27]
E. Benham, A. Mortimer

"We Do the Dirty Work"
S. Jarvis, J. Whittell

Ensemble
Company

---

[25]Program note: The action of Act 2 will not be interrupted by Musical Numbers.

[26]Interpolated during the subsequent tour:
"Down in My Heart" (Duet)
Charles King, Elizabeth Brice
(*Music and Lyrics by* Irving Berlin.)

[27]Dropped during the run.

"Characteristic Waltz"
G. M. Cohan, L. Rhodes
"Drill of the Seventh"
Gentlemen of the Chorus
"Any Place the Old Flag Flies"
G. M. Cohan, Chorus

ACT 3
"The Musical Moon"
E. Benham, Chorus
"Oh, You Wonderful Girl"
S. Jarvis, J. Whittell
"Barnum Had the Right Idea"
G. M. Cohan
"The Dancing Wedding"
G. M. Cohan, L. Rhodes, G. Parsons, Chorus
Finale
Company

1911.34 THE REVUE OF REVUES

A Series of Musical Satires (Musical Revue) in Two Acts, 10 Scenes and a Prologue. Sketches by Jean Havez, Edgar Smith, Leo Donnelly. Music by Louis A. Hirsch, Melville Gideon. Lyrics by Jean Havez, Leo Donnelly, Harold Atteridge. Staged by Lewis Morton. Dances arranged by Gus Sohlke, William J. Wilson. Scenery by H. Robert Law. Costumes by Melville Ellis. Orchestra under the direction of Silvio Hein. Produced by the Winter Garden Company (Messrs. Shubert). Opened 27 September 1911 at the Winter Garden and closed 11 November 1911 after 55 performances.

CAST: GABY DESLYS, DOROTHY JARDON, LYDIA BARRY, HAROLD CRANE, CLARENCE HARVEY, DORIS CAMERON, GEORGIO MAJERONI, ERNEST HARE, MAUD RAYMOND, LOS MALIGINITAS, FRANK TINNEY, HARRY JOLSON, Mabel DeYoung, Edward DeNoyer, Edward Cutler, Kate Elinore, Mlle. (Albertina) Rasch, James B. Carson, Leeds and Lemar, Mlle. Rayo, Sam Williams, Kathryn Kerwan.

ACT 1

IN THE LIMELIGHT, an Up-to-the-Minute Satire de Luxe, a Prologue, Two Acts and 6 Scenes. Book by Edgar Smith, Leo Donnelly, Jean Havez. Lyrics by Harold Atteridge, Jean Havez, Leo Donnelly. Music by Louis A. Hirsch and Melville Gideon. Folies Begeabers scenes originated and suggested by Lew Fields. Staged by Lewis Morton. Musical numbers staged by Gus Sohlke. Carmen number staged by William J. Wilson. Costumes designed by Melville Ellis.

CAST (in order of appearance): *Colonel John Pastor*: HAROLD CRANE. *Nobody*: Georgio Majeroni. *Miss Liberty*: LYDIA BARRY. *Anthony Contalk*: CLARENCE HARVEY. *Barker and Policeman*: ERNEST HARE. *Lillie Braham*: DORIS CAMERON. *Lina Ratheleri*: DOROTHY JARDON. *Diamond Sim Brodsky*: James B. Carson. *Maud*: Herself. *Graham Biscuit*: Mabel DeYoung. *Jokes*, of the Ammonia Hotel: Raymond Bloomer. *Melissa*: KATE ELINORE. *Modesty*: Kathryn Kerwan. *Youth*: Edward Cutler. *Mirandy*: MAUD RAYMOND. *Henry Clay*: HARRY JOLSON. *Mister Harried*: Raymond Bloomer. *Jessie Lewsky*: Sam Williams. *Modesty*: Miss Douglas. *Rockyfeller*: Harry Sulkin. *Sam Billikins*: Edward DeNoyer. *Mrs. Billikins*: MAUD RAYMOND. *Announcer*: Leo Donnelly. *Waiter*: HARRY JOLSON. *The Inebriate*: HARRY LEEDS. *Usher*: TRIXIE LeMAR. (*Spanish Singing and Dancing Specialties* from the Bal Tabarin, Paris: LOS MALAGUENITAS.)

Spanish Girls: Misses Borreo, Kerwin, Burker, Werner, French, Cable, Goulding, Mitchell, Douglas, Courtland, Arthur. *Bathers*: Misses Crane, Burnette, Falk, Sherer, Lachere, Laboulaye, E. Prager, McLellan, Truesdale, Ward, Grayel, Sparks, Camar, Florence, Callen, Zaltz, Wallace, LaPlace, Hardy, Leichman, Dakin, H. Burnette, M. Prager. *Beauty Doctors*: Misses Cameron, Mitchell, Douglas, Cable, Burker, Courtland, Lester. *Heiresses*: Misses French, Mitchell, Miller, Bently, Kerwin, Arthur Steinhardt. *Toreadors, Guests, Waiters, etc.*: Messrs. Gray, Pomeroy, Pierce, Welch, Harold, Gurney, Dellet, Miller, Golden, Stone, George, Schomers, Gilbert, Gillis, Hartman, Georgi, Sulkin, Stanley, Moran, Kleinman, Page, Smith, Lane, Gray.

Prologue: In the Clouds outside New York Bay.

Act 1, Scene 1: Loony Park. *Scene 2*: Street Scene in New York. *Scene 3*: Mme. Ratheleri's Beauty Parlor. *Scene 4*: International Peace Panorama. *Scene 5*: Aboard the U.S.S. *"New York."*

Act 2, Scene 1: Exterior of the Folies Begeabers. *Scene 2*: Interior of the Folies Begeabers, during Cabaret Show.

ACT 1[28]
"Visit Loony Park" (Opening Chorus)
Ensemble
"(The Candy) College Boys"
H. Leeds, T. LeMar
Boxing Specialty
H. Leeds, T. LeMar
"The Carmen Girl"[29]
D. Jardon, Chorus
"The Rushing Ballet"[30]
Ballet
"On the Congo"[31]
H. Leeds, T. LeMar, Chorus
"(I Met You in) Pittsburgh, Pa."[32]
L. Barry
(*Music by* Louis A. Hirsch.)
"Shooting Show Girls and French Chauffeurs"[33]
Chorus
"The Board Walk Crawl"
M. Raymond, Chorus
(*Music by* Louis A. Hirsch.)
"Twenty Years Ago"
L. Barry
"The Minstrel Band"[34]
M. Raymond, H. Jolson
"Oriental Eyes"[35]
D. Jardon, Chorus
The Sousa Marches
H. Crane, Chorus
Finale
Ensemble

ACT 2[36]

Scene 1

NOVELTIES OF NATIONS, "NEL GIAPPONE", a Japanese Pantomime Ballet in One Act, by S. L. Bensusan. Music by Louis Ganne. Dances arranged by Ottokar Bartik.

CAST: *The Wife*: DOROTHY JARDON. *The Husband*: GEORGIO MAJERONE. *The Lover*: JOSEPH SMITH. *The Servant*: ERNEST HARE. (*Specialties*: MLLES. (ALBERTINA) RASCH, RAYO, LOS MALAGUENITAS.)
Scene: The Estate of a Samurai of Japan.

MUSICAL NUMBERS
Wooden Shoes Dance
Corps de Ballet
Fan Dance
Corps de Ballet
Flirtartion Dance Classic
Mlles. A. Rasch, Rayo
Variation
Mlle. A. Rasch
Grand Ballabile
Corps de Ballet

Scene 2
Specialty
Frank Tinney

Scene 3

LE DÉBUTS DE CHICHINE, a Comedietta in 2 Scenes. Book by

---

[28]During the run Act 1, Scene 3 of INTO THE LIMELGHT was eliminated.

[29]Replaced during the run by:
"Sombrero Land"
D. Jardon, Joseph Smith, Chorus
(*Music by* Irving Berlin. *Lyrics by* E. Ray Goetz, Ted Snyder.)

[30] Replaced during the run by an added specialty:
The Roller Skating Dancers
Reynolds and Donnegan

[31]Dropped during the run.

[32]Dropped during the run.

[33]Dropped during the run.

[34]Dropped during the run.

[35]Dropped during the run.

[36]During the run all of Act 2 of INTO THE LIMELGHT was eliminated; Belle Baker was added as a song specialty appearing prior to "Les Débuts de Chichine."

Andre Luguet and Guillardet. Music arranged by Albert Chantrier. Produced [staged] by M. Georges Wague. Mlle. Deslys' costumes by Maison Callot.

CAST: *Chichine*: Mlle. GABY DESLYS. *Rene*: Mons. Vermandele. *Flip*: Mons. Edgard Chatel. *Durton*: Harold Crane. *The Maid*: Doris Cameron.

Scene 4

ACT 2 (of INTO THE LIMELIGHT)

Opening Chorus
Ensemble

"Tony Caponi"
M. Raymond
(*Music by* Louis A. Hirsch.)

"(I Sang) Tra-La-Li"
D. Jardon, Chorus

Spanish Singing and Dancing Specialties
Los Malaguenitas

Finale
Ensemble

Scene 5

Farewell March

1911.35 THE NEVER HOMES

A Musical Kinemacolor (Comedy) in Two Acts, 6 Scenes. Words (book) by Glen MacDonough. Music by A. Baldwin Sloane. Rhymes (lyrics) by E. Ray Goetz. Staged by J. C. Huffman, William J. Wilson, Ned Wayburn. Scenery by Arthur Voegtlin. Costume plates by Cora MacGeachy. Orchestra under the direction of Hilding Anderson. Orchestrations by Hilding Anderson. Produced by Lew Fields. Opened 5 October 1911 at the Broadway Theatre and closed 23 December 1911 after 92 performances.

CAST: *Patricia Flynn*, a political boss, and proprietor of Flynn's laundry: GEORGE W. MONROE. *Herman Dinglebender*, chief of police, formerly a wig maker and hairdresser, and now running for sheriff on the Repubocrat ticket: JESS DANDY. *Daly Bunn*, proprietor of Bunn's stoneyard; monuments and headstones to order: AL LEECH. *Dr. August Breeze*, the town's most popular bachelor doctor: Denman Maley. *Webster Choate*, a young lawyer, running for district attorney on the Repubocrat ticket: JOSEPH SANTLEY. *Jimmy Louder*, a near orphan: WILL ARCHIE. *Mr. Louder*, only a husband: Edward Adams. *Pietro*, an indignant Italian: Fred Sidney.[37] *Mrs. Daly Bunn*, Daly Bunn's second wife, a woman lawyer, running for mayor on the Super-Suffragette ticket: RAY COX. *Mrs. Talkington Louder*, a local society leader devoted to "the cause": LILLIAN HERLEIN. *Wistaria Bunn*, Daly Bunn's daughter: BESSIE CLIFFORD. *Pearl White*, a colored washlady temporarily in politics: Artie Hall. *Fannie Hicks*, another near orphan: HELEN HAYES. *Pauline Panhard*, a prominent citizen of Lilydale: Vera Finlay. *Fanchon Finnegan*, a lady police captain: May Maloney. *Annie Key*, a bold fire girlie: MAUDE GRAY. *Daisy Copp*, a dashing roundsgirl: HAZEL ALLEN. *Lotta Lipp*, a ward leader: NAN BRENNAN. *Iona Mann*, the pride of the fire department: Grace Gilbert. *Lina Pipe*, lieutenant of Excelsior Hose No. 1: Elsa Rinehardt.

Of Captain Dinglebender's Command: *Bonavita Hagenbeck*: Harry Russell. *Chauncey Nightingale*: Julian Schroeder. *Uffenduffer*: Leslie Powers: *Hermann Muff*: Kenneth Ryan.

Personnel of Chorus: *Policemisses, Court Spectators, Laundry Patrons, Suffragettes, etc.*: Misses May Tormey, Nedda Nilssen, Teresa Allen, Helen Miller, Anita Francesca, Estelle Francesca, Berna Devore, Diane Oste, Elsa Reinhardt, May Willard, Lillian Hanson, Daisy Rudd. *Fire Lassies, Police Reporters, Court Stenographers, Laundresses, Suffargettes, etc.*: Misses Cassie Meade, Margaret Day, Bertie Britton, Mabel Allen, Katherine Humphrey, Amy Wilson, Bessie Cottrell, Margie Herman, Eileen Jackson, Violet Shaw, Ethel Tennis. *Fire Laddies, Court Messengers, Junior Pinkertons, White Wings, Suffragettes, etc.*: Misses Olga Harting, Mabel Woodrow, Ray Miller, Ruth Hanson, Gertrude Rutland, Lillian Foster, Aileen Pickard, Jane Houston, May Miller, Emily Price, Dolly Filley. *Small Town Chaps, Village Cutups, Rural Police, Kiss Burglars, Wine Agents, Fiances, etc.*: Messrs. Julius Schroeder, Fred Bates, John Klaboe, Kenneth Ryan, Clay Hill, Barry Delaney, Robert Hunter, Harry Russell, E. F. Taylor, William Heidloff, Harry Harrington, Leslie Powers, Morris Bodington, Alex Gibson, Herbert Dunham, Hal Frost.

Act 1, Scene 1: Public square of the town of Lilydale on the evening of election day. *Scene 2*: A street of Lilydale, two weeks later. *Scene 3*: The engine house of the new Lilydale fire department.

Act 2, Scene 1: Interior of the Lilydale court house. *Scene 2*: Exterior of the police station. *Scene 3*: Patricia Flynn's laundry.

ACT 1

Scene 1

"To-night's the Night"
L. Herlein, Chorus
(*Music by* A. Baldwin Sloane.)

"There's a Girl in Havana"
B. Clifford, J. Santley
(*Music and Lyrics by* Irving Berlin, E. Ray Goetz.[38])

Scene 2

"Take Me Along with You, Dearie"
Policemisses, Wine Agents
(*Music by* A. Baldwin Sloane.)

"I'm All for You"
A. Leech, M. Gray

Scene 3

"Fire Belles"
E. Reinhardt, Fire Laddies, Fire Lassies, Fire Ladies

"The Fire Ladies' Ball"
M. Gray, Chorus

"The Kiss Burglar"
B. Clifford, J. Santley, Chorus
(*Music by* A. Baldwin Sloane.)

ACT 2

Scene 1

"Good Morning, Judge" (Opening Chorus)
Ensemble

"First Love Days"
L. Herlein, Chorus
(*Music by* A. Baldwin Sloane.)

Scene 2[39]

"A Post Card Beau"
White Wings, Carriers

Scene 3

Opening:
"Here We Are Scrubbing"
Ensemble
"Just a Little Bit of Lingerie"
N. Brennan, H. Allen, M. Gray

"That Spooky Tune"
B. Clifford, A. Leech, J. Santley
(*Music by* A. Baldwin Sloane.)

Finale
Ensemble

1911.36 THE DUCHESS

A Comic Opera in Three Acts. Book (and lyrics) by Joseph Herbert and Harry B. Smith. Music by Victor Herbert. Production staged by J. C. Huffman. Dances and numbers staged by William J. Wilson and Gus Sohkle. Costumes designed by Melville Ellis. Orchestra under the direction of John McClure, Oscar Radin. Orchestrations by Victor Herbert. Produced by the (Messrs.) Sam S. and Lee Shubert Inc. Opened 16 October 1911 at the Lyric Theatre and closed 4 November 1911 after 24 performances.

CAST: *Aristede Boutonniere*, (proprietor of a flower shop in Paris): WILTON TAYLOR. *Rose*, his daughter: FRITZI SCHEFF. *Angelique Boutonniere*, her aunt: MAY BOLEY. *Marianne*, her cousin: LILLIAN SPENCER. *Phillipe*, Marquis de Montreville, (a soldier): GEORGE ANDERSON. *Adolphe*, Count de Paravante, a butterfly: JOHN E. HAZZARD. *Boni de Francellas*, man about town : George Graham. *Alfonso Castelet*: Madison Smith. *Lieutenant Prosper de Merimée*: ROBERT MILLIKEN. *Comte Gaston Gerome*: Raymond Bloomer. *Picotte*, footboy: M. Berenson. *Duchess de Greadfre*: Ida Bernard. *Notary*: Robert Flynn.

Shoppers: Misses Eleanor Guest, Leona Court, Belle Court, Vera Netta, Blanche Netta, Audry DeMars, Harriet DeNorma, Katherine Gray, Eleanor Ryley, Eleanor Twain, Carmen Romero. *Flowers Girls*: Misses Edna Bennett, Jewyl Taylor, Dorothy Duncan, Fannie Hudson, Vinna Mason, Mary Elder, Marie Grazia, Mildred Brown, Marie Andree, Edna Graym, Lois Meredith, Daisy Devere, Helen Glenmore, Jaine

---

[37]The character of Pietro appears to have been omitted from the opening week's playbill.

[38]Ted Snyder credited as co-author.

[39]Added to Act 2, Scene 2, in second week of run:
"The Base Ball Girl"
R. Cox

Frazier, Adele DePerry, Fern Maddox, Frisco Devere, Marie Gorty, Frances Kornwach, Mabel Devere, Dorothy Barnett. *Gentlemen of Fashion, Artists, etc.*: Messrs. Flynn, Whitcomb, Weir, Slaven, Harten, Premo, Rose, Willard, Rogers, Canova, Sullivan, Zoller, Goldie, Gordon, Ludermann, Williams.

Time: Present.

Act 1: The Flower Shop of Aristede Boutonniere.

Act 2: Grand Salon in the Chateau de Montreville.

Act 3: Hunting Lodge of the Duc de Montpensier at Versailles.

ACT 1
"Cupid, Tell Me Why" (Love That's Sincere)
F. Scheff
"The Land of the Sultans' Dreams"
G. Anderson
"It's the Bump"
M. Boley
Finale

ACT 2
"Richer Than Gold"
"The Coryphee"
Entrance of Rose (Auction Song)
"If I Should Dream of You (When Out on the Desert)"
Finale

ACT 3
"A Girlie-Land"
Hunting Song (The Chase)
"I'm Such a Romantic Girl"
"Isn't It Nasty of Papa?"
"The Latest Society Pet"
"Let Me Be Free"
"Life Is a Riddle"
"The Old Noblesse"
"Play the Game, Sally"
"Teach Me to Forget"
"There Is a Soul Mate"
"Upsi-Daisy"
"What's the Use of Moonlight?"
Finale Ultimo

1911.37 GYPSY LOVE

A Romantic Opera in Three Acts. Original Viennese libretto to the operette 'Zieguenerliebe' by A. M. Willner and Robert Bodanzky. (American) Book and lyrics by Harry B. Smith and Robert B. Smith. Music by Franz Lehár. Produced under the stage direction of George Marion. Settings designed by Ernest Albert. Costumes by Mueltzer, Paul Pieret, Mme. Sotager. Orchestra under the direction of Louis F. Gottschalk. Produced by A. H. Woods. Opened 17 October 1911 at the Globe Theatre and closed 11 November 1911 after 31 performances.

CAST: *Zorika*: MARGUERITA SYLVA; PHYLLIS PARTINGTON. *Niklas*, her father: HARRY MACDONOUGH. *Jozsi*, a gypsy musician: ARTHUR ALBRO. *Fedor*, Zorika's betrothed: CARL HAYDN. *Ilma*, a young widow: FRANCES DEMAREST. *Mikel*, proprietor of Cafe Orientale, Buda Pesth: GEORGE L. BICKEL. *Lila*, niece of Niklas, a school girl, ambitious to marry: Dorothy Webb. *Kaspar*, a bashful youth, son of the Burgomaster: ROBERT G. PITKIN. *Moschu*, a tonsorial artist and beauty doctor: Albert Hart. *Sacha*, Zorika's old nurse: Lucie Mitchell. *Magda*, a maid servant: Josephine Harmon. *Dimitri*, a waiter, Cafe Orientale: Anton Hanschmann. *Fancha*, a maid: Kittie Saville. *Henry*: Robert Smith. *Etta*: Oralla Mars.

Grand Dames: Misses Lillian Wallace, Peggy O'Neil, Naoma Malone, Leuvine Jacques, Josephine Harmon, Katherine Melton, Alice Melrose, Ray Ruddy, Mildred DeSilva, Edna Caruthers, Virginia Rhodes, Marie Kennedy, Clara Boley, Billie Davenport. *Gypsy Girls*: Misses Elinor Miles, Madaline Frain, Dodo Bernard, Constance Hoag, Grace Nelson, Gertrude Fielding, Geraldine Burton, Alma Pickard. *Bridesmaids*: Misses Peggy Merrett, Jean Hague, Alice Randolph, Marion Thompson, Ethel Fawcett, Helen McAdam, Valleaux Elliott, Charlotte Fielding. *Housemaids*: Misses Marion Brown, Alie Hall, Gertrude Thurston, Marion Watts, Jean Wallace, Winifred Ayers. *Officers*: Messrs. Albert Cody, Tom Shannon, Charles Staples, Lou Chalmers. *Court Men*: Messrs. Fred Robinson, Maurice Newmann, Edgar Evans, Irving LaPato, James C. Morris, Will P. Plummer, Arthur Snyder, Charles Schuler. *Gypsy Men*: Messrs. Albert Macklin, John Carleton, Fred Turner, Fred Kallgren, Willis McClellan, Christopher Hayes, Ber Kirsch, James T. Taylor, Walter Brown. *Water Sprites*: Misses Lillian Rockwell, Frankie DeMar, Ethel Evans, Anna Deneny, Pearl Wilkinson, Rose Maxwell, Reana Davis, Jule Sutherland, Marguerite Frances, May Delaney, Charlotte Allen, Portia Belmont.

Act 1: Park of the Chateau Niklas, Roumania.

Act 2: Palm Garden, Café Orientale, Buda Pesth.

Act 3: Same as Act 1.

ACT 1
"Defying the Storm" (Solo)
M. Sylva
"The Land of Fancy" (There Is a Land of Fancy)(Duet)
M. Sylva, A. Albro
"Wedding Guests" (Ensemble)
"Love Is Like the Rose" (Duet)
C. Haydn, M. Sylva
"Love's Sorcery" (Song)
F. Demarest, Chorus
"I Will Give You All for Love"[40] (Solo)
M. Sylva
"Lessons in Love" (Trio)
D. Webb, R. G. Pitkin, F. Demarest
Finale

ACT 2
Opening Ensemble
"Gypsy Love" (Song)
A. Albro
Ensemble
"The Melody of Love" (Song)
M. Sylva, Chorus
"When I'm Waltzing with You" (Duet)
H. Macdonough, F. Demarest
Baby Duet
D. Webb, R. G. Pitkin
Finale

ACT 3
Opening Ensemble
"I Will Give You All for Love" (Solo, reprise)
M. Sylva
"Matrimony" (Quintet)
F. Demarest, H. Macdonough, R. G. Pitkin, D. Webb, G. L. Bickel
Finale

1911.38 THE ENCHANTRESS

An Opera Comique (Comic Opera) in Two Acts. Book and lyrics by Fred DeGrésac.[41] and Harry B. Smith.[42] Music by Victor Herbert. Staged under the personal direction of Frederick G. Latham. Ensembles and dances by Frederic A. Bishop. Settings by W. M. Harvey, P. Dodd Ackerman. Costumes by Ralph Riggs. Orchestra under the direction of Gustave Salzer. Orchestrations by Victor Herbert. Produced by Joseph M. Gaites. Opened 19 October 1911 at the New York Theatre and closed 20 January 1912 after 104 peformances.[43]

CAST: *Vivien Savary*, an opera singer: KITTY GORDON. *Mamoute*, her aunt: Hattie Arnold. *Marion Love*, an American heiress: NELLIE McCOY. *Princess Diana* of Russia: IDA FITZHUGH. *Princess Stellina*: Louise Bliss. *Princess Stephanie*: VENITA FITZHUGH. *Princess Poppy*: NINA BARBOUR. *Princess Floria*: Mabel Berra. *Princess Berenice*: Dorothy Berry. *Princess Hortensia*: Clarice Gilberte. *Prince Ivan of Zergovia*: HAROLD [Hal] FORDE. *Troute*, head of the Secret Service: RALPH RIGGS. *Poff*, the Prince's tutor: Gilbert Clayton. *Miloch*, Regent of Zergovia: HARRISON BROCKBANK. *Ozir*, Minister of War: ARTHUR FORREST. *Prince Zepi*: Bertram Fox. *Mina*, maid to Vivien: KATHERINE WITCHIE.

---

[40]Dropped for subsequent tour.

[41]Nom de plume for Mrs. Victor Maurel.

[42]Contrary to the program credit, Harry B. Smith alone wrote the lyrics.

[43]Played a return engagement 1 April 1912 at the Grand Opera House for 8 performances.

Other Characters by Misses Maud Stone, Christine Campbell, Lois Dale, Carrie Burke, Olive Crosby, Louise Freeman, Anna Walcott, Adele Covert, Ruth Gribben, Madge Trapp, Georgina Neekamp, Anna Dexter, Margaret Murdock, Marjorie English, Anita Fortier, Leah Griffith, Helen Crane, Winona Wilkins. Messrs. Conroy, Harvey, Moore, Kelly, Warren, Gahn, Mortimer, Mason, Doffus, Maddern, Von Stein, Brown, Clay, Fair, Leach, Chamblain.

Act 1: Royal Palace of Zergovia. (Harvey.)

Act 2: Vivien's Villa on the Banks of the Danube. (Ackerman.)

ACT 1[44]

Opening Ensemble
Princesses
"When the Right Man Sings Tra La" (Duet)
B. Fox, V. Fitzhugh
"They All Look Good When They're Far Away" (Comic Duo)
R. Riggs, G. Clayton
Chorus and Entrance of Regent (March)
H. Brockbank, Chorus
"If You Can't Be as Happy as You'd Like to Be, Be Just as Happy as You Can" (Song)
H. Brockbank
Entrance of Prince Ivan
H. H. Forde, Chorus
"And That (Last) Little Girl Is You" (Solo)
H. H. Forde
Entrance of Vivian
Principals, Chorus
"(To the) Land of My Own Romance" (I Have a Dream by Night, by Day) (Solo)
K. Gordon
"I've Been Looking for a Perfect Man" (Song)
N. McCoy, Princesses
"Rose, Lucky Rose" (Duet)
K. Gordon, H. H. Forde
Finale
Ensemble

ACT 2

Opening Chorus
Princesses, R. Riggs, Chorus
"Art is Calling for Me" (I Want to Be a Prima Donna)(Song)
L. Bliss, Chorus
"Come Little Fishes" (Soliloquy)
K. Gordon
"Come to Sunny Spain" (Duet)
R. Riggs, H. Arnold
"One Word from You" (Duet)
K. Gordon, H. H. Forde
"Dreaming Princess" (Madrigal)
Princesses
"That Naughty Little Song" (Novelty Number)
N. McCoy, Priuncesses
Dance Extraordinaire
R. Riggs, K. Witchie
"All Your Own Am I" (Champagne Song)
K. Gordon, A. Forrest
Finale
Ensemble

1911.39 THE QUAKER GIRL

A Musical Play in Three Acts.[45] Book by James T. Tanner. Music by Lionel Monckton. Lyrics by Adrian Ross and Percy Greenbank. Produced under the direction of J. A. E. Malone. Scenery by H. Robert Law. Costumes by Maison Blum, Paris; Mrs. Field, London; Lucille, Ltd., Paris. Orchestra under the direction of Augustus Barratt. Produced by Henry B. Harris. Opened 23 October 1911 at the Park Theatre and closed 18 May 1912 after 240 performances.[46]

CAST (in order of appearance): *Jarge*, the village crier: Fred Tooze. *Mrs. Lukyn*, landlady at "The Chequers": Nellie McHenry. *William*, waiter at "The Chequers": Harold Thomas. *Nathaniel Pym*, a Quaker: LAWRENCE EDDINGER. *Rachel Pym*, a Quakeress: Eleanor Sheldon. *Phoebe*, maid to Princess Mathilde: MAY VOKES. *Princess Mathilde*, an exiled Bonapartist Princess: DAPHNE GLENNE. *Captain Cherteris*, King's Messenger: (F.) POPE STAMPER. *Madame Blum*, of the Maison Blum, Paris: MAISIE GAY. *Tony Chute*, naval attaché at the American Embassy, Paris: CLIFTON CRAWFORD. *Jeremiah*, a Quaker: PERCIVAL KNIGHT. *Prudence*, a Quaker girl: INA CLAIRE. *Toinette*, employee of Maison Blum: Viola Clark. *Monsieur Larose*, Chief of Police, Paris: Arthur Klein. *Diane*, a Parisian actress: OLGA PETROVA. *Prince Carlo*: LAWRENCE REA. *Monsieur Duhamel*, Minister of State: Edward Martyn. *Dorcas*: Elaine Hall. *Phyllis*: Irma Bertrand. *Marguerite, Germaine*, Lady Customers: Marge Wallace, Anna Nelson. *Employees of Maison Blum (4)*: *Gaby*: Stella Beardsley. *Cleo*: Blanche Malli. *Liane*: Gertrude Fayot. *Louise*: Alice Chase. *Mimi*: Nora McClory. *Fifi*: Gloria Starr *Suzette*: Belle Delmar. *Micheline*: Myrtle McCloud. *Commissionaire*: W. Metcalfe. (*Dance Specialty*: Les Bluettes, Oscar Odee.)

Villagers, Quakers, Models, Shop Girls, Mannequins, etc.: Misses Helen Drew, Dolly Shimmin, Thelma Belmont, Gertrude Williams, Florence Grant, Irene Hopping, Frances Mayer, Easter Higbee, Elizabeth Keane, Camille Mayer, Norris Pendleton, Ethel Dunn, Norma Harland, Helen Merest, Ida Hall, Gertrude Fursman, Hazel Proctor, Mae Borden, Marie Pendleton, Ada Proctor, Mae Mortimer, Adelaide Murray, Billie Grant, Ruth Mason, Dolly Sterling, Bessie Bell, Clara Heath, Maude Cannar. Messrs. M. Stephen, A. Willis, W. Metcalfe, W. Wells, H. Hall, F. Snyder, M. Cox, A. Walton, C. Dunham, W. Bradfield, R. Denny, B. Russell, J. Worden, H. Kittridge, J. Newell, F. Fitzhugh, G. Pullman.

Act 1: An English Country Village.

Act 2: Madame Blum's Dressmaking Salon, Paris.

Act 3: The Pre Catalan, outside Paris.

ACT 1

Opening Chorus (We've Such a Tale to Tell)
Solo
N. McHenry
"Quaker's Meeting" (Entrance of Quakers and Double Chorus)
Chorus
"Wonderful"[47] (Duet)
D. Glenne, P. Stamper
"A Runaway Match" (Quartet)
D. Glenne, M. Vokes, P. Stamper, C. Crawford
"A Quaker Girl" (Song)
I. Claire
"The Bad Boy and the Good Girl" (Duet)
I. Claire, C. Crawford
(*Lyrics by* Percy Greenbank.)
"Tiptoe" (Concerted Number)
(D. Glenne, I. Claire, M. Gay, M. Vokes, P. Stamper, C. Crawford, Chorus)
"Just as Father Used To Do" (Song)
P. Knight, Chorus
(*Lyrics by* Percy Greenbank.)
Finale

ACT 2

Opening Chorus (In This Abode of Madame la Mode)
"Or Thereabouts" (Song)
M. Vokes
(*Music by* Hugo Felix.)
"On Revient de Chantilly" (General Entrance and Chorus)
Chorus
"Come to the Ball" (Valse Song)
L. Rea, Chorus
"A Dancing Lesson" (Take a Step)(Duet)
I. Claire, C. Crawford
"Barbizon" (March Quintet)
(D. Glenne, M. Vokes, M. Gay, P. Stamper, P. Knight)

---

[44]For subsequent tour, "When the Right Man Sings Tra-La" moved to follow "If You Can't Be as Happy as You'd Like to Be."
[45]Billed as "The London Musical Success."

[46]Played a return engagement 2 December 1912 at the Grand Opera House for 8 performances.
[47]Dropped for subsequent tour.

"Get Away, I'm a Married Man" (Keep Away from a Married Man)
C. Crawford
(*Music and Lyrics by* Clifton Crawford.)
Finale

ACT 3
Introduction and Dance
L. Bluettes, O. Odee
"Tony from America" (Song)
I. Claire
(*Lyrics by* Lionel Monckton.)
Ensemble Dance
"Something to Tell"[48] (I Want to Tell You Something)
C. Crawford
(*Music and Lyrics by* Clifton Crawford.)
"The First Dance"[49]
I. Claire, C. Crawford
Finale

1911.40 THE WIFE HUNTERS

A Musical Production in Two Acts, 4 Scenes. Book by Edgar Allan Woolf. (Based on his book for the musical "Three Million Dollars".[50]) Music by Anatol Friedland and Malvin Franklin. Lyrics by David Kempner. Production staged and dances arranged by Ned Wayburn. Scenery painted by John H. Young. Costumes by Cora MacGeachey. Orchestra under the direction of Lee Orean Smith. Produced by Lew Fields. Opened 2 November 1911 at the Herald Square Theatre and closed 2 December 1911 after 36 performances.

CAST: *Reginald Ogden Bruce*, a young clubman: JOHN PARK. *Dudley Stephens*, his friend: JOSEPH RATLIFF. *Guernsey Bruce*, his stepfather: GEORGE A. SCHILLER. *Paul De Laperra*, Juanita's brother: ARTHUR CONRAD. *Count De Grampton*, chef at the Casino: Louis Franklin. *Homer Van Pelt*, Mrs. Van Pelt's most recent husband: Louis Merkle. *Hiram*, an old bus driver: George Keefe. *Porter* at the hotel: George Dowling. *Chauncey*, the Van Pelt's chauffeur: Frederick Thorpe. *Phil Atkin*, Reginald's valet: Louis Simon. *Juanita DeLaperra*, a Cuba heiress: EDITH DECKER. *Henrietta Lampton*, daughter of the hotel proprietor: DOROTHY BRENNER. *Miss Phoebe Lang*, still single: LILLIAN LEE. *Belle Carruthers*, a New York heiress: HAZEL KIRKE. *Mlle. Follette Folarie*, Mrs. Van Pelt's chaperone: Frances Alain. *Mabel Lang, Flora Lang*, Miss Phoebe's nieces: Madge Vincent, Frances Nelson. *Premier Danseuse*: Gladys Moore. *Mellette* of the Varieties: Veronica Marquez. *Lulu*: May Brennan. *Marie*, everybody's little friend: Harriet Richmond. *Wilfred Page, Egbert Page*, bellhops at the hotel: Olive Carr, Nora Cotter. *Mrs. Homer Van Pelt*, a buxom chorus alumna: EMMA CARUS.

Original English Pony Ballet: Misses Ada Robertson, Eva Marlowe, Nellie Wilkie, Seppie McNeil, Dorothy Marlowe, Louise Hawman. *Guests, Picknickers, Old Fashioned Girls, etc.*: Misses Emily Monte, Virginia Gunther, Gladys Coleman, Janet Burton, Lillian LeRoy, Cynthia Perot, Betty Scott, Margaret Vingut, Marjorie Gerald, Evelyn Arnold. *Maids, Havana Misses, Crinoline Girls, Colleens*: Misses Gertrude Howard, Violet DuVourn, Alma Wilson, Mabel Landers, Carmen Jordan, Ella Vincent, Rosie Wolf, Adelaide Folger, Florence Coleman, May Brennan. *Havana Maids and Boys, Picnic Kiddies, Boys of '60, Colleens, etc.*: Misses Aimee Berry, Olive Carr, Ruth Heil, Nora Cotter, Louise Owen, Stacia Leslie, Madge Parsells, Olive Horner, Opal Scott, Lee Leontine. *Vacationers, Guests, Beaux of Ante-Bellum Days, etc.*: Messrs. Deane, Foin, Rogers, Pierce, Armstrong, Finch, Horan, Graham, Mills, Bogart.

Act 1, Scene 1: Lawn in front of the Wave Crest Inn. *Scene 2*: Pine grove, back of the Inn. *Scene 3*: The picnic grove.

Act 2: The Casino at Wave Crest.

ACT 1[51]
Scene 1
"Love Waves"
E. Decker
(*Music by* Anatole Friedland.)
"Follette"
A. Conrad, F. Alain
(*Music by* Anatole Friedland.)
"(My Little) Havana Made" (My Havana Maid)
J. Park, Chorus
(*Music by* Anatole Friedland.)
Scene 2
"Honeyland"
A. Conrad, D. Brenner
"(Girls,) Girls, Keep Your Figures"
E. Carus
(*Music by* Anatole Friedland.)
Scene 3
"The Picnic Club"
Chorus
Specialty Dance
Pony Ballet
"In Your Arms"
E. Decker, J. Park
"(Down at) Mammy Jinny's"
E. Carus, Chorus
(*Music by* Anatole Friedland.)
"Let's Take Him Home in Triumph" (Finale)
Ensemble

ACT 2
"The Wave Crest Waltz"
Chorus
"Pas de Seul"
G. Moore
"The Waltz of the Wild"
Pony Ballet
"On the Avenue"
J. Ratliff, E. Decker, Chorus
"Leonora"
E. Carus, Chorus
(*Music by* Anatole Friedland.)
"Swinging with Someone"
E. Decker, Chorus
(*Music by* Anatole Friedland.)
"Little Dancing Jumping Jigger"
D. Brenner, A. Conrad, Pony Ballet, Chorus
(*Music by* Anatole Friedland.)
"Recitative"
E. Decker, J. Park
Finale
Ensemble

[48]Replaced for subsequent tour by:
"Just a Little Word Unspoken"
P. Knight (Tony)
(*Music and Lyrics by* Augustus Barratt.)

[49]Dropped for subsequent tour.

[50]THREE MILLION DOLLARS closed prior to New York in 1910; Anatol Friedland wrote its music, David Kempner its lyrics.

[51]The show was revised during the run into 3 Acts, with Act 1, Scenes 2 and 3 combined as 'The Picnic Grove.' Song order was also revised, with "Girls, Keep Your Figures" moved into Act 1 following "Follette." "Honeyland" was moved to follow the Specialty Dance. "Singing with Someone" was dropped.

1911.41 THE RED WIDOW

A Musical Play in Three Acts. Book and lyrics by Channing Pollock and Rennold Wolf. (Based on the story "My Official Wife" by Archibald Clavering Gunther.) Music by Charles J. Gebest. Produced under the direction of Frederick G. Latham. Ballet and March Numbers staged by James Gorman. Scenery painted by Ernest Albert. Gowns, millinery and costumes by Lord & Taylor, Stern Brothers, Klaw & Erlanger Costume Co. Orchestra under the direction of Charles J. Gebest. Produced by (George M.) Cohan and (Sam) Harris. Opened 6 November 1911 at the Astor Theatre and closed 24 February 1912 after 128 performances.

CAST: *Cicero Hannibal Butts*, Manufacturer of C.H.B. Corsets, and Colonel in the New York State National Guard, U.S.A.: RAYMOND HITCHCOCK. *Violet Butts*, His Wife: Jean Newcombe. *Oswald Butts*, His Son: HARRY CLARKE. *Anna Varvara*, The Red Widow: SOPHYE BERNARD. *Yvette*, a Dancer: GERTRUDE VANDERBILT. *Ivan Scorpioff*, Chief of the Third Section, Russian Secret Police: John Hendricks. *Baron Maximilian Scareovich*, His Assistant: Joseph Allen. *Dick Graham*, Manager of the Hotel l'Europe, St. Petersburg: Lincoln Plumer. *Tantul Popova*, a Waiter, President of a Group of Nihilists: GEORGE E. MACK. *Captain Basil Romanoff* of the Imperial Body Guard: THEODORE MARTIN. *Princess Sophya, Countess Alexandra*, Relatives of Butts by Marriage: Augusta Lang, Clara Schroeder. *Kirglig, Paskof, Adyk, Ovak*, Four Nihilists: Stanley Fields, Rokey Johnson, Stanley Carter, William Lafferty. *Manager of the Alcazar Music Hall*: Ralph Harlowe. *Clerk of the Hotel l'Europe*: Ralph Harlowe.

Act 1: *Patrons of the Play*: *Ladies*: Misses Helen Cheevers, Ann O'Kane, Tempy Evans, Mona Clifford, Olga Markusson, Dorothy Courtney, Lola Lorraine, Margie Melvin, Evelyn May, Julie Newell, Helen Lee, Glory Gray, Mary Gordon, Elsie Richmond, Marie Fanning, Mattie Vance, Daisy Marshall, Elsie Markert, Gladys Taylor, Constance Talbott. *Gentlemen*: Messrs. Martin Enwright, Paul McShane, William Barube, Rorkey Johnson, Stanley Fields, Ray Russell, Owen Jones, Donald Archer, Lee Carrier, William Lafferty, Harry Pond, George Rose, Edward Morrison, S. R. Sommerville, D. Dickson. *Bar Maids*: Poney Cantor, Fay Darling. *Lady Ushers*: Misses Kitty Devere, Vivian Rogers, Anna Pauly, Sylvia Clark, B. Pennington, Beck Wood, Christine Mangasarin, Dorothy Dickson. *Dancing Girls*: Misses Cantor, Clark, Darling, Devere, Dickson, Mangasarin, Pauly, Pennington, Rogers, Wood.

Act 2: *Chambermaids*: Misses Courtney, Evans, Fanning, Gordon, Grey, Lorraine, Lee, Markusson, Marshall, May, Melvin, O'Kane, Richmond, Talbott, Taylor, Vance. *Bell Boys*: Misses Cantor, Clark, Darling, Devere, Dickson, Mangasarin, Pauly, Pennington, Rogers, Wood. *Hotel Porters*: Messrs. Archer, Burube, Enwright, Jones, McShane, Ross, Russell. *Hotel Waiters*: Messrs. Carriere, Dickson, Fields, Johnson, Lafferty, Morrison, Pond, Sommerville. *Five Designing Damsels*: Misses Helen Cheevers, Elsie Markert, Julie Newell, Olga Markusson, Mona Clifford. *Ladies in Waiting*: Misses Cheevers, Clifford, Courtney, Evans, Fanning, Gordon, Gray, Lee, Lorraine, Markusson, May, Marshall, Melvin, Markert, Newell, O'Kane, Richmond, Talbott, Taylor, Vance. *Soldiers of the Czar*: Messrs. Archer, Burube, Carriere, Enwright, Fields, Dickson, Jenkins, Johnson, Jones, Lafferty, McShane, Morrison, Pond, Ross, Russell, Sommerville.

Act 3: *Ladies of the Court*: Misses Cheevers, Clifford, Courtney, Evans, Fanning, Gordon, Gray, Lee, Richmond, Talbott, Taylor, Vance. *Court Ballet*: Misses Cantor, Darling, Devere, Rogers, Pauly, Clark, Pennington, Wood, Mangasarin, Dickson. *Imperial Body Guard*: Messrs. Jenkins, Enwright, McShane, Burube, Johnson, Fields, Russell, Jones, Archer, Carriere, Lafferty, Pond, Ross, Morrison, Sommerville, Dickson.

Act 1: The Foyer of the Alcazar Music Hall, London.

Act 2: Private Parlor in the Hotel de l'Europe, St. Petersburg. Five days later.

Act 3: The Gardens of the Winter Palace, St. Petersburg, by night. One day later. The Annual "White Fête" is in progress.

ACT 1

"Patrons of the Play"
Ensemble

"Never Mind the Singing—Just Dance, My Dear"
G. Vanderbilt

"When Woman Is the Question"
S. Barnard, J. Allen, T. Martin

"I'm a Wonderful Man in Yonkers"
R. Hitchcock, Girls

"We Will Go, Go (All Aglow) to Gogo"
H. Clarke, G. Vanderbilt

"Off to Russia" (Finale)
Ensemble

ACT 2

Opening Chorus
Ensemble

"The Avenue of Palms"
S. Barnard, H. Clarke, G. Vanderbilt

"I Shall Never Look at a Pretty Girl Again"
R. Hitchcock

"In Society It's Always Dress Parade"
A. Lang, C. Schroeder, R. Hitchcock, S. Barnard, Court Ladies

"You Can't Pay the Landlord With Love"
H. Clarke, G. Vanderbilt

"I Love You, Dear"
S. Barnard, T. Martin

Finale
Ensemble

ACT 3

"The White Fête" (March)
Ensemble

"Just For You"
S. Barnard

"The Nihilists"
G. E. Mack, Conspirators

"Soldiers of the Czar"
T. Martin, S. Barnard, Ensemble

Finale
Entire Company

1911.42 THE THREE ROMEOS

An American Musical Comedy in Three Acts. Book and lyrics by R. H. Burnside. Music by Raymond Hubbell. Produced under the stage direction of R. H. Burnside. Settings by Walter Burridge, Theodore Reisig. Costumes by Lucille, Ltd. Orchestra under the direction of Anton Heindl. Orchestrations by Frank Saddler. Produced by Fellner and Dreyfuss. Opened 13 November 1911 at the Globe Theatre and closed 30 December 1911 after 56 performances.

CAST (in order of appearance): *Vera Steinway*, a School Girl: Peggy Wood. *Daisy Dean*, a School Girl: SHIRLEY KELLOGG. *Peter Poppleton*, a School Master: FRED WALTON. *Minerva Poppleton*, his Sister: Minnie Olton. *Nancy Mallory*, secretly married to Dick: ETHEL CADMAN. *Diana Mallory*, her Aunt: Mabella Baker. *Gussie Gibson*, an Actress: GEORGIA CAINE. *Titus Bellamy*, a Rounder: WILLIAM DANFORTH. *Dick Dawson*, Poppleton's nephew: ALFRED KAPPELER. *Jack Willoughby*, divorced from Gussie: FRITZ WILLIAMS. *Rose Bellamy*, in love with Bertie Montague: VIVIAN RUSHMORE. *Mrs. Bellamy*, her Mother: ELITA PROCTOR OTIS. *Timothy Stubbs*, a Florist: FRED LENNOX. *Bertie Montague*, in love with Rose: EDWARD ALFINO. *Willie Mortimer*, a Johnnie: H. P. Woodley.

School Girls: Misses Augusta Baker, May Gunderman, Anna Engel, Agnes Devereux, Dottie Van Court, Elsie Stillwell, Gladys McNally, Annette Wilson, Eleanor Carrol, Grace Edwards, Miriam Von Prague, Cecil Waldron, Glory Foraker, May McCarthy, Alice Cantwell, Cissie Dolliver, Fannie Bradshaw, Anna Harrington, Monte Mulman. *Frivolity Girls*; Misses Estelle Richmond, Althea Francis, Sophia Ralph, Hazel Robinson, Sallie Ronayne, Noette Aimes, Mary Michael, Eleanor Guest, Frankie Lee, Frankie Wilson, Tessie Goldie, Clara DeWitt, Mae Wesley, Frances Ray, Katherine Peters, Myrtle Starkey, Sybil Elwood. *Flower Girls*: Misses Carrol, Edwards, Von Prague, Waldron, Foraker, McCarthy, Cantwell, Dolliver, Bradshaw, Harrington, Langdon, Hamilton, Donlevy. *Johnnies*: Misses Baker, Gunderman, Engle, Mulman, Van Court, Stilwell, McNally, Wilson, Carroll, Edwards, Von Prague, Waldron, Foraker, McCarthy, Cantwell, Dolliver, Bradshaw, Harrington. Messrs. Paul Gascoigne, Wood Goble, Edward Alfino, Frank Wayne, Frank Gillespie, Gerald LaForest, Ned Booth, Harry Nelson, H. P. Woodley, Howard Stevens, Edward Smith, Lebold. *Society Buds*: Misses Baker, Gunderman, Engle, Bradshaw, Van Court, Stillwell, McNally, Wilson.

The action takes place at the present time.

Act 1: Reception Room in Miss Poppleton's Academy. (Burridge.)

Act 2: Flower Store on Fifth Avenue. (Reisig.)

Act 3: Bellamy's Villa at Newport. (Burridge.)

ACT 1

"Education" (Opening Chorus)
School Girls

"Oh, Romeo" (Song)
S. Kellogg, Chorus

"Humpty and Dumpty" (Duet)
F. Walton, E. Cadman

"Divorce" (Song)
G. Caine, Frivolity Girls

"(A Matter of) Experience" (Trio)
W. Danforth, G. Caine, F. Walton

"It's Nice to Have Some One to Love You" (Duet)
E. Cadman, A. Kappeler

"Off to the Matinee" (Finale)
Ensemble

ACT 2

"Oh, Fifth Avenue" (Opening Chorus)
Ensemble

"Moonlight" (Song)
S. Kellogg, Chorus

"She Didn't Seem to Care" (Song)
F. Lennox

"The Lily and the Rose" (Song)
E. Cadman, Chorus

"Along Broadway" (Quartette)
W. Danforth, F. Walton, A. Kappeler, F. Lennox

"(I've Been) Looking for a Girl Like You" (Song)
G. Caine, Chorus

"Mary Ann, (Where Are You?)" (Song)
W. Danforth, Principals

"Off to the Wedding" (Finale)
Ensemble

ACT 3

"Where's the Bridegroom?" (Opening Chorus)
Ensemble

"Mary Carey" (Duet)
G. Caine, F. Walton, Chorus

"Annabelle Jerome" (Song)
W. Danforth, Chorus

"He's Crazy" (Trio)
F. Lennox, F. Walton, W. Danforth

Finale
Ensemble

1911.43 VERA VIOLETTA

A Musical Entertainment (Comedy) in Two Acts, followed by the Continental Idea of Variété (vaudeville, dance). American book by Leonard Liebling and Harold Atteridge. Adapted from the German vaudeville of the same name by Leo Stein. Music by Edmund Eysler. Lyrics by Harold Atteridge. Staged by Lewis Morton. Dances arranged by William J. Wilson, Joseph C. Smith. Costumes designed by Melville Ellis. Orchestra under the direction of Samuel Lehman. Produced by the Winter Garden Company (Messrs. Shubert). Opened 20 November 1911 at the Winter Garden and closed 24 February 1912 after 112 performances.[52]

CAST (in order of appearance): *Manager of the Skating Rink*: Lew Quinn. *Claude*, a waiter: AL JOLSON. *Margot*: DORIS CAMERON. *Aristide de St. Cloche*: VAN RENSSELAER WHEELER. *Pierre*, a waiter: ERNEST HARE. *Professor Otto von Gruenberg*: James B. Carson. *Mlle. Angelique*, an American dancer: KATHLEEN CLIFFORD. *Morris Cohen*, Newark U.S.A., on pleasure bent: BARNEY BERNARD. *A Rounder*: BILLEE TAYLOR. *La Duchesse*: Florence Douglas. *Mme. von Gruenberg*, known as Vera Violetta: JOSÉ COLLINS. *Paul Voison*: MELVILLE ELLIS. *Mme. Adelle de St. Cloche*: GABY DESLYS. *Mme. Elise*, Adele's aunt and M. Berton's wife: STELLA MAYHEW. *Andrew Mason*: HARRY PILCER. *Marquis de Tivoli*: CLARENCE HARVEY. *Ninon*: Maidie Berker. *Lulu*: Florence Douglas. *Susanne*: Jane Lawrence. *Cavaliers, Grisettes, Skaters, Guests, etc, etc.*

The Chorus: *Patronesses of the Skating Rink*: Misses Dakin, Truesdale, Cannar, Grayel, Warde, E. Prager, Scherer, Sparks, Furlong, Wallace, Callan, E. Burnette, Falk, Sachere, Laboulaye. *Patrons of the Skating Rink*: Messrs. Dellet, Cohan, Gilbert, Austin, Hartman, Carter, Gilliss, Sohmers, Georgi, Bingham, Miller Hoffman, Godlen, Gordon. *Russian Dancers*: Misses McLelland, Zaltz, H. Burnette, Falk, Florence, LaPlace, M. Prager, Hardy. *Guests*: Misses Cameron, Lawrence, Cable, Goulding, Dell, Burker, Barnes, Harris, Bentley, DeBeers, Martin, Miller, French, Douglas, Quinn, Cummings, Parker *The Ballet in Undine*: Misses LaPlace, Lachere, E. Prager, Hardy, Callan, Walalce, H. Burnett, Warde, Laboulaye, Sparks, Florence, McLellan, Dakin, Falk, Zaltz, Crane.

The action takes place in Paris at the present time at night.

Act 1, Scene 1: Foyer of Berton's Skating Rink. *Scene 2*: The ante-room of the Skating Room and Restaurant.

ACT 1[53]

Scene 1

Opening Chorus

"Paree, Gay Paree"
V. R. Wheeler, Chorus

"Angelique of the Opera Comique"
K. Clifford, Chorus
(*Music by* Louis A. Hirsch. *Lyrics by* Melville Gideon.)

"Olga from the Volga"
J. Collins, Chorus

"Vera Violetta"
J. Collins, B. Taylor

Scene 2

Songs and Pianologue (Specialty)
M. Ellis

"(There Are) 57 Ways to Win a Man"
S. Mayhew

"Come Back to Me"
G. Deslys

"Come and Dance (with Me)"
G. Deslys, H. Pilcer
(*Music by* Louis A. Hirsch. *Lyrics by* Melville Gideon.)

"That Haunting Melody"
A. Jolson
(*Music and Lyrics by* George M. Cohan.)

"Rum Tum Tiddle"
A. Jolson
(*Music by* Jean Schwartz. *Lyrics by* Edward Madden.)

"My Lou"
S. Mayhew, B. Taylor

"I've Heard That Before"
G. Deslys, Chorus
(*Music by* Louis A. Hirsch. *Lyrics by* Melville Gideon.)

"I Wonder If It's True"
J. Collins

"The Gaby Glide"
H. Pilcer, Chorus
(*Music by* Louis Hirch. *Lyrics by* Harry Pilcer.)

Finale
Company

ACT 2: UNDINE[54]

An Idyll of Forest and Stream in One Act. Book, music and lyrics by Manuel Klein.

CAST: *The Lord of Rose Hill*: EDWARD CUTLER. *The Lady of Rose Hill*: DORIS CAMERON. *Jacqueminot*, their daughter: DOROTHY SCHERER. *Ursula*, her nurse: Maidie Berker. *Athelig*, a companion of the Nymph: Max Welly. *A Court Jester*: Clarence Harvey. *A Shepherd*: George Dellett. *Undine*, a water Nymph: ANNETTE KELLERMAN. *Shepherds and Shepherdesses*.

Scene: A wood in the heart of England on a summer's day.

VARIÉTÉ[55]

Frank Tinney; The Kaufmann Troupe

1911.44 LITTLE BOY BLUE

A Romantic Operetta in Two Acts. Original Viennese libretto to the operette "Lord Piccolo" by Rudolph Schanzer and Carl Lindau. American adaptation by A. E. Thomas and Edward A. Paulton. Music by Henri Berény. Additional lyrics by Carolyn Wells, Grant Stewart, Edward Madden, William F. Kirk. Scenery painted by Ernest M. Gros. Costumes by DeWolf, Wachner & Co. (principals), Landolff (French-Scotch dresses), Freisinger, Jack Weiner (mens'). Staged under direction of Frank Smithson. Dances arranged by Jack Mason. Orchestra under the direction of Arthur Weld. Produced by Henry W. Savage. Opened 27 November 1911 at the Lyric Theatre and closed 27 April 1912 after 176 performances.[56]

CAST: *The Earl of Goberdeen*: JOHN DUNSMURE. *Gaston*, the Marquis de la Tour: CHARLES MEAKINS. *Dupont*, a detective: OTIS HARLAN. *Captain Graham*: C. Morton Horne. *Tabarin*: Victor Kahn. *Archie*, Goberdeen's Scotch valet: Neil McNeil. *Daisy*, barmaid at the Bal Tabarin: GERTRUDE BRYAN. *Amaranth*, a seeress: MAUDE ODELL. *Kitty*, Lord Goberdeen's niece and ward: KATHERYN STEVENSON.

At the Bal Tabarin: *Dubois, Mars, Fleur*, Habitués of the Bal Tabarin: Jack Rowe, Harry Hamilton, Ivan Murchison. *Dancers (4)*: *René*: Viola Napp. *Marcelle*: Edith Warren. *Lois*: Anita Pollock. *Clementine*: Ada Ripel. *Hélène*: Mary Hamilton. *Raoul*, a chasseur: Antoinette LeComte. *Alphonse*, portier: Sam Chadwick. *Munkacs Janos*, Hungarian violinist: C. Grosskopf. *A Cabman*: Maxwell Kennedy. *Waitresses*: Misses Anita Barreto, Edith Langdon, Billie Busch, Gertrude Barreto, Margaret Cecil, Anna Sayce, Marie Kavenaugh, Charlotte Burt. *Grisettes*: Misses Mary Young, Gloria Alba, Helen Summers, Antoinette Stone, Alma Morrison, Beatrice North, Antoinette LeComte, Crystal Everett. *Cocottes*: Misses Emma Nagel, Mary Hamilton, Gwendolyn

---

[52]Settings uncredited.

[53]Added during the run:

"The Cafe Man" (after "Olga from the Volga")
M. Brown

"I Want Something New to Play With" (after "57 Ways to Win a Man")
J. Collins, B. Bernard

[54]Late in the run replaced by (a) the Courtney Sisters, followed by (b) Mikail Mordkin, Mlle. Lydia Lopoukowa, Mlle. Bronislowa Pajitzkaia in a Program of Ballet Divertissements.

[55]Though the Variete portion of the program was originally announced to open the evening, along with Los Malaguenitas (Spanish Songs and Dances), Lydia Barry and Belle Baker, Variete had been moved to the end the program as of opening night.

[56]Play a return engagement 21 April 1913 at the Grand Opera House for 8 performances.

Canfield, Florence Taylor, Lillian West, Adele Harrison, Lutie Evans, Fern Hollis. *Mannequins*: Misses Marion Wilson, Lea Leature, Mabel Gebeau, Agnes Jeppson, Marie Fredriks, Jane Warrington, Loretta Wright, Flora Gould. *Soldiers, Cabmen, Boulevardiers, Artists, etc*: Messrs. Kennedy, Sutton, Bowen, J. Hamilton, Hedge, Homan, Garretson, Sansifer, Roberts, Golden, Mulvey, Jesson, Rankin, Fletcher, Roger.

At Goberdeen Castle: *Baroness Lloyd*: Lillian West. *Lady Whitten*: Gwendolyn Canfield. *Lady Barrison*: Florence Taylor. *Willie MacTaggart*: Sam Chadwick. *A Housekeeper*: Mary Hamilton. *Writer to the Signet*: Albert Hedge. *Flunkies*: F. Roberts, J. R. Hamilton, F. Bowen. *Donald Ferguson, Ronald MacGregor*, Lord Goberdeen's Pipers: James Cooper, John Cowle.

Act 1: Dance Hall, Bal Tabarin, Paris.

Act 2, Scene 1: Ancestral Hall, Goberdeen Castle, Scotland. *Scene 2*: Courtyard and Battlements of Castle.

ACT 1[57]

Opening Chorus
Chorus

"King of the Boulevards"[58]
C. Meakins, Chorus
(*Music by* Paul Rubens. *Lyrics by* Edward A. Paulton, A. E. Thomas.)

"It Seems Somehow, They Want Me Now"[59]
G. Bryan, Chorus

"Detective" (Song)
O. Harlan, Chorus
(*Music by* Arthur Weld.)

"Love Never Dies" (Waltz Duet)
G. Bryan, C. Meakins

"The Crystal Ball" (Trio)
M. Odell, J. Dunsmure, N. McNeil

"Sandy MacDougal"
J. Dunsmure, Chorus
(*Music and Lyrics by* Edward A. Paulton.)

Finale
Ensemble

ACT 2[60]

Scene 1

Scotch Medley (arranged by Arthur Weld)
M. Young, B. North, S. Chadwick

"Aeroplane" (Duet)
K. Stevenson, C. M. Horne

"Flirt"
G. Bryan, Chorus
(*Lyrics by* William Kirk, Edward Madden.)

"You're Very Like Your Sister, Dear" (Quartette)
G. Bryan, C. Meakins, J. Dunsmure, O. Harlan

"Angus Gordon Donald Douglas Ewart John McKee"
G. Bryan, Chorus
(*Music and Lyrics by* Edward A. Paulton.)

"Little Boy Blue" (Boy in Blue)
Ensemble

Scene 2

"Kiss Me, Dearest, Kiss Me, Do"
G. Bryan, C. Meakins

"Two Cockatoos"
M. Odell, O. Harlan
(*Music and Lyrics by* Edward A. Paulton.)

"Gathering of the Clans"
Clansmen, Pipers

Finale
Ensemble

---

[57]Added during the run, after Opening Chorus:
"In the Heart of the Golden Wine" (Drinking Song)
C. Meakins, Chorus
(*Lyrics by* Grant Stewart.)

[58]Moved during the run to follow "Detective" song.

[59]Dropped during the run.

[60]Added after opening to Act 2, Scene 2, opening:
"When the Mists of the Night"
J. Dunsmure
(*Music by* Arthur Weld.)

1911.45

PEGGY

A Musical Play in Two Acts.[61] Book by George Grossmith, Jr. Based on "L'Amorçage" by Léon Xanroff and Gaston Guérin. Music by Leslie Stuart. Lyrics by C. H. Bovill. Staged by Ned Wayburn. Scenery by Ernest Albert, Lee Lash Studio. Costumes designed by Stern Brothers. Orchestra conducted by Silvio Hein. Produced by Thomas W. Ryley. Opened 7 December 1911 at the Casino Theatre and closed 6 January 1912 after 36 performances.

CAST: *Captain James Bendoyle*: FARREN SOUTAR. *Auberon Blow*, a street hawker: CHARLES BROWN. *Cecil Custard Caruthers*: HARRY FISHER. *Phonso*, barber at the New Hotel: Jules Charmettes. *Emil*, manager of the New Hotel: A. Hylton Allen. *Montagu Bartle* of Buenos Aires: JOHN W. RANSOME. *Man About Town, Official at the Casino*: Lew Quinn. *Marquis of Didsbury*: TOM DINGLE. *Aristide Picot*, collector: Jules Charmettes. *Lady Snoop*: ALVA YORK. *Peggy Barrison*: RENÉE KELLY. *Polly Polino*, the American dancer: LOUISE ALEXANDER. *Doris Bartle*: VIDA WHITMORE. *Diamond*, barmaid of New Hotel: ESTHER BISSETT. *Lady Frederick*: Rose Winter. *Miss Vooch* of Cincinnati: Margaret Rutledge. *Dolly*: Elise Hamilton. *Ruby*: Maude Brown. *Nini*: Blanche West. *Jeanette*, fleuriste: Blanche West. (*Dance Specialties*: Gladys Moore, Mons. MAURICE, MADELINE D'HARVILLE.)

Society Ladies: Misses Isabel Congleton, Betty Adams, Jeannette Clark, Adelaide Croker, Grace Williams, Ruth Cardon, Josephine Angela, Janet Marran, Kelcey Staunton, Madeleine Ottie. *Manicure Girls*: Misses Flora Ottie, Anna Watson, Billie Hunter, Olive Carr, Minerva Walton, Marguerite Dana. *Bell Boys*: Misses Laura Gaynelle, Fluffy Lichter, Margone Dayton, Irene Spencer, Helen Mooney, Hazel Mooney. *English Pony Ballet*: Misses Ada Robertson, Dorothy Marlow, Louise Hawman, Seppie McNeil, Nellie Wilkie, Eva Marlow. *Guests*: Misses Gertrude Thurston, Jane Arrol, Clara Lloyd, Marie Garland, Katharine Grant, Faith Powell, Eleanore Gray, May Thompson, Elsie Weller, Aimee Montague, Joan Sherman. Messrs. Arthur Wells, Oliver Van Der Burgh, Frank Caruso, Byron Bell, Arthur J. Richter, William J. deForest. *Officers*: Messrs. W. M. Benedict, Waldo Heinemann, Paul Riblet, Billy Faye, Angelo Caruso, Charles Gurney. *Waiters*: Messrs. Genarro Marino, Joseph Luna, Paul Profatta.

Act 1: Lounge at the New Hotel, London.

Act 2: The Plage at Trouville.

ACT 1

Opening Ensemble:
"The New Hotel"
Chorus
Dance Eccentrique
T. Dingle

"Whistle and the Girls Come (Running) 'Round"
F. Soutar, R. Winter, Chorus

"I'm a Lady"
A. York

"In Sunny Kokomo" (Kokomo)
C. Brown, B. West, Chorus

"The Lass with a Lasso"
V. Whitmore, Chorus

"Any Old Tune"
R. Kelly, A. York, F. Soutar, C. Brown, Chorus

"Come to Trouville" (Finale)
English Pony Ballet, Ensemble

ACT 2

Ensembles:
Opening Chorus
Chorus
Dance
G. Moore

"Beautiful Ocean"
V. Whitmore, E. Bissett, L. Alexander, Pony Ballet, Chorus
(*Music and Lyrics by* Irving Berlin.)

"(Go Away, Little Girl—) Go Back to School"
L. Alexander, E. Bissett, Chorus

"Ladies Beware (When the Lights Are Low)"
V. Whitmore

Dance Fascinating and Spirit of Gambling
L. Alexander, T. Dingle

(Specialty)
M. Maurice, M. d'Harville

"(I Like to Have) A Little Bit On"
A. York, Chorus

---

[61]Billed as "George Edwardes' current London Gaiety Theatre Production."

Finale
Entire Company

1911.46 BETSY, An American Widow

A Comedy with Music in Three Acts. Book by H. Kellett Chambers. (Based on the play "An American Widow" by Kitty Chambers.) Music by Alexander Johnstone. Lyrics by W. B. Johnstone. Play staged by Edward Elsner. Orchestra under the direction of Charles E. Candee, Jr. Orchestra arrangements by Domenick Sodero. Produced by Byron Chandler. Opened 11 December 1911 at the Herald Square Theater and closed 6 January 1912 after 32 performances.[62]

CAST (in order of appearance): *Frederick*, Mrs. Killigrew's servant: Donald Buchanan. *Agnes*, maid to Mrs. Killigrew: Myrtle Jersey. *Gloria Stebbins*: Lucie Carter. *Pitney Killigrew*: Worthington L. Romaine. *Teddy Bacon*: HASSARD SHORT. *Jasper Mallory*: ROBERT DEMPSTER. *Augustus Tutwiler*: GEORGE W. CALLAHAN. *Mrs. Elizabeth Killigrew*, Betsy: GRACE LaRUE. *Earl of Dexminster*: ALFRED DEERY. *Mrs. O'Leary*: Lavinia Shannon. *Abaloni*: Juliette Lange. *Charlie*: R. Saito.

Act 1: Mrs. Killigrew's Boudoir, Riverside Drive, New York City. Present time.

Act 2: Teddy Bacon's Bungalow at Magnolia Springs, New York. Four months later.

Act 3: The same. The next morning.

ACT 1
Opening Ensemble
M. Jersey, L. Carter, D. Buchanan
"Laughter and Love"
G. LaRue
"Aristocracy"
G. LaRue, A. Deery
"First Gray Hair"
G. LaRue
Finale

ACT 2
"Snoop Snoop"
G. W. Callahan, W. L. Romaine
"Composing"
R. Dempster
"Dream Love"
G. LaRue
"Only a Voice"
J. Lange
Ensemble
Company
"There Came a Vision"
G. LaRue, J. Lange, R. Dempster

ACT 3
"The Day Before the Morning After"
A. Deery
"Love's Conquests"
G. LaRue

1911.47 THE WEDDING TRIP

A Comic Opera in Three Acts. Book by Fred DeGrésac.[63] Music by Reginald DeKoven. Lyrics by Harry B. Smith. Staged by William J. Wilson. Scenery by H. Robert Law. Costumes designed by Cora MacGeachy. Musical director, Frank E. Tours. Produced by Sam S. and Lee Shubert (Inc.). Opened 25 December 1911 at the Broadway Theatre and closed 3 February 1912 after 48 performances.

CAST (in order of appearance): *Szigetti*, who composes the wedding anthem: CHARLES ANGELO. *Ignace*, father of the bride: George Madison. *Candide*, the bride's younger sister: Grace Emmons. *Celeste*, the mother of the bridegroom: DOROTHY MORTON. *Fritzi*, the bride: CHRISTINE NIELSEN. *Felix*, the bridegroom: JOHN McCLOSKEY. *Captain Josef*, who rudely interrupts the wedding: ARTHUR CUNNINGHAM. *Lieutenant Johann*, *Corporal Oscar*, who assist Captain Josef: John Rogers, Martin Delaney. *Drummer Boy*: L. Parmet. *Aza*, a gypsy: DOROTHY JARDON. *Lotta*, keeper of a tavern: FRITZI VON BUSING. *Lieutenant Niklas*: William Brandt. *Lieutenant Leo*: John Crawford. *Major Vathek*, an amateur warrior: Albert Busby. *Basilie*, wife of Felix's twin brother, Francois: Gwen Dubary. *Willie Barnett*, an American tourist: Joseph Phillips. *Mafta*, brigand and philanthropist: EDWARD MARTINDEL.

Bridesmaids: Misses Williamson, Ashton, Barnette, Money, Merritt, Hill, McKenzie, Linnell. *Peasants*: Messrs. Cryan, Jackson, Lovel, Doolan, Sachs, McCormack, Landres, Rubinroff, Edward, Gold, Cardero, Pendergast, Reese, Brunner Wilson, Nathan, Scott, Cody, Lang, Drees, Rose, Bogart, Deem. *Fishermaids*: Misses Merritt, Smith, Roche, Barnette, Linnell, Oliver, Lean, Springer, Adair, Gray, Ashton, Williamson, May, Barrie, Hill, Proctor, Loraine, Myrtle, Rothwell, Siegel, Parry, Campbell, Hill, McKenzie, Jerome, Frazer, Rudd, Thornton, Huntington, Perot, Baline, Langdon. *Soldiers*: Messrs. Doolan, Cryan, Lovie, Sachs, McCormack, Jackson, Landres, Rubinroff, Edward, Gold, Cardero, Pendergast, Reese, Brunner, Wilson, Nathan, Scott, Cody, Long, Drees, Rose, Bogart, Deem. *Bell Boys*: Misses Huntington, Parry, Perot, Rothwell, Myrtle, Oliver, Springer, Langdon. *Waitresses*: Misses Babin, Smith, Adair, May, Hill, Barnette, Mooney, Williamson. *Maids*: Misses Siegel, Rudd, Roche, McKenzie, Gray, Campbell, Thornton. *Manicures*: Misses Loraine, Jerome, Merritt, Ashton, Proctor, Barrie, Hill, Linnell. *Porters*: Messrs. Cryan, Long, Jackson, Doolan, Sachs, Cody, Scott, Reese, Edwards, Pendergast. *Waiters*: Messrs. Lovie, Bogart, Nathan, Gold, McCormack, Landres, Deem, Wilson, Rubinroff, Rose, Dreese, Brunner, Cordero.

The action takes place in Dalmatia at the present time.

Act 1: Courtyard of Ignace's house.

Act 2: Public square at Ragusa.

Act 3: In the mountains—the bandits' lair.

ACT 1
Introduction and Opening Ensemble
C. Angelo, G. Madison, Chorus
"A Lesson in Love" (Duet)
D. Morton, J. McCloskey
"The Little Bride" (Song)
C. Neilsen
"The Interrupted Love Song" (Duet and Ensemble)
C. Nielsen, J. McCloskey, D. Morton, C. Angelo, Chorus
"The Family Council" (Septette)
C. Nielsen, G. Emmons, D. Morton, C. Angelo, A. Cunningham, G. Madison
"Here Is a Tunic of a Soldier" (Scene and Quartette)
A. Cunningham, J. McCloskey, M. DeLaney, J. Rogers
"Gypsy Kiss" (Song)
D. Jardon
"Hail the Wedding Pair" (Finale)

ACT 2
Introduction and Ensemble
Fisher Girls
"The Sea Shell Telephone" (Legend)
D. Jardon, Fisher Girls
Entrance of Soldiers
"The Beau Sabreur"
D. Jardon, F. von Busing, Chorus
"Flirtation" (Duet)
G. Dubary, J. Phillips
"Ah, At Last" (Duet)
G. Dubary, J. McCloskey, C. Nielsen, A. Cunningham
"The Modern Bandit" (Modern Banditti)(Entrance and Solo)
E. Martindel, Brigands
"The Miraculous Cure" (Scene and Solo)
A. Busby, Girls
"Bivouac Song"
D. Jardon, Chorus
"The Curfew Bell Has Sounded" (Finale)

ACT 3
Opening Ensemble
"The Gentlemanly Brigands" (Song)
E. Martindel, Chorus
"Sweet Sixteen"
D. Morton
"Awakened Love" (Duet)
C. Nielsen, J. McCloskey
Finale
Ensemble

[62]Settings, costumes uncredited; Miss LaRue's gowns designed by herself.
[63]Nom de plume for Mrs. Victor Maurel.

1912.01 MODEST SUZANNE

A Viennese Operetta in Three Acts. American libretto by Harry B. Smith, Robert B. Smith. Based on the German original 'Der keusche Susanne' by Georg Okonkowsky, (adapted from a French farce 'Fils à papa' by Antony Mars and Maurice Desvallières). Music by Jean Gilbert. Staged under the direction of George Marion. Scenery by Dodge & Castle. Costumes by Mme. Francis. Orchestra under the direction of Louis F. Gottschalk. Produced by A. H. Woods, in conjunction with H. H. Frazee. Opened 1 January 1912 at the Liberty Theatre and closed 20 January 1912 after 24 performances.

CAST: *Baron Dauvray*, a newly elected member of the Academy: STANLEY G. FORDE. *Baroness Delphine Dauvray*, his wife: Kathryn Osterman. *Jacqueline*, their daughter: Florence Martin. *Hubert*, their son: LAURENCE WHEAT. *Professor Charcot*, a member of the Academy: ERNEST TORRENCE. *Mariette*, a housemaid in the home of the Baroness: Charlotte Leslay. *Rene*, a lieutenant, nephew of the Baron: ARTHUR STANFORD. *Monsieur Pomeral*, a wealthy manufacturer of Tours: John L. Kearney. *Suzanne*, his wife: SALLIE FISHER. *Rose*, Professor Charcot's wife: HARRIET BURT. *Tina, Mina, Phrynette*, stars of the Moulin Rouge: Corrine Uzzell, Claudia Clark, Millie Murray. *Gustave*, one of the regular patrons: Lester Corrish. *Alexis*, head waiter: Sherman Wade. *Emil*, a waiter: Ezra C. Walck. *Felix*, a half portion of the same profession: Joseph Zaino. *Police Sergeant*: D. Haverty. *Gendarme*: William Glynn.

Guests of the Baron, Members of the Academy, and Patrons of the Moulin Rouge: Misses Mildred Gibson, Kitty Swagne, Alice Clayton, Virginia Seinhardt, Catherine Ursprung, Mable Merlin, Lillian Baker, Josie Ursprung, Bessie Lawlor, Portia Belma, Gertrude Gibbons, Marcia Nash, Georgette Warren, Dorothy Stoy, Helen Steeves, Mabelle Glynn, Bertha Dehan. Messrs. G. Hughes, L. Corrish, W. S. Clark, D. Haverty, D. O'Leary, H. Durham, William Glynn, H. Hoffman, A. Frewn, J. Campbell, J. Miller R. Torry.

Act 1: Drawing Room of Baron Dauvray in Paris.

Act 2: Ball-room at the Moulin Rouge.

Act 3: Same as Act 1. Morning following Act 2.

ACT 1
(Opening) Ensemble
K. Osterman, F. Martin, Chorus
"Virtue Is Its Own Reward" (Entrance Song)
S. G. Forde, Chorus
"(A) Model Married Pair" [64](Duet)
S. Fisher, J. L. Kearney
"Paris" (Trio)
S. Fisher, A. Stanford, L. Wheat
Finale

ACT 2
Opening Chorus
"(I Would Like to See the) Peaches"
L. Wheat
(*Music by* Jean Schwartz. *Lyrics by* Harry B. Smith.)
"Confidence" (Duet)
S. Fisher, L. Wheat
"(The) Tangoland Tap"
A. Stanford, Chorus
(*Music by* Jean Schwartz. *Lyrics by* Grant Clarke.)
"All the World Loves a Lover" (Waltz Song)
S. Fisher, Chorus
"Father and Son" (Sextette)
S. Fisher, F. Martin, H. Burt, A. Stanford, L. Wheat, S. G. Forde
Finale
Ensemble, Chorus

ACT 3
"The Return"
L. Wheat, S. G. Forde
"Suzanne, Suzanne"
S. Fisher, S. G. Forde, L. Wheat, A. Stanford
Finale

1912.02 OVER THE RIVER

A Musical Farce in Three Acts, 4 Scenes. Book by George V. Hobart and H. A. DuSouchet. Based on DuSouchet's play 'The Man from Mexico.' Music (and lyrics) by John L. Golden. Staged by R. H. Burnside.[65] Orchestra under the direction of DeWitt Coolman. Produced by Charles Dillingham and Florenz Ziegfeld.[66] Opened 8 January 1912 at the Globe Theatre and closed 20 April 1912 after 120 performances.[67]

CAST [in order of appearance]: *George*, Head waiter: Frank M. Rainger. *Jerry Cooper*: Frank Wonderlee. *Herbert Vandersnip*: Charles L. Kelley. *Bismarck Herring*, a Poet: Harry Hermsen. *Harry Blackstone*, Ninth Assistant District Attorney: Lester Crawford. *Mrs. Madison Parke*: MAUD LAMBERT. *Myrtle Mirabeau*, an Actress: LILLIAN LORRAINE. *Hudson Rivers*, Friend of Parke: MELVILLE STEWART. *Madison Parke*: EDDIE FOY. *Sarah Parke*, his daughter: EDNA HUNTER. *Charlie Gray*, an Architect: Osborne Searle. *Lizzie*, a Maid: JOSIE SADLER. *Timothy Cook*, a Bailiff: William Sellery. *Warden Vokes*: David Andrada. *Charles Bigroll*: JOSEPH C. SMITH. *Number 89*: Leavitt James. *Street Singers*: Jeanette, Billy and Grace Methven. (*Specialties*: LAS SEVILLANITAS, THE MARVELOUS MILLERS. *Dance Specialties*: Mons. Maurice, Mlle. Madeline d'Harville, Lawrence Beck.)

Other characters by Misses Leila Benton, Marguerite St. Clair, Clementine Dundas, Estelle Richmond, Bessie Fennell, Bessie Skeer, Dal Turgeon, Selma Mantell, Vonnie Hoyt, Neil Bertrand, Claire Bertrand, Frances Leslie, Anna Stone, Mazie LeRoy, Katherine Daly, Edna Dodsworth, Mildred Manning, Dorothy Langdon. Messrs. Black, Simpson, Leavitt, Beard, Morgan, Smith, Hay, Vail, O'Neil, Fleming, DeBeen, Goodman. *THE BERLIN MADCAPS*: Gretchen Fink, Marie Neckar, Rosa Burklein, Freda Hirsch, Anna Bacherer, Fanny Bacherer, Betty Fuchs, Emma Collier.

Act 1, Scene 1: At the Café Cabaret, New York. *Scene 2*: Reception Room, Madison Parke's House, next morning.

Act 2: Warden's Room, Blackwell's Island, "Over the River."

Act 3: Garden of Mrs. Parke's Home, Inwood, near New York.

ACT 1
Scene 1
Opening Ensemble
"For de Lawd's Sake, Play a Waltz"[68] (from THE SLIM PRINCESS)
M. Lambert
(*Music and Lyrics by* Elsie Janis.)
"Los Sevillanitas"[69] (Specialty)
Cabaret Dance
Mons. Maurice, Mlle. M d'Harville
["(The) Broadway Cabaret"
(*Music by* Charles N. Grant. *Lyrics by* E. J. Griffin.)
"The Maurice Rag"
(*Music by* William H. Penn.)]
"Ring-ting-a-ling on the Telephone"
L. Lorraine
(*Music by* Jean Schwartz. *Lyrics by* William Jerome.)
"New York Isn't Such a Bad Old Town"
E. Foy
(*Music by* Jean Schwartz. *Lyrics by* William Jerome.)
Scene 2
"The Raggedy Man" (Raggity Man)
L. Lorraine, Chorus
(*Music by* Egbert Van Alstyne. *Lyrics by* Harry Williams.)
Finale

ACT 2
"I Want Him Saved"[70]
E. Hunter, Chorus

---

[64]Replaced after opening by:
"The Worldly Man" (Duet)
F. Martin, A. Stanford

[65]Burnside's credit as director did not appear in programs until the second month of the run.

[66]Toured the following season under the auspices of Werba and Luescher. Production was restaged by Frank M. Rainger, ensemble numbers staged by Charles J. Morgan, Jr. Added musical numbers:
"Save the Men" (Act 2, in place of "I Want Him Saved")
"A Gay Butterfly" (Act 2, after "The Raggedy Man")

[67]Settings, costumes uncredited.

[68]Replaced late in the run by:
"Coontown Quartette"
Mae Busch (Myrtle Mirabeau), Cavanaugh and McBride

[69]Replaced early in the run by:
(Specialty)
Hidalgo Sisters

[70]Replaced after opening by:
"Edna May"
E. Hunter, Chorus

"Chop Stick Rag"
L. Lorraine, the Berlin Madcaps
(*Music by* Jean Schwartz. *Lyrics by* Edward Clark. *At piano*: Jean Schwartz.)
"Lock-step, Two-step Slide"
Ensemble, Marvelous Millers
"Our Hero" (Finale)

ACT 3
"The Day We Celebrate"
Ensemble
"Montezuma"
J. Methven, Sisters
(*Music by* Charles Eggett. *Lyrics by* Earl Carroll.)
"The Tongo Dance"
L. Lorraine, J. C. Smith
"My Irish Senorita"[71]
M. Lambert
(*Music and Lyrics by* Edward J. Griffin, Henry B. Murtagh and John L. Golden.)
"(Way Down in) Mexico"[72]
E. Foy
"When There's No Light at All"
M. Stewart, L. Lorraine, Methven Sisters, J. Sadler, W. Sellery, E. Foy
Dancing Frolic
The Berlin Madcaps
Finale

1912.03

THE BIRD OF PARADISE

A Hawaiian Play (with Music) in Three Acts, 5 Scenes. Play by Richard Walton Tully. [Music from authentic Hawaiian sources.] Staged by Richard Walton Tully. Scenery by Ernest Gros. Lighting and storm effect by Kliegl Brothers. Produced by Oliver Morosco. Opened 8 January 1912 at Daly's Theatre, moved 22 January 1912 to Maxine Elliott's Theatre and closed 13 April 1912 after 112 performances.[73]

CAST (in order of appearance): *Liliha*, a hula dancer: Virginia Reynolds. *Makia*, a convert: Jane Meredith. *Cane-cutters (5)*: *Kanoa*: W. K. Kolomuku. *Kapule*: Ben Waiwaiole. *Naihe*: S. M. Kaiawe. *Kuakini*: A. Kawala. *Lanipule*: W. B. Aeko. *Mahumahu*, Luana's foster mother: Ida Waterman. *Kaia*, a poi maker: HERBERT FARJEON. *Hopoe*, a hula dancer: Nona Kelly. *Konia*, a woman of the old days: Nance Caldwell. *Lemule*, a graduate: Van Rensselaer Townsend. *Hewahewa*, a priest of Pele: Albert Perry. *Luana*, a Hawaiian girl: LAURETTE TAYLOR. *Paul Wilson*, a young doctor: LEWIS S. STONE. *Captain Hatch*, a planter: THEODORE ROBERTS. *Mr. Sysonby*, the missionary: W. J. Constantine. *Mrs. Sysonsby*, his wife: Estar Banks. *Diana Larned*, a university graduate: PAMELA GAYTHORNE. *"Ten Thousand Dollar" Dean*, a beachcomber: GUY BATES POST. *Hoheno*, a fisherman: Robert Harrison. *Tomoro*, a Japanese: Clyde Crawford. *Mrs. Crothers*, a widow: Margaret Nagele. *Guests at the Villa (2)*: *Mr. Jameson*, of the Sugar Company: Craig Miner. *Miss Kennedy*, a debutante: Gladys Byers.

Act 1: A beach, cave and native house on the Puna Coast. Island of Hawaii.

Act 2: Interior of the same native house. Two years later.

Act 3, Scene 1: The Cage: Lanai of Captain Hatch's Villa. Waikiki Beach, Honolulu. Ten days later. *Scene 2*: The Flight: Approaching Kilauea. *Scene 3*: Freedom: The House of Everlasting Fire.

MUSICAL NUMBERS[74]
"Burning Love" (Ahi Wela)
"Farewell to Thee" (Aloha Oe)
"Forget Me Not" (Mai Poina oe la'u)
"Song of the Lonesome Forest" (Kumukahi)
"Hula Shouting Song" (Aiaihea)
"Press Me to Thee" (Tomi Tomi)
"I Love But Thee" (Akahi Hoi)
"My Love Is Like a Blooming Flower" (Pua i Mohala)
"The Sparkling Waters" (Waialae)
"Maui Girl"
"Honolulu Tom Boy" (Sonny Cunha)
"The Bubbling Spring" (Kaua i ka Huahuai)
"The Drowsy Waters" (Wailana)
"Constancy" (Ua Like No a Like)
"Hawaii Ponoi"
"Native Plantation Song" (Kuu Home)
"Sacred Dancing Hula Song" (Mauna Kea)
"Maid of Honolulu"
"The Whirling Waters" (Kawiliwiliwai)
"Hawaiian Hula Dance Song" (Moanalua)
"We Strive to Win" (Kokohi)
"My Honolulu Hula Girl"
"Fragrance of the Lehua Wreath" (Sweet Lei Lehua)
"Wreath of Carnations" (Lei Poni Moi)
"One-Two-Three-Four"
(*Music by* Sylvester Kalama.)
"Luana Waltz"
(*Music by* Kapule Kanoa.)

1912.04

THE ROSE OF PANAMA

An Opéra-Comique in Three Acts. English libretto by John L. Shine and Sydney Rosenfeld. Based on the German original "Kreolenblut" (with libretto by Ignaz Schneitzer and Emmerich von Gatti). Music by Heinrich Berté. Staged by Frank Smithson. Scenery by Homer Emens. Costumes by Max & Mahieu. Lighting by Kleigl Brothers. Musical director, Theodore Bendix. Produced by John Cort. Opened 22 January 1912 at Daly's Theatre and closed 10 February 1912 after 24 performances.

CAST: *Remy de Valmore*, President of a Central American Republic: JOHN J. McGOWAN. *Angele*, his wife: ANNA BUSSERT. *Sever*, his secretary: Mortimer Weldon. *Andre Royan*, Colonel of the Guards: Carrick Major. *Jacinta*: CHAPINE. *Casterra*, the Pretender: TOM HADAWAY. *Hiram Query*, a reporter: WILL PHILLIPS. *Of the Guards (5)*: *Major de Molina*: Joseph Parsons. *Captain Ariza*: Gerald Gordon. *Lieutenant Pesaro*: William R. Reed. *Second Lieutenant Guirago*: William C. Reed. *Corporal*: John L. Wheeler. *Marcel Arranto*, a cowboy: FORREST HUFF. *Anita*, lady's companion to Angele: Reina Lazar. *Celine Marinter*, a stenographer and typist: FAY BAINTER. *Uncle Billy*, colored head waiter at the Officers' Club: Teddy LeDuc. *Officers, Ladies, Gentlemen, Guests, Servants, Soldiers, Populace, etc.*

Time and Place: The Present, a Central American Republic.

Act 1: Exterior of the President's Palace and the Officers' Club.

Act 2: Grand Salon of the President's Palace.

Act 3: Garden of the President's Villa.

ACT 1
Ensemble
"Tip-a-Top" (Duet)
F. Bainter, M. Weldon
"When Your Fortune Has Flown" (When Your Good Luck Has Flown)
F. Huff
"Lasso Duet"
A. Bussert, F. Huff
Ensemble and Entrance of Jacinta
"You Cannot Blame Me for My Spanish Blood" (Spanish Blood)
Chapine, Chorus
"He Has Subdued Her" (He Is Her Master)(Finale)
Tout Ensemble

ACT 2[75]
Ensemble
"Isabella and Romero" (Isabella and Ramiro)
A. Bussert, Chorus

---

[71]Replaced after opening by:
Dancing Frolic
The Berlin Madcaps

[72]May have reprised his hit song "He Goes to Church on Sunday" (from THE ORCHID) according to reviews.

[73]Costumes uncredited.

[74]Musical numbers not listed in program. Not in performance order. List prepared from published sheet music and recordings. Songs were performed by the Hawaiian Quintette: Ben Waiwaiole, S. M. Kaiawe, W. B. J. Aeko, E. K. Rose, W. K. Kolomuku.

[75]Added to Act 2 after "Love's Fond Dream" for subsequent tour:
"The Way to Jug a Hare" (Sextette)
[President, Sever, Query, Royan, Celine, Angele]

"Make a Night of It" (Trio)
F. Bainter, J. J. McCowan, M. Weldon
"Love's Fond Dream" (How Enthralling the Music's Soulful Greeting)(Waltz Song)
Chapine, F. Huff
"Thy Thought, My Thought" (Waltz Duet) (Finale)
Tout Ensemble

ACT 3
Ensemble
"The Day of Love" (Song)
Chapine
"Cupid's Flirtation" (When Cupid Makes a Target of Your Heart)
F. Bainter, M. Weldon
"Pray Tell Me" (Duet)
A. Bussert, J. J. McCowan
"Oolie Girl of Panama"[76] (Oolie Girl, from Panama)
W. Phillips
(*Music by* Herman Finck. *Lyrics by* Arthur J. Gillespie, H. S. Krouse.)
Finale
Tout Ensemble
"Waiting for You"
(*Music by* Theodore Norman. *Lyrics by* Arthur J. Gillespie.)

1912.05 THE PEARL MAIDEN

A Musical Play in Three Acts. Libretto by Earle C. Anthony and Arthur F. Kales. Music by Harry Auracher [Archer].Staged by Al. Holbrook. Dances arranged by James Gorman. Scenery by Theodore Reisig. Costumes by Orange Manufacturing Co. Orchestra under the direction of Silvio Hein. Produced by Weich and Aarons. Opened 22 January 1912 at the New York Theatre and closed 10 February 1912 after 24 performances.

CAST: *Anaka,* a native servant: Davis Wheeler. *Veritas Sharpe,* president of the International Pearl Company: CHARLES J. STINE. *Jack Sharp,* his son: RICHARD TABOR. *Loraine,* his daughter: ELSA RYAN. *Pinkerton Kerr,* the wireless operator, Mona Island: JEFFERSON DeANGELIS. *Bob Norris,* in love with Loraine: BURRELL BARBARETTO. *Peg Leg Jukes,* captain of Nadine's crew: F. Holmes. *Of the Crew (3): Cockeye Morgan*: L. J. DeBold. *Vincenzo*: Walter Lysat. *Bilge*: Henry Bergman. *Nadine,* the Pearl Maiden: FLORA ZABELLE. *Kaliko,* King of Powi Island: CHARLES PRINCE. *Talulu,* his daughter (the Cannibal Princess): DAISY LEON. *Alfonse,* Kaliko's "chef": Henry Bergman. *Gideon Slim,* a pearl trader and adventurer: Jerry McAuliffe.

Aaron's Dancing Girls: Misses Carry Poltz, Florrie Poltz, Maudie Crossland, Margie Graham, Phillis Errol, Lottie Crossland. *Middies*: Misses Ella Warner, Nellie Feltes, Ethel Lytle, Edna Richardson. *Natives, Nadine's Crew, Yachtsmen, Girls from Yacht, etc. Young Ladies from Miss Deeley's Boarding School*: Misses Martha Dean, Marie Farrell, Gloria Starr, Dorothy Dunn, Maureen Hubin, Grace Lloyd, Sadie Carr, Pattis Hamilton, Pauline Sterling, Marie Benton, Lillian Davis, Grace Wickham, Winefred Brown, Kitty Collier, Albertine Marr, Alice Gibbons, Nellie Young. *Yacht Stewards*: Misses Ella Warner, Nellie Feltes, Ethel Lytle, Edna Richardson. *Yachtsmen, Friends of Jack Sharpe*: Messrs. Dan Dale, John Walker, Thomas LeMode, Joe Murphy, Russell Price, Gordon Newman, Roy Pruette, Jr., Nat Saunders, Fred Wilson, Herbert Burnham.

Act 1: The Wireless Relay Station, Mona Island. The present time.

Act 2: A Native Village, Powi Island.

Act 3: Interior of the Wireless Station, Powi Island.

ACT 1
"Take Us 'Round the Island"
Ensemble
"Look at the Package They Handed to Me"
J. DeAngelis, C. J. Stine, T. Taber
Entrance of Girls
Ensemble
"Our Morals Are Most Refined"
Nadine's Crew
"The Pearl Maiden" (Entrance of Nadine)
F. Zabelle, Crew
"If One Little Girl Loves Me"
E. Ryan, B. Barbaretto
"You Never Can Tell Until You Try"
J. DeAngelis, F. Zabelle, E. Ryan, B. Barbaretto
"King of a South Sea Isle"
C. Prince, Ensemble
Finale

ACT 2
Opening Chorus:
Ensemble; "Taboo"
Ensemble
Lei Dance
Aaron's Dancing Girls
"The Cruise of the Boozemobile"
R. Taber
"Coral Isle"
D. Leon
Finale

ACT 3
"That Typical, Topical, Tropical Tune"
D. Leon, Chorus
"I Am Lonely for You" (Story of the Pearl)
F. Zabelle, Chorus
"Davy Jones"
J. DeAngelis, Beachcombers
"My Old Brass Band"
B. Barbaretto, Dancing Girls
Finale

[76]Replaced for subsequent tour by: "Cupid's Hour" [Celine, Sever] (*Music and Lyrics by* Art Stenkem and Sydney Rosenfeld.)

1912.06 MACUSHLA

A Play with Music (Romantic Comedy) in Four Acts.[77] Play by Rida Johnson Young. Music by Ernest R. Ball. Lyrics by J. Keirn Brennan. Staged by William Henry Miller. Produced by Augustus Pitou. Opened 5 February 1912 at the Grand Opera House and closed 24 February 1912 after 24 performances.[78]

CAST: *Sir Brian Fitzgerald*: CHAUNCEY OLCOTT. *Warren Fairchild*: CHARLES WELLESLEY. *Sandy McNabb*: ROBERT V. FERGUSON. *Thomas Wiggins*: E. H. Reardon. *Dinny O'Mara*: GEORGE BRENNAN. *Will Dorkins*: F. Gatenby Bell. *A Bookmaker*: Edmund Shalet. *Patricia Boyer*: GAIL KANE. *Mrs. Boyer*: JENNIE LAMONT. *Gwendolin Fairchild*: Katherine Clarendon. *Lady Dorothy Hammond*: Alice Farrell.

Act 1: The Garden outside Mrs. Boyer's Cottage.

Act 2: The Duncannon Stables. The day before the Steeplechase.

Act 3: Tent at the Dublin Race Track.

Act 4: A room in Duncannon Castle. A few weeks after the race.

MUSICAL NUMBERS[79]
"The Girl I'll Call My Sweetheart Must Look Like You"
(*Music and Lyrics by* Chauncey Olcott, Dan J. Sullivan.)
"Macushla"
(*Music by* Dermot MacMurrough. *Lyrics by* Josephine V. Rowe.)
"With a Twinkle in Her Eye"
(*Music by* Ernest R. Ball. *Lyrics by* Chauncey Olcott, Louis Weslyn.)
"Good-Bye My Emerald Land"
(*Music and Lyrics by* Fredeick Knight Logan, Chauncey Olcott.)
"My Land"
(*Music by* Ernest R. Ball, Chauncey Olcott. *Lyrics by* Bartley Costello.)

1912.07 HOKEY-POKEY

Weber & Fields Jubilee Company in a Pot-pourri of Weber-Fields Reminiscences in Two Acts, 4 Scenes. Book by Edgar Smith. Music by John Stromberg, A. Baldwin Sloane, W. T. Francis. Lyrics by Edgar Smith, E. Ray Goetz. Production staged by Gus Sohlke. Costumes by Cora MacGeachy.

[77]Macushla is the name of the winning horse in the play, and means "Pulse of My Heart."
[78]No credits for scenery, costumes or musical director in programs.
[79]No Musical Numbers listed in program. List prepared from reviews, published sheet music and recordings.

Settings designed by John Young. Lighting by David Atchison. Orchestra under the direction of George A. Nichols. Produced by Joe Weber and Lew Fields. Opened 8 February 1912 at the Broadway Theatre and closed 11 May 1912 after 108 performances.

CAST: *Josh Kidder*, promoter of the International Cabaret-Vaudeville Trust: WILLIAM COLLIER. *Michael Dillpickle, Meyer Bockheister*, doing Europe on a circumscribed bargain counter letter of credit: JOE WEBER, LEW FIELDS. *Jeremiah McCann*, a reform politician: JOHN T. KELLY. *Pierre Poisson*, proprietor of a bankrupt Parisian café: GEORGE BEBAN. *Mrs. Wallingford Grafter*, with Bohemian instincts and a talent for poker: LILLIAN RUSSELL. *Peachie Mullen*, in vaudeville: FAY TEMPLETON. *Clorinda McCann*, her father's daughter: HELENA COLLIER GARRICK. *Lieutenant Shapeleigh*: Frankie Bailey. *Pierre Boulmiche*, a boulevardier: Frankie Bailey. *Henri Montmartre, Aristide Lenuit, Wilhelm Blatz*, art students: Adelaide Mason, Elsie Hamilton, Fay Tincher. *Toots Hornblower, Dodge Chappelle*, American college students: Pattie Rose, Madge Vincent. *Rosie*: Gertrude Moyer. *Posie*: Edna Chase. *Henri*, a footman: Joseph Torpey.

"Le Clair de la Lune": *Pierrot de Willette*: BESSIE CLAYTON. *Harlequin*: Signor A. Romeo. *Troubadours*: Hazel Kirke, Emily Miles.

Personnel of the Chorus: *Tourists, Gendarmes, Vivandieres, etc.*: Misses Elsa Reinhardt, May Willard, May Hopkins, Gladys Breston, Hazel Robertson, Lynn D'Arcy, Edna Caruthers, Gladys Feldman, Hermione Brown, Nettie Lyon, Grace Grindell, Martha Dean. *Grisettes, Flower Girls, Clowns, etc.*: Misses Beatrice Capulet, Louise Abrams, Gertrude Moyer, Emily Miles, Clara Lloyd, Nancy Smith, Flora Russell, Libbia Diamond, Madge Vincent, Edna Chase, Frances Nelson, Sadie Carr, Marjorie Purcell, Frances Duront, Vera Olcott, Katherine O'Neill. *Chappies, Artists, etc.*: Misses Lola Curtis, Fay Tincher, Hazel Rosewood, Pattie Rose, Louise Owen, Eunice Hamilton, Adelaide Mason, Ruth Pecan, Olive Carr, Elise Hamilton, Vinnie Mason. *Minstrel Banderines*: Misses Sadie Berger, Leona Bitter, Jane Hood, Sadie Hill, Lillian Whiting, Emily Powers. *Waiters, Tourists, etc.*: Messrs. Fred Roberts, Harry Prew, George Scannell, Harry Wilcox, Malcolm Grindell, Edward McNulty.

ACT 2: BUNTY, BULLS AND STRINGS. A Parody by Edgar Smith of the comedy by Graham Moffat, "Bunty Pulls the Strings." Music by A. Baldwin Sloane. Lyrics by E. Ray Goetz. Staged by Gus Sohlke.

CAST: *Bunty Biggar*, with a talent for management: FAY TEMPLETON. *Tammas Biggar*, her "feyther," with a past: WILLIAM COLLIER. *Rab Biggar*, his son: JOE WEBER. *Weelum Grunt*: LEW FIELDS. *Susie Slimpson*, a female villain: ADA LEWIS. *Eelen Bunshop*, Tammas Biggar's past: HELENA COLLIER GARRICK. *Teenie*, her niece: George Beban. *Jeems*, janitor of the town hall: John T. Kelly. *Daniel Squirrel*, town policeman: Charles Mitchell. *Mr. MacGregor*, an aged farmer: Patrick Walsh. *Sandy*, his son: Richard Fanning. *Mr. Haggis*, a shop-keeper: Harry Wilcox. *Mr. Leggit*, a Heilander: Malcolm Grinnell. *Mr. McSwat, Mrs. McSwatt*, villagers: Harry Prew, Elsa Reinhardt.

Highland Lassies: Misses Pattie Rose, Fay Tincher, Louise Owen, Flora Russell, Amelia Abrams, Vinnie Mason, Clara Lloyd, Libbia Diamond, Beatrice Cupulet, Nancy Smith. *Highland Laddies*: Misses Adelaide Mason, Ruth Pecan, Eunice Hamilton, Edna Chase, Hazel Rosewood, Olive Carr, Elise Hamilton, Lola Curtis, Gertrude Moyer, Lynn Darcy, Nettie Lyon, Grace Grindell, Hazel Robertson, May Willard, May Hopkins, Gladys Feldman, Gladys Breston, Hermione Brown, Edna Caruthers, Elsa Reinhardt, Emily Miles, Madge Vincent, Martha Dean, Vera Olcott, Katherine O'Neil, Marjorie Purcell.

Act 1, Scene 1: Place d'l'Opera, Paris. *Scene 2*: Mrs. Wallingford Grafter's villa near Paris.

Act 2, Scene 1: Tammas Biggars' Parlor in Limpytown. *Scene 2*: Exterior of the Town Hall, Limpytown.

ACT 1[80]

"La Belle Paree" (Opening Ensemble)
Chorus

"If It Wasn't for the Irish and the Jews"
J. T. Kelly, Chorus
(*Music by* Jean Schwartz. *Lyrics by* William Jerome.)

"The Island of Roses and Love"
L. Russell, Chorus
(*Music and Lyrics by* Neil Moret and E. C. Jones.)

"The Minstrel Parade"
W. Collier, Chorus

"The Singer and the Song"
F. Templeton

"Le Claire de la Lune" (Dance)
B. Clayton

"The Garden of Yesterday"[81]
L. Russell, Chorus

"On the Stage" (Duet)
H. C. Garrick, W. Collier

Songs:
F. Templeton, Chorus
"Senorita"
"Ma' Blushin' Rosie" (from FIDDLE DEE DEE)
(*Music by* John Stromberg. *Lyrics by* Edgar Smith.)

Finale
Entire Company

ACT 2

"Heather Belles"[82]
Ensemble

"Alexander's Bagpipe Band"
F. Templeton, Chorus
(*Music and Lyrics by* Irving Berlin, E. Ray Goetz and A. Baldwin Sloane.)

Finale
Entire Company

1912.08 THE OPERA BALL

A Musical Comedy in Three Acts. (American libretto) By Sydney Rosenfeld and Clare Kummer. Adapted from the Viennese original "Der Opernball" by Victor Léon and Heinrich von Waldberg (based on the comedy "Les Dominos roses" by Alfred Hennequin and Alfred Delacour). Music by Richard Heuberger. Scenery painted by D. Frank Dodge and William Castle. Costumes by Max & Mahieu. Orchestra under the direction of Josiah Zuro. (Produced by Daniel V. Arthur.) Opened 12 February 1912 at the Liberty Theatre and closed 9 March 1912 after 32 performances.[83]

CAST (in order of appearance): *George Dumenil*, a Parisian: HARRY FAIRLEIGH. *Paul Aubier*, his friend: GEORGE LYDECKER. *Germain*, a butler: Howard Pascal. *Palmyra*, wife of Beaubisson: Evelyn Carter Carrington. *Theophilus Beaubisson*, merchant: HARRY CONOR. *Captain Henry Beaubisson*, his nephew: BURRELL BARBARETTO. *Angele*, his daughter, married to Paul: OLIVE ULRICH. *Marguerite*, wife of George: ALICE GENTLE. *Celeste Deremy*, a young widow: MARIE CAHILL. *Yvette*, maid: Hazel Kingdon. *Fleurette, Babette, Coquette*, Three Follies: Dorothy Arthur, Viola Cain, Marion Miller. *Philip*, head waiter: Frank Tierney. *Fedora*, chansonette: Mayme Gehrue.

Guests and Dancers at the Opera Ball: Misses Mignon Leris, Gertrude Adams, Maybelle Haskelle, Mae Starkey, Evelyn Inch, Bessie Clifford, Margaret Zimmerman, Evelyn Kneen, May Stockton, Elvira North, Martha Stone, Bertie Harris, Julia Kelleher, Ida Bentley, Irma Cummings, Ethel Peterson, Emma Paxton, Gladys Buckley, Beatrice Thompson, Della Forsyth. Messrs. Jack Elliott, Jack Johnson, Fenton Bolger, Philip Moore, Harry Dee, Jack Hamilton, Thomas Shields, Jack Borden, Frank Carrig, Ned Elkington, Wilson Price, George Wagner, William Croxton, Kenneth Roland.

The action takes place at the present time in Paris.

Act 1: Living room of the Dumenils, Paris.

Act 2: Foyer leading to the ball room of the Opera House.

Act 3: Same as Act 1.

ACT 1

"We Have Only One Life to Live" (Duet)
H. Fairleigh, G. Lydecker

"Paris Is a Spot So Fair" (Song)
O. Ulrich

---

[80]Performed in the show as per published sheet music:
"De Pullman Porter's Ball" (from HOITY TOITY)
W. Collier
(*Music by* John Stromberg. *Lyrics by* Edgar Smith.)
"When Chloe Sings a Song" (from WHIRL-I-GIG)
L. Russell
(*Music by* John Stromberg. *Lyrics by* Harry B. Smith.)

[81]Replaced during the run by:
"When You're Away"
(*Music by* Bert Grant. *Lyrics by* A. Seymour Brown, Joe Young.)/
"My Evening Star" (Come Down, Ma Evenin' Star)(from TWIRLY-WHIRLY)
L. Russell, Chorus
(*Music by* John Stromberg. *Lyrics by* Robert B. Smith.)

[82]Replaced during the run by:
"Mrs. Grafter's Dinner Party"
Ensemble

[83]Stage direction uncredited.

"What Are We Coming To?" (Song)
M. Cahill
Letter (Trio)
M. Cahill, A. Gentle, O. Ulrich
Finale

ACT 2
Opening Chorus
F. Tierney, Chorus
"Let Us Find a Charming Rendezvous" (Let Us Find a Cosey Little Nook)(Duet)
M. Cahill, B. Barbaretto
"Sergeant Philip of the Lancers" (Duet)
M. Gehrue, F. Tierney
(*Music by* Jerome Kern. *Lyrics by* Sydney Rosenfeld.)
"(I Want a Little Loving) Sometimes" (Song)
M. Cahill
(*Music and Lyrics by* Chris Smith.)
"Never Again" (Trio)
G. Lydecker, H. Fairleigh, B. Barbaretto
"Folly"
D. Arthur, V. Cain, M. Miller, G. Lydecker, H. Fairleigh, B. Barbaretto, Chorus
Quarrel Trio
A. Gentle, O. Ulrich, B. Barbaretto

ACT 3
Opening Scene
Quartet
A. Gentle, O. Ulrich, H. Fairleigh, G. Lydecker
"Listen to Me" (Song)
M. Cahill
"Nurses' Chorus" (Nurses Are We)
H. Conor, Chorus
(*Music by* Jerome Kern. *Lyrics by* Sydney Rosenfeld.)
"Kiss and Be Friends"[84] (Quintet)
M. Cahill, A. Gentle, O. Ulrich, G. Lydecker, H. Fairleigh
Finale

1912.09 WHIRL OF SOCIETY

A Musical Satire in One Act, preceded by a Vaudeville A NIGHT WITH THE PIERROTS, and followed by an operatic mimodrama SESOSTRA. Scenery by H. Robert Law. Costumes by Melville Ellis; Joseph; Landorff, Paris; Hugo Baruch, Berlin; Max & Mahieu, New York. Orchestra under the direction of Samuel Lehman. Produced by the Winter Garden Company (Messrs. Shubert). Opened 5 March 1912 at the Winter Garden and closed 29 June 1912 after 136 performances.

ACT 1: A NIGHT WITH THE PIERROTS

CAST: Prologue: *The Humpback*: AL JOLSON. *Sumurun*: STELLA MAYHEW. *Interlocutor*: BILLEE TAYLOR. *Bones*: AL JOLSON. *Tambo*: BARNEY BERNARD. With STELLA MAYHEW, JOSÉ COLLINS, BLOSSOM SEELEY, Kathleen Clifford, Mildred Elaine, George White, Melissa Ten Eyck, Laura Hamilton, Courtney Sisters, Doris Cameron, Clarence Harvey, ERNEST HARE, Edward Cutler, Cecil Ryan, Barney Thornton, Harry Wardell, Martin Brown, Florence Cable.

MUSICAL NUMBERS
Prologue
E. Hare
"My Sumurun Girl"
A. Jolson, S. Mayhew, Company
(*Music by* Louis A Hirsch. *Lyrics by* Al Jolson.)
Opening Chorus
Ensemble
"Oh, Mr. Dream Man"[85]
B. Taylor
"Hypnotizing Man"
L. Hamilton, G. White
"I'm Goin' Back to Dixie" (I Want to be in Dixie)
Courtney Sisters
(*Music and Lyrics by* Irving Berlin.)
"Blow on Your Piccolo"[86]
S. Mayhew
"The Villain Still Pursued Her"
A. Jolson
(*Music by* Harry von Tilzer. *Lyrics by* William Jerome.)
"How Do You Do, Miss Ragtime?"
M. Brown, Company
(*Music and Lyrics by* Louis A Hirsch.)
"The Ragtime Sextette" (from HANKY-PANKY)
J. Collins, S. Mayhew, A. Jolson, B. Taylor, C. Ryan, E. Cutler, E. Hare
(*Music and Lyrics by* Irving Berlin, based on "Chi Mi Frena" from LUCIA DI LAMMERMOOR by Gaetano Donizetti.)
Finale
Ensemble

ACT 2: WHIRL OF SOCIETY[87]

A Musical Satire of up-to-date society in One Act, 2 Scenes. Book by Harrison Rhodes. Music by Louis A. Hirsch. Lyrics by Harold Atteridge. Staged by J. C. Huffman. Musical numbers staged by William Wilson.

CAST: *Mrs. Dean*: STELLA MAYHEW. *Mr. Dean*: CLARENCE HARVEY. *Angela*, their daughter: JOSÉ COLLINS. *Gus*, their butler: AL JOLSON. *Archduke Frederich*: Lawrence D'Orsay. *Archduchess*: Mildred Elaine. *Harry Courtfield*: MELVILLE ELLIS. *Franklyn Copeland*: MARTIN BROWN. *Mrs. Vandercrief*: Doris Cameron. *Mrs. Tatters*: Florence Cable. *Mlle. Eclatante*: Dollé Dalnert. *Baron de Shine*: Barney Bernard. *At the piano*: Melville Ellis.

The Chorus: *Show Girls*: Misses Mae Allen, Eliore Dell, Maidie Burker, Bessie Frewen, Mae Dealy, Bessie Fisher, Florence Harris, Irene Clair, Leona Quinn, Marion Baker Clara DeBeers, Louise Galem, Anne Merriam, Carmen Romero, Marie Flood, Gladys Briggs, Anna Berg, Marie Barbare. *Dancers*: Misses Cannan, Callan, M. Prager, Dakin, McLellan, Richter, E. Burnett, Falk, Scherer, E. Prager, H. Burnett, Lachere, Hardy, Zaitz, Gray, Warde, Furlong, Sommerville, Dare, Jason, DeNoville, Sparks, LaPlace, Phillips, Marsden. *Men*: Messrs. Gellis, Sohmers, Sterling, Raleigh, Gilbert, Dodge, Hamilton, Cohan, Lyman, Glynn, Georgi, Holmes, Miller Gordon, Wilcox, Frewen, Hagen, Stone, Smith.

Scene 1: Drawing-room at Mrs. Dean's. *Scene 2*: Ball-room at Mrs. Dean's.

MUSICAL NUMBERS
"Hard Luck in Society"[88]
S. Mayhew
"Which Shall I Choose?"
J. Collins
Quadrille
Chorus
Song
Mlle. Dalnert

[84]Dropped after opening.

[85]Dropped during the run.

[86]Replaced during the run by:
Specialty
W. Howard, E. Howard

[87]Subsequently toured in a two-act format, wherein A NIGHT WITH THE PIERROTS formed the latter portion of the first act of WHIRL OF SOCIETY. The song order was radically revised; added were:
"Four O'Clock Tea"
Chorus
"Fol de Rol (Dol Doi)" (A Yiddish Serenade)
Fanny Brice
(*Music by* Jean Schwartz. *Lyrics by* Edward Madden.)
"I'm Saving My Kisses"
G. Deslys, H. Pilcer
"How Do You Know?"
F. Brice
"I Want Something New to Play With"
G. Deslys, A. Jolson
"The Cotillion"
Ensemble
Pianologue
M. Ellis
"Come Back to Me"
G. Deslys, M. Ellis, O. Schwarz

[88]Dropped during the run.

"(That) Society Bear"
S. Mayhew
(*Music and Lyrics by* Irving Berlin.)
"Cinderella Waltz"
M. Brown, J. Collins
Song:
A. Jolson
["Snap Your Fingers"
(*Music by* Harry von Tilzer. *Lyrics by* William Jerome.)
"Row, Row, Row"
(*Music by* James V. Monaco. *Lyrics by* William Jerome.)
"Waiting for the Robert E. Lee"
(*Music by* Lewis F. Muir. *Lyrics by* L. Wolfe Gilbert.)
"On the Mississippi"
(*Music by* Harry Carroll and Arthur Fields. *Lyrics by* Ballard Macdonald.]
"The Gaby Glide"[89]
M. Brown, Company
(*Music by* Louis A. Hirsch. *Lyrics by* Harry Pilcer.)]

ACT 3: SESOSTRA[90]

An Operatic Mimodrama in One Act, 3 Tableaux. Poem and production by Monsieur Leon Pavi. Music by Henri Hirschmann.

CAST: *Sesostra*: Mme. LINA IMPERIA. *The Slave*: Mlle. LUCY GERARD. *Ranib*: FARINA (Pantomimist).

1912.10 BARON TRENCK

A Comic Opera in Two Acts, 3 Scenes. English version (American book) by Henry Blossom. Based on the German original 'Baron Trenck der Pandur' by A. M. Wilner and Robert Bodansky. Music by Felix Albini. Lyrics by Frederick F. Schrader. Direction, ensembles and dances by Al Holbrook. Settings and costumes by Hugo Baruch & Cie., Berlin; Ernest Albert. Orchestra under the direction of Antonio DeNovellis. Produced by the Whitney Opera Company (F. C. Whitney, Director). Opened 11 March 1912 at the Casino Theatre and closed 13 April 1912 after 40 performances.

CAST: *Baron Trenck*, Colonel of Imperial Corps of Pandours: FRITZ STURMFELS. *Nikola*, the Village Dancing Master: JOHN SLAVIN. *Josef*, the Village Magistrate: Royal Cutter. *Captain Franz*, an Officer in the Imperial Corps: Mitchell Lewis. *Alla Wanja*, a Bandit Chieftain: Charles Gallagher. *Herr von Trautenbach*, Major Domo to the Empress Marie Therese: Pacie Ripple. *Marquis d'Aucuneterre*, French Ambassador to the Austrian Court: JOSEPH HERBERT. *Count Zukoski*: Charles Sherman. *A Herald*: Raymond Bloomer. *Countess Lydia von Schwalbenau* Lady in Waiting to the Empress: BLANCHE DUFFIELD. *Mariza*, a Peasant Maid: PERLE BARTI. *Frau Cornelia Stecher*, Lydia's Aunt: ETHEL DUFRE HOUSTON. *Countess von Holstein*: Jeanette Horton. *Anna*, in love with Franz: Mabel Ferry. *Ella*, in love with Josef: Ethel Hamilton.

The action takes place in 1759, during the reign of Marie Therese of Austria.

Act 1: Farmyard and Inn on the Estate of Baron Trenck in Silesia.

Act 2, Scene 1: Countess Lydia's Boudoir in the Palace of the Empress near Vienna. (Albert.) *Scene 2*: Ballroom in the Palace of the Empress.

ACT 1
Opening Chorus
"Cupid Is a Cruel Master" (Trio)
P. Barti, E. Hamilton, M. Ferry
(*Music by* Alfred G. Robyn. *Lyrics by* Henry Blossom.)
"I'd Like to Be a Soldier, Gay" (Duet)
J. Slavin, P. Barti
"I'm from the Court of the Empress Queen" (Lydia's Entrance, Valse)
B. Duffield, P. Barti, J. Slavin, R. Cutter, Chorus
"We're Bold, Bad Bandits All"
C. Gallagher, Chorus
"Trenck Is My Name" (Trenck's Entrance/March Song)
F. Sturmfels, B. Duffield, Chorus
"Incognito?" (Duet)
F. Sturmfels, B. Duffield
"This Handsome Soldier Is Too Bold" (Trio)
B. Duffield, J. Slavin, P. Barti
Finale

ACT 2
Scene 1
"With Song and Cheer" (Opening Chorus)
B. Duffield, Chorus
"In Merry Merry May" (Duet)
E. D. Houston, P. Ripple
(*Music by* Alfred G. Robyn, Felix Albini.)
"My Heart's My Own" (My Heart's Mine Own)
B. Duffield
(*Music by* Alfred G. Robyn. *Lyrics by* Henry Blossom.)
Scene 2
Introduction, Chorus, Melodrama
R. Bloomer, Chorus
"When I Get Married" (Song)
J. Herbert, Chorus
(*Music by* Alfred G. Robyn. *Lyrics by* Henry Blossom.)
"(An) Angel! At Last I Find You" (Duet)
F. Sturmfels, B. Duffield
"When the Elves Hold Masquerade" (Kola Dance and Minuet)
J. Slavin, P. Barti, B. Duffield, F. Sturmfels, J. Herbert, Chorus
Finale

1912.11 45 MINUTES FROM BROADWAY

A Revival of the Musical Play in Three Acts.[91] Book, music and lyrics by George M. Cohan. Staged by George M. Cohan. Scenery painted by Edward G. Unitt and Joseph Wickes. Gowns by Schneider-Anderson Company. Musical director, Charles J. Gebest. Produced by (George M.) Cohan and (Sam) Harris. Opened 14 March 1912 at the George M. Cohan Theatre and closed 13 April 1912 after 36 performances.

CAST [in order of appearance]: *Mary Jane Jenkins*, the housemaid: SALLIE FISHER. *Flora Dora Dean*, a footlight favorite: Louise Aichel. *Mrs. David Dean*, her mother: Lorena Atwood. *Mrs. Purdy*, a resident of New Rochelle: Ada Gilman. *Tom Bennett*, the heir-at-law: LAWRENCE WHEAT. *Kid Burns*, his secretary: GEORGE M. COHAN, JR. *James Blake*, public administrator: Elmer Booth. *Daniel Krohman*, in the mining business: George Parsons. *Andy Gray*, the butler: Edgar Halstead. *Station Master*: John Klendon. *Police Sergeant*: William Ford. *Messenger Boy*: Tom Daw. *Baggageman*: Hawley Brooks. *Fannie Fordham*: Elsie Artz. *Pauline Peekskill*: Marion Donn. *Tessie Tarrytown*: Rose Leslie. *Polly Poughkeepsie*: Sydney Martineau. *Rosie Rye*: Lydia Scott. *Minnie Melrose*: Paula Leslie. *Theresa Tuckahoe*: Dorothy Lockhart. *Winnie Wakefield*: Elizabeth Young.

---

[89]Replaced during the run by:
The Texas Tommy Dance
Original Texas Tommy Dancers

[90]By 18 March 1912 SESOSTRA had been replaced by THE CAPTIVE, an Oriental Phantasy in 2 Scenes and a Prologue. Devised and staged by William J. Wilson. Prologue by Harold Atteridge. Music by Theodore Bendix. Scenery painted by H. Robert Law. Costumes by Lansdorf, Paris.

CAST: *The Rajah*: Mlle. D. Dalneri. *The Ranee*: D. Cameron. *Chief of the Harem*: E. Cutler. *The Sayer*: C. Ryan. *Captain of the Palace Guard*: B. Angere. *The Captive*: B. Angere. *Soldiers, Guards, Peasants, Eunuchs, Princesses, African Princesses, Indian Princes, Dancing Girls, Women of the Harem, Guards, etc.*.

Prologue: Corridor of the Favorites. *Scene 1*: Interior of the Harem. *Scene 2*: Courtyard of the Palace.

MUSICAL NUMBER
"My Oriental Rose"
Mlle.D. Dalnert
(*Music by* Louis A. Hirsch.)

By 28 April 1912, THE CAPTIVE had been replaced by: Grete Wiesenthal in a program of Modern Danses, followed by THE ROSE OF ISPAHAN, a Dance Scena in 1 Act, devised and staged by William J. Wilson.

CAST: *The Caliph*: E. Hare. *Head Eunuch*: E. Cutler. *Nadir*: M. Brown. *Zuricka*: J. Collins. *Soldiers, Guards, Peasants, Eunuchs, Persian Princesses, African Princesses, Dancing Girls, Women of the Harem, etc.*

MUSICAL NUMBER
"My Oriental Rose"
Mlle.D. Dalnert
(*Music by* Louis A. Hirsch.)

[91]Originally produced in New York 1 January 1906 at the New Amsterdam Theatre for 90 performances. For Synopsis of Scenes and Musical Numbers, see original 1906 production.

1912.12 THE MAN FROM COOK'S

A Musical Comedy in Two Acts. English book and lyrics by Henry Blossom. Based on an original French story ('Un Voyage Cook') by Maurice Ordonneau. Music by Raymond Hubbell. Staged by Ben Teal. Costumes by F. Richard Anderson. Settings designed by Walter Burridge, Ernest Gros. Orchestra under the direction of Anton Heindl. Orchestrations by Frank Saddler. Produced by (Marc) Klaw and (Abraham) Erlanger. Opened 25 March 1912 at the New Amsterdam Theatre and closed 20 April 1912 after 32 performances.

CAST: *Mrs. Benton*: Marion Murray. *Marjorie Benton*: STELLA HOBAN. *Madame Leontine*: FLAVIA ARCARO. *Estelle du Bois*: ELEANOR PENDLETON. *Floria*: Rene Thorton. *Lolita*: Nonette Lyle. *Paula*: Josephine Harriman. *Mariette*: Frances Rubens. *Berthe*: May Leslie. *Jeanne*: Adele Kornau. *Louise*: Bessie Durant. *La Belle Tortino*: Bena Hoffman. *Marie*: Daisy Rudd. *Prince Victor de Champagnax*: WALTER PERCIVAL. *"Toto" Soulard*: FRED WALTON. *Zachary Benton*: JOHN DALY MURPHY. *Lord Fitz-Bertie Baffingfone*: LESLIE KENYON. *Stubbs*, his valet: Antonio Moreno. *T. Laurence O'Donnell*: John J. Dempsey. *Chauffeur*: J. T. Chaille. *Leonard de Biron*: WILLIAM PINKHAM. *Johnson*, a Cook's agent: F. A. Bishop. *Giacommetti*, hotel proprietor: J. T. Chaille. *Pietro*, a porter: William Pinkham. *Wilhelm*, a waiter: W. Hobart. *The Bell Family*: Celia, Nellie, Silvia, Richard, Albert, Edward, Charles, William, George. *Personnel of the Chorus*.

Act 1: Dining Room of Pension, Avenue d l'Opera, Paris. Afternoon. (Gros.)

Act 2: Grounds of Hotel del Vesuvio, Naples. Afternoon. Two days later. (Burridge.)

ACT 1

Opening Chorus
W. Pinkham, F. Arcaro, N. Lyle, Tuneless Tooters of the Montmartre Dental College

"Just As You Are" (Duet)
F. Walton, E. Pendleton

"My Girl of Chance" (The Girl of Chance)(Song)
W. Percival

"All for You" (Duet)
W. Percival, S. Hoban

"(A) Little Tin Soldier" (Song)
F. Walton, E. Pendleton, Chorus

"Doctor's, Doctor's" (Trio)
J. D. Murphy, F. Walton, W. Pinkham

Finale

ACT 2

Opening Chorus
Bell Family, R. Thornton, Male Octette

"You and I" (Duet)
S. Hoban, W. Percival

"We Can't Do Without (the) Men" (Song)
E. Pendleton, Tourists

Flower Fête
Ensemble

"A Little Pot of Tea" (Song)
L. Kenyon, Girls

"A Little World for Two" (Duet)
S. Hoban, W. Percival

Finale

1912.13 A WINSOME WIDOW

A Farce Comedy with Music in Three Acts, 5 Scenes. Book founded on the farce comedy "A Trip to Chinatown" by Charles Hoyt. Music by Raymond Hubbell. (Additional songs by John Golden, Jerome Kern, Nathaniel D. Ayer, Jean Schwartz, Stanley Murphy, Henry I. Marshall.) Staged by Julian Mitchell. Settings painted by Edward G. Unitt and Joseph Wickes, Ernest Albert. Musical director, Frank N. Darling. Produced by Florenz Ziegfeld. Opened 11 April 1912 at the Ziegfeld Moulin Rouge and closed 7 September 1912 after 172 performances.[92]

CAST (in order of appearance): *Members of the Purity League (4)*: *Mrs. Gadder*: Fawn Conway. *Mrs. Noyes*: Katherine Smythe. *Mrs. Howell*: Lottie Vernon. *Mrs. Flippant*: Marie Baxter. *Flirt*, the Widow's maid, who knows her way about: ETHEL [AMORITA] KELLEY. *Slavin*, the old family nuisance: HARRY KELLY. *Rashleigh Gay*, who thinks life is a joy ride: CHARLES J. ROSS. *Wilder Daly*, Ben Gay's nephew: CHARLES KING. *Ben Gay*, President of the Purity Leage: LEON ERROL. *Tony*, Ben Gay's ward: Ida Adams. *Isabel*, Ben Gay's ward: ELIZABETH BRICE. *Mrs. Duer*, a reformer: Natalie Dagwell. *Mrs. Guyer*, a winsome widow: EMMY WEHLEN. *Willie Grow*, the millionaire kid: Kathleen Clifford. *Welland Strong*, who enjoys poor health: HARRY CONOR. *Noah*, a waiter at "The Poodle Dog": FRANK TINNEY. *Bryton Early*, a man about town: SIDNEY JARVIS. *Rosie, Jenny*: THE DOLLY TWINS [Rosie, Jennie]. *Le Petite Daffy*: MAE WEST. *Mons. McGinnis, Mlle. Bridgite*, Entertainers at "The Poodle Dog": Jack Clifford, Irene Weston. *Proprietor of The Cliff House*: Charles Mitchell. *Chief of Police*: A. Brannigan. *Officer O'Mara*: J. McDermott. *Mlle. Nana, Mons. Alexis*, masquerade dancers at The Cliff House: Nana and Alexis. *Fancy Skaters*: Cathleen Pope, George Kirner.

Widows: Misses Morris, Lewis, Zell, Hilton, St. Clair, Bonner, Carlton, Sewell. *Pink Ladies*: Misses Newell, Perot, Conway, L. Vernon, Smythe, Oste, Howard, Leroy, Baxter, Hart, Dagwell, Warrington, Kenny. *Spirits of Pousse Cafe*: Misses Zell, B. Lewis, J. Lewis, St. Clair, Beaubien. *Piccolo Girls*: Misses Curzon, Sewell, Morris, H. Lewis, Warner, Lorraine, Barrett, West, Hilton, Bonner, Randall, Gabrielle. *Drummers*: Misses Bonner, E. Christy, E. Francesca, A. Francesca, Warner, Randall, West, Barrett, J. Lewis, Beaubien, Dana, LaPierre, Gabrielle, R. Bellaire, F. Bellaire, Wellington, Winthrop, Morris, H. Lewis, Curzon, St. Clair, Zell, Hilton, R. Lewis, Carlton. *Bowery Boys*: Misses Dana, Morris, Randall, Hilton. *Bowery Girls*: Misses R. Lewis, St. Clair, H. Lewis, Barrett, Zell. *Pierrots*: Misses Smythe, Hart. *Pierretts*: Misses J. Lewis, LaPierre. *Punchinello*: Misses E. Bellaire, Perot, Warrington, Conway. *Troubadors*: Misses Baxter, Oste, Barrett, Dana. *Harlequins*: Misses E. Christy, Gabrielle. *Columbines*: Misses Randall, Warner. *Press*: Marjorie Bonner. *The Ziegfeld Moulin Rouge Girl*: Lottie Vernon. *Skating Boys*: Misses E. Christy, R. Bellaire, F. Bellaire, Beaubien, Hart, West, LaPierre, Randolph. *Skating Girls*: Misses Morris, Oste, Zell, Barrett, Baxter, Curzon, Randall, Dana. *Brown Hockey Boys*: Misses Lewis, Warner, J. Lewis, E. Francesca, Winthrop. *Lavender Hockey Boys*: Misses Bonner, H. Lewis, Hilton, St. Clair, Gabrielle.

Act 1: Reception Room in Ben Gay's House, San Francisco. (Unitt & Wickes)

Act 2: Private Dining Room in "The Poodle Dog Restaurant," San Francisco. (Unitt & Wickes)

Act 3, Scene 1: Ball Room, Cliff House, San Francisco. (Albert) *Scene 2*: Ante Room, Ice Palace, San Francisco. *Scene 3*: Interior of Ice Palace Gardens, San Francisco. (Albert)

ACT 1[93]

"Teach Me Everything You Know"
E. A. Kelley, L. Errol

"You're a Regular Girl"[94]
E. Brice, C. King

"They Mean More"[95] (Waltz)
E. Wehlen, Eight Widows, Chorus

"I Take After Dad" (Song)
K. Clifford, Chorus

"Purity Brigade March"[96] (Finale)
E. Wehlen, Ensemble

ACT 2

Opening Chorus

"Pousse Cafe"[97]
S. Jarvis, Chorus

Dance
Dolly Twins

"(Toodle-oodle-oodle on Your) Piccolo"
K. Clifford, Girls
(*Music and Lyrics by* Griffin and Murtagh.)

Dance
J. Clifford, I. Weston

---

[92]Lyrics uncredited; costumes uncredited.

[93]Added during the run, after "I Take After Dad":
"Be My Little Baby Bumble Bee"
E. Brice, C. King
(*Music by* Henry I. Marshall. *Lyrics by* Stanley Murphy.)

[94]Dropped during the run.

[95]Replaced during the run by:
"A Winsome Widow Am I"
E. Wehlen, Eight Widows, Chorus
(*Music by* Gus Edwards. *Lyrics by* Edward Madden.)

[96]During the run, this was revised to read in the program:
Finale
Entire Company

[97]During the run, replaced by:
"Fascinating Girl" [from Act 3]
Bernard Granville (Rashleigh Gay)

"I Never Knew What Eyes Could Do (Till Yours Looked into Mine)"[98]
I. Adams
(*Music by* Henry Marshall. *Lyrics by* Stanley Murphy.)
"Songs of Yesterday"
E. Wehlen, H. Conor, S. Jarvis, I. Adams, Chorus
"The Frisco" (Finale)
Principals, Ensemble

ACT 3

Scene 1

Masquerade Ball—Costume Prize Contest
Dolly Twins, Ensemble
Dance
E. A. Kelley
"(Could You Love) A Girl Like Me?" (Waltz)
E. Wehlen, Ensemble
(*Lyrics by* Robert B. Smith.)
"String a Ring of Roses (Round Your Rosie)"
E. Brice, C. King, Chorus
(*Music by* Jean Schwartz. *Lyrics by* William Jerome.)
"Fascinating Girl"[99]
S. Jarvis, I. Adams
Dance
Mlle. Nana, Mons. Alexis

Scene 2

"The Skate Boy"
F. Tinney

Scene 3

Interior Ice Palace Gardens—Ice Skating Carnival (Music from GYPSY LOVE)
Entire Company
(*Music by* Franz Lehár.)
Finale
Entire Company

1912.14 THE WALL STREET GIRL

A Musical Play in Three Acts. Book by Margaret Mayo and Edgar Selwyn. Music by Karl Hoschna. Lyrics by (Benjamin) Hapgood Burt. (Additional songs by Nat D. Ayer, Jean Schwartz, A. Seymour Brown, Al Piantadosi, Joseph McCarthy, Alfred Bryan, Grant Clarke.) Staged by Charles Winninger. Dances by Gus Sohlke. Scenery painted by H. Robert Law Studio. Costumes designed by Cora MacGeachy. Orchestra under the direction of William Loraine. Produced by Frederick McKay. Opened 15 April 1912 at the George M. Cohan Theatre and closed 1 June 1912 after 56 performances.

CAST: *James Greene*, senior member of Greene & Longman: HARRY GILFOIL. *John Chester*, of Chester & Chester: CHARLES WINNINGER. *Dexter Barton*, a Western product: WILLIAM P. CARLETON. *Bertie Longman*, junior member of Longman & Longman: CLARENCE OLIVER. *Reverend Dr. Leonard*: Paul Porter. *With Greene & Longman (6)*: *Jordan*: Cyril Ring. *Pinch*: Charles Silber. *Walker*: Jack Wellekens. *Simons*: Ralph Shipman. *Harris*: William Bourn. *West*: Robert Thurston. *Mrs. Williams*, Jemima's chaperone: Maude Knowlton. *Pearl Williams*, her daughter: Florence Shirley. *Lawrence O'Connor*, who has the moving picture rights: WELLINGTON CROSS. *Sunshine Reilly*, back door keeper: LOIS JOSEPHINE. *Jemima's friends (6)*: *Glen Underwood*: Helene French. *Rosie Dale*: Ivy Paget. *Grace Sinclair*: Catherine Hurst. *Edythe Torrant*: Helen Turner. *Mazie Blackburn*: Kathryn Sainpolis. *Trixie Allen*: Cleo LeMoyne. *Jemina Greene*, also known as Jimmy, the Wall Street girl: BLANCHE RING. (*Specialties in Act 2*: WILL ROGERS [Lariat Performer], S. J. RAWSON [Expert Boomerang Thrower].)

Personnel of the Chorus: *Clerks*: Misses Ethelyn Clark, Edna Hettler, Helen Williams, Edith Kimball, Marie Earl, Estelle Wood, Alice Sullivan, Mabel Clark. *Bookkeepers*: Misses Gladyce Fox, Frankie James, Yewell Fields, Bessie Sessions, Gladys Clifton, Grace Kimball, Anna Ford, Lilette Boyce, Irene LeMay, Mary F. Greene. *Indians and Cowgirls*: Misses Ethelyn Clark, Helen Williams, Edith Kimball, Marie Earl, Estelle Wood, Edna Hettler, Alice Sullivan, Mabel Clark, Gladyce Fox, Frankie James, Yewell Fields, Bessie Sessions, Gladys Clifton, Grace Kimball, Anna Ford, Lilette Boyce, Irene LeMay, Mary F. Greene. *Cowboys*: Messrs. Ralph Shipman, Jack Wellekens, William Bourne, Herbert A. Burnham, Gordon R. Newman, Robert Thurston, Leo E. Crook, Fred Howard, John Day, Harry C. Powers.

The action takes place at the present time.

Act 1: Private Office of Greene & Longman, Wall Street brokers.

Act 2: Outside of Ring. Town near Reno, Nevada.

Act 3: Room in Mr. Green's Home on Fifth Avenue.

ACT 1

Opening Chorus
Clerks, Bookkeepers
(*Music by* Karl Hoschna. *Lyrics by* Benjamin Hapgood Burt.)
"Love Is a Peculiarity"[100]
F. Shirley, C. Oliver
(*Music by* Al Piantadosi. *Lyrics by* Joseph McCarthy.)
"(Gee!) I Should Have Been Born a Boy"
B. Ring, Ensemble
(*Music by* Nathaniel D. Ayer. *Lyrics by* A. Seymour Brown.)
"I Want a Regular Man"
B. Ring, Principals
(*Music by* Karl Hoschna. *Lyrics by* Benjamin Hapgood Burt.)
"On the Quiet"
H. Gilfoil, C. Oliver
(*Music by* Karl Hoschna. *Lyrics by* Benjamin Hapgood Burt.)
Finale
Company
(*Music by* Karl Hoschna. *Lyrics by* Benjamin Hapgood Burt.)

ACT 2[101]

Opening Chorus
Ensemble
"If You Only Will"
W. Cross, L. Josephine
(*Music and Lyrics by* Benjamin Hapgood Burt.)
"Every Day"
B. Ring, W. P. Carleton
(*Music and Lyrics by* Earl Jones and Charles Daniels.)
"The Indian Rag"
B. Ring, Ensemble
(*Music by* Nathaniel D. Ayer. *Lyrics by* A. Seymour Brown.)
"Whistle It"
B. Ring
(*Music by* Jean Schwartz. *Lyrics by* Alfred Bryan, Grant Clarke.)
Finale
Ensemble
(*Music by* Nathaniel D. Ayer. *Lyrics by* A. Seymour Brown.)

ACT 3

Opening
"You're Some Girl"[102]
W. Cross, L. Josephine
(*Music by* Nathaniel D. Ayer. *Lyrics by* A. Seymour Brown.)
"I Never Knew"
W. P. Carleton
(*Music by* Henry I. Marshall. *Lyrics by* Stanley Murphy.)
"(Come with Me to) Spoony Land"[103]
F. Shirley, C. Oliver
(*Music by* M. J. Fitzpatrick. *Lyrics by* Edward Madden.)

---

[98]Replaced during the run by:
"When You're Away"
I. Adams

[99]Dropped during the run and moved to Act 2.

[100]Replaced for subsequent tour by:
"Under the Love Tree"
Lillian Spencer (Pearl Williams), Elmer Thompson (Bertie Longman)
(*Music by* Bert Grant. *Lyrics by* A. Seymour Brown.)

[101]The running order was revised for subsequent tour, and added to Act 2 was:
"Georgia Land"
B. Ring, W. P. Carleton
(*Music by* Harry Carroll. *Lyrics by* Arthur Fields.)

[102]Dropped during the run and replaced by:
"Sweetheart Time"
L. Spencer, E. Thomas

[103]Dropped for subsequent tour.

"I Can Drink"[104]
H. Gilfoil
(*Music and Lyrics by* Benjamin Hapgood Burt.)
"Deedle-Dee-Dum" (The Deedle-Dum-Dee)
B. Ring, Chorus
(*Music by* Silvio Hein. *Lyrics by* Benjamin Hapgood Burt.)
Request Numbers
B. Ring
Finale
Entire Company
(*Music by* Karl Hoschna. *Lyrics by* Benjamin Hapgood Burt.)

1912.15 THE ROSE MAID

An Operetta in Two Acts. American libretto by Harry B. Smith and Raymond Peck. Adapted from the Viennese original 'Bub Oder Mädel' (libretto by Felix Dörmann and Adolf Altmann). Music by Bruno Granichstädten. Lyrics by Robert B. Smith. Production staged by George Marion. Dances arranged by William Rock. Settings designed by D. Frank Dodge and William Castle. Costumes designed by Will Barnes and Mme. Mank. Orchestra under the direction of Robert Hood Bowers. Produced by Louis F. Werba and Mark A. Luesher. Opened 22 April 1912 at the Globe Theatre and closed 21 September 1912 after 181 performances.

CAST: *Duke of Barchester*, a young nobleman living beyond his income and noted for his extravagant entertaining, who is sole heir to the estate of his uncle: J. HUMBIRD DUFFEY, Arthur Royd (alt.) *Sir John Portman*, a wealthy bachelor, who visits his young relative unexpectedly at his London home on the night the Duke announces his betrothal to Princess Hilda: R. E. GRAHAM. *Princess Hilda Von Lahn*, whose love for the Duke receives a shock when she learns that he is financed by, and in the clutches of Dennis, Schmuke and Chumley: EDITH DECKER. *Dennis, Schmuke, Chumley*, loan brokers and bankers whose methods are not approved by Daphne: EDWARD GALLAGHER, AL SHEAN, ARHUR LACEBY. *Daphne*, the pretty little daughter of the Duke's housekeeper, who was an officer in the regiment of Sir John. She wears the white rose of friendship, which she proves to be more enduring than the red rose of love as worn by Angela and Berenice: ADRIENNE AUGARDE. *Angela, Berenice*, friends of the Duke: Emilie Lea, May Emory. *Lieutenant Woolridge*: PHILLIP SHEFFIELD. *The Honorable Bertie Walpole*, a young cadet who while an attaché in Washington met Gwendolen Bruce: BURRELL BARBRETTO. *Gwendolen Bruce*, a young American heiress who visits Ostend during the gala cavalry carnival, with the members of the "Million Club of Heiresses": DOROTHY FOLLIS. *Myrtle Doolittle*: Louise Brunelle. *Mabel Willing*: Grace Williams. *Madge Mortimer*: Jane Rock. *Mamie Morris*: Eithel Kelley. *Madeline Miggs*: Sadie Melles. *Maude Schuyler*: Anne Raymond. *Countess Bertrand*, Chaperone to the Misses Doolittle, Willing, Mortimer, Morris, Miggs, Schuyler on the trip to Ostend: Juliette Dika. *Blatz*, at whose hotel have congregated for the cavalry tournament Officers from Russia, France, Italy and Germany: Harry Lambart. *Count Orloffsky of Russia*: Alfred Darling. *The Marquis Cassaignac of France*: Charles Wheeler. *Duke d'Este of Italy*: E. L. Spencer. *Honorary Member of German Cavalry*: F. McCullough. *Honorary Member of East Indian Lancers*: Philip Sheffield. (*Kute Kiddies Sextette*: Marie Sattler, Madelyn Ball, Marie Moore, Gertrude Gmelch, Helen Singleton, Helen Faulkner.)

Guests and Attendants: Misses May Carlisle, Helen O'Day, Cynthia Grace, Virginia Steinhart, Millie Murray, Katherine Grant, Alice Clayton, Helen Atkins, Blanche Burnham, Anna Crippen, Zamora Pierce, Eileen Spellman, Elma Decker, Mae Harris, Vivian Lawrence, Florence Flanderaux, Winnifred Ayres, Julia Mornin, Lucille Schrader, Viola Vincent, May Heagney, Eloise King. Messrs. Leslie Barnard, E. Lisle Bloodgood, Maurice Boddington, Alfred Darling, William Johns, Fred LeDeux, Harry Potter, Edward Lawrence, Percy Matson, Paul Pollock, Charles Wheeler, Alfred Walton, Stephen Fyle.

Act 1: Salon in Barchester House, London.

Act 2: At Ostend, one week later.

ACT 1
Opening Chorus
Ensemble
"Liberty Hall"
E. Decker
Dance Eccentrique
E. Lea
"Soldiers of Bohemia" (A Soldier of Bohemia)(Song)
J. H. Duffey, Guests
(*Music by* Robert Hood Bowers. *Lyrics by* Raymond Peck.)
"The Course of True Love" (Duet)
E. Decker, P. Sheffield
"Two Little Hearts" (When Two Little Hearts Beat Together)(Duet)
A. Augarde, B. Barbretto
"Roses Bloom for Lovers" (Song)
A. Augarde
"Sweethearts, Wives and Good Fellows" (Song)
J. H. Duffey, Guests
"Telephone (Song)" (Incidental)
J. H. Duffey, P. Sheffield, E. Gallagher, A. Shean, A. Laceby, Officers
Finale

ACT 2
Opening Chorus
Ensemble
"The Heiresses"
P. Sheffield, Ensemble
(*Music by* Robert Hood Bowers. *Lyrics by* Raymond Peck.)
"Money Talks" (Quintette)
P. Sheffield, E. Gallagher, A. Shean, A. Laceby, C. Halton
"The Happy Family" (Duet)
E. Decker, R. E. Graham, Kute Kiddies Sextette
"The American Heiress"
D. Follis, Heiresses
"(One Waltz) Only One Waltz" (Trio)
E. Decker, D. Follis, P. Sheffield
"Tip Your Hat to the American Millionairess"
A. Augarde, Ensemble
"I Live for You Alone" (Duet)
J. H. Duffey, A. Augarde
"The Cavalry Brigade" (March)
E. Decker, P. Sheffield, D. Follis, Ensemble of World's Riders
Pony Dance Divertissement
E. Lea
"Moon, Lovely Moon" (Song)
J. H. Duffey, Ensemble
"Now His Choice We See"[105] (Ensemble)
A. Augarde, J. H. Duffey, Company
Finale

1912.16 LET GEORGE DO IT

The Big Musical Comedy Surprise in Two Acts, 4 Scenes. Book by Aaron Hoffman. Founded on George McManus' drawings. Music and lyrics by Paul West and Nathaniel D. Ayer. Musical director, Eugene Salzer. Staged by Al. Holbrook. Produced by the Leffler-Bratton Company. Opened 22 April 1912 at the West End Theatre, moved 29 April 1912 to the Manhattan Opera House and closed 4 May 1912 after 17 performances.

CAST: *Helen Merritt*, in love with Billy Brush: IVA IRBY. *Hazel May*, a Newport society bud: MINTHORNE WORTHLEY. *Tillie Ticker*, a telegraph operator at Hotel Astor: LEONA STEPHENS. *Mrs. Georges Georges*, an automobile enthusiast: Mildred Wood. *Billy Brush*, an artist with ambitions: RUSSELL LENNON. *I. Seldom Ketchum*, a detective who seldom does: Tom Burton. *Dr. Theopholus Knutt*, a young New York physician: ABBOTT WORTHLEY. *Spike*, Tillie's brother: I. Arbuckle. *Georges Georges*, an excitable Frenchman: James Dubois. *A. Tuffold Knutt*, uncle of Dr. Knutt: Murray Bernard. *Gus Gasoline*, a chauffeur: Fay C. Peterson. *Claxton Horn*, his mechanician: Mat Kennedy. *Will Pinchem*, a policeman (honest): Ivan Arbuckle. *X. Press*, transfer man: Arthur Wilson. *Noah Tipp*, head waiter at Tulip Inn: J. H. Prescott. *Wanta Tipp*, another waiter: W. H. Rupert. *George George*, janitor of the Artists' Apartments: GEORGE P. MURPHY.

Girls in High Society (8): *Miss Ward*: Florence Campbell. *Miss Atwood*: Goldier Redding. *Miss Beechey*: Bessie Clay. *Miss Mars*: Francis Campbell. *Miss Hamilton*: Isabelle Arbor. *Miss Rogers*: Columbia DeShield. *Miss Curtis*: Mildred Stevens. *Miss Grahame-White*: Jennie Reiser. *Eight Dancing Darlings*: Helen Coyran, Lottie Wesner, Frederica Smith, Grace Howard, Julia Grant, Anna Trainer, Vera Burt, Peggy Rich.

Act 1, Scene 1: Billy Brush's Studio. New York, afternoon of 4 July. *Scene 2*: Along the Highway. *Scene 3*: The Jolly Jail.

Act 2: Tulip Inn in Tulip Town.

ACT 1
"We've Painted All the Morning" (Opening Chorus)
Artists, Models, Chorus

[104]Dropped for subsequent tour.

[105]Dropped during the run.

"Helen's Hat"
R. Lennon, I. Irby, Chorus
"Spoony Words"
A. Worthley, M. Worthley
"I'd Rather Go to Jail"
G. P. Murphy
"Waltz Me (Up) to the Altar, Waiter"
L. Stephens
"Night Time's the Right Time to Spoon with the Girl You Love"
I. Irby, R. Lennon
(*Music by* George W. Meyer. *Lyrics by* Joe Goodwin; extra verses by Jack Bratton.)
"The Gum Shoe Man"
L. Stephens, Small Folks
Finale

ACT 2
"Two Lips Are Waiting in Tulip Town" (Opening Chorus and Song)
I. Irby, Chorus
"The Band Came Back"
G. P. Murphy
(*Lyrics by* A. Seymour Brown.)
"The Dramatic Rag"
L. Stephens, J. Dubois, Chorus
"Confidence"
G. P. Murphy, Girls
"Don't You Ever Think About Me, Dearie?"
A. Worthley, M. Worthley
(*Music and Lyrics by* William Cahill.)
"In a Bungalow for Two"
I. Irby, R. Lennon, Chorus
Finale

1912.17 TWO LITTLE BRIDES

A Musical Comedy in Two Acts. Book and lyrics by Arthur Anderson, James T. Powers, Harold Atteridge. Adapted from the Viennese original ('Schneeglöckchen,' libretto) by A. M. Willner and Julius Wilhelm. Music by Gustav Kerker. Staged by J. C. Huffman. Orchestra under the direction of Max Hershfield. Produced by the Messrs. Shubert. Opened 23 April 1912 at the Casino Theatre, moved 3 June 1912 to the Lyric Theatre, and closed 15 June 1912 after 63 performances.[106]

CAST: *The King of Wurtenburg*: WALTER LAWRENCE. *Count Boris Rimanow*: FORREST WINANT. *Prince Petroff*, Russian Ambassador at the Court of Wurtenburg: George Pauncefort. *Vodka*, Janitor of the Institute: Sherman Wade. *General Audrey* of the Cossack Regiment: Tom Ferris. *A Corsican*: Louis London. *Monsieur Descamps*: Oscar Schwartz. *Captain of the Guard*: Edgar Bryde. *High Priest*: Frank Williams. *Footman*: Edward Stanley. *The Mayor*: Harry Sulkin. *The Councilman*: Joe Wells. *The Waiter*: Dave Manser. *Honorka, Tatjana*, Pupils at the School: FRANCES CAMERON, LEILA HUGHES. *Vendetta*: FLAVIA ARCARO. *Pincess Athanasia*, Directrix of Russian Imperial Institute: SALLIE SALLINGER. *Lucille*: Melissa Ten Eyck. *Polycarp Ivanovitch*: JAMES T. POWERS. *Military Guards, High Priests, Canopy Bearers, Domestics of the Institute, Townspeople, The King's Guards, Ladies and Gentlemen, Guests of the Court of Westminster, Officers of the Court. Ambassadors of Italy, England, Spain, China. Four Officers of the Wurtenburg Guard. Four Cavaliers , an Old Fashioned Lady and Gentlemen, Flower Girls, Waiters, Citizens of Wurtenburg.*

Personnel of Ensemble: *Teachers*: Gertrude Aldrich, Gloria Starr. *Pages*: Misses Taylor, Wilkins, Goodwin, Watson, Dealy, Devere, Fitzhugh, Castle, Smith, Kidstone, Strater, Dorlys, Ward, Ross, Norton, DeSoto, Latimer, Donaldsn, DeVoe, Dennison, Harris, Dunn, Doigne, Lloyd, Morse, Ormiston, Wallace, Hebron, Lawlor, Campbell, Beck. *Pupils at the School*: *Men*: Messrs. Corish, Erick, Frenic, Wells, Abercrombie, Foley, Frazer, Sulkin, Bryde, Stanley, Tuller, DeMuth, Dyer, Manser, Mansour, Torrye, Pierce, Goldstein, Hays.

Act 1: The Ladies' Institute, under the protectorate of the Empress of Russia, at St. Petersburg.

Act 2: A Court Ball at the Palace of Prince Petroff in Wurtenburg. One year later.

ACT 1
Opening Chorus
"Snowdrops and the Spring" (Snowdrops in the Spring)
L. Hughes, Chorus
"The Letter (Song)" (Meet Me at Eight in the Hall)
F. Cameron, L. Hughes
"How Do You Do"[107]
F. Winant, Girls
"Kiss Me Again Bebe"
F. Winant, L. Hughes
"Oh! Honorka"
J. T. Powers, Chorus
Finale

ACT 2[108]
Opening Chorus
"Are We Widows, Wives or What?"
F. Cameron, L. Hughes
"Buzz On Little Busy Bees"
F. Winant, Girls
"So Away with Sorrow"
W. Lawrence, Soldeirs
"I Like All Girls"
W. Lawrence, L. Hughes, F. Camern
"(You Remind Me of) Someone I Used to Know"
L. Hughes, F. Wiannt
"The Corsican"
F. Arcaro, L. London, Chorus
"The Waltz Without a Kiss"
J. T. Powers, Chorus
(*Lyrics by* James T. Powers.)
"What About It?"
J. T. Powers, F. Cameron
Finale

1912.18 PATIENCE, or Bunthorne's Bride

An All-Star Revival of the Comic Opera in Two Acts.[109] Libretto by William S. Gilbert. Music by Arthur Sullivan. Staged under the direction of William J. Wilson. Scenery by H. Robert Law. Costumes designed by Melville Ellis. Orchestra under the direction of Clarence Rogerson. Produced by the Messrs. Shubert and William A. Brady. Opened 6 May 1912 at the Lyric Theatre and closed 1 June 1912 after 32 performances.

CAST: *Reginald Bunthorne*: DeWOLF HOPPER. *Archibald Grosvenor*: CYRIL SCOTT. *Colonel Calverley*: GEORGE J. MacFARLANE. *Major Murgatroyd*: EUGENE COWLES. *Lieutenant, The Duke of Dunstable*: ARTHUR ALDRIDGE. *The Attorney*: George Romain. *Patience*: MARIE DORO. *Rapturous Maidens (4)*: *The Lady Angela*: VIOLA GILLETTE. *The Lady Saphir*: Alice Brady. *The Lady Ella*: CHRISTINE NIELSON. *The Lady Jane*: EVA DAVENPORT.

Chorus of Maids: Misses Fern Hollis, Constance Crane, Margaret Morrison, Ruth Bonner, Nora McClory, Alice Chase, Alice Stratton, Marion George, Louise MacFarland, Loretta Doyle, Rose Wertz, Nathalie Saymore, Annette Herbert, Norma Higgins, Flora Lyons, Josephine DeNoville, Dorothy Cassel, Caro DuBurgho, Florence Sommerville, May von Summerfield, Katherine Gray, Edith Buell, Sara Meredith, Harriett DeNorma, Florence Harris, Edna Lee, Marie Corty, Helen Starr, Billie Williams, Sidonia Brann, Pauline Sterling, Leonora Guest. *Chorus of Dragoon Guards*: Messrs. Henry Holt, Joseph Galton, Frank Mirose, Louis Derman, Jose Pepe, John C. Cryan, Charles Yorkshire, George Williams, Irving Lavitz, Lew Graham, Fred Walker, J. Leonard Feiner, L. Williams, Tom Bryan, Jack Evans, Parker Leonard, David Heilbron, Herbert Hall, John E. Reese, Alex. Keene, William Baumann, Lew Litchfield.

---

[106]Scenery and costumes uncredited.

[107]Replaced during the run by:
"Buzz On, Little Busy Bee" [formerly in Act 2]
W. Lawrence (as Boris)

[108]The running order was revised. Added to Act 2 during the run:
Eccentric Dance
Moon, Morris (added to cast)
"Some Time, Some Place, Some Girl" (Somehow, Sometime, Somewhere)
L. Hughes, W. Lawrence
(*Music and Lyrics by* Louis A. Hirsch.)
Ensemble (before Finale)
J. T. Powers, Chorus

[109]First presented in New York 22 September 1881 at the Standard Theatre for 177 performances. For Synopsis of Scenes and Musical Numbers, see original 1881 production.

1912.19 ROBIN HOOD

A Revival of the Comic Opera in Three Acts.[110] Book (and lyrics) by Harry B. Smith. Music by Reginald deKoven. Staged by Daniel V. Arthur. Scenery painted by Frank Gates and Edward A. Morange (Acts 1 and 3), Homer F. Emens (Act 2). Costumes designed by Will R. Barnes. Orchestra under the direction of Frank E. Tours. Produced by the deKoven Opera Company (Daniel V. Arthur, Manager). Opened 6 May 1912 at the New Amsterdam Theatre and closed 29 June 1912 after 64 performances.

CAST (in order of appearance): *Little John*: CARL GANTVOORT. *Alan-a-Dale*: FLORENCE WICKHAM. *Will Scarlet*: BASIL RUYSDAEL. *Annabel*: ANNE SWINBURNE. *Friar Tuck*: GEORGE B. FROTHINGHAM. *Dame Durden*: PAULINE HALL. *Robin Hood*: WALTER HYDE. *Maid Marian*: BELLA ALTEN. *Sheriff of Nottingham*: EDWIN STEVENS. *Guy of Gisborne*: SIDNEY BRACY. *Joan, Ned*, Morris Dancers: Dorothy Arthur, Marie Wiova. *King's Herald*: Mary Mooney. *Villagers, Milkmaids, Outlaws, King's Foresters, Archers, Pedlars, etc.*

1912.20 MAMA'S BABY BOY

A Musical Farce in Three Acts. Adaptation (book) and lyrics by Junie McCree. Based on the comedy "Mrs. Black Is Back" by George V. Hobart. Music by Hans S. Linne. Additional numbers by Will H. Becker [George Botsford]. Staged by George W. Lederer. Dances arranged by Julian Alfred. Scenery painted by D. Frank Dodge and William Castle. Costumes by Lederer's Costume Department. Orchestra conducted by Hans S. Linne. Produced by George W. Lederer. Opened 25 May 1912 at the Broadway Theatre and closed 1 June 1912 after 9 performances.

CAST (in order of appearance):[111] *Spaff Hyman*: WILL J. KENNEDY. *Celia West*: ANNA LAUGHLIN. *Carrie Beverly*: LOUISE MINK. *Fred West*: ARTHUR McWATTERS. *Helen West*: GRACE TYSON. *Ann*, the cook: SALLIE STEMBLER. *Professor Ivory*: ALBERT HART. *Lawrence McManus*: JUNIE McCREE. *Jack North*: Bobby Barry.

Athletic Girls: Misses Lethia Gray, Lea LeLand, Martha Dean, Billie West, Katheryn Beach, Betty Scott, Cecile Mayo, Minnie Monroe. *The Little Fawns*: Misses Margaret Taylor, Miriam Sanford, Vera DeFord, Edna Ford, Nettie Hamilton, Lew Page, Rita Mason, Fannie Bradshaw, Marjorie Cogan, Alice Clifford, Helen Luchs, Mittie Bright, Millie Lorraine, Anna Sayce, Frances Alaine, Cissie Shatten.

Act 1: The West's Bungalow at Huntington, Long Island. 3 P.M.

Act 2: Kitchen. 11 P.M.

Act 3: The West's Bungalow. 1 A. M.

ACT 1

Opening Chorus
Schoolgirls, W. J. Kennedy
"Capital H" (Trio)
A. Laughlin, L. Mink, A. McWatters
"Back from Thirty-Six to Twenty-Nine"
G. Tyson
"White Lies, Black Lies"
A. McWatters
"The White Man's Hope"
A. Hart
"Time Has Changed So Many Customs in the Last Decade"
A. Laughlin
Finale

ACT 2

Opening Chorus
Girls, W. J. Kennedy
Quartette
G. Tyson, L. Mink, A. McWatters, J. McCree
"Cecelia"
A. Laughlin, A. McWatters
(*Music by* Will H. Becker.)
"Lonegan"
S. Stembler, J. McCree, W. J. Kennedy
"The Kitchen Cabaret"
L. Dockstader, E. M. Murray, Howard and Howard, Others
"Demonstration Number"
A. Hart, Girls
Finale

ACT 3

Opening Chorus
"If the Man in the Moon Would Only Speak"
A. Laughlin, L. Mink, S. Stembler, A. Hart, J. McCree, W. J. Kennedy
(*Music by* Will H. Becker.)
"Hysterical Tune"
G. Tyson, A. McWatters
"Every Coon"
A. Hart
Finale
Entire Company

[110]Originally presented in New York 28 September 1891 at the Standard Theatre for 77 performances in two separate engagements. For Synopsis of Scenes and Musical Numbers, see original 1891 production.

[111]On opening night, specialty guest appearances were made by Lew Dockstader, Elizabeth Murray and Al Jolson, Howard and Howard.